# RHS PLANT FINDER 2007-2008

Devised by Chris Philip
and Realised by Tony Lord

**Consultant Editor**
Tony Lord

**RHS Editors**
James Armitage    Janet Cubey
Dawn Edwards    Neil Lancaster

**Compiler**
Judith Merrick

A Dorling Kindersley Book

London, New York, Munich, Melbourne, Delhi

Published by
Dorling Kindersley Ltd
80 Strand, London WC2R 0RL
A Penguin company


First edition April 1987
Twenty-first edition April 2007



British Library Cataloguing Publication Data.
A Catalogue record for this book is available from the British Library.

ISBN 978-1-40532-065-8

Compiled by
The Royal Horticultural Society
80 Vincent Square,
London SW1P 2PE
Registered charity no: 222879

**www.rhs.org.uk**

Royal Horticultural Society

Illustrations by Sarah Young
Maps by Alan Cooper

Produced for Dorling Kindersley Ltd by
COOLING BROWN
Printed and bound in England by Clays Ltd, St Ives Plc

**The Compiler and the Editors of the *RHS Plant Finder* have taken every care, in the time available, to check all the information supplied to them by the nurseries concerned. Nevertheless, in a work of this kind, containing as it does hundreds of thousands of separate computer encodings, errors and omissions will, inevitably, occur. Neither the RHS, the Publisher nor the Editors can accept responsibility for any consequences that may arise from such errors.**

If you find mistakes we hope that you will let us know so that the matter can be corrected in the next edition.

**Back cover photographs from top to bottom:** *Chrysanthemum* 'Brietner', *Dahlia* 'Ragged Robin', *Salvia guaranitica* 'Blue Enigma', *Nerine sarniensis, Blechnum gibbum*
**Front cover and spine:** *Centaurea cineraria*

# Contents

# INTRODUCTION

The *RHS Plant Finder* exists to put enthusiastic gardeners in touch with suppliers of plants. The book is divided into two related sections – **PLANTS** and **NURSERIES. PLANTS** includes an A–Z Plant Directory of some 77,000 plant names, against which are listed a series of nursery codes. These codes point the reader to the full nursery details contained in the **NURSERIES** section towards the back of the book.

The *RHS Plant Finder* is comprehensively updated every year and provides the plant lover with the richest source of suppliers known to us, whether you are looking for plants locally, shopping from your armchair or touring the country in search of the rare and unusual.

As you will see from the entries in the **NURSERY DETAILS BY CODE** many nurseries do not now publish a printed catalogue but produce an online version only. This is a growing trend, fuelled by the cost of printing a full catalogue.

It is important to remember when ordering that many of the nurseries listed in the book are small, family-run, businesses that propagate their own material. They cannot therefore guarantee to hold large stocks of the plants they list. Many will, however, propagate to order.

# NEW IN THIS EDITION

For the 20th Anniversary of the *Plant Finder*, Mike Grant, now editor of *The Plantsman* and formerly one of the editors of the *RHS Plant Finder*, takes a look at how plant trends have been reflected in the book over the course of its 20-year history.

One of the most frequently asked recycling questions is what can gardeners do with all the plastic flowerpots they acquire? Rebecca Matthews-Joyce, RHS Principal Environmental Policy Adviser, looks at the options. With ever-hotter summers, Guy Barter, Head of RHS Advisory Services, addresses the issue of how much we should be watering our gardens.

In this edition, revisions have occurred to many genera, incl. *Rosa, Verbena, Begonia* and the families *Araliaceae* and *Sapotaceae*. Revisions to *Fuchsia* and *Chrysanthemum* have focused around the addition of new horticultural classification codes for Encliandra and Triphylla fuchsias and Korean chysanthemums (see *Classification of Genera* pp.36–40)

Following long-considered decisions by the RHS Advisory Panel on Nomenclature & Taxonomy, readers will notice the incorporation of *Corallospartium* and *Chordospartium* within *Carmichaelia* and the split of *Eupatorium sensu lato* into *Ageratina, Ayapana, Bartlettina, Chromolaena, Conoclinium, Eupatorium,* and *Fleischmannia*. Decisions such as these are never taken lightly. We hope you will find the cross-references helpful and if you want to learn more about the split of *Eupatorium* please refer to N. Hind, Splitting *Eupatorium, The Plantsman* ns 5(3) Sep 2006.

# AVAILABLE FROM THE COMPILER

## APPLICATION FOR ENTRY

Nurseries appearing in the *RHS Plant Finder* for the first time this year are printed in bold type in the *Nursery Index by Name* starting on p.926.

If you wish your nursery to be considered for inclusion in the next edition of the *RHS Plant Finder* (2008-2009), please write for details to the Compiler at the address below.

## PLANTS LAST LISTED IN EARLIER EDITIONS

Plants cease to be listed for a variety of reasons. For more information turn to *How to Use the Plant Directory* on p.26. A listing of the 34,000 or so plants listed in earlier editions, but for which we currently have no known supplier, is available online at www.rhs.org.uk/RHSPlantFinder/documents/PF_Lastlisted_2007.pdf.

## LISTS OF NURSERIES FOR PLANTS WITH MORE THAN 28 SUPPLIERS

To prevent the book from becoming too big, we do not print the nursery codes where more than 28 nurseries offer the same plant. The plant is then listed as being "Widely available". This is detailed more fully in *How to Use the Plant Directory* on p.26.

If any readers have difficulty in finding such a plant, we will be pleased to send a full list of all the nurseries that we have on file as stockists. All such enquiries must include the full name of the plant being sought, as shown in the *RHS Plant Finder*, together with an A5 size SAE. For more than one plant, please send an A4 1st class SAE.

The above may be obtained from:
**The Compiler, *RHS Plant Finder*, RHS Garden Wisley, Woking, Surrey GU23 6QB**
**Email: plantfinder@rhs.org.uk**
This information is also available online.

## THE RHS PLANT FINDER ONLINE

The *RHS Plant Finder* is available on the Internet. Visit the Royal Horticultural Society's website **www.rhs.org.uk** and search the *RHS Plant Finder* database online.

# ACKNOWLEDGMENTS

Judith Merrick, assisted by Wendy Marsh, with help from Patty Boardman and June Skinner, compiled this edition, whilst Richard Sanford managed the editing of the plant names on the database. Rupert Wilson and Graham Hawkes administered the Horticultural Database, using the BG-BASE™ Collection Management Software, from which the book is produced.

We should like to acknowledge the help of Simon Maughan, RHS Publications, John David, RHS Head of Botany, Kerry Walter of BG-BASE (UK) Ltd., Max Phillips of Strange Software Ltd. and Alan Cooper, who produces the nursery maps.

We are greatly indebted to Peter Cooling of Cooling Brown Ltd., for enabling us to turn our mass of raw data into a published format. We are grateful to him for his patience and skill.

RHS botanists, James Armitage and Neil Lancaster, have been joined in the task of editing the plant names this *RHS Plant Finder* season by Dawn Edwards. We are also grateful to Christopher Whitehouse, Keeper of the Herbarium, for continuing to play an active role in the editing process.

Once again this year we are indebted to our colleagues on the RHS Advisory Panel on Nomenclature and Taxonomy, along with the RHS International Cultivar Registrars all of whom have provided much valuable guidance and information. Scores of nurseries have sent helpful information about plants which has proved immensely useful in verifying some of the most obscure names, as well as suggesting corrections to existing entries. Some of these suggested corrections remain to be checked and entered in our next edition and we are grateful for your patience while information is checked and processed, though those that contravene the Codes of Nomenclature may have to be rejected. We are grateful, too, to our regular correspondents.

| | |
|---|---|
| *Cistus* | R. Page ('97, '99 & '02) |
| *Clematis* | V. Matthews, former International Cultivar Registrar, RHS ('00–'06) |
| *Cotoneaster* | Jeanette Fryer, NCCPG Collection Holder ('99) |
| *Dahlia* | R. Hedge, RHS Wisley ('96–'00 & '02) |
| *Dianthus* | Dr A.C. Leslie, International Cultivar Registrar, RHS Wisley ('91–'00 & '02) |
| *Erica* | Dr E.C. Nelson, International Cultivar Registrar |
| *Geranium* | D.X. Victor, International Cultivar Registrar ('03) |
| *Hebe* | Mrs J. Hewitt ('94–'99) |
| *Ilex* | Ms S. Andrews ('92–'98) |
| *Iris* | Mrs J. Hewitt ('95–'99, '02 & '05) |
| *Jovibarba* & *Sempervivum* | P.J. Mitchell, International Cultivar Registrar, Sempervivum Society ('98) |
| *Lavandula* | Ms S. Andrews ('02, '03 & '05) |
| *Lilium* | Dr A.C. Leslie, International Cultivar Registrar, RHS Wisley ('91–'00 & '02) |
| *Liriope* | Dr P.R. Fantz ('99) |
| *Meconopsis* | Dr E. Stevens ('02, '03 & '05) |
| *Narcissus* | Mrs S. Kington, International Cultivar Registrar, RHS ('91–'00 & '02) |
| *Ophiopogon* | Dr P.R. Fantz ('99) |
| *Rhododendron* | Dr A.C. Leslie, International Cultivar Registrar, RHS Wisley ('91–'00 & '02) |
| *Sorbus* | Dr H. McAllister ('01) |
| *Thymus* | Mrs M. Easter ('03–'06) |

To all these, as well as to the many readers and nurseries who have also made comments and suggestions, we are once again extremely grateful.

Tony Lord, Consultant Editor, and Janet Cubey, RHS Principal Botanist, February 2007

# PLANT FINDER: THE FIRST 20 YEARS

This 21st edition marks the twentieth anniversary of Chris Philip's first publication of *The Plant Finder*. All gardeners, whether professional or amateur, owe him a debt of gratitude. His vision, determination and resourcefulness in achieving it has made it easier for us all to find exactly the plants we want and for nurseries to produce a wider range of plants, including some that might not have been viable before *The Plant Finder* appeared. It is remarkable that Chris devised this before he knew about or had seen similar projects such as *The Hardy Plant Directory* or *Find that Rose!*

Chris realised the value of consistent nomenclature and attached great importance to it. With as many as fifteen variants of names for a single plant, the whole project would not have been viable without trying to find the one most acceptable name for each. He recognised that thousands of hours needed to be spent checking the names in each edition. His vision and investment in this, carried forward since 1993 by Wisley's botanists, has resulted in a name set for garden plants that is perhaps more reliable than any we had before and is valued world wide.

**Tony Lord, Consultant Editor**
**Jan 07**

Chris Philip's vision has been augmented and carried forward by many others, many largely unsung.

Alan Cooper, for instance, worked with Chris Philip to prepare the maps for the book from 1988. When the RHS took over publication, Alan came with the book. Nineteen years on, he is still responsible for the maps that appear in each edition.

When the RHS assumed production of the *Plant Finder,* Clare Burgh took on the job of compiling the book and the RHS botanists, working closely with Tony Lord, began the daunting task of verifying the thousands of plant names submitted by nurseries.

The greatest credit of all, however, must go to Tony Lord who, single-handedly, carried out the editorial task until 1996. Since then, he has sustained his close involvement with the project, working alongside the RHS botanists. It is Tony who set the standard for the book's authority.

In an ever-changing age of communication, those involved with the *RHS Plant Finder* recognise the challenge in maintaining its relevance and value. It will need to continue to develop in order to serve the needs of nursery folk and plants-people alike.

We are proud of the past twenty years – but never trust an old edition!

TO AVOID DISAPPOINTMENT,
WE SUGGEST THAT YOU ALWAYS

**check with the nursery before visiting or ordering and always use the current edition of the book.**

# PLANT TRENDS 1987-2007

Twenty years ago an unassuming brown paperback book looking not unlike a small telephone directory was first published. I suspect the cover design reminded people of something from the 1970s self-sufficiency movement, even then in 1987. This was the first edition of the ***Plant Finder***, a book that quickly revolutionised the world of ornamental horticulture. It allowed keen gardeners to locate even the obscurest plants relatively easily, and its well-researched listing of plants resulted in the stabilisation of plant names. Previously, horticulturists had relied on various definitive books for accepted plant names but the annual nature of the ***Plant Finder*** allowed the listing to be kept up-to-date.

I was not aware of the ***Plant Finder*** 20 years ago and I can't say I was particularly tuned in to plant trends. I did not work in horticulture then, which could explain my lack of awareness, but I was a keen gardener. The only plant trend I can remember, and one that I did engage in, was that for large-leaved perennials – the forerunner of the exoticist movement, which is now starting to look a bit dated.

A detailed analysis of the fluxes of plant names that have appeared in the ***Plant Finder*** over the years would be fascinating. However, it would probably be too multi-dimensional to comprehend sensibly. It would reveal plant trends, but in immense detail. I have not performed any such analysis but in this short essay I intend to discuss some of the changes, not so much in gardening trends, but to focus on a few individual plants and plant groups.

**Remembering 1987**

Just to put the time period into perspective, 1987 was the year of the Great Storm (in October); the Princess of Wales Conservatory opened at Royal Botanic Gardens, Kew, and the lily beetle was still restricted to a few home counties west of London. Global warming was on the agenda, back then it was called the greenhouse effect, and gardening magazines were advocating Mediterranean planting even then. The issue of peat in horticulture was also starting to be discussed but it didn't start making an impact until 1990 when a peatland campaign was launched and the RHS did its first peat-replacement compost trials in 1990.

The Chelsea Flower Show of 1987 seemed to feature rhododendrons and hostas in a big way, and Kelways were exhibiting tree peonies but there was no sign of the fabulous Chinese cultivars we now see. A newly launched window box competition had entries composed of pelargoniums, busy lizzies, begonias, fuchsias and ivies. But the boxes lacked the present diversity of container plants we are currently spoiled with, such as *Bidens*, *Brachyscome*, *Diascia*, *Felicia*, *Sutera* and *Verbena*. It's hard to believe but even petunias were not reliable enough to plant with confidence.

In the early days the ***Plant Finder*** was not as reliable a guide to what was generally available than it is today. There were fewer nurseries included and the data gathering was not as systematic as it is now. But a glance through the 1987 edition is quite revealing. Certain genera seemed to be well represented. These include *Aubrieta*, *Campanula*, *Hebe*, *Helianthemum*, *Phlox*, *Pernettya* and *Potentilla*. The Hebe Society was formed around this time and hebes are still major garden centre fare with a rash of new cultivars in the past five years. *Phlox* have since declined in popularity but may be in for a revival, what with an imminent RHS trial, but will their pest susceptibility and general intolerance of dry soil hold them back?

In contrast there were very few *Corydalis*, *Digitalis*, *Euphorbia*, *Hamamelis*, *Kniphofia*, *Lavandula*, *Lavatera*, *Phormium*, *Pulmonaria*, *Salvia* and *Thalictrum*. There was also a limited range of bamboos, grasses and sedges (with hardly any *Calamagrostis*, *Carex*, *Miscanthus* or *Molinia*). But then again, if you had a great big dollop of pampas grass in your front garden you probably weren't ready for any more grasses. Surprisingly, quite a few of the more unusual bamboos had a reputation for tenderness at the time.

**Exotic tendencies**

The popularity of exotic gardening has certainly driven the rapid rise in availability of all sorts of obscure bamboos and palms. Both groups are still responsible for many of the new genera that are listed each year. Similarly, there has been much interest in new bananas, particularly those with hardiness potential, and *Hedychium*. However, there is one Mediterranean tree that has risen significantly in the polls but for which I've never understood the desire to plant. Unless it's a venerable, rugged specimen in a grove, the olive is one of the most boring looking trees; the flowers are insignificant, the fruits rarely appear and if they do they are hardly attractive. And worst of all, even authors who should know better ignore the fact that olives need to be subjected to complex fermentation or soaked in caustic soda to make them edible! Who's going to try that at home?

**Woody winners**

Homing in on particular species reveals a few that have made a significant impact on our gardens in the past 20 years. A shrub and a small tree, both raised in the US in the mid-1940s, suddenly became available and popular in the UK. In the 1987 edition, *Ceanothus* 'Concha' and *Cercis canadensis* 'Forest Pansy' were listed by just one and two nurseries respectively, and were outnumbered by *Ceanothus* 'Edinburgh' and *C. siliquastrum* 'Album'. Who grows the latter two now?

In the 1987 edition *Dicksonia antarctica* was only listed by one nursery, it is now imported from Australia by the container load. *Cotinus* 'Grace' was raised in the early 1980s but did not appear in the book until 1988. And then there are oddities such as Japanese *Ajania pacifica* (then better known as *Chrysanthemum pacificum*), which was introduced to the UK in 1988.

*Choisya ternata* 'Sundance' was introduced in 1986 but was already listed by seven nurseries in 1987, a testament to its rapid penetration of the market. We had yet to encounter *Rubus cockburnianus* Goldenvale ('Wyego'). While on the subject of coloured leaves, there is also a trio of variegated woody plants that were introduced between 1970 and 1980: *Acer negundo* 'Flamingo', *Photinia davidiana* 'Palette' and *Salix integra* 'Hakuro-nishiki'. All became major sellers in the late 20th century.

Staying with woody plants, we now have a much greater choice of magnolias, with several large-flowered ones from New Zealand breeders that will provide blooms at 4-5 years old. At the other extreme of the woody spectrum, New Zealand and Australian breeders have also been responsible for expanding the range of Lavandula now available. The choice of *Hamamelis* has also mushroomed and there are now some gorgeous broad-petalled cultivars in various shades of orange.

You might have thought that there was enough variety in *Clematis* to satisfy most gardeners in 1987, indeed throughout most of the 20th century. However, in the final two decades of the century several dedicated breeders vastly increased the range available. *Daphne*, too, has been the subject of much breeding although they don't find their way into mainstream production.

Also, as I mentioned above, there is now a bewildering array of tree peonies available due to the opening up of trade with China. And it's not just esoteric plants like peonies that are flooding out of China – their immense horticultural production facilities are resulting in big trade shifts away from Holland for everything from tulips to grafted Japanese maples.

**Herbaceous ascendancies**

Trends in herbaceous plants are similarly hinted at if early editions of the ***Plant Finder*** are studied. *Dahlia* 'Bishop of Llandaff' was listed by just four nurseries in 1987, outnumbered by several showbench cultivars. It has now spawned a whole series of imitators and other dahlias suited to the flower garden. *Echinacea purpurea* was listed along with 7 cultivars but with no other species. *Echinacea angustifolia* and *E. pallida* appeared in the book in 1988, but only listed by one herb nursery each, reflecting their medicinal rather than ornamental qualities. Now you can buy virtually every species in the genus and interspecific orange and yellow hybrids are set to become highly popular.

*Geranium* and *Pulmonaria* have substantially increased their presence in the past two decades, a fact supported by the fact that the Hardy Plant Society has launched specialist groups for enthusiasts of these genera. Indeed, the number of geraniums has increased to such a degree that a recent RHS trial of them had to be split into three stages and run over 6 years. Another pair of genera that have their own specialist society is *Hosta* and *Hemerocallis*. Both were well represented in 1987 but the numbers have exploded in the intervening 20 years, boosted by imports from the States. *Hemerocallis* deserve to be more widely grown but I think potential growers may be overwhelmed by the choice.

Hellebores have made great strides since 1987. Breeder Helen Ballard had exhibited a pure yellow-flowered hellebore in 1980 but she was still trying to improve the vigour of her yellow-flowered selections in 1987 and they were not commercially available. Since then several other skilled hybridists working from nurseries have taken on hellebore breeding with superb results. We now have broad, substantial sepals on outward-facing flowers with purer colours, fantastic patterning, double flowers and anemone-centred flowers. The doubles are derived from wild origin double-flowered *H. torquatus* introduced from Montenegro in 1971. But the most infamous hellebore introduction of recent decades was Chinese *H. thibetanus*. Slow to propagate, there has been deep concern that collectors have been repeatedly removing plants from the wild.

Coupled with the rise of hellebores has been a rise in popularity of woodland perennials. There have been many new *Epimedium* introductions, both of species new to science and numerous hybrids and selections. Also fitting into this category would be *Arisaema*, a genus that inspires collectors as well as concerns about the origin of some commercial material. Other woodland genera that have expanded in cultivation include *Actaea*, *Disporopsis*, *Disporum*, *Paris*, *Polygonatum*, *Roscoea*, *Smilacina* and *Tricyrtis*. Their rise has been aided by the garden-enriching collecting activities of nurseries such as Crûg Farm Plants in Wales and the recently extinguished Heronswood in the US (although Dan Hinkley continues).

Other recently introduced species include *Campanula takesimana*, which was brought from Korea in the mid 1980s and has now contributed to several hybrids. *Corydalis flexuosa* was nowhere to be seen in the UK in 1987; it was still a name confined to Chinese floras and its main introduction was in 1989. However, I was surprised to see *Verbena bonariensis* listed by 11 nurseries in the 1987 edition, I had always assumed its popularity was more recent.

**Bulbous bruisers**

One cannot talk about plant trends without mentioning *Galanthus*. Although the fascination of snowdrops passes many gardeners by, they have a loyal following. Over the past 20 years enthusiasts have recognised more and more cultivars, all wearing a slightly different livery of green and white. In complete contrast, alliums have been getting bigger and better and cheaper. Cultivars with spherical-sounding names and large flower heads in shades of pink, lilac, purple, violet or burgundy are now readily available in garden centres. Every year you seem to get more per bag.

The last two decades has been a boom period for horticulture. A wide range of genera have been subject to breeding work, wild plant collecting has just about managed to continue while respecting legislation, garden plants have been well-documented in numerous horticultural monographs and encyclopaedias, and the ***Plant Finder*** has provided an annual snapshot of what is available. Long may it continue!

**Mike Grant,**
**Editor, *The Plantsman***

# WATER IN THE GARDEN

Up to 70% of our domestic water supply is poured and sprinkled on to our gardens during peak summer periods. This huge demand is hard to sustain in a drought.

The RHS believes that much of the watering carried out in gardens is the result of a misunderstanding about how and when water needs to be applied. An excessive amount is often used, which then simply drains out of reach of the roots. On the other hand, insufficient water sprinkled on the soil merely wets the surface.

Good watering aims to supply enough water to replenish soil moisture levels without overdoing it. Apply it at a steady rate at the base of stems and beneath the canopy of foliage, as wetting the leaves is a waste. The surrounding soil should stay dry, with all the water going where it is needed – to the roots. Keeping much of the soil surface dry will also help to limit weed problems.

There is little point in applying excess water, as it will quickly drain below where the roots can reach. So always check the weather forecast and only water if not enough rain falls. Watering in the evening gives it time to sink in while evaporation rates are low. Unfortunately, summer evenings are times of peak water demand. It is often better to water early in the morning, as water pressure is high and demand low.

Plants can be watered with bath, shower, kitchen and washing machine water (but not dishwasher water), which is collectively referred to as "grey" water. A washing machine can use 50 litres per wash – over five watering cans' worth. Grey water varies in quality and usually contains some degree of contamination. However, soil and potting compost is effective at filtering out contaminants, including soaps and detergents. There should be no problem with the small-scale, short-term use of grey water to tide plants over during a summer drought.

**When to water?**
When do plants need water? The best guide comes from digging 30cm (1 foot) into the soil. If it feels damp at this depth, watering is not needed, but if it feels dry, then some plants will need a drink. Gardeners should be aware that clay feels slightly damp when all available water has been used, and sandy soil is dry to the touch even when some water is available. It just takes a little experience to get used to this.

Fruit and vegetables will usually crop adequately without watering. The quality and quantity, however, is improved by watering at times when drought would affect the part of the plant that is harvested. When leaves are the crop, such as lettuce, the plants should never go short of water. In practical terms, watering about two weeks before harvesting is usually sufficient.

Containers need frequent watering because they only hold a limited amount of water. Apply water when the surface of the compost appears dry. You can tell if you have given enough water when the excess flows out of the bottom. A saucer will retain this run-off.

**How to save water**
Help the soil to store water by digging in or mulching with organic matter, such as well-rotted manure. This can provide the equivalent of 5cm of rain or 20 day's supply. Deeply digging beds or using raised beds will increase the volume of soil from which plants can take moisture.

To reduce the water needed by containers, try grouping them together. This allows the plants to shade each other and, as a result, less moisture will be lost from their leaves. Also place a saucer under each pot to collect water that would otherwise run away. This reservoir will be absorbed by the plants.

If you have a choice, position your containers in a sheltered spot near the kitchen so it is easy to use grey water.

As well as watering by hand, containers can be connected to an automatic irrigation system set to deliver the minimum amount of water. It is economical and can water while you are on holiday. However, this is not permitted during a hosepipe ban except if it uses grey water or stored rainwater.

Mature trees and shrubs do not need watering. Likewise, a lawn can be left to brown.

Water butts are invaluable. They can store run-off from the roofs of houses, greenhouses and sheds, fit neatly against walls and can be placed near vegetable beds to make watering easy. When the butts are running low, save the water for edibles such as vegetables and herbs. Other thirsty plants, such as bedding, can be watered with grey water.

**Guy Barter**
Head of Advisory Services

For further advice on watering and to download the complete *Water in the Garden booklet*, log on to the RHS website at **www.rhs.org.uk/advice**

# Plant Pots and Sustainability

Gardening should be a highly sustainable activity. From an environmental perspective, the true beauty of a plant is its ability to replenish itself from sunlight, water, and locally available nutrients, without a scrap of waste being generated. Now it is the turn of gardeners to emulate these qualities in their own lives, as to live in a sustainable way, we are told, means eating local food, relying on renewable sources of energy, managing water carefully, and limiting the amount of waste we produce.

Gardens have become inextricably linked with sustainable, environment- conscious lifestyles, as we look to them as a place to compost, grow our own food, store and recycle water, cleanse the air, and provide shade and welcome humidity as the global temperature rises.

Gardeners however, in their haste to create the ultimate outdoor room, alongside the heaps of compost and water butts, are piling up a problem for the future, a plastic pot mountain that won't rot away and is clogging up landfill sites all around the UK.

All plastics can be recycled but not all plastics are the same. There are seven different classifications of plastic and to successfully melt down and re-use plastic it ideally has to be the same type of plastic, the same colour, and there has to be a lot of it. This is why most household recycling schemes only collect plastic milk bottles and pop bottles, because this guarantees collection of a high number of items that will all be the same. Mixed plastics have to be hand sorted, by type and colour, and there are very few facilities with trained staff to do this.

Standardising pot size, type, and colour, across the horticultural industry to offer some hope of recycling becoming easier is probably a waste of time, as the world is fast running out of the key resource that all plastics are derived from – oil. In fact it will be interesting to see which one runs out first - the space for landfilling, or the oil for manufacturing. Which ever it is, there is a need to start thinking of new alternatives to plastics.

So it is heartening to see that there are wide varieties of alternative materials that plant pots can be made from. Pots made from corn starch, pulped bamboo, paper and even seaweed are all being manufactured and the beauty of all of these is that they are biodegradable. Admittedly, some biodegrade more quickly than others – too quickly in some cases – but despite some teething problems, the standards are improving all the time and many of these products are just as good as the tried and trusted plastic version.

The horticultural industry has been slow to catch on to this. The initial difficulties with strength and longevity of product and the limited ranges available have meant that biodegradable pots haven't been the runaway success that we might have hoped. But this could change with consumer demand. No one is going to persevere with biodegradable pots unless there is a market for them and so the discerning gardener should ask for a sustainable alternative to plastic and maybe soon the pot will go into the border as well as the plant.

**Rebecca Matthews-Joyce**
RHS Principal Adviser, Environmental Policy

# CONSERVATION AND THE ENVIRONMENT

As the ***RHS Plant Finder*** demonstrates, gardens in Britain have been greatly enriched by the diversity of plants introduced to cultivation from abroad. Whilst the vast majority of those introduced have enhanced our gardens, a few have proved to be highly invasive and to threaten native habitats. Once such plants are established it is very difficult, costly and potentially damaging to native ecosystems to eradicate or control the invasive "alien" species. Gardeners can help by choosing not to buy or distribute non-native invasive plants and by taking steps to prevent them escaping into the wild and by disposing of them in a responsible way.

The top eight invasive non-native species are no longer listed in the *RHS Plant Finder*. Any cultivars or varieties of them that are listed are believed to be less invasive than the species themselves. These seven plants are:

*Azolla filiculoides* – fairy fern
*Crassula helmsii* – New Zealand pygmy weed
*Fallopia japonica* – Japanese knotweed
*Heracleum mantegazzianum* – giant hogweed
*Hydrocotyle ranunculoides* – floating pennywort
*Impatiens glandulifera* – Himalayan balsam
*Ludwigia grandiflora* – water primrose
*Myriophyllum aquaticum* – parrot's feather

**Bringing plants back from abroad**

Travelling can be a great source of inspiration for gardeners and often provides an introduction to new and interesting plants. Anyone thinking of bringing plants back into Britain from overseas must realise, however, that this is a complex matter. Various regulations are in force which apply to amateur gardeners as well as to commercial nurseries. The penalties for breaking these can be serious.

Some of the most important regulatory bodies are listed below.

**Plant Health regulations** are in place to control the spread of pests and diseases. Plants are divided into the categories of prohibited, controlled and unrestricted, but there are also limits that vary according to the part of the world you are travelling from. For full details contact the Plant Health division of DEFRA, or visit www.defra.gov.uk/planth/ph.htm

DEFRA has produced a leaflet that summarises the Horticultural Code of Practice. This is available online at www.defra.gov.uk or by phoning the helpline on 08459 335577.

**The Convention on International Trade in Endangered Species (CITES)** affects the transport of animal and plant material across international boundaries. Its aim is to prevent exploitative trade and thereby to prevent harm and the ultimate extinction of wild populations. Export and import licences are required for any plants listed on the CITES Appendices. A broad range of plants is covered in these Appendices, including *Cactaceae* and *Orchidaceae* and, although species are mentioned in the convention title, the restrictions cover all cultivars and hybrids too. Details of the plants listed in the Appendices can be found on the CITES website, www.ukcites.gov.uk/intro/cites_species.htm, or in the leaflets detailed below.

**The Convention on Biological Diversity** (CBD or the "Rio Convention") recognises the property rights of individual countries in relation to their own biodiversity. It exists to enable access to that biodiversity, but equally to ensure the sharing of any benefit derived from it. Export permits are required for plant material taken from the country of origin, with prior informed consent being gained for any uses that the material will be used for in the future. Further information on the Convention can be found on the CBD website, www.biodiv.org.

If you would like to read more about these subjects, *Conservation and Environment Guidelines* leaflets are available on request from the RHS. Please write to the Compiler at the address given on page 4 enclosing an A4 SAE, or find them online at www.rhs.org.uk/publications. Leaflets are also available on a wider range of subjects, with topics including:

*Peat and the gardener*
*Potentially harmful garden plants*
*The use of limestone in horticulture*
*Trees and timber products*
*Wild and endangered plants in cultivation*
*Wildlife in gardens*

# LINDLEY LIBRARY

The Lindley Library is the best gardening library in the world. It is essential for garden history, gardens and horticulture, with books dating from 1514 to the very latest publications.

The two main libraries at London and Wisley have extensive collections and specialist enquiry teams. They support the smaller libraries at Harlow Carr, Hyde Hall and Rosemoor.

**London - Main Library**

- History of gardening, gardens and horticulture
- Essential for students of garden history, researchers and historians
- 50,000 books from 1514 to all the latest titles
- 400 current journals
- Historical gardening journals
- 22,000 botanical drawings and illustrations
- Historical nursery, seed, tools and glasshouse catalogues
- Lending service (including postal loans)
- Full-time specialist enquiry team
- Regular book request service from Wisley

**Open** 1000-1700, Mon-Fri, Tue until 1900. Closes for two weeks in August.

**Wisley - Main Library**

- Practical gardening, garden history, garden design
- Floras, cultivated plant monographs, science of gardening
- Essential for amateur & professional gardeners and students
- 21,000 books
- 500 current journals
- Historical gardening journals
- 20th century nursery and seed catalogues
- Lending service
- Full-time specialist enquiry team
- Regular book request service from London

**Open** 1100-1600, seven days a week. Closes for two weeks in December.

**Harlow Carr Garden Library**

- 4,000 books including most new gardening titles, and key horticultural works
- All the major gardening magazines
- Lends books and videos to local RHS Members
- Operated daily by team of volunteers

**Open** 1130-1530, Mon-Fri (closed Public Holidays), 1400-1600, Sat (Mar-Oct). Closes for two weeks in December.

**Hyde Hall Garden Library**

- 1,700 books including most new gardening titles and key horticultural works
- RHS publications
- Gardening magazines
- Operated daily by team of volunteers

**Open** 1200-1600, seven days. Closes for two weeks in December.

**Rosemoor Garden Library**

- 1,300 books including most new gardening titles and key horticultural works
- RHS publications
- Gardening magazines
- Operated daily by team of volunteers

Open 1100-1600, Mon-Sat. Closes for two weeks in December.

**Library Enquiry Service**

The Library welcomes enquiries from the public on the history of gardening and all garden-related subjects. The enquiry teams can help with a selective search of the available literature, provide lists of references, and much more.

RHS Library staff at London and Wisley provide a specialist information service.

The library enquiry service is open to all.

**For information on all library services contact:**
01483 212428 (Wisley) or
020 7821 3050 (London)
or see the website at www.rhs.org.uk/libraries

# RHS Britain in Bloom

Every year over 1000 communities, from tiny rural villages to the largest cities, take on the challenge of improving their local environment by signing up to the *Britain in Bloom* campaign. Through the creative planting of trees, shrubs and flowers and by addressing local environmental issues such as litter, graffiti and vandalism, these communities work all year round to create a more beautiful and sustainable Britain.

As custodian of the campaign since 2002, the Royal Horticultural Society has worked to enhance the status of the competition, to provide sound support for entries and to contribute horticultural expertise to participating communities.

The campaign works through its 12 English regions plus Scotland, Wales, Northern Ireland, Isle of Man, Jersey and Guernsey. Entrants first compete against each other within their region or nation and from there approximately 60-80 selected entries go on to compete in the UK finals each year.

The results speak for themselves. The *Britain in Bloom* participants experience benefits such as improved community cohesion and a boost to the local economy. Through planting, floral displays and high levels of cleanliness, the campaign encourages community co-operation in order to address issues such as sustainability, recycling, minimising waste and energy conservation. By enabling local people to take control of the planning and management of their local environment the campaign instils a sense of civic pride often missing in local communities.

It is the transformation of these communities that demonstrates the power of the campaign in economic, social and environmental terms.

One such community is Scarborough, Yorkshire, which has become a true tourist attraction in recent years. The continued efforts of the *Britain in Bloom* committee to incorporate environmental and horticultural elements to tourist attractions have won Scarborough the *RHS Britain in Bloom Tourism Award* in 2006 and ensured its place as the 6th most visited place in Britain by domestic holidaymakers.

One of the most popular horticultural projects initiated by the *Britain in Bloom* group in Scarborough is the Peasholm Glen Tree Trail project. Peasholm Glen contains rare and unusual trees and the aim of this project is to conserve them.

A champion tree is the largest or tallest known example of its kind and Peasholm Glen is home to six new champions: Swedish whitebeam (*Sorbus intermedia*); a rare Caucasian alder (*Alnus subcordata*); the tallest blue Nootka cypress (*Chamaecyparis nootkatensis* "Glauca"); the tallest example of *Populus* × *canadensis* 'Robusta' and *Cotoneaster lacteus.*

The trail also includes a stunning example of Dickson's golden elm (*Ulmus minor* 'Dicksonii').

Following on from the success of *Britain in Bloom*, a non-competitive category was launched last year. The *Neighbourhood Awards* are a unique initiative aimed at small, resident-led communities that are just starting to 'green up' and clean up their local area. They encourage a sense of ownership and community renewal, building civic pride and creating places where people want to live.

**For further information about RHS Britain in Bloom please contact:**
RHS Britain in Bloom Coordinator,
80 Vincent Square, London, SW1P2PE
tel. 020 7821 3118,
email: britaininbloom@rhs.org.uk
or visit: www.rhs.org.uk/britaininbloom

# RHS QUALIFICATIONS

The RHS is a nationally accredited awarding body providing qualifications for professional horticulturalists and dedicated amateurs.

The RHS does not itself offer the teaching leading to the qualifications; this is provided by further education colleges, private teaching providers or distance-learning organisations that have been approved by the RHS and have the facilities and skilled professional staff to teach the syllabus.

**Who can study for an RHS qualification in horticulture?**
Anyone who loves plants and gardening and wants to develop their knowledge of horticulture. The qualifications are designed to interest enthusiastic gardeners and stretch committed horticulturalists.

**Where can I study?**
The teaching, learning and practical training leading to RHS qualifications are run by colleges around the UK that have been approved by the RHS Qualifications Office.

RHS qualifications can also be gained from home-based study by distance learning.

The Certificate in Horticulture, the Advanced Certificate and the Diploma are taught on a part-time basis, usually one day a week for a year.

**What sort of qualifications does the RHS offer?**
**RHS (Level 2) Certificate in Horticulture**
This is equivalent to GCSE or NVQ Level 2 set in a two-part format. A theory-based qualification, it covers a wide range of topics from plant propagation to garden planning.

**RHS (Level 3) Advanced Certificate and Diploma in Horticulture**
These 2 qualifications allow the advanced student to select a number of modules, four for the Advanced Certificate and a further two for the Diploma.

**Master of Horticulture (RHS) Award**
The Society's most prestigious qualification offered to horticultural professionals. Of degree equivalence, it usually takes three years of continuous personal study to complete.

For further information contact your local further education college or the RHS Qualifications, RHS Garden Wisley, Woking, Surrey GU23 6QB, tel: 0845 260 9000.

# RHS HERBARIUM STANDARDS

**If you have introduced a new cultivar, a sample should be sent to the world-famous RHS Herbarium at Wisley for recording as a nomenclatural standard.**

A nomenclatural standard is the designated herbarium specimen, or illustration if more appropriate, which represents the diagnostic characters of the plant and fixes the cultivar name. It is the definitive record of the named cultivar. By establishing that your plant is a 'standard', it will benefit future generations of nurserymen, horticultural taxonomists and gardeners.

We require a fresh sample (not the whole plant) displaying the characteristics of flower and foliage and/or fruit, which distinguish the new cultivar from existing ones. Living rooted plants are not needed. These samples will then be prepared as 'Standard' specimens.

Please send the following, if possible:

- dried specimen
- photographic transparency
- dated published description

Specimens should be placed individually in dry polythene bags, clearly labelled using a waterproof pen or pencil and packed in a crush-proof box/ padded envelope as appropriate.

The package should be sent by first-class post, avoiding weekends and bank holidays and marked 'Standard' to:
**The Herbarium, RHS Garden, Wisley,Woking, Surrey GU23 6QB**

# Extended Glossary

This glossary combines some of the helpful introductory sections from older editions in an alphabetical listing. A fuller, more discursive account of plant names, *Guide to Plant Names,* and a detailed guide to the typography of plant names, *Recommended Style for Printing Plant Names*, are both available as RHS Advisory Leaflets. To request a copy of either please send an A4 SAE to The Compiler at the contact address given on page 4.

## Advisory Panel on Nomenclature and Taxonomy

This Panel advises the RHS on individual problems of nomenclature regarding plants in cultivation and, in particular, use of names in the *RHS Horticultural Database*, reflected in the annual publication of the *RHS Plant Finder*.

The aim is always to make the plant names in the *RHS Plant Finder* as consistent, reliable and stable as possible and acceptable to gardeners and botanists alike, not only in the British Isles but around the world. Recent proposals to change or correct names are examined with the aim of creating a balance between the stability of well-known names and botanical and taxonomic correctness. In some cases the Panel feels that the conflicting views on the names of some groups of plants will not easily be resolved. The Panel's policy is then to wait and review the situation once a more obvious consensus is reached, rather than rush to rename plants only to have to change them again when opinions have shifted.

The Panel is chaired by Dr Alan Leslie (RHS) with Dr Janet Cubey (RHS) (Vice-Chair) and includes: Dr Crinan Alexander (RBGE), Susyn Andrews, Chris Brickell, Dr James Compton, Dr John David (RHS), Mike Grant (RHS Publications), Dr Stephen Jury (University of Reading), Sabina Knees, Dr Tony Lord, Julian Shaw (RHS) & Adrian Whiteley, with Dr Christopher Whitehouse (RHS) as Secretary.

## Authorities

In order that plant names can be used with precision throughout the scientific world, the name of the person who coined the name of a plant species (its author, or authority) is added to the plant name. Usually this information is irrelevant to gardeners, except in cases where the same name has been given to two different plants or a name is commonly misapplied. Although only one usage is correct, both may be encountered in books, so indicating the author is the only way to be certain about which plant is being referred to. This can happen equally with cultivars. Authors' names, where it is appropriate to cite them, appear in a smaller typeface after the species or cultivar name to which they refer and are abbreviated following Brummitt and Powell's *Authors of Plant Names.*

## 🏆 Award Of Garden Merit

The Award of Garden Merit (AGM) is intended to be of practical value to the ordinary gardener and is therefore awarded only after a period of assessment by the Society's Standing and Joint Committees. An AGM plant:

- must be available
- must be of outstanding excellence for garden decoration or use
- must be of good constitution
- must not require highly specialist growing conditions or care
- must not be particularly susceptible to any pest or disease
- must not be subject to an unreasonable degree of reversion

The AGM symbol is cited in conjunction with the **hardiness** rating. A full list of AGM plants may be found on the RHS website at www.rhs.org.uk/plants/award_plants.asp.

## Botanical Names

The aim of the botanical naming system is to provide each different plant with a single, unique, universal name. The basic unit of plant classification is the species. Species that share a number of significant characteristics are grouped together to form a genus (plural **genera**). The name of a species is made up of two elements; the name of the genus followed by the specific epithet, for example, *Narcissus romieuxii*.

Variation within a species can be recognised by division into subspecies (usually abbreviated to subsp.), varietas (or variety abbreviated to var.) and forma (or form abbreviated to f.). Whilst it is unusual for a plant to have all of these, it is possible, as in this example, *Narcissus romieuxii* subsp. *albidus* var. *zaianicus* f. *lutescens*.

The botanical elements are always given in italics, with only the genus taking an initial capital letter. The rank indications are never in italics. In instances where the rank is not known it is necessary to form an invalid construction by quoting a second epithet without a rank. This is an unsatisfactory situation, but requires considerable research to resolve.

## CLASSIFICATION OF GENERA

Genera that include a large number of species or with many cultivars are often subdivided into informal horticultural classifications or more formal Cultivar Groups, each based on a particular characteristic or combination of characteristics. Colour of flower or fruit and shape of flower are common examples and, with fruit, whether a cultivar is grown for culinary or dessert purposes. How such groups are named differs from genus to genus.

To help users of the *RHS Plant Finder* find the plants they want, the classifications used within cultivated genera are listed using codes and plants are marked with the appropriate code in brackets after its name in the Plant Directory. To find the explanation of each code, simply look it up under the genus concerned in the **Classification of Genera** starting on p.36. The codes relating to edible fruits are also listed here, but these apply across several genera.

## COLLECTORS' REFERENCES

Abbreviations (usually with numbers) following a plant name refer to the collector(s) of the plant. These abbreviations are expanded, with a collector's name or expedition title, in the section **Collectors' References** starting on p.28.

A collector's reference may indicate a new, as yet unnamed range of variation within a species. The inclusion of collectors' references in the *RHS Plant Finder* supports the book's role in sourcing unusual plants.

The Convention on Biological Diversity calls for conservation of biodiversity, its sustainable use and the fair and equitable sharing of any derived benefits. Since its adoption in 1993, collectors are required to have prior informed consent from the country of origin for the acquisition and commercialisation of collected material.

## COMMON NAMES

In a work such as this, it is necessary to refer to plants by their botanical names for the sake of universal comprehension and clarity. However, at the same time we recognise that with fruit and vegetables most people are more familiar with their common names than their botanical ones. Cross-references are therefore given from common to botanical names for fruit, vegetables and the commoner culinary herbs throughout the Plant Directory.

## CULTIVAR

Literally meaning cultivated variety, cultivar names are given to denote variation within species and that generated by hybridisation, in cultivation. To make them easily distinguishable from botanical names, they are not printed in italics and are enclosed in single quotation marks. Cultivar names coined since 1959 should follow the rules of the International Code of Nomenclature for Cultivated Plants (**ICNCP**).

## DESCRIPTIVE TERMS

Terms that appear after the main part of the plant name are shown in a smaller font to distinguish them. These descriptive elements give extra information about the plant and may include the **collector's reference**, **authority**, or what colour it is. For example, *Fritillaria thessala* SBEL 443, *Penstemon* 'Sour Grapes' M. Fish, *Lobelia tupa* dark orange.

## FAMILIES

**Genera** are grouped into larger groups of related plants called families. Most family names, with the exception of eight familiar names, end with the same group of letters, *-aceae*. While it is still acceptable to use these eight exceptions, the modern trend adopted in the *RHS Plant Finder* is to use alternative names with *–aceae* endings. The families concerned are *Compositae* (*Asteraceae*), *Cruciferae* (*Brassicaceae*), *Gramineae* (*Poaceae*), *Guttiferae* (*Clusiaceae*), *Labiatae* (*Lamiaceae*), *Leguminosae* (split here into *Caesalpiniaceae*, *Mimosaceae* and *Papilionaceae*), *Palmae* (*Arecaceae*) and *Umbelliferae* (*Apiceae*). Also the traditionally large family *Liliaceae* is split into a number of smaller, more natural, families that as yet may be unfamiliar to readers.

Apart from these exceptions we follow Brumitt's *Vascular Plant Families and Genera* for our family names.

## GENUS (plural – GENERA)

Genera used in the *RHS Plant Finder* are almost always those given in Brummitt's *Vascular Plant Families and Genera.* For spellings and genders of generic names, Greuter's *Names in Current Use for Extant Plant Genera* has also been consulted. See **Botanical Names**.

## Grex

Within orchids, hybrids of the same parentage, regardless of how alike they are, are given a grex name. Individuals can be selected, given cultivar names and propagated vegetatively. For example, *Pleione* Versailles gx 'Bucklebury', where Versailles is the grex name and 'Bucklebury' is a selected **cultivar**.

## Group

This is a collective name for a group of cultivars within a genus with similar characteristics. The word Group is always included and, where cited with a cultivar name, it is enclosed in brackets, for example, *Actaea simplex* (Atropurpurea Group) 'Brunette', where 'Brunette' is a distinct cultivar in a group of purple-leaved cultivars.

Another example of a Group is *Rhododendron polycladum* Scintillans Group. In this case *Rhododendron scintillans* was a species that is now botanically 'sunk' within *R. polycladum*, but it is still recognised horticulturally as a Group.

Group names are also used for swarms of hybrids with the same parentage, for example, *Rhododendron* Polar Bear Group. These were formerly treated as **grex** names, a term now used only for orchids. A single clone from the Group may be given the same cultivar name, for example, *Rhododendron* 'Polar Bear'.

## Hardiness

Hardiness ratings are shown for **Award of Garden Merit** plants. The categories used are as follows:

H1 = plants requiring heated glass in the British Isles

H2 = plants requiring unheated glass in the British Isles

H3 = plants hardy outside in some regions of the British Isles or in particular situations, or which, while usually grown outside in summer, need frost-free protection in winter (eg. dahlias)

H4 = plants hardy throughout the British Isles

H1-2, H2-3, H3-4 = plants intermediate between the two ratings given

H1+3 = requiring heated glass; may be grown outside in summer

## Hybrids

Some species, when grown together, in the wild or in cultivation, are found to interbreed and form hybrids. In some instances a hybrid name is coined, for example hybrids between *Primula hirsuta* and *P. minima* are given the name *Primula* × *forsteri*, the multiplication sign indicating hybrid origin. Hybrid formulae that quote the parentage of the hybrid are used where a unique name has not been coined, for example *Rhododendron calophytum* × *R. praevernum*. In hybrid formulae you will find parents in alphabetical order, with the male (m) and female (f) parent indicated where known. Hybrids between different genera are also possible, for example × *Mahoberberis* is the name given to hybrids between *Mahonia* and *Berberis*.

There are also a few special-case hybrids called graft hybrids, where the tissues of two plants are physically rather than genetically mixed. These are indicated by an addition rather than a multiplication sign, so *Laburnum* + *Cytisus* becomes +*Laburnocytisus*.

## ICNCP

The ICNCP is the International Code of Nomenclature for Cultivated Plants. First published in 1959, the most recent edition was published in 2004.

**Cultivar** names that do not conform to this Code, and for which there is no valid alternative, are flagged I (for invalid). This code states that the minimum requirement is for a cultivar name to be given in conjunction with the name of the genus. However, in the ***RHS Plant Finder*** we choose to give as full a name as possible to give the gardener and botanist more information about the plant.

## Notes on Nomenclature and Identification

The **Notes on Nomenclature and Identification**, starting on p.31, give further information for names that are complex or may be confusing. See also **Advisory Panel on Nomenclature and Taxonomy**.

## Plant Breeders' Rights

Plants covered by an *active* grant of Plant Breeders' Rights (PBR) are indicated throughout the Plant Directory. Grants indicated are those awarded by both UK and EU Plant Variety Rights offices. Because grants can both come into force and lapse at any time, this book can only aim to represent the situation at one point in time, but it is hoped that this will act as a useful guide to growers and gardeners. UK grants represent the position as of the end of December 2006 and EU grants as of the end of October 2006. We do not give any indication where PBR grants may be pending.

To obtain PBR protection, a new plant must be registered and pass tests for distinctness, uniformity and stability under an approved name. This approved name, under the rules of the **ICNCP**, established by a legal process, has to be regarded as the cultivar name. Increasingly however, these approved names are a code or "nonsense" name and are therefore often unpronounceable and meaningless, so the plants are given other names designed to attract sales when they are released. These secondary names are often referred to as selling names but are officially termed **trade designations**.

For further information on UK PBR contact:

**Plant Variety Rights Office, White House Lane, Huntingdon Road, Cambridge CB3 0LF**
**Tel: (01223) 342396**
**Fax: (01223) 342386.**
**Website: www.defra.gov.uk/planth/pvs/default.htm**

For details of plants covered by EU Community Rights contact:

**Community Plant Variety Office (CPVO), 3 Boulevard Maréchal Foch, BP 10121**
**FR-49101 Angers, Cedex 02, France**
**Tel: 00 33 (02) 41 25 64 00**
**Fax: 00 33 (02) 41 25 64 10**
**Website: www.cpvo.europa.eu**

The *RHS Plant Finder* takes no responsibility for ensuring that nurseries selling plants with PBR are licensed to do so.

## Reverse Synonyms

It is likely that users of this book will come across names in certain genera that they did not expect to find. This may be because species have been transferred from another genus (or **genera**). In the list of **Reverse Synonyms** on p.41, the name on the left-hand side is that of an accepted genus to which species have been transferred from the genus on the right. Sometimes all species will have been transferred, but in many cases only a few will be affected. Consulting **Reverse Synonyms** enables users to find the genera from which species have been transferred. Where the right-hand genus is found in the Plant Directory, the movement of species becomes clear through the cross-references in the nursery code column.

## Selling Names

See **Trade Designations**

## Series

With seed-raised plants and some popular vegetatively-propagated plants, especially bedding plants and pot plants such as *Petunia* or *Impatiens*, Series have become increasingly popular. A Series contains a number of similar cultivars, but differs from a **Group** in that it is a marketing device, with cultivars added to create a range of flower colours in plants of similar habit. Individual colour elements within a species may be represented by slightly different cultivars over the years. Series names are styled similarly to **Groups**.

## Species

See under **Botanical Names**

## Subspecies

See under **Botanical Names**

## Synonyms

Although the ideal is for each species or cultivar to have only one name, anyone dealing with plants soon comes across a situation where one plant has received two or more names, or two plants have received the same name. In each case, only one name and application, for reasons of precision and stability, can be regarded as correct. Additional names are known as synonyms. Further information on synonyms and why plants change names is available in *Guide to Plant Names*. See the introduction to this glossary for details of how to request a copy.

See also **Reverse Synonyms**.

## Trade Designations

A **trade designation** is the name used to market a plant when the cultivar name is considered unsuitable for selling purposes. It is styled in a different typeface and without single quotation marks.

In the case of **Plant Breeders' Rights** it is a legal requirement for the cultivar name to appear with the trade designation on a label at the point of sale. Most plants are sold under only one trade designation, but some, especially roses, are sold under a number of names, particularly when cultivars are introduced from other countries. Usually, the correct cultivar name is the only way to ensure that the same plant is not bought unwittingly under two or more different trade designations. The *RHS Plant Finder* follows the recommendations of the **ICNCP** when dealing with trade designations and PBR. These are always to quote the cultivar name and trade designation together and to style the trade designation in a different typeface, without single quotation marks.

## Translations

When a cultivar name is translated from the language of first publication, the translation is regarded as a **trade designation** and styled accordingly. We endeavour to recognise the original cultivar name in every case and to give an English translation where it is in general use.

## Variegated Plants

Following a suggestion from the Variegated Plant Group of the Hardy Plant Society, a (v) is cited after those plants which are "variegated". The dividing line between variegation and less distinct colour marking is necessarily arbitrary and plants with light veins, pale, silver or dark zones, or leaves flushed in paler colours, are not shown as being variegated unless there is an absolutely sharp distinction between paler and darker zones.

For further details of the Variegated Plant Group, please write to:

**Jerry Webb, Esq.,**
**17 Heron Way, Minster Heights,**
**Ilminster TA19 0BX**

## Variety

See under **Botanical Names** and **Cultivar**

*'The question of nomenclature is always a vexed one. The only thing certain is, that it is impossible to please everyone.'*

W.J. Bean – Preface to first edition of *Trees & Shrubs Hardy in the British Isles*

# SYMBOLS AND ABBREVIATIONS

## SYMBOLS APPEARING TO THE LEFT OF THE NAME

| | |
|---|---|
| * | Name not validated. Not listed in the appropriate International Registration Authority checklist nor in works cited in the Bibliography. For fuller discussion see p.18 |
| I | Invalid name. See *International Code of Botanical Nomenclature 2000* and *International Code of Nomenclature for Cultivated Plants 2004*. For fuller discussion see p.18 |
| N | Refer to Notes on Nomenclature and Identification on p.31 |
| § | Plant listed elsewhere in the Plant Directory under a synonym |
| × | Hybrid genus |
| + | Graft hybrid genus |

## SYMBOLS APPEARING TO THE RIGHT OF THE NAME

| | |
|---|---|
| ✿ | National Council for the Conservation of Plants and Gardens (NCCPG) National Plant Collection® exists for all or part of this genus. Provisional Collections appear in brackets. Full details of the NCCPG Plant Collections are found in the *National Plant Collections® Directory 2005* available from: www.nccpg.com or NCCPG, RHS Garden, Wisley, Woking, Surrey GU23 6QP |
| ♀H4 | The Royal Horticultural Society's Award of Garden Merit, see p.18 |
| (d) | double-flowered |
| (F) | Fruit |
| (f) | female |
| (m) | male |
| (v) | variegated plant, see p.22 |
| PBR | Plant Breeders Rights see p.20 |
| **new** | New plant entry in this edition |

For abbreviations relating to individual genera see **Classification of Genera** p.36
For **Collectors' References** see p.28
For symbols used in the **Nurseries** section see p.812

## SYMBOLS AND ABBREVIATIONS USED AS PART OF THE NAME

| | |
|---|---|
| × | hybrid species |
| aff. | affinis (akin to) |
| agg. | aggregate, a single name used to cover a group of very similar plants, regarded by some as separate species |
| ambig. | ambiguous, a name used by two authors for different plants and where it is unclear which is being offered |
| cf. | compare to |
| cl. | clone |
| f. | forma (botanical form) |
| gx | grex |
| sensu lato | in the broadest sense |
| sp. | species |
| subsp. | subspecies |
| subvar. | subvarietas (botanical subvariety) |
| var. | varietas (botanical variety) |

**IT IS NOT WITHIN THE REMIT OF THIS BOOK TO CHECK that nurseries are applying the right names to the right plants or to ensure nurseries selling plants with Plant Breeders' Rights are licensed to do so.**

*Please, never use an old edition*

# PLANTS

WHATEVER PLANT YOU ARE LOOKING FOR, MAYBE AN OLD FAVOURITE OR A MORE UNUSUAL CULTIVAR, SEARCH HERE FOR A LIST OF THE SUPPLIERS THAT ARE CLOSEST TO YOU.

# How to Use the Plant Directory

## Nursery Codes

Look up the plant you require in the alphabetical Plant Directory. Against each plant you will find one or more four-letter codes, for example WCru, each code represents one nursery offering that plant. The first letter of each code indicates the main area of the country in which the nursery is situated. For this geographical key, refer to the **Nursery Codes and Symbols** on p.812.

Turn to the **Nursery Details by Code** starting on p.816 where, in alphabetical order of codes, you will find details of each nursery which offers the plant in question. If you wish to visit any nursery, you may find its location on one of the maps (following p.935). Please note, however, that not all nurseries, especially mail order only nurseries, choose to be shown on the maps. For a fuller explanation of how to use the nursery listings please turn to p.813. **Always check that the nursery you select has the plant in stock before you set out.**

## Plants with more than 28 Suppliers

In some cases, against the plant name you will see the term 'Widely available' instead of a nursery code. If we were to include every plant listed by all nurseries, the *RHS Plant Finder* would become unmanageably bulky. We therefore ask nurseries to restrict their entries to those plants that are not already well represented. As a result, if more than 28 nurseries offer any plant the Directory gives no nursery codes and the plant is listed instead as having 'Widely available'.

You should have little difficulty in locating these in local nurseries or garden centres. However, if you are unable to find such plants, we will be pleased to send a full list of all the nurseries that we have on file as stockists. To obtain a list, please see the Introduction on p.4.

## Finding Fruit, Vegetables and Herbs

You will need to search for these by their botanical names. Common names are cross-referenced to their botanical names in the Plant Directory.

## If you have Difficulty Finding your Plant

If you cannot immediately find the plant you seek, look through the various species of the genus. You may be using an incomplete name. The problem is most likely to arise in very large genera such as *Phlox* where there are a number of possible species, each with a large number of cultivars. A search through the whole genus may well bring success. Please note that, for space reasons, the following are not listed in the Plant Directory: annuals, orchids, except hardy terrestrial orchids; cacti, except hardy cacti.

## Cross-references

It may be that the plant name you seek is a synonym. Our intention is to list nursery codes only against the correct botanical name. Where you find a synonym you will be cross-referred to the correct name. Occasionally you may find that the correct botanical name to which you have been referred is not listed. This is because it was last listed in an earlier edition as explained below.

## Plants Last Listed in Earlier Editions

It may be that the plant you are seeking has no known suppliers and is thus not listed.

The loss of a plant name from the Directory may arise for a number of reasons – the supplier may have gone out of business, or may not have responded to our latest questionnaire and has therefore been removed from the book. Such plants may well be still available but we have no current knowledge of their whereabouts. Alternatively, some plants may have been misnamed by nurseries in previous editions, but are now appearing under their correct name.

To obtain a listing of plants last listed in earlier editions please see the Introduction on p.4.

*Please, never use an old edition*

# USING THE PLANT DIRECTORY

The main purpose of the Plant Directory is to help the reader correctly identify the plant they seek and find its stockist. Each nursery has a unique identification code which appears to the right of the plant name. Turn to **Nursery Details by Code** (p.816) for the address, opening times and other details of the nursery. The first letter of each nursery code denotes its geographical region. Turn to the map on p.812 to find your region code and then identify the nurseries in your area.

Another purpose of the Directory is to provide more information about the plant through the symbols and other information. For example, if it has an alternative names, is new to this edition or has received the RHS Award of Garden Merit.

## *Euonymus* (*Celastraceae*)

| | | |
|---|---|---|
| | B&L 12543 | EPla EWes |
| | B&SWJ 4457 | WPGP |
| | CC 4522 | CPLG |
| | ***alatus*** 🏆H4 | Widely available |
| | - B&SWJ 8794 | WCru |
| | - var. ***apterus*** | EPfP |
| | - Chicago Fire | see *E. alatus* 'Timber Creek' |
| | - 'Ciliodentatus' | see *E. alatus* 'Compactus' |
| § | - 'Compactus' 🏆H4 | Widely available |
| § | - 'Fire Ball' | EPfP |
| | - Little Moses = 'Odom' | MBlu |
| * | - 'Macrophyllus' | EPfP |
| | - 'Rudy Haag' | CPMA EPfP |
| | - 'Select' | see *E. alatus* 'Fire Ball' |
| | - 'Silver Cloud' **new** | EPfP |
| § | - 'Timber Creek' | CPMA EPfP MBlu MBri NLar |
| | ***americanus*** | EPfP GIBF MBlu NLar |
| | - 'Evergreen' **new** | EPfP |
| | - narrow-leaved | EPfP NLar |
| | ***atropurpureus*** | EPfP |
| | 'Benkomoki' **new** | MGos |
| | ***bungeanus*** | CMCN EPfP EPla NLar |
| | - 'Dart's Pride' | CPMA EPfP NLar |
| | - 'Fireflame' | EPfP NLar |
| * | - var. ***mongolicus*** | EPfP |
| | - 'Pendulus' | EPfP MBlu SIFN |
| | - var. ***semipersistens*** | CPMA EPla |
| | ***carnosus*** | EPfP NLar |
| | 'Copper Wire' | EMil SPoG |
| | ***cornutus*** var. ***quinquecornutus*** | CPMA EPfP LPan MBlu NBhm NLar SIFN SPoG WPGP WPat |
| | 'Den Haag' | EPfP MBri |
| | ***echinatus*** | EPfP EPla |
| | - BL&M 306 | SLon |
| | ***europaeus*** | Widely available |
| | - f. ***albus*** | CPMA CTho EPfP LTwo NLar |
| | - 'Atropurpureus' | CMCN CTho EPfP MBlu MBri NLar SIFN |
| | - 'Atrorubens' | CPMA |
| | - 'Aucubifolius' (v) | EPfP |
| * | - 'Aureus' | CNat |
| | - 'Brilliant' **new** | EPfP |
| * | - f. ***bulgaricus*** | EPfP |
| | - 'Chrysophyllus' | EPfP MBlu NLar |
| | - 'Howard' | EPfP |
| | - var. ***intermedius*** | ENot EPfP MAsh MBlu NLar |
| | - 'Miss Pinkie' | CEnd CMCN |
| | - 'Pumilis' **new** | EPfP |
| | - 'Red Cascade' 🏆H4 | Widely available |
| | - 'Scarlet Wonder' | CPMA EPfP MBri NLar |
| | - 'Thornhayes' | CTho EPfP |
| I | - 'Variegatus' **new** | EPfP |
| | ***farreri*** | see *E. nanus* |
| | ***fimbriatus*** | EPfP |
| | ***fortunei*** Blondy = 'Interbolwi'PBR (v) | Widely available |

*ABBREVIATIONS*
*To save space a dash indicates that the previous heading is repeated. If written out in full the name would be* Euonymus alatus *'Fire Ball'.*

*NEW*
*Plant new to this edition.*

*DESCRIPTIVE TERM*
*See p.19.*

*SYMBOLS TO THE LEFT OF THE NAME*
*Provides information about the name of the plant. See p.23 for the key.*

*SYMBOLS TO THE RIGHT OF THE NAME*
*Tells you more about the plant itself, e.g.* (v) *indicates that the plant is variegated,* (F) *= fruit. See p.23 for the key.*

*SELLING NAMES*
*See p.21.*

🏆H4
*This plant has received the RHS Award of Garden Merit. See p.18.*

*CROSS-REFERENCES*
*Directs you to the correct name of the plant and the nursery codes. See p.26.*

*NURSERY CODE*
*A unique code identifying each nursery. Turn to p.816 for details of the nurseries.*

***Widely available***
*Indicates that more than 28 Plant Finder nurseries supply the plant, and it may be available locally. See p.26.*

***PBR***
*Plant Breeders' Rights. See p.20.*

# SUPPLEMENTARY KEYS TO THE DIRECTORY

## COLLECTORS' REFERENCES

Abbreviations following a plant name, refer to the collector(s) of the plant. These abbreviations are expanded below, with a collector's name or expedition title. For a fuller explanation, see p.19.

A&JW A. & J. Watson
A&L Ala, A.; Lancaster, Roy
AB&S Archibald, James; Blanchard, John W; Salmon, M.
AC Clark, Alan J.
AC&H Apold, J.; Cox, Peter; Hutchison, Peter
AC&W Albury; Cheese, M.; Watson, J.M.
ACE AGS Expedition to China (1994)
ACL Leslie, Alan C.
AER Robinson, Allan
AGS/ES AGS Expedition to Sikkim (1983)
AGSJ AGS Expedition to Japan (1988)
AH Hoog, A.
Airth Airth, Murray
Akagi Akagi Botanical Garden
AL&JS Sharman, Joseph L.; Leslie, Alan C.
ARG Argent, G.C.G.
ARJA Ruksans, J. & Siesums, A.
B Blanchard, John
B L. Beer, Len
B&L Brickell, Christopher D.; Leslie, Alan C.
B&M & BM Brickell, Christopher D.; Mathew, Brian
B&S Bird P. & Salmon M.
B&SWJ Wynn-Jones, Bleddyn; Wynn-Jones, Susan
B&V Burras, K. & Vosa, C.G.
BB Bartholomew, B.
BC Chudziak, W.
BC&W Beckett; Cheese, M.; Watson, J.M.
Beavis Beavis, Derek S.
Berry Berry, P.
Berry & Brako Berry, P. & Brako, Lois
BKBlount Blount, B.K.
BL&M University of Bangor Expedition to NE Nepal
BM Mathew, Brian F.
BM&W Binns, David L.; Mason, M.; Wright, A.
BOA Boardman, P.
Breedlove Breedlove, D.
BR Rushbrooke, Ben
BS Smith, Basil
BSBE Bowles Scholarship Botanical Expedition (1963)
BSSS Crûg Expedition, Jordan (1991)
Bu Bubert, S.
Burtt Burtt, Brian L.
C Cole, Desmond T.
C&C Cox, P.A. & Cox, K.N.E.
C&Cu Cox, K.N.E. & Cubey, J.
C&H Cox, Peter; Hutchison, Peter
C&K Chamberlain & Knott
C&R Christian & Roderick
C&S Clark, Alan; Sinclair, Ian W.J.
C&V K.N.E. Cox & S. Vergera
C&W Cheese, M.; Watson, J.M.
CC Chadwell, Christopher
CC&H Chamberlain, David F.; Cox, Peter; Hutchison, P.
CC&McK Chadwell, Christopher; McKelvie, A.
CC&MR Chadwell, Christopher; Ramsay
CCH&H Chamberlain, D.F.; Cox, P.; Hutchison, P.; Hootman, S.
CCH&H Chamberlain, Cox, Hootman & Hutchison
CD&R Compton, J.; D'Arcy, J.; Rix, E.M.
CDB Brickell, Christopher D.
CDC Coode, Mark J.E.; Dockrill, Alexander
CDC&C Compton, D'Arcy, Christopher & Coke
CDPR Compton, D'Arcy, Pope & Rix
CE&H Christian, P.J.; Elliott; Hoog
CEE Chengdu Edinburgh Expedition China 1991
CGW Grey-Wilson, Christopher
CH Christian, P. & Hoog, A.
CH&M Cox, P.; Hutchison, P.; Maxwell-MacDonald, D.
CHP&W Kashmir Botanical Expedition
CL Lovell, Chris
CLD Chungtien, Lijiang & Dali Exped. China (1990)
CM&W Cheese M., Mitchel J. & Watson, J.

| | |
|---|---|
| CN&W | Clark; Neilson; Wilson |
| CNDS | Nelson, C. & Sayers D. |
| Cooper | Cooper, R.E. |
| Cox | Cox, Peter A. |
| CPC | Cobblewood Plant Collection |
| CPN | Compton, James |
| CSE | Cyclamen Society Expedition (1990) |
| CT | Teune, Carla |
| Dahl | Dahl, Sally |
| DBG | Denver Botanic Garden, Colorado |
| DC | Cheshire, David |
| DF | Fox, D. |
| DHTU | Hinkley, D., Turkey 2000 |
| DJH | Hinkley, Dan |
| DJHC | Hinkley China |
| DM | Millais, David |
| Doleshy | Doleshy, F.L. |
| DS&T | Drake, Sharman J.; Thompson |
| DWD | Rose, D. |
| DZ | Zummell, D. |
| ECN | Nelson, E. Charles |
| EDHCH | Hammond, Eric D. |
| EGM | Millais, T. |
| EKB | Balls, Edward K. |
| EM | East Malling Research Station |
| EMAK | Edinburgh Makalu Expedition (1991) |
| EMR | Rix, E.Martyn |
| EN | Needham, Edward F. |
| ENF | Fuller, E. Nigel |
| ETE | Edinburgh Taiwan Expedition (1993) |
| ETOT | Kirkham, T.S.; Flanagan, Mark |
| F | Forrest, G. |
| F&M | Fernandez & Mendoza, Mexico |
| F&W | Watson, J.; Flores, A. |
| Farrer | Farrer, Reginald |
| FK | Kinmonth, Fergus W. |
| FMB | Bailey, F.M. |
| G | Gardner, Martin F. |
| G&K | Gardner, Martin F.; Knees, Sabina G. |
| G&P | Gardner, Martin F.; Page, Christopher N. |
| GDJ | Dumont, Gerard |
| GG | Gusman, G. |
| GS | Sherriff, George |
| Green | Green, D. |
| Guitt | Guittoneau, G.G. |
| Guiz | Guizhou Expedition (1985) |
| GWJ | Goddard, Sally; Wynne-Jones, Bleddyn & Susan |
| G-W&P | Grey-Wilson, Christopher; Phillips |
| H | Huggins, Paul |
| H&B | Hilliard, Olive M.; Burtt, Brian L. |
| H&D | Howick, C.; Darby |
| H&M | Howick, Charles; McNamara, William A. |
| H&W | Hedge, Ian C.; Wendelbo, Per W. |
| Harry Smith | Smith, K.A.Harry |
| Hartside | Hartside Nursery |
| HCM | Heronswood Expedition to Chile (1998) |
| HECC | Hutchison, Evans, Cox, P., Cox, K. |
| HH&K | Hannay, S&S & Kingsbury, N |
| HLMS | Springate, L.S. |
| HM&S | Halliwell, B., Mason, D. & Smallcombe |
| HOA | Hoog, Anton |
| Hummel | Hummel, D. |
| HW&E | Wendelbo, Per; Hedge, I.; Ekberg, L. |
| HWEL | Hirst, J.Michael; Webster, D. |
| HWJ | Crûg Heronswood Joint Expedition |
| HWJCM | Crûg Heronswood Expedition |
| HWJK | Crûg Heronswood Expedition, East Nepal (2002) |
| HZ | Zetterlund, Henrik |
| ICE | Instituto de Investigaciónes Ecológicas Chiloé & RBGE |
| IDS | International Dendrological Society |
| ISI | Int. Succulent Introductions |
| J&JA | Archibald, James; Archibald, Jennifer |
| J. Jurasek | Jurasek, J. |
| JCA | Archibald, James |
| JE | Jack Elliott |
| JJ | Jackson, J. |
| JJ&JH | Halda, J.; Halda, J. |
| JJH | Halda, Joseph J. |
| JLS | Sharman, J.L. |
| JM-MK | Mahr, J.; Kammerlander, M. |
| JMT | Mann Taylor, J. |
| JN | Nielson, Jens |
| JR | Russell, J. |
| JRM | Marr, John |
| JW | Watson, J.M. |
| K | Kirkpatrick, George |
| K&LG | Gillanders, Kenneth; Gillanders, L. |
| K&Mc | Kirkpatrick, George; McBeath, Ronald J.D. |
| K&P | Josef Kopec, Milan Prasil |
| K&T | Kurashige, Y.; Tsukie, S. |
| KC | Cox, Kenneth |
| KEKE | Kew/Edinburgh Kanchenjunga Expedition (1989) |
| KGB | Kunming/Gothenburg Botanical Expedition (1993) |
| KM | Marsh, K. |
| KR | Rushforth, K.D. |
| KRW | Wooster, K.R. (distributed after his death by Kath Dryden) |
| KW | Kingdon-Ward, F. |
| L | Lancaster, C. Roy |
| L&S | Ludlow, Francis; Sherriff, George |
| LA | Long Ashton Research Station clonal selection scheme |
| LB | Bird P., Salmon, M. |
| LEG | Lesotho Edinburgh/Gothenburg Expedition (1997) |
| Lismore | Lismore Nursery, Breeder's Number |
| LM&S | Leslie, Mattern & Sharman |
| LP | Palmer, W.J.L. |

| | |
|---|---|
| LS&E | Ludlow, Frank; Sherriff, George; Elliott, E. E. |
| LS&H | Ludlow, Frank; Sherriff, George; Hicks, J. H. |
| LS&T | Ludlow, Frank; Sherriff, George; Taylor, George |
| M&PS | Mike & Polly Stone |
| M&T | Mathew; Tomlinson |
| Mac&W | McPhail & Watson |
| McB | McBeath, R.J.D. |
| McLaren | McLaren, H.D. |
| MDM | Myers, Michael D. |
| MECC | Scottish Rock Garden Club, Nepal (1997) |
| MESE | Alpine Garden Society Expedition, Greece 1999 |
| MF | Foster, Maurice |
| MH | Heasman, Matthew T. |
| MK | Kammerlander, Michael |
| MP | Pavelka, Mojmir |
| MPF | Frankis, M.P. |
| MS | Salmon, M. |
| MS&CL | Salmon, M.; Lovell, C. |
| MSF | Fillan, M.S. |
| NJM | Macer, N.J. |
| NNS | Ratko, Ron |
| NS | Turland, Nick |
| NVFDE | Northern Vietnam First Darwin Expedition |
| Og | Ogisu, Mikinori |
| OS | Sonderhousen, O. |
| P. Bon | Bonavia, P. |
| P&C | Paterson, David S.; Clarke, Sidney |
| P&W | Polastri; Watson, J. M. |
| PB | Bird, Peter |
| PC&H | Pattison, G.; Catt, P.; Hickson, M. |
| PD | Davis, Peter H. |
| PF | Furse, Paul |
| PJC | Christian, Paul J. |
| PJC&AH | P.J. Christian & A. Hogg |
| PNMK | Nicholls, P.; Kammerlander, M. |
| Polunin | Polunin, Oleg |
| Pras | Prasil, M. |
| PS&W | Polunin, Oleg; Sykes, William; Williams, John |
| PW | Wharton, Peter |
| R | Rock, J.F.C. |
| RB | Brown, R. |
| RBS | Brown, Ray, Sakharin Island |
| RCB AM | Brown, Robert, Expedition to Armenia |
| RCB/Arg | Brown, Robert, Argentina, (2002) |
| RCB E | Brown, Robert, Expedition to Spain (Andalucia) |
| RCB/Eq | Brown, Robert, Ecuador, (1988) |
| RCB RA | Brown, Robert |
| RCB RL | Brown, Robert, Expedition to Lebanon |
| RCB/TQ | Brown, Robert, Turkey (2001) |
| RH | Hancock, R. |
| RKMP | Ruksans, J., Krumins, A., Kitts, M., Paivel, A. |
| RM | Ruksans, J. & Kitts, M. |
| RMRP | Rocky Mountain Rare Plants, Denver, Colorado |
| RS | Suckow, Reinhart |
| RSC | Richard Somer Cocks |
| RV | Richard Valder |
| RWJ | Crûg Farm-Rickards Ferns Expedition to Taiwan (2003) |
| S&B | Blanchard, J.W.; Salmon, M. |
| S&F | Salmon, M. & Fillan, M. |
| S&L | Sinclair, Ian W.J.; Long, David G. |
| S&SH | Sheilah and Spencer Hannay |
| Sandham | Sandham, John |
| SB&L | Salmon, Bird and Lovell |
| SBEC | Sino-British Expedition to Cangshan |
| SBEL | Sino-British Lijiang Expedition |
| SBQE | Sino-British Expedition to Quinghai |
| Sch | Schilling, Anthony D. |
| SD | Sashal Dayal |
| SDR | Rankin, Stella; Rankin, David |
| SEH | Hootman, Steve |
| SEP | Swedish Expedition to Pakistan |
| SF | Forde, P. |
| SG | Salmon, M. & Guy, P. |
| SH | Hannay, Spencer |
| Sich | Simmons, Erskine, Howick & Mcnamara |
| SL | Sinclair, I. & Long, D. |
| SLIZE | Swedish-Latvian-Iranian Zagros Expedition to Iran (May 1988) |
| SOJA | Kew / Quarryhill Expedition to Southern Japan |
| SS&W | Stainton, J.D.Adam; Sykes, William; Williams, John |
| SSNY | Sino-Scottish Expedition to NW Yunnan (1992) |
| T | Taylor, Nigel P. |
| T&K | Taylor, Nigel P.; Knees, Sabina |
| TH | Hudson, T. |
| TS&BC | Smythe, T and Cherry, B |
| TSS | Spring Smyth, T.L.M. |
| TW | Tony Weston |
| USDAPI | US Department of Agriculture Plant Index Number |
| USDAPQ | US Dept. of Agriculture Plant Quarantine Number |
| USNA | United States National Arboretum |
| VHH | Vernon H. Heywood |
| W | Wilson, Ernest H. |
| WM | McLewin, William |
| Woods | Woods, Patrick J.B. |
| Wr | Wraight, David & Anke |
| Yu | Yu, Tse-tsun |

# NOTES ON NOMENCLATURE AND IDENTIFICATION

These notes refer to plants in the Plant Directory that are marked with a 'N' to the left of the name. 'Bean Supplement' refers to W.J. Bean *Trees & Shrubs Hardy in the British Isles* (Supplement to the 8th edition) edited by D L Clarke 1988.

***Acer davidii*** **'Ernest Wilson' and *A. davidii* 'George Forrest'**
These cultivars should be grafted in order to retain the characteristics of the original clones. However, many plants offered under these names are seed-raised.

***Acer palmatum*** **'Sango-kaku'/ 'Senkaki'**
Two or more clones are offered under these names. *A. palmatum* 'Eddisbury' is similar with brighter coral stems.

***Achillea ptarmica*** **The Pearl Group/ *A. ptarmica* (The Pearl Group) 'Boule de Neige' / *A. ptarmica* (The Pearl Group) 'The Pearl'**
In the recent trial of achilleas at Wisley, only one of the several stocks submitted as 'The Pearl' matched the original appearance of this plant according to Graham Stuart Thomas, this being from Wisley's own stock. At rather less than 60cm (2ft), this needed little support, being the shortest of the plants bearing this name, with slightly grey, not glossy dark green, leaves and a non-invasive habit. This has been designated as the type for this cultivar and only this clone should bear the cultivar name 'The Pearl'. The Pearl Group covers all other double-flowered clones of this species, including seed-raised plants which are markedly inferior, sometimes scarcely double, often invasive and usually needing careful staking. It has been claimed that 'The Pearl' was a re-naming of Lemoine's 'Boule de Neige' but not all authorities agree: all plants submitted to the Wisley trial as 'Boule de Neige' were different from each other, not the same clone as Wisley's 'The Pearl' and referrable to The Pearl Group.

***Anemone magellanica***
According to *The European Garden Flora*, this is a variant of the very variable *A. multifida*.

***Anemone nemorosa*** **'Alba Plena'**
This name is used for several double white forms including *A. nemorosa* 'Flore Pleno' and *A. nemorosa* 'Vestal'.

***Artemisia ludoviciana*** **var. *latiloba* / *A. ludoviciana* 'Valerie Finnis'**
Leaves of the former are glabrous at maturity, those of the latter are not.

***Artemisia stelleriana*** **'Boughton Silver'**
This was thought to be the first validly published name for this plant, 'Silver Brocade' having been published earlier but invalidly in an undated publication. However, an earlier valid publication for the cultivar name 'Mori' has subsequently been found for the same plant. A proposal to conserve 'Boughton Silver' has been tabled because of its more widespread use.

***Aster amellus*** Violet Queen
It is probable that more than one cultivar is sold under this name.

***Aster dumosus***
Many of the asters listed under *A. novi-belgii* contain varying amounts of *A. dumosus* blood in their parentage. It is not possible to allocate these to one species or the other and they are therefore listed under *A. novi-belgii*.

***Aster* × *frikartii*** **'Mönch'**
The true plant is very rare in British gardens. Most plants are another form of *A.* × *frikartii*, usually 'Wunder von Stäfa'.

***Aster novi-belgii***
See note under *A. dumosus*. *A. laevis* is also involved in the parentage of most cultivars.

***Berberis buxifolia*** **'Nana'/ 'Pygmaea'**
See explanation in Bean Supplement.

***Betula utilis*** **var. *jacquemontii***
Plants are often the clones *B. utilis* var. *jacquemontii* 'Inverleith' or *B. utilis* var. *jacquemontii* 'Doorenbos'

***Brachyscome***
Originally published as *Brachyscome* by Cassini who later revised his spelling to *Brachycome*. The original spelling has been internationally adopted.

***Calamagrostis* × *acutiflora*** **'Karl Foerster'**
C. × *acutiflora* 'Stricta' differs in being 15cm taller, 10-15 days earlier flowering with a less fluffy inflorescence.

***Calceolaria integrifolia sensu lato***
Christine Ehrhart (*Systematic Botany*. (2005. 30(2):383-411) has demonstrated that this is a complex involving nine distinct species (*C. andina*, *C. angustifolia*, *C. auriculata*, *C. georgiana*, *C. integrifolia* sensu stricto, *C. rubiginosa*, *C. talcana*, *C. verbascifolia* and *C. viscosissima*). However, it is not yet clear to which species plants in cultivation belong or whether they are hybrids.

***Caltha polypetala***
This name is often applied to a large-flowered variant of C. *palustris*. The true species has more (7-10) petals.

***Camassia leichtlinii*** **'Alba'**
The true cultivar has blueish-white, not cream flowers.

***Camassia leichtlinii* 'Plena'**
This has starry, transparent green-white flowers; creamy-white 'Semiplena' is sometimes offered under this name.

***Campanula lactiflora* 'Alba'**
This refers to the pure white-flowered clone, not to blueish- or greyish-white flowered plants, nor to seed-raised plants.

***Carex morrowii* 'Variegata'**
*C. oshimensis* 'Evergold' is sometimes sold under this name.

***Carya illinoinensis***
The correct spelling of this name is discussed in *Baileya*, **10**(1) (1962).

***Cassinia retorta***
Now included within *C. leptophylla*. A valid infra-specific epithet has yet to be published.

***Ceanothus* 'Italian Skies'**
Many plants under this name are not true to name.

***Chamaecyparis lawsoniana* 'Columnaris Glauca'**
Plants under this name might be *C. lawsoniana* 'Columnaris' or a new invalidly named cultivar.

***Chrysanthemum* 'Anastasia Variegated'**
Despite its name, this seems to be derived from 'Mei-kyo', not 'Anastasia'.

***Clematis chrysocoma***
The true *C. chrysocoma* is a non-climbing erect plant with dense yellow down on the young growth, still uncommon in cultivation.

***Clematis montana***
This name should be used for the typical white-flowered variety only. Pink-flowered variants are referable to *C. montana* var. *rubens*.

***Clematis* 'Victoria'**
Raised by Cripps (1867). There is also a Latvian cultivar of this name with petals with a central white bar in the collection of Janis Ruplēns which is probably, though not certainly, of his own raising.

***Colchicum* 'Autumn Queen'**
Entries here might refer to the slightly different *C.* 'Prinses Astrid'.

***Cornus* 'Norman Hadden'**
See note in Bean Supplement, p.184.

***Cotoneaster dammeri***
Plants sold under this name are usually *C. dammeri* 'Major'.

***Cotoneaster frigidus* 'Cornubia'**
According to Hylmø this cultivar, like all other variants of this species, is fully deciduous. Several evergreen cotoneasters are also grown under this name; most are clones of *C.* × *watereri* or *C. salicifolius*.

***Crataegus coccinea***
*C. intricata*, *C. pedicellata* and *C. biltmoreana* are occasionally supplied under this name.

***Crocus cartwrightianus* 'Albus'**
The plant offered is the true cultivar and not *C. hadriaticus*.

***Dianthus* fringed pink**
*D.* 'Old Fringed Pink' and *D.* 'Old Fringed White' are also sometimes sold under this name.

***Dianthus* 'Musgrave's Pink' (p)**
This is the registered name of this white-flowered cultivar.

***Epilobium glabellum* misapplied**
Plants under this name are not *E. glabellum* but are close to *E. wilsonii* Petrie or perhaps a hybrid of it.

***Erodium glandulosum***
Plants under this name are often hybrids.

***Erodium guttatum***
Doubtfully in commerce; plants under this name are usually *E. heteradenum*, *E. cheilanthifolium* or hybrids.

***Fagus sylvatica* Cuprea Group/Atropurpurea Group**
It is desirable to provide a name, Cuprea Group, for less richly coloured forms, used in historic landscapes before the purple clones appeared.

***Fagus sylvatica* 'Pendula'**
This name refers to the Knap Hill clone, the most common weeping form in English gardens. Other clones occur, particularly in Cornwall and Ireland.

***Fuchsia loxensis***
For a comparison of the true species with the hybrids 'Speciosa' and 'Loxensis' commonly grown under this name, see Boullemier's Check List (2nd ed.) p.268.

***Geum* 'Borisii'**
This name refers to cultivars of *G. coccineum* Sibthorp & Smith, especially *G.* 'Werner Arends' and not to *G.* × *borisii* Kelleper.

***Halimium alyssoides* and *H. halimifolium***
Plants under these names are sometimes *H.* × *pauanum* or *H.* × *santae*.

***Hebe* 'Carl Teschner'**
See note in Bean Supplement, p.264.

***Hebe glaucophylla***
A green reversion of the hybrid *H.* 'Glaucophylla Variegata' is often sold under this name.

***Hedera helix* 'Caenwoodiana' / 'Pedata'**
Some authorities consider these to be distinct cultivars while others think them different morphological forms of the same unstable clone.

***Hedera helix* 'Oro di Bogliasco'**
Priority between this name and 'Jubiläum Goldherz' and 'Goldheart' has yet to be finally resolved.

***Helleborus* × *hybridus* / *H. orientalis* misapplied**
The name *H.* × *hybridus* for acaulescent hellebore hybrids does not seem to follow the *International Code of Botanical Nomenclature* Article H.3.2 requiring one of the parent species

to be designated and does not seem to have been typified, contrary to Article 7 of the Code. However, the illustration accompanying the original description in Vilmorin's *Blumengärtnerei* 3(1): 27 (1894) shows that one parent of the cross must have been *H. guttatus*, now treated as part of *H. orientalis*. Taking this illustration as the type for this hybrid species makes it possible to retain *H.* × *hybridus* formally as a hybrid binomial (rather than *H. hybridus* as in a previous edition), as the Code's requirement to distinguish one parent is now met.

***Hemerocallis fulva*** **'Kwanso', 'Kwanso Variegata', 'Flore Pleno' and 'Green Kwanso'**

For a discussion of these plants see *The Plantsman*, 7(2).

***Heuchera villosa*** **'Palace Purple'**

This cultivar name refers only to plants with deep purple-red foliage. Seed-raised plants of inferior colouring should not be offered under this name.

***Hosta montana***

This name refers only to plants long grown in Europe, which differ from *H. elata*.

***Hydrangea macrophylla*** **Teller Series**

This is used both as a descriptive common name for Lacecap hydrangeas (German *teller* = plate, referring to the more or less flat inflorescence) and for the series of hybrids raised by Wädenswil in Switzerland bearing German names of birds. It is not generally possible to link a hydrangea described by the series name plus a colour description (e.g. Teller Blau, Teller Rosa, Teller Rot) to a single cultivar.

***Hypericum fragile***

The true *H. fragile* is probably not available from British nurseries.

***Hypericum*** **'Gemo'**

Either a selection of *H. prolificum* or *H. prolificum* × *H. densiflorum*.

***Ilex*** × ***altaclerensis***

The argument for this spelling is given by Susyn Andrews, *The Plantsman*, 5(2) and is not superseded by the more recent comments in the Supplement to Bean's Trees and Shrubs.

***Iris***

Apart from those noted below, cultivar names marked 'N' are not registered. The majority of those marked 'I' have been previously used for a different cultivar.

***Iris histrioides*** **'Major'**

Two clones are offered under this name, the true one pale blue with darker spotting on the falls, the incorrect one violet-blue with almost horizontal falls.

***Juniperus*** × ***media***

This name is illegitimate if applied to hybrids of *J. chinensis* × *J. sabina*, having been previously used for a different hybrid (P.A. Schmidt, *IDS Yearbook 1993*, 47-48). Because of its importance to gardeners, a proposal to conserve its present use was tabled but subsequently rejected.

***Lavandula spica***

This name is classed as a name to be rejected (*nomen rejiciendum*) by the *International Code of Botanical Nomenclature*.

***Lavatera olbia*** **and** ***L. thuringiaca***

Although *L. olbia* is usually shrubby and *L. thuringiaca* usually herbaceous, both species are very variable. Cultivars formally ascribed to one species or the other have been shown to be hybrids and are referable to the recently-named hybrid species *L.* × *clementii*.

***Lobelia*** **'Russian Princess'**

This name, originally for a pink-flowered, green-leaved cultivar, is now generally applied to a purple-flowered, dark-leaved cultivar that seems to lack a valid name.

***Lonicera periclymenum*** **'Serotina'**

See note in Bean Supplement, p.315.

***Lonicera sempervirens*** **f.** ***sulphurea***

Plants in the British Isles usually a yellow-flowered form of *L. periclymenum*.

***Malus domestica*** **'Dummellor's Seedling'**

The phonetic spelling 'Dumelow's Seedling' contravenes the ICBN ruling on orthography, i.e. that, except for intentional latinizations, commemorative names should be based on the original spelling of the person's name (Article 60.11). The spelling adopted here is that used on the gravestone of the raiser in Leicestershire.

***Meconopsis*** **Fertile Blue Group**

This Group comprises seed-raised and intrinsically perennial tall blue poppies of as yet indeterminate origin. The only cultivars so far established are 'Lingholm' (synonyms 'Blue Ice' and 'Correnie') and 'Kingsbarns'.

***Meconopsis napaulensis*** **misapplied**

In his revision of the evergreen monocarpic species, Dr C. Grey-Wilson has established that *M. napaulensis* DC., a dwarfish yellow-flowered species not usually more than 1.1m tall and endemic to C Nepal, is not currently in cultivation. The well-known plants of gardens which pass for *M. napaulensis* are hybrids, for the present to be known as *M. napaulensis* misapplied. The parents of the hybrids are *M. staintonii* (from W Nepal) and *M. paniculata* (a yellow-flowered species with a purple stigma) or *M. staintonii* and *M. regia* or a complex mixture of all three species. *M. staintonii*, newly described by C. Grey-Wilson (*Bot. Mag.* (2006) 23(2):176-209), is a tall (to 2.5m), robust species with red or pink flowers and a dark green stigma, near in appearance to *M. napaulensis* of gardens, but less so to true *M. napaulensis*. As *M. staintonii*, like its near relatives, readily hybridises in cultivation, it is rarely seen in an unadulterated form.

***Melissa officinalis* 'Variegata'**
The true cultivar of this name had leaves striped with white.

***Nemesia caerulea* 'Joan Wilder'**
The lavender-blue clone 'Joan Wilder', described and illustrated in *The Hardy Plant,* **14(1)**, 11-14, does not come true from seed; it may only be propagated from cuttings.

***Osmanthus heterophyllus* 'Gulftide'**
Probably correctly *O.* × *fortunei* 'Gulftide'.

***Papaver orientale* agg.**
Plants listed as *P. orientale* agg. (i.e. aggregate) or as one of its cultivars may be *P. orientale* L., *P. pseudo-orientale* or *P. bracteatum* or hybrids between them.

***Pelargonium* 'Lass o' Gowrie'**
The American plant of this name has pointed, not rounded leaf lobes.

***Pelargonium quercifolium***
Plants under this name are mainly hybrids. The true species has pointed, not rounded leaf lobes.

***Penstemon* 'Taoensis'**
This name for a small-flowered cultivar or hybrid of *P. isophyllus* originally appeared as 'Taoense' but must be corrected to agree in gender with *Penstemon* (masculine). Presumably an invalid name (published in Latin form since 1958), it is not synonymous with *P. crandallii* subsp. *glabrescens* var. *taosensis*.

***Pernettya***
Botanists now consider that *Pernettya* (fruit a berry) is not separable from *Gaultheria* (fruit a capsule) because in some species the fruit is intermediate between a berry and a capsule. For a fuller explanation see D. Middleton, *The Plantsman*, **12(3)**.

***Pinus ayacahuite***
*P. ayacahuite* var. *veitchii* (syn. *P. veitchii)* is occasionally sold under this name.

***Pinus nigra* 'Cebennensis Nana'**
A doubtful name, possibly a synonym for *P. nigra* 'Nana'.

***Polemonium archibaldiae***
Usually sterile with lavender-blue flowers. A self-fertile white-flowered plant is sometimes sold under this name.

***Prunus laurocerasus* 'Castlewellan'**
We are grateful to Dr Charles Nelson for informing us that the name 'Marbled White' is not valid because although it has priority of publication it does not have the approval of the originator who asked for it to be called 'Castlewellan'.

***Prunus serrulata* var. *pubescens***
See note in Bean Supplement, p.398.

***Prunus* × *subhirtella* 'Rosea'**
Might be *P. pendula* var. *ascendens* 'Rosea', *P. pendula* 'Pendula Rosea', or *P.* × *subhirtella* 'Autumnalis Rosea'.

***Rheum* × *cultorum***
The name *R.* × *cultorum* was published without adequate description and must be abandoned in favour of the validly published *R.* × *hybridum*.

***Rhododendron* (azaleas)**
All names marked 'N', except for the following, refer to more than one cultivar.

***Rhododendron* 'Hinomayo'**
This name is based on a faulty transliteration (should be 'Hinamoyo') but the spelling 'Hinomayo' is retained in the interests of stability.

***Rhus typhina***
Linnaeus published both *R. typhina* and *R. hirta* as names for the same species. Though *R. hirta* has priority, it has been proposed that the name *R. typhina* should be conserved.

***Rosa gentiliana***
Plants under this name are usually the cultivar 'Polyantha Grandiflora' but might otherwise be *R. multiflora* 'Wilsonii', *R. multiflora* var. *cathayensis, R. henryi* or another hybrid.

***Rosa* 'Gros Choux de Hollande' hort. (Bb)**
It is doubtful if this name is correctly applied.

***Rosa* 'Jacques Cartier' hort.**
For a discussion on the correct identity of this rose see *Heritage Rose Foundation News*, Oct. 1989 & Jan. 1990.

***Rosa* 'Kazanlik'**
For a discussion on the correct identity of this rose see *Heritage Roses,* Nov. 1991.

***Rosa* Sweetheart**
This is not the same as the Sweetheart Rose, a common name for *R.* 'Cécile Brünner'.

***Rosa wichurana***
This is the correct spelling according to the ICBN 1994 Article 60.11 (which enforces Recommendation 60C.1c) and not *wichuraiana* for this rose commemorating Max Wichura.

***Rubus fruticosus* L. agg.**
Though some cultivated blackberries do belong to *Rubus fruticosus* L. *sensu stricto,* others are more correctly ascribed to other species of *Rubus* section *Glandulosus* (including *R. armeniacus, R. laciniatus* or *R. ulmifolius)* or are hybrids of species within this section. Because it is almost impossible to ascribe every cultivar to a single species or hybrid, they are listed under *R. fruticosus* L. agg. (i.e. aggregate) for convenience.

***Salvia microphylla* var. *neurepia***
The type of this variety is referable to the typical variety, *S. microphylla* var. *microphylla*.

***Salvia officinalis* 'Aurea'**
*S. officinalis* var. *aurea* is a rare variant of the common sage with leaves entirely of gold. It is represented in cultivation by the cultivar 'Kew Gold'. The plant usually offered as *S. officinalis* 'Aurea' is the gold variegated sage *S. officinalis* 'Icterina'.

***Sambucus nigra* 'Aurea'**
Plants under this name are usually not *S. nigra.*

***Sedum nevii***
The true species is not in cultivation. Plants under this name are usually either *S. glaucophyllum* or occasionally *S. beyrichianum.*

***Skimmia japonica* 'Foremanii'**
The true cultivar, which belongs to *S. japonica* Rogersii Group, is believed to be lost to cultivation. Plants offered under this name are usually *S. japonica* 'Veitchii'.

***Spiraea japonica* 'Shirobana'**
Shirobana-shimotsuke is the common name for *S. japonica* var. *albiflora.* Shirobana means white-flowered and does not apply to the two-coloured form.

***Staphylea holocarpa* var. *rosea***
This botanical variety has woolly leaves. The cultivar 'Rosea', with which it is often confused, does not.

***Stewartia ovata* var. *grandiflora.***
Most, possibly all, plants available from British nurseries under this name are not true to name but are derived from the improved Nymans form.

***Thymus* Coccineus Group**
Thymes under this have dark crimson (RHS 78A) flowers whereas those of 'Alan Bloom' are purplish-pink (RHS 78C).

***Thymus serpyllum* cultivars**
Most cultivars are probably correctly cultivars of *T. polytrichus* or hybrids though they will remain listed under *T. serpyllum* pending further research.

***Thymus* 'Silver Posie'**
The cultivar name 'Silver Posie' is applied to several different plants, not all of them *T. vulgaris.*

***Tricyrtis* Hototogisu**
This is the common name applied generally to all Japanese *Tricyrtis* and specifically to *T. hirta.*

***Tricyrtis macropoda***
This name has been used for at least five different species.

***Uncinia rubra***
This name is also misapplied to *U. egmontiana* and *U. uncinata.*

***Verbena***
Entries marked (G) are considered by some botanists to belong to a separate genus, *Glandularia.*

***Verbena* 'Kemerton'**
Origin unknown, not from Kemerton.

***Viburnum opulus* 'Fructu Luteo'**
See note below.

***Viburnum opulus* 'Xanthocarpum'**
Some entries under this name might be the less compact *V. opulus* 'Fructu Luteo'.

***Viburnum plicatum***
Entries may include the 'snowball' form, *V. plicatum* f. *plicatum* (syn. *V. plicatum* 'Sterile'), as well as the 'lacecap' form, *V. plicatum* f. *tomentosum.*

***Viola labradorica***
See Note in *The Garden*, **110**(2): 96.

***Wisteria floribunda*** 'Violacea Plena' and *W. floribunda* 'Yae-kokuryū'
We are grateful to Yoko Otsuki, who has established through Engei Kyokai (the Horticultural Society of Japan) that there are two different double selections of *Wisteria floribunda.* 'Violacea Plena' has double lavender/lilac flowers, while 'Yae-kokuryū' has more ragged and tightly double flowers with purple/indigo centres. Each is distinctive but it is probable that both are confused in the British nursery trade. 'Yae-fuji' might be an earlier name for 'Violacea Plena' or a Group name covering a range of doubles but, as *fuji* is the Japanese common name for the species, it would not be a valid name under ICNCP.

# Classification of Genera

Genera including a large number of species, or with many cultivars, are often subdivided into informal horticultural classifications, or formal cultivar groups in the case of *Clematis* and *Tulipa*. The breeding of new cultivars is sometimes limited to hybrids between closely-related species, thus for *Saxifraga* and *Primula*, the cultivars are allocated to the sections given in the infrageneric treatments cited. Please turn to p.19 for a fuller explanation.

## Actinidia

(s-p) Self-pollinating

## Begonia

(C) Cane-like
(R) Rex Cultorum
(S) Semperflorens Cultorum
(T) × *tuberhybrida* (Tuberous)

## Chrysanthemum

(By the National Chrysanthemum Society)
(1) Indoor Large (Exhibition)
(2) Indoor Medium (Exhibition)
(3a) Indoor Incurved: Large-flowered
(3b) Indoor Incurved: Medium-flowered
(3c) Indoor Incurved: Small-flowered
(4a) Indoor Reflexed: Large-flowered
(4b) Indoor Reflexed: Medium-flowered
(4c) Indoor Reflexed: Small-flowered
(5a) Indoor Intermediate: Large-flowered
(5b) Indoor Intermediate: Medium-flowered
(5c) Indoor Intermediate: Small-flowered
(6a) Indoor Anemone: Large-flowered
(6b) Indoor Anemone: Medium-flowered
(6c) Indoor Anemone: Small-flowered
(7a) Indoor Single: Large-flowered
(7b) Indoor Single: Medium-flowered
(7c) Indoor Single: Small-flowered
(8a) Indoor True Pompon
(8b) Indoor Semi-pompon
(9a) Indoor Spray: Anemone
(9b) Indoor Spray: Pompon
(9c) Indoor Spray: Reflexed
(9d) Indoor Spray: Single
(9e) Indoor Spray: Intermediate
(9f) Indoor Spray: Spider, Quill, Spoon or Any Other Type
(10a) Indoor, Spider
(10b) Indoor, Quill
(10c) Indoor, Spoon
(11) Any Other Indoor Type
(12a) Indoor, Charm
(12b) Indoor, Cascade
(13a) October-flowering Incurved: Large-flowered
(13b) October-flowering Incurved: Medium-flowered
(13c) October-flowering Incurved: Small-flowered
(14a) October-flowering Reflexed: Large-flowered
(14b) October-flowering Reflexed: Medium-flowered
(14c) October-flowering Reflexed: Small-flowered
(15a) October-flowering Intermediate: Large-flowered
(15b) October-flowering Intermediate: Medium-flowered
(15c) October-flowered Intermediate: Small-flowered
(16) October-flowering Large
(17a) October-flowering Single: Large-flowered
(17b) October-flowering Single: Medium-flowered
(17c) October-flowering Single: Small-flowered
(18a) October-flowering Pompon: True Pompon
(18b) October-flowering Pompon: Semi-pompon
(19a) October-flowering Spray: Anemone
(19b) October-flowering Spray: Pompon
(19c) October-flowering Spray: Reflexed
(19d) October-flowering Spray: Single
(19e) October-flowering Spray: Intermediate
(19f) October-flowering Spray: Spider, Quill, Spoon or Any Other Type
(20) Any Other October-flowering Type
(21a) Korean: Anemone
(21b) Korean: Pompon
(21c) Korean: Reflexed
(21d) Korean: Single
(21e) Korean: Intermediate
(21f) Korean: Spider, Quill, Spoon, or any other type
(22a) Charm: Anemone
(22b) Charm: Pompon
(22c) Charm: Reflexed
(22d) Charm: Single
(22e) Charm: Intermediate
(22f) Charm: Spider, Quill, Spoon or Any Other Type
(23a) Early-flowering Outdoor Incurved: Large-flowered

| | |
|---|---|
| (23b) | Early-flowering Outdoor Incurved: Medium-flowered |
| (23c) | Early-flowering Outdoor Incurved: Small-flowered |
| (24a) | Early-flowering Outdoor Reflexed: Large-flowered |
| (24b) | Early-flowering Outdoor Reflexed: Medium-flowered |
| (24c) | Early-flowering Outdoor Reflexed: Small-flowered |
| (25a) | Early-flowering Outdoor Intermediate: Large-flowered |
| (25b) | Early-flowering Outdoor Intermediate: Medium-flowered |
| (25c) | Early-flowering Outdoor Intermediate: Small-flowered |
| (26a) | Early-flowering Outdoor Anemone: Large-flowered |
| (26b) | Early-flowering Outdoor Anemone: Medium-flowered |
| (27a) | Early-flowering Outdoor Single: Large-flowered |
| (27b) | Early-flowering Outdoor Single: Medium-flowered |
| (28a) | Early-flowering Outdoor Pompon: True Pompon |
| (28b) | Early-flowering Outdoor Pompon: Semi-pompon |
| (29a) | Early-flowering Outdoor Spray: Anemone |
| (29b) | Early-flowering Outdoor Spray: Pompon |
| (29c) | Early-flowering Outdoor Spray: Reflexed |
| (29d) | Early-flowering Outdoor Spray: Single |
| (29e) | Early-flowering Outdoor Spray: Intermediate |
| (29f) | Early-flowering Outdoor Spray: Spider, Quill, Spoon or Any Other Type |
| (30) | Any Other Early-flowering Outdoor Type |

## Clematis

(Cultivar Groups as per Matthews, V. (2002) *The International Clematis Register & Checklist 2002*, RHS, London.)

| | |
|---|---|
| (A) | Atragene Group |
| (Ar) | Armandii Group |
| (C) | Cirrhosa Group |
| (EL) | Early Large-flowered Group |
| (F) | Flammula Group |
| (Fo) | Forsteri Group |
| (H) | Heracleifolia Group |
| (I) | Integrifolia Group |
| (LL) | Late Large-flowered Group |
| (M) | Montana Group |
| (T) | Texensis Group |
| (Ta) | Tangutica Group |
| (V) | Viorna Group |
| (Vb) | Vitalba Group |
| (Vt) | Viticella Group |

## Dahlia

(By the National Dahlia Society with corresponding numerical classification according to the RHS's International Register)

| | |
|---|---|
| (Sin) | 1 Single |
| (Anem) | 2 Anemone-flowered |
| (Col) | 3 Collerette |
| (WL) | 4 Waterlily (unassigned) |
| (LWL) | 4B Waterlily, Large |
| (MWL) | 4C Waterlily, Medium |
| (SWL) | 4D Waterlily, Small |
| (MinWL) | 4E Waterlily, Miniature |
| (D) | 5 Decorative (unassigned) |
| (GD) | 5A Decorative, Giant |
| (LD) | 5B Decorative, Large |
| (MD) | 5C Decorative, Medium |
| (SD) | 5D Decorative, Small |
| (MinD) | 5E Decorative, Miniature |
| (SBa) | 6A Small Ball |
| (MinBa) | 6B Miniature Ball |
| (Pom) | 7 Pompon |
| (C) | 8 Cactus (unassigned) |
| (GC) | 8A Cactus, Giant |
| (LC) | 8B Cactus, Large |
| (MC) | 8C Cactus, Medium |
| (SC) | 8D Cactus, Small |
| (MinC) | 8E Cactus, Miniature |
| (S-c) | 9 Semi-cactus (unassigned) |
| (GS-c) | 9A Semi-cactus, Giant |
| (LS-c) | 9B Semi-cactus, Large |
| (MS-c) | 9C Semi-cactus, Medium |
| (SS-c) | 9D Semi-cactus, Small |
| (MinS-c) | 9E Semi-cactus, Miniature |
| (Misc) | 10 Miscellaneous |
| (Fim) | 11 Fimbriated |
| (SinO) | 12 Single Orchid (Star) |
| (DblO) | 13 Double Orchid |
| (B) | Botanical |
| (DwB) | Dwarf Bedding |
| (Lil) | Lilliput (in combination) |

## Dianthus

(By the RHS)

| | |
|---|---|
| (b) | Carnation, border |
| (M) | Carnation, Malmaison |
| (pf) | Carnation, perpetual-flowering |
| (p) | Pink |
| (p,a) | Pink, annual |

## FRUIT

(B) Black (*Vitis*), Blackcurrant (*Ribes*)
(Ball) Ballerina (*Malus*)
(C) Culinary (*Malus, Prunus, Pyrus, Ribes*)
(Cider) Cider (*Malus*)
(D) Dessert (*Malus, Prunus, Pyrus, Ribes*)
(F) Fruit
(G) Glasshouse (*Vitis*)
(O) Outdoor (*Vitis*)
(P) Pinkcurrant (*Ribes*)
(Perry) Perry (*Pyrus*)
(R) Red (*Vitis*), Redcurrant (*Ribes*)
(S) Seedless (*Citrus, Vitis*)
(W) White (*Vitis*), Whitecurrant (*Ribes*)

## FUCHSIA

(E) Encliandra
(T) Triphylla

## GLADIOLUS

(B) Butterfly
(E) Exotic
(G) Giant
(L) Large
(M) Medium
(Min) Miniature
(N) Nanus
(P) Primulinus
(S) Small
(Tub) Tubergenii

## HYDRANGEA MACROPHYLLA

(H) Hortensia
(L) Lacecap

## IRIS

(By the American Iris Society)
(AB) Arilbred
(BB) Border Bearded
(Cal-Sib) Series *Californicae* × Series *Sibiricae*
(CH) Californian Hybrid
(DB) Dwarf Bearded (not assigned)
(Dut) Dutch
(IB) Intermediate Bearded
(J) Juno (subgenus) *Scorpiris*
(La) Louisiana Hybrid
(MDB) Miniature Dwarf Bearded
(MTB) Miniature Tall Bearded
(SDB) Standard Dwarf Bearded
(Sino-Sib) Series *Sibiricae*, chromosome number 2n=40
(SpH) Species Hybrid
(Spuria) Spuria
(TB) Tall Bearded

## LILIUM

(Classification according to *The International Lily Register* (ed. 3, 1982) with amendments from Supp. 10 (1992), RHS)
(I) Early-flowering Asiatic Hybrids derived from *L. amabile, L. bulbiferum, L. cernuum, L. concolor, L. davidii, L. × hollandicum, L. lancifolium, L. leichtlinii, L. × maculatum* and *L. pumilum*
(Ia) Upright flowers, borne singly or in an umbel
(Ib) Outward-facing flowers
(Ic) Pendant flowers
(II) Hybrids of Martagon type, one parent having been a form of *L. hansonii* or *L. martagon*
(III) Hybrids from *L. candidum, L. chalcedonicum* and other related European species (excluding *L. martagon*)
(IV) Hybrids of American species
(V) Hybrids derived from *L. formosanum* and *L. longiflorum*
(VI) Hybrid Trumpet Lilies and Aurelian hybrids from Asiatic species, including *L. henryi* but excluding those from *L. auratum, L. japonicum, L. rubellum* and *L. speciosum*.
(VIa) Plants with trumpet-shaped flowers
(VIb) Plants with bowl-shaped flowers
(VIc) Plants with flat flowers (or only the tips recurved)
(VId) Plants with recurved flowers
(VII) Hybrids of Far Eastern species as *L auratum, L. japonicum, L. rubellum* and *L. speciosum* (Oriental Hybrids)
(VIIa) Plants with trumpet-shaped flowers
(VIIb) Plants with bowl-shaped flowers
(VIIc) Plants with flat flowers
(VIId) Plants with recurved flowers
(VIII) All hybrids not in another division
(IX) All species and their varieties and forms

## MALUS *SEE* FRUIT

## NARCISSUS

(By the RHS, revised 1998)
(1) Trumpet
(2) Large-cupped

| | |
|---|---|
| (3) | Small-cupped |
| (4) | Double |
| (5) | Triandrus |
| (6) | Cyclamineus |
| (7) | Jonquilla and Apodanthus |
| (8) | Tazetta |
| (9) | Poeticus |
| (10) | Bulbocodium |
| (11a) | Split-corona: Collar |
| (11b) | Split-corona: Papillon |
| (12) | Miscellaneous |
| (13) | Species |

## NYMPHAEA

| | |
|---|---|
| (H) | Hardy |
| (D) | Day-blooming |
| (N) | Night-blooming |
| (T) | Tropical |

## PAEONIA

| | |
|---|---|
| (S) | Shrubby |

## PELARGONIUM

| | |
|---|---|
| (A) | Angel |
| (C) | Coloured Foliage (in combination) |
| (Ca) | Cactus (in combination) |
| (d) | Double (in combination) |
| (Dec) | Decorative |
| (Dw) | Dwarf |
| (DwI) | Dwarf Ivy-leaved |
| (Fr) | Frutetorum |
| (I) | Ivy-leaved |
| (Min) | Miniature |
| (MinI) | Miniature Ivy-leaved |
| (R) | Regal |
| (Sc) | Scented-leaved |
| (St) | Stellar (in combination) |
| (T) | Tulip (in combination) |
| (U) | Unique |
| (Z) | Zonal |

## PRIMULA

(Classification by Section as per Richards. J. (2002) *Primula* (2nd edition). Batsford, London)

| | |
|---|---|
| (Ag) | *Auganthus* |
| (Al) | *Aleuritia* |
| (Am) | *Amethystinae* |
| (Ar) | *Armerina* |
| (Au) | *Auricula* |
|   (A) | Alpine Auricula |
|   (B) | Border Auricula |
|   (S) | Show Auricula |
|   (St) | Striped Auricula |
| (Bu) | *Bullatae* |
| (Ca) | *Capitatae* |
| (Cf) | *Cordifoliae* |
| (Ch) | *Chartaceae* |
| (Co) | *Cortusoides* |
| (Cr) | *Carolinella* |
| (Cu) | *Cuneifoliae* |
| (Cy) | *Crystallophlomis* |
| (Da) | *Davidii* |
| (De) | *Denticulatae* |
| (Dr) | *Dryadifoliae* |
| (F) | *Fedtschenkoanae* |
| (G) | *Glabrae* |
| (Ma) | *Malvaceae* |
| (Mi) | *Minutissimae* |
| (Mo) | *Monocarpicae* |
| (Mu) | *Muscarioides* |
| (Ob) | *Obconicolisteri* |
| (Or) | *Oreophlomis* |
| (Pa) | *Parryi* |
| (Pe) | *Petiolares* |
| (Pf) | *Proliferae* |
| (Pi) | *Pinnatae* |
| (Pr) | *Primula* |
|   (Poly) | Polyanthus |
|   (Prim) | Primrose |
| (Pu) | *Pulchellae* |
| (Py) | *Pycnoloba* |
| (R) | *Reinii* |
| (Si) | *Sikkimenses* |
| (So) | *Soldanelloides* |
| (Sp) | *Sphondylia* |
| (Sr) | *Sredinskya* |
| (Su) | *Suffrutescentes* |
| (Y) | *Yunnannenses* |

## PRUNUS *SEE* FRUIT

## PYRUS *SEE* FRUIT

## RHODODENDRON

| | |
|---|---|
| (A) | Azalea (deciduous, species or unclassified hybrid) |
| (Ad) | Azaleodendron |
| (EA) | Evergreen azalea |
| (G) | Ghent azalea (deciduous) |
| (K) | Knap Hill or Exbury azalea (deciduous) |
| (M) | Mollis azalea (deciduous) |
| (O) | Occidentalis azalea (deciduous) |
| (R) | Rustica azalea (deciduous) |
| (V) | Vireya rhododendron |
| (Vs) | Viscosa azalea (deciduous) |

## RIBES *SEE* FRUIT

## ROSA

(A) Alba
(Bb) Bourbon
(Bs) Boursault
(Ce) Centifolia
(Ch) China
(Cl) Climbing (in combination)
(D) Damask
(DPo) Damask Portland
(F) Floribunda or Cluster-flowered
(G) Gallica
(Ga) Garnette
(GC) Ground Cover
(HM) Hybrid Musk
(HP) Hybrid Perpetual
(HT) Hybrid Tea or Large-flowered
(Min) Miniature
(Mo) Moss (in combination)
(N) Noisette
(Patio) Patio, Miniature Floribunda or Dwarf Cluster-flowered
(Poly) Polyantha
(Ra) Rambler
(RH) Rubiginosa hybrid (Hybrid Sweet Briar)
(Ru) Rugosa
(S) Shrub
(SpH) Spinosissima Hybrid
(T) Tea

## SAXIFRAGA

(Classification by Section from Gornall, R.J. (1987). *Botanical Journal of the Linnean Society,* **95**(4): 273-292)
(1) *Ciliatae*
(2) *Cymbalaria*
(3) *Merkianae*
(4) *Micranthes*
(5) *Irregulares*
(6) *Heterisia*
(7) *Porphyrion*
(8) *Ligulatae*
(9) *Xanthizoon*
(10) *Trachyphyllum*
(11) *Gymnopera*
(12) *Cotylea*
(13) *Odontophyllae*
(14) *Mesogyne*
(15) *Saxifraga*

## TULIPA

(Classification by Cultivar Group from *Classified List and International Register of Tulip Names* by Koninklijke Algemeene Vereening voor Bloembollenculture 1996)
(1) Single Early Group
(2) Double Early Group
(3) Triumph Group
(4) Darwinhybrid Group
(5) Single Late Group (including Darwin Group and Cottage Group)
(6) Lily-flowered Group
(7) Fringed Group
(8) Viridiflora Group
(9) Rembrandt Group
(10) Parrot Group
(11) Double Late Group
(12) Kaufmanniana Group
(13) Fosteriana Group
(14) Greigii Group
(15) Miscellaneous

## VERBENA

(G) Species and hybrids considered by some botanists to belong to the separate genus *Glandularia.*

## VIOLA

(C) Cornuta Hybrid
(dVt) Double Violet
(ExVa) Exhibition Viola
(FP) Fancy Pansy
(PVt) Parma Violet
(SP) Show Pansy
(T) Tricolor
(Va) Viola
(Vt) Violet
(Vtta) Violetta

## VITIS *SEE* FRUIT

# REVERSE SYNONYMS

The following list of reverse synonyms is intended to help users find from which genus an unfamiliar plant name has been cross-referred. For a fuller explanation see p.21.

*Abelmoschus – Hibiscus*
*Abutilon – Corynabutilon*
*Acacia – Racosperma*
*Acca – Feijoa*
× *Achicodonia – Eucodonia*
*Achillea – Anthemis*
*Achillea – Tanacetum*
*Acinos – Calamintha*
*Acinos – Clinopodium*
*Acinos – Micromeria*
*Acmella – Spilanthes*
*Actaea – Cimicifuga*
*Actaea – Souliea*
*Aethionema – Eunomia*
*Agapetes – Pentapterygium*
*Agarista – Leucothoe*
*Agastache – Cedronella*
*Agathosma – Barosma*
*Agave – Manfreda*
*Agrostis – Eragrostis*
*Aichryson – Aeonium*
*Ajania – Chrysanthemum*
*Ajania – Dendranthema*
*Ajania – Eupatorium*
*Albizia – Acacia*
*Alcea – Althaea*
*Allardia – Waldheimia*
*Allocasuarina – Casuarina*
*Aloysia – Lippia*
*Althaea – Malva*
*Alyogyne – Anisodontea*
*Alyogyne – Hibiscus*
*Alyssum – Ptilotrichum*
× *Amarygia – Amaryllis*
*Amaryllis – Brunsvigia*
*Amomyrtus – Myrtus*
*Amsonia – Rhazya*
*Anacamptis – Orchis*
*Anaphalis – Gnaphalium*
*Anchusa – Lycopsis*
*Androsace – Douglasia*
*Androstoma – Cyathodes*
*Anemanthele – Oryzopsis*
*Anemanthele – Stipa*
*Anemone – Eriocapitella*
*Anisodontea – Malvastrum*
*Anisodus – Scopolia*
*Anomatheca – Freesia*
*Anomatheca – Lapeirousia*
*Anredera – Boussingaultia*
*Antirrhinum – Asarina*
*Aphanes – Alchemilla*
*Apium – Apium* × *Petroselinum*
*Arctanthemum – Chrysanthemum*
*Arctostaphylos – Arbutus*
*Arctotis – Venidium*
*Arctotis –* × *Venidioarctotis*
*Arenga – Didymosperma*
*Argyranthemum – Anthemis*
*Argyranthemum – Chrysanthemum*
*Armoracia – Cochlearia*
*Arnoglossum – Cacalia*
*Arundinaria – Pseudosasa*
*Asarina – Antirrhinum*
*Asarum – Hexastylis*
*Asparagus – Myrsiphyllum*
*Asparagus – Smilax*
*Asperula – Galium*
*Asphodeline – Asphodelus*
*Asplenium – Camptosorus*
*Asplenium – Ceterach*
*Asplenium – Phyllitis*
*Asplenium – Scolopendrium*
*Aster – Crinitaria*
*Aster – Doellingeria*
*Aster – Erigeron*
*Aster – Microglossa*
*Aster – Symphyotrichum*
*Astilboides – Rodgersia*
*Asyneuma – Campanula*
*Athanasia – Hymenolepis*
*Atropanthe – Scopolia*
*Aurinia – Alyssum*
*Austrocedrus – Libocedrus*
*Austromyrtus – Myrtus*
*Azorella – Bolax*
*Azorina – Campanula*

*Bambusa – Arundinaria*
*Bashania – Arundinaria*
*Bassia – Kochia*
*Beaucarnea – Nolina*
*Bellevalia – Muscari*
*Bellis – Erigeron*
*Bignonia – Campsis*
*Blechnum – Lomaria*
*Blepharocalyx – Temu*
*Bolax – Azorella*
*Bolboschoenus – Scirpus*
*Bonia – Indocalamus*
*Borago – Anchusa*
*Bothriochloa – Andropogon*
*Bouteloua – Chondrosum*
*Boykinia – Telesonix*
*Brachyglottis – Senecio*
*Brimeura – Hyacinthus*
*Brodiaea – Triteleia*
*Brugmansia – Datura*
*Brunnera – Anchusa*
*Buglossoides – Lithospermum*
*Bulbine – Bulbinopsis*

*Cacalia – Adenostyles*
*Calamagrostis – Stipa*
*Calamintha – Clinopodium*
*Calamintha – Thymus*
*Calibrachoa – Petunia*
*Callisia – Phyodina*
*Callisia – Tradescantia*
*Calocedrus – Libocedrus*
*Calomeria – Humea*
*Caloscordum – Nothoscordum*
*Calylophus – Oenothera*
*Calytrix – Lhotzkya*
*Camellia – Thea*
*Campanula – Campanula* × *Symphyandra*
*Campanula – Symphyandra*
*Cardamine – Dentaria*
*Carpobrotus – Lampranthus*
*Cassiope – Harrimanella*
*Cedronella – Agastache*
*Centaurium – Erythraea*
*Centella – Hydrocotyle*
*Centranthus – Kentranthus*
*Centranthus – Valeriana*
*Cephalaria – Scabiosa*
*Ceratostigma – Plumbago*
*Chaenomeles – Cydonia*
*Chaenorhinum – Linaria*
*Chamaecytisus – Cytisus*
*Chamaedaphne – Cassandra*
*Chamaemelum – Anthemis*
*Chamerion – Chamaenerion*
*Chamerion – Epilobium*
*Chasmanthium – Uniola*
*Cheilanthes – Notholaena*
*Chiastophyllum – Cotyledon*
*Chimonobambusa – Arundinaria*
*Chimonobambusa – Qiongzhuea*
*Chionohebe - Parahebe*
*Chionohebe – Pygmea*
× *Chionoscilla – Scilla*
*Chlorophytum – Diuranthera*

*Chordospartium – Carmichaelia*
*Chromolaena – Eupatorium*
*Chrysanthemum – Dendranthema*
*Chrysopsis – Heterotheca*
*Cicerbita – Lactuca*
*Cissus – Ampelopsis*
*Cissus – Parthenocissus*
× *Citrofortunella – Citrus*
*Clarkia – Eucharidium*
*Clarkia – Godetia*
*Clavinodum – Arundinaria*
*Claytonia – Calandrinia*
*Claytonia – Montia*
*Clematis – Atragene*
*Clematis – Clematopsis*
*Cleyera – Eurya*
*Clinopodium – Calamintha*
*Clytostoma – Bignonia*
*Clytostoma – Pandorea*
*Cnicus – Carduus*
*Conoclinium – Eupatorium*
*Codonopsis – Campanumoea*
*Consolida – Delphinium*
*Corallospartium – Carmichaelia*
*Cordyline – Dracaena*
*Cornus – Chamaepericlymenum*
*Cornus – Dendrobenthamia*
*Coronilla – Securigera*
*Cortaderia – Gynerium*
*Corydalis - Capnoides*
*Corydalis – Fumaria*
*Corydalis – Pseudofumaria*
*Cosmos – Bidens*
*Cotinus – Rhus*
*Cotula – Leptinella*
*Crassula – Rochea*
*Crassula – Sedum*
*Crassula – Tillaea*
*Cremanthodium – Ligularia*
*Crinodendron – Tricuspidaria*
*Crocosmia – Antholyza*
*Crocosmia – Curtonus*
*Crocosmia – Montbretia*
*Cruciata – Galium*
*Ctenanthe – Calathea*
*Ctenanthe – Stromanthe*
× *Cupressocyparis – Chamaecyparis*
× *Cupressocyparis -* × *Cuprocyparis*
*Cupressus – Chamaecyparis*
*Cyclosorus – Pneumatopteris*
*Cymbalaria – Linaria*
*Cymophyllus – Carex*
*Cyperus – Mariscus*
*Cypripedium – Criogenes*
*Cyrtanthus – Anoiganthus*
*Cyrtanthus – Vallota*
*Cyrtomium – Phanerophlebia*
*Cyrtomium – Polystichum*
*Cytisus – Argyrocytisus*
*Cytisus – Genista*
*Cytisus – Lembotropis*
*Cytisus – Spartocytisus*

*Daboecia – Menziesia*
*Dacrycarpus – Podocarpus*
*Dactylorhiza – Orchis*
*Dalea – Petalostemon*
*Danae – Ruscus*
*Darmera – Peltiphyllum*
*Datura – Brugmansia*
*Davallia – Humata*
*Delairea – Senecio*
*Delosperma – Lampranthus*
*Delosperma – Mesembryanthemum*
*Desmodium – Lespedeza*
*Deuterocohnia – Abromeitiella*
*Dicentra – Corydalis*
*Dichelostemma – Brodiaea*
*Dicliptera – Barleria*
*Dicliptera – Justicia*
*Diervilla – Weigela*
*Dietes – Moraea*
*Diplazium – Athyrium*
*Dipogon – Dolichos*
*Disporopsis – Polygonatum*
*Dracaena – Pleomele*
*Dracunculus – Arum*
*Dregea – Wattakaka*
*Drepanostachyum – Bambusa*
*Drepanostachyum – Chimonobambusa*
*Drepanostachyum – Gelidocalamus*
*Drepanostachyum – Thamnocalamus*
*Drimys – Tasmannia*
*Duchesnea – Fragaria*
*Dypsis – Chrysalidocarpus*
*Dypsis – Neodypsis*

*Echeveria – Cotyledon*
*Echinacea – Rudbeckia*
*Echinospartum – Genista*
*Edraianthus – Wahlenbergia*
*Egeria – Elodea*
*Elatostema – Pellionia*
*Eleutherococcus – Acanthopanax*
*Elliottia – Botryostege*
*Elliottia – Cladothamnus*
*Elymus – Agropyron*
*Elymus – Leymus*
*Ensete – Musa*
*Epipremnum – Philodendron*
*Epipremnum – Scindapsus*
*Episcia – Alsobia*
*Eranthis – Aconitum*
*Eremophila – Myoporum*
*Erepsia - Semnanthe*
*Erigeron – Haplopappus*
*Erysimum – Cheiranthus*
*Eucalyptus – Corymbia*
*Eupatorium – Ageratina*
*Eupatorium – Ayapana*
*Eupatorium – Bartlettina*
*Euphorbia – Poinsettia*
*Euryops – Senecio*
*Eustachys – Chloris*
*Eustoma – Lisianthus*

*Fallopia – Bilderdykia*
*Fallopia – Polygonum*
*Fallopia – Reynoutria*
*Farfugium – Ligularia*
*Fargesia – Arundinaria*
*Fargesia – Borinda*
*Fargesia – Semiarundinaria*
*Fargesia – Sinarundinaria*
*Fargesia – Thamnocalamus*
*Fatsia – Aralia*
*Felicia – Agathaea*
*Felicia – Aster*
*Fibigia – Farsetia*
*Filipendula – Spiraea*
*Foeniculum – Ferula*
*Fortunella – Citrus*

*Galium – Asperula*
*Gaultheria – Chiogenes*
*Gaultheria – Pernettya*
*Gaultheria –* × *Gaulnettya*
*Gelasine – Sisyrinchium*
*Genista – Chamaespartium*
*Genista – Cytisus*
*Genista – Echinospartum*
*Genista – Teline*
*Gethyum – Ancrumia*
*Geum – Sieversia*
*Gladiolus – Acidanthera*
*Gladiolus – Anomalesia*
*Gladiolus – Homoglossum*
*Gladiolus – Petamenes*
*Glebionis – Chrysanthemum*
*Glebionis – Xanthophthalmum*
*Glechoma – Nepeta*
*Gloxinia – Seemannia*
*Gomphocarpus – Asclepias*
*Gomphocarpus – Asclepias*
*Goniolimon – Limonium*
*Graptopetalum – Sedum*
*Graptopetalum – Tacitus*
*Greenovia – Sempervivum*
*Gymnadenia – Nigritella*
*Gymnospermium – Leontice*

*Habranthus – Zephyranthes*
*Hacquetia – Dondia*
× *Halimiocistus – Cistus*
× *Halimiocistus – Halimium*
*Halimione – Atriplex*
*Halimium – Cistus*
*Halimium – Helianthemum*
*Halimium –* × *Halimiocistus*
*Halocarpus – Dacrydium*
*Hanabusaya – Symphyandra*
*Hedychium – Brachychilum*
*Helianthella – Helianthus*
*Helianthemum – Cistus*
*Helianthus – Coreopsis*
*Helianthus – Heliopsis*
*Helichrysum – Gnaphalium*
*Helicodiceros – Dracunculus*
*Helictotrichon – Avena*
*Helictotrichon – Avenula*
*Hepatica – Anemone*
*Herbertia – Alophia*
*Hermodactylus – Iris*
*Heterocentron – Schizocentron*
*Heteromeles – Photinia*
*Heterotheca – Chrysopsis*
× *Heucherella – Heuchera*
× *Heucherella – Tiarella*
*Hibbertia – Candollea*
*Hieracium – Andryala*
*Himalayacalamus – Arundinaria*
*Himalayacalamus – Chimonobambusa*
*Himalayacalamus – Drepanostachyum*
*Himalayacalamus – Drepanostachyum*
*Himalayacalamus – Thamnocalamus*
*Hippocrepis – Coronilla*
*Hippolytia – Achillea*
*Hippolytia – Tanacetum*
*Hoheria – Plagianthus*
*Homalocladium – Muehlenbeckia*
*Howea – Kentia*
*Hyacinthoides – Endymion*
*Hyacinthoides – Scilla*
*Hylomecon – Chelidonium*
*Hymenocallis – Elisena*
*Hymenocallis – Ismene*
*Hymenoxys – Dugaldia*
*Hymenoxys – Helenium*
*Hyophorbe – Mascarena*
*Hypoxis – Rhodohypoxis*

*Incarvillea – Amphicome*
*Indocalamus – Sasa*
*Iochroma – Acnistus*
*Iochroma – Cestrum*
*Iochroma – Dunalia*
*Ipheion – Tristagma*
*Ipheion – Triteleia*
*Ipomoea – Calonyction*
*Ipomoea – Mina*
*Ipomoea – Pharbitis*
*Ipomopsis – Gilia*
*Ischyrolepis – Restio*
*Isolepis – Scirpus*
*Isotoma – Laurentia*
*Isotoma – Solenopsis*

*Jamesbrittenia – Sutera*
*Jeffersonia – Plagiorhegma*
*Jovibarba – Sempervivum*
*Juncus – Scirpus*
*Jurinea – Jurinella*
*Justicia – Beloperone*
*Justicia - Duvernoia*
*Justicia – Jacobinia*
*Justicia – Libonia*

*Kalanchoe – Bryophyllum*
*Kalanchoe – Kitchingia*
*Kalimeris – Aster*
*Kalimeris – Asteromoea*
*Kalimeris – Boltonia*
*Kalopanax – Acanthopax*
*Kalopanax – Eleutherococcus*
*Keckiella - Penstemon*
*Keckiella – Penstemon*
*Kitagawia – Peucedanum*
*Knautia – Scabiosa*
*Kniphofia – Tritoma*
*Kohleria – Isoloma*
*Krascheninnikovia – Ceratoides*
*Kunzea – Leptospermum*

*Lablab – Dolichos*
*Lagarosiphon – Elodea*
*Lagarostrobos – Dacrydium*
*Lamium – Galeobdolon*
*Lamium – Lamiastrum*
*Lampranthus – Mesembryanthemum*
*Lavatera – Malva*
*Ledebouria – Scilla*
× *Ledodendron – Rhododendron*
*Ledum – Rhododendron*
*Leontodon – Microseris*
*Lepechinia – Sphacele*
*Lepidothamnus – Dacrydium*
*Leptecophylla – Cyathodes*
*Leptinella – Cotula*
*Leptodactylon – Gilia*
*Leucanthemella – Chrysanthemum*
*Leucanthemella – Leucanthemum*
*Leucanthemopsis – Chrysanthemum*
*Leucanthemum – Chrysanthemum*
*Leucocoryne – Beauverdia*
*Leucophyta – Calocephalus*
*Leucopogon – Cyathodes*
*Leucopogon – Styphelia*
× *Leucoraoulia – Raoulia*
× *Leucoraoulia – Raoulia* × *Leucogenes*
*Leymus – Elymus*
*Ligularia – Senecio*
*Ligustrum – Parasyringa*
*Lilium – Nomocharis*
*Limonium – Statice*
*Linanthus – Linanthastrum*
*Lindelofia – Adelocaryum*
*Lindera – Parabenzoin*
*Lindernia – Ilysanthes*
*Liriope – Ophiopogon*
*Lithodora – Lithospermum*
*Lobelia – Monopsis*
*Lophomyrtus – Myrtus*
*Lophospermum – Asarina*
*Lophospermum – Maurandya*
*Lotus – Dorycnium*
*Lotus – Tetragonolobus*
*Ludwigia – Jussiaea*
*Luma – Myrtus*
× *Lycene – Lychnis*
*Lychnis – Agrostemma*
*Lychnis – Silene*
*Lychnis – Viscaria*
*Lycianthes – Solanum*
*Lytocaryum – Cocos*
*Lytocaryum – Microcoelum*

*Macfadyena – Bignonia*
*Macfadyena – Doxantha*
*Machaeranthera – Xylorhiza*
*Machaerina – Baumea*
*Mackaya – Asystasia*
*Macleaya – Bocconia*
*Maclura - Cudrania*
*Macropiper – Piper*
*Magnolia – Parakmeria*
*Mahonia – Berberis*
*Maianthemum – Smilacina*
*Mandevilla – Dipladenia*
*Mandragora – Atropa*
*Marrubium – Ballota*
*Matricaria – Tripleurospermum*
*Maurandella – Asarina*
*Maurandya – Asarina*
*Melanoselinum – Thapsia*
*Melicytus – Hymenanthera*
*Melinis – Rhynchelytrum*
*Mentha – Preslia*
*Merremia – Ipomoea*
*Mimulus – Diplacus*
*Minuartia – Arenaria*

*Moltkia – Lithodora*
*Moltkia – Lithospermum*
*Morina – Acanthocalyx*
*Morina – Acanthocalyx*
*Mukdenia – Aceriphyllum*
*Muscari – Hyacinthus*
*Muscari – Leopoldia*
*Muscari – Muscarimia*
*Muscari – Pseudomuscari*
*Myrteola – Myrtus*

*Naiocrene – Claytonia*
*Naiocrene – Montia*
*Nectaroscordum – Allium*
*Nematanthus – Hypocyrta*
*Nemesia – Diascia* × *Linaria*
*Neolitsea – Litsea*
*Neopaxia – Claytonia*
*Neopaxia – Montia*
*Neoregelia – Nidularium*
*Nepeta – Dracocephalum*
× *Niduregelia – Guzmania*
*Nipponanthemum – Chrysanthemum*
*Nipponanthemum – Leucanthemum*
*Nolina – Beaucarnea*
*Notospartium – Carmichaelia*
*Nymphoides – Villarsia*

*Ochagavia – Fascicularia*
*Oemleria – Osmaronia*
*Oenothera – Chamissonia*
*Olsynium – Sisyrinchium*
*Onixotis – Dipidax*
*Onoclea – Matteuccia*
*Ophiopogon – Convallaria*
*Orchis – Anacamptis*
*Orchis – Dactylorhiza*
*Oreopteris – Thelypteris*
*Orostachys – Sedum*
*Oscularia – Lampranthus*
*Osmanthus – Phillyrea*
*Osmanthus* – × *Osmarea*
*Othonna – Hertia*
*Othonna – Othonnopsis*
*Ozothamhus – Helichrysum*

*Pachyphragma – Cardamine*
*Pachyphragma – Thlaspi*
*Pachystegia - Olearia*
*Packera – Senecio*
*Paederota – Veronica*
*Pallenis – Asteriscus*
*Papaver – Meconopsis*
*Parahebe – Derwentia*
*Parahebe – Hebe*
*Parahebe – Veronica*
*Paraserianthes – Albizia*
*Paris – Daiswa*
*Parthenocissus – Ampelopsis*
*Parthenocissus – Vitis*
*Passiflora – Tetrapathaea*
*Paxistima – Pachystema*
*Pecteilis – Habenaria*
*Pelargonium – Geranium*
*Peltoboykinia – Boykinia*
*Penstemon – Chelone*
*Penstemon – Nothochelone*
*Penstemon – Pennellianthus*
*Pentaglottis – Anchusa*
*Pericallis – Senecio*
*Persea – Machilus*
*Persicaria – Aconogonon*
*Persicaria – Antenoron*
*Persicaria – Bistorta*
*Persicaria – Polygonum*
*Persicaria – Tovara*
*Petrocoptis – Lychnis*
*Petrophytum – Spiraea*
*Petrorhagia – Tunica*
*Petroselinum – Carum*
*Phegopteris – Thelypteris*
*Phoenicaulis – Parrya*
*Photinia – Stransvaesia*
*Photinia* – × *Stravinia*
*Phuopsis – Crucianella*
*Phyla – Lippia*
*Phymatosorus – Microsorum*
*Phymosia – Sphaeralcea*
*Physoplexis – Phyteuma*
*Physostegia – Dracocephalum*
*Pieris – Arcterica*
*Pilosella – Hieracium*
*Platycladus – Thuja*
*Plecostachys – Helichrysum*
*Plectranthus – Coleus*
*Plectranthus – Solenostemon*
*Pleioblastus – Arundinaria*
*Pleioblastus – Sasa*
*Podophyllum – Dysosma*
*Podranea – Tecoma*
*Polygonum – Persicaria*
*Polypodium – Phlebodium*
*Polyscias – Nothopanax*
*Poncirus – Aegle*
*Potentilla – Comarum*
*Pratia – Lobelia*
*Prenanthes – Nabalus*
*Pritzelago – Hutchinsia*
*Prumnopitys – Podocarpus*
*Prunus – Amygdalus*
*Pseudocydonia – Chaenomeles*
*Pseudogynoxys – Senecio*
*Pseudopanax – Metapanax*
*Pseudopanax – Neopanax*
*Pseudosasa – Arundinaria*
*Pseudotsuga – Tsuga*
*Pseudowintera – Drimys*
*Pterocephalus – Scabiosa*
*Pteryxia - Cymopterus*
*Ptilostemon – Cirsium*
*Pulicaria – Inula*
*Pulsatilla – Anemone*
*Purshia – Cowania*
*Puschkinia – Scilla*
*Pyrrocoma – Aster*
*Pyrrocoma – Haplopappus*

*Reineckea – Liriope*
*Retama – Genista*
*Retama – Lygos*
*Rhamnus – Frangula*
*Rhapis – Chamaerops*
*Rhodanthe – Helipterum*
*Rhodanthemum – Argyranthemum*
*Rhodanthemum – Chrysanthemopsis*
*Rhodanthemum – Chrysanthemum*
*Rhodanthemum – Leucanthemopsis*
*Rhodanthemum – Leucanthemum*
*Rhodanthemum – Pyrethropsis*
*Rhodiola – Clementsia*
*Rhodiola – Rosularia*
*Rhodiola – Sedum*
*Rhododendron – Azalea*
*Rhododendron – Azaleodendron*
*Rhododendron – Rhodora*
*Rhododendron – Therorhodion*
*Rhododendron – Tsusiophyllum*
*Rhodophiala – Hippeastrum*
× *Rhodoxis – Hypoxis* × *Rhodohypoxis*
× *Rhodoxis – Rhodohypoxis*
*Rhus – Toxicodendron*
*Rhyncospora – Dichromena*
*Rosularia – Cotyledon*
*Rosularia – Sempervivella*
*Rothmannia – Gardenia*
*Ruellia – Dipteracanthus*

*Saccharum – Erianthus*
*Sagina – Minuartia*
*Sanguisorba – Dendriopoterium*
*Sanguisorba – Poterium*
*Sasa – Arundinaria*
*Sasaella – Arundinaria*
*Sasaella – Pleioblastus*
*Sasaella – Sasa*
*Sauromatum – Arum*
*Scadoxus – Haemanthus*
*Schefflera – Brassaia*
*Schefflera – Dizygotheca*

*Schefflera – Heptapleurum*
*Schizachyrium – Andropogon*
*Schizostachyum – Arundinaria*
*Schizostachyum – Thamnocalamus*
*Schizostylis – Hesperantha*
*Schoenoplectus – Scirpus*
*Scilla – Oncostema*
*Scirpoides – Scirpus*
*Sedum – Hylotelephium*
*Sedum – Sedastrum*
*Semiaquilegia – Aquilegia*
*Semiaquilegia – Paraquilegia*
*Semiarundinaria – Arundinaria*
*Semiarundinaria – Oligostachyum*
*Senecio – Cineraria*
*Senecio – Kleinia*
*Senecio – Ligularia*
*Senna – Cassia*
*Seriphidium – Artemisia*
*Shortia – Schizocodon*
*Sibbaldiopsis – Potentilla*
*Silene – Lychnis*
*Silene – Melandrium*
*Silene – Saponaria*
*Sinacalia – Ligularia*
*Sinacalia – Senecio*
*Sinningia – Gesneria*
*Sinningia – Rechsteineria*
*Sinobambusa – Pleioblastus*
*Sinobambusa – Pseudosasa*
*Siphocranion – Chamaesphacos*
*Sisymbrium – Hesperis*
*Sisyrinchium – Phaiophleps*
*Smallanthus – Polymnia*
*Solanum – Lycianthes*
*Soleirolia – Helxine*
*Solenostemon – Coleus*
× *Solidaster – Aster*
× *Solidaster – Solidago*
*Sophora – Styphnolobium*
*Sorbaria – Spiraea*
*Sparaxis – Synnotia*
*Sphaeralcea – Iliamna*
*Sphaeromeria – Tanacetum*
*Spirodela – Lemna*
*Stachys – Betonica*
*Stemmacantha – Centaurea*
*Stemmacantha – Leuzea*
*Stenomesson – Urceolina*
*Stewartia – Stuartia*
*Stipa – Achnatherum*
*Stipa – Agrostis*
*Stipa – Calamagrostis*
*Stipa – Lasiagrostis*
*Stipa – Nassella*
*Strobilanthes – Parachampionella*
*Strobilanthes – Pteracanthus*
*Succisa – Scabiosa*
*Sutera – Bacopa*
*Syagrus – Arecastrum*
*Syagrus – Cocos*
*Syncarpha - Helipterum*
*Syzygium – Caryophyllus*

*Talbotia – Vellozia*
*Tanacetum – Achillea*
*Tanacetum – Balsamita*
*Tanacetum – Chrysanthemum*
*Tanacetum – Matricaria*
*Tanacetum – Pyrethrum*
*Tanacetum – Spathipappus*
*Tecoma – Tecomaria*
*Telekia – Buphthalmum*
*Tetradium – Euodia*
*Tetraneuris - Actinella*
*Tetraneuris – Actinella*
*Tetraneuris – Hymenoxys*
*Tetrapanax – Fatsia*
*Thamnocalamus – Arundinaria*
*Thlaspi – Hutchinsia*
*Thlaspi – Noccaea*
*Thlaspi – Vania*
*Thuja – Thujopsis*
*Thymus – Origanum*
*Tiarella* – × *Heucherella*
*Tonestus – Haplopappus*
*Toona – Cedrela*
*Trachelium – Diosphaera*
*Trachycarpus – Chamaerops*
*Tradescantia – Rhoeo*
*Tradescantia – Setcreasea*
*Tradescantia – Zebrina*
*Trichopetalum – Anthericum*
*Tripetaleia – Elliottia*
*Tripogandra – Tradescantia*
*Tristaniopsis – Tristania*
*Triteleia – Brodiaea*
*Tritonia – Crocosmia*
*Tritonia – Montbretia*
*Trochiscanthes – Angelica*
*Tropaeolum – Nasturtium hort.*
*Tulipa – Amana*
*Tupistra – Campylandra*
*Tutcheria – Pyrenaria*
*Tweedia – Oxypetalum*

*Ugni – Myrtus*
*Utricularia – Polypompholyx*
*Uvularia – Oakesiella*

*Vaccaria – Melandrium*
*Vaccinium – Oxycoccus*
*Verbascum – Celsia*
*Verbascum* – × *Celsioverbascum*
*Verbena – Glandularia*
*Verbena – Lippia*
*Veronicastrum – Veronica*
*Vigna – Phaseolus*
*Viola – Erpetion*
*Vitaliana – Androsace*
*Vitaliana – Douglasia*

*Wedelia – Zexmenia*
*Weigela – Diervilla*
*Weigela – Macrodiervilla*

*Xanthorhiza – Zanthorhiza*
*Xerochrysum – Bracteantha*
*Xerochrysum – Helichrysum*

*Yushania – Arundinaria*
*Yushania – Sinarundinaria*
*Yushania – Thamnocalamus*

*Zantedeschia – Calla*
*Zauschneria – Epilobium*
*Zephyranthes* – × *Cooperanthes*
*Zephyranthes – Cooperia*

# The Plant Directory

# A

## *Abelia* ✿ (*Caprifoliaceae*)

| | | |
|---|---|---|
| | ***chinensis*** misapplied | see *A.* x *grandiflora* |
| § | ***chinensis*** R.Br. | EBee ECre EPfP EWTr GKir MAsh MMuc SDnm SEND SPer SPla SPoG SRms WBod WFar WHCG WLeb WPat |
| | 'Edward Goucher' | CDoC CDul CMac CSBt CWSG CWib EBee ECrN ELan EPfP LBMP LPan LRHS LSRN MGos MRav NBir NHol SEND SPer SPlb SRGP SWvt WDin WFar WPat WSHC |
| | ***engleriana*** | CPLG CWan EBee EPfP LRHS NLar WFar |
| | ***floribunda*** ♀$^{H3}$ | CBcs CDul CMac CSBt CSam CWib EBee ECre ELan EPfP LRHS NLar SDnm SPer SPoG SSpi WAbe WBod WFar WGob WPat WPic |
| § | x ***grandiflora*** ♀$^{H4}$ | Widely available |
| | - 'Aurea' | see *A.* x *grandiflora* 'Gold Spot' |
| | - 'Compacta' | LRHS WFar |
| | - Confetti = 'Conti'$^{PBR}$ (v) | Widely available |
| | - dwarf | CDoC |
| § | - 'Francis Mason' (v) | Widely available |
| § | - 'Gold Spot' | CWSG EBee EMil EPfP LRHS MGos MWat MWhi NMun SSto WGob |
| | - 'Gold Strike' | see *A.* x *grandiflora* 'Gold Spot' |
| | - 'Goldsport' | see *A.* x *grandiflora* 'Gold Spot' |
| | - 'Hopleys'$^{PBR}$ (v) | CBcs CDoC CMac CSBt CWib EBee EPfP LHop LRHS MAsh MGos NHol SLim WFar WGob WHar WLeb |
| | - 'Kaleidoscope' (v) **new** | EMil LRHS MAsh MGos SPoG |
| | - 'Mardi Gras' (v) **new** | LRHS |
| | - 'Panache' (v) | MGos MRav WPat |
| | - 'Prostrate White' | ECrN MAsh |
| | - 'Semperflorens' **new** | EMil |
| | - 'Sherwoodii' | CWSG EBee EHig EPfP SWvt WFar WPat |
| | - 'Sunrise'$^{PBR}$ (v) | CDoC CSBt EBee ELan EPfP EQua ERas MGos NLar SBod SHBN SLim SLon SPla |
| | - 'Tanya' | EBee |
| | - 'Variegata' | see *A.* x *grandiflora* 'Francis Mason' |
| | ***mosanensis*** | CMCN LRHS MBri NLar |
| | ***rupestris*** misapplied | see *A.* x *grandiflora* |
| | ***rupestris*** Lindl. | see *A. chinensis* R.Br. |
| | ***schumannii*** ♀$^{H4}$ | Widely available |
| | - 'Saxon Gold'$^{PBR}$ | EBee LRHS SLim SPoG SSto |
| | ***spathulata*** | WFar |
| | ***triflora*** | CAbP CPLG CWib EBee ECre EPfP LAst LHop MMuc NLar SLon WFar WGob |

## *Abeliophyllum* (*Oleaceae*)

| | | |
|---|---|---|
| | ***distichum*** | Widely available |
| | - Roseum Group | CBcs CDoC CPLG CPMA EBee ELan EPfP GBuc LAst LHop LRHS MAsh MGos MRav NSti SHBN SLon SPoG WFar |

## *Abelmoschus* (*Malvaceae*)

| | | |
|---|---|---|
| § | ***manihot*** | CFir |

## *Abies* (*Pinaceae*)

| | | |
|---|---|---|
| | ***alba*** | IFFs MBar NWea WMou |
| | - 'Compacta' | CKen |
| | - 'King's Dwarf' | CKen |
| | - 'Microphylla' | CKen |
| | - 'Münsterland' | CKen NLar |
| | - 'Nana' misapplied | see *Picea glauca* 'Nana' |
| | - 'Nana' ambig. | CKen |
| | ***amabilis*** | NWea |
| | ***arizonica*** | see *A. lasiocarpa* var. *arizonica* |
| | x ***arnoldiana*** | NLar |
| | ***balsamea*** | CDul NWea WMou |
| | - Hudsonia Group ♀$^{H4}$ | CDoC CKen CMac ECho EHul EMil GKir IMGH LRHS MBar NDlv NHol NLar NMen SLim SPoG |
| | - 'Jamie' | CKen NLar |
| | - 'Le Feber' | CKen |
| | - 'Nana' | CKen CRob ECho EHul EOrn MAsh NLar WDin WFar |
| | - var. ***phanerolepis*** 'Bear Swamp' | CKen NLar |
| | - 'Piccolo' | CKen ECho EHul IMGH LRHS NLar SLim SPoG WFar WGor |
| | - 'Prostrata' | ECho EHul |
| | - 'Renswoude' | CKen |
| | - 'Tyler Blue' | CKen |
| | - 'Verkade's Prostrate' | CKen |
| * | ***borisii-regis*** 'Pendula' | CKen |
| | ***brachyphylla*** dwarf | see *A. homolepis* 'Prostrata' |
| | ***bracteata*** | GKir |
| | ***cephalonica*** | CDul NWea |
| I | - 'Compacta' | SPoG |
| | - 'Greg's Broom' | CKen ECho |
| § | - 'Meyer's Dwarf' | CDoC EBrs ECho EHul GKir LRHS MBar NLar SCoo SLim SPoG |
| | - 'Nana' | see *A. cephalonica* 'Meyer's Dwarf' |
| | ***concolor*** ♀$^{H4}$ | CBcs CDul CTho EHul EMac EWTr GKir IFFs LMaj LPan MBar MMuc NWea SPer WDin |
| | - 'Archer's Dwarf' | CKen ECho LRHS MGos NLar SLim |
| I | - 'Argentea' Niemetz, 1903 | CKen |
| | - 'Aurea' | MGos |
| | - 'Birthday Broom' | CKen NLar |
| | - 'Blue Cloak' | NLar |
| | - 'Blue Sapphire' | CKen |
| | - 'Blue Spreader' | CKen MGos |
| § | - 'Compacta' ♀$^{H4}$ | CDoC CKen EBrs ECho EOrn GKir LRHS MAsh MBar MGos NHol NLar SCoo SLim SPoG WFar |
| | - 'Creamy' (Lowiana Group) | CKen |
| | - 'Fagerhult' | CKen NLar |
| | - 'Gable's Weeping' | CKen |
| | - 'Glauca' | see *A. concolor* Violacea Group |
| | - 'Glauca Compacta' | see *A. concolor* 'Compacta' |
| | - 'Hillier Broom' | see *A. concolor* 'Hillier's Dwarf' |
| § | - 'Hillier's Dwarf' | CKen |
| | - 'Husky Pup' | CKen |

| | | |
|---|---|---|
| | - 'Masonic Broom' | CKen NLar |
| | - 'Mike Stearn' | CKen NLar |
| | - 'Mora' | CKen |
| | - 'Ostrov nad Ohri' | CKen |
| | - 'Piggelmee' | CKen NLar |
| | - 'Pygmy' **new** | CKen |
| | - 'Scooter' | CKen NLar |
| | - 'Sherwood's Blue' | ECho |
| * | - 'Swift's Silver' | LRHS WBVN |
| § | - Violacea Group | CKen ECho MAsh MBar MBri MGos SCoo SLim WFar |
| | - 'Wattez Prostrate' | LRHS NLar SCoo SLim SPoG WFar |
| | - 'Wattezii' | CKen ECho |
| | - 'Wintergold' | CKen EBrs ECho GKir MGos NLar |
| | ***delavayi*** | CMCN MGos NWea |
| | - SDR 3269 | GKev |
| I | - 'Nana' | CKen |
| | ***fargesii*** | NLar |
| | - var. ***faxoniana*** | GKir |
| | ***firma*** | GKir |
| | ***forrestii*** | CKen |
| | - var. ***ferreana*** SF 95168 | ISea |
| | - - SF 95226 | ISea |
| | ***fraseri*** | CTri IFFs MBar MMuc SCoo WMou |
| | - 'Blue Bonnet' | CKen |
| | - 'Raul's Dwarf' | CKen ECho |
| | ***grandis*** | CBcs CDul EMac IFFs MBar NWea SCoo SHBN WDin WMou |
| | - 'Compacta' | CKen |
| | - 'Van Dedem's Dwarf' | CKen NLar |
| | ***holophylla*** | NLar NWea |
| | ***homolepis*** | CDul NLar NWea |
| § | - 'Prostrata' | CKen |
| | ***koreana*** | Widely available |
| | - 'Alpin Star' | CKen |
| | - 'Aurea' | see *A. koreana* 'Flava' |
| | - 'Blaue Zwo' | CKen MAsh NLar |
| | - 'Blauer Eskimo' | CDoC CKen MBlu NLar SLim |
| | - 'Blauer Pfiff' | CKen ECho NLar |
| | - 'Blinsham Gold' | CKen |
| | - 'Blue Emperor' | CKen NLar |
| | - 'Blue Magic' | CKen NLar |
| | - 'Blue 'n' Silver' | ECho NLar |
| | - 'Bonsai Blue' | NLar |
| | - 'Cis' | CDoC CKen NLar SCoo SLim |
| | - 'Compact Dwarf' | ECho EPot MAsh MBar MGos NLar |
| | - 'Crystal Globe' | CKen NLar |
| | - 'Dark Hill' | NLar |
| | - 'Doni Tajuso' | CKen |
| § | - 'Flava' | CKen EMil IMGH MBar MGos NLar SCoo |
| | - 'Frosty' | NLar SLim SPoG |
| | - 'Gait' | CKen ECho NLar |
| | - 'Golden Dream' | CKen |
| | - 'Golden Glow' | NLar WFar |
| | - 'Green Carpet' | CKen GKir NLar SLim |
| | - 'Grübele' witches' broom | CKen |
| | - 'Inverleith' | CKen |
| | - 'Knospenkönigin' | NLar |
| | - 'Kohout' | CKen NLar |
| | - 'Lippetal' | CKen |
| | - 'Luminetta' | CKen MGos NLar SLim |
| | - 'Nadelkissen' | CKen |
| | - 'Nisbet' | ECho IMGH SCoo SLim WGor |
| | - 'Oberon' | CKen MAsh NLar SLim |
| | - 'Piccolo' | CKen |
| | - 'Pinocchio' | CDoC CKen |
| | - 'Prostrata' | see *A. koreana* 'Prostrate Beauty' |
| § | - 'Prostrate Beauty' | ECho EOrn WFar WGor |
| | - 'Schneestern' | NLar |
| | - 'Silberkugel' | CKen ECho SLim |
| | - 'Silberlocke' $\Upsilon^{H4}$ | CDoC CKen CRob EBrs ECho EMil LPan LRHS MBar MBlu MBri MGos NBea NLar SCoo SLim SPer SPoG SSpi WFar WOrn |
| | - 'Silbermavers' | CKen |
| | - 'Silberperl' | CKen NLar |
| | - 'Silberschmelze' | ECho |
| | - 'Silver Show' | CKen NWea |
| | - 'Taiga' | NLar |
| | - 'Threave' | CKen |
| | - 'Tundra' | NLar |
| | - 'Winter Goldtip' | ECho |
| | ***lasiocarpa*** | CDul NWea |
| | - 'Alpine Beauty' **new** | CKen |
| § | - var. ***arizonica*** | CDul |
| | - - 'Compacta' Hornibr. $\Upsilon^{H4}$ | CDoC CKen CMac EBrs ECho EHul ELan GKir LRHS MAsh MBar MBri MGos SCoo SHBN SLim SPoG WFar WGor |
| | - - 'Kenwith Blue' | CKen ECho MGos NLar WFar |
| | - 'Compacta' Beissn. | NHol WFar |
| | - 'Day Creek' | CKen |
| | - 'Duflon' | CKen |
| | - 'Green Globe' | CKen ECho LRHS MBar NLar |
| | - 'Joe's Alpine' | CKen |
| * | - 'King's Blue' | CKen |
| | - 'Logan Pass' | CKen NLar |
| | - 'Mulligan's Dwarf' | CKen ECho |
| | - 'Prickly Pete' | CKen |
| | - 'Toenisvorst' | CKen |
| | ***magnifica*** | GKir NWea |
| I | - 'Nana' | CKen NLar |
| | - witches' broom | CKen |
| | ***nobilis*** | see *A. procera* |
| | ***nordmanniana*** $\Upsilon^{H4}$ | CDul CTri EHul EMac EPfP EWTr GKir IFFs LBuc LMaj LPan MBar MGos MMuc NWea SHBN SPer SPoG WDin WMou |
| | - 'Arne's Dwarf' | CKen |
| | - 'Barabits' Compact' | MBar MBri MGos NLar |
| | - 'Barabits' Spreader' | CKen |
| | - subsp. ***equi-trojani*** | NWea |
| | - - 'Archer' | CKen |
| | - 'Golden Spreader' $\Upsilon^{H4}$ | CDoC CKen EBrs ECho EOrn GKir LRHS MAsh MBar MBri MGos NLar SCoo SLim SPoG WFar |
| | - 'Hasselt' | CKen |
| | - 'Jakobsen' | CKen |
| | - 'Pendula' | LPan |
| | - 'Silberspitze' | CKen |
| | ***numidica*** | LPan |
| | - 'Glauca' | CKen |
| | - 'Lawrenceville' | ECho WFar |
| | ***pindrow*** | ECho NWea |
| | ***pinsapo*** | GKir IFFs MBar NWea SEND |
| | - 'Aurea' | CKen EBrs ECho MGos NLar SLim WFar |
| I | - 'Aurea Nana' | CKen |
| | - 'Fastigiata' | MPkF |
| | - 'Glauca' $\Upsilon^{H4}$ | CDoC CKen CTho ECho EHul ELan GKir LMaj LPan MBar MBlu NLar SCoo SLim SPoG WDin WMou |
| | - 'Hamondii' | CKen |
| I | - 'Horstmann' | CKen ECho GKir NLar |
| | - 'Pendula' | MGos MPkF NLar |
| | - 'Quicksilver' | CKen |
| § | ***procera*** $\Upsilon^{H4}$ | CBcs CDoC CDul EHul EMac IFFs MBar NWea WBVN WDin WMou |
| | - 'Bizarro' | ECho NLar |
| | - 'Blaue Hexe' | CKen ECho NLar SLim SPoG WFar |
| | - Glauca Group | CDoC CMac CTho LPan MAsh MBar MBlu MBri MGos SHBN WFar WOrn |
| | - - 'Glauca Prostrata' | CRob ECho LPan MBar MGos SCoo WFar |
| | - 'La Graciosa' | NLar |

| | | |
|---|---|---|
| | - 'Noble's Dwarf' | ECho GKir |
| | - 'Obrighofen' | NLar |
| | - 'Seattle Mount' | NLar |
| | - 'Sherwoodii' | CKen ECho |
| | ***recurvata*** | NLar |
| | - var. ***ernesti*** | GKir |
| | Rosemoor hybrid | CKen |
| | ***sibirica*** | NWea |
| | ***squamata*** | CDoC |
| | ***veitchii*** | CBcs CDul GKir NWea |
| | - 'Heddergott' | CDoC CKen ECho MGos NLar |
| | - 'Heine' | CKen |
| I | - 'Pendula' | CKen |
| | - 'Rumburg' | CKen |

## *Abromeitiella* (*Bromeliaceae*)

| | | |
|---|---|---|
| | ***brevifolia*** ♀H1 | WCot |

## *Abrotanella* (*Asteraceae*)

| | | |
|---|---|---|
| | sp. | ECho EDAr |

## *Abutilon* ✿ (*Malvaceae*)

| | | |
|---|---|---|
| | 'Ashford Red' | CBcs CCCN CWGN ELan MAsh SAga SKHP SOWG WKif |
| * | 'Benary's Giant' | CPLG |
| | 'Boule de Neige' | CHal ELon SOWG |
| | 'Canary Bird' ♀H2 | CBcs CCCN CHEx CHal ELon MLan SAga WBod |
| | 'Cannington Carol' (v) ♀H2 | CCCN LSRN SRGP |
| | 'Cannington Peter' (v) ♀H2 | CCCN LSRN |
| | 'Cannington Sally' (v) | MLan SRGP |
| | 'Cloth of Gold' | SOWG |
| | 'Cynthia Pike' (v) | LRHS |
| | 'Flamenco' **new** | LRHS |
| | 'Hinton Seedling' | CCCN CRHN |
| | x ***hybridum*** | CHEx |
| | apricot-flowered | |
| | - red-flowered | CHEx |
| | ***indicum*** | CCCN |
| | 'Isles of Scilly' **new** | CCCN |
| | 'Jacqueline Morris' | MAsh SPoG SSta |
| | 'John Thompson' **new** | CCCN CWGN |
| | 'Kentish Belle' ♀H2-3 | CBcs CCCN CDoC CHEx CHal CMHG CMac CRHN EBee ECGP ECot ELan ELon EPfP ERas LRHS LSRN NPal SCoo SPer SPlb WFar |
| I | 'Kentish Belle Variegatum' (v) | ELan |
| | 'Marion' ♀H2 | CRHN LRHS LSRN SOWG SPoG WCot |
| | 'Master Michael' | CMac |
| | ***megapotamicum*** ♀H3 | CBcs CCCN CHEx CMHG CRHN CSBt CTri EBee ELan EPfP EPla EShb GQui LRHS MAsh MGos MLan MRav SOWG SPer SPoG SRms WBod WFar WHar WSHC |
| | - 'Variegatum' (v) | CBcs CCCN CSBt ELan EPfP GQui LRHS MAsh MGos SBod SOWG SPer SPoG SWvt WFar |
| | - 'Wisley Red' | CRHN |
| | x ***milleri*** hort. ♀H2 | CMac CRHN MLan WWlt |
| | - 'Variegatum' (v) | CCCN CHEx CMac SEND SPoG |
| | 'Nabob' ♀H2 | CCCN CDoC CHal CRHN EShb LRHS MLan SOWG SPoG |
| | 'Orange Vein' | CHal EShb WPrP |
| | 'Patrick Synge' | CCCN CMHG EShb SOWG SPhx |
| | ***pictum*** | CHal |
| | - 'Thompsonii' (v) | CHEx CHal EShb MJnS WDyG |
| | 'Pink Lady' | CHal EShb |
| | 'Russels Dwarf' **new** | CCCN |
| | 'Savitzii' (v) ♀H2 | CHal MCot SOWG |
| | 'Simcox White' | CCCN WEas |
| | 'Souvenir de Bonn' (v) ♀H2 | CHal EShb LSou MLan SAga |
| | x ***suntense*** | CBcs CCCN CMHG CPLG CSBt EPfP ERas GKev LHyd LRHS LSou MJnS NPer SChF SOWG WBod |
| | - 'Jermyns' ♀H3 | EBee EPfP GCra LRHS LSRN MBri SCoo SPoG SSpi WFar |
| | - Ralph Gould seedling **new** | ECGP |
| | - 'Violetta' | CEnd CHEx WKif |
| | 'Tango' **new** | LRHS |
| | ***theophrasti*** | MSal |
| | variegated, salmon-flowered (v) | LAst |
| | 'Victory' | SKHP |
| | ***vitifolium*** | CBcs CCCN ECot EPfP EQua GGar MGos NBid NLar SPad SPer WKif |
| | - var. ***album*** | CBcs CDul EPfP GCal LHyd MLan SEND SSpi WBor WFar WSHC |
| | - 'Buckland' | CGHE CHll |
| | - 'Tennant's White' ♀H3 | CAbP CCCN EPfP ERas GGal LRHS MBri NBur |
| | - 'Veronica Tennant' ♀H3 | CPLG ELon SAga WKif |
| | 'Wakehurst' | WCot |
| | 'Waltz' **new** | LRHS |
| | 'Westfield Bronze' | CRHN |

## *Acacia* ✿ (*Mimosaceae*)

| | | |
|---|---|---|
| | ***acinacea*** | SPlb |
| | ***adunca*** | SPlb |
| | ***alpina*** | WCel |
| | ***armata*** | see *A. paradoxa* |
| | ***baileyana*** ♀H2 | CBcs CCCN CDul CGHE CSBt CTrG ECot ELan EMil EPfP EWTr ISea LRHS MGos SBig SCoo SEND SOWG SPer SPlb SWvt WFar WPat |
| | - var. ***aurea*** | SPlb |
| | - 'Purpurea' ♀H2 | Widely available |
| | ***boormanii*** | WCel |
| | ***brachybotrya*** | CDTJ |
| | ***cultriformis*** | CCCN CTrC CTsd |
| | ***cyanophylla*** | see *A. saligna* |
| | ***dealbata*** ♀H2 | Widely available |
| | - 'Gaulois Astier' | LRHS LSRN MBri MGos MREP WBrE WCot |
| | - subsp. ***subalpina*** | WCel WPGP |
| | ***erioloba*** | CPLG |
| | Exeter hybrid | CSBt |
| | ***filicifolia*** | WCel |
| | ***fimbriata*** | CRHN |
| | ***floribunda*** 'Lisette' | EPfP |
| | ***frigescens*** | WCel |
| | ***julibrissin*** | see *Albizia julibrissin* |
| | ***juniperina*** | see *A. ulicifolia* |
| | ***karroo*** | CArn CCCN CDTJ CPLG SKHP |
| | ***kybeanensis*** | EBee WCel WPGP |
| | ***longifolia*** | CBcs CCCN CDTJ CTsd EBee EPfP LRHS SEND SPer SRms |
| | - subsp. ***sophorae*** | CCCN GGar |
| | ***macradenia*** | SPlb |
| | ***mearnsii*** | CCCN CSec WCel |
| | ***melanoxylon*** | CDTJ CTrC CTsd EBee GGar WCel WHer |
| | ***motteana*** | ECot |
| | ***mucronata*** | CTrC EShb |
| | ***obliquinervia*** | WCel |
| § | ***paradoxa*** ♀H2 | CCCN ECou ESwi LRHS WPat |
| | ***pataczekii*** | EBee EPfP EWes LRHS SKHP |
| | ***pendula*** | IDee |
| | ***podalyriifolia*** | EBee IDee SPlb |
| | ***pravissima*** ♀H2-3 | Widely available |
| | - 'Bushwalk Baby' | SOWG |
| | ***retinodes*** ♀H2 | CBcs CCCN CDoC CRHN CTrC CTsd EBee EPfP ESwi LRHS LSRN |

| | |
|---|---|
| | MREP MTPN SEND SLim SWvt WCFE |
| ***riceana*** | CCCN CTrG CTsd |
| ***rubida*** | EBee IDee MGos MREP SPlb WCel |
| § ***saligna*** | CDTJ CSec EBee SBLw |
| ***sentis*** | see *A. victoriae* |
| ***spectabilis*** | CCCN SPlb |
| ***suaveolens*** | SPlb |
| § ***ulicifolia*** | CPLG CSBt CTrG |
| ***verticillata*** | CBcs CCCN CDTJ CHll CSec CTrG CTsd EBee GGar MTPN SOWG |
| - riverine | CTrC LRHS SKHP |
| § ***victoriae*** | ECre |

## *Acaena* (*Rosaceae*)

| | |
|---|---|
| RCB RA B-3 **new** | WCot |
| ***adscendens*** misapplied | see *A. affinis*, *A. magellanica* subsp. *magellanica*, *A. saccaticupula* 'Blue Haze' |
| ***adscendens*** Vahl | see *A. magellanica* subsp. *laevigata* |
| ***adscendens*** ambig. 'Glauca' | EHoe NBir |
| § ***affinis*** | EBee ECha SDix |
| ***anserinifolia*** misapplied | see *A. novae-zelandiae* |
| § ***anserinifolia*** (Forst. & Forst. f.) Druce | EBee GGar NHol |
| ***buchananii*** | CSpe CTri EBee ECho EDAr EHoe GAbr GGar MLLN NBro NLar SRms STre WFar WPer |
| ***caerulea*** hort. | see *A. caesiiglauca* |
| § ***caesiiglauca*** | CTri EBee GAbr GGar GQue MLHP NBid SGar WEas WPer |
| ***caespitosa*** | GKev |
| - F&W 93 **new** | EBee |
| ***fissistipula*** | WMoo |
| ***glaucophylla*** | see *A. magellanica* subsp. *magellanica* |
| ***inermis*** | MLLN MMuc SPlb |
| - 'Purpurea' | EBee ECha EDAr EGoo EHoe EShb GAbr GBin GGar GKev GQue LRHS NLar SIng SPlb WHoo WMoo WPtf |
| ***macrocephala*** | EBee |
| ***magellanica*** **new** | EBee GKev |
| § - subsp. ***laevigata*** | GGar |
| § - subsp. ***magellanica*** | EBee |
| ***microphylla*** 🏆$^{H4}$ | CSam CTri EAlp EBee ECho EDAr GAbr GGar LBee NLar NMen SIng SPlb SRms WFar |
| - Copper Carpet | see *A. microphylla* 'Kupferteppich' |
| - 'Glauca' | see *A. caesiiglauca* |
| - 'Grüner Zwerg' **new** | EBee |
| § - 'Kupferteppich' | EBee ECho EHoe ETod GAbr GGar GKir GQue MBri MMuc MRav NBir NDov NLar NVic SBch WMoo WPat WPer |
| ***myriophylla*** | EBee ECho EDAr |
| § ***novae-zelandiae*** | CSec CTri EBee GGar SDix WMoo WPer |
| ***ovalifolia*** | EBee ECho MCot |
| 'Pewter' | see *A. saccaticupula* 'Blue Haze' |
| ***pinnatifida*** | NBro WCot |
| ***profundeincisa*** | see *A. anserinifolia* (Forst. & Forst. f.) Druce |
| 'Purple Carpet' | see *A. microphylla* 'Kupferteppich' |
| 'Purple Haze' | CSpe |
| ***saccaticupula*** | NLar WFar |
| § - 'Blue Haze' | CMoH EBee ECha ECho EDAr EHoe EShb GGar GKir LRHS MLLN MRav NVic SIng SPer SPlb SRms WFar WHoo WMoo |
| ***sanguisorbae*** | see *A. anserinifolia* (Forst. & Forst. f.) Druce |
| ***splendens*** | SIng |
| ***viridior*** | see *A. anserinifolia* (Forst. & Forst. f.) Druce |

## *Acalypha* (*Euphorbiaceae*)

| | |
|---|---|
| ***hispida*** 🏆$^{H1}$ | LRHS MBri MJnS |
| ***pendula*** | see *A. reptans* |
| § ***reptans*** | CHal |

## *Acanthocalyx* see *Morina*

## *Acantholimon* (*Plumbaginaceae*)

| | |
|---|---|
| ***androsaceum*** | see *A. ulicinum* |
| § ***ulicinum*** | EPot NWCA |

## *Acanthopanax* see *Eleutherococcus*

| | |
|---|---|
| ***ricinifolius*** | see *Kalopanax septemlobus* |

## *Acanthus* ✿ (*Acanthaceae*)

| | |
|---|---|
| ***balcanicus*** misapplied | see *A. hungaricus* |
| 'Candelabra' | WHil |
| ***dioscoridis*** | CAby EBee EGle EMon MAvo SMHy |
| - var. ***perringii*** | CDes EBee ECha GBin LHop MAvo MNrw MSte NChi WCot WFar WHil WPGP WSHC |
| - smooth-leaved | WHil |
| ***eminens*** **new** | WHil |
| ***hirsutus*** | EMon LPio NBre SPav WCot |
| - f. ***roseus*** | WFar |
| - subsp. ***syriacus*** | EBee EHrv EMon GCal MSte NBre NLar WCot WFar WHil |
| - - JCA 106.500 | SPhx |
| 'Hollande du Nort' | EBee |
| § ***hungaricus*** | CArn CHar CHid EBee EBla EBrs ECtt EGle ELan EMon EShb EWTr GCal GKir LBMP LRHS MCot MRav MSte NCGa NLar SDix SPav SPer SWat WCot WFar WHil WMnd |
| - AL&JS 90097YU | EMon |
| - MESE 561 | EPPr |
| ***longifolius*** Host | see *A. hungaricus* |
| ***mollis*** | Widely available |
| - 'Fielding Gold' | see *A. mollis* 'Hollard's Gold' |
| - free-flowering | GCal MSte WHil |
| § - 'Hollard's Gold' | Widely available |
| - 'Jefalba' | see *A. mollis* (Latifolius Group) 'Rue Ledan' |
| - Latifolius Group | EBee ECrN EPfP MCot MRav MSte NHol SPer SRms WHil WHoo WTin |
| § - - 'Rue Ledan' | EBee EMon EPPr IPot LPio MAvo MDKP MSte NLar SMHy SPhx SUsu WCot WFar WHil WTin |
| - - 'Sjaak' | EBee WHil |
| 'Morning Candle' **new** | EBee |
| ***pubescens*** **new** | WHil |
| ***sennii*** | CMdw SKHP SMad SPhx WHil WSHC |
| ***spinosus*** L. 🏆$^{H4}$ | Widely available |
| - Ferguson's form | WCot WHil |
| - 'Lady Moore' (v) | EMon IBlr IPot MCCP NLar SBch WCot WHil |
| - 'Royal Haughty' | GCal MSte WHil |
| - Spinosissimus Group | CBct CMHG ECha EHrv ELan ELon EMon GCal LEdu LPio MCCP MRav NChi SAga SPhx SWat WCot WFar WHil WMnd WTin |
| 'Summer Beauty' | EBee GCal GKir LHop LPio LRHS MAvo MBri MSte NBre NLar WCot WFar WHil |

## *Acca* (*Myrtaceae*)

| | |
|---|---|
| sp. | SBLw SWvt WBod |
| ***sellowiana*** (F) | CBcs CDul CMHG CPLG CSBt CSam CTrG EBee ELan EPfP ERom |

| | |
|---|---|
| | GQui LAst LHop LPan LRHS MCCP MGos MREP SLim SOWG SPer SPlb SPoG SVic WBod WFar WSHC |
| - 'Apollo' (F) | EBee |
| - 'Coolidge' (F) | CAgr |
| - 'Mammoth' (F) | CAgr CBcs CCCN |
| - 'Marian' (F) **new** | EBee |
| - 'Triumph' (F) | CAgr CBcs CCCN |
| - 'Unique' (F) **new** | CAgr |
| - 'Variegata' (F/v) | CHid ELan LAst SPoG |

## *Acer* ✿ (*Aceraceae*)

| | |
|---|---|
| HWJK 2040 from Nepal | WCru |
| SDR 4944 **new** | GKev |
| ***albopurpurascens*** | WPGP |
| ***argutum*** | IMGH |
| ***barbinerve*** | CMCN EPfP |
| ***buergerianum*** | CDul CLnd CMCN CMen CPMA IArd LMaj MBlu MBri MMuc MPkF NLar SBLw SBir SCoo |
| - 'Integrifolium' | see *A. buergerianum* 'Subintegrum' |
| - 'Mino-yatsubusa' | MPkF |
| - 'Miyasama-yatsubusa' | MPkF |
| - 'Naruto' | CMCN MPkF |
| § - 'Subintegrum' | CMCN |
| ***calcaratum*** | CDul CMCN |
| ***campbellii*** B&SWJ 7685 | WCru |
| * - var. ***fansipanense*** B&SWJ 8270 | WCru |
| - - HWJ 569 | WCru |
| § - subsp. ***flabellatum*** B&SWJ 8057 | WCru |
| - - var. ***yunnanense*** | CBcs EBee ECrN EHig IMGH WHCr |
| ***campestre*** 🏆H4 | Widely available |
| - 'Carnival' (v) | CDul CEnd CMCN CPMA CWib EBee ECrN EHig EMil EPla LRHS MAsh MBlu MBri MPkF NHol NLar SMad SPer SPoG SPur SWvt WMou WPGP |
| - 'Commodore' | LPan |
| - 'Elsrijk' | CCVT CLnd EBee LMaj SBLw SCoo |
| - 'Evelyn' | see *A. campestre* 'Queen Elizabeth' |
| - 'Evenly Red' | MBlu |
| - 'Pendulum' | CEnd ECrN |
| - 'Postelense' | CEnd CMCN CPMA MBlu MGos MPkF |
| - 'Pulverulentum' (v) | CEnd CMCN CPMA MGos SSta |
| § - 'Queen Elizabeth' | LMaj MGos |
| - 'Red Shine' | GKir MGos |
| - 'Royal Ruby' | CWSG MGos WFar |
| * - 'Ruby Glow' | CEnd ECrN |
| - 'Schwerinii' | CDul |
| I - 'Silver Celebration' (v) | CPMA |
| - 'William Caldwell' | CEnd CTho ECrN |
| ***capillipes*** 🏆H4 | Widely available |
| - B&SWJ 10845 **new** | WCru |
| - 'Candy Stripe' | see *A.* x *conspicuum* 'Candy Stripe' |
| - 'Gimborn' | WPGP |
| - 'Honey Dew' | NLar |
| ***cappadocicum*** | CCVT CDul CEnd CMCN CSam ECrN GKir LMaj MLan MMuc NWea SBLw SBir WDin |
| - 'Aureum' 🏆H4 | Widely available |
| - subsp. ***divergens*** | MPkF |
| - var. ***mono*** | see *A. pictum* |
| - 'Rubrum' 🏆H4 | CBcs CDul CLnd CMCN EBee ECrN EPfP GAuc GKir LAst LBuc LMaj LPan MBlu MBri MGos MRav SBLw SLim SPer WDin WFar WHer WOrn |
| - subsp. ***sinicum*** | EPfP GBin WFar WPGP |
| - - var. ***tricaudatum*** | CPLG WPGP |
| ***carpinifolium*** | CBcs CMCN EWTr IArd MPkF NLar SBir |

| | |
|---|---|
| - B&SWJ 10955 **new** | WCru |
| - B&SWJ 11124 **new** | WCru |
| ***catalpifolium*** | see *A. longipes* subsp. *catalpifolium* |
| § ***caudatifolium*** | CMCN SBir WPGP |
| - B&SWJ 6734 | WCru |
| § ***caudatum*** GWJ 9279 | WCru |
| - HWJK 2338 **new** | WCru |
| - subsp. ***ukurunduense*** | CMCN MPkF |
| ***circinatum*** | CBcs CDoC CDul CLnd CMCN CPMA ECrN EPfP MBlu MBri MLan MMuc MPkF NBea NLar NWea SCoo SHBN SSta WDin WFar |
| - B&SWJ 9565 | WCru |
| - 'Little Gem' | CPMA |
| - 'Little Joe' | CPMA |
| - 'Monroe' | CPMA |
| - 'Pacific Fire' | CPMA |
| - 'Sunglow' | CPMA NLar |
| ***circinatum* x *palmatum*** | GKir SBig |
| ***cissifolium*** | CBcs CMCN EPfP IArd MBri NLar |
| - B&SWJ 10801 **new** | WCru |
| § x ***conspicuum*** 'Candy Stripe' | CBcs CLnd CPMA GKir NLar SLim SSpi SSta |
| - 'Elephant's Ear' | CPMA EPfP NLar |
| - 'Mozart' | SHBN |
| I - 'Phoenix' | CBcs CEnd CMCN CPMA EPfP MAsh MBlu MBri NLar SSpi WDin WPat |
| - 'Red Flamingo' **new** | MGos |
| - 'Silver Ghost' | MGos MPkF |
| § - 'Silver Vein' | CDoC CDul CEnd CMCN CPMA EBee EPfP MGos MWea NLar SPur SSpi SSta WPGP |
| ***crataegifolium*** B&SWJ 11036 **new** | WCru |
| - 'Meuri-keade-no-fuiri' (v) | MPkF |
| - 'Meuri-no-ōfu' (v) | MPkF |
| - 'Veitchii' (v) | CMCN CPMA EPfP MBlu MBri MPkF NLar SBig SSpi |
| ***creticum*** L., non F. Schmidt. | see *A. sempervirens* |
| ***dasycarpum*** | see *A. saccharinum* |
| ***davidii*** | Widely available |
| - B&SWJ 8183 | WCru |
| § - 'Canton' | CPMA MPkF |
| - 'Cantonspark' | see *A. davidii* 'Canton' |
| - 'Chinese Temple' **new** | SBir |
| N - 'Ernest Wilson' | CBcs CMCN CSBt EBee MBlu NLar |
| N - 'George Forrest' 🏆H4 | Widely available |
| - 'Hagelunie' | MPkF SBir |
| - 'Karmen' | CBcs CGHE CPMA EBee MPkF SBir WPGP |
| - 'Madeline Spitta' | CMCN CPMA GKir MBlu MBri MPkF |
| - 'Purple Bark' | SBir |
| - 'Rosalie' | CBcs CPMA EPfP MBlu MBri SBir |
| - 'Serpentine' 🏆H4 | CBcs CDoC CMCN CPMA EBee EPfP EPla IDee MBlu MBri NLar SBir SSpi SSta WFar WOrn WPGP |
| - 'Silver Vein' | see *A.* x *conspicuum* 'Silver Vein' |
| ***divergens*** | CMCN |
| ***elegantulum*** | CDoC CPMA GBin LLHF WPGP |
| ***erianthum*** | CLnd WHCr |
| ***fabri*** | CBcs |
| ***flabellatum*** | see *A. campbellii* subsp. *flabellatum* |
| ***forrestii*** | CMCN EPfP NBea NHol |
| - BWJ 7515 **new** | WCru |
| - 'Alice' | CBcs CDul CEnd CPMA |
| § - 'Sirene' | CPMA |
| § - 'Sparkling' | CPMA |
| x ***freemanii*** | CMCN |
| - 'Armstrong' | SBLw WFar |
| - Autumn Blaze = 'Jeffersred' | CBcs CCVT CDoC CDul CMCN EPfP LMaj MBlu MGos |

| | |
|---|---|
| | MMuc SBLw SCoo SMad WDin WFar WPat |
| - Autumn Fantasy = 'Dtr 102' | MBlu SCoo |
| - Celebration = 'Celzam' | MGos WFar |
| - 'Elegant' | SBLw |
| - 'Indian Summer' | see *A.* x *freemanii* 'Morgan' |
| § - 'Morgan' | CEnd CPMA SBir |
| ***fulvescens*** | see *A. longipes* |
| ***ginnala*** | see *A. tataricum* subsp. *ginnala* |
| ***globosum*** | see *A. platanoides* 'Globosum' |
| ***grandidentatum*** | see *A. saccharum* subsp. *grandidentatum* |
| ***griseum*** ♀H4 | Widely available |
| ***grosseri*** | CDul CMCN CTri |
| - var. ***hersii*** ♀H4 | CBcs CCVT CDoC CDul CLnd CSBt CWib EBee ECrN EHig EPfP EPla GKir LRHS MAsh MRav NBea NLar NWea SBLw SPer SWvt WBVN WDin WFar WHCr WOrn WPGP |
| - 'Leiden' | EPfP MBlu |
| ***heldreichii*** | CMCN EPfP |
| ***henryi*** | CDul CLnd CMCN EPfP LMaj NLar |
| ***hyrcanum*** | CMCN |
| ***japonicum*** | CMCN MBar MMuc SSta WHCr |
| - B&SWJ 5950 | WCru |
| § - 'Aconitifolium' ♀H4 | Widely available |
| - 'Ao-jutan' | CPMA |
| - 'Attaryi' | MPkF |
| - 'Aureum' | see *A. shirasawanum* 'Aureum' |
| - 'Ezo-no-momiji' | see *A. shirasawanum* 'Ezo-no-momiji' |
| - 'Filicifolium' | see *A. japonicum* 'Aconitifolium' |
| - 'Green Cascade' | CBdw CEnd CMCN CPMA ECho LRHS MPkF NLar SBig WPGP WPat |
| - 'Kalmthout' | CBdw |
| - 'King's Copse' | LRHS SPoG |
| - 'Laciniatum' | see *A. japonicum* 'Aconitifolium' |
| - f. ***microphyllum*** | see *A. shirasawanum* 'Microphyllum' |
| - 'Ogurayama' | see *A. shirasawanum* 'Ogurayama' |
| - 'Ō-isami' | EPfP MPkF SBig |
| - 'Ō-taki' | CPMA |
| - 'Vitifolium' ♀H4 | CDoC CEnd CMCN CPMA CSBt ECho ELan EPfP LPan LRHS MBlu MBri MGos MPkF NBea NLar NPal SBig SPer SPoG SSpi SSta WDin WPGP WPat |
| ***kawakamii*** | see *A. caudatifolium* |
| ***laevigatum*** | CMCN |
| ***laxiflorum*** | EBee EPla |
| - HWJK 2240 | WCru |
| ***leucoderme*** | see *A. saccharum* subsp. *leucoderme* |
| ***lobelii*** Bunge | see *A. turkestanicum* |
| ***lobelii*** Tenore | CLnd WPGP |
| § ***longipes*** | CMCN |
| - Sich 731 | WPGP |
| § - subsp. ***catalpifolium*** | CMCN |
| ***macrophyllum*** | CDul CMCN CTho EPfP LHyd |
| ***mandschuricum*** | EPfP MBri MPkF WDin |
| § ***maximowiczianum*** | CBcs CMCN CTho ELan MPkF WFar |
| ***maximowiczii*** | ECrN MPkF NWea WHCr |
| ***micranthum*** | CDoC CEnd CGHE CMCN EBee EPfP LLHF MBlu MBri MPkF NLar SHGN SSpi WPGP |
| ***miyabei*** | MPkF |
| ***mono*** | see *A. pictum* |
| ***monspessulanum*** | CDul CLnd CMCN EBee SEND |
| ***morifolium*** | EBee MPkF |
| ***morrisonense*** | see *A. caudatifolium* |
| ***negundo*** | CDul CLnd CMCN CWib ECrN LMaj NWea SBLw |

| | |
|---|---|
| - IDS 2000 | WHCr |
| - 'Argenteovariegatum' | see *A. negundo* 'Variegatum' |
| - 'Auratum' | CMCN MBar SBLw WDin |
| - 'Aureomarginatum' (v) | ECrN LAst LMaj WOrn |
| - 'Aureovariegatum' (v) | CBcs MBar |
| § - 'Elegans' (v) | CDul CEnd CLnd CMCN ECrN EPfP LRHS NHol SCoo SHBN SPer WFar |
| - 'Elegantissimum' | see *A. negundo* 'Elegans' |
| - 'Flamingo' (v) | Widely available |
| - 'Kelly's Gold' | CBcs CWSG LRHS MAsh MBri MGos NLar NMun NPro NWea SCoo SLim SPoG WDin WFar WHar WOrn |
| - subsp. ***mexicanum*** F&M 48 | WPGP |
| § - 'Variegatum' (v) | CLnd ECrN LAst LRHS SBLw SPer WDin WFar |
| - var. ***violaceum*** | CEnd CMCN |
| - 'Winter Lightning' | CPMA LPan |
| ***nikoense*** | see *A. maximowiczianum* |
| ***oblongum*** | CDul CMCN WPGP |
| - HWJK 2422 | WCru |
| - var. ***concolor*** HWJ 869 **new** | WCru |
| § ***obtusifolium*** | WCot |
| ***oliverianum*** | EBee EPfP WPGP |
| - subsp. ***formosanum*** B&SWJ 6773 **new** | WCru |
| - - B&SWJ 6797 | WCru |
| - - RWJ 9912 | WCru |
| ***opalus*** | CMCN SEND |
| ***orientale*** | see *A. sempervirens* |
| ***orizabense*** | EBee |
| ***palmatum*** | Widely available |
| - 'Abigail Rose' (v) | CBdw |
| - 'Akane' | CBdw CMen MPkF |
| § - 'Aka-shigitatsu-sawa' | CBcs CMCN CMac CMen CPMA ECho LMil LRHS MGos MPkF NLar SPer WBod WFar WHar |
| - 'Akebono' | CBdw CPMA |
| - 'Akegarasu' | CMen NLar |
| - 'Alpenweiss' | CPMA |
| - 'Alpine Sunrise' | CBdw |
| - 'Alpine Surprise' | CPMA |
| - 'Amagi-shigure' | CBdw CPMA |
| - 'Aoba-jo' | CMen CPMA ECho MPkF NLar |
| - 'Ao-kanzashi' (v) | CBdw MPkF |
| - 'Aoshime-no-uchi' | see *A. palmatum* 'Shinobuga-oka' |
| - 'Aoyagi' | CEnd CMCN CMen CPMA ECho EPfP LMil LRHS MBri MGos NHol WFoF |
| § - 'Arakawa' | CEnd CMCN CMen ECho MPkF |
| - 'Arakawa-ukon' | CPMA |
| - 'Aratama' | CBdw CPMA LRHS MGos SCoo WBod WPat |
| - 'Ariake-nomura' | CMen MPkF |
| - 'Asahi-zuru' (v) | CBcs CBdw CDoC CMCN CMen CPMA EBee ECho LPan LRHS MBri MGos MPkF NHol NLar SPer WDin WFar WFoF WHar WPat |
| - 'Ashurst Wood' | SBig |
| - 'Atrolineare' | CMen MPkF NBPN NBea NLar WPat |
| - 'Atropurpureum' | Widely available |
| - 'Atropurpureum Novum' | MPkF |
| - 'Atsugama' | CBdw |
| - 'Attraction' | CMCN |
| - 'Aureum' | CBdw CMCN CMen CWib ECho EPfP LMil LRHS MAsh MBlu MGos MPkF NHol NLar SBod SSpi WFar |
| - Autumn Glory Group | CEnd CPMA ECho |
| - 'Autumn Red' | ECho LPan |
| * - 'Autumn Showers' | CEnd CPMA |
| - 'Azuma-murasaki' | CMen CPMA ECho MPkF NLar |
| - 'Beni-chidori' | CMen ECho |

| | | |
|---|---|---|
| | - 'Beni-gasa' | CPMA |
| | - 'Beni-hime' | MBri MPkF NLar |
| | - 'Beni-hoshi' | CBdw WPat |
| | - 'Beni-kagami' | CEnd CMCN CPMA EPfP MBlu MPkF NBPN NBea NLar |
| | - 'Beni-kawa' | CBdw CMen CPMA ECho LMil MPkF SBig SSpi WPat |
| | - 'Beni-komachi' | CBcs CEnd CMCN CMac CMen CPMA ECho EPfP LMil LRHS MBri MGos MPkF NLar WHar WPat |
| | - 'Beni-maiko' | CBdw CEnd CMCN CMen CPMA CWib ECho EPfP GKir LBuc LMil LRHS MBri MGos MPkF MWea NBlu NLar SBig SCoo SWvt WBVN WBod WDin WHar WPGP WPat |
| | - 'Beni-musume' | CBdw MPkF |
| | - 'Beni-otake' | CBcs CBdw CLnd CMCN CMen CPMA ECho EPfP LMil LRHS MBri MGos MPkF NLar SBig WPat |
| | - 'Beni-schichihenge' (v) | CBcs CBdw CEnd CMCN CMen CPMA CWCL CWGN ECho EPfP LRHS MAsh MBri MGos MPkF NHol SBig SCoo SPoG WBod WPGP WPat |
| | - 'Beni-shi-en' | CBdw CPMA MPkF NLar |
| | - 'Beni-shigitatsu-sawa' | see *A. palmatum* 'Aka-shigitatsu-sawa' |
| | - 'Beni-tsukasa' (v) | CBdw CEnd CMen CPMA ECho LMil LRHS MPkF SPoG SSpi WPGP |
| | - 'Beni-ubi-gohon' | CPMA MPkF NLar |
| | - 'Beni-zuru' | CBdw |
| | - 'Bloodgood' ΨH4 | Widely available |
| | - 'Bonfire' misapplied | see *A. palmatum* 'Seigai' |
| | - 'Bonfire' ambig. | CPMA |
| | - 'Bonnie Bergman' | CPMA |
| | - 'Boskoop Glory' | ECho |
| | - 'Brandt's Dwarf' | CBdw MPkF WPat |
| | - 'Burgundy Lace' ΨH4 | Widely available |
| | - 'Butterfly' (v) | Widely available |
| | - 'Calico' | CBdw CPMA |
| | - 'Carlis Corner' | CPMA |
| | - 'Carminium' | see *A. palmatum* 'Corallinum' |
| | - 'Chikuma-no' | MPkF |
| | - 'Chirimen-nishiki' (v) | CMCN MPkF |
| | - 'Chishio' | see *A. palmatum* 'Shishio' |
| | - 'Chishio Improved' | see *A. palmatum* 'Shishio Improved' |
| | - 'Chishio-hime' | CBdw |
| | - 'Chitose-yama' ΨH4 | CEnd CMCN CMen CPMA CWCL CWib EBee ECho EPfP LRHS MBar MBri MGos MLan MPkF MRav NHol NLar SCoo SLim SSpi SSta WBod WFar WPat |
| § | - 'Chiyo-hime' | CBdw ELan MGos NLar |
| | - 'Coonara Pygmy' | CBdw CMCN CMen CPMA ECho IDee LRHS MGos MPkF NLar SBod SCoo WFar WPat |
| | - 'Coral Pink' | CBdw CMen CPMA ECho MPkF |
| § | - 'Corallinum' | CEnd CMCN CMen CPMA ECho MPkF NLar NPal WDin WPat |
| | - var. ***coreanum*** | CMCN LMil |
| | - - B&SWJ 8606 | WCru |
| | - - 'Korean Gem' | CPMA ECho MPkF |
| | - 'Crimson Carol' | CBdw |
| | - 'Crimson Prince' | CBcs ECho EMac LRHS MPkF SBod SCoo |
| | - 'Crippsii' | CBcs CMen ECho EMil LRHS MBri MGos MPkF SCoo WFar |
| | - 'Demi-sec' | CBdw |
| | - 'Deshōjō' | CBdw CMCN CMen CWib ECho LPan MBar MBlu MGos MLan MPkF NHol NLar SCoo SHBN |
| | - 'Deshōjō-nishiki' | CBdw |
| | - 'Diana' | CMen MPkF NLar |

| | | |
|---|---|---|
| | - 'Diane Verkade' | CBdw |
| | - var. ***dissectum*** ΨH4 | Widely available |
| | - - 'Ao-shidare' | CBdw CPMA |
| | - - 'Ariadne' (v) | CBdw CEnd CPMA CWib LRHS MBri MGos MPkF NLar SBig SCoo WPat |
| | - - 'Autumn Fire' | CBdw CPMA |
| | - - 'Baby Lace' | CBdw CPMA MBri NLar |
| | - - 'Balcombe Green' | SBig |
| | - - 'Baldsmith' | CBdw CPMA LRHS MGos WPat |
| | - - 'Barrie Bergman' | CBdw CPMA |
| | - - 'Beni-fushigi' | CBdw MPkF NLar WPat |
| | - - 'Beni-shidare Tricolor' (v) | CBdw CMen ECho MPkF NLar |
| | - - 'Beni-shidare Variegated' (v) | CMCN CPMA ECho |
| | - - 'Beni-tsukasa-shidare' | CBdw |
| | - - 'Berrima Bridge' | CBdw CPMA |
| | - - 'Bewley's Red' | CBdw CPMA |
| | - - 'Brocade' | CBdw MPkF WPat |
| | - - 'Bronzewing' | CPMA |
| | - - 'Chantilly Lace' | CBdw CPMA ECho |
| | - - 'Crimson Queen' ΨH4 | Widely available |
| | - - Dissectum Atropurpureum Group | CBcs CCVT CPMA CTri CWCL ELan EPfP LCro LHyd LRHS MGan MGos NBea NHol NLar NWea SBig SCoo SHBN SLim SReu SSpi SSta WDin WFar WHCr WOrn |
| | - - 'Dissectum Flavescens' | CBdw CEnd CMac CPMA ECho MBlu MPkF |
| § | - - 'Dissectum Nigrum' | CPMA CTri CWSG ECho MAsh MPkF NBPN NBea NBee NHol NLar SSpi WPat |
| | - - 'Dissectum Palmatifidum' | CDoC CLnd ECho EQua LRHS MPkF SCoo SPer WFar WPat |
| | - - 'Dissectum Rubrifolium' | ECho |
| § | - - 'Dissectum Variegatum' (v) | CBcs CPMA EPfP MPkF |
| | - - Dissectum Viride Group | CBcs CMCN CMen CPMA CSBt CWSG ECho ELan EMui EPfP GKir LMil LPan LRHS MAsh MGos MSwo NBea NWea SBod SLim SPer SPla SSta WFar WOrn |
| | - - 'Doctor Baker' | CBdw |
| | - - 'Ellen' | CBdw CPMA WPat |
| | - - 'Emerald Lace' | CPMA LRHS MBlu MPkF NLar WCFE |
| | - - 'Felice' | CBdw CPMA MPkF WPat |
| | - - 'Filigree' (v) | CBdw CMCN CMen CPMA CWCL ECho EPfP LMil LRHS MGos MPkF NLar SBig SSpi WDin WPGP WPat |
| | - - 'Garnet' ΨH4 | Widely available |
| | - - 'Goshiki-shidare' (v) | CEnd CMen CPMA ECho MPkF |
| | - - 'Green Globe' | CBdw LPan NLar |
| | - - 'Green Hornet' | CPMA |
| | - - 'Green Lace' | LPan MPkF |
| | - - 'Green Mist' | CBdw CPMA WPat |
| | - - 'Hanzel' | WPat |
| | - - 'Inaba-shidare' ΨH4 | Widely available |
| I | - - 'Kawaii' | CPMA |
| | - - 'Kiri-nishiki' | CMen CPMA ECho MPkF NLar |
| | - - 'Lemon Chiffon' | CBdw |
| * | - - 'Lionheart' | CBdw CDoC CPMA ECho EMac EMil LPan LRHS MGos MPkF NLar SBod SCoo SPer WFar WHar WPat |
| | - - 'Mioun' | CBdw |
| | - - 'Octopus' | CBdw CPMA |
| | - - 'Orangeola' | CBcs CBdw CPMA ECho LRHS MAsh MGos MPkF NHol NLar SBig SCoo SPoG WPat |
| | - - 'Ornatum' | CDoC CDul CMCN CMen CWCL CWib ECho ELon EPfP IMGH LMil LPan MBar MGos MPkF MRav NBea |

| | |
|---|---|
| | SCoo SHBN WCFE WDin WFar WHCr WHar |
| - - 'Otto's Dissectum' | CBdw CPMA |
| - - 'Pendulum Julian' | CMCN MPkF SBod |
| - - 'Pink Ballerina' (v) | CPMA |
| - - 'Pink Filigree' | CBdw LPan MPkF |
| - - 'Raraflora' | CBdw CPMA |
| - - 'Red Autumn Lace' | CBdw CPMA LPan WPat |
| - - 'Red Dragon' | CDoC CMen CPMA ECho EQua LPan LRHS MPkF NLar SBig SBod WHar WPat |
| - - 'Red Feather' | CPMA |
| - - 'Red Filigree Lace' | CBdw CEnd CMCN CMen CPMA CWGN ECho EPfP MBlu MGos NHol SBig WPat |
| - - 'Red Select' | ECho MPkF |
| - - 'Red Strata' | CBdw |
| - - 'Rilas Red' | CBdw |
| - - 'Seiryū' ♀$^{H4}$ | Widely available |
| § - - 'Shōjō-shidare' | CBdw CDul CEnd CPMA ECho NLar |
| - - 'Spring Delight' | CBdw CPMA MPkF NLar |
| - - 'Sumi-shidare' | CBdw |
| - - 'Sunset' | CBdw CPMA EMui MPkF WPat |
| - - 'Tamukeyama' | CBcs CLnd CMCN CMen CPMA CWCL EBee ECho ELan EMac LMil LPan LRHS MGos MPkF NLar SBod SCoo SLau SPoG WFar WPat |
| - - 'Toyama-nishiki' (v) | CMCN CMen ECho LRHS WPat |
| - - 'Waterfall' | CMCN CPMA ECho |
| - - 'Watnong' | CBdw CPMA |
| - - 'Zaaling' | CMen ECho |
| - 'Dormansland' | LMil SBig SCoo |
| - 'Dragon's Fire' | CBdw EMui |
| - 'Eddisbury' | CEnd CMen CPMA MPkF NBea NLar SSta WBod WOrn WPat |
| - 'Edna Bergman' | CPMA |
| - 'Effegi' | see *A. palmatum* 'Fireglow' |
| - 'Eimini' | CBdw MPkF WPat |
| - 'Elegans' | CMen ECho EPfP MPkF NLar WDin |
| - Emperor 1 | see *A. palmatum* 'Wolff' |
| - 'Englishtown' | CBdw WPat |
| - 'Enkan' | CBdw CPMA MBri MPkF NLar WPat |
| - 'Eono-momiji' | CMen |
| - 'Ever Red' | see *A. palmatum* var. *dissectum* 'Dissectum Nigrum' |
| - 'Fall's Fire' | CBdw CPMA |
| - 'Fascination' | CBdw CPMA |
| - 'Filigree Rouge' | CBdw |
| - 'Fior d'Arancio' | CPMA MPkF NBea NLar |
| § - 'Fireglow' | CBcs CDoC CEnd CLnd CMCN CMen CPMA CSBt CWCL CWib ECho EMil LMaj LPan LRHS MBlu MBri MGos MPkF NBea NLar SCoo WFar WHar WPGP WPat |
| - 'First Ghost' | CBdw CPMA |
| - 'Fjellheim' | CPMA MPkF |
| - 'Frederici Guglielmi' | see *A. palmatum* var. *dissectum* 'Dissectum Variegatum' |
| - 'Fūhjin' | CBdw |
| - 'Garyū' | MPkF |
| - 'Gassho' | CBdw |
| - 'Geisha' | CBdw CPMA MGos MPkF |
| - 'Gekkō-nishiki' | CBdw |
| - 'Germaine's Gyration' | CBdw CPMA |
| - 'Glowing Embers' | WPat |
| - 'Golden Pond' | CBdw CPMA |
| - 'Goshiki-kotohime' (v) | CMCN CPMA LRHS MPkF |
| - 'Goten-nomura' | CBdw |
| - 'Green Star' | CBdw |
| - 'Green Trompenburg' | CMCN CMen ECho MGos MPkF NLar |
| § - 'Hagoromo' | CDoC CMen ECho MPkF SCoo WFar |

| | |
|---|---|
| - 'Hanami-nishiki' | ECho MPkF WPat |
| - 'Harusame' (v) | MPkF |
| - 'Hatsukoi' (v) | CBdw |
| - 'Hazeroino' (v) | MPkF |
| - 'Heartbeat' | CBdw CPMA |
| - var. ***heptalobum*** | CMCN |
| § - 'Heptalobum Elegans' | CMCN LRHS MBlu SSpi |
| - 'Heptalobum Elegans Purpureum' | see *A. palmatum* 'Hessei' |
| - 'Herbstfeuer' | CPMA MPkF |
| § - 'Hessei' | CEnd CMCN CWCL ECho MBlu NBea NLar |
| - 'Higasayama' (v) | CBcs CEnd CMCN CMen CPMA ECho GKir LRHS MGos MPkF NHol SCoo WHar WPGP WPat |
| - 'Hino-tori-nishiki' | CMen |
| - 'Hi-no-tsukasa' | CBdw |
| - 'Hōgyoku' | CMCN CMen CPMA MPkF |
| - 'Hondoshi' | CBdw |
| - 'Hooftman A' | CBdw |
| - 'Hoshi-kuzu' | CBdw MPkF |
| - 'Hubbs Red Willow' | CBdw |
| - 'Ibo-nishiki' | CMen MPkF |
| - 'Ichigyōji' | CEnd CMCN CMen CPMA ECho LMil LRHS SBig SChF WPGP WPat |
| - 'Inazuma' | CBcs CDoC CMCN CMen CPMA ECho EPfP LRHS MPkF NBPN NLar SBod SCoo SLau WFar WPat |
| - 'Irish Lace' | CBdw CPMA |
| - 'Issai-nishiki' | ECho MPkF |
| * - 'Issai-nishiki-kawazu' | MPkF |
| - 'Itami-nishiki' | CBdw |
| - 'Jane' | MPkF |
| - 'Japanese Sunrise' | CPMA MPkF |
| - 'Jerre Schwartz' | MGos NLar WPat |
| - 'Jirō-shidare' | CBdw CPMA EPfP MPkF NLar SBig |
| - 'Julia D.' | CPMA NLar |
| - 'Kaba' | CMen MPkF |
| - 'Kagero' (v) | MPkF WFar |
| § - 'Kagiri-nishiki' (v) | CBcs CDul CMCN CMen CPMA CWSG ECho LRHS MPkF NHol NLar WFar |
| - 'Kamagata' | CBdw CEnd CMCN CMen CPMA ECho EPfP IDee LMil LRHS MBri MGos MPkF NHol NLar SCoo SPer WPGP WPat |
| - 'Kandy Kitchen' | CPMA LRHS MGos MPkF |
| - 'Karaori-nishiki' (v) | CMen ECho MBlu MPkF NLar |
| - 'Karasugawa' (v) | CBdw CMen CPMA ECho MGos MPkF NLar |
| - 'Kasagiyama' | CBdw CEnd CMCN CMen CPMA ECho LMil MPkF NBea NLar WBod WPGP |
| - 'Kasen-nishiki' | CBdw CMen ECho MPkF |
| - 'Kashima' | CEnd CMCN CMen CPMA ECho MPkF NLar WFar |
| - 'Kashima-yatsubusa' | CBdw |
| - 'Katja' | CMen |
| - 'Katsura' ♀$^{H4}$ | Widely available |
| - 'Ki-hachijō' | CMCN CMen CPMA ECho EPfP MBri NLar WPat |
| - 'Kingsville Variegated' (v) | CBdw |
| - 'Kinran' | CMCN CMen ECho MPkF |
| - 'Kinshi' | CBdw CEnd CMCN CMen CPMA ECho EPfP LRHS MPkF NBea NHol SPoG SSta WPat |
| - 'Kiyohime' | CBdw CDoC CMCN CMen ECho MBlu MPkF NBea WFar WPat |
| - 'Koba-shōjō' | CBdw |
| - 'Ko-chidori' | CBdw |
| - 'Kogane-nishiki' | ECho |
| - 'Kogane-sakae' | CPMA |

| | | |
|---|---|---|
| | – 'Kokobunji-nishiki' (v) | CBdw |
| | – 'Komache-hime' | CBdw CMen CPMA ECho WPat |
| * | – 'Komaru' | NLar |
| | – 'Komon-nishiki' (v) | CBdw CMen CPMA ECho MPkF |
| | – 'Koriba' | CBdw CPMA MPkF NLar |
| § | – 'Koshimino' | CPMA |
| | – 'Kotohime' | CAbP CBdw CMCN CMen CPMA LRHS MBri MPkF NLar SBig SCoo SPoG |
| | – 'Koto-ito-komachi' | CBdw CMen CPMA ECho LRHS MPkF NLar WPat |
| | – 'Koto-maru' | MPkF |
| | – 'Koto-no-ito' | CBdw CMCN LRHS MBri MGos MPkF NLar WHar WPat |
| | – 'Koya-san' | CBdw CMen MPkF |
| | – 'Koyō-ao-shidare' | CBdw |
| | – 'Krazy Krinkle' | CPMA |
| | – 'Kurabu-yama' | CMen MPkF |
| | – 'Kurui-jishi' | CBdw MGos MPkF WPat |
| | – 'Kyra' | CMen MPkF |
| | – 'Lemon Lime Lace' | CBdw |
| | – 'Linearilobum' | ECho EPfP LHyd LMil MBlu MGos MPkF NBea NLar SCoo WFar WHar WPat |
| | – 'Linearilobum Atropurpureum' | NBea |
| | – 'Lin-ling' | LMil |
| | – 'Little Princess' | see *A. palmatum* 'Chiyo-hime' |
| | – 'Lozita' | WPat |
| | – 'Lutescens' | ECho MPkF |
| | – 'Lydia' | MPkF |
| | – 'Maiko' | CMen ECho MPkF |
| | – 'Mama' | CMen ECho |
| | – 'Manyō-no-sato' (v) | CBdw |
| | – 'Mapi-no-machihime' | CBdw CEnd CMCN CMen CPMA ECho ELan LMil LRHS MAsh MBri MGos MPkF NHol WPGP WPat |
| | – 'Marakumo' | MPkF |
| | – 'Mardi Gras' | CPMA |
| | – 'Marjan' | NLar |
| | – 'Masamurasaki' | CMen WPat |
| | – 'Masukagami' (v) | CEnd CPMA MPkF NLar |
| | – 'Matsuga-e' (v) | CMen ECho MPkF |
| | – 'Matsukaze' | CMCN CMen CPMA ECho |
| | – 'Meihō-nishiki' | CBdw CPMA |
| | – 'Melanie' | CPMA SBig |
| | – 'Meoto' | CBdw |
| | – 'Midori-no-teiboku' | CBdw |
| | – 'Mikawa-yatsubusa' | CBdw CMCN CMen CPMA ECho EPfP LRHS MGos MPkF NBhm NLar SPoG WPat |
| | – 'Mimaye' | CPMA |
| | – 'Mirte' | CPMA MPkF SBig WFar WPat |
| | – 'Mischa' | CBdw |
| | – 'Misty Moon' | CBdw |
| | – 'Mitsuba-yama' | CBdw |
| | – 'Mizuho-beni' | CPMA ECho |
| | – 'Mizu-kuguri' | CMCN MPkF NLar |
| | – 'Momenshide' | CBdw |
| | – 'Momoiro-koya-san' | CBdw CPMA MPkF WPat |
| | – 'Mon Papa' | CPMA |
| | – 'Monzukushi' | CPMA MPkF |
| | – 'Moonfire' | CMCN CPMA EPfP LMil LRHS MPkF NLar SPoG WPat |
| | – 'Mr Sun' | CPMA |
| * | – 'Muncaster' | LMil SBig |
| | – 'Murasaki-hime' | MPkF |
| | – 'Murasaki-kiyohime' | CBdw CEnd CMCN CMen CPMA ECho GBin LRHS MPkF WPat |
| | – 'Murasaki-shikibu' | CBdw |
| | – 'Mure-hibari' | CMCN CPMA MPkF |
| | – 'Murogawa' | CPMA ECho |
| | – 'Nanase-gawa' | MPkF |

| | | |
|---|---|---|
| | – 'Nicholsonii' | CMCN CMen CTri ECho EPfP LMil MPkF NLar WFar WPat |
| | – 'Nigrum' 🏆$^{H4}$ | CMCN ECho LPan SHBN WPat |
| | – 'Nishiki-gasane' (v) | MPkF |
| § | – 'Nishiki-gawa' | CBdw CEnd CMCN CMen CPMA ECho MPkF WPGP |
| | – 'Nishiki-momiji' | CMen |
| | – 'Nomura' | CMen CPMA |
| | – 'Nomurishidare' misapplied | see *A. palmatum* var. *dissectum* 'Shojo-shidare' |
| | – 'Nomurishidare' Wada | MAsh SSpi |
| | – 'Nuresagi' | CBdw CEnd CPMA |
| | – 'Ōgi-nagashi' (v) | CBdw |
| | – 'Ōgon-sarasa' | CPMA MPkF |
| | – 'Ojishi' | CMen MPkF |
| | – 'Ō-kagami' | CBcs CDoC CEnd CMen CPMA ECho GKir LMil LRHS MPkF NLar SCoo WPGP |
| | – 'Okukuji-nishiki' | CBdw CPMA |
| | – 'Okushimo' | CBdw CEnd CMCN CMen CPMA ECho MBri MPkF NHol NLar WPGP WPat |
| | – 'Omato' | CPMA MPkF SBig WFar |
| | – 'Omurayama' | CBcs CDoC CEnd CMCN CMen CPMA ECho EPfP LRHS MGos MPkF NBhm NLar SCoo SPer SSta WFar WPat |
| | – 'Orange Dream' | Widely available |
| | – 'Oregon Sunset' | CBdw MPkF WPat |
| | – 'Oridono-nishiki' (v) | CBcs CDoC CDul CEnd CMCN CMen CPMA CWCL ECho ELan EPfP LMil LRHS MAsh MBar MBlu MGos MPkF NLar SCoo SPer SPoG SSta WBod WFar WHar WOrn |
| | – 'Ori-zuru' | CBdw |
| | – 'Ōsakazuki' 🏆$^{H4}$ | Widely available |
| | – 'Ōshio-beni' | CMen CPMA ECho |
| | – 'Ōshu-shidare' | CBdw CMen CPMA ECho EPfP MPkF WFar |
| | – 'Oto-hime' | CPMA ECho MPkF |
| | – 'Otome-zakura' | CMen CPMA ECho MPkF WPat |
| | – 'Peaches and Cream' (v) | CBdw CMen CPMA ECho MPkF NLar SPer WPat |
| | – 'Peve Chameleon' **new** | MPkF |
| | – 'Peve Dave' | MPkF NLar |
| | – 'Peve Multicolor' | CBdw CMen CPMA MGos MPkF NLar |
| | – 'Phoenix' | CBdw MBri MPkF |
| | – 'Pine Bark Maple' | see *A. palmatum* 'Nishiki-gawa' |
| | – 'Pixie' | CBdw CMen CPMA MGos MPkF NLar WPat |
| | – 'Pung-kil' | CBdw MPkF |
| | – 'Purple Ghost' | CBdw |
| | – 'Red Baron' | CPMA |
| | – 'Red Cloud' | CBdw MPkF NLar |
| | – 'Red Embers' | CWib |
| | – 'Red Emperor' | NLar |
| | – 'Red Flash' | LPan WPat |
| | – 'Red Jonas' | NBPN NLar WPat |
| | – 'Red Pygmy' 🏆$^{H4}$ | Widely available |
| | – 'Red Spider' | CPMA |
| | – 'Red Wood' | CDoC CPMA ECho GBin MBri MPkF SBod SCoo SLau SPer WPat |
| | – 'Reticulatum' | see *A. palmatum* 'Shigitatsu-sawa' |
| | – 'Ribesifolium' | see *A. palmatum* 'Shishigashira' |
| * | – 'Rigassii' **new** | LMaj |
| | – 'Rising Sun' | CPMA |
| | – 'Rokugatsu-en-nishiki' | CBdw WPat |
| | – 'Roseomarginatum' | see *A. palmatum* 'Kagiri-nishiki' |
| | – 'Roseum Ornatum' | CBdw |
| | – 'Rough Bark Maple' | see *A. palmatum* 'Arakawa' |
| | – 'Royle' | CBdw CPMA |
| | – 'Rubrum' | CMen ECho |
| I | – 'Rubrum Kaiser' | CPMA ECho |

| | | |
|---|---|---|
| | – 'Ruby Ridge' **new** | CPMA |
| | – 'Ruby Star' | CPMA MPkF NLar |
| | – 'Ryōkū-ryū' | CMen |
| | – 'Ryuto' | CBdw |
| | – 'Ryuzu' | CPMA MPkF WPat |
| | – 'Sagara-nishiki' (v) | CBdw CEnd CMen CPMA ECho |
| | – 'Saint Jean' | CBdw |
| | – 'Samidare' | CPMA EPfP MPkF NLar |
| | – 'Sandra' | CMen MPkF |
| N | – 'Sango-kaku' 𝕐$^{H4}$ | Widely available |
| | – 'Saoshika' | CMen CPMA ECho MPkF |
| | – 'Sa-otome' | CMen ECho MPkF |
| | – 'Satsuki-beni' | ECho |
| | – 'Sawa-chidori' | CBdw |
| | – 'Sazanami' | CDoC CEnd CPMA CWCL ECho MPkF NBea NLar WPGP WPat |
| | – 'Scolopendriifolium' | CBcs CDoC GBin LMil LRHS MPkF SCoo SLau WFar WPat |
| § | – 'Seigai' | CPMA MPkF |
| | – 'Seigen' | CBdw CEnd CMCN CMen CPMA ECho MPkF WPGP |
| I | – 'Seigen Aureum' | CPMA |
| | – 'Seiun-kaku' | CBdw CMen CPMA MBri WPat |
| | – 'Sekimori' | CBdw CPMA SBig |
| | – 'Sekka-yatsubusa' | CMCN CMen ECho |
| N | – 'Senkaki' | see *A. palmatum* 'Sango-kaku' |
| | – 'Septemlobum Elegans' | see *A. palmatum* 'Heptalobum Elegans' |
| | – 'Septemlobum Purpureum' | see *A. palmatum* 'Hessei' |
| | – 'Sessilifolium' dwarf | see *A. palmatum* 'Hagoromo' |
| | – 'Sessilifolium' tall | see *A. palmatum* 'Koshimino' |
| | – 'Shaina' | CBcs CDoC CEnd CMen CPMA CWCL CWib ECho LPan LRHS MBri MGos MPkF NBhm NLar NPal SBod SCoo WFar WHar |
| | – 'Sharp's Pygmy' | CBdw CMen CPMA ECho GBin LRHS MPkF WPat |
| | – 'Sherwood Flame' | CDoC CMCN CMen CPMA CWib ECho LRHS MAsh MBlu MGos MPkF NLar SCoo WFar WPat |
| | – 'Shichigosan' | CMen |
| | – 'Shidava Gold' | CBdw CPMA |
| | – 'Shi-en' | MPkF |
| | – 'Shigarami' | CPMA MPkF |
| | – 'Shigi-no-hoshi' | CBdw |
| § | – 'Shigitatsu-sawa' (v) | CBcs CBdw CEnd CMCN CMen CPMA ECho EMil LPan LRHS MGos MPkF NBea NLar SBig SHBN |
| | – 'Shigure-bato' | CPMA MPkF |
| | – 'Shigurezome' | CMCN MPkF |
| | – 'Shikageori-nishiki' | CMen CPMA ECho MPkF |
| | – 'Shime-no-uchi' | CMCN CPMA LMil MPkF SBig |
| | – 'Shindeshōjō' | Widely available |
| § | – 'Shinobuga-oka' | CBcs CMCN CMen CPMA ECho LRHS MPkF SCoo SLau |
| | – 'Shinonome' | CPMA MPkF |
| | – 'Shirazz' (v) **new** | MPkF |
| | – 'Shiro-fu-nishiki' | CBdw |
| § | – 'Shishigashira' | CDoC CMCN CMen CPMA EBee ECho EPfP LMil LRHS MBar MBlu MBri MDun MGos MPkF NBea NLar SCoo SPoG WBod WDin WFar WPat |
| | – 'Shishigashira-no-yatsubusa' | CBdw |
| § | – 'Shishio' | CBcs CMCN CMen ECho LAst LHyd LRHS MPkF SBig SSpi WPat |
| § | – 'Shishio Improved' | CBdw CEnd CMCN CPMA CTho CWSG ECho EPfP MBlu MGos MPkF NBhm NHol NLar SBig SWvt WBod WHar |
| | – 'Shōjō' | CMCN CPMA WFar |
| | – 'Shōjō-no-mai' | CBdw |
| | – 'Shōjō-nomura' | CAbP CEnd CMen MGos MPkF NBea NLar WPGP WPat |
| | – 'Sister Ghost' | CBdw CPMA |
| | – 'Skeeter's Broom' | CBcs CBdw CPMA ECho LRHS MBri MGos MPkF NBPN SBig SCoo WPat |
| * | – 'Sode-nishiki' | CBdw CPMA MPkF NLar |
| | – 'Stella Rossa' | CBdw CEnd CPMA LPan MBlu MPkF NBea NLar WPat |
| | – 'Suminagashi' | CBcs CDoC CMCN CMen CWCL ECho LMil LRHS MGos MPkF NBPN NLar SBod SChF SCoo SLau WBod WPat |
| I | – 'Summer Gold' | LPan MBri SPoG SWvt |
| * | – 'Sunago' | NLar |
| | – 'Suruga-nishiki' (v) | CBdw |
| | – 'Susan' | MPkF |
| | – 'Taiyō-nishiki' | CBdw CPMA MPkF |
| | – 'Takinogawa' | LRHS |
| | – 'Tamahime' | CMen CPMA ECho |
| | – 'Tana' | CBdw CMCN CPMA EPfP MPkF WFar WPat |
| | – 'Tarō-yama' | CBdw CPMA WPat |
| | – 'Tatsuta' | ECho MPkF WHar |
| | – 'Taylor'$^{PBR}$ (v) | CEnd EMil LRHS MBri MPkF NLar SCoo SPoG |
| | – 'Tennyo-no-hoshi' | CMen ECho MPkF NLar |
| | – 'Tiger Rose' | CBdw CPMA |
| | – 'Tiny Tim' | CBdw CPMA |
| | – 'Trompenburg' 𝕐$^{H4}$ | Widely available |
| | – 'Tsuchigumo' | CMen CPMA ECho MPkF NLar |
| | – 'Tsukubane' | WPat |
| | – 'Tsukushigata' | MPkF |
| | – 'Tsuma-beni' | CBdw CMCN CMen EPfP LRHS MPkF |
| | – 'Tsuma-gaki' | CBdw CDoC CMCN CMen CPMA ECho EPfP MBri MGos MPkF NLar WPat |
| | – 'Tsuri-nishiki' | CBdw CMen CPMA ECho MPkF NLar |
| | – 'Ueno-homare' | CBdw MPkF SCoo WPat |
| | – 'Ueno-yama' | CBcs CBdw CPMA GBin MGos MPkF WPat |
| | – 'Ukigumo' (v) | Widely available |
| | – 'Ukon' | CBdw CMCN CMen CPMA ECho EMil GBin LMil MPkF SBod SCoo |
| | – 'Umegae' | CPMA |
| | – 'Uncle Ghost' | CPMA |
| | – 'Usu-midori' | CPMA |
| | – 'Utsu-semi' | CPMA MPkF |
| | – 'Van der Akker' | CPMA |
| | – 'Vanderhoss Red' | ECho |
| | – 'Vens Red' | WPat |
| | – 'Versicolor' (v) | CBdw CEnd CMCN CPMA LRHS SHBN |
| | – 'Vic Broom' | CBdw |
| | – 'Vic Pink' | CBdw CPMA WPat |
| | – 'Villa Taranto' | CBcs CBdw CDoC CEnd CMCN CMen CPMA ECho EPfP LMil LRHS MAsh MBlu MBri MGos MPkF NBea NHol NLar SCoo SSpi SSta WHar WPGP WPat |
| | – 'Volubile' | CMCN CMen ECho EPfP |
| | – 'Wabito' | CMCN CPMA ECho LRHS MPkF |
| | – 'Waka-midori' | ECho |
| | – 'Waka-momiji' (v) | CBdw CPMA |
| | – 'Wakehurst Pink' (v) | CMCN MPkF WPat |
| | – 'Wendy' | CMen CPMA MPkF NLar WPat |
| | – 'Wetumpka Red' | CPMA |
| | – 'Whitney Red' | CMen |
| | – 'Will D' **new** | CPMA |
| | – 'Wilson's Pink Dwarf' | CBdw CEnd CMen CPMA CWib ECho LRHS MBri MGos MPkF NLar SCoo SPoG WPat |

| | | |
|---|---|---|
| | – 'Winter Flame' | CBdw CPMA LRHS MLan NHol NLar WHar WPat |
| § | – 'Wolff' | MPkF WPat |
| | – 'Wolff's Broom' | CBdw WPat |
| | – 'Wou-nishiki' | CBdw CMCN CMen ECho MPkF |
| | – 'Yana-gawa' | CMen ECho |
| | – 'Yasemin' | CBdw CMen CPMA MPkF NLar SBig |
| | – 'Yezo-nishiki' | CBdw CMCN CMen MPkF WFar |
| | – 'Yūba e' | MPkF WFar WPat |
| | – 'Yūgure' | MPkF NLar WFar |
| | ***papilio*** | see *A. caudatum* |
| | ***paxii*** | CMCN |
| | ***pectinatum*** 'Sirene' | see *A. forrestii* 'Sirene' |
| | – 'Sparkling' | see *A. forrestii* 'Sparkling' |
| | ***pensylvanicum*** ♀$^{H4}$ | Widely available |
| | – 'Erythrocladum' | CEnd CMCN CPMA EPfP LRHS MAsh MBri NBea NHol NLar SBig SLim SPur SSpi SSta WFar |
| | ***pentaphyllum*** | CMCN SBig SBir SPur SSpi |
| * | ***phlebanthum*** B&SWJ 9751 | WCru |
| § | ***pictum*** | CMCN |
| | – subsp. ***okamotoanum*** | CMCN WPGP |
| | – – B&SWJ 8516 | WCru |
| | – 'Shufu-nishiki' | CMCN |
| | – 'Usugomo' | WPat |
| | ***platanoides*** ♀$^{H4}$ | CBcs CCVT CDoC CDul CLnd CMCN CSBt CTri CWib EBee ECrN EMac EPfP LBuc MGos MMuc MSwo NBee NWea SBLw SPer STre WDin WFar WHar WMou |
| | – 'Charles Joly' | LMaj |
| | – 'Cleveland' | CBcs |
| | – 'Columnare' | CCVT CDul CLnd CMCN CWib ECrN SBLw SCoo WOrn |
| | – 'Crimson King' ♀$^{H4}$ | Widely available |
| | – 'Crimson Sentry' | CDoC CDul CEnd CLnd CMCN CWib EBee ECrN ELan EPfP IArd LAst LCro LPan MAsh MBlu MBri MGos MLan MRav NBee SCoo SLim WDin WFar WHar |
| | – 'Cucullatum' | CMCN |
| | – 'Deborah' | CBcs CTho LMaj LPan SBLw SCoo WOrn |
| | – 'Drummondii' (v) | Widely available |
| | – 'Emerald Queen' | CCVT CLnd CWib ECrN LMaj SBLw SHBN WDin |
| | – 'Faassen's Black' | CPMA SBLw |
| § | – 'Globosum' | CLnd CMCN EBee ECrN EHig LBuc LCro LMaj LPan NLar SBLw SWvt |
| | – 'Goldsworth Purple' | CDul CLnd |
| | – 'Laciniatum' | CEnd CMCN ECrN |
| | – 'Lorbergii' | see *A. platanoides* 'Palmatifidum' |
| | – 'Marit' | WPat |
| § | – 'Palmatifidum' | CLnd |
| | – Princeton Gold = 'Prigo'PBR | CDoC CDul ELan EMil LPan LRHS MAsh MGos SCoo SPoG |
| | – 'Red Lace' | WOrn |
| | – 'Reitenbachii' | CDul LMaj |
| | – 'Royal Red' | CBcs CDul CWib EBee ECrN LMaj LPan MRav NBPN NLar SCoo |
| | – 'Schwedleri' ♀$^{H4}$ | CDul CMCN ECrN EPfP MGos NWea SBLw WDin |
| | – 'Tharandt' | CMCN |
| | – 'Walderseei' | CLnd |
| | ***pseudoplatanus*** | CBcs CCVT CDul CLnd CMCN CSBt CTri ECrN EMac LBuc LPan MBar MGos NBee NWea SBLw SPer WDin WFar WHar WMou |
| § | – 'Atropurpureum' | CDoC CDul CLnd EWTr NBee NWea SBLw WDin WHar |
| | – 'Brilliantissimum' ♀$^{H4}$ | Widely available |
| | – 'Corstorphinense' | CMCN |
| | – 'Erectum' | WFar |
| | – 'Gadsby' | CDul |
| | – 'Prinz Handjéry' | CBcs CDul CEnd CLnd CMCN CSBt CTri CWib LPan MAsh MBar MGos NHol NLar NWea SBLw SPer SPoG SSpi WHar |
| | – f. ***purpureum*** | SEND |
| | – 'Spaethii' misapplied | see *A. pseudoplatanus* 'Atropurpureum' |
| | – 'Sunshine' | LBuc LRHS MGos |
| | – f. ***variegatum*** 'Esk Sunset' (v) | CBcs CDul ECho LRHS MBri MGos MPkF NLar |
| | – – 'Leopoldii' Vervaene (v) | SCrf |
| | – – 'Leopoldii' ambig. (v) | CBcs CDul CLnd CMCN EBee ECrN ELan LAst LPan NBee SBLw SCoo SEND SHBN SPer SWvt WDin WFar WOrn |
| | – – 'Nizetii' (v) | CMCN SBLw |
| | – – 'Simon-Louis Frères' (v) | CCVT CDul CEnd CLnd CMCN CWSG CWib EBee ECrN EMui LAst LPan LRHS MAsh MBar MBri MGos NBee NLar SBod SCrf SPer SPoG SWvt WFar WFoF WHar WOrn |
| | – 'Worley' | CBcs CCVT CDul CLnd CMCN CSBt CTri EBee ECrN LRHS MAsh MBar MRav NBee NWea SBLw SCrf SEND SHBN SLim SPer WDin WHar WOrn |
| | ***pseudosieboldianum*** | CMCN CPMA IDee MBlu |
| | – var. ***microsieboldianum*** B&SWJ 8766 | WCru |
| | ***pycnanthum*** | EPfP |
| | ***rubescens*** | CPMA WPGP |
| | – B&SWJ 6735 | WCru |
| | – RWJ 9840 **new** | WCru |
| | – variegated seedlings (v) | CPMA WPGP |
| | ***rubrum*** | Widely available |
| | – 'Autumn Spire' | CPMA |
| | – 'Bowhall' | SBir |
| | – 'Brandywine' | CPMA GKir MAsh MBri SPoG SSpi |
| | – 'Candy Ice' (v) | CPMA |
| | – 'Columnare' | CMCN EPfP |
| | – 'Embers' | CPMA |
| | – Fireball = 'Firzam' **new** | CPMA |
| | – 'Firedance' | CPMA |
| | – 'New World' **new** | NLar |
| | – 'Northwood' | CPMA |
| | – 'October Glory' ♀$^{H4}$ | Widely available |
| | – 'Red King' **new** | CPMA |
| | – 'Red Rocket' **new** | SPoG SSpi |
| | – Red Sunset = 'Franksred' | CDoC CDul CEnd CMCN CPMA CTho EBee EPfP GKir LMaj LPan LRHS MBlu NLar SBir SCoo SMad SSta WPGP |
| | – 'Scanlon' | CBcs CDoC CDul CEnd CMCN CPMA CTho EBee ECho EPfP LAst LMaj LPan MBlu SBLw SPer WOrn |
| | – 'Schlesingeri' | CEnd CMCN CMac CPMA EPfP |
| | – 'Somerset' | CPMA MBri |
| | – 'Summer Red' **new** | CPMA |
| | – 'Sun Valley' | CPMA MAsh |
| | – 'Tilford' | CPMA SBir SSta |
| § | ***rufinerve*** ♀$^{H4}$ | CBcs CCVT CDoC CDul CLnd CMCN CTho CTri EBee ECrN EHig EPfP EPla LCro LMaj LRHS MAsh MBri NBea NLar NWea SBLw SCoo SPer WBVN WDin WOrn WPGP |
| | – 'Albolimbatum' | see *A. rufinerve* 'Hatsuyuki' |
| | – 'Albomarginatum' | see *A. rufinerve* 'Hatsuyuki' |
| | – 'Erythrocladum' | CBcs CPMA |
| § | – 'Hatsuyuki' (v) | CEnd CMCN CPMA SBig WPGP |
| | – 'Winter Gold' | CPMA CTho EPfP LRHS NLar SPur SSpi |

| | |
|---|---|
| § ***saccharinum*** | CBcs CCVT CDoC CDul CLnd CMCN CTri CWib EBee ECrN ELan EMac EPfP LRHS MGos MLan MMuc MWat NBee NWea SBLw SCoo SHBN SPer WDin WFar WHar |
| - 'Born's Gracious' | CPMA EMil |
| - 'Fastigiatum' | see *A. saccharinum* f. *pyramidale* |
| - f. ***laciniatum*** | CMCN EBee LAst MBlu MGos MMuc SPer WDin |
| - 'Laciniatum Wieri' | CDul CMCN EBee ECrN LAst LPan SBLw WDin |
| - f. ***lutescens*** | CDul CMCN MBlu SBLw |
| § - f. ***pyramidale*** | CDoC CLnd CMCN EBee ECrN LMaj SBLw SPer WDin |
| ***saccharum*** | CAgr CBcs CDoC CDul CLnd CMCN CTho ECrN EPfP MBlu MLan NWea SBLw SHBN SPer |
| - 'Adirondak' | CPMA |
| - 'Arrowhead' | CPMA |
| - subsp. ***barbatum*** | see *A. saccharum* subsp. *floridanum* |
| - 'Brocade' | CPMA MPkF SBir |
| - 'Caddo' | CPMA |
| - 'Fiddlers Creek' | CPMA |
| § - subsp. ***floridanum*** | CMCN |
| § - subsp. ***grandidentatum*** | CMCN MBlu NLar |
| - 'Green Mountain' | CPMA LPan |
| - 'Legacy' | LPan |
| § - subsp. ***leucoderme*** | CMCN |
| - 'Majesty' | CPMA |
| - subsp. ***nigrum*** | CMCN |
| - - 'Greencolumn' | CPMA |
| - 'Sugar Cone' | CPMA |
| § ***sempervirens*** | CGHE EBee LEdu WPGP |
| 'Sensu' | CPMA |
| ***serrulatum*** B&SWJ 6760 | WCru |
| ***shirasawanum*** | CMCN |
| § - 'Aureum' ♀H4 | Widely available |
| - 'Autumn Moon' | CBcs CBdw CEnd CPMA EPfP LRHS MBri MPkF NLar SCoo |
| § - 'Ezo-no-momiji' | CMCN CMen CPMA MPkF NLar |
| - 'Johin' | CPMA |
| - 'Jordan'$^{PBR}$ | CEnd LPan MBri NLar |
| - 'Lovett' | CPMA |
| § - 'Microphyllum' | CMCN ECho MPkF |
| § - 'Ogurayama' | CBdw CPMA ECho |
| - 'Palmatifolium' | CBdw CMCN CPMA |
| - 'Susanne' | CPMA |
| ***sieboldianum*** | CDul CMCN CMen CTri ECho ECrN SSpi WHCr WHar WPat |
| - 'Sode-no-uchi' | CMCN CMen |
| 'Silver Cardinal' (v) | CBcs CDul CEnd CMCN CPMA EBee EHig EPfP LRHS MBlu MGos MPkF NBhm NLar SMad WHar |
| 'Silver Vein' | see *A.* x *conspicuum* 'Silver Vein' |
| ***sinense*** | SSpi |
| ***spicatum*** | EPfP NLar |
| § ***stachyophyllum*** | GAuc GQui |
| § ***sterculiaceum*** | CMCN EBee WPGP |
| - subsp. ***franchetii*** | NLar |
| - subsp. ***sterculiaceum*** GWJ 9317 **new** | WCru |
| ***syriacum*** | see *A. obtusifolium* |
| ***takesimense*** | MBri |
| - B&SWJ 8500 | WCru |
| ***tataricum*** | CMCN |
| § - subsp. ***ginnala*** | CBcs CDul CLnd CMCN CTri CWSG ECrN EMac EPfP EWTr LMaj MAsh MGos NBea NPal NWea SBLw SHBN SPer WDin WPat |
| - - 'Flame' | CPMA CWSG EBee EHig ELan EPfP LRHS MGos MMuc NLar NWea SPoG |
| - - 'Red Wing' **new** | CPMA |
| ***tegmentosum*** | CBcs CMCN CPMA EPfP LPan MBlu MBri |
| - B&SWJ 8421 | WCru |
| - subsp. ***glaucorufinerve*** | see *A. rufinerve* |
| ***tetramerum*** | see *A. stachyophyllum* |
| ***trautvetteri*** | CMCN EPfP |
| ***triflorum*** ♀H4 | CBcs CDul CMCN CPMA CSBt CTho EPfP LMaj LPan LRHS MBri NBea NLar SSpi WDin WFar |
| ***truncatum*** | CMCN ISea MPkF |
| - 'Akikaze-nishiki' (v) | CPMA MPkF |
| ***tschonoskii*** | GQui |
| - subsp. ***koreanum*** | MPkF |
| § ***turkestanicum*** | CMCN EBee WFar |
| ***velutinum*** | CMCN |
| - var. ***vanvolxemii*** | WPGP |
| ***villosum*** | see *A. sterculiaceum* |
| 'White Tigress' | CPMA CTho MBlu NLar WPGP |
| ***wilsonii*** | CDul CSam |
| x ***zoeschense*** | CMCN |
| - 'Annae' | NHol SBLw |

## *Aceriphyllum* see *Mukdenia*

## x *Achicodonia* (*Gesneriaceae*)

| | |
|---|---|
| 'Dark Velvet' | WDib |

## *Achillea* (*Asteraceae*)

| | |
|---|---|
| ***ageratifolia*** ♀H4 | EBla ECho ECtt EDAr EOHP LBee MTho NBre NLar SRms WClo WFar |
| - subsp. ***serbica*** | EDAr |
| § ***ageratum*** | CArn CHby CPrp ELau GBar GPoy MHer MNHC MSal NGHP NPri NTHB SIde SRms WGwG WHer WJek WLHH WPer |
| Anthea = 'Anblo'$^{PBR}$ | CKno CWCL EAEE EBee EBla EBrs ECtt EGle GBBs LPio LRHS LSRN MBri MCot MLLN MRav MSte NChi NCob NLar SPer SRGP SRkn SRms WFar |
| Appleblossom | see *A. millefoium* 'Apfelblüte' |
| ***argentea*** misapplied | see *A. clavennae*, *A. umbellata* |
| ***argentea*** Lamarck | see *Tanacetum argenteum* |
| ***aurea*** | see *A. chrysocoma* |
| 'Breckland Bouquet' | ECtt EWes |
| 'Breckland Ruby' | ECtt EWes |
| 'Brilliant' | LRHS |
| 'Carmina Burana' **new** | CAbx MSte |
| 'Caroline' | LRHS |
| ***cartilaginea*** | see *A. salicifolia* |
| § ***chrysocoma*** | ECho EDAr MWat WMoo |
| - 'Grandiflora' | CHar EBee ECha ELan LPla NGdn |
| 'Citrona' **new** | NBHF |
| § ***clavennae*** | ECho EDAr LPio MLLN MWat SMrm SRms WAbe WFar |
| ***clypeolata*** Sibth. & Sm. | EBee EPPr EShb LHop LPio NBre NLar SPhx SPlb SRms WOut |
| ***coarctata*** | NBir WPer |
| 'Coronation Gold' ♀H4 | CDoC CPrp CTca CWCL EBee EBla ECtt ELan EPfP GMac LAst LRHS MBri MNFA MRav MWat SAga WCAu WCot WEas WFar |
| 'Cranberry Fool' **new** | EBee |
| ***crithmifolia*** | GKir |
| ***decolorans*** | see *A. ageratum* |
| ***erba-rotta*** | WPer |
| - subsp. ***moschata*** | ECho NBro |
| ***filipendulina*** | GKir SWal WHrl |
| - 'Cloth of Gold' ♀H4 | Widely available |
| - 'Gold Plate' ♀H4 | Widely available |
| - 'Parker's Variety' ♀H4 | EBee GQue MLan NBre WFar |
| Flowers of Sulphur | see *A.* 'Schwefelblüte' |

| | | |
|---|---|---|
| | ***fraasii*** | MDKP |
| | 'Gartenzwerg' | EMon |
| | ***glaberrima*** hybrid | WCot |
| | 'Gloria Jean' | CSli SHar |
| | 'Gold and Grey' | CSli |
| | 'Goldstar' | EBee LRHS NBHF NBPC NDov WFar |
| | ***grandifolia*** misapplied | see *Tanacetum macrophyllum* (Waldst. & Kit.) Sch.Bip. |
| § | ***grandifolia*** Friv. | CElw CFwr COlW CSam CSec EBee EGle GBuc MRav MSte NBro SMad SSvw WAul WBor WFar WHer WHil WMnd WMoo WOld |
| | 'Great Expectations' | see *A. millefolium* 'Hoffnung' |
| | 'Grey and Gold' | SMrm |
| | 'Hannelore Pahl' | NBHF NBre |
| | 'Hartington White' | GBuc |
| | x ***huteri*** | CLyd EAlp EAro EBee EBla ECho ECtt EDAr EPfP LBee LRHS MHer MRav SPoG WClo WEas WFar |
| | 'Inca Gold' | EAEE EBee EBla ECha ECtt EGle EHrv EPPr EShb GBuc GQue LRHS MRav NBro NCob NGdn NHol NPro SAga SPav |
| | 'Jacqueline' | EWll MAvo NBHF |
| | 'Judith' | WOut |
| | x ***kellereri*** | NLar |
| | 'King Alfred' | LAst MMuc |
| | x ***kolbiana*** | LSou MWat NMen SRms |
| § | - 'Weston' | NBre |
| | x ***lewisii*** | NMen |
| | - 'King Edward' ΥH4 | CSam EAlp ECha ECho EDAr EPfP GBin GMaP LPio NBir SIng SPoG WFar |
| | ***ligustica*** | WCot |
| | 'Lucky Break' ΥH4 | EBla ECha SDix SMHy SUsu |
| | ***macrophylla*** | NBre |
| | 'Martina' ΥH4 | CDoC CKno CMMP CPrp CSli EBee ECtt EGle EPPr EPfP GAbr GBuc IPot LAst LBMP LHop LRHS MCot MLLN MRav MSte NCGa NDov NGdn NHol NOrc NPro SRGP |
| | ***millefolium*** | CArn COld CWan EBWF ELau GBar GPoy MNHC NLan NMir NSco SECG SPlb WHer WJek WLHH WSFF |
| | - 'Alabaster' | CDes CSli EBee GBuc NBHF NDov SPhx |
| § | - 'Apfelblüte' (Galaxy Series) | CPrp CSBt CSli CWCL EAEE EBee EBla ECha ECtt EGle ELan LBMP LLWG LRHS LSRN MRav NCGa NDov NGdn NHol SEND SPer WCAu WFar WMnd WPer |
| | - 'Apricot Beauty' | CSli CTca EBee ECtt GBBs GMaP GQue LSRN NHol NPro SSvw |
| | - 'Bahama' | EPPr GBin GQue MAvo NBHF NBre NBro |
| | - 'Belle Epoque' ΥH4 | CSli EBee MAvo NBHF |
| | - 'Bloodstone' | CSli EBee ECtt EWes GBar MRav NBHF WOut |
| | - 'Bright Cerise' | WFar |
| | - 'Carla Hussey' | WFar |
| | - 'Cassis' | CCVN CSpe EAro ECGP GQue LDai LRHS MNHC NBre NGBl SDnm SPav SWal WFar WOut |
| § | - 'Cerise Queen' | Widely available |
| | - 'Cherry King' **new** | MCot |
| | - 'Christel' | CCVN CSli EWes GBin MAvo SUsu |
| | - 'Christine' | CSpe GBin NBre |
| | - 'Christine's Pink' ΥH4 | CKno CSli EPPr EShb NBHF SUsu |
| | - Colorado Group | CWCL EAro GAbr LRHS NBre NChi NHol SPav WFar WHrl |
| | - 'Credo' ΥH4 | Widely available |
| | - dark red | CSli |
| | - 'Excel' | EBee |

| | | |
|---|---|---|
| § | - 'Fanal' | Widely available |
| | - 'Faust' | CDes CHar CSli EBla ELon NBHF SMrm SPhx STes SUsu WPGP WPrP |
| | - 'Feuerland' | CSam CSli EBee EBla ECha ECtt ELon EPfP LRHS MLLN MRav NBir NDov NGdn NSti SMad SPer SUsu SWat WCAu WCot WFar WHil WPer |
| | - 'Fire King' | CElw CHal |
| | - (Forncett Series) 'Forncett Beauty' | CSli NBHF |
| | - - 'Forncett Bride' | CSli NBHF NBre NDov WHil |
| | - - 'Forncett Candy' | CSli NBHF NDov |
| | - - 'Forncett Citrus' | CSli EBee MAvo NBHF NBre WPGP |
| | - - 'Forncett Fletton' | Widely available |
| | - - 'Forncett Ivory' | CSli EPPr MSte NBHF NBre WHil |
| | - 'Harlekin' | EBee NBHF |
| | - 'Heidi' ΥH4 | CCVN CSli GBri |
| | - 'Hella Glashoff' ΥH4 | CDes CMea CSli CWCL CWan EBee EBrs ECho ECtt EGle EGoo EPPr GBin LRHS MWea NDov WCot WHoo |
| § | - 'Hoffnung' | CPrp CSli CWCL EBee EBla ECtt EGle LRHS MRav NPro SPer WCAu WMnd WPer |
| | - 'Kelwayi' ΥH4 | CSli |
| | - Kirschkönigin | see *A. millefolium* 'Cerise Queen' |
| § | - 'Lachsschönheit' (Galaxy Series) ΥH4 | Widely available |
| | - 'Lansdorferglut' ΥH4 | CKno CSli EBee EBrs EPPr LRHS MBri MRav NDov NPro SPhx SUsu |
| | - 'Lavender Beauty' | see *A. millefolium* 'Lilac Beauty' |
| § | - 'Lilac Beauty' | CBgR CHar CMHG COlW CSli EBrs ECha EHrv ELon EPPr EWTr GMaP IPot LCro LRHS LSRN MRav NBir NDov NGHP NHol NPri NSti SPav WFar WHoo WPer |
| * | - 'Lilac Queen' | CSli MArl |
| | - 'Lollypop' | LDai |
| | - 'Marie Ann' | CPar CWCL EBee ECtt GBri GQue LPio LSRN MAvo MLLN NBHF NBPC NBhm NLar NPro NSti SPhx SRGP |
| | - 'Marmalade' | CSli LSou NDov SMrm WMnd WPGP |
| | - 'McVities' | CSli CWCL EBee ECtt EPPr LEdu MLLN NPro SDnm SPav STes WCAu WCra WMnd WTin |
| | - 'Oertels Rose' | WFar |
| | - 'Old Brocade' | CSli EBee EShb NBre NDov NGby SPhx WPGP WPtf |
| | - 'Paprika' (Galaxy Series) | Widely available |
| * | - 'Pastel Shades' | GKir IFoB WMoo |
| | - 'Prospero' | WCot WCra |
| | - 'Raspberry Ripple' | GBin |
| | - 'Red Beauty' | CMHG CSli CWCL EBee LSou NBro SMad SRms SWat |
| | - 'Red Velvet' | Widely available |
| | - 'Rose Madder' | Widely available |
| | - 'Rosie' | GBar |
| | - 'Rougham Beauty' | CSli |
| | - 'Rougham Cream' | CSli |
| | - 'Rougham White' | CSli |
| | - 'Ruby Port' | WFar |
| | - 'Salmon Pink' | WFar |
| | - 'Salmon Queen' | NGHP NHol WCra |
| | - 'Sammetriese' | CBgR CSli CWan EBee EGle GBuc LRHS MNrw MSte NCGa SMad WCAu WCot WFar WTin |
| | - 'Schneetaler' | EBee GBin |
| | - 'Serenade' | EBee EBla NBHF WFar |
| | - 'Summer Berries' | NBHF WRHF |
| | - 'Summertime' | LAst SBod SPav |
| | - 'Terracotta' | Widely available |
| | - 'Tickled Pink' | WPer |

| | | |
|---|---|---|
| § | - 'Wesersandstein' | CDes CFir CHar CKno CSli CWCL EBee ECtt EPPr EShb GMaP MAvo MLLN NBir NHol NPro SAga STes WCot WFar WPer WTin |
| | - 'White Queen' | EBee LBMP NBHF WPer |
| | - 'Yellowstone' | EWes LAst LDai MBri WCra |
| | 'Mondpagode' ♀$^{H4}$ | CHar CMHG CPrp CSli EAEE EBee ECGP EGle EPPr LRHS LSRN MAvo MBNS MNFA MRav MSte NCGa NGdn NPro SMHy SPhx SUsu WPtf |
| * | 'Moonbeam' | EBla |
| | 'Moonshine' ♀$^{H3}$ | Widely available |
| | 'Moonwalker' | CAbP EBee MLLN NBre NGBl SIde SPav WCot WFar WPer |
| | ***nobilis*** subsp. ***neilreichii*** | CSli CSpe EBee EBla ECGP EGoo EHoe EHrv GBri MLLN MNFA NSti SPer WCot WHal WPrP WTin |
| | 'Nostalgia' | EBee NBHF |
| | ***odorata*** | EBee |
| | 'Old Rose' | MAvo |
| | 'Peardrop' | NBre |
| | 'Peter Davis' | see *Hippolytia herderi* |
| | 'Petra' **new** | EBee |
| | ***pindicola*** subsp. ***integrifolia*** | EWes |
| | 'Pink Lady' | EBee EBla GBBs MBri SPoG |
| | pink-flowered from Santa Cruz Island | CKno CWCL |
| | 'Pretty Belinda' | EBee EPfP GMac IPot NBPC NPri SHBN WBor WWlt |
| | 'Pretty Flamingo' | WOut |
| | ***ptarmica*** | CArn CBre EBWF ELau EMFW GBar MHer MSal NMir NPri SECG SHBN SIde WLHH |
| * | - 'Ballerina' | EHig NBre NDov NLar WOut |
| | - Innocence | see *A. ptarmica* 'Unschuld' |
| | - 'Major' | GMaP NBre |
| | - 'Nana Compacta' | CSli CSpe EBee EBla ECha IGor MLLN NBir NCGa SPlb SPoG SUsu WCFE WFar WHil WWlt |
| | - 'Perry's White' | CBcs CBre EBee ECha LRHS MNFA MNrw NGHP NGdn NHol SRGP WCot |
| | - 'Stephanie Cohen' | see *A. sibirica* 'Stephanie Cohen' |
| N | - The Pearl Group seed-raised (d) | CTri ELan GMaP LAst NPri NVic SPlb SPoG SWat WFar WMoo WPer WTin |
| N | - - 'Boule de Neige' (clonal) (d) | CHal EPfP GKir MBri MRav NBre NCob NPer NSti SPer SPet SPla WFar |
| N | - - 'The Pearl' (clonal) (d) ♀$^{H4}$ | Widely available |
| § | - 'Unschuld' | NBir |
| | - 'Weihenstephan' | EBee |
| | 'Rougham Bright Star' | CSli |
| | 'Rougham Salmon' | CSli |
| | 'Ruby Wine' **new** | CSli |
| § | ***salicifolia*** | CSli EPPr NBHF NBre SPav WFar WMoo |
| | - 'Silver Spray' | EBee GQue NBre NLar SDnm SPav WPtf |
| | 'Sally' | NBre |
| | Salmon Beauty | see *A. millefolium* 'Lachsschönheit' |
| | 'Sandstone' | see *A. millefolium* 'Wesersandstein' |
| § | 'Schwefelblüte' | MRav NBir SBch SMrm |
| | 'Schwellenburg' | CDes CHar CSli EBee NBre WPGP |
| | ***sibirica*** | SRGP |
| | - subsp. ***camschatica*** **new** | WPtf |
| | - - 'Love Parade' | CSec CSli CTca EAEE EBee EPfP ITim MMuc MNFA MNHC MRav NBPC NGdn SPad SPer SRGP SSvw WFar WMoo |
| § | - 'Stephanie Cohen' | CPrp EBee ECtt GBin MLLN MSte NBhm NGdn WCot WFar |
| | 'Stephanie' | EBee ECtt EPPr EWes LSRN NBHF NBre |
| | 'Summer Glory' | NCob |
| | Summer Pastels Group | CHrt GKir LRHS MNHC NBir NHol NOrc SPav SPoG SRms SWal WFar WHil WRha |
| | 'Summerwine' ♀$^{H4}$ | Widely available |
| | 'Sunbeam' | CSli SHar |
| I | 'Taygetea' | CSam CSli CTca EAEE EBee EBla ELan EPfP EShb LRHS MSte SDix SPer WCAu WFar WKif WPer WSHC |
| | 'The Beacon' | see *A. millefolium* 'Fanal' |
| | ***tomentosa*** ♀$^{H4}$ | CTri ECha ECho ECtt EPfP |
| § | - 'Aurea' | EBla ECho ELau MSCN NBlu NBre NBro |
| | - 'Maynard's Gold' | see *A. tomentosa* 'Aurea' |
| § | ***umbellata*** | EBee GBri WBrk |
| | - 'Weston' | see *A.* x *kolbiana* 'Weston' |
| | 'W.B. Childs' | CSli CSpe ECha ELan GBuc MArl MCot MNrw NDov SHar WCot WEas |
| | 'Walther Funcke' | Widely available |
| | 'Wilczekii' | NBre NChi SRms |
| | 'Yellowstone' | EBee MBri |

## x *Achimenantha* (*Gesneriaceae*)

| | |
|---|---|
| 'Aries' | WDib |
| 'Inferno' ♀$^{H1}$ | EABi WDib |
| 'Tyche' | EABi |

## *Achimenes* (*Gesneriaceae*)

| | |
|---|---|
| 'Ambroise Verschaffelt' ♀$^{H1}$ | EABi LAma WDib |
| 'Blue David' | EABi |
| 'Blue Sparkles' | EBrs |
| 'Boy David' | EABi |
| 'Cattleya' | LAma |
| 'Charity' | WDib |
| 'Clouded Yellow' | EABi |
| 'Coral Cameo Mix' | EABi |
| 'Crummock Water' | WDib |
| 'Donna' | EABi |
| 'Dot' | EABi |
| 'English Waltz' | EABi |
| ***erecta*** | WDib |
| 'Extravaganza' | WDib |
| 'Glory' **new** | WDib |
| ***grandiflora*** 'Robert Dressler' | EABi |
| 'Harry Williams' | LAma WDib |
| 'Hilda Michelssen' ♀$^{H1}$ | WDib |
| 'India' | EShb |
| 'Jennifer Goode' | EABi |
| 'Jubilee Gem' | EABi |
| 'Just Divine' | EABi |
| 'Kim Blue' **new** | WDib |
| 'Little Beauty' | SWal WDib |
| ***longiflora*** | EABi |
| 'Luneberg' | EABi |
| 'Maxima' | LAma |
| 'Mozelle' | EABi |
| 'Orange Delight' | WDib |
| (Palette Series) 'Palette Mix Lilac' | EABi |
| - 'Palette Mix Red Dwarf' | EABi |
| - 'Palette Mix Salmon' | EABi |
| - 'Palette Mix White' | EABi |
| - 'Palette Red Mix' | EABi |
| 'Patens Major' | WDib |
| 'Peach Blossom' | EBrs LAma |

| | | |
|---|---|---|
| | 'Pearly Queen' | EABi |
| | 'Pink Beauty' | EABi |
| | 'Platinum' | EABi |
| I | 'Purple Hybrid' | EABi |
| | 'Purple King' | SWal |
| | 'Red Giant' | EABi |
| | 'Rose Dream' | EABi |
| | 'Stan's Delight' (d) ♀H1 | EABi WDib |
| | 'Summer Sunset' | EABi |
| | 'Tarantella' | EABi WDib |
| | 'Teresa' | EABi |
| | (Tetra Series) 'Tetra Verschaffelt' | EABi |
| | - 'Tetra Wine Red Charm' | EABi |
| | 'Trailing Yellow' | EABi |
| | 'Vivid' | EABi |
| | 'Weinrot Elfe' **new** | WDib |
| | 'Wetterflow's Triumph' | EABi WDib |
| | 'Yellow Beauty' | WDib |

## *Achlys* (*Berberidaceae*)

| | | |
|---|---|---|
| | ***japonica*** | WCru |
| | ***triphylla*** | GGar WCru |

## *Achnatherum* see *Stipa*

## *Achyranthes* (*Amaranthaceae*)

| | | |
|---|---|---|
| | ***bidentata*** | CArn MSal |

## *Acidanthera* see *Gladiolus*

## *Acinos* (*Lamiaceae*)

| | | |
|---|---|---|
| § | ***alpinus*** | CArn CPBP EAlp EAro EBee EDAr EPot GJos GPWP ILad ITim LLHF LRHS NLar SBch WJek |
| § | ***arvensis*** | MHer MSal |
| § | ***corsicus*** | NLAp NMen NWCA WHoo |

## *Aciphylla* (*Apiaceae*)

| | | |
|---|---|---|
| | ***aurea*** | EBee GBin GCal GGar NLar NWCA SMad SPlb |
| | ***dieffenbachii*** | EUJe |
| | ***glaucescens*** | ECou NLar SMad |
| | ***pinnatifida*** | GGar |
| | ***squarrosa*** | CTrC EUJe |
| | ***subflabellata*** | ECou |

## *Acis* (*Amaryllidaceae*)

| | | |
|---|---|---|
| § | ***autumnalis*** ♀H4 | Widely available |
| | - 'Cobb's Variety' | EBee WCot |
| | - var. ***oporantha*** | CSsd CStu CWCL ERos MSte |
| * | - - from Morocco | ECho |
| | - var. ***pulchella*** | EBrs ECho ERos GKev |
| § | ***longifolia*** | ECho ERos |
| | ***nicaeensis*** ♀H2-3 | CLyd CPBP CStu EBrs EBur ECho ERos GKev ITim MTho SCnR WAbe WCot |
| § | ***rosea*** | CLyd CStu EBur ERos NMen NWCA SCnR WAbe |
| § | ***tingitana*** | CBro EBrs ECho WCot |
| § | ***trichophylla*** | EBrs ECho LLHF SCnR WCot |
| | - f. ***purpurascens*** | EBrs ECho WCot |
| § | ***valentina*** | CBro CPBP EBrs ECho EPot SCnR SRot WCot |

## *Acmella* (*Asteraceae*)

| | | |
|---|---|---|
| § | ***oleracea*** | CArn EOHP MSal SCoo |

## *Acmena* (*Myrtaceae*)

| | | |
|---|---|---|
| | ***smithii*** | EShb |

## *Acnistus* (*Solanaceae*)

| | | |
|---|---|---|
| | ***australis*** | see *Iochroma australe* |

## *Acoelorrhaphe* (*Arecaceae*)

| | | |
|---|---|---|
| | ***wrightii*** | EAmu LPal |

## *Aconitum* (*Ranunculaceae*)

| | | |
|---|---|---|
| | ACE 1449 | GBuc |
| | B&SWJ 2954 from Nepal | WCru |
| | B&SWJ 8488 from Korea | WCru |
| | CNDS 036 from Burma | WCru |
| | GWJ 9393 from northern India | WCru |
| | GWJ 9417 from northern India | WCru |
| | SDR 4842 **new** | EBee GKev |
| | SDR 4912 **new** | EBee GKev |
| | SDR 4948 **new** | EBee |
| | ***alboviolaceum*** | GCal |
| | - var. ***alboviolaceum*** f. ***albiflorum*** B&SWJ 4105 | WCru |
| | - - B&SWJ 8444 | WCru |
| | ***anglicum*** | see *A. napellus* subsp. *napellus* Anglicum Group |
| | ***anthora*** | NBHF WCot |
| | ***arcuatum*** | see *A. fischeri* var. *arcuatum* |
| | ***austroyunnanense*** | EBee |
| | - BWJ 7902 | WCru |
| | ***autumnale*** misapplied | see *A. carmichaelii* Wilsonii Group |
| | ***autumnale*** Rchb. | see *A. fischeri* Rchb. |
| | x ***bicolor*** | see *A.* x *cammarum* 'Bicolor' |
| | 'Blue Opal' | CDes EBee ECtt EWes WPGP |
| | 'Blue Sceptre' | EGle GBin LDai MBri NLar NMoo WHlf |
| | 'Bressingham Spire' ♀H4 | Widely available |
| § | x ***cammarum*** 'Bicolor' ♀H4 | Widely available |
| | - 'Eleanora' | CFir EBee ECtt EGle EPPr EPfP EWes GBuc GCra LHop MAvo MBri MLLN NBPC NGHP NGdn NLar NMoo NSti SPer SSvw WFar WMoo |
| | - 'Grandiflorum Album' | CAby LPla MSte |
| | - 'Pink Sensation' | EBee ECtt EGle GBin LLHF MBNS NBPC NBre NDov NGHP NSti SMrm SPoG WCAu |
| | ***carmichaelii*** | CArn CMea EBee GKir IFoB IFro MBri NBro NOrc SPet SRms WBod WCot WFar WHoo WTin |
| | - Arendsii Group | ECtt LBMP SRot |
| | - - 'Arendsii' ♀H4 | Widely available |
| | - 'Blue Bishop' | LSou |
| | - 'Redleaf' PBR | see *A. carmichaelii* 'Royal Flush' |
| § | - 'Royal Flush' PBR | CFir CMil EBee ECtt EGle MAvo MBNS MLLN NCob NGdn NLar WClo WCot |
| | - var. ***truppelianum*** HWJ 732 | WCru |
| § | - Wilsonii Group | CPrp EBee GGar GKir MCot MLLN MRav MSte MWat NDov SPhx WFar WPGP WPer |
| | - - 'Barker's Variety' | CFir CKno CPou EBee EGle ELon EPfP GBuc GCal GMac LPio MSte NDov NHol NLar NSti SMrm WCot WSHC |
| | - - 'Kelmscott' ♀H4 | EBee ECtt EGle EMon EWes GMac MCot MRav MSte SAga SDix SMHy SMrm SSvw WFar WRHF |
| | - - 'Spätlese' | CAbP EBee ECtt EGle ELon EMon GCal LHop MCot MLLN MNFA MSte NBHF NBir NDov NGdn SAga SMHy SMrm SPer STes SUsu WClo WCot |
| | - - 'The Grim Reaper' | EMon SSvw |
| | ***chiisanense*** B&SWJ 4446 | WCru |
| | ***chuanum*** | WCot |

| | | |
|---|---|---|
| | ***cilicicum*** | see *Eranthis hyemalis* Cilicica Group |
| | 'Cloudy' | EBee MSCN NBPC NGdn SPer |
| | ***compactum*** | see *A. napellus* subsp. *vulgare* |
| | ***elwesii*** | EBee NBre |
| | ***episcopale*** | WCru WFar |
| | aff. ***episcopale*** | WSHC |
| | - CLD 1426 | GBuc WFar |
| | ***ferox*** | EBee ELon EWes GBin MLLN |
| | - HWJK 2217 | WCru |
| § | ***fischeri*** misapplied | see *A. carmichaelii* |
| § | ***fischeri*** Rchb. | CSpe CWib NMoo |
| § | - var. ***arcuatum*** B&SWJ 774 | WCru |
| | ***formosanum*** | LEdu |
| | - B&SWJ 3057 | WCru |
| | ***fukutomei*** | NBre |
| | - B&SWJ 337 | GBin WCru |
| | ***fukutomei*** x ***japonicum*** subsp. ***subcuneatum*** | EBee |
| | ***gammiei*** GWJ 9418 | WCru |
| | ***grossedentatum*** | EBee GBin |
| § | ***hemsleyanum*** | CBgR CPLG CPrp CRHN CSec CWGN EBee EPfP GCra MDun MHar MMuc NBid NGHP NHol SGar SMad WBrE WCot WCru WFar |
| | ***hyemale*** | see *Eranthis hyemalis* |
| | 'Ivorine' | Widely available |
| | ***jaluense*** B&SWJ 8741 | WCru |
| | ***japonicum*** | EBee GCal WFar |
| | - var. ***hakonense*** | EBee |
| § | - subsp. ***napiforme*** | EBee EWes SAga WPGP WPnP |
| | - - B&SWJ 943 | ELon SMeo WCru |
| § | - subsp. ***subcuneatum*** | EBee |
| | - - B&SWJ 6228 | WCru |
| | ***krylovii*** | WCot |
| | ***laciniatum*** GWJ 9254 | WCru |
| | ***lamarckii*** | see *A. lycoctonum* subsp. *neapolitanum* |
| | ***longecassidatum*** B&SWJ 4277 | WCru |
| | - B&SWJ 8486 | WCru |
| | ***lycoctonum*** | GKir NLar SRms WBVN WCAu WCot |
| | - 'Darkeyes' | CAbP CFir EBee EGle LSou MCot NCob NDov NGdn SPoG WCot WGwG |
| | - 'Graupe' | WCot |
| | - 'Langhuso' | WCot |
| § | - subsp. ***lycoctonum*** | MSal SRms |
| | - subsp. ***moldavicum*** | EBee |
| § | - subsp. ***neapolitanum*** | EBee ECtt EGle ELan EPfP EWTr GCal GKir GMaP MLLN NGHP NGdn NLar SEND WFar |
| | - 'Russian Yellow' | EWld GCal |
| § | - subsp. ***vulparia*** | CArn CPrp CSam EBee GMac GPoy LPio MNFA MRav MSal NDov WAul WCot WEas WPer |
| | ***nagarum*** BWJ 7644 | WCru |
| | ***napellus*** | Widely available |
| | - 'Albiflorus' | see *A. napellus* subsp. *vulgare* 'Albidum' |
| | - 'Bergfürst' | CAby EBrs EGle MBri NDov SMHy SPhx |
| | - 'Blue Valley' | EBee EGle EPfP EQua EWes NPro WFar |
| | - 'Carneum' | see *A. napellus* subsp. *vulgare* 'Carneum' |
| | - 'Gletschereis' | GBin |
| | - subsp. ***napellus*** | LEdu |
| § | - - Anglicum Group | CRow CSev CWan GBuc MCot MSal MSte NLar WCot WPen |
| | - 'Rubellum' | CDWL EBee EGle ELan EPfP LAst MCot NBir NBro NPri WBor WMnd |
| | - 'Schneewittchen' | EBee SSvw |
| | - 'Sphere's Variety' | NOrc |
| § | - subsp. ***vulgare*** new | WFar |
| § | - - 'Albidum' | EBee EGle EHrv ELan EPfP GAbr GMaP GMac LEdu LRHS MCot MRav MWat NBid NDov NGHP NHol NLar NPri NSti SPer SPet WAul WBrE WCAu WFar |
| § | - - 'Carneum' | EGle GCra MLLN WFar WHer WKif |
| | ***napiforme*** | see *A. japonicum* subsp. *napiforme* |
| | ***neapolitanum*** | see *A. lycoctonum* subsp. *neapolitanum* |
| | 'Newry Blue' | CMea CSam EBee ELan EMon GBuc MSte MWhi NBHF NBir NHol NLar SGar SRms WFar WPer |
| | ***orientale*** misapplied | see *A. lycoctonum* subsp. *vulparia* |
| | ***orientale*** ambig. | NPro |
| | ***paniculatum*** | see *A. variegatum* subsp. *paniculatum* |
| | - 'Roseum' | EBee WFar |
| | ***pendulum*** new | EBee |
| | 'Pink Sensation'[PBR] | CFir ECtt EPfP GQue IPot LPio NLar |
| | ***proliferum*** B&SWJ 4107 | WCru |
| | ***pseudolaeve*** | EWld |
| | - B&SWJ 8663 | WCru |
| | - var. ***erectum*** B&SWJ 8466 new | WCru |
| | ***pyrenaicum*** | see *A. lycoctonum* subsp. *neapolitanum* |
| | ***ranunculifolius*** | see *A. lycoctonum* subsp. *neapolitanum* |
| | ***scaposum*** new | EBee |
| | - var. ***vaginatum*** new | EBee |
| | ***sczukinii*** | EMon |
| | ***seoulense*** B&SWJ 694 | WCru |
| | - B&SWJ 864 | WCru |
| | ***septentrionale*** | see *A. lycoctonum* subsp. *lycoctonum* |
| | 'Spark's Variety' ♀H4 | Widely available |
| | ***spicatum*** | GKir |
| | - GWJ 9418 | WCru |
| | 'Stainless Steel' | Widely available |
| | ***subcuneatum*** | see *A. japonicum* subsp. *subcuneatum* |
| | x ***tubergenii*** | see *Eranthis hyemalis* Tubergenii Group |
| | ***uchiyamai*** | NLar |
| | - B&SWJ 1005 | WCru |
| | - B&SWJ 1216 | ELon WCru |
| | ***variegatum*** | EBee |
| § | - subsp. ***paniculatum*** | EBee MBri NBre WCot |
| | ***volubile*** misapplied | see *A. hemsleyanum* |
| | ***volubile*** Pall. | EBee GCal NTHB |
| | ***vulparia*** | see *A. lycoctonum* subsp. *vulparia* |
| | ***yamazakii*** | WCru |
| | ***yezoense*** new | GCal |

## *Aconogonon* see *Persicaria*

## *Acorus* ✿ (*Acoraceae*)

| | | |
|---|---|---|
| | ***calamus*** | CArn CBen CDWL CRow CWat EHon ELau EMFW GKir GPoy LCro LPBA MCCP MSKA MSal NPer SWat WHer |
| | - 'Argenteostriatus' (v) | CBen CRow CWat EBee ECha ECtt EHon EMFW LPBA NOrc SWat WMAq |
| * | ***christophii*** | EBee ELon EPPr EWes SApp WMoo |
| | ***gramineus*** | ELau LPBA MLan MNHC MSKA NPer SWat WHer WMoo WTin |
| | - 'Golden Delight' | CKno |
| | - 'Golden Edge' (v) | EBee NHol WMoo |

| | | |
|---|---|---|
| | - 'Hakuro-nishiki' (v) | CEnd EBee ECtt EHoe EHul EMil EOrn EPPr GBuc GKir LPBA LRHS MBar MCCP MGos MMoz NBid NHol SHBN SRms SWvt WMoo |
| | - 'Kinchinjunga' (v) **new** | IFro |
| | - 'Licorice' | EAlp EBee EPPr GCal MBNS MDKP MSal NHol WCHb WLeb WMoo WPnP |
| | - 'Masamune' (v) | EBee EPla GBin IFro MSCN NHol SApp WMoo WTin |
| | - 'Minimus Aureus' | CBre GCal |
| | - 'Oborozuki' misapplied | see *A. gramineus* 'Ogon' |
| | - 'Oborozuki' (v) | CKno EBee EHoe EPla |
| § | - 'Ogon' (v) | Widely available |
| | - 'Omogo' **new** | EBee |
| | - var. ***pusillus*** | EBee EPla NBro |
| | - 'Variegatus' (v) | Widely available |
| | - 'Yodo-no-yuki' (v) | EBee EPla IFro |
| | 'Intermedius' | NPer |

## *Acradenia* (*Rutaceae*)

| | | |
|---|---|---|
| | ***frankliniae*** | CBcs CCCN CMHG CPne CTrC CTrG CTsd EBee EWTr GGar GKir IDee SEND SSpi WBod WFar WPGP WSHC |

## *Actaea* (*Ranunculaceae*)

| | | |
|---|---|---|
| | SDR 3042 **new** | EBee GKev |
| | ***alba*** misapplied | see *A. pachypoda, A. rubra* f. *neglecta* |
| | ***arizonica*** | CAby CLAP EBee EBrs GCal WCru |
| | ***asiatica*** | CDes CLAP EBee WPGP |
| | - B&SWJ 616 | WCru |
| | - B&SWJ 6351 from Japan | WCru |
| | - B&SWJ 8694 from Korea | WCru |
| | - BWJ 8174 from China | WCru |
| | ***atropurpureum*** 'Mountain Wave' | see *A. simplex* (Atropurpurea Group) 'Mountain Wave' |
| | ***biternata*** | CLAP MSte |
| | - B&SWJ 5591 | WCru |
| § | ***cimicifuga*** | CDes CLAP EBee GCal GPoy MSte |
| | - B&SWJ 2657 | WCru |
| § | ***cordifolia*** | EBee GBin GMaP LPBA MLLN MSal WBor |
| | - 'Blickfang' | CLAP WCot |
| | ***dahurica*** | EBee GKir MSal NLar SWat |
| | - B&SWJ 8426 | WCru |
| | - B&SWJ 8573 | WCru |
| | - B&SWJ 8653 | GEdr |
| | - tall **new** | GCal LPla |
| | ***erythrocarpa*** | see *A. rubra* |
| | ***europaea*** | EBee GCal SPhx |
| | ***frigida*** B&SWJ 2966 | WCru |
| | ***heracleifolia*** B&SWJ 8843 | WCru |
| § | ***japonica*** | CLAP CMea CRow GCal LEdu NCGa WCot WFar |
| | - B&SWJ 5828 | WCru |
| | - var. ***acutiloba*** B&SWJ 6257 | WCru |
| | - compact | GBin |
| | - - B&SWJ 8758A | WCru |
| | ***mairei*** ACE 2374 **new** | WCot |
| | - BWJ 7635 | WCru |
| | - BWJ 7939 | WCru |
| § | ***matsumurae*** | CPLG |
| § | - 'Elstead Variety' ♀H4 | CPLG CRow GBin GCal MBri MRav NBre |
| | - 'Frau Herms' | CLAP |
| | - 'White Pearl' | Widely available |
| § | ***pachypoda*** ♀H4 | CBro COld EBee ECGP ECha EWTr GBBs GBuc GCal GGar GKir GPoy IGor MCot MSal MSte NBid NLar NMen WBVN WCru |
| | - f. ***rubrocarpa*** | EBee GCal |
| § | ***podocarpa*** | LPla MSal SPlb SRms |
| § | ***racemosa*** ♀H4 | CArn COld CRow CSam EBee ELan EPfP EWTr GCal GPoy LFur MHer MLLN MSal NBid NGdn NSti SPer WCAu WFar WMnd |
| § | ***rubra*** ♀H4 | CAby CBro CHid CMHG EBee ECha ELan EWTr GAbr GBBs GBuc GGar GKir MCot MRav MSte NBid SMad WCru WEas WFar WPGP |
| | - B&SWJ 9555 | WCru |
| | - ***alba*** | see *A. pachypoda, A. rubra* f. *neglecta* |
| § | - f. ***neglecta*** | CDes EBee GBuc GEdr NLar SMad WCru |
| | ***simplex*** | CSam CSec EBee ECha EWTr GCra GKir NPri SWat |
| | - B&SWJ 8664 | WCru |
| § | - Atropurpurea Group | Widely available |
| | - - 'Bernard Mitchell' | CFir |
| | - - 'Black Negligee' | NBhm |
| | - - 'Brunette' ♀H4 | Widely available |
| | - - 'Hillside Black Beauty' | CCVN CLAP EBee ECtt EGle GMaP IPot LHop MLLN MNrw NBir NCob NDov WBor WCAu WCot |
| | - - 'James Compton' | Widely available |
| § | - - 'Mountain Wave' | CLAP EBee IPot WFar |
| | - 'Pink Spike' | Widely available |
| § | - 'Prichard's Giant' | CLAP EBee EBrs ECha GBin GBuc GKir MBri MRav MSte SPhx WFar |
| | - ***ramosa*** | see *A. simplex* 'Prichard's Giant' |
| | - 'Scimitar' | SMeo |
| | - 'Silver Axe' | GCal NBre |
| | - variegated (v) **new** | WCot |
| | ***spicata*** | COld CSec EBee GBin GBuc GCra GEdr GKir GPoy MSal MSte NLar WCot WCru |
| | - from England | GCal WCru |
| | ***taiwanensis*** | CLAP |
| | - B&SWJ 343 | CLAP |
| | - B&SWJ 3413 | WCru |
| | - RWJ 9996 | WCru |
| | ***yesoensis*** | CFir GCal |
| | - B&SWJ 6355 | WCru |
| | ***yunnanensis*** | EBee GCal |
| | - ACE 1880 | GBuc |

## *Actinella* see *Tetraneuris*

## *Actinidia* (*Actinidiaceae*)

| | | |
|---|---|---|
| | BWJ 8161 from China | WCru |
| | ***arguta*** (f/F) | CAgr EMui NLar WPGP |
| | - (m) | EMui SHBN |
| | - B&SWJ 569 | WCru |
| | - 'Issai' (s-p/F) | CBcs CCCN CDul EPfP LBuc MGos NLar |
| | - 'Kiwai Vert' (f/F) | CAgr |
| | - LL#1 (m) | CAgr |
| | - LL#2 (f/F) | CAgr |
| | - LL#3 (m) | CAgr |
| | - 'Shoko' (F) **new** | WCru |
| | - 'Unchae' (F) **new** | WCru |
| | - 'Weiki' | MGos |
| | ***callosa*** var. ***ephippioidea*** B&SWJ 1790 | WCru |
| | - var. ***formosana*** B&SWJ 3806 | WCru |
| | ***chinensis*** misapplied | see *A. deliciosa* |
| § | ***deliciosa*** | EBee ERom EUJe MGos WFar WSHC |
| | - (f/F) | MRav SHBN |
| | - 'Atlas' (m) | CAgr ECrN MREP NLar WBVN |
| * | - 'Boskoop' | EUJe LBMP MWat |
| | - 'Hayward' (f/F) | CAgr CBcs CCCN CDoC CHEx EBee ECrN ELan EMil EMui EPfP |

| | |
|---|---|
| | LRHS LSRN MREP NLar NPal SDea SHBN SPer SWvt WBVN WCru WFar |
| - 'Jenny' (s-p/F) | CAgr CDul CSut CTri ECrN EMui LAst LBuc LRHS MAsh MBri MCoo MGos MLan SDea SKee SLim SLon SPoG SVic WBVN |
| - 'Solo' | CCCN CDoC ECrN EPfP LRHS MREP NLar SEND WPGP |
| - 'Tomuri' (m) | CBcs CCCN CDoC CHEx EBee ELan EMil EMui EPfP LRHS LSRN NLar NPal SHBN SPer SWvt WCru |
| ***hypoleuca*** B&SWJ 5942 | WCru |
| ***kolomikta*** $\Upsilon^{H4}$ | Widely available |
| - (m) | CAgr MBlu NScw |
| - B&SWJ 4243 | WCru |
| - 'Tomoko' (F) | WCru |
| - 'Yazuaki' (m) | WCru |
| ***latifolia*** B&SWJ 3563 | WCru |
| ***petelotii*** HWJ 628 | WCru |
| ***pilosula*** | CBcs CCCN CSPN CWGN EBee EMil EPfP EWTr GCal GGal GKir LEdu LHop LRHS LSRN MAsh MBri MGos SCoo SLon SPoG WCru WPGP WPat WSHC |
| ***polygama*** (F) | EWld GCal IDee |
| - B&SWJ 5444 | WCru |
| - B&SWJ 8525 from Korea | WCru |
| - B&SWJ 8923 from Japan | WCru |
| ***purpurea*** (f/F) | CAgr |
| ***rubricaulis*** B&SWJ 3111 | WCru |
| ***rufa*** B&SWJ 3525 | WCru |
| aff. ***strigosa*** HWJK 2367 | WCru |
| ***tetramera*** B&SWJ 3564 | WCru |

## *Adansonia* (*Bombacaceae*)

| | |
|---|---|
| ***gregorii*** | SPlb |

## *Adelocaryum* see *Lindelofia*

## *Adenia* (*Passifloraceae*)

| | |
|---|---|
| ***glauca*** | LToo |
| ***spinosa*** | LToo |

## *Adenium* (*Apocynaceae*)

| | |
|---|---|
| ***obesum*** $\Upsilon^{H1}$ | CSec LToo |
| - subsp. ***boehmianum*** | LToo |
| - 'Petra Pink' new | LRHS |
| - 'Scooby'$^{PBR}$ new | LRHS |

## *Adenocarpus* (*Papilionaceae*)

| | |
|---|---|
| ***complicatus*** new | SEND |
| ***decorticans*** | SPlb |

## *Adenophora* (*Campanulaceae*)

| | |
|---|---|
| BWJ 7696 from China | WCru |
| 'Afterglow' | see *Campanula rapunculoides* 'Afterglow' |
| ***asiatica*** | see *Hanabusaya asiatica* |
| ***aurita*** | CFir MLLN NCGa WCot WPrP |
| ***bulleyana*** | CDMG CSec EBee EGle ELan EWTr GBuc GJos NBid SDnm SPav SPet SPlb WCot WFar WPer |
| ***capillaris*** subsp. ***leptosepala*** BWJ 7986 new | WCru |
| ***coelestis*** | CSec EBee NBre SPhx |
| - ACE 2455 | GBuc |
| - B&SWJ 7998 | WCru |
| ***confusa*** | CSec LDai LHop MDKP NBre SAga SPav WFar WHer WSHC |
| * ***cymerae*** | CSec GQue LDai |
| ***divaricata*** | WFoF |
| ***forrestii*** | NBre WFar |
| ***grandiflora*** B&SWJ 8555 | WCru |
| ***himalayana*** | GBri |
| ***jasionifolia*** BWJ 7946 | WCru |
| ***khasiana*** | CFir GMac LLHF MDKP NLar WPrP |
| ***koreana*** | NBre SPav |
| ***lamarkii*** B&SWJ 8738 | WCru |
| ***latifolia*** misapplied | see *A. pereskiifolia* |
| ***latifolia*** ambig. white-flowered new | MMuc |
| ***latifolia*** Fischer | WFar |
| ***liliifolia*** | CMoH CSec ECtt ELan GJos NBPC NCGa NPer NSti SMad SPav SPet WFar WHal WTin |
| ***morrisonensis*** RWJ 10008 | WCru |
| § ***nikoensis*** | CSec GAuc NBid |
| § - var. ***stenophylla*** | NBre |
| ***nipponica*** | see *A. nikoensis* var. *stenophylla* |
| § ***pereskiifolia*** | EWes NBre SHar SPlb WCot WFar WPer |
| ***polyantha*** | CHar CSec EHrv GAbr GBuc NLar SBod SRms WFar |
| ***polymorpha*** | see *A. nikoensis* |
| ***potaninii*** | CFir EBee EHrv ELan GBuc SEND SGar SPav SPoG WCHb WFar WHal |
| - pale-flowered | EHrv WHal |
| ***remotiflora*** | CSec |
| - B&SWJ 8562 | WCru |
| - B&SWJ 11016 new | WCru |
| ***stricta*** | EBee |
| - subsp. ***sessilifolia*** | CSec GBuc NBre SPla |
| ***sublata*** | CSec WFar |
| ***takedae*** var. ***howozana*** | LHop MLHP |
| ***taquetii*** | EBee GKev |
| - B&SWJ 1303 | WCru |
| ***tashiroi*** | CMHG CPrp CSec ECtt EPfP GBuc NLar NPro WCHb |
| ***triphylla*** | NBir SPav WFar |
| - B&SWJ 10916 new | WCru |
| - var. ***hakusanensis*** | LLHF NBre |
| - var. ***japonica*** | CSec LDai |
| - - B&SWJ 8835 | WCru |
| ***uehatae*** B&SWJ 126 | WCru |

## *Adenostyles* see *Cacalia*

## *Adiantum* ✿ (*Adiantaceae*)

| | |
|---|---|
| § ***aleuticum*** $\Upsilon^{H4}$ | CBcs CLAP EBee ELan EMon EWld MAvo NBid NBro NHol NLar WAbe WFib WPGP WRic |
| - 'Imbricatum' | CBcs CElw CLAP EBee ECha ELon MGos NHol NLar NMyG SDix SPla SRms WCot WFar WFib WRic |
| § - 'Japonicum' | CLAP CMil EBee ELan MAvo NBir NHol SRms WFar WHal WPGP |
| - 'Laciniatum' | SRms |
| - 'Miss Sharples' | CDTJ CLAP CMil EBee ELan LRHS MAsh MGos NLar SRms WFar WRic |
| § - 'Subpumilum' $\Upsilon^{H4}$ | CLAP CWsd EBee MRav SRms WAbe WFib WRic |
| ***bonatianum*** new | CFwr |
| ***capillus-veneris*** | CHEx EShb SChr WCot WFib WRic |
| ***cuneatum*** | see *A. raddianum* |
| ***fulvum*** | WRic |
| ***hispidulum*** | CCCN CMil EBee EShb LRHS NLar SKHP SRms WRic |
| - 'Bronze Venus' | CCCN EBee LRHS SKHP |
| ***pedatum*** misapplied | see *A. aleuticum* |
| ***pedatum*** ambig. | CWsd EBee GKir |
| ***pedatum*** L. $\Upsilon^{H4}$ | CBcs CHEx CLAP ECha EFer ELan EPfP GEdr GMaP LPBA LRHS MAsh MAvo MBri MMoz NHol NMoo NVic SApp SMad SPer SSpi SWat WFar WPGP |

| | | |
|---|---|---|
| | – Asiatic form | see *A. aleuticum* 'Japonicum' |
| | – 'Japonicum' | see *A. aleuticum* 'Japonicum' |
| | – 'Roseum' | see *A. aleuticum* 'Japonicum' |
| | – var. ***subpumilum*** | see *A. aleuticum* 'Subpumilum' |
| | ***pubescens*** | MBri WRic |
| § | ***raddianum*** ♀H2 | CHal |
| | – 'Brilliantelse' ♀H2 | LRHS |
| | – 'Fragrans' | see *A. raddianum* 'Fragrantissimum' |
| § | – 'Fragrantissimum' | LRHS MBri |
| | – 'Fritz Lüthi' ♀H2 | CHal LRHS MBri |
| | – 'Micropinnulum' | WRic |
| | – 'Monocolor' | MBri |
| | ***reniforme*** **new** | CFwr |
| | ***venustum*** ♀H4 | CGHE CHEx CLAP CWsd EBee EFer EGle EMon EPot MCot MWat NVic SChr SDix SKHP SRms SSpi SWat WAbe WCot WEas WFar WFib WHal WIvy WPGP WRic |

## *Adina* (*Rubiaceae*)

| | | |
|---|---|---|
| | ***rubella*** | NLar |

## *Adlumia* (*Papaveraceae*)

| | | |
|---|---|---|
| | ***fungosa*** | CSpe |

## *Adonis* (*Ranunculaceae*)

| | | |
|---|---|---|
| | ***aestivalis*** | MCot |
| | ***amurensis*** misapplied | see *A.* 'Fukujukai', *A. multiflora* |
| | ***amurensis*** ambig. | CMea CSec EBee EPot LAma LLHF MBri SCnR WCot WFar |
| | – 'Pleniflora' | see *A. multiflora* 'Sandanzaki' |
| | ***brevistyla*** | EBee GBuc GKir WAbe |
| § | 'Fukujukai' | EBee ECha GEdr WFar WWst |
| § | ***multiflora*** | EBee WFar |
| § | – 'Sandanzaki' (d) | EBee EPot EWes MBri NLar WFar |
| | ***vernalis*** | EBee GKir GPoy NLar NSla |

## *Adoxa* (*Adoxaceae*)

| | | |
|---|---|---|
| | ***moschatellina*** | CRWN EBWF NMen WAbe WHer WPnP WSFF WShi |

## *Adromischus* (*Crassulaceae*)

| | | |
|---|---|---|
| | ***cooperi*** | WCot WEas |

## *Aechmea* (*Bromeliaceae*)

| | | |
|---|---|---|
| | sp. | XBlo |
| | ***caudata*** var. ***variegata*** | CHEx |
| | ***chantinii*** ♀H1 | LRHS |
| | ***fasciata*** ♀H1 | LRHS MBri XBlo |
| | 'Maya'PBR **new** | LRHS |
| | ***ramosa*** | LRHS XBlo |
| | 'Romero' | LRHS |
| | ***victoriana*** | XBlo |

## *Aegle* (*Rutaceae*)

| | | |
|---|---|---|
| | ***sepiaria*** | see *Poncirus trifoliata* |

## *Aegopodium* (*Apiaceae*)

| | | |
|---|---|---|
| | ***podagraria*** 'Bengt' | EMon |
| | – 'Dangerous' (v) | CHid CNat WCHb |
| | – gold-margined (v) | EMon EPPr |
| | – 'Variegatum' (v) | CDoC COlW CRow EBee ECha ECrN EHoe EHrv EMon EPPr EPla GMaP LHop LRHS MBri MRav MSCN NBid NPri NSti NVic SPer SPoG WCAu WCFE WCot WMoo |

## *Aeonium* (*Crassulaceae*)

| | | |
|---|---|---|
| | RCB RL C-5 **new** | WCot |
| | ***arboreum*** ♀H1 | CAbb CDTJ CHEx CTsd EShb LPio LRHS NPal WCor WRos |
| | – 'Albovariegatum' (v) | LPio MSCN |
| | – 'Atropurpureum' ♀H1 | CAbb CHEx CHVG EAmu EBee EPfP EShb MBri MLan NPer SEND SWal WCor WCot |
| | – green-leaved | SEND |
| I | – 'Magnificum' | EBee EPfP EShb SAPC SArc |
| | – 'Variegatum' (v) | EShb NPer |
| | ***balsamiferum*** | CAbb CCCN CHEx CSpe EBee EPfP SAPC SArc SChr WCot |
| | 'Black Cap' | CCCN LRHS |
| | 'Blush' | EBee |
| | 'Blushing Beauty' | CAbb LRHS |
| | ***canariense*** | CBrP CCCN CDTJ CHEx LPio LRHS |
| | – var. ***palmense*** | EBee |
| | ***castello-paivae*** | EBee EShb |
| | 'Cristata Sunburst' | WCot |
| | ***cuneatum*** | MLan SChr SEND SPet WCor |
| | ***decorum*** | SEND |
| * | – 'Variegatum' (v) | CBow LPio WCot |
| | 'Dinner Plate' | CHEx CTsd |
| | 'Dinner Plate' x ***haworthii*** | CHEx |
| | x ***domesticum*** | see *Aichryson* x *domesticum* |
| | ***gomerense*** **new** | STre |
| | ***goochiae*** | CBow EBee |
| | ***haworthii*** ♀H1 | CArn CBrP CHEx CHal LPio LRHS MSCN SBHP SEND |
| | – 'Variegatum' (v) | EBee EShb LPio SChr |
| | ***holochrysum*** Webb & Berth. | CAbb |
| | ***lindleyi*** | SChr |
| | – var. ***viscatum*** | EBee |
| * | ***multiflora*** | EBee |
| * | – 'Variegata' (v) | EBee |
| | ***nobile*** | CBrP |
| | ***percarneum*** | EShb |
| | ***simsii*** | CHal EBee |
| | – variegated (v) | EShb |
| | ***tabuliforme*** ♀H1 | CAbb CCCN CSpe LRHS |
| | ***urbicum*** | CHEx |
| | 'Zwartkop' ♀H1 | Widely available |

## *Aeschynanthus* (*Gesneriaceae*)

| | | |
|---|---|---|
| | 'Big Apple' | CHal WDib |
| | Black Pagoda Group | WDib |
| | 'Carina' **new** | LRHS |
| | 'Caroline' **new** | LRHS |
| | 'Fire Wheel' | WDib |
| | ***hildebrandii*** | WDib |
| | 'Holiday Bells' | WDib |
| | 'Hot Flash' | CSpe WDib |
| | ***longicalyx*** | WDib |
| § | ***longicaulis*** ♀H1 | WDib |
| | ***marmoratus*** | see *A. longicaulis* |
| | 'Mona' | MBri |
| | 'Mona Lisa' **new** | LRHS |
| | ***radicans*** ♀H1 | MBri WDib |
| | 'Scooby Doo' | WDib |
| | ***speciosus*** ♀H1 | CHal EShb WDib |
| | 'Twister'PBR **new** | LRHS |

## *Aesculus* ✿ (*Hippocastanaceae*)

| | | |
|---|---|---|
| | ***arguta*** | see *A. glabra* var. *arguta* |
| | x ***arnoldiana*** | CDul CMCN SBir |
| | – 'Autumn Splendor' | EPfP |
| § | x ***bushii*** | CMCN CTho MGos NLar |
| | ***californica*** | CMCN EBee EPfP ERod WPGP |
| | x ***carnea*** | CDul CTri ELan MBar SBLw |
| | – 'Aureomarginata' (v) | CTho ERod LLHF SMad WHar WPat |
| | – 'Briotii' ♀H4 | Widely available |
| | – 'Marginata' (v) | MBlu |
| | – 'Plantierensis' | CDul ECrN MBlu SBLw |
| * | – 'Variegata' (v) | CBcs CDul CMCN MGos |
| | ***chinensis*** | CMCN |

| | | |
|---|---|---|
| | 'Dallimorei' (graft-chimaera) | SMad WPat |
| | ***flava*** 🏆$^{H4}$ | CCVT CMCN CTho EBee ECrN EHig EPfP GKir LMaj LPan MMuc MWat NWea SBLw SHBN SLim SSpi WFar WPGP |
| | - f. ***vestita*** | CDoC CDul MBlu |
| | ***georgiana*** | see *A. sylvatica* |
| | ***glabra*** | CDul CMCN CTho EGFP GKir |
| § | - var. ***arguta*** | CMCN GKir |
| | - 'Autumn Blaze' | EPfP MBlu MBri SMad |
| | - 'October Red' | EPfP MBlu MBri WPGP |
| | ***glaucescens*** | see *A.* x *neglecta* |
| | ***hippocastanum*** 🏆$^{H4}$ | Widely available |
| § | - 'Baumannii' (d) 🏆$^{H4}$ | CDoC CDul CLnd EBee ECrN EPfP ERod GKir LMaj LPan MGos MSwo NWea SBLw SHBN SPer WDin WFar |
| | - 'Digitata' | CDul CMCN SBLw |
| | - 'Flore Pleno' | see *A. hippocastanum* 'Baumannii' |
| | - 'Hampton Court Gold' | CBcs CDoC CDul CMCN NBhm |
| | - 'Honiton Gold' | CTho |
| | - f. ***laciniata*** | CDul CMCN ERod IArd MBlu NLar SMad WPat |
| | - 'Memmingeri' | SBir |
| | - 'Monstrosa' | MBri SMad |
| | - 'Pyramidalis' | CDul SBLw |
| | - 'Wisselink' | CDul CLnd CMCN ECrN MBlu SMad |
| | ***indica*** | CDul CHEx CLnd CMCN CTho EBee ECrN EHig ELan EMil EPfP GKir IArd ISea LMaj SHBN SMHT SSpi WDin WPGP |
| | - 'Sydney Pearce' 🏆$^{H4}$ | CDul CEnd CMCN ECrN EPfP ERod GKir MBlu MBri MGos NLar SMad SSpi WDin WPGP |
| | x ***marylandica*** | CDul |
| | x ***mississippiensis*** | see *A.* x *bushii* |
| | x ***mutabilis*** 'Harbisonii' | NLar |
| | - 'Induta' | CLnd CMCN EBee EPfP IArd MBlu MBri NLar NSti SDix SMad SSpi WFar |
| § | - 'Penduliflora' | CDul CEnd CTho EPfP LRHS MBlu |
| § | x ***neglecta*** | CLnd CMCN |
| | - 'Autumn Fire' | MBlu MBri |
| | - 'Erythroblastos' 🏆$^{H4}$ | CBcs CDul CEnd CLnd CMCN EBee EPfP ERod GKir LRHS MAsh MBlu MBri NLar SBir SCoo SHBN SLim SMad SSpi SSta WDin WPGP WPat |
| | ***parviflora*** 🏆$^{H4}$ | Widely available |
| § | ***pavia*** 🏆$^{H4}$ | CBcs CDul CLnd CMCN CTho EPfP SSpi WCru WDin |
| | - 'Atrosanguinea' | CDul CEnd CLnd CMCN EBee EPfP ERod MBlu MBri NPal SMad |
| | - var. ***discolor*** | SBLw |
| | - - 'Koehnei' | CDul CMCN LRHS MBlu MBri NLar SPoG |
| | - 'Penduliflora' | see *A.* x *mutabilis* 'Penduliflora' |
| | - 'Purple Spring' | MBlu |
| | - 'Rosea Nana' | CMCN WPat |
| | ***splendens*** | see *A. pavia* |
| § | ***sylvatica*** | CMCN CTho LRHS |
| | ***turbinata*** | CDul CMCN GKir ISea SSpi |
| | - var. ***pubescens*** | WPGP |
| | ***wilsonii*** | CDul CTho WPGP |

## *Aethionema* (*Brassicaceae*)

| | | |
|---|---|---|
| | ***glaucinum*** | GKev |
| § | ***grandiflorum*** 🏆$^{H4}$ | CSec GEdr GKev NBro SRms WFar WPer |
| | - Pulchellum Group 🏆$^{H4}$ | CSpe GKev |
| | ***iberideum*** | MDKP MWat SRms |
| * | ***kotschyi*** hort. | ECho EDAr NMen WAbe |
| | ***membranaceum*** | ECho EDAr WFar |
| | ***oppositifolium*** | CLyd MWat WHoo |
| | ***pulchellum*** | see *A. grandiflorum* |
| | ***saxatile*** | GKev |
| | - red-flowered **new** | GKev |
| | ***schistosum*** | GKev LLHF WAbe |
| | ***spicatum*** | WFar |
| | 'Warley Rose' 🏆$^{H4}$ | ECho ELan EPot GKir GMaP LHop LRHS MWat NLAp NMen SBch SIng SRms WFar |
| | 'Warley Ruber' | CMea CPBP NBir NMen WAbe WFar |

## *Afrocarpus* (*Podocarpaceae*)

| | | |
|---|---|---|
| | ***falcatus*** | CTrC ECou GGar |

## *Agapanthus* ✿ (*Alliaceae*)

| | | |
|---|---|---|
| | sp. | XPde |
| | from Johannesburg | ECha |
| | 'Aberdeen' | CPne XPde |
| | 'Adonis' | CPrp IBal IBlr |
| | 'African Moon' | CPne |
| § | ***africanus*** 🏆$^{H1}$ | CElw CWib EBee ECho EHrv ELan EPfP EUJe GAbr LCro LEdu LPan LRHS MNHC NBlu SAPC SArc SBod SPad SPav SPer SSwd SVic SWat WBor WBrE WFar WPer |
| * | - 'Albus' 🏆$^{H1}$ | CBcs CDoC CKno CTca EBee EBrs ECho EPfP IFoB LCro LRHS NBlu SBod SEND SMeo SPad SPav SPer WFar WGwG WPer |
| | 'Albatross' | CPne ECha GCra |
| | 'Albus' ambig. | CPLG ECrN GMaP LPan MGos MHer MWat SAga SHom |
| I | 'Albus Nanus' | ECho LPan |
| | 'Amsterdam' | CPen NHoy XPde |
| | 'Angela' | CPne NHoy XPde |
| | 'Anthea' | CPne XPde |
| | 'Aphrodite' | IBlr |
| | 'Apple Court' | XPde |
| | 'Aquamarine' | CAvo CFFs NHoy SBch |
| | 'Arctic Star' | CPLG CPne XPde |
| | Ardernei hybrid | CDes CPne CPrp EBee ECha ECtt EGle EWes GCal GQue IBal IBlr LFur LPio LSou MBri MSte SAga SRos SUsu WBor WCFE WCot WGwG WPGP XPde |
| § | 'Argenteus Vittatus' (v) 🏆$^{H1}$ | CDes CPen CPne CPrp ELan EPfP LRHS NHoy NOrc WPGP |
| | 'Arosa' **new** | CPne |
| | 'Atlas' | IBlr |
| | 'Aureovittatus' (v) | NHoy |
| | 'Baby Blue' | see *A.* 'Blue Baby' |
| | 'Back in Black' | CPne CSpe CWCL EBee ELan EPfP ESwi EWes GAbr IBal IPot LCro LPio MBNS NBPC NBPN NCob NHoy NOrc SHBN |
| | 'Ballyrogan' | IBlr |
| | 'Balmoral' | CPne |
| | 'Bangor Blue' | CPrp IBal IBlr |
| | 'Basutoland' | LRHS |
| | 'Beatrice' | CPne XPde |
| | 'Beeches Dwarf' | CPne ELan NHoy |
| | 'Ben Hope' | GBuc IBal IBlr NHoy SDnm SPav WCot XPde |
| | 'Beth Chatto' | see *A. campanulatus* 'Albovittatus' |
| | 'Bethlehem Star' | CBgR CPne SRos |
| | 'Bianco' | XPde |
| | 'Bicton Bell' | CPne IBlr |
| | 'Big Blue' | EBee LRHS LSRN NMun SEND SRkn |
| | 'Black Buddhist' **new** | EBee NHoy WHlf |
| | 'Black Pantha' PBR | Widely available |
| § | 'Blue Baby' | CCCN CLyd COIW CPen CPrp EBee ELan ELon EPfP IBal IBlr LAst LRHS NHoy WFar XPde |

| | | |
|---|---|---|
| | 'Blue Bird' | CPne XPde |
| | 'Blue Boy' | XPde |
| | 'Blue Brush' | CPne CSBt EBee EMil IBal NHoy SCoo SEND |
| | 'Blue Cascade' | IBlr |
| | 'Blue Companion' | CPne CPrp IBlr NHoy SMrm WMnd |
| | 'Blue Diamond' ambig. | EHrv NHoy SRos |
| | 'Blue Dot' | CPrp EBee LBMP LRHS NBsh |
| | 'Blue Formality' | CPne IBal IBlr |
| | 'Blue Giant' | CBcs CBro CCVN CPen CPrp EBee EPfP IBlr LRHS MBri MNFA MSte NGby NHoy SAga SWat WCFE WFar WPGP |
| | 'Blue Globe' | CHid CMMP EBee GMaP LAst MSCN STes WCAu |
| | 'Blue Gown' | CPne CSam |
| | 'Blue Haze' | SRos XPde |
| | 'Blue Heaven'PBR | CPne EBee EWTr NHoy |
| | 'Blue Ice' | CPne |
| | 'Blue Imp' | CBro CPne EBee GBuc IBlr LRHS NHol SApp SKHP |
| | 'Blue Lakes' | XPde |
| | 'Blue Méoni' | XPde |
| | 'Blue Moon' | CAvo CBro CPen EBee ECha IBal IBlr LRHS NHoy SAga WCot |
| | 'Blue Nile' | CPne XPde |
| | 'Blue Prince' | CPen CPrp EBee LBuc LRHS NHoy |
| | 'Blue Ribbon' | CPne XPde |
| | 'Blue Skies' ambig. | NCGa NHoy XPde |
| I | 'Blue Skies' Dunlop | IBlr |
| | 'Blue Spear' | CPen |
| | 'Blue Triumphator' | CPne CSec CTca EBee EBrs EPfP EWll GMaP IBlr LRHS NGby NHoy NScw SMeo XPde |
| | 'Blue Umbrella' | EBee LRHS NHoy |
| | 'Blue Velvet' | CPne XPde |
| | 'Bressingham Blue' | CBro CPne CPrp CTri EBrs ECho ECtt EWes GCal GKir IBal IBlr IFoB LRHS MAvo MRav MSte NHoy NVic SMHy SWat XPde |
| | 'Bressingham Bounty' | CPne EBrs LRHS XPde |
| | 'Bressingham White' | CPne EBee ECGP ECtt EHrv LEdu LRHS MBri MRav NCGa NHoy SWat XPde |
| | 'Bristol' | XPde |
| | 'Buckingham Palace' | CBro CDes CPne CPrp EBee ECho EWes GAbr IBlr NHoy WCot WPGP XPde |
| | 'Cally Blue' | GAbr GCal |
| | 'Cambridge' | CPne XPde |
| | ***campanulatus*** | CPLG CPrp CWCL EAEE EBee EBla ECho ELan EPfP IBlr IGor ITim LPio LRHS MCot MRav NCob NHoy SWat WAbe WCot WFar WPGP |
| | - var. ***albidus*** | Widely available |
| § | - 'Albovittatus' | CPrp CSam ECho EWTr LPio MCot NHoy |
| | - 'Albus Nanus' | see *A.* 'Albus Nanus' |
| | - 'Beth Chatto' (v) | CPrp EBla IBal |
| | - bright blue | CWCL GCal |
| | - 'Buckland' | IBlr |
| | - 'Cobalt Blue' | EAEE EBee ECha LRHS NGdn NHoy |
| | - dark blue-flowered **new** | XPde |
| | - 'Oxford Blue' | CPen CPrp EBrs ECGP GBri GBuc IBal IBlr NHoy SRos WPGP XPde |
| | - subsp. ***patens*** ♀H3 | CPrp CSec CWsd EBla EPfP GBin GBri GBuc IBal LPio SWat WPGP |
| | - - deep blue-flowered | CFir CPrp IBlr NHoy XPde |
| | - 'Profusion' | CBro EBrs ECha IBal IBlr NHoy SRos WFar XPde |
| | - variegated (v) | EBla ECha NPer |
| | - 'Wedgwood Blue' | CPrp EBee EBrs IBal IBlr LRHS NHoy SRos XPde |
| | - 'Wendy' | CPne CPrp IBal IBlr LRHS NHoy XPde |
| | - 'White Hope' | IBal IBlr SRos |
| | 'Carefree' | CPrp |
| | 'Castle of Mey' | CBro CPne CPrp EBee GAbr GBuc IBlr LPio LPla LRHS MTho NHoy SPav SRos WPGP XPde |
| | 'Catharina' | CPne XPde |
| § | ***caulescens*** ♀H1 | EBee EBrs GBuc IBlr IGor WCot WPGP XPde |
| | - subsp. ***angustifolius*** | EBee IBlr WCot WPGP |
| | - subsp. ***caulescens*** | CPne IBlr SWat |
| | 'Cedric Morris' | IBlr LPio NHoy SRos XPde |
| | 'Chandra' | IBlr |
| | 'Charlotte' | EBee NHoy XPde |
| | 'Cheney's Lane' **new** | SMHy |
| | 'Cherry Holley' | CPne SRos XPde |
| | 'Clarence House' | CBro CPne XPde |
| | ***coddii*** | CPLG CPne EWes IBlr WCot WHil XPde |
| | 'Columba' | CPen CPne CPrp CTca EBee LAma LDai NHoy XPde |
| | ***comptonii*** | see *A. praecox* subsp. ***minimus*** |
| | 'Cool Blue' | CPne XPde |
| | 'Corina' **new** | EBee |
| | 'Cornish Sky' | CPne |
| | 'Crystal Drop' | CPne SWat |
| | 'Dainty Lady' | NHoy |
| | Danube | see *A.* 'Donau' |
| | 'Dark Star' | WFar |
| | 'Dartmoor' | CPne |
| | 'Davos' | CPne |
| | 'Dawn Star' | XPde |
| | 'Debbie' | XPde |
| | 'Delft' | CPrp IBlr |
| | 'Density' | IBlr |
| | 'Devon Dawn' | CPne |
| | 'Diana' | XPde |
| | 'Dnjepr' | XPde |
| | 'Dokter Brouwer' | CPen EBee IBal MCot MDKP NHoy SKHP SPoG WGwG XPde |
| § | 'Donau' | CBro CDoC CPen CPne CSec EBee EBrs NBir NHoy NOrc SWat WFar XPde |
| | 'Dorothy Kate' | CPne |
| | 'Double Diamond' | CPen NHoy |
| | 'Dublin' | CPne |
| | 'Duivenbrugge Blue' | CPne XPde |
| | 'Duivenbrugge White' | XPde |
| | ***dyeri*** | see *A. inapertus* subsp. *intermedius* |
| | 'Ed Carman' (v) | WCot |
| | 'Elisabeth' | CPne XPde |
| | 'Enigma' | CAbb CPar CPne CWGN EBee IBal LRHS NHoy SRkn SWat |
| | 'Essence of Summer' **new** | WCot |
| | 'Ethel's Joy' | CPen |
| | 'Eve' | EBee IBlr XPde |
| | 'Evening Star' | CPne ECha XPde |
| | 'Exmoor' | CPne |
| | 'Far Horizon' | CPne |
| | 'Farncombe' **new** | NCot |
| | 'Fast Track' | WCot |
| | 'Findlay's Blue' | EBee GBuc WHil WPGP |
| | 'Finnline' **new** | CPne |
| | 'Flanders Giant' | XPde |
| | 'Gayle's Lilac' | Widely available |
| | 'Gem' | CPne |
| | 'Getty White' | GBin |
| I | 'Giganteus Albus' | XPde |
| | 'Glacier Stream' | CBro CCVN CPen EBee EHrv NHoy |

| | | |
|---|---|---|
| | 'Glen Avon' | CAbb CBro CFir CPne CPrp EBee EMil IBal LCro LRHS LSRN NBPC NHoy NLar SApp SCoo SEND XPde |
| | 'Golden Rule' (v) | CBow CDes CPne CPrp EBee EHoe GBuc IBal IBlr WPGP XPde |
| | 'Goldfinger' (v) | CPne |
| | 'Grey Ruler' **new** | WCot |
| | 'Harvest Blue' | CPne XPde |
| | Headbourne hybrid dwarf | LRHS |
| § | Headbourne hybrids | Widely available |
| | 'Heavenly Blue' | CPne |
| | 'Helen' | IBlr |
| | 'Holbeach' | CPen CPne XPde |
| | 'Holbrook' | CSam XPde |
| | 'Hydon Mist' | XPde |
| | 'Ice Blue Star' | CPne SRos XPde |
| | 'Ice Lolly' | CBro CPen EBee XPde |
| | ***inapertus*** | CBro CPLG CPrp EWes GGal IGor ITim LPio MHer SMHy SWat WCot WPGP XPde |
| | - dwarf | IBlr |
| | - subsp. ***hollandii*** | CPne CSpe CWsd GCal IBal IBlr MAvo MSte NHoy SKHP SWat WCot WHil XPde |
| | - - 'Zealot' | IBlr |
| | - subsp. ***inapertus*** | IBlr SWat WCot |
| I | - - 'Albus' | IBlr |
| | - - 'Cyan' | IBlr |
| | - - 'White' | CPne |
| § | - subsp. ***intermedius*** | CBgR CBro CPne CPrp EBee IBal IBlr NHoy SKHP SWat WCot |
| | - 'Midnight Cascade' | CPne SUsu SWat |
| | - subsp. ***parviflorus*** | IBlr |
| | - subsp. ***pendulus*** | CAby CDes CFir CPne EBrs GCal IBlr IPot WPGP |
| | - - 'Graskop' | CPne IBlr |
| | - - 'Violet Dusk' | IBlr |
| | 'Innocence' | IBlr |
| | 'Intermedius' Leichtlin | XPde |
| I | 'Intermedius' van Tubergen | EBee |
| | 'Isis' | CAvo CBro CFir CPne CPrp CSam CTri EBee EBla EBrs ECha GBuc IBal IBlr NHoy SRos XPde |
| | 'Jack Elliott' | SMHy SMeo |
| | 'Jack's Blue' | Widely available |
| | 'Jersey Giant' | NHoy XPde |
| | 'Jodie' | CPne XPde |
| | 'Johanna' | CPne EBee XPde |
| | 'Jolanda' | CPne |
| | 'K. Wiley' | SUsu |
| | 'Kew White' | SDix |
| | 'Kingston Blue' | CPne CPrp EBee ECha EHrv IBal IBlr LSou MLLN NHoy SRGP WFar WPrP WSHC XPde |
| | 'Kirstenbosch' | CPne |
| | 'Kirsty' | CPne |
| | 'Kobold' | CPne EGle NHoy WFar |
| | 'Lady Edith' | IBlr |
| § | 'Lady Grey' | IBlr |
| | 'Lady Moore' | EGle IBlr IGor SMHy XPde |
| | 'Lady Wimborne' | CPne |
| | 'Latent Blue' | IBlr |
| | 'Lavender Haze' | EBee IBal NHoy |
| | 'Leicester' | XPde |
| | 'Lilac Bells' | CPne |
| | 'Lilac Mist' | EBee |
| | 'Lilac Time' | CPne EBee IBlr XPde |
| | 'Lilliput' | Widely available |
| | 'Limoges' | XPde |
| | 'Little Diamond' | LRHS SPoG |
| | 'Loch Hope' ♀H3 | CBro CDoC CPne CPrp EBee EBrs EGle GAbr GGar IBal IGor LAst LRHS MAvo MLLN NCob NHoy SApp SPav SPer SRos WCot WHoo WPnn XPde |
| | 'Lorna' | CPne |
| | 'Lowland Nursery' | XPde |
| | 'Luly' | CPne NHoy SWat XPde |
| | 'Lydenburg' | CPne IBlr |
| | 'Lyn Valley' | CPne |
| | 'Mabel Grey' | see *A.* 'Lady Grey' |
| | 'Magnifico' | IBlr |
| | 'Majorie' | CPne |
| | 'Malaga' | XPde |
| | 'Malvern Hills' | XPde |
| | 'Marchant's Lapis Cascade' **new** | SMHy |
| | 'Marcus' | CPne |
| | 'Marianne' **new** | CPne XPde |
| | 'Mariètte' | CPen CPne EBee XPde |
| | 'Marjorie' | SApp XPde |
| | 'Martine' | CPne EBee |
| | 'Meibont' (v) | CPne WCot XPde |
| | 'Mercury' | CPne IBlr |
| | 'Middleburg' | CPne |
| | Midknight Blue = 'Monmid' | EBee MWte NHoy |
| | 'Midnight' | EWes SAga WSHC |
| | 'Midnight Blue' P. Wood | CPrp GCal IBlr |
| | 'Midnight Blue' ambig. | COlW CWsd ECha ELan GBuc IBal IGor MSte SPav WFar |
| § | 'Midnight Star' | Widely available |
| | 'Miniature Blue' | SWat |
| | mixed seedlings | CPen CPne EPfP IBal MGos NOrc SRos WHil XPde |
| | mixed whites | WCFE |
| | 'Montreal' | XPde |
| | 'Mood Indigo' **new** | CPne |
| * | 'Mooreanus' misapplied | EBee EPfP IBlr NBid WPGP XPde |
| | 'Morning Star' | CPne SRos |
| | 'Mount Stewart' | IBal IBlr |
| | 'Navy Blue' | see *A.* 'Midnight Star' |
| | 'New Love' | EBee |
| | 'New Orleans' **new** | XPde |
| | 'Newa' | XPde |
| | 'Nikki' | CPne |
| | 'Norman Hadden' | IBlr |
| | ***nutans*** | see *A. caulescens* |
| | - 'Polar White' | NHoy |
| | 'Nyx' | IBlr |
| | 'NZ Blue' | XPde |
| | 'NZ White' | XPde |
| | 'Offenham Cream' | WCot |
| | 'Oslo' | CPne NHoy XPde |
| | 'Oxbridge' | IBlr |
| | Palmer's hybrids | see *A.* Headbourne hybrids |
| | 'Paris' | CPen XPde |
| | 'Patent Blue' | CPrp IBlr |
| | 'Patriot' **new** | LRHS |
| | 'Penelope Palmer' | CPrp IBal IBlr |
| | 'Penny Slade' | SAga SRos XPde |
| | 'Peter Pan' ambig. | Widely available |
| | 'Peter Pan American' | GKev |
| | 'Phantom' | CDes CPne CPrp GCal IBlr XPde |
| | 'Pinchbeck' | CPne XPde |
| | 'Pinky' | XPde |
| | 'Pinocchio' | CPen CWib EBee ECho NHol NHoy XPde |
| | 'Plas Merdyn Blue' | IBal IBlr |
| | 'Plas Merdyn White' | CFir IBal IBlr NHoy XPde |
| | 'Podge Mill' | IBlr SMHy XPde |
| | 'Polar Ice' | CFir CPen CPne EBee GBin IBlr WFar WHlf XPde |
| | 'Porcelain' | IBlr |
| | ***praecox*** | CPrp EBee EBrs EShb GAbr IBlr LRHS NHoy |
| | - 'Blue Storm' | LBuc |

| | | |
|---|---|---|
| | - 'Dwarf White' | see *A.* white dwarf hybrids |
| | - 'Flore Pleno' (d) | CDes CDoC CPne CPrp EBee ECha EHrv ELan EMon IBal IBlr LRHS NBPC NCob NGdn NHoy NLar SPoG WCot WFar WKif WPGP WPrP XPde |
| | - 'Floribundus' | SWat |
| | - 'Maximus Albus' | CPou IBal IBlr WBrE |
| § | - subsp. ***minimus*** | CElw CPne CPou IBlr LPio NHoy SWat WCot WHil XPde |
| | - - 'Adelaide' | EBee SWat |
| | - - blue-flowered | SWat |
| | - - 'Grootkans' **new** | CPne |
| | - - white-flowered | CPne SWat |
| | - 'Neptune' | IBlr |
| § | - subsp. ***orientalis*** | CCCN CPne CSut EHrv GGar IBlr SWat WPic |
| | - - var. ***albiflorus*** | CBro CDes CPne CPou CSut EBee LAst LBMP NHoy XPde |
| | - - 'Weaver' | CPne |
| | - subsp. ***praecox*** | IBlr IGor |
| | - - azure-flowered | SWat |
| | - - 'Variegatus' | see *A.* 'Argenteus Vittatus' |
| | - 'Saturn' | IBlr |
| | - Slieve Donard form | IBlr |
| | - 'Storms River' | SWat |
| | - 'Uranus' | IBlr |
| | - 'Venus' | IBlr |
| | - 'Vittatus' (v) | NHoy WCot WFar |
| | - 'White Storm' **new** | LBuc |
| | 'Premier' | CPrp EBee EBrs IBal IBlr LRHS NHoy SRos WPGP |
| | 'Princess Margaret' | CPne XPde |
| | 'Proteus' | EBee XPde |
| § | 'Purple Cloud' | Widely available |
| | 'Purple Haze' | CWGN |
| | 'Purple Star' | EBee |
| | 'Queen Anne' | NHoy |
| | 'Queen Elizabeth The Queen Mother' | CPne CPrp XPde |
| | 'Quink Drops' **new** | SMHy |
| | 'Raveningham Hall' | XPde |
| | 'Regal Beauty' | CPar CPne CSpe EBee IBal LSRN LSou NHoy SPoG SRkn |
| | 'Rhone' | CPne IBlr XPde |
| | rich blue-flowered | XPde |
| | 'Rosemary' | CPne XPde |
| | 'Rosewarne' | CCCN CKno CPne CPrp IBal IBlr NCGa NHoy XPde |
| | 'Rotterdam' | CPen CPne NHoy XPde |
| | 'Royal Blue' | CBro CHar CPne GBuc GMaP MSte NHol NHoy |
| | 'Royal Lodge' | XPde |
| | 'Royal Purple' | XPde |
| | 'Saint Pauls Waldenbury' | CPne |
| | 'Sally Anne' **new** | CPne |
| | 'San Gabriel' (v) | XPde |
| | 'Sandringham' | CDes CPne EBee EWes IBlr WPGP XPde |
| | 'Sapphire' | IBal IBlr XPde |
| | 'Sarah'PBR | CAbb NCGa |
| | 'Sea Coral' | CCCN CFir CPne CPrp EBee EMil GGar IBal LLWG LRHS MBNS NBsh NHoy NSti SHom |
| | 'Sea Foam' | CPen CPne CPrp EBee IBal MSte NLar XPde |
| | 'Sea Mist' | CCCN CPne EBee EMil IBal |
| | 'Sea Spray' | CCCN CPne EBee EMil IBal LSRN NHoy XPde |
| | 'Septemberhemel' | CPen XPde |
| | 'Sevilla' | XPde |
| | 'Silver Baby' | CAbb CPen CPne CWGN LRHS MNrw MSte NHoy SRos |
| | 'Silver Jubilee' | XPde |

| | | |
|---|---|---|
| | 'Silver Mist' | CPne EBee IBlr SWat XPde |
| | Silver Moon = 'Notfred'PBR (v) | CBow EBee EHrv ELan EPfP GQue LRHS LSou MBNS MGos NCob NHoy WCot XPde |
| | 'Silver Sceptre' | IBlr |
| | 'Sky' | CAbb CPar CPne CWGN EBee IBal IBlr LBuc LRHS LSRN MSte SHar SWat |
| | 'Sky Rocket' | CPne CPrp IBlr |
| | 'Sky Star' | CPne XPde |
| | 'Slieve Donard' | IBlr WFar |
| | 'Sneeuwwitje' | XPde |
| | 'Snow Cloud' | CAbb CBro CPne EBee ELon IBal NHoy SRkn XPde |
| | 'Snow Pixie' | CBro CPne CSBt CSpe CWGN EBee LSRN NHoy |
| | 'Snow Princess' | CPen CPne IBal LBuc LRHS |
| | 'Snowball' | CAby CBcs CDoC COIW CPne CPrp EBee ECho EMil EWTr GAbr IBal LSou MSte NBPC NHoy WClo XPde |
| | 'Snowdrops' | CBro CPne CPrp EBee EGle EHrv EPyc GAbr GBuc IBal LHop LSRN MLLN MNrw MSte NCob SApp SBod SDnm SKHP SMrm SPav SPla WCot WFar |
| | 'Snowstorm'PBR | LBuc |
| | 'Southern Star' | CPne |
| | 'Spokes' | IBlr |
| | 'Starburst' | IBlr |
| | 'Stéphanie' | CPne XPde |
| | 'Stéphanie Charm' | CPen XPde |
| | 'Storm Cloud' (d) | CBro CFir |
| | 'Storm Cloud' Reads | see *A.* 'Purple Cloud' |
| | 'Streamline' | Widely available |
| | 'Summer Clouds' | CPne EBee ELan IBal MBNS NHoy |
| | 'Summer Skies' | CPne IBal NHoy SRos |
| | 'Summer Snow' | CPne |
| | 'Sunfield' | CKno CPen CPrp EBee GBin GBuc LAma NHoy NLar NPer XPde |
| | 'Super Star' | CPne XPde |
| I | 'Supreme' | IBlr |
| | 'Suzan' | XPde |
| | 'Sylvia' **new** | NHoy |
| | 'Sylvine' | CPen XPde |
| | 'Tall Boy' | IBlr |
| | 'Tarka' | CPne |
| | 'Taw Valley' | CPne |
| | 'Thorn' | CPne |
| | 'Thumbelina' | CBro CPne CSpe EBee NHoy |
| | 'Timaru' | Widely available |
| | 'Tinkerbell' (v) | Widely available |
| | 'Tiny Tim' | EBee XPde |
| | 'Titan' | IBlr |
| | 'Torbay' | CPne CPrp EAEE EBee ECtt IBlr LRHS MBNS MWte NBsh NCGa NHol SRos XPde |
| | 'Tornado' **new** | NBhm |
| | Tresco hybrid | CHEx |
| | 'Tresco Select' | NHoy |
| | 'Trudy' | XPde |
| | 'Twilight' | IBlr |
| | ***umbellatus*** L'Hérit. | see *A. africanus* |
| | ***umbellatus*** Redouté | see *A. praecox* subsp. *orientalis* |
| | 'Underway' | EWes GCal IBlr XPde |
| | 'Vague Bleue' **new** | XPde |
| | 'Velvet Night' | CPen |
| | 'Virginia' | XPde |
| | 'Wembworthy' **new** | CPne |
| § | white dwarf hybrids | CBro CPen EBee ECha ECtt EPfP EShb GBuc NBre WFar |
| | 'White Heaven'PBR | CKno CPne EBee NHoy SWat |
| | 'White Ice' | CBcs CPne SApp |

| | | |
|---|---|---|
| | 'White Ice' **new** | NBsh |
| | 'White Orb' | EBee IBal NHoy SPoG |
| | 'White Star' | XPde |
| | 'White Starlet' | NHoy XPde |
| | 'White Superior' | CMMP CPne CSpe EBee GMaP LAst SHBN SPet WCAu XPde |
| | 'White Triumphator' | WCot |
| | 'White Umbrella' | LRHS |
| | white-flowered | CHEx GGar NCob |
| | 'Whitney' PBR | IBlr |
| | 'Wholesome' | IBal |
| | 'Windlebrooke' | CPne EBee ECha XPde |
| | 'Windsor Castle' | CPen CPrp IBal IBlr XPde |
| | 'Windsor Grey' | Widely available |
| | 'Winsome' | IBlr |
| | 'Winter Sky' | CPne XPde |
| | 'Wolga' | EBee |
| | 'Wolkberg' Kirstenbosch | CPne IBlr |
| | 'Yellow Tips' | CPne XPde |
| | 'Yolande' | LAma |
| | 'Yves Klein' | CPrp IBlr |
| | 'Zachary' | CPne |
| | 'Zella Thomas' | CPne EBee LHyd XPde |

## *Agapetes* (*Ericaceae*)

| | | |
|---|---|---|
| | 'Ludgvan Cross' ♀H1-2 | CCCN WPic |
| | ***serpens*** ♀H1 | CCCN CHEx CWib EShb SLon WPic |
| | - 'Scarlet Elf' | CCCN EMil SKHP |
| | ***smithiana*** var. ***major*** | GGGa |

## *Agarista* (*Ericaceae*)

| | | |
|---|---|---|
| § | ***populifolia*** | WFar |

## *Agastache* (*Lamiaceae*)

| | | |
|---|---|---|
| | RCB RA X-1 **new** | WCot |
| | Acapulco Purple = 'Kiegapur' PBR (Acapulco Series) | EBee LHop LRHS |
| | 'After Eight' PBR | EBee |
| | ***anethiodora*** | see *A. foeniculum* (Pursh) Kuntze |
| | ***anisata*** | see *A. foeniculum* (Pursh) Kuntze |
| | ***aurantiaca*** | CHFP EAro GCal LHop NLar SPhx WFar |
| | - 'Apricot Sprite' | EAro EBee LDai LRHS MHav MHer NHol SDnm SPav SPoG SRkn WCHb WFar |
| | 'Black Adder' | Widely available |
| | 'Blue Delight' **new** | SBch |
| | 'Blue Fortune' ♀H3-4 | CBcs EBee ECha EPfP GBri LCro LPio LRHS MBri MCot MLLN MSCN NDov NMoo SMrm SPer WFar WHlf |
| § | ***cana*** | EAro ECtt LDai MLLN WFar |
| | - 'Cinnabar Rose' | NBir WFar |
| | - 'Purple Pygmy' | EBee ECtt LRHS MAsh |
| | 'Firebird' | EAEE EBee EBla ECtt EHrv ELan LHop LRHS MBri MNrw NBir NCGa NDov SGar SMrm SPer SPla SUsu SWat SWvt WAul WCAu WCot WFar WHil |
| | ***foeniculum*** misapplied | see *A. rugosa* |
| § | ***foeniculum*** (Pursh) Kuntze | CArn CChe CMea CPrp EBee ECha ELan GMaP GPoy MHer MNHC MRav NDov NGHP SPav SPhx SRms WCAu WFar WPer |
| | - 'Alabaster' | CBcs EAro EBee SPhx WCHb |
| | - 'Alba' | ECrN MLLN NBre NGHP SHDw SPav WFar |
| | - Apache Fuchsia = 'Puragaat52' **new** | NPri |
| * | 'Fragrant Delight' | SRms |
| | 'Globetrotter' | LHop SAga SPhx SUsu |
| | 'Glowing Embers' | ECtt EPfP |
| | 'Hazy Days' | EBee LSou SPhx |
| | 'Heather Queen' | SRkn |
| | 'Linda' **new** | NDov |
| § | ***mexicana*** | EAro EBee LDai LPio MSal SDnm SPav |
| | - 'Champagne' | WCHb |
| | - 'Marchant's Pink' | SMrm |
| | - 'Red Fortune' PBR | EAEE EBee EBla ECtt LBuc LHop LLWG MBri NBsh NCGa SPoG |
| | - 'Rosea' | see *A. cana* |
| * | - 'Toronjil Morado' | LHop |
| | ***nepetoides*** | CArn CSec EAro EPPr MSal NLar SDnm SPav SPhx SSvw WCHb |
| | 'Painted Lady' | CSpe EBee ECtt LPio MNrw MWea SAga SBch SMrm SPhx |
| | ***pallidiflora*** var. ***neomexicana*** 'Lavender Haze' | EBee |
| | ***palmeri*** | LHop |
| | 'Pink Panther' | LHop |
| | 'Pink Pop' | EAro EBee |
| | ***pringlei*** | EAro EBee WMoo |
| | 'Purple Candle' | EWes SPla |
| | 'Purple Haze' | NDov |
| § | ***rugosa*** | CArn CFir CSec GKir GPoy MCot MLLN MNHC MSal SDnm SMeo SPav SPhx SUsu SWat WJek WMoo WPer |
| | - B&SWJ 4187 from Korea | WCru |
| | - f. ***albiflora*** | NBre SDnm WCAu |
| | - - 'Liquorice White' | EBee LRHS NBre NLar SPav SPer |
| | - 'Golden Jubilee' | Widely available |
| | - 'Honey Bee Blue' | LRHS NHol |
| | - 'Korean Zest' | EBee EGoo WCru |
| | - 'Liquorice Blue' | CSec EAEE EAro EBla ECrN LRHS MCot MLan NChi NGBl NGdn NLar NOrc SAga SDnm SGar SPav SPer SPhx WFar WMoo WPer |
| | - pink-flowered | CEnt |
| | ***rupestris*** | CMdw CSpe EAro LHop NLar SPhx SPur WKif |
| | - 'Apache Sunset' | CBow LEdu MBri NTHB SDnm SGar SPav SPlb WHal |
| | ***scrophulariifolia*** | CSec WCHb |
| | 'Serpentine' | EBee NDov SPhx SSvw |
| | 'Spicy' | MSte |
| | 'Tangerine Dreams' ♀H3 | EAEE EAro EBee EBla ECtt LRHS NCGa NCob SCoo SPoG |
| | 'Tutti-frutti' | EBee ECtt EHrv LDai LHop SDnm SPav SUsu |
| | ***urticifolia*** | CSec CSpe MSal NBre |
| | - 'Alba' | CSec CSpe EAro GQue NBre NLar WPer |
| | - 'Liquorice' | CTca EBee SAga WFar |

## *Agathaea* see *Felicia*

## *Agathis* (*Araucariaceae*)

| | | |
|---|---|---|
| | ***australis*** | CDoC |

## *Agathosma* (*Rutaceae*)

| | | |
|---|---|---|
| | ***ovata*** | CCCN |
| | - 'Igoda' | EShb |

## *Agave* ✿ (*Agavaceae*)

| | | |
|---|---|---|
| | F&M 120 **new** | WPGP |
| | ***acicularis*** **new** | MAga |
| | ***aktites*** **new** | MAga |
| | ***albescens*** **new** | MAga |
| | ***albomarginata*** | CDTJ MAga |
| | ***amaniensis*** | MAga |
| | ***americana*** ♀H1 | Widely available |
| | - var. ***expansa*** | MAga |
| | - 'Marginata' (v) ♀H3-4 | CBrP CDTJ CHal CHII IBlr MAga MREP SDnm SSwd |

| | | |
|---|---|---|
| | - 'Mediopicta' misapplied | see *A. americana* 'Mediopicta Alba' |
| | - 'Mediopicta' (v) 🏆$^{H1}$ | CDTJ CHEx MAvo SAPC SArc SBig WEas |
| § | - 'Mediopicta Alba' (v) 🏆$^{H1}$ | CBrP CDTJ EAmu ESwi MAga SChr WCot |
| | - 'Mediopicta Aurea' (v) | MAga |
| | - var. ***oaxacensis*** | MAga |
| | - subsp. ***protamericana*** | MAga WPGP |
| | - subsp. ***protamericana*** x ***scabra*** NJM 05.057 **new** | WPGP |
| | - 'Striata' (v) | EShb MAga MCot WCot |
| | - 'Variegata' (v) 🏆$^{H1}$ | Widely available |
| | ***angustiarum*** | MAga |
| | ***angustifolia*** | see *A. vivipara* var. *vivipara* |
| | ***asperrima*** | CDTJ MREP |
| § | - subsp. ***maderensis*** | MAga |
| | - subsp. ***potosiensis*** | MAga |
| § | - subsp. ***zarcensis*** | MAga |
| | ***attenuata*** | CAbb CBrP CHEx EAmu EWll MAga SAPC SArc SBig |
| | ***attenuata*** x ***shawii*** | MAga |
| | ***aurea*** **new** | MAga |
| | ***beauleriana*** | EAmu MAga |
| | ***boldinghiana*** | MAga WCot |
| | ***bovicornuta*** | MAga |
| | ***bracteosa*** | CCCN MAga MREP SChr |
| | ***brittoniana*** | MAga |
| | ***cantala*** | MAga |
| | ***capensis*** | MAga |
| | ***celsii*** | see *A. mitis* var. *mitis* |
| | ***cerulata*** subsp. ***nelsonii*** | MAga |
| | ***chiapensis*** | MAga |
| | ***chrysantha*** | CCCN CTrC EBee MAga SChr SEND WLeb WPGP |
| | - 'Black Canyon' **new** | WCot |
| | ***chrysoglossa*** | MAga |
| | ***colimana*** | see *A. ortgiesiana* |
| | ***colorata*** | CCCN CDTJ |
| | - dwarf | MAga |
| | ***congesta*** **new** | MAga |
| | ***cupreata*** | MAga |
| | ***dasylirioides*** | MAga |
| | ***datylio*** | MAga |
| | ***decipiens*** | MAga |
| | - dwarf | MAga |
| | ***delamateri*** | MAga |
| | ***deserti*** | CBrP WCot |
| | - var. ***simplex*** variegated (v) | MAga |
| | ***desmetiana*** **new** | EAmu MAga |
| | - var. ***marginata*** **new** | MAga |
| | ***difformis*** | MAga |
| | ***durangensis*** | MAga |
| | ***eggersiana*** | MAga |
| | ***ellemeetiana*** **new** | MAga |
| | ***elongata*** | see *A. vivipara* var. *vivipara* |
| | ***ensifera*** | MAga |
| | - var. ***marginata*** **new** | MAga |
| | ***evadens*** | MAga |
| | ***felgeri*** | CDTJ MAga |
| | ***ferdinandi-regis*** | see *A. victoriae-reginae* |
| | ***ferox*** | see *A. salmiana* var. *ferox* |
| | ***filifera*** 🏆$^{H1}$ | CBcs CCCN CDTJ CHEx MAga SChr |
| | - 'Compacta' | MAga |
| | - subsp. ***microceps*** ISI 1184 | MAga |
| | ***flexispina*** | MAga |
| | ***fortiflora*** **new** | MAga |
| | ***fourcroydes*** | MAga MREP |
| | ***funkiana*** | MAga |
| | - blue-leaved | MAga |

| | | |
|---|---|---|
| | ***garciae-mendozae*** **new** | CDTJ |
| | - NJM 05.073 **new** | WPGP |
| | ***geminiflora*** | CBcs CCCN CDTJ EAmu EShb MAga WCot |
| | ***gentryi*** | MAga |
| | - F&M 213A **new** | WPGP |
| | ***ghiesbreghtii*** | MAga MREP |
| | ***gigantea*** | see *Furcraea foetida* |
| | ***gigantensis*** | MAga |
| | x ***glomeruliflora*** | MAga |
| | ***goldmaniana*** | see *A. shawii* subsp. *goldmaniana* |
| | x ***gracilipes*** | MAga WPGP |
| | ***guadalajarana*** | CDTJ MAga |
| | - dwarf | MAga |
| | - 'Trelease' | MREP |
| | ***guiengola*** | MAga |
| | ***gypsophila*** **new** | MAga |
| | ***havardiana*** | CTrC EAmu MAga WCot |
| | - dwarf | MAga |
| | ***hiemiflora*** | MAga |
| | ***hookeri*** **new** | MAga |
| | ***horrida*** | MAga |
| | - 'Perotensis' | EShb |
| | ***hurteri*** | CDTJ MAga |
| | ***inaequidens*** | MAga |
| | ***karwinskii*** | MAga |
| | ***kerchovei*** | MAga WCot |
| § | ***lechuguilla*** | EBee MAga SChr WPGP |
| | ***lechuguilla*** x ***univittata*** | MAga |
| | ***lechuguilla*** x ***victoria-reginae*** | MAga |
| | ***lophantha*** | see *A. univittata* |
| | ***lurida*** Aiton | see *A. vera-cruz* |
| | ***macroacantha*** | CDTJ MAga |
| | ***mapisaga*** | MAga |
| | - NJM 05.036 **new** | WPGP |
| | - var. ***lisa*** **new** | MAga |
| | ***maximilliana*** | MAga |
| | - 'Katharinae' | MAga |
| | ***missionum*** from The Virgin Islands | MAga |
| | ***mitis*** var. ***albidior*** | MAga |
| § | - var. ***mitis*** | CBrP CHEx EShb MAga SAPC SArc SChr |
| | ***montana*** | CGHE EAmu EBee MAga |
| | - F&M 221 | WPGP |
| | ***moranii*** **new** | MAga |
| | ***multifilifera*** | MAga |
| | ***neglecta*** | MAga |
| | ***neomexicana*** | CCCN EAmu IDee MAga |
| | x ***nigra*** hort. **new** | EAmu |
| | ***nizandensis*** | CHEx MAga |
| | ***obscura*** | CDTJ MAga MREP |
| | ***ocahui*** | MAga |
| | - var. ***longifolia*** | MAga |
| | ***ornithobroma*** | MAga |
| | ***oroensis*** | MAga |
| § | ***ortgiesiana*** **new** | MAga |
| | ***ovatifolia*** **new** | EAmu MAga SKHP |
| | ***pachycentra*** | MAga |
| | ***palmeri*** | CCCN CTrC MAga |
| | ***panamana*** | see *A. vivipara* var. *vivipara* |
| | ***parrasana*** | EAmu MAga SKHP |
| | - dwarf | MAga |
| | ***parryi*** | CBcs CDTJ CDoC CSpe EAmu EWll GKev MAga SChr WLeb WPGP |
| | - var. ***huachucensis*** | CDTJ CTsd |
| | - var. ***parryi*** | CBrP CDTJ CFir MAga MREP SKHP WPGP |
| | ***parvidentata*** | MAga |
| | - blue-leaved | MAga |
| | ***parviflora*** 🏆$^{H1}$ | MAga SChr |
| | - subsp. ***flexiflora*** | MAga |

| | |
|---|---|
| - - dwarf | MAga |
| x ***peacockii*** | MAga |
| ***pedunculifera*** | MAga |
| ***pelona*** | MAga |
| ***pendula*** new | MAga |
| ***petiolata*** new | MAga |
| ***polianthiflora*** | MAga |
| ***polyacantha*** | MAga |
| - var. ***xalapensis*** | see *A. obscura* |
| ***potatorum*** ♀H1 | SChr |
| - var. ***potatorum*** | MAga |
| - var. ***verschaffeltii*** | MREP |
| - - dwarf | MAga |
| ***promontorii*** | MAga |
| ***pumila*** | MAga |
| ***pygmaea*** | see *A. seemanniana* |
| ***rhodacantha*** | MAga |
| ***salmiana*** | CDTJ EAmu MAga SBig |
| - var. ***angustifolia*** | MAga |
| - subsp. ***crassispina*** | MAga |
| § - var. ***ferox*** | CBrP CDTJ CTrC EAmu EWll LCro MAga MREP SAPC SArc SBig SChr |
| - - 'Marginata' (v) new | MAga |
| - - variegated (v) | MAga |
| ***scabra*** | CCCN EBee MAga |
| - subsp. ***maderensis*** | see *A. asperrima* subsp. *maderensis* |
| - subsp. ***zarcensis*** | see *A. asperrima* subsp. *zarcensis* |
| ***scabra*** x ***univittata*** new | MAga |
| ***scaposa*** | MAga |
| ***schidigera*** | CBrP MAga WCot |
| ***schottii*** | CDTJ MAga |
| - var. ***treleasei*** | MAga |
| ***sebastiana*** | MAga |
| § ***seemanniana*** | MAga |
| ***shawii*** | MAga |
| § - subsp. ***goldmaniana*** | MAga |
| ***shrevei*** subsp. ***matapensis*** | MAga |
| ***sisalana*** | EAmu MAga |
| I - f. ***armata*** | MAga |
| ***sobria*** | MAga |
| - subsp. ***frailensis*** new | MAga |
| - subsp. ***sobria*** | MAga |
| § ***spicata*** | MAga |
| ***striata*** | CTrC IDee |
| - subsp. ***falcata*** | MAga |
| * - ***rubra*** | CDTJ |
| ***stricta*** ♀H1 | CCCN CDTJ MAga MREP SKHP |
| - dwarf | CBrP MAga |
| - 'Nana' | CDTJ |
| - 'Nana' blue-leaved | MAga |
| ***stringens*** | MAga |
| ***subsimplex*** | MAga |
| ***tecta*** | MAga |
| ***tenuifolia*** | MAga |
| ***tequilana*** blue-leaved | MAga |
| - green-leaved | MAga |
| - variegated (v) new | WCot |
| ***thomasae*** | MAga |
| ***titanota*** | MAga |
| ***toumeyana*** | MAga SChr WCot |
| - var. ***bella*** | CDTJ MAga |
| ***triangularis*** | MAga |
| ***underwoodii*** | MAga |
| § ***univittata*** | CDTJ MAga WCot |
| ***utahensis*** ♀H1 | MAga SEND |
| - var. ***discreta*** | MAga |
| - dwarf | MAga |
| - var. ***eborispina*** | MAga |
| - var. ***nevadensis*** | MAga |
| § ***vera-cruz*** | MAga MREP |
| ***victoriae-reginae*** ♀H1 | CBrP CCCN CDTJ EShb EWll MAga SChr SWal |
| - dwarf | MAga |
| - f. ***ornata*** | MAga |
| - variegated (v) | SChr |
| ***vilmoriniana*** | MAga |
| ***vivipara*** | MAga |
| - var. ***letonae*** | MAga |
| - 'Marginata' | MAga |
| - var. ***nivea*** | MAga |
| - var. ***sargentii*** | MAga |
| § - var. ***vivipara*** | MAga WCot |
| ***vizcainoensis*** | MAga |
| ***warelliana*** | MAga |
| ***weberi*** | MAga |
| ***wendtii*** | MAga |
| ***wercklei*** | MAga |
| x ***winteriana*** | MAga |
| ***wocomahi*** new | MAga |
| ***xylonacantha*** | MAga SChr |
| ***yuccifolia*** | see *A. spicata* |
| ***zebra*** | MAga |

## *Ageratina* (*Asteraceae*)

| | |
|---|---|
| § ***altissima*** | CHid EBee EGle ELan EPfP GBar MCot NLar SPav SPhx SSvw WCHb WTin |
| - 'Braunlaub' | CPrp EBee ECtt EMon LRHS NBre NGdn SWat WCAu WHrl WMnd |
| - 'Brunette' | EHrv GKir |
| - 'Chocolate' ♀H4 | Widely available |
| § ***aromatica*** | CRow EBee MLLN MRav NBre NBro SWat WCHb WPer WSFF |
| § ***glechonophylla*** | MAvo MDKP |
| § ***ligustrina*** ♀H3 | Widely available |
| § ***occidentalis*** NNS 94-53 | WCot |

## *Ageratum* (*Asteraceae*)

| | |
|---|---|
| ***corymbosum*** | CHll CSec CSpe |

## *Aglaomorpha* (*Polypodiaceae*)

| | |
|---|---|
| ***coronans*** | WRic |

## *Aglaonema* (*Araceae*)

| | |
|---|---|
| 'Christina' new | LRHS |
| 'Cleopatra' PBR new | LRHS |
| ***crispum*** 'Marie' | MBri |
| 'Greenlight' PBR new | LRHS |
| 'Maria Christina' new | LRHS |
| 'Silver Queen' ♀H1 | MBri |

## *Agonis* (*Myrtaceae*)

| | |
|---|---|
| ***flexuosa*** | CCCN CTrC |

## *Agoseris* (*Asteraceae*)

| | |
|---|---|
| ***glauca*** var. ***dasycephala*** new | CSec |

## *Agrimonia* (*Rosaceae*)

| | |
|---|---|
| ***eupatoria*** | CArn COld CRWN EBWF EBee GPoy MHer MNHC NMir SECG SIde SWat WHer |
| * - var. ***alba*** | NBre NLar |
| ***grandiflora*** | EBee NBre |
| ***gryposepala*** | EBee |
| ***odorata*** misapplied | see *A. procera* |
| ***odorata*** (L.) Mill. | see *A. repens* |
| ***pilosa*** | CArn EBee MSal |
| § ***procera*** | EBWF |
| § ***repens*** | GBar MSal WCHb WMoo |

## *Agropyron* (*Poaceae*)

| | |
|---|---|
| ***glaucum*** | see *Elymus hispidus* |

**magellanicum** see *Elymus magellanicus*
**pubiflorum** see *Elymus magellanicus*

## *Agrostemma* (*Caryophyllaceae*)

**coronaria** see *Lychnis coronaria*
**githago** CArn
– 'Ocean Pearl' **new** CSpe

## *Agrostis* (*Poaceae*)

**calamagrostis** see *Stipa calamagrostis*
§ **canina** 'Silver Needles' (v) CBre EHul EWes GKir MMoz NBir WFar WRos
**karsensis** see *A. stolonifera*
'Lago Lago' EBee
**nebulosa** CKno
– 'Fibre Optics' **new** CSpe
§ **stolonifera** EBWF

## *Aichryson* (*Crassulaceae*)

§ x **domesticum** CHal SEND
– 'Variegatum' (v) ΨH1 CHal EBak EBee WCot
**tortuosum** CFee

## *Ailanthus* (*Simaroubaceae*)

§ **altissima** CBcs CCVT CDul CHEx CLnd CPLG CTho EBee ECrN EHig EMil EPfP EWTr LAst LPan MBlu NWea SAPC SArc SBLw SCoo SDnm SPer SPlb SWvt WBVN WDin
– var. **tanakae** B&SWJ 6777 WCru
**glandulosa** see *A. altissima*

## *Ainsliaea* (*Asteraceae*)

**acerifolia** B&SWJ 4795 WCru
– B&SWJ 6059 WCru
**cordifolia** **new** EBee
**fragrans** EBee
**macroclinidioides** **new** EBee

## *Aiphanes* (*Arecaceae*)

**aculeata** LPal

## *Ajania* (*Asteraceae*)

§ **pacifica** CHal EBee WHer
– 'Silver Edge' EBee
**tibetica** JJH 9308103 NWCA

## *Ajuga* (*Lamiaceae*)

**ciliata** var. **villosior** CFir EPPr GBin WOut
**genevensis** EPPr EShb WOut
– 'Tottenham' WOut
**incisa** EBee GCal
– 'Bikun' (v) CMoH EBee EShb SRGP
– 'Blue Enigma' CLAP EBee EWes NCGa NHol WOVN
– 'Blue Ensign' LDai
'Little Court Pink' see *A. reptans* 'Purple Torch'
**metallica** hort. see *A. pyramidalis*
'Pink Spires' NCot
§ **pyramidalis** CFee EBee GKir WHer
– 'Metallica Crispa' CBct CBow CStu EBee ECho ECtt EPfP EWes LAst LRHS MBNS NBPC NHol NLar SPoG SRms SSvw SWvt WFar
**reptans** CRWN CTri CWan EBWF EBee ECtt GKev GKir GPoy LPBA MCot MHer MNHC MSal NMir NSco SGar WFar
– f. **albiflora** 'Alba' CArn CWan EBee ECtt EPfP GGar MNrw MRav MSCN NBro SRms WAlt WCAu WCHb WFar WLHH WMoo
– – 'Sanne' **new** EBee
– – 'Silver Shadow' NChi WTin
– 'Arctic Fox' (v) CCVN CWGN EBee ECho EHrv GBuc LHop LRHS MAvo MNrw MRav NRya SAga SWvt WBrk WCot WFar WHer
– 'Argentea' see *A. reptans* 'Variegata'
§ – 'Atropurpurea' CCVT CHrt CTca CWan EBee ECha ECho ELan EMFW EPfP GGar LBMP LCro LPBA LRHS MAvo MCot MGos MLHP NHol NVic SPer SPlb SRms SWvt WBrE WBrk WFar
– Black Scallop = 'Binblasca' CBgR CHFP EBee ECtt EPPr ETod GKir LBMP LRHS MAvo MGos MMHG MWhi NBPN NBsh NDov NHol NSti SPer SRot WFar
– 'Braunherz' Widely available
– 'Brean Down' CNat
– 'Burgundy Glow' (v) Widely available
§ – 'Catlin's Giant' ΨH4 Widely available
– 'Chocolate Chip' see *A. reptans* 'Valfredda'
– 'Delight' (v) ECho ECot WEas
– 'Ebony' EBee LRHS LSRN
– 'Ermine' (v) MNrw MTPN SAga
– 'Evening Glow' GGar
– 'Flisteridge' CNat WAlt
– 'Golden Beauty' EBee ECtt EWes GBar LAst NHol
– 'Grey Lady' GBuc
– 'Harlequin' (v) SWvt WBrE
– 'John Pierpoint' EBee LRHS SHar
– 'Jumbo' see *A. reptans* 'Jungle Beauty'
§ – 'Jungle Beauty' CSev EAEE EBee EPfP GBar LRHS MRav NCob WCAu WFar
– 'Lush Blue' **new** WAlt
– 'Macrophylla' see *A. reptans* 'Catlin's Giant'
§ – 'Multicolor' (v) CArn CBcs CChe EBee ECho ELan GKir LBMP LHop LPBA LRHS MAvo MBar MCot NHol SBod SPer SPlb SPoG SRms SWal SWvt WFar WMoo
– 'Palisander' EAEE EBee LRHS NLar
– 'Pink Elf' CChe CMHG ECho MRav NBro SWat WBrk WFar
– 'Pink Splendour' NBre NChi
– 'Pink Surprise' EBee ECtt EHoe GBar GBuc LAst MHer MLHP NRya SSvw WFar WGwG WMoo
– 'Purple Brocade' EHoe
§ – 'Purple Torch' EBee GKir LBMP LBuc LRHS NBsh WEas WOut
– 'Purpurea' see *A. reptans* 'Atropurpurea'
– 'Rainbow' see *A. reptans* 'Multicolor'
– 'Rosea' EAEE EBee WAlt WMoo
– 'Rowden Amethyst' CRow
– 'Rowden Appleblossom' CRow
– 'Rowden Royal Purple' CRow
– 'Silver Carpet' EBee
– 'Silver Queen' EBee ECtt
– 'Tricolor' see *A. reptans* 'Multicolor'
§ – 'Valfredda' CEnt EAlp EBee ECtt EPfP EShb GBar GGar GKev LAst LBMP LSou MAvo NLar NPro SHar WCot WGwG WMoo WOut
– 'Vanilla Chip' (v) EBee
§ – 'Variegata' (v) CBct EBee ECho ECtt EPfP EShb LBMP LHop MNHC NBid NPri SBod SPer SPoG SRms SWat WEas WFar
– 'Wild Purple' **new** WAlt

## *Akebia* (*Lardizabalaceae*)

**longeracemosa** CBcs LEdu NLar SKHP WCot
– B&SWJ 3606 WCru
x **pentaphylla** EBee EPfP LEdu LRHS MAsh WSHC
– B&SWJ 2829 WCru

| | |
|---|---|
| ***quinata*** | Widely available |
| - B&SWJ 4425 | WCru |
| - 'Alba' | CBcs CSPN CWGN NLar WPat |
| - 'Amethyst Glow' | EPfP LRHS MBri SPer SPoG |
| - cream-flowered | EBee EPfP LRHS MWea SPer SPoG SSta SWvt WCru WPGP |
| - variegated (v) | CBcs CBow LLHF WCru WPat |
| - 'White Chocolate' | NLar WCru WSHC |
| ***trifoliata*** | CBcs CHEx EBee EPfP GKir LRHS SLim |
| - B&SWJ 2829 | WCru |
| - B&SWJ 5063 | WCru |

## *Alangium* (*Alangiaceae*)

| | |
|---|---|
| ***chinense*** | CBcs EPla WBVN |
| ***platanifolium*** | CAbP CPLG MBlu MBri NLar WPGP |
| - var. ***macrophyllum*** | WPGP |
| - var. ***platanifolium*** | NLar |

## *Albizia* (*Mimosaceae*)

| | |
|---|---|
| ***distachya*** | see *Paraserianthes lophantha* |
| § ***julibrissin*** | CArn CDTJ CTrC EAmu EPfP IDee LAst LMaj LPan LRHS MJnS SBLw SPlb WDin |
| - Ombrella = 'Boubri'[PBR] | EMil LRHS MREP SBLw SCoo |
| - f. ***rosea*** ♀H2-3 | Widely available |
| - 'Rouge d'Été' | EBee |
| - 'Rouge Selection' **new** | SKHP |
| ***lophantha*** | see *Paraserianthes lophantha* |

## *Albuca* (*Hyacinthaceae*)

| | |
|---|---|
| J&JA 15856 **new** | NWCA |
| from Lesotho | GCal |
| ***altissima*** | CStu EBee |
| ***angolensis*** | CPou WHil |
| ***aurea*** | WHil WPrP |
| * ***batliana*** | ECho |
| ***batteniana*** | CFir EBee EBrs ECho |
| ***canadensis*** | CStu EBee WHil |
| ***clanwilliamigloria*** | WHil WPrP |
| 'Dirk Wallace' | CPLG CSec |
| ***fastigiata*** | WHil |
| - f. ***floribunda*** | WCot |
| ***humilis*** | CDes CPLG CStu EBee ECho NMen WAbe WCot WPrP |
| ***juncifolia*** | EBee |
| ***maxima*** | CPou WCot WHil |
| ***nelsonii*** | CAvo EBee EBrs WPGP |
| ***rupestris*** | WCot WHil |
| ***setosa*** | EBee |
| ***shawii*** | CAvo CBgR CBro CDes CFFs CPou CPrp CSec CStu EAEE EBee EBla EBrs ECho EMil ERos LRHS MHer NSla NWCA SGar SPad SPet SPoG SSvw WAbe WPGP WPrP |
| ***trichophylla*** | WCot |

## *Alcea* (*Malvaceae*)

| | |
|---|---|
| 'Apple Blossom' (d) | NBHF |
| 'Arabian Nights' | MBri NBHF SPav |
| 'Blackcurrant Whirl' | NBHF SPav |
| ***ficifolia*** | GCra LCro MCCP NChi SDnm SPav WFar WMoo |
| 'Happy Lights' | CWib |
| 'Peaches 'n' Dreams' | CWib EBee NGBl WRHF |
| § ***rosea*** | GKir LAst NBlu SECG SVic WFar |
| - 'Black Beauty' | NBur |
| - Chater's Double Group (d) | CWib ECtt EPfP MBri MLan MWat SRms WRHF |
| - - chamois (d) | GKir |
| - - pink (d) | ECtt EPfP NPri SPer |
| - - purple (d) | EPfP SPer |
| - - red (d) | ECtt EPfP NPri |
| - - salmon pink (d) | EPfP |
| - - scarlet (d) | EPfP |
| - - violet (d) | EPfP SPer |
| - - white (d) | EPfP NPri SPer |
| - - yellow (d) | ECtt EPfP NPri SPer |
| - 'Crème de Cassis' | EPfP MWat NGBl SPav |
| - double apricot-flowered (d) | NBHF NBur |
| - double pink-flowered (d) | MHer |
| - double red-flowered (d) | MHer |
| - double rose-flowered (d) | EBee SPer |
| - double scarlet-flowered (d) | SPer SPla |
| - double white-flowered (d) | MHer |
| - double yellow-flowered (d) | EBee MHer |
| - 'Lemon Light' | LHop NBur |
| - 'Nigra' | CArn CMea CSpe EBee ECtt EHrv ELan EPfP GMaP LCro LHop LRHS LSRN MHer MSte MWat NGBl NGdn NPri SGar SMad SPer WCAu WFar |
| - 'Queeny Purple' **new** | CWCL |
| - single-flowered | MWat |
| - Summer Carnival Group | CWCL CWib LAst SRms |
| § ***rugosa*** | CMea LHop MCot MSte SPav WPGP |

## *Alcea* × *Althaea* (*Malvaceae*)

| | |
|---|---|
| 'Parkallee' (d) | CBgR CDes CSpe EBee ECtt EMon GBri LCro LDai LSou MAvo MBNS MCCP MCot NSti SPhx SUsu WCot WHoo WWFP WWlt |
| 'Parkfrieden' (d) | CSpe EBee ECtt EMon SPhx WCot |
| 'Parkrondell' (d) | CBgR EBee ECha ECtt EMon GBri MAsh MAvo MBNS MSCN SPoG WCot |

## *Alchemilla* ✿ (*Rosaceae*)

| | |
|---|---|
| ***abyssinica*** | EBee WHrl |
| ***alpina*** misapplied | see *A. conjuncta, A. plicatula* |
| ***alpina*** ambig. | EOHP MCot |
| ***alpina*** L. | CEnt CFee EBla ECho ECrN EHoe EPfP GKir LEdu LRHS MRav MWat NGHP NMir SBch SIng SPet SRms SWat WFar WKif WMoo WPer |
| ***aroanica*** | EBee EBla |
| ***arvensis*** | see *Aphanes arvensis* |
| § ***conjuncta*** | Widely available |
| ***elisabethae*** | EMon WCHb |
| ***ellenbeckii*** | CFee CMCo EBee ECho EDAr EPfP GBar GGar LAst MTho NChi WCHb WFar WPGP |
| ***epipsila*** | EBee EShb EWes MSte NLar SPhx WPer WPtf |
| ***erythropoda*** ♀H4 | Widely available |
| ***faeroensis*** | CMCo WMoo WPer WPtf |
| - var. ***pumila*** | EBla GEdr NMen |
| ***filicaulis*** **new** | EBWF |
| - 'Minima' | CNat |
| § ***fulgens*** | LEdu |
| ***glaucescens*** | CNat EBla |
| ***hoppeana*** misapplied | see *A. plicatula* |
| ***iniquiformis*** | EBee WPGP |
| ***lapeyrousei*** | EBee EPPr |
| ***mollis*** ♀H4 | Widely available |
| * - 'Robusta' | EBee MMuc NBur SEND SPlb SWat WFar WMoo WPnP |
| - 'Thriller' | EBee IBal NBur |
| ***monticola*** | WPer |
| 'Mr Poland's Variety' | see *A. venosa* |
| ***pedata*** | EBee NChi |
| ***pentaphylla*** | EBee |
| § ***plicatula*** | WPer |
| ***psilomischa*** | EMon |
| ***pumila*** | NBre |

| | | |
|---|---|---|
| | ***saxatilis*** | EDAr IFoB LBMP WPer |
| * | ***sericophylla*** new | EBee |
| | ***splendens*** misapplied | see *A. fulgens* |
| | ***straminea*** | EBee MRav NBre |
| § | ***venosa*** | CMoH |
| | aff. ***venosa*** | EPla |
| | ***vetteri*** | EBee WHrl |
| | ***vulgaris*** misapplied | see *A. xanthochlora* |
| § | ***xanthochlora*** | CArn CWan EBee GBar GPoy MSal NBre NLar NSco SRms WFar WHer WPer |

## *Aldrovanda* (*Droseraceae*)

| | | |
|---|---|---|
| | ***vesiculosa*** | EFEx |

## alecost see *Tanacetum balsamita*

## *Alectorurus* (*Liliaceae*)

| | | |
|---|---|---|
| | ***yedoensis*** var. ***platypetalus*** new | EBee |

## *Alectryon* (*Sapindaceae*)

| | | |
|---|---|---|
| | ***excelsus*** | CBcs ECou |

## *Aletris* (*Melanthiaceae*)

| | | |
|---|---|---|
| | ***spicata*** | EBee |

## *Alisma* (*Alismataceae*)

| | | |
|---|---|---|
| | ***plantago-aquatica*** | CBen CDWL CRow EBWF EHon EMFW LPBA MSKA NPer NSco SWat WFar WMAq WPnP |
| | - var. ***parviflorum*** | CBen CDWL LPBA MSKA SPlb SWat WMAq |

## *Alkanna* (*Boraginaceae*)

| | | |
|---|---|---|
| | ***tinctoria*** | MSal |
| | - HH&K 345 | CMdw |

## *Allamanda* (*Apocynaceae*)

| | | |
|---|---|---|
| § | ***blanchetii*** | SOWG |
| | ***cathartica*** | MBri MJnS |
| | - 'Birthe' | MBri |
| | - 'Cherry Red' | MJnS |
| | - 'Halley's Comet' | SOWG |
| | 'Cherries Jubilee' | SOWG |
| | 'Jamaican Sunset' | SOWG |
| | ***neriifolia*** | see *A. schottii* |
| § | ***schottii*** ♀H1 | SOWG |
| | ***violacea*** | see *A. blanchetii* |

## *Alliaria* (*Brassicaceae*)

| | | |
|---|---|---|
| | ***petiolata*** | CArn EBWF GPoy NLan WHer WSFF |

## *Allium* ✿ (*Alliaceae*)

| | | |
|---|---|---|
| § | ***acuminatum*** | CPom EBee ECho GBin NBir NMen SPhx |
| I | - 'Album' | ECho |
| | ***aflatunense*** misapplied | see *A. hollandicum* |
| | ***aflatunense*** ambig. | CSec IBal LSRN WCot WFar |
| | ***aflatunense*** B.Fedtsch. | EMon LHop SApp |
| I | - 'Alba' | EBee EBrs |
| | ***akaka*** | NWCA |
| | 'Akbulak' | EBee ECho ERCP LAma MSte |
| | ***albopilosum*** | see *A. cristophii* |
| | ***altaicum*** | CSec |
| | ***altissimum*** 'Goliath' | CGrW CTca EBee EBrs LRHS WCot |
| | ***amabile*** | see *A. mairei* var. *amabile* |
| | 'Ambassador' new | CBro CMea EBee ERCP LRHS MNrw |
| | ***amethystinum*** | CPom |
| | ***ampeloprasum*** | EBWF EBee EBrs ECha ECho LAma NGHP WHer WShi |
| | - var. ***babingtonii*** | CAgr CArn CHFP CNat GPWP GPoy ILis LEdu MLLN WHer WShi |
| § | - 'Elephant' | CArn |
| | ***amphibolum*** | EBee EBrs ECho EHrv |
| | ***amplectens*** | EBee EBrs |
| § | ***angulosum*** | CAvo CMea EBee EBrs ECho EMon LAma SMrm WCot |
| | ***angustitepalum*** | see *A. jesdianum* subsp. *angustitepalum* |
| | ***anisopodium*** | EBee |
| | ***atropurpureum*** | CPom EBee EBrs ECha EHrv ELan EMon EPfP ERCP LAma LEdu LRHS MLLN SPer SPhx WBor |
| | ***atroviolaceum*** | EBee EMon |
| | ***azureum*** | see *A. caeruleum* |
| | ***backhousianum*** new | MPoH |
| | 'Beau Regard' ♀H4 | CTca CWCL EBee EBrs ERCP LAma |
| | ***beesianum*** misapplied | see *A. cyaneum* |
| | ***beesianum*** W.W. Smith | CLyd GEdr NBir NRya SMeo |
| | - 'Album' | EBrs |
| | ***bidentatum*** new | EBee |
| | ***blandum*** | see *A. carolinianum* |
| | ***bolanderi*** | EBee |
| | ***brevistylum*** new | EBee |
| | ***bucharicum*** | ERos |
| | ***bulgaricum*** | see *Nectaroscordum siculum* subsp. *bulgaricum* |
| § | ***caeruleum*** ♀H4 | Widely available |
| | - ***azureum*** | see *A. caeruleum* |
| | ***caesium*** ♀H4 | EBrs ECho IPot |
| | ***caespitosum*** new | EBee |
| | ***callimischon*** | CBro |
| | - subsp. ***callimischon*** | EBrs ECho MPoH SPhx |
| | - subsp. ***haemostictum*** | CBgR EBrs ECho NMen |
| | ***canadense*** | CArn CSec EBee GPWP SHar |
| | ***cardiostemon*** | MPoH |
| | ***caricoides*** | EBee |
| § | ***carinatum*** | ECho |
| § | - subsp. ***pulchellum*** ♀H4 | Widely available |
| | - - f. ***album*** ♀H4 | CAvo CBgR CBro CSWP EBee EBrs ECha ECho EGle ELon EMon EPot ERCP LEdu LLWP MNrw NMen SBch SMeo SMrm SPhx WBor WCot WHil |
| | - - 'Tubergen' | ECho |
| § | ***carolinianum*** | EBee WCot |
| | ***cassium*** subsp. ***hirtellum*** | LRHS |
| | ***cepa*** Aggregatum Group | GPoy ILis |
| | - 'Kew White' | WCot |
| | - 'Perutile' | CArn CHby GBar GPoy ILis LEdu MHer SHDw |
| | - Proliferum Group | CArn CBod CHby CPrp CSev CWan EOHP GBar GPoy ILis LEdu MHer MNHC NGHP NTHB SIde WCHb WGwG WHer WJek WLHH |
| | - var. ***viviparum*** | EBrs ECho LAma |
| | ***cernuum*** | Widely available |
| § | - 'Hidcote' ♀H4 | CSam EMon MSte WBVN WKif |
| | - 'Major' | see *A. cernuum* 'Hidcote' |
| | - pink-flowered | EBrs |
| | ***cirrhosum*** | see *A. carinatum* subsp. *pulchellum* |
| | ***cowanii*** | see *A. neapolitanum* Cowanii Group |
| | ***crenulatum*** | EBee EBrs |
| § | ***cristophii*** ♀H4 | Widely available |
| | ***cupanii*** | EBee EBrs ECho |
| | ***cupuliferum*** | EBee |
| § | ***cyaneum*** ♀H4 | CGra CLyd CPBP CPom CSec EBee ECho ERos GEdr LBee LRHS MPoH NChi NMen NRya WCot |
| | ***cyathophorum*** | CSec ECho NWCA |
| § | - var. ***farreri*** | CArn CBgR CBre CBro CSec EBee EBrs ECho EPot ERos GAuc GEdr GKir LBee LEdu LLWP MLHP MRav |

| | | |
|---|---|---|
| | | MSte NChi NRya SBch WBVN WCot WPrP |
| | ***darwasicum*** RM 8274 new | MPoH |
| | ***decipiens*** | EBee |
| | ***delicatulum*** | EBee |
| | ***dichlamydeum*** | CPom ERos |
| § | ***drummondii*** | CPom ERos |
| | 'Early Emperor' | ERCP |
| | ***elatum*** | see *A. macleanii* |
| | 'Emir' new | EBee |
| | ***ericetorum*** | EBee ERos WCot |
| | ***eusperma*** | LAma |
| | ***falcifolium*** | EBee EBrs ECho EPot LAma NMen NMin |
| | ***farreri*** | see *A. cyathophorum* var. *farreri* |
| | ***fasciculatum*** | LAma |
| | ***fimbriatum*** | ECho |
| | 'Firmament' | CAvo CBro CFFs EBee EBrs ECha ECho EMon ERCP IHer IPot LAma LRHS MSte SPhx WCot |
| | ***fistulosum*** | CArn CHby CHrt CWan EBee EBrs ECho ELau GBar GPoy ILis LAma LEdu MHer MMuc MNHC NGHP NHol NPri SIde SMrm WCHb WGwG WPer |
| | - 'Red Welsh' | ILis WJek |
| | - red-flowered | CPrp NGHP |
| | ***flavidum*** new | EBee |
| | ***flavum*** ♀H4 | CArn CBro CSec CTca ECha ECho EGle ERCP IFoB LAma MRav SBch SHBN SMad WGor WGwG |
| § | - 'Blue Leaf' | ECho ERos MLLN NBir SMrm |
| | - subsp. ***flavum*** | EBee EBrs ECho LEdu MMHG MNrw |
| | - - var. ***minus*** | EBee ECho MTho NWCA |
| | - 'Glaucum' | see *A. flavum* 'Blue Leaf' |
| | - var. ***nanum*** | EBrs GEdr GKir |
| | - subsp. ***tauricum*** | EBee EBrs ECho SPhx |
| | ***forrestii*** | EBee GBin MDKP WCot |
| | ***galanthum*** | EBee |
| | ***geyeri*** | EBee ECho WCot |
| | ***giganteum*** ♀H4 | Widely available |
| | 'Gladiator' ♀H4 | CFir CTca CWCL EBee EBrs ECtt EMon ERCP LAma LRHS MLLN MNrw MRav MSte NOrc SMad SPad SPet SPhx |
| | ***glaucum*** | see *A. senescens* subsp. *montanum* var. *glaucum* |
| | 'Globemaster' ♀H4 | Widely available |
| | ***globosum*** | EBee ECho |
| | 'Globus' | CTca EBee EBrs IBal LAma |
| | ***goodingii*** | CPom EBee EBrs ECho GMaP |
| | 'Guna' | LRHS |
| | ***guttatum*** subsp. ***dalmaticum*** | EBee |
| | - - AH 9114 new | MPoH |
| | - subsp. ***sardoum*** | EBee |
| | - - CH 859 new | MPoH |
| | ***gypsaceum*** ARJA 9836 new | MPoH |
| | ***haematochiton*** | WCot |
| | - NNS 95-23 new | EBee |
| | 'Hair' | see *A. vineale* 'Hair' |
| | ***heldreichii*** | EBee EBrs ECho MPoH |
| * | ***hirtifolium*** var. ***album*** | EBee EBrs ECho LAma |
| | 'His Excellency' | CFir EBee EBrs ERCP IBal LAma LRHS MSte |
| § | ***hollandicum*** ♀H4 | CAvo CBro CFFs CHar CKno CTca CWCL EBee EBrs ECha ECtt EHrv EPfP GKev GKir LAma MLLN MNrw MWat NOrc SPer SPlb WBor WFar WPer |
| | - 'Purple Sensation' ♀H4 | Widely available |
| | - 'Purple Surprise' ♀H4 | GKir |
| | ***hookeri*** ACE 2430 | EBee WCot |
| | - var. ***muliense*** | GEdr |
| | ***humile*** | EBee GEdr |
| | ***hyalinum*** | EBrs |
| | - pink-flowered | EBee WCot WPrP |
| | ***hymenorrhizum*** new | EBee |
| § | ***insubricum*** ♀H4 | EBrs ECho LEdu NBir NHol NMen |
| | ***jajlae*** | see *A. rotundum* subsp. *jajlae* |
| | ***jesdianum*** | CBro ECho EMon LRHS |
| § | - subsp. ***angustitepalum*** | EBee EBrs |
| | - 'Michael Hoog' | see *A. rosenorum* 'Michael H. Hoog' |
| | - 'Purple King' | CMdw CPom EBee EBrs LAma MNrw MSte |
| | - white-flowered | EBee EBrs |
| | ***kansuense*** | see *A. sikkimense* |
| | ***karataviense*** ♀H3 | Widely available |
| | - 'Ivory Queen' | CAvo CBro CFFs CMea CTca EBee EBrs ECha ECho ECtt EMon EPfP ERCP GKev IBal LAma LCro LRHS LSRN MSte SPlb WAul WFar |
| | ***kazemunii*** new | MPoH |
| | ***kharputense*** | EBee |
| | ***komarovianum*** | see *A. thunbergii* |
| | ***ledebourianum*** | EBrs ECho MPoH |
| | ***lenkoranicum*** | CAvo EBee EBrs ECho MPoH |
| | ***libani*** | WPer |
| § | ***lineare*** | EBee |
| | 'Lucy Ball' | EBee EBrs EMon EPot ERCP LAma LEdu LRHS MLLN MSte NBir NLar SUsu |
| § | ***macleanii*** | CArn EBee EBrs ECho LAma LRHS |
| | ***macranthum*** | EBee EBrs ECho GEdr LRHS MMHG MSte WCot |
| | - S&L 5369 new | MPoH |
| | ***macropetalum*** new | EBee |
| | ***mairei*** | EBee EBrs ECho ERos LHop LLWP LRHS NMen NRya WTin |
| § | - var. ***amabile*** | CLyd CSec EBee ERos GEdr LBee NChi NRya NSla WThu |
| | 'Mars' | see *A. stipitatum* 'Mars' |
| | ***maximowiczii*** | EBee EBrs ECho |
| | 'Mercurius' new | CMea EBee ERCP LRHS SPhx |
| | ***meteoricum*** | MPoH |
| | ***moly*** | CArn CBro CWCL EBee EBrs ECho EPfP GKir IFoB LAma MBri MRav NBPC NGHP NRya SRms WCHb WCot WHil WTin |
| | - 'Jeannine' ♀H4 | CBro CMea CTca EBee EBrs ECho EPot LAma LRHS MLLN MMHG SPhx |
| | ***mongolicum*** new | EBee |
| | 'Mont Blanc' | CMea EBee EBrs ELan ERCP GBin IPot LAma LRHS MNrw |
| | 'Mount Everest' | see *A. stipitatum* 'Mount Everest' |
| | ***multibulbosum*** | see *A. nigrum* |
| | ***murrayanum*** misapplied | see *A. unifolium* |
| | ***murrayanum*** Reg. | see *A. acuminatum* |
| | ***myrianthum*** new | EBee |
| | ***narcissiflorum*** misapplied | see *A. insubricum* |
| § | ***narcissiflorum*** Villars | ECho LEdu NWCA |
| | ***neapolitanum*** | CArn CSec EBee ECho EPot GBuc LAma LBee LRHS MBri MCot SMrm SPer SRms WGwG |
| § | - Cowanii Group | CBro CSec CTca EBee EBrs ECho EHrv EWTr LRHS WCot |
| | - 'Grandiflorum' | CSam EBee EBrs ECho LRHS MLLN SPhx WBrE |
| | ***nevskianum*** | CTca EBee EBrs ECho LAma LRHS |
| § | ***nigrum*** | CArn CAvo CBro CFFs CSec CTca EBee EBrs EHrv EMon EPot ERCP |

| | | |
|---|---|---|
| | | LAma LRHS MLLN MRav MSte NBir SPhx SSto WCot WRos |
| | ***nutans*** | CBod CPrp EBee EBrs ECho LAma LEdu MHer NGHP SHDw WHal WJek |
| | ***nuttallii*** | see *A. drummondii* |
| § | ***obliquum*** | CArn CAvo CSec EBee EBrs ECha ECho EGle ERCP LRHS MSte WCot WPrP WTin |
| | ***odorum*** L. | see *A. ramosum* L. |
| | ***oleraceum*** | EBee ECho WHer |
| § | ***oreophilum*** | CArn CAvo CBro CFFs CMea CSam CTca EBee EBrs ECha ECho ECtt EHrv EPfP LAma LRHS MLLN MWat NRya NWCA SPer SRms STes WCot WHoo WTin |
| | - 'Agalik Giant' **new** | LRHS |
| | - 'Zwanenburg' ♀H4 | ECho EPot NMen WCot |
| | ***oreoprasum*** | EBee |
| | ***ostrowskianum*** | see *A. oreophilum* |
| | ***ovalifolium*** var. ***leuconeurum*** | WCot |
| | ***pallasii*** | EBee MPoH |
| | ***pallens*** | CBre CWsd NBir |
| § | ***paniculatum*** | EBee EBrs GKir SCnR |
| | - Hoa 0129 **new** | EBee |
| | ***paradoxum*** | LEdu NBir |
| | - var. ***normale*** | CBgR CBro CDes EBee EBrs ECho EMon EPot ERCP MMHG NMen WCot |
| | ***pedemontanum*** | see *A. narcissiflorum* Villars |
| | ***pendulinum*** **new** | EBee |
| | ***peninsulare*** | CPBP |
| | 'Pinball Wizard' | CBro EBee ERCP MNrw |
| | ***platycaule*** | WCot |
| | ***plummerae*** | EBee EBrs ECho MPoH |
| | ***plurifoliatum*** | LAma |
| | ***polyphyllum*** | see *A. carolinianum* |
| | ***polyrrhizum*** | EBee |
| | ***prattii*** | EBee |
| | ***przewalskianum*** | MPoH |
| | ***pskemense*** RKMP 8207 **new** | MPoH |
| | ***pulchellum*** | see *A. carinatum* subsp. *pulchellum* |
| | 'Purple Giant' | CBro ERCP |
| | 'Purple Pride' | SPhx |
| | ***pyrenaicum*** misapplied | see *A. angulosum* |
| | ***pyrenaicum*** Costa & Vayreda | ELan |
| | ***ramosum*** Jacquin | see *A. obliquum* |
| § | ***ramosum*** L. | EBee EBrs ECho LAma LEdu NBre NCob NGHP WPer |
| | 'Renaissance' | ERCP |
| | 'Rien Poortvliet' | CArn LAma |
| | ***robustum*** | EBrs |
| | ***rosenbachianum*** misapplied | see *A. stipitatum* |
| | ***rosenbachianum*** Regel | CArn CBro EBee EMon EPot LAma MLLN |
| | - 'Akbulak' | EBrs ECho LRHS MSte |
| | - 'Album' | EBee EBrs ECha ECho EPot ERCP LAma LRHS MLLN WCot |
| | - 'Michael Hoog' | see *A. rosenorum* 'Michael H. Hoog' |
| | - 'Purple King' | ECho |
| | - 'Shing' | EBee EBrs IBal LAma LRHS |
| § | ***rosenorum*** 'Michael H. Hoog' | EBee EBrs ECho EPot LAma LRHS |
| | ***roseum*** | CArn CMea CPBP EBee EBrs ECho ECtt EPfP ERos LAma LLWP MDKP |
| § | - var. ***bulbiferum*** | CSec |
| | - 'Grandiflorum' | see *A. roseum* var. *bulbiferum* |
| | ***rotundum*** | CSec MPoH |
| § | - subsp. ***jajlae*** | EBee LLWP LRHS MPoH |

| | | |
|---|---|---|
| | 'Round and Purple' | CPom EBee EBrs ERCP IPot MMHG |
| | ***rubellum*** | ERos |
| | ***sarawschanicum*** 'Bright Boy' **new** | EBee |
| | - 'Chinoro' | EBrs |
| | ***sativum*** | CArn MHer MNHC NPri SIde SPoG SVic |
| | - 'Albigensian Wight' | NGHP |
| | - 'Arno' ♀H4 | CPrp |
| | - 'Cristo' ♀H4 | CPrp |
| | - 'Elephant' | see *A. ampeloprasum* 'Elephant' |
| | - golden | GPoy |
| | - 'Iberian Wight' | NGHP |
| | - 'Lautrec' **new** | NGHP |
| | - 'Mediterranean Wight' | NGHP |
| | - var. ***ophioscorodon*** | EBee ECho GPoy ILis LAma |
| | - - 'Early White' ♀H4 | NGHP |
| | - - 'Purple Wight' | NGHP |
| | - 'Purple Heritage Moldovan' **new** | NGHP |
| | - 'Solent White' ♀H4 | NGHP |
| | - 'Sprint' | CPrp |
| | ***saxatile*** | EBee EBrs ECho ERos |
| | ***schmitzii*** | EMon |
| | ***schoenoprasum*** | Widely available |
| | - f. ***albiflorum*** | CArn CBgR CPbn CPrp CSWP EBrs ECha ECrN GMaP GPWP LEdu MHer MSte NBir NCGa NHol SIde SSvw WCHb WEas WHer |
| | - 'Black Isle Blush' | CPbn GPoy MHer SMHy |
| | - 'Corsican White' | EMon LEdu |
| | - fine-leaved | ELau |
| | - 'Forescate' | CBgR CBod CPrp CTca EBee EBla EBrs ECha ECho EWes GBar LAma LAst LHop LRHS MLLN MRav SBch SIde SPet SPla SSvw WCHb WHil |
| | - 'Forncett Forescate' | CBgR SMrm |
| | - medium-leaved | ELau |
| | - 'Netherbyres Dwarf' | CArn |
| | - 'Pink Perfection' | CHFP GPoy MHer SMHy |
| | - 'Polyphant' | CBre WCHb WRha |
| | - var. ***sibiricum*** | GBar GGar SDix WShi |
| | - 'Silver Chimes' | CDes CWan EBee MRav SHDw WLHH |
| | - thick-leaved | NPri |
| | - 'Wallington White' | GBar |
| | ***schubertii*** | Widely available |
| | ***scorodoprasum*** | EBWF EBee SIde WCHb WJek |
| | - subsp. ***jajlae*** | see *A. rotundum* subsp. *jajlae* |
| | - subsp. ***scorodoprasum*** | EBrs ECho LAma LEdu |
| | ***semenowii*** **new** | EBee |
| | ***senescens*** | CArn CBro CTri EBee ECGP ECho ERos EWsh LAma LRHS MRav MSte NChi SApp SBch SEND SIng SRms SSvw WTin |
| | - var. ***calcareum*** | CSec EBee |
| § | - subsp. ***montanum*** | CBro EBla ECha ECho EGoo EPot ERCP GAuc LAma LEdu LPio NBre NMen SDix SIng SMHy WAbe WMoo |
| § | - - var. ***glaucum*** | Widely available |
| | - subsp. ***senescens*** | EBee EBrs ECho EMon LEdu LPio MLLN WPrP |
| | ***setifolium*** **new** | EBee |
| | ***sewerzowii*** ARJA 9883 **new** | MPoH |
| | ***sibthorpianum*** | see *A. paniculatum* |
| | ***siculum*** | see *Nectaroscordum siculum* |
| | ***sieheanum*** | EBee |
| § | ***sikkimense*** | CSsd CWCL EAEE EBee EBla ECho ERos GEdr LBee LRHS MDKP NSla SPet SPla SSvw WCot WPer WPrP |

| | |
|---|---|
| 'Silver Spring' | CAvo CBgR CMea CPom EBee ERCP IPot LRHS SMeo |
| ***sinkiangense*** | EBee |
| ***sphaerocephalon*** | Widely available |
| ***splendens*** | EBrs ECho ERos |
| ***stellatum*** | WGwG |
| ***stellerianum*** | WPer |
| - var. ***kurilense*** | CLyd WThu |
| § ***stipitatum*** | EBrs ECho EMon ERCP LAma LRHS SPhx WCot |
| - 'Album' | CArn CBro EBee EBrs ECho EMon EPot LRHS |
| - 'Glory of Pamir' | LRHS |
| § - 'Mars' | CFir EBee EBrs ERCP LRHS MLLN NLar |
| § - 'Mount Everest' | CArn CAvo CBro CFFs CFir CTca EBee EBrs ECho EMon EPot ERCP EWTr GKev GMaP LAma LEdu LRHS MLLN MSte NBPC NPri SPer SPhx WShi |
| § - 'Violet Beauty' | CBgR CMdw CWCL EBee LAma LRHS SMeo SPhx WCot |
| § - 'White Giant' | EBee EBrs ECho MSte SMeo SPhx |
| ***stracheyi*** | WCot |
| ***strictum*** Ledeb. | see *A. szovitsii* |
| ***strictum*** Schrad. | see *A. lineare* |
| ***subtilissimum*** new | EBee |
| ***subvillosum*** | ERos WCot |
| 'Summer Beauty' | see *A. senescens* subsp. *montanum* |
| 'Sweet Discovery' | EBee EBrs ECho LAma |
| § ***szovitsii*** | EBee |
| ***teretifolium*** new | EBee |
| ***textile*** | ERos |
| § ***thunbergii*** ♀H4 | CAvo EBee EBrs ECho NBir NDlv NRya |
| - 'Nanum' | CPom CSsd |
| - 'Ozawa' | EBee LBee NMen SIng WCot |
| ***tibeticum*** | see *A. sikkimense* |
| * ***tournefortii*** | EBee |
| ***tricoccum*** | EBee |
| ***triquetrum*** | CStu CTca EBee EBrs ECho ELan ELau EPfP EPot GGar GPWP IBlr ILis LAma LBMP LEdu NBir NSti NTHB SIng SPhx WCot WHer WMoo |
| ***tuberosum*** | Widely available |
| - B&SWJ 8881 | WCru |
| - purple/mauve-flowered | CHby ELau |
| § ***unifolium*** ♀H4 | Widely available |
| ***ursinum*** | CArn CBgR CHby CWan EBWF EBee EBrs ECho EOHP EWTr GPWP GPoy LAma MNHC MWat NGHP NTHB SVic WAul WCHb WFar WJek WPtf WShi |
| 'Valerie Finnis' | CPBP |
| ***victorialis*** | EBrs ECho |
| - 'Cantabria' ARMEH 7827 | EBee |
| - 'Kemerovo' | EBee |
| ***vineale*** | CArn EBWF EBee NMir WHer |
| § - 'Hair' | CAby EBee EBrs ECho EPfP ERCP LAma MBri SGar SMad WHil WRos |
| ***violaceum*** | see *A. carinatum* |
| 'Violet Beauty' | see *A. stipitatum* 'Violet Beauty' |
| ***virgunculae*** | CPBP EBee WAbe |
| ***wallichii*** | CLyd EBee EBrs ECho EMon GAuc GBin GMaP MBNS NBir NChi WCot WTin |
| - ACE 2458 | WCot |
| - purple-flowered | GEdr |
| 'White Giant' | see *A. stipitatum* 'White Giant' |
| 'World Cup' | LRHS |
| ***zaprjagajevii*** | WCot |
| ***zebdanense*** | EBee EBrs ECho ERos LAma LRHS |

## *Allocasuarina* (*Casuarinaceae*)

| | |
|---|---|
| ***monilifera*** | ECou |
| ***nana*** | IDee |

## *Allowissadula* (*Malvaceae*)

| | |
|---|---|
| ***holosericea*** new | CSec |

## almond see *Prunus dulcis*

## *Alnus* ✿ (*Betulaceae*)

| | |
|---|---|
| ***cordata*** ♀H4 | Widely available |
| ***cremastogyne*** | EGFP NLar |
| ***crispa*** | see *A. viridis* subsp. *crispa* |
| ***fauriei*** from Niigata, Japan | CSto |
| ***firma*** | CDul CMCN CSto IDee |
| - var. ***sieboldiana*** | see *A. sieboldiana* |
| ***glutinosa*** | CBcs CCVT CDoC CDul CLnd CRWN CSBt CTri EBee ECrN EMac EPfP EWTr GKir LBuc LMaj MGos NBee NBlu NWea SBLw SHBN SPer WDin WMou WOrn |
| - from Corsica | CSto |
| - 'Aurea' | CDul CEnd CLnd CTho CWib ECrN GKir MBlu MGos SBLw SPer |
| - var. ***barbata*** | CSto |
| - 'Imperialis' ♀H4 | CCVT CDoC CDul CEnd CPMA CTho EBee ECrN ELan EPfP GKir IMGH LBuc LPan LRHS MAsh MBlu MBri MDun MMuc NBee NPal NWea SBLw SPer SPoG WDin WOrn |
| - 'Laciniata' | CDoC CDul CTho ECrN GKir MBlu MDun MGos NBlu SBLw WFar |
| ***hirsuta*** | CMCN CSto |
| ***incana*** | CDoC CDul CLnd CMCN CWib EBee ECrN EMac GKir LBuc MBar MGos MMuc NWea SBLw SHBN SPer WDin WMou |
| - 'Aurea' | Widely available |
| - 'Laciniata' | CTho LPan MGos NLar SBLw SCoo WDin WFar |
| - 'Pendula' | CTho LRHS SBLw |
| ***japonica*** | CLnd CSto NLar |
| ***maximowiczii*** | CSto NLar |
| ***nitida*** | CMCN CSto IDee |
| ***oregana*** | see *A. rubra* |
| ***pendula*** | CSto |
| - B&SWJ 10895 new | WCru |
| ***rhombifolia*** | CMCN |
| § ***rubra*** | CCVT CDoC CDul CLnd CMCN ECrN ELan EMac GKir NWea SBLw WDin WMou |
| - 'Pinnatifida' | see *A. rubra* f. *pinnatisecta* |
| § - f. ***pinnatisecta*** | CMCN CTho MBlu |
| § ***rugosa*** | CMCN |
| ***serrulata*** | see *A. rugosa* |
| § ***sieboldiana*** | CSto |
| ***sinuata*** | see *A. viridis* subsp. *sinuata* |
| x ***spaethii*** | CDoC EWTr GKir LRHS MBri MMuc SBLw |
| ***subcordata*** | CLnd CSto |
| ***viridis*** | CAgr CMCN CSto ECrN NWea SBLw |
| § - subsp. ***crispa*** | CSto GKir |
| - - var. ***mollis*** | CMCN |
| § - subsp. ***sinuata*** | CAgr GAuc GKir |

## *Alocasia* ✿ (*Araceae*)

| | |
|---|---|
| x ***amazonica*** ♀H1 | MBri XBlo |
| - 'Polly' | LRHS |
| - 'Polly Bambino' new | LRHS |
| 'Calidora' | CDTJ EUJe MJnS |
| ***cucullata*** | XBlo |

| | |
|---|---|
| ***gageana*** | CDTJ CKob EAmu |
| ***macrorrhiza*** | CDTJ CKob EAmu MJnS SBig |
| - 'Variegata' (v) ♀H1 | MJnS |
| ***odora*** | CDTJ EAmu EUJe XBlo |
| - from Yunnan | MJnS |
| ***plumbea*** | XBlo |
| 'Portodora' | EAmu MJnS |
| ***robusta*** new | CDTJ |
| ***wentii*** | CDTJ EAmu LRHS |

## *Aloe* (*Aloaceae*)

| | |
|---|---|
| ***aculeata*** | CAbb EShb WCot |
| ***africana*** new | CAbb |
| ***alooides*** | CAbb |
| ***arborescens*** | CAbb CBrP CDTJ CHEx EShb EWll SChr |
| ***aristata*** ♀H1 | CAbb CHEx CHal MBri SAPC SArc SChr SEND SWvt WCor WGwG WPGP |
| ***barbadensis*** | see *A. vera* |
| ***barberae*** | CAbb CCCN EShb |
| ***branddraaiensis*** | WCot |
| ***brevifolia*** ♀H1 | CAbb CBrP EShb SAPC SArc |
| ***broomii*** | CAbb CCCN EPfP SChr |
| ***camperi*** 'Maculata' | SChr |
| ***castanea*** | CAbb |
| ***ciliaris*** | EShb SChr |
| ***comptonii*** | CAbb EShb |
| ***cooperi*** | CAbb CCCN CDTJ EShb |
| ***dewetii*** new | CAbb |
| ***dichotoma*** | CAbb EShb |
| ***distans*** | SEND |
| ***ecklonis*** | CAbb CCCN CTrC SPlb |
| ***ferox*** | CAbb CBod CBrP CCCN CDTJ CTrC EShb GPoy LRHS MSal SBig SChr SEND SWal |
| ***fosteri*** | CAbb CBrP CDTJ |
| ***globuligemma*** | CAbb |
| ***greatheadii*** | CTrC |
| - var. ***davyana*** | CAbb |
| ***humilis*** | CBrP CTrC SChr |
| ***immaculata*** | WCot |
| ***krapohliana*** new | CAbb |
| ***littoralis*** | CAbb |
| ***maculata*** | CDTJ CHEx CTrC |
| ***marlothii*** | CAbb CCCN EShb |
| ***microstigma*** | CAbb CCCN |
| ***mitriformis*** | CBrP EPfP LCro SChr SEND |
| ***mutabilis*** | CHEx CTrC SChr |
| ***peglerae*** new | CAbb |
| ***petricola*** new | CAbb |
| ***plicatilis*** | CAbb CCCN CDTJ EShb |
| ***polyphylla*** | WPGP |
| ***pratensis*** | CCCN CDTJ CFir SChr |
| ***ramosissima*** | EShb |
| ***reitzii*** | CAbb CTrC |
| ***speciosa*** | CAbb EShb |
| ***spicata*** new | CAbb |
| x ***spinosissima*** | SChr |
| ***striata*** | CAbb CCCN EShb SChr |
| ***striatula*** | CAbb CBrP CDTJ CGHE CHEx CTrC EAmu EBee EShb EUJe IBlr LPJP LRHS SAPC SArc SBHP SBig SChr SEND WCot WPGP |
| - var. ***caesia*** | IBlr |
| ***succotrina*** | CAbb |
| ***thraskii*** | CAbb |
| ***variegata*** (v) ♀H1 | CSpe EShb SWal SWvt |
| § ***vera*** ♀H1 | CArn CCCN CDoC CHby COld CSpe EOHP EShb GPWP GPoy IFro ILis LRHS MNHC MSal NPer NPri NScw SBch SIde SVic SWal WCot |
| ***wickensii*** | CAbb |

## *Alonsoa* (*Scrophulariaceae*)

| | |
|---|---|
| ***acutifolia*** | CSec |
| 'Bright Spark' | CSpe |
| ***incisifolia*** new | CCCN |
| ***meridionalis*** | CCCN CSec |
| - 'Rebel' | LSou SVil |
| 'Pink Beauty' | CSpe NBur |
| ***unilabiata*** | CSpe |
| ***warscewiczii*** | CCCN CHll ELan |
| - 'Peachy-keen' | CSpe |

## *Alopecurus* (*Poaceae*)

| | |
|---|---|
| ***alpinus*** | see *A. borealis* |
| § ***borealis*** | MMoz |
| - subsp. ***glaucus*** | CSpe EAlp EBee EHoe ELan EPPr GBin NSti SIng SPer |
| ***geniculatus*** | CRWN |
| ***lanatus*** | NBea |
| ***pratensis*** | EBWF NOrc |
| - 'Aureovariegatus' (v) | CWan EBee EHoe EPPr EPla GKir GMaP MBar MMoz NBPC NBid NHol SApp SLim SPer WFar WMoo |
| - 'Aureus' | ECha GBin MRav NBro NSti SPlb WFar |
| - 'No Overtaking' (v) | EPPr |

## *Alophia* (*Iridaceae*)

| | |
|---|---|
| ***drummondii*** | ERos |
| ***lahue*** | see *Herbertia lahue* |

## *Aloysia* (*Verbenaceae*)

| | |
|---|---|
| ***citriodora*** | see *A. triphylla* |
| ***gratissima*** | EOHP |
| § ***triphylla*** ♀H2 | Widely available |

## *Alpinia* (*Zingiberaceae*)

| | |
|---|---|
| B&SWJ 3775 | CKob WPGP |
| ***conchigera*** new | MJnS |
| ***formosana*** | LEdu |
| ***galanga*** | CArn |
| ***japonica*** | CKob CPLG EBee LEdu MSal |
| - B&SWJ 8889 | WCru |
| ***malaccensis*** | CKob |
| ***officinarum*** | CArn |
| ***suishanensis*** new | EBee |
| ***zerumbet*** 'Variegata' (v) | CKob EAmu EShb MJnS XBlo |

## *Alsobia* see *Episcia*

## *Alstroemeria* (*Alstroemeriaceae*)

| | |
|---|---|
| 'Adonis' new | WViv |
| 'Aimi' | CFir LRHS MBri SWal SWvt WFar WViv |
| 'Alexis' new | WViv |
| 'Angelina' | LRHS SWvt |
| 'Apollo' ♀H4 | CBcs CFir CTsd LRHS MBNS MBri MNrw NBre SPer SWvt WViv |
| ***aurantiaca*** | see *A. aurea* |
| § ***aurea*** | CTri GGar MRav NBPC NLar SRms WHer WMoo |
| - 'Apricot' | GCal |
| - 'Dover Orange' | CBod IGor SCoo SEND |
| - 'Lutea' | EBrs EWll NBre SPlb |
| - 'Orange King' | CBod CTsd EBee EBrs ELan EPfP EWll NLar WCot |
| 'Avanti' new | WViv |
| 'Blushing Bride' | CFir MBNS MBri SPer SWvt WWlt |
| 'Bolero' new | WViv |
| 'Bonanza' | SPer |
| ***brasiliensis*** | CFir CTsd CWsd EBee EShb GCal LHop MNrw NChi WCot WSHC |
| Butterfly hybrids | SWal |
| 'Candy Floss' | EBee |

| | | |
|---|---|---|
| | 'Charm' | WFar WViv |
| | 'Coronet' ♀H4 | MBNS WViv |
| | 'Dandy Candy' | EBrs NLar WCot |
| | 'Devotion' **new** | MGos |
| | Diana, Princess of Wales = 'Stablaco' | EMui |
| | ***diluta*** subsp. ***chrysantha*** F&W 8700 | WCot |
| | Doctor Salter's hybrids | ECGP LLHF NSla SRms |
| | 'Dutch Pink' **new** | SEND |
| | 'Dwarf Lemon' **new** | SEND |
| | 'Dwarf Pink' **new** | SEND |
| | 'Elvira' | SPer |
| | 'Eternal Love' | EMui |
| | 'Evening Song' | CFir MBNS SPer SWal SWvt |
| | aff. ***exserens*** | WCot |
| | 'Flaming Star' | CBcs LRHS MBri WCot WViv |
| | 'Freedom' | EBee ECtt ELon GBin LAst MBNS NBPC NGdn SPoG SUsu WCot WGwG |
| | 'Friendship' ♀H4 | CBcs CTsd LRHS NBre SWvt WViv |
| | ***garaventae*** | NLar |
| | 'Gloria' | MBNS SWvt WViv |
| | 'Glory of the Andes' (v) | CWGN LAst NLar |
| | 'Golden Delight' | LRHS MBri SPer SPla WViv |
| | 'Golden Queen' | WFar |
| | H.R.H. Princess Alexandra = 'Zelblanca' ♀H2 | EMui |
| § | H.R.H. Princess Alice = 'Staverpi' ♀H2 | EMui GKir WFar |
| | ***haemantha*** | EBrs MDKP |
| I | 'Hatch Hybrid' | GCal |
| | 'Hawera' | GCal |
| | ***hookeri*** | EBee ECho GCal GGar NLar SCnR |
| | - subsp. ***cummingiana*** | LLHF WCot |
| | 'Inca Blaze' | see *A.* 'Mini Bell' |
| | Inca Devotion = 'Konevotio' | WViv |
| | Inca Exotica = 'Koexotica' | LRHS MGos WViv |
| | Inca Glow = 'Koglow'PBR | MGos WViv |
| | Inca Ice = 'Koice' | LRHS MGos WViv |
| | Inca Moonlight = 'Komolight' | WViv |
| | Inca Obsession = 'Koobsion' | WViv |
| | Inca Pulse = 'Konpulse' | WViv |
| | Inca Serin = 'Koserin' | WViv |
| | Inca Tropic = 'Kotrop' | LRHS MGos WViv |
| | Jubilee = 'Stalilas' **new** | EMui |
| | ***kingii*** | see *A. versicolor* |
| | ***ligtu*** hybrids | CAvo CFFs CSBt EBrs ECha ELan EPfP IFoB LAst LHop MDun MNrw NPer NVic SPoG SRms SRot SWal SWvt WBVN WBrE WFar WHoo |
| | - var. ***ligtu*** | SMHy SPhx WCot |
| | 'Lilac Wonder' | EBee NBhm |
| | 'Little Eleanor' | EBee GBin WCot WFar WViv |
| | 'Little Miss Charlotte' | WFar WViv |
| | 'Little Miss Christina' | LRHS MBNS SWvt WViv |
| | 'Little Miss Isabel' | WViv |
| | 'Little Miss Matilda' | WViv |
| | 'Little Miss Natalie' | NPri WViv |
| | 'Little Miss Olivia' | WViv |
| | 'Little Miss Rosanna' | WViv |
| | 'Little Miss Roselind' | see *A.* 'Roselind' |
| | 'Little Miss Sophie' | MBNS SWvt WHlf WViv |
| | 'Little Miss Tara' | MBNS SWvt WHlf WViv |
| | 'Little Miss Veronica' | MBNS WViv |
| | 'Lucinda' | CBcs MBri SPer SWvt WViv |
| | ***magnifica*** | WCot |
| | - subsp. ***magnifica*** | WCot |
| | Manon | see *A.* Princess Marie-Louise = 'Zelanon' |
| | Marie-Louise | see *A.* Princess Marie-Louise = 'Zelanon' |
| | 'Marina' | MBNS |
| | 'Marissa' | GMaP |
| | 'Mars' | GKir SWal |
| | Meyer hybrids | MTho |
| § | 'Mini Bell' | WViv |
| | Monika = 'Stalmon' **new** | EMui |
| | 'Moulin Rouge' | LRHS MBNS MBri WViv |
| | 'Neptune' **new** | LRHS |
| | 'Orange Gem' ♀H4 | MBNS WFar WViv |
| | 'Orange Glory' ♀H4 | GKir GMaP IArd LRHS MBNS SPla SWvt WFar WViv WWlt |
| | 'Orange Supreme' **new** | WViv |
| | 'Oriana' | LRHS SWvt WViv |
| | ***pallida*** | CPBP |
| | ***pelegrina*** | EBrs ECho MTho |
| | - 'Alba' | ELan |
| | - 'Rosea' | ELan |
| | 'Perfect Blue' | SPoG WViv |
| | 'Perfect Love' | EMui MNrw |
| | ***philippii*** | WCot |
| | 'Phoenix' (v) | CFir SPla SWal SWvt |
| | 'Pink Perfection' | NLar |
| | 'Pink Sensation' **new** | WViv |
| | 'Polka' | MBNS WViv |
| | ***presliana*** RB 94103 | WCot |
| | - subsp. ***australis*** | CPou |
| | Princess Aiko = 'Zapriko'PBR | EBee EMui LRHS SPla |
| | Princess Alice | see *A.* H.R.H. Princess Alice = 'Staverpi' |
| | Princess Angela = 'Staprilan'PBR | CBcs EMui LRHS MBNS NLar SCoo |
| | Princess Anouska = 'Zaprinous'PBR | EBee EMui MNrw |
| | Princess Astrid = 'Stabopink' | EMui |
| | Princess Beatrix = 'Stadoran' | EMui GKir WFar |
| | Princess Camilla = 'Stapricamil'PBR | CBcs EMui LRHS SPoG |
| | Princess Carmina = 'Stasilva' | EMui |
| § | Princess Caroline = 'Stakaros' | EMui |
| § | Princess Charlotte = 'Staprizsa'PBR | EMui GKir |
| | Princess Daniela = 'Stapridani'PBR | EBee EMui SCoo SPoG |
| | Princess Elizabeth | see *A.* Queen Elizabeth The Queen Mother = 'Stamoli' |
| | Princess Ella = 'Staprirange'PBR | EBee EMui LRHS NLar |
| | Princess Emily = 'Staprimil' | EMui |
| | Princess Fabiana = 'Zaprifabi'PBR **new** | LRHS SPoG |
| * | Princess Freckles | EMui |
| | Princess Frederika = 'Stabronza' | EMui GKir |
| | Princess Grace = 'Starodo' | EMui GKir |
| | Princess Ileana = 'Stalvir' | EMui |
| | Princess Isabella = 'Zapribel'PBR | EBee EMui |
| | Princess Ivana = 'Staprivane'PBR | EMui LRHS NLar SPoG |
| | Princess Juliana = 'Staterpa' | EMui SPla SPoG |
| | Princess Julieta = 'Zaprijul'PBR | EMui SPoG |
| | Princess Leyla = 'Stapriley'PBR | CBcs EBee EMui LRHS MBNS MNrw SPoG |
| | 'Princess Margaret' | EMui GKir NLar |

| | |
|---|---|
| 'Princess Margarita' | EMui |
| § Princess Marie-Louise = 'Zelanon' | EMui |
| Princess Marilene = 'Staprilene'[PBR] | EBee EMui LRHS MBNS |
| Princess Mira = 'Stapripur' | EMui |
| Princess Monica = 'Staprimon'[PBR] | EBee EMui GKir MBNS SPla SPoG |
| Princess Morana = 'Staprirana' | EMui |
| Princess Oxana = 'Staprioxa'[PBR] | EBee EMui MNrw NLar SCoo |
| Princess Pamela = 'Stapripame' | EMui |
| Princess Paola = 'Stapripal'[PBR] | EBee EMui MBNS MNrw SCoo SPla |
| Princess Ragna | see *A.* Princess Stephanie = 'Stapirag' |
| Princess Sara = 'Staprisara'[PBR] **new** | SPoG |
| Princess Sarah = 'Stalicamp' | EBee EMui MBNS |
| Princess Sissi = 'Staprisis'[PBR] | EMui SPoG |
| § Princess Sophia = 'Stajello' | EMui SPoG |
| § Princess Stephanie = 'Stapirag' | EMui GKir NLar SPla |
| Princess Susana = 'Staprisusa'[PBR] | EMui NLar SCoo SPoG |
| Princess Victoria[PBR] | see *A.* 'Victoria' |
| 'Princess Violet' | EMui |
| Princess Zavina = 'Staprivina'[PBR] | CBcs CFir EMui MBNS MNrw NLar |
| Princess Zsa Zsa[PBR] | see *A.* Princess Charlotte = 'Staprizsa' |
| § ***psittacina*** | Widely available |
| - 'Mona Lisa' | EShb EWll LLHF NLar WCot WViv |
| - 'Royal Star' (v) | CBro CWCL EBee EBla ELan ELon EMon EPPr EPfP EPla GCal MRav NLar SHar WCot WFar WHil WHoo WPrP WSHC |
| ***pulchella*** Sims | see *A. psittacina* |
| ***pulchra*** | LLHF |
| 'Purple Rain' | MBri MNrw SWvt WViv |
| ***pygmaea*** | MTho |
| § Queen Elizabeth The Queen Mother = 'Stamoli' | EMui GKir |
| 'Red Beauty' (v) | see *A.* 'Spitfire' |
| 'Red Beauty' | GKir GMaP LRHS MBNS MBri NBir SPer SPlb SWvt WCot |
| 'Red Elf' | MBNS NBre SWvt WFar |
| 'Regina'[PBR] | see *A.* 'Victoria' |
| 'Rhubarb and Custard' | EBee |
| § 'Roselind' | CFir MBNS NPri SWvt WHlf WViv |
| 'Rosy Wonder' | NMoo |
| 'Selina' | GBin MBNS NBre SWal WFar WViv |
| 'Serenade' | CBcs WViv |
| 'Short Purple' | CDes WCot |
| 'Sirius' **new** | LRHS |
| 'Solent Candy' | WFar |
| 'Solent Crest' | WFar |
| 'Solent Dawn' | WFar |
| 'Solent Pride' | WFar |
| 'Solent Wings' | WFar |
| 'Sonata' **new** | WViv |
| 'Sovereign' | MDKP |
| § 'Spitfire' (v) | GKir LRHS MBri SWvt WViv |
| 'Spring Delight' (v) | WCot |
| 'Staroko' | see *A.* Princess Caroline = 'Stakaros' |
| 'Strawberry Lace' | EBee |
| 'Sunrise' | WWlt |
| 'Sunstar' | GMaP |
| 'Sweet Laura'[PBR] | GGar LAst LLHF LSRN NLar SPoG |
| 'Tanya' | WViv |
| 'Tapestry' | SWal |
| 'Tessa' | LRHS MBNS NBre WViv |
| 'Turkish Delight' | EBee |
| 'Uranus' **new** | LRHS |
| 'Ventura' **new** | WViv |
| § ***versicolor*** | WCot |
| § 'Victoria'[PBR] | EMui GKir |
| 'White Apollo' | SPla |
| 'White Queen' **new** | WViv |
| 'Yellow Friendship' ♀H4 | MBNS NLar SPlb SWvt WFar WViv |
| Yellow King | see *A.* Princess Sophia = 'Stajello' |

## *Alternanthera* (*Amaranthaceae*)

| | |
|---|---|
| ***dentata*** 'Purple Knight' | EShb LRHS |

## *Althaea* (*Malvaceae*)

| | |
|---|---|
| ***armeniaca*** | EBee EMon LBMP NLar WCot |
| ***cannabina*** | CAby CFir CSpe EBee ELan EMon GBri GCal GQui WBor WHal WHoo WHrl WKif WOld WSHC |
| ***officinalis*** | CArn CPrp CSev CWan EBWF EBee ELan EMon GBar GMac GPoy ILis MHer MNHC MSal SECG SIde WGwG WPer |
| - ***alba*** | LSou NLar WHer |
| § - 'Romney Marsh' | EBee EDAr EWll GCal MRav NCot SBHP SMad WKif WSHC |
| ***rosea*** | see *Alcea rosea* |
| ***rugosostellulata*** | see *Alcea rugosa* |

## *Altingia* (*Hamamelidaceae*)

| | |
|---|---|
| ***gracilipes*** | WPGP |

## x *Alworthia* (*Aloaceae*)

| | |
|---|---|
| 'Black Gem' | CBct EBee EShb EWll LSou SKHP |

## *Alyogyne* (*Malvaceae*)

| | |
|---|---|
| ***hakeifolia*** | CSpe ECou |
| - 'Elle Maree' | ECou SOWG |
| - 'Melissa Anne' | ECou SOWG |
| § ***huegelii*** | CBcs CSec EBee ECou ERas LRHS SPoG SRkn WDyG |
| - 'Lavender Lass' | ECou |
| - 'Santa Cruz' | CCCN CHll CMdw CSec CSpe EBee EMil LHop SEND SMad SOWG WPGP WRos |

## *Alyssoides* (*Brassicaceae*)

| | |
|---|---|
| ***utriculata*** | CSec GAbr WPer |

## *Alyssum* (*Brassicaceae*)

| | |
|---|---|
| ***argenteum*** misapplied | see *A. murale* |
| ***atlanticum*** **new** | CSec |
| ***corymbosum*** | see *Aurinia corymbosa* |
| ***montanum*** | ECha ECho NBlu SPlb SRms WMoo |
| § - 'Berggold' | ECho EPfP |
| - 'Luna' **new** | EAlp EDAr |
| - Mountain Gold | see *A. montanum* 'Berggold' |
| § ***murale*** | CSec NLar |
| ***oxycarpum*** | WAbe |
| ***repens*** | EDAr |
| ***saxatile*** | see *Aurinia saxatilis* |
| ***scardicum*** | LLHF |
| ***serpyllifolium*** | NWCA |
| ***spinosum*** | WFar |
| § - 'Roseum' ♀H4 | CSec CSpe CTri ECha ELan EPot GMaP LBee MLHP MWat NMen NWCA WAbe WCot WFar WPer |

| | | |
|---|---|---|
| * | - 'Roseum Variegatum' | EPot |
| | - 'Strawberries and Cream' | WAbe WFar |
| | ***tortuosum*** | SEND WMoo |
| | ***wulfenianum*** | GAbr GEdr IFoB LLHF NLar SEND STre |

## *Amana* see *Tulipa*

## *Amaranthus* (*Amaranthaceae*)

| | | |
|---|---|---|
| | ***caudatus*** new | CSec |
| | ***hypochondriacus*** | CSpe |
| | 'Pygmy Torch' ♀H3 | |

## x *Amarcrinum* (*Amaryllidaceae*)

| | | |
|---|---|---|
| | 'Dorothy Hannibal' | WCot |
| | ***memoria-corsii*** | CPrp CTca ECho |
| | - 'Howardii' | CFir EBee EBrs ECho EShb LEdu LPio LRHS WCot |

## x *Amarine* (*Amaryllidaceae*)

| | | |
|---|---|---|
| | ***tubergenii*** | CAvo |
| | - 'Zwanenburg' | CAby EBee LRHS WCot |

## x *Amarygia* (*Amaryllidaceae*)

| | | |
|---|---|---|
| § | ***parkeri*** 'Alba' | CAvo CBro EBee EBrs ECho LPio MSte WCot |
| | - 'Rosea' | EBrs |

## *Amaryllis* ✿ (*Amaryllidaceae*)

| | | |
|---|---|---|
| § | ***belladonna*** ♀H2-3 | CAby CBcs CBro CHEx CPne CPrp CTca CWsd EBee EBrs ECho EMon EPfP ERCP EShb LAma LEdu LRHS MBri MSte NBPC NCGa SChr SDnm SMrm SPav WCot WHil |
| | - 'Bloemfontein' | CAvo |
| | - 'Johannesburg' | CAvo EMon WCot |
| | - 'Kimberley' | CPne EMon |
| | - 'Major' | CAvo |
| | - 'Parkeri Alba' | see x *Amarygia parkeri* 'Alba' |
| | - 'Purpurea' | EBrs EMon LRHS WCot |
| | - white-flowered | EBee ECho WCot |
| | - 'Windhoek' | CAvo |

## *Amberboa* (*Asteraceae*)

| | | |
|---|---|---|
| § | ***moschata*** | WCot |

## *Ambrosina* (*Araceae*)

| | | |
|---|---|---|
| | ***bassii*** | EBrs |
| | - from Tunisia | ECho WCot |

## *Amelanchier* ✿ (*Rosaceae*)

| | | |
|---|---|---|
| | ***alnifolia*** | EPla |
| | - 'Forestburg' | MBri |
| | - 'Obelisk' PBR | CAbP CDul EBee EHig LBuc LLHF LRHS MAsh MBri MGos NLar SCoo SPoG SSta |
| § | - var. ***pumila*** | LHop MSte WTin |
| | - 'Smokey' | CDul NLar |
| § | ***arborea*** | SRms |
| | ***bartramiana*** | CTho LRHS SSta |
| | - 'Eskimo' | EBee NLar |
| | ***canadensis*** K. Koch | see *A. lamarckii* |
| | ***canadensis*** Sieb. & Zucc. | see *A. arborea* |
| | ***canadensis*** ambig. | GAuc GKir NPri WBod |
| | ***canadensis*** (L.) Medik. | Widely available |
| | ***denticulata*** F&M 176 | WPGP |
| | x ***grandiflora*** 'Autumn Brilliance' | CDul CEnd MAsh NHol NLar |
| | - 'Ballerina' ♀H4 | Widely available |
| | - 'Princess Diana' | LRHS MAsh NLar |
| | - 'Robin Hill' | CBcs CWSG EBee ECrN EHig ELon EMil GKir LBuc LPan LRHS MBlu MGos MRav NLar SBLw SCoo SHBN SLim SPoG WFar |
| | - 'Rubescens' | CDul CEnd CPMA EBee GKir LPan LRHS SLon |
| | ***humilis*** | GAuc |
| | 'La Paloma' | CWSG GKir LRHS MBri SCoo |
| | ***laevis*** | CBcs CDul CTri EPfP LPan MGos NLar SPer STre WGor |
| | - 'Cumulus' | MBri NLar |
| | - 'Prince Charles' | MBri NLar |
| | - 'R.J. Hilton' | GKir MBri MLan SCoo |
| | - 'Snow Cloud' | CDoC |
| | - 'Snowflakes' | CDoC CEnd CPMA CWSG EBee GKir LRHS MAsh MDun MGos MLan NHol SLim SPoG |
| § | ***lamarckii*** ♀H4 | Widely available |
| | ***ovalis*** Medik. | SPlb |
| | - 'Edelweiss' | CEnd CPMA EBee LPan LRHS MBlu MGos NLar SCoo |
| | - 'Helvetia' | CEnd WEas |
| | ***pumila*** | see *A. alnifolia* var. *pumila* |
| | ***spicata*** | ECrN |

## x *Amelasorbus* (*Rosaceae*)

| | | |
|---|---|---|
| | ***raciborskiana*** new | MBlu |

## *Amicia* (*Papilionaceae*)

| | | |
|---|---|---|
| | ***zygomeris*** | CHEx CHll CMdw CPom CSpe EBee ELon EWes EWld GBuc GCal MCot SAga SBHP SMad SMrm WCot WSHC |

## *Ammi* (*Apiaceae*)

| | | |
|---|---|---|
| | ***majus*** | CArn CSec MCot MSal SDix |
| | ***visnaga*** | CArn CBre CSpe MSal WHal |

## *Ammocharis* (*Amaryllidaceae*)

| | | |
|---|---|---|
| | ***coranica*** | WCot WVal |

## *Ammophila* (*Poaceae*)

| | | |
|---|---|---|
| | ***arenaria*** | CRWN EBWF GFor GQui |

## *Amomyrtus* (*Myrtaceae*)

| | | |
|---|---|---|
| § | ***luma*** | CAgr CDoC CDul CHEx CPrp CTrG CTri EBee ELan GQui IDee SArc WFar WPic |

## *Amorpha* (*Papilionaceae*)

| | | |
|---|---|---|
| | ***canescens*** | CBcs EBee GKir MBri SKHP SPlb WBVN WSHC |
| | ***fruticosa*** | CBcs EShb EWTr LEdu MBlu MBri NLar SEND SPlb WSHC |
| | ***herbacea*** | NLar |
| | ***ouachitensis*** | NLar |
| | ***paniculata*** | NLar |

## *Amorphophallus* ✿ (*Araceae*)

| | | |
|---|---|---|
| | ***albus*** | CKob LEdu WCot |
| | ***bulbifer*** | CDTJ CDes CKob CSec EAmu EBee EBrs EUJe LAma LRHS SBig WPGP |
| | ***dunnii*** | CKob EBee |
| | ***henryi*** | CKob |
| | ***kerrii*** | CExc EBee WCot |
| | ***kiusianus*** B&SWJ 4845 new | WCru |
| | ***konjac*** | CDTJ CDes CExc CGHE CHEx CKob EBee EUJe LEdu SHaC SKHP WCot WPGP WPat |
| | ***nepalensis*** | CDTJ CKob EBee EBrs EUJe |
| | ***paeoniifolius*** | MJnS SBig |
| | ***rivieri*** | EBee EBrs GCal |

| | |
|---|---|
| ***stipitatus*** | CAby WCot |
| ***titanum*** | WVal |
| ***tonkinensis*** | CKob |
| ***yunnanensis*** | EBee |

## *Ampelocalamus* (*Poaceae*)

| | |
|---|---|
| ***scandens*** | CGHE EPla WPGP |

## *Ampelocissus* (*Vitaceae*)

| | |
|---|---|
| ***sikkimensis*** HWJK 2066 | WCru |

## *Ampelodesmos* (*Poaceae*)

| | |
|---|---|
| ***mauritanica*** | CHar CHrt CKno COIW CSam EBee ECha EHoe EPPr EShb EWes GFor NLar SEND SMHy SMad SPlb WCot |

## *Ampelopsis* (*Vitaceae*)

| | |
|---|---|
| ***aconitifolia*** | EBee ELon MGos NLar |
| - 'Chinese Lace' | EBee LRHS NLar WPGP |
| § ***brevipedunculata*** | CRHN ELan LHop SCoo SGar SLim SPer WDin WFar |
| - 'Citrulloides' | WCru |
| § - var. ***maximowiczii*** 'Elegans' (v) | CBcs CHEx CMac CWib EBee ELan EPfP EShb LAst LHop LRHS MBar MGos MRav MSwo NBro NPri SAga SHBN SPer SPla SPoG STes SWvt WCot WDin WPat WSHC |
| ***delavayana*** | EBee |
| ***glandulosa*** var. ***brevipedunculata*** | see *A. brevipedunculata* |
| - - 'Tricolor' | see *A. brevipedunculata* var. *maximowiczii* 'Elegans' |
| - var. ***hancei*** B&SWJ 3855 | WCru |
| ***henryana*** | see *Parthenocissus henryana* |
| ***megalophylla*** | CHEx EBee ELan EPfP EShb GCal IDee MBlu MBri NCGa NLar SPer WBVN WCru WFar WOVN |
| ***sempervirens*** | see *Cissus striata* |
| ***tricuspidata*** 'Veitchii' | see *Parthenocissus tricuspidata* 'Veitchii' |

## *Amphicome* see *Incarvillea*

## *Amsonia* (*Apocynaceae*)

| | |
|---|---|
| ***ciliata*** | CFir EBee ELan WFar WPer |
| ***elliptica*** new | EBee |
| ***hubrichtii*** | CAby CEnt CMdw CPom EBee EBrs ECha EGle EPPr GBuc GMac LBMP LHop MSte NDov SMad SMrm SPhx WCot WHoo WPer WPnP |
| - from Hans Kramer new | SMHy |
| ***illustris*** | CAbP CEnt CPom EBee EBrs EHig GKir GMac LRHS MSte NDov SHar WHoo WHrl WPer WTin |
| § ***orientalis*** | Widely available |
| ***tabernaemontana*** | Widely available |
| - var. ***salicifolia*** | CEnt EGle GKir LRHS MSte NBPC NDov WAbb WCAu WRos WTin |

## *Amygdalus* see *Prunus*

## *Anacamptis* (*Orchidaceae*)

| | |
|---|---|
| x ***callithea*** new | NLAp |
| ***champagneuxii*** new | NLAp |
| § ***laxiflora*** | NLAp SHdy |
| ***longicornu*** x ***morio*** new | NLAp |
| § ***morio*** | EBee GAuc NLAp SHdy |
| - ***alba*** x ***sancta*** new | NLAp |
| ***morio*** x ***papilionacea*** new | NLAp |
| ***palustris*** new | NLAp |
| ***pyramidalis*** | EFEx NLAp SHdy WHer |
| ***sancta*** new | NLAp |

## *Anacyclus* (*Asteraceae*)

| | |
|---|---|
| ***pyrethrum*** | GPoy |
| - var. ***depressus*** | CTri EBee ECho ELan EPfP GKir GMaP LRHS NTHB NVic NWCA SIng SPlb WCFE WFar WHoo WPer |
| - - 'Garden Gnome' | CTri ECho MSCN NTHB SRms WFar |
| - - 'Silberkissen' | EDAr |

## *Anagallis* (*Primulaceae*)

| | |
|---|---|
| ***arvensis*** | MHer MSal |
| ***monellii*** Blue Compact = 'Wesanacomp' | LSou SVil |
| - subsp. ***linifolia*** 'Blue Light' | CSpe |
| - 'Skylover' | CCCN LAst NPri |
| - 'Sunrise' | LAst SUsu |
| ***tenella*** 'Studland' | CEnt EPot GAbr NWCA SIng WAbe |

## *Anagyris* (*Papilionaceae*)

| | |
|---|---|
| ***foetida*** | WCot |

## *Ananas* (*Bromeliaceae*)

| | |
|---|---|
| ***comosus*** (F) | CCCN LRHS |
| - var. ***variegatus*** (v) | LRHS MBri |
| 'Elyne' new | LRHS |

## *Anaphalioides* (*Asteraceae*)

| | |
|---|---|
| § ***bellidioides*** | CTri ECha ECou GAbr GGar |

## *Anaphalis* (*Asteraceae*)

| | |
|---|---|
| sp. | EDAr |
| ***alpicola*** | NMen |
| ***margaritacea*** | CBcs CSBt EBee ECha ECrN ECtt EWTr GMaP LRHS MLLN MMuc NBid SRms WFar WMoo WPtf |
| § - 'Neuschnee' | CTri CWan EBee GJos NBPC NBre NGdn NMir NPri SPla WFar WPer |
| - New Snow | see *A. margaritacea* 'Neuschnee' |
| - var. ***yedoensis*** ♀H4 | CTri EBee ECot MCot MLHP NBre SDix SGar SPer WBrE WCAu WTin |
| § ***nepalensis*** var. ***monocephala*** | ELan EMon MCot NBre NSti WCAu |
| ***nubigena*** | see *A. nepalensis* var. *monocephala* |
| ***sinica*** 'Moon's Silver' | EBee |
| ***transnokoensis*** | EBee EWes |
| § ***trinervis*** | CPLG |
| ***triplinervis*** ♀H4 | Widely available |
| - 'Silberregen' | EBee |
| § - 'Sommerschnee' ♀H4 | EBee ECha ECot ECtt EGle EPfP GKir LBMP LRHS MBri MCot MNFA MRav NDov SPer WMnd WPer |
| - Summer Snow | see *A. triplinervis* 'Sommerschnee' |

## *Anchusa* (*Boraginaceae*)

| | |
|---|---|
| ***angustissima*** | see *A. leptophylla* subsp. *incana* |
| § ***azurea*** | CTca EBee EWTr WPer |
| - 'Dropmore' | CTri EBee ELan EPfP LAst LRHS MAvo MLHP MNHC NBPC NOrc SMrm SPad SPav SRms SSth WPer |
| - 'Feltham Pride' | CSBt EBee GKir GMaP LRHS MBri MSte SPav SRms SWvt WFar WHil WHoo WPGP WPer |
| - 'Little John' | EBee ECot ELon SRms |
| - 'Loddon Royalist' ♀H4 | Widely available |
| - 'Opal' | EAEE EBee ECot ECtt EPfP ETod GCal LRHS MMHG MWat NBsh SPla WCAu |
| - 'Royal Blue' | CElw GKir |
| ***capensis*** | CSec SGar |
| - 'Blue Angel' | CSec MNHC SWvt WFar |

| | |
|---|---|
| ***cespitosa*** misapplied | see *A. leptophylla* subsp. *incana* |
| ***cespitosa*** Lam. | ECho ELan EWes LLHF SIng WAbe |
| ***italica*** | see *A. azurea* |
| ***laxiflora*** | see *Borago pygmaea* |
| § ***leptophylla*** subsp. ***incana*** | SBch |
| - - F&W 9550 | MDKP |
| - 'Sapphire Blue' | NBHF |
| ***myosotidiflora*** | see *Brunnera macrophylla* |
| ***officinalis*** | CArn MSal SPav |
| ***sempervirens*** | see *Pentaglottis sempervirens* |

## *Ancylostemon* (*Gesneriaceae*)

| | |
|---|---|
| ***convexus*** B&SWJ 6624 | WCru |

## *Andrachne* (*Euphorbiaceae*)

| | |
|---|---|
| ***colchica*** | EBee WCot |

## *Androcymbium* (*Colchicaceae*)

| | |
|---|---|
| ***gramineum*** | ECho |

## *Andrographis* (*Acanthaceae*)

| | |
|---|---|
| ***paniculata*** | CArn |

## *Andromeda* (*Ericaceae*)

| | |
|---|---|
| ***glaucophylla*** | MBar |
| ***polifolia*** | CMHG ECho GKev NWCA WDin WFar |
| - 'Alba' | ECho GBin LRHS MAsh MBar NBlu NLAp NRya SPer SPlb SPoG SWvt WFar |
| - 'Blue Ice' | CWib ELan EPfP GKir LRHS MAsh MBri MNHC NHar NLAp NLar NMen SPer SPoG SSpi WAbe WFar WPat |
| - 'Compacta' $\Upsilon^{H4}$ | CDoC CWib EBee ECho EPfP GEdr GKir LRHS LSRN MBar MBri MMuc NHol NMen SPer SPoG SRms SWvt WGwG WSHC |
| - 'Compacta Alba' $\Upsilon^{H4}$ | ECho |
| - 'Grandiflora' | ECho GBin GEdr GGar GKev LRHS |
| - 'Kirigamine' | GKir LRHS MAsh NHol |
| - 'Macrophylla' $\Upsilon^{H4}$ | ECho GBin GEdr NHar WAbe WPat |
| - 'Nana' | CSBt ELan EPfP GKev LRHS MAsh NMen |
| - 'Nikko' | CWib NHol |
| - 'Shibutsu' | NMen |

## *Andropogon* (*Poaceae*)

| | |
|---|---|
| ***gerardii*** | CKno CRWN EHoe EHul EPPr EPla EWsh GFor LEdu MWhi SApp WDyG |
| ***ischaemum*** | see *Bothriochloa ischaemum* |
| ***saccharoides*** | EBee |
| ***scoparius*** | see *Schizachyrium scoparium* |

## *Androsace* (*Primulaceae*)

| | |
|---|---|
| CD&R 2477 from China | WCru |
| ***albana*** | GKev NLAp |
| ***alpina*** | CGra WAbe |
| ***armeniaca*** var. ***macrantha*** | CSec |
| ***barbulata*** | WAbe |
| ***bisulca*** var. ***aurata*** | GKev |
| ***bulleyana*** | GKev WAbe |
| ***caduca*** | WAbe |
| ***cantabrica*** | EDAr |
| ***carnea*** | CPBP ECho EDAr GKev |
| - ***alba*** | NWCA |
| - subsp. ***brigantiaca*** | CSec EDAr GKev ITim NLAp NSla WAbe WHoo |
| - subsp. ***laggeri*** $\Upsilon^{H4}$ | ECho EPot GKev LLHF NLAp NSla WAbe WFar |
| ***carnea*** x ***pyrenaica*** | ECho EPot NMen SIng |
| ***chamaejasme*** | ECho |
| ***ciliata*** | WAbe |
| ***cylindrica*** | CGra ITim LRHS NLAp NMen WAbe WFar |
| ***cylindrica*** x ***hirtella*** | ECho ITim LRHS WAbe |
| ***delavayi*** | GKev NLAp WAbe |
| ***fedtschenkoi*** new | CSec |
| ***geraniifolia*** | EBee ECha GKev SRms WCru |
| ***globifera*** | EPot WAbe |
| ***gracilis*** PB 99/20 | EPot |
| ***hedraeantha*** | CLyd ITim NRya NSla WAbe |
| ***himalaica*** | CPBP EPot GEdr NMen WAbe |
| ***hirtella*** | CGra ITim NMen WAbe |
| ***idahoensis*** | WAbe |
| ***incana*** | WAbe |
| ***jacquemontii*** | see *A. villosa* var. *jacquemontii* |
| ***kosopoljanskii*** | WAbe |
| ***lactea*** | WAbe |
| ***laevigata*** | NMen WAbe |
| - from Columbia River Gorge, USA | WAbe |
| - var. ***ciliolata*** | NWCA |
| - - NNS 03-242 new | GKev |
| - 'Gothenburg' | GKev WAbe |
| - 'Saddle Mount' | WAbe |
| ***lanuginosa*** $\Upsilon^{H4}$ | CLyd CMea ECho EDAr EPot NMen NPri NWCA SMrm SRms SRot WAbe WFar |
| - 'Leichtlinii' | GKev |
| ***lehmannii*** | GKev |
| ***limprichtii*** | see *A. sarmentosa* var. *watkinsii* |
| ***mariae*** SDR 4768 new | GKev |
| - SDR 5169 new | GKev |
| x ***marpensis*** | EPot WAbe |
| ***mathildae*** | ITim |
| ***microphylla*** | see *A. mucronifolia* G.Watt |
| 'Millstream' | CPBP |
| § ***mollis*** | CPBP |
| ***montana*** | WAbe |
| ***mucronifolia*** misapplied | see *A. sempervivoides* |
| § ***mucronifolia*** G.Watt | EPot WAbe |
| ***mucronifolia*** x ***sempervivoides*** | EPot |
| ***muscoidea*** | GKev WAbe |
| - 'Breviscapa' | EPot |
| - Schacht's form | WAbe |
| ***nivalis*** 'Chumstick Form' | CGra |
| - var. ***nivalis*** | CGra |
| - - NNS 00-268 | NWCA |
| ***ochotensis*** | WAbe |
| ***primuloides*** | see *A. studiosorum* |
| ***pubescens*** | CGra ITim LLHF LRHS NMen |
| ***pyrenaica*** | CGra ECho ITim LRHS NLAp NMen SIng WAbe |
| ***rigida*** | WAbe |
| - KGB 168 | EPot |
| ***robusta*** subsp. ***purpurea*** | WAbe |
| ***rotundifolia*** | EWld GEdr GKev WCru |
| ***sarmentosa*** misapplied | see *A. studiosorum* |
| ***sarmentosa*** ambig. | EAlp GJos |
| ***sarmentosa*** Wall. | GKev SRms WHoo |
| - from Namche, Nepal | EPot WAbe |
| - Galmont's form | see *A. studiosorum* 'Salmon's Variety' |
| - 'Sherriffii' | EPot GEdr SRms WHoo |
| § - var. ***watkinsii*** | EPot NMen |
| - var. ***yunnanensis*** Knuth | see *A. mollis* |
| - var. ***yunnanensis*** misapplied | see *A. studiosorum* |
| ***selago*** | WAbe |
| § ***sempervivoides*** $\Upsilon^{H4}$ | CLyd ECho EDAr EPot GJos GKev GMaP LHop LRHS NDlv NHol NLAp NMen NWCA SPlb SRms WPat |

| | |
|---|---|
| - CC 4622 | GKev |
| - CC 4631 new | GKev |
| - 'Greystone' | EPot NMen |
| - 'Susan Joan' (v) | CPBP EPot GEdr GKev WAbe |
| ***septentrionalis*** 'Stardust' | ECho |
| ***sericea*** | WAbe |
| ***strigillosa*** | WAbe |
| § ***studiosorum*** 🏆H4 | ECho EDAr GEdr GKev |
| - 'Chumbyi' | GEdr LLHF NHol NLAp NWCA SRms WPat |
| - 'Doksa' | CPBP EPot GKev NLAp WAbe WPat |
| § - 'Salmon's Variety' | CMea CTri ECho WAbe |
| ***tapete*** | WAbe |
| - ACE 1725 | EPot |
| ***vandellii*** | ITim WAbe |
| ***villosa*** | EDAr |
| § - var. ***jacquemontii*** | CPBP EDAr NHar NWCA |
| - - lilac-flowered | EPot |
| - - pink-flowered | EPot GKev NLAp WAbe |
| ***vitaliana*** | see *Vitaliana primuliflora* |
| ***watkinsii*** | see *A. sarmentosa* var. *watkinsii* |
| ***yargongensis*** | WAbe |
| ***zambalensis*** | GKev NLAp WAbe |

## *Andryala* (*Asteraceae*)

| | |
|---|---|
| ***agardhii*** | WPat |
| ***lanata*** | see *Hieracium lanatum* |

## *Anemanthele* (*Poaceae*)

| | |
|---|---|
| § ***lessoniana*** 🏆H4 | Widely available |
| - 'Gold Hue' | EAlp EBee |

## *Anemarrhena* (*Anthericaceae*)

| | |
|---|---|
| ***asphodeloides*** | CArn MSal WCot |

## *Anemone* ✿ (*Ranunculaceae*)

| | |
|---|---|
| Chen Yi T49 new | WCot |
| SDR 4623 new | GKev |
| ***aconitifolia*** Michx. | see *A. narcissiflora* |
| ***altaica*** | GAbr MSal NLar NSum SRms WBVN |
| ***amurensis*** | EBla |
| ***apennina*** 🏆H4 | CAvo CLAP GEdr IBlr WShi WTin |
| - var. ***albiflora*** | CDes CFwr CLAP EBee EBrs EPot ERCP ERos GEdr IBlr LRHS MAvo MSte NDov SMeo WCot WPnP |
| - 'Ballyrogan Park' | IBlr |
| - double-flowered (d) | EBla IBlr NDov SMHy WCru |
| - 'Petrovac' | CLAP EBee EBrs EPot IBlr LLHF WCot |
| ***baicalensis*** | EWll |
| ***baldensis*** | CSec EBee ECho EDAr GKev ITim LRHS NBre NBur SRms |
| ***barbulata*** | EWes GAuc GBuc GEdr NLar SHar WBVN WSHC |
| ***blanda*** 🏆H4 | EBrs GKir IHer LAma LBMP LHop LRHS MBri MLHP MNHC NBlu NChi SEND SWal WBor WFar WShi |
| - blue shades | CHFP CSam CTca EBrs ECGP ECho ELon EPfP ERCP GKev GMaP IGor LRHS SMeo SPer SPhx WRHF |
| - 'Blue Star' | ECho |
| - blue-flowered | CAvo CBro CFFs CMea CTri ELan EPot GAbr LAma LBMP LRHS MBri MNFA SMrm SPoG SRms WFar |
| - 'Charmer' | CMea EBrs ECho EPot LHop NMen SMeo WHil |
| - 'Ingramii' | MCot WCot |
| - 'Pink Charmer' | ECho |
| - 'Pink Star' | CBro EBrs ECho ERCP LAma LRHS MCot NBir WBor |
| - 'Radar' 🏆H4 | CAvo CFFs EBrs ECho EPot ERCP LAma MNrw NBir WAbe |
| - var. ***rosea*** 🏆H4 | EBrs ECho ELan EPfP LAma MLLN SMrm SPer SPoG WFar |
| - 'Violet Star' | CMdw EBrs ECho EPot ERCP LRHS SMeo |
| - 'White Charmer' new | WHil |
| - 'White Splendour' 🏆H4 | Widely available |
| blue-flowered from China | CDes |
| ***canadensis*** | CHar CLAP CMea CSec EBee ELon EPPr GAbr GBuc ITim MNrw MSte NBur NSum WBVN WCot |
| ***caroliniana*** | EBee ECho GBuc GKev GKir LRHS |
| ***chapaensis*** HWJ 631 | WCru |
| ***coronaria*** 'Bicolor' | EBrs NBur |
| - De Caen Group | EBrs EPfP LAma LHop LRHS SPoG SWal WFar |
| § - - 'Die Braut' | CMea EBrs LBMP LRHS NBir NBur WFar |
| - - 'His Excellency' | see *A. coronaria* (De Caen Group) 'Hollandia' |
| § - - 'Hollandia' | CMea EBrs LBMP LRHS SPer |
| - - 'Mister Fokker' | CTca EBrs ERCP LAma LBMP WFar |
| - - The Bride | see *A. coronaria* (De Caen Group) 'Die Braut' |
| - - 'The Governor' | CTca EBrs LRHS NBur WFar WRHF |
| - Jerusalem hybrids | WFar |
| - Saint Bridgid Group (d) | EBrs EPfP LAma LRHS SPet WFar |
| - - 'Lord Lieutenant' (d) | CMea EBrs ERCP LRHS NBir NBur WFar WRHF |
| - - 'Mount Everest' (d) | EBrs ERCP LRHS NBir NBur |
| - - 'Saint Bridgid' (d) | EBrs |
| - - 'The Admiral' (d) | EBrs LRHS NBir NBur SWal WFar |
| - 'Sylphide' (Mona Lisa Series) | EBrs ERCP LBMP LRHS NBir SPer WFar |
| ***crinita*** | GBuc WBVN |
| ***cylindrica*** | CMHG CSam CSec MDKP MNrw NBre NLar |
| ***decapetala*** | NChi |
| ***deltoidea*** NNS 04-38 new | EBee |
| ***demissa*** | GBuc GKev NBid WCot |
| - SDR 3307 | EBee GKev |
| - SDR 4769 new | GKev |
| ***dichotoma*** | SSvw |
| ***drummondii*** | CSec GKev NBur NChi WBVN |
| ***elongata*** B&SWJ 2975 | WCru |
| ***eranthoides*** | EBee EBrs ECho WHil |
| ***fanninii*** new | GCal |
| ***fasciculata*** | see *A. narcissiflora* |
| ***flaccida*** | CBro CDes CLAP EBee EHrv EPPr GBuc GEdr GMac LRHS MSte SPhx WCot WCru WFar WHal WSHC |
| x ***fulgens*** | ECha |
| - 'Annulata Grandiflora' | ECGP |
| - 'Multipetala' | CMil CSpe EBrs WCot |
| - Saint Bavo Group | SMHy |
| ***globosa*** | see *A. multifida* Poir. |
| 'Green Apples' | WMoo |
| 'Guernica' | CSec EBee ECho EWes WBVN |
| 'Hatakeyama Double' (d) | CMdw GCal LPla |
| 'Hatakeyama Single' | CDes CMdw LPla |
| ***hepatica*** | see *Hepatica nobilis* |
| § ***hortensis*** | NBre SPhx |
| - ***alba*** | CLAP |
| - subsp. ***heldreichii*** | CDes |
| § ***hupehensis*** | CPLG EBee GBBs GMaP IGor NOrc WBod WFar WPer |
| - BWJ 8190 | WCru |
| - f. ***alba*** | CDes CLAP CMil CSpe EBla WCot WPGP |
| § - 'Bowles' Pink' 🏆H4 | CElw CPLG EBee EPPr IGor MAvo MWat SPet WBrk WCru WPGP WTin |
| - 'Crispa' | see *A.* x *hybrida* 'Lady Gilmour' Wolley-Dod |
| - 'Eugenie' | EBee GBuc MBNS NBir NHol |

| | | |
|---|---|---|
| | - 'Hadspen Abundance' 🏆$^{H4}$ | Widely available |
| | - 'Hadspen Red' | WFar |
| | - var. ***japonica*** | CPou EWTr NCob |
| | - - B&SWJ 4886 | WCru |
| | - - 'Bodnant Burgundy' | CDes CPrp EBee ECtt EGle WBod WCAu WPGP |
| § | - - 'Bressingham Glow' | CMHG CPLG EAEE EBee ECtt EGle ELan EPfP EPot LHop LRHS MBri MNrw MRav NBir NHol NOrc NVic SHBN SPer SPet WAbb WBrk WCAu WFar |
| § | - - 'Pamina' 🏆$^{H4}$ | Widely available |
| | - - Prince Henry | see *A. hupehensis* var. *japonica* 'Prinz Heinrich' |
| § | - - 'Prinz Heinrich' 🏆$^{H4}$ | Widely available |
| § | - - 'Rotkäppchen' | EBee EBla EBrs ECtt EGle GAbr GBin LBMP LRHS LSou MAvo MRav NBur NGby NGdn NHol SMrm WCot |
| | - - 'Splendens' | CMHG COIW EBee EBrs ELon GBBs GBuc LAst LCro LHop MCot MRav NCGa SPoG SPur SWal SWvt WAbb WFar WHal |
| | - 'Ouvertüre' | CDes EBee MAvo WPGP |
| | - 'Praecox' | CMea EAEE EBee EBla EHrv EPfP GBBs GBri GBuc LRHS MAvo MBNS NBPC NBir NGdn NHol NPri NSti SPoG SWvt WAbb WFar WHal WHil WMnd |
| | - 'September Charm' | see *A.* x *hybrida* 'September Charm' |
| | - 'Superba' | WKif |
| § | x ***hybrida*** | MWat NChi NCob SGar WFar WMoo |
| | - 'Alba Dura' | see *A. tomentosa* 'Albadura' |
| | - 'Alba' misapplied (UK) | see *A.* x *hybrida* 'Honorine Jobert' |
| | - 'Albert Schweitzer' | see *A.* x *hybrida* 'Elegans' |
| | - 'Andrea Atkinson' | Widely available |
| | - 'Bowles' Pink' | see *A. hupehensis* 'Bowles' Pink' |
| | - 'Bressingham Glow' | see *A. hupehensis* var. *japonica* 'Bressingham Glow' |
| | - 'Coupe d'Argent' | EBee NBre |
| § | - 'Elegans' 🏆$^{H4}$ | CSam CWCL EBee ECtt GMaP MRav NBir NCGa SWat SWvt WCru WFar WHil |
| § | - 'Géante des Blanches' | CHar IGor LPla LRHS WFar WHoo |
| § | - 'Honorine Jobert' 🏆$^{H4}$ | Widely available |
| § | - 'Königin Charlotte' 🏆$^{H4}$ | Widely available |
| | - 'Kriemhilde' | EBee GBin |
| § | - 'Lady Gilmour' Wolley-Dod | CBgR CSam CSpe EBee ECtt EGle EHrv EMil EPfP GCra GKir GMac LEdu LRHS MAvo MBri MCot MRav NBPC NBir NCGa NChi NGdn SAga SHBN SPoG SRGP WCot WCru WFar |
| | - 'Lady Gilmour' misapplied | see *A.* x *hybrida* 'Montrose' |
| | - 'Loreley' | CMea CPrp EBee GBuc MSte MWat |
| | - 'Luise Uhink' | CPou IGor NBir |
| | - 'Margarete' Kayser & Seibert | CPLG CPar EBee EBrs ELan EPPr IBlr LAst MBri MWat SMrm WCot WCru WFar |
| | - 'Max Vogel' | see *A.* x *hybrida* 'Elegans' |
| | - 'Monterosa' | see *A.* x *hybrida* 'Montrose' |
| § | - 'Montrose' | CPou CSpe EBee EHrv EWes GAbr GCal GKir GMaP LSou NBir SRms SWat WFar |
| | - 'Pamina' | see *A. hupehensis* var. *japonica* 'Pamina' |
| | - 'Prinz Heinrich' | see *A. hupehensis* var. *japonica* 'Prinz Heinrich' |
| | - 'Profusion' | CTri LBuc SHBN WHal |
| | - Queen Charlotte | see *A.* x *hybrida* 'Königin Charlotte' |
| | - 'Richard Ahrens' | EBee ECtt EGle GBuc GCal GKir GMaP IBlr LHop LRHS MLHP NHol NOrc SAga SMeo SPla SWat WCAu WCru WFar WMnd |

| | | |
|---|---|---|
| § | - 'Robustissima' | Widely available |
| | - 'Rosenschale' | EBee EGle LRHS WCru WFar |
| | - 'Rotkäppchen' | see *A. hupehensis* var. *japonica* 'Rotkäppchen' |
| § | - 'September Charm' 🏆$^{H4}$ | Widely available |
| | - 'Serenade' | CChe CMHG CPar CSam EBee ECtt EPfP MLLN MRav NBir NCGa SHBN SMrm SPad SPoG SRkn SSvw WCAu WFar WHil WHoo WMoo |
| | - Tourbillon | see *A.* x *hybrida* 'Whirlwind' |
| § | - 'Whirlwind' | Widely available |
| | - 'White Queen' | see *A.* x *hybrida* 'Géante des Blanches' |
| | - Wirbelwind | see *A.* x *hybrida* 'Whirlwind' |
| | ***japonica*** | see *A.* x *hybrida*, *A. hupehensis* |
| | ***keiskeana*** | GEdr WCru |
| § | x ***lesseri*** | CBro CFir CSpe EBee ECha ECho ECtt EDAr EHrv ELan GKev MHer SPhx SRms WFar WHoo |
| | ***leveillei*** | Widely available |
| | - BWJ 7919 | WCru |
| § | x ***lipsiensis*** | Widely available |
| | - 'Pallida' 🏆$^{H4}$ | CPMA CWsd EBee EBla ECho ERos GBuc GEdr GKev IGor LLWP MAvo MNFA WAbe WCot |
| | ***lyallii*** | EBee GBuc WBrE |
| N | ***magellanica*** hort. ex Wehrh. | see *A. multifida* Poir. |
| | ***matsudae*** B&SWJ 1452 | WCru |
| | - 'Taiwan's Tiny Treasure' | WCru |
| | ***mexicana*** B&SWJ 8414 | WCru |
| | ***multifida*** misapplied, red-flowered | see *A.* x *lesseri* |
| § | ***multifida*** Poir. | Widely available |
| | - RCB/Arg RA-F-5 | WCot |
| | - 'Major' | CFir CHar CMea CSpe CWsd EPfP MCot NCob NPro NWCA SMrm SPhx WBVN WFar |
| | - pink-flowered | GBuc LBMP |
| * | - 'Rubra' | CBgR CPrp CSec EAEE EBee EDAr EHrv EPfP EWll GAbr GBuc LBMP LRHS MAvo MBNS MNrw NBPC NBir NDlv NWCA SPet SPoG |
| | - yellow-flowered | GBBs NSum |
| § | ***narcissiflora*** | EHrv GBuc IGor NBir NBre NChi WFar WSHC |
| | - var. ***citrina*** | CWsd |
| | ***nemorosa*** 🏆$^{H4}$ | Widely available |
| N | - 'Alba Plena' (d) | CBro CSWP CSam CStu EBee EBla EBrs ECha ECho EPPr ERos GBuc GEdr GGar GMac LRHS MTho NMen SIng WAbb WCru WEas WFar WPnP WSHC |
| | - 'Allenii' 🏆$^{H4}$ | CBro CHFP EBee EBrs ECha ECho ELon ERos GBuc GEdr GMaP ITim MAvo MNFA MRav NMen NRya SIng WAbe WCot WCru WPGP WPnP WShi |
| | - 'Amy Doncaster' | CLAP |
| | - 'Atrocaerulea' | CLAP GBuc IBlr NLar WCru WFar |
| | - 'Atrorosea' | EBee |
| | - 'Bill Baker's Pink' | CDes CLAP MAvo |
| | - 'Blue Beauty' | CLAP CPMA CWsd EBee ELon ERos GBuc GMaP IBlr MAvo NMen SBch WAbe WCru |
| | - 'Blue Bonnet' | CElw ECho GBuc IGor ITim MAvo MNrw |
| | - 'Blue Eyes' (d) | CAby CDes CElw CLAP CStu EBee EBla EGle GBuc GEdr GMaP IBlr IGor ITim MAvo MSte NBir NDov |

| | |
|---|---|
| | NMen NSla WAbe WCot WCru WPGP |
| - 'Blue Queen' | EBee GAbr GBuc |
| - 'Bowles' Purple' | Widely available |
| - 'Bracteata' | ECho EHrv ERos GEdr NDov NMen |
| - 'Bracteata Pleniflora' (d) | CBow CLAP CStu EBee EBla EBrs ECho EGle GBuc GMaP IBlr IGor LHop MAvo MNFA MNrw NBir NMen WAbe WCot WCru WFar WHal |
| - 'Buckland' | CDes CFwr CLAP CWsd EBee EHrv EPfP EPot IBlr MAvo SKHP WCru WFar |
| - 'Cedric's Pink' | CLAP CPMA EBee EPPr ERos IBlr IGor LLHF MNrw WCru WFar |
| - 'Celestial' | EBee EBla ECho EPPr GBuc |
| - 'Dee Day' | CLAP CWsd EBee EHrv GBuc MAvo MNrw NDov SCnR WAbe WCru WFar |
| - 'Evelyn Meadows' ♀H4 | CLAP |
| - 'Flore Pleno' (d) | CAby CDes EBee EBla ECho GAbr GKir NBir NDov NMen WPGP |
| - 'Frühlingsfee' | NLar |
| - 'Gerda Ramusen' | CLAP ECho LLHF |
| - 'Glenroy Blush' | WAbe |
| - 'Green Dream' **new** | SKHP |
| - 'Green Fingers' | CLAP EBla ECho EHrv EPPr GBuc GEdr GMaP IGor ITim MAvo MNrw NDov NGby SCnR WAbe WCot WCru WIvy |
| - 'Hannah Gubbay' | CLAP GBuc IBlr IGor MAvo MNrw MSte WAbe |
| - 'Hilda' | EBee EBrs ECho EGle EPot ERos GBuc GEdr IPot MAvo MNrw NDlv NDov NLAp NMen NRya NSla WAbe |
| - 'Ice and Fire' | MAvo |
| - 'Jack Brownless' | CLAP ITim WCot |
| - 'Kentish Pink' | GBBs GBuc GMaP |
| - 'Knightshayes Vestal' (d) | CLAP EBee MRav NHol WCot WIvy |
| - 'Lady Doneraile' | CDes CLAP CWsd EPot GBuc NBir NLar SSvw WCru WFar |
| - 'Latvian Pink' **new** | EPot |
| - 'Leeds' Variety' | CLAP CWsd EGle GMaP GMac IGor ITim MAvo MNrw MTho NDov NMen NSla |
| - 'Lismore Blue' | EBee EPPr EPot |
| - 'Lismore Pink' | EHrv GBuc GEdr |
| - 'Lucia' **new** | EPot |
| - 'Lychette' | CAvo CHid CMea EBee ECho EGle EHrv EPot GAbr GBuc IBlr ITim LPio MAvo NDov NSla NWCA SHar WAbe WCot WCru WFar |
| - 'Martin' | CStu |
| - 'Mart's Blue' | GBuc |
| - 'Miss Eunice' **new** | CLAP CWsd |
| - 'Monstrosa' | EBee EBrs ECho EPot GBuc MAvo WCot |
| - 'New Pink' | CLAP CPom CWsd EBee IBlr |
| - 'Parlez Vous' | CWsd EBee EHrv EPPr GEdr LPio MAvo MNrw NDov NMen SCnR SKHP SSvw WCru WFar |
| - 'Pat's Pink' **new** | WShi |
| - 'Pentre Pink' | IBlr MAvo MNrw MSSP MTho WBVN WCru WFar WIvy |
| - 'Picos Pink' | EHrv GBuc SCnR |
| - 'Pink Carpet' | GBuc GEdr |
| - pink-flowered | CLAP WCru |
| - 'Polar Star' **new** | CLAP CWsd |
| - 'Robinsoniana' ♀H4 | Widely available |
| - 'Rosea' | CLAP EBrs ECho GEdr GMac MNFA MSte WAbe WCru |
| - 'Royal Blue' | Widely available |
| - 'Rubra' **new** | EPot |

| | |
|---|---|
| - 'Salt and Pepper' **new** | MAvo |
| - 'Slack Top Pink' **new** | NSla |
| - 'Super Allenii' | EBee |
| - 'Tinney's Blush' | CLAP |
| - 'Tomas' | CLAP EBee GBin GEdr MAvo NHar NWCA SPoG SUsu |
| - 'Vestal' (d) ♀H4 | Widely available |
| - 'Virescens' ♀H4 | Widely available |
| - 'Viridiflora' | CFwr CLAP ECho EGle EPfP GAbr GBuc LHop MNrw MRav MTho NBir NSti SSvw WCot WCru WFar WSHC |
| - 'Westwell Pink' | CDes CLAP CSpe EBee LLHF MAvo MSSP MSte WCot WPGP |
| - 'Wilks' Giant' | CLAP ITim MAvo WCru WFar |
| - 'Wilks' White' | CLAP EBee EBla EGle ELon EPPr GEdr LBuc NSla WCru WFar |
| - 'Wyatt's Pink' | CLAP CWsd ELon EPot GBuc ITim MAvo NCGa NSla WAbe WCru WFar WPnP WTin |
| - 'Yerda Ramusem' | EBee ECho EPPr MAvo |
| ***nemorosa* x *ranunculoides*** | see *A.* x *lipsiensis* |
| ***obtusiloba*** | CLAP GBuc GKir MTho SRms WAbe |
| - CLD 1549 | GEdr |
| - ***alba*** | GMac WAbe |
| - var. ***polysepala*** | GEdr |
| I - 'Sulphurea' | CDes GEdr NMen |
| - yellow-flowered | GBuc WAbe |
| ***palmata*** | CFwr CHFP CLAP CSec EBee EDAr EWTr GKir LDai MDKP MWea NBre SKHP SMad WCru WFar WRos |
| ***parviflora*** | CSec EBee GBuc GKev |
| ***patens*** | see *Pulsatilla patens* |
| ***pavonina*** | CAby CPMA CSpe EBee ECha ERos LRHS MAsh MAvo MBri MSSP MTho NBir SPoG WCru |
| - 'Grecian Sunset' | MAsh WPGP |
| ***polyanthes*** | EBee WCot |
| - HWJK 2337 | WCru |
| ***prattii*** | CLAP EBee GEdr WHal |
| ***pseudoaltaica*** | EBee GEdr WCot WCru WWst |
| - pale blue-flowered | CLAP |
| - 'Yuki-no-sei' (d) **new** | GEdr |
| ***pulsatilla*** | see *Pulsatilla vulgaris* |
| ***quinquefolia*** | CLAP WAbe WCot |
| ***raddeana*** | EBee EBrs ECho |
| ***ranunculoides*** ♀H4 | Widely available |
| - 'Frank Waley' | WCot |
| * - ***laciniata*** | CLAP GBuc MSte NMen WCot |
| - 'Pleniflora' (d) | CAvo CFwr CLAP EBla EBrs ECha ECho EHrv GBBs GKev GMaP MRav NLar NMen WCot WFar WIvy |
| - subsp. ***ranunculoides*** | CSec EBrs |
| - 'Semi Plena' | EBrs |
| - subsp. ***wockeana*** | CDes EBee ECho |
| ***reflexa*** **new** | EBee GKev |
| ***riparia*** | see *A. virginiana* var. *alba* |
| ***rivularis*** | Widely available |
| - BWJ 7611 | WCru |
| - GWJ 9391 | WCru |
| - SDR 4229 **new** | GKev |
| - 'Glacier' **new** | WPer |
| ***rockii*** | GEdr |
| ***rupicola*** | CSec EBee GMac NBir |
| x ***seemannii*** | see *A.* x *lipsiensis* |
| ***smithiana*** | CExc |
| ***stellata*** | see *A. hortensis* |
| ***stolonifera*** double-flowered (d) | CAby CDes CElw EBee ITim WCot |
| ***sulphurea*** | see *Pulsatilla alpina* subsp. *apiifolia* |

***sylvestris*** Widely available
- 'Elise Fellmann' (d) CHFP CLAP EBee EPfP GBri GBuc IGor MAvo MWea NSti SPoG WCot
- 'Flore Pleno' (d) CDes CLAP EBee WCot
- 'Macrantha' CDes CLAP CPrp EBee EPfP GAbr WBrE WPGP WPrP

***tetrasepala*** CLAP WCot WPGP
§ ***tomentosa*** EBee ECha GGar GKev IGor LBMP LRHS MWhi NBre SDix SPoG SRms SWat WBVN WFar
§ - 'Albadura' EBee NBre
- 'Robustissima' see *A.* x *hybrida* 'Robustissima'
- 'September Glanz' EBee

***trifolia*** CDes CWsd EPPr ERos GBuc NBid NDov SCnR SRms WCot WPGP WPat
- pink-flowered CLAP MSte WFar

***trullifolia*** EBee EPfP GAbr GBin GBuc GCra GEdr GGar GKev GKir GMaP GMac LAst LRHS MMHG MRav NSla
- ***alba*** GMac
- var. ***coelestina*** GBuc NBir
- var. ***linearis*** GMac

***vernalis*** see *Pulsatilla vernalis*
***virginiana*** CSec CSpe EBee EPPr GAbr ILad LDai MDKP MSte NBid NBur WBVN WFar WOut
§ - var. ***alba*** EBee EHig NLar WBVN WPrP
***vitifolia*** misapplied see *A. tomentosa*
***vitifolia*** DC. GKev
- B&SWJ 2320 WCru
- B&SWJ 8202 from Vietnam WCru
- GWJ 9434 WCru
- HWJK 2044 WCru

## *Anemonella* (*Ranunculaceae*)

***thalictroides*** CBct CElw CFir CLAP CTca EBee ECho EFEx EHrv EPot GEdr GGar ITim LAma LPio MAvo NDov NHar NMen NRya NWCA WAbe WCru WFar WPrP
- 'Alba Plena' (d) ECho GBuc
- 'Amelia' CLAP GEdr NHar SCnR WAbe
- 'Babe' **new** WWst
- 'Betty Blake' (d) ECho GEdr NHar
- 'Big' **new** WWst
- 'Cameo' CLAP EBee EFEx GEdr MAvo NHar SCnR WCru WWst
- 'Charlotte' NHar WWst
- 'Double Green' (d) CLAP EBee EFEx GEdr WCot
- 'Full Double White' (d) EFEx GEdr
- 'Green Hurricane' (d) EBee EFEx GEdr ITim
- 'Jade Feather' CElw
- f. ***rosea*** CAby CElw CLAP CPom CWCL EPot GBuc MAvo WAbe WCru
- - 'Oscar Schoaf' (d) CLAP EBee GBuc GEdr ITim WAbe WWst
- - semi-double pink-flowered (d) CElw CLAP EHrv GKir NLar WWst
- semi-double white-flowered (d) CElw CLAP EBee EHrv EPot GBuc NMen WAbe WCot
- 'Tairin' EBee GEdr WWst
- 'White Bells' NHar

## *Anemonopsis* (*Ranunculaceae*)

***macrophylla*** CDes CElw CLAP CMoH CWsd EBee ECha ECho EPot GBuc GCal GEdr GKir GMac IGor MNrw MSte MTho NLar SPhx WAbe WCru WSHC
- 'White Swan' WCru

## *Anemopsis* (*Saururaceae*)

***californica*** CDes EBee IFoB LLWG MSKA NLar WPGP

## *Anethum* (*Apiaceae*)

***graveolens*** CArn GKir GPoy MHer MNHC SECG SIde SPoG SWal
- 'Dukat' CSev ELau NGHP
- 'Vierling' **new** WLHH

## angelica see *Angelica archangelica*

## *Angelica* (*Apiaceae*)

***acutiloba*** CSpe EBee EWll MHer MLLN MMHG NDov NGHP NLar WFar WPrP
- var. ***iwatensis*** B&SWJ 11197 **new** WCru

***anomala*** B&SWJ 10886 **new** WCru
***archangelica*** Widely available
- subsp. ***archangelica*** GAuc
- 'Corinne Tremaine' (v) NGHP NTHB WCHb

***atropurpurea*** CArn CBct EBee ECtt EShb EWll GKev LRHS MHer MNHC MNrw MRav NBur NCGa NChi NDov NGHP NLar SMrm SWat WCAu WCHb WFar WJek WMnd
***dahurica*** EBee MSal
- B&SWJ 8603 WCru

***decursiva*** CArn EBee MSal NDov WCot
- B&SWJ 5746 WCru

'Ebony' MDKP
***edulis*** B&SWJ 10968 **new** WCru
***florentii*** CDes WPGP
***gigas*** Widely available
- B&SWJ 4170 WCru

***hispanica*** see *A. pachycarpa*
***japonica*** B&SWJ 8816a WCru
***montana*** see *A. sylvestris*
***morii*** RWJ 9802 WCru
§ ***pachycarpa*** Widely available
***pubescens*** MSte NDov SPhx
- B&SWJ 5593 WCru
- var. ***matsumurae*** B&SWJ 6387 WCru

***sachalinensis*** EBee
***sinensis*** CHFP GAuc GPoy WCHb
'Summer Delight' see *Ligusticum scoticum*
§ ***sylvestris*** CArn CHrt CRWN EBWF GBar NSco NTHB WCHb
- 'Boraston Pink Lace' **new** WCHb
* - 'Purpurea' CKno CSpe CWsd EWes SDnm WPGP
- 'Vicar's Mead' CHFP CWan EBee IPot LCro LEdu LHop LPla LSRN MDKP MLLN NBPC NBPN NBid NCGa NChi NDov NGHP NLar NSti SPhx SRkn WBrk WCHb WPtf WSHC

***taiwaniana*** CArn CWan EBee ELan LRHS NGHP NLar SGar WOut WPer
***ursina*** MDKP
- B&SWJ 10829 **new** WCru
- RBS 0205 WBVN

## *Angelonia* (*Scrophulariaceae*)

(Angelface Series) Angelface Blue = 'Anzwei'PBR CSpe SVil
- Angelface Blue Bicolour = 'Anstern' LAst NPri

| | |
|---|---|
| ***angustifolia*** (AngelMist Series) Angel Mist Lavender Pink = 'Balanglapi' | LAst |
| - - AngelMist Light Pink = 'Balangpili' new | NPri |

## *Anigozanthos* (*Haemodoraceae*)

| | |
|---|---|
| 'Big Red' | SOWG |
| (Bush Gems Series) 'Bush Eclipse' | SOWG |
| - 'Bush Haze' | SOWG |
| ***flavidus*** | CHEx CSec CTrC ECre EOHP MBri SOWG SPlb |
| - 'Illusion' | CCCN |
| - 'Opal' | CCCN |
| - 'Orange Cross' | SOWG |
| - 'Pearl' | CCCN |
| - 'Splendour' | CCCN |
| - yellow | WBrE |
| 'Galileo' new | LRHS |
| ***humilis*** Lindl. ♀H1 | SOWG |
| ***manglesii*** ♀H1 | CTrC MCot SOWG SPlb |
| - 'Bush Dawn' (Bush Gems Series) | SOWG |
| 'Regal Claw' | SOWG |
| 'Royal Cheer' | SOWG |

## anise see *Pimpinella anisum*

## *Anisodontea* (*Malvaceae*)

| | |
|---|---|
| § ***capensis*** | CCCN EBee ELan EShb GKir LAst MAsh MCot NBir SBod SChF SLim SMrm SOWG SRkn SRms SWvt WDyG |
| - 'Tara's Pink' | CSpe EBee EWes IFoB LRHS MAsh MBNS SAga SMrm SPhx SRGP |
| ***elegans*** | LHop |
| 'Elegant Lady' | GFai |
| ***huegelii*** | see *Alyogyne huegelii* |
| x ***hypomadara*** misapplied | see *A. capensis* |
| § x ***hypomadara*** (Sprague) D.M. Bates | ECtt SRms |
| ***julii*** | SPlb |
| ***scabrosa*** | CChe |

## *Anisodus* (*Solanaceae*)

| | |
|---|---|
| § ***luridus*** | EWld GCal MSal |

## *Anisotome* (*Apiaceae*)

| | |
|---|---|
| ***lyallii*** new | GBin |

## *Annona* (*Annonaceae*)

| | |
|---|---|
| ***cherimola*** (F) | CCCN MREP XBlo |

## *Anoiganthus* see *Cyrtanthus*

## *Anomalesia* see *Gladiolus*

## *Anomatheca* (*Iridaceae*)

| | |
|---|---|
| ***cruenta*** | see *A. laxa* |
| ***grandiflora*** | CHII CPLG ECho ERos |
| § ***laxa*** ♀H2-3 | Widely available |
| - var. ***alba*** ♀H2-3 | CPLG CPom CRHN CSpe CStu EBee ECho EDif EHrv ELan ERos ITim LEdu MCot MTho MWea NMen SBch WAbe WBrk WCFE |
| - blue-flowered | CRHN ECho ERos WAbe |
| - 'Joan Evans' | CPom CRHN CSec CStu EBee ECho ELan ERos EShb LLHF NDlv NMen NWCA SHom SRms WAbe WBrk WHrl |
| - red-spotted | CPLG ECho EDif ITim SGar |
| - ***viridiflora*** | ECho |
| ***viridis*** | CPLG CPou EBee ECho ERos WBrk WPGP |

## *Anopterus* (*Escalloniaceae*)

| | |
|---|---|
| ***glandulosus*** | IBlr WPGP WSHC |

## *Anredera* (*Basellaceae*)

| | |
|---|---|
| § ***cordifolia*** | CRHN EBrs ECho EShb LEdu LRHS |

## *Antennaria* (*Asteraceae*)

| | |
|---|---|
| ***aprica*** | see *A. parvifolia* |
| ***dioica*** | CArn CEnt CTri EDAr GJos GKir GPoy MHer SPlb SRms WFar |
| - 'Alba' | EDAr EHoe WFar |
| - 'Alex Duguid' | GMaP LBee NLAp |
| - 'Aprica' | see *A. parvifolia* |
| - 'Minima' | ECho MWat NBro NMen SIng WAbe |
| - 'Nyewoods Variety' | NLAp |
| - red-flowered | ECho |
| - var. ***rosea*** | see *A. rosea* |
| * - 'Rubra' | CSec CTri ECha ECho EDAr GBin LRHS MHer NMen NWCA WFar WRos |
| 'Joy' | WAbe |
| ***macrophylla*** hort. | see *A. microphylla* |
| § ***microphylla*** | ECho MBar SRms WEas |
| § ***parvifolia*** | CTri ECho MBar NLar NPri SRms WPer |
| - var. ***rosea*** | see *A. microphylla* |
| ***plantaginifolia*** | EBee |
| 'Red Wonder' | CMea NLar |
| § ***rosea*** ♀H4 | ECho GKir LRHS MSCN NHol NLAp NMen NVic SPlb SRms WFar |

## *Antenoron* see *Persicaria*

## *Anthemis* ✿ (*Asteraceae*)

| | |
|---|---|
| from Turkey | ECtt EWes LLWP SUsu |
| § 'Beauty of Grallagh' | EBee ECtt GBuc GCal GMac IGor MDKP SDix SUsu |
| 'Cally Cream' | GCal |
| 'Cally White' | GCal |
| ***carpatica*** | MAvo NBro |
| - 'Karpatenschnee' | EBee LRHS NBre |
| § ***cretica*** subsp. ***cretica*** | NWCA |
| 'Daisy Bee' | EBee LRHS |
| ***frutescens*** hort. & Siebert & Voss. | see *Argyranthemum frutescens* |
| 'Grallagh Gold' misapplied, orange-yellow | see *A.* 'Beauty of Grallagh' |
| 'Grallagh Gold' | CMoH EBee EBla ECha ECtt EMon EWes LDai MRav MWat NPer SPhx WFar |
| § ***marschalliana*** | CPBP EAlp EBee ECha ECho ECtt EDAr EPot LBee LRHS MSte SMrm SPlb |
| ***montana*** | see *A. cretica* subsp. *cretica* |
| ***nobilis*** | see *Chamaemelum nobile* |
| ***punctata*** | WCor |
| - subsp. ***cupaniana*** ♀H3-4 | Widely available |
| - - 'Nana' | EMon MSte NPer SHar |
| ***rudolphiana*** | see *A. marschalliana* |
| ***sancti-johannis*** | CBgR CWib EAEE EAro EBee EBla EHig IGor LDai LRHS MBri MSal NPer SDix SMad SPoG SRms WFar WMoo WPer |
| 'Sauce Béarnaise' | GCra WMnd |
| Susanna Mitchell = 'Blomit' | CHar EBee EBla ECtt ELon EPfP EShb EWll GKir GMaP GMac LRHS LSRN MAvo MLHP |

| | |
|---|---|
| | MNrw NBir NCob NDov SMrm SRGP SUsu WCAu WMnd WSHC WTin |
| 'Tetworth' | EBee EBla ECha ECtt EHrv ELan EMon GBuc LSRN MAvo MBNS MRav MSte NOrc SMad WFar WPer |
| ***tinctoria*** | CArn CHby EAro EBee EMon GPoy MHer NPer SPet SWvt WAbe WJek WSFF |
| - from Judaea | EMon |
| - 'Alba' | EBee GKir NBre NCGa WClo WFar WPer |
| - 'Charme'PBR **new** | EBee SUsu |
| - 'Compacta' | EWes GCal NBre NCob NGdn WOut |
| - dwarf | EBee EBla MAvo MHar SBri WAbe WFar |
| - 'E.C. Buxton' | Widely available |
| - 'Eva' | EBee EMon LRHS NBre NCob NLar WEas |
| I - 'Golden Rays' | MDKP NPro SDix |
| - 'Kelwayi' | CEnt CPrp CSBt CTri EBee EPfP EShb GKir GMaP LRHS NBPC NBro NCob NPer SPer SPla SPoG SRms WFar WMoo |
| - 'Lemon Maid' | CFir GBin NBre NBur NCob NDov SMrm |
| - 'Powis White' **new** | MSCN |
| - 'Pride of Grallagh' | see *A.* 'Beauty of Grallagh' |
| - 'Sauce Hollandaise' | Widely available |
| - subsp. ***tinctoria*** | EMon |
| - 'Wargrave Variety' | Widely available |
| 'Tinpenny Sparkle' | EBee WCot WTin |
| ***triumfettii*** | NPer |
| ***tuberculata*** | NChi SAga |
| 'White Water' | WAbe WFar |

## *Anthericum* (*Anthericaceae*)

| | |
|---|---|
| ***algeriense*** | see *A. liliago* |
| ***baeticum*** | EBee ERos |
| § ***liliago*** | CBro EBee ECho ELan ERas ERos EWTr GCal GKev GMaP GMac IFoB LHop MAvo MCot MLLN MRav MSte NCGa WHrl WPer |
| - 'Major' ♀H4 | CAvo CDes ECha ECho EHrv GBuc IGor MLHP NBre SPhx WPGP |
| ***ramosum*** | CSec CSpe EBee ECha ECho ELan EPot ERos EWes GCal GKev GMac MBrN MLLN NBid NBir NCGa NWCA SPhx WPGP WPer |
| - ***plumosum*** | see *Trichopetalum plumosum* |
| ***saundersiae*** | CPLG CPne SHom |
| ***undulatum*** | ERos |

## *Antholyza* (*Iridaceae*)

| | |
|---|---|
| ***coccinea*** | see *Crocosmia paniculata* |
| x ***crocosmioides*** | see *Crocosmia* x *crocosmioides* |
| ***paniculata*** | see *Crocosmia paniculata* |

## *Anthoxanthum* (*Poaceae*)

| | |
|---|---|
| ***odoratum*** | CArn CRWN EBWF GBar GPoy |

## *Anthriscus* (*Apiaceae*)

| | |
|---|---|
| ***cerefolium*** | CArn CSev EPfP GPoy ILis MDun MHer MNHC SPoG WJek WLHH |
| ***sylvestris*** | CArn EBWF NSco |
| - 'Broadleas Blush' | CNat WAlt |
| - 'Kabir' | CNat |
| - 'Moonlit Night' | EHoe |
| - 'Ravenswing' | Widely available |

## *Anthurium* (*Araceae*)

| | |
|---|---|
| ***amazonicum*** | MBri |
| ***andraeanum*** ♀H1 | MBri MJnS |
| - 'Glowing Pink' | XBlo |
| - 'Red Heart' | XBlo |
| - 'Tivolo' | XBlo |
| 'Aztec' | XBlo |
| Baleno = 'Anthauf4'PBR **new** | LRHS XBlo |
| 'Caribo' | LRHS XBlo |
| 'Charme'PBR **new** | CPrp |
| ***clarinervium*** **new** | LRHS |
| ***crenatum*** | XBlo |
| 'Crimson' | XBlo |
| 'Fantasy Love' **new** | LRHS |
| 'Magenta' | XBlo |
| 'Maxima Elegancia' **new** | LRHS |
| 'Mikra' **new** | XBlo |
| 'Octavia' | XBlo |
| 'Olivia' **new** | LRHS |
| 'Orange Love'PBR **new** | LRHS |
| 'Pico Bello' | XBlo |
| 'Pink Champion' **new** | LRHS XBlo |
| 'Polaris White' **new** | LRHS |
| 'Porcelaine White' | XBlo |
| Red Champion = 'Anthbnena'PBR **new** | LRHS XBlo |
| 'Red Love'PBR **new** | LRHS |
| 'Rima' **new** | LRHS |
| 'Robino Red' **new** | LRHS |
| ***scherzerianum*** ♀H1 | MBri |
| 'Sharada' **new** | LRHS |
| 'Sugar Love'PBR **new** | LRHS |
| 'Sunny Love' **new** | LRHS |
| 'Tender Love'PBR **new** | LRHS |
| 'Texan Rose' **new** | LRHS |
| 'Tricolor' **new** | LRHS |
| 'Vitara' **new** | LRHS XBlo |
| 'Vitara Red' **new** | LRHS |
| 'White Butterfly' **new** | LRHS |
| White Champion = 'Anthefaqyr'PBR **new** | LRHS XBlo |

## *Anthyllis* (*Papilionaceae*)

| | |
|---|---|
| ***barba-jovis*** | CSpe |
| ***hermanniae*** 'Compacta' | see *A. hermanniae* 'Minor' |
| § - 'Minor' | NLar NMen |
| ***montana*** 'Rubra' ♀H4 | ECho EPot EWes LHop LLHF NMen WThu |
| ***vulneraria*** | CFee EBWF ECho NMir NRya NSco SECG WSFF |
| - var. ***coccinea*** | CHar CSec CSpe CSsd EBee GAbr GGar GKev ITim MCCP MLLN MSCN MSte MTho NLar NSla NWCA SGar WAbe WCFE WFar WHal WHil |

## *Antigonon* (*Polygonaceae*)

| | |
|---|---|
| ***leptopus*** | MJnS SOWG |

## *Antirrhinum* (*Scrophulariaceae*)

| | |
|---|---|
| ***asarina*** | see *Asarina procumbens* |
| ***australe*** **new** | CSec |
| ***barrelieri*** | SEND |
| ***braun-blanquetii*** | CHal CSec EBee MLLN NLar SAga SEND WCot WPtf |
| 'Candy Stripe' | CSec LSou |
| ***glutinosum*** | see *A. hispanicum* subsp. *hispanicum* |
| § ***hispanicum*** | CSec |
| - 'Avalanche' | CHal ECtt |
| § - subsp. ***hispanicum*** | SRot |
| - - 'Roseum' | CMea CPom CSpe SBHP |
| (Luminaire Series) | LAst |
| Luminaire Deep Purple = 'Balumdepur'PBR **new** | |

- Luminaire Yellow = 'Balumyell'$^{PBR}$ LAst NPri
***majus*** 'Black Prince' CSec CSpe ECtt EShb LHop LSou
- 'Candy Snap'$^{PBR}$ (v) LSou
- 'Night and Day' CSpe
***molle*** CPom CSpe ECtt MCot MSte NBir NPer NWCA SAga SChF SRot SUsu WAbe
- pink MSte WAbe
***pulverulentum*** LHop SAga WAbe
***sempervirens*** SAga WAbe
***siculum*** CSec EBee WMoo

## **añu** see *Tropaeolum tuberosum*

## *Aphanes* (*Rosaceae*)

§ ***arvensis*** MSal

## *Aphelandra* (*Acanthaceae*)

***squarrosa*** CHal MBri
- 'Citrina' XBlo
- 'Dania' (v) LRHS

## *Aphyllanthes* (*Aphyllanthaceae*)

***monspeliensis*** CFee EBee ECho

## *Apios* (*Papilionaceae*)

§ ***americana*** CAgr CMdw CPom EBee EBrs ECho EMon GBin LEdu NBir NLar NSti WBVN WCot WCru WSHC
***tuberosa*** see *A. americana*

## *Apium* (*Apiaceae*)

***graveolens*** CArn CBgR CBod CPrp EBWF ELau GPoy MHer MNHC MSal NPri SIde WJek
- (Secalinum Group) 'Par-cel' MHer NGHP
***nodiflorum*** EBWF

## *Apium* x *Petroselinum* (*Apiaceae*)

hybrid, misapplied see *A. graveolens* Secalinum Group

## *Apocynum* (*Apocynaceae*)

***cannabinum*** CArn COld GPoy MSal

## *Aponogeton* (*Aponogetonaceae*)

***distachyos*** CDWL CRow CWat EHon EMFW EPfP LPBA MSKA NPer SCoo SVic SWat WFar WMAq WPnP

## **apple** see *Malus domestica*

## **apricot** see *Prunus armeniaca*

## *Aptenia* (*Aizoaceae*)

***cordifolia*** 🏆$^{H1-2}$ CCCN CSev NPer SChr SDnm SEND SPet WCor
- 'Variegata' (v) CCCN MRav

## *Aquilegia* ✿ (*Ranunculaceae*)

***akitensis*** misapplied see *A. flabellata* var. *pumila*
'Alaska' (State Series) 🏆$^{H3-4}$ SMrm
* ***alba variegata*** (v) ECho WEas
***alpina*** CMea CPrp CSec EBee ECho ECtt EPfP GEdr LCro MHer MLan MNHC MRav SPer SPet SRms WFar WMoo WPer WRHF
***amaliae*** see *A. ottonis* subsp. *amaliae*
***amurensis*** CLAP
'Apple Blossom' MCot
***aragonensis*** see *A. pyrenaica*
§ ***atrata*** CLAP CPou CSec EBee ECho EDAr MDKP MDun MWea NBre SMHy WBVN WHil WPer
***atrovinosa*** MWea SPad
***aurea*** misapplied see *A. vulgaris* golden-leaved
***barnebyi*** EBee GKev NLAp
***bertolonii*** 🏆$^{H4}$ ECho GKev LHop LRHS NDlv NMen NRya SRms WHoo
- ***alba*** NWCA
Biedermeier Group CSec EBee ECho GKir LRHS MAvo NOrc SPoG WFar WPer
'Blue Berry' WPat
'Blue Jay' (Songbird Series) GKir MHer NPri SMrm SPer SWvt
'Blue Star' (Star Series) CSam EAEE EBee ELan EPfP LRHS NCGa SDix SPoG WPer
'Bluebird' (Songbird Series) 🏆$^{H2}$ NPer
***brevistyla*** new CSec
***buergeriana*** GEdr MDKP NChi STes WPer
- 'Calimero' CHFP CSsd LBMP MDKP MSte NLar NPri SUsu WFar WHil
- var. ***oxysepala*** see *A. oxysepala*
'Bunting' (Songbird Series) 🏆$^{H2}$ NLar SSvw WFar
'Cally Spice' GCal
***canadensis*** 🏆$^{H4}$ CLAP CMHG CSpe EBee EDAr ELan GKev GQue LBMP MSte NBid NBir NBro NWCA SGar SRms SWal WPer
- SDR 1068 GKev
- 'Corbett' CLAP GBuc MDKP WHil
- 'Little Lanterns' CLAP CSam CTsd CWCL ECtt EPPr GKev LBMP MDKP MSte NLar NSum SPad SVil WFar WHil
- 'Nana' GBuc GKev MDKP MWea WThu
'Cardinal' (Songbird Series) EWll GKir MBri MHer NLar NPri SPer WFar
***cazorlensis*** see *A. pyrenaica* subsp. *cazorlensis*
***chaplinei*** NBir SBch
***chrysantha*** CSam GBuc GKev MLLN MNFA NBre SPad SRms WAbe WBrE WEas WPer
- 'Denver Gold' new EHig
I - 'Flore Pleno' (d) MDKP
- 'Yellow Queen' CHrt COlW CPLG CPrp CSec CWCL EBee EGoo ENor EPPr EPfP GMaP LBMP LHop MAvo MDKP NBre NLar NMoo SMrm SPhx SPla SPur SSvw STes SWal WCFE WHil
***clematiflora*** see *A. vulgaris* var. *stellata*
Clementine Series SPoG
***coerulea*** 🏆$^{H4}$ MDKP SRms
- var. ***coerulea*** GKev
- 'Himmelblau' EBee EGoo NBre
'Colorado' (State Series) CHFP EWll
'Crimson Star' EBee EPfP GKir MBNS MDKP SPer SPoG SPur WMoo
'Debutante' EBee LLWP MDKP MWea WGwG
***desertorum*** MDKP
***discolor*** LHop LLHF NMen
'Double Chocolate' LRHS
'Double Rubies' (d) GCra LSRN SHar WMoo
'Dove' (Songbird Series) 🏆$^{H2}$ CHFP EWll MBri MHer NLar NPri SHar SMrm SPer WFar
I 'Dragonfly' CBcs CTsd CWib EPfP MNHC NBlu NBre NMir SPer SPet SPoG SPur WFar
***ecalcarata*** see *Semiaquilegia ecalcarata*
***einseleana*** CSec EBee
***elegantula*** MWea
***eximia*** CWsd
'Firewheel' see *A. vulgaris* var. *stellata* 'Firewheel'
***flabellata*** 🏆$^{H4}$ GCra GGar GKir WAbe WKif WPer

| | |
|---|---|
| - f. ***alba*** | CTri ECho ELan NWCA WEas |
| * - - 'White Angel' | NHol WPer |
| - - 'White Jewel' (Jewel Series) | GKev SPla |
| - 'Amethyst' (Jewel Series) | GKir |
| - 'Blue Angel' | CBcs NHol WPer |
| - 'Blue Jewel' (Jewel Series) | ECho SPla |
| - Cameo Series | EWll LBMP WFar WGor WHil |
| - - 'Cameo Blue and White' | CWib ECho MWat NCGa WFar |
| - - 'Cameo Blue' | ECho |
| - - 'Cameo Blush' | WFar |
| - - 'Cameo Pink and White' | ECho MHer NCGa WFar |
| - - 'Cameo Rose' | NBir |
| - 'Georgia' (State Series) $\Upsilon^{H3-4}$ | SMrm |
| - Jewel Series | ECho WPer |
| - 'Ministar' | CSec EAlp ECho EPfP GKir LRHS MHer NBlu NVic WBrE WFar WHil WPer |
| - 'Nana Alba' | see *A. flabellata* var. *pumila* f. *alba* |
| - 'Pink Jewel' (Jewel Series) | SPla |
| § - var. ***pumila*** $\Upsilon^{H4}$ | CSam CSec CWCL EBee ECha ECho EHig EPfP GAbr GKir LHop MDKP NLAp NPri SIng WFar WPer |
| § - - f. ***alba*** $\Upsilon^{H4}$ | ECha ECho GEdr GKev LHop LRHS MSte NLAp SIng SRms WHil |
| - - 'Flore Pleno' | ECho |
| - - f. ***kurilensis*** | MSte |
| - 'Vermont' (State Series) | CHFP SMrm |
| 'Flamboyant' **new** | WTou |
| ***flavescens*** | WPer |
| 'Florida' (State Series) $\Upsilon^{H2}$ | SMrm |
| ***formosa*** | CMea EBee ECho GGar LBMP MDKP NChi NPri NWCA WGwG WKif WPer |
| - var. ***truncata*** | EBee GBuc GCal MLLN WOut |
| § ***fragrans*** | CDMG CHrt CLAP COIW CPrp EBee EHig EPfP GEdr LBMP MTho MWat NWCA SGar STes WGwG WHoo WPnP WRha |
| - white-flowered | ELan |
| ***glandulosa*** | NDlv NLar WEas |
| ***glauca*** | see *A. fragrans* |
| 'Golden Guiness' | WPnP WTou |
| 'Goldfinch' (Songbird Series) | EWll MHer NBir NPri SMrm SPer |
| ***grata*** | MDKP |
| 'Heavenly Blue' **new** | MAvo WHil |
| 'Hensol Harebell' $\Upsilon^{H4}$ | CSWP EBee GBuc SRms WPtf |
| 'Irish Elegance' | EGoo WRha |
| ***japonica*** | see *A. flabellata* var. *pumila* |
| ***jonesii*** | CPBP GKev |
| ***jonesii*** x ***saximontana*** | GKev NLAp |
| 'Koralle' | COIW CSam MDKP NBre WFar WHil |
| 'Kristall' | EBee EShb ITim LCro LSRN MDKP NBre SSvw STes WHil |
| ***laramiensis*** | CPBP NWCA |
| 'Little Plum' | WHil |
| ***longissima*** $\Upsilon^{H4}$ | CHar CMea EHig EShb GBuc ILad MAsh MDKP MHer MLLN MWea SHar STes WEas WGwG WHoo WPen |
| 'Louisiana' (State Series) $\Upsilon^{H2}$ | CHFP |
| ***lutea*** **new** | CSec |
| 'Magpie' | see *A. vulgaris* 'William Guiness' |
| x ***maruyamana*** | CSec |
| 'Maxi' | MDKP NBre WHil |
| McKana Group | CTri EAEE ELan ELon EPfP GJos GMaP LAst LBMP LHop LRHS MLHP MNHC NGdn NVic SPer SPlb SPoG SRms SWal WMnd WMoo WWlt |
| 'Milk and Honey' | CBre EBee MRav |
| ***moorcroftiana*** | EBee |
| Mrs Scott-Elliot hybrids | CSBt LHop MLan SGar SPer SPet WFar WRHF WWlt |
| Music Series | SRms |
| 'Nightingale' (Songbird Series) **new** | NPri |
| ***nigricans*** | see *A. atrata* |
| ***nivalis*** | LLHF |
| ***olympica*** | EWes WPer |
| 'Oranges and Lemons' | EDAr LSou |
| Origami Series | GAbr WFar |
| ***ottonis*** | LHop |
| § - subsp. ***amaliae*** | CSec GEdr |
| § ***oxysepala*** | CPLG EBee GCal WCru WPrP |
| - B&SWJ 4775 | WCru |
| ***parviflora*** | EBee |
| 'Petticoats' | WTou |
| 'Purple Emperor'$^{PBR}$ | LRHS SPoG |
| § ***pyrenaica*** | EBee GKev |
| § - subsp. ***cazorlensis*** | CSec |
| 'Red Hobbit' | CBcs CBct CSpe EAEE EBee GAbr GGar GKir ITim LRHS MDKP NBre SIng WBrE WFar WHoo |
| 'Red Star' (Star Series) | CPrp EAEE EBee EPfP NCGa SHar WHil WPer |
| 'Robin' (Songbird Series) | EWll MHer NPri SMrm WFar |
| ***rockii*** | CHrt CLAP CSam EBee EWes GCal GKev GKir LHop MDKP MSte SSvw WHil |
| - B&SWJ 7965 | WCru |
| 'Roman Bronze' | see *Aquilegia* x *Semiaquilegia*, 'Roman Bronze' |
| 'Rose Queen' | COIW CSam EBee ITim MAvo MDKP NBre SSvw WHil WHoo |
| ***saximontana*** | CGra CSec GEdr GKev NLAp NLar NWCA WPer |
| § 'Schneekönigin' | GMaP WPer |
| ***scopulorum*** | CGra WAbe |
| ***shockleyi*** | CSec GBuc |
| ***sibirica*** | LLHF MAvo WPer |
| 'Silver Queen' | ELan MDKP |
| ***skinneri*** | CDMG CHrt CPLG CSec CSpe EBee EShb LHop MWat NCGa SPoG WMnd WMoo WRha WRos |
| - 'Tequila Sunrise' | CWib ECtt EWsh NHol NPri WPer |
| Snow Queen | see *A.* 'Schneekönigin' |
| Songbird Series | COIW MLLN NPri WFar |
| 'Spitfire' | EBee LBuc MBNS |
| 'Spring Magic Blue and White' (Spring Magic Series) | LBuc NNor |
| ***stellata*** | see *A. vulgaris* var. *stellata* |
| 'Stoulton Blue' | EBee |
| 'Sunburst Ruby' | CSec EBee EDAr LHop MDKP MWat NPro WMoo WTou |
| 'Sweet Lemon Drops' | LSou |
| 'Tequila Sunrise' | EBee |
| ***triternata*** | NWCA |
| 'Virginia' (State Series) | CHFP |
| ***viridiflora*** | CLAP CPom CSec EBee EHig EPfP GBuc GCal LBMP MAvo SGar SMHy SSvw WCot WEas WFar WGwG WHil WMnd WPGP WPer |
| - 'Chocolate Soldier' | CEnt CSpe ENor LEdu LSou MWea SPoG |
| ***vulgaris*** | CArn CMHG CRWN CWCL EPfP GPoy LLWP NBro NSco SGar SPlb WCAu WMoo WPer WShi WTin |
| - 'Adelaide Addison' | ECha GBri GBuc SUsu WEas WFar WHoo |

| | | |
|---|---|---|
| | - var. ***alba*** | CMea EBee LBMP LCro LLWP MNFA SMrm WCAu |
| | - 'Altrosa' | NBre |
| * | - 'Anemoniflora' | CSec |
| | - 'Aureovariegata' | see *A. vulgaris* Vervaeneana Group |
| | - 'Blue Streak' **new** | WTou |
| | - 'Burnished Rose' | ECtt WHil WTou |
| | - ***clematiflora*** | see *A. vulgaris* var. *stellata* |
| | - 'Clyne Woodside' (v) **new** | WTou |
| | - var. ***flore-pleno*** (d) | LLWP WPer |
| | - - black-flowered (d) | WCot |
| | - - 'Blue Bonnet' (d) | WHil |
| | - - blue-flowered (d) | WCot |
| | - - Dorothy Series (d) | GBuc LHop |
| | - - - 'Dorothy Rose' (d) | LSRN SPad |
| | - - 'Double Pleat' blue/white-flowered (d) | CPrp CWCL WHil WPer |
| | - - - pink/white-flowered (d) | CPrp NGdn WPer |
| * | - - 'Frilly Dilly Rose' (d) | WTou |
| | - - 'Jane Hollow' (d) | CPou |
| | - - pale blue-flowered (d) | LLWP |
| | - - 'Pink Bonnet' (d) | WFar |
| | - - pink-flowered (d) | GGar |
| | - - purple-flowered (d) | LLWP |
| | - - 'Strawberry Ice Cream' (d) | GBri NBro NBur SPad WBrE |
| | - - (Tower Series) 'Tower Light Blue' (d) | EGoo WTou |
| | - - - 'Tower White' (d) | EGoo |
| * | - - 'White Bonnet' (d) | MBNS SPer SRos |
| | - - white-flowered (d) | LLWP |
| | - 'Foggy Bottom Blues' | GKir |
| § | - golden-leaved | ECho WOut WTou |
| | - 'Heidi' | NBre |
| | - 'Mellow Yellow' | CSec CTsd GBuc GCra ILad MDKP SDix WHil WMoo WPer WRos WTou |
| | - Munstead White | see *A. vulgaris* 'Nivea' |
| | - subsp. ***nevadensis*** **new** | EBee |
| § | - 'Nivea' ♀H4 | COlW CPou CSpe EBee ECGP ECha LAst LCro NChi SPoG |
| | - 'Pink Spurless' | see *A. vulgaris* var. *stellata* pink-flowered |
| | - (Pom Pom Series) 'Pom Pom Crimson' | NBro NBur WCot |
| | - - 'Pom Pom White' | WTou |
| | - scented | WTou |
| § | - var. ***stellata*** | CHrt CSec ELan EWsh GBuc GKev LEdu NBro NChi WBVN WMoo WPer WTou |
| | - - Barlow Series (d) | WFar WRHF WTou |
| | - - - 'Black Barlow' (d) | Widely available |
| | - - - 'Blue Barlow' (d) | CHFP COlW CSpe EBee ECtt EPfP EShb GCal GMaP IBal LCro LSRN NBre SMrm SPad SPer SPhx WMnd WPer WRHF |
| | - - 'Blue Fountain' **new** | WTou |
| | - - 'Christa Barlow' (Barlow Series) (d) | EBee GGar LRHS MDKP NBre |
| | - - double-flowered (d) | WTou |
| § | - - 'Firewheel' | CSec MBNS WMoo WTou |
| | - - 'Gisela Powell' | EBee |
| | - - 'Greenapples' (d) | CBre EBee EWll GCra GKev SMHy SPad WCot |
| | - - 'Nora Barlow' (Barlow Series) (d) ♀H4 | Widely available |
| § | - - pink-flowered | LLWP |
| | - - purple-flowered | LLWP MGos |
| | - - red-flowered | ELan LLWP MGos |
| | - - 'Rose Barlow' (Barlow Series) (d) | EPfP IBal LCro SPad WMnd WRHF |
| | - - 'Royal Purple' (d) | LSou NBro SPoG WBVN WTou |
| | - - 'Ruby Port' (d) | Widely available |
| | - - 'Ruby Port' crimped (d) | WPnP |
| | - - 'Sunlight White' (d) | WPer |
| § | - - white-flowered | CSpe GCra LHop NBro WFar |
| | - variegated foliage | see *A. vulgaris* Vervaeneana Group |
| § | - Vervaeneana Group (v) | CMHG CSam CWCL ECtt EPfP EWll IBal LBMP MCot MNrw NBir NBre NPer SMrm SPer SPla SPlb SPoG SRms SWat WFar WHoo WMoo WRha WRos WTou |
| | - - 'Graeme Iddon' (v) | GBuc |
| | - - 'Woodside' | see *A. vulgaris* Vervaeneana Group |
| | - - 'Woodside Blue' (v) | ECtt EGoo GKir NHol WOut WTou |
| | - - 'Woodside Pink' (v) | MGos |
| | - - 'Woodside Red' (v) | WTou |
| | - - 'Woodside White' (v) | NBir WBrk WOut |
| | - 'White Spurless' | see *A. vulgaris* var. *stellata* white-flowered |
| § | - 'William Guiness' | Widely available |
| | - 'William Guiness Doubles' (d) | EShb WMoo WTou |
| | 'White Star' (Star Series) | CPrp EBee EPfP LAst LCro MRav NCGa WHil WPer |
| | Winky Series | ECtt |
| | - 'Winky Blue-White' | NBre NLar NPri SPoG WCFE WFar WHil |
| | - 'Winky Double White-White' (d) **new** | NPri WHil |
| | - 'Winky Pink' | NLar |
| | - 'Winky Purple-White' | NBre NPri WFar WHil |
| | - 'Winky Red-White' | NBre NPri SPoG SWvt WCot WFar WHil |
| | - 'Winky Rose-Rose' | NBre |
| | ***yabeana*** | CDMG EBee EGoo GGar GKev ILad |

## *Aquilegia* x *Semiaquilegia* (*Ranunculaceae*)

| | | |
|---|---|---|
| | hybrid, blue-flowered | WCru |
| § | 'Roman Bronze' | CSec CWCL EBee ILad LSou MHer WMoo WTou |

## *Arabis* (*Brassicaceae*)

| | | |
|---|---|---|
| | ***aculeolata*** | GAuc |
| | - NNS 01-28 | EPPr |
| | ***albida*** | see *A. alpina* subsp. *caucasica* |
| | ***alpina*** | SPlb |
| § | - subsp. ***caucasica*** | ECho NBlu WFar |
| | - - 'Corfe Castle' | ECho ECtt |
| | - - 'Douler Angevine' (v) | NPri SPoG |
| | - - 'Flore Pleno' (d) ♀H4 | CDow CSpe CTri CWCL ECha ECho ECtt ELan GAbr GMaP MTho SRms WBrk WEas WFar WHoo |
| | - - 'Pink Pearl' | ECho |
| | - - 'Pinkie' | ECho |
| | - - 'Pixie Cream' **new** | EDAr |
| | - - 'Rosea' | GJos MBNS NBir NPri SRms WFar WMoo |
| § | - - 'Schneehaube' ♀H4 | CTri CWib ECho ECtt EPfP EShb GKir GMaP MBNS MBar NMir NPri SPoG SRms WMoo |
| | - - Snowcap | see *A. alpina* subsp. *caucasica* 'Schneehaube' |
| | - - 'Snowdrop' | MRav WFar |
| | - - 'Variegata' (v) | ECho ECtt ELan GMaP LBee LHop MHer NPri SAga SPoG SRms WEas WFar |
| | - 'Revolution' | WCot |
| | ***androsacea*** | CSec SRms WFar |
| | x ***arendsii*** 'Compinkie' | SPlb SRms |
| | ***blepharophylla*** | CSec EPfP SIng WCot WFar |
| § | - 'Frühlingszauber' ♀H4 | CWib GJos GKir NBir NBlu NPri SPoG SRms WFar |
| | - 'Rote Sensation' **new** | CMea NPri WRHF |

| | |
|---|---|
| - Spring Charm | see *A. blepharophylla* 'Frühlingszauber' |
| ***bryoides*** | NMen |
| ***caucasica*** | see *A. alpina* subsp. *caucasica* |
| ***cypria*** | LSou |
| double white-flowered (d) | CFee |
| ***ferdinandi-coburgi*** | ECho WEas |
| - 'Aureovariegata' (v) | CMea CTri ECho ECtt EDAr SPet SWvt |
| - 'Old Gold' | ECho EDAr EHoe EPfP GKir LBee LRHS MBar MHer NHol NPri SPoG SRms SWvt WCFE WFar WHoo |
| - 'Variegata' | see *A. procurrens* 'Variegata' |
| ***glabra*** | EBWF WPer |
| § ***procurrens*** 'Variegata' (v) ♀H4 | CMoH CTri ECha ECho ECtt EHoe ELan EPfP EWes GKev LBee LEdu LRHS MBar MBrN MHer NBlu NHol NPri SHGN SPlb SPoG SRms |
| ***pumila*** <u>new</u> | CSec |
| ***purpurea*** <u>new</u> | GKev |
| § ***scabra*** | CNat |
| Snow Cap | see *A. alpina* subsp. *caucasica* 'Schneehaube' |
| ***stricta*** | see *A. scabra* |
| 'Tu Tu' | NLar |
| x ***wilczekii*** <u>new</u> | EPot |

## *Arachniodes* (*Dryopteridaceae*)

| | |
|---|---|
| ***simplicior*** | CCCN EBee LRHS SKHP WCot WRic |
| ***standishii*** | WRic |

## *Araiostegia* (*Davalliaceae*)

| | |
|---|---|
| ***hymenophylloides*** | WCot |

## *Aralia* ✿ (*Araliaceae*)

| | |
|---|---|
| CD&R 2289 from China | WCru |
| EDHCH 9720 from China | WCru |
| ***apioides*** EDHCH 9720 <u>new</u> | WCru |
| ***armata*** RWJ 10060 | WCru |
| ***cachemirica*** | CDTJ CDes CLAP EWes EWld GCal GKev NBid NLar SDix SMad SPlb WHal WPGP |
| ***californica*** | COld EBee GCal GPoy LEdu MSal MSte NLar SDix WCru |
| ***chapaensis*** HWJ 723 | WCru |
| ***chinensis*** misapplied | see *A. elata*, *A. stipulata* |
| ***chinensis*** L. | MSal WBVN |
| - BWJ 8102 | WCru |
| ***continentalis*** | CLAP EPPr EShb LEdu NLar WCot |
| - B&SWJ 4152 | WCru |
| - B&SWJ 8524 | WCru |
| ***cordata*** | EBee EWes GAbr GCal LEdu MSal NLar |
| - B&SWJ 5511 | WCru |
| ***decaisneana*** RWJ 9910 | WCru |
| § ***elata*** ♀H4 | Widely available |
| - B&SWJ 5480 | WCru |
| - 'Albomarginata' | see *A. elata* 'Variegata' |
| - 'Aureo-marginata' (v) <u>new</u> | EHig |
| - 'Aureovariegata' (v) | CBcs CDoC ELan EWes MBlu NLar NMoo NPal SCoo WDin WOrn |
| - 'Golden Umbrella' (v) | CDoC NLar WDin |
| - 'Silver Umbrella' | CDoC CDul MGos NLar |
| § - 'Variegata' (v) ♀H4 | CBcs CDoC CDul EHig ELan EPfP MBlu MGos NLar NMoo NPal SCoo SHBN SPoG WCot WDin |
| ***foliolosa*** B&SWJ 8360 | WCru |
| ***fragrans*** HWJK 2385 | WCru |
| ***kansuensis*** BWJ 7650 <u>new</u> | WCru |
| ***montana*** B&SWJ 6719 | WCru |
| - RWJ 10101 | WCru |
| ***nudicaulis*** | GPoy |
| ***papyrifera*** | see *Tetrapanax papyrifer* |
| ***racemosa*** | CArn EBee GPoy LEdu MLLN MNrw MSal MSte NLar SRms WFar |
| - B&SWJ 9570 | WCru |
| ***sieboldii*** | see *Fatsia japonica* |
| ***spinosa*** L. | MBlu NLar SPlb |
| § ***stipulata*** | NLar WPGP |

## *Araucaria* (*Araucariaceae*)

| | |
|---|---|
| ***angustifolia*** | CDoC ECho WPGP |
| § ***araucana*** | Widely available |
| ***cunninghamii*** | ECho ECou |
| ***excelsa*** misapplied | see *A. heterophylla* |
| § ***heterophylla*** ♀H1 | CCCN CDoC CTsd EShb LRHS MBri SAPC SArc SEND |
| ***imbricata*** | see *A. araucana* |

## *Araujia* (*Asclepiadaceae*)

| | |
|---|---|
| ***sericifera*** | CMac CRHN CTrG EMil EShb GQui SDnm SGar SPav WFoF WSHC |

## *Arbutus* ✿ (*Ericaceae*)

| | |
|---|---|
| ***andrachne*** | EPfP WBod |
| x ***andrachnoides*** ♀H4 | CAbP CBcs CDul CPMA CTri EBee ELan EPfP GGal LRHS LSRN MAsh SAPC SArc SDnm SMad SPer SPoG SReu SSpi SSta WHCG WPGP WPat |
| ***glandulosa*** | see *Arctostaphylos glandulosa* |
| 'Marina' | CAbP CDoC CDul CEnd CPMA CSam EBee ELan EPfP LHop LRHS MAsh MBlu SEND SMad SPer SPoG SRGP SReu SSpi SSta SWvt WFar WPGP WPat |
| ***menziesii*** ♀H3 | CBcs CDoC CEnd CMCN CTho EBee ECrN EPfP LRHS LSRN MAsh MGos NLar SLon SMad SPer SSpi WDin WFar WPGP WPat |
| ***unedo*** ♀H4 | Widely available |
| - 'Atlantic' | CCCN ECrN LCro LPan LRHS LSRN MGos SPoG SWvt WPat |
| - 'Compacta' | CBcs CCCN CDoC EMil GKir LPan LRHS MAsh MGos SWvt WCFE WDin |
| - 'Elfin King' | ELan EPfP LHop LRHS MAsh SDnm SPoG SSta SWvt |
| - 'Quercifolia' | CPMA EBee ELan EPfP NLar SDnm SReu SSta WBod WPat |
| - f. ***rubra*** ♀H4 | Widely available |
| ***xalapensis*** F&M 206 <u>new</u> | WPGP |

## *Archontophoenix* (*Arecaceae*)

| | |
|---|---|
| ***alexandrae*** | EAmu LPal |
| ***cunninghamiana*** ♀H1 | CBrP EAmu LPal XBlo |

## *Arctanthemum* (*Asteraceae*)

| | |
|---|---|
| § ***arcticum*** | CKno EBee ECha NBre WPer |
| - 'Roseum' | EBee GBin |
| - 'Schwefelglanz' | EBee NCGa |

## *Arcterica* see *Pieris*

## *Arctium* (*Asteraceae*)

| | |
|---|---|
| ***lappa*** | CArn GBar GPoy MHer MSal NMir SIde SVic |
| - 'Takinogawa Long' | MNHC |
| ***minus*** | EBWF MSal NSco |
| - 'Plus' | WAlt |

## *Arctostaphylos* (*Ericaceae*)

| | |
|---|---|
| § ***glandulosa*** | SAPC SArc |
| x ***media*** 'Wood's Red' | MBar WFar |
| ***myrtifolia*** | MBar |

| | |
|---|---|
| ***stanfordiana*** C&H 105 | GGGa |
| ***uva-ursi*** | GPoy MBar NLar NMen SHBN SLon SPlb SSta WBod WDin |
| - 'Massachusetts' | GKir LRHS MAsh NLar |
| - 'Snowcap' | MAsh NHol |
| - 'Vancouver Jade' | CDoC EBee GKir LRHS LSRN MAsh MBar MBri SCoo SPer SPoG SReu SRms SSta SWvt |

## *Arctotis* (*Asteraceae*)

| | |
|---|---|
| ***acaulis*** **new** | CSec |
| ***adpressa*** | CPBP |
| Hannah = 'Archnah'PBR | CHVG CSpe MBNS SVil |
| Hayley = 'Archley'PBR | CCCN LAst MBNS SVil |
| x ***hybrida*** hort. 'Apricot' | CCCN CHEx LAst MLan SAga SMrm |
| - 'China Rose' | SMrm |
| - cream-flowered | CHEx SAga |
| - 'Flame' ♀H1+3 | CAby CCCN LAst MBNS MLan SAga SCoo SMrm WHlf |
| - 'Harlequin' | CSec |
| * - 'Mahogany' ♀H1+3 | LSou |
| - 'Red Devil' | CCCN CHEx LAst MBNS MLan SAga SCoo SMrm SPoG SVil |
| - 'Wine' | CCCN CHEx LAst LSou MBNS MLan SCoo SMrm SRkn SVil |
| 'Prostrate Raspberry' | CSpe SAga |

## *Ardisia* (*Myrsinaceae*)

| | |
|---|---|
| ***crenata*** | LRHS MBri |
| ***japonica*** B&SWJ 1841 **new** | WCru |
| - B&SWJ 3809 | WCru |
| - var. ***angusta*** | WCot |
| - 'Miyo-nishiki' (v) | WCot |
| ***maclurei*** B&SWJ 3772 | LRHS |
| ***pusilla*** **new** | CBcs |

## *Areca* (*Arecaceae*)

| | |
|---|---|
| ***catechu*** | MBri |
| ***triandra*** | XBlo |
| ***vestiaria*** | LPal |

## *Arecastrum* see *Syagrus*

## *Arenaria* (*Caryophyllaceae*)

| | |
|---|---|
| ***balearica*** | CWCL ECho EWes GKir LBee LEdu LRHS SIng SPlb SRms |
| ***capillaris*** | CTri |
| ***festucoides*** | ITim NLAp |
| ***ledebouriana*** | EDAr EPot GEdr NLar |
| ***magellanica*** | see *Colobanthus quitensis* |
| ***montana*** ♀H4 | Widely available |
| - 'Avalanche' | WFar |
| ***pinifolia*** | see *Minuartia circassica* |
| ***purpurascens*** | ECho EDAr EPot EWes LLHF NMen SRms SRot WFar |
| - 'Elliott's Variety' | WPat |
| ***serpyllifolia*** | EDAr |
| ***tetraquetra*** | MWat NLAp |
| - subsp. ***amabilis*** | EPot MBar NMen NSla SIng |
| ***tmolea*** | NMen |
| ***verna*** | see *Minuartia verna* |

## *Arenga* (*Arecaceae*)

| | |
|---|---|
| ***engleri*** | LPal |

## *Argemone* (*Papaveraceae*)

| | |
|---|---|
| ***grandiflora*** | SBch SPav |
| ***mexicana*** | ELan SPav |
| ***pleiacantha*** | SPav |

## *Argyranthemum* ✿ (*Asteraceae*)

| | |
|---|---|
| 'Anastasia' | MAJR |
| 'Apricot Surprise' | see *A.* 'Peach Cheeks' |
| 'Beth' | MAJR |
| 'Blanche' (Courtyard Series) | MAJR |
| Blazer Primrose = 'Supanova' (Daisy Crazy Series) | MAJR |
| Blazer Rose = 'Supaglow'PBR (Daisy Crazy Series) | MAJR |
| § 'Blizzard' (d) | MAJR |
| Blushing Rose = 'Supaellie' (Daisy Crazy Series) | MAJR |
| 'Bofinger' | MAJR |
| 'Bon Bon' **new** | MBNS SVil |
| 'Bridesmaid' | CCCN MAJR |
| Bright Carmine = 'Supalight'PBR (Daisy Crazy Series) | LSou MAJR |
| ***broussonetii*** | MAJR |
| Butterfly = 'Ulyssis' ♀H1+3 | MAJR WGor |
| Camara = 'Ohmadcama' (Madeira Series) | MAJR |
| 'Camilla Ponticelli' | MAJR |
| ***canariense*** hort. | see *A. frutescens* subsp. *canariae* |
| 'Champagne' | MAJR |
| 'Cheek's Peach' | see *A.* 'Peach Cheeks' |
| Cherry Love (Daisy Crazy Series) | CCCN EPfP MAJR |
| 'Christy Bell' | MAJR |
| 'Citronelle' **new** | SVil |
| * ***compactum*** | MAJR |
| 'Comtesse de Chambord' | MAJR SPet |
| 'Cornish Gold' ♀H1+3 | CCCN LSou MAJR SVil |
| ***coronopifolium*** | MAJR |
| 'Donington Hero' ♀H1+3 | MAJR MHom |
| double white-flowered (d) | MAJR |
| 'Edelweiss' (d) | MAJR MHom |
| 'Ella'PBR | MAJR |
| 'Flamingo' | see *Rhodanthemum gayanum* |
| § ***foeniculaceum*** misapplied | CTri ELan GKir WKif |
| - pink-flowered | see *A.* 'Petite Pink' |
| § ***foeniculaceum*** (Willd.) Webb & Sch.Bip. | CHal MAJR MCot |
| § - 'Royal Haze' ♀H1+3 | CCCN CHll MAJR NPer |
| 'Frosty' | MAJR MBNS |
| § ***frutescens*** | CHEx MAJR |
| § - subsp. ***canariae*** ♀H1+3 | CCCN MAJR |
| - subsp. ***succulentum*** | MAJR |
| - - 'Margaret Lynch' | MAJR |
| 'Fuji Sundance' | MAJR |
| 'George' | MAJR |
| 'Gill's Pink' | CCCN MAJR MHom WPnn |
| 'Golden Treasure' | MAJR |
| ***gracile*** | CHll |
| - 'Chelsea Girl' ♀H1+3 | CCCN CHEx COIW MAJR MCot MHom WKif WPnn |
| 'Gretel' | MAJR |
| 'Guernsey Pink' | MAJR MHom |
| Gypsy Rose = 'M9/18d' | CCCN |
| 'Harvest Snow' | LAst MBNS |
| 'Henriette'PBR | MAJR |
| 'Icknield Jubilee' | MAJR |
| 'Icknield Lemon Ice' | MAJR |
| 'Icknield Pink' | MAJR |
| 'Icknield Surprise' | MAJR |
| 'Icknield Sylvia' | MAJR |
| 'Icknield Yellow' | MAJR |
| 'Jamaica Primrose' ♀H1+3 | CHEx CSpe CTri ECtt MAJR MHar SDix WPnn |
| 'Jamaica Snowstorm' | see *A.* 'Snow Storm' |
| 'Julieanne' | LAst MAJR MBNS SMrm |
| 'Lemon Chiffon' | MAJR |
| 'Lemon Delight' | CHal LAst MAJR |

| | | |
|---|---|---|
| | 'Lemon Meringue' (d) | CCCN MAJR |
| | 'Lemon Soufflé' | MAJR |
| | ***lemsii*** | MAJR |
| § | 'Levada Cream' ♀H1+3 | MAJR MHom |
| | 'Libby Brett' | MAJR |
| | 'Lilliput' | MAJR |
| | Machio Double Pink = 'Ohar01245' (Madeira Series) **new** | MAJR |
| | Madelana = 'Ohmadmade'PBR (Madeira Series) | SVil |
| | Monte = 'Ohar01241'PBR (Madeira Series) | MAJR |
| § | ***maderense*** ♀H1+3 | CHll GCal MAJR |
| | - pale-flowered | MAJR |
| | 'Mary Cheek' (d) ♀H1+3 | CCCN MAJR SPet SRGP |
| | 'Mary Wootton' (d) | ECtt MAJR MHom |
| | ***mawii*** | see *Rhodanthemum gayanum* |
| | 'Mike's Pink' | MAJR |
| | 'Millennium Star' | MAJR |
| | 'Mini-snowflake' | see *A.* 'Blizzard' |
| | Molimba Duplo Pearl = 'Argydupea' | MAJR |
| § | 'Mrs F. Sander' (d) | MAJR MCot |
| | 'Nevada Cream' | see *A.* 'Levada Cream' |
| | ***ochroleucum*** | see *A. maderense* |
| | 'Pacific Gold' **new** | SVil |
| § | 'Peach Cheeks' (d) | CCCN |
| § | 'Petite Pink' ♀H1+3 | CCCN ECtt LAst MAJR MHom |
| | Ping-Pong = 'Innping' (d) | CBcs CCCN MBNS |
| | 'Pink Australian' (d) | CCCN MAJR MHom |
| | 'Pink Delight' | see *A.* 'Petite Pink' |
| | 'Pink Pixie' | MAJR |
| | Pink Wonder = 'Supalily' (Daisy Crazy Series) | MAJR |
| | ***pinnatifidium*** subsp. ***succulentum*** | MAJR |
| | Polly = 'Innpolly' | SMrm SVil |
| | 'Pomponette Pink' **new** | SVil |
| | 'Porto Moritz' **new** | MAJR |
| | 'Powder Puff' (d) | ECtt MAJR |
| | 'Primrose Petite'PBR (Courtyard Series) | MAJR |
| | prostrate double pink-flowered (d) | MAJR |
| | 'Qinta White' (d) ♀H1+3 | MAJR |
| | 'Rising Sun' | MAJR |
| | 'Rosa Dwarf' | MAJR |
| | 'Royal Haze' | see *A. foeniculaceum* L. 'Royal Haze' |
| | 'Saimi' | MAJR |
| | Santana = 'Ohmadsant' (Madeira Series) | MAJR SVil |
| | Santa Catarina = 'Ohmadsaca' (Madeira Series) **new** | MAJR |
| | São Martinho = 'Ohmadsaom' (Madeira Series) | MAJR SVil |
| | São Vicente = 'Ohmadsavi'PBR (Madeira Series) | MAJR |
| | 'Silver Leaf' | MAJR |
| | 'Silver Queen' | see *A. foeniculaceum* misapplied |
| § | 'Snow Storm' ♀H1+3 | LAst MAJR MHom WClo WPnn |
| | 'Snowball' | MAJR |
| | 'Snowflake' misapplied | see *A.* 'Mrs F. Sander' |
| | 'Starlight' | MAJR |
| | Strawberry Pink = 'Suparosa'PBR (Daisy Crazy Series) | EPfP |
| | 'Sugar and Ice'PBR | CCCN MAJR |
| | 'Sugar Baby'PBR | CCCN MAJR |
| | Sugar Cheer = 'Cobeer' | MAJR |
| | 'Sugar Lace' | MAJR |
| | Sultan's Dream = 'Supadream'PBR (Daisy Crazy Series) | EPfP |
| | Sultan's Lemon = 'Supalem'PBR (Daisy Crazy Series) | EPfP MAJR |
| | Sultan's Pride = 'Cosupri' (Daisy Crazy Series) | MAJR |
| | 'Summer Angel' (d) | MAJR |
| | 'Summer Cloud' **new** | MCot |
| | 'Summer Eyes' | MAJR |
| | 'Summer Melody'PBR (d) | CCCN CSpe MAJR |
| | 'Summer Pink'PBR | CCCN LAst LSou MAJR SMrm |
| | 'Summer Stars'PBR (Daisy Crazy Series) | MAJR |
| | Summersong Lemon = 'Supa601'PBR (Daisy Crazy Series) **new** | LSou |
| | Summersong White = 'Supa594'PBR (Daisy Crazy Series) **new** | LSou |
| | 'Summertime' | MAJR |
| | Summit Pink = 'Cobsing'PBR (Daisy Crazy Series) | EPfP MAJR |
| | 'Sweety' | MAJR WPnn |
| | 'Tony Holmes' | MAJR |
| | 'Tweeny' | MAJR |
| | 'Tweety' | MAJR |
| | 'Vancouver' (d) ♀H1+3 | CCCN CHll CWCL ECtt EShb LAst SBHP SEND SPet |
| | Vanilla Ripple = 'Supabright' (Daisy Crazy Series) | MAJR |
| * | 'Vera' | CCCN MAJR |
| | 'Wellwood Park' | CCCN |
| | 'Weymouth Pink' | MAJR |
| | 'Weymouth Surprise' | MAJR |
| | White Blush = 'Supamorni' (Daisy Crazy Series) | MAJR |
| | White Crystal = 'Supagem' (Daisy Crazy Series) | MAJR |
| | 'White Spider' | CCCN ELan MAJR MHom |
| | 'White Star' (d) | MAJR |
| | 'Whiteknights' ♀H1+3 | MAJR |
| | 'Yellow Australian' (d) | CCCN MAJR |

## *Argyrocytisus* see *Cytisus*

## *Argyroderma* (*Aizoaceae*)

| | | |
|---|---|---|
| | ***testiculare*** **new** | LRHS |

## *Arisaema* (*Araceae*)

| | | |
|---|---|---|
| | ACE 2408 | GBuc |
| | C&H 7026 | NMen |
| | CC 4904 | CPLG |
| | CC 5511 **new** | CPLG |
| | Chen Yi 14 | WCot |
| | Chen Yi 35 | MLul |
| | Chen Yi 38 | MLul WCot |
| | Chen Yi 41 | WCot |
| | SDR 3276 **new** | GKev |
| | ***album*** **new** | EBee WVal |
| | ***amurense*** | CLAP CStu EBee ECho EPot GAuc GBuc GCal GGar LAma LFur MLLN MMoz WCot WFar WPnP |
| | - B&SWJ 947 | WCru |
| § | - subsp. ***robustum*** | CStu ECho LFur NMen WCot |
| * | ***angustatum*** var. ***amurense*** | LAma |
| | - var. ***serratum*** | see *A. serratum* |

| | |
|---|---|
| ***asperatum*** | EBee LAma MLul |
| ***austroyunnanense*** | EBee |
| ***bathycoleum*** | EBee |
| ***biauriculatum*** | see *A. wattii* |
| * ***bijinagensis*** new | EBee |
| ***brachyspathum*** | see *A. heterophyllum* |
| ***brevipes*** | NLAp |
| ***calcareum*** | EBee |
| ***candidissimum*** ♀H4 | Widely available |
| - green-flowered | WCot |
| - pink-flowered | MLul |
| - white-flowered | GEdr LAma MLul WCot |
| ***ciliatum*** | CBro CDes CPom CSpe CStu EBee EBla GBuc GEdr LAma LFur MHar MLLN MLul MMoz MNrw NLar SRot WCot WSHC |
| - var. ***liubaense*** | CFwr CGHE CLAP CWsd EBee EPfP EUJe GEdr MMoz WIvy WPGP |
| - - CT 369 | SCnR SKHP WCot |
| * ***coenobialis*** | MLul |
| ***concinnum*** | CFir CStu EBee EBrs EPot GAuc GBin GEdr GGar LAma MLul NHol NLar WPnP |
| ***consanguineum*** | Widely available |
| - B&SWJ 071 | WCru |
| - CC 3635 | WCot |
| - GG 92112 | WCot |
| - PJ 277 | WCot |
| - SDR 2850 | GKev |
| - SDR 3214 | GKev |
| - dark new | WVal |
| - subsp. ***kelung-insulare*** B&SWJ 256 | WCru |
| - marble-leaf red | WCot |
| - 'Qinling' | WCot |
| ***costatum*** | CCCN CHEx CKob CLAP CPom EBee EBrs ECho EPot EUJe GBuc GEdr GGar GKev LAma MLul MMoz NHol NMen WCot WPGP WVal |
| - CC 2924 | WCot |
| - CC 3237 | WRos |
| ***dahaiense*** | EBee LAma MLul |
| ***dilatatum*** | LAma MLul |
| ***dracontium*** | CLAP EBee EBrs ECho EPot LAma NLar NMen |
| ***du-bois-reymondiae*** | EBee LAma |
| ***ehimense*** | WWst |
| ***elephas*** | EBee ECho LAma MLul WCot WWst |
| ***engleri*** | MLul |
| ***erubescens*** | CPom CStu EBee EPot ERos MLul NLar WBVN |
| - marbled-leaved | GEdr |
| aff. ***erubescens*** | WCot |
| ***exappendiculatum*** | CDes EBee MMoz SKHP WPGP |
| ***fargesii*** | CLAP EBee EBrs ECho EPot GEdr LAma MLul MMoz SChF WCot WWst |
| ***fimbriatum*** new | WVal |
| ***flavum*** | Widely available |
| - CC 1782 | WCot |
| - subsp. ***abbreviatum*** | EUJe WCot |
| - - GG 84193 | WWst |
| * - ***minus*** | NWCA |
| - tall | CLAP ECho |
| - subsp. ***tibeticum*** | EBee |
| ***formosanum*** B&SWJ 280 | WCru |
| - B&SWJ 390 | CPou |
| - var. ***bicolorifolium*** B&SWJ 3528 | WCru |
| - f. ***stenophyllum*** B&SWJ 1477 | WCru |
| § ***franchetianum*** | EBee GEdr LAma MLul WCot |
| ***fraternum*** | WWst |
| ***galeatum*** | EBee ECho EPot LAma MLul NHol WCot |
| ***grapsospadix*** B&SWJ 7000 new | WCru |
| § ***griffithii*** | CMil CSec EBee EBrs ECho EPot ERCP GAuc GEdr GGar LAma LRHS MLul NHol SKHP WPnP WVal |
| - 'Numbuq' | GCra |
| - var. ***pradhanii*** | EBee GAuc MLul WVal |
| ***handelii*** | CPom |
| ***helleborifolium*** | see *A. tortuosum* |
| § ***heterophyllum*** | EBee GEdr LFur WWst |
| ***inkiangense*** | LAma |
| ***intermedium*** | EBee EBrs ECho GEdr LAma MLul MNrw NHol NMen SKHP |
| ***iyoanum*** | EBee WCru |
| - subsp. ***nakaianum*** | GEdr WWst |
| ***jacquemontii*** | CBro CLAP EBee EBla EBrs ECho GBuc GEdr GGar GKir MHar NLar NMen SPhx WCot WPGP |
| - GG 88172 | WCot |
| - GG 94120 | WCot |
| aff. ***jacquemontii*** MECC 29 | EBee NMen |
| - MECC 76 | NMen |
| ***japonicum*** Blume | see *A. serratum* var. *mayebarae* |
| ***japonicum*** Komarov | see *A. serratum* |
| ***jinshajiangense*** | EBee LAma MLul |
| ***kishidae*** | EBee |
| ***kiushianum*** | EBee EFEx GEdr LAma MMoz WWst |
| ***leschenaultii*** | EBee LAma WVal WWst |
| ***lichiangense*** | GEdr LAma |
| ***lingyunense*** | EBee |
| § ***lobatum*** | EBee LAma LFur MLul |
| ***maximowiczii*** | EBee GEdr WWst |
| ***meleagris*** | EBee LAma MLul |
| ***multisectum*** | CFir |
| ***negishii*** | EBee WCru WWst |
| § ***nepenthoides*** | CBro EBee EBrs ECho EHrv EPot GBin GEdr ITim LAma LFur MLul MNrw NHol WPnP |
| ***ochraceum*** | see *A. nepenthoides* |
| ***omeiense*** | EBee NLar |
| ***onoticum*** | see *A. lobatum* |
| ***petelotii*** B&SWJ 9706 new | WCru |
| ***pianmaense*** new | EBee |
| ***polyphyllum*** B&SWJ 3904 | WCru |
| ***prazeri*** | EBee |
| ***propinquum*** | CLAP CPom EBee EBrs ECho EPot GBin GBuc GGar LAma MLul NMen SKHP WCot |
| ***purpureogaleatum*** | see *A. franchetianum* |
| ***rhizomatum*** | EBee LAma |
| ***rhombiforme*** | EBee LAma MLul WWst |
| ***ringens*** misapplied | see *A. amurense* subsp. ***robustum*** |
| ***ringens*** (Thunberg) Schott | CDes EBee EFEx EPot EUJe GEdr GKev LAma MLul WWst |
| - f. ***praecox*** B&SWJ 1515 | WCru |
| - f. ***sieboldii*** | EBrs |
| - - B&SWJ 551 | WCru |
| ***robustum*** | see *A. amurense* subsp. ***robustum*** |
| ***saxatile*** | EBee LAma MLul WCot WWst |
| ***sazensoo*** | EBee GEdr LAma WWst |
| § ***serratum*** | CDes EBee EBrs ECho LAma MMoz MNrw WCot WPGP |
| - var. ***mayebarae*** new | EBee WWst |
| ***sikokianum*** | CBro EBee EBrs ECho EFEx EHrv EPPr EPot EUJe GEdr LAma LFur LRHS MLul SPoG WCru WVal |
| - var. ***serratum*** | CFir |
| - variegated (v) | EBee GEdr WWst |
| ***speciosum*** | CHEx CKob CPLG CSec EBee EBrs ECho EPot EUJe GBuc GEdr GGar |

| | |
|---|---|
| | IHer LAma MLul NHol NMen SPlb WFar WPnP WVal |
| - CC 3100 | WCot |
| * - var. ***magnificum*** | EBee EHrv GBin GEdr MLul NHol |
| - var. ***mirabile*** | WVal |
| * - var. ***sikkimense*** | LAma |
| ***taiwanense*** | CFwr CLAP CPom GEdr SKHP WCot |
| - B&SWJ 269 | WCru |
| - B&SWJ 356 | CPou |
| - var. ***brevipedunculatum*** B&SWJ 1859 | WCru |
| - f. ***cinereum*** B&SWJ 19121 | WCru |
| - silver-leaved | WCot |
| ***tashiroi*** | EBee GEdr WWst |
| ***ternatipartitum*** | EBee GEdr WWst |
| - B&SWJ 5790 | WCru |
| ***thunbergii*** | CPom EFEx EPPr LRHS SPoG |
| - subsp. ***autumnale*** B&SWJ 1425 | WCru |
| - subsp. ***urashima*** | CLAP EBee EBrs EFEx GEdr LAma LFur MLul WVal WWst |
| § ***tortuosum*** | CArn CBro CLAP CPLG EBee EBrs ECho ERos EUJe GBin GEdr GGar IHer LAma MLul MNrw MTho NHol NLar NWCA SChF SPhx WAbe WCot WPGP WPnP WVal |
| - CC 1452 | CPou |
| - from high altitude | GBuc NMen |
| - var. ***helleborifolium*** CC 3641 | WCot |
| ***tosaense*** | EBee GEdr WWst |
| ***triphyllum*** | CLAP CPLG CPom CSec EBee EBrs ECho EPot GBuc GEdr GGar GKev ITim LAma MHar MSal MTho NHol NWCA SMad WFar WPGP WPnP |
| - subsp. ***stewardsonii*** | EBee EBrs GGar NMen WWst |
| - subsp. ***triphyllum*** var. ***atrorubens*** | CLAP |
| § ***utile*** | CSec EBee EBrs ECho EPot GAuc GEdr LAma MLul WPnP WVal |
| ***verrucosum*** | see *A. griffithii* |
| - var. ***utile*** | see *A. utile* |
| § ***wattii*** | EBee LAma MLul WCot |
| ***yamatense*** | EBee WWst |
| - subsp. ***sugimotoi*** | LAma |
| - - B&SWJ 5092 | WCru |
| * ***yingjiangense*** new | EBee |
| ***yunnanense*** | CLAP EBee LAma |

## *Arisarum* (*Araceae*)

| | |
|---|---|
| ***proboscideum*** | Widely available |
| ***vulgare*** | ECho WCot |
| * - f. ***maculatum*** | ECho |
| - subsp. ***simorrhinum*** | CStu EBee EBrs ECho WCot |
| - subsp. ***vulgare*** | EBee WCot WHal |

## *Aristea* (*Iridaceae*)

| | |
|---|---|
| sp. | CStu GGal |
| ***ecklonii*** | CBod CHEx CPLG CPou CTrC CTsd EShb IGor MCot MHar SChr SHom WCot WDyG WOut WPic |
| ***ensifolia*** | CMdw MWea SAga WSHC |
| ***grandis*** | CFir WCot |
| ***inaequalis*** new | CDes |
| § ***major*** | CHll CTrC |
| - pink-flowered | CDes WPGP |
| ***thyrsiflora*** | see *A. major* |

## *Aristolochia* (*Aristolochiaceae*)

| | |
|---|---|
| ***baetica*** | CArn CPLG SKHP WPGP |
| ***californica*** | LEdu |
| ***chilensis*** | CCCN |
| ***clematitis*** | CArn EBee EBrs ECho GPoy LEdu MSal |
| ***contorta*** | EBee |
| ***cucurbitifolia*** B&SWJ 7043 new | WCru |
| ***delavayi*** | CHEx |
| ***durior*** | see *A. macrophylla* |
| ***elegans*** | see *A. littoralis* |
| ***gigantea*** | CCCN CHll CSpe |
| ***grandiflora*** | CCCN MJnS |
| ***griffithii*** B&SWJ 2118 | WCru |
| ***heterophylla*** | see *A. kaempferi* f. *heterophylla* |
| ***kaempferi*** | WSHC |
| - B&SWJ 293 | WCru |
| § - f. ***heterophylla*** B&SWJ 3109 | WCru |
| x ***kewensis*** | CCCN |
| § ***labiata*** | CSec |
| § ***littoralis*** 🏆H1 | LRHS SOWG |
| ***longa*** new | WThu |
| § ***macrophylla*** | CBcs CCCN CHEx EBee EPfP GKir MBri MRav NPal SHBN SLim WDin |
| ***manshuriensis*** | WDin |
| - B&SWJ 962 | WCru |
| ***moupinensis*** BWJ 8181 | WCru |
| ***onoei*** B&SWJ 4960 | WCru |
| ***pearcei*** | CCCN |
| ***ringens*** Link & Otto non Vahl. | see *A. labiata* |
| ***rotunda*** | SKHP |
| ***sempervirens*** | SKHP WDin WSHC |
| ***sipho*** | see *A. macrophylla* |
| ***tomentosa*** | IDee SKHP |

## *Aristotelia* (*Elaeocarpaceae*)

| | |
|---|---|
| § ***chilensis*** | LEdu |
| - 'Variegata' (v) | CCCN CWib EBee GQui IDee SEND SPlb |
| ***fruticosa*** (f) | ECou |
| - (m) | ECou |
| - black-fruited (f) | ECou |
| - white-fruited (f) | ECou |
| ***macqui*** | see *A. chilensis* |
| ***peduncularis*** | CPLG |
| ***serrata*** | ECou |
| - (f) | ECou |
| - (m) | ECou |

## *Armeria* (*Plumbaginaceae*)

| | |
|---|---|
| § ***alliacea*** | CSpe ECha |
| - f. ***leucantha*** | SRms WMoo |
| § ***alpina*** | GAuc |
| ***arenaria*** new | EBWF |
| Bees' hybrids | WMoo |
| 'Bees' Ruby' | WPer |
| 'Bloodgood' | ECho |
| 'Brutus' | CDes MAvo |
| ***caespitosa*** | see *A. juniperifolia* |
| - 'Bevan's Variety' | see *A. juniperifolia* 'Bevan's Variety' |
| ***euscadiensis*** | CSpe EMon |
| § ***girardii*** | EPot |
| Joystick Series | CHrt ECho GJos NVic |
| - 'Joystick Lilac Shades' | EBee EGoo EShb NLar |
| - 'Joystick Pink' | SWal |
| - 'Joystick Red' | EBee EPPr EShb GKir SBri WHil |
| - 'Joystick White' | EGoo EShb GKir NLar |
| § ***juniperifolia*** 🏆H4 | CLyd CMea ECho EDAr ELan EPfP GMaP LBee LRHS NHol NMen NVic NWCA SIng SPoG SRms |
| - 'Alba' | CMea ECho ELan EPfP EPot GBin GKev MMuc NBlu NMen NPri NRya |

| | | |
|---|---|---|
| | | SIng SPoG SRms WAbe WFar WHoo WThu |
| § | - 'Bevan's Variety' ♀H4 | EAlp ECha ECho ECtt ELan EPfP EPot GGar GKir GMaP LEdu LRHS MLHP MMuc MWat NLAp NMen NPri NRya SPoG SRms SRot WAbe WFar WHoo WPat |
| | - 'Brookside' | EPot |
| | - dark-flowered | EWes WAbe |
| | - rose-flowered | ITim |
| § | ***maritima*** | CArn EBWF ECho EPfP GJos GKev GKir LAst LRHS MBar MCot MNHC NBlu NChi SPet WCFE WFar WGwG WMoo |
| | - 'Alba' | Widely available |
| | - subsp. ***alpina*** | see *A. alpina* |
| | - 'Bloodstone' | CTri ECho ECot ELan MWat |
| | - 'Corsica' | CTri ECha NBir NRya WFar |
| | - Düsseldorf Pride | see *A. maritima* 'Düsseldorfer Stolz' |
| § | - 'Düsseldorfer Stolz' | CElw EAlp ECha ECho ECtt EDAr ELan EPfP GGar GKev GKir GMaP ITim LHop LRHS MCot MLHP NLAp NMen NPri SPoG |
| | - 'Glory of Holland' | EPot |
| | - 'Laucheana' | WHoo WMoo |
| * | - 'Pink Lusitanica' | ECho |
| | - 'Rossi' **new** | NHol |
| I | - 'Rubrifolia' | CFir CMea CMil CSpe EAlp EBee ECho ECtt EDAr EHoe EPPr EShb GEdr GGar GKev GMaP LAst MAvo MHer NLAp NLar NRya SPoG WAbe WFar WHoo WPat |
| | - 'Ruby Glow' | CTri LBuc |
| | - 'Splendens' | CBcs CHrt COIW CTri ECho EDAr EMil EPfP GGar GMaP LAst LBMP MGos NBlu NMir NNor NRya NVic SBch SPoG SWal WFar WMoo WPer |
| | - 'Splendens Alba' | EDAr |
| | - 'Vindictive' ♀H4 | CMea CTri EPfP |
| | ***morisii*** | SBch |
| | 'Nifty Thrifty' (v) | CBod CMea CTri EAlp EBee ECho ECtt EHoe EWes LRHS MHer NLAp NRya SCoo SIde SPoG SRot WFar WPat WWFP |
| | 'Ornament' | ECtt |
| | ***plantaginea*** | see *A. alliacea* |
| | ***pseudarmeria*** | CHrt EBee ELan EPfP MLan MWhi NBlu |
| | - 'Drumstick Red' | ECho WPer |
| | - 'Drumstick White' | WPer |
| | - hybrids | CTri ELan GGar NMir SPad |
| | ***setacea*** | see *A. girardii* |
| | ***vulgaris*** | see *A. maritima* |
| | ***welwitschii*** | IFoB SRms |
| | 'Westacre Beauty' | EWes |

## *Armoracia* (*Brassicaceae*)

| | | |
|---|---|---|
| § | ***rusticana*** | CArn CBod COld CPrp CSev CTri ELau EPfP GPoy ILis MBri MHer MNHC MSal NPer NPri NTHB SEND SIde SVic WHer WJek WLHH |
| | - 'Variegata' (v) | CHid CPrp ELau EMon GCal IFoB LHop LRHS MAvo NSti SMad SPla WCHb WHer WMoo |

## *Arnica* (*Asteraceae*)

| | | |
|---|---|---|
| | ***angustifolia*** subsp. ***alpina*** | SRms |
| | - subsp. ***iljinii*** | EBee NBir |
| | ***chamissonis*** Schmidt | see *A. sachalinensis* |
| | ***chamissonis*** Less. | CHby EBee GBar MNHC MSal NBre NLar WHil WJek WPer |
| | ***longifolia*** | EBee NBre |
| | ***montana*** | CArn CSam EBee GBar GPWP GPoy MHer MNHC SRms SWat WPer |
| § | ***sachalinensis*** | NBre |
| | - RBS 0206 | EPPr |
| | ***unalaschkensis*** | EBee |

## *Aronia* (*Rosaceae*)

| | | |
|---|---|---|
| | ***arbutifolia*** | CBcs CDul CTri EMil EPfP LSRN MBlu MGan NBlu SHBN SLon SPer SPlb WBod WDin WOrn |
| | - 'Erecta' | EBee ECrN ELan EPfP GBin LHop MBNS MBlu MBri NLar SLPl SPoG SRms SSpi WFar |
| | ***melanocarpa*** | CBgR CDul CMCN CMHG CSpe CTsd CWib EBee ELan EMil EPfP EWTr GKir LEdu LRHS MAsh MBar MBlu MRav SSpi WDin WFar WHCG |
| | - 'Autumn Magic' | CBcs CDoC CPMA EBee EPfP GBin LAst LRHS MAsh MBlu NMyG SCoo SLPl SPoG |
| | - var. ***grandifolia*** | CPMA |
| | - 'Hugin' | CAgr CPMA NLar |
| | x ***prunifolia*** | CDoC CDul CMHG EBee EWTr GKir LEdu WHCG |
| | - 'Aron' (F) | CPMA |
| | - 'Brilliant' | CDoC CTri EBee EMil LAst LRHS MAsh SCoo SPer SPur |
| | - 'Nero' (F) | CAgr |
| | - 'Serina' (F) | CPMA |
| | - 'Viking' (F) | CAgr CPMA EBee ECrN EMil EPfP GKir LBuc MBlu NScw SCoo WDin |

## *Aronia* x *Sorbus* (*Rosaceae*)

| | | |
|---|---|---|
| § | 'Burka' | WPat |

## *Arracacia* (*Apiaceae*)

| | | |
|---|---|---|
| | B&SWJ 9023 from Guatemala **new** | WCru |

## *Arrhenatherum* (*Poaceae*)

| | | |
|---|---|---|
| | ***elatius*** var. ***bulbosum*** | WFar |
| | - - 'Variegatum' (v) | CSpe EAlp EBee EHoe ELan GBin GMaP LEdu LRHS MMoz MWhi NBid NHol NOak NOrc SWal WFar WMoo |

## *Artemisia* ✿ (*Asteraceae*)

| | | |
|---|---|---|
| | RBS 0207 | CPLG EPPr |
| | from Taiwan | WHer |
| § | ***abrotanum*** ♀H4 | Widely available |
| | ***absinthium*** | CArn CPbn CSev CWan EEls ELau GPWP GPoy MBar MHer MLLN MNHC NSti NTHB SAdn SECG SIde SVic SWat WPer |
| | - 'Corinne Tremaine' (v) | WHer |
| | - 'Lambrook Giant' | EEls |
| | - 'Lambrook Mist' ♀H3-4 | CSev EBee EBla EEls ELan EPfP GBar GBri GCal GKir GMaP GMac LRHS MRav NBre SBch SWat WCAu WMnd |
| | - 'Lambrook Silver' ♀H4 | Widely available |
| | - 'Silver Ghost' | EEls |
| | ***afra*** | CArn EBee EEls GBar IFro |
| § | ***alba*** | CSev EEls EMon EOHP GBar GPoy ILis MHer MSal NBur SIde SMad WPer WRha |
| § | - 'Canescens' ♀H4 | CArn CSam CTri EBee ECha ECtt EEls EGle EHrv EPfP GBar GMaP LAst LBMP LRHS MHer MRav SDix SPer SWvt WAul WCFE WCot WFar WHCG WMnd WPer |
| | ***annua*** | EEls GPoy MSal SIde |
| | ***anomala*** | EEls |

| | | |
|---|---|---|
| | ***arborescens*** ♀H3 | CArn CMHG ECrN EEls ERas SDix SPer WDin WHer WKif |
| | - 'Brass Band' | see *A.* 'Powis Castle' |
| | - 'Faith Raven' | EBee EEls EPfP GBin GBuc MBNS WFar |
| | - 'Little Mice' | EBee EEls SSvw WGwG |
| | - 'Porquerolles' | EAro EEls |
| | ***arctica*** | EEls |
| | ***argyi*** | EEls |
| § | ***armeniaca*** | ECho EEls NSti |
| | ***assoana*** | see *A. caucasica* |
| | ***atrata*** | EEls |
| | ***barrelieri*** | EEls |
| | ***brachyloba*** | MLLN WCHb |
| | ***caerulescens*** | see *Seriphidium caerulescens* |
| | ***californica*** | EEls |
| | - 'Canyon Gray' | EEls |
| | ***campestris*** subsp. ***borealis*** | EEls WRha |
| | - subsp. ***campestris*** | EEls |
| | - subsp. ***maritima*** | EEls |
| | - - from Wales | EEls |
| | ***camphorata*** | see *A. alba* |
| | ***cana*** | see *Seriphidium canum* |
| | ***canariensis*** | see *A. thuscula* |
| | ***canescens*** misapplied | see *A. alba* 'Canescens' |
| | ***canescens*** Willd. | see *A. armeniaca* |
| | ***capillaris*** | EEls MSal |
| § | ***caucasica*** ♀H3-4 | ECho EEls EWes MBrN MHer SChF SPhx SRms SRot WCHb WEas WPer |
| | - ***caucasica*** | EEls WFar |
| | ***chamaemelifolia*** | EBee EEls GPWP IGor MHer NBre WJek |
| | ***cretacea*** | see *Seriphidium nutans* |
| | ***discolor*** Dougl. ex Besser | see *A. michauxiana* |
| | ***douglasiana*** | EEls |
| | - 'Valerie Finnis' | see *A. ludoviciana* 'Valerie Finnis' |
| | ***dracunculus*** | ECha GAbr MBar MCot MNHC MRav NBlu NVic SPlb WBrk WFar WLHH WPer |
| | - French | CArn CBod CHby CHrt CSev CWan EEls ELau GBar GPoy LEdu MHer NGHP NPri SBch SIde WGwG |
| | - Russian | CArn EEls GBar GJos SVic |
| | ***ferganensis*** | see *Seriphidium ferganense* |
| | ***filifolia*** | EEls |
| | ***fragrans*** Willd. | see *Seriphidium fragrans* |
| | ***frigida*** ♀H3-4 | EEls GBar WHCG |
| | ***genipi*** | EEls MSal |
| | ***glacialis*** | EEls |
| | ***gmelinii*** | CArn EBee EEls GBar |
| | ***gnaphalodes*** | see *A. ludoviciana* |
| | ***gorgonum*** | EBee EEls EWes |
| | ***herba-alba*** | EAro EEls |
| | 'Huntington' | EEls WFar |
| | ***kawakamii*** B&SWJ 088 | EEls WCru |
| | ***kitadakensis*** | EEls |
| | - 'Guizhou' | see *A. lactiflora* Guizhou Group |
| | ***laciniata*** | EEls |
| | ***lactiflora*** ♀H4 | EBee ECha ECtt EEls ELan GBar GMaP MRav NGdn NOrc SDix SRms WFar WMoo WTin |
| | - dark | see *A. lactiflora* Guizhou Group |
| | - 'Elfenbein' | EBee GBin GCal LHop LPla |
| § | - Guizhou Group | Widely available |
| | - - 'Dark Delight' **new** | EWes |
| | - 'Jim Russell' | CBow CDes CElw EWes NBre NDov |
| | - ***purpurea*** | see *A. lactiflora* Guizhou Group |
| | - 'Stonyford' **new** | MSCN |
| | - 'Variegata' | see *A. vulgaris* 'Variegata' |
| | - 'Weisses Wunder' | EBee |
| | ***lagocephala*** | EEls LSou |
| | ***lanata*** Willd. non Lam. | see *A. caucasica* |

| | | |
|---|---|---|
| | ***laxa*** | see *A. umbelliformis* |
| § | ***ludoviciana*** | EEls ELan GBar IFoB MRav NOrc NPer SBch SGar SRms WCFE |
| | - var. ***latifolia*** | see *A. ludoviciana* subsp. *ludoviciana* var. *latiloba* |
| N | - var. ***latiloba*** | see *A. ludoviciana* subsp. *ludoviciana* var. *latiloba* |
| | - subsp. ***ludoviciana*** var. ***incompta*** | EBee EEls LAst MRav |
| § | - - var. ***latiloba*** | EBee EEls EHoe GBar GBuc LHop LRHS MRav NBro NSti SBch SWvt WBod WCot WEas WHoo WPer |
| | - subsp. ***mexicana*** var. ***albula*** | EEls WFar |
| | - 'Silver Queen' ♀H4 | Widely available |
| N | - 'Valerie Finnis' ♀H4 | Widely available |
| | ***manshurica*** | LSou |
| | ***maritima*** | see *Seriphidium maritimum* |
| § | ***michauxiana*** | EBee EEls NBur NSti WHer |
| | ***molinieri*** | EEls |
| | ***mutellina*** | see *A. umbelliformis* |
| | ***niitakayamensis*** | EEls EOHP GBar |
| | ***nitida*** | EEls |
| | ***nutans*** | see *Seriphidium nutans* |
| | ***palmeri*** hort. | see *A. ludoviciana* |
| | ***pamirica*** | EEls |
| | aff. ***parviflora*** CLD 1531 | EEls |
| | ***pedemontana*** | see *A. caucasica* |
| | ***pontica*** | CWan EBee ECha ECrN EEls EHoe ELan GBar GMaP GPWP GPoy LRHS MBNS MHer MNFA MRav NBro NSti SDix SPer SSvw WFar WHoo WPer |
| § | 'Powis Castle' ♀H3 | Widely available |
| | ***princeps*** | CArn EEls GPWP MSal SIde WTou |
| | ***procera*** Willd. | see *A. abrotanum* |
| | ***purshiana*** | see *A. ludoviciana* |
| | ***pycnocephala*** | EEls |
| | - 'David's Choice' | EEls |
| | ***ramosa*** | EEls |
| | 'Rosenschleier' | CAby EBee EMon EPPr EWes LPla NBre WFar WPGP WTin |
| | ***sachalinensis*** | EEls |
| * | ***sancti-johannis*** **new** | SMrm |
| | ***schmidtiana*** ♀H4 | ECha ECot EEls MWat NLAp NOrc SRms |
| | - 'Nana' ♀H4 | Widely available |
| | ***selengensis*** | EEls |
| | ***splendens*** misapplied | see *A. alba* 'Canescens' |
| | ***splendens*** Willd. | EEls ELan SPhx |
| | - var. ***brachyphylla*** | MAsh |
| | ***stelleriana*** | EBee ECha EDAr EEls EWTr GKev IFoB LHop MAvo MHer NBro NPri SPer SPhx SRms WCAu |
| | - RBS 0207 | EEls NLar |
| N | - 'Boughton Silver' | CHrt EBee ECtt EEls EGle EGoo EHoe ELan EPfP GBri GGar GMaP GMac LDai LRHS MAsh MRav NSti SPer SRms SWvt WFar WMnd |
| N | - 'Mori' | see *A. stelleriana* 'Boughton Silver' |
| | - 'Nana' | EEls SWvt |
| | - 'Prostrata' | see *A. stelleriana* 'Boughton Silver' |
| | - 'Silver Brocade' | see *A. stelleriana* 'Boughton Silver' |
| | ***taurica*** | EEls |
| § | ***thuscula*** | EEls |
| | ***tridentata*** | see *Seriphidium tridentatum* |
| § | ***umbelliformis*** | EEls |
| | ***vallesiaca*** | see *Seriphidium vallesiacum* |
| | ***verlotiorum*** | EEls GBar |
| | ***vulgaris*** L. | CArn CPrp EBWF EEls ELau GBar GPoy MHer MNHC WHer WLHH |
| | - 'Cragg-Barber Eye' (v) | EBee EEls NBid NPro SAga WCHb WRha |

| | |
|---|---|
| - Oriental Limelight = 'Janlim' (v) | COIW EBee ECtt EDAr EEls EHoe EPfP EWTr GAbr LEdu LHop MCCP MWhi NBir NOrc NPri SHar SPoG SWal SWvt WCAu WFar WHer WJek |
| § - 'Variegata' (v) | CEnt EBee EEls MMuc NBir NSti SMad WAlt WCHb WFar WHer WMoo WPer WRha |
| - 'Woolaston' (v) | WAlt |
| x ***wurzellii*** | EEls |

## *Arthropodium* (*Anthericaceae*)

| | |
|---|---|
| ***candidum*** | CStu EBee EBrs ECha ECho ECou MSCN NWCA SHBN SRot WFar WPer WPtf |
| - 'Cappucino' new | CBcs |
| - 'Capri' | EBee |
| - ***maculatum*** | GEdr LEdu SPlb |
| - ***purpureum*** | CAbb CSec EAlp EBee EWll GBri GGar NBsh NWCA WCot WFar WPGP |
| ***cirratum*** | CHEx ECou GGar IDee LEdu SBch |
| - 'Matapouri Bay' | CAbP CAbb CBcs CDes CHEx EBee ECre EMil WPGP |
| ***minus*** new | CPLG |

## *Arthrostylidium* (*Poaceae*)

| | |
|---|---|
| ***naibuense*** | CDTJ CGHE EBee WPGP |

## artichoke, globe see *Cynara cardunculus* Scolymus Group

## artichoke, Jerusalem see *Helianthus tuberosus*

## *Arum* (*Araceae*)

| | |
|---|---|
| ***alpinum*** | see *A. cylindraceum* |
| ***besserianum*** | EBee ECho |
| 'Chameleon' | CDes EMon LFur MAvo MNrw MSte MTho NBir NLar SKHP SMad SPer WCot WCru WFar WHil WPGP WPrP WTin |
| § ***concinnatum*** | CStu EBee EBrs ECho SChr SKHP WCot WPrP |
| - black-spotted | EBee |
| - variegated (v) | WCot |
| ***cornutum*** | see *Sauromatum venosum* |
| ***creticum*** | CArn CBgR CBro CFir CSpe CWsd EBee ECha GBuc GCal LEdu MHar MNrw MRav MTho SCnR SRot WBor WCot WFar |
| - MS 696 | MNrw |
| - FCC form | EBrs ECho WCot WPGP |
| - 'Marmaris White' | SCnR WCot |
| - white-spotted | MNrw MTho |
| - yellow-spotted | NBir WFar WIvy |
| ***creticum*** x ***italicum*** | MAvo MDKP WCot WFar |
| § ***cylindraceum*** | EBee EBrs ECho NLar |
| ***cyrenaicum*** | CStu EBee ECho EWld LEdu MNrw MTho SKHP WCot WPGP |
| - from Crete | ECho WCot |
| ***cyrenaicum*** x ***concinnatum*** | EBrs ECho GKev |
| ***dioscoridis*** | CPom CSec CStu EBrs ECho EWes GKev MTho NLar WCot |
| - JCA 195.197 | WCot |
| - var. ***cyprium*** | EBee EBrs ECho |
| § - var. ***dioscoridis*** | EBee ERos LFur WCot |
| - - JCA 195200 | WPrP |
| - var. ***liepoldtii*** | see *A. dioscoridis* var. *dioscoridis* |
| - var. ***smithii*** | see *A. dioscoridis* var. *dioscoridis* |
| ***dracunculus*** | see *Dracunculus vulgaris* |
| ***elongatum*** | EBrs WCot |
| - RS 274/87 | EBee |
| ***hygrophilum*** | EBrs |
| ***idaeum*** | EBrs |
| ***italicum*** | CArn CLAP ECho GAbr GKev GKir LAma LBMP MTho NBPC NLar SBod SEND SWat WCot WFar WPnP WSHC WShi |
| - subsp. ***albispathum*** | CDes CHid CStu EBee ECho EDAr EMon WCot WFar WPGP |
| - black-spotted | SCnR WFar |
| - giant | WHil |
| - 'Green Marble' | CBct WFar |
| - subsp. ***italicum*** | CBct EBee EBrs ECho EPla EShb GKev LFur NWCA WBrk |
| - - 'Bill Baker' | EMon WFar |
| - - 'Cyclops' EAF 7701 | CHid WCot |
| § - - 'Marmoratum' $\mathbb{Y}^{H4}$ | Widely available |
| - - 'Sparkler' | EBee MAvo WCot |
| - - 'Spotted Jack' | EBee LFur MAvo MNrw NBre WCot WCru |
| - - 'Tiny' | CFir EMon GCal SCnR SMHy |
| § - - 'White Winter' | CElw EBee ECGP EMon GBuc MAvo NCGa WCot |
| - 'Nancy Lindsay' | EMon MAvo |
| - subsp. ***neglectum*** | CSec SChr WFar |
| - - 'Castle Brissac' new | MAvo |
| - - 'Miss Janay Hall' (v) | EBee EWes LFur LLHF WCot |
| - 'Pictum' | see *A. italicum* subsp. *italicum* 'Marmoratum' |
| - 'Splish Splash' | CAvo CBow |
| - 'Tresahor Beauty' new | MAvo |
| ***jacquemontii*** | ECho |
| ***korolkowii*** | WCot |
| ***maculatum*** | CArn CRWN CSec EBrs ECho EPot GPoy LAma MCot MHer MRav MSal NLar WHer WPrP WShi |
| - 'Painted Lady' (v) | MAvo WCot |
| - 'Pleddel' | MRav WCot |
| - Tar Spot Group | CNat |
| ***nickelii*** | see *A. concinnatum* |
| § ***nigrum*** | EBrs ECho EWes LLHF WGwG |
| - CE&H 524 | EBee |
| ***orientale*** | EPot WCot |
| - subsp. ***amoenum*** | MNrw |
| ***petteri*** misapplied | see *A. nigrum* |
| ***pictum*** | CBgR CDes CLAP CPLG EBrs ECho ERos EWes GEdr LEdu WCot WWst |
| - 'Taff's Form' | see *A. italicum* subsp. *italicum* 'White Winter' |
| ***purpureospathum*** | CPom EBee EBrs ECho WCot WPGP WWst |
| ***rupicola*** var. ***rupicola*** | WWst |
| - var. ***virescens*** | SBig WCot |
| ***sintenisii*** | EBee WCot |
| 'Streaked Spectre' | EMon |

## *Aruncus* ✿ (*Rosaceae*)

| | |
|---|---|
| AGSJ 214 | NHol |
| ***aethusifolius*** $\mathbb{Y}^{H4}$ | Widely available |
| - 'Little Gem' | ECho WCru |
| ***asiaticus*** | EBee |
| - B&SWJ 8624 | WCru |
| § ***dioicus*** | Widely available |
| - (m) $\mathbb{Y}^{H4}$ | CDoC CRow ECha ELan EPla MBNS MRav NBro NHol NSti SGar SMad SMrm SPer SRms SWat WFar WMoo WPer |
| - CC 5185 new | ITim |
| - var. ***acuminatus*** | EBee |
| - Child of Two Worlds | see *A. dioicus* 'Zweiweltenkind' |
| - 'Glasnevin' | CRow CSev ECtt MRav WFar |
| - var. ***kamtschaticus*** | EWes MCCP MGos NBre NHol NLar SWal WPGP WPnP |
| - - AGSJ 238 | NHol |
| - - RBS 0208 | MHar NGdn WBVN |

| | | |
|---|---|---|
| | - 'Kneiffii' | Widely available |
| § | - 'Zweiweltenkind' | CEnt EBee EHrv MAvo NBre NLar SMad |
| | 'Horatio' | EMon GBin IPot NDov NLar SMeo SPhx |
| | 'Johannifest' | CDes EBee EMon GBin WPGP |
| | 'Noble Spirit' | CEnt EBee EBla EPPr NGdn NLar SWat |
| | 'Perlehuhn' | EMon |
| | ***plumosus*** | see *A. dioicus* |
| | ***sinensis*** | NBre WFar |
| | ***sylvestris*** | see *A. dioicus* |
| | 'Woldemar Meier' | EMon GBin NDov |

## *Arundinaria* ✿ (*Poaceae*)

| | | |
|---|---|---|
| | ***amabilis*** | see *Pseudosasa amabilis* (McClure) Keng f. |
| | ***anceps*** | see *Yushania anceps* |
| | ***auricoma*** | see *Pleioblastus viridistriatus* |
| | ***chino*** | see *Pleioblastus chino* |
| | ***disticha*** | see *Pleioblastus pygmaeus* 'Distichus' |
| | ***falconeri*** | see *Himalayacalamus falconeri* |
| | ***fargesii*** | see *Bashania fargesii* |
| | ***fastuosa*** | see *Semiarundinaria fastuosa* |
| | ***fortunei*** | see *Pleioblastus variegatus* |
| | ***funghomii*** | see *Schizostachyum funghomii* |
| § | ***gigantea*** | MWht |
| | - subsp. ***tecta*** | CBcs MGos |
| | ***hindsii*** | see *Pleioblastus hindsii* |
| | ***hookeriana*** misapplied | see *Himalayacalamus falconeri* 'Damarapa' |
| | ***hookeriana*** Munro | see *Himalayacalamus hookerianus* |
| | ***humilis*** | see *Pleioblastus humilis* |
| | ***japonica*** | see *Pseudosasa japonica* |
| | ***jaunsarensis*** | see *Yushania anceps* |
| | ***maling*** | see *Yushania maling* |
| | ***marmorea*** | see *Chimonobambusa marmorea* |
| | ***murielae*** | see *Fargesia murielae* |
| | ***nitida*** | see *Fargesia nitida* |
| | ***oedogonata*** | see *Clavinodum oedogonatum* |
| | ***palmata*** | see *Sasa palmata* |
| | ***pumila*** | see *Pleioblastus argenteostriatus* f. *pumilus* |
| | ***pygmaea*** | see *Pleioblastus pygmaeus* |
| | ***quadrangularis*** | see *Chimonobambusa quadrangularis* |
| | ***simonii*** | see *Pleioblastus simonii* |
| | ***spathiflora*** | see *Thamnocalamus spathiflorus* |
| | ***tessellata*** | see *Thamnocalamus tessellatus* |
| | ***vagans*** | see *Sasaella ramosa* |
| | ***variegata*** | see *Pleioblastus variegatus* |
| | ***veitchii*** | see *Sasa veitchii* |
| | ***viridistriata*** | see *Pleioblastus viridistriatus* |
| | 'Wang Tsai' | see *Bambusa multiplex* 'Floribunda' |

## *Arundo* (*Poaceae*)

| | | |
|---|---|---|
| | ***donax*** | Widely available |
| | - 'Golden Chain' | CKno EBee EPPr EWes SMad |
| | - 'Macrophylla' | CGHE CKno CRow EPPr ETod LEdu LPJP SApp WPGP |
| | - 'Variegata' | see *A. donax* var. *versicolor* |
| § | - var. ***versicolor*** (v) | Widely available |
| I | - - 'Aureovariegata' | CDTJ EUJe IPot MDKP |
| | - - yellow-variegated (v) | CDes EShb SEND SPoG |
| | ***formosana*** | CKno CMCo EBee EPPr |
| | - 'Golden Showers' | EAlp |
| | ***pliniana*** | CRow EPla WPGP |

## *Asarina* (*Scrophulariaceae*)

| | | |
|---|---|---|
| | ***antirrhiniflora*** | see *Maurandella antirrhiniflora* |
| | ***barclayana*** | see *Maurandya barclayana* |
| | ***erubescens*** | see *Lophospermum erubescens* |
| | ***hispanica*** | see *Antirrhinum hispanicum* |
| | ***lophantha*** | see *Lophospermum scandens* |
| | ***lophospermum*** | see *Lophospermum scandens* |
| § | ***procumbens*** | CDMG CEnt CMea CSec CTri EBee ECho EPfP MNFA MTho NRya SGar SIng SRms WFar WGwG |
| | ***scandens*** | see *Maurandya scandens* |
| | 'Victoria Falls' | see *Maurandya* 'Victoria Falls' |

## *Asarum* ✿ (*Aristolochiaceae*)

| | |
|---|---|
| ***albomaculatum*** B&SWJ 1726 | WCru |
| ***arifolium*** | CLAP EHrv EPPr GBBs NLar |
| ***asaroides*** | CKob EBee WWst |
| ***asperum*** | EPot |
| ***campaniflorum*** | CLAP EBee ECho EHrv LAma MLul WCru WWst |
| ***canadense*** | CArn CBct CHEx CSec EBee ECho EHrv EPPr EPot ERos GBBs GPoy LRHS MSal NLar WCru |
| ***caudatum*** | CAvo CDes CLAP CRow CStu EBee EBrs ECho EMon GBuc GEdr LEdu NBro NHol NLar NSti NWCA SRms WCot WCru WFar WPGP |
| - white-flowered | CLAP EBee EHrv EPPr WCru |
| ***caudigerum*** | EBee MLul WCot |
| - B&SWJ 1517 | WCru |
| ***caulescens*** | CLAP EBee ECho EHrv EPPr LAma LEdu MLul WCru WWst |
| - B&SWJ 5886 | WCru |
| ***celsum*** new | EBee |
| ***costatum*** | CLAP |
| ***delavayi*** | CKob EBee EHrv LAma MLul WCot WCru |
| ***dimidiatum*** new | EBee |
| ***epigynum*** | EBee |
| - B&SWJ 3443 | WCru |
| - 'Kikko' new | EBee GEdr |
| - 'Silver Web' | CLAP WCru |
| ***europaeum*** | Widely available |
| ***fauriei*** | WCru |
| ***forbesii*** | EBee ECho EHrv MLul NLar WWst |
| ***geophilum*** | MLul |
| ***hartwegii*** | CLAP EBee EBrs EHrv GBuc GGar GKev NLar WCru WPGP |
| - NNS 00-74 | EPPr |
| ***hatsushimae*** new | EBee GEdr |
| ***heterotropoides*** var. ***mandshuricum*** | EBee |
| ***hexalobum*** | EBee |
| ***hirsutisepalum*** | EBee |
| ***hypogynum*** B&SWJ 3628 | WCru |
| ***ichangense*** | EBee |
| ***infrapurpureum*** B&SWJ 1994 | WCru |
| ***insigne*** | EBee |
| ***kiusianum*** | EBee |
| ***kumageanum*** | EBee WCot |
| ***lemmonii*** | LEdu WCru |
| ***leptophyllum*** B&SWJ 1983 | WCru |
| ***longirhizomatosum*** | MLul WCru |
| ***macranthum*** | WCot |
| - B&SWJ 1691 | WCru |
| ***maculatum*** B&SWJ 1114 | WCru |
| ***magnificum*** | CKob CLAP EBee EHrv LAma MLul WCru WWst |
| ***maximum*** | CFwr CKob CLAP EBee EBrs ECho EHrv ERCP GAbr LAma MLul NMen WCot WCru |
| - 'Silver Panda' | CBct EBee EHrv EUJe GEdr LSou SPoG WCot |

| | |
|---|---|
| ***megacalyx*** | EBee GEdr |
| ***minamitanianum*** | EBee |
| ***naniflorum*** 'Eco Decor' | CBct CLAP EBee EBla EHrv GEdr LAst LSou MBNS NLar NMyG WClo WCot |
| ***nipponicum*** | EBee GEdr |
| - var. ***kooyanum*** new | EBee |
| ***petelotii*** B&SWJ 9706 | WCru |
| ***porphyronotum*** new | EBee |
| ***pulchellum*** | EBee EHrv WCot WCru WWst |
| ***rigescens*** | EHrv EPot |
| ***satsumense*** new | EBee GEdr |
| ***savatieri*** new | EBee |
| ***shuttleworthii*** | CLAP NLar |
| ***sieboldii*** | CLAP EBee GEdr WCru |
| ***simile*** new | EBee GEdr |
| ***splendens*** | Widely available |
| ***subglobosum*** | EBee |
| ***taipingshanianum*** B&SWJ 1688 | WCot WCru |
| - yellow-flowered B&SWJ 1746 new | WCru |
| ***taitonense*** | WWst |
| ***takaoi*** | CKob EBee |
| ***tamaense*** new | EBee |
| ***unzen*** new | EBee GEdr |
| ***viridiflorum*** new | GEdr |
| ***wulingense*** | EBee |
| ***yakusimense*** new | EBee |

## *Asclepias* (*Asclepiadaceae*)

| | |
|---|---|
| 'Cinderella' | EBee LBuc SSvw |
| ***curassavica*** | CCCN CSev EShb EWld MNrw NBre SBig SPav SRkn WRos |
| ***incarnata*** | CEnt CMoH CPom CSec ELan EPau IFoB MRav NBre SPav SPlb WPer |
| - 'Alba' | ELan EMon MMuc |
| - 'Ice Ballet' | CPrp EBee ELan IFoB LHop LRHS NBPC NBre NTHB SAga SBig SPoG WPer |
| - 'Soulmate' | EBee ELan EPfP MLLN MMHG MMuc NBPC NBre NBsh NCGa NGdn NTHB SPad |
| - 'White Superior' | EBee |
| ***physocarpa*** | see *Gomphocarpus physocarpus* |
| ***purpurascens*** | CArn EMon |
| ***speciosa*** | EMon NBre NLar |
| ***sullivantii*** | NBre SPav |
| ***syriaca*** | CArn CPom EBee MSal NBre SPav |
| ***tuberosa*** | CArn CBcs CPom CWib EBee EBrs EShb GKir GPoy LHop MHer MNrw MSal NBsh NDov SPet SPoG |
| - Gay Butterflies Group | NBre NGdn |
| ***verticillata*** | NBre |

## *Asimina* (*Annonaceae*)

| | |
|---|---|
| ***triloba*** (F) | CBcs CDTJ MBlu MBri NLar SPlb |
| - 'Davis' (F) | CAgr |
| - 'Sunflowers' | CCCN |

## *Asparagus* (*Asparagaceae*)

| | |
|---|---|
| ***asparagoides*** ♀H1 | EShb |
| § - 'Myrtifolius' | CHal |
| ***crassicladus*** | EShb |
| ***densiflorus*** 'Mazeppa' | EShb |
| - 'Myersii' ♀H1 | CHal EShb SEND |
| - Sprengeri Group ♀H1 | CHal LRHS MBri |
| - - 'Variegatus' | EShb |
| ***denudatus*** | EShb |
| ***falcatus*** | EShb SEND |
| ***filicinus*** var. ***giraldii*** | EBee |
| ***officinalis*** | MNHC SEND WFar WOut |
| * - 'Amarus' | EMui |
| - 'Backlim' ♀H4 | ECrN EMil EMui |
| - 'Butler' | SDea |
| - 'Cito' (m) | EMil LRHS MAsh SDea |
| - 'Connover's Colossal' ♀H4 | CSBt CWan ECrN SEND |
| - 'Dariana' | EMil SDea |
| - 'Eros' | EMui |
| - 'Franklim' | SEND WFar |
| - 'Gijnlim' ♀H4 | ECrN EMil EMui SDea WHil |
| - 'Grolim'PBR | EMil |
| - 'Guelph Millennium' | EMui |
| - 'Jersey Giant' (m) | EMui |
| - 'Jersey Knight' new | EMui SVic |
| - 'Mary Washington' new | SVic |
| - 'Pacific Purple' | EMui |
| - 'Purple Jumbo' | EBee ECrN |
| ***plumosus*** | see *A. setaceus* |
| ***pseudoscaber*** 'Spitzenschleier' | EBee EShb MAvo SDix |
| ***retrofractus*** | EShb WPGP |
| ***scandens*** | EShb |
| ***schoberioides*** | LEdu |
| § ***setaceus*** ♀H1 | CHal EShb LRHS MBri |
| - 'Pyramidalis' ♀H1 | MBri |
| ***suaveolens*** | EShb |
| ***tenuifolius*** | EMon |
| ***virgatus*** | EShb WPGP |

## *Asperula* (*Rubiaceae*)

| | |
|---|---|
| § ***arcadiensis*** ♀H3 | ECho WThu |
| ***aristata*** subsp. ***scabra*** | CSpe EBee ECha ELan EMon |
| - subsp. ***thessala*** | see *A. sintenisii* |
| ***boissieri*** | ECho |
| ***cyanchica*** | MSal |
| ***daphneola*** | ECho EWes WAbe |
| ***gussonei*** | CMea ECho EPot MWat NLAp NMen NWCA WAbe |
| ***lilaciflora*** | ECho |
| - var. ***caespitosa*** | see *A. lilaciflora* subsp. *lilaciflora* |
| § - subsp. ***lilaciflora*** | ECho NMen |
| ***nitida*** | ECho |
| - subsp. ***puberula*** | see *A. sintenisii* |
| ***odorata*** | see *Galium odoratum* |
| ***orientalis*** | CSec WPGP |
| ***scutellaris*** | EBee |
| § ***sintenisii*** ♀H2-3 | CLyd CMea CPBP ECho EPot NMen WAbe WHoo WThu |
| ***suberosa*** misapplied | see *A. arcadiensis* |
| ***suberosa*** Sibth. & Sm. | ECho |
| ***taurina*** new | EBee |
| - subsp. ***caucasica*** | CMoH NLar WCHb |
| ***tinctoria*** | CArn GBar GPoy MHer MSal NDov SRms WCHb |

## *Asphodeline* (*Asphodelaceae*)

| | |
|---|---|
| RCB/TQ C-2 | WCot |
| § ***brevicaulis*** | GAuc |
| Cally Hybrids | EDAr |
| ***damascena*** | CPBP EBee |
| ***liburnica*** | CAvo CBro CMoH EBee ECha ELan ERos GAbr MRav SEND WCAu WCot WFar WHal WHoo WPer |
| § ***lutea*** | Widely available |
| § - 'Gelbkerze' | GKir NBre |
| - Yellow Candle | see *A. lutea* 'Gelbkerze' |
| ***taurica*** | CMHG EBee ECho GAuc LBMP MBNS NBre WPer |

## *Asphodelus* (*Asphodelaceae*)

| | |
|---|---|
| ***acaulis*** | ECho SCnR WAbe WCot |
| § ***aestivus*** | GAuc GCal MRav NBur SPhx SSvw WPer |
| ***albus*** | CArn CSpe EBee EBrs ECha EPPr EPyc GAuc GBuc IFoB LBMP MCot |

| | |
|---|---|
| | NBid NCGa SPer SPlb SRms WAul WPer |
| ***brevicaulis*** | see *Asphodeline brevicaulis* |
| ***cerasiferus*** | see *A. ramosus* |
| ***fistulosus*** | NBir WPrP |
| ***lusitanicus*** | see *A. ramosus* |
| ***luteus*** | see *Asphodeline lutea* |
| ***microcarpus*** | see *A. aestivus* |
| - Cally Spear | GCal NCGa |
| § ***ramosus*** | CAby CPar EBee ECho GAuc GCal LEdu MCot MNrw MTho NCGa WBVN WCot WPer |

## *Aspidistra* (*Convallariaceae*)

| | |
|---|---|
| from China | WCot |
| ***attenuata*** | CKob IBlr |
| - B&SWJ 377 | WCru |
| ***caespitosa*** new | CKob |
| - 'Jade Ribbons' | IBlr WCot |
| 'China Star' | CKob EBee IBlr WCot |
| 'China Sun' | CKob WCot |
| ***daibuensis*** | CKob IBlr |
| - B&SWJ 312b | WCru |
| ***elatior*** ♀H1 | CBct CHEx CHal CKob CTsd EBak EBee EShb IBlr LRHS MBri NLar NPal NScw SAPC SArc SEND SMad STre WCot |
| - 'Akebono' (v) | WCot |
| - 'Asahi' (v) | IBlr WCot |
| - 'Hoshi-zora' (v) | EBee IBlr WCot |
| - 'Milky Way' (v) | CBct CBow CHid EBee EShb IBlr MTho SEND SMad WCot |
| - 'Morning Frost' new | IBlr |
| - 'Okame' (v) | WCot |
| - 'Sekko-kan' new | EBee |
| - 'Variegata' (v) ♀H1 | CBct CHEx CHal CKob EShb IBlr IFoB IFro MTho NBir WCot |
| - 'Variegata Exotica' | XBlo |
| ***flaviflora*** new | EBee |
| ***leshanensis*** (v) | IBlr |
| ***linearifolia*** 'Leopard' | IBlr WCot |
| ***longiloba*** | EBee WCot |
| ***lurida*** | CBct EBee IBlr |
| - 'Amanogawa' (v) | EBee IBlr |
| - 'Fuji-no-mine' (v) | IBlr |
| - 'Ginga' (v) new | EBee |
| - 'Irish Mist' (v) | IBlr |
| - 'Seiun' (v) new | EBee |
| ***minutiflora*** | EBee WCot |
| ***omeiensis*** | EBee WCot |
| ***punctata*** | IBlr |
| ***saxicola*** 'Uan Fat Lady' | CKob WCru |
| ***sichuanensis*** | EBee |
| ***typica*** | IBlr |
| ***urceolata*** | IBlr |
| ***zongbayi*** | EBee WCot |

## *Asplenium* ✿ (*Aspleniaceae*)

| | |
|---|---|
| ***adiantum-nigrum*** | GKir SRms WAbe |
| ***australe*** 'Redondo' | WFib |
| ***bulbiferum*** misapplied | see *A.* x *lucrosum* |
| ***bulbiferum*** ambig. 'Suze' new | EBee |
| ***bulbiferum*** ambig. x ***oblongifolium*** | EUJe WRic |
| § ***ceterach*** | CLAP EBee EFer LRHS SRms WAbe WFib WHer WRic |
| ***daucifolium*** new | EOHP |
| x ***ebenoides*** | LRHS WRic |
| ***flaccidum*** | WRic |
| ***fontanum*** | EBee |
| ***friesiorum*** | SKHP |
| § x ***lucrosum*** ♀H1-2 | CDTJ CTrC ESwi WFib |
| ***lyallii*** | WRic |
| 'Maori Princess' | WFib |
| ***nidus*** ♀H1 | MBri XBlo |
| ***oblongifolium*** | WRic |
| ***obovatum*** subsp. ***lanceolatum*** | WRic |
| ***platyneuron*** | EBee |
| ***polyodon*** new | WRic |
| ***ruprechtii*** | WRic |
| ***ruta-muraria*** | EFer SRms |
| § ***scolopendrium*** ♀H4 | Widely available |
| - 'Angustatum' | Widely available |
| - 'Apple Court' | CLAP |
| - 'Capitatum' | MDun |
| * - 'Circinatum' | WPGP |
| - 'Conglomeratum' | SRms |
| - Crispum Group | CBgR CLAP EFer ELan MRav NHol SApp SRms SRot WAbe WFib WPGP WPtf |
| - - 'Crispum Bolton's Nobile' ♀H4 | WFib WPGP |
| - - 'Golden Queen' | CLAP |
| - Crispum Cristatum Group | CLAP NVic |
| - Crispum Fimbriatum Group | CLAP GQui |
| - Cristatum Group | Widely available |
| - Fimbriatum Group | CLAP WRic |
| - 'Furcatum' | CFwr CLAP CPrp EBee GEdr NHol NLar WRic |
| - 'Kaye's Lacerated' ♀H4 | CLAP EBee EFer WFib WRic |
| - Laceratum Group | CLAP SRms |
| - Marginatum Group | EFer SWat WPGP |
| - - 'Irregulare' | SRms |
| - 'Muricatum' | CFwr CLAP ELan GBin MRav NBid NHol SRms WFib WTin |
| - 'Ramocristatum' | CLAP |
| - Ramomarginatum Group | CLAP ELan SRms WFar WRic |
| - (Sagittatocristatum Group) 'Apple Court' | CBgR |
| - - 'Sagittatocristatum' | SRms WPGP |
| - 'Sagittatoprojectum Sclater' | WFib |
| * - 'Sagittatum' | SRms |
| - 'Stagshorn' | SRms |
| - Undulatum Group | CBgR CLAP EAEE EBee ECha EPfP MAsh MMoz NBir NHol NLar NMyG NSti SPla SRms SWat WIvy WPnP WRic |
| - Undulatum Cristatum Group | CLAP |
| ***septentrionale*** | SRms |
| ***trichomanes*** ♀H4 | Widely available |
| - Cristatum Group | SRms |
| - Incisum Group | CLAP EBee LRHS MAvo NOrc SRms WCot |
| - 'Ramocristatum' | WAbe |
| ***viride*** | EBee EFer SRms |

## *Astelia* (*Asteliaceae*)

| | |
|---|---|
| ***alpina*** | IBlr |
| ***banksii*** | CBcs CDoC CHEx CHll CTrC EBee ECou EUJe GBin GCal GGar IBal LRHS LSRN MBri WDyG |
| § ***chathamica*** ♀H3 | Widely available |
| - 'Silver Spear' | see *A. chathamica* |
| ***chathamica*** x ***fragrans*** | ECou |
| ***cunninghamii*** | see *A. solandri* |
| ***fragrans*** | CSpe ECou GGar IBlr LEdu WCot WDyG |
| ***graminea*** | GCal IBlr |
| ***grandis*** | IBlr LEdu |

| | | |
|---|---|---|
| | ***nervosa*** | CAbb CTrC CWsd ECou GKir IBlr LEdu SAPC SArc WPat WPic |
| | - 'Bronze Giant' | IBlr |
| | - 'Westland' | CAbb CBcs CBod CDoC CPen CTrC EBee EMil EPla EUJe GAbr GCal GKir IBlr LEdu LRHS MBri MGos MRav SEND SPoG WCot WLeb WPic |
| | ***nivicola*** 'Red Gem' | GCal LEdu |
| | ***petriei*** | IBlr |
| § | ***solandri*** | IBlr |
| | ***trinervia*** | IBlr |

## *Aster* ✿ (*Asteraceae*)

| | | |
|---|---|---|
| | ***acris*** | see *A. sedifolius* |
| | ***alpinus*** 𝕐H4 | CTri EAlp ECho EPfP GJos GKir MWat SRms WFar WPer |
| | - var. ***albus*** | EBee EDAr EMil EPfP GKev NBre NBro SPoG SRGP WPer |
| | - Dark Beauty | see *A. alpinus* 'Dunkle Schöne' |
| | - var. ***dolomiticus*** | GKev |
| § | - 'Dunkle Schöne' | EBee ECho LDai MHar NBre NVic SPoG SRGP SRms WFar WPer |
| | - 'Goliath' | EBee ECho MMHG NBre NBro SPlb WFar |
| | - 'Happy End' | CMMP EAlp ECho EMil LDai NBre NBro NLar SPoG SRGP SRms WFar |
| | - 'Märchenland' (d) | CPBP NBre |
| | - 'Pinkie' | CSam EBee GKev NBre NHol NLar SMad WOut |
| | - 'Trimix' | ECho GAbr NBir SRms WFar |
| | - violet-flowered | WPer |
| | - 'White Beauty' | SRms |
| * | - 'Wolfii' | SRms WFar |
| | ***amelloides*** | see *Felicia amelloides* |
| | ***amellus*** | CSec LSou SPer WMoo |
| | - 'Blue King' | EBee EWsh MLLN SMrm SWvt WCAu |
| | - 'Breslau' | EBee |
| | - 'Brilliant' | CPrp EBee EBla ECtt EGle GBuc LAst LSou MAvo MLLN MNFA MRav MWat SPer SRGP WIvy WOld |
| | - 'Butzemann' | EBee GBin |
| | - 'Forncett Flourish' | WOld WOut |
| | - 'Framfieldii' 𝕐H4 | SMHy WFar WOld |
| | - 'Gründer' | WOld |
| | - 'Jacqueline Genebrier' 𝕐H4 | CHar EGle WCot WIvy WSHC |
| | - 'Joseph Lakin' | WFar |
| | - 'King George' 𝕐H4 | Widely available |
| | - 'Kobold' | EBrs WFar |
| | - 'Lac de Genève' | EBee LCro MRav NLar WCot WFar WOld |
| | - 'Lady Hindlip' | CSam WFar |
| | - 'Louise' | MBrN SUsu |
| | - 'Moerheim Gem' | WIvy |
| | - 'Nocturne' | WCot WIvy WOld |
| | - Pink Zenith | see *A. amellus* 'Rosa Erfüllung' |
| § | - 'Rosa Erfüllung' | CPrp EBee EBla ECtt EPfP EShb GBuc GMaP GMac LAst LHop MCot MRav NDov SAga SPet SPla SRGP SWvt WCot WMnd WOld WPer |
| | - 'Rotfeuer' | NGby WCot |
| | - 'Rudolph Goethe' | EBee EMil EPyc LAst LRHS MLLN MRav MSte NVic SHBN SRGP WCAu WFar WMoo WOld |
| | - 'Silbersee' | CSam EMon NDov |
| | - 'Sonia' | EBee EGle MRav NGby NLar |
| | - 'Sonora' | CPrp ECGP EGle LHop LPla MSte NBre NDov SMrm SRGP WKif WOld |
| | - 'Sternkugel' | GMac WOld |
| | - 'Ultramarine' | WFar |
| | - 'Vanity' | GBuc WOld |

| | | |
|---|---|---|
| § | - 'Veilchenkönigin' 𝕐H4 | Widely available |
| N | - Violet Queen | see *A. amellus* 'Veilchenkönigin' |
| | - 'Weltfriede' | WOld |
| | 'Anja's Choice' | EBee EMon EWsh NBre WCot WOld |
| | ***asper*** | see *A. bakerianus* |
| | ***asperulus*** | CWsd EBrs LPla MHar SMeo SPhx SUsu |
| | ***asteroides*** | GKev |
| § | ***bakerianus*** | WFar |
| | ***capensis*** 'Variegatus' | see *Felicia amelloides* variegated |
| § | ***carolinianus*** | EShb |
| | 'Cassandra' | WOld |
| | 'Climax' misapplied | see *A. laevis* 'Calliope', *A. laevis* 'Arcturus' |
| | 'Climax' ambig. | CBnk CElw EBee GBuc GCal MRav NBid NSti SAga SMrm |
| | 'Climax' Vicary Gibbs | WOld |
| | ***coelestis*** | see *Felicia amelloides* |
| | ***coloradoensis*** | CPBP LLHF NSla |
| | 'Connecticut Snow Flurry' | see *A. ericoides* f. *prostratus* 'Snow Flurry' |
| | 'Coombe Fishacre' 𝕐H4 | CAby CHrt COlW CPrp CSam EBee EPPr GBuc GCal LPla MCot MRav MSte NBre SAga SMrm SPla SPoG SSvw SUsu WCot WFar WOld WTin |
| | ***cordifolius*** | WFar |
| | - 'Blutenregen' **new** | EBee |
| | - 'Chieftain' 𝕐H4 | IGor MNFA MNrw SAga SPhx WIvy WOld |
| | - 'Elegans' | CAby EBee IGor MSte WIvy WMnd WMoo WOld |
| | - 'Ideal' | EBee NLar WOld |
| | - 'Silver Queen' | WHil WOld |
| | - 'Silver Spray' | CPrp EBee ECtt GMaP GMac GQue MHom MLLN MWat NBre SRGP WOld WPer |
| | - 'Sweet Lavender' 𝕐H4 | CWsd WOld |
| | ***corymbosus*** | see *A. divaricatus* |
| | 'Cotswold Gem' | WCot WOld |
| § | 'Dark Pink Star' | WOld |
| | 'Deep Pink Star' | see *A.* 'Dark Pink Star' |
| | ***delavayi*** | EBee SUsu |
| | ***diffusus*** | see *A. lateriflorus* |
| | ***diplostephioides*** | CAby CSec EBee EDAr EPPr EShb GCal LBMP MMHG NBre NHol NLar SGar SPlb WAul WPer WPtf |
| § | ***divaricatus*** | Widely available |
| § | - 'Eastern Star' | NCGa WBVN WCot WOld |
| | - Raiche form | see *A. divaricatus* 'Eastern Star' |
| | ***drummondii*** | EBee |
| N | ***dumosus*** | CPLG WFar WPer |
| | - 'Biteliness' | NBre NLar |
| | - Sapphire = 'Kiesapphire'PBR | CBow MBNS NPri SPoG |
| | ***ericoides*** | CKno EShb MCot NBre NOrc NWCA WFar |
| | - 'Blue Star' 𝕐H4 | CPrp CSam EBee EBrs GBuc IGor LRHS MLLN MSte NBPC NBid NLar SHGN SPer SPoG WCAu WCot WMnd WOld |
| | - 'Brimstone' 𝕐H4 | IGor MRav NBre WOld |
| | - 'Cinderella' | COlW CPrp GBuc GMac NSti WOld |
| | - 'Cirylle' | MLLN NBre |
| | - 'Constance' | WOld |
| | - 'Erlkönig' | EBee GCal LAst MRav MSte NGdn NLar SPla SWat WMnd WOld WPer |
| | - 'Esther' | CPrp EBee ECha ELan MSte SMrm WOld |
| | - 'Golden Spray' 𝕐H4 | EBee GMaP GQue NLar NSti SPer WFar WMnd WOld |
| | - 'Herbstmyrte' | MLLN |
| | - 'Hon. Edith Gibbs' | WOld |
| | - 'Hon. Vicary Gibbs' | see *A.* 'Hon. Vicary Gibbs' |

| | | |
|---|---|---|
| | - 'Monte Cassino' | see *A. pilosus* var. *pringlei* 'Monte Cassino' |
| | - 'Pink Cloud' ♀$^{H4}$ | Widely available |
| | - f. ***prostratus*** | EBee EMon EPot SGar SHGN WFar |
| § | - - 'Snow Flurry' ♀$^{H4}$ | CMea CSam EBee ECha ECtt GMac IGor MAvo MLLN MNFA MNrw SDix SMrm SPhx SPla SUsu WCAu WCot WEas WMnd WOld WOut |
| | - 'Rosy Veil' | CKno GMac IGor MHom NBir NGdn |
| | - 'Schneegitter' | EBee MLLN MSte WCot WFar WOld |
| | - 'Schneetanne' | NBre |
| | - 'Sulphurea' | MWat |
| | - 'Vimmer's Delight' | WCot |
| | - 'White Heather' | CPrp GQue IGor MNFA NLar WIvy WMnd WOld WPer WRHF |
| | - 'Yvette Richardson' | CWsd MHom MSte SMHy WOld |
| | ***falcatus*** | EBee |
| | - var. ***commutatus*** | WCot |
| | 'Fanny's Fall' | see *A. oblongifolius* 'Fanny's' |
| § | ***flaccidus*** | WRos |
| | ***foliaceus*** | WHil |
| | - from Montana | EPPr |
| | x ***frikartii*** | CPrp EBee EGle ELan EPfP EShb MRav SAga SHBN SMrm SRms SWvt WEas WOld WSHC |
| | - 'Eiger' | WOld |
| | - 'Flora's Delight' | GCal WOld |
| | - 'Jungfrau' | CWGN EBee EPPr GMaP GMac LPio MRav MSte NLar SMrm WOld WSHC |
| N | - 'Mönch' ♀$^{H4}$ | Widely available |
| | - Wonder of Stafa | see *A.* x *frikartii* 'Wunder von Stäfa' |
| § | - 'Wunder von Stäfa' ♀$^{H4}$ | CEnd CKno CPLG EBee ECtt ELan ELon EPfP GBuc GKir GMaP LHop LPio LRHS MAvo MBNS MCot MRav NBlu NLar SMrm WCot WMnd WOld WPGP |
| | ***glaucodes*** | EBee |
| | ***greatae*** **new** | EBee |
| | ***hayatae*** | GEdr |
| | - B&SWJ 8790 | WCru |
| | 'Herfstweelde' | CPrp EBee EMon GBuc LRHS MAvo MSte SMad WFar WOld |
| | x ***herveyi*** | EBla EBrs EMon SPhx WOld |
| | ***himalaicus*** | EShb SRms |
| | 'Hittlemaar' | WHil |
| § | 'Hon. Vicary Gibbs' (*ericoides* hybrid) | MNFA MSte WCot WOld WOut |
| | ***hybridus luteus*** | see x *Solidaster luteus* |
| | 'Ivy House' **new** | ECtt |
| | 'Kylie' ♀$^{H4}$ | CAby CHVG CPrp EMon GBuc GMac IGor MHom MSte NCGa SPhx SRGP WBor WCot WFar WOld WRHF WTin |
| | ***laevis*** | MSte NBre NLar WPer WTin |
| | - 'Anneke Van der Jeugd' **new** | EBee |
| § | - 'Arcturus' | CFir MHom MLLN MSte NBir NBre NCGa NSti SSvw WCot WFar WWlt |
| | - 'Blauhügel' | LPla |
| | - 'Blue Bird' **new** | EMon |
| § | - 'Calliope' | CElw CKno CMea CSam CWan EBee ECtt GCal GMaP LPio MAvo MCot MHom MNFA MWat NDov NSti SAga SMad SMrm SPhx WBor WEas WFar WHoo WIvy WKif WOld |
| | - var. ***geyeri*** | MAvo MHar MNrw |
| | - 'Nightshade' | MHar WOld WRHF |
| | ***lanceolatus*** Willd. | NCGa WCot |
| | - 'Edwin Beckett' | CBre MHom WOld |
| § | ***lateriflorus*** | EBee WOld WPer |
| | - 'Bleke Bet' | WCot WOld |
| | - 'Buck's Fizz' | CHrt EBee ELan NLar WOld |
| | - 'Chloe' | NCGa |
| | - 'Datschi' | WFar |
| | - 'Delight' | MLLN |
| | - var. ***horizontalis*** ♀$^{H4}$ | Widely available |
| | - 'Jan' | WOld |
| | - 'Lady in Black' | Widely available |
| | - 'Lovely' | EBee EBrs LRHS MLLN NBre NCGa NNor SRGP |
| | - 'Prince' | Widely available |
| | ***laterifolius*** 'Snow Flurry' | see *A. ericoides* f. *prostratus* 'Snow Flurry' |
| § | ***linosyris*** | EBee EWes GBin NBre NLar SMrm WHer WOld |
| | - 'Goldilocks' | see *A. linosyris* |
| | 'Little Carlow' (*cordifolius* hybrid) ♀$^{H4}$ | Widely available |
| | 'Little Dorrit' (*cordifolius* hybrid) | EWsh MLLN WOld |
| | ***macrophyllus*** | CPou ELan EMon LRHS NLar WOld |
| | - 'Albus' | EBee EMon EPPr GBin WFar WIvy WOld |
| | - 'Twilight' | CHVG CMoH CSam EBee ECha ECtt EGle ELan EPfP EPla EWsh GCal LBMP LLWP MHar MLLN MSte NDov NSti SDix SRGP WCAu WCot WHil WIvy WMnd WOld |
| | ***mongolicus*** | see *Kalimeris mongolica* |
| | 'Mrs Dean' **new** | ECtt |
| | ***natalensis*** | see *Felicia rosulata* |
| | 'Noreen' | MAvo |
| | ***novae-angliae*** | CArn NBPC NBre WOld |
| | - 'Alex Deamon' | WOld |
| | - 'Andenken an Alma Pötschke' | Widely available |
| | - 'Andenken an Paul Gerber' | EBee EMon MAvo MHom MNrw NGby WBrk WOld |
| | - 'Annabelle de Chazal' | WOld |
| | - Autumn Snow | see *A. novae-angliae* 'Herbstschnee' |
| | - 'Barr's Blue' | CAby CDow EBee EMon EWsh GCra GQue LRHS MAvo MBNS MMuc MSte MWat NLar SPer SRms WBrk WCAu WMoo WOld |
| | - 'Barr's Pink' | CBre CDow EBee ECtt EMon MCot MHer MHom MLHP MRav MWat NLar SEND WBrk WCAu WFar WHrl WOld WPer WSFF |
| * | - 'Barr's Purple' | WCFE WOld |
| | - 'Barr's Violet' | CAby CHVG CWan EGle EPPr MAvo MHom SRms WBrk WCot WHal WHoo WHrl WMoo WOld WPer WTin |
| | - 'Bishop Colenso' | NBre |
| | - 'Christopher Harbutt' | CAbx EGle NPro SRGP WOld |
| | - 'Colwall Constellation' | WOld |
| | - 'Colwall Galaxy' | MAvo WOld |
| | - 'Colwall Orbit' | WOld |
| | - 'Crimson Beauty' | EMon EPPr MAvo MHom MSte MWat WBrk WOld |
| | - 'Evensong' | WOld |
| | - 'Festival' | CAbx |
| | - 'Harrington's Pink' ♀$^{H4}$ | Widely available |
| | - 'Helen Picton' | MBrN MHar MWat WOld |
| § | - 'Herbstschnee' | Widely available |
| | - 'Indian Summer' **new** | GJos |
| | - 'James Ritchie' | LLHF WHoo WOld |
| | - 'John Davies' | MAvo WOld |
| | - 'Lachsglut' | MAvo SMrm WCot |
| | - 'Lou Williams' | MAvo MHar MWat WOld |
| I | - 'Lucida' | WBrk WHal WOld |
| | - 'Lye End Beauty' | CKno CWan ECtt EGle EMon EPyc LLWP LRHS MAvo MHom MNFA |

| | | |
|---|---|---|
| | | MRav MSte MWat MWte SMrs WBrk WCot WHoo WMoo WOld WTin |
| | – 'Marina Wolkonsky' | EBee ECtt EWes WBrk WCot WOld |
| | – 'Millennium Star' | MSte WOld |
| | – 'Miss K.E. Mash' | MHom SRGP WBrk WOld |
| | – 'Mrs S.T. Wright' | CAby CDow CTri ECtt EGle EMon EWes MBrN MHom MSte SRGP WFar WOld |
| | – 'Mrs S.W. Stern' | WOld |
| | – 'Pink Parfait' | EBrs ECtt GMac NBre NGdn SRms WCot WOld |
| | – 'Pink Victor' | CTri EPPr SEND SRms WMoo |
| | – 'Primrose Upward' | CAby EWsh MSte WBrk WCot WOld |
| | – 'Purple Cloud' | EMon GMac LHop MHer MHom MWat NBre NGdn WBrk WHal WOld |
| I | – 'Purple Dome' | Widely available |
| | – 'Quinton Menzies' | CAbx MSte WOld |
| | – 'Red Cloud' | NBre SMrm WOld |
| | – 'Rosa Sieger' ♀H4 | CAbx CAby CBre CPrp EBee ECtt EGle EMon GMac MAvo MHom MSte NGdn SMrs SPhx SUsu WBor WBrk WOld |
| | – 'Rose Williams' | MAvo WOld |
| | – 'Roter Stern' | ECtt |
| | – 'Rubinschatz' | EBee MAvo MHom MSte NBre SRms WOld |
| | – 'Rudelsburg' | EMon WBrk |
| | – 'Sayer's Croft' | CAbx CWan EBee EGle EMon MHom MWat NBre WBrk WCot WHil WHoo WOld WTin |
| | – September Ruby | see *A. novae-angliae* 'Septemberrubin' |
| § | – 'Septemberrubin' | CAbx CAby CDow CMea CSsd EBee ECtt ELon EMon EWsh IFoB LHop MHer MHom MNFA MRav MSte NSti SPhx SRGP SUsu WFar WMoo WOld WPrP |
| | – 'Treasure' | CAbx CBre EMon NBre SMrm WMoo WOld |
| | – 'Violet Haze' **new** | CAbx |
| | – 'Violetta' | CAbx EBrs ECtt EGle EMon LSou MAvo MHom MNFA MSte MWea SPhx WBrk WFar WHoo WOld WTin |
| | – 'W. Bowman' | WOld |
| | – 'Wow' | NBre SMrm |
| N | ***novi-belgii*** | NSco WHer |
| | – 'Ada Ballard' | CBnk EBee LDai NBre NGdn SMrs SPer SPet SPoG SRGP WOld |
| | – 'Albanian' | CBnk WOld |
| | – 'Alderman Vokes' | WOld |
| | – 'Alex Norman' | CBnk WOld |
| | – 'Algar's Pride' | CBnk CHrt ECtt WOld |
| | – 'Alice Haslam' | CBnk EBee ECtt GBri MCCP NOrc NPri SPoG SRGP SRms WOld WPer |
| | – 'Alpenglow' | CBnk |
| | – 'Angela' | CBnk |
| | – 'Angela Peel' | CBnk |
| | – 'Anita Ballard' | CBnk WOld |
| | – 'Anita Webb' | CBnk GBri NBir WOld |
| | – 'Anneke' | CBnk EBee SRGP |
| | – 'Apollo' | CBnk NBre NLar NPri WOld |
| | – 'Apple Blossom' | CBnk WOld |
| | – 'Arctic' | CBnk |
| | – 'Audrey' | CBnk CEnt EBee ECtt GMaP LRHS LSRN MLLN NGdn NOrc SMrs SPla SRGP STes WFar WOld |
| | – 'Autumn Beauty' | CBnk CHVG WOld |
| | – 'Autumn Days' | CBnk WOld |
| | – 'Autumn Glory' | CBnk WOld |
| | – 'Autumn Rose' | CBnk WOld |
| | – 'Baby Climax' | CBnk WOld |
| | – 'Bahamas' | CBnk SGar |

| | |
|---|---|
| – 'Barbados' | CBnk MBri |
| – 'Beauty of Colwall' | CBnk WOld |
| – 'Beechwood Challenger' | CBnk WOld |
| – 'Beechwood Charm' | CBnk CWsd WOld |
| – 'Beechwood Rival' | CBnk CTri EBee MHar MSte |
| – 'Beechwood Supreme' | CBnk WOld |
| – 'Beth' | CBnk |
| – 'Bewunderung' | CBnk WOld |
| – 'Blandie' | CBnk CTri EBee MBNS MSte SRGP WCAu WOld |
| – 'Blauglut' | CBnk WOld |
| – 'Blue Baby' | CBnk WPer |
| – 'Blue Bouquet' | CBnk CTri SRms WOld |
| – 'Blue Boy' | MAvo WBrk WOld |
| – 'Blue Danube' | CBnk WOld |
| – 'Blue Eyes' | CBnk CElw EMon SAga SMrs WOld |
| – 'Blue Gown' | CBnk CMdw GCal WOld WOut |
| – 'Blue Lagoon' | CBnk CMea ELan MBri NOrc SMrs SRGP WOld |
| – 'Blue Patrol' | CBnk WOld |
| – 'Blue Radiance' | CBnk WOld |
| – 'Blue Whirl' | WOld |
| – 'Bonanza' | WOld |
| – 'Boningale Blue' | CBnk WOld |
| – 'Boningale White' | CBnk WOld |
| – 'Bridesmaid' | CBnk WOld |
| – 'Bridgette' | NBPC |
| – 'Bright Eyes' | CBnk SRGP |
| – 'Brightest and Best' | CBnk WOld |
| – 'Cairo' **new** | CBnk |
| – 'Calgary' **new** | CBnk |
| – 'Cameo' | CBnk WOld |
| – 'Cantab' | CBnk WOld |
| – 'Cantonese Queen' (v) | EPPr |
| – 'Carlingcott' | CBnk WOld |
| – 'Carnival' | CBnk CMMP EBee ECtt LDai MBNS MMHG NOrc SRGP WOld |
| – 'Cecily' | CBnk WOld |
| – 'Charles Wilson' | CBnk WOld |
| – 'Chatterbox' | CBnk COIW CPrp EPfP LRHS MRav MWat NLar SRms WOld |
| – 'Chelwood' | CBnk WOld |
| – 'Chequers' | CBnk CMMP EBee ECot MBNS MSte SMrs SRGP WOld |
| – 'Chicago' **new** | CBnk |
| – 'Christina' | see *A. novi-belgii* 'Kristina' |
| – 'Christine Soanes' | CBnk WOld |
| – 'Cliff Lewis' | CBnk WOld |
| – 'Climax Albus' | see *A.* 'White Climax' |
| – 'Cloudy Blue' | CBnk WOld |
| – 'Colonel F.R. Durham' | CBnk |
| – 'Coombe Delight' | CBnk |
| – 'Coombe Gladys' | CBnk WOld |
| – 'Coombe Joy' | CBnk WOld |
| – 'Coombe Margaret' | CBnk WOld |
| – 'Coombe Pink' | CBnk |
| – 'Coombe Queen' | WOld |
| – 'Coombe Radiance' | CBnk MSte WOld |
| – 'Coombe Ronald' | CBnk MWat WOld |
| – 'Coombe Rosemary' | CBnk EBrs ECtt LRHS NLar WBor WOld |
| – 'Coombe Violet' | CBnk MWat WOld |
| – 'Countess of Dudley' | CBnk WOld WPer |
| – 'Court Herald' | CBnk WOld |
| – 'Crimson Brocade' | CAby CBnk EBee LCro MRav MWea NLar SPhx SPoG SRGP WOld |
| – 'Dandy' | CBnk EBee ECot ELan NBir NGdn SPoG SRGP WFar WOld |
| – 'Daniela' | CBnk SRms WBrk WOld |
| – 'Daphne Anne' | CBnk WOld |
| – 'Dauerblau' | CBnk WOld |
| – 'Davey's True Blue' | CBnk CTri LCro MSte SMrs WOld |
| – 'David Murray' | CBnk WOld |

- 'Dazzler' CBnk CWsd WOld
- 'Destiny' CBnk WOld
- 'Diana' CBnk EWsh WOld
- 'Diana Watts' CBnk WOld
- 'Dietgard' CBnk WOld
- 'Dolly' CBnk NBir SRms WOld
- 'Dora Chiswell' CBnk WOld
- 'Dusky Maid' CBnk WBor WOld
- 'Elizabeth' CBnk CElw WOld
- 'Elizabeth Bright' CBnk WOld
- 'Elizabeth Hutton' CBnk WOld
- 'Elsie Dale' CBnk WOld
- 'Elta' CBnk WOld
- 'Erica' CBnk CElw MWat WOld
- 'Ernest Ballard' CBnk WOld
- 'Eva' CBnk SRms WOld
- 'Eventide' CAby CBnk CElw CTri EBee WOld WRHF
- 'F.M. Simpson' CBnk
- 'Fair Lady' CBnk CHVG MWat WOld
- 'Faith' CBnk WOld
- 'Farncombe Lilac' CBnk EBrs
- 'Farrington' CBnk WOld
- 'Fellowship' ♀H4 CAby CBgR CBnk CDes CFir CMoH COlW EBee ECtt MAvo MBri MSte MWat NCGa SAga SHar SPhx SRGP SRms WBrk WCot WOld
- 'Flamingo' CBnk
- 'Fontaine' CBnk WOld
- 'Freda Ballard' CBnk ECtt EWll GMaP MBNS MWat NGdn SMrs SRGP WCAu WOld
- 'Freya' CBnk WOld WSHC
- 'Fuldatal' CBnk WOld
- 'Gayborder Blue' CBnk WOld
- 'Gayborder Royal' CBnk CFir WOld
- 'Glory of Colwall' CBnk WOld
- 'Goliath' CBnk WOld
- 'Grey Lady' CBnk WOld
- 'Guardsman' CBnk WOld
- 'Gulliver' CBnk WOld
- 'Gurney Slade' CBnk WOld
- 'Guy Ballard' CBnk
- 'Harrison's Blue' CBnk NBre SAga SPhx WBrk WOld WPer
- 'Heinz Richard' CBnk CMMP COlW EBee ECha LBMP MSte NBir NBre NCGa NGdn SBch SPet SRGP SRms WOld
- 'Helen' CBnk WOld
- 'Helen Ballard' CBnk CMoH LCro NBre SRms WBrk WOld
- 'Herbstgruss vom Bresserhof' CBnk NBre
- 'Herbstpurzel' CBnk WOld
- 'Hilda Ballard' CBnk NBre WOld
- 'Ilse Brensell' CBnk MSte WOld
- 'Irene' CBnk WOld
- 'Isabel Allen' CBnk WOld
- 'Janet Watts' CBnk WOld
- 'Jean' CBnk MWat SRms WOld
- 'Jean Gyte' CBnk WOld
- 'Jeanette' CBnk SRms WOld
- 'Jenny' CBnk COlW CSBt EBee ECtt EPfP GKev GMaP LBMP LRHS MBri MRav MWat NBir NGdn SHBN SPer SPoG SRGP SRms STes WBrk WEas WFar WMnd WOld
- 'Jollity' CBnk WOld
- 'Judith' CBnk
- 'Julia' CBnk WOld
- 'Karminkuppel' CBnk NBre WOld
- 'Kassel' CBnk SRms WOld
- 'King of the Belgians' CBnk WOld
- 'King's College' CBnk WOld

§ - 'Kristina' CBnk COlW CWan EBee ECha MBri MRav SPet SPoG WCot WOld
- 'Lady Evelyn Drummond' WOld
- 'Lady Frances' CBnk SRms WOld
- 'Lady in Blue' Widely available
- 'Lady Paget' CBnk WOld
- 'Lassie' CBnk CElw LLWP MWat SBri WCot WOld
- 'Lavender Dream' CBnk WOld
- 'Lawrence Chiswell' CBnk WOld
- 'Lilac Time' CBnk WOld
- 'Lisa Dawn' CBnk WOld
- 'Little Boy Blue' CAby CBnk NBre SHBN SRms WOld
- 'Little Man in Blue' CBnk WOld
- 'Little Pink Beauty' CBnk CEnt COlW CPrp EBee ECtt ELan LHop LRHS MBNS MRav NBid NGdn NVic SPer SRGP SRms STes WFar WOld
- 'Little Pink Lady' CBnk SRms WOld
- 'Little Pink Pyramid' CBnk SRms
- 'Little Red Boy' CBnk WOld
- 'Little Treasure' CBnk WOld
- 'Lucy' CBnk WOld
- 'Madge Cato' CBnk MAvo WOld
- 'Malvern Queen' CBnk
- 'Mammoth' CBnk WOld
- 'Margaret Rose' CBnk WOld
- 'Margery Bennett' CBnk GBri WOld
- 'Marie Ballard' CBnk COlW CSBt EBee EPfP GKir GMaP MBri MHer MRav MWat MWhi NCGa NGdn NOrc NPer SHBN SMrm SPer SPoG SRGP SRms SWat WBrk WCAu WOld WPer
- 'Marie's Pretty Please' CBnk WOld
- 'Marjorie' CBnk SPoG WOld
- 'Marjory Ballard' CBnk WOld

* - 'Mark Ballard' NBre
- 'Martonie' WOld WPer
- 'Mary' CBnk
- 'Mary Ann Neil' CBnk WOld
- 'Mary Deane' CBnk MSte WOld WPer
- 'Mauve Magic' CBnk SRms WOld
- 'Melbourne Belle' CBnk WOld
- 'Melbourne Magnet' CBnk WOld
- 'Michael Watts' CBnk WOld
- 'Midget' CBnk
- 'Mistress Quickly' CBnk GBri MCot SMrs WOld
- 'Mount Everest' CAby CBnk SPhx WOld WPer
- 'Mrs J. Sangster' **new** CBnk
- 'Mrs Leo Hunter' CBnk WOld
- 'Nesthäkchen' CBnk WOld
- 'Newton's Pink' CBnk
- 'Niobe' CBnk
- 'Nobilis' WOld
- 'Norman's Jubilee' CBnk EBee NBir WOld
- 'Nursteed Charm' CBnk WOld
- 'October Dawn' **new** CBnk
- 'Oktoberschneekuppel' EBee LRHS WOld
- 'Orlando' CBnk WOld
- 'Pamela' CBnk WOld
- 'Patricia Ballard' CBcs CBnk CElw CPrp CSBt EBrs GCra GMaP MBri MWat NLar NPer SMrs SPer SPoG SRGP WCAu WFar WOld WPer
- 'Peace' CBnk WOld
- 'Percy Thrower' CBnk WOld
- 'Peter Chiswell' CBnk SRms WOld
- 'Peter Harrison' CBnk GMaP GMac NBir WMnd WOld WPer
- 'Peter Pan' CBnk CStu EBee WOld
- 'Picture' CBnk NBre WOld
- 'Pink Gown' WOld

| | | |
|---|---|---|
| | - 'Pink Lace' | CBnk MBNS MLLN WOld WPer |
| | - 'Pink Pyramid' | WOld |
| | - 'Plenty' | CBnk MBri WOld |
| | - 'Porzellan' | CAby CBnk CElw CMMP COIW EBee ECtt EGoo MAvo MBNS NGdn SMrs SRGP WCot |
| | - 'Pride of Colwall' | CBnk WBrk |
| | - 'Princess Marie Louise' **new** | CBnk |
| | - 'Priory Blush' | CBnk SPhx WOld |
| | - 'Professor Anton Kippenberg' | CBnk CEnt CWan EBee EPfP GKir GMaP LLWP LRHS MBri MHer MRav NBre SPer SRGP WMnd WOld |
| | - 'Prosperity' | CBnk NBre WOld |
| * | - 'Prunella' | CBnk WOld |
| | - 'Purple Dome' | CBnk COIW ECha LCro LEdu LSRN MCCP MHer NMoo SHar SPoG WOld WOut |
| | - 'Queen Mary' | CBnk WOld |
| | - 'Queen of Colwall' | CBnk WOld |
| | - 'Ralph Picton' | CBnk WOld |
| | - 'Raspberry Ripple' | CBnk ECot WOld |
| | - 'Rector' | see *A. novi-belgii* 'The Rector' |
| | - 'Red Robin' | MWat |
| | - 'Red Sunset' | CBnk SRms WOld |
| | - 'Rembrandt' | CBnk ECtt EWll LDai NGdn SMrs SRGP |
| | - 'Remembrance' | CBnk SRms WBrk WOld |
| | - 'Reverend Vincent Dale' | WOld |
| | - 'Richness' | CBnk MAvo SAga WOld |
| | - 'Robin Adair' | WOld |
| | - 'Roland Smith' | CBnk WOld |
| | - 'Rose Bonnet' | CBnk CSBt MWat SHBN SPlb |
| | - 'Rose Bouquet' | WOld |
| | - 'Roseanne' | CBnk |
| | - 'Rosebud' | CBnk WBrk WOld |
| | - 'Rosenwichtel' | CBnk MBri MMuc NLar WBrk WOld |
| | - 'Royal Blue' | CBnk |
| | - 'Royal Ruby' | CBnk EBee EBrs ECtt LIMB WOld |
| | - 'Royal Velvet' | WOld |
| | - 'Rozika' | CBnk WOld |
| | - 'Rufus' | CBnk WOld |
| | - 'Sailor Boy' | CBnk EBee WOld |
| | - 'Saint Egwyn' | CBnk WOld |
| | - 'Sam Banham' | CBnk WOld |
| | - 'Samoa' | CBnk |
| | - 'Sandford White Swan' | CBnk GBuc MHom WBrk WEas WPer |
| | - 'Sapphire' | SVil |
| | - 'Sarah Ballard' | CBnk MBri SRGP WOld |
| § | - 'Schneekissen' | CBnk CPrp CStu EBee ECtt EGoo EPfP GMaP MHer NPri SRGP STes SWvt WFar WOld |
| | - 'Schöne von Dietlikon' | CBnk CKno MAvo WOld |
| | - 'Schoolgirl' | CBnk WOld |
| | - 'Sheena' | CBnk SRGP WOld |
| | - 'Silberblaukissen' | CBnk GBin |
| § | - 'Silberteppich' | GMac |
| | - Silver Carpet | see *A. novi-belgii* 'Silberteppich' |
| | - 'Sir Edward Elgar' | CBnk |
| | - Snow Cushion | see *A. novi-belgii* 'Schneekissen' |
| | - 'Snowdrift' | CBnk WOld |
| | - 'Snowsprite' | CBcs CBnk CSBt ELan EPfP MWat NLar NOrc NPro SRGP SRms SWat WBrk WOld |
| | - 'Sonata' | GMaP WOld |
| | - 'Sophia' | CBnk WBrk WOld |
| | - 'Starlight' | CBnk EBee NMoo WFar WOld WRHF |
| | - 'Steinebrück' | CBnk WOld |
| | - 'Sterling Silver' | CBnk WOld |
| | - 'Sunset' | CBnk WOld |
| | - 'Susan' | CBnk WOld |
| | - 'Sweet Briar' | CBnk CElw WOld |
| | - 'Tapestry' | CBnk WOld |
| | - 'Terry's Pride' | CBnk WOld |
| | - 'The Archbishop' | CBnk ECtt WOld |
| | - 'The Bishop' | CBnk WOld |
| | - 'The Cardinal' | CBnk WOld |
| | - 'The Choristers' | CBnk WOld |
| | - 'The Dean' | CBnk WOld |
| § | - 'The Rector' | CBnk WOld |
| | - 'The Sexton' | CBnk WOld |
| | - 'Thundercloud' | CBnk WBrk WOld |
| | - 'Timsbury' | CBnk CWsd SRms WBrk WOld |
| | - 'Tony' | CBnk WOld |
| | - 'Tovarich' | CBnk WOld |
| | - 'Trudi Ann' | CBnk NBir WOld |
| | - 'Twinkle' | CBnk WOld |
| | - 'Victor' | CBnk WOld |
| | - 'Vignem' | NSti |
| | - 'Violet Lady' | CBnk WOld |
| | - 'Violetta' | LCro |
| | - 'Waterperry' | CBnk MWat |
| | - 'Weisses Wunder' | CBnk WOld WOut |
| | - 'White Ladies' | CAby CBcs CBnk ECtt GCra GMaP LLWP MWat NLar NOrc SPer SPoG SRGP |
| | - 'White Swan' | CAby ECtt EPPr SPhx WOld |
| | - 'White Wings' | CBnk WOld |
| | - 'Winston S. Churchill' | CBnk CMMP CMoH COIW CTri EBee ELan EPfP GMaP LRHS MCot MWat SHBN SPer SPlb SPoG SRGP WOld |
| | ***oblongifolius*** | GCal WOld WPer |
| § | - 'Fanny's' | CPrp EBee EBla ECtt MNFA SMrm SPet SPoG SRGP WCAu WCot WFar WOld |
| | 'Ochtendgloren' (*pringlei* hybrid) ♀H4 | CPrp CSam EBee ECtt EGle EMon EPPr EWes GBuc MAvo MNFA MNrw MSte NCGa SMrm WCAu WCot WFar WHal WOld WOut |
| | Octoberlight | see *A.* 'Oktoberlicht' |
| § | 'Oktoberlicht' | EMon SMrm WOld |
| | ***oolentangiensis*** | EBee |
| | 'Orchidee' | EBee ECtt EWes |
| | 'Orpheus' | EMon |
| | ***pappei*** | see *Felicia amoena* |
| | 'Pearl Star' | WOld |
| | ***petiolatus*** | see *Felicia petiolata* |
| | 'Photograph' ♀H4 | EBrs GMac MAvo MHom MSte SMrm SUsu WCot WFar WIvy WMnd WOld |
| § | ***pilosus*** var. ***demotus*** ♀H4 | ECha EWes MLLN MRav MSte WFar WOld WTin |
| § | - var. ***pringlei*** 'Monte Cassino' ♀H4 | CHid CSBt EBee EBla ECtt EPfP LHop LRHS MBNS MLLN MRav MWat NBPC NCGa SMrm SPav SPer SPhx SRGP WCAu WFar WMoo WOld |
| | - - 'October Glory' | CMdw WFar |
| | - - 'Phoebe' | WOld |
| | - - 'Pink Cushion' | CMHG WCot |
| | 'Pink Cassino' | WCAu |
| | 'Pink Star' | CAby CMea CMoH ECtt GMac MRav MWat NSti SBch SPhx WBrk WFar WHoo WOld WTin |
| | 'Pixie Dark Eye' (*ericoides* hybrid) | WCot |
| | 'Pixie Red Eye' (*ericoides* hybrid) | WCot |
| | 'Plowden's Pink' | WOld |
| | 'Prairie Lavender' | WOld |
| | 'Prairie Pink' | MSte WOld |
| | 'Prairie Violet' | WOld |

| | |
|---|---|
| ***prenanthoides*** from Pennsylvania, USA | EPPr |
| 'Primrose Path' | WCot |
| § ***ptarmicoides*** | CSam EBee EBla EMon LBMP MLLN NBre WOld WPer |
| - 'Mago' **new** | EBee |
| ***puniceus*** | NBre |
| ***purdomii*** | see *A. flaccidus* |
| ***pyrenaeus*** 'Lutetia' | CPrp CSam EBee ECha GBuc GCal GMaP MAvo MHom MNFA MSte NCGa NDov NLar SRGP WCAu WCot WFar WHil WOld |
| ***radula*** | EBee EMon EWes MAvo MNrw NBre NLar NSti WOld WSHC |
| 'Ringdove' (*ericoides* hybrid) ♀H4 | CKno CPrp EBee EBla ECGP ECtt EPfP GMac LRHS MCot MHom MNFA MNrw NDov NSti SMrs SRGP STes WCAu WCot WIvy WOld |
| 'Rosa Star' | WOld |
| ***rotundifolius*** 'Variegatus' | see *Felicia amelloides* variegated |
| ***rugulosus*** 'Asrugo' | EBee |
| x ***salignus*** | WOld |
| - Scottish form | WOld |
| § ***scaber*** | EBee EWsh WCot WPGP |
| ***scandens*** | see *A. carolinianus* |
| ***schreberi*** | EBee EPPr EWsh MAvo MHar MHom MLLN NBre NCGa WCot WOld |
| § ***sedifolius*** | CAby EBee ECtt ELan LPio LRHS MDKP MSte MWat NBid SDix SEND SPla WCot WFar WHil WMnd WOld WPer |
| - RCB AM -5 **new** | WCot |
| - 'Nanus' | CPLG CSam ELan GCal MLLN MNFA MRav MSte NBir NLar SPer WAbe WCot WFar WMnd WOld WOut WTin |
| - 'Snow Flurries' | see *A. ericoides* f. *prostratus* 'Snow Flurry' |
| § ***sibiricus*** | EShb NBre NLar |
| 'Snow Flurry' | see *A. ericoides* f. *prostratus* 'Snow Flurry' |
| 'Snow Star' | WOld |
| ***souliei*** | EBee EBrs |
| - B&SWJ 7655 | WCru |
| ***spectabilis*** | WOld |
| ***subcaeruleus*** | see *A. tongolensis* |
| 'Sunhelene' | CBgR EBee WCot |
| 'Sunqueen' | EBee WCot |
| ***tataricus*** | MSal |
| - 'Jindai' | EBee WFar |
| ***thomsonii*** | WFar WOld |
| - 'Nanus' | CAby CMdw CMoH ERas GGar GMaP MCot MSte MWea SAga SPhx WCot WOld WSHC |
| ***tibeticus*** | see *A. flaccidus* |
| Tonga = 'Dasfour' | CBnk |
| § ***tongolensis*** | SBHP SRms WFar WWFP |
| - 'Berggarten' | CHar EBee LDai MBri NMoo WAbe WFar |
| - 'Dunkleviolette' | GBuc NBro SRms |
| - 'Lavender Star' | GBuc |
| - 'Napsbury' | EBee MBri WPGP |
| - 'Wartburgstern' | CPrp EBee EPfP NGdn STes WCFE WFar WPer |
| ***tradescantii*** misapplied | see *A. pilosus* var. *demotus* |
| ***tradescantii*** L. | EBee ELan MBNS MRav NBre NHol NSti SMad WBrk WCot WOld WTin |
| ***trinervius*** subsp. ***ageratoides*** | CPou WFar WOld |
| - - 'Asran' | CWan EBee ECtt EMon EWes LSou SHGN SSvw WFar WOld |
| - - 'Harry Smith' **new** | EBee |
| - - 'Stardust' | EBee MSte |
| - var. ***harae*** | MHar SSvw WOld |
| ***tripolium*** | EBWF WHer |
| 'Triumph' | EBee WCot |
| ***turbinellus*** misapplied ♀H4 | CAby CKno CWsd EBee EMon EPfP GBuc MSte SDix SMHy SPhx SUsu WCot WFar WHoo WOld WPtf WTin |
| ***turbinellus*** Lindl. | CSam EPPr EPfP ERas WBrk |
| - hybrid | CWsd WFar |
| ***umbellatus*** | CBre CWsd EBee EMon GBin GQue MNFA NBre NCGa NDov NLar NSti SMrm SRms WCot WOld WPrP WTin |
| 'Vasterival' | EBee NDov SMHy SUsu |
| * ***verticallis*** | EMon |
| ***vimineus*** Lam. | see *A. lateriflorus* |
| - 'Ptarmicoides' | see *A. ptarmicoides* |
| § 'White Climax' | EBee MHom MSte WBrk WCot |
| 'Wood's Pink' | EBee |
| ***yunnanensis*** | WSHC |
| 'Yvonne' | CBre |

## *Asteranthera* (*Gesneriaceae*)

| | |
|---|---|
| ***ovata*** | CGHE EBee GGGa GGar LSou MAsh SKHP SPoG WAbe WBod WPGP |

## *Asteriscus* (*Asteraceae*)

| | |
|---|---|
| 'Gold Coin' | see *Pallenis maritima* |
| ***maritimus*** | see *Pallenis maritima* |
| ***spinosus*** | CSec |

## *Asteromoea* (*Asteraceae*)

| | |
|---|---|
| ***mongolica*** | see *Kalimeris mongolica* |
| ***pinnatifida*** | see *Kalimeris pinnatifida* |

## *Asteropyrum* (*Ranunculaceae*)

| | |
|---|---|
| ***cavaleriei*** | EBee GEdr WCru |

## *Asterotrichion* (*Malvaceae*)

| | |
|---|---|
| ***discolor*** | ECou GGar |

## *Astilbe* ✿ (*Saxifragaceae*)

| | |
|---|---|
| CC 5201 **new** | CPLG |
| 'Alive and Kicking' | MBri |
| 'Amerika' (x *arendsii*) | CMHG CSBt ECtt GBri |
| 'Amethyst' (x *arendsii*) | CMHG EMFW LRHS MRav NBir NBlu NBre SApp SPer SPoG SRGP WCAu WFar WHoo WMoo |
| 'Angel Wings' | NPro |
| 'Anita Pfeifer' (x *arendsii*) | CMHG EBrs GBin GKir LPBA LRHS WFar WPnP |
| 'Aphrodite' (*simplicifolia* hybrid) | CBcs CWCL GCal GKir LAst MDKP MLHP NBre NGdn NHol NPro WBrE WGor |
| x ***arendsii*** | IFoB NBre WMoo WPer |
| ***astilboides*** | CMHG NHol SWvt |
| 'Atrorosea' (*simplicifolia* hybrid) | NCot SRms |
| 'Avalanche' | CSBt GAbr GBin GKir NHol WMnd |
| Bella Group (x *arendsii*) | NBre SPet WMnd |
| 'Bergkristall' (x *arendsii*) | CMHG |
| 'Betsy Cuperus' (*thunbergii* hybrid) | CMHG EBee GBin LRHS MRav MSte NBre SApp SRGP WCAu |
| ***biternata*** | EBee EMon |
| 'Bonn' (*japonica* hybrid) | CWCL CWat NBlu SCoo SRms |
| § 'Brautschleier' (x *arendsii*) ♀H4 | CBgR CMHG CMMP CMac CPrp CTri EBrs ECtt EPfP GCra LAst LSRN NGdn NLar NPri SRGP WPnP WPtf |
| 'Bremen' (*japonica* hybrid) | CMHG CMMP EBrs GBin LPBA NHol |

| | | |
|---|---|---|
| | 'Bressingham Beauty' (x *arendsii*) | CMHG CPrp CSam CWCL EBrs ECtt ELan EMFW EPfP EPla GKir GMaP LCro LPBA LRHS MCot MRav NGdn NHol NPro SPer SPoG SWvt WFar WMoo |
| | Bridal Veil (x *arendsii*) | see *A.* 'Brautschleier' |
| § | 'Bronce Elegans' (*simplicifolia* hybrid) ΨH4 | CMHG EBee ECha EPfP GBin GBuc GKir GMaP LAst LRHS MRav NHol NOrc NPro SPoG WCAu WFar WMoo |
| | 'Broncelaub' (x *arendsii*) | GBin GKir |
| | 'Bronze Sprite' (*simplicifolia* hybrid) | WFar |
| * | ***bumalda*** 'Bronze Pygmy' | EBee NHol STes |
| | 'Bumalda' (x *arendsii*) | CBcs CFir CSBt CWCL GMaP LLWG LRHS NChi NDlv NGdn NMyG NOrc NPro SPlb WFar WMoo |
| | 'Burgunderrot' (x *arendsii*) | CWCL GAbr MBri MNrw WBor |
| | 'Carnea' (*simplicifolia* hybrid) | CMHG |
| | 'Catherine Deneuve' | see *A.* 'Federsee' |
| | 'Cattleya' (x *arendsii*) | CMHG CSam EBrs GBri NBPC NLar NMoo WFar WMoo |
| | 'Cattleya Dunkel' (x *arendsii*) | CMHG WFar |
| | 'Ceres' (x *arendsii*) | CMHG NHol |
| | 'Cherry Ripe' | see *A.* 'Feuer' |
| | ***chinensis*** | CMHG ECho IBlr LRHS NBre WFar WSHC |
| | - B&SWJ 8178 | WCru |
| | - from Russia | GCal |
| | - 'Brokat' | GBin |
| | - 'Christian' | GBin |
| | - var. ***davidii*** | CMHG |
| | - - B&SWJ 8583 | WCru |
| | - - B&SWJ 8645 | WCru |
| | - 'Diamonds and Pearls' **new** | MWea |
| | - 'Finale' | CHar COIW EMFW NCGa NHol NPro SPer WFar |
| | - 'Frankentroll' | CMHG |
| | - 'Intermezzo' | GCal GMaP |
| | - 'Milk and Honey' **new** | MBNS |
| § | - var. ***pumila*** ΨH4 | Widely available |
| | - - 'Serenade' | CMac LRHS MBri NGdn WFar |
| | - 'Purple Glory' | CMHG GKir |
| | - 'Spätsommer' | CMHG |
| | - var. ***taquetii*** | CMac EBee NBre NSti SRms |
| | - - Purple Lance | see *A. chinensis* var. *taquetii* 'Purpurlanze' |
| § | - - 'Purpurlanze' | Widely available |
| § | - - 'Superba' ΨH4 | CMHG CMac CRow CTri ECha EPfP GGar MCCP MCot MLHP MLLN MSte NBro NGdn NHol SDix SPer SPoG SRms STes WEas WFar WMoo WPGP |
| | - 'Troll' | GBin |
| | - 'Veronika Klose' | CMHG EBee GBin GKir NLar NPro WCAu |
| | - 'Vision in Pink'[PBR] | CWCL MBNS NBhm |
| | - 'Vision in Red'[PBR] | CBgR CWCL CWat GBin GGar MBNS MBri MNrw MSCN NBhm NLar NMyG WBor WFar |
| | - 'Visions' | CMHG CMac CWCL EBee EBrs GBin GQue LRHS MBNS MBri MSte NBro NGdn NMyG NPro STes WFar |
| | Cologne | see *A.* 'Köln' |
| | 'Colorflash' **new** | LPBA |
| | 'Crimson Feather' | see *A.* 'Gloria Purpurea' |
| | x ***crispa*** | ECho IBlr WFar |
| | - 'Gnom' | EMFW NHar |
| | - 'Lilliput' | CBcs GBin GBri GEdr GGar GKir LRHS NDlv NHar NLar NPro NRya |
| § | - 'Perkeo' ΨH4 | CBcs ECho ELan EPfP GEdr GGar GKir GMaP LHop LRHS MSte NBir NHar NLar NMen NPri NPro NSla SRms WAul WBVN WFar WMoo |
| | - 'Peter Pan' | see *A.* x *crispa* 'Perkeo' |
| | - 'Snow Queen' | LRHS NBir NHar NMen NPro WFar |
| | 'Darwin's Dream' | NLar NPri WFar |
| | 'Darwin's Favourite' (x *arendsii*) | CWCL |
| | 'Deutschland' (*japonica* hybrid) | Widely available |
| § | 'Diamant' (x *arendsii*) | CMHG EBrs EShb GAbr LRHS NGdn NHol WFar |
| | Diamond (x *arendsii*) | see *A.* 'Diamant' |
| | 'Drayton Glory' (x *arendsii*) | see *A.* x *rosea* 'Peach Blossom' |
| | 'Dunkelachs' (simplicifolia hybrid) | CBgR NMyG WAbe WFar |
| | 'Dusseldorf' (*japonica* hybrid) | CMHG CSam CWCL EBrs GKir LLWG NHol |
| | 'Eden's Odysseus' | EBee GBin NHol |
| | 'Elegans' (*simplicifolia* hybrid) | CMHG GKir WFar |
| | Elizabeth Bloom = 'Eliblo'[PBR] (x *arendsii*) | EBee EBrs EPla GKir LLWG LRHS MRav NHol WFar |
| | 'Elizabeth' (*japonica* hybrid) | CMHG EBee |
| | 'Ellie' (x *arendsii*) | CMHG CWCL GBin LSRN MBNS MBri NBPC NBhm NGdn NHol WBor WPtf |
| | 'Else Schluck' (x *arendsii*) | ECha |
| | 'Erica' (x *arendsii*) | CMHG CTri EWll GKir LRHS MBri MRav NPro WFar WMnd WMoo |
| | 'Etna' (*japonica* hybrid) | CBcs CMHG CSam EBee GBri LLWG LRHS NGdn NHol NLar NPro SRms WPnP |
| | 'Europa' (*japonica* hybrid) | CMHG CMac CSBt ECtt EMFW GBin GKir LHop MRav SPla SPoG WFar WMoo |
| | 'Fanal' (x *arendsii*) ΨH4 | Widely available |
| | 'Fata Morgana' (x *arendsii* hybrid) | CMHG |
| § | 'Federsee' (x *arendsii*) | CBcs CDWL CMHG EBrs ECha ELan EMil EPyc GKir LLWG LRHS MBNS NBPC NBre NBro NGdn NPro SPer WFar |
| § | 'Feuer' (x *arendsii*) | CMCo CMHG CMMP CMac CPrp ELan EPfP GBuc GKir LBMP LLWG LRHS NGdn NHol NOrc NPro NVic WBor WMoo |
| | Fire | see *A.* 'Feuer' |
| | 'Flamingo'[PBR] (x *arendsii*) | GBin MAvo MBNS NCGa |
| | 'Gertrud Brix' (x *arendsii*) | CBcs CWat GKir NBir NGdn NPro SPla |
| § | ***glaberrima*** | NBid NHol NMen |
| § | - var. ***saxatilis*** ΨH4 | CLyd CRow EBee EPfP GBin GGar IFro LSou NHar NSla SPla WAbe WHal WThu |
| | - ***saxosa*** | see *A. glaberrima* var. *saxatilis* |
| | - - ***minor*** | see *A. glaberrima* var. *saxatilis* |
| * | ***glaberrima*** x 'Saxosa' | NHar |
| | 'Gladstone' (x *arendsii*) | see *A.* 'W.E. Gladstone' |
| | 'Gloria' (x *arendsii*) | CMHG CMac CTri EBrs LPBA MRav WFar |
| § | 'Gloria Purpurea' (x *arendsii*) | CDWL CMHG GKir LRHS NHol NMoo NMyG SRGP WMoo |
| | Glow (x *arendsii*) | see *A.* 'Glut' |
| § | 'Glut' (x *arendsii*) | CMHG CWCL EBrs ECtt GBin GKir GQue LRHS MAvo NGdn NHol NMyG SRms WFar |
| | 'Granat' (x *arendsii*) | CMHG CMMP CMac EMFW LLWG NBir NBre NHol NPro WMoo |
| * | Grande Group (x *arendsii*) | NBre |
| | ***grandis*** | CMHG WHer |

| | | |
|---|---|---|
| | 'Grete Püngel' (x *arendsii*) | ECha GBin GBri GKir MLLN WFar |
| | 'Harmony' (x *arendsii*) | CMHG |
| | 'Heart and Soul' PBR | EPfP MBri MWea |
| | 'Hennie Graafland' (*simplicifolia* hybrid) | CBcs CChe CMHG CWCL EBrs EMil GBin GKir NLar |
| | 'Holden Clough' (*japonica* hybrid) | NHol |
| | Hyacinth (x *arendsii*) | see *A.* 'Hyazinth' |
| § | 'Hyazinth' (x *arendsii*) | CMHG CPLG CPrp EBrs EMFW GMaP LBMP LLWG LRHS LSou NGdn NHol NPro SPoG WFar |
| | 'Inshriach Pink' (*simplicifolia* hybrid) | CBcs CCVN CMHG CPrp EHoe ELan EMFW GBin GKir MBri NBir NHar NHol SAga SBch SHGN WFar WHal |
| | 'Irrlicht' (x *arendsii*) | CMHG CSBt EBrs ELan EMFW EPfP EPla EShb GGar GKir LHop LLWG LPBA MCot MGos NHol SPer SWat WAul WPnP |
| | ***japonica*** | CPLG |
| * | - 'Pumila' | NBir NGdn |
| | - var. ***terrestris*** | see *A. glaberrima* |
| | 'Jo Ophorst' (*davidii* hybrid) | CMHG GBin GBuc LRHS MRav NGdn NHol NLar NPro SPer WFar |
| | 'Jump and Jive' PBR | GGar NCGa |
| | 'Koblenz' (*japonica* hybrid) | CMHG CWCL MDKP NMyG |
| § | 'Köln' (*japonica* hybrid) | CMHG CWat GBin LPBA NMyG WFar |
| | ***koreana*** | GGar WCot WPGP |
| | - B&SWJ 8611 | WCru |
| | - B&SWJ 8680 | WCru |
| | 'Kriemhilde' | CMHG MSCN |
| | 'Kvële' (x *arendsii*) | CMHG GKir WFar WMoo |
| § | 'Lachskönigin' (x *arendsii*) | CMHG GKir |
| | 'Lilli Goos' (x *arendsii*) | CMHG GBin |
| | 'Lollipop' | GBin MBNS MBri NBhm NPro |
| | ***longicarpa*** B&SWJ 6711 | WCru |
| | ***macroflora*** | GCal |
| | 'Maggie Daley' | CHFP CMMP EBee LAst MBri NBro NPro WMoo |
| | 'Mainz' (*japonica* hybrid) | CMHG ELan LPBA |
| | 'Mars' (x *arendsii*) | CMHG |
| | ***microphylla*** | CMHG NHol |
| | - B&SWJ 11085 **new** | WCru |
| | - pink-flowered | CMHG NHol |
| | 'Moerheim Glory' (x *arendsii*) | CMMP GBin LAst MSCN NBre NGdn |
| | 'Moerheimii' (*thunbergii* hybrid) | CMHG GKir |
| | 'Mont Blanc' (x *arendsii*) | CMHG |
| | 'Montgomery' (*japonica* hybrid) | CMHG CWCL EBrs GAbr GBin GKir LLWG LRHS LSRN MAvo MBNS MBri MCot MRav MWat NBro NGdn NHol SPad WBVN WFar |
| | 'Obergärtner Jürgens' (x *arendsii*) | CMMP GBin |
| | Ostrich Plume | see *A.* 'Straussenfeder' |
| | 'Paul Gaärder' (x *arendsii*) | CMHG |
| | 'Peaches and Cream' | EBee GKir LRHS MMHG MRav NBro NLar WPnP |
| | 'Peter Barrow' (*glaberrima* hybrid) | GBin SRms |
| | 'Pink Lightening' PBR (*simplicifolia* hybrid) | CBow CWCL EBee EShb MAvo MBNS NBPC NBhm NLar NOrc SMrm WBor |
| | Pink Pearl (x *arendsii*) | see *A.* 'Rosa Perle' |
| | 'Poschka' | CFir NPro |
| I | 'Poschka Alba' | CFir NMyG NPro |
| | 'Professor van der Wielen' (*thunbergii* hybrid) | CMHG CMil EBee EMon GGar GKir LAst MSte MWte NHol SDix SPer SRms WCAu WFar |
| | ***pumila*** | see *A. chinensis* var. *pumila* |
| * | 'Queen' | LPBA |
| | 'Radius' | CBgR CMMP EBee GBin LPBA NGdn WPnP |
| | Red Light (x *arendsii*) | see *A.* 'Rotlicht' |
| | 'Red Sentinel' (*japonica* hybrid) | CBcs CMMP CWCL CWat EBrs EMFW GBin GMaP LAst LLWG NBro NCGa NGdn NHol NPro SMrm SPoG WBor WFar |
| | 'Rheinland' (*japonica* hybrid) 🏆H4 | CBcs CMHG CMMP CWCL CWat EPfP LLWG LPBA MAvo NPri SRot STes WCAu WEas WFar WHoo WPnP |
| | ***rivularis*** | CMHG EBee GBin WCot |
| | - GWJ 9366 | WCru |
| | - var. ***myriantha*** | NBre |
| | - - BWJ 8076a | WCru |
| | 'Rock and Roll' PBR **new** | LPBA |
| § | 'Rosa Perle' (x *arendsii*) | CMHG CSam NHol |
| | 'Rose of Cimarron' **new** | NPro |
| § | x ***rosea*** 'Peach Blossom' | CBcs CBgR CMHG CMMP CMoH EBrs GBuc GKir LPBA NBir NHol NPro SPoG WFar WHoo WMoo |
| | - 'Queen Alexandra' | WFar |
| | 'Rosea' (*simplicifolia* hybrid) | EBrs NHol WFar |
| | Rosemary Bloom = 'Rosblo' | EBee NHol |
| | 'Rot Straussenfeder' (x *arendsii*) | GBin |
| § | 'Rotlicht' (x *arendsii*) | CMHG EBrs ECot GKir LLWG NHol NMyG NPro WFar WGor |
| | Salmon Queen (x *arendsii*) | see *A.* 'Lachskönigin' |
| | 'Salmonea' (*simplicifolia* hybrid) | CMHG |
| | 'Saxosa' | see *A. glaberrima* var. *saxatilis* |
| | Showstar Group (x *arendsii*) | NBre SEND SPoG |
| | ***simplicifolia*** 🏆H4 | CRow WFar |
| | - 'Alba' | CMHG NPro |
| | - Bronze Elegance | see *A.* 'Bronce Elegans' |
| | - 'Darwin's Snow Sprite' | CMac GBin GQue MBri MSte NHol NLar NPri WFar |
| | - 'Jacqueline' | EBee NHol NLar WFar |
| * | - 'Nana Alba' | NPro |
| | - 'Praecox Alba' | CMCo EBee GBin |
| | - 'Sheila Haxton' | EBrs NHar |
| | 'Snowdrift' (x *arendsii*) | CMHG CWat EBrs EPla EWTr GKir GMaP LBMP LLWG MBNS MDKP MWat NBir NCGa NOrc NPro SPer SWat WFar |
| | 'Solferino' (x *arendsii*) | CMHG |
| | 'Spartan' (x *arendsii*) | see *A.* 'Rotlicht' |
| | 'Spinell' (x *arendsii*) | CWCL MDun NOrc WFar WPnP |
| | 'Sprite' (*simplicifolia* hybrid) 🏆H4 | Widely available |
| | 'Stand and Deliver' | MBri |
| § | 'Straussenfeder' (*thunbergii* hybrid) 🏆H4 | CBcs CDWL CMHG CTri EBrs EPfP EPla GKir GMaP LAst LBMP LHop LRHS NBid NBir NBro NHol NOrc SPer SPla SPoG WAul WCAu WFar WMoo WPnP WPtf |
| | 'Sugar Plum' (*simplicifolia* hybrid) | EBee LAst NGdn |
| | 'Superba' | see *A. chinensis* var. *taquetii* 'Superba' |
| | ***thunbergii*** | CEnt CPLG |
| | - var. ***hachijoensis*** | EBee |
| | - - B&SWJ 5622 | WCru |
| | - var. ***terrestris*** B&SWJ 6125 | WCru |
| | 'Venus' (x *arendsii*) | CDWL CHar CSam ECha ECtt EMFW GGar GMaP LPBA MCot MSte NHol NOrc NVic SPer SWat WFar WMoo |
| | 'Vesuvius' (*japonica* hybrid) | CBcs CDWL MDKP NBlu NBro |

| | | |
|---|---|---|
| § | 'W.E. Gladstone' (*japonica* hybrid) | CWat MSte NBlu NHol NPro WAbe WGor |
| | 'Walküre' (x *arendsii*) | CMHG |
| | 'Walter Bitner' | GBin LLWG LRHS MBNS NHol SRGP |
| | 'Washington' (*japonica* hybrid) | CBcs EBee LAst MDKP NGdn |
| § | 'Weisse Gloria' (x *arendsii*) | CMHG CMac CTca EBrs ECha GBuc GKir LPBA NBPC NBro NHol NMyG NOrc SCoo SPad SRGP WBor WMoo WTin |
| | 'Weisse Perle' (x *arendsii*) | GKir |
| | White Gloria (x *arendsii*) | see *A.* 'Weisse Gloria' |
| | 'White Queen' (x *arendsii*) | NHol |
| | 'White Wings'PBR (*simplicifolia* hybrid) | NLar |
| | 'William Reeves' (x *arendsii*) | CMHG NHol |
| | 'Willie Buchanan' (*simplicifolia* hybrid) | CBcs CDWL CMHG CPrp EHoe GKev GKir GMaP LBMP LRHS MBar NHar NHol NMen SApp SIng SPer SPla SRms WAbe WFar WMoo |
| | 'Zuster Theresa' (x *arendsii*) | CBgR CMHG EBee EBrs GKir LPBA MBNS MSCN NBPC NBro SMrm WFar |

## *Astilboides* (*Saxifragaceae*)

| | | |
|---|---|---|
| § | ***tabularis*** | Widely available |

## *Astragalus* (*Papilionaceae*)

| | | |
|---|---|---|
| | ***canadensis*** | GKir SPhx |
| | ***candelarius*** | SPhx |
| | ***glycyphyllos*** | CArn LLHF |
| | ***membranaceus*** | CArn ELau MSal |
| | - var. ***mongholicus*** | MSal |
| | ***sempervirens*** **new** | LLHF |

## *Astrantia* ✿ (*Apiaceae*)

| | | |
|---|---|---|
| | ***bavarica*** | CCge EBee GCal MDKP WFar |
| | 'Bloody Mary' | EBee GBin IBal NBPC NGdn NLar NSti SHBN SPer |
| | 'Buckland' | Widely available |
| | ***carniolica*** | EMon EPyc |
| | - ***major*** | see *A. major* |
| | - var. ***rubra*** | see *A. carniolica* 'Rubra' |
| § | - 'Rubra' | CBcs EBee GKev MMuc MNFA NBre WHal WSHC |
| | - 'Variegata' | see *A. major* 'Sunningdale Variegated' |
| | 'Dark Shiny Eyes' | CBct EBee LCro MBNS NBhm NCGa NGdn NLar |
| | 'Hadspen Blood' | Widely available |
| | Harptree hybrid | CHar |
| | 'Helen' | NLar |
| | ***helleborifolia*** misapplied | see *A. maxima* |
| | 'Madeleine' | EBee NBhm WCra |
| | 'Magnum Blush' | NBhm SPoG |
| § | ***major*** | Widely available |
| | - 'Abbey Road'PBR | CBct CDWL EBee EBla ECGP EWTr LHop LSou MAvo MGos NBPC NLar NPro SMrm SPoG STes WAul |
| * | - ***alba*** | CBcs CMHG CPrp CWCL EBee EBla ECha EGle EHrv EMon GMac IBal LCro MCot MNFA MSte NBir NGdn NPer WMnd WMoo |
| | - 'Ann Cann' | CBct |
| | - 'Berendien Stam' | CCge EBee EMon MAvo |
| | - subsp. ***biebersteinii*** | CCge EBee EBla EMon NBir NBre |
| | - 'Bo-Ann' | CWCL EBla IBal MAvo MBri NCob NLar SHBN WAul |
| | - 'Celtic Star' | EBee EBla GBuc LHop NCob NGdn SPla WCAu |
| | - 'Claret' | Widely available |
| | - 'Côte d'Azur' | CBct |
| | - 'Cottage Herbery' **new** | WCHb |
| | - 'Cyril James' | CBct |
| | - 'Dulcie Scott' | WOut |
| | - dwarf | WFar |
| | - 'Gill Richardson' | Widely available |
| | - 'Gracilis' **new** | EBee |
| | - 'Greenfingers' | EWes |
| | - 'Gwaun Valley' | WFar |
| | - 'Hillview Red' | CCge CElw |
| | - subsp. ***involucrata*** | EBee EBla EHrv LRHS SWat WFar |
| | - - 'Barrister' | CHFP CSam EMon GBuc NLar WFar WPGP |
| | - - 'Canneman' | CBct EBee EBla EMon EWes LPla SMHy SMeo SPhx SUsu WCAu WCot WFar |
| | - - 'Jumble Hole' | NDov |
| | - - 'Margery Fish' | see *A. major* subsp. *involucrata* 'Shaggy' |
| | - - 'Moira Reid' | Widely available |
| | - - 'Orlando' | CHFP EBee EMon |
| § | - - 'Shaggy' ♀H4 | Widely available |
| | - 'Jade Lady' | WFar |
| | - 'Jitse' **new** | EBee NCot |
| | - 'Lars' | Widely available |
| | - 'Little Snowstar' | EHrv IBal |
| | - 'Lola' **new** | EBee NCGa NCot WCra |
| | - 'Major Gardner' **new** | WOut |
| | - 'Montelolor' | WFar |
| | - 'Paper Moon' | WFar |
| | - 'Pink Pride' **new** | EBee |
| | - 'Primadonna' | CBct CCge EBee EBla EHrv EWsh MNFA NHol NLar SPlb WFar WPer |
| | - 'Reverse Sunningdale Variegated' **new** | MAvo |
| | - 'Roma'PBR | Widely available |
| | - 'Rosa Lee' | CWCL EBee IBal NCob NLar WAul |
| | - var. ***rosea*** | CBre CHFP COIW CPrp EBee EBla EHrv EPfP GBBs IBal LCro LHop LRHS LSRN MCot MRav MWat MWhi NDlv NGdn SMrm SPer SPla WCAu WFar WMoo |
| | - - George's form | CBct CKno CSam EAEE EBee EBla EWTr IPot LAst LLWG LSRN MBNS NBsh NCGa NCob NHol |
| | - 'Rosensinfonie' | EBee EBla GMaP MAvo NBro NGdn NPro WFar WMnd |
| § | - 'Rubra' | Widely available |
| | - 'Ruby Cloud' | CCge CHid EBee EBla EHrv IBal MCot MNrw MRav NBro NGdn NLar NSti SRot WFar WFoF WHlf WMnd WPnP |
| | - 'Ruby Wedding' | Widely available |
| | - 'Silver Glow' | EBee IBal NBPC NGdn NLar NMyG SHBN SPer SRot WFar |
| | - 'Star of Summer' **new** | EBee |
| | - 'Starburst' | WFar |
| | - 'Sue Barnes' (v) | EMon GCal |
| § | - 'Sunningdale Variegated' (v) ♀H4 | Widely available |
| | - 'Temptation Star' | NLar |
| | - 'Titoki Point' | MAvo WCot |
| | - 'Variegata' | see *A. major* 'Sunningdale Variegated' |
| § | ***maxima*** ♀H4 | Widely available |
| | - 'Mark Fenwick' | NBir |
| * | - ***rosea*** | EBla ECtt MCot MDKP MWhi NBir NGdn SAga |
| | ***minor*** | CPrp EBee WCru WFar |
| | 'Moulin Rouge' | Widely available |
| | 'Queen's Children' | EBee NBhm |
| | 'Rainbow' | NLar |
| | ***rubra*** | see *A. major* 'Rubra' |
| | 'Snow Star'PBR | CWCL CWib EBee EHrv GBin IPot LCro MBri SMrm |

| | | |
|---|---|---|
| | 'Venice' **new** | NBhm |
| | 'Warren Hills' | EBee EBla |

## *Astrodaucus* (*Apiaceae*)

| | | |
|---|---|---|
| | ***orientalis*** | SPhx |

## *Asyneuma* (*Campanulaceae*)

| | | |
|---|---|---|
| | ***canescens*** | CDMG CEnt LSou NBre SGar SWal |
| | ***pulvinatum*** | CPBP EPot SIng WAbe |

## *Asystasia* (*Acanthaceae*)

| | | |
|---|---|---|
| | ***bella*** | see *Mackaya bella* |
| § | ***gangetica*** | CSev EShb |
| | ***violacea*** | see *A. gangetica* |

## *Athamanta* (*Apiaceae*)

| | | |
|---|---|---|
| | ***turbith*** subsp. ***haynaldii*** | EBee |

## *Athanasia* (*Asteraceae*)

| | | |
|---|---|---|
| § | ***parviflora*** | SPlb |

## *Atherosperma* (*Monimiaceae*)

| | | |
|---|---|---|
| | ***moschatum*** | CBcs CHII SKHP WSHC |

## *Athrotaxis* (*Cupressaceae*)

| | | |
|---|---|---|
| | ***cupressoides*** | CDoC CDul CKen GKir MBar WThu |
| | ***laxifolia*** | CDoC CKen EMil GKir MBar WThu |
| | ***selaginoides*** | CDoC CDul CTrG |

## *Athyrium* ✿ (*Woodsiaceae*)

| | | |
|---|---|---|
| | 'Branford Beauty' | CCCN CDes CLAP EBee LRHS NLar WRic |
| | 'Branford Rambler' | CLAP WRic |
| | ***filix-femina*** ♀H4 | Widely available |
| | - var. ***angustum*** 'Lady in Red' | CCCN CDes CElw CLAP EBee EMil LLHF MAvo MBri MGos NBid NLar SPad WMoo WRic |
| | - 'Corymbiferum' | GQui SRms |
| | - 'Crispum Grandiceps Kaye' | SRms |
| | - Cristatum Group | CLAP EBee EFer ELan EMon MMoz SWat WAbe WFib |
| § | - Cruciatum Group | CBgR CFwr CLAP EBee ELan EMon MMoz NHol SPer SRms WCot WFib WMoo WRic |
| | - 'Fieldii' | CLAP SRms |
| | - 'Frizelliae' ♀H4 | Widely available |
| | - 'Frizelliae Capitatum' | CLAP WFib WPGP |
| | - 'Frizelliae Cristatum' | SRms |
| | - 'Grandiceps' | CLAP EBee SRms |
| | - 'Minutissimum' | CBgR CDes CGHE CLAP EBee ECha ELan EMon MMoz WPGP |
| * | - 'Nudicaule' | SRms |
| | - 'Percristatum' | EMon |
| | - Plumosum Group | CLAP CWsd GBri GQui WAbe WFib |
| * | - - 'Plumosum Aureum' | NBhm |
| | - - 'Plumosum Axminster' | CLAP CMil EFer EWsh |
| | - - 'Plumosum Cristatum' | CLAP |
| | - - 'Plumosum Divaricatum' | SRms |
| | - - 'Plumosum Druery' | CLAP CWsd |
| | - Red Stem | see *A. filix-femina* 'Rotstiel' |
| § | - 'Rotstiel' | CFwr CLAP EBee MMoz WFar WMoo WPnP WRic |
| | - 'Vernoniae' ♀H4 | CLAP CWCL EBee ELan EMon EWsh LPBA MAsh NHol NLar WRic |
| | - 'Vernoniae Cristatum' | CLAP NHol WFib |
| | - 'Victoriae' | CCCN CDes CFwr CPrp CWCL EBee EWTr GEdr GMaP LPBA MAsh NBPC NBid NHol NLar STes |
| | - Victoriae Group | see *A. filix-femina* Cruciatum Group |
| | 'Ghost' | CCCN CDes CLAP EBee LRHS MAvo MGos NLar WPat WRic |
| | ***goeringianum*** 'Pictum' | see *A. niponicum* var. *pictum* |
| | ***grammitoides*** var. ***oldhamii*** **new** | EBee |
| | ***mackinnoniorum*** **new** | CFwr |
| | ***niponicum*** | WHal |
| | - f. ***metallicum*** | see *A. niponicum* var. *pictum* |
| § | - var. ***pictum*** ♀H3 | Widely available |
| | - - 'Apple Court' | CCCN EBee NLar WRic |
| | - - 'Burgundy Glow' | CBow |
| | - - 'Burgundy Lace' PBR | CBcs CLAP NPri SMrm STes WPtf |
| * | - - 'Cristatoflabellatum' | CLAP ELan EMon |
| | - - 'Red Beauty' | CFwr CLAP EBee ECha EFer EPfP GAbr GBin GCal MAvo NHol NLar SMad WCot WPnP |
| | - - 'Silver Falls' | CBcs CCVN CElw CHid CLAP CMil EBee EFer EShb MAvo NCob NMyG WCot WHal WPGP |
| | - - 'Soul Mate' | CLAP |
| | - - 'Ursula's Red' | CBcs CCVN CElw CEnd CFwr CLAP CTrC EShb GBin IBal LHop LSou MAvo MSte NBPN NBid NBir NMoo NMyG NPri SMrm SPad SPer WCot WFar WPGP WPat |
| | - - 'Wildwood Twist' | CLAP |
| | ***otophorum*** ♀H4 | EMon NBid NHol SRms WIvy WPGP WRic |
| | - var. ***okanum*** | Widely available |
| | ***vidalii*** | CFwr CLAP EBee MMoz NLar NMyG WFib WRic |

## *Atractylodes* (*Asteraceae*)

| | | |
|---|---|---|
| | ***japonica*** | EFEx |
| | ***macrocephala*** | CArn EFEx |

## *Atragene* see *Clematis*

## *Atriplex* (*Chenopodiaceae*)

| | | |
|---|---|---|
| | ***canescens*** | NLar WDin |
| | ***cinerea*** | ECou |
| | ***halimus*** | CArn CBcs CDul EBee ECha EHoe EPPr MBlu MBri MRav NLar SLon SPlb WCot WDin WHer WKif WPat WTin |
| | ***hortensis*** var. ***rubra*** | CArn CEnt CSec CSpe ELan LSou MHer MNHC MWte NDov NGHP SIde WCHb WCot WEas WJek WLHH WTou |

## *Atropa* (*Solanaceae*)

| | | |
|---|---|---|
| | ***bella-donna*** | CArn CSec GBar GPoy MSal WTin |
| | - var. ***lutea*** | MSal |
| | ***mandragora*** | see *Mandragora officinarum* |

## *Atropanthe* (*Solanaceae*)

| | | |
|---|---|---|
| § | ***sinensis*** | MSal |

## *Aubrieta* ✿ (*Brassicaceae*)

| | | |
|---|---|---|
| | 'Alba' | see *A.* 'Fiona' |
| | ***albomarginata*** | see *A.* 'Argenteovariegata' |
| | 'Alix Brett' | CMea CPBP ECho SPoG |
| | 'Ann Kendall' **new** | ECtt |
| | 'April Joy' (d) | ECot |
| § | 'Argenteovariegata' (v) ♀H4 | ECho ELan GKir WAbe WHoo |
| | 'Astolat' (v) | ECho NSla SRms WAbe WEas |
| § | 'Aureovariegata' (v) ♀H4 | CMea ECho ELan GKir LRHS MHer NPer NWCA WAbe WFar |
| | 'Belisha Beacon' | ECho |
| | Blaue Schönheit | see *A.* 'Blue Beauty' |
| | 'Blaumeise' | GKir |
| § | 'Blue Beauty' | ECtt NBlu WRHF |
| | 'Blue Chip' **new** | ECtt |
| | 'Blue Emperor' | MAvo |

| | | |
|---|---|---|
| | 'Blue Gown' | GKir |
| § | 'Bob Saunders' (d) | CMea ECho LLHF |
| | 'Bonfire' | ECho |
| | 'Bressingham Pink' (d) ♀H4 | ECtt ELan EPfP LRHS SPoG WFar |
| | 'Bressingham Red' | ECho EPfP GKir LRHS SIng SPoG |
| | ***canescens*** subsp. ***cilicica*** | GKev |
| | Cascade Series | GJos GKir SPoG |
| | - 'Blue Cascade' | ECtt EPfP GKir IBal MBNS NNor SPlb SPoG WGor |
| | - 'Lilac Cascade' | SPoG |
| | - 'Purple Cascade' | CTri CWCL CWib ECtt EPfP IBal LRHS MBNS MWat SPlb SPoG SRms WGor |
| | - 'Red Cascade' ♀H4 | CTri CWib ECtt EPfP MBNS NNor SPlb SPoG |
| | ***deltoidea*** | GKev |
| | - 'Nana Variegata' (v) | CMea CPBP ECtt EPot WGor |
| | - Variegata Group (v) | ECtt NSla WFar |
| | - - 'Shaw's Red' new | GKir |
| | 'Doctor Mules' ♀H4 | ECtt GKir SIng SRms |
| | 'Doctor Mules Variegata' (v) | CTri EAlp ECho ECtt EPfP LAst MHer NPri SPoG SWvt WFar |
| | 'Dream' | SIng |
| | 'Eila' (d) | STre |
| | 'Elsa Lancaster' | ECtt NMen NSla |
| § | 'Fiona' | SIng |
| § | 'Frühlingszauber' | SRms |
| | ***glabrescens*** | WAbe |
| | 'Gloriosa' | ECho GAbr SIng |
| | 'Golden King' | see *A.* 'Aureovariegata' |
| | ***gracilis*** | WAbe |
| | - 'Kitte Rose' new | EAlp |
| * | 'Graeca' | NPri |
| | 'Greencourt Purple' ♀H4 | CMea ECho ELan MHer MWat SIng |
| | 'Gurgedyke' | SRms |
| | 'Hamburger Stadtpark' | CWCL EAlp ECho EPfP |
| | 'Harknoll Red' | ECtt |
| | 'Hartswood' | SIng |
| | 'Hemswell Purity' PBR | see *A.* 'Snow Maiden' |
| | 'Hendersonii' | SRms |
| | 'J.S. Baker' | SRms |
| | 'Joy' (d) | ECtt LLHF NSla SIng |
| | 'Kitte' | ECho EPfP LAst NLar SPoG |
| | 'Leichtlinii' | NLar |
| | 'Lemon and Lime' | ECho |
| | ***macedonica*** | EAlp EPot |
| | 'Magician' | ECho WCFE |
| | 'Mrs Lloyd Edwards' | ECho |
| | 'Mrs Rodewald' ♀H4 | ECho SRms |
| | 'Novalis Blue' | SRms |
| | 'Oakington Lavender' | GKir |
| | ***pinardii*** | GKev NSla |
| | 'Pink Beauty' new | ECtt |
| | 'Purple Charm' | SRms |
| | 'Purple Emperor' | SIng |
| | 'Red Carpet' | ECho ECtt ELan EPot LRHS MAvo MHer SIng SPoG SRms |
| | 'Red Carpet Variegated' (v) | CMea |
| | 'Red Dyke' | SIng |
| | 'Riverslea' | SIng |
| | 'Rosanna Miles' | SIng |
| | 'Rose Queen' | CMea CPBP LRHS SAga |
| | Royal Series | COIW |
| | - 'Royal Blue' | EPfP WFar WMoo |
| | - 'Royal Lavender' | WFar |
| | - 'Royal Lilac' | WFar |
| | - 'Royal Red' | EPfP NPri SRms WFar WGor WMoo |
| | - 'Royal Rose' | WFar |
| | - 'Royal Violet' | CTri NHol WFar WMoo WPer |
| | 'Schofield's Double' | see *A.* 'Bob Saunders' |
| | 'Silberrand' | ECha ECtt NSla |
| § | 'Snow Maiden' PBR | ECtt LRHS NPri |
| | 'Somerfield Silver' | MBar NPri |
| | 'Somerford Lime' (v) | ECtt MBar NPri |
| | Spring Charm | see *A.* 'Frühlingszauber' |
| | 'Swan Red' (v) | ECtt LAst LIMB NPro NSla SPoG WAbe WFar WHoo |
| | 'Toby Saunders' | ECho |
| | 'Triumphante' | ECtt LLHF |
| | 'Wanda' | SIng |
| | 'Whitewell Gem' | EAlp ECho NHol SRms WMoo |

## *Aucuba* ✿ (*Aucubaceae*)

| | | |
|---|---|---|
| | ***japonica*** (f) | WDin |
| | - (m) | SReu |
| | - 'Angelon' | EMil |
| | - var. ***borealis*** | EMil |
| | - 'Crassifolia' (m) | EPla EQua SAPC SArc |
| | - 'Crotonifolia' (f/v) ♀H4 | Widely available |
| | - 'Crotonifolia' (m/v) | CTca LBMP MAsh SRms |
| | - 'Dentata' | CHEx SPoG |
| | - 'Gold Splash' (v) | GKir |
| | - 'Golden King' (m/v) ♀H4 | CDoC CMac CSBt CWib EBee ELan ELon EPfP GKir LRHS MAsh MGos MWat NLar SLim SPla SPoG WBrE WFar |
| | - 'Golden Spangles' (f/v) | CBcs CDoC EBee ECot ERas NLar NMun SWvt |
| | - 'Goldstrike' (v) | EBee |
| | - 'Hillieri' (f) | EQua |
| | - f. ***longifolia*** ♀H4 | CMac NHol NLar SAPC SArc SDix WCru |
| | - - 'Lance Leaf' (m) | EPla EQua SLon |
| | - - 'Salicifolia' (f) | CHEx EPla LAst MRav NLar SLon SPla WCru WDin WFar WPGP |
| | - 'Maculata' hort. | see *A. japonica* 'Variegata' |
| | - 'Marmorata' | EPla LRHS |
| | - 'Mr Goldstrike' (m/v) new | SPoG |
| | - 'Nana Rotundifolia' (f) | EPla |
| | - Pepper Pot = 'Shilpot' | SSta |
| | - 'Pepperpot' (m/v) | CHEx EPfP MAsh SPoG |
| | - 'Picturata' (m/v) | CBow CDul CHEx CMac CSBt EBee ELan GKir LRHS MAsh MGan MGos MRav NHol SHBN SLim SPer SPoG WFar |
| | - 'Rozannie' (f/m) ♀H4 | Widely available |
| | - 'Speckles' | NLar |
| | - 'Sulphurea Marginata' (f/v) | CBcs CBow CMac CTri EBee EMil EPla NPro SPoG WBod |
| § | - 'Variegata' (f/v) | Widely available |
| | - Windsor form (f) | EPla EQua MBri |
| | ***omeiensis*** BWJ 8048 | WCru |

## *Aurinia* (*Brassicaceae*)

| | | |
|---|---|---|
| § | ***corymbosa*** | LLHF |
| § | ***saxatilis*** ♀H4 | CSec ECho EPfP LAst MBar SPlb WFar |
| | - 'Argentea' | ECho |
| § | - 'Citrina' ♀H4 | ECha ECho ECtt MWat SRms |
| | - 'Compacta' | CTri ECho ECtt GJos |
| | - 'Dudley Nevill' | ECho MWat SIng |
| | - 'Dudley Nevill Variegated' (v) | ECha ECho ECtt EWes GMaP LIMB MHer NBir SIng WFar |
| | - 'Flore Pleno' (d) | ECho |
| | - Gold Ball | see *A. saxatilis* 'Goldkugel' |
| | - 'Gold Dust' | ECho ECtt SRms |
| | - 'Golden Queen' | ECtt MHer |
| § | - 'Goldkugel' | ECho GKir LRHS NBlu SPoG SRms WFar WRHF |
| | - 'Silver Queen' | WEas |
| | - 'Variegata' (v) | NPri SPoG |

## *Austrocedrus* (*Cupressaceae*)

| | | |
|---|---|---|
| § | ***chilensis*** | CKen CTho IDee LRHS |
| | - 'Thornhayes Ghost' | CTho |

## *Austromyrtus* (*Myrtaceae*)

| | | |
|---|---|---|
| § | ***dulcis*** | ECou |

## *Avena* (*Poaceae*)

| | | |
|---|---|---|
| | ***candida*** | see *Helictotrichon sempervirens* |
| | ***sativa*** 'French Black' | CSpe |

## *Avenula* see *Helictotrichon*

## avocado see *Persea americana*

## *Ayapana* (*Asteraceae*)

| | | |
|---|---|---|
| § | ***triplinervis*** | MSte |

## *Azalea* see *Rhododendron*

## *Azara* ✿ (*Flacourtiaceae*)

| | | |
|---|---|---|
| | ***dentata*** | CBcs CHll CMac EBee GGal GKir LAst SPoG WDin WFar |
| | - 'Variegata' | see *A. integrifolia* 'Variegata' |
| * | ***integerrima*** | GQui |
| | ***integrifolia*** | CCCN |
| | - 'Uarie' | CCCN |
| § | - 'Variegata' (v) | EBee SDnm |
| | ***lanceolata*** | CDul CMCN CPLG CTri EBee ECrN GGal IDee LEdu NSti SLon SPer WFar WPic |
| | ***microphylla*** ♀H3 | CBcs CChe CDul CLnd CMCN CMHG CPLG CPSs CSBt CTri EBee EPfP GKir LAst NSti SArc SDnm SPer SSpi WBod WFar WPGP WSHC |
| | - 'Gold Edge' (v) | LBuc WFar |
| | - 'Variegata' (v) | Widely available |
| | ***paraguayensis*** | CDoC GGar SDnm WFar |
| | ***petiolaris*** | EPfP WPic |
| | - G&P 5026 | WPGP |
| | ***serrata*** ♀H3 | CBcs CDul CEnd CMCN CSBt CWib EBee EPfP EPla GGar GKir IDee ISea NCGa SAga SDix SGar SPer SPoG SRms SSta WBod WBor WDin WFar WHar WSHC |
| | - 'Patagonica' | GKir |
| | ***uruguayensis*** | CCCN CPLG EBee GBin |

## *Azorella* (*Apiaceae*)

| | | |
|---|---|---|
| | ***filamentosa*** | ECou |
| | ***glebaria*** misapplied | see *A. trifurcata* |
| | ***glebaria*** A. Gray | see *Bolax gummifer* |
| | ***gummifer*** | see *Bolax gummifer* |
| | ***lycopodioides*** | GEdr |
| * | ***speciosa*** | EPot |
| § | ***trifurcata*** | CPar CSpe CTri ECho ECtt GAbr GEdr GKev GKir NLAp NWCA SIng SPlb WPer |
| | - 'Nana' | ECho EDAr GGar MWat WPat WThu |

## *Azorina* (*Campanulaceae*)

| | | |
|---|---|---|
| § | ***vidalii*** | CSpe EShb IDee SAPC SArc SGar |
| | - 'Rosea' | CKob WCot |

# B

## *Babiana* (*Iridaceae*)

| | | |
|---|---|---|
| | ***ambigua*** | CStu |
| | ***angustifolia*** | CGrW CPLG GGar |
| | 'Blue Gem' | EBrs ECho |
| | ***disticha*** | see *B. plicata* |
| | ***ecklonii*** | WCot |
| | ***framesii*** | CStu |
| | - var. ***kamiesbergensis*** | CPLG |
| | ***nana*** | CGrW CPBP CStu WCot |
| | ***odorata*** | WCot |
| § | ***plicata*** | CGrW |
| | ***pygmaea*** | WCot |
| | ***ringens*** | CPLG WCot |
| | ***rubrocyanea*** | WCot |
| | ***sambucina*** | CStu WCot |
| | ***sinuata*** | CGrW WCot |
| | ***stricta*** ♀H1-2 | CCCN CPLG CStu EBrs ECho SBch WCot WRos |
| | - var. ***erectifolia*** | WPrP |
| | - 'Purple Star' | CPLG EBrs ECho |
| | - 'Tubergen's Blue' | EBrs ECho |
| | ***truncata*** | CStu WCot |
| | ***vanzyliae*** | CStu WCot |
| | ***villosa*** | WCot |
| | 'Zwanenburg's Glory' | EBrs ECho |

## *Baccharis* (*Asteraceae*)

| | | |
|---|---|---|
| | ***genistelloides*** | SMad |
| | ***glomeruliflora*** | MBri |
| | ***halimifolia*** | CBcs CTrC EBee GQui IFFs SEND SLon |
| | ***magellanica*** | EBee |
| | ***patagonica*** | EBee GGar MMuc SAPC SArc SKHP WPat |
| | ***salicifolia*** | WCot |
| | 'Sea Foam' | SMad |

## *Bacopa* (*Scrophulariaceae*)

| | | |
|---|---|---|
| | 'Cinderella Strawberry' | NPri |
| | 'Snowflake' | see *Sutera cordata* 'Snowflake' |

## *Baeckea* (*Myrtaceae*)

| | | |
|---|---|---|
| | ***densifolia*** | ECou |
| | ***gunniana*** | CPLG |
| | ***linifolia*** | SPlb |
| | ***virgata*** | CBcs CTrC ECou SPlb |

## *Baillonia* (*Verbenaceae*)

| | | |
|---|---|---|
| | ***juncea*** | WSHC |

## *Balbisia* (*Geraniaceae*)

| | | |
|---|---|---|
| | ***peduncularis*** | CCCN |

## *Baldellia* (*Alismataceae*)

| | | |
|---|---|---|
| | ***ranunculoides*** | CRow EMFW WMAq |
| | - f. ***repens*** | LLWG |

## *Ballota* ✿ (*Lamiaceae*)

| | | |
|---|---|---|
| | ***acetabulosa*** ♀H3-4 | EBee ECha EGoo EWes SBch SDix WCot WKif |
| | 'All Hallow's Green' | see *Marrubium bourgaei* var. *bourgaei* 'All Hallow's Green' |
| | ***nigra*** | CArn EBWF GPoy MHer MNHC MSal NMir SECG WMoo |
| § | - 'Archer's Variegated' (v) | CBow EWes LDai |
| | - 'Variegata' | see *B. nigra* 'Archer's Variegated' |
| | - 'Zanzibar' (v) | EMon |
| | ***pseudodictamnus*** ♀H3-4 | Widely available |
| | - from Crete | ECha |
| | ***rupestris*** 'Frogswell Carolyn' (v) | IFro |

## *Balsamita* see *Tanacetum*

## *Balsamorhiza* (*Asteraceae*)

| | | |
|---|---|---|
| | ***deltoidea*** | GEdr SPhx |
| | ***sagittata*** | ECho |

## *Bambusa* ✿ (*Poaceae*)

| | | |
|---|---|---|
| | ***glaucescens*** | see *B. multiplex* |
| | ***gracilis*** | see *Drepanostachyum falcatum* |
| § | ***multiplex*** | EFul XBlo |
| | - 'Alphonso-Karrii' | CGHE EPla LEdu SBig WPGP |
| | - 'Elegans' | see *B. multiplex* 'Floribunda' |
| | - 'Fernleaf' | see *B. multiplex* 'Floribunda' |
| § | - 'Floribunda' | CHEx EBee EFul EShb XBlo |
| | - 'Golden Goddess' | XBlo |
| | - 'Silverstripe' | see *B. multiplex* 'Variegata' |
| | - 'Tiny Fern' | WPGP |
| § | - 'Variegata' (v) **new** | XBlo |
| | - 'Wang Tsai' | see *B. multiplex* 'Floribunda' |
| | ***pubescens*** | see *Dendrocalamus strictus* |
| | ***ventricosa*** | SBig XBlo |
| | ***vulgaris*** | XBlo |
| | - 'Vittata' | XBlo |
| | ***vulgaris*** 'Variegata' (v) | CArn CHal CMoH CSec EBee LDai MAvo MLan MNHC NBro NCob SPav WCHb WCot WMoo |
| | - 'Variegated Winter Cream' (v) | WFar |

## banana see *Musa*

## *Banksia* (*Proteaceae*)

| | |
|---|---|
| ***aemula*** | SOWG |
| ***burdettii*** | SOWG |
| ***canei*** | CTrC SPlb |
| ***coccinea*** | SOWG |
| ***ericifolia*** | LRHS WBor |
| - var. ***ericifolia*** | CBcs CCCN CTrC SOWG SSta |
| - var. ***macrantha*** | SPlb |
| ***grandis*** | CCCN LRHS SOWG |
| ***integrifolia*** | CBcs CCCN CTrC ECou SOWG SSta |
| ***marginata*** | CTrC ECou SOWG SPlb |
| - mauve-flowered | SOWG |
| ***media*** | SPlb |
| ***oblongifolia*** | CTrC SPlb |
| ***occidentalis*** | SOWG |
| ***paludosa*** | CTrC SPlb |
| ***robur*** | CCCN LRHS SPlb WBor |
| ***serrata*** | SOWG SPlb |
| ***speciosa*** | SPlb |
| ***spinulosa*** | CTrC WBor |
| - var. ***collina*** | CTrC SOWG SPlb |
| - pink-flowered | SOWG |
| - var. ***spinulosa*** | CBcs CCCN |
| ***violacea*** | SPlb |

## *Baptisia* (*Papilionaceae*)

| | | |
|---|---|---|
| § | ***alba*** | EBee NLar |
| | - var. ***alba*** 'Wayne's World' **new** | IPot |
| § | - var. ***macrophylla*** | CMdw EWes LPla NBir NDov NLar SDix WCot |
| | ***australis*** ♀H4 | Widely available |
| | - 'Caspian Blue' | CWCL LHop MLan MMHG SPla WFar WHil WSHC |
| | - 'Exaltata' | ELan GBuc LHop |
| | - var. ***minor*** | NLar WCot |
| | - 'Nelson's Navy' **new** | LRHS SMrs |
| § | ***bracteata*** var. ***leucophaea*** | LSou WFar |
| | 'Carolina Moonlight' | IPot |
| | ***lactea*** | see *B. alba* var. *macrophylla* |
| | ***leucantha*** | see *B. alba* var. *macrophylla* |
| | ***leucophaea*** | see *B. bracteata* var. *leucophaea* |
| | ***megacarpa*** | SKHP |
| | ***pendula*** | see *B. alba* |
| | 'Purple Smoke' | EBee SMHy |
| | ***tinctoria*** | CArn |

## *Barbarea* (*Brassicaceae*)

| | | |
|---|---|---|
| | ***praecox*** | see *B. verna* |
| § | ***verna*** | CArn GPoy MHer NGHP |

## *Barleria* (*Acanthaceae*)

| | |
|---|---|
| ***micans*** | CCCN |
| ***obtusa*** 'Amethyst Lights' (v) **new** | EShb |
| ***suberecta*** | see *Dicliptera sericea* |

## *Barosma* see *Agathosma*

## *Bartlettina* (*Asteraceae*)

| | | |
|---|---|---|
| § | ***sordida*** | CCCN CKob EBee |

## *Bashania* (*Poaceae*)

| | | |
|---|---|---|
| | ***faberi*** Og 94053 | EPla |
| § | ***fargesii*** | CDoC ENBC EPla ERod MRav MWht SEND |
| I | ***qingchengshanensis*** | CGHE EBee EPla WPGP |

## basil see *Ocimum basilicum*

## *Bauera* (*Cunoniaceae*)

| | |
|---|---|
| ***rubioides*** var. ***alba*** | ECou |
| - 'Candy Stripe' | SOWG |
| - pink-flowered | ECou SOWG |
| - 'Ruby Glow' | SOWG |
| ***sessiliflora*** | SOWG |

## *Bauhinia* (*Caesalpiniaceae*)

| | |
|---|---|
| ***acuminata*** **new** | CSec |
| ***corymbosa*** | SOWG |
| ***galpinii*** | EShb SOWG SPlb |
| ***monandra*** | SOWG |
| ***natalensis*** | EShb SPlb |
| ***tomentosa*** | CCCN EShb |
| ***yunnanensis*** | SOWG WSHC |

## *Baumea* see *Machaerina*

## bay see *Laurus nobilis*

## *Beaucarnea* (*Dracaenaceae*)

| | |
|---|---|
| ***recurvata*** ♀H1 | CTrC LPal MBri NScw WFar |

## *Beaufortia* (*Myrtaceae*)

| | |
|---|---|
| ***sparsa*** | SOWG |
| ***squarrosa*** | SPlb |

## *Beaumontia* (*Apocynaceae*)

| | |
|---|---|
| ***grandiflora*** | SOWG |

## *Beauverdia* see *Leucocoryne*

## *Beccariophoenix* (*Arecaceae*)

| | |
|---|---|
| ***madagascariensis*** | LPal |

## *Beesia* (*Ranunculaceae*)

| | |
|---|---|
| ***calthifolia*** | CBct CFir CLAP EBee EHrv EWld GBBs LLHF WCot WCru WPGP |
| - DJHC 98447 | CDes |
| ***deltophylla*** | WCot |

## *Begonia* ✿ (*Begoniaceae*)

| | |
|---|---|
| B&SWJ 6881 from Taiwan | WCru |
| BWJ 7840 from China | WCru |
| B&SWJ 10279 from Mexico **new** | WCru |
| B&SWJ 10442 from Guatemala **new** | WCru |

| | | |
|---|---|---|
| | B&SWJ 10479 from Costa Rica **new** | WCru |
| | Chen Yi 5 | WCot |
| | DJHC 580 | WCot |
| | from China | NShi |
| | from Ruwenzori, Uganda | NShi |
| | from Sikkim, India | WCot |
| | from Vietnam | ERhR NShi |
| | 'Abel Carrière' | CHal ERhR NShi WDib |
| | ***acetosa*** | NShi |
| | ***acida*** | ERhR NShi |
| | ***aconitifolia*** (C) | ERhR EShb NShi |
| | ***acutifolia*** | ERhR NShi |
| | 'Aladdin' | ERhR NShi |
| | 'Alamo III' | ERhR NShi |
| | ***albopicta*** (C) | CHal EBak ERhR NShi SAdn |
| | - 'Rosea' (C) | CHal EShb NShi WDib |
| | 'Albuquerque Midnight Sky' (R) | NShi |
| | ***alice-clarkiae*** | ERhR NShi |
| | 'Alleryi' (C) | ERhR NShi |
| | ***alnifolia*** | ERhR |
| | 'Alto Scharff' $\Upsilon^{H1}$ | ERhR NShi |
| | 'Alzasco' (C) | ERhR NShi |
| | 'Amazon Delta'$^{PBR}$ (R) | LRHS |
| | 'Amigo Pink' (C) | ERhR NShi |
| | ***ampla*** | NShi |
| | 'Anita Roseanna' (C) | ERhR NShi |
| | 'Ann Anderson' (C) | ERhR NShi |
| | 'Anna Christine' (C) | ERhR NShi |
| § | ***annulata*** | ERhR NShi |
| | 'Aquarius' | ERhR NShi |
| | 'Arabian Sunset' (C) | ERhR NShi |
| | ***arborescens*** var. ***arborescens*** | ERhR |
| | 'Arctic Breeze'$^{PBR}$ (R) | LRHS |
| | 'Argentea' (R) | EBak MBri NShi |
| | 'Argenteo Guttata' (C) | CHal ERhR EShb NShi |
| | 'Aries' | ERhR NShi |
| | 'Art Monday' (C) | NShi |
| | 'Arthur Mallet' | ERhR NShi |
| | 'Aruba' | ERhR |
| | 'Atlanta Jazz' (R) | NShi |
| | 'Autumn Glow' (T) | ERhR NShi |
| | 'Avalanche' (T) | ERhR NShi |
| | 'Axel Lange' (R) | NShi |
| | 'Aya' (C) | NShi WDib |
| | 'Baby Perfection' | NShi WDib |
| | 'Bahamas' | ERhR NShi |
| | 'Bantam Delight' | ERhR NShi |
| | 'Barbara Ann' (C) | ERhR |
| | 'Barbara Hamilton' (C) | ERhR |
| | 'Barbara Parker' (C) | ERhR |
| | 'Barclay Griffiths' | ERhR NShi |
| | 'Beatrice Haddrell' | CHal ERhR NShi WDib |
| * | ***benichoma*** | WDib |
| | 'Benigo' (C) **new** | NShi |
| | 'Benitochiba' (R) | ERhR NShi WCot |
| | 'Bess' | ERhR NShi |
| | 'Bessie Buxton' | ERhR NShi |
| | 'Bethlehem Star' | ERhR NShi WDib |
| § | 'Bettina Rothschild' (R) | CHal ERhR GGar LRHS NShi WDib |
| | 'Beverly Jean' | ERhR NShi |
| | 'Big Boy' (R) **new** | NShi |
| | 'Big Mac' | ERhR NShi |
| | 'Bill's Beauty' | ERhR NShi |
| | 'Bishop's Irish Eyes' (C) | NShi |
| | 'Black Beauty' (R) **new** | NShi |
| | 'Black Jack' (C) | ERhR NShi |
| | 'Black Knight' (R) | CHal NShi |
| | 'Black Raspberry' | ERhR NShi |
| | 'Black Velvet' | NShi |
| | 'Blanc de Neige' | ERhR NShi |
| | 'Blue Vein' | ERhR NShi |
| | 'Blue Wave' | NShi |
| | 'Bokit' | ERhR NShi WDib |
| | 'Bokit' x ***imperialis*** | NShi WDib |
| | ***boliviensis*** (T) | CDes CDoC GCal NShi WCot WCru |
| | 'Bonaire' | CHal |
| | 'Bonfire' | LBuc LRHS SPer |
| | 'Boomer' (C) | ERhR NShi |
| | 'Botato' | NShi |
| | ***bowerae*** | CHal ERhR LRHS NShi |
| § | - var. ***nigramarga*** | ERhR NShi |
| | 'Boy Friend' | ERhR NShi |
| | ***bracteosa*** | ERhR |
| | ***bradei*** | ERhR |
| | ***brevirimosa*** | ERhR NShi |
| | 'Bronze King' (R) | NShi |
| | 'Brown Lace' | NShi |
| | 'Brown Twist' | NShi WDib |
| | 'Bunchii' | ERhR NShi |
| | 'Burgundy Velvet' | ERhR NShi WDib |
| | 'Burle Marx' $\Upsilon^{H1}$ | CHal ERhR EShb NShi SDix WDib |
| | 'Bush Baby' | CHal NShi |
| | 'Butter Cup' | NShi |
| | 'Calico Kew' | ERhR |
| | 'Calla Queen' (S) | ERhR NShi |
| | 'Can-can' (R) | see *B.* 'Herzog von Sagan' |
| | 'Candy Floss' | NShi WCru |
| | 'Captain Nemo' (R) | ERhR NShi |
| | ***cardiocarpa*** | ERhR NShi |
| | 'Carol Mac' | ERhR NShi |
| | 'Carolina Moon' (R) $\Upsilon^{H1}$ | ERhR NShi |
| | ***carolineifolia*** | CHal NShi WDib |
| | ***carrieae*** | ERhR NShi |
| | x ***carrierei*** | see *B.* Semperflorens Cultorum Group |
| | 'Cathedral' | ERhR GGar NShi WDib |
| | 'Champagne' | SPer |
| | 'Chantilly Lace' | CHal ERhR NShi |
| * | ***chapaensis*** | NShi |
| | - HWJ 642 | WCru |
| | 'Charles Chevalier' | ERhR NShi |
| | 'Charles Jaros' | ERhR NShi |
| | 'Charm' (S) | CHal ERhR NShi WDib |
| | (Cheimantha Group) 'Gloire de Lorraine' | NShi |
| | 'Cherry Feast' | CHal |
| | 'Cherry Jubilee' (C) | NShi |
| | 'Cherry Red' **new** | NShi |
| | 'Cherry Sundae' | ERhR |
| | 'Chesson' | ERhR NShi |
| | 'China Curl' (R) $\Upsilon^{H1}$ | ERhR LRHS NShi |
| | 'China Doll' | NShi |
| | ***chitoensis*** | CKob |
| | - B&SWJ 1954 | WCru |
| | ***chloroneura*** | ERhR WDib |
| | 'Chocolate Box' | ERhR |
| | 'Chocolate Chip' | ERhR NShi |
| | 'Christine' | NShi |
| | 'Christmas Candy' | ERhR WDib |
| | 'Christy White' | NShi |
| | 'Chuck Jaros' | NShi |
| | 'Chumash' | ERhR NShi |
| | 'Cilia' **new** | NShi |
| | ***circumlobata*** | EBee |
| | 'Cistine' | ERhR NShi |
| | 'Clara' (R) | MBri NShi |
| | 'Cleopatra' $\Upsilon^{H1}$ | CHal ERhR MRav NShi WDib |
| | 'Clifton' | ERhR NShi |
| | ***coccinea*** (C) | ERhR NShi WDib |
| | 'Coconut Ice' | LAst |
| | 'Comte de Lesseps' (C) | NShi WDib |
| | ***conchifolia*** f. ***rubrimacula*** | ERhR NShi |

| | | |
|---|---|---|
| | 'Concord' | ERhR NShi |
| | 'Connee Boswell' | ERhR NShi WDib |
| | ***convolvulacea*** | ERhR NShi |
| | ***cooperi*** | ERhR NShi |
| | 'Cora Anne' | ERhR |
| | 'Cora Miller' (R) | ERhR NShi |
| § | ***corallina*** (C) | EBak NShi |
| § | - 'Lucerna' (C) | CHal EBak ERhR |
| | - 'Lucerna Amazon' (C) | CHal ERhR NShi |
| | 'Corbeille de Feu' | CHal ERhR NShi |
| | 'Cosie' (C) | NShi |
| | 'Cowardly Lion' (R) | ERhR NShi |
| | 'Cracklin' Rosie' (C) | ERhR NShi |
| | ***crassicaulis*** | ERhR NShi |
| | 'Crestabruchii' | ERhR NShi |
| | 'Crystal Brook' | ERhR NShi |
| § | ***cubensis*** | ERhR NShi |
| | ***cucullata*** (S) | CHal ERhR NShi |
| | 'Curly Fireflush' (R) | ERhR NShi WDib |
| | 'Curly Locks' (S) | CHal |
| | 'Curly Merry Christmas' (R) | NShi |
| | 'Dales' Delight' (C) | ERhR NShi |
| | 'Dancin' Fred' | ERhR NShi |
| | 'Dancing Girl' | ERhR NShi |
| | 'Dannebo' | MBri |
| | 'D'Artagnan' | ERhR NShi |
| | 'David Blais' (R) ♀H1 | NShi WDib |
| | 'Dawnal Meyer' (C) | ERhR NShi WDib |
| I | 'de Elegans' | ERhR NShi WDib |
| | 'Decker's Select' | ERhR NShi |
| | 'Deco Diamond Dust' | ERhR |
| | ***decora*** | ERhR NShi |
| | ***deliciosa*** | ERhR NShi |
| | 'Delray Silver' | NShi |
| | 'Dewdrop' (R) ♀H1 | ERhR NShi WDib |
| | ***diadema*** | ERhR NShi |
| | 'Di-anna' (C) | ERhR NShi |
| | ***dichotoma*** | ERhR NShi |
| | ***dichroa*** (C) | ERhR NShi |
| | 'Dielytra' | ERhR NShi |
| | 'Di-erna' | ERhR NShi |
| | ***dietrichiana*** | ERhR NShi |
| | 'Digswelliana' | ERhR NShi |
| | ***dipetala*** | ERhR |
| | ***discolor*** | see *B. grandis* subsp. *evansiana* |
| | ***domingensis*** misapplied | see *B. obliqua* |
| | ***domingensis*** ambig. | ERhR NShi |
| | 'Don Miller' (C) | ERhR NShi WDib |
| | 'Doublet Pink' | ERhR |
| | 'Doublet Red' | ERhR |
| | 'Doublet White' | ERhR |
| | 'Douglas Nisbet' (C) | ERhR |
| § | ***dregei*** (T) ♀H1 | ERhR GCal NShi |
| | - 'Bonsai' | NShi STre |
| | - var. ***dregei*** (T) | ERhR EShb NShi |
| | - 'Glasgow' | ERhR NShi |
| | - var. ***macbethii*** (T) | NShi |
| | 'Druryi' | ERhR NShi |
| | 'Dwarf Houghtonii' | ERhR NShi |
| | 'Earl of Pearl' | ERhR NShi |
| * | 'Ebony' (C) | CHal ERhR NShi |
| | ***echinosepala*** | ERhR NShi |
| | ***echinosepala*** x ***sanguinea*** | NShi |
| | ***edmundoi*** (C) | ERhR |
| | ***egregia*** | ERhR |
| | 'Elaine' | ERhR NShi |
| | 'Elaine Ayres' (C) | ERhR NShi |
| § | 'Elaine Wilkerson' | ERhR NShi |
| | 'Elaine's Baby' | see *B.* 'Elaine Wilkerson' |
| | 'Elda' | ERhR NShi |
| | 'Elda Haring' (R) | ERhR NShi |

| | | |
|---|---|---|
| | 'Elizabeth Hayden' | ERhR NShi |
| | 'Elsie M. Frey' | ERhR NShi |
| | ***emeiensis*** | CKob |
| | - DJHC 98479 **new** | SKHP |
| | 'Emerald Beauty' (R) ♀H1 | ERhR NShi |
| | 'Emerald Giant' (R) | ERhR NShi WDib |
| | 'Emerald Isle' | NShi |
| | 'Emerald Princess' | NShi |
| | 'Emma Watson' | CHal ERhR NShi |
| | 'Enchantment' | ERhR NShi |
| | 'Enech' | ERhR NShi |
| | 'English Knight' | ERhR NShi |
| | 'English Lace' | ERhR NShi |
| | ***epipsila*** | ERhR NShi |
| | 'Erythrophylla' | EShb NShi |
| | 'Erythrophylla Bunchii' | ERhR NShi |
| § | 'Erythrophylla Helix' | CHal ERhR NShi |
| | 'Escargot' (R) ♀ | GGar LRHS NShi WDib |
| | 'Essie Hunt' | ERhR NShi |
| | 'Esther Albertine' (C) ♀H1 | CHal ERhR NShi |
| | 'Evening Star' | ERhR NShi |
| | 'Exotica' | ERhR |
| | 'Fairy' | ERhR NShi |
| | ***feastii*** 'Helix' | see *B.* 'Erythrophylla Helix' |
| | ***fernando-costae*** | ERhR NShi |
| § | 'Feuerkönigin' (S) | ERhR NShi |
| | 'Fever' (R) | NShi |
| | 'Filigree' | ERhR NShi |
| | ***fimbriata*** Liebm. | EBrs |
| | ***fimbristipula*** | EBee |
| | 'Fire Flush' | see *B.* 'Bettina Rothschild' |
| | 'Fireworks' (R) ♀ | ERhR LRHS NShi WDib |
| | 'Five and Dime' | ERhR NShi |
| | 'Flamboyant' (T) | ERhR LSou MBri NShi SVil WGor |
| | Flaming Queen | see *B.* 'Feuerkönigin' |
| | 'Flamingo' | ERhR NShi |
| | 'Flamingo Queen' | ERhR NShi |
| | 'Flo'Belle Moseley' (C) | CHal ERhR NShi WDib |
| | 'Florence Carrell' | ERhR NShi |
| | 'Florence Rita' (C) | ERhR NShi |
| | 'Flying High' | ERhR NShi |
| | ***foliosa*** | CHal ERhR NShi WDib |
| | - var. ***amplifolia*** | see *B. holtonis* var. *holtonis* |
| § | - var. ***miniata*** ♀H1 | CDTJ CDoC CTsd EBak ERhR EShb LPio MArl NShi SDix WDib |
| § | - - pink-flowered | CCCN GGar LAst LSou NShi WFar |
| § | - - red-flowered | CCCN WFar |
| | - - 'Rosea' | CDoC CHal NShi |
| | ***formosana*** | NShi |
| | - B&SWJ 7041 | WCru |
| | 'Frances Lyons' | ERhR NShi |
| | 'Frau Hoffman' (R) | NShi |
| | 'Freckles' (R) | ERhR NShi |
| | 'Fred Bedson' | ERhR NShi |
| | 'Fred Martin' (R) | NShi |
| | ***friburgensis*** | ERhR |
| | 'Friendship' | ERhR NShi |
| | 'Frosty' (T) | NShi WDib |
| | 'Frosty Fairyland' | ERhR |
| | 'Frosty Knight' | ERhR NShi |
| | 'Fuchsifoliosa' | ERhR NShi |
| | ***fuchsioides*** | see *B. foliosa* var. *miniata* |
| | ***fusca*** | ERhR NShi |
| | 'Fuscomaculata' | ERhR NShi |
| | 'Gaystar' | NShi |
| | ***gehrtii*** | ERhR NShi |
| | ***geranioides*** (T) | ERhR |
| | ***glabra*** | ERhR |
| | ***glandulosa*** misapplied | see *B. multinervia* |
| | ***glandulosa*** ambig. | ERhR |

| | | |
|---|---|---|
| | ***glaucophylla*** | see *B. radicans* Vell. |
| | 'Glen Daniels' | NShi |
| | 'Gloire de Sceaux' | ERhR NShi |
| | ***goegoensis*** | ERhR NShi |
| | 'Good 'n' Plenty' | ERhR NShi |
| § | ***gracilis*** (T) | NShi |
| | - var. ***martiana*** | see *B. gracilis* |
| | 'Granada' | ERhR NShi |
| | ***grandis*** | NShi |
| § | - subsp. ***evansiana*** ♀H3-4 | CAvo CHEx CKob CSam CSpe CStu EBee EMon ERhR EShb EWld GCal LEdu LPio LPla MLLN MSte MTho NShi SBch SDix SMad SPlb WCot WCru WFar WMoo |
| | - - var. ***alba*** hort. | CAby CHal CMdw EMon ERhR EShb GCal LPla MSte MTho SMad SSpi WCot WPGP |
| | - - 'Claret Jug' | EBee EMon LPio NShi WCot WPGP |
| | - - hybrid | NShi |
| | - - 'Pink Parasol' | EBee NShi WCru |
| | - - 'Simsii' | NShi WFar |
| | - 'Maria' | EBee WCot |
| | - 'Sapporo' | EBee EPPr GCal LPio LPla MSte NShi WCru |
| § | - subsp. ***sinensis*** | EBee NShi |
| | - - B&SWJ 8011A | NShi |
| | - - BWJ 8011 | NShi WCru |
| § | - aff. subsp. ***sinensis*** | NShi |
| | - - BWJ 8133 | WCru |
| * | 'Great Beverly' | ERhR NShi |
| | 'Green Acres' | ERhR |
| | 'Green Gold' (R) | NShi WDib |
| | 'Green Lace' | ERhR NShi |
| | 'Grey Feather' | ERhR NShi |
| | ***griffithii*** | see *B. annulata* |
| | 'Gustav Lind' (S) | CHal ERhR NShi |
| | 'Guy Savard' (C) | NShi WDib |
| | 'Gypsy Maiden' (T) | NShi |
| | ***haageana*** hort. ex W. Watson | see *B. scharffii* |
| | ***handelii*** | ERhR NShi |
| * | 'Happy Heart' | ERhR NShi |
| | 'Harbison Canyon' | NShi |
| * | 'Harry's Beard' | ERhR NShi |
| | 'Hastor' | ERhR NShi |
| | ***hatacoa*** | ERhR NShi |
| | - silver-leaved | CHal ERhR NShi |
| | - spotted-leaved | ERhR NShi |
| | 'Hazel's Front Porch' (C) | ERhR NShi |
| | 'Helen Lewis' ♀H1 | ERhR NShi |
| | 'Helen Teupel' (R) | ERhR NShi WDib |
| | 'Helene Jaros' | ERhR NShi |
| | ***hemsleyana*** | NShi |
| | 'Her Majesty' (R) | ERhR NShi |
| § | ***heracleifolia*** | CHal ERhR NShi |
| | - var. ***longipila*** | see *B. heracleifolia* |
| | - var. ***nigricans*** | see *B. heracleifolia* |
| | - 'Wisley' | NShi |
| § | 'Herzog von Sagan' (R) | ERhR NShi |
| | 'Hilo Holiday' (R) ♀ | NShi |
| | ***hispida*** var. ***cucullifera*** | ERhR NShi |
| | 'Holmes Chapel' | ERhR NShi |
| § | ***holtonis*** var. ***holtonis*** | CHal ERhR NShi |
| | ***homonyma*** (T) | see *B. dregei* |
| | 'Honeysuckle' (C) | ERhR NShi |
| | 'Hot Tamale' | ERhR NShi |
| | 'Hottentot' | NShi |
| | 'Houston Fiesta' (R) | NShi |
| | ***hydrocotylifolia*** | ERhR NShi |
| | ***hypolipara*** | see *B. sericoneura* |
| | (Illumination Series) 'Illumination Apricot' | SCoo |
| | - 'Illumination Rose' | SCoo |
| | - 'Illumination Salmon Pink' ♀H2-3 | SCoo |
| | - 'Illumination White' | SCoo |
| | ***imperialis*** | ERhR NShi |
| | 'Inca Fire'PBR (R) | LRHS |
| | ***incarnata*** | ERhR NShi |
| | - 'Metallica' | see *B. metallica* |
| | 'Indian Summer'PBR (R) | LRHS |
| | 'Ingramii' | ERhR NShi |
| | 'Interlaken' (C) | ERhR NShi |
| | 'Irene Nuss' (C) ♀H1 | ERhR NShi |
| | 'Ironstone' (R) ♀H1 | NShi |
| | 'Ivy Ever' | ERhR NShi |
| | 'Jade' | NShi |
| | 'Jelly Roll Morton' | ERhR |
| | 'Jenney' (R) **new** | NShi |
| | 'Joe Hayden' | CHal ERhR NShi |
| | 'John Tonkin' (C) | ERhR NShi |
| | ***johnstonii*** | ERhR |
| | 'Joy Porter' (C) | NShi |
| | 'Jubilee Mine' | ERhR |
| | ***juliana*** | ERhR NShi |
| | 'Jumbo Jeans' | ERhR NShi |
| | 'Jumbo Jet' (C) | ERhR NShi |
| | 'Kagaribi' (C) | ERhR NShi |
| | ***kellermanii*** | ERhR NShi |
| | 'Ken Lau Ren' (C) | NShi |
| | ***keniensis*** | GCal |
| | 'Kentwood' (C) | ERhR NShi |
| | ***kenworthyae*** | ERhR |
| | ***kingiana*** | NShi WDib |
| | 'Kit Jeans' | ERhR NShi |
| | 'Kit Jeans Mounger' | ERhR NShi |
| | 'Knutsford' | NShi |
| | 'Kyoto' | NShi |
| | 'La Paloma' (C) | NShi WDib |
| | 'Lacewing' | ERhR |
| | 'Lady Clare' | ERhR NShi |
| * | 'Lady France' | ERhR MBri |
| | 'Lady Snow' | CHal |
| | 'Lalome' (R) **new** | NShi |
| | 'Lana' (C) | ERhR NShi |
| | 'Langeana' | NShi |
| | 'Laurie's Love' (C) | ERhR |
| | 'Lawrence H. Fewkes' | ERhR NShi |
| | 'Lazy River' (R) | NShi |
| | ***leathermaniae*** (C) | ERhR NShi |
| | 'Legia' | ERhR |
| | 'Lenore Olivier' (C) | ERhR NShi |
| | 'Leopard' | ERhR MBri NShi |
| | 'Lexington' | ERhR |
| | 'Libor' (C) | ERhR |
| | 'Lillian' (R) | NShi |
| | 'Lime Swirl' | ERhR NShi |
| | ***limmingheana*** | see *B. radicans* Vell. |
| | 'Linda Dawn' (C) | ERhR NShi |
| | 'Linda Harley' | ERhR |
| | 'Linda Myatt' | ERhR NShi |
| | ***lindeniana*** | ERhR NShi |
| | ***listada*** ♀H1 | CHal ERhR MBri NShi WDib |
| | 'Lithuania' | ERhR |
| | 'Little Brother Montgomery' ♀H1 | ERhR EShb GGar NShi SDix WDib |
| | 'Little Darling' | ERhR NShi |
| | 'Little Iodine' | NShi |
| | 'Little Red' (R) **new** | NShi |
| | 'Lois Burks' (C) | CHal ERhR NShi WDib |
| | 'Loma Alta' | ERhR |
| | 'Looking Glass' (C) | ERhR NShi WDib |
| | 'Lospe-tu' | ERhR NShi |
| | 'Lubbergei' (C) | ERhR NShi |
| | 'Lucerna' | see *B. corallina* 'Lucerna' |

| | | |
|---|---|---|
| | 'Lucy Closson' (R) | NShi |
| | 'Lulu Bower' (C) | ERhR NShi |
| | ***luxurians*** ♀H1 | CHll CKob CSpe ERhR NShi WCot |
| | - 'Ziesenhenne' | ERhR NShi |
| | ***lyman-smithii*** | ERhR NShi |
| | 'Mabel Corwin' | ERhR NShi |
| | 'Mac MacIntyre' | NShi |
| | ***macduffieana*** | see *B. corallina* |
| | 'Mac's Gold' | ERhR NShi |
| | ***maculata*** (C) ♀H1 | ERhR NShi |
| | - 'Wightii' (C) | CHal CSpe ERhR NShi WDib |
| | 'Mad Hatter' | ERhR NShi |
| | 'Madame Butterfly' (C) | ERhR NShi |
| | 'Magic Carpet' | ERhR NShi |
| | 'Magic Lace' | ERhR NShi |
| | 'Manacris' | ERhR NShi |
| | 'Mandarin Orange' (C) | NShi |
| | ***manicata*** | ERhR NShi WDib |
| | 'Maori Haze'PBR (R) | LRHS |
| | 'Maphil' | MBri NShi |
| | 'Mardi Gras' (R) | NShi |
| | 'Margaritae' | ERhR NShi |
| * | 'Marginata Crispa White' | SPer |
| | 'Marmaduke' ♀H1 | CHal CTsd NShi WDib |
| | 'Marmorata' (T) | LRHS |
| | 'Martha Floro' (C) | ERhR |
| | 'Martin Johnson' (R) ♀H1 | ERhR NShi WDib |
| | 'Martin's Mystery' | ERhR NShi |
| | ***masoniana*** ♀H1 | CTsd ERhR NShi WDib |
| | - light-leaved | NShi |
| | 'Maurice Amey' | ERhR NShi |
| | 'Maverick' | ERhR NShi |
| | ***mazae*** | ERhR NShi |
| | 'Medora' (C) | ERhR NShi |
| | 'Melissa' (T) | NShi |
| | 'Merry Christmas' (R) ♀H1 | ERhR NShi WDib |
| | ***metachroa*** | ERhR NShi |
| § | ***metallica*** ♀H1 | CHal ERhR EShb NShi |
| | 'Meteor' (R) | NShi |
| | 'Michaele' | ERhR |
| | 'Midnight Magic' (R) ♀H1 | NShi |
| | 'Midnight Sun' | ERhR NShi |
| | 'Midnight Twister' | ERhR NShi |
| | 'Mikado' (R) ♀H1 | ERhR NShi |
| | Million Kisses | see *B.* 'Passion' |
| | 'Mini Merry Christmas' (R) **new** | NShi |
| | ***minor*** | ERhR |
| | 'Mirage' ♀H1 | ERhR NShi |
| | 'Miss Priss' (C) | NShi |
| | ***mollicaulis*** | ERhR |
| | 'Moon Maid' | ERhR |
| | 'Mr Kartuz' (T) | NShi |
| | 'Mrs Hashimoto' (C) | ERhR NShi |
| | 'Mrs Hatcher' (R) | ERhR NShi |
| | 'Mrs Schinkle' (C) | NShi |
| | 'Mrs T' **new** | NShi |
| § | ***multinervia*** | ERhR |
| | 'Munchkin' ♀H1 | CHal ERhR NShi WDib |
| | 'My Best Friend' | NShi |
| * | 'Mystic' | ERhR NShi |
| | 'Mystique' | ERhR NShi |
| | 'Namur' (R) ♀H1 | NShi WDib |
| | 'Nancy Cummings' | ERhR |
| | ***natalensis*** (T) | see *B. dregei* |
| | 'Nebula' **new** | NShi |
| | 'Nelly Bly' | ERhR |
| | ***nelumbiifolia*** | ERhR NShi |
| | ***nigramarga*** | see *B. bowerae* var. *nigramarga* |
| | ***nigritarum*** | ERhR NShi |
| | ***nitida alba*** | see *B. obliqua* |
| | 'Nokomis' (C) | ERhR NShi |
| | 'Norah Bedson' | ERhR NShi |
| | 'Northern Lights' (S) | ERhR NShi |
| § | ***obliqua*** | ERhR NShi |
| | ***obscura*** | ERhR NShi |
| | 'Obsession' | ERhR |
| | ***odorata*** | see *B. obliqua* |
| | 'Odorata Alba' | ERhR NShi |
| | 'Odorata Rosea' | NShi |
| | ***olbia*** | ERhR |
| | 'Old Gold' (T) | ERhR |
| | 'Oliver Twist' | ERhR |
| | 'Orange Dainty' | ERhR |
| | 'Orange Pinafore (C)' | ERhR |
| | 'Orange Rubra' (C) ♀H1 | CHal ERhR NShi |
| | 'Orient' (R) | ERhR NShi |
| | 'Orococo' | NShi |
| | 'Orpha C. Fox' (C) | ERhR NShi |
| | 'Orrell' (C) | ERhR NShi |
| | 'Othello' | ERhR NShi |
| | 'Otto Forster' | NShi |
| | 'Pachea' (R) | NShi |
| | ***paleata*** | ERhR NShi |
| | ***palmata*** | CDes EBee EBla GCal LSou MHar NCGa NShi SKHP WCot WPGP |
| | - B&SWJ 2692 from Sikkim | WCru |
| | - from China | EBla NShi |
| | - var. ***palmata*** | CKob NShi |
| | 'Palomar Prince' | ERhR NShi |
| | 'Panasoffkee' | ERhR NShi |
| | 'Pantaloon' | NShi |
| | 'Panther' | ERhR NShi |
| | 'Papillon' (T) | ERhR NShi |
| | ***paranaënsis*** | ERhR NShi |
| | ***parilis*** | ERhR NShi |
| | ***partita*** | see *B. dregei* |
| | 'Passing Storm' | ERhR NShi |
| § | 'Passion' **new** | SVil |
| | 'Patricia Ogdon' | ERhR NShi |
| | 'Paul Harley' | ERhR NShi |
| | 'Paul Henry' | NShi |
| | 'Paul-bee' | ERhR NShi |
| | ***paulensis*** | ERhR NShi |
| | ***pavonina*** | NShi |
| | 'Peace' (R) | NShi |
| | 'Peach Parfait' (C) | ERhR NShi |
| | ***pearcei*** (T) | ERhR NShi |
| | 'Pearl Ripple' | ERhR NShi |
| | 'Pearls' (C) | ERhR NShi |
| | ***pedatifida*** | EBee |
| | - DJHC 98473 **new** | WCru |
| | 'Peggy Stevens' (C) | ERhR |
| | ***peltata*** | ERhR NShi |
| * | 'Penelope Jane' | ERhR |
| | 'Persian Brocade' | ERhR NShi |
| | 'Petite Marie' (C) | ERhR |
| | 'Phil Corwin' (R) | NShi |
| | 'Piccolo' | ERhR NShi |
| | 'Pickobeth' (C) | ERhR NShi |
| | 'Picotee' (T) | CSut |
| | 'Pinafore' (C) ♀H1 | ERhR NShi |
| | 'Pink Basket' | NShi |
| | 'Pink Champagne' (R) ♀H1 | NShi WDib |
| | 'Pink Frosted' (R) | NShi |
| | 'Pink Jade' (C) | NShi |
| | 'Pink Lady' (R) | NShi WCru |
| | 'Pink Nacre' | CHal ERhR NShi |
| | 'Pink Parade' (C) | ERhR NShi |
| | 'Pink Parfan' | NShi |
| | 'Pink Shasta' (C) | NShi |
| | 'Pink Slate' (C) | NShi |
| | 'Pink Spot Lucerne' (C) | ERhR NShi |
| | 'Pink Taffeta' | ERhR NShi |
| | ***plagioneura*** | see *B. cubensis* |
| | 'Plum Rose' | ERhR NShi |

| | |
|---|---|
| ***plumieri*** | ERhR |
| ***polyantha*** | ERhR NShi |
| ***polygonoides*** | ERhR |
| ***popenoei*** | ERhR |
| 'Posy Wahl' (C) | NShi |
| 'Potpourri' | ERhR |
| 'Président Carnot' (C) | ERhR NShi |
| 'Pretty Rose' | ERhR |
| 'Preussen' | ERhR NShi |
| 'Pride of Saint Albans' (R) **new** | NShi |
| 'Princess of Hanover' (R) ♀$^{H1}$ | ERhR LRHS NShi WDib |
| 'Princessa Rio de Plata' | ERhR NShi |
| ***prismatocarpa*** | ERhR NShi |
| ***procumbens*** | see *B. radicans* Vell. |
| 'Purple Snow' (R) | LRHS NShi |
| ***pustulata*** 'Argentea' | ERhR NShi |
| ***putii*** | NShi |
| - B&SWJ 7245 | WCru |
| 'Queen Mother' (R) | ERhR NShi |
| 'Queen Olympus' | ERhR GGar NShi WDib |
| 'Quinebaug' | ERhR NShi |
| § ***radicans*** Vell. ♀$^{H1}$ | ERhR LRHS MBri NShi |
| ***rajah*** | NShi |
| 'Raquel Wood' | ERhR NShi |
| 'Raspberry Swirl' (R) ♀$^{H1}$ | CHal ERhR NShi WDib |
| ***ravenii*** (T) | GCal NShi SKHP WCot |
| 'Raymond George Nelson' ♀$^{H1}$ | CHal ERhR NShi |
| 'Razzmatazz' (R) | NShi WDib |
| 'Red Berry' (R) | ERhR NShi |
| 'Red Dragon' (R) **new** | WDib |
| 'Red Planet' | ERhR NShi WDib |
| 'Red Reign' | ERhR NShi |
| 'Red Robin' (R) | NShi WDib |
| 'Red Spider' | ERhR NShi |
| 'Red Undies' (C) | NShi WCru |
| 'Red Wing' (R) | NShi |
| 'Regal Minuet' (R) | LRHS NShi WDib |
| 'Reine des Neiges' (R) | NShi |
| ***reniformis*** | ERhR NShi |
| ***rex*** (R) | LRHS MBri MRav NShi |
| 'Richmondensis' | ERhR EShb NShi |
| 'Ricinifolia' | ERhR GCal NShi |
| 'Ricky Minter' ♀$^{H1}$ | ERhR NShi |
| 'Rip van Winkle' | ERhR NShi |
| 'River Nile' **new** | NShi |
| 'Robert Blais' (R) | NShi |
| 'Robin' (R) | ERhR NShi |
| 'Robin's Red' (C) | ERhR NShi |
| 'Rocheart' (R) ♀$^{H1}$ | NShi WDib |
| 'Roi de Roses' (R) ♀$^{H1}$ | ERhR NShi |
| ***roxburghii*** | ERhR NShi |
| 'Royal Lustre' | ERhR NShi |
| 'Rubacon' | ERhR NShi |
| ***rubro-setulosa*** | ERhR |
| 'Sabre Dance' (R) | ERhR NShi |
| 'Sachsen' | ERhR NShi |
| 'Saint Albans Grey' | NShi |
| 'Salamander' (R) | NShi |
| 'Sal's Comet' (R) ♀ | NShi WDib |
| 'Sal's Moondust' | NShi WDib |
| 'San Diego Sunset' (R) | NShi |
| ***sanguinea*** | ERhR NShi |
| 'Savannah Pink Parfait' (R) | NShi |
| 'Scarlett O'Hara' (T) | ERhR |
| ***scharffiana*** | NShi |
| § ***scharffii*** | CHal EBak ERhR NShi SDix |
| 'Scherzo' | CHal ERhR NShi WDib |
| 'Scottish Star' | NShi |
| 'Sea Captain' | NShi |
| 'Sea Serpent' ♀$^{H1}$ | NShi |
| 'Secpuoc' | ERhR |
| ***semperflorens*** hort. | see *B.* Semperflorens Cultorum Group |
| § Semperflorens Cultorum Group (S) | MBri NShi |
| § ***sericoneura*** | ERhR NShi |
| 'Serlis' | ERhR NShi |
| ***serratipetala*** | CHal EBak ERhR EShb MBri NShi WDib |
| 'Shamus' | ERhR NShi |
| 'Shaun Henthorn' (R) | NShi |
| * ***sheperdii*** | NShi WDib |
| 'Shiloh' (R) | ERhR NShi |
| * 'Shinihart' | ERhR NShi |
| 'Shoppy' | NShi |
| 'Sierra Mist' (C) | ERhR NShi |
| ***sikkimensis*** **new** | GCal |
| 'Silbreen' | NShi |
| ***silletensis*** subsp. ***mengyangensis*** | EBee GCal |
| 'Silver Cloud' (R) ♀$^{H1}$ | ERhR NShi WDib |
| 'Silver Dawn' (R) | ERhR NShi |
| 'Silver Dollar' | NShi |
| 'Silver Dots' | NShi |
| 'Silver Giant' (R) | ERhR NShi |
| 'Silver Jewell' | NShi WDib |
| 'Silver King' (R) ♀$^{H1}$ | NShi |
| 'Silver Lace' | NShi WDib |
| 'Silver Mist' (C) | ERhR NShi |
| 'Silver Points' | ERhR NShi |
| 'Silver Queen' (R) ♀$^{H1}$ | NShi |
| 'Silver Sweet' (R) | ERhR NShi |
| 'Silver Wings' | ERhR NShi |
| 'Sinbad' (C) | ERhR NShi |
| ***sinensis*** | see *B. grandis* subsp. *sinensis* |
| * 'Sir Charles' | ERhR |
| 'Sir John Falstaff' | ERhR NShi |
| ***sizemoreae*** **new** | WDib |
| Skeezar Group | ERhR NShi |
| - 'Brown Lake' | ERhR NShi |
| 'Snow Storm' | NShi |
| * 'Snowcap' (C) ♀$^{H1}$ | ERhR EShb NShi WDib |
| ***socotrana*** (T) | ERhR |
| ***solananthera*** ♀$^{H1}$ | CHal ERhR EShb GGar LRHS NShi WDib |
| ***soli-mutata*** | NShi WDib |
| ***sonderiana*** | GCal |
| 'Sophie Cecile' (C) ♀$^{H1}$ | CHal ERhR NShi |
| 'Sophie's Jenny' | NShi |
| 'Speckled Roundabout' | NShi |
| 'Speculata' (R) | ERhR NShi |
| 'Spellbound' | ERhR NShi WDib |
| 'Spindrift' | ERhR NShi |
| 'Splotches' | ERhR NShi |
| 'Stained Glass' | NShi WDib |
| 'Stichael Maeae' | ERhR |
| ***stipulacea*** ambig. | CHal ERhR NShi |
| ***subvillosa*** | ERhR |
| 'Sugar Plum' | ERhR NShi |
| 'Summer Maid' | NShi |
| 'Sun God' | NShi |
| 'Sun Set' | NShi |
| Superba Group (C) | NShi |
| 'Superba Azella' (C) | NShi |
| ***sutherlandii*** (T) ♀$^{H1}$ | CAvo CCCN CFFs CHal EABi EBak EOHP ERhR ERos EWld GGar LPio MHar NBir NPer NShi SAdn SBch SDix WCot WDib WEas WFar WHer |
| - 'Papaya' (T) | CSpe LRHS |
| 'Swan Song' | ERhR |
| 'Sweet Magic' | CHal ERhR NShi |
| 'Swirly Top' (C) | ERhR NShi |

| | | |
|---|---|---|
| | 'Sylvan Triumph' (C) | ERhR NShi |
| | ***taiwaniana*** | NShi |
| | ***taliensis*** **new** | SKHP |
| | 'Tapestry' | ERhR NShi |
| | 'Tar Baby' (T) | ERhR NShi |
| * | ***taya*** | WDib |
| | 'Tea Rose' | ERhR NShi |
| | 'Tequesta' | NShi |
| | ***teuscheri*** | ERhR NShi |
| | 'Texastar' | ERhR NShi WDib |
| | 'The Dutchess' **new** | NShi |
| | 'The Wiz' | ERhR NShi |
| | ***thelmae*** | ERhR NShi |
| | ***thiemei*** | NShi WDib |
| | 'Think Pink' | NShi |
| | 'Thrush' (R) | NShi |
| | 'Thumotec' | ERhR |
| | 'Thunderclap' | CHal ERhR NShi |
| | 'Thurstonii' ♀H1 | ERhR EShb NShi |
| | 'Tickled Pink' | LRHS |
| | 'Tiger Kitten' **new** | NBPN |
| | 'Tiger Paws' ♀H1 | CHal CTsd ERhR MBri NShi |
| | 'Tim Anderson' (R) | NShi |
| | 'Tingley Mallet' (C) | ERhR NShi |
| | 'Tiny Bright' (R) | ERhR NShi |
| | 'Tiny Gem' | ERhR NShi |
| | 'Tom Ment' (C) | ERhR NShi |
| | 'Tom Ment II' (C) | ERhR NShi |
| | 'Tomoshiba' | ERhR NShi |
| | 'Tondelayo' (R) | ERhR NShi |
| | 'Tornado' (R) | NShi |
| | 'Tribute' | ERhR NShi |
| | 'Trinidad' | ERhR NShi |
| * | ***tripartita*** (T) | ERhR NShi WDib |
| | 'Trout' (C) | NShi |
| | 'Tucson Bonfire' (R) | NShi |
| | 'Twilight' | ERhR NShi |
| | 'Two Face' | ERhR NShi WDib |
| | ***ulmifolia*** | ERhR NShi |
| | ***undulata*** (C) | CHal ERhR NShi |
| | 'Universe' | ERhR NShi |
| | 'Valentine' (R) | NShi |
| | 'Venetian Red' (R) | ERhR NShi |
| | ***venosa*** | CHal ERhR NShi |
| | 'Venus' | CHal ERhR NShi |
| | 'Vera Wyatt' | NShi |
| | 'Verschaffeltii' | ERhR NShi |
| | ***versicolor*** | ERhR |
| | 'Vesuvius' (R) | NShi WDib |
| | 'Viaudii' | ERhR NShi |
| | 'Viau-Scharff' | ERhR |
| | 'Vista' (R) | NShi |
| | 'Wally's World' | NShi |
| | 'Wanda' | NShi |
| | 'Weltoniensis' | ERhR NShi |
| | 'Weltoniensis Alba' (T) | ERhR |
| | 'Westland Beauty' | NShi |
| | 'White Cascade' | ERhR |
| | 'Wild Fire' **new** | NShi |
| | 'Wild Fury' (R) **new** | NShi |
| | 'Wild Swan' | NShi WCru |
| | ***williamsii*** | see *B. wollnyi* |
| | 'Witch Craft' (R) | ERhR NShi |
| | 'Withlacoochee' | ERhR NShi WDib |
| § | ***wollnyi*** | ERhR NShi |
| | 'Wood Nymph' (R) | ERhR NShi |
| | 'York Town' **new** | NShi |
| | 'Zuensis' | ERhR |

## *Belamcanda* (*Iridaceae*)

| | | |
|---|---|---|
| | ***chinensis*** | CArn CBro CHFP CHll CMea CPen CSec EBee EHig ELau EShb GKev GPoy LRHS MAvo MHer MLLN MSal SDnm SPav SPlb SRms SSto WBrE WGwG WKif WPer |
| | – B&SWJ 8692B | WCru |
| | – 'Freckle Face' | EBee GBri NBPC SPad SPoG |
| | – 'Hello Yellow' | EShb GBuc MAvo |

## *Bellevalia* (*Hyacinthaceae*)

| | | |
|---|---|---|
| | ***atroviolacea*** | EBrs ECho |
| | ***brevipedicellata*** | EBrs ECho |
| | ***ciliata*** | ERos |
| | ***dubia*** | EBee ECho WCot |
| | ***forniculata*** | ERos |
| | ***hackelii*** | EBrs ECho ERos |
| | ***hyacinthoides*** | CSec CStu ECho WCot |
| | ***kurdistanica*** | ERos |
| * | ***maura*** | EBrs ECho |
| | ***nivalis*** | EBrs |
| § | ***paradoxa*** | CMea CTca EBee EBrs ECho EHrv ERCP ERos ITim LBMP LLHF LRHS |
| | – white-flowered | EBrs ECho |
| | ***pycnantha*** misapplied | see *B. paradoxa* |
| | ***romana*** | CPom CTca EBee EBrs ECho ERCP ERos MTho SPhx WCot WHil |
| | ***sarmatica*** | ERos |
| | ***tabriziana*** | ERos |
| | ***webbiana*** | ECho ERos |

## *Bellis* (*Asteraceae*)

| | | |
|---|---|---|
| § | ***caerulescens*** | GAbr NBro SIng |
| | ***perennis*** | CArn EBWF GKir NMir NSco |
| | – 'Alice' | WCot |
| | – 'Blue Moon' | WCHb |
| | – 'Changeling' **new** | WAlt |
| | – 'Dawn Raider' | EMon |
| | – 'Dresden China' | ECho EWes GAbr MTho |
| | – 'Galaxy White' (Galaxy Series) | EPfP |
| | – Hen and Chickens | see *B. perennis* 'Prolifera' |
| | – 'Hula' **new** | CNat |
| | – 'Miss Mason' | GAbr |
| | – 'Parkinson's Great White' | GAbr |
| § | – 'Prolifera' single-flowered | WAlt WHer |
| | – 'Red Buttons' | NBlu |
| | – 'Rob Roy' (d) | WCot |
| | – 'Robert' | GAbr |
| | – 'Rusher Rose' | EPfP |
| | – 'Single Blue' | see *B. caerulescens* |
| | – 'The Pearl' | WCot |
| | – 'Upper Seagry' | WAlt |
| | ***rotundifolia*** 'Caerulescens' | see *B. caerulescens* |
| | ***sylvestris*** | CArn |

## *Bellium* (*Asteraceae*)

| | | |
|---|---|---|
| * | ***crassifolium canescens*** | WPer |
| | ***minutum*** | MTho |

## *Beloperone* see *Justicia*

| | | |
|---|---|---|
| | ***guttata*** | see *Justicia brandegeeana* |

## *Bensoniella* (*Saxifragaceae*)

| | | |
|---|---|---|
| | ***oregona*** | CPLG EMon |

## *Benthamiella* (*Solanaceae*)

| | | |
|---|---|---|
| | ***patagonica*** F&W 9345 **new** | WAbe |

## *Berberidopsis* (*Flacourtiaceae*)

| | | |
|---|---|---|
| | sp. **new** | GGal |
| | ***beckleri*** | WPGP |
| | ***corallina*** | Widely available |

## *Berberis* ✿ (*Berberidaceae*)

| | | |
|---|---|---|
| | CC 4730 | CPLG |

| | | |
|---|---|---|
| | SDR 3055 | GKev |
| | SDR 3256 | GKev |
| | SDR 4219 **new** | GKev |
| | ***aetnensis*** | GAuc |
| | ***aggregata*** | EMac GKir NBir SRms |
| | ***amurensis*** var. ***latifolia*** B&SWJ 4353 | WCru |
| | ***angulosa*** **new** | GCal |
| | ***aquifolium*** | see *Mahonia aquifolium* |
| | - 'Fascicularis' | see *Mahonia* x *wagneri* 'Pinnacle' |
| | ***aristata*** Parker | see *B. glaucocarpa* |
| | ***aristata*** ambig. | CMCN |
| | ***asiatica*** | CAgr CPLG GPoy |
| | ***bealei*** | see *Mahonia japonica* Bealei Group |
| | 'Blenheim' | WFar |
| | 'Boughton Red' | MBri |
| | ***brevipaniculata*** Schneider **new** | GAuc |
| | ***brevipedunculata*** Bean | see *B. prattii* |
| | x ***bristolensis*** | SLon SPla SRms |
| | ***buxifolia*** | EPfP GKir LEdu WCFE |
| N | - 'Nana' misapplied | see *B. buxifolia* 'Pygmaea' |
| N | - 'Pygmaea' | CAbP CBcs CSBt EBee GKir LAst MAsh MBar MGos MRav NHol NLar NPri SPer WDin WFar |
| | ***calliantha*** | WFar |
| | ***candidula*** C.K. Schneid. | EBee EPfP GKir MBar MGan MSwo NHol NLar SLon SPer WDin |
| | - 'Jytte' | see *B.* 'Jytte' |
| | x ***carminea*** 'Barbarossa' | WDin |
| | - 'Buccaneer' | EPfP |
| | - 'Pirate King' | CSBt MRav SPer SWvt WFar WPat |
| | ***chrysosphaera*** | WFar |
| | ***coxii*** | GBin GGar |
| | ***darwinii*** ♀H4 | Widely available |
| I | - 'Compacta' | EBee EDAr GKir LBuc MAsh NLar SPoG |
| | ***diaphana*** | CMCN |
| | ***dictyophylla*** ♀H4 | CPMA EPfP ERas GKir MGos NLar SPer SPoG SSpi WDin WPat WSHC |
| | ***dulcis*** 'Nana' | see *B. buxifolia* 'Pygmaea' |
| | x ***frikartii*** 'Amstelveen' ♀H4 | CDoC EBee ELan EPfP GKir LAst MBNS MRav NHol NLar NPri SPoG WDin WFar |
| | - 'Telstar' | EBee ECrN LAst LBuc MGos MRav NLar NPro |
| | ***gagnepainii*** misapplied | see *B. gagnepainii* var. *lanceifolia* |
| | ***gagnepainii*** C.K. Schneid. | CMac EBee EMac GKir MGan MRav NHol SLPl |
| § | - var. ***lanceifolia*** | CTri EBee ECrN EPla GKir MBar MGos NHol NWea SLim WDin WFar |
| | - - 'Fernspray' | EPfP EPla MRav SBod SRms WBod |
| | - 'Purpure' | see *B.* x *interposita* 'Wallich's Purple' |
| | - 'Purpurea' | see *B.* x *interposita* 'Wallich's Purple' |
| | 'Georgei' ♀H4 | CMHG CWib EPfP GQui SSpi |
| § | ***glaucocarpa*** | EPfP EPla NHol |
| | 'Goldilocks' | CAbP CDul CPMA CPSs EPfP GKir LAst MBlu SSpi |
| | ***goudotii*** B&SWJ 10769 | WCru |
| | x ***hybridogagnepainii*** 'Chenaultii' | ELan NHol SPer |
| | ***hypokerina*** | CMac |
| | ***insignis*** | IDee WFar |
| | - subsp. ***insignis*** var. ***insignis*** | WFar |
| | - - - B&SWJ 2432 | WCru |
| § | x ***interposita*** 'Wallich's Purple' | CCVT EBee ECrN EPfP MBar MDun MRav MSwo NHol SPer WDin |
| | ***jamesiana*** | WPat |

| | | |
|---|---|---|
| | ***julianae*** ♀H4 | Widely available |
| | - 'Mary Poppins' | EBee |
| § | 'Jytte' | EBee EMil WDin |
| | Purple' | |
| | ***kawakamii*** | SLPl |
| | ***koreana*** | CMCN EPfP NLar |
| | - 'Rubin' | CAgr |
| | ***lempergiana*** | CMCN |
| | ***lepidifolia*** | GBin |
| | ***linearifolia*** | CMac |
| | - 'Orange King' | CBcs CDoC CMac CTri ELan EPfP GKir LRHS MAsh MBlu MGos NLar NPri SCoo SHBN SPer SPoG WDin WFar WHar WPat |
| | 'Little Favourite' | see *B. thunbergii* f. *atropurpurea* 'Atropurpurea Nana' |
| | x ***lologensis*** | MGos WDin |
| | - 'Apricot Queen' ♀H4 | CBcs CMac EBee EPfP GKir LRHS MAsh MGos MHav MRav NBlu NLar NPri SCoo SHBN SPer SPoG WDin WPat |
| | - 'Mystery Fire' | EBee GKir LRHS MAsh MBlu MBri MGos NHol NLar SCoo SPoG SWvt WDin WFar WHar |
| | - 'Stapehill' | CSam ELan EPfP GKir LRHS MAsh NHol SPoG |
| | x ***media*** Park Jewel | see *B.* x *media* 'Parkjuweel' |
| § | - 'Parkjuweel' | EBee ECrN IArd MRav NLar SCoo WDin WFar WMoo |
| | - 'Red Jewel' ♀H4 | CDoC CMac EBee EPfP LRHS MGos MRav NLar SCoo SPer SPoG WCFE WDin WFar WMoo |
| | ***mitifolia*** | NLar |
| | ***montana*** | WPGP WPat |
| | ***morrisonicola*** | GAuc |
| | x ***ottawensis*** 'Auricoma' | EBee SWvt |
| | - f. ***purpurea*** | CWib MGos SBod WDin WFar WHar |
| § | - - 'Superba' ♀H4 | Widely available |
| § | - 'Silver Miles' (v) | EHoe EQua MRav NLar WFar WPat |
| § | ***panlanensis*** | MBar SLon |
| | ***poiretii*** | CPLG NBhm NLar |
| | ***polyantha*** misapplied | see *B. prattii* |
| § | ***prattii*** | GAuc |
| | - var. ***laxipendula*** | SMad |
| | ***pruinosa*** | CDul |
| | 'Red Tears' | CPMA CSam LRHS MBlu MBri MGos MRav NLar SPer WMoo |
| | ***sanguinea*** misapplied | see *B. panlanensis* |
| | ***sargentiana*** | SLPl |
| | ***sieboldii*** | LLHF MRav WPat |
| | ***soulieana*** | EPfP MGan |
| | x ***stenophylla*** Lindl. ♀H4 | CBcs CDoC CDul CSBt CTri EBee ECrN EPfP GKir ISea LBuc LRHS MBar MBri MRav NHol NWea SCoo SPer SPoG WBod WCFE WDin WFar WHar WMoo |
| | - 'Claret Cascade' | EBee LRHS MBri MGos MRav NHol NLar SEND SPer WFar |
| | - 'Corallina Compacta' ♀H4 | CLyd ECho ELan EPfP EPot GKir LHop LRHS MAsh NRya SIng SPoG SRms WAbe WPat |
| | - 'Crawley Gem' | GBin MBar MGos NHol NLar WFar |
| | - 'Etna' | ELan LRHS MAsh SPoG |
| | - 'Irwinii' | CMac EBee ERas LAst MBar MGos MSwo SPer WFar WMoo |
| | - 'Nana' | SRms |
| | - 'Pink Pearl' (v) | CMHG MGos |
| | ***temolaica*** ♀H4 | CGHE CPMA EPfP ERas GKir LRHS MDun MGos MRav NLar NSti NWea SDnm SPoG SSpi SSta WAbe WDin WPGP WPat |
| | ***thunbergii*** ♀H4 | CBcs CDoC CDul CSBt EMac EPfP GBin GKir LBuc MAsh MRav NLar |

| | |
|---|---|
| | NWea SCoo SPer SPlb SPoG SWvt WDin WFar |
| - f. ***atropurpurea*** | CBcs CCVT CDul CSBt CTri EBee EMac EPfP ISea LAst LBuc MBar MCot MGan MGos MSwo NLar NWea SCoo SPer SPoG WBVN WDin WFar WMoo |
| - - 'Admiration' | CAbP CBcs CEnd EMil EPfP LLHF MAsh MBri MGos NCGa SPer SPoG SWvt WPat |
| § - - 'Atropurpurea Nana' $\Upsilon^{H4}$ | Widely available |
| - - 'Bagatelle' $\Upsilon^{H4}$ | Widely available |
| - - 'Carmen' | MGos |
| - - 'Dart's Purple' | WFar |
| - - 'Dart's Red Lady' | CPLG CPMA CSBt CWib EBee ECrN EHoe ELan EPfP LRHS MAsh MBri MRav NLar NPro SCoo SLim SPer SPoG SWvt WDin WFar WPat |
| - - 'Golden Ring' $\Upsilon^{H4}$ | Widely available |
| - - 'Harlequin' (v) | CBcs CDoC CSBt EBee ELan ELon EMil EPfP GKir LRHS LSRN MAsh MBri MGos MRav SLim SPer SPla SPoG SWvt WBod WDin WFar WHar WPat |
| - - 'Helmond Pillar' | Widely available |
| - - 'Red Chief' $\Upsilon^{H4}$ | CBcs CMHG EBee ECrN EHoe ELan EPfP GKir LRHS LSRN MAsh MGos MRav NPri SLim SLon SPer SPla SPoG SWvt WDin WFar WHar WMoo WPat |
| - - 'Red King' | MRav WDin |
| - - 'Red Pillar' | CDoC EBee EHoe ELan LAst LRHS MAsh MBar MGos MRav MWat NHol NLar SHBN SPla SWvt WDin WFar WPat WRHF |
| - - 'Red Rocket' | EMil MBri MCCP NLar |
| - - 'Rose Glow' (v) $\Upsilon^{H4}$ | Widely available |
| - 'Atropurpurea Superba' | see *B.* x *ottawensis* f. *purpurea* 'Superba' |
| - 'Aurea' | Widely available |
| - Bonanza Gold = 'Bogozam'PBR | CAbP CBcs CDoC EBee ELan EPfP GKir LRHS MAsh MRav NLar SLim SPer SPoG WDin WFar WPat |
| - 'Boum' **new** | EMil |
| - 'Carpetbagger' | WHar |
| - 'Coronita' | MBri |
| - 'Crimson Pygmy' | see *B. thunbergii* f. *atropurpurea* 'Atropurpurea Nana' |
| - 'Erecta' | CMac EPfP MBar MGos MRav SPer WBod WCFE WDin |
| - 'Golden Carpet' | LRHS MAsh SPoG |
| - 'Golden Pillar' | LRHS |
| - 'Golden Rocket' | LLHF MAsh SPer SPoG |
| - 'Golden Torch' | CSBt EBee EHig EMil EPfP EPla LSRN MBri MRav SPoG SWvt WPat |
| - 'Green Carpet' | EBee GKir LHop MBar MBlu NLar SPoG WFar |
| - 'Green Mantle' | see *B. thunbergii* 'Kelleriis' |
| - 'Green Marble' | see *B. thunbergii* 'Kelleriis' |
| - 'Green Ornament' | NHol |
| - 'Green Ring' | EQua |
| § - 'J.N. Variegated' (v) | SPer |
| § - 'Kelleriis' (v) | CDoC EPfP LHop MBar MGos MRav NHol NLar NPro SLon WClo WDin WFar |
| - 'Kobold' | EBee EPfP LHop LRHS MAsh MBar MGos NHol NLar SLim SPer SPla SPoG WFar |
| - 'Maria'PBR **new** | LLHF LSou MGos NCGa NHol WHar |
| - 'Pink Queen' (v) | CDul EBee ELan EPfP EWTr MAsh SPur WDin WFar WHar WPat |
| - 'Pow-wow' | CBcs EBee MGos NLar SCoo SPoG SWvt WDin |
| - 'Silver Beauty' (v) | CMHG EBee ELan MGos WDin |
| - 'Silver Mile' | see *B.* x *ottawensis* 'Silver Miles' |
| - 'Somerset' | CMac |
| - 'Starburst' (v) | CBcs CDoC CDul CSBt EMil EPfP MAsh MBri MGos SCoo SPoG SWvt |
| - Stardust | see *B. thunbergii* 'J.N. Variegated' |
| - 'Tiny Gold' | CEnd LBuc LSRN MGos SWvt |
| * - 'Tricolor' (v) | CMac MRav WFar WPat |
| ***valdiviana*** | CDul CGHE CPLG CPMA EBee EPfP EPla SKHP SMad SSpi WPGP WPat |
| ***verruculosa*** $\Upsilon^{H4}$ | CChe EBee EPfP GKir LAst LHop MBar MGan MGos NHol NLar NWea SCoo SPer SRms SWvt WCFE WDin WFar |
| - 'Hard's Rob' | NLar |
| aff. ***verticillata*** B&SWJ 10672 | WCru |
| ***virescens*** B&SWJ 2646D | WCru |
| ***vulgaris*** | CArn CNat EMac EPfP GPoy |
| - 'Wiltshire Wonder' (v) | CNat |
| ***wilsoniae*** | CBcs CDul CTri EBee EMac EPfP GKir LHop MBar MMuc NHol NWea SCoo SHBN SPer WCFE WDin WFar |
| - L 650 | CGHE WPGP |
| - blue-leaved | LRHS WFar WPat |
| - var. ***guhtzunica*** | EPla EWes |

## *Berchemia* (*Rhamnaceae*)

| | |
|---|---|
| ***racemosa*** | CMen NLar WSHC |

## bergamot see *Citrus bergamia*

## *Bergenia* (*Saxifragaceae*)

| | |
|---|---|
| 'Abendglocken' | EBee ECGP ECha ECtt EGle EMil EPfP GKir LHop LRHS MNFA MWat NGdn NSti SPla WEas WFar |
| § 'Abendglut' | Widely available |
| 'Admiral' | CBct CMoH ECha MLHP |
| * ***agavifolia*** | CBct |
| 'Apple Court White' | CBct |
| 'Autumn Magic' | CBct EBee GAbr GQue LAst LHop LSou MSte NCGa NPri SPoG WFar |
| 'Baby Doll' | Widely available |
| § 'Ballawley' clonal $\Upsilon^{H4}$ | CFir CMoH EBrs ECha GCal IBlr IGor MLHP MRav WCAu WFar WMnd |
| 'Ballawley Guardsman' | CBct EBee EHrv |
| § Ballawley hybrids | EBee SDix |
| 'Ballawley Red' | GBin |
| 'Ballawley' seed-raised | see *B.* Ballawley hybrids |
| 'Bartók' | CDes |
| ***beesiana*** | see *B. purpurascens* |
| 'Beethoven' | CBct CDes CLAP CMoH EBee ECha EGle EPla GCra IGor MRav NBir NBre SUsu WCot WPGP |
| Bell Tower | see *B.* 'Glockenturm' |
| 'Biedermeir' | ECha |
| 'Bizet' | CBct |
| 'Borodin' | CBct |
| 'Brahms' | CBct GBuc |
| 'Bressingham Beauty' | GKir |
| 'Bressingham Bountiful' | CBct |
| 'Bressingham Ruby'PBR | CBcs CBct CLAP EBee EBrs ECha ECtt EPPr GKir LAst LBMP LSRN MRav NBir NCGa SHBN WCAu WPGP |
| 'Bressingham Salmon' | CBct CHar CMoH EBee ELan GMaP MBri MRav SHBN WCot WMnd |
| 'Bressingham White' $\Upsilon^{H4}$ | Widely available |
| ***ciliata*** | CDes CFee CHEx CLAP CTca EBee EBla EBrs EShb GCal IFro LEdu |

| | |
|---|---|
| | MCot MLHP MRav MSte NBir NHol NLar SDix SUsu WCot WKif WPGP WSHC WTin |
| - f. ***ciliata*** | CBct WCot |
| - f. ***ligulata*** | see *B. pacumbis* |
| - 'Patricia Furness' | CLAP |
| - 'Wilton' | CLAP WCot |
| ***ciliata* x *crassifolia*** | see *B.* x *schmidtii* |
| 'Claire Maxine' | GCal |
| ***cordifolia*** | Widely available |
| - 'Flore Pleno' | CBct |
| - 'Jelle' | GBin |
| - 'Purpurea' ♀$^{H4}$ | CBcs CDoC EAEE EBee ECha ELan EMFW EPfP EWTr GKir LBuc LCro LRHS MLHP MNFA MRav NBir SHBN SPer SPla SRms WCAu WFar WPnP |
| - 'Rosa Schwester' | EBee ECha |
| - 'Rosa Zeiten' | GBin |
| - 'Tubby Andrews' (v) | CBct CBow EBla ECtt EGle EMon LEdu MAvo MBrN MBri MCCP MDKP MLLN NLar NPro |
| - 'Winterglut' | CHFP EBee ELan GMaP IBal IFoB NBre NGdn SPoG SWvt WFar WHil WPnP WRHF |
| ***crassifolia*** | EBee NBre SRms |
| - 'Autumn Red' | CBct CMoH ECha |
| - 'Orbicularis' | see *B.* x *schmidtii* |
| * ***cyanea*** | CLAP WCot |
| 'David' | ECha EMon EWes |
| ***delavayi*** | see *B. purpurascens* var. *delavayi* |
| 'Delbees' | see *B.* 'Ballawley' clonal |
| 'Doppelgänger' | EBee SUsu |
| 'Eden's Dark Margin' | CBct CBgR EBee NPro |
| 'Eden's Magic Carpet' | CFir |
| 'Eden's Magic Giant' | CBct EBee GBin |
| ***emeiensis*** | CDes CLAP CPom WPGP |
| - hybrid | CBct MWat WCot |
| 'Eric Smith' | CBct EBee ECha EPla GBin GCal IGor MBri WCot WMnd |
| 'Eroica' | CBct COlW CSpe EBee ECha ECtt ELan EMon EPfP GBin LAst LHop MRav NBre NSti WCAu WMnd WPtf |
| 'Evening Glow' | see *B.* 'Abendglut' |
| 'Frau Holle' | EBee MBri |
| § 'Glockenturm' | CBct |
| 'Hellen Dillon' | see *B. purpurascens* 'Irish Crimson' |
| 'Herbstblute' | EBee EMon |
| 'Jo Watanabe' | CBct MRav |
| 'Lambrook' | see *B.* 'Margery Fish' |
| § 'Margery Fish' | CBct ECha SPer |
| ***milesii*** | see *B. stracheyi* |
| § 'Morgenröte' ♀$^{H4}$ | CBcs CBct CPrp EBee EBrs ECha EMil EPfP GKir GMaP LAst LSRN MGos MRav MSte NHol SHBN SPer SRms SWvt WCFE WCot |
| 'Morning Light' | NPro |
| Morning Red | see *B.* 'Morgenröte' |
| 'Mrs Crawford' | CBct ECha |
| 'Oeschberg' | CBct GBin GCal WCAu |
| 'Opal' | CBct |
| 'Overture' | CBct EBee ECtt EGle EHrv EUJe GAbr GEdr LAst LDai LHop LSRN MAvo MBri MNFA MWat NCGa NCob NGby NGdn SUsu WCAu WCot WFar WWFP |
| § ***pacumbis*** | CBct CDes CHEx CLAP EBee GBin GEdr NBid NBre NSti SDix WCot |
| - CC 1793 | SBch |
| - CC 3616 | WCot |
| 'Perfect' | CBct EBee WMnd |
| 'Pink Dragonfly' | CWGN EBee GBin LHop NBPN NBhm SPoG |
| 'Pinneberg' | GBin |
| 'Profusion' | SPer WCAu |
| 'Pugsley's Pink' | CBct GCra SHBN |
| § ***purpurascens*** ♀$^{H4}$ | CMoH EBee EPfP GBuc GKev GMaP IFoB IGor MBrN SDix SPer WCot WTin |
| - SDR 3978 new | GKev |
| § - var. ***delavayi*** ♀$^{H4}$ | EBrs MBri NBre SRms |
| - - CLD 1366 | WPer |
| § - 'Irish Crimson' | CBct CGHE WCot |
| aff. ***purpurascens*** | SMad |
| - ACE 2175 | WCot |
| 'Red Beauty' | CMoH MGos WPnP |
| 'Reitheim' | CBct EBee |
| 'Rosi Klose' | Widely available |
| 'Rosi Ruffles' | EBee |
| 'Rotblum' | CBct EBee ECGP ECtt EHoe EPfP GMaP MAvo NBir NCob NGdn NOrc NVic WFar WPer |
| § x ***schmidtii*** ♀$^{H4}$ | CBct CMac EBee IGor NBir NBre WCot |
| 'Schneekissen' | CBct CMac CPrp EBee ECGP EGle LAst MRav WCAu |
| § 'Schneekönigin' | CBct ECha GBin MRav |
| § 'Silberlicht' ♀$^{H4}$ | Widely available |
| Silverlight | see *B.* 'Silberlicht' |
| 'Simply Sweet' | WCot |
| Snow Queen | see *B.* 'Schneekönigin' |
| § ***stracheyi*** | CBct CMoH CPLG EBee ECha EGle EGoo EMon GCal IGor MLHP MRav NBid NLar SApp SDix WCot WEas |
| - CC 4609 | GKev |
| - Alba Group | CBct CDes CMoH EBee ECha GCal MSte SUsu WPGP |
| 'Sunningdale' | CBcs CBct CMac EAEE EBee ECha ELan EMFW EPfP GCra GKir GMaP LHop LRHS MLLN MRav NBir NGdn SWvt WCAu WMnd |
| ***tianquanensis*** | EBee |
| 'Walter Kienli' | GBin |
| Winter Fairy Tales | see *B.* 'Wintermärchen' |
| § 'Wintermärchen' | CBct EBee ECha ECtt ELan EPfP GCra LRHS MGos MRav MSte NCGa NHol NPro NSti SPoG WCot WMnd |
| 'Winterzauber' | EBee |

## *Bergeranthus* (*Aizoaceae*)

| | |
|---|---|
| sp. | WThu |
| ***glenensis*** | EDAr |
| ***multiceps*** | SChr |
| ***scapiger*** | WCot |

## *Berkheya* (*Asteraceae*)

| | |
|---|---|
| ***draco*** | EWld |
| ***multijuga*** | EDAr SBHP |
| ***purpurea*** | Widely available |
| - 'Silver Spike' | EDAr EPfP LSRN MBri |
| - 'Zulu Warrior' | CEnt EDif IPot NGBl SBHP SRkn |
| ***radula*** new | EBee |

## *Berlandiera* (*Asteraceae*)

| | |
|---|---|
| ***lyrata*** | EBee |

## *Berneuxia* (*Diapensiaceae*)

| | |
|---|---|
| ***thibetica*** | IBlr |

## *Berula* (*Apiaceae*)

| | |
|---|---|
| ***erecta*** | EHon EMFW NPer |

## *Berzelia* (*Bruniaceae*)

| | |
|---|---|
| ***galpinii*** | SPlb |
| ***lanuginosa*** | CTrC GGar IDee |

## *Beschorneria* (*Agavaceae*)

sp. WPGP
**albiflora** new WPGP
**septentrionalis** CAbP CFir CGHE CSpe CTrC EAmu EBee ECGP ESwi GAbr LSou MBNS MSCN MSte WClo WCot WLeb WPGP WPat
**septentrionalis** x **yuccoides** WPGP
**tubiflora** CDTJ CHEx EBee LEdu WPGP
**wrightii** EBee WPGP
**yuccoides** ♀H3 CAbb CBcs CHEx CTrC EAmu EBee EShb ESwi IBlr IDee ISea LEdu MSte SAPC SArc SChr SDnm SEND SLim WPGP
- subsp. **dekosteriana** F&M 102 new WPGP
- 'Quicksilver' CBcs CBod CCCN CDoC CEnd CKno CTrC EBee LRHS MBri MGos MSte NVic SDix SDnm SPoG SSpi WCot WLeb WPGP

## *Bessera* (*Alliaceae*)

**elegans** CAvo CFFs CFir EBee EBrs ECho EPot LRHS WCot

## *Beta* (*Chenopodiaceae*)

**trigyna** WCot
**vulgaris** WHer
- 'Bull's Blood' CArn CHFP CSpe EBee MSte WJek
- subsp. **cicla** var. **flavescens** 'Bright Lights' ♀H3 CArn
- - - 'Rhubarb Chard' ♀H3 WJek
- subsp. **maritima** CAgr EBWF

## *Betonica* see *Stachys*

## *Betula* ✿ (*Betulaceae*)

**alba** L. see *B. pendula, B. pubescens*
**albosinensis** misapplied see *B. utilis*
**albosinensis** Burkill ♀H4 CDul CLnd CMCN CTri EBee EPfP EWTr ISea NLar NWea SBLw WDin WFar WOrn
- W 4106 CSto
- from Gansu, China new CSto
- 'Bowling Green' CPMA WPGP
- 'China Ruby' CDul CLnd CPMA GKir MBri SMad SSpi
- 'Chinese Garden' CPMA MBlu
- clone F see *B. albosinensis* 'Ness'
- 'Fascination' new LMaj
- 'K.Ashburner' CPMA CTho
- 'Kansu' CLnd CPMA GKir SBig SBir SCoo SPur SSpi WHCr
§ - 'Ness' CPMA CTho
- 'Pink Champagne' new CSto
- 'Rhinegold' new MBlu
- 'Sable' SPer
- var. **septentrionalis** ♀H4 Widely available
- - 'Purdom' CPMA GKir SBig SMad
§ **alleghaniensis** CCVT CDul CMCN CSto EBee EPfP GKir IDee NLar NWea WDin
**apoiensis** 'Mount Apoi' CPMA GKir SBig
§ x **caerulea** CPMA NLar
**caerulea-grandis** see *B.* x *caerulea*
**chichibuensis** CSto SBir WHer
**chinensis** CMCN
'Conyngham' CPMA CTho MBlu SBir SLau
**cordifolia** see *B. papyrifera* var. *cordifolia*
**costata** misapplied see *B. ermanii* 'Grayswood Hill'
**costata** ambig. EHig
**costata** Trautv. CLnd CTho EBee ELan EPfP GKir MAsh MSwo SBLw WDin WOrn
* - 'Fincham Cream' CPMA GKir SBig WHCr
I x **cruithnei** GAuc
**cylindrostachya** CExc EBee
**dahurica** Pall. CDul CMCN GAuc IArd
- 'Maurice Foster' CPMA CTho
- 'Stone Farm' CPMA
**delavayi** GKir
**ermanii** Widely available
- B&SWJ 8801 from South Korea new WCru
- from Hokkaido, Japan CSto
- 'Blush' CLnd CPMA GKir SBig SCoo SHBN WHCr
- var. **ermanii** MSF 865 EBee SKHP WPGP
§ - 'Grayswood Hill' ♀H4 CDul CEnd CLnd CMHG CPMA CTho EBee GKir GQui LCro LRHS MBlu MBri MGos NWea SCoo SHBN SLim SMad SPer SSpi WHCr WOrn WPGP
- 'Hakkoda Orange' CPMA CTho GKir MBlu MBri SCoo
- 'Holland' new LMaj
- 'Moonbeam' GKir
- 'Mount Zao' CTho
* - 'Pendula' CPMA MBlu SBig SCoo SMad
- 'Polar Bear' CPMA CWSG GKir LRHS MBri SCoo WHCr WHar
* - **ussuriensis** GKir
'Fetisowii' CDul CEnd CMCN CTho ECrN GKir LRHS MBlu SBig SCoo SSta
**fruticosa** see *B. humilis*
**globispica** EWTr SBir
'Hergest' EBee EPfP GKir LRHS MBri MGos SCoo SLau SLim WHCr WPGP
§ **humilis** GKir GQui WDin
**insignis** CExc
'Inverleith' see *B. utilis* var. *jacquemontii* 'Inverleith'
**jacquemontii** see *B. utilis* var. *jacquemontii*
**kamtschatica** see *B. humilis*
**lenta** CDul CLnd CMCN CSto EPfP IArd IDee MBlu NLar NWea WDin
**luminifera** CPMA GKir IDee NLar SBir
**lutea** see *B. alleghaniensis*
**mandshurica** GQui WHCr
§ - var. **japonica** CLnd ECrN GKir NLar NWea
- - 'Whitespire Senior' CDul
**maximowicziana** CDoC CDul CLnd CMCN CTho CWib EPfP EWTr LHop NLar NWea WDin
§ **medwedewii** CDul CMCN CSto EBee EHig EMil EPfP GQui NHol NWea SBir SCoo
- from Winkworth CTho
- 'Gold Bark' MBlu
**megrelica** see *B. medwedewii*
§ **michauxii** NLar
**nana** CDul EBee GAuc GKir MBar MGos MRav NHol NWea SIng SRms SSta STre WDin
- 'Glengarry' EPot NLar
- var. **michauxii** see *B. michauxii*
**nigra** CBcs CCVT CDoC CDul CEnd CLnd CMCN CSBt CTho CTri ECrN EMil LMaj LPan MAsh MBri SBLw SBir SHBN SPoG SSta WDin WMou WOrn
- Heritage = 'Cully' ♀H4 CDul CEnd CLnd CMCN CPMA EBee EMil LPan LRHS MBlu MGos NWea SBig SBir SCoo SLim SPoG SSta WDin WFar WHCr WMoo
- 'Little King' CPMA MBlu SPoG
- 'Summer Cascade' MBri

| | | |
|---|---|---|
| | - Wakehurst form | EPfP GKir LRHS SPer |
| | ***papyrifera*** | Widely available |
| | - var. ***commutata*** | WDin |
| § | - var. ***cordifolia*** | CSto |
| | - 'Saint George' | CPMA CTho |
| | - 'Vancouver' | CPMA CTho |
| § | ***pendula*** ♀$^{H4}$ | Widely available |
| | - 'Bangor' | CLnd CPMA |
| * | - 'Boeugh's Variety' | CEnd GBin |
| | - f. ***crispa*** | see *B. pendula* 'Laciniata' |
| | - 'Dalecarlica' misapplied | see *B. pendula* 'Laciniata' |
| | - 'Dalecarlica' ambig. | CBcs CCVT CSBt ECrN MDun MRav SCrf SLim WFar |
| | - 'Dark Prince' | CPMA |
| | - 'Fastigiata' | CDoC CDul CEnd CLnd CSBt CTho EBee ECrN ELan GKir LMaj LPan MGos NWea SBLw SCoo SLim SPer WDin WFar WMoo WOrn |
| * | - 'Golden Beauty' | CDoC CTri ECrN GKir LPan LRHS MAsh MGos NLar SCoo SLim SPer SPoG SSpi WDin WFar WHCr WOrn |
| § | - 'Laciniata' ♀$^{H4}$ | CDoC CDul CMCN CTho CWSG CWib EBee ECrN ELan EPfP GKir LAst LMaj LPan MAsh MGos MSwo NBea NBee NLar NWea SBLw SCoo SPer WDin WHar |
| | - 'Long Trunk' | CDul EBee ECrN EMil LPan MAsh MBlu |
| | - 'Purpurea' | CCVT CDul CLnd CMCN CSBt CWib EBee ECrN ELan ELon EPfP LAst LPan LRHS LSRN MGos MSwo NBea NWea SBLw SCoo SPer SPoG WDin WFar WOrn |
| | - 'Silver Cascade' | MGos |
| | - 'Silver Grace' | EBee ECrN LSRN MGos |
| | - 'Swiss Glory' **new** | CLnd LMaj |
| | - 'Tristis' ♀$^{H4}$ | Widely available |
| | - 'Youngii' | Widely available |
| | ***platyphylla*** misapplied | see *B. mandshurica* |
| | ***platyphylla*** Sukaczev | CMCN NWea |
| | - Dakota Pinnacle = 'Fargo' **new** | SPoG |
| | - var. ***japonica*** | see *B. mandshurica* var. *japonica* |
| | - subsp. ***kamtschatica*** | see *B. mandshurica* var. *japonica* |
| | - subsp. ***platyphylla*** | CMCN |
| | ***populifolia*** | CMCN CSto |
| § | ***pubescens*** | CCVT CDul CLnd CSto CTri ECrN EMil NBee NBlu NWea SBLw SLPl WDin WFar WMou |
| I | ***refugia*** | GAuc |
| | 'Royal Frost' | CDul CPMA GKir IArd MAsh NLar NPal SPoG WHar |
| | ***saposhnikovii*** | GKir |
| | ***schmidtii*** | EWTr |
| | ***szechuanica*** | GQui WDin WPGP |
| | - SF 9903 **new** | ISea |
| | - 'Liuba White' | CPMA CTho |
| | - 'Moonlight' **new** | SLau |
| | 'Trost's Dwarf' | WDin |
| § | ***utilis*** | CDul CMCN CMHG CSBt CSto EBee ECrN EMil ERas ISea LMaj MAsh MBar MRav NBee NWea SSta WDin WFar WPGP |
| | - H&M 1480 from Sichuan, China **new** | CSto |
| | - RSC 1 from Langtang, Nepal | CSto |
| | - Yu 10163 from Yunnan, China **new** | CSto |
| | - from Eastern Nepal | CSto |
| | - from Uttar Pradesh, India **new** | GAuc |
| | - 'Buckland' | ECrN |
| | - 'Darkness' | SLon |
| | - 'Fascination' | CCVT CDul CPMA EMil EPfP GKir IArd LPan LRHS MBri MGos NPal NWea SBir SCoo SLim SSpi WHCr |
| * | - 'Fastigiata' | CLnd CPMA SBig |
| | - 'Forrest's Blush' | CLnd CPMA EBee MBri SBig SBir |
| N | - var. ***jacquemontii*** | Widely available |
| | - - Polunin | WPGP |
| | - - SF 00004 | ISea |
| | - - 'Doorenbos' ♀$^{H4}$ | Widely available |
| | - - 'Grayswood Ghost' ♀$^{H4}$ | CDul CEnd CMCN CMHG CPMA CTho ECrN EPfP EWes GKir LCro LPan LRHS MBlu MDun SBig SBir SHBN SLau SLim SMad SPer SSpi |
| § | - - 'Inverleith' | CDul CEnd CLnd CPMA EBee GKir MAsh MBri SBig SBir SCoo SLim WFar WOrn WPGP |
| | - - 'Jermyns' ♀$^{H4}$ | CDul CEnd CLnd CMCN CPMA CTho CTri ECot EPfP GKir LMaj LPan LRHS MBlu MBri SCoo SLau SPer SSpi WHCr WOrn |
| | - - 'McBeath' | SLau |
| | - - 'Silver Shadow' ♀$^{H4}$ | CDul CEnd CMCN CPMA CTho CTri EBee EPfP GKir LRHS LSRN MBlu NWea SBig SBir SCoo SLau SLim SMad SPer SPoG SSpi SSta WOrn |
| | - - 'Trinity College' | CPMA EBee GKir MBri SBig SBir SSpi WHCr |
| | - 'Knightshayes' | CTho |
| | - 'Moonbeam' | CDul CLnd CPMA GKir MBri SBig SBir SCoo SPoG SPur WHCr WHar |
| | - var. ***occidentalis*** 'Kyelang' | CPMA |
| | - 'Polar Bear' | GKir |
| | - var. ***prattii*** | CEnd CTho MBlu |
| | - 'Ramdana River' | CLnd MBlu |
| | - 'Wakehurst Place Chocolate' | CDul CLnd CPMA CWSG GKir LRHS MBlu MBri MLan SBig SCoo SMad SSpi WHCr |
| | cf. ***utilis*** GWJ 9259 | WCru |
| | - HWJK 2345 | WCru |
| | ***verrucosa*** | see *B. pendula* |

## *Biarum* (*Araceae*)

| | | |
|---|---|---|
| | S&L 604 | WCot |
| | SBLBL 597 | WCot |
| | ***arundanum*** | WCot |
| | ***bovei*** | EBrs ECho WCot |
| | ***carratracense*** | WCot |
| | ***davisii*** | EBee EBrs ECho SKHP WCot |
| | - subsp. ***marmarisense*** | ECho WCot |
| | ***dispar*** | WCot |
| | ***ditschianum*** | WCot |
| | ***galianii*** PB 435 | WCot |
| | ***ochridense*** | EBrs WCot |
| | ***spruneri*** S&L 229 | SKHP |
| | ***tenuifolium*** | EBee EBrs ECho ERos SKHP WCot |
| | - subsp. ***abbreviatum*** MS 974 | WCot |
| | - - from Greece | ECho |
| | - subsp. ***idomenaeum*** | WCot |
| | - subsp. ***zelebori*** LB 300 | WCot |

## *Bidens* (*Asteraceae*)

| | | |
|---|---|---|
| | B&SWJ 10276 from Mexico | WCru |
| | ***atrosanguinea*** | see *Cosmos atrosanguineus* |
| § | ***aurea*** | CEnt EBee EBla ECtt EMon EPPr EWes GCal GGar LAst LEdu LRHS MDKP MNrw NBlu NCGa NPer SGar SPet SPhx STes WBor WFar WOld |

| | |
|---|---|
| - from Guatemala B&SWJ 9049 | WCru |
| - 'Blacksmith's Flame' | EBla |
| - cream-flowered | MNrw MSte |
| - 'Golden Drop' | EBee EWes |
| - 'Hannay's Lemon Drop' | CEnt CFwr CKno CPen CSev EBee EBla ECtt ELon EPPr GCal LHop MDKP MNrw MSte NCGa SSvw STes SUsu WHrl WMoo WPGP |
| - 'Rising Sun' | EBee EWes |
| ***ferulifolia*** Ÿ$^{H1+3}$ | ECtt NPer |
| - Golden Flame = 'Samsawae' | NBlu |
| - Peter's Gold Carpet = 'Peters Goldteppich'$^{PBR}$ | SVil |
| - Peter's Gold Rush = 'Topteppich'$^{PBR}$ | LSou NPri |
| - Solaire = 'Bidtis 1' | WGor |
| 'Golden Star' | LAst LSou |
| ***heterophylla*** misapplied | CAby CEnt CKno ECtt MCot MRav SMrm WFar WHal WHrl WMoo WPrP WWlt |
| - CD&R 1515 **new** | LPla |
| ***heterophylla*** Ortega | see *B. aurea* |
| ***humilis*** | see *B. triplinervia* var. *macrantha* |
| ***integrifolia*** | SMad |
| ***pilosa*** | EBee |
| ***triplinervia*** B&SWJ 10413 | WCru |
| - B&SWJ 10696 | WCru |
| § - var. ***macrantha*** | EBee ELon LHop |

## *Bignonia* (*Bignoniaceae*)

| | |
|---|---|
| ***capreolata*** | CCCN WCot WSHC |
| § - 'Atrosanguinea' | LRHS |
| - 'Dragon Lady' | WCot |
| ***lindleyana*** | see *Clytostoma calystegioides* |
| ***tweedieana*** | see *Macfadyena unguis-cati* |
| ***unguis-cati*** | see *Macfadyena unguis-cati* |

## *Bilderdykia* see *Fallopia*

## *Billardiera* (*Pittosporaceae*)

| | |
|---|---|
| ***cymosa*** | SOWG |
| ***erubescens*** | CSec |
| ***longiflora*** Ÿ$^{H3}$ | Widely available |
| - 'Cherry Berry' | CBcs CWan EBee ELan IArd IDee LRHS MAsh MCCP NLar SLim SPer SPoG SRms SWvt |
| - ***fructu-albo*** | CBcs EBee ELan EWes GGar IDee ITim SLim SPer SPoG SWvt |
| - red-berried | GGar |
| - white-berried | LRHS |
| ***variifolia*** **new** | CSec |

## *Billbergia* (*Bromeliaceae*)

| | |
|---|---|
| ***nutans*** | CHEx CHal CHll CPen EBak EOHP EShb IBlr IDee LEdu LRHS MBri MJnS NPal SChr SEND SRms WCor WGwG |
| - var. ***schimperiana*** | EShb |
| * - 'Variegata' (v) | CHll CSpe EShb NPal SChr WCot WGwG |
| ***pyramidalis*** Ÿ$^{H1}$ | XBlo |
| I - 'Variegata' (v) | IBlr |
| x ***windii*** Ÿ$^{H1}$ | CHEx CHal EBak SRms |

## *Bismarckia* (*Arecaceae*)

| | |
|---|---|
| ***nobilis*** | EAmu LPal SBig |

## *Bistorta* see *Persicaria*

## *Bituminaria* (*Papilionaceae*)

| | |
|---|---|
| ***bituminosa*** | WSHC |

## blackberry see *Rubus fruticosus*

## blackcurrant see *Ribes nigrum*

## *Blechnum* (*Blechnaceae*)

| | |
|---|---|
| from Chile | SKHP |
| ***alpinum*** | see *B. penna-marina* subsp. *alpinum* |
| ***auriculatum*** | EBee WRic |
| ***brasiliense*** Ÿ$^{H1}$ | WRic |
| ***chambersii*** | WRic |
| ***chilense*** Ÿ$^{H3}$ | CDes CGHE CHEx CLAP EBee EPfP GCra GGar IBlr MMoz NVic SAPC SArc SDix SKHP WCru WMoo WPGP WRic |
| ***colensoi*** | WRic |
| ***discolor*** | CBcs CLAP CTrC EUJe GBin IDee LPal WRic |
| ***fluviatile*** | CBcs CLAP CTrC EUJe GBin IDee MMoz SKHP WRic |
| ***fraseri*** **new** | WRic |
| ***gibbum*** | EShb MBri |
| - 'Silver Lady' | CTrC WRic |
| ***magellanicum*** misapplied | see *B. chilense* |
| ***magellanicum*** (Desv.) Mett. | EBee SKHP WRic |
| ***minus*** | MGos WRic |
| § ***niponicum*** **new** | EBee |
| ***novae-zelandiae*** | CBcs CDTJ CTrC EUJe GBin WRic |
| ***nudum*** | EPfP EQua NMoo WRic |
| ***penna-marina*** Ÿ$^{H4}$ | CCCN CElw CLAP CPLG EFer EMil EMon EPot GAbr GCal GGar GMaP LEdu MBri NBir NRya NVic NWCA SRms WAbe WEas WFib WMoo WRic |
| § - subsp. ***alpinum*** | CLAP EBee ECha GGar SKHP WAbe WMoo |
| - 'Cristatum' | CLAP GAbr GGar SRms WAbe |
| ***punctulatum*** | WRic |
| ***spicant*** Ÿ$^{H4}$ | Widely available |
| - 'Cristatum' | EBee |
| ***tabulare*** misapplied | see *B. chilense* |
| ***tabulare*** (Thunb.) Kuhn Ÿ$^{H1}$ | CBcs EPfP GKev NMun WPGP WRic |
| ***vulcanicum*** | CLAP WRic |
| ***wattsii*** | EAmu |

## *Blepharocalyx* (*Myrtaceae*)

| | |
|---|---|
| ***cruckshanksii*** | CPLG LRHS WPic |
| - 'Heaven Scent' | CCCN EBee LAst LRHS MCCP MLan NLar WBor |

## *Blephilia* (*Lamiaceae*)

| | |
|---|---|
| ***ciliata*** | MSal |

## *Bletilla* ✿ (*Orchidaceae*)

| | |
|---|---|
| ***hyacinthina*** | see *B. striata* |
| ***ochracea*** | EBee |
| **Penway Sunset gx** | WCot |
| ***sinensis*** | EBrs |
| § ***striata*** | CBct CBgR CDes CPom CSec CTri EBee EBrs ECho EPot IHer LAma LEdu MSal NCGa NHol NLAp NMen SHdy SMeo SPer WFar WPGP |
| - ***alba*** | see *B. striata* var. *japonica* f. *gebina* |
| - 'Albostriata' | CBct CWsd EBee EBrs ECho ELan LAma NCGa NLAp WCot |
| - var. ***japonica*** | EPot |
| § - - f. ***gebina*** | CAby CDes CMdw CMea CSec CTri EBee EBrs ECho EPot LAma LEdu LRHS NLar WCot WFar WPGP |
| - - - variegated (v) | LEdu NMen WCot |

| | | |
|---|---|---|
| | - variegated (v) | CBow |
| | - yellow-flowered | EBrs |
| | ***szetschuanica*** | EBee |

## *Bloomeria* (*Alliaceae*)

| | | |
|---|---|---|
| | ***crocea*** | ECho |
| | - var. ***aurea*** | EBee EBrs ECho ERos GKev LRHS |
| | - var. ***montana*** | ECho |

## blueberry see *Vaccinium corymbosum*

## *Blumenbachia* (*Loasaceae*)

| | | |
|---|---|---|
| | ***insignia*** | CSec |

## *Bocconia* (*Papaveraceae*)

| | | |
|---|---|---|
| | ***cordata*** | see *Macleaya cordata* (Willd.) R. Br. |
| | ***microcarpa*** | see *Macleaya microcarpa* |

## *Boehmeria* (*Urticaceae*)

| | | |
|---|---|---|
| | ***nipononivea*** 'Kogane-mushi' (u) new | EBee |
| | - 'Nichirin' (u) new | EBee |
| | ***nivea*** | MSal |
| | ***sylvatica*** | NLar |

## *Boenninghausenia* (*Rutaceae*)

| | | |
|---|---|---|
| | ***albiflora*** | CSpe EBee GKev |
| | - B&SWJ 1479 | WCru |
| | - BWJ 8141 from China | WCru |
| | - pink-flowered B&SWJ 3112 | WCru |
| | ***japonica*** B&SWJ 4876 | WCru |

## *Bolandra* (*Saxifragaceae*)

| | | |
|---|---|---|
| | aff. ***californica*** | EBee |

## *Bolax* (*Apiaceae*)

| | | |
|---|---|---|
| | ***glebaria*** | see *B. gummifer* |
| § | ***gummifer*** | ECho EPot WAbe |

## *Bolboschoenus* (*Cyperaceae*)

| | | |
|---|---|---|
| § | ***maritimus*** | CRWN EBWF GFor LPBA WFar |
| * | ***romanus*** new | EBee |

## *Boltonia* (*Asteraceae*)

| | | |
|---|---|---|
| | ***asteroides*** | CFee CSam CSpe ECtt EHrv EMon GQue LEdu MMuc NGdn NSti SMrm SPer STes SVil SWat WBVN WCAu WDyG WRHF |
| | - var. ***latisquama*** | EBee GMaP LSou MAvo MRav MSte MWat NLar SSvw WBor WFar WHal WWFP |
| | - - 'Nana' | EGoo LEdu MLLN MRav NBre WFar WPer |
| | - - 'Snowbank' | EBee EBla ELan EWsh GCal |
| | - 'Pink Beauty' | EBla EMon LEdu |
| | - var. ***recognita*** | EMon LRHS |
| | ***decurrens*** | EBee NBre |
| | ***incisa*** | see *Kalimeris incisa* |
| * | ***richardsonii*** | EBee |

## *Bomarea* (*Alstroemeriaceae*)

| | | |
|---|---|---|
| | F&M 130 new | WPGP |
| | aff. ***acuminata*** B&SWJ 10617 | WCru |
| | ***acutifolia*** B&SWJ 9094 | WCru |
| | - B&SWJ 994 new | WPrP |
| | ***boliviensis*** | EBee WCru |
| | - RCB/Arg P-18 | WCot |
| | ***caldasii*** ♀H1 | CCCN CFir CHEx CRHN EBee EShb SMad SOWG WBor WFoF WPGP WSHC |
| | ***costaricensis*** B&SWJ 10467 | WCru |
| § | ***edulis*** | CBgR CGHE CHEx CRHN EBee WCot WOut WPGP |
| | - B&SWJ 9017 | WCru |
| | - F&M 104 | WPGP |
| | aff. ***frondea*** B&SWJ 10681 new | WCru |
| | ***hirtella*** | see *B. edulis* |
| | ***isopetala*** | SKHP |
| | ***multiflora*** | CFir EBee GCal SKHP |
| | ***patacocensis*** | SKHP |
| | ***salsilla*** | CAvo CCCN CRHN SKHP WCot WCru WPGP WSHC |

## *Bongardia* (*Berberidaceae*)

| | | |
|---|---|---|
| | ***chrysogonum*** | CAvo EBrs ECho EPot WCot WHal |

## *Bonia* (*Poaceae*)

| | | |
|---|---|---|
| § | ***solida*** | CHEx ERod LPal MMoz MMuc MWht NPal SEND |

## borage see *Borago officinalis*

## *Borago* (*Boraginaceae*)

| | | |
|---|---|---|
| | ***alba*** | MNHC WCHb |
| | ***laxiflora*** | see *B. pygmaea* |
| | ***officinalis*** | CArn CBod CSev CWan ELau EPfP GKir GPoy LRHS MHer MNHC NBir NGHP NVic SBch SVic WCot WHer WLHH |
| | - 'Alba' | CBre CHFP CSev ELau ILis NGHP SBch SDnm SIde WCHb WHer WJek WLHH WRha |
| | - 'Bill Archer' (v) | CNat |
| § | ***pygmaea*** | CArn CHFP CHid CPLG CSev ELan EOHP GBar LHop MHar MHer MTho NGHP NSti STes SWat WCHb WGwG WHer WMoo WPrP |

## *Borinda* (*Poaceae*)

| | | |
|---|---|---|
| | ***albocerea*** | EPla ERod MWht |
| | - Yunnan 1 | EPla WPGP |
| | - Yunnan 2 | CDTJ EPla MMoz WPGP |
| | - Yunnan 3a | CDTJ EPla WPGP |
| | - Yunnan 4 new | CDTJ WPGP |
| | ***boliana*** | EPla SBig |
| | ***edulis*** | EPla |
| | ***frigida*** | CDTJ EPla WPGP |
| | ***grossa*** (Yi) | EPla |
| | ***lushuiensis*** | EPla |
| | ***macclureana*** | EPla |
| | - KR 5177 | MWht WPGP |
| | ***papyrifera*** | EPla WPGP |
| | - KR 7613 new | MWht |
| | ***scabrida*** | CDTJ CEnt CGHE EPla MMoz MWht WPGP |
| | - 'Asian Wonder' | NLar |

## *Boronia* (*Rutaceae*)

| | | |
|---|---|---|
| | ***citriodora*** | SOWG |
| | ***denticulata*** | ECou |
| | ***heterophylla*** | CBcs CCCN CTsd ECou SOWG |
| | - white-flowered | ECou |
| | ***megastigma*** | ECou |
| | - 'Brown Meg' | CBcs |
| | ***mollis*** | SOWG |
| | ***pinnata*** | ECou SOWG |
| | ***serrulata*** | ECou |

## *Bothriochloa* (*Poaceae*)

| | | |
|---|---|---|
| § | ***bladhii*** | EPPr MAvo |
| | ***caucasica*** | see *B. bladhii* |
| § | ***ischaemum*** | EPPr MAvo |

## *Botryostege* see *Tripetaleia*

## *Bougainvillea* (*Nyctaginaceae*)

| | | |
|---|---|---|
| | 'Alexandra' | LRHS MBri |
| | 'Apple Blossom' | see *B.* 'Elizabeth Doxey' |
| | 'Audrey Grey' | see *B.* 'Elizabeth Doxey' |
| | 'Brilliant' misapplied | see *B.* x *buttiana* 'Raspberry Ice' |
| | x ***buttiana*** 'Ametyst' | MBri |
| | - 'Audrey Grey' | see *B.* 'Elizabeth Doxey' |
| | - 'Barbara Karst' | SOWG |
| | - 'Coconut Ice' (v) | MJnS SOWG |
| § | - 'Lady Mary Baring' | SOWG |
| § | - 'Mahara' (d) | SOWG |
| | - 'Mahara Double Red' | see *B.* x *buttiana* 'Mahara' |
| § | - 'Miss Manila' 🏆$^{H1}$ | SOWG |
| § | - 'Raspberry Ice' (v) | EShb SOWG |
| § | - 'Roseville's Delight' (d) | SOWG |
| § | Camarillo Fiesta = 'Monle' (*spectabilis* hybrid) | SOWG |
| § | 'Closeburn' | SOWG |
| § | 'Elizabeth Doxey' | SOWG |
| | ***glabra*** 🏆$^{H1}$ | CMen LRHS MBri |
| § | - 'Magnifica' | SOWG |
| § | - 'Sanderiana' | LCro |
| | 'Gloucester Royal' | SOWG |
| | 'Golden Doubloon' | see *B.* x *buttiana* 'Roseville's Delight' |
| | 'Hawaiian Scarlet' | see *B.* 'San Diego Red' |
| | 'Klong Fire' | see *B.* x *buttiana* 'Mahara' |
| | 'Lady Mary Baring' | see *B.* x *buttiana* 'Lady Mary Baring' |
| | 'Little Caroline' | SOWG |
| | 'Lord Willingdon' misapplied | see *B.* 'Torch Glow' |
| | 'Magnifica' | see *B. glabra* 'Magnifica' |
| | 'Mahara Double Red' | see *B.* x *buttiana* 'Mahara' |
| | 'Mahara Orange' | see *B.* x *buttiana* 'Roseville's Delight' |
| | 'Manila Magic Red' | see *B.* x *buttiana* 'Mahara' |
| | 'Mini-Thai' | see *B.* 'Torch Glow' |
| * | 'Orange Flame' | SOWG |
| | 'Orange Glow' | see *B.* Camarillo Fiesta = 'Monle' |
| | 'Pixie' | see *B.* 'Torch Glow' |
| | 'Princess Mahara' | see *B.* x *buttiana* 'Mahara' |
| | 'Raspberry Ice' | see *B.* x *buttiana* 'Raspberry Ice' |
| | 'Rubyana' | SOWG |
| § | 'San Diego Red' 🏆$^{H1}$ | SOWG |
| | 'Sanderiana' | see *B. glabra* 'Sanderiana' |
| | Scarlett O'Hara | see *B.* 'San Diego Red' |
| | 'Smartipants' | see *B.* 'Torch Glow' |
| | 'Tango' | see *B.* x *buttiana* 'Miss Manila' |
| | 'Temple Fire' | see *B.* 'Closeburn' |
| | 'Thai Gold' | see *B.* x *buttiana* 'Roseville's Delight' |
| § | 'Torch Glow' | EAmu |
| | 'Tropical Rainbow' | see *B.* x *buttiana* 'Raspberry Ice' |
| | 'Vera Blakeman' | MJnS SOWG |
| | 'Wac Campbell' (d) | SOWG |

## *Boussingaultia* (*Basellaceae*)

| | | |
|---|---|---|
| | ***baselloides*** Hook. | see *Anredera cordifolia* |

## *Bouteloua* (*Poaceae*)

| | | |
|---|---|---|
| | ***curtipendula*** | CRWN EBee GFor |
| § | ***gracilis*** | EBee EBrs EHoe EQua EWsh GFor MWhi SUsu SWal WPGP WPer |

## *Bouvardia* (*Rubiaceae*)

| | | |
|---|---|---|
| | x ***domestica*** | EShb |
| | ***longiflora*** | SOWG |
| | ***ternifolia*** | WCot |

## *Bowiea* (*Hyacinthaceae*)

| | | |
|---|---|---|
| | ***volubilis*** | CHal EBee EBrs EShb |

## *Bowkeria* (*Scrophulariaceae*)

| | | |
|---|---|---|
| | ***cymosa*** | SPlb |
| | ***verticillata*** | WBor |

## *Boykinia* (*Saxifragaceae*)

| | | |
|---|---|---|
| | ***aconitifolia*** | CAbP EBee EBla GBuc GGar MLLN MRav NLar NRya SMad WCru WMoo WSHC |
| | ***elata*** | see *B. occidentalis* |
| | ***heucheriformis*** | see *B. jamesii* |
| § | ***jamesii*** | CGra EBee GEdr GKev NWCA |
| | ***lycoctonifolia*** | EBee |
| | ***major*** | EBee GAuc WBor |
| § | ***occidentalis*** | EBee GGar GKev WCru WMoo WPtf |
| | ***rotundifolia*** | EBee GBuc GKev NBir WCru WMoo |
| | - JLS 86269LACA | EMon |
| | ***tellimoides*** | see *Peltoboykinia tellimoides* |

## boysenberry see *Rubus* 'Boysenberry'

## *Brachychilum* see *Hedychium*

## *Brachychiton* (*Sterculiaceae*)

| | | |
|---|---|---|
| | ***acerifolius*** | CHEx EShb |
| | ***discolor*** | EShb |
| § | ***rupestris*** | EShb |

## *Brachyelytrum* (*Poaceae*)

| | | |
|---|---|---|
| | ***japonicum*** | GFor MAvo NLar |

## *Brachyglottis* ✿ (*Asteraceae*)

| | | |
|---|---|---|
| § | ***bidwillii*** | IDee |
| | - 'Basil Fox' | WAbe |
| § | ***buchananii*** | GKir WSHC |
| | - 'Silver Shadow' | GGar |
| § | ***compacta*** | ECou EPfP LRHS MAsh SPer SPoG WEas |
| | ***compacta*** x ***monroi*** | ECou LRHS |
| | 'County Park' | ECou |
| | 'Drysdale' | ELan EPfP GGar LRHS MAsh MBri MRav NPri SRGP SWvt |
| § | (Dunedin Group) 'Moira Reid' (v) | CPLG EHoe ELon |
| § | - 'Sunshine' 🏆$^{H4}$ | Widely available |
| | 'Frosty' | ECou |
| | ***greyi*** misapplied | see *B.* (Dunedin Group) 'Sunshine' |
| § | ***greyi*** (Hook. f.) B. Nord. | CTrG EBee EPfP MBar MWhi |
| | ***greyi*** x ***repanda*** | CDoC CHEx GGar SAPC SArc SKHP SSpi |
| | ***huntii*** x ***stewartii*** | GGar |
| | ***laxifolia*** misapplied | see *B.* (Dunedin Group) 'Sunshine' |
| | 'Leith's Gold' | CTrC |
| § | ***monroi*** 🏆$^{H4}$ | CSBt CWib EBee ECou EGoo EHoe ELan EPfP GGar LAst MLLN MRav SLon SPoG WDin WEas |
| | - 'Clarence' | ECou |
| | ***repanda*** | CBcs CHEx CTrG |
| § | ***rotundifolia*** | CBcs CCCN CDoC GGal GGar NLar WEas |
| | 'Silver Waves' | ECou |
| § | ***spedenii*** | GGar |
| I | 'Sunshine Improved' | CBcs EHoe NBir SWvt |
| | 'Sunshine Variegated' | see *B.* (Dunedin Group) 'Moira Reid' |
| | Walberton's Silver Dormouse = 'Walbrach'$^{PBR}$ | LBuc MAsh SPoG |

## *Brachypodium* (*Poaceae*)

***pinnatum*** EHoe
***sylvaticum*** EBWF EHul GCal GFor

## *Brachyscome* (*Asteraceae*)

***formosa*** ECou
***iberidifolia*** LAst
'Metallic Blue' NPri
'Mini Yellow' NPri
***multifida*** MBri NPri
'Pink Mist' SPet
***rigidula*** ECou
'Strawberry Mousse' CWsd LAst SPet
'Tinkerbell' SPoG

## *Brachysema* (*Papilionaceae*)

***celsianum*** SOWG

## *Brachystachyum* (*Poaceae*)

***densiflorum*** EPla NLar

## *Brachystelma* (*Asclepiadaceae*)

***angustum*** LToo
***bracteolatum*** LToo
***caffrum*** LToo
***circinatum*** LToo
***dinteri*** LToo
***filifolium*** LToo
***nanum*** LToo

## *Bracteantha* see *Xerochrysum*

## *Brahea* (*Arecaceae*)

***armata*** CAbb CBrP CDTJ EAmu EPfP EShb ETod IDee LPal MGos MREP NPal SAPC SArc SChr SPer STrG
***dulcis*** EAmu
***edulis*** CBrP EAmu LPal

## *Brainea* (*Blechnaceae*)

***insignis*** **new** WRic

## *Brassaia* see *Schefflera*

## *Brassica* (*Brassicaceae*)

***japonica*** see *B. juncea* var. *crispifolia*
§ ***juncea*** var. ***crispifolia*** CArn MNHC
***nigra*** CArn
***oleracea*** EBWF WHer
* ***rapa*** var. ***japonica*** CArn WJek
* - var. ***purpurea*** WJek

## *Bravoa* (*Agavaceae*)

***geminiflora*** see *Polianthes geminiflora*

## *Bretschneidera* (*Bretschneideraceae*)

***sinensis*** CExc

## *Brillantaisia* (*Acanthaceae*)

***kirungae*** CCCN EShb MJnS

## *Brimeura* (*Hyacinthaceae*)

§ ***amethystina*** 🏆$^{H4}$ CAvo CBgR CPLG CPom EBrs ECho ERos GBin GKev MSte NWCA SMeo SPhx WCot
- 'Alba' CAvo CBgR EBrs ECho EPfP ERos GKev MSte SMeo SPhx WCot
§ ***fastigiata*** ERos

## *Briza* (*Poaceae*)

***maxima*** CEnt CHrt CKno CSec CTri EGoo EHoe EPla LEdu LHop NGdn NSti SBch SIng WHal WHer WRos WTou
***media*** Widely available
- 'Limouzi' CElw CFir CKno EBee EBrs EGle EGoo EHoe EHrv EMon EPPr GCal GKir LRHS MAvo MBri NSti SDys SMad SPoG WPrP
- 'Russells' CElw CKno EAlp EBee EGle EPPr GBin SHom SPer
***minor*** WRos
***subaristata*** CSec EBee EPPr LRHS MWhi NBsh NLar WHrl
***triloba*** CSec EWes EWsh GBin MMHG WGwG WRos

## *Brodiaea* (*Alliaceae*)

'Blue Ocean Blend' **new** LRHS
§ ***californica*** EBee EBrs ECho ERos NMen WCot
- NNS 00-108 WCot
***capitata*** see *Dichelostemma capitatum*
***coronaria*** CPBP WCot
'Corrina' see *Triteleia* 'Corrina'
***elegans*** EBee ECho ERos WCot
***ida-maia*** see *Dichelostemma ida-maia*
***jolonensis*** ERos
***laxa*** see *Triteleia laxa*
***pallida*** WCot
***peduncularis*** see *Triteleia peduncularis*

## *Bromus* (*Poaceae*)

***erectus*** **new** EBWF
***inermis*** 'Skinner's Gold' (v) EBee EHoe EHul EMil EPPr EWes NLar NSti SMrm SPer SPoG WCot

## *Broussonetia* (*Moraceae*)

***kazinoki*** CArn CBcs EBee IDee IFFs NLar WDin WPGP
***papyrifera*** CAbP CAgr CBcs CDul CMCN EGFP ELan IDee LMaj MBri SPer WDin WPGP
- 'Laciniata' MBri NLar SMad

## *Browallia* (*Solanaceae*)

from Sikkim CSpe

## *Bruckenthalia* see *Erica*

## *Brugmansia* ✿ (*Solanaceae*)

sp. WFar
'Apricot Queen' MJnS
§ ***arborea*** CArn CDTJ CHEx SRms
§ - 'Knightii' (d) 🏆$^{H1}$ CDTJ CHal ELan EPfP LRHS MJnS SOWG
***aurea*** CCCN CHEx LRHS SAdn
'Canary Bird' MJnS
x ***candida*** CCCN CHEx
- 'Bergkönigin' (d) **new** MJnS
§ - 'Grand Marnier' 🏆$^{H1}$ CDTJ CHEx CHll ECot ELan EPfP MJnS SOWG
- 'Maya' MJnS
- 'Plena' see *B. arborea* 'Knightii'
- ***plena*** 'Mon Amoure M' (D) MJnS
§ - 'Variegata' (v) CCCN CDTJ CKob CSam
§ ***chlorantha*** CBcs
x ***cubensis*** 'Charles Grimaldi' CSam
'Dalen's Glorie' **new** MJnS
'Dark Rosetta' MJnS
'Double Apricot' (d) MJnS
'Flowerdream' (d) MJnS
'Herzenbrucke' MJnS
'Igea Pink' CSam

§ x ***insignis*** CHll
- 'Pink' CTrG
§ - pink-flowered CHEx EPfP
'Langenbuscher Garten' (d) new MJnS
***meteloides*** see *Datura inoxia*
'Mobishu' EShb
'Morgensonne' MJnS
'Pink Lady' MJnS
pink-flowered WFar
***rosei*** see *B. sanguinea* subsp. *sanguinea* var. *flava*
§ ***sanguinea*** CBcs CCCN CHEx CHll EShb IDee MSal SOWG
- 'Feuerwerk' MJnS
- red-flowered CHEx
- 'Rosea' see *B.* x *insignis* pink-flowered
§ - subsp. ***sanguinea*** var. ***flava*** CHEx
§ ***suaveolens*** ♀H1 CHEx CHll ELan SPlb
- pink-flowered EShb
- ***rosea*** see *B.* x *insignis* pink-flowered
- 'Variegata' (v) CKob EShb
- yellow-flowered EShb
***suaveolens*** x ***versicolor*** see *B.* x *insignis*
'Sunrise' MJnS
'Variegata Sunset' see *B.* x *candida* 'Variegata'
***versicolor*** misapplied see *B. arborea*
§ ***versicolor*** Lagerh. CCCN SOWG
- 'Ecuador Pink' EPfP MJnS
* 'Yellow Trumpet' EPfP
yellow-flowered WFar

## *Brunfelsia* (*Solanaceae*)

***americana*** CCCN EShb SOWG
***calycina*** see *B. pauciflora*
***jamaicensis*** SOWG
***lactea*** CCCN
§ ***pauciflora*** ♀H1 ELan LRHS MBri
- 'Floribunda' SOWG
- 'Macrantha' SOWG

## *Brunia* (*Bruniaceae*)

***albiflora*** SPlb

## *Brunnera* ✿ (*Boraginaceae*)

§ ***macrophylla*** ♀H4 Widely available
- 'Agnes Amez' CLAP SUsu
- 'Alba' see *B. macrophylla* 'Betty Bowring'
§ - 'Betty Bowring' Widely available
- 'Blaukuppel' CLAP EAEE EBee EBla EMon EWes GBin LRHS NBsh NCob NDov WFar
- 'Blue Louise' new CLAP
§ - 'Dawson's White' (v) Widely available
- 'Gordano Gold' (v) CBow EHoe EPPr WCot WHal
- 'Hadspen Cream' (v) ♀H4 Widely available
- 'Jack Frost'PBR ♀H4 Widely available
- 'Langford Hewitt' (v) MNrw
- 'Langtrees' Widely available
- 'Looking Glass'PBR Widely available
- 'Marley's White' CAbP CLAP CMea CSam EBee EGle EHrv GKev LLHF NCob NDov SMrm SUsu WCot WCra WPnP
- 'Miller White' new GAbr
- 'Silver Wings' CElw EBee EPfP
- 'Variegata' see *B. macrophylla* 'Dawson's White'
***sibirica*** CDes CLAP EBee EMon EPPr EWes GBin

## *Brunsvigia* (*Amaryllidaceae*)

***bosmaniae*** WVal
***gregaria*** WVal
***josephinae*** new WVal
***multiflora*** see *B. orientalis*
§ ***orientalis*** WVal
- red-flowered new EBee
***pulchra*** WVal
***radulosa*** WVal
***rosea*** 'Minor' see *Amaryllis belladonna*

## *Bryonia* (*Cucurbitaceae*)

***dioica*** CArn GPoy MSal

## *Bryophyllum* see *Kalanchoe*

## *Buchloe* (*Poaceae*)

***dactyloides*** CRWN

## *Buddleja* ✿ (*Buddlejaceae*)

HCM 98.017 from Chile WPGP
***agathosma*** SLon WEas WLav WPGP WSHC
***albiflora*** SLon WLav
***alternifolia*** ♀H4 Widely available
- 'Argentea' CBcs CDoC EBee ELan EPfP GKir LRHS MBNS MRav NLar NSti SHBN SMad SPer SPla SPoG SRGP SSpi WCot WHCG WLav WPat WSHC
***asiatica*** ♀H2 EShb SLon SOWG WLav
- B&SWJ 7214 WCru
***auriculata*** CBcs CBgR CMCN CPLG CPSs CTca CWib EBee EPfP ERas EShb LAst LRHS MRav NSti SDix SLon SOWG SPoG WBor WCru WHCG WLav WPGP
* 'Blue Trerice' CPLG
***caryopteridifolia*** EBee SLon
***colvilei*** CBcs CDoC CDul ELan EPfP ERas GCal GGal GKir IDee LAst MBri MRav SDnm SKHP WBor
- B&SWJ 2121 WCru
- GWJ 9399 WCru
- 'Kewensis' CPLG CRHN CSam EBee EWes GCal GCra GKir LAst NLar NSti SKHP SLon WBod WCru WLav WPGP WSHC
***cordata*** SLon
- F&M 220 new WPGP
***coriacea*** SLon
§ ***crispa*** CBcs CBgR CDul CPLG CPSs CSpe EBee ECha ELan EPfP ERas LRHS MCot MSte SDnm SHBN SLon SOWG SRkn SSpi WAbe WEas WFar WHCG WKif WPGP WSHC
***crotonoides amplexicaulis*** SLon
***curviflora*** f. ***venenifera*** SLon
- - B&SWJ 895 WCru
- - B&SWJ 6036 WCru
***davidii*** CArn NWea SGar STre WDin
- B&SWJ 8083 WCru
- Adonis Blue = 'Adokeep'PBR MGos
- 'African Queen' CAni SLon SRGP
- var. ***alba*** CWib SHBN
§ - 'Autumn Beauty' CAni SLon WSFF
- 'Bath Beauty' new CAni
- 'Beijing' see *B. davidii* 'Autumn Beauty'
- 'Bishop's Velvet' new CAni
- 'Black Knight' ♀H4 Widely available
- 'Blue Horizon' CAni CSam SEND SLon SRGP WCot WLav WMoo WRHF
- 'Border Beauty' CAni SLon
- 'Boskoop Beauty' new CAni
- 'Brown's Beauty' new CAni
- Camberwell Beauty = 'Camkeep' MGos SLon
- 'Car Wash' new CAni

| | |
|---|---|
| - 'Castle School' | CAni CSam |
| § - 'Charming' | CDul WMoo WWlt |
| - 'Clive Farrell' | see *B. davidii* 'Autumn Beauty' |
| - 'Croyde' | CSam |
| - 'Dartmoor' ♀H4 | Widely available |
| - 'Dart's Ornamental White' | MRav SLon |
| - 'Dart's Papillon Blue' | CAni SLPl SLon |
| - 'Dart's Purple Rain' | CAni |
| - 'Dubonnet' | CAni SLon WLav |
| - 'Dudley's Compact Lavender' **new** | CAni |
| - 'Ecolonia' | CAni |
| - 'Empire Blue' ♀H4 | Widely available |
| - 'Fascinating' | CAni GCal MGan MRav NBir SLon WLav |
| - 'Flaming Violet' | CAni SLon WLav |
| - 'Florence' | EBee LLHF LSou NCGa NHol NLar WFar WHar WMoo |
| - 'Fortune' | CAni |
| - 'Glasnevin Hybrid' | CAni NSti SAga SDix SLon WLav |
| - 'Gonglepod' | CAni SLon |
| - 'Greenway's River Dart' **new** | CAni |
| - 'Harlequin' (v) | Widely available |
| - 'Ile de France' | CAni CBcs CWib EBee MGos NBlu NWea SLon SRms WLav |
| - 'Jane Taylor' **new** | CAni |
| - 'Les Kneale' | CAni |
| - 'Lyme Bay' **new** | CAni |
| - 'Malvern Blue' **new** | CAni |
| - Marbled White = 'Markeep' | SLon |
| - Masquerade = 'Notbud'PBR (v) | MBri MGos MRav SLon WGor |
| § - 'Nanho Blue' ♀H4 | Widely available |
| - 'Nanho Petite Indigo' | see *B. davidii* 'Nanho Blue' |
| - 'Nanho Petite Plum' | see *B. davidii* 'Nanho Purple' |
| - 'Nanho Petite Purple' | see *B. davidii* 'Nanho Purple' |
| § - 'Nanho Purple' ♀H4 | CAni CDoC CMHG CTri CWib EBee ELan EPfP LRHS LSRN MAsh MBar MGos MRav NLar SLim SLon SPer SPla SPlb SPoG SRGP WHar |
| - Nanho White = 'Monite' | ELan EPfP GKir MBar SLon SPer SPoG SRms WFar |
| - var. ***nanhoensis*** | CAni CDul CHrt EBee SEND SIde WHCG WLav |
| - - blue-flowered | SLon SPer |
| - Operette = 'Courtabud' | EBee |
| - 'Orchid Beauty' | CAni SLon WBod WLav |
| - 'Orpheus' | CAni WLav |
| - 'Peace' | CChe CDoC CTri EBee EPfP LSRN MBri MRav SLon SPoG WLav |
| - Peacock = 'Peakeep'PBR | MGos |
| - 'Petite Indigo' | see *B. davidii* 'Nanho Blue' |
| - 'Pink Beauty' | CEnt GKir LAst SHBN SRGP WHCG |
| - 'Pink Charming' | see *B. davidii* 'Charming' |
| - 'Pink Pearl' | CAni SEND SLon WLav |
| - 'Pink Spreader' | CAni SLon |
| - 'Pixie Blue' | CAni LAst LBMP MAsh NLar NMyG NPri SRGP |
| - 'Pixie Red' | CAni LBMP MAsh NLar NMyG NPri |
| - 'Pixie White' | MAsh NLar NPri SRGP WLav |
| - Purple Emperor = 'Pyrkeep' | NBir SLon |
| - 'Purple Friend' | CAni WLav |
| - 'Purple Prince' | CAni |
| - 'Red Admiral' | CAni LLHF LRHS MAsh SPoG |
| - Rêve de Papillon = 'Minpap' **new** | EMil MAsh |
| - 'Royal Purple' | CAni SLim |
| - 'Royal Red' ♀H4 | Widely available |

| | |
|---|---|
| - 'Santana' (v) | CAni CDul EBee EHoe ELon EMil EWes LHop LRHS MGos MRav MWea NCGa NHol NLar SAga SPoG WCot WHar WMoo WPat WRHF |
| - 'Shapcott Blue' **new** | CAni |
| - 'Southcombe Splendour' **new** | CAni |
| - 'Summer Beauty' | CAni CWib EBee MGos MRav SLon SPoG WLav |
| - 'Summer House Blue' **new** | SLon |
| - 'Variegata' (v) | CAni LRHS MAsh SLon WLav WSFF |
| - var. ***veitchiana*** | CTca |
| - 'White Ball' | EBee EPfP LRHS NLar SLon |
| - 'White Bouquet' | CAni CCVT CEnt CSBt EBee EPfP GKir LAst MAsh MHer MNHC MSwo MWat NPri NWea SEND SPer SRGP SReu SWal WBod WLav |
| - 'White Cloud' | CAni ECrN GQui MGos SRms WGwG |
| - 'White Harlequin' (v) | CRow WCFE |
| - 'White Profusion' ♀H4 | Widely available |
| - 'White Wings' | SLon WLav |
| - 'Widecombe' **new** | CAni |
| § ***delavayi*** | GKir NLar WCru |
| ***fallowiana*** misapplied | see *B.* 'West Hill' |
| ***fallowiana*** Balf. f. | ELan LRHS WLav |
| - ACE 2481 | LRHS |
| - BWJ 7803 | WCru |
| - var. ***alba*** ♀H3 | CBgR CDoC EBee ECrN ELan EPfP LRHS MRav NChi NLar NSti SLon SPer SPoG WAbe WFar WPGP WSHC |
| ***forrestii*** | CRHN WCru |
| ***globosa*** ♀H4 | Widely available |
| - RCB/Arg C-11 | WCot |
| - 'Cally Orange' | GCal GGar |
| - 'Lemon Ball' | MBlu NPer SLon WLav |
| ***glomerata*** | EBee EShb SLon |
| ***heliophila*** | see *B. delavayi* |
| ***indica*** | SLon WBor |
| ***japonica*** | IFro |
| - B&SWJ 8912 | WCru |
| 'Leela Kapila' | MGos |
| x ***lewisiana*** 'Margaret Pike' | SLon SOWG |
| ***limitanea*** | SLon |
| ***lindleyana*** | Widely available |
| 'Lochinch' ♀H3-4 | Widely available |
| ***loricata*** | CBgR CHid CTca CWib EBee GQui IDee MSte SGar SKHP SLon SOWG SPlb WCFE WLav WPGP |
| ***macrostachya*** | GBin WPGP |
| - HWJ 602 | WCru |
| § ***madagascariensis*** ♀H1 | CRHN SGar SLon SOWG WCot WHar |
| ***megalocephala*** B&SWJ 9106 | WCru |
| § 'Morning Mist'PBR | CDoC EBee EMil EPfP GBin LAst LLHF LSRN LSou MAvo MGos NBir NHol NLar SLon SPoG WHar WPGP |
| ***myriantha*** | SLon |
| * - f. ***fragrans*** | EBee WCot |
| ***nappii*** | SLon |
| ***nicodemia*** | see *B. madagascariensis* |
| ***nivea*** | CPLG SLon SOWG WLav |
| - B&SWJ 2679 | WCru |
| - pink-flowered | SLon |
| - var. ***yunnanensis*** | GCal MSte SLon WCFE |
| - - B&SWJ 8146 | WCru |
| ***officinalis*** ♀H2 | CPLG CTca SLon |
| ***paniculata*** | SLon |
| ***parvifolia*** | SLon |
| - MPF 148 | WLav |

| | |
|---|---|
| x ***pikei*** 'Hever' | GCal |
| 'Pink Delight' 𝕐H4 | Widely available |
| 'Pink Perfection' | CAni WFar |
| 'Pride of Hever' new | SOWG |
| 'Pride of Longstock' new | SLon |
| 'Purple Splendour' new | GGal |
| ***saligna*** | SLon |
| 'Salmon Spheres' | SKHP SLon |
| ***salviifolia*** | CBcs CBgR CDul CPLG CRHN CSWP CSam CTca CTrG EBee ELan GGal GGar GQui IDee LAst MBlu NSti SDnm SWal WAbe WGwG WHer WLav |
| - white-flowered | CRHN IFro |
| Silver Anniversary | see *B.* 'Morning Mist' |
| ***stachyoides*** | SLon |
| ***stenostachya*** | CPLG SLon |
| ***sterniana*** | see *B. crispa* |
| ***tibetica*** | see *B. crispa* |
| ***tubiflora*** | SLon SOWG WLav |
| § 'West Hill' | SLon SRGP WLav |
| x ***weyeriana*** | CBgR CDul CRHN CSam CTca EBee ECtt EPfP GQui IFoB MGos MNrw MSwo NBir SGar SPlb SWvt WBor WBrE WDin WFar WHCG WLav WMoo |
| - 'Golden Glow' (v) | CBow CTri ECrN EPfP LSRN SLon SPoG WLav WSFF |
| - 'Honeycomb' | EShb GKir |
| - 'Lady de Ramsey' | SEND WPer |
| - 'Moonlight' | CBcs CPLG GKir IFro SLon WCot WLav |
| - 'Sungold' 𝕐H4 | CBcs CHrt CWib EBee ELan EPfP GGar GKir GQui MBlu MCCP MGan MGos MLHP MLLN MRav NBir NHol NVic SBod SLon SPer SRGP WBVN WCot WFar WHar WLav |
| 'Winter Sun' | SLon |

## *Buglossoides* (*Boraginaceae*)

| | |
|---|---|
| § ***purpurocaerulea*** | CEnt CHll CMHG CPom CSpe CWGN EBee ECha ELan LHop MLHP MSal MSte MWhi NBid NBir WAul WCot WFar WSHC |

## *Bukiniczia* (*Plumbaginaceae*)

| | |
|---|---|
| ***cabulica*** | CSpe GKev WCot |

## *Bulbine* (*Asphodelaceae*)

| | |
|---|---|
| SH 74 new | CMdw |
| ***annua*** misapplied | see *B. semibarbata* |
| ***bulbosa*** misapplied | see *B. semibarbata* |
| ***caulescens*** | see *B. frutescens* |
| § ***frutescens*** | CHll EHig MBNS WBrk WJek WPrP |
| ***latifolia*** | EShb |
| § ***semibarbata*** | CCCN CSec |

## *Bulbinella* (*Asphodelaceae*)

| | |
|---|---|
| ***angustifolia*** | ECho WCot |
| ***cauda-felis*** | WCot |
| ***eburnifolia*** | WCot |
| ***elata*** | WCot |
| ***floribunda*** | IBlr |
| ***gibbsii*** var. ***balanifera*** | ECho |
| ***hookeri*** | CPom CWsd EBee ECho ECou GEdr GGar GKir ITim NChi NDlv NLAp NWCA SRms WHal |
| ***nutans*** | CDes |
| ***setosa*** var. ***latifolia*** | CPne |

## *Bulbinopsis* see *Bulbine*

## *Bulbocodium* (*Colchicaceae*)

| | |
|---|---|
| ***vernum*** | CPBP EBrs ECho EPot ERos EWTr GKir LAma LLHF MBri NHol NMin |
| - white-flowered | ECho |

## bullace see *Prunus insititia*

## *Bunias* (*Brassicaceae*)

| | |
|---|---|
| ***orientalis*** | CAgr MSal |

## *Bunium* (*Apiaceae*)

| | |
|---|---|
| ***bulbocastanum*** | CAgr LEdu SHDw |

## *Buphthalmum* (*Asteraceae*)

| | |
|---|---|
| ***salicifolium*** | CHrt CSam CSec CSev EBee ELan EPfP GKir LAst MNFA MRav NBlu NBro NGdn SEND SHGN SPer SRms SWat WCAu WCot WFar WPer |
| - 'Alpengold' | ECha EShb GMaP NBre NLar |
| - 'Dora' | ECtt WCot |
| § - 'Golden Wonder' | GKir |
| - 'Sunwheel' | EWll GKir LRHS NBre SRms |
| ***speciosum*** | see *Telekia speciosa* |

## *Bupleurum* (*Apiaceae*)

| | |
|---|---|
| ***angulosum*** | CDes CPom CSpe NChi SMrm WFar |
| - copper-leaved | see *B. longifolium* |
| ***candollei*** GWJ 9405 | WCru |
| ***falcatum*** | CArn CElw ECha EPPr MLLN MSal NDov NLar SBri SPur WCot WFar |
| ***fruticosum*** | CBcs CSpe EBee ECGP ECtt EPfP LHop LRHS SDix SDnm SSpi SSta WCot WDin WEas WPGP WPat |
| ***gibraltaricum*** | EBee WCot |
| * ***griffithii*** | MSal |
| - 'Decor' | CSec CSpe |
| § ***longifolium*** | CElw CFee CPom CSec CSpe EBee ECha EWes GBBs GBin GBuc GKir LRHS MDKP MNrw NCGa NChi NLar WCot WHal WHoo |
| - subsp. ***aureum*** | MAvo NChi NGby SPhx WFar |
| - bronze-leaved | LSou |
| - subsp. ***shikotanense*** | EBee |
| - short bronze | WCru |
| ***longiradiatum*** B&SWJ 729 | WCru |
| ***ranunculoides*** | NLar WFar |
| ***rotundifolium*** | CSec MSal |
| - 'Copper' | MAvo NDov |
| ***spinosum*** | SMad |
| ***tenue*** | CArn |

## *Bursaria* (*Pittosporaceae*)

| | |
|---|---|
| ***spinosa*** | CCCN ECou EShb NLar |

## *Butia* (*Arecaceae*)

| | |
|---|---|
| ***bonnetii*** | EAmu ETod |
| ***capitata*** | CAbb CBcs CBrP CCCN CDTJ CHEx CPHo CTrC EAmu EPla ESwi ETod EUJe LMaj LPJP LPal LPan MGos MREP NPal SAPC SArc SBLw SChr |
| § - var. ***odorata*** | EAmu LPal |
| ***eriospatha*** | CDTJ EAmu ETod LPal |
| ***odorata*** | see *B. capitata* var. *odorata* |
| ***yatay*** | CDTJ EAmu ETod LPal SBig |

## *Butomus* (*Butomaceae*)

| | |
|---|---|
| ***umbellatus*** 𝕐H4 | CBen CDWL CRWN CRow CWat ECha ECtt EHon EMFW EPfP LPBA MCCP MRav MSKA NPer NSco SWat WFar WMAq WPnP WTin |
| - 'Rosenrot' | CRow LLWG |
| - 'Schneeweisschen' | CRow LLWG NLar |

## butternut see *Juglans cinerea*

## x *Butyagrus* (*Arecaceae*)

***nabonnandii*** **new** EAmu

## *Buxus* ✿ (*Buxaceae*)

***aurea*** 'Marginata' see *B. sempervirens* 'Marginata'
***balearica*** ♀H4 EPla EQua IDee SEND SLan SLon WPGP
***bodinieri*** EPla EQua SLan
- 'David's Gold' WPen
***colchica*** SLan
'Glencoe' SLan
'Green Gem' NGHP NHol SLan
'Green Mound' SLan
'Green Mountain' SLan
'Green Velvet' EPfP NHol SLan
***harlandii*** hort. EPla SLan SRiv
- 'Richard' SLan STre
***henryi*** MBri
***japonica*** 'Nana' see *B. microphylla*
***macowanii*** SLan
§ ***microphylla*** CSWP MHer NHol NWea SIng SLan STre
- 'Asiatic Winter' see *B. microphylla* var. *japonica* 'Winter Gem'
§ - 'Compacta' CMen LLHF SLan SRiv WCot WPat
- 'Curly Locks' EPla MHer SLan
- 'Faulkner' CCVT CSBt EBee ELan EPfP EQua LBuc LHop LPan LRHS MBNS MBlu MGos NHol SLan SPoG SRiv WDin
- Golden Dream = 'Peergold'PBR SPoG
- 'Golden Triumph'PBR SLan
- 'Grace Hendrick Phillips' SLan
- 'Green Pillow' SLan SRiv
- 'Helen Whiting' SLan
- 'Henry Hohman' SLan
- 'Herrenhausen' LPan SLan
- var. ***insularis*** see *B. sinica* var. *insularis*
- var. ***japonica*** 'Belvédère' SLan
- - 'Gold Dust' SLan
- - 'Green Beauty' SLan
- - 'Green Jade' SLan
- - 'Jim Stauffer' SLan
- - 'Morris Dwarf' SLan
- - 'Morris Midget' IArd NHol SLan
- - 'National' SLan WPGP
- - 'Sunnyside' SLan
- - 'Trompenburg' SLan
§ - - 'Winter Gem' EBee MHer MRav NHol NLar SLPl SLan
- - f. ***yakushima*** SLan
- 'John Baldwin' SLan SRiv
- 'Kagushima' SLan
- var. ***koreana*** see *B. sinica* var. *insularis*
- 'Quiet End' SLan
- var. ***riparia*** see *B. riparia*
- var. ***sinica*** see *B. sinica*
- 'Winter Gem' see *B. microphylla* var. *japonica* 'Winter Gem'
'Newport Blue' see *B. sempervirens* 'Newport Blue'
§ ***riparia*** EPla SLan
***rugulosa*** SLan
***sempervirens*** ♀H4 Widely available
- 'Abilene' SLan
- 'Agram' SLan
- 'Anderson' SLan
§ - 'Angustifolia' EPla MGos MHer NHol SLan SMad
- 'Arborescens' EQua LPan
- 'Argentea' see *B. sempervirens* 'Argenteo-variegata'
§ - 'Argenteo-variegata' (v) EPfP IFoB MRav NGHP SLan WFar
- 'Aristocrat' SLan
- 'Aurea' see *B. sempervirens* 'Aureovariegata'
- 'Aurea Maculata' see *B. sempervirens* 'Aureovariegata'
- 'Aurea Marginata' see *B. sempervirens* 'Marginata'
- 'Aurea Pendula' (v) CPMA EPla SLan SLon WDin
§ - 'Aureovariegata' (v) CBcs EBee ECrN EPfP GBar ISea MAsh MBar MCot MGan MGos MHer MNHC MRav NHol NSti SLan SPer SRiv WDin WFar WMoo
- 'Belleville' SLan
- 'Bentley Blue' NHol
- 'Berlin' SLan
- 'Blauer Heinz' ELan EMil LPan LRHS MHer NHol SLPl SLan SRiv
- 'Blue Belle' SLan
§ - 'Blue Cone' CHar NHol
- 'Blue Spire' see *B. sempervirens* 'Blue Cone'
- 'Bowles' Blue' EQua SLan
- 'Brilliantissima' **new** NHol
- 'Bullata' SLan
- 'Claverton' SLan
- clipped ball CWib EPfP LPan MGos NBlu NGHP NLar SLan SLim SRiv WFar
- clipped cone LPan
- clipped pyramid CWib EPfP LPan MGos NBlu NGHP NLar SLan SLim SRiv
- clipped spiral LPan NBlu SLan SLim SRiv
- 'Crossley' SLan
- 'Dee Runk' SLan
- 'Denmark' SLan
- 'Egremont' SLan
- 'Elegans' IFoB
§ - 'Elegantissima' (v) ♀H4 Widely available
- 'Emir' SLan
- 'Fiesta' SLan
- 'Fleur de Lys' SLan
- 'Glauca' SLan
- 'Gold Tip' see *B. sempervirens* 'Notata'
- 'Golden Frimley' (v) LHop
§ - 'Graham Blandy' MHer NHol SLan SRiv
- 'Grand Rapids' SLan
- 'Green Balloon' LBuc SLan
- 'Greenpeace' see *B. sempervirens* 'Graham Blandy'
- 'Haller' SLan
- 'Handsworthiensis' CLnd EBee ECrN LPan NHol SEND SLan SPer
- 'Handsworthiensis' blue SLan
- 'Handsworthii' CTri NWea SRms
- 'Henry Shaw' SLan
- 'Hermann von Schrenk' SLan
- 'Holland' SLan
- subsp. ***hyrcana*** SLan
- 'Ickworth Giant' SLan
- 'Inglis' SLan
- 'Ingrid' SLan
- 'Inverewe' SLan
- 'Ipek' SLan
- 'Japonica Aurea' see *B. sempervirens* 'Latifolia Maculata'
- 'Kensington Gardens' SLan
- 'King Midas' SLan
- 'Kingsville' see *B. microphylla* 'Compacta'
- 'Kingsville Dwarf' see *B. microphylla* 'Compacta'
- 'Krakow' NLar
- 'Lace' NSti SLan
§ - 'Langley Beauty' SLan
- 'Langley Pendula' see *B. sempervirens* 'Langley Beauty'
- 'Latifolia Macrophylla' SLan SLon
§ - 'Latifolia Maculata' (v) ♀H4 CAbP CDoC CWib EBee EPfP EPla LRHS MNHC NGHP NHol NPer SEND SLan SPoG SRiv STre WJek

| | | |
|---|---|---|
| * | - 'Latifolia Pendula' | NHol SLan |
| | - 'Linda' | SLan |
| | - 'Longifolia' | see *B. sempervirens* 'Angustifolia' |
| § | - 'Marginata' (v) | ECtt EPla GBar IFoB LHop MHer MRav SHBN SLan SLon SPer WBrE WHar |
| | - 'Mary Gamble' | SLan |
| | - 'Memorial' | MHer NHol SLan SMHy SRiv |
| | - 'Molesworth' | SLan |
| | - 'Myosotidifolia' | CMHG EPla NPro SLan SRiv WPGP |
| | - 'Myrtifolia' | EPla MHer NHol SLan SLon |
| | - 'Natchez' | SLan |
| § | - 'Newport Blue' | SLan |
| | - 'Northern' | SLan |
| § | - 'Notata' (v) | CSWP IFoB MAsh SPlb WDin WRHF |
| | - 'Obelisk' | SLan |
| | - 'Ornament' | SLan |
| | - 'Parasol' | MHer SLan |
| | - 'Pendula' | CMHG GKir SLan SLon |
| | - 'Pinnacle' | SLan |
| I | - 'Planifolia' | SLan |
| | - 'Prostrata' | NHol NWea SLan |
| | - 'Pyramidalis' | EBee SEND SLan WFar |
| | - 'Raket' | SLan |
| | - 'Rosmarinifolia' | MRav SLan |
| | - 'Rotundifolia' | EBee ELan MGos SEND SIde SLan WDin |
| | - 'Roy Lancaster' | SLan |
| | - 'Saint Genevieve' | SLan |
| | - 'Salicifolia Elata' | SLan |
| | - 'Sentinelle' | SLan |
| | - 'Silver Beauty' (v) | MGos |
| | - 'Silver Variegated' | see *B. sempervirens* 'Elegantissima' |
| | - 'Suffruticosa' ♀H4 | Widely available |
| I | - 'Suffruticosa Blue' | NHol |
| | - 'Suffruticosa Variegata' (v) | EBee ECrN EOHP NWea SRms SWvt |
| | - 'Sultan' | SLan |
| | - 'Sunningdale Silver' | EQua |
| | - 'Twisty' | SLan WFar |
| | - 'Undulifolia' | SLan |
| | - 'Vardar Valley' | NHol NPro SLan SLon SRiv |
| * | - 'Variegata' (v) | CTca ELan LRHS SLan SLon |
| | - 'Varifolia' | SLan |
| | - 'Waterfall' | SLan |
| | - 'Welleri' | SLan |
| | - 'William Borek' | SLan |
| | - 'Wisley Blue' | SLan |
| § | ***sinica*** | SLan |
| § | - var. ***insularis*** | MAsh NHol SLan |
| | - - 'Chegu' | SLan |
| | - - 'Filigree' | NHol SLan |
| | - - 'Justin Brouwers' | MHer SLan SRiv |
| | - - 'Pincushion' | SLan |
| | - - 'Tall Boy' | SLan |
| | - - 'Tide Hill' | SLan SRiv WFar |
| | - - 'Winter Beauty' | SLan |
| | - - 'Wintergreen' | SLan |
| | - var. ***intermedia*** | SLan |
| | ***wallichiana*** | CGHE EPla SLan WPGP |

# C

## *Cacalia* (*Asteraceae*)

| | | |
|---|---|---|
| | ***atriplicifolia*** | EBee LRHS |
| | ***corymbosa*** HWJK 2214 | WCru |
| | ***delphiniifolia*** | EBee GEdr |
| | - B&SWJ 5789 | WCru |
| | - B&SWJ 11189 new | WCru |
| | - 'Sansyoku' new | EBee |
| | ***hastata*** subsp. ***orientalis*** variegated (v) new | EBee |
| | ***muehlenbergii*** | MSal |
| | ***suaveolens*** | EBee |

## *Caesalpinia* (*Caesalpiniaceae*)

| | | |
|---|---|---|
| | ***gilliesii*** | CSec EBee LSRN NLar SOWG SPlb |
| | - RCB/Arg N-1 | WCot |
| | ***mexicana*** | WPGP |
| | ***pulcherrima*** | CCCN CSec SOWG SPlb |

## *Caiophora* (*Loasaceae*)

| | | |
|---|---|---|
| | ***prietea*** | CSec |

## *Caladium* (*Araceae*)

| | | |
|---|---|---|
| § | ***bicolor*** (v) | EBrs MBri |
| | x ***hortulanum*** | see *C. bicolor* |

## *Calamagrostis* (*Poaceae*)

| | | |
|---|---|---|
| | x ***acutiflora*** 'Avalanche' | CKno EHoe EPPr |
| N | - 'Karl Foerster' | Widely available |
| | - 'Overdam' (v) | Widely available |
| | - 'Stricta' | EPPr EWsh GKir |
| | - 'Waldenbuch' new | GBin |
| | ***argentea*** | see *Stipa calamagrostis* |
| | ***arundinacea*** | CElw COlW CPLG CSpe ECha ECou EPGN EPla LEdu MNrw NBid NHol NVic SDix SGar SPlb WFar WMoo WPGP WPer WPrP |
| | 'Avalanche' | CKno GBin |
| § | ***brachytricha*** ♀ | Widely available |
| | ***emodensis*** | CBod CFwr CKno CMil CPen EAlp EBee ECha EHoe EPla LEdu MMoz NOak SMad WLeb WPGP |
| | ***epigejos*** | CSec GFor NBre NHol WHrl WPrP WRos |
| | ***splendens*** misapplied | see *Stipa calamagrostis* |
| | ***varia*** | CKno EHoe EPPr NDov SMrm WHrl |

## *Calamintha* (*Lamiaceae*)

| | | |
|---|---|---|
| | ***alpina*** | see *Acinos alpinus* |
| § | ***ascendens*** | CArn CSec EBee MLLN SGar SPhx WMoo |
| | ***clinopodium*** | see *Clinopodium vulgare* |
| | ***cretica*** | WPer |
| § | ***grandiflora*** | CArn CSam CSec CSev EBee ECha ELan GGar GJos GPoy LEdu MHer MRav MWhi NBir NDov NPer SMad SPer SPet SPlb SSvw SWat WCAu WFar WMoo WTin |
| | - 'Elfin Purple' | EPfP |
| | - 'Variegata' (v) | CPrp CTca EAro EBee ECtt ELan ELon EMil EShb GGar LAst LSou NPri STes WCHb WFar |
| § | ***menthifolia*** | NBre NLar |
| | - HH&K 163 | GBri |
| § | ***nepeta*** | CArn CWan EBWF EBee ECha GMaP LAst LBMP LRHS MHer MNHC MSte NBir NBro NDov NPri NWCA SPhx SPlb SPoG SWal SWat WCAu WFar WMoo WPer |
| | - subsp. ***glandulosa*** | CEnt EAro EBee WMoo |
| | - - ACL 1050/90 | LRHS WHoo |
| | - - 'White Cloud' | CSpe EBee EHrv ELan GBar GBuc LLWP MBri MRav MSte NBir WCAu WMoo |
| | - 'Gottfried Kuehn' | EBee MRav MSte WCAu |
| § | - subsp. ***nepeta*** | CPrp ELan ELon EMon EPfP GBar GKir LHop MHer MLHP MRav NDov NSti SPer SUsu WCHb WClo WEas WFar WHal WTin |
| | - - 'Blue Cloud' | CSam CSec CSpe EAro EBee ECha EHrv EPfP GKev LCro MBri NBir |

| | |
|---|---|
| | NDov SAga SMeo SPhx SWat WCAu WCHb WFar WHil WMoo |
| - 'Weisse Riese' | SPhx |
| ***nepetoides*** | see *C. nepeta* subsp. *nepeta* |
| ***officinalis*** misapplied | see *C. ascendens* |
| ***sylvatica*** | see *C. menthifolia* |
| I - 'Menthe' | EBee |
| ***vulgaris*** | see *Clinopodium vulgare* |

## *Calandrinia* (*Portulacaceae*)

| | |
|---|---|
| ***colchaguensis*** | CSec |
| ***depressa*** | CSec |
| ***discolor*** | LRHS |
| ***grandiflora*** | CSec LLHF MLLN |
| ***sibirica*** | see *Claytonia sibirica* |
| ***umbellata*** | EDAr GKev LBMP NWCA WPer |
| - 'Ruby Tuesday' | NPri |

## *Calanthe* (*Orchidaceae*)

| | |
|---|---|
| ***alismifolia*** | EFEx |
| ***arisanenesis*** | EFEx |
| ***aristulifera*** | EFEx GEdr WWst |
| ***bicolor*** | see *C. striata* |
| ***caudatilabella*** | EFEx |
| ***discolor*** | EBee EBrs EFEx GEdr LAma LFur NLAp SKHP WWst |
| - subsp. ***amamiana*** | EFEx |
| - var. ***flava*** | see *C. striata* |
| - subsp. ***tokunoshimensis*** | EFEx |
| ***fargesii*** | WCot WWst |
| ***graciliflora*** | EFEx |
| **Kozu gx** | GEdr LEdu WWst |
| - red-flowered **new** | GEdr |
| ***mannii*** | EFEx |
| ***nipponica*** | CBct EFEx GEdr LAma LFur WWst |
| ***reflexa*** | EBee EBrs EFEx GEdr LAma LFur NLAp WWst |
| ***sieboldii*** | see *C. striata* |
| § ***striata*** | CBct EBee EBrs EFEx GEdr LAma SKHP WCot WWst |
| - Kawakamii Group **new** | GEdr |
| **Takane gx** | GEdr WWst |
| ***tricarinata*** | CBct EBrs EFEx GEdr LAma NLAp WWst |

## *Calathea* (*Marantaceae*)

| | |
|---|---|
| ***argyrophylla*** 'Exotica' | XBlo |
| ***crocata*** ♀H1 | LRHS MBri |
| 'Greystar' | MBri |
| ***louisae*** 'Maui Queen' | MBri XBlo |
| § ***majestica*** ♀H1 | XBlo |
| ***makoyana*** ♀H1 | MBri XBlo |
| ***metallica*** | MBri |
| ***oppenheimiana*** | see *Ctenanthe oppenheimiana* |
| ***ornata*** | see *C. majestica* |
| ***picturata*** 'Argentea' ♀H1 | MBri XBlo |
| ***roseopicta*** ♀H1 | LRHS MBri XBlo |
| ***rufibarba*** | XBlo |
| * ***stromata*** | XBlo |
| ***veitchiana*** | MBri |
| ***warscewiczii*** | MBri |
| 'Wavestar' | MBri |
| ***zebrina*** ♀H1 | MBri XBlo |
| 'Zoizia' | XBlo |

## *Calceolaria* (*Scrophulariaceae*)

| | |
|---|---|
| ***acutifolia*** | see *C. polyrhiza* Cav. |
| ***alba*** | EBee NLar |
| x ***banksii*** | EBee |
| ***bicolor*** | EBee |
| § ***biflora*** | CSec ECho EDAr EPfP GGar GKev LEdu NLar |
| - 'Goldcap' | ECho MAvo |
| - 'Goldcrest Amber' | ECho SPlb WPer |
| 'Briga Elite' | EBee LSou |
| 'Camden Hero' | GCal MAJR |
| ***chelidonioides*** | GGar MTho |
| ***corymbosa*** | GKev |
| ***falklandica*** | CSec ECho GKir ITim NLAp SPav SRms |
| ***fothergillii*** | GKev NLAp |
| 'Goldcrest' | ECho GKev LRHS SRms |
| 'Hall's Spotted' | NWCA |
| N ***integrifolia*** ♀H3 | CAbb CDTJ CHal CPLG CSpe EBee ELan GKir MSCN SBHP SEND SGar SIng SPer SPoG SRms WAbe WWlt |
| - bronze | MSCN SPer |
| - 'Gaines' Yellow' **new** | GCal |
| - 'Sunshine' ♀H2-3 | CAbb |
| 'John Innes' | ECho WRha |
| 'Kentish Hero' | CHal GCal MAJR WAbe |
| ***lagunae-blancae*** | GKev NLAp |
| ***mexicana*** | CSec |
| ***perfoliata*** B&SWJ 10638 | WCru |
| ***petiolaris*** | CSec |
| ***plantaginea*** | see *C. biflora* |
| § ***polyrhiza*** Cav. | ECho NRya |
| ***rugosa*** | see *C. integrifolia* |
| Sunset Series | EPfP NBlu |
| ***tenella*** | ECtt NWCA WAbe |
| ***uniflora*** var. ***darwinii*** | ECho NLAp |
| 'Walter Shrimpton' | ECho EDAr EPot EWes SIng WAbe |

## *Caldcluvia* (*Cunoniaceae*)

| | |
|---|---|
| ***paniculata*** | ISea |

## *Calendula* (*Asteraceae*)

| | |
|---|---|
| ***arvensis*** | CCCN CSec |
| ***meuselii*** | CFee |
| ***officinalis*** | CArn ELau GPoy MHer MNHC MSal SIde SPav WJek WLHH |
| - Fiesta Gitana Group ♀H4 | CPrp WJek |
| - 'Porcupine' | CTca |
| - 'Touch of Red' (Touch of Red Series) **new** | CSpe |

## *Calibanus* (*Dracaenaceae*)

| | |
|---|---|
| ***hookeri*** | EShb |

## *Calibrachoa* (*Solanaceae*)

| | |
|---|---|
| (Cabaret Series) Cabaret Apricot = 'Balcabapt' **new** | SVil |
| - Cabaret Cherry Rose = 'Balcabcher' **new** | SVil |
| - Cabaret Purple = 'Balcabpurp' **new** | SVil |
| - Cabaret Scarlet = 'Balcabscar' **new** | NPri |
| - Cabaret White Improved = 'Balcabwitim' **new** | SVil |
| - Cabaret Yellow = 'Balcabyel' **new** | NPri SVil |
| (Callie Series) Callie Rose = 'Cal Rose' | NBlu |
| - Callie Sunrise = 'Cal Sunre' PBR | NBlu |
| (Million Bells Series) Million Bells Apricot = 'Sunbel-ap' | LAst |
| - Million Bells Cherry = 'Sunbelchipi' PBR | LSou WGor |

| | |
|---|---|
| - Million Bells Crackling Fire = 'Sunbelfire' | LAst LSou WGor |
| - Million Bells Golden Terracotta **new** | NPri |
| - Million Bells Lemon = 'Sunbelkic' | LAst LSou WGor |
| - Million Bells Orange Glow | LSou |
| - Million Bells Red = 'Sunbelre' PBR | NBlu |
| - Million Bells Salmon = 'Sunbelpapi' PBR **new** | WGor |
| - Million Bells Trailing Blue = 'Sunbelkubu' PBR | WGor |
| - Million Bells Trailing Fuchsia = 'Sunbelrkup' ♀H3 | NBlu WGor |
| - Million Bells Trailing Ice **new** | NPri |
| - Million Bells Trailing Ice White **new** | LSou |
| - Million Bells Trailing Lavender Vein = 'Sunbelbura' PBR | WGor |
| - Million Bells Trailing Pink = 'Sunbelkupi' PBR ♀H3 | LSou |
| - Million Bells White = 'Sunbelho' | LSou |
| (Noa Series) Noa Lemon **new** | LSou |
| - Noa Orange Eye **new** | LSou |
| - Noa Ultra Purple **new** | LSou |
| (Superbells Series) Superbells Candy White = 'Uscali48' PBR | LAst LSou |
| - Superbells Imperial Purple = 'Uscali100' PBR | LAst LSou SVil |
| - Superbells Indigo = 'Uscali51' PBR | LAst LSou |
| - Superbells Light Pink = 'Uscali67' PBR | SVil |
| - Superbells Magenta = 'Uscali17' PBR | LAst LSou NPri SVil |
| - Superbells Pink = 'Uscali11' PBR ♀H3 | LAst LSou |
| - Superbells Red = 'Uscali28' PBR | LAst LSou SVil |
| - Superbells Royal Blue = 'Uscali4' PBR | LAst LSou NPri |
| - Superbells Strawberry Pink = 'Uscali47' PBR | LAst SVil |

## *Calla* (*Araceae*)

| | |
|---|---|
| ***aethiopica*** | see *Zantedeschia aethiopica* |
| ***palustris*** | CRow CWat EHon EMFW EPfP LPBA MCCP MSKA NPer SWat WFar WMAq WPnP |

## *Calliandra* (*Mimosaceae*)

| | |
|---|---|
| 'Dixie Pink' | CCCN MJnS |
| ***emarginata*** 'Minima' | LRHS SOWG |
| ***haematocephala*** | SOWG |
| ***portoricensis*** | CCCN |
| ***surinamensis*** | CCCN |
| ***tweediei*** | CCCN SOWG |

## *Callianthemum* (*Ranunculaceae*)

| | |
|---|---|
| ***coriandrifolium*** | GEdr |
| ***kernerianum*** | NMen WAbe |

## *Callicarpa* (*Verbenaceae*)

| | |
|---|---|
| ***americana*** | CPLG NLar |
| - var. ***lactea*** | CMCN |
| ***bodinieri*** | GKir NBir WFar |
| - var. ***giraldii*** | CEnt GBin MGan MRav NLar WBod WDin |
| - - 'Profusion' ♀H4 | Widely available |
| ***cathayana*** | CBcs CMCN MBri NLar |
| ***dichotoma*** | CPLG CTrG EBee ELan NLar WBod WFar |
| - 'Issai' | EMil MAsh MGos NLar |
| - 'Shirobana' | NLar |
| ***japonica*** | CPLG NLar |
| - B&SWJ 8587 | WCru |
| - 'Koshima-no-homate' | MBri NLar |
| - 'Leucocarpa' | CBcs CMac CPLG EBee ELan EPfP MRav NLar SPer SPoG WFar |
| - var. ***luxurians*** B&SWJ 8521 | WCru |
| ***kwangtungensis*** | CBcs CMCN MBri NLar |
| ***mollis*** | CPLG NLar |
| ***shikokiana*** | NLar |
| x ***shirasawana*** | NLar |
| ***yunnanensis*** | NLar |

## *Callirhoe* (*Malvaceae*)

| | |
|---|---|
| ***involucrata*** | EBee GBri GGar MWea NBur NWCA SMad WHrl |

## *Callisia* (*Commelinaceae*)

| | |
|---|---|
| ***elegans*** ♀H1 | CHal |
| § ***navicularis*** | CHal |
| ***repens*** | CHal MBri |

## *Callistemon* ✿ (*Myrtaceae*)

| | |
|---|---|
| ***acuminatus*** | CCCN |
| 'Awanga Dam' | ECou |
| 'Burgundy' | SOWG |
| * 'Burning Bush' | SOWG |
| 'Candy Pink' | SOWG |
| ***chisholmii*** | SOWG |
| ***citrinus*** | CHll CSBt CTri EBee ECot ECou EPfP ERom EShb GGar LAst MCot MSCN NHol SOWG SPad SPlb WBrE WDin WHar |
| - 'Albus' | see *C. citrinus* 'White Anzac' |
| - 'Angela' | SOWG |
| - 'Canberra' | SOWG |
| - 'Firebrand' | CDoC LRHS SOWG |
| - 'Splendens' ♀H3 | Widely available |
| § - 'White Anzac' | CMac ELan EPfP LRHS SOWG SPoG SSta |
| ***comboynensis*** | CCCN GBin SOWG |
| 'Coochy Coochy Station' | SOWG |
| 'Dawson River Weeper' | SOWG |
| 'Eureka' | SOWG |
| ***flavescens*** | SOWG |
| ***flavovirens*** | SOWG |
| ***formosus*** | SOWG |
| ***glaucus*** | see *C. speciosus* |
| 'Hannah's Child' | SOWG |
| 'Happy Valley' | SOWG |
| 'Harkness' | SOWG |
| 'Horse Paddock' | SOWG |
| 'Injune' | SOWG |
| 'Kings Park Special' | SOWG |
| ***laevis*** hort. | see *C. rugulosus* |
| ***linearis*** ♀H3 | CBcs CMac CTrC CTri ECou ECrN ELan EPfP EPla LRHS LSRN MDun MHer SCoo SLim SLon SOWG SPlb SRms SSpi SWvt WSHC |
| ***macropunctatus*** | SOWG SPlb |
| 'Mauve Mist' | CCCN CDoC CTsd EBee ELan ELon EPfP GBin LRHS MAsh SOWG SPoG |
| ***pachyphyllus*** | ECou SOWG |

| | | |
|---|---|---|
| | - var. ***viridis*** | SOWG |
| | ***pallidus*** | CCCN CHEx CMHG CMac CWib EBee ECou ELan EPfP GGar LRHS MAsh MRav SOWG SPer SPlb SPoG SSta |
| | - 'Candle Glow' | SOWG |
| | - 'Father Christmas' | SOWG |
| | ***paludosus*** | see *C. sieberi* DC. |
| | ***pearsonii*** | SOWG |
| | - prostrate | SOWG |
| | - 'Rocky Rambler' | SOWG |
| | 'Perth Pink' | CBcs CCCN CDoC ELan SOWG SPoG |
| | 'Phil May' | SOWG |
| | ***phoeniceus*** | ECou SOWG |
| | - 'Pink Ice' | SOWG |
| | ***pinifolius*** | CTsd SOWG SPlb |
| | - green-flowered | SOWG |
| | - red-flowered | SOWG |
| | - 'Sockeye' | SOWG |
| | 'Pink Champagne' | SOWG |
| § | ***pityoides*** | CPLG ECou NHol SOWG WBod |
| | - from Brown's Swamp, Australia | ECou |
| | ***polandii*** | SOWG |
| | - dwarf | SOWG |
| | 'Purple Splendour' | SOWG |
| | ***recurvus*** | SOWG |
| | 'Red Clusters' | CDoC CMac CTrG CTsd EBee ELan IArd ISea LRHS MAsh MDun NLar SBod SChF SOWG SPoG SSto SWvt |
| | 'Reeve's Pink' | SOWG |
| | ***rigidus*** | CBcs CDoC CHEx CMHG CTri CWib EBee ELan EMil EPfP GGar IArd ISea LRHS MBlu MGos MLan MRav NLar SBod SOWG SWvt WBod WDin |
| § | ***rugulosus*** | CCCN EBee EMil IFFs NCob SOWG SWvt |
| | 'Running River' | SOWG |
| | ***salignus*** ♀H3 | CBcs CCCN CDoC CHEx CTrC CTri EBee ECrN EPfP ISea LRHS MHer SEND SLim SOWG WBVN WDin |
| | - Flaming Fire = 'Flaipp' | EMil NLar |
| | ***sieberi*** misapplied | see *C. pityoides* |
| § | ***sieberi*** DC. | CDoC CMHG CTrC EBee ECou ELan EPfP GGar MMuc NBir NLar NPal SOWG SPlb SPoG WFar |
| | - purple-flowered | SOWG |
| § | ***speciosus*** | CDul EBee NLar SOWG SPlb |
| | ***subulatus*** | CDoC CHEx CTrC EBee ECou GGal MCCP NHol NLar SAPC SArc SOWG SPlb SSto WMoo |
| | - 'Crimson Tail' | CWCL EBee GBin MMuc NLar |
| | - 'Packer's Selection' | ECou SOWG |
| | 'Taree Pink' | SOWG |
| | ***teretifolius*** | SOWG |
| | ***viminalis*** | CBcs CCCN CHEx SGar SOWG SPad SPlb |
| | - 'Captain Cook' | CMac ECou LRHS NLar SOWG SRms SWvt |
| | - 'Endeavor' | CCCN |
| | - 'Hannah Ray' | EBee SOWG |
| | - 'Little John' | CBcs CDTJ CSBt CTrC CWSG EBee ECou NLar SOWG SWvt |
| | - 'Malawi Giant' | SOWG |
| | - 'Wilderness White' | SOWG |
| | 'Violaceus' | EHig |
| | ***viridiflorus*** | CTrC ECou GGal GGar GQui MCCP SOWG SPlb SWal WGwG |
| | - 'County Park Dwarf' | ECou |
| | - 'Sunshine' | ECou |
| | 'White Anzac' | see *C. citrinus* 'White Anzac' |
| | 'Wildfire' **new** | LCro |

## *Callitriche* (*Callitrichaceae*)

| | | |
|---|---|---|
| | ***autumnalis*** | see *C. hermaphroditica* |
| § | ***hermaphroditica*** | EPfP WMAq |
| § | ***palustris*** | CDWL EHon EMFW |
| | ***stagnalis*** | NSco |
| | ***verna*** | see *C. palustris* |

## *Callitris* (*Cupressaceae*)

| | | |
|---|---|---|
| | ***rhomboidea*** | CDoC CTrC GGar |

## *Calluna* ✿ (*Ericaceae*)

| | | |
|---|---|---|
| | ***vulgaris*** | EBWF |
| | - 'Aberdeen' | EHea |
| | - 'Adrie' | EHea |
| | - 'Alba Argentea' | EHea |
| | - 'Alba Aurea' | EHea MBar |
| | - 'Alba Carlton' | EHea |
| | - 'Alba Dumosa' | EHea |
| | - 'Alba Elata' | EHea MBar |
| | - 'Alba Elegans' | EHea |
| | - 'Alba Elongata' | see *C. vulgaris* 'Mair's Variety' |
| | - 'Alba Erecta' | EHea |
| | - 'Alba Jae' | EHea MBar |
| | - 'Alba Minor' | EHea |
| | - 'Alba Multiflora' | EHea |
| | - 'Alba Pilosa' | EHea |
| § | - 'Alba Plena' (d) | CSBt EHea MBar |
| | - 'Alba Praecox' | EHea |
| | - 'Alba Pumila' | EHea MBar |
| § | - 'Alba Rigida' | EHea LRHS MBar SRms |
| | - 'Alec Martin' (d) | EHea |
| | - 'Alex Warwick' | EHea |
| | - 'Alexandra' PBR ♀H4 | EHea LRHS NHol SPoG SRms |
| | - 'Alice Knight' | EHea |
| | - 'Alicia' PBR (Garden Girls Series) ♀H4 | CBcs EHea LRHS NHol SPoG |
| | - 'Alieke' | EHea |
| | - 'Alina' | EHea |
| | - 'Alison Yates' | EHea MBar |
| | - 'Allegretto' | EHea |
| | - 'Allegro' ♀H4 | EHea EPfP MBar MMuc SRms |
| | - 'Alportii' | EHea GKir MBar |
| | - 'Alportii Praecox' | EHea MBar |
| | - 'Alys Sutcliffe' | EHea |
| | - 'Amanda Wain' | EHea |
| | - 'Amethyst' PBR (Garden Girls Series) | EHea MBar NHol SPoG |
| | - 'Amilto' | CBcs EHea LRHS SRms |
| | - 'Andrew Proudley' | EHea MBar |
| | - 'Anette' PBR (Garden Girls Series) ♀H4 | EHea LRHS MBar |
| | - 'Angela Wain' | EHea |
| | - 'Anna' | EHea |
| | - 'Annabel' (d) | EHea |
| | - 'Anne Dobbin' | EHea |
| | - 'Annegret' | see *C. vulgaris* 'Marlies' |
| | - 'Anneke' | EHea |
| | - 'Annemarie' (d) ♀H4 | CSBt EHea EPfP LRHS MBar NHol SCoo SPer SPlb SRms |
| | - 'Anne's Zwerg' | EHea SRms |
| | - 'Anthony Davis' ♀H4 | EHea LRHS MBar NHol |
| | - 'Anthony Wain' | EHea |
| | - 'Anton' | EHea |
| | - 'Antrujo Gold' | EHea |
| | - 'Aphrodite' PBR (Garden Girls Series) | CBcs EHea |
| | - 'Apollo' | EHea |
| | - 'Applecross' (d) | EHea |
| | - 'Arabella' PBR | EHea LRHS SRms |
| | - 'Argentea' | EHea MBar |
| | - 'Ariadne' | EHea |
| | - 'Arina' | EHea LRHS |

| | | |
|---|---|---|
| | - 'Arran Gold' | EHea MBar |
| | - 'Ashgarth Amber' | EHea |
| | - 'Ashgarth Amethyst' | EHea |
| | - 'Ashgarth Shell Pink' | EHea |
| | - 'Asterix' | EHea |
| | - 'Atalanta' | EHea |
| | - 'Atholl Gold' | EHea |
| | - 'August Beauty' | EHea |
| | - 'Aurea' | EHea |
| | - 'Aurora' | EHea |
| | - 'Autumn Glow' | EHea |
| | - 'Babette' | EHea |
| | - 'Baby Ben' | EHea |
| | - 'Baby Wicklow' | EHea |
| | - 'Barbara' | EHea |
| | - 'Barbara Fleur' | EHea |
| | - 'Barja' | EHea |
| | - 'Barnett Anley' | EHea |
| | - 'Battle of Arnhem' | EHea MBar |
| | - 'Bayport' | EHea |
| | - 'Beechwood Crimson' | EHea |
| | - 'Bella Rosa' | EHea |
| | - 'Ben Nevis' | EHea |
| | - 'Bennachie Bronze' | EHea |
| | - 'Bennachie Prostrate' | EHea |
| | - 'Beoley Crimson' | EHea MBar |
| | - 'Beoley Crimson Variegated' (v) | EHea |
| | - 'Beoley Gold' ♀H4 | CSBt CTri EHea EPfP GKir LRHS MBar MGos NHol SRms |
| | - 'Beoley Silver' | EHea MBar |
| | - 'Bernadette' | EHea |
| | - 'Betty Baum' | EHea |
| | - 'Bispingen' | EHea |
| | - 'Blazeaway' | CTri EHea EPfP GKir LRHS MBar NHol SPer SRms |
| | - 'Blueness' | EHea |
| | - 'Bognie' | EHea |
| | - 'Bonfire Brilliance' | CSBt EHea LRHS MBar NHol |
| | - 'Bonita'[PBR] (Garden Girls Series) | EHea |
| | - 'Bonne's Darkness' | EHea |
| | - 'Bonsaï' | EHea |
| | - 'Boreray' | EHea |
| | - 'Boskoop' | EHea LRHS MBar NHol |
| | - 'Bradford' | EHea |
| | - 'Braemar' | EHea |
| | - 'Braeriach' | EHea |
| | - 'Branchy Anne' | EHea |
| | - 'Bray Head' | EHea MBar |
| | - 'Brita Elisabeth' (d) | EHea |
| | - 'Bronze Beauty' | EHea |
| | - 'Bud Lyle' | EHea |
| | - 'Bunsall' | EHea |
| | - 'Buxton Snowdrift' | EHea |
| | - 'C.W. Nix' | CSBt EHea MBar |
| | - 'Caerketton White' | EHea |
| | - 'Caleb Threlkeld' | EHea |
| | - 'Calf of Man' | EHea |
| | - 'Californian Midge' | EHea MBar NHol |
| | - 'Camla Variety' | EHea |
| | - 'Carl Röders' (d) | EHea |
| | - 'Carmen' | EHea |
| | - 'Carngold' | EHea |
| | - 'Carole Chapman' | EHea MBar |
| | - 'Carolyn' | EHea |
| | - 'Cassa' | EHea |
| | - 'Catherine' | EHea |
| | - 'Catherine Anne' | EHea |
| | - 'Celtic Gold' | EHea |
| | - 'Charles Chapman' | EHea |
| § | - 'Chernobyl' (d) | EHea NHol |
| | - 'Chindit' | EHea |
| I | - 'Christin' **new** | EHea |
| | - 'Christina' | EHea |
| | - 'Cilcennin Common' | EHea |
| | - 'Clare Carpet' | EHea |
| | - 'Coby' | EHea |
| | - 'Coccinea' | EHea MBar |
| | - 'Colette' | EHea |
| | - 'Con Brio' | EHea LRHS MMuc SRms |
| | - 'Copper Glow' | EHea |
| | - 'Coral Island' | EHea MBar |
| | - 'Corbett's Red' | EHea |
| | - 'Corrie's White' | EHea |
| | - 'Cottswood Gold' | EHea NHol SRms |
| | - 'County Wicklow' (d) ♀H4 | CBcs CTri EHea EPfP GGar GKir LRHS MBar MMuc NBlu NHol SRms |
| | - 'Craig Rossie' | EHea |
| | - 'Crail Orange' | EHea |
| | - 'Cramond' (d) | EHea MBar |
| | - 'Cream Steving' | EHea |
| | - 'Crimson Glory' | EHea LRHS MBar |
| | - 'Crimson Sunset' | EHea |
| | - 'Crinkly Tuft' | EHea |
| | - 'Crowborough Beacon' | EHea |
| | - 'Cuprea' | EHea EPfP LRHS MBar NBlu NHol |
| | - 'Dainty Bess' | EHea MBar MSwo |
| | - 'Dapiali' | EHea |
| | - 'Dark Alicia'[PBR] | EHea |
| | - 'Dark Beauty'[PBR] (d) ♀H4 | CBcs EHea EPfP LRHS MBar NDlv NHol |
| | - 'Dark Star' (d) ♀H4 | CBcs EHea EPfP LCro LRHS MBar MGos MMuc NHol SCoo SRms |
| | - 'Darkness' ♀H4 | CSBt CTri EHea EPfP LRHS MBar NHol SCoo SRms |
| | - 'Darleyensis' | EHea MBar |
| | - 'Dart's Amethyst' | EHea |
| | - 'Dart's Beauty' | EHea |
| | - 'Dart's Brilliant' | EHea |
| | - 'Dart's Flamboyant' | EHea |
| | - 'Dart's Gold' | EHea MBar NHol |
| | - 'Dart's Hedgehog' | EHea |
| | - 'Dart's Parakeet' | EHea |
| | - 'Dart's Parrot' | EHea |
| | - 'Dart's Silver Rocket' | EHea |
| | - 'Dart's Squirrel' | EHea |
| | - 'David Eason' | EHea |
| | - 'David Hagenaars' | EHea |
| | - 'David Hutton' | EHea MBar |
| | - 'David Platt' (d) | EHea |
| | - 'Denkewitz' | EHea |
| | - 'Denny Pratt' | EHea |
| | - 'Desiree' | EHea |
| | - 'Devon' (d) | EHea |
| | - 'Diana' | EHea |
| | - 'Dickson's Blazes' | EHea |
| | - 'Dirry' | EHea NHol |
| | - 'Doctor Murray's White' | see *C. vulgaris* 'Mullardoch' |
| | - 'Doris Rushworth' | EHea |
| | - 'Drum-ra' | EHea MBar SRms |
| | - 'Dunnet Lime' | EHea SPlb |
| | - 'Dunnydeer' | EHea |
| | - 'Dunwood' | EHea MBar |
| § | - 'Durford Wood' | EHea |
| | - 'Dwingeloo Delight' | EHea |
| | - 'E.F. Brown' | EHea |
| | - 'E. Hoare' | EHea MBar |
| | - 'Easter-bonfire' | EHea LRHS NBlu NHol |
| | - 'Eckart Miessner' | EHea |
| | - 'Edith Godbolt' | EHea |
| | - 'Elaine' | EHea |
| | - 'Elegant Pearl' | EHea MBar |
| | - 'Elegantissima' | EHea MMuc |
| | - 'Elegantissima Walter Ingwersen' | see *C. vulgaris* 'Walter Ingwersen' |

| | | |
|---|---|---|
| | - 'Eleonore' (d) | EHea |
| | - 'Elkstone White' | EHea MBar |
| | - 'Ellen' | EHea |
| | - 'Ellie Barbour' | EHea |
| | - 'Elly' | EHea |
| | - 'Else Frye' (d) | EHea |
| | - 'Elsie Purnell' (d) $\mathfrak{Y}^{H4}$ | CSBt EHea EPfP LRHS MBar MGos NHol SPlb SRms |
| | - 'Emerald Jock' | EHea |
| | - 'Emma Louise Tuke' | EHea |
| | - 'Eric Easton' | EHea |
| | - 'Eskdale Gold' | EHea |
| | - 'Eurosa'[PBR] | EHea |
| | - 'Fairy' | EHea |
| | - 'Falling Star' | EHea |
| | - 'Feuerwerk' | EHea |
| § | - 'Finale' | EHea MBar |
| | - 'Findling' | EHea |
| | - 'Fire King' | EHea MBar |
| | - 'Fire Star' | EHea |
| | - 'Firebreak' | EHea MBar NHol |
| | - 'Firefly' $\mathfrak{Y}^{H4}$ | CBcs CSBt EHea EPfP LRHS MBar MMuc NHol SPer SRms |
| | - 'Flamingo' | CSBt EHea LRHS MBar MMuc MSwo NHol SPer SRms |
| | - 'Flatling' | EHea |
| | - 'Flore Pleno' (d) | EHea MBar |
| | - 'Floriferous' | EHea |
| | - 'Florrie Spicer' | EHea |
| | - 'Fokko' (d) | EHea |
| | - 'Fort Bragg' | EHea |
| | - 'Fortyniner Gold' | EHea |
| | - 'Foxhollow Wanderer' | EHea MBar |
| | - 'Foxii' | EHea |
| | - 'Foxii Floribunda' | EHea MBar |
| | - 'Foxii Lett's Form' | see *C. vulgaris* 'Velvet Dome', 'Mousehole' |
| | - 'Foxii Nana' | EHea MBar NHol SRms |
| | - 'Foya' | EHea |
| | - 'Fraser's Old Gold' | EHea |
| | - 'Fred J. Chapple' | EHea LRHS MBar NBlu |
| | - 'Fréjus' | EHea |
| | - 'French Grey' | EHea |
| | - 'Fritz Kircher'[PBR] | EHea |
| | - 'Gaia' | EHea |
| | - Garden Girls Series **new** | MMuc |
| | - 'Gerda' | EHea |
| | - 'Ginkel's Glorie' | EHea |
| | - 'Glasa' | EHea |
| | - 'Glen Mashie' | EHea |
| | - 'Glencoe' (d) | EHea MBar |
| | - 'Glendoick Silver' | EHea |
| | - 'Glenfiddich' | CSBt EHea LRHS MBar NHol |
| | - 'Glenlivet' | EHea MBar |
| | - 'Glenmorangie' | EHea MBar |
| | - 'Gloucester Boy' | EHea |
| | - 'Gnome' | EHea |
| | - 'Gold Charm' | EHea |
| | - 'Gold Finch' | EHea |
| | - 'Gold Flame' | EHea MBar |
| | - Gold Hamilton | see *C. vulgaris* 'Chernobyl' |
| | - 'Gold Haze' $\mathfrak{Y}^{H4}$ | CTri EHea GKir LRHS MBar NHol SCoo SPer SRms |
| | - 'Gold Knight' | EHea EPfP MBar |
| | - 'Gold Kup' | EHea MBar |
| | - 'Gold Mist' | EHea NBlu |
| | - 'Gold Spronk' | EHea |
| | - 'Goldcarmen' | EHea |
| | - 'Golden Blazeaway' | EHea |
| | - 'Golden Carpet' | CSBt EHea MBar MGos NDlv NHol SPer SRms |
| | - 'Golden Dew' | EHea |
| | - 'Golden Dream' (d) | EHea |
| | - 'Golden Feather' | CSBt EHea MBar |
| | - 'Golden Fleece' | EHea SRms |
| | - 'Golden Max' | EHea |
| | - 'Golden Rivulet' | EHea MBar MSwo |
| | - 'Golden Turret' | EHea LRHS NHol |
| | - 'Golden Wonder' (d) | EHea |
| | - 'Goldsworth Crimson' | CSBt EHea |
| | - 'Goldsworth Crimson Variegated' (v) | EHea MBar |
| | - 'Goscote Wine' | EHea |
| | - 'Grasmeriensis' | EHea MBar |
| | - 'Great Comp' | MBar |
| | - 'Green Cardinal' | EHea |
| | - 'Grey Carpet' | EHea LRHS MBar SRms |
| | - 'Grijsje' | EHea |
| | - 'Grizabella' | EHea |
| | - 'Grizzly' | EHea |
| | - 'Grönsinka' | EHea |
| | - 'Guinea Gold' | EHea LRHS MBar |
| § | - 'H.E. Beale' (d) | CSBt CTri EHea EPfP LRHS MBar MGos NHol |
| | - 'Hamlet Green' | EHea MBar |
| | - 'Hammondii' | EHea |
| | - 'Hammondii Aureifolia' | EHea MBar SPlb |
| | - 'Hammondii Rubrifolia' | EHea MBar NBlu SRms |
| | - 'Harlekin' | EHea |
| | - 'Harry Gibbon' (d) | EHea |
| | - 'Harten's Findling' | EHea |
| | - 'Hatje's Herbstfeuer' (d) | EHea |
| | - 'Hayesensis' | EHea |
| | - 'Heidberg' | EHea |
| | - 'Heidepracht' | EHea |
| | - 'Heidesinfonie' | EHea |
| | - 'Heideteppich' | EHea |
| | - 'Heidezwerg' | EHea |
| | - 'Heike' (d) | EHea |
| | - 'Herbert Mitchell' | EHea |
| | - 'Hester' | EHea |
| | - 'Hetty' | EHea |
| | - 'Hibernica' | EHea MBar |
| | - 'Hiemalis' | EHea MBar |
| | - 'Hiemalis Southcote' | see *C. vulgaris* 'Durford Wood' |
| | - Highland Cream | see *C. vulgaris* 'Punch's Dessert' |
| | - 'Highland Rose' | EHea SPlb SRms |
| | - 'Highland Spring' | EHea |
| | - 'Hilda Turberfield' | EHea |
| | - 'Hillbrook Limelight' | EHea |
| | - 'Hillbrook Orange' | EHea MBar |
| | - 'Hillbrook Sparkler' | EHea |
| | - 'Hinton White' | EHea |
| | - 'Hirsuta Albiflora' | EHea |
| | - 'Hirsuta Typica' | EHea |
| | - 'Hollandia' | EHea |
| | - 'Holstein' | EHea |
| | - 'Hookstone' | EHea MBar |
| | - 'Hoyerhagen' | EHea |
| § | - 'Hugh Nicholson' | EHea |
| | - 'Humpty Dumpty' | EHea LRHS MBar NHol |
| | - 'Hypnoides' | EHea |
| | - 'Ide's Double' (d) | EHea |
| | - 'Inchcolm' | EHea |
| | - 'Inchkeith' | EHea |
| | - 'Ineke' | EHea MBar |
| | - 'Inge' | EHea |
| | - 'Ingrid Bouter' (d) | EHea |
| | - 'Inshriach Bronze' | EHea MBar |
| | - 'Iris van Leyen' | EHea MBar |
| | - 'Islay Mist' | EHea |
| | - 'Isle of Hirta' | EHea MBar NHol |
| | - 'Isobel Frye' | EHea MBar |
| | - 'Isobel Hughes' (d) | EHea MBar |
| | - 'J.H. Hamilton' (d) $\mathfrak{Y}^{H4}$ | CTri EHea GKir LRHS MBar NHol SRms |

| | |
|---|---|
| – 'Jan' | EHea |
| – 'Jan Dekker' | EHea LRHS MBar NBlu NHol |
| – 'Janice Chapman' | EHea MBar |
| – 'Japanese White' | EHea |
| – 'Jenny' | EHea |
| – 'Jill' | EHea |
| – 'Jimmy Dyce' (d) | EHea |
| – 'Joan Sparkes' (d) | EHea LRHS MBar |
| – 'Jochen' | EHea |
| – 'Johan Slegers' | EHea |
| – John Denver | see *C. vulgaris* 'Marleen Select' |
| – 'John F. Letts' | EHea MBar NHol SRms |
| – 'Johnson's Variety' | EHea MBar |
| – 'Jos' Lemon' | EHea |
| – 'Jos' Whitie' | EHea |
| – 'Josefine' | EHea |
| – 'Joseph's Coat' | EHea |
| – 'Joy Vanstone' ♀H4 | CSBt EHea EPfP GKir MBar MGos NHol SRms |
| – 'Julia' | EHea |
| – 'Julie Ann Platt' | EHea |
| – 'Juno' | EHea |
| – 'Kaiser' | EHea |
| – 'Karin Blum' | EHea |
| – 'Kermit' | EHea |
| – 'Kerstin' ♀H4 | EHea LRHS MBar MMuc MSwo NBlu NHol SPlb SRms |
| – 'Kerstin Jacke' **new** | NHol |
| – 'Kinlochruel' (d) ♀H4 | CBcs CSBt CTri EHea EPfP GGar GKir LRHS MBar MGos NHol SPlb SRms |
| – 'Kir Royal' | EHea |
| – 'Kirby White' | EHea LRHS MBar NDlv NHol SPlb |
| – 'Kirsty Anderson' | EHea |
| – 'Kit Hill' | EHea MBar |
| – 'Knaphill' | EHea |
| – 'Kontrast' | EHea |
| – 'Kuphaldtii' | EHea MBar |
| – 'Kuppendorf' | EHea |
| – 'Kynance' | EHea MBar |
| – 'Lady Maithe' | EHea |
| – 'Lambstails' | EHea MBar |
| – 'L'Ancresse' | EHea |
| – 'Larissa' PBR | EHea |
| – 'Lemon Gem' | EHea |
| – 'Lemon Queen' | EHea |
| – 'Leprechaun' | LRHS NHol |
| – 'Leslie Slinger' | EHea LRHS MBar NHol |
| – 'Lewis Lilac' | EHea |
| – 'Liebestraum' | EHea |
| – 'Lilac Elegance' | EHea |
| – 'Lime Glade' | EHea |
| – 'Lime Gold' | EHea |
| – 'Little John' | EHea LSRN |
| – 'Llanbedrog Pride' (d) | EHea MBar |
| – 'Loch Turret' | EHea MBar |
| – 'Loch-na-Seil' | EHea MBar |
| – 'Long White' | EHea MBar |
| – 'Loni' | EHea |
| – 'Lüneberg Heath' | EHea |
| – 'Lyle's Late White' | EHea |
| – 'Lyle's Surprise' | EHea MBar |
| – 'Lyndon Proudley' | EHea |
| – 'Macdonald of Glencoe' | EHea |
| § – 'Mair's Variety' ♀H4 | EHea MBar |
| – 'Mallard' | EHea |
| – 'Manitoba' | EHea |
| – 'Manuel' | EHea |
| – 'Marianne' | EHea |
| – 'Marie' | EHea |
| – 'Marion Blum' | EHea MBar |
| – 'Marleen' | EHea LRHS MBar NHol |
| § – 'Marleen Select' | EHea |
| § – 'Marlies' | EHea |
| – 'Martha Hermann' | EHea |
| – 'Martine Langenberg' | EHea |
| – 'Masquerade' | EHea MBar |
| – 'Matita' | EHea |
| – 'Mauvelyn' | EHea |
| – 'Mazurka' | EHea |
| – 'Melanie' (Garden Girls Series) | EHea LRHS MBar MSwo NHol |
| – 'Mick Jamieson' (d) | EHea |
| – 'Mies' | EHea |
| – 'Minima' | EHea MBar |
| – 'Minima Smith's Variety' | EHea MBar |
| – 'Miniöxabäck' | EHea |
| – 'Minty' | EHea |
| – 'Mirato' **new** | EHea |
| – 'Mirelle' | EHea |
| – 'Miss Muffet' | EHea NHol |
| – 'Molecule' | EHea MBar |
| – 'Monika' (d) | EHea |
| – 'Moon Glow' | EHea |
| – 'Mountain Snow' | EHea |
| § – 'Mousehole' | EHea MBar NHol |
| – 'Mousehole Compact' | see *C. vulgaris* 'Mousehole' |
| – 'Mrs Alf' | EHea |
| – 'Mrs E. Wilson' (d) | EHea |
| – 'Mrs Pat' | EHea LRHS MBar NHol |
| – 'Mrs Pinxteren' | EHea |
| – 'Mrs Ronald Gray' | EHea MBar |
| – 'Mullach Mor' | EHea |
| § – 'Mullardoch' | EHea MBar |
| – 'Mullion' ♀H4 | EHea MBar |
| – 'Multicolor' | EHea LRHS MBar NBlu NHol SRms |
| – 'Murielle Dobson' | EHea MBar |
| § – 'My Dream' (d) ♀H4 | CSBt EHea EPfP LRHS MBar NHol SCoo |
| – 'Nana' | EHea |
| – 'Nana Compacta' | EHea MBar |
| – 'Natasja' | EHea |
| – 'Naturpark' | EHea MBar |
| – 'Nele' (d) | EHea |
| – 'Nico' | EHea |
| – 'Nofretete' | EHea |
| – Nordlicht | see *C. vulgaris* 'Skone' |
| – 'October White' | EHea |
| – 'Odette' | EHea |
| – 'Oiseval' | EHea |
| – 'Old Rose' | EHea |
| – 'Olive Turner' | EHea |
| – 'Olympic Gold' | EHea |
| – 'Orange and Gold' | EHea |
| – 'Orange Carpet' | EHea |
| – 'Orange Max' | EHea LRHS NHol |
| – 'Orange Queen' | CSBt EHea MBar |
| – 'Öxabäck' | EHea MBar |
| – 'Oxshott Common' | EHea GQui MBar |
| – 'Pallida' | EHea |
| – 'Parsons' Gold' | EHea |
| – 'Parsons' Grey Selected' | EHea |
| – 'Pastell' (d) | EHea |
| – 'Pat's Gold' | EHea |
| – 'Peace' | EHea |
| – 'Pearl Drop' | EHea MBar |
| – 'Peggy' | EHea |
| – 'Penhale' | EHea |
| – 'Penny Bun' | EHea |
| – 'Pennyacre Gold' | EHea |
| – 'Pennyacre Lemon' | EHea |
| – 'Pepper and Salt' | see *C. vulgaris* 'Hugh Nicholson' |
| – 'Perestrojka' | EHea |
| – 'Peter Sparkes' (d) ♀H4 | CBcs CSBt EHea EPfP LRHS MBar MGos NHol SRms |
| – 'Petra' | EHea |

| | | |
|---|---|---|
| | - 'Pewter Plate' | EHea MBar |
| | - 'Pink Alicia'$^{PBR}$ (Garden Girls Series) | EHea |
| | - 'Pink Beale' | see *C. vulgaris* 'H.E. Beale' |
| | - 'Pink Dream' (d) | EHea |
| | - 'Pink Gown' | EHea |
| | - 'Pink Spreader' | EHea |
| | - 'Pink Tips' | EHea |
| | - 'Plantarium' | EHea |
| | - 'Platt's Surprise' (d) | EHea |
| | - 'Polly' | EHea |
| | - 'Poolster' | EHea |
| | - 'Porth Wen White' | EHea |
| | - 'Prizewinner' | EHea |
| * | - 'Procumbens' | EHea |
| | - 'Prostrata Flagelliformis' | EHea |
| | - 'Prostrate Orange' | EHea MBar |
| § | - 'Punch's Dessert' | EHea |
| | - 'Purple Passion' | EPfP |
| | - 'Pygmaea' | EHea MBar |
| | - 'Pyramidalis' | EHea |
| | - 'Pyrenaica' | EHea MBar |
| | - 'R.A. McEwan' | EHea |
| | - 'Radnor' (d) 🏆$^{H4}$ | CSBt EHea LRHS MBar |
| | - 'Radnor Gold' (d) | EHea MBar |
| | - 'Raket' | EHea |
| | - 'Ralph Purnell' | EHea MBar |
| | - 'Ralph Purnell Select' | EHea |
| | - 'Ralph's Pearl' | EHea |
| | - 'Ralph's Red' | EHea |
| | - 'Randall's Crimson' | EHea |
| | - 'Rannoch' | EHea |
| | - 'Rebecca's Red' | EHea SRms |
| | - 'Red Carpet' | EHea LRHS MBar |
| | - 'Red Favorit' (d) | CBcs EHea LRHS SRms |
| | - 'Red Fred' | EHea NHol |
| | - 'Red Haze' | EHea EPfP LRHS MBar NHol SPer |
| | - 'Red Max' | EHea |
| | - 'Red Pimpernel' | EHea EPfP MBar NHol |
| | - 'Red Rug' | EHea |
| | - 'Red Star' (d) | EHea LRHS MBar NHol |
| | - 'Red Wings' | EHea |
| | - 'Redbud' | EHea |
| | - 'Redgauntlet' | EHea |
| | - 'Reini' | EHea |
| | - 'Rica' | EHea |
| | - 'Richard Cooper' | EHea MBar |
| | - 'Rieanne' | EHea |
| | - 'Rigida Prostrata' | see *C. vulgaris* 'Alba Rigida' |
| | - 'Rivington' | EHea |
| | - 'Robber Knight' | EHea |
| | - 'Robert Chapman' 🏆$^{H4}$ | CSBt CTri EHea GKir LRHS MBar NHol SRms |
| | - 'Rock Spray' | EHea |
| | - 'Röding' | EHea |
| | - 'Rokoko' | EHea |
| | - 'Roland Haagen' 🏆$^{H4}$ | EHea MBar |
| | - 'Roma' | EHea MBar |
| | - 'Romina' | EHea MSwo NHol |
| | - 'Ronas Hill' | EHea |
| | - 'Roodkapje' | EHea |
| | - 'Rosalind' ambig. | CSBt EPfP MBar NHol |
| | - 'Rosalind, Crastock Heath' | EHea |
| | - 'Rosalind, Underwood's' | EHea EPfP LRHS |
| | - 'Ross Hutton' | EHea |
| | - 'Roswitha' | EHea |
| | - 'Roter Oktober' | EHea |
| | - 'Rotfuchs' | EHea |
| | - 'Ruby Slinger' | EHea LRHS MBar NHol |
| | - 'Rusty Triumph' | EHea |
| | - 'Ruth Sparkes' (d) | EHea LRHS MBar NHol |
| | - 'Sabrina' (d) | EHea |
| | - 'Saima' | EHea |
| | - 'Saint Nick' | EHea MBar |
| | - 'Salland' | EHea |
| | - 'Sally Anne Proudley' | EHea MBar |
| | - 'Salmon Leap' | EHea LRHS MBar NHol |
| | - 'Sam Hewitt' | EHea |
| | - 'Sampford Sunset' | CSam EHea |
| | - 'Sandhammaren' | EHea |
| | - 'Sandwood Bay' | EHea |
| | - 'Sandy'$^{PBR}$ (Garden Girls Series) | EHea LRHS NHol SPoG |
| | - 'Sarah Platt' (d) | EHea |
| | - 'Saskia' | EHea |
| | - 'Schneewolke'$^{PBR}$ | EHea |
| | - 'Scholje's Jimmy' | EHea |
| | - 'Scholje's Rubin' (d) | EHea |
| | - 'Scholje's Super Star' (d) | EHea |
| | - 'Schurig's Sensation' (d) | EHea LRHS MBar |
| | - 'Schurig's Wonder' (d) | EHea |
| | - 'Scotch Mist' | EHea |
| | - 'Sedloñov' | EHea |
| | - 'Sellingsloh' | EHea |
| | - 'September Pink' | EHea |
| | - 'Serlei' | EHea MBar |
| | - 'Serlei Aurea' 🏆$^{H4}$ | CSBt EHea EPfP MBar NHol SRms |
| | - 'Serlei Grandiflora' | EHea MBar |
| | - 'Serlei Purpurea' | EHea |
| | - 'Serlei Rubra' | EHea |
| | - 'Sesam' | EHea |
| | - 'Sesse' | EHea |
| | - 'Shirley' | EHea MBar |
| | - 'Silberspargel' | EHea |
| | - 'Silver Cloud' | EHea MBar |
| | - 'Silver Fox' | EHea |
| | - 'Silver King' | EHea MBar |
| | - 'Silver Knight' | CSBt EHea EPfP GGar LRHS MBar MGos NHol SPer SPlb SRms |
| | - 'Silver Pearl' | EHea |
| | - 'Silver Queen' 🏆$^{H4}$ | EHea LRHS MBar NHol SRms |
| | - 'Silver Rose' 🏆$^{H4}$ | EHea MBar |
| | - 'Silver Sandra' | EHea |
| | - 'Silver Spire' | EHea MBar |
| | - 'Silver Stream' | EHea MBar |
| | - 'Silvie' | EHea |
| | - 'Simone' | EHea |
| | - 'Sir Anthony Hopkins' | EHea |
| | - 'Sir John Charrington' 🏆$^{H4}$ | CSBt EHea EPfP LRHS MBar MGos NHol |
| | - 'Sirsson' | EHea MBar |
| | - 'Sister Anne' 🏆$^{H4}$ | CSBt EHea EPfP LRHS MMuc NHol SRms |
| | - 'Skipper' | EHea MBar NHol |
| § | - 'Skone' (v) | EHea |
| | - 'Snowball' | see *C. vulgaris* 'My Dream' |
| | - 'Snowflake' | EHea |
| | - 'Soay' | EHea MBar |
| | - 'Sonja' (d) | EHea |
| | - 'Sonning' (d) | EHea |
| | - 'Sonny Boy' | EHea |
| | - 'Sophia' (d) | EHea |
| | - 'Sparkling Stars' | EHea |
| | - 'Sphinx' | EHea |
| | - 'Spicata' | EHea |
| | - 'Spicata Aurea' | EHea MBar |
| | - 'Spicata Nana' | EHea |
| | - 'Spider' | EHea |
| | - 'Spitfire' | EHea LRHS MBar NHol |
| | - 'Spook' | EHea |
| | - 'Spring Cream' 🏆$^{H4}$ | EHea GGar GKir LRHS MBar MMuc NBlu NHol SPer SPoG |
| | - 'Spring Glow' | EHea LRHS MBar |
| | - 'Spring Torch' | CSBt EHea GGar GKir LRHS MBar NBlu NHol SCoo SPer SPoG SRms |

| | | |
|---|---|---|
| | - 'Springbank' | EHea MBar |
| | - 'Stag's Horn' | EHea |
| I | - 'Startler' | EHea |
| | - 'Stefanie' | EHea NHol SRms |
| | - 'Stranger' | EHea |
| | - 'Strawberry Delight' (d) | EHea EPfP |
| | - 'Summer Elegance' | EHea |
| | - 'Summer Gold' | SRms |
| | - 'Summer Orange' | EHea LRHS MBar NHol |
| | - 'Summer White' (d) | EHea |
| | - 'Sunningdale' | see *C. vulgaris* 'Finale' |
| | - 'Sunrise' | CSBt EHea EPfP MBar MGos NBlu |
| | - 'Sunset' ♀$^{H4}$ | CSBt EHea LRHS MBar SRms |
| | - 'Sunset Glow' | EHea |
| | - 'Talisker' | EHea |
| | - 'Tenella' | EHea |
| | - 'Tenuis' | EHea MBar |
| | - 'Terrick's Orange' | EHea |
| | - 'The Pygmy' | EHea |
| | - 'Theresa' (Garden Girls Series) | EHea |
| | - 'Tib' (d) ♀$^{H4}$ | CSBt EHea LRHS MBar SPer SRms |
| | - 'Tijdens Copper' | EHea |
| | - 'Tino' | EHea |
| | - 'Tom Thumb' | EHea MBar |
| | - 'Tomentosa Alba' | EHea |
| | - 'Torogay' | EHea |
| | - 'Torulosa' | EHea |
| | - 'Tremans' | EHea |
| | - 'Tricolorifolia' | EHea EPfP LRHS NHol SPer |
| | - 'Underwoodii' | EHea MBar |
| | - 'Unity' | EHea |
| | - 'Valorian' | EHea |
| | - 'Van Beek' | EHea |
| § | - 'Velvet Dome' | EHea MBar |
| | - 'Velvet Fascination' ♀$^{H4}$ | EHea EPfP LRHS MBar MGos NHol |
| | - 'Violet Bamford' | EHea |
| | - 'Visser's Fancy' | EHea |
| § | - 'Walter Ingwersen' | EHea |
| | - 'Waquoit Brightness' | EHea |
| | - 'Westerlee Gold' | EHea |
| | - 'Westerlee Green' | EHea |
| | - 'Westphalia' | EHea |
| | - 'White Bouquet' | see *C. vulgaris* 'Alba Plena' |
| | - 'White Carpet' | EHea MBar |
| | - 'White Coral' (d) | EHea EPfP MGos |
| | - 'White Gold' | EHea |
| | - 'White Gown' | EHea |
| | - 'White Lawn' ♀$^{H4}$ | EHea LRHS MBar MSwo NDlv NHol SRms |
| | - 'White Mite' | EHea MBar |
| | - 'White Pearl' (d) | EHea |
| | - 'White Princess' | see *C. vulgaris* 'White Queen' |
| § | - 'White Queen' | EHea MBar |
| | - 'White Star' (d) | EHea |
| | - 'Whiteness' | EHea MBar |
| | - 'Wickwar Flame' ♀$^{H4}$ | CBcs CSBt EHea EPfP LCro LRHS MBar MGos MMuc NBlu NHol SPer SPlb SRms |
| | - 'Wilma' | EHea |
| | - 'Wingates Gem' | EHea |
| | - 'Wingates Gold' | EHea |
| | - 'Winter Chocolate' | CSBt EHea EPfP LRHS MBar MSwo NDlv NHol SPer |
| | - 'Winter Fire' | EHea |
| | - 'Winter Red' | EHea |
| | - 'Wollmer's Weisse' (d) | EHea |
| | - 'Wood Close' | EHea |
| | - 'Yellow Basket' | EHea |
| | - 'Yellow Beauty'$^{PBR}$ | EHea |
| | - 'Yellow Globe' | EHea |
| | - 'Yellow One' | EHea |
| | - 'Yvette's Gold' | EHea |
| | - 'Yvette's Silver' | EHea |
| | - 'Yvonne Clare' | EHea |

## calamondin see x *Citrofortunella microcarpa*

## *Calocedrus* (*Cupressaceae*)

| | | |
|---|---|---|
| § | ***decurrens*** ♀$^{H4}$ | CBcs CDoC CDul CLnd CMac CTho CTri EHul EPfP GKir LPan LRHS MBar MBlu MBri MGos MMuc NWea SBLw SLim SPer SPoG WFar WMou |
| | - 'Aureovariegata' (v) | CBcs CWib EHul LPan LRHS MAsh MBar MBlu MBri NLar SBLw SCoo SLim SPoG WFar |
| | - 'Berrima Gold' | CDoC CKen EMil EPfP GKir LRHS MGos NLar SLim SPoG |
| | - 'Columnaris' **new** | LMaj |
| § | - 'Depressa' | CKen |
| | - 'Intricata' | CKen NLar SLim |
| | - 'Maupin Glow' (v) | NLar SLim |
| | - 'Nana' | see *C. decurrens* 'Depressa' |
| | - 'Pillar' | CKen NLar |
| | ***formosana*** | WFar |
| | ***macrolepis*** | EMon |

## *Calocephalus* (*Asteraceae*)

| | |
|---|---|
| ***brownii*** | see *Leucophyta brownii* |
| 'Silver Sand' | LSou SVil |

## *Calochortus* (*Liliaceae*)

| | |
|---|---|
| 'Cupido'$^{PBR}$ | CSec EBrs ECho EPot LAma |
| ***luteus*** Douglas ex Lindl. | EPot LAma |
| - 'Golden Orb'$^{PBR}$ | CGrW CHFP EBrs ECho LRHS |
| ***splendens*** | LAma |
| - 'Violet Queen' | CGrW ECho LAma LEdu |
| ***superbus*** | CHFP CSec EBee EBrs ECho EPot LRHS WFar |
| 'Symphony' | EBrs ECho EPot LAma |
| ***uniflorus*** | EPot |
| ***venustus*** | CGrW EBee EBrs ECho EPot LAma LEdu LRHS |

## *Calomeria* (*Asteraceae*)

| | | |
|---|---|---|
| § | ***amaranthoides*** | WJek |

## *Calonyction* see *Ipomoea*

## *Calopsis* (*Restionaceae*)

| | |
|---|---|
| ***paniculata*** | CBcs CCCN CDTJ CHEx CTrC CTsd EAmu IArd IDee WPGP |

## *Caloscordum* (*Alliaceae*)

| | | |
|---|---|---|
| § | ***neriniflorum*** | CPom EBur WAbe WCot |

## *Calothamnus* (*Myrtaceae*)

| | |
|---|---|
| ***blepharospermus*** | SOWG |
| ***gilesii*** | SOWG |
| ***homolophyllus*** | SOWG |
| ***quadrifidus*** | ECou SOWG |
| - yellow-flowered | SOWG |
| ***rupestris*** | SOWG |
| ***sanguineus*** | SOWG |
| ***validus*** | SOWG SPlb |

## *Caltha* ✿ (*Ranunculaceae*)

| | | |
|---|---|---|
| | 'Auenwald' | CLAP CRow CWsd LLWG |
| | 'Honeydew' | CDes CLAP CRow EBee WPGP |
| | ***howellii*** | see *C. leptosepala* subsp. *howellii* |
| | ***introloba*** | SWat |
| | ***laeta*** | see *C. palustris* var. *palustris* |
| | ***leptosepala*** | CLAP CRow EBee NLar |
| § | - subsp. ***howellii*** | EBee |
| | ***natans*** | CRow |
| | ***palustris*** ♀$^{H4}$ | Widely available |

| | | |
|---|---|---|
| | - var. ***alba*** | Widely available |
| | - var. ***barthei*** | CFir EBee GEdr SKHP WPnP |
| | - - f. ***atrorubra*** new | GEdr |
| | - 'Flore Pleno' (d) ♀H4 | Widely available |
| | - var. ***himalensis*** | WCot |
| | - 'Marilyn' | CLAP LLWG |
| | - 'Multiplex' (d) | EBee GBuc |
| | - Newlake hybrid new | LLWG |
| § | - var. ***palustris*** | CBre CRow ECha EHon ELan EMFW EMon GGar LPBA SWat WCra WFar |
| | - - 'Plena' (d) | CRow CWat EPfP GGar LRHS MCot MSKA WFar |
| | - subsp. ***polypetala*** | CDWL MSKA NPer SDix SMad SWat WMAq |
| | - var. ***radicans*** | CRow |
| | - - 'Flore Pleno' (d) | CRow |
| | - 'Semiplena' (d) | EMon |
| | - 'Stagnalis' | CRow MSKA |
| | - Trotter's form | GBuc |
| | - 'Tyermannii' | CRow |
| | - 'Yellow Giant' | CDWL |
| N | ***polypetala*** misapplied | see *C. palustris* var. *palustris* |
| N | ***polypetala*** Hochst. ex Lorent | CLAP CWat EBee EWll GBuc GCal GKir WBor |
| | - from Turkey | GBuc |
| | ***sagittata*** | CRow WSHC |
| | 'Susan' | CRow |

## *Calycanthus* (*Calycanthaceae*)

| | | |
|---|---|---|
| | ***fertilis*** | see *C. floridus* var. *glaucus* |
| | - var. ***laevigatus*** | see *C. floridus* var. *glaucus* |
| | - 'Purpureus' | see *C. floridus* var. *glaucus* 'Purpureus' |
| | ***floridus*** | CAgr CArn CBcs CDul CMCN CPMA CTho CWib EBee ELan EPfP EWTr IDee LAst LEdu LRHS MBNS MBlu MBri MMuc NBea SDnm SPer SPlb SPoG WBod WCFE WDin |
| | - 'Athens' | CPMA |
| § | - var. ***glaucus*** | EPfP MGos NBlu NLar WSHC |
| § | - - 'Purpureus' | CBcs CPMA MBlu MBri NLar |
| | - var. ***laevigatus*** | see *C. floridus* var. *glaucus* |
| | - 'Michael Lindsay' | CPMA |
| | ***occidentalis*** | CAgr CArn CBcs CDul CMCN CWib EPfP MBlu MMuc SGar SSpi WBVN |

## *Calyptridium* (*Portulacaceae*)

| | | |
|---|---|---|
| | ***umbellatum*** | see *Spraguea umbellata* |

## *Calystegia* (*Convolvulaceae*)

| | | |
|---|---|---|
| § | ***hederacea*** 'Flore Pleno' (d) | EBee ELan EMon NCGa NLar NSti SMad WCot WFar |
| | ***japonica*** 'Flore Pleno' | see *C. hederacea* 'Flore Pleno' |
| | ***silvatica*** 'Incarnata' | EBee EMon |
| | ***soldanella*** NNS 99-85 | WCot |

## *Calytrix* (*Myrtaceae*)

| | | |
|---|---|---|
| | ***tetragona*** | SPlb |
| | - compact, pink-flowered | SOWG |

## *Camassia* ✿ (*Hyacinthaceae*)

| | | |
|---|---|---|
| | ***biflora*** | EBee |
| | ***cusickii*** | Widely available |
| | - white-flowered | IFoB |
| | - 'Zwanenburg' | CTca EBee EBrs ERCP GKev LRHS MSte SMeo |
| | ***esculenta*** Lindl. | see *C. quamash* |
| | ***fraseri*** | see *C. scilloides* |
| | ***howellii*** | EBee |
| | ***leichtlinii*** misapplied | see *C. leichtlinii* subsp. *suksdorfii* |
| | ***leichtlinii*** (Baker) S.Watson | CSec ECho ISea SSto |
| N | - 'Alba' hort. | see *C. leichtlinii* subsp. *leichtlinii* |
| * | - 'Alba Plena' | NBPC NBir |
| | - 'Blauwe Donau' | see *C. leichtlinii* subsp. *suksdorfii* 'Blauwe Donau' |
| | - Blue Danube | see *C. leichtlinii* subsp. *suksdorfii* 'Blauwe Donau' |
| § | - subsp. ***leichtlinii*** ♀H4 | Widely available |
| | - 'Magdalen' | CAvo |
| N | - 'Plena' (d) | ECha MSte |
| | - 'Semiplena' (d) | CAvo CBro CFFs CMea CMil CTca EBee EBrs EMon EPot ERCP GGar LRHS MSte NMen NSti SDix SPhx WAul WCot WHoo |
| § | - subsp. ***suksdorfii*** | CAvo CSam ECho GBuc GCra LRHS MWat WAul |
| § | - - 'Blauwe Donau' | CTca EBee EBrs GKev MSte SMeo |
| | - - Caerulea Group | Widely available |
| | - - 'Electra' | CAvo ECha SUsu |
| § | ***quamash*** | Widely available |
| | - 'Blue Melody' (v) | CBow CBro CMea CTca EBee EBrs EMon EPot ERCP GBuc GKev GMaP GMac LRHS MCCP NMen SPhx SWal |
| | - var. ***breviflora*** | CTca EBee EBrs |
| | - 'Orion' | CBro CMea CTca EBee EBrs EMon GBuc GMac NSti SMeo SPhx WAul WCot |
| § | ***scilloides*** | WRos |

## *Camellia* ✿ (*Theaceae*)

| | | |
|---|---|---|
| | 'Adorable' (*pitardii* hybrid) | LSRN |
| | 'Annette Carol' | CDoC |
| | 'Ariel's Song' | CDoC |
| | 'Auburn White' | see *C. japonica* 'Mrs Bertha A. Harms' |
| | 'Baby Bear' | CDoC |
| | 'Barbara Clark' (*saluenensis* x *reticulata*) | CDoC CTrG LRHS LSRN MGos SCog SCoo |
| | 'Bertha Harms Blush' | see *C. japonica* 'Mrs Bertha A. Harms' |
| | 'Bett's Supreme' | CDoC |
| | 'Betty Ridley' | SImb |
| | 'Black Lace' (*reticulata* x *williamsii*) ♀H4 | CTrh CTri EPfP GLld LBuc LRHS LSRN MBri NPri SCam SCog SCoo SImb WBVN WCot WGob WMoo |
| | 'Blissful Dawn' | CTrh |
| | 'Bonnie Marie' (hybrid) | CBcs CDoC MGos SCam SCog SImb |
| | ***brevistyla*** | CBcs |
| | 'Charles Cobb' | see *C. japonica* 'Mrs Charles Cobb' |
| * | 'Chatsworth Belle' | CTrh SCam |
| | 'China Lady' (*reticulata* x *granthamiana*) | MBri |
| | 'Cinnamon Cindy' (hybrid) | CDoC SCam SCog |
| | 'Congratulations' | LSRN SPer |
| | 'Contessa Lavinia Maggi' | see *C. japonica* 'Lavinia Maggi' |
| * | 'Cornish Clay' | ISea |
| | 'Cornish Snow' (*cuspidata* x *saluenensis*) ♀H4 | CBcs CDoC CSBt CSam CTri EPfP LHyd MGos SCam SCog SHBN SImb SPur SSpi WFar |
| | 'Cornish Spring' (*japonica* x *cuspidata*) ♀H4 | CCCN CDoC CSBt CTrh EPfP LHyd SCog SPer |
| | 'Corsica' | SHBN |
| | ***cuspidata*** | LHyd |
| | 'Czar' | see *C. japonica* 'The Czar' |
| | 'Dainty Dale' (hybrid) | CDoC LRHS SCam SSta |
| | 'Delia Williams' | see *C.* x *williamsii* 'Citation' |
| | 'Diana's Charm' | CDoC LSRN |
| | 'Doctor Clifford Parks' (*reticulata* x *japonica*) ♀H2 | CDoC GLld LHyd SCam SCog |
| | 'Donckelaeri' | see *C. japonica* 'Masayoshi' |
| | 'Dorothy James' (hybrid) | SImb |
| | 'El Dorado' (*pitardii* x *japonica*) | CDoC CTrG |

| | | |
|---|---|---|
| | 'Extravaganza' (*japonica* hybrid) | CBcs CTrh IArd MBri SCog SImb |
| | 'Fairy Wand' (hybrid) | CDoC |
| | 'Faustina Lechi' | see *C. japonica* 'Faustina' |
| | 'Felice Harris' (*sasanqua* x *reticulata*) | CDoC MBri SCam SCog |
| | 'Fire 'n' Ice' | CDoC SCam SCog |
| | 'Fox's Fancy' | CDoC |
| | 'Fragrant Pink' (*japonica* subsp. *rusticana* x *lutchuensis*) | CTrh |
| | 'Francie L' (*saluenensis* x *reticulata*) ♀H3-4 | CDoC CDul EPfP LHyd SCam SCog SSta |
| | 'Frau Minna Seidel' | see *C. japonica* 'Otome' |
| | 'Freedom Bell' (hybrid) ♀H4 | CDoC CMHG CTrG CTrh GGGa GGal ISea LHyd LRHS MAsh MMuc SCam SCog SCoo SPoG |
| | 'Gay Baby' (hybrid) | CDoC |
| | 'Golden Anniversary' | see *C. japonica* 'Dahlohnega' |
| | ***grijsii*** | CTrh LHyd |
| | ***handelii*** | CBcs |
| | 'Happy Anniversary' | LSRN SPer |
| | 'Happy Birthday' (*japonica*) **new** | LSRN |
| § | ***hiemalis*** 'Bonanza' | CTrh SCam SImb |
| | - 'Chansonette' | CDoC SCam SCog SImb |
| | - 'Christmas Candles' | CSam |
| § | - 'Dazzler' | CBcs CSBt LHyd SCam SCog SImb |
| | - 'Kanjirō' | CDoC LHyd SCam SCog SImb |
| | - 'Shōwa Supreme' | SCam SImb |
| | - 'Shōwa-no-sakae' | SCog |
| § | - 'Sparkling Burgundy' ♀H3 | CBcs CDoC EPfP GLld LCro LHyd LRHS MGos SCam SCog SImb SPoG |
| | 'Hooker' | CDoC |
| | 'Howard Asper' (*reticulata* x *japonica*) | SCam |
| | 'Ice Follies' | SCam SCog |
| | 'Imbricata Rubra' | see *C. japonica* 'Imbricata' |
| | 'Innovation' (x *williamsii* x *reticulata*) | SCam SCoo SImb |
| | 'Inspiration' (*reticulata* x *saluenensis*) ♀H4 | CBcs CDoC CMHG CMac CSBt CTrG CTrh CWSG EPfP GGGa LHyd LSRN MBri MGos SBod SCam SCog SHBN SImb SSpi SVic WBod WGob |
| | ***japonica*** | CBcs WBod |
| | - 'Aaron's Ruby' | CBcs CDoC LRHS SCam SCog SImb |
| | - 'Ace of Hearts' | MBri |
| | - 'Ada Pieper' | CTrh |
| | - 'Adelina Patti' ♀H4 | CBcs CDoC CMHG CSBt CTrh LHyd LRHS SCog SCoo SImb SPoG |
| | - 'Adelina Patti' carmine sport | SImb |
| | - 'Adolphe Audusson' ♀H4 | Widely available |
| § | - 'Akashigata' ♀H4 | CDoC CMac CTrG EPfP ISea LRHS SCam SCog SCoo SImb SPer SPoG SSta WBod |
| | - 'Alba Plena' ♀H4 | CTrh CWSG LHyd MGos SCam SCog SImb WFar |
| | - 'Alba Simplex' | CDoC CDul CMac ELan EPfP LRHS MGos SCam SCog SHBN SImb SPer SSpi SSta |
| | - 'Alexander Hunter' ♀H4 | CDoC LHyd LRHS SCam SCog SImb |
| | - 'Alexis Smith' | CBcs |
| | - 'Alison Leigh Woodroof' | CDoC |
| § | - 'Althaeiflora' | CBcs CDoC MGos SCam SCog SImb |
| | - 'Ama-no-gawa' | LHyd |
| | - 'Amazing Graces' | CDoC |
| | - 'Anemoniflora' | CBcs CDoC CTrG ELan LRHS SCam SCog WBod WFar |
| | - 'Angel' | CBcs SCam SCog SImb |
| | - 'Angela Cocchi' | WBod |
| | - 'Angello' | LSou |
| | - 'Ann Sothern' | CBcs |

| | | |
|---|---|---|
| | - 'Annette Gehry' | CBcs |
| | - 'Annie Wylam' ♀H4 | CTrh LHyd SCog |
| | - 'Apollo' ambig. | CBcs CDoC CTsd LRHS MGos WBod |
| I | - 'Apollo' Paul, 1911 | CSam CTrG EPfP MGos MSwo SCam SCog SHBN SImb |
| § | - 'Apple Blossom' ♀H4 | ELan SImb WBod |
| | - 'Arajishi' misapplied | see *C. japonica* subsp. *rusticana* 'Beni-arajishi' |
| * | - 'Augustine Supreme' | CMac |
| | - 'Augusto Leal de Gouveia Pinto' | WBod |
| | - 'Australis' ♀H4 | SCam |
| | - 'Ave Maria' ♀H4 | CDoC CTrh MAsh SImb |
| | - 'Baby Pearl' | LSRN SCam |
| | - 'Baby Sis' | SCam |
| | - 'Ballet Dancer' ♀H4 | CDoC MGos SCam SCog SImb SVic |
| | - 'Bambino' | CDoC |
| | - 'Baron Gomer' | see *C. japonica* 'Comte de Gomer' |
| | - 'Baronne Leguay' | SCam SImb |
| | - 'Beau Harp' | SCam SImb |
| | - 'Bella Lambertii' **new** | NMun |
| | - 'Bella Romana' | SCam SImb |
| | - 'Benidaikagura' | SCam SImb |
| | - 'Benihassaku' | SImb |
| | - 'Benten' (v) | CTrG |
| | - 'Berenice Boddy' ♀H4 | CBcs SCam SImb |
| | - 'Berenice Perfection' | CDoC CMHG LHyd SImb WFar |
| | - 'Betty Foy Sanders' | CTrh |
| | - 'Betty Robinson' | CDoC SCam |
| | - 'Betty Sheffield' | CTrG MGos SCog SCoo SHBN SImb WFar |
| | - 'Betty Sheffield Pink' | CTrG LRHS SCam SImb |
| | - 'Betty Sheffield Supreme' | CBcs |
| | - 'Billie McCaskill' | SCam SImb |
| | - 'Black Tie' | CDoC ISea LRHS MGos SCog SImb SVic WGob |
| | - 'Blackburnia' | see *C. japonica* 'Althaeiflora' |
| | - 'Blaze of Glory' | NLar SCog |
| § | - 'Blood of China' | CBcs CDoC CSBt CWSG ISea LBuc LRHS LSou MGos MMuc SCam SCog SCoo SImb SPer WBod WFar WMoo |
| | - 'Bob Hope' ♀H4 | CBcs CDoC CTrh GLld LHyd MGos SCam SImb |
| | - 'Bob's Tinsie' ♀H4 | CDoC CMHG CSBt EPfP GBin ISea NLar SCog |
| § | - 'Bokuhan' ♀H4 | CDoC EPfP SCog |
| | - 'Bright Buoy' | CDoC |
| | - 'Brushfield's Yellow' ♀H4 | CBcs CDoC CMHG CSBt ELan EPfP GLld IArd ISea LHyd LRHS MBlu MBri MDun MGos SCam SCog SCoo SImb SPer SSta SVic WFar WGob |
| | - 'Bush Hill Beauty' | see *C. japonica* 'Lady de Saumarez' |
| § | - 'C.M. Hovey' ♀H4 | CMHG CMac MAsh SCam SHBN SImb WBod |
| | - 'C.M. Wilson' | CDoC CMac SCog SImb WBod |
| | - 'Campsii Alba' | CDoC |
| | - 'Can Can' | CBcs CDoC CTrG SCam SCog SImb |
| | - 'Candy Stripe' | CDoC |
| | - 'Canon Boscawen' | CTrG |
| | - 'Cara Mia' | CBcs CDoC SCam SImb |
| | - 'Carolina Beauty' | CDoC LRHS |
| | - 'Carter's Sunburst' ♀H4 | CBcs CDoC CTrh ELan EPfP LRHS SCam SCog SImb WGob |
| | - 'Chandleri Elegans' | see *C. japonica* 'Elegans' |
| | - 'Charlotte de Rothschild' | CTrh CTri EPfP GLld SCam |
| | - 'Cheryll Lynn' | CDoC CTrh SImb |
| | - 'Christmas Beauty' | SCam WBod |
| | - 'Cinderella' | CDoC SCog SImb |
| | - 'Clarise Carleton' | GGGa LHyd MBri |
| | - 'Clarissa' | SCam SImb |

| | | |
|---|---|---|
| | - 'Colonel Firey' | see *C. japonica* 'C.M. Hovey' |
| | - 'Commander Mulroy' ♀H4 | CDoC CTrh MBri SCam SImb |
| | - 'Compton's Brow' | see *C. japonica* 'Gauntlettii' |
| § | - 'Comte de Gomer' | CDoC ELan EPfP LRHS NPri SCam SCog SImb |
| | - 'Conspicua' | CBcs |
| | - 'Contessa Samailoff' **new** | CDoC |
| § | - 'Coquettii' ♀H4 | CBcs CDul LRHS MAsh |
| | - 'Coral Beauty' | WFar |
| | - 'Coral Pink Lotus' | CDoC SCam |
| | - 'Coral Queen' | CDoC SCam SImb |
| § | - 'Dahlohnega' | CTrh LSRN SPer |
| | - 'Daikagura' | CBcs |
| | - 'Dainty' | CBcs |
| | - 'Daitairin' | see *C. japonica* 'Dewatairin' |
| | - 'Dark of the Moon' | CDoC |
| | - 'Dear Jenny' | CBcs CTrG |
| | - 'Debutante' | CBcs CDoC CMac LHyd MAsh SCam SCog SImb WBod |
| | - 'Deep Secret' | SCog |
| | - 'Desire' ♀H4 | CBcs CDoC CMHG CTrh EPfP GLld LRHS LSRN MDun NMun SCam SCog SCoo SImb SPoG WGob |
| | - 'Devonia' | EPfP LHyd SCog |
| § | - 'Dewatairin' (Higo) | CDoC MGos SCam SCog SImb |
| | - 'Dixie Knight' | CBcs CDoC MGos SCam SCog SImb |
| | - 'Dobreei' | CMac |
| | - 'Doctor Burnside' | CBcs CDoC CMHG CTrh SCam SCog SImb |
| | - 'Doctor King' | GLld |
| | - 'Doctor Olga Petersen' | SCog |
| | - 'Doctor Tinsley' ♀H4 | CDoC GLld LRHS NPri SCam SCoo SImb |
| | - 'Dolly Dyer' | CDoC |
| | - 'Dona Herzilia de Freitas Magalhaes' | CDoC SCam SImb |
| | - 'Dona Jane Andresson' | SCam SImb |
| | - 'Donckelaeri' | see *C. japonica* 'Masayoshi' |
| | - 'Donnan's Dream' | CTrh |
| | - 'Doris Ellis' | CMHG |
| | - 'Drama Girl' ♀H2 | CBcs CDoC EPfP SBod SCam SCog SImb SVic |
| | - 'Dream Time' | CBcs |
| | - 'Duc de Bretagne' | SCog |
| | - 'Duchesse Decazes' | CBcs MBri SImb |
| | - 'Duchesse Decazes Pink' | SImb |
| | - 'Duckyls Belle' | SImb |
| | - 'Edelweiss' | CDoC MGos SCam SCog SImb |
| | - 'Effendee' | see *C. sasanqua* 'Rosea Plena' |
| | - 'Eleanor Grant' | SImb |
| | - 'Eleanor Hagood' | CBcs |
| § | - 'Elegans' ♀H4 | CBcs CDoC CMac CTrG EPfP LBuc LRHS MAsh SBod SCam SCog SCoo SHBN SImb SPer SPoG SSta WBod WFar |
| | - 'Elegans Champagne' | NPri |
| | - 'Elegans Splendor' | CDoC SImb |
| | - 'Elegans Supreme' | CDoC |
| | - 'Elegant Beauty' | see *C.* x *williamsii* 'Elegant Beauty' |
| | - 'Elisabeth' | CDoC WFar |
| | - 'Elizabeth Dowd' | CBcs SCog |
| | - 'Elizabeth Hawkins' | CTrh GLld LHyd LRHS MMuc |
| | - 'Elizabeth Rose Open' | SImb |
| | - 'Emily Wilson' | CDoC |
| | - 'Emmett Barnes' | LHyd SCam SImb |
| | - 'Emmett Pfingstl' | SCam SImb |
| | - 'Emperor of Russia' | CBcs SImb WBod |
| | - 'Erin Farmer' | CBcs |
| | - 'Eugène Lizé' | SCam |
| | - 'Evelyn' | SCam SImb |
| | - 'Eximia' | LRHS SCam SCog |
| | - 'Extravaganza Pink' | SImb |

| | | |
|---|---|---|
| | - 'Faith' | CBcs SImb |
| | - 'Fanny' | SCam |
| | - 'Fashionata' | CDoC SCam SImb |
| § | - 'Faustina' | MAsh |
| | - 'Feast Perfection' | CDoC |
| § | - 'Fimbriata' | SCam SImb |
| | - 'Fimbriata Alba' | see *C. japonica* 'Fimbriata' |
| | - 'Finlandia Variegated' | CDoC SCam SCog SImb SVic |
| | - 'Fire Falls' ♀H4 | CMHG |
| | - 'Firebird' | CBcs |
| | - 'Flame' | CBcs WBod |
| | - 'Flamingo' **new** | LHyd |
| | - 'Flashlight' | CDoC EPfP LRHS |
| § | - 'Fleur Dipater' | LSou SCam SImb WBod |
| | - 'Flora' | WBod |
| | - 'Flowerwood' | SCam SCog SImb WFar |
| | - 'Forest Green' | CDoC ELan MAsh |
| | - 'Fortune Teller' | CBcs |
| | - 'Frans van Damme' | CBcs SImb |
| | - 'Fred Sander' | CBcs CDoC GLld MGos SCam SCog SCoo SImb |
| | - 'Frizzle White' | SApp |
| | - 'Frosty Morn' | CBcs CDoC ELan |
| | - 'Furo-an' | MAsh SCam SImb |
| § | - 'Gauntlettii' | SImb |
| | - 'Geisha Girl' | SCam SCog SImb |
| § | - 'Gigantea' | SCam SImb |
| | - 'Giuditta Rosani' | CDoC |
| | - 'Giuseppina Pieri' | LHyd |
| | - 'Gladys Wannamaker' | SCog |
| | - 'Glen 40' | see *C. japonica* 'Coquettii' |
| | - 'Gloire de Nantes' ♀H4 | LRHS SCam SCog SImb WBod |
| | - 'Gold Tone' | CDoC MGos SCam SImb |
| | - 'Grace Bunton' | CBcs CDoC MGos SCam SCog SImb |
| | - 'Granada' | SCog |
| | - 'Grand Prix' ♀H4 | CDoC CTrh GLld LHyd LRHS LSRN MGos SBod SCam SCog SImb SVic |
| | - 'Grand Slam' ♀H2 | CBcs CDoC CDul CTrh EPfP MAsh SCam SCog SImb |
| | - 'Grand Sultan' | SImb |
| | - 'Guest of Honor' | CBcs CDoC GLld LSou |
| | - 'Guilio Nuccio' ♀H4 | CBcs CDoC CTrG CTri EPfP IArd LBuc MGos NPri SCam SCog SImb SPer SVic WBod |
| | - 'Gus Menard' | SCam |
| | - 'Gwenneth Morey' | CBcs CDoC ELan EPfP SCam SImb |
| | - 'H.A. Downing' | SCam SImb |
| § | - 'Hagoromo' ♀H4 | CDoC ELan EPfP LRHS SCog SHBN SImb SPer WBod WFar |
| | - 'Hakugan' **new** | EMil |
| § | - 'Hakurakuten' ♀H4 | CDoC CMHG GLld IArd ISea SCog SImb |
| | - 'Hanafūki' | CDoC MAsh MGos SCam SCog SImb |
| | - 'Hanatachibana' | SCam |
| | - 'Hatsuzakura' | see *C. japonica* 'Dewatairin' |
| | - 'Hawaii' | CDoC CMac CSBt CTrh MGos SCam SCog SImb |
| | - 'Henry Turnbull' | SImb |
| | - 'Her Majesty Queen Elizabeth II' | CDoC |
| | - Herme | see *C. japonica* 'Hikarugenji' |
| | - 'High Hat' | CBcs SCog |
| | - 'High, Wide 'n' Handsome' | CDoC SImb |
| | - 'Higo-momijigari' **new** | GLld |
| § | - 'Hikarugenji' | CDoC MGos SCog SImb |
| | - 'Hime-otome' | SCam SImb |
| | - 'Hinomaru' | CMac |
| | - 'Holly Bright' | CTrh GLld |
| | - HTB 10 | SCam |
| | - HTB 4 | SCam |
| | - 'Ichisetsu' | SCog |

| | | |
|---|---|---|
| § | - 'Imbricata' | LBuc LRHS SCog SImb |
| | - 'Imbricata Alba' | SCam SImb |
| | - 'Italiana Vera' | LRHS MAsh |
| | - 'J.J. Whitfield' | CMac SImb |
| | - 'Jack Jones Scented' | CMHG |
| | - 'Janet Waterhouse' | CBcs SCoo WFar |
| | - 'Jean Clere' | CDoC CTrG GLld MGos MWea SCog SCoo SImb |
| | - 'Jean Renaud' **new** | NBlu |
| | - 'Jennifer Turnbull' **new** | CDoC |
| | - 'Jingle Bells' | CBcs |
| | - 'Jitsugetsusei' | CDoC |
| | - 'Joseph Pfingstl' 🏆$^{H4}$ | CDoC CTri EPfP GLld LRHS MMuc NPri SCam SCog SImb WBVN |
| | - 'Joshua E. Youtz' | LHyd SCog SImb |
| | - 'Joy Sander' | see *C. japonica* 'Apple Blossom' |
| § | - 'Julia Drayton' | MAsh |
| | - 'Julia France' | SCog |
| | - 'June McCaskill' | CDoC |
| | - 'Juno' | CBcs LRHS SCam |
| I | - 'Jupiter' Paul, 1904 🏆$^{H4}$ | CBcs CDoC CMac CTri EPfP ISea LHyd LRHS LSRN MGos SCog SCoo SHBN SImb WBod |
| | - 'Justine Heurtin' | SCam SImb |
| § | - 'K. Sawada' | SCam SCog SImb |
| | - 'Katherine Nuccio' | SImb |
| | - 'Katie' | MDun SCog |
| | - 'Kay Truesdale' | SImb |
| | - 'Kellingtoniana' | see *C. japonica* 'Gigantea' |
| | - 'Kenny' | CBcs |
| | - 'Kentucky' | SCam |
| | - 'Kick-off' | CBcs CTrh SCog SCoo SImb |
| | - 'Kimberley' | CBcs CDoC EPfP GLld SCog WBVN |
| | - 'King Size' | CDoC MGos SCam SImb |
| | - 'King's Ransom' | CDoC CMac LRHS |
| | - 'Kingyoba-shiro-wabisuke' | CDoC |
| | - 'Kingyo-tsubaki' | WBod |
| | - 'Kinsekai' | see *C. japonica* subsp. *rusticana* 'Kinsekai' |
| | - 'Kitty Berry' | CTrh SImb |
| | - 'Kokinran' | CDoC SCam |
| | - 'Kōkirin' **new** | SImb |
| § | - 'Konronkoku' 🏆$^{H4}$ | CBcs CDoC LRHS MAsh SCog SImb WBod |
| | - 'Kouron-jura' | see *C. japonica* 'Konronkoku' |
| | - 'Kramer's Beauty' | SCoo |
| | - 'Kramer's Supreme' | CBcs CCCN CDoC CTrG CWSG LBuc LRHS MGos NLar SBod SCam SCog SCoo SImb WBrE WFar |
| | - 'La Graciola' | see *C. japonica* 'Odoratissima' |
| | - 'La Pace Rubra' | SCam SImb |
| | - 'Lady Campbell' | CTri NLar NMun NPri SCam SImb SPad |
| | - 'Lady Clare' | see *C. japonica* 'Akashigata' |
| § | - 'Lady de Saumarez' | CBcs CDoC CMac SImb |
| | - 'Lady Erma' | CBcs |
| | - 'Lady Loch' | CTrh LRHS MAsh MBri MGos SCam SImb |
| | - 'Lady Mackinnon' | MAsh |
| | - 'Lady McCulloch' | SCam |
| | - 'Lady Saint Clair' **new** | CDoC |
| | - 'Lady Vansittart' | CBcs CDoC CTrG ELan EPfP GLld LHyd LRHS MGos SCog SCoo SImb SPer SPoG WBod WGob |
| § | - 'Lady Vansittart Pink' | CMac SCam SHBN |
| | - 'Lady Vansittart Red' | see *C. japonica* 'Lady Vansittart Pink' |
| | - 'Lady Vansittart Shell' | see *C. japonica* 'Yours Truly' |
| | - 'Lady Vere de Vere' (d) **new** | CDoC |
| | - 'Latifolia' | GLld LRHS SCam |
| | - 'Laurie Bray' | SCog WFar |
| § | - 'Lavinia Maggi' 🏆$^{H4}$ | CBcs CDoC CTrG CTrh CTri ELan EPfP GLld ISea LBuc LHyd LPan LRHS MGos SCam SCog SCoo SHBN SImb SPer SPoG SReu SRms SSta WBVN WGob |
| | - 'L'Avvenire' | SCog |
| § | - 'Le Lys' | SCam |
| | - 'Lemon Drop' | CTrh GLld SCam |
| | - 'Leonora Novick' | CDoC SCog |
| | - 'Lily Pons' 🏆$^{H4}$ | CDoC CTrh GLld LHyd |
| | - 'Little Bit' | CBcs CDoC CMHG CTrh MGos SCam SCog SImb SPer |
| | - 'Little Slam' | CDoC |
| | - LOR 280 | SCam |
| | - 'Lotus' | see *C. japonica* 'Gauntlettii' |
| | - 'Lovelight' 🏆$^{H4}$ | CTrh |
| | - 'Ludgvan Red' | SCam |
| | - 'Lulu Belle' | SCog |
| | - 'Ma Belle' | CMHG |
| | - 'Mabel Blackwell' | SCam SImb |
| | - 'Madame de Strekaloff' | CMac CSBt SCam SImb |
| | - 'Madame Hahn' | CDoC |
| | - 'Madame Lebois' | CBcs CDoC SCam SImb |
| | - 'Madame Martin Cachet' | SCog SCoo |
| | - 'Madge Miller' | MAsh |
| | - 'Magic Moments' | SCog |
| | - 'Magnoliiflora' | see *C. japonica* 'Hagoromo' |
| | - 'Magnoliiflora Alba' | see *C. japonica* 'Miyakodori' |
| | - 'Maiden's Blush' | CMac |
| | - 'Man Size' | CDoC |
| | - 'Margaret Davis' | CCCN CDoC CSBt CTrG ELan EPfP GLld LBuc LHyd LSRN MAsh MDun MGos MWea SCam SCoo SImb SPoG SVic WGob |
| | - 'Margaret Davis Picotee' 🏆$^{H4}$ | CBcs CMHG CTrh SCog SPer SSta |
| | - 'Margaret Rose' | SCam SImb |
| | - 'Margaret Short' | CDoC |
| | - 'Margherita Coleoni' | CBcs LHyd SHBN SImb |
| | - 'Marguérite Gouillon' | CBcs CDoC ISea LHyd SCam SImb |
| | - 'Marian Mitchell' | SCam SImb |
| | - 'Mariana' | CDoC SCog SImb |
| I | - 'Marie Antoinette' **new** | NBlu |
| | - 'Marie Bracey' | CBcs SCam SImb |
| | - 'Marinka' | CBcs |
| | - 'Marjorie Magnificent' | LRHS |
| | - 'Mark Alan' | CDoC LSRN |
| | - 'Maroon and Gold' | CDoC SCog |
| | - 'Mars' 🏆$^{H4}$ | CBcs MGos SCam SCog SImb WFar |
| | - 'Mary Alice Cox' | CDoC |
| | - 'Mary Costa' | CDoC CTrh WFar |
| § | - 'Masayoshi' 🏆$^{H4}$ | CSBt CTrG GLld LHyd SCog WBod |
| | - 'Masquerade' | SImb |
| | - 'Masterpiece' | SImb |
| | - 'Mathotiana' | WBod |
| | - 'Mathotiana Alba' 🏆$^{H4}$ | CBcs CDoC CMac CSBt CTri ELan EPfP LSRN MGos SCam SCog SImb SPer WBod |
| | - 'Mathotiana Purple King' | see *C. japonica* 'Julia Drayton' |
| § | - 'Mathotiana Rosea' 🏆$^{H4}$ | CMac SCam SHBN WBod |
| | - 'Mathotiana Supreme' | CDoC SCam SCog SImb WBod |
| | - 'Matterhorn' | CTrh MAsh |
| | - 'Mattie Cole' | CDoC LHyd SCam WGob |
| | - 'Mercury' 🏆$^{H4}$ | CBcs CMac CTrG CWSG GGGa SCog SHBN WBod |
| | - 'Mercury Variegated' | CMHG |
| | - 'Mermaid' | CDoC |
| | - 'Midnight' | CBcs CDoC CMHG LBuc LRHS MAsh NPri SCam SImb WFar WGob |
| | - 'Midnight Magic' | CTrh CTri |
| | - 'Midnight Serenade' | CDoC SCam |
| | - 'Midsummer's Day' | CBcs |
| § | - 'Mikenjaku' | CBcs CTrG EPfP LBuc LRHS MAsh |

| | | |
|---|---|---|
| | | NMun SCam SCog SCoo SImb WBod WGob |
| | - 'Minnie Maddern Fiske' | SCam SImb |
| | - 'Miriam Stevenson' | SCam |
| | - 'Miss Charleston' | CBcs LHyd SCog |
| | - 'Miss Lyla' | NLar SCam SImb |
| | - 'Miss Universe' | CTrh |
| | - 'Mississippi Beauty' | CTrh |
| § | - 'Miyakodori' | EPfP |
| | - 'Mona Lisa' | SImb |
| | - 'Monsieur Faucillon' | CBcs |
| | - 'Monte Carlo' | CDoC SBod SCam SCog SImb SVic |
| | - 'Moonlight Bay' | SCog |
| | - 'Moshe Dayan' | CDoC GLld LBuc LRHS LSou NPri SCam SCog WGob |
| | - 'Moshio' | CDoC |
| § | - 'Mrs Bertha A. Harms' | CDoC MGos SCam SCog SImb SVic |
| § | - 'Mrs Charles Cobb' | LPan |
| | - 'Mrs D.W. Davis' | CBcs CDoC EPfP SCam SImb |
| | - 'Mrs Derlocquer's Beauty' | SImb |
| | - 'Mrs Lyman Clarke' | CDoC |
| | - 'Mrs Sander' | see *C. japonica* 'Gauntlettii' |
| | - 'Mrs Swan' | NPri |
| | - 'Mrs Tingley' | SImb |
| | - 'Mrs William Thompson' | SCam |
| | - 'Myrtiflora' | SImb |
| | - 'Nagasaki' | see *C. japonica* 'Mikenjaku' |
| | - 'Nigra' | see *C. japonica* 'Konronkoku' |
| | - 'Nina Avery' | CDoC |
| | - 'Nobilissima' | CDoC CMac CTrG CTrh CTri EPfP GKev ISea LCro LRHS MBlu MMuc NBlu NLar NPri SCam SCog SCoo SHBN SImb SPer SPoG WFar |
| | - 'Nuccio's Cameo' | CDoC CTrh LRHS SCoo |
| | - 'Nuccio's Gem' ♀$^{H4}$ | CDoC CMHG ELan EPfP LHyd LRHS MGos SCam SCog SImb SSta |
| | - 'Nuccio's Jewel' ♀$^{H4}$ | CBcs CDoC CTrh CWSG LBuc LHyd LRHS SCam SCog SImb SPer WBVN WMoo |
| | - 'Nuccio's Pearl' | CBcs CDoC LRHS LSou NPri SCam SCog SPoG WBVN WBod WGob WMoo |
| | - 'Nuccio's Pink Lace' | CBcs CDoC CTri |
| § | - 'Odoratissima' | CTrG |
| | - 'Olga Anderson' | CDoC MGos |
| | - 'Onetia Holland' | CBcs CDoC LSRN MGos MWea SCam SCog SCoo |
| | - 'Optima' | CBcs CDoC LRHS SCog SCoo |
| | - 'Optima Rosea' | CTrG SImb SPoG |
| § | - 'Otome' | SImb WBod |
| | - 'Patricia Ann' | LSRN |
| | - 'Paulette Goddard' | SCam SImb |
| | - 'Paul's Apollo' | see *C. japonica* 'Apollo' Paul, 1911 |
| | - 'Pax' | SImb |
| | - 'Peachblossom' | see *C. japonica* 'Fleur Dipater' |
| | - 'Pearl Harbor' | SCam SImb |
| | - 'Pensacola Red' | CDoC SCam |
| | - 'Pink Champagne' | SBod |
| | - 'Pink Clouds' | CBcs |
| | - 'Pink Perfection' | see *C. japonica* 'Otome' |
| | - 'Pope Pius IX' | see *C. japonica* 'Prince Eugène Napoléon' |
| | - 'Preston Rose' | CBcs CDoC SImb |
| | - 'Primavera' | CTrh SCam SCog SImb |
| § | - 'Prince Eugène Napoléon' | GLld SCam SImb |
| | - 'Prince Murat' | CDoC |
| | - 'Prince of Orange' | SImb |
| | - 'Princess Baciocchi' Armstrong | CBcs NLar SCam |
| | - 'Princess du Mahe' | CMac |
| | - 'Purple Emperor' | see *C. japonica* 'Julia Drayton' |
| | - 'R.L. Wheeler' ♀$^{H4}$ | CBcs CDoC CSBt CTri LHyd LRHS LSRN MWea NBlu NPri SCog SCoo SImb WBod |
| | - 'Rafia' | SCam |
| | - 'Ralph Peer Seedling' | SImb |
| | - 'Red Cardinal' | SImb |
| | - 'Red Dandy' | CDoC MGos SCam SCog SImb |
| | - 'Red Elephant' | SCam |
| | - 'Red Red Rose' | CDoC |
| | - 'Reg Ragland' | CDoC CMHG MGos SCam SCog SImb |
| | - 'Reigyoku' | see *C. japonica* subsp. *rusticana* 'Reigyoku' |
| | - 'Robert Strauss' | SCam SImb |
| | - 'Roger Hall' | CBcs CDoC LSRN SCam SCog SCoo SImb SPoG WGob |
| | - 'Rōgetsu' | SCam |
| | - 'Roman Soldier' | CBcs |
| | - 'Rosularis' | SCam SCog SImb SPur |
| | - 'Rubescens Major' ♀$^{H4}$ | CBcs LHyd SCam SImb WBod |
| | - 'Ruby Creek' | SImb |
| | - 'Ruddigore' | CTrh SCam |
| | - subsp. ***rusticana*** | SImb |
| | - - 'Arajishi' misapplied | see *C. japonica* subsp. *rusticana* 'Beni-arajishi' |
| | - - 'Arajishi' | CDoC SImb |
| § | - - 'Beni-arajishi' | CBcs CDoC CDul LRHS SCam SCog SCoo WBod WFar |
| § | - - 'Kinsekai' (v) | SImb |
| § | - - 'Reigyoku' (v) | CBcs CDoC SImb |
| § | - - 'Shiro-daikagura' | WBod |
| | - 'Sabiniana' | LRHS |
| | - 'Sacco Nova' **new** | NBlu |
| | - 'Saint André' | CMac |
| | - 'Sally Harrell' | SCam SImb |
| | - 'San Dimas' ♀$^{H4}$ | CDoC CTrh GLld SCam SCog SImb SVic |
| | - 'Saturnia' | CDoC ELon GLld LRHS |
| | - 'Sawada's Dream' | CDoC ISea SCog |
| | - 'Scented Red' | CDoC SCam SCog |
| | - 'Scentsation' ♀$^{H4}$ | CDoC CMHG CTri SCog |
| | - 'Sea Foam' | LHyd LRHS SCam SSta |
| | - 'Sea Gull' | CTrh SCam SImb |
| | - 'Senator Duncan U. Fletcher' | CDoC |
| | - 'Shikibu' **new** | CTrh |
| | - 'Shiragiku' | CBcs CDoC SCog SPer WBod |
| | - 'Shiro Chan' | CDoC MGos SCam SCog SImb |
| | - 'Shirobotan' | CDoC CTrG GQui MGos SBod SCam SCog SImb SPur SVic |
| | - 'Shiro-daikagura' | see *C. japonica* subsp. *rusticana* 'Shiro-daikagura' |
| | - 'Silver Anniversary' | CBcs CDoC CMHG CSBt CTrG CTrh CTri ELan EPfP GLld GQui ISea LHyd LRHS LSRN MAsh MGos NPri SCam SCog SCoo SImb SPer SPoG SReu SSta SVic WGob |
| | - 'Silver Moon' | see *C. japonica* 'K. Sawada' |
| | - 'Silver Ruffles' | CDoC SCam SImb |
| | - 'Simeon' | SCam |
| | - 'Snow Chan' | CMHG |
| | - 'Something Beautiful' | CDoC |
| | - 'Souvenir de Bahuaud-Litou' ♀$^{H4}$ | CBcs SCam SCog SImb WBod |
| | - 'Spencer's Pink' | CBcs CDoC SCam SImb |
| | - 'Splendens Carlyon' | LRHS SCoo |
| | - 'Spring Fever' | SCam |
| | - 'Spring Fling' | CTrh |
| | - 'Spring Formal' | CTrh |
| | - 'Spring Frill' | SCam SCog |
| | - 'Spring Sonnet' | NBlu |
| | - 'Stardust' | SImb |
| | - 'Strawberry Blonde' | SCog |
| | - 'Strawberry Swirl' | CBcs SCog |

| | | |
|---|---|---|
| | - 'Sugar Babe' | CDoC CSBt SCam SCog SImb WGob |
| | - 'Sunset Glory' | CMHG SCam |
| | - 'Sweetheart' | SCog |
| | - 'Sylva' ♀$^{H4}$ | GGGa GGal SImb SSpi WBod |
| | - 'Sylvia' | CMac |
| | - 'Tada Meibi' | CDoC |
| | - 'Takanini' | CDoC CTrh |
| | - 'Takayama' | SImb |
| | - 'Tammia' | EPfP SCam |
| | - 'Tarō'an' | GGal |
| | - 'Tear Drops' | SImb |
| | - 'Teresa Ragland' | CDoC SCam SImb |
| | - 'Teringa' | CDoC |
| § | - 'The Czar' | CBcs SCog WBod |
| | - 'The Mikado' | CDoC SCog |
| | - 'Theo's Mini' | SCam |
| | - 'Tickled Pink' | CDoC SCam |
| | - 'Tiffany' | CBcs CDoC LHyd LRHS MGos SCam SCog SCoo SHBN SImb SVic |
| | - 'Tiki' | MBri WFar |
| | - 'Tinker Bell' | CDoC MBri SCog SImb |
| | - 'Tom Thumb' ♀$^{H4}$ | CDoC CTrh LRHS SCam SImb SRms SSta WGob |
| | - 'Tomorrow' | CDoC LRHS MAsh SCam SCog |
| | - 'Tomorrow Park Hill' | CBcs SCog SImb |
| § | - 'Tomorrow Variegated' | MGos SCog |
| | - 'Tomorrow's Dawn' | SCam |
| | - 'Touchdown' | SCam SImb |
| | - 'Tregye' | CBcs |
| | - 'Trewithen White' | CDoC CSam |
| § | - 'Tricolor' ♀$^{H4}$ | CBcs CDoC CMHG CMac CSBt CTrh EPfP GLld LHyd LRHS MGos SCam SCog SCoo SHBN SImb SPer WBod WBrE WFar |
| | - 'Tricolor Red' | see *C. japonica* 'Lady de Saumarez' |
| | - 'Tricolor Superba' | WBod |
| | - 'Trinkett' | CDoC |
| | - 'Twilight' | SImb |
| | - variegated (v) | CBcs SCog |
| | - 'Victor de Bisschop' | see *C. japonica* 'Le Lys' |
| | - 'Victor Emmanuel' | see *C. japonica* 'Blood of China' |
| | - 'Ville de Nantes' | MGos |
| | - 'Ville de Nantes Red' | SCog |
| | - 'Virginia Carlyon' | CBcs CDoC GLld |
| | - 'Virginia Robinson' | SCam SImb |
| | - 'Virgin's Blush' | SCam SImb |
| | - 'Vittorio Emanuele II' | CDoC CTrh GLld LBuc LRHS MAsh MGos |
| | - 'Vosper's Rose' | CDoC |
| | - 'Warrior' | SCam SCog |
| | - 'White Nun' | SCog |
| | - 'White Swan' | CSBt GLld LRHS MAsh SCog SCoo |
| | - 'Wilamina' ♀$^{H4}$ | CDoC CMHG GLld |
| | - 'Wildfire' | SCam SImb |
| | - 'William Bartlett' | CTrh |
| | - 'William Honey' | CTrh |
| | - 'Winter Cheer' | SCog |
| | - 'Wisley White' | see *C. japonica* 'Hakurakuten' |
| § | - 'Yours Truly' | CBcs CDoC CMac CTrh GLld LHyd LRHS LSRN MDun SCam SCog |
| | - 'Yukimi-guruma' | WBod |
| | 'Jury's Yellow' | see *C.* x *williamsii* 'Jury's Yellow' |
| | 'Lasca Beauty' (*reticulata* x *japonica*) | LHyd SCam |
| | 'Lavender Queen' | see *C. sasanqua* 'Lavender Queen' |
| | 'Leonard Messel' (*reticulata* x *williamsii*) ♀$^{H4}$ | CBcs CDoC CDul CMHG CTrG CTrh EPfP GGGa GGal LHyd LRHS MDun MGos SCam SCog SCoo SHBN SImb SPer SPoG SReu SVic WBod |
| | 'Liz Henslowe' | CDoC |
| | ***lutchuensis*** | SCam |
| | 'Madame Victor de Bisschop' | see *C. japonica* 'Le Lys' |
| § | ***maliflora*** (d) | CBcs |
| | 'Maud Messel' (x *williamsii* x *reticulata*) | SCam |
| | 'Mimosa Jury' | CDoC |
| | 'Monticello' | CDoC |
| | 'Nicky Crisp' (*japonica* x *pitardii*) | CDoC GLld LHyd |
| | 'Nijinski' (*reticulata* hybrid) | CDoC |
| | 'Nonie Haydon' (*pitardii* hybrid) | CDoC |
| | ***oleifera*** | CSam SCam SCog WFar |
| | 'Phyl Doak' (*saluenensis* x *reticulata*) **new** | CDoC |
| | 'Pink Spangles' | see *C. japonica* 'Mathotiana Rosea' |
| | ***pitardii*** | SCog SImb |
| | - 'Snippet' | CDoC |
| | 'Polar Ice' (*oleifera* hybrid) | CDoC SCam SCog |
| | 'Polyanna' | CDoC SCog |
| | 'Quintessence' (*japonica* x *lutchuensis*) | CDoC GLld SCog SImb |
| | ***reticulata*** 'Arch of Triumph' | CTrG |
| | - 'Captain Rawes' | SCam |
| | - 'Les Jury' **new** | LHyd |
| | - 'Mary Williams' | NLar SCoo |
| | - 'Miss Tulare' | LHyd |
| | - 'Mystique' **new** | CDoC |
| | ***rosiflora*** 'Cascade' | SImb |
| | - 'Roseaflora Cascade' | CDoC |
| | 'Royalty' (*japonica* x *reticulata*) ♀$^{H3}$ | CTrG GLld |
| | ***saluenensis*** | SImb |
| | - 'Trewithen Red' | WBod |
| | 'Salutation' (*reticulata* x *saluenensis*) | SCam SImb WBod |
| | ***sasanqua*** Thunb. | CDul CSam ISea LPan |
| | - 'Baronesa de Soutelinho' | SCam SCog SImb |
| | - 'Bert Jones' | SImb |
| | - 'Bettie Patricia' | SCog |
| | - 'Bonanza' | see *C. hiemalis* 'Bonanza' |
| | - Borde Hill form | SCam |
| | - 'Cleopatra' | EPfP LPan MAsh |
| | - 'Cotton Candy' | CDoC |
| | - 'Crimson King' ♀$^{H3}$ | CDoC SCam SHBN SImb WBod |
| | - 'Dazzler' | see *C. hiemalis* 'Dazzler' |
| | - 'Early Pearly' | CDoC |
| I | - 'Exquisite' **new** | CDoC |
| | - 'Flamingo' | see *C. sasanqua* 'Fukuzutsumi' |
| | - 'Flore Pleno' | see *C. maliflora* |
| | - 'Fragrans' | SCog |
| | - 'Fuji-no-mine' | CTrh SCog |
| § | - 'Fukuzutsumi' | CSBt CTrG SCam SImb |
| | - 'Gay Sue' | CDoC CTrh LHyd SCam SImb |
| | - 'Hiryū' | SCam SCog |
| | - 'Hugh Evans' ♀$^{H3}$ | CAbP CBcs CDoC CTrh CTri LHyd LRHS SCam SCog SImb SPoG SSta WBod |
| | - 'Jean May' ♀$^{H3}$ | CBcs CDoC EPfP LHyd LRHS SCam SCog SCoo SImb SPer SSta WCot WGob |
| | - 'Kenkyō' | MGos SCam SCog SImb SSta |
| § | - 'Lavender Queen' | SCam SImb |
| | - 'Little Pearl' | LHyd |
| | - 'Lucinda' | LHyd SCog |
| | - 'Maiden's Blush' | CSBt ISea SCam SCog SImb WFar |
| | - 'Narumigata' | CAbP CBcs CDoC CMac CTrh EPfP LCro LHyd LRHS MBlu SCam SCog SCoo SPoG SSta WBod WGob WSHC |
| | - 'New Dawn' | SCam SCog SImb |
| | - 'Nyewoods' | CMac |
| | - 'Papaver' | SCam SCog |

| | | |
|---|---|---|
| | - 'Paradise Baby Jane' | SImb |
| | - 'Paradise Belinda'PBR | SImb |
| | - 'Paradise Blush' | CBcs SCam SCog SImb |
| | - Paradise Caroline = 'Parcaroline' | SImb |
| | - 'Paradise Glow' | SCam SCog SImb |
| | - 'Paradise Hilda' | SCog SImb |
| | - Paradise Illumination = 'Parillumination' | SImb |
| | - Paradise Jennifer = 'Parjennifer' | SImb |
| | - 'Paradise Joan' | SImb |
| | - 'Paradise Little Liane' | CBcs SCam SCog SImb |
| | - 'Paradise Pearl' | CBcs SCam SCog |
| | - 'Paradise Petite'PBR | SCog SImb |
| | - Paradise Sandra = 'Parsandra' | SImb |
| | - 'Paradise Sayaka' | SImb |
| | - 'Paradise Venessa'PBR | CBcs SCog SImb |
| | - 'Peach Blossom' | CBcs LHyd |
| | - 'Plantation Pink' | CSBt CTrh GKev LCro LRHS SCam SCog SImb SPer SPoG |
| | - 'Rainbow' | CAbP CDoC CTrG CTrh EPfP GGal GLld LRHS NMun SCam SCog SCoo SImb SSta WBod WFar WGob |
| | - 'Rosea' | SCam |
| § | - 'Rosea Plena' | CBcs CMac |
| | - 'Sasanqua Rubra' | CMac |
| | - 'Sasanqua Variegata' (v) | SCam SCog SSta |
| | - 'Setsugekka' | CDoC SCam SCog |
| | - 'Shinonome' | CBcs |
| I | - 'Shishigashira' Nihon Engei Kai Zasshi, 1894 | SCam SImb |
| | - 'Snowflake' | SCam SCog SSta |
| | - 'Sparkling Burgundy' | see *C. hiemalis* 'Sparkling Burgundy' |
| | - 'Tanya' | CDoC SImb |
| | - 'Winter's Joy' | SCam |
| | - 'Winter's Snowman' | CDoC SCam SCog |
| | 'Satan's Robe' (*reticulata* hybrid) | CDoC MGos SCam SCog SImb WFar |
| | 'Scented Sun' | CTrh |
| | 'Scentuous' (*japonica* x *lutchuensis*) | CDoC |
| | 'Show Girl' (*sasanqua* x *reticulata*) | LHyd SCam SCog |
| | 'Shōwa-wabisuke' (wabisuke) | CTrh |
| § | ***sinensis*** | CCCN CTrG CTsd GPoy LPan LRHS SCam |
| | 'Snow Flurry' (*oleifera* hybrid) | SCam SCog |
| | 'Spring Festival' (*cuspidata* hybrid) 🏆H4 | CDoC CMHG CTrh LHyd LRHS NLar SCam SCog SCoo SImb SPoG WMoo |
| | 'Spring Mist' (*japonica* x *lutchuensis*) | CDoC CMHG CTrh LHyd SCam SImb |
| | 'Strawberry Parfait' | SCog |
| | 'Sugar Dream' | CDoC |
| | 'Swan Lake' (hybrid) | CTrG SCam SCog |
| | 'Sweet Emily Kate' (*japonica* x *lutchuensis*) | CDoC |
| | 'Tarōkaja' (wabisuke) | SCam |
| | ***thea*** | see *C. sinensis* |
| | 'Tinsie' | see *C. japonica* 'Bokuhan' |
| | 'Tom Knudsen' (*reticulata* x *japonica*) 🏆H3 | CDoC CTrh SCam |
| | 'Tomorrow Supreme' | see *C. japonica* 'Tomorrow Variegated' |
| | ***transnokoensis*** | ISea SCam |
| | 'Tricolor Sieboldii' | see *C. japonica* 'Tricolor' |
| | 'Tristrem Carlyon' (*reticulata* hybrid) 🏆H4 | CBcs CDoC CTrG CTri LSou WGob |

| | | |
|---|---|---|
| | 'Usu-ōtome' | see *C. japonica* 'Otome' |
| | 'Valley Knudsen' (*saluenensis* x *reticulata*) | SCog |
| | x ***vernalis*** **new** | CBcs |
| | - 'Hiryū' | SCog SImb |
| | - 'Star Above Star' | CMHG |
| | - 'Yuletide' | CDoC SCam |
| | 'Volcano' | CDoC |
| | x ***williamsii*** 'Angel Wings' | SCam |
| | - 'Anticipation' 🏆H4 | Widely available |
| | - 'Anticipation Variegated' | GGGa |
| | - 'Ballet Queen' | CBcs CDoC CSBt MGos SCam SImb SVic WBod WFar |
| | - 'Ballet Queen Variegated' | CDoC MGos SCog SImb |
| | - 'Barbara Jane' | SImb |
| | - 'Bartley Number Five' | CMac |
| | - 'Beatrice Michael' | CMac SImb |
| | - 'Bow Bells' | CDoC CDul GKir LHyd LRHS SCam SSta |
| | - 'Bowen Bryant' 🏆H4 | CTsd GGGa GLld LRHS SCog |
| | - 'Bridal Gown' | GGGa LHyd |
| | - 'Brigadoon' 🏆H4 | CBcs CDoC CMHG CTrG EPfP GGGa GGal GKir GLld LHyd MAsh MBri MDun MGos SCam SCog SImb |
| | - 'Browncreek's Festivity' | SImb |
| | - 'Burncoose' | CBcs |
| | - 'Burncoose Apple Blossom' | CBcs |
| | - 'Buttons 'n' Bows' | CDoC SCog |
| | - 'C.F. Coates' | CDoC SCog SImb SSta |
| | - 'Caerhays' | CBcs SImb |
| | - 'Carnation' | MAsh |
| | - 'Carolyn Williams' | CBcs SCam SImb |
| | - 'Celebration' | CBcs LSRN SPer |
| | - 'Charlean' | CDoC SCam SImb |
| | - 'Charles Colbert' | CDoC |
| | - 'Charles Michael' | CBcs SImb |
| | - 'Charles Puddle' | WBod |
| | - 'China Clay' 🏆H4 | CBcs CDoC CTrG EPfP LHyd SCog WBod |
| § | - 'Citation' | CBcs CMac SCog WBod |
| | - 'Clarrie Fawcett' 🏆H4 | CDoC |
| | - 'Contribution' | CTrh |
| | - 'Crinkles' | CDoC CDul SCam SSta |
| | - 'Daintiness' 🏆H4 | CDoC LHyd SCog SImb |
| | - 'Dark Nite' | CMHG |
| | - 'Debbie' 🏆H4 | Widely available |
| | - 'Debbie's Carnation' | CDoC CMHG |
| | - 'Donation' 🏆H4 | Widely available |
| | - 'Dream Boat' | CBcs CDoC LHyd |
| | - 'E.G. Waterhouse' | CBcs CDoC CMHG CTrG CTrh CTri EPfP LAst LHyd LRHS MGos MMuc SCam SCog SCoo SImb SPoG SSta SVic WBod WGob |
| | - 'E.T.R. Carlyon' 🏆H4 | CBcs CDoC CTrh CTri CTsd EPfP GLld LBuc LHyd LRHS NLar SCam SCog SCoo SImb SPoG WBVN |
| § | - 'Elegant Beauty' 🏆H4 | CBcs CDoC CSBt CTrG CWSG GLld MDun SBod SCam SCog SImb SPer SPur SVic WBVN |
| | - 'Elizabeth Anderson' 🏆H4 | CTrh SImb |
| | - 'Elizabeth de Rothschild' | SCam SImb |
| | - 'Ellamine' | CBcs |
| | - 'Elsie Jury' 🏆H3 | CBcs CDoC CMac CTrG CTri CWSG GGar GLld GQui ISea LHyd MGos SCam SCog SImb SPer SVic WBod |
| | - 'Exaltation' | CDoC SCog |
| | - 'Francis Hanger' | CBcs CDoC CTrh LHyd MDun SCam SCog SImb SPer |
| | - 'Free Style' | SImb |
| | - 'Galaxie' 🏆H4 | CBcs CDoC SCog |
| | - 'Garden Glory' | GGGa LHyd |

| | |
|---|---|
| - 'George Blandford' ΨH4 | CMac GGal SCam |
| - 'Glenn's Orbit' ΨH4 | CBcs CDoC SCam SCog SImb |
| - 'Golden Spangles' (v) | CBcs CDoC CSBt CTrG CTrh CTsd ELan EPfP ISea LHyd LRHS MDun MGos MMuc NLar SBod SCam SCog SImb SPer SPoG SSta WGob |
| - 'Grand Jury' | LRHS SCam |
| - 'Gwavas' | CBcs CCCN CDoC GLld LHyd LRHS SCam SCog SCoo |
| - 'Hilo' | CDoC |
| - 'Hiraethlyn' | LHyd SCam SImb WBod |
| - 'Holland Orchid' **new** | SCog |
| - 'J.C. Williams' ΨH4 | CBcs CMac CSam CTri CWSG EPfP ISea LHyd MMuc SCog WBod |
| - 'Jamie' | CDoC |
| - 'Jean Claris' | CDoC SCog |
| - 'Jenefer Carlyon' | CDoC |
| - 'Jill Totty' | CTrh SCog |
| - 'Joan Trehane' ΨH4 | CTsd |
| - 'Julia Hamiter' ΨH4 | CBcs SCog SImb |
| § - 'Jury's Yellow' ΨH4 | Widely available |
| - 'Lady's Maid' | CBcs |
| - 'Laura Boscawen' | CDoC CTrG LHyd SCam SImb |
| - 'Les Jury' ΨH4 | CDoC CGHE CMHG CSBt CTrh GLld LSRN MWea SCog SPer SPoG |
| - 'Little Lavender' **new** | CDoC |
| - 'Margaret Waterhouse' | CBcs CDoC SCam SCog SImb |
| - 'Mary Christian' ΨH4 | CBcs EPfP GGal LHyd LRHS SCam SSta |
| - 'Mary Jobson' | CBcs SCam SImb |
| - 'Mary Phoebe Taylor' ΨH4 | CBcs CDoC CTrG CWSG ERas GGal GLld NLar SCam SCog SCoo SHBN SPoG WBod |
| - 'Mildred Veitch' | CSBt |
| - 'Mirage' | CDoC SImb |
| - 'Moira Reid' | CDoC |
| - 'Monica Dance' | CBcs CDoC LRHS SImb |
| - 'Muskoka' ΨH4 | CBcs CMHG SImb |
| - 'November Pink' | CBcs |
| - 'Phillippa Forward' | CBcs CMac WBod |
| - 'Red Dahlia' | CBcs |
| - 'Rendezvous' | CDoC SCog SImb SVic |
| - 'Rose Bouquet' | CDoC |
| - 'Rose Court' | WBod |
| - 'Rose Parade' | LHyd LRHS NPri |
| - 'Rose Quartz' | LRHS |
| - 'Rosemary Williams' | CBcs SCam |
| - 'Ruby Bells' | CMHG |
| - 'Ruby Wedding' | CBcs CDoC CSBt CTrh EPfP GLld GQui LHyd LRHS LSRN MAsh MWea NLar NPri SCog SCoo SImb SPer SPoG WBVN |
| - 'Saint Ewe' ΨH4 | CBcs CDoC CSBt CTrG CTrh CTri EPfP GGal GKev GLld LBuc LHyd LRHS MBri MGos MMuc SCam SCog SCoo SHBN SImb SPer SPoG WBod |
| - 'Saint Michael' | CDoC WBod |
| - 'Sayonara' | CBcs SCog |
| - 'Senorita' ΨH4 | CDoC CTrh LHyd SBod SCam SCog SImb SVic |
| - 'Shocking Pink' **new** | GLld |
| - 'Simon Bolitho' | LHyd SCog |
| - 'Sun Song' | SCog |
| - 'The Duchess of Cornwall' | CDoC |
| - 'Tiptoe' | CDoC LHyd MBri |
| - 'Tregrehan' | GLld |
| - 'Waltz Time' | CDoC SImb |
| - 'Water Lily' ΨH4 | CBcs CDoC CTrh CTri EPfP MGos SCam SImb SVic WBod |
| - 'Wilber Foss' ΨH4 | CBcs CDoC CMHG CTrh GLld LHyd MGos MMuc SCam SCog SImb |
| - 'William Carlyon' | CWSG |
| - 'Wynne Rayner' | CDoC SCam |
| - 'Yesterday' | MMuc |
| 'Winter's Charm' (*oleifera* x *sasanqua*) | SCog |
| 'Winter's Dream' (*hiemalis* x *oleifera*) | SCog |
| 'Winter's Interlude' (*oleifera* x *sinensis*) | CDoC SCam SCog |
| 'Winter's Joy' | SCog |
| 'Winter's Toughie' (*sasanqua* hybrid) | CDoC SCam SCog |
| 'Winton' (*cuspidata* x *saluenensis*) | CBcs CDoC SCam SImb WFar |
| 'Wirlinga Belle' | SCam SCog |
| 'Yoimachi' (*fraterna* x *sasanqua*) | CDoC CTrh |

## *Campanula* ✿ (*Campanulaceae*)

| | |
|---|---|
| from Iran | EBee EPPr NBre |
| ***abietina*** | see *C. patula* subsp. *abietina* |
| § ***alliariifolia*** | Widely available |
| - DHTU 0126 **new** | WCru |
| - 'Ivory Bells' | see *C. alliariifolia* |
| ***allionii*** | see *C. alpestris* |
| § ***alpestris*** | ECho |
| ***alpina*** | MDKP NBur |
| ***americana*** | CSec EWTr SPav |
| ***argyrotricha*** | NBur |
| ***armena*** | EBee ELan NLar SWal |
| ***arvatica*** | CGra CLyd ECho EPot GMaP LRHS MDKP NHar NMen |
| - 'Alba' | CGra ECho GMaP NMen NSla |
| ***aucheri*** | see *C. saxifraga* subsp. *aucheri* |
| ***autraniana*** | CGra ITim |
| 'Azure Beauty' | CSpe EBee NCGa WCot |
| § 'Balchiniana' (v) | CBow |
| ***barbata*** | CGra EBee EDAr GMaP LHop MMHG NBur NWCA WMoo WPer |
| - var. ***alba*** | NBur |
| ***bellidifolia*** | EDAr NBir NBre |
| ***besenginica*** | CGra |
| § ***betulifolia*** ΨH4 | CGra CSam NBur SDix WFar |
| 'Birch Hybrid' ΨH4 | CMHG EBee ECho ECtt EDAr ELan EPfP GKir LBee LRHS SEND SIng WBod WFar |
| ***bononiensis*** | LLHF NBre SRms STes |
| 'Bumblebee' | CGra WAbe |
| 'Burghaltii' ΨH4 | CDes CHar CPom EBee ECha EHrv ELan EMon GCal GMac LRHS MSte SBch SMrm SWat WCot WFar WMnd WPer |
| ***calaminthifolia*** | EBur |
| 'Cantata' | CGra CPBP |
| § ***carnica*** | ECho |
| ***carpatica*** ΨH4 | CSec ECho EPfP GKev GKir MBar MLHP NBre NBro NGdn SPlb SRms SWat |
| - f. ***alba*** | GKev NBre NGdn SPlb SWat |
| - - 'Snowdrift' | GKir |
| § - - 'Weisse Clips' | CSec EAEE EBee ECho ECtt ELan EPfP GGar GKir GMaP LAst LCro LHop MDun NGdn NPri SPer SPla SPoG SRms STes SWvt WFar WPer |
| § - 'Blaue Clips' | CBcs EBee ECho ECtt ELan EPfP EShb GGar GKev GKir GMaP IBal IFoB LAst LCro MDun NGdn NPri SPer SPla SPoG SRms STes SWvt WFar WPer WRHF |
| - Blue Clips | see *C. carpatica* 'Blaue Clips' |
| - 'Blue Moonlight' | EBur LRHS |
| - blue-flowered | MRav |
| - 'Chewton Joy' | CTri EAEE GKir LRHS |

| | |
|---|---|
| - 'Ditton Blue' | GMaP |
| - 'Karpatenkrone' | EBee |
| - 'Kathy' | CMoH GBuc |
| * - var. ***pelviformis*** | SMHy |
| - 'Silberschale' | NBre |
| - var. ***turbinata*** | ECho SRms |
| - - 'Foerster' | GBin GBuc LRHS MTho WHoo |
| - - 'Isabel' | LRHS |
| - - 'Jewel' | LRHS |
| - White Clips | see *C. carpatica* f. *alba* 'Weisse Clips' |
| § ***cashmeriana*** | CGra EBur NBur |
| - 'Blue Cloud' | CWib |
| ***cenisia*** | WFar |
| ***cephallenica*** | see *C. garganica* subsp. *cephallenica* |
| § ***chamissonis*** | EBee ECho GEdr LLHF NBur NSla WPat |
| - 'Alba' **new** | GEdr |
| - 'Major' | CPBP EDAr EWes LBee NBur SIng |
| - 'Oyobeni' | NBur NLAp |
| § - 'Superba' ♀$^{H4}$ | CPBP EBur ECho ELan MTho NBur NMen NSla WAbe |
| ***choruhensis*** | CGra CPBP NBur |
| § ***cochlearifolia*** ♀$^{H4}$ | CEnt CSpe CTri EBee ECho EDAr EPfP EPot GAbr GJos GKir GMaP LRHS MDun MMuc MTho MWat SBch STre WFar WHoo WPer |
| - var. ***alba*** | CSpe EDAr GMaP LRHS MHer MMuc MWat NRya SBch SRms WAbe WHoo WPer |
| - - 'Bavaria White' | ECho LBMP WFar |
| - - double white-flowered (d) | WPat |
| - - 'White Baby' (Baby Series) | ECho ECtt EPfP EPot GAbr GGar GKir NHol SPoG |
| - 'Annie Hall' | ECho |
| - 'Bavaria Blue' | ECho ITim LBMP NHol NWCA |
| - 'Blue Baby' (Baby Series) | ECho EPfP GGar GJos GKir MHer NBlu NPro SPoG SRms |
| - 'Blue Tit' | GBuc |
| - 'Cambridge Blue' | WFar |
| - 'Elizabeth Oliver' (d) | CCge CGra CTri ECho EDAr EPot GBuc GCal GGar GKev GKir GMaP LAst LHop LRHS MHer MTho NLAp NWCA SMrm SPlb SPoG SRms WAbe WFar WHoo |
| - 'Miss Willmott' | CLyd MTho NBir |
| - 'Oakington Blue' | GKir LLHF WAbe |
| - var. ***pallida*** 'Silver Chimes' | ECho ITim |
| - 'Tubby' | CLyd ECho GKev LRHS MHer MTho SRms |
| - 'Warleyensis' | see *C.* x *haylodgensis* W. Brockbank 'Warley White' |
| ***collina*** | CTri EBee LLHF NBre NBur WCFE WPer |
| 'Covadonga' | CMea EBee ECho LHop LLHF LRHS |
| ***cretica*** | GKev NBre |
| 'Crystal' | ECtt MAvo MNrw SUsu |
| ***dasyantha*** | see *C. chamissonis* |
| ***dolomitica*** | EBee GKev LLHF NLAp NMen |
| ***dzaaku*** | CGra |
| 'E.K. Toogood' | CElw CPBP EAlp ECho ECtt GKev MWat NBro NVic NWCA SRms |
| ***elatines*** | EBee |
| 'Elizabeth' | see *C. takesimana* 'Elizabeth' |
| ***erinus*** | CSec |
| ***eriocarpa*** | see *C. latifolia* 'Eriocarpa' |
| 'Faichem Lilac' | GCra LLHF MLHP NChi NLar NPro STes |
| ***fenestrellata*** | MTho NLAp NMen SRms WAbe WFar |
| ***finitima*** | see *C. betulifolia* |
| ***foliosa*** | NBur WPer |
| ***formanekiana*** ♀$^{H2-3}$ | EBur NBur |
| ***fragilis*** | CGra EBur ECho |
| - 'Hirsuta' | ECho |
| ***garganica*** ♀$^{H4}$ | ECho EPfP GAbr GGar GKev GMaP LAst MDKP MRav SIng SWvt WFar WMoo WPer |
| - 'Aurea' | see *C. garganica* 'Dickson's Gold' |
| - 'Blue Diamond' | ECho LHop NBlu WAbe WFar |
| § - subsp. ***cephallenica*** | CElw NBro |
| § - 'Dickson's Gold' | Widely available |
| - 'Hirsuta' | ECho |
| - 'Major' | EBee ECho GKir LAst SPoG WFar |
| - 'Mrs Resholt' | EWll GKir NBlu WFar |
| - 'W.H. Paine' ♀$^{H4}$ | ECho ECtt EPot LRHS MDKP NMen NSla WAbe WFar WHoo |
| 'Gaven' | IPot |
| ***glomerata*** | CElw CEnt CPLG CRWN EBWF GCra GJos LSRN MAvo MBNS MSCN NBro NLan NMir SPet SRms WBrk WEas WFar |
| - var. ***acaulis*** | CChe CHFP CPrp CStu EBee EPfP GAbr GKir LRHS NLar NPri NWCA SPla WFar WPer |
| - var. ***alba*** | Widely available |
| § - - 'Alba Nana' | LAst |
| § - - 'Schneekrone' | ECha EPfP GKir NBre WFar |
| - 'Caroline' | Widely available |
| - Crown of Snow | see *C. glomerata* var. *alba* 'Schneekrone' |
| - var. ***dahurica*** | CTri NBre NLar SPet WFar WPer WRHF |
| - 'Emerald' **new** | EBee LLHF |
| - 'Joan Elliott' | CBgR ECha GBuc LEdu MRav MWat WAul |
| - 'Nana Alba' | see *C. glomerata* var. *alba* 'Alba Nana' |
| - 'Purple Pixie' | LRHS MGos |
| - 'Superba' ♀$^{H4}$ | Widely available |
| ***grossekii*** | CSec EHrv ERCP LLHF NBre WHrl WOut |
| ***hagielia*** SDR 4003 **new** | GKev |
| 'Hallii' | LRHS |
| 'Hannah' | LRHS |
| Hannay's form | CHar |
| x ***haylodgensis*** misapplied | see *C.* x *haylodgensis* 'Plena' |
| § x ***haylodgensis*** W. Brockbank 'Marion Fisher' (d) | CCge CGra CPBP EDAr EPot WAbe WHoo |
| § - 'Plena' (d) | EBee ECho EDAr ELan EPot LBee LHop LRHS NBro NMen NPri NWCA SRms WAbe WCot WEas WFar WHoo WKif |
| § - 'Warley White' (d) | EBur ECho ELan |
| - 'Yvonne' | GMaP SMrm SPoG WFar |
| 'Hemswell Starlight' | CLyd WAbe |
| ***hercegovina*** 'Nana' | LLHF WAbe |
| ***hierapetrae*** **new** | CGra |
| 'Hilltop Snow' | CGra CPBP NMen WAbe |
| ***hofmannii*** | CSec EBee EBur ELan GGar GJos GKev MBNS NLar WFar WRha |
| § ***incurva*** | CDMG CSpe EBee EBur EWTr GAbr GKev MNrw |
| ***isophylla*** ♀$^{H2}$ | ECho EPot |
| - 'Alba' ♀$^{H2}$ | ECho |
| - 'Flore Pleno' (d) | EBur |
| - 'Mayi' misapplied | see *C.* 'Balchiniana' |
| - 'Mayi' ♀$^{H2}$ | CSpe |
| - 'Variegata' | see *C.* 'Balchiniana' |
| ***jaubertiana*** | CGra |
| 'Joe Elliott' ♀$^{H2-3}$ | CStu ECho LRHS WAbe |
| ***kemulariae*** | LLHF NBur SRms WPer |

| | | |
|---|---|---|
| | - ***alba*** | ITim |
| | 'Kent Belle' ♀H4 | Widely available |
| | ***khasiana*** | EBee GKev |
| | 'Kifu' (v) | CBow EBee |
| | ***kirpicznikovii*** | CGra |
| | ***lactiflora*** | CElw CMea CSev EBee ECha EPfP GAbr GCra GKir GMaP IFoB LCro LRHS MCot MLHP MSCN MWhi NChi NDov NVic SPer WBod WBrE WFar WHoo WMoo WPer WTin |
| | - ***alba*** | see *C. lactiflora* white-flowered |
| N | - 'Alba' ♀H4 | EBee EBla EGle GAbr GKir GMaP MAvo MDKP MLHP SMrm STes WFar WMnd |
| | - 'Avalanche' | EBrs |
| | - 'Blue Avalanche' | EBee |
| | - 'Blue Cross' | CMoH EBrs GKir LEdu LRHS NBre NLar |
| | - 'Blue Lady' | CAby NBre WFar |
| | - 'Dixter Presence' | IPot NDov SUsu |
| | - dwarf pink-flowered | EBee SHGN SHar |
| | - 'Favourite' | CFir CSpe EBee MNrw NCGa NGdn NLar STes WFar |
| | - 'Loddon Anna' ♀H4 | Widely available |
| | - 'Moorland Rose' | WMoo |
| | - 'Pouffe' | CPrp EAEE EBee EBla ECtt ELan ELon EPfP GGar GKir GMaP GMac LRHS MBri MDKP MRav NBro NGdn SMrm SPer SPet SPla SWat SWvt WFar |
| | - 'Prichard's Variety' ♀H4 | Widely available |
| | - 'Senior' | EBee MDKP |
| | - 'Superba' ♀H4 | EBee ELon SMad WClo WCot |
| | - 'Violet' | SWat WPer |
| | - 'White Pouffe' | EAEE EBee ECtt EGle ELan ELon EPfP GKev GKir GMaP GMac LRHS MBri MDKP MRav NBPC NChi NLar SAga SPer SPla SPoG STes SWat WFar |
| § | - white-flowered | ECha GKir NBir NBur NChi SPer SWat WFar WPer |
| | ***lasiocarpa*** | CGra LRHS WFar |
| | ***latifolia*** | CArn EBWF ECha GAbr GJos LRHS NBid NMir NOrc NSti NVic SPer SRms WCAu WFar WMoo |
| | - var. ***alba*** | EBee ELan GCra GJos MAvo MSte NGdn SPav SPer SRms SUsu WFar WHal WPer |
| | - - 'White Ladies' | NBur |
| * | - 'Amethyst' | SDnm SPav |
| | - 'Brantwood' | GAbr GKir GMac MRav MWhi NChi SDnm SPav SRms SWat WCot WMnd |
| | - 'Buckland' | SPav |
| § | - 'Eriocarpa' | NBur |
| | - 'Gloaming' | ECtt MCot NBur |
| | - var. ***macrantha*** | EBee ELan EPfP GMaP LHop LRHS MBri MCot MHar MSte MWat NGdn NHol NSti SPav SPer SWat SWvt WCAu WMoo WPer |
| | - - 'Alba' | CMMP CSam EBee ECha ECtt EShb GMaP LHop LRHS MCot MRav MSte SPhx WCAu WMoo WPer |
| | - 'Misty Dawn' | WCot WFar |
| | - 'Roger Wood' | GCal |
| § | ***latiloba*** | CElw CMHG GKir MWhi SBch SGar WBrk WCot WFar |
| § | - 'Alba' ♀H4 | CBre CElw EBee EGle ELan EPPr EPfP GCal GMaP MCot MDKP NChi NGdn SBch SGar SSvw WBrk WEas WOut WRHF |
| | - 'Hidcote Amethyst' ♀H4 | CElw COIW CSpe EBee ECtt EGle EHrv ELan EPfP GBuc GCal LRHS MAvo MCot MNFA MRav NBid NBir NChi NGdn SGar SPav SPla WCot WFar WKif WMnd |
| § | - 'Highcliffe Variety' ♀H4 | CSpe EBee ELan EPfP GBuc GCra MDKP MNFA SMrm SPla WCAu WCot WEas WKif WMnd |
| * | - 'Highdown' | MLLN WFar |
| § | - 'Percy Piper' ♀H4 | CSam ELan GBuc GKir LRHS MAvo MRav NBre NBro NLar WFar |
| | - 'Splash' | CElw CFee EBee MAvo WHil |
| | ***linifolia*** | see *C. carnica* |
| | ***longestyla*** 'Isabella Blue' new | EBee |
| | ***lourica*** | ITim |
| | ***makaschvilii*** | CEnt CSpe EBee ECtt GMac IGor LRHS MHer MWhi NBur NLar SAga SBod STes WCHb WCot WHrl WPer WSHC |
| | 'Marion Fisher' | see *C.* x *haylodgensis* W. Brockbank 'Marion Fisher' |
| | ***medium*** | LAst NBlu |
| | 'Milkshake' | EBee |
| | ***mirabilis*** 'Mist Maiden' | CLyd LRHS WFar |
| | ***moesiaca*** | CSec |
| | 'Molly Pinsent' | EBee |
| | 'Monic' | NBlu |
| | ***muralis*** | see *C. portenschlagiana* |
| | ***nitida*** | see *C. persicifolia* var. *planiflora* |
| | - var. ***planiflora*** | see *C. persicifolia* var. *planiflora* |
| | 'Norman Grove' | EPot |
| | ***ochroleuca*** | CMea CPom CSpe EBee GCal LRHS MCot NBur SHGN STes SWat WCFE WCot WHrl WMoo |
| | - 'White Beauty' | CWib |
| | - 'White Bells' | MWhi |
| | ***odontosepala*** | EMon |
| | 'Oliver's Choice' | WHrl |
| | ***olympica*** misapplied | see *C. rotundifolia* 'Olympica' |
| | ***oreadum*** | CGra |
| § | ***ossetica*** | CSpe EBee ECtt ELan MLHP |
| | ***pallida*** subsp. ***tibetica*** | see *C. cashmeriana* |
| | ***parviflora*** Lam. | see *C. sibirica* |
| | ***patula*** | CSec EGoo GJos NLar |
| § | - subsp. ***abietina*** | NBre NLar |
| | 'Paul Furse' | EBee ECtt LRHS MAvo MDKP MHar MLLN NBre NCGa NLar NPro NSti WCAu WHal WTin |
| | ***pelviformis*** | MNrw |
| § | ***pendula*** | CSec CSpe EPfP EWes GBuc GJos GKev NBlu NLar WFar |
| | ***persicifolia*** | Widely available |
| | - var. ***alba*** | Widely available |
| § | - 'Alba Coronata' (d) | CSec EMon GAbr GKir LRHS NBir WCAu WEas WFar |
| | - 'Alba Plena' | see *C. persicifolia* 'Alba Coronata' |
| | - Ashfield double ice blue (d) | NBre |
| | - 'Beau Belle' | EBee LSou NBPC NLar NMoo STes WHil |
| § | - 'Bennett's Blue' (d) | EBee EBla EHrv ELan EPfP GBuc IPot LAst LHop LRHS MAvo MRav NHol NSti SPer SPla SRms SWat WBrk WCra WFar WWlt |
| | - blue- and white-flowered | WHil |
| | - 'Blue Bell' | MWat |
| | - 'Blue Bloomers' (d) | CElw CHar CLAP CMil EBee ECtt EGle EMon EWes GBri GMac LLWP MAvo MHar MNFA MRav SMrm WBrk WCot WHal |
| | - blue cup-in-cup (d) | EBla MDKP WFar WPtf |
| | - blue-flowered | GKir IFoB LAst MRav SPlb WEas WFar |
| | - 'Boule de Neige' (d) | CMMP CMoH CWCL EBla ECtt LAst WEas |

- 'Caerulea Coronata' — see *C. persicifolia* 'Coronata'
§ - 'Chettle Charm' PBR ♀H4 — Widely available
- 'Cornish Mist' — CBgR EBee EHrv SPoG
§ - 'Coronata' (d) — ECtt GCra
- 'Cristine' — MDKP
- cup and saucer blue (d) — GCra
§ - cup and saucer white (d) — EBla ELan GMaP WFar WPer
§ - double blue-flowered (d) — EGle NBir NBro WEas
- double white-flowered (d) — ELan WMoo
- 'Eastgrove Blue' — NCob
- 'Fleur de Neige' (d) ♀H4 — ECtt LRHS MLLN NBre NCob WAul WBrk WCot WHoo
- 'Flore Pleno' — see *C. persicifolia* double blue-flowered
- 'Frances' (d) — CLAP EGoo EMon
- 'Frank Lawley' (d) — LRHS
- 'Gawen' — CWCL EAEE EBee GMaP GMac MAvo MNFA NBre NLar SAga WCot
- 'George Chiswell' PBR — see *C. persicifolia* 'Chettle Charm'
- 'Grandiflora' — NBre
- 'Grandiflora Alba' — EBee GBuc NBre NHol SMrm
- 'Grandiflora Caerulea' — EBee NBlu NLar
§ - 'Hampstead White' (d) — ECtt EGle EHrv GBuc GCal LAst NBro SPla STes WCAu WEas WHer WMnd
- 'Hetty' — see *C. persicifolia* 'Hampstead White'
- 'Kelly's Gold' — CFwr EBee EBla EPPr LAst LSou MCCP NBhm NBir NHol NLar NPri NPro SPav SPoG WBor WCot WFar
- 'La Belle' — EBee EPyc NLar STes
- 'La Bello' PBR **new** — EBee
- 'La Bonne Amie' — EBee
- 'Moerheimii' (d) — EAEE EBee EPfP EShb MWea NBir STes WCAu WFar
- 'Monita White' **new** — CMoH
- var. ***nitida*** — see *C. persicifolia* var. *planiflora*
- 'Perry's Boy Blue' — NPer
§ - var. ***planiflora*** — CPBP EBee EPot
- - f. ***alba*** — CMea EPot
- 'Powder Puff' (d) — CHFP CWCL EBee GBin GMac LSou NCob SMrm WBor WCot
- 'Pride of Exmouth' (d) — CCge CHar CMMP EBee ECtt EHrv ELan EShb GBuc LAst LRHS MCCP MHer MNFA WBrk WCFE WCot WMnd
- subsp. ***sessiliflora*** — see *C. latiloba*
- - 'Alba' — see *C. latiloba* 'Alba'
- - 'Highcliffe' — see *C. latiloba* 'Highcliffe Variety'
- - 'Percy Piper' — see *C. latiloba* 'Percy Piper'
- 'Snow White' (d) **new** — EPPr
- 'Snowdrift' — ELan SRms
- Takion Series **new** — CSpe
- - 'Takion Blue' **new** — MSCN WHil
- - 'Takion White' **new** — WHil
- 'Telham Beauty' misapplied — CSBt CWCL EBee ECtt ELan EPfP EShb GAbr GKir LRHS MRav MSte SMrm SPer SPla SRms SWvt WFar WMnd WPer
- 'Telham Beauty' ambig. — EAEE MSCN NGBl
- 'Telham Beauty' D.Thurston — SPoG
- 'Tinpenny Blue' — WTin
- 'White Bell' — MWat
- 'White Cup and Saucer' — see *C. persicifolia* cup and saucer white
- 'White Queen' (d) — NBur WMnd
- 'Wortham Belle' misapplied — see *C. persicifolia* 'Bennett's Blue'
- 'Wortham Belle' ambig. — CWGN EShb GBri
- 'Wortham Belle' — CPrp CWCL WFar
- 'Yellow Binstead' — EBee

***petrophila*** — CGra WAbe
***pilosa*** — see *C. chamissonis*
- 'Superba' — see *C. chamissonis* 'Superba'

'Pink Octopus' **new** — NBhm
***piperi*** 'Townsend Ridge' — CGra
- 'Townsend Violet' — CGra

***planiflora*** — see *C. persicifolia* var. *planiflora*
'Polly Henderson' — CGra CPBP
§ ***portenschlagiana*** ♀H4 — Widely available
- 'Catharina' **new** — ECtt
- 'Lieselotte' — CElw GBuc GMaP LIMB
- 'Major' — LAst WFar
- 'Resholdt's Variety' — CMea CSam EAEE EBee ECho EDAr EPfP GMaP LAst LBee LHop LRHS MRav NPri WPer

***poscharskyana*** — Widely available
- 'Blauranke' — EBee EWes
- 'Blue Gown' — EGle GMaP GMac MNFA
- 'Blue Waterfall' — EBrs LRHS WFar
- 'E.H. Frost' — CBre CElw EBee ECho ECtt EDAr EGle EPPr EPfP EWTr GMaP GMac LAst LCro LHop MBri MWat NBro NRya SAga SPer SRGP SRms SWvt WBrk WFar WMoo WPer
- 'Lilacina' — CElw EPPr
- 'Lisduggan Variety' — CElw EBee EBur ECtt EDAr EGle EPPr EWes GKir GMaP GMac LIMB MBri MNFA NBro NCGa NChi SBch WBrk WCot WFar WMoo WPer
- 'Stella' ♀H4 — EBee ECGP ECha ECho ECtt EGle LRHS LSRN MAvo MRav NBro SDix SPer SRGP SWvt WFar WMoo
- variegated (v) — EHoe IBlr
- white-flowered — ECho ELan LAst MDKP WFar

***primulifolia*** — CDMG CSec CSsd EBee EBrs ELan GAbr GKir IFro MNrw MSte SBod SHGN SRms WCHb WFar WMoo WPer
- 'Blue Oasis' — CMHG LSRN

x ***pseudoraineri*** — EBur EDAr EWes LRHS NMen
I - 'Alba' **new** — GKev

***pulla*** — CLyd CPBP CSpe CWCL EBur ECho ECtt EDAr GGar GMaP LAst LRHS MTho NRya SPoG SRot WAbe WFar
- ***alba*** — EBur ECho ECtt EDAr EPot WAbe

x ***pulloides*** hort. — EDAr
- 'G.F. Wilson' ♀H4 — EBee EBur ECho ECtt EPot LLHF WFar

***punctata*** — CMHG CSec CSpe EBee EHrv GJos GKev LEdu LRHS MCot NBPC NBro NSti SPla SWat WAul WFar WGwG WMoo WPer
- f. ***albiflora*** — CMMP LHop LRHS MLLN MNrw NChi SHar WFar WHil WMnd
- - 'Alba' — CCVN
- - 'Nana Alba' — NBur SBch
- 'Alina's Double' (d) — GMac MDKP MNrw
- var. ***hondoensis*** — GKev IGor MLHP MNrw SAga
- hose-in-hose (d) — CDes EBla MMHG NLar WFar WGwG
- 'Hot Lips' — CChe CFir CMMP EBee EBla ECtt ELan EPPr EPfP EShb LAst LHop MBri NBPC NPro NSti SPoG SRGP WCAu WPrP
- var. ***microdonta*** B&SWJ 5553 — WCru
- 'Millennium' — MAvo WFar
- 'Milly' — EMon EPPr WPGP
- 'Mottled' (v) — CSec NBre
* - 'Nana' — CCVN
- 'Pallida' — WBrE
- 'Pantaloons' (d) — CSpe EBee EBla ECtt GMac LHop LRHS LSRN MBri MDKP NChi NCob NLar SBch SHar WBor WCAu WCra

| | | |
|---|---|---|
| | - 'Pink Chimes'PBR | CCge CPou EBee EPPr GKev LHop LSou MBri NBhm NCGa NPri NPro SRot |
| | - 'Pink Eclipse' | WFar |
| | - 'Reifrock' | GMac SMrm |
| | - 'Rosea' | SRms WFar |
| | - f. ***rubriflora*** | CCVN ECtt ELan EPfP EPla GBBs GCra LBMP LHop LRHS MCot MDun MHer MNrw MWhi NHol NOrc SAga SGar SIng SMad SPer SWal WFar WHil WMnd WPer |
| | - - 'Beetroot' | EBee EBla ECtt EMon EPPr GBri GKev GKir ITim LHop LSou MBNS MSte NBur NChi NLar WHrl WPGP |
| | - - 'Bowl of Cherries'PBR | CSpe EBee EBla EPPr EShb GAbr GKir LLHF LSRN LSou MBri MMHG NLar NMoo NPri NSti SHar SPav SRkn SRot SUsu |
| | - - 'Cherry Bells' | CFir EAEE EBla ECtt EPfP GMac LAst LBMP LSRN MAvo MBri MCCP MNrw NBro NCob NLar SPav SPoG SSvw |
| | - - 'Vienna Festival' | CSBt EBee ECtt LEdu LSou NBhm NLar NSti |
| | - - 'Wine 'n' Rubies' | CElw ECtt EHrv GMac LSRN LSou MAvo MDKP MNrw SBch SHar SPav WCot |
| | - var. ***takesimana*** | see *C. takesimana* |
| | - 'Twilight Bells' | NBre |
| | - 'Wedding Bells' | Widely available |
| I | - 'White Bells' | EPPr MBNS MDKP NSti |
| | - white hose-in-hose (d) | MAvo MNFA MNrw NCob SAga WBrk WFar |
| | 'Purple Sensation'PBR | CHFP EBee EPfP GMac MNrw SPoG WCot |
| | ***pusilla*** | see *C. cochlearifolia* |
| | ***pyramidalis*** | CMoH CSec CSpe EBee ELan EPfP GJos MCCP MMuc NOrc SDnm SPav SPlb WPer |
| | - 'Alba' | CSpe CWib EBee ELan EPfP GJos MMuc NBre NLar SDnm SPav SPlb WBrE WPer |
| | - lavender blue-flowered | CWib LAst |
| | ***raddeana*** | ITim MAvo MDKP NLar WBrk WFar |
| | ***raineri*** ♀H4 | CGra EPot LRHS NMen NSla WAbe |
| * | - ***alba*** | CGra WAbe |
| | - 'Nettleton Gold' | EPot |
| § | ***rapunculoides*** | CSec EBee EGoo GKev NBHF NBre SWat WFar WMoo |
| § | - 'Afterglow' | EBee MAvo WCot WDyG WFar |
| | - 'Alba' | EMon MAvo |
| | ***rapunculus*** | ILis MLLN NBHF |
| | ***recurva*** | see *C. incurva* |
| | ***reiseri*** | NBur |
| | ***rhomboidalis*** Gorter | see *C. rapunculoides* |
| | ***rhomboidalis*** L. | EBee |
| | ***rigidipila*** | NBur |
| | ***rotundifolia*** | CArn CHrt CRWN EBWF ECho EPfP GJos GKir LAst LBMP MCot MHer NBid NBre NGBl NLan NMir NRya SIde SPlb SWat WAbe WBrk WPer WPtf |
| | - var. ***alba*** | WAbe WPer |
| | - 'Jotunheimen' | CPBP |
| § | - 'Olympica' | EBee EBur IGor MBNS MMuc NLar NPri WFar WHoo |
| | - 'Superba' | ECho |
| | - 'White Gem' | GJos LBMP NBre NChi SSvw WPtf |
| | 'Royal Wave' | NBhm |
| | ***rupestris*** | EBur LLHF |
| | 'Samantha' | CBow CSpe EBee EBla GMac LHop LRHS LSRN LSou MWea NPri SHar SMrm SPoG SRGP WOVN |

| | | |
|---|---|---|
| | 'Saragamine' **new** | EBee |
| | 'Sarastro' | Widely available |
| | ***sarmatica*** | CGra EBee ECGP EMon EPfP GAbr MSte MWhi NBid NSti SRms WCHb WPer |
| | - 'Hemelstraling' | EBee WCot |
| | ***sartorii*** | EBur |
| | ***saxifraga*** | EBur EDAr ITim NBur NMen NWCA |
| § | - subsp. ***aucheri*** | EBee EBur EDAr ITim NLAp WAbe WFar |
| | ***scabrella*** | CGra |
| | ***seraglio*** | CGra GKir |
| | ***shetleri*** | CGra |
| § | ***sibirica*** | NBHF NBre NBur |
| | - white-flowered | NLar |
| | ***siegizmundii*** | EBee NBur |
| | 'Sojourner' | CGra |
| | ***speciosa*** | CSec EBee MWhi NBHF NBre |
| | 'Stansfieldii' | CPBP EBur NMen WPat |
| | 'Summer Pearl' | GKev |
| § | 'Swannables' | CPou EBee ECtt EGle LLHF MNFA MRav NCGa NChi SAga WOut |
| § | ***takesimana*** | Widely available |
| | - B&SWJ 8499 | WCru |
| I | - 'Alba' | EBla GKir MDKP NBre SHar SSvw WMoo |
| | - 'Beautiful Trust'PBR | CLAP CSpe EBee EBla ECtt GMac LAst LHop LRHS MBNS MWea NBPC NBhm NLar NSti SHar SRkn WCru WOVN WPGP |
| § | - 'Elizabeth' | Widely available |
| | - 'Elizabeth II' (d) | CDes EPPr MAvo MDKP MTho WCot |
| | - 'White Giant' | SHar |
| | ***thyrsoides*** | CSec GJos NBre NBur SDnm SPav |
| | - subsp. ***carniolica*** | SGar |
| | 'Timsbury Perfection' | CPBP NHar |
| | ***tommasiniana*** ♀H4 | LRHS NBur WAbe |
| | ***trachelium*** | CEnt CMHG EBWF EBee EPfP GAbr GKir LCro MBNS MNrw MRav NBPC NLan SAga SGar SPad STes WFar WHer WMoo WPer |
| | - var. ***alba*** | CEnt CLAP GKir LRHS MNrw MWhi NLar STes WBrE WCot WFar WMoo WPer |
| | - 'Alba Flore Pleno' (d) | CBgR CDes CHar CLAP CMil STes WFar |
| | - 'Bernice' (d) | Widely available |
| | - 'Snowball' | EBee EShb LAst LSRN LSou MWea |
| | ***troegerae*** | GKev LRHS |
| | 'Tymonsii' | CPBP EBee EBur ECho LLHF LRHS NBir NMen WFar |
| | 'Van-Houttei' | CDes CElw CHar EBee EMon EWes GMac NLar SAga SBch WCot WFar WPer |
| | ***versicolor*** | CGra CPBP NBre |
| | - G&K 3347 | EMon |
| | ***vidalii*** | see *Azorina vidalii* |
| | ***waldsteiniana*** | CPBP LLHF LRHS WAbe WFar |
| | ***wanneri*** | CSec EBur EPfP LRHS NLar |
| | 'Warley Gem' **new** | GKir |
| | 'Warley White' | see *C.* x *haylodgensis* W. Brockbank 'Warley White' |
| | 'Warleyensis' | see *C.* x *haylodgensis* W. Brockbank 'Warley White' |
| | x ***wockei*** 'Puck' | EBur ECho ECtt EPot LLHF LRHS NLar WAbe |
| | ***zangezura*** | CHrt CSec EBee EBur GKev MLLN NGdn SGar STes |
| | ***zoysii*** | CGra LRHS WAbe |

## *Campanula* x *Symphandra* see *Campanula*

## *Campanumoea* see *Codonopsis*

## Cape gooseberry see *Physalis peruviana*

## *Campsis* (*Bignoniaceae*)

| | | |
|---|---|---|
| | ***atrosanguinea*** | see *Bignonia capreolata* 'Atrosanguinea' |
| | ***grandiflora*** | CArn CBcs CSPN CWGN EBee ELan EPfP IMGH LRHS MAsh SPer SWvt WCFE |
| | ***radicans*** | CArn CBcs CDul CMac CRHN CSBt CSec CWib EBee ECrN ELan EPfP LPan LRHS LSRN MCot MSwo SHBN SLon SPer SPlb WBVN WBrE WDin |
| | - 'Atrosanguinea' | EMil EPfP |
| | - 'Flamenco' | CDoC EBee ELan LAst LRHS MAsh NLar SAdn SBod SCoo SLim SPoG SWvt WCot WFar WGwG |
| § | - f. ***flava*** ♀H4 | CBcs CDoC CHEx CSec CTri EBee ELan ELon EPfP IMGH LHop LRHS MAsh MCCP MGos NBlu NLar NPal NScw NSti SLim SPer SPoG SSta SWvt |
| | - 'Indian Summer' | CWGN EBee EMil EPfP LRHS MBlu MBri MGos NLar SCoo SLim SPoG WCot |
| | - 'Yellow Trumpet' | see *C. radicans* f. *flava* |
| | x ***tagliabuana*** Dancing Flame = 'Huidan'PBR | EBee MGos NLar |
| | - 'Madame Galen' ♀H4 | Widely available |

## *Camptosema* (*Papilionaceae*)

| | |
|---|---|
| ***praeandinum*** | WPGP |

## *Camptosorus* see *Asplenium*

## *Camptotheca* (*Cornaceae*)

| | |
|---|---|
| ***acuminata*** | WPGP |

## *Campylandra* see *Tupistra*

## *Campylotropis* (*Papilionaceae*)

| | |
|---|---|
| ***macrocarpa*** | NLar |

## *Canarina* (*Campanulaceae*)

| | |
|---|---|
| ***canariensis*** ♀H1 | CCCN SOWG WCot WPGP |

## *Candollea* see *Hibbertia*

## *Canna* ✿ (*Cannaceae*)

| | | |
|---|---|---|
| | 'A. Eisenbarth' **new** | WCCa |
| | 'Abraham Lincoln' **new** | WCCa |
| | 'Adam's Orange' | CDTJ CHEx |
| | 'Admiral Aurellan' **new** | WCCa |
| | 'Admiral Courbet' **new** | WCCa |
| | 'Alberich' | CSam SHaC WCCa |
| | 'Albino' **new** | WCCa |
| | 'Alfred Young' **new** | WCCa |
| | 'Alice McGuigan' **new** | WCCa |
| | 'Allemania' **new** | WCCa |
| | 'Alt Württemberg' **new** | WCCa |
| | ***altensteinii*** | CDTJ WHil XBlo |
| | 'Ambassador' | EBrs LAma SHaC |
| | 'America' | EAmu LAma |
| | 'American Flag' **new** | WCCa |
| | 'Anetta Dalebö' **new** | WCCa |
| | 'Angie Summers' | CDWL |
| | 'Annaeei' ♀H3 | EAmu WCCa WHil |
| | 'Anthéor' **new** | WCCa |
| | 'Apricot Dream' | WCCa |
| | 'Aranyálom' | LAma |
| | 'Argentina' | SHaC |
| | 'Arne Dalebö' (v) **new** | WCCa |
| | 'Arthur William Paul' (v) **new** | WCCa |
| | 'Assaut' | SHaC |
| | 'Atlantis' | XBlo |
| | 'Auguste Ferrier' (v) **new** | WCCa |
| | 'Australia' | CDTJ EUJe LSou MJnS SHaC WHil XBlo |
| | 'Austria' **new** | WCCa |
| | 'Autumn Dragon' **new** | WCCa |
| | 'Avon' **new** | WCCa |
| | 'Baby Pink' | SHaC |
| | 'Baronne de Pouilly' **new** | WCCa |
| | 'Bavaria' **new** | WCCa |
| | 'Berenice Emsley' **new** | WCCa |
| | 'Bevere' **new** | WCCa |
| | 'Black Knight' | CFir EBee EBrs ECGP LAma LAst LSRN MJnS MSte SGar SHaC SPad SPet WCra WWlt XBlo |
| | 'Bonfire' | CDTJ CHEx |
| | ***brasiliensis*** | CHII CRHN XBlo |
| | 'Brillant' | CDWL LAma WDyG |
| | 'Burbank' **new** | WCCa |
| | 'Burgundia' **new** | WCCa |
| | 'Burgundy Blush' (v) **new** | WCCa |
| | 'Caballero' | SHaC |
| | 'Calimèro' | SHaC |
| | 'Canary' | XBlo |
| | 'Carnaval' | SHaC |
| | 'Carolina Gold' **new** | WCCa |
| | 'Centenaire de Rozain-Boucharlat' | CHEx SHaC |
| | 'Centurion' | LAma |
| | 'Cerise Davenport' | CFir |
| | 'Chameleon' **new** | WCCa |
| | 'Champigny' | SHaC WCCa |
| | 'Champion' | SHaC WCCa |
| | 'Chatei Grandis' **new** | WCCa |
| | Chaumes = 'Turcacha' | WCCa |
| | 'China Lady' | WCCa |
| | 'Chinese Coral' Schmid | CHEx LAma |
| | 'Chouchou' | SHaC |
| I | 'Citrina' | XBlo |
| | 'City of Gloucester' (v) **new** | WCCa |
| § | 'City of Portland' | LAma WCCa WHil |
| * | 'Cleopatra' | CCCN CFir EAmu EBrs LAma SHaC SPet WGwG XBlo |
| § | 'Colibri' | LAma |
| | 'Confetti' | see *C.* 'Colibri' |
| | 'Constitution' **new** | SHaC WCCa |
| | 'Corail' | SHaC |
| | 'Corrida' | SHaC |
| | 'Corsica' (Island Series) | EBee WCCa |
| | 'Creamy White' | CHEx SHaC XBlo |
| | 'Crimson Beauty' | EBrs LAma LAst |
| | 'Delaware' ♀H3 | WHil |
| | 'Délibáb' | CSam EBee LAma NBPN SPet WDyG |
| | 'Di Bartolo' | WCCa XBlo |
| | 'Doctor Nansen' **new** | WCCa |
| | 'Dondo' | SHaC |
| | 'Doreen Morris' **new** | WCCa |
| | 'Duchesse de Montenard' **new** | WCCa |
| | 'Durban' ambig. | CWGN EBee IHer LAma LAst LSRN SAga SMrm WGwG WPic |
| | 'Durban' Hiley, orange-flowered | see *C.* 'Phasion' |
| | ***edulis*** | CDTJ CHEx ETod EUJe WHil |
| | - purple-leaved | ETod |
| § | x ***ehemanii*** ♀H3 | CDTJ CRHN CSev EUJe MJnS SChr SDix SHaC WPGP |

| | | |
|---|---|---|
| | 'Eileen Gallo' (v) new | WCCa |
| | 'Ella Dalebö' new | WCCa |
| | 'Ellen Layden' new | WCCa |
| | 'Emblème' | SHaC |
| | 'En Avant' | CDTJ CHEx LAma SHaC SPlb |
| | 'Endeavour' | CDWL CHEx EUJe LPJP MSKA SHaC |
| | 'Epi d'Or' new | WCCa |
| | 'Erebus' ♀H3 | CDWL MSKA SDix SHaC WHil |
| | 'Ermine' | MJnS |
| | 'Espresso Festival' | EBee NBPN NGdn WCCa |
| | 'Étoile du Feu' | XBlo |
| | 'Evening Star' | LAma |
| | 'Extase' | SHaC |
| | 'Falstaff' new | WCCa |
| | 'Fatamorgana' | LAma WHil |
| | 'Felix Ragout' | LAma WCCa |
| | 'Ferrandii' new | WCCa |
| | 'Feuerzauber' | SHaC |
| | 'Fire Red' new | WCCa |
| | Firebird | see *C.* 'Oiseau de Feu' |
| | ***flaccida*** | CDWL MSKA SHaC |
| | 'Flame' | XBlo |
| | 'Flammèche' | WCCa |
| § | 'Florence Vaughan' | SHaC |
| | 'Freya' new | WCCa |
| | 'Fröken' new | WCCa |
| | 'Gaiety' | WCCa |
| | 'General Eisenhower' ♀H3 | ETod SHaC |
| | x ***generalis*** | SHaC |
| | ***glauca*** | EUJe SDix SHaC WCCa WHil |
| | 'Gnom' | SHaC WCCa |
| * | 'Gold Ader' | LAma |
| | 'Gold Dream' | LAma |
| | 'Golden Girl' | WHil |
| | 'Golden Lucifer' | CHEx EBrs ELan LAma |
| | 'Goldilocks' new | WCCa |
| | 'Gran Canaria' | SHaC |
| | 'Grand Duc' | SHaC |
| | 'Grande' | CFir MAJR MJnS SHaC WHil WPic |
| | 'Hallow' new | WCCa |
| | 'Heinrich Seidel' | CHEx |
| | 'Hellas' new | WCCa |
| | Henlade new | CDTJ |
| | 'Henri Cohn' new | WCCa |
| | 'Hercule' | CHEx SHaC |
| | 'Hilary Owen' new | WCCa |
| | 'Hiley' | ETod |
| | 'Hungaria' new | WCCa |
| | hybrids | ELan |
| | 'Ibis' | EPfP SHaC |
| | ***indica*** | CDTJ CHEx EFul EShb ETod SAPC SArc SHaC SPlb WCCa WHil |
| | - gold and orange-flowered new | WCCa |
| | - orange-flowered new | WCCa |
| | - 'Purpurea' | CDTJ CHEx EUJe LEdu MCot SChr SDix SHaC SMHy SPlb WDyG WHil WPGP |
| | - 'Red King Rupert' | CCCN |
| | - 'Russian Red' ♀H3 | SHaC WHil |
| | - 'Singapore Orange' new | WCCa |
| | ***indica*** x ***musifolia*** new | WHil |
| | 'Ingeborg' ♀H3 | LAma WCCa |
| | 'Intrigue' | SHaC WCCa WHil |
| | ***iridiflora*** misapplied | see *C.* x *ehemanii* |
| | ***iridiflora*** Ruiz & Pav. | CDTJ CDWL CHEx CSpe SAPC SArc WHil |
| | 'Iridiflora Rubra' (v) new | WCCa |
| | 'Italia' | SHaC WCCa WHil |
| | 'J.B. van der Schoot' new | WCCa |
| | ***jacobiniflora*** new | WCCa |
| | 'Jean Krupp' new | WCCa |
| | 'Jessie Dalebö' new | WCCa |
| | 'Jivago' | SHaC |
| | 'John Tulett' new | WCCa |
| | 'Joseph Bischau' new | WCCa |
| | 'Kalimpong' new | CDTJ |
| | 'Kansas City' (v) | WCCa |
| | 'Karla Dalebö' new | WCCa |
| | 'King City Gold' | WHil |
| I | 'King Humbert' (blood-red) | CBcs CDTJ CHEx EBrs EPfP LAma LAst MJnS WCCa XBlo |
| | King Humbert (orange-red) | see *C.* 'Roi Humbert' |
| | 'King Midas' | see *C.* 'Richard Wallace' |
| | 'Kings' Gold' new | WCCa |
| | 'Königin Charlotte' | SHaC SPad |
| | 'Kyneburg' new | WCCa |
| | 'La Bohème' (Grand Opera Series) | LAma |
| | 'La France' new | WCCa |
| | 'La Quintinie' | SHaC |
| | 'La Traviata' | WHil |
| | 'Laura Dalebö' new | WCCa |
| | 'Lemon Zest' | NScw |
| | 'Lenape' ♀H3 | WCCa |
| | 'Lesotho Lil' | CHll |
| | 'Liberté' | see *C.* 'Wyoming' |
| | 'Lincroft' new | WCCa |
| | 'Lippo's Kiwi' | WHil |
| | 'Llanthony' new | WCCa |
| | 'Lolita' | SHaC |
| | 'Louis Cayeux' ♀H3 | SDix SHaC |
| | 'Louis Cottin' | CBcs CCCN CDTJ CHEx EBee EBrs EPfP LAma NBPN SHaC SPad WCCa WHil |
| | 'Lucifer' | CCCN CHEx EBrs EPfP LAma LAst LRHS NPer SEND SHaC SPet SPlb SRot WBrE WHil |
| | 'Ludlow' new | WCCa |
| | ***lutea*** | CHEx XBlo |
| | 'Madame Angèle Martin' | WCCa WHil XBlo |
| | 'Madame Chabanne' new | WCCa |
| | 'Madame Legris' new | WCCa |
| | 'Madeira' (Island Series) | NScw |
| | 'Malawiensis Variegata' | see *C.* 'Striata' |
| | 'Malvern' new | WCCa |
| | 'Mandy Robinson' new | WCCa |
| | 'Marabout' | CKob SHaC WCCa |
| | 'Margaret Strange' | SHaC WCCa |
| | 'Marilyn' new | WCCa |
| | 'Mark McGuigan' new | WCCa |
| | 'Marvel' | LAma |
| | 'Mary Leyden' new | WCCa |
| | 'Maudie Malcolm' new | EPfP WCCa |
| | 'May Vince' new | WCCa |
| | 'Michelle M.' new | WCCa |
| | 'Milk Festival' new | WCCa |
| | 'Miss B. Brunner' new | WCCa |
| | 'Molly Guy' new | WCCa |
| | 'Monet' | EPfP WHil |
| | 'Montaigne' | SHaC |
| | 'Mrs Kate Gray' new | WCCa |
| | 'Mrs Oklahoma' | CSut LAma WHil |
| | 'Musifolia' ♀H3 | CDTJ CHEx CKob EAmu ETod EUJe EWes LPJP SDix SEND SHaC WDyG WPic XBlo |
| I | 'Musifolia Peruviana' new | WCCa |
| | 'Mystique' ♀H3 | EWes SDix SHaC WCCa |
| | 'Nero' new | WCCa |
| | 'Oberon' new | WCCa |
| | 'Ointment Pink' | XBlo |
| § | 'Oiseau de Feu' | LAma SHaC WCCa |
| | 'Oiseau d'Or' | SHaC |
| | 'Old Red' new | WCCa |
| | 'Ombersley' new | WCCa |
| | 'Orange Perfection' | CFir CHEx CSam LAma LAst SHaC |

| | | |
|---|---|---|
| | 'Orange Punch' | SHaC WHil |
| | 'Orchid' | see *C.* 'City of Portland' |
| | 'Osric' | CSpe WCCa |
| | 'Pacific Beauty' | LSou NGdn WCot |
| | 'Panache' | CDTJ CHEx CKob SHaC WDyG |
| | 'Panama' | SHaC |
| | ***paniculata*** **new** | SHaC |
| | 'Paprika' **new** | WCCa WHil |
| | 'Parténope' **new** | WCCa |
| | 'Peach Surprise' **new** | WCCa |
| | 'Pearlescent Pink' | XBlo |
| | 'Percy Lancaster' **new** | WCCa |
| | 'Perkeo' | LAma MJnS SPet |
| § | 'Pfitzer's Salmon Pink' | CHEx |
| § | 'Phasion' (v) ♀H3 | CHEx CHll CKob CSpe EBee EBrs ELan EPfP EUJe EWes LPJP LRHS LSRN MJnS NGdn NPer NScw NVic SDix SHBN SHaC SPoG WCCa WCot XBlo |
| | 'Picadore' | SHaC |
| | 'Picasso' ♀H3 | CBcs CCCN CDTJ CHEx CPLG EBrs EPfP LAma SEND SPet XBlo |
| | 'Pink Champagne' | XBlo |
| | 'Pink Perfection' | SHaC |
| | 'Pink Sunburst' (v) | CDTJ CSpe EUJe NGdn SHaC SPlb |
| | 'Pinky' | WHil |
| | 'Plaster Pink' | XBlo |
| | 'Porcelain Petals' **new** | WCCa |
| | 'Powick' **new** | WCCa |
| | 'Preference' **new** | WCCa |
| | 'President' | CHEx CSut EBrs EPfP LAma SHaC SPet WBrE WCCa XBlo |
| | 'President Carnot' | SHaC WCCa |
| | 'Pretoria' | see *C.* 'Striata' |
| | 'Primrose' **new** | WCCa |
| | 'Prince Charmant' | SHaC |
| | 'Princess Di' | CMdw SHaC WHil |
| | 'Professor Lorentz' | see *C.* 'Wyoming' |
| | 'Puck' | SHaC |
| | 'Puppet' **new** | WCCa |
| | 'Purpurea Floribunda' **new** | WCCa |
| | 'Ra' ♀H3 | CDWL MSKA SHaC WHil |
| | 'Red Bird' **new** | WCCa |
| | 'Red Futurity' (Futurity Series) | MJnS WHil |
| | 'Red Giant' **new** | WHil |
| | 'Red Tyrol' **new** | WCCa |
| | 'Red Wine' | SHaC WCCa |
| § | 'Richard Wallace' | CPLG CSam EBrs LAma MJnS SPlb XBlo |
| | 'Rigoletto' **new** | WCCa |
| § | 'Roi Humbert' | CSam LAst MSte SHaC SRot |
| | 'Roi Soleil' ♀H3 | CHEx LAma SHaC |
| | 'Roitelet' | CHEx |
| | 'Roma' **new** | WCCa |
| | 'Rose Futurity' (Futurity Series) | WCCa WHil |
| | 'Rosemawr' **new** | WCCa |
| | 'Rosemond Coles' | CHEx CSam CSut EBrs LAma SHaC XBlo |
| | 'Russian Lance' **new** | WCCa |
| | 'Russian Red' **new** | WCCa |
| | 'Safrano' **new** | WCCa |
| | 'Saladin' | SHaC |
| | 'Salmon Pink' | see *C.* 'Pfitzer's Salmon Pink' |
| | 'Salsa' | SHaC |
| | 'Saumur' | SHaC |
| | 'Scorch' **new** | WCCa |
| | 'Sémaphore' | EBee NBPN SHaC XBlo |
| | 'Shenandoah' ♀H3 | SHaC WCCa |
| | 'Singapore Girl' | SHaC |
| | 'Sky Hawk' **new** | WCCa |
| | 'Snow-white' | XBlo |
| | 'Sophia Young' **new** | WCCa |
| | 'Soudan' | CDTJ |
| | 'Souvenir de Madame Nardy' **new** | WCCa |
| | 'Sparks' **new** | WCCa |
| | ***speciosa*** | CDTJ XBlo |
| | 'Spritzii' **new** | WCCa |
| | 'Star of India' **new** | WCCa |
| | 'Statue of Liberty' **new** | WCCa |
| | 'Strasbourg' | CSam ETod LAma NPer |
| | 'Strawberry Pink' | XBlo |
| | 'Striata' misapplied | see *C.* 'Stuttgart' |
| § | 'Striata' (v) ♀H3 | CCCN CDTJ CHEx CKob CSev CSpe CWGN EBee EBrs EUJe LPJP LSRN MREP NGdn NMoo NScw NVic SAga SEND SHBN SHaC SMrm SPet WCCa WCot WDyG WPic XBlo |
| | 'Striped Beauty' (v) | CCCN CDTJ CDWL EBrs |
| § | 'Stuttgart' (v) | CDTJ CDWL CSpe EAmu EPfP EWes MJnS NMoo SHaC WCCa WCot |
| | 'Summer Gold' | XBlo |
| | 'Summer Joy' **new** | SHaC |
| | 'Sunbeams' **new** | WCCa |
| | 'Sundance' | NPri |
| | 'Südfunk' | SHaC |
| | 'Sunset' | CWGN NGdn SMrm WCot WGwG WWlt |
| | 'Talisman' | XBlo |
| | 'Taney' | CDWL EUJe MSKA SHaC |
| | 'Taroudant' | SHaC |
| | 'Tchad' | SHaC |
| | 'Teme' **new** | WCCa |
| | 'Temploux' **new** | WCCa |
| | 'Theresa Blakey' **new** | WCCa |
| | 'Thorvald Dalebö' **new** | WCCa |
| | 'Tirol' | EBrs NBPN WCCa |
| | 'Tricarinata' | CHEx |
| | 'Triomphe' | SHaC |
| | (Tropical Series) 'Tropical Red' | SGar |
| | - 'Tropical Rose' | LRHS MJnS SHaC SRms WCCa |
| | - 'Tropical Salmon' **new** | MJnS |
| | - 'Tropical Sunrise' | WCCa |
| | - 'Tropical White' | MJnS SGar SHaC |
| | - 'Tropical Yellow' | MJnS SGar SHaC WCCa |
| | Tropicanna | see *C.* 'Phasion' |
| | 'Ulrich Brunner' **new** | WCCa |
| | 'Uncle Sam' **new** | WCCa |
| | 'Uvurderlig' **new** | WCCa |
| | 'Valentine' | WCot WHil |
| | 'Vanilla Pink' | XBlo |
| * | 'Variegata' (v) | LAma LRHS |
| | 'Verdi' ♀H3 | CSpe LAma SHaC |
| | 'Viva' | SHaC WCCa |
| | ***warscewiczii*** | CDTJ CPLG SHaC WHil |
| | 'Weymouth' **new** | CDTJ |
| | 'Whithelm Pride' ♀H3 | SHaC |
| | 'Wine 'n' Roses' | SHaC |
| | 'Woodbridge Pink' | XBlo |
| | 'Wye' **new** | WCCa |
| § | 'Wyoming' ♀H3 | CBcs CCCN CDTJ CHEx CSam EBrs ECGP ETod EUJe LAma MCCP MSte NVic SEND SHaC WHil XBlo |
| | 'Yara' | EBrs WHil |
| | 'Yellow Humbert' misapplied | see *C.* 'Richard Wallace', *C.* 'Cleopatra', *C.* 'Florence Vaughan' |
| | 'Yellow Humbert' | LAma WCCa WHil |

## *Cantua* (*Polemoniaceae*)

| | | |
|---|---|---|
| | ***buxifolia*** ♀H2-3 | CAbb CBcs CCCN CFee CPLG EBee ECre EShb SOWG WCot WPGP WVal |
| | - 'Alba' | WVal |

## Cape gooseberry see *Physalis peruviana*

## *Capnoides* see *Corydalis*

## *Capparis* (*Capparaceae*)

| | |
|---|---|
| ***spinosa*** | CCCN |

## *Capsicum* (*Solanaceae*)

| | |
|---|---|
| ***annuum*** | CCCN CSim MBri |
| - var. ***annuum*** (Longum Group) cayenne | CCCN |
| - - 'Prairie Fire' ♀H2 | CCCN |
| - 'Apache' ♀H2 | CCCN SEND |
| ***baccatum*** | CSim |
| ***chinense*** | CSim |
| ***frutescens*** | CSim |
| ***pubescens*** | CSim |

## *Caragana* (*Papilionaceae*)

| | |
|---|---|
| CC 3945 | CPLG |
| ***arborescens*** | CAgr CArn EBee EPfP GKir MBar NWea SBLw SEND SPer SPlb WDin |
| - 'Lorbergii' | CEnd GBin GKir MBlu SCoo SPer WFoF |
| - 'Pendula' | CLnd CWib ELan EMil EPfP GKir LAst MAsh MBar MBlu NBee NHol NPri SBLw SCoo SLim SPer WDin |
| - 'Walker' | CDul CEnd CWib EBee EHig ELan EMil EPfP GKir LPan LRHS MAsh MBar MBlu MBri MGos NHol SBLw SCoo SLim SMad SPer SPoG WOrn |
| ***aurantiaca*** | MBar |
| ***jubata*** | NLar |
| ***pygmaea*** | NLar |

## *Caralluma* (*Asclepiadaceae*)

| | |
|---|---|
| 'Bufoni' **new** | CFwr |
| ***hesperidum*** **new** | CFwr |

## carambola see *Averrhoa carambola*

## caraway see *Carum carvi*

## *Cardamine* ✿ (*Brassicaceae*)

| | |
|---|---|
| ***asarifolia*** misapplied | see *Pachyphragma macrophyllum* |
| ***asarifolia*** L. | CLAP |
| ***bulbifera*** | CLAP CWsd EBee ELon EPPr GBin GBuc GEdr LEdu NRya WCru WSHC |
| ***californica*** | EBee EPPr NRya WCru WMoo |
| ***concatenata*** | CLAP NLar SKHP WCru WHal |
| ***diphylla*** | CLAP EBee LEdu MLLN WCot WCru WFar |
| - 'American Sweetheart' **new** | WCot |
| - 'Eco Cut Leaf' | CDes EBee EPPr WCru WPGP |
| - 'Eco Moonlight' | SKHP WCru |
| ***enneaphylla*** | CLAP GBuc GMaP IBlr LEdu NDov |
| ***glanduligera*** | CDes CElw EBee EGle ELon EPPr GBuc LEdu MNrw WCru WPGP WSHC |
| § ***heptaphylla*** | CAby CAvo CLAP CWsd EBee ECha ELan ELon EWTr GBuc GKir IBlr WCru |
| - 'Big White' **new** | GCal |
| - Guincho form | CDes CLAP EPPr GBin IBlr WCot WPGP |
| - white-flowered | CLAP GBBs GMaP |
| § ***kitaibelii*** | CLAP ECha GBin GBuc IBlr LEdu NPol WCru |
| ***latifolia*** Vahl | see *C. raphanifolia* |
| ***lineariloba*** | IBlr |
| ***macrophylla*** | CAby CLAP EBee EWld LEdu NLar SWat WCot WFar |
| - 'Bright and Bronzy' | GEdr WCru |
| ***maxima*** | LEdu WCru |
| § ***microphylla*** | CLAP WCru |
| ***pentaphylla*** ♀H4 | CSpe EBee EBrs ECho EGle ELan ELon EPPr ERos EWTr GBBs GBuc GEdr GGar GKir IBlr LPla MDun MNFA NBir SUsu WCot WCru WTin |
| - bright pink-flowered | CLAP NPol WCot |
| ***pratensis*** | CArn CHrt CRWN CWat EBWF EBee EHon EMFW MCot MHer MSKA NLan NPri SIde SWat WFar WHer WMoo WPtf WSFF WShi |
| - var. ***angustifolia*** | WCru |
| - 'Edith' (d) | CLAP GBin GBuc MNrw NChi |
| - 'Flore Pleno' (d) | CBre CFee CSpe CWan EBee ECha ELan IFro MHer MNrw MTho NBid NBir NBro NLar SBch SUsu SWat WAlt WFar WHoo WMoo WSFF WSHC |
| - white-flowered **new** | WAlt |
| - 'William' (d) | EPPr GBuc MNrw WFar WMoo |
| ***quinquefolia*** | CDes CElw CLAP CMea CPom EBee ECha EGle EHrv ELon GBuc IBlr LEdu MCot NMyG SBch SDys WBrk WCot WCru WFar WPGP WRha |
| § ***raphanifolia*** | CBre CDes CLAP CPom CRow EBee ECha EPPr GAbr GBuc GCal GGar IBlr IFro LEdu LLWG MRav NBid NBro NChi NSti SWat WBor WMoo WPGP WTin |
| ***trifolia*** | CSpe EBee ECha EGle EHrv EPPr EWTr GBuc GCal GEdr GGar GKir GMaP IBlr IFro MBar NBir NBro NHol NRya NVic SWat WCot WCru WFar WHer WMoo |
| * - ***digitata*** | MTho |
| ***urbaniana*** | EBee |
| ***waldsteinii*** | CAby CDes CElw CLAP CPom CSpe CWsd EBee ECho EGle EHrv GBuc LEdu NCGa NDov SBch SCnR WCru WHoo WIvy WSHC |
| ***yezoensis*** | CDes IBlr |
| - B&SWJ 4659 | WCru |

## cardamon see *Elettaria cardamomum*

## *Cardiandra* (*Hydrangeaceae*)

| | |
|---|---|
| ***alternifolia*** | CLAP |
| - B&SWJ 5719 | WCru |
| - B&SWJ 5845 | WCru |
| - B&SWJ 6354 | WCru |
| - 'Pink Geisha' **new** | WCru |
| ***amamiohshimensis*** | WCru |
| ***formosana*** | CLAP |
| - B&SWJ 2005 | WCru |
| - 'Crûg's Abundant' **new** | WCru |
| - 'Hsitou' | WCru |
| - 'Hsitou Splendour' **new** | WCru |

## *Cardiocrinum* (*Liliaceae*)

| | |
|---|---|
| ***cathayanum*** | CBct CSpe EBee GEdr WCot WPGP |
| ***cordatum*** | EBee ECho WBVN |
| - B&SWJ 4841 | WCru |
| - var. ***glehnii*** | CCCN EBee EBrs ECho GBuc GEdr GGar WWst |
| - - B&SWJ 4758 | WCru |
| - red-veined | EBrs GBuc GEdr |
| ***giganteum*** | Widely available |
| - B&SWJ 2419 | WCru |
| - HWJK 2158 from Nepal | WCru |
| - var. ***yunnanense*** | CBcs CPom EBee EBrs EPfP GAbr |

| | |
|---|---|
| | GBuc GEdr GGGa GGar GKir GMaP ITim NBid SKHP WCru WPGP |

**cardoon** see *Cynara cardunculus*

## *Carduus* (*Asteraceae*)

| | |
|---|---|
| ***benedictus*** | see *Cnicus benedictus* |
| ***nutans*** | WSFF |

## *Carex* (*Cyperaceae*)

| | | |
|---|---|---|
| | from Uganda | MMoz SApp |
| | ***acuta*** | GFor GKir MSKA NBre |
| | - 'Variegata' (v) | CBen CDWL CRow EBee EHoe EHon ELon EMFW EMon EPla EShb GMaP LPBA MAvo MMoz MMuc NBro NHol NOak SApp WAbb WCot WFar WHal WMoo WPnP |
| | ***acutiformis*** | CRWN EBWF GFor NBHF NBre NSco |
| | ***alba*** | EPPr GFor |
| | ***albida*** | EBrs EHul LRHS |
| | ***albula*** | CWsd MMoz MWhi |
| | 'Amazon Mist' | EBee GFor NPri |
| | ***appressa*** | SApp |
| | ***arenaria*** | EBWF GBin GFor NBHF NBre |
| | ***atrata*** | EBee EHoe EPla LRHS WHrl |
| | ***aurea*** | EPPr GFor IFoB NBre NHol |
| | ***baccans*** | CPLG GCal GFor NOak |
| | ***bebbii*** | EPPr |
| | ***berggrenii*** | EBee ECou EHig EHul ELan GKir LEdu LPBA LRHS NCob NWCA SPlb SWat WMoo WPer WTin |
| | ***binervis*** | CRWN EBWF |
| | ***boottiana*** | EWes |
| | ***brunnea*** | EWes SHDw |
| | - 'Jenneke' | CKno EAlp EBee EHoe LRHS MBar MBri NCGa SHDw SLim SPoG SWvt |
| | - 'Variegata' (v) | CEnt EAlp EHoe MMoz SApp SHDw WWFP |
| | ***buchananii*** ♀H4 | Widely available |
| | - 'Viridis' | ELan EPPr GBin LRHS WHer |
| | ***bushii*** | NCob |
| | ***caryophyllea*** 'The Beatles' | EBee EGoo EHoe EPPr MMoz NBir NHol |
| | ***chathamica*** | EBee MMoz |
| | 'China Blue' | EPPr MMoz SApp WMoo |
| | ***comans*** | COIW EFul EMon EPPr EShb GKir GQui LRHS NBro NHol NPol |
| | - 'Bronze Perfection' | SWal WFar |
| | - bronze-leaved | Widely available |
| | - 'Dancing Flame' | CWCL EBee EWsh MBri |
| | - 'Frosted Curls' | Widely available |
| | - green-leaved | GFor |
| | - 'Kupferflamme' | EBee |
| | - red-leaved | LAst MGos SRms |
| | - 'Small Red' | see *C. comans* 'Taranaki' |
| § | - 'Taranaki' | EBee EPfP GKir MBNS MMoz NHol SCoo SWal |
| | ***conica*** | MWat |
| | - 'Hime-kan-suge' | see *C. conica* 'Snowline' |
| | - 'Kiku-sakura' (v) | NHol |
| § | - 'Snowline' (v) | Widely available |
| | ***crinita*** | EPPr |
| | ***cristatella*** | EPPr |
| | ***curta*** | CRWN EBWF |
| * | ***cyperus*** | GKir |
| | ***dallii*** | EBee ECou EWes GBin MMoz MMuc NLar WHrl |
| | ***davisii*** | EPPr |
| | ***demissa*** | CRWN EBWF EBee EHoe |
| | ***depauperata*** | CRWN EBWF EHoe EMon |
| | ***digitata*** | CRWN EBWF |
| | ***dioica*** | CRWN EBWF |
| | ***dipsacea*** | Widely available |
| | - 'Dark Horse' | EBee GCal LLHF NHol |
| | ***divulsa*** subsp. ***divulsa*** | CRWN EBWF |
| | ***dolichostachya*** 'Kaga-nishiki' (v) | CPen CSBt EMon EPPr EPla LAst LEdu LRHS MMoz MWhi SLim WPnP WPrP |
| | ***duthiei*** | EBee GCal |
| | - KEKE 494 | MMoz WPGP |
| | ***echinata*** | CRWN EBWF |
| § | ***elata*** | GKir |
| § | - 'Aurea' (v) ♀H4 | Widely available |
| | - 'Bowles' Golden' | see *C. elata* 'Aurea' |
| | - 'Knightshayes' ♀H4 | CKno EBee EWes GBin MMoz WCot |
| | 'Evergold' | see *C. oshimensis* 'Evergold' |
| | ***firma*** 'Variegata' (v) | MWat NMen NWCA WAbe WThu |
| | ***flacca*** | CRWN EBWF EHoe EPPr GBin GFor GKir NBre WGwG |
| | - 'Bias' (v) | EMon EPPr EPla MMoz |
| § | - subsp. ***flacca*** | EBee EWes MMoz NSti WPGP |
| | ***flagellifera*** | Widely available |
| | - 'Auburn Cascade' | EBee EPfP MAvo NHol NPro SApp SPad |
| | - 'Coca-Cola' | CPen EBee NOak |
| | - 'Rapunzel' | CWsd EBee EPPr MMoz WPGP |
| | - 'Toffee Twist' **new** | EHig |
| | ***flava*** | CKno EHoe EPPr GFor |
| | ***fraseri*** | see *Cymophyllus fraserianus* |
| | ***fraserianus*** | see *Cymophyllus fraserianus* |
| | ***glauca*** Scopoli | see *C. flacca* subsp. *flacca* |
| | ***glauca*** Bosc. ex Boott | CKno CWCL EBee EPla WPGP |
| | ***granularis*** | EPPr |
| I | 'Grayassina' | CKno EPPr |
| | ***grayi*** | CKno EBee EBrs EHoe EMon EPla GBuc GFor LEdu MBlu MSCN MSKA MTho NCGa NLar NOak WCot WPer |
| § | ***hachijoensis*** | EMon LAst WFar |
| | - 'Evergold' | see *C. oshimensis* 'Evergold' |
| | 'Happy Wanderer' | SLPl |
| | ***hirta*** | CRWN EBWF NSco |
| | ***hispida*** | EHig GFor MCCP MMoz WMoo WRos |
| | ***hordeistichos*** | EBee |
| | ***hostiana*** | CRWN EBWF |
| | 'Ice Dance' (v) | CKno CMea CWGN EAlp EBee EGle EPPr EPla GGar GQue MMoz NHol NLar NOak NOrc SWvt WPGP WPrP WPtf |
| | ***kaloides*** | CSsd EAlp EBee EHoe EMon LRHS |
| | ***limosa*** **new** | EBWF |
| | ***lucida*** | NNor |
| | ***lupulina*** | NOak |
| | ***lurida*** | CKno EPfP GBin GFor MAvo MBNS NBre NLar |
| | - 'Silver' **new** | MBNS |
| | ***macloviana*** | EPPr |
| | ***macrocephala*** | GFor NBre |
| | 'Majken' | EBee GFor NBre |
| | ***maritima*** | CRWN EBWF |
| | Milk Chocolate = 'Milchoc'PBR (v) | CKno CPen CWGN EAlp EBee EPfP LBMP NMun SApp |
| | ***montana*** | EBrs LRHS |
| | ***morrowii*** misapplied | see *C. oshimensis*, *C. hachijoensis* |
| | ***morrowii*** Boott 'Evergold' | see *C. oshimensis* 'Evergold' |
| | - 'Fisher's Form' (v) | CKno CTri EBee EPPr EPla EWsh LAst LEdu LHop LRHS MMoz MMuc MRav NGdn NHol NMir SApp SWvt WFar WPGP WPer |
| | - 'Gilt' (v) | EAEE EBee EHoe EMon EPPr EPla LBMP MBNS NHol |
| | - 'Nana Variegata' (v) | CTri NBir WPGP |
| | - var. ***temnolepis*** 'Silk Tassel' | EPPr NHol |

| | | |
|---|---|---|
| N | - 'Variegata' (v) | EHoe EHrv EHul ELan EMon EPPr EPfP EPla GCal GKev GMaP LAst LPBA LRHS MBar MMoz MRav NBir NHol NSti SLPl SRms WCot WEas WFar WPnP |
| | ***muehlenbergii*** | EPPr |
| | ***muricata*** subsp. ***muricata*** | EPPr |
| | ***muskingumensis*** | Widely available |
| | - 'Ice Fountains' (v) | EBee EPPr |
| | - 'Little Midge' | CKno CWsd EBee EBrs EPPr EShb GBin GCal GKir LRHS |
| | - 'Oehme' (v) | CKno CWCL EBee EBrs EPPr EPla EPyc EShb GBin GCal LEdu MSCN NBid NHol WCot WPtf WTin |
| | - 'Silberstreif' (v) | CKno CPen EBee EPPr GBin GGar MMuc NLar SApp |
| | ***nigra*** | CRWN EBWF EHon EPPr NBHF NLar WPnP |
| § | - 'On-line' (v) | EHrv EPPr EWsh MMoz NHol SApp WMoo |
| | - 'Variegata' | see *C. nigra* 'On-line' |
| | No 1, Nanking (Greg's broad leaf) | MMoz |
| | No 4, Nanking (Greg's thin leaf) | EPPr SApp |
| | ***normalis*** | EPPr |
| | ***obnupta*** | CKno EPPr |
| | ***ornithopoda*** 'Aurea' | see *C. ornithopoda* 'Variegata' |
| § | - 'Variegata' (v) | EBee ECtt EHul EWsh GFor MBrN MMoz NBro NGdn NHol NOak SBch WFar WMoo WTin |
| § | ***oshimensis*** | EHoe |
| § | - 'Evergold' (v) ♀H4 | Widely available |
| | - 'Supergold' | EBee |
| | - 'Variegata' (v) | NBir |
| | ***otrubae*** | CRWN EBWF |
| | ***ovalis*** | CRWN EBWF SWal |
| | ***pallescens*** 'Breckland Frost' (v) | EPPr MAvo |
| | - 'Wood's Edge' (v) | CNat |
| | ***panicea*** | CKno CRWN CWCL EBWF EBee EHoe EMil EPPr EPla MMoz MSKA SApp WFar WMoo |
| | ***paniculata*** | CRWN GFor NBre NSco |
| | ***pendula*** | Widely available |
| | - 'Cool Jazz' (v) | EPPr MAvo WAlt |
| | - 'Moonraker' | CWCL EBee EHoe EPPr EPla LEdu MAvo MBNS MSKA NOak SApp WCot WMoo |
| | ***petriei*** | CWCL ECha ETod EWes GBuc LLWP MAvo MBNS MMoz NVic SWal WFar WPer WTin |
| | ***phyllocephala*** | EPPr EShb |
| | - 'Sparkler' (v) | Widely available |
| | ***pilulifera*** 'Tinney's Princess' (v) | LRHS NHol |
| | ***plantaginea*** | EBee EBrs EHoe EMon EPPr EPla GBin LEdu SApp WCot WFar WMoo WPGP |
| | ***praegracilis*** | CKno |
| | ***projecta*** | EPPr |
| | ***pseudocyperus*** | CRWN CSec EBWF EHoe EHon EPla EWsh GBin GFor GKir LPBA MMoz MMuc MSKA NNor NPer SRms SWal SWat WFar WMoo WPer WPnP |
| | ***pulicaris*** | CRWN |
| | 'Red Rooster' **new** | EHig |
| | ***remota*** | CRWN EBWF EHoe LRHS NBre |
| | ***riparia*** | CRWN EBWF EMFW LPBA MMoz MMuc MSKA NHol NPer NSco SWal SWat WFar WRos WShi |

| | | |
|---|---|---|
| | - 'Bowles' Golden' | see *C. elata* 'Aurea' |
| | ***rostrata*** | CRWN EBWF |
| | ***sabynensis*** | see *C. umbrosa* subsp. *sabynensis* |
| | ***saxatilis*** 'Ski Run' | EBee |
| * | - 'Variegata' (v) | EHoe |
| | ***secta*** | CKno ECou EPPr GFor GGar GMaP MNrw NBre SHDw WDyG WMoo WPer |
| | - from Dunedin, New Zealand | EPPr |
| | - var. ***tenuiculmis*** | see *C. tenuiculmis* |
| | ***shortiana*** | EHoe |
| | ***siderosticha*** | EPla EShb SLPl WPGP WPer |
| | - 'Banana Boat' (v) | EBee LSou MNrw NOrc SMad |
| | - 'Echigo-nishiki' (v) **new** | EPPr |
| | - 'Elaine West' (v) | EBee |
| | - 'Golden Fountains' | WCot |
| | - 'Kisokaido' (v) | EBee EPPr MWhi WCot |
| | - 'Old Barn' | EPPr |
| | - 'Shima-nishiki' (v) | CElw CHrt CPen CPrp EBee ECtt EPPr EPfP EShb LAst LEdu NOak NPro SAga SMad WFar |
| | - 'Variegata' (v) | Widely available |
| | 'Silver Sceptre' (v) | Widely available |
| | 'Silver Sparkler' | NBir |
| | ***solandri*** | CSam EWsh LEdu MAvo NLar SApp SHDw WMoo WPtf |
| | ***spissa*** | CKno MNrw |
| | ***sprengelii*** | EPPr |
| | ***stricta*** Gooden. | see *C. elata* |
| | -. 'Bowles' Golden' | see *C. elata* 'Aurea' |
| | ***stricta*** Lamarck | EPla |
| | ***sylvatica*** | CRWN EBWF GFor |
| § | ***tenuiculmis*** | CKno CWCL EAlp EBee EBrs EMon EPPr EShb EWsh LBMP MAvo NHol NOak NSti SBch SPad SWal WTin |
| | - 'Cappucino' | CKno |
| | ***testacea*** | Widely available |
| | - 'Old Gold' | EBee ELan EMil EWes MAvo NOak SMad SPlb WFar WLeb |
| | ***texensis*** | EPPr |
| | ***trifida*** | CHEx CHrt CKno EBee EHoe GFor GGar MMoz MNrw WFar WMoo WPnP |
| | - 'Chatham Blue' | CHid CKno EPPr GBin MAvo NBir SEND |
| | ***umbrosa*** subsp. ***sabynensis*** 'Thinny Thin' (v) | EBee EMon EPPr |
| | ***uncifolia*** | ECou |
| | ***viridula*** | EBWF |
| | - subsp. ***viridula*** | CRWN EBWF |
| | ***vulpina*** | EPPr NBre |
| | ***vulpinoidea*** | EPPr |

## *Carica* (*Caricaceae*)

| | | |
|---|---|---|
| | ***goudotiana*** | CKob |
| | x ***heilbornii*** (F) | CKob |
| | ***papaya*** (F) | CSec |
| | ***quercifolia*** | CKob |

## *Carissa* (*Apocynaceae*)

| | | |
|---|---|---|
| | ***grandiflora*** | see *C. macrocarpa* |
| § | ***macrocarpa*** (F) | EShb |

## *Carlina* (*Asteraceae*)

| | | |
|---|---|---|
| | ***acanthifolia*** | ECho |
| | - subsp. ***cyanara*** JJA 274.101 | NWCA |
| | ***acaulis*** | CArn CHrt ECho ELan EPfP GEdr GKir GPWP MNHC NPri NWCA SDnm SPav SPlb SRms WFar WPer |
| | - subsp. ***acaulis*** | GPoy |

| | |
|---|---|
| - bronze-leaved | EWll LDai MCCP WHil |
| - var. ***caulescens*** | see *C. acaulis* subsp. *simplex* |
| § - subsp. ***simplex*** | ECha GGar GKir GMaP LRHS NPri WFar WJek WPer |
| - - bronze-leaved | CBow EBee GMaP MAvo NChi SPhx |
| ***vulgaris*** | EBWF WPer |
| - 'Silver Star' | GEdr |

## *Carmichaelia* (*Papilionaceae*)

| | |
|---|---|
| 'Abundance' | ECou |
| 'Angie' | ECou |
| ***angustata*** 'Buller' | ECou |
| ***appressa*** | ECou GGar |
| - 'Ellesmere' | ECou |
| ***arborea*** | ECou |
| - 'Grand' | ECou |
| ***astonii*** | ECou |
| - 'Ben More' | ECou |
| - 'Chalk Ridge' | ECou |
| ***australis*** | EBee ECou WBod WSHC |
| - 'Bright Eyes' | ECou |
| - 'Cunningham' | ECou |
| - Flagelliformis Group | ECou |
| - 'Mahurangi' | ECou |
| - Ovata Group | ECou |
| - 'Solander' | ECou |
| ***carmichaeliae*** | ECou |
| - 'Hodder' | ECou |
| - 'Seymour' | ECou |
| 'Charm' | ECou |
| 'Clifford Bay' | ECou |
| 'Coral Spears' | ECou |
| ***corrugata*** | ECou |
| ***crassicaulise*** | ECou |
| - 'Jack Sprat' | ECou |
| - var. ***racemosa*** | ECou |
| 'Culverden' | ECou |
| ***curta*** | ECou |
| ***enysii*** | CCCN |
| 'Essex' | ECou |
| ***exsul*** | ECou |
| ***fieldii*** 'Westhaven' | ECou |
| ***flagelliformis*** 'Roro' | ECou |
| ***glabrescens*** | ECou |
| - 'Woodside' | ECou |
| ***glabrescens*** x ***torulosa*** | ECou |
| 'Havering' | ECou |
| 'Hay and Honey' | ECou |
| § x ***hutchinsii*** | ECou |
| - 'Butterfly' | ECou |
| - 'County Park' | ECou GGar |
| - 'Delight' | ECou |
| - 'Pink Beauty' | ECou |
| - 'Wingletye' | ECou |
| 'Joy' | ECou |
| ***juncea*** Nigrans Group | ECou |
| ***kirkii*** | ECou |
| 'Lilac Haze' | ECou |
| ***monroi*** | ECou |
| - 'Rangitata' | ECou |
| - 'Tekapo' | ECou |
| ***muritai*** | ECou |
| - 'Huia Gilpen' | ECou |
| - 'Ron Feron' | ECou |
| - 'Wayne Nichols' | ECou |
| ***nana*** | ECou |
| - 'Desert Road' | ECou |
| - 'Pringle' | ECou |
| - 'Waitaki' | ECou |
| ***nigrans*** 'Wanaka' | ECou |
| ***odorata*** | CPLG ECou |
| - Angustata Group | ECou |
| - 'Green Dwarf' | ECou |
| - 'Lakeside' | ECou |
| - 'Riverside' | ECou |
| ***ovata*** 'Calf Creek' | ECou |
| 'Parson's Tiny' | ECou |
| ***petriei*** | ECou SMad |
| - 'Aviemore' | ECou |
| - 'Lindis' | ECou |
| - 'Pukaki' | ECou |
| - Virgata Group | ECou |
| 'Porter's Pass' | ECou |
| 'Spangle' | ECou |
| ***stevensonii*** | ECou EPfP NLar WBVN |
| - hybrid | ECou |
| - 'Duncan' | ECou |
| - 'Kiwi' | ECou |
| - 'Miller' | ECou |
| 'Tangle' | ECou |
| ***torulosa*** | ECou |
| - 'Blue Butterfly' | ECou |
| - 'Malvern Hills' | ECou |
| ***uniflora*** | ECou |
| - 'Bealey' | ECou |
| 'Weka' | ECou |
| ***williamsii*** | ECou |
| 'Yellow Eyes' | ECou |

## x *Carmispartium* see *Carmichaelia*

| | |
|---|---|
| ***astens*** | see *Carmichaelia* x *hutchinsii* |

## *Carpenteria* (*Hydrangeaceae*)

| | |
|---|---|
| ***californica*** ♀H3 | CPMA CSBt EBee ELan EPfP EWTr GKir IMGH LHop MBri MGos MLan MWat NCGa NPal NPri SHBN SPer SPla SPoG SReu SSpi SSta WCot WDin WHCG WPat WSHC |
| - 'Bodnant' | CDul ELan LRHS MBri MGos MWea WBod WPGP |
| - 'Elizabeth' | CAbP CBcs CPMA CWGN ELan EPfP GKir LRHS LSRN SKHP SPer SPoG SSpi SSta WDin WPGP WPat |
| - 'Ladhams' Variety' | CBcs CPMA EBee EPfP LRHS MGos MRav NLar WKif |

## *Carpinus* ✿ (*Corylaceae*)

| | |
|---|---|
| sp. | CMen |
| ***betulus*** ♀H4 | Widely available |
| * - 'A. Beeckman' | SBLw |
| - 'Columnaris' | CLnd CTho GKir SBLw |
| * - 'Columnaris Nana' | CMCN |
| § - 'Fastigiata' ♀H4 | CBcs CCVT CDoC CDul CEnd CLnd CMCN CSBt CTho CWib EBee ECrN ELan EPfP GKir LBuc LMaj LPan MBar MGos NBee NWea SBLw SCoo WDin WFar WHar WOrn |
| - 'Frans Fontaine' | CCVT CDoC CDul CMCN CTho EBee EPfP GKir IArd LAst LMaj LPan LRHS MBlu MBri MGos NBlu SBLw SCoo SLim SPer SPoG |
| - 'Globus' **new** | MBlu |
| - 'Horizontalis' | CMCN |
| I - 'Monumentalis' **new** | LMaj |
| - 'Pendula' | CDul CEnd CLnd CTho EBee GKir LPan MBlu SBLw SPoG WDin |
| - 'Purpurea' | CBcs CDul CEnd LMaj MGos NBPN NLar SBLw |
| - 'Pyramidalis' | see *C. betulus* 'Fastigiata' |
| - 'Quercifolia' | CDul EBee SBLw |
| ***caroliniana*** | CLnd CMCN MBlu SBir |
| ***cordata*** | CMCN MBlu SBir WDin |
| ***coreana*** | CMCN MBlu |

| | |
|---|---|
| ***fangiana*** | CEnd CGHE CTho EBee EPla GKir WPGP |
| ***fargesii*** | see *C. viminea* |
| ***henryana*** | CMen SBir |
| ***japonica*** 🏆H4 | CDul CEnd CMCN CMen CTho EPfP GKir LLHF LPan MBlu SBir SCoo WDin |
| - B&SWJ 10803 **new** | WCru |
| - var. ***cordifolia*** B&SWJ 11072 **new** | WCru |
| ***laxiflora*** | CMen MBlu MPkF WFar WPGP |
| - B&SWJ 10809 **new** | WCru |
| - B&SWJ 11035 **new** | WCru |
| - var. ***longispica*** B&SWJ 8772 | WCru |
| - var. ***macrostachya*** | see *C. viminea* |
| ***orientalis*** | CMCN SBir |
| ***polyneura*** | CMCN SBir |
| ***pubescens*** | GKir WPGP |
| x ***schuschaensis*** | GKir SBir |
| ***shensiensis*** | CDul CMCN |
| ***tschonoskii*** | CMCN |
| - B&SWJ 10800 **new** | WCru |
| ***turczaninowii*** 🏆H4 | CBcs CMCN CMHG CMen GKir IDee MBlu NLar NPal NWea SBir WDin WPGP |
| § ***viminea*** | CEnd CMCN MBlu SBir WPat |

## *Carpobrotus* (*Aizoaceae*)

| | |
|---|---|
| § ***edulis*** | CCCN CDTJ CDoC CHrt EShb SAPC SArc SChr SEND WCor WHer |
| - var. ***edulis*** | CHEx |
| - var. ***rubescens*** | CCCN CHEx |
| ***muirii*** | CCCN EShb |
| ***sauerae*** | CCCN |

## *Carpodetus* (*Escalloniaceae*)

| | |
|---|---|
| ***serratus*** | CBcs CTrC |

## *Carrierea* (*Flacourtiaceae*)

| | |
|---|---|
| ***calycina*** | WPGP |

## carrot see *Daucus carota*

## *Carthamus* (*Asteraceae*)

| | |
|---|---|
| ***tinctorius*** | CArn MNHC MSal SPav |

## *Carum* (*Apiaceae*)

| | |
|---|---|
| ***carvi*** | CArn CHrt CWan GPoy MHer MNHC NPri SIde SVic WHer WJek WLHH WPer |
| ***copticum*** | MSal |
| ***petroselinum*** | see *Petroselinum crispum* |

## *Carya* ✿ (*Juglandaceae*)

| | |
|---|---|
| ***aquatica*** | CTho |
| ***cordiformis*** | CTho EPfP |
| ***glabra*** | CMCN WPGP |
| N ***illinoinensis*** (F) | CAgr CBcs CMCN |
| - 'Carlson No 3' seedling | CAgr |
| - 'Colby' seedling | CAgr |
| - 'Cornfield' | CAgr |
| - 'Lucas' (F) | CAgr |
| ***laciniosa*** (F) | CTho EPfP WPGP |
| - 'Henry' (F) | CAgr |
| - 'Keystone' seedling (F) | CAgr |
| ***ovata*** (F) | CAgr CMCN CTho EPfP MBlu WDin |
| - 'Grainger' seedling (F) | CAgr |
| - 'Neilson' seedling (F) | CAgr |
| - 'Weschke' seedling (F) | CAgr |
| - 'Yoder no 1' seedling (F) | CAgr |
| ***pallida*** | EGFP |
| ***texana*** | EGFP |
| ***tomentosa*** | EPfP |

## *Caryophyllus* see *Syzygium*

## *Caryopteris* ✿ (*Verbenaceae*)

| | |
|---|---|
| x ***clandonensis*** | EBee ECtt MGan MLHP MWat NBir WBod WCFE WDin WFar WHCG WHar |
| - 'Arthur Simmonds' 🏆H4 | CSam CTri EBee ECha EPfP GKir LHop SPer WGor |
| - 'Blaue Donau' | EBee SPoG |
| - 'Dark Night' | CHar EBee ELon LBuc LRHS MBri MWat SPur |
| - 'Ferndown' | CDoC CWib EBee EPfP GKir LHop LRHS NLar SEND SPer SPla SReu SRms |
| - 'First Choice' 🏆H3-4 | CAbP CSBt CSpe EBee ECrN ELan EPfP LHop LRHS LSRN MAsh MGos MWat NLar SPer SPoG SRkn SWvt WOVN |
| - Grand Bleu = 'Inoveris'PBR | CSBt EBee ELan EMil EQua EShb LSRN MAsh MBlu MGos MRav MSwo NLar SMad SPoG SPur WCot |
| - 'Heavenly Baby' | EBee MAsh |
| - 'Heavenly Blue' | Widely available |
| - 'Kew Blue' | Widely available |
| - 'Longwood Blue' | CMdw ELan EPfP LRHS |
| - 'Moody Blue' (v) | EPfP |
| - 'Pershore' | EBee |
| - 'Summer Gold' | GKir MRav |
| - 'Summer Sorbet'PBR (v) | CBow CDoC EBee EBrs EHoe ELan EMil EPfP EWes LBuc LHop LRHS MAsh MGos MNHC MTPN NHol NLar NPro SCoo SPoG WCFE WHar WPat |
| - 'Worcester Gold' 🏆H3-4 | Widely available |
| ***divaricata*** | EBee EMon MBri |
| - 'Electrum' | ECtt EMon LSou MDKP |
| - 'Jade Shades' | EBee ECtt EMon LSou |
| - 'Pink Butterfly' **new** | EBee |
| - 'Pink Illumination' (v) **new** | EBee |
| - variegated (v) | CBow |
| § ***incana*** | CMCN EBee ECrN EPfP SECG SPer WPat WSHC |
| - 'Autumn Pink'PBR | CBgR EBee ECrN EMil EPfP SPoG |
| - 'Blue Cascade' | GQue |
| § - 'Jason'PBR | EPfP WPat |
| - Sunshine BluePBR | see *C. incana* 'Jason' |
| - weeping | EBee ELan GBuc MRav MSte NLar WLeb |
| ***mastacanthus*** | see *C. incana* |

## *Caryota* (*Arecaceae*)

| | |
|---|---|
| ***gigas*** | EAmu |
| ***mitis*** 🏆H1 | EAmu LPal SBig |
| - 'Himalaya' | EAmu LPal |
| ***obtusa*** | LPal |
| ***ochlandra*** | LPal |
| ***urens*** | LPal |

## *Cassandra* see *Chamaedaphne*

## *Cassia* (*Caesalpiniaceae*)

| | |
|---|---|
| ***corymbosa*** Lam. | see *Senna corymbosa* |
| ***fistula*** **new** | CSec |
| ***marilandica*** | see *Senna marilandica* |
| ***obtusifolia*** | see *Senna obtusifolia* |

## *Cassinia* (*Asteraceae*)

| | |
|---|---|
| ***aculeata*** | GGar |
| ***leptophylla*** | GGar SPer |
| - 'Avalanche Creek' **new** | ECou |
| - subsp. ***fulvida*** | EBee ECou GGar MBar SPer |

| | | |
|---|---|---|
| | - subsp. ***vauvilliersii*** | GGar MCot SEND SPer |
| | - - BR 55 | GGar |
| | - - var. ***albida*** | SKHP SPer |
| | - - 'Silberschmelze' | SOWG |
| N | ***retorta*** | ECou |
| | 'Ward Silver' | CSpe ECou EHoe EWes IDee |

## *Cassinia* x *Helichrysum* (*Asteraceae*)

| | | |
|---|---|---|
| * | hybrid | WKif |

## *Cassiope* ✿ (*Ericaceae*)

| | | |
|---|---|---|
| | 'Askival Snow-wreath' | see *C.* Snow-wreath Group |
| | 'Badenoch' | ECho GAbr GEdr NDlv NLar |
| | 'Bearsden' | MBar NDlv |
| | 'Edinburgh' ♀H4 | ECho GEdr MBar NDlv NHar NHol NLar WBod |
| | ***lycopodioides*** 'Beatrice Lilley' | ECho GEdr LLHF NDlv NHar SRms |
| | - 'Jim Lever' | ITim WAbe |
| | 'Medusa' | WPat WThu |
| | ***mertensiana*** | ECho MBar NDlv SRms |
| | - var. ***gracilis*** | NLar WThu |
| | 'Muirhead' ♀H4 | ECho GEdr MBar NDlv NRya SRms WThu |
| | 'Randle Cooke' ♀H4 | ECho GEdr GGar MBar NDlv SRms WThu |
| | ***selaginoides*** | NLar |
| | - LS&E 13284 | ITim WAbe |
| § | Snow-wreath Group | ITim |
| | ***tetragona*** | MBar SRms |
| | ***wardii*** 'George Taylor' | GGGa |

## *Castanea* ✿ (*Fagaceae*)

| | | |
|---|---|---|
| | 'Bouche de Betizac' (F) | CAgr LPan |
| | ***crenata*** | CAgr |
| | ***dentata*** | EGFP |
| | ***henryi*** | CBcs |
| | 'Layeroka' (F) | CAgr |
| | 'Maraval' | CAgr CTho EMil MCoo |
| | 'Maridonne' (F) | CAgr |
| | 'Marigoule' (F) | CAgr EMil MCoo |
| | 'Marlhac' (F) | CAgr EMil MCoo |
| | 'Marsol' (F) | CAgr MCoo MREP |
| | 'Précoce Migoule' (F) | CAgr |
| | ***pumila*** | CAgr |
| | 'Rousse de Nay' (F) | CAgr |
| | ***sativa*** ♀H4 | Widely available |
| § | - 'Albomarginata' (v) ♀H4 | CDoC CDul CEnd CTho EBee EPfP LMaj MBlu MBri MDun MGos NBea SBLw SPoG WDin WFar WOrn WPat |
| | - 'Anny's Red' | MBlu |
| | - 'Anny's Summer Red' | CDul LRHS MAsh SCoo SLon |
| | - 'Argenteovariegata' | see *C. sativa* 'Albomarginata' |
| | - 'Aspleniifolia' | CDul MBlu |
| | - 'Aureomarginata' | see *C. sativa* 'Variegata' |
| | - 'Belle Epine' (F) | CAgr |
| | - 'Bournette' (F) | CAgr |
| * | - 'Doré de Lyon' | CAgr |
| | - 'Herria' (F) | CAgr |
| | - 'Laguépie' (F) | CAgr |
| | - 'Marron Comballe' (F) | CAgr |
| | - 'Marron de Goujounac' (F) | CAgr |
| | - 'Marron de Lyon' (F) | CAgr CDul CEnd CTho EMil EMui EPfP MBlu MCoo SKee SVic |
| | - 'Marron de Redon' (F) | CAgr |
| | - 'Numbo' (F) | CAgr |
| | - 'Pyramidalis' | WDin |
| § | - 'Variegata' (v) | CLnd CMCN ECrN EHig ELan EMil LMaj LPan MAsh MGos |
| | - 'Verdale' (F) | CAgr |
| | ***seguinii*** | CAgr |
| | 'Simpson' | CAgr |
| | 'Vignols' (F) | CAgr |

## *Castanopsis* (*Fagaceae*)

| | | |
|---|---|---|
| | ***platyacantha*** | CExc |
| | ***sclerophylla*** new | CBcs |

## *Castanospermum* (*Papilionaceae*)

| | | |
|---|---|---|
| | ***australe*** | CArn |

## *Castilleja* (*Scrophulariaceae*)

| | | |
|---|---|---|
| | ***elegans*** | WAbe |
| | ***hispida*** | WAbe |
| | ***miniata*** | WAbe |
| | ***sessiliflora*** | GKev |

## *Casuarina* (*Casuarinaceae*)

| | | |
|---|---|---|
| | ***cunninghamiana*** | ECou |

## *Catalpa* ✿ (*Bignoniaceae*)

| | | |
|---|---|---|
| | ***bignonioides*** ♀H4 | Widely available |
| | - 'Aurea' ♀H4 | Widely available |
| * | - 'Aurea Nana' new | MBri |
| | - 'Nana' | ECrN LMaj LRHS MBri SBLw WDin |
| | - 'Purpurea' | see *C.* x *erubescens* 'Purpurea' |
| | - 'Variegata' (v) | CLnd CTho EBee EPfP EWTr LRHS MGos SPer SSta WPat |
| | ***bungei*** | EGFP LPan MBlu MGos SAPC SArc SHGN |
| | - 'Purpurea' | ELan LAst |
| | x ***erubescens*** | SBLw |
| § | - 'Purpurea' ♀H4 | CBcs CDoC CDul CEnd CLnd CTho EAmu EBee EMil EPfP EWTr LPan LRHS MAsh MBlu MBri MGos MRav SHBN SMad SPer SSta WDin WFar WOrn WPGP WPat |
| | ***fargesii*** f. ***duclouxii*** | CBcs CDul CEnd CMCN EPfP MBlu MBri NLar WPat |
| | ***ovata*** | CMCN EGFP WBVN |
| | - 'Slender Silhouette' | MBri NLar |
| | ***speciosa*** | CDul CMCN EPfP EWTr SBLw SEND |
| | - 'Frederik' new | MBri |
| | - 'Pulverulenta' (v) | CDoC CDul CEnd CMCN EMil MGos NLar SBig SPer WOrn |

## *Catananche* (*Asteraceae*)

| | | |
|---|---|---|
| | ***caerulea*** | Widely available |
| | - 'Alba' | CMea EAEE EBee EBla ECha EPfP GKir GMac IFoB LRHS NBir NPri SGar SMrm SPer SPoG SUsu WCAu WMoo WPer |
| | - 'Bicolor' | CMMP MHer MNrw SHGN STes WFar WHoo WMoo |
| | - 'Major' ♀H4 | EBee ECrN LDai LRHS SRms |

## *Catha* (*Celastraceae*)

| | | |
|---|---|---|
| | ***edulis*** | CArn CKob GPoy WJek |

## *Catharanthus* (*Apocynaceae*)

| | | |
|---|---|---|
| | ***roseus*** ♀H1 | EOHP GPoy MBri MSal |
| | - Ocellatus Group | MBri |

## *Cathaya* (*Pinaceae*)

| | | |
|---|---|---|
| | ***argyrophylla*** | WPGP |

## *Caulophyllum* (*Berberidaceae*)

| | | |
|---|---|---|
| | ***thalictroides*** | CArn CLAP EBee GBBs GBuc GEdr GKir LEdu MSal NLar WCru WFar WMoo WPnP WSHC |
| | - subsp. ***robustum*** | CLAP WCru |

## *Cautleya* ✿ (*Zingiberaceae*)

| | | |
|---|---|---|
| | ***cathcartii*** | CLAP LEdu |

| | | |
|---|---|---|
| | - B&SWJ 2314 | CBct |
| | - 'Tenzing's Gold' | CLAP WCru |
| § | ***gracilis*** | CDTJ CKob CLAP CPrp CWsd EBee ETod GCal IBlr LEdu MJnS SBig WPic |
| | - B&SWJ 7186 | WCru WDyG |
| | - CC 1751 | WCot |
| | ***lutea*** | see *C. gracilis* |
| | ***spicata*** | CBct CCCN CDTJ CDoC CHEx CKob CSec CTsd EBee EBrs ECho EPPr EUJe IBlr SBHP SBig WCot |
| | - 'Crûg Canary' | CLAP LEdu WCru |
| * | - var. ***lutea*** | CBct CHEx CPne ETod |
| | - 'Robusta' | CAvo CGHE CHEx CLAP CPne CPrp CTca EAmu EBee EShb GCal GCra IBlr LEdu MNrw NPal SMad WBor WCru WPGP WPic WSHC |

## *Cayratia* (*Vitaceae*)

| | | |
|---|---|---|
| § | ***thomsonii*** BWJ 8123 | WCru |

## *Ceanothus* ✿ (*Rhamnaceae*)

| | | |
|---|---|---|
| | 'A.T. Johnson' | CDul EBee LAst SHBN SLim SPad SPer SRms |
| | ***americanus*** | CArn MSal |
| | ***arboreus*** | SAPC SArc |
| | - 'Trewithen Blue' ♀H3 | Widely available |
| | 'Autumnal Blue' ♀H3 | Widely available |
| * | 'Blue Carpet' | CWSG |
| | 'Blue Cushion' | CBcs CDoC CPMA CWSG EBee LHop LRHS MGos MRav NHol NLar NPri SEND SLon SWvt WBVN WBrE WFar |
| | 'Blue Dreams' | WFar |
| | 'Blue Jeans' | EBee ELan IArd LRHS SAga WLeb |
| | 'Blue Mound' ♀H3 | Widely available |
| | 'Blue Sapphire' PBR | CBcs CDoC CMHG CWGN CWSG EBee ELan EMil EPfP LAst LHop LRHS LSRN MBlu MGos MRav NCGa NLar NPri SHBN SPer SPoG SWvt |
| | 'Burkwoodii' ♀H3 | CBcs CDoC CDul CSBt CTri CWSG EPfP GKir LAst LCro LRHS MAsh MDun MGan MGos MRav NHol SCoo SHBN SPer SPoG SWvt WFar WGwG |
| | 'Cascade' ♀H3 | CBcs CTri CWSG EBee GKir LRHS MGos MWat NSti SCoo SLim SLon SPer SPlb WBod WHCG |
| | 'Centennial' | LBuc LRHS MRav |
| | 'Comtesse de Paris' | see *C.* x *delileanus* 'Comtesse de Paris' |
| | 'Concha' ♀H3 | Widely available |
| § | ***cuneatus*** var. ***rigidus*** | LRHS NHol SRms WSHC |
| | - - 'Snowball' | ELan EPfP LRHS |
| | 'Cynthia Postan' | CMHG CSBt CWSG EBee EPfP ERas IArd ISea LRHS MBlu MWat NHol NLar SCoo SDix WAbe |
| | 'Dark Star' ♀H3 | CBcs CChe CDoC CMHG CSPN CWSG EBee ELon EPfP LBMP LRHS MAsh MBlu MGos NHol NSti SCoo SEND SMad SOWG SPla SPoG SSta SWvt |
| | 'Delight' | CBcs EBee ELan EPfP EPla LRHS MGos WBod WDin WFar WRHF |
| § | x ***delileanus*** 'Comtesse de Paris' | EBee |
| | - 'Gloire de Versailles' ♀H4 | Widely available |
| | - 'Henri Desfossé' | ELan EPfP ERas LRHS LSRN MRav NCGa NLar SOWG SPer WDin WKif |
| | - 'Indigo' | EBee EPfP WKif |
| | - 'Topaze' ♀H4 | CWSG EBee ELan EMil EPfP ERas LRHS MRav NLar SLon SOWG WDin WHar |
| | ***dentatus*** misapplied | see *C.* x *lobbianus* |
| | ***dentatus*** Torr. & A.Gray | SPlb |
| | - var. ***floribundus*** | CSBt ELan LRHS SDix |
| * | - 'Superbus' | EBee |
| | 'Diamond Heights' | see *C. griseus* var. *horizontalis* 'Diamond Heights' |
| | 'Edinburgh' ♀H3 | EBee EPfP LRHS WFar |
| | 'El Dorado' (v) | MGos |
| | 'Eleanor Taylor' | EBee |
| | ***gloriosus*** | EBee EWes |
| | - 'Anchor Bay' | EBee ELan EPfP LRHS SLon SOWG |
| | - 'Emily Brown' | CBcs CDoC CSPN EBee ELan GGar LAst LSRN LSou MRav NHol NLar WFar |
| § | ***griseus*** var. ***horizontalis*** 'Diamond Heights' (v) | EBee EPfP LSRN MAsh MBri SPer WFar |
| | - - 'Hurricane Point' | WFar |
| | - - 'Silver Surprise' PBR (v) | CBcs CSPN CWGN EBee ELan EPfP LRHS LSRN MGos NLar SHBN SLim SPoG WOVN |
| | - - 'Yankee Point' | CBcs CChe CDoC CSBt CWib EBee EMil EPfP GKir ISea LRHS MGos MRav MSwo NBlu NHol SCoo SHBN SLim SPlb SPoG SWvt WDin WFar |
| | ***impressus*** | CMHG CSBt CTri EBee ECrN EPfP LRHS MAsh MBlu MRav SEND SPer SPla SWvt WCFE WFar |
| | - 'Victoria' | EBee ERas LBuc LSRN LSou MGos MHav NLar SRGP |
| N | 'Italian Skies' ♀H3 | CBcs CDoC CSBt CWSG EBee ELan EMil EPfP GKir LAst LRHS MDun MGos MRav MSwo NBlu SCoo SLim SLon SPer SPlb SPoG SWvt WDin WFar |
| | 'Julia Phelps' | CMHG EBee WEas |
| § | x ***lobbianus*** | CTri SPlb WDin WFar |
| | - 'Russellianus' | EBee SHBN |
| | 'Logan' **new** | EBee |
| | Marie Bleue = 'Minmari' **new** | MAsh |
| | x ***pallidus*** 'Marie Simon' | CWib EBee ECrN ELan EMil EPfP LAst LBMP LHop LRHS LSRN MGos SPer SPoG SRms SWvt WCFE WDin WFar WKif |
| | - 'Perle Rose' | EBee EPfP LAst LLHF LRHS MGos SHBN SOWG SPer SPla SPoG WKif WSHC |
| | ***papillosus*** var. ***roweanus*** | EBee |
| § | 'Pershore Zanzibar' PBR (v) | CBcs CChe CSBt CSPN CWSG EBee EHoe ELan EPfP GGar LAst LBuc LRHS MGos MRav MSwo MWat SAdn SCoo SHBN SPer SPoG SSto SWvt WBrE |
| | 'Pin Cushion' | CAbP CDoC CWSG CWib EBee EPfP LRHS MAsh NHol SPoG |
| | 'Point Millerton' | see *C. thyrsiflorus* 'Millerton Point' |
| | 'Popcorn' | LRHS MGos SPoG |
| | ***prostratus*** | MAsh MCot SHBN SMad |
| | 'Puget Blue' ♀H4 | Widely available |
| | ***purpureus*** | LRHS |
| | 'Ray Hartman' | NLar |
| | x ***regius*** | GKir |
| | ***repens*** | see *C. thyrsiflorus* var. *repens* |
| | ***rigidus*** | see *C. cuneatus* var. *rigidus* |
| | 'Sierra Blue' | EBee |
| | 'Snow Flurries' | see *C. thyrsiflorus* 'Snow Flurry' |
| | 'Snow Showers' | WBod |
| | 'Southmead' ♀H3 | CDoC CTri EBee ECrN ELan EMil EPfP ERas GBuc LRHS MAsh MGos MSwo MWat NHol SCoo WDin WFar WHCG WMoo |

| | | |
|---|---|---|
| | ***thyrsiflorus*** | CMac CTri CWSG CWib LBMP LRHS MAsh NHol SHBN SPer SRms SWvt WDin WHar |
| § | - 'Millerton Point' | CWSG EBee EMil EPfP LAst LRHS MBlu MGos NLar SCoo SLim SPoG WGwG |
| § | - var. ***repens*** ♀H3 | Widely available |
| | - 'Skylark' ♀H3 | CDoC CDul CWSG EBee ELan EPau EPfP GGar LCro LHop LRHS LSRN MAsh MBri MGos MLHP NPri SDix SGar SLim SSpi WDin WFar WPat |
| § | - 'Snow Flurry' | CBcs CWib EPfP MSwo SEND WAbe WFar |
| | 'Tilden Park' | EBee LRHS SPoG |
| | x ***veitchianus*** | CSBt EBee ELan LRHS MAsh MBar NHol SCoo SEND SPer WGwG |
| | ***velutinus*** | MSal |
| | 'White Cascade' | EBee |
| | 'Zanzibar' PBR | see *C.* 'Pershore Zanzibar' |

## *Cedrela* (*Meliaceae*)

| | | |
|---|---|---|
| | ***sinensis*** | see *Toona sinensis* |

## *Cedronella* (*Lamiaceae*)

| | | |
|---|---|---|
| § | ***canariensis*** | CArn CBod CHby CHrt CPrp CSec CSev EShb GBar GGar GPoy ILis MHer MNHC MSal NGHP NTHB SECG SIde SOWG SWat WCHb WHer |
| | ***mexicana*** | see *Agastache mexicana* |
| | ***triphylla*** | see *C. canariensis* |

## *Cedrus* (*Pinaceae*)

| | | |
|---|---|---|
| | ***atlantica*** | CDul CLnd CMen CSBt ECrN EHul EWTr IFFs MBar NWea SEND WBVN WMou |
| | - 'Aurea' | CDul CMac MBar MGos NLar NWea SSta WDin WHar |
| | - 'Fastigiata' | CDul CMac EHul MBar MGos NLar SCoo SLim SPoG |
| | - Glauca Group ♀H4 | Widely available |
| | - - 'Glauca Fastigiata' | CKen CMen ECho GKir |
| | - - 'Glauca Pendula' | Widely available |
| | - - 'Saphir Nymphe' | ECho NLar |
| | - - 'Silberspitz' | CKen |
| | - 'Pendula' | CMac ECho MAsh SHBN |
| | ***brevifolia*** | ECho GKir LPan MBar MGos NLar |
| | - 'Epstein' | ECho MBar MGos NLar |
| | - 'Hillier Compact' | CKen MGos NLar |
| | - 'Kenwith' | CKen ECho NLar |
| | ***deodara*** ♀H4 | Widely available |
| | - 'Albospica' (v) | SWvt |
| | - 'Argentea' | MBar MGos |
| | - 'Aurea' ♀H4 | CDoC CDul CKen CSBt CTho ECho EHul EOrn EPfP GBin GKir IMGH LMaj LPan LRHS MBar MBri MGos NWea SBLw SLim WDin WFar WOrn |
| I | - 'Aurea Pendula' | ECho |
| | - 'Blue Dwarf' | CKen ECho NLar |
| * | - 'Blue Mountain Broom' | CKen |
| | - 'Blue Snake' | CKen NLar |
| | - 'Blue Triumph' | LPan |
| | - 'Bush's Electra' | NLar |
| | - 'Cream Puff' | CSli ECho MBar MGos |
| | - 'Dawn Mist' (v) | ECho |
| | - 'Devinely Blue' | CKen SLim SPoG |
| | - 'Feelin' Blue' | CDoC CDul CKen CSli ECho EHul EPla GKir IMGH LBee LRHS MAsh MBar MBri MGos NHol SCoo SHBN SLim SPoG SWvt WFar |
| | - 'Gold Cascade' | SLim |
| | - 'Gold Cone' | ECho MGos |
| | - 'Gold Gowa' | MGos NLar |
| | - 'Gold Mound' | CKen CSBt ECho MAsh |
| | - 'Golden Horizon' | CDoC CKen CMen CSBt ECho ECrN EHul EOrn EPla IMGH LBee LPan LRHS MAsh MBar MBri MGos NBlu NHol SCoo SHBN SLim SPoG WDin WFar |
| | - 'Karl Fuchs' | EWTr GKir MAsh MBri NBlu NLar SCoo WGor |
| | - 'Kashmir' | CSli NLar |
| | - 'Kelly Gold' | EMil LPan NLar |
| | - 'Mountain Beauty' | CKen |
| | - 'Nana' | CKen |
| | - 'Nivea' | CKen |
| | - 'Pendula' | CDoC CKen ECho EHul LMaj LPan MBar MGos WGor |
| | - 'Polar Winter' | SMad |
| | - 'Pygmy' | CKen |
| | - 'Raywood's Prostrate' | CKen |
| | - 'Robusta' | SBLw |
| | - 'Roman Candle' | CSli ECho EOrn SHBN |
| | - 'Scott' | CKen |
| | - 'Silver Mist' | CKen MGos |
| | - 'Silver Spring' | EMil MGos NLar |
| | ***libani*** ♀H4 | Widely available |
| | - 'Comte de Dijon' | ECho EHul LRHS NLar |
| | - 'Fontaine' | NLar |
| | - 'Gold Tip' | NLar |
| | - 'Home Park' | CKen NLar |
| | - Nana Group | CKen ECho |
| | - 'Pampisford' | ECho NLar |
| | - 'Sargentii' | CKen ECho EHul EOrn IMGH MBar MBlu MGos NLar SHBN |
| | - 'Taurus' | MBar NLar |
| | ***libanii*** 'Green Prince' | NLar |
| | - 'Hedgehog' | NLar |

## *Celastrus* (*Celastraceae*)

| | | |
|---|---|---|
| | ***flagellaris*** B&SWJ 8572 **new** | WCru |
| | ***orbiculatus*** | CBcs CDoC CMac ELan LRHS MRav NCGa NSti SLon SReu SSta WBod WBor WFar WSHC |
| | - 'Diana' (f) | CMac NBea SSta |
| | - 'Hercules' (m) | CMac NBea NLar |
| | - Hermaphrodite Group ♀H4 | EBee SDix SEND SPer |
| | ***scandens*** | CMac EBee IMGH NScw SPlb WDin |
| | ***stephanotiifolius*** B&SWJ 4727 **new** | WCru |

## *Celmisia* ✿ (*Asteraceae*)

| | | |
|---|---|---|
| | ***allanii*** | IBlr WAbe |
| | ***alpina*** | IBlr |
| | - large-leaved | IBlr |
| | ***angustifolia*** | IBlr |
| | - silver-leaved | IBlr |
| | ***argentea*** | ECho IBlr WAbe |
| | ***armstrongii*** | ECho |
| | Ballyrogan hybrids | IBlr |
| | ***bellidioides*** | ECho EPot EWes IBlr MDKP |
| | ***bonplandii*** | IBlr |
| | ***brevifolia*** | IBlr |
| | ***coriacea*** misapplied | see *C. semicordata* |
| | ***coriacea*** Raoul | see *C. mackaui* |
| | ***coriacea*** (G.Forst.) Hook.f. | MDun |
| | ***costiniana*** | IBlr |
| | ***dallii*** | IBlr |
| | 'David Shackleton' | IBlr |
| | ***densiflora*** | IBlr |
| | - silver-leaved | IBlr |
| | ***discolor*** | IBlr |
| | ***glandulosa*** | IBlr |

| | |
|---|---|
| ***gracilenta*** | IBlr NSla |
| - CC 563 | NWCA |
| ***graminifolia*** | ECho IBlr |
| ***haastii*** | IBlr |
| § 'Harry Bryce' | IBlr |
| ***hectorii*** | IBlr ITim WAbe |
| ***hectorii* x *ramulosa*** | WAbe |
| ***holosericea*** | IBlr |
| ***hookeri*** | IBlr |
| ***incana*** | IBlr |
| Inshriach hybrids | GKir IBlr NHar |
| ***insignis*** | IBlr |
| ***latifolia*** | IBlr |
| - large-leaved | IBlr |
| ***longifolia*** large-leaved | IBlr |
| - small-leaved | IBlr |
| § ***mackaui*** | GGar IBlr |
| ***major*** var. ***brevis*** new | GKev |
| ***markii*** | IBlr |
| ***monroi*** | IBlr |
| ***prorepens*** | IBlr |
| ***pugioniformis*** | IBlr |
| ***ramulosa*** | EPot NLAp SIng |
| - var. ***tuberculata*** | IBlr NSla |
| ***saxifraga*** | IBlr ITim |
| § ***semicordata*** | GAbr GBuc GCra IBlr NLAp NSla WAbe |
| - subsp. ***aurigans*** | IBlr |
| - subsp. ***stricta*** | IBlr |
| ***sessiliflora*** | IBlr ITim |
| - 'Mount Potts' | IBlr |
| ***spectabilis*** | ECho GKir IBlr MDun |
| - 'Eggleston Silver' | GKev |
| - subsp. ***magnifica*** | GKev IBlr |
| - subsp. ***spectabilis*** var. ***angustifolia*** | IBlr |
| ***spedenii*** | IBlr |
| ***tomentella*** | IBlr |
| ***traversii*** | IBlr |
| ***verbascifolia*** | IBlr |
| § ***walkeri*** | IBlr |
| ***webbiana*** | see *C. walkeri* |

## *Celosia* (*Amaranthaceae*)

| | |
|---|---|
| ***argentea*** var. ***cristata*** | MBri |
| - - Plumosa Group | MBri |

## *Celsia* see *Verbascum*

## x *Celsioverbascum* see *Verbascum*

## *Celtica* see *Stipa*

## *Celtis* (*Ulmaceae*)

| | |
|---|---|
| ***australis*** | CBcs EHig LEdu LPan MGos MMuc SBLw |
| ***biondii*** | EGFP |
| ***bungeana*** | IDee NLar |
| ***caucasica*** | GAuc NLar |
| ***julianae*** | IArd NLar |
| ***koraiensis*** new | EGFP |
| ***occidentalis*** | CDul ELan IArd WBVN |
| ***sinensis*** | CMen LEdu NLar |
| ***tournefortii*** | EGFP |

## *Cenolophium* (*Apiaceae*)

| | |
|---|---|
| ***denudatum*** | CDes CHrt EBee ECha EPPr NChi WPGP |

## *Centaurea* ✿ (*Asteraceae*)

| | |
|---|---|
| HH&K 271 | NBid |
| RCB AM -1 new | WCot |
| RCB AM -6 new | WCot |
| RCB EA-1 new | WCot |
| from Turkey | WPGP |
| ***achtarovii*** | NWCA |
| ***alba*** | EBee LDai |
| ***alpestris*** | CSam EBee NBre NLar WPer |
| ***atropurpurea*** | EBee GQue LDai NDov NLar SPhx WHal WHoo WPer |
| ***bagadensis*** | EBee GAuc |
| ***bella*** | Widely available |
| ***benoistii*** | CDes EBee EGle EWes GBin MBri MRav NBPC NDov SMeo SPhx SUsu WHrl WPGP WSHC |
| ***cana*** hort. | see *C. triumfettii* subsp. *cana* |
| ***candidissima*** misapplied | see *C. cineraria* |
| 'Caramia' | CDes EBee MAvo SMeo SSvw |
| ***cheiranthifolia*** | CDes ECha EMon EPPr NBir WFar WPGP |
| - var. ***purpurascens*** | EMon MAvo |
| § ***cineraria*** | EBee ECre LDai SRms WEas |
| - subsp. ***cineraria*** ♀H3 | WCot |
| ***clementei*** new | CSpe |
| ***cyanus*** | CArn LCro MHer MNHC NPri WFar WJek |
| - 'Black Ball' | CSpe |
| ***cynaroides*** | see *Stemmacantha centaureoides* |
| ***dealbata*** | COIW CPrp CWib EBee EPfP GJos GKir IFoB LAst LBMP LRHS NBPC NBlu NBro NMir NOrc NPri SECG STes WBor WCot WFar WMoo WPer |
| - 'Steenbergii' | EBee EBla EGle ELan GCal GGar GKir LRHS MNFA NBid NBir NGdn NPer NSti SBch SPer SPoG WAbb WCAu WCot WFar WHoo WMnd |
| - 'Steenbergii' variegated (v) | LDai |
| ***debeauxii*** subsp. ***nemoralis*** | LDai |
| ***fischeri*** Willd. | CDes EBee EMon WPGP |
| ***glastifolia*** | CDes EBee EMon GCal MLLN NBre WCot WPGP |
| ***gymnocarpa*** | see *C. cineraria* |
| ***hypoleuca*** | NBid |
| ***jacea*** | CSam EShb GAbr NBid NLar WCot WOut WPer |
| 'John Coutts' | Widely available |
| 'Jordy' | EBee IPot LDai |
| ***kotschyana*** | CDes EBee NBid NBre WPGP |
| ***macrocephala*** | Widely available |
| ***maculosa*** | LDai |
| ***marschalliana*** | NBid |
| ***mollis*** | NBid |
| ***montana*** | Widely available |
| - 'Alba' | Widely available |
| § - 'Carnea' | CCVN CElw CPom CSam CTca EBee EBla ECha EGle EMon GMaP LLWP MAvo NBir NChi NLar SAga SMeo SPhx STes WCAu WMoo WSHC |
| - 'Gold Bullion' | CDes CSpe EBee EBla ECtt EGle ELan ELon EMon EPPr EWes GBuc GKir GMaP LDai MCCP MRav NBid NBir NLar NPro SMad SUsu WBor WCAu |
| - 'Gold Strike' | EBee |
| - 'Grandiflora' | EBee MBri |
| - 'Horwood Gold' | LHop |
| - 'Joyce' | CDes CElw CPom EBee EBla EMon LDai NBid NLar |
| - 'Lady Flora Hastings' | CBre CDes CElw CKno CMdw CPom CSam CSpe CTca EBla EMon GMac LDai LEdu MAvo NBid SUsu WPGP |

| | | |
|---|---|---|
| | - lilac-flowered | NBid |
| | - 'Ochroleuca' | EGoo EMon GBuc LDai MLLN NBid NBre |
| | - 'Parham' | CElw CMHG CPrp CSev EBee EBla ECtt ELan GBuc GCal LBMP LHop LLWG LLWP LRHS LSRN MCot MRav MSte MWat NBid NSti SPer SPla SPlb WFar WMnd |
| | - 'Purple Heart' | EBee EBla IPot NBPC NBPN NPri SMrm |
| | - 'Purple Prose' | EMon |
| | - 'Purpurea' | CDes CPom |
| | - 'Rosea' | see *C. montana* 'Carnea' |
| * | - ***violacea*** | NBid |
| | - 'Violetta' | EBee NBir WFar WMoo |
| | ***montana* x *triumfettii*** | CDes WCot |
| | ***moschata*** | see *Amberboa moschata* |
| | ***nervosa*** | see *C. uniflora* subsp. *nervosa* |
| | ***nigra*** | CArn COld CRWN EBWF EBee EBla GJos NBre NLan NMir NSco SECG WMoo WSFF |
| | - var. ***alba*** | CArn CBre NBid |
| | - subsp. ***rivularis*** | ECha LDai NBid NBre |
| | ***orientalis*** | CSpe EBee EWes LLWG MHar MMHG MNFA NBre NDov NLar SMeo SPhx WHal WPer |
| | ***pannonica*** subsp. ***pannonica*** | NBid WSHC |
| | ***phrygia*** | COlW EBee GAbr NBid NBre NLar WPer WRos |
| | - subsp. ***pseudophrygia*** | NBid |
| | ***pulcherrima*** | COlW EBee ECha EMon MLLN NBre NChi WPer |
| | 'Pulchra Major' | see *Stemmacantha centaureoides* |
| | ***rhapontica*** | see *Stemmacantha rhapontica* |
| | ***rigidifolia*** | EGle |
| | ***rothrockii*** | LDai |
| | ***rupestris*** | EBee NBre NDov SGar SPhx WPer |
| | ***ruthenica*** | EBee GQue MNFA MSte NBre NGdn NHol NLar SPer SPhx SPlb WCot WFar |
| * | - 'Alba' | MSte |
| | ***scabiosa*** | CArn CHrt CRWN CSec CWib EBWF MHer NBid NBre NDov NLan NMir NPri NSco SECG SPoG WPer |
| | - f. ***albiflora*** | EBee LRHS NDov |
| | ***simplicicaulis*** | CDes CSam CWan EBee ECrN EGle GAbr GBri MTho SRms WEas WHoo WPer WSHC |
| | ***thracica*** | EBee LDai SAga WCot |
| | ***triumfetti*** 'Blue Dreams' | CPBP EMon LDai MLLN |
| | - 'Hoar Frost' | CDes EMon NDov WPGP |
| I | - subsp. ***cana*** 'Rosea' | WBrk |
| | - subsp. ***stricta*** | CDes CPrp EBee EMon GBuc MSte NBre WFar |
| | ***uniflora*** | CDes EBee LDai |
| § | - subsp. ***nervosa*** | NBid NBre NBro WPer |
| | ***woronowii*** | LDai |

## *Centaurium* (*Gentianaceae*)

| | | |
|---|---|---|
| | ***erythraea*** | CArn EBWF GPoy MHer MSal |
| * | ***littorale*** 'Album' | CSec |
| | ***scilloides*** | CPBP MTho NLAp NMen NSla NWCA WAbe |

## *Centella* (*Apiaceae*)

| | | |
|---|---|---|
| § | ***asiatica*** | CArn EOHP GPoy ILis MSal WJek |

## *Centradenia* (*Melastomataceae*)

| | | |
|---|---|---|
| | ***inaequilateralis*** | CCCN |
| | - 'Cascade' | CHal MBri SPet |

## *Centranthus* (*Valerianaceae*)

| | | |
|---|---|---|
| § | ***lecoqii*** | ECtt EWes LPla SPhx WCot |
| § | ***ruber*** | Widely available |
| * | - 'Alba Pura' | NBPC |
| § | - 'Albus' | Widely available |
| | - 'Atrococcineus' | ECha SPoG WPer |
| | - var. ***coccineus*** | CBcs CHrt CKno EBee EDAr EGoo ELan EPfP GAbr GMaP LAst LBMP LRHS MNHC MRav MWat NBlu NPri NVic SEND SMrm SPer SPhx SPla WCAu WCot WFar |
| | - mauve-flowered | NBir |
| | - mauve-flowered misapplied | see *C. lecoqii* |
| | - 'Roseus' | WMoo WOVN |
| | - 'Snowcloud' | COlW CSev ECtt EPfP MNHC |
| | 'White Cloud' | WJek |

## *Centratherum* (*Asteraceae*)

| | | |
|---|---|---|
| | ***punctatum*** | CHrt |

## *Centropogon* (*Campanulaceae*)

| | | |
|---|---|---|
| | ***costaricae*** B&SWJ 10455 | WCru |
| | aff. ***ferrugineus*** B&SWJ 10663 new | WCru |

## *Cephalanthera* (*Orchidaceae*)

| | | |
|---|---|---|
| | ***falcata*** | EFEx GEdr |
| | ***longibracteata*** | EFEx GEdr |

## *Cephalanthus* (*Rubiaceae*)

| | | |
|---|---|---|
| | ***occidentalis*** | CWib EBee ELon EMil IDee IMGH MBNS MBlu MBri MGos NLar SMad SPer SPoG SRms WBVN WFar |

## *Cephalaria* (*Dipsacaceae*)

| | | |
|---|---|---|
| | HWJ 695 | SPhx |
| § | ***alpina*** | COlW CSec EBee EBla EHrv EPfP LRHS MHer MNrw MRav NHol NLar SBch SPhx SRms SWat WCot WFar WPer |
| | - 'Nana' | CMil EMon NMen NWCA |
| | ***ambrosioides*** | MLLN |
| | - MESE 503 | EBee |
| | ***caucasica*** | see *C. gigantea* |
| | ***dipsacoides*** | CEnt CFee CKno CSam EBee EBla ECha EMon GQue LDai LPio MHer NBre NLar SMHy SPhx SPoG STes SUsu WHal WMoo |
| § | ***flava*** | EBee NBre |
| | ***galpiniana*** | CSec SPlb |
| | - subsp. ***simplicior*** | EBee |
| § | ***gigantea*** | Widely available |
| | ***graeca*** | see *C. flava* |
| | ***leucantha*** | CArn COlW GBuc MLLN NBid NBre SPhx STes WFar WMoo |
| | ***litvinovii*** | CElw EBee EMon SPhx |
| | ***radiata*** | CSam EBee GBin NDov SPhx |
| | ***tatarica*** hort. | see *C. gigantea* |
| | ***tchihatchewii*** | EBee MLLN |
| | ***uralensis*** | EBee |

## *Cephalotaxus* (*Cephalotaxaceae*)

| | | |
|---|---|---|
| | ***fortunei*** | CDul |
| | - 'Prostrate Spreader' | EHul SLim |
| | ***harringtonii*** | ECho GKir LEdu MRav |
| | - B&SWJ 5416 | WPGP |
| | - var. ***drupacea*** | CDoC NWea |
| | - 'Fastigiata' | CBcs CDoC ECho EHul EOrn GKir IArd IDee LRHS MAsh MBar MBri MGos NPal SBLw SCoo SLim SPoG WDin WFar |

\- 'Gimborn's Pillow' IDee MBar
\- 'Korean Gold' CKen GKir NLar SLim SPoG
\- 'Prostrata' LRHS MBar
***sinensis*** CBcs CMCN

## *Cephalotus* (*Cephalotaceae*)

***follicularis*** SHmp

## *Cerastium* (*Caryophyllaceae*)

***alpinum*** ECho SRms
\- var. ***lanatum*** ECho EWes NLar
***arvense*** NDlv
***candidissimum*** EWes NLar
***tomentosum*** CHal EAlp ECho EPfP GKir NBlu NDlv NPri SPer SPet SPlb SPoG WFar
\- var. ***columnae*** ECha ECho EHoe EPfP EWes WCot
\- 'Silberteppich' LBMP
\- 'Yo Yo' WFar

## *Ceratonia* (*Caesalpiniaceae*)

***siliqua*** CBcs MSal SEND

## *Ceratophyllum* (*Ceratophyllaceae*)

***demersum*** CBen CDWL CRow CWat EHon EMFW EPfP MSKA NSco SWat WMAq

## *Ceratostigma* ✿ (*Plumbaginaceae*)

***abyssinicum*** ELan
'Autumn Blue' EPfP
***griffithii*** CChe CDoC CDul CHll CWSG EBee ECtt EHoe ELan EPfP LAst LRHS MCCP MRav MSwo SPer SPla SPoG SWal WBrE WDin WFar WKif WSHC
\- SF 149/150 ISea
§ ***plumbaginoides*** ♀H3-4 Widely available
***willmottianum*** ♀H3-4 Widely available
\- BWJ 8140 WCru
\- Desert Skies = 'Palmgold'$^{PBR}$ CBcs CSBt EBee ELan EPfP ERas GBuc LAst LCro LHop LRHS MGos NLar SCoo SHBN SLim SMad SPer SSta SSto SWvt
\- Forest Blue = 'Lice'$^{PBR}$ Widely available

## *Ceratotheca* (*Pedaliaceae*)

***triloba*** CSec

## *Cercidiphyllum* ✿ (*Cercidiphyllaceae*)

***japonicum*** ♀H4 Widely available
\- 'Boyd's Dwarf' LRHS MBri NLar
\- 'Herkenrode Dwarf' MBri NLar
\- 'Heronswood Globe' CPMA EPfP MBlu NLar SSta
\- 'Kreukenberg Dwarf' **new** CPMA
\- 'Morioka Weeping' CTho SSta
§ - f. ***pendulum*** ♀H4 CBcs CDul CEnd CLnd CMCN CPMA CWSG EBee EHig EMil EPfP GKir LRHS MAsh MBlu MGos NLar SCoo SHBN SLim SPer SPoG SSpi WDin WOrn
\- - 'Amazing Grace' CTho LLHF MBlu SSta
\- 'Raspberry' MBri
\- Red Fox see *C. japonicum* 'Rotfuchs'
§ - 'Rotfuchs' CBcs CEnd CMCN CPMA EBee EHig EPfP GKir LRHS MAsh MBlu MBri MGos NCGa NLar NPal SCoo SLim SMad SPoG SSpi SSta WPGP
\- 'Ruby' CPMA MBlu MBri NLar
\- 'Strawberry' CBcs MBlu MBri NLar
\- 'Tidal Wave' MBri NLar
***magnificum*** CBcs CDoC CDul CEnd CMCN EPfP IDee MBri NLar WCru WPGP
\- f. ***pendulum*** see *C. japonicum* f. *pendulum*

## *Cercis* (*Caesalpiniaceae*)

sp. **new** WFoF
***canadensis*** CBcs CDul CLnd CMCN EPfP MGos NHol NLar NWea SCoo SLim SPer WPat
\- f. ***alba*** 'Royal White' CPMA EPfP IArd MBlu
\- 'Appalachian Red' CPMA MBlu MBri NBhm NLar
\- 'Covey' MBri NLar
\- 'Flame' CPMA NBhm
\- 'Forest Pansy' ♀H4 Widely available
\- 'Hearts of Gold' **new** MGos
\- 'Lavender Twist' MGos NLar
§ - var. ***occidentalis*** NLar NMun SOWG
\- 'Pauline Lily' MBri NLar
\- 'Rubye Atkinson' CPMA MBri NLar SSpi
***chinensis*** CBcs NLar SPer SSta WDin
\- 'Avondale' CAbP CBcs CDoC CEnd CPMA CWib EBee EHig EMil EPfP ERas EWes IArd LRHS LSRN MAsh MBlu MBri MGos MMuc NHol NLar SCoo SLim SSpi SWvt WPGP WPat
\- 'Don Egolf' MGos MPkF
***gigantea*** NLar
***griffithii*** EGFP LLHF NLar NMun
***occidentalis*** see *C. canadensis* var. *occidentalis*
***racemosa*** IDee NLar WPGP
***reniformis*** 'Oklahoma' CPMA EBee EHig NLar
\- 'Texas White' CBcs CPMA NLar SLim
***siliquastrum*** ♀H4 Widely available
\- f. ***albida*** EBee ECrN EPfP LPan LRHS SPoG SSpi WCFE
\- 'Bodnant' EBee EHig EMil EPfP EWes LAst LLHF MBlu MBri NLar
\- 'White Swan' **new** EWes
***yunnanensis*** EBee NLar

## *Cerinthe* (*Boraginaceae*)

***glabra*** CSec NBre SPlb
***major*** LEdu WEas
\- 'Kiwi Blue' CHll LEdu MDKP
\- 'Purpurascens' CChe CHrt CMea CSec CSpe EBee EGoo EHrv ELan EPfP IFoB LBMP MCot MSCN NLar SGar SMad SMrm SPer SPoG
\- 'Yellow Gem' NLar
***retorta*** CSpe LDai

## *Ceropegia* (*Asclepiadaceae*)

***barklyi*** CHal LToo
***conrathii*** LToo
***fusca*** EShb
§ ***linearis*** subsp. ***woodii*** ♀H1 CHal EShb MBri SRms
§ - subsp. ***woodii*** 'Lady Heart' (v) EShb
\- - 'Variegata' see *C. linearis* subsp. *woodii* 'Lady Heart'
***multiflora*** LToo
***pubescens*** GWJ 9441 WCru
***woodii*** see *C. linearis* subsp. *woodii*

## *Ceroxylon* (*Arecaceae*)

***alpinum*** LPJP LPal
***ventricosum*** LPal

## *Cestrum* (*Solanaceae*)

***aurantiacum*** EShb
***auriculatum*** SOWG
x ***cultum*** CHll EShb
\- 'Cretan Purple' CBcs CHll CWan EBee ELon EPfP EShb EWTr LHop LRHS MBri SEND SMad SOWG SPoG SUsu WCFE WSHC

| | |
|---|---|
| ***diurnum*** x ***nocturnum*** | EShb |
| § ***elegans*** | CDoC CHEx CHal CHll CPLG CSev EBee LRHS MJnS SLon SOWG WCot WDin WWlt |
| ***fasciculatum*** | EShb GBin MBri SMad SOWG |
| 'Newellii' 🏆H2 | CBcs CHEx CMHG CPLG CSev CWib EBak EBee ELan ELon EPfP EShb LRHS SDnm SEND SGar SOWG WBor WPic WSHC |
| ***nocturnum*** | CBcs CDoC CDow CHal CHll EBak EOHP EShb MJnS SHBN SOWG WCFE |
| ***parqui*** 🏆H3 | CAbb CBcs CHEx CHll CMHG CWib EBee ELan EPfP EShb IDee LRHS MCot SDix SDnm SGar SLon SMad SMrm SOWG SUsu WCot WKif WSHC WWlt |
| - 'Orange Essence' | WCot |
| ***psittacinum*** | CPLG |
| ***purpureum*** misapplied | see *Iochroma cyaneum* 'Trebah' |
| ***purpureum*** (Lindl.) Standl. | see *C. elegans* |
| ***roseum*** | CPLG CSev |
| - 'Ilnacullin' | CFee |
| * ***splendens*** | SOWG |
| ***violaceum*** misapplied | see *Iochroma cyaneum* 'Trebah' |

## *Ceterach* (*Aspleniaceae*)

| | |
|---|---|
| ***officinarum*** | see *Asplenium ceterach* |

## *Chaenomeles* (*Rosaceae*)

| | |
|---|---|
| ***cathayensis*** | CTho LEdu NLar |
| § ***japonica*** | ECrN MBar WDin WFar |
| - 'Chojubai' **new** | CMen |
| - 'Cido' | CAgr LBuc |
| - 'Orange Beauty' | WFar |
| - 'Sargentii' | CMac |
| 'John Pilger' | NHol |
| ***lagenaria*** | see *C. speciosa* |
| 'Madame Butterfly' | CDoC CEnd EBee EWTr GKir LSRN MAsh MBri MRav NLar SMad SPer SPoG WLeb |
| ***maulei*** | see *C. japonica* |
| 'Orange Star' | EBee |
| ***sinensis*** | see *Pseudocydonia sinensis* |
| § ***speciosa*** | CMen CSam ISea MBar MGan NWea |
| - 'Apple Blossom' | see *C. speciosa* 'Moerloosei' |
| - 'Aurora' | LRHS |
| - 'Brilliant' | EPfP |
| - 'Contorta' | CDoC EBee SPoG |
| - 'Falconnet Charlet' (d) | MRav |
| - 'Geisha Girl' 🏆H4 | Widely available |
| - 'Grayshott Salmon' | NHol NPro WFar |
| § - 'Moerloosei' 🏆H4 | Widely available |
| - 'Nivalis' | Widely available |
| - 'Rubra Grandiflora' | WBVN |
| - 'Simonii' (d) | CBcs EBee EHig EPfP LRHS MGos MRav NHol NWea SPer WFar |
| - 'Snow' | CSBt MRav MSwo NHol |
| - 'Umbilicata' | SPer SRms |
| - 'Yukigoten' | CDoC CWib EBee LRHS NLar |
| x ***superba*** | STre |
| - 'Boule de Feu' | CTri CWib ECtt MCoo |
| - 'Cameo' (d) | CAbP CChe CEnd CSBt EBee ECrN EPfP LHop LRHS MBri MHav MRav NCGa NLar SLPl WRHF |
| - 'Clementine' | CWib EBee |
| - 'Crimson and Gold' 🏆H4 | Widely available |
| - 'Elly Mossel' | CMac CSBt CWib WFar |
| - 'Ernst Finken' | EBee NLar |
| - 'Fascination' | NLar |
| - 'Fire Dance' | CDul CWib EBee ECrN ECtt MAsh MSwo NHol NLar SPer |
| - 'Hollandia' | MGos |
| - 'Issai White' | EBee LRHS MRav |
| - 'Jet Trail' | CBcs CSBt EBee ELan EPfP LAst LRHS MAsh MGos MRav MSwo NBlu NLar NPro SLPl SPoG SSta WFar |
| - 'Knap Hill Scarlet' 🏆H4 | CDoC CDul EBee ECot EPfP GGal GKir LHop LRHS MAsh MGos MRav NHol SEND SLim SPoG SRms WDin WFar |
| - 'Lemon and Lime' | ELan EPfP MGos MRav NSti SLon SPer |
| - 'Nicoline' 🏆H4 | CBcs CDoC CDul EBee EPfP GKir LRHS MBri MRav NPri WDin WFar |
| - 'Pink Lady' 🏆H4 | Widely available |
| - 'Red Joy' | NLar SPoG |
| - 'Red Trail' | MRav |
| - 'Rowallane' 🏆H4 | EBee ECrN ELan EPfP ERas MNHC MRav SHBN |
| - 'Salmon Horizon' | MGos NLar |
| - 'Tortuosa' | EBee LHop MBNS SPoG |
| 'Toyo-nishiki' | EBee NLar |

## *Chaenorhinum* (*Scrophulariaceae*)

| | |
|---|---|
| § ***origanifolium*** | ECho GKev MBrN SBch SPlb WCot |
| - 'Blue Dream' | CEnt CSpe EBee ECho ECtt GKev NVic SPoG SWvt WFar WMoo WPer |
| - 'Summer Skies' | NPri SGar SPet WFar |

## *Chaerophyllum* (*Apiaceae*)

| | |
|---|---|
| ***hirsutum*** | CRow |
| - 'Roseum' | Widely available |
| ***temulum*** **new** | CArn |

## *Chamaebatiaria* (*Rosaceae*)

| | |
|---|---|
| ***millefolium*** | NLar |

## *Chamaecyparis* ✿ (*Cupressaceae*)

| | |
|---|---|
| 'Erecta Viridis' **new** | MHav |
| ***formosensis*** | CKen |
| ***lawsoniana*** | CDul CSBt EHul EMac MBar NWea WBVN WDin WMou |
| - 'Albospica' (v) | GKir MBar WFar |
| - 'Albospica Nana' | see *C. lawsoniana* 'Nana Albospica' |
| - 'Albovariegata' (v) | MBar SHaC |
| - 'Allumii Aurea' | see *C. lawsoniana* 'Alumigold' |
| - 'Allumii Magnificent' | CDul MAsh NLar |
| § - 'Alumigold' | CDul CSBt CWib GKir MAsh MBar MGos SCoo SHaC WDin |
| - 'Alumii' | CMac CTri EHul GKir MAsh MBar MGos NWea SHaC |
| - 'Argentea' | see *C. lawsoniana* 'Argenteovariegata' |
| § - 'Argenteovariegata' (v) | CDoC CMac GKir SHaC SPoG |
| - 'Aurea' | CDul |
| - 'Aurea Densa' 🏆H4 | CFee CKen CMac CRob CSBt CTri ECho EHul EOrn EPfP LAst MAsh MBar MGos SCoo STre WGor |
| - 'Aureovariegata' (v) | GKir MBar |
| § - 'Barabits' Globe' | MBar |
| § - 'Bleu Nantais' | CKen CMac CRob CSBt ECho EHul GKir LBee LRHS MAsh MBar MGos SCoo SHBN SLim SPoG WCFE WFar |
| - 'Blom' | CKen EHul MBri |
| § - 'Blue Gown' | EHul MBar MGos SHaC SRms |
| § - 'Blue Jacket' | NWea |
| - Blue Nantais | see *C. lawsoniana* 'Bleu Nantais' |
| - 'Blue Surprise' | CKen EHul MBar WFar |
| - 'Brégéon' | CKen NLar |
| - 'Broomhill Gold' | CDoC CMac CRob CSBt ECho EHul GKir LAst MAsh MBar MGos NHol SCoo SLim SPer SPla SPoG WDin |
| * - 'Burkwood's Blue' | MBar |
| - 'Caudata' | CKen MBar NLar |

| | | |
|---|---|---|
| | - 'Chantry Gold' | EHul SCoo |
| § | - 'Chilworth Silver' ♀H4 | CRob CSBt EHul GKir LBee LRHS MAsh MBar SCoo SHBN SHaC SLim SPer SPoG SRms WBVN WDin WFar |
| | - 'Columnaris' | CBcs CDoC CMac ECho EPfP GKir LBee LMaj LRHS MBar MBri MGos NWea SCoo SHBN SPoG WFar |
| | - 'Columnaris Aurea' | see *C. lawsoniana* 'Golden Spire' |
| N | - 'Columnaris Glauca' | CSBt CWib EHul GKir MAsh MGos SBod SCoo SHaC SPer WDin WFar |
| | - 'Crawford's Compact' | CMac |
| | - 'Cream Crackers' | EHul |
| | - 'Cream Glow' | CDoC CKen CRob CSBt GKir LRHS MGos NLar SCoo SLim SPoG WFar WGor |
| | - 'Croftway' | EHul |
| | - 'Dik's Weeping' | CDoC GKir NWea |
| | - 'Dorset Gold' | CMac |
| | - 'Duncanii' | ECho EHul |
| | - 'Dutch Gold' | EHul MAsh |
| | - 'Dwarf Blue' | see *C. lawsoniana* 'Pick's Dwarf Blue' |
| | - 'Eclipse' | CKen |
| | - 'Elegantissima' ambig. | CKen CMac MGos |
| | - 'Ellwoodii' ♀H4 | CDul CMac CSBt CTri CWib ECho EHul EPfP GKir LAst MAsh MBar MGos NBlu NWea SCoo SHaC SLim SPer SPoG WDin WFar WMoo |
| I | - 'Ellwoodii Glauca' | SPlb |
| | - 'Ellwood's Empire' | EHul GKir |
| | - 'Ellwood's Gold' ♀H4 | Widely available |
| | - 'Ellwood's Gold Pillar' | CRob ECho EHul GKir LBee MAsh MGos NHol SCoo SLim SPla SPoG WFar |
| § | - 'Ellwood's Nymph' | CKen CRob ECho GKir MAsh MBar SCoo SHBN SLim WFar WGor |
| | - Ellwood's Pillar = 'Flolar' | CDoC CMac CRob EHul GKir LAst LBee LRHS MAsh MBar MBri MGos NBlu NHol SCoo SHaC SLim SPla WCFE WDin WFar |
| | - 'Ellwood's Pygmy' | CMac ECho GKir MBar |
| | - 'Ellwood's Silver' | ECho MAsh WFar |
| | - 'Ellwood's Silver Threads' | CMac |
| | - 'Ellwood's Variegata' | see *C. lawsoniana* 'Ellwood's White' |
| § | - 'Ellwood's White' (v) | CKen CMac CSBt ECho EHul EPfP MBar SHBN WFar |
| I | - 'Emerald' | CKen MBar |
| | - 'Emerald Spire' | CMac MAsh NHol |
| | - 'Empire' | WFar |
| | - 'Erecta Aurea' | ECho EHul MGos SCoo SHaC |
| | - 'Erecta Filiformis' | MBar |
| | - 'Erecta Viridis' | CMac CTrG GKir MBar NWea SHaC WDin WFar |
| | - 'Ericoides' | EHul |
| | - 'Erika' | ECho MBar |
| | - 'Filiformis Compacta' | EHul |
| | - 'Fleckellwood' | CRob CWib EHul MAsh MBar |
| | - 'Fletcheri' ♀H4 | CMac CWib EHul GKir MBar NWea SBod SHBN SHaC WDin WFar |
| | - 'Fletcheri Aurea' | see *C. lawsoniana* 'Yellow Transparent' |
| | - 'Fletcher's White' | ECho EHul MBar |
| | - 'Forsteckensis' | CKen ECho EHul EOrn GKir MBar NLar NWea SCoo SPoG SRms WFar WGor |
| | - 'Fraseri' | CMac MBar NWea SHaC |
| | - 'Gimbornii' ♀H4 | CMac ECho EHul GKir LBee MAsh MBar SCoo SLim SRms WFar |
| | - 'Globosa' | MGos |
| | - 'Globus' | see *C. lawsoniana* 'Barabits' Globe' |
| | - 'Gnome' | CDoC CMac CRob ECho EHul EMil EOrn GEdr LAst MBar MGos SCoo SLim SPoG WGor |
| | - 'Gold Flake' | MBar MGos |
| | - 'Gold Lace' | SHaC |
| | - 'Gold Splash' | MBar |
| | - 'Golden King' | MBar NWea |
| § | - 'Golden Pot' | CDoC CRob CSBt CWib EHul GKir LBee LRHS MBar MGos NHol SCoo SPoG WDin WFar |
| § | - 'Golden Queen' | EHul |
| | - 'Golden Showers' | EHul |
| § | - 'Golden Spire' | MBar NLar SHaC WFar |
| | - 'Golden Triumph' | EHul |
| | - 'Golden Wonder' | EHul LBee MBar MGos NLar NWea SCoo SHaC SRms WDin WFar |
| | - 'Goldfinger' | CDoC |
| | - 'Grant's Gold' | EHul |
| | - 'Grayswood Feather' | CDoC CRob CSBt EHul EMil GKir LBee LRHS MAsh MBar MGos SCoo SHaC SLim SPlb |
| | - 'Grayswood Gold' | EHul GKir LBee MBar SHaC |
| | - 'Grayswood Pillar' ♀H4 | CMac EHul LRHS MBar MGos |
| * | - 'Grayswood Spire' | CMac |
| | - 'Green Globe' | CDoC CKen CRob CSBt EHul LBee LRHS MAsh MBar MGos SAga SCoo SLim WAbe WDin |
| § | - 'Green Hedger' ♀H4 | CMac CSBt MBar MHav NBlu NWea SCoo SHaC SRms WFar |
| § | - 'Green Pillar' | CRob CWib ECho LAst LBee LRHS MBar SCoo SHBN SHaC |
| | - 'Green Pinnacle' | CRob |
| | - 'Green Spire' | see *C. lawsoniana* 'Green Pillar' |
| | - 'Hillieri' | MBar |
| | - 'Hogger's Blue Gown' | see *C. lawsoniana* 'Blue Gown' |
| | - 'Imbricata Pendula' | CDoC CKen GKir IDee LRHS NLar SLim |
| | - 'Intertexta' ♀H4 | EHul |
| | - 'Ivonne' | EHul GKir MGos NBlu WOrn |
| | - 'Jackman's Green Hedger' | see *C. lawsoniana* 'Green Hedger' |
| | - 'Jackman's Variety' | see *C. lawsoniana* 'Green Pillar' |
| | - 'Jeanette' | MGos |
| | - 'Kelleriis Gold' | EHul MBar |
| | - 'Kilmacurragh' ♀H4 | GKir MBar MGos NWea WCFE |
| | - 'Kilworth Column' | CDoC CRob MGos NLar NWea SCoo |
| | - 'Knowefieldensis' | CMac ECho EHul |
| | - 'Lane' misapplied | see *C. lawsoniana* 'Lanei Aurea' |
| | - 'Lanei' misapplied | see *C. lawsoniana* 'Lanei Aurea' |
| | - 'Lanei' | CSBt CWib ECho MGos SCoo SHaC WDin WFar |
| § | - 'Lanei Aurea' ♀H4 | CMac EHul MBar MGos NWea WFar |
| | - 'Lemon Pillar' | WDin |
| | - 'Lemon Queen' | CSBt EHul LBee LRHS |
| | - 'Limelight' | MGos |
| | - 'Little Spire' ♀H4 | CDoC ECho EOrn GKir LBee LRHS MBar MBri MGos NHol SCoo SLim SPoG WGor |
| | - 'Lombartsii' | WFar |
| | - 'Lutea' ♀H4 | CMac EHul GKir MGos NWea |
| § | - 'Lutea Nana' ♀H4 | CMac EHul MAsh MBar MGos NLar SCoo |
| § | - 'Lutea Smithii' | MBar NWea |
| | - 'Luteocompacta' | LBee SHBN |
| | - 'Lycopodioides' | ECho MBar |
| * | - 'MacPenny's Gold' | CMac |
| | - 'Milford Blue Jacket' | see *C. lawsoniana* 'Blue Jacket' |
| § | - 'Minima' | MBar SRms |
| | - 'Minima Argentea' | see *C. lawsoniana* 'Nana Argentea' |
| | - 'Minima Aurea' ♀H4 | Widely available |
| | - 'Minima Densa' | see *C. lawsoniana* 'Minima' |
| | - 'Minima Glauca' ♀H4 | CDul CMac CSBt ECho EHul EPfP GEdr GKir MAsh MBar MGos NHol NWea SCoo SHBN SLim SPla WDin WFar |
| | - 'Moonlight' | MBar MGos |

| | | |
|---|---|---|
| * | - 'Moonsprite' | ECho LRHS SCoo SLim SPoG |
| | - 'Naberi' **new** | GKir |
| | - 'Nana' | LAst MBar |
| § | - 'Nana Albospica' (v) | CRob ECho EHul EOrn LBee LRHS MBar SCoo SPoG WFar WGor |
| § | - 'Nana Argentea' | CKen CMac EHul EPfP SCoo WFar WGor |
| | - 'Nana Lutea' | see *C. lawsoniana* 'Lutea Nana' |
| | - 'New Silver' | MGos SPoG |
| | - 'Nicole' | ECho LAst MAsh SCoo SLim SPoG WGor |
| | - 'Nidiformis' | EHul MBar NWea SCoo SRms |
| | - 'Nyewoods' | see *C. lawsoniana* 'Chilworth Silver' |
| | - 'Nymph' | see *C. lawsoniana* 'Ellwood's Nymph' |
| | - 'Pagoda' **new** | CRob |
| | - 'Parsons' | CDoC |
| § | - 'Pelt's Blue' ♀H4 | CBcs CDoC CDul CKen CSBt EHul LBee LRHS MBar MGos NLar SCoo SHBN SHaC SLim SPoG WDin WFar WOrn |
| | - 'Pembury Blue' ♀H4 | CDoC CDul CMac CSBt CWib ECho EHul EPfP GKir LBee LRHS MAsh MBar MGos NBlu NWea SBod SCoo SHBN SHaC SLim SPer SPoG WDin WFar |
| | - 'Pendula' | CDoC MBar |
| § | - 'Pick's Dwarf Blue' | MBar MGos NHol SCoo WGor |
| | - Pot of Gold | see *C. lawsoniana* 'Golden Pot' |
| | - 'Pottenii' | CMac CSBt ECho EHul GKir LBee LRHS MAsh MBar MGos NWea SCoo SHBN SHaC WDin WFar |
| | - 'Pygmaea Argentea' (v) ♀H4 | CKen CMac CWib ECho EHul EOrn EPfP GKir LBee LRHS MAsh MBar MBri MGos NBlu NHol SLim SPoG SRms WCFE WDin WFar |
| | - 'Pygmy' | EHul GKir MBar NHol NLar SCoo SLim |
| | - 'Rijnhof' | EHul LBee |
| | - 'Rimpelaar' **new** | CDoC MGos |
| | - 'Rogersii' | MBar SRms WFar |
| | - 'Romana' | MBri |
| | - 'Royal Gold' | EHul |
| | - 'Silver Queen' (v) | CKen MBar |
| | - 'Silver Threads' (v) | CMac CRob ECho EHul GKir LBee LRHS MAsh MBar WFar |
| | - 'Silver Tip' (v) | ECho EHul SCoo SLim |
| | - 'Slocock' | SHBN |
| | - 'Smithii' | see *C. lawsoniana* 'Lutea Smithii' |
| | - 'Snow Flurry' (v) | CKen ECho EHul WFar |
| | - 'Snow White' PBR (v) | CRob ECho EHul GKir LBee LRHS MAsh MBar MBri MGos NHol SCoo SLim SPla SPoG WFar WGor |
| | - 'Somerset' | CMac MBar MGos |
| | - 'Springtime' PBR | CDoC CRob EHul LBee SCoo SLim SPoG WGor |
| | - 'Stardust' ♀H4 | CBcs CDoC CDul CMac CRob CSBt CTri CWib EHul GKir LPan MAsh MBar MBri NBlu SBod SCoo SHBN SHaC SLim SPer SPoG WDin |
| | - 'Stewartii' | CDul CTri MBar NWea SBod SCoo SHBN SHaC |
| | - 'Stilton Cheese' | MBar NHol SCoo |
| * | - 'Summer Cream' | EHul |
| | - 'Summer Snow' (v) | CDoC CDul CMac CRob ECho EHul EPfP GKir LBee LRHS MAsh MBar MGos NHol SCoo SLim SPla SRms WFar |
| | - 'Sunkist' | CSBt SCoo SLim WFar |
| | - 'Tamariscifolia' | CDoC EHul MBar WCFE WDin WFar |
| | - 'Tharandtensis Caesia' | EOrn MBar WFar |
| | - 'Tilford' | EHul |

| | | |
|---|---|---|
| | - 'Treasure' (v) | CRob CSBt CSli ECho EHul EPfP LBee LRHS MAsh MBar NHol SCoo SLim SPoG WFar |
| | - 'Triomf van Boskoop' | MBar |
| | - 'Van Pelt' | see *C. lawsoniana* 'Pelt's Blue' |
| | - 'Van Pelt's Blue' | see *C. lawsoniana* 'Pelt's Blue' |
| | - 'Versicolor' (v) | MBar |
| | - 'Waterfall' | SMad |
| | - 'Westermannii' (v) | CMac EHul SCoo SLim |
| | - 'White Edge' | WFar |
| | - 'White Spot' (v) | ECho EHul GKir LBee LRHS MBar MBri NBlu SCoo SHaC SLim SPoG WBVN WFar |
| | - 'White Wonder' | MGos |
| | - 'Winston Churchill' | CSBt MBar MGos SBod |
| | - 'Wisselii' ♀H4 | CDoC CKen CMac CTrG ECho EHul EMil GKir LBee MBar MBri NLar NWea SCoo SHaC SRms WDin WFar WMoo |
| | - 'Wisselii Nana' | CKen EHul |
| | - 'Wissel's Saguaro' | CDoC CKen NLar SLim |
| | - 'Witzeliana' | CDul CSBt ECho EOrn MBar MGos NLar WOrn |
| | - 'Wyevale Silver' | MBar |
| | - 'Yellow Queen' | see *C. lawsoniana* 'Golden Queen' |
| | - 'Yellow Success' | see *C. lawsoniana* 'Golden Queen' |
| § | - 'Yellow Transparent' | MBar SCoo SHBN SHaC SPoG |
| | - 'Yvonne' | CDul CRob ECho GKir LRHS MAsh MBar MGos NHol SCoo SLim SPoG |
| | ***leylandii*** | see x *Cupressocyparis leylandii* |
| | ***nootkatensis*** | ECho MBar SHaC |
| | - 'Aurea' | GKir WDin |
| | - 'Aureovariegata' (v) | EHul |
| | - 'Compacta' | CTri MBar |
| | - 'Glauca' | CTho MBar NWea |
| | - 'Gracilis' | EHul |
| | - 'Green Arrow' | CKen ECho SCoo SLim |
| | - 'Jubilee' | SCoo SLim |
| | - 'Kanada' | NLar |
| | - 'Lutea' | CTri MBar NWea |
| | - 'Nidifera' | MBar |
| | - 'Nordkroken' | NLar |
| | - 'Pendula' ♀H4 | CDoC CDul CKen ECho ELan EOrn EPfP GKir LMaj LPan LRHS MAsh MBar MBri MGos NBlu NWea SCoo WCFE WDin WFar WOrn |
| | - 'Strict Weeper' | CKen NLar SLim SPoG |
| | - 'Variegata' (v) | LRHS MBar |
| | ***obtusa*** 'Albospica' (v) | EHul |
| | - 'Albovariegata' (v) | CKen |
| | - 'Arneson's Compact' | CKen |
| | - 'Aurea' | CDoC SCoo |
| | - 'Aureovariegata' | see *C. obtusa* 'Opaal' |
| | - 'Aurora' | CKen CRob ECho EMil EOrn MBri MGos SPoG |
| * | - 'Autumn Gold' | MBar |
| | - 'Bambi' | CKen EOrn MGos NLar WThu |
| | - 'Barkenny' | CKen |
| | - 'Bartley' | CKen |
| | - 'Bassett' | CKen |
| | - 'Bess' | CKen |
| | - 'Brigitt' | CKen |
| | - 'Buttonball' | CKen |
| | - 'Caespitosa' | CKen |
| | - 'Chabo-yadori' | CDoC ECho EHul EOrn GKir LRHS MBar MGos SCoo SLim SPoG WFar |
| | - 'Chilworth' | CKen MBar MGos NLar |
| | - 'Chima-anihiba' | CKen |
| | - 'Chirimen' | CDoC CKen MGos NLar |
| | - 'Clarke's Seedling' | CDoC NLar |
| | - 'Confucius' | CDoC CRob EHul MGos NHol |
| | - 'Contorta' | EOrn MBar NLar |
| § | - 'Coralliformis' | CMac ECho EOrn MBar |

| | | |
|---|---|---|
| § | – 'Crippsii' 🏆H4 | CBcs CDoC CDul EHul EOrn GKir MBar MGos NHol SCoo SLim |
| | – 'Crippsii Aurea' | see *C. obtusa* 'Crippsii' |
| | – 'Dainty Doll' | CKen EOrn NLar |
| | – 'Densa' | see *C. obtusa* 'Nana Densa' |
| | – 'Draht' | CDoC MBar NLar SCoo |
| | – 'Draht Hexe' | CKen |
| | – 'Elf' | CKen |
| | – 'Ellie B' | CKen EOrn |
| | – 'Ericoides' | CKen ECho EOrn |
| | – 'Erika' | ECho EOrn |
| | – 'Fernspray Gold' | CDoC CKen CMac CRob CTri ECho EHul EOrn GKir MAsh MBar SBod SCoo SLim SPla SPoG WFar |
| | – 'Flabelliformis' | CKen |
| | – 'Gimborn Beauty' | CDoC |
| | – 'Gnome' | CKen CMen GKir |
| | – 'Gold Fern' | CKen WFar |
| | – 'Gold Tip' | EOrn |
| | – 'Golden Fairy' | CKen EOrn WAbe |
| | – 'Golden Filament' (v) | CKen |
| | – 'Golden Nymph' | CKen EOrn MGos NLar |
| | – 'Golden Sprite' | CDoC CKen MGos NLar |
| | – 'Goldilocks' | EHul |
| | – 'Gracilis Aurea' | CKen |
| | – 'Graciosa' | see *C. obtusa* 'Loenik' |
| | – 'Green Diamond' | CKen |
| | – 'Hage' | CKen EOrn |
| | – 'Hypnoides Nana' | CKen EOrn |
| | – 'Intermedia' | CDoC CKen EOrn MGos WAbe |
| | – 'Ivan's Column' | CKen |
| | – 'Junior' | CKen |
| | – 'Juniperoides' | CKen EOrn WThu |
| | – 'Juniperoides Compacta' | CKen WAbe |
| | – 'Kamarachiba' | CDoC CKen ECho LBee LRHS NLar SCoo SLim SPoG WFar |
| | – 'Kanaamihiba' | MBar NLar |
| | – 'Kerdalo' | NLar SLim SPoG |
| | – 'Konijn' | ECho EHul EOrn |
| | – 'Kosteri' | CDoC CKen CMac CRob ECho EHul ELan EOrn LBee MAsh MBar NHol SCoo SHBN SLim |
| | – 'Kyoto Creeper' | CKen |
| | – 'Leprechaun' | NLar |
| | – 'Limerick' | CKen |
| | – 'Little Markey' | CKen EOrn |
| § | – 'Loenik' | EOrn MBar SCoo |
| | – 'Lycopodioides' | ECho EOrn MGos |
| | – 'Lycopodioides Aurea' | SCoo |
| | – 'Marian' | CKen MGos NLar |
| § | – 'Mariesii' (v) | CKen EOrn LBee SCoo SHBN |
| | – 'Melody' | CKen NLar |
| | – 'Minima' | CKen MGos |
| | – 'Nana' 🏆H4 | CDoC CKen CMac CMen CRob LBee MBar MGos NHol |
| | – 'Nana Aurea' 🏆H4 | CDoC CRob ECho EHul EOrn EPfP GKir MAsh MBar MGos NHol SHBN SPla WBrE WFar |
| | – 'Nana Compacta' | EOrn |
| I | – 'Nana Confucius' | MGos |
| § | – 'Nana Densa' | CDoC CKen CMac NLar WBVN |
| | – 'Nana Gracilis' 🏆H4 | CDoC CDul CKen CMen CSBt CSli ECho EHul ELan EOrn EPfP GEdr GKir MAsh MBar MBri MGos NBlu NHol NWea SCoo SHBN SLim SPla SPoG STre WDin WFar |
| I | – 'Nana Gracilis Aurea' | EHul |
| I | – 'Nana Lutea' | CDoC CKen CRob CSBt ECho EHul EOrn EPfP GKir LBee LRHS MAsh MBar MGos NDlv NHol NWea SCoo SLim SPla SPoG |
| | – 'Nana Pyramidalis' | LBee |
| | – 'Nana Rigida' | see *C. obtusa* 'Rigid Dwarf' |
| | – 'Nana Variegata' | see *C. obtusa* 'Mariesii' |
| § | – 'Opaal' (v) | MBar |
| | – 'Pygmaea' | CSBt ECho EHul EOrn MBar MGos SCoo SLim SPoG |
| | – 'Pygmaea Aurescens' | MBar |
| § | – 'Rigid Dwarf' | CDoC CKen ECho EHul EOrn LBee LRHS MBar NLar SCoo SPoG |
| | – 'Saffron Spray' | CKen SLim |
| | – 'Snowflake' (v) | CDoC CKen CRob ECho EOrn WFar |
| | – 'Snowkist' (v) | CKen |
| | – 'Spiralis' | CKen MBar |
| | – 'Stoneham' | CKen MBar |
| | – 'Suirova-hiba' | SLim |
| | – 'Tempelhof' | CKen CSBt ECho EHul EOrn GKir LRHS MAsh MBar MGos MHav NLar SCoo SLim |
| | – 'Tetragona Aurea' | CBcs CFee CMac ECho EHul EOrn MBar MGos SCoo SLim |
| | – 'Tonia' (v) | CKen EHul EOrn GKir NHol NLar SCoo SLim SPoG WGor |
| | – 'Topsie' | CKen NLar |
| | – 'Torulosa' | see *C. obtusa* 'Coralliformis' |
| | – 'Tsatsumi' | CDoC EMil SCoo |
| | – 'Tsatsumi Gold' | CDoC CKen ECho NLar SCoo SLim SPoG |
| | – 'Verdon' | CKen |
| | – 'Wissel' | CKen EOrn |
| | – 'Wyckoff' | CKen |
| | – 'Yellowtip' (v) | CKen ECho EHul MBar MGos NLar |
| | ***pisifera*** 'Aurea Nana' misapplied | see *C. pisifera* 'Strathmore' |
| | – 'Avenue' | EHul |
| | – 'Baby Blue' | ECho EPfP SCoo SLim |
| | – 'Blue Globe' | CKen EOrn |
| | – 'Boulevard' 🏆H4 | CBcs CDoC CSBt CTri CWib ECho EHul EPfP GKev GKir LBee LRHS MAsh MBar MGos MHav NBlu NWea SHaC SLim SPer SRms STre WBVN WDin WFar WMoo |
| | – 'Compacta' | EOrn |
| | – 'Compacta Variegata' (v) | ECho EOrn MBar NDlv |
| | – 'Curly Tops' | CRob CSBt ECho GKir MGos SCoo SLim |
| | – 'Devon Cream' | CDul CRob ECho LBee LRHS MAsh MBar SCoo WFar |
| | – 'Filifera' | CMac CSBt GKir MBar SCoo WFar |
| | – 'Filifera Aurea' 🏆H4 | CKen CMac CSBt CWib ECho EHul EOrn GKir LBee LRHS MAsh MBar MGos NHol NWea SCoo SPoG SRms WCFE WDin WFar |
| | – 'Filifera Aureovariegata' (v) | CMac EHul MBar SCoo SPoG |
| | – 'Filifera Nana' | ECho EHul ELan EOrn MBar SLim SPoG STre WDin WFar |
| | – 'Filifera Nana Aurea' | see *C. pisifera* 'Golden Mop' |
| | – 'Filifera Sungold' | see *C. pisifera* 'Sungold' |
| | – 'Fuiri-tsukomo' | CKen |
| * | – 'Gold Cascade' | MGos |
| | – 'Gold Cushion' | CKen |
| | – 'Gold Dust' | see *C. pisifera* 'Plumosa Aurea' |
| | – 'Gold Spangle' | CKen ECho EHul MBar WFar |
| § | – 'Golden Mop' 🏆H4 | CKen EHul GKir MAsh |
| | – 'Green Pincushion' | CKen CMen |
| | – 'Hime-himuro' | CKen |
| | – 'Hime-sawara' | CKen CMen EOrn |
| | – 'Margaret' | CKen |
| | – 'Nana' | CKen CMen ECho EHul EPfP MAsh MBar MGos NDlv NHol WFar |
| I | – 'Nana Albovariegata' (v) | CDoC ECho EOrn MAsh MBar SPoG WFar WThu |
| | – 'Nana Aureovariegata' (v) | CDoC CMac CRob CSBt ECho EHul LBee LRHS MAsh MBar NDlv NHol SCoo SLim SPer WFar |

| | | |
|---|---|---|
| I | - 'Nana Compacta' | CMac SRms |
| | - 'Nana Variegata' (v) | LBee LRHS MBar SCoo SLim WFar |
| I | - 'Parslorii' | CKen |
| | - 'Pici' | CKen |
| | - 'Plumosa Albopicta' (v) | MBar |
| § | - 'Plumosa Aurea' | CKen EHul GKir MBar WDin WFar |
| | - 'Plumosa Aurea Compacta' | CKen CMac NDlv |
| I | - 'Plumosa Aurea Compacta Variegata' (v) | CMac |
| | - 'Plumosa Aurea Nana' | CRob ECho MBar MGos NDlv NHol WFar |
| I | - 'Plumosa Aurea Nana Compacta' | CMac |
| | - 'Plumosa Aurescens' | CDoC CMac |
| § | - 'Plumosa Compressa' | CDoC CFee CKen CRob ECho EHul EOrn MAsh MBar SCoo SLim WFar WGor |
| | - 'Plumosa Densa' | see *C. pisifera* 'Plumosa Compressa' |
| | - 'Plumosa Flavescens' | EHul MBar SCoo |
| I | - 'Plumosa Juniperoides' | CKen ECho EHul EOrn MBar SCoo SLim WFar WGor |
| | - 'Plumosa Purple Dome' | see *C. pisifera* 'Purple Dome' |
| I | - 'Plumosa Pygmaea' | MGos NDlv WGor |
| § | - 'Plumosa Rogersii' | CRob EHul EOrn MBar NHol WGor |
| | - 'Pompom' | CRob |
| § | - 'Purple Dome' | EHul EOrn MBar |
| I | - 'Pygmaea Tsukumo' | MGos |
| | - 'Rogersii' | see *C. pisifera* 'Plumosa Rogersii' |
| | - 'Silver and Gold' (v) | EHul MBar |
| | - 'Silver Lode' (v) | CKen EOrn |
| | - 'Snow' (v) | CKen CMac EOrn MBar |
| | - 'Snowflake' | CKen ECho EHul |
| | - 'Spaan's Cannon Ball' | CKen ECho |
| § | - 'Squarrosa' | MBar WDin WFar |
| | - 'Squarrosa Dumosa' | CKen EHul MBar |
| | - 'Squarrosa Intermedia' | MBar |
| I | - 'Squarrosa Lombarts' | CMac CSBt ECho EHul EOrn GKir MBar SCoo |
| | - 'Squarrosa Lutea' | CKen MBar |
| | - 'Squarrosa Sulphurea' | CSBt ECho EHul EOrn EPfP LRHS MAsh MBar SLim SPer SPla STre WBVN WDin WFar |
| | - 'Squarrosa Veitchii' | see *C. pisifera* 'Squarrosa' |
| § | - 'Strathmore' | CKen EHul MBar NHol WDin |
| § | - 'Sungold' | CDoC CKen CRob CSBt ECho EHul GKir LRHS MAsh MBar SCoo SLim SPla SPoG |
| | - 'Tama-himuro' | CKen |
| | - 'Teddy Bear' | MBri NLar NScw |
| | - 'True Blue' | MBri MGos |
| | - 'White Beauty' (v) | SLim |
| * | - 'White Brocade' | CMac |
| | - 'White Pygmy' | EOrn |
| | ***thyoides*** 'Andelyensis' | CFee CMac CRob CSBt ECho EHul EOrn GKir MBar SCoo WFar |
| | - 'Andelyensis Nana' | CKen |
| | - 'Aurea' | EHul MBar |
| | - 'Conica' | CKen |
| | - 'Ericoides' 🏆H4 | CKen CMac CRob CTri ECho EHul EOrn GKir LBee MBar SPlb WDin WFar |
| § | - 'Glauca' | EOrn |
| | - 'Kewensis' | see *C. thyoides* 'Glauca' |
| | - 'Little Jamie' | CKen |
| | - 'Red Star' | see *C. thyoides* 'Rubicon' |
| § | - 'Rubicon' | CMac CRob CSBt ECho EHul EOrn EPfP GKir LBee LRHS MAsh MBar MGos SLim SPla SPoG WFar |
| | - 'Top Point' | CDoC CRob ECho EOrn LBee MAsh MGos SCoo SLim SPoG |
| | - 'Variegata' (v) | EHul MBar |

## *Chamaecytisus* (*Papilionaceae*)

| | | |
|---|---|---|
| § | ***albus*** | GQui WDin |
| § | ***hirsutus*** | MBri WPGP |
| | - var. ***demissus*** | see *C. polytrichus* |
| | ***palmensis*** | CSec |
| § | ***polytrichus*** | WAbe |
| | ***prolifer*** | CPLG NLar |
| § | ***purpureus*** | CBgR CSBt EBee ELan EPfP GKir LRHS MAsh MRav NLar NPri NWea SBod SHBN SPer WBVN WCFE WDin WFar WPat |
| | - f. ***albus*** | CBcs EPfP SHBN SPer |
| § | - 'Atropurpureus' 🏆H4 | CBcs SPer |
| | - 'Incarnatus' | see *C. purpureus* 'Atropurpureus' |
| § | ***supinus*** | CPLG SRms |

## *Chamaedaphne* (*Ericaceae*)

| | | |
|---|---|---|
| | ***calyculata*** | CBcs EBee LRHS SPer WSHC |
| | - 'Nana' | CMHG MBar |

## *Chamaedorea* (*Arecaceae*)

| | | |
|---|---|---|
| | ***elegans*** 🏆H1 | CTsd LPal MBri |
| | ***erumpens*** | see *C. seifrizii* |
| | ***linearis*** | LPal |
| | ***metallica*** misapplied | see *C. microspadix* |
| | ***metallica*** O.F. Cook ex H.E. Moore 🏆H1 | LPal SBig |
| § | ***microspadix*** | CPHo EAmu LPJP LPal SChr |
| | ***radicalis*** | CBrP CPHo EAmu LPJP LPal |
| § | ***seifrizii*** 🏆H1 | LPal |

## *Chamaelirium* (*Melanthiaceae*)

| | | |
|---|---|---|
| | ***luteum*** | CArn |

## *Chamaemelum* (*Asteraceae*)

| | | |
|---|---|---|
| § | ***nobile*** | CArn CHby CPrp CSev CTri CWan ECho ELau EPfP GBar GKir GMac GPoy MBri MHer MNHC NGHP NGdn NPri SPlb SRms SVic WJek WPer |
| | - dwarf | GBar SVic |
| | - dwarf, double-flowered (d) | GBar |
| | - 'Flore Pleno' (d) | Widely available |
| | - 'Treneague' | Widely available |

## *Chamaenerion* see *Chamerion*

## *Chamaepericlymenum* see *Cornus*

## *Chamaerops* (*Arecaceae*)

| | | |
|---|---|---|
| | ***excelsa*** misapplied | see *Trachycarpus fortunei* |
| | ***excelsa*** Thunb. | see *Rhapis excelsa* |
| | ***humilis*** 🏆H3 | Widely available |
| § | - var. ***argentea*** | CBrP CDTJ CPHo CTrC EAmu EPla ETod LPJP LPal MGos NPal |
| | - var. ***cerifera*** | see *C. humilis* var. *argentea* |
| | - 'Vulcano' | CDTJ EAmu LCro MBri MGos SChr SKHP |

## *Chamaespartium* see *Genista*

## *Chamaesphacos* (*Lamiaceae*)

| | | |
|---|---|---|
| | ***ilicifolius*** misapplied | see *Siphocranion macranthum* |

## *Chambeyronia* (*Arecaceae*)

| | | |
|---|---|---|
| | ***macrocarpa*** | LPal |

## *Chamelaucium* (*Myrtaceae*)

| | | |
|---|---|---|
| | ***axillare*** | SOWG |
| | ***uncinatum*** | EShb LRHS SOWG |

## *Chamerion* (*Onagraceae*)

| | | |
|---|---|---|
| § | ***angustifolium*** | EBWF GBar NSco SWat WSFF |

| | |
|---|---|
| § - 'Album' | Widely available |
| - 'Isobel' | CSpe MLLN MRav WCot |
| - 'Stahl Rose' | CHid CMea CWsd EBee EWes MSte NSti SMrm SPhx SSvw STes SUsu SWat WPGP WSHC |
| § ***dodonaei*** | CSec ELan LHop MTho SPhx WFar WSHC |

## *Chasmanthe* (*Iridaceae*)

| | |
|---|---|
| ***aethiopica*** | CPou GGar |
| ***bicolor*** | CPLG CPou EBee IDee |
| ***floribunda*** | CAbb CHEx CPrp CSec CTca EBee EBrs WOut |
| - var. ***duckittii*** | CPrp CSec EBee EBrs ECho EPfP WPGP |
| - - 'Golden Wave' | EBrs |
| - 'Saturnes' | EBee |
| - 'Venus' | EBee EBrs |

## *Chasmanthium* (*Poaceae*)

| | |
|---|---|
| § ***latifolium*** | Widely available |

## *Cheilanthes* (*Adiantaceae*)

| | |
|---|---|
| ***argentea*** | CLAP WAbe WRic |
| ***distans*** | SRms WAbe WRic |
| ***eatonii*** | WAbe |
| - f. ***castanea*** | WAbe |
| ***eckloniana*** | WAbe |
| ***lanosa*** | CCCN CLAP EBee EFer EShb EWes NMyG SRms WCot |
| ***lindheimeri*** | WAbe WCot |
| ***microphylla*** new | LRHS WAbe |
| ***myriophylla*** | WAbe |
| ***nivea*** | WAbe |
| ***sieberi*** | WAbe |
| ***sinuata*** | CLAP |
| ***tomentosa*** | CCCN CLAP SKHP SRms WRic |

## *Cheiranthus* see *Erysimum*

## *Chelidonium* (*Papaveraceae*)

| | |
|---|---|
| ***japonicum*** | see *Hylomecon japonica* |
| ***majus*** | CArn CRWN EBWF GPoy GQui MHer MNHC MSal WCHb WHer WSFF |
| - 'Flore Pleno' (d) | CBre NBid NBro WCFE WCHb WHer WTou |
| - var. ***laciniatum*** | CSec EMon GBar WCot |

## *Chelone* (*Scrophulariaceae*)

| | |
|---|---|
| ***barbata*** | see *Penstemon barbatus* |
| § ***glabra*** | Widely available |
| ***lyonii*** | EBee LEdu MDKP NBre NGdn NLar SPad SPet WMoo WPer WPnP WShi |
| - 'Pink Temptation' new | EBee |
| ***obliqua*** | Widely available |
| - var. ***alba*** | see *C. glabra* |
| - 'Forncett Foremost' | GQui |
| - 'Forncett Poppet' | CBgR NBre |
| - 'Ieniemienie' | EMon |
| - 'Pink Sensation' | EBee MBri NBre WFar |
| * - ***rosea*** | EBee MLLN MMHG NBPC WGwG |

## *Chelonopsis* (*Lamiaceae*)

| | |
|---|---|
| ***moschata*** | CDes CLAP CPom EBee LEdu MHar SMad WMoo WPGP WPrP |
| ***yagiharana*** | CHFP EBee ELon GGar MBri MCCP MDKP MWea NBPC NBhm NBid NSti SBHP WMoo |

## *Chengiopanax* (*Araliaceae*)

| | |
|---|---|
| ***sciadophylloides*** B&SWJ 4728 | WCru |

## *Chenopodium* (*Chenopodiaceae*)

| | |
|---|---|
| ***bonus-henricus*** | CAgr CArn CBod CHby CPrp CWan GBar GPoy ILis MHer MNHC NTHB SIde WCHb WHer WLHH |
| ***botrys*** | MSal |
| ***giganteum*** | ILis MNHC WJek |

## cherimoya see *Annona cherimola*

## cherry, Duke see *Prunus* x *gondouinii*

## cherry, sour or morello see *Prunus cerasus*

## cherry, sweet see *Prunus avium*

## chervil see *Anthriscus cerefolium*

## chestnut, sweet see *Castanea sativa*

## *Chiastophyllum* (*Crassulaceae*)

| | |
|---|---|
| § ***oppositifolium*** ♀H4 | Widely available |
| - 'Frosted Jade' | see *C. oppositifolium* 'Jim's Pride' |
| - 'Jane's Reverse' | EBee WCot |
| § - 'Jim's Pride' (v) | Widely available |
| ***simplicifolium*** | see *C. oppositifolium* |

## *Chiliotrichum* (*Asteraceae*)

| | |
|---|---|
| ***diffusum*** | CWib GGar |
| - 'Siska' | CBcs GBin IFFs SMad WCot |

## *Chilopsis* (*Bignoniaceae*)

| | |
|---|---|
| ***linearis*** | CArn CSec |

## *Chimonanthus* (*Calycanthaceae*)

| | |
|---|---|
| ***fragrans*** | see *C. praecox* |
| ***nitens*** | CBcs NLar |
| § ***praecox*** | Widely available |
| - 'Grandiflorus' ♀H4 | CEnd CPMA EPfP LRHS MAsh MBri SPoG SSpi SSta WPGP WPat |
| - 'Luteus' ♀H4 | CEnd CPMA ECrN ELan EPfP LRHS MAsh MBri MGos MRav NLar SPer SSpi SSta WPGP WPat |
| - 'Sunburst' new | CPMA |
| - 'Trenython' | CEnd CPMA |
| ***yunnanensis*** | NLar |

## *Chimonobambusa* (*Poaceae*)

| | |
|---|---|
| ***falcata*** | see *Drepanostachyum falcatum* |
| ***hejiangensis*** | EPla |
| ***hookeriana*** misapplied | see *Himalayacalamus falconeri* 'Damarapa' |
| ***macrophylla*** f. ***intermedia*** | EPla |
| § ***marmorea*** | CDTJ CMCo EAmu EPla ERod LPal MMoz MWht NPal SBig WDyG WPGP |
| - 'Variegata' (v) | CDTJ EFul EPla ERod MMoz SLPl WPGP |
| § ***quadrangularis*** | CBcs CDTJ CDoC CGHE CHEx CTrG EBee EFul EPfP EPla ERod ESwi LEdu MAvo MMoz MWht NPal SBig WPGP |
| - 'Nagaminei' (v) | EPla |
| - 'Suow' (v) | CDTJ CGHE EBee EPla WPGP |
| - 'Tatejima' | EPla |
| ***tumidissinoda*** | CAbb CDTJ CGHE CMCo EPla ERod ESwi MMoz NPal SBig WDyG WPGP |

## Chinese chives see *Allium tuberosum*

## *Chiogenes* see *Gaultheria*

## *Chionanthus* (*Oleaceae*)

| | |
|---|---|
| ***foveolatus*** | EShb |
| ***retusus*** | CBcs CDul CMCN EPfP IDee LRHS MBri MPkF NLar SLon SSpi WDin |
| ***virginicus*** | CBcs CDoC CDul CEnd CMCN CPMA EBee ELan EPfP ERas EWTr IArd IDee IMGH LRHS MBlu MBri MMuc MRav SPlb SSpi SSta WDin WHCG WOrn WPGP |

## *Chionochloa* (*Poaceae*)

| | |
|---|---|
| ***conspicua*** | CAby CGHE CKno CSec EBee EWsh GCal GFor GQue LBMP MAvo NBir NBsh NLar WPGP |
| - subsp. ***conspicua*** | GGar |
| - 'Rubra' | see *C. rubra* |
| ***flavescens*** | EBee EGoo EHoe GBin MAvo |
| ***flavicans*** | CHrt CKno EBee EWsh GBin GFor MMuc SGar WCot |
| § ***rubra*** | CElw CGHE CKno CSpe EBee EHoe ELan EPla EWes EWsh GCal GFor GMaP LBMP LEdu LHop MAvo MMoz MRav NChi SApp SHBN WMoo WPGP WTin |
| - subsp. ***cuprea*** | EBee GBin GGar |

## *Chionodoxa* ✿ (*Hyacinthaceae*)

| | |
|---|---|
| ***cretica*** | see *C. nana* |
| § ***forbesii*** | CBro CTca CWCL EBrs ECGP ECho EPfP EPot LRHS NBir SMrm SPer SRms WFar WShi |
| - 'Alba' | ECho LAma |
| - 'Blue Giant' | EBrs ECho EPot ERCP LRHS |
| - 'Rosea' | EBrs ECho LAma |
| - Siehei Group | see *C. siehei* |
| ***gigantea*** | see *C. luciliae* Gigantea Group |
| ***lochiae*** | EBrs |
| ***luciliae*** misapplied | see *C. forbesii* |
| ***luciliae*** ambig. | IHer |
| ***luciliae*** Boiss. ♀H4 | CAvo CBro EPfP EPot LAma MBri SPer |
| - 'Alba' | CBro EBrs ECho GGar LRHS SMrm SPer SPhx |
| § - Gigantea Group | CHar EBrs ECho ELan EPot GKev LAma SPhx |
| - - 'Alba' | EPot GKev |
| § ***nana*** | ECho |
| 'Pink Giant' | CAvo CBro CTca EBrs ECho ELan EPfP EPot ERCP EWTr GGar GKev LAma LHop LRHS MAvo SMrm WCot WHil |
| ***sardensis*** ♀H4 | CBgR CBro CTca EBrs ECho EPot ERCP LAma LHop LRHS SGar SPhx WCot WRHF WShi |
| § ***siehei*** ♀H4 | CBro |

## *Chionographis* (*Melanthiaceae*)

| | |
|---|---|
| ***japonica*** | EFEx WCru |

## *Chionohebe* (*Scrophulariaceae*)

| | |
|---|---|
| ***pulvinaris*** | WAbe |

## x *Chionoscilla* (*Hyacinthaceae*)

| | |
|---|---|
| § ***allenii*** | EBrs ECho EPot SPhx WCot |

## *Chirita* (*Gesneriaceae*)

| | |
|---|---|
| 'Aiko' | LRHS WDib |
| 'Chastity' | CSpe LRHS WDib |
| 'Diane Marie' | LRHS WDib |
| ***dielsii*** | CFir |
| ***heterotricha*** | LRHS WDib |
| 'Keiko' | CSpe LRHS WDib |
| * ***latifolia*** x ***linearifolia*** | WDib |
| ***linearifolia*** | LRHS WDib |
| ***linearifolia*** x ***sinensis*** | LRHS WDib |
| ***longgangensis*** | LRHS WDib |
| 'New York' | CSpe LRHS WDib |
| ***sinensis*** ♀H1 | CHal LRHS WDib |
| - 'Hisako' | CSpe LRHS WDib |
| ***speciosa*** HWJ 1056 | WCru |
| - 'Crûg Cornetto' **new** | WCru |
| 'Stardust' | LRHS WDib |
| ***tamiana*** | CSpe LRHS WDib |

## *Chironia* (*Gentianaceae*)

| | |
|---|---|
| ***baccifera*** | SPlb |

## x *Chitalpa* (*Bignoniaceae*)

| | |
|---|---|
| ***tashkentensis*** | CBcs CEnd CMCN CTho EBee EHig EPfP IDee MBlu MBri NLar WPGP |
| - 'Pink Dawn' | IArd IFFs LRHS MBri NLar |
| - 'Summer Bells' | CDoC EBee EMil LRHS MAsh MGos SBig SCoo WCot |

## chives see *Allium schoenoprasum*

## *Chlidanthus* (*Amaryllidaceae*)

| | |
|---|---|
| ***fragrans*** | CCCN CMdw CSec CStu EBrs ECho EShb |

## *Chloranthus* (*Chloranthaceae*)

| | |
|---|---|
| ***erectus*** **new** | EBee |
| ***fortunei*** | CDes CLAP EBee WPGP |
| - 'Domino' **new** | WCot |
| ***henryi*** | EBee |
| ***japonicus*** | CLAP EBee LFur WCru |
| - 'Aojiku' **new** | EBee |
| ***oldhamii*** | CLAP LEdu |
| - B&SWJ 2019 | WCru |
| ***serratus*** | CLAP EBee WCru |
| ***sessilifolius*** **new** | EBee |
| - var. ***austrosinensis*** | EBee |
| ***spicatus*** **new** | EBee |

## *Chloris* (*Poaceae*)

| | |
|---|---|
| ***distichophylla*** | see *Eustachys distichophylla* |

## *Chlorophytum* (*Anthericaceae*)

| | |
|---|---|
| ***comosum*** | EShb SEND SVic |
| - 'Aureomarginata' **new** | SEND |
| - 'Mandanum' (v) | CHal |
| - 'Variegatum' (v) ♀H1+3 | CDTJ CHal LRHS MBri SEND SRms |
| - 'Vittatum' (v) ♀H1+3 | EShb SRms SWal |
| ***krookianum*** | CFir EBee WCot |
| ***macrophyllum*** | EShb |
| ***majus*** | WCot |
| ***nepalense*** | WCot |
| - B&SWJ 2393 | WCru |
| - B&SWJ 2528 **new** | WCru |
| ***orchidastrum*** | EShb |

## *Choisya* (*Rutaceae*)

| | |
|---|---|
| 'Aztec Pearl' ♀H4 | Widely available < |
| ***dumosa*** | LHop |
| Goldfingers = 'Limo'PBR | CBcs CDul CEnd EBee ECrN ELan EPfP LAst LCro LHop LRHS LSRN MAsh MBri MGos MRav MSwo NHol NLar NPri SCoo SHBN SLim SLon SPer SPoG SSta SWvt |
| ***ternata*** ♀H4 | Widely available |
| - 'Brica'PBR | see *C. ternata* Sundance = 'Lich' |
| - Moonshine = 'Walcho'PBR | EBee GBin LRHS NHol NLar SLon |
| - MoonsleeperPBR | see *C. ternata* Sundance = 'Lich' |
| § - Sundance = 'Lich'PBR ♀H3 | Widely available |

## *Chondropetalum* (*Restionaceae*)

| | |
|---|---|
| * ***elephantinum*** | CSpe |
| ***mucronatum*** | CBcs CTrC EAmu WPGP |
| ***tectorum*** | CAbb CBcs CBct CDoC CFir CHEx CKno CPen CSpe CTrC EAmu EBee IDee LSRN MGos NOak NScw SApp SHDw SKHP SPer SPlb WHal WPGP WPrP |
| - dwarf | CTrC WPGP |

## *Chondrosum* (*Poaceae*)

| | |
|---|---|
| ***gracile*** | see *Bouteloua gracilis* |

## *Chordospartium* see *Carmichaelia*

## *Chorisia* (*Bombacaceae*)

| | |
|---|---|
| ***speciosa*** | CCCN EAmu |

## *Chorizema* (*Papilionaceae*)

| | |
|---|---|
| ***cordatum*** ♀H1 | CSec ECou |
| ***ilicifolium*** | CBcs CCCN CSPN EBee EMil SKHP |

## *Chromolaena* (*Asteraceae*)

| | |
|---|---|
| ***arnottiana*** RCB/Arg L2 **new** | CDes |
| - 'Salsipuede' **new** | WCot |

## *Chronanthus* see *Cytisus*

## *Chrysalidocarpus* (*Arecaceae*)

| | |
|---|---|
| ***decipiens*** | CBrP |
| ***lutescens*** ♀H1 | LPal LRHS MBri XBlo |

## *Chrysanthemopsis* see *Rhodanthemum*

| | |
|---|---|
| ***hosmariense*** | see *Rhodanthemum hosmariense* |

## *Chrysanthemum* ✿ (*Asteraceae*)

| | |
|---|---|
| 'Agnes Ann' (21d) | MNrw |
| 'Albert's Yellow' (21d) | MAvo |
| 'Alec Bedser' (25a) | NHal |
| 'Alehmer Rote' (21) | EMon |
| 'Alexandra' | NHal |
| 'Aline' (21) | MNrw |
| 'Allison '88' (21) | MNrw |
| 'Allouise' (25b) ♀H3 | NHal |
| ***alpinum*** | see *Leucanthemopsis alpina* |
| 'Anastasia' ambig. | CWsd |
| 'Anastasia' (21c) | CHid EBee ECtt EMon EPPr MNrw MRav NSti SRms WCot WFar WIvy WPer |
| N 'Anastasia Variegated' (28/v) | EMon |
| 'Anastasia White' (28) | SSvw WCot WIvy |
| 'Angela Blundell' | WCot |
| 'Anja's Bouquet' | EBee |
| 'Anne Ratsey' (21) | CSam |
| 'Anne, Lady Brocket' (21d) | EWsh MNrw NCGa |
| 'Apollo' (21) | EBee EMon EWll LDai SPhx SSvw WCot |
| 'Apricot' (21) | CPrp EBee EPPr MRav SSvw |
| 'Apricot Chessington' (25a) | NHal |
| 'Apricot Courtier' (24a) | NHal |
| 'Apricot Enbee Wedding' | see *C.* 'Bronze Enbee Wedding' |
| ***arcticum*** L. | see *Arctanthemum arcticum* |
| ***argenteum*** | see *Tanacetum argenteum* |
| 'Astro' | NHal |
| 'Aunt Millicent' (21d) | LLHF MNrw |
| 'Balcombe Perfection' (5a) | NHal |
| ***balsamita*** | see *Tanacetum balsamita* |
| Barbara = 'Yobarbara'^PBR (22) | EPfP NHal |
| 'Beacon' (5a) ♀H2 | NHal |
| 'Beppie Purple' (29) | NHal |
| 'Beppie Red' (29) | NHal |
| 'Bernadette Wade' (23a) | NHal |
| 'Bethanie Joy' (25b) | NHal |
| 'Betty' (21) | MNrw |
| 'Bill Wade' (25a) | NHal |
| 'Billy Bell' (25a) | NHal |
| 'Bo-peep' (28) | EMon |
| Bravo = 'Yobra' (22c) ♀H3 | EPfP MNrw NHal |
| * 'Breitner's Supreme' | MNrw WCAu |
| 'Brietner' (24b) ♀H3 | NHal |
| 'Bright Eye' (21b) | MNrw WMnd |
| 'Brightness' (21) | SUsu |
| 'Bronze Beauty' (25b) | WFar |
| 'Bronze Cassandra' (5b) ♀H2 | NHal |
| 'Bronze Dee Gem' (29c) | NHal |
| § 'Bronze Elegance' (28b) | CSam EBee EBrs EMon MLLN NBir NGdn NSti SPla SRms WEas WIvy WMnd |
| § 'Bronze Enbee Wedding' (29d) ♀H3 | NHal |
| 'Bronze Margaret' (29c) ♀H3 | NHal |
| 'Bronze Matlock' (24b) | NHal |
| 'Bronze Max Riley' (23b) ♀H3 | NHal |
| 'Bronze Mayford Perfection' (5a) ♀H2 | NHal |
| 'Bronze Mei-kyo' | see *C.* 'Bronze Elegance' |
| 'Bruera' (24b) | NHal |
| 'Capel Manor' **new** | EBee WCot |
| 'Carmine Blush' (21) | EBee WBrk WCot WHoo |
| 'Cassandra' (5b) ♀H2 | NHal |
| 'Chelsea Physic Garden' **new** | EBee MNrw WCot |
| 'Cherry Chessington' (25a) | NHal |
| 'Christine's Pink' **new** | MAvo |
| 'Christopher Lawson' (24b) | NHal |
| 'Cinderella' | WMnd |
| ***cinerariifolium*** | see *Tanacetum cinerariifolium* |
| 'Clapham Delight' (23a) | NHal |
| 'Clara Curtis' (21d)) | Widely available |
| 'Clive Skinner' (25b) **new** | NHal |
| ***coccineum*** | see *Tanacetum coccineum* |
| 'Columbine' (21d) | MNrw |
| 'Cornetto' (25b) | NHal |
| ***corymbosum*** | see *Tanacetum corymbosum* |
| 'Cottage Apricot' | EBrs LDai LHop MBNS MLHP MNrw WEas |
| 'Cottage Bronze' | MNrw |
| 'Cottage Lemon' | MNrw |
| 'Cottage Pink' | see *C.* 'Emperor of China' |
| 'Cottage Yellow' | MSte WCot WHoo |
| 'Courtier' (24a) | NHal |
| 'Cousin Joan' **new** | EBee LDai WCot |
| 'Cream Patricia Millar' (14b) | NHal |
| Dana = 'Yodana' (25b) ♀H3 | NHal |
| 'Daniel Cooper' (21) | MNrw |
| 'Darren Pugh' (3b) | NHal |
| Debonair = 'Yodebo'^PBR (22c) ♀H3 | EPfP |
| 'Dee Gem' (29c) ♀H3 | NHal |
| § 'Doctor Tom Parr' (21c) | CPLG EBee ELan EMon GCal IGor LHop MNrw SUsu WPtf |
| 'Doreen Statham' (4b) | NHal |
| 'Dorothy Stone' (25b) | NHal |
| 'Dorridge Crystal' (24a) | NHal |
| 'Duchess of Edinburgh' (21d) | CPrp CSam EBee EBrs ECtt ELan EShb LRHS MRav SSvw WCAu WMnd |

| | | |
|---|---|---|
| | 'Edelweiss' (21) | CAby EMon WCot |
| | 'Egret' (23b) | NHal |
| | 'Elaine Johnson' (3b) | NHal |
| | 'Elizabeth Lawson' (5b) | NHal |
| | 'Elizabeth Shoesmith' (1) | NHal |
| | 'Ellen' (29c) | CHrt NHal |
| * | 'Emma Jane' (25a) | NHal |
| § | 'Emperor of China' (21) | CAby CElw CSam EBee ECha ECtt EMon EPPr GCal IGor LRHS MNrw MRav MSte NCGa SSvw WBor WCot WFar WMnd |
| | 'Enbee Wedding' (29d) ♀H3 | NHal |
| | 'Esther' (21d) | EMon MNrw |
| | 'Fairie' (28a) ♀H3 | MNrw |
| * | 'Fairy Rose' (21) | MNrw |
| | ***foeniculaceum*** misapplied | see *Argyranthemum foeniculaceum* misapplied |
| | ***foeniculaceum*** (Willd.) Desf. | see *Argyranthemum foeniculaceum* (Willd.) Webb & Sch. Bip. |
| | 'Fred Raynor' | MNrw |
| | ***frutescens*** | see *Argyranthemum frutescens* |
| | 'Gambit' (24a) | NHal |
| | 'Geof Brady' (5a) | NHal |
| | 'Geoff Sylvester' (25a) | NHal |
| | 'George Griffiths' (24b) ♀H3 | NHal |
| | 'Gigantic' (1) | NHal |
| | 'Gladys' (24b) | ELan SRGP |
| | 'Gladys Emerson' (3b) | NHal |
| | 'Gloria' (21c) | MNrw |
| § | 'Gold Margaret' (29c) ♀H3 | NHal |
| | 'Golden Cassandra' (5b) ♀H2 | NHal |
| | 'Golden Courtier' (24a) | NHal |
| | 'Golden Gigantic' (1) | NHal |
| | 'Golden Margaret' | see *C.* 'Gold Margaret' |
| | 'Golden Mayford Perfection' (5a) ♀H2 | NHal |
| | 'Golden Plover' (22) | NHal |
| | 'Golden Seal' (7b) | EMon |
| | 'Golden William Florentine' (15a) **new** | NHal |
| | 'Goldengreenheart' (21) | MNrw |
| | 'Goldmarianne' (21) | GBin |
| | 'Gompie Bronze' | NHal |
| | 'Gompie Red' | NHal |
| I | 'Gompie Rose' | NHal |
| | 'Grace Wade' (25b) | NHal |
| | 'Grandchild' (21c) | LLHF MNrw |
| § | x ***grandiflorum*** | SRms |
| | - 'Corinna' **new** | GBin |
| | 'Hanenburg' | NHal |
| | ***haradjanii*** | see *Tanacetum haradjanii* |
| | 'Harold Lawson' (5a) | NHal |
| | 'Harry Gee' (1) | NHal |
| | 'Heather James' (3b) | NHal |
| | 'Hebe' **new** | EBee |
| | 'Heide' (29c) ♀H3 | NHal |
| | 'Hesketh Knight' (5b) | NHal |
| | Holly = 'Yoholly' (22b) ♀H3 | NHal |
| | 'Honey Enbee Wedding' (29d) | NHal |
| | 'Horningsea Pink' (19d) | ECGP WBor |
| | ***hosmariense*** | see *Rhodanthemum hosmariense* |
| | 'Innocence' (21) | CAby CSam EBee ECtt ELan EMon IGor MNrw MRav NGdn NSti SAga SPla WHoo |
| | 'Jante Wells' (21b) | EMon WEas |
| | 'Jessie Cooper' | see *C.* 'Mrs Jessie Cooper' |
| | 'John Harrison' (25b) | NHal |
| | 'John Hughes' (3b) | NHal |
| | 'John Riley' (14a) | NHal |
| | 'John Wingfield' (14b) | NHal |
| | 'Joyce Fountain' (24a) **new** | NHal |
| | 'Joyce Frieda' (23b) | NHal |
| | 'Julia' (28) | EPPr SRGP |
| | 'Julia Peterson' **new** | WCot |
| | Julia = 'Yojulia' | EBee |
| | 'Julie Lagravère' (28) | WPtf |
| | 'Juweeltja' | NHal |
| | 'Kay Woolman' (13b) | NHal |
| | 'Kimberley Marie' (15b) | NHal |
| | x ***koreanum*** | see *C.* x *grandiflorum* |
| | 'Lady in Pink' (21) | LDai |
| | 'Lakelanders' (3b) | NHal |
| | 'Le Bonheur Red' | NHal |
| | 'Lemon Margaret' (29c) ♀H3 | NHal |
| | 'Leo' (21b) | EMon |
| | ***leucanthemum*** | see *Leucanthemum vulgare* |
| | 'Lilac Chessington' (25a) | NHal |
| | Linda = 'Lindayo'PBR (22c) ♀H3 | NHal |
| | 'Lorna Wood' (13b) | NHal |
| | 'Louise' (25b) | MNrw |
| | 'Lucy' (29a) ♀H2 | NHal |
| | 'Lucy Simpson' (21d) | MNrw |
| | 'Lundy' (2) | NHal |
| | 'Luv Purple' | NHal |
| | 'Lynn Johnson' (15a) | NHal |
| | Lynn = 'Yolynn'PBR (22c) ♀H3 | NHal |
| | ***macrophyllum*** | see *Tanacetum macrophyllum* (Waldst. & Kit.) Sch.Bip. |
| | 'Malcolm Perkins' (25a) | NHal |
| | 'Mancetta Comet' (29a) | NHal |
| | ***maresii*** | see *Rhodanthemum hosmariense* |
| | 'Margaret' (29c) ♀H3 | NHal |
| | 'Marion' (25a) | LDai WCot |
| | 'Mark Woolman' (1) | NHal |
| | 'Mary' (21f) | LDai MNrw |
| | 'Mary Stoker' (21d)) | CHrt CSam EBee EBrs ECtt ELan EShb LRHS MNFA MNrw MRav MSte NCGa NSti SPer SRGP SSvw WAul WBor WBrk WCAu WFar WHoo WMnd |
| | 'Matador' (14a) | NHal |
| | 'Matlock' (24b) | NHal |
| | 'Mauve Gem' (21f) | MNrw |
| | ***mawii*** | see *Rhodanthemum gayanum* |
| | 'Max Riley' (23b) ♀H3 | NHal |
| | ***maximum*** misapplied | see *Leucanthemum* x *superbum* |
| | ***maximum*** Ramond | see *Leucanthemum maximum* (Ramond) DC. |
| | - 'Aglaia' | see *Leucanthemum* x *superbum* 'Aglaia' |
| | - 'T.E. Killin' | see *Leucanthemum* x *superbum* 'T.E. Killin' |
| | - 'Wirral Supreme' | see *Leucanthemum* x *superbum* 'Wirral Supreme' |
| | 'Maxine Johnson' (25b) | NHal |
| | 'May Shoesmith' (5a) ♀H2 | NHal |
| | 'Mayford Perfection' (5a) ♀H2 | NHal |
| | 'Mei-kyo' (28b) | CMea EBee ECtt EMon IGor MLLN MRav SPla SRms WBor WFar WHil |
| | 'Membury' (24b) | NHal |
| | 'Michelle Preston' (13b) | NHal |
| | 'Millennium' (25b) | NHal |
| | 'Moonlight' (29d/K) | MRav |
| § | 'Mrs Jessie Cooper' (21) | CAby ELan EWsh GQue MNrw MSte NBir NLar SSvw WCot WHil WHoo WPtf WTin |
| | 'Mrs Jessie Cooper No 1' | SSvw |

| | |
|---|---|
| 'Mrs Jessie Cooper No 2' | MNrw |
| 'Music' (23b) | NHal |
| 'Nancy Perry' (21d) | CSam ELan EMon MNrw MRav SSvw |
| § ***nankingense*** | WFar |
| 'Nantyderry Sunshine' (28b) ♀H4 | CPrp CSam CWsd EBee LLHF LRHS MNrw SPla WCot WEas WMnd WPer WRha |
| 'Nell Gwyn' (21d) | MNrw |
| 'Netherhall Moonlight' | EMon |
| Nicole = 'Yonicole' (22c) ♀H3 | NHal |
| ***nipponicum*** | see *Nipponanthemum nipponicum* |
| 'Orange Allouise' (25b) | NHal |
| 'Orange Enbee Wedding' (29d) | NHal |
| 'Oury' | EMon |
| ***pacificum*** | see *Ajania pacifica* |
| 'Parkfield Tigger' (29c) | NHal |
| ***parthenium*** | see *Tanacetum parthenium* |
| 'Patricia Millar' (14b) | NHal |
| 'Paul Boissier' (30Rub) | CAby EMon NSti SPhx WCot WMnd |
| 'Payton Dale' (29c) ♀H3 | NHal |
| 'Payton Prince' (29c) ♀H3 | NHal |
| 'Payton Toffee' (29c) | NHal |
| 'Peach Courtier' (24a) | NHal |
| 'Peach Enbee Wedding' (29d) ♀H3 | NHal |
| 'Peach John Wingfield' (14b) | NHal |
| 'Pennine Bullion' | NHal |
| 'Pennine Gift' (29c) | NHal |
| 'Pennine Marie' (29a) ♀H3 | NHal |
| 'Pennine Oriel' (29a) ♀H3 | NHal |
| 'Pennine Polo' (29d) ♀H3 | NHal |
| 'Pennine Ranger' (29d) | NHal |
| 'Pennine Swan' (29c) | NHal |
| 'Pennine Toy' (19d) | NHal |
| 'Perry's Peach' (21a) | LLHF MNrw NPer SSvw |
| 'Peter Rowe' (23b) | NHal |
| 'Peterkin' | CPrp ECGP ECtt EMon MNrw |
| 'Phil Houghton' (1) | NHal |
| 'Pink John Wingfield' (14b) | NHal |
| 'Pink Progression' | NBir |
| 'Polar Gem' (3a) | NHal |
| 'Primrose Allouise' (24b) ♀H3 | NHal |
| 'Primrose Courtier' | see *C.* 'Yellow Courtier' |
| 'Primrose Dorothy Stone' (25b) | NHal |
| 'Primrose Enbee Wedding' (29d) ♀H3 | NHal |
| 'Primrose John Hughes' (3b) | NHal |
| 'Primrose Mayford Perfection' (5a) ♀H2 | NHal |
| 'Primrose West Bromwich' (14a) | NHal |
| 'Princess' (21d) | LLHF MNrw SSvw |
| 'Promise' (25a) | NHal |
| 'Purleigh White' (28b) | CPrp MNrw NSti SPla WRha |
| 'Purple Chempak Rose' (14b) | NHal |
| 'Purple Fairie' (28b) | MNrw |
| 'Purple Margaret' (29c) | NHal |
| 'Raquel' (21) | EPfP MNrw |
| 'Red Balcombe Perfection' (5a) | NHal |
| 'Red Bruno' **new** | NHal |
| 'Red Pennine Gift' (29c) | NHal |
| 'Red Shirley Model' (3a) | NHal |
| 'Regal Mist' (25b) | NHal |
| 'Richmond' (3b) **new** | NHal |
| 'Rita McMahon' (29d) ♀H3 | NHal |
| Robin = 'Yorobi'PBR (22c) | NHal |
| 'Roen Sarah' (29c) | NHal |
| 'Romany' (2) | CElw WEas |
| 'Rose Enbee Wedding' (29d) | NHal |
| 'Rose Madder' **new** | WCot |
| 'Rose Mayford Perfection' (5a) ♀H2 | NHal |
| 'Rose Patricia Millar' (14b) | NHal |
| ***roseum*** | see *Tanacetum coccineum* |
| 'Royal Command' (21) | MNrw WCot |
| ***rubellum*** | see *C. zawadskii* |
| 'Ruby Enbee Wedding' (29d) ♀H3 | NHal |
| 'Ruby Mound' (21c) ♀H3 | LLHF MNrw SSvw WEas |
| 'Ruby Raynor' (21) | MNrw |
| 'Rumpelstilzchen' (21d) | CMea ECtt MNrw WPer |
| 'Salmon Allouise' (25b) | NHal |
| 'Salmon Blenda' **new** | NHal |
| 'Salmon Enbee Wedding' (29d) ♀H3 | NHal |
| 'Sam Vinter' (5a) | NHal |
| 'Sarah Louise' (25b) | NHal |
| 'Sarah's Yellow' | CAby CSam |
| 'Sea Urchin' (21f) ♀H3 | MNrw |
| 'Shining Light' (21f) | LLHF MNrw SSvw |
| 'Shirley Primrose' (1) | NHal |
| 'Silver Gigantic' (1) | NHal |
| ***sinense*** | see *C.* x *grandiflorum* |
| 'Skylark' (22a) | NPri |
| 'Smokey' (29) | NHal |
| 'Sonnenschein' | EWTr LHop |
| 'Sophie Elizabeth' (24a) | NHal |
| 'Southway Shiraz' (29d) | NHal |
| 'Southway Snoopy' (29d) | NHal |
| 'Southway Strontium' (29d) | NHal |
| 'Spartan Seagull' (21d) | MNrw SSvw |
| 'Starlet' (21f) | LLHF MNrw SSvw |
| 'Stockton' (3b) ♀H2 | NHal |
| 'Sunbeam' (28) | EBee |
| Sundoro = 'Yosun' (22d) | NHal |
| 'Syllabub' | ECtt |
| 'Tapestry Rose' (21d) | CMea CWsd EMon IGor LDai MCot MNrw NCGa SSvw WBor |
| 'Thoroughbred' (24a) | NHal |
| 'Tom Parr' | see *C.* 'Doctor Tom Parr' |
| 'Tom Snowball' (3b) | NHal |
| 'Tommy Trout' (28/K) | MNrw |
| 'Tracy Waller' (24b) | NHal |
| Triumph = 'Yotri' (22) | NHal |
| ***uliginosum*** | see *Leucanthemella serotina* |
| 'Uri' | LPla SAga SPhx |
| 'Vagabond Prince' | MNrw MSte WHoo |
| 'Venice' (24b) | NHal |
| 'Venus' (21) | WCot |
| 'Venus One' **new** | LDai |
| 'Wedding Day' (21) | EBee MNrw NCGa WCAu WTin |
| 'Wedding Sunshine' (21) | LDai LRHS MNrw |
| 'Wembley' (24b) | NHal |
| 'Wessex Eclipse' (29c) | NHal |
| 'West Bromwich' (14a) | NHal |
| ***weyrichii*** | EBee ECho ECtt EShb GKev LEdu MTho NRya SAga SRms |
| 'White Allouise' (25b) ♀H3 | NHal |
| 'White Cassandra' (5b) | NHal |
| 'White Enbee Wedding' (29d) | NHal |
| 'White Gloss' (21e) | LLHF LRHS MNrw SSvw |
| 'White Margaret' (29c) ♀H3 | NHal |
| 'White Skylark' (22) | NHal |
| 'White Tower' | MNrw |
| 'Wilder Charms' | WHil |
| 'William Florentine' (15a) | NHal |
| 'Winning's Red' (21) | EMon LHop MNrw SMad |
| 'Woolman's Star' (3a) | NHal |

| | |
|---|---|
| 'Woolman's Venture' (4b) | NHal |
| 'Yellow Billy Bell' (15a) | NHal |
| § 'Yellow Courtier' (24a) | NHal |
| 'Yellow Egret' (23b) | NHal |
| 'Yellow Ellen' (29c) | NHal |
| 'Yellow Enbee Wedding' (29d) | NHal |
| 'Yellow Harold Lawson' (5a) | NHal |
| 'Yellow Heide' (29c) ♀H3 | NHal |
| 'Yellow John Hughes' (3b) ♀H2 | NHal |
| 'Yellow John Wingfield' (14b) | NHal |
| 'Yellow May Shoesmith' (5a) | NHal |
| 'Yellow Mayford Perfection' (5a) ♀H2 | NHal |
| 'Yellow Pennine Oriel' (29a) ♀H3 | NHal |
| 'Yellow Ralph Lambert' (1) | NHal |
| 'Yellow Rylands Gem' (24b) | NHal |
| 'Yellow Starlet' (21f) | LLHF MNrw SSvw |
| ***yezoense*** ♀H4 | CSam CStu ELan |
| - 'Roseum' | CSam ECtt NSti WBor |
| § ***zawadskii*** | WFar |

## *Chrysocephalum* (*Asteraceae*)

| | |
|---|---|
| 'Desert Flame' **new** | LSou |

## *Chrysocoma* (*Asteraceae*)

| | |
|---|---|
| ***ciliata*** JJH 9401633 | NWCA |

## *Chrysogonum* (*Asteraceae*)

| | |
|---|---|
| ***australe*** | EBee |
| ***virginianum*** | CMea CPrp EBee ECha EShb EWes LRHS MRav SBch WFar WMoo |

## *Chrysopogon* (*Poaceae*)

| | |
|---|---|
| ***gryllus*** | EBee SApp WPGP |

## *Chrysopsis* (*Asteraceae*)

| | |
|---|---|
| § ***mariana*** | EMon WOld |
| ***villosa*** (Pursh) Nutt. ex DC. | see *Heterotheca villosa* |

## *Chrysosplenium* (*Saxifragaceae*)

| | |
|---|---|
| ***alternifolium*** | EMFW |
| ***davidianum*** | CBre CSam EBee ECha EPot EWld GEdr GGar GJos GKev MNFA NBir NSla WBor WCot WCru WFar WMoo WPrP WPtf |
| ***flagelliferum*** B&SWJ 8902 | WCru |
| ***lanuginosum*** var. ***formosanum*** B&SWJ 6979 | WCru |
| ***macrophyllum*** | CBct CExc EBee EWld WCot WCru |
| ***macrostemon*** var. ***shiobarense*** | EPot |
| - - B&SWJ 6173 | WCru |
| ***oppositifolium*** | EBWF EBee GPWP WHer WShi |

## *Chrysothemis* (*Gesneriaceae*)

| | |
|---|---|
| ***pulchella*** ♀H1 | CHal |

## *Chusquea* ✿ (*Poaceae*)

| | |
|---|---|
| ***breviglumis*** misapplied | see *C. culeou* 'Tenuis' |
| ***breviglumis*** Phil. | NMoo |
| ***culeou*** ♀H4 | CAbb CBcs CDoC CEnd CEnt CGHE CHEx CPSs EBee EFul ENBC EPfP EPla LAst LEdu LPal MGos MMoz MWht NBea NMoo SArc SBig SDix SSta WPGP |
| - 'Breviglumis' | see *C. culeou* 'Tenuis' |
| - 'Purple Splendour' | EPla WPGP |
| § - 'Tenuis' | EPla ERod |
| - weeping **new** | CDTJ WPGP |
| ***cumingii*** | EBee |
| ***delicatula*** from Machu Picchu, Peru **new** | WPGP |
| ***gigantea*** | CDTJ EPla LEdu MMoz MWht SBig WPGP |
| - 'Bracken Hill' | MMoz |
| ***macrostachya*** | EBee EPla WPGP |
| ***montana*** | EBee EPla |
| ***mulleri*** F&M 104A from Mexico **new** | WPGP |
| ***nigricans*** | EPla |
| ***quila*** | EPla MMoz WPGP |
| ***valdiviensis*** | EPla WPGP |

## *Cibotium* (*Dicksoniaceae*)

| | |
|---|---|
| ***glaucum*** **new** | WRic |

## *Cicerbita* (*Asteraceae*)

| | |
|---|---|
| sp. | ECtt |
| BWJ 7891 from China | WCru |
| § ***alpina*** | EBee NBid NLar SGar SPlb |
| ***plumieri*** | EWes GAbr SPhx WCot WFar WHrl WPtf WRos |

## *Cichorium* (*Asteraceae*)

| | |
|---|---|
| ***intybus*** | CArn CHby CHrt CPrp EBWF EBee EBla ELan ELau GAbr GPoy LHop MAvo MNHC NBir NGHP NMir NPri SECG SIde SPer SPlb SPoG WCHb WFar WJek WMoo |
| - f. ***album*** | CBod CPrp EBee EBla ECha ECtt EPfP GMac LHop MAvo MRav NCGa NCob NGdn SBch SWat WCAu WCHb |
| - var. ***foliosum*** | EBee |
| - 'Roseum' | CBod CPrp CSpe CWCL EBee EBla ECha ECot ECtt ELan EPfP GMac LHop MAvo MRav NCGa NCob NGdn SBch SWat WCAu WCHb |

## *Cimicifuga* see *Actaea*

| | |
|---|---|
| ***acerina*** | see *Actaea japonica* |
| ***americana*** | see *Actaea podocarpa* |
| ***cordifolia*** (DC.) Torrey & A.Gray | see *Actaea cordifolia* |
| ***cordifolia*** Pursh | see *Actaea podocarpa* |
| ***foetida*** | see *Actaea cimicifuga* |
| ***racemosa*** var. ***cordifolia*** | see *Actaea cordifolia* |
| - 'Purpurea' | see *Actaea simplex* Atropurpurea Group |
| ***ramosa*** | see *Actaea simplex* 'Prichard's Giant' |
| ***rubifolia*** | see *Actaea cordifolia* |
| ***simplex*** var. ***matsumurae*** | see *Actaea matsumurae* |

## *Cineraria* (*Asteraceae*)

| | |
|---|---|
| ***maritima*** | see *Senecio cineraria* |
| ***saxifraga*** | EShb |

## *Cinnamomum* (*Lauraceae*)

| | |
|---|---|
| ***camphora*** | CBcs CHEx CPLG CTrG |
| ***japonicum*** | WPGP |
| ***micranthum*** | WPGP |

## *Cionura* (*Asclepiadaceae*)

| | |
|---|---|
| ***oreophila*** | EBee WPGP WSHC |

## *Circaea* (*Onagraceae*)

| | |
|---|---|
| ***alpina*** | EBee |
| ***lutetiana*** | EBWF MSal NSco WHer |

| | |
|---|---|
| - 'Caveat Emptor' (v) | CBow CHid EBee NBid WCot WHer |

## *Cirsium* (*Asteraceae*)

| | |
|---|---|
| ***acaule*** | NBre NLar |
| ***arvense*** | WSFF |
| * ***atroroseum*** | SWat |
| ***ciliatum*** | EBee |
| ***diacantha*** | see *Ptilostemon diacantha* |
| ***eriophoroides*** | WCot |
| ***eriophorum*** | LDai NLar |
| ***falconeri*** | NBur |
| ***helenioides*** | see *C. heterophyllum* |
| § ***heterophyllum*** | CDes CPom EBee EMon EWld GBri LDai LEdu NBre NBur NLar SHar SPhx SUsu WCot WPGP WTin |
| ***japonicum*** | GKir |
| - 'Early Pink Beauty' | LDai NBre |
| - 'Early Rose Beauty' | ILad NBre |
| - 'Pink Beauty' | LHop |
| - 'Rose Beauty' | EBee ECrN LRHS SPur |
| - variegated (v) **new** | EMon |
| ***kamtschaticum*** B&SWJ 10927 **new** | WCru |
| 'Mount Etna' | CSam EAEE EBee EBla GBri LBMP LHop LLWG LRHS MBNS NCob NGdn |
| ***oleraceum*** | LEdu NBid NBre NLar |
| ***palustre*** | EBWF |
| - 'Love and Hate' **new** | WAlt |
| ***purpuratum*** | MNrw WCot WPGP |
| ***rivulare*** | CSam GKir |
| - 'Atropurpureum' | Widely available |
| ***subcoriaceum*** pink-flowered B&SWJ 10245 | WCru |
| - yellow-flowered B&SWJ 10471 | WCru |
| ***tuberosum*** | CAby NDov SPhx |
| ***vulgare*** | WSFF |

## *Cissus* (*Vitaceae*)

| | |
|---|---|
| ***antarctica*** ♀$^{H1}$ | CCCN EShb MBri SEND |
| ***discolor*** | CHal |
| ***pedata*** B&SWJ 2371 | WCru |
| ***rhombifolia*** ♀$^{H1}$ | EOHP MBri SEND |
| - 'Ellen Danica' ♀$^{H1}$ | CHal SEND |
| § ***striata*** | CBcs CDoC CHEx CTrC CWCL EBee ELon EMil EShb IMGH LRHS MRav SEND SLim SWvt WSHC |

## *Cistus* ✿ (*Cistaceae*)

| | |
|---|---|
| ***acutifolius*** misapplied | see *C. inflatus, C.* x *pulverulentus* |
| x ***aguilarii*** | CBcs CSBt CTri EPfP EWTr LAst MRav SKHP WOut WSHC |
| - 'Maculatus' ♀$^{H3}$ | CDoC CDul CPLG CSam EBee ELan EPfP GGar GKir LCro LRHS LSRN NPri SCoo SLPl SPer SPla SPoG SWvt WAbe WBod WCFE WHCG WKif |
| ***albidus*** | CArn EGoo WKif |
| ***algarvensis*** | see *Halimium ocymoides* |
| 'Ann Baker' | SLPl |
| 'Anne Palmer' | see *C.* x *fernandesiae* 'Anne Palmer' |
| x ***argenteus*** 'Blushing Peggy Sammons' | CDoC CSBt |
| - Golden Treasure = 'Nepond' (v) | CBow EPfP EQua SWvt |
| - 'Paper Moon' | LSRN |
| § - 'Peggy Sammons' ♀$^{H3}$ | Widely available |
| - 'Silver Pink' ambig. | Widely available |
| ***atriplicifolius*** | see *Halimium atriplicifolium* |
| 'Blanche' | see *C. ladanifer* 'Blanche' |
| x ***bornetianus*** 'Jester' | CSBt EBee LRHS SPla |
| x ***canescens*** | EBee |
| - f. ***albus*** | CWib EBee EQua WEas WHCG WKif |
| § ***clusii*** | NLar SPla |
| x ***corbariensis*** | see *C.* x *hybridus* |
| ***creticus*** | CDoC CPLG EQua LAst MAsh MBri MGos MLHP NMun SGar SLon SPoG SSto WBVN WPGP |
| § - subsp. ***creticus*** | EBee ELan ELon EPfP LRHS MRav MSte SCoo SPer WAbe |
| - - 'Lasithi' | WAbe |
| § - subsp. ***incanus*** | WHCG WPat |
| § x ***crispatus*** 'Warley Rose' | GMaP SHBN WKif |
| ***crispus*** misapplied | see *C.* x *pulverulentus, C.* x *purpureus* |
| § ***crispus*** L. | EBee MRav WEas |
| - 'Prostratus' | see *C. crispus* L. |
| - 'Sunset' | see *C.* x *pulverulentus* 'Sunset' |
| § x ***cyprius*** ♀$^{H4}$ | CArn CDul EBee ECtt ELan EPfP LHop MCot MGos MNHC MRav MWat SDix SEND SHBN SPer SRms WDin WFar |
| - f. ***albiflorus*** | MSte |
| § - var. ***ellipticus*** 'Elma' ♀$^{H3}$ | EBee ELan EPfP ERas LHop LRHS MAsh MCot SPer SPla WBod WEas WHCG WPGP |
| § x ***dansereaui*** | CMHG CSBt CWib EBee MGos MRav MSte WFar |
| - 'Albiflorus' | see *C.* x *dansereaui* 'Portmeirion' |
| - 'Decumbens' ♀$^{H4}$ | CBcs CChe CDul CMHG CTri EBee ELan EPfP LBMP MAsh MBNS MRav MSwo SArc SCoo SHBN SPer SPla SPoG SWvt WDin WHCG WPGP |
| - 'Jenkyn Place' | CDoC EBee GMaP MBNS MBri MGos SLPl SPoG SUsu WKif |
| § - 'Portmeirion' | WFar |
| x ***dubius*** | EBee |
| 'Elma' | see *C.* x *cyprius* var. *ellipticus* 'Elma' |
| 'Enigma' **new** | CDoC EBee |
| § x ***fernandesiae*** 'Anne Palmer' | CBgR CDoC EBee EPfP LLHF LSRN SEND SPoG SRGP WBod WFar |
| x ***florentinus*** misapplied | see x *Halimiocistus* 'Ingwersenii' |
| § x ***florentinus*** Lam. | CAbP EBee |
| - 'Fontfroide' | EBee WAbe |
| ***formosus*** | see *Halimium lasianthum* subsp. *formosum* |
| 'Gordon Cooper' | CWan EBee LSRN MMuc SCoo |
| x ***heterocalyx*** 'Chelsea Bonnet' | EBee GMaP MSte SCoo SLim SPoG WPGP WPen |
| ***hirsutus*** Lam. 1786 | see *C. inflatus* |
| - var. ***psilosepalus*** | see *C. inflatus* |
| § x ***hybridus*** | Widely available |
| - Gold Prize = 'Wyecis' (v) | EBee ELan ELon MBri MGos NLar SPoG SWvt WFar WHar WLeb |
| ***incanus*** | see *C. creticus* subsp. *incanus* |
| § ***inflatus*** | WHar |
| ***ingwerseniana*** | see x *Halimiocistus* 'Ingwersenii' |
| 'Jessamy Beauty' | EBee SLPl |
| 'Jessamy Bride' | SLPl |
| 'Jessamy Charm' | SPhx |
| ***ladanifer*** misapplied | see *C.* x *cyprius* |
| ***ladanifer*** L. ♀$^{H3}$ | CDoC CSBt CTri ECha ECrN ELan EPfP ERas EWTr GCra IMGH LRHS MRav MSal MSwo SGar SPer WBod WEas WFar WHar WSHC |
| - var. ***albiflorus*** | EQua SKHP |
| § - 'Blanche' | CBgR EBee LLHF WKif |
| § - 'Paladin' | EBee |
| - Palhinhae Group | see *C. ladanifer* var. *sulcatus* |
| - 'Pat' | EBee ELan EPfP LRHS LSRN MAsh NBir SPoG |
| § - var. ***sulcatus*** | CDoC CHar EBee ELan EPfP LHop MSte SPoG WBod WFar |
| - - f. ***bicolor*** | EBee |

| | |
|---|---|
| ***lasianthus*** | see *Halimium lasianthum* |
| ***laurifolius*** 🏆H4 | CDoC CHar EBee EPfP MGos MNrw MRav NBir NLar NSti SKHP SLPl SPoG WHar WPnn |
| x ***laxus*** | WAbe |
| - 'Snow White' | CAbP CDoC EBee EPfP LAst LHop LRHS MCot MGos MSte NPer NPro SLPl SLim SLon SPoG SRms WKif WLeb |
| x ***ledon*** | SLPl |
| § x ***lenis*** 'Grayswood Pink' 🏆H4 | Widely available |
| x ***longifolius*** | see *C.* x *nigricans* |
| x ***loretii*** misapplied | see *C.* x *dansereaui* |
| x ***loretii*** Rouy & Foucaud | see *C.* x *stenophyllus* |
| x ***lusitanicus*** Maund | see *C.* x *dansereaui* |
| 'May Snow' | LRHS MBNS SPoG |
| 'Merrist Wood Cream' | see x *Halimiocistus wintonensis* 'Merrist Wood Cream' |
| ***monspeliensis*** | CAbP EBee EPfP EQua GGar LRHS MAsh SPer SPoG WFar |
| - CMBS 62 | WPGP |
| - 'Vicar's Mead' | CCCN CDoC EBee ELan MAsh MBNS SEND SPla SPoG SRms |
| § x ***nigricans*** | EBee ELan |
| x ***obtusifolius*** misapplied | see *C.* x *nigricans* |
| x ***obtusifolius*** ambig. | EAlp |
| x ***obtusifolius*** Sweet | CAbP EPfP EWes SLPl WEas |
| § - 'Thrive' | MBri SCoo |
| ***ochreatus*** | see *C. symphytifolius* subsp. *leucophyllus* |
| ***ocymoides*** | see *Halimium ocymoides* |
| 'Paladin' | see *C. ladanifer* 'Paladin' |
| ***palhinhae*** | see *C. ladanifer* var. *sulcatus* |
| ***parviflorus*** misapplied | see *C.* x *lenis* 'Grayswood Pink' |
| ***parviflorus*** Lam. | WSHC |
| 'Peggy Sammons' | see *C.* x *argenteus* 'Peggy Sammons' |
| x ***platysepalus*** | EBee SLPl SPhx |
| ***populifolius*** | CMHG ECha LLHF LRHS SKHP SPer WAbe WBod WPGP |
| - var. ***lasiocalyx*** | see *C. populifolius* subsp. *major* |
| § - subsp. ***major*** 🏆H3 | CBgR EBee EPfP LSRN WPGP |
| ***psilosepalus*** | see *C. inflatus* |
| § x ***pulverulentus*** | CPLG CTri EBee ECha EPfP MMHG SWal WDin WSHC |
| § - 'Sunset' 🏆H3 | Widely available |
| - 'Warley Rose' | see *C.* x *crispatus* 'Warley Rose' |
| § x ***purpureus*** 🏆H3 | Widely available |
| - 'Alan Fradd' | Widely available |
| - var. ***argenteus*** f. ***stictus*** | EBee LSRN WAbe |
| - 'Betty Taudevin' | see *C.* x *purpureus* |
| - var. ***holorhodos*** | EBee |
| x ***rodiaei*** 'Jessabel' | CBgR EBee MAsh SCoo SEND SPoG WAbe WLeb |
| - 'Jessica' | CDoC EBee LAst NLar WAbe |
| ***rosmarinifolius*** | see *C. clusii* |
| 'Ruby Cluster' | CCCN CDoC EBee LSRN SRms |
| ***sahucii*** | see x *Halimiocistus sahucii* |
| ***salviifolius*** | CAbP CArn CCCN ERas LRHS WFar WHCG |
| - 'Avalanche' | EBee MRav WAbe |
| - 'Gold Star' | EBee SPoG |
| - 'Prostratus' | ELan LRHS SPoG WPGP |
| ***salviifolius*** x ***monspeliensis*** | see *C.* x *florentinus* Lam. |
| 'Silver Pink' misapplied | see *C.* x *lenis* 'Grayswood Pink' |
| x ***skanbergii*** 🏆H3 | Widely available |
| 'Snow Fire' 🏆H4 | CAbP CBgR CCCN CDoC CSBt EBee EPfP LRHS LSRN MGos MMuc NPro SCoo SLPl SPla SPoG SSpi WLeb |
| § x ***stenophyllus*** | CWib SPer |
| ***symphytifolius*** | WPGP |
| § - subsp. ***leucophyllus*** MSF 98.019 | WPGP |
| 'Thornfield White' | EBee |
| 'Thrive' | see *C.* x *obtusifolius* 'Thrive' |
| ***tomentosus*** | see *Helianthemum nummularium* subsp. *tomentosum* |
| x ***verguinii*** | LHop SDix |
| - f. ***albiflorus*** | EBee |
| - var. ***albiflorus*** misapplied | see *C.* x *dansereaui* 'Portmeirion' |
| ***villosus*** | see *C. creticus* subsp. *creticus* |
| ***wintonensis*** | see x *Halimiocistus wintonensis* |

## *Citharexylum* (*Verbenaceae*)

| | |
|---|---|
| ***spicatum*** | CPLG |

## x *Citrofortunella* (*Rutaceae*)

| | |
|---|---|
| sp. | CCCN |
| § ***microcarpa*** (F) 🏆H1 | CCCN CDoC EMui EPfP LRHS MBri NLar SPoG |
| § - 'Tiger' (v/F) 🏆H1 | EPfP LRHS |
| - 'Variegata' | see x *C. microcarpa* 'Tiger' |
| ***mitis*** | see x *C. microcarpa* |

## **citron** see *Citrus medica*

## *Citrullus* (*Cucurbitaceae*)

| | |
|---|---|
| ***colocynthis*** | CArn |

## *Citrus* ✿ (*Rutaceae*)

| | |
|---|---|
| ***aurantiifolia*** (F) | CCCN SVic |
| - key lime (F) | CDoC |
| ***aurantium*** 'Bouquet de Fleurs' | CCCN |
| calamondin | see x *Citrofortunella microcarpa* |
| 'Fukushu' | CCCN EMui |
| ***hystrix*** | CCCN CKob EMui NScw |
| ***japonica*** | see *Fortunella japonica* |
| 'Kulci' | CCCN |
| kumquat | see *Fortunella margarita* |
| 'La Valette' (F) | EPfP |
| ***latifolia*** (F/S) | CCCN EMui EPfP LRHS MREP |
| ***limetta*** | CCCN |
| ***limettoides*** (F) | CArn |
| ***limon*** (F) | CHEx CTsd EPfP LPan MREP SPoG STrG SVic |
| - 'Four Seasons' | CCCN NLar |
| § - 'Garey's Eureka' (F) | CDoC CKob EPfP |
| - 'Mosquito' (v) | CHll |
| - 'Quatre Saisons' | see *C. limon* 'Garey's Eureka' |
| - 'Toscana' | EPfP |
| - 'Variegata' (F/v) 🏆H1 | CCCN EMui |
| 'Lipo' | CCCN MJnS NLar |
| ***madurensis*** | see *Fortunella japonica* |
| ***medica*** (F) | CHll |
| - 'Cidro Digitado' | see *C. medica* var. *digitata* |
| § - var. ***digitata*** (F) | CKob EMui |
| - var. ***sarcodactylis*** | see *C. medica* var. *digitata* |
| x ***meyeri*** | CHEx |
| - 'Improved Meyer' (F) | EMui |
| - 'Meyer' (F) 🏆H1 | CBcs CCCN CHll CKob CTsd EPfP LRHS MJnS NLar SPer |
| ***microcarpa*** Philippine lime | see x *Citrofortunella microcarpa* |
| ***mitis*** | see x *Citrofortunella microcarpa* |
| x ***nobilis*** Ortanique Group (F) | EPfP |
| x ***paradisi*** (F) | CCCN MREP SPoG SVic |
| - 'Star Ruby' (F/S) | EMui |
| 'Pursta' | CCCN |
| ***reticulata*** (F) | CCCN MREP |
| - Mandarin Group (F) | CDoC |

| | | |
|---|---|---|
| | – – 'Clementine' (F) | CDoC |
| | ***sinensis*** (F) | CCCN LPan LRHS SPoG SVic |
| | – 'Navelina' (F/S) | CDoC |
| | – 'Valencia' (F) | ECot EMui |
| | – 'Washington' (F/S) | EPfP |
| | ***unshiu*** 'Miyagawa' | CCCN |

## *Cladothamnus* see *Elliottia*

## *Cladrastis* (*Papilionaceae*)

| | | |
|---|---|---|
| § | ***kentukea*** | CArn CBcs CDul CLnd CMCN ELan EPfP MBlu MBri NLar SEND SHBN SSpi WDin |
| § | – 'Perkins Pink' | MBlu MBri SSpi |
| | – 'Rosea' | see *C. kentukea* 'Perkins Pink' |
| | ***lutea*** | see *C. kentukea* |
| | ***sinensis*** | CBcs CGHE EBee EPfP EPla IDee IFFs MBlu SKHP SSpi WPGP |

## *Clarkia* (*Onagraceae*)

| | | |
|---|---|---|
| * | ***repens*** | CSpe LCro |

## *Clavinodum* (*Poaceae*)

| | | |
|---|---|---|
| § | ***oedogonatum*** | EPla MWht |

## *Claytonia* (*Portulacaceae*)

| | | |
|---|---|---|
| | ***alsinoides*** | see *C. sibirica* |
| | ***australasica*** | see *Neopaxia australasica* |
| | ***caroliniana*** | NLar |
| § | ***perfoliata*** | CArn GPoy ILis WCHb WHer |
| § | ***sibirica*** | CAgr CArn CElw CSec LSou |
| | – 'Alba' | CElw WCot WMoo |
| | ***virginica*** | EHrv LAma WFar WMoo |

## *Clematis* ✿ (*Ranunculaceae*)

| | | |
|---|---|---|
| | BWJ 7630 from China | WCru |
| | BWJ 8169 from China | WCru |
| | CC 711 | CPLG |
| | CC 4167 **new** | GKev |
| | CC 4710 | CPLG |
| | SDR 2863 **new** | GKev |
| | SDR 3060 **new** | GKev |
| | SDR 4939 **new** | GKev |
| | WJS 8910 from Japan | WCru |
| | 'Abundance' (Vt) ♀H4 | CDoC CElw CRHN CSPN CWCL EBee EPfP ESCh ETho LCro LRHS MBri MRav NBea NHol NTay SDix SHBN SPer SPet |
| | ***acuminata*** var. ***sikkimensis*** B&SWJ 7202 | WCru |
| | ***addisonii*** | CBcs CSPN CWGN EBee ESCh MWhi NHaw WSHC |
| | ***aethusifolia*** | CSPN |
| | ***afoliata*** | CSPN EBee ECou WThu |
| | ***afoliata*** x ***forsteri*** | ECou |
| | 'Ai-Nor' (EL) | ETho |
| | 'Akaishi' (EL) | CWGN EBee ESCh ETho NTay |
| | ***akebioides*** | LRHS SHBN |
| | Alabast = 'Poulala'PBR (EL) ♀H4 | CSPN EBee ESCh ETho MAsh NBea NHaw NPri NTay SCoo SMDP SPoG SWCr |
| | 'Alba Luxurians' (Vt) ♀H4 | Widely available |
| | 'Albatross' | ESCh |
| | 'Albiflora' (A) | CSPN ECtt ESCh LCro NSti |
| | 'Albina Plena' (A/d) | ESCh ETho MAsh SMDP |
| | 'Aleksandrit' (EL) | CWGN NHaw |
| | 'Alice Fisk' (EL) | CSPN EBee ESCh ETho LSRN MSwo NBea NHaw NTay SHBN SSto WGor |
| | 'Alionushka' (I) ♀H4 | CElw CRHN CSam EBee ELan ELon EPfP ESCh ETho LRHS LSRN MAsh MBri MGos NBea NHol NPri NTay SAga SPer SPla SPoG SWCr WCra |
| | 'Allanah' (LL) | EBee ELon EPfP ETho LSRN MGos NHaw NTay SCoo SPoG WFar |
| | ***alpina*** ♀H4 | ECtt EPfP ESCh GGal GKir LCro MBar MRav MWhi NBlu NHaw NPer SHBN SPlb WBVN WFar |
| | – 'Albiflora' | see *C. sibirica* |
| | – 'Columbine White' | see *C.* 'White Columbine' |
| | – 'Jan Lindmark' | see *C.* 'Jan Lindmark' |
| I | – 'Odorata' | CSPN MGos NHaw |
| § | – 'Pamela Jackman' ♀H4 | CDoC CSPN CWSG EBee ELan ESCh GKir LAst LRHS MAsh MGos NBea NHol NSti NTay SBod SCoo SDix SPer SPoG SWvt WFar |
| | – pink-flowered | GKir |
| | – subsp. ***sibirica*** | see *C. sibirica* |
| | – 'Stolwijk Gold' | ESCh ETho MGos NTay |
| | ***alternata*** | CWGN ESCh ETho |
| | 'Amelia Joan' (Ta) | MWat |
| | 'Ameshisuto' (EL) | ESCh ETho |
| | 'Andromeda' (EL) | CSPN EBee ESCh ETho NBea NHaw NTay SGar WFar |
| | Angelique = 'Evipo017' (EL) | MAsh SPoG SWCr |
| | ***angustifolia*** | ETho |
| | 'Anita' (Ta) | EPfP ESCh ETho NHaw |
| | 'Anna' (EL) | ESCh NTay |
| | 'Anna Carolina' | ESCh |
| | Anna Louise = 'Evithree'PBR (EL) ♀H4 | CSPN CWCL EBee ESCh ETho IBal LRHS MBri NPri NTay SCoo SPoG SWCr |
| | 'Annabel' (EL) | CSPN |
| | 'Annemieke' (Ta) | ESCh MGos |
| | Anniversary = 'Pynot'PBR (EL) | ESCh LSRN SCoo |
| | ***anshunensis*** | see *C. clarkeana* H. Lév. & Vaniot |
| | 'Anti' (LL) | ESCh NBea |
| | 'Aotearoa' (LL) | ESCh NHaw |
| | Aphrodite = 'Aphrodite Elegafumina' | CRHN ESCh NBea NHaw |
| | ***apiifolia*** | MWhi |
| | – B&SWJ 4838 | WCru |
| | 'Apple Blossom' (Ar) ♀H4 | Widely available |
| | 'Apulejus' (A) | ESCh |
| | 'Arabella' (I) ♀H4 | CElw CPou CRHN CSPN CSam CWCL EBee ELan EPfP ESCh ETho LAst LCro LRHS LSRN MAsh MBri NBea NPri NTay SPer SPet SPoG SWCr SWvt WCra WFar |
| § | Arctic Queen = 'Evitwo'PBR (EL) ♀H4 | CSPN CWCL EBee ESCh ETho IBal LCro LRHS LSRN MAsh MBNS NPri NTay SCoo SPer SPoG SWCr WFar |
| | ***armandii*** | Widely available |
| | – 'Enham Star' | LBuc LRHS MBri MGos |
| § | – 'Little White Charm' | CSPN MBlu NLar SHBN SPoG |
| | – 'Meyeniana' | see *C. armandii* 'Little White Charm' |
| § | – 'Snowdrift' | CBcs CBgR CSBt CSPN CSam CWSG EBee ELan ELon EPfP ESCh ETho LCro LRHS MAsh MGos MLan NSti NTay SHBN SPer SPoG SRms |
| | x ***aromatica*** | CBcs CPrp CSPN CSam CWGN EAEE EBee ELan EPfP ESCh ETho LCro LFol LPio LRHS MBNS MCot MRav NBea NCGa NSti NTay SCoo SPoG |
| § | 'Asagasumi' (EL) | ESCh ETho NTay |
| | 'Asao' (EL) | CElw CFir CRHN EBee ELan EPfP ESCh ETho LAst LCro LRHS MGos MRav NTay SCoo SPer SPet SPoG SWCr |
| | 'Ascotiensis' (LL) | CBcs CRHN CSPN EBee EPfP ESCh ETho LRHS NHaw NTay SCoo SPer SPoG SWCr WFar |
| | 'Ashva' | CWGN ESCh ETho |

| | | |
|---|---|---|
| | 'Aureolin' (Ta) | CSPN CWSG EBee EPfP ESCh ETho LRHS MBar NHol SCoo WPGP |
| | Avant-garde = 'Evipo033'$^{PBR}$ (Vt) | CWGN ETho MAsh SPoG |
| § | 'Bagatelle' (LL) | CRHN CSPN ESCh LSRN MAsh NHaw SMDP SPad SPoG WFar |
| | 'Bal Maiden' (Vt) | CRHN |
| § | 'Ballerina in Blue' (A/d) | ESCh NHaw |
| | 'Ballet Skirt' (A/d) ♀H4 | ESCh LRHS MGos NHaw |
| | 'Bałtyk' (EL) | CSPN ESCh NTay |
| | 'Barbara' (LL) | ESCh ETho MRav NHaw NTay |
| | 'Barbara Dibley' (EL) | CTri CWSG ELon ESCh LRHS MBNS NBea NTay SCoo SDix SPet |
| | 'Barbara Harrington'$^{PBR}$ (LL) | ESCh MAsh NHaw |
| | 'Barbara Jackman' (EL) | CSam EBee ECtt ETho GKir LCro LRHS LSRN MAsh MBar MGos MRav MSwo NBea NTay SCoo SLim SPer SPoG SWCr WFoF |
| | ***barbellata*** | EBee |
| | 'Basil Bartlett' (Fo) | ECou |
| | 'Beata' (LL) | CWGN ESCh NBea |
| | 'Beauty of Richmond' (EL) | CWSG ESCh |
| | 'Beauty of Worcester' (EL) | CFir CSPN CWSG ELan ELon EPfP ESCh ETho GKir LAst LRHS LSRN MBar MSwo NBea NHaw NTay SCoo SDix SPer SPoG WFar |
| | 'Bees' Jubilee' (EL) | Widely available |
| | 'Bella' (EL) | EBee ESCh ETho NHaw SMDP |
| | 'Belle Nantaise' (EL) | EBee LRHS SCoo SPet |
| | 'Belle of Woking' (EL) | CRHN CSPN CWSG EBee ECtt ELan ELon EPfP ESCh ETho LCro LRHS LSRN MAsh MBar MRav NBea NTay SCoo SDix SHBN SLim SPet SPoG SWCr WBVN |
| | 'Benedictus' (EL) | ESCh |
| | 'Berry Red' (A) | CWGN |
| § | 'Beth Currie' (EL) | CSPN EBee ESCh MAsh NPri |
| | 'Betina' | see *C.* 'Red Beetroot Beauty' |
| | 'Betty Corning' (Vt) ♀H4 | CRHN CSPN CWGN EBee ELan ELon EPfP ESCh ETho LCro LFol LRHS MAsh MBri MGos NBea NPri NTay SCoo SLim SLon SWCr WFar WGwG |
| | 'Betty Risdon' (EL) | ESCh ETho LRHS |
| | 'Big Bird' (A/d) | ESCh |
| | 'Bill MacKenzie' (Ta) ♀H4 | Widely available |
| | 'Black Prince' (Vt) | CRHN CWGN EBee ELan ESCh ETho LCro LRHS LSRN NBea NHaw NLar NTay SLon SMDP |
| | 'Black Tea' (LL) | ESCh NBPN NHaw NTay |
| § | 'Błękitny Anioł' (LL) ♀H4 | CElw CRHN CSPN ESCh ETho LRHS MAsh MGos NBea NLar NPri NTay SCoo SPer SPet SPoG WFar |
| | Blue Angel | see *C.* 'Błękitny Anioł' |
| | 'Blue Belle' (Vt) | CPou CRHN ELan LCro LRHS NBea NSti NTay SLon SMDP SPet SPoG WFar |
| | 'Blue Bird' (A/d) | CBcs CWCL CWSG EBee ECtt ESCh GKir LCro NBea NHol SMDP SPoG |
| | Blue Blood | see *C.* 'Königskind' |
| | 'Blue Boy' (I) | see *C.* x *diversifolia* 'Blue Boy' (I) |
| | 'Blue Boy' | see *C.* 'Elsa Späth' |
| | 'Blue Dancer' (A) | CElw EBee EPfP ESCh EShb ETho IBal MAsh MGos NBea NLar NTay SPet SWCr |
| | 'Blue Eclipse' (A) | CSPN CWGN ETho LRHS MAsh MBri NHaw |
| | 'Blue Eyes' (EL) | CSPN EBee ESCh ETho LCro LSRN NHaw NTay SPoG |
| | 'Blue Fizz' **new** | ESCh |
| § | 'Blue Light'$^{PBR}$ (EL/d) | CSPN ELan ESCh ETho MGos NLar NTay WFar |

| | | |
|---|---|---|
| | Blue Moon = 'Evirin'$^{PBR}$ (EL) | ESCh ETho LAst LRHS LSRN MAsh MBNS NLar NPri NTay SCoo SWCr WFar |
| | Blue Pirouette = 'Zobluepi'$^{PBR}$ (I) | CWGN EBrs ESCh ETho MAsh NLar SMDP SPoG |
| | Blue Rain | see *C.* 'Sinii Dozhd' |
| | 'Blue Ravine' (EL) | EBee EPfP ESCh MGos NLar NTay SCoo SPoG |
| | 'Blue Tapers' (A) | ESCh NHaw |
| § | 'Blushing Ballerina' (A/d) | ESCh |
| | Bonanza = 'Evipo031'$^{PBR}$ **new** | ESCh MAsh SPoG |
| § | x ***bonstedtii*** 'Campanile' (H) | NBir |
| | - 'Crépuscule' (H) | CMdw SMDP SRms WCot |
| | 'Boskoop Beauty' (EL) | ESCh NHaw NTay |
| | Bourbon = 'Evipo018'$^{PBR}$ **new** | ETho LRHS MAsh |
| | 'Bowl of Beauty' (Ar) | MGos |
| | 'Bracebridge Star' (EL) | ECtt ESCh NBea |
| | 'Brocade' (Vt) | CRHN CSPN ESCh ETho SMDP |
| | 'Broughton Bride' | CSPN CWGN ESCh ETho MAsh NHol |
| | 'Broughton Star' (M/d) ♀H4 | Widely available |
| | 'Brunette' (A) | CSPN EBee ELan EPfP ESCh ETho MAsh MGos NBPN NHaw NLar NTay SHBN SMDP SPoG SWCr |
| | ***buchananiana*** Finet & Gagnep. | see *C. rehderiana* |
| | ***buchananiana*** DC. | EBee |
| | - B&SWJ 8333a | WCru |
| | 'Buckland Beauty' (V) | ESCh ETho |
| | 'Buckland Longshanks' (H) | SMDP |
| | 'Burford Princess' (Vt) | NHaw |
| I | 'Burford Variety' (Ta) | ESCh |
| | 'Burford White' (A) | CSPN EBee EPfP NLar |
| | 'Burma Star' (EL) | CWGN EPfP ESCh ETho NBea NHaw NTay |
| | 'C.W. Dowman' (EL) | ETho |
| | Caddick's Cascade = 'Semu' | CSPN CWGN ESCh ETho NHaw |
| | 'Caerulea Luxurians' (Vt) | CRHN CWGN ESCh NHaw NTay WSHC |
| | ***calycina*** | see *C. cirrhosa* var. *balearica* |
| § | ***campaniflora*** | CMea CRHN CSPN EShb ETho GCal NBea NHaw NWCA WCru WPGP |
| | 'Campanile' | see *C.* x *bonstedtii* 'Campanile' |
| | 'Candida' (EL) | EBee ESCh |
| | 'Candleglow' (A) | CElw CSPN EBee MAsh MBri |
| | 'Candy Stripe' | EBee ESCh NTay SCoo SPoG SWCr |
| | 'Capitaine Thuilleaux' | see *C.* 'Souvenir du Capitaine Thuilleaux' |
| | 'Cardinal Wyszyński' | see *C.* 'Kardynał Wyszyński' |
| | 'Carmencita' (Vt) | CRHN CSPN EBee ESCh ETho NBea NHaw NTay SCoo SDix SLon SPet WFar |
| | 'Carnaby' (EL) | CSPN CWCL CWSG EBee ELan EPfP ESCh ETho LAst LRHS LSRN MAsh MBar MBri MGos NBea NTay SCoo SLim SPoG SSto SWCr WPGP |
| | 'Carnival Queen' | CSPN CWSG ESCh NTay |
| | 'Caroline' (LL) | CSPN CWGN EBee ESCh ETho NHaw NTay SMDP |
| * | x ***cartmanii*** hort. (Fo) | SAga |
| | - 'Avalanche'$^{PBR}$ (Fo/m) ♀H3 | CSPN ELan ESCh ETho GBin LBuc LRHS MGos NCGa NLar NPri NTay SCoo SHBN SLim SPer SPoG |
| | - 'Joe' (Fo/m) | CBcs EBee ELan EPfP EPot ESCh ETho EWes GEdr ITim LRHS LSRN MAsh MGos MLan MRav NHol SCoo SPoG SWCr WCot WHil |

| | | |
|---|---|---|
| | - 'Joe' x ***marmoraria*** (Fo) | ECho MGos |
| | - 'Snow Valley'PBR (Fo) | NCGa |
| | - 'White Abundance'PBR (Fo/f) | ESCh ETho NLar SPoG |
| | x ***cartmanii*** hort x ***petriei*** (Fo) | ECho |
| | Cassis = 'Evipo020'PBR new | ETho MAsh NTay |
| | Cezanne = 'Evipo023'PBR (EL) | ETho LBuc MAsh SPoG SWCr |
| | 'Chacewater' (Vt) | CRHN |
| | 'Chalcedony' (EL) | CSPN CWGN ESCh ETho MGos |
| | 'Charissima' (EL) | CBcs CSPN CSam CWGN EPfP ETho MAsh MGos NLar NTay SCoo SPet SPoG SWCr WFar |
| | 'Chatsworth' (Vt) | LRHS MAsh |
| | ***chiisanensis*** | CSPN MWhi |
| | - B&SWJ 4560 | WCru |
| | - B&SWJ 8706 | WCru |
| | - 'Korean Beauty' new | CHFP |
| | - 'Lemon Bells' (A) | ELan EPfP ETho LRHS MAsh SCoo SMDP SPoG SWCr |
| | - 'Love Child' (A) | CElw CSPN EBee ELan ESCh MBlu NTay SLim SPer WCot |
| | 'China Blue' new | SMDP |
| | ***chinensis*** misapplied | see *C. terniflora* |
| | ***chinensis*** Osbeck RWJ 10042 | WCru |
| | Chinook = 'Evipo013'PBR | ESCh LRHS MAsh NTay |
| | 'Christian Steven' (LL) | CSPN ESCh |
| | ***chrysantha*** | see *C. tangutica* |
| | ***chrysocoma*** misapplied | see *C. spooneri* |
| N | ***chrysocoma*** Franch. | EPfP MAsh MBar NHol SMDP WCru |
| | - ACE 1093 | CPou |
| | - B&L 12237 | NBea |
| | 'Cicciolina' (Vt) | ETho NHaw |
| | ***cirrhosa*** | CTri ELan GKir LRHS MAsh MCot MGos MWhi NTay SArc SWCr |
| § | - var. ***balearica*** | Widely available |
| | - 'Ourika Valley' | EBee EPfP ESCh ETho MAsh NBea NLar NTay SWCr WFar |
| | - var. ***purpurascens*** 'Freckles' ♀H3 | Widely available |
| | - - 'Jingle Bells' | CRHN EBee EPfP ESCh ETho LCro LRHS MAsh NBea NHol SCoo SLim SPoG SWCr WFar |
| | - - 'Lansdowne Gem' | CSPN CWGN CWib SMDP |
| | - 'Wisley Cream' ♀H3 | Widely available |
| | 'Citra' | see *C.* 'Claudius' |
| | 'Claire de Lune' | EBee EPfP NPri SPoG |
| | ***clarkeana*** misapplied | see *C. urophylla* 'Winter Beauty' |
| § | ***clarkeana*** H. Lév. & Vaniot | ETho |
| § | 'Claudius' (A) | EBee SMDP |
| | 'Clochette Pride' (A/d) | ESCh |
| | 'Colette Deville' (EL) | NTay |
| | ***columbiana*** var. ***tenuiloba*** 'Ylva' (A) | WAbe |
| | 'Columbine' (A) | CWSG EBee ETho GGar MBar MSwo NBea NHol SDix SPer SPoG |
| | 'Columella' (A) | ESCh ETho NHaw NLar |
| | 'Comtesse de Bouchaud' (LL) ♀H4 | Widely available |
| | Confetti = 'Evipo036'PBR new | ESCh ETho LRHS LSRN MAsh NTay |
| | ***confusa*** HWJK 2200 | WCru |
| | ***connata*** | ESCh GQui |
| | - GWJ 9386 | WCru |
| | - HWJCM 132 | WCru |
| | aff. ***connata*** GWJ 9431 from West Bengal | WCru |
| | - HWJK 2176 from Nepal | WCru |
| | 'Constance' (A) ♀H4 | CElw CRHN CSPN CWCL EBee EPfP ESCh ETho LCro LRHS NBea NHaw NPri NSti NTay SCoo SPer SPoG SRms SWCr WBor WPGP |
| | 'Continuity' (M) | CWGN EBee MAsh NTay SDix SPla |
| | 'Corona' (EL) | CSPN ELan EPfP ETho LAst LRHS MAsh MBar NBea NHaw NTay SBod SCoo SPoG WFar |
| | 'Corry' (Ta) | ESCh NLar |
| | 'Côte d'Azur' (H) | CMdw GCal MAvo MCCP SPer WPtf |
| | 'Countess of Lovelace' (EL) | CBcs CSPN CWSG EBee ELan EPfP ESCh ETho LRHS MAsh MBar MBri MGos MRav NBea NTay SCoo SLim SPet SSto SWCr WFar |
| | County Park hybrids (Fo) | ECou |
| | 'Cragside' (A) | ESCh ETho NBea |
| | ***crassifolia*** B&SWJ 6700 | WCru |
| § | 'Crimson King' (LL) | ESCh ETho NHaw NTay WGor |
| | 'Crinkle' (M) | CCCN ESCh SMDP SPoG |
| § | ***crispa*** | CElw CPou CSPN ESCh GAuc IFro MWhi NBea WSHC |
| § | Crystal Fountain = 'Evipo038'PBR (EL) | CWCL CWGN ESCh ETho LCro LRHS MAsh NPri NTay SCoo SPoG SWCr |
| | x ***cylindrica*** | CSPN EBee |
| | 'Danae' (Vt) | CRHN NHaw |
| | 'Daniel Deronda' (EL) ♀H4 | CDoC CDul CSPN CWSG ECtt ELan ESCh ETho GKir LCro LRHS LSRN MAsh MGos MRav NBea NBir NPri NTay SCoo SDix SHBN SLim SPoG SWCr WFar |
| | 'Darius' (EL) | ESCh |
| | 'Dark Secret' (A) | CSPN EBee EPfP MAsh MBri |
| | 'Dawn' (EL) | CCCN CSPN ELon ESCh ETho LRHS LSRN MAsh NBea NTay SCoo SPoG SWCr |
| | 'Débutante' (EL) | ESCh NHaw |
| | 'Denny's Double' (EL/d) | CSPN CWGN CWSG ESCh ETho MAsh NTay |
| | 'Diana' (LL) | ESCh ETho |
| | ***dioica*** | EBee |
| | - F&M 100 | WPGP |
| | ***dioscoreifolia*** | see *C. terniflora* |
| § | x ***diversifolia*** | CRHN EBee ESCh LRHS MBNS MGos MSte NHaw NHol SDix SGar SHBN |
| § | - 'Blue Boy' (I) | CElw CMoH CRHN CSPN CSam EBee EPfP ESCh MGos NHaw NTay |
| | - 'Floris V' (I) | ESCh LPio NLar NTay |
| | - 'Heather Herschell' (I) | CElw CRHN CSPN EBee ESCh NBea NHaw NLar SMDP SPet |
| § | - 'Hendersonii' (I) | CPrp CSam EAEE EBee ELan EPfP ESCh ETho GGar GKir LAst LHop LPio LRHS MCot MRav MSwo NBea NBir NHol NSti NTay SDix SPer SWat |
| § | - 'Olgae' (I) | CMoH CPLG CSPN ETho NBea NTay SMDP WGwG |
| | 'Docteur Le Bêle' (LL) | NTay |
| | 'Doctor Penelope' (M) | ESCh |
| | 'Doctor Ruppel' (EL) | Widely available |
| | 'Dominika' (LL) | CSPN CWGN ESCh ETho NHaw NTay |
| | 'Dorath' | ESCh |
| | 'Dorothy Tolver' (EL) | ESCh ETho |
| | 'Dorothy Walton' | see *C.* 'Bagatelle' |
| | 'Double Cross' | ECou |
| | 'Dubysa' | ESCh |
| | 'Duchess of Albany' (T) | CSPN CTri CWSG CWib EBee ELan EPfP ESCh ETho IBal LAst LCro LRHS LSRN MAsh MBar NBea NHol NSti NTay SGar SHBN SLim SPer SPet SWCr WFar |
| | 'Duchess of Edinburgh' (EL) | Widely available |

| | | |
|---|---|---|
| | 'Duchess of Sutherland' (EL) | LRHS MGos NHaw SDix SPet |
| | 'Dulcie' | NHaw |
| | x ***durandii*** ♀H4 | CBcs CRHN CSPN CWCL EBee ELan EPfP ESCh ETho LRHS LSRN MAsh MBar MBri MRav NBea NHol NPri NSti SCoo SLim SPer SPla SPoG SWCr WFar |
| | 'Dusky Star' (M) | CWGN ESCh |
| | 'Early Sensation' (Fo/f) | Widely available |
| | 'East Malling' (M) | ESCh NHaw |
| | 'Edith' (EL) ♀H4 | ECtt ESCh ETho LSRN NBea NHaw NTay WGor |
| | 'Edomurasaki' (EL) | ESCh ETho |
| | 'Edouard Desfossé' (EL) | ESCh |
| | 'Edward Prichard' | CMoH CSPN EBee EPfP ESCh ETho MAvo MWea NBea NHaw SMDP |
| | 'Eetika' (LL) | ESCh ETho |
| | 'Ekstra' (LL) | EBee ESCh ETho |
| | 'Eleanor' (Fo/f) | ECou |
| | Eleanor of Guildford = 'Notpy'PBR (EL) | ESCh |
| | 'Elfin' (Fo/v) | ECou |
| | 'Elizabeth' (M) ♀H4 | Widely available |
| § | 'Elsa Späth' (EL) | Widely available |
| | 'Elten' (M) | CSPN CWGN SMDP |
| | 'Elvan' (Vt) | CRHN ESCh NHaw NLar SPet |
| | 'Emajõgi' (LL) | ESCh |
| | 'Emerald Stars' | ESCh |
| | 'Emilia Plater' (Vt) | CRHN CSPN ESCh ETho NBea NHaw NTay SLon |
| | Empress = 'Evipo011'PBR (EL) | LRHS |
| | 'Entel' (Vt) | CWGN ETho NHaw |
| | 'Erik' (A) | ESCh |
| | x ***eriostemon*** | see *C.* x *diversifolia* |
| | 'Ernest Markham' (LL) ♀H4 | Widely available |
| | 'Esperanto' (LL) | EBee ESCh NBea SMDP |
| | 'Essex Star' (Fo) | ECou |
| | 'Étoile de Malicorne' (EL) | ESCh NTay WGor |
| | 'Étoile de Paris' (EL) | ESCh |
| | Etoile Nacrée | see *C.* 'Sakurahime' |
| | 'Étoile Rose' (Vt) | CRHN CSPN CTri CWCL ELan EPfP ESCh ETho GKir LAst LRHS LSRN MAsh MRav NBea NHol NTay SCoo SDix SLim SPer SWCr WFar WPGP |
| | 'Étoile Violette' (Vt) ♀H4 | Widely available |
| | 'Eva' (LL) | ESCh NBea |
| | Evening Star = 'Evista'PBR | EPfP NTay WFar |
| | 'Eximia' | see *C.* 'Ballerina in Blue' |
| | 'Fair Rosamond' (EL) | EBee ELon EPfP ESCh LRHS NBea NHaw NTay SPet |
| | 'Fairy' (Fo/f) | ECou |
| | Fairy BluePBR | see *C.* Crystal Fountain = 'Evipo038' |
| | 'Fairy Queen' (EL) | ESCh ETho |
| | ***fargesii*** var. ***souliei*** | see *C. potaninii* var. *potaninii* |
| | x ***fargesioides*** | see *C.* 'Paul Farges' |
| | ***fasciculiflora*** | CMHG CRHN CSPN EBee IDee LRHS SAga SSpi |
| | - L 657 | WCru WPGP |
| | 'Fascination'PBR (I) | CWGN EBrs EPfP ESCh ETho LRHS NHaw SMDP |
| | ***fauriei*** | WSHC |
| | ***finetiana*** misapplied | see *C. paniculata* J.G.Gmel. |
| | 'Firefly' (EL) | ESCh MGos |
| | 'Fireworks' (EL) | CSPN CWGN EBee ECtt EPfP ESCh ETho LAst LCro LRHS LSRN MAsh MBri MGos MRav NBea NPri NTay SWCr WFar WFoF WGor |
| | 'Flamingo' (EL) | CWCL CWSG |
| | ***flammula*** | Widely available |
| | - 'Rubra Marginata' | see *C.* x *triternata* 'Rubromarginata' |
| § | 'Floral Feast' (A/d) | CSPN ESCh NBea NTay SPoG |
| | 'Floralia' | see *C.* 'Floral Feast' |
| | ***florida*** | CSPN CWGN ESCh |
| | - 'Bicolor' | see *C. florida* var. *sieboldiana* |
| | - var. ***flore-pleno*** (d) | CCCN CFir CSPN EBee ELan EPfP ESCh ETho LAst LCro LRHS MAsh NBea NHol NTay SHBN SPer SPla SPoG SWCr WCot WFar WGwG |
| | - Pistachio = 'Evirida'PBR (LL) | CCCN CSPN CWGN EBee EMil EPfP ESCh ETho IBal LBuc LCro LSRN MAsh MBNS NLar NTay SMDP SPer SWCr WFar |
| § | - var. ***sieboldiana*** (d) | Widely available |
| | - 'Thorncroft' (LL) | ETho |
| | 'Florida Blue' **new** | ESCh |
| | ***foetida*** | CBcs CSPN |
| | ***foetida*** x 'Lunar Lass' (Fo) | ECho ECou |
| | ***foetida*** x ***petriei*** | ECho ECou |
| | 'Fond Memories' (EL) | ETho LSRN |
| | 'Forever' | ESCh ETho |
| I | 'Forget-me-not' **new** | LSRN |
| | ***forrestii*** | see *C. napaulensis* |
| § | ***forsteri*** | CBcs CSPN ESCh ETho IDee LFol WPGP WSHC |
| | 'Foxtrot' (Vt) | CRHN ESCh NBea |
| | 'Foxy' (A) ♀H4 | CBcs EBee NBea NHaw NTay SLon SPoG WGob |
| | 'Fragrant Joy' (Fo/m) | ECou |
| | 'Fragrant Oberon' **new** | ECou |
| | 'Fragrant Spring' (M) | CSPN CWGN ECtt ETho MGos NHaw NLar SBod SMDP WFar WGwG |
| | 'Frances Rivis' (A) ♀H4 | Widely available |
| | 'Francesca' (A) | ESCh MGos |
| | 'Frankie' (A) ♀H4 | CSPN EBee ELan ESCh ETho LCro LRHS LSRN MAsh NTay SCoo SPoG SWCr |
| | Franziska Marie = 'Evipo008' (EL) | ESCh LRHS MAsh NPri NTay |
| | 'Frau Mikiko' (EL) | ESCh ETho |
| | 'Freda' (M) ♀H4 | CRHN CTri CWSG EBee ECtt ELan EPfP ESCh ETho LCro LRHS MAsh MBlu MBri MGos MRav NBea NHol NSti NTay SDix SGar SHBN SPer SPoG SWCr WCru |
| | 'Fryderyk Chopin' (EL) | CSPN ESCh ETho LCro NHaw NLar NTay |
| | 'Fuji-musume' (EL) ♀H4 | CSPN CWGN ESCh ETho NBea NHaw NLar NTay SPet SPoG SWCr WFar |
| | 'Fujinami' (EL) | ESCh |
| | 'Fukuzono' (I) | ETho NHaw |
| | ***fusca*** misapplied | see *C. japonica* |
| | ***fusca*** Turcz. | WIvy WSHC |
| | - dwarf | CWGN NHaw |
| § | - var. ***fusca*** | ESCh ETho WSHC |
| | - var. ***kamtschatica*** | see *C. fusca* Turcz. var. *fusca* |
| | 'Fuyu-no-tabi' (EL) | ESCh ETho |
| | 'G. Steffner' (A) | ESCh |
| | 'Gabrielle' (EL) | CSPN ESCh LSRN NHaw NTay SPoG |
| | Gazelle = 'Evipo014'PBR | ESCh LRHS MAsh NTay SPoG |
| | 'Gemini' | ESCh |
| | 'Generał Sikorski' (EL) | CBcs CMac CRHN CSPN CWSG ECtt ELan EPfP ESCh ETho LAst LCro LRHS LSRN MAsh MBri MGos NBea NTay SCoo SDix SHBN SLim SPer SPet SPoG SWCr |
| | ***gentianoides*** | ETho WCot |
| | 'Georg' (A/d) | ESCh MGos NHaw |
| | 'Georg Ots' (LL) | ESCh |
| | 'Giant Star' | CWGN ESCh LRHS MAsh MGos NLar NPer SMDP SPoG SSto |

| | | |
|---|---|---|
| | 'Gillian Blades' (EL) $\Upsilon^{H4}$ | CRHN CSPN EBee ELan EPfP ESCh ETho LAst LCro LRHS MAsh NBea NHaw NPri NTay SCoo SPer SPet SPoG SWCr |
| § | 'Gipsy Queen' (LL) $\Upsilon^{H4}$ | CBcs CSPN CWCL CWSG EBee ECtt ELan EPfP ESCh ETho GKir LCro LRHS LSRN MAsh MBar MRav NBea NPri NTay SDix SHBN SPet SPoG SWCr WFar |
| | 'Girenas' | ESCh |
| | 'Gladys Picard' (EL) | ESCh NHaw NTay WFar |
| | ***glauca*** Turcz. | see *C. intricata* |
| | ***glaucophylla*** | WCru WSHC |
| | 'Glynderek' (EL) | ESCh |
| | 'Golden Harvest' (Ta) | ESCh NHol NLar WFar |
| | Golden Tiara = 'Kugotia'PBR (Ta) $\Upsilon^{H4}$ | CSPN CWGN ESCh ETho LRHS MBri MGos NBea NLar NTay |
| | 'Gothenburg' (M) | EBee ESCh NBea NHaw WFar |
| I | 'Gothenburg Superba' **new** | SMDP |
| | 'Grace' (Ta) | CRHN CSPN EBee ESCh ETho NHaw NLar SMDP |
| I | 'Grandiflora' (F) | LCro WFar |
| | 'Grandiflora Sanguinea' Johnson | see *C.* 'Södertälje' |
| | ***grata*** misapplied | see *C.* x *jouiniana* |
| | ***grata*** Wall. B&SWJ 6774 | WCru |
| | 'Gravetye Beauty' (T) | Widely available |
| § | 'Grażyna' | ESCh NTay |
| | 'Green Velvet' (Fo/m) | ECou |
| | ***grewiiflora*** | SMDP |
| | - B&SWJ 2956 | WCru |
| | 'Guernsey Cream' (EL) | CFir CSPN CSam CWSG EBee EMil ESCh ETho LAst LCro LRHS MAsh MBri NBea NTay SCoo SDix SHBN SLim SPet SPoG SWCr WFar |
| | 'Guiding Star' (EL) | ETho NHaw |
| | 'H.F. Young' (EL) | CSPN CWSG EBee ELan EPfP ESCh ETho GKir LRHS LSRN MAsh MBar MBri MGos NBea NTay SCoo SDix SHBN SLim SPer SPet SPoG SWCr |
| | 'Hagley Hybrid' (LL) | Widely available |
| | 'Haku-ōkan' (EL) | CSPN EBee EPfP ESCh ETho LRHS MAsh NBea NLar NTay SCoo SPoG |
| | 'Hakuree' (I) | ESCh ETho SMDP |
| | 'Hanaguruma' (EL) | CSPN ESCh ETho NBea NHaw NTay SPoG WFar |
| | 'Hanajima' (I) | ESCh ETho SMDP |
| | 'Hania' | CWGN ESCh ETho |
| | 'Happy Anniversary' (EL) | ETho LCro LSRN NTay |
| | Harlow Carr = 'Evipo004'PBR | CWGN ESCh ETho LRHS MBri SCoo SPoG SWCr |
| | 'Harmony' (EL/d) | ESCh |
| | 'Haruyama' (EL) | ESCh |
| | Havering hybrids (Fo) | ECou |
| | 'Helen Cropper' (EL) | ESCh ETho MAsh |
| | 'Helios' (Ta) | CSPN EPfP ESCh ETho LRHS MGos NBea NSti NTay SCoo SPer SPoG WGwG |
| | 'Helsingborg' (A) $\Upsilon^{H4}$ | CBcs CSPN EBee ECtt ELan EPfP ESCh ETho LAst LCro LRHS MAsh NBea NHol NSti NTay SCoo SPla SPoG SWCr |
| | ***hendersonii*** Koch | see *C.* x *diversifolia* 'Hendersonii' |
| | ***hendersonii*** Stand. | see *C.* x *diversifolia* |
| I | 'Hendersonii' (I) | CSam ETho LRHS LSRN MSte NHol NTay SPla SRkn |
| | 'Hendersonii Rubra' (Ar) | CSPN NLar |
| | 'Hendryetta'PBR (I) | CWGN EBrs EPfP ESCh ETho MAsh NTay SMDP SPoG SRkn |
| | ***henryi*** | LSRN MAsh SBod |
| | - B&SWJ 3402 | WCru |
| | - var. ***morii*** | ESCh |
| | 'Henryi' (EL) $\Upsilon^{H4}$ | Widely available |

| | | |
|---|---|---|
| | - - B&SWJ 1668 | WCru |
| | ***heracleifolia*** | CBcs CBgR CFir CPou CSec CWCL ECtt ESCh GAuc GGar MAsh MWhi NHol NLar WMoo WPer |
| | - Alan BloomPBR | see *C. tubulosa* Alan Bloom = 'Alblo' |
| I | - 'Alba' (H) | LPio |
| | - 'Blue Dwarf' | ESCh ETho MGos SMDP |
| | - 'Campanile' | see *C.* x *bonstedtii* 'Campanile' |
| | - 'Cassandra' | CPrp EAEE ECtt EPfP ESCh ETho GCal MAvo MCot NCGa NHol NLar NOrc SAga SMDP |
| | - 'China Purple' | CBgR CSpe EBee ESCh LPio MBNS MHer MNrw NLar WHoo WPtf |
| | - var. ***davidiana*** | see *C. tubulosa* |
| | - 'Pink Dwarf' | CWGN ESCh ETho NLar SMDP |
| | - 'Roundway Blue Bird' | ESCh LHop LRHS NHaw |
| | 'Herbert Johnson' (EL) | ESCh |
| | ***hexapetala*** misapplied | see *C. recta* subsp. *recta* var. *lasiosepala* |
| | ***hexapetala*** Forster | see *C. forsteri* |
| | ***hexasepala*** | see *C. forsteri* |
| | 'Hikarugenji' (EL) | CSPN ESCh NHaw NTay |
| | ***hirsutissima*** | CGra |
| | - var. ***scottii*** | EBee GKev |
| | 'Honora' (LL) | CSPN CWGN ESCh NTay SCoo SPoG |
| | 'Horn of Plenty' (EL) | ESCh LRHS NBea NHaw SPet |
| | 'Huldine' (LL) $\Upsilon^{H4}$ | CBcs CElw CRHN CSPN EBee ELan EPfP ESCh ETho LAst LCro LRHS MBar MRav NBea NSti NTay SDix SPer SPet SPoG SSto SWCr WWlt |
| | 'Huvi' (LL) | CWGN ESCh ETho NHaw |
| | 'Hybrida Sieboldii' (EL) | CRHN EBee ESCh NTay SCoo WCot |
| | Hyde Hall = 'Evipo009'PBR | CWGN EBee EPfP ESCh ETho IBal LRHS MBri SPoG SWCr |
| | 'Hythe Egret' (Fo) | ECho ESCh LLHF SIng |
| | I am a Little Beauty = 'Zolibe' (Vt) | CWGN ESCh NHaw |
| | I am Red Robin = 'Zorero' (A) | ESCh SMDP |
| | ***ianthina*** | ESCh WPGP WSHC |
| | - var. ***kuripoensis*** B&SWJ 700 | WCru |
| | 'Ibi' (EL) **new** | ESCh |
| | Ice Blue = 'Evipo003'PBR (Prairie Series) (EL) | ETho MAsh NPri |
| | 'Ice Maiden' (EL) | NTay |
| | 'Ice Queen' (EL) | LRHS MAsh |
| | 'Ilka' (EL) | ESCh |
| | 'Imperial' (EL) | ESCh ETho NHaw |
| | ***indivisa*** | see *C. paniculata* J.G. Gmel. |
| | 'Inglewood' (EL) | NTay |
| | Inspiration = 'Zoin'PBR (I) | CSPN EBrs ELan EPfP ESCh ETho LCro MGos NLar NTay SCoo SMDP |
| | ***integrifolia*** | Widely available |
| I | - 'Alba' | CBcs CElw CSPN EBee ECtt ESCh ETho GBuc LAst LHop LPio LSRN MBNS MDKP MSte NBea NBir NHaw NTay SCoo SPer SPoG |
| | - 'Budapest' | ESCh NHaw NTay |
| | - 'Cora' (I) | CWGN |
| | - 'Hendersonii' Koch | see *C.* x *diversifolia* 'Hendersonii' |
| | - var. ***latifolia*** | CElw ESCh |
| | - mid-blue-flowered **new** | ESCh |
| | - 'Olgae' | see *C.* x *diversifolia* 'Olgae' |
| | - 'Ozawa's Blue' | CPrp EAEE EBee ESCh ETho LPio MBNS MSte NSti |
| | - white-flowered | see *C. integrifolia* 'Alba' |
| § | ***intricata*** | CBcs CPLG CSPN EBee MGos SGar |
| | - 'Harry Smith' (Ta) | ESCh SMDP |
| | 'Iola Fair' (EL) | CSPN ESCh ETho NHaw NTay |
| | ***ispahanica*** | SGar |

| | |
|---|---|
| 'Iubileinyi-70' (LL) | EBee ESCh |
| 'Ivan Olsson' (EL) | CSPN ESCh ETho NBea |
| 'Jackmanii' (LL) ♀H4 | CBcs CMac CTri EBee EPfP ESCh ETho GKir LCro LRHS LSRN MAsh MGos NBea NBlu NWea SCoo SLim SPer SPet SPoG SWCr WFar |
| 'Jackmanii Alba' (EL) | ELan EPfP ETho LAst LRHS LSRN MAsh MBar NBea NTay SCoo SLim SPet SWCr |
| 'Jackmanii Rubra' (EL) | ETho NBea |
| 'Jackmanii Superba' misapplied | see *C.* 'Gipsy Queen' |
| 'Jackmanii Superba' ambig. (LL) | Widely available |
| 'Jacqueline du Pré' (A) ♀H4 | CBcs CSPN CSam CWCL EBee ELan EPfP ESCh ETho MGos NBea NHaw NTay SMDP |
| 'Jacqui' (M/d) | ETho LRHS MGos NHaw NLar |
| 'James Mason' (EL) | CSPN ESCh ETho NBea NHaw NTay |
| 'Jan Fopma' PBR (I) | CWGN ESCh ETho NBPN SMDP |
| § 'Jan Lindmark' (A/d) | CBcs EBee EPfP ESCh ETho LCro LRHS MGos NBea NHol NLar NSti NTay SCoo SMDP SWCr WFar |
| § 'Jan Paweł II' (EL) | CWSG EBee ECtt ELan EPfP ESCh ETho GKir LRHS NBea SBod SCoo SPer SPet SSto |
| 'Janina' | CWGN ESCh |
| 'Janny' (A) **new** | ESCh |
| § ***japonica*** | CSPN ESCh ETho NHaw SMDP |
| - B&SWJ 11204 **new** | WCru |
| § - var. ***obvallata*** B&SWJ 8900 | WCru |
| 'Jasper' | ESCh |
| 'Jefferies' (Ar) | NLar |
| 'Jenny' (M) | CWGN EBee ESCh ETho MAsh MGos NHaw NLar SMDP |
| 'Jenny Caddick' (Vt) | CSPN ESCh ETho NHaw NTay SMDP |
| 'Jerzy Popiełuszko' | ETho |
| 'Joan Gray' (EL) | ESCh |
| 'Joan Picton' (EL) | CWSG ESCh NBea NTay |
| 'John Gudmundsson' (EL) | ESCh |
| 'John Huxtable' (LL) ♀H4 | CDoC CRHN EPfP ESCh ETho LRHS NBea NHaw NPri NTay SPoG SWCr WGor |
| John Paul II | see *C.* 'Jan Paweł II' |
| 'John Treasure' (Vt) | CRHN EBee ESCh ETho NHaw NLar |
| 'John Warren' (EL) | CWSG EBee ESCh ETho LRHS MAsh NHaw NTay SCoo SPer SPoG SWCr WFar |
| Josephine = 'Evijohill' PBR (EL) ♀H4 | CSPN CWCL EBee EPfP ESCh ETho LAst LCro LRHS LSRN MAsh MBNS NLar NPri NTay SCoo SPer SPoG SWCr WFar |
| § x ***jouiniana*** | EBee MBlu MRav NHol WGwG WSHC |
| - 'Chance' (H) | ESCh NHaw NTay |
| 'Julka' (EL) | ESCh ETho NHaw |
| 'June Pyne' | ESCh ETho LRHS |
| 'Justa' (Vt) | CWGN ESCh |
| 'Juuli' (I) | ESCh LSRN NTay |
| 'Kaaru' (LL) | CRHN CSPN ESCh ETho |
| 'Kacper' (EL) | CSPN ESCh ETho MGos NHaw |
| 'Kaiu' (V) | ESCh NHaw SPoG |
| § 'Kakio' (EL) | EBee ESCh ETho LAst LCro LSRN MGos NBea NTay SPer SPet SPoG SSto WFar |
| 'Kalina' (EL) | ESCh ETho NHaw |
| 'Kamilla' (EL) | CWGN ESCh |
| § 'Kardynał Wyszyński' (EL) | EBee ETho GKir MGos NBea SCoo SMDP SPoG |
| 'Karin' | ESCh |

| | |
|---|---|
| § 'Kasmu' (Vt) | ESCh ETho |
| 'Katharina' (EL) | ESCh |
| 'Kathleen Dunford' (EL) | LAst LRHS LSRN NBea NHaw SCoo SMDP SPoG |
| 'Kathleen Wheeler' (EL) | NTay |
| 'Kathryn Chapman' (Vt) | CRHN ESCh |
| 'Keith Richardson' (EL) | ESCh NTay |
| 'Ken Donson' (EL) ♀H4 | EBee EPfP ESCh MGos NTay SCoo SPoG |
| 'Kermesina' (Vt) ♀H4 | Widely available |
| 'Kiev' (Vt) | ESCh NHaw |
| 'Killifreth' (Vt) | CRHN |
| 'King Edward VII' (EL) | EBee EPfP ESCh LRHS MAsh NBea NTay SPoG SWCr WGor |
| King Fisher = 'Evipo037' **new** | ETho LRHS MAsh |
| 'King George V' (LL) | ESCh |
| 'Kiri Te Kanawa' (EL) | CSPN EBee ELon ESCh ETho LAst LSRN NBea NHaw NTay SMDP |
| ***kirilovii*** | ESCh |
| 'Kirimäe' (LL) | ESCh |
| 'Kjell' (EL) | ESCh |
| 'Kommerei' (LL) | ESCh ETho NHaw |
| § 'Königskind' (EL) | CSPN ESCh ETho NBea NTay |
| ***koreana*** | NHol SMDP WCru WSHC |
| - var. ***lutea*** | EBee GGar SMDP WCru |
| 'Kosmicheskaia Melodiia' (LL) | CSPN ESCh NTay |
| 'Kuba' (LL) | ESCh |
| 'Küllus' (LL) | CWGN ESCh ETho NTay |
| 'Kunpū' | ESCh |
| ***kweichowensis*** | ETho |
| ***ladakhiana*** | CSPN CSec ETho GQui MWhi NHaw SMDP WPtf |
| 'Lady Betty Balfour' (LL) | CElw CSPN CWSG ESCh ETho LRHS MBNS NTay SCoo SDix SGar SPet SPoG WFar |
| 'Lady Bird Johnson' (T) | EBee ESCh ETho MAsh NPri NTay SCoo SPoG SWCr |
| 'Lady Caroline Nevill' (EL) | ESCh NBea NTay SWCr |
| 'Lady Londesborough' (EL) | EBee EPfP ESCh LRHS NBea NHaw NTay SCoo SDix SPoG |
| 'Lady Northcliffe' (EL) | CSPN CTri CWSG EPfP ESCh ETho LRHS MAsh NBea NTay SDix SPet SWCr |
| 'Lambton Park' (Ta) ♀H4 | CFir CRHN EBee EPfP ETho LRHS NBea NHaw NLar NTay SMDP |
| ***lasiandra*** | NHaw |
| - B&SWJ 6252 **new** | WCru |
| - B&SWJ 6775 | WCru |
| 'Last Dance' (Ta) | CRHN |
| Lasting Love | see *C.* 'Grażyna' |
| 'Lasurstern' (EL) ♀H4 | CBcs CPLG CRHN CSPN CTri EBee ECtt ELan EPfP ESCh ETho GKir LAst LCro LRHS LSRN MAsh MBar MBri MLan MRav NTay SDix SWCr WFar |
| 'Laura' (LL) | ESCh NHaw |
| 'Laura Denny' (EL) | ESCh ETho SMDP |
| 'Lavender Lace' | ESCh |
| 'Lawsoniana' (EL) | CElw CRHN CWSG ETho LAst MBar NTay SSto |
| 'Lech Wałęsa' | ETho |
| 'Lemon Chiffon' (EL) | CSPN EBee EMil ESCh ETho MAsh NHaw NTay SPoG SWCr |
| 'Leoni' | ESCh |
| Liberation = 'Evifive' PBR (EL) | ESCh LAst LRHS MAsh SCoo SPoG SWCr |
| § ***ligusticifolia*** | NHaw |
| 'Liisu' (LL) | ESCh |
| 'Lilacina Floribunda' (EL) | CBcs EBee LRHS MBNS MBar NHaw |
| 'Lilactime' (EL) | ESCh NHaw |

| | | |
|---|---|---|
| | 'Lincoln Star' (EL) | CRHN EPfP ESCh GKir LAst LRHS MBar MGos NBea NTay SDix SPer SPet SPoG |
| | 'Lincolnshire Lady' (A) | NTay |
| | 'Little Bas' (Vt) | CRHN CSPN ESCh NHaw NLar NTay SLon |
| | 'Little Butterfly' (Vt) | CRHN ESCh NHaw NTay |
| | 'Little Nell' (Vt) | CCCN CElw CRHN CSPN ELan ESCh ETho GKir LRHS MRav NBea NHol NTay SCoo SDix SPer SPet SPoG WFar |
| | 'Lord Herschell' | ETho SMDP |
| | 'Lord Nevill' (EL) | CRHN CWSG EPfP ESCh ETho LRHS NBea NTay SDix SPoG SSto WFar |
| | 'Louise Pummell' **new** | ECou |
| | 'Louise Rowe' (EL) | CElw EBee ELan ESCh ETho LRHS LSRN MGos NBea NHaw NTay SPoG |
| | ***loureiroana*** HWJ 663 | WCru |
| | 'Love Jewelry' | CWGN ESCh ETho NHaw NTay |
| | 'Lucey' (LL) | ESCh |
| | 'Lucie' (EL) | NBea |
| | 'Lunar Lass' (Fo/f) | ECho EPfP ESCh ETho ITim NBea NLAp NSla SIng WPGP |
| I | 'Lunar Lass Variegata' (Fo/v) | ECho LLHF |
| | 'Luther Burbank' (LL) | ESCh NTay |
| § | 'M. Johnson' (A) | ESCh |
| § | 'M. Koster' (Vt) | CDoC CRHN CSam EBee EPfP ESCh ETho LRHS NBea NHaw SPer |
| | ***macropetala*** (d) | CBcs CSBt CSec EBee ELan EPfP ESCh ETho LAst LCro LRHS MBar MGan MGos MRav MWhi NBea SDix SGar SPer SPet SWCr WBrE WFar |
| | - 'Alborosea' | see *C.* 'Blushing Ballerina' |
| | - 'Blue Lagoon' | see *C. macropetala* 'Lagoon' Jackman 1959 |
| | - 'Lagoon' Jackman 1956 | see *C. macropetala* 'Maidwell Hall' Jackman |
| | - 'Lagoon' ambig. | LCro SPet |
| § | - 'Lagoon' Jackman 1959 (A/d) Ψ$^{H4}$ | CSPN EBee ETho LRHS LSRN MSwo NBea NHol NSti NTay SCoo SLim SPoG SWCr |
| § | - 'Maidwell Hall' Jackman (A/d) | CSPN CTri CWSG EBee ECtt EPfP ESCh ETho LRHS LSRN MAsh MGos NBea NHol SHBN SWCr WPGP WSHC |
| | - 'Maidwell Hall' O.E.P. Wyatt (A) | MAsh MRav SCoo |
| | - 'Wesselton' (A/d) Ψ$^{H4}$ | CSPN EPfP ESCh ETho LCro MAsh MBri MGos NBea NHaw NHol WFar |
| | - 'White Moth' | see *C.* 'White Moth' |
| | 'Madame Baron-Veillard' (LL) | ECtt ESCh LAst LCro LRHS MBar NTay SCoo SDix SPoG WFar |
| | 'Madame Edouard André' (LL) | CRHN CSPN EPfP ESCh LRHS MAsh NBea NTay SCoo SDix SPet SPoG SWCr WFar |
| | 'Madame Grangé' (LL) Ψ$^{H4}$ | CSPN EPfP ESCh LCro LRHS NBea NHaw NTay SCoo SPoG SWCr |
| | 'Madame Julia Correvon' (Vt) Ψ$^{H4}$ | Widely available |
| | 'Madame le Coultre' | see *C.* 'Mevrouw Le Coultre' |
| | 'Madame van Houtte' (EL) | ESCh |
| | 'Madeleine' (A) | ESCh |
| | 'Magnus Johnson' | see *C.* 'M. Johnson' |
| | 'Majojo' (Fo) | LLHF |
| § | ***mandschurica*** | ETho GCal NHaw |
| | - B&SWJ 1060 | WCru |
| | 'Marcel Moser' (EL) | NTay |
| | 'Marcelina' (EL) **new** | CWGN ESCh |
| | 'Margaret Hunt' (LL) | CSPN ELan ESCh ETho LRHS LSRN NBea NHaw SPla |
| | 'Margaret Jones' (M/d) | EBee ESCh NHaw |
| | 'Margaret Wood' (EL) | NTay |
| | 'Margot Koster' | see *C.* 'M. Koster' |
| | 'Maria Louise Jensen' (EL) | NTay |
| | 'Marie Boisselot' (EL) Ψ$^{H4}$ | Widely available |
| | 'Marinka' (H) | ESCh MAvo SMDP |
| | 'Märjamaa' (LL) | ESCh |
| | 'Marjorie' (M/d) | Widely available |
| | 'Markham's Pink' (A/d) Ψ$^{H4}$ | Widely available |
| | ***marmoraria*** Ψ$^{H2-3}$ | CMoH EAEE ECho LHop LRHS SIng WFar |
| | - hybrid (Fo) | ITim |
| | ***marmoraria* x *petriei*** | ECho |
| | 'Marmori' (LL) | CWGN ESCh ETho NHaw |
| | 'Mary Whistler' (A) | ESCh |
| | 'Mary-Claire' (EL/d) | ESCh |
| § | 'Maskarad' (Vt) | CSPN ESCh |
| | Masquerade (Vt) | see *C.* 'Maskarad' |
| I | 'Masquerade' (EL) | ETho LRHS MBri NTay |
| | 'Matilda' (EL) | ESCh |
| | 'Matka Siedliska' (EL) | CSPN NTay |
| | 'Maureen' (LL) | CSPN CWGN CWSG ETho |
| | ***maximowicziana*** | see *C. terniflora* |
| | 'Mayleen' (M) Ψ$^{H4}$ | CPou CSBt CWSG EBee ECtt EPfP ESCh ETho LCro LRHS MAsh MBri MGos MRav NBea NTay SAga SBod SCoo SHBN SLim SPer SPet SPoG SSto SWCr WFar |
| | Medley = 'Evipo012'$^{PBR}$ | ESCh LRHS MAsh NTay |
| | 'Meeli' (LL) | EBee ESCh |
| | 'Meloodia' (LL) | NBea |
| § | 'Mevrouw Le Coultre' (EL) | MGan NBlu |
| | ***microphylla*** | ECou |
| | 'Mikelite' (Vt) | ESCh ETho NHaw |
| | 'Miniseelik' (LL) | ESCh ETho NTay SMDP |
| | 'Minister' (EL) | ESCh ETho SPoG |
| | 'Minuet' (Vt) Ψ$^{H4}$ | CRHN CSPN ELon EPfP ESCh ETho GKir LRHS MSwo NBea NHol NTay SCoo SDix SPer SPla SPoG |
| | 'Miriam Markham' (EL) | ESCh NBea NHaw |
| | 'Miss Bateman' (EL) Ψ$^{H4}$ | Widely available |
| | 'Miss Christine' (M) | ESCh ETho LCro LSRN WFar |
| | 'Miss Crawshay' (EL) | NHaw |
| N | ***montana*** | CBcs CPLG CSBt EBee ECtt GGal GQue MBar MGos NBea NHol SBod SDix SHBN SPet SSta WFar |
| | - B&SWJ 6724 from Taiwan | WCru |
| | - B&SWJ 6930 | WCru |
| | - BWJ 8189b from China | WCru |
| | - HWJK 2156 from Nepal | WCru |
| | - ***alba*** | see *C. montana* |
| | - 'Alexander' | CPou CWSG LRHS MAsh MBNS MGos SWCr |
| | - var. ***grandiflora*** Ψ$^{H4}$ | Widely available |
| I | - 'Lilacina' | ESCh MAsh |
| | - 'Peveril' | CSPN ESCh ETho |
| | - 'Prosperity' | ESCh |
| | - var. ***rubens*** E.H.Wilson | Widely available |
| I | - - 'Odorata' | EBee ESCh ETho LFol MGos MRav SBod SCoo SLim SPoG WGor WGwG |
| | - - 'Pink Perfection' | CDoC CWSG EBee ECtt ELan EPfP ESCh LAst LBMP LCro LRHS LSRN MAsh NBea NBlu NHol NTay SCoo SPer SPoG SSto SWCr WFar |
| | - - 'Tetrarose' Ψ$^{H4}$ | Widely available |
| | - - 'Veitch' | ESCh |
| I | - 'Rubens Superba' | CMHG CTri CWSG EBee ECtt ESCh LBuc MGan NPri SHBN SLim WBVN WFar |
| | - var. ***sericea*** | see *C. spooneri* |
| | - 'Spooneri' | see *C. spooneri* |

| | | |
|---|---|---|
| § | - var. ***wilsonii*** | Widely available |
| | - - DJHC 0540 **new** | WCru |
| | - - DJHC 795 | ETho SMDP |
| | 'Monte Cassino' (EL) | CSPN CWGN EBee ESCh ETho NBea SMDP SPoG |
| | 'Moonbeam' (Fo) | CMHG CPrp EAEE EBee ECou ELan EPot ESCh GEdr GKev ITim MGos MRav MSte NBea NOrc NTay SLon WCot |
| § | 'Moonlight' (EL) | CElw CSPN ESCh LRHS NTay |
| | 'Moonman' (Fo) | LLHF |
| | Morning Cloud | see *C.* 'Yukikomachi' |
| | 'Morning Yellow' (M) | CCCN MAsh SMDP |
| | 'Mrs Bush' (LL) | LRHS |
| | 'Mrs Cholmondeley' (EL) ♀H4 | CMac CSPN CWSG EBee ELan EPfP ESCh ETho GKir LAst LCro LRHS LSRN MAsh MBar MBri MGan MGos MSwo NBea NBlu NPri NTay SDix SLim SPoG SWCr WFar |
| | 'Mrs George Jackman' (EL) ♀H4 | CSPN ESCh ETho LCro MGos NBea NLar NTay SCoo SPla SPoG |
| | 'Mrs Hope' (EL) | ESCh |
| | 'Mrs James Mason' (EL) | ELon ESCh ETho NBea NHaw NTay SMDP SPoG |
| | 'Mrs N.Thompson' (EL) | CMac CSPN CTri EBee ELan ESCh ETho LAst LCro LRHS LSRN MAsh MBar MBri MGos NBea NBir NPer NTay SDix SHBN SPer SPoG WFar |
| | 'Mrs P.B.Truax' (EL) | ESCh LRHS NBea NTay SDix SMDP SPoG |
| | 'Mrs. P.T. James' (EL) | ESCh |
| | 'Mrs Robert Brydon' (H) | CChe IPot MBNS NBPC NHol NLar NSti NTay SRGP STes WCot WFar |
| | 'Mrs Spencer Castle' (EL) | CSPN ESCh ETho NBea NTay |
| | 'Mrs T. Lundell' (Vt) | CRHN CSPN EBee ESCh ETho NTay |
| | 'Multi Blue' (EL) | Widely available |
| | 'My Angel'PBR (Ta) | CSPN ELan ESCh MGos NBPN NHaw NLar NTay SPer |
| | 'Myōjō' (EL) | CSPN EBee ESCh LRHS SPoG |
| | 'Nadezhda' (LL) | ESCh NBea SMDP |
| § | ***napaulensis*** | CSPN CTri ESCh ETho LFol LRHS NTay WCru WFar WSHC |
| I | 'Natacha' (EL) | CElw EBee ESCh MAsh NBea NHaw NTay SCoo SPet |
| | 'Natascha' (EL) | LSRN SPoG |
| | 'Neapolitan' | ESCh |
| | 'Negritianka' (LL) | CSPN EBee ESCh NBPN NBea NHaw NTay SPoG |
| | 'Negus' (LL) | ESCh |
| | 'Nelly Moser' (EL) ♀H4 | Widely available |
| | 'Nelly Moser Neu' (EL) **new** | NTay |
| | 'New Dawn' (M) | CSPN LCro NHaw |
| | 'New Love'PBR (H) | CSPN CWGN ESCh ETho LHop LSRN MBlu MGos NHaw NLar NSti |
| | New Zealand hybrids (Fo) | ECou |
| | 'Nikolai Rubtsov' (LL) | CSPN ESCh SMDP |
| | 'Niobe' (EL) ♀H4 | Widely available |
| | 'Norfolk Queen' (EL) | ESCh |
| | 'North Star' (EL) **new** | NTay |
| | North Star (LL) | see *C.* 'Põhjanael' |
| | 'Nuit de Chine' (EL) | CWGN ESCh |
| | ***nutans*** var. ***thyrsoidea*** | see *C. rehderiana* |
| | ***obvallata*** | see *C. japonica* var. *obvallata* |
| | 'Ocean Pearl' (A) | ETho NLar NTay |
| | ***ochotensis*** | CSPN SDys |
| | 'Odoriba' (V) | CWGN ESCh ETho NLar |
| | 'Ola Howells' (A/d) | ESCh NBea |
| | 'Olga' (M) | ESCh |
| | 'Olimpiada-80' (EL) | ESCh |
| | 'Omoshiro' (EL) | CWGN ESCh ETho MGos NBea NHaw NTay |
| | 'Oonagare Ichigoo' (Vt) | ESCh |
| | Opaline | see *C.* 'Asagasumi' |
| | ***orientalis*** misapplied | see *C. tibetana* subsp. *vernayi* |
| | ***orientalis*** L. | CElw CSec EBee GCra LRHS NHol SCoo WFar |
| | - 'Orange Peel' | see *C. tibetana* subsp. *vernayi* var. *vernayi* 'Orange Peel' |
| | 'Otto Fröbel' (EL) | CSPN ESCh NTay |
| | 'Pagoda' (Vt) ♀H4 | CDoC CRHN EBee EPfP ESCh ETho LAst LRHS MAsh MBri MRav NBea NHol NSti NTay SCoo SPla SRms SWCr |
| | Palette = 'Evipo034'PBR **new** | MAsh SPoG |
| | 'Pamela' (F) | CSPN ESCh ETho LBuc NHaw NTay |
| | 'Pamela Jackman' | see *C. alpina* 'Pamela Jackman', *C.* 'Pamela Jackman' (Vt) |
| § | 'Pamela Jackman' (Vt) **new** | GKir SPet |
| | 'Pamiat Serdtsa' (I) | EBee ESCh ETho NHaw |
| | 'Pamina' (EL) | ETho |
| | 'Pangbourne Pink' (I) ♀H4 | CSPN CWCL EBee EPfP ESCh ETho GBuc LRHS MAsh NBea NHaw NTay SCoo SPoG |
| | ***paniculata*** Thunb. | see *C. terniflora* |
| § | ***paniculata*** J.G.Gmel. | CSPN LRHS WPGP |
| | - (f) | ETho |
| | - var. ***lobata*** | LCro NLar |
| | 'Paola' (EL/d) | ESCh |
| | 'Paradise Queen' (EL) | ESCh LBuc NLar WFar |
| | 'Parasol' (EL) | CSPN ESCh |
| | Parisienne = 'Evipo019'PBR | LBuc MAsh SPoG SWCr |
| | ***parviflora*** DC. | see *C. campaniflora* |
| | ***parviloba*** var. ***bartlettii*** B&SWJ 6788 | WCru |
| | 'Pastel Blue' (I) | ESCh ETho NBea SMDP |
| | 'Pastel Pink' (I) | ESCh SMDP |
| | 'Pastel Princess' (EL) | NHaw NTay |
| | 'Pat Coleman' (EL) | ETho |
| | ***patens*** 'Korean Moon' (EL) | WCru |
| § | - 'Manshuu Ki' (EL) | CDoC CElw CRHN CSPN CWSG EBee ECtt EPfP ESCh ETho GKir LCro MRav NBea NTay SGar SHBN SPer SPla SPoG |
| | - 'Nagoya' (EL) | ESCh |
| | - 'Sanda' (EL) | ESCh |
| | - 'Yukiokoshi' (EL) | ESCh ETho NTay |
| | Patricia Ann Fretwell = 'Pafar' (EL) | CSPN LRHS |
| § | 'Paul Farges' (Vt) ♀H4 | CSPN CWGN EBee ETho MBlu NHol NSti NTay SMDP |
| | 'Pauline' (A/d) ♀H4 | CBcs CWSG EBee ESCh ETho LRHS LSRN NBea NTay SCoo SWCr |
| | 'Pearl Rose' (A/d) | CWSG |
| | 'Pendragon' (Vt) | CRHN CWGN ESCh NHaw |
| | 'Pennell's Purity' (LL) | NBea NHaw NTay |
| | 'Perle d'Azur' (LL) | Widely available |
| | 'Perrin's Pride' (Vt) | ESCh LRHS MAsh MGos NBea NLar NTay SCoo SWCr |
| | Petit Faucon = 'Evisix'PBR (I) ♀H4 | EBee ECtt EPfP ETho LAst LRHS LSRN MAsh MBNS MBri NBea NPri NSti NTay SCoo SLim SPer SPoG SWCr WPGP |
| | ***petriei*** | ECou GBBs GGar |
| | - 'Princess' (Fo/f) | ECou SIng |
| | - 'Steepdown' (Fo/f) | ECou |
| | 'Peveril Pearl' (EL) | ESCh ETho NTay |
| | 'Peveril Profusion' (T) **new** | MAsh SPoG |
| | 'Phoenix' (EL) | ESCh NTay |
| | Picardy = 'Evipo024'PBR (EL) | ETho LBuc LRHS MAsh SPoG SWCr |
| I | 'Picton's Variety' (M) | CTri EBee ESCh NHaw NHol SHBN SMDP WFar |
| | ***pierotii*** B&SWJ 6281 | WCru |

| | | |
|---|---|---|
| | 'Piilu' (EL) | CSPN CWGN ELan ESCh ETho LBuc LCro LRHS LSRN MAsh MBNS MBri MWea NBea NHaw NPri NTay SCoo SMDP SPad SPoG SWCr |
| | 'Pink Celebration' | CWGN ESCh ETho |
| | 'Pink Champagne' | see *C.* 'Kakio' |
| | 'Pink Delight'PBR **new** | CWGN |
| | 'Pink Fantasy' (LL) | CRHN CSPN CTri CWSG ESCh ETho LCro LRHS MBar NBea NTay SCoo SLim SPoG SRkn SWCr |
| | 'Pink Flamingo' (A) ♀H4 | CSPN CWCL EBee ECtt ELan EPfP ESCh ETho LCro LRHS NSti NTay SBod SCoo SPet SPoG SRkn SWCr WBrE |
| | 'Pink Ice' (I) | ESCh |
| | 'Pink Pearl' (EL) | ESCh NTay |
| | 'Pink Starlight' (M) | ESCh SMDP |
| | 'Pirko' (Vt) | ESCh NHaw |
| § | ***pitcheri*** | ESCh ETho WSHC |
| | 'Pixie' (Fo/m) | CSPN ECou ELan EPfP ESCh ETho GGar ITim LRHS MAsh MGos NHaw NHol NLar NTay SBod SCoo SPoG |
| I | 'Pleniflora' (M/d) | ESCh MGos NHaw |
| § | 'Plum Beauty' (A) | CSPN ESCh NHaw |
| § | 'Põhjanael' (LL) | CSPN CWSG ESCh MGos NBea |
| | 'Pointy' (A) | ESCh |
| | Polar BearPBR | see *C.* Arctic Queen |
| | 'Poldice' (Vt) **new** | CRHN |
| | 'Polish Spirit' (LL) ♀H4 | Widely available |
| | 'Polonez' (Vt) | ETho |
| | ***potaninii*** | CSPN ECtt EPPr ETho GCra MWhi SBod WPtf WSHC |
| § | - var. ***potaninii*** | NTay |
| | - var. ***souliei*** | see *C. potaninii* var. *potaninii* |
| | - 'Summer Snow' | see *C.* 'Paul Farges' |
| | 'Praecox' (H) ♀H4 | CPrp CRHN CWCL EAEE EBee ECtt ELan EPfP ESCh ETho LAst LHop LRHS MAvo MBar MBri NBea NBir NHol NSti SDix SPet SWCr WCot |
| * | 'Prairie' | LRHS |
| | 'Prairie River' (A) | ETho |
| | Pretty in Blue = 'Zopre'PBR (F) | EBee ESCh ETho NTay SHBN SMDP |
| | 'Pribaltika' (LL) | ESCh |
| | 'Primrose Star' (M) | CDoC CSPN CWGN EBee EPfP ESCh ETho LRHS MAsh MBlu MGos MRav MSwo NHol NLar SPoG SSto WFar |
| | 'Prince Charles' (LL) ♀H4 | CElw CPou CRHN CSPN CTri EBee ELan EPfP ESCh ETho LCro LRHS LSRN NBea NTay SCoo SDix SLim SPer SPoG SWCr WFar WGwG |
| | 'Prince Philip' (EL) | ESCh NTay WFar |
| § | 'Princess Diana' (T) ♀H4 | Widely available |
| § | 'Princess of Wales' (EL) | CSam CWCL EPfP ESCh LRHS LSRN MBNS NLar NPri NSti WFar |
| | 'Prins Hendrik' (EL) | WGor |
| | 'Prinsesse Alexandra'PBR | EBee ESCh ETho NTay SPad |
| | 'Propertius' (A) | CWGN EBee ESCh ETho NHaw SMDP SPoG |
| | 'Proteus' (EL) | CSPN ELan EPfP ESCh ETho LAst LCro LRHS MAsh MBNS NBea NTay SCoo SDix SPet |
| | 'Pruinina' | see *C.* 'Plum Beauty' |
| | ***psilandra*** | SMDP |
| | 'Purple Haze' (Vt) | CRHN |
| | 'Purple Princess' (H) | ESCh MAvo NCGa |
| | 'Purple Rain' (A) **new** | MAsh |
| | 'Purple Spider' (A/d) | CSPN EBee ESCh ETho MBlu NHaw NHol NLar NTay SCoo SPer SPoG |
| | 'Purpurea Plena Elegans' (Vt/d) ♀H4 | Widely available |
| | ***quadribracteolata*** | ECou |
| | - 'Nancy's Lookout' | ECou |
| | 'Queen Alexandra' (EL) | ESCh |
| | 'Queen of Holland'PBR **new** | CWGN ESCh |
| | 'Radar Love' (Ta) | GMaP LLHF NLar WBrE |
| | 'Radost' (EL) | ESCh |
| | 'Ragamuffin' (EL/d) | ESCh |
| | 'Rahvarinne' (LL) | ESCh ETho |
| | 'Ramona' (LL) | ETho LSRN MAsh NHaw |
| | ***recta*** | CSPN ECtt EPfP ETho GKir LPio LRHS MCot MLLN MNrw MWhi NBea NLar WPer WTin |
| § | - 'Lime Close' (F) | LPio MSte |
| I | - 'Peveril' (F) | CPrp ESCh MSte NBea SMDP |
| | - 'Purpurea' (F) | Widely available |
| § | - subsp. ***recta*** var. ***lasiosepala*** | CSPN |
| | - Serious Black | see *C. recta* 'Lime Close' |
| | - 'Velvet Night' (F) | CMHG CPrp CWGN EAEE ECtt ESCh LHop NCGa NHol NLar SMDP SPoG WAul |
| | 'Red Ballon' (Ta) | ESCh SMDP |
| § | 'Red Beetroot Beauty' (A) | CSPN ESCh |
| | 'Red Cooler' | see *C.* 'Crimson King' |
| | 'Red Pearl' (EL) | ESCh ETho MGos NTay |
| § | ***rehderiana*** ♀H4 | Widely available |
| | - BWJ 7700 | WCru |
| | 'Remembrance' (LL) **new** | ETho LSRN |
| | ***repens*** | see *C. montana* var. *wilsonii* |
| | 'Rhapsody' ambig. | EPfP ETho LRHS MAsh MGos NTay SCoo SPoG SSto SWCr WFar |
| I | 'Rhapsody' B. Fretwell (EL) | CSPN LSRN NHaw |
| | 'Richard Pennell' (EL) ♀H4 | EBee ESCh ETho LRHS MAsh NBea NTay SDix SPoG SWCr |
| | 'Rodomax' (A) | ESCh |
| | 'Roko-Kolla' (LL) | CSPN EBee ESCh ETho NBea |
| | 'Romantika' (LL) | CSPN EBee ELan ELon ESCh ETho LCro NBPN NBea NHaw NTay SCoo SPer SPoG |
| | 'Roogoja' (LL) | ESCh |
| | 'Rooguchi' (I) | EBee ESCh ETho LRHS MAsh SMDP SPoG SWCr |
| | 'Rosa Königskind' (EL) | ESCh ETho |
| | 'Rose Supreme' (EL) | ESCh ETho |
| I | 'Rosea' (I) ♀H4 | CBcs CPrp CSPN EAEE EBee EPfP ESCh ETho LAst LHop LSRN MSte MTho NBea NChi NSti NTay SPoG |
| | Rosebud = 'Robud'PBR (M/d) | EBee ESCh NLar NPer SMDP |
| | Rosemoor = 'Evipo002'PBR | CWCL CWGN EPfP ETho IBal LRHS MAsh MBri SCoo SWCr |
| | 'Rosy O'Grady' (A) ♀H4 | CWCL EBee ELan ETho MBar MBri MGos NHol NLar NSti |
| | 'Rosy Pagoda' (A) | EBee ELan EPfP ESCh LCro LRHS MBri NBea NBir NHaw NLar |
| | 'Rouge Cardinal' (LL) | Widely available |
| | 'Royal Velours' (Vt) ♀H4 | CDoC CElw CRHN CSPN CTri EBee ELan EPfP ESCh ETho GKir LCro LRHS LSRN MAsh MWhi NBea NHol NSti SCoo SDix SHBN SLim SPer SPet SWCr |
| | Royal Velvet = 'Evifour'PBR (EL) | CSPN CWCL EPfP ESCh ETho IBal LAst LSRN MBri NTay SCoo SLim SPoG |
| | 'Royalty' (EL) ♀H4 | CElw CSPN ELan EPfP ESCh IBal LRHS LSRN MAsh NBir NPri NTay SCoo SLim SPer SPoG SWCr |
| | 'Rozalia' (EL) | ESCh |
| | 'Rubens Superba' | see *C. montana* 'Rubens Superba' |
| | 'Ruby' (A) | CMHG CSPN CWSG EBee EPfP ETho LCro LRHS LSRN MAsh MGos NBea NBlu NHol NSti SCoo SHBN SPer SPoG |

| | | |
|---|---|---|
| | 'Ruby Glow' (EL) | EPfP ESCh LSRN NTay SCoo SPoG |
| | 'Rüütel' (EL) | ESCh ETho NBea NHaw NTay SCoo SMDP SPoG |
| | 'Saalomon' (LL) | ESCh ETho |
| | 'Sakala' (EL) | ESCh |
| § | 'Sakurahime' (EL) | EBee ESCh |
| | 'Sally Cadge' (EL) | ESCh NTay |
| | 'Samantha Denny' (EL) | CSPN ESCh ETho NBea NHaw |
| | 'Sander' (H) | CSPN ESCh ETho SMDP |
| | 'Sandra Denny' (EL) | ETho |
| | 'Sano-no-murasaki' (EL) | ESCh |
| | Saphyra Indigo = 'Cleminov51' **new** | MAsh |
| | 'Satsukibare' (EL) | ESCh MGos |
| I | 'Saturn' (LL) | ESCh NBea SPla |
| | 'Saturn' (EL) | ESCh |
| | Savannah = 'Evipo015'$^{PBR}$ (Vt) **new** | MAsh NTay |
| | 'Scartho Gem' (EL) | EPfP ESCh NTay SCoo SPoG |
| | 'Sealand Gem' (EL) | ESCh ETho LAst NBea NHaw NTay |
| | 'Serenata' (EL) | ESCh |
| | ***serratifolia*** | CElw ESCh ETho MDKP MLLN MWhi SDix SMDP SWal WBVN WFar |
| | - B&SWJ 8458 from Korea | WCru |
| | 'Sheila Thacker' (EL) | ETho |
| | 'Shin-shigyoku' (EL) | CWGN ESCh MGos NTay |
| | 'Shirayukihime' (LL) | CSPN ESCh |
| § | 'Shiva' (A) | MAsh MBri |
| | 'Sho-un' (EL) | EBee ESCh |
| | 'Sialia' (A/d) | ESCh |
| § | ***sibirica*** | SPla |
| | 'Signe' (EL) **new** | ETho |
| | 'Signe' (Vt) | see *C.* 'Kasmu' |
| | 'Silmakivi' (EL) | ESCh |
| | 'Silver Lady' | SPoG |
| | 'Silver Moon' (EL) | CSPN ESCh ETho LCro NBea NLar NTay SCoo |
| | 'Simplicity' (A) | CSPN EBee MAsh MBri |
| | ***simsii*** Small | see *C. pitcheri* |
| | ***simsii*** Sweet | see *C. crispa* |
| | 'Sinee Plamia' (LL) | ESCh NHaw |
| § | 'Sinii Dozhd' (I) | CSPN ESCh |
| | 'Sir Eric Savill' (M) | ESCh |
| | 'Sir Garnet Wolseley' (EL) | ESCh SDix |
| | 'Sir Trevor Lawrence' (T) | CSPN EBee ESCh ETho LAst LRHS MAsh NBea NHaw NHol NSti NTay SCoo SPer SPoG SWCr WFar |
| | 'Sizaia Ptitsa' (I) | ESCh ETho |
| | 'Sky Blue' **new** | ESCh |
| | 'Snow Queen' (EL) | CSPN EBee ELon EPfP ESCh ETho LRHS MBri MGos NBea NTay SPet |
| | 'Snowbird' (A/d) | CSPN ELon ESCh NHaw NHol |
| | 'Snowdrift' | see *C. armandii* 'Snowdrift' |
| § | 'Södertälje' (Vt) | CRHN ESCh ETho NBea SCoo SPoG WFar |
| | 'Solidarność' (EL) | ETho |
| | ***songarica*** | ESCh NHol |
| | 'Sonnette' | ESCh |
| | 'Souvenir de J.L. Delbard' (EL) | ESCh |
| § | 'Souvenir du Capitaine Thuilleaux' (EL) | ESCh GKir LAst MAsh MGos NBea NTay |
| | 'Special Occasion' (EL) | CSPN CWGN EBee ESCh ETho LBuc LSRN MAsh MBNS NBea NHaw NLar NPri NTay SCoo SPoG WFar |
| § | ***spooneri*** | CElw CTri CWSG ECtt EPfP ESCh GQui MAsh MGan SCoo SRms SWCr WFoF |
| | 'Sputnik' (I) | CSPN CWGN ESCh NHaw NTay |
| | Stanislaw Moniuszko = 'Moniuszko' | CWGN ESCh |

| | | |
|---|---|---|
| | ***stans*** | CElw CPLG CPou EPfP ESCh IFro LRHS NLar SIng SMDP |
| | - B&SWJ 5073 **new** | WCru |
| | - B&SWJ 6345 | WCru |
| | 'Star of India' (LL) | CElw CRHN EBee EPfP ESCh ETho LCro LRHS MGos MRav NBea NTay SCoo SPer SPoG SSto SWCr WFar |
| | 'Starfish' (EL) | ESCh NHaw |
| | 'Stasik' (LL) | ESCh NHaw |
| | 'Stephanie' (A) | ESCh |
| | 'Strawberry Roan' (EL) | ESCh |
| | Sugar Candy = 'Evione'$^{PBR}$ (EL) | ESCh IBal LAst MBri NTay SCoo SPoG |
| | Summer Snow | see *C.* 'Paul Farges' |
| | 'Sundance' | CSPN EBee ESCh |
| | 'Sunrise'$^{PBR}$ (M/d) | CSPN CWGN EBee ESCh ETho LBuc MSwo NHaw NLar WFar |
| | 'Sunset' (EL) ♀$^{H4}$ | ESCh LCro LRHS MAsh MBri NBea NLar NPri NTay SCoo SPoG SWCr WFar |
| | 'Sunstar' | SWal |
| | 'Suruga' (EL) | ESCh |
| | 'Susan Allsop' (EL) | ESCh |
| | 'Swedish Bells' (I) | ETho |
| | 'Sylvia Denny' (EL) | CWSG EBee ELan EPfP ESCh ETho GKir LAst LRHS MBar MRav NBea NTay SPer SPet |
| | 'Sympatia' (LL) | ESCh NHaw |
| | 'Syrena' (LL) | ESCh NBea NHaw |
| | ***szuyuanensis*** B&SWJ 6791 | WCru |
| | 'Tage Lundell' (A) | CSPN EBee EPfP ETho MGos NBea SMDP |
| | 'Tamula' | ESCh |
| | 'Tango' (Vt) | CElw CRHN EBee ESCh NBea NHaw NTay SMDP |
| § | ***tangutica*** | Widely available |
| | 'Tapestry' (I) | SMDP |
| | 'Tartu' (EL) | CSPN ESCh ETho |
| | ***tashiroi*** purple-flowered B&SWJ 7005 | WCru |
| | - 'Yellow Peril' | WCru |
| | 'Tateshina' (EL) | NTay |
| | 'Tentel' (LL) | ESCh ETho |
| § | ***terniflora*** | CBcs EBee EPfP ESCh ETho LFol LRHS NHaw NSti |
| | - B&SWJ 5751 | WCru |
| | - var. ***mandshurica*** | see *C. mandschurica* |
| | - var. ***robusta*** | see *C. terniflora* var. *terniflora* |
| § | - var. ***terniflora*** | LFol |
| | 'Teshio' (EL) | CSPN EBee ESCh ETho NHaw SPoG |
| | ***texensis*** | CBcs CElw IFro |
| | - 'The Princess of Wales' | see *C.* 'Princess Diana' |
| | 'The Bride' (EL) | CSPN CWGN ESCh ETho LSRN NBea NHaw NTay |
| | 'The First Lady' (EL) | CSPN ESCh ETho LBuc NTay SPoG |
| | 'The President' (EL) ♀$^{H4}$ | Widely available |
| | 'The Princess of Wales' | see *C.* 'Princess of Wales' (EL) |
| | 'The Princess of Wales' (T) | see *C.* 'Princess Diana' (T) |
| | 'The Vagabond' (EL) | CSPN CWSG ELan ESCh ETho MAsh MGos NBea NHaw NLar NTay SCoo SPet |
| | 'Theydon Belle' (EL) | ESCh |
| | ***thunbergii*** misapplied | see *C. terniflora* |
| | ***thunbergii*** Steud. | see *C. triloba* |
| | 'Thyrislund' (EL) | CSPN EBee ESCh ETho |
| | 'Tibetan Mix' (Ta) | CSPN SMDP |
| | ***tibetana*** | MBar MNrw NHaw SPer |
| | - 'Black Tibet' | ESCh SMDP |
| § | - subsp. ***vernayi*** | CMHG GKir MSte |
| | - - var. ***laciniifolia*** | NHol |
| § | - - var. ***vernayi*** 'Orange Peel' | CBcs CDoC ESCh ETho GKir LRHS MRav NHol SGar SLim WFar |

| | |
|---|---|
| Timpany NZ hybrids (Fo) | ITim |
| 'Tinkerbell' | see *C.* 'Shiva' |
| 'Titania' (EL) | ESCh |
| 'Toki' (EL) | CWGN EBee ESCh |
| ***tongluensis*** GWJ 9358 | WCru |
| - HWJCM 076 | WCru |
| - HWJK 2368 | WCru |
| 'Treasure Trove' (Ta) | CSPN NHol SMDP |
| 'Trianon' (EL) | ESCh |
| 'Triibu' (LL) | ESCh |
| 'Trikatrei' (LL) | ESCh |
| § ***triloba*** | ETho |
| § x ***triternata*** 'Rubromarginata' ♀H4 | CDoC CFir CRHN CSPN CWGN EBee ELan EPfP ESCh ETho LAst LCro LFol LRHS LSRN MAsh MBri MGos MRav NBea NHol NSti SDix SPer SPla SPoG SRkn SWCr |
| 'True Blue' new | ESCh |
| 'Tsuzuki' (EL) | CSPN EBee ESCh NBea |
| § ***tubulosa*** | CSPN EBee ESCh ETho MGos NHol SBch SMDP SRms |
| § - Alan Bloom = 'Alblo'PBR (H) | EBrs GKir LRHS |
| - 'Wyevale' (H) ♀H4 | CPrp CSPN EAEE ELan EPfP ETho LHop LRHS MAvo MBlu MRav NHol NTay SAga SCoo SDix SMad SPer SPla WCot WEas WHil |
| 'Tuchka' (EL) | ESCh |
| 'Twilight' (EL) | CSPN ESCh ETho LCro MAsh NTay WFar |
| ***uncinata*** | SDix |
| - B&SWJ 1893 | WCru |
| § ***urophylla*** 'Winter Beauty' | ESCh ETho MGos MRav SHBN SPoG |
| ***urticifolia*** | WSHC |
| - B&SWJ 8651 | WCru |
| - B&SWJ 8852 new | WCru |
| 'Valge Daam' (LL) | CWGN ESCh ETho NHaw NTay |
| 'Vanessa' (LL) | CRHN ESCh |
| 'Vanilla Cream' (Fo) | ECou |
| 'Vanso'PBR | see *C.* 'Blue Light' |
| x ***vedrariensis*** 'Hidcote' (M) | ESCh NHaw SMDP |
| 'Venosa Violacea' (Vt) ♀H4 | Widely available |
| 'Vera' (M) | CElw CSPN EBee ECtt ESCh ETho LRHS LSRN NTay SCoo SPet SPla SPoG WFar |
| ***vernayi*** | see *C. tibetana* subsp. *vernayi* |
| 'Veronica's Choice' (EL) | CRHN CSPN ELan ELon ESCh LRHS MGos MRav NBea NHaw NTay SPet |
| Versailles = 'Evipo025'PBR (EL) | ETho |
| ***versicolor*** | ESCh |
| Vesuvius = 'Evipo032'PBR new | ETho MAsh SPoG |
| Victor Hugo = 'Evipo007'PBR | ESCh ETho IBal MAsh NLar NTay SCoo |
| N 'Victoria' (LL) ♀H4 | CRHN CSPN ESCh ETho LAst LRHS LSRN MAsh MRav NBea NHaw NTay SCoo SDix SPoG SWCr |
| 'Vilhelmīne' | ESCh |
| 'Ville de Lyon' (LL) | Widely available |
| 'Vince Denny' (Ta) | ESCh ETho SMDP |
| 'Vino' | IBal LRHS NHaw NTay SCoo SPoG |
| I 'Viola' (LL) | CSPN EBee ESCh ETho LCro MBri NBea NHaw NTay WFar |
| 'Violet Charm' (EL) | CWSG ESCh NTay |
| 'Violet Elizabeth' (EL) | ESCh MRav |
| 'Violet Purple' (A) | ESCh MGos NHaw |
| 'Violetta' (EL) | ESCh |
| ***viorna*** | ESCh ETho WSHC |
| ***virginiana*** misapplied | see *C. vitalba* |
| ***virginiana*** Hook. | see *C. ligusticifolia* |
| ***virginiana*** L. | CElw |
| § ***vitalba*** | CArn CRWN EBWF ESCh ETho MBar NHaw SECG WGwG WHer |
| ***viticella*** ♀H4 | CElw CRHN CWib ESCh ETho MBri NBea NHaw SDix WSHC |
| § - 'Flore Pleno' | CRHN ESCh ETho LAst MAsh NHaw SWCr |
| - 'Hågelby Pink' | CWGN ESCh ETho |
| - 'Hågelby White' | CWGN ETho NHaw |
| - 'Hanna' (Vt) | ESCh ETho LRHS NHaw |
| - 'Mary Rose' | see *C. viticella* 'Flore Pleno' |
| 'Vivienne' | see *C.* 'Beth Currie' |
| 'Vivienne Lawson' (LL) | ESCh |
| 'Voluceau' (Vt) | CPou CRHN ELan ESCh GKir LAst MGos MRav NBea SPer |
| 'Vostok' (LL) | ESCh |
| 'Vyvyan Pennell' (EL) | Widely available |
| 'W.E. Gladstone' (EL) | CRHN ESCh ETho GKir LRHS NBea NTay SDix |
| 'Wada's Primrose' | see *C. patens* 'Manshuu Ki' |
| 'Walenburg' (Vt) | CRHN CWGN ESCh ETho NBea NHaw SLon |
| 'Walter Pennell' (EL) | CBcs CWSG EBee ESCh ETho IBal NBea NTay SCoo SLim WGor |
| 'Warsaw' (Ta) | NPri |
| 'Warszawska Nike' (EL) ♀H4 | CRHN EBee ELan EPfP ESCh ETho LAst LCro MAsh MBri MGos NBea NTay SCoo SHBN SPad SPer SPet SSto |
| 'Warwickshire Rose' (M) | CRHN CSPN CWGN CWSG ECtt ESCh ETho GKir LSRN MAsh MGos NBea NHaw NHol NTay SPoG WFar WPGP |
| 'Waterperry Star' (Ta) | MWat |
| 'Wedding Day' (EL) | ETho LCro LSRN NLar |
| 'Wee Willie Winkie' (M) | CWGN ESCh MAsh SCoo SMDP SPoG |
| 'Western Virgin' (Vb) | NTay |
| 'Westerplatte' (EL) | CRHN CSPN CWGN EPfP ESCh ETho LRHS MAsh MGos NBea NHaw NTay SMDP WFar |
| 'Whirligig' (A) | CSPN |
| § 'White Columbine' (A) ♀H4 | EBee EPfP ESCh ETho NBea NSti SDix SPet |
| 'White Lady' (A/d) | ESCh NHaw NTay |
| 'White Magic' (Vt) | CWGN ESCh ETho MGos |
| § 'White Moth' (A/d) | CSPN CWSG EBee ELan ESCh ETho LRHS MAsh MGos MRav NHaw NHol SPer SPla SPoG SRms |
| 'White Swan' (A/d) | CSPN EPfP ESCh LRHS MBri MGos NBea NHol NSti SCoo SPla WFoF |
| 'White Tokyo' (A/d) | MGos |
| 'White Wings' (A/d) | EBee ESCh SPet |
| 'Wilhelmina Tull' (EL) | CSPN ESCh |
| 'Will Goodwin' (EL) ♀H4 | CBcs CWCL EBee ELan ELon EPfP ESCh ETho LAst LRHS MBri NBea SWCr |
| 'William Kennett' (EL) | CWSG EBee ELan EPfP ESCh ETho LAst LRHS MBNS MBar MBri MGan MGos NTay SDix SSto SWCr |
| ***williamsii*** | ESCh |
| 'Willy' (A) | Widely available |
| Wisley = 'Evipo001'PBR | CBcs EPfP ESCh IBal LRHS MAsh MBri NLar SPer SPoG SWCr |
| 'Xerxes' misapplied | see *C.* 'Elsa Späth' |
| 'Yaichi' (EL) | ESCh |
| Yalta Study = 'Ialtinskii Etiud' (LL) | ESCh |
| 'Yellow Jester' (A) | CWGN |
| 'Yellow Queen' Holland | see *C. patens* 'Manshuu Ki' |
| 'Yellow Queen' Lundell/ Treasures | see *C.* 'Moonlight' |
| 'Yorkshire Pride' (EL) | ESCh |

| | |
|---|---|
| § 'Yukikomachi' (EL) | CSPN ESCh ETho NBea NHaw NTay |
| 'Yvette Houry' (EL) | ESCh NHaw NLar NTay |

## *Clematopsis* see *Clematis*

## *Clementsia* see *Rhodiola*

## *Cleome* (*Capparaceae*)

| | |
|---|---|
| 'Senorita Rosalita' new | SVil |

## *Clerodendrum* (*Verbenaceae*)

| | |
|---|---|
| ***bungei*** | Widely available |
| - 'Herfstleu' | MGos |
| - 'Pink Diamond' (v) | CCCN CDoC CDul EBee EMil EPfP EWes LBuc LRHS LSRN MAsh MGos MPkF NLar NPri NSti SMad SPer SPoG WCot WFar |
| § ***chinense*** var. ***chinense*** (d) ♀H1 | CCCN |
| - 'Pleniflorum' | see *C. chinense* var. *chinense* |
| ***fragrans*** var. ***pleniflorum*** | see *C. chinense* var. *chinense* |
| * ***mutabile*** B&SWJ 6651 | WCru |
| ***myricoides*** 'Ugandense' ♀H1 | CCCN CHII CKob CRHN CSpe CTsd ELan EShb MJnS SAga SMrm SOWG |
| ***philippinum*** | see *C. chinense* var. *chinense* |
| ***quadriloculare*** | CCCN |
| x ***speciosum*** | LRHS SOWG |
| ***splendens*** ♀H1 | SOWG |
| ***thomsoniae*** ♀H1 | ELan LRHS MBri MJnS SOWG |
| ***trichotomum*** | Widely available |
| - B&SWJ 4896A | WCru |
| - 'Carnival' (v) | CAbP CBcs CCCN CDul CPMA EBee ELan EPfP EPla EWes IArd LRHS MAsh MBlu MBri NCGa NLar SLim SMad SPer SPoG SSta WPat |
| - var. ***fargesii*** ♀H4 | Widely available |
| - 'Purple Haze' | MBri |
| - white calyx B&SWJ 4896 | WCru |
| ***wallichii*** | CSpe EShb LRHS SOWG |

## *Clethra* ✿ (*Clethraceae*)

| | |
|---|---|
| ***acuminata*** | EPfP |
| ***alnifolia*** | CBcs CDul CEnd CMCN CMHG CPLG CTrC CTrG EBee EHig EPfP IDee MBar SPer SRms WBor WCFE WDin WFar |
| - 'Anne Bidwell' | MBri NLar |
| - 'Creel's Calico' (v) | MBri NLar |
| - 'Fern Valley Pink' | CCCN CSBt LLHF MBri MDun NLar |
| - 'Hokie Pink' | MBri NLar |
| - 'Hummingbird' | CCCN CDoC CEnd CPLG EBee ELan EPfP GGGa GKir LRHS MAsh MBlu MBri MGos NLar SPoG SSpi SWvt WBVN WFar WSHC |
| - 'Paniculata' ♀H4 | CDoC EBee EPfP GKir LRHS SPoG SPur WFar |
| - 'Pink Spire' | CBcs CDoC CDul EBee ECrN ELon EPfP GGGa MRav NBlu NLar NPal SCoo WDin WFar WOrn |
| - 'Rosea' | CTri GQui IMGH MBar MBlu MGos MMHG SHBN SPer WFar |
| - 'Ruby Spice' | CBcs CCCN CEnd EBee ELan EMil EPfP GGGa GKir IDee LAst LRHS MAsh MBlu MBri MDun MGos NLar SPoG SSpi SSta SWvt WBVN WBod WGob |
| - 'September Beauty' | MBri NLar |
| - 'Sixteen Candles' | NLar |
| ***arborea*** | CBcs CHEx CMHG CTrC NLar SSpi |
| ***barbinervis*** ♀H4 | CBcs CMCN CPLG EBee EPfP GAuc IDee LRHS MBlu NLar SPer WBod WFar WSHC |
| - B&SWJ 5416 | WPGP |
| - B&SWJ 8915 | WCru |
| ***delavayi*** Franch. | CBcs CCCN CDoC EPfP EWes GGGa GQui NLar SKHP |
| ***fargesii*** | EPfP IMGH MBri MGos NLar WBVN |
| ***monostachya*** | NLar |
| ***pringlei*** | NLar WSHC |
| ***tomentosa*** | MBri |
| - 'Cottondale' | MBri NLar |

## *Cleyera* (*Theaceae*)

| | |
|---|---|
| ***fortunei*** | see *C. japonica* 'Fortunei' |
| - 'Variegata' | see *C. japonica* 'Fortunei' |
| § ***japonica*** 'Fortunei' (v) | CCCN CMac CWib EBee SSta WFar |
| - var. ***japonica*** | CGHE WPGP |
| - 'Tricolor' (v) | CDoC EBee IDee |
| - var. ***wallichii*** | EBee WPGP |

## *Clianthus* (*Papilionaceae*)

| | |
|---|---|
| ***maximus*** | ECou |
| § ***puniceus*** ♀H2 | CAbb CBcs CHEx CHII CPLG CPne CSBt CSec CSpe CWib EBee ECou EMil EPfP GGar LHop LRHS MLan SAga SGar SOWG SPer SPlb SPoG WCru WPGP WPic WSHC |
| § - 'Albus' ♀H2 | CHEx CHII CPLG CTsd CWib EBee EMil EPfP LRHS SGar SOWG SPer SPoG WPGP |
| - 'Flamingo' | see *C. puniceus* 'Roseus' |
| - 'Kaka King' | CBcs |
| - 'Red Admiral' | see *C. puniceus* |
| - 'Red Cardinal' | see *C. puniceus* |
| § - 'Roseus' | CBcs CPLG EBee EMil LRHS SPoG WPGP |
| - 'White Heron' | see *C. puniceus* 'Albus' |

## *Clinopodium* (*Lamiaceae*)

| | |
|---|---|
| ***acinos*** | see *Acinos arvensis* |
| ***ascendens*** | see *Calamintha ascendens* |
| ***calamintha*** | see *Calamintha nepeta* |
| ***georgianum*** | SKHP |
| ***grandiflorum*** | see *Calamintha grandiflora* |
| § ***vulgare*** | CArn CRWN EBWF EBee GBar MHer NGHP NMir NSco SECG SGar SIde WDyG WMoo WOut WPtf |

## *Clintonia* (*Convallariaceae*)

| | |
|---|---|
| ***andrewsiana*** | CLAP EBee ECho EHrv EWes GBuc GEdr GGGa GGar GMaP MNrw WCot WCru |
| ***borealis*** | SCnR WCru |
| I ***dulongensis*** new | EBee |
| ***udensis*** | EBee WCru |
| - HWJK 2339 from Nepal new | WCru |
| ***umbellulata*** | CLAP GCal WCru |
| ***uniflora*** | CLAP EBee EBrs ECho EHrv EWes GBuc GEdr GGar MNrw WCru |

## *Clitoria* (*Papilionaceae*)

| | |
|---|---|
| ***ternatea*** | CSec |

## *Clivia* ✿ (*Amaryllidaceae*)

| | |
|---|---|
| ***caulescens*** | WCot WVal |
| ***gardenii*** | WCot WVal |
| ***gardenii*** x ***miniata*** | WCot |
| ***miniata*** ♀H1 | CBcs CBgR CHal CSpe CTca CTsd ECho EShb LRHS MLan SMrm SRms WCot WVal |
| - 'Aurea' ♀H1 | CSpe |
| - var. ***citrina*** ♀H1 | CFwr CTca ECho LAma WCot WVal |
| - 'Citrina Spider' new | CFwr |

| | |
|---|---|
| - hybrids | MBri NPal SEND |
| - 'Orange Spider' new | CFwr |
| - pastel shades new | CFwr |
| - 'Striata' (v) | CFwr WVal |
| - 'Viscy Yellow' new | CTsd |
| - 'Wide Leaf Monk' new | WCot |
| ***mirabilis*** new | WVal |
| ***nobilis*** ♀H1 | WCot WVal |
| ***robusta*** new | WVal |
| 'Solomone Yellow' new | WCot |

## *Clusia* (*Clusiaceae*)

| | |
|---|---|
| ***rosea*** | CCCN |

## *Clypeola* (*Brassicaceae*)

| | |
|---|---|
| ***jonthlaspi*** | WCot |

## *Clytostoma* (*Bignoniaceae*)

| | |
|---|---|
| § ***calystegioides*** | CHll CRHN EShb |

## *Cneorum* (*Cneoraceae*)

| | |
|---|---|
| ***tricoccon*** | SKHP WSHC |

## *Cnicus* (*Asteraceae*)

| | |
|---|---|
| § ***benedictus*** | CArn GPoy MHer MSal SIde SPav |

## *Coaxana* (*Apiaceae*)

| | |
|---|---|
| ***purpurea*** B&SWJ 9028 new | WCru |

## *Cobaea* (*Cobaeaceae*)

| | |
|---|---|
| ***lutea*** B&SWJ 9142A | WCru |
| ***pringlei*** | CSec WPGP WSHC |
| ***scandens*** ♀H3 | CCCN CDTJ CSpe EBee ELan EShb IFoB SGar SPer |
| - f. ***alba*** ♀H3 | CSec CSpe SPer |

## cobnut see *Corylus avellana*

## *Coccothrinax* (*Arecaceae*)

| | |
|---|---|
| ***argentea*** (Lodd. ex Schult. & Schult.f.) Sarg. ex Becc. | EAmu |
| ***crinita*** | LPal |

## *Cocculus* (*Menispermaceae*)

| | |
|---|---|
| § ***orbiculatus*** | CPLG |
| - B&SWJ 535 | WCru |
| ***trilobus*** | see *C. orbiculatus* |

## *Cochlearia* (*Brassicaceae*)

| | |
|---|---|
| ***armoracia*** | see *Armoracia rusticana* |
| ***glastifolia*** | MSal |
| ***officinalis*** | CArn EBWF MHer MSal SECG WHer |

## *Cocos* (*Arecaceae*)

| | |
|---|---|
| ***plumosa*** | see *Syagrus romanzoffiana* |
| ***weddelliana*** | see *Lytocaryum weddellianum* |

## *Codiaeum* ✿ (*Euphorbiaceae*)

| | |
|---|---|
| ***variegatum*** var. ***pictum*** 'Excellent' (v) | LRHS |
| - - 'Petra' (v) | LRHS MBri |

## *Codonanthe* (*Gesneriaceae*)

| | |
|---|---|
| ***gracilis*** | WDib |
| 'Paula' | WDib |

## x *Codonatanthus* (*Gesneriaceae*)

| | |
|---|---|
| 'Golden Tambourine' | WDib |
| 'Sunset' | WDib |
| 'Tambourine' | WDib |

## *Codonopsis* ✿ (*Campanulaceae*)

| | |
|---|---|
| GWJ 9442 from India new | WCru |
| HWJK 2105 from Nepal new | WCru |
| ***affinis*** HWJCM 70 | WCru |
| - HWJK 2151 | WCru |
| ***benthamii*** | EBee |
| - GWJ 9352 | WCru |
| ***bhutanica*** | WCot |
| ***bulleyana*** | EBee GKir IGor NLar |
| ***cardiophylla*** | EBee EWld GCal |
| ***celebica*** HWJ 665 | WCru |
| ***clematidea*** | CHar CSec CSpe EBee ECha ECho ECtt EPfP GCal GKev ITim LHop MCCP MTho MWhi NBid NChi NSum SAga SMad SPhx SPlb SRms SWvt WBVN WCru WFar WKif |
| - 'Lilac Eyes' | MCCP NBre NSti SPad |
| ***convolvulacea*** misapplied | see *C. grey-wilsonii* |
| ***convolvulacea*** Kurz | CPne GBuc IGor ITim MTho NSla WPGP |
| - J&JA 4.220.705 | NWCA |
| - 'Alba' | see *C. grey-wilsonii* 'Himal Snow' |
| - Forrest's form | see *C. forrestii* Diels |
| - var. ***hirsuta*** B&SWJ 7812 | WCru |
| 'Dangshen' | see *C. pilosula* |
| ***dicentrifolia*** HWJCM 267 | WCru |
| ***forrestii*** misapplied | see *C. grey-wilsonii* |
| § ***forrestii*** Diels | EBee GKev GKir NHar |
| - BWJ 7776 | WCru |
| - BWJ 7847 new | WCru |
| § ***grey-wilsonii*** ♀H4 | CAby CHFP CLAP EBee EBrs ECho GEdr IGor ITim MAvo NSum WCot WFar WIvy |
| - B&SWJ 7532 | WCru |
| § - 'Himal Snow' | CAby CLAP GEdr GKev ITim MDKP SPhx |
| ***handeliana*** | see *C. tubulosa* |
| ***javanica*** B&SWJ 8145 | WCru |
| ***kawakamii*** | EBee |
| - B&SWJ 1592 | WCru |
| - RWJ 10007 new | WCru |
| § ***lanceolata*** | CAby CPne EWld IGor LFur NSti |
| - B&SWJ 562 | WCru |
| ***lancifolia*** B&SWJ 3835 | WCru |
| ***meleagris*** Diels | IGor ITim |
| ***mollis*** | ECho NBre NGby NLar NSum WFar |
| ***nepalensis*** Grey-Wilson | see *C. grey-wilsonii* |
| ***obtusa*** | EBee EWld GKir NChi |
| ***ovata*** | CFir GBuc IGor ITim MTho NBro NChi SPhx SRms |
| § ***pilosula*** | CAby CSec EBee EWld GKev GPoy IGor MNrw MSal MTho NLar SPhx |
| - BWJ 7910 | WCru |
| § ***rotundifolia*** var. ***angustifolia*** | EBee GKev IGor MDKP |
| - var. ***grandiflora*** | EBee GKev |
| ***silvestris*** | see *C. pilosula* |
| ***subscaposa*** | EBee |
| ***tangshen*** misapplied | see *C. rotundifolia* var. *angustifolia* |
| ***tangshen*** Oliv. | CAby CArn EBee GKir ITim MNrw MSal MTho |
| ***thalictrifolia*** | NSla |
| - MECC 93 | WCru |
| § ***tubulosa*** | EBee ITim LRHS |
| ***ussuriensis*** | see *C. lanceolata* |
| ***vinciflora*** | CPne GEdr IGor WBVN WCot WIvy WSHC |
| ***viridiflora*** | WCru |
| ***viridis*** HWJK 2435 | WCru |

## *Coffea* (*Rubiaceae*)

| | |
|---|---|
| ***arabica*** | CCCN MJnS |

## coffee see *Coffea*

## *Coix* (*Poaceae*)

| | | |
|---|---|---|
| | ***lacryma-jobi*** | MSal SWal |

## *Colchicum* ✿ (*Colchicaceae*)

| | | |
|---|---|---|
| | ***agrippinum*** ♀H4 | CAvo CBro CFee CTca EBla EBrs ECha ECho EPot GGar ITim MRav NBir NMen NRya SPhx WHoo WTin |
| | 'Antares' | CAvo ECha NBir |
| | ***atropurpureum*** | EBrs ECho EPot GEdr LAma |
| | - Drake's form | ECho |
| | 'Attlee' | LAma |
| | 'Autumn Herald' | EBrs ECho LAma |
| N | 'Autumn Queen' | CTca EBrs ECho LAma SPhx |
| § | ***autumnale*** | CArn CAvo CBro CFee CSec EBrs ECho EPot GAuc GKir GPoy ITim LAma LRHS NMen NRya WFar WShi |
| * | - 'Albopilosum' | NBir |
| | - 'Alboplenum' | CBro CHFP EBrs ECho EPot ERCP LAma WTin |
| | - 'Album' | CAvo CBro CTca EBrs ECho EPot ERCP GEdr GGar LAma LRHS NBir SPer SPhx WFar WGwG WHoo WShi WTin |
| | - var. ***major*** hort. | see *C. byzantinum* Ker Gawl. |
| | - var. ***minor*** hort. | see *C. autumnale* |
| § | - 'Nancy Lindsay' ♀H4 | CBro EBla EBrs EPot MSte WCot |
| | - 'Pannonicum' | see *C. autumnale* 'Nancy Lindsay' |
| § | - 'Pleniflorum' (d) | EBrs ECho EPot GEdr LAma MMHG WFar |
| | - 'Roseum Plenum' | see *C. autumnale* 'Pleniflorum' |
| | ***baytopiorum*** | GAuc GEdr |
| | - from Turkey | ECho |
| § | ***bivonae*** | CWsd EBrs ECha LAma |
| | - 'Apollo' | EBrs ECho GKev |
| | Blom's hybrid | WTin |
| § | ***boissieri*** | CWsd EBrs ECho EPot ERos |
| | - MFF 2192 | WCot |
| | ***bornmuelleri*** misapplied | see *C. speciosum* var. *bornmuelleri* hort. |
| | ***bornmuelleri*** Freyn | CBro ECho EPot GAuc GEdr LAma |
| | ***bowlesianum*** | see *C. bivonae* |
| § | ***byzantinum*** Ker Gawl. ♀H4 | CBro CTca EBrs EPot LAma LRHS MSte NBir WTin |
| | - ***album*** | see *C. byzantinum* 'Innocence' |
| § | - 'Innocence' | CBro EBla EBrs EPot GAuc |
| | ***cilicicum*** | CBro EPot LAma WHoo |
| | - 'Purpureum' | EBrs ECho LAma LRHS WWst |
| | 'Conquest' | see *C.* 'Glory of Heemstede' |
| | ***corsicum*** | EBrs ECho ERos NMen WThu |
| | ***crocifolium*** | EBrs |
| | ***cupanii*** | CPBP EBrs ECho EPot GKev WWst |
| | - var. ***pulverulentum*** | EBrs ECho |
| | 'Daendels' | LAma |
| | 'Dick Trotter' | EBrs ECho EPot LAma MBri MSte |
| | 'Disraeli' | CBro EBrs ECho GEdr GKev |
| | ***doerfleri*** | see *C. hungaricum* |
| | 'E.A. Bowles' | GEdr LAma |
| | ***falcifolium*** | WWst |
| § | ***giganteum*** | EBrs EPot GAuc GEdr LAma |
| § | 'Glory of Heemstede' | EBrs GKev |
| | 'Gracia' | EBrs |
| | ***graecum*** | EBrs WWst |
| | 'Harlekijn' | CTca EBrs ERCP GEdr |
| § | ***hungaricum*** | CFee EBrs ECho WWst |
| | - f. ***albiflorum*** | EBrs ECho EPot GAuc |
| | ***illyricum*** | see *C. giganteum* |
| | 'Jochem Hof' | EBrs |
| | ***kesselringii*** | GAuc WWst |
| | ***kotschyi*** | EPot WWst |
| | ***laetum*** misapplied | see *C. parnassicum* |
| | ***laetum*** Stev. | GAuc |
| | 'Lilac Bedder' | EBrs EPot |
| | 'Lilac Wonder' | CBro EBrs EPfP EPot GKev LAma LRHS MRav SPer WCot WFar |
| | ***lusitanum*** | GAuc LAma |
| | ***luteum*** | EBrs ECho GAuc WWst |
| | ***macrophyllum*** | EBrs ECho GAuc LAma |
| | ***parlatoris*** | EBrs ECho |
| § | ***parnassicum*** | CBro EBrs ECha ECho WWst |
| | ***peloponnesiacum*** | EBrs |
| | 'Pink Goblet' ♀H4 | CBro LAma |
| | 'Poseidon' | EBrs |
| | ***procurrens*** | see *C. boissieri* |
| | ***pusillum*** | EBrs |
| | 'Rosy Dawn' ♀H4 | CAvo CBro CTca EBrs ECha ECho GGar GKev LAma SPhx |
| | ***sfikasianum*** | EBrs |
| | ***sibthorpii*** | see *C. bivonae* |
| | ***speciosum*** ♀H4 | CAvo CBro CSec EBrs ECho EPot GEdr GKev GKir LAma LRHS NBir |
| | - 'Album' ♀H4 | CAvo CBro CFee EBla EBrs ECha ECho EPfP EPot GEdr LAma LRHS MBri MSte NBir SPhx |
| | - 'Atrorubens' | CAvo ECha LAma MBri |
| I | - var. ***bornmuelleri*** hort. | GEdr WWst |
| | - var. ***illyricum*** hort. | see *C. giganteum* |
| | - 'Maximum' | LAma MBri |
| | - 'Ordu' | EBrs ECho LEdu |
| | ***szovitsii*** Fisch. & B. Mey. | EBrs WWst |
| | - white-flowered **new** | ECho |
| | ***tenorei*** ♀H4 | EBrs ECho EPot GAuc GKev LAma NBir SPhx |
| | 'The Giant' | CAvo CBro EBrs ECho EPot GKev LAma LRHS WCot |
| | ***triphyllum*** | EBrs WWst |
| | ***troodi*** ambig. | ERos |
| | ***variegatum*** | LAma |
| | 'Violet Queen' | CBro EBrs ECho EPot LAma LRHS |
| | 'Waterlily' (d) ♀H4 | CAvo CBro CHFP CLyd CTca EBla EBrs ECho ELan EPfP EPot ERCP GAbr GGar GKev LAma LRHS NBir SPhx WCot WGwG WHoo |
| | 'William Dykes' | EBla EBrs GEdr LAma |
| | 'Zephyr' | ECho LAma |

## *Coleonema* (*Rutaceae*)

| | | |
|---|---|---|
| § | ***pulchellum*** | CCCN CHEx CSpe NSti |
| | ***pulchrum*** misapplied | see *C. pulchellum* |
| | 'Sunset Gold' | CSpe CTrC LHop LPio |

## *Coleus* see *Solenostemon*

## *Colignonia* (*Nyctaginaceae*)

| | | |
|---|---|---|
| | ***ovalifolia*** B&SWJ 10644 | WCru |

## *Colletia* (*Rhamnaceae*)

| | | |
|---|---|---|
| | ***armata*** | see *C. hystrix* |
| | ***cruciata*** | see *C. paradoxa* |
| § | ***hystrix*** | CBcs CHEx CTrG CTri CTsd EBee GBin GGar SAPC SArc SLon SMad SOWG WBor WSHC |
| | - 'Rosea' | CTrC EBee GCal SKHP |
| § | ***paradoxa*** | CBcs CCCN CHEx GCal LPJP MBri NLar SAPC SArc SMad |
| | ***paradoxa*** x ***spinosissima*** | SMad |

## *Collinsonia* (*Lamiaceae*)

| | | |
|---|---|---|
| | ***canadensis*** | CArn ELan MSal |

## *Collomia* ✿ (*Polemoniaceae*)

| | | |
|---|---|---|
| | ***debilis*** | NPol |
| | ***grandiflora*** | CSec CSpe NPol WCot |

***mazama*** NPol

## *Colobanthus* (*Caryophyllaceae*)

***canaliculatus*** NMen
§ ***quitensis*** ECho

## *Colocasia* (*Araceae*)

***affinis*** var. ***jeningsii*** CDTJ CKob EAmu
***antiquorum*** see *C. esculenta*
§ ***esculenta*** ♀H1 CBct CDTJ CDWL CHEx CKob EAmu EBrs EUJe MJnS MSKA SDix XBlo
- 'Black Magic' CAby CBct CDTJ CDWL CHEx CSam EAmu EBee ECtt EUJe LRHS LSou MJnS MNrw MSKA SAPC SArc SBig SDix SMad WCot WGwG WPrP XBlo
- 'Black Marble' CDTJ
- 'Black Ruffles' CDTJ EUJe
- burgundy-stemmed CDTJ EUJe SBig
- 'Chicago Harlequin' CDTJ CDWL EUJe
- 'Elepaio Keiki' (v) MJnS
- 'Fontanesii' CDTJ CHEx CKob EAmu EUJe MJnS SKHP
- 'Hilo Beauty' XBlo
- 'Illustris' CDTJ CHEx CKob EUJe MJnS
- 'Nancy's Revenge' CDTJ CDWL
- 'Nigrescens' EAmu
- 'Ruffles' EUJe

***fallax*** CDWL CFir CKob EAmu EUJe SKHP WPrP
***formosana*** CKob
- B&SWJ 6909 WCru

***gigantea*** CDTJ CDWL EAmu EUJe MSKA SBig

## *Colquhounia* (*Lamiaceae*)

***coccinea*** CArn CHEx CHal CHll CTrC EShb GQui MRav NLar SGar SLon WBod WCru WPGP WSHC
- Sch 2458 WPGP
§ - var. ***mollis*** B&SWJ 7222 WCru
- var. ***vestita*** misapplied see *C. coccinea* var. *mollis*
- var. ***vestita*** ambig. CBcs CTsd CWib EBee EPfP GGar IMGH LHop LRHS MSte MWea SEND WBor

## *Columnea* (*Gesneriaceae*)

'Aladdin's Lamp' WDib
'Apollo' WDib
x ***banksii*** ♀H1 CHal EOHP WDib
'Bold Venture' WDib
§ 'Broget Stavanger' (v) WDib
'Chanticleer' ♀H1 CHal MBri WDib
I 'Firedragon' WDib
'Gavin Brown' EOHP WDib
***gloriosa*** EBak
***hirta*** ♀H1 MBri WDib
- 'Variegata' see *C.* 'Light Prince'

'Inferno' WDib
'Katsura' MBri WDib
I 'Kewensis Variegata' (v) ♀H1 MBri
§ 'Light Prince' (v) WDib
'Merkur' WDib
***microphylla*** 'Variegata' (v) MBri
I 'Midnight Lantern' WDib
'Rising Sun' WDib
'Robin' WDib
***schiedeana*** CHal EOHP EShb MBri WDib
'Stavanger' ♀H1 CHal WDib
'Stavanger Variegated' see *C.* 'Broget Stavanger'
Yellow Dragon Group CHal

## *Colutea* (*Papilionaceae*)

***arborescens*** CArn CBcs CPLG CWib EBee ELan GKir LHop LRHS MBlu MGos MSal NWea SHBN SPer SPlb SPoG WDin
§ ***buhsei*** NLar SOWG
x ***media*** GKir MBlu SGar SHGN
- 'Copper Beauty' CBcs EMil GKir MBri MGos MRav NLar SPer WPat

***orientalis*** CCCN LHop
***persica*** misapplied see *C. buhsei*

## *Colysis* (*Polypodiaceae*)

***wrightii*** f. ***laciniata*** new EBee

## *Comarum* see *Potentilla*

## *Combretum* (*Combretaceae*)

***fruticosum*** new CCCN
***kraussii*** new CSec

## *Commelina* (*Commelinaceae*)

***coelestis*** see *C. tuberosa* Coelestis Group
***dianthifolia*** EBee GCal LPio MCot MTho SHGN SRms WPer
- 'Electric Blue' EAlp
- 'Sapphirino' EMon

***robusta*** EBee LPio WCot
***tuberosa*** EBrs ELan EPfP LPio MSte WBrE
- B&SWJ 10353 WCru
- 'Alba' ELan GCal LPio WPer
- 'Axminster Lilac' EMon WPer
§ - Coelestis Group CEnt CSec CSpe CStu EBee ECha IGor MAvo MCot SGar SRkn SRms WFar WPGP WPer WPtf WSHC
- - 'Hopleys Variegated' (v) CBow CSec EBee
- - 'Sleeping Beauty' LRHS

## *Comptonia* (*Myricaceae*)

***peregrina*** NLar WCru WRos

## *Conandron* (*Gesneriaceae*)

***ramondoides*** B&SWJ 8929 WCru

## *Conanthera* (*Tecophilaeaceae*)

***campanulata*** EBee ECho WHil

## *Conicosia* (*Aizoaceae*)

***pugioniformis*** CTrC

## *Coniogramme* (*Adiantaceae*)

***emeiensis*** WCot
***intermedia*** WRic

## *Conioselinum* (*Apiaceae*)

***morrisonense*** B&SWJ 173 WCru
***schugnanicum*** EBee WSHC

## *Conium* (*Apiaceae*)

***maculatum*** CArn MSal

## *Conoclinium* (*Asteraceae*)

***coelestinum*** EBee EShb EWes GKir LHop MDKP NBre SMad WFar WSFF
***dissectum*** SKHP WSFF

## *Conopodium* (*Apiaceae*)

***majus*** CRWN CSec EBWF WShi

## *Conradina* (*Lamiaceae*)

***verticillata*** NLAp WPat

## *Consolida* (*Ranunculaceae*)

| | | |
|---|---|---|
| § | ***ajacis*** | MNHC MSal |
| | ***ambigua*** | see *C. ajacis* |

## *Convallaria* ✿ (*Convallariaceae*)

| | | |
|---|---|---|
| | ***japonica*** | see *Ophiopogon jaburan* |
| | ***keiskei*** | EBla EPPr GAuc |
| | ***majalis*** Y$^{H4}$ | Widely available |
| | - 'Albostriata' (v) | CBct CBow CFwr CLAP CRow EBee EBla EBrs ECha ECho EHoe EHrv ELan EPPr EPfP GKir MRav MTho NBir NSti SIng WCHb WCot WEas WFar WHer WPGP WSHC |
| | - 'Berlin Giant' | EBee EBla NBre NRya |
| | - 'Bordeaux' **new** | CHid EBee |
| | - 'Dorien' | CBct CBre EBee MAvo |
| | - 'Flore Pleno' (d) | EBee EHrv MAvo MTho |
| | - 'Fortin's Giant' | CBct CBro CFir CLAP CRow EBla EMon EPla EPot GCal GEdr MRav NBir NBre NGby SMad WCot WPGP |
| | - 'Gerard Debureaux' | see *C. majalis* 'Green Tapestry' |
| § | - 'Green Tapestry' (v) | CBct CBow CLAP CRow EMon |
| | - 'Haldon Grange' (v) | CLAP EMon SMad |
| | - 'Hardwick Hall' (v) | CBct CBow CLAP CMdw CRow EBee EBla ECha ECho EHoe EHrv EPla EPot MAvo NBre WCot WTin |
| | - 'Hofheim' (v) | CLAP CRow |
| | - 'Marcel' (v) **new** | CLAP |
| | - 'Prolificans' | CAvo CBct CBgR CBro CFir CLAP CMdw CRow EBee EBrs ECho EMon EPPr ERos MRav NBir SSvw WCot |
| | - var. ***rosea*** | Widely available |
| | - 'Variegata' (v) | CAvo CBgR CHar CMea EBee EBla EPla LHop NMen SBch SMad SSvw WHil |
| | - 'Vic Pawlowski's Gold' (v) | CDes CLAP CPLG CRow CStu CWsd EBee EPPr MAvo WCHb |
| | ***montana*** | LRHS NLar |
| | ***transcaucasica*** | EBee ECho EPot WCot |

## *Convolvulus* (*Convolvulaceae*)

| | | |
|---|---|---|
| | ***althaeoides*** | CMea ECGP ECho ELan EShb LRHS NBir SMrm SPhx WAbb WEas WPGP WPtf |
| § | - subsp. ***tenuissimus*** | CSWP CSpe CWsd EBee ECtt EWes WCFE |
| § | ***boissieri*** | CGra EPot WPat |
| | ***cantabricus*** | CHll MDKP |
| | ***chilensis*** | CBod CCCN LSou |
| | ***cneorum*** Y$^{H3}$ | Widely available |
| | - 'Snow Angel' | CSpe EBee GBin LBuc LSou MRav NCGa SWvt |
| | ***elegantissimus*** | see *C. althaeoides* subsp. *tenuissimus* |
| | ***humilis*** | ECho |
| | ***lineatus*** | EBee ECho EWes LRHS MTho NMen NWCA |
| | ***mauritanicus*** | see *C. sabatius* |
| | ***nitidus*** | see *C. boissieri* |
| § | ***sabatius*** Y$^{H3}$ | Widely available |
| | - dark-flowered | CCCN CSpe ECho ELan GCal MSte SMrm SUsu |
| | - 'Moroccan Beauty'PBR | CSpe |

## x *Cooperanthes* see *Zephyranthes*

## *Cooperia* see *Zephyranthes*

## *Copernicia* (*Arecaceae*)

| | | |
|---|---|---|
| | ***alba*** | LPal |

## *Coprosma* ✿ (*Rubiaceae*)

| | | |
|---|---|---|
| | ***acerosa*** 'Hawera' | CBcs |
| | - 'Live Wire' (f) | ECou |
| | - 'Red Rocks' | CBcs CTrC |
| | ***areolata*** (m) | ECou |
| | ***atropurpurea*** (f) | ECou NWCA |
| | - (m) | ECou |
| | 'Autumn Orange' (f) | ECou |
| | 'Autumn Prince' (m) | ECou |
| | ***baueri*** misapplied | see *C. repens* |
| | 'Beatson's Gold' (f/v) | CBcs CDTJ CHal CHll CTrG CTsd EBee ELan EPfP GGar ISea MSCN SEND STre WDin WLeb WSHC |
| | 'Black Cloud' | CTrC |
| | 'Blue Pearls' (f) | ECou |
| | 'Brunette' (f) | ECou |
| | ***brunnea*** | CTrC ECou |
| | - 'Blue Beauty' (f) | ECou |
| | - 'Violet Fleck' (f) | ECou |
| | 'Bruno' (m) | ECou |
| | 'Cappuccino'PBR | CBcs EBee GBin IFFs LSou |
| | ***cheesemanii*** (f) | ECou |
| | - (m) | ECou |
| | - 'Hanmer Red' (f) | ECou |
| | - 'Mack' (m) | ECou |
| | - 'Red Mack' (f) | ECou |
| | 'Chocolate Soldier' (m) | ECou |
| | 'Clearwater Gold' | CTrC |
| | 'Coppershine' | CPLG CTrC |
| | ***crassifolia*** x ***repens*** (m) | ECou |
| | ***crenulata*** | WPic |
| | x ***cunninghamii*** (f) | ECou |
| | (x ***cunninghamii***) x ***macrocarpa*** (m) | ECou |
| | 'Cutie' (f) | CTrC ECou |
| | ***depressa*** | ECou |
| | - 'Orange Spread' (f) | ECou |
| | 'Evening Glow'PBR (f/v) | CBgR CCCN CDTJ CDoC CSBt EBee ECou ELan EMil EPfP ERas IFFs LHop LRHS LSou MAsh MGos SKHP SLim |
| | 'Fire Burst'PBR | CBcs CCCN CDoC ELan EMil EPfP ERas IFFs LSou MRav SLim WCFE |
| | 'Green Girl' (f) | ECou |
| | 'Green Globe' | CHll |
| | 'Hinerua' (f) | ECou |
| | 'Indigo Lustre' (f) | ECou |
| | 'Jewel' (f) | ECou |
| | 'Karo Red'PBR (v) | CDoC CTrC EBee EPfP IFFs LRHS MAsh MGos |
| | x ***kirkii*** 'Gold Edge' | ECou |
| I | - 'Kirkii' (f) | CHll ECou STre |
| I | - 'Kirkii Variegata' (f/v) | CBcs CDoC CHal CTrC CTsd EBee ECou NScw SOWG STre WBrE WSHC |
| | 'Kiwi' (m) | ECou |
| | 'Kiwi Red' | GGar |
| | 'Kiwi-gold' (m/v) | ECou |
| | 'Lemon Drops' (f) | ECou |
| | ***linariifolia*** (m) | ECou |
| | ***lucida*** (f) | ECou |
| | - 'Mount White' (m) | ECou |
| | - 'Wanaka' (f) | ECou |
| | ***macrocarpa*** (f) | ECou |
| | - (m) | CTrC ECou |
| | 'Middlemore' | CDoC |
| | ***nitida*** (f) | ECou |
| | ***parviflora*** (m) | ECou |
| | - purple-fruited (f) | ECou |
| | - red-fruited (f) | ECou |
| | - white-fruited (f) | ECou |
| | 'Pearl Drops' (f) | ECou |
| | 'Pearl's Sister' (f) | ECou |

| | |
|---|---|
| 'Pearly Queen' (f) | ECou |
| ***petriei*** | ECou WThu |
| - 'Don' (m) | ECou |
| - 'Lyn' (f) | ECou |
| 'Pride' | CDoC CTrG MHav |
| ***propinqua*** | WSHC |
| - (f) | ECou |
| - (m) | ECou |
| - var. ***latiuscula*** (f) | ECou |
| - - (m) | ECou |
| 'Prostrata' (m) | ECou |
| ***pseudocuneata*** (m) | ECou |
| ***quadrifida*** | ECou |
| 'Rainbow Surprise'PBR (v) | CCCN CDoC CSBt EBee ELan ERas IFFs LRHS LSou MAsh MGos MRav SLim |
| § ***repens*** | CPLG EShb |
| - (f) | ECou |
| - (m) | ECou |
| - 'Apricot Flush' (f) | ECou |
| - 'County Park Plum' (v) | ECou |
| - 'County Park Purple' (f) | ECou |
| - 'County Park Red' | ECou |
| - 'Exotica' (f/v) | ECou |
| - 'Marble King' (m/v) | ECou |
| - 'Marble Queen' (m/v) 🏆H1-2 | CBcs CHll ECou MGos WFar |
| - 'Orangeade' (f) | ECou |
| - Pacific Night = 'Hutpac' | ECou EPfP LBuc MGos NBPN SPoG |
| - 'Painter's Palette' (m) | CBcs EBee ECou GGar WDin |
| - 'Picturata' (m/v) 🏆H1-2 | EBee ECou EShb |
| - 'Pink Splendour' (m/v) | CBcs CDoC EBee ECou LHop MGos MHav WDin |
| - 'Rangatiri' (f) | ECou |
| - 'Silver Queen' (m/v) | ECou |
| - 'Variegata' (m/v) | ECou WBod |
| ***rigida*** | ECou |
| - 'Ann' (f) | ECou |
| - 'Tan' (m) | ECou |
| ***robusta*** | ECou |
| - 'Cullen's Point' (f) | ECou |
| - 'Sally Blunt' (f) | ECou |
| - 'Steepdown' (f) | ECou |
| - 'Tim Blunt' (m) | ECou |
| - 'Variegata' (m/v) | ECou |
| - 'William' (m) | ECou |
| - 'Woodside' (f) | ECou |
| ***rotundifolia*** | ECou |
| 'Roy's Red' (m) | CBgR CDoC EBee ECou GGar LSRN |
| ***rugosa*** **new** | CPLG |
| - (f) | ECou |
| 'Snowberry' (f) | ECou |
| 'Taiko' | CTrC |
| ***tenuifolia*** (m) | ECou |
| 'Translucent Gold' (f) | ECou |
| 'Violet Drops' (f) | ECou |
| ***virescens*** (f) | ECou |
| 'Walter Brockie' | CHll CTrC |
| 'White Lady' (f) | ECou |
| 'Winter Bronze' (f) | ECou |
| 'Yvonne' | MGos |

## *Coptis* (*Ranunculaceae*)

| | |
|---|---|
| ***japonica*** | WCru |
| - var. ***dissecta*** | EBee WCru |
| - var. ***major*** | CDes EBee WCru WSHC |
| ***omeiensis*** **new** | WCru |
| ***quinquefolia*** | EBee |
| - B&SWJ 1677 | WCru |
| ***ramosa*** B&SWJ 6000 | WCru |
| - B&SWJ 6030 **new** | WCru |

## *Corallospartium* see *Carmichaelia*

## *Cordyline* ✿ (*Agavaceae*)

| | |
|---|---|
| ***australis*** 🏆H3 | Widely available |
| - 'Albertii' (v) 🏆H3 | CBcs CCCN CTrC LHop MBri NMoo SAPC SArc SEND |
| - 'Atropurpurea' | CDoC IFoB SSto WDin WFar |
| - 'Black Night' | CCCN CTrC |
| - 'Black Tower' | CDoC MGos |
| - 'Cardinal' **new** | CBcs |
| - 'Claret' **new** | CBcs |
| - 'Coffee Cream' | CBcs EAmu EBee ELan EPfP SPer WDin WFar |
| - 'Olive Fountain' | CCCN EBee |
| - 'Peko'PBR | CCCN MGos |
| - 'Pink Champagne' | CBcs CCCN EMil LBuc LRHS LSRN MGos SPoG SSto |
| § - 'Pink Stripe' (v) | CBcs CDTJ CDoC EBee ELan EPfP ISea LRHS LSRN MBri MCCP NBlu NScw SEND SLim SPla SSto SWvt WFar |
| - 'Purple Heart' | CCCN CTrC MSwo |
| - Purpurea Group | CBcs CChe CDTJ CDul CMHG CTrC CWSG EAlp EBee ELan EPfP GKir ISea LAst LRHS MGos NBlu SBLw SEND SHBN SPer SPlb WFar |
| - 'Red Sensation' | CHEx CTrC CTsd EBee LRHS NBPN SWvt |
| - 'Red Star' | CAbb CBcs CDoC CSBt CTrC CWSG CWib EBee ELan EPfP GKir LAst LBMP LCro LRHS MCCP MLan MRav MSwo NPer NPri SPoG SWvt WBVN WBrE WCot WFar WGwG |
| - 'Sparkler' | CBcs ESwi LBuc LRHS MGos |
| - 'Sundance' 🏆H3 | Widely available |
| - 'Torbay Dazzler' (v) 🏆H3 | Widely available |
| - 'Torbay Red' 🏆H3 | CAbb CBcs CDoC CMHG CWSG EBee ELan EPfP LHop LPan LRHS LSRN MAsh MBri MJnS NPri SPla SWvt WFar |
| - 'Torbay Sunset' | CCCN CDoC CTrC ELan LRHS |
| 'Autumn' | WFar |
| ***banksii*** | CTsd GCal GGar ISea WPic |
| 'Dark Star' | CBcs CCCN CDTJ CDoC EBee SLim |
| ***fruticosa*** 'Atom' | MBri |
| - 'Baby Ti' (v) | MBri |
| - 'Calypso Queen' | MBri |
| - 'Kiwi' | MBri |
| - 'Orange Prince' | MBri |
| - 'Red Edge' 🏆H1 | MBri XBlo |
| - 'Yellow King' | MBri |
| 'Green Goddess' | CTrC GGar |
| § ***indivisa*** | CDTJ EAmu EBak GGar LMaj LPan LRHS MBri SBig SPlb WPGP |
| 'Jurassic Jade' | CBcs CTrC |
| 'Jurassic Jasper' **new** | CTrC |
| ***kaspar*** | CCCN CHEx CTsd SAPC SArc |
| ***obtecta*** | CCCN |
| 'Pacific Coral' | LBuc |
| 'Pacific Sunset' | LBuc |
| 'Pink Stripe' | see *C. australis* 'Pink Stripe' |
| 'Purple Sensation' | CBcs CCCN CTrC NPri |
| 'Purple Tower' 🏆H3 | CDoC CHEx EMil EPfP MGos NBPN NPri SLim SPad WCot |
| 'Red Bush' | XBlo |
| 'Red Fountain' | ESwi WCot |
| § ***stricta*** | CHEx MBri |
| ***terminalis*** | see *C. fruticosa* |

## *Coreopsis* (*Asteraceae*)

| | |
|---|---|
| 'Astolat' | EAEE EBee EMon LHop MNFA SPer |
| ***auriculata*** Cutting Gold | see *C.* 'Schnittgold' |
| - 'Elfin Gold' | EBee EDAr LBMP WFar |
| - 'Nana' | EBee NBre WFar |

| | |
|---|---|
| - 'Superba' | EBee |
| - 'Zamphir' | EBee EPfP MNrw NBhm SMrm |
| 'Autumn Blush' new | NBhm |
| 'Baby Gold' | see *C. lanceolata* 'Sonnenkind' (unblotched) |
| Baby Sun | see *C.* 'Sonnenkind' |
| ***basalis*** 'Sunshine' | WPer |
| 'Calypso' (v) | EBee ECtt EWes LRHS SCoo SMad |
| 'Cutting Edge' | CEnt |
| ***grandiflora*** | NBlu |
| - 'Badengold' | EBee EMil |
| - 'Bernwode' (v) | EBee LSou NLar SPoG SWvt |
| - 'Domino' | EBee LHop NBre SMrm |
| - 'Early Sunrise' ♀H4 | CSBt EBee ECrN ECtt EPfP GMaP LBMP LDai LRHS MBri MHer MWat NBir NGBl NMir NPer SAga SGar SPet SPoG STes SWal SWvt WFar WPer WWFP |
| - Flying Saucers = 'Walcoreop'PBR | EBee GKir LRHS SCoo SPoG |
| - 'Heliot' | SAga |
| - 'Mayfield Giant' | CSBt EBee EShb LHop LRHS MNrw NPri SPer SPoG SRms SWvt |
| - 'Rising Sun' | EBee MBri NPri SPhx WPer |
| - 'Sunburst' | EBee EPfP LRHS NBre WPer |
| - 'Sunfire' new | WHil |
| - 'Sunray' | CBcs CDoC CSBt CWib EBee ECtt EPfP EShb GKir LAst LRHS LSRN MBri NGdn NPri SMrm SPad SPla SPlb SPoG SRms SWvt WFar WMoo WPer |
| - 'Tetra Riesen' | NBre |
| ***heterophylla*** | see *Iostephane heterophylla* |
| ***lanceolata*** | NBre NSti |
| - 'Goldfink' | GKir MRav SRms |
| - 'Little Sundial' new | EBee |
| § - 'Sonnenkind' (unblotched) | EBee EPfP NBlu NNor SWvt WFar |
| - 'Walter' | EAEE EBee LRHS MBri |
| 'Limerock Ruby'PBR | EBee GQue MNrw NDov NPri SPoG WCot WFar |
| ***major*** new | CSam |
| ***maximiliani*** | see *Helianthus maximiliani* |
| ***palmata*** | MDKP |
| 'Pinwheel' new | NBhm |
| ***pubescens*** | EBee LSou |
| - 'Sunshine Superman' | CSam EDAr LSou |
| ***pulchra*** | EBee |
| ***rosea*** | NLar WFar WPer |
| - 'American Dream' | CSBt EBee ELan EMil EPfP EShb GKir LAst LBMP LRHS LSRN MCot NGdn NPri SGar SPad SPer SPlb SPoG SRms SWal SWvt WBrE WFar |
| - 'Heaven's Gate'PBR | EBee EPfP MAvo NBPC NDov SUsu |
| - 'Sweet Dreams'PBR | EBee EBrs WFar |
| § 'Schnittgold' | CWan EBee NBre WFar WPer WRHF |
| 'Snowberry' new | NBhm |
| I 'Sonnenkind' (red-blotched) | EBee ECtt EMil LBMP MHer NBre WPer |
| 'Sterntaler' | CFir EBee EMil EPPr EPau EShb GKir LRHS MBri MWat NCGa NPri NVic SMad SPad SPet SPhx SWvt WPer |
| Sun Child | see *C.* 'Sonnenkind' |
| 'Tequila Sunrise' (v) | EBee NMoo SMrm |
| ***tripteris*** | CAby CPou EMon LPla MDKP MSte MWea NBre SAga SMad SPhx SUsu WMoo WPer |
| - 'Mostenveld' | EBee |
| - 'Pierre Bennerup' | EMon EPPr SUsu |
| ***verticillata*** | EBee ECha EHrv EPfP GCal LRHS MBrN MDun MGos MHer MWat NPer SDix SRms WFar WHal |
| - Crème Brûlée = 'Crembru'PBR | EBee EBrs SUsu |
| I - 'Golden Gain' | EBee ECtt GBri LHop LRHS MArl MLLN NGdn WFar WMnd |
| - 'Golden Shower' | see *C. verticillata* 'Grandiflora' |
| § - 'Grandiflora' ♀H4 | CBcs COIW CPrp CTca EAEE EBee EBrs ELan EPfP GMaP MNFA MRav NCGa NGdn NHol NVic SMad SPer SPla WCAu WCot WFar WMnd |
| - 'Moonbeam' ♀H4 | Widely available |
| - 'Old Timer' ♀H4 | SDix SUsu |
| - 'Ruby Red' new | CAbP CCVN CHFP ECtt LSou SMrm SUsu WClo |
| - 'Zagreb' ♀H4 | Widely available |

## coriander see *Coriandrum sativum*

## *Coriandrum* (*Apiaceae*)

| | |
|---|---|
| ***sativum*** | CArn CSev GPoy ILis LRHS MHer MNHC NBlu NVic SIde SPoG WLHH |
| - 'Leisure' | NPri SVic |
| - 'Santo' | ELau NGHP WJek |
| - 'Slobolt' new | NGHP |

## *Coriaria* ✿ (*Coriariaceae*)

| | |
|---|---|
| ***arborea*** | WCru |
| ***intermedia*** B&SWJ 019 | WCru |
| ***japonica*** | IDee IFFs NLar WCot WCru |
| - B&SWJ 2833 | WCru |
| - subsp. ***intermedia*** B&SWJ 3877 | WCru |
| ***kingiana*** | CDes ECou WCru |
| § ***microphylla*** | WCru |
| - B&SWJ 8999 | WCru |
| ***myrtifolia*** | EBee NLar WCru WFar |
| ***nepalensis*** | EWld NLar WCru |
| - BWJ 7755 | WCru |
| ***pteridoides*** | WCru |
| ***ruscifolia*** | WCru |
| - HCM 98178 | WCru |
| ***sarmentosa*** | WCru |
| ***terminalis*** var. ***xanthocarpa*** | CBcs CDes CMdw CTrG EBee EPfP GBuc GCal GGar LSou NLar WCot WCru WPGP |
| - - GWJ 9204 | WCru |
| - - HWJK 2112c | WCru |
| ***thymifolia*** | see *C. microphylla* |

## *Cornus* ✿ (*Cornaceae*)

| | |
|---|---|
| ***alba*** L. | CCVT CDoC CDul CLnd CTrG ECrN EMac ISea MHer MRav NWea SRms WDin WMou |
| - 'Alleman's Compact' | CPMA |
| - 'Argenteovariegata' | see *C. alba* 'Variegata' |
| - 'Aurea' ♀H4 | Widely available |
| - Chief Bloodgood = 'Chblzam' | CPMA |
| - 'Cream Cracker'PBR (v) | MAsh MGos NHol WPat |
| - 'Elegantissima' (v) ♀H4 | Widely available |
| - 'Gouchaultii' (v) | CBcs CMac CPMA EBee ECrN EMac EPfP GKir LPan LRHS MAsh MBar MRav MWat NLar NPri SLim SPer SRms WDin WFar |
| - 'Hessei' misapplied | see *C. sanguinea* 'Compressa' |
| - 'Hessei' | MRav WPat |
| - Ivory Halo = 'Bailhalo'PBR | EBee EMil EPfP LRHS MAsh MBNS MBri MGos MRav NPri NWea SPer SPoG SRms |
| - 'Kesselringii' | Widely available |
| - Red Gnome = 'Regnzam' | CPMA LLHF WPat |
| - 'Ruby' | CPMA |
| - 'Siberian Pearls' | CBcs CPMA ELan MBlu MGos SSta |

| | | |
|---|---|---|
| § | - 'Sibirica' ♀H4 | Widely available |
| | - 'Sibirica Variegata' (v) | CBow CDoC CMac CPMA EBee EPfP EPla GCra LPan LRHS LSRN MAsh MBar MBlu MGos NCGa NPri SHBN SLim SPer SPoG SSpi SSta SWvt WCFE WFar |
| | - 'Snow Pearls' | CPMA |
| | - 'Spaethii' (v) ♀H4 | Widely available |
| § | - 'Variegata' (v) | CBcs ECho EQua LAst MGos |
| | - 'Westonbirt' | see *C. alba* 'Sibirica' |
| | ***alternifolia*** | CBcs CMCN ELan EWTr MDun SSpi WPat |
| § | - 'Argentea' (v) ♀H4 | Widely available |
| | - 'Brunette' **new** | NLar |
| | - 'Silver Giant' (v) | CPMA |
| | - 'Variegata' | see *C. alternifolia* 'Argentea' |
| | ***amomum*** | CAbP NHol NLar WFar |
| | - 'Blue Cloud' | CPMA |
| | - 'Lady Jane' **new** | NLar |
| | - subsp. ***obliqua*** | WPGP |
| | ***angustata*** | SPer |
| § | 'Ascona' | CBcs CEnd CPMA ELan EPfP IMGH LRHS MBlu MBri NLar SSpi SSta WPat |
| | Aurora = 'Rutban' (Stellar Series) | CPMA MBlu MPkF NLar SKHP |
| | ***canadensis*** ♀H4 | Widely available |
| | ***candidissima*** Marshall | see *C. racemosa* |
| | ***capitata*** | CAgr CBcs CBgR CDoC CDul CEnd CMac CPne CSBt CTho CTrG EPfP GGar ITim LRHS SEND SGar SKHP SSpi WBVN WCot WCru WFar WPGP WPat |
| | - subsp. ***emeiensis*** | SSpi |
| § | Celestial = 'Rutdan' (Stellar Series) | CPMA MPkF NLar |
| | 'Centennial' | LRHS SSpi |
| | ***chinensis*** | LMil SWvt |
| | 'Constellation' (Stellar Series) | CPMA SKHP |
| | ***controversa*** | Widely available |
| | - 'Candlelight' **new** | NLar |
| § | - 'Frans Type' (v) | CBcs CEnd CPMA ELan ERom LSRN SHBN SReu SSta WDin WHCG |
| I | - 'Marginata Nord' | NLar NPal WPGP |
| | - 'Pagoda' | EPfP MBlu MBri NBhm NLar NPal SSpi |
| | - 'Troya Dwarf' **new** | NLar |
| | - 'Variegata' (v) ♀H4 | Widely available |
| | - 'Variegata' Frans type | see *C. controversa* 'Frans Type' |
| | - 'Winter Orange' | CPMA NLar |
| | 'Eddie's White Wonder' ♀H4 | Widely available |
| | ***excelsa*** F&M 057 **new** | WPGP |
| | ***florida*** | CCVT CDul CLnd CMCN CTho EBee EWTr LAst LRHS MBar NBlu SPer WBVN WDin WHCr |
| | - 'Alba Plena' (d) | CPMA NLar |
| | - 'Andrea Hart' | CPMA |
| | - 'Apple Blossom' | CMac CPMA ECho |
| | - 'Autumn Gold' **new** | CPMA |
| | - Cherokee Brave = 'Comco No 1' | CPMA CWib ECho LRHS MGos MPkF NLar SSpi |
| | - 'Cherokee Chief' ♀H4 | CAbP CBcs CDul CEnd CPMA CSBt CTri CWib ECho EWTr IMGH LRHS LSRN MGos MPkF NLar SBLw SHBN SPer SSta WBod WDin WFar WGob WHar WOrn WPat |
| | - 'Cherokee Daybreak' | see *C. florida* 'Daybreak' |
| | - 'Cherokee Princess' | CPMA ECho LRHS MAsh MPkF SPoG |
| | - 'Cherokee Sunset' | see *C. florida* 'Sunset' |
| | - 'Cloud Nine' | CBcs CDoC CPMA EBee ECho MGos MPkF NLar WOrn |
| | - 'Daniela' (v) | NLar |
| § | - 'Daybreak' (v) | CBcs CEnd CPMA CSBt CWib ECho LSRN MAsh MBri MGos MPkF SPer SSta |
| I | - 'Eternal Dogwood' (d) **new** | MGos |
| | - 'Firebird' **new** | MGos |
| | - 'First Lady' (v) | CMac CPMA ECho WGob |
| | - 'Fragrant Cloud' | ECho |
| | - 'G.H. Ford' (v) | CPMA |
| | - 'Golden Nugget' (v) | CPMA ECho |
| | - 'Junior Miss' | CEnd CPMA EMil |
| | - 'Junior Miss Variegated' (v) | CPMA |
| | - 'Moonglow' | CPMA LMaj |
| | - 'Pendula' | CBcs CPMA MPkF |
| | - f. ***pluribracteata*** (d) | NLar |
| | - var. ***pringlei*** **new** | CPMA |
| | - 'Purple Glory' | CBcs CPMA ECho MBri NLar SSta |
| | - 'Pygmaea' | NLar |
| | - 'Rainbow' | CAbP CBcs CPMA CSBt CWib EBee GKir LRHS MBri MGos MPkF SBod SHBN SPer SPla SSpi WDin |
| | - 'Red Giant' | CAbP CBcs CPMA ELan LMil LRHS MBri NLar |
| | - f. ***rubra*** | CBcs CSBt CTri CWib ECho ELan EWTr GKir LAst LMaj LRHS MBri MGos MMuc MWea SBLw SPer SPoG WDin WFar |
| | - 'Spring Day' | ECho WGob |
| | - 'Spring Song' | CMac CPMA ECho NLar |
| | - 'Springtime' | CPMA ECho NLar |
| | - 'Stoke's Pink' | CEnd CPMA ECho |
| § | - 'Sunset' (v) | CEnd CPMA CSBt CWib ECho MGos MPkF NLar SBLw SHBN SPer SPoG SSta SWvt |
| | - 'Sweetwater' | CBcs CEnd CPMA EMil |
| | - 'Tricolor' | see *C. florida* 'Welchii' |
| | - 'Variegata' | SBLw |
| | - 'Weaver's White' | CBcs ECho MPkF |
| § | - 'Welchii' (v) | CEnd CPMA |
| | - 'White Cloud' | CPMA ELan MBri MPkF |
| | - 'Xanthocarpa' | MPkF |
| | 'Gloria Birkett' | CAbP LMil LRHS SSpi WGob |
| | ***hemsleyi*** | EPla |
| | ***hessei*** misapplied | see *C. sanguinea* 'Compressa' |
| | ***hongkongensis*** HWJ 1033 | WCru |
| | - subsp. ***tonkinensis*** HWJ 1022 **new** | WCru |
| | 'Kelsey Dwarf' | see *C. sericea* 'Kelseyi' |
| | 'Kenwyn Clapp' | CPMA |
| | ***kousa*** | CDoC CDul CMCN CMac CPne CTho ECho ECrN EHig ELan EMac EPfP ERom GKir ISea LMaj LRHS MBar MBri MDun MLan NBlu NLar SHBN SPer SPlb WDin WFar WHCG WHar |
| | - B&SWJ 5494 | WCru |
| | - 'Aget' | CPMA |
| | - 'Akabana' | CPMA |
| | - 'Akatsuki' | CPMA |
| | - 'All Summer' | CPMA |
| | - 'Autumn Rose' | CPMA EPfP NLar |
| | - 'Beni-fuji' | CPMA NLar |
| | - 'Big Apple' | CPMA |
| | - 'Blue Shadow' | CPMA IDee MBri NLar |
| | - 'Bonfire' (v) | CPMA |
| I | - 'Bultinck's Beauty' | LRHS NLar |
| | - 'Bush's Pink' | CPMA |
| | - 'Cherokee' | CPMA |
| | - 'China Dawn' (v) | CPMA |
| | - var. ***chinensis*** ♀H4 | Widely available |
| | - - 'Bodnant Form' | CEnd CPMA GKir NLar WPGP |

| | | |
|---|---|---|
| | - - 'China Girl' | CAbP CDul CEnd CPMA CWib EBee ELan EPfP GKir LBuc LMil LRHS MBlu MBri MGos MSwo SHBN SPer SSpi SSta WBod WDin WOrn WPGP WPat |
| | - - 'Claudia' | MBri |
| | - - 'Greta's Gold' (v) | CPMA |
| | - - 'Milky Way' | CMCN CPMA CWib EBee ECho LBuc MBlu MBri MPkF NLar SHBN WPat |
| | - - 'Snowflake' | CPMA |
| | - - Spinners form | CPMA |
| | - - 'Summer Stars' | CPMA WPat |
| | - - 'White Dusted' | CPMA EPfP SPoG |
| | - - 'White Fountain' | MBlu MBri MPkF NLar |
| | - - 'Wieting's Select' | CPMA MBri MPkF |
| | - - 'Wisley Queen' | CAbP CPMA LRHS SPoG SSpi |
| | - 'Claudine' | CPMA |
| | - 'Doctor Bump' | CPMA |
| | - 'Doubloon' | CPMA ECho |
| | - 'Dwarf Pink' | CPMA NLar |
| | - 'Ed Mezitt' | CPMA |
| | - 'Elizabeth Lustgarten' | CPMA SSta |
| | - 'Fanfare' | CPMA |
| | - 'Galilean' | CPMA |
| | - 'Gay Head' | CPMA |
| I | - 'Girard's Nana' | CPMA |
| | - 'Gold Cup' (v) | CPMA MPkF |
| | - 'Gold Star' (v) | CAbP CBcs CEnd CMCN CMac CPMA CSBt CWib EBee ECho ELan EMil EPfP LBuc LMil LRHS MAsh MBlu MBri MGos NLar SHBN SPla SSpi |
| | - 'Greensleeves' | CPMA |
| | - 'Heart Throb' | CPMA MGos NLar |
| | - 'Highland' | CPMA |
| | - 'John Slocock' | SSpi |
| | - 'Kreus Dame' | CPMA MBri MPkF |
| | - 'Little Beauty' | CPMA |
| | - 'Lustgarten Weeping' | CPMA LRHS NLar |
| | - 'Madame Butterfly' | CEnd CPMA LRHS MAsh MBlu MBri NLar WGob |
| | - 'Milky Way Select' | CBcs CPMA ECho LMaj LPan MGos |
| | - 'Minuma' | NLar |
| | - 'Miss Petty' | CPMA MPkF NLar |
| | - 'Moonbeam' | CPMA MBri MPkF WPat |
| | - 'Mount Fuji' | CPMA MBri NLar |
| | - 'National' | CDul CPMA ECho LMil MBlu MGos MPkF NLar SSpi WPat |
| | - 'Nicole' | CDoC NLar WDin WGob WPat |
| | - 'Peve Limbo' (v) | CPMA MPkF NLar |
| | - 'Polywood' | CPMA |
| | - 'Radiant Rose' | CPMA MPkF NLar SSpi |
| | - 'Rasen' | CPMA MBri NLar |
| | - 'Rel Whirlwind' | CPMA |
| | - 'Rosea' | CPMA |
| | - Samaratin = 'Samzam' (v) | CEnd CPMA MBri MGos MPkF |
| | - 'Satomi' $\mathbb{Y}^{H4}$ | Widely available |
| | - 'Schmetterling' | CPMA MBri WPat |
| | - 'Snowbird' | CPMA |
| | - 'Snowboy' (v) | CBcs CEnd CPMA LRHS NLar |
| | - 'Southern Cross' | CPMA |
| | - 'Square Dance' | CPMA |
| | - 'Steeple' | CPMA |
| | - 'Summer Fun' | CPMA |
| | - 'Summer Majesty' | CPMA |
| | - 'Sunsplash' (v) | CPMA |
| | - 'Temple Jewel' (v) | CPMA LRHS |
| | - 'Teutonia' | CPMA MBri MPkF |
| | - 'Tinknor's Choice' | CPMA |
| | - 'Trinity Star' | CPMA |
| | - 'Triple Crown' | CPMA |
| | - 'Tsukubanomine' | CPMA NLar |
| | - 'U.S.A.' | MPkF |
| | - 'Vale Milky Way' (v) | NLar |
| | - 'Weaver's Weeping' | CPMA MPkF |
| | - 'Weisse Fontäne' | CPMA |
| | - 'White Dream' **new** | CPMA NLar |
| | - 'White Giant' **new** | CPMA |
| | - 'Wolf Eyes' (v) | CPMA MBlu MPkF SSpi SSta WPat |
| | ***kousa* x *florida* 'Aurea'** | MPkF |
| | ***macrophylla*** Wall. | CMCN EPfP WPGP |
| | ***mas*** | Widely available |
| | - 'Aurea' (v) | CAbP CDul CPMA EBee EHig ELan EPfP LRHS MAsh MBri MGos MRav NLar SLim SPer SPoG SSpi SSta WDin WPat |
| § | - 'Aureoelegantissima' (v) | CEnd CGHE CPMA CWib EHig MBri NLar SPer SPoG SSpi WFar WPGP WPat WSHC |
| | - 'Devin' **new** | NLar |
| | - 'Elegantissima' | see *C. mas* 'Aureoelegantissima' |
| | - 'Golden Glory' $\mathbb{Y}^{H4}$ | CBcs CPMA EPfP MBlu MBri NLar |
| | - 'Hillier's Upright' **new** | CPMA |
| | - 'Jolico' | CPMA MBlu MBri NLar |
| | - 'Pioneer' | CPMA |
| | - 'Redstone' | CPMA |
| | - 'Spring Glow' | CPMA NLar |
| | - 'Titus' **new** | NLar |
| | - 'Variegata' (v) $\mathbb{Y}^{H4}$ | CAbP CBcs CMCN CMac CPMA EBee EPfP EPla LRHS MAsh MBlu MBri MGos NHol NLar NPal SPer SPoG SSpi WDin WFar WPat |
| | - 'Xanthocarpa' | CPMA NLar |
| N | 'Norman Hadden' $\mathbb{Y}^{H4}$ | Widely available |
| | ***nuttallii*** | CCVT CDul CSBt CTho CTri CWib ELan EPfP EWTr IMGH LRHS MGos SHBN SPer SWvt WDin WFar |
| | - B&SWJ 9651 | WCru |
| | - 'Ascona' | see *C.* 'Ascona' |
| | - 'Colrigo Giant' | CPMA MPkF WPat |
| | - 'Gold Spot' (v) | CMac CPMA ECho LRHS MGos NWea |
| | - 'Monarch' | CPMA CTho NLar |
| | - 'North Star' | CPMA MBri NLar |
| | - 'Pink Blush' | MPkF NLar |
| | - 'Portlemouth' | CEnd CPMA LRHS SSpi WGob WPat |
| | - 'Zurico' | CPMA MPkF NLar |
| | ***officinalis*** | CAgr CDul CMCN CMac EBee ECrN EMil EPfP LPan LRHS MAsh MBri MWea NLar WDin |
| | 'Ormonde' | CPMA ECho LRHS NLar SKHP SSpi WGob |
| | 'Pink Blush' | CPMA |
| | 'Porlock' $\mathbb{Y}^{H4}$ | CDul CMCN CPMA EPfP GKir LRHS MBri NLar SSpi WDin |
| | ***pumila*** | CPMA NLar WDin |
| § | ***racemosa*** | NLar WFar |
| | ***rugosa*** | NLar |
| | x ***rutgersiensis*** Galaxy | see *C.* Celestial = 'Rutdan' |
| § | Ruth Ellen = 'Rutlan' (Stellar Series) | CPMA NLar |
| | ***sanguinea*** | CBcs CCVT CDul CLnd CRWN CTri ECrN EMac EPfP LBuc LMaj MRav MSwo NWea SPer SVic WBVN WDin WHar WMou |
| | - 'Anny' | MAsh MBlu |
| § | - 'Compressa' | EBee EPfP NLar WFar |
| | - 'Magic Flame' | EBee MAsh MBri NHol |
| | - 'Midwinter Fire' | Widely available |
| | - 'Winter Beauty' | CDoC CPMA CSBt CWib EBee EPfP ERas MAsh MBlu NLar NWea SHBN SLon SWvt WCFE WFar WPat |
| § | ***sericea*** | CArn EMac EPla GKir SRms WMoo |

| | | |
|---|---|---|
| | - 'Budd's Yellow' | GKir LRHS MBlu MBri |
| | - 'Cardinal' | EPfP LRHS MBri NLar |
| | - 'Coral Red' | CPMA |
| | - 'Flaviramea' ♀H4 | Widely available |
| | - 'Hedgerows Gold' (v) | CPMA CSBt EBee EMil LBuc LHop LRHS MAsh NPri SPoG SPur WPat |
| | - 'Isanti' | CPMA |
| § | - 'Kelseyi' | CBgR CMac CPMA EBee EPla LRHS MBNS MBar MRav NPri SBod SLPl SPer SPoG WDin WMoo |
| | - Kelsey's Gold = 'Rosco' | MAsh SLon WPat |
| | - subsp. ***occidentalis*** 'Sunshine' | CPMA CSpe NLar NPro |
| § | - 'White Gold' (v) ♀H4 | CBow CDoC CPMA EBee ECrN EHoe EPla MAsh MBri MRav MSwo NPro SLon SPer WDin WFar WMoo |
| | - 'White Spot' | see *C. sericea* 'White Gold' |
| | Stardust = 'Rutfan' (Stellar Series) | CPMA |
| | Stellar Pink = 'Rutgan' (Stellar Series) | CPMA CWib MBri MPkF NLar SKHP SSpi |
| | ***stolonifera*** | see *C. sericea* |
| | - 'White Spot' | see *C. sericea* 'White Gold' |
| | ***suecica*** | NHar |
| | Venus = 'Kn30-8' | MPkF |
| | ***walteri*** | CBcs CMCN WFar |
| | ***wilsoniana*** | CBcs CMCN |

## *Corokia* (*Escalloniaceae*)

| | | |
|---|---|---|
| | ***buddlejoides*** | CBcs CDoC CMHG CTca CTsd CWib EBee ECou GGar GKir SEND SOWG SPoG WFar |
| | 'Coppershine' | CMHG |
| | ***cotoneaster*** | CAbP CMac CTri EBee ECho ECou ELan EPfP LRHS MGos SLon SMad SPer SPoG SWvt WBod WBrE WCot WFar WPat |
| | - 'Boundary Hill' | ECou |
| | - 'Brown's Stream' | ECou |
| | - 'Hodder River' | ECou |
| | - 'Little Prince' | GGar |
| | - 'Ohau Scarlet' | ECou |
| | - 'Ohau Yellow' | ECou |
| | - 'Swale Stream' | ECou |
| | - 'Wanaka' | ECou |
| | ***macrocarpa*** | CDoC ECou ISea SDix |
| * | ***parviflora*** new | CTrC |
| | x ***virgata*** | CAbP CBcs CDoC CMHG CMac CTrC CTri ECou ELan EPfP ISea LRHS MBlu MCCP NScw SAPC SArc SPer SWvt WBVN WBod WHar WSHC |
| | - 'Bronze King' | CDoC EBee SOWG SPer |
| | - 'Bronze Lady' | ECou |
| | - 'Cheesemanii' | ECou GGar |
| | - 'County Park Lemon' | ECou SOWG |
| | - 'County Park Orange' | ECou |
| | - 'County Park Purple' | ECou |
| | - 'County Park Red' | ECou |
| | - 'Envy' | ECou |
| | - 'Everglades' | ECou |
| | - 'Frosted Chocolate' | CBcs CDoC CSam CTrC CTsd EBee ECou EPfP LBMP LHop LLHF MGos SKHP SOWG SPoG SSta SWvt WCot WDin WFar |
| | - 'Geenty's Green' | CTrC ECou |
| | - 'Havering' | ECou |
| | - 'Mangatangi' | CTrC MGos |
| | - 'Pink Delight' | CDoC EBee ECou EPfP LBMP MRav SSta |
| | - 'Red Wonder' | CDoC CMHG CMac CPen CTrC EBee GGar LRHS MMHG SEND SOWG SPoG WDin |
| | - 'Sandrine' | ECou |
| | - 'Silver Ghost' | CDoC ECou |
| | - 'Sunsplash' (v) | CBcs CDoC CTrC CTsd EBee ECou LBMP LHop LLHF LRHS MGos SEND SPoG SWvt |
| I | - 'Virgata' | CChe ECou MGos |
| | - 'Wingletye' | ECou |
| | - 'Yellow Wonder' | CBcs CDoC CMHG CPen CTrC EBee ECot ECou GGar MGos NLar SBod SPoG SWvt WBod WDin |

## *Coronilla* (*Papilionaceae*)

| | | |
|---|---|---|
| | ***comosa*** | see *Hippocrepis comosa* |
| | ***emerus*** | see *Hippocrepis emerus* |
| | ***glauca*** | see *C. valentina* subsp. *glauca* |
| | ***minima*** | WAbe |
| | ***scorpioides*** new | CSec |
| | ***valentina*** | CDMG CDoC CRHN CSPN EBee EMil LHop SDix |
| § | - subsp. ***glauca*** ♀H3 | CBgR CDul CFee CMac CSBt CSec CTca CTri CWib EBee ELan EPfP LAst LRHS SGar SPer SPoG SRms SWvt WAbe WBod WFar WHCG WKif WPat |
| | - - 'Brockhill Blue' | CWGN EBee SKHP |
| | - - 'Citrina' ♀H3 | Widely available |
| * | - - 'Pygmaea' | WCot WWFP |
| | - - 'Variegata' (v) | CBcs CDoC CMac CSPN CSec CTca CTri CWCL CWib EBee ELan EMil EPfP LRHS MAsh MCot SBod SLim SLon SPer SPla SPoG SSto WAbe WCot WFar |
| | ***varia*** | CArn EBee IFoB NLar NPri SEND SRms |

## *Correa* (*Rutaceae*)

| | | |
|---|---|---|
| | ***alba*** | CCCN CDoC CPLG CTrC EBee ECou EPfP LBMP WGwG |
| | - 'Pinkie' ♀H2 | CBcs CPLG ECou SHGN SOWG WCot |
| | ***backhouseana*** ♀H2 | CAbb CBcs CDoC CPLG CTrG CTri EBee ECou EPfP GGar IDee LHop NLar SAga SBod SGar SLon SOWG SPoG WCot WGwG WSHC |
| | - 'Peaches and Cream' | CSBt SRkn |
| | ***baeuerlenii*** | ECou SOWG |
| | ***decumbens*** | CAbb CTrC ECou SEND SOWG |
| | 'Dusky Bells' ♀H2 | CBcs CCCN CDMG CDoC CHll CSWP CTrC CTri EBee ECou EPfP GGar LBMP LHop SAga SMrm SOWG SPoG SRkn |
| | 'Dusky Maid' | CCCN CPLG WAbe |
| | 'Federation Belle' | CDoC ECou SOWG |
| | ***glabra*** | SOWG |
| | - red-flowered | ECou |
| | 'Gwen' | CDoC ECou SOWG |
| | 'Harrisii' | see *C.* 'Mannii' |
| | 'Inglewood Gold' | ECou |
| | 'Ivory Bells' | ECou |
| | ***lawrenceana*** | CDoC ECou SEND WAbe |
| § | 'Mannii' ♀H2 | CBcs CDoC CMdw CPLG CPom CTsd EBee ECou EPfP SKHP SOWG SPoG WSHC |
| | 'Marian's Marvel' ♀H2 | CBgR CCCN CDoC CMHG CPLG CTrC ECou LBMP SGar SOWG SRkn WAbe |
| | 'Peachy Cream' | CDoC EPfP |
| | 'Pink Mist' | CDoC ECou |
| | 'Poorinda Mary' | ECou SOWG |
| | ***pulchella*** ♀H2 | CDoC CPLG CTri SOWG |
| | - orange-flowered | ECou |
| | ***reflexa*** ♀H2 | CDoC CPLG ECou SOWG WAbe |
| | - var. ***nummulariifolia*** | ECou LBMP WAbe WCot |
| | - var. ***reflexa*** | CPLG |

| | | |
|---|---|---|
| | - - 'Mary's Choice' **new** | CDoC |
| | - var. ***scabridula*** 'Yanakie' | ECou SOWG |
| * | - ***virens*** | CPLG WEas |
| | ***schlechtendalii*** | ECou |

## *Cortaderia* ✿ (*Poaceae*)

| | | |
|---|---|---|
| | sp. | EBee |
| | RCB/Arg K2-2 | WCot |
| | ***argentea*** | see *C. selloana* |
| | ***fulvida*** misapplied | see *C. richardii* (Endl.) Zotov |
| § | ***fulvida*** (Buchanan) Zotov | CBcs CHrt CKno EBee EWes EWsh GFor IDee MNrw SMad WDin |
| | ***jubata*** 'Candy Floss' | CKno |
| | 'Point du Raz' | CKno NLar |
| | ***richardii*** misapplied | see *C. fulvida* (Buchanan) Zotov |
| | ***richardii*** ambig. | CFir CSec EHoe EPau |
| § | ***richardii*** (Endl.) Zotov 🏆$^{H3-4}$ | CBcs CKno CMCo EPPr EPla EWes EWsh GGar GMaP IBlr LBMP MAvo NVic SAPC SArc SMad SWal WCot WCru WMnd |
| | - BR 26 | GGar |
| § | ***selloana*** | CBcs CDul CHEx CSBt CTrG CTri CWib EHul EPfP GKir MAvo MBar MGos MRav NBir NBlu NGBl SAPC SArc SPlb SWal WBVN WFar WMoo |
| § | - 'Albolineata' (v) | CBcs CBct EBee EHoe ELon EMil EWes EWsh MWht NOak SEND SLim SPer SPoG SSta SSto SWvt WLeb WPat |
| § | - 'Aureolineata' (v) 🏆$^{H3}$ | CBcs CDoC CMac EBee EHoe ELan EPfP EWsh GKir LRHS MAsh MGos MMoz MWhi NLar NOak SLim SPer SPoG SSto SWvt WFar WLeb WPGP WPat |
| | - 'Cool Ice' | CKno CPen |
| | - 'Evita' **new** | CKno |
| | - 'Gold Band' | see *C. selloana* 'Aureolineata' |
| | - 'Golden Comet' | GKir |
| | - 'Icalma' | CPen CPrp EPPr LBMP NBsh |
| | - 'Monstrosa' | SMad |
| | - 'Patagonia' | EHoe EPPr |
| | - 'Pink Feather' | EBee EPfP GKir NPri SAdn SApp SPer WFar |
| | - 'Pumila' 🏆$^{H4}$ | Widely available |
| | - 'Rendatleri' | CBcs CDoC ELan EPfP EWsh GKir LRHS LSRN SCoo SLim SMad SPer SPoG WDin |
| | - 'Rosea' | EAlp EBee EPfP LBMP LCro LRHS MBar MGos NBPC NBlu NGdn WBrE WFar |
| | - 'Silver Comet' | GKir |
| | - Silver Feather = 'Notcort' (v) | EWsh |
| | - 'Silver Fountain' (v) | ELan EPfP LRHS MAsh SPer |
| | - 'Silver Stripe' | see *C. selloana* 'Albolineata' |
| | - 'Splendid Star'PBR (v) | CBcs CDTJ CDoC CKno EBee EHoe GBin LBuc LHop MAsh MBri MGos NLar NOak SAdn SMad SPoG SWvt |
| | - 'Sunningdale Silver' 🏆$^{H3}$ | Widely available |
| * | - 'White Feather' | CChe COlW EBee MWhi NGdn NPri SApp SLim WFar WMoo |
| | Toe Toe | see *C. richardii* (Endl.) Zotov |

## *Cortia* (*Apiaceae*)

| | |
|---|---|
| SDR 3922 **new** | EBee |
| SDR 3952 **new** | EBee |

## *Cortiella* (*Apiaceae*)

| | |
|---|---|
| aff. ***hookeri*** HWJK 2291 | WCru |

## *Cortusa* (*Primulaceae*)

| | |
|---|---|
| ***altaica*** | GKev |
| ***brotheri*** | ECho |
| - CC 2987 **new** | EBee |
| - CC 5247 **new** | GKev |
| - CC 5272 **new** | GKev |
| ***matthioli*** | CElw CPom EBee ECho EPfP EWld GBBs GKev GKir NMen NWCA SRms WBVN WFar WRos |
| - BWJ 7740 **new** | WCru |
| - 'Alba' | EBee ECho GBuc GEdr GKir NHol NMen NWCA SRms |
| - subsp. ***pekinensis*** | CFir CLyd ECho EDAr GBuc GCal GEdr GGar GKir NHol NLar NMen SPet SRms WFar |
| - var. ***yezoensis*** | EBee |
| ***turkestanica*** | ECho GAuc LLHF |

## *Corydalis* ✿ (*Papaveraceae*)

| | | |
|---|---|---|
| | CLD 385 | EMon |
| | from Sichuan, China | CPom MDKP NCot |
| | ***alexeenkoana*** subsp. ***vittae*** | see *C. vittae* |
| | ***ambigua*** misapplied | see *C. fumariifolia* |
| | ***ambigua*** Cham. & Schldlt. | WWst |
| | ***angustifolia*** | NDlv |
| | - white-flowered | WWst |
| | ***anthriscifolia*** | CLAP CSec EBee |
| | ***aurea*** | WHil |
| | 'Berry Exciting' **new** | CBow |
| | 'Blackberry Wine' | CSpe EBee GBri GBuc MDKP NPri SPur WFar |
| | 'Blue Panda' | see *C. flexuosa* 'Blue Panda' |
| | ***bulbosa*** misapplied | see *C. cava* |
| | ***bulbosa*** (L.) DC. | see *C. solida* |
| | ***buschii*** | CDes CLAP EBee EBrs ECho ERos GBuc GEdr NHar NRya SCnR WPGP WWst |
| | ***cashmeriana*** | CLAP GEdr GKir NHar NMen WAbe WHal |
| | - 'Kailash' | CLAP EMon GBuc MAvo NLar |
| | ***cashmeriana*** x ***flexuosa*** | CBro CLAP WAbe |
| | ***caucasica*** | ERos GBuc NMen |
| | - var. ***alba*** misapplied | see *C. malkensis* |
| § | ***cava*** | CHid CLAP CPom EBee EBrs ECho EPot LAma SHGN SPhx WFar WShi |
| | - 'Albiflora' | CLAP CSsd EBrs ECho EPot SPhx |
| | - subsp. ***cava*** | ECho |
| | ***chaerophylla*** | IBlr |
| | - B&SWJ 2951 | WCru |
| | ***cheilanthifolia*** | CBcs CRow CSpe EBee ECha EDAr EHrv EPfP GEdr LBMP LRHS MSCN SGar SIng SPhx SRms WEas WFar WPGP WPnn WTin |
| | ***chionophila*** | WWst |
| | 'Craigton Blue' | GBuc NHar |
| | ***curviflora*** subsp. ***rosthornii*** | CWsd EWes SSvw |
| | ***davidii*** | CExc |
| I | ***decipiens*** misapplied 🏆$^{H4}$ | CPom EBrs ECho EPPr EPot |
| I | - purple-flowered | EBee EBrs ECho WWst |
| | ***decipiens*** Schott, Nyman & Kotschy | see *C. solida* subsp. *incisa* |
| | ***densiflora*** | ECho WWst |
| | 'Early Bird' | EWes |
| | ***elata*** | Widely available |
| | - 'Blue Summit' | CLAP EBee EBrs EPPr MSte |
| | ***elata*** x ***flexuosa*** clone 1 | CLAP CMdw CPom EGle GEdr WPrP |
| | 'Electric Blue' (V) | NBhm |
| | ***erdelii*** | EBrs ECho WWst |
| | ***flexuosa*** 🏆$^{H4}$ | CFee CMil CSpe EBee ECho EDAr EGle EPfP EPot IFro LAst MArl MLHP MNrw MTho NCob SGar WAbe WBor WFar WSHC |

| | | |
|---|---|---|
| | - CD&R 528 | MRav NRya |
| | - 'Balang Mist' | CLAP |
| | - 'Blue Dragon' | see *C. flexuosa* 'Purple Leaf' |
| § | - 'Blue Panda' | CWsd EBee EGle EWes GBuc GMaP MDun NHar NLar WFar |
| | - 'China Blue' | Widely available |
| | - 'Copperhead' | ECho |
| | - 'Golden Panda'$^{PBR}$ (v) | CBct CBow CHid EBee ECho LHop MCCP MMHG NLar SPoG WCot |
| | - 'Hale Cat' | EPPr |
| | - 'Hidden Purple' | CHid |
| | - 'Nightshade' | ECtt GBuc MCot NBid NCob WCot WFar WPrP |
| I | - 'Norman's Seedling' | ECtt EPPr WPGP |
| | - 'Père David' | Widely available |
| § | - 'Purple Leaf' | Widely available |
| § | ***fumariifolia*** | EBee EBrs ECho GKev MTho |
| | ***glauca*** | see *C. sempervirens* |
| | ***glaucescens*** | ECho WWst |
| | - 'Early Beauty' | EBrs ECho |
| | ***gracilis*** | WWst |
| | ***henrikii*** | WWst |
| | ***heterocarpa*** | CSec |
| | ***incisa*** | ECho ERCP |
| | - B&SWJ 4417 | WCru |
| | ***integra*** | WWst |
| | 'Kingfisher' | CDes CLAP EWes NHar NLar SBch WAbe WFar |
| | ***kusnetzovii*** | WWst |
| | ***ledebouriana*** | EBrs ECho EPot NMen WWst |
| | ***leucanthema*** | CLAP EBee |
| | - DJHC 752 | CDes WPrP |
| | - 'Silver Spectre' (v) | CBow CWsd EBee LLHF NSti SKHP SPoG WFar |
| | ***lineariloba*** | NCot |
| | ***linstowiana*** | CWsd EMon SPhx |
| | - CD&R 605 | CLAP |
| § | ***lutea*** | CBcs CRWN EBee EPfP GBuc IBlr IFoB IFro MMuc MSCN NBir NCob NPer NVic SEND SRms WCot WMoo |
| | ***macrocentra*** | WWst |
| | ***magadanica*** | LBMP LFur |
| § | ***malkensis*** ♀$^{H4}$ | CAvo CMea EBee ECho ERos GBin GBuc NBir NMen NRya SCnR WThu |
| | ***maracandica*** new | WWst |
| | ***moorcroftiana*** | CExc |
| | ***muliensis*** | CExc NCot |
| | ***nariniana*** | WWst |
| | ***nobilis*** | CHrt CSec CSpe EBrs ECho MLLN SPhx WFar |
| | ***nudicaulis*** | EBrs ECho WWst |
| | ***ochotensis*** B&SWJ 917 | WCru |
| § | ***ochroleuca*** | CElw CRow CSpe EBee EPot GCal GKir LPla MSCN MTho NPol WFar WMoo |
| | ***ophiocarpa*** | CSec CSpe CSsd EGoo EHoe ELan GCal IBlr MBNS MRav NBur WMoo |
| | ***oppositifolia*** | WWst |
| | - subsp. ***kurdica*** | WWst |
| | ***ornata*** | WWst |
| | ***paczoskii*** | EBrs ECho ERos GBuc GKev GKir NDlv NMen |
| | - RS 12180 | EBee |
| | ***pallida*** | CSec |
| | ***paschei*** | WWst |
| | ***popovii*** | EPot MTho SCnR |
| | ***pseudofumaria alba*** | see *C. ochroleuca* |
| | ***pumila*** | EBee |
| | ***quantmeyeriana*** 'Chocolate Stars' | CBow EBee ELon LLHF LSou MAvo MBNS NBPN SMrm WFar |
| | ***raddeana*** B&SWJ 11057 new | WCru |
| | 'Rainier Blue' | CWsd |
| | ***repens*** | WWst |
| | ***rosea*** | IBlr |
| | - 'American Dream' new | CWCL |
| § | ***saxicola*** | EBee |
| | ***scandens*** | see *Dicentra scandens* |
| | ***schanginii*** subsp. ***ainii*** ♀$^{H2}$ | EBrs ECho WWst |
| | - subsp. ***schanginii*** | EBrs ECho |
| | ***scouleri*** | NBir WCot |
| | ***seisumsiana*** | WWst |
| § | ***sempervirens*** | CBod CSec WRos |
| | - 'Alba' | CSec ECho WFoF |
| | ***sewerzowii*** | WWst |
| | ***siamensis*** B&SWJ 7200 | WCru |
| | ***smithiana*** | CSec WFar |
| § | ***solida*** | CAvo CBro CHFP CPom CStu EBee EBrs ECho ECtt ELan EPfP EPot GAbr IBlr ITim LAma MRav NMen NRya SIng SPhx WBVN WCot WFar WPnP WShi WTin |
| | - BM 8499 | NHol |
| | - 'Alcombe' new | MPoH |
| | - 'Firecracker' | CBro EBrs ECho ITim LRHS |
| | - 'First Kiss' | WWst |
| | - 'Grove Seedling' new | MPoH |
| | - 'Harkov' | MPoH WWst |
| § | - subsp. ***incisa*** ♀$^{H4}$ | EBee EBrs ECho GKev MNrw MTho SPhx WCot WShi |
| | - 'Margaret' | WWst |
| | - 'Merlin' | WWst |
| | - Nettleton seedlings | EPot |
| | - 'Purple Beauty' | EBee EBrs WWst |
| | - 'Snowlark' | WWst |
| § | - subsp. ***solida*** | CLAP CMil EBrs ECho EPot GGar LRHS NBir NDov NRya SPhx |
| | - - from Penza, Russia | GBuc ITim LRHS MPoH NCot |
| | - - 'Alba' | NSla |
| | - - 'Beth Evans' | CAvo CMea CPBP EBee EBrs ECha ECho EPPr EPot ERCP GBin GEdr GKev GMaP IPot LAma LEdu LLHF NHar NMen SCnR SPhx WCot |
| | - - 'Blue Giant' | MPoH |
| | - - 'Dieter Schacht' ♀$^{H4}$ | EBee ECho GBin ITim LAma NLar NMen WCot |
| | - - 'George Baker' ♀$^{H4}$ | CBct CBro CMea CPBP CPom EBee EBrs ECho EPot ERCP GBuc GEdr GKev GMaP IPot LAma LFur LLHF LRHS MTho NDov NMen NSla SPhx SUsu WCot WWst |
| | - - 'Lahovice' | ITim NMen WCot |
| | - - 'Nettleton Pink' | EBrs |
| | - - Prasil Group | EBrs GKev IPot SPhx |
| | - - 'Snowstorm' | MPoH |
| | - f. ***transsylvanica*** | see *C. solida* subsp. *solida* |
| | - 'White King' | WWst |
| | - 'White Swallow' | EBrs ECho GKev WWst |
| | 'Spinners' | CDes CElw CLAP EPPr GCal GKev SBch SMeo SPhx SSvw SUsu WPGP WPrP WSHC |
| | ***taliensis*** | CSec EBee LBMP |
| | ***tauricola*** | WWst |
| | ***thalictrifolia*** Franch. | see *C. saxicola* |
| | ***tomentella*** | GKev |
| | 'Tory MP' | CDes CEnt CHid CLAP CPne CPom CSam EBee GAbr GBuc GEdr GMac MDKP MNrw NBid NChi NHar WHoo WMnd WPGP WPrP |
| | ***trachycarpa*** | NCot |
| | ***transsylvanica*** | see *C. solida* subsp. *solida* |
| | ***triternata*** ♀$^{H4}$ | EPot |
| | ***turtschaninovii*** | WWst |
| § | ***vittae*** | ECho EPot WWst |

| | |
|---|---|
| ***vivipara*** | ECho |
| ***wendelboi*** | EBrs ECho EPot |
| - subsp. ***congesta*** | WWst |
| 'Wildside Blue' new | CLAP CWsd |
| ***wilsonii*** | GEdr IBlr IGor WEas |
| ***zetterlundii*** | GBuc NDlv WWst |

## *Corylopsis* ✿ (*Hamamelidaceae*)

| | |
|---|---|
| ***glabrescens*** | CPMA IMGH LRHS |
| - var. ***gotoana*** | EPfP LRHS NLar SPoG SSpi SSta |
| - - 'Chollipo' | CBcs LRHS MAsh SSta |
| ***glandulifera*** | NLar |
| ***himalayana*** | NLar |
| ***pauciflora*** 🏆H4 | Widely available |
| ***platypetala*** | see *C. sinensis* var. *calvescens* |
| - var. ***laevis*** | see *C. sinensis* var. *calvescens* |
| ***sinensis*** | WPGP |
| § - var. ***calvescens*** | CBcs CPMA NLar WPGP |
| § - - f. ***veitchiana*** 🏆H4 | CPMA ELan EPfP IDee NLar SSpi WDin |
| - - - purple-leaved | CPMA |
| - 'Golden Spring' | NLar |
| § - var. ***sinensis*** 🏆H4 | CBgR CDoC CMHG CPMA EBee EPfP IDee IMGH LAst MAsh SLon SPoG SReu WAbe WDin WFar |
| - - 'Spring Purple' | CAbP CBcs CEnd CGHE CMac CPMA EBee EPfP LRHS MBri NLar SKHP SPla SPoG SSpi SSta WDin WFar WPGP |
| ***spicata*** | CBcs CPMA EBee IDee LRHS MBlu MRav NLar SLim SSpi |
| - 'Red Eye' | MBri NLar |
| ***veitchiana*** | see *C. sinensis* var. *calvescens* f. *veitchiana* |
| ***willmottiae*** | see *C. sinensis* var. *sinensis* |

## *Corylus* ✿ (*Corylaceae*)

| | |
|---|---|
| ***avellana*** (F) | CBcs CCVT CDoC CDul CLnd CRWN CTri ECrN EMac EPfP EWTr GAbr GKir LAst LBuc LRHS MAsh MBar MBri MGos NLar NWea SPer SVic WDin WHar WMou WOrn |
| - 'Anny's Compact Red' | MAsh NHol |
| - 'Anny's Red Dwarf' | WPat |
| - 'Aurea' | CBcs CDul CEnd CLnd CSBt CTho CTri EBee ECrN ELan EPfP EWTr GKir LBuc LRHS MAsh MBlu MBri MGos MRav NHol NWea SLim SPer SSta SWvt WDin WFar |
| - 'Bollwylle' | see *C. maxima* 'Halle'sche Riesennuss' |
| - 'Casina' (F) | CAgr CTho |
| - 'Contorta' | Widely available |
| - 'Corabel' (F) | CAgr MCoo |
| - 'Cosford Cob' (F) | CAgr CCVT CDoC CDul CSBt CTho CTri ECrN EMui GKir GTwe LBuc LRHS MBlu MBri MGos SDea SKee SPer |
| - Emoa Series new | MCoo |
| - 'Fortin' (F) | ECrN |
| § - 'Fuscorubra' (F) | GKir MRav |
| - 'Gustav's Zeller' (F) | CAgr MBri MCoo |
| § - 'Heterophylla' | CEnd CTho EBee EPfP GKir MBri NLar WMou |
| - 'Laciniata' | see *C. avellana* 'Heterophylla' |
| § - 'Lang Tidlig Zeller' | CAgr MCoo |
| - 'Merveille de Bollwyller' | see *C. maxima* 'Halle'sche Riesennuss' |
| - 'Nottingham Prolific' | see *C. avellana* 'Pearson's Prolific' |
| - 'Pauetet' (F) | CAgr |
| § - 'Pearson's Prolific' (F) | CAgr CSBt GTwe LBuc SDea SKee |
| - 'Pendula' | GKir LPan MBlu MBri SBLw SCoo SLim WPat |
| - 'Purpurea' | see *C. avellana* 'Fuscorubra' |
| - 'Red Majestic' PBR | Widely available |
| - 'Tonda di Giffoni' | CAgr MBri MCoo |
| - 'Webb's Prize Cob' (F) | CAgr CDoC CDul ECrN GTwe MBlu NLar SBLw SDea SEND SKee SVic WMou |
| ***chinensis*** | EGFP |
| ***colurna*** 🏆H4 | CAgr CCVT CDul CLnd CMCN CTho EBee ECrN EPfP EWTr GKir LPan LRHS MGos NBee NLar NWea SBLw SCoo SPer WBVN WDin WMou |
| x ***colurnoides*** 'Laroka' (F) | ECrN |
| Early Long Zeller | see *C. avellana* 'Lang Tidlig Zeller' |
| ***ferox*** GWJ 9293 | WCru |
| ***maxima*** (F) | CLnd CTri ECrN EMac EMui GTwe MSwo NWea SDea WDin |
| - 'Butler' (F) | CAgr CTho CTri ECrN GTwe LRHS MBri SKee |
| - 'Ennis' (F) | CAgr ECrN GTwe SDea SKee |
| - 'Fertile de Coutard' | see *C. maxima* 'White Filbert' |
| - 'Frizzled Filbert' (F) | ECrN |
| - 'Frühe van Frauendorf' | see *C. maxima* 'Red Filbert' |
| - 'Garibaldi' (F) | MBlu |
| - 'Grote Lambertsnoot' | see *C. maxima* 'Kentish Cob' |
| - 'Gunslebert' (F) | CAgr CCVT CSBt CTho ECrN GTwe LRHS MBri SDea SKee |
| - Halle Giant | see *C. maxima* 'Halle'sche Riesennuss' |
| § - 'Halle'sche Riesennuss' (F) | CAgr ECrN GTwe MMuc SEND SKee |
| § - 'Kentish Cob' (F) | CAgr CBcs CDoC CDul CSBt CTho CWSG ECrN EPfP GTwe LBuc LRHS MBlu MBri MGan MGos SDea SKee SPer SRms WHar WOrn |
| - 'Lambert's Filbert' | see *C. maxima* 'Kentish Cob' |
| - 'Longue d'Espagne' | see *C. maxima* 'Kentish Cob' |
| - 'Monsieur de Bouweller' | see *C. maxima* 'Halle'sche Riesennuss' |
| - 'Purple Filbert' | see *C. maxima* 'Purpurea' |
| § - 'Purpurea' (F) 🏆H4 | Widely available |
| § - 'Red Filbert' (F) | CEnd CTho CWSG EMil GTwe LRHS MAsh MBlu MBri NLar SCoo SKee SLim WPat |
| - 'Red Zellernut' | see *C. maxima* 'Red Filbert' |
| - 'Spanish White' | see *C. maxima* 'White Filbert' |
| § - 'White Filbert' (F) | CDoC GTwe SKee WHar |
| - 'White Spanish Filbert' | see *C. maxima* 'White Filbert' |
| - 'Witpit Lambertsnoot' | see *C. maxima* 'White Filbert' |
| 'Te Terra Red' | CMCN GKir LPan MBlu MBri SBLw SMad SSpi WMou |

## *Corymbia* see *Eucalyptus*

## *Corynabutilon* see *Abutilon*

## *Corynephorus* (*Poaceae*)

| | |
|---|---|
| ***canescens*** | CHrt CKno EBee GFor GQue MBar NBir |

## *Corynocarpus* (*Corynocarpaceae*)

| | |
|---|---|
| ***laevigatus*** | CHEx ECou MBri |

## *Cosmos* (*Asteraceae*)

| | |
|---|---|
| § ***atrosanguineus*** | Widely available |
| - 'Chocamocha' | CBcs CCCN CSpe CWCL EPfP GBin LAst LCro LHop LRHS LSou NBhm NPri SMrm SRot STes SUsu WOVN |
| ***bipinnatus*** Bright Lights mixed (d) | CSpe |
| - 'Purity' | CSpe MCot |
| - 'Sonata Carmine' | NPri |
| - 'Sonata Pink' | NPri SPoG |

| | | |
|---|---|---|
| | - 'Sonata White' | CSpe LAst NPri SPoG |
| § | ***peucedanifolius*** | CAvo CSpe EBee SUsu |
| | - 'Flamingo' | EBee GBri NBhm |
| | ***pucidanifolia*** | see *C. peucedanifolius* |
| | ***sulphureus*** | MSal |

## *Cosmos* x *Dahlia* (*Asteraceae*)

| | |
|---|---|
| 'Mexican Black' new | WCot |

## costmary see *Tanacetum balsamita*

## *Costus* (*Costaceae*)

| | |
|---|---|
| ***barbatus*** | MJnS |
| ***speciosus*** | CKob MJnS |

## *Cotinus* ✿ (*Anacardiaceae*)

| | | |
|---|---|---|
| | ***americanus*** | see *C. obovatus* |
| § | ***coggygria*** $\Upsilon^{H4}$ | Widely available |
| | - 'Foliis Purpureis' | see *C. coggygria* Rubrifolius Group |
| | - Golden Spirit = 'Ancot'PBR | Widely available |
| | - Green Fountain = 'Kolcot'PBR | LBuc |
| | - 'Kanari' | CPMA EBee EMil NLar WPat |
| | - 'Nordine' | NLar WPat |
| | - 'Notcutt's Variety' | ELan EPfP GKir MGos MRav NSti |
| | - 'Pink Champagne' | CBcs CPMA EPfP MBri NLar SSpi WPat |
| | - Purpureus Group | GKir |
| | - 'Red Beauty' | CPMA NLar |
| | - Red Spirit = 'Firstpur' | NLar |
| | - 'Royal Purple' $\Upsilon^{H4}$ | Widely available |
| § | - Rubrifolius Group | CBcs CMac EBee EPfP MAsh NHol SPer SWvt WDin WFar |
| | - Smokey Joe = 'Lisjo' | MAsh SPoG SSta |
| | - 'Smokey Joe Purple' new | LSou |
| | - 'Velvet Cloak' | CAbP CPMA EBee ELan EPfP EWTr GKir LRHS MBri MGos MRav NLar SLon SPer SPla SWvt WHCG |
| | - 'Young Lady'PBR | CBcs CDoC CWSG EBee EMil EPfP EWes GBin LAst MAsh MBlu MBri MPkF NBea NHol NLar NPal SCoo SPer WDin WFar WHar |
| | 'Flame' $\Upsilon^{H4}$ | CAbP CBcs CDul CPMA EBee ELan EPfP GKir LRHS MAsh MBlu MBri MGos MRav NLar SLim SPer SPla SPoG SSpi WHCG WPat |
| | 'Grace' | Widely available |
| § | ***obovatus*** $\Upsilon^{H4}$ | EPfP IArd IDee MBlu MRav NLar SPer SSta WPat |

## *Cotoneaster* ✿ (*Rosaceae*)

| | | |
|---|---|---|
| | CC&McK 465 | NWCA |
| | ***acuminatus*** | EMac SRms |
| | ***adpressus*** $\Upsilon^{H4}$ | EPfP MGos MSwo WFar |
| § | - 'Little Gem' | ECho MGos NLar |
| | - var. ***praecox*** | see *C. nanshan* |
| | - 'Tom Thumb' | see *C. adpressus* 'Little Gem' |
| | ***affinis*** | SRms SSpi |
| | ***albokermesinus*** | SRms |
| | ***amoenus*** | SLPl SRms |
| | - 'Fire Mountain' | NPro WFar |
| § | ***apiculatus*** | MAsh SRms |
| § | ***ascendens*** | SRms |
| | ***assamensis*** | SRms |
| § | ***astrophoros*** | CMac GKir MBlu |
| | ***atropurpureus*** | SRms |
| § | - 'Variegatus' (v) $\Upsilon^{H4}$ | Widely available |
| | ***boisianus*** | SRms |
| | ***bradyi*** | SRms |
| § | ***bullatus*** $\Upsilon^{H4}$ | CDul CLnd CTri EMac EPfP GKir MGos MMuc NLar SGar SPer SRms WOrn |
| | - 'Firebird' | see *C. ignescens* |
| | - f. ***floribundus*** | see *C. bullatus* |
| | - var. ***macrophyllus*** | see *C. rehderi* |
| | - 'McLaren' | SRms |
| | ***bumthangensis*** | SRms |
| | ***buxifolius*** blue-leaved | see *C. lidjiangensis* |
| | - 'Brno' | see *C. marginatus* 'Brno' |
| | - f. ***vellaeus*** | see *C. astrophoros* |
| | ***camilli-schneideri*** | SRms |
| | ***canescens*** | SRms |
| § | ***cashmiriensis*** $\Upsilon^{H4}$ | MGos |
| | ***cavei*** | SRms |
| | ***cinnabarinus*** | SRms |
| § | ***cochleatus*** | EBee LAst MBar MGos NMen SRms |
| § | ***congestus*** | CSBt CWib EBee EDAr GKir MBar MGos MRav MSwo MWat NHol SPlb SRms WBod WDin WHar |
| | - 'Nanus' | CMea CTri ELan EOrn MGos NDlv NHol NLAp |
| | ***conspicuus*** | CBcs SRms |
| | - 'Decorus' $\Upsilon^{H4}$ | CCVT CDoC CSBt CWSG EBee ECrN EPfP GKir LRHS MBar MGan MGos MMuc MRav MSwo NHol NPri NWea SLim SPer SPlb SPoG SWal WDin WMoo |
| | - 'Flameburst' | SHBN |
| | - 'Leicester Gem' | SRms |
| | - 'Red Glory' | CMac |
| | ***cooperi*** | SRms |
| | ***cornifolius*** | SRms |
| N | ***dammeri*** $\Upsilon^{H4}$ | Widely available |
| § | - 'Major' | LAst LBuc |
| § | - 'Mooncreeper' | MBri SCoo |
| | - 'Oakwood' | see *C. radicans* 'Eichholz' |
| | - var. ***radicans*** misapplied | see *C. dammeri* 'Major' |
| | - var. ***radicans*** C.K. Schneid. | see *C. radicans* |
| | - 'Streib's Findling' | see *C.* 'Streib's Findling' |
| | ***dielsianus*** | EMac NWea SRms |
| | ***distichus*** var. ***tongolensis*** | see *C. splendens* |
| | ***divaricatus*** | EMac EPfP NLar NWea SLon SRms WFar |
| | ***duthieanus*** 'Boer' | see *C. apiculatus* |
| | ***elatus*** | SRms |
| | ***elegans*** | SRms |
| | ***emeiensis*** | SRms |
| | 'Erlinda' | see *C.* x *suecicus* 'Erlinda' |
| | ***falconeri*** | EBee SRms |
| | ***fangianus*** | EMac |
| | ***fastigiatus*** | SRms |
| | ***flinckii*** | SRms |
| | ***floccosus*** | NWea |
| | ***floridus*** | SRms |
| | ***forrestii*** | SRms |
| | ***franchetii*** | Widely available |
| | - var. ***cinerascens*** | SRms |
| | - var. ***sternianus*** | see *C. sternianus* |
| | ***frigidus*** | NWea SRms WDin |
| N | - 'Cornubia' $\Upsilon^{H4}$ | Widely available |
| | - 'Notcutt's Variety' | ELan EPfP |
| | - 'Saint Monica' | MBlu |
| | ***gamblei*** | SRms |
| | ***ganghobaensis*** | LLHF SRms |
| | ***glabratus*** | SLPl SRms |
| | ***glacialis*** | SRms |
| | ***glaucophyllus*** | IArd SEND SRms |
| § | ***glomerulatus*** | MBar SRms |
| | ***gracilis*** | SRms |
| | ***granatensis*** | SRms |
| | ***harrovianus*** | SLPl SRms |
| | ***harrysmithii*** | GAuc GKir |
| | ***hebephyllus*** | NLar |

| | | |
|---|---|---|
| I | ***hedegaardii*** 'Fructu Luteo' | SRms |
| | ***henryanus*** | CDoC SRms |
| | 'Herbstfeuer' | see *C. salicifolius* 'Herbstfeuer' |
| | 'Highlight' | see *C. pluriflorus* |
| § | ***hjelmqvistii*** | LBuc SRms |
| | - 'Robustus' | see *C. hjelmqvistii* |
| | - 'Rotundifolius' | see *C. hjelmqvistii* |
| | ***hodjingensis*** | SRms |
| | ***horizontalis*** ♀H4 | Widely available |
| | - 'Variegatus' | see *C. atropurpureus* 'Variegatus' |
| | - var. ***wilsonii*** | see *C. ascendens* |
| | ***hualiensis*** | SRms |
| | ***humifusus*** | see *C. dammeri* |
| | ***hummelii*** | SRms |
| § | 'Hybridus Pendulus' | Widely available |
| § | ***hylmoei*** | SLPl SRms |
| | ***hypocarpus*** | SRms |
| | ***ignavus*** | SLPl SRms |
| § | ***ignescens*** | NWea SRms |
| | ***ignotus*** | SRms |
| | ***induratus*** | SLPl SRms |
| | ***insculptus*** | SRms |
| | ***integerrimus*** | SRms |
| § | ***integrifolius*** ♀H4 | EBee EPfP EPla MBar NMen SCoo SRms STre WMoo |
| | - 'Silver Shadow' | EBee NLar |
| | ***kangdingensis*** | SRms |
| | ***lacteus*** ♀H4 | Widely available |
| | - 'Variegatus' (v) | CEnd |
| | ***lancasteri*** | SRms |
| | ***langei*** | SRms |
| | ***laxiflorus*** | SRms |
| § | ***lidjiangensis*** | SRms |
| § | ***linearifolius*** | GCra GKir |
| | ***lucidus*** | LBuc SPer SRms |
| | ***ludlowii*** | SRms |
| | ***magnificus*** | SRms |
| § | ***mairei*** | SRms |
| | ***marginatus*** | SRms |
| § | - 'Blazovice' | SRms |
| § | - 'Brno' | SRms |
| | ***marquandii*** | EPla GKir SRms |
| § | ***meiophyllus*** | MBlu |
| | ***meuselii*** | SRms |
| | ***microphyllus*** misapplied | see *C. purpurascens* |
| | ***microphyllus*** Wall. ex Lindl. | CDul CTri EBee MBar MGos MRav NBlu NScw NWea SDix SHBN SPer SPoG STre WDin WMoo |
| | - var. ***cochleatus*** misapplied | see *C. cashmiriensis* |
| | - var. ***cochleatus*** (Franch.) Rehd. & Wils. | see *C. cochleatus* |
| | - 'Donard Gem' | see *C. astrophoros* |
| | - 'Ruby' | SRms |
| | - 'Teulon Porter' | see *C. astrophoros* |
| | - var. ***thymifolius*** misapplied | see *C. linearifolius* |
| | - var. ***thymifolius*** (Lindl.) Koehne | see *C. integrifolius* |
| | ***milkedandai*** | SRms |
| | ***miniatus*** | SRms |
| | ***mirabilis*** | SRms |
| | ***monopyrenus*** | SRms |
| | 'Mooncreeper' | see *C. dammeri* 'Mooncreeper' |
| | ***morrisonensis*** | SRms |
| | ***moupinensis*** | SRms |
| | ***mucronatus*** | SRms |
| | ***multiflorus*** Bunge | SRms |
| § | ***nanshan*** | CAbP NLar NWea SRms |
| | - 'Boer' | see *C. apiculatus* |
| | ***newryensis*** | SRms |
| | ***nitens*** | SRms |

| | | |
|---|---|---|
| | ***nitidifolius*** | see *C. glomerulatus* |
| | ***nohelii*** | SRms |
| | ***notabilis*** | SRms |
| | ***nummularioides*** | SRms |
| | ***nummularius*** | SRms |
| | ***obscurus*** | SRms |
| | ***obtusus*** | SRms |
| | ***pangiensis*** | SRms |
| | ***pannosus*** | SLPl SRms WFar |
| | - 'Speckles' | SRms |
| | ***paradoxus*** | SRms |
| | ***parkeri*** | SRms |
| | ***pekinensis*** | SRms |
| | ***permutatus*** | see *C. pluriflorus* |
| | ***perpusillus*** | SRms WFar |
| § | ***pluriflorus*** | SRms |
| | ***poluninii*** | SRms |
| | ***polycarpus*** | SRms |
| | ***praecox*** 'Boer' | see *C. apiculatus* |
| | ***procumbens*** | SLon SRms WDin |
| | - 'Queen of Carpets' | CDoC CDul EBee EPfP EQua ERas GKir LRHS LSRN MAsh MGos MRav MWhi NLar SCoo SLim SPoG SRms SWvt WMoo |
| | - 'Streib's Findling' | see *C.* 'Streib's Findling' |
| | ***prostratus*** | SRms |
| | ***przewalskii*** | SRms |
| | ***pseudo-obscurus*** | SRms |
| § | ***purpurascens*** | GKir MGos NPri WFar |
| | ***pyrenaicus*** | see *C. congestus* |
| | ***qungbixiensis*** | SRms |
| | ***racemiflorus*** | SRms |
| § | ***radicans*** | LRHS |
| § | - 'Eichholz' | EBee MGos NHol NLar SPoG WDin |
| § | ***rehderi*** | CMHG NLar SRms |
| | ***roseus*** | SRms |
| | 'Rothschildianus' | see *C. salicifolius* 'Rothschildianus' |
| | ***rotundifolius*** | NLar SLon |
| | ***rubens*** new | GKir |
| | ***rugosus*** | SRms |
| | ***salicifolius*** | EBee GKir MSwo SPer SRms WDin WFar |
| | - Autumn Fire | see *C. salicifolius* 'Herbstfeuer' |
| § | - 'Avonbank' | CDoC CEnd NLar |
| | - 'Bruno Orangeade' | SRms |
| | - 'Elstead' | MRav |
| | - 'Exburyensis' | CBcs CDoC CDul EBee EPfP ERas GKir LAst LRHS MAsh MBri MGos MRav NLar SEND SHBN SPla WDin WFar WHCG |
| | - 'Gnom' | CChe CDul CMac EBee ELan EPfP EQua LRHS MAsh MBar MBlu MGos MRav NBir SPer SPoG SRms WDin WFar WMoo |
| § | - 'Herbstfeuer' | LAst MGos MRav MSwo SRms WDin WFar |
| | - 'Merriott Weeper' | CDoC |
| | - Park Carpet | see *C. salicifolius* 'Parkteppich' |
| § | - 'Parkteppich' | NWea |
| | - 'Pendulus' | see *C.* 'Hybridus Pendulus' |
| | - 'Repens' | CDoC CWib EPfP MGan MWhi NHol NScw NWea SPer SPoG SRms SSto WDin WFar |
| § | - 'Rothschildianus' ♀H4 | Widely available |
| | - var. ***rugosus*** hort. | see *C. hylmoei* |
| | - 'Scarlet Leader' | CMac |
| | ***salwinensis*** | SLPl SRms |
| | ***sandakphuensis*** | SRms |
| | ***scandinavicus*** | SRms |
| | ***schantungensis*** | SRms |
| | ***schlechtendalii*** 'Blazovice' | see *C. marginatus* 'Blazovice' |
| | - 'Brno' | see *C. marginatus* 'Brno' |

***schubertii*** SRms
***serotinus*** misapplied see *C. meiophyllus*
***serotinus*** Hutchinson NLar SLPl SRms
***shannanensis*** SRms
***shansiensis*** SRms
***sherriffii*** SRms
aff. ***sichuanensis*** new GAuc
***sikangensis*** GBin SLon SRms
***simonsii*** ♀H4 CCVT CDoC CDul CLnd CMac CTri EBee EHig ELan EMac EPfP GKir LAst LBuc LRHS MAsh MBar MGos NHol NScw NWea SCoo SPer SPoG SRms WDin WFar WHar
§ ***splendens*** GKir SRms WFar
- 'Sabrina' see *C. splendens*
***spongbergii*** SRms
***staintonii*** SRms
§ ***sternianus*** ♀H4 EBee EPfP LRHS MBar SLPl SRms
§ 'Streib's Findling' EBee MAsh NLar
***suavis*** SRms
***subacutus*** SRms
***subadpressus*** SRms
x ***suecicus*** 'Coral Beauty' Widely available
§ - 'Erlinda' (v) CEnd CWib NBlu NLar SCoo SRms
- 'Ifor' SLPl SRms
- 'Juliette' (v) CWib EHoe EMil ERas LBMP LSRN MAsh MBar NBlu NLar NPro SCoo SPoG WFar WOrn
- 'Skogholm' CBcs CWSG CWib EBee GKir MBar MGos NWea SCoo SPer SRms WDin WFar WHar
***taoensis*** SRms
***tardiflorus*** SRms
***tauricus*** SRms
***teijiashanensis*** SRms
***tengyuehensis*** SRms
***thimphuensis*** SRms
***tomentellus*** WCFE
***tomentosus*** SRms
***turbinatus*** SLPl SRms
'Valkenburg' SRms
***vandelaarii*** SRms
***veitchii*** MBri NLar SRms
***verruculosus*** SRms
***villosulus*** EHig SRms
***vilmorinianus*** SRms
***wardii*** misapplied see *C. mairei*
***wardii*** W.W.Sm. GGal SRms
x ***watereri*** CCVT CWib EBee MSwo NWea WDin WJas
- 'Avonbank' see *C. salicifolius* 'Avonbank'
- 'Corina' SRms
- 'Cornubia' see *C. frigidus* 'Cornubia'
- 'John Waterer' ♀H4 EPfP LRHS MGos SPer SPoG WFar
- 'Pendulus' see *C.* 'Hybridus Pendulus'
- 'Pink Champagne' CAbP CMac EQua
***wilsonii*** SRms
***yallungensis*** SRms
***yinchangensis*** SRms
***zabelii*** SRms

## *Cotula* (*Asteraceae*)

C&H 452 NWCA
***atrata*** see *Leptinella atrata*
- var. ***dendyi*** see *Leptinella dendyi*
***coronopifolia*** CBen CWat EDAr EHon EMFW LPBA NPer SWat
§ ***hispida*** Widely available
***lineariloba*** ECha ECho EWes LBee LRHS
***minor*** see *Leptinella minor*
'Platt's Black' see *Leptinella squalida* 'Platt's Black'
***potentilloides*** see *Leptinella potentillina*
***pyrethrifolia*** see *Leptinella pyrethrifolia*
***rotundata*** see *Leptinella rotundata*
***sericea*** see *Leptinella albida*
***serrulata*** see *Leptinella serrulata*
***squalida*** see *Leptinella squalida*

## *Cotyledon* (*Crassulaceae*)

***chrysantha*** see *Rosularia chrysantha*
***gibbiflora*** var. ***metallica*** see *Echeveria gibbiflora* var. *metallica*
***oppositifolia*** see *Chiastophyllum oppositifolium*
***orbiculata*** CHEx CWsd SDix SEND
- B&SWJ 723 WCru
- var. ***oblonga*** EBee WCot WEas
- 'Silver Waves' new MCot
***simplicifolia*** see *Chiastophyllum oppositifolium*
***tomentosa*** subsp. ***ladismithensis*** EShb

## *Cowania* see *Purshia*

## *Crambe* (*Brassicaceae*)

***cordifolia*** ♀H4 Widely available
***filiformis*** WHal
***maritima*** ♀H4 CArn CSev CSpe EBWF EBee ECGP ECha EPfP GMaP GPoy LAst MCot MLLN MRav MSal NSti SMad SPer SPhx SVic SWat WCot WFar WJek WMnd WPer
- 'Lilywhite' CAgr ILis WCot
***tatarica*** NLar SHar WPer

## cranberry see *Vaccinium macrocarpon, V. oxycoccos*

## *Crassula* (*Crassulaceae*)

***anomala*** see *C. atropurpurea* var. *anomala*
***arborescens*** EShb SRms STre
***argentea*** see *C. ovata*
§ ***atropurpurea*** var. ***anomala*** SChr
- subsp. ***arborescens*** 'Blue Mist' new SEND
***coccinea*** EShb
***dejecta*** EShb
§ ***exilis*** subsp. ***cooperi*** STre
***lactea*** CHal STre
***lycopodioides variegata*** see *C. muscosa* 'Variegata'
***multicava*** CHEx
***muscosa*** EShb SChr SRot STre
§ - 'Variegata' (v) EShb
***obtusa*** SRot
§ ***ovata*** ♀H1 CHEx CHal CTsd EBak EOHP EPfP LRHS MBri NPer NScw SWal WCor WThu
- 'Gollum' STre
- 'Hummel's Sunset' (v) ♀H1 CHal MAvo STre SWal
* - ***nana*** STre
- 'Obliqua' new STre
- 'Variegata' (v) CHal EBak WCot
***pellucida*** subsp. ***marginalis*** CHal
* - - 'Variegata' (v) CHal
***perfoliata*** var. ***falcata*** ♀H1 CTsd EShb MBri SRot
***perforata*** CHal WCor
- 'Variegata' (v) CHal EWll LSou SRot
***picturata*** see *C. exilis* subsp. *cooperi*
***portulacea*** see *C. ovata*
***rupestris*** ♀H1 MBri
§ ***sarcocaulis*** CHEx CHal CStu CTri EAlp ECho ELan ELon EWll GEdr GMaP MTho

| | | |
|---|---|---|
| | | NLAp NMen NVic NWCA SGar SIng SPlb SPoG SRms SRot STre WAbe WEas WFar WPat WSHC |
| I | - ***alba*** | CHal GEdr NLAp STre WPer |
| | - 'Ken Aslet' | STre |
| | ***schmidtii*** | CHal MBri |
| | ***sedifolia*** | see *C. setulosa* 'Milfordiae' |
| | ***sediformis*** | see *C. setulosa* 'Milfordiae' |
| § | ***setulosa*** 'Milfordiae' | CTri ECho GKir NBir |
| | ***socialis*** | EPot |
| | - 'Major' **new** | SChr |
| | ***tetragona*** | SEND |
| * | ***tomentosa*** 'Variegata' (v) | EShb |
| | 'Très Bon' | STre |

## + *Crataegomespilus* (*Rosaceae*)

| | | |
|---|---|---|
| | 'Dardarii' | MBri |
| | 'Jules d'Asnières' | MBri NLar |

## x *Crataegosorbus* (*Rosaceae*)

| | | |
|---|---|---|
| § | 'Granatnaja' **new** | IArd |
| § | ***miczurinii*** 'Ivan's Belle' | CAgr |

## *Crataegus* ✿ (*Rosaceae*)

| | | |
|---|---|---|
| | F&M 196 | WPGP |
| | ***altaica*** **new** | GKir |
| | ***arnoldiana*** | CAgr CDul CEnd CLnd CTri EBee ECrN EPfP GKir IMGH LRHS MCoo MLan NWea SCoo SEND SLPl SPer WOrn |
| | 'Autumn Glory' | CEnd CLnd EBee ECrN GKir WFar |
| | ***azarolus*** | CAgr CLnd EPfP MBri |
| | ***champlainensis*** | CLnd |
| | ***chrysocarpa*** | EPfP |
| N | ***coccinea*** misapplied | see *C. intricata* |
| N | ***coccinea*** ambig. | NWea |
| § | ***coccinea*** L. | CAgr CLnd CTho EPfP GKir MAsh MBri MCoo SCoo |
| | ***coccinioides*** | EPfP |
| | ***cordata*** | see *C. phaenopyrum* |
| | ***crus-galli*** misapplied | see *C. persimilis* 'Prunifolia' |
| | ***crus-galli*** L. | CCVT CDoC CDul CLnd CTho EBee ECrN EPfP LAst MAsh NWea SPer WDin WFar WJas |
| | - thornless | MBlu |
| | ***dahurica*** | EPfP |
| | x ***dippeliana*** | EPfP |
| | ***douglasii*** | EPfP GAuc |
| | ***dsungarica*** | EPfP |
| | x ***durobrivensis*** | CAgr CDul CLnd EPfP GKir MBri MCoo NLar |
| | ***ellwangeriana*** | CAgr ECrN EPfP |
| | ***eriocarpa*** | CLnd |
| | ***flabellata*** | CEnd GKir |
| | ***gemmosa*** | CEnd GKir MAsh MBlu MBri MCoo NLar NWea SSpi |
| | ***greggiana*** | EPfP |
| | x ***grignonensis*** | CBcs CCVT CDul CLnd CTho ECrN EMil LMaj MAsh SBLw SEND SPer WJas |
| § | ***intricata*** | EPfP |
| | ***irrasa*** | EPfP |
| | ***jonesiae*** | EPfP |
| | ***laciniata*** Ucria | see *C. orientalis* |
| § | ***laevigata*** | GKir NWea |
| | - 'Coccinea Plena' | see *C. laevigata* 'Paul's Scarlet' |
| | - 'Crimson Cloud' | CDoC CDul CEnd CLnd CWSG CWib EBee ECrN ELan EMui EPfP GKir LBuc LRHS MAsh MBri MGos MSwo NWea SCoo SCrf SLim SLon SPer SPoG WHar WJas WOrn |
| | - 'Flore Pleno' | see *C. laevigata* 'Plena' |
| | - 'Gireoudii' | CBcs CDul CEnd CPMA CWib LAst MBlu MGos NLar NSti WPat |
| | - 'Mutabilis' | CLnd CTri SBLw |
| § | - 'Paul's Scarlet' (d) ♀H4 | Widely available |
| | - 'Pink Corkscrew' | EPfP GKir LLHF MAsh MBlu MBri MGos NHol SMad WPat |
| § | - 'Plena' (d) | CBcs CDoC CDul CLnd CSBt CTho CTri CWib EBee ECrN GKir LAst LRHS MGos MSwo MWat NWea SBLw SCrf SHBN SLim SPer WDin WHar WOrn |
| | - 'Punicea' | GKir |
| | - 'Rosea' | GKir |
| | - 'Rosea Flore Pleno' (d) ♀H4 | Widely available |
| | x ***lavalleei*** | CCVT CDul CLnd CTri EBee ECrN EPfP GKir LMaj MSwo NWea SCoo SPer SPur WDin |
| | - 'Carrierei' ♀H4 | CDoC CTho EHig EPfP EWTr GKir LMaj MAsh MBlu MBri NWea SBLw SCoo WOrn |
| | ***lobulata*** | EPfP |
| | ***mexicana*** | see *C. pubescens* f. *stipulacea* |
| | ***mollis*** | CAgr CTho ECrN EPfP |
| | ***monogyna*** | CArn CBcs CCVT CDoC CDul CLnd CRWN CTri ELan EMac EPfP GKir LAst LBuc LRHS MAsh MBar MBri MGos NBlu NPri NWea SPer SPoG WDin WFar WMou |
| § | - 'Biflora' | CDul CEnd CLnd CTho CTri EBee ECrN EHig GKir MAsh MCoo MGos NWea SCoo SLim SPoG |
| | - 'Compacta' | MBlu NLar |
| | - 'Flexuosa' | MGos |
| | - 'Praecox' | see *C. monogyna* 'Biflora' |
| | - 'Stricta' | CCVT CDul CLnd CSBt EBee ECrN EHig EPfP GKir LMaj MBlu SBLw SPoG |
| | - 'Variegata' (v) | ECrN MRav |
| | x ***mordenensis*** 'Toba' (d) | CDul CLnd EPfP MBri SBLw |
| | ***nigra*** | EPfP |
| § | ***orientalis*** | CCVT CDul CEnd CLnd CMCN CTho CTri EBee ECrN EPfP GKir IArd IDee LPan LRHS MBlu MBri MCoo MGos NWea SCoo SHBN SLPl SLim SSpi WJas WMou WOrn |
| | ***oxyacantha*** | see *C. laevigata* |
| | ***pedicellata*** | see *C. coccinea* L. |
| | ***pentagyna*** | EPfP |
| § | ***persimilis*** 'Prunifolia' ♀H4 | Widely available |
| | - 'Prunifolia Splendens' | CCVT GBin GKir MBri MCoo SBLw SCoo WPat |
| § | ***phaenopyrum*** | CDul CLnd CTho EPfP IDee MGos SLPl SMad |
| | ***pinnatifida*** | EPfP GKir |
| | - var. ***major*** | CDul CEnd EBee EPfP MBri MCoo NWea SCoo |
| | - - 'Big Golden Star' | CAgr CLnd CTho ECrN GKir MAsh MBri MCoo NLar SCoo |
| | 'Praecox' | see *C. monogyna* 'Biflora' |
| | ***prunifolia*** | see *C. persimilis* 'Prunifolia' |
| | ***pseudoheterophylla*** | EPfP |
| * | ***pubescens*** f. ***major*** | CAgr |
| § | - f. ***stipulacea*** | CDul CLnd CTho EPfP MBri |
| | ***punctata*** | CTho SLPl |
| | - f. ***aurea*** | EPfP |
| | ***sanguinea*** | EPfP |
| | ***schraderiana*** | CAgr CDul CLnd CTho EBee EPfP GKir MBri MCoo NWea SCoo SPoG |
| | ***sorbifolia*** | EPfP |
| | ***succulenta*** | EPfP GKir |
| | - var. ***macracantha*** | EPfP GKir SMad |

***suksdorfii*** EPfP
***tanacetifolia*** CAgr CDul CTho EPfP GKir LLHF MBlu MBri SPer
* - 'Fructu Albo' **new** GKir
***triflora*** **new** MBri
***turkestanica*** EPfP
***viridis*** 'Winter King' CDoC EPfP GKir MAsh MBlu MCoo SLim
***wattiana*** EHig EPfP

## x *Crataemespilus* (*Rosaceae*)

***grandiflora*** CBcs CDul CEnd CLnd CTho

## *Crawfurdia* (*Gentianaceae*)

***speciosa*** B&SWJ 2138 WCru

## *Cremanthodium* (*Asteraceae*)

***angustifolium*** EBee
- SDR 1831 **new** GKev
***ellisii*** CC 4642 **new** EBee
aff. ***ellisii*** HWJK 2262 WCru
***reniforme*** GWJ 9407 WCru

## x *Cremnosedum* (*Crassulaceae*)

§ 'Little Gem' CStu EPot NMen

## *Crenularia* see *Aethionema*

## *Crepis* (*Asteraceae*)

***aurea*** EBee
***incana*** 🏆H4 CMea CMoH EBee ECho EGoo GBri LRHS MTho NChi NSla NWCA SIng SPhx SRms WAbe WPat
- 'Pink Mist' GBin MBri NLar
***rubra*** LRHS

## *Crinitaria* see *Aster*

## *Crinodendron* (*Elaeocarpaceae*)

***hookerianum*** 🏆H3 Widely available
- 'Ada Hoffmann' CBcs CDoC EBee ELan GBin ISea LRHS MBlu MBri MREP NDlv NLar NMun SKHP
***patagua*** CBcs CCCN CSam CWib EBee EHig GGar GQui IArd ISea MBri NLar SLon WBod WFar WPic WSHC

## *Crinum* (*Amaryllidaceae*)

***americanum*** CDWL
***amoenum*** CCCN CSec CTca EBee EBrs ECho WCot
***asiaticum*** WCot
- DJHC 970606 WCot
- var. ***sinicum*** WCot
§ ***bulbispermum*** CFir EBee ELan WCot
***capense*** see *C. bulbispermum*
'Carolina Beauty' WCot
'Elizabeth Traub' WCot
'Ellen Bosanquet' CCCN CDes CFir CTca EBee WCot
'Emma Jones' WCot
***erubescens*** WCot
'Hanibal's Dwarf' CDes EBee WCot
'Heja Lodge' WCot
***latifolium*** EBee
***macowanii*** WCot
***moorei*** CDes CFir CTca EBee EBrs ECho LEdu LPio SChr WCot WPGP
- f. ***album*** CAvo CCCN EBee LPio WCot
'Ollene' WCot
§ x ***powellii*** 🏆H3 Widely available
- 'Album' 🏆H3 CAvo CHEx CTca CTri EBee EBrs ECha ECho ELan EShb EWes GCra GKir LAma LEdu LHop LPio LRHS MBri MRav MWte SSpi WCot WFar WHil WPGP WPic
- 'Harlemense' SSpi
- 'Longifolium' see *C. bulbispermum*
- 'Roseum' see *C.* x *powellii*
'Regina's Disco Lounge' WCot
***variabile*** EBee WCot
***yemense*** WCot

## *Criogenes* see *Cypripedium*

## *Crithmum* (*Apiaceae*)

***maritimum*** CArn EBWF GPoy MSal NLar NTHB SECG SPlb WJek

## *Crocosmia* ✿ (*Iridaceae*)

'Alistair' ECtt
'Anniversary' CTca IBlr
'Apricot' **new** CTca
***aurea*** misapplied see *C.* x *crocosmiiflora* 'George Davison' Davison
***aurea*** ambig. CTca EShb GCal
***aurea*** (Pappe ex Hook.f.) Planch. CPne CPou ECtt IBlr NHol
- subsp. ***aurea*** CTca IBlr
- - 'Maculata' IBlr
- subsp. ***pauciflora*** IBlr
'Auricorn' IBlr NCot NHol
'Auriol' IBlr
'Aurora' CHVG NGdn
'Beth Chatto' CPrp CTca
Bressingham Beacon = 'Blos' EBee IBlr LRHS WRHF
'Bressingham Blaze' CBre CMHG CTca EBee EBla EBrs ECtt GKir IBlr LRHS NBre NGdn NHol WCot
Bridgemere hybrid NHol
'Cadenza' IBlr NCot
'Carnival' ECtt IBlr
'Cascade' IBlr NCot
'Chinatown' IBlr MAvo NCot NHol WHil
'Citronella' misapplied see *C.* x *crocosmiiflora* 'Honey Angels'
'Comet' Knutty CPrp CTca EBrs GBuc IBlr NCot NHol
§ x ***crocosmiiflora*** CHEx CTca CTri EBee EPla IBlr LAst MCot NHol SIng SPlb SRms WBrk WCot WFar WMoo WShi
- 'A.E.Amos' ECtt
- 'A.J. Hogan' CPrp CTca GBin IBal IBlr NHol SMrs WHil
- 'Amber Sun' IBlr
- 'Amberglow' CBgR CElw CMea CPrp ECho GKir IBal IBlr NBre NHol NPer WFar
- 'Apricot Queen' CTca IBlr MAvo NHol
- 'Autumn Gold' IBlr
- 'Baby Barnaby' CBre CDes CTca EBee ECtt IBlr NHol SBch WPGP
- 'Babylon' Widely available
- 'Best of British' **new** CHVG
- 'Bicolor' CPrp CTca IBal IBlr NHol
- 'Burford Bronze' CAbx CPrp CTca IBal IBlr MAvo NCot NHol
- 'Buttercup' CTca EWll GAbr GBri GKev IBlr MAvo MLLN NBre NHol WBor WFar
- 'Canary Bird' CBro CPne CPrp CRow CSam CTca EBee ECho ECtt GAbr GMac IBal IBlr NBPC NGdn NHol WBrk WHil WRHF
- 'Cardinale' IBlr
- 'Carmin Brillant' 🏆H3-4 Widely available
- 'Carminea' CTca
- 'Citrina' CTca GKir

- 'Citronella' J.E. Fitt — CBgR CBro CPLG CPrp CSam CTca CTri EBee EBla EBrs ECha EPfP GKev GMaP GQue LAst LBMP LRHS MRav NGdn NHol SAga WBVN WCot WRha
§ - 'Coleton Fishacre' — Widely available
§ - 'Columbus' — CPar CSam EBee GBin IBal IBlr LHop LRHS MWea NHol SGar WBor WCot WFar WHil WMnd
- 'Colwall' — IBlr NCot
- 'Constance' — CBgR CBre CBro CElw CPrp CSam CTca EBee EBrs GGar GKir IBal IBlr LRHS MAvo MBri MNrw NBid NGdn NHol SRGP SRos WFar WHil
- 'Corona' — CPrp CTca EBee IBal IBlr MAvo NCot NHol
- 'Corten' — IBlr
§ - 'Croesus' — CTca GBri IBlr MAvo MRav NCot
- 'Custard Cream' — CAbx CPrp CSpe CTca ECtt GBin IBlr LRHS MAvo NHol SRos WFar WRHF
- 'D.H. Houghton' — IBlr
- 'Debutante' — CPrp CTca EBee EBrs ECtt IBal IBlr MAvo MHar NHol WCot WHoo WPGP WSHC
§ - 'Diadème' — CSam MAvo NHol
- 'Dusky Maiden' — Widely available
§ - 'E.A. Bowles' — CPou CPrp CTca IBlr
- 'Eastern Promise' — CAbx CBre CMea CPrp CTca EBee IBal IBlr MAvo MSte NCot SMrm SUsu
- 'Eclatant' — IBlr
- 'Elegans' — CBre CElw CTca EBrs ECtt IBlr
- 'Emberglow' — Widely available
§ - 'Emily McKenzie' — Widely available
- 'Etoile de Feu' — IBlr
- 'Fantasie' — CBgR IBal
- 'Festival Orange' — CTca IBlr MAvo
- 'Firebrand' — IBlr NCot
- 'Fireglow' — ECho ECtt GKir IBlr NCot WFar WPer
- 'Flamethrower' — IBlr MAvo
- 'George Davison' misapplied — see *C.* x *crocosmiiflora* 'Golden Glory' ambig., 'Sulphurea'
§ - 'George Davison' Davison — Widely available
- 'Gloria' — CTca IBlr
- 'Golden Glory' misapplied — see *C.* x *crocosmiiflora* 'Diadème'
§ - 'Golden Glory' ambig. — CPLG CWCL EHrv ELan IBal IBlr MSwo NBir NHol SPlb SRos WCot WFar WHil
- 'Goldfinch' — CTca IBlr NCot NHol WHil
- 'Goldie' **new** — CTca
- 'Hades' — CPrp IBlr MAvo NCot WHil
- 'Harvest Sun' — IBlr
- 'His Majesty' — CAbx CBro CPne CPou CPrp CSam CSpe CTca ECtt IBal IBlr LRHS NHol SDys WFar WPer
- 'Hoey Joey' **new** — GMac
§ - 'Honey Angels' — Widely available
- 'Honey Bells' — CElw CTca WBrk
- 'Irish Dawn' — CPrp GBin GBri IBlr NBre NCot NHol
§ - 'Jackanapes' — CPne CPrp CRow CTca CWCL EBee EBrs ECtt EHrv ELan ELon GCal GGar GKir IBal IBlr LCro LRHS MBri MGos MLHP NHol SDys SUsu WFar
- 'James Coey' J.E. Fitt — CHar COIW CPrp CRow EAEE EBee EBla ECha EHoe EHrv EPfP IFoB LRHS MLHP NDov NGdn NHol SIng SRGP SWvt WFar WMoo WWlt
- 'Jesse van Dyke' — IBlr
§ - 'Jessie' — CElw CTca IBlr LPio MAvo SMrm WPer
- 'Judith' **new** — IBlr NCot
- 'Kapoor' — IBlr
- 'Kiautschou' — CHVG CTca CWCL EBee EBrs ECtt GMac IBlr MAvo NBre NHol SDys WHil
- 'Lady Hamilton' — Widely available
- 'Lady McKenzie' — see *C.* x *crocosmiiflora* 'Emily McKenzie'
- 'Lady Oxford' — CPrp CTca IBlr LRHS NHol WHil
- 'Lambrook Gold' — CAvo IBlr
- 'Lord Nelson' — CPrp CTca MAvo
- 'Loweswater' — MAvo SUsu
- 'Lutea' — CTca EBee ECtt IBlr NHol
- 'Marjorie' — MAvo WCot
- 'Mars' — CElw CPrp CTca EBla EWes EWll GAbr GBuc GCal GGar GMac IBal IBlr IFoB LPio LRHS MWhi NHol SPlb SRGP WFar WPGP WPer
- 'Mephistopheles' — CPrp CTca IBlr MAvo NCot NHol
- 'Merryman' — CTca GAbr
- 'Météore' — CBgR CHFP CPrp CTca EBrs EPot GGar IBal MBNS NBre NHol NPri SBch WPrP
- 'Morgenlicht' — CTca ECtt GBin IBal IBlr NHol WCot
- 'Mount Usher' — CFir CMdw CTca ECtt GAbr GCal IBlr MAvo NHol WFar WOut
- 'Mrs David Howard' — SApp
§ - 'Mrs Geoffrey Howard' — CDes CMea CPrp CSam CTca ECtt IBal IBlr MAvo NHol SUsu WCru WPGP WPrP
- 'Mrs Morrison' — see *C.* x *crocosmiiflora* 'Mrs Geoffrey Howard'
- Newry seedling — see *C.* x *crocosmiiflora* 'Prometheus'
- 'Nimbus' — CPrp CTca EBee IBal IBlr WCot WHil
§ - 'Norwich Canary' — CBgR CMHG COIW CTca EBee EBla ECha EPPr EPfP EShb GBuc IBlr LCro LEdu LRHS MRav NBir NGdn NHol NPri NSti SMrm WBod WBrk WCot WCra WHil WMoo
- 'Olympic Fire' — IBlr NCot
- 'Pepper' — IBlr
- 'Plaisir' — CTca IBlr MAvo NBid NHol WFar WPrP
- 'Polo' — CBgR CSam CTca
- 'Princess' — see *C. pottsii* 'Princess'
- 'Princess Alexandra' — IBlr
- 'Prolificans' — IBlr
§ - 'Prometheus' — CPrp CTca IBal IBlr NHol SMrs WHil
§ - 'Queen Alexandra' J.E. Fitt — CTca ECha IBlr LEdu LHop NHol WHal WMoo WPer
- 'Queen Charlotte' — CPrp CTca IBal IBlr
- 'Queen Mary II' — see *C.* x *crocosmiiflora* 'Columbus'
- 'Queen of Spain' — CPrp CTca EBrs GKir IBlr LRHS MDKP MLLN NHol WHil
- 'Rayon d'Or' — CDes IBlr WPGP
- 'Red King' — CPrp EBee EBla EBrs EPfP EPot IBal IBlr MWea SGar WFar WHil WRHF
- 'Red Knight' — CAbx CBgR CHVG CMMP GAbr IBlr MAvo MBNS NCot NHol SMHy WCot
- 'Rheingold' misapplied — see *C.* x *crocosmiiflora* 'Diadème'
- 'Rose Queen' — IBlr NCot
- 'Saint Clements' — IBlr
- 'Saracen' — CBcs CHFP CHVG CSpe CTca EBee ECtt EGle EShb GCal GKir GMac IBal IBlr IPot LAst MAvo MBNS MCot NBre NCob NLar SMrm SPla SPoG WBrk WCot WFar
- 'Sir Mathew Wilson' — CDes EBee EBrs GBri GKir IBal IBlr WCot WPGP

| | |
|---|---|
| - 'Solfatare' 𝕐H3 | Widely available |
| - 'Solfatare Coleton Fishacre' | see *C.* x *crocosmiiflora* 'Coleton Fishacre' |
| - 'Star of the East' 𝕐H3 | Widely available |
| - 'Starbright' | IBlr |
| - 'Starfire' | ECtt |
| - 'Sultan' | CDes CElw CTca IBlr NCot WCot WFar WPGP |
| - 'Venus' | CBgR CBre CPen CPou CTca EBee EBrs ECtt EShb EWll GBuc IBal IBlr LRHS MAvo NBre NHol NLar SRGP SRos WFar WMoo WPrP |
| - 'Vesuvius' W. Pfitzer | CElw GCal IBlr WFar |
| - 'Vic's Yellow' | SGar SMrm |
| - 'Voyager' | CPrp CTca EBee EBrs ECtt EPot ERCP IBal IBlr LRHS MBri NHol SGar SWal WBor WPer |
| - 'Zeal Tan' | CElw CHFP CPar CPen CPrp CSam CTca EBee ECGP ECtt ELan ELon EPPr GBin GCal GKir GMac IBlr MAvo MBNS MDKP NCGa SMrm SPla SUsu WBrk WCot WWlt |
| § x ***crocosmioides*** | IBlr |
| - 'Castle Ward Late' | CBgR CHFP CPou CRow CTca EAEE ECha GAbr GBuc GCal IBal IBlr LRHS MBNS MSte NBre NCGa NHol SUsu WMoo WSHC |
| - 'Mount Stewart Late' | IBlr |
| - 'Vulcan' Leichtlin | IBlr NHol WHil |
| 'Darkleaf Apricot' | see *C.* x *crocosmiiflora* 'Coleton Fishacre' |
| 'Devil's Advocate' | MAvo |
| 'Doctor Marion Wood' | EBee MAvo NCot |
| 'Eldorado' | see *C.* x *crocosmiiflora* 'E.A. Bowles' |
| 'Elegance' | EBee IBlr |
| 'Elizabeth' | NHol |
| 'Ellenbank Canary' | CBgR GMac MAvo |
| 'Ellenbank Firecrest' | CBgR GMac MAvo WOut |
| 'Ellenbank Skylark' | CBgR GMac MAvo |
| 'Fandango' | IBlr NCot |
| 'Fernhill' | IBlr |
| * 'Feuerser' | ECtt |
| 'Fire Jumper' | CDes |
| 'Fire King' misapplied | see *C.* x *crocosmiiflora* 'Jackanapes' |
| 'Fire King' ambig. | CBgR ERCP IBal NBPC WHil |
| 'Fire Sprite' | IBlr |
| 'Firefly' | IBlr NCot NHol |
| 'Flaire' | IBlr |
| 'Fleuve Jaune' | CPne ECtt |
| ***fucata*** | IBlr |
| - 'Jupiter' | see *C.* 'Jupiter' |
| ***fucata*** x ***paniculata*** | CHFP CPrp CTca NHol |
| 'Fugue' | IBlr |
| 'Fusilade' | IBlr |
| 'Gold Sprite' | IBlr NCot |
| 'Golden Dew' | CTca EBee ECtt EGle GAbr GKir GQue LSou MBNS NCGa NChi NCot WBrk WCot WGor WHil |
| Golden Fleece *sensu* Lemoine | see *C.* x *crocosmiiflora* 'Coleton Fishacre' |
| 'Harlequin' | CElw CTca |
| 'Highlight' | IBlr MAvo NCot NHol |
| 'Irish Flame' | GKir NHol |
| 'Irish Sunset' | GKir NHol |
| 'Jennine' | CAbx EBee NCot NHol SRGP |
| Jenny Bloom = 'Blacro'PBR | COlW EBrs GBuc GKir LRHS NBir NChi SMHy SMrs WRHF |
| 'John Boots' | CPrp CTca EBee EBrs EHrv GBuc IBal IBlr LPio MBNS NCGa NHol SRGP WFar WHil |
| § 'Jupiter' | CAbx CBre CDes CPou CPrp CSam CTca CWCL GAbr GBuc GMac IBal IBlr MAvo MMuc MRav NChi NHol SApp WFar WHil |
| 'Kathleen' | GSec |
| 'Krakatoa' | CPrp EBee IBal LCro LLHF MLan MWea SPoG SRkn |
| 'Lady Wilson' misapplied | see *C.* x *crocosmiiflora* 'Norwich Canary' |
| 'Lana de Savary' | CPrp CTca EBee GBin GCal IBal IBlr NCot NHol WCot |
| 'Late Cornish' | see *C.* x *crocosmiiflora* 'Queen Alexandra' J.E. Fitt |
| 'Late Lucifer' | CHEx CTri GCal IBlr LSRN SDix SMHy |
| x ***latifolia*** | see *C.* x *crocosmioides* |
| 'Limpopo' | CHFP CKno CSpe CTca EBee ECtt EGle GAbr GQue LSou MAvo MBNS NCot SMad SPer SPoG WCot WWlt |
| 'Lucifer' 𝕐H4 | Widely available |
| 'Mandarin' | IBlr |
| 'Marcotijn' | CTca ECtt GGar IBlr IGor LPio NHol WHil WOut |
| ***masoniorum*** 𝕐H3 | Widely available |
| - 'African Dawn' | CPen ECtt EGle GQue MAvo NCot |
| - 'Amber' | IBlr |
| - 'Dixter Flame' | ECtt IBlr IFoB LPio SDix WOut |
| - 'Firebird' | EBrs GBuc IBlr IGor LRHS MBri NBre NHol SRos |
| - 'Flamenco' | IBlr |
| - 'Golden Swan' | ECtt |
| - 'Kiaora' | IBlr |
| - 'Moira Reid' | IBlr NHol |
| - red-flowered | IBlr |
| - 'Rowallane Apricot' | IBlr |
| - 'Rowallane Orange' | CTca GAbr IBlr NHol |
| - 'Rowallane Yellow' 𝕐H3-4 | CDes CTca CWsd EBrs ECtt GBri GCal GKir IBlr IGor LRHS MAvo MBri MSte NCGa NHol SMHy SMrm SRos WCot WOut |
| - 'Tropicana' | IBlr |
| ***mathewsiana*** | IBlr |
| 'Mex' | WCot |
| 'Minotaur' | IBlr |
| 'Mistral' | CAbx CBgR CMea CPrp CSec CTca EBee EBrs EPfP EPot EWll GBuc GMac IBal IBlr MAvo MNrw NBre NHol WBor WFar WMoo |
| 'Mount Stewart' | see *C.* x *crocosmiiflora* 'Jessie' |
| 'Mr Bedford' | see *C.* x *crocosmiiflora* 'Croesus' |
| 'Mullard Pink' | CTca MAvo |
| 'Okavango' | CBre CBro CPen CSpe CTca EBee ECGP ECtt EGle GAbr GBri GQue LSou MAvo MBNS MSte NCot NLar SHar SMrm SPoG WCot WRHF |
| Old Hat | see *C.* 'Walberton Red' |
| 'Orange Devil' | CAbx CBre EBee ECtt IBlr MAvo MBri |
| 'Orange Lucifer' | CTca NBre NCot WPrP |
| 'Orange Spirit' | WFar |
| 'Orangeade' | CTca EBrs ECtt GBin GBri IBal IBlr NCot NHol SMrm SMrs SUsu |
| 'Pageant' | NCot |
| § ***paniculata*** | CHEx CPne CPou CTca EBla ECtt GAbr GGar LPla LRHS MNFA MNrw NBid NHol NOrc SAPC SPet WBor WBrk WCot WMoo WPen WShi WTin |
| - brown/orange-flowered | IBlr |
| - 'Cally Greyleaf' | GCal |
| - 'Cally Sword' | GCal |
| - 'Major' | CTri IBlr |
| - 'Natal' | CPrp CTca EBee ECtt NHol WFar |
| - red-flowered | IBlr SWvt |
| - triploid | IBlr |
| aff. ***paniculata*** | ECtt IBlr |

| | | |
|---|---|---|
| | ***pearsei*** | IBlr |
| | 'Phillipa Browne' | CTca EBee EGle GAbr LSou MAvo NCGa NCot NDov SRGP WCot WMoo |
| § | ***pottsii*** | CBgR CFee CHVG CRow CTca ECtt EPla GBin IBlr NHol WFar |
| | - CD&R 109 | CPou |
| | - 'Culzean Pink' | CBgR CHVG CPrp CTca EBee ECha ELon GAbr GBin GBuc GCal GMac IBal IBlr LPla MAvo MRav NBir NCob NCot NHol SMrm SMrs WHil WOut WPGP |
| | - deep pink-flowered | IBlr IGor WMoo |
| | - 'Grandiflora' | CTca IBlr |
| § | - 'Princess' **new** | MAvo |
| | 'Quantreau' | IBlr NCot |
| | 'R.W. Wallace' | CPrp NHol |
| | 'Red Devils' | NHol |
| | 'Red Star' | CTca |
| | 'Roman Gold' | IBlr |
| | ***rosea*** | see *Tritonia disticha* subsp. *rubrolucens* |
| | 'Rowden Bronze' | see *C.* x *crocosmiiflora* 'Coleton Fishacre' |
| | 'Rowden Chrome' | see *C.* x *crocosmiiflora* 'George Davison' Davison |
| | 'Ruby Velvet' | IBlr |
| | 'Rubygold' | IBlr |
| | 'Sabena' | MAvo |
| | 'Saffron Queen' | IBlr |
| | 'Saturn' | see *C.* 'Jupiter' |
| | 'Scarlatti' | GAbr IBlr NCot NHol |
| | 'Severn Sunrise' 🏆$^{H3-4}$ | Widely available |
| | 'Shocking' | IBlr NCot NHol |
| | 'Short Red' | CTca |
| | 'Son of Lucifer' | WFar |
| | 'Sonate' | CTca NHol SPlb WPer |
| | 'Spitfire' | Widely available |
| § | 'Sulphurea' | CHFP CPou CPrp CRow CSam CTca ECtt IBal IBlr MCot NHol SDix SIng SMrm WBrk WCot WEas WHal WHil WPer |
| | 'Sunzest' | MAvo WFar |
| | 'Tangerine Queen' | CAbx CTca EBrs ECtt GAbr IBal IBlr NCot NHol SUsu WCot |
| | 'Tiger' | CAbx CElw CTca EBee IBlr |
| I | 'Vulcan' A. Bloom | CPen CPrp CTca EBee EBrs ECtt GAbr GGar IBal IBlr LRHS MAvo NHol SAga WCot WFar |
| § | 'Walberton Red' | CAbx CTca EWes IBlr MAvo MBri SAga SApp SMHy SMad SUsu WCot |
| | Walberton Yellow = 'Walcroy'$^{PBR}$ | SApp SMHy SUsu WCot |
| | 'Zambesi' | CKno CTca EBee ECtt EGle EHrv GAbr GMac GQue LHop LSou MAvo MBNS NCGa NCot NLar SMad SPer WCot WWlt |
| | 'Zeal Giant' | CRow CTca ECtt IBlr MAvo |
| | Zeal unnamed | CPrp CTca EBee IBlr NHol |

## *Crocus* ✿ (*Iridaceae*)

| | | |
|---|---|---|
| | ***abantensis*** | ERos |
| | ***adanensis*** | ERos |
| | 'Advance' | see *C. chrysanthus* 'Advance' |
| | ***albiflorus*** | see *C. vernus* subsp. *albiflorus* |
| | ***ancyrensis*** | EPot LAma SGar |
| | - 'Golden Bunch' | EBrs EPfP LRHS WShi |
| § | ***angustifolius*** 🏆$^{H4}$ | ERos |
| | - bronze-tinged | NMin |
| | - 'Minor' | EBrs |
| | ***asturicus*** | see *C. serotinus* subsp. *salzmannii* |
| | ***asumaniae*** | EBrs ECho ERos |
| | ***aureus*** | see *C. flavus* subsp. *flavus* |
| | ***banaticus*** 🏆$^{H4}$ | CBro EBrs ECho ERos GEdr LLHF MSSP NHar NMen |
| | - ***albus*** | ERos |
| | ***baytopiorum*** | ERos |
| | ***biflorus*** subsp. ***adamii*** | EBrs ERos |
| | - subsp. ***alexandri*** | ERos |
| | - subsp. ***biflorus*** | EBrs ERos |
| § | - - 'Parkinsonii' | EPot ERos |
| | - - 'Serevan' | NMin |
| | - subsp. ***crewei*** | ERos |
| | - subsp. ***isauricus*** | EBrs ECho ERos |
| | - subsp. ***melantherus*** | EBrs ECho ERos WWst |
| | - 'Miss Vain' | EBrs EPot GKev LAma MBri |
| | - var. ***parkinsonii*** | see *C. biflorus* subsp. *biflorus* 'Parkinsonii' |
| | - subsp. ***tauri*** | ECho LRHS WWst |
| | - subsp. ***weldenii*** 'Albus' | EBrs EPot ERos LAma |
| | - - 'Fairy' | EBrs ERos LAma LRHS |
| | ***boryi*** | EBrs ECho LLHF WCot |
| | ***cambessedesii*** | EBrs ECho ERos SCnR |
| § | ***cancellatus*** subsp. ***cancellatus*** | EBrs ECho ERos LAma |
| | - var. ***cilicicus*** | see *C. cancellatus* subsp. *cancellatus* |
| | - subsp. ***lycius*** | EBrs ECho |
| | - subsp. ***mazziaricus*** | ERos |
| | - subsp. ***pamphylicus*** | ECho ERos |
| | ***candidus*** **new** | ECho |
| | - var. ***subflavus*** | see *C. olivieri* subsp. *olivieri* |
| § | ***cartwrightianus*** 🏆$^{H4}$ | ECho |
| | - 'Albus' misapplied | see *C. hadriaticus* |
| N | - 'Albus' Tubergen 🏆$^{H4}$ | EBrs ECho EPot ERos LRHS |
| § | ***chrysanthus*** 'Advance' | CBro EBrs ECho EGoo EPfP EPot LAma LRHS MBri SPer |
| | - 'Ard Schenk' | EBrs EPot GKev LAma LRHS SGar |
| | - 'Aubade' | EBrs EPot |
| | - 'Blue Bird' | CBro EBrs ECho EPot LAma LRHS MSte |
| | - 'Blue Pearl' 🏆$^{H4}$ | CAvo CBro CFFs CMea EBrs EPfP EPot GKev LRHS MBri MSte NBir SBch SMeo SPer SPhx WShi |
| | - 'Cream Beauty' 🏆$^{H4}$ | CAvo CBro CFFs CMea EBrs ECho EPfP EPot GKev LAma LRHS MBri MSte NBir SMeo SPhx |
| | - 'Dorothy' | EBrs LAma LRHS |
| | - 'E.P. Bowles' | CAvo CBro EBrs EPot LAma MBri |
| | - 'Ego' | WWst |
| | - 'Elegance' | EBrs LRHS |
| | - 'Eye-catcher' | MCot |
| | - var. ***fuscotinctus*** | EBrs EPot LAma MBri MCot |
| | - 'Gipsy Girl' | CAvo CBro CFFs EBrs EPot LAma MBri MSte |
| | - 'Goldilocks' | EBrs LAma LRHS |
| | - 'Herald' | CAvo EBrs EPot LAma MSte |
| | - 'Jeannine' | EBrs EPot |
| | - 'Ladykiller' 🏆$^{H4}$ | CAvo CBro CFFs EBrs EPot ERCP LAma LRHS MBri MSte SGar |
| | - 'Milea' | EBrs |
| | - 'Moonlight' | LAma |
| | - 'Prins Claus' | EBrs EPot LAma LRHS MBri SPer |
| | - 'Romance' | CAvo CFFs EBrs EPot GKev LAma LRHS MBri MCot SPer |
| | - 'Saturnus' | EBrs EPot LAma |
| | - 'Skyline' | EBrs |
| | - 'Snow Bunting' 🏆$^{H4}$ | CAvo CBro CFFs CTca EBrs EGoo EPfP EPot LAma LRHS NBir SMeo SPer SPhx WShi |
| | - 'Sunspot' | EPot |
| | - 'Uschak Orange' | EBrs |
| | - 'White Triumphator' | LAma |
| | - 'Zenith' | EPot |
| | - 'Zwanenburg Bronze' 🏆$^{H4}$ | EBrs EPfP EPot LAma LRHS MCot MSte SMeo |

| | | |
|---|---|---|
| | 'Cloth of Gold' | see *C. angustifolius* |
| | ***clusii*** | see *C. serotinus* subsp. *clusii* |
| | ***corsicus*** ♀H4 | EBrs ECho EPot ERos LRHS |
| | ***dalmaticus*** | EPot |
| | ***danfordiae*** | ERos |
| | 'Dutch Yellow' | see *C.* x *luteus* 'Golden Yellow' |
| | ***etruscus*** ♀H4 | ERos |
| | - 'Rosalind' | EBrs ECho EPot |
| | - 'Zwanenburg' | EBrs EPot LAma MCot |
| | ***flavus*** | WWst |
| § | - subsp. ***flavus*** ♀H4 | EBrs ECho EPot LAma LRHS WShi |
| | ***fleischeri*** | EBrs EPot ERos LAma LRHS |
| | ***gargaricus*** | ERos SCnR WWst |
| | - subsp. ***gargaricus*** | ERos |
| | - subsp. ***herbertii*** | ERos |
| | 'Golden Mammoth' | see *C.* x *luteus* 'Golden Yellow' |
| | ***goulimyi*** ♀H4 | CBro EBrs ECho EPot ERos LAma MSte NMen WCot |
| | - 'Albus' | see *C. goulimyi* subsp. *goulimyi* 'Mani White' |
| § | - subsp. ***goulimyi*** 'Mani White' ♀H4 | ERos SCnR |
| | - subsp. ***leucanthus*** | ERos |
| § | ***hadriaticus*** ♀H4 | EBrs ECho ERos LAma NMin |
| | - var. ***chrysobelonicus*** | see *C. hadriaticus* |
| | ***imperati*** ♀H4 | ERos |
| | - subsp. ***imperati*** 'De Jager' | EPot ERCP LAma |
| | - subsp. ***suaveolens*** | EBrs ERos |
| | x ***jessoppiae*** | EBrs ECho EPot ERos LRHS WWst |
| | ***karduchorum*** | EPot LAma |
| | ***korolkowii*** | CGrW EBrs ECho ERos LAma LRHS |
| | - 'Kiss of Spring' | EBrs EPot |
| | - 'Lemon Queen' **new** | ECho |
| | ***kosaninii*** | EBrs EPot ERos NMin |
| | ***kotschyanus*** ♀H4 | ECho NRya SPer |
| | - 'Albus' | EBrs ECho |
| § | - subsp. ***kotschyanus*** | CBro EBrs EPot LAma |
| | - var. ***leucopharynx*** | EBrs ECho LRHS |
| | - 'Reliance' | EBrs ECho |
| | ***kotschyanus*** x ***ochroleucus*** | EBrs ECho |
| | ***laevigatus*** ♀H4 | ECho MSte |
| | - from Crete | EBrs |
| | - 'Fontenayi' | CBro EBrs ECho EPot ERCP |
| | - white-flowered | EBrs ECho |
| | 'Large Yellow' | see *C.* x *luteus* 'Golden Yellow' |
| | ***ligusticus*** | EBrs |
| | ***longiflorus*** ♀H4 | CBro EBrs ECho ERos GEdr LLHF |
| § | x ***luteus*** 'Golden Yellow' ♀H4 | CAvo CFFs EBrs EPfP LAma WShi |
| § | - 'Stellaris' | EBrs ERos |
| | ***malyi*** ♀H2-4 | EBrs ECho EPot ERos |
| | - 'Ballerina' **new** | ECho |
| | 'Mammoth Yellow' | see *C.* x *luteus* 'Golden Yellow' |
| | ***mathewii*** | EBrs EPot WCot |
| | ***medius*** ♀H4 | CBro EPot ERos LAma |
| | ***michelsonii*** | WWst |
| | ***minimus*** | EBrs EPot ERCP ERos LAma |
| | ***niveus*** | CBro EBrs ECho EPot ERos LAma WCot |
| | ***nudiflorus*** | CBro EBrs ECho EPot ERos LAma NMen WCot |
| | ***ochroleucus*** ♀H4 | EBrs EPot ERos LRHS MSte SPhx |
| | ***olivieri*** | ERos |
| | - subsp. ***balansae*** | EBrs ERos |
| | - - 'Zwanenburg' | CMea EBrs EPot |
| § | - subsp. ***olivieri*** | EBrs ECho EPot ERos |
| | - - 'Little Tiger' | EBrs ECho |
| | ***oreocreticus*** | EBrs |
| | ***pallasii*** | EBrs ECho |
| | - subsp. ***pallasii*** | ERos |
| | ***pestalozzae*** | EBrs ERos |
| | - var. ***caeruleus*** | EPot ERos SCnR |
| | ***pulchellus*** ♀H4 | CHFP EBrs ECho EPot ERCP ERos LAma LRHS NWCA SPhx |
| | - ***albus*** | EBrs ECho EPot |
| | - 'Inspiration' | EBrs |
| | - 'Michael Hoog' | EBrs ECho |
| | 'Purpureus' | see *C. vernus* 'Purpureus Grandiflorus' |
| | ***reticulatus*** | WWst |
| | ***rujanensis*** | ERos |
| | ***salzmannii*** | see *C. serotinus* subsp. *salzmannii* |
| | ***sativus*** | CArn CAvo CBod CBro CGrW CPrp CTca EBrs ECho ELan EOHP EPot ERCP GPoy IHer LAma LRHS MMHG MSal NBir NGHP SPer |
| | - var. ***cartwrightianus*** | see *C. cartwrightianus* |
| | - var. ***cashmirianus*** | EBrs ECho |
| | ***scepusiensis*** | see *C. vernus* subsp. *vernus* var. *scepusiensis* |
| § | ***serotinus*** subsp. ***clusii*** | CBro EBrs ECho EPot LAma LRHS |
| § | - subsp. ***salzmannii*** | CBro EBrs ECho EPot ERos LAma |
| | - - 'Erectophyllus' | EBrs ECho |
| | ***sibiricus*** | see *C. sieberi* |
| § | ***sieberi*** ♀H4 | EPot ERos |
| § | - 'Albus' ♀H4 | CAvo CBro CFFs EBrs ECho EPot MBri MSte |
| | - subsp. ***atticus*** | EBrs LAma LRHS |
| | - 'Bowles' White' | see *C. sieberi* 'Albus' |
| | - 'Firefly' | CBro EBrs EPot GKev LAma LRHS MSte |
| | - 'Hubert Edelsten' ♀H4 | EBrs ERos LAma |
| | - 'Ronald Ginns' | EPot |
| | - subsp. ***sublimis*** 'Tricolor' ♀H4 | CAvo CBro CFFs CGrW CTca EBrs ECho EPfP EPot ERos GKev LAma MBri NBir NMen SBch SPer |
| | - 'Violet Queen' | CBro EBrs LAma MBri MSte |
| | ***speciosus*** ♀H4 | CAvo CBro CTca EBrs EPot LAma LRHS MLHP NBir SPer WCot WHoo WShi |
| | - 'Aino' | EBrs ECho |
| | - 'Aitchisonii' | CBro CGrW EBrs ECho EPot LAma LRHS MSte SPhx |
| | - 'Albus' ♀H4 | CAvo CBro EBrs ECho EPot LRHS MSte SPhx |
| | - 'Artabir' | CBro EBrs ECho EPot LRHS |
| | - 'Cassiope' | EBrs ECho EPot LAma LRHS |
| | - 'Conqueror' | CBro EBrs ECho EPot LAma LRHS MCot MSte WBor |
| | - 'Lithuanian Autumn' | WWst |
| | - 'Oxonian' | EBrs EPot LAma LRHS MCot MSte SPhx |
| | - subsp. ***speciosus*** | EBrs ECho |
| | x ***stellaris*** | see *C.* x *luteus* 'Stellaris' |
| | - 'Golden Yellow' | see *C.* x *luteus* 'Golden Yellow' |
| | ***susianus*** | see *C. angustifolius* |
| | ***suterianus*** | see *C. olivieri* subsp. *olivieri* |
| | ***tommasinianus*** ♀H4 | CAvo CBro CFFs CGrW CMea CTca EBrs ECho EPot LAma LLWP LRHS MBri MRav NBir SRms WShi |
| | - f. ***albus*** | EBrs EPot LAma LRHS |
| | - 'Barr's Purple' | EBrs EGoo EPot LAma LRHS SPhx |
| | - 'Claret' **new** | EPot |
| | - 'Lilac Beauty' | EBrs EPfP EPot LAma SPer |
| | - var. ***pictus*** | EBrs EPot ERos LAma NMen |
| | - var. ***roseus*** | CAvo CMea EBrs EPot ERos LAma LRHS NMen WCot |
| | - 'Ruby Giant' | CAvo CBro EBrs EPfP EPot GKev LAma LRHS MBri MCot NBir SGar SMeo SPer SPhx WShi |
| | - 'Whitewell Purple' | CAvo CBro CFFs EBrs ECho EPot LAma MBri NBir SMeo SPhx WShi |
| | ***tournefortii*** ♀H2-4 | CBro EBrs ECho ERos WCot |
| * | - 'Albus' **new** | ECho |

| | | |
|---|---|---|
| § | 'Vanguard' ♀H4 | CBro EBrs EPot ERCP LAma LRHS MCot SBch |
| | ***veluchensis*** | EBrs EPot WWst |
| | ***veneris*** | EBrs ECho |
| § | ***vernus*** subsp. ***albiflorus*** | CGrW EBrs ECho EPot ERos |
| | - 'Fantasy' | EBrs |
| | - 'Flower Record' | EBrs EPfP GKev LRHS MBri NBir |
| | - 'Graecus' | EBrs ECho EPot ERos WWst |
| | - 'Grand Maître' | CAvo CFFs EBrs LAma MBri |
| | - 'Haarlem Gem' | EBrs LRHS |
| | - 'Jeanne d'Arc' | CAvo CBro CFFs EBrs EPfP EPot LAma LRHS MBri MCot NBir WShi |
| | - 'King of the Striped' | EBrs SPer |
| | - 'Michael's Purple' | EBrs ECho |
| | - 'Negro Boy' | EBrs EPot |
| | - 'Pickwick' | CAvo CFFs EBrs EPfP EPot LAma LRHS MBri NBir WShi |
| § | - 'Purpureus Grandiflorus' | CBro |
| | - 'Queen of the Blues' | CAvo CBro CFFs EBrs EPot |
| | - 'Remembrance' | EBrs EPfP EPot LAma NBir SPhx WShi |
| | - Uklin Strain **new** | ECho |
| | - 'Vanguard' | see *C.* 'Vanguard' |
| | - subsp. ***vernus*** 'Grandiflorus' | 'Purpureus Grandiflorus' |
| | - - Heuffelianus Group | EBrs EPot WWst |
| | - - - 'Dark Eyes' | WWst |
| | - - var. ***neapolitanus*** | ERos |
| | - - 'Oradea' | WWst |
| § | - - var. ***scepusiensis*** | EBrs ERos |
| * | ***versicolor*** | ERos |
| | - 'Picturatus' | EBrs EPot ERCP ERos LAma LLHF LRHS |
| | ***vitellinus*** | EBrs ECho EPot |
| | 'Yellow Mammoth' | see *C.* x *luteus* 'Golden Yellow' |
| | 'Zephyr' ♀H4 | CBro ECho EPot ERos LAma LRHS |
| | ***zonatus*** | see *C. kotschyanus* subsp. *kotschyanus* |

## *Croomia* (*Stemonaceae*)

| | | |
|---|---|---|
| | ***heterosepala*** | WCru |

## *Crotalaria* (*Papilionaceae*)

| | | |
|---|---|---|
| | ***laburnifolia*** | CCCN |

## *Crowea* (*Rutaceae*)

| | | |
|---|---|---|
| | ***exalata*** x ***saligna*** | CPLG |

## *Crucianella* (*Rubiaceae*)

| | | |
|---|---|---|
| | ***stylosa*** | see *Phuopsis stylosa* |

## *Cruciata* (*Rubiaceae*)

| | | |
|---|---|---|
| § | ***laevipes*** | CNat EBWF NMir |

## *Cryptanthus* (*Bromeliaceae*)

| | | |
|---|---|---|
| | ***bivittatus*** ♀H1 | CHal |
| | - 'Roseus Pictus' | CHal |
| | ***bromelioides*** | MBri |

## *Cryptogramma* (*Adiantaceae*)

| | | |
|---|---|---|
| | ***crispa*** | SRms WCot WHer WRic |

## *Cryptomeria* (*Cupressaceae*)

| | | |
|---|---|---|
| | ***fortunei*** | see *C. japonica* var. *sinensis* |
| | ***japonica*** ♀H4 | CDul CMen GKir IFFs ISea STre |
| | - Araucarioides Group | CDoC EHul NLar |
| | - 'Atawai' | NLar |
| | - 'Aurea' | NHol |
| | - 'Bandai' | LBuc |
| | - 'Bandai-sugi' ♀H4 | CKen CMac CMen ECho EHul EOrn EPfP GKir LRHS MBar MGos SCoo SLim SPla WGor WRHF |
| | - 'Barabits Gold' | MBar MGos |
| | - 'Compressa' | CDoC CKen CSli ECho EHul EPfP LBee MAsh MBar MGos SCoo SLim WGor |
| § | - 'Cristata' | CBcs CDoC CMac ECho ELan EOrn MBar MGos NPal SCoo SLim SPoG |
| * | - 'Cristata Compacta' | EOrn |
| | - 'Dacrydioides' | CDoC SLim |
| | - Elegans Group | Widely available |
| | - 'Elegans Aurea' | CBcs CDoC CTri ECho ECrN EHul EMil MAsh MBar SPoG STre WDin |
| | - 'Elegans Compacta' ♀H4 | CDoC CRob CSBt CWib ECho EHul EOrn GBin IMGH LBee LRHS MAsh MBar MBri SCoo SLim SPoG WBVN |
| | - 'Elegans Nana' | LBee LRHS SRms |
| | - 'Elegans Viridis' | ELan LBuc LRHS MBar SCoo SLim SPer SPoG |
| | - 'Globosa' | EOrn |
| | - 'Globosa Nana' ♀H4 | CDoC ECho EHul EPfP ERom LAst LBee LPan LRHS MAsh MBar MBri MGos NLar SCoo SHBN SLim SPoG WFar WGor |
| | - 'Golden Promise' | CDoC CRob EOrn MAsh NHol SCoo SLim SPer SPoG WGor |
| | - Gracilis Group | CDoC |
| | - 'Jindai-sugi' | CMac ECho MBar NLar |
| | - 'Kilmacurragh' | CDoC CKen EHul MBar NWea SLim WThu |
| | - 'Knaptonensis' (v) | CDoC MGos |
| | - 'Kohui-yatsubusa' | CKen |
| * | - 'Konijn-yatsubusa' | CKen |
| | - 'Koshiji-yatsubusa' | EOrn MBar |
| | - 'Koshyi' | CKen EMil NLar |
| | - 'Little Champion' | CDoC CKen NLar SCoo SLim |
| | - 'Little Diamond' | CKen |
| | - 'Littleworth Dwarf' | see *C. japonica* 'Littleworth Gnom' |
| § | - 'Littleworth Gnom' | NLar |
| | - 'Lobbii Nana' hort. | see *C. japonica* 'Nana' |
| § | - 'Mankichi-sugi' | MBri NHol NLar |
| | - 'Monstrosa' | MBar |
| | - 'Monstrosa Nana' | see *C. japonica* 'Mankichi-sugi' |
| | - 'Mushroom' | MGos WFar |
| § | - 'Nana' | CDoC CMac CTri EHul EOrn EPfP SPoG WFar |
| | - 'Osaka-tama' | CKen |
| | - 'Pipo' | CKen NLar |
| | - 'Pygmaea' | MBar MGos SCoo SRms |
| | - 'Rasen' **new** | EMil |
| | - 'Rasen-sugi' | LBuc MBar NLar NPal SCoo SLim SMad SPoG |
| | - 'Sekkan-sugi' | CBcs CCVN CDoC CDul CSli ECho EHul EOrn EPfP GBin IDee LAst LBee LRHS MAsh MBar MGos NHol NLar SCoo SLim SPoG WFar |
| | - 'Sekka-sugi' | see *C. japonica* 'Cristata' |
| § | - var. ***sinensis*** | CMCN LAst |
| * | - - 'Vilmoriniana Compacta' | EOrn |
| § | - 'Spiralis' | CDoC CKen CMac CRob ECho EHul EOrn EPfP LBee LRHS MAsh MBar MGos NHol NPal SCoo SLim SPer SPla SPoG WFar |
| § | - 'Spiraliter Falcata' | CDoC MBar NLar |
| § | - 'Tansu' | CDoC CKen ECho EOrn MBar MGos |
| | - 'Tenzan-sugi' | CDoC CKen MAsh MGos SLim WThu |
| | - 'Tilford Cream' | ECho LAst |
| | - 'Tilford Gold' | ECho EHul EOrn MBar MGos NHol WFar WGor |
| | - 'Toda' | CKen |
| | - 'Vilmorin Gold' | CKen EMil EOrn WFar |
| | - 'Vilmoriniana' ♀H4 | CDoC CKen CMen CRob CSli CTri ECho EHul EOrn EPfP GKir IMGH |

| | | |
|---|---|---|
| | | LBee LRHS MBar MGos NHol SCoo SHBN SIng SLim SPer SPoG WDin WFar |
| | - 'Viminalis' | NHol |
| | - 'Winter Bronze' | CKen |
| | - 'Yatsubusa' | see *C. japonica* 'Tansu' |
| | - 'Yore-sugi' | see *C. japonica* 'Spiralis', 'Spiraliter Falcata' |
| | - 'Yoshino' | CKen LRHS SLim |
| | ***sinensis*** | see *C. japonica* var. *sinensis* |

## *Cryptostegia* (*Asclepiadaceae*)

| | | |
|---|---|---|
| | ***grandiflora*** | CCCN |

## *Cryptotaenia* (*Apiaceae*)

| | | |
|---|---|---|
| | ***canadensis*** | MRav |
| | ***japonica*** | CPou MHer MNHC MSal WHer WJek |
| | - f. ***atropurpurea*** | CArn CSpe EBee EHoe GGar LBMP LEdu NSti WCHb WFar |

## *Ctenanthe* (*Marantaceae*)

| | | |
|---|---|---|
| § | ***amabilis*** 🏆H1 | CHal |
| | ***lubbersiana*** 🏆H1 | CHal XBlo |
| § | ***oppenheimiana*** | LRHS XBlo |

## *Cucubalus* (*Caryophyllaceae*)

| | | |
|---|---|---|
| | ***baccifer*** | CSec EBee NLar WPer WPrP |

## *Cudrania* see *Maclura*

## cumin see *Cuminum cyminum*

## *Cuminum* (*Apiaceae*)

| | | |
|---|---|---|
| | ***cyminum*** | CArn MNHC SIde SVic |

## *Cunninghamia* (*Cupressaceae*)

| | | |
|---|---|---|
| § | ***lanceolata*** | CBcs CDoC CDul CGHE CMCN CTho EMil EPla GKir IArd IDee LRHS MBlu SCoo SLim SMad SPoG SSta STre WPGP |
| § | - 'Bánó' | CMac EOrn |
| | - 'Compacta' | see *C. lanceolata* 'Bánó' |
| | - 'Glauca' | CTho WPGP |
| | - 'Little Leo' | CKen |
| | ***sinensis*** | see *C. lanceolata* |
| | ***unicaniculata*** | see *C. lanceolata* |

## *Cunonia* (*Cunoniaceae*)

| | | |
|---|---|---|
| | ***capensis*** | CPLG CTrC EShb GKir |

## *Cuphea* (*Lythraceae*)

| | | |
|---|---|---|
| | ***caeciliae*** | CHal |
| * | ***compacta*** | LAst |
| | ***cyanea*** | CMHG SDix SOWG WWlt |
| | 'Harlequin' | NPri |
| | ***hirtella*** | LHop SOWG |
| | ***hyssopifolia*** 🏆H1 | CHal CHll EShb LRHS SOWG SWvt |
| | - 'Alba' | CCCN SOWG SWvt |
| | - pink-flowered | CCCN |
| | - red-flowered | CCCN |
| | - 'Rosea' | SWvt |
| § | ***ignea*** 🏆H1 | CDMG CHal CWib EBee MBri MLLN SOWG SUsu WWlt |
| | - 'Variegata' (v) | CHal SOWG |
| | ***lanceolata*** | CSec |
| § | ***llavea*** 'Georgia Scarlet' | CCCN EBee LAst LSou NPri SPoG SUsu WWlt |
| | - 'Tiny Mice' | see *C. llavea* 'Georgia Scarlet' |
| I | ***macrophylla*** hort. | CHll |
| | ***miniata*** hort. | see *C.* x *purpurea* |
| | ***platycentra*** | see *C. ignea* |
| § | x ***purpurea*** | CSec |
| | ***viscosissima*** | MCot |

## x *Cupressocyparis* ✿ (*Cupressaceae*)

| | | |
|---|---|---|
| § | ***leylandii*** 🏆H4 | CBcs CCVT CChe CDoC CDul CMac CTri EHul EPfP LBuc LPan LRHS LSRN MAsh MBar MBri MGos NBlu NWea SLim SPer SWvt WDin WHar WMou |
| § | - 'Castlewellan' | CBcs CCVT CChe CDoC CDul CMac CTri EHul EPfP ERom LBuc LPan LRHS LSRN MAsh MBar MBri MGos NBlu NWea SLim SPer SWvt WDin WFar WHar WMou |
| | - 'Douglas Gold' | CRob |
| | - 'Galway Gold' | see x *C. leylandii* 'Castlewellan' |
| | - 'Gold Rider' 🏆H4 | CDoC EHul EPfP LRHS MAsh MBar MGos NWea SCoo SPer SWvt WDin WHar |
| § | - 'Harlequin' (v) | CBcs MBar SEND SWvt |
| | - 'Herculea' | CDoC LPan MAsh |
| | - 'Naylor's Blue' | CMac SEND |
| | - 'Olive's Green' | EHul SWvt |
| | - 'Robinson's Gold' 🏆H4 | CMac EHul GQui LRHS MBar MMuc NWea SLim WFar |
| | - 'Silver Dust' (v) | WFar |
| | - 'Variegata' | see x *C. leylandii* 'Harlequin' |
| | - 'Winter Sun' | WCFE |
| | ***ovensii*** | EHul |

## *Cupressus* (*Cupressaceae*)

| | | |
|---|---|---|
| | ***arizonica*** var. ***arizonica*** | MGos |
| § | - - 'Arctic' | CDoC |
| | - 'Conica Glauca' | MBar |
| § | - var. ***glabra*** | WPGP |
| | - - 'Aurea' | ECho EHul EMil LRHS MBar MGos SLim WFar |
| | - - 'Blue Ice' 🏆H3 | CBcs CDoC CDul CRob CTho ECho EHul EMil EOrn LRHS MAsh MBar MGos SCoo SLim SPer SPoG SWvt WFar |
| | - - 'Compacta' | CKen |
| | - - 'Conica' | CKen |
| I | - - 'Fastigiata' | CCVT CDoC ECrN EHul EPfP LMaj LPan MBar SCoo |
| | - - 'Glauca' | ECho EPfP MBlu WBVN |
| * | - - 'Lutea' | ECho EOrn SPoG |
| | - var. ***nevadensis*** new | GAuc |
| | - 'Pyramidalis' 🏆H3 | CMac ECrN EPfP SEND |
| I | - 'Sulfurea' | MAsh NLar |
| | ***cashmeriana*** 🏆H2 | CBcs CDTJ CDoC CTho ELan LPan LRHS SLim WFar |
| | ***glabra*** | see *C. arizonica* var. *glabra* |
| | - 'Arctic' | see *C. arizonica* var. *arizonica* 'Arctic' |
| | ***guadalupensis*** | CMHG |
| | ***lusitanica*** 'Brice's Weeping' | CKen SLim |
| | - 'Brookhall' | IDee |
| | - 'Glauca Pendula' | CDoC CKen EPfP |
| | - var. ***lusitanica*** | CMCN |
| | - 'Pygmy' | CKen |
| | ***macrocarpa*** | CBcs CCVT CDoC CDul CTho EHul IFFs SEND |
| | - 'Compacta' | CKen |
| | - 'Donard Gold' | CBcs CMac CSBt EOrn MBar |
| | - 'Gold Spread' | CRob ECho EHul EMil EOrn SCoo SLim SPoG WFar |
| | - 'Goldcrest' 🏆H3 | Widely available |
| | - 'Golden Cone' | CKen CSBt ECho |
| | - 'Golden Pillar' 🏆H3 | CDoC CRob EHul EMil EOrn MAsh MBar SPoG SWvt WDin WFar |
| | - 'Golden Spire' | WFar |
| | - 'Greenstead Magnificent' | ECho LRHS MAsh SCoo SLim |
| | - 'Horizontalis Aurea' | EHul MBar |

| | |
|---|---|
| - 'Lohbrunner' | CKen |
| - 'Lutea' | CDoC ECho WFar |
| - 'Pygmaea' | CKen |
| - 'Sulphur Cushion' | CKen |
| - 'Wilma' | ECho EHul LAst LBee LRHS MAsh MGos SCoo SLim SPoG SWvt |
| - 'Woking' | CKen |
| ***sargentii*** | GKir |
| ***sempervirens*** | CDul CMCN CPMA ECrN EHul ELan ERom ETod ISea LPan NLar SPlb STrG WFar |
| - 'Agrimed' new | LMaj |
| - 'Bolgheri' | SBig |
| - 'Garda' | CDoC |
| - 'Green Pencil' | CKen EPfP |
| - 'Pyramidalis' | see *C. sempervirens* Stricta Group |
| - var. ***sempervirens*** | see *C. sempervirens* Stricta Group |
| § - Stricta Group ♀H3 | CArn CBcs CCVT CKen CMCN CSWP CTho ECho EHul EPfP LPan MAsh NBlu NLar SAPC SArc SBLw SCoo WOrn |
| - 'Swane's Gold' | CBcs CDoC CFee CKen ECho EHul EMil EOrn EPfP LRHS NPal SCoo SLim SPoG WFar |
| - 'Totem Pole' | CDoC CKen CSBt CTho CTri ECho EHul EMil EOrn EPfP LAst LBee LPan LRHS MGos NScw SCoo SEND SLim SPoG WGor |
| ***torulosa*** | EGFP IDee |

## x *Cuprocyparis* see x *Cupressocyparis*

## *Curculigo* (*Hypoxidaceae*)

| | |
|---|---|
| ***capitulata*** | CKob XBlo |
| ***crassifolia*** B&SWJ 2318 | WCru |

## *Curcuma* (*Zingiberaceae*)

| | |
|---|---|
| ***alismatifolia*** | LRHS |
| ***amada*** | CKob |
| ***angustifolia*** | CKob |
| ***aromatica*** | CKob |
| 'Blue Top' | CKob |
| 'Cobra' | CKob |
| ***elata*** | CKob |
| ***longa*** | CArn CKob MSal |
| ***ornata*** | CKob |
| ***petiolata*** 'Emperor' (v) | CKob |
| 'Red Fire' | CKob |
| ***roscoeana*** | LAma |
| 'Ruby' | CKob |
| 'Siam Silver' | LRHS |
| 'Siam Suzy' | LRHS |
| ***zedoaria*** | CKob EShb LAma LRHS |
| - 'Bicolor Wonder' new | CCCN |
| - 'Pink Wonder' | CCCN |
| - 'White Wonder' new | CCCN |

## *Curtonus* see *Crocosmia*

## *Cuscuta* (*Convolvulaceae*)

| | |
|---|---|
| ***chinensis*** | MSal |

## *Cussonia* (*Araliaceae*)

| | |
|---|---|
| ***paniculata*** | CDTJ CKob EShb WCot |
| ***spicata*** | CKob EShb |
| ***transvaalensis*** | CKob EShb |
| ***zuluensis*** new | CKob |

## custard apple see *Annona cherimola*, *A. reticulata*

## *Cyananthus* (*Campanulaceae*)

| | |
|---|---|
| SDR 3098 new | GKev |
| SDR 4908 new | GKev |
| ***integer*** misapplied | see *C. microphyllus* |
| ***lobatus*** ♀H4 | ECho GBuc GMaP NMen NSla |
| - 'Albus' | EPot EWes GKev WAbe WIvy |
| - dark | WAbe |
| - 'Dark Beauty' | ECho |
| - giant | EPot GEdr |
| - 'Midnight' new | GEdr |
| ***lobatus*** x ***microphyllus*** | NWCA WAbe |
| ***macrocalyx*** | WIvy |
| § ***microphyllus*** ♀H4 | CPBP ECho EPot GEdr GJos GKev GMaP NLAp NSla WAbe |
| ***sherriffii*** | EPot GKev NMen WAbe WFar |

## *Cyanella* (*Tecophilaeaceae*)

| | |
|---|---|
| ***lutea*** | ECho |

## *Cyanotis* (*Commelinaceae*)

| | |
|---|---|
| ***somaliensis*** ♀H1 | CHal |

## *Cyathea* (*Cyatheaceae*)

| | |
|---|---|
| ***australis*** | CDTJ EAmu ESwi ETod LPal MGos NPal WFib WPGP WRic |
| ***brownii*** | WRic |
| ***cooperi*** | CDTJ EAmu WFib WRic |
| * - 'Brentwood' | WRic |
| ***cunninghamii*** | CDTJ EAmu |
| ***dealbata*** | CBcs CDTJ CTrC EAmu EUJe LPal MGos WRic |
| ***dregei*** | SPlb WRic |
| ***incisoserrata*** | WRic |
| ***medullaris*** | CBcs CDTJ EAmu ETod EUJe MGos WRic |
| ***milnei*** | WRic |
| ***robusta*** | WRic |
| ***smithii*** | CBcs CDTJ CTrC EAmu WRic |
| ***tomentosissima*** | WRic |

## *Cyathodes* (*Epacridaceae*)

| | |
|---|---|
| ***colensoi*** | see *Leucopogon colensoi* |
| ***fasciculata*** | see *Leucopogon fasciculatus* |
| ***fraseri*** | see *Leucopogon fraseri* |
| ***juniperina*** | see *Leptecophylla juniperina* |
| ***parviflora*** | see *Leucopogon parviflorus* |
| ***parvifolia*** | see *Leptecophylla juniperina* subsp. *parvifolia* |

## *Cycas* (*Cycadaceae*)

| | |
|---|---|
| ***circinalis*** | LPal |
| ***media*** | LPal |
| ***panzhihuaensis*** | CBrP CKob LPal SPlb |
| ***revoluta*** ♀H1 | CAbb CBrP CCCN CDoC CHEx CKob CTrC EAmu EPfP EUJe LPal LRHS MBri MREP NLar NPal SAPC SArc SChr SEND SMad STrG |
| ***revoluta*** x ***taitungensis*** | CBrP |
| § ***rumphii*** | CBrP CKob EAmu LPal LRHS |
| ***taitungensis*** | CBrP |
| ***thouarsii*** | see *C. rumphii* |

## *Cyclamen* ✿ (*Primulaceae*)

| | |
|---|---|
| ***africanum*** | CBro EBrs ECho EJWh ITim LAma LRHS MAsh NWCA STil WCot |
| ***africanum*** x ***hederifolium*** | CWCL ECho |
| § ***alpinum*** | CBro CWoo EBee EBrs ECho EJWh GKev LAma LLHF LRHS MAsh STil |
| ***balearicum*** | CBro CPBP EBee EBrs ECho EJWh LAma LRHS MAsh NMen STil |
| ***cilicium*** ♀H2-4 | CBro CLAP CStu EBla EBrs ECho EJWh EPot ERCP ERos LAma LRHS MAsh MCot MHer MSSP MTho NMen STil WAbe WFar WIvy WPat WShi |

| | Plant | Suppliers |
|---|---|---|
| | - f. ***album*** | CBro CWoo EBee EBrs ECho EJWh EPot ERos GKir LAma LRHS MAsh NMen STil |
| | - patterned-leaved | NBir |
| | ***colchicum*** | ECho SKHP STil |
| § | ***coum*** ♀H4 | Widely available |
| | - from Turkey | ERos |
| | - var. ***abchasicum*** | see *C. coum* subsp. *caucasicum* |
| § | - subsp. ***caucasicum*** | ERos GBuc STil |
| | - subsp. ***coum*** | CBro ECho MAsh |
| | - - f. ***albissimum*** 'Golan Heights' | MAsh STil WIvy |
| | - - f. ***coum*** Nymans Group | CWCL MAsh WFar |
| | - - - Pewter Group ♀H2-4 | CPMA CWCL EBrs ECGP ECho ERos GKev MAsh MTho WIvy |
| | - - - - bicoloured | EJWh |
| | - - - - 'Blush' | CPMA GBuc STil |
| | - - - - 'Maurice Dryden' | CAvo CBro CLAP CPMA CWCL EBrs ECGP ECho EHrv GBuc LAma LRHS MAsh STil |
| | - - - - red-flowered | LAma WPat |
| | - - - - 'Tilebarn Elizabeth' | CDes CSsd CWCL EHrv MAsh NBir STil WHoo |
| | - - - - white-flowered | GBuc MAsh |
| | - - - plain-leaved red | STil |
| | - - - 'Roseum' | CWCL EBrs GBuc STil |
| | - - - Silver Group | CBro CPMA CWoo EBee ECho EHrv GEdr GKir LRHS NHol NRya NSla WHoo WPGP |
| | - - - - red-flowered | CAvo EPot MTho STil WHoo |
| | - - magenta-flowered | CWCL WHoo |
| | - - f. ***pallidum*** 'Album' | CAvo CPMA CWCL EBrs ECho EPot ERos LAma MAsh SIng STil WAbe WCot WHoo WPat |
| | - - - 'Marbled Moon' | MAsh STil |
| | - dark pink-flowered | CAvo CLAP ECho ITim WAbe WHoo |
| | - subsp. ***elegans*** | see *C. elegans* |
| | - hybrid new | ERCP |
| | - marble-leaved | CWCL ECho LHop WHoo |
| | - plain-leaved | CLAP EBla EPot WAbe |
| | - red-flowered | CLAP ECho |
| I | - 'Rubrum' | EBrs |
| | - 'Tilebarn Graham' | MAsh |
| | ***creticum*** | ECho EJWh MAsh STil |
| | ***creticum*** x ***repandum*** | see *C.* x *meiklei* |
| | ***cyprium*** | CBro CWCL EBrs ECho EJWh LRHS MAsh STil WIvy |
| | - 'E.S.' | MAsh STil WFar |
| | x ***drydeniae*** | CPMA |
| § | ***elegans*** | EJWh MAsh STil |
| | ***europaeum*** | see *C. purpurascens* |
| | ***fatrense*** | see *C. purpurascens* subsp. *purpurascens* from Fatra, Slovakia |
| | ***graecum*** | CBro CWCL CWoo EBla EBrs ECho EJWh EPot LRHS MAsh NMen STil WAbe WCot WIvy |
| | - f. ***album*** | CBro EBrs EJWh EPot LRHS MAsh STil |
| | - subsp. ***anatolicum*** | STil |
| | - subsp. ***candicum*** | MAsh STil |
| | - subsp. ***graecum*** f. ***graecum*** 'Glyfada' | STil |
| § | ***hederifolium*** ♀H4 | Widely available |
| | - arrow-head | CLAP |
| | - var. ***confusum*** | MAsh STil WCot |
| | - var. ***hederifolium*** f. ***albiflorum*** | Widely available |
| | - - - 'Album' | CWCL EBrs |
| | - - - Bowles' Apollo Group | GBuc |
| § | - - - - 'Artemis' | MAsh STil |
| | - - - - 'White Bowles' Apollo' | see *C. hederifolium* var. *hederifolium* f. *albiflorum* (Bowles' Apollo Group) 'Artemis' |
| | - - - 'Linnett Stargazer' | WCot |
| | - - - 'Nettleton Silver' | see *C. hederifolium* var. *hederifolium* f. *albiflorum* 'White Cloud' |
| | - - - 'Perlenteppich' | GBuc GMaP |
| | - - - 'Tilebarn Helena' | STil |
| § | - - - 'White Cloud' | CLAP EBla EPot MAsh NSla STil WHoo WIvy |
| | - - f. ***hederifolium*** Bowles' Apollo Group | CHid CLAP CWCL ECGP GBuc MAsh STil |
| | - - - 'Fairy Rings' | MAsh |
| | - - - 'Rosenteppich' | EBee GBuc GMaP |
| | - - - 'Ruby Glow' | CWCL GBuc MAsh NBir WCot WPat |
| | - - - 'Silver Cloud' | CBro CHid CLAP EHrv GBuc MAsh NBir STil WAbe WCot WHoo WIvy WPGP WPat |
| | - - - 'Stargazer' | MAsh |
| | - - 'Tilebarn Silver Arrow' | CPMA STil |
| | - long-leaved | CPMA |
| | - 'Pewter Mist' new | LAma |
| | - 'Rose Pearls' new | EAlp |
| | - 'San Marino Silver' | GEdr |
| | - scented | NHol STil |
| | - silver-leaved | CAvo CPMA CWoo EBla EBrs ECGP ECho EPot LHop LRHS MAsh NWCA SRot STil WFar |
| | x ***hildebrandii*** | WIvy |
| | ***ibericum*** | see *C. coum* subsp. *caucasicum* |
| | ***intaminatum*** | CBro CWCL CWoo EBee EBrs ECho EJWh EPot ERos GKir LAma LRHS MAsh NMen STil WIvy |
| | - patterned-leaved | CWCL EJWh MAsh STil |
| | - pink-flowered | MAsh NMen STil |
| | - plain-leaved | MAsh STil WThu |
| | ***latifolium*** | see *C. persicum* |
| | ***libanoticum*** | CBro CPBP EBrs ECho EJWh LAma LRHS MAsh NMen STil WFar |
| § | x ***meiklei*** | CBro |
| | ***mirabile*** ♀H2-3 | CBro CPBP CWCL CWoo EBee EBla EBrs ECho EJWh LAma LRHS MAsh NMen STil WAbe WIvy WThu |
| | - f. ***niveum*** new | EJWh |
| | - 'Tilebarn Anne' | MAsh STil |
| | - 'Tilebarn Jan' | CPMA MAsh STil |
| | - 'Tilebarn Nicholas' | CWoo EBla MAsh STil |
| | ***neapolitanum*** | see *C. hederifolium* |
| | ***orbiculatum*** | see *C. coum* |
| | ***parviflorum*** | EJWh MAsh STil |
| § | ***peloponnesiacum*** ♀H2-3 | EJWh ERos MAsh |
| | - subsp. ***peloponnesiacum*** | CBro CWCL CWoo STil |
| | - subsp. ***rhodense*** | MAsh STil |
| | - subsp. ***vividum*** | STil |
| | - white-flowered | STil |
| § | ***persicum*** | CBro CStu CWCL EBrs ECho EJWh LRHS MAsh NMen STil |
| | - CSE 90560 | STil |
| | - var. ***persicum*** f. ***puniceum*** from Lebanon | STil |
| | - - - 'Tilebarn Karpathos' | STil |
| | - white-flowered | MAsh |
| | ***pseudibericum*** ♀H2-3 | CBro CWCL CWoo EBee EBrs ECho EJWh EPot LAma LRHS MAsh STil |
| | - 'Roseum' | MAsh NMen STil |
| § | ***purpurascens*** ♀H4 | CBro EJWh EPot GBuc GKir LLHF LRHS MAsh MSSP NMen NWCA STil WFar WHoo WIvy WPat |
| | - var. ***fatrense*** | see *C. purpurascens* subsp. *purpurascens* from Fatra, Slovakia |
| | - 'Lake Garda' | MAsh WPGP |
| § | - subsp. ***purpurascens*** from Fatra, Slovakia | MAsh STil |
| | - silver-leaved | STil |

| | | |
|---|---|---|
| | ***repandum*** | CAvo CBro CWCL EBrs ECho EHrv EJWh ERos LAma LRHS MAsh MSSP NMen SCnR STil WCot WHer |
| | - subsp. ***peloponnesiacum*** | see *C. peloponnesiacum* |
| | - 'Pelops' misapplied | see *C. peloponnesiacum* subsp. *peloponnesiacum* |
| | - subsp. ***repandum*** f. ***album*** | CLAP EJWh MAsh STil |
| | ***rohlfsianum*** | CBro EJWh LRHS MAsh STil WThu |
| | x ***saundersii*** | EJWh MAsh STil |
| | ***trochopteranthum*** | see *C. alpinum* |
| | x ***wellensiekii*** | MAsh STil |
| | x ***whiteae*** new | MAsh |

## *Cyclanthera* (*Cucurbitaceae*)

| | | |
|---|---|---|
| | ***pedata*** 'Fat Baby' new | WTou |

## *Cydonia* ✿ (*Rosaceae*)

| | | |
|---|---|---|
| | ***japonica*** | see *Chaenomeles speciosa* |
| | ***oblonga*** (F) | ECrN LMaj |
| | - 'Agvambari' (F) | SKee |
| | - 'Champion' (F) | CAgr CBcs ECrN LBuc SKee SVic WJas |
| | - 'Early Prolific' (F) | ECrN LAst |
| | - 'Ekmek' (F) | SKee |
| | - 'Isfahan' (F) | SKee |
| | - 'Krymsk' (F) | CAgr |
| | - 'Leskovac' (F) | NLar |
| § | - 'Lusitanica' (F) | CAgr CDoC CDul GTwe MCoo SKee SPer WJas |
| | - 'Meech's Prolific' (F) | CAgr CDul CLnd CTho CTri ECrN EMil EMui GTwe LRHS MBlu MBri MGos MWat NLar SDea SKee SPer SPoG |
| | - pear-shaped (F) | CDul ECrN MCoo |
| | - Portugal | see *C. oblonga* 'Lusitanica' |
| | - 'Rea's Mammoth' (F) new | NLar |
| | - 'Shams' (F) | SKee |
| | - 'Sobu' (F) | SKee |
| | - 'Vranja' (F) ♀H4 | Widely available |

## *Cymbalaria* (*Scrophulariaceae*)

| | | |
|---|---|---|
| | ***aequitriloba*** 'Alba' | GGar |
| § | ***hepaticifolia*** | LRHS WPer |
| § | ***muralis*** | EAlp EBWF ECho ECtt GGar MHer NPri WGor |
| | - 'Albiflora' | see *C. muralis* 'Pallidior' |
| § | - 'Globosa Alba' | CHal |
| | - 'Kenilworth White' | WMoo |
| | - 'Nana Alba' | NPri SEND WPer |
| § | - 'Pallidior' | ECho |
| | - 'Rosea' | WFar |
| § | ***pallida*** | CEnt CMea CPBP NSla SBch SPlb WFar WMoo WPer |
| § | ***pilosa*** | ECtt NLar |
| | - 'Alba' | WFar |

## *Cymbopogon* (*Poaceae*)

| | | |
|---|---|---|
| | ***citratus*** | CArn CBod CCCN CDow CHby COld CSev GPoy MNHC MSal NGHP NPri NTHB SHDw SIde SPoG SVic WCHb WJek WLHH |
| | ***flexuosus*** | MHer |
| | ***martini*** | CArn GPoy MSal |
| | ***nardus*** | CArn GPoy MSal |

## *Cymophyllus* (*Cyperaceae*)

| | | |
|---|---|---|
| § | ***fraserianus*** | CHEx EShb GBin |

## *Cynanchum* (*Asclepiadaceae*)

| | | |
|---|---|---|
| | ***acuminatifolium*** | GCal |

## *Cynara* (*Asteraceae*)

| | | |
|---|---|---|
| § | ***baetica*** subsp. ***maroccana*** | LDai |
| | ***cardunculus*** ♀H3-4 | Widely available |
| | - ACL 380/78 | SWat |
| I | - 'Cardy' | EBee LCro MCot NBre NCGa SPoG SWat WBrE |
| | - dwarf | SMHy WCot |
| I | - 'Florist Cardy' | IGor MWat NLar WCot |
| | - 'Gobbo di Nizza' | EBee ELau WHer |
| § | - Scolymus Group | CBcs CHEx CKno CWan EBee EHoe EMil EPfP EWes GPoy IGor ILis LRHS LSRN MBri MLan MNHC MRav NPri SDnm SMrm SPav SPhx SPoG WFar WHer WHoo |
| | - - 'Blanco Arois' new | EBee |
| | - - 'Carciofo Violetto Precoce' | WHer |
| | - - 'Gigante di Romagna' | WHer |
| | - - 'Gros Camus de Bretagne' | MAvo WCot |
| | - - 'Gros Vert de Lâon' | CBcs ECha ELan NBhm SBig SMHy WCot WPGP |
| | - - 'Imperial Star' new | WHil |
| | - - 'Large Green' | NLar NScw |
| | - - 'Purple Globe' | CArn CPrp CSBt ELau SMrm |
| | - - 'Romanesco' | EBee ELau SVic |
| | - - 'Vert Globe' | CBod CHar CPrp CSBt CSev EBee ELau IFoB MWat NPer NVic SMrm SVic |
| | - - 'Violetto di Chioggia' | CSev EBee ELau WHer |
| | - white-flowered | WCot |
| | ***hystrix*** misapplied | see *C. baetica* subsp. *maroccana* |
| | ***scolymus*** | see *C. cardunculus* Scolymus Group |

## *Cynodon* (*Poaceae*)

| | | |
|---|---|---|
| | ***aethiopicus*** | CMHG EBee EHoe GBin LEdu SHDw SKHP SPhx |

## *Cynoglossum* (*Boraginaceae*)

| | | |
|---|---|---|
| | ***amabile*** ♀H4 | GKev NCGa SEND |
| | - f. ***roseum*** 'Mystery Rose' | WPGP |
| | - - 'Pink Shower' | EDif |
| | ***creticum*** | EMon |
| | ***dioscoridis*** | NLar WKif WPer |
| | ***nervosum*** | EBee ECtt ELan EMil EPPr EPfP GKir LAst LHop LRHS MCot MLHP MRav NChi NGdn NWCA SPad SPer SPoG SWat WCAu WCHb WCot WFar WPnn |
| | ***officinale*** | CArn CSec EBWF MHer MSal NSti WCHb WHer |
| | ***zeylanicum*** 'Chill Out' new | GJos |

## *Cynosurus* (*Poaceae*)

| | | |
|---|---|---|
| | ***cristatus*** | EBWF |
| | - viviparous | CNat |

## *Cypella* (*Iridaceae*)

| | | |
|---|---|---|
| § | ***coelestis*** | EDif |
| | ***herbertii*** | EDif WFar |
| | ***plumbea*** | see *C. coelestis* |

## *Cyperus* (*Cyperaceae*)

| | | |
|---|---|---|
| § | ***albostriatus*** | CCCN CHEx CHal EShb MBri |
| | ***alternifolius*** misapplied | see *C. involucratus* |
| | ***alternifolius*** L. | CBen EAmu LPBA MSKA WMAq |
| | - 'Compactus' | see *C. involucratus* 'Nanus' |
| | 'Chira' | CHrt CSec EWsh MBNS WGwG |
| § | ***cyperoides*** | MBri |
| | ***diffusus*** misapplied | see *C. albostriatus* |

§ ***eragrostis*** CArn CHal CMil CPom CRow CSec EHoe EWsh MCCP MMuc SDix SPlb SWal SWat WAbb WLeb WMAq WMoo
***esculentus*** CArn SWal
***fuscus*** MDKP WFar WHal WMoo
§ ***giganteus*** CDWL
***glaber*** EAlp EBee EPGN EUJe LDai MBNS MBar MNHC NBre
***haspan*** misapplied see *C. papyrus* 'Nanus'
***haspan*** L. CDWL EShb MSKA
§ ***involucratus*** ♀H1 CBen CHEx CHal CRow CWCL EBak EHon EShb EUJe LPBA MBri MSKA SArc SWal SWat WFar WMnd WMoo
- 'Gracilis' EBak MBri
§ - 'Nanus' LPBA MSCN SWal
- 'Variegatus' (v) MJnS
***longus*** CBen CHrt CWat EHoe EHon EMFW EMon EPGN EPPr EWsh GAuc GCal LPBA MBar MLHP MMuc NNor NPer SWal SWat WFar WHal WMAq WPnP WPrP
'Medina Sedonia' **new** MMuc
***papyrus*** ♀H1 CDTJ CDow CHEx CKno CMCo EAmu GKir LPan LRHS MBri MJnS MSKA SAPC SArc SBig SMad WHal XBlo
- 'Mexico' see *C. giganteus*
§ - 'Nanus' ♀H1 CDWL CHEx LPal XBlo
***prolifer*** LLWG
***rotundus*** CRow MCCP NLar SBch SWal WTou
***sumula*** hort. see *C. cyperoides*
***ustulatus*** CKno MDKP
***vegetus*** see *C. eragrostis*

## *Cyphomandra* (*Solanaceae*)

***abutiloides*** MJnS
***betacea*** (F) CCCN SVic
***corymbiflora*** CKob MJnS SKHP

## *Cypripedium* (*Orchidaceae*)

***acaule*** SHdy
**Aki gx** CAvo GEdr NLAp SHdy WWst XFro
- 'Light' SHdy
- 'Pastel' GEdr WWst XFro
***arietinum*** SHdy
x ***barbeyi*** see *C.* x *ventricosum*
***bardolphianum*** **new** SHdy
***calceolus*** CFir EHrv EPot MDun NLAp SHdy WCot WWst
- from Korea **new** NLAp
- from Kurilen Island **new** NLAp
- from Lake Baikal **new** NLAp
***calcicolum*** NLAp SHdy
***californicum*** NLAp SHdy
***candidum*** SHdy
***cordigerum*** SHdy
***corrugatum*** see *C. tibeticum*
***debile*** GEdr NLAp SHdy
**Emil gx** CAvo GEdr NLAp SHdy WWst XFro
***fargesii*** SHdy
***farreri*** SHdy
***fasciolatum*** NLAp SHdy
***flavum*** CFir GBin MDun NLAp SHdy WCot
- white-flowered CFir SHdy WCot
§ ***formosanum*** GAuc LAma SHdy SKHP
***forrestii*** NLAp
***franchetii*** SHdy
**Gisela gx** CAvo GEdr LAma NLAp WWst XFro
- 'Pastel' GEdr NLAp SHdy WWst XFro
- 'Yellow' LAma
***guttatum*** NLAp SHdy WWst
**Hank Small gx** NLAp SHdy WWst XFro
***henryi*** EBee LAma NLAp SHdy
***himalaicum*** NLAp
**Inge gx** NLAp WWst XFro
**Ingrid gx** GEdr NLAp SHdy WWst XFro
***japonicum*** GBin GEdr NLAp SHdy WWst
- var. ***formosanum*** see *C. formosanum*
***kentuckiense*** CCCN CFir GEdr MDun NLAp SHdy SKHP WCot
***lichiangense*** SHdy
***macranthos*** EHrv NLAp SHdy WWst
- from Lake Baikal **new** NLAp
- f. ***albiflorum*** NLAp SHdy
***manchuricum*** red-flowered **new** NLAp
- white-flowered **new** NLAp
***margaritaceum*** SHdy
**Maria gx** XFro
**Michael gx** NLAp WWst XFro
***montanum*** SHdy
***palangshanense*** SHdy
***parviflorum*** NLAp
- var. ***makasin*** NLAp
§ - var. ***pubescens*** GBin LAma NLAp SHdy
**Philipp gx** WWst XFro
***plectrochilum*** SHdy
**Princess gx** GKev
***pubescens*** see *C. parviflorum* var. *pubescens*
***reginae*** CCCN CFir EBee EHrv EPot EWes GAuc GEdr GKev LAma MDun NCGa NLAp SHdy SKHP WCot
- f. ***albolabium*** SHdy
**Sabine gx** GEdr NLAp WWst XFro
***segawae*** LAma SHdy
§ ***tibeticum*** NLAp SHdy
**Ulla Silkens gx** EBee GEdr LAma NLAp SHdy WWst XFro
§ x ***ventricosum*** NLAp SHdy WWst
**Ventricosum gx** **new** XFro
***wardii*** SHdy
***yunnanense*** SHdy

## *Cyrilla* (*Cyrillaceae*)

***parvifolia*** SKHP
***racemiflora*** MBri

## *Cyrtanthus* (*Amaryllidaceae*)

from high altitude WCot
'Alaska' EBrs LRHS
§ ***brachyscyphus*** CSpe EBee EBrs ECho ERos EShb GGar WPrP
***breviflorus*** CDes EBee ECho SKHP WPGP
'Edwina' CCCN ECho EShb SPer
§ ***elatus*** ♀H1 CHal CSev CSpe CStu CTca EBrs EShb LAma LEdu LRHS MCCP SEND SIng WCot WGwG WHer WHil
- 'Cream Beauty' EBrs ECho
- 'Pink Diamond' EBrs LRHS WCot
'Elizabeth' CCCN ECho SPer
***falcatus*** ♀H1 EBee EBrs
§ ***luteus*** WAbe
***mackenii*** CDes CPne EBee ECho WGwG WPGP
- var. ***cooperi*** WCot
- cream-white-flowered **new** CCCN
- 'Himalayan Pink' CCCN EBee WHil
- pink-flowered WPrP
- red-flowered CCCN EBee
- white-flowered EBee EBrs WHil
- yellow-flowered WPrP
***montanus*** EBee EBrs ECho WCot
***obliquus*** WCot
***parviflorus*** see *C. brachyscyphus*
***purpureus*** see *C. elatus*
***sanguineus*** ECho WCot WPGP
***speciosus*** see *C. elatus*

## *Cyrtomium* (*Dryopteridaceae*)

| | |
|---|---|
| § **caryotideum** | CLAP EBee GQui WRic |
| § **falcatum** ♀H3 | CFwr CHEx CHal CLAP CMHG CTrC EBee ELan EPfP GCal GMaP IBal LRHS NHol NMoo NMyG NOrc NSti SEND SPad SPla SPoG SRms SRot WFar WMoo WPnP WRic |
| - 'Rochfordianum' | CBcs CCCN EBee WFib |
| § **fortunei** ♀H4 | Widely available |
| - var. **clivicola** | CFwr CPrp CWCL EBee EPfP EShb GCal MAsh MGos MRav NDlv NHol NLar NMoo SRot WRic |
| **lonchitoides** | CLAP EBee |
| **macrophyllum** | CLAP EBee |
| **tukusicola** new | CFwr |

## *Cystopteris* ✿ (*Woodsiaceae*)

| | |
|---|---|
| **bulbifera** | CLAP EBee GQui |
| **dickieana** | CLAP EBee EMon GBin GGar NHol NVic SRms WCot WFib WRic |
| **fragilis** | EBee ECha EFer GQui SRms WFib |
| - 'Cristata' | CLAP |
| **moupinensis** B&SWJ 6767 | WCru |
| **tennesseensis** | WRic |

## *Cytisus* (*Papilionaceae*)

| | |
|---|---|
| **albus** misapplied | see *C. multiflorus* |
| **albus** Hacq. | see *Chamaecytisus albus* |
| 'Amber Elf' | LRHS MBri SRms WBod |
| 'Andreanus' | see *C. scoparius* f. *andreanus* |
| 'Apricot Gem' | LRHS MAsh MBar MGos NLar NPri SPoG WFar |
| **battandieri** ♀H4 | Widely available |
| - 'Yellow Tail' ♀H4 | CEnd LRHS MBri WPGP |
| x **beanii** ♀H4 | EBee ELan EPfP GKir LRHS MAsh MBar SLon SRms SSto WDin WFar |
| 'Boskoop Glory' | GKir NLar |
| 'Boskoop Ruby' ♀H4 | CBgR CDoC CSBt EPfP EWTr GGar GKir LAst LRHS LSRN NPri SPad SPer SPoG SWvt WFar |
| 'Burkwoodii' ♀H4 | CBcs CDoC CDul CSBt CWSG EBee ELan EPfP GKir LAst LRHS LSRN MRav MSwo MWat NHol SPoG WBod WFar |
| **canariensis** | see *Genista canariensis* |
| 'Compact Crimson' | CDoC EBee SPoG |
| 'Cottage' | EPot MAsh WAbe |
| 'Crimson King' | WBod |
| 'Daisy Hill' | CSBt |
| § **decumbens** | CLyd MAsh NLar SSto |
| **demissus** | see *Chamaecytisus polytrichus* |
| 'Donard Gem' | CDoC EBee LRHS |
| 'Dorothy Walpole' | WFar |
| 'Dukaat' | EBee GKir SHBN |
| 'Firefly' | CBcs CSBt NBlu NBro NLar |
| 'Fulgens' | CSBt EPfP LRHS MBar |
| 'Golden Cascade' | CBcs CDoC EBee ELan LAst LRHS |
| 'Golden Sunlight' | CSBt EBee EPfP SHBN |
| 'Goldfinch' | CDoC CHar CSBt CWSG EBee ELan GKir MAsh MBri MNHC MSwo NBlu NLar NPri SWal WBod |
| **hirsutus** | see *Chamaecytisus hirsutus* |
| 'Hollandia' ♀H4 | CBcs CDoC CSBt CTsd CWSG EBee EPfP EWTr GKir LBMP MBar MGos MMuc MRav NBro NHol NPri SHBN SPer WDin WFar |
| x **kewensis** ♀H4 | CBcs CWSG EBee ELan EPfP GKir LRHS MAsh MBar MGos MRav SHBN SPer SPoG SRms WDin |
| - 'Niki' | EBee EPfP LRHS MAsh MGos NHol SPer SPoG |
| 'Killiney Red' | ELan MBri MGos MMuc WBod |
| 'Killiney Salmon' | GGar LSRN MRav NBlu SSto WFar |
| 'La Coquette' | CDoC EBee MAsh MBar SPlb SPoG |
| 'Lena' ♀H4 | CDoC CHar CSBt EBee ELon EPfP GGar GKir LAst LRHS LSRN MBar MBri MGos MRav MWat NHol NLar NPri WBod WFar |
| **leucanthus** | see *Chamaecytisus albus* |
| 'Luna' | EBee LRHS WFar |
| **maderensis** | see *Genista maderensis* |
| 'Maria Burkwood' | EPfP MGos NBlu NLar SHBN |
| 'Minstead' | CDoC ELan EPfP GGar SPoG WAbe |
| **monspessulanus** | see *Genista monspessulana* |
| 'Moonlight' | NBro |
| 'Moyclare Pink' | CMHG |
| 'Mrs Norman Henry' | NLar |
| § **multiflorus** ♀H4 | SRms |
| **nigrescens** | see *C. nigricans* |
| § **nigricans** | WPGP |
| - 'Cyni' | CTsd ELan IArd LAst LRHS MAsh SEND SPer SPoG SSpi |
| 'Palette' | LAst LRHS MBar |
| 'Porlock' | see *Genista* 'Porlock' |
| x **praecox** | CPSs CSBt EWTr LAst LRHS MAsh NBlu NHol SPlb WBVN WBod WFar |
| - 'Albus' | CDoC CDul CHar EBee ECrN ELan EPfP GGar GKir LAst LRHS MAsh MBar MGos MRav NBlu NHol NPri SHBN SPer WBod WFar |
| - 'Allgold' ♀H4 | Widely available |
| - 'Canary Bird' | see *C.* x *praecox* 'Goldspeer' |
| - 'Frisia' | MBar MRav NBro WBod WFar |
| § - 'Goldspeer' | CSBt SEND |
| - 'Lilac Lady' | LRHS |
| - 'Warminster' ♀H4 | EBee EPfP LRHS MBar MBri MRav MWat NBlu NWea SRms |
| **purpureus** | see *Chamaecytisus purpureus* |
| - 'Atropurpureus' | see *Chamaecytisus purpureus* 'Atropurpureus' |
| **racemosus** | see *Genista* x *spachiana* |
| Red Favourite | see *C.* 'Roter Favorit' |
| 'Red Wings' | NHol SPer WBod |
| § 'Roter Favorit' | EPfP MBar MGos MNHC NScw WGor |
| **scoparius** | CArn CDul CRWN EBWF NWea SRms WDin WTou |
| § - f. **andreanus** ♀H4 | CDoC EPfP MGos NWea SPer SPoG WFar |
| - - 'Splendens' | CBgR SSto |
| - 'Cornish Cream' | CDoC CDul ECot EPfP GKir SPer WFar |
| § - subsp. **maritimus** | SLPl |
| - Monarch strain new | GJos |
| - var. **prostratus** | see *C. scoparius* subsp. *maritimus* |
| x **spachianus** | see *Genista* x *spachiana* |
| **supinus** | see *Chamaecytisus supinus* |
| 'Windlesham Ruby' | CDoC CPLG EBee ELan EPfP GKir LAst LRHS MBar NLar NPri SPer WBVN WBod WDin WFar |
| 'Zeelandia' ♀H4 | CBcs EBee EPfP GKir LAst LRHS MBar MRav MWat NBlu NPri SPer SPoG WBod WFar |

# D

## *Daboecia* ✿ (*Ericaceae*)

| | |
|---|---|
| § **cantabrica** f. **alba** | CSBt EHea MBar MBri NHol SPer SRms |
| - - 'Alba Globosa' | CCCN EHea MBar MSwo |
| - - 'Creeping White' | EHea |
| - - 'David Moss' ♀H4 | EHea MBar |
| - - 'Early Bride' | EHea |

| | |
|---|---|
| - - 'Snowdrift' | EHea MBar |
| - - 'White Carpet' | EHea |
| - 'Arielle' 𝕐H4 | EHea |
| - 'Atropurpurea' | CCCN CSBt EHea NHol SPer |
| - 'Barbara Phillips' 𝕐H4 | EHea MBar |
| - 'Bellita' | EHea |
| - 'Bicolor' 𝕐H4 | EHea |
| - 'Blueless' | EHea |
| - f. ***blumii*** 'Pink Blum' | EHea |
| - - 'Purple Blum' | EHea |
| - - 'White Blum' | EHea |
| - 'Bubbles' | EHea |
| - 'Celtic Star' | EHea |
| - 'Chaldon' | EHea |
| - 'Charles Nelson' (d) | EHea MBar |
| - 'Cherub' | EHea |
| - 'Cinderella' | EHea MBar |
| - 'Cleggan' | EHea |
| - 'Clifden' | EHea |
| - 'Covadonga' | EHea MBar |
| - 'Cupido' | CTsd EHea |
| § - 'Donard Pink' | EHea MBar |
| - 'Eskdale Baron' | EHea |
| - 'Eskdale Blea' | EHea |
| - 'Eskdale Blonde' | EHea |
| - 'Glamour' | EHea |
| - 'Globosa Pink' | EHea |
| - 'Harlequin' | EHea |
| - 'Heather Yates' | EHea |
| - 'Heraut' | EHea |
| - 'Hookstone Purple' | CCCN EHea MBar |
| - 'Irish Shine' | EHea |
| - 'Johnny Boy' | EHea |
| - 'Lilac Osmond' | EHea MBar |
| - 'Pink' | see *D. cantabrica* 'Donard Pink' |
| - 'Pink Lady' | EHea MBar |
| - 'Polifolia' | EHea SRms |
| - 'Porter's Variety' | EHea MBar |
| - 'Praegerae' | CCCN CTri EHea MBar |
| - 'Purpurea' | EHea MBar |
| - 'Rainbow' (v) | EHea MBar |
| - 'Rodeo' 𝕐H4 | EHea |
| - 'Rosea' | EHea MBar |
| - 'Rubra' | EHea |
| - subsp. ***scotica*** 'Bearsden' | EHea MBar |
| - - 'Ben' | EHea |
| - - 'Cora' | EHea MBar |
| - - 'Golden Imp' | EHea |
| - - 'Goscote' | EHea MGos |
| - - 'Jack Drake' 𝕐H4 | EHea MBar MBri |
| - - 'Katherine's Choice' | CBcs EHea |
| - - 'Red Imp' | EHea |
| - - 'Robin' | EHea |
| - - 'Silverwells' 𝕐H4 | CBcs EHea MBar MBri |
| - - 'Tabramhill' | EHea MBar |
| - - 'William Buchanan' 𝕐H4 | EHea GGar MBar MBri NHol |
| - - 'William Buchanan Gold' (v) | CCCN EHea MBar MBri |
| - 'Tom Pearce' | CCCN |
| - 'Waley's Red' 𝕐H4 | EHea GQui MBar NHol |
| - 'Wijnie' | EHea |

## *Dacrycarpus* (*Podocarpaceae*)

| | |
|---|---|
| § ***dacrydioides*** | CBcs ECou LEdu |
| - 'Dark Delight' | ECou |

## *Dacrydium* (*Podocarpaceae*)

| | |
|---|---|
| ***bidwillii*** | see *Halocarpus bidwillii* |
| ***cupressinum*** | CAbb CBcs CDoC CTrC |
| ***franklinii*** | see *Lagarostrobos franklinii* |
| ***laxifolium*** | see *Lepidothamnus laxifolius* |

## *Dactylis* (*Poaceae*)

| | |
|---|---|
| ***glomerata*** | WSFF |
| - 'Variegata' (v) | CPen EBee EMon EPPr MBlu MCCP NBid NHol SEND SHDw WFar |

## *Dactylorhiza* (*Orchidaceae*)

| | |
|---|---|
| ***alpestris*** | CFir EBee GEdr MDun NLAp WCot |
| ***aristata*** | EFEx GEdr WWst |
| x ***braunii*** | ECha |
| - dark | ECha |
| § ***elata*** 𝕐H4 | EMon GAbr GKev GQui IBlr LAma MBri NLAp SPhx SUsu WCot |
| - 'Lydia' | GCra SPhx |
| **Foliorella gx** new | NLAp |
| § ***foliosa*** 𝕐H4 | CBro CCCN CDes CTsd CWsd EPot ERas ERos GCra GKir IBlr MDun MNrw MTho NLAp NSum WCot WFar WOld |
| § ***fuchsii*** | CCCN CMil CSec EBee EBla EPot ERos GBuc GKev ITim MAvo MDun MGos MNrw NLAp NMen NRya NSla NSum SCnR SHdy SUsu WCot WHer WPnP WTin |
| - pink-flowered | CFir |
| - white-flowered | CFir NLAp SHdy |
| x ***grandis*** | CWsd EBla EMon IBlr SCnR |
| hybrids | GKir NLAp |
| ***incarnata*** | CFir GAuc MDun NBid NLAp |
| § ***maculata*** | CFir CHid EBee EHrv ELan EPfP GAbr GAuc GKir LAma MDun NCGa NLAp NSum SHdy WBor WCot WFar WHer WHlf WPnP |
| - subsp. ***ericetorum*** | NLAp |
| ***maderensis*** | see *D. foliosa* |
| § ***majalis*** | CFir CLAP EPot GAuc LAma MDun NLAp SHdy WFar WPnP |
| - subsp. ***praetermissa*** | see *D. praetermissa* |
| - subsp. ***sphagnicola*** | EBee MAvo MDun NLAp WCot |
| ***mascula*** | see *Orchis mascula* |
| § ***praetermissa*** | CCCN CFir CLAP EBee GEdr GKev MAvo MDun NCGa NLAp SHdy WCot WFar WPnP |
| - 'Copenhaven' | NLAp |
| ***purpurella*** | CFir CLAP EBee MAvo MDun NLAp NRya SHdy WCot WFar WPnP |
| - 'Palmengarten' | NLAp |
| ***sambucina*** | GAuc NLAp |

## *Dahlia* ✿ (*Asteraceae*)

| | |
|---|---|
| NJM 05.008 new | WPGP |
| NJM 05.072 new | WPGP |
| NJM 05.085 new | WPGP |
| 'A la Mode' (LD) | CWGr |
| 'Abba' (SD) | CWGr ECtt |
| 'Abingdon Ace' (SD) | CWGr |
| 'Abridge Alex' (SD) | CWGr |
| 'Abridge Ben' (MinD) | CWGr |
| 'Abridge Florist' (SWL) | CWGr |
| 'Abridge Fox' (MinD) | CWGr |
| 'Abridge Natalie' (SWL) | CWGr |
| 'Abridge Primrose' (SWL) | CWGr MSHN |
| 'Abridge Taffy' (MinD) | CWGr MSHN |
| 'Adelaide Fontane' (LD) | CWGr |
| 'Admiral Rawlings' (SD) | CBgR CWGr MAJR WHal WWlt |
| 'Aimie' (MinD) | CWGr |
| 'Aitara Cloud' (MinC) | NHal |
| 'Aitara Diadem' (MD) | CWGr |
| 'Aitara Majesty' (GS-c) | CWGr |
| 'Akita' (Misc) | CWGr MBri SPer |
| 'Albert Schweitzer' (MS-c) | CWGr |
| 'Alden Regal' (MinC) | CWGr |
| 'Alfred C' (GS-c) | CWGr |

| | | |
|---|---|---|
| | 'Alfred Grille' (MS-c) | CWGr LRHS SPer |
| | 'Alice Ireland' (MinD) | CWGr |
| | 'Alice May' **new** | MSHN |
| | 'Aljo' (MS-c) | CWGr |
| | 'All Triumph' (MinS-c) | CWGr |
| | 'Allan Snowfire' (MS-c) | MSHN NHal |
| | 'Allan Sparkes' (SWL) ♀H3 | CWGr |
| I | 'Allegro' (LS-c) | CWGr |
| | 'Alloway Cottage' (MD) | CWGr NHal |
| | 'Alltami Apollo' (GS-c) | CWGr |
| | 'Alltami Cherry' (SBa) | CWGr |
| | 'Alltami Classic' (MD) | CWGr |
| | 'Alltami Corsair' (MS-c) | CWGr MSHN |
| | 'Alltami Cosmic' (LD) | CWGr |
| | 'Alltami Dandy' (SD) | CWGr |
| | 'Alltami Joy' (MD) | CWGr |
| | 'Alltami Ruby' (MS-c) | CWGr |
| * | 'Allyson' (MinBa) | CWGr |
| | 'Almand's Climax' (GD) ♀H3 | CWGr MSHN |
| | 'Alpen Beauty' (Col) | CWGr |
| | 'Alpen Fern' (Fim) | CWGr |
| | 'Alpen Flame' (MinC) | CWGr |
| | 'Alpen Mildred' (SS-c) | CWGr |
| | 'Alpen Sun' (MinS-c) | CWGr |
| | 'Alstergruss' (Col) | CWGr |
| | 'Alva's Doris' (SS-c) ♀H3 | CWGr |
| | 'Alva's Lilac' (SD) | CWGr |
| | 'Alva's Supreme' (GD) ♀H3 | CWGr MSHN NHal |
| | 'Amanda Jarvis' (SC) | CWGr |
| | 'Amanjanca' (MinS-c) | CWGr |
| | 'Amaran Candyfloss' (SD) | CWGr |
| | 'Amaran Pentire' (SS-c) | CWGr |
| | 'Amaran Pico' (MD) | CWGr |
| | 'Amaran Relish' (LD) | CWGr |
| | 'Amaran Return' (GD) | CWGr |
| | 'Amaran Royale' (MinD) | CWGr |
| | 'Amaran Troy' (SWL) | CWGr |
| I | 'Amazone' (DwB) | LAst |
| | 'Amber Banker' (MC) | CWGr |
| | 'Amber Festival' (SD) | CWGr MSHN NHal |
| | 'Amber Vale' (MinD) | CWGr |
| | 'Amberglow' (MinBa) | CWGr |
| | 'Amberley Jean' (SD) | CWGr |
| | 'Amberley Joan' (SD) | CWGr |
| | 'Amberley Nicola' (SD) | CWGr |
| | 'Amberley Victoria' (MD) | CWGr |
| | 'Ambition' (SS-c) | CWGr ERCP |
| | 'Amelia's Surprise' (LD) | CWGr |
| | 'American Copper' (GD) | CWGr |
| | 'Amgard Coronet' (MinD) | CWGr MSHN |
| | 'Amgard Delicate' (LD) | CWGr |
| | 'Amgard Rosie' (SD) | CWGr |
| | 'Amira' (SBa) | CWGr NHal |
| | 'Amorangi Joy' (SC) | CWGr |
| | 'Ananda' (S-c) **new** | CFir |
| | 'Ananta Patel' (SD) | CWGr |
| * | 'Anatol' (LD) | CWGr |
| | 'Anchorite' (SD) | CWGr |
| | 'Andrea Clark' (MD) | CWGr MSHN NHal |
| | 'Andrea Lawson' **new** | MSHN |
| | 'Andrew Lockwood' (Pom) | CWGr |
| | 'Andrew Magson' (SS-c) ♀H3 | CWGr |
| | 'Andrew Mitchell' (MS-c) | CWGr NHal |
| | 'Andries' Amber' (MinS-c) | CWGr LBut |
| | 'Andries' Orange' (MinS-c) | CWGr LBut MSHN |
| | 'Angora' (SD/Fim) | CWGr |
| | 'Ann Breckenfelder' (Col) ♀H3 | EBee ECtt EHrv MAvo MSHN NHal SDix SMrm WCot |
| | 'Anna Lindh' (MWL) **new** | MSHN |
| | 'Anniversary Ball' (MinBa) | CWGr |
| | 'Apache' (MS-c/Fim) | CWGr SPer |
| | ***apiculata*** | CWGr |
| | 'Appetizer' (SS-c) | CWGr |
| I | 'Appleblossom' (Col) | CWGr |
| | 'Apricot Beauty' (MS-c) | CWGr |
| | 'Apricot Honeymoon Dress' (SD) | CWGr |
| | 'Apricot Jewel' (SD) | CWGr |
| | 'Apricot Parfait' (SS-c) | CWGr |
| | 'April Dawn' (MD) | CWGr |
| | 'April Heather' (Col) | MSHN NHal |
| | 'Arab Queen' (GS-c) | CWGr |
| | 'Arabian Night' (SD) | Widely available |
| | 'Arc de Triomphe' (MD) | CWGr |
| | 'Arlequin' (LD) | CWGr |
| | 'Arnhem' (SD) | CWGr |
| | 'Arthur Godfrey' (GD) | CWGr |
| | 'Arthur Hankin' (SD) | CWGr |
| | 'Arthur Hills' (SC) | CWGr |
| | 'Arthur's Delight' (GD) | CWGr |
| | 'Asahi Chohje' (Anem) ♀H3 | CWGr |
| | 'Askwith George' (MinD) | CWGr |
| | 'Aspen' (Dwf) | CWGr MWea |
| | 'Athalie' (SC) | CWGr |
| | 'Athelston John' (SC) | CWGr |
| | 'Atilla' (SD) | CWGr |
| | 'Audacity' (MD) | CWGr |
| | 'Audrey Grace' (SD) | CWGr |
| | 'Audrey R' (SWL) | CWGr |
| | 'Aurora's Kiss' (MinBa) | CWGr LBut NHal |
| | 'Aurwen's Violet' (Pom) | CWGr NHal |
| | ***australis*** | EBee WPGP |
| | - B&SWJ 10358 | WCru |
| | - B&SWJ 10389 **new** | WCru |
| | 'Autumn Lustre' (SWL) ♀H3 | CWGr |
| | 'Avoca Comanche' (SS-c) **new** | MSHN NHal |
| | 'Avoca Salmon' (MD) | NHal |
| | 'Awaikoe' (Col) | CWGr |
| | 'B.J. Beauty' (MD) | CWGr MSHN NHal |
| | 'Babette' (S-c) | LBut |
| | 'Baby Fonteneau' (SS-c) | CWGr |
| | 'Babylon' (GD) | EPfP |
| | 'Babylon Bronze' **new** | CSut |
| | 'Babylon Purple' (SD) | WBor |
| | 'Bacchus' (MS-c) | CWGr |
| | 'Bach' (MC) | CWGr LRHS |
| | 'Balcombe' (SD) | CWGr |
| | 'Ballego's Glory' (MD) | CWGr |
| | 'Bambino' (Lil) | CWGr |
| | 'Banker' (MC) | CWGr |
| | 'Bantling' (MinBa) | CWGr ECtt |
| | 'Barb' (LC) | CWGr |
| | 'Barbara' (MinBa) | CWGr |
| | 'Barbara Schell' (GD) | CWGr |
| | 'Barbara's Pastelle' (MS-c) | CWGr MSHN |
| | 'Barbarossa' (LD) | CWGr |
| | 'Barbarry Ball' (SBa) | CWGr |
| | 'Barbarry Banker' (MinD) | CWGr |
| | 'Barbarry Bluebird' (MinD) | NHal |
| | 'Barbarry Cadet' (MinD) | CWGr |
| | 'Barbarry Carousel' (SBa) | CWGr |
| | 'Barbarry Cascade' (SD) | CWGr |
| | 'Barbarry Centrepoint' (SD) **new** | MSHN |
| | 'Barbarry Challenger' (MinD) | CWGr |
| | 'Barbarry Chevron' (MD) | CWGr |
| | 'Barbarry Clover' (SB) | CWGr |
| | 'Barbarry Cosmos' (SD) | CWGr MSHN |
| | 'Barbarry Dominion' (MinD) | CWGr |

| | |
|---|---|
| 'Barbarry Drifter' (SD) | CWGr |
| 'Barbarry Flag' (MinD) | CWGr |
| 'Barbarry Gateway' (MinD) | MSHN |
| 'Barbarry Gem' (MinBa) | CWGr |
| 'Barbarry Ideal' (MinD) | CWGr |
| 'Barbarry Monitor' (MinBa) | CWGr |
| 'Barbarry Noble' (MinD) | CWGr |
| 'Barbarry Olympic' (SBa) | CWGr |
| 'Barbarry Oracle' (SD) | CWGr |
| 'Barbarry Pimpernel' (SD) | CWGr |
| 'Barbarry Pinky' (SD) | CWGr |
| 'Barbarry Pointer' (SD) | NHal |
| 'Barbarry Polo' (MinD) | CWGr MSHN |
| 'Barbarry Quest' (MinD) | CWGr |
| 'Barbarry Red' (MinD) | CWGr |
| 'Barbarry Riviera' (MinD) | CWGr |
| 'Barbarry Stockton' (SD) | CWGr |
| 'Barbarry Triumph' (MinD) | CWGr |
| 'Barbette' (MinD) | CWGr |
| 'Bareham's Beauty' (SD) | CWGr |
| 'Baret Joy' (LS-c) | CWGr NHal |
| 'Bargaly Blush' (MD) | NHal |
| 'Baron Ray' (SD) | CWGr |
| 'Barry Williams' (MD) | CWGr |
| 'Bart' (SD) | CWGr |
| 'Barton Memory' (S-c) | NHal |
| 'Baseball' (MinBa) | CWGr |
| 'Bassingbourne Beauty' (SD) | CWGr |
| 'Bayswater Red' (Pom) | CWGr |
| 'Baywatch' (Anem) | CWGr |
| 'Beach Boy' (SD) | CWGr |
| 'Beacon Light' (SD) | CWGr |
| I 'Beatrice' (MinBa) | CWGr |
| 'Beatrice' (MinD) | CWGr |
| 'Bedford Sally' (MD) | CWGr |
| 'Bednall Beauty' (Misc/DwB) ♀H3 | CBgR CHll CMoH COlW CSpe CWGr EBee ECtt EHrv ELan EMil EShb EWes LHop MBri MRav NPri SDnm SDys SPav SUsu WBrk WCot WDyG |
| 'Bell Boy' (MinBa) | CWGr |
| 'Bella S' (GD) | CWGr |
| 'Belle Epoque' (MC) | CWGr |
| 'Belle Moore' (SD) | CWGr |
| 'Bell's Delight' (MSC) | CWGr |
| 'Beretta' (MD) | CWGr |
| 'Berger's Rekord' (S-c) | CSut CWGr EPfP LRHS |
| 'Berliner Kleene' (MinD/DwB) | CWGr LRHS |
| 'Bernice Sunset' (SS-c) | CWGr MSHN |
| 'Berolina' (MinD) | CWGr |
| 'Berwick Banker' (SBa) | CWGr |
| 'Berwick Wood' (MD) | CWGr MSHN NHal |
| 'Bess Painter' (SD) | CWGr |
| 'Betty Ann' (Pom) | CWGr |
| 'Betty Bowen' (SD) | CWGr |
| 'Biddenham Fairy' (MinD) | CWGr |
| 'Biddenham Strawberry' (SD) | CWGr |
| 'Biddenham Sunset' (MS-c) | CWGr |
| 'Big Red' (MD) | CWGr |
| 'Bill Homberg' (GD) | CWGr |
| 'Bill Sanderson' (Sin/DwB) | CWGr |
| 'Bingley' (SD) | CWGr |
| 'Bingo' (MinD) | CWGr |
| 'Bishop of Auckland'[PBR] (Misc) | EBee ECtt LRHS MSHN NBsh WCot |
| 'Bishop of Canterbury' (Misc) | CBgR CWGr EBee ECtt LRHS NBPN NBsh NGdn NHal |
| 'Bishop of Dover' **new** | SGar |
| 'Bishop of Lancaster' (Misc) | CWGr LRHS |
| 'Bishop of Leicester' (Misc) | CBgR CSpe ECtt EPfP MWea NBPN |

| | |
|---|---|
| 'Bishop of Llandaff' (Misc) ♀H3 | Widely available |
| 'Bishop of Oxford' (Misc) | CBgR CSpe EBee EPfP MSte MWea NBPC NBsh NGdn |
| 'Bishop of York' (Misc) | CAvo CBgR CSpe CWGr EBee ECtt EPfP ERCP MSte MWea NBPC NBPN NBsh NGdn SWal WBrk |
| 'Bishop Peter Price' (Sin) | CHar CMil |
| 'Bishop's Children' | MSHN |
| 'Bitsa' (MinBa) | CWGr |
| 'Bitter Lemon' (SD) | CWGr |
| 'Black Fire' (SD) | CWGr |
| * 'Black Knight' (MD) | CWGr |
| 'Black Monarch' (GD) | CWGr NHal |
| 'Black Narcissus' (MC) | CHVG CWGr WWlt |
| 'Black Spider' (SS-c) | CWGr |
| 'Black Tucker' (Pom) | CWGr |
| 'Blaisdon Red' (SD) | CWGr |
| 'Blaze' (MD) | CWGr |
| 'Blewbury First' (SWL) | CWGr |
| 'Bliss' (SWL) | CWGr |
| 'Blithe Spirit' (LD) | CWGr |
| 'Bloemfontein' (SD) | LRHS |
| 'Bloodstone' (SD) | CWGr |
| 'Bloommaster' (MinD) **new** | NHal |
| 'Bloom's Amy' (MinD) | CWGr |
| 'Bloom's Graham' (SS-c) | CWGr |
| 'Bloom's Kenn' (MD) | CWGr |
| I 'Blossom' (Pom) | CWGr |
| 'Blue Beard' (SS-c) | CWGr |
| 'Blue Diamond' (MC) | CWGr |
| 'Bluesette' (SD) | CWGr |
| 'Blushing Princess' (SS-c) | CWGr |
| 'Blyton Lady in Red' (MinD) **new** | NHal |
| 'Blyton Softer Gleam' (MinD) **new** | NHal |
| 'Bob Fitzjohn' (GS-c) | CWGr |
| 'Bokay' (SWL) | CWGr |
| 'Bonaventure' (GD) | MSHN NHal |
| 'Bonesta' (MinD) | CSut CWGr |
| 'Bonne Espérance' (Sin/Lil) | CWGr MSHN |
| 'Bonny Blue' (SBa) | CWGr |
| 'Bonny Brenda' (MinD) | CWGr |
| 'Boogie Woogie' (Anem) | CSut CWGr |
| 'Bora Bora' (SS-c) | CWGr |
| 'Border Princess' (SC/DwB) | CWGr |
| 'Border Triumph' (DwB) | CWGr |
| 'Boy Scout' (MinBa) | CWGr |
| 'Bracken Lorelei' (SWL) **new** | MSHN |
| 'Brackenhill Flame' (SD) | CWGr |
| 'Brackenridge Ballerina' (SWL) | CSam CWGr MSHN NHal |
| 'Brandaris' (MS-c) | CWGr MSHN |
| 'Brandysnap' (SD) | CWGr |
| 'Brian R' (SD) | CWGr |
| 'Brian's Dream' (MinD) | MSHN NHal |
| 'Bride's Bouquet' (Col) | CWGr ERCP |
| 'Bridge View Aloha' (MS-c) ♀H3 | CWGr EPfP MSHN |
| 'Bridgette' (SD) | CWGr |
| 'Bright Star' (SC) | CWGr |
| 'Brilliant Eye' (MinBa) | CWGr |
| 'Bristol Petite' (MinD) | CWGr |
| 'Brookfield Delight' (Sin/Lil) ♀H3 | CWGr SUsu |
| 'Brookfield Deirdre' (MinBa) | CWGr |
| 'Brookfield Judith' (MinD) | NHal |
| 'Brookfield Rachel' (MinBa) | CWGr |

| | | |
|---|---|---|
| | 'Brookfield Rene' (Dwf MinD) | CWGr |
| | 'Brookfield Snowball' (SBa) | CWGr |
| | 'Brookfield Sweetie' (DwB/Lil) | CWGr |
| | 'Brookside Cheri' (SC) | CWGr |
| | 'Brookside Snowball' (SB) | CWGr |
| | 'Brunello' (Misc) | CWGr |
| | 'Bryce B. Morrison' (SD) | CWGr |
| | 'Bryn Terfel' (GD) | MSHN NHal |
| | 'Bud Flanagan' (MD) | CWGr |
| | 'Butterball' (MinD/DwB) | CWGr |
| * | 'Buttercup' (Pom) | CWGr |
| | 'Buttermere' (SD) | CWGr |
| | 'By George' (GD) | CWGr |
| | 'Cabo Bell' (MSC) | CWGr |
| | 'Café au Lait' (GD) | CBgR CWGr SEND SPer |
| | 'Calgary' (SD) | CWGr |
| | 'Camano Ariel' (MC) | CWGr |
| | 'Camano Choice' (SD) | CWGr |
| | 'Camano Passion' (MS-c) | CWGr |
| | 'Camano Poppet' (SBa) | CWGr |
| | 'Camano Regal' (MS-c) | CWGr |
| | 'Cameo' (WL) | CSam CWGr LBut MSHN NHal |
| | 'Campos Billy M' (LS-c) | CWGr |
| | 'Campos Hush' (SS-c) | CWGr |
| | 'Campos Philip M' (GD) | CWGr |
| * | 'Canary Fubuki' (MD) | CWGr |
| I | 'Candlelight' (GD) | CWGr NHal |
| I | 'Candy' (SD) | CWGr |
| | 'Candy Cane' (MinBa) | CWGr |
| | 'Candy Cupid' (MinBa) 🏆$^{H3}$ | CWGr LBut |
| | 'Candy Eyes' **new** | CBcs NBPN |
| | 'Candy Hamilton Lilian' (SD) | CWGr |
| | 'Candy Keene' (LS-c) | CWGr MSHN NHal |
| | 'Caproz Jerry Garcia' (MD) | CWGr |
| | 'Capulet' (SBa) | CWGr |
| | 'Cara Tina' (Misc/DwO) | CWGr |
| | 'Careless' (SD) | CWGr |
| | 'Caribbean Fantasy' | CSut EBee SPer |
| | 'Carole Melville' (MinBa) | CWGr |
| I | 'Carolina' (Dwf) | CWGr |
| | 'Carolina Moon' (SD) | CSam CWGr NHal |
| | 'Carstone Cobblers' (SBa) | CWGr |
| | 'Carstone Ruby' (SD) | CWGr NHal |
| | 'Carstone Sunbeam' (SD) | CWGr |
| | 'Carstone Suntan' (MinC) | CWGr MSHN NHal |
| | 'Castle Drive' (MD) | CWGr MSHN |
| | 'Catherine Bateson' (MinWL) 🏆$^{H3}$ | CWGr |
| | 'Catherine Deneuve' (Misc) | CWGr ECtt |
| | 'Catherine Ireland' (MinD) | CWGr |
| | 'Cerise Prefect' (MS-c) | CWGr |
| | 'Cha Cha' (SS-c) | CWGr |
| | 'Chanson d'Amour' (SD) | CWGr |
| | 'Chantal' (MinBa) | CWGr |
| | 'Charles de Coster' (MD) | CWGr |
| | 'Charlie Briggs' (SBa) | NHal |
| | 'Charlie Dimmock' (SWL) 🏆$^{H3}$ | CWGr NHal |
| | 'Charlie Kenwood' (MinD) | CWGr MSHN |
| | 'Charlie Two' (MD) | CWGr MSHN NHal |
| | 'Charlotte Bateson' (MinBa) | CWGr |
| | 'Chat Noir' (MS-c) | CAvo CSec CSut CWGr EBee ERCP LCro NBsh |
| | 'Chee' (SWL) | CWGr |
| | 'Cheerio' (SS-c) | CWGr |
| | 'Cheerleader' (GS-c) | CWGr |
| | 'Cherokee Beauty' (GD) | CWGr |
| | 'Cherry Pop' (Fim) **new** | MSHN |
| | 'Cherry Wine' (SD) | CWGr MSHN |
| | 'Cherrywood Millfield' (MS-c) | CWGr |
| | 'Cherrywood Stoddard' (MD) | CWGr |
| | 'Cherrywood Turnpike' (SD) | CWGr |
| | 'Cherrywood Wilderness' (MD) | CWGr |
| | 'Cherubino' (Col) | CWGr |
| | 'Cherwell Goldcrest' (SS-c) | CWGr NHal |
| | 'Cherwell Siskin' (MD) | CWGr |
| | 'Cherwell Skylark' (SS-c) 🏆$^{H3}$ | CWGr MSHN NHal |
| | 'Chessy' (Sin/Lil) 🏆$^{H3}$ | CWGr EPfP LRHS NHal |
| | 'Chic' (MinBa) | EBee ECtt NBPN |
| | 'Chic en Rouge' | NBPC NBPN |
| | 'Chilson's Pride' (SD) | CWGr |
| | 'Chiltern Amber' (SD) | CWGr |
| | 'Chiltern Fantastic' (SC) | CWGr |
| | 'Chiltern Herald' (MS-c) | CWGr |
| | 'Chiltern Sylvia' (MinS-c) | CWGr |
| | 'Chimacum Topaz' (MS-c) | CWGr |
| | 'Chimborazo' (Col) | CWGr SDix |
| | 'Chislehurst Charisma' (SD) | CWGr |
| | 'Chocolate Orange' (Sin) | WCot |
| | 'Chorus Girl' (MinD) | CWGr |
| | 'Christine' (SD) | SPer |
| I | 'Christine' (SWL) | CWGr |
| | 'Christmas Carol' (Col) | CWGr EBee ECtt MSHN |
| | 'Christmas Star' (Col) | CWGr |
| | 'Christopher Nickerson' (MS-c) | CWGr |
| | 'Christopher Taylor' (SWL) | CWGr MSHN NHal |
| | 'Clair de Lune' (Col) 🏆$^{H3}$ | CHFP CWCL CWGr EBee ECtt LAst MCot MSHN NDov NHal SMrm SPav WCot WGwG WHrl |
| | 'Claire Diane' (SD) | CWGr |
| | 'Claire Louise Kitchener' (MWL) | CWGr |
| | 'Clara May' (MS-c/Fim) | CWGr |
| | 'Clarence' (S-c) | CWGr |
| | 'Clarion' (MS-c) | CSpe LRHS NPri WCot |
| | 'Clarion' **new** | ERCP |
| | 'Clarion 79' (DwB) **new** | SUsu |
| | 'Classic A.1' (MC) | CWGr |
| | 'Classic Elise' (Misc) | CWGr |
| | 'Classic Masquerade'$^{PBR}$ (Misc) | CBgR EBee |
| | 'Classic Poème'$^{PBR}$ (Misc) | CBgR EBee |
| | 'Classic Rosamunde'$^{PBR}$ (Misc) | CBgR EBee NBPN NGdn SWal |
| | 'Classic Summertime' (Misc) | CBgR CWGr EBee |
| | 'Classic Swanlake'$^{PBR}$ (Misc) | CBgR CWGr EBee |
| | 'Clearview Arla' (MinS-c) | CWGr |
| | 'Clearview Irene' (MS-c) | CWGr |
| | 'Clyde's Choice' (GD) | CWGr |
| | ***coccinea*** (B) | CBgR CGHE CHFP CHll CSpe CWGr EBee EBrs EHrv GCal IHer LAst MCot MSte NCob SDix SHGN SMHy SPav WCot WDyG WHrl WPGP |
| | - B&SWJ 9126 | WCru |
| | - var. ***palmeri*** | CBgR CSpe EBee MHar WPGP |
| | ***coccinea*** x ***merckii*** (B) | EBee EBla EWes |
| | 'Cocktail' (S-c) | CWGr |
| | 'Colac' (LD) | CWGr |
| | 'Color Spectacle' (LS-c) | CWGr |
| | 'Colour Magic' (LS-c) | CWGr |
| | 'Coltness Gem' (Sin/DwB) | CWGr |
| | 'Comet' (Misc Anem) | CWGr |
| | 'Como Polly' (LD) | CWGr |

| | | |
|---|---|---|
| I | 'Concordia' (SD) | CWGr |
| | 'Connie Bartlam' (MD) | CWGr |
| | 'Connoisseur's Choice' (MinBa) | CWGr |
| | 'Constance Bateson' (SD) | CWGr |
| | 'Constantine' (MD) | CWGr |
| | 'Contessa' (SWL) | CWGr |
| | 'Conway' (SS-c) | CWGr |
| | 'Coral Jupiter' (GS-c) | MSHN |
| | 'Coral Puff' (DwAnem) | CWGr LRHS |
| | 'Coral Relation' (SC) | CWGr |
| | 'Coral Strand' (SD) | CWGr |
| | 'Corali' (SD) **new** | MSHN |
| | 'Coralle' (MD) | CWGr |
| | 'Cornel' (SBa) | CWGr LBut MSHN NHal |
| | 'Corona' (SS-c/DwB) | CWGr |
| | 'Coronella' (MD) | CWGr |
| | 'Cortez Silver' (MD) | CWGr |
| | 'Cortez Sovereign' (SS-c) | CWGr |
| | 'Corton Bess' (SD) | CWGr |
| | 'Corton Olympic' (GD) | CWGr |
| | 'Corydon' (SD) | CWGr |
| | 'Cottesmore' (MD) | CWGr |
| | 'Cottonrail' (Col) | CWGr |
| | 'Country Boy' (MS-c) | CWGr |
| | 'Crazy Legs' (MinD) | CWGr |
| | 'Cream Alva's' (GD) $\Upsilon^{H3}$ | CWGr |
| | 'Cream Delight' (SS-c) | CWGr |
| | 'Cream Klankstad' (SC) | CWGr |
| | 'Cream Linda' (SD) | CWGr |
| | 'Cream Moonlight' (MS-c) | CWGr MSHN |
| | 'Cream Reliance' (SD) | CWGr |
| | 'Crève Coeur' (GD) | CWGr |
| | 'Crichton Cherry' (MinD) | CWGr |
| | 'Crichton Honey' (SBa) | CWGr |
| | 'Croesus' (GS-c) | CWGr |
| | 'Crossfield Allegro' (SS-c) | CWGr |
| | 'Crossfield Anne' (MinD) | CWGr |
| | 'Crossfield Ebony' (Pom) | CWGr |
| | 'Crossfield Festival' (LD) | CWGr |
| | 'Croydon Jumbo' (GD) | CWGr |
| | 'Croydon Snotop' (GD) | CWGr |
| | 'Croydon Superior' (GD) | CWGr |
| | 'Crushed Velvet' (MinD) | CWGr |
| | 'Cryfield Harmony' (MinBa) | CWGr MSHN |
| | 'Cryfield Jane' (MinBa) | CWGr |
| | 'Cryfield Keene' (LS-c) | CWGr |
| | 'Cryfield Max' (SC) | CWGr |
| | 'Cryfield Rosie' (SBa) | CWGr |
| | 'Crystal Ann' (MS-c) | CWGr |
| | 'Curate' (Misc) | CWGr |
| | 'Curiosity' (Col) | CWGr |
| | 'Currant Cream' (SBa) | CWGr |
| | 'Cyclone' (MD) | CWGr |
| | 'Cycloop' (SS-c) | CWGr |
| | 'Cynthia Chalwin' (MinBa) | CWGr |
| | 'Cynthia Louise' (GD) | CWGr |
| | 'Czardas' | GCal |
| | 'D. Day' (MS-c) | CWGr |
| | 'Daddy's Choice' (SS-c) | CWGr |
| | 'Dad's Delight' (MinD) | CWGr |
| | 'Daleko Adonis' (GS-c) | CWGr |
| | 'Daleko Gold' (MD) | CWGr |
| | 'Daleko Jupiter' (GS-c) | CWGr MSHN NHal |
| | 'Daleko National' (MD) | CWGr |
| | 'Daleko Tangerine' (MD) | CWGr |
| | 'Dana' (SS-c) | CWGr |
| | 'Dana Champ' (MinS-c) | CWGr |
| | 'Dana Dream' (MinS-c) | CWGr |
| | 'Dana Iris' (SS-c) | CWGr |
| | 'Dana Sunset' (SC) | CWGr |
| | 'Dancing Queen' (S-c) | CWGr |
| | 'Danjo Doc' (SD) | CWGr |
| | 'Danum Belle' (SD) | CWGr |
| | 'Danum Cherry' (SD) | CWGr |
| | 'Danum Chippy' (SD) | CWGr |
| | 'Danum Cream' (MS-c) | CWGr |
| | 'Danum Fancy' (SD) | CWGr |
| | 'Danum Gail' (LD) | CWGr |
| | 'Danum Hero' (LD) | CWGr |
| | 'Danum Julie' (SBa) | CWGr |
| | 'Danum Meteor' (GS-c) | CWGr |
| | 'Danum Rebel' (LS-c) | CWGr |
| | 'Danum Rhoda' (GD) | CWGr |
| | 'Danum Salmon' (MS-c) | CWGr |
| | 'Danum Torch' (Col) | CWGr |
| | 'Dark Desire'$^{PBR}$ (Sin/DwB) | CBct CBgR CFir CHFP CSpe CWCL EBla ECtt LAst LCro LHop MBri SCoo SDnm SMrm WOVN |
| | 'Dark Splendour' (MC) | CWGr |
| | 'Dark Stranger' (MC) $\Upsilon^{H3}$ | CWGr |
| | 'Darlington Diamond' (MS-c) | CWGr |
| | 'Darlington Jubilation' (SS-c) | CWGr |
| | 'Dauntless' (GS-c) **new** | MSHN |
| | 'Davar Donna' (MS-c) $\Upsilon^{H3}$ | CWGr |
| | 'Davar Hayley' (SC) | CWGr |
| | 'Davar Jim' (SS-c) $\Upsilon^{H3}$ | CWGr |
| | 'Davenport Anita' (MinD) | CWGr |
| | 'Davenport Honey' (MinD) | CWGr |
| | 'Davenport Lesley' (MinD) | CWGr |
| | 'Davenport Sunlight' (MS-c) | CWGr |
| | 'Dave's Snip' (MinD) | CWGr |
| | 'David Digweed' (SD) | CWGr NHal |
| | 'David Howard' (MinD) $\Upsilon^{H3}$ | Widely available |
| | 'David Shaw' (MD) | CWGr |
| | 'David's Choice' (MinD) | CWGr |
| | 'Dawn Chorus' (MinD) | CWGr |
| | 'Daytona' (SD) | CWGr |
| | 'Dazzler' (MinD/DwB) | CWGr |
| | 'Deborah's Kiwi' (SC) | CWGr MSHN NHal |
| | 'Debra Anne Craven' (GS-c) | CWGr MSHN NHal |
| | 'Decorette' (DwB/SD) | CWGr |
| | 'Decorette Bronze' (MinD/DwB) | CWGr |
| | 'Decorette Rose' (MinD/DwB) | CWGr |
| | 'Deepest Yellow' (MinBa) | CWGr |
| | 'De-la-Haye' (MS-c) **new** | MSHN |
| | 'Dentelle de Venise' (MC) | CWGr |
| | 'Deuil du Roi Albert' (MD) | CWGr |
| | 'Deutschland' (MD) | CWGr |
| I | 'Devon Elegans' | CWGr |
| | 'Devon Joy' (MinD) | CWGr |
| | 'Diamond Rose' (Anem/DwB) | CWGr |
| | 'Diana Gregory' (Pom) | MSHN |
| | 'Dick Westfall' (GS-c) | CWGr |
| | 'Dinah Shore' (LS-c) | CWGr |
| | 'Director' (SD) | CWGr |
| | ***dissecta*** | WPGP |
| | – F&M 191 **new** | WPGP |
| | 'Doc van Horn' (LS-c) | CWGr |
| | 'Doctor Anne Dyson' (SC) | CWGr |
| | 'Doctor Arnett' (GS-c) | CWGr |
| | 'Doctor Caroline Rabbitt' (SD) | CWGr |
| | 'Doctor John Grainger' (MinD) | CHVG CWGr |
| | 'Don Hill' (Col) $\Upsilon^{H3}$ | MSHN NBsh NHal |
| | 'Don's Delight' (Pom) | CWGr |
| | 'Doris Bacon' (SBa) | CWGr |
| | 'Doris Day' (SC) | CWGr LBut MSHN NHal |
| | 'Doris Knight' (SC) | LBut |
| | 'Doris Rollins' (SC) | CWGr |
| | 'Dottie D.' (SBa) | CWGr |

| | |
|---|---|
| 'Downham Royal' (MinBa) | CWGr |
| 'Drummer Boy' (LD) | CWGr |
| 'Duet' (MD) | CWGr EPfP LRHS |
| 'Dusky Harmony' (SWL) | CWGr |
| 'Dutch Baby' (Pom) | CWGr |
| 'Dutch Boy' (SD) | CWGr |
| 'Dutch Triumph' (LD) | CWGr |
| 'Earl Haig' (LD) | CWGr |
| 'Earl Marc' (SC) | CWGr |
| 'Early Bird' (SD) | CWGr |
| 'Easter Sunday' (Col) | CWGr MSHN |
| 'Eastwood Moonlight' (MS-c) | CWGr MSHN NHal |
| 'Eastwood Star' (MS-c) | CWGr |
| 'Ebbw Vale Festival' (MinD) | CWGr |
| 'Edge of Gold' (GD) | CWGr |
| 'Edgeway Joyce' (MinBa) | CWGr MSHN |
| 'Edinburgh' (SD) | CWGr ERCP MSHN SWal |
| 'Edith Holmes' (SC) | CWGr |
| 'Edith Mueller' (Pom) | CWGr |
| 'Edna C' (MD) | CWGr |
| 'Eileen Denny' (MS-c) | CWGr |
| 'Eisprinzessin' (MS-c) | CWGr |
| 'El Cid' (SD) | CWGr |
| 'El Paso' (SD) | CSut CWGr MBri |
| 'Eldon Wilson' (Misc/O) | CWGr |
| 'Eleanor Fiesta' (MinS-c) | CWGr |
| 'Elgico Leanne' (MC) | CWGr |
| 'Elise' (MinD) | SPer |
| 'Elizabeth Hammett' (MinD) | CWGr |
| 'Elizabeth Snowden' (Col) | CWGr MSHN |
| 'Ella Britton' (MinD) | LRHS |
| 'Ellen Huston' (Misc/DwB) 🏆H3 | CBgR CWGr EBee EBrs ECtt ERCP LPio LRHS MBri MSHN NHal WCot |
| 'Elma E' (LD) | CWGr MSHN NHal |
| 'Elmbrook Chieftain' (GD) | CWGr |
| 'Elmbrook Rebel' (GS-c) | CWGr |
| 'Embrace' (SC) | MSHN NHal |
| 'Emma's Coronet' (MinD) | CWGr MSHN |
| 'Emmental' (SD) **new** | MSHN |
| 'Emmie Lou' (MD) | CWGr |
| 'Emory Paul' (LD) | CWGr |
| 'Emperor' (MD) | CWGr |
| 'Enfield Salmon' (LD) | CWGr |
| 'Engadin' (MD) | CWGr |
| 'Engelhardt's Matador' (MD) | CBgR EBee ECtt LAst LSou WCot WGwG WHrl |
| 'Enid Adams' (SD) | CWGr |
| 'Epping Forest' (GD) | CWGr |
| 'Eric's Choice' (SD) | CWGr |
| 'Ernie Pitt' (SD) | CWGr |
| 'Esau' (GD) | CWGr |
| 'Eunice Arrigo' (LS-c) | CWGr |
| 'Eveline' (SD) | CBgR CWGr EBrs EPfP LRHS MBri |
| 'Evelyn Foster' (MD) | CWGr MSHN |
| 'Evelyn Rumbold' (GD) | CWGr |
| 'Evening Lady' (MinD) | CWGr |
| ***excelsa*** (B) | CHll |
| - B&SWJ 10233 | WCru |
| 'Excentrique' (Misc) | CWGr |
| 'Exotic Dwarf' (Sin/Lil) | CFir CWGr EBee ECtt LSou NGdn NHal WCot |
| 'Explosion' (SS-c) | CWGr |
| 'Extase' (MD) | CWGr LRHS |
| 'Eye Candy' | LRHS |
| 'Fabula' (Col) | CWGr |
| 'Fairfield Frost' (Col) | NHal |
| 'Fairway Pilot' (GD) | CWGr |
| 'Fairway Spur' (GD) | NHal |
| 'Fairy Queen' (MinC) | CWGr |
| 'Falcon's Future' (MS-c) | CWGr |
| 'Fascination' (SWL/DwB) 🏆H3 | CBgR CHar CHrt COlW CSam EBee EBrs ECtt EWll LPio LSou MAJR MCot MWea NBPN NGdn NPri SMrm WHoo |
| I 'Fascination' (Misc) | CSec CWGr MSHN |
| 'Fascination Aus' (Col) | CWGr |
| 'Fashion Monger' (Col) | CWGr EBee ECtt EHrv NGdn NHal SMrm WCot |
| 'Fata Morgana' (Anem) | CWGr |
| 'Federwolke' (LD) | CWGr |
| 'Fermain' (MinD) | CWGr MSHN |
| 'Fern Irene' (MWL) | CWGr MSHN |
| 'Ferncliffe Fuego' (MC) | CWGr |
| 'Ferncliffe Illusion' (LD) | CWGr |
| 'Fernhill Champion' (MD) | CWGr |
| * 'Fernhill Suprise' (SD) | CWGr |
| 'Festivo' (Col) | CWGr LRHS |
| 'Feu Céleste' (Col) | CWGr |
| 'Fidalgo Blacky' (MinD) | CWGr |
| 'Fidalgo Bounce' (SD) | CWGr |
| 'Fidalgo Climax' (LS-c/Fim) | CWGr |
| 'Fidalgo Magic' (MD) | CWGr |
| 'Fidalgo Snowman' (GS-c) | CWGr |
| 'Fidalgo Splash' (MD) | CWGr |
| 'Fidalgo Supreme' (MD) | CWGr |
| 'Fiesta Dance' (SC) | CWGr |
| 'Figurine' (SWL) 🏆H3 | CWGr MSHN |
| 'Fille du Diable' (LS-c) | CWGr |
| 'Finchcocks' (SWL) 🏆H3 | CWGr |
| 'Fiona Stewart' (SBa) | CWGr |
| 'Fire Magic' (SS-c) | CWGr |
| 'Fire Mountain' (MinD) | MSHN NHal WCot |
| 'Firebird' (MS-c) | see *D.* 'Vuurvogel' |
| 'Firebird' (Sin) | CWGr LRHS |
| 'First Lady' (MD) | CWGr |
| 'Fleur' (MinD) | SPer |
| 'Fleur Mountjoy' (Col) | CWGr |
| 'Flevohof' (MS-c) | CWGr |
| 'Floorinoor' (Anem) | CWGr SPer |
| 'Flutterby' (SWL) | CWGr |
| 'Foreman's Jubilee' (GS-c) | CWGr |
| 'Formby Supreme' (MD) | CWGr |
| 'Forncett Furnace' (B) | GCal |
| 'Forrestal' (MS-c) | CWGr |
| 'Frank Holmes' (Pom) | CWGr MSHN |
| 'Frank Hornsey' (SD) | CWGr |
| 'Frank Lovell' (GS-c) | CWGr |
| 'Franz Kafka' (Pom) | CWGr ECtt |
| 'Frau Louise Mayer' (SS-c) | CWGr |
| 'Fred Wallace' (SC) | CWGr |
| 'Freelancer' (LC) | CWGr |
| 'Freestyle' (SC) | CWGr |
| § 'Freya's Paso Doble' (Anem) 🏆H3 | CWGr MSHN |
| 'Friendship' (LC) | CWGr |
| 'Frigoulet' | CWGr |
| 'Fringed Star' (MS-c) | LRHS |
| * 'Friquolet' | ERCP |
| 'Frits' (MinBa) | CWGr |
| 'Frivolous Glow'[PBR] (Misc) | CBgR |
| 'Funfair' (MD) | CWGr |
| 'Funny Face' (Misc) | CWGr |
| 'Fusion' (MD) 🏆H3 | CWGr |
| 'Fuzzy Wuzzy' (MD) | CSut CWGr |
| 'G.F. Hemerik' (Sin) | CWGr |
| 'Gala Parade' (SD) | CWGr |
| 'Gale Lane' (Pom) | CWGr |
| 'Gallery Art Deco'[PBR] (SD) 🏆H3 | CWGr NHal SUsu |
| 'Gallery Art Fair'[PBR] (MinD) 🏆H3 | NHal |
| 'Gallery Art Nouveau'[PBR] (MinD) 🏆H3 | CWGr ECtt MBri NHal SUsu WCot WCra |

| | |
|---|---|
| 'Gallery Cézanne'[PBR] (MinD) | CWGr |
| 'Gallery Leonardo'[PBR] (SD) ♀H3 | CWGr |
| 'Gallery Matisse' (SD) | SPer |
| 'Gallery Monet'[PBR] (SD) ♀H3 | CWGr |
| 'Gallery Rembrandt'[PBR] (MinD) ♀H3 | CWGr |
| 'Gallery Renoir'[PBR] (SD) ♀H3 | CWGr NHal |
| 'Gallery Singer'[PBR] (MinD) ♀H3 | CWGr |
| 'Gallery Vermeer'[PBR] (MinD) | CWGr |
| 'Gallery Vincent'[PBR] (MinD) ♀H3 | CWGr |
| 'Gamelan' (DwAnem) | CWGr |
| 'Garden Festival' (SWL) | CWGr |
| 'Garden Party' (MC/DwB) ♀H3 | CWGr |
| 'Garden Princess' (SC/DwB) | CWGr |
| 'Garden Wonder' (SD) | ECtt EPfP LRHS |
| 'Gargantuan' (GS-c) | CWGr |
| 'Gateshead Angel' (MD) | CWGr |
| Gateshead Festival | see *D.* 'Peach Melba' (SD) |
| 'Gaudy' (GD) | CWGr |
| 'Gay Mini' (MinD) | CWGr |
| 'Gay Princess' (SWL) | CWGr |
| 'Gay Triumph' (GS-c) | CWGr |
| 'Geerlings' Cupido' (SWL) | CWGr |
| 'Geerlings' Indian Summer' (MS-c) ♀H3 | NHal |
| 'Geerlings' Jewel' (MD) | CWGr |
| 'Geerlings' Moonlight' (MD) | CWGr |
| 'Geerlings' Sorbet' (MS-c) | CWGr |
| 'Geerlings' Star' (SS-c) | CWGr |
| 'Geerlings' Yellow' (SS-c) | CWGr |
| 'Gelber Vulkan' (LS-c) | CWGr |
| 'Gemma Darling' (GD) | CWGr MSHN |
| 'Gemma's Place' (Pom) | CWGr |
| 'Genève' (MD) | CWGr |
| 'Gentle Giant' (GD) | CWGr |
| 'Geoffrey Kent' (MinD) ♀H3 | MSHN NHal |
| 'Gerald Grace' (LS-c) | CWGr |
| 'Gerlos' (MD) | CWGr |
| 'Gerrie Hoek' (SWL) | CSam CWGr LBut LRHS MSHN |
| 'Gill's Pastelle' (MS-c) | CWGr |
| 'Gillwood Violet' (Pom) **new** | MSHN |
| 'Gilt Edge' (MD) | CWGr |
| 'Gilwood Pip' (SD) | CWGr |
| 'Gilwood Terry G' (SC) | CWGr |
| 'Gina Lombaert' (MS-c) | CWGr LRHS SEND |
| 'Ginger Willo' (Pom) | CWGr |
| 'Giraffe' (Misc) | CWGr MSHN |
| 'Giselle' | SPer |
| 'Gitts Perfection' (GD) | CWGr |
| 'Gitty' (SBa) | CWGr |
| 'Glad Huston' (DwSS-c) | CWGr |
| 'Glenafton' (Pom) | CWGr |
| 'Glenbank Honeycomb' (Pom) | CWGr MSHN |
| 'Glenbank Paleface' (Pom) | CWGr |
| 'Glenbank Twinkle' (MinC) | CWGr |
| 'Glengarry' (SC) | CWGr |
| 'Globular' (MinBa) | CWGr |
| 'Gloria Romaine' (SD) | CWGr |
| 'Glorie van Heemstede' (SWL) ♀H3 | CSam CWGr LBut LPio LRHS MWte NHal SEND WHrl |
| 'Glorie van Noordwijk' (Min S-c) | CWGr |
| 'Glory' (LD) | CWGr |
| 'Glow Orange' (MinBa) | CWGr |
| 'Go American' (GD) | CWGr MSHN NHal |
| 'Gold Ball' (MinBa) | CWGr |
| 'Gold Crown' (LS-c) | CWGr EPfP |
| 'Gold Mine' (SS-c) | CWGr |
| 'Gold Standard' (LD) | CWGr |
| 'Goldean' (GD) | CWGr |
| 'Golden Emblem' (MD) | CWGr ECtt |
| 'Golden Explosion' (MC) | CWGr |
| 'Golden Fizz' (MinBa) | CWGr |
| 'Golden Glitter' (MS-c) | CWGr |
| 'Golden Heart' (MS-c) | CWGr |
| 'Golden Horn' (MS-c) | CWGr |
| 'Golden Impact' (MS-c) | CWGr |
| 'Golden Jubilee' (D) | EPfP SPer |
| 'Golden Leader' (SD) | CWGr |
| 'Golden Scepter' (MinD) | CWGr EPfP |
| 'Golden Symbol' (MS-c) | CWGr |
| 'Golden Turban' (MD) | CWGr |
| 'Golden Willo' (Pom) | CWGr |
| 'Goldilocks' (S-c) | CWGr |
| 'Goldorange' (SS-c) | CWGr |
| 'Good Earth' (MC) | CWGr |
| 'Good Hope' (MinD) | CWGr |
| 'Good Intent' (MinBa) | CWGr |
| 'Goshen Beauty' (SWL) | CWGr |
| 'Goya's Venus' (SS-c) | CWGr |
| 'Grace Nash' (SD) | CWGr |
| 'Grace Rushton' (SWL) | CWGr |
| 'Gracie S' (MinC) | NHal |
| 'Grand Duc' (Col) | CWGr MSHN |
| 'Grand Prix' (GD) | CWGr SWal |
| 'Grenadier' (Misc) | CWGr |
| 'Grenadier' (SWL) ♀H3 | CBgR EBee ECtt LSou SDix SDys SPav WCot |
| 'Grenidor Pastelle' (MS-c) | CWGr MSHN NHal |
| 'Gretchen Heine' (SD) | CWGr |
| 'Grock' (Pom) | CWGr |
| 'Gryson's Yellow Spider' (SC) **new** | MSHN |
| 'Gunyuu' (GD) | CWGr |
| 'Gurtla Twilight' (Pom) | CWGr MSHN NHal |
| 'Gute Laune' (Min S-c) | CWGr |
| 'Gwyneth' (SWL) | CWGr MSHN |
| 'Gypsy Boy' (LD) | CWGr |
| 'Hallmark' (Pom) | CWGr MSHN |
| 'Hallwood Asset' (MinD) | CWGr |
| 'Hallwood Coppernob' (MD) | CWGr |
| 'Hallwood Satin' (MD) | CWGr |
| 'Hallwood Tiptop' (MinD) | CWGr |
| 'Hamari Accord' (LS-c) ♀H3 | CWGr MSHN |
| 'Hamari Bride' (MS-c) ♀H3 | CWGr |
| 'Hamari Girl' (GD) | CWGr NHal |
| 'Hamari Gold' (GD) ♀H3 | CWGr MSHN NHal |
| 'Hamari Katrina' (LS-c) | CWGr LRHS MSHN |
| 'Hamari Rosé' (MinBa) ♀H3 | CWGr MSHN NHal |
| 'Hamari Sunshine' (LD) ♀H3 | CWGr NHal |
| 'Hamilton Amanda' (SD) | CWGr |
| 'Hamilton Lillian' (SD) ♀H3 | CWGr |
| 'Hans Ricken' (SD) | CWGr |
| 'Happy Caroline' (MinD) | CWGr LRHS |
| 'HS First Love' (Sin) **new** | ERCP |
| 'HS Party' (Sin) **new** | ERCP |
| (Happy Single Series) | ERCP NBPN |
| Happy Single Juliet = 'HS Juliet' (Sin) | |
| - Happy Single Kiss = 'HS Kiss' | NOrc |

| | | |
|---|---|---|
| | - Happy Single Party = 'HS Party' **new** | SUsu |
| | 'Haresbrook' (Sin) | EShb LAst MSte NGdn SPav |
| | 'Harvest' (LS-c/Fim) | CWGr |
| | 'Harvest Amanda' (Sin/Lil) ♀H3 | CWGr |
| | 'Harvest Brownie' (Sin/Lil) | CWGr |
| | 'Harvest Dandy' (Sin/Lil) | CWGr |
| § | 'Harvest Imp' (Sin/Lil) | CWGr |
| § | 'Harvest Inflammation' (Sin/Lil) ♀H3 | CWGr |
| § | 'Harvest Samantha' (Sin/Lil) ♀H3 | CWGr NHal |
| § | 'Harvest Tiny Tot' (Misc/Lil) ♀H3 | CWGr |
| | 'Haseley Bridal Wish' (MC) | CWGr |
| | 'Haseley Goldicote' (SD) | CWGr |
| | 'Haseley Miranda' (SD) | CWGr |
| | 'Haseley Triumph' (SD) | CWGr |
| | 'Haseley Yellow Angora' (SD) | CWGr |
| | 'Hayley Jayne' (SC) | CWGr SPer |
| | 'Heather Huston' (MD) | CWGr |
| | 'Heidi' (SSC) | CWGr |
| | 'Helga' (MS-c) | CWGr ECtt |
| | 'Helma Rost' (SS-c) | CWGr |
| | 'Henri Lweii' (SC) | CWGr |
| | 'Henriette' (MC) | CWGr |
| | 'Herbert Smith' (D) | CWGr SEND |
| | 'Heronista' **new** | WCot |
| | 'Hexton Copper' (SBa) | CWGr |
| | 'Hi Ace' (LC) | CWGr |
| | 'Higherfield Champion' (SS-c) | CWGr |
| | 'Highgate Bobby' (SBa) | CWGr |
| | 'Highness' (MinS-c) | CWGr |
| | 'Hilda Clare' (Col) | CWGr |
| | 'Hildepuppe' (Pom) | CWGr |
| | 'Hillcrest Albino' (SS-c) | CWGr |
| | 'Hillcrest Amour' (SD) | CWGr |
| | 'Hillcrest Blaze' (SS-c) | CWGr |
| | 'Hillcrest Bobbin' (SBa) | CWGr |
| | 'Hillcrest Camelot' (GS-c) | CWGr |
| | 'Hillcrest Carmen' (SD) | CWGr |
| | 'Hillcrest Contessa' (MinBa) | CWGr |
| | 'Hillcrest Delight' (MD) | NHal |
| | 'Hillcrest Desire' (SC) ♀H3 | CWGr |
| | 'Hillcrest Divine' (MinD) | MSHN |
| | 'Hillcrest Fiesta' (MS-c) | CWGr |
| | 'Hillcrest Hannah' (MinD) | MSHN NHal |
| | 'Hillcrest Heights' (LS-c) | CWGr MSHN |
| | 'Hillcrest Hillton' (LS-c) | CWGr |
| | 'Hillcrest Kismet' (MD) | MSHN NHal |
| | 'Hillcrest Pearl' (MD) | CWGr |
| | 'Hillcrest Regal' (Col) ♀H3 | CWGr MSHN |
| | 'Hillcrest Royal' (MC) ♀H3 | CWGr NHal SDix |
| | 'Hillcrest Suffusion' (SD) | CWGr MSHN |
| | 'Hillcrest Ultra' (SD) | CWGr |
| | 'Hill's Delight' (MS-c) | CWGr |
| | 'Hindu Star' (MinBa) | CWGr |
| | 'Hit Parade' (MS-c) | CWGr |
| | 'Hockley Maroon' (SD) | CWGr |
| | 'Hockley Nymph' (SWL) | CWGr |
| | 'Holland Festival' (GD) | CWGr |
| | 'Homer T' (LS-c) | CWGr |
| | 'Honest John' (LD) | CWGr |
| | 'Honey' (Anem/DwB) | CWGr LRHS |
| | 'Honka' (Misc) ♀H3 | CBgR CWGr MSHN |
| | 'Hot Chocolate' (MinD) | CWGr EPfP WBrk WCot WHoo |
| | 'Hugh Mather' (MWL) | CWGr MSHN |
| | 'Hulin's Carnival' (MinD) | CWGr |
| | 'Huston Legacy' (GS-c) | CWGr |
| | 'Hy Clown' (SD) | CWGr |
| | 'Hy Fire' (MinBa) | CWGr |
| | 'Ice Queen' (SWL) | CWGr |
| | 'Ida Gayer' (LD) | CWGr |
| | 'I-lyke-it' (SS-c) | CWGr |
| | 'Imp' | see *D.* 'Harvest Imp' |
| | ***imperialis*** (B) | CDTJ CHEx CHll CWGr EBee EMon EShb EUJe EWes LRHS MJnS SBig WBVN WDyG WHal |
| | - B&SWJ 8997 | WCru |
| | - 'Alba' (B) | EMon |
| I | - 'Tasmania' (B) | GCal |
| | aff. ***imperialis*** | MSHN |
| | - B&SWJ 10238 | WCru |
| | 'Impression Famosa' | MBri |
| | 'Impression Fantastico' | MBri |
| | 'Impression Festivo' | MBri |
| | 'Impression Flamenco' (Col/DwB) | CWGr LRHS |
| | 'Impression Fortuna' (Col/DwB) | CWGr |
| | 'Inca Concord' (MD) | CWGr |
| | 'Inca Dambuster' (GS-c) | CWGr MSHN NHal |
| | 'Inca Matchless' (MD) | CWGr |
| | 'Inca Metropolitan' (LD) | CWGr |
| | 'Inca Panorama' (MD) | CWGr |
| | 'Inca Royale' (LD) | CWGr |
| | 'Inca Spectrum' (GS-c) | CWGr |
| | 'Inca Streamline' (S-c) | CWGr |
| | 'Inca Vanguard' (GD) | CWGr |
| | 'Inca Vulcan' (GS-c) | CWGr |
| | 'Indian Summer' (SC) | CWGr |
| | 'Inflammation' | see *D.* 'Harvest Inflammation' |
| | 'Inglebrook Jill' (Col) | CWGr |
| | 'Inland Dynasty' (GS-c) | CWGr |
| | 'Inn's Gerrie Hoek' (MD) | CWGr |
| | 'Inskip' (SC) | CWGr |
| | 'Invader' (SC) | CWGr |
| | 'Iola' (LD) | CWGr |
| | 'Irene Ellen' (SD) | CWGr |
| | 'Irene van der Zwet' (Sin) | CWGr MSHN |
| | 'Iris' (Pom) | CWGr MSHN |
| | 'Irisel' (MS-c) | CWGr |
| | 'Islander' (LD) | CWGr |
| | 'Ivanetti' (MinBa) | CWGr NHal |
| | 'Ivor's Rhonda' (Pom) | MSHN |
| | 'Jack Hood' (SD) | CWGr |
| | 'Jack O'Lantern' (Col) | CWGr |
| | 'Jackie Magson' (SS-c) | CWGr |
| | 'Jack's Pastelle' (MS-c) **new** | MSHN |
| | 'Jacqueline Tivey' (SD) | CWGr |
| | 'Jake's Coronet' (MinD) | CWGr |
| | 'Jaldec Jerry' (GS-c) | CWGr |
| | 'Jaldec Joker' (SC) | CWGr |
| | 'Jaldec Jolly' (SC) | CWGr |
| | 'Jamaica' (MinWL) | CWGr |
| | 'Jamie' (SS-c) | CWGr |
| | 'Jan Carden' | CWGr |
| I | 'Jan van Schaffelaar' (Pom) | CWGr |
| | 'Janal Amy' (GS-c) | MSHN NHal |
| | 'Jane Cowl' (LD) | CWGr |
| | 'Jane Horton' (Col) | CWGr |
| | 'Janet Beckett' (LC) | CWGr |
| | 'Janet Clarke' (Pom) | CWGr |
| | 'Janet Howell' (Col) | CWGr |
| | 'Janet Jean' (SWL) | CWGr |
| | 'Japanese Waterlily' (SWL) | CWGr |
| | 'Jazzy' (Col) | CWGr |
| | 'Je Maintiendrai' (GD) | CWGr |
| | 'Jean Fairs' (MinWL) ♀H3 | CWGr LBut MSHN |
| | 'Jean Marie' PBR (MD) | CWGr LRHS |
| | 'Jean Melville' (MinD) | CWGr |
| | 'Jeanette Carter' (MinD) ♀H3 | CWGr |

| | | |
|---|---|---|
| | 'Jeanne d'Arc' (GC) | CSut CWGr EPfP |
| | 'Jeannie Leroux' (SS-c/Fim) | CWGr |
| | 'Jean's Carol' (Pom) | CWGr |
| | 'Jennie' (MS-c/Fim) | CWGr |
| | 'Jenny Smith' (Col) | CWGr |
| | 'Jersey Beauty' (MD) | CBgR CWGr |
| | 'Jescot Buttercup' (SD) | CWGr |
| | 'Jescot India' (MinD) | CWGr |
| | 'Jescot Jess' (MinD) | CWGr LBut |
| | 'Jescot Jim' (SD) | CWGr |
| | 'Jescot Julie' (O) | CWGr MSHN SMeo |
| | 'Jescot Lingold' (MinD) | CWGr |
| | 'Jescot Nubia' (SS-c) | CWGr |
| | 'Jescot Redun' (MinD) | CWGr |
| | 'Jessica' (S-c) | CWGr |
| | 'Jessie G' (SBa) | CWGr MSHN |
| | 'Jessie Ross' (MinD/DwB) | CWGr |
| | 'Jet' (SS-c) | CWGr |
| | 'Jill Day' (SC) | CWGr LBut |
| | 'Jill Doc' (MD) | CWGr |
| | 'Jill's Blush' (MS-c) | CWGr |
| | 'Jill's Delight' (MD) | CWGr |
| | 'Jim Branigan' (LS-c) | CWGr NHal |
| | 'Jive' (Anem) | CWGr |
| | 'Jo Anne' (MS-c) | CWGr |
| | 'Joan Beecham' (SWL) | CWGr MSHN |
| | 'Jocondo' (GD) | CWGr NHal |
| | 'Johann' (Pom) | CWGr NHal |
| | 'Johanna Preinstorfer' (LC) | CWGr |
| | 'John Prior' (SD) | CWGr |
| | 'John Street' (SWL) ♀$^{H3}$ | CWGr MSHN |
| | 'John's Champion' (MD) | CWGr |
| | 'Joicie' (MinD) | NHal |
| | 'Jomanda' (MinBa) ♀$^{H3}$ | CWGr LBut MSHN NHal |
| | 'Jorja' (MS-c) | CWGr |
| | 'Jo's Choice' (MinD) | CWGr LBut |
| | 'Joy Donaldson' (MC) | CWGr |
| | 'Joyce Green' (GS-c) | CWGr |
| | 'Joyce Margaret Cunliffe' (SD) | CWGr |
| | 'Juanita' (MS-c) | CWGr |
| | 'Judy Tregidden' (MWL) | CSam |
| | 'Jules Dyson' (Misc) | SDys |
| | 'Julie One' (Misc/O) | CWGr |
| | 'Julio' (MinBa) | CWGr MSHN |
| | 'Jura' (SS-c) | CWGr EPfP |
| | 'Just Jill' (MinD) | CWGr |
| | 'Justin' (Fim) **new** | MSHN |
| | 'Juul's Allstar' (Misc) ♀$^{H3}$ | CWGr |
| | 'Kaftan' (MD) | CWGr |
| | 'Kaiser Wilhelm' (SBa) | CWGr |
| | 'Kaiserwalzer' (Col) | CWGr |
| | 'Karenglen' (MinD) ♀$^{H3}$ | CWGr LBut MSHN NHal |
| | 'Kari Blue' (SWL) | CWGr |
| | 'Kari Quill' (SC) | CWGr |
| | 'Karma Amanda' (SD) | CWGr LRHS |
| | 'Karma Corona'$^{PBR}$ (SC) | CWGr |
| | 'Karma Lagoon'$^{PBR}$ | CWGr LRHS |
| | 'Karma Maarten Zwaan'$^{PBR}$ (SWL) | CWGr |
| | 'Karma Sangria'$^{PBR}$ | CWGr |
| | 'Karma Thalia'$^{PBR}$ | CWGr |
| | 'Karma Yin Yang' (SD) | CWGr |
| | 'Karras 150' (SS-c) | CWGr MSHN |
| | 'Kasasagi' (Pom) | CWGr |
| | 'Kate Mountjoy' (Col) | CWGr |
| | 'Kathleen's Alliance' (SC) ♀$^{H3}$ | NHal |
| | 'Kathryn's Cupid' (MinBa) ♀$^{H3}$ | CWGr MSHN SWal |
| | 'Kathy' (SC) | CWGr |
| | 'Katie Dahl' (MinD) | CWGr NHal |
| | 'Katisha' (MinD) | CWGr |
| | 'Kay Helen' (Pom) | CWGr |
| | 'Kayleigh Spiller' (Col) | CWGr |
| | 'Keith's Choice' (MD) | CWGr NHal |
| | 'Kelsea Carla' (SS-c) ♀$^{H3}$ | CWGr NHal |
| | 'Keltie Peach' (MD) | MSHN |
| | 'Kelvin Floodlight' (GD) | CWGr EPfP |
| | 'Kenn Emerland' (MS-c) | CSut EPfP |
| | 'Kenora Canada' (MS-c) | CWGr |
| | 'Kenora Challenger' (LS-c) | CWGr MSHN NHal |
| | 'Kenora Christmas' (SBa) | CWGr |
| | 'Kenora Clyde' (GS-c) | CWGr |
| | 'Kenora Fireball' (MinBa) | MSHN |
| | 'Kenora Jubilee' (LS-c) | MSHN NHal |
| | 'Kenora Lisa' (MD) | CWGr MSHN |
| | 'Kenora Macop-B' (MC/Fim) | CSut EBee |
| | 'Kenora Ontario' (LS-c) | CWGr |
| | 'Kenora Peace' (MinBa) | CWGr |
| | 'Kenora Sunburst' (LS-c) | CWGr |
| | 'Kenora Sunset' (MS-c) ♀$^{H3}$ | CWGr LBut MSHN NHal |
| | 'Kenora Superb' (LS-c) | CWGr MSHN NHal |
| | 'Kenora Valentine' (LD) ♀$^{H3}$ | CWGr MSHN NHal |
| | 'Ken's Choice' (SBa) | MSHN NHal |
| | 'Ken's Coral' (SWL) | CWGr |
| | 'Ken's Flame' (SWL) | CWGr |
| | 'Kidd's Climax' (GD) ♀$^{H3}$ | CWGr MSHN |
| | 'Kilmorie' (SS-c) | CWGr MSHN NHal |
| | 'Kim Willo' (Pom) | CWGr |
| | 'Kimberley B' (MinD) | CWGr |
| | 'Kingston' (MinD) | CWGr |
| | 'Kismet' (SBa) | CWGr |
| | 'Kiss' (MinD) | CWGr NBPN |
| | 'Kit Kat' (LC) | CWGr |
| | 'Kiwi Brother' (SS-c) | CWGr |
| | 'Kiwi Cousin' (SC) | CWGr |
| | 'Kiwi Gloria' (SC) | MSHN NHal |
| | 'Klankstad Kerkrade' (SC) | CWGr MSHN |
| | 'Klondike' (MS-c) | CWGr |
| I | 'Knockout' (Sin) **new** | CBcs CPar NBPN |
| * | 'Kogano Fubuki' (MD) | CWGr |
| | 'Korgill Meadow' (MD) | CWGr |
| | 'Kotare Jackpot' (SS-c) | CWGr |
| | 'Kung Fu' (SD) | CWGr |
| I | 'Kyoto' (SWL) | CWGr |
| | 'L.A.T.E.' (MinBa) | CWGr MSHN NHal |
| | 'La Cierva' (Col) | CWGr |
| | 'La Corbière' (MinBa) | CWGr |
| | 'La Gioconda' (Col) | CWGr |
| | 'Lady Day' (S-c) | CWGr |
| | 'Lady Jane' (SWL) | CWGr |
| | 'Lady Kerkrade' (SC) | CWGr MSHN |
| | 'Lady Linda' (SD) | CWGr LBut NHal |
| | 'Lady Orpah' (SD) | CWGr |
| | 'Lady Sunshine' (SS-c) | CWGr |
| | 'L'Ancresse' (MinBa) | CWGr MSHN NHal |
| | 'Larkford' (SD) | CWGr |
| | 'Last Dance' (MD) | CWGr |
| | 'Laura Marie' (MinBa) | CWGr |
| | 'Laura's Choice' (SD) | CWGr |
| | 'Laurence Fisher' (MS-c) | CWGr |
| | 'Lauren's Moonlight' | see *D.* 'Pim's Moonlight' |
| | 'Lavendale' (MinD) | CWGr |
| | 'Lavender Athalie' (SC) | CWGr |
| | 'Lavender Chiffon' (MS-c) | CWGr |
| | 'Lavender Freestyle' (SC) | CWGr |
| | 'Lavender Leycett' (GD) | CWGr |
| | 'Lavender Line' (SC) | CWGr MSHN NHal |
| | 'Lavender Nunton Harvest' (SD) | CWGr MSHN |
| | 'Lavender Perfection' (GD) | CSut CWGr EPfP |
| | 'Lavender Prince' (MD) | CWGr |

| | | |
|---|---|---|
| | 'Lavender Symbol' (MS-c) **new** | MSHN |
| | 'Lavengro' (GD) | CWGr |
| | 'Le Baron' (SD) **new** | ERCP |
| | 'Le Batts Premier' (SD) | CWGr |
| | 'Le Castel' (D) $\mathbb{Y}^{H3}$ | CWGr |
| | 'Le Patineur' (MD) | CWGr |
| | 'Le Vonne Splinter' (GS-c) | CWGr |
| | 'Leander' (GS-c) | CWGr |
| | 'Lecta' (MS-c) | CWGr |
| | 'Lemon' (Anem) | CWGr |
| | 'Lemon Cane' (Misc) | CWGr MSHN |
| | 'Lemon Elegans' (SS-c) $\mathbb{Y}^{H3}$ | CWGr LBut MSHN NHal |
| | 'Lemon Meringue' (SD) | CWGr |
| * | 'Lemon Puff' (Anem) | CWGr |
| | 'Lemon Symbol' (MS-c) | CWGr |
| | 'Lemon Zing' (MinBa) | NHal |
| * | 'Lenny' (MinD) | CWGr |
| | 'Lexington' (Pom) | CWGr |
| | 'Leycett' (GD) | CWGr |
| | 'Libretto' (Col) | CWGr MSHN |
| | 'Life Force' (GD) | CWGr |
| | 'Life Size' (LD) | CWGr |
| | 'Light Music' (MS-c) | CWGr |
| | 'Lilac Athalie' (SC) | CWGr |
| | 'Lilac Marston' (MinD) $\mathbb{Y}^{H3}$ | CWGr MSHN NHal |
| | 'Lilac Shadow' (S-c) | CWGr |
| § | 'Lilac Taratahi' (SC) $\mathbb{Y}^{H3}$ | CSam CWGr |
| | 'Lilac Time' (MD) | CWGr LRHS SPer |
| | 'Lilac Willo' (Pom) | CWGr |
| | 'Lilian Alice' (Col) | NHal |
| | 'Lillianne Ballego' (MinD) | CWGr |
| | 'Linda's Chester' (SC) | CWGr LBut MSHN |
| | 'Linda's Diane' (SD) | CWGr |
| | 'Lisa'[PBR] | CWGr |
| | 'Lismore Canary' (SWL) | CSam |
| | 'Lismore Carol' (Pom) | CWGr MSHN NHal |
| | 'Lismore Moonlight' (Pom) | NHal |
| | 'Lismore Peggy' (Pom) | CWGr MSHN |
| | 'Lismore Robin' (MinD) | NHal |
| | 'Lismore Sunset' (Pom) | CWGr MSHN |
| | 'Lismore Willie' (SWL) $\mathbb{Y}^{H3}$ | CWGr LBut MSHN |
| | 'Little Dorrit' (Sin/Lil) $\mathbb{Y}^{H3}$ | CWGr |
| | 'Little Glenfern' (MinC) | CWGr |
| | 'Little Jack' (MinS-c) | CWGr |
| | 'Little John' (Sin/Lil) | CWGr |
| | 'Little Lamb' (MS-c) | CWGr |
| | 'Little Laura' (MinBa) | CWGr |
| | 'Little Matthew' (Pom) | CWGr |
| | 'Little Reggie' (SS-c) | CWGr |
| | 'Little Robert' (MinD) | CWGr |
| | 'Little Sally' (Pom) | CWGr |
| | 'Little Scottie' (Pom) | CWGr |
| | 'Little Shona' (MinD) | CWGr |
| | 'Little Snowdrop' (Pom) | CWGr MSHN |
| | 'Little Tiger' (MinD) | CWGr MBri MSHN |
| | 'Little Treasure' | CWGr EPfP |
| I | 'Little William' (MinBa) | ECtt |
| | 'Littledown Tango' (DwB) | CWGr |
| | 'Liz' (LS-c) | CWGr |
| | 'Lois Walcher' (MD) | CWGr |
| | 'Lollypop' (SBa) | CWGr |
| | 'Lombada' (Misc) | CWGr |
| | 'Long Island Lil' (SD) | CWGr |
| | 'Longwood Dainty' (DwB) | CWGr |
| | 'Loretta' (SBa) | CWGr |
| | 'Loud Applause' (SC) | CWGr |
| | 'Louis V' (LS-c/Fim) | CWGr |
| | 'Louise Bailey' (MinD) | CWGr |
| | 'Lucky Devil' (MD) | CWGr |
| | 'Lucky Number' (MD) | CWGr |
| | 'Ludwig Helfert' (S-c) | CWGr ERCP LRHS SEND |
| | 'Lupin Dixie' (SC) | CWGr |
| | 'Luther' (GS-c) | CWGr |
| | 'Lyn Mayo' (SD) | CWGr |
| | 'Lyndsey Murray' (MinD) | CWGr |
| | 'Mabel Ann' (GD) | CWGr MSHN NHal |
| | 'Madame de Rosa' (LS-c) | NHal |
| | 'Madame Elisabeth Sawyer' (SS-c) | CWGr |
| | 'Madame J. Snapper' | NBsh |
| | 'Madame Simone Stappers' (WL) | CWGr LPio MMHG |
| | 'Madame Vera' (SD) | CWGr LBut |
| | 'Madelaine Ann' (GD) | CWGr |
| | 'Maelstrom' (SD) | CWGr |
| | 'Mafolie' (GS-c) | CWGr |
| | 'Magenta Magic' (Sin/DwB) | NHal |
| | 'Magic Moment' (MS-c) | CWGr |
| | 'Magnificat' (MinD) | CWGr |
| | 'Maisie' (SD) | CWGr |
| | 'Maisie Mooney' (GD) | CWGr |
| | 'Majestic Athalie' (SC) | CWGr |
| | 'Majestic Kerkrade' (SC) | CWGr |
| | 'Majjas Symbol' (MS-c) | CWGr |
| | 'Malham Honey' (SD) | CWGr |
| | 'Malham Portia' (SWL) | CWGr |
| | 'Maltby Fanfare' (Col) | CWGr |
| | 'Mandy' (MinD) | CWGr |
| | 'Marble Ball' (MinD) | CWGr |
| | 'March Magic' (MinD) | CWGr |
| | 'Margaret Ann' (MinD) | CWGr |
| | 'Margaret Brookes' (LD) | CWGr |
| | 'Margaret Haggo' (SWL) | CSam CWGr NHal |
| | 'Marie' (SD) | CWGr |
| | 'Marie Schnugg' (Misc) $\mathbb{Y}^{H3}$ | CWGr MSHN |
| | 'Mariposa' (Col) | CWGr MSHN |
| | 'Marissa' (SWL) **new** | MSHN |
| | 'Mark Damp' (LS-c) | CWGr |
| | 'Mark Lockwood' (Pom) | CWGr |
| | 'Market Joy' (SS-c) | CWGr |
| | 'Marla Lu' (MC) | CWGr |
| | 'Marlene Joy' (MS-c/Fim) | CWGr MSHN |
| | 'Maroen'[PBR] (Misc) | CWGr |
| | 'Mars' (Col) | CWGr |
| | 'Marshmello Sky' (Col) | CWGr |
| | 'Marta' (GD) | CWGr |
| | 'Martina' (5d) **new** | NHal |
| | 'Martin's Red' (Pom) | CWGr |
| | 'Martin's Yellow' (Pom) | NHal |
| | 'Mary Eveline' (Col) | ECtt NHal |
| | 'Mary Jennie' (MinS-c) | CWGr |
| | 'Mary Layton' (Col) | CWGr |
| | 'Mary Lunns' (Pom) | CWGr |
| | 'Mary Magson' (SS-c) | CWGr |
| | 'Mary O' (SS-c) | NHal |
| | 'Mary Partridge' (SWL) | CWGr |
| | 'Mary Pitt' (MinD) | CWGr |
| | 'Mary Richards' (SD) | CWGr |
| | 'Mary's Jomanda' (SBa) $\mathbb{Y}^{H3}$ | CWGr MSHN NHal |
| | 'Master David' (MinBa) | CWGr |
| | 'Master Michael' (Pom) | CWGr |
| | 'Match' (SS-c) | CWGr MSHN |
| | 'Matilda Huston' (SS-c) | CWGr NHal |
| | 'Matt Armour' (Sin) | CWGr |
| | 'Maureen Hardwick' (GD) | CWGr |
| | 'Maureen Kitchener' (SWL) | CWGr |
| | 'Maxine Bailey' (SD) | CWGr |
| | 'Maya' (SD) | CWGr |
| | 'Megan Dean' (MInBa) | NHal |
| | 'Meiro' (SD) | CWGr |
| | 'Melanie Jane' (MS-c) | CWGr |
| | 'Melody Dixie'[PBR] (MinD) | CWGr |
| | 'Melody Dora'[PBR] (SD) | CWGr |
| | 'Melody Gipsy'[PBR] (SS-c) | CWGr |

| | |
|---|---|
| 'Melody Latin'[PBR] | CWGr |
| 'Melody Lisa' | CWGr |
| 'Melody Swing'[PBR] | CWGr |
| 'Melton' (MinD) | CWGr |
| ***merckii*** (B) | CBgR CFir CGHE CMdw CSpe CWGr EBee EGoo EWes GMac LFur LPio LRHS MCot MNrw MSHN MSte SAga SMad SUsu WDyG WPGP WSHC |
| - F&M 222 | WPGP |
| - ***alba*** (B) | CSpe LPio MSte SUsu WCru |
| - compact (B) | WPGP |
| 'Meredith's Marion Smith' (SD) | CWGr |
| 'Mermaid of Zennor' (Sin) | CFir CWGr EBee MCot |
| 'Merriwell Topic' (MD) | CWGr |
| 'Mi Wong' (Pom) | CWGr MSHN |
| 'Miami' (SD) | CWGr |
| 'Michael J' (MinD) | CWGr |
| 'Michigan' (MinD) | CWGr |
| 'Mick' (SC) | CWGr |
| 'Mick's Peppermint' (MS-c) | CWGr |
| 'Midas' (SS-c) | CWGr |
| 'Midnight' (Pom) | CWGr |
| 'Mies' (Sin) | CWGr |
| 'Mignon Roxy' (Sin/DwB) | NBPN |
| 'Mignon Silver' (DwSin) | CWGr |
| 'Minder' (GD) | CWGr |
| 'Mingus Alex' (MS-c/Fim) | CWGr |
| 'Mingus Gregory' (LS-c) | CWGr |
| 'Mingus Kyle D' (SD) | CWGr |
| 'Mingus Nichole' (LD) | CWGr |
| 'Mingus Tracy Lynn' (SS-c) | CWGr |
| 'Mingus Whitney' (GS-c) | CWGr |
| 'Mini' (Sin/Lil) | CWGr |
| 'Mini Red' (MinS-c) | CWGr |
| 'Minley Carol' (Pom) ♀H3 | CWGr MSHN NHal |
| 'Minley Linda' (Pom) | CWGr MSHN |
| 'Miramar' (SD) | CWGr |
| 'Mish-Mash' (Fim/MS-c) **new** | MSHN |
| 'Miss Blanc' (SD) | CWGr |
| 'Miss Ellen' (Misc) ♀H3 | CWGr |
| 'Miss Rose Fletcher' (SS-c) | CWGr |
| 'Miss Swiss' (SD) | CWGr |
| 'Misterton' (MD) | CWGr |
| 'Mistill Beauty' (SC) | CWGr MSHN |
| 'Mistill Delight' (MinD) | CWGr |
| 'Mistral' (MS-c/Fim) | CWGr ECtt |
| 'Molly Trotter' (Sin) | CHar |
| 'Mom's Special' (LD) | CSut CWGr |
| I 'Mon Trésor' (Min SC) | CWGr |
| 'Monk Marc' (SC) | CWGr |
| 'Monkstown Diane' (SC) | CWGr |
| 'Monrovia' (MinBa) | CWGr |
| 'Moonfire' (Misc/DwB) ♀H3 | Widely available |
| 'Moonglow' (LS-c) | CWGr ERCP |
| 'Moor Place' (Pom) | MSHN NHal |
| 'Moray Susan' (SWL) | CWGr MSHN |
| 'Moret' (SS-c) | CWGr |
| 'Morley Lady' (SD) | CWGr |
| 'Morley Lass' (SS-c) | CWGr |
| 'Morning Dew' (SC) | CWGr MSHN |
| 'Motto' (LD) | CWGr |
| 'Mount Noddy' (Sin) | CWGr |
| 'Mrs A. Woods' (MD) | CWGr |
| 'Mrs Black' (Pom) | CWGr |
| 'Mrs Clement Andries' (MS-c) | CWGr |
| 'Mrs George Le Boutillier' (LD) | CWGr |
| 'Mrs H. Brown' (Col) | CWGr |
| 'Mrs McDonald Quill' (LD) | CWGr |
| 'Mrs Silverston' (SD) | CWGr |
| 'Mummy's Favourite' (SD) | CWGr |
| 'München' (MinD) | CWGr NGdn |
| 'Murdoch' | CBgR CHFP EBee ECtt EPfP SDys SPav WCot WGwG WHrl |
| 'Muriel Gladwell' (SS-c) | CWGr |
| 'Murillo' | CWGr MBri WCot |
| 'Murray May' (LD) | CWGr |
| 'Musette' (MinD) | CWGr ECtt |
| 'My Beverley' (MS-c/Fim) | CWGr NHal |
| 'My Joy' (Pom) | CWGr |
| 'My Love' (SS-c) | CSut CWGr EPfP LAst LRHS MWea SEND SPer |
| 'My Valentine' (SD) | CWGr |
| 'Mystery Day' (MD) | CBgR CWGr ECtt EPfP MBri |
| 'Nagano' (MinD) | CWGr |
| 'Nancy H' (MinBa) | CWGr |
| 'Nankyoku' (GD) | CWGr |
| 'Nargold' (MS-c/Fim) | CWGr MSHN |
| 'Natal' (MinBa) | CAby ECtt EPfP SPer |
| 'National Vulcan' (MinD) | CWGr |
| 'Nationwide' (SD) | CWGr |
| 'Neal Gillson' (MD) | CWGr |
| ***neglecta*** NJM 05.023 **new** | WPGP |
| 'Nellie Birch' (MinBa) | CWGr |
| 'Nellie Geerlings' (Sin) | CWGr |
| 'Nenekazi' (MS-c/Fim) | CWGr MSHN |
| 'Nepos' (SWL) | CWGr LBut MSHN |
| 'Nescio' (Pom) | CWGr EPfP |
| 'Nessit Inferno' (MinD) **new** | MSHN |
| 'Nessit Pink' (MinWL) **new** | MSHN |
| 'Nettie' (MinBa) | CWGr |
| 'New Baby' (MinBa) | CWGr LRHS |
| 'New Dimension' (SS-c) | CWGr EPfP SPer |
| 'New Look' (LS-c) | CWGr |
| 'Newby' (MinD) | CWGr |
| 'Newchurch' (MinD) | CWGr |
| 'Newsham Wonder' (SD) | CWGr |
| 'Nichola Higgo' (MC/Fim) | CWGr |
| 'Nicola' (SS-c) | CWGr |
| 'Nicolette' (MWL) | CWGr |
| 'Night Editor' (GD) | CWGr |
| 'Night Life' (SC) | CWGr |
| I 'Night Queen' (Pom) | EPfP |
| 'Nijinsky' (SBa) | CWGr |
| 'Nina Chester' (SD) | CWGr MSHN |
| 'Nippon' (Sin) | CBgR EBee MWea |
| 'Nonette' (SWL) | CBgR CHFP CWGr EBee ECtt LAst WCot WGwG |
| 'Norbeck Dusky' (SS-c) | CWGr |
| 'Noreen' (Pom) | CWGr NHal |
| 'Norman Lockwood' (Pom) | CWGr |
| 'North Sea' (MD) | CWGr |
| 'Northland Primrose' (SC) | CWGr |
| 'Northwest Cosmos' (Sin) | CWGr |
| * 'Nuit d'Eté' (MS-c) | CWGr EBee ERCP LPio LRHS MWea SEND |
| Nunton form (SD) | CWGr |
| 'Nunton Harvest' (SD) | CWGr |
| 'Nutley Sunrise' (MC) | CWGr |
| 'Nymphenburg' (SD) | CWGr |
| 'Oakwood Diamond' (SBa) | CWGr LBut |
| 'Oakwood Goldcrest' (SS-c) | CWGr |
| 'Old Boy' (SBa) | CWGr |
| 'Old Gold' (SD) | CWGr |
| 'Omo' (Sin/Lil) ♀H3 | CWGr MSHN |
| 'Onesta' (SD) | CSam CWGr |
| 'Only Love' (MS-c) | CWGr |
| 'Onslow Michelle' (SD) | CWGr |
| 'Onslow Renown' (LS-c) | CWGr |
| 'Oosterbeek Remembered' (Misc) | CWGr |
| 'Opal' (SBa) | CWGr |
| 'Optic Illusion' (SD) | CWGr |
| 'Opus' (SD) | CWGr |

| | | |
|---|---|---|
| | 'Orange Berger's Record' (MS-c) | CWGr |
| | 'Orange Cushion' (MinD) | CWGr |
| | 'Orange Fire' (MS-c) | CWGr |
| | 'Orange Jewel' (SD) | CWGr |
| | 'Orange Keith's Choice' (MD) | CWGr |
| | 'Orange Mullett' (MinD/DwB) | CWGr |
| | 'Orange Nugget' (MinBa) | CWGr LRHS |
| I | 'Orange Queen' (MC) | CWGr |
| | 'Orange Sun' (LD) | CWGr |
| | 'Oranjestad' (SWL) | CWGr |
| | 'Orchid Lace' (MC) | CWGr |
| | 'Orel' (Col) | CWGr |
| | 'Oreti Classic' (MD) | NHal |
| | 'Oreti Duke' (Pom) | MSHN |
| | 'Oreti Jewel' (MinS-c) ♀H3 | CWGr |
| | 'Oreti Star' (MinC) **new** | NHal |
| | 'Orfeo' (MC) | CWGr ECtt ERCP SWal |
| I | 'Orion' (MD) | CWGr |
| | 'Ornamental Rays' (SC) | CWGr |
| | 'Osaka' (SD) | CWGr |
| | 'Oterilla' | CWGr |
| | 'Othello' (MS-c) | CWGr |
| | 'Pacific Argyle' (SD) | NHal |
| | 'Paint Box' (MS-c) | CWGr |
| | 'Palm Springs' (SD) **new** | EPfP |
| | 'Palomino' (MinD) | CWGr |
| | 'Pam Houdin' | CWGr |
| | 'Pam Howden' (SWL) **new** | MSHN NHal |
| | 'Pamela' (SD) | CWGr |
| | 'Papageno' | CWGr |
| | 'Pari Taha Sunrise' (MS-c) | CWGr |
| | 'Park Princess' (SC/DwB) | CSut CWGr LRHS NGdn |
| | 'Paroa Gillian' (SC) | CWGr |
| | 'Party' | NBPN |
| | 'Party Girl' (MS-c/Fim) | NHal |
| | 'Paso Doble' misapplied (Anem) | see *D.* 'Freya's Paso Doble' |
| | 'Passion' (MinD) | CWGr |
| | 'Pat Knight' (Col) | CWGr |
| | 'Pat Mark' (LS-c) | CWGr |
| | 'Pat 'n' Dee' (SD) | CWGr |
| | 'Pat Seed' (MD) | CWGr |
| | 'Patricia' (Col) | NHal |
| | 'Paul Chester' (SC) | CWGr MSHN |
| | 'Paul Critchley' (SC) | CWGr |
| | 'Paul Magson' (SS-c) **new** | NHal |
| | 'Paul Smith' (SBa) | CWGr |
| | 'Peace Pact' (SWL) | CWGr |
| | 'Peach Athalie' (SC) | CWGr |
| | 'Peach Cupid' (MinBa) ♀H3 | CWGr LBut MSHN |
| § | 'Peach Melba' (SD) | MSHN |
| | 'Peaches and Cream'PBR (MinD) | CWGr |
| | 'Peachette' (Misc/Lil) ♀H3 | CWGr |
| | 'Pearl Hornsey' (SD) | CWGr |
| | 'Pearl of Heemstede' (SD) ♀H3 | CWGr NHal |
| | 'Pearl Sharowean' (MS-c) | CWGr |
| | 'Pearson's Benn' (SS-c) | CWGr MSHN |
| | 'Pearson's Mellanie' (SC) | CWGr |
| | 'Pearson's Patrick' (S-c) | CWGr |
| | 'Pembroke Pattie' (Pom) | CWGr |
| | 'Pennsclout' (GD) | CWGr |
| | 'Pennsgift' (GD) | CWGr |
| | 'Pensford Marion' (Pom) | CWGr |
| | 'Perfectos' (MC) | CWGr |
| | 'Periton' (MinBa) | CWGr |
| | 'Peter' (MinD) | CWGr ECtt |
| I | 'Peter' (LD) | LRHS |
| I | 'Peter' (SS-c) | EPfP |
| | 'Peter Nelson' (SBa) | CWGr |
| | 'Petit Bôt' (SS-c) | CWGr |
| | 'Petit Byoux' (DwCol) | CWGr |
| | 'Philis Farmer' (SWL) | CWGr |
| | 'Phill's Pink' (SD) ♀H3 | CWGr |
| I | 'Phoenix' (MD) | CWGr |
| | 'Pianella' (SS-c) | CWGr |
| § | 'Pim's Moonlight' (MS-c) | CWGr MSHN NHal |
| | 'Pineholt Princess' (LD) | CWGr |
| | 'Pinelands' Morgenster' (MS-c/Fim) | CWGr |
| | 'Pinelands Pam' (MS-c) | CWGr |
| | 'Pinelands Pixie' (MinC/Fim) **new** | NHal |
| | 'Pink Attraction' (MinD) | CWGr |
| | 'Pink Breckland Joy' (MD) | CWGr |
| | 'Pink Carol' (Pom) | CWGr |
| | 'Pink Giraffe' (O) ♀H3 | CWGr EBla ERCP MSHN |
| | 'Pink Honeymoon Dress' (SD) | CWGr |
| | 'Pink Jean Fairs' (MinWL) **new** | MSHN |
| | 'Pink Jewel' (MinD) | CWGr |
| | 'Pink Jupiter' (GS-c) | CWGr NHal |
| | 'Pink Katisha' (MinD) | CWGr |
| | 'Pink Kerkrade' (SC) | CWGr MSHN |
| | 'Pink Leycett' (GD) | CWGr |
| | 'Pink Loveliness' (SWL) | CWGr |
| | 'Pink Newby' (MinD) | CWGr |
| | 'Pink Pastelle' (MS-c) ♀H3 | CWGr NHal |
| | 'Pink Preference' (SS-c) | CWGr |
| | 'Pink Robin Hood' (SBa) | CWGr |
| | 'Pink Sylvia' (MinD) | CWGr |
| | 'Pink Worton Ann' (MinD) | CWGr |
| | ***pinnata*** B&SWJ 10240 | WCru |
| | 'Piperoo' (MC) | CWGr |
| | 'Piper's Pink' (SS-c/DwB) | CWGr MSHN |
| | 'Playa Blanca' | CWGr LRHS |
| | 'Playboy' (GD) | CWGr |
| | 'Plum Surprise' (Pom) | CWGr |
| | 'Poème' | CSpe SPer |
| | 'Polar Sight' (GC) | CWGr |
| | 'Polly Bergen' (MD) | CWGr |
| | 'Polly Peachum' (SD) | CWGr |
| | 'Polventon Supreme' (SBa) | CWGr MSHN |
| | 'Pontiac' (SC) | CWGr |
| | 'Pooh' (Col) | CWGr MSHN NHal |
| | 'Pop Willo' (Pom) | CWGr MSHN |
| I | 'Poppet' (Pom) | CWGr |
| | 'Popular Guest' (MS-c/Fim) | CWGr |
| | 'Porcelain' (SWL) ♀H3 | LBut |
| | 'Pot Black' (MinBa) | CWGr |
| | 'Potgieter' (MinBa) | CWGr |
| | 'Pot-Pourri' (MinD) | CWGr |
| | 'Prefect' (MS-c) | CWGr |
| | 'Prefere' (Sin) | CWGr LRHS |
| | 'Preference' (SS-c) | CWGr SWal |
| | 'Preston Park' (Sin/DwB) ♀H3 | CSam CWGr NHal |
| | 'Pretty in Pink' **new** | CSut |
| | Pride of Berlin | see *D.* 'Stolz von Berlin' |
| | 'Prime Minister' (GD) | CWGr |
| | 'Primeur' (MS-c) | CWGr |
| | 'Primrose Accord' (LS-c) | CWGr |
| | 'Primrose Pastelle' (MS-c) | CWGr NHal |
| | 'Primrose Rustig' (MD) | CWGr |
| | 'Prince Valiant' (SD) | CWGr |
| | 'Princess Beatrix' (LD) | CWGr |
| | 'Princess Marie José' (Sin) | CWGr |
| | 'Pristine' (Pom) | CWGr |
| | 'Procyon' (SD) | CBgR CWGr EPfP LRHS |
| | 'Prom' (Pom) | CWGr |
| | 'Promise' (MS-c/Fim) | CWGr ECtt |

| | | |
|---|---|---|
| | 'Punky' (Pom) | CWGr |
| | 'Purbeck Lydia' (LS-c) | CWGr |
| | 'Purbeck Princess' (MinD) | CWGr |
| I | 'Purity' (SS-c) | CWGr |
| | 'Purper R'O'Sehen' (SD) | CWGr |
| | 'Purpinca' (Anem) | CWGr |
| | 'Purple Cottesmore' (MWL) | CWGr MSHN |
| | 'Purple Gem' (SS-c) | CWGr EPfP LRHS |
| | 'Purple Joy' (MD) | CWGr |
| | 'Purple Sensation' (SS-c) | CWGr |
| | 'Purple Tai Hei Jo' (GD) | CWGr |
| | aff. ***purpusii*** B&SWJ 10321 | WCru |
| | 'Pussycat' (SD) | CWGr |
| | 'Quel Diable' (LS-c) | CWGr |
| | 'Quick Step' (Anem) | CWGr |
| | 'Rachel's Place' (Pom) | CWGr |
| | 'Radfo' (SS-c) | CWGr |
| | 'Radiance' (MC) | CWGr |
| | 'Raffles' (SD) | CWGr |
| | 'Ragged Robin'$^{PBR}$ (Misc) | CBgR CSpe CWCL EBee EBla ECtt ERCP LCro MBri WCot WHrl WOVN WWlt |
| | 'Raiser's Pride' (MC) | CWGr NHal |
| | 'Raspberry Ripple' (SS-c) | CWGr |
| | 'Rebecca Lynn' (MinD) | CWGr |
| | 'Red Admiral' (MinBa) | CWGr MSHN |
| | 'Red Alert' (LBa) | CWGr |
| | 'Red and White' (SD) | CWGr |
| | 'Red Arrows' (SD) | CWGr |
| | 'Red Balloon' (SBa) | CWGr |
| | 'Red Beauty' (SD) | CWGr |
| | 'Red Bird' **new** | CMoH |
| | 'Red Cap' (MinD) | CWGr |
| | 'Red Carol' (Pom) | CWGr MSHN |
| | 'Red Diamond' (MD) | CWGr NHal |
| | 'Red Highlight' (LS-c) | CWGr |
| | 'Red Kaiser Wilhelm' (SBa) | CWGr |
| | 'Red Majorette' (SS-c) | CWGr SWal |
| | 'Red Pimpernel' (SD) | CWGr |
| | 'Red Pygmy' (SS-c) | CWGr MBri |
| | 'Red Riding Hood' (MinBa) | CWGr |
| | 'Red Schweitzer' (MinD) | CWGr |
| | 'Red Sensation' (MD) | CWGr |
| | 'Red Sunset' (MS-c) | CWGr |
| | 'Red Triumph' (SD) | CWGr |
| | 'Red Velvet' (SWL) | CWGr MSHN |
| | 'Red Warrior' (Pom) | CWGr |
| | 'Reddy' (DwLil) | CWGr |
| | 'Reedly' (SD) | CWGr |
| | 'Reese's Dream' (GD) | CWGr |
| | 'Regal Boy' (SBa) | CWGr |
| | 'Reginald Keene' (LS-c) | MSHN NHal |
| | 'Reliance' (SBa) | CWGr |
| | 'Rembrandt USA' (DwSin) | CWGr MBri |
| | 'Renato Tozio' (SD) | CWGr |
| | 'Reputation' (LC) | CWGr |
| | 'Requiem' (SD) | CSut CWGr ERCP |
| | 'Reverend P. Holian' (GS-c) | CWGr |
| | 'Reverend Roy Gardiner' (LS-c) | CWGr |
| | 'Rhonda' (Pom) | CWGr MSHN NHal |
| | 'Rhonda Suzanne' (Pom) ♀$^{H3}$ | MSHN |
| | 'Richard Howells' (MinD) | CWGr |
| | 'Richard Marc' (SC) | CWGr |
| | 'Richard S' (LS-c) | NHal |
| | 'Riisa' (MinBa) | CWGr |
| | 'Rip City' (SS-c) | CSpe CWGr LCro MCot |
| | 'Risca Miner' (SBa) | CWGr |
| | 'Rita Easterbrook' (LD) | CWGr |
| | 'Rita Hill' (Col) | CWGr |
| | 'Roan' (MinD) | CWGr |
| | 'Robann Royal' (MinBa) | CWGr |
| | 'Robbie Huston' (LS-c) | CWGr |
| | 'Robert Catterini' (Dw) | CWGr |
| | 'Robert Too' (MinD) | CWGr |
| | 'Robin Hood' (SBa) | CWGr |
| | 'Rockcliffe Gold' (MS-c) | CWGr |
| | 'Rokesly Mini' (MinC) | CWGr |
| | 'Rokesly Radiant' (MinD) | CWGr |
| | 'Rokewood Candy' (MS-c) | CWGr |
| | 'Rokewood Opal' (SC) | CWGr MSHN |
| | 'Romeo' | LRHS NBPN |
| | 'Roodkapje' (Sin) | CWGr |
| | 'Rosalinde' (S-c) | CWGr |
| | 'Rose Cupid' (MinBa) | CWGr |
| | 'Rose Jupiter' (GS-c) | CWGr LRHS NHal |
| | 'Rose Tendre' (MS-c) | CWGr |
| | 'Rosella' (MD) | CWGr EPfP LRHS |
| | 'Rosemary Webb' (SD) | CWGr |
| | 'Rossendale Luke' (SD) | CWGr MSHN |
| | 'Rossendale Natasha' (MinBa) | MSHN NHal |
| | 'Rossendale Peach' (SD) **new** | MSHN |
| | 'Rossendale Ryan' (SD) | CWGr |
| | 'Rosy Cloud' (MD) | CWGr |
| | 'Rothesay Castle' (MinD/DwB) | CWGr |
| | 'Rothesay Herald' (SD/DwB) | CWGr |
| | 'Rothesay Reveller' (MD) | CWGr |
| | 'Rothesay Robin' (SD) | CWGr MSHN |
| | 'Rothesay Rose' (SWL) | CWGr |
| | 'Rothesay Snowflake' (SWL) | CWGr |
| | 'Rotonde' (SC) | CWGr |
| | 'Rotterdam' (MS-c) | CWGr |
| I | 'Roxy' (Sin/DwB) | CBgR CHVG CMMP CWGr EBee ECtt EHrv ELan EMil EPfP LAst LCro LRHS MAvo MBri MSHN NGdn NVic SPav SPla WCot WGwG |
| | 'Royal Blood'$^{PBR}$ (Misc) | CSpe MBri |
| | 'Royal Ivory' (SWL) **new** | MSHN |
| | 'Royal Visit' (SD) | CWGr |
| | 'Royal Wedding' (LS-c) | CWGr |
| | 'Ruby Red' (MinBa) | CWGr |
| | 'Ruby Wedding' (MinD) | CWGr |
| | 'Ruskin Andrea' (SS-c) | MSHN NHal |
| | 'Ruskin Belle' (MS-c) | CWGr |
| | 'Ruskin Buttercup' (MinD) | CWGr |
| | 'Ruskin Charlotte' (MS-c) | CWGr MSHN NHal |
| | 'Ruskin Delight' (SS-c) | CWGr |
| | 'Ruskin Diana' (SD) | CWGr LBut MSHN NHal |
| | 'Ruskin Dynasty' (SD) | CWGr |
| | 'Ruskin Emil' (SS-c) | CWGr |
| | 'Ruskin Gypsy' (SBa) | CWGr |
| | 'Ruskin Marigold' (SS-c) | CWGr LBut NHal |
| | 'Ruskin Myra' (SS-c) | MSHN NHal |
| | 'Ruskin Orient' (SS-c) | CWGr |
| | 'Ruskin Petite' (MinBa) | CWGr |
| * | 'Ruskin Tangerine' (SBa) | CWGr NHal |
| | 'Russell Turner' (SS-c) | CWGr |
| | 'Rustig' (MD) | CWGr |
| | 'Rusty Hope' (MinD) | CWGr |
| | 'Rutland Gem' (MinD) | CWGr |
| | 'Rutland Water' (SD) | CWGr |
| | 'Ryecroft Claire' (MinD) **new** | NHal |
| | 'Ryecroft Crystal' | CWGr |
| | 'Ryecroft Delight' (MinBa) **new** | NHal |
| | 'Ryecroft Dream' (S-c) | CWGr |
| | 'Ryecroft Gem' (MinBa) **new** | NHal |
| | 'Ryecroft Jan' (MinBa) ♀$^{H3}$ | MSHN NHal |

'Ryecroft Magnum' (MD) **new** NHal
'Ryecroft Zoe' (SS-c) **new** NHal
'Ryedale King' (LD) CWGr
'Ryedale Pinky' (SD) CWGr
'Ryedale Rebecca' (GS-c) CWGr
'Ryedale Sunshine' (SD) CWGr
'Safe Shot' (MD) CWGr
'Sailor' (MS-c) CWGr
'Saint Croix' (GS-c) CWGr
'Saint Moritz' (SS-c) CWGr
'Saint-Saëns' SEND
'Sakura Fubuki' **new** ERCP
'Saladin' (Misc) CWGr
'Salmon Carpet' (MinD) CWGr
'Salmon Hornsey' (SD) CWGr
'Sam Hopkins' (SD) CSam NHal SMeo
'Sam Huston' (GD) CWGr
'Samantha' see *D.* 'Harvest Samantha'
'Sans Souci' (GC) CWGr
'Santa Claus' (MD) CWGr
'Sarabande' (MS-c) CWGr
'Sarah G' (LS-c) CWGr
'Sarah Louise' (SWL) CWGr
'Sarum Aurora' (SD) CWGr
'Sarum Queen' (SD) CWGr
'Sascha' (SWL) ♀H3 CWGr MSHN NHal
'Sassy' (MinD) CWGr
'Satellite' (MS-c) CWGr
'Saynomore' (SWL) CWGr
'Scarborough Ace' (MD) CWGr
'Scarborough Fair' (MS-c) NHal
'Scarlet Comet' (Anem) CWGr
'Scarlet Fern' **new** CBcs
'Scarlet Kokarde' (MinD) CWGr
'Scarlet Rotterdam' (MS-c) CWGr
'Scaur Princess' (SD) CWGr
'Scaur Swinton' (MD) CWGr NHal
'Schloss Reinbek' (Sin) CWGr
'Schweitzer's Kokarde' (MinD) CWGr
'Scottish Impact' (MinS-c) CWGr
'Scott's Delight' (SD) CWGr
'Scura' (DwSin) CWGr
'Sean C' (Col) **new** NHal
'Seattle' (SD) CWGr LRHS
'Senior Ball' (SBa) CWGr
'Senzoe Brigitte' (MinD) CWGr
'Senzoe Ursula' (SD) CWGr
'Severin's Triumph' (LD) CWGr
'Shandy' (SS-c) CWGr NHal
'Shannon' (SD) CWGr SPer
'Sharon Ann' (LS-c) CWGr
'Sheila Mooney' (LD) CWGr
***sherffii*** CWGr EBla MNrw SIng
'Sherwood Monarch' (GS-c) CWGr
'Sherwood Standard' (MD) CWGr
'Sherwood Sunrise' (SD) CWGr
'Sherwood Titan' (GD) CWGr
'Sherwood's Peach' (LD) CWGr
'Shining Star' (SC) CWGr
'Shirley' (LD) CWGr
'Shirley Alliance' (SC) CWGr
'Shooting Star' (LS-c) CWGr SPer
* 'Show and Tell' CWGr
'Shy Princess' (MC) CWGr
'Siedlerstolz' (SD) CWGr
'Siemen Doorenbos' (Anem) CWGr
'Silver City' (LD) CWGr MSHN NHal
'Silver Slipper' (SS-c) CWGr
'Silver Years' (MD) CWGr MSHN
'Sir Alf Ramsey' (GD) CWGr MSHN NHal
'Sisa' (SD) CWGr
'Skipley Spot' (SD) CWGr
'Skipper Rock' (GD) CWGr
'Sky High' (SD) CWGr
'Small World' (Pom) ♀H3 NHal
'Smart Boy' (LS-c) CWGr
'Smokey' CWGr EPfP LRHS SEND SPer SWal
'Smoky O' (MS-c) CWGr
'Smoots' (SC/Fim) CWGr
'Sneezy' (Sin) CWGr ELan LRHS
'Snip' (MinS-c) CWGr
'Snoho Barbara' (MS-c) CWGr
'Snoho Christmas' CWGr
'Snoho Peggy' (SBa) CWGr
'Snoho Tammie' (MinBa) CWGr
'Snow Cap' (SS-c) CWGr
'Snow Fairy' (MinC) CWGr
'Snow White' (DwSin) CWGr
'Snowflake' (SWL) CWGr
'Snowstorm' (MD) CSut CWGr
'Snowy' (MinBa) CWGr
'So Dainty' (MinS-c) ♀H3 CWGr
'Sondervig' (SD) CWGr
'Song of Olympia' (SWL) CWGr
'Sonia' CWGr
'Sonia Henie' (SBa) CWGr
'Sorbet' (MS-c) NHal
***sorensenii*** CWGr
'Sorrento Girl' (SS-c) MSHN
'Soulman' (Anem) CWGr
'Sourire de Crozon' (SD) CWGr
'Souvenir d'Eté' (Pom) CWGr
'Sparkler' CWGr
'Spartacus' (LD) CWGr MSHN NHal
'Spassmacher' (MS-c) CWGr
'Spectacular' (SD) CWGr
'Spencer' (SD) CWGr
'Spennythorn King' (SD) CWGr
'Spikey Symbol' (MS-c) CWGr
'Sprinter' CWGr
'Staleen Condesa' (MS-c) ♀H3 MSHN NHal
'Star Child' (Misc/O) CWGr
'Star Elite' (MC) CWGr LRHS
'Star Spectacle' (MS-c) CWGr
'Star Surprise' (SC) CWGr
'Starburst' **new** LRHS
'Starry Night' (MinS-c) CWGr
'Star's Favourite' (MC) CWGr
'Star's Lady' (SC) CWGr
'Stefan Bergerhoff' (Dwf D) CWGr
'Stella J' (SWL) CWGr
'Stella's Delight' (SD) CWGr
'Stellyvonne' (LS-c/Fim) CWGr
'Stephanie' (SS-c) CWGr
'Sterling Silver' (MD) CWGr
'Stevie D' (SD) ♀H3 CWGr
§ 'Stolz von Berlin' (MinBa) CWGr ECtt EPfP
'Stoneleigh Cherry' (Pom) CWGr
'Stoneleigh Joyce' (Pom) CWGr
'Storm Warning' (GD) CWGr
'Streets Ahead' (MinD) NHal
'Stylemaster' (MC) CWGr
'Sue Mountjoy' (Col) CWGr
'Sue Willo' (Pom) CWGr
'Suffolk Fantasy' (SD) CWGr
'Suffolk Punch' (MD) CWGr LBut SPer
'Sugartime Sunrise' (MinD) NHal
'Suitzus Julie' (Lil) CWGr MSHN
'Summer Festival' (SD) CWGr
I 'Summer Night' (SC) CWGr ECGP LCro MCot NHal SPer
'Summer's End' CWGr
'Summertime' SPer

| | | |
|---|---|---|
| | 'Sungold' (MinBa) | CWGr |
| | 'Sunlight' (SBa) | CWGr |
| | 'Sunlight Pastelle' (MS-c) | CWGr |
| | 'Sunny Boy' (MinD) | CWGr LRHS |
| | 'Sunray Glint' (MS-c) | CWGr |
| | 'Sunray Silk' (MS-c) | CWGr |
| I | 'Sunshine' (Sin) | ECtt |
| | 'Sunstruck' (MS-c) | CWGr |
| | 'Super Rays' (MC) | CWGr |
| | 'Super Trouper' (SD) | CWGr |
| | 'Superfine' (SC) | CWGr |
| | 'Supermarket' (MS-c) | CWGr |
| | 'Sure Thing' (MC) | CWGr |
| | 'Susan Willo' (Pom) | CWGr |
| | 'Susannah York' (SWL) | CWGr |
| | 'Susan's Pride' (GD) | CWGr |
| | 'Suzette' (SD/DwB) | CWGr |
| | 'Swallow Falls' (SD) | CWGr |
| | 'Swan Lake' (SD) | EShb SPer |
| | 'Swanvale' (SD) | CWGr MSHN |
| | 'Sweet Content' (SD) | CWGr |
| | 'Sweet Sensation' (MS-c) | MSHN |
| | 'Sweetheart' (SD) | CBgR EBrs ECtt LRHS |
| | 'Swiss Miss' (MinBa/O) | CWGr |
| I | 'Sylvia' (SBa) | CWGr EPfP |
| | 'Sylvia's Desire' (SC) | CWGr |
| | 'Symbol' (MS-c) | CWGr |
| | 'Syston Harlequin' (SD) | CWGr |
| | 'Syston Sophia' (LBa) | CWGr |
| | 'Tahiti Sunrise' (MS-c) | CWGr |
| | 'Tally Ho' (Misc) 🏆H3 | CBgR CMMP CSam CWGr EBee EBla ECtt EHrv GCal LCro LRHS MAvo MBri MRav MSHN NCob SDys SMad SPav SPla WCot |
| | 'Tam Tam' | SWal |
| | 'Taratahi Lilac' | see *D.* 'Lilac Taratahi' |
| | 'Taratahi Ruby' (SWL) 🏆H3 | CWGr LBut MSHN NHal |
| | 'Taratahi Sunrise' (MS-c) | CWGr |
| | 'Tartan' (MD) | CWGr |
| | 'Teesbrooke Audrey' (Col) | CWGr ECtt NHal |
| | 'Teesbrooke Red Eye' (Col) 🏆H3 | CWGr MSHN NHal |
| | 'Tempo' (MD) | CWGr |
| | 'Temptress' (SS-c) | CWGr |
| | 'Tender Moon' (SD) | CWGr |
| | ***tenuicaulis*** | CDTJ CWGr EBee SBig |
| | - F&M 99 **new** | WPGP |
| | aff. ***tenuicaulis*** | MSHN |
| | 'Thais' (Col) | CWGr |
| | 'Thames Valley' (MD) | CWGr |
| | 'That's It!' (SD) | CWGr |
| | 'The Baron' (SD) | CWGr |
| | 'Thelma Clements' (LD) | CWGr |
| | 'Theo Sprengers' (MD) | CWGr |
| | 'Thomas A. Edison' (MD) | CSut CWGr EPfP ERCP SWal |
| | 'Thoresby Jewel' (SD) | CWGr |
| I | 'Tiara' (SD) | CWGr |
| | 'Tiffany Lynn' (Misc/O) | CWGr |
| | 'Tiger Eye' (MD) | CWGr |
| | 'Tiger Tiv' (MD) | CWGr |
| | 'Tina B' (SBa) | MSHN |
| | 'Tinker's White' (SD) | CWGr |
| | 'Tiny Tot' (Lil) | see *D.* 'Harvest Tiny Tot' |
| | 'Tioga Spice' (MS-c/Fim) | CWGr NHal |
| | 'Tiptoe' (MinD) | NHal |
| | 'Toga' (SWL) | CWGr |
| | 'Tohsuikyou' (Misc/O) | CWGr |
| | 'Tommy Doc' (SS-c) | CWGr |
| | 'Tommy Keith' (MinBa) | CWGr |
| | 'Tomo' (SD) | MSHN NHal |
| | 'Top Affair' (MS-c) | CWGr |
| | 'Top Totty' (MinD) | MSHN NHal |
| * | 'Topaz Puff' | LRHS |
| | 'Toto' (Anem) | CWGr |
| | 'Tout-à-Toi' (SD) | CWGr |
| | 'Towneley Class' (SD) | CWGr |
| | 'Tramar' (SC) | CWGr |
| | 'Trampolene' (SS-c) | CWGr |
| | 'Trelawny' (GD) | CWGr |
| | 'Trelyn Kiwi' (SS-c) 🏆H3 | CWGr MSHN NHal |
| | 'Trengrove Autumn' (MD) | CWGr MSHN |
| | 'Trengrove d'Or' (MD) | CWGr |
| | 'Trengrove Jill' (MD) | CWGr |
| | 'Trengrove Millennium' (MD) | CWGr MSHN NHal |
| | 'Trengrove Summer' (MD) | CWGr |
| | 'Trengrove Tauranga' (MD) | CWGr |
| | 'Trengrove Terror' (GD) | CWGr |
| | 'Trevor' (Col) | CWGr |
| | 'Trinidad' (GS-c) | CWGr |
| | 'Tropical Sunset' (SD) | CWGr EPfP SPer |
| | 'Troy Dyson' (Misc) | SDys |
| | 'Tsuki-yorine-shisha' (MC) | CWGr |
| | 'Tu Jays Nicola' (Misc) 🏆H3 | CWGr |
| | 'Tu Tu' (MS-c) | CWGr |
| | 'Tudor 1' (DwB) | NHal |
| | 'Tui Avis' (MinC) | CWGr MSHN |
| | 'Tui Orange' (SS-c) | CWGr MSHN |
| | 'Tui Ruth' (SS-c) | CWGr |
| | 'Tula Rosa' (Pom) | CWGr |
| | 'Tutankhamun' (Pom) | CWGr |
| | 'Twiggy' (SWL) | CWGr LRHS |
| | 'Twilight Time' (MD) | CWGr ECtt EPfP LRHS MMHG |
| | 'Twyning's After Eight' (Sin) 🏆H3 | CAby CBgR CHFP CSam CWGr EBee MBNS MBri MCot MSte SDix SMrm SUsu WCot WGwG WHoo WRHF |
| | 'Twyning's Afternoon Tea' **new** | WCra |
| | 'Twyning's Aniseed' (Sin) | CWGr |
| | 'Twyning's Candy' (Sin) 🏆H3 | CWGr |
| | 'Twyning's Chocolate' (Sin) 🏆H3 | CSam CWGr |
| | 'Twyning's Cookie' (Sin) | CWGr |
| | 'Twyning's Peppermint' (Sin) | CWGr |
| | 'Twyning's Pink Fish' (Col) 🏆H3 | CWGr |
| | 'Twyning's Smartie' (Sin) 🏆H3 | CWGr |
| | 'Twyning's White Chocolate' (Sin) | CWGr |
| | 'Uchuu' (GD) | CWGr |
| | 'Union Jack' (Sin) | CBgR CWGr EMon |
| | 'United' (SD) | CWGr |
| | 'Utrecht' (GD) | CWGr |
| | 'Vader Abraham' (MinD) | CWGr |
| | 'Vaguely Noble' (SBa) | CWGr |
| | 'Valentine Lil' (SWL) | CWGr |
| | 'Valley Pop' (MinD) | CWGr |
| | 'Vancouver' (Misc) | CBgR CWGr |
| | 'Vanquisher' (GS-c) | CWGr |
| | 'Velda Inez' (MinD) | CWGr |
| | 'Vera's Elma' (LD) | CWGr |
| | 'Vesuvius' (MD) | CWGr |
| | 'Vicky Baum' (SBa) | CWGr |
| | 'Vicky Crutchfield' (SWL) | LBut |
| | 'Vicky Jackson' (SWL) | CWGr |
| | 'Victory Day' (LC) | CWGr |
| | 'Vidal Rhapsody' (MS-c) | CWGr |
| | 'Vigor' (SWL) | CWGr |
| | 'Vinovium' (MinBa) | CWGr |
| | 'Violet Davies' (MS-c) | CWGr |
| | 'Vivex' (Pom) | CWGr |
| | 'Volkskanzler' (Sin) | CWGr |
| | 'Vrouwe Jacoba' (SS-c) | CWGr |

'Vulcan' (LS-c) CWGr
§ 'Vuurvogel' (MS-c) CWGr
'Walter Hardisty' (GD) CWGr
'Walter James' (SD) CWGr
'Wanborough Gem' (SBa) CWGr
'Wanda's Aurora' (GD) NHal
'Wanda's Capella' (GD) CWGr MSHN
'Wanda's Moonlight' (GD) CWGr
'Wandy' (Pom) ♀H3 CWGr
'War of the Roses' WHer
'Warkton Willo' (Pom) CWGr
'Warmunda' (MinBa) LRHS
I 'Washington' CWGr
'Waveney Pearl' (SD) CWGr
'Welcome Guest' (MS-c) CWGr
'Welsh Beauty' (SBa) CWGr
'Wendy Spencer' (MinD) CWGr
'Wendy's Place' (Pom) CWGr
'Weston Aramac' (SS-c) CWGr
'Weston Dove' (MinS-c) CWGr
'Weston Flamingo' (MinC) CWGr
'Weston Forge' (SC) CWGr
'Weston Kelpie' (MinC) **new** MSHN
'Weston Miss' (MinS-c) CWGr MSHN NHal
'Weston Nugget' (MinC) CWGr
'Weston Pandora' (S-c) CWGr
'Weston Perky' (MinC) CWGr
'Weston Pirate' (MinC) ♀H3 CWGr MSHN NHal
'Weston Princekin' (MinS-c) CWGr
'Weston Spanish Dancer' (MinC) ♀H3 CWGr LBut MSHN NHal
'Weston Sunup' (MinC) CWGr MSHN
'Weston Teatime' (DwfC) CWGr
'Whale's Rhonda' (Pom) MSHN
'Wheel' (Col) CWGr
'Whiston Sunrise' (MS-c) CWGr
'White Alva's' (GD) ♀H3 CWGr MSHN NHal
'White Aster' (Pom) EPfP
'White Ballerina' (SWL) CSam MSHN NHal
'White Ballet' (SD) ♀H3 CWGr MSHN NHal
'White Cameo' CWGr MSHN
'White Charlie Two' (MD) MSHN NHal
'White Hunter' (SD) CWGr
'White Katrina' (LS-c) **new** MSHN
'White Knight' (MinD) NHal
'White Linda' (SD) CWGr NHal
'White Mathilda' (Dw) CWGr
'White Merriwell' (SD) CWGr
'White Moonlight' (MS-c) LBut MSHN NHal
'White Nettie' (MinBa) CWGr
'White Pastelle' (MS-c) CWGr MSHN
'White Perfection' (LD) CWGr EPfP
'White Polventon' (SBa) CWGr
'White Rustig' (MD) CWGr
'White Star' (MS-c) CWGr LRHS
'White Swallow' (SS-c) NHal
'Wicky Woo' (SD) CWGr
'Wildwood Marie' (SWL) CWGr MSHN
'Willemse Glory' (Misc Orch) CWGr
'William B' (GD) CWGr
'William Gregory' (Pom) CWGr MSHN
'Williamsburg' (SS-c) CWGr
'Willo's Borealis' (Pom) CWGr NHal
'Willo's Night' (Pom) CWGr
'Willo's Surprise' (Pom) CWGr MSHN NHal
'Willo's Violet' (Pom) CWGr MSHN NHal
'Willowfield Jackie' (MinD) CWGr
'Willowfield Matthew' (MinD) MSHN NHal
'Willowfield Mick' (LD) CWGr
'Winholme Diane' (SD) CWGr MSHN NHal
'Winkie Colonel' (GD) CWGr
'Winnie' (Pom) CWGr
'Winsome' (SWL) CWGr
'Winston Churchill' (MinD) CWGr LBut
'Winter Dawn' (SWL) CWGr
'Wise Guy' (GD) CWGr
'Wisk' (Pom) CWGr
'Wittem' (MD) CWGr
'Wittemans Superba' (SS-c) ♀H3 CWGr NHal SDix
'Wootton Cupid' (MinBa) ♀H3 CWGr LBut MSHN NHal
'Wootton Impact' (MS-c) ♀H3 MSHN NHal
'Wootton Phebe' (SD) CWGr
'Wootton Tempest' (MS-c) CWGr
'Wootton Windmill' (Col) CWGr
'Worton Blue Streak' (SS-c) CWGr
'Worton Revival' (MD) CWGr
'Worton Superb' (SD) CWGr
'Wundal Horizon' (LS-c) CWGr
'Yellow Abundance' (SD) CWGr
'Yellow Baby' (Pom) CWGr
I 'Yellow Bird' (Col) CWGr
'Yellow Galator' (MC) CWGr
'Yellow Hammer' (Sin/DwB) ♀H3 CWGr NHal
'Yellow Impact' (MS-c) MSHN
'Yellow Linda's Chester' (SC) CWGr
'Yellow Pages' (SD) CWGr
'Yellow Pet' (SD) CWGr
'Yellow Spiky' (MS-c) CWGr
'Yellow Star' (MS-c) CWGr
'Yellow Symbol' (MS-c) CWGr LBut
'Yelno Enchantment' (SWL) CWGr
'Yelno Firelight' (SWL) CWGr
'Yelno Harmony' (SD) ♀H3 CWGr LBut
'Yelno Petite Glory' (MinD) CWGr
'Yin Yang' **new** ERCP
'York and Lancaster' (MD) CBgR CTca CWGr EMon IGor
'Yorkie' (MS-c) CWGr
'Young Bees' (MD) CWGr
'Yukino' (Col) CWGr
'Zagato' (MinD) CWGr
* 'Zakuro-fubuki' (MD) CWGr
'Zakuro-hime' (SD) CWGr
I 'Zelda' (LD) CWGr
'Zest' (MinD) CWGr
'Zing' (LS-c) CWGr
'Zorro' (GD) ♀H3 CWGr NHal
'Zurich' (SS-c) CWGr

## *Dais* (*Thymelaeaceae*)
***cotinifolia*** EShb

## *Daiswa* see *Paris*

## *Dalechampia* (*Euphorbiaceae*)
***dioscoreifolia*** CCCN
***spathulata*** CCCN

## *Damasonium* (*Alismataceae*)
***alisma*** **new** CNat

## damson see *Prunus insititia*

## *Danae* (*Ruscaceae*)
§ ***racemosa*** CBcs CTri EBee ELan EMon EPfP EPla GCal GKir LCro LRHS MGos MRav SAPC SArc SEND SPer SRms SSpi WCot WDin WPGP WPat

## *Daphne* ✿ (*Thymelaeaceae*)

| | | |
|---|---|---|
| | DJHC 98164 from China | WCru |
| | ***acutiloba*** | CPMA ECho EPot GKev WPGP WSHC |
| | - 'Fragrant Cloud' | CPMA EWes SChF |
| | ***albowiana*** | CPMA EWes LLHF LRHS SAga SChF SCoo |
| | ***alpina*** | CPMA EPot WThu |
| | ***altaica*** | CPMA |
| | ***arbuscula*** 🏆$^{H4}$ | CPMA ECho EPot LLHF NMen WAbe |
| | - subsp. ***arbuscula*** f. ***albiflora*** | CPMA |
| | - 'Jurasek' **new** | EPot |
| | - 'Muran Pride' | CPMA |
| | - f. ***radicans*** | CPMA |
| | ***arbuscula*** x ***cneorum*** var. ***verlotii*** | CPMA |
| | ***arbuscula*** x 'Leila Haines' | see *D.* x *schlyteri* |
| | ***bholua*** | CAbP CBcs CHll CPMA EPfP LAst LHop LRHS MGos SReu SSpi SSta WAbe WBod WCru |
| I | - 'Alba' | CEnd CLAP CPMA ECho ELan EPfP GAbr GEdr GGGa LRHS MGos SCoo SSta WBVN WCru WGob WPGP |
| | - 'Darjeeling' | CBcs CLAP CPMA EPfP LRHS NLar SCoo SKHP SSpi SSta WGob WPGP |
| | - var. ***glacialis*** | WCru |
| | - - 'Gurkha' | CBct CGHE CPMA EBee ELan EPfP SKHP WPGP |
| | - 'Glendoick' | EPfP GGGa |
| | - 'Jacqueline Postill' 🏆$^{H3}$ | Widely available |
| | - 'Limpsfield' **new** | LRHS SCoo |
| | - 'Peter Smithers' | CBcs CBct CLAP CPMA GGGa LRHS SChF SCoo SReu SSpi SSta WGob WPGP |
| | ***blagayana*** | CPMA ECho EPot GAbr GKev MGos SRms WFar WPGP |
| | - 'Brenda Anderson' | ITim |
| | 'Bramdean' | see *D.* x *napolitana* 'Bramdean' |
| | x ***burkwoodii*** 🏆$^{H4}$ | SAga SHBN WBod WDin |
| | - 'Albert Burkwood' | CPMA LRHS |
| | - 'Astrid' (v) | CBcs CBow CPMA EBee LAst LRHS MGos SCoo SIng SMrm SPoG SSta WBod WDin |
| § | - 'Carol Mackie' (v) | CPMA LHop MGos |
| | - 'G.K.Argles' (v) 🏆$^{H4}$ | CPMA MAsh MGos WBod WFar |
| | - 'Gold Strike' (v) | CPMA |
| | - 'Golden Treasure' | CPMA LRHS SChF |
| | - 'Lavenirei' | CPMA |
| | - 'Somerset' | CBcs CPMA EBee ELan EPfP LAst MGos MSwo NWea SAga SCoo SHBN SLim SPla WBod WDin WOrn |
| § | - 'Somerset Gold Edge' (v) | CPMA |
| I | - 'Variegata' (v) | MGos |
| | - 'Variegata' broad gold edge | see *D.* x *burkwoodii* 'Somerset Gold Edge' |
| | - 'Variegata' narrow gold edge | see *D.* x *burkwoodii* 'Carol Mackie' |
| | ***caucasica*** | CPMA |
| | ***cneorum*** | CPMA EPfP MGos NMen WBod WDin |
| | - f. ***alba*** | CPMA SChF |
| | - 'Benaco' | CPMA |
| | - 'Blackthorn Triumph' | CPMA |
| | - 'Eximia' 🏆$^{H4}$ | CPMA ECho EPot GAbr LHop MDun MGos SHBN SIng SRms WAbe |
| | - 'Grandiflora' | see *D.* x *napolitana* 'Maxima' |
| | - 'Puszta' | CPMA SAga WAbe |
| | - var. ***pygmaea*** | CPMA EPot |
| | - - 'Alba' | CPMA |
| | - 'Rose Glow' | CPMA ECho |
| | - 'Ruby Glow' | CPMA ECho |
| | - 'Variegata' (v) | CPMA ECho EPot MGos NWCA SIng WAbe |
| | - 'Velký Kosir' | CPMA SChF WAbe |
| | ***collina*** | see *D. sericea* Collina Group |
| | ***genkwa*** | LRHS WBod |
| | ***giraldii*** | CPMA CSec |
| | aff. ***giraldii*** | NMen |
| | x ***hendersonii*** | CPMA |
| | - 'Appleblossom' | CPMA ECho LHop WAbe |
| | - 'Aymon Correvon' | CPMA |
| | - 'Blackthorn Rose' | CPMA |
| | - 'Ernst Hauser' | CPMA ECho ELon GAbr GEdr LHop LLHF MGos WAbe |
| | - 'Fritz Kummert' | CPMA WAbe |
| | - 'Kath Dryden' | CPMA |
| | - 'Marion White' | CPMA |
| | - 'Rosebud' | CPMA |
| | 'Hinton' | CPMA |
| | x ***houtteana*** | CPMA ECho LLHF MGos NBir WBod |
| | x ***hybrida*** | CPMA |
| | ***japonica*** 'Striata' | see *D. odora* 'Aureomarginata' |
| | ***jasminea*** | CPMA ECho NMen WAbe |
| | ***jezoensis*** | CPMA LRHS SSta WCru |
| | ***juliae*** | CPMA |
| | ***kamtschatica*** | CPMA |
| | ***kosaninii*** | CPMA |
| | x ***latymeri*** 'Spring Sonnet' | CPMA |
| | ***laureola*** | CPMA CSWP EPfP GKev GPoy LRHS MBri MGos MMHG MSte NBir NPer WCFE WPGP |
| | - 'Margaret Mathew' | CPMA EPfP EPot MGos NLar |
| | - subsp. ***philippi*** | CBgR CPMA CWSG EBee ELan EPfP LAst LRHS MBlu MBri MGos NDlv NMen SSta WBod WFar |
| | 'Leila Haines' | CPMA |
| | ***longilobata*** 'Peter Moore' | CPMA |
| | x ***mantensiana*** | MGos |
| | - 'Audrey Vockins' | CPMA |
| | - 'Manten' | CPMA ECho LHop |
| | x ***mauerbachii*** 'Perfume of Spring' | CPMA ECho LHop |
| | 'Meon' | see *D.* x *napolitana* 'Meon' |
| | ***mezereum*** | CDul CSBt CTri EBee ECho EPfP EPot GAbr GKev GKir GPoy IFoB ITim LRHS MBar MBri MGos MRav NChi NPri NWea SHBN SLim SWvt WDin WFar WHar WPGP |
| | - f. ***alba*** | CPMA CWib ECho ERas GAbr GKir LHop LRHS MGos NChi SRms SWvt WAbe WBod |
| | - - 'Bowles' Variety' | CPMA GAbr NBid |
| | - 'Rosea' | ECho SRms |
| | - var. ***rubra*** | CBcs CPMA CWSG CWib ECho ELan EPfP EWTr GKir LRHS MGan MGos MSwo NBlu SPer SPoG WAbe WDin WFar WGwG WOrn |
| | x ***napolitana*** 🏆$^{H4}$ | CPMA ECho EPfP EPot GAbr MGos SChF SHBN SKHP WBod WGob |
| § | - 'Bramdean' | CPMA ECho LHop |
| § | - 'Maxima' | MGos |
| § | - 'Meon' | CPMA ECho LHop LLHF MAsh WAbe WGob |
| | ***odora*** | CBcs CPMA EBee EPot LRHS MGos MSwo NMen SLim SSta WBod WDin |
| § | - f. ***alba*** | CCCN CPMA ECho GAbr GEdr GKir MGos MWea NLar SPer |
| | - - 'Sakiwaka' | CCCN CPMA ECho GEdr LLHF SKHP WGob |
| § | - 'Aureomarginata' (v) 🏆$^{H3-4}$ | Widely available |
| | - 'Clotted Cream' (v) | CPMA |
| | - 'Geisha Girl' (v) | ELan MAsh MGos SPoG |

| | |
|---|---|
| - var. ***leucantha*** | see *D. odora* f. *alba* |
| - 'Mae-jima' (v) | ELan EPfP LLHF LRHS MAsh SLon SPoG |
| - 'Marginata' | see *D. odora* 'Aureomarginata' |
| - var. ***rubra*** | CBcs CCCN CFir CPMA ECho GAbr GEdr GKev LLHF MLan NLar SKHP SPer WBod WGob |
| - 'Walberton' (v) | GKir LRHS MGos SPoG |
| ***oleoides*** | CPMA GKev |
| ***papyracea*** | GGGa |
| ***petraea*** | WAbe |
| - 'Alba' | see *D. petraea* 'Tremalzo' |
| - 'Garnet' | WAbe |
| - 'Grandiflora' | CPMA EPot SChF WAbe |
| - 'Michele' | CPMA |
| - 'Persebee' | CPMA |
| - 'Punchinello' | CPMA |
| § - 'Tremalzo' | SKHP |
| - 'Tuflungo' | CPMA |
| ***petraea* x *sericea*** Collina Group | SSta |
| ***pontica*** $\Upsilon^{H4}$ | CBcs CGHE CPMA EBee ECho EPfP EPla GKir LRHS MAsh MBri NLar NMen SDix SKHP SPer SPoG SSpi WPGP |
| ***pseudomezereum*** | WCru |
| ***retusa*** | see *D. tangutica* Retusa Group |
| 'Richard's Choice' | CPMA |
| ***rodriguezii* x *sericea*** | CPMA |
| x ***rollsdorfii*** 'Arnold Cihlarz' | CPMA EPot LRHS WAbe |
| - 'Wilhelm Schacht' | CPMA ECho EPot LHop SChF WAbe |
| 'Rossetii' | CPMA |
| 'Rosy Wave' | CPMA SChF WAbe |
| § x ***schlyteri*** | CPMA |
| - 'Lovisa Maria' | CPMA WAbe |
| ***sericea*** | CPMA |
| § - Collina Group | CPMA EPfP SRms WAbe WBod |
| 'Stasek' (v) | CPMA WThu |
| ***sureil*** GWJ 9200 | WCru |
| x ***susannae*** 'Anton Fahndrich' | EPot |
| - 'Anton Fahndrich' x ***sericea*** Collina Group | CPMA |
| - 'Cheriton' | CPMA ECho EPfP EPot LHop LLHF LRHS SChF |
| - 'Tichborne' | CPMA EPot LLHF MAsh NMen SChF WAbe WThu |
| ***tangutica*** $\Upsilon^{H4}$ | Widely available |
| § - Retusa Group $\Upsilon^{H4}$ | CPMA ECho ELan EPot GAbr GGar GKev GKir GMaP ITim LHop MAsh MBri NLAp NMen NRya SHBN SRms WAbe WBod WCru WSHC |
| - - SDR 3024 | GKev |
| x ***thauma*** | NMen |
| x ***transatlantica*** 'Beulah Cross' (v) | CAbP CPMA ELan LLHF LRHS MAsh SPer SPoG SSpi |
| - Eternal Fragrance = 'Blafra'$^{PBR}$ | CAbP ELan LLHF LRHS MAsh MGos SPer SPoG SSpi |
| 'Valerie Hillier' | CPMA |
| ***velenovskyi*** | CPMA |
| x ***whiteorum*** 'Beauworth' | CPMA ECho LLHF LRHS WAbe |
| - 'Kilmeston' | CPMA NMen |
| - 'Warnford' | CPMA |
| ***wolongensis*** 'Kevock Star' | GKev |

## *Daphniphyllum* (*Daphniphyllaceae*)

| | |
|---|---|
| ***calycinum*** B&SWJ 8225 | WCru |
| ***glaucescens*** B&SWJ 4058 | WCru |
| - subsp. ***oldhamii*** var. ***kengii*** B&SWJ 6872 | WCru |
| - - var. ***oldhamii*** B&SWJ 7056 | WCru |
| § ***himalaense*** subsp. ***macropodum*** | CBcs CCCN CGHE CHEx CWib EBee EPfP EPla MBri NLar SAPC SArc SDix SKHP SLPl SMad SSpi WCru WFar WPGP |
| - - B&SWJ 581 | WCru |
| - - B&SWJ 2898 | WCru |
| - - B&SWJ 6809 from Taiwan | WCru |
| - - B&SWJ 8763 from Cheju-Do | WCru |
| - - dwarf | WCru |
| ***humile*** | see *D. himalaense* subsp. *macropodum* |
| ***teijsmannii*** B&SWJ 3805 | WCru |
| - B&SWJ 11110 from Japan **new** | WCru |

## *Darlingtonia* (*Sarraceniaceae*)

| | |
|---|---|
| ***californica*** $\Upsilon^{H1}$ | CSWC EFEx MCCP SHmp WSSs |
| - 'Siskiyou Dragon' | SKHP |

## *Darmera* (*Saxifragaceae*)

| | |
|---|---|
| § ***peltata*** $\Upsilon^{H4}$ | Widely available |
| - 'Nana' | CHEx EBee EBla ECha GBuc NBid NLar SWat WFar WMoo WPnP |

## *Darwinia* (*Myrtaceae*)

| | |
|---|---|
| ***fascicularis*** | SOWG |
| ***taxifolia*** | SOWG |

## *Dasylirion* (*Dracaenaceae*)

| | |
|---|---|
| sp. | SBLw |
| § ***acrotrichum*** | CDTJ LPan SAPC SArc SChr |
| ***cedrosanum*** | CDTJ |
| ***glaucophyllum*** | EAmu MREP |
| ***gracile*** Planchon | see *D. acrotrichum* |
| ***longissimum*** | CAbb CBrP CTrC EAmu EShb SChr |
| ***miquihuanense*** NJM 05.062 **new** | WPGP |
| ***serratifolium*** | EAmu |
| ***texanum*** | CTrC LEdu |
| ***wheeleri*** $\Upsilon^{H1}$ | CBrP CTrC EAmu SChr |

## *Dasyphyllum* (*Asteraceae*)

| | |
|---|---|
| ***diacanthoides*** | WPGP |

## date see *Phoenix dactylifera*

## *Datisca* (*Datiscaceae*)

| | |
|---|---|
| ***cannabina*** | CArn CDTJ CDes CFir CFwr CHid CSec EBee ECha GBin GCal NChi NLar SDix SMHy SMrm SPhx WCot WMoo WPGP |

## *Datura* (*Solanaceae*)

| | |
|---|---|
| ***arborea*** | see *Brugmansia arborea* |
| ***chlorantha*** | see *Brugmansia chlorantha* |
| ***cornigera*** | see *Brugmansia arborea* |
| § ***inoxia*** $\Upsilon^{H3}$ | MSal |
| ***meteloides*** | see *D. inoxia* |
| ***rosea*** | see *Brugmansia* x *insignis* pink-flowered |
| ***rosei*** | see *Brugmansia sanguinea* |
| ***sanguinea*** | see *Brugmansia sanguinea* |
| ***stramonium*** | CArn CSec MSal |
| - var. ***chalybaea*** | MSal |
| - var. ***inermis*** | MSal |
| ***suaveolens*** | see *Brugmansia suaveolens* |
| ***versicolor*** | see *Brugmansia versicolor* Lagerh. |
| - 'Grand Marnier' | see *Brugmansia* x *candida* 'Grand Marnier' |

## *Daucus* (*Apiaceae*)

| | |
|---|---|
| ***carota*** | CArn CHrt CRWN EBWF NMir NSco |

| | |
|---|---|
| - 'Ballydowling Lace' | CNat |
| - 'Jane's Lace' | CNat |

## *Davallia* (*Davalliaceae*)

| | |
|---|---|
| ***canariensis*** 𝕐H1 | SEND |
| ***mariesii*** 𝕐H3 | CMen CTsd SMad WCot |
| - var. ***stenolepis*** | CMen WRic |
| ***tasmanii*** | WRic |
| ***trichomanoides*** | CMen |
| - f. ***barbata*** | CMen |

## *Davidia* (*Cornaceae*)

| | |
|---|---|
| ***involucrata*** 𝕐H4 | Widely available |
| - 'Sonoma' | MBlu |
| - var. ***vilmoriniana*** 𝕐H4 | CBcs CDoC CWCL EBee EHig ELan EPfP EWTr GKir IMGH LRHS MBlu MCCP MGan MGos NBlu SHBN SPer WOrn |

## *Daviesia* (*Papilionaceae*)

| | |
|---|---|
| ***brevifolia*** | SPlb |
| ***ovalifolia*** new | SPlb |

## *Decaisnea* (*Lardizabalaceae*)

| | |
|---|---|
| ***fargesii*** | Widely available |
| - B&SWJ 8070 | WCru |
| ***insignis*** | WPGP |

## *Decodon* (*Lythraceae*)

| | |
|---|---|
| ***verticillatus*** | EMon |

## *Decumaria* (*Hydrangeaceae*)

| | |
|---|---|
| ***barbara*** | EBee EMil LRHS MMuc NLar NSti SHBN SLim SSta WCru WFar WSHC |
| - 'Vicki' | NLar |
| ***sinensis*** | EBee EPfP LRHS MAsh MMuc SPoG SSpi WCru WSHC |

## *Degenia* (*Brassicaceae*)

| | |
|---|---|
| ***velebitica*** | EDAr |

## *Deinanthe* (*Hydrangeaceae*)

| | |
|---|---|
| ***bifida*** | CDes CLAP EBee EWes GEdr LEdu LFur WCru WPGP |
| - B&SWJ 5012 | WCru |
| - B&SWJ 5436 | EWld GEdr SBig |
| - B&SWJ 5655 | WCru |
| - 'Pink Kii' new | WCru |
| - 'Pink-Shi' | CLAP LEdu WCru |
| ***bifida* x *caerulea*** | CLAP CWsd |
| - x - 'Blue Blush' new | WCru |
| ***caerulea*** | CLAP CMil EBee GEdr IGor LEdu MHar NLar WCru WPGP |
| - 'Blue Wonder' | CLAP EBee EPPr |
| - pale-flowered | GEdr |

## *Delonix* (*Caesalpiniaceae*)

| | |
|---|---|
| ***regia*** | CSec SOWG SPlb |

## *Delosperma* (*Aizoaceae*)

| | |
|---|---|
| § ***aberdeenense*** 𝕐H1 | CHEx |
| * ***album*** | EDAr |
| ***ashtonii*** | CCCN EDAr WPer |
| ***basuticum*** | NSla |
| 'Basutoland' | see *D. nubigenum* |
| ***congestum*** | EAlp ECho EDAr EPot EShb EWll GEdr WClo |
| - 'Gold Nugget' | LRHS |
| ***cooperi*** | CCCN CSec EAlp ECho ECtt EDAr EWll GEdr ITim LRHS NLAp SEND SIng SPlb WDyG WFar WPer |
| ***ecklonis*** | EDAr |
| ***harazianum*** | CPBP |
| * ***jamesonii*** | EDAr |
| ***lineare*** | NBir |
| ***lydenburgense*** | CHEx SChr |
| § ***nubigenum*** | EAlp ECho ECtt EDAr ELan EPfP EPot GEdr GGar GKev ITim SBHP SEND SPoG WFar WPer |
| ***sutherlandii*** | EAlp ECho EDAr EShb EWll GGar |
| - 'Peach Star' | EAlp EDAr |

## *Delphinium* ✿ (*Ranunculaceae*)

| | |
|---|---|
| HWJK 2179 from Nepal | WCru |
| HWJK 2263 from Nepal | WCru |
| from Nepal | GKir |
| 'After Midnight' | CNMi |
| 'Ailsa' | CNMi |
| 'Alice Artindale' (d) | EMon EWes IFoB MWte SAga SMrm WCot WPGP |
| 'Alie Duyvensteyn' | EBee |
| 'Amadeus' | LCro |
| ***ambiguum*** | see *Consolida ajacis* |
| 'Angela Harbutt' | CNMi |
| 'Ann Woodfield' | CNMi |
| 'Anne Kenrick' | CNMi |
| 'Ariel' ambig. | LRHS |
| Astolat Group | CBcs COIW CSBt CTri CWCL CWib EBee ELan EPfP GKir GMaP LBMP LRHS MBri MWat NBPC NBir NCob NLar NPri SMrm SPer SPoG WCAu WFar WHoo |
| 'Atholl' 𝕐H4 | ELar |
| 'Augenweide' | EBee |
| Barbaskyblue = 'Dashsix' new | EBee |
| 'Bella Light Blue' new | EBee |
| Belladonna Group | IFoB |
| - 'Atlantis' 𝕐H4 | EBee ECha ELar EPPr LRHS NGby NLar SMeo SMrm SWat WCot |
| - 'Balaton' | ELar |
| - 'Blue Shadow' | CWCL |
| - 'Capri' | EBee |
| - 'Casa Blanca' | EBee ELar GMaP NLar SMrm SWat WPer |
| - 'Cliveden Beauty' | CWCL EBee GBri LHop MRav MSte NLar SMrm SPoG SWat WPer |
| - 'Delft Blue' PBR | EBee EPfP MLLN NMoo NSti SMrm |
| § - 'Janny Arrow' PBR | LRHS |
| - 'Moerheimii' | MRav NGby SMrm |
| - 'Piccolo' | ECha NLar SWat |
| - 'Pink Sensation' | see *D.* x *ruysii* 'Pink Sensation' |
| - 'Völkerfrieden' 𝕐H4 | ELar MCot MRav NGby NPro |
| x ***bellamosum*** | NLar WPer |
| 'Berghimmel' | EBee NGby |
| 'Beryl Burton' | CNMi |
| Black Knight Group | Widely available |
| 'Black Velvet' new | EBee NBPN SPoG |
| 'Blackberry Ice' | CNMi |
| 'Blauwal' | GBin |
| 'Blue Arrow' ambig. | LCro |
| 'Blue Arrow' | see *D.* 'Blue Max Arrow', *D.* (Belladonna Group) 'Janny Arrow' |
| Blue Bird Group | CBcs CSBt CTri CWCL EBee ELan EPfP GMaP LBMP LRHS MRav MWat NBPC NCGa NLar NMir NPri SPer SPla SPoG WCAu WFar WHoo |
| 'Blue Butterfly' | see *D. grandiflorum* 'Blue Butterfly' |
| 'Blue Dawn' 𝕐H4 | CNMi ELar |
| Blue Fountains Group | CSBt EPfP GKir LRHS LSRN SPer SPet SPoG SRms |
| 'Blue Hex' | WCot |
| 'Blue Jay' | CBcs CTri EBee ECtt EPfP GKir LCro LRHS LSRN MWat NBir NLar NPri SPer SPoG |
| § 'Blue Max Arrow' | LRHS |

| | |
|---|---|
| 'Blue Mirror' | SRms |
| 'Blue Nile' ♀H4 | CNMi |
| 'Blue Oasis' | CNMi |
| Blue River **new** | CBcs EBee SPoG |
| 'Blue Skies' | ECtt GKir NLar |
| Blue Springs Group | NGdn NLar |
| 'Blue Tit' | CNMi LCro |
| 'Blue Triumphator' | EBee |
| 'Bruce' ♀H4 | CNMi ELar WCFE |
| ***brunonianum*** | WThu |
| 'Butterball' | CNMi ELar |
| Cameliard Group | CBcs CSBt EBee ECtt ELan EPfP GKir LBMP LRHS MWat NBPC NCGa NLar NPri SPer SPoG WHoo |
| 'Can-Can' ♀H4 | CNMi ELar |
| ***cardinale*** | EHrv |
| ***cashmerianum*** | EBee GEdr GKev |
| 'Cassius' ♀H4 | CNMi LCro |
| ***caucasicum*** | see *D. speciosum* |
| 'Centurion Sky Blue' (Centurion Series) | LRHS NBHF |
| ***ceratophorum*** var. ***ceratophorum*** BWJ 7799 | WCru |
| 'Chelsea Star' | CNMi GBin |
| 'Cher' | CNMi |
| 'Cherry Blossom' | EPfP NLar |
| 'Cherub' ♀H4 | ELar LCro |
| ***chinense*** | see *D. grandiflorum* |
| 'Christel' | LRHS LSRN NGby |
| ***chrysotrichum*** var. ***tsarongense*** **new** | EBee GKev |
| 'Clack's Choice' | CNMi |
| 'Claire' ♀H4 | CNMi ELar |
| Clear Springs Series | SGar |
| 'Clifford Sky' ♀H4 | ELar |
| Connecticut Yankees Group | SMrm SRms |
| 'Conspicuous' ♀H4 | CNMi ELar |
| 'Constance Rivett' ♀H4 | ELar |
| 'Coral Sunset'PBR (d) | NMoo WCot |
| 'Crown Jewel' | ELar WCFE |
| 'Cupid' | CNMi ELar |
| 'Darling Sue' | CNMi LCro |
| 'Darwin's Blue Indulgence'PBR | EPfP MLLN SMrm |
| 'Darwin's Pink Indulgence'PBR | MLLN |
| ***delavayi*** | EBee GKev WCot |
| - B&SWJ 7796 | WCru |
| 'Demavand' | CNMi |
| 'Diamant'PBR | LRHS |
| 'Dreaming Spires' | SRms |
| ***drepanocentrum*** HWJK 2263 | WCru |
| 'Dunsden Green' | CNMi |
| 'Dusky Maiden' | IFoB STes |
| dwarf dark blue-flowered | LRHS |
| dwarf lavender-flowered | LRHS |
| dwarf pink-flowered | LRHS |
| dwarf sky blue-flowered | LRHS |
| 'Eelkje' | EBee |
| ***elatum*** | EBee GCal IFoB NGdn SRms |
| 'Elisabeth Sahin' | CNMi ELar |
| 'Elizabeth Cook' ♀H4 | CNMi ELar |
| 'Elmhimmel' | GKir |
| 'Emily Hawkins' ♀H4 | CNMi |
| 'F.W. Smith' | EBee |
| 'Fanfare' | CNMi ELar |
| 'Faust' ♀H4 | CNMi LCro MRav |
| 'Fenella' ♀H4 | CNMi ELar LCro WCFE |
| 'Filique Arrow' | CFir |
| 'Finsteraarhorn' | EBee GBin LRHS MCot NGby WCot |
| 'Florestan' | CNMi |
| cf. ***forrestii*** **new** | EBee |
| 'Foxhill Nina' | CNMi ELar |
| 'Franjo Sahin' | CNMi |
| Galahad Group | Widely available |
| 'Galileo' ♀H4 | CNMi |
| 'Gemma' | CNMi |
| 'Gillian Dallas' ♀H4 | ELar LCro |
| 'Giotto' ♀H4 | CNMi |
| ***glaciale*** HWJK 2299 | WCru |
| 'Gordon Forsyth' | CNMi |
| 'Gossamer' | CNMi |
| § ***grandiflorum*** | CWCL |
| § - 'Blauer Zwerg' | SPoG |
| § - 'Blue Butterfly' | CSpe EBrs EBur LEdu LRHS SCoo SPlb SPoG WPer WSHC |
| - Blue Dwarf | see *D. grandiflorum* 'Blauer Zwerg' |
| (Guardian Series) 'Guardian Blue' **new** | NPri |
| - 'Guardian Lavender' | NPri |
| - 'Guardian White' **new** | CWCL NPri |
| Guinevere Group | CBcs CSBt CWCL CWib EBee ECtt EPfP EWTr LBMP LCro LRHS MBri NBPC NBir NLar NPri SPad SPer SPla SPoG WCAu WFar |
| 'Guy Langdon' | CNMi |
| ***hansenii*** **new** | LLHF |
| 'Harlekijn' | NLar |
| 'Heavenly Blue' | NLar |
| 'Holly Cookland Wilkins' | CNMi |
| 'Hordon Blue' | NBHF |
| I 'Independence' | LRHS |
| Ivory Towers Group | ECtt |
| 'Jenny Agutter' | CNMi |
| 'Jill Curley' ♀H4 | CNMi ELar LCro |
| 'Joan Edwards' | CNMi |
| 'Kathleen Cooke' | CNMi |
| 'Kennington Calypso' | CNMi |
| 'Kennington Classic' | CNMi |
| 'Kestrel' ♀H4 | CNMi ELar |
| King Arthur Group | CBcs CSBt EBee ECtt ELan EPfP LBMP LSRN MRav MWat NBPC NCGa NLar NPri SPer SPoG WCAu WFar |
| 'Lady Guinevere' | EBee |
| 'Langdon's Orpheus' | LCro |
| § 'Langdon's Royal Flush' ♀H4 | CNMi ELar |
| 'Lanzenträger' | LRHS SMeo |
| ***laxiflorum*** | CSec WCot |
| 'Leonora' | CNMi ELar |
| 'Lillian Basset' | CNMi |
| 'Lily Radley' **new** | ELar |
| 'Loch Leven' ♀H4 | CNMi GBin |
| 'Loch Nevis' | CNMi |
| 'Lord Butler' ♀H4 | CNMi ELar LRHS |
| 'Lucia Sahin' ♀H4 | CNMi ELar |
| ***maackianum*** | EWld GCal |
| Magic Fountains Series | CSam GMaP IFoB MRav NPri SPlb SPoG SRot WFar WGor WRHF |
| - 'Magic Fountains Cherry Blossom' | SMrm SPoG WFar |
| - 'Magic Fountains Dark Blue' | EPfP GMaP LSRN NLar SMrm SPoG WFar |
| - 'Magic Fountains Deep Blue' | NLar |
| - 'Magic Fountains Lavender' | EPfP |
| - 'Magic Fountains Lilac Pink' | SPoG |
| - 'Magic Fountains Lilac Rose' | NLar NVic WFar |
| - 'Magic Fountains Pure White' | EPfP NBHF NLar SMrm WFar |

| | |
|---|---|
| – 'Magic Fountains Sky Blue' | EPfP LRHS NVic SPoG WFar |
| ***menziesii*** | CSec |
| 'Merlin' ambig. | LRHS LSRN |
| 'Michael Ayres' $\Upsilon^{H4}$ | CNMi ELar |
| ***micropetalum*** CNDS 031 | WCru |
| 'Mighty Atom' | CNMi LCro WCot |
| 'Min' $\Upsilon^{H4}$ | CNMi ELar |
| 'Moonbeam' | ELar |
| 'Mrs Newton Lees' | EBee MRav |
| 'Mulberry Rose' | NBHF |
| New Century hybrids | CBcs |
| 'Nicolas Woodfield' | CNMi |
| 'Nobility' | ELar LCro |
| ***nudicaule*** | ECho SPoG |
| – 'Fox' | WHil |
| – 'Laurin' | ECho WFar |
| 'Olive Poppleton' $\Upsilon^{H4}$ | CNMi LCro SAga |
| 'Oliver' $\Upsilon^{H4}$ | CNMi |
| 'Our Deb' $\Upsilon^{H4}$ | CNMi ELar |
| Pacific hybrids | CWCL EPfP GJos LRHS LSRN MHer MLHP NBlu NLar SPet SRms SWal SWvt WFar |
| 'Pagan Purples' (d) | ELar IFoB |
| 'Pandora' | CNMi ELar LCro |
| 'Patricia Johnson' | ELar |
| Percival Group | LRHS NLar |
| 'Pericles' | LCro |
| 'Perlmutterbaum' | SMeo |
| 'Pink Petticoat' (d) | EMon |
| Pink River = 'Barfourtythree' **new** | CBcs EBee |
| 'Pink Ruffles' | CNMi ELar |
| Princess Caroline = 'Odabar'PBR | CBcs EBee |
| 'Purple Princess' **new** | EBee SPoG |
| 'Purple Ruffles' | EPfP SMrm |
| 'Purple Velvet' $\Upsilon^{H4}$ | CNMi ELar LCro |
| 'Red Caroline' | CBcs EBee SPoG |
| ***requienii*** | CBgR CBre CSec CSpe EWTr EWld SBHP SBch WCot WEas |
| 'Rona' | CNMi |
| 'Rosemary Brock' $\Upsilon^{H4}$ | ELar |
| Round Table Mixture | CTri |
| 'Royal Aspirations' (New Millennium Series) **new** | ELar |
| 'Royal Flush' | see *D.* 'Langdon's Royal Flush' |
| § x ***ruysii*** 'Pink Sensation' | CFir CWCL EPPr EWTr GBri NGby NLar NPro SMrm WFar WPGP |
| 'Sandpiper' $\Upsilon^{H4}$ | CNMi |
| 'Sarita'PBR | NSti SMrm SUsu |
| 'Schildknappe' | EBee |
| 'Secret'PBR | LRHS |
| 'Sentinel' | CNMi |
| ***siamense*** B&SWJ 7278 | WCru |
| 'Silver Jubilee' | CNMi ELar |
| 'Sir Harry Secombe' | CNMi |
| 'Sky Sensation' **new** | NLar |
| 'Skyline' | CNMi EBee |
| 'Snow Queen Arrow' | LRHS |
| 'Snowdon' | CNMi |
| § ***speciosum*** | EBee GKev |
| 'Spindrift' $\Upsilon^{H4}$ | CNMi ELar |
| ***stapeliosmum*** B&SWJ 2954 | WCru |
| ***staphisagria*** | CArn ECGP EOHP MSal MSte |
| 'Starmaker' | EPfP |
| 'Strawberry Fair' | CNMi |
| Summer Skies Group | CBcs CSBt CTri CWCL EBee ECtt ELan EPfP EWTr LBMP LHop LRHS MBri MWat NBir NCGa NLar NPri SPer SPoG WBrE WCAu WFar WHoo |
| 'Summer Wine' | ELar |
| 'Summerfield Miranda' $\Upsilon^{H4}$ | CNMi |
| 'Summerfield Oberon' | CNMi ELar |
| 'Sungleam' $\Upsilon^{H4}$ | EBee ELar LCro NLar |
| 'Sunkissed' $\Upsilon^{H4}$ | CNMi ELar LCro |
| 'Sunny Skies' (New Millennium Series) | ELar |
| 'Susan Edmunds'PBR (d) $\Upsilon^{H4}$ | EMil |
| ***sutchuenense*** | CSec EWld NCGa |
| – BWJ 7867 | CHFP WCru |
| ***tatsienense*** | EBee SRms WCru |
| ***tenii*** BWJ 7693 | WCru |
| – BWJ 7906 | WCru |
| 'Tiddles' $\Upsilon^{H4}$ | ELar LCro |
| 'Tiger Eye' | CNMi ELar |
| 'Tiny Tim' | CNMi |
| 'Titania' | LCro |
| ***tricorne*** | CLAP |
| 'Vanessa Mae' | CNMi |
| 'Vespers' | ELar |
| ***vestitum*** | ECtt EWld SBch |
| ***viscosum*** HWJK 2268 | WCru |
| 'Walton Beauty' | CNMi |
| 'Walton Benjamin' | CNMi |
| 'Walton Gemstone' $\Upsilon^{H4}$ | CNMi ELar |
| White River **new** | CBcs EBee |
| 'White Ruffles' | CNMi ELar |
| 'Wishful Thinking'PBR | SMrm |
| Woodfield strain | WHrl |
| ***yunnanense*** | EBee GKev |
| 'Yvonne' | LSRN NLar |

## *Dendranthema* see *Chrysanthemum*

| | |
|---|---|
| ***pacificum*** | see *Ajania pacifica* |

## *Dendriopoterium* see *Sanguisorba*

## *Dendrobenthamia* see *Cornus*

## *Dendrocalamus* (*Poaceae*)

| | |
|---|---|
| ***asper*** | XBlo |
| ***giganteus*** | XBlo |
| § ***strictus*** | XBlo |

## *Dendromecon* (*Papaveraceae*)

| | |
|---|---|
| ***rigida*** | CBcs EBee EPfP LRHS MBri MWea NLar SAga SKHP SMad SSpi WPGP WSHC |

## *Dendropanax* (*Araliaceae*)

| | |
|---|---|
| ***trifidus*** B&SWJ 11230 **new** | WCru |

## *Dennstaedtia* (*Dennstaedtiaceae*)

| | |
|---|---|
| ***punctilobula*** | CLAP EBee WCot WRic |

## *Dentaria* see *Cardamine*

| | |
|---|---|
| ***pinnata*** | see *Cardamine heptaphylla* |
| ***polyphylla*** | see *Cardamine kitaibelii* |

## *Dermatobotrys* (*Scrophulariaceae*)

| | |
|---|---|
| ***saundersii*** | ECre |

## *Derwentia* see *Parahebe*

## *Deschampsia* (*Poaceae*)

| | |
|---|---|
| ***cespitosa*** | CHrt CKno COIW CRWN CSam CWib EBWF EPPr EPfP GFor LBuc LCro MBar MWat SPlb WCFE WCot WDin WGwG WMnd WMoo WPnP WTin |
| – subsp. ***alpina*** | LEdu |
| – Bronze Veil | see *D. cespitosa* 'Bronzeschleier' |

| | |
|---|---|
| § - 'Bronzeschleier' | Widely available |
| - brown | SApp |
| - 'Fairy's Joke' | see *D. cespitosa* var. *vivipara* |
| - 'Fose' | SApp |
| - Gold Dust | see *D. cespitosa* 'Goldstaub' |
| - Golden Dew | see *D. cespitosa* 'Goldtau' |
| - Golden Pendant | see *D. cespitosa* 'Goldgehänge' |
| - Golden Shower | see *D. cespitosa* 'Goldgehänge' |
| - Golden Veil | see *D. cespitosa* 'Goldschleier' |
| § - 'Goldgehänge' | CSam EBee EHoe EHul EPPr EPfP EPla MMHG NBir NLar NPro SLPl |
| - 'Goldschatt' **new** | EBee |
| § - 'Goldschleier' | CPrp CSam EBee EBrs ECha EMon EPPr EPla EWsh GCal GGar GKir GMaP GQue LCro LEdu NGdn SApp SPhx WMoo WPGP |
| § - 'Goldstaub' | EPPr |
| § - 'Goldtau' | Widely available |
| - 'Morning Dew' | WFar |
| - 'Northern Lights' (v) | CWCL EAlp EBee ELan GGar GKir LEdu LHop MAvo MWhi SApp SLim SPer SPla SPoG SRms SWvt WPGP |
| - 'Schottland' | EBee GBin |
| - 'Tardiflora' | EBee |
| - 'Tauträger' | MSte |
| § - var. ***vivipara*** | EBee EHoe EMon EPPr EPla NBid NBro NBsh NHol NLar WRos |
| - 'Waldschatt' | EBee |
| - 'Willow Green' | GCal MRav SCoo |
| ***flexuosa*** | COIW EHoe EWsh GFor MWat NBir |
| - 'Tatra Gold' | Widely available |

## *Desfontainia* (*Loganiaceae*)

| | |
|---|---|
| § ***spinosa*** ♀H3 | Widely available |
| - 'Harold Comber' | CMac MDun WBod WCru |
| - f. ***hookeri*** | see *D. spinosa* |

## *Desmanthus* (*Mimosaceae*)

| | |
|---|---|
| ***illinoensis*** | MSal |

## *Desmodium* (*Papilionaceae*)

| | |
|---|---|
| ***callianthum*** | CMac EBee EPfP LRHS WSHC |
| ***canadense*** | EBee NLar SBHP |
| § ***elegans*** ♀H4 | CBcs CHEx EBee ELan EPfP MBri NLar WBod WHer WPGP WSHC |
| ***praestans*** | see *D. yunnanense* |
| ***tiliifolium*** | see *D. elegans* |
| § ***yunnanense*** | CHEx EPfP LRHS WSHC |

## *Deutzia* ✿ (*Hydrangeaceae*)

| | |
|---|---|
| CC 4548 | CPLG |
| CC 4550 | CPLG |
| ***calycosa*** | GQui WPat |
| - BWJ 8007 **new** | WCru |
| - 'Dali' | CDoC CExc SDys WPGP |
| ***chunii*** | see *D. ningpoensis* |
| ***compacta*** | SLon WBod WFar WPGP |
| - GWJ 9202 **new** | WCru |
| - 'Lavender Time' | CDoC CMac CPLG EBee LRHS WCFE |
| ***cordatula*** B&SWJ 6917 | WCru |
| ***coreana*** BWJ 8588 | WCru |
| ***corymbosa*** | CDoC |
| ***crenata*** B&SWJ 8896 | WCru |
| - B&SWJ 8879 **new** | WCru |
| - 'Flore Pleno' | see *D. scabra* 'Plena' |
| - var. ***heterotricha*** B&SWJ 5805 **new** | WCru |
| - 'Nakaiana' | SIng WPat |
| - var. ***nakaiana*** 'Nikko' | see *D. gracilis* 'Nikko' |
| § - 'Pride of Rochester' (d) | CBcs CMCN CWib EBee GKir MBar MGos MMuc MRav NLar SLim SLon SPad SPoG SWvt WDin WHar |
| 'Dark Eyes' **new** | GGGa |
| ***discolor*** 'Major' | CPLG |
| x ***elegantissima*** | MRav SRms |
| - 'Fasciculata' | EBee EPfP SPer WLeb |
| - 'Rosealind' ♀H4 | CBcs CMac CPLG CTri EBee ECrN EPfP EWTr LHop LRHS MBri MGos MRav NCGa NSti SPer SPoG SRms SSpi SWvt WBod WKif WSHC |
| ***glabrata*** B&SWJ 617 | GQui WCru |
| ***glomeruliflora*** BWJ 7742 **new** | WCru |
| ***gracilis*** | CDoC CHar CSBt EBee ELan EPfP GQui LBMP MBar MGos MRav MSwo SDix SPer SPoG WBod WDin WFar WGwG |
| - 'Aurea' | CBcs |
| - 'Carminea' | see *D.* x *rosea* 'Carminea' |
| § - 'Marmorata' (v) | CBow CPMA EBee NLar SLon WCot WHCG |
| § - 'Nikko' | CAbP CBcs CMCN CPLG CTri EBee ECho EMil EWTr EWes MBar MGos MHer MMuc NHol NLar NPro SPlb WDin WHCG WKif WRHF WSHC |
| - var. ***ogatae*** B&SWJ 8911 **new** | WCru |
| - 'Rosea' | see *D.* x *rosea* |
| - 'Variegata' | see *D. gracilis* 'Marmorata' |
| ***hookeriana*** | EBee LRHS WFar |
| - KW 6393 | WPGP |
| x ***hybrida*** 'Contraste' | CMac SPer |
| - 'Joconde' | CPLG GKir MBri WFar WKif |
| - 'Magicien' | CDoC CDul CMHG CPLG CSBt CSam CWib EBee ECrN EPfP GQui LHop MAsh MBri MRav MSwo NBir SHBN SLon SMrm SPer SWvt WBod WFar WHCG WHar WPat |
| - 'Mont Rose' ♀H4 | Widely available |
| § - 'Strawberry Fields' ♀H4 | CBcs CGHE CPLG CTri EBee ELan ELon EPla GKir LAst LBMP LBuc LRHS LSRN MAsh MBar MBlu MBri MGos NPri SBod SLon SPoG WBVN WBod WFar WKif WPGP |
| 'Iris Alford' | SLon |
| x ***kalmiiflora*** | CMac CPLG CPMA CSBt CTri EBee GQui LRHS MBar MBri MRav SLPl SPer SPoG SRms WBod |
| ***longifolia*** 'Veitchii' ♀H4 | CSBt ERas GQui MRav WCFE |
| - 'Vilmoriniae' | CDul MRav |
| x ***magnifica*** | CBcs CDul EBee ELan EPfP GQui MBri SRms WDin WHCG WHar |
| - 'Rubra' | see *D.* x *hybrida* 'Strawberry Fields' |
| ***monbeigii*** | CDoC CPLG GKir WKif |
| - BWJ 7728 | WCru |
| § ***ningpoensis*** ♀H4 | CAbP CBrd CPLG EBee GBin GQui LRHS SLPl SMrm SPer WBod WPGP |
| ***parviflora*** var. ***barbinervis*** B&SWJ 8478 **new** | WCru |
| 'Pink Pompon' | see *D.* 'Rosea Plena' |
| ***pulchra*** | CAbP CDoC CHar CMCN CPom EBee EPfP IDee MRav NPro SKHP SLon SMrm SPer SSpi WFar WHCG WPGP |
| - B&SWJ 3870 | WCru |
| - B&SWJ 6908 | WCru |
| ***purpurascens*** BWJ 7859 **new** | WCru |
| § x ***rosea*** | CDul CWib EBee ECrN EPfP LAst LRHS MBar SHBN SPoG SRms WBod WFar WKif |
| - 'Campanulata' | CPLG EPfP |
| § - 'Carminea' | MSwo NCGa SPlb SRms WDin WFar WMoo WPat |

| | | |
|---|---|---|
| § | 'Rosea Plena' (d) | CDoC CPLG CSBt CWib EBee EPfP MAsh MGos MMuc NLar SLim SPoG SSta WBod WFar WGwG WPat WRHF |
| | ***scabra*** | CDul CTri IFFs |
| | - B&SWJ 8924 **new** | WCru |
| § | - 'Candidissima' (d) | CMac ECrN GQui MRav NLar SPer WBod |
| | - 'Codsall Pink' | MRav |
| § | - 'Plena' (d) | CPLG EBee ECtt ELan EPfP GKir IMGH LRHS MRav SHBN SPer SPur WBod |
| | - 'Pride of Rochester' | see *D. crenata* 'Pride of Rochester' |
| | - 'Punctata' (v) | EBee EHoe MMuc SRms WFar |
| | - 'Variegata' (v) | CDul CMac |
| | ***setchuenensis*** | CMac EPfP GQui SSpi WHCG WPat WSHC |
| | - var. ***corymbiflora*** ♀H4 | CBcs CDoC CDul CGHE CSam CTri EBee EPfP ERas EWTr GKir IDee LRHS MBri MSwo SPoG WFar WKif WPGP |
| | ***taiwanensis*** | EBee EMil NLar |
| | - B&SWJ 6858 | WCru |
| | 'Tourbillon Rouge' | CDoC EBee EQua WDin |
| * | ***vidalii*** **new** | GGal |
| | x ***wellsii*** | see *D. scabra* 'Candidissima' |
| | x ***wilsonii*** | SRms |

## *Dianella* ✿ (*Phormiaceae*)

| | | |
|---|---|---|
| | ***brevicaulis*** **new** | ECou |
| | ***caerulea*** | CMac CWsd ECha ECou ELan GBuc IFoB IGor NBir SOWG |
| | - Breeze = 'Dcnco' | ECou ELan EPPr NBsh NOak |
| | - Cassa Blue = 'Dbb03' | CBgR CPrp EBee ELan EPPr EWes GEdr GGar LHop NBhm NBsh NOak |
| | - 'Kulnura' | ECou |
| | - Little Jess = 'Dcmp01' | CBgR CPrp EBee EPPr EPla GEdr GGar LEdu LRHS NBsh NOak |
| | - var. ***petasmatodes*** | EPPr WCot |
| | - 'Variegata' | see *D. tasmanica* 'Variegata' |
| | ***intermedia*** | CTrC EWld IBlr WPic |
| | - 'Variegata' (v) | IBlr |
| | ***nigra*** | CBcs CFir CPen CPou CTrC ECou LEdu NCGa WFar |
| | - 'Margaret Pringle' (v) | CPen CTrC EMil NOak |
| | - 'Taupo' | ECou |
| | ***revoluta*** | CFir ECou IBlr |
| | - 'Baby Bliss' | ECou NOak |
| | - 'Hartz Mountain' | ECou |
| | - Little Rev = 'Dr5000'PBR | CPrp EBee ECou ELan EPPr EPfP GEdr GGar LHop MMHG NBsh NOak |
| | ***tasmanica*** | Widely available |
| | - 'Emerald Arch' | ELan NBsh NOak |
| | - 'Prosser' | ECou |
| | - Tasred = 'Tr20' | EBee ELan EPPr EPfP GBin GEdr LEdu LRHS MCot MMHG NOak WAul |
| § | - 'Variegata' (v) | CBct CDTJ CFir CSpe CStu EBee ECou ELan GBuc IBlr LHop MSte WCot |

## *Dianthus* ✿ (*Caryophyllaceae*)

| | | |
|---|---|---|
| | ACW 2116 | GEdr LBee |
| | 'Adam James' (b) | SAll |
| | 'Admiral Crompton' (pf) | CNMi |
| | 'Alan Titchmarsh' (p) | CCge EAEE EBee ECtt EPfP EWll LSRN MMHG NCGa NPri SPoG SWvt |
| | 'Albus' | LBMP |
| | 'Aldridge Yellow' (b) | SAll |
| | 'Alice' (p) | LSRN SAll |
| | 'Alice Lever' (p) | WAbe |
| | 'Allspice' (p) | MRav SBch SSvw WEas WHoo |
| | Allwoodii Alpinus Group (p) | SRms WFar |
| | 'Allwood's Crimson' (pf) | SAll |
| | ***alpinus*** ♀H4 | CLyd ECho GKev LRHS NBlu NMen SRms WFar WPer |
| | - 'Albus' | ECho GKev LRHS WAbe |
| § | - 'Joan's Blood' ♀H4 | GBuc LHop LSRN NHar NHol SMad WAbe WFar WRHF |
| | - 'Millstream Salmon' | CLyd |
| | 'Alyson' (p) | SAll |
| | ***amurensis*** | CSec ECho EPPr LCro LRHS NDov SSvw WGwG WPer |
| | - 'Siberian Blue' | GBin |
| | ***anatolicus*** | CSec CTri ECho EDAr LRHS MHer NDlv NGdn NWCA SSvw WOut WPer |
| | 'Andrew Morton' (b) | SAll |
| | 'Angelo' (b) | SAll |
| | 'Annabelle' (p) | ECho LRHS |
| | 'Anne Jones' (b) | EPfP |
| | 'Annette' (pf) | EBee ECho ECtt EDAr GKev LRHS LSRN MWat SWvt |
| | 'Annie Claybourne' (pf) | CNMi |
| | 'Apricot Sue' (pf) | CNMi |
| | 'Arctic Star' (p) | CMea CTri EBee ECho GMaP LAst NLar NPri SPet SPoG SRot SWvt WFar |
| | ***arenarius*** | EWTr GKev SPlb SSvw WPer |
| | 'Argus' | IGor SSvw |
| | ***armeria*** | CSec WHer WOut WTou |
| | 'Arthur Leslie' (b) | SAll |
| § | x ***arvernensis*** (p) ♀H4 | EAlp ECha ECho EPot |
| | - 'Albus' | ECho |
| | 'Autumn Tints' (b) | SAll |
| | 'Auvergne' | see *D.* x *arvernensis* |
| | 'Averiensis' | SAll |
| | 'Baby Treasure' (p) | ECho SRot |
| | 'Bailey's Anniversary' (p) | SEND |
| | 'Bailey's Celebration' (p) | CBgR EPfP SRGP |
| § | 'Bailey's Daily Mail' (p) ♀H4 | CBcs EBee SPoG |
| | 'Barbara Norton' (p) **new** | ECtt |
| | ***barbatus*** | CHrt GAuc SECG |
| | - 'Black Adder' | CSpe |
| | - Nigrescens Group (p,a) ♀H4 | CBre CHrt CMea CSpe EMon SAga SPhx |
| I | - 'Sooty' (p,a) | CSec EBee ELan EWld GBri NDlv NGdn WCFE WFar |
| | - 'Tuxedo Black' | MWea |
| | - 'Woodfall' | WBor |
| | 'Bath's Pink' (p) | LRHS |
| § | 'Bat's Double Red' (p/d) | IGor SAll SSvw |
| | 'Becky Robinson' (p) ♀H4 | SAll |
| | 'Bella' (p) | CPBP |
| | 'Berlin Snow' | CLyd CPBP ECho EPot GKev MSte |
| | 'Betty Morton' (p) ♀H4 | ECtt IFoB MWea SSvw WFar WKif WThu |
| | 'Binsey Red' (p) | SSvw |
| | Black and White Minstrels Group | CLyd |
| | 'Blue Hills' (p) | CLyd ECho GKev MWea SIng |
| | 'Blue Ice' (b) | SAll |
| | 'Blush' | see *D.* 'Souvenir de la Malmaison' |
| | 'Bobby' (p) | SAll |
| | 'Bob's Highlight' (pf) | CNMi |
| | 'Bookham Heroine' (b) | SAll |
| | 'Bookham Lad' (b) | SAll |
| | 'Bookham Sprite' (b) | SAll |
| | 'Border Special' (b) | SAll |
| | 'Bouquet Purple' (p) **new** | CSpe |
| | 'Bourboule' | see *D.* 'La Bourboule' |

| | | |
|---|---|---|
| | 'Bovey Belle' (p) $\mathbb{Y}^{H4}$ | CBcs LRHS |
| | 'Bressingham Pink' (p) | ECtt |
| | 'Brian Tumbler' (b) $\mathbb{Y}^{H4}$ | SAll |
| | 'Bridal Veil' (p) | SAll SBch SSvw WHer |
| | 'Brigadier' (p) | ECho |
| | 'Brilliance' (p) | ECho WMoo |
| | 'Brilliant' | see *D. deltoides* 'Brilliant' |
| | 'Brilliant Star' (p) $\mathbb{Y}^{H4}$ | CBgR ECho LBee SPet SWvt WWFP |
| | 'Brymos' (p) | CWsd |
| | 'Brympton Red' (p) | ECha MRav SSvw WEas |
| | 'Bryony Lisa' (b) $\mathbb{Y}^{H4}$ | SAll |
| | ***caesius*** | see *D. gratianopolitanus* |
| | ***callizonus*** | GEdr GKev NMen |
| | 'Calypso Star' (p) $\mathbb{Y}^{H4}$ | CPBP EBee ECho ECtt GBuc GMaP SPet SPoG STes |
| | 'Camilla' (b) | SSvw |
| | 'Can-can' (pf) | ECho ECtt |
| | 'Candy Clove' (b) | SAll |
| | Candy Floss = 'Devon Flavia' (p) | CBgR ECtt EWll GKir LBMP SPoG |
| | 'Candy Spice'$^{PBR}$ (p) | MRav |
| | 'Carmine Letitia Wyatt'$^{PBR}$ (p) $\mathbb{Y}^{H4}$ | EBee LBMP SPoG |
| | ***carthusianorum*** | CArn CKno IGor LCro LDai LPla MNFA MSte NDlv NDov SAga SGar SMeo SPhx SSvw SWat WEas WOut WPGP WPer |
| | - var. ***humilis*** **new** | CSec |
| | ***caryophyllus*** | CArn GBar MNHC NBlu |
| | 'Casser's Pink' (p) | GBuc |
| | 'Charles' (p) | SAll |
| | 'Charles Edward' (p) | SAll |
| | 'Charles Musgrave' | see *D.* 'Musgrave's Pink' |
| | 'Chastity' (p) | WHoo |
| | Cheddar pink | see *D. gratianopolitanus* |
| | 'Cherly' **new** | LSRN |
| | 'Cherry Clove' (b) | SAll |
| | 'Cherry Moon' | LRHS |
| | 'Cherry Pie' (p) | EAEE EBee EPfP SPoG WMnd |
| | 'Cheryl' | see *D.* 'Houndspool Cheryl' |
| | 'Chianti' (pf) | NGdn |
| | ***chinensis*** (p,a) | CArn |
| | - 'Black and White' | CSpe |
| | 'Chris Crew' (b) $\mathbb{Y}^{H4}$ | SAll |
| | 'Christopher' (p) | LRHS SAll |
| | 'Clara' (pf) | CNMi |
| | 'Clara's Lass' (pf) | CNMi |
| | 'Clare' (p) | SAll |
| | 'Claret Joy' (p) $\mathbb{Y}^{H4}$ | CBcs CFir EPfP LAst NPri SAll SEND |
| § | 'Cockenzie Pink' (p) | IGor NChi SAll SSvw WEas |
| | 'Coconut Sundae' (p) | CBgR ECtt EWll WBor |
| | 'Constance' (p) | SAll |
| | 'Constance Finnis' | see *D.* 'Fair Folly' |
| | 'Consul' (b) | SAll |
| | 'Conwy Silver' | WAbe |
| | 'Conwy Star' | CPBP WAbe |
| | 'Cornish Snow' (p) | NChi |
| | 'Corona Cherry Magic' $\mathbb{Y}^{H3}$ | LRHS |
| | 'Coronation Ruby' (p) $\mathbb{Y}^{H4}$ | CBcs SAll |
| | 'Coste Budde' (p) | IGor WEas WSHC |
| | 'Cranmere Pool' (p) $\mathbb{Y}^{H4}$ | CCge CMea EBee ECtt ELan EPfP LAst LRHS NPri SPoG SWvt WFar WMnd |
| | ***cretaceus*** | NWCA |
| | 'Crimson Chance' (p) | NSla |
| | 'Crompton Classic' (pf) | CNMi |
| | ***cruentus*** | MSte NDov SPhx SSvw WPer |
| | 'Dad's Favourite' (p) | CCge CEnt IGor SAll SRms SSvw WEas |
| | 'Daily Mail' (p) | see *D.* 'Bailey's Daily Mail' |
| | 'Dainty Dame' (p) $\mathbb{Y}^{H4}$ | CPBP CSpe CTri ECho GBuc MNHC MSte MWea SEND SPoG SRot WFar |
| | 'Damask Superb' (p) | IGor |
| | 'Daphne' (p) | SAll |
| | 'Dark Star' (p) | ECho |
| | 'Dartington Double' (p) | ECho |
| | 'David' (p) | LSRN SAll |
| | 'David Russell' (b) $\mathbb{Y}^{H4}$ | SAll |
| | 'Dawlish Joy' (p) | EBee SPoG SRGP |
| | 'Dawn' (b) | SAll |
| | 'Dawn' (pf) | ECho |
| | 'Dedham Beauty' | WCot |
| | ***deltoides*** $\mathbb{Y}^{H4}$ | CArn CEnt CSec CSev EBWF ECha ECho ELau EPfP GBar NSco SECG SHGN SPlb SRms WFar WJek WLHH |
| | - 'Albus' | ECha EPfP GBar MNHC NBlu NPri SSvw SWat WMoo WRos |
| | - 'Arctic Fire' | CWib ECho LBMP NGdn WFar WMoo |
| | - 'Bright Eyes' | CCge ECho |
| § | - 'Brilliant' | CTri ECho EPau MDun MNHC NPri NVic SAll SRms SWat WFar WGor |
| | - 'Canta Libra' | SWal |
| | - 'Dark Eyes' (p) | EWes |
| | - 'Erectus' | EPfP |
| | - Flashing Light | see *D. deltoides* 'Leuchtfunk' |
| § | - 'Leuchtfunk' | CHrt EAlp ECho ECtt EPfP GGar IBal LAst LBMP LRHS NBlu NMir NNor SPoG SWal WFar WMoo WRHF WRos |
| I | - 'Luneburg Heath Maiden Pink' **new** | SSvw |
| | - 'Microchip' | WFar WMoo |
| | - 'Nelli' (p) | ECho SSvw |
| | - red | NBlu SVic |
| | - 'Vampir' | EHig |
| | 'Denis' (p) | LSRN SAll |
| | 'Desert Song' (b) | SAll |
| | 'Devon Charm' (p) | LRHS |
| | 'Devon Cream'$^{PBR}$ (p) | EAEE EBee ECtt LRHS NDov NPri SPoG WMnd WRHF |
| | 'Devon Dove'$^{PBR}$ (p) $\mathbb{Y}^{H4}$ | CBgR CMea CSBt EAEE EBee EPfP LAst NCGa NDov SPoG WWFP |
| § | 'Devon Flores' (p) **new** | LRHS |
| | 'Devon General'$^{PBR}$ (p) | CTri EBee ECtt SPoG |
| | 'Devon Glow' (p) $\mathbb{Y}^{H4}$ | EBee EPfP LBMP LRHS SPoG |
| | 'Devon Joy' (p) | LRHS |
| | 'Devon Magic'$^{PBR}$ (p) | EBee ELan SPoG WFar |
| | 'Devon Pearl'$^{PBR}$ (p) | EBee LHop WMnd |
| | 'Devon Pink Pearl' | LBMP |
| | 'Devon Wizard'$^{PBR}$ (p) $\mathbb{Y}^{H4}$ | CBgR EAEE EBee EPfP LBMP LRHS NDov SPoG WCAu WFar |
| | 'Devon Yvette'$^{PBR}$ $\mathbb{Y}^{H4}$ | CCge |
| | 'Dewdrop' (p) | CMea CTri EBee ECho ECtt EPot MHer NBir NGdn NPro SAll SEND WFar WPer |
| | 'Diana' | see *D.* Dona = 'Brecas' |
| | 'Diane' (p) $\mathbb{Y}^{H4}$ | EBee ECtt ELan EPfP GKir SAll SPla SPoG SWvt WMnd |
| | 'Diplomat' (b) | SAll |
| § | Dona = 'Brecas' (pf) | EAEE LRHS SRGP |
| | 'Dora' (p) | LRHS |
| | 'Doris' (p) $\mathbb{Y}^{H4}$ | CBcs CMea CTri CWan EBee ECtt EPfP GKir LAst LBMP LCro LHop LRHS LSRN MRav NPri SAll SPer SPla SPlb SPoG SRGP SRms SSvw SWvt WCAu WKif WMnd |
| | 'Doris Allwood' (pf) | CNMi CSBt EMal SAll |
| | 'Doris Elite' (p) | SAll |
| | 'Doris Galbally' (b) | SAll |
| | 'Doris Majestic' (p) | SAll WFar |
| | 'Doris Ruby' | see *D.* 'Houndspool Ruby' |
| | 'Doris Supreme' (p) | SAll |
| | 'Double North' | NWCA |
| § | 'Dubarry' (p) | CTri CWan ECho ECtt WGor WPer |

| | | |
|---|---|---|
| | 'Duchess of Westminster' (M) | EMal SAll |
| | 'Duke of Norfolk' (pf) | EMal |
| | 'Earl of Essex' (p) | SAll SSvw |
| | 'Edenside Scarlet' (b) | SAll |
| | 'Edenside White' (b) | SAll |
| | 'Edna' (p) | SAll |
| | 'Edward Allwood' (pf) | SAll |
| | 'Eileen' (p) | SAll |
| | 'Eileen Lever' (p) | CPBP EPot ITim WAbe WFar |
| | 'Eleanor Parker' (p) **new** | WAbe |
| | 'Eleanor's Old Irish' (p) | WCot WHoo WTin |
| | 'Elfin Star' (p) | ECho MSte SPet |
| | 'Elizabeth' (p) | CEnt WEas |
| | 'Elizabethan' (p) | CFee CTca GMac |
| * | 'Elizabethan Pink' (p) | SAll |
| | 'Emma James' (b) | SAll |
| | 'Emperor' | see *D.* 'Bat's Double Red' |
| | ***erinaceus*** | EAlp ECho EDAr GKev LRHS NWCA SRot WAbe |
| | - var. ***alpinus*** | EPot ITim |
| | 'Erycina' (b) | SAll |
| | 'Ethel Hurford' (p) | WHoo |
| | 'Eva Humphries' (b) | SAll |
| | 'Evening Star' (p) ♀H4 | CBgR EAlp EBee ECho LBee SPet SPoG SWvt |
| | 'Excelsior' (p) | SSvw |
| | 'Exquisite' (b) | SAll |
| § | 'Fair Folly' (p) | SAll SSvw |
| | 'Fanal' (p) | NBir |
| | 'Farnham Rose' (p) | SSvw |
| | 'Fenbow Nutmeg Clove' (b) | MBrN SDix WMnd |
| | ***ferrugineus*** | MSte |
| | 'Fettes Mount' (p) | SSvw WCot |
| | 'Feuerhexe' (p) | LRHS NPro |
| | 'Fiery Cross' (b) | SAll |
| | 'Fimbriatus' (p) | WHoo |
| | 'Fiona' (p) | SAll |
| | 'Fireglow' (b) | SAll |
| | 'Firestar' (p) | EAlp GAbr LBee NPri SPet SWvt |
| | 'First Lady' (b) | ECho SAll |
| | 'Flanders' (b) ♀H4 | SAll |
| | 'Fleur' (p) | SAll |
| | 'Forest Princess' (b) **new** | SAll |
| | 'Forest Sprite' (b) | SAll |
| | 'Forest Treasure' (b) | SAll |
| | 'Forest Violet' (b) | SAll |
| | 'Fortuna' (p) | SAll |
| | 'Fountain's Abbey' (p) | IGor |
| | 'Fragrant Ann' (pf) ♀H1 | CNMi |
| * | ***fragrantissimus*** | LRHS |
| | 'Frances Isabel' (p) | SAll |
| | 'Freda' (p) | SAll |
| | ***freynii*** | CLyd ECho EPot EWes GKev WAbe |
| * | - var. ***nana*** | GKev |
| N | fringed pink | see *D. superbus* |
| | ***furcatus*** | GKev |
| | 'Fusilier' (p) | CElw CMea CTri EAlp EBee ECho EDAr EPfP GMaP LAst LHop LRHS MBar MSte NWCA SAll SRot SWvt WBVN WFar WPat |
| | 'Gail Graham' (b) | SAll |
| | 'Garland' (p) | CMea CTri LRHS WGor |
| | 'Gaydena' (b) | SAll |
| | 'George Allwood' (pf) | SAll |
| | ***giganteus*** | CSec CSpe MSte MWea WGwG WSHC |
| | 'Gingham Gown' (p) | CPBP EPot NBir SPoG |
| | ***glacialis*** | SSvw |
| * | - ***elegans*** | GKev |
| | 'Gold Fleck' | EPot MSte SBch SIng |
| | 'Grandma Calvert' (p) | SAll |
| | ***graniticus*** | EPot |
| | 'Gran's Favourite' (p) ♀H4 | CBcs CCge CEnt CMea CSBt CTri EAEE EBee ECtt EPfP LAst LBMP LRHS LSRN NPri SAll SEND SPlb SPoG SRGP SRms SWvt WBor WEas WFar |
| § | ***gratianopolitanus*** ♀H4 | CArn CBod CMea CSec CTri EPfP EPot GKev LRHS MHer MNHC MNrw MRav NBid NChi NWCA SRms WAbe WGwG |
| | - 'Albus' | EPot MHer |
| | - 'Compactus Eydangeri' (p) | GBin |
| | - 'Flore Pleno' (d) | SHGN SSvw |
| | - 'Grandiflorus' | SHGN WFar |
| I | - 'Radicans' **new** | CSec |
| § | - 'Tiny Rubies' (p) | MSte WAbe |
| | 'Gravetye Gem' (b) | SRms |
| | 'Green Lane' (p) | CHll |
| | 'Grenadier' (p) | ECho |
| | 'Grey Dove' (b) ♀H4 | SAll |
| | 'Gypsy Star' (p) | EBee ECho GMaP SPet SPoG |
| | ***haematocalyx*** | NMen NWCA SSvw WAbe WFar WPer |
| | - 'Alpinus' | see *D. haematocalyx* subsp. *pindicola* |
| § | - subsp. ***pindicola*** | GAuc GKev LLHF NMen |
| | 'Harkell Special' (b) | SAll |
| | 'Harlequin' (p) | WPer |
| | 'Harmony' (b) | SAll |
| | 'Haytor' | see *D.* 'Haytor White' |
| | 'Haytor Rock' (p) ♀H4 | EBee EPfP |
| § | 'Haytor White' (p) ♀H4 | CWib EPfP GKir LAst LRHS MRav SAll SRms WCot WEas |
| | 'Hazel Ruth' (b) ♀H4 | SAll |
| | 'Heidi' (p) | LBuc SHGN |
| | 'Helen' (p) | LSRN SAll |
| | 'Helena Hitchcock' (p) | SAll |
| | 'Hereford Butter Market' (p) | EBee |
| | 'Hidcote' (p) | CLyd CTri LRHS NMen WFar |
| | 'Hidcote Red' | ECho LBee LRHS MSte MWat |
| | 'Highland Fraser' (p) | SRms WEas WKif |
| | 'Hope' (p) | SSvw |
| | 'Horsa' (b) | SAll |
| | 'Hot Spice'PBR (p) ♀H4 | SPoG |
| § | 'Houndspool Cheryl' (p) ♀H4 | CTri EBee EPfP LRHS SAll SRGP SRms WFar |
| § | 'Houndspool Ruby' (p) ♀H4 | CBgR EPfP LBMP SAll WCAu WEas |
| | 'Ian' (p) | LSRN SAll |
| | 'Iceberg' (p) | ECho |
| | 'Icomb' (p) | CLyd SRms WHoo WPer |
| | 'Ina' (p) | EGoo LBuc SRms |
| | 'Inchmery' (p) | SAll SHGN SSvw WEas WHoo WTin |
| | 'India Star'PBR (p) ♀H4 | CBgR CCge CTri EAlp EBee ECho LAst SPet STes |
| | 'Inglestone' (p) | CTri NHol WPer |
| | 'Inshriach Dazzler' (p) ♀H4 | CPBP EAlp ECho ECtt GAbr GGar GMaP LBee LHop LRHS MHer MSte MWea NDlv NHar NHol NRya SIng SRot WAbe |
| | 'Inshriach Startler' (p) | CLyd CMea |
| | 'Ipswich Pink' (p) | LRHS MNHC SRms |
| | 'Jacqueline Ann' (pf) ♀H1 | CNMi |
| | 'James Portman' (p) | CBcs CBgR EBee WMnd |
| | 'Jane Austen' (p) | WPer |
| | 'Jane Barker' (b) | SAll |
| | 'Janelle Welch' (pf) | CNMi |
| | 'Janet Walker' (p) | GMaP |
| | ***japonicus*** | CSec |
| | - f. ***albiflorus*** | EHig |
| | 'Jess Hewins' (pf) | CNMi SAll |
| * | 'Jewel' | ECho |
| | 'Joan Schofield' (p) | ECho SBch SPoG |
| | 'Joanne's Highlight' (pf) | CNMi |
| | 'Joan's Blood' | see *D. alpinus* 'Joan's Blood' |
| | 'Joe Vernon' (pf) | CNMi |

| | | |
|---|---|---|
| | 'John Ball' (p) | SSvw |
| | 'Joy' (p) $\mathbb{Y}^{H4}$ | EBee ECho ECtt EPfP GKir LAst LRHS SAll SPoG |
| | 'Julian' (p) | SAll |
| | 'Julie Ann Davis' (b) | SAll |
| | 'Kessock Charm' | MNrw |
| | 'Kesteven Chamonix' (p) | WPer |
| | 'Kesteven Kirkstead' (p) $\mathbb{Y}^{H4}$ | CSWP MNrw |
| | ***kitaibelii*** | see *D. petraeus* subsp. *petraeus* |
| | 'Kiwi Far North' | SHGN |
| | ***knappii*** | EBee LDai LHop NDov NLar NVic SMeo SRms SSvw WMoo WPer |
| | - 'Yellow Harmony' (p,a) | EHig LRHS SGar |
| | ***kusnezovii*** **new** | GKev |
| § | 'La Bourboule' (p) $\mathbb{Y}^{H4}$ | CMea CTri ECho EDAr EPot GAbr LRHS MBar MWat NHol NMen NPri SRms WFar WPat |
| | 'La Bourboule Alba' (p) | CTri ECho ECtt EDAr EPot WFar WGor |
| | 'Laced Hero' (p) | IGor NWCA |
| | 'Laced Joy' (p) | SAll |
| | 'Laced Monarch' (p) | CBcs CEnt EAEE EBee ECtt GCra GKir LRHS NCGa NLar SAll SEND SMrm SPlb SPoG |
| | 'Laced Mrs Sinkins' (p) | SAll SHGN |
| | 'Laced Prudence' | see *D.* 'Prudence' |
| | 'Laced Romeo' (p) | SAll |
| | 'Laced Treasure' (p) | SAll |
| | 'Lady Granville' (p) | IGor SAll SBch SHGN SSvw |
| | Lady in Red = 'WP04 Xanthe' (p) | CBgR LBMP |
| | 'Lady Madonna' (p) | CBgR CSBt SSvw |
| § | 'Lady Wharncliffe' (p) | IGor SBch |
| | 'Lady Windermere' (M) | EMal |
| | ***langeanus*** NS 255 | NWCA |
| | 'Laura' (p) | SAll |
| | 'Lemsii' (p) $\mathbb{Y}^{H4}$ | ECho ECtt NMen WPer |
| | 'Leslie Rennison' (b) | SAll |
| | 'Letitia Wyatt' (p) $\mathbb{Y}^{H4}$ | CMea EBee EPfP LBMP SPoG SRGP |
| | 'Leuchtkugel' | ECho LLHF NHar NMen SIng |
| | ***leucophaeus*** var. ***leucophaeus*** | EPot |
| I | 'Lily the Pink' (p) | CBgR |
| | 'Linfield Annie's Fancy' (pf) | CNMi |
| | 'Linfield Dorothy Perry' (p) $\mathbb{Y}^{H4}$ | SAll |
| | 'Linfield Isobel Croft' (p) | SAll |
| | 'Lionheart' (p) | LRHS |
| | 'Little Ben' (p) | SAll |
| | 'Little Jock' (p) | CCge CPBP ECho ECtt EDAr EPot GGar GMaP LRHS MBar MHer MRav MWat SAll SIng SPlb SPoG SRms WEas WFar |
| | 'Little Miss Muffet' (p) | CHll |
| | 'London Brocade' (p) | SHGN SSvw |
| | 'London Glow' (p) | SAll |
| | 'London Lovely' (p) | SAll SHGN SSvw |
| | 'London Poppet' (p) | NDlv SAll SSvw |
| | 'Loveliness' (p,a) | CBre |
| | ***lumnitzeri*** | ECho LLHF WPer |
| | 'Lustre' (b) | SAll |
| | 'Madame Dubarry' | see *D.* 'Dubarry' |
| | 'Madonna' (p) **new** | SSvw |
| | 'Madonna' (pf) | EPfP |
| | 'Maggie' (p) **new** | LSRN |
| | 'Maisie Neal' (b) $\mathbb{Y}^{H4}$ | SAll |
| | 'Mandy' (p) | SAll |
| | 'Marjery Breeze' | SAll |
| | 'Marmion' (M) | EMal SAll |
| | 'Mars' (p) | ECho ECtt NDlv |
| | 'Matthew' (p) | WHoo |
| | 'Maudie Hinds' (b) | SAll |

| | | |
|---|---|---|
| | 'Maybole' (b) | SAll |
| | 'Maythorne' (p) | SRms |
| | 'Mendip Hills' (b) | SAll |
| | Mendlesham Minx = 'Russmin'$^{PBR}$ (p) | EBee ECho EDAr GBuc GGar SAll SEND SPet SWvt |
| | 'Messines Pink' (p) | SAll SSvw |
| | 'Michael Saunders' (b) $\mathbb{Y}^{H4}$ | SAll |
| | ***microlepis*** | CGra ECho GKev ITim NGdn WAbe |
| | - 'Leuchtkugel' | ECho WAbe |
| | - var. ***musalae*** | CLyd ECho ITim LLHF NHar NMen WAbe |
| | 'Mike Briggs' (b) | SAll |
| | 'Miss Sinkins' (p) | ECtt SPet SPla |
| | 'Monica Wyatt' (p) $\mathbb{Y}^{H4}$ | EAEE EBee ECtt EPfP GKir LRHS NCGa SPoG |
| | ***monspessulanus*** | GKev NDlv SSvw WMoo WPer |
| | 'Montrose Pink' | see *D.* 'Cockenzie Pink' |
| | Morning Star = 'Devon Winnie'$^{PBR}$ | LBee SPet |
| | 'Moulin Rouge' (p) $\mathbb{Y}^{H4}$ | CBgR CEnt EBee LBMP SHGN SPoG WWFP |
| | 'Mrs Clark' | see *D.* 'Nellie Clark' |
| | 'Mrs Macbride' (p) | SAll |
| | 'Mrs N. Clark' | see *D.* 'Nellie Clark' |
| | 'Mrs Perkins' (b) | SAll |
| | 'Mrs Roxburgh' (p) | CSam |
| | 'Mrs Sinkins' (p) | CMea COlW CSam EBee ECha ELan EPfP GMaP LAst LCro LHop LRHS LSRN MHer MLHP MNHC MRav SAll SMrm SPer SPoG SRms SSvw SWvt WCAu WFar WMnd |
| | 'Murray Douglas' (p) | SSvw |
| N | 'Musgrave's Pink' (p) | ECha MRav SAga SAll SBch SSvw WEas |
| | 'Musgrave's White' | see *D.* 'Musgrave's Pink' |
| | ***myrtinervius*** | CLyd CPBP CSec ECho GBin GEdr MAvo NLar NWCA SHGN SRms |
| | - subsp. ***caespitosus*** | NHar |
| | 'Mystic Star' | CMea EAlp ELan |
| | 'Napoleon III' (p) | SSvw |
| | ***nardiformis*** | SPhx SSvw WPer |
| | 'Natalie Saunders' (b) $\mathbb{Y}^{H4}$ | SAll |
| | 'Nautilus' (b) | SAll |
| | ***neglectus*** | see *D. pavonius* |
| § | 'Nellie Clark' (p) | CLyd ECho MWat |
| | 'Neon Star'$^{PBR}$ (p) $\mathbb{Y}^{H4}$ | EBee ECho EDAr ELan GKev SPoG WFar |
| | 'Night Star' (p) $\mathbb{Y}^{H4}$ | CBgR EAlp EBee ECho ELan GKev GMaP LSou MNrw SPet SRot WBVN WFar |
| | ***nitidus*** | CLyd CSec NBir NWCA SSvw WPer |
| | ***noeanus*** | see *D. petraeus* subsp. *noeanus* |
| | 'Northland' (pf) | CNMi EMal SAll |
| | 'Nyewoods Cream' (p) | CMea CTri ECho MBar MHer MRav MSte NHol NMen NPri SIng WPer WTin |
| § | 'Oakington' (p) | CTri LRHS MRav NPri NWCA |
| | 'Oakington Rose' | see *D.* 'Oakington' |
| | 'Old Blush' | see *D.* 'Souvenir de la Malmaison' |
| | 'Old Dutch Pink' (p) | IGor SSvw |
| | 'Old French Red' (pf) | EMal |
| | 'Old Irish' (p) | IGor |
| | 'Old Mother Hubbard' (p) | CFee CHll |
| | 'Old Red Clove' (p) | WCot WEas |
| § | 'Old Square Eyes' (p) | MNrw SAll SSvw WEas WFar |
| | 'Old Velvet' (p) | GCal MNrw SAll |
| | 'Oliver' (p) | SAll |
| | 'Orange Maid' (b) | SAll |
| | 'Oscar' (b) | SAll |
| | 'Painted Lady' (p) | IGor SAll |
| | 'Paisley Gem' (p) | SSvw |
| § | ***pavonius*** $\mathbb{Y}^{H4}$ | CLyd EWes GKev NGdn NLar NWCA WPer |

| | | |
|---|---|---|
| | - 'Nancy Lindsay' (p) | SSvw |
| | - ***roysii*** | see *D.* 'Roysii' |
| § | ***petraeus*** | EWes |
| § | - subsp. ***noeanus*** | EPot GKev LLHF WHal WPer |
| § | - subsp. ***petraeus*** | WPer |
| | 'Petticoat Lace' (p) | SAll |
| | 'Pheasant's Eye' (p) | SAll SSvw WHer |
| * | 'Picton's Propeller' (p) | GBuc |
| | 'Pike's Pink' (p) ♀H4 | CCge CSpe CTri EBee ECho ECtt EDAr ELan EPfP GGar LHop MHer MRav MWat NMen SAll SEND SIng SPet SPoG SRms SSvw WBVN WEas |
| | ***pindicola*** | see *D. haematocalyx* subsp. *pindicola* |
| | ***pinifolius*** | NLar |
| | 'Pink Devon Pearl'PBR | CBgR SAll |
| | 'Pink Fantasy' (b) | SAll |
| | 'Pink Jewel' (p) | CLyd CMea EAlp ECho ECtt EPot LRHS NMen SAll WEas |
| | 'Pink Mrs Sinkins' (p) | ECha MHer MLHP SAll |
| | 'Pixie' (b) | EPot |
| | 'Pixie Star'PBR (p) ♀H4 | ECho EPfP GMaP SPoG SRot |
| | ***plumarius*** | CArn SAll SECG SRms SSvw WHer WMoo |
| | ***pontederae*** | WPer |
| | 'Popstar' | EWll |
| | 'Pretty' (p) | LRHS |
| | 'Pretty Lady' (p) | ECho |
| | 'Prince Charming' (p) | EAlp ECho EPot NPri SRms WPer |
| | 'Princess of Wales' (M) | EMal SAll |
| | 'Priory Pink' (p) | SAll |
| § | 'Prudence' (p) | SAll |
| | 'Pudsey Prize' (p) | CLyd CPBP WAbe |
| | 'Pummelchen' (p) | EPot ITim WAbe |
| | 'Purple Jenny' (p) | SAll |
| | ***pygmaeus*** | NBro |
| | 'Queen of Hearts' (p) | CTri ECho LRHS NWCA SEND WPer |
| § | 'Queen of Henri' (p) | ECho ECtt GEdr LRHS MHer SHGN SHar WBVN WFar |
| | 'Queen of Sheba' (p) | SHGN SSvw WKif |
| | 'Rachel' (p) | ECtt WPat |
| | 'Rainbow Loveliness' (p,a) | SAll SRms WHil |
| | 'Ralph Gould' (p) | ECho |
| | 'Raspberry Sundae' (p) | CBgR ECtt LBMP |
| | 'Rebecca' (b) | SAll |
| | 'Red Star'PBR ♀H4 | EAlp ELan GGar MMHG MSte SPet SRot |
| | 'Red Velvet' | CLyd |
| | 'Reine de Henri' | see *D.* 'Queen of Henri' |
| | 'Revell's Lady Wharncliffe' | see *D.* 'Lady Wharncliffe' |
| | 'Richard Gibbs' (p) | MOne |
| | 'Rivendell' (p) | CLyd CPBP ECho NMen WAbe |
| | 'Robert Allwood' (pf) | SAll |
| | 'Robin Ritchie' (p) | WHoo |
| | 'Robina's Daughter' | GAbr |
| | 'Roodkapje' (p) | SSvw |
| | 'Rose de Mai' (p) | CSam SAll SBch SHGN SSvw WHoo |
| | 'Rose Devon Pearl'PBR | EPfP NCGa |
| | 'Rose Joy' (p) ♀H4 | EBee EPfP NLar |
| § | 'Roysii' (p) | WPer |
| | 'Rubin' (pf) | WEas |
| | 'Ruby' | see *D.* 'Houndspool Ruby' |
| | 'Ruby Doris' | see *D.* 'Houndspool Ruby' |
| | 'Rudheath Ruby' (b) | SAll |
| | aff. ***ruprechtii*** JJ 0448 **new** | MSte |
| | 'Saint Nicholas' (p) | SSvw |
| | 'Sam Barlow' (p) | SAll SSvw |
| | ***sanguineus*** | NDov |
| | 'Santa Claus' (b) | SAll |
| | Scarlet Beauty = 'Hilbeau' | NBlu |
| | ***scopulorum perplexans*** | ITim |
| | ***seguieri*** | SSvw |
| | ***serotinus*** | EPot SSvw WCot |
| | ***shinanensis*** | GKev |
| | Shooting Star | see *D.* 'Devon Flores' |
| | 'Shot Silk' (pf) | SAll |
| | 'Show Aristocrat' (p) | SAll |
| | 'Show Beauty' (p) | ECtt SAll |
| | 'Show Glory' (p) | SAll |
| | 'Show Harlequin' (p) | SAll |
| | 'Show Satin' (p) | SAll |
| | 'Shrimp' (b) | CWib |
| * | 'Six Hills' | NHol WPat |
| | 'Slap 'n' Tickle' **new** | LSRN |
| | 'Snowflake' (p) | ECho |
| | 'Snowshill Manor' (p) | WPer |
| | 'Solomon' (p) | SSvw |
| | 'Sops-in-wine' (p) | CSam ECha ECtt GBuc SAll |
| | 'Southmead' (p) | ECho |
| § | 'Souvenir de la Malmaison' (M) | EMal SAll |
| | 'Spangle' (b) | SAll |
| | 'Spencer Bickham' (p) | MNrw SHGN |
| | ***spiculifolius*** | EPot GAuc NWCA SPhx SSvw WFar |
| | 'Spring Beauty' (p) | NBir WHer |
| | 'Spring Star' (p) | ECtt SRot |
| | 'Square Eyes' | see *D.* 'Old Square Eyes' |
| | ***squarrosus*** | ECho EPot NWCA |
| * | - ***alpinus*** | ECho |
| | - 'Nanus' | ECho ELan EWes LBee |
| | 'Starburst' **new** | CMea EAlp |
| | 'Stardust' **new** | EAlp |
| | Starlight = 'Hilstar' | CMea |
| | 'Starry Eyes' (p) ♀H4 | CMea EAlp ELan EPfP GMaP MWea SRot STes SWvt WFar |
| | 'Storm' (pf) | EMal SAll |
| | 'Strawberries and Cream' (p) | EAEE EBee ECtt GKir LAst LRHS NCGa NOrc SPla SPoG WMnd |
| | 'Strawberry Kiss' | LRHS |
| * | ***strictus*** subsp. ***pulchellus*** | CPBP |
| | ***subacaulis*** | NGdn NLar |
| | - subsp. ***brachyanthus*** | NMen WAbe |
| | - - 'Murray Lyon' | WThu |
| | ***suendermannii*** | see *D. petraeus* |
| | 'Summerfield Adam' (p) | SAll |
| | 'Summerfield Amy Francesca' (p) | SAll |
| | 'Summerfield Blaze' (p) | SAll |
| | 'Summerfield Debbie' (p) | SAll |
| | 'Summerfield Emma Louise' (p) | SAll |
| | 'Summerfield Rebecca' (p) | SAll |
| | 'Sunray' (b) | SAll |
| | 'Sunstar' (b) | SAll |
| § | ***superbus*** | EGoo EWTr MNFA MSal NDov WHal WHer WMoo WPer WRHF |
| | - 'Crimsonia' | MBrN WOut |
| | - var. ***longicalycinus*** | MNrw MSte WHer |
| I | - 'Primadonna' | WPer |
| | - subsp. ***speciosus*** | CSec GKev |
| | 'Susan' (p) | SAll |
| | 'Susannah' (p) | SAll |
| * | 'Susan's Seedling' (p) | SAll |
| | 'Swanlake' (p) | SAll |
| | 'Sway Lass' (p) | SEND |
| | 'Sweet Sophie' (pf) | CNMi |
| | 'Sweet Sue' (b) | SAll |
| | 'Sweetheart Abbey' (p) | GBuc IGor SSvw |
| | ***sylvestris*** | CSec SSvw |
| | - dwarf **new** | EPot |
| * | - subsp. ***frigidus*** **new** | GKev |
| | 'Tamsin Fifield' (b) ♀H4 | SAll |
| | 'Tatra Blush' (p) | GCal |
| | 'Tatra Fragrance' (p) | CMdw GCal SAll |
| | 'Tatra Ghost' (p) | GCal SAll |

'Tayside Red' (M) — EMal SAll
'Thora' (M) — EMal SAll
Tickled Pink = 'PP11' — CBgR ECtt ELan EWll GKir LAst LBMP LSRN SPoG
'Tiny Rubies' — see *D. gratianopolitanus* 'Tiny Rubies'
'Tony's Choice' (pf) — CNMi
'Treasure' (p) — ECho
'Trevor' (p) — SAll
***turkestanicus*** — CSec NBir WGwG
Tyrolean trailing carnations — SAll
'Unique' (p) — MNrw SAll SSvw
'Ursula Le Grove' (p) — IGor SSvw
'Valda Wyatt' (p) ♀H4 — CBcs EAEE EBee ELan EPfP GKir LAst LRHS NCGa SAll SBch SPla SPoG SRGP SWvt WMnd
'Vic Masters' — SPhx
'W.A. Musgrave' — see *D.* 'Musgrave's Pink'
'W.H. Brooks' (b) — SAll
'Waithman Beauty' (p) — CTri ECtt MBar SAll WHoo WPer WTin
'Waithman's Jubilee' (p) — GMaP SAll SRms WSHC
'Warden Hybrid' (p) — CMea CTri ECho ECtt EPfP GMaP LAst LRHS MWea SHGN SPoG SWvt WAbe WFar
'Waterloo Sunset' **new** — CMea
'Wedding Bells' (pf) — SAll
'Weetwood Double' (p) — CFee
***weyrichii*** — CLyd ECho
'Whatfield Anona' (p) — SAll
'Whatfield Beauty' (p) — CPBP ECho ECtt ELan LRHS
'Whatfield Brilliant' (p) — ECho
'Whatfield Cancan' (p) ♀H4 — CMea ECho ECtt LHop LRHS MNHC NPri NWCA SAll SBch SPoG SWvt WWFP
'Whatfield Cream Lace' — NWCA
'Whatfield Cyclops' (p) — CLyd ECho LRHS SAll
'Whatfield Dawn' (p) — CLyd ECho
'Whatfield Dorothy Mann' (p) — ECho SAll
'Whatfield Doug's Choice' (p) **new** — NWCA
'Whatfield Fuchsia Floss' (p) — CLyd SAll
'Whatfield Gem' (p) — CLyd CPBP ECho ECtt ELan GEdr LAst MSte MWat NPri SAll SPoG SWvt WBVN WFar WPer
'Whatfield Joy' (p) — CLyd ECho ECtt ELan EPfP GMaP LBee LRHS MHer NMen SAll SPoG WFar WHoo WPat
'Whatfield Magenta' (p) ♀H4 — CLyd ECho ELan EPfP EPot LBee LEdu LRHS MWat NMen NWCA SAll SPoG WAbe WEas
'Whatfield Mini' (p) — SAll SRms WPer
'Whatfield Miss' (p) — SAll
'Whatfield Misty Morn' (p) — ECho SAll SEND
'Whatfield Peach' (p) — SAll
'Whatfield Pretty Lady' (p) — ECho SAll
'Whatfield Rose' (p) — ECho EPot
'Whatfield Ruby' (p) — ECho ELan LAst LRHS NWCA SAll WFar WPer
'Whatfield Supergem' (p) — CLyd ECho ECtt EPot
'Whatfield White' (p) — ECho ECtt LRHS SAll SRms
'Whatfield White Moon' (p) — ECho
'Whatfield Wisp' (p) — CPBP CTri EAlp ECho EPot GEdr MRav NBir NMen NWCA SPoG
'White and Crimson' (p) — SAll
'White Joy'PBR (p) ♀H4 — MRav
'White Ladies' (p) — ELan MRav SAll
'Whitecliff' (b) — SAll
'Whitehill' (p) ♀H4 — ECho EPot MHer NMen
'Whitesmith' (b) ♀H4 — SAll
'Widecombe Fair' (p) ♀H4 — CCge CTri CWan EBee ECtt ELan LRHS SAll SPoG SRms
'William Brownhill' (p) — SSvw
'Zebra' (b) — SAll
***zonatus*** — NWCA

## *Diarrhena* (*Poaceae*)

***americana*** — EPPr GFor
***japonica*** — EPPr GFor
* ***mandschurica*** — EPPr
***obovata*** — EPPr

## *Diascia* ✿ (*Scrophulariaceae*)

'Appleby Apricot' — NDov
'Apricot' — see *D. barberae* 'Hopleys Apricot'
Apricot Delight = 'Codicot' (Sun Chimes Series) — WFar
***barberae*** 'Belmore Beauty' (v) — CCge ECtt EWes LIMB LSou WAbe
- 'Blackthorn Apricot' ♀H3-4 — EAEE EAlp ECha ECtt EDAr ELan EPfP GBuc LAst LRHS MRav MSte NDov SPav SPer SPlb SPoG SWvt WFar WPer WSHC
§ - 'Fisher's Flora' ♀H3-4 — EPyc NDov WFar
- 'Fisher's Flora' x 'Lilac Belle' — ECtt
§ - 'Hopleys Apricot' — EPfP
§ - 'Ruby Field' ♀H3-4 — CMea ECha ECtt EDAr ELan EPfP LAst LRHS MRav SPer SPla SPoG SRms SWvt WCFE WFar
Blue Bonnet = 'Hecbon' — ECtt SWvt WFar
'Blush' — see *D. integerrima* 'Blush'
Blush Delight = 'Codiush' (Sun Chimes Series) — WFar
'Coldham' — CMdw
Coral Belle = 'Hecbel'PBR ♀H3-4 — ECtt EPfP EWes LHop LRHS LSou MSte SIng SMrm SPav WFar
***cordata*** misapplied — see *D. barberae* 'Fisher's Flora'
***cordifolia*** — see *D. barberae* 'Fisher's Flora'
Eclat = 'Heclat' — ECtt WFar
***elegans*** misapplied — see *D. fetcaniensis, D. vigilis*
'Emma' — SWvt
***felthamii*** — see *D. fetcaniensis*
§ ***fetcaniensis*** — CMHG CMea EPfP EShb SPer WBrk WCFE WClo WHal WKif
- 'Daydream' — LBuc LRHS WHil
***flanaganii*** misapplied — see *D. vigilis*
***flanaganii*** Hiern — see *D. stachyoides*
(Flying Colours Series) Flying Colours Appleblossom = 'Diastara'PBR — NBlu SPoG
- Flying Colours Apricot = 'Diastina'PBR — SPoG
- Flying Colours Coral = 'Diastis'PBR — SPoG
- Flying Colours Red = 'Diastonia'PBR — SPoG
'Frilly' ♀H3-4 — ECtt
'Hector Harrison' — see *D.* 'Salmon Supreme'
'Hector's Hardy' ♀H3-4 — MSte
Ice Cracker = 'Hecrack' — CMea ECtt ELan LHop LRHS SHGN SPav
Ice Cream = 'Icepol' — LAst NLar SCoo SMrm
Iceberg = 'Hecice'PBR — SWvt
§ ***integerrima*** ♀H3-4 — CSam ECha ELan ELon LLWP SGar SPla WCot
- 'Alba' — see *D. integerrima* 'Blush'
§ - 'Blush' — CSpe EGoo MSte SGar
- 'Ivory Angel' — see *D. integerrima* 'Blush'
***integrifolia*** — see *D. integerrima*
'Jack Elliott' — see *D. vigilis* 'Jack Elliott'
'Jacqueline's Joy' — CMea MSte NPer SBch WFar
'Joyce's Choice' ♀H3-4 — EWes LRHS MSte SBri WFar

| | |
|---|---|
| 'Kate' | LRHS |
| 'Katherine Sharman' (v) | ECtt EWes LSou SAga WAbe |
| 'Lady Valerie' ♀H3-4 | EWes MSte WPer |
| 'Lilac Belle' ♀H3-4 | CCge CMea ECtt EDAr ELan EPfP LRHS MHar MMuc NBir NGdn SBch SPla SPlb SPoG WFar WPer |
| 'Lilac Mist' ♀H3-4 | NPer |
| ***lilacina*** x ***rigescens*** | CCge |
| Little Dancer = 'Pendan' PBR | LAst LSou SCoo SIng WGor |
| Little Dreamer = 'Pender' PBR | LAst SMrm SVil |
| Little Drifter **new** | LSou SVil WRHF |
| Little Maiden = 'Penmaid' **new** | SVil WGor |
| Little Tango **new** | LSou SVil |
| 'Miro' | NLar |
| ***patens*** | CHll |
| ***personata*** | LHop SDys |
| Pink Delight = 'Codiink' | WFar |
| Pink Panther = 'Penther' PBR | ECtt LHop NLar SCoo SMrm SPav SPoG SWvt |
| 'Pink Queen' | ECtt SRms |
| 'Pink Spires' | CElw |
| Prince of Orange = 'Hopor' PBR | LHop NLar |
| Red Ace = 'Hecrace' PBR | EPfP LAst LHop MAvo NPer SPav SPoG SWvt |
| Redstart = 'Hecstart' | ECtt EPfP LHop NGdn SPet SWvt WFar |
| ***rigescens*** ♀H3 | CHEx COIW CPrp CSpe CWCL ECtt ELan EPfP EShb ISea LHop MHer MLLN MRav MWte NPer SAga SPlb SUsu SWvt WAbe WCFE WFar WPGP WSHC |
| § - 'Anne Rennie' | EBee ECtt SWvt |
| - pale-flowered | see *D. rigescens* 'Anne Rennie' |
| 'Ruby Field' | see *D. barberae* 'Ruby Field' |
| 'Rupert Lambert' ♀H3-4 | GBuc LLWP NDov SBri WPer |
| § 'Salmon Supreme' | ECtt ELan EPfP LAst LRHS NGdn NPer SPet SPhx SPoG SRms WFar WMoo WPer |
| § ***stachyoides*** | SBch |
| Susan = 'Winsue' PBR | WFar |
| ***tugelensis*** | WFar |
| 'Twinkle' ♀H3-4 | ECtt EPfP LAst LRHS NBir NGdn NPer SPet WFar |
| * 'Twins Gully' | GCal |
| § ***vigilis*** ♀H3 | CFee CMHG CPLG ECha EDAr EPfP GMaP LRHS MCot NBro SGar WHal |
| § - 'Jack Elliott' | MAvo SPla WCFE |
| (Whisper Series) Whisper Apricot Improved = 'Balwhisaptim' PBR | NBlu NPri SCoo |
| - Whisper Cranberry Red = 'Balwhiscran' PBR | SCoo |
| - Whisper Tangerine = 'Balwhistang' PBR | LSou SGar |
| - Whisper White = 'Balwhiswhit' PBR | NPri SGar |
| 'White Belle' **new** | LSou |
| 'White Cloud' | WHil |
| (Wink Series) Wink Garnet = 'Balwingarn' | SGar |
| - Wink Orange = 'Balwinorg' | NPri |
| - Wink Pink Improved = 'Balwinlapi **new** | NPri |

# *Dicentra* ✿ (*Papaveraceae*)

| | |
|---|---|
| CC 4452 | CPLG |
| 'Adrian Bloom' | EBee EBrs ECtt EHrv EPfP EPla MBNS MCot NBPC NCob NPri SCoo SMrm SPer SWvt WBrE WFar WMoo |
| 'Bacchanal' ♀H4 | Widely available |
| 'Boothman's Variety' | see *D.* 'Stuart Boothman' |
| 'Bountiful' | EAEE EBee GMaP LRHS MBNS MLLN MNFA MRav NCob NGdn SPer SPla SWvt |
| 'Brownie' | CMoH EBee GBuc |
| ***canadensis*** | CLAP EBee EPot GBuc MAvo MTho NLar NSti WCot WCru WHal |
| 'Candy Hearts' PBR | EBee ECtt ELan EPfP IPot MBNS NBro NCob NGdn NLar NSti WFar |
| 'Coldham' | EBee WCru WSHC |
| ***cucullaria*** | CElw CLAP CMea CRow CStu CWCL EBee EBrs ECho EPot ERos GBuc GEdr GGar LRHS MRav MTho NDov NMen NWCA SPhx SPoG WAbe WBVN WCru |
| - 'Pittsburg' | EBee EPPr GBuc SCnR WCot |
| * 'Dark Stuart Boothman' | ECho |
| ***eximia*** misapplied | see *D. formosa* |
| ***eximia*** (Ker Gawl.) Torr. | CSpe EBee LBMP |
| - 'Alba' | see *D. eximia* 'Snowdrift' |
| § - 'Snowdrift' | CLAP EBee ECtt EHrv ELan EPfP MBri MCot MDun MSte MTho NGdn SMrm SPoG SRms WFar WMoo WPnP WPrP |
| § ***formosa*** | Widely available |
| - ***alba*** | CTri ECha GMaP NBir SPla SRms WCAu WCru WFar |
| - 'Aurora' | CSec EBee EBrs ELon EPPr GBin LAst LCro LRHS MRav NBPC NGdn SPer SPet SPoG SWvt WFar WPnP |
| - 'Cox's Dark Red' | CLAP EBee EWes GBin GBuc NMen WMoo |
| - dark | WMoo |
| - 'Furse's Form' | CMoH |
| - subsp. ***oregana*** | CLAP EBee EPPr GBuc GGar NBre NChi NMen WCru WHal |
| - - 'Rosea' | EPPr |
| - 'Spring Gold' | ECha WMoo |
| 'Ivory Hearts' PBR | CLAP EBee ECtt ELan EPPr EPfP GBri LAst LRHS LSRN MAvo MBNS MCot NBro NCGa NCob NLar NSti SMrm SPer |
| 'Katy' **new** | EPPr |
| 'King of Hearts' | Widely available |
| 'Langtrees' ♀H4 | Widely available |
| ***lichiangensis*** | EWld WCru |
| - GWJ 9376 | WCru |
| 'Luxuriant' ♀H4 | CBcs COIW CSBt CSec EAEE EBee EBrs ECtt ELan EPfP GAbr MAvo MLLN MRav NCob NPri SMrm SPer SPoG SRms SWvt WBor WCAu WFar WMoo WPnP |
| ***macrantha*** | CAby CDes CEnt CLAP CMoH CRow EBee ECha EPfP GBuc GCra LAma MTho SMad WCru WPGP WSHC |
| ***macrocapnos*** | CBcs CFir CRow EBee EMil EPfP GBuc GCal GQui IDee MDKP MTho NSti WCru WTou |
| 'Paramount' | GBin |
| 'Pearl Drops' | CElw CRow EHrv ELan GBuc GGar GMaP MCot MRav NBid NGdn NMen SPla SRms WAbb WEas WMoo |
| ***peregrina*** | EDAr GEdr |
| - ***alba*** | EDAr GEdr |
| § ***scandens*** | CMHG CRHN CRow CSam CSpe EBee ECho EPfP GCal ITim LAst MCCP MSCN MTho NCob NLar SHGN SUsu WSHC |
| - GWJ 9438 | WCru |
| - 'Shirley Clemo' | CPLG |

| | |
|---|---|
| 'Silver Beads' | EBee ECho |
| Snowflakes = 'Fusd' | EBee EWes MRav NBre |
| ***spectabilis*** ♀H4 | Widely available |
| - 'Alba' ♀H4 | Widely available |
| - 'Gold Heart' PBR | CBow CSec EBee EBrs EPfP GBri MAsh MGos MRav NLar NSti SPoG WFar |
| 'Spring Morning' | CElw CMHG CMoH CSam ECtt EHrv EPPr LRHS MHar NBre NSti WEas WRHF |
| § 'Stuart Boothman' ♀H4 | Widely available |
| ***thalictrifolia*** | see *D. scandens* |
| ***torulosa*** | CSec WTou |
| - B&SWJ 7814 | WCru |

## *Dichelostemma* (*Alliaceae*)

| | |
|---|---|
| § ***capitatum*** NNS 95-213 | WCot |
| ***congestum*** | CAvo CFFs EBee EBrs ECho EPot ERos GAuc LEdu WCot |
| § ***ida-maia*** | CAvo CBro CFFs CGrW CTca EBee EBrs ECho EPot ILad LEdu LRHS |
| - 'Pink Diamond' | CBro EBee EBrs ECho LEdu WCot |
| ***multiflorum*** | WCot |
| ***pulchellum*** | see *D. capitatum* |
| ***volubile*** | EBee ECho WCot |
| - NNS 95-220 | WCot |

## *Dichondra* (*Convolvulaceae*)

| | |
|---|---|
| ***argentea*** 'Silver Falls' | CSpe EShb LAst LSou NPri SCoo SPoG |
| § ***micrantha*** | EShb |
| ***repens*** misapplied | see *D. micrantha* |

## *Dichopogon* (*Anthericaceae*)

| | |
|---|---|
| ***strictus*** | ECou |

## *Dichorisandra* (*Commelinaceae*)

| | |
|---|---|
| * ***pendula*** | MJnS |
| ***thyrsiflora*** | MJnS |

## *Dichroa* (*Hydrangeaceae*)

| | |
|---|---|
| Guiz 48 | CKob |
| ***febrifuga*** | CAbb CBcs CDoC CHEx CHll CKob CMil CTsd CWGN CWib EBee ELan EWes LRHS MAsh NPri SOWG WCot WCru WOVN WPGP |
| - B&SWJ 2367 | WCru |
| - BL&M 347 new | CKob |
| - HWJK 2430 | WCru |
| - pink-flowered | CHEx |
| aff. ***hirsuta*** B&SWJ 8207 from Vietnam | WCru |
| - B&SWJ 8371 from Lao | WCru |
| - from Thailand | CKob |
| ***versicolor*** | CKob |
| - B&SWJ 6565 | WCru |
| - B&SWJ 6605 from Thailand new | WCru |
| aff. ***versicolor*** | WPGP |
| - Guiz 48 | WPGP |
| aff. ***yunnanensis*** B&SWJ 9734 new | WCru |

## *Dichromena* see *Rhynchospora*

## *Dicksonia* ✿ (*Dicksoniaceae*)

| | |
|---|---|
| ***antarctica*** ♀H3 | Widely available |
| ***berteriana*** | WRic |
| ***fibrosa*** ♀H3 | CBcs CDTJ CTrC EAmu ETod IDee SPoG WRic |
| ***sellowiana*** | WRic |
| ***squarrosa*** ♀H2 | CBcs CCCN CDTJ CTrC ETod LPan NMoo SAPC SArc SPoG WRic |

## *Dicliptera* (*Acanthaceae*)

| | |
|---|---|
| § ***sericea*** | CDes CHal CHll CMdw EBee EShb GCal LHop LSou MWea SEND SMrm SOWG SRkn WCot WDyG WHil WPGP WSHC |
| ***suberecta*** | see *D. sericea* |

## *Dicoma* (*Asteraceae*)

| | |
|---|---|
| ***anomala*** | SPlb |

## *Dicranostigma* (*Papaveraceae*)

| | |
|---|---|
| ***lactucoides*** CC 3756 | WRos |
| ***leptopodum*** | CSpe |

## *Dictamnus* ✿ (*Rutaceae*)

| | |
|---|---|
| ***albus*** | Widely available |
| § - var. ***purpureus*** ♀H4 | Widely available |
| * - ***turkestanicus*** | GCal |
| ***caucasicus*** | SMHy |
| ***fraxinella*** | see *D. albus* var. *purpureus* |
| ***tadshikorum*** | EBee |

## *Didymochlaena* (*Dryopteridaceae*)

| | |
|---|---|
| ***lunulata*** | see *D. truncatula* |
| § ***truncatula*** | CHal MBri XBlo |

## *Dieffenbachia* (*Araceae*)

| | |
|---|---|
| 'Camille' (v) ♀H1 | LRHS |
| 'Compacta' (v) | LRHS |

## *Dierama* ✿ (*Iridaceae*)

| | |
|---|---|
| ***ambiguum*** | CStu EWld GAbr NChi WCot |
| ***argyreum*** | CBgR CCCN CElw EBee GKev IBlr LFur MCot NChi NFir WCot WKif |
| 'Ariel' | IBlr |
| 'Ballerina' | CFir |
| 'Black Knight' | CPrp IBlr |
| 'Blush' | IBlr |
| 'Candy Stripe' | CRow GBri STes |
| 'Castlewellan' | WCra |
| 'Cherry Chimes' | CPen MGos |
| ***cooperi*** | CElw CPou CPrp EBee GBri IBlr WCot |
| 'Coral Bells' | CDes GCal WPGP |
| ***dissimile*** | EBee NFir |
| 'Donard Legacy' | GBri IBlr SKHP |
| § ***dracomontanum*** | Widely available |
| - JCA 3.141.100 | WPGP |
| - Wisley Princess Group | MBri |
| ***dracomontanum*** x ***pulcherrimum*** | SMad |
| ***dubium*** | IBlr |
| ***ensifolium*** | see *D. pendulum* |
| ***erectum*** | CBgR CCCN CHid GAbr IBlr MCot NLar WCot |
| 'Fairy Bells' | CPen EBee IPot NCob |
| 'Fireworks' new | NChi |
| ***floriferum*** | CBro IBlr |
| ***formosum*** | CGHE WPGP |
| ***galpinii*** | CGHE NFir NLar STes WPGP |
| ***grandiflorum*** | CPBP CPou ECho IBlr WCru |
| 'Guinevere' | Widely available |
| ***igneum*** | Widely available |
| - CD&R 278 | CPou |
| ***insigne*** | EBee WCot |
| 'Iris' | IBlr |
| ***jucundum*** | CPne EBee GBri GBuc MLLN WCot |
| 'Knee-high Lavender' | CDes CSpe EPla SAga WPGP |
| 'Lancelot' | Widely available |
| ***latifolium*** | CGHE CHid IBlr NFir SMad |
| ***luteoalbidum*** | CDes CStu EBee WPGP |
| 'Mandarin' | CDes IBlr WPGP |

| | |
|---|---|
| ***medium*** | CGHE CPen CWsd EBee ELon NCGa SUsu SWat WCot WPGP |
| 'Milkmaid' | CPrp IBlr NCot |
| 'Miranda' | CAby CPen CSpe EBee ECtt GBuc GEdr GKev GQue MBNS NCGa NCob NCot NFir NGdn NSti SDnm SMad SMrm SPoG WCot |
| ***mossii*** | CCCN EBee ELon GAbr GKev IBlr MCot NBre NLar SPlb SPoG WPGP |
| ***nixonianum*** | IBlr |
| 'Oberon' | EBee MRav |
| 'Pamina' | CPrp IBlr |
| 'Papagena' | IBlr |
| 'Papageno' | IBlr |
| ***pauciflorum*** | CBgR CBro CFir CGHE CHid CPLG CPrp CStu CWCL CWib EBee EDAr ERos GEdr MHar MHer NBir NFir NLAp NLar SMrm SUsu SWat WAbe WPGP WSHC |
| - CD&R 197 | CPBP MDKP |
| § ***pendulum*** | Widely available |
| - var. ***pumilum*** | CMoH |
| 'Petite Fairy' | CPen |
| ***pictum*** | IBlr |
| Plant World hybrids | GGar |
| 'Pretty Flamingo' | CPrp IBlr |
| 'Puck' | CDes CPen EBee GCal IBlr IGor MLLN MRav WPGP |
| ***pulcherrimum*** | Widely available |
| - var. ***album*** | CBro CCCN CGHE CHar CLAP ECho ELan GBuc GKev IBlr IPot LPio LRHS MCot MNrw NCGa NCob NFir STes SWal WAul WPGP |
| - 'Blackbird' | Widely available |
| - dark pink-flowered | GKev |
| - dwarf | GKev IPot |
| - 'Falcon' | IBlr |
| - 'Flamingo' | IBlr |
| - 'Flaring Tips' | IPot |
| - lilac-flowered | GAbr |
| - 'Merlin' | Widely available |
| - 'Pearly Queen' | CRow EBee |
| - 'Peregrine' | WPGP |
| - 'Red Orr' | ITim |
| - 'Redwing' | IBlr |
| - Slieve Donard hybrids | CLAP CWCL EBee ECho ECtt GBri IPot ITim LAst LHop LRHS MCot MHer SPet WFar WHrl WMnd |
| ***pumilum*** misapplied | see *D. dracomontanum* |
| 'Purple Passion' | CPen CWGN LBuc |
| 'Queen of the Night' | IBlr |
| ***reynoldsii*** | CAbb CBgR CBro CDes CGHE CHid CKno CPrp EBee GAbr GBuc GKev IBlr LAst LFur LRHS MCot MLLN NChi NFir SGar SPlb SPoG STes WHoo WKif WMnd WPGP |
| ***robustum*** | CGHE CPou CSpe GBri IBlr NFir WBVN WPGP |
| 'Sarastro' | CPrp IBlr |
| 'September Charm' | IBlr |
| ***sertum*** | CBro EBee |
| 'Spring Dancer' **new** | MCot |
| 'Tamino' | IBlr |
| 'Tiny Bells' | CDes EBee ECha EDAr GCal GKev WPGP |
| 'Titania' | CPen IBlr |
| ***trichorhizum*** | CBgR CCCN CFir CGHE CPBP CWCL EBee ECho GAbr GBri IBlr LFur MNrw NFir NLar SAga SPoG WSHC |
| 'Tubular Bells' | IBlr |
| ***tyrium*** **new** | NFir |
| 'Violet Ice' | IBlr |
| 'Westminster Chimes' | CDes IBlr WPGP |
| Wilside hybrids | CWsd |
| 'Zulu Bells' | ELon |

## *Diervilla* ✿ (*Caprifoliaceae*)

| | |
|---|---|
| ***lonicera*** | CHar SLon |
| ***middendorffiana*** | see *Weigela middendorffiana* |
| ***rivularis*** 'Troja Black' | NLar |
| § ***sessilifolia*** | CBcs CHar CMac EBee GAuc IDee LAst MRav SGar SLon WBVN WBod WCot WFar WMoo WPat |
| - 'Butterfly' | CMac |
| x ***splendens*** | CAbP CMHG CPLG CWib EBee EHoe ELan EPfP LHop LRHS MBNS MBar MGos MRav MSwo NHol SEND SGar SLPl SPer SPla SPoG WDin |

## *Dietes* (*Iridaceae*)

| | |
|---|---|
| ***bicolor*** | CAbb CDes CHEx CPen CPne CTrC EShb LEdu LPio LSou SDnm SHom |
| ***grandiflora*** | CAbb CArn CDes CFee CMdw CPen CPne EBee ECho EDif EShb LEdu LPio SBch SHom WBor WCot WThu |
| § ***iridioides*** | CDes CPne CSWP EBee EBrs ECho EShb GBin LPio MSte WCot WPGP |

## *Digitalis* ✿ (*Scrophulariaceae*)

| | |
|---|---|
| RCB/TQ 059 from İkizdere **new** | WCru |
| ***ambigua*** | see *D. grandiflora* |
| apricot hybrids | see *D. purpurea* 'Sutton's Apricot' |
| ***cariensis*** | SPav |
| ***ciliata*** | CFir EBee ELan GCal MLLN SPav |
| ***davisiana*** | CPLG GBuc MNHC SPav SPhx STes WCHb WHrl WMoo |
| ***dubia*** | EBee EPfP ERCP NBir SDnm SPav WAbe |
| 'Elsie Kelsey' | CEnt CSec EBee ECtt EShb SDnm SPav SPoG SWvt WHil |
| ***eriostachya*** | see *D. lutea* |
| ***ferruginea*** ♀H4 | Widely available |
| - 'Gelber Herold' | EBee GMaP LRHS MDKP MSte NBre NLar WFar |
| - 'Gigantea' | EBee GQue LRHS MBNS MBri NBPC NChi NPri NSti SSvw SWat WCot |
| - var. ***schischkinii*** | SDnm SPav WBor |
| 'Flashing Spires' | see *D. lutea* 'Flashing Spires' |
| * ***floribunda*** | SPav |
| ***fontanesii*** | CEnt CSec EPPr GBuc NBur WCot |
| x ***fulva*** | MLLN NBir |
| 'Glory of Roundway' | CDes EBee EBla MHer WFar |
| § ***grandiflora*** ♀H4 | Widely available |
| - 'Carillon' | CWan EBee EPau EShb IFoB LDai MBNS MSte NBir NGHP NLar NPri SPhx WGor WPer |
| - 'Cream Bell' **new** | LRHS |
| - 'Dwarf Carillon' | ECtt EWld |
| - 'Temple Bells' | WFar WPer |
| ***heywoodii*** | see *D. purpurea* subsp. *heywoodii* |
| 'John Innes Tetra' | CSec EBee EShb LRHS SWat WPGP |
| ***kishinskyi*** | see *D. parviflora* |
| ***laevigata*** | CEnt CHar CHrt CSam EBee EBla EBrs MCot MSte NBro NGHP SDnm SPav SPet WCHb WMnd WMoo WPer |
| - subsp. ***graeca*** | CSec |
| ***lamarckii*** misapplied | see *D. lanata* |
| ***lamarckii*** Ivanina | EBee NBPC |
| § ***lanata*** | Widely available |
| - 'Café Crème' | LSou MNHC NBPC |
| § ***lutea*** | Widely available |

| | |
|---|---|
| § - subsp. ***australis*** | CSec EBla LDai MAvo SDnm SPav |
| § - 'Flashing Spires' (v) | CBow GBri NBHF |
| - 'Yellow Medley' | EBee WCot |
| ***macedonica*** from Macedonia | CSec |
| x ***mertonensis*** 𝕐$^{H4}$ | Widely available |
| - 'Raspberry Rose' **new** | ITim |
| - 'Summer King' | CBcs ECtt LSRN MWat NBre NGHP WGor |
| ***micrantha*** | see *D. lutea* subsp. *australis* |
| ***nervosa*** | SPav |
| ***obscura*** | EBee ECho EHrv ERCP EShb GEdr GKev MCot NBir NCob NGHP NPri SDnm SEND SIde SPav SPet WCHb WGor WMnd |
| * - 'Dusky Maid' | NBHF |
| ***orientalis*** | see *D. grandiflora* |
| § ***parviflora*** | Widely available |
| - 'Milk Chocolate' | CBcs CMHG ECtt EPfP GQue LFur LSRN MCot MHer MNHC NBPN NBre SBHP SIde SPet WFar WPnP |
| ***purpurea*** | CArn CSec EBWF EBee ECtt GKir GPoy LCro MHer MLHP MNHC NBlu NCob NLan NMir NPri SECG SIde SPlb SPoG WMoo WWFP |
| - 'Alba' | see *D. purpurea* f. *albiflora* |
| § - f. ***albiflora*** | Widely available |
| - - 'Anne Redetzky'$^{PBR}$ | NSti WMnd |
| - - unspotted | CWan |
| - Camelot Series | NGHP WHil WRHF |
| - - 'Camelot Cream' | EAEE NPri SWvt |
| - - 'Camelot Lavender' | NPri SWvt WCot |
| - - 'Camelot Rose' | NPri SWvt |
| - - 'Camelot White' **new** | NPri |
| - Excelsior Group | CBcs CCVT CHrt CSBt CSam CSec CTri EAEE ECtt EPfP GJos GKir GMaP LAst LCro MBri MNHC MWat NMir NVic SPer SPoG SRms SWal SWvt WFar WGor |
| - - (Suttons; Unwins) 𝕐$^{H4}$ | ECtt MRav |
| - Foxy Group | CWib ECtt EHrv SPet SPoG SRms WFar |
| - - 'Foxy Apricot' | CBcs CSec NCGa SPla SWvt WOVN |
| - - 'Foxy Pink' | NCGa SPla |
| - - 'Foxy Primrose' | NPri |
| - Giant Spotted Group | ECtt EHrv EPfP LCro LHop LRHS SCoo |
| - Glittering Prizes Group | SWat |
| - Gloxinioides Group | ELan NCob WFar |
| - - 'The Shirley' 𝕐$^{H4}$ | ECtt SGar WGor |
| § - subsp. ***heywoodii*** | EBee ELan GBuc SDnm SPav WCHb WMoo |
| - - 'Silver Fox' | ECtt LSRN SPer |
| - 'Jellito's Apricot' | CSam |
| - 'Pam's Choice' | CPLG CSpe EAEE EBee EBla ECtt EWTr IPot LAst LHop LRHS LSRN MAvo MGos MNFA MWat MWea NBPC NChi NGBl SPer SRGP WFar WHrl WMnd WMoo WPnP WWlt |
| - peloric | CSec WCHb |
| - 'Primrose Carousel' | EBee ECtt MWat WWlt |
| - 'Snow Thimble' | EBee ECtt GAbr MBri MNFA NLar NVic WCot |
| § - 'Sutton's Apricot' 𝕐$^{H4}$ | Widely available |
| 'Red Skin' | CPom MAvo |
| 'Saltwood Summer' | LCro |
| x ***sibirica*** | EBee SPhx WCHb |
| 'Silver Anniversary' | LBuc |
| * ***spaniflora*** | CSec NLar SPhx |
| 'Spice Island' | EBee LBuc SPoG |
| * ***stewartii*** | CDMG CHar ECtt ELan EWes GCra LDai LFur MBNS MHar NBPC NBur SPad SPav WMoo |
| ***thapsi*** | CArn CSec ECtt ERCP GKev MBNS MLLN NBPC NBur NPri NWCA SDnm SEND SIde SPav WCHb WMoo WPer WWFP |
| - JCA 410.000 | EBee |
| - 'Spanish Peaks' | EBee |
| ***trojana*** | ECtt SGar |
| Vesuvius Group | CEnt |
| ***viridiflora*** | CHrt CPLG EBee ECtt EDAr EShb MBNS MDKP NBro NChi SBHP SGar SPav SPhx SWat WCHb WFar WPer |
| - 'Moss Green' | NBHF |

## *Dimorphocarpa* (*Brassicaceae*)

| | |
|---|---|
| ***wislizeni*** **new** | CSec |

## *Dimorphotheca* (*Asteraceae*)

| | |
|---|---|
| ***pluvialis*** **new** | CSec |

## *Dionaea* (*Droseraceae*)

| | |
|---|---|
| ***muscipula*** | CHew CSWC EECP LRHS MCCP SHmp WSSs |
| - 'Akai Ryu' | CSWC EECP WSSs |
| - 'Royal Red' | CHew CSWC |
| - shark-toothed | CSWC EECP |
| - 'Spider' | CSWC EECP |

## *Dionysia* (*Primulaceae*)

| | |
|---|---|
| 'Annielle' | WAbe |
| ***aretioides*** 𝕐$^{H2}$ | WAbe |
| - 'Bevere' | WAbe |
| - 'Gravetye' | ECho |
| - 'Phyllis Carter' | ECho |
| ***bazoftica*** | WAbe |
| 'Bernd Wetzel' | WAbe |
| ***bryoides*** | WAbe |
| 'Charlson Moonglow' | WAbe |
| 'Charlson Primrose' **new** | WAbe |
| 'Charlson Terri' | WAbe |
| ***curviflora*** | WAbe |
| 'Emmely' | WAbe |
| 'Eric Watson' | WAbe |
| 'Ewesley Iota' | WAbe |
| ***gaubae*** | WAbe |
| 'Harlekin' **new** | WAbe |
| ***janthina*** | WAbe |
| 'Monika' | CPBP WAbe |
| 'Orion' | WAbe |
| ***tapetodes*** | WAbe |
| - 'Brimstone' | WAbe |
| - farinose | ECho |

## *Dioon* (*Zamiaceae*)

| | |
|---|---|
| ***califanoi*** | CBrP |
| ***caputoi*** | CBrP |
| ***edule*** 𝕐$^{H1}$ | CBrP LPal |
| - var. ***angustifolium*** | CBrP |
| ***mejiae*** | CBrP LPal |
| ***merolae*** | CBrP |
| ***rzedowskii*** | CBrP LPal |
| ***spinulosum*** | CBrP LPal SBig |

## *Dioscorea* (*Dioscoreaceae*)

| | |
|---|---|
| ***alata*** **new** | EBee |
| ***araucana*** | LSou |
| ***batatas*** | ELau LEdu MSal |
| ***deltoidea*** | CPLG EWld |
| ***japonica*** | CAgr EShb WBVN |
| ***nipponica*** | EBee MSal |
| ***opposita*** | EBee |
| ***pentaphylla*** | EBee |
| ***villosa*** | CArn ELau MSal |

## *Diosma* (*Rutaceae*)

| | |
|---|---|
| ***ericoides*** | SEND SWvt |
| - 'Pink Fountain' | EBee LBuc SPoG |
| - 'Sunset Gold' | EBee LBuc SCoo SPoG |
| ***hirsuta*** 'Silver Flame' | LBuc |

## *Diosphaera* (*Campanulaceae*)

| | |
|---|---|
| ***asperuloides*** | see *Trachelium asperuloides* |

## *Diospyros* (*Ebenaceae*)

| | |
|---|---|
| ***austroafricana*** | SPlb |
| * ***hyrcanum*** | NLar |
| ***kaki*** (F) | CAgr CBcs CMCN CTho EPfP ERom LPan MREP NLar WDin |
| - 'Fuyu' | CAgr |
| - 'Kostata' | CAgr |
| - 'Mazelii' | CAgr |
| ***lotus*** | CAgr CBcs CLnd CMCN CTho LEdu MBri NLar SPlb WFar WPGP |
| - (f) | CAgr |
| - (m) | CAgr |
| ***lycioides*** | EShb SPlb |
| ***rhombifolia*** | WPGP |
| ***virginiana*** (F) | CAgr CMCN CTho EHig EPfP NLar SSpi |

## dill see *Anethum graveolens*

## *Dipcadi* (*Hyacinthaceae*)

| | |
|---|---|
| ***serotinum*** | EBee ITim |
| - subsp. ***lividum*** | WPGP |

## *Dipelta* (*Caprifoliaceae*)

| | |
|---|---|
| ***floribunda*** ♀H4 | CBcs CDul CMCN CPMA ELan EMil EPfP ERas LHop LRHS MBlu MBri NLar SSta WBod WPGP WPat |
| ***ventricosa*** | CAbP CBcs CGHE CPMA EPfP LRHS MAsh MBlu MBri NLar SSpi WFar WPGP WPat |
| ***yunnanensis*** | CBcs CPMA CTri EBee ELan EMil EPfP LRHS MBri MWea NLar SSpi SSta WPGP WPat |

## *Diphylleia* (*Berberidaceae*)

| | |
|---|---|
| ***cymosa*** | CLAP ECha GEdr MRav MSal SPhx WCot WCru WTin |
| ***grayi*** | CLAP EBee GEdr WCru |
| ***sinensis*** | CLAP GEdr WCru |

## *Dipidax* see *Onixotis*

## *Diplacus* see *Mimulus*

## *Dipladenia* see *Mandevilla*

## *Diplarrhena* (*Iridaceae*)

| | |
|---|---|
| § ***latifolia*** | GBBs GBin GCal GGar IBlr |
| - Helen Dillon's form | IBlr |
| ***moraea*** | CAbP CMac CMea CWCL CWsd EBee ECha ECho EGle GBBs GCal GKir GMac IBlr IFoB ITim LRHS MDun NCGa NLAp SAga WAbe WBrE WPGP WSHC |
| - ***minor*** | IBlr |
| - 'Slieve Donard' | IBlr |
| - West Coast form | see *D. latifolia* |

## *Diplazium* (*Woodsiaceae*)

| | |
|---|---|
| ***tomitaroanum*** new | EBee |
| ***wichurae*** | EBee EPPr |

## *Diplolaena* (*Rutaceae*)

| | |
|---|---|
| ***dampieri*** | SOWG |

## *Diplostephium* (*Asteraceae*)

| | |
|---|---|
| ***alveolatum*** B&SWJ 10686 | WCru |

## *Diplotaxis* (*Brassicaceae*)

| | |
|---|---|
| ***muralis*** | CArn ELau WJek |
| ***tenuifolia*** | MNHC NGHP NPri |

## *Dipsacus* (*Dipsacaceae*)

| | |
|---|---|
| § ***fullonum*** | CArn CPrp CWan EBWF EDAr EPfP GBar GPWP IFro MBri MHer MNHC NBid NMir NPri NVic SBch SECG SIde WHer WJek WSFF |
| ***inermis*** | CSam EBee ECha EMon NBid NDov NLar SPhx WFar |
| ***japonicus*** | MSal |
| - HWJ 695 | WCru |
| ***pilosus*** | CPom EBWF NDov |
| ***sativus*** | CSec GPWP NLar |
| ***strigosus*** | CSec SPhx |
| ***sylvestris*** | see *D. fullonum* |

## *Dipteracanthus* see *Ruellia*

## *Dipteronia* (*Aceraceae*)

| | |
|---|---|
| ***sinensis*** | CGHE CMCN EBee EPla LRHS MBri NLar WPGP |

## *Disanthus* (*Hamamelidaceae*)

| | |
|---|---|
| ***cercidifolius*** ♀H4 | CAbP CBcs CMCN EPfP GKir IDee LRHS MBlu NLar SSpi WPGP |
| - 'Ena-nishiki' (v) | NLar |

## *Discaria* (*Rhamnaceae*)

| | |
|---|---|
| ***chacaye*** | LEdu WPGP |

## *Diselma* (*Cupressaceae*)

| | |
|---|---|
| ***archeri*** | CDoC CKen GKir MBar SCoo |
| - 'Read Dwarf' | CKen |

## *Disphyma* (*Aizoaceae*)

| | |
|---|---|
| ***crassifolium*** | SChr |

## *Disporopsis* (*Convallariaceae*)

| | |
|---|---|
| ***aspersa*** | CDes CLAP CWsd EBee EPPr EWld LEdu MAvo MHar WCru WPGP |
| - tall | CBct WCru |
| ***fuscopicta*** | CBct CExc CLAP EBee EHrv EPPr MAvo WCru WTin |
| ***longifolia*** | CLAP |
| - B&SWJ 5284 | WCru |
| * ***luzoniensis*** | CBct GEdr |
| - B&SWJ 3891 | WCru |
| 'Min Shan' | ELon |
| * ***nova*** | EBee EPPr |
| § ***pernyi*** | Widely available |
| - B&SWJ 229 new | WCru |
| - B&SWJ 1864 | CBct EPPr WCru |
| - 'Bill Baker' | EBee MAvo |
| 'Shina-no-tsuki' (v) new | EBee |
| ***taiwanensis*** | CBct |
| - B&SWJ 3388 | WCru |
| ***undulata*** | LEdu WCru |

## *Disporum* (*Convallariaceae*)

| | |
|---|---|
| ***austrosinense*** B&SWJ 9777 | WCru |
| ***bodinieri*** | CDes EBee LEdu |
| aff. ***bodinieri*** | WPGP |
| ***calcaratum*** | EBee |

| | | |
|---|---|---|
| | ***cantoniense*** | CDes CFir CLAP CPom EBee GEdr LEdu WCru WFar WPGP WPrP WWst |
| | - B&L 12512 | CLAP |
| | - B&SWJ 1424 | WCru |
| | - B&SWJ 9715 **new** | WCru |
| | - DJHC 98485 | CDes |
| I | - 'Aureovariegata' | CBct CDes EBee WCot |
| | - var. ***cantoniense*** f. ***brunneum*** B&SWJ 5290 | WCru |
| | - 'Green Giant' | CDes CLAP EBee IFoB |
| | - var. ***kawakamii*** B&SWJ 350 | WCru |
| | - - RWJ 10103 **new** | WCru |
| | - 'Night Heron' | CLAP EBee IFoB SKHP WCot |
| | ***flavens*** | CBct CDes CGHE CLAP CPom CStu EBee EBrs ECho EPfP EPla GKir IFoB LEdu NBid SBch SMHy WFar WPGP WSHC WTin |
| | - B&SWJ 872 | WCru |
| * | ***flavum*** | CAvo ECho GKir LRHS SUsu |
| | ***hookeri*** | CLAP CPom EBee EBrs ECho EPot GGar GKir NMen WCot WCru |
| | - var. ***oreganum*** | EBee EPPr IBlr IFoB WCru |
| | ***lanuginosum*** | CBct EPPr GEdr MAvo WCot WCru |
| | ***leschenaultianum*** B&SWJ 9484 | WCru |
| | - B&SWJ 9505 **new** | WCru |
| | ***leucanthum*** | WFar |
| | - B&SWJ 2389 | WCru |
| | ***longistylum*** L 1564 | WCru |
| | ***lutescens*** | EBee WCru |
| | ***maculatum*** | CAby CBct CLAP IFoB WCru |
| | ***megalanthum*** | CLAP EBee EHrv WCot WCru |
| | - CD&R 2412B | EPPr |
| | ***nantouense*** | CStu IFoB LEdu WCot WFar WPGP |
| | - B&SWJ 359 | CBct WCru |
| | - B&SWJ 6812 **new** | WCru |
| | ***sessile*** | EBee ECho GGar GMaP LEdu MSCN WCru |
| | - AGSJ 146 | NMen |
| | - B&SWJ 2824 | WCru |
| I | - 'Aureovariegatum' (v) | ECho WCru |
| | - 'Awa-no-tsuki' (v) **new** | EBee |
| | - 'Cricket' | EBee GEdr |
| | - 'Ginsekai' **new** | EBee |
| | - 'Kinga' (v) **new** | EBee GEdr |
| I | - 'Robustum Variegatum' | EBee MAvo |
| | - variegated (v) **new** | EBee |
| | - 'Variegatum' (v) | CAvo CHEx CRow EBee EBrs ECha ECho ELan EPPr EPfP EPla EPot GEdr GMaP LEdu LRHS MRav NBid WCot WCru WFar WHil WPGP WPnP |
| | - 'White Lightning' (v) | WCot |
| | ***shimadae*** B&SWJ 399 | WCru |
| | ***smilacinum*** | NLar WCru WFar |
| | - B&SWJ 713 | WCru |
| * | - 'Aureovariegatum' (v) | LEdu MAvo WCot WCru |
| | - 'Dai-setsurei' (v) **new** | EBee |
| | - double-flowered (d) | EBee GEdr WCru |
| | - 'Kino-tsukasa' **new** | EBee |
| | - 'Kogane-tsuki' (v) **new** | EBee |
| | - pink-flowered | WCru |
| | ***smithii*** | CBct CPom CStu EBee EBrs ECho EPfP ERos GBuc GEdr GGar GKev GKir LEdu NBir NMen SUsu WCot WCru WFar WPGP |
| | ***taiwanense*** B&SWJ 1513 | WCru |
| | - B&SWJ 2018 | WCru |
| | ***trabeculatum*** 'Nakafu' | WCru |
| | ***trachycarpum*** **new** | CLAP |

| | | |
|---|---|---|
| | ***uniflorum*** | CBct CWsd LEdu WCru |
| | - B&SWJ 651 | WCot WCru |
| | - B&SWJ 4100 **new** | WCru |
| | ***viridescens*** | CBct LEdu SKHP WCru |
| | - B&SWJ 4598 | WCru |

## *Distictis* (*Bignoniaceae*)

| | | |
|---|---|---|
| | ***buccinatoria*** | SOWG |
| | 'Mrs Rivers' | SOWG |

## *Distylium* (*Hamamelidaceae*)

| | | |
|---|---|---|
| | ***myricoides*** | CMCN NLar WFar |
| | ***racemosum*** | CBcs CMac EPfP LRHS MBlu MBri NLar SHBN SLPl SLon SReu SSta WBVN WFar WSHC |

## *Diuranthera* see *Chlorophytum*

## *Dizygotheca* see *Schefflera*

## *Dobinea* (*Podoaceae*)

| | | |
|---|---|---|
| | ***vulgaris*** B&SWJ 2532 | WCru |

## *Dodecatheon* (*Primulaceae*)

| | | |
|---|---|---|
| | ***alpinum*** | EBee NHar SRms WAbe |
| | - subsp. ***majus*** | EBee |
| | ***amethystinum*** | see *D. pulchellum* |
| | 'Aphrodite' PBR | EBee MBri NLar |
| | ***austrofrigidum*** | GKev NHar |
| | ***clevelandii*** | MDKP |
| | - subsp. ***insulare*** | EBee LRHS NWCA |
| | - - NNS 03-236 **new** | GKev |
| | - subsp. ***patulum*** | GBuc LRHS |
| | ***cusickii*** | see *D. pulchellum* subsp. *cusickii* |
| | ***dentatum*** 🏆H4 | CElw EBee GBuc GEdr MDKP MTho NHar WAbe WFar |
| | ***frigidum*** | WAbe |
| § | ***hendersonii*** 🏆H4 | GBuc NMen SRms |
| | ***integrifolium*** | see *D. hendersonii* |
| § | ***jeffreyi*** | CSec EBee EBrs EPPr LRHS MAvo MBri NBPC NBid NLAp NLar NMen NMyG WAbe WBor WFar |
| | - NNS 05-250 **new** | NWCA |
| | - 'Rotlicht' | SRms WPer |
| * | x ***lemoinei*** | WAbe |
| § | ***meadia*** 🏆H4 | Widely available |
| | - f. ***album*** 🏆H4 | CBro CFwr CSWP CSec CTri EBee EBrs ECho EGle ELan EPfP EPot GAuc GEdr GGar GKev LAma LHop LRHS MTho NHol NMen NMyG NWCA SRms SWvt WPnP |
| | - from Cedar County | WAbe |
| | - 'Aphrodite' | NBrd WBor |
| * | - 'Goliath' | NLar WFar WMoo |
| | - membranaceous | WAbe |
| | - 'Queen Victoria' | EBee EBrs ECho LEdu SMeo SRGP WFar WPnP |
| | ***pauciflorum*** misapplied | see *D. pulchellum* |
| | ***pauciflorum*** (Dur.) E. Greene | see *D. meadia* |
| | ***poeticum*** NNS 00-259 **new** | GKev |
| § | ***pulchellum*** 🏆H4 | CBro EBee GEdr GGar GKev LHop LLWG LRHS MNrw NLAp NMen SIng WPer |
| § | - subsp. ***cusickii*** | SRms |
| | - subsp. ***pulchellum*** 'Red Wings' | CMea EBee EBla EBrs ECho EPot GEdr MDKP NBir NMen NSla SMeo WFar WHoo WPnP |
| | - ***radicatum*** | see *D. pulchellum* |
| | - 'Sooke's Variety' | CStu WAbe |
| | ***radicatum*** | see *D. pulchellum* |
| | ***redolens*** | EBee NHar |
| | ***tetrandrum*** | see *D. jeffreyi* |

## *Dodonaea* (*Sapindaceae*)

| | |
|---|---|
| ***viscosa*** | CArn CSec CTrC ECou SPlb |
| - (f) | ECou |
| - (m) | ECou |
| - 'Picton' (f) | ECou |
| - 'Purpurea' | CAbb CBcs CDoC CPLG CPne CTrC EBee ECou EShb ISea LSou |
| - 'Purpurea' (f) | ECou |
| - 'Purpurea' (m) | ECou |
| - 'Red Wings' (f) | ECou |

## *Doellingeria* (*Asteraceae*)

| | |
|---|---|
| ***scabra*** | see *Aster scaber* |

## *Dolichos* (*Papilionaceae*)

| | |
|---|---|
| ***purpureus*** | see *Lablab purpureus* |

## *Dombeya* (*Sterculiaceae*)

| | |
|---|---|
| ***burgessiae*** | IDee SOWG |
| ***calantha*** | CCCN |
| x ***cayeuxii*** | CCCN |

## *Dondia* see *Hacquetia*

## *Doodia* (*Blechnaceae*)

| | |
|---|---|
| ***aspera*** | WRic |
| § ***caudata*** | WRic |
| ***media*** | GBin LLHF MGos WRic |
| ***squarrosa*** | see *D. caudata* |

## *Doronicum* (*Asteraceae*)

| | |
|---|---|
| ***austriacum*** | MSCN NBid NBre |
| ***cataractarum*** | NBre |
| ***caucasicum*** | see *D. orientale* |
| § ***columnae*** | CBcs EBee GKev |
| ***cordatum*** | see *D. columnae* |
| § x ***excelsum*** 'Harpur Crewe' | CPSs CPrp EBee LEdu MRav NBre NPer NVic WCAu WEas WHil |
| 'Finesse' | EBee EDAr GBuc NBre SPoG SRms WMoo |
| 'Little Leo' | COIW EBee ELan GJos GMaP LHop LSRN NLar NPri NVic SAga SPet SPoG SRGP STes WBVN WBrE |
| § ***orientale*** | CWan EBee EPfP GJos GKir LRHS NBid NBlu SPer SPoG SWat |
| - 'Goldcut' | NBre NGdn |
| - 'Leonardo' | LAst |
| - 'Magnificum' | CSBt ECGP EDAr EPfP GMaP LRHS MBri MHer NGBl NMir SPoG SRms SWal WFar |
| ***pardalianches*** | CMea ECha NBre NSco WCot WRHF |
| - 'Goldstrauss' | EBee |
| ***plantagineum*** 'Excelsum' | see *D.* x *excelsum* 'Harpur Crewe' |
| 'Riedels Goldkranz' | WCot |

## *Doryanthes* (*Doryanthaceae*)

| | |
|---|---|
| ***excelsa*** | CHEx |
| ***palmeri*** | CHEx |

## *Dorycnium* see *Lotus*

## *Doryopteris* (*Adiantaceae*)

| | |
|---|---|
| ***pedata*** | MBri |

## *Douglasia* see *Androsace*

| | |
|---|---|
| ***vitaliana*** | see *Vitaliana primuliflora* |

## *Dovea* (*Restionaceae*)

| | |
|---|---|
| ***macrocarpa*** | CCCN |

## *Dovyalis* (*Flacourtiaceae*)

| | |
|---|---|
| ***caffra*** (F) | XBlo |

## *Doxantha* see *Macfadyena*

## *Draba* (*Brassicaceae*)

| | |
|---|---|
| ***acaulis*** | CSec |
| ***aizoides*** | CSec ECho LRHS MWat SPlb SPoG SRms |
| - subsp. ***beckeri*** new | CSec |
| ***aizoon*** | see *D. lasiocarpa* |
| ***alticola*** | EPot |
| ***athoa*** new | CSec |
| ***bruniifolia*** | EBur ECho EWes GKev LRHS |
| - subsp. ***olympica*** | WFar |
| ***bryoides*** | see *D. rigida* var. *bryoides* |
| ***carinthiaca*** new | CSec |
| ***compacta*** | see *D. lasiocarpa* Compacta Group |
| ***crassifolia*** | ECho |
| ***cretica*** | ECho NMen |
| ***cuspidata*** | EPot |
| ***dedeana*** | ECho EWes |
| ***fladnizensis*** new | CSec EHig |
| ***hispanica*** | CSec |
| § ***lasiocarpa*** | SGar |
| § - Compacta Group | ECho NWCA |
| ***longisiliqua*** ♀H2 | ITim |
| - EMR 2551 | EPot |
| ***mollissima*** | EPot WAbe |
| ***oligosperma*** subsp. ***subsessilis*** | NWCA |
| ***ossetica*** | GKev |
| ***paysonii*** var. ***treleasei*** | WAbe |
| ***polytricha*** | GAuc WAbe |
| § ***rigida*** var. ***bryoides*** | ECho WThu |
| - var. ***imbricata*** f. ***compacta*** | EPot |
| x ***salomonii*** | EPot |
| ***scardica*** | see *D. lasiocarpa* |
| ***shiroumana*** | CSec |
| ***ventosa*** | WAbe |
| ***yunnanensis*** | EPot |

## *Dracaena* ✿ (*Dracaenaceae*)

| | |
|---|---|
| ***congesta*** | see *Cordyline stricta* |
| ***draco*** ♀H1 | CArn CTrC EShb XBlo |
| ***fragrans*** | MBri |
| - (Compacta Group) 'Compacta Purpurea' | MBri |
| - - 'Compacta Variegata' (v) | MBri |
| - (Deremensis Group) 'Lemon Lime' (v) ♀H1 | LRHS MBri |
| - - 'Warneckei' (v) ♀H1 | MBri |
| - - 'Yellow Stripe' (v) ♀H1 | MBri |
| * - ***glauca*** | MBri |
| - 'Janet Craig' | MBri |
| - 'Massangeana' (v) ♀H1 | MBri |
| ***indivisa*** | see *Cordyline indivisa* |
| 'Lemon Lime Tips' | XBlo |
| ***marginata*** (v) ♀H1 | LRHS MBri XBlo |
| - 'Colorama' (v) | MBri |
| - 'Tricolor' (v) ♀H1 | XBlo |
| ***sanderiana*** (v) ♀H1 | LRHS MBri |
| * ***schrijveriana*** | MBri |
| ***steudneri*** | MBri |
| ***stricta*** | see *Cordyline stricta* |

## *Dracocephalum* (*Lamiaceae*)

| | |
|---|---|
| sp. | LLHF |
| ***altaiense*** | see *D. imberbe* |
| ***argunense*** | CAby CWCL GEdr GKev NLAp SAga SGar SPhx SRms WPat WPer |
| - 'Fuji Blue' | CEnt EBee LSRN NLar |
| - 'Fuji White' | CEnt EBee GEdr LSRN SHGN SPad SPhx WPer |

| | |
|---|---|
| ***austriacum*** | WPer |
| ***botryoides*** | LLHF NWCA SHGN WMoo WPer |
| ***grandiflorum*** | CBod CEnt CHar CMHG CMea EBee GKev GKir LLHF MHar MMHG SAga SBHP SPhx WFar WPer |
| ***hemsleyanum*** | LLHF |
| § ***imberbe*** | MLLN |
| ***isabellae*** | EBrs |
| ***mairei*** | see *D. renatii* |
| ***moldavica*** | SIde |
| ***nutans*** | NLar |
| ***peregrinum*** 'Blue Dragon' | NPri |
| ***prattii*** | see *Nepeta prattii* |
| § ***renatii*** | CEnt CSec GEdr LLHF SPhx WPer |
| ***rupestre*** | CAby EBee EWld GBri MBri |
| ***ruyschiana*** | ELan GEdr LRHS MLLN MRav NLar NWCA SEND |
| - 'Blue Moon' | SPad |
| ***sibiricum*** | see *Nepeta sibirica* |
| * ***tataricum*** | EBee |
| ***virginicum*** | see *Physostegia virginiana* |
| ***wendelboi*** | MLLN NBir |

## *Dracunculus* (*Araceae*)

| | |
|---|---|
| ***canariensis*** | CStu WCot |
| ***muscivorus*** | see *Helicodiceros muscivorus* |
| § ***vulgaris*** | CArn CHid CMea CPom CSec CSpe CStu EBee EBrs ECho EHrv EMon EPot EUJe GGar LEdu LRHS MCCP MRav NWCA SDix SEND SMrm SPad WCot WFar WHil WPnP |
| - var. ***creticus*** | WCot |
| - white-flowered | WCot WPnP |

## *Dregea* (*Asclepiadaceae*)

| | |
|---|---|
| ***sinensis*** | CCCN CHEx CHll CRHN EBee ELan EPfP EShb EWes LRHS MAsh SOWG SPoG WCot WFar WPGP WSHC |
| - 'Variegata' (v) | EWes WCot |

## *Drepanocladus* (*Amblystegiaceae*)

| | |
|---|---|
| ***revolvens*** | EMFW |

## *Drepanostachyum* (*Poaceae*)

| | |
|---|---|
| § ***falcatum*** | CAbb GKir |
| ***falconeri*** | see *Himalayacalamus falconeri*, *Himalayacalamus falconeri* 'Damarapa' |
| ***hookerianum*** | see *Himalayacalamus hookerianus* |
| § ***khasianum*** | CDTJ CGHE EPla WPGP |
| § ***microphyllum*** | EPla WPGP |

## *Drimiopsis* (*Hyacinthaceae*)

| | |
|---|---|
| ***maculata*** | CStu LToo WCot |

## *Drimys* (*Winteraceae*)

| | |
|---|---|
| ***aromatica*** | see *D. lanceolata* |
| ***colorata*** | see *Pseudowintera colorata* |
| ***granadensis*** var. ***grandiflora*** B&SWJ 10777 new | WCru |
| ***granatensis*** | CGHE WPGP |
| § ***lanceolata*** | Widely available |
| - (f) | CTrC ECou GGar NCGa SPer |
| - (m) | CDoC CTrC ECou GGar SPer |
| - 'Inverewe Prolific' (f) new | GGar |
| - 'Mount Wellington' | GBin GCal |
| - 'Suzette' (v) | MBlu MGos |
| * ***latifolia*** | CBcs CHEx |
| ***winteri*** ♀H4 | Widely available |
| - var. ***andina*** | CPLG EBee EPfP EPla SKHP WPGP |
| § - var. ***chilensis*** | CPLG EBee EPfP GGar ISea LRHS SKHP SPoG SSpi WBod WCru WPGP |
| - Latifolia Group | see *D. winteri* var. *chilensis* |

## *Drosanthemum* (*Aizoaceae*)

| | |
|---|---|
| ***hispidum*** | EAlp ECho EDAr ELan EPfP EPot GMaP ITim LRHS MTho NMen NWCA SBHP SIng SPlb SPoG |
| ***speciosum*** | ECho |
| * ***sutherlandii*** | ECho |

## *Drosera* ✿ (*Droseraceae*)

| | |
|---|---|
| ***admirabilis*** | CHew CSWC |
| ***aliciae*** | CHew CSWC EECP SHmp |
| ***andersoniana*** | EFEx |
| ***androsacea*** | CHew |
| ***anglica*** | CHew CSWC |
| ***ascendens*** | CHew |
| ***binata*** | CHew EECP SHmp |
| § - subsp. ***dichotoma*** | CHew CSWC |
| - 'Extrema' | CHew |
| - 'Multifida' | CHew MCCP |
| ***browniana*** | EFEx |
| ***bulbigena*** | EFEx |
| ***bulbosa*** subsp. ***bulbosa*** | EFEx |
| - subsp. ***major*** | EFEx |
| ***callistos*** | CHew EECP |
| ***capensis*** | CHew CSWC LRHS MCCP SHmp |
| - 'Albino' | CHew EECP MCCP |
| - red | CSWC |
| ***citrina*** | CHew |
| ***closterostigma*** new | CHew |
| ***dichotoma*** | see *D. binata* subsp. *dichotoma* |
| ***dichrosepala*** | CHew EECP |
| ***ericksoniae*** new | CHew |
| ***erythrorhiza*** | EFEx |
| - subsp. ***collina*** | EFEx |
| - subsp. ***erythrorhiza*** | CHew EFEx |
| - subsp. ***magna*** | EFEx |
| - subsp. ***squamosa*** | EFEx |
| ***filiformis*** var. ***filiformis*** | CHew CSWC EECP |
| ***gigantea*** | EFEx |
| ***graniticola*** | EFEx |
| ***helodes*** new | CHew |
| ***heterophylla*** | EFEx |
| ***lasiantha*** | CHew |
| ***loureiroi*** | EFEx |
| ***macrantha*** | EFEx |
| - subsp. ***macrantha*** | EFEx |
| ***macrophylla*** subsp. ***macrophylla*** | EFEx |
| ***mannii*** | EECP |
| ***marchantii*** subsp. ***prophylla*** | EFEx |
| ***menziesii*** subsp. ***basifolia*** | EFEx |
| - subsp. ***menziesii*** | EFEx |
| - subsp. ***thysanosepala*** | EFEx |
| ***modesta*** | EFEx |
| ***nidiformis*** | CHew |
| ***orbiculata*** | EFEx |
| ***paleacea*** subsp. ***trichocaulis*** new | CHew |
| ***peltata*** | CSWC EFEx |
| ***platypoda*** | EFEx |
| ***ramellosa*** | EFEx |
| ***roseana*** new | CHew |
| ***rosulata*** | EFEx |
| ***rotundifolia*** | CSWC SHmp WHer |
| ***salina*** | EFEx |
| ***sargentii*** new | CHew |
| ***scorpioides*** | CHew CSWC EECP SHmp |
| ***slackii*** | CHew CSWC |

| | | |
|---|---|---|
| | ***spatulata*** | CSWC SHmp |
| | ***stelliflora*** | CHew |
| | ***stolonifera*** subsp. ***compacta*** | EFEx |
| | - subsp. ***humilis*** | EFEx |
| | - subsp. ***porrecta*** | EFEx |
| | - subsp. ***rupicola*** | EFEx |
| | - subsp. ***stolonifera*** | EFEx |
| | ***tubaestylus*** | EFEx |
| | ***zonaria*** | EFEx |

## *Drosophyllum* (*Droseraceae*)

| | | |
|---|---|---|
| | ***lusitanicum*** | CHew |

## *Dryandra* (*Proteaceae*)

| | | |
|---|---|---|
| | ***formosa*** | SPlb |

## *Dryas* (*Rosaceae*)

| | | |
|---|---|---|
| | ***drummondii*** | ECho EDAr WAbe WFar |
| § | ***integrifolia*** | NMen |
| | - 'Greenland Green' | WAbe |
| | ***octopetala*** 🏆H4 | CMea CSam CSec EAlp ECho EDAr EPfP GJos GKev GMaP ITim LHop LRHS MWat NLAp NVic SIng SPoG SRms WFar |
| § | - dwarf **new** | EWTr |
| | - 'Harry Bush' | GJos |
| | - 'Minor' 🏆H4 | ECho NMen WAbe |
| | x ***suendermannii*** 🏆H4 | EPfP GMaP LRHS NMen WAbe |
| | ***tenella*** misapplied | see *D. octopetala* dwarf |
| | ***tenella*** Pursh | see *D. integrifolia* |

## *Dryopteris* ✿ (*Dryopteridaceae*)

| | | |
|---|---|---|
| | from Emei Shan, China | WPGP |
| | ***aemula*** | SRms WRic |
| § | ***affinis*** 🏆H4 | CFwr CLAP EBee ECha EMFW EMon EPfP ERod GMaP LBuc LPBA MAsh MCot MGos MMoz MRav NHol NMoo SPer SRms SSto WFib WRic WShi |
| § | - subsp. ***borreri*** | SRms STre |
| | - subsp. ***cambrensis*** 'Crispa Barnes' | WPGP |
| | - - 'Insubrica' | EFer |
| | - 'Congesta' | CLAP EBee |
| | - 'Congesta Cristata' | CLAP CWCL EFer EPfP GMaP LPBA MAsh NHol NSti SPla SRot WBrE |
| | - Crispa Group | CLAP EWsh LAst MMoz |
| § | - 'Crispa Gracilis' 🏆H4 | CFwr CLAP CPrp EFer ELan EPPr ERod GBin MCCP NBir WRic |
| * | - 'Crispa Gracilis Congesta' | NHol WFib WPat |
| § | - 'Cristata' 🏆H4 | Widely available |
| | - 'Cristata Angustata' 🏆H4 | CChe CFwr CLAP CPrp EBee EFer ELan EMon EPfP ETod GBin MAsh MMoz NBid NDlv NHol SRms WFib WMoo WPGP WPrP WRic |
| | - 'Cristata The King' | see *D. affinis* 'Cristata' |
| | - 'Grandiceps Askew' | EFer SRms WFib |
| | - 'Pinderi' | CLAP EBee EFer ELan GBin NHol SEND SRms WRic |
| | - Polydactyla Group | CLAP GQui MDun SPer WFar |
| | - 'Polydactyla Dadds' | CFwr CLAP EQua LLHF NLar NMyG |
| | - 'Polydactyla Mapplebeck' 🏆H4 | CLAP GBin LPBA NBid NHol SRms WFib WRic |
| | - 'Revolvens' | CLAP EFer EWsh SRms |
| | ***atrata*** misapplied | see *D. cycadina* |
| | ***atrata*** | CWCL EBee LRHS MAsh NMoo SPoG |
| | x ***australis*** | CLAP WRic |
| | ***austriaca*** | see *D. dilatata* |
| | ***bissetiana*** | WRic |
| | ***blanfordii*** | WPGP WRic |
| | ***borreri*** | see *D. affinis* subsp. *borreri* |
| | ***buschiana*** | CLAP EBee MRav NLar |
| | ***carthusiana*** | CLAP EBee EFer GBin NLar SRms WPtf WRic |
| | - 'Cristata' | EFer |
| | ***celsa*** | WRic |
| | ***championii*** | CCCN CLAP EBee LRHS WRic |
| | ***clintoniana*** | CFwr CLAP EBee EFer GBin MAsh WPGP WRic |
| | x ***complexa*** 'Stablerae' | CFwr CLAP GBin WFib WPGP WRic |
| | - - crisped | WFib |
| | ***coreanomontana*** | MAsh |
| | ***crassirhizoma*** | CCCN CLAP EBee GBin WRic |
| | ***cristata*** | CFwr CLAP CWCL EBee EFer EMon EPfP WMoo WRic |
| § | ***cycadina*** 🏆H4 | Widely available |
| | ***dickinsii*** | EMon |
| § | ***dilatata*** 🏆H4 | CBgR CRWN ECha EFer ELan EMon EPfP ERod MAsh MRav MSte NHol SRms WFib WHal WRic WShi |
| | - 'Crispa Whiteside' 🏆H4 | CBgR CFwr CLAP CPrp CWCL EBee EFer EMon EPfP ERod MAsh MBri MRav MSte NHol NLar NMyG SPlb SRms WFib WMoo WPGP WRic |
| | - 'Grandiceps' | CLAP EFer EMon NHol WFib |
| | - 'Jimmy Dyce' | CLAP EBee |
| | - 'Lepidota Crispa Cristata' | CLAP EBee EWsh LRHS WPat |
| | - 'Lepidota Cristata' 🏆H4 | CChe CFwr CLAP CMHG CWCL ELan EMon ERod GBin IMGH MAsh NHol NMyG NVic SRms WFar WFib WMoo WPrP WRic |
| | - 'Lepidota Grandiceps' | CFwr CLAP |
| * | - 'Recurvata' | CLAP EBee LLHF NLar WRic |
| | - recurved **new** | CMil |
| | ***erythrosora*** 🏆H4 | Widely available |
| | - 'Brilliance' | CCCN CLAP EBee NLar |
| | - 'Prolifera' | see *D. erythrosora* var. *prolifica* |
| § | - var. ***prolifica*** 🏆H4 | CChe CLAP EBee MAsh MGos MMoz MSte NBir NDlv NHol NLar NMyG NSti SPla WCot WFib WPat WRic |
| | ***expansa*** | EBee EMon |
| | ***filix-mas*** 🏆H4 | Widely available |
| | - 'Barnesii' | CFwr CLAP CWCL EBee EFer ERod ETod EWsh GBin GCal MAsh MSte NDlv NLar NMoo SEND SPlb SPoG WRic |
| | - 'Crispa' | CLAP EBee EHon NHol SRms WFib |
| | - 'Crispa Congesta' | see *D. affinis* 'Crispa Gracilis' |
| | - 'Crispa Cristata' | CBgR CChe CFwr CLAP CPrp CWCL EBee EFer ELan EMon EPfP ERod GMaP LCro MAsh MBri MDun NBid NBir NHol NSti SPoG SRms SWat WFib WGor WRic |
| | - Cristata Group | EFer WRic |
| | - - 'Fred Jackson' | CLAP NHol WFib |
| | - 'Cristata' 🏆H4 | CFwr CLAP EBee EFer ELan GKir MMoz NMyG NOrc SRms SWat WBVN WMoo |
| * | - 'Cristata Grandiceps' | EFer |
| | - 'Cristata Jackson' | CLAP SPlb |
| | - 'Cristata Martindale' | CFwr CLAP NBid NHol SRms WFib |
| | - 'Depauperata' | CLAP WPGP |
| | - 'Euxinensis' | CLAP |
| * | - 'Furcans' | CLAP EBee WRic |
| | - 'Grandiceps Wills' 🏆H4 | EMon NBid NHol WFib |
| | - 'Linearis' | CMHG EBee EFer EHon ELan EMon EWsh LAst LPBA MGos NHol SRms WFib |
| | - 'Linearis Congesta' | WPGP |
| | - 'Linearis Cristata' | WRic |
| | - 'Linearis Polydactyla' | CBgR CFwr CLAP CWCL EBee EFer EPfP GBin GKir IMGH LRHS MAsh |

| | | |
|---|---|---|
| | | MMoz MSte NBlu NHol NMoo NMyG SPoG WAbe WFar WIvy WMoo WPtf |
| | - 'Parsley' | CLAP |
| * | - Polydactyla Group | MGos MRav |
| I | ***filix-mas*** 'Revolvens' | WFib |
| | ***goldieana*** | CFwr CLAP CMHG EBee EFer GBin GMaP LRHS MAsh NBir NCob NLar NMyG WFar WFib WMoo WPnP WRic |
| | ***hirtipes*** misapplied | see *D. cycadina* |
| | ***hondoensis*** | WRic |
| | 'Imperial Wizard' | CFir |
| | ***intermedia*** | WRic |
| | ***lacera*** | WRic |
| | ***ludoviciana*** | EBee WRic |
| | ***marginalis*** | CFwr CLAP EBee GBin LRHS MMoz NHol NLar WMoo WRic |
| | ***oreades*** | SRms WAbe |
| | ***pacifica*** | CLAP |
| | ***paleacea*** | CLAP |
| | ***pseudofilix-mas*** | WRic |
| | ***pseudomas*** | see *D. affinis* |
| | ***pycnopteroides*** | WRic |
| | x ***remota*** | EBee SRms WRic |
| | ***sieboldii*** | CBcs CFwr CHEx CLAP CWCL EBee EFer ELan EMon ERod EShb GEdr IMGH LRHS MAsh MAvo MSte NDlv NHol NMyG SRms WAbe WBor WCot WFib WMoo WPGP WRic |
| | ***stewartii*** | CLAP EBee GBin LLHF NMyG WRic |
| | ***tokyoensis*** | CDes CFwr CLAP EBee GBin MSte NHol NLar WPGP WRic |
| | ***uniformis*** | CLAP ELan EMon |
| | ***villarii*** **new** | EBee |
| | ***wallichiana*** ♀H4 | Widely available |
| | - F&M 107 **new** | WPGP |

## *Duchesnea* (*Rosaceae*)

| | | |
|---|---|---|
| | ***chrysantha*** | see *D. indica* |
| § | ***indica*** | CSWP CSec EHig ELon GAbr IGor LEdu MRav WMoo WOut |
| § | - 'Harlequin' (v) | CPLG CSec EBee GBar MCCP MTho |
| * | - 'Snowflake' (v) | CRow EBee WMoo |
| | - 'Variegata' | see *D. indica* 'Harlequin' |

## *Dudleya* (*Crassulaceae*)

| | |
|---|---|
| ***farinosa*** | CHEx |
| ***lanceolata*** | WCot |

## *Dugaldia* (*Asteraceae*)

| | |
|---|---|
| ***hoopesii*** | see *Hymenoxys hoopesii* |

## *Dulichium* (*Cyperaceae*)

| | |
|---|---|
| ***arundinaceum*** | GKir LLWG |

## *Dunalia* (*Solanaceae*)

| | |
|---|---|
| ***australis*** | see *Iochroma australe* |
| - blue-flowered | see *Iochroma australe* 'Bill Evans' |
| - white-flowered | see *Iochroma australe* 'Andean Snow' |

## *Duranta* (*Verbenaceae*)

| | | |
|---|---|---|
| § | ***erecta*** | EShb LRHS |
| | - 'Geisha Girl' | CCCN EShb |
| | ***plumieri*** | see *D. erecta* |
| | ***repens*** | see *D. erecta* |

## *Duvalia* (*Asclepiadaceae*)

| | | |
|---|---|---|
| | from Mierenfontein **new** | CFwr |
| | hybrid **new** | CFwr |
| * | ***speciosa*** **new** | CFwr |

## *Duvernoia* see *Justicia*

## *Dyckia* (*Bromeliaceae*)

| | |
|---|---|
| ***frigida*** | EBee WCot |
| ***marnier-lapostollei*** | WCot |
| 'Morris Hobbs' | WCot |
| ***remotiflora*** | SChr |
| ***velascana*** | CHEx |

## *Dymondia* (*Asteraceae*)

| | |
|---|---|
| ***margaretae*** | CFee WAbe WRos |

## *Dypsis* see *Chrysalidocarpus*

| | |
|---|---|
| ***decaryi*** | see *Neodypsis decaryi* |

## *Dysosma* see *Podophyllum*

# E

## *Ebenus* (*Papilionaceae*)

| | |
|---|---|
| ***cretica*** | LEdu |

## *Ecballium* (*Cucurbitaceae*)

| | |
|---|---|
| ***elaterium*** | CArn CDTJ CSec LEdu MSal SGar SIde WPGP |

## *Eccremocarpus* (*Bignoniaceae*)

| | | |
|---|---|---|
| | ***ruber*** | see *E. scaber* 'Ruber' |
| | ***scaber*** | CBcs CDul CEnt CRHN CTrG ELan EPfP LBMP MBri MNrw NPer SGar SLim SRms WBrE |
| | - 'Aureus' | EPfP SPoG |
| | - 'Carmineus' | CSec EPfP EWld GGar SGar SPoG |
| | - cream-flowered | LRHS |
| | - orange-flowered | CSec EBee SPoG |
| I | - 'Roseus' | EBee NLar SPoG |
| § | - 'Ruber' **new** | EBee |
| | - Tresco Series **new** | CTsd |
| | - - 'Tresco Cream' | CSpe IDee LBMP |

## *Echeandia* (*Liliaceae*)

| | |
|---|---|
| ***formosa*** B&SWJ 9147 | WCru |

## *Echeveria* ✿ (*Crassulaceae*)

| | | |
|---|---|---|
| | B&SWJ 10277 from Mexico | WCru |
| | B&SWJ 10396 from Guatemala | WCru |
| | ***affinis*** | EBrs MBri |
| | ***agavoides*** ♀H1 | MRav |
| * | - 'Metallica' | MBri |
| * | 'Black Prince' | CAbb CBow CDoC CTca EBee NPer SMrm SPlb SRot WCot WDyG WFar |
| | 'Blue Prince' **new** | LRHS |
| * | ***cana*** | CBct EWll SRot |
| | ***coccinea*** **new** | ELan |
| | 'Crûg Ice' | WCru |
| | x ***derosa*** | EPfP |
| | - 'Worfield Wonder' ♀H1 | WEas |
| | 'Duchess of Nuremberg' | CDoC EBee SRot WCot WFar |
| | ***elegans*** ♀H1 | CHEx CHal EBee EPfP GAbr LSou MBri SAPC SIng WBrE WCot WDyG WGwG |
| § | ***gibbiflora*** var. ***cristata*** | GAbr |
| § | - var. ***metallica*** ♀H1 | EPfP WEas |
| * | x ***gilva*** 'Red' ♀H1 | WEas |
| | ***glauca*** Baker | see *E. secunda* var. *glauca* |
| | **- *cristata*** | see *E. gibbiflora* var. *cristata* |
| | ***harmsii*** ♀H1 | CDoC CHal CSWP WGwG |

| | |
|---|---|
| 'Hens and Chicks' | CHEx |
| 'Little Rose' **new** | STre |
| 'Mahogany' | MAvo SUsu WCot WLeb |
| 'Mauna Loa' **new** | WCot |
| 'Meridian' | CHEx |
| ***nodulosa*** | WCot |
| 'Paul Bunyon' | CHal |
| ***peacockii*** | EBee EOHP LRHS MSCN SMrm SPet SPoG SWal WRos |
| 'Perle d'Azur' | CHEx WCot |
| 'Perle von Nürnberg' ΥH1 | CAbb SMad SPet |
| 'Pinky' **new** | WCot |
| ***pulidonis*** ΥH1 | EPfP WCot |
| ***pulvinata*** ΥH1 | CHal |
| ***rosea*** | WCot |
| 'Ruby Lips' **new** | CAbb |
| ***runyonii*** 'Topsy Turvy' | CDoC CHEx EBee EOHP EPfP SMrm SPet SRot |
| ***secunda*** | CAbb STre SWal |
| § - var. ***glauca*** ΥH1 | CDTJ CHEx CTsd EAmu EBee ELan EPfP EShb ETod LPJP MAvo NBir SArc STre SUsu WCot WGwG |
| * - - 'Gigantea' | NPer |
| ***setosa*** ΥH1 | EPfP MSCN |
| - var. ***ciliata*** | EShb |
| ***shaviana*** | CAbb CBow EBee EWll |
| 'Violet Queen' **new** | CAbb |

## *Echidnopsis* (*Asclepiadaceae*)

| | |
|---|---|
| ***cereiformis*** **new** | CFwr |
| ***dammanniana*** **new** | CFwr |

## *Echinacea* ✿ (*Asteraceae*)

| | |
|---|---|
| After Midnight | see *E.* 'Emily Saul' |
| ***angustifolia*** | CArn CBod EBee EBla EPfP GPoy LPio LRHS MHer MLLN MNHC MSal NGHP SUsu WCAu WHil |
| § 'Art's Pride' PBR | Widely available |
| § 'Emily Saul' (Big Sky Series) **new** | CPar |
| 'Evan Saul' (Big Sky Series) | CBcs CPar EAEE EPfP IPot MWea NBhm NBsh NMoo SPhx SPoG SRkn WCot WCra |
| 'Green Envy' | CBct CKno CPar CWGN EBee ELon GQue LSou MBNS NDov NGdn SMrm SPoG SUsu WClo WCot WCra |
| Mango Meadowbrite = 'CBG Cone3' | EBee MSte NBhm NBsh WCot |
| 'Matthew Saul' (Big Sky Series) | Widely available |
| Orange Meadowbrite PBR | see *E.* 'Art's Pride' |
| ***pallida*** | Widely available |
| - 'Hula Dancer' **new** | EBee NPri |
| ***paradoxa*** | Widely available |
| - 'Yellow Mellow' | EPfP NLar WCra |
| Pixie Meadowbrite = 'CBG Cone 2' | CWGN EBee ECtt EGle LFur NDov WCot WCra WWlt |
| § ***purpurea*** | Widely available |
| - 'Alaska' PBR **new** | NCGa |
| - 'Alba' | EBla ECtt EShb GKir LBMP MNHC NVic |
| - 'Augustkönigin' | CKno EBee EGle EHrv MSte NBir NCob |
| - Bressingham hybrids | EAEE EBee EBla ELan LAst LRHS MRav SPer WFar |
| - 'Coconut Lime' **new** | WHlf |
| - dark-stemmed | SAga SPhx |
| - Doppelganger | see *E. purpurea* 'Doubledecker' |
| § - 'Doubledecker' | CHll CWCL EBee ECtt EDAr ILad LBMP LLHF MDKP NChi NGHP SMad SPhx STes WFar WHil WPer |
| - Elton Knight = 'Elbrook' ΥH3 | EBee IPot LRHS MBri MWea SPhx SRkn |
| - 'Fancy Frills' | EBee EBla ECtt GAbr IPot LSou MDKP NBhm NDov NGHP NGdn SPoG WCot WCra |
| - 'Fatal Attraction' | CKno CPar EBee ECtt EGle EHrv GQue IPot LPio LRHS LSou MAvo MBNS MNrw MWea NBsh NDov NGHP NGdn NMoo SMrs SPoG WCot WCra |
| - 'Fragrant Angel' PBR | CKno EBee EBla ECtt EGle ELon GAbr IPot LSRN LSou MDKP MWea NDov NGHP SHar SMrm SPhx SPoG WCot WCra |
| - 'Green Eyes' | NBhm NGHP |
| - 'Hope' | IPot MMHG |
| - 'Indiaca' | EBee MBNS NGHP SMrm |
| - 'Jade' | CKno CWGN EBee ECtt EGle EHrv EPfP GQue LCro LPio LRHS LSRN LSou MBNS MBri NDov NGdn NLar SMrs SPoG WCot WCra |
| - 'Kim's Knee High' PBR | Widely available |
| - 'Kim's Mop Head' | CKno EBee EBla EBrs ECtt EHrv EWes GKir LAst LCro LHop LRHS MSte NCob NGHP NPri SHar SPav SPla SPoG SUsu WCra WFar |
| § - 'Leuchtstern' | CKno EBee GJos NBir NBre NGHP NGdn NLar SWat WHal WMnd WPer |
| - 'Little Giant' | EBee NBhm |
| - 'Little Magnus' **new** | CKno |
| - 'Magnus' ΥH4 | Widely available |
| - 'Maxima' | CAbP EBee EBrs ECtt EHrv LPio LRHS MLLN NCob NDov WCot WGwG |
| - 'Pica Bella' | EBee NGdn SPoG |
| - 'Pink Double Delight' **new** | WHlf |
| - 'Prairie Frost' (v) | NGHP |
| - 'Primadonna Deep Rose' | CEnt EBee NBre NGBl NGHP |
| - 'Razzmatazz' PBR (d) | Widely available |
| - 'Robert Bloom' | EBee EBla ECtt EGle EHrv GQue LHop MCot MLLN MNFA NBir NCob NGdn SMrm WCAu WCot WGwG WWlt |
| - 'Rubinglow' | CElw CHFP CHar CWCL EBee EBla ECtt EGle EHrv IBal IPot LAst LHop MDKP MSte NBir NCGa NCob NDov NGHP NLar SPhx SPoG SWvt WCAu WCot |
| - 'Rubinstern' ΥH4 | Widely available |
| - 'Ruby Giant' ΥH4 | Widely available |
| - 'The King' | CKno EBee ECtt IBal LRHS NGdn |
| - 'Verbesserter Leuchtstern' | NBre NGHP NLar |
| - 'Vintage Wine' PBR | CHFP CKno CWCL CWGN EBee EBrs ECtt EGle EHrv ELan GBri GQue IBal IPot LCro LRHS MLLN NCob NDov NGHP NGdn NSti SMad SMrs SPhx SPoG WCot WCra |
| - 'White Lustre' | CHFP EBee ECha EPfP LPio NBre NDov NMoo SPav WFar |
| - 'White Swan' | Widely available |
| 'Starlight' | see *E. purpurea* 'Leuchtstern' |
| 'Sunrise' PBR (Big Sky Series) | Widely available |
| 'Sunset' PBR (Big Sky Series) | Widely available |
| ***tennesseensis*** | CArn EShb GPoy |
| - 'Rocky Top' | Widely available |
| 'Twilight' (Big Sky Series) | CBcs CPar EBee EPfP IPot MWea NBhm NDov NOrc SPhx SUsu WCot WCra |

## *Echinops* (*Asteraceae*)

| | |
|---|---|
| RCB AM -14 **new** | WCot |
| ***albus*** | see *E.* 'Nivalis' |
| ***araneosus*** | EBee |
| ***babatagensis*** **new** | EBee |
| § ***bannaticus*** | CBcs EBee GKir NBid WFar |

| | | |
|---|---|---|
| * | - 'Albus' | EPfP EWll LAst LRHS NBre NGdn SPoG |
| | - 'Blue Globe' | CMHG EBee EHoe ELon EPfP EShb EWTr GCal GKir GMaP LAst LBMP LCro LRHS LSRN MBri MCot NBPC NChi NGdn SCoo SMrm STes WBrE WCAu WFar WMnd WPer |
| | - 'Blue Pearl' | EBee WCot |
| | - 'Taplow Blue' ♀H4 | Widely available |
| | ***commutatus*** | see *E. exaltatus* |
| § | ***exaltatus*** | LPla NBir NBre WGwG |
| | ***maracandicus*** | EBee GCal WCot |
| § | 'Nivalis' | CBre EBee SEND |
| | ***ritro*** misapplied | see *E. bannaticus* |
| § | ***ritro*** L. ♀H4 | Widely available |
| | - 'Moonstone' | CRow |
| | - subsp. ***ruthenicus*** ♀H4 | ECGP ELan IGor MRav NBre SDix WPGP |
| | - - 'Platinum Blue' | CWCL EBee GKir NBPC NLar SPet WMnd WPer |
| | - 'Sea Stone' new | EBee |
| | - 'Veitch's Blue' misapplied | see *E. ritro* L. |
| | - 'Veitch's Blue' | Widely available |
| | ***sphaerocephalus*** | GQue NBid NBir NBre NBur SPlb WPer |
| | - 'Arctic Glow' | Widely available |
| | ***strigosus*** | EBee NBre |
| | ***terscheckii*** | EAmu |
| | ***tjanschanicus*** | EBee LDai NLar NMoo |
| | ***tournefortii*** | GBin |

## *Echinospartum* see *Genista*

## *Echium* (*Boraginaceae*)

| | | |
|---|---|---|
| | ***acanthocarpum*** new | XPde |
| | ***aculeatum*** | XPde |
| | - 'Bicolor' | XPde |
| | - 'Rosea' | XPde |
| | ***amoenum*** | CFir NWCA |
| | ***boissieri*** | CCCN CSec ELan WOut XPde |
| | ***brevirame*** | XPde |
| | ***callithyrsum*** new | XPde |
| § | ***candicans*** ♀H2-3 | CAbb CBcs CCCN CFir CHEx CSec CTrC EBee ECre EShb GGal IDee LRHS MGos MREP NBur SAPC SArc WCHb WFar XPde |
| | ***decaisnei*** subsp. ***decaisnei*** new | XPde |
| | ***famarae*** new | XPde |
| | ***fastuosum*** | see *E. candicans* |
| | - 'Ciel' | XPde |
| | - 'Marine' | XPde |
| | - 'Rouge' | XPde |
| | ***gentianoides*** | XPde |
| | - 'Dark Globe' new | XPde |
| | - 'Maryvonne' | XPde |
| | - 'Pablina' | XPde |
| | ***giganteum*** | CHll XPde |
| | ***handiense*** | XPde |
| | ***italicum*** | CCCN CSec EBee NLar SIde XPde |
| | ***lusitanicum*** | CCCN CSec |
| | - subsp. ***polycaulon*** | WHil WOut XPde |
| | ***onosmifolium*** | CHll XPde |
| § | ***pininana*** ♀H2-3 | CAbb CBcs CDoC CHEx COlW CSec CTrC EAmu EBee ECre ELan EWll GGal IDee LRHS NBur NVic SAPC SArc SChr SDnm SGar SIde SPav SPhx WCHb WHer XPde |
| | - 'Pink Fountain' | CCCN EBee ECre ELan ILad NLar XPde |
| | - 'Snow Tower' | CCCN CDTJ CSec CTsd EBee ELan GKev XPde |
| | ***pinnifolium*** | see *E. pininana* |
| | ***plantagineum*** | CCCN CSec XPde |
| | ***rossicum*** | SPlb |
| | ***rosulatum*** | CCCN CSec WOut XPde |
| | ***russicum*** | CCCN CHFP CSec CSpe EBee IFro LAst NBPC NChi NLar SDnm SGar SIde SPad SPav WAul WCHb WCot WPer XPde |
| | ***simplex*** | CCCN XPde |
| | ***strictum*** | CCCN CSec XPde |
| | ***sventenii*** | XPde |
| | ***tuberculatum*** | CCCN CFir SBod SPhx WMoo XPde |
| | ***vulgare*** | CArn CCCN CSec EBWF EGoo ELan EOHP GPWP MHer MNHC MSal NLar NMir NPri NSco SBch SECG SIde WBrE WCHb WHer WJek WPnn |
| | - 'Blue Bedder' new | WSFF |
| | - Drake's form | SGar |
| | ***webbii*** | MMHG XPde |
| | ***wildpretii*** ♀H2-3 | CBow CCCN CDTJ CSec EBee ELan ILad XPde |
| | - subsp. ***wildpretii*** | CSec SPav |

## *Eclipta* (*Asteraceae*)

| | | |
|---|---|---|
| | ***alba*** | see *E. prostrata* |
| § | ***prostrata*** | MSal |

## *Edgeworthia* (*Thymelaeaceae*)

| | | |
|---|---|---|
| § | ***chrysantha*** | CBcs CPMA CTri CWib EPfP LBuc LPan LRHS MBri MGos NPal SBig SChF SKHP SPer WBod WSHC |
| | - B&SWJ 1048 | WCru |
| I | - 'Grandiflora' | CPMA MBri MGos NLar NPal |
| § | - 'Red Dragon' | CPMA |
| | - f. ***rubra*** hort. | see *E. chrysantha* 'Red Dragon' |
| | ***gardneri*** | NLar WCot |
| | ***papyrifera*** | see *E. chrysantha* |

## *Edraianthus* (*Campanulaceae*)

| | | |
|---|---|---|
| | ***croaticus*** | see *E. graminifolius* |
| | ***dalmaticus*** | GKev |
| | ***dinaricus*** | NMen NSla |
| § | ***graminifolius*** | EBee ECho NLAp NMen WFar |
| | ***owerinianus*** | GKev |
| § | ***pumilio*** ♀H4 | CGra ECho GKev ITim LRHS NLAp NMen SRms WAbe |
| § | ***serpyllifolius*** | ECho NMen |
| | - 'Major' | NMen WAbe |

## *Ehretia* (*Boraginaceae*)

| | | |
|---|---|---|
| | ***anacua*** new | CBcs |
| | ***dicksonii*** | CBcs CHEx MBri WPGP |

## *Ehrharta* (*Poaceae*)

| | | |
|---|---|---|
| | ***thunbergii*** | EPPr |

## *Eichhornia* (*Pontederiaceae*)

| | | |
|---|---|---|
| | ***crassipes*** | CBen CWat EMFW LPBA MSKA SCoo |
| | - 'Major' | CDWL NPer |

## *Elaeagnus* ✿ (*Elaeagnaceae*)

| | | |
|---|---|---|
| | ***angustifolia*** | CAgr CDul EBee ECrN EMac EPfP LMaj MBar MBlu MCoo MGos MRav NLar NWea SHBN SPer SRms WBVN WDin WFar |
| | - Caspica Group | see *E.* 'Quicksilver' |
| | ***argentea*** | see *E. commutata* |
| § | ***commutata*** | CBcs CMCN CMac EBee ECrN EHoe EPfP IMGH LEdu LHop MBlu MWhi NLar SPer WDin WPen |
| | - 'Zempin' | ECrN EMil |
| § | x ***ebbingei*** | Widely available |

| | |
|---|---|
| - 'Coastal Gold' (v) | CAbP CBcs CDoC CDul CSBt EBee EQua LBMP LRHS LSRN MAsh MGos SLim SLon SPoG SRms WBod |
| - 'Gilt Edge' (v) ♀H4 | Widely available |
| * - 'Gold Flash' | LAst |
| - Gold Splash = 'Lannou' (v) | CDoC CWSG EBee EMil EPfP EQua ERas LRHS MAsh MBri SArc SWvt |
| - 'Lemon Ice' (v) | NLar |
| - 'Limelight' (v) | Widely available |
| - 'Salcombe Seedling' | CCCN NLar |
| ***glabra*** | EPfP GGal |
| - 'Reflexa' | see *E.* x *reflexa* |
| ***macrophylla*** | CMac EPfP WMoo |
| ***multiflora*** | CDul IDee MBri SPer WPGP |
| ***parvifolia*** | CCCN EPfP |
| ***pungens*** | ERom NBir |
| - 'Argenteovariegata' | see *E. pungens* 'Variegata' |
| - 'Aureovariegata' | see *E. pungens* 'Maculata' |
| - 'Dicksonii' (v) | CBcs CBow CWib EBee LRHS NLar SLon SPer SRms WFar |
| - 'Forest Gold' (v) | CAbP ELan EPfP LRHS MAsh |
| - 'Frederici' (v) | CBcs CDoC CMHG CMac EBee EHoe ELan EPfP EPla ERas LBMP LHop LRHS MAsh MRav SHBN SPer SPla SPoG WBor WDin WHCG WPat |
| - 'Goldrim' (v) ♀H4 | CMac EPfP MGos SHBN SLim WDin |
| - 'Hosuba-fukurin' (v) | LLHF SLon SPoG |
| § - 'Maculata' (v) | Widely available |
| § - 'Variegata' (v) | CBcs CMac EPla EQua NBir SHBN SPer WHCG |
| § 'Quicksilver' ♀H4 | Widely available |
| § x ***reflexa*** | CBcs EPla WHCG WPGP |
| x ***submacrophylla*** | see *E.* x *ebbingei* |
| ***umbellata*** | CAgr CBcs CPLG EBee ECrN EMac EPfP MBlu MBri NLar SPer WHCG WSHC |
| - var. ***borealis*** 'Polar Lights' | MBri |

## *Elatostema* (*Urticaceae*)

| | |
|---|---|
| ***repens*** var. ***pulchrum*** ♀H1 | CHal MBri |
| - var. ***repens*** | CHal |
| ***rugosum*** | CHEx |

## elderberry see *Sambucus nigra*

## *Elegia* (*Restionaceae*)

| | |
|---|---|
| ***capensis*** | CAbb CBcs CBct CCCN CDoC CFir CHEx CPen CTrC EAmu EBee EShb ESwi IDee SPlb WDyG WPGP |
| ***cuspidata*** | EShb |
| ***spathacea*** | CFir |

## *Eleocharis* (*Cyperaceae*)

| | |
|---|---|
| ***acicularis*** | CWat EMFW EPfP WPnP |
| ***dulcis*** variegated (v) | CRow |
| ***palustris*** | CRWN EBWF EMFW |

## *Elettaria* (*Zingiberaceae*)

| | |
|---|---|
| ***cardamomum*** | CArn EOHP EShb GPoy LEdu MBri MSal SHDw WJek |

## *Eleutherococcus* (*Araliaceae*)

| | |
|---|---|
| ***hypoleucus*** B&SWJ 5532 | WCru |
| ***nakaianus*** B&SWJ 5027 | WCru |
| ***pictus*** | see *Kalopanax septemlobus* |
| ***senticosus*** | GPoy |
| - B&SWJ 4528 | WCru |
| ***septemlobus*** | see *Kalopanax septemlobus* |
| ***sessiliflorus*** B&SWJ 8457 | WCru |
| ***sieboldianus*** | CBcs MGos MRav WDin WFar |
| - 'Variegatus' (v) | CBcs CSpe EBee EHoe ELan EPfP EQua IDee LAst MBlu MGos MRav NLar NMun WHer WSHC |
| ***trifoliatus*** RWJ 10108 | WCru |

## *Elingamita* (*Myrsinaceae*)

| | |
|---|---|
| ***johnsonii*** | ECou |

## *Elisena* (*Amaryllidaceae*)

| | |
|---|---|
| ***longipetala*** | see *Hymenocallis longipetala* |

## *Elliottia* (*Ericaceae*)

| | |
|---|---|
| ***bracteata*** | see *Tripetaleia bracteata* |
| * ***paniculata latifolia*** | NLar |

## *Ellisiophyllum* (*Scrophulariaceae*)

| | |
|---|---|
| ***pinnatum*** | CFee WBor WMoo |
| - B&SWJ 197 | WCru WPrP |

## *Elmera* (*Saxifragaceae*)

| | |
|---|---|
| ***racemosa*** | WPtf |

## *Elodea* (*Hydrocharitaceae*)

| | |
|---|---|
| ***canadensis*** | EHon EMFW MSKA NBir WMAq |
| ***crispa*** | see *Lagarosiphon major* |

## *Elsholtzia* (*Lamiaceae*)

| | |
|---|---|
| ***ciliata*** | MSal |
| ***fruticosa*** | CArn |
| ***stauntonii*** | CArn CBcs EBee ECha EPPr GPoy LRHS MHer SPer WBor |
| - 'Alba' | CArn CBcs |

## *Elymus* (*Poaceae*)

| | |
|---|---|
| ***arenarius*** | see *Leymus arenarius* |
| ***canadensis*** | CRWN EHoe EPPr |
| - f. ***glaucifolius*** | CFir GCal |
| ***cinereus*** from Washington State, USA | CDes WPGP |
| ***elongatus*** | SApp |
| ***giganteus*** | see *Leymus racemosus* |
| ***glaucus*** misapplied | see *E. hispidus* |
| § ***hispidus*** | CBod EAlp EBee EHig EHoe EPPr EPau EWsh LRHS MBlu MBri MLHP MMoz MREP NDov NPri NSti SPer SPla WCFE WCot WRos |
| ***magellanicus*** | Widely available |
| - 'Blue Sword' | NBPC WPtf |
| ***repens*** subsp. ***repens*** 'Julie Ann' (v) | WCot |
| ***riparius*** | EPPr |
| ***sibiricus*** | EPPr |
| ***solandri*** | EHoe EWes GBin GFor NNor |
| - JCA 5.345.500 | WPGP |
| ***villosus*** | EPPr |
| - var. ***arkansanus*** | EPPr MAvo |
| ***virginicus*** | EBee EPPr |

## *Elytrigia* (*Poaceae*)

| | |
|---|---|
| ***atherica*** new | EBWF |

## *Embothrium* ✿ (*Proteaceae*)

| | |
|---|---|
| ***coccineum*** | CBcs CGHE CSec CTrG CTri EBee EPfP GKev MAsh MGos MPhe SPlb SReu WBrE WPGP WPat |
| - Lanceolatum Group | CDoC CDul CEnd CHid CSBt ELan EPfP GCal GGar ISea LRHS MBlu MDun NPal SAPC SArc SHBN SPer SPoG SSpi SSta WDin WFar WPic |
| - - 'Inca Flame' | CBcs CCCN CDoC CPMA CSBt ELan EPfP ISea MDun NLar SSta SWvt |
| - - 'Ñorquinco' ♀H3 | CBcs CDoC GGal GGar WBod |
| - Longifolium Group | CCCN GGal IBlr ISea |

## *Eminium* (*Araceae*)

| | |
|---|---|
| ***albertii*** | EBee EBrs ECho |

## *Emmenopterys* (*Rubiaceae*)

| | |
|---|---|
| ***henryi*** | CBcs CCCN CGHE CMCN EBee EPfP IArd MBri NLar SPoG WPGP WSHC |

## *Empetrum* (*Empetraceae*)

| | |
|---|---|
| ***luteum*** | MBar |
| ***nigrum*** | GAuc GPoy MBar NLar WThu |
| ***rubrum*** 'Tomentosum' | WThu |

## *Empodium* (*Hypoxidaceae*)

| | |
|---|---|
| ***plicatum*** | EBrs ECho |

## *Enantiophylla* (*Apiaceae*)

| | |
|---|---|
| B&SWJ 10318 from Guatemala **new** | WCru |
| ***heydeana*** B&SWJ 9114 **new** | WCru |

## *Enceliopsis* (*Asteraceae*)

| | |
|---|---|
| ***covillei*** | GKev |

## *Encephalartos* ✿ (*Zamiaceae*)

| | |
|---|---|
| ***altensteinii*** | CBrP |
| ***caffer*** | CBrP |
| ***cycadifolius*** | CBrP LPal |
| ***friderici-guilielmi*** | CBrP |
| ***ghellinckii*** | LPal |
| ***horridus*** | CBrP |
| ***kisambo*** | LPal |
| ***lanatus*** | CBrP |
| ***lebomboensis*** | CBrP |
| ***lehmannii*** | CBrP LPal |
| ***natalensis*** | CBrP LPal |
| ***senticosus*** | LPal |
| ***umbeluziensis*** | CBrP |
| ***villosus*** | CBrP LPal |

## *Endymion* see *Hyacinthoides*

## *Enkianthus* ✿ (*Ericaceae*)

| | |
|---|---|
| ***campanulatus*** ♀H4 | Widely available |
| - var. ***campanulatus*** f. ***albiflorus*** | CBcs LRHS NLar |
| I - 'Hollandia' | CBcs CPMA MBri |
| - var. ***palibinii*** | EPfP GGGa LRHS MAsh MGos NLar SSpi SSta WBrE |
| - 'Red Bells' | CBcs CDoC CDul CMac EPfP GBin LRHS MAsh MBri MGos NLar SPoG SSpi SSta SWvt WFar |
| - 'Red Velvet' | MBri NLar |
| - 'Ruby Glow' | MBri NLar |
| - var. ***sikokianus*** | CAbP CBcs EPfP GGGa NLar |
| - 'Tokyo Masquerade' | CPMA NLar |
| * - 'Variegatus' (v) | LRHS MAsh SPoG |
| - 'Venus' | CBcs NLar |
| - 'Victoria' | CBcs NLar |
| - 'Wallaby' | CBcs MBri NLar |
| ***cernuus*** f. ***rubens*** ♀H4 | CBcs CMac EPfP GGGa LRHS MBri NBea WBod WDin WPic |
| ***chinensis*** | EPfP GGGa IMGH LRHS MAsh SPoG |
| ***deflexus*** | CDul CMCN LRHS SSpi WPGP |
| - GWJ 9225 | WCru |
| ***perulatus*** ♀H4 | CDul CMac EPfP WFar |

## *Ensete* (*Musaceae*)

| | |
|---|---|
| ***gilletii*** **new** | XBlo |
| ***glaucum*** | CDTJ CKob EAmu EUJe MJnS |
| ***superbum*** | MJnS |
| § ***ventricosum*** ♀H1+3 | CCCN CDTJ CDoC CKob EAmu EUJe LPal MJnS SAPC SArc SChr XBlo |
| § - 'Maurelii' | CBrP CCCN CDTJ CDoC CHEx CHll CKob CSpe CTsd EAmu EShb ESwi ETod EUJe LRHS MJnS MREP NScw SAPC SArc SChr SDix WCot WPGP |
| - 'Montbeliardii' | CKob EUJe |
| - 'Rubrum' | see *E. ventricosum* 'Maurelii' |

## *Entelea* (*Tiliaceae*)

| | |
|---|---|
| ***arborescens*** | CHEx ECou EShb |

## *Eomecon* (*Papaveraceae*)

| | |
|---|---|
| ***chionantha*** | Widely available |

## *Epacris* (*Epacridaceae*)

| | |
|---|---|
| ***longiflora*** | SOWG |
| ***microphylla*** | ITim |
| ***paludosa*** | ECou |
| ***serpyllifolia*** | ECou WThu |

## *Ephedra* (*Ephedraceae*)

| | |
|---|---|
| sp. | SAPC SArc |
| ***chilensis*** 'Mellow Yellow' | EBee |
| - 'Quite White' | EBee WCot |
| ***distachya*** | GPoy MSal |
| ***equisetina*** | IFro MSal |
| ***gerardiana*** | EBee GEdr |
| - var. ***sikkimensis*** | EPla NLar WBod WOld WPer |
| ***intermedia*** RCB/TQ K-1 | WCot |
| § ***major*** | WHer |
| ***minima*** | GEdr NWCA WThu |
| ***minuta*** | CKen SMad |
| ***nebrodensis*** | see *E. major* |
| ***nevadensis*** | GPoy MSal |
| ***sinica*** | CArn MSal |
| ***viridis*** | CArn MSal |

## *Epigaea* (*Ericaceae*)

| | |
|---|---|
| ***gaultherioides*** | GGGa |

## *Epilobium* (*Onagraceae*)

| | |
|---|---|
| ***angustifolium*** | see *Chamerion angustifolium* |
| - f. ***leucanthum*** | see *Chamerion angustifolium* 'Album' |
| ***californicum*** misapplied | see *Zauschneria californica* |
| ***canum*** | see *Zauschneria californica* subsp. *cana* |
| ***crassum*** | CSec GBuc |
| ***dodonaei*** | see *Chamerion dodonaei* |
| ***garrettii*** | see *Zauschneria californica* subsp. *garrettii* |
| N ***glabellum*** misapplied | CSpe GMaP SUsu WEas WWlt |
| ***hirsutum*** | EBWF SECG |
| - 'Album' | SPoG WAlt |
| - 'Caerphilly Castle' (d) | WAlt |
| - 'Cheryl's Blush' | CRow |
| - 'Pistils at Dawn' | CNat |
| - ***roseum*** | WRha |
| - 'Spring Lime' | WAlt |
| - 'Well Creek' (v) | MLLN WAlt WCHb WCot WHrl |
| ***microphyllum*** | see *Zauschneria californica* subsp. *cana* |
| ***rosmarinifolium*** | see *Chamerion dodonaei* |
| ***septentrionale*** | see *Zauschneria septentrionalis* |
| ***villosum*** | see *Zauschneria californica* subsp. *mexicana* |

## *Epimedium* ✿ (*Berberidaceae*)

| | |
|---|---|
| from Yunnan, China | CDes CLAP CPom |
| ***acuminatum*** | CDes CElw CLAP CMoH CWsd EBee EFEx ELon LPio MLul MNFA SUsu WAbe WPGP WSHC |
| - L 575 | EHrv MSte |

| | |
|---|---|
| - 'Galaxy' | CLAP CPMA CWsd |
| 'Akakage' | CHid EBee |
| 'Akebono' | CDes CLAP CMil CPMA EBee NLar |
| ***alpinum*** | CMac EBee EBla EPPr GBuc GKir NHol WMoo WSHC |
| 'Amanogawa' | CDes CLAP CPMA CWsd |
| 'Amber Queen' **new** | CWsd |
| 'Anju' **new** | EBee |
| Asiatic hybrids | CElw CLAP CPMA WHal WPnP |
| 'Beni-chidori' | CLAP EBee GEdr |
| 'Beni-goromo' **new** | EBee |
| 'Beni-kujaku' | CLAP CPMA EBee GBuc GEdr |
| 'Beni-yushima' **new** | EBee |
| ***brachyrrhizum*** | CDes CLAP CMil CPMA CPom CWsd EBee LLHF WPGP |
| ***brevicornu*** | CDes CLAP CPMA CPom EBee WPGP |
| - Og 82.010 | EBee |
| 'Buckland Spider' | CDes CLAP CWsd EBee WPGP |
| ***campanulatum*** | CPMA LLHF |
| x ***cantabrigiense*** | CBro CMac ECtt EPla GGar GMaP LRHS MRav NBre NHol |
| ***chlorandrum*** | CDes CLAP EBee SUsu WPGP |
| ***cremeum*** | see *E. grandiflorum* subsp. *koreanum* |
| ***davidii*** | CDes CMoH CPMA CWsd EBee ECha EGle GBri GEdr MNFA MSte NLar WAbe WFar WHal WHoo WPGP WSHC |
| - EMR 4125 | CElw CLAP EHrv |
| ***diphyllum*** | CPom CPrp CWsd EBee EGle EHrv ELan SAga WBVN WHal |
| - 'White Splash' **new** | EBee GEdr |
| ***dolichostemon*** | CElw CLAP CPMA EGle MSte |
| ***ecalcaratum*** | CDes CLAP CPMA CPom CWsd EBee WPGP |
| ***elongatum*** | CLAP GEdr |
| 'Enchantress' | CLAP CPMA CPom CWsd ECha EGle EHrv GBuc MSte SAga WAbe WHal WHoo |
| ***epsteinii*** | CDes CLAP CPMA CPom CWsd EBee EPPr LLHF WPGP |
| ***fargesii*** | CDes CMil CWsd EBee EHrv GEdr WCot WPGP |
| - 'Pink Constellation' | CDes CLAP CPMA CPom CWsd SBch |
| 'Fire Dragon' **new** | CWsd |
| ***flavum*** | CDes CLAP CPMA CWsd EHrv WPGP |
| ***franchetii*** | CPom |
| - 'Brimstone Butterfly' | CDes CLAP CPMA CWsd EBee EGle WAbe WHil WHoo WPGP |
| 'Fukujuji' **new** | EBee LFur |
| 'Golden Eagle' | CBow CLAP CPMA EBee EWes EWld WPrP |
| § ***grandiflorum*** 🏆$^{H4}$ | CBcs CElw CMac CTri EBee EHrv ELan ELon EPfP EWTr GEdr GKev GKir LBMP NBir NLar NMen SAga SPer WAbe WCAu WFar WPnP |
| - 'Album' | CLAP CWsd EBee |
| - 'Crimson Beauty' | CLAP CPMA GBuc MRav WHal WHoo WSHC |
| - 'Crimson Queen' | CBow CDes WPGP |
| - 'Elfenkönigin' | WAbe |
| - 'Freya' | EGle |
| § - var. ***higoense*** | CDes CPMA WCot WHal |
| - 'Jennie Maillard' | SUsu |
| - 'Koji' | CLAP EGle MSte NLar WSHC |
| § - subsp. ***koreanum*** | CLAP CWsd ECha EFEx WAbe |
| - - 'La Rocaille' | CDes CLAP EGle |
| - lilac-flowered | CLAP WFar WHal |
| - 'Lilacinum' | CDes |
| - 'Lilafee' | Widely available |
| - 'Mount Kitadake' | CLAP WAbe |
| - 'Nanum' 🏆$^{H4}$ | CDes CLyd CMil CPMA CPom CWsd EBee ECho EGle EHrv GKir NMen NWCA WAbe WPGP |
| - 'Pallidum' | NMyG |
| - pink-flowered | EHrv |
| - 'Purple Prince' | CLAP |
| - 'Queen Esta' | CDes CLAP CWsd WPGP |
| - 'Red Beauty' | CLAP GAbr MSte NLar |
| - 'Rose Queen' 🏆$^{H4}$ | CMMP CPrp EBee ECha EHrv ELan EPfP GBuc GGar GMaP LAst LRHS MAvo MBri MRav NBir NMyG NSti SPoG SUsu SWvt WCAu WMoo |
| - 'Roseum' | CHid CLAP CMil CWsd GBri NMen WSHC |
| - 'Rubinkrone' | EBee GMaP NHol WOVN |
| - 'Shikinomai' | CLAP CPMA EGle WAbe |
| - 'Sirius' | CDes CLAP CPMA EBee |
| - var. ***thunbergianum*** variegated **new** | EBee |
| - f. ***violaceum*** | CFir CLAP CPMA CPrp CWsd WAbe WSHC |
| - 'White Beauty' | EGle WSHC |
| - 'White Queen' 🏆$^{H4}$ | CElw CFir CPMA CPrp EBee EHrv EPPr MRav NMyG WAbe WHal |
| - 'Wildside Red' **new** | CWsd |
| - 'Yellow Princess' | CDes CLAP CPMA WCot |
| - 'Yubae' | EBee GEdr WWst |
| 'Hagoromo' **new** | EBee LFur |
| 'Hakubai' **new** | EBee |
| ***higoense*** | see *E. grandiflorum* var. *higoense* |
| ***ilicifolium*** | CDes WPGP |
| 'Jean O'Neill' **new** | CDes |
| 'Jujisei' **new** | EBee |
| 'Kaguyahime' | CBow CLAP CWsd EHrv EPPr MSte WAbe |
| 'Koharu' **new** | EBee |
| 'Koki' **new** | EBee GEdr |
| 'Kozakura' **new** | EBee |
| ***latisepalum*** | CBow CDes CLAP CMil CPMA CPom EBee EHrv GEdr WCot WPGP |
| ***leptorrhizum*** | CDes CElw CLAP CPMA CWsd EBee EGle EHrv GBuc MNFA SUsu WAbe WHal WSHC |
| - 'Mariko' | CLAP CWsd |
| ***lishihchenii*** | CDes CLAP WPGP |
| 'Little Shrimp' | CLyd CPMA CTri EGle ELon GBuc LLHF MNFA NLar WPat |
| ***macranthum*** | see *E. grandiflorum* |
| ***membranaceum*** | CDes CLAP CPMA LLHF SUsu WHal WPGP |
| 'Mine-no-fubuki' **new** | EBee |
| 'Murasaki-komachi' **new** | EBee |
| ***myrianthum*** | CBow CDes CPMA WPGP |
| ***ogisui*** | CDes CLAP CPMA CPom EBee EGle EHrv MSte SMHy WPGP WThu |
| - Og 91.001 | CWsd WAbe |
| § x ***omeiense*** 'Akame' | CBow CDes CLAP CMil CPMA CWsd EBee EPPr WPGP |
| - 'Emei Shan' | see *E.* x *omeiense* 'Akame' |
| - 'Myriad Years' **new** | SMHy |
| - 'Pale Fire' **new** | EWld |
| - 'Pale Fire Sibling' | CDes CPom |
| - 'Stormcloud' | CDes CLAP CMil CPMA CPom CWsd EBee WPGP |
| ***pauciflorum*** | CLAP CPMA EPPr WHil |
| x ***perralchicum*** 🏆$^{H4}$ | CBro CMac CPMA CTri GBuc GKev GKir MLHP NLar SGar SLPl WBVN WPnP |
| - 'Frohnleiten' | Widely available |
| - 'Lichtenberg' | CDes SUsu |
| - 'Wisley' | CElw CPMA CSam EHrv EWes |

| | |
|---|---|
| ***perralderianum*** | CHEx CSam EBee EGle ELan GMaP MCot SRms WAbe WHal WPnP |
| 'Pink Elf' | CWsd GBuc LBMP LRHS NOrc SPla |
| ***pinnatum*** | EBrs ECho GMaP WHal WRha |
| § - subsp. ***colchicum*** 🏆H4 | Widely available |
| - - 'Black Sea' | CLAP CPMA EBee EHrv NCGa NLar SAga |
| - ***elegans*** | see *E. pinnatum* subsp. *colchicum* |
| ***platypetalum*** | CBow CLAP CPMA CWsd SMHy WCot |
| - Og 93.085 | EGle |
| - ***album*** | EBee |
| ***pubescens*** | CMil CPMA EBee EHrv SAga |
| ***pubigerum*** | CHid COIW CPMA CSam EBee ECha EGle EHrv EWTr GAbr GBuc GEdr GKir MLan MNFA NHol NMyG NPri WCAu WHal WPtf |
| ***rhizomatosum*** | CDes CLAP CPom EBee EPPr LLHF WCot WPGP |
| - Og 92.114 | CPMA |
| x ***rubrum*** 🏆H4 | Widely available |
| ***sagittatum*** | CLAP EBee EFEx |
| 'Sakura-maru' new | EBee GEdr |
| 'Sasaki' | CLAP EBee GBuc NMyG |
| ***sempervirens*** | CLAP CPMA EBee WHal |
| - 'Cream Sickle' new | EBee |
| - var. ***sempervirens*** | CLAP |
| x ***setosum*** | CPMA CPom CWsd EBee ECha EHrv MSte NLar WAbe WHal |
| 'Shigure' new | EBee |
| 'Sizukagozen' new | EBee |
| ***stellulatum*** 'Wudang Star' | CDes CLAP CMil CPMA CPom CWsd EHrv EWes GEdr WPGP |
| 'Suzuka' new | EBee GEdr |
| 'Tama-no-genpei' | CPMA CPom |
| 'Tanima-no-yuki' new | EBee |
| x ***versicolor*** | CBow CPLG WMoo |
| - 'Cupreum' | CLAP CPom EBee |
| § - 'Discolor' | CDes CLAP CPom CWsd EBla EHrv NBir SAga |
| - 'Neosulphureum' | CBro CDes CLAP CMMP SLPl WThu |
| - 'Sulphureum' 🏆H4 | Widely available |
| - 'Versicolor' | see *E.* x *versicolor* 'Discolor' |
| x ***warleyense*** | Widely available |
| - 'Orangekönigin' | CElw CMoH CPom CWCL EBee EBla EGle GBBs GBuc LPio MBri MNFA MRav NBro NLar NMyG NSti SEND SPla WAbe WBor WCAu WHal WPnP |
| Wendy Perry's hybrid new | CDes |
| 'William Stearn' new | CWsd |
| ***wushanense*** | CLAP CPMA CWsd LEdu |
| - 'Caramel' | CBow CDes CFee CLAP CMil CPMA CPom CWsd EBee EHrv LEdu WPGP |
| 'Yokihi' new | EBee |
| x ***youngianum*** | CBcs CMac EGle |
| - 'Merlin' | CLAP CMil CPMA CWsd EBee ECha EHrv EPfP NLar NMyG NSti WAbe WCAu WHal WSHC |
| - 'Niveum' 🏆H4 | Widely available |
| - 'Roseum' | Widely available |
| - 'Shikinomai' new | CPMA |
| - 'Tamabotan' | CBow CDes CLAP CWsd GBuc |
| § - 'Typicum' | CLAP EGle WAbe WSHC |
| - white-flowered | NMen |
| - 'Yenomoto' | CLAP CPMA EGle |
| - 'Youngianum' | see *E.* x *youngianum* 'Typicum' |
| ***zhushanense*** | EBee GEdr |

## *Epipactis* (*Orchidaceae*)

| | |
|---|---|
| ***gigantea*** | Widely available |
| ***gigantea*** x ***veratrifolia*** | see *E.* Lowland Legacy gx |
| ***helleborine*** | WHer |
| § **Lowland Legacy gx** | NLAp |
| - 'Irène' | WWst |
| ***mairei*** new | WWst |
| ***palustris*** | EBee EBla EPot GEdr IPot NLAp NLar NMyG NWCA SHdy WHer |
| ***purpurata*** new | EBee |
| 'Renate' | WWst |
| **Sabine gx** | NLAp SHdy WWst |
| * - 'Frankfurt' | NMen |
| ***thunbergii*** | EFEx GEdr LFur NLAp WWst |
| - yellow-flowered new | GEdr WWst |
| ***veratrifolia*** | NLAp SHdy WWst |

## *Epipremnum* (*Araceae*)

| | |
|---|---|
| § ***aureum*** 🏆H1 | MBri |
| § ***pinnatum*** | LRHS MBri |
| - 'Aureum' | see *E. aureum* |
| - 'Marble Queen' (v) | CHal LRHS XBlo |

## *Episcia* (*Gesneriaceae*)

| | |
|---|---|
| 'Country Kitten' | CHal EOHP |
| ***cupreata*** | CHal EOHP |
| ***dianthiflora*** | CHal SRms WDib |
| 'Pink Panther' | CHal EOHP |
| 'San Miguel' | CHal WDib |

## *Equisetum* ✿ (*Equisetaceae*)

| | |
|---|---|
| ***arvense*** | CArn MSal |
| 'Bandit' (v) | CBow CNat CRow EMon MSKA SMad |
| x ***bowmanii*** | CNat |
| * ***camtschatcense*** | CBgR CDes CMCo CNat CRow EBee IDee SBig SMad |
| x ***dycei*** | CNat |
| ***fluviatile*** | CNat MSKA NLar |
| ***hyemale*** | CDWL CKno CMil CNat CTrC EHoe EPfP EPla LCro MHar MSKA NOak NPer NSti SAPC SArc SPlb WDyG WFar WMoo WPrP |
| § - var. ***affine*** | CBgR CNat CRow EBee ELan EMon EPla GCal LEdu LSou MBlu MSKA SMad SPur WMAq |
| - var. ***robustum*** | see *E. hyemale* var. *affine* |
| ***pratense*** new | CNat |
| ***ramosissimum*** | CNat |
| - var. ***japonicum*** | EMFW LPBA MCCP NScw SWat WPnP |
| ***robustum*** new | CTrC |
| ***scirpoides*** | CDWL CNat CTrC EBee EFer EHoe EMFW EMil EMon EPfP LPBA MCCP MSKA NHol NPer SPlb SWat WMAq WMoo WPrP |
| ***sylvaticum*** | CNat |
| ***telmateia*** | CNat SMad |
| ***variegatum*** | EBee NVic |

## *Eragrostis* (*Poaceae*)

| | |
|---|---|
| RCB/Arg S-7 | WCot |
| ***airoides*** | CHar CHrt CKno EBee EWsh GQui MWat NPro SMad SPoG SUsu WHrl WMnd WMoo WRos |
| ***chloromelas*** | EPPr MSte WPGP |
| ***curvula*** | Widely available |
| - S&SH 10 | MSte WPGP |
| - 'Totnes Burgundy' | CAby CDes CKno CPen CWCL EAlp EBee ECha EHoe EPPr LEdu MAvo MMoz MNrw NOak SPhx SUsu WHal WHrl WMoo WPGP WPrP |
| ***elliottii*** | CHrt CKno EBee EGoo EPPr GFor MAvo MSte NCGa SPad WFar WHrl |
| 'Silver Needles' | see *Agrostis canina* 'Silver Needles' |

| | |
|---|---|
| ***spectabilis*** | CFir CHrt CKno EBee EHoe EPPr EWTr GFor ILad LDai MDKP MMHG MWea MWhi NBHF NCGa NChi NDov NLar SMad SPur WFar WMoo |
| ***trichodes*** | CFir CKno EBee EGoo EHig EHoe LDai LEdu MAvo NBre NDov SMad SUsu WHrl WPer |

## *Eranthemum* (*Acanthaceae*)

| | |
|---|---|
| ***pulchellum*** 𝕐H1 | ECre |

## *Eranthis* (*Ranunculaceae*)

| | |
|---|---|
| ***cilicica*** | see *E. hyemalis* Cilicica Group |
| § ***hyemalis*** 𝕐H4 | CBro CMea CTca CTri EBrs ECho EHrv ELan EMon EPfP EPot ERCP GKev IHer ITim LAma MAvo MBri MCot MRav MWat SGar SPer SPhx WCot WFar WGwG WShi |
| § - Cilicica Group | CBro EBrs ECho EHrv ELan EMon EPot ERCP GKev GMaP ITim LAma LHop LRHS SPhx |
| § - Tubergenii Group | WAbe |
| - - 'Guinea Gold' 𝕐H4 | CBro EBrs ECho |
| ***pinnatifida*** | EBrs EFEx WCru |
| ***stellata*** | WCot |
| x ***tubergenii*** | see *E. hyemalis* Tubergenii Group |

## *Ercilla* (*Phytolaccaceae*)

| | |
|---|---|
| ***volubilis*** | CFee CPLG CRHN EBee EMil EWes NSti WCot WCru WSHC |

## *Eremophila* (*Myoporaceae*)

| | |
|---|---|
| ***bignoniiflora*** | SOWG |
| § ***debilis*** | ECou |
| ***glabra*** 'Burgundy' | SOWG |
| - orange-flowered | ECou |
| 'Kilbara Carpet' | ECou SOWG |
| ***maculata*** | ECou |
| - var. ***brevifolia*** | SOWG |
| - pale pink-flowered | SOWG |
| - 'Peaches and Cream' | SOWG |
| * 'Summer Blue' | SOWG |
| 'Yellow Trumpet' | ECou |

## *Eremurus* (*Asphodelaceae*)

| | |
|---|---|
| ***altaicus*** JCA 0.443.809 | WCot |
| 'Brutus' | EBee EBrs LAma LRHS MSte |
| ***bungei*** | see *E. stenophyllus* subsp. *stenophyllus* |
| 'Emmy Ro' | EBee EBrs LAma LRHS MSte NLar SPur WCot |
| 'Helena' | EBee LAma NLar SPur |
| ***himalaicus*** | CAvo CBro CFFs CMea CTca EBee EBrs ECho EHrv ELan EPot ERCP LAma LAst LRHS MHer MSte SPer WCra WHil |
| 'Image' | EBee EBrs LFur LRHS |
| x ***isabellinus*** 'Cleopatra' | Widely available |
| - 'Obelisk' | EBee EBrs ELan ERCP LAma LRHS SPhx WCot |
| - 'Pinokkio' | CAvo EBee EBrs ECho EGoo EPot LAma LRHS MAvo MHer SPhx |
| - Ruiter hybrids | CMea CSWP EBee EBrs ECot ELan EMon EPfP LAma LAst LFur LRHS MGos MLLN SPer SPet SPhx SPoG WBVN WClo WFar |
| - Shelford hybrids | CAvo CBcs CBct CFFs EBee EBrs ELan EMon LAma LBMP LRHS MLLN MNrw SPhx WBVN WFar |
| - 'Tropical Dream' | EBee |
| 'Jeanne-Claire' | EBee LAma NLar SPur |
| 'Joanna' | EBee LAma LCro LSRN NLar |
| 'Line Dance' | LAma |
| 'Luca Ro' | EBee |
| 'Moneymaker' | EBee EBrs EPot LAma LRHS MSte NLar |
| 'Oase' | CAvo CBro CHFP CTca EBee EBrs ECho EHrv ELan LAma LFur LRHS MSte NLar SPer |
| 'Rexona' | EBee EBrs LAma LRHS |
| ***robustus*** 𝕐H4 | Widely available |
| 'Roford' | CMea EBee EBrs ECho LAma NMoo |
| 'Romance' | CAvo CHFP CTca EBee EBrs ELon EMon EPot ERCP LAma LRHS MNrw MSte |
| 'Rumba' | LAma NLar |
| 'Samba' | EBee LAma |
| ***sogdianus*** | EBrs |
| - JCA 0.444/090 | WCot |
| ***stenophyllus*** 𝕐H4 | CBro CFFs CSec CTca CTri CWib EBrs EPot ERCP LBMP LCro LHop LRHS MAvo SPhx SPoG WFar |
| § - subsp. ***stenophyllus*** | CAvo CBcs CMea EBee EHrv EMon EPfP EShb GMaP LAma LAst MHer MLLN MNrw MRav NBPC NPer NPri SPad SPer WBVN WCra WFar |
| 'Tap Dance' | LAma |
| ***tauricus*** | EBrs |
| 'Yellow Giant' | EBee EBrs ECho WCot WHil |
| ***zenaidae*** | WCot |

## *Erianthus* see *Saccharum*

## *Erica* ✿ (*Ericaceae*)

| | |
|---|---|
| 'African Fanfare' | EHea |
| x ***afroeuropaea*** | EHea |
| ***alopecurus*** | SPlb |
| ***arborea*** | CTrG SPlb |
| § - 'Albert's Gold' 𝕐H4 | CBcs CSBt CTri EHea ELan EPfP LRHS MAsh MBar MBri MGos MSwo NHol SPer SPla SPoG SRms WBod WFar |
| - var. ***alpina*** 𝕐H4 | CDoC CTri EHea EPfP LRHS MBar NHol SPer SPoG SRms |
| - 'Arbora Gold' | see *E. arborea* 'Albert's Gold' |
| - 'Arnold's Gold' | see *E. arborea* 'Albert's Gold' |
| - 'Estrella Gold' 𝕐H4 | CBcs CDoC CSBt CTri EHea ELan EPfP LRHS MAsh MBar MGos NHol SLon SPer SPla SPoG SRms |
| - 'Picos Pygmy' | EHea |
| - 'Spanish Lime' | EHea |
| - 'Spring Smile' | EHea |
| ***australis*** 𝕐H4 | MBar |
| - 'Castellar Blush' | EHea |
| - 'Holehird' | EHea |
| - 'Mr Robert' 𝕐H3 | EHea EPfP MBar |
| - 'Riverslea' 𝕐H4 | CTri EHea MAsh MBar WBod |
| ***caffra*** | EHea IDee SPlb |
| ***canaliculata*** 𝕐H3 | CBcs EHea |
| ***carnea*** | ELan |
| - 'Accent' | EHea |
| - 'Adrienne Duncan' 𝕐H4 | EHea MBar NDlv NHol |
| - 'Alan Coates' | EHea MBar |
| - 'Alba' | EHea |
| - 'Altadena' | EHea MBar |
| - 'Amy Doncaster' | see *E. carnea* 'Treasure Trove' |
| - 'Ann Sparkes' 𝕐H4 | CSBt CTri EHea EPfP LRHS MBar MSwo NHol SPla SRms |
| - 'Atrorubra' | EHea MBar |
| - 'Aurea' | CSBt EHea MBar NHol SRms |
| - 'Barry Sellers' | EHea |
| § - 'Bell's Extra Special' | EHea EPfP |
| - 'Beoley Pink' | EHea |
| - 'C.J. Backhouse' | EHea |
| I - 'Carnea' | EHea MBar |

| | | |
|---|---|---|
| | - 'Catherine Kolster' | EHea |
| | - 'Cecilia M. Beale' | EHea MBar |
| | - 'Challenger' ♀H4 | EHea EPfP MBar MGos NHol SCoo SPer SPla SRms |
| | - 'Christine Fletcher' | EHea |
| | - 'Clare Wilkinson' | EHea |
| | - 'David's Seedling' | EHea |
| | - 'December Red' | CSBt EHea EPfP LRHS MBar MSwo NHol SPer SPla SRms |
| | - 'Dømmesmoen' | EHea |
| | - 'Dwingeloo Pride' | EHea |
| | - 'Early Red' | EHea |
| | - 'Eileen Porter' | EHea MBar NHol |
| | - 'Eva' | CBcs EHea |
| | - 'Foxhollow' ♀H4 | CBcs CSBt CTri EHea EPfP IArd LRHS MBar MGos MSwo MWat NHol SPla SRms |
| | - 'Foxhollow Fairy' | EHea MBar SRms |
| | - 'Gelber Findling' | EHea |
| | - 'Gelderingen Gold' | EHea |
| | - 'Golden Starlet' ♀H4 | CTri EHea EPfP LRHS MBar MGos NBlu NHol SPer SPla SRms |
| | - 'Gracilis' | EHea MBar |
| | - 'Hamburg' | EHea |
| | - 'Heathwood' | EHea MBar NHol SCoo SPla SRms |
| | - 'Hilletje' | EHea SRms |
| | - 'Ice Princess' ♀H4 | EHea EPfP LRHS NHol SCoo SPer SPla SRms |
| | - 'Isabell' ♀H4 | CBcs EHea EPfP LRHS SCoo SPla SRms |
| | - 'Jack Stitt' | EHea MBar |
| | - 'James Backhouse' | CTri EHea |
| | - 'January Sun' | EHea |
| | - 'Jason Attwater' | EHea |
| | - 'Jean' | EHea |
| | - 'Jennifer Anne' | EHea MBar |
| | - 'John Kampa' | EHea MBar NHol |
| | - 'John Pook' | EHea |
| | - 'King George' | CSBt CTri EHea LRHS MBar NHol |
| § | - 'Kramer's Rubin' | EHea |
| | - 'Lake Garda' | EHea |
| | - 'Late Pink' | EHea |
| | - 'Lena' | see *E.* x *darleyensis* 'Lena' |
| | - 'Lesley Sparkes' | CSBt EHea MBar |
| | - 'Little Peter' | EHea |
| | - 'Lohse's Rubin' | EHea LRHS NHol |
| | - 'Lohse's Rubinfeuer' | EHea |
| | - 'Lohse's Rubinschimmer' | EHea |
| | - 'Loughrigg' ♀H4 | CSBt CTri EHea MBar NHol SPla SRms |
| | - Madame Seedling | see *E. carnea* 'Weisse March Seedling' |
| | - 'March Seedling' | EHea EPfP MBar NHol NPri SRms |
| | - 'Margery Frearson' | EHea |
| | - 'Martin' | EHea |
| | - 'Moonlight' | EHea |
| | - 'Mrs Sam Doncaster' | EHea MBar |
| | - 'Myretoun Ruby' ♀H4 | CBcs CSBt CTri EBrs EHea EPfP LCro LRHS MBar MGos MWat NBlu NDlv NHol NPri SPer SPla SRms |
| | - 'Nathalie' ♀H4 | EHea LRHS MSwo NHol SCoo SRms |
| | - 'Netherfield Orange' | EHea |
| | - 'Oriënt' | EHea SRms |
| | - 'Pallida' | EHea |
| | - 'Pink Beauty' | see *E. carnea* 'Pink Pearl' |
| | - 'Pink Cloud' | EHea |
| | - 'Pink Mist' | EHea LRHS SPer SRms |
| § | - 'Pink Pearl' | EHea MBar |
| | - 'Pink Spangles' ♀H4 | CBcs CSBt CTri EHea MBar MGos MSwo NHol SRms |
| | - 'Pirbright Rose' | EHea SRms |
| | - 'Polden Pride' | EHea |
| | - 'Porter's Red' | EHea MBar |

| | | |
|---|---|---|
| | - 'Praecox Rubra' ♀H4 | EHea EPfP MBar NHol |
| | - 'Prince of Wales' | EHea |
| | - 'Queen Mary' | EHea |
| | - 'Queen of Spain' | EHea |
| | - 'R.B. Cooke' ♀H4 | EHea EPfP MBar SCoo SPla SRms |
| | - 'Red Rover' | EHea |
| | - 'Robert Jan' | EHea |
| | - 'Romance' | EHea |
| | - 'Rosalie' ♀H4 | CBcs EHea EPfP IArd LCro LRHS MSwo SCoo SPer SPla SRms |
| | - 'Rosalinde Schorn' | EHea |
| | - 'Rosantha' | EHea SRms |
| | - 'Rosea' | SPlb |
| | - 'Rosy Gem' | EHea MBar |
| | - 'Rosy Morn' | EHea |
| | - 'Rotes Juwel' | EHea |
| | - 'Rubinteppich' | EHea SRms |
| | - 'Ruby Glow' | EHea LRHS MBar MSwo NHol SPla |
| | - 'Scatterley' | EHea |
| | - 'Schatzalp' | EHea |
| | - 'Schneekuppe' | EHea |
| | - 'Schneesturm' | EHea SRms |
| § | - 'Sherwood Creeping' | EHea MBar |
| | - 'Sherwoodii' | see *E. carnea* 'Sherwood Creeping' |
| | - 'Smart's Heath' | EHea |
| | - 'Sneznik' | EHea |
| | - 'Snow Prince' | EHea |
| | - 'Snow Queen' | EHea MBar |
| | - 'Spring Cottage Crimson' | EHea MBar |
| | - 'Spring Day' | EHea MSwo |
| | - 'Springwood Pink' | CSBt CTri EHea LRHS MBar NHol SRms |
| | - 'Springwood White' ♀H4 | CSBt CTri EBrs EHea EPfP LRHS MBar MGos MSwo MWat NHol SPer SPla SRms |
| I | - 'Startler' | EHea LRHS MBar NHol |
| | - 'Sunshine Rambler' ♀H4 | EHea MBar |
| | - 'Thomas Kingscote' | EHea MBar |
| § | - 'Treasure Trove' | EHea |
| | - 'Tybesta Gold' | EHea |
| | - 'Urville' | see *E. carnea* 'Vivellii' |
| | - 'Viking' | EHea NHol |
| § | - 'Vivellii' ♀H4 | CSBt CTri EHea LRHS MBar MWat NDlv NHol SRms |
| | - 'Vivellii Aurea' | EHea |
| | - 'Walter Reisert' | EHea |
| | - 'Wanda' | EHea MBar |
| § | - 'Weisse March Seedling' | EHea |
| | - 'Wentwood Red' | EHea |
| | - 'Westwood Yellow' ♀H4 | CSBt EHea LRHS MBar MGos NHol SPer SPla SRms |
| | - Whisky | see *E. carnea* 'Bell's Extra Special' |
| | - 'Whitehall' | EHea LCro LRHS NHol SRms |
| | - 'Winter Beauty' | EHea MGos NDlv NHol |
| | - 'Winter Gold' | EHea |
| | - 'Winter Melody' | EHea |
| | - Winter Rubin | see *E. carnea* 'Kramer's Rubin' |
| | - 'Winter Snow' | EHea SCoo SRms |
| | - 'Winter Sport' | EHea |
| | - 'Winterfreude' | EHea |
| | - 'Wintersonne' | CBcs EHea EPfP SRms |
| | ***ciliaris*** 'Aurea' | EHea MBar SRms |
| | - 'Bretagne' | EHea |
| | - 'Camla' | EHea MBar |
| | - 'Corfe Castle' | EHea MBar |
| | - 'David McClintock' | EHea MBar |
| | - 'Fada das Serras' | EHea |
| | - 'Globosa' | EHea |
| | - 'Mawiana' | EHea |
| | - 'Mrs C.H. Gill' ♀H4 | EHea |
| | - 'Ram' | EHea |
| | - 'Rotundiflora' | EHea |
| | - 'Stapehill' | EHea |

| | |
|---|---|
| - 'Stoborough' $\mathbb{Y}^{H4}$ | EHea MBar |
| - 'White Wings' | EHea |
| - 'Wych' | EHea |
| ***cinerea*** f. ***alba*** 'Alba Major' | CSBt EHea MBar |
| - - 'Alba Minor' $\mathbb{Y}^{H4}$ | EHea MBar NBlu NHol |
| - - 'Celebration' | EHea MBar NBlu NHol |
| - - 'Doctor Small's Seedling' | EHea |
| - - 'Domino' | EHea MBar |
| - - 'Godrevy' | EHea |
| - - 'Hookstone White' $\mathbb{Y}^{H4}$ | EHea MBar NDlv |
| - - 'Jos' Honeymoon' | EHea |
| - - 'Marina' | EHea |
| - - 'Nell' | EHea MBar |
| - - 'Snow Cream' | EHea MBar |
| - - 'White Dale' | EHea MBar |
| - 'Alette' | EHea |
| - 'Alfred Bowerman' | EHea |
| - 'Alice Ann Davies' | EHea |
| - 'Angarrack' | EHea |
| - 'Anja Bakker' | EHea |
| - 'Anja Blum' | EHea |
| - 'Anja Slegers' | EHea |
| - 'Ann Berry' | EHea MBar |
| - 'Apple Blossom' | EHea |
| - 'Apricot Charm' | CSBt EHea MBar MSwo |
| - 'Aquarel' | EHea |
| - 'Ashdown Forest' | EHea |
| - 'Ashgarth Garnet' | EHea MBar |
| - 'Atropurpurea' | EHea MBar |
| - 'Atrorubens' | EHea MBar SRms |
| - 'Atrorubens, Daisy Hill' | EHea |
| - 'Atrosanguinea' | MBar |
| - 'Atrosanguinea Reuthe's Variety' | EHea |
| - 'Atrosanguinea Smith's Variety' | EHea |
| I - 'Aurea' new | MMuc |
| - 'Baylay's Variety' | EHea MBar |
| - 'Bemmel' | EHea |
| - 'Blossom Time' | EHea MBar |
| - 'Bucklebury Red' | EHea |
| - 'C.D. Eason' $\mathbb{Y}^{H4}$ | CBcs CSBt CTri EHea EPfP MBar NBlu NHol SRms |
| § - 'C.G. Best' $\mathbb{Y}^{H4}$ | ECho EHea MBar |
| - 'Cairn Valley' | EHea |
| - 'Caldy Island' | EHea MBar |
| - 'Cevennes' | EHea MBar |
| - 'Champs Hill' $\mathbb{Y}^{H4}$ | EHea |
| - 'Cindy' $\mathbb{Y}^{H4}$ | EHea MBar NHol |
| - 'Coccinea' | EHea |
| - 'Colligan Bridge' | EHea MBar |
| - 'Constance' | EHea MBar |
| - 'Contrast' | EHea MBar |
| - 'Crimson Glow' | EHea |
| - 'Discovery' | EHea |
| - 'Duncan Fraser' | EHea MBar |
| - 'Eden Valley' $\mathbb{Y}^{H4}$ | EHea MBar NHol SRms |
| - 'Eline' | EHea |
| - 'England' | EHea |
| - 'Felthorpe' | EHea |
| - 'Fiddler's Gold' $\mathbb{Y}^{H4}$ | EHea MBar NHol |
| - 'Flamingo' | EHea |
| - 'Foxhollow Mahogany' | EHea MBar |
| - 'Frances' | EHea |
| - 'Frankrijk' | EHea |
| - 'Fred Corston' | EHea |
| - 'G. Osmond' | EHea MBar |
| - 'Geke' | EHea |
| - 'Glasnevin Red' | EHea MBar |
| - 'Glencairn' | EHea MBar NHol |
| - 'Golden Charm' | EHea NHol |
| - 'Golden Drop' | CSBt EHea MBar NHol |
| - 'Golden Hue' $\mathbb{Y}^{H4}$ | EHea MBar NHol |
| - 'Golden Sport' | EHea |
| - 'Golden Striker' | EHea |
| - 'Golden Tee' | EHea |
| - 'Goldilocks' | EHea |
| - 'Graham Thomas' | see *E. cinerea* 'C.G. Best' |
| - 'Grandiflora' | EHea MBar |
| - 'Guernsey Lime' | EHea MBar |
| - 'Guernsey Pink' | EHea |
| - 'Guernsey Plum' | EHea |
| - 'Guernsey Purple' | EHea |
| - 'Hardwick's Rose' | EHea MBar |
| - 'Harry Fulcher' | EHea |
| - 'Heatherbank' | EHea |
| - 'Heathfield' | EHea |
| - 'Heidebrand' | EHea MBar |
| - 'Hermann Dijkhuizen' | EHea |
| - 'Honeymoon' | EHea MBar |
| - 'Hookstone Lavender' | EHea |
| - 'Hutton's Seedling' | EHea |
| - 'Iberian Beauty' | EHea |
| - 'Jack London' | EHea |
| - 'Janet' | EHea MBar |
| - 'Jersey Wonder' | EHea |
| - 'Jiri' | EHea |
| - 'John Ardron' | EHea |
| - 'John Eason' | EHea |
| - 'Jos' Golden' | EHea |
| - 'Joseph Murphy' | EHea MBar |
| - 'Josephine Ross' | EHea MBar |
| - 'Joyce Burfitt' | EHea |
| - 'Katinka' | CBcs EHea MBar MSwo NHol |
| - 'Kerry Cherry' | EHea |
| - 'Knap Hill Pink' $\mathbb{Y}^{H4}$ | EHea MBar |
| - 'Lady Skelton' | EHea MBar |
| - 'Lavender Lady' | EHea |
| - 'Lilac Time' | EHea MBar |
| - 'Lilacina' | EHea MBar |
| - 'Lime Soda' $\mathbb{Y}^{H4}$ | EHea |
| - 'Lorna Anne Hutton' | EHea |
| - 'Michael Hugo' | EHea |
| - 'Miss Waters' | EHea MBar |
| - 'Mrs Dill' | EHea MBar |
| - 'Mrs E.A. Mitchell' | EHea NHol SPlb |
| - 'Mrs Ford' | EHea MBar |
| - 'My Love' | EHea MBar |
| - 'Neptune' | EHea |
| - 'Newick Lilac' | EHea MBar |
| - 'Next Best' | EHea MBar |
| - 'Novar' | EHea |
| - 'Old Rose' | EHea |
| - 'P.S. Patrick' $\mathbb{Y}^{H4}$ | EHea MBar |
| - 'Pallas' | EHea |
| - 'Pallida' | EHea |
| - 'Paul's Purple' | EHea |
| - 'Peñaz' | EHea |
| - 'Pentreath' $\mathbb{Y}^{H4}$ | EHea MBar |
| - 'Pink Foam' | EHea MBar |
| - 'Pink Ice' $\mathbb{Y}^{H4}$ | CTri EHea EPfP MBar MSwo NHol |
| - 'Plummer's Seedling' | EHea MBar |
| - 'Promenade' | EHea |
| - 'Prostrate Lavender' | EHea |
| - 'Providence' | EHea |
| - 'Purple Beauty' | EHea MBar |
| - 'Purple Robe' | EHea |
| - 'Purple Spreader' | EHea |
| - 'Purpurea' | EHea |
| - 'Pygmaea' | EHea MBar |
| - 'Red Pentreath' | EHea |
| - 'Robert Michael' | EHea |
| - 'Rock Pool' | EHea MBar NHol |
| - 'Rock Ruth' | EHea |
| - 'Romiley' | EHea MBar |
| - 'Rose Queen' | EHea |

| | | |
|---|---|---|
| | – 'Rosea' | EHea |
| I | – 'Rosea Splendens' | EHea |
| | – 'Rosy Chimes' | EHea MBar |
| | – 'Rozanne Waterer' | EHea |
| | – 'Ruby' | EHea MBar |
| | – 'Sandpit Hill' | EHea MBar |
| | – 'Schizopetala' | EHea MBar |
| | – 'Screel' | EHea |
| | – 'Sea Foam' | EHea MBar |
| | – 'Sherry' | EHea MBar NHol |
| | – 'Smith's Lawn' | EHea |
| | – 'Spicata' | EHea |
| | – 'Splendens' | EHea |
| | – 'Startler' | EHea |
| | – 'Stephen Davis' ♀H4 | EHea MBar NHol |
| | – 'Strawberry Bells' | EHea |
| | – 'Sue Lloyd' | EHea |
| | – 'Summer Gold' | EHea LRHS NDlv |
| | – 'Tilford' | EHea |
| | – 'Tom Waterer' | EHea MBar |
| | – 'Underwood Pink' | EHea |
| | – 'Uschie Ziehmann' | EHea |
| | – 'Velvet Night' ♀H4 | CSBt EHea MBar NHol SRms |
| | – 'Victoria' | EHea MBar |
| | – 'Violacea' | EHea |
| | – 'Violetta' | EHea |
| | – 'Vivienne Patricia' | EHea MBar |
| | – 'W.G. Notley' | EHea |
| | – 'West End' | EHea |
| | – 'Windlebrooke' ♀H4 | EHea MBar NHol |
| | – 'Wine' | EHea |
| | – 'Yvonne' | EHea |
| | ***curviflora*** | EHea SPlb |
| | x ***darleyensis*** | CBcs |
| | – 'Ada S. Collings' | EHea MBar |
| | – 'Alba' | see *E.* x *darleyensis* 'Silberschmelze' |
| | – 'Archie Graham' | EHea |
| | – 'Arthur Johnson' ♀H4 | CSBt CTri EHea LRHS MBar NHol SRms |
| | – 'Aurélie Brégeon' | EHea SRms |
| | – 'Cherry Stevens' | see *E.* x *darleyensis* 'Furzey' |
| § | – 'Darley Dale' | CSBt EHea EPfP LRHS MBar NHol SCoo SPer SRms |
| | – 'Dunreggan' | EHea |
| | – 'Dunwood Splendour' | MBar |
| | – 'Epe' | EHea |
| | – 'Erecta' | EHea |
| | – 'Eva' | see *E. darleyensis* 'Eva Gold' |
| | – 'Eva Gold' PBR | EHea LRHS NHol NPri SRms |
| § | – 'Furzey' ♀H4 | CSBt EHea EPfP LCro LRHS MBar MGos NHol SCoo SPer SRms |
| | – 'George Rendall' | CSBt CTri EHea EPfP LRHS NHol SCoo SPla |
| | – 'Ghost Hills' ♀H4 | CSBt EHea EPfP LRHS MBar MSwo NHol SCoo SPer SRms |
| | – 'J.W. Porter' ♀H4 | EHea EPfP LCro MBar NDlv SCoo SEND SPla SRms |
| | – 'Jack H. Brummage' | CSBt CTri EHea IArd LRHS MBar MGos MSwo NHol SPla SRms |
| | – 'James Smith' | EHea MBar |
| | – 'Jenny Porter' ♀H4 | CSBt EHea EPfP LRHS MBar |
| | – 'Kramer's Rote' ♀H4 | CBcs CSBt CTri EBrs EHea EPfP LRHS MBar MGos NBlu NDlv NHol SPer SPla SRms |
| § | – 'Lena' | EHea |
| | – 'Margaret Porter' | CSBt EHea EPfP SPer SPla |
| | – 'Mary Helen' | CSBt EHea EPfP LCro LRHS NHol SCoo SPer SPla SRms |
| | – Molten Silver | see *E.* x *darleyensis* 'Silberschmelze' |
| | – 'Moonshine' | LRHS NHol |
| | – 'Mrs Parris' Red' | EHea |
| | – 'N.R. Webster' | EHea |
| | – 'Pink Perfection' | see *E.* x *darleyensis* 'Darley Dale' |
| § | – 'Silberschmelze' | CSBt CTri EHea EPfP LRHS MBar MGos MMuc MSwo NDlv NHol NPri SPer SRms |
| | – 'Spring Surprise' PBR | EHea EPfP LRHS |
| | – 'Tweety' | CBcs EHea |
| | – 'W.G. Pine' | EHea |
| | – 'White Fairy' | EHea |
| | – 'White Glow' | CSBt CTri EHea NHol SPla |
| | – 'White Perfection' ♀H4 | CBcs CSBt EHea EPfP IArd LRHS MBar NHol NPri SCoo SPla SRms |
| | ***discolor*** | EHea |
| | ***erigena*** 'Alba' | EHea MBar |
| | – 'Brian Proudley' | EHea MBar |
| | – 'Brightness' | CSBt EHea EPfP MBar MSwo MWat NHol SCoo |
| | – 'Coccinea' | EHea |
| | – 'Ewan Jones' | EHea MBar |
| | – 'Glauca' | EHea |
| | – 'Golden Lady' ♀H4 | CSBt EHea LRHS MBar MSwo NHol SCoo |
| | – 'Hibernica' | EHea |
| | – 'Hibernica Alba' | EHea MBar |
| | – 'Irish Dusk' ♀H4 | CBcs CSBt CTri EHea EPfP MBar MGos NHol SCoo SPla SRms |
| | – 'Irish Salmon' | CSBt EHea MBar |
| | – 'Irish Silver' | EHea MBar |
| | – 'Ivory' | EHea |
| | – 'Maxima' | EHea |
| | – 'Mrs Parris' Lavender' | EHea |
| | – 'Mrs Parris' White' | EHea |
| | – 'Nana' | EHea |
| | – 'Nana Alba' | EHea MBar |
| | – 'Nana Compacta' | EHea |
| | – 'Rosea' | EHea MBar |
| | – 'Rosslare' | EHea |
| | – 'Rubra' | EHea |
| | – 'Superba' | EHea MBar MGos SRms |
| | – 'Thing Nee' | EHea |
| | – 'W.T. Rackliff' ♀H4 | CBcs CSBt EHea EPfP MBar MGos MSwo NBlu NHol SCoo SPer SPla SRms |
| | – 'W.T. Rackliff Variegated' (v) | EHea |
| | x ***garforthensis*** 'Tracy Wilson' | EHea |
| | ***glauca*** var. ***glauca*** | SPlb |
| | ***gracilis*** | SPoG |
| | x ***griffithsii*** 'Ashlea Gold' | EHea |
| | – 'Elegant Spike' | EHea |
| § | – 'Heaven Scent' | EHea LRHS |
| | – 'Jaqueline' | EHea NHol SPla SRms |
| | – 'Valerie Griffiths' | EHea LRHS MBar NHol SCoo SRms |
| | 'Heaven Scent' | see *E.* x *griffithsii* 'Heaven Scent' |
| | 'Hélène' | EHea |
| | x ***hiemalis*** hort. | SPoG |
| | – 'Ghislaine' | EHea |
| | x ***krameri*** 'Otto' | EHea |
| | – 'Rudi' | EHea |
| | ***lusitanica*** ♀H3 | CTrG EHea MAsh MBar SPer SPoG |
| | – 'George Hunt' | EHea ELan EPfP LRHS MAsh NHol SLon SPer SPla SPoG |
| | – 'Sheffield Park' | EHea ELan LRHS SPer |
| | ***mackayana*** subsp. ***andevalensis*** | EHea |
| | – – f. ***albiflora*** | EHea |
| | – 'Ann D. Frearson' (d) | EHea |
| | – 'Doctor Ronald Gray' | EHea MBar |
| | – 'Donegal' | EHea |
| | – 'Errigal Dusk' | EHea |
| | – 'Galicia' | EHea |
| | – 'Lawsoniana' | EHea |
| | – 'Maura' (d) | EHea |

| | | |
|---|---|---|
| | - 'Plena' (d) | EHea MBar |
| | - 'Shining Light' | EHea SDys |
| | - 'William M'Calla' | EHea |
| | ***mammosa*** | SPlb |
| | ***manipuliflora*** | MBar |
| | - 'Aldeburgh' | EHea |
| § | - 'Cascades' | EHea |
| | - 'Corfu' | EHea |
| | - 'Don Richards' | EHea |
| | - 'Ian Cooper' | EHea |
| | - 'Korçula' | EHea |
| | - 'Toothill Mustard' | EHea |
| | - 'Waterfall' | see *E. manipuliflora* 'Cascades' |
| | ***mediterranea*** | see *E. erigena* |
| | ***multiflora*** 'Formentor' | EHea |
| | x ***oldenburgensis*** 'Ammerland' | EHea |
| | - 'Oldenburg' | EHea |
| § | ***patersonii*** | SPlb |
| | x ***praegeri*** | see *E.* x *stuartii* |
| | ***racemosa*** | EHea |
| | ***scoparia*** subsp. ***azorica*** | EHea |
| | - subsp. ***maderincola*** 'Madeira Gold' | EHea |
| | - subsp. ***platycodon*** | EHea |
| § | - subsp. ***scoparia*** 'Minima' | EHea MBar |
| | - - 'Pumila' | see *E. scoparia* subsp. *scoparia* 'Minima' |
| | ***spiculifolia*** | MBar WThu |
| | - f. ***albiflora*** | EHea |
| | - 'Balkan Rose' | EHea GCal |
| * | 'Spring Field White' **new** | MMuc |
| | ***straussiana*** | SPlb |
| § | x ***stuartii*** | MBar |
| | - 'Charles Stuart' | EHea |
| | - 'Connemara' | EHea |
| | - 'Irish Lemon' $\mathbb{Y}^{H4}$ | CSBt EHea EPfP LRHS MBar MSwo NHol |
| | - 'Irish Orange' | CSBt EHea LRHS MBar NBlu NHol |
| | - 'Irish Rose' | EHea |
| | - 'Nacung' | EHea |
| | - 'Pat Turpin' | EHea |
| | ***subdivaricata*** | EHea |
| § | ***terminalis*** $\mathbb{Y}^{H4}$ | EHea MBar SRms |
| | - 'Golden Oriole' | EHea |
| | - ***stricta*** | see *E. terminalis* |
| | - 'Thelma Woolner' | EHea MBar |
| | ***tetralix*** | SRms |
| | - 'Alba' | EHea |
| | - 'Alba Mollis' $\mathbb{Y}^{H4}$ | CSBt EHea MBar NHol |
| | - 'Alba Praecox' | EHea |
| | - 'Allendale Pink' | EHea |
| | - 'Ardy' | EHea |
| | - 'Bala' | EHea |
| | - 'Bartinney' | EHea MBar |
| | - 'Con Underwood' $\mathbb{Y}^{H4}$ | CSBt EHea LRHS MBar MSwo NHol SRms |
| | - 'Curled Roundstone' | EHea |
| | - 'Dänemark' | EHea |
| | - 'Daphne Underwood' | EHea |
| | - 'Darleyensis' | EHea |
| | - 'Dee' | EHea |
| | - 'Delta' | EHea MBar |
| | - 'Foxhome' | EHea MBar |
| | - 'George Fraser' | EHea |
| | - 'Gratis' | EHea |
| | - 'Hailstones' | EHea MBar |
| | - 'Helma' | EHea |
| | - 'Helma Variegated' (v) | EHea |
| | - 'Hookstone Pink' | EHea MSwo |
| | - 'Humoresque' | EHea |
| | - 'Jos' Creeping' | EHea |

| | | |
|---|---|---|
| | - 'Ken Underwood' | EHea MBar |
| | - 'L.E. Underwood' | EHea MBar NHol |
| | - 'Mary Grace' | EHea |
| | - 'Melbury White' | EHea MBar |
| | - 'Morning Glow' | see *E.* x *watsonii* 'F. White' |
| | - 'Pink Glow' | EHea |
| | - 'Pink Pepper' | EHea |
| | - 'Pink Star' $\mathbb{Y}^{H4}$ | EHea MBar NHol SRms |
| | - 'Renate' | EHea |
| | - 'Riko' | EHea SRms |
| | - 'Rosea' | EHea |
| | - 'Rubra' | EHea |
| § | - 'Ruby's Variety' | EHea MBar |
| | - 'Ruby's Velvet' | see *E. tetralix* 'Ruby's Variety' |
| | - 'Ruth's Gold' | EHea MBar NHol |
| | - 'Salmon Seedling' | EHea |
| | - 'Samtpfötchen' | EHea |
| | - 'Silver Bells' | CSBt EHea MBar |
| | - 'Stikker' | EHea |
| | - 'Swedish Yellow' | EHea |
| | - 'Terschelling' | EHea |
| | - 'Tina' | EHea |
| | - 'Trixie' | EHea |
| | - 'White House' | EHea |
| | ***umbellata*** | EHea MBar |
| | - 'Anne Small' | EHea |
| | - 'David Small' | EHea |
| | ***vagans*** f. ***alba*** **new** | MMuc |
| | - 'Alba Nana' | see *E. vagans* 'Nana' |
| | - 'Bianca' | EHea |
| | - 'Birch Glow' $\mathbb{Y}^{H4}$ | EHea EPfP |
| | - 'Carnea' | EHea |
| | - 'Charm' | EHea |
| | - 'Chittendenii' | EHea |
| | - 'Cornish Cream' $\mathbb{Y}^{H4}$ | EHea EPfP MBar NHol |
| | - 'Cream' | EHea |
| | - 'Diana Hornibrook' | EHea MBar |
| | - 'Diana's Gold' | EHea |
| | - 'Fiddlestone' | EHea MBar |
| | - 'French White' | EHea MBar |
| | - 'George Underwood' | EHea MBar |
| | - 'Golden Triumph' | EHea MBar |
| | - 'Grandiflora' | EHea MBar |
| | - 'Holden Pink' | EHea |
| | - 'Hookstone Rosea' | EHea MBar |
| | - 'Ida M. Britten' | EHea MBar |
| | - 'J.C. Fletcher' | EHea |
| | - 'Kevernensis Alba' $\mathbb{Y}^{H4}$ | EHea MBar |
| | - 'Leucantha' | EHea |
| | - 'Lilacina' | EHea MBar |
| | - 'Lyonesse' $\mathbb{Y}^{H4}$ | CTri EHea MBar MGos MMuc MSwo NHol SRms |
| | - 'Miss Waterer' | EHea MBar |
| | - 'Mrs D.F. Maxwell' $\mathbb{Y}^{H4}$ | CBcs CSBt CTri EHea MBar MGos MSwo NHol SPer SRms |
| | - 'Mrs Donaldson' | EHea |
| § | - 'Nana' | EHea MBar |
| | - 'Pallida' | EHea |
| | - 'Peach Blossom' | EHea MBar |
| | - 'Pyrenees Pink' | EHea MBar |
| | - 'Rosea' | EHea |
| | - 'Rubra' | EHea MBar |
| | - 'Saint Keverne' | CSBt CTri EHea IArd MBar NHol |
| | - 'Summertime' | EHea MBar |
| | - 'Valerie Proudley' $\mathbb{Y}^{H4}$ | CSBt EHea MBar MGos MWat NHol SPer SRms |
| | - 'Valerie Smith' | EHea |
| | - 'Viridiflora' | EHea MBar |
| | - 'White Lady' | EHea MBar |
| | - 'White Rocket' | EHea MBar |
| | - 'White Spire' | EHea |
| | - 'Yellow John' | CBcs EHea MBar |
| | x ***veitchii*** 'Brockhill' | EHea |

| | | |
|---|---|---|
| | - 'Exeter' ♀H3 | CSBt EHea ELan EPfP LRHS MAsh MBar NHol SPer SPoG WFar |
| | - 'Gold Tips' ♀H4 | CSBt EHea EPfP MAsh MBar NHol |
| | - 'Pink Joy' | EHea |
| | ***ventricosa*** | SPoG |
| | ***versicolor*** | SPlb |
| | ***verticillata*** | EHea |
| | ***viridescens*** | EHea |
| | x ***watsonii*** 'Cherry Turpin' | EHea |
| | - 'Dawn' ♀H4 | EHea MBar |
| | - 'Dorothy Metheny' | EHea |
| | - 'Dorset Beauty' | EHea |
| § | - 'F. White' | EHea MBar |
| | - 'Gwen' | EHea MBar |
| | - 'H. Maxwell' | EHea |
| | - 'Mary' | EHea |
| | - 'Pink Pacific' | EHea |
| | - 'Rachel' | EHea |
| | - 'Truro' | EHea |
| | x ***williamsii*** 'Cow-y-Jack' | EHea |
| | - 'Croft Pascoe' | EHea |
| | - 'David Coombe' | EHea |
| | - 'Gew Graze' | EHea |
| | - 'Gold Button' | EHea MBar |
| | - 'Gwavas' | EHea MBar |
| | - 'Jean Julian' | EHea |
| | - 'Ken Wilson' | EHea |
| | - 'Lizard Downs' | EHea |
| | - 'Marion Hughes' | EHea |
| | - 'P.D. Williams' ♀H4 | EHea MBar |
| I | 'Winter Fire' (*oatesii* hybrid) | EHea |

## *Erigeron* ✿ (*Asteraceae*)

| | | |
|---|---|---|
| | from Bald Mountains, USA | NWCA |
| | from Big Horn, USA | NMen |
| | ***acer*** | EBWF |
| | 'Adria' | EBee EBla ECtt GBuc LLHF MBNS SPer SPla WFar WMnd |
| § | ***alpinus*** | NLAp |
| | ***annuus*** | NDov |
| | ***aurantiacus*** | EBee EDAr EPfP MBNS NBre NBro NPri |
| § | ***aureus*** | GKev NSla |
| | - 'Canary Bird' ♀H4 | CPBP EPfP NBir NMen NSla WAbe WFar |
| | - 'The Giant' new | CGra |
| | 'Azure Beauty' | EBee EPfP |
| | Azure Fairy | see *E.* 'Azurfee' |
| § | 'Azurfee' | CSBt EBee ELan EPfP GKir GMaP MBNS MWat NBir NLar NPri SGar SPer SPla SPoG SWvt WMoo WPer |
| | Black Sea | see *E.* 'Schwarzes Meer' |
| | 'Blue Beauty' | SRms |
| | 'Charity' | EBee LRHS MRav WBrE |
| | ***chrysopsidis*** | GKev |
| | - var. ***brevifolius*** | GKev |
| | - 'Grand Ridge' | EPfP LHop LLHF LRHS WAbe |
| | ***compositus*** | CPBP CTri SRms WPer |
| § | - var. ***discoideus*** | EBur GKev NBre NLar NMen SPlb WPer |
| | - 'Rocky' | ECho SPoG SRot |
| | Darkest of All | see *E.* 'Dunkelste Aller' |
| | deep pink-flowered | CHEx |
| | 'Dignity' | EBee EBla EGle ELan LHop LLHF MWat NBro SMrm SUsu WCot WFar |
| | 'Dimity' | CMea ECha NBre SAga WBrk WFar WHal WSFF |
| | 'Dominator' | GBin |
| I | 'Dunkelste Aller' ♀H3 | CPrp CSam EBee EBla ELan EPfP GMaP LBMP LHop LRHS MBri MRav SBch SPer SPoG SRms SWvt WBrE WCAu WCot WEas WFar WHlf |
| | ***elegantulus*** | CMea |
| * | ***ereganus*** | NBre |
| | 'Felicity' | EBee |
| | ***flettii*** | GKev NLAp WPat |
| | 'Foersters Liebling' ♀H4 | EBee EBla EPfP GBin NGdn WAul WCAu |
| | ***formosissimus*** | GBin |
| | 'Four Winds' | EBee ECtt ELan EWes GKev LHop MRav NGdn NMen SEND WPer |
| | ***frigidus*** | NMen |
| | 'Gaiety' | NBre |
| | ***glaucus*** | CHrt CSBt EBee EWll GAbr GGar GJos MRav NBre NGdn NVic SIng SMad WBrk WCot WFar WHoo |
| | - 'Albus' | EBee EShb LHop SMad WFar WPer |
| | - 'Elstead Pink' | CTri EBee ECtt ELan NCGa SAga SPla WFar WSHC |
| | - pink-flowered | SPla |
| | - 'Roger Raiche' | MRav SMrm |
| | - 'Roseus' | CBcs CHal |
| | - 'Sea Breeze' | CPrp ENor GGar GMaP LHop MBNS MBri MCot NBre NCGa NLar NPri SPoG WCot |
| | ***howellii*** | EBee NBre |
| § | ***karvinskianus*** ♀H3 | Widely available |
| | - 'Stallone' | CSec WFar |
| | ***leiomerus*** | LBee LLHF |
| | ***linearis*** | LLHF NBre NMen |
| | 'Mrs F.H. Beale' | EBee EBla ECtt LRHS SRGP |
| | ***mucronatus*** | see *E. karvinskianus* |
| | ***multiradiatus*** | WFar |
| | 'Nachthimmel' | EBla ECtt LAst NBre NGdn WFar |
| | ***nanus*** | NWCA WPer |
| | ***ochroleucus*** var. ***scribneri*** new | LLHF |
| | 'Offenham Excellence' | WCot |
| § | ***peregrinus*** subsp. ***callianthemus*** | CPBP |
| | ***philadelphicus*** | CElw CMea IGor NBir NBro |
| | - 'Lilac Sky' | SKHP |
| | Pink Jewel | see *E.* 'Rosa Juwel' |
| | ***pinnatisectus*** | GKev NWCA WFar WPer |
| | 'Profusion' | see *E. karvinskianus* |
| | ***pumilus*** new | CDes |
| | ***pyrenaicus*** misapplied | see *E. alpinus* |
| | ***pyrenaicus*** Rouy | see *Aster pyrenaeus* |
| | 'Quakeress' | CPrp CSam EBee EBla EBrs ECtt EPfP GMaP GMac LAst LBMP LEdu MBri MCot MRav NBro NGdn SMrm SPoG SUsu WAul WCot WEas WFar WOut |
| § | 'Rosa Juwel' | CSBt CTri EBee ECtt ELan EPfP GJos GMaP LAst LBMP MBNS MRav NBir NPri SPer SPla SPoG SRms SWvt WMnd WMoo WPer |
| | 'Rotes Meer' | CPrp EBee EBla ELan MRav WBrk WCot WFar |
| | ***rotundifolius*** 'Caerulescens' | see *Bellis caerulescens* |
| | ***salsuginosus*** misapplied | see *Aster sibiricus, E. peregrinus* subsp. *callianthemus* |
| § | 'Schneewittchen' | CMMP EBee EBla ELan EPfP GMac LHop MRav MWat NCGa NVic SPet SPla SPoG SWvt WCAu |
| § | 'Schwarzes Meer' | EBee NGdn SPer WFar |
| | ***scopulinus*** | CPBP WPat |
| | ***simplex*** | CSec LRHS |
| | 'Sincerity' | WFar |
| | 'Snow Queen' | WFar |
| | Snow White | see *E.* 'Schneewittchen' |
| | 'Sommerabend' | EBee |
| | 'Sommerneuschnee' | EBee ECha GBin LCro WMnd |
| | ***speciosus*** 'Grandiflora' | NBre |
| | - var. ***macranthus*** | EBee |

| | | |
|---|---|---|
| | 'Strahlenmeer' | CPrp EBee EWTr NBre NGdn WFar |
| | ***thunbergii*** var. ***glabratus*** | CSec |
| | ***trifidus*** | see *E. compositus* var. *discoideus* |
| | ***uniflorus*** | LLHF SRms |
| | ***vagus*** | CPBP LLHF |
| | 'Wayne Roderick' | EBee SRGP |
| | 'White Quakeress' | CMea EGle GBuc MRav SIng WCot WRHF |
| | 'Wuppertal' | EBee MRav NBro NGdn |

## *Erinacea* (*Papilionaceae*)

| | | |
|---|---|---|
| § | ***anthyllis*** ♀H4 | EPot SIng |
| | ***pungens*** | see *E. anthyllis* |

## *Erinus* (*Scrophulariaceae*)

| | | |
|---|---|---|
| | ***alpinus*** ♀H4 | CSec CTri ECho ECtt EPfP GJos GKev GMaP LBMP MLHP MSCN MWat NBlu NHol NLAp NPri NWCA SIng SPet SRms WEas WFar WPer |
| | - var. ***albus*** | ECho NHol NLAp NLar NMen SIng SRms WHoo WPer |
| | - 'Doktor Hähnle' | ECho EDAr ITim LRHS NLar NMen SRms WFar WHoo WPer |
| | - 'Mrs Charles Boyle' | NMen |

## *Eriobotrya* (*Rosaceae*)

| | | |
|---|---|---|
| | ***deflexa*** | CHEx |
| | - 'Coppertone' | EPfP SAPC SArc SBLw SCoo |
| | ***japonica*** (F) ♀H3 | CAbb CBcs CDow CDul CHEx CWGN EAmu EBee EPfP ERom EShb GQui LEdu LMaj LPan LRHS MREP SArc SBLw SCoo SPer SVic WHer WPat WSHC |

## *Eriocapitella* see *Anemone*

## *Eriocephalus* (*Asteraceae*)

| | | |
|---|---|---|
| | ***africanus*** | SPlb WJek |

## *Eriogonum* (*Polygonaceae*)

| | | |
|---|---|---|
| | ***cespitosum*** | CGra NLAp |
| | ***flavum*** | WPer |
| | - var. ***piperi*** | CGra |
| | ***gracilipes*** new | NLAp |
| | ***jamesii*** | NLAp WPat |
| | ***kennedyi*** | CGra |
| | - var. ***alpigenum*** | NLAp |
| | ***ovalifolium*** var. ***nivale*** | NWCA |
| | ***siskiyouense*** | NLAp |
| | ***thymoides*** | CGra |
| | ***umbellatum*** | ECho EShb LRHS NLAp |
| | - subsp. ***covillei*** | CMea |
| | - var. ***humistratum*** | WPat |
| | - var. ***torreyanum*** | CMea GEdr NLAp |
| | - var. ***umbellatum*** | LBee |

## *Eriophorum* (*Cyperaceae*)

| | | |
|---|---|---|
| | ***angustifolium*** | CBen CRWN CWat EBWF EGle EHoe EHon EMFW EPla GFor LPBA MCCP MSKA SPlb SWat WHer WMAq WMoo WPer WPnP WSFF |
| | ***latifolium*** | GFor LPBA MSKA |
| | ***vaginatum*** | CRow EHig EHoe GFor MSKA NSco WSFF |

## *Eriophyllum* (*Asteraceae*)

| | | |
|---|---|---|
| | ***lanatum*** | EBee ECha EPfP EShb MDKP NBid NBre NGBl SAga SPhx WPen |
| * | - 'Pointe' | EHig |

## *Eritrichium* (*Boraginaceae*)

| | | |
|---|---|---|
| § | ***canum*** | CSec |
| | ***rupestre*** | see *E. canum* |
| * | ***sibiricum*** | CSec EDif |
| | ***strictum*** | see *E. canum* |

## *Erodium* (*Geraniaceae*)

| | | |
|---|---|---|
| | SDR 2951 new | GKev |
| | ***absinthoides*** | EPot |
| | - var. ***amanum*** | see *E. amanum* |
| § | ***acaule*** | LLHF NLar WFar |
| § | ***amanum*** | EBee EWes LRHS |
| | 'Ardwick Redeye' | GCal SUsu |
| | ***balearicum*** | see *E.* x *variabile* 'Album' |
| | 'Bidderi' | MOne WAbe |
| | 'Carmel' | NLAp WAbe |
| | 'Caroline' | LPio |
| | ***carvifolium*** | CElw EBee GKev LRHS NLAp NWCA SBch WFar |
| § | ***castellanum*** | EBee LLHF NBre NBro NLAp NMen SHGN SRms WFar |
| | - 'Dujardin' | SPhx |
| | ***celtibericum*** | NLAp |
| | 'Cézembre' | MOne |
| | ***chamaedryoides*** | see *E. reichardii* |
| | - 'Roseum' | see *E.* x *variabile* 'Roseum' |
| | ***cheilanthifolium*** 'David Crocker' | NMen WAbe |
| | ***chrysanthum*** | Widely available |
| | - pink-flowered | CSpe ECha EPot NMen SPhx SRot |
| | ***corsicum*** | EBee EBur ECho MTho NMen NWCA WAbe |
| | - 'Album' | EBee ECho LAst LLHF NLar NMen WAbe |
| | 'County Park' | CMea EBee ECha ECou EWTr MLHP MOne NLAp SHar SRms |
| | ***daucoides*** misapplied | see *E. castellanum* |
| | ***daucoides*** Boiss. | EBee |
| | 'Eileen Emmett' | WAbe |
| | 'Florida' | MAga |
| | ***foetidum*** | EGle NMen |
| | - 'Pallidum' | see *E.* 'Pallidum' |
| | 'Fran's Choice' | see *E.* 'Fran's Delight' |
| § | 'Fran's Delight' | CMea CSpe GCal GMaP LRHS MLHP NDlv NLAp NMen WHoo |
| | 'Fripetta' | MOne WAbe |
| | 'Géant de Saint Cyr' | ECtt |
| N | ***glandulosum*** ♀H4 | EBee ECho EPfP LHop MHer MWea SRms SRot SUsu WFar WKif WPat |
| | ***gruinum*** | CSpe EBee MCot SPhx |
| | ***guttatum*** misapplied | see *E.* 'Katherine Joy' |
| N | ***guttatum*** (Desf.) Willd. | CWCL ECho EWTr MWat NMen SRms |
| | ***hymenodes*** L'Hér. | see *E. trifolium* |
| | ***jahandiezianum*** | NWCA |
| | 'Julie Ritchie' | CMea WHoo |
| § | 'Katherine Joy' | CElw EBee EWes MHer MOne NDlv NLAp SRGP SRot WAbe |
| | x ***kolbianum*** | NDlv NLAp SMHy WAbe WFar WHoo WKif |
| | - 'Natasha' | CMHG EAlp EBee ECtt EPot EWes GBuc GGar GKir GMaP LBee LRHS MHer NLAp NMen SPoG SRGP WAbe WFar WKif |
| | 'Las Meninas' | SUsu |
| | 'Lilac Wonder' | MOne |
| | x ***lindavicum*** 'Charter House' | CMoH |
| | ***macradenum*** | see *E. glandulosum* |
| | ***manescavii*** | Widely available |
| | 'Marchant's Mikado' new | SMHy |
| | 'Merstham Pink' | CMHG CMoH GMaP NDlv NLAp NLar SMrm SRms |
| | ***moschatum*** | ECho |
| | 'Nunwood Pink' | MOne NWCA |

| | | |
|---|---|---|
| § | 'Pallidum' | CSam |
| | ***pelargoniiflorum*** | CSec CSpe EBee EPfP EWTr LPio MCot MTho NBro NChi NDov NLar SBod SEND SMad SMrm SRms STes WEas WFar WKif WPer WPnP WWFP |
| | 'Peter Vernon' | NWCA |
| | ***petraeum*** subsp. ***glandulosum*** | see *E. glandulosum* |
| | 'Pickering Pink' | EBee LIMB NDlv NLAp NMen |
| | 'Pippa Mills' | CElw |
| | 'Princesse Marion' | LPio MLHP NChi |
| * | 'Purple Haze' | CSpe EBee SRms SRot WFar |
| § | ***reichardii*** | CTri ECho ECtt LRHS MBrN MHer MTho NLAp NWCA SPet SPoG SRms WCFE WFar |
| | - 'Album' | CEnt CHrt EAlp ECho GEdr NMen SPet SPoG WFar WHoo |
| | - 'Bianca' | EBee SUsu |
| | - 'Pipsqueak' | NWCA |
| * | - 'Rubrum' | CElw ECho |
| | 'Robertino' | WAbe |
| | 'Robespierre' | SPhx |
| | ***rodiei*** | EBee EWes |
| | ***romanum*** | see *E. acaule* |
| § | ***rupestre*** | EBee ECho ECtt GMaP MOne MWea NDlv NWCA SRms SRot |
| | ***sebaceum*** 'Polly' | NWCA |
| | 'Spanish Eyes' | GKir NLAp SRot SUsu WAbe WCot WFar |
| | 'Stephanie' | CElw CMHG ECho EWes GMaP LBee LSRN MHer NDlv NLAp SRot SUsu SWal |
| | ***supracanum*** | see *E. rupestre* |
| | 'Tiny Kyni' | NLAp WAbe WFar |
| | ***tordylioides*** | EBee |
| | ***trichomanifolium*** L'Hér. | EWes LBee |
| § | ***trifolium*** | CBgR CHrt ECho ELan EPfP EPot MHer NSla SGar SIng WCru |
| | x ***variabile*** | ECtt NLAp |
| § | - 'Album' | CMea EBee ECho EDAr EPot GBuc MBar MHer MTho NPri NWCA SRms SRot WAbe WBrk WFar WPat WPer |
| I | - 'Bishop's Form' | Widely available |
| | - 'Candy' | EAlp EDAr MHer SRot |
| | - 'Derek' | ECho |
| | - 'Flore Pleno' (d) | EBee ECho EDAr ELan EWes MHer NLAp NMen SIng SRms SRot WBrk WFar WPer |
| | - 'Red Rock' | EBee SIng |
| § | - 'Roseum' 🏆$^{H4}$ | EAlp ECho ECtt EDAr ELan EPfP GGar LBee LRHS NLAp NWCA SEND SPlb SRms WBrk WFar WPer |
| I | 'Westacre Seedling' | EWes |
| | 'Whitwell Superb' | CDes CElw WPGP |
| | x ***willkommianum*** | NWCA |

## *Erpetion* see *Viola*

## *Eruca* (*Brassicaceae*)

| | |
|---|---|
| ***vesicaria*** | CWan |
| - subsp. ***sativa*** | CSpe ELau GPoy MHer MNHC MSal NGHP SIde SPoG WJek WLHH |

## *Eryngium* ✿ (*Apiaceae*)

| | | |
|---|---|---|
| | F&M 208 **new** | WPGP |
| | F&M 224 | WPGP |
| | PC&H 268 | NLar |
| | from Isfahan, Iran **new** | GKev |
| § | ***agavifolium*** | Widely available |
| | ***alpinum*** 🏆$^{H4}$ | Widely available |
| | - SDR 3512 **new** | GKev |
| | - 'Amethyst' | EBee GBuc IPot LRHS MBri MRav MSte NBro SMrm |
| | - 'Blue Jacket' | NSti WBrE |
| | - 'Blue Star' | CElw CHar CSpe EBee EBla EDAr EHrv ELan EPfP GAbr GMac MCot MNFA MRav MSte MWat NChi NDov NGBl NHol SPhx SPla WCot WFar WHil WHoo WPer WTin |
| | - 'Holden Blue' | MAvo SUsu |
| | - 'Slieve Donard' | see *E.* x *zabelii* 'Donard Variety' |
| | - 'Superbum' | CSpe CWCL ECtt EHrv GAbr GBri GBuc MBri MNrw NCob NLar SPer SPla SRms SWat WGwG |
| | ***amethystinum*** | CMdw EBee EBla EGoo EHrv LPio MAvo MCot MNrw SPla WFar WPer |
| | ***biebersteinianum*** | see *E. caeruleum* |
| | 'Blue Jackpot' | CWCL EBee EHrv EWes GMac MBri MLLN NBhm NCob NMoo SWat |
| | 'Blue Steel' | MAvo MDKP NChi |
| | ***bourgatii*** | Widely available |
| | - Graham Stuart Thomas's selection | Widely available |
| | - 'Oxford Blue' 🏆$^{H4}$ | CEnt CSpe EBee EHrv ENor GGar GMaP GMac LAst MCot MHer NLar SGar SPoG SWvt WEas WOld |
| | - 'Picos Amethyst' | CBcs CMac CWGN EBee EBrs EGle GBri LCro LHop LRHS LSRN NCGa NLar NSti SCoo SPhx SPoG SVil WOVN |
| | - 'Picos Blue'$^{PBR}$ | Widely available |
| | ***bromeliifolium*** misapplied | see *E. agavifolium, E. eburnium* |
| § | ***caeruleum*** | GBuc GMac MNrw NChi |
| | ***campestre*** | EWll MDKP MHer NGby NLar WFar WOut WPer |
| | ***caucasicum*** | see *E. caeruleum* |
| | 'Cobalt Star' | GMac |
| | ***creticum*** | NBro NChi |
| | ***cymosum*** B&SWJ 10267 **new** | WCru |
| | ***decaisneanum*** misapplied | see *E. pandanifolium* |
| | ***deppeanum*** NJM 05.031 **new** | WPGP |
| | ***dichotomum*** | NChi |
| | Dove Cottage hybrid **new** | NDov |
| | ***ebracteatum*** | CSpe EBla IGor LPio MCot |
| | - CD&R 3248 **new** | WCru |
| | - var. ***poterioides*** | NDov SMHy SMad SPhx |
| § | ***eburneum*** | CBcs CFir CGHE CKno EBee EBrs ECha EPfP EWes GBuc GCal GMaP LPio LRHS NBro NChi NHol NSti SMad SPad WCot WFar WPic |
| | aff. ***eburneum*** | WPGP |
| | ***elegans*** var. ***elegans*** CDPR 3076 | WPGP |
| | ***foetidum*** | CArn |
| § | ***giganteum*** 🏆$^{H4}$ | Widely available |
| | - 'Silver Ghost' 🏆$^{H4}$ | Widely available |
| | ***glaciale*** | EBee |
| | ***guatemalense*** | CGHE WPGP |
| | - B&SWJ 8989 | WCru |
| | - B&SWJ 10322 **new** | WCru |
| | - B&SWJ 10420 **new** | WCru |
| | ***horridum*** misapplied | see *E. eburneum* |
| | ***horridum*** ambig. | EBee EWes GKir LEdu LPio LRHS MNrw NChi SAPC SArc WCAu WFar WMnd WPGP |
| | ***horridum*** Malme | GKir WCot |
| | ***maritimum*** | CArn CPou EBWF EBee EGoo GPoy ITim MDKP MHer NLar SPlb WCot WFar |
| | Miss Willmott's ghost | see *E. giganteum* |
| | ***monocephalum*** | WPGP |
| | x ***oliverianum*** 🏆$^{H4}$ | Widely available |
| | ***palmatum*** | NChi |

| | | |
|---|---|---|
| § | ***pandanifolium*** ♀H4 | CFir CHEx CMHG CSec CTrG EBee EPfP EWes GCal LPio NSti SAPC SArc SGar SMad SPav SPlb SPoG SWvt WCot WMnd WPGP |
| | - 'Physic Purple' | CAby SMHy SPhx WCot |
| | ***paniculatum*** | EBee WPGP |
| | ***pectinatum*** | CSec |
| | - B&SWJ 9109 | WCru |
| | ***petiolatum*** | CSec MNrw |
| | ***planum*** | Widely available |
| | - 'Bethlehem' ♀H4 | EBee LRHS MBri NBro NLar SWat |
| § | - 'Blauer Zwerg' | CKno EBee LCro LHop MGos SPla SWat WFar WHlf |
| | - 'Blaukappe' | CHar CMea CSec EBee EBrs ELon GBBs GBri GMac LCro LDai LRHS NLar SMrm SPet SPhx WAul WBrE WFar WGwG WHil WSHC |
| * | - 'Blue Candle' | EBee NLar WFar |
| | - Blue Dwarf | see *E. planum* 'Blauer Zwerg' |
| | - 'Blue Ribbon' | EBee EBla LAst LRHS LSou MRav NGdn SWat |
| | - 'Flüela' | EBee EBla EWes GMaP LRHS LSRN NBro SBch SCoo SPhx SPla SWat WFar WTin |
| | - 'Hellas' | EBee NLar |
| | - 'Jade Frost' (v) new | CWGN EBee ELon LPio LSou MBNS NChi NSti SPoG |
| | - 'Paradise Jackpot' | EBee NCGa NGdn SPer |
| | - 'Seven Seas' | CFir EBee EBla ECtt LRHS MBNS MBri NBro NGdn SPhx SPla SWat WPer |
| | - 'Silver Stone' | EBee EBla GMaP LDai LRHS MBri MDKP NBre NBro NPri SPhx WCAu |
| | - 'Tetra Petra' | CBcs EBee GBri MAvo WHil WPer |
| | - 'Violet Blue' | GCal |
| § | ***proteiflorum*** | EBee EDAr GCal LPio LRHS MAvo MDKP NCGa NDov NSti SMad SPlb WCot WGwG WHil |
| | ***serbicum*** | MAvo |
| | ***serra*** | EBee EBrs EDAr EWes GBuc LDai LRHS MAvo NChi WBor |
| | - RB 90454 | MDKP |
| | ***spinalba*** | SPhx |
| | ***strotheri*** | CSec |
| | - B&SWJ 9109 | WCru |
| | - B&SWJ 10392 new | WCru |
| | ***tricuspidatum*** | CSec EBrs ECtt GKir LRHS WPer |
| | x ***tripartitum*** ♀H4 | Widely available |
| * | ***umbelliferum*** | CBcs EBee EDAr GCal GKir MBNS MDKP NChi NPri NSti SPhx SPoG |
| | ***variifolium*** | Widely available |
| | ***venustum*** | CDes LPio MAvo SMrm WFar WOut |
| | ***yuccifolium*** | CArn CHEx CKno EBee EBla EBrs EPfP EWes GCal GKir LEdu LPio NHol NVic SDix SDnm SMrm SPav SPhx SPlb SWvt WBrE WFar WHoo WTin |
| | x ***zabelii*** | CAby ECha GMac LPio MAvo NBir NChi NDov SMeo SPhx WPGP |
| | - 'Blaue Ritter' new | SWat |
| § | - 'Donard Variety' | EBla ECtt GCal GMac IPot ITim LRHS MDKP NLar SWat |
| | - 'Forncett Ultra' | CDes EMon GCal GMac MAvo NChi SMeo WPGP |
| | - 'Jewel' | CDes MAvo SApp SMHy SUsu SWat |
| | - 'Jos Eijking' | EBrs ELon GKir GMac LRHS MRav NLar SMad WBor |
| | - 'Spring Hill Seedling' | MAvo |
| | - 'Violetta' | ECha ELan GBuc GMac IGor MAvo MBri MSte NGby SWat WFar WHoo WPen |

## *Erysimum* (Brassicaceae)

| | | |
|---|---|---|
| | from Madeira | CPLG ELon |
| | ***allionii*** misapplied | see *E.* x *marshallii* |
| | ***amoenum*** | LLHF |
| | 'Apricot Delight' | see *E.* 'Apricot Twist' |
| § | 'Apricot Twist' | Widely available |
| | ***arkansanum*** | see *E. helveticum* |
| | 'Bowles' Mauve' ♀H3 | Widely available |
| | 'Bowles' Purple' | MCot NCob SRms SWvt WBVN |
| | 'Bowles' Yellow' | GBuc |
| | 'Bredon' ♀H3 | EBee EPfP LRHS MAsh NPer WHoo WKif |
| | ***brevistylum*** | GKev |
| | 'Butterscotch' | CFee ECtt EGoo MMHG NCob SAga WEas WHoo WTin |
| | 'Butterscotch Variegated' (v) | GBri NCob |
| | ***cheiri*** | CArn MHer NSco WCot |
| | - 'Blood Red' | CSpe SMeo |
| | - 'Bloody Warrior' (d) | CElw ECtt |
| | - 'Fire King' | SMeo |
| § | - 'Harpur Crewe' (d) | CFee CTri EBee ELan ELon EPfP EShb GMaP LRHS MTho NPer SRms SUsu WCot WPnn |
| | - 'Jane's Derision' | CNat |
| | - 'Orange Bedder' (Bedder Series) new | NBir |
| | 'Chelsea Jacket' | EBee ECtt EPfP GBri LHop SUsu WEas |
| | 'Constant Cheer' | Widely available |
| | 'Cotswold Gem' (v) | CElw EBee ECtt EHoe ELan ELon EMil EPPr EPfP EShb GBri LAst LBMP LDai MAsh MHer NBPC NCob NPer SBri SHBN SLim SMrm SPoG SWvt WCot WGwG WWlt |
| | 'Cream Delight' | EBee |
| | 'Dawn Breaker' | CElw CWGN EBee ECtt EWes GAbr GBin GBri LSou MAsh NBPC NCob SPoG SUsu WCot |
| | 'Devon Gold' | see *E.* 'Plant World Gold' |
| | 'Devon Sunset' | GBri MRav SUsu |
| | 'Dorothy Elmhirst' | see *E.* 'Mrs L.K. Elmhirst' |
| | dwarf lemon | WHoo |
| | 'Ellen Willmott' | GBin |
| | 'Golden Gem' | NBlu NDlv WFar WPer |
| | 'Golden Jubilee' | EAlp ECho ECtt GGar LIMB WFar |
| | 'Hector's Gatepost' | EBee LCro LSRN LSou NBPC SPoG SRGP SRkn |
| § | ***helveticum*** | CMdw ECho IFro ILad SAga SRms |
| | 'Jacob's Jacket' | ECtt EPyc EWTr MBNS MHer NPer WEas |
| | 'Jaunty Joyce' | GBri |
| | 'Joan Adams' | EBee LHop SAga |
| | 'John Codrington' | EBee GBri LHop NPer SUsu WKif WWFP |
| | 'Joseph's Coat' | LIMB |
| | 'Jubilee Gold' | GAbr WCot |
| | 'Julian Orchard' | CHll CSpe SSth |
| | ***kotschyanum*** | CPBP ECho ECtt EPot GEdr LBee MOne NMen NWCA SRms |
| | ***linifolium*** | EBur SRms WFar WGor |
| § | - 'Variegatum' (v) | CArn CCCN CSBt CWan EBee ECtt ELan EPfP GGar LRHS NPer NPri SPer SPoG SRot STes WPGP |
| § | x ***marshallii*** ♀H4 new | EWTr |
| | 'Mayflower' | NCob |
| | 'Moonlight' | EBee ECtt EPot GBuc GMaP LCro MHer MTho NBir NDov SRms WBVN |
| § | 'Mrs L.K. Elmhirst' | ELon LSou MDKP MMHG NDov NPer WCot WHoo WWFP |
| | ***mutabile*** | CBgR CTri EBee EGoo MAsh MRav SIde SUsu WHal |

| | |
|---|---|
| 'My Old Mum' **new** | GBri |
| 'Orange Flame' | CMea EAlp EBee ECha ECho ECtt EPot GGar LAst LHop MHer NHol NPer NWCA WFar WPer |
| 'Parish's' | CMdw CSpe ECtt EWTr MRav SAga |
| 'Parkwood Gold' **new** | EDAr GJos |
| 'Pastel Patchwork' | CSpe EBee LSou NBPC |
| Perry's hybrid | NPer |
| 'Perry's Peculiar' | NPer |
| § 'Plant World Gold' | CElw |
| 'Plant World Lemon' | CPLG EBee ECtt GBri LSou MBri SDnm SRot |
| § ***pulchellum*** | CSec ECha SRot |
| - 'Variegatum' (v) | WBrE WSFF |
| ***pumilum*** DC. | see *E. helveticum* |
| ***rupestre*** | see *E. pulchellum* |
| 'Ruston Royal' | EBee |
| 'Sissinghurst Variegated' | see *E. linifolium* 'Variegatum' |
| 'Sprite' | CLyd CMea CTri ECho ECtt EDAr EPot NPer |
| 'Starbright' **new** | SPoG |
| 'Stars and Stripes' | CWGN EBee LSou |
| 'Sunshine' | SWal |
| 'Sweet Sorbet' | CHrt EBee ECtt EPfP MBri MSte NBPC NDov NPri SMrm SPav SPoG SRkn SWvt WHoo |
| 'Turkish Bazaar' | ECho |
| Walberton's Fragrant Sunshine = 'Walfrasun' | LRHS MAsh SCoo SPoG |
| 'Wenlock Beauty' | GBin LDai SRms |
| 'Winter Joy' | CBow EBee LLHF LSou MBNS |
| ***witmannii*** | SSth |

## *Erythraea* see *Centaurium*

## *Erythrina* (*Papilionaceae*)

| | |
|---|---|
| x ***bidwillii*** | CCCN |
| ***crista-galli*** | CAbb CBcs CCCN CDTJ CHEx CSpe CWCL ELan GQui IDee LRHS MREP MWea SOWG SPlb WPGP WPat WSHC |
| - 'Compacta' | MBri SMad |
| § ***humeana*** | CDTJ |
| ***latissima*** | CDTJ |
| ***princeps*** | see *E. humeana* |

## *Erythronium* ✿ (*Liliaceae*)

| | |
|---|---|
| ***albidum*** | CLAP CWsd EBee ECho EPot GAuc GBuc IBlr LAma NMen SGar |
| ***americanum*** | CAby CArn CLAP CWoo EBee EBrs ECho EPot GBuc IBlr LAma MLLN MSSP NHol NMen WCru |
| 'Apple Blossom' | CWsd |
| 'Beechpark' | IBlr |
| 'Blush' | CWsd GBuc IBlr |
| 'Brimstone' | CWsd |
| 'Californian Star' | IBlr |
| ***californicum*** ♀H4 | CAby CFir CLAP CWoo CWsd EBee EBrs ECho GBuc ITim SCnR WAbe WCru |
| - J&JA 1.350.209 | CWoo |
| - J&JA 13216 | CLAP |
| - JCA 1.350.200 | WWst |
| * - var. ***candidum*** MS 01/009 | WWst |
| - 'Harvington Snowgoose' | CLAP EHrv LRHS WWst |
| - Plas Merdyn form | IBlr |
| § - 'White Beauty' ♀H4 | Widely available |
| ***californicum*** x ***hendersonii*** | IBlr |
| ***caucasicum*** | CLAP |
| ***citrinum*** | CWoo CWsd GBuc NMen |
| - J&JA 1.350.410 | CWoo |
| - J&JA 13462 | CLAP CWoo WWst |
| - var. ***roderickii*** **new** | EBee |
| ***citrinum*** x ***hendersonii*** | CAvo IBlr |
| 'Citronella' | CBro CLAP CWsd EHrv GBuc GKev IBlr ITim MSSP NDlv NMen WAbe WCru WFar |
| ***cliftonii*** hort. | see *E. multiscapoideum* Cliftonii Group |
| ***dens-canis*** ♀H4 | Widely available |
| - JCA 470.001 | CLAP |
| - from Slovenia | CLAP |
| - 'Charmer' | EBee GEdr WWst |
| - 'Frans Hals' | CLAP CWsd EBee EBrs ECho EPot ERos GBuc GEdr GGar MNFA MTho WCru WHal |
| - 'Lilac Wonder' | CWsd EBee EBrs ECho EPot EWTr GEdr GMaP LAma LEdu LRHS MNrw MTho NHol WWst |
| * - 'Moerheimii' (d) | IBlr WWst |
| - var. ***niveum*** | ERos IBlr |
| - 'Old Aberdeen' | CLAP CWsd EBee IBlr MNrw WWst |
| - 'Pink Perfection' | CHFP EBee EBrs ECho EPot ERos GEdr GGar LEdu LRHS NHol WCru |
| - 'Purple King' | CHFP CWsd EBee EBrs ECGP ECho EPot ERos GBuc GEdr GMaP LAma LRHS MNrw NHol WCru |
| - 'Rose Queen' | CAby CBro CFir CMil EBee EBrs ECho EPot ERos GAbr GBuc GGar GMaP LAma MAvo MTho NHol NLAp SPhx WHal |
| * - 'Semi-plenum' (d) | IBlr |
| - 'Snowflake' | CHFP CLAP CMea CTca EBee EBrs ECha ECho EPot ERos GBuc GEdr GGar GKev LAma LRHS MNFA MNrw NBir NMen WAbe WCru |
| - 'White Splendour' | CBro ECho ERos IBlr MNrw WWst |
| 'Diana Chappell' **new** | SKHP |
| ***elegans*** | CWsd EBee EBrs ECho EHrv GBuc WWst |
| 'Flash' | IBlr |
| § ***grandiflorum*** | CLAP EBee EBrs ECho EPot GBuc GEdr NMen |
| - M&PS 007 | CLAP |
| - M&PS 96/024 | NMen |
| - var. ***candidum*** M&PS 01/001 **new** | EBee |
| - subsp. ***chrysandrum*** | see *E. grandiflorum* |
| ***helenae*** | CLAP CWoo CWsd IBlr |
| - J&JA 11678 | WWst |
| ***hendersonii*** | CLAP CPom CWoo CWsd ECho EHrv MSSP WAbe WWst |
| - J&JA 1.351.301 | CWoo |
| - J&JA 12945 | CLAP CWoo |
| - JCA 11116 | CLAP |
| ***howellii*** | CLAP CWsd |
| - J&JA 13428 | WWst |
| - J&JA 13441 | CLAP |
| 'Janice' | CWsd |
| ***japonicum*** | CBcs EBee EBrs ECho EFEx EPot GAuc GBuc GEdr GGar LAma MNrw NCot NHol NMen WCru WFar |
| 'Jeanette Brickell' | CLAP CWsd IBlr WWst |
| 'Jeannine' | CWsd GBuc IBlr WCru |
| 'Joan Wiley' | CWsd |
| 'Joanna' | CWsd GBuc IBlr MNrw NMen WWst |
| 'Kondo' | CTri EBee EBrs ECho EPfP EPot ERos GBuc GEdr GGar GMaP IBlr ITim LAma LEdu LRHS MTho NBir NHol NMen SPer WAbe WCot WCru WFar |
| 'Margaret Mathew' | CLAP CWsd IBlr WAbe WWst |
| 'Minnehaha' | CWsd WWst |

| | | |
|---|---|---|
| | ***montanum*** | ECho EHrv WWst |
| § | ***multiscapoideum*** | CLAP CWoo CWsd EBee ECho GBuc WCot |
| | - JCA 1.352.100 | WWst |
| | - NNS 99-163 | WWst |
| § | - Cliftonii Group | CAvo CLAP CWsd EBrs WAbe |
| | 'Oregon Encore' | IBlr |
| | ***oregonum*** | CLAP CWoo EBrs ECho EHrv GBuc GGar IBlr ITim MNrw MSSP SKHP |
| | - subsp. ***leucandrum*** | CLAP CWsd WWst |
| | - - J&JA 13494 | CWoo |
| | - - JCA 4.352.400 | WWst |
| | - subsp. ***oregonum*** | WCot |
| I | - 'Sulphur Form' | CLAP |
| | - yellow-flowered | CWsd |
| | 'Pagoda' ♀H4 | Widely available |
| | ***pluriflorum*** | EBrs |
| | ***purdyi*** | see *E. multiscapoideum* |
| | ***revolutum*** ♀H4 | CAby CAvo CBro CLAP CMea CPom CSec CWoo EBee EBrs ECho EHrv EPot GBuc GGar GKev GMaP IBlr ITim MNrw MSSP NMen SCnR SKHP SRot WAbe WCru |
| | - from God's Valley | WWst |
| | - early-flowering | CWsd |
| | - 'Guincho Splendour' | IBlr |
| | - Johnsonii Group | CWoo EBee WAbe WCru WWst |
| | - 'Knightshayes' | CWsd SKHP |
| | - 'Knightshayes Pink' | CLAP EHrv GBuc IBlr NBir WShi |
| | - late-flowering | CWsd |
| | - Plas Merdyn form | IBlr |
| | - 'Rose Beauty' | EBrs NMen |
| | - 'White Beauty' | see *E. californicum* 'White Beauty' |
| | - 'Wild Salmon' | CLAP |
| | 'Rippling Waters' | IBlr |
| | 'Rosalind' | CWsd IBlr SCnR |
| | ***sibiricum*** | EBee EBrs ECho NMen WWst |
| | - from Siberia | MPhe |
| * | - subsp. ***altaicum*** new | WWst |
| | - white-flowered | WWst |
| | 'Sundisc' | CAby ECha ECho GBuc IBlr MSSP MTho NMen WAbe WWst |
| | 'Susannah' | CWsd WWst |
| | ***taylorii*** new | CWsd EBee WWst |
| | ***tuolumnense*** ♀H4 | CBro CLAP CTca CWCL CWsd EBee EBrs ECho EHrv EPot ERos GAuc GBuc GEdr GGar GKev GMaP IBlr IHer LAma LEdu MCot NMen SKHP SPoG WAbe |
| | - EBA clone 2 | WAbe |
| | - EBA clone 3 | WAbe |
| | - 'Spindlestone' | CWsd IBlr WWst |
| | ***umbilicatum*** | IBlr MSSP WWst |

## *Escallonia* ✿ (*Escalloniaceae*)

| | | |
|---|---|---|
| | 'Alice' | EBee SLPl SPer |
| | 'Apple Blossom' ♀H4 | Widely available |
| § | ***bifida*** ♀H3 | CDoC CDul CFee EQua LRHS WFar WPat WSHC |
| | 'C.F. Ball' | CBcs CSBt CTri EBee ELan GGar LBMP LBuc MGan MSwo NBlu NScw NWea SEND SPad SRms WBVN WDin WFar WMoo |
| | 'Compacta Coccinea' | CBcs |
| | 'Dart's Rosy Red' | NHol SLPl |
| | 'Donard Beauty' | EBee SRms WBod |
| | 'Donard Radiance' ♀H4 | CBcs CDoC CDul CSBt CSam CWib EBee ELan EPfP LHop LRHS LSRN NHol NWea SBod SLim SPer SPla SPoG SRms SWvt WBod WDin WFar WMoo |
| | 'Donard Red' new | GGal |
| | 'Donard Seedling' | Widely available |
| | 'Donard Star' | CSBt CWib EBee EPfP LAst NWea SLPl WCFE |
| | 'Edinensis' | EBee EPfP ERas MBar NLar SBch SEND SLim WDin WFar WMoo |
| | 'Erecta' | EPfP SHGN |
| | 'Everest' | LBuc LRHS MAsh SLon |
| | x ***exoniensis*** | SRms |
| | 'Gwendolyn Anley' | SLPl WFar |
| | 'Hopleys Gold' PBR | see *E. laevis* 'Gold Brian' |
| | ***illinita*** | EBee LLHF NLar |
| | 'Iveyi' ♀H3 | Widely available |
| § | ***laevis*** | WFar |
| § | - 'Gold Brian' PBR | CDul CMHG EBee EHoe ELan EPau EPfP GGar LRHS LSRN MAsh MGos MWat SCoo SPer SPoG SWal WBod WFar WHar |
| | - 'Gold Ellen' (v) | CBcs CChe CSBt CTri CWSG EBee ELan EPfP LAst LBMP LRHS MAsh MGos MRav MSwo NHol NPri SAga SCoo SEND SLim SPer SPla SPoG SRms SWvt WBod WMoo |
| | 'Langleyensis' ♀H4 | CBcs CSBt CTri CWib GGal NWea WDin WFar WHar |
| | 'Little Treasure' | SPoG |
| | ***mexicana*** | WFar |
| | x ***mollis*** | SPer |
| | ***montevidensis*** | see *E. bifida* |
| | ***organensis*** | see *E. laevis* |
| | 'Peach Blossom' ♀H4 | CBcs CDoC CDul CSam CWib EBee ECrN ELan EMil EPfP GGar LRHS MAsh MBNS MBri MLHP MSwo NBir NPri SCoo SHBN SLPl SLim SPer SPoG SRms SSto WFar |
| | 'Pink Elf' | MSwo NHol |
| | 'Pride of Donard' ♀H4 | CBcs CDoC CPLG CSBt EBee EPfP GGar MAsh MGan NPri SRms SSto WBod |
| | ***punctata*** | see *E. rubra* |
| | 'Red Dream' | CSBt CWSG EBee ERas LAst LBMP LRHS MAsh MBri MGos MSwo NBlu NHol NLar NPri SAga SCoo SPoG SRms SWvt WFar |
| | 'Red Elf' | CCVT EBee ELan EPfP GGar LAst LRHS MAsh MBar MBri MGos MRav MWat NHol SCoo SLPl SPer SPlb SPoG SRms SWvt WBVN WFar |
| | 'Red Hedger' | CDoC CSBt CTrG CTsd CWib ELan GGal LRHS MRav SCoo SRms |
| | 'Red Robin' | CBcs SPoG |
| | ***resinosa*** | CBcs CPLG SAPC SArc WHCG WJek |
| § | ***rubra*** | MLHP |
| | - 'Crimson Spire' ♀H4 | Widely available |
| | - 'Ingramii' | CSBt CWib EBee NWea SEND SHBN |
| | - var. ***macrantha*** | CBcs CCVT CChe CDoC CDul CSBt CWSG CWib EBee ECrN ELan EPfP GGar IArd LAst LRHS MHer NBir NBlu NWea SCoo SLim SPer SPoG WDin WFar WMoo |
| * | - - ***aurea*** | NScw |
| | - 'Pygmaea' | see *E. rubra* 'Woodside' |
| § | - 'Woodside' | ECho EPfP LLHF MLHP NHol SRms WHCG |
| | 'Silver Anniversary' | MSwo |
| | 'Slieve Donard' | EBee EPfP MRav NHol NWea SLPl SLim SLon SRms WFar |

## *Eschscholzia* (*Papaveraceae*)

| | | |
|---|---|---|
| | ***caespitosa*** 'Sundew' | CSec CSpe |
| | ***californica*** ♀H4 | GKir |
| | - 'Jersey Cream' | CSec CSpe |
| | ***lobbii*** | CSpe |

## *Etlingera* (*Zingiberaceae*)

***elatior*** 'Pink Torch' new WVal
- 'Red Sceptre' new WVal
- 'Red Torch' new WVal
- 'Red Tulip' new WVal
- 'White Torch' new WVal
- 'Yamamoto' new WVal

## *Eucalyptus* ✿ (*Myrtaceae*)

***aggregata*** CCVT SAPC SArc WCel
***alpina*** SPlb
***apiculata*** WCel
***approximans*** subsp. ***approximans*** WCel
***archeri*** CCVT CDTJ CDoC CDul CTho EBee ECrN EPfP GQui LRHS MMuc MWhi WCel WOVN WPGP
***baeuerlenii*** WCel
§ ***bridgesiana*** WCel
***caesia*** SPlb
***camaldulensis*** SPad SPlb
***camphora*** CCCN CTho WCel
***cinerea*** GQui SBig SPlb WCel
***citriodora*** CWib EOHP GQui MHer MNHC NGHP SPlb WCel
***coccifera*** CBcs CCVT CDoC CDul CMHG CSBt CTho EBee ELan EPfP GGar LMaj LRHS MCCP MLan NPer SBig SPlb SPoG WCel WDin WPGP
- silver-leaved LPan
***cordata*** CCVT CDul WCel
***cosmophylla*** WCel
***crenulata*** CTrC GQui WCel
***crucis*** subsp. ***crucis*** SPlb
***cypellocarpa*** SPlb
***dalrympleana*** ♀H3 CAbb CBcs CCVT CDoC CDul CMHG EBee ECrN ELan EPfP EWes LRHS MGos MSwo NBea NPer SBig SCoo SLim SPer SPoG SRms WCel WDin WHar WPGP
***deanei*** WCel
***debeuzevillei*** see *E. pauciflora* subsp. *debeuzevillei*
***delegatensis*** CMHG EBee NPer WCel
- subsp. ***tasmaniensis*** GGar
***divaricata*** see *E. gunnii* subsp. *divaricata*
***erythrocorys*** SPlb
***eximia*** SPlb
***ficifolia*** CBcs CDTJ
***fraxinoides*** SPlb WCel
***gamophylla*** SPlb
***glaucescens*** CCVT CMHG CTho CWCL ELan EPfP EWes GQui LRHS NPri SAPC SArc SPer WCel WPGP
***globulus*** CHEx MNHC MSal SBLw WCel WFar
***goniocalyx*** EPfP WCel
§ ***gregsoniana*** CCVT CDoC CTho EPfP GGal SPlb WCel WPGP
***gunnii*** ♀H3 Widely available
§ - subsp. ***divaricata*** CCVT EPfP GQui LRHS MBri WCel
***johnstonii*** CDul CMHG CTrC EBee ECrN NLar SPer WCel
***kitsoniana*** GGar WCel
***kruseana*** SPlb
***kybeanensis*** CCVT GQui MGos WCel
§ ***lacrimans*** WCel WPGP
***lehmannii*** SOWG
***leucoxylon*** WCel
- subsp. ***megalocarpa*** SPlb
* - - 'Rosea' MCot
***ligustrina*** WCel
'Little Boy Blue' CWib LSRN
***macarthurii*** WCel
***macrocarpa*** SPlb
***macroryncha*** SPlb
***mannifera*** subsp. ***elliptica*** WCel
***mitchelliana*** WCel WDin
* ***moorei nana*** CDTJ MHer
***neglecta*** EPfP WCel
***nicholii*** CCVT CDul EBee EPfP ERas EWes GQui LHop LRHS MGos NLar SCoo SPoG WCel WOVN WPGP
***niphophila*** see *E. pauciflora* subsp. *niphophila*
***nitens*** CCVT CDTJ CMHG SAPC SArc SBig SCoo SPlb WBVN WCel
§ ***nitida*** GGar WCel
***nova-anglica*** CMHG
***obliqua*** GGar
***olsenii*** WCel
***ovata*** GGar
***paliformis*** WCel
***parviflora*** WBVN
***parvifolia*** ♀H4 CBcs CCCN CCVT CDoC CDul CLnd CMHG EPfP LRHS MWhi SCoo SEND WCel WPGP
***pauciflora*** CCCN CCVT CDoC CSBt CTho ELan EPfP MGos MMuc NLar SPer WCel
- subsp. ***acerina*** WCel
§ - subsp. ***debeuzevillei*** CCVT CDoC CDul CMHG CTho EBee EPfP EWes GQui LMaj LPan MAsh MGos SAPC SArc SBig WCel WPGP
- subsp. ***hedraia*** NPri WCel
- var. ***nana*** see *E. gregsoniana*
§ - subsp. ***niphophila*** ♀H4 Widely available
- - 'Pendula' see *E. lacrimans*
- subsp. ***pauciflora*** LPan
***perriniana*** Widely available
***phoenicea*** SOWG
***pulchella*** WCel
***pulverulenta*** CDul LRHS SPlb
- 'Baby Blue' MBri MGos WCel
***regnans*** GGar
***risdonii*** GGar
***rodwayi*** GGar
***rubida*** CCCN CMHG WCel
***sideroxylon*** SPlb
- 'Rosea' SPlb
***simmondsii*** see *E. nitida*
***stellulata*** WCel
***stuartiana*** see *E. bridgesiana*
***subcrenulata*** CCVT CMHG EPfP GGar GQui LHop WCel
***tetraptera*** SPlb
***torquata*** SPlb
***urnigera*** CCVT CDoC EBee LHop LRHS SCoo WCel WDin
***vernicosa*** CCVT GGar WCel
***viminalis*** CArn CHEx WCel WDin

## *Eucharidium* see *Clarkia*

## *Eucharis* (*Amaryllidaceae*)

§ ***amazonica*** ♀H1 CCCN CSec EBrs ECho EShb LAma LRHS SPav
***grandiflora*** misapplied see *E. amazonica*

## *Eucodonia* (*Gesneriaceae*)

'Adele' EABi WDib
***andrieuxii*** 'Naomi' WDib
***verticillata*** CSpe

## *Eucomis* ✿ (*Hyacinthaceae*)

| | |
|---|---|
| ***autumnalis*** misapplied | see *E. zambesiaca* |
| § ***autumnalis*** (Mill.) Chitt. ♀H2-3 | Widely available |
| - subsp. ***amaryllidifolia*** | WPGP |
| - subsp. ***autumnalis*** | WPGP |
| - - 'Peace Candles' | CPen |
| - subsp. ***clavata*** | CTca EBee |
| ***bicolor*** ♀H2-3 | Widely available |
| - 'Alba' | CAvo CPLG CTca EAmu EBee EBrs ECho EPot LPio LRHS SDnm |
| - 'Stars and Stripes' | WCru |
| 'Cabernet Candles' | CPen |
| § ***comosa*** | CAvo CBgR CBro CDWL CDes CFFs CHEx CHll CPrp CRHN CSam CTca EBee EBrs ERCP EShb GAbr LAma LEdu LPio LRHS SDnm SMad SPav WTin |
| - 'Cornwood' | CAvo CFFs CTca |
| - 'First Red' | CDes CPou WPGP |
| - green-leaved **new** | CTca |
| - purple-leaved | CTca EShb |
| - 'Sparkling Burgundy' | Widely available |
| - 'Tarzan's Trail' **new** | WHil |
| ***humilis*** | CPen |
| hybrid | SDix |
| 'John Treasure' | WHil |
| 'Joy's Purple' | CBro CPar CPen LBuc LRHS |
| ***montana*** | CBro CFwr CPen EBee ERCP WPGP |
| ***pallidiflora*** ♀H4 | CAvo CDes CGHE CHEx CPen EBee LEdu SMHy WHil WPGP |
| ***pole-evansii*** | CBro CDes CFir CHEx CPLG CPen CRHN CTca EAEE EBee EBrs ECGP ERCP EShb EUJe LPio LRHS MLLN MMHG MRav SPla WPGP WTin |
| - bronze-leaved | CPne |
| I - 'Purpurea' | GCal |
| ***punctata*** | see *E. comosa* |
| * ***reichenbachii*** | CTca |
| 'Swazi Pride' | CTca |
| ***undulata*** | see *E. autumnalis* (Mill.) Chitt. |
| ***vandermerwei*** | CAvo CBro CDes CFwr CPLG CPen CTca EBee LRHS WHil WPGP WTin |
| - 'Octopus' | CPen CPrp CTca EBee EShb IPot SPoG WCot |
| § ***zambesiaca*** | CPen EBee GCal LPio SSvw |
| - 'White Dwarf' | CStu ECho EShb MLan SPer |
| 'Zeal Bronze' | CAbb CBcs CDes CGHE CMHG CMil CTca EBee ELan EPfP GCal LPio NSti SPhx WPGP |

## *Eucommia* (*Eucommiaceae*)

| | |
|---|---|
| ***ulmoides*** | CBcs CCCN CDul CMCN EPfP GKir MBlu NLar WPGP |

## *Eucrosia* (*Amaryllidaceae*)

| | |
|---|---|
| ***bicolor*** **new** | EBee |

## *Eucryphia* ✿ (*Eucryphiaceae*)

| | |
|---|---|
| ***cordifolia*** | CAbP CBcs CGHE CMac CWib GGar GKir ISea LAst NMun SSpi WBod WDin |
| - Crarae hardy form | GGGa |
| § ***cordifolia* x *lucida*** | CBcs CCCN ELan GGal ISea SPer SRot WDin WPGP WPat |
| ***glutinosa*** ♀H4 | CCCN CDul EPfP IMGH LRHS MAsh MBar MBri MDun NBea SSpi SSta WBod WDin WFar WOrn WPat |
| - Plena Group (d) | WPat |
| x ***hillieri*** 'Winton' | CMHG GQui |
| x ***intermedia*** | CPLG CTrC CTrG CWSG EBee ELan EPfP GGGa LRHS NPal NVic SHBN SPer SRms SRot SSpi WDin WFar WPat |
| - 'Rostrevor' ♀H3 | CBcs CDul CMHG CMac CPMA CSBt CWib EBee ELan EPfP GAbr GQui IMGH LHyd LRHS LSRN MAsh MBlu MDun MGos NCGa SReu SSta WBod WFar WPGP WPat WSHC |
| 'Leatherwood Cream' | NHol |
| ***lucida*** | CCCN CDoC CTrC CTsd EBee ELan EPfP GGar IArd IMGH MDun NLar WBod WFar |
| - 'Ballerina' | CMHG CMac CPMA ELon GGar ISea LRHS MAsh MGos NVic SCoo SKHP SPoG SRot SSpi SSta WAbe WFar |
| - 'Dumpling' | CGHE EBee SKHP WPGP |
| - 'Gilt Edge' (v) | CBcs CTrC CWGN EBee ISea LLHF LRHS MAsh SHBN |
| - 'Leatherwood Cream' (v) | EBee ISea |
| - 'Pink Cloud' | Widely available |
| - 'Pink Whisper' | see *E. milliganii* 'Pink Whisper' |
| - 'Spring Glow' (v) | CWGN EMil ISea LLHF LRHS SKHP SPoG SSta |
| ***milliganii*** | CAbP CBcs CDoC CPMA CTrC EBee ELan EPfP GGar GQui LHop LRHS MBlu NPal SBod SHBN SRms SSpi SSta WAbe WBod WPGP |
| § - 'Pink Whisper' | WPGP |
| ***moorei*** | CCCN CMac GQui LRHS WBod |
| x ***nymansensis*** | CTrG CWib MLan SAPC SArc SDnm SKHP SReu SRms SSpi WBVN WFar WHCG |
| - 'George Graham' | GGGa IMGH WBod |
| - 'Mount Usher' | WBod |
| - 'Nymans Silver' (v) **new** | ELan LLHF LRHS MAsh SPoG SSpi |
| - 'Nymansay' ♀H3 | Widely available |
| - 'Nymansay Variegated' (v) **new** | CPMA |
| 'Penwith' misapplied | see *E. cordifolia* x *lucida* |
| 'Penwith' ambig. | CDoC CTsd GQui SPer WBrE WDin WFar WMoo |

## *Eugenia* (*Myrtaceae*)

| | |
|---|---|
| ***uniflora*** | CCCN |

## *Eunomia* see *Aethionema*

## *Euodia* (*Rutaceae*)

| | |
|---|---|
| ***daniellii*** | see *Tetradium daniellii* |
| ***hupehensis*** | see *Tetradium daniellii* Hupehense Group |

## *Euonymus* ✿ (*Celastraceae*)

| | |
|---|---|
| B&L 12543 | EPla EWes |
| B&SWJ 4457 | WPGP |
| CC 4522 | CPLG |
| ***alatus*** ♀H4 | Widely available |
| - B&SWJ 8794 | WCru |
| - var. ***apterus*** | EPfP MAsh |
| - Chicago Fire | see *E. alatus* 'Timber Creek' |
| - 'Ciliodentatus' | see *E. alatus* 'Compactus' |
| § - 'Compactus' ♀H4 | Widely available |
| § - 'Fire Ball' | CPMA EPfP MBri |
| - Little Moses = 'Odom' | MBlu |
| * - 'Macrophyllus' | CPMA EPfP MBri |
| - 'Rudy Haag' | CPMA EPfP MBri |
| - 'Select' | see *E. alatus* 'Fire Ball' |
| - 'Silver Cloud' | EPfP |
| § - 'Timber Creek' | CPMA EPfP GKir MBlu MBri NLar |
| ***americanus*** | CBcs EPfP MBlu MBri |
| - 'Evergreen' | EPfP |
| - narrow-leaved | EPfP |

| | | |
|---|---|---|
| | ***atropurpureus*** | EPfP |
| | 'Benkomoki' | EMil |
| | ***bungeanus*** | EPfP EPla WPat |
| | - 'Dart's Pride' | CPMA EPfP NLar |
| | - 'Fireflame' | CPMA EPfP NLar |
| * | - var. ***mongolicus*** | EPfP |
| | - 'Pendulus' | CPMA EPfP MBlu SCoo |
| | - var. ***semipersistens*** | CPMA |
| | ***carnosus*** | EPfP NLar |
| | ***chibae*** B&SWJ 11159 new | WCru |
| | 'Copper Wire' | EMil |
| | ***cornutus*** var. ***quinquecornutus*** | CPMA ELan EPfP GKir IDee LPan MBlu NBhm NLar WPGP WPat |
| | 'Den Haag' | EPfP MBri |
| | ***echinatus*** | EPfP EPla |
| | - BL&M 306 | SLon |
| | ***europaeus*** | Widely available |
| | - f. ***albus*** | CPMA CTho EPfP EQua NLar |
| | - 'Atropurpureus' | CMCN CTho EPfP MBlu MBri NLar |
| | - 'Atrorubens' | CPMA |
| | - 'Aucubifolius' (v) | CMac EPfP |
| * | - 'Aureus' | CNat |
| | - 'Brilliant' | CPMA EPfP |
| * | - f. ***bulgaricus*** | EPfP |
| | - 'Chrysophyllus' | EPfP MBlu NLar |
| | - 'Howard' | EPfP |
| | - var. ***intermedius*** | EPfP MAsh MBlu NLar |
| | - 'Miss Pinkie' | CEnd GKir |
| | - 'Red Cascade' 🏆H4 | Widely available |
| | - 'Scarlet Wonder' | CPMA EPfP MBri NLar |
| | - 'Thornhayes' | CTho EPfP MBri |
| I | - 'Variegatus' | EPfP |
| | ***europeaus*** 'Pumilis' | EPfP |
| | ***farreri*** | see *E. nanus* |
| | ***fimbriatus*** | CPMA EPfP |
| | ***fortunei*** | LEdu NHol |
| | - Blondy = 'Interbolwi'PBR (v) | Widely available |
| | - 'Canadale Gold' (v) | EBee EPfP EPla EQua LRHS MAsh MGos NHol SPoG WDin WFar |
| | - 'Coloratus' | CMac EBee EPfP MBar MSwo NHol SHBN SLon SPer WDin |
| | - 'Dart's Blanket' | CDul ECrN EHig ELan EPla MRav WDin WFar |
| | - 'Emerald Cushion' | CDul |
| | - 'Emerald Gaiety' (v) 🏆H4 | Widely available |
| * | - 'Emerald Green' | IFoB |
| | - 'Emerald 'n' Gold' (v) 🏆H4 | Widely available |
| | - 'Emerald Surprise' (v) 🏆H4 | EBee EPfP SRGP |
| | - 'Gold Spot' | see *E. fortunei* 'Sunspot' |
| | - 'Gold Tip' | see *E. fortunei* Golden Prince |
| | - 'Golden Harlequin' (v) | EMil LRHS |
| § | - 'Golden Pillar' (v) | EHoe EPla WFar |
| § | - Golden Prince (v) | CMac EHoe EPfP EPla MBar MGos MRav MSwo SLim SRms WGor |
| | - 'Harlequin' (v) | Widely available |
| | - 'Kewensis' | CDoC CMac CWib EBee EPfP MBar MRav MWhi SAPC SArc SBod SLon SPoG WCru WFar |
| | - 'Minimus' | CDul CTri EPPr EPla MGos NHol NPro WFar |
| * | - 'Minimus Variegatus' (v) | ECho SPlb |
| | - 'Perrolino' | EBee |
| § | - var. ***radicans*** | MGan |
| | - - 'Variegatus' (v) | MAsh |
| | - 'Sheridan Gold' | CMac CTri EHoe EPla MRav SHBN |
| | - 'Silver Gem' | see *E. fortunei* 'Variegatus' |
| | - 'Silver Pillar' (v) | CPLG EBee EHoe WFar |
| | - 'Silver Queen' (v) | Widely available |
| | - 'Silverstone'PBR (v) | EPfP LRHS NHol NPro SPoG |
| | - 'Sunshine' (v) | CAbP ELan LRHS MAsh MGos SPoG |
| § | - 'Sunspot' (v) | CBcs CWSG EBee ECrN ELan EPla IFoB LAst LBMP MBar MGos MSwo NHol SLim SRms WDin WFar WHar WRHF |
| | - 'Tustin' 🏆H4 | EPla SLPl |
| § | - 'Variegatus' (v) | MBar SRms STre WDin |
| | - var. ***vegetus*** | EPla |
| | - 'Wolong Ghost' | LRHS SKHP |
| | ***frigidus*** | EPfP WPGP |
| | ***grandiflorus*** | CPMA EPfP GKir MBlu NLar SCoo SSpi WFar |
| | - 'Red Wine' | CPMA CTho EBee EMil EPfP SEND WPGP WPat |
| | - f. ***salicifolius*** | CPMA EPfP |
| | ***hamiltonianus*** | CMCN EPfP SSpi WAbe WFar |
| I | - 'Calocarpus' | CPMA GKir SCoo |
| | - 'Coral Chief' | SLon |
| | - 'Fiesta' | EPfP |
| | - subsp. ***hians*** | see *E. hamiltonianus* subsp. *sieboldianus* |
| | - 'Indian Summer' | CPMA EBee EHig EPfP GKir LRHS MAsh MBri MWea NLar SCoo SKHP SSpi SSta WPGP |
| | - 'Koi Boy' | CPMA GKir LRHS MAsh MGos SPoG |
| | - 'Miss Pinkie' | CDul CPMA EPfP GKir LRHS MAsh MGos NLar SCoo SSpi SSta WPat |
| | - 'Pink Delight' | CPMA EPfP |
| | - 'Poort Bulten' | CPMA EPfP |
| | - 'Popcorn' | CPMA EPfP MBri |
| | - 'Rainbow' | CPMA EPfP MBri NLar |
| | - 'Red Chief' | CPMA EPfP |
| | - 'Red Elf' | CPMA EPfP MBri |
| | - 'Rising Sun' | CPMA EPfP MBri |
| § | - subsp. ***sieboldianus*** | CDul CMCN CMen CPLG CPMA CTho EPfP GAuc MAsh MRav SLPl WFar WPat |
| | - - B&SWJ 10941 new | WCru |
| | - - 'Calocarpus' | EPfP |
| | - - 'Coral Charm' | CPMA EPfP |
| | - - Semiexsertus Group | EPfP |
| * | - - var. ***yedoensis*** f. ***koehneanus*** | EPfP |
| | - 'Snow' | CPMA EPfP MBri NLar WPat |
| | - 'Winter Glory' | CPMA EPfP GKir LRHS WPat |
| | - var. ***yedoensis*** | see *E. hamiltonianus* subsp. *sieboldianus* |
| | ***hibarimisake*** | see *E. japonicus* 'Hibarimisake' |
| | ***japonicus*** | CBcs CCVT CDoC CDul ECrN EPfP SAPC SArc SPer WDin |
| | - 'Albomarginatus' | CBcs CChe CTri EPfP NBlu SEND SRms |
| | - 'Aureopictus' | see *E. japonicus* 'Aureus' |
| | - 'Aureovariegatus' | see *E. japonicus* 'Ovatus Aureus' |
| § | - 'Aureus' (v) | CBcs CDoC CDul CSBt CWib EBee ECrN NPri SCoo SHBN SLon SPer SSto WDin WHar WRHF |
| | - 'Benkomasaki' | EPfP |
| | - 'Bravo' | CDoC EBee ECrN EHoe EMil ERas LAst LPan LRHS MGos MWea NLar SCoo SLim SPer SPoG SWvt WDin WFar |
| | - 'Chollipo' 🏆H4 | ELan EPfP EPla LRHS MAsh MGos |
| | - 'Compactus' | SAPC SArc SCoo |
| | - 'Duc d'Anjou' misapplied | see *E. japonicus* 'Viridivariegatus' |
| | - 'Duc d'Anjou' Carrière (v) | CBcs CHrt EBee EHoe ELan EPla EWes LPan MRav NHol SEND SPoG |
| | - Exstase = 'Goldbolwi'PBR (v) | EMil SPoG |
| | - 'Francien' (v) | SPoG |
| | - 'Golden Maiden' | ELan EPfP LRHS MAsh SLim SLon SPoG SWvt |
| | - 'Golden Pillar' | see *E. fortunei* 'Golden Pillar' |

| | | |
|---|---|---|
| | - 'Green Rocket' new | EPfP |
| | - 'Green Spider' | SPoG |
| | - 'Grey Beauty' | EBee NLar |
| § | - 'Hibarimisake' | EPfP |
| | - 'Kathy'PBR | ERas MGos SPoG SRGP |
| § | - 'Latifolius Albomarginatus' | CDul ELan EPfP EPla MRav MSwo SPer SPoG WDin |
| | - 'Luna' | see *E. japonicus* 'Aureus' |
| | - 'Macrophyllus Albus' | see *E. japonicus* 'Latifolius Albomarginatus' |
| | - 'Maiden's Gold' | CSBt EBee |
| | - 'Marieke' | see *E. japonicus* 'Ovatus Aureus' |
| | - 'Microphyllus' | CDoC MRav STre WFar |
| § | - 'Microphyllus Albovariegatus' (v) | CBcs CChe CDoC CDul CMea CSBt CTri CWSG ELan ELon EMil EPfP EPla LAst LRHS MBar MGos NHol SHBN SLim SPla SPoG SRms SWvt WDin WFar WHCG WPat |
| § | - 'Microphyllus Aureovariegatus' (v) | CDoC CMea ELan EMil EPfP MGos NLar WPat |
| | - 'Microphyllus Aureus' | see *E. japonicus* 'Microphyllus Pulchellus' |
| § | - 'Microphyllus Pulchellus' (v) | CBcs CDoC CSBt CWSG EBee ECrN ELon EPfP EPla LHop MBar MRav NHol SPoG SWvt WDin WHCG |
| | - 'Microphyllus Variegatus' | see *E. japonicus* 'Microphyllus Albovariegatus' |
| § | - 'Ovatus Aureus' (v) ♀H4 | CChe CDoC CDul CPLG CSBt CTri CWSG EBee ECrN EPfP LAst LRHS MBar MGos MRav MSwo NBlu NPri SLim SPer SPlb SPoG SRms SWvt WBod WDin WFar |
| | - 'Président Gauthier' (v) | CDoC EBee ECrN EQua MGos MWea SCoo SLim SWvt WCFE WDin |
| | - 'Pulchellus Aureovariegatus' | see *E. japonicus* 'Microphyllus Aureovariegatus' |
| I | - 'Pyramidatus' | EPfP |
| | - 'Robustus' | EPfP EPla |
| | - 'Royal Gold' | SPoG |
| | - 'Silver Krista' (v) | SPoG |
| | - Silver Princess = 'Moness' | SHBN |
| | - 'Susan' | CDoC EPla EQua SRGP |
| § | - 'Viridivariegatus' (v) | LRHS |
| | ***kiautschovicus*** | EPfP GKir |
| | - 'Berry Hill' | EPfP NLar |
| | - 'Manhattan' | EPfP NLar |
| | ***latifolius*** | CMCN CPMA EPfP GKir |
| | ***macropterus*** | CPMA EPfP |
| | ***maximowiczianus*** | EPfP MBlu WPat |
| | ***morrisonensis*** | EPfP |
| | - B&SWJ 3700 | WCru |
| | ***myrianthus*** | CBcs CPMA EPfP EWes MBlu NLar |
| § | ***nanus*** | CWib EHig EPfP EPla NHol NLar |
| | - var. ***turkestanicus*** | EPfP EPla LHop MBri SLon SRms WFar |
| | ***obovatus*** | EPfP NLar |
| | ***occidentalis*** | EPfP |
| | ***oresbius*** | CPMA EPfP |
| | ***oxyphyllus*** | CMCN CPMA EPfP GKir IArd NLar SCoo SSpi WCru WDin |
| | - 'Angyo Elegant' (v) | EPfP |
| | - 'Waasland' | CPMA EPfP MBri |
| | ***pauciflorus*** | EPfP MBri |
| | ***pendulus*** | CBcs CHll CPLG |
| | ***phellomanus*** ♀H4 | CDul CEnd CTho CWSG EBee EPfP EWTr GKir LHop LRHS MBar MBlu MGos MRav NLar SCoo SHBN SPoG WDin WFar WPGP WPat |
| | - 'Silver Surprise' (v) | CPMA EPfP NLar WPat |
| | Pierrolino = 'Heespierrolino'PBR | SCoo SPoG |
| § | ***planipes*** ♀H4 | Widely available |
| | - 'Dart's August Flame' | CPMA EPfP |
| | - 'Gold Ore' | EPfP |
| | - 'Sancho' | CPMA EPfP MBri |
| | ***quelpaertensis*** | EPfP |
| | ***radicans*** | see *E. fortunei* var. *radicans* |
| | 'Rokojō' | CLyd NWCA |
| | ***rongchuensis*** | EPfP MBri |
| | ***rosmarinifolius*** | see *E. nanus* |
| | ***sachalinensis*** misapplied | see *E. planipes* |
| | ***sacrosanctus*** | CPMA EPfP |
| | ***sanguineus*** | CPMA EPfP NLar SSpi |
| | ***sieboldianus*** var. ***sanguineus*** B&SWJ 11140 new | WCru |
| | ***spraguei*** | EPfP |
| | ***tingens*** | CBcs EPfP GKir NLar SKHP SSpi |
| | ***trapococcus*** | EPfP NLar |
| | ***vagans*** | EPfP |
| | - L 551 | EPla SLon |
| | ***velutinus*** | EPfP NLar |
| | ***verrucosus*** | CPMA EPfP EPla GKir NLar |
| | ***vidalii*** | EPfP |
| | ***wilsonii*** | NLar |
| | ***yedoensis*** | see *E. hamiltonianus* subsp. *sieboldianus* |

## *Eupatoriadelphus* see *Eupatorium*

## *Eupatorium* ✿ (*Asteraceae*)

| | | |
|---|---|---|
| | B&SWJ 9052 from Guatemala | WCru |
| § | ***album*** | NBid SWat WPer |
| | ***altissimum*** | MSal SRms |
| | ***aromaticum*** | see *Ageratina aromatica* |
| | ***atrorubens*** | see *Bartlettina sordida* |
| | ***cannabinum*** | Widely available |
| | - 'Album' | EMon NDov SPhx |
| | - 'Flore Pleno' (d) | CPrp CSev EBee ECha ECtt EGle ELan EPfP MHer MLLN MRav MSte NDov NGdn NSti SAga SPhx SWat WAul WCAu WCot WCra WFar WMnd WPtf WSFF WTin |
| | - 'Spraypaint' | CNat EPPr |
| | ***capillifolium*** ♀H3 | ELon EShb LSou MCot MLLN SDix SDys WCot WPGP |
| | - 'Elegant Feather' | CAby CSpe EBee ECtt EWes GBin LHop MDKP SAga SHar SMad SMrm SPhx SUsu WHil |
| | ***fistulosum*** | CSec NGdn |
| | ***fortunei*** | CArn SKHP |
| I | - 'Variegatum' (v) | CBow CKno EBee LSou MAvo MDKP MHer MLHP WCot WPGP WSFF |
| | ***glechonophyllum*** | see *Ageratina glechonophylla* |
| | ***japonicum*** new | EBee GPoy |
| | ***ligustrinum*** | see *Ageratina ligustrina* |
| | ***lindleyanum*** | CKno EBee |
| | ***maculatum*** | CAby EBee EHrv EMon MDKP NGHP NGdn NLar SBri STes WFar WHil WHrl WPer |
| | - 'Album' | EBee EMon NBir NDov NSti SMad |
| | - 'Atropurpureum' ♀H4 | Widely available |
| | - 'Augustrubin' | NDov |
| | - 'Berggarten' | EBee GCal MSte |
| | - 'Carin' | WSFF |
| | - 'Gateway' | CRow EBee EBrs GCal WTin |
| | - 'Glutball' | CHVG CKno EBee EBrs GCal LPla MNrw NChi SMad |
| | - 'Orchard Dene' ♀H4 new | SPur |
| | - 'Phantom' new | MBri |

| | |
|---|---|
| – 'Purple Bush' 🏆$^{H4}$ | CKno CSam EBee ECha ELon EMon GCal MDKP MSte NBre NDov SMad SPhx SSvw WSFF |
| – 'Riesenschirm' 🏆$^{H4}$ | CKno CSam EBee ECGP ECtt EGle EPPr EWes GBin GCal LRHS MNFA MSCN MSte NCGa NDov SDix SPhx SWat WCAu WCot |
| ***makinoi*** var. ***oppositifolium*** B&SWJ 8449 **new** | WCru |
| 'Massive White' | CFir GCal |
| ***micranthum*** | see *Ageratina ligustrina* |
| ***occidentale*** | see *Ageratina occidentalis* |
| ***perfoliatum*** | CArn GPoy MNrw MSal NBre NLar SPav |
| 'Phantom' | CHFP EBee IPot NDov |
| ***purpureum*** | Widely available |
| – 'Album' | CTri MLLN SPhx |
| – 'Ankum's August' **new** | NDov |
| – 'Bartered Bride' | CKno EBee EBrs ECtt EWes GCal MSte |
| – 'Joe White' | WSFF |
| – 'Little Red' | WSFF |
| ***rugosum*** | see *Ageratina altissima* |
| – ***album*** | see *E. album* |
| ***triplinerve*** | see *Ayapana triplinervis* |
| I ***variabile*** 'Variegatum' (v) | EWes MDKP |
| ***weinmannianum*** | see *Ageratina ligustrina* |

## *Euphorbia* ✿ (*Euphorbiaceae*)

| | |
|---|---|
| 'Abbey Dore' | WCot WSHC |
| ***altissima*** | MSte |
| ***ambovombensis*** | LToo |
| ***amygdaloides*** | EBla ECtt GKir SWat SWvt WOut |
| – 'Bob's Choice' | EMon EWes |
| – 'Brithembottom' | CSam |
| – 'Craigieburn' | CDes EBee EBla EWes GBri GCal GCra LBMP LRHS MGos MRav NDov NSti SUsu WCra WPGP |
| – 'Mark's Red' | WCot |
| § – 'Purpurea' | Widely available |
| § – var. ***robbiae*** 🏆$^{H4}$ | Widely available |
| – – dwarf | EWes |
| – – 'Pom Pom' | CDes EBee LSou WPGP |
| – – 'Redbud' | EBee EPla EWes GCal LSou SLPl |
| – 'Rubra' | see *E. amygdaloides* 'Purpurea' |
| – 'Variegata' (v) | GBuc |
| – 'Winter Glow' | CSpe |
| ***ankarensis*** | LToo |
| ***aureoviridiflora*** | LToo |
| ***barrelieri*** | WCot |
| ***baselicis*** | CBod CBow CMea CPom CSpe CTca CWsd EBee EWll GAbr LPio WHoo WHrl WPer |
| ***biglandulosa*** Desf. | see *E. rigida* |
| Blackbird = 'Nothowlee'[PBR] | CSpe CWGN EBee EBrs ELan EPfP EWes GBin IPot LAst LBuc LCro LLHF LRHS LSRN MAsh MAvo MBNS MBri MGos NBPN NSti SLim SPoG SWvt WCot |
| 'Blue Haze' | CDes SMeo |
| 'Blue Lagoon' | NBhm |
| ***bulbispina*** | LToo |
| ***canariensis*** | EPfP |
| ***capitulata*** | EWes MTho |
| ***cashmeriana*** | GKev NWit |
| – CC&McK 607 | EWes |
| – CC&McK 724 | GBin |
| ***ceratocarpa*** | CFwr EBee EMon EPPr EWes GBuc GMaP MAvo MBri NWit SEND SMad WCot WPGP WSHC |
| ***characias*** | CBcs CHEx CWCL EBee EBla ECtt EPfP GKir MCot MLHP MRav NChi NPer NPri NVic SMrm SPer SRms SWvt WBrk WCot WFar WMnd WPer |
| – Ballyrogan hybrids | IBlr NBhm |
| – 'Black Pearl' | CBcs CTca CWCL EBee EPfP LAst MAvo MCCP MGos MSte NBPC NCGa NSti SDnm SEND SMrm SPav SPer SPoG SWvt WFar WOVN |
| – 'Blue Wonder' | CSpe CWCL EBee ECtt EHrv ELan EPfP GMaP LCro LHop LRHS MAvo MCCP MSte NLar NWit SAga SDnm SPav WCot WGwG WHoo |
| – subsp. ***characias*** | CPrp CWCL EHrv GMaP MGos SMHy SPoG |
| – – 'Blue Hills' | ECtt EGle GBuc GCal NWit |
| – – 'Burrow Silver' (v) | CFir CTca EBee GMaP LDai MRav SDnm SPav SPer SWvt WFar |
| – – 'Green Mantle' | IBlr |
| – – 'H.E. Bates' | NBir |
| – – 'Humpty Dumpty' | EBee ECtt EHrv ELan EPfP GBBs GMaP LAst LCro LHop LPio LRHS MBri MCCP MGos NGdn NPer NPri SDnm SPav SPer SPoG SRms SSto SWvt WCFE WFar WOVN |
| – – 'Perry's Winter Blusher' | ECtt NWit |
| – dwarf | SMrm |
| – 'Forescate' | CSWP CWCL EBee EMil EPfP GMaP LPio LSRN MSte NWit SDnm SPav WFar |
| – 'Goldbrook' | EBla EHoe LBMP LHop MBNS MRav MSte SHBN |
| – 'Kestrel' (v) | WCot |
| – 'Portuguese Velvet' 🏆$^{H4}$ | Widely available |
| – Silver Swan = 'Wilcott'[PBR] (v) | CBcs CMdw CSpe CWGN EBee EBrs ELan EMil EPfP EWes LAst LBuc LRHS LSRN MAsh MBNS MGos MRav NCGa NSti SDix SPoG SWvt |
| – 'Sombre Melody' | IBlr |
| – 'Spring Splendour' | EWes NWit |
| – 'Starbright' | EBee GBin |
| – 'Whistleberry Jade' | NWit |
| – subsp. ***wulfenii*** 🏆$^{H3-4}$ | Widely available |
| – – 'Bosahan' (v) | CBcs GCra NWit |
| – – dwarf **new** | WOut |
| – – 'Emmer Green' (v) | CBow CSpe EBee EHrv EWTr EWes GBri GCal GMaP MSte MWea NWit SHBN SPoG WCot WFoF |
| – – 'Jayne's Golden Giant' | SMad |
| – – 'Jimmy Platt' | EGle ERCP MTho SRms WBrE WCot WGwG WPic |
| § – – 'John Tomlinson' 🏆$^{H3-4}$ | CMoH EBee EGle EHrv EWes GBin LSRN MRav MWhi WCot |
| – – Kew form | see *E. characias* subsp. *wulfenii* 'John Tomlinson' |
| – – 'Lambrook Gold' 🏆$^{H3-4}$ | CSam ECtt EGle EPfP GCra MRav MWat NLar NPer SMad WFar WGwG WMnd |
| – – 'Lambrook Gold' seed-raised | see *E. characias* subsp. *wulfenii* Margery Fish Group |
| – – 'Lambrook Yellow' | EBee EWsh GBuc GCal |
| § – – Margery Fish Group | CPrp EBee EGle LBMP NBir SPer |
| – – 'Perry's Tangerine' | EWes NPer NWit |
| § – – 'Purple and Gold' | CSpe EBee EWes GMaP NCGa NLar NWit SHBN SWvt WCot |
| – – 'Purpurea' | see *E. characias* subsp. *wulfenii* 'Purple and Gold' |
| – – 'Thelma's Giant' | NWit |
| ***clavarioides*** var. ***truncata*** | WCot |
| 'Copton Ash' | CSpe EBee EPPr EWes MAvo NWit SKHP |
| ***corallioides*** | CSsd EBee ECha GCal IBlr LRHS NPer NSti SPav SRms WBrE WHer WPnP |

| | Name | Suppliers |
|---|---|---|
| § | ***cornigera*** ♀H4 | CElw CHrt EAEE EBee ECha EPfP GBBs GBin GBuc GMac IBlr LPio LRHS MAvo MCot MRav NBid NCGa NDov NGdn NLar NSti NWit SWat WCru WHoo WPGP WPen |
| | - 'Goldener Turm' | CMoH EBee GBuc MAvo WCot WCra |
| | ***corollata*** | EBee |
| | ***croizatii*** | LToo |
| | ***cylindrifolia*** var. ***tubifera*** | LToo |
| | ***cyparissias*** | CArn CBcs CHrt EBee ECha ELan LRHS MLHP MRav NBir NGdn NMen SMrm SPav SRms WBrk WEas WFar WFoF WPer WTin |
| | - 'Baby' | WFar |
| | - 'Betten' | see *E.* x *gayeri* 'Betten' |
| | - 'Bushman Boy' | GBri IBlr SMrm |
| | - 'Clarice Howard' | see *E. cyparissias* 'Fens Ruby' |
| § | - 'Fens Ruby' | Widely available |
| | - 'Orange Man' | CTca EBee EBla EHig EMon EPfP EPla EWes GBin IBlr LAst LBMP LRHS NBro NHol SMrm SPla SWat SWvt WAul WFar |
| | - 'Purpurea' | see *E. cyparissias* 'Fens Ruby' |
| | - 'Red Devil' | CBre IBlr NWit SMrm |
| | - 'Tall Boy' | EMon EWes IBlr SMrm |
| | ***deflexa*** | EBee GKev |
| | 'Despina'PBR | NLar |
| § | ***donii*** | EBee EGle EWes IBlr NDov NWit SDix SMHy WFar |
| | - HWJK 2405 | WCru |
| | - 'Amjillasa' | EBee SAga SDix SUsu |
| | ***dulcis*** | CBre CStu ECtt NBro NWit |
| | - 'Chameleon' | Widely available |
| | 'Efanthia'PBR | CCVN CEnd CMil CPrp CSpe EBee EWes LHop LSou MBri NLar NPri SMrm SPoG SVil |
| | ***enopla*** | EPfP |
| | ***epithymoides*** | see *E. polychroma* |
| | ***esula*** Baker's form | NWit |
| | Excalibur = 'Froeup'PBR ♀H4 | CMHG CWCL EBee ELan GBin GBuc LHop LRHS MBNS MBri MCCP MRav MSte NBir NHol NSti SHBN WFar WSHC |
| | ***flavicoma*** | GCal |
| | ***fragifera*** | EBee NWit |
| | 'Garblesham Enchanter' | EPPr |
| § | x ***gayeri*** 'Betten' | EBee |
| | ***glauca*** | CFir ECou NWit SKHP |
| | 'Golden Foam' | see *E. stricta* |
| | ***gottlebei*** | LToo |
| | ***griffithii*** | CHll GGal IFoB NBro SPav SWat WFar WMoo |
| | - 'Dixter' ♀H4 | Widely available |
| | - 'Dixter Flame' | NWit |
| | - 'Fern Cottage' | CElw CWCL EBee EHrv EWes GAbr SUsu WMnd |
| | - 'Fireglow' | Widely available |
| | - 'King's Caple' | EBee ELon EWes GBin MBNS NWit SWal WCru |
| | - 'Wickstead' | EBee GAbr GBin MLHP NLar |
| | 'Helena'PBR (v) | EBee LHop LLHF NLar NPri SPoG STes SVil WCot WOVN |
| | ***hirta*** | CLyd |
| | ***hyberna*** | GBri IBlr LLHF MLLN NMen NWit SWat |
| | ***hypericifolia*** Diamond Frost = 'Inneuphe' | CCVN CSpe EPfP LHop LSou SVil WOVN |
| | ***ingens*** | NScw |
| | ***jacquemontii*** | EBee ECha LPio MLLN MNrw MRav NChi NWit |
| | 'Jade Dragon' | CSpe EBee MWat SPoG SPur |
| | 'Jessie' | EBee MAvo |
| | ***jolkinii*** | EBee GKev |
| | - SDR 4307 **new** | GKev |
| | Kalipso = 'Innkalff'PBR | EBee EPfP NLar SVil |
| | ***lambii*** | EShb |
| | 'Lambrook Silver' | SRkn |
| | ***lathyris*** | CArn CBre ILad MDun MHer MLHP NLar NPer NWit SRms WEas |
| | ***longifolia*** misapplied | see *E. cornigera* |
| | ***longifolia*** D. Don | see *E. donii* |
| | ***longifolia*** Lam. | see *E. mellifera* |
| | ***margalidiana*** | EWes |
| | x ***martini*** ♀H3 | Widely available |
| | - 'Aperitif'PBR | CBow EBee EPfP WCot |
| | - 'Baby Charm' | EBee LBuc LRHS WCot |
| | - dwarf | CFir GCal |
| | - 'Helen Robinson' | WCot |
| | - 'Kolibri' **new** | LSou |
| | - 'Signal' | EMon |
| | - 'Tiny Tim' | EMil EWTr LSRN MWat SPoG SWvt |
| | - 'Walberton's Rudolf' **new** | SPoG |
| § | ***mellifera*** ♀H3 | Widely available |
| | ***milii*** ♀H1 | CHal EBak |
| | - yellow-flowered | CHal |
| | ***moratii*** | LToo |
| | ***myrsinites*** ♀H4 | Widely available |
| | ***nereidum*** | EWes NWit |
| | ***nicaeensis*** | CDes EBee EMon GCal NWit SEND SMrm SPhx WCot WPGP WSHC |
| | - subsp. ***glareosa*** | NWit |
| | ***oblongata*** | EBee EWes IBlr NWit |
| | 'Orange Grove' | NBhm |
| | ***pachypodioides*** | LToo |
| | ***palustris*** ♀H4 | Widely available |
| | - 'Walenburg's Glorie' | CMHG CWCL EAEE EBee EBla ECha ELan EWTr GBin LRHS MBri MNrw MRav NCGa NSti NWit SMad SWat WKif |
| | - 'Zauberflöte' | CHrt SRms WFar |
| | x ***paradoxa*** | NWit |
| | ***paralias*** | NWit WCot WHer |
| | x ***pasteurii*** | CBgR CDTJ CFir CPom EBee EMon EWes LSou MAvo NWit WPGP |
| | - 'John Phillips' | EBee WPGP |
| | ***pekinensis*** | MSal SKHP |
| | ***pilosa*** 'Major' | see *E. polychroma* 'Major' |
| | ***piscatoria*** | WPGP |
| | ***pithyusa*** | CBgR CPom CSpe EBee ECha ECtt ELan EPfP LRHS MAvo MRav NGdn SHBN |
| § | ***polychroma*** ♀H4 | Widely available |
| § | - 'Candy' | CHar COIW CWCL EBee ECha EHrv ELan EPfP MCCP NCGa SEND SPla WCot WFar WMnd |
| | - compact | LBuc |
| | - 'Emerald Jade' | IBlr NWit WPGP |
| § | - 'Lacy' (v) | CDoC CWCL EBee ECtt EHoe EHrv EWes GCal LAst LBMP MCCP MRav NBir NCob NGdn NSti NWit SMad SPla SPoG WCot WFar |
| § | - 'Major' ♀H4 | CMHG CPLG MWte SAga SPer SPhx WCot WKif |
| | - 'Midas' | EGle GBin MAvo MNrw NWit SMrm SUsu |
| | - 'Purpurea' | see *E. polychroma* 'Candy' |
| * | - 'Senior' | MGos NWit |
| | - 'Sonnengold' | EWes WSHC |
| | - 'Variegata' | see *E. polychroma* 'Lacy' |
| | ***portlandica*** | NWit WHer |
| § | x ***pseudovirgata*** | IBlr NWit |
| | 'Purple Preference' | EPPr |
| | Redwing = 'Charam'PBR ♀H4 | CBcs EBee ELan EMil EPfP LBuc LCro LRHS LSou MAsh MBri MGos |

| | |
|---|---|
| | MRav NDov NLar NWit SCoo SPer SPoG SWvt |
| ***reflexa*** | see *E. seguieriana* subsp. *niciciana* |
| § ***rigida*** ♀$^{H4}$ | CBro CDes CSpe EBee ECGP EHrv ELan EPfP EPyc EWes GKir LPio MAvo MLLN NSti NVic SKHP SMad SMrm SPhx SUsu WCot WFar WHoo WPGP WSHC |
| - 'Sardis' | NWit |
| ***robbiae*** | see *E. amygdaloides* var. *robbiae* |
| 'Rosies Surprise' | EHig LLHF MTho |
| ***rothiana*** GWJ 9479a | WCru |
| 'Roundway Titan' | SSpi |
| 'Royal Velvet' **new** | CBow |
| ***sarawschanica*** | EBee ECha GBBs GBin GKev GQue NWit SMad SPhx |
| ***schillingii*** ♀$^{H4}$ | CMHG CPrp EBee EHoe ELan EPfP GAbr GCra GMaP LPio MRav SDix SMrm SPer SPoG SUsu SWal WCot WCru WFar WGwG WHoo WPGP WTin |
| ***seguieriana*** | CSec ECha NLar WPer |
| § - subsp. ***niciciana*** | CBow CMoH EMon EWsh GBin SDix |
| ***serrulata*** Thuill. | see *E. stricta* |
| ***sikkimensis*** ♀$^{H4}$ | CBow CHrt CMHG CMea CPLG CPom CSam EBee ECha ELan GAbr GCal GKev LPio NPer SMrm SPav SRms WCru WEas WFar WHoo |
| - GWJ 9214 | WCru |
| ***soongarica*** | MSte NWit |
| ***spinosa*** | NWit SPlb |
| § ***stricta*** | EBee MCCP WRos WTin |
| ***stygiana*** | CHid CMil CSam CSpe EBee ELon EPla EWes GCal LPio MAvo MSte NWit SAga SKHP SMeo WCot WPGP WSHC |
| - 'Devil's Honey' | WCot |
| ***symmetrica*** | LToo |
| ***tirucalli*** | EShb |
| ***uralensis*** | see *E.* x *pseudovirgata* |
| ***valdevillosocarpa*** | WCot WPer |
| ***verrucosa*** | NWit WFar |
| - Baker's form | EPPr |
| ***viguieri*** ♀$^{H1}$ | LToo |
| ***villosa*** Waldst. & Kit. ex Willd. | NWit |
| § ***virgata*** | EWes NWit SPav |
| x ***waldsteinii*** | see *E. virgata* |
| ***wallichii*** misapplied | see *E. donii* |
| ***wallichii*** Kohli | see *E. cornigera* |
| ***wallichii*** Hook. f. | CPLG EBee GCal GKir IBlr MBri NOrc WPGP |
| - 'Lemon and Lime' | CWib LSou WFar |
| 'Whistleberry Garnet' | EBee LCro LLHF LSou MWea SDix SPoG |

## *Euptelea* (*Eupteleaceae*)

| | |
|---|---|
| ***franchetii*** | see *E. pleiosperma* |
| § ***pleiosperma*** | EBee EPfP NLar SSpi |
| ***polyandra*** | EPfP NLar WPGP |

## *Eurya* (*Theaceae*)

| | |
|---|---|
| ***japonica*** | WPGP |
| - 'Moutiers' (v) | WPat |
| - 'Variegata' misapplied | see *Cleyera japonica* 'Fortunei' |

## *Euryale* (*Nymphaeaceae*)

| | |
|---|---|
| ***ferox*** **new** | CDWL |

## *Euryops* (*Asteraceae*)

| | |
|---|---|
| ***abrotanifolius*** | CCCN CTrC |
| § ***acraeus*** ♀$^{H4}$ | CMea CSBt ECho EPfP EPot GKev LHop LRHS MWat NLAp NMen NWCA SAga SIng WAbe WFar |
| ***candollei*** | CTrC |
| § ***chrysanthemoides*** | CCCN CHEx CSam EShb MSte |
| - 'Sonnenschein' | CHal EBee SPet |
| ***evansii*** | see *E. acraeus* |
| ***lateriflorus*** | SPlb |
| ***pectinatus*** ♀$^{H2}$ | CBcs CCCN CDTJ CDoC CHEx CHrt CPLG CSam CTrC CTrG CTri EBee EPfP EShb GGal GGar LRHS MNrw MRav NPri SBod SGar SHBN SOWG WCFE WHer WPic |
| ***tysonii*** | CTrC EBee GCal GEdr SPlb WCot |
| ***virgineus*** | CBcs CCCN CPLG CTrC CTrG EBee GGar IDee |

## *Eustachys* (*Poaceae*)

| | |
|---|---|
| § ***distichophylla*** | EBee EWsh MAvo WCot WPrP |

## *Eustoma* (*Gentianaceae*)

| | |
|---|---|
| § ***grandiflorum*** | LRHS MBri |
| ***russellianum*** | see *E. grandiflorum* |

## *Eustrephus* (*Philesiaceae*)

| | |
|---|---|
| ***latifolius*** | ECou |

## *Eutaxia* (*Papilionaceae*)

| | |
|---|---|
| ***obovata*** | ECou |

## *Euthamia* (*Asteraceae*)

| | |
|---|---|
| ***gymnospermoides*** | EWes |

## *Eutrochium* see *Eupatorium*

## *Ewartia* (*Asteraceae*)

| | |
|---|---|
| ***planchonii*** | CPBP WAbe |

## *Exacum* (*Gentianaceae*)

| | |
|---|---|
| ***affine*** ♀$^{H1+3}$ | LRHS MBri |
| - 'Rococo' | MBri |

## *Exochorda* (*Rosaceae*)

| | |
|---|---|
| ***giraldii*** | WGwG |
| - var. ***wilsonii*** | CPLG CSam EBee EPfP GBin IMGH LHop MBNS MBlu NLar SLim SPoG SSta SWvt |
| x ***macrantha*** | EBee MNHC |
| - 'Irish Pearl' **new** | CPLG |
| - 'The Bride' ♀$^{H4}$ | Widely available |
| ***racemosa*** | EPfP MGos NBlu NLar SHBN SPer WDin WHCG |
| ***serratifolia*** | EPfP GAuc SPoG |
| - 'Snow White' | CPMA EBee EWes IArd LBuc MBlu MBri NLar |

# F

## *Fabiana* (*Solanaceae*)

| | |
|---|---|
| ***imbricata*** | CAbP EMil EPfP GQui LLHF LRHS SAga SLon SPer |
| - 'Prostrata' | EBee EPfP LRHS SSpi WAbe WBod |
| - f. ***violacea*** ♀$^{H3}$ | CBcs CFee CSBt CTri EBee EPfP GQui LLHF LRHS MMuc SPer WKif |

## *Fagopyrum* (*Polygonaceae*)

| | |
|---|---|
| ***cymosum*** | see *F. dibotrys* |
| § ***dibotrys*** | EBee ECha ELan EWld LEdu WMoo |
| - 'Variegatum' | CBow |

## *Fagus* ✿ (*Fagaceae*)

| | | |
|---|---|---|
| § | ***crenata*** | CMCN CMen NWea WDin |
| | - 'Mount Fuji' | SBir |
| | ***engleriana*** | CMCN SBir |
| | ***grandifolia*** | CMCN |
| | - subsp. ***mexicana*** | SBir |
| | ***japonica*** | CMCN SBir |
| | - var. ***multinervis*** **new** | SBir |
| | ***lucida*** | CMCN |
| | ***orientalis*** | CMCN ECrN SBir |
| | - 'Iskander' **new** | MBlu |
| | ***sieboldii*** | see *F. crenata* |
| | ***sylvatica*** ♀H4 | Widely available |
| § | - 'Albomarginata' (v) | CMCN |
| | - 'Albovariegata' | see *F. sylvatica* 'Albomarginata' |
| | - 'Ansorgei' | CEnd CMCN MBlu |
| N | - Atropurpurea Group | Widely available |
| | - - 'Friso' | CEnd CMCN |
| | - 'Aurea Pendula' | CEnd CMCN ECrN GKir MBlu SBLw SBir |
| | - 'Bicolor Sartini' | MBlu |
| | - 'Birr Zebra' | CEnd |
| | - 'Black Swan' | CEnd CMCN ECrN GKir IArd LPan MAsh MBlu NLar SBLw SBir SLon |
| | - 'Bornyensis' | SBir |
| | - 'Brathay Purple' | MBlu |
| | - 'Cochleata' | CMCN |
| | - 'Cockleshell' | CDul CMCN MBlu MBri SBir SHBN |
| | - 'Comptoniifolia' | see *F. sylvatica* var. *heterophylla* 'Comptoniifolia' |
| | - 'Cristata' | MBlu |
| N | - Cuprea Group | NWea |
| § | - 'Dawyck' ♀H4 | Widely available |
| | - 'Dawyck Gold' ♀H4 | Widely available |
| | - 'Dawyck Purple' ♀H4 | Widely available |
| | - 'Fastigiata' misapplied | see *F. sylvatica* 'Dawyck' |
| | - 'Felderbach' | MBlu SBir SLon |
| | - 'Franken' (v) | MBlu SBir |
| | - 'Grandidentata' | CMCN LPan SLon |
| | - 'Greenwood' | MBlu |
| | - 'Haaren' | CMCN SBir |
| | - var. ***heterophylla*** | CLnd CSBt CTho ECho ISea NWea WOrn |
| | - - 'Aspleniifolia' ♀H4 | CBcs CDoC CDul CEnd CMCN ECrN EHig ELan EMil EPfP GKir IMGH LPan LRHS MBar MBlu MBri MGos SBLw SBir SCoo SHBN SLau SLon SPer SPoG WDin WMou |
| § | - - 'Comptoniifolia' | SBir |
| | - - f. ***laciniata*** | CMCN GKir MBlu |
| | - 'Horizontalis' | CMCN MBlu SLon |
| | - 'Incisa' **new** | MBlu |
| | - f. ***latifolia*** | SBLw |
| | - 'Leith' | SBir |
| | - 'Luteovariegata' (v) | CDul CEnd CMCN |
| | - 'Mercedes' | CDoC CMCN MBlu SBir WPat |
| | - 'Miltonensis' | IArd LPan |
| N | - 'Pendula' ♀H4 | Widely available |
| | - 'Prince George of Crete' | CDul CEnd CMCN SBir |
| | - 'Purple Fountain' ♀H4 | CDoC CDul CEnd CMCN EBee ELan EMil GKir LAst LPan LRHS MAsh MBar MBlu MBri MGos NBPN NLar SBLw SBir SLau SLim SPoG WFar WOrn |
| | - Purple-leaved Group | see *F. sylvatica* Atropurpurea Group |
| | - 'Purpurea Latifolia' **new** | LMaj |
| | - 'Purpurea Nana' | NPri |
| | - 'Purpurea Pendula' | Widely available |
| § | - 'Purpurea Tricolor' (v) | CDoC CDul CEnd CMCN ECrN MBlu MBri MGos NBea SBir SCoo SCrf SHBN SPer WDin WOrn |
| | - 'Quercifolia' | CMCN MBlu |
| I | - 'Quercina' | SBir SLon |
| | - 'Red Obelisk' | see *F. sylvatica* 'Rohan Obelisk' |
| | - 'Riversii' ♀H4 | Widely available |
| | - 'Rohan Gold' | CDul CEnd CMCN EBee MBlu |
| § | - 'Rohan Obelisk' | CDul CEnd CMCN EBee ELan IArd MBlu MGos NLar SBir WOrn |
| I | - 'Rohan Pyramidalis' | CEnd CMCN |
| | - 'Rohan Trompenburg' | CMCN MBlu |
| | - 'Rohan Weeping' | MBlu SBir |
| | - 'Rohanii' | CAbP CBcs CDoC CDul CEnd CLnd CMCN CTri EBee ECho ECrN EHig ELan EMil EPfP IMGH LPan NBee SCoo SCrf SHBN WDin WFar WHar WOrn |
| | - 'Roseomarginata' | see *F. sylvatica* 'Purpurea Tricolor' |
| | - 'Rotundifolia' | CDoC CDul LPan MBlu |
| | - 'Silver Wood' | CMCN |
| | - 'Spaethiana' | CMCN EWTr NBPN |
| | - 'Striata' | SBir |
| | - 'Tortuosa Purpurea' | CDul MBlu |
| | - 'Tricolor' (v) misapplied | see *F. sylvatica* 'Purpurea Tricolor' |
| | - 'Tricolor' (v) ambig. | SLau WFoF |
| | - 'Tricolor' (v) | CBcs CLnd CMac CSBt CWib EBee ELan LPan SBLw SHBN WDin |
| | - 'Viridivariegata' (v) | CMCN |
| | - 'Zlatia' | CBcs CDoC CDul CLnd CMCN CSBt CWib ELan EMil EPfP GKir MBar MBlu MGos MSwo NBee NWea SBLw SBir SCoo SHBN SLau SPer SPoG WDin WOrn |

## *Fallopia* (*Polygonaceae*)

| | | |
|---|---|---|
| | ***aubertii*** | see *F. baldschuanica* |
| § | ***baldschuanica*** | Widely available |
| | x ***bohemica*** 'Spectabilis' (v) | CBow CRow EMon |
| § | ***japonica*** var. ***compacta*** | CRow NBre NLar WFar WMoo |
| | - - 'Fuji Snow' | see *F. japonica* var. *compacta* 'Milk Boy' |
| § | - - 'Milk Boy' (v) | CBow CRow EShb |
| | - - f. ***rosea*** hort. | CSpe |
| | - - 'Variegata' misapplied | see *F. japonica* var. *compacta* 'Milk Boy' |
| | - 'Crimson Beauty' | CRow EMon SMHy |
| § | ***multiflora*** | CArn EOHP MSal |
| | - var. ***hypoleuca*** | EBee MCCP SCoo SPoG |
| | - - B&SWJ 120 | WCru |
| | ***sachalinensis*** | CRow EMon NLar |

## *Farfugium* (*Asteraceae*)

| | | |
|---|---|---|
| § | ***japonicum*** | CHEx EPPr MTho |
| | - B&SWJ 884 | WCru |
| | - 'Argenteum' (v) | CFir CHEx WCot WFar |
| § | - 'Aureomaculatum' (v) ♀H1 | CAbb CFir CHEx CKob EBee EPfP LFur MCCP MTho SBHP SBig SDnm SPav WFar WHer |
| | - 'Crispatum' | CAbP CAbb CBct CBod CBow CDWL CFir CHEx CKob EBee ECtt ELan EMil EPPr EPfP EWll LAst LEdu LFur MCCP NSti SDnm SMad SPav SPer WCot WFar WHil |
| | - double-flowered (d) **new** | WCru |
| | - var. ***formosanum*** B&SWJ 7125 | WCru |
| | - var. ***giganteum*** | CHEx WCot |
| | - 'Kagami-jishi' (v) | EPPr WCot |
| | - 'Kinkan' (v) | WCot |
| I | - 'Nanum' | CHEx |
| | - 'Ryuto' | EBee EPPr SMad WCot |
| I | - 'Tsuwa-buki' | WCot |
| | ***tussilagineum*** | see *F. japonicum* |
| | - 'Aureomaculatum' | see *F. japonicum* 'Aureomaculatum' |

## *Fargesia* (*Poaceae*)

| | | |
|---|---|---|
| | from Jiuzhaigou, China | CEnt ETod MBri MMoz MMuc NLar |
| | ***adpressa*** | EPla |
| | ***angustissima*** | CDTJ ENBC EPla MWht SBig WPGP |
| | 'Baby' **new** | STre |
| | ***confusa*** **new** | CDTJ |
| | ***denudata*** | CEnt ENBC EPla SBig |
| | - L 1575 | CGHE MMoz MWht WPGP |
| | - Xian 1 | EPla MMoz WPGP |
| | - Xian 2 **new** | EPla |
| | ***dracocephala*** | CAbb CDoC CEnt CGHE EBee EPfP EPla GBin LEdu MAvo MBrN MBri MMoz MMuc MWht NGdn SBig SLPl SPoG WMoo WPGP |
| | ***ferax*** | EPla WPGP |
| | ***fungosa*** | EPla WPGP |
| § | ***murielae*** ♀$^{H4}$ | Widely available |
| | - 'Amy' | NLar NMoo |
| | - 'Bimbo' | CEnt CHEx COIW EBee EPfP EPla ETod EWsh GBin LAst MWht NPal WMoo WPGP |
| | - 'Grüne Hecke' | MWht SBig |
| | - 'Harewood' | CWSG EBee GBin MMoz MWht NMoo SWvt WFar WPGP |
| | - 'Joy' | GBin NLar WMoo WPnP |
| | - 'Jumbo' | Widely available |
| | - 'Kranich' | NLar |
| | - 'Lava' | MBri |
| | - 'Little John' | ENBC |
| | - 'Mae' | CDTJ EBee MWht |
| | - 'Novecento' | ELan |
| | - 'Pinocchio' | EBee MBri |
| | - 'Simba' ♀$^{H4}$ | Widely available |
| | - 'Vampire' | EBee MBri MGos SBig |
| | - 'Willow' | EBee MBri |
| * | ***nepalensis*** **new** | CDTJ |
| § | ***nitida*** | Widely available |
| * | - from Jiuzhaigou, China | CDTJ EMui EPla EWsh GBin MWht SBig WPGP |
| | - 'Anceps' | EPla MWht |
| | - 'Chennevières' | EPla |
| | - 'Eisenach' | EBee EPla GKir MAvo MMoz WFar WMoo |
| | - Gansu 2 | CGHE EPla GKir |
| | - 'Great Wall' | ENBC ETod GBin MBri MWht |
| | - 'Jiuzhaigou 1' **new** | EPla |
| | - 'Jiuzhaigou 2' **new** | EPla |
| | - 'Jiuzhaigou 4' **new** | EPla |
| | - 'Nymphenburg' ♀$^{H4}$ | CEnd CPMA ENBC EPla GKir MBar MBri MMoz MWhi MWht NLar NMoo SBig WFar WMoo WPGP |
| | - 'Wakehurst' | EPla MWht NLar |
| | ***nujiangensis*** **new** | EPla |
| | ***perlonga*** **new** | EPla |
| | - Yunnan 95/6 | MMoz WPGP |
| | ***robusta*** | CAbb CBcs CDTJ CEnd CEnt EBee EFul ENBC EPfP EPla ETod LPal MBrN MBri MMoz MWht NGdn NLar NMoo SBig SLPl WDyG |
| | - 'Ming Yunnan' | LEdu |
| | - 'Pingwu' | CEnt EBee ENBC ERas ETod GBin MBri MWht NLar SBig |
| | - 'Red Sheath' | CEnt EPla ERod MMoz MWht NPal SEND WPGP |
| | - 'Wolong' | CDoC EPla GBin MMoz MWht WPGP |
| | ***rufa*** | CAbb CEnt CTca EBee EMil ENBC EPPr EPfP EPla EShb LMaj MAvo MBar MBrN MBri MCCP MMoz MMuc MWhi MWht NLar NPal SBig WPGP |
| | - variegated (v) **new** | EPla |
| | ***spathacea*** misapplied | see *F. murielae* |
| | ***utilis*** | CEnt EPla ERod LEdu MAvo MMoz MWht NLar NPal SEND WPGP |
| | ***yulongshanensis*** | EPla MWht |
| | aff. ***yulongshanensis*** | EPla |

## *Farsetia* (*Brassicaceae*)

| | | |
|---|---|---|
| | ***clypeata*** | see *Fibigia clypeata* |

## *Fascicularia* (*Bromeliaceae*)

| | | |
|---|---|---|
| | ***andina*** | see *F. bicolor* |
| § | ***bicolor*** | Widely available |
| § | - subsp. ***canaliculata*** | CHEx EBee EPla IBlr LEdu LPio SChr WCot WPGP WPic |
| | ***kirchhoffiana*** | see *F. bicolor* subsp. *canaliculata* |
| | ***litoralis*** | see *Ochagavia litoralis* |
| | ***pitcairniifolia*** misapplied | see *F. bicolor* |
| | ***pitcairniifolia*** (Verlot) Mez | see *Ochagavia* sp. |

## x *Fatshedera* (*Araliaceae*)

| | | |
|---|---|---|
| | ***lizei*** ♀$^{H3}$ | CBcs CDoC CDul CHEx CTri EBee EPfP EPla GQui IDee LRHS MAsh MREP MRav NPal SAPC SArc SDix SPer SPla SPlb SPoG SWvt WCFE WDin WFar |
| § | - 'Annemieke' (v) ♀$^{H3}$ | CBcs CBow CDoC CHEx EBee EPfP LHop MREP MRav SMad SPer SPoG |
| § | - 'Aurea' (v) | ELan LRHS MAsh SEND |
| | - 'Aureopicta' | see x *F. lizei* 'Aurea' |
| | - 'Lemon and Lime' | see x *F. lizei* 'Annemieke' |
| | - 'Maculata' | see x *F. lizei* 'Annemieke' |
| | - 'Variegata' (v) ♀$^{H3}$ | CAbb CHEx EBee ELan EPfP ERas LAst LRHS MAsh MGos NPal SEND SHGN SPer SPla SPoG SWvt WCFE WDin WFar |

## *Fatsia* (*Araliaceae*)

| | | |
|---|---|---|
| § | ***japonica*** ♀$^{H4}$ | Widely available |
| | - 'Golden Handshake' | CBow |
| | - 'Moseri' | CAbP CMdw CSam CTrC EBee ECtt EUJe IBal LHop MSte NGdn NLar SWvt WCot WGwG WPat |
| | - 'Murakumo-nishiki' (v) | NPal |
| | - 'Spider's Web' (v) | CBow EUJe LHop LSou NBhm NGdn SPer SPoG WCot WGwG |
| | - 'Variegata' (v) ♀$^{H3}$ | CBcs EBee EPfP LRHS MBri MGos MRav NPal SArc SLim SPer SPoG |
| | ***papyrifera*** | see *Tetrapanax papyrifer* |
| | ***polycarpa*** | CDTJ CHEx EAmu EBee EPla SKHP WPGP |
| | - B&SWJ 7144 | WCru |
| | - RWJ 10133 | WCru |

## *Faucaria* (*Aizoaceae*)

| | | |
|---|---|---|
| | ***tigrina*** ♀$^{H1}$ | EPfP |

## *Fauria* see *Nephrophyllidium*

## *Feijoa* see *Acca*

## *Felicia* (*Asteraceae*)

| | | |
|---|---|---|
| | ***aethiopica*** | GFai |
| § | ***amelloides*** | CHEx EShb LAst LRHS MCot MLan SGar SPlb |
| | - 'Astrid Thomas' | see *F. amelloides* 'Read's Blue' |
| § | - 'Read's Blue' | SDnm SGar |
| | - 'Read's White' | SDnm |
| | - 'Santa Anita' ♀$^{H3}$ | CHal CTri |
| § | - variegated (v) | CHal ECtt ELon LAst MBri MCot MSte NPer SPet |
| § | ***amoena*** | CTri SRms |
| | - 'Variegata' (v) | CTri |
| | ***capensis*** | see *F. amelloides* |

- 'Variegata' see *F. amelloides* variegated
***coelestis*** see *F. amelloides*
***erigeroides*** CHal GFai
***filifolia*** SPlb
***fruticosa*** CHll
***natalensis*** see *F. rosulata*
***pappei*** see *F. amoena*
§ ***petiolata*** CTri EBee NSti WCot WEas WWFP
§ ***rosulata*** CPBP ECho EMon MBrN MHer MTho NBro SFgr SKHP SRms SRot
***uliginosa*** ECho EWes GEdr GGar LRHS MTho WFar

## fennel see *Foeniculum vulgare*

## fenugreek see *Trigonella foenum-graecum*

## *Ferraria* (*Iridaceae*)

§ ***crispa*** ECho
***undulata*** see *F. crispa*

## *Ferula* (*Apiaceae*)

***assa-foetida*** CArn LDai LEdu MSal
***chiliantha*** see *F. communis* subsp. *glauca*
§ ***communis*** CArn CMea CSpe EBee ECGP ECha ELan IDee LEdu LPio MSte NBid NLar NSti SDix SDnm SMad SPav SPlb WCAu WCot WFar WJek WPGP
- 'Gigantea' see *F. communis*
§ - subsp. ***glauca*** CMea EWes SDix SGar SMHy SPhx WCot WHal WPGP
'Giant Bronze' see *Foeniculum vulgare* 'Giant Bronze'
***tingitana*** CSec
- 'Cedric Morris' EBee ECha SDix WSHC

## *Festuca* (*Poaceae*)

***actae*** SGar
***amethystina*** CKno CWCL CWib EBee EHoe EMon GFor LEdu MNHC MNrw MWhi NGdn NHol NNor SPer WMoo WPer WTin
- 'Aprilgrün' EPPr
***arenaria*** new EBWF
***arundinacea*** CRWN EBWF
***californica*** CKno EPPr
***coxii*** MAvo WCot
***curvula*** subsp. ***crassifolia*** EPla EShb EWsh NHol
***elegans*** EPPr
***eskia*** CKno EAEE EBee EHoe EHul EPPr NHol SPer SPla WDyG
***filiformis*** EHoe
'Fromefield Blue' EHul
§ ***gautieri*** EBee GBin GFor MBar NBre NGdn NHol
- 'Pic Carlit' EMon GBin
***gigantea*** GFor NBre
***glauca*** Widely available
I - 'Auslese' CPLG EPPr GFor NGdn NPro
- 'Azurit' EAlp EBee EHoe EPPr EWes EWsh LAst NHol SPad SPoG
§ - 'Blaufuchs' ♀H4 Widely available
§ - 'Blauglut' EAEE EAlp EBee EHul EPPr EPfP EPla LRHS MBri MRav NHol
- Blue Fox see *F. glauca* 'Blaufuchs'
- Blue Glow see *F. glauca* 'Blauglut'
- 'Bofinger' new EBee
- 'Elijah Blue' Widely available
- 'Euchre' LSRN
- 'Golden Toupee' CWSG EAEE EAlp EBee ECha ELan EPfP EWes GKir LAst LRHS MBar MBlu MGos MMoz MRav NBir NHol NPri NSti SLim SPer SPlb SWvt WCot WDin WFar
- 'Harz' EBee EHoe EHul MBar SApp
* - ***minima*** CCCN SPoG
- 'Pallens' see *F. longifolia*
- Sea Urchin see *F. glauca* 'Seeigel'
§ - 'Seeigel' EAlp EBee EHoe EPPr GKir MMoz NHol NPro
- Select see *F. glauca* 'Auslese'
- 'Seven Seas' see *F. valesiaca* 'Silbersee'
- 'Silberreiher' EBee EPPr
- 'Uchte' CWCL EBee WPtf
'Hogar' EHoe
***idahoensis*** EShb
§ ***longifolia*** EBee EPPr
***mairei*** CKno EBee ECha EHig EHoe EMon EPPr GFor GQue NBHF SPhx SWal
***novae-zelandiae*** CWCL NNor
***ovina*** CWan EBWF GFor WPer WSFF
- var. ***duriuscula*** CRWN
- var. ***gallica*** new EWsh
I - 'Kulturform' NNor
- 'Söhrewald' EPPr WMoo
* - 'Tetra Gold' SWvt
***paniculata*** CKno EHoe EMon EPPr EWsh WMoo
***punctoria*** GFor WMoo
***rubra*** CRWN EBWF WSFF
***scoparia*** see *F. gautieri*
'Siskiyou Blue' CKno EAlp EBee
***tatrae*** EBee WCot
***valesiaca*** SGar WFar
- var. ***glaucantha*** CWib EBee EPPr GFor MNHC NBre NGdn NLar
§ - 'Silbersee' EBee EHoe EPPr EWsh LRHS MBar MSte NHol SRms WFar
- Silver Sea see *F. valesiaca* 'Silbersee'
***violacea*** EBee EHoe EPPr NNor SIng SWal
***vivipara*** CNat CPrp EBWF EGoo EHoe EMon LEdu NBid WRos
* 'Willow Green' SLim SPlb

## *Fibigia* (*Brassicaceae*)

§ ***clypeata*** CSec LDai SGar
- 'Select' CSpe

## *Ficus* ✿ (*Moraceae*)

***australis*** misapplied see *F. rubiginosa* 'Australis'
***benghalensis*** MBri
***benjamina*** ♀H1 CHal LRHS MBri SRms
- 'Exotica' CHal LRHS MBri
- 'Golden King' (v) LRHS MBri
- 'Starlight' (v) ♀H1 LRHS MBri
***carica*** (F) CCCN ETod LMaj LPan MBri MREP SArc SLon SPad
- 'Abbey Slip' (F) CHEx
- 'Bourjassotte Grise' (F) SDea
- 'Brogiotto' (F) CCCN NLar
- 'Brown Turkey' (F) ♀H3 Widely available
- 'Brunswick' (F) CAgr CCCN CHll CWib EMui GTwe MCoo NGHP SLim WCot
- 'Castle Kennedy' (F) GTwe
- 'Colummaro Black Apulia' (F) CCCN
- 'Colummaro White Apulia' (F) CCCN
- 'Dalmatie' (F) ELan LRHS MCoo
I - 'Digitata' (F) MBlu
- 'Filacciano' (F) CCCN
- 'Goutte d'Or' (F) SDea SEND
- 'Kadota' (F) NLar
* - 'Laciniata' (F) MBri SMad
- 'Malta' (F) GTwe

| | | |
|---|---|---|
| | - 'Marseillaise' (F) | GTwe SDea |
| | - 'Melanzana' (F) | CCCN |
| | - 'Newlyn Coombe' (F) | CHEx |
| | - 'Newlyn Harbour' (F) | CHEx |
| | - 'Noire de Carombe' (F) | EMil MCoo |
| | - 'Osborn's Prolific' (F) | ECrN EMil SWvt |
| | - 'Porthminster' (F) | CHEx |
| | - 'Précoce de Dalmatie' (F) | EMil MAsh NLar WPGP |
| | - 'Rouge de Bordeaux' (F) | CCCN EMil SDea |
| | - 'Violette Dauphine' (F) | EMil EPfP |
| | - 'White Genoa' | see *F. carica* 'White Marseilles' |
| § | - 'White Marseilles' (F) | CCCN CWib ECrN EMui EPfP MBri MCoo NGHP SDea |
| | ***cyathistipula*** | MBri |
| | ***deltoidea*** var. ***diversifolia*** | MBri |
| | ***elastica*** | LRHS |
| | - 'Robusta' | MBri |
| | ***foveolata*** Wallich | see *F. sarmentosa* |
| | ***lyrata*** ♀H1 | MBri |
| | ***microcarpa*** 'Hawaii' (v) | CHal |
| | ***pubigera*** | CPLG |
| | ***pumila*** ♀H1 | CHEx CHal LRHS MBri |
| | - 'Minima' | CFee |
| | - 'Sonny' (v) | MBri |
| | - 'Variegata' (v) | CHal MBri |
| | ***radicans*** 'Variegata' | see *F. sagittata* 'Variegata' |
| § | ***rubiginosa*** 'Australis' | MBri |
| | - 'Variegata' (v) ♀H1 | CHal |
| § | ***sagittata*** 'Variegata' (v) | MBri |
| § | ***sarmentosa*** | MBri |

## fig see *Ficus carica*

## filbert see *Corylus maxima*

## *Filipendula* ✿ (*Rosaceae*)

| | | |
|---|---|---|
| | ***alnifolia*** 'Variegata' | see *F. ulmaria* 'Variegata' |
| | ***camtschatica*** | CFir CMCo CRow EBee ECha ELan LEdu MCot NBid NLar NMir NPol WFar WMoo WPGP |
| | - B&SWJ 10828 new | WCru |
| | - 'Rosea' | LHop MRav SMad |
| | ***digitata*** 'Nana' | see *F. multijuga* |
| | ***formosa*** B&SWJ 8707 | WCru |
| | ***hexapetala*** | see *F. vulgaris* |
| | - 'Flore Pleno' | see *F. vulgaris* 'Multiplex' |
| | 'Kahome' | CMCo CPrp CRow EBee EBrs EPla EShb GBuc GGar GKir GMaP IFoB LAst LHop LRHS NBir NGdn NLar NMir NOrc SPer SPla SWat WFar WHoo WMoo WPnP |
| | ***kiraishiensis*** B&SWJ 1571 | EBee WCru |
| § | ***multijuga*** | CRow EWTr GCal GGar IFoB NHol WFar WMoo |
| | ***palmata*** | ECha MBri MLHP NBre SWat WFar WMoo |
| | - 'Digitata Nana' | see *F. multijuga* |
| | - dwarf | CLAP MLHP |
| | - 'Elegantissima' | see *F. purpurea* 'Elegans' |
| | - 'Nana' | see *F. multijuga* |
| | - ***purpurea*** | see *F. purpurea* |
| | - 'Rosea' | NBir WCHb |
| | - 'Rubra' | CTri GCra MRav NGdn |
| § | ***purpurea*** ♀H4 | CKno CRow CSBt ECha ELon EPfP EWTr GGar IBlr LPBA LRHS MBri WBVN WCru WFar WMoo WPnP |
| | - f. ***albiflora*** | EBee MBri NPri WMoo WOut |
| § | - 'Elegans' | CRow EBee ECha EMil GGar GMac LAst MLHP MSte NBPC NBid NHol NPri NSti SPet SWat WFar WMoo |
| | - 'Nephele' | EBee GMac SMHy |
| | - 'Pink Dreamland' | EBee SAga |
| * | - 'Plena' (d) | NLar |
| | 'Queen of the Prairies' | see *F. rubra* |
| § | ***rubra*** | CRow CSec GAbr LAst LSRN MCot NBid WBVN WFar WSFF |
| § | - 'Venusta' ♀H4 | Widely available |
| | - 'Venusta Magnifica' | see *F. rubra* 'Venusta' |
| | ***rufinervis*** B&SWJ 8611 | WCru |
| § | ***ulmaria*** | Widely available |
| | - 'Aurea' | CArn CRow EBee EBrs ECha ECtt EGle EHoe ELan EPla GAbr GBar GBuc GMaP MLHP MRav NBid NGHP NPri SAga SMad SRms WEas WFar WMoo WSHC WTin |
| | - 'Flore Pleno' (d) | CBre CRow EBee EBrs LAst LHop LRHS MRav NBid NBre NGdn SIde SPer SWat WCAu WCot WFar WTin |
| | - 'Rosea' | CDes IBlr WPGP |
| § | - 'Variegata' (v) | Widely available |
| § | ***vulgaris*** | CArn CFee CRWN CTri CWan EBWF ECtt GBar GKir MLHP MNHC MSal NBlu NBro NMir NNor SWat WPer |
| | - 'Alba' | EBee |
| | - 'Flore Pleno' | see *F. vulgaris* 'Multiplex' |
| | - 'Grandiflora' | CBre GKir |
| § | - 'Multiplex' (d) | CRow EBee EBrs ECha EGle ELan EWTr GGar GKir GMaP LRHS MBri MHer MLLN MRav NBid NBir NPri NRya SPer SRms WAul WEas WFar WHlf WMoo WTin |
| | - 'Plena' | see *F. vulgaris* 'Multiplex' |
| | - 'Rosea' | EBee NBre |

## *Firmiana* (*Sterculiaceae*)

| | | |
|---|---|---|
| | ***simplex*** | CHEx EShb WPGP |

## *Fittonia* (*Acanthaceae*)

| | | |
|---|---|---|
| | ***albivenis*** Argyroneura Group ♀H1 | CHal EShb LRHS |
| I | - - 'Nana' | CHal |
| § | - Verschaffeltii Group ♀H1 | CHal EShb |
| | ***verschaffeltii*** | see *F. albivenis* Verschaffeltii Group |

## *Fitzroya* (*Cupressaceae*)

| | | |
|---|---|---|
| | ***cupressoides*** | CBcs CDoC CMac CTho GKir IDee IFFs LRHS MBar SCoo SLim WThu |

## *Fockea* (*Asclepiadaceae*)

| | | |
|---|---|---|
| | ***edulis*** | EShb |

## *Foeniculum* (*Apiaceae*)

| | | |
|---|---|---|
| | ***vulgare*** | Widely available |
| | - 'Bronze' | see *F. vulgare* 'Purpureum' |
| | - var. ***dulce*** | CSev SIde |
| § | - 'Giant Bronze' | CChe EBee ELan LCro SMad SPhx |
| § | - 'Purpureum' | Widely available |
| | - 'Smokey' | ECha MRav |

## *Fontanesia* (*Oleaceae*)

| | | |
|---|---|---|
| | ***phillyreoides*** | CBcs |

## *Fontinalis* (*Fontinalaceae*)

| | | |
|---|---|---|
| | sp. | LPBA |
| | ***antipyretica*** | MSKA WFar |

## *Forsythia* ✿ (*Oleaceae*)

| | | |
|---|---|---|
| | 'Arnold Dwarf' | ECrN NBir NLar SRms |
| | 'Beatrix Farrand' ambig. | CTri CWSG EBee LRHS MGos MWat SPer SRms WBod |
| | 'Beatrix Farrand' K. Sax | GKir IMGH NLar |
| | 'Fiesta' (v) | CPMA CWSG EBee ELon EPfP LAst LRHS MAsh MBar MGos MRav MSwo NWea SLim SPer SPoG WCot WDin WFar |

| | |
|---|---|
| ***giraldiana*** | EBee GKir MSwo SLon SRms WBod |
| Gold TidePBR | see *F.* Marée d'Or = 'Courtasol' |
| 'Golden Nugget' | EBee ELan EPfP LRHS MAsh MBri SCoo SLon SPoG WCFE |
| 'Golden Times' (v) | EBee ERas EWes LBuc LSRN MAsh MGos NLar SCoo SPoG SWal SWvt WBod WDin WFar |
| x ***intermedia*** | ECrN |
| - 'Arnold Giant' | MBlu WBod |
| - 'Goldrausch' | LAst MAsh MBri MGos |
| - 'Goldzauber' | NWea |
| - 'Josefa' (v) | ELan LBuc MAsh SPoG |
| - 'Lynwood Variety' ♀H4 | Widely available |
| - 'Lynwood Variety' variegated (v) | CWib |
| - Minigold = 'Flojor' | CSBt EPfP LAst MGos MSwo MWat NBlu SRms WBVN |
| - Show Off = 'Mindor'PBR **new** | MAsh |
| - 'Spectabilis' | CDul EBee EMac EPfP LBuc MBar NWea SCoo SLim WBod WDin WFar |
| - 'Spectabilis Variegated' (v) | CBow MBNS NPro |
| - 'Spring Glory' | EBee MHer |
| - 'Variegata' (v) | NWea WBod WGwG |
| - Week-End = 'Courtalyn'PBR ♀H4 | CWSG EBee EPfP LBuc LSou MAsh MBri MGos NLar NPri SEND SLPl SLim SLon SPlb SPoG WDin WFar |
| § Marée d'Or = 'Courtasol'PBR ♀H4 | CWSG ECrN EMil LRHS MAsh MBri MGos MRav NLar NWea SLon SPoG WDin |
| Mêlée d'Or = 'Courtaneur' | LRHS SCoo SPer |
| Melissa = 'Courtadic' | NLar NWea |
| ***ovata*** 'Tetragold' | EBee EMil MBar NWea |
| 'Paulina' | NLar |
| ***suspensa*** | CArn CTri CWib EOHP EPfP GKir LRHS MSal NWea SHBN SPer SPlb SRms |
| - f. ***atrocaulis*** | CDul NWea |
| - 'Decipiens' | WBod |
| - var. ***fortunei*** | MBri |
| - 'Nymans' | EPfP GKir MBri MRav NSti |
| § - 'Taff's Arnold' (v) | CPLG CPMA EBee |
| - 'Variegata' | see *F. suspensa* 'Taff's Arnold' |
| 'Tremonia' | ECrN NLar WGwG |
| 'Verfors Minor Gold' | MBri |
| ***viridissima*** | NWea |
| - 'Bronxensis' | ECho GEdr LLHF MAsh NBir NLar WPat |
| - var. ***koreana*** 'Kumsom' (v) | EMil MAsh |
| - 'Weber's Bronx' | NLar |

## Fortunatia see *Oziroë*

| | |
|---|---|
| ***biflora*** | see *Oziroë biflora* |

## Fortunella (*Rutaceae*)

| | |
|---|---|
| § ***japonica*** (F) | EPfP |
| § ***margarita*** (F) | CDoC MBri |

## Fothergilla (*Hamamelidaceae*)

| | |
|---|---|
| ***gardenii*** | CBcs CPMA ELan EPfP EWTr MBlu MBri MGos MRav NLar SPer SPoG SSpi WDin |
| - Beaver Creek = 'Klmtwo' | NLar |
| - 'Blue Mist' | CAbP CDoC CEnd CPMA CWSG EBee ELan EPfP LRHS NLar SMad SPer SPla SReu SSta WBod WDin WFar WPat |
| - 'Harold Epstein' | NLar |
| - 'Suzanne' | NLar |
| - 'Zundert' | NLar |
| 'Huntsman' | CCCN EBee WFar |
| ***major*** ♀H4 | CBcs CDul CEnd CPMA CSam CWib EBee ELan EPfP LCro LRHS LSRN MBri MGos MLan NBlu NLar NPri SHBN SPer SPoG SReu SSpi WBod WDin WFar WPat |
| - 'Bulkyard' | MBri |
| - Monticola Group | CDoC CEnd CPMA CSBt CWSG EBee ELan EPfP IMGH LCro LRHS MAsh MBar MDun MGos MMuc NPal SHBN SLim SSpi SSta SWvt WBrE WFar |
| - 'Red Licorice' | CPMA MBri |
| - 'Seaspray' | CPMA |
| 'Mount Airy' | CMCN CPMA EBee EPfP NLar SPoG SSpi |

## Fragaria (*Rosaceae*)

| | |
|---|---|
| from Taiwan | WHer |
| ***alpina*** | see *F. vesca* 'Semperflorens' |
| - 'Alba' | see *F. vesca* 'Semperflorens Alba' |
| x ***ananassa*** 'Alice'PBR (F) ♀H4 | CAgr CSut EMui LBuc MCoo |
| - 'Aromel' (F) ♀H4 | CSBt EPfP GTwe LRHS SDea SEND |
| - 'Bogota' (F) | LRHS |
| - 'Bolero' (F) | EMui MBri |
| - 'Calypso'PBR (F) | CSBt EMui LBuc LRHS SDea SEND |
| - 'Cambridge Favourite' (F) ♀H4 | CAgr CSBt CTri EMui EPfP GTwe LBuc LRHS MBri MCoo MGan MGos NPri SDea |
| - 'Cambridge Late Pine' (F) | EMui LRHS |
| - 'Cambridge Rival' (F) | LRHS |
| - 'Cambridge Vigour' (F) | GTwe LRHS SDea |
| - 'Challenger' (F) | EMui |
| - 'Chelsea Pensioner' (F) | EMui |
| - 'Christine' (F) **new** | EMil |
| - 'Darselect'PBR (F) | EMui |
| - 'Elsanta'PBR (F) | CSBt CTri EMui EPfP GKir GTwe IArd LBuc LRHS MGan NPri SDea SEND SPer |
| - 'Elvira' (F) | EMui |
| * - 'Emily' (F) | GTwe |
| - 'Eros'PBR (F) | EMui GTwe LBuc |
| - 'Everest'PBR (F) | EMil LBuc |
| - 'Flamenco'PBR (F) | CSut EMil EMui |
| - 'Florence'PBR (F) | CAgr CSBt EMil EMui GTwe LBuc LRHS MBri SPer |
| - Fraise des Bois | see *F. vesca* |
| - 'Gariguette' (F) | EMui |
| - 'Hampshire Maid' (F) | LRHS |
| - 'Hapil' (F) ♀H4 | CTri EMui EPfP GTwe LBuc LRHS NBlu |
| - 'Honeoye' (F) ♀H4 | CAgr CSBt EMui GTwe LBuc LRHS MBri SEND SPer |
| - 'Judibell' (F) **new** | EMil EMui |
| - 'Korona'PBR (F) | EMui |
| - 'Kouril' (F) | LRHS |
| - 'Loran' (F) | WHlf |
| - 'Mae'PBR (F) | CSut EMui |
| - 'Malling Pearl' (F) | EMil EMui |
| - 'Maxim' (F) | EMui |
| - 'Pantagruella' (F) | LRHS |
| - 'Pegasus'PBR (F) ♀H4 | CAgr CSBt EMui GTwe LRHS NPri |
| - Pink Panda = 'Frel'PBR (F) | CBcs EAEE EBee ELan LBuc MRav NHol NLar SIng SPer SPoG SSto WCAu WEas WFar WWFP |
| - pink-flowered (F) | CFee EMui |
| - Red Ruby = 'Samba'PBR | EAEE EBee MNrw NGdn NLar SIng SPer SPoG WCAu |
| - 'Redgauntlet' (F) | EPfP GTwe LRHS |
| - 'Rhapsody' (F) ♀H4 | GTwe LBuc LRHS |
| - 'Rosie'PBR (F) | EMui SDea |
| - 'Royal Sovereign' (F) | GTwe LBuc LRHS MGan |
| - 'Sonata'PBR (F) **new** | CSut EMui |
| - 'Sophie'PBR (F) | CAgr LRHS |

| | |
|---|---|
| - 'Symphony' PBR (F) 𝕐H4 | CAgr CSBt EMil EMui EPfP LBuc MBri SEND |
| - 'Tamella' (F) | EMui LRHS |
| - 'Tenira' (F) | EMui |
| - 'Totem' (F) | GTwe |
| § - 'Variegata' (v) | CArn EBee EMon EPla LDai LHop MCCP MHar MRav SIng SPer SPoG WMoo WRha |
| - 'Viva Rosa' (F) | EMui LBuc LRHS |
| 'Bowles' Double' | see *F. vesca* 'Multiplex' |
| ***chiloensis*** (F) | CAgr EMon ILis LEdu SHar |
| - 'Chaval' | CHid EBee ECha EGoo EHrv EMon EPPr MRav WMoo |
| - 'Variegata' misapplied | see *F.* x *ananassa* 'Variegata' |
| ***daltoniana*** | GCra |
| ***indica*** | see *Duchesnea indica* |
| 'Lipstick' | EBee NLar WRos |
| ***moschata*** | CAgr |
| ***nubicola*** | GPoy |
| - 'Mount Omei' **new** | EBee |
| 'Variegata' | see *F.* x *ananassa* 'Variegata' |
| § ***vesca*** (F) | CAgr CArn CRWN CWan EAlp EBWF EPfP GPoy LRHS MHer MNHC NGHP NMir NPri SECG SIde SPlb SVic WGwG WJek WPer WSFF WShi |
| - 'Alexandra' (F) | CArn CBod CPrp ELau GAbr LRHS NVic SIde WCHb |
| - 'Baron Solemacher' (F) | SHDw |
| - 'Flore Pleno' | see *F. vesca* 'Multiplex' |
| - 'Fructu Albo' (F) | CAgr CArn CBre CHFP CRow CWan EBee NLar WLHH WMoo WPer |
| - 'Golden Alexandra' | EAlp EBee ECha EHoe ELau EWes LSou WHer |
| - 'Golden Surprise' **new** | SHDw |
| - 'Mara des Bois' PBR (F) | EMui |
| - 'Monophylla' (F) | CRow EMon IGor SIde WHer |
| § - 'Multiplex' (d) | CRow CSev EMon ILis MRav NGHP NHol NLar WAlt WCHb WHer WOut WRHF |
| § - 'Muricata' | CBre CPou CRow IGor ILis LEdu WAlt WHer |
| - 'Pineapple Crush' | WHer |
| - 'Plymouth Strawberry' | see *F. vesca* 'Muricata' |
| - 'Rügen' (F) | IGor |
| § - 'Semperflorens' (F) | ILis WAlt |
| § - 'Semperflorens Alba' (F) | CAgr CSec |
| - 'Variegata' misapplied | see *F.* x *ananassa* 'Variegata' |
| * - 'Variegata' ambig. (v) | EHoe EHrv NGHP WFar WHrl WPer |
| ***virginiana*** | CAgr |
| - subsp. ***glauca*** | EPPr |
| ***viridis*** | CAgr |

## *Francoa* (*Saxifragaceae*)

| | |
|---|---|
| ***appendiculata*** | CAbP CSec EBla EHig GQui MDKP NBre SGar WFar WHer WHrl WMoo WPnP |
| - red-flowered | CDes CKno EBee |
| Ballyrogan strain | IBlr |
| 'Confetti' | CBct CDes CHFP CKno CPLG ELan ELon GMaP MAvo MCot MNrw NCob SWal WCot WFar WPGP |
| 'Purple Spike' | see *F. sonchifolia* Rogerson's |
| ***ramosa*** | CCVN CMCo CTri EHrv GBuc IBlr MHav MLan MNrw NBro SAga SDix SHGN SPav WFar WMoo |
| * - 'Alba' | CSpe |
| ***sonchifolia*** | Widely available |
| - 'Alba' | MDKP SMrm SUsu WFar WHrl WMoo |
| - 'Culm View Lilac' | CCVN |
| - 'Doctor Tom Smith' | WCot |
| - 'Molly Anderson' | EBee MAvo SUsu |
| § - Rogerson's | CCVN CElw CKno CSam CSec EBee EDAr EHrv GBuc GGar LBMP MAvo MDKP NChi NHol SAga SBod SDix SGar STes SUsu SWal WCot WHil WMoo WSHC |

## *Frangula* see *Rhamnus*

| | |
|---|---|
| § ***alnus*** | CArn CCVT CDul CLnd CRWN EMac LBuc MBlu NWea SLPl STre WDin WFar WMou WSFF |
| - 'Aspleniifolia' | CBgR CTho EBee EMil EPfP LBuc MBlu MBri MMuc MRav NLar WDin WFar WPat |
| - 'Columnaris' | EMil SLPl |
| - 'Minaret' | MBri |

## *Frankenia* (*Frankeniaceae*)

| | |
|---|---|
| ***laevis*** | SRms |
| ***thymifolia*** | CTri EAlp ECho GGar MBar MHer MWat NBlu NPri SPlb WFar WTin |

## *Franklinia* (*Theaceae*)

| | |
|---|---|
| ***alatamaha*** | CBcs CPMA EPfP LHyd MBlu MBri SEND WFar |

## *Fraxinus* ✿ (*Oleaceae*)

| | |
|---|---|
| ***americana*** | CDul CMCN EPfP SBLw WDin |
| - 'Autumn Purple' | CDul CEnd CMCN CTho EBee ECrN EHig EPfP LRHS MAsh MBlu SBLw SLon |
| - 'Rosehill' | CTho |
| ***angustifolia*** | CMCN EGFP |
| - 'Raywood' 𝕐H4 | Widely available |
| * - 'Variegata' (v) | MGos |
| ***bungeana*** | EGFP |
| ***chinensis*** | CLnd CMCN EGFP |
| ***elonza*** | CLnd |
| ***excelsior*** | CBcs CCVT CDoC CDul CLnd CRWN CSBt CTri CWib EBee ECrN EMac EPfP GKir LAst LBuc LPan MBar MGos NBee NWea SBLw SHBN SLim STre WDin WMou WOrn |
| - 'Allgold' | CEnd |
| - 'Aurea' | SBLw |
| - 'Aurea Pendula' | CCVT CDul CEnd CWib EBee ECrN LRHS MBlu MGos NPal SBLw SPoG |
| - 'Crispa' | MBlu NLar SBLw |
| - f. ***diversifolia*** | CDul CLnd |
| - 'Globosa' | SBLw |
| - 'Jaspidea' 𝕐H4 | Widely available |
| - 'Nana' | EMon LMaj SBLw WPat |
| - 'Pendula' 𝕐H4 | CCVT CDoC CDul CEnd CLnd CTho EBee ECrN ELan LAst LMaj LPan LRHS MBlu NBee NPal NWea SBLw SHBN SLim SPer SPoG WDin WJas WMou WOrn |
| - 'R.E. Davey' | CDul CNat |
| - variegated (v) | ECrN |
| - 'Westhof's Glorie' 𝕐H4 | CCVT CDoC CDul CLnd EBee ECrN LMaj SBLw WDin WFar WJas WOrn |
| ***insularis*** var. ***henryana*** | CDul CMCN WPGP |
| ***latifolia*** | CLnd |
| ***mandshurica*** | MBri |
| ***mariesii*** | see *F. sieboldiana* |
| ***nigra*** 'Fallgold' | CEnd |
| ***ornus*** 𝕐H4 | CArn CCVT CDul CLnd CMCN CTri EBee ECrN ELan EMac EPfP EWTr GKir IMGH LAst LMaj MSwo NPal NWea SBLw SPer WDin WFar WMoo WOrn |
| - 'Arie Peters' | CDul LPan SBLw |
| - 'Mecsek' | MBlu |
| - 'Obelisk' | LMaj MAsh NLar SMad |

| | | |
|---|---|---|
| | - 'Rotterdam' | EBee SBLw |
| | **pennsylvanica** | CDul CLnd |
| | - 'Cimmaron' | see *F. pennsylvanica* 'Cimmzam' |
| § | - 'Cimmzam' new | CDul |
| | - 'Variegata' (v) | CLnd EBee GKir MAsh WPat |
| | **quadrangulata** | WDin |
| | **richardi** new | CDul |
| § | **sieboldiana** | CDoC CDul CLnd CMCN CPMA EPfP MBlu MBri NLar SSpi WPGP WPat |
| | **velutina** | CDul CLnd SLPl |
| | **xanthoxyloides** var. **dumosa** | WPGP |

## *Freesia* ✿ (*Iridaceae*)

| | | |
|---|---|---|
| | sp. new | WHil |
| | 'Amulet' (d) new | LRHS |
| | 'Beethoven' (d) new | LRHS |
| | 'Blue Heaven' new | LRHS |
| | hybrids | EBrs |
| | - yellow-flowered new | WHil |
| | **laxa** | see *Anomatheca laxa* |
| | 'Marianne' (d) new | LRHS |
| | **xanthospila** | EBee EBrs WCot |

## *Fremontodendron* (*Sterculiaceae*)

| | | |
|---|---|---|
| | 'California Glory' ♀H3 | Widely available |
| | **californicum** | CSec CTri CWib EBee ELan EMil MBri NBlu SHBN SLim SOWG SPlb WBod WDin WFar |
| | **mexicanum** | NLar |
| | 'Pacific Sunset' | CPMA EPfP LHop MGos MREP MRav SPer SPoG |
| | 'Tequila Sunrise' | CBcs CDoC CPMA EBee GBin ISea LLHF MGos MRav NLar NMun SPoG SRkn |

## *Freylinia* (*Scrophulariaceae*)

| | | |
|---|---|---|
| | **cestroides** | see *F. lanceolata* |
| | **densiflora** | GFai |
| § | **lanceolata** | CBcs CCCN CTrC CWib EShb |
| | **tropica** | CHII GFai |
| | **visseri** | GFai SOWG |

## *Fritillaria* ✿ (*Liliaceae*)

| | | |
|---|---|---|
| | **acmopetala** ♀H4 | CAvo CBro CFFs CMea CPom CWCL EBrs ECho EPot ERCP ERos GBuc GEdr ITim LAma LRHS MSSP MSte MTho NMen SPhx WCot |
| | - 'Brunette' | EBrs ECho EPot MSte SPhx WWst |
| | - subsp. **wendelboi** | EBrs ECho EPot LAma SPhx WCot |
| | **affinis** | CWCL ECho GBin GBuc GGar GKev ITim LAma MPoH MSSP NMen WCot |
| | - 'Limelight' | ECho |
| | - 'Sunray' | EBrs ECho GEdr ITim SKHP |
| § | - var. **tristulis** | ERos NMen |
| | - 'Vancouver Island' | EBrs ECho EPot |
| | **alburyana** | ECho |
| | **alfredae** subsp. **glaucoviridis** | ITim WCot |
| | **arabica** | see *F. persica* |
| | **ariana** new | WWst |
| | **armena** | EBrs ECho |
| | - MP 8146 new | MPoH |
| | **assyriaca** | EPot GBuc |
| | **aurea** | ECho MPoH MSSP NMen WCot WWst |
| | - 'Golden Flag' | EBrs ECho EPfP EPot GKev LLHF SPhx |
| | **biflora** | ECho EPot GEdr MPoH |
| | - 'Martha Roderick' | EBrs ECho ERCP LAma MSSP NMen |
| § | **bithynica** | CSec EBrs ECho EPot GEdr ITim LAma MPoH MSSP |
| | **bucharica** | CPBP EBee ECho GKev |
| | - 'Nurek Giant' | ECho |
| | **camschatcensis** | CAvo CBro CPom CWCL EBrs ECha ECho EFEx EPfP EPot ERCP GAuc GEdr GGar GKir GMaP LAma LRHS MSSP MTho NBir NHar NMen NWCA SPhx WAbe WCru |
| I | - **alpina aurea** | GEdr |
| | - 'Aurea' | ECho GBuc NHar NMen SPhx WWst |
| | - black-flowered | ECho GBuc |
| | - double-flowered (d) | CFir EBrs ECho NMen |
| | - f. **flavescens** | EBrs ECho EFEx GEdr LAma |
| | - green-flowered | MSSP NMen |
| | **carduchorum** | see *F. minuta* |
| | **carica** | EBrs ECho GEdr LRHS MSSP NMen |
| | - NS 2181 new | MPoH |
| | - brown-flowered | ECho |
| | **caucasica** | EBrs ECho NMen |
| | **cirrhosa** | EBrs ECho GEdr GKir WWst |
| | - brown-flowered | EBrs ECho GEdr NMen WWst |
| | - green-flowered | GEdr NMen WWst |
| | **citrina** | see *F. bithynica* |
| § | **collina** | ECho NMen |
| | **conica** | NMen WCot |
| | **crassifolia** | ECho LAma MSSP |
| | - subsp. **crassifolia** | CGra |
| § | - subsp. **kurdica** | EBrs EPot NMen WCot WWst |
| | **davidii** | ECho |
| | **davisii** | CHFP CPBP EBrs ECho EPot ERCP GBuc GEdr LAma LRHS NMen WCot |
| | **delavayi** | CExc WCot |
| | **delphinensis** | see *F. tubiformis* |
| | **drenovskii** | WWst |
| | **eduardii** | EBrs ECho MPoH WWst |
| | **elwesii** | CHFP CHid EBee EBrs ECho EPot ERCP GEdr MPoH NMen WCot |
| | **ferganensis** | see *F. walujewii* |
| | **frankiorum** | WCot |
| | **gentneri** | SKHP WCot |
| | **glauca** | LAma MPoH MSSP WCot |
| * | - 'Golden Flag' | ECho |
| | - 'Goldilocks' | EBrs ECho EPot ERCP NMen |
| | **graeca** | CBro EBrs ECho EPot GBuc GKev LRHS MTho NMen NMin |
| | - subsp. **ionica** | see *F. thessala* |
| | **gussichiae** | EBrs MSSP NMen WWst |
| | **hermonis** subsp. **amana** | CTca CWCL EBrs ECho EPot ERCP GEdr GKev ITim LAma LLHF LPio LRHS NMen WCot |
| | - - 'Cambridge' ♀H4 | WCot |
| | - - yellow-flowered | EPot |
| | **hispanica** | see *F. lusitanica* |
| | **imperialis** | ECGP GKir IHer MBri WBVN WTin |
| | - 'Argenteovariegata' (v) | GKir |
| | - 'Aureomarginata' (v) | EBee EBrs LAma |
| | - 'Aurora' | EBee EBrs EPot ERCP EWTr GKev LAma LRHS NGHP NLar NPer NPri SMeo SMrm SPer SPhx WFar |
| | - 'Garland Star' | EBee EBrs LAma |
| | - 'Inodora Purpurea' | CTca |
| | - var. **inodora** | EBee EBrs |
| | - 'Lutea' | CAvo CMea CSam CTca EBrs ELan EPfP ERCP LRHS MSte NBPC NPri SMeo SMrm SPad SPhx SPoG WFar |
| | - 'Lutea Maxima' | see *F. imperialis* 'Maxima Lutea' |
| | - 'Maxima' | see *F. imperialis* 'Rubra Maxima' |
| § | - 'Maxima Lutea' ♀H4 | CBro ELan EMon EPfP EPot LAma NLar SMrm SPer |
| | - 'Orange Brilliant' | EBee EBrs LRHS MSte |
| | - 'Prolifera' | CTca EBee EBrs ECho LAma NLar WCot WHer |

| | |
|---|---|
| - 'Rubra' | CTca EBee EBrs ECho ERCP GKev LAma LRHS NLar NPri SBch SMeo SMrm SPer WFar |
| § - 'Rubra Maxima' | CBro EBee EBrs ELan EPfP EPot LAma LRHS MSte SMeo SPad SPhx |
| - 'Slagzwaard' | EBee EBrs |
| - 'Sulpherino' | EBee EBrs EMon LAma |
| - 'The Premier' | EBee EBrs ECho EMon LAma WCot |
| - 'William Rex' | CAvo CFFs CWCL EBee EBrs EPot ERCP LAma SPoG |
| - yellow-flowered | CFFs |
| ***involucrata*** | EBrs ECho MPoH |
| ***ionica*** | see *F. thessala* |
| ***japonica*** var. ***koidzumiana*** | EBrs EFEx GEdr WWst |
| ***karadaghensis*** | see *F. crassifolia* subsp. *kurdica* |
| ***kotschyana*** | EBrs ECho EPot GEdr MPoH NMen |
| ***lanceolata*** | see *F. affinis* var. *tristulis* |
| ***latakiensis*** | EBrs ECho EPot GEdr MPoH |
| § ***latifolia*** | GEdr MPoH |
| - var. ***nobilis*** | see *F. latifolia* |
| § ***lusitanica*** | MPoH MSSP NMen SKHP |
| ***lutea*** Bieb. | see *F. collina* |
| ***maximowiczii*** | ECho |
| ***meleagris*** | Widely available |
| - var. ***unicolor*** subvar. ***alba*** 🏆H4 | CBro CMea EBrs ECGP ECho EWTr GBri GBuc LAma LEdu LRHS MBri MMHG MSSP MWat NHol NLAp SPer WAul WCot WShi |
| - - - 'Aphrodite' | EPot GBuc NBir WCot |
| ***meleagroides*** | EBrs WCot |
| § ***messanensis*** | MPoH MSSP WCot |
| - subsp. ***gracilis*** | ITim MSSP |
| - subsp. ***messanensis*** | CBro |
| ***michailovskyi*** 🏆H2 | CAvo CBro CFFs CHFP CHid CTca CTri EBrs ECho EPfP EPot ERCP GBuc GEdr GGar GKev LAma LRHS MNrw MTho NHol NLAp NMen SRms WFar WHil |
| § ***minuta*** | EBrs ECho EPot ERCP MPoH NMen NMin |
| ***montana*** | EBrs ECho NMen WCot |
| ***nigra*** Mill. | see *F. pyrenaica* |
| ***obliqua*** | WCot |
| § ***orientalis*** | ECho WCot WWst |
| ***pallidiflora*** 🏆H4 | Widely available |
| § ***persica*** | CTca EBee EBrs ECha ECho ECtt EHrv ELon EPfP EPot ERCP LAma LHop LRHS MAvo MBri NBPC NMen NPri SGar SMeo SPad SPer SPhx SPoG WCot WFar WHil |
| - 'Adiyaman' 🏆H4 | CAvo CBro CTca EBrs ELan EMon SMeo SPhx |
| - 'Alba' **new** | MPoH |
| - 'Ivory Bells' | EBrs ECho EPot ERCP LAma LPio MSte SPhx WWst |
| - 'Ivory Queen' | CBro |
| * - 'Senkoy' **new** | MPoH |
| ***pinardii*** | ECho EPot NMen |
| ***pontica*** 🏆H4 | CBro CLAP CSec CWCL EBee EBrs ECho EPot ERCP ERos GBuc GEdr GKev ITim LAma LPio LRHS MLLN MSSP MTho NMen NSla SMeo SPhx WCru WPnP |
| - subsp. ***substipilata*** | WCot |
| ***pudica*** | EBrs ECho GBuc GEdr GKev ITim LAma MSSP MTho NMen WAbe |
| * - 'Fragrant' | ECho MPoH NMen SPhx |
| - 'Giant' | EBrs ECho EPot |
| - 'Richard Britten' | NMen |
| ***puqiensis*** | CExc |
| ***purdyi*** | EBrs ECho MSSP |

| | |
|---|---|
| § ***pyrenaica*** 🏆H4 | CLAP CSec CWCL EBrs ECho ERos GCra GEdr LPio MSSP NMen SPhx WCot WCru WTin WWst |
| - 'Cedric Morris' | MSSP |
| ***raddeana*** | CHFP EBee EBrs ECho EMon EPot ERCP LAma SPhx WWst |
| ***recurva*** | EBrs ECho SKHP |
| ***regelii*** **new** | WWst |
| ***rhodocanakis*** | EBrs ECho MPoH NMen NMin |
| - subsp. ***argolica*** | ECho NMen |
| - - OS 864 **new** | MPoH |
| ***rubra major*** | see *F. imperialis* 'Rubra Maxima' |
| ***ruthenica*** | EBrs ECho ERos MSSP NMen |
| ***sewerzowii*** | EBrs ECho MPoH WCot WWst |
| ***sibthorpiana*** | ECho |
| ***sphaciotica*** | see *F. messanensis* |
| ***stenanthera*** | EBrs ECho EPot LAma NMen WWst |
| ***stribrnyi*** | EBrs |
| ***tachengensis*** | see *F. yuminensis* |
| ***tenella*** | see *F. orientalis* |
| § ***thessala*** | EBrs ECho GBuc MSSP MTho NMen SPhx |
| ***thunbergii*** | CAvo EBee EBrs ECho EPot GEdr NMen WCot |
| ***tortifolia*** | NMen |
| § ***tubiformis*** | EBrs ECho GEdr MPoH MSSP |
| ***tuntasia*** | WCot |
| ***unibracteata*** var. ***unibracteata*** | CExc |
| ***uva-vulpis*** | CBro CHFP CMea CTca EBrs ECrN ECtt EHon EPot GBuc GEdr GKev LAma LHop LPio LRHS MNrw MTho NBir NChi NMen SPad SPhx WCot WFar |
| ***verticillata*** | CBro CMea CPBP EBrs ECha ECho EHrv EPot ERCP GEdr LAma MTho NMen SPhx WCru |
| § ***walujewii*** | EPot GEdr MSSP WCot |
| ***whittallii*** | EBrs ECho EPot MSSP NMen |
| - 'Green Light' | EBrs NMin |
| § ***yuminensis*** | ECho WCot |
| - var. ***roseiflora*** | GEdr |

## *Fuchsia* ✿ (*Onagraceae*)

| | |
|---|---|
| 'A.M. Larwick' | CSil EBak EKMF SRiF |
| 'A.W. Taylor' | EBak |
| 'A1' (d) **new** | CTsd |
| 'Aalt Groothuis' (d) | SRiF WPBF |
| 'Aart Verschoor' (d) | WPBF |
| 'Abbé Farges' (d) | CDoC CLoc CSil CWVF EBak EKMF EPts SLBF SPet SRiF SVic WFFs WFuv WRou |
| 'Abbigayle Reine' (v) | SRiF |
| 'Abigail' | CWVF EKMF WRou |
| 'Abigail Storey' | CSil |
| 'Abundance' | CSil |
| 'Acclamation' (d) | WPBF |
| 'Achievement' 🏆H4 | CDoC CLoc CSil EKMF LCla MJac SPet SVic WFFs WPBF |
| 'Adagio' (d) | CLoc |
| 'Adelaide Hoodless' | WRou |
| 'Adinda' (T) | CDoC EKMF EPts LCla MHav MWar SLBF SRiF WRou |
| 'Admiration' | CSil EKMF |
| 'Adrienne' (d) | MHav |
| 'Agnes de Ridder' (d) **new** | WPBF |
| 'Aiguillette' | WPBF |
| 'Ailsa Garnett' (d) | EBak |
| 'Aintree' | CTsd CWVF |
| 'Airedale' | CWVF WFFs |
| 'Aisen' | WRou |
| 'Ajax' (d) | SRiF |
| 'Aladna's Sander' (d) | CWVF SRiF WPBF |

| | | |
|---|---|---|
| | 'Alan Ayckbourn' | CWVF |
| | 'Alan Dyos' | SRiF |
| | 'Alan Titchmarsh' | CDoC EKMF EPts LCla MHav MWar SLBF |
| | 'Alaska' (d) | CLoc EBak EKMF SVic |
| | 'Albertina' | SRiF SVic WFuv WRou |
| | 'Albertus Schwab' | LCla |
| | 'Alde' | CWVF |
| | 'Alderford' | SLBF WPBF |
| | 'Alf Thornley' (d) | CTsd CWVF WPBF |
| | 'Alfred Rambaud' (d) | CDoC CSil SRiF |
| | 'Ali' (d) | EKMF |
| | 'Alice Ashton' (d) | EBak EKMF |
| | 'Alice Blue Gown' (d) | CWVF |
| | 'Alice Doran' | CDoC CSil EKMF LCla SRiF |
| | 'Alice Hoffman' (d) ♀H3-4 | Widely available |
| | 'Alice Mary' (d) | EBak |
| | 'Alice Sweetapple' (d) | CWVF SRiF |
| | 'Alice Travis' (d) | EBak |
| | 'Alipat' | EBak EKMF |
| | 'Alisha Jade' | SRiF |
| | 'Alison Ewart' | CLoc CWVF EBak EKMF MJac SPet SVic |
| | 'Alison Patricia' ♀H3 | CWVF EBak EKMF LAst MJac MWar SLBF SRGP WFFs WFuv WPBF WRou |
| | 'Alison Reynolds' (d) | CWVF WPBF |
| | 'Alison Ruth Griffin' (d) | MJac |
| | 'Alison Ryle' (d) | EBak |
| | 'Alison Sweetman' ♀H1+3 | CSil CWVF EKMF MJac |
| | 'Allen Jackson' **new** | MWar |
| | 'Allure' (d) | CWVF |
| | 'Alma Hulscher' (d) | CWVF |
| | Aloha = 'Sanicomf' PBR (Sunangels Series) | SLBF SRiF |
| | 'Alpengluhn' **new** | WPBF |
| § | ***alpestris*** | CDoC CSil EBak LCla SRiF WPBF |
| | - Berry 64-87 | EKMF |
| | 'Alton Waters' (d/v) | MWar |
| | 'Alwin' (d) | CWVF SRiF |
| | 'Alyce Larson' (d) | CTsd CWVF EBak MHav MJac SRiF SVic |
| | 'Amanda Bridgland' (d) | EKMF |
| | 'Amanda Jones' | EKMF |
| | 'Amaranth' **new** | WPBF |
| | 'Amazing Maisie' (d) | MWar WPBF |
| | 'Ambassador' | CTsd EBak MHav SPet SRiF SVic |
| | 'Ambiorix' | WFuv |
| | 'Amelie Aubin' | CLoc CWVF EBak EKMF SVic |
| | 'America' | CWVF |
| | 'Amethyst Fire' (d) | CSil SRiF |
| | 'Amigo' ambig. | EBak SRiF |
| § | ***ampliata*** | EKMF LCla |
| | 'Amy' | MJac |
| | 'Amy Lye' | CLoc CSil EBak EKMF MHav SVic |
| | 'Amy Ruth' | CWVF |
| § | 'Andenken an Heinrich Henkel' (T) | CDoC CLoc CWVF EBak EKMF WRou |
| | 'Andenken an R Heinke' **new** | SLBF |
| | 'André Le Nostre' (d) | CWVF EBak SRiF |
| | 'Andreas Schwab' | LCla |
| | ***andrei*** | CDoC LCla |
| | - Berry 4637 | EKMF |
| | 'Andrew' | CDoC EBak EKMF |
| | 'Andrew Carnegie' (d) | CLoc |
| | 'Andrew George' | MJac |
| | 'Andrew Hadfield' | CWVF EKMF MWar SVic WRou |
| I | 'Andromeda' De Groot | CSil |
| | 'Andy Jordens' (d) | WFuv |
| | 'Angela Dawn' **new** | WPBF |
| | 'Angela Leslie' (d) | CLoc CWVF EBak SRiF SVic |
| | 'Angela Rippon' | CWVF MJac |
| | 'Angelika Fuhrmann' (d) | WPBF |
| | 'Angel's Flight' (d) | EBak |
| | 'Anita' (d) | CCCN CLoc CWVF EKMF EPts LAst MHav MJac SLBF SVic WFFs WFuv WGor WPBF WRou |
| | 'Anjo' (v) | CWVF MHav SLBF SRiF |
| | 'Ann Howard Tripp' | CDoC CLoc CWVF MBri MJac SRiF SVic WFuv WPBF WRou |
| | 'Ann Lee' (d) | EBak |
| | 'Ann Marie Batty' **new** | EKMF |
| | 'Anna Louise' | EKMF MWar |
| | 'Anna of Longleat' (d) | CCCN CTsd CWVF EBak MJac SPet WFuv |
| | 'Anna Silvena' | CCCN MHav |
| | 'Annabel' (d) ♀H3 | CCCN CDoC CLoc CTri CTsd CWVF EBak EKMF EPts LAst LCla MBri MJac MWar SLBF SPet SRGP SVic WFFs WFuv WPBF WRou |
| | 'Annabelle Stubbs' (d) | SRGP |
| | 'Anneke de Keijzer' | LCla |
| | 'Annie Den Otter' | WPBF |
| | 'Annie Earle' | EKMF |
| | 'Annie M.G. Schmidt' | EPts WPBF |
| | 'Another Storey' | CSil |
| | 'Anthea Day' (d) | CLoc |
| | 'Anthony Heavens' | SRiF WFFs |
| | 'Antigone' | SLBF SRiF WPBF |
| | ***apetala*** DG 1044 | EKMF |
| | 'Aphrodite' (d) | CLoc CWVF EBak SRiF |
| | 'Applause' (d) | CLoc CWVF EBak EKMF EPts LVER SPet SVic |
| | 'Apple Blossom' | EKMF |
| | ***aprica*** misapplied | see *F.* x *bacillaris* |
| | ***aprica*** Lundell | see *F. microphylla* subsp. *aprica* |
| | 'Apricot Ice' **new** | CLoc |
| | 'Aquarius' | SRiF |
| | 'Arabella' | CWVF |
| | 'Arabella Improved' | CWVF EKMF SVic |
| | ***arborea*** | see *F. arborescens* |
| § | ***arborescens*** | CBcs CDoC CHEx CLoc CSil CWVF EBak EKMF EShb LCla LRHS SRiF SVic WRou WWlt |
| | 'Arcadia Gold' (d) | CWVF SVic |
| | 'Arcady' | CLoc CWVF |
| | 'Ariel' (E) | CDoC CSil SRiF SVic WRou |
| | 'Arlendon' (d) | CWVF |
| | 'Army Nurse' (d) ♀H4 | CDoC CLoc CSil CWVF EKMF EPts MAsh MGos MSmi NBir NDlv SLBF SPet SVic WFFs WFuv |
| | 'Aronst Hoeck' | WPBF |
| | 'Art Deco' (d) | WPBF |
| | 'Arthur Baxter' | EBak SRiF |
| | 'Ashley' | CDoC CTsd LCla |
| | 'Ashley and Isobel' | CWVF |
| | 'Ashtede' | SLBF |
| | 'Athela' | EBak SRiF |
| | 'Atlantic Star' | CWVF EKMF MJac WPBF |
| | 'Atlantis' (d) | CWVF MJac |
| | 'Atlas' | SRiF |
| | 'Atomic Glow' (d) | EBak SVic |
| | 'Aubergine' | see *F.* 'Gerharda's Aubergine' |
| | 'Aubrey Harris' (d) | SRiF |
| | 'Audrey Booth' (d) | SRiF |
| | 'Audrey Dahms' | SRiF |
| | 'Audrey Hepburn' | CWVF |
| | 'Augustin Thierry' (d) | EKMF |
| | 'Aunt Juliana' (d) | EBak |
| | 'Auntie Jinks' | CCCN CDoC CWVF EBak EKMF LAst LCla MJac SPet SVic WFuv WRou |
| | 'Auntie Kit' | SRiF |
| | 'Aurora Superba' | CLoc CTsd CWVF EBak EKMF MHav SRiF WRou |

| | | |
|---|---|---|
| | 'Australia Fair' (d) | CWVF EBak SRiF |
| § | ***austromontana*** | EBak SRiF |
| | 'Autumnale' Y$^{H1+3}$ | CCCN CDoC CHEx CLoc CWVF EBak EKMF EPts LAst LCla LVER NVic SLBF SMrm SPet SPoG SVic WFuv WPBF WRou |
| | 'Avalanche' ambig. (d) | CDoC CLoc CSil EBak EKMF SLBF |
| | 'Avocet' | CLoc EBak SRiF |
| | 'Avon Celebration' (d) | CLoc |
| | 'Avon Gem' | CLoc CSil SRiF |
| | 'Avon Glow' (d) | CLoc |
| | 'Avon Gold' | CLoc |
| | ***ayavacensis*** | CDoC LCla |
| | - Berry 3601 | EKMF |
| | 'Aylisa Rowan' (E) | EKMF |
| | 'Azure Sky' (d) | EKMF MJac WPBF |
| | 'Babette' (d) | EKMF SRiF |
| | 'Baby Blue Eyes' Y$^{H3-4}$ | CDoC CSil CWVF EKMF MAsh WFFs WFuv WRou |
| | 'Baby Blush' | CSil |
| | 'Baby Bright' | CDoC CWVF MHav MWar SLBF SRiF WFFs WRou |
| | 'Baby Chang' | LCla SRiF WPBF |
| | 'Baby Girl' | WFuv |
| | 'Baby Love' **new** | WPBF |
| | 'Baby Pink' (d) | CWVF |
| | 'Baby Thumb' (d/v) | EPts |
| | 'Baby van Eijk' **new** | WPBF |
| | 'Babyface' Tolley (d) **new** | SVic |
| § | x ***bacillaris*** (E) | CChe CDoC CDul CEnt CSil EBak EWes GCal ITim MBlu SEND SLBF SPoG SRms WPBF |
| § | - 'Cottinghamii' (E) | CDoC CSil EKMF IDee WSHC |
| | - 'Oosje' | see *F.* 'Oosje' |
| § | - 'Reflexa' (E) | CAbP CCCN CTrC GQui LAst LSou WFFs |
| | 'Baden Powell' (E) | SRiF SVic |
| | 'Bagworthy Water' | CLoc |
| | 'Bahia' **new** | WPBF |
| | 'Baker's Tri' (T) | EBak |
| | 'Balkonkönigin' | CLoc CWVF EBak SRiF WFuv |
| | 'Ballerina' | CDoC |
| | Ballerina Blue | see *F.* 'Blaue Ballerina' |
| | 'Ballet Girl' (d) Y$^{H1+3}$ | CHrt CLoc CWVF EBak EKMF SLBF SRiF |
| | 'Balmoral' (d) | SRiF |
| | 'Bambini' | CWVF EPts SRiF |
| | 'Banks Peninsula' | GBin GQui |
| | 'Barbara' | CLoc CSil CTsd CWVF EBak EKMF EPts MJac MWar SPet SRiF SVic WEas WFuv WPBF WRou |
| | 'Barbara Evans' | EKMF MWar SLBF SRiF WRou |
| | 'Barbara Norton' | CCCN |
| | 'Barbara Pountain' (d) | CWVF |
| | 'Barbara Windsor' | CWVF MJac SRiF |
| | 'Barbara's Gem' (d) | SRiF |
| | 'Baron de Ketteler' (d) | CSil CTsd EKMF SRiF |
| | 'Baroness van Dedem' | SRiF |
| | 'Barry M. Cox' | WPBF |
| | 'Barry's Queen' | see *F.* 'Golden Border Queen' |
| | 'Bart Comperen' (d) | WPBF |
| | 'Bartje' | WPBF |
| | 'Bashful' (d) | CDoC CSil EPts LCla LRHS SPet SVic WFFs WPBF |
| | 'Beacon' | CDoC CLoc CSil CWVF EBak EKMF ELon EPts LAst MBri MJac NDlv SPet SPoG SRGP SVic WFFs WFuv WRou |
| | 'Beacon Rosa' | CCCN CDoC CLoc CSil CWVF EKMF EPts MBri MJac NDlv SLBF SPet SPoG SVic WFuv WRou |
| | 'Beacon Superior' | CSil |
| | 'Bealings' (d) | CLoc CWVF MBri MHav SRiF SVic WFuv |
| | 'Beau Nash' | CLoc |
| | 'Beauty of Bath' (d) | CLoc EBak |
| | 'Beauty of Bexley' (d) | SRiF |
| | 'Beauty of Cliff Hall' Monk | EKMF |
| | 'Beauty of Clyffe Hall' Lye | CSil EBak |
| | 'Beauty of Exeter' (d) | CWVF EBak EKMF |
| | 'Beauty of Prussia' (d) | CLoc CSil CWVF |
| | 'Beauty of Swanley' | EBak |
| | 'Beauty of Trowbridge' | CWVF LCla |
| | 'Beckey' (d) | SRiF WPBF |
| | 'Becky Jane' | CSil |
| | 'Becky Reynolds' | MWar SRiF |
| | 'Belinda Jane' | WPBF |
| | 'Bella Forbes' (d) Y$^{H1+3}$ | CLoc CSil EBak EKMF MSmi |
| | 'Bella Harris' (d) | SRiF |
| | 'Bella Rosella' (California Dreamers Series) (d) | CCCN CWVF EKMF EPts LAst MJac SCoo SLBF WFuv WPBF |
| | 'Bellbottoms' | SRiF |
| | 'Belsay Beauty' (d) | CWVF MJac SRiF SVic |
| | 'Belvoir Beauty' (d) | CLoc |
| | 'Ben de Jong' (T) | CDoC CTsd LCla SRiF WRou |
| | 'Ben Jammin' | CBgR CDoC CLoc CSil CWVF EPts LAst LCla LSou MJac MWar SPoG SRiF SVic WFFs WFuv WGor WRou |
| | 'Ben Turner' (d) | SRiF |
| | 'Beninkust' **new** | WPBF |
| I | 'Béranger' Lemoine, 1897 (d) | CSil EBak EKMF |
| | 'Berba's Coronation' (d) | WPBF |
| | 'Berba's Happiness' (d) | CWVF |
| | 'Bergnimf' (T) | CTsd SRiF WRou |
| | 'Berliner Kind' (d) | CSil CWVF EBak |
| | 'Bermuda' (d) | CWVF SRiF |
| | 'Bernadette' (d) | CWVF |
| | 'Bernie's Big-un' (d) | MJac |
| | 'Bernisser Hardy' Y$^{H3-4}$ | CDoC CSil EKMF EPts LCla WFFs |
| | 'Bert de Jong' (T) | WPBF |
| | 'Bertha Gadsby' | EKMF |
| | 'Beryl Shaffery' | WPBF |
| | 'Beryl's Choice' (d) | SRiF |
| | 'Berys Elizabeth' | EKMF MWar |
| | 'Bessie Girl' **new** | WPBF |
| | 'Bessie Kimberley' (T) | CDoC EKMF LCla WPBF |
| | 'Beth Robley' (d) | CWVF |
| | 'Betsy Huuskes' **new** | WPBF |
| | 'Betsy Ross' (d) | EBak |
| | 'Bette Sibley' (d) | SRiF |
| | 'Betty Jean' (d) | MWar WPBF |
| | Betty = 'Shabetty'$^{PBR}$ (Shadowdancer Series) | LAst MHav NPri |
| | 'Beverley' | CSil CWVF EBak EKMF EPts SPet SRiF WFFs |
| | 'Bewitched' (d) | EBak |
| | 'Bianca' (d) | CWVF SVic WPBF |
| | 'Bicentennial' (d) | CCCN CDoC CLoc CTsd CWVF EBak EKMF EPts LSou LVER MJac MWar SPet SVic WFuv |
| | 'Big Slim' (T) | SRiF WPBF |
| | 'Bill Gilbert' | SRiF |
| | 'Bill Stevens' (d) | CTsd |
| | 'Billy'$^{PBR}$ | CDoC SRGP |
| | 'Billy Green' (T) Y$^{H1+3}$ | CDoC CLoc CWVF EBak EPts LCla MHer MJac MWar SLBF SPet SRiF SVic WFuv WPBF WRou |
| | 'Bishop's Bells' (d) | CWVF SVic |
| | 'Bits' (d) | CTsd SRiF |
| | 'Bittersweet' (d) | SVic |
| | 'Black Beauty' (d) | CWVF |
| | 'Black Prince' | CDoC CWVF MHav MWar SRiF SVic WFuv |
| | 'Black to the Future' **new** | LAst |
| | 'Blackmore Vale' (d) | CWVF |

| | | |
|---|---|---|
| | 'Blacky' (d) | CCCN EBak LAst MHav SPet SVic WFFs |
| I | 'Blanche Regina' (d) | CWVF MJac |
| | 'Bland's New Striped' | CDoC EBak EKMF EPts SLBF SRiF |
| § | 'Blaue Ballerina' (d) | LAst |
| | 'Blauer Engel' | WPBF |
| | 'Blaze Away' (d) | LAst MBri MJac |
| | 'Bliss' (d) | WPBF |
| | 'Blood Donor' (d) | EKMF MJac |
| | 'Blowick' | CDoC CWVF MBri MJac SPet |
| | 'Blue Beauty' (d) | CSil EBak EKMF |
| | 'Blue Boy' | WFuv WPBF |
| | 'Blue Bush' | CSil CWVF EKMF EPts MJac SVic |
| | 'Blue Butterfly' (d) | CWVF EBak SRiF SVic |
| | 'Blue Eyes' (d) | CDoC MHav NBlu SPet |
| | 'Blue Gown' (d) | CDoC CLoc CSil CWVF EBak EKMF LRHS LVER MGos SPet SVic WFFs WRou |
| | 'Blue Lace' (d) | CSil WFuv |
| | 'Blue Lagoon' ambig. (d) | CWVF |
| | 'Blue Lake' (d) | CWVF LVER |
| | 'Blue Mink' | EBak SRiF |
| | 'Blue Mirage' (d) | CLoc CTsd CWVF EKMF MHav MJac SRiF SVic WFuv |
| | 'Blue Mist' (d) | EBak |
| | 'Blue Pearl' (d) | CDoC CWVF EBak MHav SRiF |
| | 'Blue Pinwheel' | CWVF EBak |
| | 'Blue Sails' | SRiF WPBF |
| | 'Blue Sleighbells' **new** | WPBF |
| | 'Blue Tit' | CSil LCla |
| | 'Blue Veil' (d) | CCCN CLoc CTsd CWVF EKMF LVER MHav MJac SCoo SRiF SVic WFuv |
| | 'Blue Waves' (d) | CLoc CSBt CTsd CWVF EBak MJac MWar SPet SRiF SVic |
| | 'Blush o' Dawn' (d) | CLoc CTsd CWVF EBak EKMF EPts LVER SRiF SVic |
| | 'Blythe' (d) | SRiF |
| | 'Bob Bartrum' | EKMF |
| | 'Bob Pacey' | CWVF |
| | 'Bobby Boy' (d) | EBak |
| | 'Bobby Dazzler' (d) | CWVF EKMF SRiF |
| | 'Bobby Shaftoe' (d) | EBak SRiF WPBF |
| | 'Bobby Wingrove' | EBak |
| | 'Bobby's Girl' | EPts |
| | 'Bobolink' (d) | EBak |
| | 'Bob's Best' (d) | CWVF EPts MJac SRiF |
| | 'Boerhaave' | EBak SRiF |
| | ***boliviana*** Britton | see *F. sanctae-rosae* |
| | ***boliviana*** ambig. | CTsd |
| § | ***boliviana*** Carrière | CDoC CHEx CLoc CWVF EBak EKMF LCla SRiF WRou |
| § | - var. ***alba*** ♀H1+3 | CDoC CLoc EBak EKMF EPts LCla SRiF SVic WRou |
| | - var. ***boliviana*** | CRHN SVic |
| | - f. ***puberulenta*** Munz | see *F. boliviana* Carrière |
| | - var. ***luxurians*** 'Alba' | see *F. boliviana* Carrière var. *alba* |
| | 'Bomber Command' (d) **new** | EKMF |
| | 'Bon Accorde' | CLoc CWVF EBak EKMF EPts SLBF SRiF SVic WFuv WRou |
| | 'Bon Bon' (d) | CTsd CWVF EBak SVic |
| | 'Bonita' (d) | CWVF MJac SVic |
| | 'Bonnie Bambini' | SRiF |
| | 'Bonnie Lass' (d) | EBak |
| | 'Bonny' (d) | CLoc |
| | 'Bora Bora' (d) | CTsd CWVF EBak EKMF SVic |
| | 'Borde Hill' (d) | EPts SLBF |
| | 'Border Princess' | EBak SRiF |
| | 'Border Queen' ♀H3-4 | CDoC CLoc CSil CTsd CWVF EBak EKMF EPts LCla MJac MWar SPet SRiF SVic WFFs WRou |
| | 'Border Raider' | MWar |

| | | |
|---|---|---|
| | 'Border Reiver' | CWVF EBak SVic |
| | 'Börnemann's Beste' | see *F.* 'Georg Börnemann' |
| | 'Boson's Norah' | SRiF |
| | 'Boswinning' | WPBF |
| | 'Bouffant' | CLoc SVic |
| I | 'Bountiful' Munkner (d) | CLoc CWVF EKMF SPet |
| | 'Bouquet' (d) | CDoC CSil EKMF SRiF |
| | 'Bow Bells' | CDoC CLoc CWVF MJac SPet SVic WFuv |
| | 'Boy Marc' (T) | LCla SRiF |
| | 'Braamt's Glorie' | WPBF |
| | ***bracelinae*** | CDoC CSil EKMF |
| | 'Brancaster' | SRiF |
| | 'Brandt's 500 Club' | CLoc EBak SPet |
| | 'Brann's Blossom' | SRiF |
| | 'Breakaway' | SRiF |
| | 'Brechtje' | WPBF |
| | 'Breckland' | EBak SRiF |
| | 'Breeders' Delight' | CSil CWVF MBri SRiF WFFs WFuv |
| | 'Breeder's Dream' (d) | EBak |
| | 'Breevis Electo' (d) **new** | WPBF |
| | 'Breevis Evelien' (d) | WPBF |
| | 'Breevis Homerus' (d) | WPBF |
| | 'Breevis Iris' (d) | WPBF |
| | 'Breevis Lucina' (d) **new** | WPBF |
| | 'Breevis Minimus' | SLBF |
| I | 'Breevis Nobilis' (d) | WPBF |
| | 'Breevis Panclione' (d) **new** | WPBF |
| | 'Breevis Rubi' (d) **new** | WPBF |
| | 'Breevis Selene' (d) | WPBF |
| | 'Breevis Varuna' (d) **new** | WPBF |
| | 'Breevis Zagreus' (d) **new** | WPBF |
| | 'Brenda' (d) | CLoc CWVF EBak WFFs |
| | 'Brenda White' | CDoC CLoc CWVF EBak SVic WRou |
| | 'Brentwood' (d) | EBak |
| | ***brevilobis*** | CSil WPBF |
| | - Berry 4445 | EKMF |
| | 'Brian C. Morrison' (T) | EKMF LCla SRiF |
| | 'Brian G. Soanes' | EBak SRiF |
| | 'Brian Hilton' | MWar |
| | 'Brian Kimberley' (T) | EKMF LCla |
| | 'Bridal Pink' (d) | CTsd |
| | 'Bridal Veil' (d) | EBak |
| | 'Bridesmaid' (d) | CWVF EBak SPet SRiF SVic |
| | 'Brigadoon' (d) | EBak |
| | 'Bright Lights' | EKMF WPBF |
| | 'Brighton Belle' (T) | CDoC CWVF SRiF |
| | 'Brilliant' ambig. | CWVF MHav NDlv WFuv |
| I | 'Brilliant' Bull, 1865 | CDoC CLoc CSil EBak EKMF LCla |
| | 'Briony Caunt' | CSil EKMF |
| | 'British Jubilee' (d) | CWVF EKMF SVic |
| | 'British Sterling' (d) | SRiF |
| | 'Brixham Orpheus' | CWVF |
| | 'Brodsworth' | CSil EKMF |
| | 'Bronze Banks Peninsula' | CSil EKMF |
| | 'Brookwood Belle' (d) | CTsd CWVF EPts LCla MJac SLBF WFFs |
| | 'Brookwood Joy' (d) | CWVF MHav MJac SLBF |
| | 'Brutus' ♀H4 | CDoC CLoc CSil CWVF EBak EKMF EPts LAst LRHS MWat SPet SPoG SVic WBod WFFs WFuv |
| | 'Bryan Breary' (E) | LCla SRiF |
| | 'Bubba Jack' | SLBF |
| | 'Bubble Hanger' | SRiF |
| | 'Buddha' (d) | EBak |
| | 'Bugle Boy' | LCla MWar |
| | 'Bunny' (d) | CWVF EBak SLBF SRiF SVic |
| | 'Burning Bush' **new** | CTsd |
| | 'Burstwick' | CSil |
| | 'Burton Brew' | MJac |
| | 'Buster' (d) | EKMF LCla |
| | 'Buttercup' | CLoc CTsd CWVF EBak MHav SVic |

| | |
|---|---|
| 'C.J. Howlett' | CSil EBak EKMF SRiF |
| 'Caballero' (d) | EBak |
| 'Caesar' (d) | CWVF EBak |
| 'Caitlin' | WPBF |
| 'Caledonia' | CSil EBak EKMF |
| 'California' | WRou |
| 'Callaly Pink' | CWVF |
| 'Cambridge Louie' | CWVF EBak MBri MWar SPet SRiF |
| 'Camcon' | MWar |
| 'Camelot' | SRiF |
| ***campii*** | EKMF |
| ***campos-portoi*** | CDoC CSil CTsd LCla |
| - Berry 4435 | EKMF |
| 'Candlelight' (d) | CLoc CTsd EBak |
| 'Candy Stripe' | CLoc |
| ***canescens*** misapplied | see *F. ampliata* |
| ***canescens*** Benth. | EKMF |
| 'Cannell's Gem' | SRiF |
| 'Canny Bob' | MJac |
| 'Canopy' (d) | CWVF |
| 'Capri' (d) | CTsd CWVF EBak |
| 'Cara Mia' (d) | CLoc CTsd CWVF SPet |
| 'Caradela' (d) | CLoc EKMF MJac MWar |
| 'Cardinal' | CLoc CTsd EKMF WPBF |
| 'Cardinal Farges' (d) | CLoc CSil CWVF EKMF MHav SLBF SPet SRiF SVic WFuv |
| 'Careless Whisper' | LCla SLBF WPBF |
| 'Carioca' | EBak |
| 'Carisbrooke Castle' (d) | EKMF SRiF |
| 'Carl Drude' (d) | CSil CTsd SVic |
| 'Carl Wallace' (d) | EKMF SRiF |
| 'Carla Johnston' 🏆$^{H1+3}$ | CDoC CLoc CWVF EKMF EPts LVER MBri MJac MWar SVic WFuv WPBF WRou |
| 'Carla Knapen' (d) **new** | WPBF |
| 'Carleton George' | MWar |
| 'Carlisle Bells' | WPBF |
| 'Carmel Blue' | CCCN CDoC CLoc CTsd LAst LCla LSou SPet SVic WFuv WGor WRou |
| 'Carmen' Lemoine (d) | CDoC CSil EKMF |
| 'Carmine Bell' | CSil EKMF |
| 'Carnea' | CSil CWib |
| 'Carnival' (d) | CTsd |
| 'Carnoustie' (d) | EBak |
| 'Carol Grace' (d) | CLoc |
| 'Carol Lynn Whittemore' (d) | SRiF |
| 'Carol Nash' (d) | CLoc |
| 'Carol Roe' | EKMF |
| 'Carole Hipkin' **new** | EKMF |
| 'Caroline' | CLoc CWVF EBak EKMF EPts SVic WFuv WPBF WRou |
| 'Caroline's Joy' | CCCN LAst MHav MJac MWar SCoo |
| 'Carol's Choice' **new** | WPBF |
| 'Caron Keating' | WPBF |
| 'Cascade' | CCCN CDoC CLoc CWVF EKMF EPts LAst MBri MJac SPet WFuv WPBF |
| 'Caspar Hauser' (d) | CWVF SLBF SRiF SVic |
| 'Catharina' (T) | SRiF |
| 'Catherine Bartlett' | CWVF EKMF |
| 'Cathie MacDougall' (d) | EBak |
| 'Cecil Glass' | CSil EKMF SRiF |
| 'Cecile' (d) | CCCN CDoC CTsd CWVF EKMF EPts LAst LCla MJac SRGP SVic WFuv WPBF WRou |
| 'Celadore' (d) | CWVF LVER SRiF SVic |
| 'Celebration' (d) | CLoc CWVF |
| 'Celia Smedley' 🏆$^{H3}$ | CCCN CDoC CLoc CSil CTsd CWVF EBak EKMF EPts LCla LVER MBri MJac MWar SLBF SPet SVic WFFs WFuv WRou |
| 'Celine' | MWar |
| 'Centerpiece' (d) | EBak |

| | | |
|---|---|---|
| | 'Ceri' | CLoc |
| | 'Cerrig' | SVic |
| | 'Chameleon' | SPet |
| | 'Champagne Celebration' | CLoc |
| | 'Champagne Gold' | SRiF |
| | 'Champion' | SRiF |
| | 'Chancellor' (d) | CWVF |
| | 'Chandleri' | CWVF EKMF SLBF SVic |
| | 'Chang' 🏆$^{H1+3}$ | CLoc CTsd CWVF EBak EKMF LCla MWar SLBF SVic WPBF |
| | 'Chantry Park' (T) | LCla SRiF |
| | 'Charisma' | SVic |
| § | 'Charles de Gaulle' | SRiF WPBF |
| | 'Charles Edward' (d) | CSil EKMF SRiF |
| | 'Charles Lester' | SRiF |
| | 'Charles Welch' | EPts |
| | Charlie Dimmock = 'Foncha'$^{PBR}$ (d) | CLoc LAst WPBF |
| | 'Charlie Gardiner' | CWVF EBak |
| | 'Charlie Girl' (d) | EBak SVic |
| | 'Charlie Pridmore' (d) | SRiF |
| | 'Charlotte Clyne' | SRiF |
| | 'Charm of Chelmsford' | LCla |
| | 'Charming' | CDoC CLoc CSil CWVF EBak EKMF MJac MWar SPet SVic WRou |
| | 'Chase Delight' (v) | CDoC |
| | 'Chase Royal' **new** | CTsd |
| | 'Chatt's Delight' | EKMF |
| | 'Checkerboard' 🏆$^{H3}$ | CCCN CLoc CSil CTsd CWVF EBak EKMF EPts LCla LVER MJac MWar SLBF SPet SVic WFFs WFuv WPBF |
| | 'Cheeky Chantelle' (d) | SLBF WPBF |
| | 'Cheerio' (d) | SRiF |
| | 'Cheers' (d) | CWVF EKMF WFuv |
| | 'Chelsea Louise' | EPts |
| | 'Chenois Godelieve' | WPBF |
| | 'Cherry'$^{PBR}$ Götz | LAst |
| | 'Cherry Pie' | SRiF |
| | 'Chessboard' | CLoc |
| | 'Chillerton Beauty' 🏆$^{H3}$ | CLoc CSil CTri CWVF EKMF EPts LCla LRHS MAsh MJac SLBF SPer SPet SVic WBod WMnd WPBF WRou |
| | 'China Doll' (d) | CWVF EBak SVic |
| | 'China Lantern' | CLoc CSil CTsd CWVF EBak EKMF SRiF SVic |
| | 'Chomal' (d) | SRiF |
| | 'Chor Echo' | WPBF |
| | 'Chris' | WPBF |
| | 'Chris Nicholls' (d) | CSil EKMF |
| | 'Christina Becker' | SRiF SVic |
| | 'Christine Bamford' | CDoC CSil CTsd CWVF MHav WFFs |
| | 'Christmas Gem' (T) | WPBF |
| | 'Churchtown' | CWVF SRiF |
| | ***cinerea*** | LCla |
| | - Berry 004-86 | EKMF |
| | 'Cinnabarina' (E) | CLoc SLBF SRiF |
| | 'Cinnamon' (d) | WPBF |
| | 'Cinque Port Liberty' (d) | SLBF SRiF |
| | 'Cinvenu' | LCla |
| | 'Cinvulca' | LCla |
| | 'Circe' (d) | CWVF EBak EKMF SVic |
| | 'Circus' | EBak |
| | 'Circus Spangles' (d) | CLoc EKMF LAst |
| | 'Citation' | CLoc CWVF EBak SVic |
| | 'City Lights' **new** | SLBF |
| | 'City of Adelaide' (d) | CLoc |
| | 'City of Leicester' | CWVF MHer SPet |
| | 'Clair de Lune' | CDoC CWVF EBak MHav SVic WRou |
| | 'Claire' | WRou |
| | 'Claire Evans' (d) | CWVF |
| | 'Claire Oram' | CLoc |

| | | |
|---|---|---|
| | 'Clare Frisby' | EKMF WPBF |
| | 'Claudia' (d) | LAst LCla MHav MJac MWar WFuv WRou |
| | 'Cliantha' (d) | CCCN EKMF MJac WFuv WRou |
| | 'Clifford Gadsby' (d) | CTsd EBak SRiF |
| | 'Cliff's Hardy' | CSil EKMF LCla MSmi WFFs |
| | 'Cliff's Own' | SVic |
| | 'Cliff's Unique' (d) | CWVF EPts |
| | 'Clifton Beauty' (d) | CTsd CWVF MJac |
| | 'Clifton Belle' (d) | CWVF |
| | 'Clifton Charm' | CSil EKMF EPts LCla MJac SVic |
| | 'Clipper' | CSil CWVF |
| | 'Cloth of Gold' | CLoc CWVF EBak MHav MJac SPet SRiF SVic |
| | 'Cloverdale Jewel' (d) | CDoC CTsd CWVF EBak MHav SPet SVic |
| | 'Cloverdale Joy' | EBak |
| | 'Cloverdale Pearl' | CTsd CWVF EBak EKMF EPfP SPet SPoG SVic WFFs WPBF |
| | 'Coachman' ♀H4 | CLoc CWVF EBak EKMF EPts LCla MWar SLBF SPet SVic WFuv WRou |
| | 'Cobalt' **new** | SLBF |
| | ***coccinea*** | CDoC CSil CTsd EKMF LCla |
| | 'Codringtonii' | CSil |
| | x ***colensoi*** | CDoC CSil ECou EKMF LCla |
| | 'Colibri' | SRiF |
| | 'Collingwood' (d) | CLoc CWVF EBak |
| | 'Colne Fantasy' (v) | EKMF SRiF |
| | 'Come Dancing' (d) | CDoC CTsd CWVF MHav SPet SVic |
| | 'Comet' Banks | CWVF |
| I | 'Comet' Tiret (d) | CDoC CLoc EBak SPet |
| | 'Comperen Alk' **new** | WPBF |
| | 'Comperen Groenling' **new** | WPBF |
| | 'Comperen Havik' (d) **new** | WPBF |
| | 'Comperen Lineola' (d) **new** | WPBF |
| | 'Comperen Lutea' (d) **new** | WPBF |
| | 'Conchilla' | EBak SRiF |
| | 'Condor' | WPBF |
| | 'Confection' (d) | CTsd |
| | 'Congreve Road' (d) | SRiF |
| | 'Connie' (d) | CSil EBak EKMF SRiF SVic WPBF |
| | 'Conspicua' ♀H3-4 | CSil CWVF EBak EKMF SVic |
| | 'Constable Country' (d) | CWVF SRiF |
| | 'Constance' (d) | CDoC CLoc CSil CTsd CWVF EKMF EPts LCla MJac NDlv SLBF SPet SVic WFFs WPBF WRou |
| | 'Constance Comer' | MJac |
| | 'Constellation' ambig. | CTsd CWVF |
| I | 'Constellation' Schnabel, 1957 (d) | CLoc EBak |
| | 'Continental' (d) | WFuv |
| | 'Coombe Park' | MJac |
| | 'Copycat' | CSil |
| | 'Coquet Bell' | CWVF EBak WPBF |
| | 'Coquet Dale' (d) | CWVF EBak SRiF |
| | 'Coquet Gold' (d/v) | SRiF |
| | 'Coral Baby' (E) | LCla |
| | 'Coral Rose' (d) | SVic |
| | 'Coral Seas' | EBak |
| § | 'Coralle' (T) | CCCN CDoC CLoc CWVF EBak EKMF EPts LCla MHer MJac SLBF SRiF SVic WFuv WRou |
| | 'Corallina' ♀H3-4 | CDoC CLoc CSil CTsd EBak EKMF MHav SPet SVic WFar |
| I | 'Corallina Variegata' (v) | CSil WPBF |
| * | ***cordata*** B&SWJ 9095 | WCru |
| | ***cordifolia*** misapplied | see *F. splendens* |
| | ***cordifolia*** Benth. | CBcs EBak EKMF WRou |
| | - B&SWJ 10325 **new** | WCru |
| | 'Core'ngrato' (d) | CLoc CWVF EBak |
| | ***coriacifolia*** | EKMF |
| | 'Cornelia Smith' (T) | LCla |

| | |
|---|---|
| 'Cornwall Calls' (d) | EBak |
| 'Corrie Barten' (d) **new** | WPBF |
| 'Corsage' (d) | CWVF SVic |
| 'Corsair' (d) | EBak SVic |
| ***corymbiflora*** misapplied | see *F. boliviana* Carrière |
| ***corymbiflora*** Ruíz & Pav. | CDoC EBak EKMF SVic |
| - Berry 4688 | EKMF |
| - ***alba*** | see *F. boliviana* Carrière var. *alba* |
| 'Cosmopolitan' (d) | EBak |
| 'Costa Brava' | CLoc EBak |
| 'Cotta Bright Star' | CWVF EKMF LCla WFFs |
| 'Cotta Carousel' | EKMF LCla |
| 'Cotta Christmas Tree' (T) | CDoC EKMF LCla SLBF SRiF |
| 'Cotta Fairy' | CWVF EKMF |
| 'Cotta Two Thousand' | EKMF SRiF |
| 'Cotta Vino' | EKMF SRiF SVic |
| 'Cottinghamii' | see *F.* x *bacillaris* 'Cottinghamii' |
| 'Cotton Candy' (d) | CLoc CWVF LCla SVic |
| 'Countdown Carol' (d) | EPts |
| 'Countess of Aberdeen' | CLoc CSil CWVF EBak EKMF SLBF SRiF WFuv |
| 'Countess of Maritza' (d) | CLoc CWVF |
| 'County Park' | CTsd ECou |
| 'Court Jester' (d) | CLoc EBak |
| 'Cover Girl' (d) | EBak EPts MJac SPet WPBF |
| 'Coxeen' | EBak |
| 'Crackerjack' | CLoc EBak |
| ***crassistipula*** Berry 3553 | EKMF |
| 'Cream Puff' **new** | CTsd |
| 'Creampuff' (d) | CDoC |
| 'Crescendo' (d) | CLoc CWVF |
| 'Crinkley Bottom' (d) | EPts LVER MJac SLBF SRiF WFuv |
| 'Crinoline' (d) | EBak |
| 'Crosby Serendipity' | CLoc |
| 'Crosby Soroptimist' | CWVF MJac MWar SRiF WFFs WRou |
| 'Cross Check' | CWVF MBri MJac SRiF WFuv |
| 'Crusader' (d) | CWVF |
| 'Crystal Blue' | EBak SVic |
| 'Crystal Stars' (d) | SVic |
| 'Cupid' | CSil EBak |
| 'Curly Q' | EBak SPet SVic |
| 'Curtain Call' (d) | CLoc CTsd CWVF EBak SVic |
| 'Cutie Karen' (d) | SRiF |
| x ***cuzco*** | EKMF |
| ***cylindracea*** misapplied | see *F.* x *bacillaris* |
| ***cylindracea*** Lindl. (E) | CSil LCla SRiF |
| - (m/E) BRE 43908 | EKMF |
| 'Cymon' (d) | CWVF SRiF |
| 'Cymru' (d) | SVic |
| 'Cyndy Robyn' (d) | SRiF WPBF |
| ***cyrtandroides*** | CSil |
| - Berry 4628 | EKMF |
| 'Dainty' | EBak |
| 'Dainty Lady' (d) | EBak |
| 'Daisy Bell' | CDoC CLoc CTsd CWVF EBak EKMF LCla MJac SPet SVic WRou |
| 'Dalton' | EBak |
| 'Dana Samantha' | EPts |
| 'Dancing Bloom' | EPts |
| 'Dancing Elves' (d) | WPBF |
| 'Dancing Flame' (d) ♀H1+3 | CCCN CHrt CLoc CTsd CWVF EBak EKMF EPts LAst LCla LVER MBri MJac MWar SLBF SPet SVic WFFs WFuv WPBF |
| 'Daniel Reynolds' **new** | MWar WPBF |
| 'Danielle' | WRou |
| 'Danielle Frijstein' | WPBF |
| 'Danish Pastry' | CTsd CWVF SPet |
| 'Danny Boy' (d) | CLoc CWVF EBak EKMF SVic WFuv WPBF |
| 'Danny Kaye' (d) | WPBF |
| 'Danson Belle' (d) | SRiF |

| | |
|---|---|
| 'Dark Eyes' (d) $\Upsilon^{H4}$ | CCCN CLoc CSil CTsd CWVF EBak EKMF LAst MBri MJac SLBF SPet SSea SVic WFuv WPBF |
| 'Dark Night' (d) | CSil |
| 'Dark Secret' (d) | EBak |
| 'Dark Treasure' (d) | CDoC CTsd EKMF |
| 'Darreen Dawn' (d) | WPBF |
| 'Daryn John Woods' | CDoC LCla SRiF |
| 'Dave's Delight' | EKMF WPBF |
| 'David' $\Upsilon^{H3-4}$ | CDoC CLoc CSil CWVF EKMF EOHP EPts LAst LCla LSou SLBF SPoG SRGP SRiF WFFs WFuv WGor WRou |
| 'David Alston' (d) | CLoc CWVF EBak |
| 'David Lockyer' (d) | CLoc CWVF SVic |
| 'David Savage' (d) | LCla |
| 'David Ward' (d) | WPBF |
| 'Dawn' | EBak |
| 'Dawn Carless' (d) | CDoC WPBF |
| 'Dawn Fantasia' (v) | CLoc EKMF EPts MHav MWar WPBF |
| 'Dawn Mist' (d) **new** | WFuv |
| 'Dawn Redfern' (d) | CWVF |
| 'Dawn Sky' (d) | EBak |
| 'Dawn Star' (d) | CCCN CTsd CWVF MHav MJac SVic WFuv |
| 'Dawn Thunder' (d) | CTsd SVic |
| 'Day by Day' | CSil |
| 'Day Star' | EBak SRiF |
| 'De Groot's Beauty' | WPBF |
| 'De Groot's Black Beauty' (d) | WPBF |
| 'De Groot's Lady' **new** | WPBF |
| 'De Groot's Moonlight' | WPBF |
| 'De Groot's Parade' | WPBF |
| 'De Groot's Regenboog' | WPBF |
| 'Deal Marine' (d) | SRiF |
| 'Debby' (d) | EBak |
| 'Deben Petite' (E) | LCla |
| 'Deben Rose' | CTsd SRiF |
| 'Deborah Street' (d) | CLoc |
| § ***decussata*** Ruíz & Pav. | CDoC EBak |
| - Berry 3049 | EKMF |
| 'Dee Copley' (d) | EBak |
| 'Dee Star' (d) | SVic |
| 'Deep Purple' (d) | CCCN CDoC CLoc CWVF EKMF LAst MJac SCoo SLBF SPoG WFuv WPBF |
| 'Delilah' (d) | CWVF |
| 'Delta's Angelique' | WPBF |
| 'Delta's Bride' | SLBF |
| 'Delta's Dream' | CTsd CWVF WPBF |
| 'Delta's Drop' | SLBF SRiF SVic WPBF |
| 'Delta's Groom' | LCla WRou |
| 'Delta's Ko' (d) | SVic |
| 'Delta's Matador' | CCCN MHav |
| 'Delta's Paljas' | WPBF |
| 'Delta's Parade' (d) | EPts |
| 'Delta's Pim' | WPBF |
| 'Delta's Rien' | SVic |
| 'Delta's Sara' | LAst LRHS MAsh WPBF |
| 'Delta's Song' | WPBF WRou |
| 'Delta's Symphonie' (d) | CWVF |
| 'Delta's Wonder' | CSil SVic |
| 'Demi van Roovert' | WPBF |
| § ***denticulata*** | CDoC CLoc CWVF EBak EKMF EPts LCla MHer SLBF SRiF SVic WPBF WRou |
| ***dependens*** | EKMF |
| 'Derby Imp' | CWVF SRiF WFFs |
| 'Desperate Daniel' | EPts |
| 'Devonshire Dumpling' (d) | CCCN CDoC CLoc CTsd CWVF EBak EKMF EPts LAst LVER MBri MJac MWar SLBF SPet SVic WFuv WPBF |
| 'Diablo' (d) | EBak |
| 'Diamond Celebration' (d) | EKMF MWar |
| 'Diamond Wedding' | SRiF SVic |
| 'Diana' (d) | EBak |
| 'Diana Princess of Wales' **new** | LAst LSou MJac STes SVil WFuv |
| 'Diana Wills' (d) | CWVF |
| 'Diana Wright' | CSil EKMF |
| 'Diane Brown' | CWVF EKMF WFuv WPBF |
| 'Diane Marie' | EKMF |
| 'Dick Swinbank' (d) | SRiF |
| § 'Die Schöne Wilhelmine' | SLBF SVic WFuv WPBF |
| 'Dilly-Dilly' (d) | CWVF |
| 'Dimples' (d) | CSil MBri SRiF |
| 'Dipton Dainty' (d) | CLoc EBak MHav SRiF SVic |
| 'Display' $\Upsilon^{H4}$ | CCCN CDoC CLoc CSil CWVF EBak EKMF EPts LAst LCla LVER MBri MJac NPer SLBF SPet SPoG SSea SVic WFFs WFar WFuv WPBF WRou |
| 'Doc' | CDoC CSil EPts MHav SPet SVic WFuv |
| 'Docteur Topinard' | CLoc EBak EKMF |
| 'Doctor' | see *F.* 'The Doctor' |
| 'Doctor Brenden Freeman' | CDoC |
| 'Doctor Foster' $\Upsilon^{H4}$ | CDoC CLoc CSil CTri EBak EKMF EPfP SVic WEas |
| 'Doctor Mason' | CWVF |
| 'Doctor Olson' (d) | CLoc EBak SRiF |
| 'Doctor Robert' | CWVF EKMF EPts MBri MJac SRiF SVic WFuv |
| 'Dodo' | WPBF |
| § 'Dollar Prinzessin' $\Upsilon^{H4}$ | CCCN CDoC CLoc CSil CWVF EBak EKMF EPfP EPts LAst LCla MAsh MBri MJac MWar NDlv NPer SLBF SPet SPlb SVic WBVN WFFs WFar WFuv WPBF |
| 'Dollie Pausch' **new** | WPBF |
| 'Dolly Daydream' (d) | EKMF |
| 'Domacin' (d) | CDoC |
| 'Dominique' (d) | EKMF |
| 'Dominyana' | CSil CTsd EBak EKMF LCla |
| 'Don Peralta' | EBak |
| 'Dopy' (d) | CDoC CSil EPts SPet SVic WFuv |
| 'Doreen Redfern' | CLoc CTsd CWVF MHav MJac SPet SVic WRou |
| 'Doreen Stroud' (d) | CWVF |
| 'Doretteke' **new** | WPBF |
| 'Dorian Brogdale' | SRiF |
| 'Doris Deaves' | SLBF |
| 'Doris Joan' | SLBF WPBF |
| 'Dorking Blue' (d) | SRiF |
| 'Dorking Delight' | SRiF |
| 'Dorothea Flower' | CLoc CSil CWVF EBak EKMF |
| 'Dorothy' | CSil EKMF LCla SLBF SPet WFFs |
| 'Dorothy Ann' | LCla SLBF WPBF |
| 'Dorothy Cheal' | CWVF |
| 'Dorothy Day' (d) | CLoc |
| 'Dorothy Hanley' (d) | CBgR CCCN CLoc CSil EKMF EPts LAst LSRN LSou MAsh MBri MJac SLBF SPet SPoG SRiF SVic WFFs WFuv WGor WPBF WRou |
| 'Dorothy Oosting' (d) | WPBF |
| 'Dorothy Shields' (d) | CWVF MHav MJac |
| 'Dorrian Brogdale' (T) | LCla |
| 'Dorset Abigail' | CWVF |
| 'Dorset Delight' (d) | CWVF |
| 'Dot Woodage' | SRiF |
| 'Double Trouble' **new** | WPBF |
| 'Douglas Boath' (d) **new** | WFuv |
| 'Dove House' | EKMF |
| 'Dragon Fang' **new** | WPBF |
| 'Drake 400' (d) | CLoc |
| 'Drama Girl' (d) | CWVF |
| 'Drame' (d) | CDoC CSil CWVF EBak EKMF LCla SPet SRiF SVic WRou |

| | | |
|---|---|---|
| | 'Drum Major' (d) | EBak |
| | 'Du Barry' (d) | EBak |
| | 'Duchess of Albany' | CLoc EBak |
| | 'Duchess of Cornwall' (d) | CSil EPts SRiF |
| | 'Duet' (d) | CTsd SRiF SVic |
| I | 'Duke of Wellington' Haag, 1956 (d) | CLoc |
| | 'Dulcie Elizabeth' (d) | CWVF EBak MJac SPet |
| | 'Dunrobin Bedder' | CSil |
| | 'Dusky Beauty' | CWVF SVic WRou |
| | 'Dusky Rose' (d) | CLoc CWVF EBak MHav MJac SVic |
| | 'Dutch Mill' | CLoc CWVF EBak SRiF |
| | 'Duyfken' | CTsd CWVF SRiF |
| | 'Dying Embers' | CLoc |
| | 'Dymph Werker van Groenland' (E) | EKMF LCla MWar WPBF |
| | 'Earre Barré' | SRiF WPBF |
| | 'East Anglian' | CLoc EBak SRiF |
| | 'Easter Bonnet' (d) | CLoc CWVF |
| | 'Ebanflo' | EBak MWar |
| | 'Ebbtide' (d) | CLoc EBak |
| | 'Echo' | CLoc CWVF |
| | 'Ectors Nursery' | WPBF |
| | 'Ed Largarde' (d) | EBak EKMF |
| | 'Eden Lady' | CDoC CLoc CTsd SPet SRiF WRou |
| | 'Eden Princess' | CWVF MJac |
| | 'Eden Rock' (d) | SRGP |
| | 'Edie Lester' | SRiF |
| | 'Edith' ambig. | EPts NDlv WRou |
| | 'Edith' Banks | SRiF |
| | 'Edith' Brown (d) | CSil EKMF LCla SLBF |
| | 'Edith Emery' (d) | SPet SRiF |
| | 'Edna May' | CWVF |
| | 'Edna W. Smith' | CWVF |
| | 'Edwin J. Jones' | SLBF |
| | 'Eileen Drew' | SLBF |
| | 'Eileen Raffill' | EBak |
| | 'Eileen Saunders' | CSil EBak |
| | 'Eileen Storey' | EKMF |
| | 'Eisleban' | SRiF |
| | 'El Camino' (d) | CWVF LAst |
| | 'El Cid' | CLoc CSil EBak EKMF SRiF SVic |
| | 'Elaine Ann' | EPts MJac |
| | 'Elaine Taylor' (d) | MJac |
| | 'Eleanor Clark' | WPBF |
| | 'Eleanor Leytham' | CWVF EBak EKMF LCla SRiF SVic WRou |
| | 'Eleanor Rawlins' | CSil EBak EKMF SRiF |
| | 'Elf' | CSil |
| | 'Elfin Glade' | CLoc CSil CWVF EBak SRiF |
| | 'Elfrida' (d) | CSil EKMF WPBF |
| | 'Elfriede Ott' (T) | CLoc EBak LCla SRiF WPBF |
| | 'Elizabeth' ambig. | CTsd |
| I | 'Elizabeth' Whiteman, 1941 | EBak EKMF |
| I | 'Elizabeth' Tiret, 1970 (d) | WPBF |
| | 'Elizabeth Broughton' | EKMF |
| | 'Elizabeth Haverkamp' | LCla |
| | 'Elizabeth Honnorine' | SVic |
| | 'Elizabeth Tompkins' (d) | MJac |
| | 'Elizabeth Travis' (d) | EBak |
| | 'Ellen Morgan' (d) | CWVF EBak |
| | 'Elma' | LCla |
| | 'Elsa' (d) | CWVF LRHS SPet SVic |
| | 'Elsie Maude' (d) | CWVF SRiF |
| | 'Elsie Mitchell' (d) | CTsd CWVF SPet SRiF WRou |
| | 'Elsie Vert' (d) | WPBF |
| | 'Elsstar' (d) | SRiF WPBF |
| | 'Elysée' | CSil EKMF |
| § | 'Emile de Wildeman' (d) | CWVF EBak EKMF LVER SPet WFuv |
| | 'Emile Zola' | CSil |
| | 'Emily' | WPBF |
| | 'Emily Austen' (T) | CWVF |
| | 'Emma Alice' (d) | CWVF |
| | 'Emma Margaret' | SLBF |
| | 'Emma Massey' | SRiF |
| | 'Emmakins' (d) **new** | EKMF |
| | 'Empress of Prussia' Υ$^{H4}$ | CDoC CLoc CSil CWVF EBak EKMF EPts ERas LAst LRHS SLBF SPet SVic WMnd WPBF WRou |
| | 'Enchanted' (d) | CWVF EBak MWar |
| | ***encliandra*** subsp. ***encliandra*** (E) | CDoC EKMF WRou |
| * | - var. ***gris*** (E) | CSil |
| | - subsp. ***microphylloides*** (E) Berry & Brako 7592 | EKMF |
| § | - subsp. ***tetradactyla*** (E) | EKMF |
| § | 'Enfant Prodigue' (d) | CDoC CLoc CSil EKMF SDix SLBF SMrm SVic WMnd |
| | 'English Rose' (d) | CWVF SRiF WPBF |
| | 'Enstone' | see *F. magellanica* var. *molinae* 'Enstone' |
| | 'Eric's Everest' (d) | EKMF |
| | 'Eric's Majestic' (d) | EKMF MJac SRiF |
| | 'Erik' | SLBF |
| | 'Erika Köth' (T) | LCla SRiF |
| | 'Ernest Rankin' | CSil SVic |
| | 'Ernie'$^{PBR}$ | EKMF LAst SLBF SRGP |
| | 'Ernie Bromley' | CSil CWVF SLBF SRiF |
| | 'Ernie Wise' (d) | LAst MJac SCoo |
| | 'Eroica' | SVic |
| | 'Errol' (d) | CLoc |
| | 'Esmerelda' | MJac |
| | 'Estafette' (d) | SRiF |
| | 'Estelle Marie' | CLoc CWVF EBak EKMF MBri MWar SLBF SPet SVic WFuv WRou |
| | 'Eternal Flame' (d) | CTsd CWVF EBak EPts MBri SVic WFuv |
| | 'Ethel' ambig. | WPBF |
| | 'Ethel May' (d) | MJac |
| | 'Ethel Wilson' | CSil |
| | 'Eureka Red' (Californian Dreamers Series) (d) | CWVF |
| | 'Eurofuchsia' (d) **new** | WPBF |
| | 'Eurydice' (d) | CLoc |
| | 'Eusebia' (d) | CTsd MJac SRiF SVic |
| | 'Eva Boerg' | CCCN CLoc CSil CTri CWVF EBak EKMF LAst LCla MBri SPet SVic WFFs WFuv WKif WPBF |
| | 'Evelyn Stanley' (d) | CWVF |
| § | 'Evelyn Steele Little' | EBak |
| | 'Evening Sky' (d) | EBak SRiF |
| | 'Evensong' | CLoc CTsd CWVF EBak SVic WFuv |
| | 'Everbeur' (d) **new** | WPBF |
| | ***excorticata*** | CBcs CDoC CPLG CSil CTsd EKMF SPlb |
| | 'Exmoor Woods' | CSil |
| | 'Expo '86' (d) | SRiF WFuv |
| | 'Eynsford' (d) | SRiF |
| | 'Fabian Franck' (T) | CDoC LCla MHav SRiF |
| | 'Fairy Falls' | WRou |
| | 'Falklands' (d) | CSil SLBF SRiF |
| | 'Falling Stars' | CLoc CTsd CWVF EBak SVic |
| | 'Fan Dancer' (d) | EBak |
| | 'Fancy Free' (d) | MBri |
| | 'Fancy Pants' (d) | CLoc CWVF EBak SVic |
| | 'Fanfare' (T) | CDoC EBak EKMF LCla SVic WRou |
| | 'Farningham' | SRiF |
| | 'Fascination' | see *F.* 'Emile de Wildeman' |
| | 'Fashion' (d) | EBak |
| | 'Favourite' | EBak |
| | 'Felicity Kendal' (d) | MJac SCoo |
| | 'Feltham's Pride' | CWVF EKMF |
| | 'Fenman' | CWVF SRiF SVic |
| | 'Fergie' (d) | SRiF |
| | 'Festival Lights' (E) | SLBF |
| | 'Festoon' | EBak |

| | |
|---|---|
| 'Fey' (d) | CWVF EKMF MHav SRiF WFuv |
| 'Ffion' | EPts |
| 'Fiery Spider' | EBak SVic |
| 'Fighter Command' **new** | EKMF |
| 'Finn' | CWVF EPts MHav |
| 'Fiona' | CDoC CLoc CWVF EBak MHav SPet SRiF SVic |
| 'Fiona Pitt' (E) | SRiF |
| 'Fiorelli Flowers' (d) | WPBF |
| 'Fire Mountain' (d) | CLoc MHav SVic |
| 'Firecracker'PBR | see *F.* 'John Ridding' |
| 'Firefly' | LAst SVic |
| 'Firelite' (d) | EBak |
| 'Firenza' (d) | CWVF SRiF |
| 'First Kiss' (d) | CWVF |
| 'First Lady' (d) | CTsd CWVF |
| 'First Lord' | CWVF |
| 'First of the Day' | SRiF |
| 'First Success' (E) | CDoC CTsd CWVF EKMF LCla SRiF SVic WRou |
| 'Flair' (d) | CLoc CWVF |
| 'Flame' | EBak |
| 'Flamenco Dancer' (California Dreamers Series) (d) | CLoc CWVF |
| 'Flament Rose' **new** | WPBF |
| 'Flamingo' (d) **new** | SVic |
| 'Flash' ♀H3-4 | CLoc CSil CTri CWVF EBak EKMF EPfP EPts LCla MJac SLBF SPet SRiF SVic WFFs WFuv WRou |
| 'Flashlight' | CDoC CSil CWVF EPfP EWld LAst LSou MHav MJac WFFs WPBF |
| 'Flashlight Amélioré' | CSil |
| 'Flat Jack o' Lancashire' (d) | CSil EKMF SLBF |
| 'Flavia' (d) | EBak |
| 'Fleur de Picardie' | SLBF |
| 'Flirtation Waltz' (d) | CLoc CTsd CWVF EBak EKMF LVER MJac SPet SRiF SVic WFuv |
| 'Flocon de Neige' | CSil EBak |
| 'Flor Izel' (d) **new** | WPBF |
| 'Floral City' (d) | CLoc EBak |
| 'Florence Mary Abbott' | WPBF |
| 'Florence Taylor' (d) | CWVF |
| 'Florence Turner' | CSil EBak EKMF SRiF |
| 'Florentina' (d) | CLoc CWVF EBak EKMF SVic |
| 'Florrie Lester' (d) | SRiF |
| 'Florrie's Gem' (d) | SLBF |
| 'Flowerdream' (d) | CWVF |
| 'Flyaway' (d) | EBak |
| 'Fly-by-night' (d) | CWVF |
| 'Flying Cloud' (d) | CLoc CSil CWVF EBak EKMF MBri SVic |
| 'Flying Scotsman' (d) | CCCN CDoC CLoc CTsd CWVF EBak EKMF EPts MJac SCoo SVic WFuv WRou |
| 'Folies Bergères' (d) | EBak |
| 'Foline' | SVic |
| 'Foolke' | CSil EBak SRiF |
| 'Forfar's Pride' (d) | CSil SRiF |
| 'Forget-me-not' | CLoc CSil CWVF EBak EKMF SVic WFFs WPBF |
| 'Forgotten Dreams' **new** | WPBF |
| 'Fort Bragg' (d) | CWVF EBak SRiF |
| 'Fort Royal' | WRou |
| 'Forward Look' | SRiF |
| 'Fountains Abbey' (d) | CWVF |
| 'Four Farthings' (d) | EKMF EPts |
| 'Foxgrove Wood' ♀H3-4 | CSil CWVF EBak EKMF EPts SLBF WFFs |
| 'Foxtrot' (d) | CWVF |
| 'Foxy Lady' (d) | CWVF EKMF WPBF |
| 'Frances Haskins' | CSil SRiF WRou |
| 'Frank Saunders' | CWVF LAst LCla WPBF |
| 'Frank Unsworth' (d) | CWVF EKMF EPts MJac SPet WFuv WPBF |
| 'Frankie's Magnificent Seven' (d) | EPts |
| 'Franz von Zon' **new** | LCla |
| 'Frau Hilde Rademacher' (d) | CDoC CSil CWVF EBak EKMF EPts MHav MSmi SLBF SRiF SVic |
| 'Frauke' | SVic |
| 'Fred Hansford' | CSil CWVF |
| 'Fred Shepherd' | SRiF |
| 'Fred Swales' (T) | WPBF |
| 'Frederick Woodward' (T) | EKMF |
| 'Fred's First' (d) | CDoC CSil EKMF SRiF |
| 'Freefall' | EBak |
| 'Friendly Fire' (d) | CLoc |
| 'Frosted Flame' | CCCN CDoC CLoc CTsd CWVF EBak EKMF LAst LCla MJac SPet SSea |
| 'Frühling' (d) | CSil EBak EKMF |
| 'Fuchsiade' | WRou |
| 'Fuchsiade '88' | CLoc CSil CTsd CWVF EBak EKMF |
| 'Fuchsiarama '91' (T) | CWVF WRou |
| 'Fuji-San' | CDoC ELon EPts SRiF |
| 'Fuksie Foetsie' (E) | CDoC CSil SRiF |
| ***fulgens*** ♀H1+3 | CDoC EKMF GCal LCla WFFs WPBF WRou |
| * - var. ***minuata*** | EKMF |
| * - 'Variegata' (T/v) | CDoC CLoc EKMF EPts LCla SRiF WRou |
| 'Fulpila' (T) | EKMF LCla SLBF SRiF |
| ***furfuracea*** | EKMF |
| 'Für Elise' (d) | EBak |
| 'Gala' (d) | EBak |
| 'Galadriel' | WPBF |
| 'Ganzenhof' | LCla |
| 'Garden News' (d) ♀H3-4 | CCCN CDoC CLoc COlW CSil CWVF EKMF EPts LAst LCla LRHS LVER MAsh MJac MWar NPer SLBF SPet SVic WFFs WFar WMnd WPBF WRou |
| 'Garden Week' (d) | CTsd CWVF SVic |
| 'Gartenmeister Bonstedt' (T) ♀H1+3 | CCCN CDoC CLoc CWVF EBak EKMF LCla SPet SRiF SSea SVic |
| 'Gary Rhodes' (d) | EBak MJac SCoo WFuv |
| 'Gay Fandango' (d) | CLoc CTsd CWVF EBak SPet |
| 'Gay Future' | EKMF |
| 'Gay Parasol' (d) | CCCN CLoc LAst MJac SVic WFuv WRou |
| 'Gay Paree' (d) | EBak |
| 'Gay Senorita' | EBak |
| 'Gay Spinner' (d) | CLoc |
| 'Geeskie Guskie' | SRiF |
| ***gehrigeri*** | EBak EKMF |
| ***gehrigeri*** x ***nigricans*** | EKMF |
| 'Gemma Fisher' (d) | EPts |
| Gene = 'Goetzgene'PBR (Shadowdancer Series) | LAst LSou MHav NPri SCoo WCot |
| 'Général Charles de Gaulle' | see *F.* 'Charles de Gaulle' |
| 'Général Monk' (d) | CDoC CSil CTsd CWVF EBak EKMF EPts LAst MBri SRGP SRiF SVic |
| 'Général Voyron' | CSil |
| 'General Wavell' (d) | CTsd SRiF SVic |
| 'Genii' ♀H4 | Widely available |
| 'Geoff Oke' **new** | MWar WPBF |
| 'Geoffrey Smith' (d) | CSil EKMF EPts MSmi |
| § 'Georg Börnemann' (T) | CLoc CWVF EBak SRiF WFFs WPBF |
| 'George Allen White' | CDoC CWVF WPBF |
| 'George Barr' | EKMF LRHS SRiF WPBF |
| 'George Johnson' | CDoC CTsd SPet |
| 'George Travis' (d) | EBak SRiF |
| 'Gerald Drewitt' | CSil |
| § 'Gerharda's Aubergine' | CDoC CLoc CSil CWVF EKMF SRiF |
| 'Gesneriana' | CDoC CLoc EBak SRiF WWlt |

| | | |
|---|---|---|
| | 'Ghislaine' (d) | MHav |
| | 'Giant Pink Enchanted' (d) | CLoc EBak |
| | 'Gilda' (d) | CWVF MJac SVic |
| | 'Gillian Althea' (d) | CDoC CTsd CWVF SRGP SRiF WFuv |
| | 'Gilt Edge' (v) | CLoc |
| | 'Gimlie' | WPBF |
| I | 'Gina' | WPBF |
| | 'Gina Bowman' (E) | LCla SLBF |
| | 'Ginger' | MHav |
| | Ginger = 'Goetzginger' PBR (Shadowdancer Series) | LAst LSou NPri SCoo |
| | 'Gingham Girl' (d) | SRiF |
| | 'Giovanna and Wesley' (d) | SRiF |
| | 'Gipsy Princess' (d) | CLoc |
| | 'Girls' Brigade' | CWVF EKMF |
| | 'Gitana' | WPBF |
| | 'Gladiator' (d) | EBak EKMF LCla SVic |
| | 'Gladys Godfrey' | EBak |
| | 'Gladys Lorimer' | CWVF EPts |
| | 'Gladys Miller' | CLoc |
| | ***glazioviana*** (T) | CDoC CSil CTsd CWVF EKMF LCla MHer SLBF SRiF WRou |
| | 'Glenby' (d) | CWVF SRiF |
| | 'Glendale' | CWVF |
| | 'Glitters' | CWVF EBak |
| § | 'Globosa' | CAgr CSil EBak EKMF SRiF |
| | 'Gloria Johnson' | EKMF |
| | 'Glow' | CSil EBak EKMF |
| | 'Glowing Embers' | EBak |
| | Glowing Lilac (d) | EPts WFuv |
| | 'Glyn Jones' (d) | EKMF |
| | 'Gold Brocade' | CSil MBri SPet SPoG SSto |
| | 'Gold Crest' | EBak |
| | 'Gold Leaf' | CWVF |
| | 'Golden Amethyst' (d) | SRiF |
| | 'Golden Anniversary' (d) | CLoc CWVF EBak EKMF LVER MJac SVic WFuv WPBF |
| | 'Golden Arrow' (T) | CDoC LCla SRiF SVic |
| § | 'Golden Border Queen' | CLoc CSil EBak SPet |
| | 'Golden Dawn' | CLoc CWVF EBak SPet SRiF SVic |
| | 'Golden Girl' | SLBF |
| | 'Golden Herald' | CSil SLBF |
| | 'Golden la Campanella' (d/v) | CLoc MBri |
| | 'Golden Lena' (d/v) | CSil CWVF |
| | 'Golden Margaret Roe' (v) | CSil |
| | 'Golden Marinka' (v) 🏆H3 | CCCN CLoc EBak EKMF LAst LRHS LSou MBri SPet SVic WPBF |
| | 'Golden Melody' (d) | CSil SRiF |
| | 'Golden Peppermint Stick' (d) | CTsd SRiF |
| | 'Golden Swingtime' (d) | CTsd MBri MHav MJac SPet SSea SVic WFuv |
| | 'Golden Treasure' (v) | CLoc CSil CWVF EKMF MBri MWar |
| | 'Golden Vergeer' (v) | SLBF |
| | 'Golden Wedding' | EKMF SVic |
| | 'Goldsworth Beauty' | CSil SRiF |
| | 'Golondrina' | CSil CWVF EBak |
| | 'Goody Goody' | EBak SRiF SVic |
| | 'Gooseberry Hill' | SRiF |
| | 'Goosebery Belle' | SRiF WRou |
| | 'Gordon Boy' (d) | CSil |
| | 'Gordon Thorley' | CSil EKMF |
| | 'Gordon's China Rose' | LCla |
| | 'Gota' | WPBF |
| | 'Gottingen' (T) | EBak EKMF SRiF WPBF |
| | 'Gouden Pater' (d) **new** | WPBF |
| | 'Governor Pat Brown' (d) | EBak |
| | 'Grace Darling' | CWVF EBak |
| | ***gracilis*** | see *F. magellanica* var. *gracilis* |
| | 'Graf Witte' | CDoC CSil CWVF EKMF SPet SRiF SVic |
| | 'Granada' (d) | SRiF |
| | 'Grand Duchess' | WPBF |
| | 'Grand Duke' (T/d) | CWVF |
| | 'Grand Prix' (d) | CTsd SVic |
| | 'Grand Slam' (d) | CTsd SVic |
| | 'Grandad Hobbs' (d) | LCla SLBF |
| | 'Grandma Hobbs' | LCla |
| | 'Grandma Sinton' (d) | CLoc CTsd CWVF MBri |
| | 'Grandpa George' (d) | LCla SRiF |
| | 'Grandpa Jack' (d) | SLBF |
| | 'Grasmere' (T) | SRiF |
| | 'Grayrigg' | CDoC CSil CTsd EKMF EPts LCla SRiF |
| | 'Great Ouse' (d) | EPts |
| | 'Great Scott' (d) | CLoc CTsd |
| | 'Green 'n' Gold' | EBak |
| | 'Greenpeace' | CDoC CTsd EKMF SVic |
| | 'Greta' (T) | MWar SRiF WPBF |
| | 'Gretna Chase' | MBri SRiF |
| | 'Grey Lady' (d) | CSil SRiF SVic |
| | 'Gris' | SRiF |
| | 'Groene Boelvaar' (d) | WPBF |
| | 'Groenekan's Glorie' | CTsd EKMF SVic WPBF |
| | 'Groovy' **new** | WPBF |
| | 'Grumpy' | CDoC CSil CWVF EPts LRHS MHav SPet SVic WFuv |
| | 'Grumpy Gord' **new** | MWar |
| | 'Gruss aus dem Bodethal' | CLoc CWVF EBak EKMF EPts SRiF |
| | 'Guinevere' | CWVF EBak |
| | 'Gustave Doré' (d) | CSil EBak EKMF |
| | 'Guy Dauphine' (d) | EBak |
| | 'Guy-Ann Mannens' **new** | WPBF |
| | 'Gwen Dodge' | LCla SRiF SVic WPBF |
| | 'Gwend-a-ling' | SRiF |
| | 'Gwendoline Clare' **new** | WPBF |
| | 'Gypsy Girl' (d) | CWVF |
| | 'H.G. Brown' | CSil EBak EKMF SRiF |
| | 'Hagelander' **new** | WPBF |
| | 'Halsall Beauty' (d) | MBri |
| | 'Halsall Belle' (d) | MBri SRiF |
| | 'Halsall Pride' (d) | MBri |
| | 'Hamadryad' (a) **new** | WPBF |
| | 'Hampshire Blue' | CDoC CWVF SVic WFuv |
| | 'Hampshire Prince' (d) | LVER |
| | 'Hanna' (d) | SRGP |
| | 'Hanna Improved' | SRiF |
| | 'Hannah Gwen' (d) | EKMF |
| | 'Hannah Louise' (d) | EPts |
| | 'Hannah Rogers' | MWar |
| | 'Hans Callaars' | LCla |
| | 'Hansi' **new** | WPBF |
| | 'Happiness' (d) | SVic |
| | 'Happy' | CDoC CSil CTsd CWVF EPts LCla MHav SPet SVic WFuv WPBF |
| | 'Happy Anniversary' | CLoc SVic WFFs WPBF |
| | 'Happy Fellow' | CDoC CLoc CSil EBak MHav NDlv SRiF |
| | 'Happy Wedding Day' (d) | CDoC CLoc CWVF EKMF EPts LAst MJac SCoo SPet SRGP SVic WFuv |
| | 'Hapsburgh' | EBak SRiF |
| | 'Harbour Lites' | MWar SLBF WPBF WRou |
| | 'Harlow Car' | CDoC CWVF EKMF EPts SRiF |
| | 'Harlow Perfection' | EKMF |
| I | 'Harmony' Niederholzer, 1946 | EBak |
| | 'Harnser's Flight' | CSil SRiF |
| | 'Harold Smith' | SRiF |
| | 'Harriett' (d) | WPBF |
| | 'Harry Dunnett' (T) | EBak |
| | 'Harry Gray' (d) | CCCN CLoc CTsd CWVF EBak EPts LAst MBri MJac SPet SRGP SVic WFuv |
| | 'Harry Pullen' | EBak |
| | 'Harry Taylor' (d) | EPts |
| | 'Harry's Sunshine' | SLBF |

| | |
|---|---|
| 'Harti's Olivia' **new** | WPBF |
| ***hartwegii*** | CDoC CSil EKMF LCla MHer |
| 'Harvey's Reward' | SLBF |
| 'Hathersage' (d) | EBak |
| ***hatschbachii*** | CDoC CSil CTsd LCla MHer SDix SRiF |
| - Berry 4464 | EKMF |
| - Berry 4465 | EKMF |
| 'Haute Cuisine' (d) | CLoc EKMF SVic |
| 'Hawaiian Sunset' (d) | CLoc CWVF EPts LCla SLBF SRiF WFuv WPBF |
| 'Hawkshead' ♀H3-4 | Widely available |
| 'Hazel' (d) | CCCN CWVF MHav SVic |
| 'Hazerland' **new** | WPBF |
| 'Heart Throb' (d) | EBak |
| 'Heavenly Hayley' (d) | SLBF SRiF |
| 'Hebe' | EBak |
| 'Heemaeer' **new** | WPBF |
| 'Heidi Ann' (d) ♀H3 | CCCN CDoC CHrt CLoc CSil CWVF EBak EKMF EPts LAst MAsh MBri NBlu SLBF SPet SVic WFFs WFuv WPBF |
| 'Heidi Blue' (d) | SLBF |
| 'Heidi Joy' | CSil |
| § 'Heidi Weiss' (d) | CDoC CLoc CSil CWVF MBri SPet WFuv WPBF |
| 'Heinrich Henkel' | see *F.* 'Andenken an Heinrich Henkel' |
| 'Heirloom' (d) | EKMF |
| 'Helen Clare' (d) | CLoc CWVF EBak |
| 'Helen Elizabeth' (d) | EKMF |
| 'Helen Gair' (d) | CWVF |
| 'Helen Nicholls' (d) | EKMF WPBF |
| 'Helen Spence' (d) | EKMF |
| 'Helena Rose' | EKMF |
| 'Hellen Devine' | CWVF |
| 'Hello Moideer' | SRiF |
| 'Hemsleyana' | see *F. microphylla* subsp. *hemsleyana* |
| 'Henk Kaspers' (d) **new** | WPBF |
| 'Henkelly's Athena' | WPBF |
| 'Henkelly's Elisabeth' | WPBF |
| 'Henkelly's Tim' **new** | WPBF |
| 'Henning Becker' ♀H3 | CWVF |
| 'Henri Poincaré' | EBak EKMF |
| 'Herald' ♀H4 | CDoC CSil CWVF EBak EKMF MHav SLBF SRiF SVic WFuv |
| 'Herbé de Jacques' | see *F.* 'Mr West' |
| 'Heritage' (d) | CLoc CSil EBak EKMF SRiF |
| 'Herman de Graaff' (d) | EKMF WPBF |
| 'Hermiena' | CLoc CTsd CWVF EPts MHav MWar SLBF SVic WFFs WFuv WPBF |
| 'Hermienne' | WRou |
| 'Heron' | CSil EBak EKMF SRiF |
| 'Herps Bongo' **new** | WPBF |
| 'Herps Cornu' **new** | WPBF |
| 'Herps Kwikstep' | WPBF |
| 'Herps Pierement' | SLBF |
| 'Hessett Festival' (d) | CWVF EBak WFuv |
| 'Heston Blue' (d) | CWVF EKMF |
| 'Heydon' | CWVF |
| 'Hi Jinks' (d) | EBak SVic |
| ***hidalgensis*** | see *F. microphylla* subsp. *hidalgensis* |
| 'Hidcote Beauty' | CDoC CLoc CTsd CWVF EBak EKMF LCla MHav SLBF SPet SVic WFFs WPBF |
| 'Hidden Treasure' | MWar WFFs WPBF |
| 'Highland Pipes' | EKMF LCla |
| 'Hilda May Salmon' | CWVF |
| 'Hindu Belle' | EBak SRiF |
| 'Hinnerike' (T) | CSil CWVF LCla SVic WPBF WRou |
| 'Hiroshige' (T) | LCla |

| | |
|---|---|
| 'His Excellency' (d) | EBak |
| 'Hobo' (d) | CSil SRiF |
| 'Hobson's Choice' (d) | CWVF SLBF |
| 'Holly's Beauty' (d) | CDoC CLoc EKMF EPts LAst LSou MWar SRGP WFuv |
| 'Hollywood Park' (d) | EBak |
| 'Hot Coals' | CLoc CWVF EKMF EPts MCot MJac MWar SRiF SVic WPBF WRou |
| 'Howerd Hebden' | CDoC |
| 'Howlett's Hardy' ♀H3-4 | CDoC CLoc CSil CWVF EBak EKMF LRHS MHav NLar SRiF SVic WMnd WRou |
| 'Huckeswagen' | SLBF |
| 'Huet's Calamijn' (d) **new** | WPBF |
| 'Huet's Kwarts' **new** | WPBF |
| 'Huet's Topaas' **new** | WPBF |
| 'Huet's Uvardiet' (d) **new** | WPBF |
| 'Hugh Morgan' (d) | SRiF |
| 'Hula Girl' (d) | CDoC CTsd CWVF EBak EKMF MJac MWar SPet SRiF |
| 'Humboldt Holiday' (d) | EKMF |
| 'Huntsman' (d) | CCCN CDoC EKMF LAst MHav MJac |
| 'Ian Brazewell' (d) | CLoc |
| 'Ian Leedham' (d) | CTsd EBak EKMF |
| 'Ian Storey' | CSil EKMF |
| 'Ice Cool' (d) **new** | MSmi |
| 'Ice Cream Soda' (d) | EBak |
| 'Ice Maiden' ambig. (d) | WPBF |
| 'Iceberg' | CWVF EBak SVic |
| 'Icecap' | CWVF EKMF MBri SVic |
| 'Iced Champagne' | CLoc CWVF EBak LAst MJac |
| 'Ichiban' (d) | CLoc CTsd SRiF |
| 'Icicle' (d) | WPBF |
| 'Ida' (d) | EBak |
| 'Igloo Maid' (d) | CLoc CWVF EBak EKMF SPet SVic WFuv |
| 'Ijzerwinning' (d) **new** | WPBF |
| 'Illusion' | WPBF |
| 'Impala' (d) | CWVF WPBF |
| 'Imperial Fantasy' (d) | CWVF |
| 'Improved Hanna' **new** | EKMF |
| 'Impudence' | CLoc CWVF EBak SPet |
| 'Impulse' (d) | CLoc |
| 'Ina Jo Marker' | SRiF |
| 'Indian Maid' (d) | CWVF EBak LVER |
| ***inflata*** | EKMF |
| 'Ingram Maid' | WPBF |
| 'Insulinde' (T) | CDoC CFee CTsd CWVF EPts LCla MJac MWar SLBF |
| 'Interlude' (d) | EBak |
| 'Iolanthe' (T) | CWVF |
| 'Irene L. Peartree' (d) | CWVF LCla SRiF |
| 'Irene Sinton' (d) | CCCN MJac |
| 'Iris Amer' (d) | CDoC CLoc CWVF EBak |
| 'Irish Dawn' | MWar |
| 'Irving Alexander' (d) | WPBF |
| 'Isabel Ryan' | CSil |
| 'Isis' Lemoine | CSil |
| 'Isle of Mull' | CDoC CSil SPet |
| 'Isle of Purbeck' | SRiF SVic |
| 'Italiano' (d) | CWVF MJac SVic |
| 'Ivana van Amsterdam' | SLBF |
| 'Ivy Grace' | CSil |
| 'Jack Acland' | CWVF |
| 'Jack Coast' | SRiF |
| 'Jack King' | SRiF |
| 'Jack Shahan' ♀H3 | CCCN CDoC CHrt CLoc CSil CTsd CWVF EBak EKMF LAst LCla MBri MJac SPet SRGP WFFs WFuv WPBF |
| 'Jack Stanway' (v) | CDoC CWVF EKMF MWar SRiF WPBF |
| 'Jack Wilson' | CSil |

| | |
|---|---|
| 'Jackie Bull' (d) | CWVF EBak |
| 'Jackpot' (d) | EBak |
| 'Jackqueline' (T) | CWVF |
| 'Jam Roll' (d) | LVER |
| 'Jamboree' (d) | EBak |
| 'James Eve' (d) | SRiF |
| 'James Hammond' | SRiF |
| 'James Lye' (d) | CWVF EBak EKMF SRiF |
| 'James Travis' (E/d) | CDoC CSil EBak EKMF LCla SRiF |
| 'Jan Bremer' | SVic |
| 'Jan Murray' | SLBF |
| 'Jandel' | CWVF MHav |
| 'Jane Amanda' (d) | SRiF |
| 'Jane Humber' (d) | CWVF EKMF |
| 'Jane Lye' | EBak |
| 'Janet Williams' (d) | CSil |
| 'Janice Ann' | EKMF LCla MWar WFFs WPBF |
| 'Janice Perry's Gold' (v) | CCCN CLoc MHav MJac SRiF |
| 'Janie' (d) | EPfP MAsh |
| 'Janneke Brinkman-Salentijn' | SRiF |
| 'Janske Vermeulen' **new** | WPBF |
| 'Jap Vantveer' (T) | LCla WPBF |
| 'Jaspers Kameleon' **new** | WPBF |
| 'Jaunty Jack' | SLBF |
| 'Jayess Helen' (d) | SRiF |
| 'Jean Baker' | CSil |
| 'Jean Campbell' | EBak |
| 'Jean de Fakteur' (d) **new** | WPBF |
| 'Jean Frisby' | CLoc |
| 'Jeane' | EKMF |
| 'Jef van der Kuylen' (d) | WPBF |
| 'Jelle Veemen' **new** | WPBF |
| 'Jennie Rachael' (d) | SRiF WFuv |
| 'Jennifer' | EBak |
| 'Jennifer Ann Porter' **new** | MWar |
| 'Jennifer Hampson' (d) | CSil |
| 'Jennifer Lister' (d) | CSil EKMF |
| 'Jenny May' | CLoc EPts |
| 'Jenny Sorensen' | CWVF EKMF SRiF WFuv WPBF WRou |
| 'Jess' | LCla SLBF |
| 'Jessica Reynolds' | SRiF WPBF |
| 'Jessie Pearson' | CWVF |
| 'Jessimae' | CWVF SPet SRiF |
| 'Jester' Holmes (d) | CLoc CSil |
| 'Jet Fire' (d) | EBak |
| 'Jezebel' | SRiF SVic WPBF |
| 'Jiddles' (E) | EKMF LCla SRiF WRou |
| 'Jill Holloway' (T) **new** | SLBF |
| 'Jill Whitworth' | CDoC |
| 'Jim Coleman' | CWVF SRiF SVic |
| 'Jim Dodge' (d) | EPts |
| 'Jim Hawkins' | EBak SRiF |
| 'Jim Muncaster' | CWVF EKMF |
| 'Jim Todd' | SRiF |
| 'Jim Watts' | CDoC CTsd EKMF WPBF |
| ***jimenezii*** | CDoC LCla |
| 'Jimmy Carr' (d) | EKMF |
| 'Jimmy Cricket' (E) | CDoC |
| 'Jingle Bells' | CTsd |
| 'Jinlye' | EKMF |
| 'JJ Roberts' **new** | MWar |
| 'Joan Barnes' (d) | CTsd CWVF SRiF |
| 'Joan Cooper' | CLoc CSil CWVF EBak EKMF SLBF SRiF |
| 'Joan Gilbert' (d) | MHav SRiF |
| 'Joan Goy' | CWVF EKMF MJac SVic WFuv |
| 'Joan Knight' | CLoc |
| 'Joan Leach' | CSil |
| 'Joan Margaret' (d) | MJac |
| 'Joan Morris' | SLBF |
| 'Joan Pacey' | CWVF EBak EKMF SRiF |
| 'Joan Paxton' (d) | LCla |

| | | |
|---|---|---|
| | 'Joan Smith' | EBak SRiF |
| | 'Joan Waters' (d) | CWVF |
| | 'Jo-Anne Fisher' (d) | EPts |
| | 'Joan's Delight' | WPBF |
| | 'Jody Goodwin' **new** | WPBF |
| | 'Joe Kusber' (d) | CWVF EBak WFuv |
| | 'Joe Nicholls' (d) | EKMF |
| | 'Joel' | CLoc WPBF |
| | 'Joergen Hahn' | WPBF |
| | 'Johannes Nowinski' | SRiF |
| | 'John Bartlett' | CLoc |
| | 'John Boy' (d) | EKMF |
| | 'John E. Caunt' ♀H3-4 | CSil EKMF |
| | 'John Green' | EKMF |
| | 'John Grooms' (d) | CLoc WFuv WRou |
| | 'John Lockyer' | CLoc CWVF EBak SRiF |
| | 'John Maynard Scales' (T) | CDoC CWVF LCla MJac WPBF WRou |
| § | 'John Ridding' PBR (T/v) | CLoc EPts LSou SPoG SVil WPBF |
| | 'John Suckley' (d) | EBak |
| | 'John Wright' | CSil EKMF LCla |
| | 'Joke's Albino' **new** | WPBF |
| | 'Jolanda Weeda' **new** | WPBF |
| | 'Jomam' ♀H3 | CLoc CWVF MWar |
| | 'Jon Oram' | CLoc CWVF |
| | 'Jorma van Eijk' (d) | WPBF |
| | 'Jose Tamerus' (d) | WPBF |
| | 'Jose's Joan' (d) | CWVF SVic |
| | 'Joy Bielby' | EKMF |
| | 'Joy Patmore' | CLoc CTsd CWVF EBak EKMF MBri SLBF SPet WFuv WPBF |
| | 'Joyce' | WPBF |
| | 'Joyce Adey' (d) | CWVF SRiF |
| | 'Joyce Sinton' | CWVF MBri WFuv |
| | 'Joyce Wilson' (d) | EPts |
| | 'Jubie-Lin' (d) | WPBF |
| | 'Jubilee Quest' | EKMF MWar WPBF |
| | 'Judith Coupland' | CWVF |
| | 'Judith Lissenden' **new** | EKMF |
| | 'Jülchen' | CWVF |
| | 'Jules Daloges' (d) | EBak EKMF SRiF |
| | 'Julia' (d) | EKMF WPBF |
| | 'Julie Ann Goodwin' **new** | WPBF |
| | 'Julie Horton' (d) | WPBF |
| | 'Julie Marie' (d) | CWVF MJac |
| | 'June Gardner' | CWVF EKMF |
| | 'Jungle' | LCla |
| I | 'Juno' Kennett | EBak |
| | ***juntasensis*** | EKMF |
| | 'Jupiter Seventy' | EBak SRiF |
| | 'Jus For You' **new** | MJac |
| | 'Just William' | SRiF |
| | 'Justin's Pride' | CDoC CSil EKMF SRiF |
| | 'Kaboutertje' | EKMF |
| | 'Kaleidoscope' (d) | EBak |
| | 'Kara Faye' | EKMF |
| | 'Karen Isles' (E) | CDoC EKMF LCla WRou |
| | 'Karen Louise' (d) | CLoc |
| | 'Karin de Groot' | SVic WFuv |
| | 'Karin Siegers' | CSil |
| | 'Kate Taylor' (d) | SLBF WPBF |
| | 'Kate Wylie' | MWar |
| | 'Kath Kirk' | EKMF |
| | 'Kath van Hanegem' | SLBF SRiF WPBF WRou |
| | 'Kathleen Galea' | SRiF |
| | 'Kathleen Muncaster' (d) | EKMF |
| | 'Kathleen Smith' (d) | EKMF |
| | 'Kathleen van Hanegan' | CLoc EKMF MWar |
| | 'Kathryn Maidment' | SVic |
| | 'Kathy Louise' (d) | WPBF |
| | 'Kathy's Pipes' | EKMF |
| | 'Kathy's Prince' | EKMF |
| | 'Kathy's Sparkler' (d) | EKMF |
| | 'Katie Elizabeth Ann' (d) | MWar |

| | | |
|---|---|---|
| | 'Katie Reynolds' (d) | MWar SRiF |
| | 'Katie Rogers' | EPts |
| | 'Katie Susan' | LCla SLBF |
| | 'Katinka' (E) | CDoC CWVF LCla SRiF WPBF |
| | 'Katjan' | CSil EKMF LCla SLBF |
| | 'Katrina' (d) | CLoc EBak |
| | 'Katrina Thompsen' | CLoc CWVF EKMF EPts MWar SRiF WFuv |
| | 'Katy James' | EKMF MWar |
| | 'Katy M' | WPBF |
| | 'Keepsake' (d) | CLoc EBak |
| | 'Kees van Eijk' (d) new | WPBF |
| | 'Keesje' | CTsd |
| | 'Kegworth Carnival' (d) | CWVF SRiF |
| | 'Ken Goldsmith' (T) | CWVF |
| | 'Ken Jennings' | CWVF |
| | 'Ken Shelton' | SRiF |
| | 'Kenny Dalglish' (d) | CSil EKMF |
| | 'Kenny Holmes' | CWVF |
| | 'Kenny Walkling' | SLBF |
| | 'Kernan Robson' (d) | CLoc CWVF EBak SRiF |
| | 'Kevin Stals' | see *F.* 'Stals Kevin' |
| | 'Keystone' | EBak SRiF |
| | 'Kim Nicholls' | EKMF |
| | 'Kimberley Hadfield' | MWar |
| | 'Kimberly' (d) | EBak |
| | 'King of Bath' (d) | EBak |
| | 'King of Hearts' (d) | EBak |
| | 'King's Ransom' (d) | CLoc CTsd CWVF EBak EKMF LRHS SPet SVic |
| | 'Kiss 'n' Tell' | CWVF MJac SRiF |
| | 'Kit Oxtoby' (d) | CCCN CDoC CHrt CWVF EKMF LCla LVER MJac WFuv WPBF |
| | 'Kiwi' (d) | EBak |
| | 'Knockout' (d) | CWVF EKMF SVic |
| | 'Kobold' new | WPBF |
| | 'Kolding Perle' | CWVF EKMF MHav SPet SRiF |
| | 'Komeet' | EKMF SEND |
| | 'Kon-Tiki' (d) | CLoc CTsd SPet |
| | 'Koog Aan de Zaan' new | WPBF |
| | 'Koralle' | see *F.* 'Coralle' |
| | 'Kwintet' | CWVF EBak MJac SPet SRiF |
| | 'Kyoto' | CWVF EKMF |
| | 'La Bianca' | EBak |
| | 'La Campanella' (d) 🏆H3 | CCCN CDoC CHrt CLoc CWVF EBak EKMF EPts LAst LCla LSou MBri MJac MWar NVic SPet SVic WFFs WPBF |
| | 'La Fiesta' (d) | EBak |
| | 'La France' (d) | EBak EKMF |
| | 'La Neige' ambig. | CTsd CWVF |
| | 'La Neige' Lemoine (d) | EBak EKMF |
| | 'La Porte' (d) | CLoc CWVF |
| | 'La Rosita' (d) | EBak SLBF SRiF |
| I | 'La Traviata' Blackwell (d) | EBak SRiF |
| | 'Lace Petticoats' (d) | EBak EKMF SVic |
| | 'Lady Bacon' | EPts EWes MBri SDys SLBF SMHy |
| | 'Lady Bartle Frere' (d) | SRiF |
| | 'Lady Beth' (d) | MHav SVic |
| | 'Lady Boothby' | CDoC CHEx CPLG CSil CWVF EBak EKMF EShb LAst LRHS LSou SLBF SMrm SPet SPlb SPoG SVic WBor WFuv WPBF |
| | 'Lady Framlingham' (d) | EPts |
| | 'Lady Heytesbury' | EKMF |
| | 'Lady in Grey' (d) | CCCN EKMF LAst MHav MJac SRiF SVic WPBF |
| | 'Lady Isobel Barnett' | CLoc CTsd CWVF EBak EKMF MBri MJac SPet SVic WFuv WPBF |
| | 'Lady Kathleen Spence' | CWVF EBak SPet SVic |
| | 'Lady Lupus' | EPts |
| | 'Lady Patricia Mountbatten' | CWVF EKMF MJac SVic WRou |
| | 'Lady Ramsey' | EBak SRiF |
| | 'Lady Rebecca' (d) | CLoc |
| | 'Lady Thumb' (d) 🏆H3 | Widely available |
| | 'Lady's Smock' | EKMF |
| | 'Laing's Hybrid' | CWVF EBak |
| | 'Lakeland Princess' | EBak |
| | 'Lakeside' | EBak |
| | 'Laleham Lass' | EKMF |
| | 'Lambada' | EKMF LAst MWar SRiF WPBF WRou |
| | 'Lancambe' | CSil |
| | 'Lancashire Lad' (d) | CTsd MWar |
| | 'Lancashire Lass' | CWVF MBri |
| | 'Lancelot' | EBak SRiF |
| | 'Land van Beveren' | MWar SLBF |
| | 'Langsford' | SRiF |
| | 'Lapshead White' | CPLG |
| | 'Lark' (T) | CWVF |
| | 'Lassie' (d) | CDoC CLoc CWVF EBak |
| | 'Last Chance' (E) | SLBF |
| | 'Laura' ambig. | CWVF WFuv WRou |
| I | 'Laura' (Dutch) | CLoc EPts LCla SLBF SRiF |
| I | 'Laura' Martin (d) | EKMF |
| | 'Laura Biolcati-Rinaldi' (d) new | WPBF |
| | 'Laura Cross' (E) | EKMF |
| | 'Lavaglut' | WPBF |
| | 'Lavender Beauty' (d) | SRiF |
| | 'Lavender Heaven' (d) new | WPBF |
| | 'Lavender Kate' (d) | CLoc CWVF EBak |
| | 'Lazy Lady' (d) | CWVF EBak |
| | 'Lechlade Apache' | CDoC LCla |
| | 'Lechlade Bullet' new | LCla |
| | 'Lechlade Chinaman' (T) | CDoC SRiF SVic WFFs |
| | 'Lechlade Debutante' | CDoC LCla SLBF SRiF |
| | 'Lechlade Fire-eater' (T) | CDoC LCla SRiF |
| | 'Lechlade Gorgon' | CDoC CDow CWVF EKMF LCla SLBF WFFs |
| | 'Lechlade Magician' | CDoC CSil CTsd EKMF EPts LCla MHav SPet SRiF SVic WFFs |
| | 'Lechlade Maiden' | CWVF LCla SRiF |
| | 'Lechlade Martianess' | LCla SRiF SVic |
| | 'Lechlade Potentate' | LCla |
| | 'Lechlade Tinkerbell' (E) | LCla SLBF SRiF |
| | 'Lechlade Violet' (T) | CSil EKMF LCla SRiF SVic |
| | ***lehmanii*** | LCla |
| | 'Len Bielby' (T) | CDoC CWVF LCla |
| | 'Lena' (d) 🏆H3 | CDoC CLoc CSil CTri CTsd CWVF EBak EKMF EPts MBri MJac SPer SPet SRGP SSea SVic WEas WPBF |
| | 'Lena Dalton' (d) | CLoc CWVF EBak EKMF SRiF SVic |
| | 'Leonhart von Fuchs' | WPBF |
| | 'Leonie Boffe' (d) | WPBF |
| | 'Leonora' | CDoC CLoc CSil CTsd CWVF EBak EKMF MBri SLBF SPet SRiF SVic WFuv WRou |
| | 'Lesley' (T) | CWVF LCla WPBF |
| | 'Leslie Drew' new | SLBF |
| | 'Lett's Delight' (d) | CWVF EPts |
| | 'Letty Lye' | EBak SRiF |
| | 'Leverhulme' | see *F.* 'Leverkusen' |
| § | 'Leverkusen' (T) | CDoC CLoc EBak LCla MJac WRou |
| | 'Li Kai Lin' | CSil SRiF |
| I | 'Liebesträume' Blackwell (d) | EBak |
| | 'Liebriez' (d) 🏆H3-4 | CSil CTsd EBak EKMF SPet SRiF SVic |
| | 'Liemers Lantaern' | CWVF |
| | 'Likalin' | CWVF |
| | 'Lilac' | CSil EBak |
| | 'Lilac Dainty' (d) | CSil |
| | 'Lilac Lustre' (d) | CLoc CWVF EBak SPet SVic |
| | 'Lilac Queen' (d) | EBak |
| | 'Lilac Tint' new | WPBF |
| | 'Lilian' | EKMF |

| | | |
|---|---|---|
| | 'Lillian Annetts' (d) | CCCN CDoC CWVF EKMF LAst LCla MJac MWar SLBF SRiF WFuv WPBF WRou |
| | 'Lillibet' (d) | CDoC CLoc CWVF EBak |
| | 'Lillydale' (d) | SRiF |
| | 'Lilo Vogt' (T) | SRiF |
| | 'Lime Lite' (d) | MJac |
| I | 'Limelight' Weston **new** | SLBF |
| | 'Lincoln Castle' **new** | EKMF MWar |
| | 'Linda Goulding' | CTsd CWVF EBak SVic WFuv WRou |
| | 'Linda Grace' | EKMF MJac MWar |
| | 'Linda Mary Nutt' | MWar |
| | 'Linda Rosling' (d) | CDoC EKMF |
| | 'Lindisfarne' (d) | CLoc CWVF EBak EKMF MJac SPet WPBF |
| | 'Lindsey Victoria' (d) **new** | SVic |
| | 'Linlithgow Lass' | MWar |
| | 'Lionel' | CSil SRiF WPBF |
| | 'Lisa' (d) | CDoC EPts SPet WPBF |
| | 'Lisa Ashton' | SRiF |
| | 'Lisa Rowe' (d) | WPBF |
| | 'Little Annie Gee' | MWar |
| | 'Little Baby' | EKMF SRiF |
| | 'Little Beauty' | CDoC CSil CWVF EKMF SVic |
| | 'Little Boy Blue' | EPts |
| | 'Little Brook Gem' | SLBF |
| | 'Little Catbells' (E) | SLBF |
| | 'Little Gene' | EBak |
| | 'Little Jewel' | CTsd SPet SRiF |
| | 'Little Nan' | SLBF |
| | 'Little Orphan Annie' | LCla |
| | 'Little Ouse' (d) | CWVF |
| | 'Little Ronnie' (d) | SRiF WPBF |
| | 'Little Snow Queen' | WPBF |
| | 'Little Witch' | EKMF SLBF SRiF |
| | 'Liz' (d) | CSil EBak EKMF WPBF |
| | Liza = 'Goetzliza'[PBR] (Shadowdancer Series) | CDoC LAst LSou NPri |
| | 'Liza Todman' (d) | SRiF |
| | 'Lochinver' (d) | CWVF |
| | 'Loeky' | CLoc CWVF EBak SPet SRiF SVic WPBF |
| | 'Logan Garden' | see *F. magellanica* 'Logan Woods' |
| | 'Lolita' (d) | CWVF EBak |
| | 'London 2000' | LCla MJac MWar SLBF SRiF WPBF WRou |
| | 'London in Bloom' | SLBF WPBF |
| | 'Lonely Ballerina' (d) | CLoc CWVF |
| | 'Long Distance' (T) | LCla WPBF |
| | 'Long John' **new** | WPBF |
| | 'Long Wings' | EKMF LCla SVic |
| | 'Longfellow' | WPBF |
| | 'Lonneke' | WPBF |
| | 'Lord Byron' | CLoc EBak EKMF SRiF |
| | 'Lord Derby' | CSil |
| | 'Lord Jim' | CDoC LCla |
| | 'Lord Lloyd Webber' (d) | MJac |
| | 'Lord Lonsdale' | CWVF EBak EPts LCla MHav SVic WFuv WRou |
| | 'Lord Roberts' | CLoc CSil CWVF SLBF |
| | 'Lorna Fairclough' | MJac |
| | 'Lorna Florence' | SLBF |
| | 'Lorna Swinbank' | CLoc CWVF SRiF SVic |
| | 'Lorraine's Delight' (d) | SVic |
| | 'Lottie Hobby' (E) ♕H1+3 | CDoC CDow CLoc CSil CTsd CWVF EKMF EPfP EPts EShb ISea LCla MLHP SIng SPet SVic WFFs WFuv WRou |
| | 'Louise Emershaw' (d) | CWVF EBak MJac SVic |
| | 'Louise Nicholls' | EKMF MJac MWar SLBF SRiF |
| | 'Loulabel' **new** | SVic |
| | 'Lovable' (d) | EBak |
| | 'Loveliness' | CLoc CWVF EBak EKMF SRiF SVic |
| | 'Lovely Les' (d) | SRiF |
| | 'Lovely Linda' | SLBF |
| | 'Love's Reward' ♕H1+3 | CLoc CWVF EKMF MJac MWar SLBF SVic WFFs WFuv WPBF WRou |
| | 'Lower Raydon' | EBak |
| | ***loxensis*** misapplied | see *F.* 'Speciosa', *F.* 'Loxensis' |
| | ***loxensis*** HBK Berry 3233 | EKMF |
| | - DG 1001 | EKMF |
| I | 'Loxensis' | CDoC CWVF EBak EKMF SVic |
| | 'Loxhore Herald' | CSil |
| | 'Loxhore Lullaby' (E) | CSil LCla |
| | 'Loxhore Mazurka' (T) | SRiF WPBF WRou |
| | 'Loxhore Minuet' (T) | CDoC LCla WRou |
| | 'Loxhore Posthorn' (T) | LCla |
| | 'Lucinda' | CWVF |
| | 'Lucky Strike' (d) | CLoc EBak |
| | Lucy = 'Goetzlucy' (Shadowdancer Series) | EBak NPri WPBF |
| | 'Lucy Locket' | MJac |
| | 'Lukas' | WPBF |
| | 'Lunter's Trots' (d) | WPBF |
| | 'Luscious Lisa' | WPBF |
| | 'Lustre' | CWVF EBak SVic |
| | 'Lut' (d) | WPBF |
| | 'Luuk van Riet' (d) **new** | WPBF |
| | ***lycioides*** misapplied | see *F.* 'Lycioides' |
| § | ***lycioides*** Andrews | EBak EKMF |
| I | 'Lycioides' | LCla |
| | 'Lydia' **new** | WPBF |
| | 'Lye's Elegance' | CSil EKMF SRiF |
| | 'Lye's Excelsior' | EBak SRiF |
| | 'Lye's Own' | EBak SPet |
| | 'Lye's Perfection' | EKMF |
| | 'Lye's Unique' ♕H1+3 | CCCN CDoC CHrt CLoc CSil CWVF EBak EKMF EPts LCla MJac MWar SLBF SPet SRiF SVic WFuv WRou |
| | 'Lynette' (d) | CLoc |
| | 'Lynn Ellen' (d) | CDoC CTsd CWVF EBak |
| | 'Lynne Marshall' | CSil |
| | 'Lynne Patricia' **new** | MWar |
| | 'Maartje' | SRiF |
| | 'Mabel Greaves' (d) | CWVF |
| | 'Mac Wagg' | WRou |
| | 'Machu Picchu' | CLoc CWVF EKMF EPts LCla MHav WPBF WRou |
| | ***macrophylla*** | CDoC WMoo |
| | - BEA 922539 | EKMF |
| | - Berry 3080 | EKMF |
| | - Berry 80-539 | EKMF |
| | - Berry 80-541 | EKMF |
| | 'Madame Aubin' | CSil EKMF |
| | 'Madame Butterfly' (d) | CLoc |
| | 'Madame Cornélissen' (d) ♕H3 | Widely available |
| | 'Madame Eva Boye' | EBak |
| | 'Madeleine Sweeney' (d) | EKMF MBri |
| | 'Maes-y-Groes' | CSil EKMF |
| | 'Maet Suycker' **new** | WPBF |
| | ***magellanica*** | CDoC COld CSil CTrG CTsd CWib EKMF GGar MLHP NChi NPer NWea SPer SVic WFar WPnn WRha |
| | - Dahl, S. | EKMF |
| | - 'Alba' | see *F. magellanica* var. *molinae* |
| I | - 'Alba Aureovariegata' (v) | CBgR CDoC CWan EPfP LAst MBri SPer SVic WFar |
| | - 'Alba Variegata' (v) | CSil NPol |
| | - 'Americana Elegans' | CDoC CSil WPBF |
| | - 'Comber' | CSil |
| | - var. ***conica*** | CDoC CSil EKMF |
| | - var. ***discolor*** | CSil |
| | - 'Duchy of Cornwall' | CDoC |
| | - 'Exmoor Gold' (v) | CSil |

| | | |
|---|---|---|
| § | - var. ***gracilis*** 🏆H3 | CAgr CDoC CHEx CLoc CSil CTri CWVF EKMF LRHS MLHP SCoo SVic WPnn |
| | - - 'Aurea' 🏆H3-4 | CBcs CDoC CSil CTsd CWVF EBee EKMF ELan ELon EPfP GAbr GQui ISea LAst LCla LRHS MHer MRav SAga SCoo SDix SLBF SPer SPet SPla SPoG WFar WRou |
| § | - - 'Tricolor' (v) 🏆H3 | CDoC CSil CTsd EKMF EPts EWes GAbr LCla LRHS SLBF SRms WCFE WFFs WPnn WRou |
| | - - 'Variegata' (v) 🏆H3 | CDoC CSil EBak EKMF EPfP GGar LCla LRHS LSou MGos MRav SAga SDix SIng SPet SRiF WFFs WFuv WPnn |
| | - 'Guiding Star' | CDoC |
| | - 'Lady Bacon' | CDoC CSil EKMF GCal LPla MCot MSte |
| § | - 'Logan Woods' | CDoC CSil EKMF GBuc ISea SLBF SMrm |
| | - 'Longipedunculata' | CDoC CSil EKMF SLPl WPBF |
| | - 'Lyonesse Lady' | CDoC |
| | - var. ***macrostema*** | CSil EKMF |
| § | - var. ***molinae*** | Widely available |
| § | - - 'Enstone' (v) | EHoe EKMF LAst SRiF |
| | - - 'Enstone Gold' | EKMF |
| | - - 'Golden Sharpitor' (v) | CBgR CCCN LAst MDKP MHav WAbe |
| | - - 'Mr Knight's Blush' | GBuc |
| § | - - 'Sharpitor' (v) | Widely available |
| | - var. ***myrtifolia*** | CDoC CSil CTsd EKMF |
| * | - var. ***prostrata*** | CSil |
| | - var. ***pumila*** | CAby CBgR CDoC CEnt CSil EWes GCal ITim LAst MHer MLHP SCoo SHGN SIng SMHy SRot SVic WAbe WBor |
| | - 'Sea King' | CDoC |
| | - 'Sea Spray' | CDoC |
| | - 'Seahorse' | CDoC |
| § | - 'Thompsonii' 🏆H3-4 | CDoC CSil ECGP EKMF SBch SMHy |
| § | - 'Versicolor' (v) | Widely available |
| | 'Magenta Flush' | CDoC CTsd CWVF |
| | 'Maggie Rose' | MWar SLBF |
| | 'Magic Flute' | CLoc CWVF MJac SVic |
| | 'Maharaja' (d) | EBak SRiF |
| | 'Majebo' (d) | SRiF |
| | 'Major Heaphy' | CWVF EBak EKMF MSmi SRiF WPBF |
| | 'Malibu Mist' (d) | CWVF LVER SRiF WPBF |
| | 'Mama Bleuss' (d) | EBak SRiF WFuv |
| | 'Mancunian' (d) | CTsd CWVF |
| I | 'Mandarin' Schnabel | EBak |
| | 'Mandi' (T) | LCla |
| | 'Mandy Oxtoby' (T) | SRiF |
| | 'Mantilla' (T) | CDoC CLoc CWVF EBak EKMF LCla MJac SVic |
| | 'Maori Maid' | SRiF WPBF |
| | 'Maori Pipes' (T) | WPBF |
| | 'Marbled Sky' | SVic |
| | 'Marcel Michiels' (d) | WPBF |
| | 'Marcia' PBR (Shadowdancer Series) | LAst LSou NPri |
| | 'Marcus Graham' (d) | CCCN CLoc CTsd CWVF EBak EKMF MWar SCoo SRiF SVic WFuv WPBF WRou |
| | 'Marcus Hanton' (d) | CWVF EKMF LCla SRiF |
| | 'Mardi Gras' (d) | CTsd EBak SRiF |
| | 'Margaret' (d) 🏆H4 | CDoC CLoc CSil CTri CTsd CWVF EBak EKMF EPts ISea LCla LVER MWar NDlv SLBF SPet SVic WFuv |
| | 'Margaret Bird' | LCla |
| | 'Margaret Brown' 🏆H4 | CDoC CLoc CSil CTri CWVF EBak EKMF LCla SLBF SMrm SPet SRGP SRiF SVic WRou |
| | 'Margaret Davidson' (d) | CLoc |
| | 'Margaret Hazelwood' | EKMF SRiF |
| | 'Margaret Lowis' | MWar |
| | 'Margaret Pilkington' | CTsd CWVF SRiF SVic |
| | 'Margaret Roe' | CDoC CSil CWVF EBak EKMF MJac SPet SRiF WPBF |
| | 'Margaret Susan' | EBak |
| | 'Margaret Tebbit' | CCCN LAst |
| | 'Margarite Dawson' (d) | CSil |
| | 'Margery Blake' | CSil EBak SRiF |
| | 'Margharita' (d) | SRiF |
| | 'Margrit Willimann' | WPBF |
| | 'Maria Landy' | CWVF EKMF LCla MJac MWar WRou |
| | 'Maria Mathilde' (d) | SLBF |
| | 'Maria Merrills' (d) | MHav SRiF |
| | 'Marie Elizabeth' (d) | WPBF |
| | 'Marielle van Dummelen' (d) | WPBF |
| | 'Marie-Louise Luyckx' (d) | WPBF |
| | 'Marilyn Jane' **new** | EKMF |
| | 'Marilyn Olsen' | CWVF |
| | 'Marin Belle' | EBak SRiF |
| | 'Marin Glow' 🏆H3 | CLoc CWVF EBak SLBF SPet SVic WFuv |
| | 'Marina Kelly' | WRou |
| | 'Marinka' 🏆H3 | CCCN CHrt CLoc CWVF EBak EKMF EPts LAst LCla LVER MBri MJac NBlu SLBF SPet SVic WFuv WPBF |
| | 'Marion Hilton' | MWar |
| | 'Mark Kirby' (d) | CWVF EBak EKMF |
| | 'Marlea's Schouwpijpke' | WPBF |
| | 'Marlies de Keijzer' (E) | LCla SLBF WPBF |
| | 'Mart' **new** | WPBF |
| | 'Martien A. Soeters' **new** | WPBF |
| | 'Martin Beije' | WPBF |
| | 'Martina' | SLBF |
| | 'Martin's Delight' (d) | WPBF |
| | 'Martin's Double Delicate' (d) | WPBF |
| | 'Martin's Inspiration' | LCla MWar |
| | 'Martin's Little Beauty' **new** | WPBF |
| | 'Martin's Yellow Surprise' (T) | LCla SLBF |
| | 'Martinus' (d) | WPBF |
| | 'Marty' (d) | EBak |
| | 'Mary' (T) 🏆H1+3 | CDoC CLoc CWVF EKMF EPts LCla LRHS SLBF SVic |
| | 'Mary Jones' (d) | EKMF |
| | 'Mary Lockyer' (d) | CLoc CTsd EBak SRiF |
| | 'Mary Poppins' | CWVF SVic |
| | 'Mary Reynolds' (d) | CWVF |
| | 'Mary Shead' (d) | MWar |
| | 'Mary Sturman' (E) | SRiF |
| | 'Mary Thorne' | CSil EBak EKMF SRiF |
| | 'Mary's Millennium' | CWVF |
| | 'Masquerade' (d) | EBak SVic |
| | ***mathewsii*** | EKMF |
| | 'Maud Murphy' **new** | WPBF |
| | 'Maureen Ward' | EKMF |
| | 'Mauve Beauty' (d) | CSil CWVF EKMF SLBF |
| | 'Mauve Lace' (d) | CSil SRiF |
| | 'Mauve Wisp' (d) | SVic |
| | 'Max Jaffa' | CSil CWVF SRiF |
| I | 'Maxima' | EKMF EPts LCla WFuv WPBF |
| | 'Maxima's Baby' | WPBF |
| | 'Maybe Baby' | WPBF |
| | 'Mayblossom' (d) | CWVF SPet |
| | 'Mayfayre' (d) | CLoc |
| | 'Mayfield' | CWVF |
| | 'Mazda' | CWVF SRiF |
| | 'Meadow Lark' (d) **new** | CTsd |
| | 'Meadowlark' (d) | CWVF EBak SRiF |
| | 'Mechtildis de Lechy' | WPBF |
| | 'Medard's Hersinde' **new** | WPBF |

| | |
|---|---|
| 'Medard's Koning Nobel' **new** | WPBF |
| 'Medard's Krieke Putte' **new** | WPBF |
| 'Medard's Reinaertsland' **new** | WPBF |
| 'Meditation' (d) | CLoc CSil |
| 'Megeti' **new** | WPBF |
| 'Melanie' | CDoC CTsd MHav SVic WFuv WPBF |
| 'Melissa Heavens' | CWVF |
| 'Melody' | EBak SPet SRiF SVic |
| 'Melody Ann' (d) | EBak |
| 'Melting Moments' (d) | EKMF SCoo WFuv |
| 'Mendocino Mini' (E) | WPBF |
| 'Mendocino Rose' **new** | SVic |
| 'Menna' | WPBF |
| 'Mephisto' | CSil CWVF |
| 'Mercurius' | CSil |
| 'Merlin' | CDoC CSil EKMF LCla SRiF |
| 'Merry Mary' (d) | CWVF EBak EKMF |
| I 'Mexicali Rose' Machado | CLoc |
| 'Michael' (d) | CWVF EPts |
| 'Michael Wallis' (T) | EKMF LCla SLBF SRiF |
| 'Michelle Wallace' | SVic |
| ***michoacanensis*** misapplied | see *F. microphylla* subsp. *aprica* |
| ***michoacanensis*** Sessé & Moç. (E) B&SWJ 8982 | WCru |
| - B&SWJ 9027 **new** | WCru |
| - B&SWJ 9148 **new** | WCru |
| 'Micky Goult' ♀H1+3 | CDoC CLoc CWVF EKMF EPts LCla MJac SPet SRiF SVic WFuv WPBF WRou |
| 'Microchip' (E) | CSil LCla |
| ***microphylla*** (E) | CBcs CBgR CBrd CDoC CElw CLoc CPLG CSil CTsd CWVF EBak ELon GGar LRHS MLan MSCN NChi SCoo STre SVic WBor WCru |
| - B&SWJ 9101 | WCru |
| - B&SWJ 10331 **new** | WCru |
| § - subsp. ***aprica*** (E) | CDoC LCla |
| - - B&SWJ 9101 **new** | WCru |
| - - BRE 69862 | EKMF |
| § - subsp. ***hemsleyana*** (E) | CDoC CPLG CSil EKMF LCla SRiF WOut |
| - - B&SWJ 10478 **new** | WCru |
| § - subsp. ***hidalgensis*** (E) | CDoC CSil EKMF LCla |
| - subsp. ***microphylla*** (E) | CSil EKMF |
| § - subsp. ***minimiflora*** | SVic |
| - subsp. ***quercetorum*** (E) | CDoC CSil EKMF LCla |
| - 'Variegata' (E/v) | EWes MCCP |
| 'Midas' | CWVF MBri |
| 'Midnight Sun' (d) | CWVF EBak |
| 'Midwinter' | CWVF SRiF SVic WPBF |
| 'Mieke Alferink' | SRiF |
| 'Mieke Meursing' ♀H1+3 | CLoc CWVF EBak EKMF MJac SPet SRiF |
| 'Mieke Sarton' **new** | WPBF |
| 'Mien Kuypers' | WPBF |
| 'Mien van Oirschot' (d) | WPBF |
| 'Miep Aalhuizen' | CDoC LCla SRiF SVic WRou |
| 'Mike Foxton' | EKMF |
| 'Mike Oxtoby' (T) | CWVF EKMF |
| 'Mildred Wagg' | MWar |
| 'Millennium' | CLoc EBak EKMF EPts MJac SCoo WFFs |
| 'Millie' | SRiF |
| 'Millie Butler' | CWVF |
| 'Ming' | CLoc CTsd SRiF |
| 'Mini Skirt' | SRiF |
| 'Miniature Jewels' (E) | SLBF |
| ***minimiflora*** misapplied | see *F.* x *bacillaris* |
| ***minimiflora*** Hemsl. | see *F. microphylla* subsp. *minimiflora* |
| 'Minirose' | CCCN CDoC CWVF EPts MJac MWar WFuv WRou |
| 'Minnesota' (d) | EBak |
| 'Mipam' | SLBF |
| 'Miramar' **new** | EPts |
| 'Mischief' | CSil SVic |
| 'Miss California' (d) | CDoC CLoc CWVF EBak EKMF MBri |
| 'Miss Debbie' (d) | WFuv |
| 'Miss Great Britain' | CWVF |
| 'Miss Lye' | CSil EKMF SRiF |
| 'Miss Marilyn' | SRiF |
| 'Miss Muffett' (d) | CSil EPts |
| 'Miss Vallejo' (d) | CTsd EBak |
| 'Mission Bells' | CDoC CLoc CSil CTsd CWVF EBak EKMF EPts MHav SPet |
| 'Mistoque' | CTsd SRiF |
| 'Misty Blue' (d) | SVic |
| 'Misty Haze' (d) | CWVF SVic |
| 'Misty Pink' (d) | WPBF |
| 'Molenkerk' (d) **new** | WPBF |
| 'Molesworth' (d) | CWVF EBak MJac SPet |
| 'Mollie Beaulah' (d) | EKMF SRiF |
| 'Money Spinner' | CLoc EBak |
| 'Monica Dare' (T) | WPBF |
| 'Monique Comperen' | WPBF |
| 'Monsieur Thibaut' ♀H4 | CSil EKMF SPet |
| 'Monte Rosa' (d) | CWVF SRiF |
| 'Montevideo' (d) | CWVF |
| 'Monument' (d) | CSil SRiF |
| 'Mood Indigo' (d) | CTsd CWVF SVic WFuv WRou |
| 'Moonbeam' (d) | CLoc |
| 'Moonglow' | CTsd LAst MJac WFuv WPBF |
| 'Moonlight' | CCCN |
| 'Moonlight Sonata' | CLoc CWVF EBak SPet |
| 'Moonraker' (d) | CWVF SRiF SVic |
| 'More Applause' (d) | CLoc EKMF |
| 'Morning Cloud' (d) | SRiF |
| 'Morning Light' (d) | CLoc EBak SPet SVic |
| 'Morning Mist' | EBak |
| 'Morning Star' | MBri |
| 'Morrells' (d) | EBak |
| 'Morton Martianette' | EKMF |
| 'Morton Splendide' | EKMF |
| 'Moth Blue' (d) | CWVF EBak MHav SPet SRiF |
| 'Mother's Day' | SVic |
| 'Mount Edgcumbe' **new** | CTsd |
| 'Mountain Mist' (d) | CWVF EKMF SVic |
| 'Moyra' (d) | CWVF |
| 'Mr A. Huggett' | CLoc CSil CWVF EKMF EPts SLBF SPet SRiF |
| 'Mr W. Rundle' | EBak SVic |
| § 'Mr West' (v) | EKMF LSou MCot SPet SSto WRou |
| 'Mrs Churchill' | CLoc |
| 'Mrs John D. Fredericks' | CSil |
| 'Mrs Lawrence Lyon' (d) | EBak |
| 'Mrs Lee Belton' (E) **new** | SLBF |
| 'Mrs Lovell Swisher' ♀H4 | CTsd CWVF EBak EKMF LCla SPet SRiF SVic WFuv |
| 'Mrs Marshall' | CWVF EBak SLBF SPet |
| 'Mrs Popple' ♀H3 | Widely available |
| 'Mrs Susan Brookfield' (d) | SRiF |
| 'Mrs W. Castle' | CDoC CSil CTsd SVic |
| 'Mrs W.P. Wood' ♀H3 | CBgR CDoC CLoc CSil CWVF EKMF MBri SVic WFuv WRou |
| 'Mrs W. Rundle' | CLoc CSil CTsd CWVF EBak EKMF LRHS SLBF SPet |
| 'Multa' | EKMF MJac WRou |
| 'Muriel' (d) | CLoc CWVF EBak EKMF |
| 'Murru's Pierre Marie' (d) | SLBF |
| 'My Dear' (d) | WPBF |
| 'My Delight' | CWVF |
| 'My Fair Lady' (d) | CLoc CWVF EBak SPet SRiF |

| | |
|---|---|
| 'My Little Cracker' **new** | MWar WPBF |
| 'My Little Star' **new** | MWar |
| 'My Mum' | LCla SLBF WFuv |
| 'My Pat' | EKMF |
| 'My Reward' (d) | CWVF |
| 'Naaldwijk 800' | WPBF |
| 'Nananice' | SRiF |
| 'Nancy Lou' (d) | CDoC CLoc CWVF LAst LVER MJac SLBF SPet SRGP SVic WFuv WRou |
| 'Nanny Ed' (d) | CWVF EKMF MBri |
| 'Natal Bronze' | SRiF |
| 'Natalie Jones' | SRiF |
| 'Natasha Sinton' (d) | CCCN CLoc CTsd CWVF EKMF LAst LVER MBri MJac NBlu SLBF SPet WPBF WRou |
| 'Native Dancer' (d) | CWVF EBak WPBF |
| 'Naughty Nicole' (d) | WPBF |
| 'Nautilus' (d) | EBak |
| 'Navy Blue' | CSil |
| 'Neapolitan' (d) | CDoC MHav SLBF WFFs |
| 'Nectarine' **new** | EKMF |
| 'Nell Gwyn' | CLoc CWVF EBak SVic |
| 'Nellie Nuttall' ♀H3 | CLoc CWVF EBak EKMF EPts MWar SLBF SPet SRiF SVic WFuv |
| 'Neopolitan' (E) | CLoc CSil EPts MHav SVic WPBF |
| 'Nettala' | CDoC SRiF SVic WPBF |
| 'Neue Welt' | CSil CWVF EBak EKMF |
| 'New Fascination' (d) | EBak |
| 'New Millennium' | LSou LVER |
| 'Nice 'n' Easy' (d) | MBri MJac NBlu SRiF |
| 'Nicki's Findling' | CDoC CTsd CWVF EKMF EPts LCla MJac WFuv WRou |
| 'Nicky Veerman' | WPBF |
| 'Nicola' | EBak |
| 'Nicola Claire' **new** | MHav |
| 'Nicola Jane' (d) | CDoC CSil CTsd CWVF EBak EKMF EPts LCla MBri MJac SHar SLBF SPet SVic WFuv WRou |
| 'Nicola Storey' | EKMF |
| 'Nicolette' | CWVF MJac |
| 'Nightingale' (d) | CLoc EBak WPBF |
| § ***nigricans*** | CDoC EKMF |
| 'Nimue' | SRiF |
| 'Nina Wills' | EBak |
| 'Niobe' (d) | EBak |
| 'Niula' | CDoC EKMF LCla |
| 'No Name' (d) | EBak |
| 'Noel van Steenberghe' (d) **new** | WPBF |
| 'Nonchalance' | LCla |
| 'Nora' (d) | WPBF |
| 'Norfolk Ivor' (d) | WPBF |
| 'Normandy Bell' | EBak SPet SVic |
| 'North Cascades' (d) | WPBF |
| 'Northern Dancer' (d) | EKMF |
| 'Northilda' | SVic |
| 'Northumbrian Belle' | EBak SRiF |
| 'Northumbrian Pipes' | LCla |
| 'Northway' | CLoc CWVF MJac SPet SVic |
| 'Norvell Gillespie' (d) | EBak |
| 'Novato' | CTsd EBak SRiF |
| 'Novella' (d) | CWVF EBak |
| 'Noyo Star' (d) | SRiF |
| 'Nuance' | LCla WPBF |
| 'Nunthorpe Gem' (d) | CDoC CSil MHav SRiF |
| 'O Sole Mio' **new** | SVic |
| ***obconica*** (E) | CSil EKMF LCla |
| 'Obcylin' (E) | CDoC EKMF LCla SRiF WRou |
| 'Obergärtner Koch' (T) | CDoC EKMF LCla SLBF |
| 'Ocean Beach' | CDoC CTsd EPts SRiF WPBF |
| 'Oddfellow' (d) | SRiF |
| 'Oetnang' (d) | CTri SCoo |
| 'Old Somerset' (v) | CCCN CDoC CTsd LCla SRiF SVic WPBF |
| 'Oldbury' | SRiF |
| 'Oldbury Gem' | SRiF |
| 'Oldbury Pearl' | SRiF |
| 'Olive Moon' (d) | WPBF |
| 'Olive Smith' | CWVF EPts LCla MJac MWar SRiF WFFs WPBF WRou |
| 'Olympia' | EKMF |
| 'Olympic Lass' (d) | EBak |
| 'Omeomy' | SRiF |
| 'Onward' | CSil EKMF WFFs WPBF |
| § 'Oosje' (E) | CDoC CSil LCla SLBF SRiF SVic WFFs WPBF WRou |
| 'Opalescent' (d) | CLoc CWVF SVic |
| 'Orange Crush' | CCCN CDoC CLoc CTsd CWVF EBak MHav MJac SPet WFuv |
| 'Orange Crystal' | CCCN CWVF EBak EKMF MJac SVic WPBF |
| 'Orange Drops' | CLoc CTsd CWVF EBak EKMF EPts SVic WFuv |
| 'Orange Flare' | CLoc CWVF EBak MHav SLBF SRiF SVic WFuv WRou |
| 'Orange Heart' **new** | LCla |
| 'Orange King' (d) | CLoc CWVF |
| 'Orange Mirage' | CLoc CTsd CWVF EBak EKMF LAst MHav SPet SVic WFuv WRou |
| 'Orangeblossom' | CDoC MHav SLBF SRiF |
| 'Oranje van Os' | CWVF |
| 'Orient Express' (T) | CCCN CDoC CWVF MJac SVic WFFs WFuv WPBF WRou |
| 'Oriental Flame' | EKMF |
| 'Oriental Lace' | SRiF |
| 'Oriental Sunrise' | CWVF |
| 'Ornamental Pearl' | CLoc CWVF EBak SRiF |
| 'Ortenburger Festival' | WFuv |
| 'Orwell' (d) | CWVF |
| 'Oso Sweet' | CWVF SRiF |
| 'Other Fellow' | CWVF EBak EKMF EPts LCla MJac SLBF SPet SRiF SVic WFFs WFuv |
| 'Oulton Empress' (E) | SLBF |
| 'Oulton Fairy' (E) | SLBF WFFs |
| 'Oulton Painted Lady' | WRou |
| 'Oulton Red Imp' (E) | LCla SLBF |
| 'Oulton Travellers Rest' (E) | SLBF |
| 'Our Boys' | WPBF |
| 'Our Darling' | CWVF SRiF |
| 'Our Debbie' | MWar |
| 'Our Nan' (d) | MJac |
| 'Our Pamela' **new** | MJac |
| 'Our Ted' (T) | EBak EPts LCla SRiF |
| 'Our William' | SLBF WPBF |
| 'Overbecks' | see *F. magellanica* var. *molinae* 'Sharpitor' |
| 'Overbecks Ruby' | GBuc |
| 'P.J.B.' (d) | WPBF |
| 'Pabbe's Kiervaalr' **new** | WPBF |
| 'Pabbe's Kopstubber' (d) **new** | WPBF |
| 'Pabbe's Premeur' **new** | WPBF |
| 'Pabbe's Siepeltrien' **new** | WPBF |
| 'Pabbe's Torreldöve' | WPBF |
| 'Pabbe's Wikwief' **new** | WPBF |
| 'Pacemaker' | MGos |
| 'Pacific Grove' Greene | see *F.* 'Evelyn Steele Little' |
| 'Pacific Grove' Niederholzer (d) | EBak |
| 'Pacific Queen' (d) | EBak |
| 'Pacquesa' (d) | CDoC CTsd CWVF EBak SPet SRiF SVic |
| 'Padre Pio' (d) | CWVF EBak MJac |
| 'Pallas' | CSil |
| ***pallescens*** | EKMF |

| | |
|---|---|
| 'Pam Plack' | CSil EKMF LCla SLBF |
| 'Pamela Knights' (d) | EBak |
| 'Pam's People' | LCla |
| 'Pan' | MWar SRiF |
| 'Pan America' (d) | EBak |
| 'Panache' (d) | LCla |
| 'Pangea' (T) | EKMF LCla |
| ***paniculata*** (T) ♀$^{H1+3}$ | CCCN CDoC CEnd CFee CHrt CRHN CTsd CWVF EBak EKMF EPts LCla MHer SLBF SRiF WCru WPBF |
| - B&SWJ **new** | WCru |
| 'Panique' | CDoC LCla |
| 'Pantaloons' (d) | EBak |
| 'Pantomine Dame' (d) | CWVF |
| 'Panylla Prince' | CDoC LCla SRiF WRou |
| 'Papa Bleuss' (d) | CWVF EBak SRiF |
| 'Papoose' (d) | CDoC CSil EBak EKMF LCla SRiF SVic WFFs |
| 'Papua' (d) | SLBF |
| 'Paramour' | SRiF |
| 'Parasol' | WPBF |
| 'Parkstone Centenary' (d) | CWVF |
| 'Party Frock' | CDoC CLoc CTsd CWVF EBak LVER |
| 'Party Time' (d) | CWVF |
| ***parviflora*** misapplied | see *F.* x *bacillaris* |
| ***parviflora*** Lindl. | see *F. lycioides* Andrews |
| 'Pastel' | EBak |
| 'Pat Meara' | CLoc EBak SRiF |
| 'Pat Rogers' (d) **new** | MWar WPBF |
| 'Pathétique' (d) | CLoc |
| 'Patience' (d) | CWVF EBak |
| 'Patio King' | EBak EKMF |
| 'Patio Princess' (d) | CCCN CLoc CWVF EPts LAst LSou MBri NBlu SSea WFFs WFuv WGor |
| 'Patricia' Wood | CSil EBak |
| 'Patricia Hodge' | MHav WRou |
| 'Pat's Smile' | SLBF |
| 'Patty Evans' (d) | CWVF EBak |
| 'Patty Sue' (d) | EKMF MBri SRiF WFFs WRou |
| 'Paul Berry' (T) | EKMF LCla |
| 'Paul Cambon' (d) | EBak EKMF SRiF |
| 'Paul Fisher' **new** | WPBF |
| 'Paul Kennes' | EKMF WPBF |
| 'Paul Pini' (d) | SRiF |
| 'Paul Roe' (d) | MJac |
| 'Paul Storey' | CSil EKMF WPBF |
| 'Paula Jane' (d) | CCCN CDoC CLoc CTsd CWVF LAst LCla MBri MJac SLBF SRGP SVic WFuv WGor WPBF WRou |
| 'Pauline Rawlins' (d) | CLoc EBak |
| 'Paulus' | WPBF |
| 'Peace' (d) | EBak |
| 'Peachy' (California Dreamers Series) (d) | CCCN CDoC CLoc EKMF LAst MJac SCoo WFuv WPBF |
| 'Peachy Keen' (d) | EBak |
| 'Peacock' (d) | CLoc |
| 'Pearly Queen' (d) **new** | WPBF |
| 'Pee Wee Rose' | CSil EBak EKMF SVic |
| 'Peggy Belle G' (T) | EKMF LCla |
| 'Peggy Burford' (T) | EKMF LCla |
| Peggy = 'Goetzpeg'PBR (Shadowdancer Series) | CDoC LAst LSou MHav NPri SCoo |
| 'Peggy King' | CDoC CSil CTsd EBak EKMF SPet SVic WPBF |
| 'Peloria' (d) | CLoc EBak |
| 'Pennine' | MBri WFuv |
| 'People's Princess' | MJac |
| 'Peper Harow' | EBak SRiF |
| 'Pepi' (d) | CLoc CWVF EBak SPet SRiF |
| 'Peppermint Candy' (d) | CDoC CWVF EKMF MHav MJac |

| | |
|---|---|
| 'Peppermint Stick' (d) | CDoC CLoc CWVF EBak EKMF LRHS MBri SPet SVic WFuv WRou |
| 'Perky Pink' (d) | CWVF EBak EPts SPet SRiF |
| 'Perry Park' | CWVF EBak MBri MJac SRiF SVic |
| 'Perry's Jumbo' | NBir NPer |
| ***perscandens*** | CBcs CPLG CSil EKMF LCla WGwG |
| 'Personality' (d) | EBak |
| 'Peter Bellerby' (d) | EKMF |
| 'Peter Bielby' (d) | CWVF EKMF MWar SRiF |
| 'Peter Crookes' (T) | CWVF SRiF |
| 'Peter Grange' | EBak |
| 'Peter Hornby' | SRiF |
| 'Peter James' (d) | CSil EKMF SRiF |
| 'Peter Pan' | CSil CWVF |
| 'Peter Peeters' (d) | WPBF |
| 'Peter Shaffery' | LCla |
| ***petiolaris*** | CDoC LCla SVic WFFs |
| - Berry 3142 | EKMF |
| 'Petit Four' | CWVF SRiF WPBF |
| 'Petite' (d) | EBak |
| 'Petra van Britsom' | SLBF |
| 'Petronella' (d) | SRiF |
| 'Pfaffenhutchen' (d) | WPBF |
| 'Phaidra' | CDoC LCla |
| 'Pharaoh' | CLoc |
| 'Phénoménal' (d) | CDoC CSil CWVF EBak EKMF SRiF WPBF |
| 'Philippe' | WPBF |
| 'Phillip Taylor' | MJac WPBF |
| 'Phryne' (d) | CSil EBak EKMF SRiF SVic |
| 'Phyllis' (d) ♀$^{H4}$ | CAgr CDoC CLoc CSil CTsd CWVF EBak EKMF EPts LCla MJac SHar SLBF SPet SRGP SVic WFFs WFar WFuv WRou |
| 'Piet G. Vergeer' | WRou |
| 'Piet van der Sande' | CDoC LCla MWar |
| ***pilaloensis*** | EKMF |
| x ***pilcopata*** | LCla |
| 'Pinch Me' (d) | CWVF EBak LVER MHav SPet SVic |
| 'Pink Aurora' | CLoc |
| 'Pink Ballet Girl' (d) | CLoc EBak SVic |
| 'Pink Bon Accorde' | CDoC CLoc CTsd CWVF SVic WPBF |
| 'Pink Cascade' **new** | CTsd |
| 'Pink Cloud' | CLoc CTsd EBak SRiF |
| 'Pink Cornet' | LCla SRiF |
| 'Pink Darling' | CLoc EBak |
| 'Pink Dessert' | CTsd EBak |
| 'Pink Domino' (d) | CSil EKMF |
| 'Pink Fairy' (d) | EBak SPet |
| 'Pink Fandango' (d) | CLoc |
| 'Pink Fantasia' | CCCN CDoC CLoc CWVF EBak EKMF EPts LAst LCla MJac MWar SRiF SVic WFuv WPBF |
| 'Pink Flamingo' (d) | CLoc EBak |
| 'Pink Galore' (d) | CCCN CLoc CTsd CWVF EBak EKMF LAst LCla LVER MBri MJac SPet SVic WFuv WPBF |
| 'Pink Goon' (d) | CDoC CSil EKMF LCla SLBF SRiF SVic |
| 'Pink Haze' | CSil SVic |
| 'Pink Ice' (d) **new** | MSmi |
| 'Pink Jade' | CWVF EBak |
| 'Pink la Campanella' | CWVF EBak LAst MBri MWar WFFs WGor |
| 'Pink Lace' (d) | CSil SPet |
| 'Pink Marshmallow' (d) ♀$^{H1+3}$ | CCCN CDoC CLoc CWVF EBak LAst LCla LVER MJac SLBF SSea SVic WFuv WPBF |
| 'Pink Panther' (d) | EKMF SVic WFFs |
| 'Pink Pearl' Bright (d) | CSil EBak EKMF LVER |
| 'Pink Poppet' | EKMF |
| 'Pink Profusion' | EBak |

| | | |
|---|---|---|
| | 'Pink Quartet' (d) | CLoc CWVF EBak MHav SPet SRiF |
| | 'Pink Rain' | CWVF EKMF MJac WFFs WFuv WPBF WRou |
| | 'Pink Slippers' | CLoc |
| | 'Pink Spangles' | CCCN CWVF MBri SVic |
| | 'Pink Surprise' (d) | CTsd |
| | 'Pink Temptation' | CLoc CWVF EBak LAst SVic |
| | 'Pinkmost' (d) | EKMF |
| | 'Pinto de Blue' (d) | EKMF MHav MWar SRiF WPBF |
| | 'Pinwheel' (d) | CLoc EBak SRiF |
| | 'Piper' (d) | CDoC CWVF SRiF |
| | 'Piper's Vale' (T) | CCCN LAst LSou MJac SLBF SRiF |
| | 'Pippa Rolt' | EKMF |
| | 'Pirbright' | CWVF EKMF |
| | 'Pixie' | CDoC CLoc CSil CTsd CWVF EBak EKMF MHav MJac SLBF SPet SVic |
| | 'Playboy' **new** | SVic |
| | 'Playford' | CWVF EBak SRiF |
| | 'Plenty' | CSil EBak SVic |
| | 'Plumb Bob' (d) | CWVF EKMF |
| | 'Pol Jannie' (d) | WPBF |
| | 'Pole Star' | CSil SRiF |
| | 'Polskie Fuksji' **new** | WPBF |
| | 'Pop Whitlock' (v) | CWVF EKMF MCot SPet SVic |
| | 'Poppet' | CWVF |
| | 'Popsie Girl' | CDoC MWar SLBF WPBF WRou |
| | 'Port Arthur' (d) | CSil EBak SRiF |
| | 'Postiljon' | CCCN CTsd CWVF EBak MJac SPet WFFs |
| | 'Powder Puff' ambig. | CWVF MBri WFuv |
| I | 'Powder Puff' Tabraham (d) | CSil |
| | 'Powder Puff' Hodges (d) | CLoc LVER SVic |
| | 'Prelude' ambig. | SVic |
| | 'Prelude' Blackwell | CLoc CSil |
| I | 'Prelude' Kennett (d) | EBak EKMF |
| | 'President' | CDoC CSil EBak EKMF |
| | 'President B.W. Rawlins' | EBak SRiF |
| § | 'President Elliot' | CSil EKMF SRiF |
| | 'President George Bartlett' (d) | CCCN CDoC CLoc CSil EKMF EPts LAst LCla MJac MWar SLBF WFFs WFuv WPBF WRou |
| | 'President Jim Muil' | SLBF WPBF |
| | 'President Joan Morris' (d) | EKMF SLBF |
| | 'President Leo Boullemier' | CSil CWVF EBak EKMF MJac SPet SVic WPBF |
| | 'President Margaret Slater' | CLoc CTsd CWVF EBak LCla MHav SPet SVic WPBF |
| | 'President Moir' (d) | SLBF WPBF |
| | 'President Norman Hobbs' | CWVF EKMF |
| | 'President Roosevelt' (d) | CDoC MSmi |
| | 'President Stanley Wilson' | CWVF EBak EPts SPet |
| | 'President Wilf Sharp' (d) | SRiF SVic |
| | 'Preston Guild' 🏆H1+3 | CDoC CLoc CSil CTsd CWVF EBak EKMF LRHS MWar NPer SLBF SPet SRiF SVic WFFs WPBF WRou |
| | 'Prickly Heat' | EKMF |
| | 'Pride of Ipswich' | SRiF WPBF |
| | 'Pride of Roualeyn' | WRou |
| | 'Pride of the West' | CSil EBak EKMF |
| | 'Pride of Windsor' | EKMF |
| | 'Prince of Orange' | CLoc CSil CWVF EBak EKMF SVic WPBF |
| | 'Prince of Peace' (d) | SRiF |
| | 'Prince Syray' | SRiF |
| | 'Princess Dollar' | see *F.* 'Dollar Prinzessin' |
| | 'Princess of Bath' (d) | CLoc |
| | 'Princess Pamela' (d) | SLBF |
| | 'Princessita' | CDoC CTsd CWVF EBak MHav SPet |
| | ***procumbens*** | CBcs CCCN CDoC CHEx CLoc CPLG CSil CTrC CWVF EBak ECou EKMF EPts EShb EWld GCal GGar IDee ITim LCla MHer NWCA SLBF SRiF WBod WDyG WPBF WRou |
| | - 'Argentea' | see *F. procumbens* 'Wirral' |
| | - 'Variegata' | see *F. procumbens* 'Wirral' |
| § | - 'Wirral' (v) | CDoC CLoc CSil CTrC CTsd EKMF ELon EQua ITim SRiF WBor WFFs WPBF WPrP |
| | 'Prodigy' | see *F.* 'Enfant Prodigue' |
| | 'Profusion' ambig. | SVic |
| I | 'Profusion' Wood | SRiF |
| | 'Prosperity' (d) 🏆H3 | CDoC CLoc CSil CWVF EBak EKMF EPfP EPts LCla LRHS LVER MJac MRav NDlv SPet SVic WFuv WRou |
| | 'Pumila' | CPLG CWib EKMF ELan EPfP EPts SDix SLBF SPer SPet SPoG SVic WPBF WRou |
| | 'Purbeck Mist' (d) | CWVF EKMF |
| | 'Purperklokje' | CSil CWVF EBak SVic WPBF |
| | 'Purple Ann' | EKMF |
| | 'Purple Emperor' (d) | CLoc |
| | 'Purple Heart' (d) | CLoc EBak |
| | 'Purple Lace' | CSil SRiF SVic |
| | 'Purple Patch' | MBri |
| | 'Purple Pride' | MBri |
| | 'Purple Rain' | CLoc EKMF EPts LCla WFuv WRou |
| | 'Purple Showers' | SRiF |
| | 'Purple Splendour' (d) | CDoC CSil SRiF |
| | 'Pussy Cat' | CLoc CWVF EBak SRiF SVic |
| | 'Putney Pride' | EPts |
| | 'Put's Folly' | CWVF EBak MJac SLBF SPet WFFs WFuv |
| | ***putumayensis*** | CSil EBak EKMF SRiF |
| | 'Quasar' (d) | CCCN CDoC CLoc CTsd CWVF EKMF EPts LAst LCla LSou LVER MJac SLBF SPet SVic WFuv WPBF WRou |
| | 'Queen Elizabeth II' (T) | EKMF |
| | 'Queen Esther' **new** | CTsd |
| | 'Queen Mabs' | EBak |
| | 'Queen Mary' | CLoc CSil EBak EKMF |
| | 'Queen of Bath' (d) | EBak SVic |
| | 'Queen of Derby' (d) | CSil CTsd CWVF |
| | 'Queen of Hearts' Kennett (d) | SVic |
| | 'Queen Victoria' Smith (d) | EKMF |
| | 'Queen's Park' (d) | EBak |
| | 'Query' | CSil EBak SRiF SVic |
| | 'R.A.F.' (d) | CCCN CLoc CTsd CWVF EBak EKMF EPts LCla MWar SLBF SPet SVic WFFs WFuv |
| | 'Rachel Craig' (d) | MWar |
| | 'Rachel Sinton' (d) | MBri SRGP WRou |
| | 'Radcliffe Bedder' (d) | CSil EKMF |
| | 'Radings Gerda' (E) | LCla SLBF |
| | 'Radings Inge' (E) | EKMF LCla |
| | 'Radings Karin' | CDoC EKMF |
| | 'Radings Mapri' | WPBF |
| | 'Radings Michelle' | CSil CWVF |
| | 'Rahnee' | CWVF SRiF |
| | 'Rainbow' | CWVF |
| | 'Raintree Legend' (d) | SRiF |
| | 'Rakastava' (d) **new** | WPBF |
| | 'Ralph Oliver' (d) | WPBF |
| | 'Ralph's Delight' (d) | CCCN CTsd CWVF EKMF LAst SRiF WFuv |
| | 'Rambling Rose' (d) | CLoc CWVF EBak MJac |
| | 'Rams Royal' (d) | CDoC CWVF SRiF |
| | 'Raspberry' (d) | CLoc CTsd CWVF EBak SVic WFuv |
| | 'Raspberry Punch' (d) **new** | WFuv |
| | 'Raspberry Sweet' (d) | CWVF |
| | 'Ratae Beauty' | CWVF |
| | 'Ratatouille' (d) | CTsd EKMF SRiF SVic WFuv WPBF |
| | ***ravenii*** | CSil LCla |
| | 'Ravensbarrow' | CSil |
| | 'Ravenslaw' | CSil EKMF |

| | |
|---|---|
| 'Ray Redfern' | CWVF |
| 'Razzle Dazzle' (d) | EBak |
| 'Reading Show' (d) | CSil CWVF EKMF EPts SRiF |
| 'Rebecca Williamson' (d) | CWVF MJac WPBF |
| 'Rebeka Sinton' | CLoc CTsd EBak MBri |
| 'Red Ace' (d) | CSil |
| 'Red Imp' (d) | CSil |
| 'Red Jacket' (d) | CWVF EBak |
| 'Red Petticoat' | CWVF |
| 'Red Rain' | CWVF LCla SRiF WRou |
| 'Red Ribbons' (d) | EBak |
| 'Red Rover' | MWar SRiF |
| 'Red Rum' (d) | SPet |
| 'Red Shadows' (d) | CLoc CWVF EBak |
| 'Red Spider' | CCCN CLoc CTsd CWVF EBak EKMF LAst MWar SCoo SPet SVic WFuv WGor WPBF |
| 'Red Sunlight' | WPBF |
| 'Red Wing' | CLoc |
| 'Reflexa' | see *F.* x *bacillaris* 'Reflexa' |
| 'Reg Gubler' | SLBF |
| 'Regal' | CLoc |
| 'Regal Robe' (d) | CDoC |
| ***regia*** | CSil |
| - var. ***alpestris*** | see *F. alpestris* |
| - var. ***radicans*** | CSil |
| - subsp. ***regia*** | CDoC CSil CTsd LCla SRiF |
| - - Berry 4450 | EKMF |
| - - Berry 77-87 | EKMF |
| - - Berry 87-87 | EKMF |
| - subsp. ***reitzii*** | CSil LCla |
| - - Berry 04-87 | EKMF |
| - - Berry 67A-87 | EKMF |
| - subsp. ***serrae*** | CDoC CSil |
| - - Berry 11-87 | EKMF |
| - - Berry 4504 | EKMF |
| - - Berry 49-87 | EKMF |
| 'Remember Eric' | CSil EKMF WPBF |
| 'Remembrance' (d) | CSil EKMF EPts LCla SLBF |
| 'Remus' (d) | SVic |
| 'Remy Kind' (d) | SRiF |
| 'Rene Schwab' | LCla |
| 'Requiem' | CLoc |
| 'Reverend Doctor Brown' (d) | EBak |
| 'Reverend Elliott' | see *F.* 'President Elliot' |
| 'Revival' | SRiF |
| 'Rhapsody' ambig. | SVic |
| I 'Rhapsody' Blackwell (d) | CLoc |
| 'Rhombifolia' | CSil |
| 'Rianne Foks' | SRiF |
| 'Riant' (d) | SRiF |
| 'Riccartonii' 🏆$^{H3}$ | Widely available |
| 'Richard John' (v) | SRiF SVic |
| 'Richard John Carrington' | CSil |
| 'Ridestar' (d) | CLoc CWVF EBak SRiF |
| 'Rigoletto' **new** | SVic |
| 'Rijs 2001' (E) | EKMF MWar SLBF |
| 'Ringwood Gold' **new** | SVic |
| 'Ringwood Market' (d) | CSil CWVF EPts MJac SCoo SPet SRiF SVic |
| 'Rita Mary' | SRiF |
| 'Riverside' (d) | SRiF |
| 'Robbie' | EKMF WPBF |
| 'Robert Lutters' | SVic |
| 'Robin Hood' (d) | CSil |
| 'Rocket' | WPBF |
| 'Rocket Fire' (California Dreamers Series) (d) | CWVF LAst MJac WFuv |
| 'Roesse Auriga' (d) **new** | WPBF |
| 'Roesse Blacky' | CDoC EKMF WFuv WPBF |
| 'Roesse Cancer' **new** | WPBF |
| 'Roesse Cetus' (d) **new** | WPBF |
| 'Roesse Crux' (d) **new** | WPBF |
| 'Roesse Esli' | WPBF |
| 'Roesse Hydrus' (d) **new** | WPBF |
| 'Roesse Indus' (d) **new** | WPBF |
| 'Roesse Lacerta' (d) **new** | WPBF |
| 'Roesse Peacock' (d) | WPBF |
| 'Roesse Pictor' (d) **new** | WPBF |
| 'Roesse Piscus' (d) **new** | WPBF |
| 'Roesse Sextans' **new** | WPBF |
| 'Roger de Cooker' | CLoc LCla MWar WPBF |
| 'Rohees Alioth' (d) | WPBF |
| 'Rohees Emperor' (d) | WRou |
| 'Rohees King' | WPBF |
| 'Rohees Lava' | SLBF |
| 'Rohees Leada' (d) | SLBF |
| 'Rohees New Millennium' (d) | SLBF SRiF WPBF |
| 'Rohees Nunki' | WPBF |
| 'Rohees Tethys' (d) | SLBF |
| 'Rolla' (d) | CWVF EBak EKMF WPBF |
| 'Rolt's Bride' (d) | SRiF |
| 'Rolt's Ruby' (d) | CSil CWVF EKMF SRiF SVic |
| 'Roman City' (d) | CLoc MHav SRiF SVic |
| 'Romance' (d) | CWVF WFuv |
| 'Romany Rose' | CLoc |
| 'Ron Chambers Love' | MWar |
| 'Ron Ewart' | WFuv WRou |
| 'Ron Holmes' | SRiF |
| 'Ronald L. Lockerbie' (d) | CLoc CTsd CWVF EKMF SVic |
| 'Rondo' | MJac |
| 'Ron's Ruby' | CSil EKMF LCla |
| 'Roos Breytenbach' (T) | CCCN CDoC EKMF LAst LCla MJac SRiF WPBF WRou |
| 'Rooster' | EKMF |
| 'Rosamunda' | CLoc |
| 'Rose Aylett' (d) | EBak |
| 'Rose Bradwardine' (d) | EBak |
| 'Rose Churchill' (d) | MBri MJac |
| 'Rose Fantasia' | CCCN CDoC CLoc CWVF EKMF EPts LAst LCla MJac MWar SLBF WFuv |
| 'Rose Marie' (d) | CLoc |
| 'Rose of Castile' | CDoC CLoc CSil CTsd EBak EKMF LCla LRHS MJac MWat SEND SVic WFFs WFuv WRou |
| 'Rose of Castile Improved' 🏆$^{H4}$ | CSil CWVF EBak EKMF LCla MJac SPet SRiF WPBF |
| 'Rose of Denmark' | CCCN CLoc CSil CTsd CWVF EBak EKMF LAst MBri MJac NBlu SCoo SPet WFuv WGor WPBF |
| 'Rose Reverie' (d) | EBak |
| 'Rose van der Bergh' **new** | WPBF |
| 'Rose Winston' (d) | LAst SCoo |
| ***rosea*** misapplied | see *F.* 'Globosa' |
| ***rosea*** Ruíz & Pav. | see *F. lycioides* Andrews |
| 'Rosebud' (d) | EBak |
| 'Rosecroft Beauty' (d) | CSil CWVF EBak SRiF SVic |
| 'Rosella' | SLBF |
| Rosella = 'Goetzrose'$^{PBR}$ (Shadowdancer Series) | LAst NPri WPBF |
| 'Rosemarie Higham' | CCCN MHav MJac SCoo |
| 'Rosemary Day' | CLoc |
| 'Rosemoor' (T) | SRiF |
| 'Roslyn Lowe' (d) | CDoC |
| 'Ross Lea' (d) | CSil |
| 'Roswitha' | SLBF WPBF |
| 'Rosy Bows' | CWVF |
| 'Rosy Frills' (d) | CWVF MJac SVic WFuv |
| 'Rosy Morn' (d) | CLoc EBak |
| 'Rosy Ruffles' (d) | EKMF |
| 'Rothbury Beauty' | CTsd SRiF |
| 'Rough Silk' | CLoc CWVF EBak MHav |
| 'Roy Castle' (d) | CWVF |

| | |
|---|---|
| 'Roy Walker' (d) | CLoc CWVF LVER WFuv |
| 'Royal Academy' | EPts WRou |
| 'Royal and Ancient' | CWVF |
| 'Royal Mosaic' (California Dreamers Series) (d) | CCCN CDoC CWVF LAst MHav MJac SRiF WFuv |
| 'Royal Orchid' | EBak |
| 'Royal Parade' (d) | WRou |
| 'Royal Purple' (d) | CSil EBak EKMF MBri |
| 'Royal Ruby' | SRiF |
| 'Royal Serenade' (d) | CWVF |
| 'Royal Touch' (d) | EBak |
| 'Royal Velvet' (d) $\mathbb{Y}^{H3}$ | CCCN CLoc CTsd CWVF EBak EKMF EPts LCla LVER MJac MWar NBlu SLBF SPet SVic WFuv WRou |
| 'Royal Welsh' | WRou |
| 'Rubra Grandiflora' | CWVF EBak EKMF LCla SLBF SRiF WRou |
| 'Ruby Wedding' (d) | CWVF EKMF SLBF |
| 'Ruddigore' | CWVF |
| 'Ruffles' (d) | CWVF EBak |
| § 'Rufus' $\mathbb{Y}^{H3-4}$ | CDoC CLoc CSil CTsd CWVF EBak EKMF EPfP EPts LCla LRHS MJac NDlv SLBF SPet SVic WFar WFuv WRou |
| 'Rufus the Red' | see *F.* 'Rufus' |
| 'Ruth' | CSil SVic |
| 'Ruth Brazewell' (d) | CLoc |
| 'Ruth King' (d) | CWVF EBak MHav |
| 'Sabrina' | WFuv WRou |
| 'Sailor' | EPts SVic WFFs |
| 'Sally Bell' | CSil |
| 'Salmon Cascade' | CTsd CWVF EBak EKMF EPts LCla MJac SLBF WFuv WRou |
| 'Salmon Glow' | CWVF MJac SVic |
| 'Salmon Perfection' | WPBF |
| 'Salmon Queen' | WPBF |
| 'Sam' (d) | WPBF |
| 'Sam Sheppard' | SLBF |
| 'Samantha Reynolds' | MWar |
| 'Samba' (d) | LAst |
| 'Sammy Girl' | SRiF |
| 'Samson' (d/v) | EBak |
| 'San Diego' (d) | CTsd CWVF |
| 'San Francisco' | EBak |
| 'San Leandro' (d) | EBak |
| 'San Mateo' (d) | EBak |
| § ***sanctae-rosae*** | CDoC CTsd EBak EKMF LCla SRiF |
| 'Sandboy' | CWVF EBak |
| 'Sanguinea' | CSil EKMF |
| 'Sanrina' | CDoC EKMF |
| 'Santa Cruz' (d) | CSil CTsd CWVF EBak EKMF MHav SLBF SVic |
| 'Santa Lucia' (d) | CLoc EBak |
| 'Santa Monica' (d) | EBak WPBF |
| 'Santorini Sunset' | WPBF |
| 'Sapphire' (d) | EBak |
| 'Sara Helen' (d) | CLoc EBak |
| 'Sarah Eliza' (d) | CCCN MHav SCoo WFuv |
| 'Sarah Jane' (d) | CSil EBak SVic |
| 'Sarah Louise' | CWVF |
| 'Sarina' | SRiF |
| 'Sarong' (d) | EBak |
| 'Satellite' | CLoc CWVF EBak EKMF |
| 'Saturnus' | CSil CWVF EBak SPet |
| 'Saxondale Sue' **new** | SVic |
| 'Scabieuse' | CSil |
| ***scabriuscula*** | CDoC EKMF LCla |
| ***scandens*** | see *F. decussata* Ruíz & Pav. |
| 'Scarcity' | CDoC CSil CWVF EBak EKMF SPet SRiF SVic |
| 'Scarlet Cascade' | EKMF |
| 'Schiller' ambig. | EKMF WPBF |
| 'Schlosz Bentheim' | WPBF |
| 'Schneeball' (d) | CDoC CSil EBak EKMF SVic |
| 'Schneewitcher' | CDoC EKMF EPts |
| 'Schneewittchen' Hoech | CSil EKMF |
| 'Schneewittchen' Klein | CSil EBak |
| 'Schönbrunner Schuljubiläum' | EBak |
| 'Schöne Hanaurin' | SLBF |
| 'Schöne Wilhelmine' | see *F.* 'Die Schöne Wilhelmine' |
| 'Scotch Heather' (d) | CWVF MSmi |
| 'Sea Shell' (d) | CWVF EBak |
| 'Seaforth' | EBak EKMF SRiF |
| 'Sealand Prince' | CDoC CSil CTsd CWVF EKMF LCla SRiF SVic WPBF |
| 'Sebastopol' (d) | CLoc |
| 'Selma Lavrijsen' **new** | WPBF |
| ***serratifolia*** Hook. | see *F. austromontana* |
| ***serratifolia*** Ruíz & Pav. | see *F. denticulata* |
| ***sessilifolia*** | EKMF |
| 'Seventh Heaven' (d) | CCCN CLoc CTsd CWVF LAst LSou MJac SCoo SVic WPBF |
| 'Shady Blue' | CWVF |
| 'Shangri-La' (d) | EBak |
| 'Shanley' | CWVF SVic |
| 'Sharon Allsop' (d) | CWVF SRiF |
| 'Sharon Caunt' (d) | CSil EKMF |
| 'Sharon Leslie' | WRou |
| 'Sharonelle' | EKMF |
| 'Sharpitor' | see *F. magellanica* var. *molinae* 'Sharpitor' |
| 'Shauna Lindsay' | LCla |
| 'Shawna Ree' (E) | EKMF |
| 'Sheila Crooks' (d) | CWVF EBak MHav |
| 'Sheila Kirby' | CWVF MJac |
| 'Sheila Mary' (d) | EKMF |
| 'Sheila Steele' (d) | CWVF |
| 'Sheila's Love' | MJac |
| 'Sheila's Surprise' (d) | WPBF |
| 'Shelford' | CDoC CLoc CWVF EBak EKMF EPts MJac MWar SLBF SVic WFFs WRou |
| 'Shell Pink' | SVic |
| 'Shelley Lyn' (d) | SRiF WPBF |
| 'Shirley Halladay' (d) | EKMF LCla WPBF |
| 'Shirley' $^{PBR}$ (Shadowdancer Series) | CDoC LAst LSou NPri SCoo SLBF |
| 'Shooting Star' (d) | EBak |
| 'Showfire' | EBak |
| 'Showtime' (d) | CWVF |
| 'Shrimp Cocktail' **new** | LRHS MAsh |
| 'Shuna Lindsay' **new** | WPBF |
| 'Shy Lady' (d) | CTsd |
| 'Siberoet' (E) | LCla SLBF |
| 'Sierra Blue' (d) | CDoC CLoc CWVF EBak MHav |
| 'Silver Anniversary' (d) | EKMF SVic |
| 'Silver Dawn' (d) | EKMF MHav |
| 'Silver Dollar' | SVic WPBF |
| 'Silver Pink' | CSil |
| 'Silverdale' | CDoC CSil EKMF EPts |
| 'Simon J. Rowell' | EKMF LCla SRiF |
| 'Simple Simon' | SRiF |
| ***simplicicaulis*** | CDoC EBak EKMF LCla WPBF |
| 'Sincerity' (d) | CLoc |
| 'Sinton's Standard' | MBri |
| 'Siobhan' | CWVF |
| 'Siobhan Evans' (d) | MWar SLBF |
| 'Sipke Arjen' | WRou |
| 'Sir Alfred Ramsey' | CWVF EBak |
| 'Sir David Jason' **new** | MJac WFuv |
| 'Sir Matt Busby' (d) | CTsd EKMF EPts LAst MHav MJac WPBF WRou |
| 'Sir Steve Redgrave' (d) | MJac |
| 'Sir Thomas Allen' | SLBF |

| | | |
|---|---|---|
| | 'Siren' Baker (d) | EBak |
| | 'Sister Ann Haley' | EKMF EPts |
| | 'Sister Sister' (d) | SLBF |
| | 'Six Squadron' | EKMF |
| | 'Sjan Schilders' (d) | WPBF |
| | 'Sleepy' | CSil CTsd EPts MHav SPet SVic WFuv WPBF |
| | 'Sleigh Bells' | CLoc CTsd CWVF EBak EKMF SPet SVic |
| | 'Small Pipes' | CWVF EKMF LCla SRiF WFuv |
| | 'Smokey Mountain' (d) | MWar SVic WFuv |
| | 'Sneezy' | CSil EPts MHav SVic WFuv WPBF |
| | 'Snow Burner' (California Dreamers Series) (d) | CCCN CDoC CLoc CWVF LAst MHav |
| | 'Snow Pearls' **new** | WPBF |
| | 'Snow White' (d) | SPet SVic WPBF |
| | 'Snowbird' (d) | SLBF |
| § | 'Snowcap' (d) 🏆$^{H3-4}$ | CBgR CCCN CDoC CLoc CSil CTsd CWVF EBak EKMF EPts LCla LVER MAsh MBri MGos MJac MWar NPer SCoo SLBF SPet SPla SVic WFFs WFar WFuv WRou |
| | 'Snowdon' (d) | CWVF |
| | 'Snowdrift' Colville (d) | CLoc |
| | 'Snowdrift' Kennett (d) | EBak |
| | 'Snowfall' | CWVF |
| | 'Snowfire' (d) | CLoc CWVF EKMF SCoo SVic WFuv |
| | 'Snowflake' (E) | EKMF LCla SLBF WBor WRou |
| | 'Snowstorm' (d) | SPet WPBF |
| | 'So Big' (d) | EKMF SRiF |
| | 'Softpink Jubelteen' | WPBF |
| | 'Software' (d) | WPBF |
| | 'Son of Thumb' 🏆$^{H4}$ | CDoC CLoc CSil CTsd CWVF EKMF EPfP EPts LAst MAsh MBar MGos MJac NDlv SIng SLBF SLim SPet SSto SVic WFar WFuv WPBF WRou |
| | 'Sonata' (d) | CLoc CWVF EBak SVic |
| | 'Sophie Louise' | CWVF EKMF EPts MWar WFuv WPBF WRou |
| | 'Sophie's Silver Lining' | MJac |
| | 'Sophisticated Lady' (d) | CLoc CWVF EBak EKMF EPts MSmi SPet SVic |
| | 'Soroptimist International' | WRou |
| | 'Source du Loiret' **new** | EKMF |
| | 'South Gate' (d) | CLoc CTsd CWVF EBak EKMF EPts LAst MBri MJac MWar SPet SVic WPBF |
| | 'South Lakeland' | CSil |
| | 'South Seas' (d) | EBak SVic |
| | 'Southern Pride' | SLBF |
| | 'Southlanders' | EBak |
| | 'Southwell Minster' | EKMF |
| | 'Space Shuttle' | CLoc EKMF LCla SLBF SRiF |
| | 'Sparky' (T) | CLoc CWVF EPts LCla MHav SRiF WRou |
| § | 'Speciosa' | CDoC EBak EKMF LCla SRiF WRou |
| | 'Spion Kop' (d) | CCCN CTsd CWVF EBak EKMF LAst SPet WFuv WGor |
| § | ***splendens*** 🏆$^{H1+3}$ | CCCN CDoC CLoc CSil EBak EKMF IDee LCla MCot MHer NPer SLBF SRiF WRou |
| | - B&SWJ 10469 | WCru |
| | - 'Karl Hartweg' | CDoC |
| | 'Squadron Leader' (d) | CWVF EBak EPts |
| | 'Square Peg' (d) | SRiF |
| | 'Stad Genk' (d) | WPBF |
| | 'Stadt Telc' | SLBF |
| § | 'Stals Kevin' (T) | WPBF |
| | 'Stan' | WPBF |
| | 'Stanley Cash' (d) | CLoc CTsd CWVF EKMF LVER MWar SPet SVic WFuv |
| | 'Star Wars' | CLoc EPts LAst MBri MHav MJac MWar SRiF WPBF WRou |
| | 'Stardust' | CDoC CWVF EBak MHav MJac |
| | 'Steeley' (d) | SVic |
| | 'Steirerblut' (T) | SRiF WPBF |
| | 'Stella Ann' (T) | CWVF EBak EPts LCla SRiF WFuv WPBF |
| | 'Stella Marina' (d) | EBak |
| | 'Stevie Doidge' (d) **new** | WPBF |
| | 'Stewart Taylor' | MJac |
| | ***steyermarkii*** DG 1057 | EKMF |
| | 'Stolze von Berlin' (d) | SRiF |
| | 'Stoney Creek' (d) | SRiF |
| | 'Storeytime' | EKMF |
| | 'Straat Fiji' | LCla |
| | 'Straat Fuknoka' **new** | LCla |
| | 'Straat Futami' (e) | EKMF LCla |
| | 'Straat Kobe' (T) | EKMF LCla WPBF |
| | 'Straat La Plata' **new** | LCla |
| | 'Straat Magelhaen' | LCla |
| | 'Straat Messina' **new** | LCla |
| | 'Straat Moji' | WPBF |
| | 'Straat of Plenty' | LCla SLBF |
| | 'Straat Red Sea' **new** | LCla |
| | 'Straat Van Diemen' | LCla |
| | 'Strawberry Daiquiri' (d) **new** | WPBF |
| | 'Strawberry Delight' (d) | CLoc CWVF EBak EKMF MHav MJac SPet SVic WFuv |
| | 'Strawberry Fizz' | MHav |
| | 'Strawberry Sundae' (d) | CLoc CWVF EBak |
| | 'Strawberry Supreme' (d) | CSil EKMF |
| | 'String of Pearls' | CLoc CWVF EKMF LCla MJac SLBF SPet SVic |
| | 'Stuart Joe' | CWVF EKMF |
| * | ***subparamosis*** Green 1006 | EKMF |
| | 'Sue' | CTsd SLBF |
| | 'Sugar Almond' (d) | CWVF |
| | 'Sugar Blues' (d) | EBak |
| | 'Summerdaffodil' | WPBF |
| | 'Summerwood' (d) | SRiF |
| | (Sunbeam Series) 'Sunbeam Ernie' | WPBF |
| | - 'Sunbeam Hillary' | WPBF |
| | 'Sunkissed' (d) | EBak |
| | 'Sunlight Path' | WPBF |
| | 'Sunningdale' (T) | CWVF LCla |
| | 'Sunny' | SRiF |
| | 'Sunny Jim' **new** | SVic |
| | 'Sunny Smiles' | CSil CWVF EKMF SPet SRiF |
| | 'Sunray' (v) | CLoc CWVF EBak EKMF GGar LBuc LRHS MAsh MWar MWat SCoo SLim SPla SPoG |
| | 'Sunset' | CLoc CWVF EBak SPer |
| | 'Sunset Boulevard' (d) | WPBF |
| | 'Supersport' (d) | SVic |
| | 'Superstar' | CWVF EPts SVic |
| | 'Susan Drew' | SLBF |
| | 'Susan Ford' (d) | CWVF SPet SRiF |
| | 'Susan Green' | CSil CWVF EBak EKMF MJac MWar SPet |
| | 'Susan McMaster' | CLoc |
| | 'Susan Olcese' (d) | CWVF EBak |
| | 'Susan Skeen' | MJac WPBF |
| | 'Susan Travis' | CLoc CSil CWVF EBak EKMF MAsh SPet SRiF SVic |
| | 'Susanna D. Dijkman' | WPBF |
| | 'Suzanna' | WPBF |
| | 'Swanley Gem' 🏆$^{H3}$ | CLoc CWVF EBak EKMF SLBF SPet SVic WRou |
| | 'Swanley Pendula' | CLoc MHav |
| | 'Swanley Yellow' | CWVF EBak SVic |

| | | |
|---|---|---|
| | 'Sweet Leilani' (d) | CLoc EBak |
| | 'Sweet Sarah' (E) | SLBF |
| | 'Sweet Sixteen' (d) | CLoc |
| I | 'Sweetheart' van Wieringen | EBak |
| | 'Swingtime' (d) 🏆$^{H3}$ | CCCN CLoc CTsd CWVF EBak EKMF EPts LAst LCla LVER MGos MJac MWar NBlu SLBF SPet SVic WFuv WPBF |
| | 'S'Wonderful' (d) | CLoc EBak |
| | ***sylvatica*** misapplied | see *F. nigricans* |
| | 'Sylvia' Veitch (d) | SRiF |
| | 'Sylvia Barker' | CWVF LCla MWar WFFs WFuv WPBF WRou |
| | 'Sylvia Rose' (d) | CWVF SRiF |
| | 'Sylvia's Choice' | EBak |
| | 'Symphony' | CLoc CWVF EBak |
| | 'T. Heivrouwke' (d) **new** | WPBF |
| | 'T.S.J.' (E) | LCla |
| | 'Taco' | CDoC LCla |
| | 'Taddle' | CWVF SLBF |
| | 'Taffeta Bow' (d) | CLoc LVER SVic |
| | 'Taffy' | EBak |
| | 'Tam O'Shanter' (d) | CTsd WFuv |
| | 'Tamerus Hop' (d) | WPBF |
| | 'Tamerus Nandoe' | WPBF |
| | 'Tamerus Toerako' | WPBF |
| | 'Tamworth' | CLoc CTsd CWVF EBak MJac SVic |
| | 'Tangerine' | CLoc CWVF EBak MHav SVic WRou |
| | 'Tanja's Blue Bells' (d) **new** | WPBF |
| | 'Tantalising Tracy' (d) | WPBF |
| | 'Tanya' | CLoc EKMF SPet |
| | 'Tanya Bridger' (d) | EBak |
| | 'Tarra Valley' (T) | LCla SRiF SVic WPBF |
| | 'Task Force' | CWVF SRiF SVic |
| | 'Tasty Tracey' | SRiF |
| | 'Tausendschön' (d) | CLoc |
| | 'Ted Perry' (d) | CWVF |
| | 'Ted's Tribute' | EKMF |
| | 'Television' (d) | CTsd |
| | 'Temptation' ambig. | CTsd CWVF SPet |
| | 'Temptation' Peterson | CLoc EBak |
| | 'Tennessee Waltz' (d) 🏆$^{H3}$ | CDoC CLoc CSil CTsd CWVF EBak EKMF EPts LRHS LVER MJac MWar SLBF SPet SVic WEas WFFs WFuv WRou |
| | 'Tequila Sunrise' **new** | WPBF |
| | 'Tessa Jane' | CSil |
| | ***tetradactyla*** misapplied | see *F. x bacillaris* |
| | ***tetradactyla*** Lindl. | see *F. encliandra* subsp. *tetradactyla* |
| | 'Texas Longhorn' (d) | CLoc CWVF EBak EKMF SVic WPBF |
| | 'Thalia' (T) 🏆$^{H1+3}$ | Widely available |
| | 'Thamar' | CDoC CLoc CWVF EKMF EPts WPBF WRou |
| | 'That's It' (d) | EBak SVic WPBF |
| | 'The Aristocrat' (d) | CLoc EBak |
| | 'The Boys' | WPBF |
| | 'The Cannons' (d) | SRiF |
| § | 'The Doctor' | CLoc CSil CWVF EBak |
| | 'The Jester' (d) | EBak |
| | 'The Madame' (d) | CTsd CWVF EBak |
| | 'The Tarns' | CSil CWVF EBak EKMF SRiF SVic |
| | 'Therese Dupois' | CSil |
| | 'Théroigne de Méricourt' | EBak EKMF SRiF |
| | 'Thilco' | CDoC CSil EKMF |
| | 'Think Pink' | CTsd |
| | 'This England' (d) | SRiF |
| | 'Thistle Hill' (d) | CSil EKMF |
| | 'Thomas' (d) | EPts |
| | 'Thomas Pips' | WPBF |
| | 'Thompsonii' | see *F. magellanica* 'Thompsonii' |

| | | |
|---|---|---|
| | 'Thornley's Hardy' | CSil EKMF MRav SPet SRiF SVic WPBF |
| | 'Three Cheers' | CLoc EBak |
| | 'Three Counties' | EBak |
| | 'Thunderbird' (d) | CLoc CWVF EBak |
| | ***thymifolia*** (E) | CWVF EAlp EBee EDAr GCra GQui LHop LRHS MHer SHGN WKif |
| | - subsp. ***minimiflora*** (E) | CSil EKMF LCla |
| | - subsp. ***thymifolia*** (E) | CDoC CSil EKMF LCla |
| | 'Tiara' (d) | EBak |
| | 'Tickled Pink' | MWar WRou |
| | 'Tiffany' Reedstrom (d) | EBak |
| | ***tillettiana*** | EKMF |
| | 'Tillingbourne' (d) | CSil SLBF |
| | Tilly = 'Goetztil'$^{PBR}$ (Shadowdancer Series) | LAst NPri |
| | 'Time After Time' **new** | WRou |
| | 'Timlin Brened' (T) | CWVF EBak SRiF WPBF |
| | 'Timothy Titus' (T) | LCla MWar SLBF SRiF |
| | 'Ting-a-ling' | CLoc CTsd CWVF EBak EKMF SLBF SPet SVic WFuv WPBF |
| | 'Tinker Bell' Hodges | EBak SVic WPBF |
| I | 'Tinker Bell' Tabraham | CSil EKMF |
| | 'Tintern Abbey' | CWVF |
| | 'Tiny Whisper' | WPBF |
| | 'Titania' **new** | WPBF |
| | 'Tjinegara' | CDoC LCla |
| | 'Toby Bridger' (d) | CLoc EBak |
| | 'Toby Foreman' **new** | SLBF |
| | 'Tolling Bell' | CTsd CWVF EBak EKMF SPet WPBF WRou |
| | 'Tom Goedeman' | LCla |
| | 'Tom H. Oliver' (d) | EBak |
| | 'Tom Knights' | EBak SPet |
| | 'Tom Thorne' | EBak |
| | 'Tom Thumb' 🏆$^{H3}$ | Widely available |
| | 'Tom West' misapplied | see *F.* 'Mr West' |
| | 'Tom West' Meillez (v) | CDoC CHEx CLoc CMHG CSBt CSil CWVF CWib EBak EKMF EPts LAst LCla LHop LVER MAsh MHer MJac MWar NVic SDix SLBF SRiF SSea WFar WFuv WPBF |
| | 'Tom Woods' | CWVF |
| | 'Tommy Struck' (d) **new** | WPBF |
| | 'Tommy Tucker' | SRiF |
| | 'Ton Ten Hove' **new** | LCla |
| | 'Tony Galea' | SRiF |
| | 'Tony's Treat' (d) | EPts |
| | 'Toon's Tuinklokje' **new** | WPBF |
| | 'Toos' | SVic |
| | 'Topaz' (d) | CLoc EBak |
| | 'Topper' (d) | CWVF |
| | 'Torch' (d) | CLoc CWVF EBak SVic |
| | 'Torchlight' | CWVF EPts LCla WFuv WRou |
| | 'Torvill and Dean' (d) | CCCN CLoc CTsd CWVF EKMF EPts LAst LRHS LVER MJac SPet WFuv WGor WRou |
| | 'Tosca' | CWVF |
| | 'Town Crier' | SLBF |
| | 'Tracid' (d) | CLoc CSil |
| | 'Tracie Ann' (d) | EKMF |
| | 'Trail Blazer' (d) | CLoc CWVF EBak MJac SPet |
| | 'Trailing Queen' | EBak EKMF MJac |
| | 'Transport Command' **new** | EKMF |
| | 'Trase' (d) | CDoC CSil CTsd CWVF CWib EBak EKMF MHav SRiF SVic |
| | 'Traudchen Bonstedt' (T) | CDoC CLoc CWVF EBak EKMF LCla SLBF SPet SRiF SVic WPBF |
| | 'Traviata' | see *F.* 'La Traviata' Blackwell |
| | 'Treasure' (d) | EBak |
| | 'Tresco' | CSil |
| | 'Treslong' | WPBF |
| | 'Tric Trac' | WPBF |

'Tricolor' see *F. magellanica* var. *gracilis* 'Tricolor'
'Tricolorii' see *F. magellanica* var. *gracilis* 'Tricolor'
'Trientje' LCla SLBF
'Trimley Bells' EBak
'Trio' (d) CLoc
***triphylla*** (T) EBak LRHS MHer
'Tripi' **new** EKMF
'Trish's Triumph' EPts
'Tristesse' (d) CLoc CWVF EBak SRiF
'Troika' (d) EBak EKMF
'Troon' CWVF
'Tropic Sunset' (d) CTsd MBri
'Tropicana' (d) CLoc CWVF EBak SVic WPBF
'Troubador' Waltz (d) CLoc
'Troutbeck' CSil
'Trudi Davro' CCCN LAst MHav MJac SCoo
'Trudy' CSil CWVF EBak EKMF SPet SVic
'Truly Treena' (d) LCla SLBF
'Trumpeter' ambig. CDoC CWVF MHav WFuv
'Trumpeter' Fry SRiF SVic
'Trumpeter' Reiter (T) CLoc EBak EKMF EPts LCla MJac
'Tsjiep' CDoC SRiF WPBF
'Tubular Bells' (T) EKMF LCla SRiF
'Tumbling Waters' (d) LVER
'Tuonela' (d) CLoc CWVF EBak WPBF
'Turandot' WPBF
'Turkish Delight' LAst MWar WRou
'Tutone' (d) SRiF
'Tutti-frutti' (d) CLoc
'T'Vöske' (d/v) WPBF
'Twinkling Stars' CWVF MJac SVic
'Twinney' CWVF
'Twinny' EKMF EPts LCla MWar
'Twirling Square Dancer' (d) WPBF
'Twist of Fate' (d) CSil EKMF
'Two Tiers' (d) CSil CWVF EKMF WPBF
'Twydale' SRiF
'U.B.' (d) SRiF
'U.F.O.' CTsd CWVF SVic
'Ullswater' (d) CWVF EBak
'Ultramar' (d) EBak
'Uncle Charley' (d) CDoC CLoc CSil EBak EKMF MSmi
'Uncle Jinks' SPet
'Uncle Steve' (d) CTsd EBak SVic
'University of Liverpool' CLoc MJac WPBF
'Upward Look' EBak EKMF
'Valda May' (d) CWVF
'Vale of Belvoir' SRiF
'Valentine' (d) EBak
'Valerie' **new** WFuv
'Valerie Ann' (d) EBak EKMF SPet SVic
'Valerie Hobbs' (d) LCla
'Valerie Tooke' (d) LCla
'Valiant' EBak
'Van Eijk Bello' (a) **new** WPBF
'Van Eijk Sheltie' (d) **new** WPBF
'Vanessa Jackson' CLoc CWVF MHav MJac SVic
'Vanity Fair' (d) CLoc EBak
'Variegated Brenda White' (v) EKMF
'Variegated Lottie Hobby' (E/v) CSil CTsd EKMF SRiF
'Variegated Pink Fantasia' (v) **new** WFuv
'Variegated Pink Fascination' WRou
'Variegated Pixie' CSil EKMF
'Variegated Procumbens' see *F. procumbens* 'Wirral'
'Variegated Superstar' (v) MBri
'Variegated Swingtime' (v) EBak LAst
'Variegated Triphylla' (T/v) SRiF
'Variegated Vivienne Thompson' (d/v) MBri
'Variegated Waveney Sunrise' (v) MBri
'Variegated White Joy' (v) EKMF
'Veenlust' CCCN EBak SRiF WPBF WRou
'Vendeta' CDoC LCla
'Venus Victrix' (T) CSil EBak EKMF SLBF SRiF WPBF
***venusta*** CDoC CTsd EBak EKMF LCla
'Versicolor' see *F. magellanica* 'Versicolor'
'Vespa' SRiF
'Vesuvio' EKMF
'Vicky' EKMF
'Victorian' (d) SVic
'Victory' Reiter (d) EBak
'Vielliebchen' CDoC CSil
'Vienna Waltz' (d) WFuv
'Vincent van Gogh' WPBF
'Vintage Dovercourt' LCla
'Violet Bassett-Burr' (d) CLoc EBak
'Violet Gem' (d) CLoc
'Violet Lace' (d) CSil
'Violet Rosette' (d) CTsd CWVF EBak SVic
Violetta = 'Goetzviol'[PBR] (Shadowdancer Series) CDoC LAst LSou NPri SCoo SVil WPBF
'Viva Ireland' EBak
'Vivien Colville' CLoc EKMF
'Vivienne Thompson' (d) WFFs
'Vobeglo' CWVF
'Vogue' (d) EBak
'Voltaire' CSil EBak EKMF SRiF
'Voodoo' (d) CCCN CDoC CLoc CWVF EBak EKMF EPts LAst LSou SCoo SLBF SVic WRou
***vulcanica*** CDoC EKMF LCla SRiF
* - subsp. ***hitchcockii*** EKMF
'Vyvian Miller' CWVF
'W.P. Wood' CDoC CSil
§ 'Wagtails White Pixie' CSil EBak EPfP
'Waldfee' (E) CCVN CDoC CSil EKMF LCla SRiF WFFs WPBF
'Waldis Geisha' (d) SLBF
'Waldis Junella' (d) **new** SLBF
'Waldis Laura' **new** SLBF
'Waldis Maja' **new** WPBF
'Waldis Ovambo' SLBF
'Waldis Simon' WPBF
'Waldis Spezi' CDoC LCla
'Waldis Speziella' **new** SLBF
'Wally Yendell' (v) SRiF WPBF
'Walsingham' (d) CWVF EBak WPBF
'Walton Jewel' EBak SRiF
'Waltz Harp' **new** MHav
'Walz Banjo' WPBF
'Walz Bella' LCla WFuv WPBF
'Walz Blauwkous' (d) CWVF
'Walz Cello' WPBF
'Walz Cimbaal' SRiF
'Walz Cocktail' WPBF
'Walz Duimelot' SRiF
'Walz Epicurist' WPBF
'Walz Fagot' SRiF
'Walz Fanclub' LCla WPBF
'Walz Fluit' CCCN MJac WRou
'Walz Fonola' WPBF
'Walz Freule' CWVF EKMF MJac
'Walz Harp' CDoC CWVF SRiF SVic WPBF
'Walz Hoorn' WPBF
'Walz Jubelteen' CDoC CLoc CTsd CWVF EKMF EPts LCla MJac MWar SLBF SSea SVic WFuv WPBF WRou
'Walz Klarinet' WPBF
'Walz Klokkenspel' **new** WFuv

| | |
|---|---|
| 'Walz Lucifer' | CWVF LCla MWar |
| 'Walz Mandoline' (d) | CWVF SVic |
| 'Walz Orgelpijp' | WPBF |
| 'Walz Panfluit' | LCla WPBF |
| 'Walz Polka' | LCla |
| 'Walz Ratel' **new** | WPBF |
| 'Walz Saxofoon' **new** | WPBF |
| 'Walz Spinet' | WPBF |
| 'Walz Triangel' (d) | EKMF SVic WPBF |
| 'Walz Trombone' | WPBF |
| 'Walz Tuba' (T) | SRiF WPBF |
| 'Walz Viool' **new** | WPBF |
| 'Walz Wipneus' | WPBF |
| 'Wapenveld's Bloei' | CDoC LCla SLBF |
| 'War Paint' (d) | CLoc CTsd EBak |
| 'Warke' (a) **new** | WPBF |
| 'Warton Crag' | CWVF SVic |
| 'Water Nymph' | CLoc SLBF WPBF |
| 'Wave of Life' | CWVF EKMF |
| 'Waveney Gem' | CDoC CWVF EBak EKMF LAst LCla MJac MWar SLBF SPet WFFs WFuv WPBF |
| 'Waveney Queen' | CWVF SVic |
| 'Waveney Sunrise' | CTsd CWVF MHav MJac MWar SPet SVic |
| 'Waveney Unique' | CWVF |
| 'Waveney Valley' | CWVF EBak MJac |
| 'Waveney Waltz' | CWVF EBak |
| 'Waxen Beauty' | WPBF |
| 'Wedding Bells' ambig. | SVic WFuv |
| 'Welsh Dragon' (d) | CLoc CWVF EBak SRiF |
| 'Wendy' Catt | see *F.* 'Snowcap' |
| 'Wendy Atkinson' (d) | EKMF |
| 'Wendy Leedham' (d) | EKMF |
| 'Wendy van Wanten' | WPBF |
| 'Wendy's Beauty' (d) | CCCN CLoc EBak EPts MHav MJac SRiF WFuv WRou |
| 'Wentworth' | CWVF SVic WPBF |
| 'Wessex Belle' (d/v) | CWVF |
| 'Wessex Hardy' | CSil EKMF |
| 'Westham' | LCla |
| 'Westminster Chimes' (d) | CLoc CWVF SPet SVic |
| 'Wharfedale' ♀H3 | CSil MJac SLBF SRiF SVic |
| 'Whickham Blue' | CWVF MWar |
| 'Whirlaway' (d) | CLoc CWVF EBak SVic |
| 'White Ann' | see *F.* 'Heidi Weiss' |
| 'White Clove' | CDoC CSil MHav SRiF SVic WPBF |
| 'White Fairy' | WPBF |
| 'White Galore' (d) | CWVF EBak EKMF LVER SVic |
| 'White Général Monk' (d) | CDoC CSil MHav |
| 'White Gold' (v) | EBak |
| 'White Haven' **new** | SVic |
| 'White Heidi Ann' (d) | CSil CTsd |
| 'White Joy' | EBak EKMF |
| 'White King' (d) | CLoc CTsd CWVF EBak EKMF LVER SPet SVic WFuv WRou |
| 'White Lace' | CSil |
| 'White Pixie' ♀H3-4 | CDoC CSil EKMF EPts LVER MHav MJac SLBF SPer SPet SVic |
| 'White Pixie Wagtail' | see *F.* 'Wagtails White Pixie' |
| 'White Princess' | SRiF |
| 'White Queen' ambig. | CWVF |
| 'White Queen' Doyle | EBak |
| 'White Spider' | CLoc CWVF EBak SPet SVic |
| 'White Veil' (d) | CWVF |
| 'Whiteknights Amethyst' | CDoC CSil EKMF |
| 'Whiteknights Blush' | CChe CDoC CMdw CPLG CSil EWes GCal GGar GQui SMrm WPBF |
| 'Whiteknights Cheeky' (T) | CWVF EBak EPts LCla SRiF SVic |
| 'Whiteknights Green Glister' | CDoC CSil EKMF EPfP |
| 'Whiteknights Pearl' ♀H1+3 | CDoC CSil CTsd CWVF ECha EKMF EPfP EPts LCla SLBF SMHy SPet SVic WFFs WFuv WPBF |
| 'Whiteknights Ruby' (T) | LCla SRiF WFFs |
| 'Whitney' | SRiF |
| 'Whitton Starburst' | LCla |
| 'Wicked Queen' (d) | CSil SRiF SVic WPBF |
| 'Widow Twanky' (d) | CWVF WPBF |
| 'Wiebke Becker' | EKMF |
| 'Wigan Pier' (d) | LCla MWar SLBF WRou |
| 'Wight Magic' (d) | MJac WFuv |
| 'Wild and Beautiful' (d) | CTsd CWVF EKMF SPet SRiF SVic |
| 'Wilf Langton' | MWar WPBF WRou |
| 'Wilhelmina Schwab' | CDoC LCla |
| 'Willeke Smit' (d) **new** | WPBF |
| 'William Caunt' | EKMF |
| 'Willie Tamerus' | WPBF |
| 'Willy Winky' | CSil SRiF |
| 'Wilma van Druten' (T) | CDoC EKMF LCla |
| 'Wilma Versloot' | WPBF |
| 'Wilson's Colours' | EPts |
| 'Wilson's Joy' | LCla MJac |
| 'Wilson's Pearls' (d) | CWVF SLBF SPet |
| 'Wilson's Sugar Pink' | EPts LCla MJac |
| 'Win Oxtoby' (d) | CWVF EKMF |
| 'Windhapper' | LCla WFuv WPBF |
| 'Windmill' | CWVF |
| 'Wine and Roses' (d) | EBak |
| 'Wingrove's Mammoth' (d) | SVic |
| 'Wings of Song' (d) | CWVF EBak |
| 'Winston Churchill' (d) ♀H3 | CCCN CLoc CTsd CWVF EBak EKMF LAst LVER MBri MJac MWar NBlu NVic SCoo SPet SPlb SSea SVic WFuv |
| 'Winter Yellow' **new** | WPBF |
| 'Winter's Touch' | EKMF WPBF |
| 'Witchipoo' | SLBF |
| 'Woodnook' (d) | CWVF |
| 'Woodside' (d) | CSil SVic |
| ***wurdackii*** | EKMF |
| 'Xmas Tree' | WPBF |
| 'Yellow Heart' **new** | WPBF |
| 'Ymkje' | EBak |
| 'Yolanda Franck' | CDoC WRou |
| 'York Manor' **new** | WRou |
| 'Yours' | SRiF |
| 'Youth' | EKMF |
| 'Yvonne Priest' | SRiF |
| 'Yvonne Schwab' | CDoC LCla SRiF |
| 'Zeebrook' | SRiF SVic |
| 'Zellertal' | WPBF |
| 'Zeta' **new** | WPBF |
| 'Zets Bravo' | CDoC CTsd SRiF |
| 'Ziegfield Girl' (d) | EBak SRiF SVic |
| 'Zifi' | SLBF |
| 'Zulu King' | CDoC CDow CSil SRiF SVic WFFs |
| 'Zulu Queen' | SVic |
| 'Zwarte Snor' (d) | CWVF |

## *Fumaria* (*Papaveraceae*)

| | |
|---|---|
| ***lutea*** see *Corydalis lutea* | |
| ***officinalis*** | CArn MSal |

## *Furcraea* (*Agavaceae*)

| | |
|---|---|
| ***bedinghausii*** | CAby CBct CCCN CHll EBee LEdu MAga WPGP |
| § ***foetida*** | CCCN |
| ***gigantea*** | see *F. foetida* |
| ***longaeva*** | CAbb CDTJ CFir CHEx CPen CTrC CTsd EAmu EBee GGar LEdu SAPC SArc SChr SDix WCot WPGP |
| ***parmentieri*** NJM 05.081 **new** | WPGP |
| ***selloa*** | MAga |
| – var. ***marginata*** (v) | CDoC MAga |

# G

## *Gagea* (*Liliaceae*)

| | |
|---|---|
| ***lutea*** | CExc EPot |
| ***pratensis*** | EPot |

## *Gaillardia* (*Asteraceae*)

| | |
|---|---|
| ***aristata*** 'Maxima Aurea' | EBee EBla LAst LRHS NBre NPri NVic SPhx WCAu |
| 'Arizona Sun' | EBee ECtt LRHS LSou MHer NPri |
| 'Bijou' | EBee MBri NBre NVic SWvt |
| 'Dwarf Goblin' | LAst NGBl SPet |
| § 'Fackelschein' | NBre SRms |
| 'Fanfare'PBR | EBee ELon ENor LBuc LSou MBri MMHG MWea NDov SCoo SPer SPoG WCot |
| Goblin | see *G.* x *grandiflora* 'Kobold' |
| x ***grandiflora*** 'Amber Wheels' | CSam EDAr LBMP LLHF NPri STes |
| - 'Aurea' | LRHS |
| - 'Bremen' | EBee MBri |
| - 'Burgunder' | COIW CSBt CSpe EBee EBla ECtt EHrv ELan EPfP EShb LAst LHop LRHS LSRN MBri NGBl NMir NPri NVic SMrm SPer SPhx SPla SPoG SRms SWvt WCAu WPer |
| - 'Dazzler' 🏆H4 | CSBt EAEE EBee EBla ECtt ELan EPfP LAst LBMP LRHS NLar NPri NVic SECG SMrm SPer SPoG WCAu WPer |
| § - 'Kobold' | CBcs COIW CSBt CSam EBla ECtt EPfP GJos GKir GMaP LAst LBMP LHop LRHS MBri NBlu NBre NPri SMrm SPad SPer SPla SPlb SPoG SRms SWal SWvt WFar |
| - 'Summer's Kiss' **new** | EBee |
| - 'Tokajer' | EBee EPfP LBMP NBre NLar SPhx |
| 'Mandarin' | LRHS SRms |
| * giant hybrids **new** | WFar |
| § 'Oranges and Lemons'PBR | EBee LSou SHar SPoG |
| Saint ClementsPBR | see *G.* 'Oranges and Lemons' |
| 'Sunshine Yellow' | CSec |
| Torch Red Ember = 'Baltoredem'PBR | SPoG |
| Torchlight | see *G.* 'Fackelschein' |

## *Galactites* (*Asteraceae*)

| | |
|---|---|
| ***tomentosa*** | CSec CSpe EBee EHrv ELan EPfP EPyc EWTr LDai LRHS MWea NBur NDov SBHP SDnm SGar SPav WEas |
| - white-flowered | CBod EGoo NBur |

## *Galanthus* ✿ (*Amaryllidaceae*)

| | |
|---|---|
| x ***allenii*** | CBro MAsh WIvy |
| ***alpinus*** | CLAP |
| - var. ***alpinus*** | LAma LFox MTho NMen |
| - - late-flowering | LRHS |
| - var. ***bortkewitschianus*** | LFox |
| § ***angustifolius*** | CBro |
| 'Annette' **new** | LAma |
| 'Armine' | CAvo CSna LFox |
| 'Atkinsii' 🏆H4 | CAvo CBgR CBro CElw CFFs CLAP CWCL ECha ECho EHrv EMon EPot GEdr GKev IHer LAma LFox LRHS MAsh MAvo MHom MRav NBir SChr WCot WPGP WShi WTin |
| 'Barbara's Double' (d) | CLAP CWsd LRHS |
| 'Benhall Beauty' | CSna LFox MAsh WTin |
| 'Bertram Anderson' | LFox MAsh |
| 'Brenda Troyle' | CBro CLAP ECha EHrv EPot GEdr IGor LFox LRHS MAsh MHom NPol WCot WIvy |
| ***byzantinus*** | see *G. plicatus* subsp. *byzantinus* |
| ***caucasicus*** misapplied | see *G. elwesii* var. *monostictus* |
| - 'Comet' | see *G. elwesii* 'Comet' |
| - var. ***hiemalis*** Stern | see *G. elwesii* var. *monostictus* Hiemalis Group |
| ***cilicicus*** | EBrs WCot |
| 'Clare Blakeway-Phillips' | CLAP |
| 'Colesborne' | EHrv |
| ***corcyrensis*** spring-flowering | see *G. reginae-olgae* subsp. *vernalis* |
| - winter-flowering | see *G. reginae-olgae* subsp. *reginae-olgae* Winter-flowering Group |
| 'Cordelia' (d) | CLAP EMon LFox LRHS MAvo |
| 'Cowhouse Green' | EHrv |
| 'Desdemona' (d) | CBro CLAP EPot LFox LRHS WCot WIvy |
| 'Dionysus' (d) | CBgR CBro CLAP CPLG EHrv EPot ERos GEdr LFox MHom NBir WBrk WTin |
| § ***elwesii*** 🏆H4 | Widely available |
| - 'Cedric's Prolific' | ECha |
| § - 'Comet' | CElw EMon MAsh |
| - 'David Shackleton' | EHrv |
| - Edward Whittall Group | CLAP |
| - var. ***elwesii*** 'Kite' | MAsh |
| - - 'Magnus' | CLAP |
| - - 'Maidwell L' | CAvo CSna EHrv LFox MAsh |
| * - 'Flore Pleno' (d) | EBrs LFox |
| - 'J. Haydn' | CElw ECho IHer LAma WWst |
| § - var. ***monostictus*** 🏆H4 | CAvo EBrs ECho EHrv EMon MAsh WBrk WIvy |
| - - from Ukraine | MPhe |
| - - 'G. Handel' | IHer LAma WWst |
| * - - 'Green Tips' | NPol |
| - - 'H. Purcell' | CElw ECho IHer LAma WWst |
| § - - Hiemalis Group | CBro ECha EHrv EMon EPot LRHS WCot |
| - (Hiemalis Group) 'Barnes' | EHrv |
| - 'Selborne Green Tips' | EMon |
| - 'Sickle' **new** | CDes |
| - 'Zwanenburg' | EMon LRHS |
| 'Faringdon Double' (d) | EHrv |
| ***fosteri*** | CBro EBrs ECho EHrv SCnR |
| 'Galatea' | CLAP CSna EHrv EMon LFox LRHS MAsh MHom WIvy |
| 'Gill Gregory' **new** | MNrw |
| 'Ginns' | CDes CLAP LFox LRHS |
| § ***gracilis*** | CBgR CBro CLAP CPLG ERos LFox MTho NPol |
| - 'Highdown' | CAvo CElw CLAP MHom |
| - Kew **new** | CElw |
| - 'Vic Horton' | GEdr WThu |
| ***graecus*** misapplied | see *G. gracilis* |
| ***graecus*** Orph. ex Boiss. | see *G. elwesii* |
| Greatorex double (d) | CLAP |
| 'Greenfields' | CAvo LRHS |
| 'Heffalump' (d) | LRHS |
| 'Hill Poë' (d) | CBro CDes CElw CLAP EPot IFoB IGor LFox MAsh |
| 'Hippolyta' (d) | CAvo CBro CElw CLAP CWsd ECha EHrv ELon EPot GEdr LAma LFox MAsh WCot WIvy |
| x ***hybridus*** 'Merlin' | CElw CWsd IGor LFox MAsh MHom WCot WIvy |
| - 'Robin Hood' | CAvo CDes CFee CLAP EHrv ERos LFox LRHS MAsh |
| § ***ikariae*** Bak. | CElw EPfP EPot ERos IGor LRHS SGar WFar |
| - subsp. ***ikariae*** Butt's form | NPol |

| | |
|---|---|
| - Latifolius Group | see *G. platyphyllus* |
| - subsp. ***snogerupii*** | see *G. ikariae* Bak. |
| 'Imbolc' | CAvo |
| 'Jacquenetta' (d) | CBro CDes CElw CLAP EHrv MAsh MHom WPGP WTin |
| 'James Backhouse' | WHoo |
| 'John Gray' | CBro CSna EMon LFox LRHS MAsh |
| 'Ketton' | CAvo CBro CElw LFox MAsh MHom NRya WIvy |
| 'Kingston Double' (d) | CBgR CLAP |
| 'Lady Beatrix Stanley' (d) | CAvo CBro CElw CLAP ECha EHrv EMon EPot ERos GEdr LFox LLWP LRHS MAsh MTho |
| ***lagodechianus*** | EBrs ECho MPhe |
| 'Lapwing' | CSna |
| ***latifolius*** Rupr. | see *G. platyphyllus* |
| 'Lavinia' (d) | CAvo CElw CLAP |
| 'Lerinda' | EHrv |
| 'Limetree' | CBgR CLAP EHrv LFox NPol |
| 'Little John' | EHrv |
| ***lutescens*** | see *G. nivalis* Sandersii Group |
| 'Lyn' | EHrv |
| 'Magnet' ♀H4 | CAvo CBro CElw CFFs CFee CLAP CWsd ECha ELon EMon EPot GEdr IGor LAma LFox LRHS MAsh MHom NPol WBrk WHoo WPGP WWst |
| 'Mighty Atom' | CDes CFee CLAP EHrv LFox MAsh WBrk |
| 'Moccas' | CBgR CElw |
| 'Modern Art' | CSna |
| 'Mrs Backhouse No 12' | EHrv |
| 'Mrs Thompson' | CElw EHrv LRHS WIvy |
| 'Neill Fraser' | LFox |
| ***nivalis*** ♀H4 | Widely available |
| - 'Anglesey Abbey' | CAvo EMon |
| - var. ***angustifolius*** | see *G. angustifolius* |
| - 'April Fool' | LFox MHom |
| - 'Bitton' | CBro CLAP LFox NPol |
| - 'Chedworth' | WBrk |
| - dwarf | GAbr ITim LFox |
| - 'Greenish' | CAvo CSna MAsh |
| - subsp. ***imperati*** | CPLG |
| - 'Lutescens' | see *G. nivalis* Sandersii Group |
| - 'Maximus' | WShi |
| - 'Melvillei' | EMon |
| - f. ***pleniflorus*** (d) | CTca GKev MAsh WAbe |
| - - 'Bagpuize Virginia' (d) **new** | CSna |
| - - 'Blewbury Tart' (d) | CAvo CLAP CSna MAsh WBrk |
| - - 'Flore Pleno' (d) ♀H4 | CBro CPLG CStu CTri CWCL EBrs EPfP EPla EPot GAbr IFoB LAma LFox LHop LLWP LRHS NRya SMrm SPer SRms WBrk WCot WFar WHoo WShi |
| - - 'Hambutt's Orchard' (d) | LFox |
| - - 'Lady Elphinstone' (d) | CAvo CBgR CBro CDes CLAP CRow CSna EHrv LFox LRHS MAsh MTho NRya WIvy |
| - - 'Pusey Green Tip' (d) | CAvo CBro CElw CLAP EPot GEdr LFox MHom WCot WPGP WTin |
| - - 'Walrus' (d) | LRHS |
| - Poculiformis Group | CLAP EMon LRHS |
| § - Sandersii Group | CBro |
| § - Scharlockii Group | CAvo CBgR CBro CElw CWsd EBrs EMon IGor LFox LRHS MAsh WBrk |
| - 'Tiny' | MHom |
| - 'Tiny Tim' | EBrs ITim NRya |
| - 'Virescens' | CLAP |
| - 'Viridapice' | CAvo CBgR CBro CElw CPLG EBrs ECha ECho EMon EPot GEdr LAma LFox LRHS MAsh MWat NMen NPol SGar WCot WFar WHoo WPGP WShi WTin |
| - 'Warei' | LFox |
| 'Nothing Special' **new** | LRHS |
| 'Ophelia' (d) | CAvo CBro EPot IGor LFox LRHS MAsh MHom WBrk WHoo |
| 'Peg Sharples' | CSna MAsh |
| ***peshmenii*** | EBrs ECho EPot SCnR WCot |
| § ***platyphyllus*** | CPLG EBrs LFox |
| ***plicatus*** ♀H4 | CAvo CElw CFee ECho EHrv EMon EPot GEdr LFox LRHS MHom NMen WBrk WShi WTin |
| - from Ukraine | MPhe |
| - 'Augustus' | CAvo CDes CElw CFee CSna EHrv ERos LFox MAsh MHom WBrk WIvy |
| - 'Baxendale's Late' | CAvo CLAP |
| § - subsp. ***byzantinus*** | CBro ERos LFox WThu |
| - - 'Ron Ginns' | LFox |
| - 'Diggory' **new** | CSna |
| - 'Edinburgh Ketton' | CSna EHrv |
| - 'Florence Baker' | EHrv |
| - large-flowered | NPol |
| - 'Sally Passmore' | CAvo |
| - 'Sophie North' | CLAP |
| - 'The Pearl' | EHrv |
| - 'Three Ships' | EHrv |
| - 'Trym' | CLAP WFar |
| - 'Walter Fish' **new** | CSna |
| - 'Warham' | CBro CWsd EHrv EPot GEdr LRHS WPGP |
| - 'Wendy's Gold' | CDes CSna CWsd EMon LRHS |
| ***reginae-olgae*** | CAvo CBro EBrs EHrv ERos MAsh WThu |
| - subsp. ***reginae-olgae*** ♀H2-4 | ECho |
| - - 'Cambridge' | EBrs MAsh |
| § - - Winter-flowering Group | CBro LFox |
| § - subsp. ***vernalis*** | EBrs ECho LRHS |
| - - 'John Marr' **new** | LRHS |
| ***rizehensis*** | CAvo CLAP EHrv GEdr |
| 'S. Arnott' ♀H4 | Widely available |
| 'Saint Anne's' | CAvo CDes CElw CSna LRHS WIvy |
| 'Sally Ann' | LFox |
| 'Scharlockii' | see *G. nivalis* Scharlockii Group |
| 'Seagull' | CSna |
| 'Silverwells' | CElw CSna EHrv GEdr |
| § 'Straffan' | CAvo CBro CElw EPot GEdr IGor LFox LRHS MAsh MHom NPol WCot |
| 'Sutton Courtenay' **new** | CDes CSna |
| 'The Apothecary' | EHrv |
| 'The O'Mahoney' | see *G.* 'Straffan' |
| 'Titania' (d) | CBro EHrv |
| 'Trotter's Merlin' | CSna MAsh |
| 'Tubby Merlin' | CAvo CElw CLAP CSna LFox MAsh WIvy |
| 'Washfield Warham' | CSna ECha EMon ITim MAsh |
| 'White Wings' | CSna |
| 'William Thomson' | CSna EMon LFox |
| 'Winifrede Mathias' | CLAP LFox |
| 'Wisley Magnet' | ECha |
| ***woronowii*** ♀H4 | CBro CElw CLAP CTca EBrs ECho EMon GKev LAma LRHS MHom WBrk WCot WFar |

## *Galax* (*Diapensiaceae*)

| | |
|---|---|
| ***aphylla*** | see *G. urceolata* |
| § ***urceolata*** | IBlr WSHC |

## *Galega* (*Papilionaceae*)

| | |
|---|---|
| ***bicolor*** | MLLN NBir NBre SRms SWat WFar |
| 'Duchess of Bedford' | CFir CFwr EBee GBin |
| x ***hartlandii*** | CPLG IBlr |

| | |
|---|---|
| - 'Alba' ♀H4 | EBee EGle EHrv ELon EWes GBri IBlr MArl MBri MCot MRav SMHy SPhx SWat WCot WHoo WPrP WSHC |
| - 'Candida' | NBir |
| - 'Lady Wilson' ♀H4 | CElw CPom EBee ECtt EGle ELon EWes MArl MBri MLHP MRav WCot WCra WFar WFoF WHoo WOut WPen |
| - 'Spring Light' (v) | EWes LSou |
| 'Her Majesty' | see *G.* 'His Majesty' |
| § 'His Majesty' | CKno ECtt EGle ELon GBri GMac MArl MBri MCot MDKP MLHP MRav NBre NCob NGby SAga SMrm WCot WFar WHoo WPGP WWlt |
| ***officinalis*** | Widely available |
| - 'Alba' ♀H4 | CBgR CPrp EBee ECtt ELan ELau EPfP MBrN MCot MHer MNHC NCob SMrm SWal WCHb WFar WHer WHrl WMoo WOut |
| - Coconut Ice = 'Kelgal'PBR (v) | CAbP NCob SPer WHer |
| - 'Lincoln Gold' | CSpe EBee MTPN |
| ***orientalis*** | CDes CFir EBee ECha ECtt EPPr EWes MArl MCot MLLN MRav SPhx WAbb WCot WMoo WOut WPGP WSHC |

## *Galeobdolon* see *Lamium*

## *Galium* (*Rubiaceae*)

| | |
|---|---|
| ***aristatum*** | EBee ECha MLLN |
| ***boreale*** | EBWF |
| ***cruciata*** | see *Cruciata laevipes* |
| ***mollugo*** | CArn CRWN EBWF MSal NSco SIde WCHb |
| § ***odoratum*** | Widely available |
| ***palustre*** | EBWF |
| ***verum*** | CArn CRWN EBWF EBee GPoy MCoo MHer MSal NLan NMir NPri NSco SECG SIde WCHb WFar WHer WLHH |

## *Galtonia* ✿ (*Hyacinthaceae*)

| | |
|---|---|
| ***candicans*** ♀H4 | Widely available |
| - 'Moonbeam' (d) | EBee |
| ***princeps*** | CBro CDes EBrs ECha ERos GBuc WPGP WTin |
| ***regalis*** | CPLG ERos GEdr WPGP |
| ***viridiflora*** | Widely available |

## *Galvezia* (*Scrophulariaceae*)

| | |
|---|---|
| ***speciosa*** | EBee |

## *Garcinia* (*Clusiaceae*)

| | |
|---|---|
| ***mangostana*** | CCCN |

## *Gardenia* (*Rubiaceae*)

| | |
|---|---|
| ***augusta*** | see *G. jasminoides* |
| ***florida*** L. | see *G. jasminoides* |
| ***grandiflora*** | see *G. jasminoides* |
| § ***jasminoides*** ♀H1 | CBcs CCCN EBak LRHS MBri |
| - 'Kleim's Hardy' | CDTJ CHll CSBt EBee ELan EPfP EShb EWes GKir LAst LRHS MAsh NLar SAPC SArc SKHP SOWG SPoG SSta WHlf |
| - 'Star' | SOWG |
| - 'Veitchiana' | EShb |
| ***magnifica*** | SOWG |
| ***thunbergia*** | EShb SPlb |

## garlic see *Allium sativum*

## garlic, elephant see *Allium ampeloprasum* 'Elephant'

## *Garrya* ✿ (*Garryaceae*)

| | |
|---|---|
| F&M 215 | WPGP |
| ***congdonii*** | NLar |
| ***elliptica*** | CBcs CDul EBee ECrN EMui EPfP GGal ISea LPan LRHS LSRN MBri MGos NHol NPri NWea SPlb WFar WHar WPat |
| - (f) | MSwo SWvt |
| - (m) | CCVT CDoC CSBt CTri GGar MAsh MGan NBlu SLim SPoG WBod WFar |
| - 'James Roof' (m) ♀H4 | Widely available |
| ***fremontii*** | NLar |
| x ***issaquahensis*** 'Glasnevin Wine' | CAbP CDul CPMA EBee ELan EPfP LRHS MAsh MBlu MBri MGos NHol NLar NSti SCoo SLim SPoG WFar |
| - 'Pat Ballard' (m) | CPMA EPfP NHol NLar |
| x ***thuretii*** | CBcs MBri MGos NLar WDin WFar |

## *Gasteria* ✿ (*Aloaceae*)

| | |
|---|---|
| ***nitida*** var. ***nitida*** variegated (v) | WCot |
| ***verrucosa*** | EShb WCor |

## x *Gaulnettya* see *Gaultheria*

## *Gaultheria* ✿ (*Ericaceae*)

| | |
|---|---|
| sp. | MGan MGos WFar |
| ***adenothrix*** | NMen |
| ***antarctica*** | WThu |
| ***antipoda*** 'Adpressa' **new** | WThu |
| ***cardiosepala*** | GEdr |
| - CLD 1351 | GEdr |
| ***cumingiana*** B&SWJ 1542 | WCru |
| ***cuneata*** ♀H4 | ECho GEdr GKev GKir LRHS MAsh MBar SPoG WThu |
| - 'Pinkie' | ECho LRHS |
| ***depressa*** var. ***novae-zelandiae*** **new** | NHol |
| ***hispida*** from Hartz Mountains, Tasmania **new** | WThu |
| ***hispidula*** | ECho |
| ***hookeri*** | IBlr |
| ***itoana*** | ECho GEdr GKev GKir MBar |
| 'Jingle Bells' | EMil MGos SPoG |
| ***macrostigma*** | WThu |
| - BR 67 | GGar |
| § ***mucronata*** | CDul EPfP GKir MBar NWea SPlb WDin WGwG |
| - (m) | CDoC CSBt CTri CWSG EPfP LAst MAsh MBar MGos NBlu NHol SPer SPoG SRms |
| - 'Alba' (f) | MBar MGos |
| § - 'Bell's Seedling' (f/m) ♀H4 | CBcs CDoC CDul CTri CWSG EPfP GGar GKir LRHS MAsh NBir SPer SPoG SReu SSta |
| § - 'Crimsonia' (f) ♀H4 | CBcs EPfP MBar SPer SPur SRms |
| - 'Indian Lake' | NHol |
| - 'Lilacina' (f) | CBcs |
| - 'Lilian' (f) | CSBt CWSG EBee EPfP LAst NHol SPer |
| - Mother of Pearl | see *G. mucronata* 'Parelmoer' |
| § - 'Mulberry Wine' (f) ♀H4 | CSBt CTri EPfP LRHS MGos NHol SPer SPoG |
| § - 'Parelmoer' (f) | CSBt EBee LAst SPer SPoG SPur |
| § - 'Pink Pearl' (f) ♀H4 | MAsh SRms |
| - 'Rosea' (f) | MBar MGos |
| - 'Rosie' (f) | SBod |
| § - 'Signaal' (f) | CBcs EPfP LAst LRHS MAsh MGos NHol SPer |

| | |
|---|---|
| - Signal | see *G. mucronata* 'Signaal' |
| § - 'Sneeuwwitje' (f) | CBcs CWSG EBee EPfP LAst LRHS MAsh NBir SPer SPoG SPur |
| - Snow White | see *G. mucronata* 'Sneeuwwitje' |
| - 'Thymifolia' (m) | EPfP |
| - white-berried (f) | MMuc NBlu |
| § - 'Wintertime' (f) ♀H4 | MGos SRms |
| * ***mucronifolia*** dwarf | NWCA |
| § ***myrsinoides*** | GKev |
| ***nummularioides*** | GEdr GGGa GGar NHol NLar |
| 'Pearls' | GKir NHol WThu |
| ***procumbens*** ♀H4 | Widely available |
| ***prostrata*** | see *G. myrsinoides* |
| - ***purpurea*** | see *G. myrsinoides* |
| ***pumila*** | GAbr LEdu MBar NHol |
| - 'E.K. Balls' | NHol |
| ***shallon*** | CAgr CBcs CSBt EBee EMil EPfP MBar MGos MMuc SHBN SPer SRms SWvt WDin WFar |
| ***sinensis*** | NHar |
| - lilac-berried | WThu |
| ***tasmanica*** | ECou |
| ***trichophylla*** | NHar |
| x ***wisleyensis*** | LRHS SLon SRms SSta |
| - 'Pink Pixie' | ECho GKir LRHS MAsh MBar NLar SSta |
| - 'Wisley Pearl' | CBcs EBee IBlr IDee MBar NLar SCoo SReu WFar |
| ***yunnanensis*** | SReu |

## *Gaura* (*Onagraceae*)

| | |
|---|---|
| ***lindheimeri*** ♀H4 | Widely available |
| - 'Ballerina Rose' **new** | SGar |
| - Cherry Brandy = 'Gauchebra' PBR | EBee ECtt EPfP EWes EWll LBMP LHop NLar SPer SWat SWvt WFar |
| - 'Corrie's Gold' (v) | CWSG EAEE EBee ECha ECtt EHoe ELan EPfP LAst LBMP LRHS MHer SGar SPav SPer SPoG WCFE WMnd |
| - 'Crimson Butterflies' PBR | EBee ECtt EPfP EWTr LRHS MAvo MCCP SPoG |
| § - 'Heather's Delight' PBR | SHar |
| - 'Heaven's Harmony' | EBee |
| - In the Pink PBR | see *G. lindheimeri* 'Heather's Delight' |
| - 'Jo Adela' (v) | ELan EPfP SUsu |
| - Karalee Petite = 'Gauka' | CWCL EBee EPfP LAst LHop NLar SCoo SIng |
| - Karalee Petite Improved | see *G. lindheimeri* Lillipop Pink |
| - Karalee Pink | MBri |
| - Karalee White = 'Nugauwhite' PBR | CSpe CWCL LAst LHop LSou MBri NLar SCoo SIng SPoG |
| § - Lillipop Pink = 'Redgapi' **new** | ECtt LAst LSou NPri SPoG STes SVil |
| - 'Madonna' (v) | CBow |
| - 'My Melody' (v) | CWCL EBee EWll NLar SPoG |
| - 'Passionate Blush' | EBee ENor LAst LSRN LSou SPoG |
| - 'Passionate Pink' PBR | CBcs |
| - 'Passionate Rainbow' (v) | EBee EPfP LSou SPoG |
| - 'Pink Dwarf' | EPfP |
| - short | LSou SGar |
| - 'Siskiyou Pink' | Widely available |
| - 'Sunset Dreams' | NBPN |
| - 'The Bride' | CEnt CSec CTri EAEE EBee ECtt EPfP GCal LRHS LSRN LSou MRav MWat SPav SPet SPla SRGP STes SWal SWvt WBVN WHil WMnd |
| - 'Whirling Butterflies' | CKno CSpe CWCL EBee ECrN ECtt ELan EMil EPfP GMaP LCro MAvo SBod SMad SMrm SPav SPer SPoG SWat SWvt WMnd |
| - 'White Heron' | MNrw |
| ***sinuata*** **new** | CAby |
| I 'Variegata' (v) | CWCL |

## *Gaussia* (*Arecaceae*)

| | |
|---|---|
| ***maya*** | LPal |

## *Gaylussacia* (*Ericaceae*)

| | |
|---|---|
| ***baccata*** (F) | NLar |
| ***brachycera*** | GGGa |

## *Gazania* (*Asteraceae*)

| | |
|---|---|
| 'Aztec' ♀H1+3 | CCCN CHal |
| 'Bicton Cream' | CHal |
| 'Bicton Orange' | CCCN COlW LSou MAJR SCoo |
| 'Blackberry Ripple' | CCCN COlW GGar LAst MAJR SAga SCoo SMrm |
| 'Blackcurrant Ice' | MCot |
| 'Christopher' | CHal GGar MSte SCoo |
| 'Christopher Lloyd' | CCCN COlW LAst MAJR NPri SMrm |
| 'Cookei' ♀H1+3 | EBee MAJR MSte SAga |
| 'Cornish Pixie' | CCCN CHal |
| 'Cream Beauty' | MCot MSte |
| 'Cream Dream' | LAst |
| cream-flowered | CHal |
| Daybreak Series | WFar |
| double bronze-flowered | CHal |
| 'Garden Sun' | MLan |
| * ***grayi*** | CHal |
| * 'Hazel' | MSte |
| (Kiss Series) 'Kiss Bronze Star' | SGar |
| - 'Kiss Rose' | SGar |
| - 'Kiss Yellow' | SGar |
| ***krebsiana*** | CCCN |
| ***linearis*** 'Colorado Gold' | CFir |
| 'Magic' | CCCN COlW LAst MAJR NPri SCoo |
| 'Northbourne' ♀H1+3 | GGar MSte |
| 'Orange Beauty' | CHEx ELan |
| 'Red Velvet' | CHEx MSte SAga |
| ***rigens*** var. ***uniflora*** ♀H1+3 | MSte |
| - 'Variegata' (v) ♀H1+3 | CBow CCCN COlW ELan LAst LSou |
| 'Silverbrite' | CHal |
| Sunset Jane = 'Sugaja' PBR | CCCN |
| 'Talent' | SEND |
| 'Tiger Eye' | CCCN CHVG LSou WHlf |
| 'Torbay Silver' | CHEx |

## *Gelidocalamus* (*Poaceae*)

| | |
|---|---|
| ***fangianus*** | see *Drepanostachyum microphyllum* |

## *Gelsemium* (*Loganiaceae*)

| | |
|---|---|
| ***rankinii*** | MBri NLar |
| ***sempervirens*** ♀H1-2 | CArn CCCN CHll CRHN EBee EShb IDee LSRN MSal SOWG SPoG WBor |

## *Genista* (*Papilionaceae*)

| | |
|---|---|
| ***aetnensis*** ♀H4 | CBcs CCVT CEnd CTri EBee ECrN ELan EPfP LRHS MDun NLar SAPC SArc SDix SHBN SPer SRms WDin WPat |
| § ***canariensis*** | CPLG CSBt CWib NBlu WBrE |
| ***cinerea*** | WCFE |
| ***decumbens*** | see *Cytisus decumbens* |
| ***delphinensis*** | see *G. sagittalis* subsp. *delphinensis* |
| 'Emerald Spreader' | see *G. pilosa* 'Yellow Spreader' |
| ***fragrans*** | see *G. canariensis* |
| ***hispanica*** | CBcs CDul CSBt CTri EBee ECrN ELan EPfP GGal GGar LRHS MBar MGos MNHC NWea SHBN SLim SPer SPoG SRms SWvt WCFE WDin WFar WHar |
| ***humifusa*** | see *G. pulchella* |
| ***lydia*** ♀H4 | Widely available |

| | | |
|---|---|---|
| § | ***maderensis*** | EWes SMrm WPic |
| | ***monosperma*** | see *Retama monosperma* |
| § | ***monspessulana*** | ECho |
| | ***pilosa*** | CTri ISea MBar NMen |
| | - 'Goldilocks' | MMuc |
| | - 'Lemon Spreader' | see *G. pilosa* 'Yellow Spreader' |
| | - var. ***minor*** | NLar NMen |
| | - 'Procumbens' | CMea MDKP MHer WPat |
| | - 'Vancouver Gold' | CBcs CSBt ELan EPfP GGar GKir MGos MMuc MRav SPer SPoG SRms WDin WFar WGor |
| § | - 'Yellow Spreader' | CBcs CMHG CSBt GEdr MSwo |
| § | 'Porlock' ♀H3 | CBcs CDoC CDul CPLG CSBt CSPN CWSG EBee GGal LRHS MAsh MBri MRav SEND WBod WDin |
| § | ***pulchella*** | CTri WAbe |
| | ***sagittalis*** | CTri EBee MMuc NBir NLar NWCA SPer WTin WWFP |
| § | - subsp. ***delphinensis*** ♀H4 | GKir NMen |
| | - ***minor*** | see *G. sagittalis* subsp. *delphinensis* |
| § | x ***spachiana*** ♀H1 | CTri SPoG |
| | ***tenera*** 'Golden Shower' | SLPl |
| | ***tinctoria*** | CArn EOHP GBar GPoy ILis MHer MSal SIde WHer WSFF |
| § | - 'Flore Pleno' (d) ♀H4 | ECho GEdr MGos NMen NPro SRot |
| | - 'Humifusa' | EPot GEdr NWCA |
| | - 'Plena' | see *G. tinctoria* 'Flore Pleno' |
| | - 'Royal Gold' ♀H4 | CWSG CWib EPfP MGos MRav SHBN SPer SPlb WBod |
| | ***villarsii*** | see *G. pulchella* |

## *Gentiana* ✿ (*Gentianaceae*)

| | | |
|---|---|---|
| § | ***acaulis*** ♀H4 | CStu EBee ECho ELan EPot GKev GMaP ITim LHop LRHS MWat NGdn NHol NLAp NMen NRya SIng SPlb SRms WAbe WCFE WEas WFar WPat |
| | - f. ***alba*** | LLHF NLAp WThu |
| | - - 'Snowstorm' **new** | GKev |
| | - 'Belvedere' | EPot GCal NMen WAbe |
| | - 'Coelestina' | WThu |
| | - 'Dinarica' | see *G. dinarica* |
| | - 'Holzmannii' | NMen |
| | - 'Krumrey' | EPot GKev |
| I | - 'Maxima Enzian' | EPot |
| | - 'Rannoch' | EPot GEdr NMen |
| | - 'Stumpy' | EPot |
| | - 'Trotter's Variety' | EPot WAbe |
| | - 'Undulatifolia' | EPot |
| | ***affinis*** | NLAp |
| | 'Alex Duguid' | GEdr |
| | 'Amethyst' | GEdr GMaP SIng WAbe |
| | ***angulosa*** misapplied | see *G. verna* 'Angulosa' hort. |
| | ***angustifolia*** | GKev WAbe |
| | - 'Rannoch' | GKev |
| | 'Ann's Special' | GEdr |
| | ***asclepiadea*** ♀H4 | Widely available |
| | - var. ***alba*** | CLAP EBee EWld GBuc GCal GGar GKev GMaP IGor MDKP MTho NBid SRms WTin |
| | - 'Knightshayes' | CLAP EBee GKev GKir LLHF NLAp |
| I | - 'Nana' | EBee GKev GKir |
| | - pale blue-flowered | WPGP |
| | - 'Phyllis' | CFir EBee GBuc GKev |
| | - 'Pink Swallow' | CLAP GBuc WFar |
| | - 'Rosea' | GBuc GMaP MDKP MNrw WPGP |
| | ***atuntsiensis*** | EBee GKev |
| | 'Balmoral' PBR **new** | GMaP |
| | 'Barbara Lyle' | WAbe |
| | ***bavarica*** var. ***subacaulis*** | EPot SPlb |
| | x ***bernardii*** | see *G.* x *stevenagensis* 'Bernardii' |
| | 'Berrybank Dome' | CSam GMaP NHar NHol |
| | 'Berrybank Sky' | GMaP NHar NHol |
| | 'Berrybank Star' | GMaP NHar |
| | ***bisetaea*** | SRms |
| | 'Blue Silk' | EWes GBin GBuc GKev NHar NHol NLAp SIng WAbe |
| | ***brachyphylla*** | WAbe |
| | - subsp. ***favratii*** | WAbe |
| | 'Braemar' PBR **new** | GMaP |
| * | ***buglossoides*** | WSHC |
| | 'Cairngorm' | GEdr NDlv |
| | 'Cambrian White' | WAbe |
| | x ***caroli*** | WAbe |
| | 'Christine Jean' | SIng |
| | ***clusii*** | EPot GKev WAbe |
| | - purple-flowered | WAbe |
| | 'Compact Gem' | GEdr NHar NHol NLAp SIng WAbe |
| § | ***cruciata*** | EAlp EBee MMHG MTho |
| § | ***dahurica*** | EBee ECho GEdr NGdn NHol SSto |
| | 'Dark Hedgehog' | GEdr |
| | ***decumbens*** | EBee NLAp |
| | ***dendrologi*** | WHil |
| | ***depressa*** | EPot MTho WAbe |
| | 'Devonhall' | GEdr NHol WAbe |
| | 'Diana' PBR **new** | EBee LRHS |
| § | ***dinarica*** | CLyd ECho EPot MTho NLAp NMen WFar |
| | - 'Colonel Stitt' | GEdr WThu |
| | - 'Frocheneite' | EPot WThu |
| | 'Dumpy' | CPBP GEdr NLAp WAbe |
| | 'Elehn' | NHar |
| | 'Elizabeth' | GEdr |
| | 'Ettrick' | GEdr NHol |
| | 'Eugen's Allerbester' (d) | GEdr GKev LLHF NHar NHol WAbe |
| | 'Eugen's Bester' | NHar SIng |
| | ***farreri*** | EWes WAbe |
| | - 'Duguid' | GEdr NHol WAbe |
| | - hybrids | WAbe |
| | ***fetissowii*** | see *G. macrophylla* var. *fetissowii* |
| | ***gelida*** | LLHF |
| | 'Gellerhard' | NHar |
| | 'Gewahn' | NHar |
| | Glamis strain | GEdr NHar |
| | 'Glen Isla' | EWes |
| | 'Glendevon' | WAbe |
| § | ***gracilipes*** | ECho LRHS MWat SPlb SRms |
| | - 'Yuatensis' | see *G. macrophylla* var. *fetissowii* |
| | x ***hascombensis*** | see *G. septemfida* var. *lagodechiana* 'Hascombensis' |
| | 'Henry' | WAbe |
| | ***hexaphylla*** | WAbe |
| | - SDR 5003 **new** | GKev |
| | 'Indigo' | WAbe |
| | 'Inverleith' ♀H4 | EWes GEdr NHol NLAp SPlb |
| | 'Iona' PBR **new** | GMaP |
| | 'Kirriemuir' | EWes NDlv |
| | ***kochiana*** | see *G. acaulis* |
| | ***kurroo*** | NLAp |
| | - var. ***brevidens*** | see *G. dahurica* |
| | ***lagodechiana*** | see *G. septemfida* var. *lagodechiana* |
| | 'Little Diamond' **new** | LRHS |
| | 'Lucerna' | GEdr GKev NDlv NHol NLAp |
| | ***lutea*** | CArn EBee ECho GKev GPoy MAvo NBid NChi SDix SMad SRms WAul WCAu WPer |
| | x ***macaulayi*** ♀H4 | SIng SRms |
| | - 'Elata' | NHol |
| | - 'Kidbrooke Seedling' | CTri EWes GEdr GKev GMaP NDlv NHol SPer WAbe |
| | - 'Kingfisher' | CTri GEdr GKev NBir SIng WAbe |
| § | - 'Praecox' | GEdr |
| § | - 'Wells's Variety' | WAbe |

| | | |
|---|---|---|
| § | ***macrophylla*** var. ***fetissowii*** | EBee GKev LLHF |
| | ***makinoi*** 'Marsha'[PBR] **new** | EBee EMil |
| | - 'Royal Blue' | GBin GBri GCal IDee |
| | 'Margaret' | WAbe |
| | 'Maryfield' | GEdr |
| | 'Melanie' | GEdr NHar NHol |
| * | ***nepaulensis*** | GAuc |
| § | ***nubigena*** | CSec |
| | ***occidentalis*** | EPot |
| | ***olgae*** **new** | EBee GKev |
| | ***paradoxa*** | EBee GKev LLHF NLAp WAbe WPat |
| | - 'Blauer Herold' | MWat |
| | ***phlogifolia*** | see *G. cruciata* |
| | ***pneumonanthe*** | EBee SPlb |
| | ***prolata*** | GKev NLAp |
| | ***przewalskii*** | see *G. nubigena* |
| | ***pumila*** subsp. ***delphinensis*** | WAbe WPat |
| | ***purdomii*** | see *G. gracilipes* |
| | 'Robyn Lyle' | WAbe |
| | 'Saphir Select' | GEdr NHol |
| | ***saxosa*** | GGar GKev ITim NBir |
| | ***scabra*** 'Zuikorindo' | EBee NLar |
| | 'Sensation' | GEdr NHar |
| | ***septemfida*** $\mathbb{Y}^{H4}$ | CEnt EAEE GAbr GEdr GKev GKir ITim LBee LHop LRHS MBri MTho MWat NBir SIng SPlb SRms WHoo |
| | - 'Alba' | GKev GKir NBir |
| § | - var. ***lagodechiana*** $\mathbb{Y}^{H4}$ | EBee GKir NMen SRms WBVN WFar |
| § | - - 'Hascombensis' | ECho |
| | 'Serenity' | GEdr NHol SIng WAbe |
| | 'Shot Silk' | CSam CTri EWes GEdr GGar GJos GKev GMaP NBir NHol SPer SUsu WAbe |
| | 'Silken Giant' | GEdr WAbe |
| | 'Silken Night' | WAbe |
| | 'Silken Seas' | GEdr NHol WAbe |
| | 'Silken Skies' | GBuc GEdr WAbe |
| | ***sino-ornata*** $\mathbb{Y}^{H4}$ | CTri EBee ECho EMil GGar GKev GKir LSRN MBri NBlu NLAp NMen SIng SPer SRms WAbe WBVN WFar |
| | - CLD 476B | GEdr |
| | - 'Alba' | NHol WFar |
| | - 'Angel's Wings' | GEdr NHol |
| | - 'Bellatrix' | GEdr NHar NHol |
| | - 'Brin Form' | SRms WAbe |
| | - 'Downfield' | GKev GMaP NHol |
| | - 'Edith Sarah' | GEdr SRms |
| | - 'Mary Lyle' | GEdr WAbe |
| | - 'Praecox' | see *G.* x *macaulayi* 'Praecox' |
| | - 'Purity' | WAbe |
| | - 'Starlight' | NHar |
| I | - 'Trotter's Form' | EWes |
| | - 'Weisser Traum' | GEdr NHar NHol |
| | - 'White Wings' | EWes |
| | ***siphonantha*** | CSec |
| | 'Sir Rupert' | NHar |
| | 'Soutra' | GEdr |
| | x ***stevenagensis*** $\mathbb{Y}^{H4}$ | CTri SIng |
| § | - 'Bernardii' | GEdr SIng WAbe |
| | - dark | WAbe WFar |
| | - 'Frank Barker' | WAbe |
| | ***straminea*** | EBee GKev LLHF MDKP |
| | 'Strathmore' $\mathbb{Y}^{H4}$ | CSam CTri EWes GEdr GGar GKev GMaP NHar NHol NLAp SIng SPer SPlb WAbe |
| | 'Suendermannii' | LLHF |
| | ***szechenyii*** SDR 4938 **new** | GKev |
| | ***ternifolia*** 'Cangshan' | GEdr WAbe |
| | - 'Dali' | GEdr GKev NBir NHar NHol |
| | ***tibetica*** | CArn CSec EBee GEdr GPoy MWat NBid WAul WCAu WEas WPer WTin |
| | ***trichotoma*** SDR 4746 **new** | GKev |
| | ***triflora*** | GBuc WFar WPGP |
| | - 'Alba' | GBuc |
| | - var. ***japonica*** | GBri GBuc |
| | - 'Royal Blue' | EBee WCot |
| | ***venusta*** | GKev |
| | ***verna*** | EAEE EBee ECho EMil EPfP EPot EWes GKev ITim LHop LRHS LSRN MTho NMen NSla SIng SPoG WAbe WFar WHoo WPat |
| | - 'Alba' | GKev NLAp WAbe WFar WPat |
| | - 'Angulosa' hort. $\mathbb{Y}^{H4}$ **new** | ITim |
| | - subsp. ***balcanica*** | CLyd MTho NLAp SRms WPat |
| | - subsp. ***oschtenica*** | NSla WAbe |
| | - slate blue | WPat |
| | - subsp. ***tergestina*** | ITim NLAp |
| | 'Violette' | GEdr NDlv NHol |
| | ***waltonii*** | ECho EWes |
| | ***wellsii*** | see *G.* x *macaulayi* 'Wells's Variety' |
| | ***wutaiensis*** | see *G. macrophylla* var. *fetissowii* |

# *Geranium* ✿ (*Geraniaceae*)

| | | |
|---|---|---|
| | from Bambashata Altai Mountains **new** | NCot |
| | from Pamirs, Tadzhikistan | WPnP |
| | from Sikkim | NWCA |
| | ***aconitifolium*** misapplied | see *G. palmatum* |
| | ***aconitifolium*** L'Hér. | see *G. rivulare* |
| | 'Alan Mayes' | CElw CPrp CSev EAEE EBee EBla ECtt EPPr MAvo MSte NGdn SRGP WCra WWpP |
| | 'Alaska' | CMCo |
| | ***albanum*** | CCge CElw EBee EPPr EWsh GAbr LLWP MNrw SDix SRGP WMoo WPtf WWpP |
| | - 'Pink and Stripes' | EBee |
| | ***albiflorum*** | CCge CMCo EPPr WMoo WPnP WWpP |
| | ***anemonifolium*** | see *G. palmatum* |
| | 'Ann Folkard' $\mathbb{Y}^{H4}$ | Widely available |
| | 'Ann Folkard' x ***psilostemon*** | LSRN NChi |
| | 'Anne Thomson' $\mathbb{Y}^{H4}$ | Widely available |
| | x ***antipodeum*** | SRms |
| | - 'Black Ice' | GBuc WCru |
| | - 'Chocolate Candy'[PBR] | EPfP MGos |
| § | - Crûg strain | CMoH EHrv LRHS MDKP MDun NGdn NWCA SHBN WCru |
| | - 'Elizabeth Wood' | LSou |
| | - 'Kahlua' | EHrv EPfP |
| | - 'Pink Spice'[PBR] | EBla ECtt MGos |
| | - 'Sea Spray' | CMHG ECtt GCra GGar LRHS MCot MNrw MSte NBro WCru WMnd WWpP |
| | - 'Stanhoe' | EBee ECtt SRot WBrk WFar |
| | ***antrorsum*** | ECou |
| | ***aristatum*** | CDes CPou EBee EBla EPPr EWes GCal GGar MNFA MNrw MRav NBir NCot SPav SRGP STes WCru WMoo WPnP WPtf WWpP |
| | - NS 649 | NWCA |
| | ***armenum*** | see *G. psilostemon* |
| | ***asphodeloides*** | CBre CElw CHid CSsd GAbr IFro LLWP MBNS MNFA MNrw MWhi NBid NBir NCot SPav SRGP WBrk WFar WHCG WMnd WMoo WPnP WTin WWpP |
| | - subsp. ***asphodeloides*** | EBee EPPr GCal WCra WPnP |
| | 'Prince Regent' | WWpP |
| | - - white-flowered | EBee EBla EPPr SRGP STes WFar WMoo WWpP |

| | |
|---|---|
| - 'Starlight' | CMoH EBee GCal NBid |
| ***atlanticum*** Hook. f. | see *G. malviflorum* |
| 'Aussie Gem' | CFwr EBee WWpP |
| 'Aya' | LPio |
| 'Baby Blue' | see *G. himalayense* 'Baby Blue' |
| 'Bertie Crûg' | CCge CHVG CSpe EBee EBla ECtt EHrv GAbr LAst LLHF NBir NMoo SMrm SPoG SRms SRot SWat SWvt WCru WFar WWpP |
| 'Bill Baker' | GKir |
| ***biuncinatum*** | IFro WPnP |
| 'Blue Boy' | MNFA NLar |
| 'Blue Cloud' ♀H4 | Widely available |
| 'Blue Haze' new | CWsd |
| 'Blue Pearl' | EPPr MAvo NBir NSti SRGP SVil WCra WMoo WPnP WWpP |
| § Blue Sunrise = 'Blogold'PBR ♀H4 | Widely available |
| 'Bob's Blunder' | CCge CElw CMHG EBee EBla ECtt EGle LSRN MAvo MBNS NCob NLar SMrm SPla SWvt WCot WFar WHoo WRHF |
| ***bohemicum*** | CCge CSec EBla NCot SRGP WBrk WHer |
| - 'Orchid Blue' | EPfP SWvt WFar |
| 'Brookside' ♀H4 | Widely available |
| ***brycei*** | MNrw |
| 'Buckland Beauty' | CWsd EBee SBch |
| 'Buxton's Blue' | see *G. wallichianum* 'Buxton's Variety' |
| ***caeruleatum*** | EBee EBla EPPr GCal SUsu WWpP |
| ***caffrum*** | CSec SRGP WOut WWpP |
| ***canariense*** | see *G. reuteri* |
| ***candicans*** misapplied | see *G. lambertii* |
| § x ***cantabrigiense*** | CSBt ECtt EShb GAbr IBlr LAst MHer MNrw NBid NBir NBro NPer NSti SGar SRms WBrk WCru WFar WHCG WMoo |
| - 'Berggarten' | CDes CElw CMCo EBee EPPr SBch SRGP WPtf WWpP |
| - 'Biokovo' | Widely available |
| - 'Cambridge' | Widely available |
| - 'Harz' new | EPPr |
| - 'Karmina' | CElw CMCo EBee EBla EPPr EPfP EPla EPot GKir MWhi SBch SPoG WHoo WMoo WPnP WWpP |
| - 'Rosalina' new | NCot |
| - 'Show Time' | CMCo EBla WWpP |
| - 'St Ola' | Widely available |
| - 'Vorjura' new | EPPr |
| - 'Westray'PBR | CCge CHVG CHid COlW EBee EPPr EShb GAbr GBuc GQue MCCP MDun MSte NGdn SMrm SPoG SRms STes SVil SWvt WCra |
| ***cataractarum*** | MLLN |
| 'Chantilly' | CElw CMCo EBee EBla EPPr GBuc GCal MAvo MNFA MNrw NBir NPro SBch WCru WMoo WPnP WPtf WWpP |
| ***christensenianum*** B&SWJ 8022 | WCru |
| ***cinereum*** | CCge EBla ECho |
| - 'Album' | CCge GKir NChi |
| - 'Apple Blossom' | see *G.* x *lindavicum* 'Apple Blossom' |
| - 'Ballerina' | see *G.* (Cinereum Group) 'Ballerina' |
| - 'Elizabeth' new | CCge |
| I - 'Heather' | CCge EBla EGle EPPr LRHS MBNS |
| - 'Hidgate's Emily' new | EBla |
| - 'Janette' | LRHS SUsu |
| - subsp. ***ponticum*** | see *G. ponticum* |
| - 'Purple Pillow' | Widely available |
| - Rothbury Gem = 'Gerfos'PBR ♀H4 | CCge EBee EBla NChi |
| - 'Sateene'PBR | CCge CElw EBee EBla EPPr LAst NMoo NSti SRot SUsu WCra |
| - 'Signal' | EBee EBla NLar |
| - 'Souvenir de René Macé' | LBuc MBri |
| - subsp. ***subcaulescens*** var. ***ponticum*** | see *G. ponticum* |
| (Cinereum Group) 'Alice'PBR | EBee EBla EPPr IPot LLHF LSRN MAvo MBNS MWea NGdn NSti WCra |
| § - 'Ballerina' ♀H4 | Widely available |
| - 'Carol' | CCge CDes EAEE EBee EBla EPPr EWes GKir LRHS LSRN MAvo MBNS MBri NLar NSti SUsu SWvt WCra WFar WPnP |
| - 'Giuseppii' | CCge EAEE EBee EBla ECtt EPPr EShb GGar GKir LSou MNFA MNrw MRav NBro NCot NDov NPri SPla SRGP SRot WBrE WCra WFar WPnP WRHF |
| - 'Laurence Flatman' | Widely available |
| - 'Prima Ballerina' new | EBee |
| 'Claridge Druce' | see *G.* x *oxonianum* 'Claridge Druce' |
| ***clarkei*** 'Kashmir Blue' | see *G.* 'Kashmir Blue' |
| - 'Kashmir Pink' | Widely available |
| § - 'Kashmir White' ♀H4 | Widely available |
| - 'Mount Stewart' | WCru WPGP |
| - (Purple-flowered Group) 'Gulmarg' new | NCot |
| - - 'Kashmir Purple' | Widely available |
| 'Coffee Time' | WWpP |
| ***collinum*** | EPPr GAbr MNrw NBir NCot SRGP WBrk WPnP WWpP |
| 'Coombland White' | CDes CSam CSpe EBee EBla ECtt EGle EPPr EWsh LAst LPio MAvo MBri MNFA MNrw NLar NSti SPoG SRGP STes SVil WCot WCra WCru WHoo WMoo WPnP WWpP |
| 'Criss Canning' new | EPPr |
| Crûg strain | see *G.* x ***antipodeum*** Crûg strain |
| 'Cyril's Fancy' | EBee EBla EPPr MAvo MNFA SUsu WPtf WWpP |
| ***dahuricum*** | WCru |
| ***dalmaticum*** ♀H4 | Widely available |
| - 'Album' | CBod CPrp CSsd EBee EBla ECho ECtt ELan EPPr EPot LRHS MRav MTho NRya SIng SPer SRGP SRms SRot SWat WAbe WCra WCru WFar WHCG WWpP |
| - 'Bressingham Pink' | EPPr WPnP WWpP |
| - 'Bridal Bouquet' | EBee GBri LLHF NChi NMen NSla WAbe WHer |
| - 'Croftlea' new | GKir |
| - 'Stades Hellrosa' new | EPPr |
| ***dalmaticum*** x ***macrorrhizum*** | see *G.* x ***cantabrigiense*** |
| ***delavayi*** misapplied | see *G. sinense* |
| ***delavayi*** Franch. | EBee |
| 'Dilys' ♀H4 | CCge CElw EBee EBla EGle ELan EPPr GMac LPio MAvo MLHP MNFA MNrw MSte NBir NChi NGdn SRGP SUsu WCru WFar WHal WMoo WPnP WWpP |
| ***dissectum*** | CHll MSal |
| 'Distant Hills' | CDes CMCo EBee EBla EPPr MAvo SRGP SUsu WWpP |
| 'Diva' | CElw CSam EBee EBla EPPr LLHF MAvo MNrw SBch SRGP WCru WPnP WWpP |
| 'Dragon Heart' | EBee LSRN NLar NSti SPoG WWpP |
| 'Dusky Crûg' | Widely available |
| 'Dusky Gem' | SUsu |

| | | |
|---|---|---|
| | 'Dusky Rose' | CLAP CMoH CSpe ELan EPfP LAst LRHS MGos NLar SRot |
| | 'Edith May' **new** | GSec |
| | 'Eleanor Fisher' | SUsu |
| | 'Elizabeth Ross' | MAvo MNrw WCru WHoo WRha WWpP |
| | 'Elke' | CCge CElw EBee EPPr EPfP MWea NGdn SPer WHlf |
| | 'Ella' | CWGN |
| | 'Elworthy Dusky' | CCge CElw |
| | 'Elworthy Eyecatcher' | CCge CElw MAvo SBch SUsu |
| | 'Elworthy Tiger' | CElw |
| | 'Emily' | SRGP WWpP |
| | ***endressii*** $\Upsilon^{H4}$ | CBre CElw CSec CSev EBee EBla ECha ECho EHrv EPPr EPfP GAbr GKir GMaP MBNS MHer NBro NPer SGar SPlb SRGP SRms SWvt WFar WMoo WWpP |
| | - 'Album' | see *G.* 'Mary Mottram' |
| | - 'Betty Catchpole' | EPPr |
| | - 'Castle Drogo' $\Upsilon^{H4}$ | EBee EBla EPPr MAvo SRGP WWpP |
| | - 'Prestbury White' | see *G.* x *oxonianum* 'Prestbury Blush' |
| | - 'Priestling's Red' | CMCo |
| | - 'Rose' | WPer WWpP |
| | - 'Wargrave Pink' | see *G.* x *oxonianum* 'Wargrave Pink' |
| | - white-flowered | WPtf |
| | ***erianthum*** | CCge GBuc GCal GMaP GMac MLHP NBre NLar SRGP STes WCru WWpP |
| | - 'Calm Sea' | EBla GBuc SUsu WCru WMoo WWpP |
| | - f. ***leucanthum*** 'Undine' | SUsu |
| | - 'Neptune' | EPPr MNFA NCot SUsu WCru WWpP |
| | ***eriostemon*** Fischer | see *G. platyanthum* |
| | 'Eva' | EBee WPnP |
| | 'Expression'[PBR] | see *G.* 'Tanya Rendall' |
| | 'Farncombe Cerise Star' | EBee EPPr NCot |
| § | ***farreri*** | EAEE EBla EGle GBri GBuc LHop NBir NChi SIng WEas |
| | 'Fireworks' | LRHS |
| | ***fremontii*** | EWld |
| | ***goldmannii*** | SKHP |
| | ***gracile*** | CCge EBee EPla GBuc GMaP LSou MNrw NBir NBre SRGP WBrk WCru WMoo WPnP WWpP |
| | - 'Blanche' | CElw EBee EPPr SBch SMrs WWpP |
| | - 'Blush' | CElw CMCo CWsd EBee EPPr WWpP |
| | ***grandiflorum*** | see *G. himalayense* |
| | - var. ***alpinum*** | see *G. himalayense* 'Gravetye' |
| | 'Grasmere' | ECtt |
| | ***guatemalense*** B&SWJ 10461 | WCru |
| | ***gymnocaulon*** | CCge CMCo CMHG EBee EBla EPPr LRHS MAvo SRGP WCru WWFP WWpP |
| | ***gymnocaulon*** x ***platypetalum*** | EBee WCra |
| | 'Harmony' | EBee EPPr WWpP |
| | ***harveyi*** | CMea CSpe EBla EPPr EWes GCal NChi SPhx SRGP WAbe WCru WKif WPGP WPat |
| | ***hayatanum*** | NCot |
| | - B&SWJ 164 | WCru WMoo WWpP |
| § | ***himalayense*** | Widely available |
| | - CC 1957 from Tibetan border | EPPr |
| | - CC&McK 442 | CMCo |
| | - from Tibetan border | WWpP |
| | - ***alpinum*** | see *G. himalayense* 'Gravetye' |
| § | - 'Baby Blue' | CCge CElw CSpe EBee EBla EBrs EGle EPPr GBuc GCal GCra IFro MAvo MBri MNFA MNrw NCot NGdn NSti SMrm SRGP SUsu WBrk WCru WMoo WPnP WWpP |
| | - 'Birch Double' | see *G. himalayense* 'Plenum' |
| | - 'Derrick Cook' | CElw EBee EPPr NCot SUsu WCra WWpP |
| | - 'Devil's Blue' | EPPr NCot SRGP WPtf WWpP |
| § | - 'Gravetye' $\Upsilon^{H4}$ | Widely available |
| | - 'Irish Blue' | CElw CMCo EBee EBla ECtt EGle EPPr GBuc GCal GMac LBMP MBri MNFA MSte NCot NLar NPol SRGP WAbb WCra WCru WHal WMoo WTin WWpP |
| | - ***meeboldii*** | see *G. himalayense* |
| | - 'Pale Irish Blue' | GCal |
| § | - 'Plenum' (d) | Widely available |
| | - 'Spiti Valley' | EBee NCot |
| | ***hispidissimum*** | CFee |
| | ***ibericum*** misapplied | see *G.* x *magnificum* |
| | ***ibericum*** Cav. | CCge CSBt CTri EBla EPla NBre NLar SPav SRGP STes WFar WWpP |
| | - 'Blue Springs' | ECtt |
| | - subsp. ***ibericum*** | EBee EPPr WWpP |
| | - subsp. ***jubatum*** | CElw EBla EPPr MNFA MNrw NCot SRms WCru WPnP WWpP |
| | - - 'White Zigana' | CFwr EBee EPPr MHar NCot WPnP WWpP |
| | - subsp. ***jubatum*** x ***renardii*** | SWvt |
| | - var. ***platypetalum*** Boissier | see *G. platypetalum* Fisch. & C.A. Mey. |
| | - var. ***platypetalum*** misapplied | see *G.* x *magnificum* |
| § | - 'Ushguli Grijs' | EBee EBla NCot WPnP |
| | ***ibericum*** x ***libani*** | CDes |
| | ***incanum*** | CHll CSev EBee EShb EWes MNrw NBir SGar SMrm SRGP SRot WWpP |
| | - var. ***multifidum*** | WFar |
| | - white-flowered | SRGP |
| | 'Ivan' $\Upsilon^{H4}$ | Widely available |
| | 'Jack of Kilbryde' | GBri |
| | 'Jean Armour' | CDes EAEE EBee ECtt EPPr GBuc LRHS MAvo MSte NBsh NGdn SPoG SRGP WCra WCru WPGP WWpP |
| | 'Jean's Lilac' | see *G.* x *oxonianum* 'Jean's Lilac' |
| | 'Johnson's Blue' $\Upsilon^{H4}$ | Widely available |
| | 'Jolly Bee'[PBR] | Widely available |
| | 'Jolly Pink' | EPPr |
| | 'Joy' | Widely available |
| | 'Kanahitobanawa' | CDes |
| § | 'Kashmir Blue' | CCge CDes EBee EPPr GMaP MAvo MNFA MSte NCot NGdn NLar SBch SMrs SWat WCAu WMoo WPnP WPtf |
| | 'Kashmir Green' | EBee EPPr GBin MAvo NCot WMoo WPnP |
| § | 'Kate' | EBla WCru WWpP |
| | 'Kate Folkard' | see *G.* 'Kate' |
| § | 'Khan' | CMCo EBee EBla EPPr IFro IPot MAvo MNrw NPro SDys SMHy SRGP SUsu WCru WWpP |
| | ***kishtvariense*** | EBee EBla EPPr GCal LRHS MNrw MRav NSti WCru |
| | ***koraiense*** | CDes EBla NBre WMoo WWpP |
| | - B&SWJ 797 | WCru |
| | - B&SWJ 878 | EBee WCru |
| | ***koreanum*** ambig. | CCge CDes CEnt EBla GBuc LRHS WFar WMoo |
| | ***koreanum*** Kom. B&SWJ 602 | WCru |
| § | ***kotschyi*** var. ***charlesii*** | EBee EBla EPPr WRos |
| | ***krameri*** | EBee EBla |

| | | |
|---|---|---|
| | - B&SWJ 1142 | EBla WCru |
| § | ***lambertii*** | EBla EWes GBuc GCal GCra MNrw NBir NChi |
| | - 'Swansdown' | EBla GBuc MNrw WCru WPtf WSHC |
| | 'Lambrook Helen' | CCge EBla |
| I | ***libani*** | EBee ELon EPPr GBuc GKir LLWP MTho NBid NCot NSti WBrk WCot WCru WEas WPnP WTin WWpP |
| | ***libani* x *peloponnesiacum*** | CCge CDes CWsd EBee |
| | 'Libretto' | WCru |
| § | x ***lindavicum*** 'Apple Blossom' | CLyd CMea CMoH EBee EBla EBrs GBuc LRHS MSte NMen WAbe WHCG |
| | ***linearilobum*** subsp. ***transversale*** | EPPr NCot SRot WCru |
| § | 'Little David' | EPPr SUsu WWpP |
| | 'Little Devil' | see *G.* 'Little David' |
| | 'Little Gem' | CDes CElw CMea EBee EBla EBrs LRHS MAvo NChi NDov NLar WCra WFar WWpP |
| | 'Lotusland' | LRHS |
| | ***lucidum*** | MSal NSti WPtf |
| | 'Luscious Linda'[PBR] | EBee GAbr MAvo NBPN NGdn NLar SPer WFar WPnP |
| | 'Lydia' | SRGP WWpP |
| § | ***macrorrhizum*** | Widely available |
| | - AL & JS 90179YU | CHid EPPr |
| | - 'Album' ♀H4 | Widely available |
| | - 'Bevan's Variety' | Widely available |
| | - 'Bulgaria' | CMCo EPPr WWpP |
| | - 'Camce' | EPPr |
| | - 'Czakor' | Widely available |
| I | - 'De Bilt' | EBee EWes WWpP |
| | - 'Freundorf' | EBee EPPr EWes GCal |
| | - 'Ingwersen's Variety' ♀H4 | Widely available |
| | - 'Lohfelden' | CDes EBee EPPr EWes GBuc GCal SRGP SUsu WPGP WWpP |
| | - 'Mount Olympus' | see *G. macrorrhizum* 'White-Ness' |
| | - 'Mount Olympus White' | see *G. macrorrhizum* 'White-Ness' |
| | - 'Mytikas' | EBee EPPr NCot |
| | - 'Pindus' | CBod CPrp EAEE EBee EBla EBrs EPPr GAbr NBre NCot NSti SPoG SRGP WCru WFar WWpP |
| | - 'Prionia' **new** | NCot |
| | - 'Ridsko' | CFee CMCo EPPr GBuc GCal NBro SRGP WCru WWpP |
| | - ***roseum*** | see *G. macrorrhizum* |
| | - 'Rotblut' | EPPr SRGP |
| | - 'Sandwijck' | CCge EBee EPPr NCot WWpP |
| | - 'Snow Sprite' | CBod CCge CEnt CMea COlW EPPr EPyc LBMP LSou MCCP NCot NPro SPoG STes WHrl WWpP |
| | - 'Spessart' | CCge EBee EBla ELan EPPr EPfP GMaP GQue LAst LBMP MSte NLar NPri WBVN WCra WFar WOVN WPnP WRHF WWpP |
| | - 'Variegatum' (v) | EBee EBla EHrv ELan GMaP LRHS MHer MNFA MTho NBPC NBir NSti SPer SRGP SRms WCot WEas WFar WMnd WSHC WWFP WWpP |
| | - 'Velebit' | CCge EPPr MSte SRGP WCru WWpP |
| § | - 'White-Ness' | Widely available |
| | ***macrostylum*** | CDes CPou EBrs WCot WCru WPer WWpP |
| | - MP 8103D | EBee |
| | - 'Leonidas' | EBee EBrs EPPr NCot SPhx WCot WPnP WWpP |
| | - 'Talish' | EPPr LRHS NCot |
| | - 'Uln Oag Triag' | EPPr |
| | ***maculatum*** | CElw CMea CSev EBee EBrs ECha EPfP EWTr GPoy LLWP LRHS MAvo MRav MSal NSti SRGP SWat WCra WCru WHal WPnP WWpP |
| | - from Kath Dryden | EBee EPPr WWpP |
| | - f. ***albiflorum*** | CElw CLAP EBee EBla EGle EMon EPPr MNFA MNrw MWhi MWte NBid NChi NLar NSti SMrm SRGP STes WBrk WCru WMoo WPnP WWpP |
| | - 'Beth Chatto' | Widely available |
| | - 'Elizabeth Ann' | Widely available |
| | - 'Espresso' | Widely available |
| | - purple-flowered | EPPr WWpP |
| | - 'Shameface' | EBee EPPr MSte SBch SDys SGar |
| | - 'Smoky Mountain' **new** | EBee |
| | - 'Spring Purple' | EBee EPPr NCot NLar |
| | - 'Sweetwater' | EPPr |
| | - 'Vickie Lynn' | CLAP EBee EPPr WWpP |
| | ***maderense*** ♀H2 | Widely available |
| | - white-flowered | CSpe LDai WCot |
| § | x ***magnificum*** ♀H4 | Widely available |
| | - 'Blue Blood' | CElw CLAP CWGN EBee ECtt EGle EPPr GBri IPot LSou MBri MSte MWea NCGa NCob NCot NDov NGdn NSti SPoG SRGP WCot WFar WPtf WWpP |
| | - 'Ernst Pagels' | NCot |
| | - 'Hylander' | EBee EPPr WWpP |
| | - 'Peter Yeo' | EPPr SRGP WWpP |
| | - 'Rosemoor' | CCge CElw CHid EBee EBla EHrv ELan EPPr EPfP GCal LCro LHop LPla MBri MNFA MSte NPro WMnd WWpP |
| | - 'Vital' | EBee MBri NCot WWpP |
| | ***magniflorum*** | EWes MRav MSCN NBid NGdn |
| § | ***malviflorum*** | CDes CElw CMHG ECha ELan EPPr LLWP LRHS MNFA MNrw MTho SBch SMeo SRms WAul WCot WCru WFar WHoo WPnP |
| | - from Spain | EWes WSHC |
| | - pink-flowered | CDes EBee EPPr WCru WMoo WPnP WWpP |
| § | 'Mary Mottram' | CElw CMCo EBee EPPr LDai LPio NBir NCot WEas WPnP WWpP |
| § | 'Mavis Simpson' ♀H4 | Widely available |
| | ***maximowiczii*** | CElw CMCo |
| | 'Maxwelton' | NCot |
| | 'Memories'[PBR] | CElw EBee LSRN MBNS NSti WCra WFar |
| | 'Menna Bach' | CDes MAvo WCru WPnP |
| | 'Meryl Anne' | SRGP WPtf |
| | ***microphyllum*** | see *G. potentilloides* |
| | ***molle*** | CSec NBir |
| | - white-flowered | NBir |
| | x ***monacense*** | CMCo EBee EBla ELan EPla GGar IFoB LEdu LRHS SRGP SWat WBrk WCru WHer WMoo WPnP WWpP |
| | - var. ***anglicum*** | CCge EBla EBrs ECtt EPPr GMaP MRav MWhi WMoo WPnP WWpP |
| | - 'Anne Stevens' | EBee NCot |
| | - 'Claudine Dupont' | CElw EBee EPPr IFro MAvo MNFA NCot WCot WWpP |
| | - dark-flowered | WMoo WPtf WWpP |
| | - var. ***monacense*** | EBla WFar |
| | - - 'Breckland Fever' | EBee EPPr MAvo SRGP WWpP |
| § | - - 'Muldoon' | CSev EBee EBla EBrs EPPr EPla NBir SRGP STes WFar WHCG WMoo WPer WPnP WWpP |
| | 'Monita Charm' **new** | CMoH |
| | 'Mourning Widow' | see *G. phaeum* var. *phaeum* black-flowered |
| | 'Mrs Jean Moss' **new** | EPPr |
| | ***napuligerum*** misapplied | see *G. farreri* |

| | | |
|---|---|---|
| | 'Natalie' | CDes CElw EBee EBla EPPr MAvo NChi SBch SUsu WWpP |
| | ***nepalense*** | CMCo IFro SRGP SRms WMoo WWpP |
| | 'Nicola' | CCge CElw EBee EBla EPPr GMac IFro MNFA NCob NHaw SAga SBch SRGP WWpP |
| | 'Nicola Jane' | MNFA |
| | 'Nimbus' ♀H4 | Widely available |
| | ***nodosum*** | Widely available |
| | - dark-flowered | see *G. nodosum* 'Swish Purple' |
| | - 'Julie's Velvet' | CDes MAvo MSte NCot SMrs WHoo WPGP WTin WWpP |
| | - pale-flowered | see *G. nodosum* 'Svelte Lilac' |
| | - 'Pascal' | EPPr WWpP |
| | - 'Saucy Charlie' | SBch |
| | - 'Silverwood' | CElw EBee EPPr MAvo SBch SUsu |
| | - 'Simon' | EBee WWpP |
| § | - 'Svelte Lilac' | CElw EAEE EBee EBla EGle EPPr EPfP LBMP LRHS MNFA MSte NDov NHol SRGP SWat WCAu WCot WCra WCru WFar WMoo WPnP WWpP |
| § | - 'Swish Purple' | CElw CMCo EBee EBla EPPr MNFA MSte NLar SRGP WCru WFar WMoo WPGP WPnP WWpP |
| | - 'Whiteleaf' | CCge CElw CMea EBla EPPr MAvo MNFA NPro SBch SRGP WCru WFar WHal WMoo WPnP WWpP |
| | - 'Whiteleaf' seedling | EBla EGle |
| | 'Nora Bremner' | EBee NChi SUsu WWpP |
| | 'Nunnykirk Pink' | EWes SUsu |
| | 'Nunwood Purple' | CMCo EBee EPPr MAvo NCot WPtf WWpP |
| | ***oreganum*** | CCge CMoH |
| § | ***orientalitibeticum*** | Widely available |
| | 'Orion' ♀H4 | Widely available |
| | 'Orkney Blue' | EPPr WCru |
| | 'Orkney Cherry' | EBee LAst LLHF LRHS SPoG SRkn |
| | 'Orkney Dawn' | NHaw WCru |
| | 'Orkney Pink' | CCge CDes EBee EBla ECtt EPPr EPfP GBuc GKir LHop LSRN MDun MLHP MSte NLAp NSti NWCA SAga SPer SPoG SRGP SWat WFar WHoo WWpP |
| | ***ornithopodon*** | NCot |
| | 'Out of the Blue' | WOut |
| | x ***oxonianum*** | NCot WMoo |
| | - 'A.T. Johnson' ♀H4 | Widely available |
| | - 'Anmore' | EPPr SRGP |
| | - 'Beholder's Eye' ♀H4 | CCge CHid CMCo EBee EBla ECGP EPPr GAbr GKir MNFA MSte NBre SBch SRGP WPnP WPtf WWpP |
| | - 'Breckland Sunset' | CMCo EPPr MAvo NCot SBch SRGP WPnP WWpP |
| | - 'Bregover Pearl' | CBre CElw CMCo CWsd EBee EBla EPPr NCot SRGP WMoo WWpP |
| | - 'Bressingham's Delight' | CMCo EBla ECtt LRHS SRGP WWpP |
| | - 'Buttercup' | EBee EPPr NCot SRGP WWpP |
| I | - 'Cally Seedling' | EBee EBla EWes GCal |
| § | - 'Claridge Druce' | Widely available |
| | - 'Coronet' | CCge EPPr GCal SMrm SRGP WMoo WWpP |
| | - 'David Rowlinson' | EPPr |
| | - 'Dawn Time' | WWpP |
| | - 'Diane's Treasure' | NCot NHaw |
| | - 'Dirk Gunst' | CElw |
| | - 'Elsbeth Blush' | EBla NCot WWpP |
| | - 'Elworthy Misty' | CCge CElw CMCo EBee EBla EPPr NCot SBch SRGP WWpP |
| | - 'Frank Lawley' | CElw CMCo EBee EBla EPPr GBuc GMac LLWP NBid SBch SMrm SRGP WBrk WMoo WWpP |
| § | - 'Fran's Star' (d) | EBee EBla EGoo SRGP WBrk WCru WRHF WWpP |
| | - 'Frilly Gilly' | EBee EPPr |
| | - 'Hexham Pink' | CCge CMCo EBee EPPr NChi SBch SRGP WWpP |
| | - 'Hollywood' | CCge CMCo EBee EBla ELan EPPr EPfP GBuc LRHS MBri MSte MTho NCot NLar NPer SRGP SRms WBor WBrk WCra WFar WMoo WPnP WPtf WWpP |
| I | - 'Jean's Lilac' | NCot |
| | - 'Julie Brennan' | EBee GAbr GBin GMac SMrs WWpP |
| | - 'Julie Searle' | SRos |
| | - 'Kate Moss' | EBee EBla EPPr GCai NSti SBch SRGP WCra WWpP |
| | - 'Katherine Adele' | CBod CCge CHFP EBee EBla ECtt EPPr EWes GGar IPot LSou MWea NBPN NBhm NCot NLar NSti SPoG SRGP SRms WCra WFar |
| § | - 'Kingston' | CElw CMCo EBee EPPr WWpP |
| | - 'Klaus Schult' | EPPr LPio |
| | - 'Königshof' | EBee EPPr EWes NCot NLar WWpP |
| | - 'Kurt's Variegated' PBR | see *G.* x *oxonianum* 'Spring Fling' |
| | - 'Lace Time' | CBre CCge CElw CMCo CSev EAEE EBee EBla EPPr GBuc GMac LBMP MNrw NCGa NCot NGdn NHol SBch SRGP SRms WCAu WMnd WMoo WPnP WWpP |
| | - 'Lady Moore' | CCge CMCo EBee EBla EPPr EPla GBuc MNrw NBro NCot SRGP WCra WMoo WPnP WWpP |
| | - 'Lambrook Gillian' | CCge CWsd EBee EPPr NCot SBch SRGP WBrk WPnP WPtf WWpP |
| | - 'Lasting Impression' | EBee EPPr SRGP WWpP |
| | - 'Laura Skelton' **new** | CElw NHaw |
| | - 'Little John' | EWes |
| | - 'Maid Marion' | EWes |
| | - 'Man of Mystery' | EBee |
| | - 'Miriam Rundle' | CElw CMCo EBrs EPPr MNrw NCot SRGP WCru WMoo WPnP WWpP |
| | - 'Moorland Jenny' | CElw WMoo WWpP |
| | - 'Moorland Star' | WMoo |
| | - 'Old Rose' | EBee EGle EPPr GKir LRHS SRGP WCra WCru WPnP WWpP |
| | - 'Pat Smallacombe' | CElw EBla NCot WMoo WWpP |
| | - 'Patricia Josephine' | WCAu |
| | - 'Pearl Boland' | EBee EPPr SRGP |
| | - 'Phantom' **new** | EBee EPPr |
| | - 'Phoebe Noble' | CBre CCge CElw CMCo EBee EBla EGle EPPr MNrw NCob NCot SAga SMad SRGP WCra WMoo WPnP WPtf WWpP |
| | - 'Phoebe's Blush' | EBee EBla EPPr GMac SRGP WWpP |
| | - 'Pink Cluster' **new** | CLAP |
| | - 'Pink Lace' | CCge LSou |
| § | - 'Prestbury Blush' | CBre CElw CMCo EPPr SRGP WCru WWpP |
| | - 'Prestbury White' | see *G.* x *oxonianum* 'Prestbury Blush' |
| | - 'Raspberry Ice' | EBee EBla EWes |
| | - 'Rebecca Moss' | CSev EAEE EBee EBla EPPr GBuc GCra GMac LRHS MSte NCot NSti SAga SBch SHBN SRGP WCra WFar WPnP WPtf WWpP |
| | - 'Robin's Ginger Nut' **new** | EBee |
| | - 'Rodbylund' | EBee |
| | - 'Rose Clair' | CCge CElw CMCo CTca EAEE EBee EBla EGle GKir LRHS MWhi NBir SGar SPet SRGP SRms WBrk WCru WEas WMnd WMoo WPer WWpP |
| | - 'Rosemary' | SBch WWpP |
| | - 'Rosemary Verey' | SBch |

| | |
|---|---|
| - 'Rosenlicht' | CElw CHrt CSev EAEE EBee EBla EPPr LRHS MRav NLar SRGP WCAu WCra WCru WMnd WMoo WPnP WPrP WPtf WWpP |
| - 'Rosewood' | SRos |
| - 'Rosita' **new** | NCot |
| § - 'Spring Fling' (v) | CCge EBee EBla ECtt EHrv EPPr LFur NCot NGdn NSti SPla SPoG SRGP WCAu WCot WCra WFar |
| - 'Stillingfleet' | see *G.* x *oxonianum* 'Stillingfleet Keira' |
| § - 'Stillingfleet Keira' | CMCo EBee NCot NSti SRGP WWpP |
| - 'Summer Surprise' | EBee EPPr EWes NCob NLar SBch WCru WPnP WWpP |
| - 'Susan' | EBee EBla EPPr EWes |
| - 'Susie White' | CElw CMCo EPPr MAvo SRGP WCru WWpP |
| § - f. ***thurstonianum*** | Widely available |
| - - 'Armitageae' | EBee EPPr NCot SRGP WWpP |
| - - 'Breckland Brownie' | CElw CMCo EBee EBla EPPr EWes MAvo NCot SRGP WWpP |
| - - 'Crûg Star' | CCge WCru |
| - - 'David McClintock' | CMCo EPPr SBch SRGP WFar WMoo WWpP |
| - - 'Peter Hale' | CMea SAga |
| - - 'Red Sputnik' | EBee EPPr MAvo SRGP WWpP |
| - - 'Sherwood' | CBod CCge EBee EBla ECtt EPPr GCal GQue MTho NBro NCob NVic SApp SGar SMrm SRGP WCAu WFar WMoo WPnP WPtf WWpP |
| - - 'Southcombe Double' (d) | CElw CMCo CSev EAEE EBee EBla ECtt EGle EHrv EPPr EPfP LAst LRHS NChi NCot SPer SPoG SRGP SRms WBrk WCra WCru WFar WMoo WWpP |
| § - - 'Southcombe Star' | EBee EBla EPPr GAbr GCal NBro NGdn SRGP WBrk WCru WFar WMoo WPer WPnP WWpP |
| - - 'Sue Cox' | EPPr NCot NLar |
| - 'Trevor's White' | CLAP EBee EBla EGle EPPr LLWP MNrw SBch SRGP WCru WWpP |
| - 'Wageningen' | CBre CMCo EAEE EBee EGle EPPr GCal GMac LPla MBri MNFA MSte NCot NGdn NPro SAga SMrm SRGP SRms WBrk WCra WCru WHer WMoo WPtf WWpP |
| - 'Walter's Gift' | Widely available |
| § - 'Wargrave Pink' ♀H4 | Widely available |
| - 'Waystrode' | CMCo EBla EPPr SRGP WWpP |
| - 'Whitehaven' | EBee NCot SRGP WWpP |
| - 'Winscombe' | CElw CHrt CMCo EBee GCal LLWP LRHS MRav MTho NBsh NCob SRGP WCAu WFar WMnd WMoo WWpP |
| - 'Winston Churchill' | CMCo WWpP |
| x ***oxonianum*** x ***sessiliflorum*** subsp. ***novae-zelandiae*** 'Nigricans' | EHrv |
| 'Pagoda' | CCge MNrw SUsu |
| § ***palmatum*** ♀H3 | Widely available |
| ***palmatum*** x ***maderense*** | WCru |
| ***palustre*** | CElw CMCo EBee EBla EPPr MNFA MNrw NBro NHol SRGP WFar WMoo WWpP |
| ***papuanum*** | WCru |
| 'Part Purple Hero' **new** | EBee |
| Patricia = 'Brempat' ♀H4 | Widely available |
| ***peloponnesiacum*** | EAEE EBee EPPr GGar LRHS SBch SPoG WFar |
| - NS 660 | CElw |
| 'Perfect Storm' | CWGN EBee LLHF LSou SPoG |
| ***phaeum*** | Widely available |
| - 'Album' | Widely available |
| - 'Alec's Pink' | EBla EPPr LLWP SHar WOut WWpP |
| - 'All Saints' | EBee EMon EPPr LEdu SRGP WWpP |
| - 'Angelina' | NCot |
| - 'Anne Claire' | NCot |
| - 'Aureum' | see *G. phaeum* 'Golden Spring' |
| - black-flowered | see *G. phaeum* var. *phaeum* black-flowered |
| - 'Blauwvoet' | CFwr EBee EPPr MAvo NCot WWpP |
| - 'Blue Shadow' | CDes CElw CMCo EBee EBla EPPr LLWP MAvo NCot SRGP WWpP |
| - 'Calligrapher' | CElw EBla EPPr LLHF MAvo NCot SBch SMrs SRGP SUsu WMoo WWpP |
| - 'Chocolate Chip' | CMCo EBla WWpP |
| - 'Conny Broe' (v) | CLAP EBee NCot |
| - 'Countess of Grey' **new** | SMrs |
| - dark-flowered | CElw |
| - 'David Bromley' | EBla EMon WCru WPrP |
| - 'Enid' **new** | EPPr |
| - 'Geele Samobor' | EBla |
| - 'George Stone' | EBee EBla EPPr LLHF WWpP |
| - 'Golden Samobor' | CElw |
| § - 'Golden Spring' | CCge CElw EBee EBla EPPr MAvo NChi NCot NPro SBch SRGP WWpP |
| - 'Hannah Perry' | CElw CMoH EBla EPPr LLWP WPtf |
| - 'Hector's Lavender' **new** | EBee |
| - var. ***hungaricum*** | EBee EPPr SRGP WPtf WWpP |
| - 'James Haunch' | EBla EPPr |
| - 'Klepper' | CFwr CMCo EBee EPPr GBin NCot WWpP |
| - 'Lily Lovell' | Widely available |
| - 'Lisa' | EBee EPPr NCot |
| - 'Little Boy' | CMCo EBee EBla EMon EPPr NGdn WWpP |
| - var. ***lividum*** | CBgR CBre CElw CFee GMaP LCro LLWP MAvo MRav NCot NHol NLar SRGP SRms STes WCAu WFar WPer WPnP WWpP |
| - - 'Joan Baker' | CBgR CBre CElw CSam EBee EPPr GBuc LPla MAvo MNFA NChi NCot NGdn NSti SBch SPhx SRGP WCra WCru WFar WMoo WPnP WPtf WTin WWpP |
| - - 'Majus' | CElw EBee ECtt EMon EPPr EPfP EPyc LLWP LPla WFar WMoo WPnP WWpP |
| - 'Maggie's Delight' (v) | SRGP |
| - 'Marchant's Ghost' | MAvo NGdn SMHy SMrm SPhx |
| - 'Margaret Hunt' | NLar |
| - 'Margaret Wilson' (v) | CBow CDes CElw CFir EBee EBla ECha ECtt EPPr EWes LEdu LPio MAvo NCot SBch SMrs SRGP SUsu WCot WPnP WWpP |
| - 'Mierhausen' | CElw CMCo EBee EBla EPPr EShb MAvo NCot WPtf WWpP |
| - 'Moorland Dylan' | EBla WMoo WOut WWpP |
| - 'Mourning Widow' | see *G. phaeum* var. *phaeum* black-flowered |
| - 'Mrs Charles Perrin' | CBgR CCge CElw EBee EBla EPPr MAvo STes WPtf WWpP |
| - 'Night Time' | EBee EPPr MNFA WWpP |
| - 'Our Pat' | EBee EPPr NChi NCot WWpP |
| - 'Pannonia' **new** | NCot |
| - var. ***phaeum*** | NBPN SBch WOut |
| § - - black-flowered | CFwr CMoH CSec EGle EPPr EShb GCal GKir NCob NCot NDov SGar SRGP SRms SWat WCru WMoo WWpP |

| | | |
|---|---|---|
| | - - 'Langthorns Blue' | CCge CElw CMCo CMoH CSev EBee ELan EPPr LEdu MAvo MNFA MNrw NBre SRGP WWpP |
| | - - 'Samobor' | Widely available |
| I | - 'Ploeger de Bilt' | EPPr |
| | - purple-flowered | MDun |
| | - 'Rachel's Rhapsody' | CElw CMCo EBee EBla EPPr MAvo NCot SUsu WWpP |
| | - 'Raven' | EBee EPPr SUsu WWpP |
| | - red-flowered | MRav |
| | - 'Rise Top Lilac' | CCge CMCo EBee NCot WWpP |
| | - 'Rose Air' | CMCo EBee EGoo EPPr MAvo NCot SRGP WMoo WPnP WPtf WWpP |
| | - 'Rose Madder' | CBgR CCge CElw EBee EBla EGle EPPr EPyc EWTr GBuc GCal LEdu LHop LLWP LPio LPla MNFA MNrw MSte NChi NCot SMrs SPhx SRGP SUsu WCru WMoo WWpP |
| | - 'Saturn' | EPPr WWpP |
| | - 'Séricourt' | EBee WCot WCra |
| | - 'Silver Fox' | WRha |
| | - 'Slatina' **new** | WPtf |
| | - 'Small Grey' | EBla EPPr |
| | - 'Springtime' PBR | CBod CElw EBee EPPr EPfP LLHF MAvo MSte NBPN NBhm NCot NSti SPoG WCra |
| | - 'Stillingfleet Ghost' | CBow CElw EBee EBla EPPr GKir LEdu NCot NPro NSti |
| | - 'Taff's Jester' (v) | CElw EBee EWes LPla NHol SApp SRGP WCot WWpP |
| | - 'Thorn's Blue' | EBee EBrs GKir |
| § | - 'Variegatum' (v) | Widely available |
| | - 'Walküre' | CMCo EBee EPPr EWes MAvo MSte WPtf WWpP |
| | 'Philippe Vapelle' | Widely available |
| | 'Pink Delight' | CElw EBla LPio MAvo SPhx WWpP |
| | 'Pink Ghost' | CBow |
| | 'Pink Penny' **new** | CElw EBee IPot NBhm NDov WCra WPnP |
| | 'Pink Splash' | LSou |
| § | ***platyanthum*** | CCge CWsd EBee EPPr GGar MNrw NBre SRGP WBrk WCru WHCG WMoo WPer WWpP |
| | - giant | EPPr SGar |
| | - var. ***reinii*** | WCru |
| | ***platypetalum*** misapplied | see *G.* x ***magnificum*** |
| | ***platypetalum*** Franch. | see *G. sinense* |
| § | ***platypetalum*** Fisch. & C.A. Mey. | EPPr GKev LRHS NBid NBir NBre SRGP SRms WCru WPtf WWpP |
| | - 'Georgia Blue' | MSte WCru WFar WPtf |
| | - 'Genyell' | EBee |
| § | ***pogonanthum*** | CDes CWsd GBuc NBir NChi WMoo WWpP |
| | ***polyanthes*** | GBuc WWpP |
| | - HWJCM 276 | WCru |
| § | ***ponticum*** | NSti |
| § | ***potentilloides*** | CCge GCal NBir SRGP WWpP |
| | ***pratense*** | Widely available |
| | - 'Akton' **new** | WCra WHlf |
| | - 'Bittersweet' | CHar CMCo EBee EBla EPPr NCot WWpP |
| | - Black Beauty = 'Nodbeauty' PBR | CBcs CBct CPar CSpe CWGN EBee ELan EPPr EPfP EWes LBuc LSou MGos MWea NBPN NCGa NPri SCoo SDnm SPav SPer SPoG SRot WFar WHlf |
| | - 'Candy' **new** | EBee |
| | - 'Cluden Sapphire' | CAbP EBla EPPr GKir MWhi NBre NCot NGdn NHol NPro WCru WFar WWpP |
| | - 'Else Lacey' (d) **new** | EBee |
| | - 'Feebers Double' (d) | CFee |
| | - 'Flore Pleno' | see *G. pratense* 'Plenum Violaceum' |
| I | - 'Himalayanum' | NLar |
| | - 'Hocus Pocus' | EBee EGle EHrv ELan EPfP LPio MAvo MBNS NBPN NBhm NBid NBro NLar NMoo NSti SHBN WCAu |
| | - 'Ilja' | EBee NCot |
| | - 'Janet's Special' | WHoo |
| | - 'Lichtenstein' **new** | NCot |
| | - 'Lilac Lullaby' | EBee WWpP |
| | - Midnight Reiter strain | Widely available |
| | - 'Mrs Kendall Clark' ΨH4 | Widely available |
| | - 'New Dimension' | CBcs EBee ELan EPPr EPfP GBin LRHS MGos MWea NBPN NBre NSti WCot WCra WWpP |
| | - 'Okey Dokey' | EBee NBsh WWpP |
| | - pale-flowered | EBee WPnP WWpP |
| | - 'Picotee' | EBee NCot |
| | - 'Plenum Album' | CBre CLAP ECtt EGle EPPr EWes LLHF NCob NCot NGdn NLar SMrm SMrs SPer SPoG WCra WGwG WPtf |
| | - 'Plenum Caeruleum' (d) | CHar CMHG EBee ECtt EGle EPPr GBuc GMaP MDun MRav NBid NGdn NHol NLar SHBN SPer SPla STes SWat WCru WFar WHCG WMoo WPnP WSHC WWpP |
| | - 'Plenum Purpureum' | see *G. pratense* 'Plenum Violaceum' |
| § | - 'Plenum Violaceum' (d) ΨH4 | Widely available |
| | - var. ***pratense*** f. ***albiflorum*** | CElw CSam EPPr GCra GMaP IFro MNrw NBid NCot NOrc SPer WCru WHCG WMnd WMoo WWpP |
| | - - - 'Galactic' | CCge EBee EPPr GKir NBir NBre NBsh NGby SPhx WCru WMoo WPnP WWpP |
| | - - - 'Plenum Album' (d) | CDes EBee EPPr NLar NSti WCot WPnP |
| | - - - 'Silver Queen' | CBre CCge CHar EBee EBla ECtt EPPr MNrw NBir NBre SRGP WFar WMoo WPGP WWpP |
| | - 'Purple Heron' | CDes EBee EBla ECGP EPPr LSRN MBri MCCP MNrw MSte MTPN SPla STes WFar |
| * | - 'Purple-haze' | CTca GBuc LSou MCCP NCob NLar WHrl WMoo WOut WTou WWpP |
| | - 'Rectum Album' | see *G. clarkei* 'Kashmir White' |
| § | - 'Rose Queen' | EBee EBla EPPr MNrw MRav NBir NHol NLar SRGP WCru WWpP |
| | - 'Roseum' | see *G. pratense* 'Rose Queen' |
| | - 'Splish-splash' | see *G. pratense* 'Striatum' |
| | - 'Stanton Mill' | NBid |
| | - var. ***stewartianum*** | EBee MRav |
| | - - 'Elizabeth Yeo' | EBee EBla EPPr MAvo NCot NLar SUsu WCru WWpP |
| | - - 'Purple Silk' | EPPr |
| § | - 'Striatum' | Widely available |
| | - 'Striatum' dwarf | WCru |
| | - 'Striatum' pale-flowered | CBre |
| | - Summer Skies = 'Gernic' PBR | see *G.* Summer Skies = 'Gernic' |
| § | - Victor Reiter Junior strain | Widely available |
| | - 'Wisley Blue' | CMCo EBee EBla EPPr MSte SBch SRGP WHal WWpP |
| | - 'Yorkshire Queen' | CMCo EBee EPPr NCob NGdn WCru WWpP |
| | 'Prelude' | CBre CCge CDes CElw CMCo EBee EPPr MNFA NBir NCot NPro SRGP SUsu WCra WWpP |
| | 'Priestley's Pink' | WWpP |
| | 'Prima Donna' | EBee |
| | ***procurrens*** | CBre CElw COIW CSev EBee EPPr EShb GAbr GCal GGar LLWP MLLN NBid NGdn WBrk WCru WFar WMoo WPnP WRos WWpP |

| | |
|---|---|
| § ***psilostemon*** ♀H4 | Widely available |
| - 'Bressingham Flair' | CPrp EBee EBla ECtt EGle EPfP GAbr GCra LHop LRHS MRav NBid NChi NGdn NHol NLar SRms WCAu WCru WFar WMoo WSHC |
| - 'Coton Goliath' | EPPr EWes SUsu |
| - 'Fluorescent' | NCot |
| - 'Gold Leaf' | EBee |
| - hybrid | CElw |
| - 'Jason Bloom' | EBrs GKir |
| - 'Madelon' | EBee NCot NLar |
| - 'Sumela' **new** | NCot |
| ***pulchrum*** | CHid CSpe EBee EPPr MNrw SGar SRGP WCot WPer WRos WWpP |
| ***punctatum*** hort. | see *G.* x *monacense* var. *monacense* 'Muldoon' |
| - 'Variegatum' | see *G. phaeum* 'Variegatum' |
| ***pusillum*** | MSal |
| ***pylzowianum*** | CMCo EBee GGar MRav NBid NRya SBch WFar WMoo WWpP |
| ***pyrenaicum*** | CCge CRWN CSec CSev EBWF GAbr NBre NSti WTou WWpP |
| - f. ***albiflorum*** | CCge CHrt EBee EBla GAbr IFro LLWP MNrw NBir SAga SRGP WBrk WPer WPnP WTou WWpP |
| - 'Barney Brighteye' | CCge EBee SRGP |
| - 'Bill Wallis' | Widely available |
| - 'Bright Eyes' | LLWP NCot |
| - 'Isparta' | CSec EBee EGle EPPr IFro NCot SBch SPhx SRGP SUsu WBrk WTou |
| - 'Summer Sky' | CCge EBrs EHig GBin LFur NCot SMrm SPav SRGP WPtf |
| - 'Summer Snow' | CCge EPyc LFur NCot NLar |
| 'Rachel' | CBow |
| Rambling Robin Group | CBow CSpe EBee ECre ECtt EPPr EWes LFur LSou MCCP MWhi SMad WCru |
| 'Ray's Pink' | CCge NPro WWpP |
| ***rectum*** | EPPr NBre WCru |
| - 'Album' | see *G. clarkei* 'Kashmir White' |
| 'Red Admiral' | CMCo EAEE EBee ECtt EPPr GCal GGar IPot LBMP LRHS MNFA MSte NCGa NCot NDov NLar NSti SPoG SRGP SUsu |
| ***reflexum*** | CSev EBla EPPr WFar WPrP WWpP |
| ***regelii*** | CCge CElw CHFP CMCo CSam EBee EPPr GAuc LEdu MNFA NCot WCru WMoo WPnP WWpP |
| ***renardii*** ♀H4 | Widely available |
| - 'Beldo' | EBee |
| - blue-flowered | see *G. renardii* 'Whiteknights' |
| - 'Heidi Morris' | WWpP |
| - 'Tcschelda' | CMCo CMHG EBee EBla ECha ECtt LBMP LPio NBir NCGa SBod SMrm SPla SRms WFar WMoo WPnP WWpP |
| § - 'Whiteknights' | CElw CMoH EBee EBla ECha GBuc NBir WCru |
| - 'Zetterlund' | CElw CMCo EAEE EBee EBla ECGP EGle EHrv EPPr EPfP GKir LLWP LPio MAvo MLLN MWat NPri WBrk WCAu WCra WFar WMnd WMoo WWpP |
| ***repens*** B&SWJ 9089 | WCru |
| § ***reuteri*** | CBod CCge IDee LDai SChr SDnm SGar SPav SRGP WCru WPnP WSHC |
| 'Richard John' | MNFA |
| 'Richard Nutt' **new** | EBee |
| ***richardsonii*** | CCge EBee EBla EPPr MNrw NBir NCot SRGP SRms WCru WPnP |
| x ***riversleaianum*** 'Mavis Simpson' | see *G.* 'Mavis Simpson' |
| - 'Russell Prichard' ♀H4 | Widely available |

| | |
|---|---|
| § ***rivulare*** | CCge EBla NBre WHCG WMnd WPtf WWpP |
| - 'Album' | EBla |
| ***robertianum*** | CArn CCge EBWF EPPr LLHF MHer SECG SRms WWpP |
| § - 'Album' | CBod EBla EPPr SHar SRGP SRms WAlt |
| - f. ***bernettii*** | see *G. robertianum* 'Album' |
| - 'Celtic White' | CBre CCge EMon EPPr GCal MHer NGHP SPav SRGP WAlt WOut WWpP |
| - subsp. ***celticum*** | WAlt |
| ***robustum*** | EBee EGoo EPPr MNFA MNrw MWhi NBir NBro NChi SMad SPav SRGP WCot WFar WHal WKif WPGP WSHC WWpP |
| - Hannays' form | CSev CSpe WPGP |
| 'Rosie Crûg' | CCge CHid SWvt WCru |
| ***rosthornii*** | WCru |
| Rozanne = 'Gerwat'PBR | Widely available |
| ***rubescens*** | see *G. yeoi* |
| ***rubifolium*** | WCru |
| § 'Ruprecht' | CWsd LFur |
| ***ruprechtii*** misapplied | see *G.* 'Ruprecht' |
| ***ruprechtii*** (Grossh.) Woronow | CCge CElw EBee EPPr GAuc MAvo MNrw NBre SRGP WPer WPtf WWpP |
| Sabani Blue = 'Bremigo'PBR | CSpe EBee EWes GBin LEdu LHop LRHS MSte MWea NLar NSti SPer SPoG SRkn STes WWpP |
| 'Salome' | Widely available |
| 'Sandrine' **new** | CWGN EBee EPPr GBin LLHF MNrw MSte WCot WCra WPnP WRHF |
| ***sanguineum*** | Widely available |
| - Alan Bloom = 'Bloger'PBR | EBrs LRHS SIng WCra |
| - 'Album' ♀H4 | Widely available |
| - 'Alpenglow' | EPPr SBch SRGP WWpP |
| - 'Ankum's Pride' ♀H4 | CCge CMMP EBee EBla EGle EMon EPPr IPot LAst LPio LRHS MNFA NChi NCot NDov NGdn NSti SBch SRGP SUsu SWat WCra WCru WFar WMoo WPnP WWpP |
| - 'Apfelblüte' | EBee EPPr NCot NGby NLar SSvw WCra WFar WWpP |
| - 'Aviemore' ♀H4 | EBee EPPr GBin GCal NCot SBch WWpP |
| - 'Barnsley' | CElw CPrp EPPr NBro NPro WHrl WWpP |
| - 'Belle of Herterton' | CMCo EBee EPPr MAvo MSte NBid NChi NPro SBch SUsu WCru WWpP |
| - 'Bloody Graham' | EBee EGle EPPr MAvo NHaw SBch WMoo WWpP |
| - 'Candy Pink' **new** | EPPr |
| - 'Canon Miles' | EBee EPPr GGar LRHS NCot WWpP |
| - 'Catforth Carnival' | EPPr MAvo WWpP |
| - 'Cedric Morris' | CElw EBla ECha EGle EPPr GCra LPio MAvo MTho NBid SAga SRGP WCru WPnP WWpP |
| - 'Compactum' | EAlp EBee WWpP |
| § - 'Droplet' | SRGP |
| - 'Elsbeth' | CCge CElw CMCo EBee EBla ECha ECtt EPPr EWes GBuc GCal NCot NGdn NSti SPoG SRGP WCru WFar WHal WMoo WPnP WWpP |
| - 'Feu d'Automne' | EBee EPPr WWpP |
| - 'Fran's Star' | see *G.* x *oxonianum* 'Fran's Star' |
| - 'Glenluce' | Widely available |
| - 'Hampshire Purple' | see *G. sanguineum* 'New Hampshire Purple' |
| - 'Holden' | CElw EPPr SBch WWpP |

| | | |
|---|---|---|
| | - 'Inverness' | EBee EPPr NCot WWpP |
| | - 'Joanna' | MAvo |
| | - 'John Elsley' | CElw CMCo CPrp EAEE EBee EBla ECtt EHoe EPPr GKir LAst LLWP LRHS MNFA MSCN NBro NCot NGdn NLar SRGP SWat WBVN WCra WMnd WPer WWpP |
| | - 'John Innes' | EBee EPPr NCot WWpP |
| | - 'Jubilee Pink' | CElw EBla GCal WCru |
| | - 'Kristin Jacob' new | EPPr |
| | - var. ***lancastrense*** | see *G. sanguineum* var. *striatum* |
| | - 'Leeds Variety' | see *G. sanguineum* 'Rod Leeds' |
| § | - 'Little Bead' ♀H4 | EBla ECho GKir NHol WWpP |
| | - 'Max Frei' | Widely available |
| | - 'Minutum' | see *G. sanguineum* 'Droplet' |
| | - 'Nanum' | see *G. sanguineum* 'Little Bead' |
| § | - 'New Hampshire Purple' | CCge CLAP CPrp EBee ECtt EPPr GGar LSou NBro NDov NGdn NLar NSti SSvw WCra WWpP |
| | - 'Nyewood' | EBee ECGP EMon EPPr MLLN SEND SRGP WCra WCru WWpP |
| I | - 'Plenum' (d) | EPPr WWpP |
| | - var. ***prostratum*** | see *G. sanguineum* var. *striatum* |
| | - 'Purple Flame' | see *G. sanguineum* 'New Hampshire Purple' |
| § | - 'Rod Leeds' | CLAP CMCo EBee LPio MSte MWea NPro SRGP WPnP WWpP |
| | - 'Sandra' | SRGP WWpP |
| | - 'Sara' | MAvo WPnP WWpP |
| | - 'Shepherd's Warning' ♀H4 | CCge CMea CSev CTca CTri EAEE EBee EBla ECtt EPPr GCal GKir MLLN NBir NLar SEND SRGP SUsu SWat WCra WCru WFar WHCG WHoo WTin WWpP |
| | - 'Shooting Star' | EBee |
| | - 'South Nutfield' | MAvo SUsu |
| § | - var. ***striatum*** ♀H4 | Widely available |
| | - - deep pink-flowered | CSBt MSwo SWvt WWpP |
| | - - 'Reginald Farrer' | GBuc WCru WWpP |
| | - - 'Splendens' ♀H4 | CCge CElw CEnt CSev CWib EBla ELan EPPr LBee LHop NBid NChi NCot WCru WEas WTin WWpP |
| | - 'Vision Light Pink' | LRHS SGar WPtf |
| | - 'Vision Violet' | CCge COIW EBee EBla LRHS NHol SWvt WFar WPer WWpP |
| | - 'Westacre Poppet' | EPPr EWes WWpP |
| | ***saxatile*** | EPPr |
| | 'Sea Pink' | MNrw |
| | 'Sellindge Blue' | NCot WCra WWpP |
| | ***sessiliflorum*** | ECou |
| I | - subsp. ***novae-zelandiae*** 'Nigricans' | CCge EBla ECha ECho EHrv ELan EPfP GAbr GGar IPot MCot MHer NChi NMoo NWCA SRGP WBrE WFar WHCG |
| § | - - 'Porter's Pass' | CBow CSpe CWib EBee ECho EHoe EWes GBuc MCCP MNrw NBir NChi SBch SPlb SWat WFar WHoo |
| | - - red-leaved | see *G. sessiliflorum* subsp. *novae-zelandiae* 'Porter's Pass' |
| * | - 'Rubrum' | CSec WBVN |
| | 'Sheilah Hannay' | CSpe |
| | ***shikokianum*** | CLAP LFur MCCP NLar SAga SGar SPer SRGP WHrl WWpP |
| | - var. ***kaimontanum*** | EBla WCru |
| | - var. ***quelpaertense*** | EBee EBla WPtf |
| | - - B&SWJ 1234 | WCru |
| | - var. ***yoshiianum*** | CCge CElw GBuc WMoo |
| | - - B&SWJ 6147 | WCru |
| | 'Shocking Blue' | EBee LCro NSti WWpP |
| | 'Shouting Star' | see *G.* 'Kanahitobanawa' |
| * | 'Silver Shadow' | SPhx |
| § | ***sinense*** | CDes CFir CHFP CMHG EBee EBla ECtt EPPr EPfP GCal LBMP LFur MBri MNrw NGdn NSti SPoG SRGP STes WHer WMnd WMoo WPer WPnP WWpP |
| | 'Sirak' ♀H4 | Widely available |
| | ***soboliferum*** | CWsd EBee EBla EBrs ELan EPPr GKir NBir NDlv NWCA SMrs SPla SRGP SUsu WCru WMoo WPtf WWpP |
| | - Cally strain | CDes GCal MSte |
| | - var. ***kiusianum*** new | MWea |
| | - 'Starman' | EBee |
| | 'Southcombe Star' | see *G.* × *oxonianum* f. *thurstonianum* 'Southcombe Star' |
| | 'Southease Celestial' | SMHy SSth SUsu |
| | 'Spinners' | Widely available |
| | ***stapfianum*** var. ***roseum*** | see *G. orientalitibeticum* |
| | 'Stephanie' | CDes CElw CMCo EBee EPPr EPfP EWes MAvo MWea NCot WPnP WWpP |
| | 'Strawberry Frost' | EBla LLHF |
| | ***subcaulescens*** ♀H4 | Widely available |
| | - 'Signal' | EBee |
| | - 'Splendens' ♀H4 | CTri EAEE EBee EBla ECtt EDAr EPPr EPfP LHop MDun MHer NDov NPri NSla SHBN SPla SRms SWat WFar WPat WPnP WWpP |
| | 'Sue Crûg' | Widely available |
| | 'Sue's Sister' | WCru |
| | 'Summer Cloud' | EBla EPPr NCot SRGP WHrl |
| § | Summer Skies = 'Gernic'PBR (d) | Widely available |
| | ***suzukii*** | WPtf |
| | - B&SWJ 016 | WCru |
| | ***swatense*** | MLLN |
| | 'Sweet Heidy' new | EBee LLHF MAvo MWea NCot NMoo WCra |
| | ***sylvaticum*** | CMMP CRWN CSec EBWF EBee EBla MSal NBid NGdn WBrk WMoo WPer WShi WWpP |
| | - 'Afrodite' new | EPPr |
| | - f. ***albiflorum*** | CBre CCge CElw EBee ELan NSti WCru |
| | - 'Album' ♀H4 | Widely available |
| | - 'Amy Doncaster' | Widely available |
| | - 'Angulatum' | CElw EBee EPPr MNFA NCot SBch WMoo WWpP |
| | - 'Arnoldshof' new | EPPr |
| | - 'Birch Lilac' | CElw EBee EBla EPPr GBuc GCal LCro MAvo MNFA SMrm WFar WMoo WPnP WWpP |
| | - 'Birgit Lion' | EBee NCot |
| | - 'Ice Blue' | EBla EPPr GBin NCot WWpP |
| | - 'Immaculée' | EBee EPPr MRav WCot WWpP |
| | - 'Kanzlersgrund' | CElw EPPr WWpP |
| | - 'Lilac Time' | EBla EPPr WWpP |
| | - 'Mayflower' ♀H4 | Widely available |
| | - 'Meran' | EPPr |
| | - 'Nikita' | EPPr WWpP |
| | - f. ***roseum*** | CCge EPPr GGar NBre NLar WOut WPtf |
| | - - 'Baker's Pink' | CCge CElw EBee EBla EPPr MNFA MRav NBir NCot SBch SRGP WCra WCru WFar WHCG WMoo WPnP WWpP |
| | - 'Silva' | CElw CMoH EBee ECtt EPPr MAvo MNFA MRav SWat WCru WWpP |
| | - subsp. ***sylvaticum*** var. ***wanneri*** | CCge EBee EPPr SBch WCru WWpP |
| § | 'Tanya Rendall'PBR | CCge CMHG EBee ECGP ECtt EPPr GAbr GBin GMac GQue LCro MBNS MBri MWea NBPC NBPN NBhm NMoo NSti SPer SUsu WCot WCra WFar WPnP WWFP |

'Terre Franche' EBee EPPr LHop MAvo NGby NLar SMrs SSvw WFar
'Thorn's Blue' CCge SWvt
§ ***thunbergii*** CCge CEnt CHid CSec EBla EWes LSou MSte NBid SRGP WMoo WPer WPnP WWpP
- 'Jester's Jacket' (v) CCge EBee EHig EPPr MCCP NPro SGar SPoG SRGP WCot WHrl WOut WPtf
- pink-flowered EPPr SRGP WCru
- white-flowered EPPr SRGP
***thurstonianum*** see *G.* x *oxonianum* f. *thurstonianum*
'Tinpenny Mauve' WHoo WTin
'Tiny Monster' CCge CDes CMCo EBee EBla EPPr EWes LSou MAvo MBNS MBri MWhi NGby NLar NMoo NSti SKHP SPhx WWpP
***transbaicalicum*** CFwr EBee EPPr GBin MNrw NHaw WCra WWpP
***traversii*** CWib GGar LRHS WRos
- var. ***elegans*** CFee CSpe CWib EAEE ECtt GGar LRHS MNrw WCru WEas WHCG WKif
***tuberosum*** CBro CElw CHid CHrt EBee EBla EBrs ECha ECho ELan EShb LRHS MNFA MTho NBir NBro NGdn SGar SMeo SMrs SPhx WCra WFar WPnP
- var. ***charlesii*** see *G. kotschyi* var. *charlesii*
- subsp. ***linearifolium*** WCru
- pink-flowered WCru WHal
'Ushguli Grijs' see *G. ibericum* 'Ushguli Grijs'
'Vera May' CElw SUsu
'Verguld Saffier' see *G.* Blue Sunrise
***versicolor*** CElw CMea COIW CRWN EBWF EBee EBla EPfP GAbr GGar MHer MNrw MTho NVic SPet SRms WBrk WFar WHCG WMoo WPnP WWpP
- 'Kingston' see *G.* x *oxonianum* 'Kingston'
- 'Knighton' WWpP
§ - 'Snow White' CCge CElw CMCo EBee ECtt EGoo EPPr MNrw NBre NCot SRGP WCra WCru WMoo WPnP WWpP
- 'The Bride' CMea ECtt
- 'White Lady' see *G. versicolor* 'Snow White'
'Victor Reiter' see *G. pratense* Victor Reiter Junior strain
***violareum*** see *Pelargonium* 'Splendide'
***viscosissimum*** EBla SRGP WMnd
- var. ***incisum*** EBrs MCCP NBre WWpP
- rose pink-flowered NBir
***wallichianum*** CCge CHrt CMCo CPou CSec EBee IFro MNFA NBir NChi NSti WFar WMoo
§ - 'Buxton's Variety' ♀H4 Widely available
- 'Chadwell's Pink' CCge EBee
- 'Chris' EPPr SRGP SUsu
- 'Crystal Lake' **new** EBee MWea NCot
- magenta-flowered GBuc
- pale blue-flowered CElw
- 'Pink Buxton' EBee EWes NLar
- pink-flowered EBla GBuc GCal NCot WCru WWpP
- 'Rosie' SRGP
- 'Syabru' CCge CMea EBla GBuc MNrw NCot NLar SAga WFar WMoo WPnP
'Wednesday's Child' WFar
'Welsh Guiness' WCru
***wilfordii*** misapplied see *G. thunbergii*
***wilfordii*** Maxim. EBee
Wisley hybrid see *G.* 'Khan'
'Wisley Jewel' EBee
***wlassovianum*** Widely available
- 'Blue Star' MRav NPro SRGP WCra WFar WWpP
- 'Zellertal' **new** NCot
§ ***yeoi*** CSpe EPPr MNrw NBir NBro NDov NSti SRGP WCru WOut
***yesoense*** CSec EBla EPPr GGar NBir NSti SRGP WFar WOut
- var. ***nipponicum*** WCru
- white-flowered EBee
***yoshinoi*** misapplied see *G. thunbergii*
***yoshinoi*** Makino MWhi WTou
***yunnanense*** misapplied see *G. pogonanthum*
***yunnanense*** ambig. CFir
***yunnanense*** Franchet IFro

## *Gerbera* (*Asteraceae*)

(Everlast Series) Everlast Pink = 'Amgerbpink' **new** NBhm STes WHlf
- Everlast White = 'Amgerbwhi'PBR **new** NBhm STes WHlf

## *Gesneria* (*Gesneriaceae*)

***cardinalis*** see *Sinningia cardinalis*
x ***cardosa*** see *Sinningia* x *cardosa*
* ***macrantha*** 'Compacta' EShb

## *Gethyum* (*Alliaceae*)

***atropurpureum*** EBee WCot

## *Geum* ✿ (*Rosaceae*)

'Abendsonne' CDes CElw MAvo
***aleppicum*** CFee NBre SBri
***alpinum*** see *G. montanum*
***andicola*** NBre
'Beech House Apricot' Widely available
'Bell Bank' CDes CElw CFee CLAP CSam EBee EBla EPPr GAbr GBri GJos GMac MAvo MHer MRav NBir NBre NChi NCot NDov NGby NPro SUsu WCot WMoo
'Birkhead's Creamy Lemon' CElw
'Blazing Sunset' (d) CElw EBee EBla ECtt GJos GMac IPot LAst LSou MAvo MBNS MDKP MHer MMuc MNHC MRav MWhi NBre NCob NDlv NGBl NPro SHGN SPad WFar WPnP
N 'Borisii' Widely available
'Borisii' x ***montanum*** LHop
'Bremner's Nectarine' NChi
'Brother Nigel' **new** CAbx
***bulgaricum*** CElw EBee GKir LRHS MRav NBir NLar NPro NRya WPnP WPrP WTin
'Butterscotch' EBee NCot
'Caitlin' EMon
***calthifolium*** EBee EPPr EWTr GKir MCCP MLLN MRav NBre NBro
***canadense*** EBee
***capense*** LSou NBre NPro SHGN SPlb
- JJ&JH 9401271 EBee
§ ***chiloense*** EBla LEdu
- P&W 6513 GBri NWCA
- 'Farncombe' NCot
- 'Red Dragon' EBee LLHF
'Chipchase' GJos MAvo NChi
***coccineum*** misapplied see *G. chiloense*
***coccineum*** ambig. EBla WRha
***coccineum*** Sibth. & Sm. MESE 374 EBee
- 'Cooky' CSam EAEE EBla ERCP EWll GBri GJos LRHS LSou MMuc MSCN NCGa NGBl NPri SPad SPhx SPoG SWal WHil WPer
- 'Eos' CDes EBee EBla EWes LEdu MAvo SMHy WCot

| | Name | Suppliers |
|---|---|---|
| § | – 'Werner Arends' | CMHG CSev EBee EBla GCal MAvo MNrw MRav NBro NCot SBri WCot WFar WMoo |
| | 'Coppertone' | CDes CLAP CWGN EBee EBla ECha ECtt EHrv ELan EMon LCro MAvo MNrw MRav NBir NBro NChi NRya SBri SPav WAul WHoo WMoo WPrP WTin |
| | 'Dingle Apricot' | CElw CFir ECtt GAbr GBin MAvo MNrw MRav NBir |
| | 'Dolly North' | EBee EBla EPyc GAbr GBri GGar GKir LRHS MAvo MNrw MRav NBro NGdn WAul WCAu WHal WPrP |
| | ***elatum*** | EBee EBla |
| | – CC 5253 **new** | GKev |
| | 'Elworthy Seedling' **new** | SBri |
| | 'Farmer John Cross' | CBre CDes CElw CLAP EBee EBla ECtt GJos MAvo MHar MNrw NCGa NCob NCot NLar SBri WHal WMoo |
| | ***fauriei* x *kamtschatica*** | EBee EBla |
| | 'Feuerball' | NBre NGdn |
| | 'Feuermeer' | EBee EBla MSte NLar NPro SBri |
| | 'Fire Opal' ♀H4 | CDes EBee EWes MAvo MNrw NBir NBre SUsu WGwG WMoo |
| | 'Fireball' | NBhm |
| | 'Flames of Passion' PBR | CCVN CHar EBee EBla ECtt GBin GMac MAvo MBNS MBri NBPC NLar SBri SRGP STes WAul WCAu WCot |
| | 'Fresh Woods' **new** | WPGP |
| | 'Georgenberg' | Widely available |
| | ***glaciale album*** | NBre |
| | 'Hergest Lisanne' **new** | SMHy |
| | 'Hergest Primrose' **new** | SMHy |
| | 'Herterton Primrose' | CElw CWCL ECtt GBri LLHF MAvo NCGa NGby SBri SUsu WHal WHoo |
| | 'Hilltop Beacon' | WHoo WPrP |
| * | ***hybridum luteum*** | NSti SBri |
| | x ***intermedium*** | CBre EBee EBla EGle EMon EPPr GBri MAvo MNrw NGdn NLar NPro SBri SHGN WFar WMoo |
| | – 'Diane' | CDes GJos MAvo NBre NChi WHoo |
| | ***japonicum*** | GMac |
| I | – 'Variegatum' (v) | EBee |
| | 'Karlskaer' | CElw EAEE EBee EBla ECtt EPfP EWes GBin LRHS MAvo MBri MNrw NCob NGdn SBri WCot WFar WMoo WPnP |
| | 'Kashmir' | SBri |
| | 'Kath Inman' | MAvo |
| | 'Lady Stratheden' ♀H4 | Widely available |
| | 'Lemon Drops' | Widely available |
| | 'Lionel Cox' | Widely available |
| | 'Lisanne' | CSam EBee NCGa NCot |
| | ***macrophyllum*** | EBee GBar |
| | – var. ***sachalinense*** | GAuc |
| | ***magellanicum*** | EBee EBla EWes NBre NLar |
| | 'Mandarin' | CFir EBla GAbr GCal |
| | 'Marmalade' | EBee EBla ECtt GAbr GJos MAvo MNrw NBre NLar NPro SAga SBri SDys SMHy SUsu WCra WHrl WKif WMoo |
| § | ***montanum*** ♀H4 | CEnt EBla ECho EDAr GAuc GCra GGar GKir LEdu NBir NBro NGdn NPri NRya SRms WMoo WPat |
| | – 'Diana' | EBla EMon MNrw NCot NLar NPro SBri |
| | 'Moorland Sorbet' | NCot SBri WFar WMoo |
| | 'Mrs J. Bradshaw' ♀H4 | Widely available |
| | 'Mrs W. Moore' | CBre CDes CElw CLAP CWGN EBee EBla ECtt EShb GBri GJos LBMP LDai MAvo MHer MLLN MNrw NBir NChi NCot NLar NPro SBri SRGP SUsu WClo WMoo WPrP |
| | 'Nordek' | EAEE EBee ECtt EPPr GAbr GBuc GJos IPot LAst NCob SBri SPoG |
| * | 'Orangeman' | MAvo MNrw |
| | ***parviflorum*** | GGar LEdu MLLN NBre NBro |
| | 'Paso Doble' | CElw SBri WRos |
| | ***pentapetalum*** | see *Sieversia pentapetala* |
| | – 'Flore Pleno' (d) | WAbe |
| | 'Pink Frills' | CDes CElw EBee EBla ECha GBri LBMP MAvo NCot NLar SBri SMHy SMrm STes WClo WPrP |
| | 'Poco' **new** | NPro |
| | ***ponticum*** | CSec EHig GAuc WOut |
| | 'Present' | CElw EBee EBla ECtt MAvo NBre NCGa NChi SBri |
| | 'Primrose' | GAbr GJos GQue NGdn NLar NPro |
| | 'Prince of Orange' | CElw EBla GAbr IGor MAvo MNrw NBre WFar WMoo WRha |
| | 'Prinses Juliana' | CElw EBee EBla EShb GBuc GCra GMac LAst MAvo MBri MRav NBPC NBir NCGa NCot NDov NGdn SPla STes SUsu WCAu WCot WCra WFar WMnd WMoo WPnP |
| | ***pyrenaicum*** | EBee EBla NBre |
| | ***quellyon*** | see *G. chiloense* |
| I | 'Rearsby Hybrid' | MAvo MRav SUsu |
| | 'Red Wings' | CMMP EBee EBla MRav NCGa SHar SUsu |
| § | ***reptans*** | GBin NCob |
| | x ***rhaeticum*** | EBee MNrw WMoo |
| | ***rhodopeum*** | NBre |
| | 'Rijnstroom' | CElw EBee EBla ELan EWTr LDai MAvo MWea NBPC WPtf |
| | ***rivale*** | Widely available |
| | – 'Album' | Widely available |
| | – apricot | LAst |
| | – 'Barbra Lawton' | EBla MAvo MDKP SBri WCra |
| | – 'Cream Drop' | EBla MSte NChi NCot NGby NPro SBri |
| | – cream-flowered, from Tien Shan, China | CFee |
| | – 'Leonard's Double' (d) | CPrp WFar WMoo |
| | – 'Leonard's Variety' | Widely available |
| | – 'Marika' | CBre CCVN CHid CRow EBee EBla NBre NCGa NCot SMrm SRGP WMoo |
| | – 'Marmalade' | EBla MSte NBPC NChi NCot |
| | – 'Oxford Marmalade' | CElw SApp |
| | – 'Snowflake' | NChi |
| | ***roylei*** | NBre |
| | 'Rubin' | CElw EBla ECtt EPPr EPyc GBuc MNrw NBre NBro SBch SBri SUsu WAul WCAu |
| | 'Sigiswang' | CDes CElw EBee GAbr GJos GMac MNrw MRav MSte NBre NPro SBri SMrm WMoo |
| I | 'Starker's Magnificum' | WCot |
| | 'Tangerine' | EBla GGar LSou MAvo MNrw MRav NPro SBri |
| | 'Tinpenny Orange' | CElw MAvo WTin |
| | x ***tirolense*** | EBee EBla NBre NCGa |
| | ***triflorum*** | CFwr EBee EBla EHrv MCCP MNrw NLar SPhx STes WFar WPnP WTin |
| | – var. ***campanulatum*** | GBri NChi NPro NRya |
| | ***urbanum*** | CArn EBWF GBar GPWP GPoy NLan NPri NSco SECG SWat WHer WMoo |
| | – from Patagonia | EBla MAvo MDKP |
| | 'Wallace's Peach' | SWal |
| | 'Werner Arends' | see *G. coccineum* 'Werner Arends' |

## *Gevuina* (*Proteaceae*)

| | |
|---|---|
| ***avellana*** | CBcs CHEx CTrG IDee WPGP |

## *Gilia* ✿ (*Polemoniaceae*)

| | |
|---|---|
| ***achilleifolia*** new | CSec |
| ***aggregata*** | see *Ipomopsis aggregata* |
| ***capitata*** | CSec |
| 'Red Dwarf' | NPol |
| ***rigidula*** new | CPBP |
| ***tricolor*** | NPol |

## *Gillenia* (*Rosaceae*)

| | |
|---|---|
| ***stipulata*** | CLAP EBee EGle EMon LEdu NDov NLar SUsu |
| ***trifoliata*** 🏆H4 | Widely available |
| - 'Pixie' | CLAP EBee WPGP |

## *Ginkgo* ✿ (*Ginkgoaceae*)

| | |
|---|---|
| ***biloba*** 🏆H4 | Widely available |
| - B&SWJ 8753 | WCru |
| - 'Anny's Dwarf' | MAsh SCoo |
| - 'Autumn Gold' (m) | CBcs CEnd CMCN EBee ECrN EHig MBlu MGos MPkF SBig SMad WPGP |
| I - 'Barabits Nana' | CMCN SBig |
| - 'Chase Manhattan' | NBhm |
| - 'Chi-chi' | SBig |
| - 'Chotek' | SBig |
| - 'Doctor Causton' (f) | CAgr |
| - 'Doctor Causton' (m) | CAgr |
| - 'Elsie' | SBig |
| - 'Fairmount' (m) | CMCN MBlu SBig |
| - 'Fastigiata' (m) | CLnd CMCN EPfP LPan MBlu MGos SBLw |
| - 'Golden Globe' | NLar |
| - 'Horizontalis' | CLnd CMCN CMen MBlu SBig |
| - 'Jade Butterflies' | CBcs MBlu MPkF NLar SLim |
| - 'King of Dongting' (f) | CMCN MBlu SBig |
| - 'Mariken' | EHig MAsh MGos MPkF NPal SBig SLim |
| - 'Mayfield' (m) | SBig |
| - Ohazuki Group (f) | CAgr |
| - Pendula Group | CEnd CMCN CTho ECrN EPfP IDee MPkF NPal SLim |
| - 'Princeton Sentry' (m) | MBlu SBig SMad |
| I - 'Prostrata' | CPMA |
| - 'Saratoga' (m) | CBcs CDoC CEnd CLnd CMCN CPMA CTho MBri MGos MPkF SBig SLim WPGP |
| - 'Tit' | CEnd CMCN CMen EPfP MGos NLar SBig WPGP |
| - 'Tremonia' | CMCN EPfP MBlu MPkF NLar SBig SLim |
| - 'Troll' | MBlu SBig SCoo |
| - 'Tubifolia' | CMCN CMen MBlu NLar SBig SLim SMad |
| - 'Umbrella' | CMCN SBig |
| - Variegata Group (v) | CMCN CMen CPMA MBlu MPkF NLar SBig SLim |

## ginseng see *Panax ginseng*

## *Gladiolus* (*Iridaceae*)

| | |
|---|---|
| 'About Face' (Min) | MSGs |
| ***acuminatus*** | WCot |
| ***alatus*** | EBee EBrs ECho LPio |
| - white-flowered | WCot |
| 'Alba' (N) | CGrW |
| 'Alexandra' (P) | WCot |
| 'Allosius' (S) | CGrW |
| 'Amanda P' | MSGs |
| 'American Dream' (Min) new | MSGs |
| 'Amsterdam' (G) | CGrW MSGs |
| 'Andre Viette' | LFur LLHF WCot |
| 'Angel' (P) | MSGs |
| ***angustus*** | CGrW WCot |
| 'Anna Leorah' (L) | MSGs |
| ***antakiensis*** | CPou |
| 'Antica' (L) | CGrW |
| 'Antique Lace' (L) | CGrW |
| 'Antique Rose' (M) | CGrW |
| 'Anyu S' (L) | CGrW MSGs |
| 'Arctic Day' (M/E) | CGrW |
| 'Atom' (S/P) | CBro CGrW EBee EBrs ECho WHil |
| ***atroviolaceus*** | WCot WPGP |
| 'August Days' (L) | MSGs |
| ***aurantiacus*** | WCot |
| 'Bangledesh' (M) | MSGs |
| Barnard hybrids | CGrW |
| 'Beau Rivage' (G) | MSGs |
| 'Beautiful Angel' | CGrW MSGs |
| 'Beauty Bride' (L) | CGrW MSGs |
| 'Beauty of Holland' PBR (L) | CGrW MSGs |
| 'Bella Donna' | MSGs |
| 'Bizar' | EPfP |
| 'Black Cherry' | WCot |
| 'Black Jack' | CSpe EPfP LCro NBPN |
| 'Black Pearls' (S) | MSGs |
| 'Blackbird' (S) | CGrW |
| ***blandus*** var. ***carneus*** | see *G. carneus* |
| 'Blue Clouds' (L) | CGrW |
| 'Blue Conqueror' (L) | LRHS |
| 'Blue Tropic' | CSut |
| 'Bluebird' (S) | CGrW |
| ***bonaespei*** | WCot |
| 'Bono's Memory' | LRHS |
| 'Boone' new | SMrm |
| 'Brittania' (L) | CGrW |
| 'Burgundy Queen' (M) | WCot |
| ***byzantinus*** | see *G. communis* subsp. *byzantinus* |
| ***caeruleus*** | CGrW WCot |
| ***callianthus*** | see *G. murielae* |
| 'Calliope' (L/E) | CGrW |
| ***cardinalis*** | CDes CMea CPne CPrp CWsd EBla GCal GGar IBlr SAga SChr SKHP WBor WCot WCru WPGP |
| ***carinatus*** | CDes CGrW WCot |
| ***carinatus*** × ***orchidiflorus*** | WCot |
| ***carmineus*** | CGrW CWsd EBee WCot WPGP |
| § ***carneus*** | CGrW CPou EBee EBrs GCal LPio SMeo WPGP |
| 'Carquirenne' (G) | CGrW |
| 'Carved Ivory' (M) | MSGs |
| ***caryophyllaceus*** | CPou |
| 'Charm' (N/Tub) | CAvo CBro CFFs CPrp EBee EBla |
| 'Charming Beauty' (Tub) | EBrs ECho WHil |
| 'Charming Lady' (Tub) | ECho |
| 'Chartreuse Ruffles' (S) | CGrW |
| 'Cheops' PBR new | CSut |
| 'Chinon' PBR (L) | CGrW |
| 'Christabel' (L) | ERos |
| 'Cindy' (B) | ECho |
| ***citrinus*** | see *G. trichonemifolius* |
| 'Claudia' (N) | CGrW EBrs |
| 'Clemence' (Min) | MSGs |
| × ***colvillii*** | CPne IBlr |
| - 'Albus' | EBrs EPot LPio LRHS SMeo |
| - 'The Bride' 🏆H3 | CAvo CBro CElw CFFs CHFP CPrp CWCL EBee EBla ECho ITim LAma LDai LEdu LPio LSRN |
| 'Comet' (N) | CAvo EBrs LPio WHil |
| § ***communis*** subsp. ***byzantinus*** 🏆H4 | Widely available |
| 'Contessa Queen' | CGrW |

| | | |
|---|---|---|
| | 'Coral Dream' (L) | CGrW |
| | 'Côte d'Azur' (G) | CGrW MSGs |
| | ***crassifolius*** | CFir GBuc |
| | 'Cream of the Crop' (M) | MSGs |
| | 'Cream Perfection' (L) | CGrW MSGs |
| | 'Creamy Acres' **new** | MSGs |
| | 'Creamy Yellow' (S) | MSGs |
| | 'Cristabel' | WCot |
| § | ***dalenii*** | CPou CPrp CSam EBee ERos IBlr LPio SKHP WCot WPGP |
| | - subsp. ***dalenii*** | IBlr |
| | - green-flowered | CDes IBlr |
| | - hybrids | WCot |
| | - orange-flowered | CDes WPGP |
| * | - f. ***rubra*** | IBlr WCot |
| | - yellow-flowered | CDes EBee WPGP |
| | 'Darlin' Clementine' (L) | CGrW MSGs |
| | 'Daydreamer' (L) | CGrW |
| | 'Day's End' (S) | CGrW |
| | 'Deanna' (L) | CGrW |
| | 'Deans List' (L) | CGrW MSGs |
| | 'Desirée' (B) | MSGs |
| | 'Doris Darling' (L) | MSGs |
| | 'Drama' (L) | CGrW MSGs |
| | 'Dreamcatcher' **new** | MSGs |
| | ***ecklonii*** | WPGP |
| | 'Edie' (P) | MSGs |
| | 'Ed's Conquest' **new** | MSGs |
| | 'Elegance' (G) | CGrW MSGs |
| | 'Elvira' (N) | EBee EBla EBrs ECho WPGP |
| | 'Emerald Spring' (S) | CGrW CSpe WCot |
| | 'Emir' (S) | MSGs |
| | 'Esperanto' (M) | MSGs |
| | 'Esta Bonita' (G) | CGrW MSGs |
| | 'Felicta' (L) | MSGs |
| | 'Femme Fatale' (L) | CGrW |
| | ***ferrugineus*** | LPio |
| | 'Final Touch' (G) | CGrW |
| | 'Fineline' (M) | CGrW |
| | 'Finishing Touch'$^{PBR}$ (L) | CGrW MSGs |
| | ***flanaganii*** | CPBP CSpe EBrs ECho GBin ITim LPio SChr SKHP WCot |
| | - JCA 261.000 | EBee |
| | 'Flevo Amico' (S) | WCot |
| | 'Flevo Bambino' (S) | CGrW |
| | 'Flevo Clown' (S) | WCot |
| | 'Flevo Cosmic' (Min) | LPio |
| | 'Flevo Dancer' (S) **new** | CGrW |
| | 'Flevo Eclips'$^{PBR}$ (G) | CGrW MSGs |
| | 'Flevo Eyes'$^{PBR}$ (L) | CGrW |
| | 'Flevo Frizzle' **new** | MSGs |
| | 'Flevo Jive' (S) | CGrW |
| | 'Flevo Junior' (S) | CGrW |
| | 'Flevo Party' (S) | CGrW |
| | 'Flevo Smile' (S) | CGrW MSGs |
| | 'Flevo Souvenir'$^{PBR}$ (L) | CGrW |
| | 'Flevo Sunset'$^{PBR}$ (L) | CGrW |
| | ***floribundus*** | EBee |
| | 'French Silk' (L) | CGrW |
| | 'Friend Dick' **new** | MSGs |
| | 'Friendship' (L) | LRHS |
| | ***garnieri*** | CWsd |
| | 'Gladiris' (L) | MSGs |
| | 'Gold Struck' (L) | CGrW |
| | 'Good Luck' (N) | CBro |
| | ***gracilis*** | WCot |
| | ***grandis*** | see *G. liliaceus* |
| | 'Green Isle' (M/E) | CGrW |
| | 'Green Star' (L) | CGrW MSGs |
| | 'Green with Envy' (L) | MSGs |
| | 'Green Woodpecker' (M) | EBee LAma LRHS |
| | 'Guernsey Glory' (N) | EBrs |
| | 'Gwendolyn' | MSGs |
| | 'Halley' (N) | ECho |
| | 'Hastings' (P) | CGrW |
| | 'High Society' **new** | MSGs |
| | 'Hi-Lite' (L) | CGrW |
| | 'Hint o' Mint' (S) | CGrW |
| | ***hirsutus*** | CGrW |
| | 'Honeydew' | CGrW MSGs |
| | 'Hotline' | MSGs |
| | 'Hunting Song' (L) | LAma |
| | 'Huron Dancer' (L) | CGrW |
| | 'Huron Fox' (S) **new** | CGrW |
| | 'Huron Frost' (L) | CGrW MSGs |
| | 'Huron Heaven' (L) | CGrW |
| | 'Huron Jewel' (M) | MSGs |
| | 'Huron Kisses' | MSGs |
| | 'Huron Lady' | CGrW |
| | 'Huron Meadow' (M) | CGrW MSGs |
| | 'Huron Pleasure' | CGrW |
| | 'Huron Silk' (L) | CGrW MSGs |
| | 'Huron Touch' | CGrW MSGs |
| | 'Huron White' (M) | CGrW |
| | ***huttonii*** | CGrW WCot |
| | ***huttonii*** x ***tristis*** | CPou |
| | ***huttonii*** x ***tristis*** var. ***concolor*** | WCot |
| | ***hyalinus*** | WCot |
| | 'Ice Cream' | SPer |
| | 'Ice Follies' (L) | MSGs |
| | ***illyricus*** | CPen CSam GBuc GCal WPGP |
| | ***imbricatus*** | EBee EBrs ECho ERos GBuc |
| | 'Impressive' (N) | EBrs EPot WHil |
| | 'Irish Blessing' (S) | CGrW |
| § | ***italicus*** | CGrW CPen CSec EBee EBrs ELan GCal LEdu MSte WHil |
| | 'Ivory Priscilla'$^{PBR}$ (L) | CGrW |
| | 'Ivory Queen' | MSGs |
| | 'Jayvee' (S) | CGrW |
| | 'Jean K' (M) | CGrW |
| | 'Jim S' (G) | CGrW MSGs |
| | 'Jo Ann' (L) | CGrW |
| | 'Jupiter' (B) | LRHS |
| | 'Karen P' | MSGs |
| | ***kotschyanus*** | EBrs ECho |
| | 'Kristin' (L) | CGrW MSGs |
| | 'Lady Caroline' (P) | MSGs |
| | 'Lady Helen' (P) | MSGs |
| | 'Lady in Red' (L) | MSGs |
| | 'Lady Lucille' (M) | CGrW MSGs |
| | 'Lady Millicent' (P) | MSGs |
| | 'Laura Jay' (P) | MSGs |
| | 'Lavender Flare' (S) | CGrW |
| | 'Lavender Rose' (L) | CGrW MSGs |
| | 'Lemon Drop' (S) | MSGs |
| | 'Lemon Zest' (M) | CGrW |
| § | ***liliaceus*** | CDes CGrW WCot |
| | 'Lime Green' (P) | LRHS |
| | 'Limoncello' **new** | MSGs |
| | 'Little Jude' (P) | MSGs |
| | 'Little Rainbow' (P) | WCot |
| | 'Little Wiggy' (P) | CGrW |
| | 'Loulou' (G) | CGrW |
| | 'Lowland Queen' (L) | CGrW MSGs |
| | ***maculatus*** | WPGP |
| | 'Magma' **new** | MSGs |
| | 'Manhattan' (L) **new** | CGrW |
| | 'Maria K' (L) | CGrW MSGs |
| | 'Marina' (P) **new** | MSGs |
| | 'Marj S' (L) | CGrW MSGs |
| | 'Melodrome' **new** | MSGs |
| | 'Mexico' | CSut |
| | 'Mileesh' (L) | CGrW MSGs |
| | 'Millennium' (L) | CGrW |
| | 'Mirella' (N) | CMea EBrs MRav WHil |

| | |
|---|---|
| 'Mon Amour'PBR | CSut |
| ***montanus*** | CPen |
| ***monticola*** | EBee |
| 'Moon Mirage' (G) | MSGs |
| 'Moon Shadow' (M/E) | CGrW |
| ***mortonius*** | GCal WPGP |
| 'Mother Theresa' (M) | MSGs |
| 'Mr Chris' (S) | MSGs |
| 'Mrs Rowley' (P) | GBri |
| § ***murielae*** 🏆H3 | Widely available |
| 'Murieliae' | see *G. murielae* |
| ***natalensis*** | see *G. dalenii* |
| 'Nathalie' (N) | CGrW EBee EBrs LEdu WHil |
| 'New Elegance' | MSGs |
| 'New Wave'PBR (L) | CGrW |
| 'Nicholas' (S) | MSGs |
| 'Nikita' (P) | MSGs |
| 'Nori' (M) | CGrW |
| 'Nova Lux' (L) | LAma |
| 'Nymph' (N) | CAvo CElw CFFs CMea CWCL EBee EBla EBrs ECGP EPot ITim LAma LDai LEdu LPio SPur WHil |
| 'Oasis'PBR (G) | CGrW |
| 'Obrigado' (L) | CGrW |
| ***ochroleucus*** | EBee |
| 'Of Singular Beauty' (G) | CGrW MSGs |
| 'Olivia' **new** | MSGs |
| § ***oppositiflorus*** | CDes CPou EBee SChr WPGP |
| - subsp. ***salmoneus*** | see *G. oppositiflorus* |
| ***orchidiflorus*** | CGrW |
| 'Orient Express' | MSGs |
| 'Oscar' (G) | LRHS |
| ***palustris*** | ERos |
| 'Pansy Face' | MSGs |
| ***papilio*** | Widely available |
| - 'David Hills' | NCGa WCot WHal |
| § - Purpureoauratus Group | CBro CSam EBee ERos IBlr SRms |
| - 'Ruby' | CAby CAvo CHFP CMil CPen CPou NCGa NChi SMHy SMad WHil |
| - yellow-flowered | CMea SMad |
| ***pappei*** | CDes EBee WPGP |
| 'Peach Cobbler' | CGrW |
| 'Peggy' (P) **new** | CGrW |
| ***permeabilis*** | EBee WPGP |
| 'Perth Ivory' (M) | MSGs |
| 'Perth Pearl' (M) | CGrW MSGs |
| 'Peter Pears' (L) | LRHS |
| 'Phyllis M' (L) | CGrW |
| Pilbeam hybrids | CGrW |
| 'Pink Elegance' (L) | CGrW MSGs |
| 'Pink Elf' (S) | MSGs |
| 'Pink Lady' (L) | CGrW MSGs |
| 'Pink Light' | MSGs |
| 'Pinnacle' (L) | MSGs |
| 'Plaisir' | MSGs |
| 'Plum Tart' (L) | LRHS |
| 'Pop Art' | LRHS |
| ***primulinus*** | see *G. dalenii* |
| 'Princess Margaret Rose' (Min) | LAma |
| 'Prins Claus' (N) | CBro CGrW CTca EBee EBla EBrs LRHS |
| 'Priscilla' (L) | LAma MLHP |
| 'Pulchritude' (M) | MSGs |
| ***punctulatus*** var. ***punctulatus*** | ERos |
| 'Purple Haze' | MSGs |
| 'Purple Prince' (M) | CGrW WCot |
| 'Purple Spray' | WCot |
| ***purpureoauratus*** | see *G. papilio* Purpureoauratus Group |
| 'Raspberry Swirl' (L/E) | CGrW |
| 'Red Beauty' | LRHS |
| 'Robinetta' (*recurvus* hybrid) 🏆H3 | CBro CElw CWCL EBee EBla EBrs ECho EPfP GGar LAma LDai SMeo SPur |
| 'Rose Elf' (S) | MSGs |
| 'Rose Laguna' | MSGs |
| 'Royal Spire' | CGrW |
| 'Ruth Ann' | CGrW MSGs |
| 'Sabu' | LRHS |
| 'Sailor's Delight' (L) | MSGs |
| 'Salmon Sorbet' | CGrW |
| 'San Remo'PBR (L) | CGrW |
| 'Santa Lucia' (L) | CGrW |
| 'Sarajevo' | MSGs |
| 'Satin 'n' Lace' (L) | CGrW |
| ***saundersii*** | EBee GCal WCot WPGP |
| 'Scarlet Lady' (P) | CGrW |
| seedling 95-042-03 | MSGs |
| seedling 97-309-03 **new** | MSGs |
| seedling 99-366-01 **new** | MSGs |
| seedling S361-5 **new** | MSGs |
| ***segetum*** | see *G. italicus* |
| 'Serafin' (Min) | LRHS |
| ***sericeovillosus*** | IBlr |
| 'Sharkey' (G) | CGrW |
| 'Show Chairman' (L) | MSGs |
| 'Show Star' (L) | CGrW |
| 'Show Stopper' (G) | CGrW |
| 'Shrimpboat' **new** | MSGs |
| 'Silvana' (S) | CGrW |
| 'Silver Dream' | MSGs |
| 'Silver Green' (L) | CGrW |
| 'Sirael' (L/E) | CGrW WCot |
| 'Sky High' (M) | CGrW |
| 'Smoke Stack' (L) | CGrW |
| 'Snazzy' **new** | MSGs |
| 'Snow Cap' (L) | CGrW |
| 'Snow Queen' (L) | CGrW |
| 'Snowdon' **new** | MSGs |
| 'Solveiga' (L/E) | CGrW |
| 'Sophie'PBR | CGrW |
| 'Sparkle Plenty' | MSGs |
| 'Sparkler' (M) **new** | CGrW |
| 'Spic and Span' (L) | CSut |
| ***splendens*** | CDes CGrW WCot WPGP |
| 'Spring Thaw' (L/E) | CGrW |
| 'Stolen Moments' **new** | MSGs |
| 'Stromboli' (L) | MSGs |
| 'Sue' (P) | MSGs |
| 'Sunrise' (L) **new** | CGrW |
| 'Sunset Fire' (G) | CGrW MSGs |
| 'Super High Brow' (G) | CGrW MSGs |
| 'Sylvia' | MSGs |
| ***symonsii*** **new** | EBee |
| 'Tan Royale' (P) | CGrW |
| 'Tante Ann' (M) | CGrW |
| ***teretifolius*** | WPGP |
| 'Topaz' (L) | CGrW MSGs |
| 'Trader Horn' (G) | LAma |
| § ***trichonemifolius*** | WPGP |
| ***tristis*** | CAvo CBro CElw CGHE CGrW CMea CPne CPou EBee EBrs ECha EDif ELan ELon GCal GGar GKev LPio LRHS NCGa SAga SDix SUsu WFar WHal WPGP WSHC |
| - var. ***concolor*** | CGrW CPrp EBee ERos LFur LPio WCot |
| ***undulatus*** | ERos WCot WPGP |
| 'Vanilla Swirl' (L) | MSGs |
| ***venustus*** | WPGP |
| 'Victoria' (M) | LRHS |
| 'Video' (L) | CGrW |
| 'Vienna' (L) | CGrW |
| 'Violetta' (M) | CGrW ECho SPer |

| | | |
|---|---|---|
| | ***virescens*** | WCot |
| | 'Visual Arts' (M) | CGrW |
| | 'Wandering Eyes' | MSGs |
| | ***watermeyeri*** | WPGP |
| | ***watsonioides*** | CPou ERos SKHP |
| | ***watsonius*** | WPGP |
| | 'White City' (P/S) | LRHS |
| | 'White Friendship' (L) | LAma |
| | 'White Ice' | MSGs |
| | 'White Out' (M) | CGrW |
| | 'White Prosperity' (L) | CSut LRHS |

## *Glandularia* see *Verbena*

## *Glaucidium* (*Glaucidiaceae*)

| | | |
|---|---|---|
| | ***palmatum*** 🏆H4 | EFEx GCra GEdr GKev NSla WAbe WBVN WCru WHal |
| | - 'Album' | see *G. palmatum* var. *leucanthum* |
| § | - var. ***leucanthum*** | EBee EFEx GBin GEdr NSla |

## *Glaucium* (*Papaveraceae*)

| | | |
|---|---|---|
| § | ***corniculatum*** | CSec CSpe EBee EBrs MLLN NLar SEND SMeo SPav SPhx WCot WEas |
| | ***flavum*** | CArn CHrt CSec CSpe EBWF ECha EGoo ELan LRHS MHer NLar SMad SMeo SPav |
| | - ***aurantiacum*** | see *G. flavum* f. *fulvum* |
| § | - f. ***fulvum*** | ECha SDix WCot WHil |
| | - orange-flowered | see *G. flavum* f. *fulvum* |
| | - red-flowered | see *G. corniculatum* |
| | ***grandiflorum*** | SWal |
| | ***phoenicium*** | see *G. corniculatum* |

## *Glaux* (*Primulaceae*)

| | | |
|---|---|---|
| | ***maritima*** | EBWF WPer |

## *Glebionis* (*Asteraceae*)

| | | |
|---|---|---|
| | ***coronaria*** **new** | CSec MNHC |

## *Glechoma* (*Lamiaceae*)

| | | |
|---|---|---|
| | ***hederacea*** | CArn EBWF GBar GPoy MHer NMir NSco WHer |
| | - 'Rosea' | GBar WAlt |
| § | - 'Variegata' (v) | LRHS MBri NBlu SPet |

## *Gleditsia* (*Caesalpiniaceae*)

| | | |
|---|---|---|
| | ***aquatica*** **new** | EGFP |
| | ***caspica*** | CArn SMad |
| | ***japonica*** | EPfP |
| | ***macrantha*** | EGFP |
| | ***sinensis*** | NLar |
| | ***triacanthos*** | CDul CWib ECrN EMac LEdu LPan SBLw SPlb WDin |
| | - 'Bujotii' | SBLw |
| | - 'Calhoun' | CAgr |
| | - 'Elegantissima' (v) | SPer |
| | - 'Emerald Cascade' | CDul CEnd EBee MAsh MBri WFar |
| | - f. ***inermis*** | SBLw |
| | - - Spectrum = 'Speczam' **new** | MAsh |
| | - 'Millwood' | CAgr |
| | - 'Rubylace' | Widely available |
| | - 'Shademaster' | NLar SBLw |
| | - 'Skyline' | LMaj SBLw |
| | - 'Sunburst' 🏆H4 | Widely available |

## *Globba* (*Zingiberaceae*)

| | | |
|---|---|---|
| | ***andersonii*** | CKob |
| * | ***cathcartii*** | CKob |
| | 'Emerald Isle' | LRHS |
| | ***marantina*** | CKob EBrs ECho |
| | 'Mount Everest' | EBrs |
| | ***winitii*** | LRHS |
| I | - 'Pink Dancing Girl' | ECho |
| | - 'Ruby Queen'PBR | MJnS |

## *Globularia* (*Globulariaceae*)

| | | |
|---|---|---|
| | ***bellidifolia*** | see *G. meridionalis* |
| | ***bisnagarica*** | CElw |
| | ***cordifolia*** 🏆H4 | EBee ECho EDAr EPot GEdr MTho NBir NLAp NMen SIng WFar |
| | - NS 696 | NWCA |
| | ***incanescens*** | LRHS |
| § | ***meridionalis*** | CElw CFee ECho EPot EWes GMaP MWat NLAp NMen SAga WFar WHal WPat |
| | - 'Blue Bonnets' | GEdr NHar |
| | - 'Hort's Variety' | NMen WAbe |
| | ***nana*** | see *G. repens* |
| | ***nudicaulis*** | GEdr |
| | - 'Alba' | WIvy |
| | ***punctata*** | CSpe GMaP LRHS NChi NWCA SRms |
| | ***pygmaea*** | see *G. meridionalis* |
| § | ***repens*** | CLyd CPBP EPot MTho NMen SIng WAbe WPat |
| | ***spinosa*** | NWCA |
| | ***trichosantha*** | CFee ECho SRms WFar |
| | ***valentina*** **new** | EPot |

## *Gloriosa* (*Colchicaceae*)

| | | |
|---|---|---|
| | ***lutea*** see *G. superba* 'Lutea' | |
| | ***rothschildiana*** | see *G. superba* 'Rothschildiana' |
| | ***superba*** 🏆H1 | EShb MBri WVal |
| | - 'Carsonii' | CSec WVal |
| § | - 'Lutea' | CSec EBrs LAma LRHS WVal |
| § | - 'Rothschildiana' | CBcs CRHN CSec CStu EBrs ECho EPfP LAma LRHS SOWG SPer SRms WVal |

## *Glottiphyllum* (*Aizoaceae*)

| | | |
|---|---|---|
| | ***nelii*** | CStu |

## *Gloxinia* (*Gesneriaceae*)

| | | |
|---|---|---|
| | ***nematanthodes*** 'Evita' | SKHP WCot |
| | ***sylvatica*** | CHal CSpe EShb WDib |

## *Glumicalyx* (*Scrophulariaceae*)

| | | |
|---|---|---|
| | ***flanaganii*** | GKev NLAp |
| | - HWEL 0325 | NWCA |
| | ***montanus*** | CFee |

## *Glyceria* (*Poaceae*)

| | | |
|---|---|---|
| | ***aquatica variegata*** | see *G. maxima* var. *variegata* |
| | ***maxima*** | CRWN EBWF EMFW GFor IFoB MMuc NPer SPlb |
| § | - var. ***variegata*** (v) | Widely available |
| | ***notata*** **new** | SVic |
| | ***spectabilis*** 'Variegata' | see *G. maxima* var. *variegata* |

## *Glycyrrhiza* (*Papilionaceae*)

| | | |
|---|---|---|
| | ***echinata*** | CAgr CArn MSal |
| § | ***glabra*** | CAgr CArn CBod CCCN CHby CWan ELau EShb GPWP GPoy MHer MNHC MSal NLar NTHB SIde WJek WLHH |
| | ***glandulifera*** | see *G. glabra* |
| | ***lepidota*** | MSal |
| | ***uralensis*** | CArn ELau GPoy MHer MSal |

## *Glyptostrobus* (*Cupressaceae*)

| | | |
|---|---|---|
| | ***pensilis*** | CGHE EGFP WPGP |

## *Gmelina* (*Verbenaceae*)

| | | |
|---|---|---|
| | ***hystrix*** | CCCN |

## *Gnaphalium* (*Asteraceae*)

| | | |
|---|---|---|
| | 'Fairy Gold' | see *Helichrysum thianschanicum* 'Goldkind' |
| | ***mackayi*** | EDAr |
| | ***trinerve*** | see *Anaphalis trinervis* |

## *Godetia* see *Clarkia*

## *Gomphocarpus* (*Asclepiadaceae*)

| | | |
|---|---|---|
| § | ***physocarpus*** | CArn NLar WCot |

## *Gomphostigma* (*Buddlejaceae*)

| | | |
|---|---|---|
| | ***virgatum*** | CDes CSpe EBee EPPr LFur MLLN MNFA MSte SPlb SSvw WCot WHrl WPGP WPic WSHC |
| | - 'White Candy' | LBMP SHGN |

## *Gonatanthus* (*Araceae*)

| | | |
|---|---|---|
| | ***pumilus*** | SKHP |

## *Goniolimon* (*Plumbaginaceae*)

| | | |
|---|---|---|
| | ***collinum*** 'Sea Spray' **new** | EDAr |
| § | ***incanum*** | SMrm |
| | - 'Blue Diamond' | EBee |
| § | ***tataricum*** | NBre NLar |
| § | - var. ***angustifolium*** | EBee SEND SRms WPer |
| | - 'Woodcreek' | NLar |

## *Goniophlebium* (*Polypodiaceae*)

| | | |
|---|---|---|
| § | ***subauriculatum*** 'Knightiae' **new** | WRic |

## *Goodenia* (*Goodeniaceae*)

| | | |
|---|---|---|
| | ***scaevolina*** | CSec |
| | ***scapigera*** | CSec |

## *Goodia* (*Papilionaceae*)

| | | |
|---|---|---|
| | ***lotifolia*** | CCCN |

## *Goodyera* (*Orchidaceae*)

| | | |
|---|---|---|
| | ***biflora*** | EFEx |
| | ***pubescens*** | EFEx LRHS |
| | ***schlechtendaliana*** | EFEx |

## gooseberry see *Ribes uva-crispa*

## *Gordonia* (*Theaceae*)

| | | |
|---|---|---|
| | ***axillaris*** | CCCN |

## *Gossypium* (*Malvaceae*)

| | | |
|---|---|---|
| | ***herbaceum*** | CCCN CSec MSal |

## granadilla, giant see *Passiflora quadrangularis*

## granadilla, purple see *Passiflora edulis*

## granadilla, sweet see *Passiflora ligularis*

## granadilla, yellow see *Passiflora laurifolia*

## grape see *Vitis*

## grapefruit see *Citrus* x *paradisi*

## *Graptopetalum* (*Crassulaceae*)

| | | |
|---|---|---|
| | ***bellum*** ♀$^{H1}$ | CStu |
| | ***filiferum*** | EWll SRot |
| § | ***paraguayense*** | CHal SEND |

## *Gratiola* (*Scrophulariaceae*)

| | | |
|---|---|---|
| | ***officinalis*** | CArn CSec CWan EHig EHon EMFW LLWG MHer MSKA MSal |

## *Grevillea* ✿ (*Proteaceae*)

| | | |
|---|---|---|
| | ***alpina*** | CPLG EBee SOWG |
| | - 'Olympic Flame' | CBcs CCCN CDoC CPLG CSBt CWib EBee LHop LRHS SCoo SOWG SPoG SRms WBor |
| | ***aquifolium*** | SOWG |
| | ***arenaria*** | SOWG |
| | - subsp. ***canescens*** | SOWG |
| | 'Austraflora Copper Crest' | see *G.* 'Copper Crest' |
| | ***baileyana*** | SOWG |
| | ***banksii*** 'Canberra Hybrid' | see *G.* 'Canberra Gem' |
| | - var. ***forsteri*** | SOWG |
| | ***banyabba*** | SOWG |
| | ***barklyana*** | SOWG SSta |
| | ***baueri*** | SOWG |
| | ***beadleana*** | SOWG |
| | ***bedggoodiana*** | SOWG |
| | ***bipinnatifida*** | SOWG |
| | 'Bonnie Prince Charlie' | CPLG SOWG |
| | 'Bronze Rambler' | SOWG |
| § | 'Canberra Gem' ♀$^{H3-4}$ | Widely available |
| | 'Clearview David' | CCCN CMac CPLG CTrC LBuc LRHS LSRN SCoo SLim SOWG |
| | ***confertifolia*** | SOWG |
| § | 'Copper Crest' | SOWG |
| | 'Cranbrook Yellow' | CDoC CPLG SOWG SSpi |
| | ***crithmifolia*** | SOWG SPlb |
| | ***diffusa*** subsp. ***evansiana*** | SOWG |
| | ***drummondii*** subsp. ***pimeleoides*** | SOWG |
| | ***endlicheriana*** | SOWG |
| | 'Evelyn's Coronet' | SOWG |
| | 'Fanfare' | SOWG |
| | ***fulgens*** | SOWG |
| | x ***gaudichaudii*** | SOWG |
| | 'Honeyeater Heaven' | SOWG |
| | 'Honey Gem' | SOWG |
| | ***iaspicula*** | ECou SOWG |
| | ***involucrata*** | SOWG |
| | ***johnsonii*** | CMac CTrC EShb SKHP SOWG |
| | ***juniperina*** | CBcs CCCN CMac CPLG CTsd EBee EPfP MGos SLim WBod |
| | - 'Molonglo' | CPLG LBuc |
| | - f. ***sulphurea*** | CCCN CDoC CHll CPLG CSBt CTrG EPfP SOWG SPlb WPat WSHC |
| | ***lanigera*** | CPLG ECou |
| I | - 'Lutea' | SOWG |
| | - 'Mount Tamboritha' | CBcs CCCN CDoC CMac CPLG CTrC EBee GGar IDee LBuc LHop LRHS SKHP SPoG SSto WBrE WFar |
| | - prostrate | ECou NLAp SOWG WPat |
| | - yellow-flowered | ECou |
| | ***leucopteris*** | SPlb |
| | ***levis*** | SOWG |
| | ***longistyla*** | SOWG |
| | 'Majestic' | SOWG |
| | 'Mason's Hybrid' | SOWG |
| | 'Misty Red' **new** | LRHS |
| | 'Moonlight' | SOWG |
| | ***nudiflora*** | ECou SOWG |
| | ***obtusifolia*** 'Gingin Gem' | SOWG |
| | ***olivacea*** 'Apricot Glow' | SOWG |
| | 'Orange Marmalade' | SOWG |
| | ***paniculata*** | SOWG SPlb |
| | ***parvula*** | SOWG |
| | 'Pink Lady' | ECou LRHS SOWG |
| | 'Pink Surprise' | SOWG |
| | 'Poorinda Constance' **new** | SOWG |
| | 'Poorinda Elegance' | SOWG |
| | 'Poorinda Peter' | CPLG SOWG |
| | 'Poorinda Rondeau' | CPLG |
| | ***pteridifolia*** | SOWG |

| | |
|---|---|
| ***quercifolia*** | SOWG |
| 'Red Dragon' (v) | LBuc LRHS |
| ***repens*** | SOWG |
| ***rhyolitica*** | SOWG |
| ***robusta*** 🏆H1+3 | CHal SBLw SBig SOWG SPlb SSta |
| 'Robyn Gordon' | SOWG |
| 'Rondeau' | CCCN CEnd EShb |
| ***rosmarinifolia*** 🏆H3 | Widely available |
| - 'Desert Flame' | CPLG |
| - 'Jenkinsii' | CDoC CPLG CSBt LAst SLim |
| 'Sandra Gordon' | SOWG |
| 'Scarlet Sprite' | SOWG |
| § x ***semperflorens*** | CBcs CEnd CPLG CTrC CWib EBee SCoo SOWG |
| ***sericea*** | SOWG |
| ***shiressii*** | SOWG |
| 'Sid Reynolds' | CPLG |
| 'Spider Man' | LBuc LRHS |
| 'Splendour' | SOWG |
| ***thelemanniana*** | ECou |
| - 'Silver' | CPLG |
| - Spriggs' form | SOWG |
| ***thyrsoides*** | GGal |
| ***tolminsis*** | see *G.* x *semperflorens* |
| ***venusta*** | SOWG |
| ***victoriae*** | ECou SKHP SOWG SSpi WBod WCot |
| - subsp. ***tenuinervis*** | see *G. parvula* |
| - subsp. ***victoriae*** | CPLG |
| - yellow-flowered **new** | LRHS |
| ***williamsonii*** | ECou LRHS SOWG WPat |

## *Greyia* (*Greyiaceae*)

| | |
|---|---|
| ***sutherlandii*** | CKob CTrC SGar SOWG SPlb |

## *Grindelia* (*Asteraceae*)

| | |
|---|---|
| § ***camporum*** | CWCL EBee GBar MSal NBre NLar SPlb WPer |
| ***chiloensis*** | CAbb ECha SKHP SMad WCot |
| ***integrifolia*** | CSam |
| ***robusta*** | see *G. camporum* |
| ***squarrosa*** | GBar |
| ***stricta*** | CArn |

## *Griselinia* (*Griseliniaceae*)

| | |
|---|---|
| * ***dependens*** **new** | ISea |
| ***littoralis*** 🏆H3 | Widely available |
| - 'Bantry Bay' (v) | CAbP CCCN CDoC CTsd CWSG EBee EHoe ELan ERas ESwi LRHS MAsh MSwo NCGa SEND SLim SPer SPoG SSto SWvt WFar |
| - 'Brodick Gold' | CPLG EBee EQua GGar |
| - 'Crinkles' | CPMA SLon |
| - 'Dixon's Cream' (v) | CBcs CCCN CDul CMac CSBt EBee EPfP GQui IArd IFoB MAsh MDun SAga SLon SPoG |
| - 'Green Jewel' (v) | CBcs CCCN CPMA CTrC CWib NLar SPla |
| - 'Variegata' (v) 🏆H3 | Widely available |
| ***lucida*** 'Variegata' (v) | IFoB |
| ***scandens*** | WSHC |

## guava, common see *Psidium guajava*

## guava, purple or strawberry see *Psidium littorale* var. *longipes*

## *Gueldenstaedtia* (*Papilionaceae*)

| | |
|---|---|
| ***himalaica*** B&SWJ 2631 | WCru |

## *Gunnera* (*Gunneraceae*)

| | |
|---|---|
| ***chilensis*** | see *G. tinctoria* |
| ***flavida*** | EBee GGar NWCA WGwG |
| ***hamiltonii*** | EBla ECha ECou GAbr GGar MAvo NBir NWCA WMoo |
| ***magellanica*** | Widely available |
| - 'Muñoz Gamero' | WShi |
| - 'Osorno' | EBee WPGP |
| ***manicata*** 🏆H3-4 | Widely available |
| ***monoica*** | GGar |
| ***perpensa*** | CBcs CCCN CDes |
| ***prorepens*** | CFee CStu EBla ECha ECou GEdr NBir NWCA WMoo |
| ***scabra*** | see *G. tinctoria* |
| § ***tinctoria*** 🏆 | CCCN CDWL CHEx CMHG CRow CTrG CWib EBee EBla ECha EHon ELan EPfP EPla GAbr GGar LBMP MDun NCot NVic SDix SWat SWvt WBVN WCot WFar WPGP WPat |

## *Guzmania* (*Bromeliaceae*)

| | |
|---|---|
| 'Gran Prix' | MBri |
| 'Surprise' | see x *Niduregelia* 'Surprise' |
| 'Vulkan' | MBri |

## *Gymnadenia* (*Orchidaceae*)

| | |
|---|---|
| ***conopsea*** | EFEx SHdy |

## *Gymnocarpium* (*Woodsiaceae*)

| | |
|---|---|
| ***dryopteris*** 🏆H4 | CLAP EBee EBrs EFer EMon GGar GKev GMaP LEdu MMoz NLar NWCA SRms WFib WPnP WRic WShi |
| - 'Plumosum' 🏆H4 | CFwr CLAP CWCL CWsd EBee EPfP EPla ERod GBin GQui MAsh NBid NHol NLar NVic SMad SPoG WFib WHal WMoo |
| ***fedtschenkoanum*** | WRic |
| ***oyamense*** | CLAP EFer SKHP |
| ***robertianum*** | CLAP EBee EFer EWld |

## *Gymnocladus* (*Caesalpiniaceae*)

| | |
|---|---|
| ***chinensis*** | CBcs EGFP |
| ***dioica*** | CBcs CDul CLnd CMCN EBee ELan EPfP LEdu LRHS MBlu MBri SPer SSpi WDin WPGP |

## *Gymnospermium* (*Berberidaceae*)

| | |
|---|---|
| § ***albertii*** | EBrs |

## *Gynandriris* (*Iridaceae*)

| | |
|---|---|
| ***sisyrinchium*** | CStu EBee EBrs ECho LEdu |
| * - ***purpurea*** | ECho |

## *Gynerium* (*Poaceae*)

| | |
|---|---|
| ***argenteum*** | see *Cortaderia selloana* |

## *Gynostemma* (*Cucurbitaceae*)

| | |
|---|---|
| ***pentaphyllum*** | CAgr |
| - B&SWJ 570 | WCru |
| - 'Gold Chain' **new** | EBee |

## *Gynura* (*Asteraceae*)

| | |
|---|---|
| § ***aurantiaca*** 'Purple Passion' 🏆H1 | MBri |
| ***sarmentosa*** misapplied | see *G. aurantiaca* 'Purple Passion' |

## *Gypsophila* (*Caryophyllaceae*)

| | |
|---|---|
| ***acutifolia*** | EBee ELan |
| ***aretioides*** | ECho EPot LRHS NMen WRos |
| § - 'Caucasica' | EBur ECho EPot GEdr LLHF NDlv |
| - 'Compacta' | see *G. aretioides* 'Caucasica' |
| ***briquetiana*** | WPat |
| ***cerastioides*** | CSec CSpe CTri ECho ECtt EPfP GAbr GGar LAst LBMP LHop LRHS |

| | |
|---|---|
| | MRav NDlv NLAp NMen NWCA SPlb SRms WAbe WHoo WPer WPnn |
| ***dubia*** | see *G. repens* 'Dubia' |
| ***fastigiata*** | WPer |
| - 'Silverstar' | LSou SPoG |
| 'Festival Pink' (Festival Series) | EBee ECtt LRHS SHar SPoG WFar |
| ***gracilescens*** | see *G. tenuifolia* |
| Happy Festival = 'Danghappy' (Festival Series) | LRHS |
| 'Jolien' (v) | CBow EBee ELan |
| ***muralis*** 'Garden Bride' | SWvt |
| - 'Gypsy Pink' (d) | SWvt |
| ***nana*** 'Compacta' | CPBP |
| ***oldhamiana*** | MLLN |
| 'Pacific Rose' | MRav |
| ***pacifica*** | MWea NBre NBro NLar WPer |
| ***paniculata*** | CSec EBee LAst MGos NBre NMir SECG SRms |
| - 'Bristol Fairy' (d) ♀H4 | CSBt CTri EBee ECha ECtt ELan EPfP GKir GMaP LCro LRHS NOrc SPoG SSto SWvt WCAu |
| - 'Compacta Plena' (d) | EBee ECtt EGle ELan EPfP GMaP LAst LHop MLHP MRav NDov NVic SPet SPla SRms WPer |
| - 'Fairy Perfect' | EBee |
| - 'Flamingo' (d) | CBcs EBee ECha ECot NLar SCoo SPer |
| - 'Perfekta' | CBcs EBee SPer |
| - 'Pink Star' (d) | EBee |
| § - 'Schneeflocke' (d) | EBee EShb GMaP NBre NLar SPhx SRms SSto WPer |
| - Snowflake | see *G. paniculata* 'Schneeflocke' |
| § ***petraea*** | EPot |
| * ***regia*** new | CSec |
| ***repens*** ♀H4 | CTca ECtt EMil GJos LBee MWat SBch SHGN SPlb SWvt WFar WPer |
| - 'Dorothy Teacher' | CLyd CMea ECho ECtt LBee SIng WEas WGor |
| § - 'Dubia' | EAlp ECha ECho ECtt EDAr EPot MHer SPoG SRms WPer WSHC |
| - 'Fratensis' | ECho ECtt ELan LLHF NMen |
| - Pink Beauty | see *G. repens* 'Rosa Schönheit' |
| § - 'Rosa Schönheit' | EBee ECha EPot LRHS NLar SPer |
| - 'Rosea' | CMea CPBP CTri CWib EBee ECho ECtt EDAr EPfP EShb GJos GMaP LAst LBMP MWat NWCA SAga SPet SPoG SRms SWvt WFar WHoo WTin |
| - 'Silver Carpet' (v) | LAst NBPC |
| - white-flowered | CMea CWib EBee ECho ELan EPfP LAst SPet SWvt WPer |
| § 'Rosenschleier' (d) ♀H4 | CMea EBee ECha ECtt ELan EPfP LAst MRav MWat NDov SAga SPer SRms SWvt WCAu WHoo WSHC WTin |
| 'Rosy Veil' | see *G.* 'Rosenschleier' |
| § ***tenuifolia*** | EAlp ECho EPot ITim LBee MWat NHol NMen |
| ***transylvanica*** | see *G. petraea* |
| Veil of Roses | see *G.* 'Rosenschleier' |
| 'White Festival'PBR (Festival Series) (d) | EBee SPoG WFar |

# H

## *Haberlea* (*Gesneriaceae*)

| | |
|---|---|
| ***ferdinandi-coburgii*** | CLAP ECho GBuc NMen NWCA |
| - 'Connie Davidson' | GBuc GEdr NMen |
| ***rhodopensis*** ♀H4 | CDes CElw CFee CStu CWsd ECho GEdr GGar GKev MSte MWat NLAp NMen NSla NWCA SIng SRms WAbe WPGP WTin |
| - 'Virginalis' | CElw CLAP CStu NMen NSla NWCA WThu |

## *Habranthus* ✿ (*Amaryllidaceae*)

| | |
|---|---|
| ***andersonii*** | see *H. tubispathus* |
| 'Argentine Pink' new | EDif |
| ***brachyandrus*** | CBro EDif GCal SRms |
| ***gracilifolius*** | CBro CStu ERos SIng WThu |
| ***martinezii*** | CBro CStu NWCA |
| § ***robustus*** ♀H1 | CCCN CPne CWsd EBee EBrs ECho EDif EPot EShb IHer LAma LHop LRHS WCot WHil WPGP |
| ***texanus*** | CBro CGHE ERos WAbe |
| § ***tubispathus*** ♀H1 | CBro CStu EBee ECho EDif ERos GCal NWCA SIng WCot WPrP |

## *Hackelia* (*Boraginaceae*)

| | |
|---|---|
| ***floribunda*** | EDif SBod |

## *Hacquetia* (*Apiaceae*)

| | |
|---|---|
| ***epipactis*** ♀H4 | Widely available |
| § - 'Thor' (v) | CBow CDes CLAP EBee EMon EWes GBri GEdr LLHF MAvo NChi NMen WPGP |
| - 'Variegata' | see *H. epipactis* 'Thor' |

## *Haemanthus* (*Amaryllidaceae*)

| | |
|---|---|
| sp. | CMdw |
| ***albiflos*** ♀H1 | CAbb CHEx CHal CSpe CStu CTsd ECho LAma LToo SRms WCot |
| ***amarylloides*** subsp. ***polyanthes*** | ECho |
| ***barkerae*** | ECho |
| ***coccineus*** ♀H1 | ECho |
| ***humilis*** | ECho |
| - subsp. ***hirsutus*** | WCot |
| ***katherinae*** | see *Scadoxus multiflorus* subsp. *katherinae* |
| ***pauculifolius*** | ECho WCot |
| ***pubescens*** subsp. ***leipoldtii*** | ECho |

## *Hakea* (*Proteaceae*)

| | |
|---|---|
| § ***drupacea*** | CTrC EShb |
| ***epiglottis*** | CTrC ECou |
| ***laurina*** | SPlb |
| ***lissocarpha*** | CTrC |
| § ***lissosperma*** | CDoC ECou EPfP EPla LRHS SPlb WPGP |
| ***microcarpa*** | ECou SLon |
| ***nodosa*** | CCCN CTrC |
| ***platysperma*** | SPlb |
| § ***salicifolia*** | CCCN EBee IMGH LRHS SPlb |
| - 'Gold Medal' (v) | CTrC EBee |
| ***saligna*** | see *H. salicifolia* |
| ***scoparia*** | CTrC |
| ***sericea*** misapplied | see *H. lissosperma* |
| ***sericea*** Schrad. & J.C.Wendl. | ECou |
| - pink-flowered | SPlb |
| ***suaveolens*** | see *H. drupacea* |
| ***teretifolia*** | CTrC |

## *Hakonechloa* (*Poaceae*)

| | |
|---|---|
| ***macra*** | CEnt CGHE CKno CPrp CSam EBee EBrs EHoe EPla EShb GKir LCro MAvo MMoz MRav NDov SApp SMad SPhx SPoG WCot WDyG WPGP WSHC |

| | | |
|---|---|---|
| § | - 'Alboaurea' ♀H4 | Widely available |
| | - 'Albovariegata' | CKno CWan EBee GCal GKev LEdu LHop MAvo WDyG |
| | - 'All Gold' | EBee EGle EPPr EWes GBin SMad |
| | - 'Aureola' ♀H4 | Widely available |
| * | - 'Mediopicta' (v) | SApp |
| * | - 'Mediovariegata' (v) | CGHE CWCL EPPr EPla WPGP |
| | - 'Naomi' (v) **new** | EBee GBin |
| | - 'Nicolas' **new** | EBee GBin |
| | - 'Variegata' | see *H. macra* 'Alboaurea' |

## *Halenia* (*Gentianaceae*)

| | | |
|---|---|---|
| | ***elliptica*** | EBee |
| | - SDR 4716 **new** | GKev |

## *Halesia* (*Styracaceae*)

| | | |
|---|---|---|
| § | ***carolina*** | Widely available |
| | - 'Wedding Bells' | CPMA |
| | ***diptera*** | CMCN MBlu SKHP |
| | - var. ***magniflora*** | EBee EPfP MBlu |
| | ***monticola*** | CBcs CDul CMCN EBee ELan EPfP LRHS NLar SSpi WFar |
| | - var. ***vestita*** ♀H4 | CAbP CDoC CPMA CTho EBee EPfP ERas EWTr IMGH LRHS MAsh MBlu MBri MRav NLar NVic SHBN SPoG SSpi WDin WFar WGob WHCG WPGP WPat |
| | - - f. ***rosea*** | CBcs CPMA EPfP MBlu |
| | ***tetraptera*** | see *H. carolina* |

## x *Halimiocistus* (*Cistaceae*)

| | | |
|---|---|---|
| | sp. | WBod |
| | ***algarvensis*** | see *Halimium ocymoides* |
| § | 'Ingwersenii' | CBcs CDoC CTca EBee ELan EWes LRHS SPer SPoG SRms WPer |
| | ***revolii*** misapplied | see x *H. sahucii* |
| § | ***sahucii*** ♀H4 | CBcs CBgR CDoC CSBt CTri EBee ECha ELan EPfP LAst LBMP LRHS MAsh MBNS MMuc MRav MSwo MWat NPri SDys SGar SHBN SPer SPoG SRms SWvt WDin WFar |
| | - Ice Dancer = 'Ebhals'PBR (v) | CDoC EBee EPfP LAst MAsh SPer SWvt |
| | 'Susan' | see *Halimium* 'Susan' |
| § | ***wintonensis*** ♀H3 | CBcs CDoC CSBt EBee ELan EPfP LRHS MAsh MRav SHBN SPer SPla SRms WCFE WHar WSHC |
| § | - 'Merrist Wood Cream' ♀H3 | CBcs CBgR CDoC CSBt EBee ELan EPfP LAst LHop LRHS MAsh MRav MSwo NBir SBod SPer SPla SPoG SSpi SWvt WAbe WDin WFar WKif WPat WSHC |

## *Halimium* ✿ (*Cistaceae*)

| | | |
|---|---|---|
| § | ***atriplicifolium*** | EHig WAbe |
| § | ***calycinum*** | CAbP CChe EBee ELan EPfP GKev LRHS MAsh MBri SCoo SKHP SLim SPer SPoG SWvt WAbe WBod WCFE WDin |
| | ***commutatum*** | see *H. calycinum* |
| | ***formosum*** | see *H. lasianthum* subsp. *formosum* |
| N | ***halimifolium*** misapplied | see *H.* x *pauanum* |
| § | ***lasianthum*** ♀H3 | CBcs CSBt CWib EBee ELan EPfP LRHS MBri MRav SLim WBod WBrE WCFE WEas WKif |
| | - 'Concolor' | CDoC CWib EBee EMil MSwo NPri SWvt WDin |
| § | - subsp. ***formosum*** | GGar SBod |
| | - - 'Sandling' | EBee ELan EPfP LRHS SRms |
| | - 'Hannay Silver' | SPla |
| | ***libanotis*** | see *H. calycinum* |
| § | ***ocymoides*** ♀H3 | CBcs CChe CDoC CWib ELan EPfP LRHS MMHG MSwo NPri SLon WHar WKif |
| § | x ***pauanum*** | EBee MMuc WAbe |
| | 'Sarah' | EBee LRHS |
| § | 'Susan' ♀H3 | CBgR CDoC EBee ELan EPfP ERas LHop LRHS LSou MMHG SCoo SLim SPer SPoG WAbe |
| § | ***umbellatum*** | CFul EBee LRHS SPer WHCG WKif |
| | ***wintonense*** | see x *Halimiocistus wintonensis* |

## *Halimodendron* (*Papilionaceae*)

| | | |
|---|---|---|
| | ***halodendron*** | CArn CBcs CDul EBee MBlu NBlu SPer WDin |

## *Halleria* (*Scrophulariaceae*)

| | | |
|---|---|---|
| | ***lucida*** | CCCN |

## *Halocarpus* (*Podocarpaceae*)

| | | |
|---|---|---|
| § | ***bidwillii*** | CDoC ECou |

## *Haloragis* (*Haloragaceae*)

| | | |
|---|---|---|
| | ***erecta*** | CSec |
| | - 'Rubra' | EBee WCot WPer |
| | - 'Wellington Bronze' | CBow CEnt CSec CSpe EBee ECtt EDAr EHoe EPPr GGar LEdu LRHS MBNS MCCP MLHP SBod SDys SWal WEas WHer WMoo |

## *Hamamelis* ✿ (*Hamamelidaceae*)

| | | |
|---|---|---|
| | 'Brevipetala' | CBcs CDul NHol |
| | x ***intermedia*** 'Advent' | NLar |
| | - 'Angelly' ♀H4 | CPMA MAsh MBlu MBri MGos NLar |
| | - 'Aphrodite' ♀H4 | EMil EPfP MAsh MBlu MBri MGos MRav NBhm NLar SSpi |
| | - 'Arnold Promise' ♀H4 | Widely available |
| | - 'August Lamken' | NLar |
| | - 'Aurora' ♀H4 | CPMA MBlu MBri NHol NLar |
| | - 'Barmstedt Gold' ♀H4 | EBee EPfP LRHS MAsh MBlu MBri MGos MRav NHol NLar SReu SRms SSpi SSta |
| | - 'Carmine Red' | CMac EMil MGos NLar |
| | - 'Copper Beauty' | see *H.* x *intermedia* 'Jelena' |
| | - 'Diane' ♀H4 | Widely available |
| | - 'Doerak' | MBri |
| § | - 'Feuerzauber' | CEnd CMac CSBt EBee LBuc LRHS MSwo NBlu NLar NScw SBir SPer SRms WBVN WDin WOrn WPat |
| | - Fire Cracker | see *H.* x *intermedia* 'Feuerzauber' |
| | - 'Frederic' **new** | MAsh |
| | - 'Gingerbread' | LRHS |
| | - 'Girard's Orange' | EPfP |
| | - 'Glowing Embers' | LRHS MAsh |
| | - 'Harry' | LRHS MAsh MBri NLar SBir SPoG SSpi |
| | - Hillier's clone | NHol |
| § | - 'Jelena' ♀H4 | Widely available |
| | - 'Lansing' | NLar |
| | - 'Limelight' | MBri |
| | - 'Livia' | LRHS MBri NLar SSpi |
| | - Magic Fire | see *H.* x *intermedia* 'Feuerzauber' |
| | - 'Moonlight' | CDul CPMA NLar |
| | - 'Nina' | LRHS MAsh |
| | - 'Orange Beauty' | CBcs EMil LRHS MGos NLar |
| | - 'Orange Peel' | EPfP LRHS MBri NLar |
| | - 'Pallida' ♀H4 | Widely available |
| | - 'Perfume' **new** | NLar |
| | - 'Primavera' | CWSG EMil LPan MLan NHol NLar SPla |
| | - 'Ripe Corn' | EPfP MBri SPoG |
| | - 'Robert' | LRHS MBri SPoG |
| | - 'Rubin' | MAsh MBri NLar SPoG SSpi |
| | - 'Ruby Glow' | CBcs CWib EBee ECho LMaj LSRN MGos NLar NPri NWea SPer WDin |

| | | |
|---|---|---|
| | - 'Sunburst' | EPfP LRHS MGos |
| | - 'Vesna' 𝕐H4 | CMac EBee EPfP MAsh MBlu NLar SPoG SSpi |
| § | - 'Westerstede' | CWSG EBee EMil LPan LRHS MGos MLan MRav NHol NLar NScw NWea SLim WDin WHar |
| | ***japonica*** | WFar |
| | - 'Pendula' | CPMA NLar |
| | - 'Robin' | NLar |
| | - 'Zuccariniana' | NLar |
| | ***mollis*** 𝕐H4 | Widely available |
| | - 'Boskoop' | NLar |
| | - 'Coombe Wood' | LRHS |
| | - 'Goldcrest' | CPMA |
| | - 'Jermyns Gold' 𝕐H4 | EPfP LRHS |
| | - 'Princeton Gold' | CWib |
| | - 'Select' | see *H.* x *intermedia* 'Westerstede' |
| | - 'Superba' | LRHS |
| | - 'Wisley Supreme' | CAbP ELan LRHS MAsh MBri SSpi |
| | 'Rochester' | MBri NLar |
| | ***vernalis*** | WDin |
| | - 'Amethyst' | NLar |
| | - 'Lombart's Weeping' | CFwr NLar |
| | - purple | MBlu NLar |
| | - 'Sandra' 𝕐H4 | CBcs CMCN ELan EPfP LRHS MAsh MBlu MBri MGos MRav NLar SHBN SLon SPoG SReu SSpi SSta WCot |
| | ***virginiana*** | CAgr ECrN GPoy IDee NWea WDin WFar |
| | 'Yamina' | NLar |

## *Hamelia* (*Rubiaceae*)

| | | |
|---|---|---|
| | ***patens*** | CCCN EShb |

## *Hanabusaya* (*Campanulaceae*)

| | | |
|---|---|---|
| § | ***asiatica*** | NChi WFar |

## *Haplocarpha* (*Asteraceae*)

| | | |
|---|---|---|
| | ***rueppellii*** | CFee NBro SRms SRot WPer |

## *Haplopappus* (*Asteraceae*)

| | | |
|---|---|---|
| | ***brandegeei*** | see *Erigeron aureus* |
| | ***coronopifolius*** | see *H. glutinosus* |
| § | ***glutinosus*** | EBee ECha ECho ECtt GEdr MTho NLar NWCA SEND SPlb SRms |
| | ***lyallii*** | see *Tonestus lyallii* |
| | ***prunelloides*** | GEdr NWCA |
| | - var. ***mustersii*** | CStu |
| | ***rehderi*** | MWat WFar |

## *Hardenbergia* (*Papilionaceae*)

| | | |
|---|---|---|
| | ***comptoniana*** 𝕐H1 | CPLG CSpe EBee |
| | ***violacea*** 𝕐H1 | CAbb CBcs CHll CRHN CSPN CSpe CTrC EBee ELan ERas GQui LRHS SBod SLim SPer WCot |
| | - f. ***alba*** | CBcs ECou ERas IDee |
| | - - 'White Crystal' | EBee WPGP |
| | - dwarf **new** | ECou |
| | - 'Happy Wanderer' | LRHS SChF SOWG SPoG WPGP |
| | - f. ***rosea*** | CBcs EBee |

## *Harpephyllum* (*Anacardiaceae*)

| | | |
|---|---|---|
| | ***caffrum*** (F) | XBlo |

## *Harrimanella* see *Cassiope*

## *Hastingsia* (*Hyacinthaceae*)

| | | |
|---|---|---|
| | ***alba*** | GBuc |
| | - NNS 98-310 | WCot |
| | - NNS 98-311 | WCot |

## *Haworthia* ✿ (*Aloaceae*)

| | | |
|---|---|---|
| | ***attenuata*** | SWal |
| | 'Black Prince' | EPfP |
| | ***cooperi*** **new** | STre |
| | ***cymbiformis*** | EPfP STre |
| | ***fasciata*** | EPfP |
| | ***glabrata*** var. ***concolor*** | EPfP |
| | ***radula*** | EPfP |
| | ***reinwardtii*** 𝕐H1 | CHal |

## **hazelnut** see *Corylus*

## *Hebe* ✿ (*Scrophulariaceae*)

| | | |
|---|---|---|
| | ***albicans*** 𝕐H4 | CCVT CChe ECou ELan EPfP GGar GKir IFoB LAst LRHS MBar MBri MGos MRav SCoo SHBN SPer SPoG SSto STre SWal WFar WHCG |
| | - 'Cobb' | ECou |
| | - 'Pink Elephant' | see *H.* 'Pink Elephant' |
| | - prostrate | see *H. albicans* 'Snow Cover' |
| | - 'Red Edge' | see *H.* 'Red Edge' |
| * | - 'Snow Carpet' | CCCN LRHS |
| § | - 'Snow Cover' | EWes |
| | - 'Snow Drift' | see *H. albicans* 'Snow Cover' |
| § | - 'Sussex Carpet' | STre |
| § | 'Alicia Amherst' | SPer SRms SSto |
| | ***allanii*** | see *H. amplexicaulis* f. *hirta* |
| | 'Amanda Cook' (v) | MCCP NPer |
| | ***amplexicaulis*** clone 4 | STre |
| § | - f. ***hirta*** | NDlv NHol |
| § | 'Amy' | GGal LRHS NPer SHBN SPer SPoG |
| | x ***andersonii*** | CDul |
| § | - 'Andersonii Variegata' (v) | NBur SPla SRms |
| | - 'Argenteovariegata' | see *H.* x *andersonii* 'Andersonii Variegata' |
| | 'Andressa Paula' | CCCN |
| | 'Anita' | SPoG |
| | ***anomala*** misapplied | see *H.* 'Imposter' |
| | ***anomala*** (Armstr.) Cockayne | CCCN LRHS |
| | 'Aoira' | see *H. recurva* 'Aoira' |
| § | ***armstrongii*** | ECho GGar MBar MGos SSto WDin WPer |
| | 'Arthur' | ECou |
| | ***astonii*** | ECho |
| | 'Autumn Glory' | CSBt CWSG ECho ELan EPfP GKir LAst LRHS MBar MGos MLHP MSwo NBir NPri SBod SHBN SPer SPla SPlb SPoG SWal SWvt WBod WDin |
| | ***azurea*** | see *H. venustula* |
| | 'Azurens' | see *H.* 'Maori Gem' |
| | 'Baby Marie' | CAbP CChe CSBt ECho ECot ECou ELan EPfP LAst LRHS LSRN MGos MSwo NBlu NMen NPer NPri SCoo SPla SPoG SRGP SRms SRot SSto SWvt WCFE |
| | 'Beatrice' | NDlv |
| | 'Beverley Hills' PBR | CSBt LRHS WHar |
| | 'Bicolor Wand' | CCCN CTsd |
| | ***bishopiana*** | ECou EPfP LRHS MGos SBod SCoo SSto |
| | - 'Champagne' | see *H.* 'Champagne' |
| | 'Black Beauty' | NBPN |
| | 'Blue Clouds' 𝕐H3 | LAst LLHF LRHS MSwo NDlv SPer SSto SWal WCFE |
| § | 'Blue Gem' | LRHS |
| | 'Blue Star' | LRHS MAsh SPoG |
| | Blue Star = 'Vergeer 1' PBR **new** | LSou |
| | ***bollonsii*** | GGar |
| | 'Boscawenii' | CTrG CTsd MGos |
| | 'Bouquet' PBR | SPoG |
| § | 'Bowles' Hybrid' | CCCN ECou LEdu MSwo SRms STre |
| | 'Bowles' Variety' | see *H.* 'Bowles' Hybrid' |

| | | |
|---|---|---|
| | ***brachysiphon*** | CTrC CTri EPfP MGos MRav SHBN SPer WDin WHCG |
| | ***brevifolia*** | ECou |
| | 'Bronzy Baby' (v) | SPoG |
| | ***buchananii*** | ECho GGar MBar MGos MHer MTho NDlv NPer WPer |
| § | - 'Fenwickii' | ECho WHoo |
| | - 'Minima' | ECho |
| | - 'Minor' | ECho GBin MBar NBir NDlv NWCA SIng |
| * | - 'Nana' | MGos |
| | ***buxifolia*** misapplied | see *H. odora* |
| | ***buxifolia*** (Benth.) Ckn. & Allan | NBlu NHol NWea WDin WHar |
| | - 'Champagne' | see *H.* 'Champagne' |
| § | 'Caledonia' ♀H3 | CCCN CSBt EPfP LRHS LSRN MBri MGos MSte NBrd NPer SCoo SPoG WFar |
| | 'Candy' | ECou |
| § | ***canterburiensis*** | ECou GGar |
| N | 'Carl Teschner' | see *H.* 'Youngii' |
| | 'Carnea Variegata' (v) | LRHS MGos MSCN SBod SPer WOut |
| | ***carnosula*** | GGar LRHS MGos NBir SPer WHar WPer |
| | ***catarractae*** | see *Parabebe catarractae* |
| | 'Celine' | GGar MGos SPoG SRGP |
| § | 'Champagne' | CCCN LAst LCro LRHS LSRN NBPN NBlu NHol SCoo |
| | Champion = 'Champseiont'PBR | LSou NBPN SCoo SPoG |
| | 'Charming White' | CChe EQua LRHS |
| | ***chathamica*** | ECou GGar |
| | 'Christabel' | LRHS |
| | ***ciliolata* x *odora*** | GGar |
| | 'Claymoddie Blue Seedling' **new** | GGal |
| | 'Clear Skies'PBR | CAbP ECou LRHS |
| | 'Colwall' | ECho |
| | 'Conwy Knight' | WAbe |
| | 'County Park' | ECou EWes NHol NMen |
| | 'Cranleighensis' | CTsd SSto |
| § | 'Cupins' | SWal |
| | ***cupressoides*** | NDlv SEND WDin |
| | - 'Boughton Dome' | CTri EAlp ECho EPfP ERas GGar MGos MHer MTho NMen WCFE WHoo WPer |
| | ***darwiniana*** | see *H. glaucophylla* |
| | 'Dazzler' (v) | CAbP LRHS |
| | ***decumbens*** | EWes GGar MGos NHol |
| | 'Diana' | ECou |
| | ***dieffenbachii*** | GGar |
| | ***diosmifolia*** | CAbP CDoC ELan NBlu WAbe |
| | - 'Marie' | ECou |
| | ***divaricata*** | ECou |
| * | - 'Marlborough' | ECou |
| | - 'Nelson' | ECou |
| | x ***divergens*** | NDlv |
| | 'Dorothy Peach' | see *H.* 'Watson's Pink' |
| | 'E.A. Bowles' | ECou WBVN |
| | 'E.B. Anderson' | see *H.* 'Caledonia' |
| | 'Early Blue' | CSpe NBir |
| | 'Edington' | LRHS SPer WCFE |
| | ***elliptica*** | CDul ECou |
| | - 'Anatoki' | ECou |
| | - 'Charleston' | ECou |
| | - 'Kapiti' | ECou SWal |
| | - 'Variegata' | see *H.* 'Silver Queen' |
| | 'Emerald Dome' | see *H.* 'Emerald Gem' |
| § | 'Emerald Gem' ♀H3 | CDul CTri ECho EPfP GGar GKev MAsh MBar MBri MGos MHer MMuc MSwo MWat NDlv NHol NMen NWCA SCoo SPer SPlb WBod WPat |
| | 'Emerald Green' | see *H.* 'Emerald Gem' |
| | ***epacridea*** | ECho EWes NHol |
| § | 'Eveline' | NBir SPer WCot |
| | ***evenosa*** | GGar NDlv |
| | 'Eversley Seedling' | see *H.* 'Bowles' Hybrid' |
| | 'Fairfieldii' | ERas WPat |
| | 'First Light'PBR | CWSG SCoo SPoG WHar |
| | 'Fragrant Jewel' | CWib SEND SWal |
| | x ***franciscana*** | ECou LAst |
| | - 'Blue Gem' misapplied | see *H.* x *franciscana* 'Lobelioides' |
| | - 'Blue Gem' ambig. | ECho LRHS NBir NPer SPer SPlb SRms SSto WHar |
| § | - 'Lobelioides' **new** | GGar |
| | - 'Purple Tips' misapplied | see *H. speciosa* 'Variegata' |
| | - 'Variegata' | see *H.* 'Silver Queen' |
| I | - 'White Gem' | SRms |
| | - yellow-variegated (v) | SPer |
| | 'Franjo' | ECou |
| | 'Garden Beauty' | LRHS MGos |
| | 'Gauntlettii' | see *H.* 'Eveline' |
| N | ***glaucophylla*** | SBod |
| | - 'Clarence' | ECou GGar |
| I | 'Glaucophylla Variegata' (v) | CTri NBir SCoo SPer WKif |
| | 'Glengarriff' | NHol |
| § | 'Gloriosa' | CEnt |
| | 'Gnome' | LRHS |
| | 'Godefroyana' | see *H. pinguifolia* 'Godefroyana' |
| | 'Gold Beauty' | LRHS |
| | 'Goldrush' (v) | MGos SPoG |
| | 'Gran's Favourite' | CCCN |
| | 'Great Orme' ♀H3 | Widely available |
| | 'Green Globe' | see *H.* 'Emerald Gem' |
| | 'Greensleeves' | ECou GGar |
| | 'Grethe' | SPoG |
| | 'Gruninard's Seedling' | GGar |
| | ***haastii*** | GGar NLar |
| | 'Hadspen Pink' | LRHS |
| | 'Hagley Park' | EPfP SAga WHCG |
| § | 'Hartii' | LRHS MRav |
| | 'Heartbreaker'PBR (v) | ELan LBuc LRHS MGos NPri SCoo SPoG |
| | 'Highdownensis' | SSto |
| | 'Hinderwell' | NPer |
| | 'Hinerua' | GGar NNor |
| | 'Holywell' | SBod SWal |
| | ***hookeriana*** | see *Parabebe hookeriana* |
| | ***hulkeana*** ♀H3 | ERas LRHS LSou MHer SAga SUsu SWal WEas WHCG WKif WPat WTin |
| | 'Ian Young' | ITim |
| § | 'Imposter' | SRms |
| | ***insularis*** | ECho ECou |
| | 'James Stirling' | see *H. ochracea* 'James Stirling' |
| | 'Janet' | SGar |
| | 'Jean Searle' | LAst |
| | 'Joanna' | ECou |
| | 'Just Judy' | LRHS |
| | 'Karen's Pink' | WAbe |
| | 'Karna' | SPoG |
| | 'Katrina' (v) | SPoG |
| | 'Kirkii' | EMil EPfP SCoo SPer |
| | 'Knightshayes' | see *H.* 'Caledonia' |
| § | 'La Séduisante' | ECou GGal MLHP SEND SHBN WKif WOut |
| | 'Lady Ann'PBR (v) | CWSG LRHS LSou NLar NPri WHar |
| | 'Lady Ardilaun' | see *H.* 'Amy' |
| | ***laevis*** | see *H. venustula* |
| | ***latifolia*** | see *H.* 'Blue Gem' |
| | 'Lavender Spray' | see *H.* 'Hartii' |
| | 'Lilac Wand' **new** | CTsd |
| | 'Linda' | SPoG |
| | 'Lindsayi' | ECou |
| | 'Lisa' | SPoG |
| § | 'Loganioides' | GGar |

| | | |
|---|---|---|
| | 'Lopen' (v) | ECou |
| | 'Louise' | LIMB SGar |
| | ***lyallii*** | see *Parahebe lyallii* |
| | ***lycopodioides*** | EWes WThu |
| | - 'Aurea' | see *H. armstrongii* |
| | ***mackenii*** | see *H.* 'Emerald Gem' |
| | ***macrantha*** ♀H3 | ECho EPfP GGar LRHS SPer SRms WAbe |
| | ***macrocarpa*** | ECou LRHS |
| | - var. ***latisepala*** | ECou |
| § | 'Maori Gem' | GGar NBrd SSto |
| | 'Margery Fish' | see *H.* 'Primley Gem' |
| | 'Margret'PBR ♀H4 | CSBt EMil EPfP ERas LAst LRHS LSRN MAsh MGos NPri SCoo SHBN SPer SPoG SRGP SSto |
| | 'Marie Antoinette' | LRHS |
| | 'Marjorie' | CCVT CDul CSBt ELan EPfP LRHS MGos MRav MSwo NPer NWea SBod SPer SRms SSto WDin |
| | ***matthewsii*** | WPat |
| | 'Mauvena' | SPer |
| | 'McKean' | see *H.* 'Emerald Gem' |
| | 'Megan' | ECou |
| § | 'Mercury' | ECou |
| | 'Midsummer Beauty' ♀H3 | ECou EPfP GGar ISea LAst LRHS MGos MLHP MRav NBir SBod SHBN SMad SPer SPlb SSto SWvt WDin WHar WOut WSFF |
| | 'Milmont Emerald' | see *H.* 'Emerald Gem' |
| * | ***minima*** 'Calvin' | ECho |
| | 'Miss Fittall' | ECou |
| | 'Misty' | CCCN |
| § | 'Mohawk'PBR | LBuc MGos NLar SCoo |
| | 'Monica' | NHol |
| * | 'Moppets Hardy' | SPer WHar |
| § | 'Mrs Winder' ♀H4 | Widely available |
| | 'Mystery' | ECou ELan SWal |
| | 'Mystery Red' | MGos |
| | 'Nantyderry' | CCCN GBri LRHS SPla SWal WOut |
| § | 'Neil's Choice' ♀H4 | CCCN ECou MSte STre |
| | 'Nicola's Blush' ♀H4 | Widely available |
| | ***ochracea*** | MGos |
| § | - 'James Stirling' ♀H4 | CDul CSBt ECho ELan EPfP GGar GKev LRHS LSRN MAsh MBar MBri MGos MRav MSwo MTho NBir SCoo SLim SPer SPlb SPoG SRGP STre SWvt WDin WFar |
| | 'Oddity' | LRHS |
| § | ***odora*** | ECou EPfP GGar MGos MRav WCFE |
| I | - 'Nana' | EPfP MBar |
| | - 'New Zealand Gold' | LRHS MAsh MGos MMuc NDlv SCoo SLon SSto SWal |
| | - var. ***patens*** | WHCG |
| | - 'Summer Frost' | NHol |
| | - 'Wintergreen' | MRav |
| | 'Oratia Beauty' ♀H4 | LRHS MRav NPri |
| | 'Orphan Annie'PBR (v) | CWSG LRHS MGos SPer |
| | ***parviflora*** misapplied | see *H.* 'Bowles' Hybrid' |
| § | ***parviflora*** (Vahl) Cockayne & Allan | GGar |
| | - 'Holdsworth' | LRHS SDys |
| | - 'Palmerston' | ECou |
| | - var. ***angustifolia*** | see *H. stenophylla* |
| | - var. ***arborea*** | see *H. parviflora* (Vahl) Cockayne & Allan |
| | 'Pascal' ♀H4 | CCCN ECou ELan EPfP LRHS LSRN MBri MGos MRav NBrd SCoo SPer SPoG |
| | 'Pastel Blue' | SSto |
| | ***pauciramosa*** | SRms SWal |
| | 'Pearl of Paradise'PBR | SPoG |
| | ***perfoliata*** | see *Parahebe perfoliata* |
| | 'Perry's Rubyleaf' | NPer |
| | 'Petra's Pink' | CCCN |
| | 'Pewter Dome' ♀H4 | CSBt ECou EPfP MGos MRav NDlv NHol SBod SDix SPer SPoG SRms STre WBrE |
| | ***pimeleoides*** | ECou NHol SCoo SSto |
| | - 'Glauca' | NPer |
| | - 'Glaucocaerulea' | ECou SCoo |
| | - 'Mercury' | see *H.* 'Mercury' |
| | - 'Quicksilver' ♀H4 | CSBt CTri ECou EDAr ELan EPfP GGar LAst LRHS MBar MGos MMuc MRav MSCN MSwo NBir NHol NPer SCoo SPer SPoG STre SUsu SWal WAbe WHar WPat |
| | - 'Red Tip' | ECho |
| | ***pinguifolia*** | ECou SPlb WFar |
| § | - 'Godefroyana' | SWal |
| | - 'Pagei' ♀H4 | Widely available |
| | - 'Sutherlandii' | CBcs CDoC ECho GGar LEdu MBar MGos NDlv SCoo SSto WFar WRHF |
| § | 'Pink Elephant' (v) ♀H3 | CAbP ELan EPfP LAst LBuc LRHS MAsh SPer SPla SPoG |
| | 'Pink Fantasy' | CChe LRHS MRav NHol |
| | 'Pink Goddess' | LRHS SRGP |
| | 'Pink Lady'PBR | SPoG |
| | 'Pink Paradise'PBR | CAbP ELan EPfP LRHS LSou MGos NHol SBod SPoG SSto |
| | 'Pink Payne' | see *H.* 'Eveline' |
| | 'Pink Pearl' | see *H.* 'Gloriosa' |
| | 'Pink Pixie' | LBuc LSou MBri MGos SCoo |
| | 'Pink Wand' | CTsd |
| | 'Porlock Purple' | see *Parahebe catarractae* 'Delight' |
| § | 'Primley Gem' | CCCN EQua SCoo |
| | ***propinqua*** | MHer NMen |
| | - 'Cupins' | see *H.* 'Cupins' |
| | - 'Minor' | NDlv |
| I | 'Prostrata' | CSBt NDlv |
| | 'Purple Emperor' | see *H.* 'Neil's Choice' |
| | 'Purple Paradise'PBR | EPfP LRHS LSou MBri SPoG |
| | 'Purple Pixie'PBR | see *H.* 'Mohawk' |
| | 'Purple Princess' | LRHS |
| § | 'Purple Queen' | CSBt ELan EPfP EShb GGar LIMB LRHS SPla SPoG SSto WAbe |
| | Purple Shamrock = 'Neprock'PBR (v) | EPfP LBuc LRHS LSRN MBri MGos NPri SCoo SPer SPoG |
| | 'Purple Tips' misapplied | see *H. speciosa* 'Variegata' |
| | 'Rachel' | LRHS LSRN |
| | ***rakaiensis*** ♀H4 | Widely available |
| | ***ramosissima*** | GGar NDlv |
| | ***raoulii*** | EPot NMen NWCA WAbe WFar |
| | ***recurva*** | CSam CTri EPfP GGar LAst LRHS MGos NHol SRms SWal WBrE WCot WDin |
| § | - 'Aoira' | ECou |
| | - 'Boughton Silver' ♀H3 | ELan EPfP LRHS |
| | - 'White Torrent' | ECou |
| § | 'Red Edge' ♀H4 | Widely available |
| | 'Red Rum' | ELan |
| | 'Red Ruth' | see *H.* 'Eveline' |
| | ***rigidula*** | LRHS MGos NHol |
| | 'Ronda' | ECou |
| | 'Rosie'PBR | EPfP LAst NMen SCoo SPer SSto |
| | 'Royal Purple' | see *H.* 'Alicia Amherst' |
| | ***salicifolia*** | CCCN CChe CTca ECou ELan EPfP GGar LAst LRHS MDun MRav NHol SCoo SHBN SPer SPlb SRms SSto SWal WFar WHCG |
| | - BR 30 | GGar |
| | 'Sandra Joy' | CCCN |
| | 'Sapphire' ♀H4 | ECou EPfP LRHS MBar MGos NBlu NPri SCoo SSto SWal |
| | 'Sarana' | CCCN ECou |
| | ***selaginoides*** hort. | see *H.* 'Loganioides' |
| | 'Shiraz' | LRHS |

| | | |
|---|---|---|
| | 'Silver Dollar' (v) | CAbP CCCN CMMP CSBt ELan EPfP LAst LBuc LHop LRHS LSou MAsh MGos MMuc NPri SPer SPoG SSto |
| § | 'Silver Queen' (v) ♀H2 | CDul ECou ELan EPfP MBar MGos MRav NPer SPer SSto WBod WHar WOut |
| | 'Simon Délaux' | CEnt CSBt ECou LRHS SEND SSto WOut |
| I | 'Southlandii' | ECho MWhi |
| | ***speciosa*** | ECho |
| | - 'La Séduisante' | see *H.* 'La Séduisante' |
| | - 'Purple Queen' | see *H.* 'Purple Queen' |
| | - 'Rangatira' | ECou |
| § | - 'Variegata' (v) | CHal LRHS NPer SSto WEas |
| | 'Spender's Seedling' misapplied | see *H. stenophylla* |
| | 'Spender's Seedling' ambig. | MCot |
| | 'Spender's Seedling' hort. | ECou EPfP LRHS MRav SEND SPoG SRms STre |
| | 'Spring Glory' | LRHS |
| § | ***stenophylla*** | ECou EShb GGal MSCN SAPC SArc SDix SSto |
| | ***stricta*** | ECou LRHS |
| | - var. ***egmontiana*** | ECou |
| | - var. ***macroura*** | ECou |
| | ***subalpina*** | CSBt ECho ERas NHol NPri |
| | 'Summer Blue' | EPfP LRHS MRav |
| | 'Sussex Carpet' | see *H. albicans* 'Sussex Carpet' |
| | 'Sweet Kim' (v) | LBuc LRHS |
| | 'Tina' | ECou NHol |
| | 'Tiny Tot' | MTho |
| | 'Tom Marshall' | see *H. canterburiensis* |
| | ***topiaria*** ♀H4 | CAbP CChe CSBt CSam ECho ECou EMil EPfP GGar LAst LHop LRHS MAsh MBrN MSwo NBlu NHol NPri SCoo SHBN SPer SPla SPoG STre SWal WAbe WFar |
| * | - 'Doctor Favier' | LRHS |
| | ***townsonii*** | ECou LHop LRHS SCoo |
| | ***traversii*** | ECou MSte NHol SRms SSto |
| | - 'Mason River' | ECou |
| | - 'Woodside' | ECou |
| | 'Tricolor' | see *H. speciosa* 'Variegata' |
| | 'Trixie' | CCCN ECou |
| | 'Twisty' | ELan LRHS MGos |
| | 'Valentino' PBR | LRHS SPer |
| | 'Veitchii' | see *H.* 'Alicia Amherst' |
| § | ***venustula*** | ECou GGar IArd MMuc |
| | - 'Patricia Davies' | ECou |
| | ***vernicosa*** ♀H3 | CChe CDul ECho EPfP LAst LRHS MBar MGos MHer NDlv NHol SCoo SPer SPlb SPoG SRot STre SWvt WAbe WFar WHCG |
| | 'Vogue' | EPfP LRHS SMrm |
| | 'Waikiki' | see *H.* 'Mrs Winder' |
| | 'Warley Pink' | LRHS |
| | 'Warleyensis' | see *H.* 'Mrs Winder' |
| § | 'Watson's Pink' | GGar MWea SPer WKif |
| | 'White Gem' (*brachysiphon* hybrid) ♀H4 | CCCN ECou MGos NDlv NPer SPer WFar |
| | 'White Heather' | LRHS NBir |
| | 'White Paradise' PBR | SPoG |
| | 'Willcoxii' | see *H. buchananii* 'Fenwickii' |
| | 'Wingletye' ♀H3 | CCCN ECho ECou EPot LRHS NDlv NNor WAbe WPer |
| | 'Winter Glow' | CCCN MGos SCoo |
| | 'Wiri Blush' | SHBN SWvt |
| | 'Wiri Charm' | CAbP CDul CSBt EPfP GGar LAst LBMP LRHS MGos MLan MRav MSwo NBlu SEND SHBN SSto WBrE |
| | 'Wiri Cloud' ♀H3 | CAbP CBcs EPfP GGar LRHS LSou MSwo SSto SWal |
| | 'Wiri Dawn' ♀H3 | CAbP ELan EPfP EWes LRHS LSou MGos MMuc SHBN SSto SWvt WHrl |
| | 'Wiri Desire' | CCCN |
| | 'Wiri Gem' | LRHS MRav |
| | 'Wiri Image' | CBcs CSBt LRHS |
| | 'Wiri Joy' | LRHS SEND |
| | 'Wiri Mist' | CBcs CTrC GGar LRHS MGos SCoo |
| | 'Wiri Prince' | LRHS |
| | 'Wiri Splash' | CTrC LRHS MGos SHBN SSto |
| | 'Wiri Vision' | CSBt LRHS |
| § | 'Youngii' ♀H3-4 | CSBt ELan EPfP GGar LAst LRHS MBar MGos MHer MRav MWat NBir NMen NPri SBod SPer SPlb SPoG SRms STre SWvt WHoo |

## *Hebenstretia* (*Scrophulariaceae*)

| | | |
|---|---|---|
| | ***dura*** | CPBP |
| * | ***quinquinervis*** | LSou |

## *Hechtia* (*Bromeliaceae*)

| | | |
|---|---|---|
| | F&M 188 **new** | WPGP |

## *Hedeoma* (*Lamiaceae*)

| | | |
|---|---|---|
| | ***hyssopifolia*** | SPhx |

## *Hedera* ✿ (*Araliaceae*)

| | | |
|---|---|---|
| § | ***algeriensis*** | CDoC CDul SAPC SArc WFib WGwG |
| § | - 'Gloire de Marengo' (v) ♀H3 | Widely available |
| | - 'Gloire de Marengo' arborescent (v) | SPer |
| | - 'Marginomaculata' (v) ♀H3 | CDoC EPfP EShb LRHS MAsh SMad WCot WFib |
| | - 'Montgomery' | LRHS MWht |
| | - 'Ravensholst' ♀H3 | CMac WFib |
| § | ***azorica*** | WFar WFib |
| | - 'Pico' | EPfP WFib |
| | - 'Variegata' (v) | WCot |
| | ***canariensis*** hort. | see *H. algeriensis* |
| | - 'Algeriensis' | see *H. algeriensis* |
| | - var. ***azorica*** | see *H. azorica* |
| | - 'Cantabrian' | see *H. maroccana* 'Spanish Canary' |
| | - 'Variegata' | see *H. algeriensis* 'Gloire de Marengo' |
| | ***chinensis*** | see *H. sinensis* var. *sinensis* |
| | - typica | see *H. sinensis* var. *sinensis* |
| § | ***colchica*** ♀H4 | EPfP LRHS SPer WCFE WDin WFar WFib |
| | - 'Arborescens' | see *H. colchica* 'Dendroides' |
| | - 'Batumi' | MBNS |
| § | - 'Dendroides' | WCot |
| | - 'Dentata' ♀H4 | EHoe EPla MRav MWhi WFib |
| | - 'Dentata Aurea' | see *H. colchica* 'Dentata Variegata' |
| § | - 'Dentata Variegata' (v) ♀H4 | Widely available |
| | - 'My Heart' | see *H. colchica* |
| | - 'Paddy's Pride' | see *H. colchica* 'Sulphur Heart' |
| § | - 'Sulphur Heart' (v) ♀H4 | Widely available |
| | - 'Variegata' | see *H. colchica* 'Dentata Variegata' |
| | ***cristata*** | see *H. helix* 'Parsley Crested' |
| § | ***cypria*** | WFib |
| | 'Dixie' | NLar |
| | ***helix*** | CArn CCVT CRWN CTri GKir MBar MGos NWea WDin WFar WHer WSFF |
| | - 'Adam' (v) | CWib EBee LAst MBri MTho WFib |
| | - 'Amberwaves' | MBri WFib |
| § | - 'Angularis' | ECot |
| | - 'Angularis Aurea' ♀H4 | EPfP MWht NBir SHBN WFar WFib |
| | - 'Anita' | CBgR GBin WFib WGwG |
| § | - 'Anna Marie' (v) | CMac LRHS MBri SRms WFib |
| | - 'Anne Borch' | see *H. helix* 'Anna Marie' |

| | | |
|---|---|---|
| | - 'Arborescens' | CNat EBee MGos NPal WCot WDin WSFF |
| | - 'Ardingly' (v) | MWhi WFib |
| | - 'Asterisk' | WFib |
| | - 'Atropurpurea' | CNat EPPr GBin MBar WDin WFib |
| | - 'Baby Face' | WFib |
| | - var. ***baltica*** | WFib |
| | - 'Barabits' Silver' (v) | EGoo EPla |
| | - 'Bill Archer' | GBin WFib |
| | - 'Bird's Foot' | see *H. helix* 'Pedata' |
| | - 'Blue Moon' | WFib |
| | - 'Boskoop' | WFib |
| | - 'Bowles Ox Heart' | WFib |
| | - 'Bredon' | MRav |
| § | - 'Brokamp' | MWht SLPl WFib |
| | - 'Bruder Ingobert' (v) | WHrl |
| | - 'Buttercup' | Widely available |
| | - 'Buttercup' arborescent | MAsh |
| | - 'Caecilia' (v) ♀$^{H4}$ | EPfP EQua LRHS MSwo NLar SPer SWvt WCot WFar WFib |
| N | - 'Caenwoodiana' | see *H. helix* 'Pedata' |
| | - 'Caenwoodiana Aurea' | WFib |
| | - 'Calico' (v) | WFib |
| | - 'California Gold' (v) | WFib |
| | - 'Calypso' | WFib |
| | - 'Carolina Crinkle' | CBgR GBin MWhi WFib |
| | - 'Cathedral Wall' | WFib |
| § | - 'Cavendishii' (v) | SRms WFib WRHF |
| | - 'Cavendishii Latina' | WCot |
| § | - 'Ceridwen' (v) ♀$^{H4}$ | CRHN EBee MBri SPlb WFib |
| | - 'Chalice' | EBee WFib |
| | - 'Chedglow Fasciated' | CNat WFar |
| | - 'Cheeky' | WFib |
| | - 'Cheltenham Blizzard' (v) | CNat |
| | - 'Chester' (v) | LRHS MAsh WFar WFib |
| | - 'Chicago' | CWib WFib |
| | - 'Chicago Variegated' (v) | WFib |
| | - 'Chrysophylla' | EPla MSwo |
| | - 'Clotted Cream' (v) | CMac EBee ELon LBMP LHop LRHS MAsh MWat WBod WFar WFib |
| | - 'Cockle Shell' | WFib |
| | - 'Colin' | GBin |
| § | - 'Congesta' ♀$^{H4}$ | EPla GCra MTho NBir SRms STre WFib |
| | - 'Conglomerata' | CBcs ELan EPla MBar NBir SRms WDin WFib |
| | - 'Conglomerata Erecta' | CSWP NVic SRms WCFE WFib |
| | - 'Courage' | WFib WGwG |
| | - 'Crenata' | WFib |
| | - 'Crispa' | MRav |
| | - 'Cristata' | see *H. helix* 'Parsley Crested' |
| | - 'Cristata Melanie' | see *H. helix* 'Melanie' |
| | - 'Curleylocks' | see *H. helix* 'Manda's Crested' |
| | - 'Curley-Q' | see *H. helix* 'Dragon Claw' |
| | - 'Curvaceous' (v) | WCot WFib |
| | - 'Cyprus' | see *H. cypria* |
| | - 'Dainty Bess' | CWib |
| | - 'Dead Again' | GBin WCot |
| § | - 'Dealbata' (v) | CMac WFib |
| | - 'Deltoidea' | see *H. hibernica* 'Deltoidea' |
| | - 'Discolor' | see *H. helix* 'Minor Marmorata', *H. helix* 'Dealbata' |
| § | - 'Donerailensis' | CBgR MBlu WFib |
| | - 'Don's Papillon' | CBgR CNat WAlt |
| | - 'Dovers' | WFib |
| § | - 'Dragon Claw' | EPla WFib |
| | - 'Duckfoot' ♀$^{H4}$ | CBgR CDoC CHal EDAr EShb GBin MTho MWhi WFar WFib WOut |
| | - 'Dunloe Gap' | see *H. hibernica* 'Dunloe Gap' |
| | - 'Egret' | WFib |
| | - 'Eileen' (v) | WFib |
| | - 'Elfenbein' (v) | WFib |
| | - 'Emerald Gem' | see *H. helix* 'Angularis' |
| | - 'Emerald Jewel' | WFib |
| | - 'Erecta' ♀$^{H4}$ | CBgR CTca EPPr EPfP EPla GCal LAst LRHS MBar MGos MTho NGHP NHol SHGN SPlb SPoG SSto WCot WDin WFar WFib |
| | - 'Erin' | see *H. helix* 'Pin Oak' |
| | - 'Ester' (v) | EQua LAst SRGP WFib |
| § | - 'Eva' (v) | MGos WDin WFib |
| | - 'Fanfare' | WFib |
| | - 'Fantasia' (v) | MBri MRav WFib |
| | - 'Feenfinger' | WFib WGwG |
| | - 'Ferney' | WFib |
| | - 'Filigran' | NLar WFib WHer |
| | - 'Flashback' (v) | WFib |
| | - 'Flavescens' | WFib |
| | - 'Fluffy Ruffles' | WFib |
| | - 'Forking Hell' **new** | WAlt |
| I | - 'Francis Ivy' | WFib |
| | - 'Frizzle' | WFib |
| | - 'Frosty' (v) | WFib |
| | - 'Funny Girl' | WFib |
| | - 'Gavotte' | MTho MWht WFib |
| | - 'Ghost' | WFib |
| | - 'Gilded Hawke' | WFib WGwG |
| | - 'Glache' (v) | WFib |
| | - 'Glacier' (v) ♀$^{H4}$ | Widely available |
| | - 'Glymii' | GBin WCFE WFar WFib WTin |
| | - 'Gold Harald' | see *H. helix* 'Goldchild' |
| | - 'Gold Ripple' | SEND |
| § | - 'Goldchild' (v) ♀$^{H3-4}$ | CBcs CDoC CMac CSam EBee EHoe EPfP EPla LAst LCro LRHS MAsh MBar MGos MRav MSwo NBir NHol SAga SPer SPoG SWvt WDin WFib |
| | - 'Goldcraft' (v) | WFib |
| | - 'Golden Ann' | see *H. helix* 'Ceridwen' |
| * | - 'Golden Arrow' | ELan MAsh SPoG |
| | - 'Golden Curl' (v) | CMac EPfP LRHS MAsh |
| | - 'Golden Ester' | see *H. helix* 'Ceridwen' |
| | - 'Golden Gate' (v) | LAst WFib |
| | - 'Golden Girl' | WFib |
| | - 'Golden Ingot' (v) ♀$^{H4}$ | ELan EQua LBMP MBar MWhi WFib WGwG |
| | - 'Golden Kolibri' | see *H. helix* 'Midas Touch' |
| | - 'Golden Mathilde' (v) | CHal GBin LAst |
| | - 'Golden Pittsburgh' (v) | WFib |
| | - 'Golden Snow' (v) | WFib |
| | - 'Goldfinch' | MBri WFib |
| | - 'Goldfinger' | MBri WFib |
| | - 'Goldheart' | see *H. helix* 'Oro di Bogliasco' |
| | - 'Goldstern' (v) | CBgR MRav MWhi WFib |
| | - 'Gracilis' | see *H. hibernica* 'Gracilis' |
| § | - 'Green Feather' | EGoo |
| | - 'Green Finger' | see *H. helix* 'Très Coupé' |
| § | - 'Green Ripple' | CBcs CSBt CTri CWib EBee ECrN EWTr GKir LRHS MAsh MBar MGos MRav MSwo MWht NBro NPri SEND SPer SPlb SRms WBor WDin WFar WFib |
| | - 'Greenman' | WFib WGwG |
| | - 'Hahn's Green Ripple' | see *H. helix* 'Green Ripple' |
| | - 'Halebob' | MBri WFib WGwG |
| | - 'Hamilton' | see *H. hibernica* 'Hamilton' |
| | - 'Harald' (v) | CTri CWib EBee WDin WFib |
| * | - 'Hazel' (v) | WFib |
| | - 'Hedge Hog' | WFib |
| | - 'Heise' (v) | WFib |
| | - 'Heise Denmark' (v) | WFib |
| | - 'Helvig' | see *H. helix* 'White Knight' |
| | - 'Henrietta' | WFib |
| | - 'Hester' | WFib |
| | - subsp. ***hibernica*** | see *H. hibernica* |
| | - 'Hispanica' | see *H. iberica* |
| | - 'Hite's Miniature' | see *H. helix* 'Merion Beauty' |

| | | |
|---|---|---|
| | - 'Holly' | see *H. helix* 'Parsley Crested' |
| | - 'Hullavington' | CNat |
| | - 'Humpty Dumpty' | CPLG MBar |
| | - 'Ice Cream' | MBlu |
| | - 'Imp' | see *H. helix* 'Brokamp' |
| | - 'Ingelise' (v) | WFib |
| | - 'Ingrid' (v) | WFib |
| | - 'Irish Lace' | WFar |
| | - 'Itsy Bitsy' | see *H. helix* 'Pin Oak' |
| | - 'Ivalace' ♀H4 | CBcs CRHN EBee ECha ECrN EPPr EPfP EPla MGos MNrw MRav MSwo MWhi MWht NBid SRms WDin WFib WTin |
| | - 'Jake' | MBri WFib |
| | - 'Jasper' | WFib |
| | - 'Jersey Doris' (v) | WFib |
| | - 'Jerusalem' | see *H. helix* 'Schäfer Three' |
| | - 'Jester's Gold' | ELan EPfP MBri MGos WDin WRHF |
| | - 'Jubilee' (v) | WCFE WFar WFib |
| | - 'Kaleidoscope' | WFib |
| | - 'Kevin' | WFib |
| | - 'Knülch' | WFib |
| | - 'Kolibri' (v) | CDoC CRHN CWan EBee EMil EPfP LAst MBar MBri MGos MWht SMad WFib |
| § | - 'Königer's Auslese' | CRHN WFib |
| | - 'Lalla Rookh' | MRav WFib WGwG WHrl |
| | - 'Lemon Swirl' (v) | WFib |
| | - 'Leo Swicegood' | CBgR MWhi WFib |
| | - 'Light Fingers' | LRHS SPoG WFib WGwG WHrl |
| | - 'Limey' | WFib |
| | - 'Little Diamond' (v) | CDoC CTri ELan EPfP LHop LRHS MAsh MBar MBri MWht NHol SHBN SLon SWvt WDin WFar WFib WHrl WTin |
| | - 'Little Silver' | LRHS |
| | - 'Little Witch' | EPla |
| | - 'Liz' | see *H. helix* 'Eva' |
| | - 'Lucille' | WFib |
| | - 'Luzii' (v) | EBee MBar MGos SGar SHBN WFib WGwG |
| | - 'Maculata' | see *H. helix* 'Minor Marmorata' |
| § | - 'Manda's Crested' ♀H4 | CSWP NLar WFib WGwG |
| | - 'Maple Leaf' ♀H4 | GBin WFib |
| | - 'Maple Queen' | MBri |
| | - 'Marginata' (v) | SRms |
| | - 'Marginata Elegantissima' | see *H. helix* 'Tricolor' |
| | - 'Marginata Minor' | see *H. helix* 'Cavendishii' |
| I | - 'Marmorata' Fibrex | WFib |
| | - 'Masquerade' (v) | WGor |
| | - 'Mathilde' (v) | EBee LRHS MWht WFib |
| | - 'Meagheri' | see *H. helix* 'Green Feather' |
| § | - 'Melanie' ♀H4 | ECha SRGP WCot WFib WGwG |
| | - 'Meon' | WFib |
| § | - 'Merion Beauty' | WFib |
| § | - 'Midas Touch' (v) ♀H3-4 | CWib EPfP MBri WFib |
| | - 'Midget' | CRow |
| | - 'Mini Ester' (v) | EPfP MBri |
| | - 'Mini Heron' | LAst MBri |
| | - 'Mini Pittsburgh' | LAst |
| | - 'Minikin' (v) | LLHF WCot WFib |
| | - 'Minima' misapplied | see *H. helix* 'Spetchley' |
| | - 'Minima' Hibberd | see *H. helix* 'Donerailensis' |
| | - 'Minima' M. Young | see *H. helix* 'Congesta' |
| § | - 'Minor Marmorata' (v) ♀H4 | CHal CWan WSHC |
| | - 'Mint Kolibri' | EHoe MBri |
| | - 'Minty' (v) | EPla LRHS MWht WFib |
| | - 'Misty' (v) | WFib |
| | - 'New Ripples' | MWht |
| | - 'Niagara Falls' | LRHS MAsh |
| | - 'Nigra Aurea' (v) | WFib |
| | - 'Norfolk Lace' | EWes |
| | - 'Obovata' | MRav WFib |
| N | - 'Oro di Bogliasco' (v) | Widely available |
| | - 'Ovata' | WFib |
| § | - 'Parsley Crested' ♀H4 | CMac EBee EPfP EQua MAsh MBar MGos SGar SRms WBVN WFar WFib WGwG |
| | - 'Patent Leather' | WFib |
| N | - 'Pedata' | MSwo WFib |
| | - 'Perkeo' | CHal WFib |
| | - 'Persian Carpet' | WFib |
| | - 'Peter' (v) | WFib |
| | - 'Peter Pan' | WFib WGwG |
| § | - 'Pin Oak' | SIng WDin WFar |
| | - 'Pink 'n' Curly' | WFib |
| | - 'Pink 'n' Very Curly' | WCot |
| § | - 'Pittsburgh' | MGos WFib |
| | - 'Plume d'Or' | CHal WFib |
| § | - f. ***poetarum*** | CNat EPla MBlu WFib |
| | - - 'Poetica Arborea' | ECha SDix |
| | - 'Poetica' | see *H. helix* f. *poetarum* |
| | - 'Professor Friedrich Tobler' | EBee |
| | - 'Raleigh Delight' (v) | WCot |
| | - 'Ray's Supreme' | see *H. helix* 'Pittsburgh' |
| | - subsp. ***rhizomatifera*** | WFib |
| | - 'Richard John' | WFib |
| | - 'Ritterkreuz' | WFib WGwG |
| | - 'Romanze' (v) | WFib WGwG |
| | - 'Russelliana' | WFib |
| | - 'Sagittifolia' misapplied | see *H. helix* 'Königer's Auslese' |
| | - 'Sagittifolia' Hibberd | see *H. hibernica* 'Sagittifolia' |
| | - 'Sagittifolia' ambig. | MAsh |
| | - 'Sagittifolia Variegata' (v) | EBee LRHS MBri NBea WFib WRHF |
| | - 'Saint Agnes' | LRHS MAsh |
| | - 'Sally' (v) | WFib |
| | - 'Salt and Pepper' | see *H. helix* 'Minor Marmorata' |
| § | - 'Schäfer Three' (v) | CWib MRav WFib |
| | - 'Shadow' | WFib |
| | - 'Shamrock' | EPfP MWht WFib |
| | - 'Silver Butterflies' (v) | WFib |
| | - 'Silver King' (v) | MRav MWht WFib WGwG |
| | - 'Silver Queen' | see *H. helix* 'Tricolor' |
| | - 'Spectre' (v) | WHer |
| § | - 'Spetchley' ♀H4 | CHal CMac EPla GCal MBar MRav MWhi NHol NPer SMad WCFE WCot WFib WGwG WHrl WPat WPtf WTin |
| | - 'Spiriusa' | WFib |
| | - 'Stuttgart' | WFib |
| | - 'Sunrise' | MRav WFib |
| | - 'Suzanne' | see *H. nepalensis* 'Suzanne' |
| | - 'Tanja' | WFib |
| | - 'Telecurl' | WFib |
| | - 'Tenerife' | WFib |
| | - 'Tiger Eyes' | WFib |
| | - 'Topazolite' (v) | WFib |
| § | - 'Très Coupé' | CBgR CDoC EBee LRHS MAsh SAPC SArc WDin |
| § | - 'Tricolor' (v) | CTri EBee EPfP LRHS MAsh MCot MGos MWht SHBN WCFE WFib |
| | - 'Trinity' (v) | WFib |
| | - 'Tripod' | WFib WGwG |
| | - 'Triton' | MBar WFib |
| | - 'Troll' | EDAr WFib WPat |
| | - 'Tussie Mussie' (v) | WFib |
| | - 'Ursula' (v) | WFib |
| | - 'White Heart' | MGos MRav |
| § | - 'White Knight' (v) ♀H4 | WFib |
| | - 'White Mein Herz' (v) | GBin WFib |
| | - 'William Kennedy' (v) | WFib |
| | - 'Williamsiana' (v) | WFib |
| | - 'Woeneri' | MWht WFib |
| | - 'Wonder' | WFib |
| | - 'Yellow Ripple' | MBri MRav WDin |

| | | |
|---|---|---|
| | - 'Zebra' (v) | WFib |
| § | ***hibernica*** 🏆H4 | CCVT CDul CSBt EPfP LBuc MBar MRav MSwo MWhi NBlu NWea SPer SRms WDin WFib |
| | - 'Anna Marie' | see *H. helix* 'Anna Marie' |
| | - 'Aracena' | EPla SLPl |
| | - 'Betty Allen' | WFib |
| § | - 'Deltoidea' 🏆H4 | EPla MWht WFib |
| I | - 'Digitata Crûg Gold' | WCru |
| § | - 'Dunloe Gap' | EPla |
| § | - 'Gracilis' | WFib |
| § | - 'Hamilton' | WFib |
| | - 'Harlequin' (v) | WFib |
| | - 'Lobata Major' | SRms |
| | - 'Maculata' (v) | SLPl WSHC |
| | - 'Palmata' | WFib |
| | - 'Rona' | WFib WGwG |
| § | - 'Sagittifolia' | CTri EPfP GBin LBMP LRHS MBar SRms WDin WFar |
| | - 'Sulphurea' (v) | MGos WFib |
| | - 'Tess' | EPla |
| | - 'Variegata' (v) | MBar MGos |
| § | ***iberica*** | WFib |
| | ***maderensis*** | WFib |
| | - subsp. ***iberica*** | see *H. iberica* |
| | ***maroccana*** 'Morocco' | WFib |
| § | - 'Spanish Canary' | WFib |
| | ***nepalensis*** | WFib |
| § | - 'Suzanne' | MBar WFib |
| | ***pastuchovii*** | WFib |
| | - from Troödos, Cyprus | see *H. cypria* |
| | - 'Ann Ala' | EBee EPfP GBin WFib WGwG |
| § | ***rhombea*** | WCot WFib |
| | - 'Eastern Dawn' | WFib |
| | - 'Japonica' | see *H. rhombea* |
| I | - f. ***pedunculata*** 'Maculata' | CWib |
| | - var. ***rhombea*** 'Variegata' (v) | WFib |
| § | ***sinensis*** var. ***sinensis*** | MWht WFib |
| | - - L 555 | EPla |

# *Hedychium* ✿ (*Zingiberaceae*)

| | | |
|---|---|---|
| | B&SWJ 3110 | WPGP |
| | B&SWJ 7155 | WPGP |
| | from Tresco | CKob |
| | 'Anne Bishop' | CKob MJnS WPGP |
| | ***aurantiacum*** | CBct CHEx EAmu EBee LAma LEdu MJnS NScw |
| | 'Big Betty' **new** | CKob |
| | ***brevicaule*** B&SWJ 7171 | CKob |
| | ***chrysoleucum*** | CCCN CHEx EShb LAma SHaC |
| | ***coccineum*** 🏆H1 | CBcs CDTJ CHFP CKob EAmu EBee EBrs ECho EPfP EShb ETod EUJe LRHS MJnS MNrw SSwd |
| | - B&SWJ 5238 | CKob WCru |
| | - var. ***angustifolium*** | CDes CGHE CRHN EBee EPfP WPGP |
| | - 'Disney' **new** | CDTJ |
| | - 'Tara' 🏆H3 | Widely available |
| | 'Corelli' **new** | CKob |
| | ***coronarium*** | CBct CCCN CDTJ CDes CKob EAmu EBee EBrs EShb EUJe LEdu LRHS MJnS MSte SHaC WCot WPGP |
| | - B&SWJ 8354 | WCru |
| | - 'Andromeda' | CKob |
| | - var. ***flavescens*** | see *H. flavescens* |
| | - 'Gold Spot' | CKob MJnS SKHP SSwd |
| | - var. ***maximum*** | ETod |
| | - 'Orange Spot' | EAmu |
| | - var. ***urophyllum*** **new** | IBlr |
| | - HWJ 99684 **new** | CKob |
| | ***coronarium*** x ***gardnerianum*** | MJnS SPer SSwd |
| | 'Daniel Weeks' | EBee |
| | 'Dave Case' | CKob MJnS WVal |
| | ***densiflorum*** | CBct CCCN CDTJ CDes CHEx CHll CKob CPLG CPne EAmu EBee ECha ETod EUJe IBlr LEdu MLLN NScw SDix SSpi WCru WPGP |
| | - EN 562 | CKob |
| | - 'Assam Orange' | CAvo CBct CDoC CGHE CHEx CKob CPne CRHN CSam EAmu EShb GCal IBlr IFoB LEdu MJnS MNrw MSte SChr SDix SEND SMad SSwd WBVN WCru WPGP WSHC |
| | - 'Sorung' | CKob LEdu |
| | - 'Stephen' | CAvo CBct CCCN CDTJ CDes CGHE CHEx CKob CSam EAmu EBee EPfP LEdu MJnS MNrw MSte WPGP |
| | 'Devon Cream' | CCCN CKob EAmu MJnS |
| | 'Doctor Moy' (v) | CDTJ CKob MJnS |
| | 'Double Eagle' | CKob MJnS WPGP WVal |
| | 'Elizabeth' | CDes CKob EBee EMil LEdu MJnS WPGP |
| | ***ellipticum*** | CDTJ CHEx CKob CSec EAmu EBee ETod EUJe LAma LEdu MJnS MNrw SSwd |
| | - B&SWJ 7171 | WCru |
| | - from Doi Suthep, Thailand **new** | CKob |
| | - red bracts | CKob |
| | 'Filigree' | CDes CKob EBee LEdu MJnS WPGP WVal |
| § | ***flavescens*** | CBcs CBct CDTJ CKob EAmu EBee EBrs EPfP EShb EUJe LAma LEdu LRHS MJnS MNrw SChr SSwd WCru WPGP |
| | ***forrestii*** misapplied | CKob |
| | ***forrestii*** Diels | CDes CHEx CKob CPLG EAmu EBee EMil EShb ETod EUJe GCal IBlr LPJP MJnS MNrw MREP MSte SAPC SArc WKif WPGP |
| | ***gardnerianum*** 🏆H1 | Widely available |
| | - B&SWJ 7155 | WCru |
| | - var. ***pallidum*** | CKob |
| | 'Gold Flame' | CDes CFir CKob CMdw EBee EMil LEdu MJnS MNrw WPGP |
| | ***gracile*** | CKob EAmu EUJe LEdu WCru |
| | ***gracillimum*** **new** | CKob |
| | ***greenii*** | Widely available |
| | ***griffithianum*** | CSpe EAmu EBee EUJe MJnS MNrw |
| | - white-flowered **new** | CCCN |
| | 'Hardy Exotics 1' | CHEx |
| | ***hasseltii*** | CKob |
| | ***horsfieldii*** | CKob |
| | ***infundibuliforme*** **new** | CKob |
| I | x ***kewense*** | CKob EMil SSwd |
| | 'Kinkaku' | CKob MJnS WDyG WPGP WVal |
| | 'Lemon Sherbet' | CFir CKob MJnS WVal |
| | 'Luna Moth' | CKob MJnS WPGP |
| | ***maximum*** | CKob MJnS SSwd WDyG WPGP |
| | - B&SWJ 8261A | WCru |
| | - HWJ 604 | WCru |
| | 'Nikasha-cho' | CKob |
| | 'Orange Brush' | CKob |
| | 'Palani' **new** | CKob |
| | 'Peach' **new** | CKob |
| | 'Pink Flame' | CKob LEdu MJnS WVal |
| | 'Pink Sparks' | CKob WVal |
| | 'Pink V' | CKob EBee WPGP WVal |
| | pink-flowered | CDes CKob |
| | 'Pradhan' | CFir CHEx CKob MJnS |
| | x ***raffillii*** | CKob MJnS MNrw |

| | |
|---|---|
| 'Shamshiri' | CKob MJnS |
| ***spicatum*** | CAby CBcs CDTJ CDes CFir CHEx CKob CPLG CRHN EBee EUJe GCal GPoy IBlr LEdu MNrw MSte SSwd WCFE |
| - B&SWJ 2303 | WPGP |
| - BWJ 8116 | WCru |
| - CC 1705 | CKob |
| - CC 3249 | WCot |
| - P.Bon 57188 **new** | CKob WPGP |
| - from Salween Valley, China | CKob |
| - var. ***acuminatum*** | EBee WPGP |
| - 'Singalila' | WCru |
| ***stenopetalum*** | CKob |
| 'Telstar 4' | CKob |
| ***thyrsiforme*** | CKob EAmu EBee EShb EUJe LEdu MJnS WCru |
| 'Tropic Bird' | WVal |
| ***villosum*** | CDTJ CSec EBee EBrs ECho |
| ***wardii*** | CHEx CKob EBee WPGP |
| 'White Starburst' | WVal |
| 'White Wings' **new** | CKob |
| ***yunnanense*** | CDes CHEx CRHN EBee IBlr LEdu MJnS MNrw SBig WPGP |
| - B&SWJ 9717 **new** | WCru |
| - BWJ 7900 | CKob WCru |
| - L 633 | CKob |

## *Hedysarum* (*Papilionaceae*)

| | |
|---|---|
| ***coronarium*** | CArn CSpe EHrv ELan EPfP MBrN MCot NBur WCot WKif |
| ***multijugum*** | CBcs EBee MBlu SPer |

## *Heimia* (*Lythraceae*)

| | |
|---|---|
| ***salicifolia*** | CArn EHig EOHP IDee MBlu MSal SGar |
| - RCB/Arg P-7 | WCot |

## *Helenium* ✿ (*Asteraceae*)

| | | |
|---|---|---|
| | ***aromaticum*** **new** | CSec |
| | 'Autumn Lollipop' | EBee IBal MBNS MCCP MSCN NLar NOrc SBig SPav |
| | ***autumnale*** | CSBt CSam CTri EGoo EPPr GKir LDai LSRN MLHP MNHC MSal NChi SMrm SPet SWvt WBVN WFar WGwG WMoo |
| | - 'All Gold' | SWvt |
| I | - 'Cupreum' | SBch |
| | - Helena Series, mixed | LBMP SWvt |
| | - - 'Helena Gold' | EBee EDAr NBre WPer |
| | - - 'Helena Rote Töne' | EBee LBMP MWhi NBHF SPhx WPer |
| | 'Baronin Linden' | CSam MAvo |
| | 'Baudirektor Linne' ♀H4 | CSam |
| | 'Biedermeier' | CAbx CAby CSam CWCL EBee EBla ECtt EShb LAst LHop MLLN NCob NGdn SPla |
| | ***bigelovii*** | EBrs |
| | 'Blütentisch' ♀H4 | CHVG CMHG CMea COlW CPrp CSam EBee GMaP MNFA NCGa NLar NVic SPoG SPur SUsu WHal WMnd |
| | 'Bressingham Gold' | CSam EBrs MAvo MNrw WBrk WHrl |
| | 'Bruno' | CAby CHar CWCL EBrs EGle ELan ELon GKir GMac MArl NGby NLar |
| | 'Butterpat' ♀H4 | EBee ECtt EHrv EPfP GCra GKir GMaP GMac LBMP MRav NCGa NPri NSti SDix SMrm |
| | 'Can Can' | CSam |
| | 'Chelsey' | EBee EHrv ELan EPfP IBal IPot LCro LSRN MBNS MBri MLLN NBPC NBhm NChi NLar NMoo NPri NSti SPoG WWlt |
| | 'Chipperfield Orange' | CElw CSam ECtt GBri LHop MArl MHar MRav NBre NGdn NVic WOld WOut |
| | 'Coppelia' | CAbx CSam CTca EBrs LBMP NBir NGdn |
| | Copper Spray | see *H.* 'Kupfersprudel' |
| | 'Crimson Beauty' | CAby EBee ECtt ELan LRHS MLLN MRav |
| | Dark Beauty | see *H.* 'Dunkelpracht' |
| | 'Dauerbrenner' | CSam MAvo |
| | 'Die Blonde' | EBee NBre NDov SMHy SPhx |
| | 'Double Trouble'PBR | EBee EHrv EPfP GBri IPot LLHF MAvo MBNS MWea NBPC NBsh NPri SPoG WCot |
| § | 'Dunkelpracht' | CElw CMHG CSam CWGN EBee ECtt EGle EHrv EWll LAst LHop LSRN MCot MLLN MNFA MSte NCob NDov NGdn NLar NSti SMrm WFar WGwG WOld |
| | 'El Dorado' **new** | CSam |
| | 'Fata Morgana' **new** | EBee |
| | 'Feuersiegel' ♀H4 | CAby CSam EBee NBre NDov WOld |
| | 'Fiesta' | CSam EBee |
| | 'Flammendes Käthchen' | CAby CKno CSam CWCL EBee EBrs IPot LRHS NBre NDov SAga SMrm SPhx |
| | 'Flammenrad' | CSam EBee SDys |
| | 'Flammenspiel' | ECtt LRHS MCot MNFA MNrw MRav NGby |
| | ***flexuosum*** | EBee EShb NBre WOut WPer |
| | 'Gartensonne' ♀H4 | CSam NBre SMrm |
| | 'Gay-go-round' | CSam |
| | 'Gold Fox' | see *H.* 'Goldfuchs' |
| | 'Gold Intoxication' | see *H.* 'Goldrausch' |
| | Golden Youth | see *H.* 'Goldene Jugend' |
| § | 'Goldene Jugend' | CElw CMea CSam ECtt ELan MRav WCot WEas WHal |
| § | 'Goldfuchs' | CSam CWCL SDys WCot |
| § | 'Goldlackzwerg' | EBrs GKir MAvo MBri NBre |
| § | 'Goldrausch' | CHar CPrp CSam EAEE EBee EBla ECtt LEdu MDKP MHar MWat NBre NBsh NGdn WOld |
| | 'Goldreif' | CAbx CSam |
| | 'Hartmut Reiger' | CSam |
| | 'Helena' | NLar WPer |
| | ***hoopesii*** | see *Hymenoxys hoopesii* |
| | 'Indianersommer' | CElw CSam CWCL EBee EBla ECtt EGle EHrv GMaP IBal LCro LDai MBNS MLLN NCGa NLar NOrc SMrm SUsu WFar |
| | 'Jam Tarts' | EBee WCot |
| | 'July Sun' | NBir |
| | 'Kanaria' | CAby CHVG CPrp EAEE EBee EBrs EMil EWll LRHS NBsh NCob NLar SMrm SMrs SPoG WMnd WOld |
| | 'Karneol' ♀H4 | CSam LHop NBre SUsu |
| | 'Kleiner Fuchs' | CAby CSam EHrv NLar |
| | 'Kokarde' | CSam |
| | 'Königstiger' | CPrp CSam EAEE EBee EBrs ECtt GMac LRHS MNrw NBre NCGa NDov SMrm SMrs |
| | 'Kugelsonne' | LCro NBre |
| | 'Kupfersiegel' **new** | CSam |
| § | 'Kupfersprudel' | CSam MAvo MRav |
| | 'Kupferzwerg' | CAbx CElw CSam CWCL EBee IPot NBre NDov WEas |
| | 'Loysder Wieck' **new** | NCGa NDov |
| | 'Luc' | CSam |
| | 'Mahagoni' | CSam GBin |
| | 'Mahogany' | see *H.* 'Goldlackzwerg' |
| | 'Margot' | CAbx CAby CSam CWCL NBre SDys SUsu |
| | 'Marion Nickig' | CSam |

| | |
|---|---|
| 'Meranti' | CMea CSam SMrs |
| 'Moerheim Beauty' ♀H4 | Widely available |
| 'Orange Beauty' | EBee |
| Pipsqueak = 'Blopip' | CWCL ECtt GBri GKir LRHS NBre |
| 'Potter's Wheel' | CSam IPot MAvo NCGa NDov SMrs |
| ***puberulum*** | SPav |
| 'Pumilum Magnificum' | CDes CHar CSam CTca CWCL EBee EPfP EWTr GQue LEdu LHop LRHS MWat SPer WFar WPGP |
| 'Ragamuffin' | CSam |
| 'Rauchtopas' | CAbx CAby CDes CSam IBal IPot MAvo NDov SDys SUsu WPGP |
| Red and Gold | see *H.* 'Rotgold' |
| 'Red Army' | EBee GMac IBal LRHS MAvo MNrw MSCN NCGa NGdn |
| 'Red Glory' | EBee EHrv |
| 'Red Jewel' **new** | MAvo WCot |
| 'Ring of Fire' ♀H4 | CSam IPot |
| 'Riverton Beauty' | CSam LLHF WCot WHoo |
| 'Riverton Gem' | CSam ECtt EHrv LLHF NBre NChi WHoo |
| § 'Rotgold' | CMea ECGP ECtt LSRN NBre NChi SGar SRms WFar WMoo WPer |
| 'Rotkäppchen' | CSam |
| 'Rubinkuppel' | CAby NCGa NDov SPhx |
| 'Rubinzwerg' ♀H4 | Widely available |
| 'Ruby Thuesday' PBR | CElw EBee EHrv GQue LLHF LSRN MBNS MWea NOrc NSti SPoG |
| 'Sahin's Early Flowerer' ♀H4 | Widely available |
| 'Septemberfuchs' | GMac LEdu MCot NBre |
| 'Sonnenwunder' | EBee ECha LEdu MLHP NBre |
| 'The Bishop' | COIW CSam EBee EBla ECtt EPfP GMac IBal LAst LEdu LHop LRHS MDKP MLLN MRav MSCN MSte NBro NCGa NPri SPer SRGP SWvt WCAu WFar WMnd |
| 'Tip Top' | EBee EDAr LBMP NHol WHil |
| 'Tresahor Red' **new** | CAbx |
| 'Vivace' | CAbx CSam SMrs |
| 'Wagon Wheel' **new** | EBee WCot |
| 'Waltraut' ♀H4 | Widely available |
| 'Wesergold' ♀H4 | CSam EBee EBla LLHF LSou NDov SMHy SPoG |
| 'Wyndley' | Widely available |
| 'Zimbelstern' | CAby CDes CElw CMdw EBee ECha ECtt LHop LRHS MCot MNFA MRav NDov SMrm SMrs SPhx WAul WFar WPGP |

# *Heliamphora* (*Sarraceniaceae*)

| | |
|---|---|
| ***minor*** | SHmp |
| ***nutans*** | SHmp |

# *Helianthella* (*Asteraceae*)

| | |
|---|---|
| § ***quinquenervis*** | EBee GBin GCal LLHF NLar WFar |

# *Helianthemum* ✿ (*Cistaceae*)

| | |
|---|---|
| 'Albert's Brick' | CFul LIMB |
| 'Albert's Gold' | CFul LIMB |
| 'Albert's Pink' | CFul |
| 'Alice Howarth' | CFul LIMB WHoo |
| ***alpestre serpyllifolium*** | see *H. nummularium* subsp. *glabrum* |
| 'Amabile Plenum' (d) | CFul EPfP GAbr GCal GEdr LIMB MBNS NLar |
| 'Amber' | CFul |
| 'Amy Baring' ♀H4 | CFul CTri ECtt GAbr LIMB LRHS NHol WPer |
| 'Annabel' (d) | CFul ECho ECtt IGor NGby NHol WPer |
| ***apenninum*** | CFul LLHF SRms |
| - var. ***roseum*** | ECho |
| 'Apricot' | CFul CTri LIMB SPer |
| 'Apricot Blush' | CFul LIMB WAbe |
| I 'Aurantiacum' | CFul |
| 'Avalanche' | CFul |
| 'Baby Buttercup' | CFul CLyd CMea LIMB |
| 'Banwy Copper' | CFul LIMB |
| 'Banwy Velvet' | LIMB WBVN |
| 'Beech Park Red' | CFul ECho ECtt LIMB MHer WAbe WFar WHoo WKif |
| 'Ben Afflick' | CFul ECho LIMB LRHS MBNS SPer SRms WFar |
| 'Ben Alder' | CFul ECho LIMB MHer |
| 'Ben Attow' | CFul LIMB |
| 'Ben Dearg' | CFul CMea ECho ECtt LIMB SRms |
| 'Ben Fhada' | CBcs CFul CMea COIW CPBP CTca CTri ECho ECtt EPfP GAbr GKev GKir GMaP LBee LIMB LRHS MHer SPer SPoG SRms WAbe WBVN WBod WBrE WFar WPer |
| 'Ben Heckla' | CFul CSam CTri ECho ECtt EPfP LIMB LRHS MSte WPer |
| 'Ben Hope' | CFul ECho ECtt EPfP GAbr LIMB NHol SPer SRGP |
| 'Ben Lawers' | CFul |
| § 'Ben Ledi' | CBcs CFul COIW CPBP ECho ECtt EPfP GAbr GMaP LHop LIMB MBar MHer MSCN NChi NHol NSla SIng SPad SPer SPoG SRms WAbe WFar WPer |
| 'Ben Lomond' | CFul ECho GAbr LIMB |
| 'Ben Lui' | CFul |
| 'Ben Macdhui' | CFul GAbr LIMB |
| 'Ben More' | CBcs CFul COIW ECho ECtt EPfP GAbr GJos LHop LIMB LRHS MSCN MSwo MWat NBir SPer SPoG SRGP SRms WFar |
| 'Ben Nevis' | CFul CTri ECho GAbr LIMB SPer SRms WFar |
| 'Ben Vane' | CFul GAbr LIMB LRHS |
| 'Bentley' | CFul |
| 'Big Orange' **new** | CFul LIMB |
| 'Birch White' | CFul |
| 'Bishopsthorpe' | CFul |
| 'Blutströpfchen' | CFul LIMB |
| 'Boughton Double Primrose' (d) | CFul CPBP ECho ELan EWes GMaP LHop WEas WHoo WSHC WTin |
| 'Braungold' | CFul LIMB |
| 'Brilliant' | CFul NBir |
| 'Bronzeteppich' | LLHF |
| 'Broughty Beacon' | CFul GAbr LIMB WGor |
| 'Broughty Orange' | LIMB |
| 'Broughty Sunset' | CFul CSam ECtt GAbr LIMB NBir NHol WHoo |
| 'Bunbury' | CFul COIW GAbr LIMB MBrN NBir SPoG SRms |
| * 'Butter and Eggs' | CTca LIMB |
| 'Butterball' (d) | CFul |
| 'Captivation' | CFul GAbr LIMB |
| I 'Carminium Plenum' | CFul LIMB |
| 'Cerise Queen' (d) | CFul CTri EAlp ECha ECho ECtt EDAr GEdr GKev LHop LIMB MMHG MSwo SDix SPer SRms WBVN WHoo |
| ***chamaecistus*** | see *H. nummularium* |
| 'Cheviot' | CFul CMea GAbr LIMB NBir SAga WEas WHoo WPer |
| 'Chichester' | CFul LIMB |
| 'Chocolate Blotch' | CFul ECho GAbr GCra GEdr LHop LIMB LRHS NChi NHol SEND SPla SRms WPer |
| 'Coppernob' | CFul |
| 'Cornish Cream' | CFul CTca ECho GAbr LBee LIMB LRHS |

| | | |
|---|---|---|
| | ***croceum*** | LLHF |
| | ***cupreum*** | CFul GAbr |
| | 'David' | CFul EGoo LIMB |
| | 'David Ritchie' | LIMB LLHF WHoo |
| | 'Devon Cream' | CFul CTca |
| | 'Diana' | CMea LIMB SAga |
| | 'Die Braut' | CFul |
| | 'Dompfaff' | CFul LIMB |
| | 'Dora' | CFul LIMB |
| | double apricot-flowered (d) | GAbr LIMB |
| | double cream-flowered (d) | ECho SPer |
| | double primrose-flowered (d) | CHVG GAbr LIMB |
| | double red-flowered (d) | NChi |
| | 'Eisbar' | CFul LIMB |
| | 'Elfenbeinglanz' | CFul LIMB NGby |
| | 'Elisabeth' | CFul EGoo |
| | 'Ellen' (d) | CMea LIMB |
| | 'Etna' | CFul LIMB STre |
| | 'Everton Ruby' | see *H.* 'Ben Ledi' |
| | 'Fairy' | CFul ECho GAbr LIMB LLHF |
| | 'Feuerbraund' | CFul LIMB |
| § | 'Fire Dragon' ♀$^{H4}$ | CFul CMea ECho EPfP GAbr GEdr GMaP GQue LIMB LRHS MGos NBir NWCA SAga SEND SRms WAbe |
| | 'Fireball' | see *H.* 'Mrs C.W. Earle' |
| | 'Firegold' | CFul LIMB WAbe WFar |
| | 'Flame' | CFul LIMB |
| | 'Frau Bachtaler' | CFul LIMB |
| | 'Gelber Findling' (d) | CFul |
| | 'Georgeham' | CFul CMea CPBP CTca EAlp ECho ECtt ELon EPfP GAbr LBee LHop LIMB LRHS NBir SAga SRms WEas WGor WHoo WPer |
| | 'Gloiriette' | CFul |
| § | 'Golden Queen' | CFul ECho ECtt EPfP GAbr LBMP LIMB MBNS MSwo NLar WFar WPer |
| | 'Goldring' | CFul |
| | 'Hampstead Orange' | CTri |
| | 'Hartshorn' | CFul LIMB |
| | 'Henfield Brilliant' ♀$^{H4}$ | CFul CHVG CPBP CPLG CTca ECho ECtt EPfP GAbr LHop LIMB LRHS MRav MSCN NBir NHol SMad SPer SPla SRms WCot WEas WHoo WPer WSHC |
| | 'Hidcote Apricot' | CFul SPer |
| | 'Highdown' | CFul GAbr SRms |
| | 'Highdown Apricot' | CTca EAlp LHop LIMB LLHF SIng SPoG WFar |
| | 'Highdown Pink' | CFul |
| | 'Honeymoon' | CFul ECtt GAbr GEdr LIMB NHol |
| | 'Ilna's Master' (d) | CFul LIMB |
| | 'Ilona' (d) **new** | LIMB |
| | 'John Lanyon' | CFul |
| | 'Jubilee' (d) ♀$^{H4}$ | CFul COIW CTca CTri ECho ECtt ELan EPfP GAbr LAst LHop LIMB NBir NChi SDix SPoG SRms WEas WFar WKif |
| I | 'Jubilee Variegatum' (v) | CFul GAbr LIMB |
| | 'Karen's Silver' | CFul LIMB WAbe |
| | 'Kathleen Druce' (d) | CFul ECho ECtt EWes GAbr LIMB MWat NHol SAga WHoo |
| | 'Kathleen Mary' | CMea LIMB |
| | 'Lawrenson's Pink' | CFul ECho ECtt GAbr GEdr LAst LIMB MBNS SPoG SRGP WClo WPer |
| | 'Lemon Queen' | CFul CWan LIMB |
| | 'Loxbeare Gold' | CFul |
| | 'Lucy Elizabeth' | CFul GAbr LIMB |
| | ***lunulatum*** | CFul CLyd CMea ECtt GKir LIMB LLHF LRHS NLAp NMen WAbe WPat |
| I | 'Lunulatum Mutabile' | CFul |
| | 'Magnificum' | CFul MWat |
| | 'Marianne' | CFul LIMB |
| | 'Mette' | CFul LIMB |
| § | 'Mrs C.W. Earle' (d) ♀$^{H4}$ | CFul COIW CTca CTri ECGP ECho ECtt ELan EPfP GAbr GBuc LAst LIMB MBNS MWat NHol SDix SRms WFar WPer |
| | 'Mrs Clay' | see *H.* 'Fire Dragon' |
| | 'Mrs Croft' | LIMB WPer |
| | 'Mrs Hays' | CFul LIMB |
| | 'Mrs Jenkinson' | CFul LIMB |
| | 'Mrs Lake' | CFul GAbr LIMB |
| | 'Mrs Moules' | CFul LIMB SRms |
| | ***mutabile*** | CEnt CFul SPhx SPlb |
| § | ***nummularium*** | EBWF GPoy MHer MNHC NMir NSco SHGN WAbe WPat WSFF |
| § | - subsp. ***glabrum*** | CFul NHol NLAp SIng WPat |
| | - subsp. ***grandiflorum*** | CFul |
| | - subsp. ***pyrenaicum*** | CFul |
| § | - subsp. ***tomentosum*** | CFul GAbr MWat NHol |
| I | 'Oblongatum' | CFul LIMB |
| | ***oelandicum*** | NHol NWCA SRms WAbe |
| | - subsp. ***alpestre*** | CFul CLyd NMen WPer |
| | - subsp. ***piloselloides*** | CLyd WAbe |
| | 'Old Gold' | CFul EGoo ELon GAbr LIMB NHol SRms WAbe WPer |
| | 'Orange Phoenix' (d) | CFul EPfP GAbr LIMB MBNS NHol NPri SRot WFar |
| | 'Orange Surprise' **new** | LIMB |
| | 'Ovum Supreme' | CFul GAbr LIMB |
| | 'Peach' | CFul LIMB |
| | 'Pershore Orange' | CFul LIMB |
| I | 'Pilosum Rosea' | CFul |
| | 'Pink Angel' (d) | CBow CFul LIMB MBNS WPer |
| | 'Pink Beauty' | CFul LIMB |
| | 'Pink Glow' | CFul GAbr LIMB WPer |
| | 'Praecox' | CFul CMea CTri CWan ECho GAbr LBee LIMB SRms WHoo WPer |
| | 'Prima Donna' | CFul ECGP NBir |
| | 'Prostrate Orange' | CFul LIMB SRms |
| | 'Raspberry Ripple' | CBow CFul EAlp ECho ECtt ELan EPfP EPot LAst LHop LIMB LRHS NGby NHol SPoG SRms WAbe WFar WHoo |
| | 'Ravens Oranje' | CFul |
| | 'Razzle Dazzle' (v) | CBow CFul LAst LHop LIMB LLHF MAvo SRms SRot WFar |
| | 'Red Dragon' | CFul EAlp EPot LIMB WAbe |
| | 'Red Orient' | see *H.* 'Supreme' |
| | 'Regenbogen' (d) | CFul GCal LIMB SEND |
| § | 'Rhodanthe Carneum' ♀$^{H4}$ | Widely available |
| § | 'Rosakönigin' | CFul CTca ECho ECtt GAbr LIMB MHer WAbe |
| | 'Rose of Leeswood' (d) | CFul CMea CPBP CTca CTri GMaP LBee LIMB NChi SAga SPoG SRms WEas WFar WHoo WKif WSHC |
| | Rose Queen | see *H.* 'Rosakönigin' |
| | 'Roxburgh Gold' | CFul SRms |
| | 'Rubin' (d) **new** | LIMB |
| | 'Rushfield's White' | CFul LIMB |
| | 'Ruth' | CFul LIMB |
| | 'Saint John's College Yellow' | CFul CSam ECho GAbr LIMB LRHS |
| | 'Salmon Beauty' | CFul |
| | 'Salmon Bee' | CFul |
| | 'Salmon Queen' | CFul ECho ECtt GAbr LHop LIMB LRHS NPri SRms WPer |
| * | ***scardicum*** | CFul CMea NLAp |
| | 'Schnee' (d) | CFul EGoo LIMB |
| | ***serpyllifolium*** | see *H. nummularium* subsp. *glabrum* |
| | 'Shot Silk' | CFul CPBP ECtt EWes |
| | 'Snow Queen' | see *H.* 'The Bride' |
| | 'Southmead' | CFul ECho LIMB |
| | 'Sterntaler' | CFul GAbr GEdr LIMB LLHF SRms |

| | | |
|---|---|---|
| | 'Sudbury Gem' | CFul CTri ECha ECho GAbr GKir LIMB LRHS |
| | 'Sulphur Moon' | CFul LLHF |
| | 'Sulphureum Plenum' (d) | CFul ECtt EPfP GEdr LIMB |
| | 'Summertime' | CFul |
| | 'Sunbeam' | CFul CSam ECho GAbr LIMB SRms |
| | 'Sunburst' | CFul LIMB |
| § | 'Supreme' | CFul ECho ELan EPfP EWes GEdr LIMB SRms |
| | 'Tangerine' | CFul ECtt LIMB NHol |
| § | 'The Bride' ♀H4 | Widely available |
| | 'Tigrinum Plenum' (d) | CFul EWes LIMB |
| | 'Tomato Red' | CFul NSla |
| | ***tomentosum*** | see *H. nummularium* subsp. *tomentosum* |
| | ***umbellatum*** | see *Halimium umbellatum* |
| | 'Venustum Plenum' (d) | CFul LIMB WEas |
| | 'Victor' (d) | CFul LIMB |
| | 'Voltaire' | CFul ECho ECtt EPfP GAbr LIMB LLHF NHol |
| | 'Watergate Rose' | CFul ECho ECtt LIMB MWat NBir |
| | 'Watfield Mist' | CHar |
| | 'Welsh Flame' | CFul LIMB WAbe WFar |
| | 'Windmill Gold' | CFul LIMB |
| | 'Wisley Pink' | see *H.* 'Rhodanthe Carneum' |
| | 'Wisley Primrose' ♀H4 | Widely available |
| | 'Wisley White' | CFul CTri EAlp ECha ECho ECtt EGoo EPfP GAbr LIMB |
| | 'Wisley Yellow' | ECtt GKir |
| | 'Yellow Queen' | see *H.* 'Golden Queen' |
| I | 'Zonatus' | CFul LIMB |

## *Helianthus* (*Asteraceae*)

| | | |
|---|---|---|
| | RCB/Arg CC-3 | WCot |
| | ***angustifolius*** | WFar WPer |
| | ***atrorubens*** | EBee LRHS MRav NBro WFar |
| | 'Bronze Teppich' | CFul |
| | 'Capenoch Star' ♀H4 | CElw CPrp EBee EBrs ECha ECtt GBuc GMaP LEdu LPio MAvo MLLN MRav NBPC NBro NLar SDix SEND SMrm SPoG WCAu WFar WMoo WOld |
| | 'Capenoch Supreme' | EBee EBrs ECtt |
| | ***decapetalus*** | CHar WHal |
| | - 'Maximus' | SRms |
| | - Morning Sun | see *H.* 'Morgensonne' |
| | ***divaricatus*** | NBre |
| | x ***doronicoides*** | SRms |
| | ***giganteus*** 'Sheila's Sunshine' | CAby CBre CElw GBri MAvo MNFA MSte NDov WOld |
| | ***gracilentus*** | NBre |
| | 'Gullick's Variety' ♀H4 | CAby CBre EBee ECtt EPfP LLWP NBro NChi STes WOld |
| | 'Happy Days' **new** | EBee MAvo WCot |
| | 'Hazel's Gold' | EBee ECtt NBre |
| | ***hirsutus*** | EBee NBre |
| | x ***kellermanii*** | CAby EBee EMon NBre NDov SAga |
| § | x ***laetiflorus*** | EBee ELan GAbr LPio MDKP MMuc MWhi NBre NLar NOrc WPer |
| * | - 'Superbus' | IBlr |
| § | 'Lemon Queen' ♀H4 | Widely available |
| | 'Limelight' | see *H.* 'Lemon Queen' |
| | 'Loddon Gold' ♀H4 | CElw CHar EBee ECtt ELan EPfP EShb MAvo MRav MSCN NBir NPri NVic SAga SRGP WBrE WBrk WCot WFar |
| § | ***maximiliani*** | EBee ELon EShb LDai LEdu LPio MDKP MSte SPav SWal WPer |
| | ***microcephalus*** | CSam EBee |
| | 'Miss Mellish' ♀H4 | CWan EBee MSCN WBrk WCot WHoo |
| | ***mollis*** | EBee EShb NBre SPav WPer |
| | 'Monarch' ♀H4 | CMea CSam EBee GMac MDKP MRav MSte NBre NCGa SDix SMad SMrm WCot WOld |
| § | 'Morgensonne' | CPrp ECtt EHrv MAvo MWat WCot WFar |
| | x ***multiflorus*** | MBri |
| | 'Anemoniflorus Flore Pleno' | |
| | - 'Meteor' | EBee ECtt MAvo NBre NChi |
| | ***occidentalis*** | WPer |
| | ***orgyalis*** | see *H. salicifolius* |
| | ***quinquenervis*** | see *Helianthella quinquenervis* |
| | ***rigidus*** misapplied | see *H.* x *laetiflorus* |
| § | ***salicifolius*** | EBee ECtt ELon EMon EPPr EShb LEdu LPio LPla LRHS MBri MMuc MSte NBPC NCGa SDix SMad SMrm WCot WCra WFar WHlf WMnd WMoo WPGP WTin |
| | - 'Hot Chocolate' | WCot |
| | - 'Low Down' PBR | EBee MCCP NLar NMoo |
| | - 'Table Mountain' **new** | EBee |
| | ***scaberrimus*** | see *H.* x *laetiflorus* |
| | 'Soleil d'Or' | EBee EBrs ECtt IPot WCAu WHal |
| | ***strumosus*** | WCot |
| | 'Triomphe de Gand' | GBri MRav MWat WFar WOld |
| | ***tuberosus*** | CArn EBee EBrs GPoy SVic |
| | - 'Fuseau' | LEdu SWal |
| | - 'Garnet' | LEdu |
| | - 'Sugarball' | LEdu |

## *Helichrysum* (*Asteraceae*)

| | | |
|---|---|---|
| | from Drakensberg Mountains, South Africa | NWCA |
| | ***adenocarpum*** | SPlb |
| | ***alveolatum*** | see *H. splendidum* |
| | ***amorginum*** Ruby Cluster = 'Blorub' PBR | EBee WFar |
| | ***angustifolium*** | see *H. italicum* |
| | - from Crete | see *H. microphyllum* (Willd.) Cambess. |
| | - 'Nanum' **new** | SEND |
| | ***arenarium*** | ECho |
| § | ***arwae*** | EPot WAbe |
| | ***basalticum*** | WAbe |
| | ***bellidioides*** | see *Anaphalioides bellidioides* |
| | ***bellum*** | NWCA |
| | ***chionophilum*** | EPot WAbe |
| | 'Coco' | see *Xerochrysum bracteatum* 'Coco' |
| | ***coralloides*** | see *Ozothamnus coralloides* |
| | 'County Park Silver' | see *Ozothamnus* 'County Park Silver' |
| | 'Dargan Hill Monarch' | see *Xerochrysum bracteatum* 'Dargan Hill Monarch' |
| | ***depressum*** | EDAr EPot |
| | 'Elmstead' | see *H. stoechas* 'White Barn' |
| | ***fontanesii*** | WHer |
| | ***frigidum*** | CPBP LRHS WAbe |
| | ***heldreichii*** NS 127 | NWCA |
| | ***hookeri*** | see *Ozothamnus hookeri* |
| § | ***hypoleucum*** | CSpe ECha GGar WHer |
| § | ***italicum*** ♀H3 | CArn CEnt CWan ECha ELau GPoy MBar MHer MLHP MNHC NBlu NGHP NPri SECG SPet SPoG SRms WDin WGwG WHCG |
| | - from Crete | GEdr NWCA |
| | - 'Dartington' | CHFP EBee EOHP NGHP SIde WJek |
| I | - 'Glaucum' | CWib |
| | - 'Korma' PBR | CAbP EBee ELan EPfP EWTr LSRN LSou MAsh NGHP NPri SIde SLon SPoG STes WJek |
| | - subsp. ***microphyllum*** | see *H. microphyllum* (Willd.) Cambess. |

| | | |
|---|---|---|
| | - 'Nanum' | see *H. microphyllum* (Willd.) Cambess. |
| § | - subsp. ***serotinum*** | CBcs EBee EGoo EHoe EPfP EPot GGar GPoy MAsh MCot MRav NPri SLim SPer SPla SRms STre SWal SWvt WDin WPer WRHF |
| | ***lanatum*** | see *H. thianschanicum* |
| | ***ledifolium*** | see *Ozothamnus ledifolius* |
| | ***marginatum*** misapplied | see *H. milfordiae* |
| § | ***microphyllum*** (Willd.) Cambess. | EPot GBar MHer MNHC SIde SPer WJek |
| § | ***milfordiae*** 🏆$^{H2-3}$ | ECho EPot GEdr NSla SRms WAbe WPat |
| | ***orientale*** | EBee EPot SPoG |
| | ***pagophilum*** | CPBP |
| § | ***petiolare*** 🏆$^{H2}$ | EBak ECtt MCot NBlu SGar SPer |
| | - 'Aureum' | see *H. petiolare* 'Limelight' |
| | - 'Goring Silver' 🏆$^{H2-3}$ | SPet |
| § | - 'Limelight' 🏆$^{H2}$ | CHal ECtt MCot NBlu NPri SPer SPet |
| | - 'Variegatum' (v) 🏆$^{H2}$ | CHal ECtt MCot NPri SPet SPoG |
| | ***petiolatum*** | see *H. petiolare* |
| | ***plumeum*** | ECou EPot |
| | ***populifolium*** misapplied | see *H. hypoleucum* |
| | ***rosmarinifolium*** | see *Ozothamnus rosmarinifolius* |
| § | 'Schwefellicht' | EBee ECha EGle EPPr EPfP EShb LRHS MLHP MNFA NDov SPer WCAu WEas WKif WSHC |
| | ***selago*** | see *Ozothamnus selago* |
| | ***serotinum*** | see *H. italicum* subsp. *serotinum* |
| | ***sessile*** | see *H. sessilioides* |
| § | ***sessilioides*** | EPot WAbe |
| § | ***sibthorpii*** | ECho LRHS NWCA |
| | 'Skynet' | see *Xerochrysum bracteatum* 'Skynet' |
| § | ***splendidum*** 🏆$^{H3}$ | EPfP NBro SKHP SLon WBrE WDin WPer |
| | ***stoechas*** | CArn |
| § | - 'White Barn' | CSpe EBee WCot |
| | Sulphur Light | see *H.* 'Schwefellicht' |
| § | ***thianschanicum*** | EShb SRms |
| | - Golden Baby | see *H. thianschanicum* 'Goldkind' |
| § | - 'Goldkind' | EPfP NBir |
| | ***thyrsoideum*** | see *Ozothamnus thyrsoideus* |
| | ***trilineatum*** | see *H. splendidum* |
| | ***tumidum*** | see *Ozothamnus selago* var. *tumidus* |
| | ***virgineum*** | see *H. sibthorpii* |
| | ***wightii*** B&SWJ 9503 new | WCru |
| | ***woodii*** | see *H. arwae* |

## *Helicodiceros* (*Araceae*)

| | | |
|---|---|---|
| § | ***muscivorus*** | CHid CStu EBee WCot |

## *Heliconia* ✿ (*Heliconiaceae*)

| | | |
|---|---|---|
| | ***aemygdiana*** | MJnS |
| | ***angusta*** 'Holiday' | MJnS |
| | - 'Yellow Christmas' | MJnS |
| | ***caribaea*** 'Burgundy' | see *H. caribaea* 'Purpurea' |
| § | - 'Purpurea' | XBlo |
| | 'Golden Torch' | MJnS XBlo |
| | ***indica*** 'Spectabilis' | XBlo |
| | ***latispatha*** 'Orange Gyro' | MJnS XBlo |
| * | - 'Red Gyro' | XBlo |
| | ***metallica*** | XBlo |
| | ***psittacorum*** | CCCN MJnS |
| | ***rostrata*** | CCCN EAmu MJnS XBlo |
| | ***stricta*** 'Dwarf Jamaican' | MJnS |

## *Helictotrichon* (*Poaceae*)

| | | |
|---|---|---|
| | ***pratense*** | EBWF EHoe |
| § | ***sempervirens*** 🏆$^{H4}$ | Widely available |
| | - var. ***pendulum*** | EBee EMon GBin MAvo MLLN |
| | - 'Saphirsprudel' | CKno CMdw EBee GBin LRHS WCot WPGP |

## *Heliophila* (*Brassicaceae*)

| | | |
|---|---|---|
| | ***carnosa*** | SPla |
| | ***longifolia*** | CSpe |

## *Heliopsis* (*Asteraceae*)

| | | |
|---|---|---|
| | Golden Plume | see *H. helianthoides* var. *scabra* 'Goldgefieder' |
| | ***helianthoides*** | EMon LRHS MLHP NBre |
| | - 'Limelight' | see *Helianthus* 'Lemon Queen' |
| | - Loraine Sunshine = 'Helhan'[PBR] (v) | LRHS |
| | - var. ***scabra*** | MDKP SRot WMnd WWFP |
| | - - 'Asahi' | EBee EBla ECtt ELan MCCP NLar NSti WHoo WWlt |
| | - - Ballerina | see *H. helianthoides* var. *scabra* 'Spitzentänzerin' |
| | - - 'Benzinggold' 🏆$^{H4}$ | MRav SMrm |
| | - - Golden Plume | see *H. helianthoides* var. *scabra* 'Goldgefieder' |
| § | - - 'Goldgefieder' 🏆$^{H4}$ | EBee EBla EPfP LRHS NBre NBro SMrm WFar |
| | - - Goldgreenheart | see *H. helianthoides* var. *scabra* 'Goldgrünherz' |
| § | - - 'Goldgrünherz' | EBee EBrs NBre |
| | - - 'Hohlspiegel' | EBee LPla NBre |
| | - - 'Incomparabilis' | MRav WCAu |
| | - - 'Karat' | EBee |
| | - - 'Lohfelden' | EBee |
| | - - 'Mars' | EBee |
| | - - 'Patula' | EBee NBro |
| | - - 'Prairie Sunset'[PBR] new | EBee MWea |
| § | - - 'Sommersonne' | CSBt EBee ECtt GKir LBMP MRav MSCN MWhi NBro NGBl NHol NPer SMrm SPer SRms WCAu WFar WMnd WPtf |
| | - - 'Sonnenschild' | EBee |
| § | - - 'Spitzentänzerin' 🏆$^{H4}$ | EBee EBla NBre NGby |
| | - - 'Summer Nights' | CSam EBee LBMP LDai MDKP MNFA MSte NDov NHol SPhx |
| | - - Summer Sun | see *H. helianthoides* var. *scabra* 'Sommersonne' |
| | - - 'Venus' | EBee EBla EBrs ECtt GBri LAst NBhm NLar NSti WCAu WFar |
| | ***orientalis*** | CSec |

## *Heliotropium* ✿ (*Boraginaceae*)

| | | |
|---|---|---|
| § | ***amplexicaule*** | SDys |
| | ***anchusifolium*** | see *H. amplexicaule* |
| § | ***arborescens*** | CArn EPfP EShb MAJR MCot MHom |
| | - 'Chatsworth' 🏆$^{H1}$ | CAby CCCN CSev CSpe ECre ECtt EShb MAJR MHom MSte SDnm SMad WFar |
| | - 'Chequerboard' | MAJR |
| | - 'Dame Alice de Hales' | CHal MAJR MHom |
| | - 'Florence Nightingale' | MAJR |
| | - 'Fowa' | MAJR |
| | - 'Gatton Park' | MAJR MHom MRav SMrm |
| | - 'Lord Roberts' | MAJR MHom WWlt |
| | - 'Marine' | ECtt SGar SPav WGor |
| | - 'Marino 2000' | MAJR |
| | - 'Mary Fox' | MAJR MHom |
| | - 'Mrs J.W. Lowther' | MAJR MHom |
| | - 'President Garfield' | MAJR MHom SMrm WFar |
| | - 'Princess Marina' 🏆$^{H1}$ | CSpe LAst LRHS LSou MAJR MSte NLar SDys SPav |
| | - 'Reva' | MAJR MHom |
| | - 'Seifel' | MAJR |
| | - 'The Queen' | ECtt MAJR |
| | - 'The Speaker' | MAJR MHom |

| | |
|---|---|
| - 'White Lady' | CCCN CHal CSpe ECtt LSou MAJR MHom NLar |
| - 'White Queen' | ECtt MAJR MHom |
| - 'Woodcote' | MAJR MHom |
| 'Baby Blue' **new** | NPri |
| ***peruvianum*** | see *H. arborescens* |

# *Helipterum* see *Syncarpha*

| | |
|---|---|
| ***anthemoides*** | see *Rhodanthe anthemoides* |
| 'Paper Cascade'PBR | see *Rhodanthe anthemoides* 'Paper Cascade' |
| ***roseum*** 'Blanche' | see *Rhodanthe chlorocephala* subsp. *rosea* 'Blanche' |

# *Helleborus* ✿ (*Ranunculaceae*)

| | |
|---|---|
| ***abruzzicus*** WM 0227 **new** | MPhe |
| ***abschasicus*** | see *H. orientalis* Lam. subsp. *abchasicus* |
| § ***argutifolius*** ♀H4 | Widely available |
| - from Italy | EHrv |
| - 'Janet Starnes' (v) | MAsh |
| - mottled-leaved | see *H. argutifolius* 'Pacific Frost' |
| § - 'Pacific Frost' (v) | CBow CLAP EBee EBla EWes MAsh NPro |
| - 'Silver Lace'PBR | CBod CBow CFir CHid CMHG CSpe CWCL EBee ELan ELon EPfP GKir LCro LDai LHop LSRN MCCP MGos MSte NBir NHol NLar NMyG NSti SPer SPoG WPtf |
| ***atrorubens*** misapplied | see *H. orientalis* Lam. subsp. *abchasicus* Early Purple Group |
| ***atrorubens*** Waldst. & Kit. | CDes WPGP |
| - WM 9028 from Slovenia | MPhe |
| - WM 9216 from Slovenia | WCru |
| - WM 9805 from Croatia | MPhe |
| - from Croatia | EBee EBrs |
| - from Slovenia | GBuc |
| - spotted | MPhe |
| x ***ballardiae*** | CLAP MAsh WAbe WFar |
| - double-flowered (d) | CLAP |
| ***bocconei*** subsp. ***bocconei*** | see *H. multifidus* subsp. *bocconei* |
| ***colchicus*** | see *H. orientalis* Lam. subsp. *abchasicus* |
| ***corsicus*** | see *H. argutifolius* |
| - 'Marble' (v) **new** | CSpe |
| ***croaticus*** | GBuc MAsh WFar |
| - WM 9313 | MPhe |
| - WM 9416 | MPhe |
| - WM 9810 from Croatia | MPhe |
| ***cyclophyllus*** | EBrs GBin GBuc GEdr GKir GMaP MAsh MHom MPhe SPer WFar |
| ***dumetorum*** | EBee EBrs GBuc GKir GMaP MAsh NLar WCru WFar |
| - WM 9209 from Hungary | MPhe |
| - WM 9209 from Slovenia | MPhe |
| - WM 9627 from Croatia | MPhe |
| § x ***ericsmithii*** | Widely available |
| - 'Bob's Best' **new** | WCot |
| ***foetidus*** ♀H4 | Widely available |
| - 'Chedglow' | CNat |
| - 'Gold Bullion' | CBow CMHG CSpe MAsh NCGa NHol NSti WFar |
| - 'Green Giant' | MTho |
| - 'Pewter' | CLAP |
| - scented | MHom |
| - 'Sopron' | CLAP |
| - Wester Flisk Group | Widely available |
| N x ***hybridus*** | Widely available |
| - 'Agnes Brook' | WFib |
| - 'Alys Collins' | WFib |
| - anemone-centred | CLAP EHrv NRar WFar |
| - 'Angela Tandy' | WFib |
| - 'Antique Shades' | WFar |
| - 'Apple Blossom' | EHrv WFar |
| - apricot-flowered | CLAP EHrv GBuc SPla WFar WTin |
| - Ashwood Garden hybrids | CPMA EBrs EHrv EPPr EPfP LRHS MAsh MGos MRav SCoo SHBN |
| - Ashwood Garden hybrids, anemone-centred | CPMA MAsh |
| - Ashwood Garden hybrids, double-flowered (d) | MAsh |
| - 'Baby Black' | ECot |
| - Ballard's Group | CBod CLAP EBee GEdr MBri MNFA NCGa NRar SPer WCru WFar WMnd |
| - 'Black Beauty' | GKev MCot WBVN |
| - black-flowered | CLAP EHrv EPPr GBuc SSth WFar WHoo WTin |
| - 'Blue Lady' | CBcs CHFP CWCL EBee EBrs EPfP GBin GEdr LAst MBNS MGos MNFA MSte MWea NMoo SMad STes WBVN |
| - 'Blue Metallic Lady' | CHFP CSpe CWCL EBee LAst MBNS SHBN |
| - blue-grey-flowered | EHrv |
| - Blumen Group | MBri |
| - Bradfield hybrids | EHrv MCot |
| - Bradfield hybrids, anemone-centred | EHrv MCot |
| - Bradfield Star Group | EHrv |
| - Caborn hybrids | LLWP |
| - 'Carlton Hall' | WFib |
| - 'Cheerful' | NBir WCru |
| - 'Cherry Davis' | WFib |
| - 'Citron' | CLAP |
| - 'Clare's Purple' | GBin LSRN WBor |
| - cream-flowered | CLAP CPMA MCCP WFar WTin |
| - 'David's Star' (d) | CFir |
| - deep red-flowered | CLAP NHol WFar WTin |
| - 'Double Vision' (d) | EPPr |
| - double, black-flowered (d) | MDun NRar |
| - double, red-flowered (d) | MDun |
| - double, yellow-flowered (d) | GBin MDun |
| - double-flowered (d) | CLAP GBuc LHop MDun NRar SHBN WFar WHoo |
| - 'Dove Cottage Double Pink' | NDov |
| - 'Dusk' | WCru |
| - 'Elizabeth Coburn' | WFib |
| - 'Fibrex Black' | WFib |
| - 'Fred Whitsey' | WFib |
| - 'Garnet' | WFar |
| - 'Gertrude Raithby' | WFib |
| - 'Gladys Burrow' | WFib |
| - 'Good Little Green' | NDov |
| - 'Good Little Yellow' | NDov |
| - 'Green Ripple' | WFar |
| - 'Greencups' | WCru |
| - green-flowered | WFar |
| - 'Harvington Apricots' | NBir NLar SPoG |
| - 'Harvington Double Pink' (d) **new** | LCro SPoG |
| - 'Harvington Double Purple' (d) | LCro NBir NLar SPoG |
| - 'Harvington Double Red' (d) | GKir LCro NBir NLar SPoG |
| - 'Harvington Double White' (d) | NBir NLar SPoG |
| - 'Harvington Double Yellow' (d) | NBir NLar SPoG |
| - 'Harvington Picotee' | GKir MGos NBir NLar SPoG |
| - 'Harvington Pink' | GKir LCro LRHS MGos MHer NLar SPoG |
| - 'Harvington Pink Speckled' | GKir LCro MGos NLar SPoG |
| - 'Harvington Red' | GKir LCro LRHS MGos MHer NLar SPoG |

| | |
|---|---|
| – 'Harvington Shades of the Night' | GKir LCro MGos MHer NLar SPoG |
| – 'Harvington Smokey Double' (d) new | LCro |
| – 'Harvington Speckled' | LRHS MHer SPoG |
| – 'Harvington Speckled White' | LCro |
| – 'Harvington White' | GKir LRHS MGos MHer NLar SPoG |
| – 'Harvington Yellow' | GKir LCro LRHS MGos MHer NLar SPoG |
| – 'Harvington Yellow Speckled' | MGos MHer NLar |
| – 'Hazel Key' | WFib |
| – 'Helen Ballard' | GKev |
| – 'Helena Hall' | WFib |
| – 'Hidcote Double' (d) | NRar |
| – 'Ian Raithby' | WFib |
| – ivory-flowered | WFar |
| – 'John Raithby' | WFib |
| – Joy hybrids | EBee MBri |
| – Kaye's garden hybrids | EPfP NBPC WMnd |
| – 'Lady Macbeth' | EWes |
| – Lady Series | NSum SHBN |
| – large, pink-flowered | WTin |
| – 'Le Max Creme' | EBee |
| – maroon-flowered | NRar SPla WFar |
| – 'Mary Petit' | WFib |
| – 'Maureen Key' | WFib |
| – 'Monita Nightshades' new | CMoH |
| – 'Mrs Betty Ranicar' (d) | CBro CHFP CPen EPfP ERas EWes GBin LAst LBuc LRHS MBNS MMHG MNFA NBPC NLar NSum SHBN SPoG WCot WFar |
| – 'Mystery' | WCru |
| – 'Pamina' | EHrv |
| § – Party Dress Group (d) | CHid EHrv ELan ELon EPfP LRHS SPoG WFar |
| – picotee Group | SSth |
| – 'Picotee' | CLAP EHrv GBuc NDov NRar SPla WFar WHoo |
| – 'Pink Lady' | EBee EBrs EPfP GBin GQue SHBN SPer |
| – pink-flowered | CLAP CPMA GBuc MBNS MCCP NRar SPla SSth WAbe WFar WHoo WTin |
| – plum-flowered | CLAP EHrv SSth WFar WTin |
| – primrose-flowered | CLAP ELan GBuc NRar SPla WAbe WFar WTin |
| – 'Purple Haze' | CBcs |
| – purple-flowered | CLAP CPMA NHol NRar SSth WAbe WBor WFar WHoo |
| * – 'Purpurascens' | MCCP |
| – 'Queen of the Night' | CLAP EPfP IBal SPad |
| – 'Ray Peters' | WFib |
| – 'Red Lady' | CBcs CHFP CWCL EAEE EBee EPfP GBin GQue IBal MBNS MGos MSte MWea NMoo NOrc SHBN |
| – 'Rosina Cross' | WFib |
| – 'Shades of Night' | EHrv LRHS |
| – slaty blue-flowered | CLAP EHrv GBuc SSth WFar |
| – slaty purple-flowered | GBuc NRar WFar |
| – 'Smokey Blue' | LCro WPtf |
| – smokey purple-flowered | ELan WFar WPtf |
| – 'Snow Queen' | EHrv |
| – 'Speckled Draco' | CPLG |
| – spotted | CLAP EPfP GAbr GBuc LAst MCCP WCot WCru WHoo WTin |
| – 'Spotted Lady' | GBin SHBN |
| – spotted, cream | CLAP NBir SSth WTin |
| – spotted, green | CLAP WFar WTin |
| – spotted, ivory | CLAP |
| – spotted, pink | CLAP GBuc NBir NDov NHol NRar SEND SPla WFar WHoo WTin |
| – spotted, pink, double (d) | GBin |
| – spotted, primrose | CLAP ELan GBuc WFar WTin |
| – spotted, white | GBuc NBir NDov NRar SPla SSth WAbe WFar WTin |
| – spotted, white, double (d) | GBin |
| – 'Sunny' | WCru |
| – Sunshine selections | GKev IBal |
| – 'Tricastin' | CHid SPad |
| – 'Ushba' | CLAP |
| – 'Victoria Raithby' | WFib |
| – Washfield double-flowered (d) | SPoG |
| – 'White Lady' | COIW EBee GEdr GQue MBNS MGos MWea SHBN SPer |
| – 'White Lady Spotted' | CWCL EBee EPfP GQue MSte NBPC NGHP SMad |
| – white-flowered | NRar SSth WCFE WCru WFar WHoo WTin |
| – white-veined | WFar |
| – 'Yellow Lady' | CBcs EBee GQue MBNS MNFA MSte MWea SPer |
| – yellow-flowered | CBow CSec NDov SSth WFar WHoo WTin |
| – Zodiac Group | EBla GBuc LBuc |
| ***liguricus*** WM 0230 new | MPhe |
| ***lividus*** ♀H2-3 | CAby CBro CHar CLAP CSpe EAEE ECho EPfP EWes GKir LHop LRHS MPhe NBir SMrs SPhx SSth SWat WAbe WFar |
| – subsp. ***corsicus*** | see *H. argutifolius* |
| 'Moonshine'PBR | GCai NHol NLar WCot |
| ***multifidus*** | EBee GKir NBir SWal WFar |
| § – subsp. ***bocconei*** | EBee EHrv MAsh MHom WFar |
| – – WM 9719from Italy | MPhe |
| – – WM 9905 from Sicily new | MPhe |
| – subsp. ***hercegovinus*** | EHrv MDun WFar |
| – – WM 0020 | MPhe |
| – – WM 0622 new | MPhe |
| – subsp. ***istriacus*** | CBro GBuc MAsh WFar |
| – – WM 9225 | WCru |
| – – WM 9322 | MPhe |
| – – WM 9324 | MPhe |
| – subsp. ***multifidus*** | EHrv MHom SMHy |
| – – WM 9529 | MPhe |
| – – WM 9748from Croatia | MPhe |
| – – WM 9833 | MPhe |
| ***niger*** ♀H4 | Widely available |
| – Ashwood marble leaf | MAsh |
| – Ashwood strain | CLAP MAsh |
| – Blackthorn Group | CBow CLAP EHrv LRHS |
| – 'Double Fantasy' (d) new | MAsh |
| – double-flowered (d) | ELan |
| – Harvington hybrids | EHrv GKir LRHS MAsh MCot MHer SPoG |
| § – subsp. ***macranthus*** | EBee NCGa NGHP NMoo |
| – ***major*** | see *H. niger* subsp. *macranthus* |
| – 'Maximus' | CLAP COIW EBee EWes NCGa WFar |
| – 'Potter's Wheel' | CDes CLAP CMoH CPMA EBee ECot ELan EPfP GBuc GKir LRHS MRav NBir SHBN SPla |
| – 'Praecox' | CWan EBee EPPr EPfP EWes GBin SHBN SPur |
| – 'Ras Buis' | NMoo |
| – Sunset Group WM 9113 | GBuc |
| – 'White Christmas' | LRHS |
| – 'White Magic' | CPMA GMaP MGos MNrw |
| × ***nigercors*** ♀H4 | CDes CElw CHFP CSam EBrs ECha ECtt EHrv GBin GBuc GEdr GKir GMaP LHop MBri MCot WAbe WCot WFar WPGP |
| – double-flowered (d) | EHrv IBal LSou |

| | | |
|---|---|---|
| | - 'HGC Green Corsican'PBR | LCro |
| | - 'Pink Beauty' | LBuc SHBN |
| | - 'Vulcan Beauty' | SHBN |
| | x ***nigristern*** | see *H.* x *ericsmithii* |
| | ***odorus*** | EHrv EWes GMaP IFoB MAsh MPhe SPer WFar WPGP |
| | - WM 0312 from Bosnia | MPhe |
| | - WM 9202 | WCru |
| | - WM 9310 | GBuc |
| | - WM 9415 | MPhe |
| | - WM 9728 from Hungary | MPhe |
| N | ***orientalis*** misapplied | see *H.* x *hybridus* |
| | ***orientalis*** Lam. | CBcs CChe CSec EPot EWes LAst LCro MPhe MSwo STre |
| § | - subsp. ***abchasicus*** | EBee GEdr MAsh SRms |
| § | - - Early Purple Group | CAvo CBre CTri GCal MRav WFar |
| | - subsp. ***guttatus*** misapplied | see *H.* x *hybridus* spotted |
| | - subsp. ***guttatus*** (A. Braun & Sauer) B. Mathew | EBee GGar NHol SPla SRkn WCru |
| | 'Pink Beauty'PBR | CBcs EPfP MBri NLar |
| | ***purpurascens*** | CSsd EBee EBrs EHrv EPPr GBuc GEdr IFoB MAsh MBNS MNFA MRav NBir SPer WBrE WFar WPnP |
| | - WM 9211 from Hungary | MPhe WCru |
| | - WM 9412 | MPhe WCru |
| | - WM 9922 | EPot |
| | - from Hungary | WCAu |
| | Snowdon strain | GCai LBuc SHBN |
| | x ***sternii*** | Widely available |
| | - Aberconwy strain **new** | CLAP |
| | - Ashwood strain | MAsh |
| | - 'Beatrice le Blanc' | MAsh |
| | - Blackthorn Group ♀H3-4 | CBcs CPMA CSpe EHrv EPfP GAbr GBuc MBri MRav MSte SPoG WBrk WCru WFar WHoo WPGP |
| | - Blackthorn dwarf strain | CLAP EBee GBuc SHBN |
| | - Boughton Group | MAsh |
| | - 'Boughton Beauty' | CAvo CLAP CMea EBee EHrv ELan GBuc LHop MTho NSum |
| | - dwarf | WFar |
| | - 'Joy's Purple' | CPen EBla LAst LRHS |
| | - pewter-flowered | CAby CSpe EBrs |
| | ***thibetanus*** | CFir CLAP EBee EBrs EFEx EHrv EPot EWes GBuc GEdr LAma MPhe WCru |
| | ***torquatus*** | CBro EBee EBla EBrs EHrv MAsh MPhe MTho SPer WFar WTin |
| | - WM 0609 from Montenegro **new** | MPhe |
| | - WM 0617 from Serbia **new** | MPhe |
| | - WM 9106 from Montenegro | GBuc MPhe WCru |
| | - WM 9745 | EHrv |
| | - WM 9820 from Bosnia | MPhe |
| | - Caborn hybrids | LLWP |
| | - 'Dido' (d) | WFar |
| | - double-flowered hybrids (d) | WFar |
| | - double-flowered, from Montenegro (d) | WFar |
| | - - WM 0620 **new** | MPhe |
| | - hybrids | ECGP EHrv WFar |
| | - Party Dress Group | see *H.* x *hybridus* Party Dress Group |
| | - semi-double-flowered (d) | WFar |
| | - Wolverton hybrids | WFar |
| | ***vesicarius*** | EHrv EWes |
| | ***viridis*** | EBee EHrv EPfP GKir IFoB SRms WCru WFar WTin |
| | - WM 0444 | MPhe |
| | - subsp. ***occidentalis*** | CBro EHrv MAsh MHom |
| | - - WM 9401 | MPhe |
| | - - WM 9502 from Germany | MPhe |
| | - subsp. ***viridis*** WM 9723 from Italy | MPhe |
| | 'White Beauty'PBR | CBcs CPen EPPr EPfP EWes LBuc MBri MRav NLar SHBN |

## *Helonias* (*Melanthiaceae*)

| | | |
|---|---|---|
| | ***bullata*** | GEdr IBlr WCot |

## *Heloniopsis* (*Melanthiaceae*)

| | | |
|---|---|---|
| | ***acutifolia*** | GEdr |
| | - B&SWJ 218 | WCru |
| | - B&SWJ 6817 | WCru |
| | ***japonica*** | see *H. orientalis* |
| § | ***kawanoi*** | CDes CLAP CWsd GEdr NMen SKHP WCot WCru |
| § | ***orientalis*** | CBro CLAP CWsd ECho GBri GBuc GCal GEdr GGar LRHS NMen NSla SIng WCot WCru |
| | - var. ***breviscapa*** | CWsd EBee WCru WPGP |
| | - B&SWJ 822 from Korea | WCru |
| | - B&SWJ 956 from Korea | WCru |
| | - B&SWJ 4173 from Korea | WCru |
| | - B&SWJ 5873 from Japan | WCru |
| | - B&SWJ 6380 from Japan | WCru |
| | - from Korea | EBee GEdr SKHP |
| | - variegated (v) | GEdr WCru |
| | - var. ***yakusimensis*** | see *H. kawanoi* |
| | ***umbellata*** | CDes CLAP EBee GEdr SKHP |
| | - B&SWJ 1839 | WCru |
| | - B&SWJ 6836 | WCru |
| | - B&SWJ 6846 **new** | WCru |
| | - B&SWJ 7117 **new** | WCru |

## *Helwingia* (*Helwingiaceae*)

| | | |
|---|---|---|
| | ***chinensis*** | CSam IDee MBri NLar SSpi WBor |
| | ***himalaica*** | CGHE WPGP |
| | ***japonica*** | EFEx NLar WFar |

## *Helxine* see *Soleirolia*

## *Hemerocallis* ✿ (*Hemerocallidaceae*)

| | | |
|---|---|---|
| | 'Aabachee' | CAbx SApp |
| | 'Absolute Zero' | MHar SRos |
| | 'Added Dimensions' | SApp |
| | 'Addie Branch Smith' | EGol |
| | 'Admiral' | CHar WCAu |
| | 'Adoration' | SPer |
| | 'African Chant' **new** | ELan |
| | 'Age of Miracles' | SPol |
| | 'Ah Youth' | SApp |
| | 'Ahoya' **new** | CBgR |
| | 'Alan' | ECtt MRav |
| | 'Alaqua' | CFir EGle EMar LAst MBNS MNrw SApp SHBN SPer WFar |
| | 'Albany' | SMrs |
| | 'Alec Allen' | SRos |
| | 'Alien Encounter' | SPol |
| | 'All American Baby' | EBee MBNS SPol |
| | 'All American Chief' **new** | CAbx |
| | 'All American Plum' | CWCL EMar EPfP GBin IPot MBNS WAul WHrl |
| | 'All American Tiger' | SRos |
| | 'All American Windmill' **new** | CAbx |
| | 'All Fired Up' | EMar SPol |
| | 'Allegiance' **new** | WNHG |
| | 'Alma Atha' (d) **new** | EMar |
| | 'Alpine Rhapsody' | SPol |
| | 'Alpine Snow' | SRos |
| | ***altissima*** | CHEx EBee EMon EPla MNFA MNrw SMrm SPhx |

| | |
|---|---|
| 'Always Afternoon' | CKel EBee EBla EMar GBuc MBNS NCGa SApp SPol SRos WAul WCAu WHrl |
| 'Amadeus' | SApp |
| 'Amazon Amethyst' | WCAu |
| 'Ambassador' | CBgR |
| 'Amber Classic' | SApp |
| 'American Revolution' | CBgR CPar CSpe CWGN EBee ECtt EGle EHrv EPPr LCro MBNS MCCP MCot MNFA MSte NChi SApp SDnm SHBN SMad SPav SPol SRos WAul WCAu WCot WMoo WTin |
| 'Amersham' | EGle MNFA SApp |
| 'Amerstone Amethyst Jewel' **new** | SApp |
| 'Andrew Christian' | SPol |
| 'Angel Artistry' | SApp |
| 'Angel Curls' | EGol |
| 'Angel Rodgers' **new** | SApp |
| 'Angel Unawares' | SApp WTin |
| 'Ann Kelley' | MHar MSte SApp |
| 'Annabelle's Ghost' **new** | CAbx |
| 'Annie Welch' | ELon EPla MBNS NBre |
| 'Antarctica' | SApp |
| 'Antique Rose' | CKel EMar |
| 'Anzac' | COIW ECha ECtt EHrv EMar EPla GMac LRHS NBre NGdn NHol NPri SAga SApp SPav SRos SWvt WMoo |
| 'Apache Uprising' | SRos |
| 'Apollodorus' | EMar |
| 'Apple Court Chablis' | SApp SPol |
| 'Apple Court Champagne' | SApp |
| 'Apple Court Damson' | SApp SPol |
| 'Apple Court Ruby' | SApp SPol |
| 'Apple Crisp' | SApp |
| 'Après Moi' | EBla EMar MBNS MLLN NLar WBrE WCAu |
| 'Apricot Angel' | SApp |
| 'Apricot Beauty' (d) | ECho EMar MBNS NBsh |
| 'Apricotta' | WCot WPnP |
| 'Aquamarine Seedling' **new** | SApp |
| 'Arctic Snow' | CBgR CBro CSec EBee EGle EMar LAst MLan MNrw NBPC NLar SDnm SPav SPoG SRos SUsu SWal WAul |
| 'Ariadne' | CWsd |
| 'Arriba' | MNFA NBro |
| 'Arthur Vincent' **new** | SPol |
| 'Artistic Gold' | WTin |
| 'Asiatic Pheasant' | SPol |
| 'Aten' | MNFA WAul |
| 'Atlanta Bouquet' | SRos |
| 'Atlanta Fringe' | SApp |
| 'August Frost' **new** | CAbx CBgR |
| 'August Orange' | MNFA |
| 'Augusto Bianco' **new** | SApp |
| 'Autumn Red' | CBcs CBgR EBla EMar MBNS MNrw NBir SPol WCot |
| 'Ava Michelle' | SApp |
| 'Avant Garde' | SApp SPol |
| 'Avon Crystal Rose' **new** | WNHG |
| 'Awakening Dream' | SRos |
| 'Awash With Color' | SRos |
| 'Awesome Blossom' | GBin MBNS NMoo |
| 'Azor' | CWsd |
| 'Baby Blues' | SPol |
| 'Baby Talk' | CFir GBuc LRHS |
| 'Badge of Honor' **new** | SApp |
| 'Bailey Hay' | see *H.* 'Bali Hai' |
| 'Baja' | MNFA WFar |
| 'Bald Eagle' | CMCo EGle |
| § 'Bali Hai' | CEnt EMar GBin MBNS MSCN WHrl |
| 'Ballerina Girl' | SRos |
| 'Bamboo Blackie' | EMar SPol |
| 'Bamboo Ruffles' **new** | EMar |
| 'Banbury Cinnamon' | MBNS |
| 'Bandolero' (d) | EBee |
| 'Bangkok Belle' | CWat |
| 'Barbara Mitchell' | MBNS MNFA MNrw NMoo SApp SHar SRos WAul |
| 'Barbary Corsair' | SApp |
| 'Barley Hay' | MSte |
| 'Baronet's Badge' | SPol |
| 'Baroni' | ECha SMrm |
| 'Battle Hymn' | WCAu |
| 'Beat the Barons' | SPol SRos |
| 'Beautiful Edgings' | SRos |
| 'Beauty Bright' | WCAu |
| 'Beauty to Behold' | SApp SRos |
| 'Becky Lynn' | ECtt MBNS SApp |
| 'Bed of Roses' | MNFA |
| 'Bejewelled' | EGol EPla NMoo SApp WTin |
| 'Bela Lugosi' | Widely available |
| 'Beloved Returns' $\Upsilon^{H4}$ | WCAu |
| 'Benchmark' | EMar MNFA SApp SRos |
| 'Berlin Lemon' $\Upsilon^{H4}$ | MNFA |
| 'Berlin Maize' | SApp |
| 'Berlin Oxblood' | MNFA WAul |
| 'Berlin Red' $\Upsilon^{H4}$ | CPrp EBla ECha EGle EMar EPla LBMP MNFA SApp |
| 'Berlin Red Velvet' $\Upsilon^{H4}$ | MNFA |
| 'Berlin Tallboy' | SApp |
| 'Berlin Watermelon' | MBNS |
| 'Berlin Yellow' | CAbx |
| 'Berliner Premiere' | MNFA |
| 'Bernard Thompson' | EMar MNFA SApp SRos |
| 'Bertie Ferris' | NLar SRos |
| 'Bess Ross' | CMHG MNFA WCAu |
| 'Bess Vestale' | GBuc MWat NHol |
| 'Bette Davis Eyes' | CBgR EMar SApp SPol SRos |
| 'Betty Benz' | SRos |
| 'Betty Jenkins' | SRos |
| 'Betty Lyn' | SApp |
| 'Betty Warren Woods' | SRos |
| 'Betty Woods' (d) | SRos |
| 'Beyond' **new** | SApp |
| 'Big Apple' | SApp SPol SRos |
| 'Big Bird' | CMCo CPar EBee LSRN MBNS MWea NCGa SApp SHBN SHar WAul |
| 'Big City Eye' | MBNS SApp |
| 'Big Smile' | CWCL EBee EMar IPot MAvo MBNS MNrw MWea NBPC NBro NMoo WFar |
| 'Big Snowbird' | EMar SRos |
| 'Big Time Happy' | MBNS SPoG |
| 'Big World' | MNFA |
| 'Bill Norris' | SApp SRos |
| 'Bird Bath Pink' | SPol |
| 'Bitsy' | EGle EGol MNFA MSte SPet WMnd |
| 'Black Briar Bay' **new** | EMar |
| 'Black Emmanuella' | CDWL EBee ECho EMar ERCP LDai MBNS MNrw SBch |
| 'Black Eye' **new** | WNHG |
| 'Black Eyed Stella' | CKel MBNS |
| 'Black Knight' | NLar SRms |
| 'Black Magic' | CBro CHar CTri CWat EBee EBla EGol ELan EMar EPla GMaP GMac LRHS LSRN MRav MWat NBir NGdn NHol SAga SMrs SPer SPoG WHer WHrl WMoo |
| 'Black Plush' | SPol SRos |
| 'Black Prince' | CFir EBee MBNS NBPN NBlu NBre NBro WAul |
| 'Blackberry Candy' | MBNS WAul WCAu |
| 'Blaze of Fire' | WCAu |

| | |
|---|---|
| 'Blessing' | SRos |
| 'Blonde Is Beautiful' | SRos |
| 'Blue Diana' **new** | CAbx |
| 'Blue Moon' | SApp |
| 'Blue Sheen' | CFir CPar EBee ECtt EGle EGol EMar GMaP MBNS MCCP MSte NGdn WCAu WFar WMoo WRHF |
| 'Blueberry Candy' | EBee MBNS SApp WAul |
| 'Blueberry Cream' | CWCL EPfP MBNS MMHG MNrw MWea SPad WWlt |
| 'Blushing Belle' | CMil EBla ECGP EMar LRHS MBNS MNFA NBro SApp |
| 'Bold Courtier' | CBgR WCAu |
| 'Bold One' | CMHG SPol SRos |
| 'Bold Ruler' | SPol |
| 'Bonanza' | Widely available |
| 'Boney Maroney' | SApp SRos |
| 'Booger' | SRos |
| 'Bookmark' | EMar |
| 'Boom Town' | EMar |
| 'Born Yesterday' | SApp |
| 'Bourbon Kings' | EBee EGol EMar MBNS NBre SPav WHrl |
| 'Bowl of Roses' | SApp WCAu |
| 'Bradley Bernard' **new** | SPol |
| 'Brand New Lover' | SApp |
| 'Brass Buckles' | see *H.* 'Puddin' |
| 'Brenda Newbold' | SPol |
| 'Bridget' | ELan |
| 'Bright Banner' | WCAu |
| 'Bright Beacon' **new** | SPol |
| 'Bright Spangles' | SApp SRos WEas |
| 'Brilliant Circle' | SApp |
| 'Bristol Fashion' **new** | SApp |
| 'Broadway Valentine' | SApp |
| 'Brocaded Gown' | ELan SApp SRos |
| 'Brookwood Wow' | SApp |
| 'Brunette' | MHar SAga SApp |
| 'Bruno Müller' | MNFA SApp |
| 'Brutus' | EMar |
| 'Bubbling Brown Sugar' **new** | SRos |
| 'Bubbly' | SApp SRos |
| 'Bud Producer' | SPol |
| 'Buffy's Doll' | EBee EMar MBNS MNFA SApp SRos WGob |
| 'Bull Durham' **new** | EMar |
| 'Bumble Bee' | CWat EMar GKir MBNS NBre SApp |
| 'Burlesque' | CWsd SPol |
| 'Burning Daylight' ♀H4 | CWsd EBee EBrs ECtt EHrv EMar EPfP EPla GAbr LRHS MNFA MNrw MRav NBre NHol SMad SPer SRms WCFE WCot WFar WWHy |
| 'Burning Embers' **new** | SApp |
| 'Burning Inheritance' **new** | SRos |
| 'Bus Stop' | SApp SPol |
| 'Butterfly Ballet' | SRos |
| 'Butterscotch' | WFar |
| 'Buzz Bomb' | CWat EAEE ECtt EGle EHrv EMFW EMar LRHS LSRN MHar MNFA MSte NCob NGdn SApp SPer SRos WCAu |
| 'Caballero' | CAbx |
| 'Calico Spider' | SRos |
| 'California Sunshine' | SApp SRos |
| 'Camden Glory' | SApp |
| 'Camden Gold Dollar' | EGol SApp SRos |
| 'Cameron Quantz' | SApp |
| 'Campfire Embers' | GBin |
| 'Canadian Border Patrol' | CWCL EMar EPfP IBal IPot MBNS MNrw MWea NLar SApp SPol SRos WFar WHrl |
| 'Canary Feathers' | SApp |
| 'Canary Glow' | CTri SMrm SRos WFar |
| 'Canary Wings' | CBgR |
| 'Candide' | SApp |
| 'Cantique' | SApp SPol |
| 'Cap and Bells' | EMar |
| 'Capernaum Cocktail' | SPol |
| 'Captain Ahab' **new** | SApp |
| 'Captive Audience' | SRos |
| 'Cara Mia' | CBgR EMar MBNS WFar |
| 'Caramba' **new** | CAbx |
| 'Carmine Monarch' | SRos |
| 'Carolicolossal' | SPol |
| 'Carolina Cranberry' **new** | ELan |
| * 'Caroline' | WHrl |
| 'Carolipiecrust' | SApp |
| 'Cartwheels' ♀H4 | EBee EBla EHrv EMFW EMar EPfP EPla ERas GBuc GMaP LRHS MBNS MNFA NBro SBch SPer SPla SRos WCAu WFar WMoo WTin |
| 'Casino Gold' | SRos |
| 'Castle Strawberry Delight' | SPol |
| 'Catherine Neal' | SPol SRos |
| 'Catherine Woodbery' | Widely available |
| 'Cathy's Sunset' | CKel CSam EBee EBla ECtt EMar EPla EWTr MBNS MSte MWat NBre NBro NGdn SRGP |
| 'Cedar Waxwing' | EGol MSte |
| 'Cedric Morris' **new** | EBrs |
| 'Cee Tee' | SRos |
| 'Celebration of Angels' **new** | SApp |
| 'Cerulean Star' | SApp |
| 'Challenger' | EMar |
| 'Champagne Memory' | SApp |
| 'Chance Encounter' | MBNS |
| 'Chantilly Lace' | CMHG |
| 'Charbonier' | MNFA |
| 'Charles Johnston' | CBgR CKel CMMP EMar LAst MBNS MNrw SApp SRos WAul |
| 'Charlie Pierce Memorial' | EMar MBNS SPol SRos |
| 'Chartreuse Magic' | CMHG EGol EPla SPer |
| 'Cheerful Note' **new** | WNHG |
| 'Cherry Cheeks' | CFir ECtt EGol ELan EPfP LRHS MBNS MBri MHar MRav NBPC NHol SApp SPav SRos WAul WCAu WCot WFar WGob |
| 'Cherry Eyed Pumpkin' | SRos |
| 'Cherry Kiss' | SRos |
| 'Cherry Ripe' | EQua |
| 'Cherry Smoke' | SApp |
| 'Cherry Tiger' | MBNS |
| 'Cherry Valentine' | EBee MBNS SApp |
| 'Chesières Lunar Moth' | SApp SPol SRos |
| 'Chestnut Lane' | SApp SRos |
| 'Chewonki' | EMar |
| 'Chic Bonnet' | SPer |
| 'Chicago Apache' | CDWL CFir EGle EMar EPfP GBuc MBNS MNFA MSte NBir NHol SApp SPer SPol SRos SUsu WAul |
| 'Chicago Aztec' **new** | CAbx |
| 'Chicago Blackout' | CFir CWat EGol EPfP MBNS NBPN NHol SApp WCAu |
| 'Chicago Cattleya' | CFir EGle EGol MRav SApp WAul |
| 'Chicago Cherry' | WNHG |
| 'Chicago Fire' | EGol EPfP GKir MBNS MHar NBPC NBhm SHar |
| 'Chicago Heirloom' | CFir EGle EGol MBNS WAul WCAu |
| 'Chicago Jewel' | CFir EGle EGol NSti WAul |
| 'Chicago Knobby' | EMar MBNS |
| 'Chicago Knockout' | CFir EGle EGol ELan EPfP LPio MBNS SPer WAul WCAu |
| 'Chicago Mist' **new** | WNHG |
| 'Chicago Peach' | IPot MBNS NBir WCAu |
| 'Chicago Petticoats' | EGol NHol SApp |

| | |
|---|---|
| 'Chicago Picotee Lace' | EGle EGol EPfP NGdn SApp WCAu |
| 'Chicago Picotee Memories' | EBee EGle MBNS WCAu |
| 'Chicago Picotee Promise' **new** | WNHG |
| 'Chicago Picotee Queen' | SApp SMrs |
| 'Chicago Princess' | EGle EGol |
| 'Chicago Queen' | GKir WMnd WNHG |
| 'Chicago Rainbow' | CBgR MBNS WAul |
| 'Chicago Rosy' | EGol |
| 'Chicago Royal' | ELon |
| 'Chicago Royal Crown' | ECtt EMar MBNS NBsh |
| 'Chicago Royal Robe' | CWCL CWat EBrs EGol EPla EWll LLWP MBNS MNFA MRav MSte NBid NCGa SWal SWat WCot WTin |
| 'Chicago Ruby' | SApp WWHy |
| 'Chicago Silver' | CFir COIW EGle EGol IPot MBNS SMrm WCAu |
| 'Chicago Star' | SRos WNHG |
| 'Chicago Sunrise' | EBee EBla EBrs EGol EMar EPla GKir GMaP IBlr LPio LRHS MBNS MBri MNFA MRav NGdn NHol NMoo NOrc SApp SPet SRos SWvt WCot WPer |
| 'Chicago Violet' | WCAu |
| 'Chicago Weathermaster' | EMar |
| 'Chief Sarcoxie' $\Upsilon^{H4}$ | SApp SRos WCAu |
| 'Child of Fortune' | SApp |
| 'Children's Festival' | CSpe CWat EBee ECtt EGle EGol EMar EMil EWTr GKir GMaP LPBA LRHS MBNS MRav NLar SApp SRos SWvt WFar WMoo WPer |
| 'China Bride' | SApp SRos |
| 'China Lake' | EMar |
| 'Chinese Autumn' | SApp SRos |
| 'Chinese Cloisonne' | EMar SApp |
| 'Chinese Imp' | NLar |
| 'Chocolate Cherry Truffle' **new** | SApp |
| 'Chorus Line' | SApp SRos WNHG |
| 'Chosen Love' | SApp |
| 'Christine Lynn' **new** | WNHG |
| 'Christmas Carol' | SApp |
| 'Christmas Is' | CBgR EBee EBla EGol EMar MBNS MNFA NMoo SApp SDnm SPav SPhx SPol WAul WCAu WGob |
| 'Christmas Island' | CDWL EMil NBre NCGa |
| 'Christmas Tidings' **new** | SApp |
| 'Churchill Downs' | MNFA |
| 'Ciao' | EMar SApp |
| 'Ciel d'Or' | GKir |
| 'Cimarron Knight' | SPol |
| 'Circle of Beauty' | SPol |
| ***citrina*** | CBgR CHid CPLG CWsd EBee LCro LRHS MCot MNFA MSte NGdn WCot WHrl WTin |
| ***citrina*** x (x ***ochroleuca***) | SMHy |
| 'Civil Rights' | SRos |
| 'Classic Caper' **new** | WNHG |
| 'Classic Simplicity' | WCAu |
| 'Classic Spider' | SApp |
| 'Claudine' | SApp |
| 'Cleopatra' | CPar SRos WAul |
| 'Cloth of Gold' | WCot |
| 'Clothed in Glory' | CWCL MBNS NMoo SApp WCot |
| 'Coburg Fright Wig' | EMar |
| 'Colonial Dame' | WTin |
| 'Colour Me Yellow' | SApp |
| 'Comanche Eyes' | SApp |
| 'Comet Flash' | SPol |
| 'Coming Up Roses' | CPar SApp SRos |
| 'Commandment' | EMar |
| 'Condilla' (d) | SApp |
| 'Contessa' | CBro EBrs |

| | |
|---|---|
| 'Cool It' | CKel EBee EGle EMar GBuc IPot LRHS MBNS NBre NCGa NMoo SApp WCAu WHrl |
| 'Cool Jazz' | EMar SApp SRos |
| 'Copper Dawn' | NChi SApp |
| 'Copper Windmill' **new** | CAbx EMar SPol SRos |
| 'Copperhead' | SPol |
| 'Coral Crab' | SApp |
| 'Coral Mist' | MBNS NBre |
| 'Coral Sparkler' **new** | WNHG |
| 'Coral Spider' **new** | EMar |
| 'Corky' $\Upsilon^{H4}$ | Widely available |
| 'Cornwall' | EMar |
| 'Corryton Pink' | SPol |
| 'Corsican Bandit' | CMMP |
| 'Cosmic Hummingbird' | SApp |
| 'Cosmopolitan' | MBNS |
| 'Country Club' | EGle EGol MBNS NHol SApp WCAu |
| 'Country Melody' | SRos |
| 'Court Magician' | EMar SApp SRos WCra |
| 'Court Troubadour' | SPol |
| 'Crackling Rosie' | EMar |
| 'Cranberry Baby' | CWan EGle EMar SRos WHoo WNHG WTin |
| 'Cranberry Coulis' **new** | MBNS |
| 'Crawleycrow' | EMar |
| 'Crazy Pierre' | EMar SPol |
| 'Cream Drop' | CPrp EBee EBla ECtt EGle EGol EMar EPPr GMaP LFur LRHS MCot MHer MRav NBro NGdn NLar NSti SApp SDnm SPav SPer WAul WCAu WCot WMoo WTin |
| 'Creative Art' | SRos |
| 'Creative Edge' | SDnm SPav WAul |
| 'Creature of the Night' **new** | SApp |
| 'Crimson Icon' | MSte WTin |
| 'Crimson Pirate' | CBgR CBre CHFP EBee ELon EMar EMil EPPr GKev LRHS LSRN MBNS MHer MNFA NBir NBlu NHol NMoo NOrc NPro SApp SPlb SPoG SWat WHrl WTin |
| 'Crimson Wind' | SApp |
| 'Croesus' | NHol SRms |
| 'Crystalline Pink' | SRos |
| 'Cupid's Bow' | EGol |
| 'Cupid's Gold' | SRos |
| 'Curls' | MBNS |
| 'Curly Cinnamon Windmill' | CAbx SRos |
| 'Curly Ripples' | SApp |
| 'Curly Rosy Posy' | SRos |
| 'Custard Candy' | CWCL MBNS MBri NBir NMoo SApp SRos SUsu WAul WCAu |
| 'Cute As Can Be' **new** | MBNS |
| 'Cynthia Mary' | EGle EMar EQua LRHS MBNS MNFA NBro SRGP WFar |
| 'Dad's Best White' | EMar WTin |
| 'Daily Bread' | EMar |
| 'Daily Dollar' | EBee EBla LRHS MBNS NBsh NGdn SApp |
| 'Dainty Pink' | EGol |
| 'Dallas Spider Time' | MNFA |
| 'Dallas Star' | EMar SApp SPol |
| 'Dan Mahony' | MBNS |
| 'Dan Tau' | CKel |
| 'Dance Ballerina Dance' | EBee SRos |
| 'Dancing Dwarf' | SApp |
| 'Dancing Shiva' | SApp |
| 'Dancing Summerbird' | SApp SPol SRos |
| 'Daring Deception' | CFir CKel EMar IPot LAst MBNS MLLN MWea NCGa NMoo SApp WFar WHrl |
| 'Daring Dilemma' | SPol |
| 'Darius' **new** | WNHG |

'Dark Avenger' CSpe MBNS
'Dark Elf' SApp
'Darker Shade' SRos
'Darkest Night' **new** SApp
'David Holman' **new** WNHG
'David Kirchhoff' IPot SApp WAul WCAu
'Davidson Update' **new** WNHG
'Dazzle' SApp
'Decatur Ballerina' **new** WNHG
'Decatur Captivation' **new** WNHG
'Decatur Dictator' **new** WNHG
'Decatur Imp' EGol
'Decatur Rhythm' **new** WNHG
'Decatur Supreme' **new** WNHG
'Decatur Treasure Chest' **new** WNHG
'Dee Dee Mac' SApp
'Deep Fire' SRos
'Delicate Design' SApp
'Delightsome' SRos
'Demetrius' MNFA MWea SApp
'Desdemona' CMil
'Desert Bandit' **new** SApp
'Designer Gown' SApp
'Designer Jeans' SPol SRos
'Destined to See' CBcs CDWL CFir CHFP CMHG CPar CWGN CWan EBee ECtt EGle EHrv EMar LDai LHop LSou MBNS NBro NCob SAga SApp SPav SPer WBVN WCot WHrl
'Devil's Footprint' SPol
'Devonshire' SApp SRos
'Dewberry Candy' SRos
'Diamond Dust' CKel EBee EGle EMar EPla LRHS MBNS MSte NLar SApp SPer SPhx WTin
'Dido' CTri GBuc
'Diva Assoluta' SApp
'Divertissment' CBgR ELon EMar SApp
'Dixie Stampede' **new** CAbx
'Doll House' SRos
'Dominic' CPar EBee EMar SApp SRos WMoo
'Dorethe Louise' CBgR SPol SRos
'Dorothy McDade' COIW
'Dottie's Rompers' EMar
'Double Action' (d) SPol
'Double Coffee' (d) SApp SPav SPol
'Double Confetti' (d) SApp
'Double Corsage' (d) SApp SPol
'Double Cutie' (d) CMCo MBNS NBre NLar WAul
'Double Daffodil' (d) WCAu
'Double Dream' (d) EMar GBuc
'Double Entendre' **new** EMar
'Double Firecracker' (d) CBcs CWCL CWat EMar IBal MBNS NBro NLar NMoo SMrm WHrl
'Double Grapette' (d) SApp
'Double Oh Seven' (d) ELon SApp
'Double Passion' (d) **new** MBNS
'Double Pink Treasure' (d) SApp
'Double Pompon' (d) WCAu
'Double Red Royal' (d) **new** EMar
'Double River Wye' (d) CBgR CDWL CFir COIW CWat EBee ECtt EGol EMar EMil IPot MBNS MNrw MSte NGdn NPri SApp SHBN SHar SPoG SPol SRos SWat WAul WCot WHoo WMnd WTin
§ 'Doubloon' COIW GBuc NHol
'Dragon Dreams' SApp
'Dragon King' SPol
'Dragon Lore' **new** MBNS
'Dragon Mouth' EGol
'Dragon's Eye' CWat SApp
'Dragon's Orb' CKel
'Dream Baby' NBre
'Dreamy Cream' SRos
'Dresden Doll' SPer
'Driven Snow' SApp
'Duke of Durham' MBNS SApp SMeo
***dumortieri*** CBro CSam ECha EGol EHrv ELan EMar EPla GBri GGar LFur MCot MNFA MNrw MRav NBid NBir NHol NSti NVic SPer WCot WHrl WTin
– B&SWJ 1283 WCru
'Dune Needlepoint' SPol
'Dutch Beauty' EMar EPla WFar
'Dutch Gold' MNrw NBro
'Dynasty Pink' SApp
'Earl Barfield' **new** EMar
'Earl of Warwick' **new** CAbx
'Earlianna' CAbx SPol
'Earth Angel' SApp SPol
'Easy Ned' EMar SRos WTin
'Ed Kirchhoff' **new** EMar
'Ed Murray' GBin MNFA NBPN SRos WAul WCAu
'Edgar Brown' MBNS
'Edge Ahead' MBNS
'Edge of Darkness' CKel CWGN EGle EPfP IPot MWea NBro NLar NSti SApp SDnm SPav WAul WCAu WFar
'Edna Spalding' EBrs SApp SRos
'Eenie Allegro' CBgR CBro EGol IBal MBNS SPer SPla WHil WMnd
'Eenie Fanfare' EGle EGol LRHS MBNS MLan MNFA NBir WAul
'Eenie Gold' LRHS
'Eenie Weenie' CBro CFee EBla ECtt EGle EGol EPla ERos GKir IBal MBNS MHar MNFA NBro NBur SAga SApp SHBN SPer SRms WPer
'Eenie Weenie Non-stop' CMoH EPPr
'Eggplant Escapade' EMar SPol SRos
'Egyptian Ibis' WMnd WNHG
'Egyptian Queen' SRos
'El Desperado' Widely available
'El Glorioso' EMar
'El Padre' SApp
'Elaine Strutt' EGol MBNS MNFA MNrw NCGa NMoo SApp SRos SWvt
'Elegant Candy' CKel EBee MBNS MLan NMoo SApp SRos WGob
'Eleonor' **new** SApp
'Elizabeth Salter' CWCL EBee IPot MBNS NLar NMoo SApp SPol SRos SUsu WCAu
'Elizabeth Yancey' EGol
'Elsie Spalding' **new** GKir
'Embuscade' EMar
'Emerald Enchantment' SApp
'Emerald Lady' SRos
'Emily Anne' SApp
'Emily Jaye' SApp
'Emmaus' **new** SApp
'Emperor Butterfly' SApp
'English Toffee' SApp
'Entransette' SApp
'Entrapment' MBNS
'Erin Prairie' SApp
***esculenta*** SMad
'Eternal Blessing' SPol SRos
'Ethel Smith' SApp
'Etruscan Tomb' SPol
'Etrusque' **new** EMar
'Evelyn Lela Stout' SApp
'Evening Bell' SApp

| | Name | Suppliers |
|---|---|---|
| | 'Evening Enchantment' **new** | SRos |
| | 'Evening Glow' | SApp SRos |
| | 'Ever So Ruffled' | SRos |
| | 'Eye-yi-yi' | SPol |
| | 'Ezekiel' | EMar |
| | 'Fabergé' | SApp |
| | 'Fabulous Paradise' **new** | EMar |
| | 'Fabulous Prize' | SApp SRos |
| | 'Fairest Love' | EBee EMar LDai MBNS |
| | 'Fairy Charm' | SApp |
| | 'Fairy Summerbird' | SApp SRos |
| | 'Fairy Tale Pink' | MNFA SApp SPol SRos |
| | 'Fairy Wings' | SPer |
| | 'Faith Nabor' | EMar SRos |
| | 'Fall Farewell' **new** | WNHG |
| | 'Fall Guy' | SApp |
| | 'Fama' | GKir SRos |
| | 'Fan Club' | EMar GKir |
| | 'Fan Dancer' | EGol |
| | 'Fandango' | LPla MNFA |
| | 'Farmer's Daughter' | SApp SRos |
| | 'Fashion Model' | SApp WPer |
| | 'Fazzle' | SApp |
| | 'Feather Down' | SPol |
| | 'Feathered Fascination' **new** | SApp |
| | 'Feelings' | SApp |
| | 'Femme Osage' | SRos |
| | 'Ferris Wheel' | CBgR SApp |
| | 'Festive Art' | SRos |
| | 'Final Touch' | CBgR IPot MBNS MLLN MWea NBhm NBro WGob |
| | 'Finlandia' | MNFA |
| | 'Fire Dance' | SRos |
| | 'Fire from Heaven' | SApp |
| | 'Fire Tree' | CBgR SPol |
| | 'Firestorm' | CAbx SApp SPol |
| | 'First Formal' | SPer |
| | 'Flames of Fantasy' | SRos |
| | 'Flaming Sword' | EBee GBuc NHol WRHF |
| | ***flava*** | see *H. lilioasphodelus* |
| | 'Fleeting Fancy' | SRos |
| | 'Flight of the Dragon' **new** | SApp |
| | 'Flint Lace' | SApp |
| | 'Flower Pavilion' **new** | SPol |
| | 'Flutterbye' | SRos |
| | 'Fly Catcher' | CBgR EMar SRos |
| | 'Flyaway Home' | SPol |
| | 'Fol de Rol' | SRos |
| | 'Fooled Me' | CAbx EBee MWea SRos |
| | 'Forgotten Dreams' | CWCL MBNS MWea SPoG |
| | ***forrestii*** | CExc |
| | - 'Perry's Variety' | EMon |
| | 'Forsyth Tangerine Ruffles' | GKir |
| | 'Forsyth White Sentinal' | SRos |
| | 'Forty Second Street' | CFir EBee MBNS MLLN NCGa NMoo SApp WFar |
| | 'Fragrant Bouquet' | SRos |
| | 'Fragrant Pastel Cheers' | SRos |
| | 'Frances Fay' | SPol SRos WAul |
| | 'Frandean' | MNFA |
| | 'Frank Gladney' | MNFA SApp SRos |
| | 'Frans Hals' | Widely available |
| | 'French Doll' | SApp |
| | 'Frosted Encore' | SApp |
| | 'Frozen Jade' | SRos |
| | 'Fuchsia Dream' | EMar |
| | 'Fuchsia Fashion' | SApp |
| | 'Full Reward' | WCAu |
| | ***fulva*** | CTri ELan LRHS MHar NBir NBre SGar SHBN SPol SRms WBrk WHrl |
| N | - 'Flore Pleno' (d) | Widely available |
| N | - 'Green Kwanso' (d) | CBgR CPLG CSWP ECGP ECha EMon EPla LBMP MMHG NVic SMad SPla WAul WFar WPnP WRha WTin |
| | - var. ***kwanso*** B&SWJ 6328 | WCru |
| * | - 'Kwanso' ambig. (d) | NOrc |
| | - var. ***littorea*** | EPla |
| | - var. ***rosea*** | EMon MNFA SMHy WCot |
| § | - 'Variegated Kwanso' (d/v) | CBow CRow EBee EGle EMon EPPr GCal GCra MRav MTho NBir SBod SPav SUsu WCot WFar WHer WHoo |
| | 'Fun Fling' **new** | SPol |
| | 'Funky Fuchsia' | SPol |
| | 'Gadsden Goliath' | SPol |
| | 'Gadsden Light' | SPol |
| | 'Gala Gown' | SApp |
| | 'Garden Portrait' | CMil SRos |
| | 'Gaucho' | MNFA |
| | 'Gauguin' **new** | EMar |
| | 'Gay Music' | SPoG |
| | 'Gay Octopus' | CAbx CBgR EMar SPol SRos |
| | 'Gay Rapture' | SPer |
| | 'Gemini' | SRos |
| | 'Gentle Country Breeze' | SApp SPol SRos |
| | 'Gentle Shepherd' | Widely available |
| | 'George Cunningham' | ECtt EGol EHrv ELan MNFA MRav NBir SMrs SPol SRos SUsu WCAu WFar |
| | 'Georgetown Lovely' **new** | SRos |
| | 'Georgette Belden' | EBee EBla ECGP ECtt EMar MBri MMHG NBsh NHol SPol WTin |
| | 'German Ballerina' | SPol |
| | 'Get All Excited' **new** | SPol |
| | 'Giant Moon' | CMHG EBee EBrs ELan EMar EPla LRHS MBNS NHol SPer SRms WFar WHal |
| | 'Gingerbread Man' | SApp |
| | 'Girl Scout' | SApp SRos |
| | 'Glacier Bay' | CBgR LHop MBNS NCGa |
| | 'Glazed Heather Plum' | SApp |
| | 'Gleber's Top Cream' | SApp |
| | 'Glomunda' | SApp |
| | 'Glory's Legacy' | SRos |
| | 'Glowing Gold' | WCAu |
| | 'Glowing Heart' **new** | SApp |
| | 'Gold Dust' | SRos |
| | 'Gold Imperial' | NBre |
| | 'Golden Bell' | NGdn NHol |
| | 'Golden Chance' | WCAu |
| | 'Golden Chimes' $\Upsilon^{H4}$ | Widely available |
| | 'Golden Empress' | SApp |
| | 'Golden Ginkgo' | LRHS MBri MNFA SApp |
| | 'Golden Orchid' | see *H.* 'Doubloon' |
| | 'Golden Peace' | SRos |
| | 'Golden Prize' | CBgR EPla GQue MNFA NGdn NPri SApp SRos WCot WFar |
| | 'Golden Scroll' | SApp SRos |
| | Golden Zebra = 'Malja'$^{PBR}$ (v) | CWGN ELan EPfP LBuc MBNS MGos MRav NLar NSti SDnm SPoG WFar |
| | 'Goldeneye' | SApp |
| | 'Golliwog' | CBgR |
| | 'Good Looking' | EGol |
| | 'Grace and Favour' | SPol |
| | 'Graceful Eye' | SApp SRos |
| | 'Graceland' | EMar |
| | 'Grain de Lumière' | EMar |
| | 'Grand Masterpiece' | CMMP IPot NGdn SPet WAul |
| | 'Grand Palais' | SApp SRos |
| | 'Grape Magic' | EGol SRos WTin |

| | |
|---|---|
| 'Grape Velvet' | CHar CPar CSpe EGle EGol MBNS MCCP MHar MNFA NBre NMyG NSti SApp SRos WAul WCAu WMnd |
| 'Great Northern' | SApp |
| 'Green Dolphin Street' | SRos |
| 'Green Drop' | SAga WFar |
| 'Green Eyed Giant' | MNFA |
| 'Green Flutter' ♀H4 | EBee EPfP GCal LPio LPla LRHS LSRN MBNS MNFA NBir NBre NGdn NSti SApp SPhx SPol SRos WWlt |
| 'Green Glitter' | MNFA |
| 'Green Gold' | CMHG |
| 'Green Puff' | NBir |
| 'Green Spider' | SRos |
| 'Green Valley' | MNFA |
| 'Grumbly' | ELan WPnP |
| 'Guardian Angel' | WCFE WTin |
| 'Gusto' | WCAu |
| 'Gypsy Ballerina' **new** | SApp |
| 'Happy Hopi' **new** | SApp |
| 'Happy Returns' | CBgR CHid CSBt CTri EBee EBla ECha EGol ELan EMar IBal LAst LSRN MBNS MBri MHar MNFA MSte NGdn SApp SRGP SRos WCAu WCFE WTin |
| 'Harbor Blue' | SApp |
| 'Harvest Hue' | MHar |
| 'Havana Banana' **new** | SApp |
| 'Hawaiian Punch' | EGol |
| 'Hawaiian Purple' | EGol |
| 'Hawk' | SApp SPol |
| 'Hazel' | SRos |
| 'Hazel Monette' | EGol |
| 'Heartthrob' | WCAu |
| 'Heather Green' | SApp |
| 'Heavenly Treasure' | SApp SRos |
| 'Heidi Eidelweiss' | CPLG |
| 'Heirloom Lace' | WCAu WFar |
| 'Helen Boehm' | EMar |
| 'Helle Berlinerin' ♀H4 | MNFA SApp SPol SRos |
| 'Helter Skelter' | EMar |
| 'Her Majesty's Wizard' | MAvo MBNS MHer NBro SPol |
| 'Hercules' | NBre |
| 'Hey There' | SRos |
| 'High Energy' | SApp |
| 'High Mogul' **new** | EMar |
| 'High Tor' | GBin GQui MNFA SPol WTin |
| 'Highland Belle' | SApp |
| 'Highland Lord' (d) | EPfP MBNS SApp |
| 'Highland Summerbird' **new** | SApp |
| 'Holiday Mood' | ELan SApp |
| 'Holly Dancer' | CAbx SPol |
| 'Honey Jubilee' | SPol |
| 'Honey Redhead' | SRos |
| 'Hope Diamond' | WCAu |
| 'Hornby Castle' | CBro EBrs LRHS NHol WPer |
| 'Hot Chocolate' PBR **new** | CFwr CSec |
| 'Hot Ticket' | SApp SRos |
| 'Hot Town' | ELan |
| 'Hot Wheels' | EMar |
| 'Hot Wire' | SRos |
| 'Houdini' | EGle EGol WCAu WMnd |
| 'House of Orange' | SApp SPol |
| 'Howard Goodson' | MNFA |
| 'Humdinger' | SRos |
| 'Hummingbird' **new** | CAbx |
| 'Hyperion' | CBgR CPrp CSev CTri CWat EBee ECha ECtt EGol EPfP LAst LCro LEdu MLan MNFA MRav NGdn NHol SApp SHBN SMrs SPer SPla SPoG SRos SUsu WCot |

| | |
|---|---|
| 'Ice Carnival' | CKel EBee EGle ELon EPfP LAst LCro LDai LRHS MBNS MNFA NBhm NBre NGdn NOrc SApp SPet SPoG |
| 'Ice Castles' | CTri SApp |
| 'Ice Cool' | SApp SRos |
| 'Icecap' | CBgR WAul WFar WMoo WPnP |
| 'Icy Lemon' | SRos |
| 'Ida Duke Miles' | SRos |
| 'Ida Munson' | EGol |
| 'Ida's Magic' | EBee SApp WFar |
| 'Imperator' | EPla LPBA NHol |
| 'Imperial Lemon' | SApp |
| 'In Depth' (d) | EPfP MBNS NBro NCGa NLar SWal WCot |
| 'In Strawberry Time' **new** | WNHG |
| 'Indian Chief' **new** | WHoo |
| 'Indian Paintbrush' | EGle LHop MBri MHar NBir SPol WCAu |
| 'Indian Sky' | SRos |
| 'Indigo Moon' | SApp |
| 'Inky Fingers' **new** | SApp |
| 'Inner View' | ECtt MBNS NLar SApp WMnd |
| 'Inspired Word' | SRos |
| 'Invicta' | SRos |
| 'Irish Elf' | ELon GBuc GMac SApp WTin |
| 'Isle of Capri' | SRos |
| 'Isle of Dreams' | SPol |
| 'Isolde' **new** | CAbx |
| 'Ivelyn Brown' **new** | CAbx SRos |
| 'Jake Russell' | CWsd LCro MNFA SAga |
| 'James Marsh' | CBgR EGle EPfP EWes MBNS MBri MNFA MNrw NCGa NSti SApp SRos WAul WCAu WCot WMnd |
| 'Janet Gordon' | SPol SRos |
| 'Janice Brown' | CKel CWCL EMar MBNS MNFA NLar NMoo SApp SPol SRos |
| 'Jan's Twister' | MNrw SApp SRos |
| 'Jason Salter' | SApp WAul |
| 'Jay Turman' | SApp |
| 'Jazz Diva' | EMar |
| 'Jean Swann' | MBNS |
| 'Jedi Brenda Spann' | SApp |
| 'Jedi Dot Pierce' | SApp SRos |
| 'Jedi Irish Spring' | SApp |
| 'Jedi Rose Frost' | SApp |
| 'Jedi Rust Frost' | SApp |
| 'Jenny Wren' | EBee EBla EMar EPPr EPla ETod MBNS MNFA NBre NBro NHol SRGP WAul WCAu |
| 'Jersey Spider' | EMar |
| 'Jerusalem' | SRos |
| 'Jesse James' | SApp SPol |
| 'Jo Jo' | WCAu |
| 'Joan Cook' | EGle |
| 'Joan Senior' | Widely available |
| 'Jocelyn's Oddity' | SApp |
| 'Jock Randall' | MNFA |
| 'Jockey Club' (d) | EMar MBNS |
| 'Joe Marinello' **new** | SPol |
| 'Jogolor' **new** | CAbx |
| 'John Bierman' | SRos |
| 'John Robert Biggs' | SApp |
| 'Jolyene Nichole' | SApp SRos |
| 'Jovial' | SApp SRos |
| 'Judah' | SApp SRos |
| 'Judge Roy Bean' | SPol SRos |
| 'Jungle Beauty' **new** | CBgR |
| 'Justin George' **new** | SPol |
| 'Kate Carpenter' | SRos |
| 'Kathleen Salter' | SRos |
| 'Katie Elizabeth Miller' | SRos |
| 'Kazuq' | SApp |

| | |
|---|---|
| 'Kecia' | MNFA |
| 'Kelly's Girl' | SRos |
| 'Kempion' | EMar |
| 'Kent's Favorite Two' | SRos |
| 'Kimmswick' | SApp |
| 'Kindly Light' | EMar MNFA SPol SRos WCAu |
| 'King Haiglar' | EGol SApp SPhx SRos |
| N 'Kwanso Flore Pleno' | see *H. fulva* 'Green Kwanso' |
| N 'Kwanso Flore Pleno Variegata' | see *H. fulva* 'Variegated Kwanso' |
| 'Lacy Doily' new | MBNS |
| 'Lacy Marionette' | EMar SApp SPol SRos |
| 'Lady Cynthia' | CKel |
| 'Lady Fingers' | CBgR EMar MNFA |
| 'Lady Hillary' | SApp |
| 'Lady Inma' | SApp |
| 'Lady Liz' | MNFA |
| 'Lady Mischief' | SApp |
| 'Lady Neva' | CBgR CPar SApp SRos |
| 'Ladykin' | SApp SPol SRos |
| 'Lake Norman Spider' | MNFA SApp |
| 'Land of Cotton' new | EMar |
| 'Land's End' new | CAbx |
| 'Lark Song' | EBrs EGol SRos WFar |
| 'Laughing Giraffe' new | CAbx |
| 'Lauren Leah' | SRos |
| 'Lavender Arrowhead' new | SApp |
| 'Lavender Bonanza' | WCAu WCFE |
| 'Lavender Deal' | EBee EMar MNrw WNHG |
| 'Lavender Flushing' | SApp |
| 'Lavender Illusion' | SApp |
| 'Lavender Silver Cords' | SPol |
| 'Lavender Spider' | SApp |
| 'Leebea Orange Crush' | EMar |
| 'Lemon Bells' ♀H4 | EBee EBla ECGP ECha EGle EMFW EMar EPfP GMaP MBNS MNFA NBro NCGa NGdn SApp SRos WCAu |
| 'Lemon Dessert' | SRos |
| 'Lemon Mint' | EGol SRos |
| 'Lemon Starfish' | SApp |
| 'Lenox' | SRos |
| 'Leonard Bernstein' | SApp SRos |
| 'Licorice Candy' new | SRos |
| 'Light the Way' | ECha GBin |
| 'Light Years Away' | MBNS NBro SApp |
| 'Lil Ledie' | SApp |
| § ***lilioasphodelus*** ♀H4 | Widely available |
| - 'Rowden Golden Jubilee' (v) | CRow |
| 'Lillian Frye' | EGol |
| 'Lilting Belle' | SRos |
| 'Lilting Lady' | SApp |
| 'Lilting Lady Red' | SApp |
| 'Lime Frost' | EMar SRos |
| 'Limoncello' | SApp |
| 'Linda' | EWll MRav NHol SRos |
| * 'Liners Moon' | EGol |
| 'Lipstick Print' | SRos |
| 'Little Angel' | SApp |
| 'Little Audrey' | EGle MHar SApp |
| 'Little Bee' | NBre |
| 'Little Beige Magic' | EGol |
| 'Little Bugger' | CMoH NGby NLar |
| 'Little Bumble Bee' | CFir COIW EGol EMar EMil MBNS MNFA SApp WCAu |
| 'Little Business' | MBNS SApp WAul |
| 'Little Cadet' | MNFA |
| 'Little Cameo' | EGol |
| 'Little Carpet' | MBNS SPer SPet |
| 'Little Carrot Top' | WCAu |
| 'Little Cranberry Cove' | EGol |
| 'Little Dandy' | EGol |
| 'Little Deeke' | COIW MHar MNFA SApp SRos |
| 'Little Fantastic' | EGol |
| 'Little Fat Cat' new | SApp |
| 'Little Fat Dazzler' | SApp SPol SRos |
| 'Little Fellow' | MBNS |
| 'Little Fruit Cup' | SApp |
| 'Little Grapette' | CPrp EGle EGol EMil EPfP GCra GQue MBNS MNFA NLar NSti SApp SMrs SRos WAul WBrk WCAu WCot WTin |
| 'Little Greenie' | EMar |
| 'Little Gypsy Vagabond' | CWat SRos |
| 'Little Heavenly Angel' | SPol |
| 'Little Lassie' | MBNS |
| 'Little Lavender Princess' | EGol |
| 'Little Maggie' | MHar MSte SApp SPol |
| 'Little Missy' | CBgR CHFP CWat EMar EMil LAst MBNS NBre SPet WGob WHoo |
| 'Little Monica' | SApp |
| 'Little Pumpkin Face' | EGol |
| 'Little Rainbow' | EGol |
| 'Little Red Hen' | CSam EBla ECGP EMar GBuc MBNS MNFA NBro NGdn SUsu |
| 'Little Show Stopper' | EWTr MBNS NBro NLar NMoo |
| 'Little Sweet Sue' | MNFA |
| 'Little Sweet Talk' | SRos |
| 'Little Tawny' | WCAu |
| 'Little Toddler' | SApp |
| 'Little Violet Lace' | SApp |
| 'Little Wart' | EGol MNFA |
| 'Little Wine Cup' | Widely available |
| 'Little Wine Spider' | SApp |
| 'Little Women' | MBNS |
| 'Lochinvar' | GBuc MRav SRos |
| 'Lonesome Dove' | SPol |
| 'Long John Silver' | SRos |
| 'Long Stocking' | SPol SRos |
| 'Longfield Purple Edge' | EBee |
| 'Longfield's Beauty' | EGle MBNS NCGa |
| 'Longfield's Glory' | MBNS NBre NMoo WGob |
| 'Longfield's Pearl' new | MBNS |
| 'Longfield's Pride' | CDWL ECho MBNS |
| 'Longfield's Purple Eye' | NLar NMoo |
| 'Longfield's Tropica' new | MBNS |
| 'Longfield's Twins' | MAvo MBNS NMoo WCot |
| ***longituba*** B&SWJ 4576 | WCru |
| 'Look Away' | SApp |
| 'Love Glow' | CFir |
| 'Loving Memories' | SApp |
| 'Lowenstine' | SApp |
| 'Lucille Lennington' new | WNHG |
| 'Lucretius' | MNFA |
| 'Luke Senior Junior' | SApp |
| 'Lullaby Baby' | EGle EGol ELan MBNS NLar SApp SPol SRos |
| 'Luscious Honeydew' new | WNHG |
| 'Lusty Lealand' | CDWL EGle EGol EMar MBNS SRos |
| 'Luverne' | SRos |
| 'Luxury Lace' | CPrp CSpe CWat EBla ECho ECtt EGle EGol ELan EMar EPfP EPla LRHS MNFA NBir NGdn NHol NPri SPer SPol SRos WAul WCAu WCFE WFar WMoo WPnP WTin |
| 'Lydia Bechtold' | SRos |
| 'Lynn Hall' | EGol MBNS NLar |
| 'Mabel Fuller' | CBgR MRav SRos WHrl |
| 'Macbeth' | EPfP MBNS SPad |
| 'Mae Graham' | SApp |
| 'Maggie Fynboe' | SPol |
| 'Magic Amethyst' new | CAbx |
| 'Magic Carpet Ride' | EMar SPol |
| 'Magic Lace' | SRos |
| 'Magnificent Eyes' | EMar |

| | |
|---|---|
| 'Mahogany Magic' | SRos |
| 'Malaysian Masquerade' | SApp |
| 'Malaysian Monarch' | SRos WMnd WNHG |
| 'Malaysian Spice' **new** | WNHG |
| 'Mallard' | CWat ECGP ECtt EGol EHrv EMar EPla LLWP LRHS MBNS MRav NBsh SApp SPer SRos SWat WCra |
| 'Manchurian Apricot' | SRos |
| 'Marble Faun' | SApp SRos |
| 'Margaret Perry' | CFee GBin MHar MNrw WAul |
| 'Marietta Delight' **new** | CAbx |
| 'Marion Caldwell' | SPol |
| 'Marion Vaughn' ♀H4 | CSev CWsd ECot EGle EGol EHrv ELan EPfP GMaP LBMP LHop LRHS MNFA NSti SBch SDix SPer SRGP SRos SSpi WCAu WFar |
| 'Mariska' | SApp SRos WNHG |
| 'Mark My Word' | SApp |
| 'Marse Connell' | SRos |
| 'Mary Todd' | EGle EGol MBNS MNFA SApp WCAu WMnd |
| 'Mary's Gold' | SPol SRos |
| 'Mask Ball' | SRos |
| 'Matt' | SRos |
| 'Mauna Loa' | CWGN EBee EGle EMar GQue MBNS MNFA MNrw MSte MWea NBre SApp WAul WCAu WCot |
| 'May Hall' | CMCo |
| 'May May' | SApp SPol |
| 'Meadow Mist' | EGle EGol |
| 'Meadow Sprite' | SRos |
| 'Medieval Guild' | SApp |
| 'Mega Stella' | SApp |
| 'Melody Lane' | CMCo EGol MNFA |
| 'Ménage Enchanté' **new** | EMar |
| 'Meno' | EGol |
| 'Merlot Rouge' | WAul |
| 'Merryn' **new** | CAbx |
| 'Metallica' **new** | CAbx |
| 'Metaphor' | EMar SApp SRos |
| 'Michele Coe' | CMMP EBee EBla EGol EHrv EMar EQua LPla LRHS MBNS MNFA NBre NBro NCGa NGdn SApp SPav SRGP SRos WCAu WMoo |
| ***middendorffii*** | CAvo EBee EMon GMaP MNFA NSti SMrm WCAu WFar WHrl |
| - 'Elfin' | EMon |
| - var. ***esculenta*** | EMon |
| - 'Major' | CFee |
| 'Midnight Dynamite' | MBNS |
| 'Midnight Magic' | EMar |
| 'Mikado' | CBgR LRHS |
| 'Milady Greensleeves' | SPol SRos |
| 'Mildred Mitchell' | EBee EWTr MBNS NLar SApp |
| 'Millie Schlumpf' | EMar SApp SPol SRos |
| 'Mimosa Umbrella' | CAbx SPol |
| 'Ming Porcelain' | CMil SApp SRos |
| 'Mini Pearl' | CBgR CMMP EGol EPfP LRHS MBNS MBri MSCN SApp SRos WPer |
| 'Mini Stella' | CBro CMea ECtt IBal MBNS NBre NOrc SPet WAul WFar |
| miniature hybrids | SRms |
| ***minor*** | CBro CWsd EBrs EGol EMon GBin NGdn SRms |
| - B&SWJ 8841 | WCru |
| 'Miracle Maid' **new** | WNHG |
| 'Miss Amelia' | SRos |
| 'Miss Jessie' | CAbx SRos |
| 'Missenden' ♀H4 | MNrw SApp SRos |
| 'Mission Moonlight' | EGol MHar WCAu |
| 'Missouri Beauty' | EBee LRHS MBNS SApp |
| 'Missouri Memories' | SRos |
| 'Mojave Mapeor' | SApp |
| 'Mokan Cindy' | EMar |
| 'Moment of Truth' | EBee NBre |
| 'Monica Marie' | SRos |
| 'Monita Gold Stripe' **new** | CMoH |
| 'Moon Witch' | SPol SRos |
| 'Moonbeam' | SApp |
| 'Moonlight Masquerade' | CDWL CHFP CWat EBee EPfP NLar SApp |
| 'Moonlight Mist' | SApp SPol SRos |
| 'Moonlit Caress' | EBee EMar IPot MBNS NBro SApp SRos WAul WFar |
| 'Moonlit Crystal' | CSpe SApp SPol |
| 'Moonlit Masquerade' | CPar CWGN EGle EMar GBuc MBNS MBri MCCP MLLN NCGa SBch SDnm SPav SPer SPet SRos WAul WCAu WGob WHrl |
| 'Moonlit Pirouette' **new** | SApp |
| 'Mormon Spider' | SApp SPol SRos |
| 'Morning Dawn' | EGle |
| 'Morning Sun' | EMar MBNS NBre NLar WCot |
| 'Morocco' | SPol |
| 'Morocco Red' | CBro CMdw CTri ELan EPla NBre |
| 'Morrie Otte' | SPol |
| 'Mount Joy' | SPer |
| 'Mountain Laurel' | EBee ECGP ECtt LDai LRHS LSRN MBNS MCot MHar MNFA MRav NBsh SApp SPol WFar |
| 'Mountain Violet' **new** | SApp |
| 'Mrs David Hall' | CMdw |
| 'Mrs Hugh Johnson' | CSev EBee ECot EWTr GCra LAst MSte NHol SHBN |
| ***multiflora*** | EMon MNFA NHol |
| 'Mumbo Jumbo' | SApp |
| 'My Belle' | SApp SRos |
| 'My Darling Clementine' | SApp SRos |
| 'My Sweet Rose' | SRos |
| 'Mynelle's Starfish' | EMar SPol SRos |
| 'Mysterious Veil' | EGol |
| 'Nairobi Dawn' | SRos |
| ***nana*** | CFir EPot |
| 'Nanuq' | SApp SRos |
| 'Naomi Ruth' | EGle EGol LAst MBNS SApp WCAu WTin |
| 'Nashville' | CBro ELan IBlr WHrl |
| 'Nashville Lights' | CBgR SPol |
| 'Natural Veil' | SPol |
| 'Navajo Princess' | EPfP MBNS MNrw |
| 'Neal Berrey' | SApp SRos |
| 'Nefertiti' | CBgR CMCo ELon LHop MBNS NBir NCGa SAga SPer WAul WCAu WTin |
| 'Neon Rose' | EBla SRos |
| 'Netsuke' | SApp SMrm |
| 'New Swirls' | SApp |
| 'Neyron Rose' ♀H4 | CHar EGol EMar EPfP EPla LAst MBNS MNFA NBre NGdn SRos WCAu WMoo |
| 'Night Beacon' | CBgR CPar ECho ECtt EGol EMar EWes EWll IBal MBNS MBri MLLN MNFA MNrw NLar NMoo SApp SRos WGob WHrl |
| 'Night Hawk' | CWsd |
| 'Night Raider' | EMar SApp SRos |
| 'Night Wings' | SApp |
| 'Nigrette' | CBen LPBA NHol |
| 'Nile Crane' | CBgR MBNS MNrw NCGa SApp SPer WAul |
| 'Nile Grave' | SApp |
| 'Nile Plum' | SApp |
| 'Nina Winegar' | SRos |
| 'Nivia Guest' | SApp |
| 'Nob Hill' | CMdw EGol EPla GBin MNFA SApp SRos WHrl |

| | |
|---|---|
| 'Nona's Garnet Spider' **new** | SApp SRos |
| 'Nordic Night' | EMar |
| 'North Star' | LPla SApp |
| 'Norton Eyed Seedling' **new** | WNHG |
| 'Norton Orange' | MNFA SAga WFar |
| 'Nosferatu' | EMar |
| 'Nova' ♀H4 | CPrp CWsd MNFA SApp SRos |
| 'Nuka' | EMar |
| 'Ocean Rain' | EMar SApp SRos |
| 'Octopus Hugs' | SRos |
| 'Old Tangiers' | EMar SRos |
| 'Old-fashioned Maiden' | EMar |
| 'Olive Bailey Langdon' | EGol SApp SRos |
| 'Olive's Odd One' | EMar |
| 'Olympic Showcase' | SRos |
| 'Omomuki' | SApp SRos |
| 'On and On' | EBee MBNS |
| 'On Silken Thread' **new** | SRos |
| 'On the Web' **new** | SApp |
| 'Oom Pah Pah' | ECha |
| 'Open Hearth' | SPol SRos |
| 'Orange Prelude' | SApp |
| 'Orange Velvet' | SApp SRos |
| 'Orangeman' hort. | EBla EPla MBNS NGdn NHol |
| 'Orchard Sprite' **new** | SApp |
| 'Orchid Beauty' | ECha MLHP WMoo |
| 'Orchid Candy' | MBNS NBir WAul |
| 'Orchid Corsage' | CAbx SApp |
| 'Oriental Ruby' | EGol MNFA SRos |
| 'Ostrich Plume' **new** | CAbx SRos |
| 'Ouachita Beauty' | SPol |
| 'Outrageous' | SApp SRos WNHG |
| 'Paige Parker' | EGol |
| 'Paige's Pinata' | EBee MBNS NBPC SApp SRos |
| 'Paint Your Wagon' | SApp |
| 'Painted Lady' | MNFA SApp |
| 'Painted Trillium' | CMil |
| 'Painter Poet' | EMar |
| 'Palace Guard' | MNFA |
| 'Palantir' **new** | SApp |
| 'Pamela Williams' **new** | EMar |
| 'Panama Hattie' **new** | EMar |
| 'Pandora's Box' | Widely available |
| 'Pantaloons' | SApp |
| 'Pantherette' | SApp SPol |
| 'Paper Butterfly' | EMar SPol SRos |
| 'Paradise Prince' | EGol |
| 'Pardon Me' | CMHG CMMP ECho EGle EGol ELan EMar GMaP MBNS MNFA NCGa NGdn NHol SApp SPol SRos SWal WAul WBor WCAu |
| 'Pardon Me Boy' **new** | SPol |
| 'Parfait' | CAbx CBgR EMar SPol |
| 'Pas de Deux' | SApp |
| 'Pastel Ballerina' | SRos |
| 'Pastel Classic' | SApp SRos |
| 'Pastilline' | SPol |
| 'Pat Mercer' | SApp |
| 'Patchwork Puzzle' | SRos |
| 'Patricia' | EPfP MBNS |
| 'Patricia Fay' | SApp SRos |
| 'Patsy Bickers' | SApp |
| 'Paul Weber' | SApp |
| 'Peach Jubilee' **new** | SPol |
| 'Peach Petticoats' | SRos |
| 'Peacock Maiden' | EMar SApp SPol |
| 'Pear Ornament' | SRos |
| 'Pemaquid Light' | CMHG |
| 'Penelope Vestey' | EBla EGle EMar GBuc LRHS MBNS MNFA NCGa SApp SPol SRGP SRos |
| 'Penny's Worth' | EBrs EGol MBNS NOrc WAul WCot WFar WHoo |
| 'Perfect Pleasure' | MBNS |
| 'Persian Princess' | CMCo |
| 'Persian Ruby' | EMar SPol |
| 'Piano Man' | EMar MBNS MWea NLar NMoo WAul WGob WNHG |
| 'Piccadilly Princess' | SRos |
| 'Pink Attraction' | SApp |
| 'Pink Ballerina' | EGol |
| 'Pink Charm' | COIW EBee ECha ECtt EMar EPPr GMaP LPBA LRHS MHar NBro NBsh NGdn NHol SHBN SPla SPol SRos WCAu |
| 'Pink Cotton Candy' | SRos |
| 'Pink Damask' ♀H4 | Widely available |
| 'Pink Dream' | EMar EQua LRHS MBNS NBir NBre NHol SPol WCAu |
| 'Pink Glow' | CMMP |
| 'Pink Grace' | SPol |
| 'Pink Heaven' | EGol |
| 'Pink Lady' | MNrw MRav NBur SHBN SRms |
| 'Pink Lavender Appeal' | EGol WCAu |
| 'Pink Monday' **new** | WNHG |
| 'Pink Prelude' | EBee EMar MBNS MNFA MWat NBro |
| 'Pink Puff' | MBNS NBir NBre NLar WGob |
| 'Pink Salute' | SRos |
| 'Pink Sundae' | ECha |
| 'Pink Super Spider' | MNFA SRos |
| 'Pink Windmill' | SPol |
| 'Pinocchio' | NMoo |
| 'Pirate Treasure' | MBNS |
| 'Pirate's Patch' | SPol SRos |
| 'Pixie Parasol' | WMnd WNHG |
| 'Pixie Pipestone' | SApp |
| 'Plum Beauty' | NLar |
| 'Pocket Size' | SApp |
| 'Poinsettia' **new** | CAbx |
| 'Pompeian Purple' | EGol |
| 'Pony' | EGol SRos |
| 'Ponytail Pink' | EGol |
| 'Pookie Bear' | SApp |
| 'Prague Spring' | EMar MNFA SPol SRos WCAu |
| 'Prairie Belle' | CBcs CSWP MBNS NBre SApp SPol WCAu WFar |
| 'Prairie Blue Eyes' | ECha ECho ECtt EGle EGol LFur LRHS MBNS MNFA NMoo NPri SApp SPlb SPol SRos WAul WCAu WCot WHrl WMnd |
| 'Prairie Charmer' | SEND WHrl |
| 'Prairie Moonlight' | SRos |
| 'Prairie Sunset' | WCAu |
| 'Prelude to Love' | EMar |
| 'Pretty Miss' | EMar MBri |
| 'Pretty Peggy' | MNFA |
| 'Preview Party' **new** | WNHG |
| 'Primal Scream' **new** | SApp |
| 'Primrose Mascotte' | NBir |
| 'Prince of Purple' | EMar SRos |
| 'Prince Redbird' | SRos |
| 'Princess Blue Eyes' | SPol |
| 'Princess Eden' | SApp |
| 'Princess Ellen' | SApp |
| 'Princess Lilli' **new** | MBNS |
| 'Princeton Point Lace' | SApp |
| 'Princeton Silky' | SRos |
| 'Prize Picotee Deluxe' | SPol SRos |
| 'Prize Picotee Elite' | EMar SPol SRos WTin |
| § 'Puddin' | CWat NHol WAul |
| 'Pudgie' | SApp |
| 'Pug Yarborough' **new** | SPol |
| 'Pumpkin Kid' | SApp SRos |
| 'Puppet Lady' | SApp |
| 'Pure and Simple' | SPol SRos |
| 'Purple Bicolor' | WHrl |

| | |
|---|---|
| 'Purple Corsage' | SApp |
| 'Purple Oddity' **new** | SPol |
| 'Purple Pinwheel' | SPol |
| 'Purple Rain' | CWat MBNS MWea SApp SPol SRos SWvt |
| 'Purple Rain Dance' | SPol |
| 'Purple Waters' | EMar EPfP EWll LRHS MBNS NBre NOrc NPri SPol WAul WPnP |
| 'Pursuit of Excellence' | EMar SRos |
| 'Pyewacket' | SApp |
| 'Queen Lily' **new** | WNHG |
| 'Queen of May' | SApp WCot |
| 'Queen Priscilla' **new** | CAbx |
| 'Queens Fancy' | SApp |
| 'Queen's Gift' | SApp |
| 'Queensland' | SApp |
| 'Quick Results' | SApp SRos |
| 'Quilt Patch' | SRos |
| 'Quinn Buck' | EMar |
| 'Ra Hansen' | SRos |
| 'Radiant' | CBcs |
| 'Radiant Greetings' | MNFA |
| 'Rainbow Candy' | LLHF MAvo MBNS NMoo SPad |
| 'Raindrop' | EGol |
| 'Rajah' | CBgR EMar MBNS NBro SPer WHrl |
| 'Randall Moore' **new** | SPol |
| 'Raspberry Candy' | ECho EMar EWll GCra MBNS MLLN MNrw NBhm NBro NCGa NHol NOrc SApp SRos WCAu WGob WHrl |
| 'Raspberry Pixie' | EGol SPol |
| 'Raspberry Wine' | MHar |
| 'Rave On' **new** | SApp |
| 'Real Wind' | EMar MNFA SApp SPol SRos |
| 'Red Butterfly' | EMar |
| 'Red Joy' | SApp |
| 'Red Precious' ♀H4 | EGol EMar MNFA MNrw SApp SMHy SRos |
| 'Red Rain' **new** | CAbx EMar |
| 'Red Ribbons' | SPol SRos |
| 'Red Ruby' | ERCP |
| 'Red Rum' | CBgR EWll NBro SMrm WPnP |
| 'Red Suspenders' | CAbx MBNS |
| 'Red Torch' | CWsd |
| 'Red Volunteer' | EMar SPol SRos |
| 'Regal Vision' **new** | SApp |
| 'Regency Dandy' | SApp |
| 'Renee' | MNrw |
| 'Respighi' | SApp SRos |
| 'Return Trip' | SPol |
| 'Rhapsody in Time' **new** | EMar |
| 'Ribbonette' | EBee MBNS NMoo |
| 'Ringlets' | MNFA |
| 'Riptide' | SApp |
| 'Robert Coe' | SRos |
| 'Robin Coleman' | MNFA |
| 'Rocket Booster' **new** | CAbx |
| 'Rocket City' | ELan SRos |
| 'Roger Grounds' | SApp SPol |
| * 'Romantic Rose' | EMar MBNS NLar |
| 'Ron Rousseau' | SApp |
| 'Root Beer' | SRos WTin |
| 'Rose Emily' | SApp SRos |
| 'Rose Festival' | WCAu |
| 'Rose Roland' | NBre |
| 'Rosella Sheridan' | SRos |
| 'Roses in Snow' **new** | MBNS |
| 'Rosewood Flame' | SRos |
| 'Rosewood Rainbow End' | SRos |
| 'Rosewood Snowflakes' | SRos |
| 'Roswitha' | SApp SPol |
| 'Rosy Returns' | MBNS MWea NLar NMoo |
| 'Round Midnight' **new** | SPol |

| | |
|---|---|
| 'Royal Braid' | EGle EPfP MBNS MNrw NCGa NLar SApp SPer WCot |
| 'Royal Charm' | SRos |
| 'Royal Corduroy' | SRos |
| 'Royal Occasion' | SRos |
| 'Royal Palace Prince' | EMar GAbr |
| 'Royal Prestige' | SApp |
| 'Royal Robe' | CTri SPhx |
| 'Ruby Spider' | SRos |
| 'Ruffled Antique Lavender' | WCAu |
| 'Ruffled Apricot' | CKel LBMP MBNS MNFA SPav SRos WCAu WNHG |
| 'Ruffled Carousel' **new** | WNHG |
| 'Rumble Seat Romance' **new** | WNHG |
| 'Russian Easter' | SRos |
| 'Russian Rhapsody' | CKel SApp SPol SRos |
| 'Rutilans' | CFee |
| 'Sabie' | SApp |
| 'Sabine Baur' | CHFP EBee IBal IPot MBNS MWea SApp WAul WCra WFar |
| 'Sabra Salina' | SRos |
| * 'Sagamore' | SApp |
| 'Salmon Sheen' | SPer SRos |
| 'Sammy' | CAbx |
| 'Sammy Russell' | Widely available |
| 'Sandra Walker' | EGol |
| 'Santiago' | SPol |
| 'Sari' | SApp |
| 'Satin Clouds' | EGol |
| 'Satin Glass' | EBrs MNFA |
| 'Satin Glow' | ECha MLHP |
| 'Scarlet Chalice' | SApp |
| 'Scarlet Flame' | ECha WMoo |
| 'Scarlet Oak' | LRHS MBri MNFA SRos |
| 'Scarlet Orbit' | SApp SHar SRos |
| 'Scarlet Ribbons' | SPol |
| 'Scarlock' | MNFA |
| 'Scatterbrain' | CKel |
| 'Schnickel Fritz' **new** | NCGa |
| 'Schoeppinger Anfang' | EBee |
| 'School Girl' | EBrs |
| 'Scorpio' | CBgR EMar MNFA SPol |
| 'Scotland' | IBal SApp |
| 'Screaming Demon' **new** | CAbx |
| 'Searcy Marsh' | EGol |
| 'Sebastian' | SApp SRos |
| 'Secret Splendor' | SPol |
| 'Segramoor' **new** | SApp |
| 'Selma Longlegs' | CAbx SRos |
| 'Serena Dark Horse' **new** | SRos |
| 'Serena Sunburst' | SPol SRos |
| 'Serene Madonna' | CFir GBin MWea |
| 'Serenity Morgan' | EBee EPfP MBNS |
| 'Shadowed Pink' **new** | WNHG |
| 'Shaman' | SApp SRos |
| 'Sherry Fair' | SApp |
| 'Sherry Lane Carr' | SPol SRos |
| 'Shimek September Morning' | SPol |
| 'Shimmering Elegance' **new** | SRos |
| 'Shogun' | MBNS |
| 'Shooting Star' | CWsd SPla |
| 'Shotgun' | SPol SRos |
| 'Show Amber' | SApp SRos |
| 'Significant Other' | SApp |
| 'Silent Sentry' | SApp |
| 'Silken Fairy' | EGol |
| 'Silken Touch' | SApp SRos |
| 'Siloam Amazing Grace' | SApp SRos |
| 'Siloam Baby Talk' | EGle EGol ELon EMar LAst MNFA NBir SApp SRos WAul WHoo WMoo WPnP WTin |

| | |
|---|---|
| 'Siloam Bertie Ferris' | MBNS |
| 'Siloam Bo Peep' | EGol SApp WAul |
| 'Siloam Brian Hanke' | SRos |
| 'Siloam Button Box' | EBee EGol MBNS WAul WHrl |
| 'Siloam Bye Lo' | EGol |
| 'Siloam Cinderella' | EGol SRos |
| 'Siloam David Kirchhoff' | EMar MBNS SRos |
| 'Siloam Doodlebug' | EGol SRos |
| 'Siloam Double Classic' (d) | EGol EMar SPol SRos |
| 'Siloam Dream Baby' | EPPr MBNS NCGa |
| 'Siloam Edith Sholar' | EGol |
| 'Siloam Ethel Smith' | EGol MNFA SApp SPol SRos |
| 'Siloam Fairy Tale' | CWat EGol |
| 'Siloam French Doll' | MBNS NLar SApp |
| 'Siloam French Marble' | SRos |
| 'Siloam Frosted Mint' | SApp |
| 'Siloam Gold Coin' | SApp |
| 'Siloam Grace Stamile' | CFir EMar MBNS SApp SRos WGob |
| 'Siloam Harold Flickinger' | SRos |
| 'Siloam Jim Cooper' | SRos |
| 'Siloam Joan Senior' | EGol MBNS |
| 'Siloam June Bug' | EGol ELan MNFA SApp WCAu |
| 'Siloam Justine Lee' | MBNS |
| 'Siloam Kewpie Doll' | EGol |
| 'Siloam Little Angel' | EGol SApp SPol |
| 'Siloam Little Girl' | EGol SRos |
| 'Siloam Mama' | SApp SRos |
| 'Siloam Merle Kent' | EMar MNFA SApp SPol SRos |
| 'Siloam New Toy' | EGol |
| 'Siloam Nugget' | SApp |
| 'Siloam Orchid Jewel' | EGol |
| 'Siloam Paul Watts' | SApp SPol SRos |
| 'Siloam Peewee' | EGol |
| 'Siloam Penny' | SApp |
| * 'Siloam Pink' | LAst |
| 'Siloam Pink Glow' | EGle EGol SWat WAul |
| 'Siloam Pink Petite' | EGol |
| 'Siloam Plum Tree' | EGol SApp |
| 'Siloam Pocket Size' | EGol MSte SApp |
| 'Siloam Powder Pink' | SApp |
| 'Siloam Prissy' | EGol SApp |
| 'Siloam Purple Plum' | EGol |
| 'Siloam Queen's Toy' | SPol |
| 'Siloam Ra Hansen' | SApp |
| 'Siloam Red Ruby' | EGol |
| 'Siloam Red Toy' | EGol |
| 'Siloam Red Velvet' | EGol |
| 'Siloam Ribbon Candy' | EGol SApp WNHG |
| 'Siloam Rose Dawn' | SApp SPol SRos |
| 'Siloam Royal Prince' | EBee EGle EGol EPfP MNFA NHol SApp |
| 'Siloam Shocker' | EGol |
| 'Siloam Show Girl' | CMCo EGle EGol EMar MBNS NBsh NCGa SApp |
| 'Siloam Sugar Time' | EGol |
| 'Siloam Sunburst' | EMar |
| 'Siloam Tee Tiny' | EGol |
| 'Siloam Tinker Toy' | EGol |
| 'Siloam Tiny Mite' | EGol |
| 'Siloam Toddler' | EGol |
| 'Siloam Tom Thumb' | CBgR EGol EMar MBNS WCAu WGob |
| 'Siloam Ury Winniford' | CBro CHFP CWan ECho EGol EMar EMil MBNS MCCP MNFA NBre NLar NMoo SApp WAul WHoo WPnP WTin |
| 'Siloam Virginia Henson' | EGol NCGa SApp SRos WCAu |
| 'Siloam Wendy Glawson' | SApp |
| 'Silver Ice' | SApp SRos |
| 'Silver Lance' | SRos |
| 'Silver Quasar' | CAbx SRos |
| 'Silver Trumpet' | EGol |
| 'Silver Veil' | WFar |
| 'Sinbad Sailor' | EMar NLar |
| 'Sir Blackstem' | ELon SApp SRos |
| 'Sir Modred' | CAbx |
| 'Sirius' | NHol |
| 'Sirocco' | EBee WTin |
| 'Sitting on a Rainbow' **new** | CAbx |
| 'Sixth Sense' | MBNS SPad |
| 'Slender Lady' | SRos |
| 'Smoky Mountain Autumn' | EMar MHar SApp SPol SRos |
| 'Smoky Mountain Bell' | SApp |
| 'Smuggler's Gold' | SApp |
| 'Snappy Rhythm' | MNFA |
| 'Snowed In' | SRos |
| 'Snowy Apparition' | EBla ECtt EMar EWTr GKir MBNS MNFA MSte MWat MWea NHol SApp SPol |
| 'Snowy Eyes' | EGle EGol EMar GBuc GMac IPot MBNS NCGa NHol SApp SWat WHrl |
| 'So Lovely' | SApp |
| 'Solano Bulls Eye' | MLHP |
| 'Solid Scarlet' | SRos |
| 'Someone Special' | SPol SRos |
| 'Song Sparrow' | CBro GMac SApp WPer |
| 'Sovereign Queen' | EGol WNHG |
| 'Spacecoast Scrambled' | EPfP MBNS |
| 'Spacecoast Starburst' | EGle EMar MBNS NBro SApp WCAu WCot WFar |
| 'Spanish Fandango' **new** | CAbx |
| 'Spanish Glow' | SRos |
| 'Spanish Sketch' | SRos |
| 'Speak of Angels' | SApp |
| 'Spider Breeder' | SApp |
| 'Spider Man' | SApp SRos WCAu |
| 'Spider Miracle' | MNFA SPol |
| 'Spider Spirits' **new** | EMar |
| 'Spilled Milk' | SPol |
| 'Spin Master' **new** | CAbx |
| 'Spindazzle' | SPol |
| 'Spinne in Lachs' | SRos |
| 'Spiral Charmer' | SApp |
| 'Spode' | SApp |
| 'Spooner' **new** | CBgR |
| 'Spring Ballerina' | SApp |
| 'Stafford' | Widely available |
| 'Staghorn Sumac' | EBla EMar LEdu MBNS NBsh NHol |
| 'Star of Fantasy' **new** | EMar |
| 'Starling' | CFir CPar EGle EGol MNFA MSte SApp WAul WCAu |
| 'Stars and Stripes' | MNFA |
| 'Starstruck' **new** | WNHG |
| 'Startle' | CFir CWGN EPfP MAvo MBNS MNrw SApp SPoG WCot |
| 'Statuesque' | WFar |
| 'Stella de Oro' | Widely available |
| 'Stoke Poges' ♀H4 | CAvo CBgR CBro EBee EBla EGle EGoo EMFW EMar EPPr EPfP EPla LAst LBMP LHop LRHS LSRN MBNS MNFA NGdn SAga SApp SPer SPoG SRos STes SWat WCAu |
| 'Stoplight' | CAbx EBla ELon EMar SApp SPol SRos |
| 'Strawberry Candy' | CMMP CWGN ECtt EMar EMil EWll GKir LAst LSRN MBNS MBri NCGa NGdn SApp SPad SPer SPet SPoG SRos WAul WCAu WHoo WHrl |
| 'Strawberry Fields Forever' | MBNS NLar SHar SPol SRos |
| 'Strawberry Swirl' | MNFA |
| I 'Streaker' B. Brown (v) | WCot |
| 'Street Urchin' | SPol |
| 'Strider Spider' **new** | SApp |
| 'Strutter's Ball' | CPar EGle IPot MBNS MNFA NGdn SApp SPer SPol SRos SWat WAul WCAu WHoo WMnd |

| | |
|---|---|
| 'Sugar Cookie' | SApp SRos |
| 'Summer Dragon' | EBee MBNS NMoo |
| 'Summer Interlude' | WCAu WMoo |
| 'Summer Jubilee' | SApp |
| 'Summer Wine' | CSam CWat ECha EGle EGol EMar EPfP EPla LAst LRHS MBNS MCot MNFA NBir NBro NMoo NPri NSti SApp SPer SUsu WAul WBVN WBor WCAu WCot WHoo WMnd |
| 'Sunday Gloves' | EGol SRos WNHG |
| 'Sungold Candy' **new** | SApp |
| 'Super Purple' | CKel SApp |
| 'Superlative' | SApp SRos |
| 'Susan Weber' | SApp SRos |
| 'Suzie Wong' | MNFA SRos |
| 'Svengali' | SPol |
| 'Sweet Pea' | EGol |
| 'Taffy Tot' | SApp |
| 'Taj Mahal' | ELon SApp WFar |
| 'Tall Boy' | SApp |
| 'Tang' | LFur MBNS NMoo NOrc WCAu |
| 'Tango Noturno' | SApp SPol |
| 'Tarantella' **new** | CBgR |
| 'Tarantula' | SApp |
| 'Tasmania' | SPer |
| 'Techny Peach Lace' | SRos |
| 'Techny Spider' | SRos |
| 'Tejas' | CElw EBee NBre |
| 'Ten to Midnight' **new** | SApp |
| 'Tender Shepherd' | EGol WCAu |
| 'Tennessee Flycatcher' | EMar SPol |
| 'Tetraploid Stella de Oro' | MBri |
| 'Tetrina's Daughter' ♀H4 | CBgR EPfP NHol SApp SRos |
| 'Texas Sunlight' | WAul |
| 'Texas Toffee' | SRos |
| 'Thai Silk' | SApp |
| 'Thanks a Bunch' | SPol |
| 'Theresa Hall' | WFar |
| 'Thumbelina' | ECha MNFA WMoo |
| § ***thunbergii*** | CWsd ECha EMon GCal MNFA MNrw WCAu |
| - 'Ovation' | MBNS |
| 'Thundercloud' **new** | WHrl |
| 'Thundering Ovation' **new** | MWea |
| 'Thy True Love' | SApp |
| 'Tigerling' | SRos |
| 'Tigger' | CDWL |
| 'Time Lord' | EMar SApp |
| 'Timeless Fire' | SApp SRos |
| 'Tinker Bell' | MSte SRos |
| 'Tiny Talisman' | SApp |
| 'Tis Midnight' **new** | WNHG |
| 'Tom Collins' | SRos |
| 'Tom Wise' | SPol SRos |
| 'Tomorrow's Song' | SApp |
| 'Tone Poem' **new** | WNHG |
| 'Tonia Gay' | LCro SApp SPol SRos |
| 'Toothpick' **new** | EMar SPol |
| 'Tootsie Rose' | SPol SRos |
| 'Top Honors' **new** | SPol |
| 'Torpoint' | EBla EMar MBNS MNFA MRav NBsh NCob |
| 'Towhead' | EGol MRav |
| 'Toyland' | EGol EMar EPfP NBir NGdn NLar NPri SPol |
| 'Trahlyta' | CPar SApp SPol SRos WTin |
| 'Trog' **new** | CAbx |
| 'Tropical Heat Wave' | SApp |
| 'True Glory' | SApp |
| 'True Grit' | SApp |
| 'Tuolumne Fairy Tale' | SPol |
| 'Turkish Turban' **new** | SPol |
| 'Tuscawilla Blackout' | SApp SRos |
| 'Tuscawilla Tigress' | CDWL ECho EMar NCGa SRos WAul WHrl |
| 'Tutankhamun' | MNFA |
| 'Tuxedo' | SApp SPol |
| 'Twenty Third Psalm' | WHal |
| 'Twist of Lemon' | SRos |
| 'Two Faces of Love' | SPol |
| 'Umbrella Parade' | CBgR |
| 'Unchartered Waters' **new** | MBNS |
| 'Uniquely Different' | SPol |
| 'Upper Class Peach' | SRos |
| 'Uptown Girl' | SRos |
| 'Valiant' | EMar MBNS |
| 'Valley Monster' **new** | EMar |
| 'Vanessa Arden' | SApp |
| 'Vanilla Candy' | SRos |
| 'Varsity' | CPLG EBrs EGol GMac NBir SPer SRos WCAu |
| 'Veiled Beauty' | WCAu |
| 'Vendetta' **new** | WNHG |
| 'Vera Biaglow' | MNFA SApp SPol SRos |
| 'Very Berry Ice' **new** | SPol |
| 'Vespers' | CAbP WFar |
| ***vespertina*** | see *H. thunbergii* |
| 'Vi Simmons' | SRos |
| 'Victoria Aden' | CBro |
| 'Victoria Elizabeth Barnes' **new** | WNHG |
| 'Victorian Collar' | SApp |
| 'Victorian Ribbons' | SPol |
| 'Video' | SApp SRos |
| 'Vino di Notte' | EMar SRos |
| 'Vintage Bordeaux' | ELan SApp WAul |
| 'Vintage Burgundy' **new** | WNHG |
| 'Viracocha' | SApp WMnd WNHG |
| 'Virgin's Blush' | SPer |
| 'Vision of Beauty' | SApp |
| 'Vohann' | SApp SRos |
| 'Waiting in the Wings' | SRos |
| 'Walking on Sunshine' | SApp SRos |
| 'Wally Nance' | SApp |
| 'Watch Tower' **new** | CBgR |
| 'Water Witch' | CWat EGol SApp |
| 'Wayside Green Imp' | EGle EGol MNrw MSte SApp |
| 'Web Browser' **new** | CAbx |
| 'Wedding Band' | SRos |
| 'Wee Chalice' | EGol |
| 'Welchkins' | WAul |
| 'Welfo White Diamond' | SApp SPol |
| 'Wendy Glawson' | SApp |
| 'Whichford' ♀H4 | CBro CMMP CSam EBee ECGP ECha ECtt EGol ELan EMar EPla LRHS MBNS MNFA NCob SPer SPhx SPla SRos WCAu |
| 'Whirling Fury' **new** | SApp |
| 'Whiskey on Ice' | SApp |
| 'White Coral' | EMar LRHS LSRN MBNS MNFA NBro |
| 'White Dish' | EGol |
| 'White Edged Madonna' | EMar SBch WHrl |
| 'White Lemonade' **new** | SApp |
| 'White Pansy' | SRos |
| 'White Temptation' | CFir CMMP EGol EPfP MBNS NCGa NGdn SApp SRos WAul WHoo WMnd WNHG |
| 'White Tie Affair' | SApp SRos |
| 'White Zone' | SRos |
| 'Whooperee' | SRos |
| * 'Wide Eyed' | EPla MNFA |
| 'Wild about Sherry' | SPol |
| 'Wild and Wonderful' **new** | SRos |
| 'Wild Horses' **new** | SPol |
| 'Wild Mustang' | MBNS |

| | |
|---|---|
| 'Wild One' | SApp |
| 'Wild Welcome' | WCAu |
| 'Wildest Dreams' **new** | SRos |
| 'Wildfire Tango' | SApp |
| 'Wilson Spider' | SApp SPol |
| 'Wind Frills' | EMar SApp SPol |
| 'Wind Song' | SApp SRos |
| 'Window Dressing' | EGol |
| 'Windsor Castle' | SApp |
| 'Windsor Tan' | WCAu WCFE |
| 'Wine Bubbles' | EGol SApp |
| 'Wine Merchant' | EMar MNFA |
| 'Wineberry Candy' | CPar EGle EPfP MBNS MLLN NLar SApp WAul WCAu |
| 'Wings on High' **new** | SApp |
| 'Winnetka' | WCAu |
| 'Winnie' | EMar |
| 'Winsome Lady' | ECha EMar LRHS MBNS WHrl |
| 'Wisest of Wizards' | MBNS NCGa WHrl |
| 'Wishing Well' | WCot |
| 'Witch Hazel' | WCAu |
| 'Witches Brew' | CBgR |
| 'Women's Work' | SApp |
| 'Wood Duck' | EGle SApp |
| 'Woodside Velour' | EMar |
| 'Xia Xiang' | SRos |
| 'Yabba Dabba Doo' | CAbx EMar SApp SPol SRos |
| 'Yearning Love' | SApp |
| 'Yellow Angel' | SApp SPol |
| 'Yellow Explosion' | SApp SRos |
| 'Yellow Lollipop' | MNFA SApp SRos |
| 'Yellow Spider' | SApp |
| 'Yellow Submarine' | MBNS |
| 'Yesterday Memories' | SRos |
| 'You Angel You' **new** | MBNS SApp |
| 'Young Countess' | CMCo |
| 'Yuma' **new** | WNHG |
| 'Zagora' | CAbx WCAu |
| 'Zampa' | CAbx |
| 'Zara' | CAbx SPer |
| 'Zarahemla' | EMar |

## *Hemiorchis* (*Zingiberaceae*)

| | |
|---|---|
| ***pantlingii*** | CKob |

## *Hemizygia* (*Lamiaceae*)

| | |
|---|---|
| ***obermeyerae*** | CPne |

## *Hepatica* ✿ (*Ranunculaceae*)

| | |
|---|---|
| ***acutiloba*** | CBro CLAP EBee EBrs ECho EPot GBuc GEdr GKir LAma MAsh NBir NHol NLar NSla WAbe WCru |
| - blue-flowered **new** | WCru |
| - white-flowered **new** | WCru |
| ***americana*** | CLAP CWsd EBee EBrs ECho EHrv ELan GBuc MAsh NBir NLar WCru WPnP |
| ***angulosa*** | see *H. transsilvanica* |
| ***henryi*** | EBee EPot LAma WCru |
| ***insularis*** | CLAP EBee |
| - B&SWJ 859 | WCru |
| ***maxima*** | EBee GEdr NSla |
| - B&SWJ 4344 | WCru |
| x ***media*** 'Ballardii' | GBuc GEdr GKir IBlr MNFA |
| - 'Harvington Beauty' | CLAP EHrv GBuc IBlr MAsh MHom NBir WCot |
| 'Miyuki' (d) | GEdr |
| § ***nobilis*** ♀H4 | Widely available |
| - var. ***asiatica*** | MAsh |
| - - variegated (v) **new** | EBee |
| - blue-flowered | ECho GBuc GEdr MAsh NLAp NSla NWCA WAbe WCru |
| - 'Cobalt' | CLAP ECho NSla WAbe |
| - dark blue-flowered | CLAP MAsh |
| - double pink-flowered | see *H. nobilis* 'Rubra Plena' |
| - dwarf white | GKir |
| - var. ***japonica*** | EPfP EWes GBuc LAma MAsh NBir NHol WCru |
| - - 'Akane' | EBee ECho GEdr |
| - - 'Akebono' **new** | GEdr |
| - - 'Aniju' **new** | GEdr |
| - - 'Benikanzan' **new** | EBee GEdr |
| - - 'Benioiran' **new** | GEdr |
| - - 'Dewa' (d) | GEdr |
| - - 'Echigobijin' **new** | EBee GEdr |
| - - 'Fujimusume' **new** | GEdr |
| - - 'Gosyozakuro' **new** | GEdr |
| - - 'Gyousei' | EBee ECho GBuc GEdr |
| - - 'Harukaze' (d) | GEdr |
| - - 'Haruno-awayuki' (d) | GEdr |
| - - 'Isaribi' | EBee ECho GEdr |
| - - 'Kasumino' | EBee ECho GEdr |
| - - 'Koshino-maboroshi' **new** | GEdr |
| - - 'Kougyoku' | GEdr |
| - - 'Koushirou' **new** | GEdr |
| - - f. ***magna*** dark blue-flowered **new** | EBee |
| - - - double, blue-flowered (d) **new** | EBee |
| - - - double, magenta-flowered (d) **new** | EBee |
| - - - double, pink-flowered (d) **new** | EBee |
| - - - double, white-flowered (d) **new** | EBee |
| - - - 'Hohobeni' **new** | GEdr |
| - - - 'Kimon' **new** | GEdr |
| - - - 'Kuukai' **new** | GEdr |
| - - - 'Murasaki-shikibu' **new** | GEdr |
| - - - 'Seizan' **new** | GEdr |
| - - - 'Shikouryuu' **new** | GEdr |
| - - - 'Taeka' **new** | GEdr |
| - - - 'Toki' **new** | GEdr |
| - - (Nidan Group) 'Hakurin' (d) **new** | GEdr |
| - - 'O-mwasaki' | ECho GEdr |
| - - 'Orihime' | GEdr |
| - - 'Ryokuun' **new** | GEdr |
| - - 'Ryougetsu' | EBee GEdr |
| - - 'Sadobeni' **new** | EBee GEdr |
| - - 'Saichou' | GEdr |
| - - 'Sakuragari' | EBee GEdr |
| - - 'Sawanemidori' **new** | EBee GEdr |
| - - 'Sayaka' | EBee GEdr |
| - - 'Senhime' **new** | GEdr |
| - - 'Shihou' | GEdr |
| - - 'Shikouden' | GEdr |
| - - 'Shirayuki' **new** | GEdr |
| - - 'Shoujyouno-homare' | GEdr |
| - - 'Sougetsu' | EBee ECho GEdr |
| - - 'Subaru' (d) **new** | GEdr |
| - - 'Tamao' **new** | EBee GEdr |
| - - 'Tamasaburou' **new** | EBee GEdr |
| - - 'Tensei' **new** | GEdr |
| - - 'Touryoku' | GEdr |
| - - 'Toyama-chiyoiwai' **new** | GEdr |
| - - 'Yahikomuasaki' **new** | EBee GEdr |
| - - 'Yoshinosato' (d) **new** | GEdr |
| - - 'Yukishino' **new** | EBee GEdr |
| - - 'Yumegokochi' **new** | GEdr |
| - - 'Yuunami' **new** | EBee GEdr |
| - var. ***japonica*** x ***yamatutai*** | MAsh |
| - large, pale blue-flowered | NLAp |

- lilac-flowered MTho
- mottled leaf CSsd ECho EHrv MTho
- Picos strain CWsd
- pink-flowered CLAP ECho EPot GKir MAsh NLar NWCA SIng WCru
* - var. ***pyrenaica*** GBuc LEdu MAsh
* - - 'Apple Blossom' CLAP MAsh NBir WAbe
- 'Pyrenean Marbles' CLAP GKir
- red-flowered ECho GKir WAbe
- Rene's form WFar
- var. ***rubra*** CLAP ECho NLAp NMen NSla
§ - 'Rubra Plena' (d) EPot GKir MAsh MHom NSla
- 'Tabby' ECho
- violet-flowered MAsh
- white-flowered CLAP ECho MAsh NLAp NMen NSla SIng WAbe WCru

'Sakaya' ECho
§ ***transsilvanica*** ♀H4 CBro CLAP CMea EBee ECho GAbr GBuc GKir LAma LHop MAsh MCot NHol NMen WAul WCru WHal WTin
- 'Ada Scott' GEdr WSHC
- 'Blue Eyes' CTca EBee EBrs ECho GEdr
- 'Blue Jewel' CFir CLAP CTca EBee EBrs ECho GBBs GEdr MCot MHom NLar NMen SMeo WPnP
- blue-flowered IBlr MAsh
- 'Buis' CBod CLAP CTca EBee EBrs ECho EPot GEdr GKev MAsh MCot MHom NLAp NLar SPhx WPnP
- 'Eisvogel' CLAP CTca EBrs ECho EPot GEdr NMen
- 'Elison Spence' (d) GEdr IBlr MAsh MCot
- 'Lilacina' ECho GEdr MAsh NSla
- 'Loddon Blue' IBlr
- pink-flowered CLAP CTca EBrs ECho MAsh
- white-flowered ECho MAsh
- 'Winterfreude' EBee

***triloba*** see *H. nobilis*
'Wakana' EBee GEdr
***yamatutai*** EBee EBrs EPot

## *Heptacodium* (*Caprifoliaceae*)

***jasminoides*** see *H. miconioides*
§ ***miconioides*** Widely available

## *Heptapleurum* see *Schefflera*

## *Heracleum* (*Apiaceae*)

***lanatum*** 'Washington Limes' (v) EPPr EWes
***lehmannianum*** CBct EBee NBPC NSti WCot
***sphondylium*** 'Hoggin' the Limelight' WAlt
- pink-flowered CNat

## *Herbertia* (*Iridaceae*)

§ ***lahue*** CDes CStu EBrs ECho LRHS WPGP

## *Hereroa* (*Aizoaceae*)

***odorata*** EShb

## *Hermannia* (*Sterculiaceae*)

***candicans*** see *H. incana*
***erodioides*** JCA 15523 CPBP
***flammea*** SPlb
§ ***incana*** CHal
***pinnata*** CPBP WAbe
***pulchella*** CPBP NWCA WAbe
***stricta*** CPBP NWCA WAbe

## *Hermodactylus* (*Iridaceae*)

§ ***tuberosus*** CAby CArn CAvo CBro CFFs CSpe CTri CWCL EBee EBrs ECGP ECha ECho ELon EPfP ERCP LAma LRHS MCot SBch SMeo SMrm SPhx WCot WTin
- BS 348 WCot
- MS 76 WCot
- MS 729 WCot
- MS 731 WCot
- MS 821 WCot
- MS 964 WCot
- PB WCot

## *Herniaria* (*Illecebraceae*)

***glabra*** CArn GBar GPoy MSal NGHP SIde

## *Herpolirion* (*Anthericaceae*)

***novae-zealandiae*** ECou

## *Hertia* see *Othonna*

## *Hesperaloe* (*Agavaceae*)

***parviflora*** CTrC IDee LEdu SBig SChr WCot

## *Hesperantha* (*Iridaceae*)

§ ***baurii*** CLyd CStu EBee EBrs ECho GBuc GGar NMen
***buhrii*** see *H. cucullata* 'Rubra'
***coccinea*** see *Schizostylis coccinea*
***cucullata*** EBee EBrs
* - 'Rubra' NWCA
***falcata*** EBee
***grandiflora*** EBee ECho
***huttonii*** EBee ECho GKev MSCN NBir NCGa
***mossii*** see *H. baurii*
§ ***radiata*** GGar
***tysonii*** see *H. radiata*
***woodii*** CFir

## *Hesperis* (*Brassicaceae*)

***lutea*** see *Sisymbrium luteum*
***matronalis*** Widely available
- ***alba*** see *H. matronalis* var. *albiflora*
§ - var. ***albiflora*** CCge CHrt CPrp CSpe CTri EBee ELau EPfP EWTr GMaP LCro LRHS MAvo MCot NGHP NGdn SIde SPer SPoG SSvw STes SWat WBrk WCAu WFar WMnd WMoo WPer
- - 'Alba Plena' (d) CAbP CCge CSpe EBee ECtt ELan GBuc LRHS MNrw NBir NCGa NCob WBrk WCot WFar WHer
- - 'Edith Harriet' (d/v) LLHF
- double-flowered (d) NCob NGdn
- 'Frogswell Doris' CBow
- 'Lilacina' SWat
- 'Lilacina Flore Pleno' (d) CCge NBre
***steveniana*** SMrm

## *Heterolepis* (*Asteraceae*)

***aliena*** SGar

## *Heteromeles* (*Rosaceae*)

***arbutifolia*** see *H. salicifolia*
§ ***salicifolia*** EShb

## *Heteromorpha* (*Apiaceae*)

***arborescens*** CPLG SPlb

## *Heteropappus* (*Asteraceae*)

***altaicus*** GAuc

## *Heteropolygonatum* (*Convallariaceae*)

***roseolum*** EBee

## *Heteropyxis* (*Myrtaceae*)

| | |
|---|---|
| ***natalensis*** | EShb |

## *Heterotheca* (*Asteraceae*)

| | |
|---|---|
| ***mariana*** | see *Chrysopsis mariana* |
| ***pumila*** | NWCA |
| § ***villosa*** | CSec WCot |

## *Heuchera* ✿ (*Saxifragaceae*)

| | |
|---|---|
| 'Amber Waves'PBR | Widely available |
| § ***americana*** | CEnt ECha GBar MRav NBir |
| - Dale's strain | CChe EBee EHoe IFoB LFur MNrw NLar SPlb SPur SWvt WClo WGor WHrl WMnd WPnP |
| - 'Eco-magnififolia' | CLAP |
| - 'Harry Hay' | CDes EBee EPPr MSte NDov WCot WPGP WSHC |
| - 'Ring of Fire' | EBee EBla ECtt EGle EPfP IBal LHop LRHS MDun MGos MSte NPri NSti SApp SDnm SPav SPla SPoG SWvt WCot WFar WPnP |
| 'Amethyst Myst' | CMMP COlW ECtt EPfP ERas LAst LRHS LSRN MGos NCob NLar NPri NScw SDnm SMeo SMrm SPav SPer SRkn SRot WFar WGor |
| 'Autumn Haze'PBR **new** | NHol |
| 'Baby's Breath' | ECho |
| 'Beauty Colour' | Widely available |
| 'Black Beauty' | see *H.* 'Dark Beauty' |
| * 'Black Velvet' | CDWL EBee EPfP NBre |
| 'Blackbird' ♀H4 | CMac EBee LBuc LFCN MBNS SApp SDnm SPav SPoG SRkn SSto SWvt WMnd |
| 'Blood Red' | LSou NBhm |
| 'Blood Vein' | CBow LBMP NBre |
| Bressingham hybrids | CWib GJos IFoB LBMP LRHS MLHP NBir NBlu NMir SEND SPer SRms WFar WPer |
| 'Brownfinch' | SMHy SUsu |
| 'Burgundy Frost' ♀H4 | WCot |
| 'Cafe Ole' **new** | GCai |
| 'Can-can' ♀H4 | Widely available |
| 'Canyon Duet' | EAEE EBee LRHS MSte NOrc |
| 'Canyon Pink' | NSti |
| 'Cappuccino' | EBee ECtt ELan MBNS MLLN NBro NPri SDnm SPav SWvt WCFE WFar |
| 'Caramel' | Widely available |
| 'Cascade Dawn' | EBee ECtt GBuc IBal LAst LBMP LHop LRHS MRav MSte NBir NLar SPav SPer SWvt WBrk WFar |
| 'Champagne Bubbles'PBR | EBee MBNS SPoG |
| 'Cherries Jubilee'PBR | CAbP CFir CHar EAEE EBee EBla EUJe GMaP LBMP LRHS MBNS MBri MGos MLLN NHol SHar SPav WBrk WFar WGor |
| 'Chiqui' | SUsu |
| ***chlorantha*** | NBre |
| 'Chocolate Ruffles'PBR | Widely available |
| 'Chocolate Veil' ♀H4 | EPfP |
| 'Citronelle' **new** | CBow CWCL EBee GCai MAvo MWea NMoo |
| 'City Lights' | LSou |
| 'Color Dream'PBR | GKir IBal SHBN |
| coral bells | see *H. sanguinea* |
| 'Coral Bouquet' | EBee GBri LAst LSou MBNS MLLN SHar WCot WCra |
| 'Coral Cloud' | MRav |
| Crème Brûlée = 'Tnheu041' (Dolce Series) | Widely available |
| 'Crème Caramel' | SHar |
| 'Crimson Curls' | EBee GKir SWvt |
| 'Crispy Curly' | MBNS NBre NBur |
| ***cylindrica*** | EBee EPfP LLWP MBNS MRav MSte NBre WPer |
| - var. ***alpina*** | NWCA |
| § - 'Greenfinch' | CWan EBee ECha EGle ELan EPfP GKev LBMP LRHS MLHP MRav MWhi NBir NOrc SPav SPer SWat WCAu WFar WMnd WPer |
| 'Dark Beauty'PBR | CBcs CBct EBee EWll GCai GJos LSou NCGa NHol NLar NPri SMrm SPoG SRot WGor |
| 'David' | CBow |
| 'Dennis Davidson' | see *H.* 'Huntsman' |
| Ebony and Ivory = 'E and I'PBR | Widely available |
| 'Eden's Aurora' | EBee SHBN WMnd |
| 'Eden's Mystery' | ECtt NBPN |
| 'Emperor's Cloak' | CEnt CHar CSsd ECGP LEdu NBur NDlv NLar SWvt WMoo |
| 'Emperor's Cloak' green-leaved | CEnt |
| 'Fantasia' | CBow |
| 'Firebird' | NBir NVic |
| Firefly | see *H.* 'Leuchtkäfer' |
| 'Fireworks'PBR ♀H4 | CBow CHFP EBee ECtt ERas GQue LSou MBNS MLLN NCob NLar NPri SAga SHar SPer SPla WBrk WClo WCot WFar WGor |
| 'Florist's Choice' | CAbP IBal MBNS MNFA SHar WCot |
| 'Frosted Violet'PBR | see *H.* 'Frosted Violet Dream' |
| § 'Frosted Violet Dream'PBR | CBow CHar EBee EBrs GCai LAst LSRN |
| 'Ginger Ale' | GCai LSou NBhm NHol |
| ***glauca*** | see *H. americana* |
| 'Green Ivory' | LRHS MRav NSti SBch |
| 'Green Spice' | CBct CWCL EBee ECtt EWll GBin LAst LHop LSou NCGa NHol NScw SMrm SPav SPer SPoG SRot SWvt WGor |
| 'Greenfinch' | see *H. cylindrica* 'Greenfinch' |
| ***grossulariifolia*** | WPer |
| 'Guardian Angel' **new** | EBee |
| 'Gypsy Dancer'PBR (Dancer Series) | LBuc |
| 'Helen Dillon' (v) | CBow EBee GCra LAst MLLN NBir NPri SPla SRGP SWvt WFar |
| 'Hercules'PBR | EBee ECtt EPfP |
| ***hispida*** | MSte WPer |
| 'Hollywood' | CBow LBuc NBhm |
| § 'Huntsman' | ECha ELan GBuc MBNS MRav WFar WMnd |
| 'Ibis' | EBee |
| 'Jade Gloss' **new** | EBee |
| 'Jubilee' | EBee |
| Key Lime Pie = 'Tnheu042'PBR (Dolce Series) | CBcs CBct CBod CWCL ECtt EWll GCai LAst LHop LRHS MBri MGos MWea NBro NCGa NPri NScw SDnm SPoG SRot STes SVil WGor |
| 'Lady in Red' | NBre |
| § 'Leuchtkäfer' | COlW CWat EBee ECtt EPfP GBuc GJos GMaP LAst LBMP LRHS MHer MRav MWat MWhi NBir NMir NOrc SPad SPer SPlb SPoG SRms WFar WMnd WMoo WPer WPtf |
| Licorice = 'Tnheu044' (Dolce Series) | CBod ECtt EWll GCai LRHS MBNS MBri MGos NCGa NLar NPri SDnm SPoG SRot SVil WGor WHoo |
| 'Lime' | LSou |
| 'Lime Rickey'PBR (Rainbow Series) | CBow CMac CWCL CWGN EBee GCai LBuc LSou MBri MGos NBhm NHol NLar SHar SPoG SRGP WHer |
| 'Little Tinker' | CHid LAst LSou NBir SPhx STes WBrk |

| | |
|---|---|
| 'Magic Color' | CBow NMoo |
| 'Magic Wand'PBR 🏆H4 | CAbP EBee MBNS SHar WCot |
| 'Marmalade'PBR | CMac EBee ENor EPfP EUJe GCai LBuc LCro LSRN LSou MBNS MBri MGos MLHP MWea NBhm SHar SPoG SRkn SWvt WFar |
| 'Mars' | EPfP MBNS SPav WCot |
| ***maxima*** | EMon |
| 'Mercury' | NMoo SPav WCot |
| 'Metallica' | MWat NGBl NLar WMoo |
| ***micans*** | see *H. rubescens* |
| ***micrantha*** | EBee GCal MLHP SRms |
| - var. ***diversifolia*** misapplied | see *H. villosa* |
| § - 'Ruffles' | ECha LRHS |
| 'Midnight Burgundy' **new** | GCai |
| 'Midnight Rose' **new** | CBow GCai |
| 'Mini Mouse' | EWes |
| 'Mint Frost'PBR | EBee EBrs ECtt ELan EPfP LAst LHop LRHS MGos MLLN MRav NGdn NHol NPri SDnm SPav SPer SPoG SWvt WCot WFar |
| 'Mocha' **new** | EBee GCai MNrw MWea NBPN NMoo |
| 'Molly Bush' 🏆H4 | EBee NMoo WCot |
| 'Monet' | see *H. sanguinea* 'Monet' |
| 'Monita Lime' **new** | CMoH |
| 'Montrose Ruby' | NBre |
| 'Moonlight' **new** | GCai |
| 'Mother of Pearl' | ECtt |
| 'Neptune' | EBee EPfP MAvo NMoo SPav |
| 'Oakington Jewel' | EBee EBrs ELan LRHS SHBN |
| 'Obsidian'PBR | Widely available |
| 'Painted Lady' | GBuc |
| ***parishii*** NNS 93-384 | NWCA |
| 'Peach Flambé' | CBow CWCL CWGN EBee ECtt GBin GCai LSRN LSou MAvo MBNS MMHG NBhm NDov SMrm SPoG WCra WGor |
| 'Peach Pie' **new** | NScw |
| 'Peachy Keen' | NBhm WCot |
| 'Peppermint Spice' (21st Century Collection Series) | LSou |
| 'Persian Carpet' | CHEx ECha ECtt EHrv GMaP LHop LRHS MDun MLLN NBir NGdn NPri SDnm SWvt WCot WFar WPtf |
| (Petite Series) 'Petite Marbled Burgundy' | CHFP EBee ECtt EGle EHoe GBri GKev GKir LAst LLHF MSte NDov NGdn NLar SWvt WAul WCot WFar |
| - 'Petite Pearl Fairy' | CAbP CBct CBow EBee ECtt EGle EHoe ELan EMil MSte NGdn NLar SPla SWvt WFar WGor |
| - 'Petite Pink Bouquet' | CBct EBee ECtt EHoe MBNS NLar SPla |
| 'Pewter Moon' | EBee ECtt ELan EMil EPfP LAst LCro LRHS MGos MRav NBir SDnm SHBN SPer SSto WBrk WFar WTin |
| 'Pewter Veil'PBR | EBee EPfP LAst MBNS MDun NPri SPer SPoG WFar WMnd |
| ***pilosissima*** | NBre |
| § 'Pluie de Feu' | CFir CWCL EBee EBrs ECtt EPPr EPfP GBri GKir MRav SSto WFar |
| 'Plum Pudding'PBR | Widely available |
| 'Prince' | CDWL EBee EBrs ELan EPfP GCai LFCN LSRN MBNS NBPN NMoo SApp SPoG SRkn SWvt WPtf |
| 'Prince of Silver' | MBNS NMoo |
| ***pringlei*** | see *H. rubescens* |
| * x ***pruhoniciana*** Doctor Sitar's hybrids | SRms |
| - 'Sancyl' | SRms |
| ***pubescens*** | EBee |
| ***pulchella*** | CBow CPBP CSsd EBee EDAr LRHS MHer MWat SRms |
| - JCA 9508 | NMen |
| 'Purple Mountain Majesty' | EBee ECtt LFCN MCot NBPN WBrk WCot |
| 'Purple Petticoats' 🏆H4 | CBcs EBee EPfP GCai LAst LSou MDun MLHP MLLN NBre NCob NDlv NGdn NHol NLar NPri SHar SMrm SRot WFar |
| 'Quick Silver' | EBla MNFA NBir SWvt WFar |
| 'Quilter's Joy' 🏆H4 | NBre |
| 'Rachel' | CAbP CMea CSev CWCL EBee EBrs ECtt EGle ELan GCal GMaP IFoB LRHS LSRN MRav MWat NBir SPer SPla SRGP SWvt WAul WBrk WFar WTin |
| Rain of Fire | see *H.* 'Pluie de Feu' |
| 'Raspberry Ice' | GKir |
| 'Raspberry Regal' 🏆H4 | ECtt MBNS MLLN MRav NBir NSti SWvt WAul WFar |
| 'Rave On' **new** | CWGN EBee GCai LSou |
| 'Red Spangles' | EPfP LRHS NBir |
| 'Regina' 🏆H4 | CAbP EBee ECGP ECtt EPfP LFCN LSRN NBro SHar SWvt WFar |
| ***richardsonii*** | MNrw |
| 'Robert' | MBNS |
| Rosemary Bloom = 'Heuros'PBR | EBee LRHS |
| § ***rubescens*** | CAbP ECho MTho NBro NMen WPer WThu |
| 'Ruby Veil' | EBee |
| 'Ruffles' | see *H. micrantha* 'Ruffles' |
| § ***sanguinea*** | CSBt LRHS MRav NBir WPer |
| - 'Alba' 🏆H4 | EMon SMHy |
| - 'Geisha's Fan' | CBow EAEE EBee LSou NBhm NHol SHar SPer SWvt |
| § - 'Monet' (v) | CBow EBee EPfP MLHP |
| - var. ***pulchra*** | CPBP |
| - 'Ruby Bells' | EAEE NPri SGar SPoG WBor |
| - 'Sioux Falls' | EWes NBre WPnP |
| § - 'Snow Storm' (v) | CBow CMoH ELan EPfP MGos MRav SPer SPlb WFar WMnd |
| - 'Taff's Joy' (v) | CBow EMon EWes |
| - 'White Cloud' (v) | EBee NBre SRms WPer |
| 'Saturn' | MBNS NMoo NSti SWvt |
| 'Scarlet Flame' | EBee |
| 'Schneewittchen' | EPfP MRav |
| 'Scintillation' 🏆H4 | CMoH ECtt NBre SRms |
| 'Shamrock' | NBre |
| 'Silver Indiana'PBR | EBee LSRN |
| 'Silver Lode' | EBee |
| 'Silver Scrolls'PBR | Widely available |
| 'Silver Shadows' | ETod MBrN |
| 'Silver Streak' | see x *Heucherella* 'Silver Streak' |
| 'Snow Angel' | EBee EPfP MBNS NBrd |
| 'Snow Storm' | see *H. sanguinea* 'Snow Storm' |
| 'Snowfire' (v) | GCai |
| 'Sparkling Burgundy' | GCai LSou |
| 'Starry Night' | SHar |
| 'Steel City' **new** | EBee |
| 'Stormy Seas' | CMHG COlW EBee EHoe ELan EPfP EPla EWsh GCra LRHS MLHP MLLN MNFA MRav NBir NDov NPri SGar SHBN SPer SPoG SWvt WBrk WCAu WCot WFar |
| 'Strawberries and Cream' (v) | EHrv MCot WHer |
| 'Strawberry Candy'PBR | CBow CWCL EBee ELon GCai GJos LAst LSou MWea NHol NLar SPoG SRkn |
| 'Strawberry Swirl' | CHar EBee EBla ECtt GMaP LAst MLLN MRav MSte NBir NDov NLar NPri NSti SPoG SWvt WCAu WCot WFar WOVN WPtf |

| | |
|---|---|
| Sugar Frosting = 'Pwheu0104' new | LAst NScw SRot SVil |
| 'Swirling Fantasy'PBR | CBow EPfP EShb GJos MBNS NMoo |
| 'Van Gogh' | MBNS |
| 'Veil of Passion' | NBre |
| 'Velvet Night' | CBow EBee EPfP EUJe EWsh LRHS MBri NBPN NBir NBre NHol WFar WMnd WPtf |
| 'Venus' | CHFP CMHG CWGN EBrs ECtt EPfP GQue LFur LSou MBNS NDov NGdn SHBN SMrm SPur SUsu WBrE WBrk WCot WCra WHoo |
| § ***villosa*** | ECha MRav |
| - 'Autumn Bride' | EBee LAst WRHF |
| - Bressingham Bronze = 'Absi'PBR | EPla ETod LBMP LRHS SPer SPla WFar |
| - 'Brownies' | MBNS |
| - 'Chantilly' new | EBee |
| - var. ***macrorhiza*** | EShb NBre WClo WMnd WPer WPnP |
| N - 'Palace Purple' | Widely available |
| - 'Palace Purple Select' | CTri CWCL CWat CWib LAst MCot SHBN SWvt WFar |
| - 'Royal Red' | ECha GBuc |
| 'White Marble' | LBMP NSti SHar |
| 'White Spires' | EBrs LBMP SHar |
| 'Winter Red' | EAEE EBee LAst LBMP MBNS SPur WCAu |
| 'Yeti' | WPnP |
| 'Zabeliana' | GBri |

## x *Heucherella* (*Saxifragaceae*)

| | |
|---|---|
| ***alba*** 'Bridget Bloom' | CPrp EBee EBla EBrs ECGP ECha ELan GMaP LBMP MRav NOrc SRms WCAu WFar |
| § - 'Rosalie' | CBow EBee EBla ECha GJos GKev GKir LRHS MBri MRav MSte NBir NBro NPro SPlb WBrk WFar WMoo |
| 'Birthday Cake' | EBee LSou |
| 'Burnished Bronze'PBR | CBct CBow EBee EBla ECtt GCai LRHS LSou MLLN MSte NBro NGdn NHol NLar NScw SDnm SHar SPav SPoG SRot SWvt WCot WFar |
| 'Chocolate Lace'PBR | EBee MLLN SHar |
| 'Cinnamon Bear' | EBee |
| 'Dayglow Pink'PBR | CBct EBla EPPr EShb GJos GMaP LSou MBri NBro NHol SHar SMrm SRkn SRot WFar WGor |
| Gold Strike = 'Hertn041' | CBow EWll GJos LAst SVil WGor |
| 'Heart of Darkness'PBR | EBee |
| 'Kimono'PBR ♀H4 | CDWL CWCL EAEE EBee ECtt EHrv ERas EUJe GCai GMaP GQue LAst LBMP LPla LSou MAvo MLLN MSte NBro NCGa NGdn NHol NLar NMyG NPri SHar SRot WCot |
| 'Ninja'PBR | see *Tiarella* 'Ninja' |
| 'Party Time'PBR | LSou |
| 'Pink Frost' | EBla GBuc |
| Pink Whispers = 'Hertn042' | CBow LFur SVil |
| 'Quicksilver' | CBct EBee EBla EHrv EMil EWTr GBuc GJos GMaP LAst MDun MSte NGdn NPri SWvt WCAu WCot WFar |
| 'Ring of Fire' | CMoH WFar |
| § 'Silver Streak' | CBow EBee EBla LFur MSte NBro SPla SPoG SWvt WFar WMoo |
| 'Stoplight' | Wideldy |
| 'Sunspot' (v) | EAEE EBee ECtt EMil EPfP EUJe LRHS MGos NBro NMyG NSti SHar SPoG WBor WCot WHer |
| ***tiarelloides*** ♀H4 | EBee EPfP LRHS WMnd |
| § 'Viking Ship'PBR | Widely available |

## *Hexastylis* see *Asarum*

## *Hibanobambusa* (*Poaceae*)

| | |
|---|---|
| 'Kimmei' | EBee |
| ***tranquillans*** | CEnt CMCo EFul EPla MBrN MMoz MMuc MWht WPGP |
| - 'Shiroshima' (v) ♀H4 | CAbb CDTJ CDoC CEnt CGHE EAmu EBee ENBC EPla ERod LPal MAvo MBrN MBri MCCP MMoz MWhi MWht NMoo NPal NVic SApp SBig WPGP |

## *Hibbertia* (*Dilleniaceae*)

| | |
|---|---|
| ***aspera*** | CBcs CCCN CRHN EBee ECre LRHS SKHP WFar WSHC |
| § ***cuneiformis*** | MAsh |
| ***procumbens*** | WAbe |
| § ***scandens*** ♀H1 | CBcs CCCN CHEx CHll CRHN CTsd ECou ELan SOWG WCot |
| ***stricta*** | ECou |
| ***tetrandra*** | see *H. cuneiformis* |
| * ***venustula*** | ECou |
| ***volubilis*** | see *H. scandens* |

## *Hibiscus* ✿ (*Malvaceae*)

| | |
|---|---|
| ***acetosella*** 'Red Shield' | CSpe |
| ***cannabinus*** | SIde |
| ***coccineus*** | EShb MSte SMad SOWG |
| ***fallax*** | CHll |
| ***hamabo*** | ELan |
| ***huegelii*** | see *Alyogyne huegelii* |
| 'Kopper King'PBR new | LRHS MAsh |
| ***leopoldii*** | SPer SRms |
| ***manihot*** | see *Abelmoschus manihot* |
| 'Moesiana' | MBri |
| ***moscheutos*** | CArn CFir MSte SMad SVic |
| - 'Galaxy' | EShb WHil |
| - Southern Belle Group | CHEx |
| ***mutabilis*** | CSec SOWG |
| ***paramutabilis*** | EWes SMad |
| 'Pyranees Pink' | EMil |
| ***rosa-sinensis*** | EBak EShb LRHS MBri SOWG |
| - 'All Aglow' | SOWG |
| - 'Bimbo' | SOWG |
| - 'Casablanca' | MBri |
| - 'Cockatoo' | SOWG |
| - 'Cooperi' (v) ♀H1 | CHal SOWG |
| - Full Moon = 'Monoon' (d) | SOWG |
| - 'Gina Marie' | SOWG |
| - 'Great White' | SOWG |
| - 'Hawaiian Sunset' | SOWG |
| - 'Holiday' | MBri |
| - 'Jewel of India' | SOWG |
| - 'Kardinal' | MBri |
| - 'Kim Ellen' | SOWG |
| - 'Kinchen's Yellow' | SOWG |
| - 'Königer' | MBri |
| - 'Lady Flo' | SOWG |
| - 'Lemon Chiffon' (d) | SOWG |
| - 'Molly Cummings' | SOWG |
| - 'Mrs Andreasen' | SOWG |
| - 'Norman Lee' | SOWG |
| - 'Pink Mist' | SOWG |
| - 'Sprinkle Rain' | SOWG |
| - 'Tarantella' | SOWG |
| - 'Ten Thirty Seven' | SOWG |
| - 'Thelma Bennell' | SOWG |
| - 'Tivoli' | MBri |
| - 'Weekend' | SOWG |
| - 'Wings Away' | SOWG |
| ***sabdariffa*** | MSal |
| ***schizopetalus*** ♀H1 | MJnS SBig SOWG |

| | |
|---|---|
| ***sinosyriacus*** | EPfP |
| – 'Lilac Queen' | LRHS SPoG WPGP |
| – 'Ruby Glow' | MGos WPGP |
| ***syriacus*** | EHig MNHC WFar |
| – 'Admiral Dewey' (d) | EBee MGos SPla |
| – 'Aphrodite' | CPMA EBee MRav |
| – 'Ardens' (d) | CEnd CSBt ELon EMui EPfP LAst MAsh MGos NLar SPer |
| – Blue Bird | see *H. syriacus* 'Oiseau Bleu' |
| – 'Boule de Feu' (d) | ELan SEND |
| – 'Bredon Springs' ♀H4 | MRav |
| – 'Caeruleus Plenus' (d) | MGos |
| – 'China Chiffon' | EMil MAsh |
| – 'Coelestis' | MGos SPer |
| – 'Diana' ♀H4 | EBee EMil EPfP EQua LRHS LSRN MAsh MGos MRav NPri SLon |
| – 'Dorothy Crane' | CEnd LRHS MAsh MGos |
| – 'Duc de Brabant' (d) | CSBt EBee ELon EMil EMui EPfP SHBN SPer |
| – 'Elegantissimus' | see *H. syriacus* 'Lady Stanley' |
| – 'Eleonore' **new** | EMil |
| – 'Freedom' | EBee EMil |
| – 'Hamabo' ♀H4 | CDul CSBt CTri EBee EMil EPfP LAst LPan LRHS LSRN MAsh MBri MGos MWat NLar SCoo SHBN SLim SPer SPla SPoG SWvt WDin WFar |
| – 'Helene' | ELan EMil EQua LRHS LSRN MAsh MBlu MRav |
| – 'Jeanne d'Arc' (d) | EMil SLon |
| § – 'Lady Stanley' (d) | EBee LRHS MAsh MGan SCoo SPer |
| – Lavender Chiffon = 'Notwoodone'PBR ♀H4 | EBee ELan EMil EPfP EWes LRHS MGos NPri SCoo SPer SPoG |
| – 'Lenny' ♀H4 | MAsh MGos |
| – 'Leopoldii' | EQua |
| – 'Marina' | EMil EMui EPfP MAsh MRav |
| – 'Meehanii' misapplied | see *H. syriacus* 'Purpureus Variegatus' |
| – 'Meehanii' (v) ♀H4 | CDul CEnd CSBt EMil EPfP LRHS MAsh MGos SCoo SPer SPla SPoG |
| – 'Monstrosus' | EBee NLar |
| § – 'Oiseau Bleu' ♀H4 | Widely available |
| – Pastelrose = 'Minpast' **new** | MAsh |
| – Pink Giant = 'Flogi' | EBee ELan EPfP EQua LRHS MBri MGos SLon SPer |
| § – 'Purpureus Variegatus' (v) | CSBt LAst MGos SPoG |
| – 'Red Heart' ♀H4 | CEnd CPMA CSBt CTri EBee ELan EPfP LAst LRHS MAsh MBri MCCP NLar NPri SPer SPla SPoG SRms SWvt WCFE WDin |
| – Rosalbane = 'Minrosa' | EBee EMil |
| – 'Roseus Plenus' (d) | WDin |
| – Russian Violet = 'Floru' | CBcs CEnd EBee ELan EMil EPfP LAst MGos |
| – 'Sanchon Yo' | EPfP |
| – 'Shintaeyang' **new** | MGos |
| – 'Souvenir de Charles Breton' | EMil |
| – 'Speciosus' | EMui SLon SPer |
| – 'Totus Albus' | CSBt SPoG |
| – 'Variegatus' | see *H. syriacus* 'Purpureus Variegatus' |
| – White Chiffon = 'Notwoodtwo'PBR (d) ♀H4 | EBee ELan EMil EPfP EWes LRHS LSRN MGos MRav SCoo SPer SPoG |
| – 'William R. Smith' ♀H4 | CPMA EBee ELan EMil LAst MSwo SEND SHBN SLon SPer WDin |
| – 'Woodbridge' ♀H4 | Widely available |
| ***trionum*** | CSec CSpe SBch SUsu WKif |
| – 'Sunny Day' | ELan |

## hickory, shagbark see *Carya ovata*

## *Hieracium* (*Asteraceae*)

| | |
|---|---|
| ***aurantiacum*** | see *Pilosella aurantiaca* |
| ***brunneocroceum*** | see *Pilosella aurantiaca* subsp. *carpathicola* |
| ***bupleuroides*** **new** | CSec |
| § ***glaucum*** | WEas |
| § ***lanatum*** | CSpe ECho MDKP NBir WEas WRos |
| ***longifolium*** CC 4346 **new** | CSec |
| ***maculatum*** | see *H. spilophaeum* |
| ***pilosella*** | see *Pilosella officinarum* |
| ***praecox*** | see *H. glaucum* |
| ***scabrum*** **new** | CSec |
| ***scullyi*** | EPPr |
| § ***spilophaeum*** | CSec EHoe GGar LRHS NBid NPer WOut WPer WRos |
| – 'Leopard' | CEnt CSsd EBee SGar |
| ***umbellatum*** | EBWF WOut |
| ***villosum*** | CSec CSpe EBee ECho EHoe GGar LRHS MDun NBro WHer WRos |
| ***waldsteinii*** | MDKP |
| ***welwitschii*** | see *H. lanatum* |

## *Hierochloe* (*Poaceae*)

| | |
|---|---|
| ***odorata*** | GBin GFor GPoy MBNS |

## hildaberry see *Rubus* 'Hildaberry'

## *Himalayacalamus* (*Poaceae*)

| | |
|---|---|
| ***asper*** | CDTJ CGHE EPla ERod WPGP |
| * ***equatus*** **new** | EPla |
| § ***falconeri*** | CDTJ CEnt EFul EPfP EPla MAsh MMoz SDix WPGP |
| § – 'Damarapa' | CDTJ EPla MMoz WDyG |
| § ***hookerianus*** | EAmu EPla |
| ***porcatus*** | CDTJ CGHE WPGP |

## *Himantoglossum* (*Orchidaceae*)

| | |
|---|---|
| ***hircinum*** | SHdy |

## x *Hippeasprekelia* (*Amaryllidaceae*)

| | |
|---|---|
| 'Red Beauty' | CFwr EBrs |
| 'Red Star' **new** | CCCN |

## *Hippeastrum* (*Amaryllidaceae*)

| | |
|---|---|
| x ***acramannii*** | WCot WVal |
| ***advenum*** | see *Rhodophiala advena* |
| 'Alfresco'PBR **new** | WVal |
| 'Amalfi' **new** | WVal |
| 'Amoretta' | LRHS |
| 'Amputo' | LAma LRHS WVal |
| 'Apple Blossom' | EBrs LAma LRHS MBri SGar |
| ***aulicum*** | WVal |
| 'Baby Doll' **new** | WVal |
| 'Benfica' **new** | LAma |
| ***bifidum*** | see *Rhodophiala bifida* |
| 'Black Pearl' **new** | WVal |
| ***blossfeldiae*** **new** | WVal |
| 'Blossom Peacock' (d) | EBrs LAma |
| 'Bogota' **new** | LAma WVal |
| 'Bordeaux' **new** | WVal |
| 'Bouquet' **new** | LAma |
| 'Britney' **new** | LAma |
| 'Calimero' | EBrs |
| 'Candy Floss' **new** | WVal |
| 'Charisma' | EBrs |
| 'Chico' | LAma LRHS WVal |
| 'Christmas Gift' | EBrs |
| 'Clown' | EBrs |
| 'Dancing Queen' | LAma |
| 'Double Record' (d) | EBrs |
| 'Elvas' | EBrs |
| 'Emerald' | LAma LRHS |

| | |
|---|---|
| 'Estella' **new** | LAma WVal |
| 'Fairytale' | EBrs MBri WVal |
| 'Firecracker' **new** | WVal |
| 'Giraffe' **new** | WVal |
| ***gracile*** 'Pamela' | CStu LAma |
| 'Grand Duchess' **new** | WVal |
| 'Grandeur' | LAma LRHS WVal |
| 'Green Goddess' | LAma |
| 'Hercules' | LRHS MBri |
| 'Inca' | LAma |
| 'Intokazi' **new** | WVal |
| 'Jade Serpent' **new** | WVal |
| 'Jewel' (d) | EBrs MBri |
| x ***johnsonii*** **new** | CPLG |
| 'Jungle Star' | EBrs |
| 'La Paz' | LAma LRHS |
| 'Lady Jane' | LRHS MBri |
| 'Lemon Lime' | EBrs LAma |
| 'Lima' | LAma LRHS WVal |
| 'Little Devil' **new** | WVal |
| 'Little Star' **new** | WVal |
| 'Lovely Garden' | LAma |
| 'Loyalty' **new** | LAma |
| 'Ludwig Dazzler' | LRHS |
| 'Magic Green' **new** | WVal |
| 'Mary Lou' (d) | EBrs |
| 'Melusine' | WVal |
| 'Merengue' | EBrs LAma WVal |
| 'Minerva' | LRHS |
| 'Misty' **new** | LAma WVal |
| 'Mount Blanc' | LRHS |
| 'Naughty Lady' **new** | LAma |
| 'Orange Souvereign' 𝕐H1 **new** | WVal |
| ***papilio*** 𝕐H1 | CTca IHer LAma LRHS MMHG WVal |
| ***petiolatum*** **new** | WVal |
| 'Philadelphia' (d) | EBrs LRHS |
| 'Picotee' | EBrs LAma |
| 'Pink Floyd' | EBrs LAma WVal |
| 'Pink Star' | EBrs |
| ***psittacinum*** **new** | WVal |
| ***puniceum*** | WVal |
| 'Quito' **new** | LAma |
| 'Rebecca' **new** | LAma |
| 'Red Lion' | EBrs LAma LRHS |
| 'Red Peacock' (d) | LAma LRHS |
| 'Reggae' | LAma WVal |
| 'Rembrandt van Rijn' **new** | LAma |
| 'Rilona' **new** | LAma |
| 'Rock and Roll' **new** | WVal |
| 'Roma' | LRHS |
| 'Rosario' **new** | WVal |
| 'Royal Velvet' | LAma WVal |
| 'Ruby Meyer' | LAma LRHS |
| ***rutilum*** **new** | WVal |
| - var. ***fulgidum*** | WVal |
| * 'San Antonio Rose' | CDes WCot WPGP WVal |
| 'Santa Cruz' **new** | WVal |
| 'Santiago' **new** | LAma |
| 'Santos' **new** | WVal |
| 'Scarlet Baby' | LRHS |
| 'Solomon' | EBrs |
| ***striatum*** | WCot WVal |
| ***stylosum*** | EBrs |
| 'Sweet Surrender' **new** | LAma |
| 'Tango' | LAma |
| 'Toledo' | WVal |
| 'Toughie' | CDes CMdw CSpe EBee LLHF WCot WPGP WVal |
| 'Trentino' **new** | WVal |
| 'Unique' (d) | EBrs |
| 'Vera' | LRHS |
| 'Vesuvius' **new** | WVal |
| ***vittatum*** | CBgR CSec EBrs |
| 'White Christmas' **new** | LAma |
| 'White Dazzler' | LAma |
| 'White Peacock' (d) | LRHS |
| 'Yellow Goddess' | EBrs EShb |
| 'Zombie' **new** | WVal |

## *Hippocrepis* (*Papilionaceae*)

| | |
|---|---|
| § ***comosa*** | CRWN EBWF |
| § ***emerus*** | CBcs CBgR CCCN CMHG CPLG EBee ELan EPfP LAst LHop MBri MGos NLar SPoG SSto STre WAbe WRHF WSHC WTou |

## *Hippolytia* (*Asteraceae*)

| | |
|---|---|
| § ***herderi*** | EOHP |

## *Hippophae* (*Elaeagnaceae*)

| | |
|---|---|
| ***rhamnoides*** 𝕐H4 | CArn CBcs CCVT CDul CLnd CRWN CSBt CSpe CTri EBee ECrN EHoe ELan EMac EPfP LBuc MBar MBlu MCoo NWea SPlb WDin WFar WMou |
| - 'Askola' (f) | MGos |
| - 'Frugna' (f) | CAgr |
| - 'Hergo' (f) | CAgr MBri MCoo |
| - 'Hikal Dafo' (m) | CAgr |
| - 'Hikul' | EMil |
| - 'Juliet' (f) | CAgr |
| - 'Leikora' (f) | CAgr ELan MBlu MCoo MGos NLar SPer |
| - 'Matt' (m) | MCoo |
| - 'Pollmix' (m) | CAgr ELan MBlu MBri MGos NLar SPer |
| - 'Romeo' (m) | CAgr |
| ***salicifolia*** | CAgr |
| - GWJ 9221 | WCru |

## *Hippuris* (*Hippuridaceae*)

| | |
|---|---|
| ***vulgaris*** | CBen EHon EMFW MSKA NPer WFar WMAq |

## *Hirpicium* (*Asteraceae*)

| | |
|---|---|
| ***armerioides*** | NWCA |

## *Histiopteris* (*Dennstaedtiaceae*)

| | |
|---|---|
| ***incisa*** | WRic |

## *Hoheria* ✿ (*Malvaceae*)

| | |
|---|---|
| § ***angustifolia*** | ECou EPfP SSpi |
| 'Borde Hill' | CPMA CWsd EBee ECou EPfP LRHS SSpi WHCG WPat |
| 'County Park' | ECou |
| ***glabrata*** | CBcs CWsd ECou EPfP GGal GGar GKir NBir NPal WPGP |
| - 'Silver Stars' | EPfP |
| 'Glory of Amlwch' 𝕐H3 | CAbb CDul CPMA CSam CTho CWsd ECou EPfP MRav SSpi WKif WPGP |
| 'Hill House' | CHll |
| 'Holbrook' | CSam |
| § ***lyallii*** 𝕐H4 | CBcs CCCN CDoC CDul CPLG EBee ECou ELan EMil EPfP IDee LRHS LSRN SHBN SPer SSpi SSta WBod WDin |
| - 'Chalk Hills' | ECou |
| - 'Swale Stream' | ECou |
| ***microphylla*** | see *H. angustifolia* |
| ***populnea*** | CBcs CCCN IDee SGar |
| - 'Alba Variegata' (v) | CDoC CTrC ECou |
| - 'Moonlight' | CDoC |
| - 'Purple Shadow' | ECou |
| - 'Sunshine' (v) | CDoC SSta |

| | |
|---|---|
| - 'Variegata' | ECou |
| 'Purple Delta' | ECou |
| ***sexstylosa*** | CAbb CDoC CDul CHEx CHid CMHG CSpe CTri EBee ECou EHig ELan EPfP EWTr IMGH ISea LHop LRHS MGos SEND SPoG SPur SSta SWvt |
| - 'Pendula' | CBcs WDin |
| - 'Stardust' ♀H4 | Widely available |

## *Holarrhena* (*Apocynaceae*)

| | |
|---|---|
| ***pubescens*** | CCCN |

## *Holboellia* (*Lardizabalaceae*)

| | |
|---|---|
| ***angustifolia*** | MBri NLar WCru |
| - subsp. ***obtusa*** DJHC 506 **new** | WCru |
| ***chapaensis*** HWJ 1023 | WCru |
| ***coriacea*** | CBcs CHEx CHll CSam EBee EPfP IDee LEdu LRHS MGos MRav NLar SAPC SArc SOWG SSta WBor WCru |
| ***fargesii*** | WCru WSHC |
| ***grandiflora*** B&SWJ 8223 | WCru |
| ***latifolia*** | CBcs CHEx CRHN CSBt CSam CTrG CTri EBee ELan EPfP GGal LPan LRHS MTPN NLar SAPC SArc SEND SLPl SLim SOWG SPoG WCFE WFar WPGP |
| - HWJK 2014 | WCru |
| - HWJK 2213 **new** | WCru |
| - SF 95134 | ISea |

## *Holcus* (*Poaceae*)

| | |
|---|---|
| ***lanatus*** | EBWF WSFF |
| ***mollis*** 'Albovariegatus' (v) | CWCL EBee ECha EHoe ELan EPPr EPfP GMaP LRHS MBar MWhi NBid NBro NGdn NPer NSti SPlb SPoG WEas WFar WMoo WPer WTin |
| - 'Jackdaw's Cream' (v) | EPPr |
| - 'White Fog' (v) | CChe EBee EHul EPPr MBlu NHol SApp SEND WFar |

## *Holodiscus* (*Rosaceae*)

| | |
|---|---|
| ***discolor*** | CBcs CDul EBee ELan EPfP EWes GQui IDee LRHS MBlu MBri MRav NSti SCoo SHBN SLon SMad SPer SPlb SPoG SSpi SSta WDin WHCG |
| - var. ***ariifolius*** | EPfP EWTr |
| ***dumosus*** | EBee NLar WPGP |

## *Homalocladium* (*Polygonaceae*)

| | |
|---|---|
| § ***platycladum*** | CHal EShb |

## *Homeria* (*Iridaceae*)

| | |
|---|---|
| ***breyniana*** | see *H. collina* |
| - var. ***aurantiaca*** | see *H. flaccida* |
| § ***collina*** | ECho ERos |
| § ***flaccida*** | EBrs ECho |
| ***ochroleuca*** | CSec EBrs ECho |

## *Homoglossum* see *Gladiolus*

## *Hordeum* (*Poaceae*)

| | |
|---|---|
| ***chilense*** | EBee |
| ***jubatum*** | CBod CHrt CKno CSpe CWCL CWib EAlp EHoe EPla EWes GKev LHop MSCN MWat MWhi NChi NDov NGdn NHol SApp SEND SIng SPhx SPoG SUsu WRos |
| - from Ussuri | NGBl |

## *Horkeliella* (*Rosaceae*)

| | |
|---|---|
| ***purpurascens*** NNS 98-323 | WCot |

## *Horminum* (*Lamiaceae*)

| | |
|---|---|
| ***pyrenaicum*** | CSec EBee ECho GAbr MAvo MMuc SRms WFar WMoo WOut WPer WPtf WRos WTin |
| - pale blue-flowered | MDKP MSte |

## horseradish see *Armoracia rusticana*

## *Hosta* ✿ (*Hostaceae*)

| | |
|---|---|
| AGSJ 302 | CDes |
| 'A Many-Splendored Thing' | IBal |
| 'Abba Dabba Do' (v) | CBdn EGol EMic EPGN LBuc NHol NMyG SApp |
| 'Abba Irresistable' (v) **new** | EMic |
| 'Abba Showtime' | EMic IBal |
| 'Abby' (v) | CBdn CBgR EGol EMic EPGN IBal MBNS NMyG SApp |
| 'Abiqua Ariel' | CBdn EMic SApp |
| 'Abiqua Blue Crinkles' | CBdn EMic NBir SApp |
| 'Abiqua Blue Edger' | EMic |
| 'Abiqua Blue Madonna' **new** | EMic |
| 'Abiqua Blushing Recluse' **new** | EMic |
| 'Abiqua Drinking Gourd' | CBdn EBee EGol EMic EPGN GBin IBal MHom MIDC NMyG SApp |
| 'Abiqua Ground Cover' | EGol IBal |
| 'Abiqua Moonbeam' (v) | CBdn CFir EMic EPGN IBal MSwo NGdn NMyG SApp |
| 'Abiqua Recluse' | EGol EMic SApp |
| 'Abiqua Trumpet' | CBdn EGol EMic IBal NGdn NLar NMyG SApp |
| 'Abiqua Zodiac' | CBdn |
| 'Academy Fire' (v) **new** | EMic |
| ***aequinoctiiantha*** | EGol |
| 'Afternoon Delight' (v) **new** | EMic |
| 'Aksarben' | EMic |
| ***albomarginata*** | see *H. sieboldii* 'Paxton's Original' |
| § 'Albomarginata' (*fortunei*) (v) | CBcs CBdn CWib EBee EGol EMic EQua GKir MBar MNrw NBir NMyG SHBN SPoG SWvt WBrE |
| 'Alex Summers' | EBee EMic IBal NBhm WFar |
| ***alismifolia*** **new** | IBal |
| 'Allan P. McConnell' (v) | CBdn EGol EMic EPGN GCra WHal |
| 'Allegan Emperor' (v) **new** | IBal |
| 'Allegan Fog' (v) | CBdn EGol EMic IBal |
| 'Alligator Shoes' (v) | EGol EMic IBal |
| 'Alpine Aire' | EMic |
| 'Alpine Dream' **new** | IBal |
| 'Alvatine Taylor' (v) | CBdn EGol EMic |
| 'Amanuma' | EGol EMic IBal MHom |
| 'Amber Maiden' (v) | EGol |
| 'Amber Tiara' | EMic |
| 'American Dream' (v) | CBdn EBee EGol EMic EPGN GSec IBal NMyG |
| 'American Halo' | EMic IBal MIDC NBPC NLar SPoG |
| 'American Icon' **new** | IBal |
| 'American Sweetheart' | IBal |
| 'Amy Elizabeth' (v) | CBdn EGol EMic IBal |
| 'Angel Feathers' (v) | EGol |
| 'Ann Kulpa' (v) | CBdn EMic EPGN IBal NMyG |
| 'Anne' (v) | CBdn EGol EMic IBal LSRN |
| 'Anne Arett' (*sieboldii*) (v) | EPGN |
| 'Antioch' (*fortunei*) (v) | CBdn EGol EMic GQue IBal MIDC MRav MSte NMyG WFar |
| 'Aoki' (*fortunei*) | EMic EPGN NHol |
| 'Aphrodite' (*plantaginea*) (d) | EBee EGol EHrv EMic IBal LSou MBNS MCot MHom MSte NCob NGdn NLar NMoo SApp SMrm SPer SPoG WCot WGwG |
| 'Apollo' | NNor |
| 'Apple Court' | SApp |

| | |
|---|---|
| 'Apple Green' | EMic IBal MMiN |
| 'Apple Pie' | SApp |
| 'Aqua Velva' | EGol IBal |
| 'Arc de Triomphe' **new** | EMic IBal |
| 'Archangel' | EGol |
| 'Argentea Variegata' (*undulata*) | see *H. undulata* var. *undulata* |
| 'Aristocrat' (Tardiana Group) (v) | CBdn EGol EMic EPGN IBal NMyG SApp |
| 'Asian Beauty' | EGol |
| 'Aspen Gold' (*tokudama* hybrid) | EMic SApp |
| 'Athena' (v) **new** | IBal |
| 'Atlantis' **new** | EMic IBal |
| 'August Beauty' | CBdn EMic |
| 'August Moon' | Widely available |
| ***aureafolia*** | see *H.* 'Starker Yellow Leaf' |
| 'Aureoalba' (*fortunei*) | see *H.* 'Spinners' |
| 'Aureomaculata' (*fortunei*) | see *H. fortunei* var. *albopicta* |
| * 'Aureomarginata' ambig. (v) | CPrp GKev GKir SCoo |
| 'Aureomarginata' (*montana*) (v) | CBdn EGol EHoe ELan EMic EPGN EWsh GCal GMaP IBal MIDC MMiN NCGa NGdn NHol NLar NMyG SApp SMrm SPla WFar WTin |
| 'Aureomarginata' (*rohdeifolia*) (v) **new** | EMic |
| § 'Aureomarginata' (*ventricosa*) (v) ♀H4 | CBdn CBro ECha EGol EMic EPfP IBal LRHS MIDC MMiN MWat NGdn NVic SApp WFar WTin |
| 'Aureostriata' (*tardiva*) | see *H.* 'Inaho' |
| 'Aurora Borealis' (*sieboldiana*) (v) | EGol |
| 'Austin Dickinson' (v) | EGol EMic IBal LBuc |
| 'Avalanche' **new** | IBal |
| 'Avocado' **new** | IBal |
| 'Awesome' (*venusta*) **new** | EMic |
| 'Azure Snow' | CBdn EGol EMic |
| 'Babbling Brook' | EGol |
| 'Baby Blue' (Tardiana Group) **new** | EMic |
| 'Baby Blue Eyes' **new** | IBal |
| 'Baby Bunting' | CBdn EGol EMic EPGN IBal MBNS NBro NLar NPro |
| 'Ballerina' | EGol IBal |
| 'Banana Boat' (v) | EGol EMic IBal |
| 'Band of Gold' | IBal |
| 'Banyai's Dancing Girl' | EGol EMic MMiN |
| 'Barbara Ann' (v) | CBdn EMic EPGN IBal MBri |
| 'Barbara May' **new** | IBal |
| 'Barbara White' | EGol IBal |
| 'Baue's Boat' **new** | EMic |
| 'Bea's Colossus' | SApp |
| 'Beauty Little Blue' | EGol |
| 'Beauty Substance' | CBdn EGle EGol EMic EPGN NMyG |
| 'Beckoning' **new** | IBal |
| 'Bedford Blue' | IBal |
| 'Bell Bottom Blues' **new** | IBal |
| ***bella*** | see *H. fortunei* var. *obscura* |
| 'Bennie McRae' | EGol |
| 'Betcher's Blue' | EGol EMic |
| 'Betsy King' | EBee EGol EMic MRav NHol NMyG |
| 'Bette Davis Eyes' | EGol |
| 'Betty' | EGol IBal |
| 'Bianca' | SApp |
| 'Biddy's Blue' **new** | IBal |
| 'Big Boy' (*montana*) | EGol GSec NNor |
| 'Big Daddy' (*sieboldiana* hybrid) (v) | Widely available |
| 'Big Mama' | CDWL EGol EMic EUJe IBal LRHS NBhm NLar |
| 'Bigfoot' | EGol EMic |
| 'Biggie' **new** | IBal |
| 'Bill Brinka' (v) | EGol EMic |
| 'Bill Dress's Blue' | EMic IBal |
| 'Bingo' (v) **new** | EMic |
| 'Birchwood Blue' | EGol |
| 'Birchwood Blue Beauty' **new** | IBal |
| 'Birchwood Elegance' | CBdn SApp |
| 'Birchwood Gem' **new** | IBal |
| § 'Birchwood Parky's Gold' | CBdn CMHG CMoH EAEE EBee EGol EMic EPfP EWTr GMaP IBal LBMP MBNS MIDC MMiN NCob NGdn NHol SApp SHBN SPoG |
| 'Birchwood Ruffled Queen' | EGol EMic |
| 'Bitsy Gold' | EGol EMic IBal |
| 'Bitsy Green' | EGol |
| 'Bizarre' **new** | EMic IBal |
| 'Black Beauty' | EGol EMic EPGN IBal |
| 'Black Hills' | CBdn CWib EGol EMic IBal MBNS NMyG |
| 'Blackfoot' | EGol EMic |
| 'Blaue Venus' | EGol IBal |
| 'Blauspecht' **new** | IBal |
| 'Blazing Saddles' | EMic IBal MBNS MIDC |
| 'Blonde Elf' | EGol EMic IBal NGdn NHol NMyG SApp |
| 'Blue Angel' misapplied | see *H. sieboldiana* var. *elegans* |
| 'Blue Angel' (*sieboldiana*) ♀H4 | Widely available |
| 'Blue Arrow' | CBdn EGol EPGN IBal LPla SApp |
| 'Blue Beard' | IBal |
| 'Blue Belle' (Tardiana Group) | CBdn EGol EMic MMiN MSte NGdn NPro WHoo WTin |
| 'Blue Blazes' | EMic LRHS |
| 'Blue Blush' (Tardiana Group) | CBdn EGol EMic GSec NGdn |
| 'Blue Boy' | CBdn CWsd EGol EMic EWes MMiN NHol NMyG |
| 'Blue Cadet' | CBcs CBdn EAEE EGol EMic EMil GEdr IBal IFoB LAst LPBA MBar MLHP MMiN NBir NGdn NLar NMyG SApp SBod SHBN SMrm SPoG WCAu WFar WMnd |
| 'Blue Canoe' | EMic IBal SApp |
| 'Blue Chip' | CBdn EMic EPGN IBal |
| 'Blue Clown' | IBal |
| 'Blue Cup' (*sieboldiana*) | CBdn EMic MRav |
| 'Blue Danube' (Tardiana Group) | CBdn EGol EMic IBal MHom MMiN |
| 'Blue Diamond' (Tardiana Group) | CBdn EGol EMic EPGN IBal MMiN WFar |
| 'Blue Dimples' (Tardiana Group) | CBdn EGol EMic IBal LRHS MMiN NMoo |
| 'Blue Edger' | CBdn CTca EMic NBir |
| 'Blue Eyes' | IBal |
| 'Blue Flame' | EMic IBal |
| 'Blue Haired Lady' **new** | IBal |
| 'Blue Hawaii' **new** | IBal |
| 'Blue Heart' (*sieboldiana*) | EMic |
| 'Blue Ice' (Tardiana Group) | CBdn EGol EMic EPGN IBal |
| 'Blue Impression' | EMic |
| 'Blue Jay' (Tardiana Group) | CBdn EGol EMic IBal |
| 'Blue Lady' | CBdn EMic |
| 'Blue Mammoth' (*sieboldiana*) | CBdn EGol EMic IBal LRHS |
| 'Blue Monday' | EMic |
| 'Blue Moon' (Tardiana Group) | CBdn CMea EGol EMic EPGN EPfP IBal MHom NGdn NHol WAul |
| 'Blue Mountains' | IBal LBuc |
| 'Blue Mouse Ears' | CBdn EGol EMic EPGN GBin IBal NMyG |
| 'Blue Seer' (*sieboldiana*) | CBdn EGol EMic IBal |
| 'Blue Shadows' (*tokudama*) (v) | CBdn EMic EPGN ESwi IBal LRHS MIDC SApp SHBN |

| | |
|---|---|
| 'Blue Skies' (Tardiana Group) | CBdn EGol EMic IBal MHom SApp |
| 'Blue Sophistication' **new** | EMic |
| 'Blue Umbrellas' (*sieboldiana* hybrid) | CBdn CDWL CMoH EGol ELan EMic EPGN EPfP IBal LRHS MHom MMiN NGdn NHol NLar NMyG SMrm |
| 'Blue Veil' | EGol |
| 'Blue Velvet' | CBdn MMiN |
| 'Blue Vision' | EMic EPGN LRHS |
| 'Blue Wedgwood' (Tardiana Group) | CBdn CBro CPrp EBee EGol ELan EMic GKir IBal LAst LCro LPBA NGdn NHol NMyG SApp SPla SPoG WHil |
| 'Blueberry Tart' **new** | IBal |
| 'Blütenwunder' | SApp |
| 'Bob Deane' (v) **new** | EMic |
| 'Bob Olson' (v) | EGol EMic IBal |
| 'Bobbie Sue' (v) | EGol |
| 'Bodacious Blue' **new** | IBal |
| 'Bold Edger' (v) | CBdn EGol |
| 'Bold Ribbons' (v) | CBdn EGol EMic GAbr IBal MMiN WTin |
| 'Bold Ruffles' (*sieboldiana*) | EGol LRHS SApp |
| 'Bolt out of the Blue' | EMic IBal |
| 'Bonanza' | EMic MMiN |
| 'Border Bandit' (v) | EGol |
| 'Borsch 1' | CBdn |
| § 'Borwick Beauty' (*sieboldiana*) (v) | CBdn CBgR CDWL EGle EGol EMic EPGN IBal LAst MMiN NBPC NCGa NGdn NLar NMyG SApp SPer WAul |
| 'Bountiful' | EGol EMic MMiN |
| 'Bouquet' | EGol |
| 'Brash and Sassy' **new** | IBal |
| 'Brave Amherst' (v) **new** | EMic |
| 'Bread Crumbs' | IBal |
| 'Brenda's Beauty' (v) | EGol EMic IBal |
| 'Bressingham Blue' | CBdn CDWL CPrp CSBt EBee EBrs ECtt EGol GQue IBal LRHS MIDC MRav NMyG SWvt WCAu WFar WMnd |
| 'Bridal Veil' **new** | IBal |
| 'Bridegroom' **new** | EGol EMic |
| 'Bridgeville' **new** | IBal |
| 'Brigadier' | EGol |
| 'Bright Glow' (Tardiana Group) | EGol EMic |
| 'Bright Lights' (*tokudama*) (v) | CBdn CBgR EGol EMic EPGN GBBs GSec IBal LAst NGdn NMyG WFar |
| 'Brim Cup' (v) | CBdn CSBt EBee EGol EMic EPGN IBal LAst MBNS MBri MIDC MMiN NBro NGdn NMyG NOrc SApp SMrm SPer SPoG |
| 'Brooke' | EGol EMic IBal NMyG |
| 'Brother Ronald' (Tardiana Group) | CBdn EGol EMic IBal LRHS SApp |
| 'Brother Stefan' **new** | IBal |
| 'Bruce's Blue' | EGol EMic |
| 'Bubba' **new** | IBal |
| 'Buckshaw Blue' | CBdn EGol EMic EPGN GSec IBal MDKP MMiN NBir NGdn NPro |
| 'Bunchoko' | IBal |
| 'Burke's Dwarf' | IBal |
| 'Butter Rim' (*sieboldii*) (v) | EGol |
| 'Cadillac' (v) | CBdn MIDC |
| 'Caliban' | SApp |
| 'Calypso' (v) | CBdn EGol EMic EPGN IBal LBuc |
| 'Camelot' (Tardiana Group) | CBdn EGol EMic IBal LRHS NGdn |
| 'Cameo' | EGol EMic IBal |
| 'Canadian Blue' | EMic |
| 'Candy Hearts' | CBdn CMHG CSam CWsd EGol EMic EPGN MHom MMiN MWat WTin |
| ***capitata*** | EMic |
| - B&SWJ 588 | WCru |
| 'Captain Kirk' (v) | CBdn EBee IBal NMyG |
| ***caput-avis*** | see *H. kikutii* var. *caput-avis* |
| 'Carder Blue' | EMic |
| 'Carnival' (v) | CBdn EGol EMic EPGN IBal MIDC NBPC NCGa SApp |
| 'Carol' (*fortunei*) (v) | CBdn EGol EMic EWsh IBal MSte NMyG NNor SApp WHal |
| 'Carolina Blue' | IBal |
| 'Carolina Sunshine' (v) **new** | EMic |
| 'Carousel' (v) | EGol EMic |
| 'Carrie Ann' | see *H.* 'Carrie' |
| § 'Carrie' (*sieboldii*) (v) | EGol SApp |
| 'Cascade Mist' (v) **new** | EMic |
| 'Cascades' (v) | CBdn EGol EMic EPGN IBal |
| 'Catherine' **new** | IBal |
| 'Cat's Eyes' (v) | CBdn EGol EMic EPGN IBal |
| 'Cavalcade' (v) | EMic |
| 'Celebration' (v) | EGol ELan EMic EPGN LRHS MDKP MMiN WHal |
| 'Celestial' | IBal |
| 'Center of Attention' | EMic IBal |
| 'Challenger' | EMic |
| 'Change of Tradition' (*lancifolia*) (v) | CBdn EMic |
| 'Chantilly Lace' (v) | CBdn EGol EMic IBal NMyG SApp WTin |
| 'Chartreuse Waves' | EGol |
| 'Chartreuse Wiggles' (*sieboldii*) | IBal LRHS NHar |
| 'Cheatin' Heart' | EGol EMic IBal |
| 'Chelsea Babe' (*fortunei*) (v) | EGol IBal |
| 'Cherish' | EGol EMic GBin IBal |
| 'Cherry Berry' (v) | CBdn CMHG EGol EMic EPGN IBal MBNS MIDC MMiN NBro NCob NGdn NLar NMyG NPro SApp WAul WBor WFar |
| 'Cherub' (v) | CBdn EGol |
| * 'China' (*plantaginea*) | EMic |
| 'Chinese Sunrise' (v) | CBdn CWsd EGol EMic EPGN IBal LBuc MBNS MHom MMiN NHol NMyG WHal |
| 'Chiquita' | EGol |
| 'Chodai Ginba' **new** | IBal |
| § 'Chōkō Nishiki' (*montana*) (v) | CBdn EGle EGol EMic EPGN EQua IBal MIDC MMiN NGdn NMyG NNor SApp SMad SPoG |
| 'Choo Choo Train' | EGol EMic |
| 'Christmas Candy'PBR | EMic EPGN GAbr IBal NBhm NCob |
| 'Christmas Cookies' **new** | IBal |
| 'Christmas Pageant' (v) | EMic IBal |
| 'Christmas Tree' (v) | CBdn CMMP EGle EGol EMic EPGN GBri IBal IFoB IPot LRHS MIDC MMiN NGdn NMyG SApp |
| 'Cinderella' **new** | IBal |
| 'Cinnamon Sticks' | IBal |
| 'Citation' (v) | EGol |
| 'City Lights' | EGol EMic |
| 'Clarence' | MMiN |
| ***clausa*** var. ***normalis*** | CBdn CMoH EGol GQui NBir NGdn NLar NMyG |
| 'Clifford's Forest Fire' | EMic EPGN IBal MBNS MIDC NMyG SPoG WFar |
| 'Clifford's Stingray' **new** | EMic IBal |
| 'Climax' (v) | IBal |
| 'Cody' | EMic IBal |
| 'Collector's Banner' | EGol |
| 'Collector's Choice' | EGol IBal |
| 'Color Glory' | see *H.* 'Borwick Beauty' (*sieboldiana*) |
| 'Colossal' | EGol EMic |

| | |
|---|---|
| 'Columbus Circle' (v) | CBdn EGol EMic |
| 'Concubine' **new** | EMic |
| 'Cookie Crumbs' (v) | CBdn EGol EMic IBal SApp |
| 'Cool Hand Luke' (*tokudama*) (v) **new** | EMic |
| 'Coquette' (v) | CBdn EGol EMic |
| 'Corkscrew' | EMic IBal SApp |
| 'Corona' (v) | EMic |
| 'Corryvreckan' **new** | EMic |
| 'Cotillion' (v) | CBdn EGol EMic IBal MMiN SApp |
| 'Counter Point' (v) **new** | EMic |
| 'County Park' | CBdn EGol EMic IBal |
| 'Cracker Crumbs' (v) | CBdn EGol EMic EPGN IBal SApp |
| 'Craig's Temptation' | CBdn |
| 'Cream Cheese' (v) | EGol IBal |
| 'Cream Delight' (*undulata*) | see *H. undulata* var. *undulata* |
| 'Cream Edge' | see *H.* 'Fisher Cream Edge' |
| 'Crepe Soul' (v) | EGol IBal |
| 'Crepe Suzette' (v) | CBdn EGol EPGN LRHS |
| 'Crested Reef' | CBdn CMoH EGol EMic NMyG |
| 'Crested Surf' (v) | EGol EMic EPGN IBal |
| 'Crinoline Petticoats' | EGol |
| § ***crispula*** (v) 𝕐$^{H4}$ | CBdn EGol EMic EPfP MBar MCot MHom MMiN MRav NChi NCob NMyG SHBN |
| 'Crown Jewel' (v) | EPGN IBal |
| 'Crown Prince' (v) | CBdn EGol EMic EPGN IBal |
| § 'Crowned Imperial' (*fortunei*) (v) | CBdn CWat EMic MMiN NHol |
| 'Crumples' (*sieboldiana*) | EGol EMic |
| 'Crusader' (v) | CBdn EGol EMic EPGN IBal LRHS MMiN NMyG SApp WFar |
| 'Crystal Charm' **new** | IBal |
| 'Crystal Chimes' **new** | IBal |
| 'Cupboard Love' | SApp |
| 'Cupid's Dart' (v) | EGol |
| 'Curlew' (Tardiana Group) | CBdn EGol EMic IBal MMiN |
| 'Cutting Edge' | IBal |
| 'Dance with Me' | EMic IBal |
| 'Dancing in the Rain' (v) | EBee EMic MAvo MBNS NBro NBsh WFar |
| 'Dark Shadows' **new** | IBal |
| 'Dark Star' (v) | CBdn EGol EMic EPGN IBal SApp |
| 'Dark Victory' **new** | IBal |
| 'Dartmoor Forest' | CBdn |
| 'Darwin's Standard' (v) | CBdn |
| 'Dawn' | CBdn EGol EMic GSec IBal |
| 'Daybreak' | CBdn EGol EMic EPGN IBal LAst LRHS MBri NBro SApp |
| 'Day's End' (v) | EGol EMic IBal |
| 'Deane's Dream' | EMic IBal |
| ***decorata*** | CBdn EGol EMic MBar MMiN |
| 'Deep Blue Sea' | CBdn EMic IBal |
| 'Deep Pockets' **new** | IBal |
| 'Déjà Blu' (v) **new** | CBdn |
| 'Delia' (v) | EPGN |
| 'Delta Dawn' | IBal |
| 'Delta Desire' **new** | IBal |
| 'Deluxe Edition' **new** | IBal |
| 'Designer Genes' **new** | IBal |
| 'Devon Blue' (Tardiana Group) | CBdn CBgR EGol MMiN |
| 'Devon Desire' (*montana*) | CBdn EMic |
| 'Devon Discovery' | CBdn |
| 'Devon Giant' | CBdn EMic |
| 'Devon Gold' | CBdn EMic |
| 'Devon Green' | CBdn CTca ELan EMic EPGN GBri IBal IPot MHom MLLN MMiN MSte NBro NCGa NCob NGdn NLar NMyG NNor NPro SApp WAul WFar WHal |
| 'Devon Hills' | CBdn |
| 'Devon Mist' | CBdn MMiN |
| 'Devon Tor' | CBdn EMic MMiN |
| 'Dew Drop' (v) | CBdn EGol EMic IBal NMyG |
| 'Diamond Tiara' (v) | CBdn EGol EMic EPGN IBal LAst LRHS MBNS MIDC MMiN NBir NGdn NMyG |
| 'Diana Remembered' | CBdn EGol EMic EPGN GKir IBal MBNS WBor |
| 'Dick Ward' | EMic IBal |
| 'Dillie Perkeo' **new** | IBal |
| 'Dimple' | EMic |
| 'Dinky Donna' **new** | IBal |
| 'Diva' **new** | EMic |
| 'Dixie Chick' (v) | EGol EMic IBal |
| 'Dixieland Heat' **new** | IBal |
| 'Doctor Fu Manchu' **new** | IBal |
| 'Domaine de Courson' | CBdn EMic EPGN IBal WFar |
| 'Don Stevens' (v) | CBdn EGol |
| 'Donahue Piecrust' | CBdn EGol EMic GSec |
| 'Dorothy' | EMic IBal |
| 'Dorset Blue' (Tardiana Group) | CBdn EGol EMic EPGN IBal LRHS SApp |
| 'Dorset Charm' (Tardiana Group) | CBdn EGol MMiN |
| 'Dorset Flair' (Tardiana Group) | EGol EMic IBal |
| 'Doubloons' | EGol EMic |
| 'Dragon Tails' **new** | IBal |
| 'Dragon Wings' **new** | EMic |
| 'Drawn Butter' **new** | EMic |
| 'Dream Queen' (v) | EMic IBal |
| 'Dream Weaver' (v) | CBgR CWib EBee EGol EMic IBal MNrw NBro NGdn NMyG SApp SPer SPoG WFar |
| 'Dress Blues' | EMic IBal |
| 'Drummer Boy' | CBdn EGol EMic |
| 'Duchess' (*nakaiana*) (v) | EMic |
| 'DuPage Delight' (*sieboldiana*) (v) | CBdn EGol IBal MMiN NGdn NLar |
| 'Dust Devil' (*fortunei*) (v) | EGol IBal |
| 'Dustin' (v) **new** | EMic |
| 'Dylan's Dillie' (v) | EMic IBal |
| 'Earth Angel' (v) | CBdn EGol EMic IBal |
| 'Ebb Tide' (*montana*) (v) **new** | EMic |
| 'Edge of Night' | CBdn EGol EMic |
| 'Edwin Bibby' | EMic |
| 'El Capitan' (v) | CBdn EGol EMic EPGN IBal LRHS |
| 'El Niño'$^{PBR}$ (Tardiana Group) (v) | CBdn CWGN EGol EMic IBal MHom MIDC MNrw MSte NBro NGdn SApp WFar |
| § ***elata*** | EBee EGol EMic SApp |
| 'Elatior' (*nigrescens*) | CBdn EMic |
| 'Eldorado' | see *H.* 'Frances Williams' |
| 'Eleanor Lachman' (v) | EGol EMic IBal |
| 'Eleanor Roosevelt' | IBal |
| 'Electrum Stater' (v) | CBdn EMic |
| 'Elegans' | see *H. sieboldiana* var. *elegans* |
| 'Elfin Power' (*sieboldii*) (v) | EGol |
| 'Elisabeth' | CBdn EMic GBin IBal LSRN NMyG |
| 'Elizabeth Campbell' (*fortunei*) (v) | CBdn EGol EMic IBal MMiN MSte |
| 'Ellen' | EMic |
| 'Ellerbroek' (*fortunei*) (v) | EGol EMic IBal MMiN |
| 'Elsley Runner' | EGol IBal |
| 'Elvis Lives' | CBdn EDAr EGol EMic EPGN GBin IBal LAst NGdn NLar NMyG NNor NPro |
| 'Embroidery' (v) | EMic |
| 'Emerald Carpet' | EGol IBal |
| 'Emerald Necklace' (v) | EGol |
| 'Emerald Ruff Cut' **new** | IBal |
| 'Emerald Skies' | EGol |

| | | |
|---|---|---|
| | 'Emerald Tiara' (v) | CBdn EGol EMic EPGN GSec LRHS MIDC MLHP MMiN NMyG SApp WTin |
| | 'Emeralds and Rubies' | EGol EMic IBal |
| | 'Emily Dickinson' (v) | CBdn EBee EGol EMic IBal MMuc SApp SPad |
| | 'Enterprise' | EMic IBal |
| | 'Eric Smith' (Tardiana Group) | CBdn EGol EMic EPGN IBal MHom NMyG WFar |
| | 'Eric's Gold' | EPGN |
| | 'Erie Magic' (v) **new** | EGol |
| | 'Eskimo Pie' (v) | CBdn EBee EMic GBin IBal NBsh WFar |
| | 'Essence of Summer' **new** | EPfP IBal |
| | 'Eternal Flame' | EMic IBal |
| | 'Eternity' **new** | GSec |
| | 'Evelyn McCafferty' (*tokudama* hybrid) | EGol |
| | 'Evening Magic' (v) | EGol EMic |
| | 'Eventide' (v) | EGol |
| | 'Everlasting Love' (v) | EGol |
| | 'Excitation' | CBdn EGol EMic GSec |
| | 'Eye Catcher' **new** | EMic |
| | 'Fair Maiden' (v) | CBdn EMic IBal |
| | 'Faithful Heart' (v) | EMic IBal |
| | 'Fall Bouquet' (*longipes* var. *hypoglauca*) | EGol |
| | 'Fall Emerald' | CBdn EMic |
| | 'Fallen Angel' | IBal |
| | 'Falling Waters' (v) | EGol IBal |
| | 'Fan Dance' (v) | EGol EMic IBal |
| | 'Fantabulous' (v) | EMic EPGN IBal |
| | 'Fantastic' (*sieboldiana* hybrid) | EGol LRHS |
| | 'Fantasy Island' (v) | EMic IBal |
| | 'Fatal Attraction' | EMic IBal |
| | 'Feather Boa' | EGol EMic IBal |
| | 'Fenman's Fascination' | EMic MMiN |
| | 'Fiesta' (v) **new** | IBal |
| | 'Fire and Ice' (v) | Widely available |
| | 'Fire Island' | CBdn EGol EMic EPGN GBin IBal SApp |
| | 'Fireworks' (v) | EBee EGol EMic EPGN GBin IBal MAvo MBNS NBro NMyG SMrm |
| | 'First Frost' (v) | CBdn EMic IBal |
| | 'First Mate' (v) **new** | IBal |
| § | 'Fisher Cream Edge' (*fortunei*) (v) | CBdn EMic MMiN |
| | 'Five O'Clock Shadow' (v) | EMic IBal |
| | 'Five O'Clock Somewhere' (v) | IBal |
| | 'Flame Stitch' (*ventricosa*) (v) | EGol EMic IBal |
| | 'Flemish Sky' | EMic IBal |
| | 'Floradora' | CBdn EGol EMic IBal NMyG |
| | 'Flower Power' | CBdn EGol GSec |
| | 'Fond Hope' | CBdn MMiN |
| | 'Fool's Gold' (*fortunei*) | CBdn EMic IBal MMiN |
| | 'Forest Shadows' | EMic IBal |
| | 'Formal Attire' (*sieboldiana* hybrid) (v) | CBdn EGol EMic IBal LRHS |
| | 'Forncett Frances' (v) | EGol EMic IBal MMiN |
| | 'Fort Knox' **new** | EMic |
| | 'Fortis' | see *H. undulata* var. *erromena* |
| | ***fortunei*** | CBdn CMMP EGol EMic GKev MIDC NHol NNor WEas WFar |
| § | - var. ***albopicta*** (v) ♀H4 | Widely available |
| | - - f. ***aurea*** ♀H4 | CBdn CMHG ECha EGol EHoe ELan EMic EPla LRHS MBar MIDC NLar NMyG SPla SRms WFar WHal |
| | - - - dwarf | EMic |
| § | - var. ***aureomarginata*** ♀H4 | Widely available |
| | - var. ***gigantea*** | see *H. montana* |
| | - var. ***hyacinthina*** ♀H4 | CBdn EGol EMic EPfP IBal LRHS MBar MRav NMyG SApp SHBN WFar WPtf |
| | - - variegated (v) | see *H.* 'Crowned Imperial' |
| § | - var. ***obscura*** | CBdn EGol EMic |
| | - var. ***rugosa*** | EMic |
| | 'Foundling' **new** | EMic |
| | 'Fountain' | NHol |
| | 'Fourth of July' | EGol |
| | 'Fragrant Blue' | CBdn EBee EGol EMic GBBs IBal LRHS NBro NGdn NMyG SApp SCoo SPoG |
| | 'Fragrant Bouquet' (v) | CBdn CMHG CWib EGol ELan EMic EPGN GAbr IBal LAst LRHS LSRN MMiN NCGa NGdn NHol NLar NMyG WPtf |
| | 'Fragrant Dream' | CBdn EGol EMic EPfP IBal NLar |
| | 'Fragrant Fire' | EMic IBal |
| | 'Fragrant Gold' | EGol EMic MMiN |
| | 'Fragrant King' | IBal |
| | 'Fragrant Star' | EMic IBal |
| | 'Fragrant Surprise' (v) | IBal |
| | 'Fran Godfrey' | EPGN |
| | 'Francee' (*fortunei*) (v) ♀H4 | Widely available |
| § | 'Frances Williams' (*sieboldiana*) (v) ♀H4 | Widely available |
| | 'Frances Williams Improved' (*sieboldiana*) (v) | CTca EGol EPfP MMiN MWat |
| | 'Freising' (*fortunei*) | EBee |
| | 'Fresh' (v) | EGol EMic EPGN SApp |
| | 'Friar Tuck' **new** | EMic |
| | 'Fried Bananas' | CBdn EGol EMic MMiN SPoG |
| | 'Fried Green Tomatoes' | CBdn EGol EMic GBin MIDC NLar NMyG |
| | 'Fringe Benefit' (v) | EGol EMic GAbr MMiN SApp |
| | 'Frosted Dimples' | EMic IBal |
| | 'Frosted Jade' (v) | CBdn CWib EBee EGol EMic EPGN MMiN NLar NMyG SApp SMrm SRGP WTin |
| | 'Frozen Margarita' **new** | IBal |
| | 'Frühlingsgold' (v) **new** | IBal |
| | 'Fujibotan' (v) | EGol IBal |
| | 'Fulda' | EGol EMic |
| | 'Gaiety' (v) | EGol EPGN |
| | 'Gaijin' (v) | CBdn EGol EMic IBal SApp |
| | 'Gala' (*tardiflora*) (v) | CBdn NMyG |
| | 'Galaxy' | IBal |
| | 'Garden Party' (v) **new** | IBal |
| | 'Garden Treasure' **new** | EGol EMic |
| | 'Garnet Prince' **new** | EGol |
| | 'Gay Blade' (v) | EGol SApp |
| | 'Gay Feather' (v) | EMic IBal LAst NMyG SApp |
| | 'Gay Search' (v) | EPGN IBal |
| | 'Geisha' (v) | CBdn EGol EPGN IBal MBNS MCCP NGdn NMyG NPro SApp WHal |
| | 'Gemini Moon' (v) **new** | IBal |
| | 'Gene's Joy' | EMic EPGN |
| | 'Ghost Spirit' | EBee IBal WFar |
| | 'Gigantea' (*sieboldiana*) | see *H. elata* |
| | 'Gilt by Association' | IBal |
| | 'Gilt Edge' (*sieboldiana*) (v) | CWat EMic NMyG |
| | 'Gin and Tonic' (v) **new** | EMic |
| | 'Gingee' **new** | IBal |
| | 'Ginko Craig' (v) | Widely available |
| | 'Ginsu Knife' (v) **new** | IBal |
| | 'Glass Hearts' | EMic IBal |
| | ***glauca*** | see *H. sieboldiana* var. *elegans* |
| | 'Glitter' | EMic IBal |
| | 'Glockenspiel' | CBdn EGol |
| I | 'Gloriosa' (*fortunei*) (v) | EGol EMic WFar |

| | |
|---|---|
| 'Glory' | CBdn EGol |
| 'Goddess of Athena' (*decorata*) (v) | EGol |
| 'Gold Drop' (*venusta* hybrid) | CBdn EGol EMic IBal NHol |
| 'Gold Edger' | CBdn CBro CMea CPrp EGol EHoe ELan EMic EPfP ERos GEdr GMaP LRHS MIDC MMiN MRav MSte NBir NGdn NHol NMyG NNor NSti SApp SPer SPla WFar WTin |
| 'Gold Edger Surprise' (v) **new** | EMic |
| 'Gold Flush' (*ventricosa*) | EMic MMiN |
| § 'Gold Haze' (*fortunei*) | CBdn EGol EMic EPGN IBal MHom NBir NCGa NHol NMyG |
| 'Gold Leaf' (*fortunei*) | EGol |
| 'Gold Regal' | CBdn EBee EGol EMic EPGN MHom MSte NMyG WFar WMnd |
| 'Gold Rush' | CBdn EMic GSec NMyG |
| 'Gold Standard' (*fortunei*) (v) | Widely available |
| 'Goldbrook' (v) | EGol EMic IBal WTin |
| 'Goldbrook Galleon' | EGol IBal |
| 'Goldbrook Gayle' (v) | EGol |
| 'Goldbrook Gaynor' | EGol IBal |
| 'Goldbrook Genie' | EGol IBal |
| 'Goldbrook Ghost' (v) | EGol |
| 'Goldbrook Girl' | EGol IBal |
| 'Goldbrook Glamour' (v) | EGol IBal |
| 'Goldbrook Glimmer' (Tardiana Group) (v) | EGol IBal |
| 'Goldbrook Gold' | EGol IBal |
| 'Goldbrook Grace' | EGol IBal |
| 'Goldbrook Gratis' (v) | EGol IBal |
| 'Goldbrook Grayling' | EGol IBal |
| 'Goldbrook Grebe' | EGol IBal |
| 'Goldbrook Greenheart' **new** | IBal |
| 'Golden Age' | see *H.* 'Gold Haze' |
| 'Golden Anniversary' | CBdn EGol IBal MBNS NHol |
| 'Golden Bullion' (*tokudama*) | CBdn EGol GBri |
| 'Golden Fascination' | EGol |
| 'Golden Fountain' **new** | EMic |
| 'Golden Friendship' | EGol |
| 'Golden Gate' | EGol EMic |
| 'Golden Guernsey' (v) | EMic |
| 'Golden Isle' | EGol IBal |
| 'Golden Meadows' | EPGN IBal NCob |
| 'Golden Medallion' (*tokudama*) | CBdn CMHG EGol ELan EMic IBal MBNS NGdn NHol NMyG SHBN WFar |
| 'Golden Nakaiana' | see *H.* 'Birchwood Parky's Gold' |
| 'Golden' (*nakaiana*) | see *H.* 'Birchwood Parky's Gold' |
| 'Golden Oriole' | CBdn EGol EMic |
| 'Golden Prayers' | CMea ECtt EHoe IBal MIDC NLar WFar WHal |
| 'Golden Prayers' (*tokudama*) | CBdn ECtt EGol ELan EPGN ERos LRHS MIDC MRav NBir NBro NGdn NHol NOrc SPla WSHC |
| 'Golden Scepter' | CBdn EGol EMic EPGN GSec IBal MMiN NHol NMyG SApp WFar |
| 'Golden Sculpture' (*sieboldiana*) | CBdn EGol LRHS |
| 'Golden Spades' **new** | EMic |
| 'Golden Spider' | EGol EMic |
| 'Golden Sunburst' (*sieboldiana*) | CBdn CPrp EGol ELan EMic IBal MMiN NGdn NHol WFar |
| 'Golden Tiara' (v) $\mathbb{Y}^{H4}$ | Widely available |
| 'Golden Waffles' | CMHG |
| 'Golden Years' **new** | EMic |
| 'Goldpfeil' | EMic |
| 'Goldsmith' | EGol MMiN SApp |

| | |
|---|---|
| 'Gone Fishin'' (v) **new** | IBal |
| 'Goober' **new** | IBal |
| 'Good as Gold' | EMic EPGN IBal NMyG |
| 'Gorgeous George' **new** | IBal |
| 'Gorgon' **new** | IBal |
| 'Gosan Gold Midget' **new** | EMic |
| 'Gosan Gold Mist' | EMic |
| 'Gosan Hildegarde' **new** | EMic GSec |
| 'Gosan Leather Strap' | EMic IBal |
| 'Gosan Mina' **new** | EMic |
| 'Gosan' (*takahashii*) | EGol |
| ***gracillima*** | EMic EPGN IBal NRya |
| 'Granary Gold' (*fortunei*) | CBdn EGol EPGN GSec LRHS |
| 'Grand Finale' | IBal |
| 'Grand Marquee' (v) | EMic GBin IBal SApp WFar |
| 'Grand Master' | EGol EMic IBal MDKP SApp |
| 'Grand Prize' (v) | EMic IBal |
| 'Grand Slam' | EGol |
| 'Grand Tiara' (v) | CBdn EGol EMic EPGN GSec IBal NMyG SApp |
| 'Gray Cole' (*sieboldiana*) | CBdn EGol EMic IBal LBuc NMyG |
| 'Great Arrival' | IBal |
| 'Great Expectations' (*sieboldiana*) (v) | Widely available |
| 'Great Lakes Gold' | IBal |
| 'Green Acres' (*montana*) | EMic LEdu MMiN MSte SMeo WFar |
| 'Green Angel' (*sieboldiana*) | EGol |
| 'Green Dwarf' | NWCA WFar |
| 'Green Eyes' (*sieboldii*) (v) | EGol EMic IBal |
| 'Green Fountain' (*kikutii*) | CBdn EGol EMic MIDC MSte |
| 'Green Gold' (*fortunei*) (v) | CBdn EMic |
| 'Green Lama' **new** | IBal |
| 'Green Mouse Ears' **new** | IBal |
| 'Green Piecrust' | CBdn EGol EMic MMiN |
| 'Green Sheen' | EGol EPGN NMyG |
| 'Green Summer Fragrance' | CBdn MMiN |
| 'Green Velveteen' | CBdn EGol |
| 'Green with Envy' (v) | CBdn EGol EMic IBal SApp |
| 'Greenwood' | EMic |
| 'Grey Ghost' | EMic IBal |
| 'Grey Piecrust' | EGol IBal |
| 'Ground Cover Trompenburg' | SApp |
| 'Ground Master' (v) | CBdn CMHG EBee ECtt EGol ELan EPfP GCra GMaP IBal IFoB LPBA LRHS MRav MSwo NBro NGdn NHol NMyG NSti SPer WFar |
| 'Ground Sulphur' | EGol EMic |
| 'Grünherz' **new** | IBal |
| 'Guacamole' (v) | CBdn CBgR EGle EGol EMic EPGN EPfP GBin IBal IPot MIDC MMiN NGdn NLar NMyG SApp WAul WTin |
| 'Guardian Angel' (*sieboldiana*) | CBdn EGol EMic EPGN IBal |
| 'Gum Drop' | CBdn EMic |
| 'Gun Metal Blue' | EGol IBal |
| 'Gypsy Rose' | EBee EMic EPGN NMyG WFar |
| 'Hadspen Blue' (Tardiana Group) | Widely available |
| 'Hadspen Dolphin' (Tardiana Group) | MMiN |
| 'Hadspen Hawk' (Tardiana Group) | EGol IBal NMyG SApp |
| 'Hadspen Heron' (Tardiana Group) | CBdn EGol MHom MWat NMyG WCot |
| 'Hadspen Nymphaea' | EGol IBal |
| 'Hadspen Rainbow' | CBdn IBal |
| 'Hadspen Samphire' | CWsd EGol EMic EPGN MHom NBir |
| 'Hadspen White' (*fortunei*) | EMic |
| 'Haku-chu-han' (*sieboldii*) (v) | CBdn EMic |
| 'Hakujima' (*sieboldii*) | EGol IBal |

| | |
|---|---|
| § 'Halcyon' (Tardiana Group) ♀H4 | Widely available |
| 'Halo' | EGol |
| 'Hampshire County' (v) | IBal |
| 'Hanky Panky' (v) **new** | GBin IBal |
| 'Happiness' (Tardiana Group) | CBdn EGol EHoe EMic MHom MRav NMyG |
| 'Happy Camper' (v) **new** | IBal |
| 'Happy Hearts' | EGol EMic |
| 'Happy Valley' (v) **new** | IBal |
| 'Harlequin' | SApp |
| 'Harmony' (Tardiana Group) | CBdn EGol EMic |
| 'Harrison' | EMic |
| 'Harry van de Laar' | CBdn EMic IBal |
| 'Harry van Trier' | EMic GBin |
| 'Hart's Tongue' | IBal |
| 'Harvest Glow' | EGol |
| 'Harvest Moon' | EMic GKir MMiN |
| 'Hazel' | EMic IBal |
| 'Heart Ache' | EGol |
| 'Heart and Soul' (v) | EGol SApp |
| 'Heart Broken' **new** | IBal |
| 'Heartleaf' | EMic MMiN |
| 'Heart's Content' (v) | CBdn EGol |
| 'Heartsong' (v) | EGol EMic NMyG |
| 'Heatwave' **new** | EPGN IBal |
| 'Heavenly Beginnings' (v) **new** | IBal |
| 'Heideturm' | EBee EGol |
| 'Helen Doriot' (*sieboldiana*) | EGol EMic |
| 'Helen Field Fischer' (*fortunei*) | EMic IBal |
| ***helonioides*** f. ***albopicta*** | see *H. rohdeifolia* |
| 'Herifu' (v) | CBdn EGol EMic MMiN |
| 'Herkules' **new** | EMic |
| 'Hertha' (v) | EMic |
| 'Hidden Cove' (v) | EGol EMic IBal |
| 'High Kicker' | EGol IBal |
| 'High Noon' **new** | EMic |
| 'High Society' | GBin IBal MHom MNrw NGdn NMyG |
| 'Hi-ho Silver' (v) | EPGN IBal |
| 'Hilda Wassman' (v) | EGol EMic |
| 'Hillbilly Blues' (v) **new** | EMic IBal |
| 'Hippodrome' (v) **new** | IBal |
| 'Hirao Elite' | IBal |
| 'Hirao Grande' **new** | GSec |
| 'Hirao Majesty' | CBdn EGol |
| 'Hirao Splendor' | EGol NMyG |
| 'Hirao Supreme' | CBdn EGol |
| 'Hirao Tetra' | CBdn |
| 'His Honor' (v) | EMic IBal |
| 'Hoarfrost' | EMic MMiN |
| 'Holly's Honey' | EGol EMic |
| 'Holstein' | see *H.* 'Halcyon' |
| 'Holy Molé' (v) **new** | IBal |
| 'Honey Moon' | CBdn EGol |
| 'Honeybells' ♀H4 | Widely available |
| 'Honeysong' (v) | CBdn EGol EMic EPGN |
| 'Hoosier Harmony' (v) | CBdn EGol EMic |
| 'Hoosier Homecoming' | CBdn SApp |
| 'Hope' (v) | EGol EMic IBal SApp |
| 'Hotspur' (v) | EGol EMic IBal SApp |
| 'Hush Puppie' **new** | IBal |
| 'Hyacintha Variegata' (*fortunei*) (v) | CMHG GBri NNor |
| 'Hydon Gleam' | EGol EMic IBal |
| 'Hydon Sunset' (*nakaiana*) | CBdn CMHG CMMP CMea ECtt EGol EMic EPGN GCra GKir IBal MIDC MMiN NBir NHol NMyG NRya NSti NWCA SApp WHal WMnd WPtf WTin |
| ***hypoleuca*** | EGol |
| 'Hyuga Urajiro' (v) **new** | IBal |
| 'Ice Age Trail' (v) **new** | IBal |
| 'Ice Cream' (*cathayana*) (v) | EGol EMic |
| 'Iced Lemon' (v) | CBdn EMic IBal |
| 'Illicit Affair' | EGol EMic IBal |
| 'Ilona' (v) | EGol |
| § 'Inaho' | CBdn EGol EPGN MMiN NMyG |
| 'Inca Gold' | EGol EMic IBal |
| 'Independence' (v) | EMic EPGN IBal NBro NMyG WFar |
| 'Inniswood' (v) | CBdn CWCL CWib EGle EGol EPGN EPfP IBal IPot LRHS MBNS MBri MMiN NBro NGdn NLar NSti SApp WFar WMnd |
| 'Invincible' | CBdn CBgR EGle EGol EMic EPGN IBal LAst LRHS MIDC MMiN NGdn NLar NMyG NNor SApp SPoG WPtf WTin |
| 'Iona' (*fortunei*) | CBdn EGol EMic EPGN MMiN NMyG |
| 'Irische See' (Tardiana Group) | EGol |
| 'Irish Eyes' (v) **new** | IBal |
| 'Iron Gate Delight' (v) | CBdn MMiN |
| 'Iron Gate Glamour' (v) | EGol MMiN |
| 'Iron Gate Special' (v) | EMic |
| 'Iron Gate Supreme' (v) | MMiN |
| 'Island Charm' (v) | CBdn EGol EMic EPGN IBal NBhm NLar SApp |
| 'Island Forest Gem' **new** | IBal |
| 'Iszat U Doc' **new** | GSec |
| 'Ivory Necklace' (v) **new** | EMic IBal |
| 'Iwa Soules' | EGol EMic |
| 'Jack of Diamonds' | EMic IBal |
| 'Jade Beauty' | CBdn |
| 'Jade Cascade' | CBdn EGol ELan EMic MSte NBir NHol NLar NMyG SApp WOVN |
| 'Jade Scepter' (*nakaiana*) | EGol EMic GSec |
| 'Jadette' (v) | EGol GBin |
| 'Janet Day' (v) | EMic SApp |
| 'Janet' (*fortunei*) (v) | CBdn EBee EGol EMic GMaP NGdn |
| 'Janet's Green Sox' **new** | IBal |
| 'Japan Girl' | see *H.* 'Mount Royal' |
| 'Jester' | SApp |
| 'Jewel of the Nile' (v) | EMic IBal |
| 'Jim Mathews' | IBal |
| 'Jimmy Crack Corn' | CBdn EGol EMic IBal |
| 'John Wargo' | EGol |
| 'Joker' (*fortunei*) (v) | CBdn |
| 'Jolly Green Giant' (*sieboldiana* hybrid) | EMic |
| 'Joseph' | EGol EMic IBal |
| 'Josephine' (v) | NNor |
| 'Journeyman' | EBrs EGol EMic IBal |
| 'Journey's End' (v) **new** | IBal |
| 'Joyce Trott' (v) | IBal |
| 'Joyful' (v) **new** | IBal |
| 'Judy Rocco' | IBal |
| 'Julia' (v) | EGol EMic IBal |
| 'Julie Morss' | CBdn EGol EMic EPGN GMaP IBal MHom MMiN MWat NMyG SApp |
| 'Jumbo' (*sieboldiana*) | EMic MMiN |
| 'June' $^{PBR}$ (Tardiana Group) (v) ♀H4 | Widely available |
| 'June Beauty' (*sieboldiana*) | EWsh MGos MMiN |
| 'June Fever' $^{PBR}$ (Tardiana Group) | EMic ESwi GBin GKir IBal NBhm NBro NLar NMoo SApp |
| 'June Moon' (v) **new** | EMic |
| 'Just So' (v) | CBdn EGol EMic IBal |
| 'Kabitan' | see *H. sieboldii* var. *sieboldii* f. *kabitan* |
| 'Kabuki' | IBal |
| 'Karin' | CBdn EGol EMic |

| | | |
|---|---|---|
| | 'Katherine Lewis' (Tardiana Group) (v) | CBdn ECtt EMic IBal LSRN NHol |
| | 'Kath's Gold' | EMic |
| | 'Katie Q' (v) **new** | EMic IBal |
| | 'Katsuragawa-beni' (v) **new** | IBal |
| | 'Kelly' | EMic GSec |
| | 'Kelsey' | EGol EMic |
| | 'Key Lime Pie' | IBal |
| | 'Ki Nakafu Otome' (*venusta*) | IBal |
| | 'Kifukurin' (*kikutii*) | see *H.* 'Kifukurin Hyuga' |
| | 'Kifukurin' (*pulchella*) (v) | CBdn EGol EMic |
| § | 'Kifukurin Hyuga' (v) | CBdn IBal |
| | 'Kifukurin Ko Mame' (*gracillima*) (v) | CBdn EMic |
| | 'Kifukurin Ubatake' (*pulchella*) (v) | CBdn EGol EPGN IBal |
| | ***kikutii*** | EGol EMic NWCA WTin |
| § | - var. ***caput-avis*** | EGol EMic |
| | - - 'Chabo-unazuki' **new** | EBee |
| | - var. ***kikutii*** f. ***leuconota*** **new** | SApp |
| | - var. ***polyneuron*** | EGol SApp |
| | - var. ***pruinosa*** | SApp |
| § | - var. ***yakusimensis*** | CBdn CPBP EGol EMic GBin GKir IBal |
| | 'Kinbotan' (v) | EGol EMic IBal |
| | 'King James' | IBal |
| | 'Kingfisher' (Tardiana Group) | EGol |
| § | 'Kirishima' | CBdn EMic |
| | 'Kisuji' | see *H.* 'Mediopicta' (*sieboldii*) |
| | 'Kitty Cat' **new** | EMic IBal |
| | 'Kiwi Black Magic' | EGol EMic IBal |
| | 'Kiwi Blue Baby' | EGol IBal |
| | 'Kiwi Blue Ruffles' | IBal |
| | 'Kiwi Blue Sky' | IBal |
| | 'Kiwi Canoe' | IBal |
| | 'Kiwi Cream Edge' (v) | EMic |
| | 'Kiwi Forest' | IBal |
| | 'Kiwi Fruit' | SApp |
| | 'Kiwi Full Monty' (v) | EMic IBal |
| | 'Kiwi Gold Rush' | IBal |
| | 'Kiwi Hippo' | EGol IBal |
| | 'Kiwi Jordan' | IBal |
| | 'Kiwi Kaniere Gold' **new** | IBal |
| | 'Kiwi Leap Frog' | IBal |
| | 'Kiwi Minnie Gold' | IBal |
| | 'Kiwi Parasol' | IBal |
| | 'Kiwi Skyscraper' **new** | IBal |
| | 'Kiwi Spearmint' | EMic IBal |
| | 'Kiwi Splash' | IBal |
| | 'Kiwi Sunlover' | IBal |
| | 'Kiwi Sunshine' | IBal |
| | 'Kiwi Treasure Trove' | IBal |
| | ***kiyosumiensis*** | NHol |
| | 'Klopping Variegated' (v) | EGol EMic |
| | 'Knockout' (v) | CBdn EGol IBal MBNS MIDC MNrw NBPC NBro NGdn NLar NMyG NNor SApp |
| | 'Komodo Dragon' | WTin |
| | 'Kong' **new** | IBal |
| | 'Korean Snow' | IBal |
| I | 'Koreana Variegated' (*undulata*) **new** | EMic |
| | 'Koriyama' (*sieboldiana*) (v) | CBdn EMic IBal LBuc MMiN |
| | 'Krinkled Joy' | EMic |
| | 'Krossa Cream Edge' (*sieboldii*) (v) | EMic IBal |
| | 'Krossa Regal' 🏆$^{H4}$ | Widely available |
| | 'Krugerrand' | IBal |
| | 'Lacy Belle' (v) | CBdn EGol EMic GSec IBal NBro NGdn NMyG NPro SPoG |
| | 'Lady Godiva' | IBal |
| | 'Lady Guineverre'$^{PBR}$ | EMic IBal |
| | 'Lady Helen' | EMic |
| | 'Lady Isobel Barnett' (v) | CBdn EMic IBal MMiN NMyG SApp |
| | ***laevigata*** | EGol EMic SApp |
| | 'Lake Hitchock' | EGol EMic IBal |
| | 'Lakeside Accolade' | EGol IBal NMyG |
| | 'Lakeside April Snow' (v) | EMic |
| | 'Lakeside Baby Face' (v) | EMic IBal |
| | 'Lakeside Black Satin' | CBdn EMic IBal SApp |
| | 'Lakeside Blue Cherub' | EMic GSec IBal |
| | 'Lakeside Butter Ball' **new** | IBal |
| | 'Lakeside Cha Cha' (v) | CBdn EGol EMic |
| | 'Lakeside Cindy Cee' (v) **new** | IBal |
| | 'Lakeside Coal Miner' | EMic IBal |
| | 'Lakeside Contender' **new** | IBal |
| | 'Lakeside Cupcake' (v) | CBdn EMic IBal |
| | 'Lakeside Delight' | EPGN |
| | 'Lakeside Down Sized' (v) **new** | IBal |
| | 'Lakeside Dragonfly' (v) | IBal |
| | 'Lakeside Elfin Fire' | EMic IBal |
| | 'Lakeside Feather Light' (v) **new** | IBal |
| | 'Lakeside Iron Man' **new** | IBal |
| | 'Lakeside Kaleidoscope' | CBdn EGol EMic IBal LBuc |
| | 'Lakeside Legal Tender' | IBal |
| | 'Lakeside Lime Time' **new** | IBal |
| | 'Lakeside Little Gem' | IBal |
| | 'Lakeside Little Tuft' (v) | IBal |
| | 'Lakeside Lollipop' | EGol EMic |
| | 'Lakeside Looking Glass' | CBdn EMic IBal |
| | 'Lakeside Love Affaire' | EGol EMic IBal |
| | 'Lakeside Meadow Ice' (v) **new** | IBal |
| | 'Lakeside Meter Maid' (v) | GSec IBal |
| | 'Lakeside Miss Muffett' (v) | IBal |
| | 'Lakeside Neat Petite' | EGol GSec IBal |
| | 'Lakeside Ninita' (v) | EGol EMic EPGN GSec IBal NMyG |
| | 'Lakeside Premier' | CBdn EGol EMic |
| | 'Lakeside Rhapsody' (v) | IBal |
| | 'Lakeside Ring Master' (v) **new** | IBal |
| | 'Lakeside Ripples' **new** | IBal |
| | 'Lakeside Rocky Top' (v) **new** | IBal |
| | 'Lakeside Roy El' (v) | EMic IBal |
| | 'Lakeside Sapphire Pleats' **new** | EMic |
| | 'Lakeside Shadows' (v) **new** | IBal |
| | 'Lakeside Shockwave' (v) **new** | IBal |
| | 'Lakeside Shoremaster' (v) | IBal |
| | 'Lakeside Small Fry' (v) | IBal |
| | 'Lakeside Sparkle Plenty' (v) **new** | IBal |
| | 'Lakeside Spruce Goose' (v) | IBal |
| | 'Lakeside Symphony' (v) | EGol EMic |
| | 'Lakeside Zinger' (v) | EMic IBal |
| | ***lancifolia*** 🏆$^{H4}$ | CBdn CBro CMHG CTca EBee ECha EGol EHrv ELan EMic GMaP LCro MIDC MMiN MRav NGdn NHol NMyG NSti SApp SBod SRms WAul WGwG WTin |
| | 'Last Dance' (v) | IBal |
| | 'Lavender Lace' **new** | IBal |
| | 'Leading Lady' **new** | EMic |
| | 'Leather Sheen' | EGol EMic EPGN |
| | 'Leatherneck' **new** | IBal |
| | 'Lederhosen' | IBal |

| | |
|---|---|
| 'Lee Armiger' (*tokudama* hybrid) | EGol |
| 'Lemon Delight' | CBdn EGol EMic EPGN GSec MMiN NMyG |
| 'Lemon Frost' | EMic IBal |
| 'Lemon Lime' | CBdn CBgR EGol EMic IBal MHom MMiN MNrw NMyG NPro SIng WBrk WPat WTin |
| 'Lemon Meringue' **new** | EMic |
| 'Lemonade' | GBin |
| 'Leola Fraim' (v) | CBdn EGol EMic IBal MMiN NMyG |
| 'Leviathan' | EMic MMiN |
| 'Libby' **new** | IBal |
| 'Liberty'$^{PBR}$ (v) | CBcs CBdn EGol EMic EPGN GBin GBri IBal NBro WFar |
| 'Li'l Abner' (v) **new** | EMic IBal |
| * ***lilacina*** | WFar |
| 'Lily Pad' | EPGN |
| 'Lime Fizz' **new** | EMic SApp |
| 'Lime Krinkles' | MMiN |
| 'Lime Piecrust' | EGol |
| 'Lime Shag' (*sieboldii* f. *spathulata*) | EGol |
| 'Limey Lisa' | EGol EMic EPGN IBal |
| 'Little Aurora' (*tokudama* hybrid) | EGol EMic EPGN IBal |
| 'Little Bit' **new** | EMic |
| 'Little Black Scape' | EGol EMic EPGN GBin IBal LSRN MHom NCob NGdn NHol NLar NMyG NPro |
| 'Little Blue' (*ventricosa*) | EGol EMic |
| 'Little Bo Beep' (v) | EGol |
| 'Little Caesar' (v) | CBdn EGol EMic EPGN IBal |
| 'Little Doll' (v) | EGol |
| 'Little Miss Magic' | IBal |
| 'Little Razor' | EGol |
| 'Little Red Rooster' | IBal NMyG |
| 'Little Stiffy' | EMic SApp |
| 'Little Sunspot' (v) | CBdn EGol EMic IBal |
| 'Little Town Flirt' (v) **new** | IBal |
| 'Little White Lines' (v) | CBdn EGol EPGN IBal |
| 'Little Wonder' (v) | CBdn EGol EMic EPGN IBal |
| 'Lochness Monster' (v) **new** | EMic |
| 'Lonesome Dove' (v) **new** | IBal |
| ***longipes*** | EGol GSec SApp |
| - var. ***latifolia*** **new** | EMic |
| ***longissima*** | CMHG WCru |
| 'Louisa' (*sieboldii*) (v) | ECha MSte |
| 'Love Pat' ♀$^{H4}$ | CBdn CBgR CFir EBee EGol EMic EPGN EPfP GBin IBal LAst MCCP MIDC MMiN MRav NCGa NGdn NMyG NNor SApp SPla |
| 'Loyalist'$^{PBR}$ (v) | CBdn EMic NLar WFar |
| 'Lucky Charm' | EMic |
| 'Lucy Vitols' (v) | CBdn EGol EMic IBal |
| 'Lunar Eclipse' (v) | CHid EGol GSec MMiN SApp |
| 'Lunar Orbit' (v) | CBdn |
| 'Mack the Knife' | IBal |
| 'Maekawa' | EGol EMic |
| 'Magic Fire' (v) | EMic EPGN EPfP GSec IBal MNrw |
| 'Majesty' | EGol IBal NGdn |
| 'Mama Mia' (v) | CWat EGol EMic EPGN EQua IBal MBNS NBro NHol SPoG SRGP |
| 'Maple Leaf' (*sieboldiana*) (v) | EMic |
| 'Maraschino Cherry' | EGol EMic EWTr GBin IBal NMyG SApp |
| 'Marble Rim' (v) **new** | EGol |
| 'Margin of Error' (v) | EGol EPGN NMyG |
| 'Marginata Alba' misapplied | see *H. crispula*, *H.* 'Albomarginata' |
| 'Marginata Alba' ambig. (v) | ECha LPBA |
| 'Marilyn' | EGol EMic GSec LRHS |
| 'Marilyn Monroe' **new** | EMic IBal |
| 'Marquis' (*nakaiana* hybrid) | EGol GSec |
| 'Maruba Iwa' (*longipes* var. *latifolia*) | CBdn |
| 'Maruba' (*longipes* var. *latifolia*) | EGol |
| 'Mary Joe' | EMic IBal |
| 'Mary Marie Ann' (*fortunei*) (v) | CBdn EGol EMic EPGN IBal NMyG |
| 'Masquerade' (v) | CBdn EGol EMic EPGN IBal NHar SApp WFar WHal |
| 'Maui Buttercups' **new** | SApp |
| 'May' | IBal |
| § 'Mediopicta' (*sieboldii*) **new** | EMic |
| 'Mediovariegata' (*undulata*) | see *H. undulata* var. ***undulata*** |
| 'Medusa' (v) | EGol EMic IBal WCot |
| 'Memories of Dorothy' | EMic IBal |
| 'Mentor Gold' | EGol EMic |
| 'Mesa Fringe' (*montana*) | CBdn EMic MMiN |
| 'Metallic Sheen' | CBdn LRHS |
| 'Metallica' | CBdn |
| 'Midas Touch' | CBdn EGol NHol NLar |
| 'Middle Ridge' | NHol |
| 'Midnight Ride' **new** | IBal |
| 'Midwest Gold' | MHom SApp |
| 'Midwest Magic' (v) | CBdn CWib EGol EMic IBal MMiN NLar SApp |
| 'Mikawa-no-yuki' **new** | EGol IBal |
| 'Miki' **new** | IBal |
| 'Mildred Seaver' (v) | CBdn EGol EMic GAbr IBal MMiN NMyG |
| 'Millennium' | EMic |
| 'Millie's Memoirs' (v) | EGol |
| 'Ming Jade' | GSec SApp |
| 'Ming Treasure' (v) **new** | IBal |
| 'Minnie Bell' (v) | EGol |
| 'Minnie Klopping' | EMic |
| ***minor*** misapplied f. ***alba*** | see *H. sieboldii* var. ***alba*** |
| § ***minor*** Maekawa | CBdn CBro EBee EGol EMic EPGN ERos EWTr GEdr GGar ITim MTho NHol NMyG WCot WFar |
| - from Korea | EGol IBal |
| - Goldbrook form | EGol IBal |
| 'Minor' (*ventricosa*) | see *H. minor* Maekawa |
| 'Mint Julep' (v) **new** | EMic IBal |
| 'Minuet' (v) **new** | IBal |
| 'Minuteman' (*fortunei*) (v) | CBdn EGle EMic EPGN EPfP GAbr IBal IPot LAst LRHS MBNS MIDC MSte NBPC NCGa NGdn NMyG NNor NOrc SApp SHBN SPad SPla SPoG WFar WGor WTin |
| 'Miss Saigon' (v) **new** | EMic |
| 'Mississippi Delta' | EMic |
| 'Mister Watson' **new** | IBal |
| 'Misty Waters' (*sieboldiana*) | EMic MMiN |
| 'Moerheim' (*fortunei*) (v) | CBdn EGol EMic EPGN IBal LRHS MBar MIDC NHol WHal |
| N ***montana*** | CWib EGol EMic MMiN NHol WBrE |
| - B&SWJ 4796 | WCru |
| - B&SWJ 5585 | WCru |
| - 'Kinkaku' **new** | EPGN |
| - f. ***macrophylla*** | EGol IBal |
| 'Moon Glow' (v) | EGol EMic NMyG |
| 'Moon Lily' **new** | EMic |
| 'Moon River' (v) | CBdn EGol EMic EPGN MMiN NMyG SApp |
| 'Moon Shadow' (v) | EGol |
| 'Moon Waves' | EGol |
| 'Moonbeam' | CBdn EShb |
| 'Moonlight' (*fortunei*) (v) | CBdn EBee EGol EMic EPGN GMaP GSec MMiN NMyG SApp |
| 'Moonlight Sonata' | CBdn EGol EMic |
| 'Moonstruck' (v) | CBdn EGol EMic EPGN IBal |

| | |
|---|---|
| 'Morning Light'PBR | CBdn EBee EGol EMic EPGN EPfP IBal MAvo MBNS MBri NBhm NBro NGdn NMoo NMyG SApp SRkn WBor |
| 'Moscow Blue' | EGol EMic LRHS |
| 'Mount Everest' | CBdn EMic IBal |
| 'Mount Fuji' (*montana*) | EGol IBal MMiN |
| 'Mount Hope' (v) | EGol |
| 'Mount Kirishima' (*sieboldii*) | see *H.* 'Kirishima' |
| § 'Mount Royal' (*sieboldii*) | NHol |
| 'Mount Tom' (v) | EGol IBal |
| 'Mountain Snow' (*montana*) (v) | CBdn CWat EGol EMic LRHS MMiN NMyG SApp |
| 'Mountain Sunrise' (*montana*) | EGol |
| 'Mourning Dove' (v) **new** | IBal |
| 'Mrs Minky' | EBrs EMic EPGN |
| 'Muffie' (v) **new** | EMic |
| 'Munchkin' (*sieboldii*) | CBdn EMic WPat |
| 'My Child Insook' (v) **new** | EMic |
| 'My Claire' (v) **new** | IBal |
| 'My Friend Nancy' (v) | EGol |
| 'Myerscough Magic' | CBdn MSte |
| 'Naegato' | SApp |
| ***nakaiana*** | EBee EMic GEdr NDlv |
| 'Nakaimo' | CBdn EMic NHol |
| 'Nameoki' | NHol |
| 'Nana' (*ventricosa*) | see *H. minor* Maekawa |
| § 'Nancy Lindsay' (*fortunei*) | CBdn CTri EGol EMic NGdn SApp |
| 'Nancy Minks' | CBdn EMic IBal |
| 'Neat and Tidy' | IBal |
| 'Neat Splash' (v) | CBdn NBir NHol |
| 'New Wave' | EGol EMic |
| 'Niagara Falls' | CBdn CFir EGol EMic GBin IBal NGdn |
| 'Nicola' | EGol EMic EPGN IBal MHom NMyG |
| 'Night before Christmas' (v) | Widely available |
| ***nigrescens*** | CBdn EBee EGol EMic EPGN |
| - 'Cally White' | GCal NCGa |
| 'Nokogiryama' | EMic |
| 'None Lovelier' (v) **new** | IBal |
| 'North Hills' (*fortunei*) (v) | CBdn CMoH EAEE EBee EGol EMic LRHS NBir NCob NGdn SWvt |
| 'Northern Exposure' (*sieboldiana*) (v) | CFir EGol EMic IBal MMiN NGdn NMyG SApp SPoG |
| 'Northern Halo' (*sieboldiana*) (v) | EGol EMic |
| 'Northern Lights' (*sieboldiana*) | EGol |
| 'Northern Mist' (*sieboldiana*) **new** | EMic |
| 'Nouzang' | IBal |
| 'Nutty Professor' (v) **new** | IBal |
| 'Obscura Marginata' (*fortunei*) | see *H. fortunei* var. *aureomarginata* |
| 'Obsession' | EGol IBal |
| 'Ocean Isle' (v) **new** | IBal |
| 'Oder' **new** | IBal |
| 'O'Harra' | EGol |
| 'Okazuki Special' | CBdn |
| 'Old Faithful' | CBdn EGol EMic |
| 'Old Glory'PBR (v) | EGol IBal |
| 'Olga's Shiny Leaf' | EGol EMic |
| 'Olive Bailey Langdon' (*sieboldiana*) (v) | CBdn EMic IBal SApp |
| 'Olive Branch' (v) | EGol EMic IBal |
| 'Olympic Edger' | EMic IBal |
| 'Olympic Glacier' (v) | EMic IBal SApp |
| 'Olympic Sunrise' (v) | CBdn EMic IBal |
| 'On Stage' | see *H.* 'Choko Nishiki' |
| 'One Man's Treasure' | EMic EPGN GBin IBal MBNS SPoG |
| 'Ooh La La' (v) **new** | IBal |
| 'Ophir' | IBal |
| ***opipara*** | MMiN |
| 'Ops' (v) | EMic IBal |
| 'Orange Crush' (v) **new** | IBal |
| 'Orange Marmalade' | EMic IBal |
| 'Oriana' (*fortunei*) | EGol EMic IBal |
| 'Orphan Annie' (*venusta*) (v) **new** | EMic |
| 'Osprey' (Tardiana Group) | EGol LRHS |
| 'Outhouse Delight' (v) **new** | EMic |
| 'Oxheart' | EMic |
| ***pachyscapa*** | EMic |
| 'Pacific Blue Edger' | CBdn CBgR CFir CMMP EGol EMic EPGN MMiN NGdn NPri SApp WAul |
| 'Pandora's Box' (v) | CBdn CWib EGol EMic EPGN GBin GEdr IBal NHar NMyG SApp WCot |
| 'Paradigm' (v) | CBdn EBee EBrs EGol EMic EPGN IBal NMyG |
| 'Paradise Backstage' (v) | CBdn EMic |
| 'Paradise Beach' | EMic |
| 'Paradise Expectations' (*sieboldiana*) (v) **new** | EMic |
| 'Paradise Glory' | EMic |
| 'Paradise Gold Line' (*ventricosa*) (v) **new** | EMic |
| 'Paradise Joyce'PBR | CBdn EGol EMic EPGN IBal MIDC NLar NMyG |
| 'Paradise on Fire' (v) | CBdn EMic IBal |
| 'Paradise Passion' (v) **new** | EMic |
| 'Paradise Power'PBR | CBdn EGol EMic IBal |
| 'Paradise Puppet' (*venusta*) | CBdn EMic EPGN IBal |
| 'Paradise Red Delight' (*pycnophylla*) | CBdn EMic |
| 'Paradise Standard' (d) | CBdn EMic |
| 'Paradise Sunset' | EGol EMic IBal |
| 'Party Dress' **new** | MMiN |
| 'Party Favor' **new** | GSec |
| 'Pastures Green' | EGol IBal |
| 'Pastures New' | EGol EMic EQua MHom NHol NMyG SApp |
| 'Pathfinder' (v) | EGol EMic IBal |
| 'Patricia' | EMic |
| 'Patrician' (v) | EGol EMic EPGN IBal NMyG |
| 'Patriot' (v) | Widely available |
| 'Patriot's Fire' (v) **new** | IBal |
| 'Paul Revere' (v) | EMic IBal |
| 'Paul's Glory' (v) | CBdn EGol EMic EPGN EQua GAbr GBin GMaP IBal LAst LPBA LRHS MBri NBhm NBir NGdn NMyG SApp WFar |
| 'Peace' (v) | EGol EMic EPGN IBal |
| 'Peacock Strut' **new** | IBal |
| 'Peanut' | IBal |
| 'Pearl Lake' | CBdn EBee EGol EMic EPGN GEdr MHom MMiN MSte MWat NBir NCob NGdn NHol NLar NMyG SApp SRGP WTin |
| 'Peedee Absinth' | EMic GSec |
| 'Peedee Elfin Bells' (*ventricosa*) **new** | GSec |
| 'Peedee Gold Flash' (v) | CBdn EMic NMyG |
| 'Peedee Laughing River' (v) **new** | EMic |
| 'Pelham Blue Tump' | EGol EMic GSec |
| 'Peppermint Ice' (v) | EGol IBal |
| 'Percy' | IBal |
| 'Peridot' (Tardiana Group) **new** | GSec |
| 'Permanent Wave' | EGol GSec |
| 'Perry's True Blue' | CBdn EMic MMiN |
| 'Peter Pan' | CBdn EGol EMic GBin |

| | |
|---|---|
| 'Pete's Dark Satellite' **new** | EMic IBal |
| 'Pewterware' **new** | IBal |
| 'Phantom' | EMic SApp |
| 'Phoenix' | EGol EMic GBin SApp |
| 'Photo Finish' (v) | EGle EGol EMic |
| 'Phyllis Campbell' (*fortunei*) | see *H.* 'Sharmon' |
| 'Picta' (*fortunei*) | see *H. fortunei* var. *albopicta* |
| 'Piecrust Power' | CBdn EGol |
| 'Piedmont Gold' | CBdn EGol EMic EPGN IBal MMiN MSte |
| 'Pilgrim' (v) | CBdn EBee EGol ELan EMic EPGN IBal NBPC NBro NMyG SApp WFar |
| 'Pineapple Poll' | CBdn EGol EMic EPGN MIDC MMiN NMyG WTin |
| 'Pineapple Upside Down Cake' (v) | EMic EPGN IBal NBhm NBro NLar NMyG WCot WFar |
| 'Pinky' **new** | IBal |
| 'Pinwheel' (v) **new** | IBal |
| 'Pistachio Cream' **new** | EMic |
| 'Pizzazz' (v) | CBdn CDWL EGle EGol EMic IBal MHom MIDC MMiN NGdn NHol NLar NMyG SApp SHBN WFar WHil |
| ***plantaginea*** | CBdn CBgR EGol EMic IBal LEdu LPla MHom NMyG SSpi WCru WFar WKif |
| - var. ***grandiflora*** | see *H. plantaginea* var. *japonica* |
| § - var. ***japonica*** 🏆H4 | CDes ECha EHrv EMic EPGN IBal SApp WCAu WCFE WFar WPGP |
| 'Platinum Tiara' (v) | CBdn EGol EMic EPGN GSec IBal MMiN NBir NMyG |
| 'Plug Nickel' | IBal |
| 'Polar Moon' (v) **new** | IBal |
| 'Pooh Bear' (v) | CBdn EGol EMic |
| 'Popcorn' | CBdn IBal |
| 'Popo' | CBdn EGol EMic EPGN IBal SApp |
| 'Porky's Prize' (v) **new** | EGol |
| 'Potomac Pride' | CBdn EGol EMic EPGN NMyG SApp |
| 'Powder Blue' (v) **new** | IBal |
| 'Powderpuff' **new** | IBal |
| 'Prairie Sky' **new** | IBal |
| 'Praying Hands' (v) | CBdn EGol EMic EPGN GBin IBal IPot |
| 'Pretty Flamingo' | EMic IBal MMiN |
| 'Prima Donna' | EMic |
| 'Primavera Primrose' | SApp |
| 'Prince of Wales' | CBdn EMic IBal LAst NMyG SApp SPoG SRkn |
| 'Princess of Wales' | EBee |
| 'Puck' | EGol |
| 'Punky' (v) **new** | IBal |
| 'Purple and Gold' | CBdn EMic |
| 'Purple Dwarf' | CBdn EGol EMic NGdn NHol NLar WHal |
| 'Purple Glory' | EMic |
| 'Purple Lady Finger' | GSec |
| 'Purple Passion' | EGol EMic |
| 'Purple Profusion' | EGol EMic |
| ***pycnophylla*** | EGol |
| 'Queen Josephine' (v) | CBdn EGol EMic EPGN IBal IPot MBri MHom NCGa NGdn NMyG NPro SApp SPoG SRGP WFar |
| 'Queen of Islip' (*sieboldiana*) (v) | CBdn |
| 'Queen of the Seas' | IBal |
| 'Quill' **new** | EMic |
| 'Quilting Bee' | EGol |
| 'Radiant Edger' (v) | CBdn EGol EMic EPGN GCra IBal LRHS MMiN NHol |
| 'Radio Waves' | EMic IBal |
| 'Rain Forest' | IBal |
| 'Rainforest Sunrise' | EMic IBal |
| 'Raleigh Remembrance' | EGol EMic |
| 'Rascal' (v) | CBdn EGol EMic LRHS |
| 'Raspberry Sorbet' | EGol EPGN IBal |
| ***rectifolia*** | NHol NNor |
| - 'Kinbuchi Tachi' (v) **new** | IBal |
| - 'Ogon Tachi' (v) **new** | IBal |
| 'Red Hot Flash' (v) **new** | IBal |
| 'Red Neck Heaven' (*kikutii* var. *caput-avis*) | CBdn EGol GSec SApp WTin |
| 'Red October' | CBdn CMHG EBee EBrs EGol EMic EPGN EPfP GAbr GBin IBal MBNS MBri NGdn NLar NMoo NMyG WFar |
| 'Red Salamander' | EGol |
| 'Regal Rhubarb' | EGol EMic IBal |
| 'Regal Splendor' (v) | CBdn EGol EMFW EMic EPGN IBal LRHS MHom MMiN NBro NCGa NGdn NHol NMyG SApp SHBN SPla WAul WMnd |
| 'Regalia' **new** | EMic |
| 'Reginald Kaye' | EMic |
| 'Remember Me'PBR | CBdn CBgR CWGN EDAr EGol ELan EMic EPGN IBal LSRN MBNS MCCP MDun NCob NGdn NHol NLar NMyG NNor SApp WFar WGor |
| 'Reptilian' **new** | EGol GSec |
| 'Resonance' (v) | EPGN GKir MMiN NGdn NLar NPro |
| 'Reversed' (*sieboldiana*) (v) | CBdn CWat EBee EGol ELan EMic EPGN EWsh MDKP MIDC MMiN MSte NBro NGdn NHol NNor WHal |
| 'Revolution'PBR (v) | CBdn CWGN CWib EBee EBrs EGle EGol EMic EPGN GKir IBal IPot LSRN MBri MIDC NBPC NBro NCob NHol NLar NMyG NOrc SApp WAul WFar |
| 'Rhapsody' (*fortunei*) (v) | EGol EMic |
| 'Rhapsody in Blue' | EGol |
| 'Rhein' (*tardiana*) **new** | EMic |
| 'Rheingold' (v) **new** | IBal |
| 'Rhino' (v) **new** | EMic |
| 'Rhythm and Blues' **new** | IBal |
| 'Rich Uncle' **new** | IBal |
| 'Richland Gold' (*fortunei*) | CBdn EGol EMic EPGN GSec NMyG |
| 'Richmond' (v) **new** | EMic |
| 'Rickrack' **new** | IBal |
| 'Rim Rock' | EMic |
| 'Rippled Honey' | CBdn EGol EMic EPGN GSec IBal NCob NMyG NPro SApp |
| 'Rippling Waves' | EGol EMic |
| 'Riptide' | CBdn EMic |
| 'Rising Sun' | EGol |
| 'Risky Business' (v) | CBdn IBal |
| 'Robert Frost' (v) | CBdn EGol EMic IBal WTin |
| 'Robin Hood' | EMic IBal SApp |
| 'Robusta' (*fortunei*) | see *H. sieboldiana* var. *elegans* |
| 'Robyn's Choice' (v) **new** | EMic |
| 'Rock Island Line' (v) **new** | IBal |
| 'Rock Princess' **new** | IBal |
| 'Rocky Mountain High' (v) **new** | EMic |
| § ***rohdeifolia*** (v) | LRHS |
| - f. ***albopicta*** | CBdn EGol ELan NHol |
| 'Roller Coaster Ride' **new** | IBal |
| 'Ron Damant' | EPGN IBal |
| 'Rosedale Golden Goose' | IBal |
| 'Rosedale Knox' | IBal |
| 'Rosedale Melody of Summer' (v) **new** | IBal |
| 'Rosedale Misty Pathways' (v) **new** | EMic |

| | |
|---|---|
| 'Rosedale Richie Valens' **new** | EMic IBal |
| 'Rosemoor' | CBdn EGol EMic IBal |
| 'Rotunda' | EGol |
| 'Rough Waters' | MMiN SApp |
| 'Roxsanne' | EMic |
| 'Royal Flush' (v) **new** | EMic |
| 'Royal Golden Jubilee' | EMic EPGN IBal NMyG |
| § 'Royal Standard' ♀$^{H4}$ | Widely available |
| 'Royal Tapestry' (v) **new** | IBal |
| 'Royal Tiara' (*nakaiana*) (v) **new** | EGol |
| 'Royalty' | EGol |
| ***rupifraga*** | EGol EMic |
| 'Ryan's Big One' | EMic IBal |
| § 'Sagae' (v) ♀$^{H3-4}$ | CBdn CMoH CWat EBee EBrs EGle EGol EMic EPGN EPfP IBal IPot MBri MHom MIDC MMiN MNrw MSte NGdn NMyG SApp SDix SPla SPoG WAul WFar WHoo |
| 'Saint Elmo's Fire' (v) | CBdn CHid EGol EMic EPGN IBal NCGa SApp SPla |
| 'Saint Fiacre' | CBdn |
| 'Saint Paul' | IBal |
| 'Saishu Jima' (*sieboldii* f. *spathulata*) | EMic NHol WCru |
| 'Saishu Yahite Site' (v) | EGol |
| 'Salute' (Tardiana Group) | CBdn EGol GSec |
| 'Samual Blue' | EGol |
| 'Samurai' (*sieboldiana*) (v) | CBdn EBee EGol EMic IBal IPot MRav NBir NBro NGdn NLar SApp |
| 'Sand Pebbles' (v) **new** | EMic |
| 'Sarah Kennedy' (v) | EPGN |
| 'Satisfaction' (v) | EMic |
| 'Savannah' | EGol |
| 'Sazanami' (*crispula*) | see *H. crispula* |
| 'Schwan' **new** | GBin |
| 'Scooter' (v) | CBdn EGol EMic EPGN MMiN NMyG |
| 'Sea Beacon' (v) **new** | EGol EMic |
| 'Sea Bunny' | EGol |
| 'Sea Dream' (v) | CBdn EGol EMic MMiN NMyG |
| 'Sea Drift' | EGol |
| 'Sea Fire' | EGol |
| 'Sea Frolic' | EGol |
| 'Sea Gold Star' | CBdn EGol MMiN NMyG |
| 'Sea Gulf Stream' | EMic IBal |
| 'Sea Hero' | EGol |
| 'Sea Lotus Leaf' | CBdn EGol EMic LLWP NLar NMyG |
| 'Sea Mist' (v) | CBdn |
| 'Sea Monster' | EGol |
| 'Sea Octopus' | EGol GSec |
| 'Sea Sapphire' | EGol |
| 'Sea Sprite' (v) | GBin MMiN |
| 'Sea Sunrise' | EPGN |
| 'Sea Thunder' (v) | CBdn EGol EMic EPGN IBal |
| 'Sea Yellow Sunrise' | CBdn EGol EMic IBal MMiN SApp |
| 'Second Wind' (*fortunei*) (v) | CBdn EGol EMic EPGN NMyG SApp |
| 'Secret Love' | IBal |
| 'See Saw' (*undulata*) | EGol EMic MMiN SApp |
| 'Seersucker' **new** | MMiN |
| 'September Sun' (v) | CBdn EGol GSec IBal LRHS MMiN NMyG |
| 'September Surprise' **new** | MMiN |
| 'Serena' (Tardiana Group) | IBal MMiN SApp |
| 'Serendipity' | CBdn EGol EMic MHom |
| 'Shade Beauty' (v) | EGol |
| 'Shade Fanfare' (v) ♀$^{H4}$ | CBdn CChe EBrs EGol ELan EMic EPGN EPfP IBal LAst LBMP LCro LRHS MBNS MBri MIDC MMiN MRav NBir NGdn NLar NMyG NSti SApp SPer WFar WMnd WTin |
| 'Shade Master' | CBdn EGol EMic NHol |
| 'Shamoa' | SApp |
| § 'Sharmon' (*fortunei*) (v) | CBdn CWat CWsd EGol EMic EPGN IBal MBNS NHol NMyG SApp |
| 'Sharp Dressed Man' **new** | IBal |
| 'Sheila West' | CBdn EMic |
| 'Shelleys' (v) | EGol IBal |
| 'Sherborne Profusion' (Tardiana Group) | CBdn EMic IBal |
| 'Sherborne Songbird' (Tardiana Group) | EGol EMic IBal MMiN |
| 'Sherborne Swan' (Tardiana Group) | EGol EMic IBal MMiN |
| 'Sherborne Swift' (Tardiana Group) | CBdn EGol EMic |
| 'Shere Khan' (v) | EGol EMic |
| 'Shining Tot' | CBdn EGol LLHF |
| 'Shiny Penny' (v) | EGol EMic IBal |
| 'Shirley Vaughn' (v) | EGol |
| 'Shogun' (v) | EGol |
| 'Showboat' (v) | CBdn EGol EMic IBal NMyG |
| ***sieboldiana*** | ECha EGol ELan EMic EPfP GCra GMaP LLWP MMuc MRav MSwo NChi NHol SPlb SRms WFar WGwG |
| § - var. ***elegans*** ♀$^{H4}$ | Widely available |
| - 'George Smith' | EMic IBal SApp |
| - var. ***mira*** | EMic |
| - var. ***sieboldiana*** **new** | GAuc |
| ***sieboldiana*** x ***sieboldii*** f. ***kabitan*** | CWsd |
| ***sieboldii*** | CWat |
| § - var. ***alba*** | EGol IBal |
| § - 'Paxton's Original' (v) ♀$^{H4}$ | CTca CWib EGol EHrv MBar SRms |
| § - var. ***sieboldii*** f. ***kabitan*** (v) | CBdn EGol EPGN MIDC NMyG NSti SApp WTin |
| - - f. ***shiro-kabitan*** (v) | EGol EMic EPGN |
| - f. ***spathulata*** **new** | EMic |
| 'Silberpfeil' **new** | EMic |
| 'Silk Kimono' (v) | EGol EMic |
| 'Silver and Gold' | MMiN |
| 'Silver Bowl' | EGol |
| 'Silver Crown' | see *H.* 'Albomarginata' |
| 'Silver Lance' (v) | CBdn EGol EMic EPGN NMyG |
| 'Silver Lining' **new** | IBal |
| 'Silver Shadow' (v) | CBdn CHid EMic EPGN GBin IBal NCob NHol NMyG SApp WPtf |
| 'Silver Spray' (v) | EGol IBal |
| 'Silverado' (v) **new** | IBal |
| 'Silvery Slugproof' (Tardiana Group) | CBdn MMiN MWat NMyG SApp |
| 'Sitting Pretty' (v) | EGol EPGN |
| 'Sky Dancer' | EMic IBal |
| 'Sleeping Beauty' | EMic IBal NMyG SPoG |
| 'Slick Willie' | EGol |
| 'Slim Polly' | CBdn |
| 'Small Sum' | IBal |
| 'Snow Cap' (v) | CBdn EBee EGle EGol EMic IBal MBri MIDC MMiN NGdn NLar NMoo NMyG NNor NPro SApp SHBN WAul WCra |
| 'Snow Crust' (v) | CBdn EGol EMic LRHS MMiN |
| 'Snow Flakes' (*sieboldii*) | CBdn EGol EPGN EPfP EWTr LRHS MBar NBro NGdn NHol NMyG NPro SBod SHBN WFar WGwG |
| 'Snow White' (*undulata*) (v) | EGol |
| 'Snowbound' (v) **new** | IBal |
| 'Snowden' | CBdn CMHG ECha EGol EMic EPGN ETod GMaP GMac IBal MMiN MWat NBir NCob NGdn NHol NMyG SApp SSpi WCru |
| 'Snowstorm' (*sieboldii*) | CBdn NHol |

| | |
|---|---|
| 'So Sweet' (v) | CBdn COlW CTca EBee EGol EHoe ELan EMFW EMic EMil EPGN IBal LBMP LPBA MHom MIDC MMiN MSte MSwo NBro NGdn NHol NMyG SApp SPad SPoG SRGP |
| 'Solar Flare' | EGol |
| 'Soldier Boy' **new** | EMic |
| 'Something Blue' | CBdn EMic |
| 'Something Different' (*fortunei*) (v) | EGol EPGN |
| 'Sophistication' (v) **new** | EGol |
| 'Sparkling Burgundy' | CBdn EGol |
| 'Sparky' (v) | EGol EMic IBal |
| 'Spartan Glory' (v) **new** | IBal |
| 'Special Gift' | CBdn CTca EGol EMic |
| 'Spellbound' (v) **new** | IBal |
| 'Spilt Milk' (*tokudama*) (v) | CBdn EGol EMic EPGN IBal SApp SPoG WHoo |
| § 'Spinners' (*fortunei*) (v) | CBdn ECha EGol EMic MMiN |
| 'Spinning Wheel' (v) | EGol |
| 'Spring Fling' | EMic IBal |
| 'Spritzer' (v) | CBdn EGol EMic GSec MMiN NMyG SApp |
| 'Squash Casserole' | EGol |
| 'Squiggles' (v) | EGol |
| 'Stained Glass' | EGol EMic EPGN IBal NGdn WFar |
| 'Standing Ovation' (v) **new** | EMic |
| 'Star Kissed' **new** | IBal |
| 'Starburst' (v) | EGol |
| 'Starburst' stable (v) **new** | IBal |
| § 'Starker Yellow Leaf' | EMic |
| 'Stenantha' (*fortunei*) | EMic |
| 'Stenantha Variegated' (*fortunei*) (v) | NHol |
| 'Step Sister' | EMic IBal |
| 'Stepping Out' (v) **new** | EMic IBal |
| 'Stetson' (v) | EGol |
| 'Stiletto' (v) | Widely available |
| 'Stirfry' | EGol GSec |
| 'Stonewall' | IBal |
| 'Striker' (v) **new** | EGol IBal |
| 'Striptease' (*fortunei*) (v) | CBdn CBgR EGol EMic EPGN GBin GQue IBal LAst MBNS MIDC MMiN NGdn NHol NLar SApp SHBN WFar WHoo |
| 'Sugar and Cream' (v) | CMMP CWat EGol EMic LRHS MMiN MWat NGdn |
| 'Sugar Babe' (v) **new** | EMic |
| 'Sugar Daddy' | EMic IBal |
| 'Sugar Plum Fairy' (*gracillima*) | EGol |
| 'Sultana' (v) | EMic IBal |
| 'Sum and Substance' ♀H4 | Widely available |
| 'Sum Cup-o-Joe' (v) **new** | EMic |
| 'Sum it Up' (v) **new** | EMic |
| 'Sum of All' (v) | CBdn EMic |
| 'Summer Breeze' (v) | EGol EMic IBal |
| 'Summer Fragrance' | CBdn EGol EMic LRHS MMiN NMyG |
| 'Summer Gold' **new** | MMiN |
| 'Summer Joy' | EMic |
| 'Summer Music' (v) | CBdn EGle EGol EMic EPGN IBal MBNS MBri NMyG SApp |
| 'Summer Serenade' (v) | CBdn EGol EMic IBal |
| 'Summer Warrior' **new** | EMic |
| 'Sun Glow' | EGol EMic MMiN |
| 'Sun Kissed' (v) | IBal |
| 'Sun Power' | CBdn EGol EMic EPfP GBin IBal LRHS MBNS MIDC NBro NGdn NLar NMyG NSti SApp SPoG SRGP |
| 'Sun Worshipper' **new** | IBal |
| 'Sundance' (*fortunei*) (v) | EGol MMiN |
| 'Sunlight Child' **new** | IBal |
| 'Sunny Delight' **new** | EMic |
| 'Sunny Disposition' **new** | EMic |
| 'Sunshine Glory' | EGol EMic |
| 'Super Bowl' | EGol MMiN |
| 'Super Nova' (v) | CBdn EGol EMic IBal SApp |
| 'Surprised by Joy' (v) | EGol EMic IBal |
| 'Susy' | IBal |
| 'Suzuki Thumbnail' | EMic |
| 'Sweet Bo Beep' | EGol GSec |
| 'Sweet Bouquet' | EMic |
| 'Sweet Home Chicago' (v) | EGol EMic IBal |
| 'Sweet Marjorie' | EGol |
| 'Sweet Standard' | MMiN |
| 'Sweet Sunshine' | EGol |
| 'Sweet Susan' | EGol EMic GBin GSec LSRN MBNS SApp SPer SPoG SWvt |
| 'Sweet Tater Pie' | CBdn EGol |
| 'Sweetheart' | EMic |
| 'Sweetie' (v) | CBdn EGol EMic IBal SApp |
| 'Swirling Hearts' | EGol GSec |
| 'Swizzle Sticks' **new** | IBal |
| 'Swoosh' | EPGN |
| 'Tall Boy' | CBdn CSev ECha EGol EMic EPla NBir NNor SPoG |
| 'Tall Twister' | EMic |
| 'Tamborine' (v) | CBdn CWat EGol EMic EPGN MMiN NMyG SApp |
| 'Tango' | EMic IBal |
| Tardiana Group | CBdn EGol ELan MHom NGdn NHol |
| - pink-flowered | MMiN |
| ***tardiflora*** | CBdn CWsd EGol ERos SApp WCot WPGP |
| ***tardiva*** | CBdn CWsd GKir |
| 'Tattoo'PBR (v) | CBdn CWGN EDAr EGol EMic EPGN IBal LSRN MBNS MIDC MNrw NLar NMoo NMyG SApp SPoG |
| 'Tea and Crumpets' (v) | CBdn EPGN |
| 'Teaspoon' | EMic IBal SApp |
| 'Teeny-weeny Bikini' (v) **new** | IBal |
| 'Templar Gold' **new** | IBal |
| 'Temple Bells' | EGol |
| 'Temptation' | EMic IBal |
| 'Tenryu' | EGol |
| 'Tequila Sunrise' **new** | IBal |
| 'Terry Wogan' | IBal |
| 'The Twister' | EGol EMic IBal |
| 'Theo's Blue' | EMic IBal |
| 'Thomas Hogg' | see ***H. undulata*** var. ***albomarginata*** |
| 'Thumb Nail' | CBdn ECha EGol EMic IBal SApp |
| 'Thumbelina' | IBal |
| 'Thunderbolt'PBR (*sieboldiana*) | CBdn CWat EGol EPGN IBal MIDC NCob NLar WFar |
| ***tibae*** | CBdn EMic |
| 'Tick Tock' (v) | IBal |
| 'Tidewater' **new** | IBal |
| 'Tijuana Brass' **new** | EMic |
| 'Time Tunnel'PBR (*sieboldiana*) (v) **new** | EMic |
| 'Tiny Tears' | CBdn CStu EGol IBal |
| 'Titanic'PBR | IBal |
| ***tokudama*** | EGol EMic IBal LRHS MHom NBir NGdn NHol NNor NSti SApp WFar |
| § - f. ***aureo-nebulosa*** (v) | CBdn EGol EMic EPGN IBal LRHS MMiN MSte NGdn NMyG NSti WMnd |
| 'Tokudama Blue' **new** | SApp |
| - f. ***flavocircinalis*** (v) | CBdn CBgR CPrp EGol EMic EPGN GMaP IBal LRHS NBPC NBro NMyG SApp WFar WHoo WMnd |

| | | |
|---|---|---|
| | 'Tom Rex' | IBal |
| | 'Tom Schmid' (v) **new** | EGol EMic |
| | 'Tom Thumb' **new** | EMic IBal |
| | 'Topaz' **new** | EMic IBal |
| | 'Topscore' | NNor |
| | 'Torchlight' (v) | CBdn EGol EMic GSec LRHS |
| | ***tortifrons*** | EBee EMic IBal |
| | 'Tortilla Chip' | IBal |
| | 'Tot Tot' | EGol IBal |
| | 'Touch of Class'[PBR] (v) | CBdn EMic IBal |
| | 'Touchstone' (v) | CBdn GSec IBal NMyG SApp SWvt |
| | 'Toy Soldier' | CBdn EMic IBal |
| | 'Trail's End' | EMic |
| | 'Tranquility' (v) **new** | EMic |
| | 'Treasure Island' **new** | IBal |
| | 'Trill' | SApp |
| | 'Trixi' (v) **new** | IBal |
| | 'True Blue' | CBdn CBgR EBee EGol EMic IBal SApp |
| | 'Tsugaru Komachi' | EMic |
| | 'Tsugaru Komachi Kifukurin' (v) **new** | IBal |
| | ***tsushimensis*** **new** | EMic |
| | 'Turning Point' | EGol |
| | 'Tutu' | EGol EPGN MIDC |
| | 'Twiggie' | EMic MMiN SApp |
| | 'Twilight' (*fortunei*) (v) | CBdn CDWL CWib EBee EGol EMFW EMic EPGN IBal MBNS NLar NMyG SApp SWvt WClo WRHF |
| | 'Twilight Time' | IBal |
| | 'Twinkle Toes' | EGol EMic |
| | 'Twinkles' | MIDC |
| | 'Twist of Lime' (v) | CBdn EGol EMic IBal |
| | 'Ultramarine' | EMic IBal |
| | 'Ultraviolet Light' | EGol |
| | 'Unchained Melody' | IBal |
| | ***undulata*** | ECha MIDC NNor WFar |
| § | - var. ***albomarginata*** | Widely available |
| § | - var. ***erromena*** ♀H4 | CBdn EHon EMic GMaP IBal LPBA NBid NHol SPer |
| § | - var. ***undulata*** (v) ♀H4 | CBdn EBee EHrv ELan EMFW EMic EPGN EPfP GMaP IBal LAst LPBA MCot MIDC MMiN MRav MSwo NGdn NMyG NVic SIng SPer SPoG WEas WFar |
| | - var. ***univittata*** (v) ♀H4 | CBro ECha EGol EMic GKev IBal MHom MMiN MWhi NBir NPro WBrk WFar WMoo |
| | 'Unforgettable' | EMic IBal NMyG |
| | 'Urajiro' (*hypoleuca*) | EGol |
| | 'Urajiro' (*longipes*) **new** | EMic |
| | 'Urajiro Hachijo' (*longipes* var. *latifolia*) | EGol IBal |
| | 'Uzo-no-mai' **new** | EBee |
| | 'Valentine Lace' | CBdn EBee EGol EMic |
| | 'Van Wade' (v) | CBdn EGol EMic EPGN MMiN |
| | 'Vanilla Cream' (*cathayana*) | EGol EMic NMyG |
| | 'Variegata' (*gracillima*) | see *H.* 'Vera Verde' |
| | 'Variegata' (*tokudama*) | see *H. tokudama* f. *aureo-nebulosa* |
| | 'Variegata' (*undulata*) | see *H. undulata* var. *undulata* |
| | 'Variegata' (*ventricosa*) | see *H.* 'Aureomarginata' |
| | 'Variegated' (*fluctuans*) | see *H.* 'Sagae' |
| | 'Velvet Moon' (v) | IBal |
| | ***ventricosa*** ♀H4 | CBcs CBdn CBro EGol EGoo EMic EPfP GMaP LPBA MIDC MRav MWhi NHol SGar WBrk WCFE WFar |
| | - var. ***aureomaculata*** | CBdn EGol EMic MMiN NBir NSti WFar |
| | - BWJ 8160 from Sichuan | WCru |
| I | 'Venucosa' | EGol EMic WFar |
| | 'Venus' (d) **new** | IBal SPoG |

| | | |
|---|---|---|
| | 'Venus Star' | EGol NMyG |
| | ***venusta*** ♀H4 | Widely available |
| | - B&SWJ 4389 | WCru |
| | - dwarf | CSWP GCal |
| | - 'Porter' **new** | EMic IBal |
| | - 'Red Tubes' **new** | IBal |
| | - ***yakusimensis*** | see *H. kikutii* var. *yakusimensis* |
| § | 'Vera Verde' (v) | CBdn EPGN GCra GQui IBal MHom NBir NMyG |
| | 'Verkade's No 1' **new** | IBal |
| | 'Verna Jean' (v) | CBdn EGol |
| | 'Veronica Lake' (v) | CBdn EGol EMic GSec IBal WHal |
| | 'Victory' | EMic IBal |
| | 'Viette's Yellow Edge' (*fortunei*) (v) | EMic MMiN |
| | 'Vilmoriniana' | EGol EMic IBal |
| | 'Viridis Marginata' | see *H. sieboldii* var. *sieboldii* f. *kabitan* |
| | 'Wagtail' (Tardiana Group) | CBdn EGol EMic IBal |
| | 'Wahoo' (*tokudama*) (v) | EGol MMiN |
| | 'War Paint' | EMic IBal |
| | 'War Party' **new** | EMic |
| | 'Warwick Ballerina' **new** | EGol |
| | 'Warwick Choice' (v) | CBdn |
| | 'Warwick Comet' (v) | IBal |
| | 'Warwick Curtsey' (v) | EGol EMic GSec IBal |
| | 'Warwick Delight' (v) | EGol EMic IBal |
| | 'Warwick Edge' (v) | CBdn EGol IBal |
| | 'Warwick Essence' | EGol EMic |
| | 'Warwick Sheen' | IBal |
| | 'Waving Winds' (v) | EGol IBal |
| | 'Waving Wuffles' | EMic |
| | 'Wayside Blue' | EMic MMiN |
| | 'Wayside Perfection' | see *H.* 'Royal Standard' |
| | 'Weihenstephan' (*sieboldii*) | EGol EMic |
| | 'Weser' | EGol |
| | 'Wheaton Blue' | CBdn EMic |
| | 'Whirligig' (v) **new** | EMic |
| | 'Whirling Dervish' (v) **new** | EMic IBal |
| | 'Whirlwind' (*fortunei*) (v) | CBcs CBdn CBgR CWib EDAr EGol EMic EPGN GBin GQue IBal IPot MBri MIDC MNrw MSte NBro NGdn NMyG NNor NOrc SApp SMad WAul WMnd |
| | 'Whirlwind Tour' (v) | EGol IBal SApp |
| | 'Whiskey Sour' | EMic IBal SApp |
| | 'White Bikini' (v) **new** | IBal |
| | 'White Christmas' (*undulata*) (v) | EGle EGol EMic EPGN EQua |
| | 'White Fairy' (*plantaginea*) (d) | CBdn IBal NMyG |
| | 'White Feather' (*undulata*) | CBdn EMic IBal NBir |
| | 'White Gold' | CBdn EGol NMyG |
| | 'White On' (Montana) | EMic |
| | 'White Tacchi' | EMic EMon |
| | 'White Triumphator' (*rectifolia*) | CBdn EGol EMic EPGN GBin IBal NBPC NMyG |
| | 'White Trumpets' | EMic |
| | 'White Vision' | EGol |
| | 'Wide Brim' (v) ♀H4 | Widely available |
| | 'Wily Willy' **new** | IBal |
| | 'Wind River Gold' | EGol EMic |
| | 'Windsor Gold' | see *H.* 'Nancy Lindsay' |
| | 'Winfield Blue' | CMHG EGol EMic IBal |
| | 'Winfield Gold' | CBdn EGol IBal |
| | 'Winfield Mist' (v) **new** | IBal |
| | 'Winsome' (v) | EGol EMic IBal |
| | 'Winter Snow' (v) **new** | CBdn |
| | 'Wintergreen' (v) **new** | IBal |
| | 'Wintersnow' | EMic IBal |
| | 'Wogon Giboshi' | see *H.* 'Wogon' |
| § | 'Wogon' (*sieboldii*) | CBdn CMMP EMic GEdr GMaP NDlv NHol NMen NSti |

| | | |
|---|---|---|
| | 'Wogon's Boy' | CBdn EGol EMic EPGN IBal |
| | 'Wolverine' (v) | CBdn EBee ECtt EGol EHoe EMic EPGN GAbr GEdr IBal LPla LSou MBNS MHom MIDC NGdn NMyG SWvt WCot |
| | 'Woolly Mammoth' (v) **new** | IBal SKHP |
| | 'Wrinkles and Crinkles' | EGol EMic IBal |
| | 'Wylde Green Cream' | EGol EMic IBal |
| | 'Xanadu' (v) | EMic IBal |
| | 'X-rated' (v) **new** | IBal |
| | 'X-ray' (v) **new** | IBal |
| | 'Yakushima-mizu' (*gracillima*) | CBdn EGol IBal MMiN |
| * | ***yakushimana*** | NMen |
| | 'Yang' **new** | IBal |
| | 'Yankee Blue' **new** | IBal |
| | 'Yellow Boa' | EGol EMic |
| | 'Yellow Edge' (*fortunei*) | see *H. fortunei* var. *aureomarginata* |
| | 'Yellow Edge' (*sieboldiana*) | see *H.* 'Frances Williams' |
| | 'Yellow River' (v) | CBdn EGol EMic IBal MBri MMiN NGdn NMyG SApp |
| | 'Yellow Splash' (v) | CBdn CMoH ECha EPGN LRHS MHom NMyG |
| | 'Yellow Splash Rim' (v) | EGol MMiN NCGa |
| | 'Yellow Splashed Edged' (v) | EMic |
| | 'Yellow Submarine' | IBal |
| | 'Yellow Waves' | CBdn |
| | 'Yin' (v) | IBal |
| | ***yingeri*** | EGol SApp WPGP |
| | - B&SWJ 546 | WCru |
| | 'Yucca Ducka Do' (v) **new** | EGol |
| | 'Zager Blue' | EMic |
| | 'Zager Green' | EMic |
| | 'Zager White Edge' (*fortunei*) (v) | EGol EMic IBal NMyG SApp WTin |
| | 'Zippity Do Dah' (v) **new** | IBal |
| | 'Zitronenfalter' **new** | EGol IBal |
| | 'Zodiac' (*fortunei*) (v) **new** | EMic |
| | 'Zounds' | CBdn CBgR CMHG EBee ECtt EGol ELan EMic EPGN EPfP EShb GKir IBal LRHS MDun MIDC MRav NHol NMyG NOrc NSti SApp SHBN SPla WBor WFar |

## *Hottonia* (*Primulaceae*)

| | | |
|---|---|---|
| | ***palustris*** | CDWL CWat EHon ELan EMFW LPBA MMuc MSKA NPer NSco NVic SWat WPnP |

## *Houstonia* (*Rubiaceae*)

| | | |
|---|---|---|
| | ***caerulea*** misapplied | see *H. michauxii* |
| | ***caerulea*** L. | ECho EDAr NPri SIng |
| | - var. ***alba*** | SPer SPlb |
| | ***longifolia*** | EWes |
| § | ***michauxii*** | SPer SPoG |
| | - 'Fred Mullard' | EWes |
| | ***serpyllifolia*** | ECho |

## *Houttuynia* (*Saururaceae*)

| | | |
|---|---|---|
| | ***cordata*** | GBar GKev SDix SWat WFar |
| § | - 'Boo-Boo' (v) | CDWL EPfP EPla LBMP LSou NBro SMrm WFar |
| § | - 'Chameleon' (v) | Widely available |
| | - 'Fantasy' | EBee |
| | - 'Flame' (v) | CBcs CWCL MAsh MBri NPri SIng |
| | - 'Flore Pleno' (d) | CBen CRow EBee ECha EHon ELan EMFW EPfP EPla GBar LPBA MCCP MRav NBir NPer SGar SIde SPer SPlb SPoG SRms SWat WFar WPnP WTin |
| | - 'Joker's Gold' | EBee ECtt EPPr EPfP EPla EShb LBMP LSou NBro NVic SMrm |
| | - 'Pied Piper' | CDoC EBee EPla EWll LRHS SPad |
| | - 'Sunshine' | EBee |
| | - 'Tequila Sunrise' | CHEx |
| | - 'Terry Clarke' | see *H. cordata* 'Boo-Boo' |
| | - 'Tricolor' | see *H. cordata* 'Chameleon' |
| | - Variegata Group (v) | EBla GBar LPBA NBro SIng |

## *Hovea* (*Papilionaceae*)

| | | |
|---|---|---|
| | ***celsii*** | see *H. elliptica* |
| § | ***elliptica*** | SPlb |

## *Hovenia* (*Rhamnaceae*)

| | | |
|---|---|---|
| | ***dulcis*** | CAgr CBcs CMCN EPfP LEdu MBlu NLar WBVN |
| | - B&SWJ 11024 **new** | WCru |

## *Howea* (*Arecaceae*)

| | | |
|---|---|---|
| § | ***belmoreana*** ♀H1 | LPal |
| § | ***forsteriana*** ♀H1 | CCCN LPal LRHS MBri NScw XBlo |

## *Hoya* (*Asclepiadaceae*)

| | | |
|---|---|---|
| § | ***australis*** | SOWG |
| | ***bella*** | see *H. lanceolata* subsp. *bella* |
| | ***carnosa*** ♀H1 | CBcs CRHN EBak EOHP SEND SRms SWal WWFP |
| * | - 'Hindu Rope' | NPer |
| * | - 'Krinkle' | NPer |
| | - 'Red Princess' | MBri SAdn |
| | - 'Tricolor' | NPer |
| | - 'Variegata' (v) | MBri |
| | ***cinnamomifolia*** | SOWG |
| * | ***compacta*** 'Tricolor' | NPer |
| | ***darwinii*** misapplied | see *H. australis* |
| | ***lacunosa*** | CCCN LRHS |
| § | ***lanceolata*** subsp. ***bella*** ♀H1 | CHal EShb SRms |
| | ***linearis*** | SOWG |
| | ***multiflora*** | SOWG |

## huckleberry, garden see *Solanum scabrum*

## *Huernia* (*Asclepiadaceae*)

| | | |
|---|---|---|
| | ***aspera*** **new** | CFwr |
| | ***campanulata*** **new** | CFwr |
| | ***confusa*** | see *H. insigniflora* |
| | ***hallii*** **new** | CFwr |
| § | ***insigniflora*** **new** | CFwr |
| | 'Kwa Sandile' **new** | CFwr |
| | ***loesneriana*** **new** | CFwr |
| | - 'Middleburgh' **new** | CFwr |
| | ***macrocarpa*** **new** | CFwr |
| | ***occulta*** **new** | CFwr |
| | ***pendula*** **new** | CFwr |
| | ***schneideriana*** **new** | CFwr |
| | ***thurettii*** **new** | CFwr |

## *Huerniopsis* (*Asclepiadaceae*)

| | | |
|---|---|---|
| | ***decipiens*** **new** | CFwr |

## *Humata* (*Davalliaceae*)

| | | |
|---|---|---|
| | ***tyermannii*** | CMen WFib WRic |

## *Humea* see *Calomeria*

| | | |
|---|---|---|
| | ***elegans*** | see *Calomeria amaranthoides* |

## *Humulus* (*Cannabaceae*)

| | | |
|---|---|---|
| | ***japonicus*** | MSal |
| | ***lupulus*** | CArn CBcs CRWN EPfP GBar GPoy ILis MNHC MSal NGHP SIde WDin WHer |
| | - 'Aureus' ♀H4 | Widely available |
| | - 'Aureus' (f) | CRHN ELon EOHP GBar GCal GGar GKev MCCP MREP SPla SPoG WCot WWFP |

| | |
|---|---|
| - 'Aureus' (m) | MCCP |
| * - ***compactus*** | CHFP GPoy |
| - 'Fuggle' | CAgr GPoy SDea |
| - 'Golden Tassels' (f) | CAgr CDul EBee ELon EMui EPfP LBuc LHop LRHS MAsh MBri MGos MREP NGHP SLim SPoG SSto WHlf |
| - (Goldings Group) 'Cobbs' | SDea |
| - - 'Mathons' | CAgr SDea |
| - 'Hallertauer' | SDea |
| - 'Hip-hop' | EMon |
| - var. ***neomexicanus*** | EWes |
| - 'Prima Donna' | CAgr CDul CSBt EBee EMui GBin LHop MCoo NLar SCoo SIde SPoG SWvt |
| - 'Taff's Variegated' (v) | EMon EWes MAvo NGHP WSHC |
| - 'Wye Challenger' | CAgr GPoy |
| - 'Wye Northdown' | CAgr SDea |

## *Hunnemannia* (*Papaveraceae*)

| | |
|---|---|
| ***fumariifolia*** | CSpe |

## *Huodendron* (*Styracaceae*)

| | |
|---|---|
| ***biaristatum*** | WPGP |
| ***tibeticum*** | WPGP |

## *Hutchinsia* see *Pritzelago*

## *Hyacinthella* (*Hyacinthaceae*)

| | |
|---|---|
| ***acutiloba*** | ERos |
| ***dalmatica*** | ERos |
| - 'Grandiflora' | ECho WWst |
| ***glabrescens*** | WCot |
| ***heldreichii*** | EBrs ECho ERos |
| ***lazuliria*** | ERos |
| ***leucophaea*** | EBrs ECho ERos WWst |
| ***millingenii*** | EBrs ECho ERos |
| ***pallens*** | CBgR CTca EBrs ECho |

## *Hyacinthoides* (*Hyacinthaceae*)

| | |
|---|---|
| § ***hispanica*** | EBrs ECho IBlr NBir |
| - subsp. ***algeriensis*** | WCot |
| - 'Dainty Maid' | EBrs ECho WCot |
| - 'Excelsior' | EBrs ECho |
| - 'Miss World' | EBrs ECho WCot |
| - 'Queen of the Pinks' | EBrs ECho WCot |
| - 'Rosea' | ECho |
| - 'White City' | EBrs ECho WCot |
| § ***italica*** ♀H4 | CPom ECho SIng SPhx WCot WShi |
| § ***non-scripta*** | CArn CAvo CBct CBro CFFs CTca CTri EBWF EBrs ECho EPot IBlr IHer LAma MHer MMuc NBir NPri SECG SMrm SPad SPer SRms SVic WHer WHil WPtf WShi |
| - 'Alba' | EBrs ECho MMuc NBir |
| - 'Bracteata' | CNat |
| - 'Rosea' | EBrs ECho MMuc WHil |
| - 'Wavertree' | EBrs ECho |
| § ***vicentina*** | ERos |
| - 'Alba' | ERos |

## *Hyacinthus* ✿ (*Hyacinthaceae*)

| | |
|---|---|
| ***amethystinus*** | see *Brimeura amethystina* |
| ***azureus*** | see *Muscari azureum* |
| ***comosus*** 'Plumosus' | see *Muscari comosum* 'Plumosum' |
| ***fastigiatus*** | see *Brimeura fastigiata* |
| multi-flowered blue | CAvo CTca EBrs |
| multi-flowered pink | CTca EBrs |
| multi-flowered white | CAvo CTca EBrs |
| ***orientalis*** | CBgR EBrs SMeo |
| - 'Aiolos' | LRHS SPer |
| - 'Amethyst' | LAma |
| - 'Amsterdam' | LAma |
| - 'Anna Liza' | LRHS MBri |
| - 'Anna Marie' ♀H4 | CBro EBrs LAma LRHS MBri |
| - 'Atlantic' | LRHS |
| - 'Ben Nevis' (d) | LAma |
| - 'Blue Festival' | LRHS SPer |
| - 'Blue Giant' | LAma |
| - 'Blue Jacket' ♀H4 | CBro EBrs LAma LRHS MBri |
| - 'Blue Star' | LAma |
| - 'Carnegie' | CAvo CBro EBrs EPfP LAma LRHS SMeo |
| - 'China Pink' | SPer |
| - 'City of Haarlem' ♀H4 | CAvo CBro EBrs EPfP LAma LRHS MBri SMeo |
| - 'Crystal Palace' (d) | LAma |
| - 'Delft Blue' ♀H4 | CAvo CBro EBrs EPfP LAma LRHS MBri SPer |
| - 'Fondant' | LAma LRHS |
| - 'General Köhler' (d) | LAma |
| - 'Gipsy Princess' | LAma |
| - 'Gipsy Queen' ♀H4 | EBrs LAma LRHS MBri SPer |
| - 'Hollyhock' (d) | LAma WCot |
| - 'Jan Bos' | EBrs EPfP LAma LRHS MBri SPer |
| - 'Lady Derby' | LAma LRHS |
| - 'L'Innocence' ♀H4 | CBro EPfP LAma |
| - 'Odysseus' | LAma |
| - 'Ostara' ♀H4 | EPfP LAma MBri |
| - 'Peter Stuyvesant' | EBrs LAma |
| - 'Pink Festival' | LRHS SPer |
| - 'Pink Pearl' ♀H4 | EBrs EPfP LAma LRHS MBri |
| - 'Pink Royal' (d) | LAma |
| - 'Purple Sensation'PBR | EBrs |
| - 'Red Magic' | LAma |
| - 'Rosette' (d) | LAma |
| - 'Sky Jacket' | LRHS |
| - 'Splendid Cornelia' | EBrs LRHS SPer |
| - 'White Festival' | LRHS SPer |
| - 'White Pearl' | CAvo LAma MBri |
| - 'Woodstock' | CAvo EBrs LAma LRHS SMeo SPer WCot |

## *Hydrangea* ✿ (*Hydrangeaceae*)

| | |
|---|---|
| BWJ 8120 from Sichuan, China **new** | WCru |
| ***angustipetala*** | see *H. scandens* subsp. *chinensis* f. *angustipetala* Hayata, 1911 |
| - f. ***formosana*** | see *H. scandens* subsp. *chinensis* f. *formosana* Koidzumi |
| ***anomala*** subsp. ***anomala*** B&SWJ 2411 | WCru |
| - - BWJ 8052 from China | WCru |
| - - 'Winter Glow' | WCru |
| - subsp. ***glabra*** B&SWJ 3117 | WCru |
| - - B&SWJ 6804 **new** | WCru |
| - - 'Crûg Coral' **new** | WCru |
| § - subsp. ***petiolaris*** ♀H4 | Widely available |
| - - B&SWJ 6081from Yakushima | WCru |
| - - B&SWJ 6337 | WCru |
| § - - var. ***cordifolia*** | EBee MBNS NLar |
| § - - - 'Brookside Littleleaf' | NLar |
| - - dwarf | see *H. anomala* subsp. *petiolaris* var. *cordifolia* |
| - - 'Mirranda' **new** | NBro |
| * - - var. ***tiliifolia*** | EBee SHyH WFar WSHC |
| - - - B&SWJ 8497 | WCru |
| - - 'Yakushima' | WCru WPGP |
| * - subsp. ***quelpartensis*** B&SWJ 8799 | WCru |
| - 'Winter Surprise' **new** | MBri |
| § ***arborescens*** | CArn CPLG MRav WFar WPGP |
| - 'Annabelle' ♀H4 | Widely available |
| - 'Astrid Lindgren' | MBri |
| § - subsp. ***discolor*** | WCru WPat |

| | |
|---|---|
| - - 'Sterilis' | GGGa SHyH SPla WPGP |
| - 'Grandiflora' ♀H4 | CBcs CMac ELan EPfP EQua LSRN MRav NBro SPer WDin WHCG WPGP WSHC |
| - 'Hills of Snow' | NLar |
| - subsp. ***radiata*** | CAbP LRHS MAsh SPoG SSpi WFar WPGP |
| - White Dome = 'Dardom'PBR | MBri NBro WCot |
| ***aspera*** | CHEx CTri MGos SHyH SLon SSpi SSta WCru WKif WPGP |
| - BWJ 8188 new | WCru |
| - from Gongshan, China | WPGP |
| - 'Anthony Bullivant' | IArd LRHS MBri NLar SKHP SSpi WPat |
| - Farrell form new | SHyH |
| - Kawakamii Group | CGHE CHEx CMil CSpe EPla NLar SSpi WCru WPGP |
| - - B&SWJ 1420 | WCru |
| - - B&SWJ 3456 new | WCru |
| - - B&SWJ 3462 | WCru |
| - - B&SWJ 6702 new | WCru |
| - - B&SWJ 6714 new | WCru |
| - - B&SWJ 6827 | WCru |
| - - B&SWJ 7025 | WCru |
| - - B&SWJ 7101 | WCru |
| - - 'August Abundance' | WCru |
| - - 'September Splendour' | WCru |
| - 'Macrophylla' ♀H3 | CWib EPfP EWTr GCal MRav NBlu NPal SHyH SMad SPer SSpi WCru WFar WPGP |
| - 'Mauvette' | CMil MAsh MBlu NLar NPal SHyH SPer WCru WPGP |
| - 'Peter Chappell' | CMil SSpi WPGP |
| § - subsp. ***robusta*** | SHyH SLPl WBod WCru WPGP |
| - 'Rocklon' | CMil MBri NLar WPGP |
| - 'Rosthornii' | see *H. aspera* subsp. *robusta* |
| - 'Sam MacDonald' | GKir NLar SSpi WPGP |
| § - subsp. ***sargentiana*** ♀H3 | Widely available |
| - - large-leaved | WCot WCru |
| - 'Spinners' | MBri |
| - subsp. ***strigosa*** | CDul CMil EPfP SKHP WCru WPGP |
| - - B&SWJ 8201 | WCru |
| - - HWJ 653 new | WCru |
| - - HWJ 737 new | WCru |
| - - from Gong Shan, China new | CGHE |
| - 'Taiwan' | EQua |
| - 'Taiwan Pink' | EPfP MBri NLar |
| - 'Velvet and Lace' | LBuc LRHS NLar |
| § - Villosa Group ♀H3 | Widely available |
| ***cinerea*** | see *H. arborescens* subsp. *discolor* |
| 'Cohhii' | ECre |
| 'Compact Red' | ERas |
| 'First Red' new | NBrd |
| ***glandulosa*** B&SWJ 4031 | WCru |
| § ***heteromalla*** | CGHE CMHG CTrG EPfP EWTr GGal GKir SLPl SSpi WPGP |
| - B&SWJ 2142 from India | WCru |
| - B&SWJ 2602 from Sikkim | WCru |
| - BWJ 7657 from China | WCru |
| - HWJCM 180 | WCru |
| - HWJK 2127 from Nepal | WCru |
| - SF 338 | ISea |
| - Bretschneideri Group | EPfP GQui MBlu NLar SHyH WBod WCru WFar |
| - 'Fan Si Pan' | WCru |
| - 'Snowcap' | EPfP GQui IArd NLar SHyH SLPl SSpi WPGP |
| * ***heterophylla*** | EWTr MGos |
| ***hirta*** B&SWJ 5000 | WCru |

| | |
|---|---|
| ***indochinensis*** B&SWJ 8307 | WCru |
| ***integerrima*** | see *H. serratifolia* |
| ***integrifolia*** | GGGa NLar WPGP |
| - B&SWJ 022 | WCru |
| - B&SWJ 6967 | WCru |
| ***involucrata*** | EPfP LLHF LRHS MMHG WDin |
| - dwarf | WCru |
| - 'Hortensis' (d) ♀H3-4 | CMac CMil EPfP MGan MRav SDix SMad SSpi WAbe WBod WCru WKif WPGP WSHC |
| - 'Plena' (d) | CLAP CMil GAbr LRHS MSte SKHP SPoG SSta WCot WCru WFar WPGP |
| - 'Sterilis' | EPfP |
| - 'Viridescens' | LLHF SKHP WCru WPGP |
| ***involucrata*** x ***aspera*** Kawakamii Group | GGGa WPGP |
| ***lobbii*** | see *H. scandens* subsp. *chinensis* |
| ***longipes*** | GQui WCru WPGP |
| - BWJ 8188 | WCru |
| ***luteovenosa*** | WCru WPGP |
| - B&SWJ 5602 | WCru |
| - B&SWJ 5929 new | WCru |
| - B&SWJ 6317 new | WCru |
| * ***macrocephala*** | SKHP |
| ***macrophylla*** | CTrG |
| - 'AB Green Shadow'PBR | MAsh SPoG |
| - 'Adria' (H) | SHyH |
| - 'Aduarda' | see *H. macrophylla* 'Mousmée' |
| - 'All Summer Beauty' (H) | CMil |
| - Alpen Glow | see *H. macrophylla* 'Alpenglühen' |
| § - 'Alpenglühen' (H) | CBcs CPLG CSBt ELan SHBN SHyH SRms WBod WPGP |
| - 'Altona' (H) ♀H3-4 | CBcs EPfP IArd ISea LRHS MAsh MGos MRav NBir NBlu NPri SHyH SPer WPGP |
| - 'Amethyst' (H/d) | CGHE WPGP |
| - 'Ami Pasquier' (H) ♀H3-4 | CDoC CMac CSBt CTri EBee ELan EPfP GGal GKir LRHS LSRN MRav MSwo SBod SCoo SGar SHyH SLim SPla SSpi SWvt WPGP |
| * - 'Aureomarginata' (v) | EPfP SHyH WCot |
| - 'Aureovariegata' (L/v) | ELan |
| - 'Ave Maria' (H) | EQua ERas GGGa |
| § - 'Ayesha' (H) | CBcs CDoC CDul CEnd CMHG CMac CPLG CWGN EBee ECtt EPfP EWTr GGal MAsh MGos MRav SDix SHBN SHyH SPer SPla SPoG SWvt WBod WBor WDin WPGP WWlt |
| - 'Bachstelze' (Teller Series) (L) | MAsh SSpi |
| - 'Beauté Vendômoise' (L) | CGHE CMil NLar SSpi WPGP |
| - 'Benelux' (H) | CBcs EMil SHyH |
| - 'Bicolor' | see *H. macrophylla* 'Harlequin' |
| § - 'Blauer Prinz' (H) | CSam MAsh SHBN SHyH WBod |
| - 'Blauer Zwerg' (H) | MGos |
| § - 'Bläuling' (Teller Series) (L) | CDoC EPfP MGos SHyH |
| § - 'Blaumeise' (Teller Series) (L) | CDoC CMHG CMil CSBt EPfP EQua GGGa GKir MAsh MBri MDKP MGos MRav NBlu NSti SCoo SHyH SLim SLon SPoG SSpi SWvt WBod WDin WPGP |
| - 'Blue Bonnet' (H) | CChe EPfP LSRN SHyH SPer |
| - Blue Butterfly | see *H. macrophylla* 'Bläuling' |
| - Blue Prince | see *H. macrophylla* 'Blauer Prinz' |
| - Blue Sky | see *H. macrophylla* 'Blaumeise' |
| - Blue Tit | see *H. macrophylla* 'Blaumeise' |
| - 'Blue Wave' | see *H. macrophylla* 'Mariesii Perfecta' |
| - 'Bluebird' misapplied | see *H. serrata* 'Bluebird' |
| - Bluebird | see *H. macrophylla* 'Bläuling' |

| | | |
|---|---|---|
| | - Blushing Bride = 'The Bride' **new** | MAsh |
| | - 'Bodensee' (H) | MBri SPla WBVN |
| | - 'Bouquet Rose' (H) | CWib ECtt LBMP WBod |
| | - 'Bridal Bouquet' (H) | CDoC |
| | - 'Brügg' (H) | MAsh SHyH WPGP |
| | - 'Buchfink' (Teller Series) (L) | SSpi WPGP |
| | - Cardinal | see *H. macrophylla* 'Kardinal' (Teller Series) |
| § | - 'Cardinal Red' (H) | ECre |
| | - 'Colour Fantasy' (H) | SPoG |
| | - 'Cordata' | see *H. arborescens* |
| | - 'Dart's Song' **new** | NLar |
| | - 'Decatur Blue' (H) | MAsh |
| | - 'Deutschland' (H) | CTri |
| | - 'Domotoi' | see *H. macrophylla* 'Setsuka-yae' |
| | - 'Doctor Jean Varnier' (L) **new** | MAsh |
| | - Dragonfly | see *H. macrophylla* 'Libelle' |
| * | - 'Dwaag Pink' | MRav |
| | - 'Early Sensation' (H) | SPoG |
| | - 'Eco Royal Velvet' | SKHP |
| | - 'Eldorado' (H) | SHyH |
| | - Endless Summer = 'Bailmer' (H) | EBrs EMil EPfP LBuc LRHS MAsh MGos |
| § | - 'Enziandom' (H) | CBcs CPLG CSBt CWsd GGal MAsh SHyH WAbe WBod WPGP |
| | - Eternity = 'Youmetwo'$^{PBR}$ (H/d) | EMil SPoG |
| | - 'Etoile Violette' | EQua MAsh |
| | - 'Europa' (H) ♀H3-4 | CBcs CMac CPLG EMil LRHS MGos SEND SHyH WBod |
| § | - 'Fasan' (Teller Series) (L) | EQua WPGP |
| | - Firelight | see *H. macrophylla* 'Leuchtfeuer' |
| | - Fireworks | see *H. macrophylla* 'Hanabi' |
| | - Fireworks Blue | see *H. macrophylla* 'Jōgasaki' |
| | - Fireworks Pink | see *H. macrophylla* 'Jōgasaki' |
| | - Fireworks White | see *H. macrophylla* 'Hanabi' |
| | - 'Forever Pink' (H) | MAsh NLar |
| § | - 'Frau Fujiyo' (Lady Series) (H) | CPLG LRHS |
| § | - 'Frau Katsuko' (Lady Series) (H) | LRHS SPer |
| § | - 'Frau Mariko' (Lady Series) (H) | LRHS |
| § | - 'Frau Nobuko' (Lady Series) (H) | LRHS |
| § | - 'Frau Taiko' (Lady Series) (H) | LRHS SPer |
| | - 'Frillibet' (H) | CAbP CDoC EPfP WPGP |
| | - 'Gartenbaudirektor Kühnert' (H) | SHyH |
| § | - 'Générale Vicomtesse de Vibraye' (H) ♀H3-4 | CDoC CEnd CMHG CTri EBee EPfP GGal GKir LRHS MAsh MBar SDix SEND SHBN SHyH SLim SPer SSpi WBVN WBod WPGP |
| | - Gentian Dome | see *H. macrophylla* 'Enziandom' |
| | - 'Geoffrey Chadbund' | see *H. macrophylla* 'Möwe' |
| | - 'Gerda Steiniger' (H) | SHyH |
| | - 'Gertrud Glahn' (H) | SHyH WFar |
| | - 'Gimpel' (Teller Series) (L) | MAsh |
| | - 'Glowing Embers' (H) | IArd MBNS WPGP |
| | - Goldrush = 'Nehyosh' (v) | LRHS SPoG |
| | - 'Goliath' (H) | EPfP |
| § | - 'Grant's Choice' (L) | EQua NBro SHyH |
| | - 'Hamburg' (H) | CEnd CTri EBee ECtt EPfP LRHS MGos MRav NPri SDix SHyH SLim WBod WFar |
| § | - 'Hanabi' (L/d) | CBcs CDoC CLAP CMil ECre EPla EQua MBlu NLar |
| § | - 'Harlequin' (H) | MAsh WCot WPGP |
| | - 'Harry's Red' (H) | MAsh |
| | - 'Hatsu-shime' (L) | NLar |
| | - 'Heinrich Seidel' (H) | CBcs WMoo |
| | - 'Hobella'$^{PBR}$ (Hovaria Series) | WBod |
| | - 'Hobergine'$^{PBR}$ (Hovaria Series) (H) | SHyH |
| | - 'Homigo'$^{PBR}$ (Hovaria Series) (H) | SHyH |
| | - 'Izu-no-hana' (L/d) | CBcs CLAP CMil ELon LRHS MAsh MBlu NLar SHyH SPoG SSpi WBor WPGP |
| | - 'James Grant' | see *H. macrophylla* 'Grant's Choice' |
| | - 'Jofloma' | EQua NLar |
| § | - 'Jōgasaki' (L/d) | CBcs CLAP CPLG MAsh MBlu NLar SHyH WPGP |
| | - 'Joseph Banks' (H) | CBcs CTri |
| | - 'Kardinal' (H) | see *H. macrophylla* 'Cardinal Red' (H) |
| § | - 'Kardinal' (Teller Series) (L) | ERas MAsh |
| | - 'King George' (H) | CBcs CDoC CDul CSBt EBee LAst LRHS MBar MGos MRav NPri SHyH SLim SPer SPoG SWvt WFar WMoo |
| § | - 'Klaveren' | CMil GGGa MAsh NBro |
| | - 'Kluis Superba' (H) | CBcs CTri GGal MAsh MRav SHyH |
| | - 'La France' (H) | CTri EBee LRHS MBar MRav SHyH WFar |
| | - 'Lady Fujiyo' | see *H. macrophylla* 'Frau Fujiyo' |
| | - Lady Katsuko | see *H. macrophylla* 'Frau Katsuko' |
| | - 'Lady Mariko' | see *H. macrophylla* 'Frau Mariko' |
| | - 'Lady Nobuko' | see *H. macrophylla* 'Frau Nobuko' |
| | - 'Lady Taiko Blue' | see *H. macrophylla* 'Frau Taiko' |
| | - 'Lady Taiko Pink' | see *H. macrophylla* 'Frau Taiko' |
| * | - 'Lanarth' blue-flowered **new** | GGal |
| | - 'Lanarth White' (L) ♀H3-4 | CBcs CDoC CPLG CSBt CTri EBee ELan EPfP EWTr GGal LBMP MAsh MRav MSwo SBod SHBN SHyH SLPl SLim SPer SRms SSpi WBod WBor WKif WPGP |
| | - 'Lemon Wave' (L/v) | NLar |
| § | - 'Leuchtfeuer' (H) | EMil MGos SHyH WBod |
| § | - 'Libelle' (Teller Series) (L) | CBcs CDoC EBee EPfP ISea MGos MRav NBlu SBod SHyH SLim SPer SPoG SSpi WBVN WBod WKif |
| | - 'Lilacina' | see *H. macrophylla* 'Mariesii Lilacina' |
| | - 'Love You Kiss'$^{PBR}$ (Hovaria Series) (L) | CBcs EMil MAsh SCoo SHyH SPoG SRGP |
| § | - 'Maculata' (L/v) | ELan GQui SGar WBod WGwG |
| | - 'Madame A. Riverain' (H) | SHyH |
| | - 'Madame Emile Mouillère' (H) ♀H3-4 | Widely available |
| | - 'Maréchal Foch' (H) | CTri GGal NLar |
| | - 'Mariesii' (L) | CMHG CTri CTsd ELan GGal ISea LRHS MMuc MSwo NMun SDix SPer WGwG WKif |
| § | - 'Mariesii Grandiflora' (L) ♀H3-4 | CTsd EPfP GGal LRHS MBar NBro NPri SHBN SHyH SPer SRms WDin WFar WMoo WPGP |
| § | - 'Mariesii Lilacina' (L) ♀H3-4 | EPfP SEND SLon SPer WKif WMoo WPGP |
| § | - 'Mariesii Perfecta' (L) ♀H3-4 | Widely available |
| | - 'Mariesii Variegata' (L/v) | CWib |
| | - 'Masja' (H) | EBee IArd LRHS MAsh MGos MRav MSwo NBlu NBro SHBN SHyH |
| | - 'Mathilde Gütges' (H) | CDoC MAsh SHyH SSpi WPGP |
| | - 'Max Löbner' (H) | SHyH |
| | - 'Merveille Sanguine' (H) | CDoC CGHE CMHG CMil EMil GCal GGal IArd MBri MRav NLar WCot WLeb WPGP WPat |
| | - 'Messalina' (L) | MGos |

| | | |
|---|---|---|
| | - 'Mirai'PBR (H) | MAsh SCoo SHyH WCot |
| | - 'Miss Belgium' (H) | CMac CTri EQua |
| § | - 'Mousmée' (L) | IArd SSpi |
| | - 'Mousseline' (H) | MAsh |
| § | - 'Möwe' (L) ♀H3-4 | CBcs CDoC CEnd CMil CPLG EBee ECtt ELon GGal LHop MAsh NLar SBod SCoo SDix SGar SHBN SHyH SLim SPer SRms SSpi SSta WPGP |
| | - 'Mrs W.J. Hepburn' | CSBt SHyH SPer |
| § | - 'Nachtigall' (Teller Series) (L) | CMil EBee GGal MAsh |
| | - 'Niedersachsen' (H) | CDoC CTri MRav SHyH WPGP |
| | - Nightingale | see *H. macrophylla* 'Nachtigall' |
| | - 'Nigra' (H) ♀H3-4 | CBcs CChe CMil CPLG CWib EBee ELan EPfP EPla GGGa MAsh MBri MGos MSCN NBro SDix SHBN SHyH SPer SPoG WClo WFar WGwG WLeb WPGP |
| | - 'Nikko Blue' (H) | CBcs CTsd EPfP MBar MHav NBlu |
| | - var. ***normalis*** (L) | CPLG |
| | - 'Oregon Pride' (H) | GGGa MAsh WPGP |
| | - 'Otaksa' (H) | NLar |
| | - 'Papagei' (Teller Series) | SPer |
| | - 'Parzifal' (H) ♀H3-4 | CDul GGGa SHyH WPGP |
| | - 'Pfau' (Teller Series) (L) | ELon MAsh SSpi |
| | - Pheasant | see *H. macrophylla* 'Fasan' |
| | - 'Pia' (H) | CBgR CDoC CPLG CStu ELan LBuc MAsh MGos MRav NWCA SMad SPer SPla SRms WAbe WBor WCru WFar |
| | - Pigeon | see *H. macrophylla* 'Taube' |
| | - 'Pink Wave' (L) | NPri |
| | - 'Prinses Beatrix' (H) | SHyH |
| | - 'Quadricolor' (L/v) | CAbb CMac CMil CPLG EHoe GCal GGal LRHS MAsh MRav SDix SGar SHBN SHyH SLim SPer SPla SPlb SRms WCot WHCG WSHC |
| | - 'R.F. Felton' (H) | CBcs SHyH |
| | - 'Red Baron' | see *H. macrophylla* 'Schöne Bautznerin' |
| | - 'Red Red'PBR (H) | MAsh |
| | - Redbreast | see *H. macrophylla* 'Rotkehlchen' |
| | - 'Regula' (H) | SHyH |
| | - 'Renate Steiniger' (H) | MGos SHyH WBod WGwG |
| | - 'Romance' | NBrd SPoG |
| | - 'Rosita' (H) | EMil MAsh WFar |
| | - 'Rotdrossel' (L) **new** | MAsh |
| § | - 'Rotkehlchen' (Teller Series) (L) | CDoC CSBt EPfP GKir NBlu SCoo SPlb SPoG SWvt WDin |
| | - 'Rotschwanz' (Teller Series) (L) | CMil EQua ERas MAsh SSpi WPGP |
| | - 'Sabrina' (H) | CBcs MAsh MBri MGos SPoG |
| | - 'Saint Claire' (H) | CBcs SHyH |
| | - 'Sandra' (Dutch Ladies Series) (L) | ELon |
| | - 'Schneeball' (H) | MAsh MGos |
| § | - 'Schöne Bautznerin' | ERas MWea WClo |
| | - 'Schwan' (H) **new** | MAsh |
| | - 'Sea Foam' (L) | EBee NBlu |
| | - 'Selina' | CBcs LSRN MAsh MDKP MGos SPoG |
| | - 'Selma'PBR (Dutch Ladies Series) (L) | CBcs MAsh MBri |
| § | - 'Setsuka-yae' (L/d) | CMil |
| | - 'Sheila' (Dutch Ladies Series) (L) | CBcs LSRN MBri |
| | - 'Sibilla' (H) | CBcs EMil WPGP |
| | - Sister Therese | see *H. macrophylla* 'Soeur Thérèse' |
| § | - 'Soeur Thérèse' (H) | CSBt EBee EMil MAsh MGos SHyH SWvt WGwG WPGP |
| | - 'Soraya'PBR (Dutch Ladies Series) (L) | CBcs |
| | - 'Sumida-no-hanabi' (L/d) | MAsh WPGP |
| * | - 'Sunset' (L) | CBcs |
| § | - 'Taube' (Teller Series) (L) | CBcs CDoC CMHG CPLG EPfP GGal GQui MAsh NBlu SCoo SWvt |
| | - 'Teller Pink' | see *H. macrophylla* 'Taube' |
| | - 'Teller Red' | see *H. macrophylla* 'Rotkehlchen' (Teller Series) |
| N | - Teller variegated | see *H. macrophylla* 'Tricolor' |
| N | - Teller Weiss | see *H. macrophylla* 'Libelle' |
| | - var. ***thunbergii*** | see *H. serrata* var. *thunbergii* |
| | - 'Tokyo Delight' (L) ♀H3-4 | CChe CDoC CGHE CLAP CMil CPLG CTsd EBee MAsh SHyH WPGP |
| | - 'Tovelit' (H) | GGGa |
| § | - 'Tricolor' (L/v) | CBcs CDoC CDul CTri EBee EMil EQua ERas LAst LRHS MGos NPri SHyH SLon SPer SPoG WFar WKif WMoo |
| | - 'Trophee'PBR | SPoG |
| | - 'Variegata' | see *H. macrophylla* 'Maculata' |
| | - 'Veitchii' (L) ♀H3-4 | CBcs CMHG CMil CPLG CSBt EPfP GGal MAsh MRav MSwo SDix SGar SHyH SPer SPoG SSpi WPGP |
| | - 'Vicomte de Vibraye' | see *H. macrophylla* 'Générale Vicomtesse de Vibraye' |
| | - 'Violetta' (H) | MAsh |
| | - 'Westfalen' (H) ♀H3-4 | CMac IArd SDix SPla |
| I | - 'White Lace' (L) | ELan SHyH |
| | - 'White Mop' (H) | CWib |
| | - 'White Wave' | see *H. macrophylla* 'Mariesii Grandiflora' |
| | - 'Zaunkoenig' (L) | MAsh |
| | - 'Zhuni Hito' | NLar |
| | - 'Zorro'PBR **new** | LRHS SCoo SPoG |
| | ***microphylla*** 'Dove' **new** | WBod |
| | ***paniculata*** | CMCN |
| | - B&SWJ 3556 from Taiwan | WCru |
| | - B&SWJ 5413 from Japan | WCru |
| | - 'Ammarin' | LLHF NLar WPat |
| | - 'Big Ben' | EPfP MBri NLar |
| | - 'Brussels Lace' | CAbP EBee EPfP GKir LRHS LSRN MAsh MBri MRav NLar SHyH SLon SPla SPoG SSpi |
| | - 'Burgundy Lace' | CBcs EQua MBlu MBri SHyH |
| | - Dart's Little Dot = 'Darlido'PBR | LLHF NLar WPat |
| | - 'Dharuma' | LLHF LRHS |
| | - 'Everest' | CAbP CMil EPfP LRHS MAsh SHyH |
| | - 'Floribunda' | CGHE ELan EPfP EWTr LRHS MAsh WBod WPGP WPat |
| | - 'Grandiflora' ♀H4 | Widely available |
| | - 'Great Escape' **new** | NLar |
| | - 'Greenspire' | LRHS MAsh MBlu MBri |
| | - 'Harry's Souvenir' | MBri NLar |
| | - 'Kyushu' ♀H4 | Widely available |
| | - 'Limelight'PBR | CBcs CMil CSBt CWGN EBee EMil EPfP EQua ERas GQui LAst LBuc LEdu MAsh MBlu MBri MGos NCGa NHol NLar SHyH SKHP SRkn WBrE WFar WOVN WPat |
| | - 'Mount Aso' | CMil NBro NLar WPGP |
| | - 'October Bride' | EBee MBri NLar WPGP |
| | - 'Papillon' **new** | WPat |
| | - 'Pee Wee' **new** | LLHF |
| | - 'Phantom' | CMil EPfP GGGa LRHS MAsh MBlu MBri MDKP NCGa NLar SHyH WCot WPGP WPat |
| | - Pink Diamond = 'Interhydia' ♀H4 | Widely available |
| | - 'Pink Jewel' | CWib LLHF WPat |
| | - Pinky-Winky = 'Dvppinky'PBR | EMil LLHF MGos NLar SPoG |
| | - 'Praecox' | GQui MAsh MRav SLon SPer WPat |

| | | |
|---|---|---|
| | - 'Silver Dollar' | EPfP MAsh MBri |
| | - 'Tardiva' | CBcs CChe CDoC CMac EBee EPfP GQui LPan LRHS MAsh MGos MRav NBro NCGa NPri SDix SHyH SPer SRms WBod WDin WFar WHCG WPGP WPat |
| | - 'Tender Rose' **new** | NLar |
| | - 'Unique' ♀H4 | CBcs CBgR CDoC CGHE CSpe EBee EPfP GQui LEdu LHop LRHS MAsh MBri MRav NBro NCGa SHyH SPer SPla SSpi WBod WBor WDin WFar WPGP WPat |
| | - Vanillé Fraise = 'Hp100' **new** | MAsh MBri |
| | - 'Waterfall' | CLAP |
| | - 'White Lace' | MBlu |
| | - 'White Lady' | CBcs MAsh |
| | - 'White Moth' | CBcs CWGN EBee EQua LLHF MAsh NBro NLar SHyH SKHP WBod WPat |
| | ***petiolaris*** | see *H. anomala* subsp. *petiolaris* |
| § | 'Preziosa' ♀H3-4 | Widely available |
| | ***quelpartensis*** | CRHN GQui |
| | - B&SWJ 4400 | WCru |
| | ***quercifolia*** ♀H3-4 | Widely available |
| | - 'Alice' | CPMA EPfP EPla MAsh SRGP SSpi WPGP |
| | - 'Alison' | EPfP |
| I | - 'Amethyst' Dirr | MBri |
| | - 'Back Porch' | NLar |
| | - 'Burgundy' | CBcs CPMA EPfP MBri NLar WPGP |
| | - 'Flore Pleno' | see *H. quercifolia* Snowflake = 'Brido' |
| | - 'Harmony' | CMil CPMA EPfP IArd MBri NLar SSta WHCG WPGP WPat |
| | - 'Lady Anne' | EBee EPla WPGP |
| | - 'Little Honey' | MAsh |
| * | - 'Pee Wee' | CDoC CMil CPMA EBee EMil EPfP LRHS MAsh NLar SHyH SLon SPoG SReu SSta WPGP WPat |
| | - 'Sike's Dwarf' | CEnd CPMA EBee GCal MGos NLar WPat |
| | - Snow Queen = 'Flemygea' | CBcs CDoC CDul CKno CMac CPMA EBee ELan EPfP EWTr ISea LCro MAsh MGos MRav MSte NLar SHyH SLim SPer SPla SWvt WFar WHCG WPGP WPat |
| | - 'Snowdrift' | CPMA |
| § | - Snowflake = 'Brido' (d) | CAbP CBcs CDoC CEnd CHar CMil CPMA CSPN CWGN EBee ELan EMil EPfP GKir LRHS MAsh MGos MRav SLon SPer SPla SPoG SSpi SSta WBod WHCG WPGP WPat |
| | - 'Tennessee Clone' | EBee MBri NLar |
| | ***sargentiana*** | see *H. aspera* subsp. *sargentiana* |
| | ***scandens*** B&SWJ 5448 **new** | WCru |
| | - B&SWJ 5481 **new** | WCru |
| | - B&SWJ 5496 **new** | WCru |
| | - B&SWJ 5523 | WCru |
| | - B&SWJ 5602 **new** | WCru |
| | - B&SWJ 5893 | WCru |
| | - B&SWJ 5929 **new** | WCru |
| | - B&SWJ 6159 **new** | WCru |
| | - B&SWJ 6317 **new** | WCru |
| § | - subsp. ***chinensis*** | CPLG WFar |
| | - - B&SWJ 1488 | WCru |
| | - - B&SWJ 3214 | WCru |
| | - - B&SWJ 3410 from Taiwan **new** | WCru |
| | - - B&SWJ 3420 | WCru |
| § | - - f. ***angustipetala*** Hayata, 1911 | WPGP |
| | - - - B&SWJ 3454 | WCru |
| | - - - B&SWJ 3553 **new** | WCru |
| | - - - B&SWJ 3667 **new** | WCru |
| | - - - B&SWJ 3733 **new** | WCru |
| | - - - B&SWJ 3814 | WCru |
| | - - - B&SWJ 6038 from Yakushima | WCru |
| | - - - B&SWJ 6041 from Yakushima **new** | WCru |
| | - - - B&SWJ 6056 from Yakushima **new** | WCru |
| | - - - B&SWJ 6787 **new** | WCru |
| | - - - B&SWJ 6802 **new** | WCru |
| | - - - B&SWJ 7121 | WCru |
| | - - - B&SWJ 7128 **new** | WCru |
| § | - - f. ***formosana*** Koidzumi | NLar |
| | - - - B&SWJ 1488 **new** | WCru |
| | - - - B&SWJ 3271 **new** | WCru |
| | - - - B&SWJ 3423 from Taiwan | WCru |
| | - - - B&SWJ 7058 **new** | WCru |
| | - - - B&SWJ 7097 | WCru |
| | - - - BWJ 8000 from Sichuan | WCru |
| | - - f. ***macrosepala*** B&SWJ 3423 **new** | WCru |
| | - - - B&SWJ 3476 | WCru |
| | - - f. ***obovatifolia*** B&SWJ 3487b | WCru |
| | - - - B&SWJ 3683 **new** | WCru |
| | - - - B&SWJ 7121 **new** | WCru |
| | - subsp. ***liukiuensis*** | WCru |
| | - - B&SWJ 6022 | WCru |
| | - 'Splash' (v) | CMil |
| | ***seemannii*** | Widely available |
| | ***serrata*** | CPLG CWib WDin WKif |
| | - B&SWJ 4817 | WCru |
| | - B&SWJ 6241 | WCru |
| | - 'Acuminata' | see *H. serrata* 'Bluebird' |
| | - 'Aigaku' (L) | CLAP CPLG WPGP |
| | - Amacha Group | CGHE |
| | - - 'Amagi-amacha' (:) | CMil NBro |
| | - - 'Ō-amacha' | CMil |
| | - 'Amagyana' (L) | CGHE CPLG WPGP |
| | - 'Belle Deckle' | see *H. serrata* 'Blue Deckle' |
| | - 'Beni-gaku' (L) | CLAP CMil CPLG CTsd EBee GGGa MAsh NBro NLar SHyH WPGP |
| | - 'Beni-yama' (L) | CGHE CMil WPGP |
| | - 'Blue Billow' (L) | GGGa NBro NLar |
| § | - 'Blue Deckle' (L) | CMHG CMac CWsd EQua GGal MAsh MRav NBro SHyH SPla WPGP |
| § | - 'Bluebird' (L) ♀H3-4 | CDul EBee ELan EPfP GKir GQui LCro LRHS MAsh MBar MBlu MGos MMuc MRav MSwo SBod SDix SHBN SHyH SLim SPer SWvt WBVN WBrE WFar WMoo |
| | - 'Diadem' (L) ♀H3-4 | CMil CPLG EBee EPfP EQua NBro SDix WPGP |
| | - dwarf white-flowered (L) | WCru |
| | - Fuji Snowstorm | see *H. serrata* 'Fuji-no-shirayuki' |
| | - 'Fuji Waterfall' (L/d) | see *H. serrata* 'Fuji-no-taki' |
| § | - 'Fuji-no-shirayuki' (L/d) | CMil |
| § | - 'Fuji-no-taki' (L/d) | CAbP CMil LLHF LSou MSte NCGa SMad WBor WCot WFar |
| | - 'Golden Showers' (L) | CMil GGGa MAsh NBro |
| | - 'Golden Sunlight'PBR (L) | CBcs CDoC SMad SPoG SWvt |
| | - 'Graciosa' (L) | CMil MAsh WPGP |
| | - 'Grayswood' (L) ♀H3-4 | CBcs CEnd CMac CSBt EPfP EQua ERas GGal GKir GQui LRHS MAsh MRav NBro SDix SGar SHyH SPer SSpi WBor WKif WPGP |

| | |
|---|---|
| - 'Hallasan' misapplied | see *H. serrata* 'Maiko', 'Spreading Beauty' |
| - 'Hallasan' ambig. | CMil |
| - 'Hime-benigaku' (L) | CLAP CMil |
| - 'Intermedia' (L) | CPLG NBro |
| - 'Kiyosumi' (L) | CDoC CEnd CGHE CLAP CMil CPLG ECre ELon GGGa GGal GQui MAsh WCru WPGP |
| - 'Klaveren' | see *H. macrophylla* 'Klaveren' |
| - 'Koreana' (L) | EQua GGGa MAsh |
| - 'Kurenai' (L) | NBro NLar SKHP SSpi |
| - 'Kurenai-nishiki' (L/v) | CMil |
| - 'Kurohime' (L) **new** | NBro |
| - 'Macrosepala' (L) | MAsh SHyH |
| § - 'Maiko' (L) | IArd |
| - 'Midora' | CPLG |
| - 'Miranda' (L) 🏆$^{H3-4}$ | CBow CBrd CPLG CSam CWsd MAsh NBro SHyH SMad SSpi WFar |
| - 'Miyama-yae-murasaki' (L/d) | CGHE CLAP CMil EQua LRHS MAsh SHyH SKHP WPGP |
| - 'Pretty Maiden' | see *H. serrata* 'Shichidanka' |
| - 'Preziosa' | see *H.* 'Preziosa' |
| - 'Professeur Iida' (L) | WPGP |
| § - 'Prolifera' (L/d) | CGHE CMil WPGP |
| - 'Pulchella' | see *H. serrata* 'Prolifera' |
| - 'Ramis Pictis' (L) | ERas NBro NLar WPGP |
| - 'Rosalba' (L) 🏆$^{H3-4}$ | CLAP CPLG EPfP GGal NBro SPer SPla WFar WSHC |
| § - 'Shichidanka' (L/d) **new** | NBro |
| - 'Shichidanka-nishiki' (L/d/v) | CDoC CGHE CPLG ECre LRHS SHyH WBor |
| - 'Shinonome' (L/d) | CLAP CMil GQui WPGP |
| - 'Shirofuji' (L/d) | CLAP CMil LRHS WPGP |
| - 'Shiro-gaku' (L) | MAsh NBro |
| - 'Shirotae' (L/d) | CMil GGGa WPGP |
| § - 'Spreading Beauty' (L) | CMil WPGP |
| § - var. ***thunbergii*** (L) | CMHG GQui WFar WPGP |
| * - - 'Plena' (L/d) | WCru |
| - 'Tiara' (L) 🏆$^{H3-4}$ | CAbb CMil CWsd GGGa GGal LCro LSRN MAsh NBro NLar SDix SHyH SSpi WPGP |
| - 'Uzu-azisai' | WPGP |
| - 'Yae-no-amacha' (L/d) | SHyH WPGP |
| § ***serratifolia*** | CHEx EPfP EPla SPoG SSpi SSta WCru WFar WPGP |
| - HCM 98056 **new** | WCru |
| ***sikokiana*** | CLAP |
| - B&SWJ 5035 | WCru |
| - B&SWJ 5855 | WCru |
| 'Silver Slipper' | see *H. macrophylla* 'Ayesha' |
| ***tiliifolia*** | see *H. anomala* subsp. *petiolaris* |
| ***villosa*** | see *H. aspera* Villosa Group |
| 'Water Wagtail' | ERas |
| ***xanthoneura*** | see *H. heteromalla* |
| 'You and Me' | SCoo |

## *Hydrastis* (*Ranunculaceae*)

| | |
|---|---|
| ***canadensis*** | CArn COld GBuc GPoy WCru |

## *Hydrocharis* (*Hydrocharitaceae*)

| | |
|---|---|
| ***morsus-ranae*** | CDWL CRow EHon EMFW LPBA NPer NSco SWat WPnP |

## *Hydrocleys* (*Limnocharitaceae*)

| | |
|---|---|
| ***nymphoides*** | XBlo |

## *Hydrocotyle* (*Apiaceae*)

| | |
|---|---|
| ***asiatica*** | see *Centella asiatica* |
| ***sibthorpioides*** | CBow |
| - 'Crystal Confetti' | EBee EDAr EPPr EShb LLWG SIng WCHb WPer |
| ***vulgaris*** | CWat EBWF EMFW |

## *Hydrophyllum* (*Hydrophyllaceae*)

| | |
|---|---|
| ***canadense*** | CLAP EBee |
| ***macrophyllum*** | EBee |
| ***virginianum*** | CLAP EBee MSal |

## *Hylomecon* (*Papaveraceae*)

| | |
|---|---|
| * ***hylomecoides*** | EBee WCru |
| § ***japonica*** | CFwr CLAP CMea EBee ECho ELan GBBs GBuc GCra GEdr GKev GKir MSte NBir NDov NMen NRya SHGN WAbe WCru WFar WPnP WTin |

## *Hylotelephium* see *Sedum*

## *Hymenanthera* see *Melicytus*

## *Hymenocallis* (*Amaryllidaceae*)

| | |
|---|---|
| 'Advance' | EBrs ECho LAma LRHS |
| § ***caroliniana*** | ECho |
| x ***festalis*** 🏆$^{H1}$ | CCCN ECho EPfP IHer LAma LRHS MBri SPav WCot WFar |
| - 'Zwanenburg' | CSec EBrs ECho WHil |
| ***harrisiana*** | CCCN EBrs ECho LRHS WCot |
| ***latifolia*** | WCot |
| § ***longipetala*** | EBrs ECho LRHS WCot |
| ***occidentalis*** | see *H. caroliniana* |
| 'Sulphur Queen' 🏆$^{H1}$ | EBrs ECho LRHS SPav WCot WHil |

## *Hymenolepis* (*Asteraceae*)

| | |
|---|---|
| ***parviflora*** | see *Athanasia parviflora* |

## *Hymenosporum* (*Pittosporaceae*)

| | |
|---|---|
| ***flavum*** | SOWG |

## *Hymenoxys* (*Asteraceae*)

| | |
|---|---|
| ***cooperi*** var. ***canescens*** **new** | CPBP |
| ***grandiflora*** | see *Tetraneuris grandiflora* |
| § ***hoopesii*** | CMHG EBee EBla EHig EHrv ELan EPfP EShb GAbr GKir GMaP LBMP LHop LRHS NBir NChi NPri NSti SECG SPer SPhx SRms WCot WFar WMnd WMoo WPer |

## *Hyophorbe* (*Arecaceae*)

| | |
|---|---|
| ***lagenicaulis*** | LPal |
| ***verschaffeltii*** | LPal |

## *Hyoscyamus* (*Solanaceae*)

| | |
|---|---|
| ***albus*** | CSpe MSal |
| ***aureus*** RCB RL -16 **new** | WCot |
| ***niger*** | CArn CSec GPoy MCot MSal |

## *Hypericum* ✿ (*Clusiaceae*)

| | |
|---|---|
| CC 4131 | CPLG |
| CC 4544 | CPLG |
| ***acmosepalum*** | WPGP WPat |
| ***aegypticum*** | CLyd ECho ECtt EPot MHer NMen NWCA SIng SRot WAbe WFar WOld WPat WPer |
| ***androsaemum*** | CArn CRWN CSec EAro ECha EHig ELan ELau MHer MRav MSal MSwo NPer NSco WDin WMoo WOut |
| § - 'Albury Purple' | CElw CSec EHig EShb GBuc LDai MRav WHrl WMoo |
| - 'Autumn Blaze' | CBcs MGos |
| § - 'Dart's Golden Penny' | SPer |
| - 'Excellent Flair' | MGos NLar |
| - 'Orange Flair' | MGos |
| § - f. ***variegatum*** 'Mrs Gladis Brabazon' (v) | EAro NBir NLar NScw NSti SBod WHrl |
| ***ascyron*** | CSec |

| | Name | Suppliers |
|---|---|---|
| | ***athoum*** | CLyd NBir WAbe WThu |
| | ***atomarium*** | EBee WPGP |
| | ***attenuatum*** | CSec |
| | ***balearicum*** | EHrv MTho WAbe WPGP |
| | ***barbatum*** | WFar |
| § | ***beanii*** | GAuc WBod |
| | ***bellum*** | EBee SLon |
| | - subsp. ***latisepalum*** | SLon |
| | ***calycinum*** | CBcs CDul CTri CWan EBee ECho ECrN ELan EPfP LBuc MBar MGos MRav MWat NBlu NWea SHBN SWvt WDin WGwG WMoo |
| | - 'Rising Sun' **new** | LRHS |
| | ***cerastioides*** | CMea CTri CWib SIng SPoG SRms WAbe WFar WPer |
| | ***coris*** | ECho EWes LRHS MTho MWat SRms |
| | ***crux-andreae*** | EBee |
| | ***cuneatum*** | see *H. pallens* |
| | x ***cyathiflorum*** 'Gold Cup' | CMac MAsh NPri |
| | x ***dummeri*** 'Peter Dummer' | NLar |
| | ***elatum*** | see *H.* x *inodorum* |
| | ***elodes*** | EMFW LLWG MSKA |
| | ***empetrifolium*** | EBee ECho |
| | - 'Prostatum' | see *H. empetrifolium* subsp. *tortuosum* |
| § | - subsp. ***tortuosum*** | ECho EWes |
| § | ***forrestii*** ♀H4 | EBee EPfP LRHS MMuc WFar WPGP |
| | - B&L 12469 | WPGP |
| | - Hird 54 | WPGP |
| N | ***fragile*** hort. | see *H. olympicum* f. *minus* |
| | ***frondosum*** 'Buttercup' | NLar |
| | - 'Sunburst' | EBee EPfP WFar |
| N | 'Gemo' | ECrN MGos |
| | 'Gold Penny' | see *H. androsaemum* 'Dart's Golden Penny' |
| | 'Golden Beacon' | CBow CElw EBee EHig LAst LSou MAsh NLar NPri SMad SPer SPoG WCot |
| | ***grandiflorum*** | see *H. kouytchense* |
| | ***henryi*** L 753 | SRms |
| | 'Hidcote' ♀H4 | Widely available |
| | 'Hidcote Variegated' (v) | CBow MAsh MCCP NPri SLim SPer SRms WFar |
| | ***hircinum*** subsp. ***cambessedesii*** | LRHS |
| | ***hirsutum*** | EBWF NMir |
| § | x ***inodorum*** | NBir |
| | - 'Albury Purple' | see *H. androsaemum* 'Albury Purple' |
| | - 'Autumn Surprise' PBR **new** | MMuc NHol |
| | - 'Dream' | NLar |
| | - 'Elstead' | EBee ECrN ECtt ELan EPfP MBar MGos MMHG MRav SHBN SRms WDin WHCG |
| | - 'Hysan' | GGar |
| | - 'Rheingold' **new** | EMil |
| | - 'Ysella' | MRav MSwo MTPN |
| | ***japonicum*** | ECho EWes |
| | ***kalmianum*** | EWes |
| | ***kamtschaticum*** | ECho |
| § | ***kiusianum*** var. ***yakusimense*** | MBar MTho NPro |
| § | ***kouytchense*** ♀H4 | CBcs CDul CMCN EBee EPfP EQua EWes GQui LRHS MAsh MMuc MRav NLar SPoG WBVN WCFE WHrl WPat |
| | ***lancasteri*** | EBee EPfP LRHS MAsh SEND WPat |
| | ***leschenaultii*** misapplied | see *H.* 'Rowallane' |
| | ***leschenaultii*** Choisy | CMCN |
| | ***linarioides*** | EBee |
| | ***maclarenii*** | EWes WPGP |
| | 'Magic Berry Pink' **new** | EHig |
| | 'Magic Berry Red' **new** | EHig |
| | Magical Beauty = 'Kolmbeau' PBR | NLar |
| | Magical Red = 'Kolmred' PBR | NLar SPoG |
| | x ***moserianum*** ♀H4 | EBee EPfP LBMP MBar MRav NPer SHBN SLon SPer SRms WDin |
| § | - 'Tricolor' (v) | Widely available |
| | - 'Variegatum' | see *H.* x *moserianum* 'Tricolor' |
| | 'Mrs Brabazon' | see *H. androsaemum* f. *variegatum* 'Mrs Gladis Brabazon' |
| | ***nummularium*** | NBir WAbe |
| | ***oblongifolium*** | CPLG WCot |
| | ***olympicum*** ♀H4 | CEnt CHrt CSec CTri ECha ECho ELan EPfP GJos GMaP LRHS MBrN MWat SHGN SPer SRms WAbe WDin WFar |
| | - 'Grandiflorum' | see *H. olympicum* f. *uniflorum* |
| § | - f. ***minus*** | CTri EBee ECho ECtt SPlb SRms WFar WHrl WPer |
| § | - - 'Sulphureum' | CChe CPrp ECho EWes GMaP LRHS MHar MLHP MLLN NBir SPer SRms WCFE WFar |
| § | - - 'Variegatum' (v) | CBow CWan EWes LBee NBir NLAp SPoG WPat |
| § | - f. ***uniflorum*** | ECho MBar NBlu NBro NPri NVic SEND |
| | - - 'Citrinum' ♀H4 | CMea EBee ECha ECtt EPfP LBee MRav MWat NBro NDlv NLAp SPoG WAbe WCot WEas WHoo WKif WPGP WPat |
| | ***orientale*** | EWes |
| § | ***pallens*** | ECho NMen WAbe |
| | ***patulum*** var. ***forrestii*** | see *H. forrestii* |
| | - var. ***henryi*** Rehder & hort. | see *H. pseudohenryi* |
| | - var. ***henryi*** Veitch ex Bean | see *H. beanii* |
| | ***perforatum*** | CArn CBod CHby CWan EBWF EBee ELau EPfP GBar GPoy MHer MNHC NMir SEND SIde WHer WJek WLHH WMoo |
| | - 'Topaz' | MSal |
| | ***polyphyllum*** | see *H. olympicum* f. *minus* |
| | - 'Citrinum' | see *H. olympicum* f. *minus* 'Sulphureum' |
| | - 'Grandiflorum' | see *H. olympicum* f. *uniflorum* |
| | - 'Sulphureum' | see *H. olympicum* f. *minus* 'Sulphureum' |
| | - 'Variegatum' | see *H. olympicum* f. *minus* 'Variegatum' |
| | ***prolificum*** | ECtt EPla MMHG WCFE |
| § | ***pseudohenryi*** L 1029 | GBuc |
| | ***pseudopetiolatum*** var. ***yakusimense*** | see *H. kiusianum* var. *yakusimense* |
| | 'Purple Smoke' **new** | EMil |
| | ***quadrangulum*** L. | see *H. tetrapterum* |
| | ***reptans*** misapplied | see *H. olympicum* f. *minus* |
| | ***reptans*** Dyer | CMea ECho EWes |
| § | 'Rowallane' ♀H3 | CPSs EPfP GCal SDix SHBN SMrm SSpi WBod |
| | 'Smoulder' **new** | WCot |
| | ***stellatum*** | EMon WFar |
| | ***subsessile*** | CPLG |
| | 'Sungold' | see *H. kouytchense* |
| § | ***tetrapterum*** | CArn EBWF MSal NSco |
| | ***trichocaulon*** | EDAr EWes WAbe WPat |
| | ***uralum*** HWJ 520 | WCru |
| | ***xylosteifolium*** | SLon |
| | ***yakusimense*** | see *H. kiusianum* var. *yakusimense* |

## *Hypocalymma* (*Myrtaceae*)

**angustifolium** ECou SOWG
**cordifolium** 'Golden Veil' (v) ECou

## *Hypocalyptus* (*Papilionaceae*)

**sophoroides** SPlb

## *Hypochaeris* (*Asteraceae*)

**maculata** WHer
**radicata** EBWF NMir

## *Hypocyrta* see *Nematanthus*

## *Hypoestes* (*Acanthaceae*)

**aristata** CPLG EShb
§ **phyllostachya** (v) ♀H1 EShb MBri
- 'Bettina' (v) MBri
- 'Carmina' (v) MBri
- 'Purpuriana' (v) MBri SEND
- 'Wit' (v) MBri SEND
**sanguinolenta** misapplied see *H. phyllostachya*

## *Hypolepis* (*Dennstaedtiaceae*)

**ambigua** new WRic
**millefolium** GGar WCot
**punctata** EFer
**rufobarbata** new WRic

## *Hypoxis* (*Hypoxidaceae*)

**hirsuta** CPen CWsd ECho
**hygrometrica** EBee EBrs ECho ECou NMen WAbe WThu
**krebsii** ECho LLHF
**obtusa** new LLHF
**parvula** CFee CTca NMen
- var. **albiflora** EBrs ITim
§ - - 'Hebron Farm Biscuit' CBro ECho EWes GEdr WAbe WFar
- pink-flowered EBrs
**villosa** ECho

## *Hypoxis* x *Rhodohypoxis* see x *Rhodoxis*

**H. parvula** x **R. baurii** see x *Rhodoxis hybrida*

## *Hypsela* (*Campanulaceae*)

sp. CFee
**longiflora** see *H. reniformis*
§ **reniformis** ECho EDAr GGar LAst LBee LRHS MRav NWCA SIng SPoG WFar
- 'Greencourt White' ECho GBuc

## *Hypseocharis* (*Oxalidaceae*)

**pimpinellifolia** WCot

## *Hyptis* (*Lamiaceae*)

**emoryi** new CArn

## *Hyssopus* ✿ (*Lamiaceae*)

**officinalis** Widely available
- f. **albus** CSev CWan EBee ECha ELau EPfP GPoy MHer MNHC NGHP SBch SGar SHGN SIde SPlb WCHb WJek WPer
- subsp. **aristatus** CArn CBod CHFP CHrt EBee ECho ELau GCal GPoy LLWP MHer MNHC NChi SIde SPoG WCHb WJek
- 'Blaue Wolke' GBin
- subsp. **canescens** EAro
- 'Roseus' CEnt CHrt CSev EBee ECha ELau EPfP GPoy LLWP MBNS MHer MNHC NGHP SBch SEND SHGN SIde SPoG WCHb WJek WKif WPer
- white-flowered SPoG
* **schugnanicus** EBee MHar

## *Hystrix* (*Poaceae*)

**patula** CHrt CKno EHoe EMon EShb GFor ILad LLWP MCCP MMoz MNrw MWhi NHol SEND SPlb WPer WRos WTin

# I

## *Iberis* (*Brassicaceae*)

**aurosica** 'Sweetheart' GBin GEdr
**candolleana** see *I. pruitii* Candolleana Group
**commutata** see *I. sempervirens*
'Dick Self' LRHS
**gibraltarica** ECho NPri SRms WGor
- 'Betty Swainson' CHrt ELon GBri SPhx SUsu
'Golden Candy' SPoG WFar
§ **pruitii** Candolleana Group ECho WAbe WFar
**saxatilis** ECho EDAr GKev LRHS
- **candolleana** see *I. pruitii* Candolleana Group
**semperflorens** WCFE
§ **sempervirens** ♀H4 CTri CWib ECho ELan EPfP GKir IFoB LAst MCot MHer MWat NBlu NBro NHol NOrc NVic SEND SRms WBrE WCFE WFar WHoo WPer
- 'Compacta' ECho
- 'Little Gem' see *I. sempervirens* 'Weisser Zwerg'
- 'Pygmaea' ECho NMen WAbe
- Schneeflocke see *I. sempervirens* 'Snowflake'
§ - 'Snowflake' ♀H4 ECho EPfP GAbr GEdr IFoB LRHS MWat NPri SBch SPer SPoG SWvt WFar
§ - 'Weisser Zwerg' CMea ECha ECho ECtt ELan LAst LBee LRHS MHer MRav MWat NMen NRya SPoG SRms WAbe WHoo
**umbellata** new CSec

## *Idesia* (*Flacourtiaceae*)

**polycarpa** CAbP CDul CMCN EPfP IDee LHop MMuc NLar SSpi WBVN WDin WFar WPGP WPat

## *Ilex* ✿ (*Aquifoliaceae*)

N x **altaclerensis** SHHo
- 'Atkinsonii' (m) SHHo WWHy
- 'Balearica' (f) SHHo
- 'Barterberry' (f) WWHy
- 'Belgica' (f) SHHo
§ - 'Belgica Aurea' (f/v) ♀H4 CBcs CDoC CPMA CSBt CTho EBee EPfP EQua ERas LRHS MBar MBri MSwo NHol NWea SHBN SHHo WFar WWHy
- 'Camelliifolia' (f) ♀H4 CDul CSBt CTho EBee ELan EPfP ERas GKir IFoB LMaj MBlu MBri MWat NLar NWea SHHo SPla WFar WWHy
- 'Golden King' (f/v) ♀H4 Widely available
- 'Hendersonii' (f) SHHo WWHy
- 'Hodginsii' (m) ♀H4 CTri ECot MBar MRav SEND SHHo WFar WWHy
- 'Howick' (f/v) SHHo
- 'James G. Esson' (f) SBir SHHo
- 'Jermyns' (m) SHHo
- 'Lady Valerie' (f/v) SHHo WWHy
- 'Lawsoniana' (f/v) ♀H4 Widely available

| | | |
|---|---|---|
| | – 'Maderensis Variegata' | see *I. aquifolium* 'Maderensis Variegata' |
| | – 'Marnockii' (f) | SHHo WWHy |
| | – 'Moorei' (m) | SHHo |
| | – 'Mundyi' (m) | SHHo |
| | – 'N.F. Barnes' (f) | SHHo |
| | – 'Purple Shaft' (f) | EQua MRav SHHo |
| | – 'Ripley Gold' (f/v) | MAsh NHol SHHo WWHy |
| | – 'Silver Sentinel' | see *I.* x *altaclerensis* 'Belgica Aurea' |
| | – 'W.J. Bean' (f) | SHHo WWHy |
| | – 'Wilsonii' (f) | EBee EPfP ERas LPan SHHo WWHy |
| | ***aquifolium*** 🏆H4 | Widely available |
| | – 'Alaska' (f) | CDoC CDul CMCN ECrN EMil LAst LBuc NBlu NHol NLar NPri NSti SBir SHHo SWvt WFar WWHy |
| | – 'Amber' (f) 🏆H4 | CTri EQua SHHo SMad WWHy |
| | – 'Angustifolia' (f) | EPla MAsh WCFE WFar WWHy |
| | – 'Angustifolia' (m or f) | EPfP MBar MWat SHHo SPoG WBVN WFar |
| | – 'Angustimarginata Aurea' (m/v) | SHHo |
| | – 'Argentea Longifolia' (m/v) | WWHy |
| § | – 'Argentea Marginata' (f/v) 🏆H4 | Widely available |
| § | – 'Argentea Marginata Pendula' (f/v) | CDoC CTri ELan EMil EPfP ERas GKir LPan LRHS MAsh MRav NHol NLar SHHo SPer SRms WFar WPat WWHy |
| | – 'Argentea Pendula' | see *I. aquifolium* 'Argentea Marginata Pendula' |
| | – 'Argentea Variegata' | see *I. aquifolium* 'Argentea Marginata' |
| | – 'Atlas' (m) | CBcs CDoC LBuc WWHy |
| | – 'Aurea Marginata' (f/v) | CDul CTho EBee EPfP LBuc MGos NHol NWea SCoo SHBN SHHo WCFE WDin WFar WPat |
| | – 'Aurea Marginata Pendula' (f/v) | CDoC MAsh NHol WPat |
| | – 'Aurea Marginata Stricta' (f/v) | WWHy |
| | – 'Aurea Ovata' | see *I. aquifolium* 'Ovata Aurea' |
| | – 'Aurea Regina' | see *I. aquifolium* 'Golden Queen' |
| | – 'Aureovariegata Pendula' | see *I. aquifolium* 'Weeping Golden Milkmaid' |
| | – 'Aurifodina' (f) | IMGH SHHo WWHy |
| | – 'Bacciflava' (f) | Widely available |
| | – 'Bella' (f) | SHHo |
| | – 'Bokrijk' (f/v) | SHHo WWHy |
| | – 'Bowland' (f/v) | NHol |
| | – 'Chris Whittle' **new** | NHol |
| | – 'Cookii' (f) | SHHo WWHy |
| | – 'Crassifolia' (f) | CWib EPla SHHo SMad WWHy |
| | – 'Crispa' (m) | EBee MBlu NHol SBir SHHo WWHy |
| | – 'Crispa Aureomaculata' | see *I. aquifolium* 'Crispa Aureopicta' |
| § | – 'Crispa Aureopicta' (m/v) | SHHo WWHy |
| | – 'Elegantissima' (m/v) | LRHS SCoo SHHo WWHy |
| | – 'Ferox' (m) | CDul ELan EPfP LRHS SHHo SPoG WDin WGwG WWHy |
| | – 'Ferox Argentea' (m/v) 🏆H4 | Widely available |
| * | – 'Ferox Argentea Picta' (m/v) | LRHS WFar WWHy |
| | – 'Ferox Aurea' (m/v) | CDoC CPMA CSBt CWib EBee ELan ELon EPfP ERas LAst MAsh NHol SHHo SPla WWHy |
| § | – 'Flavescens' (f) | EBee EMil EPfP EQua GKir NHol SHHo |
| | – 'Frogmore Silver' (m/v) | EQua SHHo |
| | – 'Gold Flash' (f/v) | EBee LRHS MBri MGos NBlu NHol NLar SHHo WDin WWHy |
| I | – 'Golden Hedgehog' | SHHo SPoG WWHy |
| | – 'Golden Milkboy' (m/v) | EBee ELan EPfP GKir MBlu MGos SHHo WDin WPat WWHy |
| § | – 'Golden Queen' (m/v) 🏆H4 | CDoC CWSG CWib EBee LRHS MGos NBir NHol SHHo SPer SRms WPat WWHy |
| | – 'Golden Tears' (f/v) | SHHo WWHy |
| | – 'Golden van Tol' (f/v) | CBcs CDoC CSBt CTri EBee ECrN ELan ELon EPfP GKir LAst LRHS MAsh MBar MBlu MGos MSwo NBlu NHol NLar SCoo SHBN SHHo SRms WBVN WDin WMoo WWHy |
| § | – 'Green Pillar' (f) | EPfP MBar SHHo WWHy |
| | – 'Green Spire' | see *I. aquifolium* 'Green Pillar' |
| | – 'Handsworth New Silver' (f/v) 🏆H4 | Widely available |
| | – 'Harpune' (f) | SHHo WWHy |
| § | – 'Hascombensis' | CDoC EDAr GKir LHop MGos NHol NMen WFar WWHy |
| | – 'Hastata' (m) | CWib IArd WWHy |
| | – 'Ingramii' (m/v) | SBir SHHo WWHy |
| | – 'Integrifolia' (f) | WWHy |
| | – 'J.C. van Tol' (f) 🏆H4 | Widely available |
| | – 'Latispina' (f) | SHHo WWHy |
| | – 'Laurifolia Aurea' (m/v) | SHHo |
| | – 'Lichtenthalii' (f) | IArd SHHo |
| | – 'Madame Briot' (f/v) 🏆H4 | Widely available |
| § | – 'Maderensis Variegata' (f/v) | SHHo |
| | – 'Monstrosa' (m) | SHHo |
| | – moonlight holly | see *I. aquifolium* 'Flavescens' |
| | – 'Myrtifolia' (m) | ELan EPfP ERas LPan MBar MBlu MGos MRav NBlu NLar SCoo SHHo SMad SPoG WFar WMoo WWHy |
| | – 'Myrtifolia Aurea' (m/v) | GKir SWvt WFar |
| § | – 'Myrtifolia Aurea Maculata' (m/v) 🏆H4 | CDoC CSam EBee ELan EPfP IMGH LAst LRHS MAsh MRav NHol NWea SHHo SMad SPer SPoG SWvt WBVN WFar WPat WWHy |
| | – 'Myrtifolia Aureovariegata' | see *I. aquifolium* 'Myrtifolia Aurea Maculata' |
| | – 'Ovata' (m) | WWHy |
| § | – 'Ovata Aurea' (m/v) | SHHo WWHy |
| | – 'Pendula' (f) | EPfP GKir SHHo |
| | – 'Pendula Mediopicta' | see *I. aquifolium* 'Weeping Golden Milkmaid' |
| § | – 'Pyramidalis' (f) 🏆H4 | CDoC CDul CSBt CTri EBee ELan IFoB LRHS MAsh MBar MBri MGos NHol NLar NWea SHHo SPer SRms WDin WFar WMoo WWHy |
| | – 'Pyramidalis Aureomarginata' (f/v) | CDoC LRHS MBri MGos NLar SHHo |
| | – 'Pyramidalis Fructu Luteo' (f) 🏆H4 | MBar NWea SHHo |
| | – 'Recurva' (m) | SHHo WWHy |
| | – 'Rederly' (f) **new** | WWHy |
| | – 'Rubricaulis Aurea' (f/v) | ERas NHol NLar SHHo WWHy |
| | – 'Scotica' (f) | GKir NWea SHHo WWHy |
| | – Siberia = 'Limsi'PBR (f) | EBee SHHo WWHy |
| | – 'Silver King' | see *I. aquifolium* 'Silver Queen' |
| | – 'Silver Lining' (f/v) | SHHo |
| | – 'Silver Milkboy' (f/v) | EHoe ELan GKir LRHS MBlu MGos WFar WWHy |
| | – 'Silver Milkmaid' (f/v) | CDoC CWSG EBee EPfP LAst LBMP LRHS MBar MRav NHol SHBN SHHo SLim SPer SPla SWvt WMoo WWHy |
| § | – 'Silver Queen' (m/v) 🏆H4 | Widely available |
| | – 'Silver Sentinel' | see *I.* x *altaclerensis* 'Belgica Aurea' |
| | – 'Silver van Tol' (f/v) | CDoC ELan LAst LRHS NHol NLar NPer NWea SHHo WFar WWHy |
| | – 'Somerset Cream' (f/v) | CPMA CWib NLar WWHy |
| § | – 'Watereriana' (m/v) | MAsh SHHo |
| | – 'Waterer's Gold' | see *I. aquifolium* 'Watereriana' |

| | | |
|---|---|---|
| § | - 'Weeping Golden Milkmaid' (f/v) | SHHo WPat |
| | x ***aquipernyi*** | EBee SHHo |
| | - Dragon Lady = 'Meschick' (f) | LPan MBri NLar SHHo WWHy |
| | - 'San Jose' (f) | CMCN SHHo |
| | x ***attenuata*** | WFar |
| | - 'Sunny Foster' (f/v) | CDoC CMCN EPfP EPla MGos SHHo WFar |
| § | ***bioritsensis*** | CMCN CTri NWea |
| | China Boy = 'Mesdob' (m) | LMaj SHHo |
| | China Girl = 'Mesog' (f) | SHHo |
| | ***ciliospinosa*** | CMCN WPGP |
| | ***colchica*** | CMCN SHHo |
| | ***corallina*** | CBcs CMCN |
| | ***cornuta*** | EPfP ERom LPan LRHS SHHo WFar |
| | - 'Anicet Delcambre' | SHHo |
| * | - 'Aurea' | SHHo |
| | - 'Burfordii' (f) | SHHo |
| § | - 'Dazzler' (f) | LPan SHHo |
| | - 'Fine Line' (f) | SHHo |
| | - 'Ira S. Nelson' (f/v) | SHHo |
| | - 'O. Spring' (f/v) | SHHo |
| | - 'Rotunda' (f) | SHHo |
| | ***crenata*** | CMCN CTri EDAr ERom GCra GKir MBar MGos NWea SAPC SArc SHHo STrG WDin WFar |
| * | - 'Akagi' | WFar |
| | - 'Aureovariegata' | see *I. crenata* 'Variegata' |
| | - 'Cole's Hardy' (f) | SHHo |
| | - 'Convexa' (f) ♀H4 | EMil EPfP GKir IMGH LPan MAsh MBar MRav MSwo NBlu NHol NWea WFar WGwG WPat |
| | - 'Convexed Gold' (f/v) | EMil MBri MGos SPoG |
| | - 'Fastigiata' (f) | CDoC ECrN EPfP EPla GKir LAst LRHS MAsh MBar MBri MGos NBlu NLar SCoo SHHo SPer SPoG WBod WFar WPic |
| | - 'Fukarin' | see *I. crenata* 'Shiro-fukurin' |
| * | - 'Glory Gem' (f) | CBcs LPan |
| | - 'Golden Gem' (f/v) ♀H4 | Widely available |
| * | - 'Green Hedge' | EMil |
| | - 'Green Island' (m) | SHHo |
| | - 'Green Lustre' (f) | SHHo |
| | - 'Helleri' (f) | EPfP EPla MBar SHHo WPat |
| | - 'Hetzii' (f) | NLar SHHo |
| | - 'Ivory Hall' (f) | EPla |
| | - 'Kobold' (m) | SHHo |
| | - 'Korean Gem' | SHHo |
| | - 'Luteovariegata' | see *I. crenata* 'Variegata' |
| | - 'Mariesii' (f) | CMac EBee IMGH MBlu SIng |
| I | - 'Pyramidalis' (f) | NHol NWea |
| § | - 'Shiro-fukurin' (f/v) | CMCN CMHG ELan EPfP LAst LRHS SHHo |
| | - 'Snowflake' | see *I. crenata* 'Shiro-fukurin' |
| | - 'Stokes' (m) | EMil NHol NLar |
| § | - 'Variegata' (v) | CMCN CMac EPla LRHS MBar |
| | 'Dazzler' | see *I. cornuta* 'Dazzler' |
| | ***decidua*** | CMCN |
| | ***dimorphophylla*** | CBcs CDoC CMCN CMac SHHo SMad |
| | - 'Somerset Pixie' (f) | SHHo |
| | ***dipyrena*** | CBcs |
| | 'Doctor Kassab' (f) | CMCN SHHo |
| | 'Drace' (f) | SHHo |
| | 'Elegance' (f) | WFar |
| | ***ficoidea*** | CMCN |
| | ***glabra*** | SHHo |
| | 'Good Taste' (f) | SHHo WFar WWHy |
| | ***hascombensis*** | see *I. aquifolium* 'Hascombensis' |
| | ***hookeri*** | SHHo |
| | 'Indian Chief' (f) | MBlu SMad WFar |
| | ***insignis*** | see *I. kingiana* |
| | 'John T. Morris' (m) | SHHo |
| § | ***kingiana*** | WFar WPGP |
| | x ***koehneana*** | CDul ELan |
| | - 'Chestnut Leaf' (f) ♀H4 | CCVT CDoC CLnd CMCN ECrN EMil EPfP EQua GKir MRav SHHo SMad WFar WLeb WPGP WWHy |
| | - 'Wirt L. Winn' (f) | WWHy |
| | ***latifolia*** | CBcs CHEx CMCN EMil SHHo SMad WPGP |
| | 'Lydia Morris' (f) | CSam SHHo WFar |
| | 'Mary Nell' (f) | SBir SHHo |
| | ***maximowicziana*** var. ***kanehirae*** | CBcs WWHy |
| | x ***meserveae*** | SHHo |
| | - 'Blue Angel' | CBcs CDoC CDul EBee ELan EMil EPfP IFoB IMGH LPan MBar MBri MLan MWat NBlu NHol NLar NWea SHHo SPoG SRms WDin WFar WMoo WPat WWHy |
| | - Blue Maid = 'Mesid' (f) | WWHy |
| | - Blue Prince (m) | CBcs CDoC EBee ELan GKev LBuc LPan MBar MBlu NBlu NHol NLar NPri NWea SHBN SHHo SLim SPoG WDin WFar WWHy |
| | - Blue Princess = 'Conapri' (f) | CBcs ELan EPfP GKir LBuc LPan MBar MBlu MRav NHol NLar NPri NSti NWea SCoo SHBN SHHo SLim SPer SPoG WDin WMoo WWHy |
| | - Golden Girl = 'Mesgolg' (f) | WWHy |
| | - 'Goliath' (f) | WWHy |
| | ***myrtifolia*** | ECot MLan MRav NPri |
| | 'Nellie R. Stevens' (f) | EMil LMaj LPan NWea SCoo WWHy |
| | ***opaca*** | CMCN |
| | ***paraguariensis*** | EOHP |
| | ***pedunculosa*** | CMCN |
| | ***perado*** subsp. ***perado*** | CBcs GKir |
| | - subsp. ***platyphylla*** | CBcs CHEx CMCN MBlu SAPC SArc SHHo WWHy |
| | ***pernyi*** | CMCN CMac CTrG CTri EPfP GKir LRHS SHHo SLon SPoG WFar WPic WWHy |
| | - var. ***veitchii*** | see *I. bioritsensis* |
| | ***purpurea*** | CMCN SPla |
| | 'Pyramidalis' | see *I. aquifolium* 'Pyramidalis' |
| | ***rugosa*** | WWHy |
| | 'September Gem' (f) | CMCN |
| | ***serrata*** | CMen |
| | - 'Leucocarpa' **new** | CMen |
| | ***suaveolens*** | CMCN |
| | ***verticillata*** | CMCN WDin WFar |
| | - (f) | EPfP NLar NWea WFar |
| | - (m) | EPfP NLar |
| | - 'Christmas Cheer' (f) | WFar |
| | - 'Maryland Beauty' (f) | CPMA |
| | - 'Southern Gentleman' (m) | CPMA |
| | - 'Winter Red' (f) | CMCN CPMA EBee |
| | ***vomitoria*** | CMCN EShb SHHo |
| | x ***wandoensis*** | CMCN SHHo WWHy |
| | 'Washington' (f) | SHHo WWHy |
| | ***yunnanensis*** | CMCN SHHo |

## *Iliamna* see *Sphaeralcea*

## *Illicium* (*Illiciaceae*)

| | | |
|---|---|---|
| | ***anisatum*** | CArn CBcs CPLG CWsd EPfP NLar SSpi WFar WPGP WSHC |
| | ***floridanum*** | CBcs EBee EPfP MBri NLar SKHP SSpi SSta WPat |
| | - f. ***album*** **new** | EPfP |
| I | - 'Compactum' | WPGP |

- 'Halley's Comet' NLar
***henryi*** CDoC CGHE CMCN CMHG CPLG CWib EBee EPfP NLar SKHP SSpi WPGP WSHC
aff. ***henryi*** CBcs
***mexicanum*** SKHP
***parviflorum*** SKHP
***simonsii*** CExc
- BWJ 8024 WCru

## *Ilysanthes* see *Lindernia*

## *Impatiens* ✿ (*Balsaminaceae*)

CC 4980 CPLG
'African Snow' **new** CKob
***apiculata*** CKob EBee GCal WPrP
***arguta*** CDes CFir CLAP CPLG CPom CSpe EBee EPPr EShb GCal LSou MCCP MDKP WCot WPGP WPrP
***auricoma*** EBak WCot
***auricoma* x *bicaudata*** WDib
***balfourii*** CSec EHrv EMon
Butterfly Salmon Eye = 'Bufly Saley' LSou
***congolensis*** CCCN EPfP
double-flowered (d) EBak
***flanaganae*** CFir EMon
***forrestii*** CLAP
aff. ***forrestii*** WPrP
'Fusion Sunset' LAst
***glandulifera*** 'Candida' EMon
- 'Mien Ruys' EMon
***gomphophylla*** CFir
(Harmony Series) Harmony Dark Red = 'Danhardkrd' WGor
- Harmony Orange Blaze = 'Danharoblaze' WGor
- Harmony Pink Smile **new** WGor
- Harmony Salmon = 'Danharsal' WGor
- Harmony Violet = 'Danharvio' WGor
***hawkeri*** see *I. schlechteri*
***keilii*** WDib
***kerriae*** B&SWJ 7219 WCru
***kilimanjari*** subsp. ***kilimanjari*** CSpe
***kilimanjari* x *pseudoviola*** CDoC CFee CSpe EBee
***langbianensis*** HWJ 1054 WCru
***macrophylla*** B&SWJ 10157 WCru
***namchabarwensis*** **new** CSec
New Guinea Group see *I. schlechteri*
***niamniamensis*** CHll CTca EBak EShb WCot WDib
- 'Congo Cockatoo' CDTJ CDoC CHEx CHal CSec CTsd EOHP GCal MJnS NPer SRms
- 'Golden Cockatoo' (v) CDTJ CDoC CHal CSec EBak EShb MJnS
***noli-tangere*** WSFF
***omeiana*** CCCN CFir CHEx CKob CLAP CPom CSpe CWsd EBee EPPr EWld GCal LEdu LHop MCCP MNrw SBch SBig WBor WCot WCru WPGP WPrP WSHC
- DJHC 98492 CWsd
- silver-leaved CHEx CKob CLAP LFur LSou MCCP MDKP MHar WCot WPGP WPrP
***parasitica*** WDib
***platypetala*** B&SWJ 9722 WCru WPrP
***pseudoviola*** SDix
***puberula*** WPrP
- HWJK 2063 WCru
§ ***schlechteri*** EBak LSou
***sodenii*** CDTJ CKob CSpe EShb SBHP
***stenantha*** CFir
***sultani*** see *I. walleriana*
* ***sutherlandii*** **new** CFir
***tinctoria*** CDoC CFir CGHE CHEx CHll CKob CPLG CSpe EBee EMon EShb GCal GCra LFur MCCP MNrw WCot WPGP WPrP WWlt
- subsp. ***elegantissima*** CFee
- subsp. ***tinctoria*** IFro
***tuberosa*** WDib
***ugandensis*** GCal
***uniflora*** CFir LHop LSou MCCP
Velvetea = 'Secret Love'[PBR] CCCN
***walkeri*** CFee
§ ***walleriana*** EBak MBri
-(Fiesta Series) Fiesta Appleblossom = 'Balfieplos' (d) NPri SVil
- - Fiesta Coral Bells = 'Balfiecobl' (d) NPri
- - Fiesta Olé Frost = 'Balolefro' (d) NPri
- - Fiesta Olé Peach = 'Balolepeac' **new** (d) NPri
- - Fiesta Olé Peppermint = 'Balolepep' (d/v) LAst
- - Fiesta Olé Purple = 'Balolepurp'[PBR] (d) **new** LAst
- - Fiesta Olé Rose = 'Balolerose'[PBR] (d) NPri
- - Fiesta Olé Salmon = 'Balolesal' (d) NPri
- - Fiesta Olé Stardust = 'Balolestop' (d) NPri
- - Fiesta Sparkler Cherry = 'Balfiespary' (d) NPri
- - 'Lavender Orchid'[PBR] (d) NPri
- 'Impulse Orange' **new** MWar
- 'Musica Spicy Red' (Double Musica Series) (d) **new** LSou
- 'Peach Ice' (Summer Ice Series) (d/v) CHal
- (Spellbound Series) Spellbound Dark Red = 'Imtradared' **new** WGor
- - Spellbound Pink = 'Imtrarepu' **new** WGor

## *Imperata* (*Poaceae*)

***cylindrica*** CMen MSal
- 'Red Baron' see *I. cylindrica* 'Rubra'
§ - 'Rubra' Widely available

## *Incarvillea* (*Bignoniaceae*)

sp. CSec
***arguta*** CKob EShb LLHF LPio
***brevipes*** see *I. mairei*
***compacta*** MDKP
- ACE 1455 EBee
- BWJ 7620 WCru
***delavayi*** Widely available
- SDR 4711 **new** GKev
- 'Alba' see *I. delavayi* 'Snowtop'
- 'Bees' Pink' CAby CSpe EBee EBrs ECho EDAr GBuc GGar GKir SHGN

| | |
|---|---|
| § - 'Snowtop' | CDWL CElw EBee EBrs ECho ELan EPfP EPot GBuc GMaP MDun MLLN NBPC NBir NLar SPer SPla SWvt WBrE WFar WPGP |
| ***forrestii*** | EBee ECho GKev LPio |
| ***grandiflora*** | ELan |
| ***himalayensis*** 'Frank Ludlow' | GBuc |
| - 'Nyoto Sama' | EBee GBuc |
| ***lutea*** BWJ 7784 | WCru |
| § ***mairei*** | CAby CTsd EBee EBrs ECho EGoo EPfP GEdr GKir LHop LPio LRHS MLLN NLar WPer |
| - SDR 3028 | GKev |
| - SDR 4336 **new** | GKev |
| - SDR 4807 **new** | GKev |
| - var. ***mairei*** | GBuc |
| - - f. ***multifoliata*** | see *I. zhongdianensis* |
| - pink-flowered | GCal GKir |
| ***olgae*** | EBee LPio MLLN NLar |
| ***sinensis*** 'Cheron' | CSpe |
| ***younghusbandii*** | GEdr |
| § ***zhongdianensis*** | CPBP EBee ERos GBuc GEdr GKev MDKP NWCA WAbe |
| - BWJ 7692 | WCru |
| - BWJ 7978 | WCru |

## *Indigofera* (*Papilionaceae*)

| | |
|---|---|
| ***amblyantha*** ♀H4 | CBcs EBee ELon EPfP IMGH LHop LRHS MAsh MBlu MBri NLar SBod SEND SKHP SPlb SPoG SSpi WDin WKif WSHC |
| ***australis*** | SOWG |
| ***balfouriana*** BWJ 7851 | WCru |
| ***cassioides*** | WCru |
| ***cytisoides*** | GFai |
| ***decora*** f. ***alba*** | EPfP |
| ***dielsiana*** | CWGN EBee EPfP MWea WKif WPGP |
| 'Dosua' | SEND SLPl |
| ***gerardiana*** | see *I. heterantha* |
| ***hebepetala*** | EPfP WDin WPGP WSHC |
| § ***heterantha*** ♀H4 | Widely available |
| ***himalayensis*** | EBee SKHP |
| - Yu 10941 | WPGP |
| - 'Silk Road' | LBuc MBri |
| ***kirilowii*** | EBee EPfP NLar SKHP SOWG WPGP WSHC |
| ***pendula*** | EBee EPfP IDee MAsh SEND SSpi WPGP WSHC |
| - B&SWJ 7741 | WCru |
| ***potaninii*** | EPfP SHBN SKHP WHer |
| ***pseudotinctoria*** | CCCN EMil EPfP MBri NLar SRms |
| ***splendens*** | EPfP MBri |
| ***subverticillata*** | EBee WPGP WSHC |
| ***tinctoria*** | CArn MSal WSFF |

## *Indocalamus* (*Poaceae*)

| | |
|---|---|
| ***latifolius*** | EBee EPPr EPla ERod MMoz MMuc MWht NLar |
| - 'Hopei' | EPla |
| ***longiauritus*** | EPla |
| ***solidus*** | see *Bonia solida* |
| § ***tessellatus*** ♀H4 | Widely available |
| - f. ***hamadae*** | CMCo EPla ERod MMoz MWht |

## *Inula* (*Asteraceae*)

| | |
|---|---|
| ***acaulis*** | WCot |
| ***afghanica*** | EBee |
| ***barbata*** | MLLN NBre |
| ***britannica*** var. ***chinensis*** | NBre |
| ***crithmoides*** | WHer |
| ***dysenterica*** | see *Pulicaria dysenterica* |
| ***ensifolia*** | CBcs ELan EPfP GJos LEdu MBNS MDKP MLLN MRav MSte MTho NBro NWCA SLPl WCAu WFar |
| - 'Compacta' | ECho |
| - 'Gold Star' | EBee ECho EPfP GKir MLLN MNFA MWat NBid NBir SPet WFar WMnd WPer |
| ***glandulosa*** | see *I. orientalis* |
| 'Golden Beauty' | see *Buphthalmum salicifolium* 'Golden Wonder' |
| ***helenium*** | Widely available |
| - 'Goliath' | MLLN SMrm |
| ***helianthus-aquatilis*** | MLLN |
| ***hirta*** | MLLN NBre WPer |
| ***hookeri*** | Widely available |
| - GWJ 9033 | WCru |
| ***macrocephala*** misapplied | see *I. royleana* |
| ***macrocephala*** Boiss. & Kotschy ex Boiss. | MLLN |
| ***magnifica*** | Widely available |
| - 'Sonnenstrahl' ♀H4 | SPhx |
| ***oculus-christi*** | CDes EBee EWes MLLN NBre WPtf |
| - MESE 437 | EPPr |
| § ***orientalis*** | CHrt CKno CSec EBee EPfP GJos MBri MNFA MWat NBre NGBl SHGN SMad SPad SPoG WBrE WCAu WFar WMnd WPGP WPer |
| ***racemosa*** | CSec EMon EPPr EPla EShb EWes GBin GCal IBlr MNrw MSte NBid SMrm SPlb SRms WFar |
| - 'Sonnenspeer' | GMac NBre NLar SLPl WPer WPtf |
| ***rhizocephala*** | ECho MDKP WPer |
| § ***royleana*** | CEnt EDAr GBuc GCal GMac MDKP MNrw MRav MSte NBre NLar WPtf |
| ***salicina*** | EBee |
| ***verbascifolia*** | ECho |

## *Iochroma* (*Solanaceae*)

| | |
|---|---|
| 'Ashcott Red' **new** | CKob |
| § ***australe*** | CHEx CHll CKob CSec CSpe SGar SOWG SPad |
| § - 'Andean Snow' | CHll CKob CPLG EShb |
| § - 'Bill Evans' | CKob CPLG EShb |
| ***cyaneum*** | CCCN CDoC CKob CTri SOWG |
| - 'John Miers' | CKob |
| - 'Karl Hartweg' **new** | CKob |
| - purple-flowered | CHll |
| § - 'Trebah' | CDTJ CKob |
| ***gesnerioides*** 'Coccineum' | CCCN CDoC CHll CKob CSec |
| § ***grandiflorum*** | CCCN CDoC CHEx CHll CKob CSev SGar SOWG |
| 'Purple Haze' | CKob |
| ***violaceum*** hort. | see *I. cyaneum* 'Trebah' |
| ***warscewiczii*** | see *I. grandiflorum* |

## *Iostephane* (*Asteraceae*)

| | |
|---|---|
| § ***heterophylla*** **new** | MMuc |

## *Ipheion* ✿ (*Alliaceae*)

| | |
|---|---|
| 'Alberto Castillo' | Widely available |
| ***dialystemon*** | CStu EBee EBrs ECho EPot LPio SIng WAbe |
| ***hirtellum*** | EBee EBrs WCot |
| 'Jessie' | CMea EBee EBrs ECho EPot ERCP GBuc LAma NMin SPhx WCot |
| 'Rolf Fiedler' ♀H2-3 | Widely available |
| ***sellowianum*** | MAsh SCnR SUsu WCot |
| § ***uniflorum*** | CBro CSpe CStu CTri EBee EBrs ECha ECho LAma LEdu MNrw MRav NMen NWCA SIng SPer SRms WAbb WAul WCot WFar WPer WPnP WTin |

| | |
|---|---|
| - 'Album' | CBro CPom EBee EBrs ECha ECho EPPr EPot ERCP ERos EWes LAma LEdu LPio LRHS MAsh MRav MTho SIng SPhx WCot WHal WHil |
| - 'Charlotte Bishop' | Widely available |
| - 'Froyle Mill' ♀H4 | Widely available |
| - 'Wisley Blue' ♀H4 | Widely available |
| yellow-flowered | CDes SUsu |

## *Iphigenia* (*Colchicaceae*)

| | |
|---|---|
| ***indica*** | EBee |

## *Ipomoea* (*Convolvulaceae*)

| | |
|---|---|
| ***acuminata*** | see *I. indica* |
| ***alba*** | CCCN |
| ***batatas*** 'Blackie' | CSpe EShb WFar |
| - 'Margarita' | NPri |
| ***carnea*** | CCCN SOWG |
| ***coccinea*** | CSec |
| - var. ***hederifolia*** | see *I. hederifolia* |
| § ***hederifolia*** | CCCN |
| x ***imperialis*** 'Sunrise Serenade' | CCCN |
| § ***indica*** ♀H1 | CCCN CHEx CHal CHll CKob EPfP EShb LRHS MJnS MREP SOWG SPer |
| ***learii*** | see *I. indica* |
| § ***lobata*** | CSpe LBMP LRHS LSou SGar |
| 'Milky Way' | CCCN |
| ***muellerii*** | CCCN |
| x ***multifida*** | CSpe |
| ***nil*** 'Scarlett O'Hara' | CSec |
| ***purpurea*** | CSec LBMP |
| - 'Feringa' | LRHS |
| - 'Grandpa Otts' | LRHS |
| - 'Kniola's Purple-black' | CSpe SBch |
| - 'Shira' | LRHS |
| ***quamoclit*** | CSpe |
| ***tricolor*** | CSec |
| ***tuberosa*** | see *Merremia tuberosa* |
| ***versicolor*** | see *I. lobata* |

## *Ipomopsis* (*Polemoniaceae*)

| | |
|---|---|
| § ***aggregata*** | NPol |
| ***rubra*** | EBee NPol |

## *Iresine* (*Amaranthaceae*)

| | |
|---|---|
| ***herbstii*** | CHal EBak EShb |
| - 'Aureoreticulata' | CHal EShb |
| - 'Brilliantissima' | CHal |
| ***lindenii*** ♀H1 | CHal |
| 'Shiny Rose Purple' | LBuc |

## *Iris* ✿ (*Iridaceae*)

| | |
|---|---|
| CLD 1399 | NHol |
| AC 4413 from Tibet **new** | GAuc |
| AC 4450 from Tibet **new** | GAuc |
| AC 4471 from Tibet **new** | GAuc |
| AC 4490 from Tibet **new** | GAuc |
| AC 4623 from Tibet | GAuc |
| AC 4674 from Tibet **new** | GAuc |
| 'Aah Soo' (TB) | EFam |
| 'Abbey Road' (TB) | WCAu |
| 'About Town' (TB) | EFam |
| 'Abracadabra' (SDB) | SMrm |
| 'Acadian Miss' (La) | WCAu |
| 'Ace' (MTB) | ESgI |
| 'Acoma' (TB) | EFam WCAu |
| 'Action Front' (TB) | EAEE EBee EBla EHrv ESgI ETod IPot LAst LFCN MAvo MSte NGdn SDnm SPla WCra |
| 'Actress' (TB) | CWGN EAEE EBla ECGP ETod IPot LBuc LFCN LSRN MSte SPet SPla WCra |
| ***acutiloba*** subsp. ***lineolata*** | WWst |
| 'Adobe Rose' (TB) | ESgI |
| 'Adrienne Taylor' (SDB) ♀H4 | WCAu |
| 'African Queen' **new** | ERCP |
| 'After Dark' | CKel |
| 'After the Dawn' (TB) | LRHS |
| 'After the Storm' (TB) | ECho EFam |
| 'Afternoon Delight' (TB) | CWCL ESgI MRav WCAu |
| 'Agatha Christie' (IB) | WCAu |
| 'Agatha Dawson' (Reticulata/v) | EMon |
| 'Aggressively Forward' (TB) | WCAu |
| 'Agnes James' (CH) ♀H3 | CBro |
| 'Ahead of Times' (TB) | EFam |
| 'Airy Fancy' (Spuria) | ESgI |
| 'Alabaster Unicorn' (TB) **new** | ESgI |
| 'Albatross' (TB) | SMrm |
| ***albicans*** ♀H4 | CMea EBrs ECho LEdu WCAu |
| 'Alcazar' (TB) | ESgI LSRN NMoo SWat WFar WMnd |
| 'Aldo Ratti' (TB) | ESgI |
| 'Alene's Other Love' (SDB) | EFam |
| 'Alexia' (TB) ♀H4 | CKel |
| 'Alice Harding' (TB) | ESgI |
| 'Alida' (Reticulata) **new** | ERCP |
| 'Alien Mist' (TB) | EFam WCAu |
| 'Alison Elizabeth' | WAul |
| 'Alizes' (TB) ♀H4 | ESgI WCAu |
| 'All American' (TB) | EFam |
| 'All Lit Up' (TB) | EFam |
| 'All Night Long' (TB) **new** | CIri |
| 'Allegiance' (TB) | WCAu |
| 'Alpine Journey' (TB) | EFam ESgI |
| 'Alpine Lake' (MDB) | WCAu |
| 'Alpine Twilight' (TB) | EFam |
| 'Alsterquelle' (SDB) | WTin |
| 'Altruist' (TB) | EFam WCAu |
| 'Amadora' (TB) | CKel ESgI |
| 'Amagita' (CH) | CWsd |
| 'Amain' (TB) | EFam |
| 'Amas' (TB) | WCAu |
| 'Ambassadeur' (TB) | EBee |
| 'Amber Queen' (DB) | EAEE EBee EBla ECtt ELan ERos MSte MWat NBir NMen SPer SPet SPla SPoG |
| 'Amber Snow' (TB) | EFam |
| 'Ambroisie' (TB) ♀H4 | CIri ESgI ETod WBIS |
| 'Amelia Chynoweth' (TB) | CKel |
| 'American Patriot' (IB) | WCAu |
| 'America's Cup' (TB) | WCAu |
| 'Amethyst Dancer' (TB) | EFam |
| 'Amethyst Flame' (TB) | ECho ESgI NBre SRms WCAu |
| 'Amherst' (SDB) | EFam |
| 'Amherst Blue' (IB) | SIri |
| 'Amherst Bluebeard' (SDB) | SIri |
| 'Amherst Caper' (SDB) | WCAu |
| 'Amherst Jester' (BB) | SIri WAul |
| 'Amherst Moon' (SDB) | SIri WCAu |
| 'Amherst Mustard' (SDB) **new** | SIri |
| 'Amherst Purple Ribbon' (SDB) | SIri WCAu |
| 'Amherst Sweetheart' (SDB) | SIri WCAu |
| 'Amigo' (TB) | ESgI |
| 'Amiguita' (CH) | CFir EBee |
| 'Amphora' (SDB) | CBro ERos GBuc |
| 'Ancient Echoes' (TB) | ESgI |
| 'Andalou' (TB) ♀H4 | CWCL ESgI SCoo WBIS |
| 'Angel Unawares' (TB) | WCAu |
| 'Angelic' (SDB) | WCAu |

| | |
|---|---|
| 'Angelic Wings' (TB) | EFam |
| 'Angel's Tears' | see *I. histrioides* 'Angel's Tears' |
| 'Angel's Touch' (TB) new | ESgI |
| ***anglica*** | see *I. latifolia* |
| 'Anna Belle Babson' (TB) | ESgI |
| 'Anna Marie' (TB) | EFam |
| 'Annabel Jane' (TB) | CKel COIW CWan ELon WCAu |
| 'Anne Elizabeth' (SDB) | CBro ERos |
| 'Annikins' (IB) $\Upsilon^{H4}$ | CKel |
| 'Anniversary Celebration' (TB) | CKel |
| 'Announcement' (TB) new | CIri |
| 'Antarctique' (IB) | ESgI |
| 'Anthology' (TB) | EFam |
| 'Antigone' (TB) | ESgI |
| 'Anvil of Darkness' (TB) | CIri WAul |
| 'Anxious' (TB) | EFam |
| 'Anything Goes' (TB) | WAul |
| ***aphylla*** | WCAu |
| - subsp. ***fieberi*** | WCot |
| 'Apollo' (Dut) | EBrs |
| 'Apparent Secret' (TB) new | WAul |
| 'Appledore' (SDB) | CBro ERos |
| 'Appointer' (SpH) | CRow GBin NChi |
| 'Apricorange' (TB) $\Upsilon^{H4}$ | CKel |
| 'Apricot Blaze' (TB) new | ESgI |
| 'Apricot Drops' (MTB) $\Upsilon^{H4}$ | ESgI WAul WCAu |
| 'Apricot Frosty' (BB) | ESgI |
| 'Apricot Silk' (IB) | CWGN SEND SMrm |
| 'Arab Chief' (TB) | CKel |
| 'Arabi Pasha' (TB) | ESgI WCAu |
| 'Arabian Story' (TB) | EFam |
| * 'Arabic Night' (IB) | WCAu |
| 'Arc de Triomphe' (TB) new | ESgI |
| 'Archie Owen' (Spuria) | WCAu |
| 'Arctic Express' (TB) new | ESgI |
| 'Arctic Fancy' (IB) $\Upsilon^{H4}$ | CKel |
| 'Arctic Snow' (TB) | WCAu |
| 'Arctic Sunrise' (TB) new | ESgI |
| 'Arctic Wine' (IB) | WCAu |
| - 'Arden' (BB) | EFam |
| ***arenaria*** | see *I. humilis* |
| * 'Argument' (J) | WWst |
| 'Argus Pheasant' (SDB) | ESgI WCAu |
| 'Armageddon' (TB) | ESgI |
| 'Arnold Sunrise' (CH) $\Upsilon^{H3}$ | GAbr |
| 'Arnold Velvet' (SDB) | EFam |
| 'Art Deco' (TB) | SIri |
| 'Art School Angel' (TB) | CIri |
| 'Artful' (SDB) | WCAu |
| 'Artistic Gold' (TB) | EFam |
| 'Artist's Whim' (TB) | EFam |
| 'As de Coeur' (TB) new | ESgI |
| 'Ascension Crown' (TB) new | ESgI |
| 'Ask Alma' (IB) | ESgI WAul WCAu |
| 'Asteroid Zone' (TB) | EFam |
| 'Astrid Cayeux' (TB) | ESgI |
| 'Astro Flash' (TB) new | ESgI |
| * 'Atlantique' (TB) | CKel |
| 'Attention Please' (TB) | CKel ELan SMrm |
| § ***attica*** | CBro CPBP EPPr EPot ERos LEdu LLHF LRHS NRya NWCA WAbe WRos WThu |
| - J&JA 583.900 new | NWCA |
| - lemon-flowered | CPBP WThu |
| § ***aucheri*** $\Upsilon^{H2}$ | EBrs ECho EPot WWst |
| ***aucheri*** x ***bucharica*** | ELon |
| 'Aunt Corley' (TB) | CIri |
| 'Aunt Josephine' (TB) | ESgI |
| 'Aunt Martha' (BB) | MBri WCAu |
| 'Aurean' (IB) | CKel |
| 'Auroralita' (SDB) | EFam |
| 'Austrian Sky' (SDB) | CSam EAEE EBee EBla LFCN MSte SPhx STes WAul WCAu |
| 'Autumn Apricot' (TB) | EFam |
| 'Autumn Bugler' (TB) | EFam |
| 'Autumn Circus' (TB) | EFam WAul WCAu |
| 'Autumn Clouds' (TB) | EFam |
| 'Autumn Echo' (TB) | EFam ESgI SPet |
| 'Autumn Encore' (TB) | COIW WBor WHlf |
| 'Autumn Jester' (SDB) | EFam |
| 'Autumn Leaves' (TB) | ESgI WCAu |
| 'Autumn Maple' (SDB) | EFam ESgI |
| 'Autumn Mists' (TB) | EFam |
| 'Autumn Orangelite' (TB) | EFam |
| 'Autumn Thunder' (TB) | EFam |
| 'Autumn Tryst' (TB) | EFam ESgI WCAu |
| 'Avalon Sunset' (TB) | ESgI |
| 'Avanelle' (IB) | NBre |
| 'Awesome Blossom' (TB) | ESgI |
| 'Az Ap' (IB) | EBee WCAu |
| 'Aztec Sun' (TB) | SIri |
| 'Babbling Brook' (TB) | ESgI |
| 'Baboon Bottom' (BB) | CIri WCAu |
| 'Baby Bengal' (BB) | WCAu |
| 'Baby Blessed' (SDB) | CBro EFam SRGP WCAu |
| 'Baby Prince' (SDB) | EFam ESgI |
| 'Baccarat' (TB) | WCAu |
| 'Back in Black' (TB) | CKel |
| 'Bahloo' (TB) | EFam |
| 'Baie Rose' (IB) new | CBgR |
| 'Bajazzo' (La) | WCAu |
| ***bakeriana*** | EBrs ECho IHer LRHS NMin |
| 'Bal Masqué' (TB) | ESgI |
| ***baldschuanica*** | WWst |
| 'Ballerina' (TB) | NBir |
| 'Ballyhoo' (TB) | WCAu |
| 'Bamba' (SDB) | EFam |
| 'Banana Cream' (TB) | EFam |
| 'Banbury Beauty' (CH) $\Upsilon^{H3}$ | CLAP |
| 'Banbury Gem' (CH) | CSam |
| 'Banbury Melody' (CH) | CFee MAvo |
| 'Banbury Ruffles' (SDB) | ESgI NMen WAul WCAu |
| 'Bandera Waltz' (TB) | WCAu |
| 'Bang' (TB) | CKel |
| 'Bangles' (MTB) | ESgI WCAu |
| 'Bantam Prince' (SDB) | EFam |
| 'Bar de Nuit' (TB) | ESgI |
| 'Barbara's Kiss' (Spuria) | CIri WBIS |
| ***barbatula*** BWJ 7663 | WCru |
| 'Baria' (SDB) | GEdr |
| 'Barletta' (TB) | WCAu |
| 'Barn Dance' (TB) | EFam |
| 'Baroque Prelude' (TB) | CKel |
| 'Batik' (BB) | LRHS WCAu WCot |
| 'Batsford' (SDB) | CBro |
| 'Baubles and Beads' (MTB) new | ESgI |
| 'Bayberry Candle' (TB) | ESgI MWea WAul WCAu |
| 'Be a Devil' (TB) | EFam |
| 'Be Mine' (TB) | EFam |
| 'Be My Baby' (BB) | WCAu |
| 'Becalmed' (IB) | EFam |
| 'Bedtime Story' (IB) | EBee GBri SSvw SWat WCot |
| 'Before the Storm' (TB) | CKel ESgI LCro MSte WCAu |
| 'Beguine' (TB) | ESgI |
| 'Being Busy' (SDB) | ESgI |
| 'Bel Azur' (IB) | CBgR ESgI |
| 'Bel Esprit' (TB) | ESgI |
| 'Belise' (Spuria) $\Upsilon^{H4}$ | WBIS |
| 'Belissinado' (Spuria) | WBIS |
| 'Belvi Cloud' (TB) | EFam |
| 'Belvi Queen' (TB) | EFam MNrw |

| | Name | Suppliers |
|---|---|---|
| | 'Ben a Factor' (MTB) **new** | ESgI |
| | 'Benton Cordelia' (TB) | ESgI |
| | 'Benton Dierdre' (TB) | SRms |
| | 'Benton Nigel' (TB) | WCAu |
| | 'Benton Sheila' (TB) | CFee ECha |
| | 'Berkeley Gold' (TB) | CSBt EAEE EBee EBla ECtt ELan EPfP EWes GKir MSte MWat NOrc NVic SCoo SHBN SPer SWat WCAu |
| | 'Berlin Tiger' (SpH) $\Upsilon^{H4}$ | CAbx CRow EPPr EPfP GBin NBhm SApp WCAu |
| | 'Bermuda Triangle' (BB) **new** | CIri |
| | 'Berry Blush' (TB) | EFam |
| | 'Bess Bergin' (TB) | EFam |
| | 'Best Bet' (TB) | EFam ESgI LRHS WCAu |
| | 'Best Man' (TB) | EFam |
| | 'Bethany Claire' (TB) | EFam ESgI |
| | 'Betty Cooper' (Spuria) | ESgI WAul WCAu |
| | 'Betty Simon' (TB) | CKel CWCL ESgI ETod |
| | 'Beverly Sills' (TB) | CPar ESgI LCro LRHS MRav MSte SRGP WAul WCAu |
| | 'Bewilderbeast' (TB) | WCAu |
| | 'Bianco' (TB) | WCAu |
| | 'Bibury' (SDB) $\Upsilon^{H4}$ | EFam WCAu |
| | 'Big Dipper' (TB) | ECtt ESgI |
| | 'Big Melt' (TB) | CKel |
| | 'Big Money' (CH) $\Upsilon^{H3}$ | GBuc |
| | ***biglumis*** | see *I. lactea* |
| | ***biliottii*** | CBro |
| | 'Billie the Brownie' (MTB) **new** | ESgI |
| | 'Billionaire' (TB) | EFam |
| | 'Bishop's Robe' (TB) | SSvw |
| N | 'Black Beauty' (Dut) | EPfP LRHS |
| | 'Black Beauty' (TB) | SPer WFar |
| | 'Black Dragon' (TB) | SPad |
| | 'Black Gamecock' (La) | CFir CWCL EPPr LPBA MBNS NBPN NBro NMoo NOrc SMrm WCAu WHlf WMAq |
| | 'Black Hills' (TB) | EBee WCAu |
| | 'Black Ink' (TB) | COIW |
| | 'Black Knight' (TB) | EWll NGdn SPoG |
| | 'Black Night' (IB) | MWea SRGP WBor |
| | 'Black Out' (TB) **new** | SIri |
| | 'Black Sergeant' (TB) $\Upsilon^{H4}$ | CKel |
| | 'Black Stallion' (MDB) | ESgI |
| | 'Black Suited' (TB) | CIri |
| | 'Black Swan' (TB) | EAEE EBla ECha ECtt ELan EPfP ESgI EShb LPio LSRN MSte NBre SDnm SHBN SPla STes WAul WCAu WEas |
| | 'Black Taffeta' (TB) | CKel |
| | 'Black Tie Affair' (TB) | ESgI MSte WCAu |
| | 'Black Ware' (TB) | EFam |
| | 'Blackalicious' (TB) **new** | CIri |
| | 'Blackbeard' (BB) $\Upsilon^{H4}$ | CKel WCAu |
| | 'Blackcurrant' (IB) | WAul |
| | 'Blackout' (TB) | EFam ESgI LRHS |
| | 'Blast' (IB) | CKel |
| | 'Blatant' (TB) | EFam ESgI WCAu |
| | 'Blazing Light' (TB) | ESgI |
| | 'Blazing Saddles' (TB) | EMic |
| | 'Blazing Sunrise' (TB) **new** | ESgI |
| | 'Blenheim Royal' (TB) | ESgI WCAu |
| | 'Blessed Again' (IB) | EFam |
| | 'Blessed Assurance' (IB) | EFam GKir |
| | 'Blitz' (SDB) | EFam |
| | 'Blitzen' (IB) | WCAu |
| N | 'Blousy Blouse' | EFam |
| | 'Blue Ballerina' (CH) $\Upsilon^{H3}$ | GBuc |
| | 'Blue Bossa' (CH) $\Upsilon^{H4}$ **new** | WBIS |
| | 'Blue Crusader' (TB) | CIri WBIS WCAu |
| | 'Blue Denim' (SDB) | CBro ECho ECtt EPfP GMaP MBNS MRav NBir NBro NMoo WCAu WCot WHoo WTin |
| | 'Blue Eyed Blond' (IB) | MWea WCAu |
| | 'Blue Eyed Brunette' (TB) | ESgI WCAu |
| | 'Blue Fin' (TB) | EFam WCAu |
| | 'Blue for You' (TB) | EFam |
| | 'Blue Hendred' (SDB) | NBir WCAu |
| | 'Blue Horizon' (TB) | ERos |
| | 'Blue Lamp' (TB) | CKel WBIS |
| | 'Blue Line' (SDB) $\Upsilon^{H4}$ | CDes NBre |
| | 'Blue Luster' (TB) $\Upsilon^{H4}$ | ESgI |
| | 'Blue Meadow Fly' (Sino-Sib) | EBee |
| | 'Blue Moonlight' (TB) | EFam |
| N | 'Blue Mystery' | WWst |
| | 'Blue Note Blues' (TB) | WCAu |
| | 'Blue Pigmy' (SDB) | CPBP CWat EBla ERos MBNS NMen NSti SBch SPer SPet |
| | 'Blue Pools' (SDB) | MBri MSte NBir WTin |
| | 'Blue Reflection' (TB) | ESgI |
| | 'Blue Rhythm' (TB) | CKel EAEE EBla EFam ELan ELon EPfP GMaP LCro MRav MSte NBre NMoo SCoo SPer SPhx WAul WCAu WMnd |
| | 'Blue Sapphire' (TB) | ESgI SHBN WCAu |
| | 'Blue Shimmer' (TB) | CSBt CWGN EAEE EBee EBla ECha ELan EPfP ESgI ETod MSte MWat NCGa NGdn SBch SHBN SPer SPet SPla SPoG SWat WCAu WCra |
| | 'Blue Staccato' (TB) | CKel ESgI SMrm WCAu |
| | 'Blue Suede Shoes' (TB) | ESgI |
| | 'Blue Velvet' (TB) | WMoo |
| * | 'Blue Warlsind' (J) | WWst |
| | 'Bluebird Wine' (TB) | WCAu |
| | 'Blushing Moon' (TB) **new** | WBIS |
| | 'Bob Nichol' (TB) $\Upsilon^{H4}$ | CKel WBIS |
| | 'Bodacious' (TB) | EFam ESgI |
| | 'Bohemia Sekt' (TB) | CKel |
| | 'Bohemian' (TB) | CWCL ESgI |
| | 'Boisterous' (BB) | WCAu |
| | 'Bold Gold' (TB) | EFam |
| | 'Bold Look' (TB) | ESgI |
| | 'Bold Pretender' (La) | EPfP MBNS MBri |
| | 'Bold Print' (IB) | CWan EAEE EBee EBla SPoG WAul WCAu WCra |
| | 'Bollinger' | see *I.* 'Hornpipe' |
| | 'Bonnie Davenport' (TB) | CIri |
| | 'Bonny' (MDB) | CBro |
| | 'Bonus Bucks' (TB) | CKel |
| | 'Bonus Mama' (TB) | EFam |
| | 'Boo' (SDB) | CKel WAul WCAu |
| | 'Bourgeois' (SDB) **new** | CIri |
| | 'Bouzy Bouzy' (TB) | ESgI |
| | ***bracteata*** | CPBP GBuc WPer |
| | – JCA 13427 | CLAP |
| | 'Braggadocio' (TB) | CWCL WCAu |
| | 'Braithwaite' (TB) | CKel EAEE EBee EBla ELan ESgI IPot MSte NBre SHBN SPer SPur SRms SWat WAul WCAu |
| | 'Brannigan' (SDB) | CBro MBri NBir NSti WPen |
| | 'Brasero' (TB) **new** | CWCL ECtt |
| | 'Brasilia' (TB) | NBir NBre |
| | 'Brass Tacks' (SDB) | EFam WCAu |
| | 'Brassie' (SDB) | CBro ERos GKir MBNS NBro NMoo SHGN |
| | 'Brave New World' (TB) $\Upsilon^{H4}$ | CIri |
| | 'Brazilian Holiday' (TB) | WAul |
| | 'Breakers' (TB) $\Upsilon^{H4}$ | CKel ESgI WCAu |
| | 'Breezy Blue' (SDB) | WCAu |
| § | 'Bride' (DB) | WMnd |
| | 'Bride's Halo' (TB) | LSRN WCAu |

| | | |
|---|---|---|
| N | 'Brigantino' (BB) | ESgI |
| | 'Bright Button' (SDB) | CBgR CKel ESgI |
| | 'Bright Chic' (SDB) | ESgI |
| | 'Bright Child' (SDB) | WCAu |
| | 'Bright Fire' (TB) | SIri |
| | 'Bright Moment' (SDB) | EFam |
| | 'Bright Vision' (SDB) | ESgI |
| | 'Bright White' (MDB) | CBro CKel ECho ERos NMen SMrm |
| N | 'Bright Yellow' (DB) | MRav |
| | 'Brighteyes' (IB) | SRms |
| | 'Brindisi' (TB) | ESgI WCAu |
| | 'Brise de Mer' (TB) | ESgI |
| | 'Broad Shoulders' (TB) **new** | WAul |
| | 'Broadleigh Angela' (CH) | CBro GKir |
| | 'Broadleigh Ann' (CH) | CBro |
| | 'Broadleigh Carolyn' (CH) $\mathbb{Y}^{H3}$ | CBro CWsd |
| N | 'Broadleigh Charlotte' (CH) | CBro |
| N | 'Broadleigh Clare' (CH) | CBro |
| | 'Broadleigh Dorothy' (CH) | CBro GGar |
| | 'Broadleigh Elizabeth' (CH) | CBro |
| N | 'Broadleigh Emily' (CH) | CBro |
| N | 'Broadleigh Jean' (CH) | CBro |
| | 'Broadleigh Joan' (CH) | CBro CWsd |
| | 'Broadleigh Joyce' (CH) | CBro |
| | 'Broadleigh Lavinia' (CH) | CBro MAvo |
| | 'Broadleigh Mitre' (CH) | CBro CElw |
| | 'Broadleigh Nancy' (CH) | CBro MAvo |
| | 'Broadleigh Peacock' (CH) | CBro CElw CWsd EShb MAvo |
| | 'Broadleigh Penny' (CH) **new** | CBro |
| N | 'Broadleigh Rose' (CH) | CBro CElw CWsd EHrv EPyc GBuc GKir MBrN MRav MWte SApp SIri SWal WSHC |
| | 'Broadleigh Sybil' (CH) | CBro GKir |
| | 'Broadleigh Victoria' (CH) | CBro GBuc |
| | 'Broadway Baby' (IB) | ESgI WAul |
| | 'Broadway Doll' (BB) | EFam |
| | 'Brom Bones' (SDB) | EFam |
| | 'Bromyard' (SDB) $\mathbb{Y}^{H4}$ | CBro WCAu |
| | 'Bronzaire' (IB) $\mathbb{Y}^{H4}$ | CKel EFam ESgI WCAu WGwG |
| I | 'Bronze Beauty' (Dut) **new** | SBch |
| | 'Bronze Beauty' Van Tubergen (*boogiana* hybrid) | EPfP LRHS MWat NBir SPer WFar |
| | 'Bronzed Aussie' (TB) | CIri |
| | 'Bronzed Violet' (TB) | CKel |
| | 'Brother Carl' (TB) | EFam |
| N | 'Brown Chocolate' (TB) | WCAu |
| | 'Brown Duet' (TB) | EFam |
| | 'Brown Lasso' (BB) $\mathbb{Y}^{H4}$ | LRHS WCAu |
| N | 'Brummit's Mauve' (TB) | WCAu |
| | 'Bruno' (TB) | LSRN |
| | 'Brussels' (TB) | ESgI |
| | ***bucharica*** misapplied | see *I. orchioides* Carrière |
| | ***bucharica*** ambig. | CAvo CTca EBla EBrs ECho IFro IHer NCGa NWCA SMrm WBor WHil WWst |
| § | ***bucharica*** Foster $\mathbb{Y}^{H3-4}$ | CBgR CBro CPom CPrp CSam EBee EBrs ECho EPfP EPot GKev LAma LRHS WCAu |
| | - 'Princess' | CTca EBrs ECho LRHS SPhx |
| N | - 'Sanglok' | WWst |
| | - 'Top Gold' | EBrs ECho WWst |
| | ***bucharica* x *orchioides*** | WWst |
| | 'Buckwheat' (TB) | EFam SIri |
| | 'Buddy Boy' (SDB) | WCAu |
| | 'Bugles and Horns' (TB) | EFam |
| | 'Bugsy' (MDB) | ESgI |
| | 'Buisson de Roses' (TB) | ESgI |
| | ***bulleyana*** | CSec ECho GAuc GBBs GKev NWCA SRms WAbe WCot |
| | - ACE 2296 | EBee GBuc |
| | - black-flowered | EBee GKev GKir |
| | 'Bumblebee Deelite' (MTB) $\mathbb{Y}^{H4}$ | CKel WCAu |
| | ***bungei*** | GAuc |
| | 'Burgundy Party' (TB) | ESgI |
| | 'Burka' (TB) | ESgI |
| | 'Burnt Toffee' (TB) | ESgI WAul |
| | 'Busy Being Blue' (TB) | EFam |
| | 'Butter Pecan' (IB) | WCAu |
| | 'Buttercup Bower' (TB) | WCAu |
| | 'Buttermere' (TB) | SRms |
| | 'Butterpat' (IB) | EFam ESgI |
| | 'Butterscotch Carpet' (SDB) | EFam WCAu |
| | 'Butterscotch Kiss' (TB) | CSBt EAEE EBee EBla ECGP ELan LDai MBNS MRav NBir SDnm SHBN SPer |
| | 'Bye Bye Blues' (TB) | EFam ESgI |
| | 'Cabaret Royale' (TB) | ESgI WCAu |
| | 'Cable Car' (TB) | CKel CWCL ECtt ESgI |
| | 'Cahoots' (SDB) | EFam |
| | 'Caliente' (TB) | COIW CWGN EPfP ESgI EWll MRav SPet WBor WCAu |
| | 'California Boy' (SDB) **new** | CIri |
| | 'California Style' (IB) | ESgI |
| § | Californian hybrids | CAby CElw CPBP CWCL EPot GCra MCot NBir WBor WCFE WCot |
| | 'Calliope Magic' (TB) | EFam |
| | 'Calm Stream' (TB) $\mathbb{Y}^{H4}$ | CKel WBIS |
| | 'Cambridge Blue' | see *I.* 'Monspur Cambridge Blue' |
| | 'Camelot Rose' (TB) | WCAu |
| | 'Cameo Blush' (BB) | EFam |
| | 'Cameo Wine' (TB) | ECtt EFam EPPr ESgI |
| | 'Cameroun' (TB) | ESgI |
| | 'Campbellii' | see *I. lutescens* 'Campbellii' |
| | ***canadensis*** | see *I. hookeri* |
| | 'Canaveral' (TB) | EFam |
| | 'Candy Clouds' (TB) | WCAu |
| | 'Candy Queen' (SDB) | EFam |
| | 'Candyland' (BB) | EFam |
| | 'Candylane' (MTB) | CKel |
| | 'Cannington Bluebird' (TB) | WCAu |
| | 'Cannington Ochre' (SDB) | CBro |
| | 'Cannington Skies' (IB) | EFam |
| | 'Cantab' (Reticulata) | CAvo CBro CFFs EBrs ECho EPot ERCP GBin GKev LAma LHop LRHS SPer SPhx |
| | 'Cantina' (TB) | EFam |
| | ***capnoides* x *orchioides*** (J) **new** | WWst |
| | 'Capricious' (TB) | ESgI |
| | 'Capricorn Cooler' (TB) | EFam |
| | 'Captain Gallant' (TB) | WCAu |
| | 'Captain Indigo' (IB) | CKel ESgI |
| | 'Caption' (TB) | ESgI |
| | 'Captive' (IB) | EFam |
| | 'Caramba' (TB) | WCAu |
| | 'Carats' (SDB) | EFam |
| | 'Carenza' (BB) | CKel |
| | 'Carilla' (SDB) | ERos |
| | 'Carnaby' (TB) | CPar EAEE EBla ESgI MBri MSte STes WCAu WWlt |
| | 'Carnival Song' (TB) | WCAu |
| | 'Carnival Time' (TB) | CWGN EAEE EBee EBla ECGP ECtt EShb IPot LAst LBuc LDai SPer STes WAul WCra |
| | 'Carnton' (TB) | WEas |
| | 'Carolyn Rose' (MTB) $\mathbb{Y}^{H4}$ | NBre |
| N | 'Caronte' (IB) | ESgI |
| | 'Carriwitched' (IB) | CKel |
| | 'Cascade Sprite' (SDB) | SRms |
| | 'Cast a Spell' (TB) | EFam |
| | 'Cat's Eye' (SDB) | CIri |

| | | |
|---|---|---|
| | 'Cayenne Capers' (TB) | ESgI |
| N | 'Cedric Morris' | EWes WEas |
| | 'Celebration Song' (TB) | CWCL ESgI WAul WCAu |
| | 'Celestial Flame' (TB) | LRHS |
| | 'Celestial Glory' (TB) | WCAu |
| | 'Celestial Happiness' (TB) | EFam |
| | 'Celsius' (SDB) | EFam |
| | 'Celtic Glory' (TB) **new** | WAul |
| | 'Cerdagne' (TB) | ESgI |
| | 'Certainly Certainly' (TB) | EFam |
| | ***chamaeiris*** | see *I. lutescens* |
| | 'Champagne Elegance' (TB) | ECtt EFam ESgI NBir WAul WCAu |
| | 'Champagne Encore' (IB) | ESgI |
| | 'Champagne Frost' (TB) | EFam WCAu |
| | 'Champagne Music' (TB) | WCAu |
| | 'Champagne Waltz' (TB) | CWCL EFam |
| | 'Chance Beauty' (SpecHybrid) 🏆H4 | WCAu |
| | 'Change of Pace' (TB) | ESgI WCAu |
| | 'Chanted' (SDB) | EFam EPPr ESgI WCAu |
| | 'Chantilly' (TB) | CMil EAEE EBee EBla ECGP ELan EPfP LPio MRav MSte NBir NGdn SDnm SPer SWat WFoF |
| | 'Chapeau' (TB) | ESgI WCAu |
| | 'Chapel Bells' (TB) | CKel |
| | 'Charlotte Maria' (TB) | CKel |
| | 'Chartreuse Ruffles' (TB) | ECtt LCro |
| | 'Char-true' (Spuria) | WCAu |
| | 'Chasing Rainbows' (TB) | WCAu |
| | 'Chaste White' (TB) | EFam ESgI |
| | 'Chatter' (TB) | EFam |
| N | 'Cherished' (TB) | EBee GBin |
| | 'Cherokee Lace' (Spuria) | WTin |
| | 'Cherry Blossom Special' (TB) | CIri |
| | 'Cherry Garden' (SDB) | CBro CKel EAEE EBee EBla ECtt EFam EGoo EHrv ELan EPfP EWes GEdr LEdu MBNS MBri MRav MSte NBir NGdn NMoo NSti NWCA WAul WBor WCot WEas |
| | 'Cherry Smoke' (TB) | WCAu |
| | 'Cherub Tears' (SDB) | WCAu |
| | 'Cherub's Smile' (TB) | ESgI |
| | 'Chevalier de Malte' (TB) **new** | ESgI |
| | 'Chickasaw Sue' (BB) | EFam |
| | 'Chickee' (MTB) 🏆H4 | CKel |
| | 'Chicken Little' (MDB) | CBro EBee NMoo |
| | 'Chief Moses' (TB) | WCAu |
| I | 'Chieftain' (SDB) | MRav |
| | 'China Dragon' (TB) | SWat |
| | 'China Nights' (TB) **new** | ESgI |
| | 'China Seas' (TB) | NBre |
| | 'Chinese Empress' (TB) | EFam |
| | 'Chinese Treasure' (TB) **new** | WAul |
| | 'Chinook Winds' (TB) | ESgI |
| | 'Chivalry' (TB) | ESgI WTin |
| | 'Chocolate Marmalade' (TB) **new** | ECtt |
| | 'Chocolate Spray' (J) **new** | WWst |
| | 'Chocolate Vanilla' (TB) | ESgI WCAu |
| | 'Chorus Girl' (TB) | CKel |
| | 'Christmas Angel' (TB) | WCAu |
| | 'Christopher Columbus' (TB) | EFam |
| | ***chrysographes*** 🏆H4 | Widely available |
| I | - 'Black Beauty' | CFir ECho EPfP |
| I | - 'Black Knight' | CMdw EDAr ELon EPfP GBuc GCal GCra GGar LHop MDun MHer MSte NBid NCGa NChi NLar SHGN SMad SWat WBor WGwG WMnd |
| | - black-flowered | Widely available |
| | - blue-flowered | EDAr |
| N | - 'Ellenbank Nightshade' | CBgR GMac |
| N | - 'Inshriach' | GBuc LEdu WAbe |
| N | - 'Kew Black' | ECho EShb LEdu NBir NChi NHol NWCA WHer WHil |
| | - 'Mandarin Purple' | CBgR GBuc GCal MBri SPer SWat WMoo |
| | - red-flowered | ECho |
| | - 'Rob'ECho | |
| § | - 'Rubella' | CRow ECho GCra MSte NCot WFar WHil WPrP |
| | - 'Rubens' **new** | GCal |
| | - 'Rubra' | see *I. chrysographes* 'Rubella' |
| N | - 'Tsiri' | NWCA |
| | - yellow-flowered | GKir |
| | ***chrysographes* x *forrestii*** | GBin GKir NBir |
| | ***chrysophylla*** | GBuc |
| | - JCA 13233 | CLAP |
| | 'Chubby Cheeks' (SDB) | CKel WCAu |
| | 'Chuck Waltermire' (TB) | EFam |
| | 'Chuckwagon' (TB) | ESgI |
| | 'Church Stoke' (SDB) | WCAu |
| N | 'Cider Haze' (TB) | CKel |
| | 'Cimarron Rose' (SDB) | EFam ESgI WCAu |
| | 'Cinnabar Red' (Spuria) | WAul |
| | 'Cinnamon Apples' (MDB) | ESgI |
| | 'Cinnamon Roll' (Spuria) | WCAu |
| | 'Cinnamon Stick' (Spuria) | CIri |
| | 'City Lights' (TB) | EFam WCAu |
| | 'Claire Doodle' (MTB) **new** | ESgI |
| | 'Clairette' (Reticulata) | ECho EPot LAma NMin |
| | 'Clara Garland' (IB) 🏆H4 | CKel EFam WCAu |
| | 'Clarence' (TB) | EFam ESgI WCAu |
| | ***clarkei*** | CPrp GKir WCot WFar |
| | - B&SWJ 2122 | WCru |
| | - CC 2751 | NWCA |
| | 'Class Act' (TB) | EFam |
| | 'Classic Hues' (TB) | ESgI |
| | 'Classic Look' (TB) | ESgI |
| | 'Classico' (TB) | EFam |
| | 'Clay's Caper' (SDB) | NBre |
| | 'Clear Morning Sky' (TB) 🏆H4 | EPfP |
| N | 'Cleo' (TB) | CKel NBir NSti |
| | 'Cleo Murrell' (TB) | ESgI |
| | 'Cliffs of Dover' (TB) | CKel EFam ESgI GCal LCro MCot SGar SIri SRms |
| N | 'Climbing Gold' | ECho |
| | 'Close Your Eyes' (TB) | EFam |
| | 'Cloud Fire' (TB) | EFam |
| | 'Cloud Mistress' (IB) | ESgI |
| | 'Cloud Pinnacle' (IB) | CKel |
| | 'Cloudcap' (TB) | SRms |
| | 'Cloudia' (TB) | EFam |
| | 'Clyde Redmond' (La) 🏆H4 | WMAq |
| | 'Coalignition' (TB) | WCAu |
| | 'Codicil' (TB) | ESgI WCAu |
| | 'Colette Thurillet' (TB) | ESgI WCAu |
| | ***collettii*** | EBee EBrs ECho |
| | 'Colonial Gold' (TB) | WCAu |
| | 'Color Brite' (BB) | EFam |
| | 'Colorific' (La) | EPPr EPfP NBro NMoo WBor WHlf |
| | 'Colortart' (TB) | LRHS |
| | 'Colorwatch' (TB) | EFam |
| | 'Combo' (SDB) | CKel |
| | 'Come to Me' (TB) | EFam |
| | 'Coming Up Roses' (TB) | WCAu |
| | 'Compact Buddy' (MDB) | ESgI |
| | 'Con Fuoco' (TB) | ESgI |
| | 'Concertina' (IB) | CIri |
| | 'Confetti' (TB) | MBri |

| | | |
|---|---|---|
| | ***confusa*** 🏆H3 | CAbP CHEx CSev EShb LEdu SAPC SArc SBig SEND SMad WBrk WFar WPic WRos WWst |
| N | – 'Martyn Rix' | CBct CDes CFwr CGHE CHEx CHid CLAP CPen CPou CSpe EBee ELon EPfP GCal IGor LFur MAvo MLHP SChr WCot WFar WGwG WHil WMnd WPGP WPer WPic |
| | 'Congo Bongo' (BB) **new** | WAul |
| | 'Conjuration' (TB) | EFam ESgI WCAu |
| | 'Connect the Dots' (MTB) | WCAu |
| | 'Constant Wattez' (IB) | CKel EBee ESgI NLar |
| | 'Cool Melodrama' (SDB) | EFam |
| | 'Copatonic' (TB) | ESgI WCAu |
| | 'Copper Classic' (TB) | ESgI WCAu |
| | 'Cops' (SDB) | ESgI |
| | 'Coquetterie' (TB) | ESgI |
| | 'Coral Chalice' (TB) | EFam LRHS |
| | 'Coral Charmer' (TB) | EFam |
| | 'Coral Joy' (TB) | EFam |
| | 'Coral Point' (TB) | EFam WCAu |
| | 'Coral Strand' (TB) | WCAu |
| | 'Cordoba' (TB) | WCAu |
| | 'Corn Harvest' (TB) | EFam |
| | 'Corps de Ballet' (TB) | CIri |
| | 'Countess Zeppelin' (Spuria) | ESgI |
| | 'County Town Red' (TB) | CIri SIri |
| | 'Court Magician' (SDB) | SIri |
| | 'Cowboy in Black' (TB) **new** | CIri |
| | 'Cozy Calico' (TB) | ESgI WCAu |
| | 'Crackles' (TB) | CKel |
| | 'Crackling Caldera' (TB) **new** | CIri |
| | 'Cranapple' (BB) 🏆H4 | CIri WAul WCAu |
| | 'Cranberry Crush' (TB) | LRHS WCAu |
| | 'Cranberry Sauce' (TB) | CIri |
| | 'Cream and Peaches' (SDB) | SIri |
| | 'Cream Beauty' (Dut) | EBrs |
| | 'Cream Pixie' (SDB) | EFam WCAu |
| | 'Cream Soda' (TB) 🏆H4 | CKel WBIS |
| | 'Creative Stitchery' (TB) | EFam |
| | 'Crème d'Or' (TB) | EFam ESgI |
| | 'Crème Glacée' (TB) | ESgI |
| | ***cretensis*** | see *I. unguicularis* subsp. *cretensis* |
| | 'Crimson Tiger' (TB) | EFam |
| | 'Crinoline' (TB) | CKel |
| | 'Crispette' (TB) | WCAu |
| | ***cristata*** 🏆H4 | CPBP GBuc LEdu NHar NLar NPro SIng SRms WCru |
| | – 'Alba' | CWsd ERos LRHS NWCA WAbe |
| | ***cristata*** x ***lacustris*** | NMen |
| | ***croatica*** | ESgI |
| | ***crocea*** 🏆H4 | GBin |
| | 'Croftway Lemon' (TB) | ELon |
| | 'Cross Current' (TB) | WCAu |
| | 'Cross Stitch' (TB) | EFam |
| | 'Crowned Heads' (TB) | CKel ESgI WAul WCAu |
| | 'Crownette' (SDB) | CKel |
| | 'Crushed Velvet' (TB) | WCAu |
| | 'Crystal Blue' (TB) **new** | LCro |
| | 'Crystal Glitters' (TB) | ESgI |
| | ***cuniculiformis*** | GAuc |
| | – ACE 2224 | GBuc |
| | 'Cup Cake' (MDB) | ESgI |
| | 'Cup Race' (TB) | WCAu |
| | 'Cupid's Cup' (SDB) | ESgI |
| | 'Curlew' (IB) | WCAu |
| | 'Curtain Up' (TB) | EFam |
| | 'Cute Orange Horn' (BB) | EFam |
| | 'Cutie' (IB) | ESgI WAul WCAu |
| | 'Cyanea' (DB) | ECho EFam |
| | ***cycloglossa*** | CPBP EBrs ECho EPot LRHS WCot WWst |
| | 'Daffodil Cloud' (TB) | EFam |
| | 'Dance Away' (TB) | ESgI WCAu |
| | 'Dance for Joy' (TB) | EFam |
| | 'Dancer's Veil' (TB) | CHar ECtt ESgI IPot MRav NBre NVic SPer WCAu |
| | 'Dancing Lilacs' (MTB) **new** | ESgI |
| | 'Dandy' (TB) **new** | ESgI |
| | 'Dandy Candy' (TB) | CIri WBIS |
| | ***danfordiae*** | CAvo CBcs CBro CFFs CTca EBrs ECho EPfP EPot GKev LAma LRHS NHol SGar SMeo SPet WFar WGwG |
| | 'Danger' (TB) | ESgI |
| | 'Dante's Inferno' (TB) | EFam |
| | 'Dardanus' (AB) | CMea EBrs ECho EPot ERCP LRHS WCot |
| | 'Dark Crystal' (SDB) | EFam ESgI |
| | 'Dark Rosaleen' (TB) 🏆H4 | NBre |
| | 'Dark Spark' (SDB) | WCAu |
| | 'Dark Twilight' (TB) | EFam |
| | 'Dark Vader' (SDB) | ESgI WCAu |
| | 'Darkling' (SDB) | EFam |
| | ***darwasica*** **new** | GAuc WWst |
| | 'Dash Away' (SDB) | ESgI SIri |
| | 'Dashing' (TB) | EFam |
| | 'Daughter of Stars' (TB) | ESgI WBIS |
| | 'Dauntless' (TB) | ESgI |
| | 'David Guest' (IB) | CKel |
| | 'Dawn of Fall' (TB) | EFam ESgI |
| | 'Dawning' (TB) 🏆H4 | CIri ESgI WBIS |
| | 'Dazzle Me' (SDB) | WCAu |
| | 'Dazzling Gold' (TB) | ESgI WCAu |
| | 'Death by Chocolate' (SDB) | CIri ESgI |
| § | ***decora*** | NWCA WCot |
| | 'Deep Black' (TB) | CKel CPar EAEE EBla EHrv ELan EPfP IPot LFCN LSRN MAvo MBNS MCot MRav MSte MWat NOrc SDnm SHBN SPer SWat WAul WCAu |
| | 'Deep Caress' (TB) | ESgI |
| | 'Deep Pacific' (TB) | MBri WCAu |
| | 'Deep Space' (TB) | WCAu |
| | 'Deft Touch' (TB) | CKel WCAu |
| | 'Deity' (TB) | EFam |
| | ***delavayi*** 🏆H4 | EBee ECho EWes GAuc GBin GMaP IBlr MLLN NLAp WPrP |
| | – SDR 50 | GKev |
| | 'Delicate Lady' (IB) 🏆H4 | CKel |
| | 'Delirium' (IB) **new** | WAul |
| | 'Delta Butterfly' (La) | WMAq |
| | 'Demelza' (TB) | CKel |
| | 'Demon' (SDB) | CKel |
| | 'Denys Humphry' (TB) | CKel WCAu |
| | 'Deputé Nomblot' (TB) | ESgI |
| | 'Derwentwater' (TB) | SRms WCAu |
| | 'Desert Country' (SDB) | EFam |
| | 'Desert Dream' (AB) | GGar |
| I | 'Desert Dream' (Sino-Sib) | GAbr |
| | 'Desert Echo' (TB) | COIW SPet |
| | 'Desert Orange' (SDB) | EFam |
| | 'Desert Song' (TB) | CKel EFam WCAu |
| | 'Destination' (Spuria) 🏆H4 **new** | CIri |
| | 'Destry Rides Again' (TB) | EFam |
| | 'Devil David' (TB) **new** | CIri |
| | 'Devil May Care' (IB) | CIri |
| | 'Devilish Nature' (SDB) **new** | CIri |
| | 'Devonshire Cream' (TB) **new** | CIri |
| | 'Diabolique' (TB) | CIri |
| | 'Diamond Doll' (BB) | EFam |
| | 'Diligence' (SDB) 🏆H4 | CKel |

| | | |
|---|---|---|
| | 'Disco Jewel' (MTB) | ESgI |
| | 'Distant Roads' (TB) | WCAu |
| | 'Ditto' (MDB) | EFam |
| | 'Diversion' (TB) **new** | ESgI |
| | 'Divine' (TB) | CKel |
| | 'Dixie Darling' (TB) | ESgI |
| | 'Dixie Pixie' (SDB) | WCAu WTin |
| | 'Doctor No' (TB) | EFam |
| | 'Dolce Acqua' (TB) | CIri |
| | ***dolichosiphon*** | GAuc |
| | aff. ***dolichosiphon*** **new** | GAuc |
| | 'Dolly Madison' (TB) | ESgI |
| | 'Don Juan' (TB) | ESgI |
| | 'Donegal' (IB) | EFam |
| | 'Don't Touch' (TB) **new** | CIri |
| | 'Doodads' (TB) | CIri ESgI WCAu |
| | 'Doodle Strudel' | EFam |
| | 'Doozey' (MDB) | ESgI |
| | 'Dorcas Lives Again' (TB) | EFam |
| | 'Double Byte' (SDB) | EFam |
| | 'Double Espoir' (TB) | ESgI SCoo |
| | 'Double Lament' (SDB) | CBro ERos |
| | 'Double Time' (TB) | EFam |
| | 'Doublemint' (TB) | EFam |
| | ***douglasiana*** ♀H4 | CPen CSec ECho EShb GCal GKev MLLN NWCA SKHP WFar WTin |
| | 'Dovedale' (TB) ♀H4 | EFam WCAu |
| | 'Dover Beach' (TB) | SGar |
| | 'Draco' (TB) | ESgI |
| | 'Dragone' (TB) **new** | CIri |
| | 'Drake Carne' (TB) | CKel |
| | 'Drama Queen' (TB) | CIri |
| | 'Drambuie' (SDB) | EFam |
| | 'Dream Indigo' (IB) | CKel WCAu |
| | 'Dream Lover' (TB) | ESgI |
| | 'Dreamsicle' (TB) | SIri |
| | 'Dresden Candleglow' (IB) | WCAu |
| | 'Driftwood' (Spuria) ♀H4 | WBIS |
| | 'Drum Song' (IB) | EFam |
| | 'Dualtone' (TB) | CKel |
| | 'Dude Ranch' (TB) | CIri |
| | 'Duke of Earl' (TB) | EFam |
| | 'Dunlin' (MDB) | CBro ERos NBir NMen |
| | 'Dural White Butterfly' (La) | CHid CSpe LAst |
| | 'Dusky Challenger' (TB) | CKel ESgI LCro MRav SCoo WAul WCAu |
| | 'Dusky Evening' (TB) **new** | ESgI |
| | 'Dutch Chocolate' (TB) | ESgI ETod LCro WCAu |
| | 'Dwight Enys' (TB) ♀H4 | CKel |
| | 'Dynamite' (TB) | WAul |
| | 'Eagle Control' (TB) | EFam |
| | 'Eagle's Flight' (TB) | CKel |
| | 'Earl of Essex' (TB) | EFam LRHS WCAu |
| | 'Early Frost' (IB) | CKel EPPr LCro WAul |
| | 'Early Light' (TB) ♀H4 | ESgI WCAu |
| | 'Earthborn' (TB) | EFam |
| | 'East Indies' (TB) | WCAu |
| | 'Easter Tide' (La) | WCAu |
| | 'Eastertime' (TB) | ECtt ESgI |
| | 'Echo Beach' (TB) | EFam |
| | 'Echo de France' (TB) | ESgI |
| | 'Ecstatic Echo' (TB) | ESgI |
| | 'Ecstatic Night' (TB) | WCAu |
| | 'Edge of Winter' (TB) | CKel SIri |
| | 'Edith Wolford' (TB) | CWCL EBee ECtt ESgI EWll GBin MWea SRGP WBor WCAu WCot WCra |
| N | 'Ed's Blue' (DB) | ELan |
| | 'Edward' (Reticulata) | CBro EBrs ECho EPfP EPot GKev LAma LRHS MWat SMrm WCAu WFar |
| | 'Edward of Windsor' (TB) | CMil ELan GMaP LPio MSte NLar SDnm SRGP WCAu WMnd |
| | 'Eggnog' (TB) | EFam |
| | 'Egyptian' (TB) | EFam |
| | 'Eileen Louise' (TB) ♀H4 | EFam WCAu |
| | 'Elainealope' (TB) | EFam |
| | 'Eleanor Clare' (IB) ♀H4 | CKel LCro |
| | 'Eleanor Hill' (Spuria) | WAul |
| | 'Eleanor's Pride' (TB) | CKel EFam ESgI WCAu |
| | 'Electrique' (TB) | WCAu |
| | ***elegantissima*** | see *I. iberica* subsp. *elegantissima* |
| | 'Elizabeth Arden' (TB) | CKel |
| | 'Elizabeth of England' (TB) | COIW EWll SPet SRGP |
| | 'Elizabeth Poldark' (TB) | ESgI WCAu |
| N | 'Ellenbank Damselfly' | CBgR GMac |
| N | 'Ellenbank Sapphire' | GMac |
| | 'Elsa Sass' (TB) | ESgI |
| N | 'Elvinhall' | CBro |
| | 'Emmanuel' (TB) | EFam |
| | 'Empress of India' (TB) | EBee |
| | 'Encircle' (CH) | GBuc |
| | 'Encre Bleue' (IB) | CBgR ESgI |
| | 'English Charm' (TB) | EFam ESgI WAul WCAu |
| | 'English Cottage' (TB) | COIW EBee EFam ELon GCal LSRN MWat NLar WCAu |
| | 'English Knight' (TB) | EFam |
| | 'Ennerdale' (TB) | SRms |
| | 'Ennoble' (TB) | CIri ESgI |
| § | ***ensata*** ♀H4 | CBcs CBro CDWL CHEx COIW ECGP ELan EMFW EPfP EWTr GKev GKir LCro LPBA LRHS MNrw MWat NBro NCob NGdn NLar SPlb SRms SWat WCAu WCFE WFar WPer |
| N | - 'Activity' | CRow NBro NGby SHar WFar WPrP |
| | - 'Alba' | ECha |
| | - 'Aicho-no-kagalaku' | CBow |
| | - 'Aldridge Prelude' | WAul |
| | - 'Aoigata' | CPrp |
| | - 'Apollo' | CBen CRow |
| | - 'Artist' | NBro |
| | - 'Asian Warrior' **new** | CElw |
| | - 'August Emperor' | CBgR LAst NBhm |
| | - 'Azuma-kagami' | CBgR CFir EBee ELan NCGa |
| | - 'Barr Purple East' ♀H4 | CHid CPrp CRow |
| | - 'Beni-tsubaki' | ESgI WAul |
| I | - 'Blue King' | MBlu NBro |
| I | - 'Blue Peter' | CBen CRow |
| | - 'Blue Pompon' **new** | NMoo |
| | - 'Blue Prince' | CBen |
| N | - 'Blush' | NBro |
| | - 'Butterflies in Flight' | CRow |
| | - 'Caprician Butterfly' ♀H4 | CMHG EPfP ESgI EWTr GAbr GBin NBhm NMoo SMrm WAul WCAu |
| N | - 'Carnival Prince' | CFir NBro SBod WFar WMoo WPnP |
| | - 'Cascade Crest' | WAul |
| | - 'Cascade Spice' | WAul |
| | - 'Center of Interest' | NCGa |
| N | - 'Chico Geisho' | ESgI WAul |
| | - 'Chitose-no-tomo' | CRow |
| | - 'Chiyodajō' | CKel |
| | - 'Crepe Paper' | WFar |
| N | - 'Cry of Rejoice' | EBee ECho EWll GBri NBhm NBre NBro SMrm SWat WAul WCAu WFar |
| | - 'Crystal Halo' | NMoo |
| | - 'Dace' | EBee GBin |
| | - 'Dancing Waves' | CRow |
| I | - 'Darling' | CPen CRow CSam EBee ECho EPfP EWTr IBlr NBro NLar SRGP SWat WAul WCAu WFar WMoo |
| | - 'Diomedes' | ESgI |
| | - 'Dramatic Moment' | GBuc SIri WFar |
| I | - 'Dresden China' | CRow |
| N | - 'Eden's Blue Pearl' | CHid CMMP EBee EGle GBin IPot NBro |

| | | |
|---|---|---|
| N | - 'Eden's Blush' | EBee MLHP SMrm WAul |
| N | - 'Eden's Charm' | EGle ELan GBin LPBA NBro NHol SPet |
| N | - 'Eden's Delight' | NHol |
| N | - 'Eden's Harmony' | EBee NBro WAul |
| N | - 'Eden's Paintbrush' | EBee EGle ELan EPfP NBro SPer |
| N | - 'Eden's Picasso' | CFir EBee EGle ELan EPfP IPot NBro |
| N | - 'Eden's Purple Glory' | CHid EGle GBin NBro WCot WTin |
| N | - 'Eden's Starship' | CFir EBee |
| | - 'Electric Rays' | WAul |
| I | - 'Emotion' | EBee EWTr NBro NGby WAul WFar WPnP |
| | - 'Flashing Koi' | ESgI |
| I | - 'Fortune' | CDWL EHrv WAul |
| | - 'Freckled Geisha' | CElw |
| | - 'Frilled Enchantment' ♀H4 | WAul |
| * | - 'Galathea' | EBee |
| | - 'Geisha Gown' | SWal |
| | - 'Gei-sho-mi' | CPrp |
| N | - 'Gipsy' | EBee WAul |
| | - 'Gold Bound' **new** | NMoo |
| N | - 'Gracieuse' | CBgR CPen EBee EGle ELan EPfP GBBs GBin GMac MBri NBro NLar SUsu SWat WAul WFar WMoo WPnP WPrP |
| | - 'Gusto' | CMHG CPen EBee EPfP IPot LDai NBhm NBro NMoo |
| | - 'Hana-aoi' | IBlr |
| | - 'Haru-no-umi' | CKel |
| | - 'Hatsu-shimo' | IBlr |
| | - 'Hegira' | WAul |
| | - 'Hercule' | CHid CPrp CRow EGle GAbr NBir |
| | - Higo hybrids | IBlr |
| | - Higo white | SPer |
| N | - 'Himatsuri' | CMHG |
| N | - 'Hokkaido' | CBen CRow ESgI IBlr |
| | - 'Hue and Cry' ♀H4 | ESgI WAul |
| | - hybrids | EHon ESgI |
| | - 'Iapetus' | ESgI |
| * | - 'Innocence' | CKel EHrv NBre NGby NLar SMrm SWat WAul WFar WMoo |
| | - 'Iso-no-nami' | EBee EWll MBlu NBro WAul WPrP |
| N | - 'Jacob's Coat' | NCot |
| | - 'Jitsugetsu' | CFir CMHG NMoo |
| N | - 'Jodlesong' | EBee WFar |
| | - 'Kalamazoo' | WFar |
| | - 'Katy Mendez' ♀H4 | WAul |
| | - 'Kiyo-tsura' | CKel |
| N | - 'Kiyozuru' | EPfP |
| N | - 'Kogesho' | EBee EPfP GBuc NBro NLar NMoo WAul |
| N | - 'Koh Dom' | SPer |
| | - 'Kongo San' | WFar |
| | - 'Kuma-funjin' | CRow IBlr |
| | - 'Kumo-no-obi' | CMHG CPrp EAEE EBee EBla GBuc LRHS NBro SWat WAul WCAu |
| N | - 'Kunshikoku' | NLar |
| N | - 'Laced' | SPer |
| | - 'Lady in Waiting' | GBin NLar |
| | - 'Landscape at Dawn' | CRow |
| N | - 'Laughing Lion' | CPen EBee EBla GKir NBro WAul WFar WMoo |
| | - 'L'Idéal' | CPen |
| | - 'Light at Dawn' | CMHG CPen EGle EPfP LDai NBPC NBhm NBro WAul WFar WMoo |
| N | - 'Lilac Blotch' | SPer |
| I | - 'Loyalty' | CDWL EBla ECho SRGP WFar |
| | - 'Manadzuru' | IBlr |
| | - 'Mancunian' ♀H4 | CKel |
| I | - 'Mandarin' | CBen CRow |
| | - 'Midnight Stars' | WAul |
| | - 'Midnight Whisper' | WAul |
| | - 'Midsummer Reverie' | CRow |
| | - 'Mist Falls' | ESgI |
| N | - 'Momozomo' | LLHF NBhm NBro NLar |
| § | - 'Moonlight Waves' | Widely available |
| | - 'Murasame' ♀H4 | CMHG WAul |
| | - 'Narihira' | IBlr |
| | - 'Ocean Mist' | CHid CMHG CPen EBee EWTr NBro NMoo |
| | - 'Oku-banri' | CHEx CPrp EShb IBlr |
| | - 'Oriental Eyes' | EBee GAbr GBin NGdn NLar NMoo WAul WCAu |
| | - pale mauve-flowered | NBir SPer |
| | - 'Pastel Princess' | WAul |
| § | - 'Peacock' | EBee |
| | - 'Pin Stripe' | MBri NBro NLar NMoo SUsu SWat WAul WBor WMoo |
| | - 'Pink Frost' | CBgR CMil CPrp CRow EBee EGle ELan EPPr EPfP EWll GBin GCal NBro NHol WAul WFar WTin |
| | - 'Pleasant Earlybird' | WAul |
| | - 'Pleasant Journey' | EHrv |
| | - 'Prairie Frost' | EBee EPfP NLar |
| | - 'Prairie Noble' | EBee NBro NLar |
| N | - 'Purple Glory' | ELan |
| | - purple-flowered | SPer |
| | - 'Ranpo' | CRow |
| I | - 'Red Dawn' | CBen |
| | - 'Reign of Glory' | WAul |
| I | - 'Reveille' | NBro SWat WAul WPtf |
| § | - 'Rose Queen' ♀H4 | Widely available |
| | - 'Rose Tower' | CMHG |
| | - 'Rowden Amir' | CRow |
| | - 'Rowden Autocrat' | CRow |
| | - 'Rowden Begum' | CRow |
| | - 'Rowden Caliph' **new** | CRow |
| | - 'Rowden Consul' **new** | CRow |
| | - 'Rowden Dauphin' | CRow |
| | - 'Rowden Dictator' **new** | CRow |
| | - 'Rowden Emperor' | CRow |
| | - 'Rowden King' | CRow |
| | - 'Rowden Knave' | CRow |
| | - 'Rowden Knight' | CRow |
| | - 'Rowden Mikado' | CRow |
| | - 'Rowden Naib' **new** | CRow |
| | - 'Rowden Nuncio' | CRow |
| | - 'Rowden Pasha' | CRow |
| | - 'Rowden Prince' | CRow |
| | - 'Rowden Queen' | CRow |
| | - 'Rowden Shah' | CRow |
| | - 'Rowden Sultana' | CRow |
| I | - 'Royal Banner' | EBee NBro SMrm WAul WFar |
| | - 'Royal Crown' | ECho |
| | - 'Royal Pageant' | CMHG EBee NBPC NBro SIri |
| I | - 'Ruby King' | WAul |
| | - 'Ruffled Dimity' | GMac IPot NBPC |
| | - 'Sapphire Star' | CKel |
| | - 'Sea of Amethyst' | ESgI |
| | - 'Sennyo-no-hora' **new** | CPrp |
| I | - 'Sensation' | CMHG CPen CWCL ECho EWTr GBin SMrm SWat WAul WCAu WPrP |
| N | - 'Shihainami' | IBlr |
| | - 'Shiro-nihonkai' | EBee NMoo |
| | - 'Snowy Hills' | WAul |
| | - 'Sorcerer's Triumph' | EBee GBin GGar WFar |
| | - 'Southern Son' ♀H4 | ESgI |
| | - var. ***spontanea*** | SPet SWat WAbe |
| | - - B&SWJ 1103 | WCru |
| | - - B&SWJ 8699 | WCru |
| | - 'Springtime Melody' | WAul |
| I | - 'Star' | CBen |
| | - 'Summer Storm' ♀H4 | CKel SPer |
| N | - 'Teleyoshi' | GBri SHar |

- 'The Great Mogul' ♀H4 CKel CRow
- 'Umi-kaze' NLar
- 'Variegata' (v) ♀H4 Widely available
N - 'Velvety Queen' CPrp WAul
- 'Waka-murasaki' EBee EGle EWll NBro
I - 'White Ladies' CSBt EWll SWat
I - 'White Pearl' CRow
- white-flowered WFar
- 'Wine Ruffles' LSRN SIri SMrm
- 'Yako-no-tama' CRow WMoo
- 'Yamato Hime' CMHG EPfP NLar NMoo
N - 'Yedo-yeman' WFar
- 'Yezo-nishiki' GBin NBro SBod
N - 'Yu Nagi' SPer
***ensata* x *pseudoacorus*** WCot
'Aicho-no-kagayaki' **new**
'Entertainer' (TB) EFam
'Entice' (TB) **new** CIri
'Epicenter' (TB) WCAu
'Eramosa Enigma' (SDB) EFam
'Eramosa Miss' (BB) EFam
'Eramosa Skies' (SDB) WCAu
'Eramosa Snowball' (SDB) EFam
'Erect' (IB) CKel EFam
'Esoteric' (SDB) ESgI
'Etched Apricot' (TB) WCAu
'Eternal Bliss' (TB) EFam
'Eternal Prince' (TB) EFam
'Evening Dress' (Spuria) CIri WBIS
'Evening Pond' (MTB) CKel
'Evening Shade' (J) **new** WWst
'Ever After' (TB) ECtt ESgI
'Ever Ready' (SDB) EFam
'Evergreen Hideaway' (TB) CIri
'Everything Plus' (TB) ESgI WCAu
'Exclusivity' (TB) ESgI
'Exotic Gem' (TB) WCAu
'Exotic Isle' (TB) ECtt ESgI
'Extra' (BB) **new** LLHF
'Eye Magic' (IB) ♀H4 CKel EFam
'Eye of Tiger' (Dut) **new** SBch
'Eye Shadow' (SDB) WCAu
'Eyebright' (SDB) ♀H4 CBro WCAu
'Fabergé' (TB) **new** CIri
'Fade to Black' (TB) **new** CIri
'Faenelia Hicks' (La) WMAq
'Fairy Meadow' (TB) EFam
'Falcon's Crest' (Spuria) ♀H4 CIri
'Fall Fiesta' (TB) ESgI
'Fall Primrose' (TB) EFam
'Fallin'' (TB) EFam
'Falling in Love' (TB) EFam
N 'Famecheck Andrew' EFam
'Famecheck Beryl' **new** EFam
'Famecheck Christine' **new** EFam
N 'Famecheck Christmas Snow' (TB) EFam
N 'Famecheck Cream Tea' (TB) EFam
'Famecheck Doreen' **new** EFam
N 'Famecheck Dream' (TB) EFam
N 'Famecheck Forever Lemon' (IB) EFam
'Famecheck Joan' **new** EFam
'Famecheck John' **new** EFam
'Famecheck Kate' **new** EFam
N 'Famecheck Lemon Repeater' (TB) EFam
'Famecheck Marjorie' **new** EFam
N 'Famecheck Muriel' (MTB) EFam
'Famecheck Norma' **new** EFam
N 'Famecheck Paul' EFam

N 'Famecheck Perpetual Joy' (TB) EFam
'Famecheck Peter' **new** EFam
N 'Famecheck Pink' (TB) EFam
N 'Famecheck Ruddy Toes' (MTB) EFam
'Famecheck Sarah' **new** EFam
N 'Famecheck Showoff' (TB) EFam
N 'Famecheck Spearhead' EFam
N 'Famecheck Taste o' Honey' (MTB) EFam
N 'Famecheck Thelma' (MTB) EFam
'Famecheck Thomas' **new** EFam
'Famecheck Victor' **new** EFam
'Famecheck William' **new** EFam
'Fancy Woman' (TB) WAul WCAu
'Fanfaron' (TB) EFam ESgI
'Faraway Places' (TB) WCAu
'Fashion Lady' (MDB) CBro ECho
'Fast Forward' (IB) **new** WAul
'Fatal Attraction' (TB) WCAu
'Feature Attraction' (TB) CIri WCAu
'Feed Back' (TB) EFam
'Feminine Charm' (TB) WCAu
***fernaldii*** GAuc
'Ferrous Fantasy' (TB) CIri
'Festive Skirt' (TB) CKel WCAu
'Feu du Ciel' (TB) ♀H4 ESgI
'Fierce Fire' (IB) ♀H4 CKel
'Fiesta Time' (TB) ECtt
***filifolia* var. *latifolia*** SF 332 SKHP
'Film Festival' (TB) ESgI
'Finalist' (TB) WAul
'Fingest' MSte
N 'Fire and Flame' (TB) NBir
'Firebeard' (TB) **new** CIri WAul
'Firebug' (IB) ESgI
'Firecracker' (TB) MRav WCAu
'Fireside Glow' (TB) EFam
'First Interstate' (TB) CWCL ESgI WCAu
'First Movement' (TB) ESgI
'First Romance' (SDB) LSRN SIri
'First Violet' (TB) WCAu
'Flambé' (IB) WAul
'Flaming Victory' (TB) ESgI
'Flareup' (TB) WCAu
***flavescens*** ESgI WCAu
'Flavours' (BB) WCAu
'Fleece As White' (BB) **new** CIri
'Fleur Collette Louise' (La) CIri
'Flight of Fancy' (La) CKel
'Flight to Mars' (TB) CIri
'Flirting' (SDB) EFam
'Flirty Mary' (SDB) MSte
'Floating World' (CH) ♀H4 **new** SIri
'Floorshow' (TB) EFam
§ 'Florentina' (IB/TB) ♀H4 CArn CBro CHby ECGP EGoo EOHP ESgI GCal GPoy ILis MHer MNHC MRav NBid NBir SEND SIde WAul WCAu WGwG WPic
'Flower Shower' (SDB) EFam
'Flumadiddle' (IB) CBro CKel
'Flushed Delight' (TB) **new** CIri
***foetidissima*** ♀H4 Widely available
- 'Aurea' WCot
- ***chinensis*** see *I. foetidissima* var. *citrina*
§ - var. ***citrina*** CBre CFir CRow CSsd ECGP EGle EPla GAbr GCal GCra GKir IBlr MRav NBid SChr SUsu WCot WEas WHoo
- 'Fructu Albo' WCot

| | | |
|---|---|---|
| | - var. ***lutescens*** | CHid EPPr IBlr |
| N | - 'Moonshy Seedling' | CSWP |
| | - 'Variegata' (v) ♀$^{H4}$ | CElw CHar CRow ECtt EGle EHrv EPfP GMaP MCCP MSCN NBir NCob NPer WCAu WCot |
| | - yellow-seeded | GCal WCot WTin |
| | 'Fogbound' (TB) | CIri WBIS |
| | 'Foggy Dew' (TB) | ECGP |
| | 'Fondation Van Gogh' (TB) | ESgI |
| | 'Foolish Fancy' (TB) | SIri |
| | 'Forest Light' (SDB) | CBro ESgI |
| | 'Forever Blue' (SDB) | EFam |
| | 'Forever Gold' (TB) | EFam |
| N | 'Forever Trevor' (CH) | SPhx |
| | 'Forever Yours' (TB) | EFam WAul |
| | 'Forge Fire' (TB) | ESgI |
| | ***formosana*** | ECho |
| | - B&SWJ 3076 | WCru |
| | ***forrestii*** ♀$^{H4}$ | CHVG CHid CMHG ECho EPfP EWTr GAbr GAuc GCal GCra GKev GKir IBlr LPBA LRHS MBri MHer NBir NBro NCob NGdn NHol SAga SPhx SRot WAbe WPtf |
| | 'Fort Apache' (TB) | ESgI EWes |
| | 'Fortunata' (TB) | EFam |
| | 'Fortune Teller' (TB) | CKel |
| | ***fosteriana*** | NWCA |
| | 'Fourfold Blue' (SpH) | GBin |
| | 'Foxy Lady' (TB) | EFam ESgI |
| | 'Frank Elder' (Reticulata) | EBrs ECho EPot ERos LAma LLHF LRHS MRav MTho NMen WCAu |
| | 'Frans Hals' (Dut) | EBrs GKev MMHG MNrw WCot |
| | 'Freedom Flight' (TB) new | CIri |
| | 'French Rose' (TB) | CKel |
| | 'Fresh Image' (TB) | WCAu |
| | 'Fresh Start' (SDB) | WAul |
| | 'Fresno Calypso' (TB) | ESgI WCAu |
| | 'Frigiya' (Spuria) new | WBIS |
| | 'Frimousee' (TB) | ESgI |
| | 'Fringe Benefits' (TB) | ESgI WCAu |
| | 'Frison-roche' (TB) | CWCL ESgI |
| | 'Frisounette' (TB) | ESgI |
| | 'Fritillary Flight' (IB) ♀$^{H4}$ | CKel LCro |
| | 'Frivolité' (TB) | ESgI |
| | 'Frontier Lady' (TB) new | CIri |
| | 'Frontier Marshall' (TB) | NMoo |
| | 'Frost and Flame' (TB) | CWCL EAEE EBla ECtt ELan EPfP EWll LBMP LFCN MBri MRav MSte MWat NGdn NLar SHBN SPer SPla SWat |
| | 'Frosted Biscuit' (TB) ♀$^{H4}$ | CKel |
| | 'Frosted Fantasy' (TB) new | CIri |
| | 'Frosted Velvet' (MTB) | EFam WAul WCAu |
| | 'Frosty Jewels' (TB) | ESgI |
| | 'Full Impact' (TB) | CIri |
| | ***fulva*** ♀$^{H3}$ | CDes CPrp CRow CWsd EBee GCal NBir NBro NSti WBor WCot WTin |
| | - 'Marvell Gold' (La) | CRow |
| | x ***fulvala*** ♀$^{H4}$ | CAby CDes CFir CWsd EBee EPPr EWes GBin NBir NSti |
| | - 'Violacea' | EBee WCot |
| | 'Fumo Negli Occhi' (TB) new | ESgI |
| | 'Furnaceman' (SDB) | CBro ERos MBri |
| | 'Fuzzy' (MDB) | ERos |
| | 'Gala Gown' (TB) | WCAu |
| | 'Galathea' | see *I. ensata* 'Galathea' |
| | 'Gallant Moment' (TB) | ECtt SIri |
| | 'Galleon Gold' (SDB) | CKel |
| | 'Galway' (IB) | SIri |
| | 'Garden Bride' (TB) | EFam |
| | 'Garden Grace' (TB) | EFam |
| | 'Garnet Dream' (TB) new | WBIS |
| | 'Gay Parasol' (TB) | LRHS MSte |
| | 'G'day Mate' (TB) | EFam |
| N | 'Gelbe Mantel' (Sino-Sib) | CHid CLAP EBee NBir NBro NGdn NHol NSti WFar WPrP |
| | 'Gemstar' (SDB) | WCAu |
| | 'Gemstone Walls' (TB) new | ESgI |
| | 'Gentius' (TB) | WMnd |
| | 'Gentle' (SDB) | WCAu |
| | 'Gentle Grace' (SDB) | ESgI |
| | 'George' (Reticulata) ♀$^{H4}$ | CAvo CBro CFFs CPrp ECho EPfP EPot ERCP ERos GAbr GKev LHop LRHS MSte NMin SPhx WHoo WRHF |
| | 'George Smith' (TB) | ESgI |
| | 'Gerald Darby' | see *I.* x *robusta* 'Gerald Darby' |
| | ***germanica*** ♀$^{H4}$ | EGoo LCro MGos WCAu |
| | - var. ***florentina*** | see *I.* 'Florentina' |
| N | - 'Mel Jope' | NBir |
| | - 'Nepalensis' | EGoo |
| N | - 'The King' | WCAu |
| | 'Ghost Train' (TB) | CIri |
| | 'Gibson Girl' (TB) | EFam WCAu |
| | 'Gilded' (TB) | EFam |
| | 'Ginger Swirl' (TB) | EFam |
| | 'Gingerbread Castle' (TB) | WCAu |
| | 'Gingerbread Man' (SDB) | CBro CMea EHrv ERos ESgI MBrN MWea NMen SWal WCAu WHoo |
| | 'Glacier' (TB) | ECho |
| | 'Glacier King' (TB) | EFam |
| | 'Glad Rags' (TB) | ESgI |
| | 'Gladys Austin' (TB) | EFam |
| | 'Glam' (IB) | EFam WCAu |
| | 'Glorious Day' (IB) | EFam |
| | 'Glowing Seraphin' (TB) | EFam |
| | 'Glowing Smile' (TB) | CIri WAul |
| | 'Gnu Rayz' (IB) | CIri |
| | 'Gnus Flash' (TB) | WCAu |
| | 'Go Between' (TB) | WCAu |
| | 'Godfrey Owen' (TB) | CKel WCAu |
| | 'God's Handiwork' (TB) | EFam |
| | 'Godsend' (TB) | CIri CKel EFam LCro WCAu |
| | 'Going My Way' (TB) | ESgI SIri WCAu |
| | 'Gold Burst' (TB) | EFam |
| | 'Gold Country' (TB) | EFam ESgI |
| | 'Gold Galore' (TB) | EFam |
| | 'Gold of Autumn' (TB) | CKel LCro SMrm |
| | 'Gold Reprise' (TB) | EFam |
| | 'Goldberry' (IB) | WCAu |
| | 'Golden Alien' (TB) | CIri |
| | 'Golden Alps' (TB) | SRms WCAu |
| | 'Golden Child' (SDB) | EFam ESgI |
| | 'Golden Ecstasy' (TB) | EFam |
| | 'Golden Encore' (TB) | CKel EFam WCAu |
| | 'Golden Fair' (SDB) | NBir |
| | 'Golden Forest' (TB) | LRHS WCAu |
| | 'Golden Immortal' (TB) | EFam |
| | 'Golden Panther' (TB) | CIri |
| | 'Golden Planet' (TB) | CKel |
| | 'Golden Violet' (SDB) | ESgI |
| | 'Goldkist' (TB) | CIri |
| | ***goniocarpa*** | EBee WAbe |
| | - var. ***grossa*** | EBee |
| | 'Good Fairy' (TB) | EFam |
| | 'Good Looking' (TB) | ESgI WCAu |
| | 'Good Show' (TB) | SCoo WAul WCAu |
| | 'Good Vibrations' (TB) | SIri |
| | 'Goodbye Heart' (TB) | ESgI |
| | 'Gordon' (Reticulata) | CAvo CFFs CSam EBrs ECho EPfP EPot ERCP GKev LAma LRHS MWat SMeo WFar |
| | ***gormanii*** | see *I. tenax* |
| | 'Gosh' (SDB) | CKel |
| | 'Gossip' (SDB) | CBro ESgI |

| | | |
|---|---|---|
| | 'Gothic' (TB) | EFam |
| | ***gracilipes*** | GKev SIng |
| | ***gracilipes* x *lacustris*** | GAuc GEdr WAbe |
| | ***graeberiana*** | EBrs ECho EPot GKev WWst |
| | - white fall | LRHS WWst |
| | - yellow fall | EBee EBrs ECho LRHS WWst |
| | ***graminea*** ♀H4 | Widely available |
| | - var. ***pseudocyperus*** | CRow GCal SDys |
| | ***graminifolia*** | see *I. kerneriana* |
| | 'Granada Gold' (TB) | SRms |
| | 'Grand Baroque' (TB) | EFam |
| | 'Grape Adventure' (TB) | EFam |
| | 'Grape Jelly' (TB) | WCAu |
| | 'Grape Reprise' (TB) | EFam |
| | 'Grapelet' (MDB) | ERos WCAu |
| | 'Grapeshot' (TB) | CIri |
| | 'Great Gatsby' (TB) | CKel EFam |
| | 'Great Lakes' (TB) | ESgI |
| | 'Grecian Goddess' (TB) | EFam |
| | 'Grecian Skies' (TB) | ESgI |
| | 'Green and Gifted' (TB) | EFam |
| | 'Green Ice' (TB) | CKel MRav |
| | 'Green Prophecy' (TB) | CKel |
| | 'Green Spot' (SDB) ♀H4 | CBgR CBro CKel CWGN EAEE EBee EBla ECtt EHrv ELan EPfP GBuc GEdr MRav NBir NCob NHol NLar NMen NWCA SPer SPhx WAul WCAu WCFE |
| | 'Green Streak' (TB) | CIri |
| | 'Gringo' (TB) | WCAu |
| | 'Guatemala' (TB) **new** | CIri |
| | 'Gudrun' (TB) | ESgI |
| | 'Gwyneth Evans' (BB) ♀H4 | CKel |
| | 'Gypsy Beauty' (Dut) | EBrs EPfP LRHS MBrN SBch SPer WCot WFar |
| | 'Gypsy Caravan' (TB) | LRHS |
| | 'Gypsy Jewels' (TB) | CKel ESgI |
| | 'Gypsy Romance' (TB) ♀H4 | ESgI SIri WCAu |
| | 'Habit' (TB) | WAul WCAu |
| | 'Hafnium' (SDB) | CKel |
| | 'Hagar's Helmet' (IB) | EFam |
| | 'Halloween Pumpkin' (TB) | EFam |
| | 'Halo in Pink' (TB) | EFam |
| | ***halophila*** | see *I. spuria* subsp. *halophila* |
| | 'Hand Painted' (TB) | EFam |
| | 'Handshake' (TB) ♀H4 | CIri |
| | 'Happenstance' (TB) | ESgI |
| | 'Happy Birthday' (TB) | ESgI |
| N | 'Happy Border' (BB) | WCAu |
| | 'Happy Mood' (IB) ♀H4 | EFam NBre WCAu |
| | 'Happy Pal' (TB) | EFam |
| | 'Harbor Blue' (TB) | MWat SWat WCAu |
| N | 'Hareknoll' | NWCA |
| | 'Harlequinade' (BB) | EFam |
| | 'Harlow Gold' (IB) | ESgI |
| | 'Harmony' (Reticulata) | CAvo CBro CFFs EBrs ECho EPfP EPot GKev LAma LRHS MBri NHol SPhx WFar WRHF |
| | 'Harriette Halloway' (TB) | CSam EAEE EBee EBla EShb ETod GMaP LPio LSRN MSte NLar SPet SRGP WCot |
| | ***hartwegii*** | ECho |
| | - subsp. ***hartwegii*** **new** | GAuc |
| | - subsp. ***pinetorum*** | GAuc |
| | 'Harvest King' (TB) | ECtt ESgI |
| | 'Harvest of Memories' (TB) | EFam ESgI |
| | 'Haut les Voiles' (TB) **new** | CWCL |
| | 'Haute Couture' (TB) | WCAu |
| | 'Haviland' (TB) | SIri |
| | 'Hawaiian Halo' (TB) | EFam |
| | 'Hazelnut Delight' (TB) | CIri |
| | 'Headcorn' (MTB) ♀H4 | CIri SIri WAul |
| | 'Headlines' (TB) | WCAu |
| | 'Heather Carpet' (SDB) | WCAu |
| | 'Heather Sky' (TB) | CIri |
| | 'Heavenly Days' (TB) | WCAu |
| | 'Heaven's Bounty' (BB) | EFam |
| | 'Heepers' (SDB) | EFam |
| | 'Helen Boehm' (TB) | ESgI |
| | 'Helen Collingwood' (TB) | ESgI |
| | 'Helen K. Armstrong' (TB) | EFam |
| | 'Helen McGregor' (TB) | ESgI |
| | 'Helen Proctor' (IB) | ESgI WCAu |
| | 'Helen Traubel' (TB) | WCAu |
| | 'Helge' (IB) | COIW ECho NBre SWat |
| | 'Hellcat' (IB) | WAul WCAu |
| | 'Hello Darkness' (TB) ♀H4 | CIri ESgI WCAu |
| | 'Hemstitched' (TB) | EFam |
| | 'Hercules' (Reticulata) | ECho EPot ERCP NMin |
| | 'Here's Heaven' (TB) | EFam |
| | 'Hey There' (MDB) | ESgI |
| | 'Hidden World' (TB) | LRHS |
| | 'High Barbaree' (TB) | WCAu |
| | 'High Blue Sky' (TB) | WCAu |
| | 'High Command' (TB) | CKel EFam |
| | 'High Energy' (TB) | EFam |
| | 'High Ho Silver' | EFam ESgI |
| | 'High Roller' (TB) ♀H4 | CIri WBIS |
| | 'High Waters' (TB) | EFam |
| | 'Highland Games' (TB) | CIri |
| | 'Highline Amethyst' (Spuria) | WAul |
| | 'Highline Halo' (Spuria) | WCAu |
| | 'Hindenburg' (TB) | EFam |
| | 'Hindu Magic' (TB) | WCAu |
| | 'Hippie' (SDB) | EFam |
| | 'Hissy-Fit' (IB) | CKel |
| | ***histrio*** | ECho GAuc |
| | - subsp. ***aintabensis*** | EBrs ECho EPot LAma |
| | ***histrioides*** | ECho GAuc WAbe |
| § | - 'Angel's Tears' (Reticulata) | CTca EBrs ECho ERCP ERos LRHS NMen NMin WWst |
| | - 'Halkis' (Reticulata) **new** | ERCP LAma NMin |
| | - 'Lady Beatrix Stanley' | CBro EBrs ECho EPot ERCP GBin LRHS NMen NMin |
| N | - 'Major' | CDes ECho EPot LAma NMin SPhx |
| N | - 'Michael Tears' | WWst |
| | - var. ***sophenensis*** | EBrs ECho |
| | 'Hocus Pocus' (SDB) | EPPr WAul |
| | 'Holden Clough' (SpecHybrid) ♀H4 | Widely available |
| | **x *hollandica*** hort. | EBrs |
| | 'Hollywood Blonde' (TB) | EFam |
| | 'Holy Fire' (TB) | CIri |
| | 'Holy Night' (TB) | CKel |
| | 'Honey Behold' (SDB) | CKel |
| | 'Honey Glazed' (IB) | ESgI WAul WCAu |
| | 'Honey Scoop' (TB) | EFam |
| | 'Honeyplic' (IB) ♀H4 | SIri WAul WCAu |
| | 'Honington' (SDB) | EFam WCAu |
| | 'Honky Tonk Blues' (TB) | CKel ESgI LSRN WAul |
| | 'Honky Tonk Hussy' (BB) | CKel |
| | 'Honorabile' (MTB) | WCAu |
| | ***hoogiana*** ♀H3 | EBrs ECho EPot GKev LRHS SPhx |
| N | - 'Gypsy Beauty' | WFar |
| | - 'Purpurea' | EBrs ECho |
| | 'Hook' (TB) **new** | WAul |
| § | ***hookeri*** | CSam CTca ELan GAuc GBin GEdr IGor WAbe WCot |
| § | 'Hornpipe' (TB) | WCAu |
| | 'Hot Fudge' (IB) | EPPr |
| | 'Hot Gossip' (TB) | WCAu |
| | 'Hot Jazz' (SDB) | WCAu |
| | 'Hot Spice' (IB) | WCAu |

| | | |
|---|---|---|
| | 'Hot to Trot' (TB) **new** | ESgI |
| | 'Hotseat' (SDB) | EFam |
| | 'Howard Weed' (TB) | EBee SPad |
| | 'Howdy Do' (TB) | EFam |
| | 'Huckleberry Fudge' (TB) | WAul |
| | 'Hugh Miller' (TB) | WCAu |
| | 'Hula Doll' (MDB) | NMen |
| | 'Hula Honey' (TB) | EFam |
| | 'Hula Moon' (TB) | ESgI |
| § | ***humilis*** | CGra |
| | ***hyrcana*** | EBrs ECho |
| | 'I Bless' (IB) | EFam |
| | 'I Do' (TB) | EFam |
| | 'I Repeat' (TB) | ESgI |
| | 'I Seek You' (TB) | ESgI |
| | ***iberica*** | ECho |
| § | - subsp. ***elegantissima*** | EBrs ECho WWst |
| | - subsp. ***iberica*** | WWst |
| § | - subsp. ***lycotis*** | WWst |
| | 'Ice Dancer' (TB) ♀H4 | CKel |
| | 'Ice Wings' (BB) | WCAu |
| | 'Iced Tea' (TB) ♀H4 | CIri WBIS |
| | 'Ida' (Reticulata) | LAma |
| | 'Ila Crawford' (Spuria) ♀H4 | WCAu |
| | ***illyrica*** | see *I. pallida* |
| | 'Imagine Me' (TB) | EFam |
| | 'Imbue' (SDB) | EFam ESgI |
| | 'Immortal Hour' (TB) | WCAu |
| | 'Immortality' (TB) | CKel CWGN EFam ESgI LRHS MSte WCAu |
| I | 'Imperator' (Dut) | ECho |
| | 'Imperial Bronze' (Spuria) | WAul WCAu |
| | 'Impetuous' (BB) ♀H4 | CKel EFam |
| | 'Imprimis' (TB) | ESgI WCAu |
| | 'In a Flash' (IB) | WCAu |
| | 'In Limbo' (IB) | CKel |
| | 'In Love' (TB) | EFam |
| | 'In Reverse' (TB) | CKel |
| | 'In the Stars' (TB) | EFam |
| | 'In Town' (TB) | ESgI |
| | 'Incentive' (TB) **new** | ECtt |
| N | 'Incoscente' (TB) | ESgI |
| | 'Indeed' (IB) | CBgR EFam |
| | 'Indian Chief' (TB) | CWCL ESgI GBin SPur WCAu |
| | 'Indian Idyll' (IB) | CKel |
| | 'Indian Pow Wow' (SDB) | CSev |
| N | 'Indiana Sunset' (TB) | CKel |
| | 'Indigo Flight' (IB) | CKel |
| | 'Indigo Princess' (TB) | CKel |
| | 'Indiscreet' (TB) | EFam WCAu |
| | 'Infernal Fire' (TB) | CIri |
| | 'Infinite Grace' (TB) | ESgI |
| | 'Innocent Devil' (TB) **new** | CIri |
| | 'Innocent Heart' (IB) ♀H4 | WCAu |
| | 'Innocent Pink' (TB) | ESgI |
| | 'Innocent Star' (TB) | EFam |
| | ***innominata*** | CWCL ECha ECho GAuc GGar GKev IBlr LHop LRHS NBir NBro NMen SRms SWal WBVN |
| | - JCA 13225 | CLAP |
| | - apricot-flowered | CPrp IBlr |
| | - Ballyrogan hybrids | IBlr |
| | - 'Bronze' **new** | MMuc |
| N | - 'Spinners' | CWsd |
| | - yellow-flowered | NMen NRya |
| | 'Interpol' (TB) | ESgI WCAu |
| | 'Intrepid' (TB) **new** | CWCL |
| | 'Invitation' (TB) | EFam ESgI |
| | 'Irish Doll' (MDB) | WCAu |
| | 'Irish Moss' (SDB) | WAul |
| | 'Irish Tune' (TB) | ESgI |
| | 'Island Sunset' (TB) | EFam ESgI SIri |
| | 'Isoline' (TB) | ESgI |
| | 'Istanbul' (TB) | EFam |
| | 'It's Magic' (TB) | EFam |
| | 'J.S. Dijt' (Reticulata) | CAvo CBro CFFs EBrs ECho EPfP EPot ERCP GKev LAma LRHS MBri MGos SPhx |
| | 'Jabal' (SDB) | SIri |
| | 'Jane Phillips' (TB) ♀H4 | Widely available |
| | 'Jane Taylor' (SDB) | CBro |
| | 'Janet Lane' (BB) | CKel |
| | 'Jangles' (IB) | WCAu |
| | 'Janice Chesnik' (Spuria) | ESgI |
| | 'Janine Louise' (TB) ♀H4 | CKel |
| | ***japonica*** ♀H3 | CHEx ECho EHrv NPer WAul WFar WOut |
| | - B&SWJ 8921 | WCru |
| | - 'Aphrodite' (v) | WTin |
| | - 'Bourne Graceful' | CWsd WCAu |
| | - 'Ledger' | CAvo CHll CKel CPrp CSpe ECha EHrv ELan EPfP IGor MRav SHom SIri SMad WPGP |
| I | - 'Purple Heart' | CAvo |
| N | - 'Rudolph Spring' | CPen GCal |
| I | - 'Snowflake' | CAvo |
| § | - 'Variegata' (v) ♀H3 | CAvo CBgR CBow CHEx CKel CPrp CSpe ECha EHrv ELon ESwi GCal GGar LRHS NBro NPer SAPC SAga SArc WAul WEas WFar WHil WPGP |
| | 'Jasper Gem' (MDB) | ERos NBir |
| | 'Jaunty Jean' (TB) | EFam |
| | 'Jay Kenneth' (IB) | CBgR |
| | 'Jazz Festival' (TB) | SIri WCAu |
| N | 'Jazz Maid' | EFam |
| | 'Jazzamatazz' (SDB) | ESgI WCAu |
| | 'Jazzed Up' (TB) | WCAu |
| | 'Jean Cayeux' (TB) | ESgI |
| | 'Jean Guymer' (TB) | EFam ESgI NBir WCAu |
| | 'Jeanne Price' (TB) | SCoo WCAu |
| | 'Jennie Grace' (SDB) | SIri |
| | 'Jephthah's Daughter' (TB) | EFam |
| | 'Jeremy Brian' (SDB) ♀H4 | WCAu |
| | 'Jersey Lilli' (SDB) | WCAu |
| | 'Jesse Lee' (SDB) | CKel |
| | 'Jesse's Song' (TB) | EFam ESgI WCAu |
| | 'Jester' (TB) | EFam |
| | 'Jeunesse' (TB) **new** | ESgI |
| | 'Jewel Baby' (SDB) | CBro CKel |
| | 'Jeweler's Art' (SDB) | WCAu |
| | 'Jiansada' (SDB) | CBro |
| | 'Jigsaw' (TB) | ESgI |
| | 'Jitterbug' (TB) | EHrv LRHS WCAu |
| | 'Joanna' (TB) | LSRN NLar |
| | 'Joanna Taylor' (MDB) | ERos NMen WCAu |
| N | 'Joe Elliott' (CH) | EGle |
| | 'John' (IB) | CKel EFam LSRN WAul |
| | 'Joli Coeur' (TB) **new** | ESgI |
| | 'Joy Boy' (SDB) | ESgI |
| | 'Joyce' (Reticulata) | CBro EBrs ECho EPot GKev LAma LRHS MBri SGar SPhx |
| | 'Joyce Terry' (TB) | CWan ESgI LRHS SPad |
| | 'Joyful' (SDB) | ESgI |
| | 'Jubilant Spirit' (Spuria) | EBee EWes |
| | 'Jubilé Rainier III' (TB) | CIri |
| | 'Jubilee Gem' (TB) | CKel |
| | 'Jud Paynter' (TB) | CKel |
| | 'Juicy Fruit' (TB) | EFam WCAu |
| | 'Julia Vennor' (TB) | CKel |
| | 'Juliet' (TB) | ESgI |
| | 'July Sunshine' (TB) | EFam |
| | 'June Prom' (IB) | LRHS SRGP WCAu |
| | 'June Rose' (IB) | WAul |
| | 'Jungle Fires' (TB) | WCAu |

| | | |
|---|---|---|
| | 'Jungle Shadows' (BB) | MRav NBir WCAu |
| | 'Jungle Warrior' (SDB) | CKel |
| | 'Jurassic Park' (TB) | ESgI WAul WBIS WCAu |
| | 'Juris Prudence' (TB) | ESgI |
| | 'Just Dance' (IB) | EFam ESgI |
| | 'Just Jennifer' (BB) | WCAu |
| | ***kaempferi*** | see *I. ensata* |
| | 'Kaibab Trail' (Spuria) | CIri WBIS |
| | 'Kangchenjunga' (TB) | ESgI |
| | 'Karen' (TB) **new** | LSRN |
| | ***kashmiriana*** | CBcs |
| | 'Katharine Hodgkin' (Reticulata) ♀H4 | Widely available |
| | 'Katie-Koo' (IB) ♀H4 | CKel |
| | 'Katmandu' (TB) | EFam |
| | 'Katy Petts' (SDB) | ESgI WCAu |
| | 'Kayleigh-Jayne Louise' (TB) | CKel |
| | 'Keeping up Appearances' (TB) | WAul WCAu |
| | 'Kelway Renaissance' (TB) | CKel |
| | ***kemaonensis*** | GAuc |
| | 'Ken's Choice' (TB) ♀H4 | CKel |
| | 'Kent Pride' (TB) | CSBt EAEE EBee EBla ECha ECtt EPfP ESgI ETod IPot MCot MRav MSte MWat SGar SHBN SIri SPer SPoG SWat WAul WCAu WCra WTin WWlt |
| | 'Kentucky Bluegrass' (SDB) | WCAu |
| § | ***kerneriana*** ♀H4 | ERos GBuc LRHS MLLN NBir WPen |
| | 'Kernewek' (TB) | EFam |
| | 'Kevin's Theme' (TB) | CIri WBIS WCAu |
| | 'Kildonan' (TB) | WCAu |
| | 'Kilt Lilt' (TB) | WCAu |
| | 'King's Rhapsody' (TB) | EFam |
| | 'Kirkstone' (TB) | WCAu |
| | 'Kiss of Summer' (TB) ♀H4 **new** | ESgI WBIS |
| | 'Kissing Circle' (TB) | EFam ESgI |
| | 'Kitt Peak' (Spuria) ♀H4 | CIri |
| | 'Kiwi Slices' (SDB) | ESgI |
| | 'Klingon Princess' (SDB) | EFam |
| | 'Knick Knack' (MDB) | CBro CMea CPBP EAEE EBee EBla ECho ELan ERos ETod GAbr LBee LRHS MRav MSte NMen SDnm SMrm SMrs SPhx SPla SPoG |
| | ***kolpakowskiana*** | WWst |
| | 'Kona Nights' (BB) | ESgI |
| | ***koreana*** **new** | GAuc |
| | ***korolkowii*** | EPot |
| | 'La Belle Aube' (TB) **new** | ESgI |
| | 'La Nina Rosa' (BB) | WCAu |
| | 'La Senda' (Spuria) | WCAu WCot |
| | 'La Vie en Rose' (TB) | ESgI |
| | 'Lace Legacy' (TB) **new** | ECtt |
| | 'Laced Cotton' (TB) | ESgI WCAu |
| | 'Laced Lemonade' (SDB) | MBri |
| § | ***lactea*** ♀H4 | EWTr NWCA |
| | ***lacustris*** ♀H4 | CBro NMen NWCA WAbe |
| | 'Lacy Snowflake' (TB) | COIW SPet |
| | 'Lady Emma' (MTB) | EFam |
| | 'Lady Essex' (TB) | EFam WCAu |
| | 'Lady Friend' (TB) | EFam ESgI WCAu |
| | 'Lady Gale' (IB) | CKel |
| | 'Lady Ilse' (TB) | WCAu |
| | 'Lady in Red' (SDB) | ESgI |
| | 'Lady Mohr' (AB) | CKel WCAu |
| | 'Lady of Fatima' (TB) | ESgI |
| | ***laevigata*** ♀H4 | CDWL CRow CWat ECha ECho EGle EHon ELan EMFW EPfP GAuc LPBA MRav NBro NPer SEND SGar SPer SWat WCAu WFar WMAq WMoo WPnP WShi |

| | | |
|---|---|---|
| | – var. ***alba*** | CBen CRow ECha ECho EHon ELan EPfP GAuc LCro LPBA MMuc SWat WAbe WFar WMoo |
| | – 'Albopurpurea' | CDWL EMFW SMrm |
| | – 'Atropurpurea' | CRow IBlr |
| | – 'Colchesterensis' | CDWL CRow EMFW LPBA NGdn NPer SWat WMAq |
| I | – 'Dorothy' | LPBA NGdn |
| N | – 'Dorothy Robinson' | SWat |
| | – 'Elegant' | see *I. laevigata* 'Weymouth Elegant' |
| N | – 'Elgar' | WMAq |
| | – 'Liam Johns' | CRow |
| | – 'Midnight' | see *I. laevigata* 'Weymouth Midnight' |
| | – 'Mottled Beauty' | CRow |
| | – 'Rashomon' | CRow |
| | – 'Regal' | CDWL CWat |
| I | – 'Reveille' | EGle |
| | – 'Richard Greaney' | CRow |
| | – 'Rose Queen' | see *I. ensata* 'Rose Queen' |
| | – 'Rowden Seaspray' **new** | CRow |
| | – 'Rowden Starlight' **new** | CRow |
| I | – 'Snowdrift' | CBen CDWL CRow CWat EHon EMFW LPBA NBir NGdn NPer SPer SWat WCAu WFar WMAq WPnP |
| | – 'Variegata' (v) ♀H4 | CBen CBow CDWL CMea CRow CSec CWat EAEE ECha ECho EHoe EHon EMFW EPfP EPla LLWG LPBA LRHS MHar NBro NGdn NPer SPer SWat WMAq WMoo WPnP WTin |
| | – 'Violet Garth' | CRow |
| | – 'Weymouth' | see *I. laevigata* 'Weymouth Blue' |
| § | – 'Weymouth Blue' | CBen CRow |
| § | – 'Weymouth Elegant' | CRow |
| § | – 'Weymouth Midnight' | CFir CMil CRow LPBA SWat |
| N | 'Langport Chapter' (IB) | CBgR CKel ESgI LCro |
| N | 'Langport Chief' (IB) | CKel |
| N | 'Langport Claret' (IB) | CBgR CKel ESgI |
| N | 'Langport Curlew' (IB) | CKel ESgI |
| N | 'Langport Duchess' (IB) | CKel ESgI WTin |
| N | 'Langport Fairy' (IB) | CBgR CKel ESgI |
| N | 'Langport Finch' (IB) | NBir |
| N | 'Langport Flame' (IB) | CBgR CKel ESgI LCro WTin |
| N | 'Langport Flash' (IB) | EFam |
| N | 'Langport Haze' (IB) | ESgI |
| N | 'Langport Hope' (IB) | CKel ESgI |
| N | 'Langport Jane' (IB) | CKel |
| N | 'Langport Lady' (IB) | CKel |
| N | 'Langport Lord' (IB) | ESgI LCro |
| | 'Langport Minstrel' (IB) | CKel ESgI LCro |
| N | 'Langport Pearl' (IB) | CKel |
| | 'Langport Phoenix' (IB) | CKel |
| N | 'Langport Pinnacle' (IB) | CKel |
| N | 'Langport Robe' (IB) | ESgI |
| N | 'Langport Smoke' (IB) | CKel |
| | 'Langport Snow' (IB) | CKel |
| N | 'Langport Song' (IB) | ESgI |
| N | 'Langport Star' (IB) | CKel ESgI LCro |
| | 'Langport Storm' (IB) | CKel CMil EAEE EBee EBla ESgI MRav MSte SHBN WAul WTin |
| N | 'Langport Sun' (IB) | CBgR CKel EFam ESgI SMrm |
| N | 'Langport Swift' (IB) | CKel |
| | 'Langport Sylvia' (IB) | CBgR CKel |
| N | 'Langport Tartan' (IB) | CKel |
| N | 'Langport Violet' (IB) | CKel ESgI |
| | 'Langport Vista' (IB) | CKel |
| | 'Langport Warrior' (IB) | CKel |
| | 'Langport Wren' (IB) ♀H4 | CBro CKel CMdw ECGP EFam EPfP ESgI GCal IPot LCro LRHS MBri MSte NBir SMrm SPhx WAul WEas WPen WTin |
| | 'Lark Rise' (TB) ♀H4 | CKel WBIS |
| | 'Larry Gaulter' (TB) | WCAu |

| | | |
|---|---|---|
| | 'Las Vegas' (TB) | WCAu |
| | 'Lascivious Dreams' (TB) | EFam |
| | 'Latest Style' | EFam |
| § | ***latifolia*** ♀H4 | ECho IHer WShi |
| | - 'Duchess of York' | ECho |
| | - 'Isabella' | EBee EBrs |
| | - 'King of the Blues' | EBrs ECho GKev |
| | - 'Mansfield' | EBee EBrs GKev WCot |
| | - 'Montblanc' | EBee EBrs |
| | - 'Queen of the Blues' (Eng) | ECho |
| | 'Latin Lady' (TB) **new** | ESgI |
| | 'Latin Lark' (TB) | ESgI |
| | 'Latin Rock' (TB) | WCAu |
| | 'Laura Louise' (La) | WHlf |
| | 'Lavender Park' (TB) **new** | ESgI |
| § | ***lazica*** ♀H4 | CAbP CBro CPen CPrp CRow CSpe EAEE EBee EMon EPPr EPfP EPot ESgI EWsh GGar GKev IBlr LEdu LFCN LRHS MRav MSte NBir NCGa NSti SIng WEas WPGP |
| | - 'Joy Bishop' | WCot |
| N | - 'Richard Nutt' | ELon WCot |
| N | - 'Turkish Blue' | CPrp GBin IBlr |
| | 'Leah Traded' (BB) | EFam |
| | 'Leda's Lover' (TB) | ESgI |
| | 'Legato' (TB) | EFam ESgI |
| | 'Lemon Brocade' (TB) | ESgI MBri WCAu |
| | 'Lemon Dilemma' (Spuria) | CIri |
| | 'Lemon Fever' (TB) | ESgI |
| | 'Lemon Flare' (SDB) | EFam MRav SRms WCAu |
| | 'Lemon Ice' (TB) | EAEE EBee EBla LBuc SPer |
| | 'Lemon Lyric' (TB) | EFam ESgI |
| | 'Lemon Mist' (TB) | ESgI |
| N | 'Lemon Peel' (IB) | CKel |
| | 'Lemon Pop' (IB) | WCAu |
| | 'Lemon Puff' (MDB) | CBro WCAu |
| | 'Lemon Tree' (TB) | WCAu |
| N | 'Lena' (SDB) | CBro |
| | 'Lenna M' (SDB) | CKel ECho |
| | 'Lenora Pearl' (BB) | ESgI WCAu |
| | 'Lent A. Williamson' (TB) | GMaP |
| | 'Lenten Prayer' (TB) | CIri |
| | 'Leprechaun's Delight' (SDB) | EFam |
| | 'Leprechaun's Purse' (SDB) | WCAu |
| | ***leptorhiza*** (J) **new** | WWst |
| | 'Let's Elope' (IB) | ESgI WCAu |
| | 'Letter from Paris' (TB) | EFam |
| | 'Liaison' (TB) | LRHS |
| | 'Licorice Fantasy' (TB) **new** | ESgI |
| | 'Light Beam' (TB) | EFam |
| | 'Light Cavalry' (IB) | ESgI |
| | 'Light Laughter' (IB) | WCAu |
| | 'Lightning Streak' (TB) | LRHS |
| | 'Lilac Stitchery' (TB) | EFam |
| | 'Lilla's Gloves' (TB) | EFam |
| | 'Lilla's Stripes' (TB) | EFam |
| | 'Lilli-white' (SDB) | CKel CWat EAEE EBee EBla EHrv ELan GEdr MBNS MRav SPhx SPoG WCAu |
| | 'Lilting' (TB) | EFam |
| | 'Lima Colada' (SDB) | NBre |
| | 'Limbo' (SpecHybrid) | CRow |
| | 'Lime Fizz' (TB) **new** | ESgI |
| | 'Limelight' (TB) | SRms |
| | 'Lingering Love' (TB) | WCAu |
| | 'Liqueur Crème' (TB) | EFam |
| N | 'Little Amoena' | ERos NMen |
| | 'Little Bev' (SDB) | EFam |
| | 'Little Black Belt' (SDB) | SIri |
| | 'Little Blackfoot' (SDB) | ESgI WCAu WHoo |
| | 'Little Blue-eyes' (SDB) | ESgI |
| | 'Little Bluets' (SDB) | ESgI |
| | 'Little Dandy' (SDB) | WCAu |
| | 'Little Dream' (SDB) | WCAu |
| | 'Little Episode' (SDB) | ESgI WCAu |
| | 'Little Firecacker' (SDB) | EFam |
| | 'Little John' (TB) | WCAu |
| | 'Little Paul' (MTB) | ESgI |
| | 'Little Rosy Wings' (SDB) | CBro CPBP EFam ERos |
| | 'Little Sapphire' (SDB) | GEdr |
| | 'Little Shadow' (IB) | MRav SRms |
| | 'Little Sheba' (AB) | WCAu |
| | 'Little Showoff' (SDB) | EFam ESgI WAul |
| | 'Little Snow Lemon' (IB) | EFam |
| | 'Little Tilgates' (CH) ♀H3 | WCot |
| | 'Live Jazz' (SDB) | WCAu |
| | 'Living Legacy' (TB) **new** | WAul |
| | 'Llanthony' (SDB) | WCAu |
| | 'Local Color' (TB) | ESgI WAul |
| | 'Lodore' (TB) | SRms WCAu |
| | 'Logo' (IB) | WCAu WGwG |
| | 'Lollipop' (SDB) | EFam ESgI SIri |
| | ***longipetala*** | EWes NBir |
| | 'Lookingglass Eyes' (Spuria) | CIri |
| | 'Loop the Loop' (TB) | EBee EPfP EWll LRHS MWea NBre SCoo SPoG SWat WCra |
| | 'Loose Valley' (MTB) ♀H4 | SIri WCAu |
| | 'Lord Warden' (TB) | CSam EAEE EBla ECtt LDai MSte SPet WAul WCAu |
| | 'Loreley' (TB) | ESgI |
| | 'Lorenzaccio de Médicis' (TB) | ESgI |
| | 'Lorilee' (TB) | ESgI |
| | 'Lothario' (TB) | WCAu WFoF |
| | 'Loud Music' (TB) | WCAu |
| | 'Louis d'Or' (TB) ♀H4 | CIri |
| | 'Louvois' (TB) | ESgI |
| | 'Love for Leila' (Spuria) ♀H4 | CIri |
| | 'Love the Sun' (TB) | EFam ESgI |
| | 'Lovebird' (TB) | EFam |
| | 'Lovely Again' (TB) | EFam MRav WCAu |
| | 'Lovely Fran' (TB) | EFam |
| | 'Lovely Leilani' (TB) | ESgI |
| | 'Lovely Light' (TB) | MBri |
| | 'Lover's Charm' (TB) | WCAu |
| | 'Love's Tune' (IB) | EAEE EBla SRGP |
| | 'Low Ho Silver' (IB) | EFam WCAu |
| | 'Loyalist' (TB) | SIri |
| | 'Lucky Devil' (Spuria) ♀H4 | CIri WBIS |
| | 'Lucy's Gift' (MTB) ♀H4 | CIri WAul |
| | 'Lugano' (TB) | ESgI |
| | 'Luli-Ann' (SDB) ♀H4 | CKel |
| | 'Lullaby of Spring' (TB) | CKel WCAu |
| | 'Lumalite' (SDB) | WAul |
| | 'Lumière d'Automne' (TB) | ESgI |
| | 'Luminosity' (TB) | EFam ESgI |
| | 'Luna di Miele' (BB) | ESgI |
| | 'Lunar Frost' (IB) | SIri |
| | 'Lurid' (TB) | EFam |
| § | ***lutescens*** ♀H4 | EBrs ECho EPot ERos GCra GEdr NSla WAbe |
| § | - 'Campbellii' | ERos MSte NMen |
| § | - 'Nancy Lindsay' | WCAu |
| | ***lycotis*** | see *I. iberica* subsp. *lycotis* |
| | 'Lyrique' (BB) | CKel WAul |
| | 'Ma Mie' (IB) | ESgI |
| | ***maackii*** from Ussuri River **new** | GAuc |
| | ***macrosiphon*** | GKev |
| | 'Madame Maurice Lassailly' (TB) | ESgI |
| | 'Madeira Belle' (TB) | ESgI WCAu |

| | | |
|---|---|---|
| | 'Magharee' (TB) | ESgI |
| | 'Magic Kingdom' (TB) | EFam |
| | 'Magic Man' (TB) | EBee |
| | 'Magic Memories' (TB) | EFam |
| | 'Magic Palette' (TB) | EFam |
| | ***magnifica*** ♀H3-4 | CBro EBrs ECho LEdu WWst |
| N | – 'Agalik' | EBrs ECho LRHS |
| | – 'Alba' | EBrs ECho WWst |
| | 'Maiden' (TB) | EFam |
| | 'Maisie Lowe' (TB) | ESgI |
| | 'Making Eyes' (SDB) | ESgI WCAu |
| | 'Mallow Dramatic' (TB) | WCAu |
| I | 'Mandarin' (TB) | ESgI |
| | 'Mandarin Purple' (Sino-Sib) | CDes EBee GGar IBlr NGdn NHol WPrP |
| | ***mandshurica*** | CPBP |
| | 'Mango Entree' (TB) | CIri |
| | 'Mango Kiss' (SDB) | EFam |
| N | 'Many Moons Tales' (TB) | EFam |
| | 'Maple Madness' (SDB) | EFam |
| | 'Maple Treat' (TB) | EFam |
| | 'Mara' (IB) | CKel |
| | 'Marcel Turbat' (TB) | ESgI |
| | 'Marche Turque' (TB) | ESgI |
| | 'Marco Polo' (TB) | ESgI |
| | 'Margarita' (TB) | WCAu |
| | 'Margot Holmes' (Cal-Sib) | CDes |
| | 'Margrave' (TB) | SIri WCAu |
| | 'Marguérite' (Reticulata/v) | EBrs ECho EPPr ERCP LRHS |
| | 'Marhaba' (MDB) | CBro ERos |
| | 'Marilyn Holloway' (Spuria) | WCAu |
| | 'Mariposa Skies' (TB) | ESgI |
| | 'Marita' (SDB) | EFam |
| | 'Marmalade Skies' (BB) | EFam WCAu |
| | 'Maroon Moon' (TB) | CIri |
| | 'Martyn Rix' | see *I. confusa* 'Martyn Rix' |
| | 'Mary Constance' (IB) ♀H4 | CKel |
| | 'Mary Frances' (TB) | ESgI WCAu |
| | 'Mary McIlroy' (SDB) ♀H4 | CBro CKel WTin |
| | 'Mary Randall' (TB) | WCAu |
| | 'Maslon' (MTB) **new** | ESgI |
| | 'Mastery' (TB) | CIri |
| | 'Matinata' (TB) | CKel |
| | 'Matrix' (TB) | EFam |
| | 'Maui Moonlight' (IB) ♀H4 | CKel EFam ESgI WAul |
| | 'Maui Surf' (BB) ♀H4 | WAul |
| | 'Mauna Loa Fire' (TB) | CIri |
| | 'Mauvelous' (TB) | CIri EFam |
| | 'May Melody' (TB) | WCAu |
| | 'Maya Mint' (MDB) | LLHF |
| | 'Meadow Court' (SDB) | CBro CKel ERos NBro WCAu |
| | 'Media Luz' (Spuria) | WCAu |
| | 'Medway Valley' (MTB) ♀H4 | SIri WAul WCAu |
| | 'Meg's Mantle' (TB) ♀H4 | CKel |
| | 'Melbreak' (TB) | WCAu |
| | 'Melissa Sue' (TB) | EFam |
| | ***mellita*** | see *I. suaveolens* |
| | 'Melon Honey' (SDB) | CKel WCAu WHoo |
| | 'Memo' (IB) | EFam |
| | 'Memphis Delight' (TB) | WCAu |
| | 'Men in Black' (TB) | WCAu |
| | 'Menton' (SDB) | CKel |
| | 'Mer du Sud' (TB) ♀H4 | ESgI |
| N | 'Merebrook Blue Lagoon' (La) | WMAq |
| | 'Merebrook Jemma J' (La) **new** | WMAq |
| N | 'Merebrook Lemon Maid' (La) | WMAq |
| | 'Merebrook Malvern Shaddow' (La) **new** | WMAq |
| | 'Merebrook Purpla' (La) **new** | WMAq |
| N | 'Merebrook Rusty Red' (La) | WMAq |
| N | 'Merebrook Snowflake' (La) | WMAq |
| | 'Merebrook Sunnyside Up' (La) **new** | WMAq |
| | 'Merit' (MTB) | EFam WCAu |
| | 'Merlot' (TB) | CIri |
| | 'Mescal' (TB) | EFam |
| | 'Mesmerizer' (TB) | CIri EFam ESgI WCAu |
| | 'Metaphor' (TB) | WCAu |
| | 'Mezza Cartuccia' (IB) | ESgI |
| | 'Michael Paul' (SDB) ♀H4 | ESgI |
| N | 'Michael's Angel' | WWst |
| | 'Midnight Caller' (TB) | EFam ESgI |
| | 'Midnight Mango' | see *I.* 'Midnight Web' |
| | 'Midnight Moonlight' (TB) | CIri |
| | 'Midnight Oil' (TB) | CIri WAul WCAu |
| | 'Midnight Pacific' (TB) | EFam |
| § | 'Midnight Web' (IB) ♀H4 | WBIS |
| | 'Mil Byers' (TB) | EFam |
| | ***milesii*** ♀H4 | CPLG CPou GBuc IGor NBir WCot WPer |
| | – CC 4590 | CHid |
| | 'Millennium Falcon' (TB) | CIri WAul |
| | 'Millennium Sunrise' (TB) | WCAu |
| | 'Ming' (IB) | WCAu |
| | 'Mini Big Horn' (IB) | CIri |
| | 'Mini Champagne' (BB) | EFam |
| | 'Mini Might' (SDB) ♀H4 | EFam |
| | 'Mini-Agnes' (SDB) | CBro |
| | 'Miss Carla' (IB) | NBre |
| | 'Miss Mauve' (IB) | CIri |
| | 'Miss Nellie' (BB) | CKel |
| | 'Miss Scarlett' (BB) | EFam |
| | 'Mission Sunset' (TB) | EHrv WCAu |
| | 'Missouri Iron Ore' (Spuria) | CIri |
| | 'Missouri Orange' (Spuria) ♀H4 | CIri WBIS |
| | 'Missouri Rainbows' (Spuria) | WBIS |
| | ***missouriensis*** ♀H4 | EBee IGor NBid |
| § | – 'Tollong' ♀H4 | MSte |
| | 'Mister Matthew' (TB) ♀H4 | CKel WBIS |
| | 'Mister Roberts' (SDB) | ESgI |
| | 'Mistigri' (IB) | CBgR WAul |
| | 'Mme Chéreau' (TB) | ESgI WCAu |
| | 'Mme Louis Aureau' (TB) | ESgI |
| N | 'Mohogang Mountain' (TB) | EFam |
| | ***monnieri*** | NLar SDix |
| N | 'Monsieur-Monsieur' (TB) **new** | ESgI |
| | Monspur Group | WCot |
| § | 'Monspur Cambridge Blue' (Spuria) ♀H4 | WCAu |
| | 'Monty's Sweet Blue' (TB) | CIri EFam |
| | 'Moon Journey' (TB) | SIri WAul |
| | 'Moon Sparkle' (IB) | CKel LCro |
| | 'Moonbeam' (TB) | CKel |
| | 'Moonlight' (TB) | EFam WCot |
| | 'Moonlight Waves' | see *I. ensata* 'Moonlight Waves' |
| | 'Moonlit Waves' (TB) | CKel |
| | 'Morning Show' (IB) | CWGN EBee |
| | 'Morning's Blush' (SDB) ♀H4 | CIri |
| | 'Morwenna' (TB) ♀H4 | CKel EFam WBIS WCAu |
| | 'Mote Park' (MTB) | SIri |
| | 'Mother Earth' (TB) | ESgI LRHS WAul |
| | 'Mountain Majesty' (TB) | ESgI |

| | | |
|---|---|---|
| | 'Mrs Horace Darwin' (TB) | CFir SWat WMnd |
| | 'Mrs Nate Rudolph' (SDB) | EBee MBri |
| | 'Mrs Tait' (Spuria) | NChi |
| | 'Mulberry Rose' (TB) | CFee NChi |
| | 'Mulled Wine' (TB) | EFam ESgI |
| | 'Murmuring Morn' (TB) | WCAu |
| | 'My Friend Jonathan' (TB) | EFam |
| | 'My Honeycomb' (TB) | WCAu |
| | 'My Kayla' (SDB) | ESgI |
| N | 'My Seedling' (MDB) | CBro ERos NMen |
| | 'Myra' (SDB) **new** | ESgI |
| | 'Mystic Beauty' (Dut) **new** | SBch |
| | 'Mystic Lover' (TB) | EFam |
| | 'Naivasha' (TB) | CKel |
| | 'Nancy' (TB) | SApp |
| | 'Nancy Hardy' (MDB) | CBro ERos NMen |
| | 'Nancy Lindsay' | see *I. lutescens* 'Nancy Lindsay' |
| | 'Nanny' (SDB) | SIri |
| | 'Naples' (TB) | ESgI |
| | ***narbutii*** (J) | WWst |
| | ***narcissiflora*** | CFir EBee |
| | 'Nashborough' (TB) | WCAu |
| | 'Natascha' (Reticulata) | EBrs ECho EPot LAma LRHS SPhx |
| | 'Natchez Trace' (TB) | MWea |
| | 'Natural Grace' (TB) | EFam |
| | 'Navajo Jewel' (TB) | ESgI LRHS WCAu |
| | 'Near Myth' (SDB) | WCAu |
| | 'Nectar' (IB) | ESgI WAul |
| | 'Needlecraft' (TB) | EFam NBre |
| | 'Needlepoint' (TB) | ESgI |
| | 'Neige de Mai' (TB) | ESgI |
| | ***nepalensis*** | see *I. decora* |
| | ***nertschinskia*** | see *I. sanguinea* |
| N | 'New Argument' (J) | WWst |
| | 'New Centurion' (TB) | WCAu |
| | 'New Day Dawning' (TB) **new** | CIri |
| | 'New Idea' (MTB) | ESgI WCAu |
| | 'New Leaf' (TB) | EFam WCAu |
| | 'New Snow' (TB) | WCAu |
| | 'Nibelungen' (TB) | ELon EPfP MWea NBre WFar |
| | 'Nice 'n' Nifty' (IB) | WTin |
| | 'Nicola Jane' (TB) ♀H4 | CKel |
| | ***nicolai*** | ECho WWst |
| | 'Nigerian Raspberry' (TB) | WCAu |
| | 'Night Edition' (TB) | ESgI |
| | 'Night Game' (TB) | WCAu |
| | 'Night Owl' (TB) | CKel COIW ELan ESgI MCot SPet WHlf |
| | 'Night Ruler' (TB) | ESgI WCAu |
| | 'Night Shift' (IB) | NBre |
| | 'Nightfall' (TB) | EBee |
| | 'Nights of Gladness' (TB) | ESgI |
| | 'Nineveh' (AB) | WCAu |
| N | 'Noces Blanches' (IB) | ESgI |
| | 'Noon Siesta' (TB) | ESgI |
| | 'Nora Eileen' (TB) ♀H4 | CKel WBIS |
| | 'Nordica' (TB) **new** | ESgI |
| | 'Norfolk Belle' (TB) ♀H4 **new** | WBIS |
| | 'Northern Flame' (TB) | EFam |
| | 'Northern Jewel' (IB) **new** | SIri |
| | 'Northwest Pride' (TB) | WCAu |
| | 'Novemberfest' (SDB) | EFam |
| | 'Nut Ruffles' (SDB) | WAul |
| | 'O Shenandoah' (TB) | EFam |
| | 'Obsidian' (TB) | CIri |
| | 'Ocean Depths' (TB) | ESgI |
| | 'Ocelot' (TB) | ESgI |
| | 'Ochraurea' (Spuria) | NGdn NSti |
| | 'Ochre Doll' (SDB) | CKel |
| | ***ochroleuca*** | see *I. orientalis* Mill. |

| | | |
|---|---|---|
| | 'O'Cool' (IB) | CKel |
| | 'October' (TB) | EFam |
| | 'October Storm' (IB) | EFam |
| | ***odaesanensis*** | EBee |
| | 'Off Broadway' (TB) | EFam |
| | 'Oh So Cool' (MTB) **new** | ESgI |
| | 'Oiseau Lyre' (TB) **new** | ESgI |
| | 'Oktoberfest' (TB) | EFam ESgI |
| | 'Ola Kalá' (TB) | EAEE EBla ECGP ESgI EWll GMaP MSte NBre NLar SPer SPoG WCAu |
| | 'Old Black Magic' (TB) | ESgI |
| | 'Olive Reflection' (TB) | EFam |
| | 'Olympiad' (TB) | ESgI |
| | 'Olympic Challenge' (TB) | ESgI WCAu |
| | 'Olympic Torch' (TB) | EFam ESgI WCAu |
| | 'Ominous Stranger' (TB) | ESgI WCAu |
| | 'One Desire' (TB) | WCAu |
| | 'Opalette' (IB) | EFam |
| | 'Open Sky' (SDB) | SIri |
| | 'Orageux' (IB) | CBgR CWCL ESgI WAul |
| | 'Orange Caper' (SDB) | EAEE EBla EGoo ESgI GBuc GEdr MRav MSte NLar SMrm WCAu |
| | 'Orange Cordial' (SDB) | EFam |
| | 'Orange Dawn' (TB) ♀H4 | EFam |
| | 'Orange Design' (SDB) | EFam |
| | 'Orange Gumdrops' (SDB) | EFam |
| | 'Orange Harvest' (TB) | EFam |
| | 'Orange Order' (TB) | WCAu |
| N | 'Orange Plaza' | ECho NMen |
| | 'Orange Pop' (BB) **new** | WAul |
| | 'Orange Popsicle' (TB) | EFam |
| | 'Orange Tiger' (SDB) | EFam WCAu |
| | 'Orangerie' (TB) | EFam |
| | 'Orchardist' (TB) | CKel |
| | 'Orchid Cloud' (TB) | EFam |
| | 'Orchidarium' (TB) | CKel |
| | 'Orchidea Selvaggia' (TB) | ESgI |
| | ***orchioides*** misapplied | see *I. bucharica* Foster |
| § | ***orchioides*** Carrière | CMea ECho ELan ERos MLHP NWCA |
| N | - 'Urungachsai' | EPot WWst |
| | 'Oregold' (SDB) | WCAu |
| | 'Oregon Skies' (TB) | ESgI ETod |
| | 'Oreo' (TB) **new** | CIri |
| N | 'Oriental Argument' (J) | WWst |
| | 'Oriental Baby' (IB) | CKel WAul |
| | 'Oriental Beauty' (TB) | GBri |
| | 'Oriental Beauty' (Dut) | EBrs GKev LRHS SBch SPer WCot WFar |
| | 'Oriental Glory' (TB) | WCAu |
| | 'Oriental Touch' (SpecHybrid) | CRow |
| | ***orientalis*** Thunb. | see *I. sanguinea* |
| | ***orientalis*** ambig. | EPyc |
| § | ***orientalis*** Mill. ♀H4 | EPPr EWTr GCal IFro MSte SGar WBVN WCAu WDyG |
| | - 'Alba' | see *I. sanguinea* 'Alba' |
| | 'Orinoco Flow' (BB) ♀H4 | CHar CKel EFam ESgI WCAu |
| | 'Orloff' (TB) | ESgI |
| | 'Oro Antico' (TB) **new** | CIri |
| | 'Osage Buff' (TB) | CKel |
| | 'Osay Canuc' (TB) **new** | CIri |
| | 'Ostrogoth' (TB) **new** | CIri |
| | 'Oulo' (TB) **new** | ESgI |
| | 'Our House' (TB) **new** | ESgI |
| | 'Out Yonder' (TB) | WCAu |
| | 'Ovation' (TB) | ESgI |
| | 'Over Easy' (SDB) | CKel |
| | 'Overjoyed' (TB) | WCAu |
| | 'O'What' (SDB) | EFam ESgI |
| | 'Owyhee Desert' (TB) | WCAu |

| | | |
|---|---|---|
| | 'Oxford Tweeds' (SDB) | ESgI |
| | 'Ozone Alert' (TB) | CIri |
| | Pacific Coast hybrids | see *I.* Californian hybrids |
| | 'Pacific Mist' (TB) | WCAu |
| | 'Pacific Panorama' (TB) | ESgI |
| | 'Pacific Tide' (TB) | EFam |
| | 'Pagan Dance' (TB) | EFam WCAu |
| | 'Pagan Goddess' (TB) | EFam |
| | 'Pagan Princess' (TB) | WCAu |
| | 'Paint It Black' (TB) | ETod |
| | 'Painted Clouds' (TB) | LRHS |
| | 'Pale Primrose' (TB) | WCAu |
| | 'Pale Shades' (IB) ♀H4 | CBro CKel ERos |
| | 'Palissandro' (TB) | ESgI |
| § | ***pallida*** | CCVT EBee EGoo ESgI GMaP LBMP MCCP MRav MSte MWat SIng WCAu WMnd |
| § | - 'Argentea Variegata' (TB/v) | CBcs CSBt CWCL CWGN EBee EBrs ECha ECho EHoe EHrv EPfP GGar GMaP LAst LRHS MBrN MBri MCot MLLN MNFA MRav NBir NSti SPer SPhx SPoG WCot WCra |
| | - 'Aurea' | see *I. pallida* 'Variegata' hort. |
| | - 'Aurea Variegata' | see *I. pallida* 'Variegata' hort. |
| | - var. ***dalmatica*** | see *I. pallida* subsp. *pallida* |
| § | - subsp. ***pallida*** ♀H4 | CKel CWan EAEE ECha ELan GCal MBri SDix SPer WAul |
| | - 'Variegata' misapplied | see *I. pallida* 'Argentea Variegata' |
| § | - 'Variegata' hort. (v) ♀H4 | Widely available |
| | 'Palo Pinto' (TB) | EFam |
| | 'Palomino' (TB) | WCAu |
| | 'Paltec' (IB) | CPou EBee |
| | 'Pane e Vino' (TB) | ESgI |
| | 'Pansy Top' (SDB) | SIri |
| | 'Paprika Fono's' (TB) | EFam |
| | 'Paradise' (TB) | CKel |
| | 'Paradise Bird' (TB) ♀H4 | EFam |
| | 'Paradise Saved' (TB) | EFam |
| | ***paradoxa*** | EBrs ECho WWst |
| | 'Paricutin' (SDB) | CBro |
| | 'Parisien' (TB) **new** | CWCL |
| | 'Party Dress' (TB) | CSBt CWGN EAEE EBee EBla ELan LAst LRHS MBNS MRav NBir NGdn NLar SPer SPet SPoG SRms SWat WCFE WCot WCra |
| | 'Passion Flower' (TB) | EFam |
| N | 'Passionata' | EFam |
| | 'Passport' (BB) | ECho |
| | 'Pastel Charm' (SDB) | CMMP MSte WMnd |
| | 'Patches' (TB) | ESgI |
| | 'Patina' (TB) | ECtt ESgI ETod WAul WCAu |
| | 'Patterdale' (TB) | NBir NBre NVic WCAu |
| | 'Paul Black' (TB) | CIri |
| | 'Pauline' (Reticulata) | CBro EBrs ECho EPfP EPot ERCP GKev LAma LRHS SMrm WFar |
| | 'Peaceful Waters' (TB) | ECtt EFam |
| | 'Peacetime' (TB) | WCAu |
| | 'Peach Brandy' (TB) | EFam |
| | 'Peach Everglow' (TB) | EFam |
| | 'Peach Eyes' (SDB) | CBro CKel ERos |
| | 'Peach Float' (TB) | WCAu |
| | 'Peach Picotee' (TB) | EFam ESgI |
| | 'Peach Reprise' (BB) | EFam |
| | 'Peach Spot' (TB) | WCAu |
| | 'Peaches ala Mode' (BB) | WCAu |
| | 'Peacock' | see *I. ensata* 'Peacock' |
| | 'Peacock Pavane' (CH) ♀H4 **new** | SIri |
| | 'Pearls of Autumn' (TB) | EFam WCAu |
| | 'Pearly Dawn' (TB) | EAEE EBee EBla ECha ECtt MCot MSte SPer SRGP SSvw SWat WAul WCot |
| | 'Pêche Melba' (TB) **new** | ESgI |
| | 'Pegaletta' | EPPr NBro |
| | 'Peggy Chambers' (IB) ♀H4 | EFam SMrm |
| | 'Pele' (SDB) | EFam ESgI WCAu |
| | 'Penny Anne' (BB) | EFam |
| | 'Penny Royal' (BB) | SKHP |
| | 'Pepita' (SDB) | SIri |
| | 'Pepper Blend' | EFam |
| | 'Perfect Interlude' (TB) | ECtt |
| | 'Perfume Counter' (TB) | EFam |
| | 'Perfume Shop' (IB) | CKel |
| | 'Persian Berry' (TB) | LRHS WCAu |
| | 'Persian Wood' (IB) **new** | WAul |
| | 'Petit Tigre' (IB) **new** | CBgR |
| | 'Petite Monet' (MTB) **new** | ESgI |
| | 'Pharaoh's Daughter' (IB) | SIri WAul |
| | 'Phil Keen' (TB) ♀H4 | CKel EFam WBIS |
| | 'Picacho Peak' (Spuria) | CIri |
| N | 'Picadee' | EAEE EBla EPfP GBuc NCob SPet |
| | 'Piero Bargellini' (TB) | ESgI |
| | 'Pigmy Gold' (IB) | EBee ERos |
| | 'Pineapple Poll' (TB) | EFam |
| N | 'Pinewood Delight' (CH) | SUsu |
| | 'Pinewood Poppet' (CH) | SUsu |
| | 'Pinewood Sunshine' (CH) | SUsu |
| | 'Pink Angel' (TB) | LCro |
| | 'Pink Attraction' (TB) | EFam ESgI |
| | 'Pink Bubbles' (BB) | WAul |
| | 'Pink Charm' (TB) | CWGN EAEE EBla EPfP IPot LBuc LRHS MWat SPet WAul WCra |
| | 'Pink Confetti' (TB) | ESgI |
| | 'Pink Fawn' (SDB) | ESgI |
| | 'Pink Formal' (TB) | ESgI |
| | 'Pink Horizon' (TB) | EPfP WFar |
| | 'Pink Kitten' (IB) | WCAu WGwG |
| | 'Pink Parchment' (BB) ♀H4 | CKel WBIS |
| | 'Pink Pele' (IB) | ESgI |
| | 'Pink Pussycat' (TB) | MBri |
| | 'Pink Reprise' (BB) **new** | WAul |
| | 'Pink Swan' (TB) | ESgI |
| | 'Pink Taffeta' (TB) | ESgI |
| | 'Pinkness' (TB) | EFam |
| N | 'Pinky Dinky' | EFam |
| | 'Pinnacle' (TB) | CKel ESgI GCal LRHS SWat WCAu |
| | 'Pipes of Pan' (TB) | ESgI MRav WCAu |
| | 'Pirate's Patch' (SDB) | ESgI |
| | 'Pirate's Quest' (TB) | EFam ESgI |
| | 'Piroska' (TB) ♀H4 | ESgI SGar |
| N | 'Piu Blue' (TB) | ESgI |
| | 'Pixie' (Reticulata) ♀H4 | EBrs ECho ELan EPot LRHS SMeo |
| | 'Pixie' (DB) | GKev |
| | 'Pixie Flirt' (MDB) | ERos |
| | ***planifolia*** | ECho SKHP |
| * | - f. ***alba*** | EBrs ECho |
| | 'Pleased as Punch' (IB) | EFam |
| | 'Pledge Allegiance' (TB) | ECtt ESgI SIri WCAu |
| | ***plicata*** | WCAu |
| | 'Plickadee' (SDB) | CBro |
| | 'Pluie d'Or' (TB) | ESgI |
| | 'Plum Lucky' (SDB) | SIri |
| | 'Plum Wine' (SDB) | CKel |
| | 'Poco Taco' (SDB) | WAul |
| | 'Poem of Ecstasy' (TB) | WCAu |
| | 'Poetess' (TB) | WCAu |
| | 'Pogo' (SDB) | CWGN EBla ECtt EFam ELan EPfP EPot ETod GBuc GMaP MBNS MMHG MRav NBir NWCA SPet SRms |
| | 'Polar Queen' (TB) | EFam |
| | 'Pond Lily' (TB) | ESgI WCAu |

| | | |
|---|---|---|
| | 'Pookanilly' (IB) | ESgI |
| | 'Portfolio' (TB) | ESgI |
| | 'Portrait of Amy' (TB) | EFam |
| | 'Posh' (IB) | EFam |
| | 'Powder Blue Cadillac' (TB) | CKel |
| | 'Power Point' (TB) **new** | CIri |
| | 'Prague' (TB) **new** | CIri |
| | 'Precious Heather' (TB) ♀H4 | CKel |
| | 'Presby's Crown Jewel' (TB) | CIri |
| | 'Presence' (TB) | EFam SIri |
| | 'Prestige Item' (TB) **new** | WAul |
| | 'Presumption' | EFam |
| | 'Pretender' (TB) | LRHS WCAu |
| | 'Pretty Please' (TB) | ESgI |
| | 'Prince Indigo' (TB) | MRav |
| | 'Prince of Burgundy' (IB) ♀H4 | WCAu |
| | 'Prince of Earl' (TB) | EFam |
| | 'Princess Beatrice' (TB) | WCAu |
| | 'Princess Pittypat' (TB) | EFam |
| | 'Princess Sabra' (TB) ♀H4 | CKel |
| | 'Princesse Caroline de Monaco' (TB) | CWCL ESgI WBIS |
| | 'Priscilla de Corinth' (TB) | EFam |
| | ***prismatica*** | EBee |
| | - ***alba*** | IGor |
| | 'Professor Blaauw' (Dut) ♀H4 | EBrs EPfP |
| | 'Progressive Attitude' (TB) | EFam WBIS WCAu |
| | 'Protocol' (IB) | CKel EFam |
| | 'Prototype' (TB) **new** | CIri |
| | 'Proud Tradition' (TB) | SIri WCAu |
| | 'Provençal' (TB) | CKel CWCL ECtt ESgI ETod LCro WAul WCAu |
| | 'Proverb' (Spuria) | WCAu |
| | 'Prudy' (BB) ♀H4 | CKel |
| | ***pseudacorus*** ♀H4 | Widely available |
| | - B&SWJ 5018 from Japan | WCru |
| | - from Korea | CRow |
| | - 'Alba' | CPrp CRow EBee GBin GCal LAst LRHS NGdn |
| | - var. ***bastardii*** | CBgR CRow CWat EBee ECha EMFW EPfP ESgI IGor LPBA NPer SLon SMHy SMrm SPer WBrk WFar WMoo WTin |
| | - 'Beuron' | CRow |
| | - cream-flowered | NBir WAul |
| N | - 'Crème de la Crème' | GBin |
| | - 'Esk' | GBin GCal |
| N | - 'Flore Pleno' (d) | CBgR CPrp CRow EBee EBrs ECho EMFW EPPr ESgI GCra LPBA MSKA NLar NPer WBrk WCot WFar |
| N | - 'Golden Daggers' | CRow |
| I | - 'Golden Fleece' | SPer |
| | - 'Golden Queen' | CRow IGor |
| | - 'Ilgengold' | CRow |
| N | - 'Ivory' | CRow |
| * | - ***nana*** | CRow |
| | - 'Roccapina' | GBin |
| | - 'Roy Davidson' ♀H4 | CBgR CDWL CKel CPrp CRow EMFW ESgI GBin GCal IBlr LPBA WFar WHil WPtf WTin |
| N | - 'Sulphur Queen' | CBgR WCot |
| | - 'Sun Cascade' | CRow |
| N | - 'Tiger Brother' | SIri WBrk |
| | - 'Tiggah' | CRow |
| N | - 'Turnipseed' | ESgI WTin |
| | - 'Variegata' (v) ♀H4 | Widely available |
| | - white-flowered, from Lake Michigan | WTin |
| * | ***pseudocapnoides*** (J) **new** | WWst |
| | ***pseudopumila*** | ERos |
| | 'Puddy Tat' (SDB) | CIri |
| | 'Pulsar' (TB) | EFam |
| | 'Pulse Rate' (SDB) | CBro |
| | ***pumila*** | CPBP EDAr GKev LRHS NHol NMen NWCA |
| | - 'Alba' (DB) | CPBP |
| | - ***atroviolacea*** | CKel ESgI SMrm WMnd |
| | - subsp. ***attica*** | see *I. attica* |
| | - blue-flowered | SWal |
| * | - 'Caerulea' **new** | GAuc |
| N | - 'Gelber Mantel' | NBir |
| N | - 'Lavendel Plicata' | EBee NBro NGdn |
| | - 'Violacea' (DB) | SRms |
| | - yellow-flowered | GAbr SWal |
| | 'Pumpin' Iron' (SDB) | CKel ESgI MSte |
| | 'Punch' (BB) **new** | WAul |
| | 'Punchline' (TB) **new** | CWCL ECtt |
| | 'Punk' (MDB) **new** | CIri |
| | 'Punkin' (TB) | EFam |
| | ***purdyi*** | GBuc |
| | 'Pure Allure' (SDB) ♀H4 | CIri |
| | 'Pure As Gold' (TB) **new** | CWCL ESgI |
| | 'Purple Duet' (TB) | EFam |
| | 'Purple Gem' (Reticulata) | EBrs ECho EPfP EPot LAma LHop LRHS MCot |
| | 'Purple People Eater' (TB) **new** | CIri |
| | 'Purple Sensation' (Dut) | ECho |
| | 'Quaker Lady' (TB) | ESgI SIri WCAu |
| | 'Quark' (SDB) | CBro CKel |
| | 'Quasar' (TB) | EFam |
| | 'Quechee' (TB) | EAEE EBee EBla ECGP EPfP ESgI ETod GMaP IPot LBuc LDai MBNS MCot MRav MSte MWat NLar SHBN STes SWat WAul WCra |
| | 'Queen in Calico' (TB) | ESgI WCAu |
| | 'Queen of May' (TB) | ESgI |
| | 'Queen's Circle' (TB) ♀H4 | CIri WBIS |
| | 'Queen's Ivory' (SDB) | SMrs WCAu |
| | 'Queen's Prize' (SDB) | SIri |
| | 'Quietly' (SDB) | EFam |
| | 'Rabbit's Foot' (SDB) | LSRN |
| | 'Radiant Angel' (TB) | EFam |
| | 'Radiant Apogee' (TB) | ECtt ESgI |
| | 'Rain Dance' (SDB) ♀H4 | ESgI WCAu |
| | 'Rainbow Goddess' (TB) | EFam |
| | 'Rainbow Rim' (SDB) | ESgI |
| | 'Rajah' (TB) | Widely available |
| | 'Rameses' (TB) | ESgI |
| | 'Rancho Rose' (TB) | CKel |
| | 'Rapture in Blue' (TB) | WAul |
| | 'Rare Edition' (IB) | CKel EFam ESgI LCro MBri NBre WAul WCAu |
| | 'Rare Quality' (TB) | WAul |
| | 'Rare Treat' (TB) | WCAu |
| | 'Raspberry Acres' (IB) | MRav WCAu |
| | 'Raspberry Blush' (IB) ♀H4 | CKel CPar EAEE EBla EFam EPfP LAst MAvo MCot MRav NBre SHBN STes SWat WAul WCAu |
| | 'Raspberry Fudge' (TB) | WCAu |
| | 'Raven Hill' (TB) | WCAu |
| | 'Razoo' (SDB) | CKel |
| | 'Real Coquette' (SDB) | SIri |
| | 'Realm' (TB) **new** | ESgI |
| | 'Recurring Dream' (TB) | EFam |
| | 'Red At Night' (TB) | WAul |

| | | |
|---|---|---|
| | 'Red Atlast' (MDB) | ESgI |
| | 'Red Canyon Glow' (TB) | CIri |
| | 'Red Duet' (TB) | EFam |
| | 'Red Flash' (TB) | ESgI |
| | 'Red Heart' (SDB) | ESgI GEdr GMaP MRav MSte STes WTin |
| | 'Red Oak' (Spuria) | ESgI WCAu |
| | 'Red Orchid' (IB) | ELan NBlu NBre WCAu |
| | 'Red Revival' (TB) | EFam MRav WCAu |
| N | 'Red Rum' (TB) | CKel |
| | 'Red Tornado' (TB) | ESgI |
| | 'Red Zinger' (IB) | ESgI WAul |
| | 'Redelta' (TB) | EFam |
| | 'Redwood Supreme' (Spuria) | WAul |
| | 'Regal Surprise' (SpecHybrid) ♀H4 | CBgR CRow WAul |
| | 'Regards' (SDB) | CBro |
| § | ***reichenbachii*** | CPBP CSsd ERos LBee LLHF NWCA WHil WThu |
| | - NS 700 | CPou |
| | 'Reincarnation' (TB) | EFam |
| | 'Remember Spring' (TB) | EFam |
| | 'Reminiscence' (MTB) **new** | ESgI |
| | 'Renown' (TB) | ESgI |
| | 'Repartee' (TB) | ESgI |
| | ***reticulata*** ♀H4 | CBcs CBro CTca EBrs ECho ELan EPfP LRHS SBch SPer SPet SPhx WCAu WFar WGwG |
| | - 'Spring Time' | EBrs ECho ERCP LAma LRHS |
| N | - 'Violet Queen' | EBrs ECho |
| | 'Return to Bayberry' (TB) | CIri |
| | 'Returning Chameleon' (TB) | EFam |
| | 'Returning Peace' (TB) | EFam |
| | 'Rime Frost' (TB) | EFam WCAu |
| | 'Ringer' (SDB) | ESgI |
| | 'Ringo' (TB) | ESgI LSRN MRav WCAu |
| | 'Rip City' (TB) | ESgI |
| | 'Ripple Chip' (SDB) | WTin |
| | 'Rippling Waters' (TB) | ESgI |
| | 'Rising Moon' (TB) | SIri |
| | 'Rive Gauche' (TB) | ESgI GEdr |
| | 'River Avon' (TB) ♀H4 | CKel WBIS WCAu |
| | 'Rivulets of Pink' (Spuria) | CIri WBIS |
| | 'Robe d'Eté' (TB) **new** | CWCL |
| § | x ***robusta*** 'Dark Aura' ♀H4 | WTin |
| § | - 'Gerald Darby' ♀H4 | Widely available |
| | - 'Mountain Brook' | CRow LLWG |
| | - 'Nutfield Blue' | WTin |
| | - 'Purple Fan' **new** | LLWG |
| | 'Rock Star' (TB) | EFam |
| | 'Rockabye' (SDB) | WAul |
| § | 'Rocket' (TB) | CMil EAEE EBla GMaP LBuc MRav MSte NBir NBre SPer |
| | 'Rocket Master' (TB) **new** | ESgI |
| | 'Role Model' (TB) | LRHS WCAu |
| | 'Roman Emperor' (TB) | EFam |
| | 'Roman Rhythm' (TB) | CWCL WCAu |
| | 'Romantic Evening' (TB) | ESgI WCAu |
| | 'Romantic Mood' (TB) | CKel |
| | 'Romp' (IB) | CKel |
| | 'Rondo' (TB) | ECtt |
| | 'Roney's Encore' (TB) | EFam |
| | 'Rosalie Figge' (TB) | EFam ESgI WCAu |
| | 'Rosé' (TB) **new** | LSRN |
| | 'Rose Queen' | see *I. ensata* 'Rose Queen' |
| | 'Rose Violet' (TB) | WCAu |
| | 'Rosemary's Dream' (MTB) | ESgI NBre |
| | ***rosenbachiana*** | EBrs ECho WWst |
| N | - 'Harangon' | ECho EPot |
| I | - 'Sina' | WWst |
| N | - 'Varzob' | WWst |
| | 'Roseplic' (TB) | ESgI |
| | 'Rosette Wine' (TB) | ESgI WCAu |
| | 'Rosy Wings' (TB) | ESgI |
| N | 'Roy Elliott' | NMen SIng |
| | 'Royal Courtship' (TB) | ESgI |
| | 'Royal Crusader' (TB) | CMdw WCAu |
| | 'Royal Elegance' (TB) | EFam SIri |
| | 'Royal Intrigue' (TB) | SIri |
| | 'Royal Magician' (SDB) | WTin |
| | 'Royal Overtime' (SDB) | EFam |
| | 'Royal Satin' (TB) | SPad |
| | 'Royal Summer' (TB) | EFam |
| | 'Royal Tapestry' (TB) | NBre |
| | 'Royal Yellow' (Dut) | LRHS |
| | 'Royalist' (TB) | CKel |
| | 'Rubacuori' (TB) | ESgI |
| | 'Ruban Bleu' (TB) | ESgI |
| | 'Rubistar' (TB) | ESgI |
| | 'Ruby Chimes' (IB) | ESgI WCAu |
| | 'Ruby Contrast' (TB) | WCAu |
| | 'Ruby Eruption' | EFam |
| | 'Ruby Morn' (TB) | CIri |
| | ***rudskyi*** | see *I. variegata* |
| | 'Ruée Vers l'Or' (TB) **new** | ESgI |
| | 'Ruffled Canary' (Spuria) | WCAu |
| | 'Ruffled Revel' (SDB) | GKir SIri |
| | 'Russet Crown' (TB) | CKel |
| | 'Rustic Cedar' (TB) | ESgI WCAu |
| | 'Rustle of Spring' (TB) **new** | CIri |
| | 'Rustler' (TB) | ESgI WAul WCAu |
| | 'Rusty Beauty' (Dut) **new** | SBch |
| | 'Ruth Black' (TB) | WCAu |
| | ***ruthenica*** | CPBP ECho ERos GBin NMen |
| | - var. ***nana*** | EBee GKev |
| | 'Ryan James' (TB) | CKel |
| | 'Sable' (TB) | EAEE EBee EBla EHrv ELan ESgI ETod GMaP LBuc LSRN MBri MCot MRav MSte MWat NGdn NOrc SCoo SEND SHBN SPer WAul WCAu WCra |
| | 'Sable Night' (TB) | CHar CKel ESgI |
| | 'Sager Cedric' (TB) | WCAu |
| | 'Saint Crispin' (TB) | EAEE EPfP GCra GMaP MRav MSte SPer SPet SPoG |
| | 'Sally Jane' (TB) | WCAu |
| | 'Salonique' (TB) | NBlu NBre NLar WCAu WFar |
| | 'Saltwood' (SDB) | CBro NBre SIri |
| | 'Sam Carne' (TB) | WCAu |
| | 'San Leandro' (TB) | MBri |
| | 'Sand Princess' (MTB) | SIri |
| | 'Sandstone Sentinel' (BB) | CIri |
| | 'Sandy Caper' (IB) | WCAu WTin |
| | 'Sangone' (IB) | ESgI |
| § | ***sanguinea*** ♀H4 | LEdu WBVN |
| § | - 'Alba' | IBlr WCot |
| | - 'Nana Alba' | GBin IBlr SIri |
| § | - 'Snow Queen' | Widely available |
| | 'Santana' (TB) | ECtt |
| | 'Sapphire Beauty' (Dut) | EPfP LRHS |
| | 'Sapphire Gem' (SDB) | CKel EFam ESgI LSRN WAul WCAu |
| | 'Sapphire Hills' (TB) | WCAu |
| | 'Sapphire Jewel' (SDB) | EPPr |
| | 'Sarah Taylor' (SDB) ♀H4 | CBro EFam WCAu |
| | 'Sarajaavo' (AB) | CKel |
| | ***sari*** | EBrs ECho |
| | 'Sass with Class' (SDB) | CKel EFam WTin |
| | 'Satin Gown' (TB) | WCAu |
| | 'Saturday Night Live' (TB) | ESgI |
| | 'Saxon' (TB) | EFam |

| | | |
|---|---|---|
| | 'Saxon Princess' (TB) | EFam |
| | 'Scented Bubbles' (TB) | EFam |
| | ***schachtii*** | CGra CPBP |
| | - J&JA 596.802 **new** | NWCA |
| | 'Scottish Warrior' (TB) | EFam |
| | 'Scribe' (MDB) | CBro NBir WCAu |
| | 'Sea Fret' (SDB) | CBro |
| | 'Sea Monster' (SDB) | EPPr SIri |
| | 'Sea Power' (TB) | CIri |
| | 'Sea Wisp' (La) | EPPr EWTr NBro |
| | 'Season Ticket' (IB) | ESgI |
| | 'Second Look' (TB) | EFam |
| | 'Second Show' (TB) | EFam |
| | 'Second Wind' (TB) | ECtt |
| | 'Secret Rites' (TB) **new** | CIri |
| | 'Secretariat' (TB) | EFam |
| | 'Self Evident' (MDB) | LLHF |
| | 'Semola' (SDB) | ESgI |
| | 'Seneca Rebound' (SDB) | EFam |
| | 'Senlac' (TB) | NLar WMnd |
| | 'Señor Frog' (SDB) | ESgI |
| | 'September Frost' (TB) | EFam |
| | 'September Replay' (TB) | EFam |
| | ***serbica*** | see *I. reichenbachii* |
| | 'Serene Moment' (TB) | SIri |
| | 'Serenity Prayer' (SDB) | WCAu |
| | 'Set to Music' (TB) | EFam |
| | ***setosa*** 🏆H4 | CBro CSec CWCL EAlp EBee ECho EMFW EPfP ERos GAuc GCra GKev GMaP IGor LEdu LPBA LRHS MHer MLan MNrw NDlv NGdn NLAp SPer WCot |
| | - ***alba*** | GBuc MSte NLar SIng |
| | - var. ***arctica*** | EBee EMon EPot GBuc LEdu MHer NMen NWCA WHoo WPer |
| | - subsp. ***canadensis*** | see *I. hookeri* |
| | - dwarf | see *I. hookeri* |
| § | - 'Hondoensis' | MSte |
| | - 'Hookeri' | see *I. hookeri* |
| | - 'Kirigamini' | see *I. setosa* 'Hondoensis' |
| | - 'Kosho-en' | MBri |
| | - var. ***nana*** | see *I. hookeri* |
| | 'Seventy-seven' (TB) | EFam |
| | 'Severn Side' (TB) 🏆H4 | CKel WBIS |
| | 'Shakespeare's Sonnet' (SDB) | ESgI |
| | 'Shameless' (IB) | NBre |
| | 'Shampoo' (IB) | CKel SIri WCAu |
| | 'Sheer Ecstasy' (TB) | CIri WBIS |
| | 'Sheila Ann Germaney' (Reticulata) | EBrs ECho EPot LLHF NHol NMen NMin WWst |
| | 'Shelford Giant' (Spuria) 🏆H4 | WBIS |
| | 'Shepherd's Delight' (TB) | WCAu |
| | 'Sherbet Lemon' (IB) 🏆H4 | CKel EFam WCAu |
| | 'Sherwood Pink' (TB) | EFam |
| | 'Sherwood Primrose' (TB) 🏆H4 | EFam |
| | 'Shindig' (SDB) | EFam WCAu |
| | 'Shocking Blue' | WWst |
| | 'Shoot the Moon' (TB) | EFam |
| | 'Short Distance' (IB) | SIri |
| | ***shrevei*** | see *I. virginica* var. *shrevei* |
| | 'Shurton Demon' (TB) **new** | LCro |
| | 'Shurton Inn' (TB) | CKel WCAu |
| | ***sibirica*** 🏆H4 | Widely available |
| | - 'Ann Dasch' | EBee |
| | - 'Annemarie Troeger' 🏆H4 | EBee NBre SMrm |
| | - 'Anniversary' | CDes CLAP EBee LRHS |
| | - 'Atlantic Crossing' | SIri WAul |
| | - 'Atoll' | SIri |
| | - 'Baby Sister' | CAby CMHG CSsd EBee EBla EGle GAbr GBin GBuc GGar GKir LRHS MBri NBre NBro SRGP SWat WAul |
| | - 'Berlin Bluebird' | SMHy |
| | - 'Berlin Purple Wine' **new** | CAbx |
| | - 'Berlin Ruffles' 🏆H4 | EWes GBin |
| | - 'Berlin Sky' | ESgI EWes |
| | - 'Berlinger Overture' **new** | GBin |
| | - 'Bickley Cape' | EBee GKir |
| | - 'Blaue Milchstrasse' 🏆H4 | CAbx GBin |
| | - 'Blaumacher' | GBuc |
| | - 'Blue Burgee' | ECha |
| I | - 'Blue Butterfly' | ELan EPfP NGdn SHBN |
| N | - 'Blue Emperor' | EBee |
| | - 'Blue King' | CHid CKel EBee EBla ELan EPfP GMaP MDun MRav NBro NGdn NMoo SMrm SPer SPoG WMnd WMoo |
| | - 'Blue Mere' | MCot |
| | - 'Blue Moon' | GBin WFar |
| | - 'Blue Pennant' | EBee GBin |
| | - 'Blue Reverie' | CAbx CPen EPPr ESgI |
| N | - 'Blue Sceptre' | IBlr |
| | - 'Blue Seraph' | GBin |
| | - 'Bournemouth Ball Gown' | SIri |
| | - 'Bracknell' | WBor |
| | - 'Bridal Jig' | EBee |
| | - 'Butter and Sugar' 🏆H4 | Widely available |
| | - 'Caesar' | CRow SDys SRms |
| | - 'Caesar's Brother' | CBgR CHid EAEE EBee EGle ELan GMaP IBlr LCro LRHS MNFA NBro SMrm SPer SPet SWal SWat WCAu |
| | - 'Cambridge' 🏆H4 | CPrp EAEE EBee EBla ECGP GBin MNFA MSte NBre SBch SWat WCAu WFar WWlt |
| | - 'Chandler's Choice' **new** | EWes |
| | - 'Chartreuse Bounty' | CHFP EBee EGle EWes GAbr GBin GQue LAst MLLN NBPC NLar NMoo NPri NSti WPtf |
| N | - 'Chateuse Belle' | WBrE |
| | - 'Circle Round' | CSpe EPPr MWte |
| | - 'Cleve Dodge' | ESgI SIri |
| | - 'Clouded Moon' | see *I. sibirica* 'Forncett Moon' |
| | - 'Coquet Waters' | NBid |
| | - 'Coronation Anthem' | WAul |
| | - cream | see *I. sibirica* 'Primrose Cream' |
| | - 'Dance Ballerina Dance' | CRow CWCL EBee GBri GGar GQue MBNS MLLN NBPC NCGa NMoo SPoG WFar WPtf |
| N | - 'Dancing Moon' | SUsu |
| | - 'Dancing Nanou' | NBre SWat |
| | - 'Dark Circle' | EBee |
| | - 'Dark Desire' | LLWG MRav |
| | - 'Dear Delight' | CElw EPPr LLHF WFar |
| | - 'Dear Dianne' | CKel ECha NBre |
| | - 'Dewful' | WFar |
| | - 'Double Standards' | CIri |
| | - 'Dreaming Spires' 🏆H4 | ESgI SIri WCot |
| | - 'Dreaming Yellow' 🏆H4 | CBre CFee COlW CSam EAEE EBee ECha EGle EHon EPfP EShb GBin GMac LLWG MMuc MNFA MRav NBro NGdn SApp SBch SHBN SMrm SPer SVic WCAu WCra WMoo |
| | - 'Dunkler Wein' **new** | EWes |

| | | |
|---|---|---|
| | – 'Ego' | CHid CWsd ECha EWTr GAbr GBin GMac NBro SWat WMoo WPen WPrP |
| | – 'Ellesmere' | NGdn |
| | – 'Emma Ripeka' | WAul |
| | – 'Emperor' | CRow CWat MSte NBre NBur NSti SWat |
| | – 'Eric the Red' | IBlr NBur |
| | – 'Ewen' | CBgR CHVG CHid CLAP CMdw CPou CRow EBee EGle GBin GBuc GKir GMaP IBlr MNrw NGdn SMrm SWat WCot WFar WPrP WWlt |
| | – 'Exuberant Encore' ♀H4 | WCAu |
| | – 'Flight of Butterflies' | Widely available |
| § | – 'Forncett Moon' | CBgR |
| | – 'Fourfold Lavender' | EBee EWes MBri WAul |
| | – 'Fourfold White' | ESgI LRHS MWte |
| | – 'Gatineau' | CLAP EBee GBuc |
| N | – 'Gerbel Mantel' | GBin SHBN SPet WFar |
| | – grey-flowered | SApp |
| | – 'Gull's Wing' | EBee |
| | – 'Harpswell Hallelujah' | EBee |
| | – 'Harpswell Happiness' ♀H4 | CHVG CLAP CPrp EBee EGle EPfP EPyc GBin GCra LLWG SWat WAul WMoo |
| | – 'Harpswell Haze' | ECha WMoo |
| | – 'Heavenly Blue' | SPer |
| | – 'Helen Astor' | CHVG CLAP CMea CRow CSam CTri EBee EGle EShb MHar MRav SApp SWat |
| N | – 'Himmel von Komi' | GBin |
| | – 'Hoar Edge' | CAbx NChi |
| | – 'Hohe Warte' ♀H4 | GBin |
| | – 'Hubbard' | CMMP CPen EShb GBin MNrw NBro NCGa NHol |
| | – 'Illini Charm' | CHid CPen NBro SSvw WFar WMoo |
| | – 'Jac-y-do' | EWes |
| | – 'Jewelled Crown' | CPen WFar |
| | – 'Kabluey' | CIri |
| | – 'Kent Arrival' | SIri WAul |
| | – 'Lady Vanessa' | CPou EBee EGle EPPr GAbr GBin GMac MBNS MRav NBro NMoo NSti WAul WHil |
| § | – 'Lake Niklas' | GBin |
| | – 'Langthorns Pink' | CMdw ELan MRav |
| | – 'Laurenbuhl' | CPLG |
| | – 'Lavendelwein' ♀H4 **new** | GBin |
| | – 'Lavender Bounty' | CHid EBee EBla EGle NBre NBro SPet WCAu |
| | – 'Limeheart' | CPou CSev EGle ELan LLHF |
| | – 'Little Blue' | EBee |
| N | – 'Little Twinkle Star' | CHid EBee GBin NPro WFar |
| | – 'Mad Magenta' | WCAu |
| | – 'Marcus Perry' | MSte |
| | – 'Marilyn Holmes' | EBee EGle WCot |
| | – 'Marshmallow Frosting' | WFar |
| § | – 'Melton Red Flare' | CMHG CPen EAEE EBee EBla EHon ELan EPPr EShb GBin LRHS MBNS SDys WCAu WFar |
| | – 'Memphis Memory' | ELan GBin GCra GMac NGdn SPer WHoo |
| | – 'Moon Silk' | EBee EPyc GBin GBuc GGar LLHF WFar |
| | – 'Mountain Lake' | CPen CSam EAEE EPPr GBin LRHS SVic SWat WCAu |
| | – 'Mrs Rowe' | CDes CFee CPou CRow EBee EBla EGle EPPr GBuc LLWP MRav MSte MWat SWat WCAu WFar WPtf |
| | – 'Navy Brass' | EGle NBre |
| | – 'Night Breeze' | SIri |
| | – 'Niklas Sea' | see *I. sibirica* 'Lake Niklas' |
| | – 'Nottingham Lace' | EBee LLHF SWat |
| | – 'Oban' ♀H4 | CHVG ESgI GBuc GMac |
| | – 'Orville Fay' | CBgR GMac WCot WFar |
| | – 'Ottawa' | CPou CRow ECGP ELan LRHS MBNS SWat WFar |
| | – 'Outset' | EBee SSvw |
| I | – 'Pageant' | WCot |
| I | – 'Painted Desert' | EBee GKir |
| | – 'Papillon' | Widely available |
| N | – 'Pearl Queen' | MCot MTPN WFar |
| | – 'Peg Edwards' | EBee |
| | – 'Percheron' | ESgI SIri |
| | – 'Perfect Vision' ♀H4 | MBri |
| | – 'Perry's Blue' | Widely available |
| I | – 'Perry's Favourite' | CFee CRow |
| | – 'Perry's Pigmy' | GBuc |
| | – 'Persimmon' misapplied | see *I. sibirica* 'Tycoon' |
| | – 'Persimmon' ambig. | CFir CHid EAEE EBee EBla ECtt EGle EMFW GCra LRHS MNFA MWat NMoo SVic SWat WFar WMoo |
| | – 'Peter Hewitt' ♀H4 **new** | WBIS |
| | – 'Pink Haze' | CRow EBee EPfP ESgI GBin GMac MAvo MBri MLLN MMuc NBro NMoo NSti SPoG WAul |
| | – 'Pirate Prince' | NPer WHoo |
| | – Plant World hybrids | MDKP |
| | – 'Plissee' ♀H4 | CBgR GBin |
| | – 'Pounsley Purple' | CPou |
| § | – 'Primrose Cream' | WCot |
| | – 'Prussian Blue' ♀H4 | GBin |
| | – 'Purple Cloak' | MSte |
| | – 'Purple Mere' | WFar |
| N | – 'Red Flag' | NHol |
| | – 'Reddy Maid' | WCAu |
| | – 'Redflare' | see *I. sibirica* 'Melton Red Flare' |
| N | – 'Regality' | CWCL EWTr GBin MHer MMuc NBro SHBN SHGN |
| | – 'Regency Belle' ♀H4 | SIri |
| | – 'Rikugi-sakura' | EBla GBin LLHF NBPC NBhm NBro WCot |
| | – 'Roanoke's Choice' | CElw EBee EWes GBin MAvo NCGa WBor WFar |
| | – 'Roaring Jelly' | CElw EWes WCAu |
| | – 'Roger Perry' | CFee |
| | – 'Rosselline' ♀H4 | CAbx |
| | – 'Royal Blue' | ECha GBuc SWat |
| | – 'Ruby Wine' | CPen GBri LEdu |
| | – 'Ruffled Velvet' ♀H4 | Widely available |
| | – 'Savoir Faire' | ECha |
| | – 'Sea Horse' | GBuc |
| | – 'Sea Shadows' | ESgI NBir WCAu |
| | – 'Shaker's Prayer' ♀H4 | EWes WAul |
| | – 'Shall We Dance' ♀H4 | EWes WAul |
| | – 'Shirley Pope' ♀H4 | CAby COIW EBee EWes GAbr GBin GKir GQue MBri MWte NMoo NSti SMeo SUsu WAul WCot WFar WMoo |
| | – 'Shirley's Choice' | GKir SIri |
| | – 'Showdown' | EBee ECtt EGle GKir GMaP NHol SAga SHBN SWat WCAu WFar |
| | – 'Shrawley' | WCAu |
| | – 'Silver Edge' ♀H4 | Widely available |
| | – 'Sky Wings' | CRow ECha GKir MArl WMoo |
| | – 'Snow Queen' | see *I. sanguinea* 'Snow Queen' |
| | – 'Snowcrest' | CBre |
| | – 'Snowflake' | CSsd |
| | – 'Soft Blue' ♀H4 | CAbx CBgR EBee LLWG NBre |
| N | – 'Southcombe White' | CRow CWsd GBin GBuc NGdn SIri |
| | – 'Sparkling Rosé' | Widely available |
| | – 'Splashdown' (Sino-Sib) | SWat |
| | – 'Star Cluster' | WFar |
| | – 'Steve' | CHVG CPar EBee EWes GMac LPio MLLN NBro SWat WAul |
| | – 'Steve Varner' | SIri WFar |

| | | |
|---|---|---|
| | - 'Summer Sky' | CAbx CBre MSCN NCGa SWat WAul WCAu WCot WPrP WRHF WTin |
| | - 'Super Ego' | WCot WTin |
| | - 'Superact' **new** | CAbx |
| | - 'Sutton Valence' | SIri WAul |
| | - 'Tal-y-Bont' | WFar |
| | - 'Tanz Nochmal' | GBin |
| | - 'Teal Velvet' | CAbx ECha SIri WCAu WFar |
| | - 'Temper Tantrum' | CKel MBNS |
| | - 'Tropic Night' | Widely available |
| § | - 'Tycoon' | EAEE EBee EShb GBin GBuc GKir IBlr LRHS NChi NHol SMrm SPer SVic WCra |
| | - 'Valda' | EBee |
| | - 'Velvet Night' | ECtt WBrE |
| | - 'Vi Luihn' | CAbx CBcs ECha WMoo |
| | - 'Viel Creme' ♀H4 | GBin |
| N | - 'Violet Skies' | EBee GBin |
| | - 'Visual Treat' | SIri |
| | - 'Walter' | EBee |
| | - 'Wealden Butterfly' ♀H4 | SIri WAul |
| | - 'Wealden Mystery' | WAul |
| | - 'Wealden Skies' | SIri WAul |
| | - 'Welcome Return' | CElw CHVG EBee GBin GQue IPot MBNS MMuc NBro NMoo SUsu SWat WFar WMoo |
| N | - 'Welfenfürstin' | GBin |
| I | - 'White Queen' | EBla ESgI SSvw SWat WBrE |
| I | - 'White Swan' | LAst |
| | - 'White Swirl' ♀H4 | Widely available |
| | - 'White Triangles' | SIri |
| | - 'Wisley White' | NBre SPer |
| | - 'Zakopane' ♀H4 **new** | CAbx EWes |
| | - 'Zweites Hundert' | NBre WFar |
| | 'Sibirica Alba' | ECha EPfP EShb GAbr GBBs LLWP SIng SWat WBrk WCFE WFar |
| | 'Sibirica Baxteri' | CFee |
| | ***sibirica*** 'Über den Wolken' | NCot |
| | 'Sibtosa Princess' **new** | CAbx |
| | ***sichuanensis*** | CExc EBee |
| | ***sieboldii*** | see *I. sanguinea* |
| | 'Sierra Blue' (TB) | ESgI |
| | 'Sierra Grande' (TB) | EFam WCAu |
| | 'Sierra Nevada' (Spuria) | SMrm |
| | 'Sign of Leo' (TB) | EFam |
| | ***sikkimensis*** | NWCA |
| | 'Silent Strings' (IB) | MBri |
| | 'Silicon Prairie' (TB) | ESgI |
| | 'Silk Romance' (TB) | EFam |
| | 'Silkirim' (TB) | CKel |
| | 'Silver Dividends' (TB) | EFam |
| | 'Silver Screen' (TB) | EFam |
| | 'Silverado' (TB) | CKel ECtt ESgI WCAu |
| | 'Silvery Beauty' (Dut) | EPfP LRHS NBir SBch SPer WFar |
| | 'Simmer' (BB) **new** | WAul |
| | ***sindjarensis*** | see *I. aucheri* |
| | 'Sindpers' (Juno) ♀H3 | WWst |
| | 'Sinfonietta' (La) **new** | LAst |
| | 'Sinister Desire' (IB) | WCAu |
| | ***sintenisii*** ♀H4 | CBro CHid CMdw CPBP EBrs ECho NWCA WTin |
| | - HH&K 172 | CMdw |
| | 'Sir Michael' (TB) | ESgI GBBs |
| | 'Sister Helen' (TB) | EFam |
| | 'Siva Siva' (TB) | MRav WCAu |
| | 'Sixtine C' (TB) **new** | SIri |
| | 'Skating Party' (TB) | CKel ESgI LRHS MSte |
| | 'Skiers' Delight' (TB) | NBre WCAu |
| | 'Skookumchuck' (TB) | EFam |
| | 'Sky Hooks' (TB) | EFam |
| | 'Skye Blue' (TB) | EFam |
| | 'Skyfire' (TB) | ESgI MWea |

| | | |
|---|---|---|
| | 'Skyline' (J) | WWst |
| | 'Slap Bang' (SDB) | ESgI |
| | 'Slovak Prince' (TB) **new** | CIri |
| | 'Small Sky' (SDB) | CBro |
| | 'Smart Aleck' (TB) **new** | ECtt |
| N | 'Smart Girl' (TB) | CKel |
| | 'Smart Move' (TB) **new** | CWCL |
| | 'Smash' (MTB) **new** | CIri |
| | 'Smell the Roses' (SDB) | EFam |
| | 'Smokey Dream' (TB) | CKel |
| | 'Sneezy' (TB) | WCAu |
| | 'Snow Plum' (IB) | SIri |
| | 'Snow Season' (SDB) | EFam |
| | 'Snow Tracery' (TB) | MBri |
| | 'Snow Troll' (SDB) | WCAu |
| | 'Snowbrook' (TB) | WCAu |
| | 'Snowcone' (IB) | ESgI |
| | 'Snowdrift' (*laevigata*) | see *I. laevigata* 'Snowdrift' |
| | 'Snow-in-Summer' (TB) | EFam |
| | 'Snowmound' (TB) | CKel ESgI WCAu |
| | 'Snowy Owl' (TB) ♀H4 | CKel WCAu |
| | 'Soaring Kite' (TB) | WCAu |
| | 'Social Event' (TB) | ESgI WCAu |
| | 'Soft Caress' (TB) | WCAu |
| | 'Solar Fire' (TB) **new** | CIri |
| | 'Solid Mahogany' (TB) | EFam MRav WCAu |
| | 'Solstice' (TB) | EFam |
| | 'Sombrero Way' (TB) | EFam |
| | 'Somerset Blue' (TB) ♀H4 | CKel LCro WBIS WCAu |
| N | 'Somerset Vale' (TB) | SMrm |
| | 'Somerton Brocade' (SDB) | CKel |
| | 'Somerton Dance' (SDB) | CBgR CKel |
| | 'Son of Sun' (Spuria) | CIri |
| | 'Sonata in Blue' (TB) | EFam |
| | 'Song of Norway' (TB) | ECtt EPPr ESgI SIri WAul WCAu |
| | 'Sonja's Selah' (BB) | WAul |
| | 'Sopra il Vulcano' (BB) | ESgI |
| | 'Sostenique' (TB) | ESgI WCAu |
| | 'Sound of Gold' (TB) | EFam |
| | 'Southern Clipper' (SDB) | MBri |
| | 'Southern Spy' (TB) | EFam |
| | 'Sovereign Crown' (TB) | EFam |
| | 'Space Cowboy' (TB) **new** | CIri |
| | 'Space Mist' (TB) | EFam |
| | 'Sparkplug' (SDB) | ESgI |
| | 'Sparks Fly' (SDB) | WCAu |
| | 'Spartan' (TB) | CKel LCro |
| | 'Spatzel' (TB) | EFam |
| | 'Special Feature' (TB) | CIri EFam |
| | 'Speck So' (MTB) **new** | ESgI |
| | 'Speed Limit' (TB) | EFam |
| | 'Spellbreaker' (TB) | ESgI |
| | 'Spice Lord' (TB) | WCAu |
| | 'Spiced Custard' (TB) | ESgI |
| | 'Spiced Tiger' (TB) | WCAu |
| | 'Spinning Wheel' (TB) | SIri |
| | 'Spirit of Fiji' (TB) | EFam |
| | 'Spirit of Memphis' (TB) | EFam |
| | 'Splashacata' (TB) | CIri |
| | 'Spot of Tea' (MDB) | ESgI |
| | 'Spreckles' (TB) | ESgI |
| | 'Spring Festival' (TB) | WCAu |
| | 'Spun Gold' (TB) | ESgI |
| | ***spuria*** | CPou WBVN |
| | - subsp. ***carthaliniae*** | GBin WPer |
| § | - subsp. ***halophila*** | GAuc GBin WCAu |
| | - 'Lilacina' | WBIS |
| | - subsp. ***ochroleuca*** | see *I. orientalis* Mill. |
| | - subsp. ***spuria*** | GBuc |
| | x ***squalens*** | WCAu |
| | 'St Louis Blues' (TB) **new** | ESgI |
| | 'Stairway to Heaven' (TB) | ESgI WAul WBIS WCAu |
| | 'Stapleford' (SDB) | CBro |

| | |
|---|---|
| 'Staplehurst' (MTB) 𝕐$^{H4}$ | SIri WAul |
| 'Star Performer' (TB) | EFam |
| 'Star Prince' (SDB) | ESgI |
| 'Star Shine' (TB) | ESgI WCAu |
| 'Starcrest' (TB) | ESgI WAul |
| 'Stardate' (SDB) | CKel |
| 'Starfrost Pink' (TB) | EFam |
| 'Starring' (TB) | CIri |
| 'Stars and Stripes' (TB) | EFam |
| 'Starship' (TB) | EFam ESgI |
| 'Starship Enterprise' (TB) | CIri LRHS |
| 'Staten Island' (TB) | ESgI MBri SRms WCAu WTin |
| 'Status Seeker' (TB) | WCAu |
| 'Stella Polaris' (TB) | CWan ELon |
| 'Stellar Lights' (TB) | MSte WCAu |
| 'Stepping Out' (TB) 𝕐$^{H4}$ | CPar EAEE EBee EBla EPfP ESgI GBin IPot LBMP LDai LRHS MWea NBre WAul WCAu |
| 'Stinger' (SDB) 𝕐$^{H4}$ | CIri |
| 'Stingray' (TB) | CIri EFam ESgI |
| 'Stitch in Time' (TB) | WCAu |
| 'Stockholm' (SDB) | CKel WPen |
| ***stolonifera*** | EBrs ECho |
| - 'Vera' | LRHS |
| - 'Zwanenburg Beauty' | EBrs ECho |
| 'Stormy Circle' (SDB) | WCAu |
| 'Stormy Night' (TB) | EFam |
| 'Strawberry Love' (IB) 𝕐$^{H4}$ | CKel |
| 'Strictly Jazz' (TB) | EFam WCAu |
| 'Study In Black' (TB) | WCAu |
| ***stylosa*** | see *I. unguicularis* |
| § ***suaveolens*** | CBro CPou NMen WIvy |
| - 'Rubromarginata' | ERos |
| * - var. ***violacea*** | ECho GCal NMen NWCA |
| ***subbiflora*** | WCot |
| ***subbiflora*** x ***timofejewii*** | WCot |
| ***subdichotoma*** | EBee |
| 'Sugar' (IB) | NSti WCAu |
| 'Sugar Blues' (TB) | EFam |
| 'Sugar Snaps' (IB) | EFam |
| 'Suky' (TB) | EFam |
| 'Sultan's Palace' (TB) | CWCL ECho ESgI EWll LCro LRHS NBPC WBor |
| 'Sumatra' (TB) | ESgI |
| 'Summer Green Shadows' (TB) | EFam |
| 'Summer Holidays' (TB) | EFam |
| 'Summer's Smile' (TB) | ESgI |
| 'Sun Doll' (SDB) 𝕐$^{H4}$ | CKel EFam |
| 'Sun King' (TB) | EFam |
| 'Sunchime' (SDB) | EFam |
| 'Sundown Red' (IB) | NBir |
| 'Sunmaster' (TB) | EFam |
| 'Sunny and Warm' (TB) | CKel |
| 'Sunny Dawn' (IB) 𝕐$^{H4}$ | CKel EFam |
| 'Sunny Day' (Spuria) | WBIS |
| 'Sunny Disposition' (TB) | EFam |
| 'Sunny Smile' (SDB) | EFam |
| 'Sunny Tyke' (MDB) | EFam |
| 'Sunset Colors' (Spuria) 𝕐$^{H4}$ | CIri |
| 'Sunshine Boy' (IB) | CKel |
| 'Superstition' (TB) 𝕐$^{H4}$ | ELan EPPr ESgI GBin LCro LRHS NBPN SIri SMrm SSvw WCAu WCot |
| 'Supreme Sultan' (TB) | CWCL EFam ESgI ETod WAul WCAu |
| 'Susan Bliss' (TB) | EBee ELan EPfP ESgI GBBs GMaP NBre WCAu |
| 'Susan Gillespie' (IB) 𝕐$^{H4}$ | CKel |
| ***susiana*** | LAma |
| 'Suspicion' (TB) **new** | CIri WBIS |
| ***svetlanae*** | WWst |
| 'Swain' (TB) | ESgI |
| 'Swaledale' (TB) | WCAu |
| 'Swazi Princess' (TB) | CKel ESgI WCAu |
| 'Sweet Kate' (SDB) 𝕐$^{H4}$ | WCAu |
| 'Sweet Lena' (TB) | ESgI |
| 'Sweet Musette' (TB) | EFam WCAu |
| 'Sweeter than Wine' (TB) | ESgI WCAu |
| 'Sweetheart Ring' (TB) | EFam |
| 'Swingtown' (TB) | WCAu |
| 'Sybil' (TB) | GBin GCra NHar |
| 'Sylvan' (TB) | EFam |
| 'Sylvia Murray' (TB) | WCAu |
| 'Symphony' (Dut) | ECho NBir |
| 'Syncopation' (TB) | ESgI WCAu |
| 'Talk' (SDB) | EFam |
| 'Tall Chief' (TB) | WCAu |
| N 'Tanex' | ECho |
| 'Tang Fizz' (TB) | EFam |
| 'Tangerine Sky' (TB) | WCAu |
| 'Tangfu' (IB) | ESgI |
| 'Tango Music' 𝕐$^{H4}$ **new** | GBin |
| 'Tantara' (SDB) | WTin |
| 'Tanzanian Tangerine' (TB) | WCAu |
| 'Tarheel Elf' (SDB) | ESgI WTin |
| 'Tarn Hows' (TB) | ESgI SRms WCAu |
| 'Tarot' (BB) 𝕐$^{H4}$ | EFam |
| 'Tatiana' (TB) | EFam |
| 'Tchin Tchin' (IB) | WAul |
| 'Tea Leaves' (TB) | EFam |
| ***tectorum*** | CMdw CSWP CSsd ERos GBin GKev MHar NWCA |
| - BWJ 8191 | WCru |
| - 'Alba' | CPBP ERos MHar WThu |
| - 'Variegata' misapplied | see *I. japonica* 'Variegata' |
| - 'Variegata' ambig. (v) | MRav |
| - 'Variegata' (v) | EAEE EBee NSti SPoG WFar |
| 'Teesdale' (TB) | EFam |
| 'Tell Fibs' (SDB) | CBro |
| 'Temple Gold' (TB) | CKel NPer |
| 'Temple Meads' (IB) | EFam ESgI WCAu |
| 'Templecloud' (IB) 𝕐$^{H4}$ | CBgR CHar CKel LCro |
| 'Tempting Fate' (TB) | WAul |
| § ***tenax*** | CLAP CPBP ECho GAuc GBuc GEdr GKir NWCA |
| 'Tender Years' (IB) | WAul |
| 'Tennessee Gentleman' (TB) | EFam |
| 'Tennessee Vol' (TB) | EFam |
| 'Tennison Ridge' (TB) | EFam WCAu |
| ***tenuissima*** | GBuc |
| - subsp. ***tenuissima*** | CPBP GAuc NMen |
| 'Terre de Feu' (TB) | ESgI |
| 'Teverlae' | LRHS |
| 'Thaïs' (TB) | ESgI |
| 'That's Red' (MTB) | WCAu |
| 'The Black Douglas' (TB) **new** | EMal |
| 'The Bride' | see *I.* 'Bride' |
| 'The Red Douglas' (TB) | ESgI |
| 'The Rocket' | see *I.* 'Rocket' |
| 'Theatre' (TB) | ESgI |
| 'Then Again' (TB) | EFam |
| 'Third Charm' (SDB) | CBro EFam |
| 'Third World' (SDB) | CBro |
| 'Thornbird' (TB) 𝕐$^{H4}$ | ECtt EFam ESgI WCAu |
| 'Three Cherries' (MDB) | CBro ECho |
| 'Three Seasons' (TB) | EFam |
| 'Thrice Blessed' (SDB) | EFam |
| 'Thriller' (TB) | ESgI WCAu |
| ***thunbergii*** | see *I. sanguinea* |
| 'Thunder Echo' (TB) | ESgI |
| 'Thundering Hills' (TB) | CKel |
| 'Tickety Boo' (SDB) **new** | CIri |
| 'Tickle Me' (MDB) | WCAu |
| 'Tide's In' (TB) | ECtt ESgI |

| | | |
|---|---|---|
| | 'Tiffany' (TB) | WTin |
| | 'Tiffany Time' (TB) | EFam |
| | 'Tiger Butter' (TB) | ESgI |
| | 'Tiger Honey' (TB) | WCAu |
| N | 'Tiger's Eye' | EPfP |
| | ***tigridia*** | EBee WCot |
| | 'Tiki Bird' (Sino-Sib) | CIri |
| | 'Tillamook' (TB) | WCAu |
| | 'Time Piece' (TB) | CKel |
| | 'Ting Tang' (SDB) | EFam |
| | ***tingitana*** var. ***fontanesii*** | EBee WPGP |
| | 'Tinkerbell' (SDB) | CPBP EAEE ECGP MSte NBir NGdn SPet |
| | 'Tintinara' (TB) ♀H4 | CKel |
| | 'Titan's Glory' (TB) ♀H4 | ELon ESgI MRav WAul WCAu WCot |
| | 'To the Point' (TB) | WCAu |
| | 'Toasted Watermelon' (TB) | WCAu |
| | 'Tol-long' | see *I. missouriensis* 'Tollong' |
| | 'Tom Johnson' (TB) ♀H4 | CIri WCAu |
| | 'Tom Tit' (TB) | WCAu |
| | 'Tomingo' (SDB) | WCAu |
| | 'Tomorrow's Child' (TB) | ESgI |
| | 'Toots' (SDB) | WTin |
| | 'Top Flight' (TB) | ELan LAst MSte SHBN SRms |
| N | 'Topolino' (TB) | CKel SAga |
| | 'Topsy Turvy' (MTB) | NBre |
| | 'Total Eclipse' (TB) | SRms |
| | 'Total Recall' (TB) | EFam |
| | 'Totally Cool' new | LSRN |
| | 'Toucan Tango' (TB) | CIri WBIS |
| | 'Touch of Mahogany' (TB) | WCAu |
| | 'Touch of Spring' (TB) | EFam |
| | 'Tracy Tyrene' (TB) | ESgI |
| | 'Trails West' (TB) new | ESgI |
| | 'Trapel' (TB) | ESgI |
| | 'Travelling North' (TB) | EFam |
| | 'Treccia d'Oro' (TB) | ESgI |
| | 'Trencavel' (TB) | ESgI |
| | 'Trenwith' (TB) | CKel |
| | 'Trick or Treat' (TB) | EFam |
| | 'Trillion' (TB) | CIri |
| | 'Triple Whammy' (TB) | EFam ESgI |
| | 'Triplet' | WAul |
| | 'True Navy' (SDB) | WCAu |
| | ***tubergeniana*** (J) new | WWst |
| | ***tuberosa*** | see *Hermodactylus tuberosus* |
| | 'Tumultueux' (TB) | ESgI |
| | 'Tut's Gold' (TB) | ECtt ESgI WCAu |
| | 'Tweety Bird' (SDB) | EFam |
| | 'Twice Told' (TB) | EFam |
| N | 'Twin' | WWst |
| | ***typhifolia*** | EBee GAuc GKev |
| | 'Tyrian Dream' (IB) | WCAu |
| § | ***unguicularis*** ♀H4 | Widely available |
| | - 'Abington Purple' | CBro CPen WCot |
| | - 'Alba' | CAvo CBct CBro |
| N | - 'Bob Thompson' | CAvo CBro EBee |
| | - subsp. ***carica*** J&JA 600.416 | NWCA |
| | - - var. ***angustifolia*** | WSHC |
| § | - subsp. ***cretensis*** | CWsd ECho EPPr GKev NMen SHGN WAbe WCot WHil |
| N | - 'Diana Clare' | WCot |
| | - 'Kilndown' | WFar |
| | - var. ***lazica*** | see *I. lazica* |
| N | - 'Marondera' | CAvo |
| | - 'Mary Barnard' ♀H4 | CAvo CBro CFee CHar CMea CPen CPou CSam ECGP ECha ECho EHrv GEdr IBlr MAvo NBir NMen SHBN WCot WHil WMnd |
| N | - 'Oxford Dwarf' | CBro EBee ECho |
| N | - 'Palette' | ELan |
| § | - 'Walter Butt' | CAvo CBro EBee ECGP ECha ECho NBir WFar WSHC |
| | 'Up Dancing' (TB) | EFam |
| | ***uromovii*** | GBuc MArl |
| | 'Ursula Warleggan' (TB) | CKel |
| | 'Vague à l'Ame' (TB) | ESgI |
| | 'Valimar' (TB) | WCAu |
| | 'Vamp' (IB) | CKel EPPr SIri WAul |
| | 'Vandal Spirit' (TB) | ESgI |
| | 'Vanity' (TB) ♀H4 | ESgI WCAu |
| | 'Vanity's Child' (TB) | WCAu |
| § | ***variegata*** ♀H4 | CMea EGoo EShb MSte WCAu WCot |
| | - var. ***reginae*** | MSte WCAu |
| I | - - 'Davidowii' | MSte |
| | 'Vegas Heat' (BB) | CIri |
| | 'Velvet Cushion' new | LCro |
| | 'Verdissant' (IB) new | CBgR |
| | 'Verity Blamey' (TB) | CKel |
| | ***verna*** | ERos NHol |
| | ***versicolor*** ♀H4 | Widely available |
| | - 'Between the Lines' | CRow |
| | - 'Candystriper' | CAbx |
| | - 'China West Lake' | CRow |
| | - 'Claret Cup' | CPou |
| | - 'Dottie's Double' | CRow |
| | - 'Georgia Bay' | CRow |
| | - 'Kermesina' | CDWL CRow CWat EBee ECha EHon ELan EMFW ESgI GBuc GGar IBlr LPBA MGos NPer NSti SRms SWat WBrk WEas WFar WMAq WMoo WPnP |
| | - 'Mysterious Monique' | CDWL CMdw CRow CWat CWsd LLWG WAul |
| | - 'Party Line' | SIri |
| | - var. ***rosea*** | CRow |
| | - 'Rowden Allegro' | CRow |
| | - 'Rowden Aria' | CRow |
| | - 'Rowden Cadenza' | CRow |
| | - 'Rowden Calypso' new | CRow |
| | - 'Rowden Cantata' | CRow |
| | - 'Rowden Concerto' | CRow LLWG |
| | - 'Rowden Harmony' new | CRow |
| | - 'Rowden Lullaby' new | CRow |
| | - 'Rowden Lyric' | CRow |
| | - 'Rowden Mazurka' | CRow |
| | - 'Rowden Melody' new | CRow |
| | - 'Rowden Nocturne' | CRow |
| | - 'Rowden Pastorale' new | CRow |
| | - 'Rowden Prelude' | CRow |
| | - 'Rowden Refrain' | CRow |
| | - 'Rowden Rondo' | CRow |
| | - 'Rowden Sonata' | CRow |
| | - 'Rowden Symphony' | CRow |
| | - 'Rowden Waltz' | CRow |
| | - 'Silvington' | CRow |
| | - 'Whodunit' | CRow |
| | 'Vert Galant' (TB) | ESgI |
| | 'Via Domitia' (TB) new | ESgI |
| | 'Vibrant' (TB) | ESgI WCAu |
| | 'Vibrations' (TB) | ESgI |
| | ***vicaria*** | EBrs ECho GKev LEdu WWst |
| | - 'Hodji-obi-Garm' | LRHS WWst |
| I | - 'Sina' | WWst |
| | 'Victoria Falls' (TB) | EFam ESgI WCAu |
| | 'Vinho Verde' (IB) ♀H4 | CKel LCro |
| | 'Vino Rosso' (SDB) | ESgI |
| | 'Vintage Press' (IB) | WCAu |
| | 'Vintage Year' (Spuria) | WCAu |
| | 'Violet Beauty' (Reticulata) | ECho EPot ERCP GKev LAma LRHS NHol SPhx |
| | 'Violet Classic' (TB) | WCAu |

| | | |
|---|---|---|
| | 'Violet Harmony' (TB) | ESgI |
| | 'Violet Icing' (TB) ♀H4 | CKel EFam |
| | 'Violet Music' (TB) | EFam |
| | 'Violet Returns' (TB) | EFam |
| | 'Violet Rings' (TB) | WCAu |
| | 'Viper' (IB) | CIri |
| | 'Virginia Bauer' (TB) | EFam |
| | ***virginica*** | LLWG |
| | - 'De Luxe' | see *I.* x *robusta* 'Dark Aura' |
| | - 'Pink Butterfly' **new** | NMoo |
| | - 'Pond Crown Point' | CRow |
| | - 'Pond Lilac Dream' | CRow |
| N | - 'Purple Fan' | CRow |
| § | - var. ***shrevei*** | CRow WCAu |
| | 'Vitafire' (TB) | ECtt |
| | 'Vitality' (IB) | ELon ESgI |
| | 'Vitrail' (IB) **new** | CBgR |
| | 'Vive la France' (TB) | ESgI |
| | 'Vizier' (TB) | WCAu |
| | 'Voilà' (IB) | ESgI |
| | 'Volts' (SDB) | CKel EFam |
| | 'Voluminous' (TB) | CIri |
| | 'Volute' (TB) | ESgI |
| | 'Wabash' (TB) | ELan ESgI EWll WBor WCAu WTin |
| | 'Wake Up' (SDB) | EFam |
| | 'Walker Ferguson' (Spuria) | WCAu |
| | 'Walter Butt' | see *I. unguicularis* 'Walter Butt' |
| | 'Waltz Across Texas' (TB) | EFam |
| | 'War Chief' (TB) | ESgI MSte WCAu |
| | 'War Sails' (TB) | SIri WCAu |
| | 'Warl-sind' (J) | WWst |
| | 'Warranty' (TB) | CIri WCAu |
| | 'Warrior King' (TB) | WCAu |
| | ***wattii*** | CExc EBee |
| | 'Way to Go' (TB) | CIri |
| | 'Wealden Canary' (Spuria) **new** | WAul |
| | 'Wealden Elegance' (Spuria) **new** | WAul |
| | 'Wealden Sunshine' (Spuria) **new** | WAul |
| | 'Wedding Candles' (TB) | WCAu |
| | 'Wedding Vow' (TB) | CKel |
| | 'Wedgwood' (Dut) | NBre |
| | 'Welch's Reward' (MTB) ♀H4 | CKel ESgI |
| | 'Westar' (SDB) ♀H4 | CBgR CKel |
| | 'Westwell' (SDB) | WCAu |
| | 'What's My Line' (TB) **new** | CIri |
| | 'Wheels' (SDB) | WTin |
| | 'Whispering Spirits' (TB) | CIri |
| | 'White City' (TB) | EAEE EBla ECGP EFam EPfP ESgI GMaP LPio MCot MRav MWat NPer SCoo SDnm SHBN SIri SPer SPoG SRms SWat WAul WCAu WMnd |
| | 'White Excelsior' (Dut) | ECho |
| | 'White Knight' (TB) | EBee ELan EPfP NBre WMnd |
| | 'White Lightning' (TB) | EFam |
| | 'White Reprise' (TB) | ESgI |
| | 'White Wine' (MTB) | WCAu |
| | 'Whiteladies' (IB) ♀H4 | EFam |
| | 'Whole Cloth' (TB) | ESgI |
| | 'Whoop 'em Up' (BB) | EFam WFar |
| N | 'Wild Echo' (TB) | CKel |
| | 'Wild Jasmine' (TB) | ECtt WCAu |
| | 'Wild Ruby' (SDB) | CKel |
| | 'Wild West' (TB) | CKel |
| | ***willmottiana*** 'Alba' | EBrs ECho WWst |
| | 'Willowmist' (SDB) | EFam |
| | ***wilsonii*** ♀H4 | EBee GBin GBuc GKir WBVN |
| | 'Windsurfer' (TB) | EFam |
| | 'Winemaster' (TB) | ECtt SIri |
| | ***winogradowii*** ♀H4 | CAvo CBro EBrs ECho EPot ERos GKev LAma LLHF NMen NMin WAbe WWst |
| | 'Winter Crystal' (TB) ♀H4 | CKel WBIS |
| | 'Winter Olympics' (TB) | CMil EAEE EBee ESgI EShb LBuc MRav |
| | 'Wirral Gold' (IB) | EFam |
| | 'Wishful Thinking' (TB) **new** | SIri |
| | 'Wisteria Sachet' (IB) | WCAu |
| | 'Witching' (TB) | EFam WCAu |
| | 'Wizard of Id' (SDB) | WTin |
| | 'Wondrous' (TB) | EFam ESgI |
| | 'Words and Music' (TB) | EFam |
| | 'Worlds Beyond' (TB) | WCAu |
| | 'Wyckhill' (SDB) | WCAu |
| | 'Xillia' (IB) | CKel |
| | ***xiphioides*** | see *I. latifolia* |
| | ***xiphium*** | EBrs ECho |
| | - var. ***lusitanica*** | SKHP |
| | 'Xmas Fires' (TB) | EFam |
| | 'Yaquina Blue' (TB) | ESgI SCoo WCAu |
| | 'Yes' (TB) | ESgI WCAu |
| | 'Young Blood' (IB) | WCAu |
| | 'Youth Dew' (TB) | EFam |
| | 'Yo-yo' (SDB) | EPPr GEdr STes |
| | 'Yvonne Pelletier' (TB) | WCAu |
| | 'Zambezi' (TB) | EFam |
| | 'Zantha' (TB) | ESgI WCAu |
| | ***zenaidae*** | WWst |
| | 'Zero' (SDB) ♀H4 | CKel |
| | 'Zinc Pink' (BB) | WCAu |
| | 'Zipper' (MDB) | ESgI WCAu |

## *Isatis* (*Brassicaceae*)

| | | |
|---|---|---|
| | ***tinctoria*** | CArn CBod CHby COld CRWN CSev EBWF EOHP GPoy ILis LRHS MHer MNHC MSal SECG SIde SPav WCHb WJek WSFF |

## *Ischyrolepis* (*Restionaceae*)

| | | |
|---|---|---|
| § | ***subverticillata*** | CAbb CHEx CTrC EAmu |

## *Ismene* see *Hymenocallis*

## *Isodon* (*Lamiaceae*)

| | | |
|---|---|---|
| | ***calycinus*** | SPlb |
| | ***longitubus*** | WCot |
| | - 'Momokaze' **new** | EBee |
| | - 'Tube Socks' **new** | EBee |
| | ***trichocarpus*** **new** | EBee |

## *Isolepis* (*Cyperaceae*)

| | | |
|---|---|---|
| § | ***cernua*** | CHal CMil CWat EAlp EBee EMFW EPfP MBri MSKA NOak SCoo SHDw WFar WMAq WPrP |

## *Isoloma* see *Kohleria*

## *Isomeris* see *Cleome*

## *Isoplexis* (*Scrophulariaceae*)

| | | |
|---|---|---|
| | ***canariensis*** | CAbb CBcs CCCN CDTJ CHEx CHll CRHN CSec CSpe EBee ECre EWll IDee SEND SGar SPlb WCFE WWlt |
| | ***chalcantha*** | CDTJ |
| | ***isabelliana*** | CCCN CDTJ EBee EShb LDai SDix |
| | ***sceptrum*** | CAbb CCCN CDTJ CHEx CHll CPLG CRHN ECre SAPC SArc WPGP |
| | - pink-flowered | WPGP |

## *Isopogon* (*Proteaceae*)

| | |
|---|---|
| ***anemonifolius*** | SPlb |
| ***anethifolius*** | SPlb |

## *Isopyrum* (*Ranunculaceae*)

| | |
|---|---|
| ***biternatum*** | GBuc NLar |
| ***nipponicum*** | CLAP EBee WCru |
| ***thalictroides*** | LLHF WAbe |

## *Isotoma* (*Campanulaceae*)

| | |
|---|---|
| sp. | LAst SWvt |
| § ***axillaris*** | CSpe IDee LRHS NPer NPri SCoo SPer SPet SPoG |
| - 'Fairy Carpet' | SPoG SRms |
| - 'Pink Star' **new** | CSec |
| ***fluviatilis*** | NLar |
| 'Sapphire Star' | LRHS |

## *Itea* (*Escalloniaceae*)

| | |
|---|---|
| ***chinensis*** | WPGP |
| ***ilicifolia*** ♀H3 | Widely available |
| * - 'Rubrifolia' | MAsh SLon SPoG |
| ***japonica*** 'Beppu' | MGos SLPl SSpi |
| ***virginica*** | CAbP CBcs CMCN EBee ELan MBlu MRav SLon SPer WBVN WFar WOrn |
| § - 'Henry's Garnet' | Widely available |
| - Little Henry = 'Sprich' PBR | CBgR CSBt EBee ELan LAst NLar SKHP |
| - 'Long Spire' | CPMA IArd WDin |
| - 'Merlot' | CPMA LRHS MGos NLar |
| - 'Sarah Eve' | CMCN CPMA EBee NLar SRGP |
| - 'Saturnalia' | NLar WDin |
| - 'Shirley's Compact' | NLar |
| - Swarthmore form | see *I. virginica* 'Henry's Garnet' |
| ***yunnanensis*** | CPLG SSpi |

## *Itoa* (*Flacourtiaceae*)

| | |
|---|---|
| ***orientalis*** SF 92300 | ISea |

## *Ixia* (*Iridaceae*)

| | |
|---|---|
| 'Blue Bird' | CFir EBrs ECho LAma WHil |
| 'Castor' | CPne CPrp EBrs ECho WHil |
| ***conferta*** **new** | EBee |
| - var. ***ochroleuca*** | WCot |
| ***flexuosa*** | EBee WCot |
| 'Giant' | EBrs ECho WHil |
| 'Hogarth' | CPrp ECho LAma WHil |
| 'Holland Glory' | ECho |
| hybrids | EBrs |
| 'Mabel' | EBrs ECho WCot WHil |
| ***maculata*** | EBee WHil |
| 'Marquette' | ECho |
| 'Panorama' | ECho WHil |
| ***purpureorosea*** 'Saldanha' | ECho |
| 'Rose Emperor' | CPrp ECho LAma WHil |
| 'Spotlight' | ECho WHil |
| ***thomasiae*** | WCot |
| 'Venus' | CFir CPne EBrs ECho LAma WHil |
| ***viridiflora*** | CBow ECho EDif WCot WVal |
| 'Vulcan' | ECho |
| 'Yellow Emperor' | CPne EBrs ECho WCot WHil |

## *Ixiolirion* (*Ixioliriaceae*)

| | |
|---|---|
| ***montanum*** | CHFP CMea ECho |
| ***pallasii*** | see *I. tataricum* |
| § ***tataricum*** | CPrp CTca EBrs ECho LAma LEdu MBri MCot NWCA SBch |
| - Ledebourii Group | CAvo CFFs EBee |

## *Ixora* (*Rubiaceae*)

| | |
|---|---|
| ***chinensis*** 'Apricot Queen' | SOWG |
| 'Golden Ball' | SOWG |
| 'Pink Malay' | SOWG |

# J

## *Jaborosa* (*Solanaceae*)

| | |
|---|---|
| ***integrifolia*** | CAby CDes CElw CFir CPLG CStu EBee ELan LFur SSvw WAul WCot WCru WPGP |

## *Jacaranda* (*Bignoniaceae*)

| | |
|---|---|
| ***acutifolia*** misapplied | see *J. mimosifolia* |
| § ***mimosifolia*** | CBcs CCCN CHII CSec ELan EShb GQui MBri MGos MREP SOWG SPlb |

## *Jacobinia* see *Justicia*

## *Jamesbrittenia* (*Scrophulariaceae*)

| | |
|---|---|
| 'Supercandy Lilac' **new** | LAst |

## *Jamesia* (*Hydrangeaceae*)

| | |
|---|---|
| ***americana*** | MBri NLar |

## x *Jancaemonda* (*Gesneriaceae*)

| | |
|---|---|
| ***vandedemii*** | GKev |

## *Jasione* (*Campanulaceae*)

| | |
|---|---|
| § ***heldreichii*** | GAbr LRHS NBir SRms |
| ***jankae*** | see *J. heldreichii* |
| § ***laevis*** | CArn CHFP ECho ECot GAbr GKev LRHS MSCN SRms WGwG WWFP |
| § - 'Blaulicht' | CMHG CWib EBee ECha EPfP LLWG LRHS MBNS MLan MMuc MNFA MWat NBPC NBlu NLar SMrm SPla SPlb WMoo |
| - Blue Light | see *J. laevis* 'Blaulicht' |
| - 'Sangster' | CSec |
| ***montana*** | EBWF ECho WFar WPnn WRHF WSFF |
| ***perennis*** | see *J. laevis* |

## *Jasminum* (*Oleaceae*)

| | |
|---|---|
| CC 4728 | CPLG |
| ***affine*** | see *J. officinale* f. *affine* |
| ***angulare*** ♀H1 | CRHN EShb SOWG |
| ***azoricum*** ♀H1 | CCCN CDoC CRHN ELan EPfP EShb NPal |
| ***beesianum*** | Widely available |
| ***bignoniaceum*** | WSHC |
| ***blinii*** | see *J. polyanthum* |
| ***dispermum*** | CRHN |
| ***farreri*** | see *J. humile* f. *farreri* |
| ***floridum*** | EBee EWes NScw |
| ***fruticans*** | CMac EBee EPfP EPla NScw |
| ***giraldii*** hort. | see *J. humile* f. *farreri* |
| ***grandiflorum*** misapplied | see *J. officinale* f. *affine* |
| ***grandiflorum*** L. | CRHN EShb SOWG |
| 'De Grasse' ♀H1 | |
| ***humile*** | CEnt CPLG EQua GAuc IMGH MGos MHer WFar WKif |
| § - f. ***farreri*** | MBri |
| - var. ***glabrum*** | see *J. humile* f. *wallichianum* |
| § - 'Revolutum' ♀H4 | Widely available |
| § - f. ***wallichianum*** B&SWJ 2559 | WCru |
| § ***laurifolium*** f. ***nitidum*** | EShb |
| § ***mesnyi*** ♀H2-3 | CEnt CMac CPLG CRHN CSBt CTri CWib EBak EBee ELan EPfP ERas IGor MCot SAga SOWG SPer STre WSHC |
| ***multipartitum*** | EShb |
| - bushy | CSpe |

| | | |
|---|---|---|
| | ***nitidum*** | see *J. laurifolium* f. *nitidum* |
| § | ***nudiflorum*** ♀H4 | Widely available |
| | - 'Argenteum' | see *J. nudiflorum* 'Mystique' |
| | - 'Aureum' | EBee ELan EPfP EPla LBMP LRHS MAsh MBNS MRav NHol NSti SLim SPer SPla SPoG WCot WPat |
| § | - 'Mystique' (v) | ELan LRHS LSou MAsh MBNS NLar SPer WCot WPat |
| | ***odoratissimum*** | EShb SOWG |
| | ***officinale*** ♀H4 | Widely available |
| § | - f. ***affine*** | CBcs CRHN CSPN CSam CTri CWSG CWib EBee ELan ELon EPfP LAst MAsh MGan MRav NHol SCoo SDix SLim SRms WCru WFar |
| § | - 'Argenteovariegatum' (v) ♀H4 | Widely available |
| | - 'Aureovariegatum' | see *J. officinale* 'Aureum' |
| § | - 'Aureum' (v) | Widely available |
| | - 'Clotted Cream' | CBcs CCCN CSBt EBee EPfP EWTr LAst LBuc LCro LRHS LSRN MAsh MBri MGos MLan MWea NHol NLar SCoo SLim SPer SPoG WBod WCot WPat |
| | - 'Crûg's Collection' | WCru |
| | - Fiona Sunrise = 'Frojas'PBR | Widely available |
| | - 'Grandiflorum' | see *J. officinale* f. *affine* |
| | - 'Inverleith' ♀H4 | CDoC CWSG EBee ELan EPfP IArd LBMP LHop LRHS MAsh MBNS MBri MCCP MLan MRav SCoo SLim SMad SPad SPer SPoG WFar WSHC |
| | - 'Variegatum' | see *J. officinale* 'Argenteovariegatum' |
| | ***parkeri*** | CBcs CBgR CFee CMea CTri EBee ECho ELon EPfP EPot GEdr GMaP IMGH LHop MBNS NLar NMen SPla WFar WPat |
| § | ***polyanthum*** ♀H1-2 | CArn CBcs CPLG CRHN CSBt CTri EBak EBee ELan EPfP ERom EShb LAst LRHS MBri NBlu NPal SLim SOWG SPer SRms WPGP |
| | ***primulinum*** | see *J. mesnyi* |
| | ***reevesii*** hort. | see *J. humile* 'Revolutum' |
| | ***sambac*** ♀H1 | CDoC CHll CRHN ELan EPfP EShb SOWG |
| | - 'Grand Duke of Tuscany' (d) | SOWG |
| | - 'Maid of Orleans' (d) ♀H1 | SOWG |
| | ***sieboldianum*** | see *J. nudiflorum* |
| | ***stenalobium*** | SOWG |
| | x ***stephanense*** | Widely available |

## *Jatropha* (*Euphorbiaceae*)

| | |
|---|---|
| ***podagrica*** ♀H1 | LToo |

## *Jeffersonia* (*Berberidaceae*)

| | |
|---|---|
| ***diphylla*** | Widely available |
| ***dubia*** | CBro CFir CLAP EBee ECho EPot ERas EWes GBuc GEdr GKev LEdu LRHS NBir NHar NMen NSla WAbe WCru |
| - B&SWJ 984 | WCru |
| - 'Alba' | EHrv |

## jostaberry see *Ribes* x *culverwellii*

## *Jovellana* (*Scrophulariaceae*)

| | |
|---|---|
| ***punctata*** | CCCN CDoC CPLG CPSs EBee IBlr MBlu |
| ***repens*** | CFir EBee |
| ***sinclairii*** | CHll CPLG EBee ECou IBlr LLHF SMrm SUsu |
| ***violacea*** ♀H3 | CAbP CAbb CBcs CCCN CDoC CEnt CPLG CPSs CTrC CWib EBee EMil GGGa GGar IBlr IDee ITim SAPC SArc SMad WBod WCru WPGP WSHC WWlt |

## *Jovibarba* ✿ (*Crassulaceae*)

| | | |
|---|---|---|
| § | ***allionii*** | CMea CTca CTri CWil EPot GAbr LBee MHer MOne NHol NPri SIng STre WAbe WFar WHal WHoo WIvy WPer WTin |
| | - 'Oki' | CWil MOne |
| | ***allionii*** x ***hirta*** | CWil GAbr MOne NHol NMen SDys SFgr |
| § | ***arenaria*** | CWil GAbr NMen |
| | - from Passo Monte Crocecar Nico | CWil |
| | 'Emerald Spring' | CTca CWil NMen SFgr |
| § | ***heuffelii*** | ECho LRHS NHol NMen WIvy WPer |
| | - 'Aga' | NHol WIvy |
| | - 'Aiolos' | NHol |
| | - 'Alemene' | NHol |
| | - 'Almkroon' | NHol |
| | - 'Angel Wings' | CWil LBee NHol NMen WHoo |
| § | - 'Apache' | CWil |
| | - 'Aquarius' | CWil WIvy |
| | - 'Artemis' | NHol |
| | - 'Aurora' | NHol |
| | - 'Be Mine' | CTca CWil |
| | - 'Beacon Hill' | CWil WIvy |
| | - 'Belcore' | CWil WIvy |
| | - 'Benjamin' | CWil NHol |
| | - 'Bermuda' | WIvy |
| | - 'Bermuda Sunset' | NHol |
| | - 'Big Red' | NHol |
| | - 'Blaze' | CWil |
| | - 'Brandaris' | NHol SDys |
| | - 'Brocade' | NHol WIvy |
| | - 'Bronze Ingot' | CWil |
| | - 'Bronze King' | WIvy |
| | - 'Bulgarien' | CWil |
| | - 'Cakor' | NHol |
| | - 'Cameo' | WIvy |
| § | - 'Cherry Glow' | CWil NHol |
| | - 'Chocoleto' | WTin |
| | - 'Cleopatra' | NHol |
| | - 'Copper King' | CWil WIvy |
| | - 'Dunbar Red' | NHol |
| | - 'Fandango' | CWil MHom WIvy |
| | - 'Gento' | NHol |
| | - 'Geronimo' | NHol |
| | - 'Giuseppi Spiny' | MHom NHol SIng WIvy WTin |
| | - var. ***glabra*** | LBee WHoo |
| | - - from Anabakanak | CWil MHom NHol WTin |
| | - - from Anthoborio | CWil NMen WIvy WTin |
| | - - from Backovo | NHol |
| | - - from Galicica | NHol |
| | - - from Haila, Montenegro/Kosovo | CWil NHol NMen SFgr WIvy |
| | - - from Jakupica, Macedonia | CWil WIvy |
| | - - from Ljuboten | CWil NHol NMen WTin |
| | - - from Osljak | CWil |
| | - - from Pasina Glava | CWil |
| | - - from Rhodope | CWil MHom NHol |
| | - - from Treska Gorge, Macedonia | CWil NMen WTin |
| | - - from Vitse, Greece | WIvy |
| § | - - 'Cameo' | NHol |
| | - 'Gold Rand' | NHol |
| | - 'Grand Slam' | CWil |
| | - 'Green Land' | CWil |
| | - 'Greenstone' | CMea CWil MHom NHol NMen WIvy WTin |

| | | |
|---|---|---|
| | - 'Harmony' | CWil NHol |
| | - 'Henry Correvon' | CWil |
| | - var. ***heuffelii*** | CWil |
| | - 'Hot Lips' | CWil |
| | - 'Hystyle' | WIvy |
| | - 'Ikaros' | NHol |
| | - 'Inferno' | MHom NHol |
| | - 'Iole' | WIvy |
| | - 'Ithaca' | NHol |
| | - 'Iuno' | CWil NHol |
| | - 'Jade' | CWil NMen WIvy |
| | - 'Kapo' | WIvy |
| | - var. ***kopaonikensis*** | CWil LBee MHom NMen |
| | - 'Mary Ann' | MHom WIvy |
| | - 'Miller's Violet' | CWil WIvy WTin |
| | - 'Mink' | CWil |
| | - 'Minuta' | CWil NHol NMen WIvy WTin |
| | - 'Mystique' | CMea CWil LBee NMen WIvy |
| | - 'Nannette' | CWil |
| | - 'Nobel' | NHol |
| | - 'Opele' | NHol |
| | - 'Orion' | CWil NHol NMen |
| | - 'Pink Skies' | CWil WIvy |
| | - 'Prisma' | CWil WIvy WTin |
| | - 'Purple Haze' | WIvy |
| | - 'Red Rose' | CWil WIvy |
| | - 'Serenade' | CWil |
| | - 'Springael's Choice' | CWil |
| | - 'Sundancer' | WIvy |
| | - 'Sungold' | NHol |
| | - 'Suntan' | CWil NHol WIvy |
| | - 'Sylvan Memory' | CWil |
| | - 'Tan' | CWil NHol WTin |
| | - 'Torrid Zone' | WIvy WTin |
| | - 'Tuxedo' | CWil |
| | - 'Vesta' | CWil |
| | - 'Violet' | SDys WIvy |
| § | ***hirta*** | CHal CWil EDAr GAbr MOne NHol NMen SFgr STre WPer |
| | - from Wintergraben | SIng SPlb |
| § | - subsp. ***borealis*** | CWil MOne NDlv NHol |
| | - subsp. ***glabrescens*** | EPot LRHS |
| | - - from Belianske Tatry | CWil MOne |
| | - - from High Tatra | CTca |
| | - - from Smeryouka | CWil SIng |
| | - 'Lowe's 66' | MOne |
| | - var. ***neilreichii*** | LRHS MHom SIng |
| | - 'Preissiana' | CTca LBee MOne NDlv NHol NMen SFgr WIvy WTin |
| § | ***sobolifera*** | CHEx CTca CWil EDAr EPot MOne NHol NMen SFgr SIng SPlb WAbe WHal WIvy WPer |
| | - 'August Cream' | CWil LBee LRHS |
| | - 'Green Globe' | CWil LRHS SDys WTin |
| | - 'Miss Lorraine' | CWil SFgr |

## *Juanulloa* (*Solanaceae*)

| | | |
|---|---|---|
| | ***aurantiaca*** | see *J. mexicana* |
| § | ***mexicana*** | SOWG |

## *Jubaea* (*Arecaceae*)

| | | |
|---|---|---|
| § | ***chilensis*** | CBrP CPHo EAmu EUJe LPJP LPal MJnS MREP SChr |
| | ***spectabilis*** | see *J. chilensis* |

## *Juglans* ✿ (*Juglandaceae*)

| | | |
|---|---|---|
| § | ***ailanthifolia*** | CMCN ECrN EGFP IDee |
| | - var. ***cordiformis*** 'Brock' (F) | CAgr |
| | - - 'Campbell Cw1' (F) | CAgr |
| | - - 'Campbell Cw3' (F) | CAgr |
| | - - 'Fodermaier' seedling | CAgr |
| | - - 'Rhodes' (F) | CAgr |
| | ***ailanthifolia*** x ***cinerea*** | see *J.* x *bixbyi* |
| § | x ***bixbyi*** | CAgr |
| | ***cinerea*** (F) | CMCN LMaj |
| | - 'Beckwith' (F) | CAgr |
| | - 'Booth' seedlings (F) | CAgr |
| | - 'Craxezy' (F) | CAgr |
| | - 'Kenworthy' seedling | CAgr |
| | - 'Myjoy' (F) | CAgr |
| | ***mandshurica*** B&SWJ 6778 | WCru |
| | - BWJ 8097 from China **new** | WCru |
| | - RWJ 9905 from Taiwan **new** | WCru |
| * | - subsp. ***sieboldiana*** B&SWJ 11026 **new** | WCru |
| | ***nigra*** (F) ♀$^{H4}$ | Widely available |
| | - 'Bicentennial' (F) | CAgr |
| | - 'Emma Kay' (F) | CAgr |
| | - 'Laciniata' | CDul MBlu WPat |
| | - 'Thomas' (F) | CAgr |
| | - 'Weschke' (F) | CAgr |
| | ***regia*** (F) ♀$^{H4}$ | Widely available |
| | - 'Broadview' (F) | CAgr CDoC CDul CEnd CTho EHig ELan EMui GTwe LRHS MAsh MBlu MBri MCoo MGos SCoo SDea SKee SPoG SVic WOrn |
| | - 'Buccaneer' (F) | CAgr CDul CTho ECrN GTwe LRHS SDea SKee |
| | - 'Corne du Périgord' (F) | CAgr |
| | - 'Ferjean' (F) | CAgr |
| | - 'Fernette'$^{PBR}$ (F) | CAgr MCoo |
| | - 'Fernor'$^{PBR}$ (F) | CAgr MCoo |
| | - 'Franquette' (F) | CAgr CDoC ECrN EMil GTwe LRHS MCoo WDin |
| | - 'Hansen' (F) | CAgr |
| | - 'Laciniata' | WPat |
| | - 'Lara' (F) | CAgr GTwe MCoo |
| | - 'Majestic' (F) | EMui |
| | - 'Mayette' (F) | CAgr ECrN EMil WDin |
| | - 'Meylannaise' (F) | CAgr |
| | - 'Parisienne' (F) | CAgr EMil |
| | - 'Plovdivski' (F) | CAgr |
| | - 'Proslavski' (F) | CAgr CDul |
| | - 'Purpurea' | CMCN MBlu MBri |
| | - 'Rita' (F) | CAgr LBuc MBri |
| | - 'Ronde de Montignac' (F) | CAgr |
| | - 'Rubis' **new** | EMui |
| | - 'Saturn' (F) | CAgr |
| | - 'Soleze' (F) | CAgr |
| | - 'Sorrento' (F) | CCCN |
| | ***sieboldiana*** | see *J. ailanthifolia* |

## jujube see *Ziziphus jujuba*

## *Juncus* (*Juncaceae*)

| | | |
|---|---|---|
| | ***acutiflorus*** | EBWF NSco |
| | ***acutus*** | EBWF GFor |
| | ***articulatus*** | EBWF |
| * | ***balticus*** 'Spiralis' | ECho |
| | ***bulbosus*** | CNat CRWN EBWF |
| | ***conglomeratus*** | EBWF |
| | 'Curly Gold Strike' (v) | CDWL ELon MSKA SPoG |
| § | ***decipiens*** 'Curly-wurly' | CDWL CDes CFee CKno CMea CMil CSpe EBee EHoe EMon EPfP EPla EWes GFor GGar LAst LHop LPBA LRHS NOak SPla SWal SWat WHal WPGP WPnP WRos |
| | - 'Spiralis' | see *J. decipiens* 'Curly-wurly' |
| I | - 'Spiralis Nana' | NWCA |
| | ***effusus*** | CHEx CRWN CWat EBWF EHon EMFW GFor LPBA MSKA NPer NSco NSti SWat WMAq |
| | - 'Carman's Japanese' | CKno |

| | | |
|---|---|---|
| | - 'Gold Strike' (v) | CWCL EPla LHop |
| § | - f. ***spiralis*** | Widely available |
| § | - - 'Unicorn'$^{PBR}$ | CBgR EBee EPPr LBMP SApp SPoG |
| | - - 'Yellow Line'$^{PBR}$ (v) | EBee WMoo |
| | ***ensifolius*** | CDWL CDes CKno CRow CWat EBee EHoe EMFW EWes GFor LPBA MAvo MMHG MSKA NHol NNor NOak NPer WFar |
| | ***filiformis*** 'Spiralis' | EAlp EBee GFor GKev SApp |
| | ***gerardii*** new | EBWF |
| | ***inflexus*** | CBen CRWN CWat EBWF EHon GFor MSKA NHol NSco SWat |
| | - 'Afro' | CBgR CKno EAlp EBee ELan EMon EPfP MBrN MCCP NBro NOak SPlb WHal |
| | ***pallidus*** | EBee EPPr NBid NNor |
| | ***patens*** 'Carman's Gray' | CFee CKno CWCL EBee EBrs EPPr EPla EWsh GCal GQue LRHS MAvo MCCP MMoz NGdn NHol NNor NOak SApp WMoo |
| | - 'Elk Blue' | CKno |
| | 'Silver Spears' | MCCP |
| | ***squarrosus*** | EBWF |
| | 'Unicorn'$^{PBR}$ | see *J. effusus* f. *spiralis* 'Unicorn' |
| | ***xiphioides*** | EHoe EPla MHar NHol |

## *Junellia* (*Verbenaceae*)

| | | |
|---|---|---|
| | ***azorelloides*** F&W 9344 | WAbe |
| | ***odonnellii*** | WAbe |
| | ***wilczekii*** | WFar |
| | - F&W 7770 | NWCA |

## *Juniperus* ✿ (*Cupressaceae*)

| | | |
|---|---|---|
| | ***chinensis*** | CMac CMen SEND |
| | - 'Aurea' ♀$^{H4}$ | CBcs CMac EHul EOrn LRHS MBar MGos SPoG |
| § | - 'Blaauw' ♀$^{H4}$ | CDoC CMac CMen ECho EHul EOrn MBar MGos SCoo SHBN SHaC STre WFar |
| | - 'Blue Alps' | CDoC ECho EHul EOrn GKir MBar MGos NHol NLar SCoo SEND SLim WDin WFar |
| | - 'Blue Point' | MBar MGos |
| | - 'Densa Spartan' | see *J. chinensis* 'Spartan' |
| | - 'Echiniformis' | CKen EOrn SHaC |
| | - 'Expansa Aureospicata' (v) | CDoC CKen CMac ECho EHul EOrn EPfP MBar MGos SEND SLim SPoG SRms |
| § | - 'Expansa Variegata' (v) | CDoC CMac CRob CWib ECho EHul EOrn EPfP GKir MAsh MBar MGos SCoo SEND SPoG SRms WDin WFar WMoo |
| | - 'Ferngold' | CDoC MGos |
| | - 'Globosa Cinerea' | MBar |
| | - 'Japonica' | EOrn MBar |
| § | - 'Kaizuka' ♀$^{H4}$ | ECho EHul EOrn GKir LBee LRHS MBar NLar SCoo SLim SMad SPoG STre |
| | - 'Kaizuka Variegata' | see *J. chinensis* 'Variegated Kaizuka' |
| | - 'Kuriwao Gold' | see *J.* x *pfitzeriana* 'Kuriwao Gold' |
| | - 'Obelisk' ♀$^{H4}$ | CDoC EHul LRHS MBar MGos |
| | - 'Oblonga' | CDoC EHul MBar STre |
| § | - 'Parsonsii' | MBar SHBN STre WCFE |
| | - 'Plumosa' | MBar |
| | - 'Plumosa Albovariegata' (v) | EOrn MBar |
| § | - 'Plumosa Aurea' ♀$^{H4}$ | EHul EOrn MBar WDin WFar |
| | - 'Plumosa Aureovariegata' (v) | CKen EOrn MBar |
| | - 'Pyramidalis' ♀$^{H4}$ | CDoC CRob ECho EHul EPfP GKir SCoo SPoG SRms WDin WFar |
| | - 'Pyramidalis Variegata' | see *J. chinensis* 'Variegata' |
| | - 'Robust Green' | CRob ECho EOrn GKir MBar SCoo SPoG |
| | - 'San José' | CDoC CMen EHul EOrn MAsh MBar SCoo SLim WDin |
| § | - var. ***sargentii*** | CMen STre |
| | - 'Shimpaku' | CKen CMen EOrn MBar NLar |
| § | - 'Spartan' | EHul |
| | - 'Stricta' | CSBt EHul LBee LRHS MAsh MBar MGos NBlu SLim SPla WDin |
| | - 'Stricta Variegata' | see *J. chinensis* 'Variegata' |
| | - 'Sulphur Spray' | see *J.* x *pfitzeriana* 'Sulphur Spray' |
| | - 'Torulosa' | see *J. chinensis* 'Kaizuka' |
| § | - 'Variegata' (v) | MBar |
| § | - 'Variegated Kaizuka' (v) | ECho EHul EOrn MBar WFar |
| | ***communis*** | CArn CRWN CTrG EHul GKir GPoy ITim MHer MNHC MSal NLar NWea SIde |
| | - (f) | SIde |
| | - 'Arnold' | CDoC CDul MBar MGos SHaC |
| | - 'Arnold Sentinel' | CKen |
| | - 'Atholl' | CKen |
| I | - 'Aureopicta' (v) | MBar |
| | - 'Barton' | MBar MGos NHol |
| | - 'Berkshire' | CKen CRob NHol WThu |
| | - 'Brien' | CDoC CKen |
| | - 'Brynhyfryd Gold' | CKen CRob |
| § | - var. ***communis*** | MBar |
| | - 'Compressa' ♀$^{H4}$ | Widely available |
| § | - 'Constance Franklin' (v) | ECho EHul MBar STre |
| | - 'Corielagan' | CKen MBar NLar |
| | - 'Cracovia' | CKen |
| | - var. ***depressa*** | GPoy MBar |
| | - 'Depressa Aurea' | CKen CMac CSBt ECho EHul GKir LBee LRHS MBar MGos SHBN WFar |
| | - 'Depressed Star' | CRob ECho EHul MBar |
| | - 'Derrynane' | EHul |
| | - 'Effusa' | CKen |
| | - 'Gelb' | see *J. communis* 'Schneverdingen Goldmachangel' |
| | - 'Gold Ball' | LBee |
| | - 'Gold Cone' | CKen CSli ECho EHul EPfP GKir LBee LRHS MAsh MBar MGos NHol SLim SPoG WDin WFar |
| | - 'Golden Showers' | see *J. communis* 'Schneverdingen Goldmachangel' |
| | - 'Goldenrod' | MGos |
| | - 'Green Carpet' ♀$^{H4}$ | CDoC CKen CRob ECho EHul EOrn EPfP GKir LBuc MAsh MBar NHol SCoo SHaC SLim SPoG WCFE WDin |
| | - 'Haverbeck' | CKen |
| | - var. ***hemispherica*** | see *J. communis* var. *communis* |
| | - 'Hibernica' ♀$^{H4}$ | CDoC CDul CSBt CTri ECho ECrN EHul EOrn EPfP GKir LAst LPan LRHS MBar MGos NWea SHBN SHaC SLPl SLim SPer SPla SPoG WBrE WDin WOrn |
| | - 'Hibernica Variegata' | see *J. communis* 'Constance Franklin' |
| | - 'Hornibrookii' ♀$^{H4}$ | CMac EHul EOrn MBar MGos NWea SBod SHBN SHaC SRms STre WDin |
| | - 'Horstmann' | MBar NLar SCoo |
| I | - 'Horstmann's Pendula' | CDoC |
| | - 'Kenwith Castle' | CKen |
| | - 'Prostrata' | WFar |
| | - 'Pyramidalis' | SPlb |
| | - 'Repanda' ♀$^{H4}$ | CBcs CDoC CMac CRob CSBt CWib ECho EHul EPfP GGar GKir LAst MAsh MBar MGos NWea SCoo SHaC SLim SPer SPla SPoG SRms WBVN WDin WFar |
| § | - 'Schneverdingen Goldmachangel' | CRob EOrn MGos NHol SLim |
| | - 'Sentinel' | CDoC ECho EHul EMil EPfP GKir LRHS MBar NHol SLim WCFE WDin |
| | - 'Sieben Steinhauser' | CKen |

- 'Silver Mist' CKen
- 'Spotty Spreader' (v) GKir SLim SPoG
- Suecica Group EHul MBar NLar NWea SLPl
- - 'Suecica Aurea' EHul EOrn
- 'Wallis' NHol
- 'Zeal' CKen
***conferta*** see *J. rigida* subsp. *conferta*
- var. ***maritima*** see *J. taxifolia*
***davurica*** EHul
- 'Expansa' see *J. chinensis* 'Parsonsii'
- 'Expansa Albopicta' see *J. chinensis* 'Expansa Variegata'
- 'Expansa Variegata' see *J. chinensis* 'Expansa Variegata'
***deppeana*** 'Silver Spire' MBar
***excelsa*** subsp. ***polycarpos*** CMen
***foetidissima*** CMen
x ***gracilis*** 'Blaauw' see *J. chinensis* 'Blaauw'
'Grey Owl' ♀H4 ECho EHul ELan EPfP MBar NWea SCoo SLim SRms STre WDin WFar
***horizontalis*** GKir NWea
§ - 'Andorra Compact' ECho MBar NLar SCoo
- 'Bar Harbor' CKen CMac EHul GKir MBar MGos NWea
§ - 'Blue Chip' CRob ECho EHul ELan EOrn EPfP GKir LBee LRHS MBar MGos NBir NBlu SCoo SLim SPer SPoG WDin
- 'Blue Moon' see *J. horizontalis* 'Blue Chip'
- 'Blue Pygmy' CKen
- 'Blue Rug' see *J. horizontalis* 'Wiltonii'
- 'Douglasii' CKen CMac EHul MBar
- 'Emerald Spreader' CKen ECho EHul ELan GKir MBar
- 'Glacier' CKen
- Glauca Group CMac EHul GKir MBar MGos NWea SPer SPoG WDin
- 'Glomerata' CKen MBar
- 'Golden Carpet' ECho ELan EOrn EPfP GKir LBuc MGos NLar SPoG
- 'Golden Spreader' CDoC
- 'Grey Pearl' CKen EHul
- 'Hughes' CMac ECho EHul LBee LRHS MBar MGos NWea SBod SPla
- Icee Blue = 'Monber' CKen CRob NLar SLim SPoG
- 'Jade River' EHul GBin GKir LRHS MGos SLim SPer SPoG
- 'Limeglow' CKen CRob ECho LAst MAsh NLar SCoo SLim
- 'Mother Lode' CKen
- 'Neumann' CKen EOrn
- 'Plumosa Compacta' see *J. horizontalis* 'Andorra Compact'
- 'Prince of Wales' CRob EHul GKir LPan LRHS MAsh MGos NLar SCoo SLim WCor
- var. ***saxatalis*** E.Murray see *J. communis* var. *communis*
- 'Turquoise Spreader' CSBt ECho EHul GKir MBar SCoo
- 'Variegata' (v) MBar
- 'Venusta' see *J. virginiana* 'Venusta'
- 'Villa Marie' CKen
- 'Webber' MBar
§ - 'Wiltonii' ♀H4 CDul EHul EOrn MGos NBlu
- 'Winter Blue' LBee SLim SPer
- 'Youngstown' CMac CRob CSWP ECho GKir MBar MGos SBod WFar
- 'Yukon Belle' CKen
N x ***media*** see *J.* x *pfitzeriana*
- 'Plumosa Aurea' see *J. chinensis* 'Plumosa Aurea'
§ x ***pfitzeriana*** CDul
- 'Armstrongii' EHul
- 'Blaauw' see *J. chinensis* 'Blaauw'
- 'Blue and Gold' (v) CKen ECho EHul MBar SHBN SPer
- 'Blue Cloud' see *J. virginiana* 'Blue Cloud'
§ - 'Carbery Gold' CBcs CDoC CMac CRob CSBt CSli ECho EHul EOrn GKir LAst LBee LRHS MAsh MBar MGos NHol SCoo SLim SPoG WFar
- 'Gold Coast' CDoC CKen CRob CSBt ECho EHul EPfP LBee LRHS MAsh MBar MBri MGos NHol NLar SLim SPer SPla WDin
- Gold Sovereign = 'Blound'PBR GKir LBee MAsh MGos NHol
- 'Gold Star' SLim
* - 'Golden Joy' SCoo SLim SPoG
- 'Golden Saucer' MBar MBri SCoo
- 'Goldkissen' CRob MGos NLar
§ - 'Kuriwao Gold' CMac EHul GKir MBar MGos NHol NLar SCoo SEND STre WFar
- 'Milky Way' (v) SCoo SPoG
- 'Mint Julep' CSBt ECho EHul GKir LAst LBee LPan LRHS MBar MGos NBlu SCoo SLim SPer WDin WFar WMoo
- 'Old Gold' ♀H4 CKen CMac ECho EHul EOrn EPfP LBee MBar MGos NBlu NHol NWea SCoo SLim SPer SPlb SPoG SRms WDin WFar
- 'Old Gold Carbery' see *J.* x *pfitzeriana* 'Carbery Gold'
- 'Pfitzeriana' see *J.* x *pfitzeriana* 'Wilhelm Pfitzer'
- 'Pfitzeriana Aurea' CMac CSBt ECho EHul EPfP GKir MBar MGos NBlu NWea SHBN SPoG WDin WFar WOrn
- 'Pfitzeriana Compacta' ♀H4 CMac EHul MBar SCoo
- 'Pfitzeriana Glauca' EHul MBar SCoo
- 'Richeson' MBar
- 'Silver Cascade' EHul
§ - 'Sulphur Spray' ♀H4 CSBt CWib ECho EHul EOrn EPla GKir LAst MAsh MBar MGos NHol SEND SHaC SLim SPer SPla SRms WBVN WCFE WDin WFar WMoo
§ - 'Wilhelm Pfitzer' EHul EPfP MBar NWea
§ ***pingii*** 'Glassell' CDoC ECho GKir MBar NLar
§ - 'Pygmaea' ECho EOrn MBar
§ - var. ***wilsonii*** CDoC CKen ECho EOrn GGar MBar
***procumbens*** 'Bonin Isles' LRHS SLim
- 'Nana' ♀H4 CDoC CKen CMac CRob CSBt ECho EHul EOrn EPfP LAst LBee LRHS MAsh MBar MGos NHol SCoo SHBN SLim SPla SPoG WCFE WDin WFar
***recurva*** 'Castlewellan' CDoC EOrn MGos NLar
- var. ***coxii*** CDoC CMac ECho EHul EOrn GGGa GKir MAsh MBar MGos SRms
§ - 'Densa' CDoC CKen ECho EHul EOrn MBar NHol SHBN
- 'Embley Park' EHul MBar
- 'Nana' see *J. recurva* 'Densa'
***rigida*** CMen EHul MBar NLar
§ - subsp. ***conferta*** GKir LBee MBar SEND SLim SPer SPoG STre
* - - 'Blue Ice' CKen EOrn SHaC SPoG WFar
- - 'Blue Pacific' CRob ECho EHul GKir MBar NLar WFar
- - 'Blue Tosho' CRob ECho GKir SLim SPoG
- - 'Emerald Sea' EHul
- - 'Schlager' SLim
- - 'Silver Mist' CKen
***sabina*** NWea
§ - 'Blaue Donau' ECho EHul MBar
- Blue Danube see *J. sabina* 'Blaue Donau'
- 'Broadmoor' EHul
- 'Buffalo' EHul
- Cupressifolia Group MBar
- 'Hicksii' CMac MBar
- 'Knap Hill' see *J.* x *pfitzeriana* 'Wilhelm Pfitzer'
- 'Mountaineer' see *J. scopulorum* 'Mountaineer'

- 'Rockery Gem' EHul EOrn SLim SPla SPoG WGor
- 'Skandia' CKen
- 'Tamariscifolia' CBcs CMac CWib ECrN EHul LBee LRHS MAsh MBar MGos NBlu NWea SEND SHBN SLim SPer SPoG WCFE WDin WFar
- 'Tripartita' see *J. virginiana* 'Tripartita'
- 'Variegata' (v) ECho EHul MBar

***sargentii*** see *J. chinensis* var. *sargentii*

***scopulorum*** CKen MBar
- 'Blue Arrow' Widely available
- 'Blue Banff' CKen
- 'Blue Heaven' EHul MAsh MBar SRms
- 'Blue Pyramid' EHul
- 'Boothman' EHul
- 'Moonglow' EHul MBar
- § 'Mountaineer' EHul
- 'Mrs Marriage' CKen
- 'Repens' MBar MGos
- 'Silver Star' (v) EHul MBar MGos
- 'Skyrocket' CBcs CDul CMac CSBt CTri CWib ECho ECrN EHul EPfP GGal GKir LAst LBee MBar MGos NBlu NHol NWea SBod SEND SPlb WBVN WCFE WDin WFar
- 'Springbank' EHul LRHS MBar WCFE
- 'Tabletop' MBar
- 'Wichita Blue' EHul EPfP

§ ***squamata*** WBVN
- 'Blue Carpet' ♀H4 Widely available
- 'Blue Spider' CKen LRHS MBar SCoo SLim
- 'Blue Star' ♀H4 Widely available
- 'Blue Star Variegated' see *J. squamata* 'Golden Flame'
- 'Blue Swede' see *J. squamata* 'Hunnetorp'
- 'Chinese Silver' EHul MBar SLim
- 'Dream Joy' CKen SCoo SLim SPoG
- var. ***fargesii*** see *J. squamata*
- 'Filborna' CKen LBee MBar SLim
- 'Glassell' see *J. pingii* 'Glassell'
- § 'Golden Flame' (v) CKen
- 'Holger' ♀H4 CDoC CDul CMac CRob CSBt ECho EHul EOrn EPfP EPla GKir LAst LBee LRHS MAsh MBar MGos SCoo SHaC SLim SPoG
- § 'Hunnetorp' EOrn MBar MGos NHol
- 'Loderi' see *J. pingii* var. *wilsonii*
- 'Meyeri' CBcs ECho EHul EOrn GKev GKir MBar NWea SCoo STre WDin WFar
- 'Pygmaea' see *J. pingii* 'Pygmaea'
- 'Wilsonii' see *J. pingii* var. *wilsonii*

§ ***taxifolia*** CDoC CRob EOrn LBee

§ ***virginiana*** 'Blue Cloud' EHul MBar SLim WGor
- 'Burkii' EHul
- I 'Compressa' new LAst
- 'Frosty Morn' CKen EHul MBar WFar
- 'Glauca' CSWP EHul NWea
- 'Golden Spring' CKen
- 'Helle' see *J. chinensis* 'Spartan'
- 'Hetzii' CMac ECho EHul MBar NLar NWea WDin WFar
- 'Hillii' MBar
- 'Hillspire' EHul
- 'Nana Compacta' MBar
- Silver Spreader = 'Mona' CKen EHul SCoo
- 'Staver' EHul
- 'Sulphur Spray' see *J.* x *pfitzeriana* 'Sulphur Spray'
- § 'Tripartita' MBar
- § 'Venusta' CKen

## *Jurinea* (*Asteraceae*)

***glycacantha*** LRHS

## *Jurinella* see *Jurinea*

## *Jussiaea* see *Ludwigia*

## *Justicia* (*Acanthaceae*)

sp. LSou MJnS

***aurea*** EShb MJnS

§ ***brandegeeana*** ♀H1 CCCN CHal EShb MBri SOWG
- 'Lutea' see *J. brandegeeana* 'Yellow Queen'
- variegated (v) EShb MJnS
- § 'Yellow Queen' CHal EShb

§ ***carnea*** CHal CSev EBak EShb MBri MJnS SMad SOWG

§ ***floribunda*** new EHig

***guttata*** see *J. brandegeeana*

'Nørgaard's Favourite' MBri

***pauciflora*** see *J. floribunda*

'Penrhosiensis' EShb

***pohliana*** see *J. carnea*

***rizzinii*** ♀H1 CCCN CHll CSev EShb SMad SOWG

***spicigera*** EShb

***suberecta*** see *Dicliptera sericea*

# K

## *Kadsura* (*Schisandraceae*)

sp. CMac

***japonica*** CBcs EShb IDee WPGP
- B&SWJ 1027 WCru
- B&SWJ 4463 from Korea new WCru
- B&SWJ 11109 from Japan new WCru
- 'Fukurin' (v) IArd NLar
- 'Variegata' (v) CCCN EPfP EShb LRHS SEND WSHC
- white fruit EPfP

## *Kaempferia* (*Zingiberaceae*)

***rotunda*** CCCN CKob LAma

## *Kalanchoe* (*Crassulaceae*)

***beharensis*** ♀H1 CAbb CCCN CDTJ CHal EShb LToo MBri SBig
- 'Fang' CDTJ
- 'Rusty' CDTJ CSpe

***blossfeldiana*** LRHS
- 'Variegata' (v) CHal

***daigremontiana*** CHal EShb SRms

§ ***delagoensis*** CCCN CHal EShb STre

***fedtschenkoi*** CHal EShb STre

***laciniata*** EShb

***manginii*** ♀H1 CDoC

***marmorata*** ♀H1 EShb

***orgyalis*** EShb

'Partridge' new LRHS

***pinnata*** new EShb

***porphyrocalyx*** new EOHP

***pubescens*** EShb

***pumila*** ♀H1 CHal EShb SBch SPet WEas

***rhombopilosa*** EShb

***sexangularis*** EShb

'Tessa' ♀H1 MBri MLan SRms STre

***thyrsiflora*** new EShb
- 'Bronze Sculpture' CSpe EWll MAvo
- 'Desert Flame' new LRHS

***tomentosa*** ♀H1 CHal EShb WCot WEas

***tubiflora*** see *K. delagoensis*

## *Kalimeris* (*Asteraceae*)

| | | |
|---|---|---|
| § | ***incisa*** | EBee GMac MMuc MRav WBor WFar WMoo WTin |
| | - 'Alba' | EBee ECha NLar SSvw WFar |
| | - 'Blue Star' | EBee ECha EMil EWll LHop MWea NLar WFar |
| | - 'Charlotte' | CSam EBee EWes NBre NDov NGby |
| | - 'Madiva' | EBee ECha |
| * | - 'Variegata' (v) | NBre |
| | ***integrifolia*** | ECha WTin |
| | ***intricifolia*** | NBre |
| § | ***mongolica*** | EBee ECha GAuc NBre WFar WPer WSHC |
| § | ***pinnatifida*** | EBee EPPr WCot |
| | - 'Hortensis' | CBod ECtt NBPC |
| § | ***yomena*** 'Shogun' (v) | CEnt EBee ECha EHoe ELan EMil EMon EPPr EPfP GBuc LBMP MLLN NBir NPri SAga SMrm SPer WFar WSHC |
| | - 'Variegata' | see *K. yomena* 'Shogun' |

## *Kalmia* ✿ (*Ericaceae*)

| | | |
|---|---|---|
| | ***angustifolia*** ♀H4 | GKev MBar SRms WDin WFar |
| | - f. ***rubra*** ♀H4 | CBcs CDoC EBee ELan EPfP LRHS MAsh MGos NDlv NPri SHBN SPer SPoG SReu SRot SSta WFar WPat |
| | ***latifolia*** ♀H4 | CBcs CEnd CPSs CTrG ELan EMil EPfP MBar MGos MLan MMuc NBlu NPri NWea SPer SPlb SReu SSpi SSta SWvt WBod WBrE WDin WFar |
| | - 'Alpine Pink' | SRot |
| | - 'Carousel' | ECho EPfP GGGa MGos NDlv WFar WGob |
| | - 'Elf' | CEnd ECho LRHS MAsh MGos MLea WBod WFar |
| | - 'Freckles' ♀H4 | ECho ELan EPfP GGGa LRHS MAsh NDlv SPoG WFar |
| | - 'Fresca' | ECho WGob |
| | - 'Galaxy' | GGGa |
| | - 'Heart of Fire' | GGGa |
| | - 'Keepsake' | GGGa |
| | - 'Little Linda' ♀H4 | ECho GGGa LRHS MAsh NDlv |
| | - 'Minuet' | CBcs CDoC CDul CEnd CWSG ECho EPfP GGGa ISea LRHS MAsh MGos MLan MLea MMuc MWea NDlv SPoG SSpi SWvt WBrE WFar |
| | - f. ***myrtifolia*** | ECho LRHS MLea WFar WGob |
| | - 'Nancy' | WBod WFar |
| | - 'Olympic Fire' ♀H4 | CEnd EPfP GGGa MGos MRav NHol SSpi |
| | - 'Ostbo Red' | CBcs CDoC CDul CPSs ECho EPfP GGGa ISea LRHS MAsh MGos MLea NDlv SHBN SPer SPoG SReu SSpi SSta SWvt W Bod WFar |
| | - 'Peppermint' | EBee GGGa |
| | - 'Pink Charm' ♀H4 | ECho GGGa MAsh |
| | - 'Pink Frost' | ECho GGGa ISea NLar WFar |
| | - 'Pinwheel' | CEnd NLar |
| | - 'Quinnipiac' | NHol |
| | - 'Raspberry Glow' | GGGa |
| | - 'Richard Jaynes' | ECho MLea WBod WBrE WFar |
| | - 'Sarah' | ECho GGGa LRHS MAsh SSpi |
| | - 'Snowdrift' | ECho LRHS NDlv NLar SSpi WBod WFar |
| § | ***microphylla*** | GGGa |
| | ***polifolia*** | CBcs EBee ECho MBar NLAp SKHP SPer WPat WThu |
| | - var. ***compacta*** | WSHC |
| | - 'Glauca' | see *K. microphylla* |
| | - f. ***leucantha*** | GGGa NLAp WPat WThu |

## *Kalmia* x *Rhododendron* (*Ericaceae*)

| | | |
|---|---|---|
| | ***K. latifolia*** x ***R. williamsianum***, 'Everlasting' | see ***Rhododendron*** 'Everlasting' |

## *Kalmiopsis* (*Ericaceae*)

| | | |
|---|---|---|
| | ***leachiana*** 'Glendoick' | GGGa |
| * | - 'Shooting Star' | ITim LLHF |

## x *Kalmiothamnus* (*Ericaceae*)

| | | |
|---|---|---|
| | ***ornithomma*** 'Cosdon' | WAbe WThu |
| | - 'Haytor' | WAbe |
| | 'Sindelberg' | ITim |

## *Kalopanax* (*Araliaceae*)

| | | |
|---|---|---|
| | ***pictus*** | see *K. septemlobus* |
| § | ***septemlobus*** | CBcs CDul CHEx ELan EPfP GBin NLar WBVN WOVN |
| | - subsp. ***lutchuensis*** B&SWJ 5947 | WCru |
| | - f. ***maximowiczii*** | CDoC EPfP EWTr MBlu NBee NLar WCot |

## *Keiskea* (*Lamiaceae*)

| | | |
|---|---|---|
| | ***japonica*** | EBee |

## *Kelseya* (*Rosaceae*)

| | | |
|---|---|---|
| | ***uniflora*** | WAbe |

## *Kennedia* (*Papilionaceae*)

| | | |
|---|---|---|
| | ***beckxiana*** | SOWG |
| | ***coccinea*** | CCCN CSec WSHC |
| | ***nigricans*** | CCCN EBee EShb SOWG |
| | ***prostrata*** | SPlb |
| | ***rubicunda*** | CCCN CHal CRHN CSec |

## *Kentia* (*Arecaceae*)

| | | |
|---|---|---|
| | ***belmoreana*** | see *Howea belmoreana* |
| | ***forsteriana*** | see *Howea forsteriana* |

## *Kentranthus* see *Centranthus*

## *Kerria* (*Rosaceae*)

| | | |
|---|---|---|
| | ***japonica*** misapplied, single | see *K. japonica* 'Simplex' |
| | ***japonica*** (d) | see *K. japonica* 'Pleniflora' |
| | - 'Albescens' | WFar |
| | - 'Golden Guinea' ♀H4 | CChe CPLG CWSG EBee ECtt ELan EPfP EWTr GGal IFro LRHS MAsh MGos MNrw MRav MSwo SCoo SPer SRms SWal SWvt WDin WFar |
| § | - 'Picta' (v) | CDul CWib EBee ECrN ELan EPfP LAst MBar MGos MRav MSwo SGar SLim SLon SPer SPoG SRms WDin WFar WSHC |
| § | - 'Pleniflora' (d) ♀H4 | Widely available |
| § | - 'Simplex' | CPLG CSBt GGal NWea WDin WFar |
| | - 'Variegata' | see *K. japonica* 'Picta' |

## *Khadia* (*Aizoaceae*)

| | | |
|---|---|---|
| | ***acutipetala*** | CCCN LRHS |

## *Kickxia* (*Scrophulariaceae*)

| | | |
|---|---|---|
| | ***spuria*** | MSal |

## *Kirengeshoma* (*Hydrangeaceae*)

| | | |
|---|---|---|
| | ***palmata*** ♀H4 | Widely available |
| | - dwarf | CDWL WCot |
| | - Koreana Group | CDWL CHFP CLAP CPLG EBee EGle EHrv ELan EPfP EWTr GBuc GCal IPot LAst MBri MDun MRav NBPC NBir NCGa SMad SPer WCot WCru WFar WGwG WHil WOVN |

## *Kitaibela* (*Malvaceae*)

| | | |
|---|---|---|
| | ***vitifolia*** | CPLG CSec EBee EDAr EHig ELan EMon GCal NBHF NBid SDnm SEND SGar SPav SPlb WPer |

## *Kitchingia* see *Kalanchoe*

## kiwi fruit see *Actinidia deliciosa*

## *Kleinia* (*Asteraceae*)

| | | |
|---|---|---|
| | ***articulata*** | see *Senecio articulatus* |
| | ***grantii*** | EShb |
| | ***repens*** | see *Senecio serpens* |
| | ***senecioides*** | WEas |
| | ***stapeliiformis*** ♀H1 | EShb |

## *Knautia* (*Dipsacaceae*)

| | | |
|---|---|---|
| § | ***arvensis*** | CArn CHll CRWN EBWF LCro MHer MLLN MNHC NLan NLar NMir NPri NSco SECG SEND SPer WFar WHer WMoo WSFF |
| | - 'Rachael' | CElw |
| | ***dipsacifolia*** | SHar SMHy |
| * | 'Gracelema' **new** | SEND |
| § | ***macedonica*** | Widely available |
| | - 'Crimson Cushion' | CSpe ECtt GAbr GBri LSou NPri SMrm SPav WCra WFar |
| | - 'Mars Midget' | CHll CSam EBee EGoo ELan EPfP EShb GQue LBMP LCro LSou MGos NLar SAga SHGN SPla SPoG SUsu SWvt WFar WHil WHoo WSHC |
| | - Melton pastels | COlW EBee EGoo EPfP EShb GJos LBMP LSRN LSou MCot MGos NCob NPer SPav SPet SPoG SRot SWat SWvt WFar |
| | - pink-flowered | CSam WWlt |
| | - 'Red Dress' | EMon |
| | - 'Red Knight' **new** | GQue |
| | - red-flowered | CWib NCob WFar |
| | - short | ECtt EHrv NCob NCot NDov STes |
| | - tall, pale-flowered | NDov SPhx |
| | ***sarajevensis*** | EBee MAvo |
| § | ***tatarica*** | NBre |

## *Knightia* (*Proteaceae*)

| | | |
|---|---|---|
| | ***excelsa*** | CBcs EUJe |

## *Kniphofia* ✿ (*Asphodelaceae*)

| | | |
|---|---|---|
| | 'Ada' | CMdw EBla EBrs EWTr EWes MLLN MRav SMrm |
| | ***albescens*** **new** | CAbb MAvo SGar |
| | 'Alcazar' | CBcs CDes CElw EBee EBla ECot ECrN ECtt EPfP GGar LPio LRHS LSRN MBri MHer MRav MSte SMrm SPer SPoG SWvt WBrE WCot WFar WMnd WPGP |
| | 'Amber' | NBre |
| | 'Amsterdam' | MWat |
| | ***angustifolia*** | SPlb |
| | 'Apricot' | EPla SMHy |
| | 'Apricot Souffle' | EBee MLLN WCot WPGP |
| | 'Atlanta' | EMon LRHS |
| | 'Barton Fever' | WCot |
| | 'Beauty of Wexford' | EBla |
| | 'Bees' Flame' | EBee |
| | 'Bee's Gold' | WCAu |
| | 'Bees' Lemon' | Widely available |
| | 'Bees' Sunset' ♀H4 | CAvo CDes EBee GAbr GBri GBuc LPla MNrw MRav SMrm SUsu WCot WPGP WPrP |
| * | ***bicolor*** | EBee ECtt NSti WPrP |
| | 'Border Ballet' | EDAr EQua EWTr LBMP LHop LRHS MNHC NBir NBre NBro NBsh NLar SWat WFar |
| | ***brachystachya*** | CPou EBee ELon GAbr GBin GCal GGar SBig SPlb WCot |
| | 'Bressingham Comet' | CWsd EBla EBrs ECtt GKir LRHS MAvo MBri MRav NBir SRms WPGP |
| | 'Bressingham Gleam' | EBrs WCot |
| | Bressingham hybrids | GKir |
| | Bressingham Sunbeam = 'Bresun' | EBee EBla EBrs NBir SMrm WCot |
| | Bridgemere hybrids | WFar |
| | 'Brimstone' ♀H4 | Widely available |
| | ***bruceae*** | CPou |
| | ***buchananii*** | CDes |
| | 'Buttercup' ♀H4 | CAvo WSHC WTin |
| | 'C.M. Prichard' misapplied | see *K. rooperi* |
| | 'C.M. Prichard' Prichard | EBee WCot |
| | 'Candlelight' | CDes CMdw COlW CWsd EBee ECtt LPio NBre SDys SUsu WPGP |
| | 'Candlemass' | EBee LPio |
| | ***caulescens*** ♀H3-4 | Widely available |
| | - from John May | CKno ECtt SPoG WCot |
| | - 'Coral Breakers' | CTca EBee ECGP ECtt GBin MLLN MSte SDix WCot |
| | - short | ECha |
| | ***citrina*** | CFir EBee EDAr EPfP GKev LAst LRHS MBrN NBre NBsh NChi NLar WCot WHil |
| | 'Cobra' | EBee EBla EBrs GBin LRHS MRav NBhm SUsu WCot |
| | 'Comet' | ECtt |
| | 'Corallina' | WFar |
| | 'Dingaan' | CAbb CPou CSam EBee ECtt EPPr GBin GMac GQue LFur MAvo MNrw NBir NPri SAga SDnm SPav WBrk WCot WFar |
| | 'Dorset Sentry' | CAbP CAbb CMdw CSam CTca EBee EBla ECtt EGle ELon GAbr GBuc GCal LAst LPio MLLN MNrw MSte NBir NCGa NLar NMyG NOrc SAga WCot WFar |
| | 'Dropmore Apricot' | CMMP SPav |
| | 'Drummore Apricot' | CMHG EAEE EBee ECha EGle ELan GBuc GCal GKir LAst LSou MLLN MRav MSte NBir NBsh NSti SAga SDnm WCot WFar WPGP WPrP |
| I | 'Earliest of All' | EBee LRHS |
| | 'Early Buttercup' | CTca EBee ECot EQua GBri MRav WCot WFar |
| | ***ensifolia*** | CDTJ CPou ECtt NGdn SRms WMnd |
| | 'Ernest Mitchell' | EBee MRav WCot |
| | Express hybrids | NBre NLar |
| | 'Fairyland' | ECGP NGBl WBrk WFar WTin |
| | 'False Maid' | MWte SMHy |
| | ***fibrosa*** | CFir SEND |
| | 'Fiery Fred' | CMil EBla EBrs ELan LRHS MRav NBre SMrm WCot |
| | 'Flamenco' | CChe CFwr COlW CWan EDAr EWll EWsh GKir NBre NGdn SPet WRHF |
| | 'Flaming Torch' | ECha |
| | ***foliosa*** | LRHS SMrm |
| | 'Frances Victoria' | WCot |
| | ***galpinii*** misapplied | see *K. triangularis* subsp. *triangularis* |
| | ***galpinii*** Baker ♀H4 | EBee GBri MRav NBre SPer SRms |
| | 'Gilt Bronze' | LFur WCot |
| | 'Gladness' | EBee ECtt LFur MRav NBir NBre NSti WCot WPrP |
| | 'Goldelse' | CWsd NBir WCot |
| | 'Goldfinch' | CMdw CSam CWsd MRav SMHy SUsu |

| | | |
|---|---|---|
| | ***gracilis*** | LEdu |
| * | ***gracilistyla*** new | EMon |
| | 'Green and Cream' | MNrw |
| | 'Green Jade' | CBct CDes CFir CMdw CRow CSpe EBee EBla ECha EPfP GBri LPio MRav MSte NBir NLar NMyG NSti SEND SGar WCAu WCot WFar WTin |
| | 'Green Lemon' | NBre |
| | 'H.E. Beale' | GCal MRav SMrm WCot |
| | 'Hen and Chickens' | WCot |
| | ***hirsuta*** | CFir CPou CSam EBee EShb GBin LPio SPad WCot |
| | - JCA 3.461.900 | WCot |
| | - 'Traffic Lights' | EWll LSou NBhm |
| | 'Hollard's Gold' | WCot |
| | 'Ice Queen' | CFir CPar CSam CSev EBee ECha ECtt EPPr GBri LPio MAvo MRav MSte NCGa NChi NGdn SEND SMad SSvw SWvt WBrE WCAu WCot WTin |
| | ***ichopensis*** | CDes GBuc WPGP |
| | 'Ingénue' | WCot |
| | 'Innocence' | EBla EBrs NBre |
| | 'Jane Henry' | CDes MAvo WPGP |
| | 'Jenny Bloom' | Widely available |
| | 'John Benary' | CHar CPou CSam CTca EBee EBla ECtt EGle GAbr GBBs GMaP IGor LHop LPio MAvo MLLN MSte NBir NGdn SMrm SPer SPoG WCot WFar WKif WTin |
| | 'Johnathan' | WCot |
| | ***laxiflora*** | CPou SKHP WPGP |
| | 'Lemon Ice' | EBee WCot |
| | 'Light of the World' | see *K. triangularis* subsp. *triangularis* 'Light of the World' |
| | ***linearifolia*** | CPou CTrC GCra GGar MAvo MLLN MNrw SHom SPlb WCot |
| | 'Little Elf' | CWsd SDys WSHC |
| | 'Little Maid' | Widely available |
| | 'Lord Roberts' | EBee ECha GCal LPio MRav SDix SMad SPav WCot |
| | 'Luna' | SMrm WCot |
| | ***macowanii*** | see *K. triangularis* subsp. *triangularis* |
| | 'Maid of Orleans' | CRow CWsd WCot |
| | 'Mermaiden' | CMHG CRow CSam ECtt GMac LAst MNrw NCob WCot WFar |
| | 'Minister Verschuur' | EBee EBla EBrs LRHS MBri NBre WFar WMnd |
| | 'Modesta' | WPGP |
| | 'Molten Lava' | EBee |
| | 'Mount Etna' | EBee SMrm WCot WPGP |
| | ***multiflora*** | CTca EBee ECtt WCot WPnP |
| | 'Nancy's Red' | Widely available |
| | ***nelsonii*** Mast. | see *K. triangularis* subsp. *triangularis* |
| | 'Nobilis' | see *K. uvaria* 'Nobilis' |
| | ***northiae*** 🏆 | CDes CFir CHEx CPou CTca CWsd EBee ECtt ELan EUJe EWes GAbr GBin GCal IFro LEdu LPio MAvo MNrw NBhm SAPC SArc SMad SPlb WCot WCru WGwG WPGP |
| | 'November Glory' | WCot |
| | 'Old Court Seedling' | EBee GGal WCot |
| | 'Orange Torch' | CPou |
| | 'Painted Lady' | CAbP CSam CTri EBee ECtt GAbr GMaP GMac MBri MRav NPri SMHy SPoG WBrk WCot WRHF |
| | ***pauciflora*** | CBro EBee ERos LHop SDys WCot WPrP |
| | 'Percy's Pride' | Widely available |
| | 'Pfitzeri' | SRms |
| | ***porphyrantha*** | WCot |
| | x ***praecox*** | GAbr MAvo SGar WCot |
| | 'Primulina' Bloom | CPou CSec EBrs LRHS |
| | 'Prince Igor' misapplied | see *K. uvaria* 'Nobilis' |
| | 'Prince Igor' Prichard | CFir EBee GAbr MLHP MWea NBir SMad WCot WHrl |
| | ***pumila*** | LLHF |
| | 'Ranelagh Gardens' | SArc |
| | 'Rich Echoes' | EBee WCot |
| | ***ritualis*** | EDAr LSou MAvo NLar WCot WPGP |
| § | ***rooperi*** 🏆H4 | Widely available |
| | - 'Cally Giant' new | GCal |
| | - 'Cally Torch' new | GCal |
| I | - 'Torchlight' | CAbb CPne CTca |
| | 'Royal Castle' | CFwr MHav MRav NBir NOrc WFar |
| | 'Royal Standard' 🏆H4 | CBcs EAEE EBee EBla ELan EPfP EShb GBri LAst LCro LRHS LSRN MCot MNrw MRav NLar SHBN SPer SPoG SRms SWvt WCot WFar WMnd |
| | ***rufa*** | CPou SMrm |
| | - CD&R 1032 new | SGar |
| | 'Safranvogel' | EBee SMad WCot |
| | 'Samuel's Sensation' 🏆H4 | CFir EBla EBrs ELan GBri LFur LRHS MNFA MRav NLar SHBN SMrm SRGP |
| | ***sarmentosa*** | EBee MAvo SGar SPlb WCot WPGP |
| | 'September Sunshine' | MRav |
| | 'Sherbet Lemon' | CHid CTca EBee ECtt EPPr GQue LFur MLLN MNrw SMrm STes WBrk WCot WRHF |
| | 'Shining Sceptre' | CSam EBee EBrs ECha ECtt LPla LRHS MLLN MRav MSte MWat MWte NLar SGar SMad SSvw SWvt WAul WEas |
| | 'Springtime' | WCot |
| | 'Star of Baden Baden' | NBir SEND SMad SMrm WCAu WCot |
| | 'Strawberries and Cream' | CAvo CBcs CFir CMoH COIW CPen CWCL EBee EBla ECha EPfP GQue LAst LPio MSte NPri SAga SMrm SPer WCot |
| | ***stricta*** | WCot |
| | 'Sunbeam' | NBir |
| | 'Sunningdale Yellow' 🏆H4 | CDes CMdw CPou EBee EBla ECha EHrv GMaP MLHP MWat MWte SMHy SMrm SRms WCot WEas WHoo WPGP |
| | 'Tawny King' | Widely available |
| | 'Tetbury Torch'[PBR] | EAEE EBee EBla ECtt LRHS MBNS NBsh NCGa SMrm WClo |
| | ***thomsonii*** var. ***snowdenii*** misapplied | see *K. thomsonii* var. *thomsonii* |
| | - var. ***snowdenii*** ambig. | CWsd SKHP SMad WPGP |
| § | - var. ***thomsonii*** | CDes CFir LPio SKHP SMHy SUsu WCot WHal WPrP WWlt |
| | 'Timothy' | Widely available |
| | 'Toffee Nosed' 🏆H4 | Widely available |
| | 'Torchbearer' | NBre WCot WFar |
| | ***triangularis*** | CMHG CPrp EPfP EShb LRHS NBsh WFar |
| § | - subsp. ***triangularis*** | CBro COIW CWCL EBee EPfP GBuc GCal LAst LRHS LSRN MRav SMrm SRms SWat WBrE |
| § | - - 'Light of the World' | CDes CHar CSpe CTca EBee ECtt EHrv GAbr GBBs LAst LPio LRHS MLLN NBPC NBir NCGa NChi NLar SPav SPoG SRms SUsu SWvt WBrk WCot WFar WGwG |
| | 'Tubergeniana' | WCot |
| | 'Tuckii' | SRms |
| | ***typhoides*** | NBir SPlb |
| | ***tysonii*** | SPlb |
| | ***uvaria*** | CPou CTrC EBrs EHig EMil LCro |

| | |
|---|---|
| | LRHS NBir NVic SRms WCot WHoo WMnd WPnP |
| - 'Grandiflora' | MWhi WFar |
| § - 'Nobilis' ƔH4 | Widely available |
| 'Vanilla' | CFir EBee LAst MAvo MRav NGdn NLar WAul |
| 'Vincent Lepage' | EBee NBhm |
| 'Wol's Red Seedling' | CAby CBct CFir CHFP EBee EBla ECtt EGle ELon EWTr GAbr LSou MAvo NBPC NCGa SPoG SUsu WCot WGwG |
| 'Wrexham Buttercup' | CDes CSam EBee EBla ECrN ECtt GAbr GBri GMaP GMac GQue IPot LSRN MAvo MCot MLLN MNFA MRav MSte SMrm SUsu WCot WHal WPrP WWlt |
| 'Yellow Cheer' | LRHS |
| 'Yellowhammer' | CSam EBee ECha NBre SEND WFar WPrP |
| 'Zululandii' | WCot |

## *Knowltonia* (*Ranunculaceae*)

| | |
|---|---|
| ***filia*** | CPLG |

## *Koeleria* (*Poaceae*)

| | |
|---|---|
| ***cristata*** | see *K. macrantha* |
| ***glauca*** | Widely available |
| § ***macrantha*** | EBee GFor NBre NLar |
| ***vallesiana*** | EBee EHoe EMon |

## *Koelreuteria* (*Sapindaceae*)

| | |
|---|---|
| ***bipinnata*** | CMCN LEdu |
| ***paniculata*** ƔH4 | Widely available |
| - 'Coral Sun' | CGHE MBlu MBri NLar WPGP WPat |
| - 'Fastigiata' | EBee EPfP LRHS MBlu MBri SCoo SSpi WHar |
| - 'Rosseels' | MBlu MGos NLar |
| - 'September' | MBlu MBri |

## *Kohleria* (*Gesneriaceae*)

| | |
|---|---|
| 'Clytie' | MBri |
| 'Cybele' | EABi WDib |
| 'Dark Velvet' | CHal WDib |
| ***eriantha*** ƔH1 | CHal EShb MBri WDib |
| ***hirsuta*** | WDib |
| 'Jester' ƔH1 | CHal EABi WDib |
| 'Marquis de Sade' new | EABi |
| 'Red Ryder' | EABi |
| 'Ruby Red' | WDib |
| 'Strawberry Fields' ƔH1 | MBri |
| § 'Sunrise' PBR new | WDib |
| 'Sunshine' PBR | see *K.* 'Sunrise' |
| ***warscewiczii*** ƔH1 | CHal EABi LRHS WDib |

## *Kolkwitzia* (*Caprifoliaceae*)

| | |
|---|---|
| ***amabilis*** | CPLG CSBt CTri ECGP ELan EMil EPfP GKir GQue LPan MGan MGos MMuc NWea SPlb SRms WCFE WDin WHCG WHar WMoo WRHF |
| - 'Maradco' | CPMA EBee EMil EPfP LRHS MAsh MRav NLar NPro SCoo SPoG SSta WPat |
| - 'Pink Cloud' ƔH4 | Widely available |

## kumquat see *Fortunella*

## *Kunzea* (*Myrtaceae*)

| | |
|---|---|
| ***ambigua*** | EBee ECou SOWG SPlb |
| - pink-flowered | ECou |
| - prostrate | ECou |
| 'Badja Carpet' | WAbe |
| ***baxteri*** | ECou SOWG |
| ***capitata*** | SOWG |
| ***ericifolia*** | SPlb |
| § ***ericoides*** | ECou GGar SOWG |
| - 'Auckland' | ECou |
| - 'Bemm' | ECou |
| ***parvifolia*** | ECou SOWG |
| ***pomifera*** | ECou |

# L

## *Lablab* (*Papilionaceae*)

| | |
|---|---|
| § ***purpureus*** | LSou |
| - 'Ruby Moon' | CSpe |

## + *Laburnocytisus* (*Papilionaceae*)

| | |
|---|---|
| 'Adamii' | CDul CLnd CPMA EBee ECrN EHig ELan EMil EPfP LBuc LPan LSRN MBlu MGos NLar SMHT SMad |

## *Laburnum* ✿ (*Papilionaceae*)

| | |
|---|---|
| ***alpinum*** | EPfP GGar NWea SPlb |
| § - 'Pendulum' | CDoC CDul CLnd EBee ELan EMil EPfP GKir LPan LRHS LSRN MAsh MBar MBri MGos SBLw SBod SCrf SLim SPer SPoG WOrn |
| § ***anagyroides*** | CDul CSec CWib ECrN EMac GKir ISea LMaj NWea SBLw SEND SRms WBVN WDin |
| - var. ***alschingeri*** | MBlu MGos |
| - 'Aureum' | GKir |
| 'Pendula' | see *L. alpinum* 'Pendulum' |
| ***vulgare*** | see *L. anagyroides* |
| I x ***watereri*** 'Fastigata' | CSec ECrN |
| - 'Vossii' ƔH4 | Widely available |

## *Lachenalia* (*Hyacinthaceae*)

| | |
|---|---|
| ***algoensis*** | WCot |
| § ***aloides*** | CBcs CBow CGrW CStu CTca EBrs ECho MBri |
| - var. ***aurea*** ƔH1 | CTca EBrs ECho LRHS MSte SBch WCot |
| I - var. ***luteola*** | ECho |
| - 'Nelsonii' | ECho LRHS WCot |
| - 'Pearsonii' | CBgR EBrs ECho LRHS |
| - var. ***quadricolor*** ƔH1 | CBgR CGrW CTca EBrs ECho GAbr IHer LRHS WCot |
| - var. ***vanzyliae*** ƔH1 | WCot |
| ***attenuata*** new | ECho |
| § ***bulbifera*** ƔH1 | CBgR CTca EBrs ECho MBri |
| ***carnosa*** | WCot |
| ***contaminata*** ƔH1 | CBgR EBrs ECho LRHS WCot |
| ***elegans*** | EBrs ECho |
| ***framesii*** | ECho |
| 'Fransie' PBR | EBrs ECho |
| ***gillettii*** | EBrs ECho |
| ***hirta*** | EBrs ECho |
| ***juncifolia*** | EBrs ECho |
| ***latimerae*** new | ECho |
| 'Lemon Ripple' | WCot |
| ***liliiflora*** | EBrs ECho |
| ***maximilianii*** | EBrs |
| ***mediana*** | CBgR EBrs ECho |
| ***montana*** | EBrs ECho |
| ***mutabilis*** | EBrs ECho LRHS WCot |
| 'Namakwa' (African Beauty Series) | CTca EBrs ECho |
| ***namaquensis*** | EBrs ECho |
| ***namibiensis*** | EBrs ECho |
| ***neilii*** | WCot |
| 'Nova' | EBrs |
| ***obscura*** new | ECho |

| | |
|---|---|
| ***orchioides*** var. ***glaucina*** | CGrW ECho WCot |
| ***orthopetala*** | EBrs ECho WCot |
| ***pallida*** | EBrs ECho |
| ***peersii*** | CGrW |
| ***pendula*** | see *L. bulbifera* |
| ***pusilla*** | ECho WCot |
| ***pustulata*** ♀H1 | CTca EBrs ECho LRHS WCot |
| - blue-flowered | CGrW CTca EBrs ECho |
| - yellow-flowered | EBrs ECho |
| ***reflexa*** | EBrs ECho WCot |
| 'Robijn' | CGrW EBrs ECho WCot |
| 'Rolina' | EBrs ECho WCot |
| 'Romaud' | EBrs ECho WCot |
| 'Romelia'PBR | EBrs ECho WCot |
| 'Ronina' | EBrs ECho WCot |
| 'Rosabeth' | EBrs WCot |
| ***rosea*** | ECho |
| ***rubida*** | CBgR EBrs ECho WCot |
| 'Rupert' (African Beauty Series) | CGrW EBrs ECho WCot |
| ***splendida*** | ECho |
| ***thomasiae*** | EBrs |
| ***tricolor*** | see *L. aloides* |
| ***unicolor*** | ECho WCot |
| ***unifolia*** | EBrs ECho |
| ***violacea*** | EBrs ECho WCot |
| ***viridiflora*** ♀H1 | CGrW ECho LRHS SBch WCot |
| ***zeyheri*** | ECho WCot |

## *Lactuca* (*Asteraceae*)

| | |
|---|---|
| ***alpina*** | see *Cicerbita alpina* |
| ***lessertiana*** | EBee |
| ***perennis*** | CSpe CWan EBee EHoe EPPr LSou MTho NDov NLar SPla SPoG WCot WHer WHrl |
| ***tenerrima*** new | WCot |
| ***virosa*** | CArn MSal |

## *Lagarosiphon* (*Hydrocharitaceae*)

| | |
|---|---|
| § ***major*** | CBen CDWL EHon EMFW EPfP MSKA WMAq |

## *Lagarostrobos* (*Podocarpaceae*)

| | |
|---|---|
| § ***franklinii*** | CBcs CDoC CTrG STre WPic |
| - 'Fota' (f) | WThu |
| - 'Picton Castle' (m) | WThu |

## *Lagerstroemia* (*Lythraceae*)

| | |
|---|---|
| ***fauriei*** B&SWJ 6023 | WCru |
| ***indica*** ♀H1 | CCCN CMen EMil EPfP ERom EShb SBLw SEND SHGN SPlb WSHC |
| - Little Chief hybrids | EShb |
| - Petite Pinkie = 'Monkie' | IDee MREP |
| - 'Red Imperator' | SEND |
| - 'Rosea' | CBcs LPan SEND |
| - 'Rubra' | MREP |

## *Lagunaria* (*Malvaceae*)

| | |
|---|---|
| ***patersonii*** | CHll WPGP |

## *Lagurus* (*Poaceae*)

| | |
|---|---|
| ***ovatus*** ♀H3 | CHrt CKno CWCL EAlp EGoo EHoe NGBl SAdn SBch SEND |

## *Lambertia* (*Proteaceae*)

| | |
|---|---|
| ***formosa*** | ECou |

## *Lamiastrum* see *Lamium*

## *Lamium* ✿ (*Lamiaceae*)

| | |
|---|---|
| ***album*** | CArn EBWF NMir |
| - 'Friday' (v) | CBow NBir NBre WHer |
| ***flexuosum*** | EPPr NBre |
| § ***galeobdolon*** | CArn CNat CTri CWib EBWF MHer MSal NSco SRms WAlt WBrE WHer WHil |
| - 'Dark Angel' new | WAlt |
| - 'Hermann's Pride' | COlW CTca EAEE EBee ECtt EHoe EPfP GKir GMaP LBMP LRHS MAvo NBir NBlu NCob NMir SAga SMad SMrm SPer SPla SRms SWvt WFar WHoo WMoo |
| - 'Kirkcudbright Dwarf' | EBee EWes GBin NBre |
| § - subsp. ***montanum*** 'Florentinum' | CHal CHrt CSBt CWan EBee ECha EPfP GKir LBMP MMuc MRav SPer WBrk WCAu WFar WPer |
| § - 'Silberteppich' | ECha ELan MRav MTho |
| - 'Silver Angel' | NBre |
| - Silver Carpet | see *L. galeobdolon* 'Silberteppich' |
| - 'Variegatum' | see *L. galeobdolon* subsp. *montanum* 'Florentinum' |
| ***garganicum*** | EPot |
| - subsp. ***garganicum*** | CPom EWes GBri LPla WPer |
| ***luteum*** | see *L. galeobdolon* |
| ***maculatum*** | CArn CHrt EGoo EPot NChi SEND SRms WFar |
| - 'Album' | EBee ELan EPfP LBMP SHar SPer SPoG SRms |
| - 'Anne Greenaway' (v) | CBow EWes GBri SPet |
| § - 'Aureum' | CArn COlW ECha EGoo EHoe ELan MTho SPet SWvt WFar WPer |
| - 'Beacon Silver' | Widely available |
| - 'Beedham's White' | NBir NSti |
| - 'Brightstone Pearl' | EBee EGoo EWes |
| - 'Cannon's Gold' | ECha ECtt ELan EPPr EWes SWvt WFar |
| - 'Chequers' ambig. | EBee LBMP LRHS NBre SPer SPla |
| - 'Elaine Franks' | CSam |
| - 'Elisabeth de Haas' (v) | CBow EWes NBre |
| - 'Forncett Lustre' | EBee EWes |
| - 'Forncett White Lustre' | NBre |
| - 'Gold Leaf' | see *L. maculatum* 'Aureum' |
| - Golden Anniversary = 'Dellam'PBR (v) | ELan LSRN NBro SPla SPoG SSto SWvt WFar |
| - 'Golden Nuggets' | see *L. maculatum* 'Aureum' |
| - 'Ickwell Beauty' (v) | EBee GBri |
| - 'James Boyd Parselle' | CBow CSam EBee MLLN NBre WHal WRHF |
| - 'Margery Fish' | SRms |
| - 'Pink Nancy' | CSpe EGoo GKir SWvt |
| - 'Pink Pearls' | CHrt CSBt NBre SHar SPet WFar WMoo |
| - 'Pink Pewter' | COlW CTca EAEE EBee ECGP ECha ECtt EHoe ELan EPfP EShb GGar GMaP LBMP LRHS SPer SPla SPlb SPoG SUsu WBrE |
| - 'Red Nancy' | EBee SWvt |
| § - 'Roseum' | CWib EBee ELan EPfP GGar GMaP LBMP MRav MWat NChi SGar SPer WCAu WPer |
| - 'Shell Pink' | see *L. maculatum* 'Roseum' |
| - 'Silver Shield' | EBee EWes |
| - 'Sterling Silver' | EBee GQue NBre WPer |
| - 'White Nancy' ♀H4 | Widely available |
| - 'Wootton Pink' | GBuc MBri MHer NBir NLar SSvw SWvt WCra WEas |
| ***microphyllum*** | WAbe |
| ***orvala*** | Widely available |
| - 'Album' | CBod CLAP EBee EHrv ELan EMon EPPr LEdu MSte NBir NLar SGar SHar SMrm WHer WPtf WTin |
| - pink-flowered | CLAP CSpe |
| - 'Silva' | CLAP CSam EBee EMon EPPr GBin LEdu NBre NGby WCot WSHC |
| ***sandrasicum*** | CPBP WAbe |

## *Lampranthus* (*Aizoaceae*)

| | |
|---|---|
| sp. | EDAr |
| ***aberdeenensis*** | see *Delosperma aberdeenense* |
| ***aurantiacus*** | CBcs CHEx SPet |
| ***aureus*** | WCor |
| 'Bagdad' | CHEx |
| ***blandus*** | CBcs CCCN |
| 'Blousey Pink' | CHEx |
| § ***brownii*** | CBcs CCCN CHEx CHal EAlp ECho ELan SEND SPet WPnn |
| ***coccineus*** | SPet |
| ***deltoides*** | see *Oscularia deltoides* |
| ***edulis*** | see *Carpobrotus edulis* |
| ***glaucus*** | CStu SEND |
| ***haworthii*** | CHal |
| ***multiradiatus*** | GGar SEND |
| ***oscularis*** | see *Oscularia deltoides* |
| ***roseus*** | CCCN CHEx EAlp LRHS SPet SPoG WCor |
| ***spectabilis*** | CBcs CCCN CHal CStu SAPC SArc SPet WBrE WCor |
| - 'Tresco Apricot' | CCCN |
| - 'Tresco Brilliant' | CCCN CHEx CStu SPet |
| - 'Tresco Fire' | CCCN CDoC CHal LRHS |
| - 'Tresco Orange' | CCCN LRHS WPnn |
| - 'Tresco Peach' | CCCN CHal CStu WCor |
| - 'Tresco Red' | CCCN ELon SEND WPnn |
| - white-flowered | CStu |
| 'Sugar Pink' | CHEx |

## *Lamprothyrsus* (*Poaceae*)

| | |
|---|---|
| ***hieronymi*** | EPPr |

## *Lantana* (*Verbenaceae*)

| | |
|---|---|
| 'Aloha' (v) | CHal LSou |
| ***camara*** | CArn ELan EPfP EShb MBri SRms WFar |
| - 'Kolibri' | LAst |
| - orange-flowered | CCCN |
| - pink-flowered | CCCN EShb |
| - red-flowered | CCCN |
| - 'Sonja' | LAst |
| - variegated | EShb |
| - white-flowered | CCCN EShb SEND |
| - yellow-flowered | EShb NPri |
| 'Goldsome' | LAst |
| § ***montevidensis*** | CHal EShb |
| - RCB/Arg AA-1 | WCot |
| * - ***alba*** | EShb |
| - 'Boston Gold' | CHal |
| 'Red and Gold' new | SEND |
| ***sellowiana*** | see *L. montevidensis* |
| 'Spreading Sunset' | SOWG |
| violet-flowered | SEND |

## *Lapageria* ✿ (*Philesiaceae*)

| | |
|---|---|
| ***rosea*** ♀H3 | CBcs CCCN CKob CPLG CPne CRHN CTsd EBee EPfP EPla EPot EShb GQui MDun NLar SAdn SChF SHBN SSpi WFar WPGP WVal |
| - var. ***albiflora*** | CRHN SAdn WVal |
| - 'Flesh Pink' | CPLG CRHN |
| - 'Nash Court' | ECot |

## *Lapeirousia* (*Iridaceae*)

| | |
|---|---|
| ***cruenta*** | see *Anomatheca laxa* |
| ***divaricata*** | CStu |
| ***laxa*** | see *Anomatheca laxa* |
| ***oreogena*** new | CStu |

## *Lapiedra* (*Amaryllidaceae*)

| | |
|---|---|
| ***martinezii*** | ECho |

## *Lappula* (*Boraginaceae*)

| | |
|---|---|
| ***squarrosa*** new | CSec |

## *Lapsana* (*Asteraceae*)

| | |
|---|---|
| ***communis*** 'Inky' | CNat WAlt |

## *Lardizabala* (*Lardizabalaceae*)

| | |
|---|---|
| ***biternata*** | see *L. funaria* |
| § ***funaria*** | CTrG |

## *Larix* ✿ (*Pinaceae*)

| | |
|---|---|
| ***decidua*** ♀H4 | CBcs CCVT CDoC CDul CMen CRWN CSBt ECrN ELan EMac EPfP GKir MBar MGos MMuc NWea SHBN SPer SPlb WDin WFar WMou |
| - 'Autumn Gold Weeping' | NHol |
| - 'Corley' | CKen ECho MBlu |
| - 'Croxby Broom' | CKen |
| § - var. ***decidua*** | WFar |
| - 'Globus' | LRHS NHol SLim |
| - 'Horstmann Recurved' | ECho GKir LRHS NLar SCoo SLim SPoG |
| - 'Krejci' | NLar SLim |
| - 'Little Bogle' | CKen MAsh NHol |
| - 'Oberförster Karsten' | CKen ECho |
| - 'Pendula' | CBcs ECho |
| - 'Puli' | CEnd ECho EHig EMil GKir LRHS MAsh MBlu MGos NHol NLar SCoo SLim |
| × ***eurolepis*** | see *L.* × *marschlinsii* |
| ***europaea*** Lam. & DC. | see *L. decidua* var. *decidua* |
| ***europaea*** Middend. | see *L. sibirica* |
| ***gmelinii*** var. ***olgensis*** | NLar |
| - var. ***principis-rupprechtii*** | GKir |
| - 'Tharandt' | CKen ECho |
| ***griffithii*** new | GKir |
| § ***kaempferi*** ♀H4 | CCVT CDoC CDul CLnd CMen CSBt CTri ECrN ELan EMac EPfP GKir LBuc LMaj LPan LRHS MAsh MBar NWea SCoo SLim SPer STre WDin WFar WMou |
| - 'Bambino' | CKen |
| - 'Bingman' | CKen |
| - 'Blue Ball' | CKen NLar |
| - 'Blue Dwarf' | CKen GKir LPan LRHS MAsh MBar MGos SCoo SLim SPoG WFar |
| - 'Blue Haze' | CKen |
| - 'Blue Rabbit' | CKen CTho |
| - 'Blue Rabbit Weeping' | GKir MGos SCoo SLim WDin |
| - 'Cruwys Morchard' | CKen |
| - 'Cupido' | NHol SLim |
| - 'Diane' | CEnd CKen ECho EPfP LRHS MAsh MBar MBlu MGos NHol NLar SBLw SLim SPoG WFar |
| - 'Elizabeth Rehder' | CKen ECho NLar |
| - 'Grant Haddow' | CKen |
| - 'Grey Green Dwarf' | NHol |
| - 'Grey Pearl' | CKen ECho EMil NLar |
| - 'Hanna's Broom' | NLar SLim |
| - 'Hobbit' | CKen |
| * - 'Jakobsen's Pyramid' | CDoC CMen LRHS MAsh NHol SCoo SLim SPoG |
| - 'Nana' | CKen ECho NLar SLim WFar |
| I - 'Nana Prostrata' | CKen |
| - 'Pendula' | CDul CEnd EBee ECho ECrN EPfP LRHS MAsh MBar MBlu MGos NHol NLar SBLw SPoG |
| - 'Peve Tunnis' | NLar |
| - 'Pulii' | ECho GKir SBLw |
| - 'Stiff Weeping' | CTri GKir MAsh MBlu NLar SCoo SLim |

| | |
|---|---|
| - 'Swallow Falls' | CKen |
| - 'Varley' | CKen |
| - 'Walter Pimven' | NLar |
| - 'Wehlen' | CKen |
| - 'Wolterdingen' | CKen ECho MBlu NLar SLim |
| - 'Yanus Olieslagers' | CKen |
| ***laricina*** 'Arethusa Bog' | CKen ECho MBlu |
| - 'Bear Swamp' | CKen |
| - 'Bingman' | CKen |
| - 'Hartwig Pine' | CKen ECho |
| - 'Newport Beauty' | CKen ECho |
| ***leptolepis*** | see *L. kaempferi* |
| § x ***marschlinsii*** | GBin GKir NWea WMou |
| - 'Domino' | CKen ECho |
| - 'Gail' | CKen |
| - 'Julie' | CKen SLim |
| - 'Newport 17' | NLar |
| ***russica*** | see *L. sibirica* |
| § ***sibirica*** | MBar |
| ***sukaczevii*** | see *L. sibirica* |
| 'Varied Directions' | SCoo SLim |

## *Larrea* (*Zygophyllaceae*)

| | |
|---|---|
| ***tridentata*** | CArn |

## *Larryleachia* (*Asclepiadaceae*)

| | |
|---|---|
| ***cactiformis*** | LToo |

## *Laserpitium* (*Apiaceae*)

| | |
|---|---|
| ***siler*** | CArn EBee GBin NDov NLar SPlb WSHC |

## *Lasiagrostis* see *Stipa*

## *Lasiospermum* (*Asteraceae*)

| | |
|---|---|
| ***bipinnatum*** | SPlb |

## *Lastreopsis* (*Dryopteridaceae*)

| | |
|---|---|
| ***glabella*** | WRic |
| ***hispida*** | WRic |
| ***microsora*** | WRic |

## *Latania* (*Arecaceae*)

| | |
|---|---|
| ***loddigesii*** | EAmu LPal |
| ***verschaffeltii*** | LPal |

## *Lathyrus* ✿ (*Papilionaceae*)

| | |
|---|---|
| ***angulatus*** | CSec |
| ***aphaca*** | CSec |
| § ***articulatus*** | CSec WCHb |
| § ***aureus*** | Widely available |
| ***azureus*** misapplied | see *L. sativus* |
| ***chilensis*** | CSpe CSsd EBee LSou NLar |
| ***chloranthus*** | SPav |
| ***cirrhosus*** | CDes EBee EMon MPet WPGP |
| ***clymenum articulatus*** | see *L. articulatus* |
| ***cyaneus*** misapplied | see *L. vernus* |
| ***cyaneus*** (Steven) K.Koch | SAga |
| ***davidii*** | EBee EMon EWes GCal WSHC |
| ***filiformis*** | WSHC |
| ***fremontii*** hort. | see *L. laxiflorus* |
| § ***gmelinii*** | NLar |
| - 'Aureus' | see *L. aureus* |
| ***grandiflorus*** | CSev EMon MSCN NLar SMrm SSvw SWat WCot |
| ***heterophyllus*** | CSpe EMon MNrw NLar |
| ***hirsutus*** | CSec WGwG |
| ***incurvus*** new | MPet |
| ***inermis*** | see *L. laxiflorus* |
| ***japonicus*** | EBWF |
| 'Lamorna's Love' new | WViv |
| ***latifolius*** ♀H4 | CArn CRHN CRWN CTca EBee EPfP GAbr GBar LAst MWat MWhi NBid NBlu NPer SDnm SPoG SRms SVic SWal WBVN WBrk WEas WFar WHer WPer |
| § - 'Albus' ♀H4 | EBee ELan NBHF SGar SPav SRms WEas |
| - 'Blushing Bride' | SPav WCot |
| - deep pink-flowered | CSec MHer NLar NSti |
| - pale pink-flowered | NSti |
| - Pink Pearl | see *L. latifolius* 'Rosa Perle' |
| - 'Red Pearl' | ECtt ELan EPfP GAbr LCro MBri MCot NPri SPav SPer SPlb SPoG SSvw WFar WPer |
| § - 'Rosa Perle' ♀H4 | CBcs CTri EBee ECtt EShb LCro LHop MBri MCot MLHP MNHC MRav MSte NBir NLar NPer NPri SPav SPer SSvw WCAu WHil WMoo |
| - Weisse Perle | see *L. latifolius* 'White Pearl' |
| - 'White Pearl' misapplied | see *L. latifolius* 'Albus' |
| § - 'White Pearl' ♀H4 | ECha EMon EPfP EShb EWTr GAbr GBuc GCal GKir LCro MBri MCot MHer MNHC MRav MSte NBir NLar NPer NPri NSti SMad SPer SPoG SSvw WCAu WFar WPer |
| § ***laxiflorus*** | CDes EBee EDAr EGle LHop MCCP MHar MNrw MTho NChi SSvw WPGP |
| ***linifolius*** | EMon NLar WCot WPGP |
| ***luteus*** (L.) Peterm. | see *L. gmelinii* |
| - 'Aureus' | see *L. aureus* |
| ***maritimus*** | NLar |
| ***montanus*** | GPoy |
| ***nervosus*** | CSpe CWsd EBee EWes MTho SRms |
| ***neurolobus*** | CPom CSec |
| ***nevadensis*** | WHil |
| ***niger*** | CSec CSpe CWCL EBee EGle EMon GBuc LHop LSou MCot MHer MLLN MMHG NLar WFar |
| ***nissolia*** | CSec |
| ***odoratus*** | NBlu SVic |
| - 'America' ♀H4 | CSec |
| - 'Black Knight' | CSec |
| - 'Black Prince' new | CSpe |
| - 'Cupani' | CHrt CSec |
| - 'Dancing Queen' | MPet |
| - 'Lightening' | MPet |
| - 'Matucana' | CSpe MWat SBch |
| - 'Queen Alexandra' new | CSec |
| ***palustris*** | NLar |
| ***polyphyllus*** | MPet NSti |
| ***pratensis*** | EBWF NMir NSco WSFF |
| ***pubescens*** | CRHN MPet |
| ***roseus*** | GCal WSHC WViv |
| ***rotundifolius*** ♀H4 | CSec MNrw MSte MTho SSvw SUsu WFar WHoo |
| - 'Tillyperone' | EMon EPPr |
| § ***sativus*** | CHid CSpe ECho ELan SBch WCHb |
| - var. ***azureus*** | see *L. sativus* |
| ***sphaericus*** | CSec |
| ***sylvestris*** | EBWF EBee EMon MLLN MNrw MSte NLar SBch SMrs WBrk |
| ***tingitanus*** | CRHN CSec WCHb |
| - 'Roseus' | CRHN CSec |
| ***transsilvanicus*** | CPom |
| ***tuberosus*** | EBee MNrw WCot |
| 'Tubro' | EMon SHar |
| ***venetus*** | CPom EBee EGle MNrw WSHC |
| § ***vernus*** ♀H4 | Widely available |
| - 'Alboroseus' ♀H4 | Widely available |
| - var. ***albus*** | CDes CLAP ECho GMaP WCot WPGP |
| - ***aurantiacus*** | see *L. aureus* |
| - 'Caeruleus' | CDes CLAP ECGP EMon LHop MNFA SUsu WPGP |

| | | |
|---|---|---|
| * | - 'Cyaneus' | SAga SWat WCot |
| I | - 'Filifolius' new | CSpe |
| | - 'Flaccidus' | CAby EGle EMon SMeo WCot WTin |
| * | - 'Gracilis' | WViv |
| | - narrow-leaved new | CSec |
| | - 'Rainbow' | CLAP ELon NWCA WFar |
| | - 'Rosenelfe' | CDes CMea EBee GBuc MDKP NPri SBod SMrm WCot WHal WHil WPGP |
| | - f. *roseus* | EBee ECha MRav NBir NCGa SRms WCot WCru |
| | - 'Spring Beauty' | CLAP |
| | - 'Spring Delight' | GKir |
| | - 'Spring Melody' | EBee MRav WCot WPat |
| | - 'Subtle Hints' | EMon |

## *Laurelia* (*Monimiaceae*)

| | | |
|---|---|---|
| § | ***sempervirens*** | CBcs SKHP WPGP |
| | ***serrata*** | see *L. sempervirens* |

## *Laureliopsis* (*Monimiaceae*)

| | | |
|---|---|---|
| | ***philippiana*** new | IDee |

## *Laurentia* see *Isotoma*

## *Laurus* (*Lauraceae*)

| | | |
|---|---|---|
| § | ***azorica*** | CBcs WFar |
| | ***canariensis*** | see *L. azorica* |
| | ***nobilis*** 🏆H4 | Widely available |
| | - f. ***angustifolia*** | CSWP EOHP EPla GGal GQui MBlu MHer NGHP NLar SAPC SArc SPoG WCHb WPGP |
| | - 'Aurea' 🏆H4 | CBcs CDul EBee ELan ELau ELon EMil EPfP GQui LHop LRHS MBlu MGos SBLw SLim SLon SPer SPoG SWvt WCHb WDin WFar WJek WMoo WPat |
| | - clipped pyramid | GKir MGos NBlu |
| | - 'Crispa' | MRav |
| | - 'Sunspot' (v) | WCot |

## *Lavandula* ✿ (*Lamiaceae*)

| | | |
|---|---|---|
| | 'After Midnight' | see *L.* 'Avonview' |
| | 'Alba' | see *L. angustifolia* 'Alba', *L.* x *intermedia* 'Alba' |
| | 'Alba' ambig. | CArn CSev CWib MHrb SAdn SIde SPer SWat WEas WPer |
| | x ***allardii*** (Gaston Allard Group) 'African Pride' | CPbn GBar |
| § | ***angustifolia*** | Widely available |
| | - 'Alba' misapplied | see *L. angustifolia* 'Blue Mountain White' |
| § | - 'Alba' | CChe CPbn EAro EPfP GPoy LBuc LSRN MHer MRav MSwo NGHP NMen SLon SPlb SSto WDin WFar |
| | - 'Alba Nana' | see *L. angustifolia* 'Nana Alba' |
| | - 'Arctic Snow' | CBcs CChe CEnt CPbn EAEE ENor LAst MAvo MHrb MSwo MWat NBPC NDov NGHP NLLv SDnm SIoW SPer SPoG WLav |
| | - 'Ashdown Forest' | CPbn CWan EBee ELon EMil GBar MAsh MHer MHrb MLHP MNHC NGHP SAdn SBch SDow SIde SIoW WHoo WJek WLav WRHF |
| | - 'Beechwood Blue' 🏆H4 | CPbn MHrb SDow WLav |
| | - 'Betty's Blue' new | SDow |
| | - Blue Cushion = 'Lavandula Schola'PBR | EPfP LRHS LSRN MHrb SDow SPad WFar WLav |
| | - 'Blue Ice' | CWSG ENor LSou MGos NBPC SDow WLav |
| | - 'Blue Mountain' | CHFP GBar ITim MHrb |
| § | - 'Blue Mountain White' | NLLv SDow WLav |
| | - 'Blue Rider' new | LRHS NGHP SWal |
| | - 'Blue River'PBR | MAsh NGHP WFar |
| § | - 'Bowles Early' | CPbn GBar NGHP SAga WFar |
| | - 'Bowles Grey' | see *L. angustifolia* 'Bowles Early' |
| | - 'Bowles Variety' | see *L. angustifolia* 'Bowles Early' |
| | - 'Cedar Blue' | CPbn CSev CWan EAro EGoo ELau EMil EPfP GBar NBur NGHP SDow SHDw SIde SIoW SPla WFar WLav WRHF |
| | - 'Coconut Ice'PBR | CWSG EMil NGHP NLLv NTHB SIoW WLav |
| | - 'Compacta' | CPbn MHrb SDow WLav |
| | - 'Crystal Lights'PBR | SIoW |
| | - 'Dwarf Blue' | CPbn EMil EPfP MBrN WFar |
| | - 'Eastgrove Dome' | WEas |
| | - 'Ellagance Ice' new | CPbn |
| | - 'Ellagance Sky' new | CPbn |
| | - 'Folgate' | CArn CPbn CWCL EBee ECtt ELau EMil EPfP GBar LAst MHer MHrb MNHC NBur NGHP SAll SDow SIde SIoW WFar WHoo WLav WMnd |
| | - 'Fring A' | SDow |
| | - 'Granny's Bouquet' | LSou SIoW |
| § | - 'Hidcote' 🏆H4 | Widely available |
| | - 'Hidcote Pink' | CEnt CPbn CWCL CWib EBee ELon EPfP GBar LSRN MHer MNHC MRav NGHP SDow WFar WKif WMnd WPer |
| | - 'Hidcote Superior' | LBMP |
| | - 'Imperial Gem' 🏆H4 | Widely available |
| | - 'Jean Davis' | see *L. angustifolia* 'Rosea' |
| | - 'Lady' | CWSG NPer SEND SHDw SSto SWal WPer |
| | - 'Lady Ann' | CWCL EMil MHrb NLLv NTHB SDow SIoW WLav |
| | - 'Lavenite Petite' | ENor EPfP LLHF LRHS LSRN MAsh MHrb NBPC NGHP NLLv NLar SDow SIoW SPoG SVil WLav |
| | - Little Lady = 'Batlad'PBR | EBee ECtt EMil EPfP LAst LRHS LSRN MAsh MHer MHrb MSwo NBPC NGHP NLLv NLar NPri SAll SIoW SSto WLav |
| | - Little Lottie = 'Clarmo' 🏆H4 | CPbn CWCL CWSG EBee EMil EPfP GBar LAst LSRN MAvo MHer SCoo SDow SIde SSto SWvt WLav |
| | - 'Loddon Blue' 🏆H4 | CEnt CHFP CPbn EBee EPfP GBar LRHS NGHP SAdn SDow SIde SIoW WHoo WLav |
| § | - 'Loddon Pink' 🏆H4 | CPbn CWan EBee ELan EPfP GBar GMaP LAst LRHS MAsh MLHP MNHC MRav NGHP NPri SAdn SSto WEas WFar WLav WPGP |
| | - 'Maillette' | CPbn MHrb NGHP SDow SIde SIoW WLav |
| | - 'Melissa Lilac' | CBcs ENor LCro LRHS LSou MAsh MHer MHrb SDow SIoW SRkn WLav WWlt |
| | - 'Middachten' | SAga |
| | - 'Miss Donnington' | see *L. angustifolia* 'Bowles Early' |
| | - 'Miss Katherine'PBR 🏆H4 | CSBt CWCL EBee ECtt ELan EMil ENor EPfP LAst LHop LRHS LSRN MAsh MHer MHrb NBPC NGHP NLar SDow SIoW SPad SPer SPoG SVil WLav |
| | - Miss Muffet = 'Scholmis' 🏆H4 | CWCL EBee EMil LLHF NLLv SDow WLav |
| | - 'Munstead' | Widely available |
| § | - 'Nana Alba' 🏆H4 | Widely available |
| | - 'Peter Pan' | CPbn CWCL EAEE ECtt EMil LLWG LSRN MAvo MHrb NDov NGHP SBch SDow SIoW WLav |
| | - 'Princess Blue' | CPbn CSBt CWCL EAro EBee ELan EMil ENor EShb GBar LRHS MAsh NPri SAga SDow SIde SIoW SSto WFar WLav WPer |

| | | |
|---|---|---|
| | - 'Rêve de Jean-Claude' | WLav |
| § | - 'Rosea' | Widely available |
| | - 'Royal Purple' | CArn CBcs CPbn EBee EMil ENor EWes GBar LCro LRHS LSou NGHP NTHB SAdn SDow SIde SIoW SSto SWvt WLav |
| | - 'Royal Velvet' **new** | SDow |
| | - 'Saint Jean' | CPbn SDow |
| | - 'Silver Mist' | GGar |
| | - 'Twickel Purple' | CHrt CWCL CWSG EBee EPfP GKir LHop LRHS LSRN MAsh MNHC MRav NGHP NPri NTHB SDow SIde SPer SPla SWvt WFar WLav |
| | - 'Walberton's Silver Edge' | see *L.* x *intermedia* Walberton's Silver Edge |
| | - 'Wendy Carlile' 🏆H4 | ENor SIoW SPoG |
| | - 'White Horse' **new** | NGHP |
| | 'Aphrodite' | WLav |
| | ***aristibracteata*** | MHer WLav |
| § | 'Avonview' | CBcs CWCL GBar MHer NGHP SDow WHoo WLav |
| | 'Badsey Starlite' | WLav |
| | 'Ballerina' | CWCL MHrb SDow |
| § | 'Bee Brilliant'PBR | CPbn NGHP SPoG WLav |
| § | 'Bee Cool'PBR | MHer MHrb NGHP NLLv SPoG WLav |
| § | 'Bee Happy' | CPbn CWCL NBir NGHP NLLv SHGN SPoG WLav |
| § | 'Bee Pretty' | CPbn NGHP |
| | (Bella Series) 'Bella Purple' | EMil |
| | - 'Bella Bridal Pink' **new** | CPbn |
| | - 'Bella Rose' | CPbn EMil |
| | - 'Bella Rouge' | EMil |
| | - 'Bella White' | CPbn EMil |
| | 'Blue Star' | EBee EPfP GBar NGHP SAll WFar WGwG |
| | 'Bowers Beauty' | LRHS MAsh WLav |
| | ***buchii*** var. ***buchii*** | CPbn SDow WLav |
| | - var. ***gracilis*** | CSpe |
| | Butterfly Garden = 'Avenue'PBR | CWSG SIoW |
| | ***canariensis*** | MHer MHrb SDow WCHb WLav |
| | x ***chaytoriae*** 'Gorgeous' | SDow |
| | - 'Richard Gray' 🏆H3-4 | CArn EBee EMil GBar LRHS LSRN MAsh MHer MHrb MNHC NGHP SDnm SDow SSvw WAbe WLav WMnd |
| § | - 'Sawyers' 🏆H4 | Widely available |
| | - 'Silver Sands' | EBee ENor LRHS LSRN LSou SPoG |
| | x ***christiana*** | CArn CPbn GBar MHrb NGHP NPri SDow SHDw WJek WKif WLav |
| | 'Cornard Blue' | see *L.* x *chaytoriae* 'Sawyers' |
| | ***dentata*** | CEnt CPbn CSev EAro EBee EShb GBar LCro MNHC NGHP SAdn SGar SMrm |
| § | - var. ***candicans*** | CSev EBee GBar LHop MHer MHrb MNHC NLLv SAga SBch SDow WCHb WLav |
| | - var. ***dentata*** 'Dusky Maiden' | CPbn CWCL MHrb SDow WLav |
| | - - 'Linda Ligon' (v) | CBow CPbn GBar MHrb NGHP WGwG WHer WJek WLav |
| | - - 'Monet' | MHrb NGHP |
| | - - 'Ploughman's Blue' | CPbn CWCL GBar MHrb WGwG WLav |
| | - - f. ***rosea*** | MHrb SDow WLav |
| | - - 'Royal Crown' 🏆H2-3 | CPbn GBar MHer WFar WLav |
| | - - 'Royal Standard' | SHBN |
| | - - 'Serenity' **new** | ENor |
| | - - 'Silver Queen' | WLav |
| | - silver-leaved | see *L. dentata* var. *candicans* |
| | 'Devonshire Compact' | CSBt CWCL EMil LSou MHer NGHP NTHB SBch WJek |
| | 'Fathead' | Widely available |
| | x ***ginginsii*** 'Goodwin Creek Grey' | CPbn CSpe MHer MHrb NLLv SDow WGwG WJek WLav WOut |
| | 'Hazel' | LRHS |
| | 'Helmsdale'PBR | Widely available |
| | ***heterophylla*** misapplied | see *L.* x *heterophylla* Gaston Allard Group |
| | ***heterophylla*** Viv. 'Devantville-Cuche' | WJek |
| § | - Gaston Allard Group | CHrt CSev GBar NGHP NLLv WLav |
| | 'Hidcote Blue' | see *L. angustifolia* 'Hidcote' |
| § | x ***intermedia*** | SPla WFar |
| | - 'Abrialii' | CHrt GBar NLLv SDow WLav |
| § | - 'Alba' 🏆H4 | CArn CHFP CMea CPbn EPfP GBar MHer MNHC SAga SDow |
| * | - 'Alexis' | WLav |
| | - 'Arabian Night' | see *L.* x *intermedia* 'Impress Purple', 'Sussex' |
| | - 'Arabian Night' ambig. | MNHC |
| | - 'Chaix' | GBar |
| § | - Dutch Group | CArn CSBt CWCL CWan CWib EBee EPfP EWTr GBar LCro LRHS MAsh MBar MRav MSwo SAga SCoo SDow SLim SPer SPoG SWat WFar WPer |
| | - 'Edelweiss' | CPbn CWan EAro EBee EMil MRav NBur NGHP NLLv SDow WLav |
| | - 'Fragrant Memories' | CPbn EBee EMil EPfP GBar MHrb NGHP SAga SDow SIde WLav |
| | - Goldburg = 'Burgoldeen'PBR (v) | CBow ELan EMil EPfP LRHS MCCP MGos MRav NGHP NLLv SPav SPer SPla SPoG SSto WLav |
| | - 'Grappenhall' misapplied | see *L.* x *intermedia* 'Pale Pretender' |
| | - 'Grey Hedge' | CPbn CWan EMil NGHP SAga WLav WRHF |
| | - 'Gros Bleu' | CPbn SDow WLav |
| | - 'Grosso' | Widely available |
| | - 'Hidcote Giant' 🏆H4 | CArn CPbn EPfP GBar LRHS MHrb NPer SAdn SAga SDow WKif WLav |
| § | - 'Impress Purple' | CPbn GBar MNHC NLLv SDow WLav |
| | - 'Lullingstone Castle' | CBod CPbn EAro GBar LHop NGHP SAga SDow SIoW WClo WGwG WJek WLav |
| | - 'Old English' | CPbn GBar MHrb SDow |
| | - Old English Group | CArn CBod ELau MNHC NGHP WHoo WJek WLav |
| § | - 'Pale Pretender' | CArn CPbn CTri EAro EBee ELon EMil GBar GKir MHer MRav MSwo NGHP SPer SWal WFar WMnd WPer WPnn |
| | - 'Seal' | CArn CPbn CPrp EAro EBee ELau GBar MHer MHrb MNHC NGHP SAga SDow SPer SPoG WFar WHCG WMnd WPer WRHF |
| | - 'Sumian' | WLav |
| § | - 'Sussex' | CPbn GBar MHrb NGHP SDow WLav |
| | - 'Twickel Purple' | CArn CPbn CWSG CWib ECtt EWes LSRN NGHP SWat WJek WMnd |
| § | - Walberton's Silver Edge = 'Walvera' (v) | CBow CPbn CSBt ENor EShb LBuc LRHS MAsh MGos MHer SBch SCoo SDow SIde SIoW SPoG |
| | 'Jean Davis' | see *L. angustifolia* 'Rosea' |
| | ***lanata*** 🏆H3 | CArn ECha GBar GPoy MHer MHrb NWCA SDow WLav |
| § | ***latifolia*** | CArn NHol |
| I | 'Lavender Lace' | CWSG NGHP SCoo |
| | 'Loddon Pink' | see *L. angustifolia* 'Loddon Pink' |
| | 'Madrid Blue' | see *L.* 'Bee Happy' |
| | 'Madrid Pink' | see *L.* 'Bee Pretty' |
| | 'Madrid Purple'PBR | see *L.* 'Bee Brilliant' |
| | 'Madrid White'PBR | see *L.* 'Bee Cool' |

| | | |
|---|---|---|
| | 'Marshwood'PBR | CTri EBee EPfP LRHS MRav SAdn SCoo SDow SIde SIoW SLim SPer SPla |
| | ***minutolii*** | CPbn MHrb SDow |
| | ***multifida*** | CPbn LDai MHer NLLv WCHb WLav |
| | - 'Blue Wonder' | CPbn GGar |
| | ***officinalis*** | see *L. angustifolia* |
| | 'Passionné' | CWSG EBee EMil LSou NGHP WLav |
| | ***pedunculata*** subsp. ***lusitanica*** | WLav |
| § | - subsp. ***pedunculata*** ♀H3-4 | Widely available |
| | - - 'James Compton' | CWib EBee ECha LRHS MAsh NBir |
| | - - 'Wine' | CBcs WLav |
| | - subsp. ***sampaiana*** | WLav |
| | - - 'Purple Emperor' | CWSG LRHS SPoG WLav |
| | - - 'Roman Candles' | WLav |
| | - 'Whero Iti' | SDow |
| § | ***pinnata*** | CHrt CPbn CSev EPfP EShb GBar MHer MHrb MNHC SDow SPoG WCHb |
| | 'Pink Perfume' | CPbn LSou |
| | 'Pippa White' | NLLv |
| | 'Pretty Polly' | CBcs ENor LSou NBPC NLLv SDow SIoW SRkn WLav |
| | ***pterostoechas pinnata*** | see *L. pinnata* |
| | 'Pukehou' | EPfP GBar LRHS MAsh MHrb NLLv SCoo SDow SIoW WLav |
| | 'Regal Splendour'PBR | CWCL EBrs ECtt ELan ENor EPfP LCro LRHS LSRN MAsh MGos MHer MHrb NGHP NLLv NPri NTHB SCoo SDow SIoW SLim SPoG WLav |
| | 'Rocky Road' | CPbn ENor LBuc LCro LRHS LSRN MAsh MGos MHrb NBPC NGHP NLLv NPri SDow SIoW SPav SPoG SRkn WLav |
| | 'Rosea' | see *L. angustifolia* 'Rosea' |
| | ***rotundifolia*** | MHer SDow |
| | 'Roxlea Park'PBR | CChe CWCL MHrb NGHP WLav |
| | 'Saint Brelade' | CPbn CWCL EPfP GBar MAsh NGHP NLLv SDow WLav |
| | 'Silver Edge' | see *L.* x *intermedia* Walberton's Silver Edge |
| | 'Somerset Mist' | WLav |
| N | ***spica*** nom. rejic. | see *L. angustifolia, L. latifolia, L.* x *intermedia* |
| | - 'Hidcote Purple' | see *L. angustifolia* 'Hidcote' |
| | ***stoechas*** ♀H3-4 | Widely available |
| | - var. ***albiflora*** | see *L. stoechas* subsp. *stoechas* f. *leucantha* |
| | - - 'Anouk'PBR | SPoG |
| | - (Barcelona Series) 'Barcelona Pink' | CPbn CWCL |
| | - - 'Barcelona Rose' | CPbn CWCL |
| | - - 'Barcelona White' | CPbn |
| | - 'Blueberries and Cream' | LRHS MAsh SCoo |
| | - 'Blueberry Ruffles' (Ruffles Series) **new** | ENor SIoW |
| | - 'Boysenberry Ruffles' (Ruffles Series) **new** | ENor SIoW |
| | - (Coco Series) 'Coco Deep Pink' | EMil LBMP |
| | - - 'Coco Deep Purple' | EMil LBMP |
| | - - 'Coco Deep Rose' | EMil |
| | - - 'Coco Deep White on Blue' | EMil |
| | - 'Fragrant Butterfly' | LSou |
| | - 'Lace' | LSRN SPoG WLav |
| | - (Little Bee Series) Little Bee Lilac = 'Florvendula Lilac' **new** | LRHS |
| | - - Little Bee Rose = 'Florevendula Rose' **new** | LRHS |
| | - subsp. ***luisieri*** 'Tickled Pink'PBR | CPbn CWCL ECtt ELan MHrb NGHP SDnm SPav |
| | - 'Madrid Rose' **new** | NLLv |
| | - 'Mulberry Ruffles' (Ruffles Series) **new** | ENor SIoW |
| | - 'Papillon' | see *L. pedunculata* subsp. *pedunculata* |
| | - 'Peachberry Ruffles' (Ruffles Series) **new** | ENor SIoW |
| | - subsp. ***pedunculata*** | see *L. pedunculata* subsp. *pedunculata* |
| | - 'Purley' **new** | CWan |
| | - 'Raspberry Ruffles' (Ruffles Series) **new** | ENor SIoW |
| | - 'Saint Marc' | EBee |
| § | - subsp. ***stoechas*** f. ***leucantha*** | CArn CPbn CSev CWCL CWan CWib ECha EPfP GBar LRHS MSwo SDow SPla WAbe WCHb WFar |
| | - - - 'Snowman' | CBcs CChe CPbn CSBt EBee EMil ENor EPfP LAst LCro LRHS MHer MHrb MTPN MWat NBPC NGHP NPri SAdn SCoo SIoW SLim SPer SPoG SSto SWvt WDin WFar |
| | - - 'Liberty' | CWCL NGHP NLLv SDow SPoG WLav |
| | - - 'Lilac Wings' | ENor LLHF LRHS LSRN NGHP SPoG WLav |
| | - - 'Provençal' | LRHS |
| | - - 'Purple Wings' | CPbn ENor LRHS MAsh SRkn |
| | - - f. ***rosea*** 'Kew Red' | Widely available |
| | - 'Sugarberry Ruffles' (Ruffles Series) **new** | ENor SIoW |
| | - 'Tapestry' **new** | CWan |
| | - 'Victory' | SPoG |
| | 'Sugar Plum' | SHGN WLav |
| | 'Tiara' | CPbn ENor LCro LSRN MAsh NBPC NGHP NLLv NPri SCoo SDow SIoW SLim WLav |
| | 'Van Gogh' | MHrb SDow |
| | ***vera*** misapplied | see *L.* x *intermedia* Dutch Group |
| | ***vera*** DC. | see *L. angustifolia* |
| | ***viridis*** | CArn CChe CPbn CSev CWCL ELan ELau EPfP GBar LRHS MHer MNHC NGHP NLLv NPer SDow SGar SPla WAbe WCHb WJek WLav |
| | 'Willow Vale' ♀H3-4 | CMea CPbn CTri CWCL EBee ELan ENor EPfP GBar LRHS LSRN MAsh MHer MHrb MLHP NLLv SAdn SAga SDow SIoW SPav SPhx SWvt WJek WPGP |
| | 'Willowbridge Calico'PBR | ELon EMil LSou SIoW WLav |

## *Lavatera* (*Malvaceae*)

| | | |
|---|---|---|
| | ***arborea*** | LEdu SChr WHer |
| | - 'Rosea' | see *L.* x *clementii* 'Rosea' |
| | - 'Variegata' (v) | CBow CDTJ CSsd ELan LSou MAvo NPer NSti SBod SDix SEND SGar WCHb WCot WEas WHer |
| | ***bicolor*** | see *L. maritima* |
| | ***cachemiriana*** | EQua GBuc IDee NBir NBur NPer WPer |
| | Chamallow = 'Inovera'PBR | EBee LBuc LSRN LSou NPri SPoG |
| | x ***clementii*** 'Barnsley' | Widely available |
| | - 'Barnsley Baby' | LBuc LRHS NLar NPer NPri SPer |
| | - 'Blushing Bride' | CDoC CWCL EBee ELon EPfP LBMP LRHS LSRN MBri MGos NLar NPri SBod SPer SPla SPoG |
| | - 'Bredon Springs' ♀H3-4 | CDoC CDul CSBt CWCL CWSG EBee ECha ECtt EMil EPfP GBri LHop LRHS LSRN MAsh MSwo NHol NScw SBod SLim SPer SPla SWvt WFar WHar |
| | - 'Burgundy Wine' ♀H3-4 | Widely available |

| | |
|---|---|
| - 'Candy Floss' ♀$^{H3-4}$ | CWCL EBee EPfP LRHS MAsh MBar MGos NBir NLar NPer SAdn WDin |
| - 'Kew Rose' | CDoC CTri EBee EMil EPfP LRHS MAsh MSwo NPer SLim SPla SRms |
| - 'Lavender Lady' | ECtt EPPr EQua GKir NPer |
| - 'Lisanne' | LRHS MAsh MHer MNrw MSwo MWhi NHol NPri SEND |
| - Memories = 'Stelav' | CHid EBee ELan EPfP GBin LRHS LSRN NLar SLim |
| - 'Pavlova' | CDoC CPLG MAsh NPri |
| - 'Poynton Lady' (v) | MGos |
| § - 'Rosea' ♀$^{H3-4}$ | CBcs CDul CWSG EBee ECtt EPfP GGar GKir LCro LRHS LSRN MAsh MBar MGos MWat NBir NBlu NHol NPri SBod SLon SPer SPoG WBVN WBod WDin WFar |
| - 'Shorty' | WFar |
| § - 'Wembdon Variegated' (v) | NPer |
| 'Dorothy' **new** | MCot |
| 'Grey Beauty' | MAsh |
| § ***maritima*** ♀$^{H2-3}$ | CDoC CHrt CMHG CPLG CRHN EBee ECtt ELan EPfP IFoB LHop MCot SEND SPer SPoG SUsu SWvt WCFE WFar WHCG WKif WSHC |
| - ***bicolor*** | see *L. maritima* |
| - 'Princesse de Lignes' | MGos |
| ***mauritanica*** | CSec |
| N ***olbia*** | CTri LAst SPlb SRms |
| - 'Eye Catcher' | EBee LRHS MSwo NLar SMrm SPer SPoG SWal |
| - 'Lilac Lady' | EBee ECha ELan EPfP LRHS LSou MAsh MCCP MWte NLar SLim SMrm SPer WFar WKif WSHC |
| § - 'Pink Frills' | EBee EQua LRHS MBar MGos MNrw NPri SMrm SPla WWlt |
| 'Peppermint Ice' | see *L. thuringiaca* 'Ice Cool' |
| 'Pink Frills' | see *L. olbia* 'Pink Frills' |
| 'Rosea' | see *L.* x *clementii* 'Rosea' |
| 'Sweet Dreams'$^{PBR}$ | LRHS NLar |
| ***tauricensis*** | NLar |
| N ***thuringiaca*** | GCal NNor WFar |
| § - 'Ice Cool' | ECha ECtt ERas GCal LAst LRHS MGos MHer SMrm WCot WFar WKif |
| - 'Red Rum' | EBee GBin LAst LBuc LLHF LRHS LSRN MAsh MBri NHol NLar NPri SEND SPoG WFar WHar WRHF |
| 'Variegata' | see *L.* x *clementii* 'Wembdon Variegated' |
| 'White Angel'$^{PBR}$ | LRHS NLar |
| 'White Satin'$^{PBR}$ | LHop SPoG |

## *Lecanthus* (*Urticaceae*)

| | |
|---|---|
| ***peduncularis*** | CHEx |

## *Ledebouria* (*Hyacinthaceae*)

| | |
|---|---|
| ***adlamii*** | see *L. cooperi* |
| ***concolor*** misapplied | see *L. socialis* |
| ***concolor*** (Baker) Jessop | EShb |
| § ***cooperi*** | CDes CHal CStu EBee ECho ELan GGar ITim LEdu LHop NCGa NLAp SUsu WPGP WPrP |
| § ***socialis*** | CBgR CHal CSWP CSpe CStu EBrs ECho ERos EShb LToo SBHP SBch SPet STre |
| ***violacea*** | see *L. socialis* |

## x *Ledodendron* (*Ericaceae*)

| | |
|---|---|
| § 'Arctic Tern' ♀$^{H4}$ | CDoC CSBt CTri ECho GGar GQui LMil LRHS MBar MGos MLea NHol NWCA SPer WBod |

## *Ledum* (*Ericaceae*)

| | |
|---|---|
| § ***groenlandicum*** | GGar MBar MLea SPer WDin WFar WSHC |
| - 'Compactum' | NLar SPoG WFar |
| - 'Lenie' **new** | NLar |
| ***macrophyllum*** | CFir |
| ***palustre*** | COld GGGa GPoy NLar WThu |

## *Leea* (*Leeaceae*)

| | |
|---|---|
| ***coccinea*** | see *L. guineensis* |
| § ***guineensis*** | MBri |

## *Leersia* (*Poaceae*)

| | |
|---|---|
| ***oryzoides*** | EBee |

## *Legousia* (*Campanulaceae*)

| | |
|---|---|
| ***pentagonica*** 'Midnight Stars' | CSpe |

## *Leiophyllum* (*Ericaceae*)

| | |
|---|---|
| ***buxifolium*** ♀$^{H4}$ | EPfP LRHS WThu |
| - var. ***hugeri*** | GBin GGar NLar |
| - 'Maryfield' | WAbe |

## *Lembotropis* see *Cytisus*

## *Lemna* (*Lemnaceae*)

| | |
|---|---|
| ***gibba*** | LPBA NPer |
| ***minor*** | CWat EHon EMFW LPBA MSKA NPer SWat |
| ***polyrhiza*** | see *Spirodela polyrhiza* |
| ***trisulca*** | CWat EHon EMFW LPBA MSKA NPer SWat |

## lemon balm see *Melissa officinalis*

## lemon grass see *Cymbopogon citratus*

## lemon see *Citrus limon*

## lemon verbena see *Aloysia triphylla*

## *Leonotis* (*Lamiaceae*)

| | |
|---|---|
| ***leonitis*** | see *L. ocymifolia* |
| ***leonurus*** | CBcs CCCN CDMG CDTJ CHEx CHll CMdw EShb EWes LRHS NSti SMad SPoG |
| - var. ***albiflora*** | CCCN |
| ***nepetifolia*** var. ***nepetifolia*** 'Staircase' | CCCN SDnm SPav WRos |
| § ***ocymifolia*** | CCCN CPLG EShb LSou WPGP |
| - var. ***ocymifolia*** | SPlb |
| - var. ***raineriana*** | CHll |

## *Leontice* (*Berberidaceae*)

| | |
|---|---|
| ***albertii*** | see *Gymnospermium albertii* |

## *Leontochir* (*Amaryllidaceae*)

| | |
|---|---|
| ***ovallei*** | CCCN EHig |

## *Leontodon* (*Asteraceae*)

| | |
|---|---|
| ***autumnalis*** | EBWF NMir |
| ***hispidus*** | EBWF NMir |
| § ***rigens*** | EBee EDAr GBri GBuc MLHP MMuc MNrw NBid SBHP SDix SMad SMrm WFar WMoo WPrP WRos |
| - 'Girandole' | see *L. rigens* |

## *Leontopodium* (*Asteraceae*)

| | |
|---|---|
| SDR 4865 **new** | GKev |
| ***alpinum*** | CArn CTri CWib ECho GEdr GKir LRHS NPri NWCA SIng SPlb SPoG SRms WPer |

- 'Mignon' CMea ECho EWes GEdr WAbe WFar WHoo
- subsp. *nivale* GKev WPat
*coreanum* EBee GKev
*jacotianum* new GKev
*kamtschaticum* ECho
§ *ochroleucum* var. *campestre* MDKP NLar WPer
*palibinianum* see *L. ochroleucum* var. *campestre*

## Leonurus (Lamiaceae)

*artemisia* see *L. japonicus*
*cardiaca* CArn CSec CWan EBWF EGoo EHig GBar GPWP GPoy LEdu MHer MSal SECG SIde
- 'Grobbebol' new CSec
§ *japonicus* CSec MMuc MSal
*macranthus* EFEx
- var. *alba* EFEx
*sibiricus* misapplied see *L. japonicus*
*sibiricus* L. CSec EBee GCal MSal SMad SPav SPhx WPer
*turkestanicus* new EBee

## Leopoldia (Hyacinthaceae)

*comosa* see *Muscari comosum*
*spreitzenhoferi* see *Muscari spreitzenhoferi*
*tenuiflora* see *Muscari tenuiflorum*

## Lepechinia (Lamiaceae)

*bella* new SDys
*chamaedryoides* CHII CPLG WOut
*floribunda* CSev
*hastata* CMdw CPom MWea SBHP
*salviae* CDTJ CDoC CSec CSpe SUsu WBor

## Lepidium (Brassicaceae)

*campestre* CArn
*latifolium* CArn MSal
*peruvianum* MSal
*ruderale* MSal
*virginicum* MSal

## Lepidothamnus (Podocarpaceae)

§ *laxifolius* WThu

## Lepidozamia (Zamiaceae)

*hopei* LPal
*peroffskyana* CBrP LPal

## Leptecophylla (Epacridaceae)

§ *juniperina* ECou
- 'Nana' WThu
§ - subsp. *parvifolia* ECou

## Leptinella (Asteraceae)

§ *albida* CStu
§ *atrata* ECho EDAr
- subsp. *luteola* EBee ECho MBrN
'County Park' ECho ECou EDAr
§ *dendyi* ECho ECou EDAr EWes MHer NLAp NMen NSla
*dioica* CTrC GBin
*filicula* ECou
*hispida* see *Cotula hispida*
§ *minor* ECou EDAr WMoo
*pectinata* var. *sericea* see *L. albida*
- subsp. *villosa* CC 475 NWCA
§ *potentillina* CTri EBee ECha ECho EHoe MBNS MRav NLar NRya SRms WMoo WPer WPtf
§ *pyrethrifolia* EBee ECho EDAr GGar NMen
- 'Macabe' ECou
§ *rotundata* ECou
§ *serrulata* ECho MBar
§ *squalida* ECha ECho EDAr GBin GGar MBar MWat NRya NSti STre WMoo
§ - 'Platt's Black' Widely available
*traillii* GGar

## Leptocarpus (Restionaceae)

*similis* BR 70 GGar

## Leptocodon (Campanulaceae)

*gracilis* EWld IGor
- HWJK 2155 WCru

## Leptodactylon ✿ (Polemoniaceae)

*pungens* GKev

## Leptogramma (Thelypteridaceae)

*himalaica* new CFwr

## Leptopteris (Osmundaceae)

*hymenophylloides* WRic
*superba* WRic

## Leptospermum (Myrtaceae)

'Centaurus'PBR CTrC CWSG MNHC NVic WFar
*citratum* see *L. petersonii*
'Confetti' ECou
'Copper Sheen' CTrC
'County Park Blush' ECou
*cunninghamii* see *L. myrtifolium*
'Electric Red'PBR (Galaxy Series) CTrC CWSG SLim
*ericoides* see *Kunzea ericoides*
*flavescens* misapplied see *L. glaucescens*
*flavescens* Sm. see *L. polygalifolium*
§ *glaucescens* CMHG ECou GGar
§ *grandiflorum* CTrC CTrG CWsd ELan EPfP GGar ISea LRHS SOWG SSpi WSHC
*grandifolium* ECou
'Havering Hardy' ECou
*humifusum* see *L. rupestre*
*juniperinum* CTrC SPlb
'Karo Pearl Star' new CBcs
'Karo Spectrobay'PBR new CBcs
*laevigatum* 'Yarrum' ECou
§ *lanigerum* CBcs CMHG CPLG CTrC CTri ECou EPfP GGar ISea SHGN SOWG SPoG
- 'Cunninghamii' see *L. myrtifolium*
- 'Wellington' ECou
*liversidgei* CChe ECou
*macrocarpum* SOWG
*minutifolium* ECou
*morrisonii* ECou
§ *myrtifolium* CTrC CTri ECou EPla EWes GGar SOWG SPer WPat
- 'Newnes Forest' ECou
*myrtifolium* x *scoparium* ECou
*nitidum* CTrC ECou SOWG SPlb
- 'Cradle' ECou
*obovatum* CMHG
§ *petersonii* CArn ECou EOHP EShb MHer SOWG
- 'Chlorinda' ECou
*phylicoides* see *Kunzea ericoides*
'Pink Surprise' ECou SOWG
§ *polygalifolium* CTrC ECou SPlb SRms
*prostratum* see *L. rupestre*
*pubescens* see *L. lanigerum*
'Red Cascade' SWvt
*rodwayanum* see *L. grandiflorum*
*rotundifolium* CTrC ECou

| | |
|---|---|
| § ***rupestre*** ℽH4 | CDoC CTri ECou EPot GGar MBar SPlb SRms WFar WSHC |
| ***rupestre*** x ***scoparium*** | ECou |
| ***scoparium*** | CArn CDul CTsd ECou ELau ERom GPWP MNHC SPlb WDin |
| - 'Adrianne' | ELan EPfP |
| - 'Album' | CTrC |
| - 'Appleblossom' | CTrC |
| - 'Autumn Glory' | CWSG EBee ISea SLim |
| - 'Avocet' | ECou |
| - 'Big Red' **new** | MMuc |
| - 'Black Robin' | SOWG |
| - 'Blossom' (d) | CBcs CTrC ECou SOWG |
| - 'Boscawenii' | CBcs |
| - 'Burgundy Queen' (d) | CBcs CSBt CTrC ECou GGar |
| - 'Chapmanii' | CMHG CTrG EBee GGar |
| - 'Coral Candy' | MMuc SOWG |
| - 'County Park Pink' | ECou |
| - 'County Park Red' | ECou |
| - 'Dove Lake' | WAbe |
| - 'Elizabeth Jane' | GGar |
| - 'Essex' | ECou |
| - 'Fantasia' | ECou |
| - 'Fred's Red' | NLAp WPat |
| - 'Gaiety Girl' (d) | CSBt |
| - var. ***incanum*** 'Keatleyi' ℽH3 | CTrC ECou SOWG |
| - - 'Wairere' | ECou |
| - 'Jubilee' (d) | CBcs ISea |
| - 'Kerry' | CAbP LRHS |
| - 'Leonard Wilson' (d) | CTri ECou |
| - 'Lyndon' | ECou |
| - 'Martini' | CDoC CSBt CTrC CTrG MMuc SOWG |
| - 'McLean' | ECou |
| - (Nanum Group) 'Huia' | CBcs |
| - - 'Kea' | CBcs ECou GGar MMuc MRav |
| - - 'Kiwi' ℽH3 | CAbP CBcs CCCN CDoC CDul CSBt CTrC CWSG ECou ELan ELon EPfP EWes GQui LRHS MAsh MDun SLim SPla WFar |
| - - 'Kompakt' | EPot |
| - - 'Nanum' | ECou NMen |
| - - 'Pipit' | EWes WAbe |
| - - 'Tui' | CSBt CTrC |
| - 'Nichollsii' ℽH3 | CTrC CTri GQui SOWG WSHC |
| - 'Nichollsii Nanum' ℽH2-3 | CMea ITim NLAp SIng SRms WPat WThu |
| - 'Pink Cascade' | CBcs CTrC CTri CWib GGar SLim |
| - 'Pink Damask' | SWvt |
| - 'Pink Falls' | ECou |
| - 'Pink Splash' | ECou |
| - var. ***prostratum*** hort. | see *L. rupestre* |
| - 'Red Damask' (d) ℽH3 | Widely available |
| - 'Red Falls' | CPLG CTrC ECou SOWG |
| - 'Redpoll' | ECou |
| - 'Rosy Morn' | ISea |
| - 'Ruby Glow' (d) | WBod |
| * - 'Ruby Wedding' | ELan EPfP LRHS MAsh SPla SPoG |
| - var. ***scoparium*** | GGar |
| - 'Silver Spire' | SOWG |
| - 'Snow Flurry' | CBcs CTrC EBee MMuc MRav SBod SLim SPoG |
| - 'Sunraysia' | CSBt |
| - 'Wingletye' **new** | ECou |
| - 'Winter Cheer' | CBcs LRHS |
| - 'Wiri Joan' (d) | CBcs |
| - 'Wiri Linda' | CBcs |
| - 'Zeehan' | ECou |
| ***sericeum*** | SOWG |
| 'Silver Sheen' ℽH3 | CEnd ECou ELan EPfP NLar SPoG WPGP |
| 'Snow Column' | ECou |
| ***spectabile*** | SOWG |
| ***sphaerocarpum*** | ECou |
| ***squarrosum*** | CTrC |
| ***turbinatum*** | ECou |
| - 'Thunder Cloud' | ECou |
| 'Wellington Dwarf' | ECou |

## *Leschenaultia* (*Goodeniaceae*)

| | |
|---|---|
| ***biloba*** | CSec ECou |
| - 'Big Blue' | SOWG |
| - 'Sky Blue' | ECou |
| * 'Eldorado' | SOWG |
| ***formosa*** red-flowered | ECou |
| - 'Scarlett O'Hara' | SOWG |
| - yellow-flowered | ECou |
| ***hirsuta*** | SOWG |
| pink-flowered | ECou |

## *Lespedeza* (*Papilionaceae*)

| | |
|---|---|
| ***bicolor*** | CAgr NPal SEND SKHP WDin WFar WHCG |
| ***buergeri*** | MBri MMHG NLar WSHC |
| ***capitata*** | MSal |
| ***floribunda*** | CMen |
| ***japonica*** | SPlb |
| ***thunbergii*** ℽH4 | CBcs CMen CWib EBee ELan EMil EPfP IDee IMGH LHop LRHS MAsh MBlu MBri MGos NBlu SEND SLon SOWG SPer SSpi SSta WDin WFar WHCG WPGP WSHC |
| - 'Albiflora' | EBee EPfP MBri MWea SKHP SPoG WPGP |
| - 'Avalanche' | NLar |
| - 'Pink Fountain' | MBri |
| - 'Summer Beauty' | CBcs CDul EPfP MBri MGos |
| ***tiliifolia*** | see *Desmodium elegans* |

## *Lesquerella* (*Brassicaceae*)

| | |
|---|---|
| ***alpina*** | CSec NWCA |

## *Leucadendron* (*Proteaceae*)

| | |
|---|---|
| ***argenteum*** | CCCN CHEx CTrC SPlb |
| ***daphnoides*** | SPlb |
| ***eucalyptifolium*** | CTrC SPlb |
| ***galpinii*** | CTrC |
| 'Inca Gold' | CBcs CTrC |
| ***laureolum*** | CCCN |
| 'Maui Sunset' | CTrC |
| 'Mrs Stanley' | CTrC |
| 'Safari Sunset' | CAbb CBcs CCCN CDoC CTrC IDee LRHS SBig |
| 'Safari Sunshine' **new** | CTrC |
| ***salignum*** | CCCN |
| - 'Early Yellow' | CAbb CTrC |
| - 'Fireglow' | CAbb CBcs CDoC CTrC IDee |
| ***strobilinum*** | CDoC CTrC |

## *Leucanthemella* (*Asteraceae*)

| | |
|---|---|
| § ***serotina*** ℽH4 | Widely available |
| - 'Herbststern' | CFir NLar |

## *Leucanthemopsis* (*Asteraceae*)

| | |
|---|---|
| § ***alpina*** | ECho |
| ***hosmariensis*** | see *Rhodanthemum hosmariense* |

## *Leucanthemum* ✿ (*Asteraceae*)

| | |
|---|---|
| ***atlanticum*** | see *Rhodanthemum atlanticum* |
| ***catananche*** | see *Rhodanthemum catananche* |
| ***graminifolium*** | MAvo NBre WPer |
| ***hosmariense*** | see *Rhodanthemum hosmariense* |
| ***mawii*** | see *Rhodanthemum gayanum* |
| ***maximum*** misapplied | see *L.* x *superbum* |
| § ***maximum*** (Ramond) DC. | NBro NPer |
| - ***uliginosum*** | see *Leucanthemella serotina* |

| | | |
|---|---|---|
| | ***nipponicum*** | see *Nipponanthemum nipponicum* |
| § | x ***superbum*** | EWsh MHer MLHP NBlu NVic WFar |
| § | - 'Aglaia' (d) ♀H4 | Widely available |
| | - 'Alaska' | CAni CPLG CWCL EBee EBla GKir LAst LEdu LHop LRHS MCot NGdn SPer SPur SWal SWvt WBor WFar WPer WRHF |
| | - 'Amelia' | EBee NBre SRGP |
| | - 'Anita Allen' (d) | CAni CElw CFee CPou EBee EBla MAvo NBre WCot WFar WPer |
| | - 'Anna Camilla' | CAni |
| | - 'Antwerp Star' | NBre NLar WBrk |
| | - 'Banwell' | CAni |
| | - 'Barbara Bush' (v/d) | ECtt ELan EPla LSou NBir NCob SPla SPoG SRGP SWvt |
| § | - 'Beauté Nivelloise' | CAni CCVN CPrp CWCL EBla ECtt EPfP MAvo MDKP MLLN MMuc NBPC NBre NLar SPoG SWat WCot WFar WPer WPrP WRha |
| | - 'Becky' | CMdw CWan EBee ECha ELon EPfP EWes LLHF LSou MAvo NBre NPro SPoG SRGP |
| | - 'Bishopstone' | CAni CSam EBee ELan LEdu MAvo NBre WEas WPer |
| | - 'Christine Hagemann' | CAni CPrp EBee EWes MAvo MDKP MRav |
| | - 'Cobham Gold' (d) | CAni CWCL EBee NBre NOrc SUsu SWal |
| | - 'Coconut Ice' | WPer |
| | - 'Colwall' | CAni |
| | - 'Crazy Daisy' | CAni CElw CMMP CTri CWib MBNS NBHF NBre NCob NLar SWal WHrl WRHF |
| | - 'Devon Mist' | CAni |
| | - 'Dipsy Daisy' | WPer |
| | - 'Droitwich Beauty' | CAni LLHF MAvo WCFE WHoo |
| | - 'Duchess of Abercorn' | CAni CSam |
| | - 'Dwarf Snow Lady' | NBre |
| | - 'Easton Lady' | CAni |
| | - 'Eclipse' | CAni MAvo |
| | - 'Edgebrook Giant' | CAni MAvo |
| | - 'Edward VII' | CAni |
| | - 'Eisstern' | CDes LEdu MAvo |
| | - 'Elworthy Sparkler' | CElw MAvo |
| | - 'Esther Read' (d) | Widely available |
| | - 'Etoile d'Anvers' | EBee |
| § | - 'Everest' | CAni CSam EBee NBre SRms |
| | - 'Exhibition' | NBre |
| | - 'Fiona Coghill' (d) | CAni CElw EAEE EBee EBla ECtt EGle GBri LBMP MAvo MDKP MLLN NCGa NChi NGdn WCot WHoo |
| | - 'Firnglanz' | CAni GBin MAvo |
| | - 'Goldrausch' PBR | EBee ECtt ELon GBri LLHF LRHS LSou MDKP NBPC NPri SPer SPoG WCot WCra WHlf WHoo WRHF |
| | - 'Gruppenstolz' | CAni EBee GBin |
| | - 'H. Seibert' | CAni CElw CEnt EBla MAvo |
| | - 'Harry' | CAni |
| | - 'Highland White Dream' PBR | EBee WFar |
| | - 'Horace Read' (d) | CAni CElw CHar CMea ELan EMon NBir SAga SBch WEas WPer |
| | - 'Jennifer Read' | CAni EBee GCal MAvo WCot |
| § | - 'John Murray' (d) | CAni EBee EShb EWes LRHS LSou MAvo MDKP NBir SMrm WAbb WCot WFar WHrl |
| | - 'Little Miss Muffet' | EAEE EBee EBla ECtt EPPr GBin GBri GGar LAst LBMP LLHF LRHS MBNS NCGa NCob NPro |
| | - 'Little Princess' | see *L.* x *superbum* 'Silberprinzesschen' |
| | - 'Majestic' | CAni |
| | - 'Manhattan' | CAni CMdw EBee EBla EBrs EWes GBin LRHS NBre |
| | - 'Margaretchen' | CAni CDes MAvo |
| | - 'Marion Bilsland' | CAni MDKP NCGa NChi |
| | - 'Marion Collyer' | CAni |
| | - 'Mayfield Giant' | CAni CTri WPer |
| | - 'Mount Everest' | see *L.* x *superbum* 'Everest' |
| | - 'Octopus' | CAni EBee MAvo |
| | - 'Old Court' | see *L.* x *superbum* 'Beauté Nivelloise' |
| | - 'Phyllis Smith' | Widely available |
| | - 'Polaris' | EBee EShb MBNS NBre WMoo |
| | - 'Rags and Tatters' | CAni EBee ECtt EWes MAvo |
| | - 'Rijnsburg Glory' | WPer |
| | - 'Schneehurken' | CAni CMac EBee EBla LLHF LSou MAvo SPoG STes SUsu |
| | - 'Shaggy' | see *L.* x *superbum* 'Beauté Nivelloise' |
| § | - 'Silberprinzesschen' | CAni CPrp EBee EBla EPfP GKir LRHS NMir NPri SPlb SRms WFar WMoo WPer |
| | - 'Silver Spoon' | GBri WPer |
| | - 'Snow Lady' | EBee EShb LRHS NMir NPer SPet SRms WFar |
| | - 'Snowcap' | EAEE EBee EBla EBrs ECha EPfP LCro LLWG LRHS MBNS MBri MRav NGdn SPer SPla SWvt WCAu WTin |
| | - 'Snowdrift' | CAni CMMP EBee EGoo MAvo NBre WCot WPer |
| § | - 'Sonnenschein' | Widely available |
| | - 'Starburst' (d) | SPhx SRms |
| | - 'Stina' | EBee |
| | - 'Summer Snowball' | see *L.* x *superbum* 'John Murray' |
| | - 'Sunny Killin' | CAni WTin |
| | - 'Sunny Side Up' PBR | EBee ECtt GBri MLLN NBPC NLar |
| | - Sunshine | see *L.* x *superbum* 'Sonnenschein' |
| § | - 'T.E. Killin' (d) ♀H4 | CElw CKno CPrp CSam EAEE EBee EBla EBrs ECha ECtt EPfP GMaP LAst LBMP LCro LHop LRHS MRav WCAu WCot WFar |
| | - 'White Iceberg' (d) | CAni WPer |
| | - 'White Knight' | EBee MBNS NBre |
| | - 'Wirral Pride' | CAni CCVN CHar EBee EGle MAvo WMnd |
| § | - 'Wirral Supreme' (d) ♀H4 | Widely available |
| | 'Tizi-n-Test' | see *Rhodanthemum catananche* 'Tizi-n-Test' |
| § | ***vulgare*** | CArn CRWN CSec EBWF EPfP GBar LEdu MHer MNHC NLan NMir NPri NSco SBch SECG SIde WBrk WHer WJek WMoo WShi |
| | - 'Avondale' (v) | NGdn |
| | - 'Filigran' | CWsd EBee EShb GMac NBre SIde |
| § | - 'Maikönigin' | EBee GAbr NBre WHrl |
| | - May Queen | see *L. vulgare* 'Maikönigin' |
| | - 'Sunny' | CBre EBla EWes WAlt |
| | 'White Knight' | MBri MCCP |

## *Leucocoryne* (*Alliaceae*)

| | | |
|---|---|---|
| | ***alliacea*** | ECho |
| | 'Andes' | CCCN EBrs ECho LRHS |
| | 'Caravelle' | EBrs ECho |
| | hybrids | EBrs ECho |
| | ***ixioides*** | ECho |
| * | - ***alba*** | EBrs ECho |
| | ***purpurea*** ♀H1 | CGrW EBrs ECho LRHS |

## *Leucogenes* (*Asteraceae*)

| | | |
|---|---|---|
| | ***grandiceps*** | NSla WAbe |
| | ***leontopodium*** | EDAr GGar NSla WAbe |
| | ***tarahaoa*** | WAbe |

## *Leucojum* (*Amaryllidaceae*)

| | |
|---|---|
| ***aestivum*** | CBcs CFee EBee EBrs ECGP ECho EPfP GCal LAma LHop LRHS MCot MDun NHol SMrm SPad SPer SRms WBod WBor WCot WEas WFar WShi |
| - 'Gravetye Giant' ♀H4 | Widely available |
| ***autumnale*** | see *Acis autumnalis* |
| ***longifolium*** | see *Acis longifolia* |
| ***roseum*** | see *Acis rosea* |
| ***tingitanum*** | see *Acis tingitana* |
| ***trichophyllum*** | see *Acis trichophylla* |
| ***valentinum*** | see *Acis valentina* |
| ***vernum*** ♀H4 | Widely available |
| - var. ***carpathicum*** | CLAP EBrs ECha ECho EHrv GEdr MRav NMen WAbe |
| - var. ***vagneri*** | CLAP EBee ECha EHrv EMon GEdr LFox LHop NPol WSHC WTin |

## *Leucophyllum* (*Scrophulariaceae*)

| | |
|---|---|
| ***frutescens*** | SOWG |

## *Leucophysalis* (*Solanaceae*)

| | |
|---|---|
| ***sinense*** BWJ 8093 | WCru |

## *Leucophyta* (*Asteraceae*)

| | |
|---|---|
| § ***brownii*** | ECou |

## *Leucopogon* (*Epacridaceae*)

| | |
|---|---|
| § ***colensoi*** | MBar MBri NLar NWCA WBod WPat WThu |
| ***ericoides*** | GKev MBar |
| § ***fasciculatus*** | ECou |
| § ***fraseri*** | ECou GEdr WThu |
| § ***parviflorus*** | ECou |

## x *Leucoraoulia* (*Asteraceae*)

| | |
|---|---|
| § ***loganii*** | NWCA WAbe |

## *Leucosceptrum* (*Lamiaceae*)

| | |
|---|---|
| ***canum*** | CPLG CTrG |
| - GWJ 9424 | WCru |
| ***japonicum*** | EBee |
| - B&SWJ 10981 new | WCru |
| - 'Golden Angel' new | EBee |
| - 'Mountain Madness' (v) new | EBee |
| ***stellipilum*** new | EBee |
| - var. ***formosanum*** | WSHC |
| - - B&SWJ 1804 | WCru |
| - - RWJ 9907 new | WCru |
| - var. ***tosaense*** B&SWJ 8892 | WCru |

## *Leucospermum* (*Proteaceae*)

| | |
|---|---|
| ***cordifolium*** | SOWG |
| 'Scarlet Ribbon' | CCCN |

## *Leucothoe* (*Ericaceae*)

| | |
|---|---|
| ***axillaris*** 'Curly Red'PBR | CBcs CWSG EBee ELan EMil EPfP LBuc LRHS MAsh MCCP MGos MMHG NLar SPoG SWvt |
| - 'Scarletta' | see *L.* Scarletta = 'Zeblid' |
| Carinella = 'Zebekot' | EMil MBri MGos SPoG |
| ***davisiae*** | EPfP |
| § ***fontanesiana*** ♀H4 | CMac EPfP GKir LRHS |
| - SDR 2249 | GKev |
| - 'Nana' | LRHS |
| - 'Rainbow' (v) | Widely available |
| - 'Rollissonii' ♀H4 | MBar MRav SRms |
| ***keiskei*** | EPfP LRHS |
| - 'Minor' | SSta |
| - 'Royal Ruby' | CWSG EBee EPfP LSou MGos NHol NLar SPoG WDin WFar WMoo |
| Lovita = 'Zebonard' | CEnd EBee MBri MGos MRav NLar SCoo |
| ***populifolia*** | see *Agarista populifolia* |
| ***racemosa*** | NLar |
| Red Lips = 'Lipsbolwi'PBR | CDoC EBee EPfP MGos NBPN NLar NScw |
| § Scarletta = 'Zeblid' | Widely available |
| ***walteri*** | see *L. fontanesiana* |

## *Leuzea* (*Asteraceae*)

| | |
|---|---|
| ***centaureoides*** | see *Stemmacantha centaureoides* |

## *Levisticum* (*Apiaceae*)

| | |
|---|---|
| ***officinale*** | CArn CBod CHby CHrt CPrp CSev ELau EPfP GBar GGar GPoy LEdu MBar MHer MNHC NBid NGHP NPri SDix SECG SEND SIde SPlb SVic SWat WBrk WHer WPer |
| I - 'Magnus' | ELau |

## *Lewisia* ✿ (*Portulacaceae*)

| | |
|---|---|
| 'Archangel' | NRya |
| Ashwood Carousel hybrids | ECho MAsh NHar |
| Birch strain | CBcs ECho ELan |
| ***brachycalyx*** ♀H2 | CGra ECho EWes GKev MTho WPer |
| ***columbiana*** | MAsh NWCA WPer |
| - subsp. ***columbiana*** | GKev |
| - 'Rosea' | GKev MAsh NLAp NSla WAbe WGor |
| - subsp. ***rupicola*** | CSec LLHF NDlv |
| - subsp. ***wallowensis*** | MAsh NMen |
| ***congdonii*** | MAsh |
| 'Constant Comment' | NBhm |
| ***cotyledon*** ♀H4 | CWCL ECho GKev GKir LLHF LRHS MNrw WBrE WFar |
| - J&JA 12959 | NWCA |
| - f. ***alba*** | GKev LHop MAsh NWCA |
| - 'Ashwood Ruby' | MAsh |
| - Ashwood strain | ECho EPfP EWes LBee LRHS LSou MAsh SRms WGor |
| - Crags hybrids | SRms |
| - 'Fransi' | NLar |
| - var. ***howellii*** | LLHF SRms WGor |
| - hybrids | CSec ECho EDAr EPot GGar GKev ITim LHop NBlu SIng SPoG WGor |
| - magenta-flowered | MAsh WGor |
| § - 'Regenbogen' mixed | EAlp SSto WGor WPer |
| - 'Snowstorm' | LLHF |
| - Sunset Group ♀H4 | LAst MHer NLar NWCA SRms WPer WRHF |
| - violet-flowered new | GKev |
| - 'White Splendour' | SIng |
| 'George Henley' | ECho EPfP EWes LLHF MAsh NMen NRya SIng WAbe WGor |
| ***glandulosa*** NNS 02-210 | NWCA |
| ***leeana*** | MAsh |
| 'Lilliput' new | GKev |
| 'Little Peach' | EDAr GKev MSte SIng WGor WPer |
| 'Little Plum' | CMea CPBP CSec EDAr EPfP GKev MDKP MSte NDlv NLar NRya NSla NWCA SIng WGor WPer |
| § ***longipetala*** | MAsh NDlv NSla |
| § ***nevadensis*** | ECho EDAr ERos GEdr GGar ITim LRHS MAsh MNrw MTho NMen NRya NWCA SRms WHoo WPer |
| - ***bernardina*** | see *L. nevadensis* |
| - 'Rosea' | EPot MAsh NWCA |
| ***oppositifolia*** | EDAr ITim MAsh |
| 'Pinkie' | CPBP LLHF NLAp NMen |
| ***pygmaea*** | CGra CSec CWCL ECho EDAr EWes GEdr GGar GKev ITim LRHS MAsh MHer MWat NBir NLAp NMen NRya WPer |

| | |
|---|---|
| - subsp. ***longipetala*** | see *L. longipetala* |
| Rainbow mixture | see *L. cotyledon* 'Regenbogen' mixed |
| 'Rawreth' | LLHF WAbe |
| ***rediviva*** | ECho EWes GEdr GKev ITim LLHF MAsh NLAp WAbe |
| - NNS 03.369 new | CPBP |
| - subsp. ***minor*** | CGra |
| ***serrata*** | GKev |
| ***sierrae*** | EDAr WPer |
| ***stebbinsii*** | NWCA |
| 'Trevosia' | SIng |
| ***tweedyi*** ♀H2 | CGra EPfP EPot GKev LHop LRHS MAsh NWCA SIng WGor |
| - 'Alba' | GKir LRHS MAsh |
| - 'Elliott's Variety' | MAsh WGor |
| - 'Rosea' | GKev LHop LRHS MAsh SIng WGor |

## Leycesteria (*Caprifoliaceae*)

| | |
|---|---|
| ***crocothyrsos*** | CAbP CArn CBcs CBod CHEx CHid CWib EBee EHig ELan EPfP GKev GQui LAst NBid SMad SPoG WSHC |
| ***formosa*** ♀H4 | Widely available |
| - brown-stemmed | IFoB |
| - Golden Lanterns = 'Notbruce'PBR | CDoC CSBt EBee EMil EPfP EPla EQua IDee LBuc MAsh MBri MGos MMHG NHol NLar SCoo SPoG WBor |
| - 'Golden Pheasant' (v) | CPMA EHoe ERas MDun |
| - 'Purple Rain' | EBee EMil EQua EWes NLar |
| 'Smouldering Embers' | WLeb |

## Leymus (*Poaceae*)

| | |
|---|---|
| from Falkland Islands | EPPr |
| § ***arenarius*** | Widely available |
| ***condensatus*** 'Canyon Prince' | CKno |
| ***hispidus*** | see *Elymus hispidus* |
| 'Niveus' | EHul |
| § ***racemosus*** | CHrt |

## Lhotzkya see *Calytrix*

## Liatris (*Asteraceae*)

| | |
|---|---|
| sp. new | CBro |
| ***aspera*** | NBre WPer |
| ***elegans*** | NBre NLar SPlb WPer |
| ***ligulistylis*** | MHar NBPC NBre NLar WPer |
| ***mucronata*** new | EBee |
| ***punctata*** | NBre |
| ***pycnostachya*** | CRWN EBee GCal MHar MLLN NLar SRms WPer |
| ***scariosa*** 'Alba' | NLar WPer |
| - 'Gracious' | EWll |
| § ***spicata*** | Widely available |
| - 'Alba' | CPrp CSBt CSpe EBee ECha ECtt ELan EPfP EShb LAma LAst LEdu LSRN MNFA MNrw NGdn SPer SPlb WBrE WCAu WHoo WPer |
| - ***callilepis*** | see *L. spicata* |
| - 'Floristan Violett' | EBee EHrv EPPr EPfP GJos GMaP LBMP LRHS MHer NPri SCoo SPlb SPoG SUsu SWvt WFar WGwG WMnd WMoo WPer |
| - 'Floristan Weiss' | CArn EBee EHrv EPPr EPfP GBuc GKir GMaP LBMP LRHS MHer MRav MWhi NBPC NCGa NPri SPad SPla SPoG SWvt WFar WGwG WMnd WMoo WPer |
| - Goblin | see *L. spicata* 'Kobold' |
| § - 'Kobold' | Widely available |

## Libertia ✿ (*Iridaceae*)

| | |
|---|---|
| HCM 98.089 | CDes EBee |
| 'Amazing Grace' | CDes CWsd EBee GCal IBlr SBch SUsu WPGP |
| 'Ballyrogan Blue' | CDes |
| Ballyrogan hybrid | IBlr |
| * ***breunioides*** | CDes CPLG |
| ***caerulescens*** | CBgR CCCN CCVN CDMG CPLG CSec EBee ECho EPla ERos GGar IFoB IGor NBid NBir NCGa NLar SGar SMad SMrm WCot WFar WHer WKif WMoo WPGP |
| ***chilensis*** | see *L. formosa* |
| ***elegans*** | CPLG GBuc IBlr |
| § ***formosa*** | Widely available |
| - brown-stemmed | IBlr IFoB |
| ***grandiflora*** ♀H4 | Widely available |
| - stoloniferous | GGar |
| ***ixioides*** | CBcs CBgR CHid CKno CSec EBee EBrs ECha ECho ECou EShb IBlr LEdu MAvo MCot NGdn NSti SBod SKHP WCFE WFoF WPGP WPic WRHF |
| - dark-leaved new | MAvo |
| - 'Goldfinger' (v) new | EBee NOak SKHP SPoG SRkn |
| - hybrid | SDix |
| - 'Tricolor' | CPen EBee ECho GBuc GGar IBlr LDai WMoo WPat |
| 'Nelson Dwarf' | ECho |
| ***paniculata*** | CPLG WSHC |
| ***peregrinans*** | Widely available |
| - from East Cape | IBlr |
| - 'Gold Leaf' | CBcs CBgR CBow CCCN CElw CPrp CTri CTsd CWsd EHrv GKir IBlr LAst SMad SUsu WCot WFar WHoo WPic WViv |
| - 'Gold Stripe' new | EPPr |
| * ***procera*** | CDes CSpe EBee EPla IBlr LEdu SKHP WPGP WSHC |
| ***pulchella*** | CWsd EBee IBlr |
| - from Tasmania | ECho |
| ***sessiliflora*** | CElw CFee CPLG EBee ECho IBlr NBir WFar WPGP |
| - RB 94073 | SMad |
| Shackleton hybrid | IBlr WFar |
| 'Taupo Blaze' new | CWGN EBee LSRN NCGa NHol SPad SPoG |
| 'Taupo Sunset'PBR | CBgR CCCN CMil EBee ETod EWes GBin MLan NBir NOak SKHP |

## Libocedrus (*Cupressaceae*)

| | |
|---|---|
| ***chilensis*** | see *Austrocedrus chilensis* |
| ***decurrens*** | see *Calocedrus decurrens* |

## Libonia see *Justicia*

## Licuala (*Arecaceae*)

| | |
|---|---|
| ***grandis*** | MBri |
| ***spinosa*** | LPal |

## Ligularia ✿ (*Asteraceae*)

| | |
|---|---|
| BWJ 7686 from China | WCru |
| ***amplexicaulis*** | EWld |
| - CC 5244 new | GKev |
| - GWJ 9404 | WCru |
| 'Britt Marie Crawford'PBR | Widely available |
| ***calthifolia*** | CRow |
| - B&SWJ 2977 new | WCru |
| 'Cheju Charmer' | LEdu WCru |
| ***clivorum*** | see *L. dentata* |
| § ***dentata*** | CRow CSec EBee ECtt GGal LBMP MMuc NBro NGby NLar SRms SWat WBVN WFar |

| | |
|---|---|
| - 'Dark Beauty' | COlW EWll MMuc MWhi NBre WMnd |
| - 'Desdemona' 𝕐$^{H4}$ | Widely available |
| - 'Orange Princess' | NPer WPer |
| - 'Orange Queen' | NBre WFar |
| - 'Othello' | Widely available |
| - 'Sommergold' | EBee ECha WFar |
| § ***fischeri*** | CBct LEdu NBre WCot WPer |
| - B&SWJ 1158 | WFar |
| - B&SWJ 2570 | WCru |
| - B&SWJ 4478 | WCru |
| - B&SWJ 5540 | WCru |
| - B&SWJ 5841 | WCru |
| ***glabrescens*** | CRow |
| § 'Gregynog Gold' 𝕐$^{H4}$ | CBct CRow EBee EBrs ECha ECtt EGle EMFW EPfP GAbr GKir GMaP LRHS MRav NBro NCGa NCob NGdn NOrc SDnm SPav SPer WCru WFar |
| x ***hessei*** | EBee GMaP MMuc NLar SWat WFar |
| ***hodgsonii*** | CKno CRow EBee EBla EPPr GKir LEdu MSte WFar WPer |
| - B&SWJ 10855 **new** | WCru |
| ***intermedia*** | WFar |
| - B&SWJ 606a | WCru |
| ***japonica*** | CHar CLAP CRow EBee ECha GCra LEdu LMaj MWhi NLar WFar |
| - B&SWJ 2883 | WCru |
| - 'Rising Sun' | CLAP WCru |
| aff. ***kaialpina*** B&SWJ 5806 | WCru |
| 'Laternchen'$^{PBR}$ | EBee NBro NMoo |
| 'Little Rocket'$^{PBR}$ | EBee ECtt GBin NBro |
| ***macrophylla*** | CRow WFar |
| 'Osiris Fantaisie' **new** | GBin |
| x ***palmatiloba*** | see *L.* x *yoshizoeana* 'Palmatiloba' |
| § ***przewalskii*** 𝕐$^{H4}$ | Widely available |
| - 'Light Fingered' | NBre |
| ***sachalinensis*** | EBee |
| ***sibirica*** | CSam GAbr MHar NLar WFar WMoo WPer |
| - B&SWJ 5806 | WCru |
| - var. ***speciosa*** | see *L. fischeri* |
| ***smithii*** | see *Senecio smithii* |
| ***speciosa*** | see *L. fischeri* |
| ***stenocephala*** | EBee EMil GKir MCot NBro NLar SWat WFar |
| - B&SWJ 283 | WCru |
| - BWJ 7964 from China | WCru |
| 'Sungold' | CBct CSam EBee EBla EBrs ECtt GBin GKir NCGa NGdn |
| ***tangutica*** | see *Sinacalia tangutica* |
| 'The Rocket' 𝕐$^{H4}$ | Widely available |
| ***tussilaginea*** | see *Farfugium japonicum* |
| - 'Aureo-maculata' | see *Farfugium japonicum* 'Aureomaculatum' |
| ***veitchiana*** | CBct CHEx CRow EBee EBla EBrs EMFW EPfP GAbr GCal GGar LAst LEdu MSte NCGa NCob SDnm SPav SWat WCAu WFar |
| ***vorobievii*** | CHar EBee GCal NLar |
| 'Weihenstephan' | GCal GKir LRHS |
| ***wilsoniana*** | CBct CHEx CRow EBee ECtt ERas LLWG MLLN MMuc MRav NBre NMun SDnm SPav SWat WCAu WFar |
| § x ***yoshizoeana*** 'Palmatiloba' | CFir CHEx EBee EBla ELan ELon EPla GCal GKir LEdu LRHS MRav NSti SDnm SPav SPhx SWat WCot WFar |
| 'Zepter' | CMHG EBee EBla ECtt GBuc GCal NLar WFar |

## *Ligusticum* (*Apiaceae*)

| | |
|---|---|
| ***lucidum*** | CDul CMCN EBee EPfP EWTr MSal SEND SPhx SUsu WFar WPGP |
| ***porteri*** | CArn MSal |
| § ***scoticum*** | CArn CHFP EOHP EWes GBar GKir GPoy ILis MCot MDKP MHer MSal NLar NSti SPav SPhx WFar WHrl WJek WLHH WOut WPtf |
| ***striatum*** B&SWJ 7259 | WCru |

## *Ligustrum* ✿ (*Oleaceae*)

| | |
|---|---|
| ***chenaultii*** | see *L. compactum* |
| § ***compactum*** | NLar |
| § ***delavayanum*** | EPfP EQua ERom LPan MBar MGos MREP SAPC SArc SBLw STrG WFar |
| ***ibota*** | NLar |
| ***ionandrum*** | see *L. delavayanum* |
| ***japonicum*** | CHEx ECrN LPan SBLw SEND SPer WDin WFar |
| I - 'Aureum' | MGos |
| - 'Coriaceum' | see *L. japonicum* 'Rotundifolium' |
| * - 'Coriaceum Aureum' | EMil LRHS |
| - 'Howardii' (v) **new** | EBee |
| - 'Macrophyllum' | EPfP MAsh |
| § - 'Rotundifolium' | CAbP CBcs CDoC CDul CHEx CPLG EBee ELan EMil EPfP EPla LRHS MAsh MGos MRav SBod SCoo SMad SPer SPoG WCFE WClo WFar |
| - 'Silver Star' (v) | CPMA EBee MGos NLar SEND SLon |
| § - 'Texanum' | EWes NLar |
| - 'Variegatum' **new** | LMaj |
| ***lucidum*** 𝕐$^{H4}$ | CDoC CSBt CTri EBee ECrN ELan LAst MBar MGos MRav MSwo NLar NWea SAPC SArc SPer SWvt WDin WFar |
| - 'Excelsum Superbum' (v) 𝕐$^{H4}$ | CAbP CBcs CDul CLnd CPMA ELan EPfP LAst LPan LRHS MAsh MBar MGos NBlu SBLw SPer SSpi |
| - 'Golden Wax' | CAbP CPMA IDee MRav |
| - 'Tricolor' (v) | CPMA EBee ELan EPfP NLar SHBN SPer SPla SPoG SSpi SWvt WDin WFar |
| ***obtusifolium*** 'Darts Perfecta' | SLPl |
| - var. ***regelianum*** | WFar |
| ***ovalifolium*** | Widely available |
| § - 'Argenteum' (v) | CBcs CCVT CDoC CDul CTri CWib EBee ECrN EHoe GKir LBuc LRHS MAsh MBar MWat NBlu NHol NPri SLim SPer SPla SPoG SWvt WDin WFar |
| - 'Aureomarginatum' | see *L. ovalifolium* 'Aureum' |
| § - 'Aureum' (v) 𝕐$^{H4}$ | Widely available |
| - 'Lemon and Lime' (v) | EBee EHoe EMil MAsh MGos SCoo SWvt |
| - 'Variegatum' | see *L. ovalifolium* 'Argenteum' |
| ***quihoui*** 𝕐$^{H4}$ | EBee ECre ELan EPfP IDee MBri MWea SDix SKHP SLon SMad SPer SPoG SSpi WFar WHCG WPat |
| ***sempervirens*** | EPfP IArd IDee NLar SLon |
| ***sinense*** | CMCN EPfP MRav WFar |
| - 'Multiflorum' | CWib WFar |
| - 'Pendulum' | EPla |
| - var. ***stauntonii*** | NLar |
| - 'Variegatum' (v) | CBgR CPMA EBee EPla EWes LHop MRav SPer |
| - 'Wimbei' | EPla WFar |
| ***strongylophyllum*** | CDoC WFar |
| ***texanum*** | see *L. japonicum* 'Texanum' |
| ***tschonoskii*** | NLar |
| ***undulatum*** 'Lemon Lime and Clippers' | CSBt EBee MWea NLar SLim SPoG WMoo |

| | |
|---|---|
| 'Vicaryi' | CPMA EBee ELan EMil EPfP EPla EQua ERas EWTr IArd LRHS MBar MGos NHol NPro SEND SPer SPla WFar |
| ***vulgare*** | CBcs CCVT CDul CRWN CTri CWan EBWF ECrN EMac EPfP LAst LBuc MSwo NWea SEND SWvt WDin WMou WSFF |
| - 'Atrovirens' | EMac |
| - 'Aureovariegatum' (v) | CNat |
| - 'Lodense' | MBar |

## *Lilium* ✿ (*Liliaceae*)

| | |
|---|---|
| Chen Yi 1 | WCot |
| 'Acapulco' (VIId) | EBrs LAma |
| African Queen Group (VIa) $\Upsilon^{H4}$ | EBrs ECot GBuc LAma SCoo SPer |
| - 'African Queen' (VIa) | CBro CSut EBrs EPfP LRHS MCri |
| 'Algarve' | MBri |
| 'Altari' **new** | LRHS |
| ***amabile*** (IX) | LRHS |
| - 'Luteum' (IX) | LRHS |
| ***amoenum*** (IX) | EPot |
| 'Apeldoorn' (Ic) | LRHS MCri NNor |
| 'Aphrodite' (Ia/d) | EBrs |
| 'Apollo' (Ia) $\Upsilon^{H4}$ | CBro EBrs GBuc GKev LAma LRHS MBri |
| 'Arena' (VIIb) | EPfP LRHS SCoo SPer WFar |
| * Asiatic hybrids (VI/VII) | LAma NGdn SGar |
| ***auratum*** (IX) | EBee EBrs ECho EFEx EPfP GBuc LRHS |
| - 'Gold Band' | see *L. auratum* var. *platyphyllum* |
| § - var. ***platyphyllum*** (IX) | GBuc MCri SBch |
| - Red Band Group (IX) | WFar |
| - var. ***virginale*** (IX) | LRHS WWst |
| 'Avignon' (Ia) | LRHS MCri |
| 'Bach' | MBri |
| Backhouse hybrids (II) | CAvo CLAP LCro |
| ***bakerianum*** (IX) | GEdr LAma |
| - var. ***aureum*** | EBee |
| - var. ***delavayi*** (IX) | EBee LAma |
| - var. ***rubrum*** | LAma |
| 'Barbados'$^{PBR}$ (VII) **new** | LRHS |
| 'Barbaresco' (VII) | SCoo SPer |
| 'Barcelona' (Ia) | LRHS MNrw NNor |
| Bellingham Group (IV) | CLAP GBuc GEdr |
| 'Bergamo' (VIId) | EPfP SCoo WFar |
| 'Bianco Uno' | MBri |
| 'Black Beauty' (VIId) | CAvo CBro CFFs CLAP EBrs EPfP ERCP GBuc GGar LAma LCro LRHS MCri MSte NNor |
| 'Black Bird' | NBPN |
| 'Black Dragon' (VIa) | MCri |
| 'Black Jack'$^{PBR}$ | NBPN |
| 'Black Tie' | MCri |
| 'Blazing Dwarf' (Ia) | MBri |
| 'Boogie Woogie' (VIIIa-b/b) **new** | LRHS |
| * 'Brasilia' | LRHS |
| 'Bright Star' (VIb) | LAma MCri |
| ***brownii*** (IX) | EBee EBrs ECho LAma MCri WWst |
| ***bulbiferum*** | ECho GBuc |
| - var. ***croceum*** (IX) | ECho |
| 'Butter Pixie'$^{PBR}$ (Ia) | LAma LRHS WGor |
| § ***canadense*** (IX) | GBuc LAma |
| - var. ***coccineum*** (IX) | GBuc |
| - var. ***flavum*** | see *L. canadense* |
| 'Cancun' (Ia) | LRHS |
| ***candidum*** (IX) $\Upsilon^{H4}$ | CArn CAvo CBcs CBro CTca CTri EBee EBrs ECha EHrv ELan EPfP EPot ERCP GAuc IHer LAma LAst LRHS MCri MHer NGHP SPer WBrE WCot |
| - 'Plenum' (IX/d) | EMon |
| ***carniolicum*** | see *L. pyrenaicum* subsp. *carniolicum* |
| 'Casa Blanca' (VIIb) $\Upsilon^{H4}$ | CAvo CBro CFFs CTca EBrs EPfP GBuc GKev LAma LRHS MCri NBir SCoo SPad SPer WFar |
| 'Casa Rosa' (V) | CSWP MCri SWat |
| 'Centrefold' | GBuc LRHS NNor |
| 'Ceres' (VI) **new** | LRHS |
| ***cernuum*** (IX) | EBee EBrs ECho GAuc LAma LRHS MCri SPer |
| * - 'Album' | EBrs LRHS SPer |
| 'Chianti' (Ia) | CSut |
| 'Chinook' (Ia) | NNor |
| 'Cinnabar' (Ia) | MCri |
| Citronella Group (Ic) | CAvo CBro EBrs ECho LAma LRHS MCri NNor WFar |
| Cobra = 'Zantricob'$^{PBR}$ (VII) **new** | LRHS |
| 'Color Parade' (VII) **new** | LRHS |
| ***columbianum*** (IX) | EBrs ECho GBuc GEdr NMen |
| - B&SWJ 9564 | WCru |
| - NNS 96-134 **new** | EBee |
| - dwarf (IX) | EBrs ECho NMen |
| 'Compass' (Ia) | MBri |
| 'Con Amore' (VIIb) | LRHS SCoo SPer WFar |
| 'Conca d'Or'$^{PBR}$ NNS 03-377 | WWst |
| 'Connecticut King' (Ia) | EPfP LAma MCri |
| 'Corina' (Ia) | GBuc NNor SGar |
| 'Costa Del Sol' (Ia/b) | EBrs |
| 'Côte d'Azur' (Ia) | CBro GKev LAma LRHS NNor SBch SRms WGor |
| 'Coulance' (VIId) | EBrs |
| 'Courier'$^{PBR}$ | CAvo CFFs |
| 'Crimson Pixie' (Ia) | CBro LRHS NPri SPet |
| x ***dalhansonii*** (IX) | CLAP SPhx WCot |
| § - 'Marhan' (II) | CLAP |
| ***dauricum*** f. ***rebunense*** **new** | EBee |
| ***davidii*** (IX) | CLAP EBee EBrs ECho GEdr LAma MCri WCru WTou |
| § - var. ***willmottiae*** (IX) | CLAP EBee WCot |
| 'Denia' (Ib) | SPoG |
| 'Diabora' | GBuc |
| ***distichum*** B&SWJ 794 | WCru |
| 'Dizzy' | LRHS MCri SPad |
| 'Doeskin' (Ic) | CLAP |
| ***duchartrei*** (IX) | CDes CFwr EBee EBrs ECho ERCP GBuc GEdr LAma NSla WAbe WCru |
| § 'Ed' (VII) | LAma NNor |
| 'Eileen North' (Ic) | CLAP GBuc |
| 'Electric' (Ia) | LRHS NNor |
| 'Elodie'$^{PBR}$ (1a/b) | CAvo CFFs LRHS |
| 'Enchantment' (Ia) | LAma MBri NNor |
| 'Eros' | CLAP |
| 'Evelina' | EBrs LRHS |
| 'Everest' (VIId) | NNor |
| 'Fairest' (Ib-c/d) | CLAP |
| 'Fancy Joy' | MBri |
| 'Fangio' (VIIIa/b) | LRHS |
| ***fargesii*** (IX) | CExc GEdr |
| 'Farolito' | LBuc LRHS |
| 'Fata Morgana' (Ia/d) $\Upsilon^{H4}$ | EBrs EPfP LRHS SCoo SPad |
| 'Feuerzauber' (Ia) | SPer |
| 'Fire King' (Ib) | EPfP LAma LRHS MCri SCoo WFar |
| ***formosanum*** (IX) | EBee EBrs ECho LFur MCri MMuc WCot |
| - B&SWJ 1589 | WCru |
| - var. ***pricei*** (IX) | CMea CWCL EBrs ECho EDAr ELan EPot GEdr GGar LRHS MHer MNrw NMen NWCA SCoo SRot WBVN WPer |

| | Name | Suppliers |
|---|---|---|
| | - 'Snow Queen' (IX) | MCri |
| | - 'White Swan' (IX) | GBuc |
| | 'Fresco' (VII) | ECho |
| | 'Garden Party' (VII) ♀$^{H4}$ | EBrs LRHS WFar |
| | 'Gibraltar' (Ia) | MCri |
| | 'Glossy Wings' | GBuc NNor |
| | 'Golden Joy' | MBri |
| | 'Golden Melody' (Ia) | MCri |
| | Golden Splendor Group (VIa) ♀$^{H4}$ | CFwr EBrs LAma LCro LRHS MCri SCoo SMeo SPer SWat |
| | 'Golden Stargazer' (VII a-b/b) **new** | CSut LRHS |
| | 'Gran Cru' (Ia) ♀$^{H4}$ | EBrs EWll LRHS MCri NNor SPad |
| | 'Gran Paradiso' (Ia) | MCri SRms |
| | 'Green Magic' (VIa) | MCri NNor |
| | ***hansonii*** (IX) | CLAP EBee EBrs ECho GEdr LAma MCri |
| | - B&SWJ 4756 | WCru |
| | 'Heloma' (Ia) | EBrs |
| | ***henryi*** (IX) ♀$^{H4}$ | CAvo CFFs CFwr CLAP CSWP EBee EBrs ECho EPfP GAuc IHer LAma LRHS MCri SMeo WCot WCru |
| | - var. ***citrinum*** | ECho |
| | 'Hit Parade' (VII) | LAma |
| | x ***hollandicum*** | MCri |
| | 'Honeymoon' (VIIIa-b/b) | SPoG |
| | 'Hotlips' | EPfP LRHS SPer |
| | 'Ibarra' | MCri |
| | Imperial Silver Group (VIIc) | LAma |
| | 'Inzell' (Ia) | EBrs |
| | 'Ivory Pixie' (Ia) | CBro SPet |
| | 'Jacqueline' | EBrs GKev LRHS |
| | 'Jacques S. Dijt' (II) | CLAP |
| | ***japonicum*** (IX) | EFEx WCru |
| | - 'Albomarginatum' (IX) | GEdr WWst |
| | 'Journey's End' (VIId) | GBuc LAma LRHS NNor |
| § | 'Joy' (VIIb) ♀$^{H4}$ | LAma LRHS MCri NNor |
| § | ***kelleyanum*** (IX) | CLAP GBuc |
| | - NNS 02-227 | WWst |
| | - NNS 98-373 | WCot WWst |
| | ***kelloggii*** (IX) | WCot |
| | - NNS 03-379 | WWst |
| | ***kesselringianum*** | EBrs |
| | 'King Pete' (Ib) ♀$^{H4}$ | EBrs |
| | 'Kiss Proof' (VIIb) | LRHS |
| | 'Lady Alice' (VI) | CLAP EBrs LRHS |
| | 'Lady Bowes Lyon' (Ic) | CWsd |
| § | ***lancifolium*** (IX) | CArn CHEx CHid CTca GBin WBVN WBrk WFar |
| | - B&SWJ 539 | WCru |
| * | - ***album*** | WBor |
| | - Farrer's form | EBee LFur WCot |
| | - var. ***flaviflorum*** (IX) | EBee EBrs GBuc MCri MSte |
| | - 'Flore Pleno' (IX/d) | CLAP CSWP CTca EBee EBrs EMon EPPr EUJe GAbr GBuc GCal GGar GKir LHop LRHS MHer MMHG NBir NSti WBrk WCot WCru WFar WHil WTin |
| * | - var. ***forrestii*** (IX) | MCri |
| | - Forrest's form (IX) | CLAP CPMA |
| | - var. ***fortunei*** (IX) | GCal |
| | - - B&SWJ 4352 | WCru |
| | - var. ***splendens*** (IX) ♀$^{H4}$ | CBro EBee EBrs ECGP ECho EPfP GAuc GKev LAma LRHS MCri NNor WBor |
| * | - ***viridulum*** | EBee |
| | 'Landini'$^{PBR}$ | LRHS NBPN |
| | ***lankongense*** (IX) | CDes CWsd GEdr LAma MCri |
| | 'Latvia' (Ia/b) | LRHS |
| | 'Le Rêve' | see *L.* 'Joy' |
| | ***ledebourii*** (IX) **new** | EBee |
| | ***leichtlinii*** | CLAP EBee EBrs ECho EPot GKev IHer LRHS MCri |
| | - B&SWJ 4519 | WCru |
| | - 'Iwashimiza' (IX) | MCri |
| | 'Lemon Pixie'$^{PBR}$ (Ia) | LAma NPri SPet |
| | 'Leslie Woodriff' (VIII) **new** | WWst |
| | ***leucanthum*** (IX) | EBee LAma |
| | - var. ***centifolium*** (IX) | MCri WCru |
| | ***lijiangense*** | GEdr MCri |
| | 'Lollypop' (Ia) | EBrs EPfP GBuc LRHS MNrw NNor SCoo |
| | ***longiflorum*** (IX) ♀$^{H2-3}$ | EBee EBrs ECho GAuc LAma LRHS MCri SCoo |
| | - B&SWJ 4885 | WCru |
| | - 'Memories' | MBri SPoG |
| § | - 'White American' (IX) | CBro CSWP EBrs ECho EPfP LRHS SPer |
| | ***lophophorum*** (IX) | EBee EPot LAma WCru WWst |
| | - var. ***linearifolium*** | GAuc |
| | 'Lovely Girl' (VIIb) | CSut EBrs LRHS |
| | 'Luxor' (Ib) | EBrs EPfP EWll LRHS MCri NBir SPer |
| | ***mackliniae*** (IX) | CDes CLAP CWCL EBee EBrs ECho GBuc GCal GCra GEdr GGGa GMac ITim NBir NMen NWCA SKHP WAbe WBVN WHal |
| | - deep pink-flowered | GGGa |
| | - robust habit | GBuc GGar SKHP WWst |
| | x ***maculatum*** Japanese double-flowered (IX/d) | EMon |
| | 'Magento' (1a) | LRHS |
| | 'Marco Polo' (Ia) | LEdu SCoo WFar |
| | 'Marhan' | see *L.* x *dalhansonii* 'Marhan' |
| | ***martagon*** (IX) ♀$^{H4}$ | Widely available |
| | - var. ***album*** (IX) ♀$^{H4}$ | CAvo CBro CFFs CLAP CSWP EBee EBrs ECha ECho EHrv ELan EPfP EPot GBuc GEdr GKev GMaP LAma LCro LRHS MTho NBir NChi SPhx SRms WAbe WShi |
| | - var. ***cattaniae*** (IX) | EPot MCri WCot |
| | - - 'The Moor' (IXb/d) | SKHP |
| | - var. ***daugava*** **new** | WWst |
| | - var. ***pilosiusculum*** (IX) | EBee |
| | - 'Plenum' (IX/d) | EMon WCot |
| | 'Maxwill' (Ic) | EBrs |
| | ***medeoloides*** (IX) | CLAP EBee EBrs ECho EFEx GBuc NMen WWst |
| | 'Mediterrannee' (VIIb/d) | LRHS |
| | 'Menton' | MCri |
| | ***michiganense*** (IX) | CSWP GBuc |
| | 'Milano' (Ia) | MCri |
| | 'Miss America' | SPad |
| | 'Miss Lucy'$^{PBR}$ (VIIa-b/b-c) | CSut LRHS |
| | 'Miss Rio' (VII) | LRHS SCoo |
| | 'Mona Lisa' (VIIb/d) | EBrs EPfP LAma LRHS MBri NNor WBVN WFar WGor |
| § | ***monadelphum*** (IX) | CWsd EBee EBrs ECho EPot GAuc GBuc GCra LAma NLar |
| | 'Montana' | LRHS |
| | 'Monte Negro' (Ia) | CAvo EBrs ECho |
| | 'Montreal' (VIIb) | LRHS |
| | 'Montreux' (Ia) | LAma |
| | 'Mr Ed' | see *L.* 'Ed' |
| | 'Mr Ruud' | see *L.* 'Ruud' |
| § | 'Mrs R.O. Backhouse' (II) | CLAP CTca EBee EBrs ECho GEdr LRHS MSte |
| | 'Muscadet'$^{PBR}$ (VII) | CSut EBrs EPfP LRHS |
| § | ***nanum*** (IX) | EBee EBrs ECho GBuc GEdr GGGa LAma NMen WCru WHal WWst |
| | - AGS/ES | WWst |
| | - EMAK 670 **new** | EBee WWst |
| | - from Bhutan (IX) | EBee EBrs ECho GBuc GEdr GGar NMen WCru |
| | - var. ***flavidum*** (IX) | EBee EBrs ECho GEdr NMen WWst |
| | - - hybrids **new** | WWst |

| | | |
|---|---|---|
| | ***nepalense*** (IX) | Widely available |
| | - B&SWJ 2985 | WCru |
| | ***nobilissimum*** (IX) | EFEx |
| | 'Noblesse' (VII) | LRHS |
| | 'Nove Cento' ♀H4 | MCri |
| | 'Odeon' | MCri |
| | 'Olivia' (Ia) | EBrs LAma MCri NNor |
| | Olympic Group (VIa) | MCri |
| | 'Orange Pixie' (Ia) | EPfP MCri SCoo SPet WGor |
| | 'Orange Triumph' (Ia) | EPfP NNor |
| | oriental hybrids | EBrs |
| * | Oriental Superb Group | NGdn |
| § | ***oxypetalum*** (IX) | EBee GBuc GGGa WWst |
| | - var. ***insigne*** (IX) | CLAP EBee EBrs ECho EPot GBin GBuc GEdr GGGa GGar NMen NSla WCru WHal WWst |
| | ***papilliferum*** | EBrs ECho LAma |
| | ***pardalinum*** (IX) ♀H4 | CBro CLAP CWCL EBee EBrs ECho ELan ERCP GKev IFro LRHS MCot MSte NSla WBVN WCot WCru WHal WPnP |
| | - var. ***giganteum*** (IX) | CLAP EPfP MCri MNrw SPer WTin |
| | - subsp. ***pardalinum*** (IX) NNS 00-488 | WCot WWst |
| | - - NNS 02=228 | WWst |
| | - subsp. ***shastense*** (IX) | CLAP EBee NMen WCot WWst |
| | - - NNS 98-374 | WWst |
| | - - NNS 00-490 | WCot |
| | - subsp. ***shastense*** x ***vollmeri*** | WWst |
| | ***parryi*** (IX) | CWsd EBee ECho GBuc WWst |
| | - NNS 03-384 | WWst |
| | ***parvum*** (IX) | EBee ECho GBuc |
| | 'Peach Pixie' (Ia) | NBir NNor NPri SCoo |
| | 'Peggy North' (Ic) | CLAP |
| | ***philippinense*** (IX) | CDes EBee MCri |
| | Pink Perfection Group (VIa) ♀H4 | CAvo CBro CFFs EBrs EPfP ERCP LAma LRHS MCri NNor SBch SCoo SPer SWat WFar |
| | 'Pink Pixie' PBR (Ia) | SGar |
| | 'Pink Tiger' (Ib) | CAvo EBrs GKev LRHS MCri NNor WGor |
| | 'Pink Twinkle' | EBrs |
| | ***pomponium*** (IX) | EBee GCal |
| | ***primulinum*** var. ***ochraceum*** | CLAP LAma WWst |
| § | ***pumilum*** (IX) ♀H4 | CLAP CTca EBee EBrs ECho ERCP GAuc GBuc GKev LAma LRHS MCri MSte MTho SBch WAul WCot |
| | ***pyrenaicum*** (IX) | CLAP EBee EBrs ECho GGar GKir IBlr IFro MCri WCot WPGP WRha WShi |
| § | - subsp. ***carniolicum*** (IX) | MCri |
| | - subsp. ***pyrenaicum*** var. ***rubrum*** (IX) | GEdr WCot |
| | 'Raspberry Butterflies' (Ic/d) | CLAP |
| | 'Red Carpet' (Ia) | EBrs LRHS MCri NBir NNor NPri WGor |
| | 'Red Dutch' (VIII) | ERCP |
| | 'Red Night' (I) | LRHS |
| | 'Red Rum' | MBri |
| | 'Red Twinkle' | CFwr EBrs LRHS |
| | 'Red Velvet' (Ib) | CLAP |
| | ***regale*** (IX) ♀H4 | Widely available |
| | - 'Album' (IX) | CAvo CFFs CSWP EBee EBrs EWTr GAuc GBuc LAma LCro LRHS MCri NNor SBch SCoo SGar WFar |
| § | - 'Royal Gold' (IX) | EPfP MCri |
| | 'Reinesse' (Ia) | MBri NPri |
| | 'Roma' (Ia) | EWll LAma LRHS NBir |
| | 'Rosefire' (Ia) | MCri NNor |
| | 'Rosemary North' (I) | CLAP |
| | Rosepoint Lace Group (Ic) | CLAP |
| | 'Rosita' (Ia) | MCri WFar |
| | ***rosthornii*** | CExc EBee GBuc GEdr WCot WCru WWst |
| | 'Royal Gold' | see *L. regale* 'Royal Gold' |
| | ***rubellum*** (IX) | EFEx GBuc |
| § | 'Ruud' (VII) | EPfP LAma LRHS |
| | ***sachalinense*** | CStu |
| | - RBS 0235 | EPPr |
| | 'Salmon Twinkle' (Ib-c/c) | EBrs WFar |
| | 'Sam' (VII) ♀H4 | EPfP GBuc LAma LRHS |
| | ***sargentiae*** (IX) | CExc EBrs GBuc GGGa MCri NMen WCot |
| | - Cox 7099 | EBee WWst |
| | ***sempervivoideum*** (IX) | EBrs ECho GEdr LAma |
| | ***shastense*** | see *L. kelleyanum* |
| | 'Siberia' PBR | EBrs |
| | 'Silly Girl' (Ia) | MCri NNor |
| § | 'Snow Crystal' (I) | EPfP |
| | ***souliei*** (IX) | CExc EBee |
| | ***speciosum*** (IX) | NSla |
| | - B&SWJ 4847 | WCru |
| | - var. ***album*** (IX) | EBee EBrs EPfP EWTr GBuc LEdu LRHS MCri NBir NNor SBch |
| | - var. ***gloriosoides*** (IX) | EBrs EPot LAma WCot |
| | - var. ***roseum*** (IX) | GBuc NNor |
| | - var. ***rubrum*** (IX) | CFwr EBee EBrs ECha ECho GAuc GBuc LAma LRHS MCri NBir NLar SPer |
| § | - 'Uchida' (IX) | EPfP MCri NNor |
| | 'Sphinx' (Ia/d) | WCot |
| | 'Staccato' (Ia) | MCri |
| | 'Star Gazer' (VIIc) | CBro CSut EBrs ECot ELan LAma LRHS MCri MHav NNor NPri SCoo SPer WFar WGor |
| | 'Starfighter' (VIId) | EBrs LRHS MCri |
| | 'Sterling Star' (Ia) | EPfP MCri NNor |
| | Stones = 'Holebobo' | LRHS NNor |
| | 'Sulphur King' | WCot |
| | ***sulphureum*** | EBee LAma MCri WWst |
| | 'Sun Ray' (Ia) | LRHS MCri |
| | ***superbum*** (IX) | EBee ECho GAuc GBuc GEdr LAma WCot WCru WPGP |
| | 'Sweet Lord' | EBrs |
| | 'Sweet Surrender' (I) | EBrs LRHS MCri NNor |
| | ***szovitsianum*** | see *L. monadelphum* |
| | ***taliense*** (IX) | EBee ECho GBuc GEdr LAma MCri WCru WWst |
| | ***tenuifolium*** | see *L. pumilum* |
| | ***tigrinum*** | see *L. lancifolium* |
| | 'Time Out' PBR | EPfP |
| | 'Tom Pouce' (VIIa/b) | LRHS |
| | 'Touch' | LRHS MCri |
| | 'Treasure' (VII) **new** | LRHS |
| | 'Triumphator' | LRHS MCri |
| | ***tsingtauense*** (IX) B&SWJ 4263 **new** | WCru |
| | - B&SWJ 519 | WCru |
| | 'Uchida Kanoka' | see *L. speciosum* 'Uchida' |
| | 'Umbria' (I) **new** | LRHS |
| | 'Vermeer' (Ia/b) | EBrs EWll WFar |
| | 'Victory Joy' | MBri |
| | 'Viking' | WThu |
| | 'Viva' (Ic) | CLAP |
| | ***vollmeri*** (IX) | CLAP NMen WCru WWst |
| | - JCA 1.500.901 | WWst |
| | - NNS 00-490 | EBee |
| | ***wallichianum*** (IX) | EBee EBrs ECho GBuc LAma LRHS |
| | ***washingtonianum*** (IX) | EBee |
| | ***wenshanense*** | EBee |
| | 'White American' | see *L. longiflorum* 'White American' |
| | 'White Butterflies' (Ic/d) | CLAP |
| | 'White Dwarf' (Ia) | EBrs GKev |

| | | |
|---|---|---|
| | 'White Heaven'[PBR] new | EPfP WGor |
| | 'White Henryi' (VId) | CLAP EBee LRHS |
| | 'White Kiss' (Ia/d) | LRHS |
| I | 'White Lace' (Ic/d) | CLAP |
| | 'White Mountain' (VIIc) | SPer |
| | 'White Paradise' (V) | SCoo |
| | 'White Pixie' (I) | see *L.* 'Snow Crystal' |
| | 'White Tiger' (Ib) | CAvo CLAP |
| | 'White Twinkle' (Ia/b) | EBrs |
| | ***wigginsii*** (IX) | CLAP EBee GEdr MCri |
| | - NNS 00-493 | WWst |
| | 'Willeke Alberti'[PBR] (VII) new | LRHS |
| | ***willmottiae*** | see *L. davidii* var. *willmottiae* |
| | 'Woodriff's Memory' (VIIb) | EBrs |
| | ***xanthellum*** var. ***luteum*** | GEdr |
| | Yellow Blaze Group (Ia) | EPfP |
| | 'Yellow Star' (Ib) | EBrs EWll LRHS NNor |
| | 'Zagora' (VII) new | LRHS |

## lime see *Citrus aurantiifolia*

## lime, djeruk see *Citrus amblycarpa*

## lime, Philippine see x *Citrofortunella microcarpa*

## *Limnanthes* (*Limnanthaceae*)

| | |
|---|---|
| ***douglasii*** ♀[H4] | CArn CHrt EPfP SECG SIde SIng |

## *Limnophila* (*Scrophulariaceae*)

| | |
|---|---|
| ***aromatica*** | MSal |

## *Limonium* (*Plumbaginaceae*)

| | | |
|---|---|---|
| | ***bellidifolium*** | CMea ECha EDAr WAbe WHoo WPer WTin |
| | ***binervosum*** | EBWF |
| | 'Blauer Diamant' | NBre |
| | ***chilwellii*** | EBee ECGP MSte NCGa SMHy SPoG |
| | ***cosyrense*** | CMea MHer NMen WAbe WPer |
| | ***dumosum*** | see *Goniolimon tataricum* var. *angustifolium* |
| | ***gmelinii*** | MLLN SPlb WClo WPer |
| * | - subsp. ***hungaricum*** | NLar |
| | ***gougetianum*** | WPer |
| | ***latifolium*** | see *L. platyphyllum* |
| | ***minutum*** | MNHC SPoG WHoo |
| | ***perezii*** | EShb WPer |
| § | ***platyphyllum*** | Widely available |
| | - 'Robert Butler' | EBee GCal GKir LRHS MRav MSte NCGa SPoG SRGP |
| | - 'Violetta' | CPrp EBee ECGP ECha ELan EPfP GCal GKir LAst LRHS MBri MRav NCGa NOrc SPer WCAu WHoo WSHC |
| | ***speciosum*** | see *Goniolimon incanum* |
| | ***tataricum*** | see *Goniolimon tataricum* |
| | ***vulgare*** | WHer |

## *Linanthastrum* see *Linanthus*

## *Linanthus* (*Polemoniaceae*)

| | |
|---|---|
| ***nuttallii*** subsp. ***floribundus*** | CPBP |

## *Linaria* (*Scrophulariaceae*)

| | | |
|---|---|---|
| | ***aeruginea*** | CSpe |
| § | - subsp. ***nevadensis*** | CSec |
| | - - 'Gemstones' | LRHS |
| | ***alpina*** | CSec CSpe ECho ECtt GGar MTho NRya SRms WEas |
| | ***amoi*** new | CSec |
| | ***anticaria*** 'Antique Silver' | EBee ECha GBuc LSou MRav WPGP WPtf |
| | Blue Lace = 'Yalin' | LSou NPri SPoG |
| | ***cymbalaria*** | see *Cymbalaria muralis* |
| § | ***dalmatica*** | CEnt CHrt CSec EBee ECha ELan EPPr IFro NBid NBro SBch SHGN SPhx WCFE WCot WKif WMoo WPer |
| | ***dalmatica*** x ***purpurea*** | WCot |
| | x ***dominii*** 'Carnforth' | LSou NBre NBro SBch WCot |
| | - 'Yuppie Surprise' | CHid LAst NBir SWvt WCot WPGP |
| | ***genistifolia*** | MDKP |
| | - subsp. ***dalmatica*** | see *L. dalmatica* |
| | ***genistifolia*** x ***triphylla*** new | SSvw |
| | 'Globosa Alba' | see *Cymbalaria muralis* 'Globosa Alba' |
| | ***hepaticifolia*** | see *Cymbalaria hepaticifolia* |
| * | ***lobata alba*** | ECho SPlb |
| | ***maroccana*** | CSec |
| | ***nevadensis*** | see *L. aeruginea* subsp. *nevadensis* |
| | - 'Grenada Sol' | MWea |
| | ***origanifolia*** | see *Chaenorhinum origanifolium* |
| | ***pallida*** | see *Cymbalaria pallida* |
| | ***pilosa*** | see *Cymbalaria pilosa* |
| | ***purpurea*** | CBgR COIW CTri EBWF EBee EHoe EHrv ELan EPfP IFoB LBMP MHer MNHC NBro NPer NPri SECG SPhx SRms WCAu WCot WMoo WPer |
| | - 'Alba' | see *L. purpurea* 'Springside White' |
| | - 'Canon Went' | Widely available |
| | - 'Radcliffe Innocence' | see *L. purpurea* 'Springside White' |
| § | - 'Springside White' | CBgR CElw COIW EBee ECha ECtt EWTr GBuc LBMP MBri MSte NBir NPri SBch SPhx SSvw WAul WCAu WCot WHil WPer WRha WWlt |
| | - 'Thurgarton Beauty' | MDKP |
| | ***repens*** | CPom MNrw WCot WHer |
| | ***reticulata*** 'Red Velvet' | CSpe |
| | x ***sepium*** | WCot |
| | 'Toni Aldiss' | SPhx |
| | ***triornithophora*** | CEnt CFir CSpe EBee ECha GBuc IGor LBMP MNFA MWea SPoG WKif WMoo WRha |
| | - 'Pink Budgies' | CDMG LSou |
| | - purple-flowered | ELan MHar WMoo |
| | ***tristis*** | CEnt |
| | ***vulgaris*** | CArn EBWF ELau LDai MDKP MHer MNHC NMir NSco SECG WHer WJek WLHH |
| | - 'Peloria' | MDKP |
| | 'Winifrid's Delight' | EPfP NBre |

## *Lindelofia* (*Boraginaceae*)

| | | |
|---|---|---|
| | ***anchusoides*** misapplied | see *L. longiflora* |
| | ***anchusoides*** (Lindl.) Lehm. | EPPr GBri NBid |
| § | ***longiflora*** | CFir EBee GBuc GCal GCra LRHS MLLN NBid |

## *Lindera* (*Lauraceae*)

| | |
|---|---|
| ***aggregata*** | CBcs |
| ***benzoin*** | CAgr CBcs CMCN EPfP GKir ISea LRHS MBri MSal NLar SSpi WDin |
| ***communis*** | WPGP |
| ***erythrocarpa*** | CBcs EPfP NLar SSpi |
| - B&SWJ 6271 | WCru |
| ***megaphylla*** | CBcs CHEx |
| ***obtusiloba*** ♀[H4] | CAbP EPfP SSpi |
| - B&SWJ 8723 new | WCru |
| ***praecox*** | EPfP WPGP |
| ***reflexa*** | CGHE EPfP NLar WPGP |
| ***sericea*** | SSpi |
| - B&SWJ 11141 new | WCru |
| ***strychnifolia*** | EPfP |
| ***triloba*** B&SWJ 5570 new | WCru |

| | |
|---|---|
| ***umbellata*** var. ***membranacea*** B&SWJ 6227 | WCru |

## *Lindernia* (*Scrophulariaceae*)

| | |
|---|---|
| ***grandiflora*** | CSpe EBee LLWG SIng |

## *Linnaea* (*Caprifoliaceae*)

| | |
|---|---|
| ***borealis*** | CStu ILis MHar WAbe |
| - subsp. ***americana*** | NHar NWCA |

## *Linum* ✿ (*Linaceae*)

| | |
|---|---|
| ***africanum*** | EShb |
| ***arboreum*** ♀H4 | LLHF SUsu WAbe WKif WPat |
| - NS 529 | NWCA |
| ***bulgaricum*** | see *L. tauricum* |
| ***campanulatum*** | WThu |
| ***capitatum*** | NSla WAbe |
| ***dolomiticum*** | WPat |
| ***flavum*** | CTri EPfP GKir |
| - 'Compactum' | EBee ECho GGar LLHF SPad SRms |
| 'Gemmell's Hybrid' ♀H4 | CLyd CMea ECho EPot EWes LRHS MDKP NBir NMen WAbe WPat |
| ***leonii*** | LRHS |
| ***monogynum*** | ECou |
| § - var. ***diffusum*** | ECou |
| - 'Nelson' | see *L. monogynum* var. *diffusum* |
| ***narbonense*** | CMdw CSec ECGP LBMP LDai LRHS NLar SBch SRms |
| - 'Heavenly Blue' | GKir |
| § ***perenne*** | CArn CRWN CTri EBee ECha ELan EPfP GKir GMaP LRHS MHer MNHC NMir SIde SPer SRms WCAu WPer |
| - 'Album' | CSec EBee ECha ELan EPfP NLar SPer WPer |
| § - 'Blau Saphir' | EBee LRHS MLLN MMHG MRav MWat NLar SRms |
| - Blue Sapphire | see *L. perenne* 'Blau Saphir' |
| - 'Diamant' | EBee LRHS |
| - 'Himmelszelt' | ELon LBMP NLar SMrm |
| - subsp. ***lewisii*** | NBir |
| - 'Nanum Diamond' | NLar |
| - 'Nanum Sapphire' | see *L. perenne* 'Blau Saphir' |
| - 'White Diamond' | NCob |
| ***sibiricum*** | see *L. perenne* |
| ***suffruticosum*** subsp. ***salsoloides*** 'Nanum' | WPat |
| - - 'Prostratum' | GBuc |
| § ***tauricum*** | SPhx |
| ***tenuifolium*** | SPhx |
| ***uninerve*** | WAbe |
| ***usitatissimum*** | CRWN MHer SIde |

## *Lippia* (*Verbenaceae*)

| | |
|---|---|
| sp. | SWvt |
| ***alba*** | MSal |
| ***canescens*** | see *Phyla nodiflora* var. *canescens* |
| ***chamaedrifolia*** | see *Verbena peruviana* |
| ***citriodora*** | see *Aloysia triphylla* |
| ***dulcis*** | CArn CFir EOHP MSal |
| ***nodiflora*** | see *Phyla nodiflora* |
| ***repens*** | see *Phyla nodiflora* |

## *Liquidambar* ✿ (*Hamamelidaceae*)

| | |
|---|---|
| ***acalycina*** | CDul CLnd CPMA EBee EHig ELan EMil EPfP GKir LPan LRHS MBlu MGos MRav NLar SBir SCoo SSpi SSta WPGP WPat |
| - 'Burgundy Flush' | CPMA |
| ***formosana*** | CDul CEnd CMCN EBee EHig EPfP IArd LPan MBlu MGos SBir SSpi SSta WPGP |
| - B&SWJ 6855 | WCru |
| - Monticola Group | CPMA EPfP SBir SSta |
| ***orientalis*** | CMCN CPMA EPfP LLHF LPan SBir SSta |
| ***styraciflua*** | Widely available |
| - 'Andrew Hewson' | CAbP CLnd CPMA EMil LRHS MAsh NLar SBir SCoo SSta |
| - 'Anja' | CPMA MBlu SBir SSta |
| - 'Anneke' | CPMA LRHS SBir SSta |
| - 'Aurea' | see *L. styraciflua* 'Variegata' Overeynder |
| - 'Aurea Variegata' | see *L. styraciflua* 'Variegata' Overeynder |
| - 'Aurora' | CPMA MBlu SBir SLim |
| - 'Burgundy' | CPMA CTho LLHF MBlu NHol SBir SSta WPGP WPat |
| - 'Elstead Mill' | CAbP |
| - 'Fastigiata' | MBlu |
| - 'Festeri' | CEnd SBir SSta WPat |
| - 'Festival' | CPMA MBlu SBLw SSta |
| - 'Frosty' (v) | CPMA |
| - 'Globe' | see *L. styraciflua* 'Gum Ball' |
| - 'Golden Treasure' (v) | CBcs CDul CMCN CPMA LRHS MAsh MBri MGos NLar WPat |
| § - 'Gum Ball' | CEnd CLnd CMCN CPMA EPfP EWes LLHF MBlu MBri MGos NLar SBir SCoo SMad SSta WPat |
| - Happidaze = 'Hapdell' | CEnd CPMA MBlu NLar WPat |
| - 'Jennifer Carol' | CPMA NLar |
| - 'Kia' | CAbP CEnd CPMA LLHF MBlu NLar SBir WPat |
| - 'Kirsten' | CPMA |
| - 'Lane Roberts' ♀H4 | CDoC CDul CLnd CMCN CSBt CTho EBee EHig EMil EPfP GKir IArd LPan LRHS MAsh MBlu MGos MLan NLar SBir SCoo SMad SReu SSta WDin WOrn WPGP WPat |
| - 'Manon' (v) | CDoC CEnd CPMA EMil LAst LPan NBhm SBir |
| - 'Midwest Sunset' | MBlu WPGP WPat |
| - 'Moonbeam' (v) | CDul CEnd CMCN CPMA EBee MBlu NLar SBir SLim SSta WPat |
| - 'Moraine' | CPMA SBLw SBir |
| - 'Naree' | CPMA NLar SBir |
| - 'Oconee' | CEnd EPfP WPat |
| - 'Paarl' (v) | CPMA |
| - 'Palo Alto' | CEnd CPMA LLHF LRHS MBlu NHol SBLw SBir SCoo SSta WPGP WPat |
| - 'Parasol' | CAbP CEnd CPMA NLar SBir SSta |
| - 'Pendula' | CLnd CMCN CPMA LRHS MBlu SBir SSta |
| - 'Penwood' | CPMA NLar SSta |
| - 'Rotundiloba' | CMCN CPMA EMil EPfP LLHF MAsh SBir SSta WPat |
| - 'Schock's Gold' | CPMA |
| - 'Silver King' (v) | CDul CLnd CMCN CPMA EBee ECrN EHig EMil EPfP IMGH LRHS MBlu MBri MGos NLar SCoo SKHP SLim SPoG SSta WFoF WOrn WPat |
| - 'Slender Silhouette' | CAbP LLHF LRHS MAsh MBlu SPoG |
| - 'Stared' | CEnd CLnd CPMA EMil LPan MBri NLar SBir SCoo SPoG WPGP WPat |
| - 'Thea' | CAbP CPMA EMil LRHS MAsh MBlu SBir SSta |
| § - 'Variegata' Overeynder (v) | CBcs CDul CLnd CPMA EBee ELan EMil EPfP LPan LRHS MAsh MGos SBir SLim SPoG SSta WDin WPat |
| - 'White Star' (v) | CPMA |
| - 'Worplesdon' ♀H4 | Widely available |

## *Liriodendron* ✿ (*Magnoliaceae*)

| | |
|---|---|
| 'Chapel Hill' | MBlu |
| ***chinense*** | CBcs CDul CGHE CLnd CMCN CTho EPfP MBlu SKHP SSpi WFar WPGP WPat |
| 'Doc Deforce's Delight' | MBlu MBri |

| | |
|---|---|
| ***tulipifera*** ♀H4 | Widely available |
| - 'Ardis' | CMCN NLar |
| - 'Aureomarginatum' (v) ♀H4 | Widely available |
| - 'Aureum' | CMCN |
| - 'Fastigiatum' | CDoC CDul CEnd CLnd CMCN CTho EBee ECrN EHig ELan EPfP IMGH LPan LRHS MAsh MBlu MBri MGos SBLw SPoG SSta WOrn WPat |
| - 'Glen Gold' | CEnd CMCN MBlu MGos NLar |
| - 'Mediopictum' (v) | CMCN CTho |
| - 'Roodhaan' | NLar |

## *Liriope* ✿ (*Convallariaceae*)

| | |
|---|---|
| HWJ 590 from Vietnam | WPGP |
| from Vietnam | WPGP |
| 'Big Blue' | see *L. muscari* 'Big Blue' |
| 'Blue Spire' | WBod |
| § ***exiliflora*** | CEnd CLAP EBee EGle NLar WFar |
| - 'Ariaka-janshige' (v) | SWat |
| - Silvery Sunproof misapplied | see *L. spicata* 'Gin-ryu', *L. muscari* 'Variegata' |
| § ***gigantea*** | CLAP EBee MBNS SWat |
| ***graminifolia*** misapplied | see *L. muscari* |
| ***hyacinthifolia*** | see *Reineckea carnea* |
| ***kansuensis*** | ERos |
| ***koreana*** | EBee EPPr GCal |
| - B&SWJ 8821 | WCru |
| 'Majestic' | CBct CHar CLAP EBee EGle SPla WBor WFar WHoo |
| § ***muscari*** ♀H4 | Widely available |
| - B&SWJ 561 | WCru |
| - 'Alba' | see *L. muscari* 'Monroe White' |
| § - 'Big Blue' | CBct CKno CLAP COIW CPrp EBee EPPr EPfP EShb LEdu LHop LRHS MRav NLar SUsu SWvt WBor WCFE WMoo |
| - 'Christmas Tree' | CLAP CPrp EPPr MBNS WHoo WMoo |
| - 'Evergreen Giant' | see *L. gigantea* |
| - 'Gold-banded' (v) | CLAP CPrp EBee EGle EMil EPfP NSti SHBN WFar |
| - 'Goldfinger' | EBee EPla WPGP |
| - 'Ingwersen' | CBgR CPrp EBee EBrs ECho ELon LBMP SMeo WHoo WLeb WPnP |
| - 'John Burch' (v) | CBct CLAP CPrp EBee ELon EShb LHop MBNS MCCP NLar SMad WLeb |
| - 'Majestic' misapplied | see *L. exiliflora* |
| § - 'Monroe White' | CBgR CEnd CLAP CPrp EBee EBla ECha ECho EGle EHrv EPfP GKir LAst LEdu MRav NLar SBod SPer SPet SPla SWat WAul WFar |
| - 'Okina' (v) | EBee WCot |
| - 'Paul Aden' | EPfP WPGP |
| - 'Pee Dee Ingot' | EBee |
| - 'Royal Purple' | CBct CHar CLAP EBee ELon EPPr EPfP GQue NBPC NGdn NLar SPla WBor WLeb |
| - 'Silver Ribbon' | CLAP CMoH CPrp EBee EBla EMil EPfP EShb LAst LSRN MBNS NBsh NSti WOut WPGP |
| - 'Silvery Midget' (v) | CPrp SUsu |
| - 'Superba' | WCot |
| § - 'Variegata' (v) | Widely available |
| - variegated, white-flowered (v) | CBcs CDes CFir ECho |
| - 'Webster Wideleaf' | EBee WHoo |
| 'New Wonder' | EHrv LEdu |
| ***platyphylla*** | see *L. muscari* |
| 'Samantha' | CPrp ECha |
| ***spicata*** | CBro EBee ECho ERos SWat |
| - 'Alba' | ECho MRav MTho WTin |
| § - 'Gin-ryu' (v) | CBct CBgR CCge CHar CLAP COIW CPLG EBee ECho ECtt EPPr EWes LEdu LSRN MAvo MCCP MSte NLar SLPl SMad SPer WCot WPGP |
| - 'Silver Dragon' | see *L. spicata* 'Gin-ryu' |

## *Lisianthius* (*Gentianaceae*)

| | |
|---|---|
| ***russelianus*** | see *Eustoma grandiflorum* |

## *Listera* (*Orchidaceae*)

| | |
|---|---|
| ***ovata*** | WHer |

## *Litchi* (*Sapindaceae*)

| | |
|---|---|
| ***chinensis*** | CCCN |

## *Lithocarpus* ✿ (*Fagaceae*)

| | |
|---|---|
| ***edulis*** | CGHE CHEx CPLG SArc WPGP |
| § ***glaber*** | CBcs |
| ***henryi*** | CExc |

## *Lithodora* (*Boraginaceae*)

| | |
|---|---|
| § ***diffusa*** | ECho NLAp SGar SRot WWlt |
| - 'Alba' | CTri ECho EPfP MGos SGar SPer SPoG WFar |
| - 'Baby Barbara' | GKev NLAp |
| - 'Cambridge Blue' | ECho SPer |
| - 'Compacta' | CWCL ECho EWes NLAp NWCA WAbe WPat |
| § - 'Grace Ward' ♀H4 | ECho GAbr MGos NLAp WAbe WFar WPat |
| § - 'Heavenly Blue' ♀H4 | Widely available |
| - 'Inverleith' | ECho EWes LLHF WFar |
| - 'Pete's Favourite' | WAbe |
| - 'Picos' | CMea ECho GKev NLAp NMen WAbe WFar WPat WThu |
| - 'Star' PBR | CMHG EPfP GGar GKev GKir LRHS NHol NLar SCoo SIng SPer SPoG SRot WBod |
| ***fruticosa*** | CArn |
| ***hispidula*** | CWCL |
| x ***intermedia*** | see *Moltkia* x *intermedia* |
| § ***oleifolia*** ♀H4 | CWCL ECho EPot LRHS NBir NMen |
| ***rosmarinifolia*** | CMoH CSpe CWCL WCFE |
| ***zahnii*** | ECho EPot LLHF WFar WPat |
| - 'Azureness' | WAbe |

## *Lithophragma* (*Saxifragaceae*)

| | |
|---|---|
| ***heterophyllum*** new | EBee |
| ***parviflorum*** | CAby CDes CPom EWes MSte MTho NLar NRya NWCA WBor WFar WPnP |

## *Lithospermum* (*Boraginaceae*)

| | |
|---|---|
| ***diffusum*** | see *Lithodora diffusa* |
| ***doerfleri*** | see *Moltkia doerfleri* |
| ***erythrorhizon*** | MSal |
| 'Grace Ward' | see *Lithodora diffusa* 'Grace Ward' |
| 'Heavenly Blue' | see *Lithodora diffusa* 'Heavenly Blue' |
| ***officinale*** | CArn EBWF GBar GPoy MSal NMir |
| ***oleifolium*** | see *Lithodora oleifolia* |
| ***purpureocaeruleum*** | see *Buglossoides purpurocaerulea* |

## *Litsea* (*Lauraceae*)

| | |
|---|---|
| ***glauca*** | see *Neolitsea sericea* |

## *Littonia* (*Colchicaceae*)

| | |
|---|---|
| ***modesta*** | CFee CRHN CSec EBrs ECho |

## *Livistona* (*Arecaceae*)

| | |
|---|---|
| ***australis*** | EAmu LPal |
| ***chinensis*** ♀H1 | CBrP CPHo EAmu LPJP LPal MREP SBig |

| | | |
|---|---|---|
| | ***decipiens*** | CPHo CTrC EAmu LPal |
| | ***mariae*** | EAmu LPal |
| | ***nitida*** | CKob |
| | ***saribus*** | EAmu |

## *Lloydia* (*Liliaceae*)

| | | |
|---|---|---|
| | ***serotina*** | WGwG |
| | ***yunnanensis*** | CExc |

## *Loasa* (*Loasaceae*)

| | | |
|---|---|---|
| | ***triphylla*** var. ***volcanica*** | EWes GCra WSHC |

## *Lobelia* (*Campanulaceae*)

| | | |
|---|---|---|
| | B&SWJ 8220 from Vietnam | WCru |
| | RCB/Arg S-4 | WCot |
| | ***angustifolia*** **new** | CDWL |
| | ***bridgesii*** | CDTJ CPLG EWes GCal GGar GKev LLHF SGar WPGP |
| § | ***cardinalis*** 🏆H3 | CArn CBen CHEx CRWN EBla EHon ELau EMFW EPfP GAbr GKir GMaP LPBA MSal NPer SMrm SPer SPet SPlb SRms SWat SWvt WEas WFar WMAq |
| | - 'Bee's Flame' | CFir CPrp CWGN EAEE EBee EPla GBuc LBMP MAvo MCot MLLN MRav MSte NBre NBsh SAga SUsu SWat |
| § | - 'Elmfeuer' | CMHG EBee EHoe EShb LAst MBNS MSte MWat NGby NLar NPri SMrm SPlb SWvt WFar |
| | - 'Eulalia Berridge' | CAby CSam CWsd EBee ECtt EGle GBuc SMrm WFar WSHC |
| | - subsp. ***graminea*** var. ***multiflora*** | CFir |
| | - 'Illumination' | GBuc |
| § | - 'Queen Victoria' 🏆H3 | Widely available |
| N | - 'Russian Princess' misapplied | WWlt |
| | ***chinensis*** | LLWG |
| | 'Cinnabar Deep Red' | see *L.* x *speciosa* 'Fan Tiefrot' |
| | 'Cinnabar Rose' | see *L.* x *speciosa* 'Fan Zinnoberrosa' |
| | Compliment Blue | see *L.* x *speciosa* 'Kompliment Blau' |
| | Compliment Deep Red | see *L.* x *speciosa* 'Kompliment Tiefrot' |
| | Compliment Purple | see *L.* x *speciosa* 'Kompliment Purpur' |
| | Compliment Scarlet | see *L.* x *speciosa* 'Kompliment Scharlach' |
| | ***dortmanna*** | EMFW |
| | ***erinus*** Big Blue = 'Weslobigblue'PBR | LAst |
| | - Blue Star = 'Wesstar'PBR | LAst |
| | - 'Kathleen Mallard' (d) | CCCN ECtt LAst SWvt |
| | - 'Pink Star' | LAst LSou |
| | - 'Richardii' | see *L. richardsonii* |
| | - 'Sailor Star' **new** | LAst SVil |
| | ***excelsa*** | CSpe EBee EShb GCra GGar MTPN NCGa SEND SPav WFar WSHC |
| | - B&SWJ 9513 | WCru |
| | Fan Deep Red | see *L.* x *speciosa* 'Fan Tiefrot' |
| | Fan Deep Rose | see *L.* x *speciosa* 'Fan Orchidrosa' |
| | Fan Salmon | see *L.* x *speciosa* 'Fan Lachs' |
| | 'Flamingo' | see *L.* x *speciosa* 'Pink Flamingo' |
| | 'Forncett Merry' | NBre |
| | ***fulgens*** | see *L. cardinalis* |
| | - Saint Elmo's Fire | see *L. cardinalis* 'Elmfeuer' |
| | x ***gerardii*** | see *L.* x *speciosa* |
| | ***gibberoa*** | CDTJ CHEx |
| | 'Gladys Lindley' | EBee |
| | ***grandidentata*** F&M 133 | WPGP |
| | 'Hadspen Purple'PBR | see *L.* x *speciosa* 'Hadspen Purple' |
| | ***inflata*** | CArn EBee EOHP GPoy MSal WCHb |
| | ***kalmii*** | WPer |
| | - 'Blue Shadow' | EBla LAst WPtf |
| | 'La Fresco' | EBee |
| | ***laxiflora*** | CHid MTho SAga SHom SPet |
| | - B&SWJ 9064 | WCru |
| | - var. ***angustifolia*** | CAby CDTJ CHEx CPrp CSam ECtt EShb GCal MSte SDnm SMrm SPav SRms SUsu WPrP WWlt |
| | 'Lena' | SWat |
| | ***linnaeoides*** | SPlb |
| | 'Lipstick' | WWlt |
| | ***longifolia*** from Chile | CFee |
| | ***pedunculata*** | see *Pratia pedunculata* |
| | ***perpusilla*** | see *Pratia perpusilla* |
| | ***polyphylla*** | ECtt MSCN SBHP SEND WOut |
| | 'Queen Victoria' | see *L. cardinalis* 'Queen Victoria' |
| | ***regalis*** | WCHb |
| § | ***richardsonii*** 🏆H1+3 | ECtt NBlu SWvt |
| | ***schaeferi*** **new** | EBee |
| | ***seguinii*** B&SWJ 7065 | WCru |
| | ***sessilifolia*** | CDWL CPLG CSec EBee GBuc LPBA MSKA WPer |
| | - B&L 12396 | EMon |
| | ***siphilitica*** | Widely available |
| | - 'Alba' | CEnt CSam EBee EBla EPfP EShb EWld GCal LPBA MLLN SPav SPoG SRms SWat SWvt WBor WCAu WCHb WFar WHoo WHrl WMnd WMoo WPer |
| | - blue-flowered | CSpe SWat SWvt |
| | - 'Rosea' | MNrw |
| | 'Sonia' | SWat |
| § | x ***speciosa*** | CEnt CHFP MHer NBre SMHy SVic SWat WBor WFar WMoo WSHC |
| | - 'Butterfly Blue' | CChe CWsd EBee LFur SPla |
| | - 'Butterfly Rose' | SRot WCHb |
| | - 'Cherry Ripe' | CPrp CWsd GCra LLHF NHol WCHb WEas |
| | - 'Cranberry Crush'PBR | SHar |
| | - dark-leaved | CMHG EBee EGle |
| | - 'Dark Crusader' | CDWL CPrp CTca CWGN CWsd EAEE EBee ECGP ECtt EGle ELan EShb LAst LBMP LRHS MCot MSCN NHol SPla SWat WCHb WEas WMnd |
| | - 'Fan Blau' | NBlu WHil |
| | - 'Fan Burgundy' | CEnt CWCL EWll WHil |
| § | - 'Fan Lachs' **new** | WHil |
| § | - 'Fan Orchidrosa' 🏆H3-4 | EPfP EShb NGdn SRot SUsu |
| | - 'Fan Scharlach' 🏆H3-4 | EHon EShb MAvo MGos NLar SGar SHar SRot SWvt WDyG WHil |
| § | - 'Fan Tiefrot' 🏆H3-4 | CChe CDWL COlW CWsd MSCN MWea NBlu NCGa SAga SHar SRms SUsu SWat SWvt WCHb WPer |
| § | - 'Fan Zinnoberrosa' 🏆H3-4 | CEnt CFir CMMP EHon LAst LRHS MHar SRms SRot SWvt WCHb WMoo WPer |
| | - 'Grape Knee-high' | EBee EPfP GCra LLHF LSRN NCGa SPoG SWat |
| § | - 'Hadspen Purple'PBR | CDWL CWCL CWGN EBee EGle ELan EPfP EWTr LSRN MBri MCCP MCot MWea NCGa NCob NSti SHar SPoG SWat WOVN WWlt |
| | - 'Kimbridge Beet' | CMac |
| § | - 'Kompliment Blau' | CFir CWat LRHS SWvt WPer |
| * | - 'Kompliment Pale Pink' | EShb |
| § | - 'Kompliment Purpur' | EShb MNrw SWvt |
| § | - 'Kompliment Scharlach' 🏆H3-4 | CSWP CTca CWsd EBee EPfP EShb LFur LHop LRHS MNrw NHol NPer SPad SPer SWvt WCHb WFar WMnd WPer WWlt |
| § | - 'Kompliment Tiefrot' | CWat EWll MNrw MWat SEND SWvt WPer |
| | - 'Monet Moment' | CBow EBee EBla EWes NBre NCGa SPoG |

| | | |
|---|---|---|
| | - 'Pauline' | ECtt |
| | - 'Pink Elephant' ♀H4 | CBow CChe CSWP CWCL CWsd EBee GCra MDKP NBre SHar WFar WRha |
| § | - 'Pink Flamingo' | CBen CMMP EBee EBla EBrs LRHS SPer SWat WCHb WFar WSHC WShi |
| | - 'Purple Towers' | EBee NBre |
| | - purple-flowered | MAvo |
| | - 'Rosenkavalier' | EBee ECtt LRHS NGby WFar |
| | - 'Ruby Slippers' | CBcs CWCL EBee EBrs ECtt ELan EPfP IPot LAst LSRN MWea SHGN SMrs SPoG SUsu SWat WFar |
| N | - 'Russian Princess' purple-flowered | Widely available |
| | - 'Sparkle deVine' | SMrm WFar |
| | - 'Tania' | Widely available |
| | - Tresahor Series | CHEx |
| § | - 'Vedrariensis' | Widely available |
| | - 'Wildwood Splendor' | NBre WFar |
| | - 'Will Scarlet' | SAga |
| | ***tenuior*** **new** | CSec |
| | ***treadwellii*** | see *Pratia angulata* 'Treadwellii' |
| | ***tupa*** | Widely available |
| | - JCA 12527 | MTPN WCot |
| | - Archibald's form | CPLG GCra |
| | ***urens*** | WPGP |
| | ***valida*** | EBee LHop SGar SWvt WFar |
| | ***vedrariensis*** | see *L.* x *speciosa* 'Vedrariensis' |
| | White Star = 'Weslowei'PBR | LSou |
| | 'Zinnoberrosa' | see *L.* x *speciosa* 'Fan Zinnoberrosa' |

## *Loeselia* (*Polemoniaceae*)

| | |
|---|---|
| ***mexicana*** | CHll |

## loganberry see *Rubus* x *loganobaccus*

## *Lomandra* (*Lomandraceae*)

| | |
|---|---|
| ***confertifolia*** | ECou |
| - 'Wingarra' | GBin MAvo |
| ***filiformis*** Savanna Blue = 'Lfm500' **new** | NOak |
| ***hystrix*** | SPlb |
| 'Little Con' | CBcs |
| 'Little Pal' | CBcs |
| ***longifolia*** | ECou GCal LEdu SPlb |
| - 'Kulnura' | ECou |
| - 'Orford' | ECou |
| - Tanika = 'Lm300'PBR | EBee EPPr GBin GGar LRHS NBsh NOak SUsu WBor |

## *Lomaria* see *Blechnum*

## *Lomatia* (*Proteaceae*)

| | | |
|---|---|---|
| | ***dentata*** | LRHS |
| | ***ferruginea*** | CBcs CHEx CTrG CWsd EPfP GBin GGal IDee SAPC SArc SKHP WCru |
| | ***fraseri*** | EPfP LHop SKHP SSpi |
| | ***longifolia*** | see *L. myricoides* |
| § | ***myricoides*** | CBcs CCCN CDoC CPSs CTrG CTsd EBee ELan EPfP LRHS MBri NLar SAPC SArc SKHP SLon SPer SSpi WPGP |
| | ***silaifolia*** | EPfP |
| | ***tinctoria*** | CBcs CDoC CPSs EPfP LRHS NLar SArc SSpi |

## *Lomatium* (*Apiaceae*)

| | |
|---|---|
| ***dissectum*** | NBhm |
| ***grayi*** | SPhx |
| ***utriculatum*** | MSal |

## *Lonicera* ✿ (*Caprifoliaceae*)

| | | |
|---|---|---|
| | B&SWJ 2654 from Sikkim | WCru |
| | F&M 207 **new** | WPGP |
| § | ***acuminata*** | EBee LRHS WGwG WPnP |
| | - B&SWJ 3480 | WCru |
| | ***alberti*** | CDul GBin MBNS MMuc MRav SLon WGwG |
| | ***alseuosmoides*** | EBee GBin IArd SAga SEND SLon SPla SPoG WCru WPGP WSHC |
| | x ***americana*** misapplied | see *L.* x *italica* Tausch |
| § | x ***americana*** (Miller) K. Koch | CBcs CRHN EPfP LRHS MAsh MGos MRav MWhi NWea SDix SGar SLim SPla WGwG WMoo |
| § | x ***brownii*** 'Dropmore Scarlet' | Widely available |
| | - 'Fuchsioides' misapplied | see *L.* x *brownii* 'Dropmore Scarlet' |
| | - 'Fuchsioides' K. Koch | WSHC |
| | ***caerulea*** | MRav STre |
| | - var. ***altaica*** | LEdu |
| | - var. ***edulis*** | CAgr LEdu |
| | - subsp. ***kamtschatica*** | CAgr NLar |
| § | ***caprifolium*** ♀H4 | CDoC CRHN EBee ELan EPfP LBuc LFol LRHS MAsh MBar MLan NBea SHBN SPer WCot |
| | - 'Anna Fletcher' | CRHN CSPN LSRN NHaw WCFE |
| | - f. ***pauciflora*** | see *L.* x *italica* Tausch |
| | ***chaetocarpa*** | WSHC |
| | ***chamissoi*** | NLar |
| | 'Clavey's Dwarf' | see *L.* x *xylosteoides* 'Clavey's Dwarf' |
| | 'Copper Beauty'PBR | CWGN LBuc |
| | ***crassifolia*** | MBri WCot |
| | ***deflexicalyx*** | EPfP NLar |
| | 'Early Cream' | see *L. caprifolium* |
| | ***elisae*** | CAbP EPfP SSpi WPat |
| | ***etrusca*** | LAst MRav |
| | - 'Donald Waterer' ♀H4 | CRHN EBee EPfP LHop LRHS LSRN NLar SPla WFar WGor |
| | - 'Michael Rosse' | EBee ELan EMil IArd LRHS MBNS MSte SKHP SRms |
| | - 'Superba' ♀H4 | CRHN EBee ECtt ELan EPfP LRHS MLLN NLar SEND SLim SPla WFar WSHC |
| | ***flexuosa*** | see *L. japonica* var. *repens* |
| | ***fragrantissima*** | Widely available |
| | ***giraldii*** misapplied | see *L. acuminata* |
| | ***giraldii*** Rehder | EBee EPfP MAsh MRav SLim |
| | ***glabrata*** | SCoo SLim |
| | - B&SWJ 2150 | WCru |
| | 'Golden Trumpet' | CWGN EBee LRHS SKHP |
| | ***gracilis*** | MBlu |
| | ***grata*** | see *L.* x *americana* (Miller) K. Koch |
| | x ***heckrottii*** | CDoC CRHN CSBt EBee ECtt MBar MGan MGos NBea NBlu NLar NSti WDin |
| § | - 'American Beauty' **new** | EBee |
| | - 'Gold Flame' misapplied | see *L.* x *heckrottii* 'American Beauty' |
| | - 'Gold Flame' ambig. | LSRN |
| | - 'Gold Flame' | CDul CMac EBee ELan EPfP GKir LAst LBuc LCro LPan LRHS MAsh MBar MBri MGos MRav NBea NBlu NHol SHBN SLim SPer SRms WBod WDin WFar WMoo WSHC |
| § | ***henryi*** | Widely available |
| | - B&SWJ 8109 | WCru |
| | - Sich 1489 | WPGP |
| | - 'Copper Beauty' | CFir EBee EQua LAst LHop LSRN MAsh MBlu MGos MRav NBPN NCGa NLar SLon SPoG WDin WPGP |
| | - var. ***subcoriacea*** | see *L. henryi* |

| | | |
|---|---|---|
| | ***hildebrandiana*** | CCCN EMil SOWG WPGP |
| | 'Hill House' | CHll |
| | 'Honey Baby' PBR | COlW EBee LLHF MAsh MBlu MBri MGos MRav NHol WPat |
| | ***implexa*** | MAsh WSHC |
| | ***insularis*** | see *L. morrowii* |
| | ***involucrata*** | CFee CMCN CMHG CPLG CPMA CWib GQui LHop MBNS MBar MBlu NChi NHol SPer WBod WCFE WDin WFar |
| | - var. ***ledebourii*** | CBgR EBee ELan EPfP GKir LAst LLHF SDys |
| | x ***italica*** ambig. | LFol LHop NPer SEND |
| § | x ***italica*** Tausch ♀H4 | COlW CRHN CSam CTri CWSG ECtt LAst LBMP LEdu LFol MSwo NPer NSti SCoo SLim SPer WDin WFar WPnn |
| § | - Harlequin = 'Sherlite' PBR (v) | CSPN EHoe EPfP LAst LHop LRHS LSRN MGos NBea NSti SGar SLim SPer SPlb SPoG SWvt |
| | ***japonica*** | CMen |
| § | - 'Aureoreticulata' (v) | CDul CMac CWib EBee ECrN EHoe ELan EPfP MBar MBri MGos MRav MWhi NPer SGar SHBN SPer SPet SRms STre WDin WEas WFar WMoo |
| | - 'Cream Cascade' | COlW EBee EMil LAst MGos MLLN MSwo NLar SCoo |
| | - 'Dart's Acumen' | CRHN |
| | - 'Dart's World' | EBee MAsh MBri SPla WFar |
| | - 'Halliana' ♀H4 | Widely available |
| | - 'Hall's Prolific' | Widely available |
| § | - 'Horwood Gem' (v) | EBee ECtt LFol LSRN MGos NLar SCoo WFar |
| | - 'Maskerade' | EBee LLHF NBro |
| | - 'Mint Crisp' PBR (v) | CBow CFwr CSBt CWGN EBee ECrN ELan EPfP LAst LRHS LSRN MBri MGos NLar SPad SPer SPoG SWvt WDin WFar |
| | - 'Peter Adams' | see *L. japonica* 'Horwood Gem' |
| | - 'Red World' | EBee |
| § | - var. ***repens*** ♀H4 | Widely available |
| | - 'Variegata' | see *L. japonica* 'Aureoreticulata' |
| | ***korolkowii*** | CBgR CPMA CSam EBee EPfP MBNS MWte NBir SEND SLon SPla SPoG WCFE WHCG WLeb WPat WSHC |
| | - 'Blue Velvet' **new** | CAgr NLar |
| | - var. ***zabelii*** misapplied | see *L. tatarica* 'Zabelii' |
| | - var. ***zabelii*** (Rehder) Rehder | ELan |
| | ***lanceolata*** BWJ 7935 **new** | WCru |
| | 'Little Honey' **new** | EMil |
| | ***maackii*** | CHll CMCN CPMA EBee EPfP MBri MRav NLar WHCG |
| | - f. ***podocarpa*** | SPoG |
| * | ***macgregorii*** | CMCN |
| | 'Mandarin' | CDoC CWSG EBee ELan GKir LBuc LRHS MAsh MBlu MGos NCGa NLar SCoo SLim SPer SSta SWvt WSHC |
| | ***maximowiczii*** var. ***sachalinensis*** | NLar |
| § | ***morrowii*** | CMCN GAuc |
| | ***myrtillus*** | GAuc NLar |
| | ***nitida*** | CBcs CCVT CDul CMen CSBt CTri ECrN EMac EPfP MRav NWea SHBN SPer SPoG STre WDin WFar WHar |
| | - 'Baggesen's Gold' ♀H4 | Widely available |
| | - 'Cumbrian Calypso' (v) | NPro |
| | - 'Eden Spring' | NPro |
| | - Edmée Gold = 'Briloni' PBR | EPfP MAsh |
| | - 'Elegant' | LBuc WDin |
| | - 'Ernest Wilson' | MBar NBlu |
| | - 'Fertilis' | SPer |
| | - 'Hohenheimer Findling' | NLar |
| | - 'Lemon Beauty' (v) | CDoC CSBt EBee EHoe EPfP EPla EShb LAst LBMP LHop LSRN MBNS MBar MGos MNHC NBir NHol NPri NScw SLPl SPer SRGP SWvt WDin WFar WHar WMoo |
| | - 'Lemon Queen' | CWib ELan MSwo |
| | - 'Lemon Spreader' | CBcs |
| § | - 'Maigrün' | CBcs CDul EMil EPfP MBri MSwo NPro SPer SWvt WDin WFar |
| | - Maygreen | see *L. nitida* 'Maigrün' |
| | - 'Red Tips' | EBee EHoe EMil EPfP EPla MGos NHol SCoo WDin WFar WMoo |
| | - 'Silver Beauty' (v) | CMHG CWib EBee ECrN EHig EHoe EPfP LAst LHop MBar MGos MLHP MRav MSwo NHol SAga SGar SPer SPlb SPoG SRms SWvt WDin WFar WMoo |
| * | - 'Silver Cloud' | NHol |
| | - 'Silver Lining' | see *L. pileata* 'Silver Lining' |
| | - 'Twiggy' (v) | CDoC CElw EDAr EHoe EMil LBuc LHop MAsh MBrN NHol NLar NPro WLeb |
| | ***periclymenum*** | CArn CDul CRWN CTri EBWF GKir GPoy MCot MDun MHer MLHP MRav NLar NSco NWea SPlb WDin WHCG WPnn WSFF |
| | - 'Belgica' misapplied | see *L.* x *italica* Tausch |
| | - 'Belgica' | Widely available |
| | - 'Florida' | see *L. periclymenum* 'Serotina' |
| | - 'Graham Thomas' ♀H4 | Widely available |
| | - 'Harlequin' PBR | see *L.* x *italica* Harlequin = 'Sherlite' |
| | - 'Heaven Scent' | LBuc LSRN MGos MNHC NLar WFar WGwG WPnn |
| | - 'Honeybush' | CDoC CPMA CSPN CWGN MAsh MBlu MBri NHol NPri SLim WMoo |
| | - 'La Gasnérie' | EBee SLim WPnn |
| | - 'Munster' | EBee WPnn WSHC |
| | - 'Purple Queen' | CChe |
| | - 'Red Gables' | CWan EBee LSRN MAsh MBNS MGos MRav MSte NLar SCoo SEND SLim SPla WCot WGor WKif WPat WPnn |
| | - 'Scentsation' PBR | MAsh MBri SCoo SLon SPoG |
| N | - 'Serotina' ♀H4 | Widely available |
| * | - ***sulphurea*** | WFar |
| | - 'Sweet Sue' | CRHN CSPN EBee ECtt ELan EPfP LAst LBuc LFol LRHS MAsh MBNS MBri MGos MLHP MSte MSwo NHol NSti SCoo SPoG SWvt WFar WMoo WPnP |
| | - 'Winchester' | EBee |
| | ***pileata*** | Widely available |
| | - 'Moss Green' | CDoC NBlu |
| | - 'Pilot' | SLPl |
| § | - 'Silver Lining' (v) | EPla SAga |
| | - 'Stockholm' | SLPl |
| | ***pilosa*** Maxim. | see *L. strophiophora* |
| | x ***purpusii*** | CBgR CDoC CPSs CRHN CTri CWSG CWib EBee ECrN EPfP EWTr GKir MBNS MBar MGos MLHP MWat NBea SPer SPla SPoG SRms WBod WCFE WFar WHCG WSHC |
| | - 'Winter Beauty' ♀H4 | Widely available |
| | ***quinquelocularis*** f. ***translucens*** | MBlu |
| | ***ramosissima*** | NLar |
| | ***rupicola*** var. ***syringantha*** | see *L. syringantha* |
| | ***saccata*** | CPMA EPfP |

| | | |
|---|---|---|
| | ***sempervirens*** ♀H4 | CRHN CSBt EPfP MBNS WFar WSHC |
| | - 'Cedar Lane' **new** | LRHS |
| | - 'Dropmore Scarlet' | see *L.* x *brownii* 'Dropmore Scarlet' |
| | - 'Leo' | CSPN CWGN |
| N | - f. ***sulphurea*** | EBee EPfP LRHS NBea WSHC |
| | - - 'John Clayton' | LRHS |
| | ***setifera*** 'Daphnis' | EPfP |
| | ***similis*** var. ***delavayi*** ♀H4 | CChe CRHN CSPN CWGN EBee ECrN ELan EPfP LRHS MAsh MBri MLan MNHC MRav NBea NSti SDix SEND SLPl SPla SPoG WCot WFar WGwG WPGP WSHC |
| | 'Simonet' | EBee |
| | 'Spring Bouquet' **new** | LRHS |
| | ***standishii*** | CTri EBee EHig MGos MRav WDin WFar WHCG WRha |
| | - 'Budapest' | MBlu MBri MGos WPat |
| | ***stenantha*** | NLar |
| | 'Stone Green' | MGos |
| § | ***strophiophora*** | EBee |
| | ***subaequalis*** | SKHP |
| | - Og 93.329 **new** | WPGP |
| § | ***syringantha*** | CArn CDul CRHN CSam EBee ELan EPfP GGar GKir LAst LEdu MAsh MBlu MGos MRav MWhi NBea NHol NPro SHBN SLPl SPer SPla WCFE WDin WFar WHCG WSHC |
| | - 'Grandiflora' | GQui SLon |
| | ***tatarica*** | CMCN CWib EBee EHig MRav WFar WHCG |
| | - 'Alba' | CPMA |
| | - 'Arnold Red' | CBcs EBee ELan EMil EPfP MBlu NBlu NLar WDin |
| | - 'Hack's Red' | CWib EBee EHig EMil EPfP EWTr GQui LHop LSou MRav MWea SAga SCoo SKHP SPer SWvt WCot WDin WFar WHCG |
| | - 'Rosea' | WCot |
| § | - 'Zabelii' | EPfP |
| | x ***tellmanniana*** | Widely available |
| | - 'Joan Sayers' | EBee LSRN MBNS SCoo SLim WCFE |
| | ***thibetica*** | MBlu SPer WFar |
| | ***tianschanica*** | GAuc |
| | ***tragophylla*** ♀H4 | CDoC CSBt EBee ELan EPfP IDee LRHS LSRN MAsh MBNS MBlu MBri MRav SCoo SLim SPer SPoG SSpi SWvt WDin WSHC |
| | - 'Maurice Foster' | EBee EMil |
| | - 'Pharaoh's Trumpet' | EPfP LRHS MAsh MBri SLon SSpi SSta |
| | ***vesicaria*** | EMon |
| | ***webbiana*** | ELan |
| | x ***xylosteoides*** | MRav WFar |
| § | - 'Clavey's Dwarf' | EBee MBlu NHol SLPl |
| | ***xylosteum*** | CArn NLar WFar |

## *Lopezia* (*Onagraceae*)

| | | |
|---|---|---|
| | ***racemosa*** | CSpe |

## *Lophomyrtus* (*Myrtaceae*)

| | | |
|---|---|---|
| § | ***bullata*** | CAbP CDTJ CTrC CTsd EBee ECou GQui SPer WCHb WPic |
| | - 'Matai Bay' | CBcs CTrC EBee |
| § | x ***ralphii*** | MHer WCHb WPic |
| | - 'Gloriosa' (v) | CDoC CTrC |
| | - 'Kathryn' | CBcs CDoC EBee EMil IDee NLar SKHP SPoG SRGP SSpi |
| | - 'Little Star' (v) | CBcs CDoC CTrC EBee GBri LRHS SKHP SPoG WPat |
| | - 'Multicolor' (v) | CBcs CTrC EBee EMil IDee |
| | - 'Pixie' | CAbP CBcs CDoC CTrC SPoG WPat |
| | - 'Red Dragon' | CBcs CTrC CTsd EBee GBri IDee LSou WFar WPat |
| | - 'Red Pixie' | CDoC |
| § | - 'Traversii' (v) | MGos SPoG |
| | - 'Tricolor' (v) | WFar |
| | - 'Variegata' (v) | MHer |
| | - 'Wild Cherry' | CBcs CTrC EBee |

## *Lophosoria* (*Dicksoniaceae*)

| | | |
|---|---|---|
| | ***quadripinnata*** | CDTJ CFir EBee WRic |

## *Lophospermum* (*Scrophulariaceae*)

| | | |
|---|---|---|
| § | ***erubescens*** ♀H2-3 | CHEx CHal CRHN MSte SBch SGar WPtf |
| | 'Magic Dragon' | MCCP |
| § | 'Red Dragon' | EShb SBch SGar |
| § | ***scandens*** | CCCN CRHN CSec ELan |
| § | - 'Pink Ice' | SOWG |

## loquat see *Eriobotrya japonica*

## *Loropetalum* (*Hamamelidaceae*)

| | | |
|---|---|---|
| | ***chinense*** | CWib |
| | - 'China Pink' | CBcs |
| | - 'Ming Dynasty' | CAbP EBee EMil MGos MREP SSta |
| | - f. ***rubrum*** | CMen CPLG CWib |
| | - - 'Blush' | CBgR CPMA |
| | - - 'Burgundy' | WCot |
| | - - 'Daybreak's Flame' | CBcs CPMA CPen EBee NBPN SSta WGob |
| | - - 'Fire Dance' | CAbP CBgR CDoC CHll CMil CPMA CPen EBee EPfP IDee MGos SEND SPoG SSta SWvt WBrE WFar WGwG WPat |
| | - - 'Pipa's Red' | CPen |
| | - 'Snowdance' | CAbP EBee |
| | - 'Tang Dynasty' | CPen EMil MGos SEND SSta |

## *Lotus* (*Papilionaceae*)

| | | |
|---|---|---|
| | ***berthelotii*** | CCCN CDTJ CFee CHEx CSpe ECtt ELan EOHP MCot SPet SPoG WCor |
| | - deep red-flowered ♀H1+3 | SWvt |
| | ***berthelotii*** x ***maculatus*** ♀H1+3 | CCCN MSCN |
| | ***corniculatus*** | CArn EBWF MCoo MHer NLan NMir NSco NTHB SECG SIde WAbe WSFF |
| | - 'Plenus' (d) | MTho NLar WPer |
| * | 'Fire Vine' (*berthelotii* x *maculatus*) | EShb LAst NPri |
| | 'Gold Flash' | CHEx LAst |
| | ***hirsutus*** ♀H3-4 | Widely available |
| | - 'Brimstone' (v) | CWib ECtt EGoo LHop LSou SPer SWvt |
| | - dwarf | LHop |
| | - 'Little Boy Blue' | EBee LRHS LSou MAsh SKHP SPoG |
| | - 'Lois' | EBee LHop MDKP WPGP |
| | ***maculatus*** | EOHP SOWG SPet |
| | ***maritimus*** | SRot |
| | ***pedunculatus*** | see *L. uliginosus* |
| | ***pentaphyllus*** | NLar |
| | 'Red Flash' | LAst |
| | ***tetragonolobus*** | SRot |
| § | ***uliginosus*** | EBWF MCoo NMir NSco WSFF |

## lovage see *Levisticum officinale*

## *Luculia* (*Rubiaceae*)

| | | |
|---|---|---|
| | ***gratissima*** ♀H1-2 | CSec |

## *Ludwigia* (*Onagraceae*)

| | | |
|---|---|---|
| | ***uruguayensis*** | LPBA |

## *Luetkea* (*Rosaceae*)

| | | |
|---|---|---|
| | ***pectinata*** | NRya WAbe |

## *Luma* (*Myrtaceae*)

| | | |
|---|---|---|
| § | ***apiculata*** ♀H3 | Widely available |
| § | - 'Glanleam Gold' (v) ♀H3 | Widely available |
| | - 'Saint Hilary' (v) **new** | WPic |
| | - 'Variegata' (v) | CMHG CTri ISea NHol SAga SLim |
| § | ***chequen*** | CBcs CFee EBee GGar IDee LEdu MHer NLar WBrE WCHb WFar WJek WMoo WPic |

## *Lunaria* (*Brassicaceae*)

| | | |
|---|---|---|
| § | ***annua*** | CTca GAbr MNHC NPri SIde SWat WHer WSFF |
| | - var. ***albiflora*** ♀H4 | CSec NBir SWat |
| I | - - 'Alba Variegata' (v) | CCge CSpe MNFA WBrk WHil WTin |
| | - 'Chedglow' **new** | CNat |
| | - 'Corfu Blue' | CSpe |
| | - 'Ken Aslet' | NHol |
| | - 'Luckington' | CNat |
| | - 'Munstead Purple' | CSpe |
| | - 'Variegata' (v) | MTho NBir SWat WEas WHer |
| | - violet-flowered | NBir |
| | ***biennis*** | see *L. annua* |
| | ***rediviva*** | Widely available |
| | - 'Partway White' | CMil |

## *Lunathyrium* (*Woodsiaceae*)

| | | |
|---|---|---|
| | ***pycnosorum*** | WRic |

## *Lupinus* ✿ (*Papilionaceae*)

| | | |
|---|---|---|
| | B&SWJ 10309 from Guatemala **new** | WCru |
| | 'African Sunset' | CWCL |
| | 'Amber Glow' | CWCL |
| | 'Animal' | CWCL |
| | ***arboreus*** ♀H4 | Widely available |
| | - ***albus*** | CSpe CWib SHGN |
| | - 'Barton-on-Sea' | CSec MAsh SPla |
| | - 'Blue Boy' | ELan ELon NSti SPla |
| | - blue-flowered | CFwr CHar CWCL CWib MAsh MCCP MCot MLHP NBPC NLar NPri SEND SPer SPlb SPoG SWvt WBrE WFar |
| | - 'Mauve Queen' | CHEx CSec SHGN |
| | - prostrate | MDKP MMHG |
| | - 'Snow Queen' | CSec MCCP NBur SPer SPoG |
| | - 'Sulphur Yellow' | SHGN SWvt |
| | - white-flowered | CWCL GGar |
| | - yellow and blue-flowered | NBir SRkn |
| | - yellow-flowered | GGar MAsh MLHP |
| | ***arboreus* x *variicolor*** | CHid |
| | ***arcticus*** | CSpe EBee EDif |
| | ***argenteus*** var. ***depressus*** | see *L. argenteus* var. *utahensis*, *L. argenteus* var. *rubricaulis* |
| § | - var. ***rubricaulis*** **new** | CWCL |
| § | - var. ***utahensis*** | EBee GKev |
| | 'Aston Villa' | CWCL |
| | 'Avalon' | CWCL |
| | Band of Nobles Series | ECtt MAvo WFar |
| | 'Beefeater' **new** | CWCL |
| | 'Beryl, Viscountess Cowdray' | EMon |
| | 'Bishop's Tipple' | CWCL EWes |
| | 'Blossom' | LCro |
| | 'Blue Moon' | CWCL |
| | 'Blue Streak' | CWCL |
| | 'Blueberry Pie' | CWCL |
| | ***bogotensis*** B&SWJ 10761 | WCru |
| | 'Brimstone' **new** | CWCL |
| | 'Bruiser' | CWCL |
| | 'Bubblegum' | CWCL |
| | 'Carmen' **new** | CWCL |
| | 'Casanova' | CWCL |
| | 'Cashmere Cream' | CWCL |
| | 'Chameleon' | CWCL LCro |
| | ***chamissonis*** | CHid CHll CSpe CWCL EBee EHrv EWes LHop LRHS MAsh MTho SEND SMrm SPer SPla SPoG SUsu WFar |
| | 'Chandelier' (Band of Nobles Series) | Widely available |
| | 'Copperlight' | CWCL |
| | ***costaricensis*** B&SWJ 10487 **new** | WCru |
| | ***densiflorus*** var. ***aureus*** | see *L. microcarpus* var. *densiflorus* |
| | 'Desert Sun' | CWCL |
| | 'Dolly Mixture' | CWCL |
| | 'Dreaming Spires' | CWCL |
| | Dwarf Gallery hybrids | GKir |
| | 'Dwarf Lulu' | see *L.* 'Lulu' |
| | Gallery Series | CSBt LAst MAvo NBlu SCoo SGar SPlb WFar |
| | - 'Gallery Blue' | ECtt EPfP GKir LSRN LSou NDlv NLar NNor NPri NVic SCoo SMrm SPoG WFar |
| | - 'Gallery Pink' | EPfP GKir LRHS LSou NDlv NLar NPri NVic SCoo SPla SPoG WFar |
| | - 'Gallery Red' | ECtt EPfP GKir LRHS NDlv NLar NPri NVic SCoo SMrm SPla SPoG WFar |
| | - 'Gallery Rose' | GKir LSRN SPoG |
| | - 'Gallery White' | EPfP GKir LRHS NDlv NLar NPri NVic SCoo SMrm SPla SPoG WFar |
| | - 'Gallery Yellow' | ECtt EPfP LRHS LSou NDlv NLar NPri NVic SCoo SMrm SPla SPoG |
| | 'Garden Gnome' | WMoo |
| | 'Gladiator' | CWCL |
| | 'Imperial Robe' | CWCL |
| | 'Ivory Chiffon' | CWCL LCro |
| | 'Le Gentilhomme' (Band of Nobles Series) **new** | MCot |
| § | 'Lulu' | ECtt LAst LRHS MRav MWat NBlu SPer SPoG SWvt WFar WMoo WRHF |
| | 'Manhattan Lights' | LCro NLar |
| § | ***microcarpus*** var. ***densiflorus*** | CWCL |
| | Minarette Group | CTri ECtt SPet SPoG SRms WFar |
| | 'Morello Cherry' | MNHC |
| | ***mutabilis*** 'Sunrise' **new** | MCot |
| | 'My Castle' (Band of Nobles Series) | Widely available |
| | 'Neptune' | CWCL |
| | 'Noble Maiden' (Band of Nobles Series) | CBcs CSBt CTri EBee ECtt ELan EPfP GKir LRHS LSRN MBri MCot MRav MWat NGBl NMir NPri SMrm SPad SPer SPoG SWal SWvt WCAu WFar WHil WMnd WMoo |
| | ***nootkatensis*** | GKir LDai |
| | 'Pauly' | CWCL |
| | 'Pen and Ink' **new** | CWCL |
| | 'Persian Slipper' | NLar |
| | 'Plummy Blue' | EDif MCCP MWea |
| | 'Pluto' **new** | CWCL |
| | 'Polar Princess' | CWCL EAEE EWes GBin SUsu SWat |
| | ***polyphyllus*** | CSec MWhi |
| | ***propinquus*** | CEnt CSec SPhx |
| | 'Queen of Hearts' | CWCL |
| | 'Red Arrow' | CWCL |
| | 'Redhead' | CWCL |
| | 'Rooster' **new** | CWCL |
| | 'Rote Flamme' | EWes SMrm |
| | 'Ruby Lantern' | CWCL |
| | Russell hybrids | CSBt EPfP LAst LHop MHer MLHP NBlu SEND SPet SPlb SRms SVic SWvt WBor WFar |
| | 'Saint George' | CWCL |

| | |
|---|---|
| 'Salmon Star' | LCro |
| 'Sand Pink' | CWCL EWes |
| 'Snowgoose' | CWCL |
| 'Sparky' | CWCL |
| 'Storm' | CWCL |
| ***succulentus*** | CWCL |
| 'Tequila Flame' | CWCL LCro |
| 'Terracotta' | CWCL |
| ***texensis*** | CSpe CWCL |
| - 'Almo Fire' | CWCL |
| 'The Chatelaine' (Band of Nobles Series) | Widely available |
| 'The Governor' (Band of Nobles Series) | Widely available |
| 'The Page' (Band of Nobles Series) | CBcs EBee ELan EPfP GKir LRHS LSRN MBri MCot MNHC MRav MWat NMir NPri SMrm SPer SPoG SWal SWvt WBVN WFar WMnd WMoo |
| 'Thundercloud' | CDes SMrm |
| 'Towering Inferno' **new** | CWCL |
| 'Tutti Frutti' | LAst MNHC SHGN WRos |
| ***variicolor*** | CArn CHid CSpe CSsd LDai MLLN SMad WBrk WHoo |

# *Luzula* (*Juncaceae*)

| | |
|---|---|
| ***alpinopilosa*** | EPPr GFor MMHG |
| x ***borreri*** | EPPr |
| - 'Botany Bay' (v) | ECtt EMon EPPr EPla GBin NHol WMoo |
| ***campestris*** | EBWF |
| ***forsteri*** | EBWF |
| ***lactea*** | EPPr |
| ***lutea*** | GFor |
| ***luzuloides*** | GFor GQui NBre NLar WPer WPtf |
| - 'Schneehäschen' | EBee EMon EWsh GBin GCal WPrP |
| ***maxima*** | see *L. sylvatica* |
| ***multiflora*** | EBWF |
| ***nivalis*** | GAbr GKir |
| ***nivea*** | Widely available |
| - 'Schattenkind' **new** | EBee |
| ***oligantha*** **new** | CSec |
| ***pilosa*** | EBWF EPla GCal NNor |
| - 'Igel' | EBee GBin SLPl |
| ***purpureosplendens*** | EMon |
| 'Ruby Stiletto' | EBee |
| ***rufa*** | ECou |
| § ***sylvatica*** | CHEx CRWN CRow CSWP CSec EBWF ELan EPPr EPfP EPla GKir LEdu MCot MLLN MMoz MMuc MRav NBro NOrc WDin WFar WHer WPGP WShi |
| - from Tatra Mountains, Czechoslovakia | EPPr |
| - 'A. Rutherford' | see *L. sylvatica* 'Taggart's Cream' |
| - 'Aurea' | Widely available |
| - 'Aureomarginata' | see *L. sylvatica* 'Marginata' |
| I - 'Auslese' | EPPr GBin GFor NLar NNor WMoo |
| - 'Barcode' (v) | CNat |
| - 'Bromel' | EBee |
| - 'Hohe Tatra' | Widely available |
| § - 'Marginata' (v) | Widely available |
| * - f. ***nova*** | ELon EPPr |
| - 'Onderbos' **new** | EBee |
| § - 'Taggart's Cream' (v) | CElw CRow EBee EBrs EHoe EPla GGar MBNS NBid NHol SApp WDyG WLeb WMoo WPrP |
| - 'Tauernpass' | EBee EHoe EPPr EPla GCal NHol |
| - 'Wäldler' | EPPr MBNS NHol |
| - 'Waulkmill Bay' | SLPl |
| ***ulophylla*** | CFir ECou GBin GFor NBre NLar NWCA |

# *Luzuriaga* (*Philesiaceae*)

| | |
|---|---|
| ***radicans*** | CCCN CFee ERos IBlr WCru WFar WSHC |

# *Lychnis* (*Caryophyllaceae*)

| | |
|---|---|
| ***alpina*** | CSec EBee ECho EDAr EPfP GKev GKir GMaP MSCN NBlu NNor NVic SGar WFar WPer |
| - 'Alba' | GKev GKir NBir |
| - 'Rosea' | NBir |
| - var. ***serpentinicola*** | CSec |
| - 'Snow Flurry' | EDAr GKev NLar |
| § x ***arkwrightii*** | ECha ELan NBre NNor SRot WFar WWlt |
| - 'Orange Zwerg' | CWCL EBee LAst LBMP LSou SMrm SPhx WHal WHlf |
| - 'Vesuvius' | CBcs CMac EAEE EBee EPfP GGar GKir LAst LBMP MNrw MWat NBPN NBir NBlu NNor SEND SPad SPav SPer SPoG SRms STes WMnd WPer |
| ***chalcedonica*** ♀H4 | Widely available |
| - var. ***albiflora*** | EBee LAst LRHS NBro SPer WBrk WFar WMoo WPer |
| - - 'Snow White' | ECtt |
| - 'Carnea' | CSec EBrs EShb NBre SPhx WBrk WPer |
| - 'Dusky Pink' | LSou |
| - 'Dusky Salmon' | MDKP NBPC NDlv |
| - 'Flore Pleno' (d) | EBee ECha ELan EShb GCal MBri MLLN NLar SMrm WCot WFar |
| - 'Morgenrot' | MCCP NNor |
| - 'Pinkie' | ELan NLar SBod |
| - 'Rauhreif' | EBee EShb NBre SPhx |
| - 'Rosea' | EBee EPfP NBir WFar WHrl WMoo WPer |
| * - 'Salmonea' | ECtt GBri NBir SRms WCAu |
| - 'Summer Sparkle Pink' | SWal |
| - 'Summer Sparkle Red' | CSec SWal |
| - 'Summer Sparkle White' | SWal |
| ***cognata*** | CDes CSec EWld GMac MDKP |
| - B&SWJ 4234 | WCru |
| § ***coronaria*** ♀H4 | Widely available |
| - 'Abbotswood Rose' | see *L.* x *walkeri* 'Abbotswood Rose' |
| - 'Alba' ♀H4 | Widely available |
| - 'Angel's Blush' | MDKP NBir SPav SPer WRha |
| - Atrosanguinea Group | CBre EBee GMaP IBlr LRHS MRav NCot NPri SPer SPoG |
| - 'Cerise' | MArl MCot MDKP NBir WRHF |
| - 'Dancing Ladies' | WMnd |
| - Gardeners' World = 'Blych' (d) | CMea CSpe EBee ECtt ELon EWes GBri LSou MBNS NGdn NSti SMrm SPer SPhx SUsu WCot |
| - 'Hutchinson's Cream' (v) | CSec NPro SBHP WCHb |
| - Oculata Group | CMHG CSec CSpe EAEE EBee ECtt EGoo GCra LEdu MCot MTho NPri SMrm SPav SPlb SPoG SWal WFar WMoo WTin |
| § ***coronata*** var. ***sieboldii*** | NBre |
| - - white-flowered **new** | EBee |
| ***dioica*** | see *Silene dioica* |
| ***flos-cuculi*** | Widely available |
| - var. ***albiflora*** | CBre CSec EBee EMFW GBar LPBA MLLN MSKA NBro NLar SSvw WCHb WHer WMnd WMoo WOut |
| - Jenny = 'Lychjen' (d) | EBee EBrs GBri |
| * - 'Little Robin' | ECho EDAr NHol |
| - 'Nana' | CSec CSpe ECho EDAr GAbr MMuc MSKA NLar WPer |
| - 'White Robin' | CBod CEnt CHFP CTca EAEE EWTr GBri GMac GQue LRHS MBNS NBsh NCGa NPri SPoG WPtf |

| | |
|---|---|
| ***flos-jovis*** $\mathbb{Y}^{H4}$ | CSec EBee ECha EPfP LRHS NBir NLar SBch SRms WMoo WPer |
| - 'Hort's Variety' | EBrs GKir MRav NBir WSHC |
| - 'Minor' | see *L. flos-jovis* 'Nana' |
| § - 'Nana' | CSec MSCN NWCA |
| - 'Peggy' | EBee EGoo LRHS MCCP NBre NLar |
| ***fulgens*** | NBre |
| x ***haageana*** | CSec EAEE EBee NBre NLar NWCA SRms |
| 'Hill Grounds' | CDes EBee WCot |
| ***lagascae*** | see *Petrocoptis pyrenaica* subsp. *glaucifolia* |
| ***miqueliana*** | CSec NBre NLar SPhx WGwG WMoo |
| 'Molten Lava' | CFir CSec EBee ECho LRHS MRav NBre NLar SGar WPer |
| ***nutans*** | MSal |
| * ***sikkimensis*** | EBee NBre |
| 'Terry's Pink' | EBee MLLN NCGa WFar |
| § ***viscaria*** | CArn CHrt CSec EBWF ECha GCra GJos LDai MSal NNor SBch SGar SHGN SWal WCot WFar WMoo WTin |
| - 'Alba' | EBee ECha MLLN NBre NBro NNor WRha |
| - ***alpina*** | see *L. viscaria* |
| § - subsp. ***atropurpurea*** | CSec ECtt EShb EWes LSou MHar NBre SBHP SRms SSvw WHrl WOut |
| - 'Feuer' | CKno EBee EWes GJos NLar NVic WMoo |
| - 'Firebird' | EWTr EWes GKir MWhi NBre NBur |
| - 'Plena' (d) | MDun |
| - 'Schnee' | MSte |
| - 'Snowbird' | CSec |
| - 'Splendens' | EPfP EQua MNFA SPad SPet |
| - 'Splendens Plena' (d) $\mathbb{Y}^{H4}$ | EBee GMac MArl NBre NBro SUsu WFar |
| § x ***walkeri*** 'Abbotswood Rose' $\mathbb{Y}^{H4}$ | IBlr WBrk |
| ***wilfordii*** | SHar |
| § ***yunnanensis*** | CHrt EBee GKev MSte NBid SIng SPav SPhx WMoo WPtf |
| - ***alba*** | see *L. yunnanensis* |

## *Lychnis* x *Silene* (*Caryophyllaceae*)

| | |
|---|---|
| 'Rollies Favourite' **new** | NDov |

## *Lycianthes* (*Solanaceae*)

| | |
|---|---|
| ***rantonnetii*** | see *Solanum rantonnetii* |

## *Lycium* (*Solanaceae*)

| | |
|---|---|
| ***barbarum*** | EWes NBlu SEND SMad SVic |
| ***chinense*** | CArn CMen NLar |

## *Lycopodium* (*Lycopodiaceae*)

| | |
|---|---|
| ***clavatum*** | GPoy |

## *Lycopsis* see *Anchusa*

## *Lycopus* (*Lamiaceae*)

| | |
|---|---|
| ***americanus*** | CArn EBee MSal |
| ***europaeus*** | CArn EBWF ELau GBar GPoy MHer MSal WGwG WHer |
| ***lucidus*** | MSal |
| ***virginicus*** | COld MSal SDys |

## *Lycoris* (*Amaryllidaceae*)

| | |
|---|---|
| ***albiflora*** | EBrs ECho WCot |
| ***aurea*** | EBee EBrs ECho LRHS |
| - from Guizhou **new** | NCot |
| - from Hubei **new** | NCot |
| ***haywardii*** | WCot |
| ***incarnata*** | ECho |
| ***radiata*** | CCCN CSec EBee EBrs ECho GBin LRHS |
| ***sanguinea*** | EBrs ECho LRHS |
| - var. ***kiusiana*** | EBee |
| ***shaanxiensis*** | EBee NCot |
| ***sprengeri*** | EBee EBrs ECho |
| ***squamigera*** | EBee EBrs ECho LRHS |

## *Lygodium* (*Schizaeaceae*)

| | |
|---|---|
| ***japonicum*** | NBid WFib WRic |

## *Lygos* see *Retama*

## *Lyonia* (*Ericaceae*)

| | |
|---|---|
| ***ligustrina*** | LRHS NLar |
| ***mariana*** | NLar |

## *Lyonothamnus* (*Rosaceae*)

| | |
|---|---|
| ***floribundus*** subsp. ***aspleniifolius*** | CAbb CCCN CDoC CGHE CPLG CPSs EBee NLar SAPC SArc SKHP SSpi WCru WFar WPGP |

## *Lysichiton* (*Araceae*)

| | |
|---|---|
| sp. **new** | GGal |
| ***americanus*** $\mathbb{Y}^{H4}$ | Widely available |
| ***americanus*** x ***camtschatcensis*** | ECha SSpi |
| ***camtschatcensis*** $\mathbb{Y}^{H4}$ | Widely available |

## *Lysimachia* ✿ (*Primulaceae*)

| | |
|---|---|
| B&SWJ 8632 from Korea | WCru |
| § ***atropurpurea*** | CHar CSpe EAro EBee EGle ELan EPfP GJos LBMP LHop LRHS MCot SPer SPlb SPoG STes WCot WFar WMnd WRos |
| - 'Beaujolais' | CBod CSec ECGP EHig GQue LCro LRHS LSRN MBNS NBPC NBPN NPri SMeo SMrm SPav SRkn WWlt |
| - 'Geronimo' | CSpe |
| ***barystachys*** | CRow EBee GMac LPla MRav SHar WFar WOut |
| ***candida*** | EBee WCot |
| ***ciliata*** | CMHG EBee ECha EHoe ELan GMaP MNrw NBir NGdn SWat WBor WCAu WCot WFar WMnd WOut WPer |
| § - 'Firecracker' $\mathbb{Y}^{H4}$ | Widely available |
| - 'Purpurea' | see *L. ciliata* 'Firecracker' |
| ***clethroides*** $\mathbb{Y}^{H4}$ | Widely available |
| - 'Geisha' (v) | CBow EBee ECtt EHoe ELon EWes GQue LLHF LSou MBNS MMHG SMrm SPer SPoG WCot |
| - 'Lady Jane' | LBMP NBur SRms |
| § ***congestiflora*** | NPer SPet |
| - HWJ 846 | WCru |
| - 'Golden Falls' | LAst |
| - 'Outback Sunset'PBR (v) | ECtt LAst NBlu |
| ***ephemerum*** | Widely available |
| ***fortunei*** | EBee MWat |
| ***henryi*** | EBee |
| ***hybrida*** | EBee WCot |
| ***japonica*** var. ***minutissima*** | CFee CStu |
| ***lichiangensis*** | CSec EBee EHig GKev GKir MBNS MLLN NBir SGar WMoo WPer |
| ***lyssii*** | see *L. congestiflora* |
| ***melampyroides*** | EBee WCot |
| ***minoricensis*** | CArn CSec EBee EEls EHrv ELan LFur MBNS SWat WPer |
| ***nemorum*** | EBWF WPer |
| - subsp. ***azorica*** | WCot |
| - 'Little Sun' | WAlt |
| - 'Pale Star' | CBre WAlt |

| | | |
|---|---|---|
| | ***nummularia*** | CHal COIW CSBt CTri CWat EBWF ECtt EHon EPfP GPoy LPBA MBar MMuc NBir SWat WBrk WCot |
| | - 'Aurea' ♀H4 | Widely available |
| | ***paridiformis*** | EBee WCot |
| | - var. ***stenophylla*** | WCot WPGP |
| | - - DJHC 704 | CDes |
| | ***punctata*** misapplied | see *L. verticillaris* |
| | ***punctata*** L. | Widely available |
| § | - 'Alexander' (v) | Widely available |
| | - 'Gaulthier Brousse' | MAvo WCot |
| | - Golden Alexander = 'Walgoldalex'^PBR (v) | CBct MBNS MBri NHol NLar SPer WFar |
| | - 'Golden Glory' (v) | WCot |
| | - 'Hometown Hero' **new** | EBee |
| | - 'Ivy Maclean' (v) | EBee LSou SWvt WCot |
| | - 'Sunspot' | EBee NBre |
| | - 'Variegata' | see *L. punctata* 'Alexander' |
| | ***- verticillata*** | see *L. verticillaris* |
| | 'Purpurea' | see *L. atropurpurea* |
| | ***pyramidalis*** | WPtf |
| | ***quadrifolia*** | EBee |
| | ***serpyllifolia*** | ECtt |
| | Snow Candles = 'L9902'^PBR | COIW EBee GBin LHop LSou SPoG |
| | ***taliensis*** BWJ 7797 | WCru |
| | ***thyrsiflora*** | CBen EBee EHon EMFW NPer SWat WCot WHer WMAq |
| § | ***verticillaris*** | CTri WCot |
| | ***vulgaris*** | CArn CRWN GBar LPBA MSKA NSco SIde WCot WFar WMoo WPer |
| | - subsp. ***davurica*** | WCot |
| | ***yunnanensis*** | CDMG CDes CSec EBee GKev GMaP MDKP SGar WPer |

## *Lysionotus* (*Gesneriaceae*)

| | |
|---|---|
| ***gamosepalus*** B&SWJ 7241 | WCru |
| aff. ***kwangsiensis*** HWJ 643 | WCru |
| 'Lavender Lady' | CSpe SEND |
| ***pauciflorus*** | SKHP WAbe |
| - B&SWJ 189 | WCru |
| - B&SWJ 303 | WCru |
| - B&SWJ 335 | WCru |
| ***serratus*** | MWea |

## *Lythrum* (*Lythraceae*)

| | | |
|---|---|---|
| | ***alatum*** | NBre |
| | ***anceps*** | NBre NLar SPhx |
| | ***salicaria*** | Widely available |
| | - 'Blush' ♀H4 | Widely available |
| | - 'Brightness' | CDWL NDov |
| § | - 'Feuerkerze' ♀H4 | Widely available |
| | - Firecandle | see *L. salicaria* 'Feuerkerze' |
| | - 'Happy' | NHol SMrm |
| | - 'Lady Sackville' | CDWL EBee ECtt EGle EMFW EPPr GBuc GMaP MCot NDov SMrm SUsu WCAu |
| | - 'Little Robert' **new** | LRHS |
| | - 'Morden Pink' | CChe CPrp EBee EGle MBri MDKP MSte NCob NGby SPhx WFar WPtf WSHC |
| | - 'Prichard's Variety' | CAby CKno EBee WPGP |
| | - 'Robert' | Widely available |
| | - 'Robin' | LLHF |
| | - 'Rose' | ELan NBir SWvt |
| | - 'Rosencaule' | EBee |
| | - 'Stichflamme' | NCob SMrm |
| | - 'Swirl' | EBee ECtt EGle LLWG MDKP NBre NDov SHar SMrm WFar |
| | - 'The Beacon' | CMHG EBee EMFW MDKP SRms |
| | - 'Zigeunerblut' | CElw CKno CMHG EBee EGle MDKP MRav MSte NGby NLar SMrm SPhx SWat |
| | ***virgatum*** | CMHG EPPr NDov SMHy SPhx SUsu WMoo WOut WSHC |
| | - 'Dropmore Purple' | CDWL CHar CSam EBee ECtt EGle EPPr LAst LBMP LHop LRHS MBri MCot MDKP MRav MSte NCob NDov SAga SPhx WCAu WFar WPnP WPtf |
| | - 'Rose Queen' | ECha ECtt GKir MDKP MRav NDov SMHy WFar WPer |
| | - 'Rosy Gem' | CHFP CMMP EBee ECtt EPfP GMaP GMac MNHC MWat MWhi NBPC NBid NBro SRGP SRms SWal SWvt WFar WHoo WPer |
| | - 'The Rocket' | CAby CMMP CSam CTri EBee EGle EPfP LAst MRav NBro NDov SPer SWvt |

## *Lytocaryum* (*Arecaceae*)

| | | |
|---|---|---|
| § | ***weddellianum*** ♀H1 | LPal MBri |

# M

## *Maackia* (*Papilionaceae*)

| | |
|---|---|
| ***amurensis*** | CBcs CDul CMCN EHig ELan EPfP GKir IArd IDee IMGH MBri MWea |
| - var. ***buergeri*** | CDul CLnd EBee |
| ***chinensis*** | CBcs CMCN IArd MBlu MBri NLar |

## *Macbridea* (*Lamiaceae*)

| | |
|---|---|
| ***caroliniana*** | WPGP |

## mace, English see *Achillea ageratum*

## *Macfadyena* (*Bignoniaceae*)

| | | |
|---|---|---|
| | ***uncata*** | SOWG |
| § | ***unguis-cati*** | CCCN CRHN CSec EShb MJnS |

## *Machaeranthera* (*Asteraceae*)

| | |
|---|---|
| ***bigelovii*** | NBre NWCA |

## *Machaerina* (*Cyperaceae*)

| | |
|---|---|
| sp **new** | CDWL |
| ***rubiginosa*** 'Variegata' (v) | CDWL CKno |

## *Machilus* see *Persea*

## *Mackaya* (*Acanthaceae*)

| | | |
|---|---|---|
| § | ***bella*** ♀H1 | CHII EShb SOWG |

## *Macleania* (*Ericaceae*)

| | |
|---|---|
| ***ericae*** | WCot |

## *Macleaya* (*Papaveraceae*)

| | | |
|---|---|---|
| | ***cordata*** misapplied | see *M.* x *kewensis* |
| § | ***cordata*** (Willd.) R. Br. ♀H4 | CArn COIW EBee ELan EPfP EWsh LHop LRHS MBri MWhi NBPC NBir NDov NOrc NPri SPer SPhx SPlb SRms SWal WCAu WCot WFar WMnd WMoo |
| | - 'Celadon Ruffles' | GBin |
| § | x ***kewensis*** | CWan EBee GAbr LBMP SMrm WHoo WPGP |
| | - 'Flamingo' ♀H4 | CPrp EBee ECha ECtt EQua GBuc LAst LBMP MBNS MRav NGdn SWvt WFar |
| § | ***microcarpa*** | CDMG SGar SWat |
| | - 'Kelway's Coral Plume' ♀H4 | Widely available |

- 'Spetchley Ruby' EBee GBin MRav NDov SPhx SUsu WCot WPGP
'Plum Tassel' EBee WCot

## *Maclura* (*Moraceae*)

***pomifera*** CArn CBcs CMCN MBri NLar SPlb WDin WFar WPGP
- 'Pretty Woman' NLar
***tricuspidata*** CAgr

## *Macrodiervilla* see *Weigela*

## *Macropiper* (*Piperaceae*)

§ ***excelsum*** CHEx ECou

## *Macroptilium* (*Papilionaceae*)

***lathyroides*** new CSec

## *Macrozamia* (*Zamiaceae*)

***communis*** CBrP CKob LPal
***diplomera*** CBrP
***dyeri*** see *M. riedlei*
***glaucophylla*** CBrP
***johnsonii*** CBrP
***lucida*** CBrP
***miquelii*** CBrP
***moorei*** CBrP ETod LPal
***mountperiensis*** CBrP
§ ***riedlei*** CBrP LPal

## *Maddenia* (*Rosaceae*)

***hypocleuca*** NLar

## *Madia* (*Asteraceae*)

***elegans*** NBur

## *Maesa* (*Myrsinaceae*)

***japonica*** CPLG
***montana*** CPLG

## *Magnolia* ✿ (*Magnoliaceae*)

***acuminata*** CBcs CDul CLnd CMCN EPfP IDee IMGH LMaj NBhm NLar WDin
- 'Golden Glow' CBcs
* - 'Kinju' CEnd NLar
- 'Koban Dori' CBcs CPMA CTho ECho
- 'Patriot' new SKHP
§ - var. ***subcordata*** EBee NLar
§ - - 'Miss Honeybee' SSpi
'Advance' CPMA
'Albatross' CBcs CDoC CEnd CTho SKHP SSpi WPGP
'Alixeed' CBcs
'Ambrosia' CBcs CPMA
***amoena*** CBcs CSdC
- 'Multiogeca' CBcs CWib
'Ann' ♀H4 CBcs CPLG CSdC MGos NLar SSpi
'Anticipation' CEnd CSdC
'Apollo' CBcs CDoC CEnd CPMA GGGa SKHP SSpi
***ashei*** see *M. macrophylla* subsp. *ashei*
'Athene' CBcs CDoC CMHG CPMA WPat
'Atlas' CBcs CDoC CEnd CMHG CPMA CTho GGGa LMil SSpi WPGP
'Banana Split' SSpi
'Betty' ♀H4 CBcs CDoC CDul CSdC IDee LPan LSRN MGos NLar NMun NScw SLim SSta WBod WDin WFar WOrn
'Big Dude' CBcs CEnd CMCN IArd
***biondii*** CBcs CSdC IDee NLar WPGP
'Black Beauty' CBcs
'Black Tulip' ELan EPfP GGGa LBuc LRHS MGos NBPN NPri SCoo SPoG SSpi WBod
x ***brooklynensis*** NPal
- 'Evamaria' CBcs CTho
- 'Hattie Carthan' CBcs WPGP
- 'Woodsman' CBcs NLar
- 'Yellow Bird' CBcs CDoC CEnd CMCN CPMA CTho EBee EPfP LRHS MAsh MBlu MBri MGos NCGa NHol NLar NPal SSpi WDin
'Butterbowl' CBcs
'Butterflies' CBcs CDoC CEnd CMHG CPMA CTho EBee ELan EMil EPfP GGGa GKir ISea LHyd LMil LRHS MBlu MDun MGos NLar SHBN SSpi SSta WBVN WBod WFar WGob WPGP
'Caerhays Belle' CBcs CPMA ECho MBri NLar SSpi
'Caerhays New Purple' CLnd ECho
'Caerhays Surprise' CBcs CPMA SKHP SSpi
***campbelli*** 'Sidbury' CBcs MBri
***campbellii*** CMCN ELan EPfP ISea LRHS SPoG SSpi WFar WPic
- Alba Group CBcs CEnd MGos WFar WPGP
- - 'Ethel Hillier' CBcs
- - 'Sir Harold Hillier' new CPMA
- - 'Strybing White' CBcs
I - - 'Trelissick Alba' CTho
- 'Betty Jessel' CPMA
- 'Darjeeling' CBcs CDoC ECho SKHP SSpi
- 'Lamellan Pink' CTho
- 'Lamellan White' CTho
- subsp. ***mollicomata*** CEnd EPfP ISea WFar
- - 'Lanarth' CBcs CEnd SKHP WBod
- - 'Maharanee' CBcs
- - 'Peter Borlase' CBcs CDoC
- (Raffillii Group) 'Charles Raffill' CAbP CBcs CDoC CDul CLnd EBee ELan EPfP LMil MAsh MBri MGos MLan SHBN SKHP SLim SPer WDin WHCr WPGP
- - 'Kew's Surprise' CBcs CDoC CPMA
'Candy Cane' LPan WPGP
'Carlos' new CBcs
***cathcartii*** HWJ 874 new WCru
'Cecil Nice' CBcs CCVT CDoC
Chameleon see *M.* 'Chang Hua'
§ 'Chang Hua' CPMA MBri NLar
'Charles Coates' CPMA CSdC EPfP MDun NLar WPGP
China Town = 'Jing Ning' MDun
'Columbus' CPMA CSdC SSpi WPGP
'Coral Lake' CPMA MDun
***cordata*** see *M. acuminata* var. *subcordata*
- 'Miss Honeybee' see *M. acuminata* var. *subcordata* 'Miss Honeybee'
***cylindrica*** misapplied see *M.* 'Pegasus'
***cylindrica*** ambig. CBcs
***cylindrica*** E.H. Wilson CMCN EPfP IArd IDee SSpi
'Daphne' CBcs
'Darrell Dean' CPMA WPGP
'David Clulow' CBcs CPMA CTho ECho SKHP SSpi
***dawsoniana*** CMCN EBee EPfP IMGH NLar
- 'Clarke' SKHP
'Daybreak' CBcs SSpi
***dealbata*** see *M. macrophylla* subsp. *dealbata*
***delavayi*** CBcs CBrP CHEx CMCN EPfP ISea LRHS SAPC SArc
§ ***denudata*** ♀H3-4 CBcs CDul CMCN CTho CWib EMil EPfP LMaj LMil LPan LRHS MGos NLar SSpi WBod WDin WFar
- 'Dubbel' CBcs MDun SKHP
- 'Forrest's Pink' CBcs
- Fragrant Cloud = 'Dan Xin' CPMA CWib MBri MDun NLar
- 'Gere' CBcs CPMA

| | | |
|---|---|---|
| | - Yellow River = 'Fei Huang' | CBcs CEnd CWib EBee MBri MDun NLar SKHP SMad SPoG WOrn |
| | 'Elizabeth' Ψ$^{H4}$ | Widely available |
| | 'Eskimo' | SKHP SSpi |
| | 'Felix Jury' | ELan EPfP SSpi |
| | 'Fireglow' | CBcs CTho |
| | 'Frank Gladney' | CPMA CTho |
| | ***fraseri*** **new** | SKHP |
| | - var. ***pyramidata*** **new** | SKHP |
| | 'Full Eclipse' | WPGP |
| | 'Galaxy' Ψ$^{H4}$ | CBcs CDoC CEnd CSdC EBee ECho EPfP EWTr GGGa IArd IMGH ISea LMil LRHS MAsh MBar MBri MGos MSte NBhm SLim SSpi SSta WBrE WDin WGob WPGP |
| | 'George Henry Kern' | CBcs CDoC EMil ERas IArd IDee LRHS MBri MSte NLar NMun SSpi SSta WCFE WDin WFar WGob WPat |
| | ***globosa*** | CBcs CPLG EBee SKHP WFar WGob WPGP |
| | - AC 5294 **new** | CSdC |
| | - from India | SKHP |
| | 'Gold Crown' | CBcs SSpi |
| | 'Gold Star' | CBcs CDoC CEnd CPMA CSdC CTho EPfP GGGa LPan LRHS MBlu MBri MGos NCGa NLar NPal SSpi WOrn |
| | 'Golden Endeavour' | CBcs |
| | 'Golden Gift' | CPMA SSpi |
| | 'Golden Pond' **new** | CBcs |
| | 'Golden Sun' | CBcs CPMA NLar |
| | ***grandiflora*** | CMCN CWib EPfP ESwi GKir LAst LCro LEdu LRHS MGos MLan MRav NBlu NLar SAPC SArc SHBN WDin WFar WOrn |
| | - 'Blanchard' | CBcs CPMA |
| | - 'Bracken's Brown Beauty' | MBri |
| | - 'Charles Dickens' | CPMA |
| | - 'Edith Bogue' | CDul CPMA ECho EQua MAsh MGos MLan NLar WBVN WGob |
| | - 'Exmouth' Ψ$^{H3-4}$ | Widely available |
| | - 'Ferruginea' | CBcs CPMA EBee MGos |
| | - 'Francois Treyve' | ECrN EMil EPfP EQua SPoG |
| | - 'Galissonnière' | CBcs CWib ECrN EPfP ERom IMGH LMaj LPan LRHS MGos NBlu SLim SSpi SWvt WDin WFar WPGP |
| I | - 'Gallissonnière Nana' | LMaj LPan SBLw |
| | - 'Goliath' | CBcs CDul CEnd CHEx CPSs ELan EPfP LPan SPer SSpi WPGP |
| | - 'Harold Poole' | CBcs CPMA |
| | - 'Kay Paris' | LRHS SKHP |
| | - 'Little Gem' | CBcs CDoC CPMA ELan EPfP LRHS MGos NLar SKHP SPoG SSpi |
| | - 'Mainstreet' | CPMA |
| | - 'Monlia' | CBcs CPMA |
| | - 'Nannetensis' | CPMA EQua |
| | - 'Overton' | CBcs CPMA |
| | - 'Russet' | CPMA |
| | - 'Saint Mary' | CBcs CPMA |
| | - 'Samuel Sommer' | CPMA SAPC SArc |
| | - 'Symmes Select' | CBcs CPMA |
| | - 'Victoria' Ψ$^{H3-4}$ | CBcs CDoC CDul CPMA CTho ELan EPfP LHyd LMil LRHS LSRN MAsh MBlu MGos NLar SLim SPoG SReu SSpi SSta WFar WGob WPGP |
| | 'Green Bee' | CBcs |
| | 'Green Mist' | CBcs CPMA |
| | 'Heaven Scent' Ψ$^{H4}$ | Widely available |
| | 'Helen Fogg' | WPGP |
| | ***heptapeta*** | see *M. denudata* |
| § | 'Hong Yur' | CEnd CPMA |
| | 'Hot Flash' | CBcs CPMA |

| | | |
|---|---|---|
| | ***hypoleuca*** | see *M. obovata* Thunb. |
| | 'Ian's Red' | CBcs CPMA SSpi |
| | 'Indian Tapestry' | MBri |
| | 'Iolanthe' | CBcs CEnd CGHE CMCN CMHG CPMA CSdC CTho ECho ELan GGGa MAsh MGos NBhm NHol NLar SPer SSpi SSta WFar WPGP |
| | 'J.C. Williams' | CBcs CDoC CPMA CTho |
| | 'Jane' Ψ$^{H4}$ | CDoC CSdC ELan EPfP LMil LRHS MAsh MBri MGos SHBN SPer |
| | 'Jersey Belle' | CPMA |
| | 'Joe McDaniel' | CPMA CSdC MLan NLar SSpi WBod |
| | 'Jon Jon' | MBri |
| | 'Judy' EMil NLar | |
| | x ***kewensis*** hort. ex Pearce 'Wada's Memory' | see *M. salicifolia* 'Wada's Memory' |
| | ***kobus*** | CBcs CDul CLnd CMCN CSBt CTho CTsd EBee EPfP IMGH LMaj LPan NLar NMoo SBLw SLdr WDin WFar WGob |
| | - var. ***borealis*** | CPMA |
| | - 'Esveld Select' | MBri SSpi |
| | - 'Janaki Ammal' | CPMA |
| § | - 'Norman Gould' | CDoC EPfP MBri NLar NScw SSta WDin |
| | 'Leda' | CMCN SSpi |
| | 'Legacy' | CBcs CPMA NLar |
| | 'Legend' | EPfP |
| § | ***liliiflora*** | CBcs MBar NBlu |
| § | - 'Nigra' Ψ$^{H4}$ | Widely available |
| | - 'Oldfield' | WPGP |
| * | 'Limelight' | CBcs CSdC |
| | x ***loebneri*** | CBcs LRHS |
| | - 'Ballerina' | CDoC NLar |
| | - 'Donna' | CBcs EPfP LRHS MGos NLar SSpi |
| | - 'Leonard Messel' Ψ$^{H4}$ | Widely available |
| | - 'Merrill' Ψ$^{H4}$ | Widely available |
| | - 'Pink Cloud' **new** | CPMA |
| | - 'Snowdrift' | NLar SSta |
| | - 'Star Bright' | CPMA |
| | - 'Willow Wood' | CPMA |
| | 'Lois' | CBcs EPfP GGGa SKHP SSpi |
| | 'Lombardy Rose' | MBri NLar |
| § | ***lotungensis*** | NLar |
| | ***macrophylla*** | CBrP CHEx CMCN EPfP IDee MBlu NLar SAPC SArc SKHP SSpi WPGP |
| § | - subsp. ***ashei*** | SKHP |
| | - subsp. ***ashei*** x ***virginiana*** | CPMA |
| § | - subsp. ***dealbata*** | WBod |
| | ***macrophylla*** x ***macrophylla*** subsp. ***ashei*** | SKHP |
| | 'Manchu Fan' | CBcs CPMA CSdC ECho EMil IArd LSRN NLar SSpi |
| | 'Margaret Helen' | CBcs CPMA ECho |
| | 'Mark Jury' | CBcs |
| | 'Maryland' | CPMA CWib EQua SSta |
| | 'Maxine Merrill' | IDee SSpi |
| | 'May to Frost' | CBcs |
| | 'Milky Way' Ψ$^{H4}$ | CBcs CDoC CGHE CMHG CPMA CTho LRHS MGos SKHP SSpi WPGP |
| | 'Moon Spire' | CBcs |
| | 'Nimbus' | SSpi |
| | ***nitida*** **new** | CBcs |
| | ***obovata*** Diels | see *M. officinalis* |
| § | ***obovata*** Thunb. Ψ$^{H4}$ | CBcs CMCN CPMA CTho EPfP IDee IMGH MGos MLan NLar SSpi SSta WDin WPGP |
| § | ***officinalis*** | CBcs CMCN EPfP NLar WBVN WFar |
| | - var. ***biloba*** | CGHE EPfP NLar SSpi WPGP |
| | 'Olivia' **new** | CBcs |

| | | |
|---|---|---|
| | 'Peachy' | CBcs NLar |
| § | 'Pegasus' | CEnd GGGa SSpi WDin |
| | 'Peppermint Stick' | CBcs CSdC ECho GGGa MGos SSta |
| | 'Peter Smithers' | CBcs CPMA CTho WFar |
| | 'Phelan Bright' | CSdC |
| | 'Phillip Tregunna' | CBcs CTho |
| | 'Pickard's Stardust' | EPfP LRHS |
| | 'Pickard's Sundew' | see *M.* 'Sundew' |
| | 'Pink Cecile Nice' **new** | CBcs |
| | 'Pinkie' ♀H4 | EMil EPfP LRHS MBri MGos NLar SSpi SSta WGob |
| | 'Pirouette' | CPMA GGGa LLHF SKHP SSpi |
| | 'Porcelain Dove' **new** | SSpi |
| | 'Princess Margaret' | CDoC CPMA ECho |
| | x ***proctoriana*** | CAbP CDoC CGHE CSdC EBee EPfP LMil NLar SKHP WPGP |
| | - Gloster form | NLar |
| I | - 'Proctoriana' | LMil |
| | - 'Robert's Dream' **new** | SSpi |
| | 'Purple Platter' | CBcs |
| | 'Purple Sensation' | CBcs CPMA |
| | ***quinquepeta*** | see *M. liliiflora* |
| | 'Randy' | CBcs EPfP MGos |
| | 'Raspberry Ice' | CBcs CDoC CMHG CSam CSdC CTho EBee EPfP ISea LMil LRHS MAsh NLar SLim WFar WGob |
| | 'Red As' **new** | CBcs |
| | 'Red as Red' **new** | CDoC |
| | 'Red Lion' **new** | CBcs |
| | 'Ricki' | CBcs CSdC EMil EPfP LSRN MBlu MGos MHav NLar NMun WFar |
| | ***rostrata*** | CGHE EBee ELan SKHP SSpi WPGP |
| | 'Rouged Alabaster' | CBcs CDoC |
| | 'Royal Crown' | CBcs CDoC CSdC EMil EQua IDee MRav NBhm NLar SLim |
| | 'Ruby' | CBcs CPMA ECho MGos |
| | 'Ruth' | CBcs SSpi |
| | ***salicifolia*** ♀H3-4 | CBcs CMCN EPfP GGal ISea LRHS SSpi SSta |
| | - 'Jermyns' | SSpi |
| | - upright | WPGP |
| § | - 'Wada's Memory' ♀H4 | CDoC CMCN CMHG CPMA CTho ELan EMil EPfP EWTr GGGa GKir IFFs LMil LRHS MAsh MBri MLan MSte NBea NLar SPer SSpi SSta WDin WFar WGob |
| | - 'Windsor Beauty' | SSpi |
| | ***sargentiana*** var. ***robusta*** | CBcs CEnd CLnd CMCN EBee ELan EPfP IMGH LMil MGos SPer SSpi SSta WDin WFar |
| | - - 'Trengwainton Glory' | SKHP SSpi |
| | 'Satisfaction' | LRHS MBri NLar |
| | 'Sayonara' ♀H4 | CBcs CPMA CSdC ECho EPfP MBri SSpi WDin WPGP WPat |
| | 'Schmetterling' | see *M.* x *soulangeana* 'Pickard's Schmetterling' |
| | 'Serene' | CBcs CEnd CMHG CPMA ECho EPfP LMil MGos SSpi SSta |
| | 'Shirazz' | CBcs CPMA SKHP |
| | ***sieboldii*** | Widely available |
| | - B&SWJ 4127 | WCru |
| | - from Korea, hardy | GGGa |
| | - 'Colossus' | SKHP SSpi |
| | - 'Michiko Renge' | NLar |
| | - 'Pride of Norway' | CBcs |
| | - subsp. ***sinensis*** | CBcs CDoC CLnd CMCN CPMA CSam CTho ELan EPfP GCra GGGa IMGH LRHS MBlu MDun SSpi WDin |
| | 'Sir Harold Hillier' **new** | CBcs |
| | 'Solar Flair' | CBcs |
| | x ***soulangeana*** | Widely available |
| § | - 'Alba' | CBcs CDoC CSBt CTri EPfP LCro LPan LRHS MBlu MGos NMun SLim SPer WBVN WFar WOrn |
| | - 'Alba Superba' | see *M.* x *soulangeana* 'Alba' |
| | - 'Alexandrina' | CBcs EPfP NLar |
| | - 'Amabilis' | MLan WGob |
| | - 'André Leroy' **new** | EMil |
| | - 'Brozzonii' ♀H3-4 | CDoC ELon EPfP ERas GGGa GKev GKir LRHS MBri MGos NLar SSpi WBVN |
| | - 'Burgundy' | CBcs CDoC ISea MGos WFar |
| | - 'Lennei' ♀H3-4 | CBcs CDoC CDul CMCN CSBt EBee EPfP IMGH LRHS MAsh MBri MGos MSwo NBea NHol SHBN SLim SPer SRms WFar WOrn |
| | - 'Lennei Alba' ♀H3-4 | CBcs CDoC CMCN CSdC LRHS SPer SSpi WFar WGob |
| | - 'Nigra' | see *M. liliiflora* 'Nigra' |
| | - 'Pickard's Ruby' | MDun |
| § | - 'Pickard's Schmetterling' | CDoC CSdC LMil MAsh |
| | - 'Pickard's Snow Queen' | MBri |
| | - 'Pickard's Sundew' | see *M.* 'Sundew' |
| | - 'Picture' | CBcs CDoC CTri NLar WDin WGob |
| | - Red Lucky | see *M.* 'Hong Yur' |
| | - 'Rosea' **new** | LMaj |
| | - 'Rubra' misapplied | see *M.* x *soulangeana* 'Rustica Rubra' |
| § | - 'Rustica Rubra' ♀H3-4 | Widely available |
| | - 'San José' | CBcs LMil LRHS MAsh MBri NLar WFar |
| | - 'Speciosa' **new** | NMun |
| | - 'Superba' **new** | NMun |
| | - 'Verbanica' | CCVT IFFs LMil LRHS MAsh NLar |
| | 'Spectrum' | CBcs CDoC CEnd CPMA CSdC EMil GGGa LMil MBri MGos NLar SKHP SSpi WPGP |
| | ***sprengeri*** | CWib |
| | - 'Copeland Court' | CBcs GGGa |
| | - var. ***diva*** | CBcs CEnd NLar SSpi WPGP |
| | - - 'Burncoose' | CBcs CDoC |
| | - - 'Claret Cup' | GGGa WBod |
| | - - 'Diva' **new** | GGal |
| | - - 'Eric Savill' | CBcs CTho SKHP SSpi SSta WPGP |
| | - - 'Lanhydrock' | CBcs CTho SSpi |
| | - - 'Westonbirt' | WPGP |
| | - 'Marwood Spring' | CMHG |
| | 'Star Wars' ♀H4 | CBcs CDoC CEnd CPMA CSdC CTho ECho ELan EMil EPfP GGGa LMil MBri MDun MGos MLan NLar SSpi SSta WBod WPGP WPat |
| | ***stellata*** ♀H4 | Widely available |
| | - 'Centennial' | CBcs CDoC CPMA CTho GGGa MBri NLar WFar |
| | - 'Chrysanthemumiflora' | LMil SSpi |
| | - 'Dawn' **new** | CPMA |
| | - 'Jane Platt' | CPMA ELan EWes GGGa MBri MGos SKHP SSpi |
| | - f. ***keiskei*** | CEnd CSdC NHol |
| | - 'King Rose' | CBcs CDoC CPMA CSdC CTsd ELon EPfP ISea LAst LRHS MSte MWat SLdr SPla |
| | - 'Norman Gould' | see *M. kobus* 'Norman Gould' |
| | - 'Rosea' | CMCN CPMA CTho ELan ELon ISea LPan LRHS MDun MGos MRav MSwo NLar SHBN SPoG WBod WDin |
| I | - 'Rosea Massey' | GBin WFar |
| | - 'Royal Star' | Widely available |
| | - 'Scented Silver' | CSdC |
| | - 'Waterlily' ♀H4 | CBcs CMCN CPMA CTho ELan ELon EMil EPfP GKev GKir IMGH LAst LRHS LSRN NLar SLdr SLim SPer SPla SPoG SSpi SSta WDin WFar WGob WPGP |

| | | |
|---|---|---|
| | - 'Wisley Stardust' **new** | LRHS |
| | 'Summer Solstice' | CBcs CPMA SSpi |
| | 'Sunburst' | CBcs |
| | 'Sundance' | CBcs CPMA MBri MGos NLar |
| § | 'Sundew' | CDoC CTsd EBee EPfP EQua IArd LMil MGos NLar WBVN WBod |
| | 'Sunsation' | CBcs SSpi |
| | 'Sunspire' | CBcs SSpi |
| | 'Susan' $\Psi^{H4}$ | Widely available |
| | 'Susanna van Veen' | CBcs |
| | 'Sweet Valentine' **new** | CPMA |
| | 'Theodora' **new** | CBcs |
| | x ***thompsoniana*** | CBcs CMCN EPfP IDee NLar |
| | 'Thousand Butterflies' | CBcs CPMA |
| | 'Tina Durio' | CBcs |
| | 'Todd Gresham' | CPMA WPGP |
| | 'Trewidden Belle' | CEnd |
| | ***tripetala*** | CBcs CHEx CPLG CTri EBee ELan EPfP IMGH LPan MDun MLan NLar SKHP SSpi SSta WBod WDin WPGP |
| | x ***veitchii*** | CDul CSBt EPfP |
| | - 'Peter Veitch' | CTho |
| | ***virginiana*** | CMCN CPMA EPfP LRHS SBig SSpi WDin WPGP |
| | - 'Henry Hicks' | SSpi |
| | - 'Moonglow' | CPMA |
| | - 'Satellite' **new** | CBcs |
| | 'Vulcan' | CBcs CEnd CMHG CPMA CTho ELan MAsh MBlu MBri MDun NHol SSpi |
| | x ***watsonii*** | see *M.* x *wieseneri* |
| § | x ***wieseneri*** | CBcs CGHE CMCN CPMA EBee ELan EPfP GKir LRHS MAsh MBlu SKHP SPer SPoG SSpi WBVN WFar WGob WPGP |
| | - 'Aashild Kalleberg' | CBcs SSpi |
| | ***wilsonii*** $\Psi^{H4}$ | Widely available |
| | - 'Gwen Baker' | CEnd |
| | 'Yellow Fever' | CBcs CMCN CPMA CTho ECho MDun SSta WBod |
| | 'Yellow Lantern' | CAbP CBcs CDoC CEnd CMCN CPMA CSdC EBee EPfP LMil LRHS LSRN MAsh MBlu NBea NLar NPal SPoG SSpi SSta |
| | ***zenii*** | CSdC |
| | - 'Pink Parchment' | CBcs CPMA |

## x *Mahoberberis* (*Berberidaceae*)

| | |
|---|---|
| ***aquisargentii*** | EBee ECrN EMil EPfP MMuc MRav NHol SEND SPoG WFar WPGP |
| 'Dart's Desire' | NLar |
| 'Dart's Treasure' | EPla WFar |
| 'Magic' | MGos NLar |
| ***miethkeana*** | EBee MBar SRms WDin |

## *Mahonia* ✿ (*Berberidaceae*)

| | | |
|---|---|---|
| | F&M 178 | WPGP |
| | F&M 193 | WPGP |
| § | ***aquifolium*** | CBcs CDul CTrG EBee ECrN EMac GKir LAst MBar MGan MGos MMuc MRav NWea SHBN SPer SPlb SReu WDin WFar |
| | - 'Apollo' $\Psi^{H4}$ | CMac CSBt CWib EBee ECrN ELan EMil EPfP GKir LAst LHop LRHS LSRN MAsh MBar MBlu MBri MGos MRav NBlu NPri SCoo SPer SPoG WDin |
| | - 'Atropurpurea' | CSBt EBee ELan EPfP EPla GKir LRHS MAsh NBPN NLar SPer SPla SPoG WDin |
| * | - 'Cosmo Crawl' | MGos |
| | - 'Euro' **new** | NLar |
| | - 'Exception' | EBee |
| | - 'Fascicularis' | see *M.* x *wagneri* 'Pinnacle' |
| | - 'Green Ripple' | CPMA EPfP MGos NLar |
| | - 'Mirena' | EBee |
| | - 'Orange Flame' | CPMA EPfP MBlu NLar |
| | - 'Smaragd' | CDoC CMac ELan EPfP LRHS LSRN MAsh MBlu MGos MRav SLPl SPoG WHCG |
| | - 'Versicolor' | EPla MBlu |
| | ***bealei*** | see *M. japonica* Bealei Group |
| | ***bodinieri*** | NLar |
| | 'Bokrafoot'$^{PBR}$ **new** | LRHS |
| | ***confusa*** | CDoC CGHE EBee EMil EPla NLar SKHP SSpi WFar WPGP |
| | ***eutriphylla*** | see *M. trifolia* |
| | ***fortunei*** | EPla MBlu NLar WSHC |
| | - 'Winter Prince' | NLar |
| | ***fremontii*** | SKHP |
| | ***gracilipes*** | CGHE EBee EPfP EPla MBlu MDun NLar SKHP SLon WPGP |
| | ***gracilis*** | WPGP |
| | ***japonica*** $\Psi^{H4}$ | Widely available |
| § | - Bealei Group | CBcs CDul CSBt EBee ELan EPfP EPla GKir LAst LRHS MAsh MBar MGos MRav MSwo NHol NPer NScw NWea SCoo SKHP SLim SPoG SWvt WBor WDin WFar WGwG |
| | - 'Gold Dust' | LAst SPer |
| | - 'Hiemalis' | see *M. japonica* 'Hivernant' |
| § | - 'Hivernant' | EBee MGos NBlu NWea WOrn |
| | ***leschenaultii*** B&SWJ 9535 | WCru |
| | ***lomariifolia*** $\Psi^{H3}$ | CBcs CHEx EBee EPfP EWes GCal LRHS SAPC SArc SKHP SPoG SSpi SSta |
| | x ***media*** 'Buckland' $\Psi^{H4}$ | CAbP CBcs CDul CMac CSBt CSam CTrC CWSG EBee EMil EPfP ERas LAst LHop LRHS MRav SDix SHBN SPer SRms WPat |
| | - 'Charity' | Widely available |
| | - 'Faith' | EPla |
| | - 'Hope' | NLar |
| | - 'Lionel Fortescue' $\Psi^{H4}$ | CBcs CEnd CMac CPSs CSBt CSam CTrC EBee ELan EPfP ISea LHop LRHS MAsh MGos MRav NPri SDix SMad SPer SPoG SSpi WBVN WFar |
| | - 'Underway' $\Psi^{H4}$ | CSam EPfP LRHS MAsh NLar SPoG |
| | - 'Winter Sun' $\Psi^{H4}$ | Widely available |
| | ***nervosa*** | CBcs EPfP EPla MBlu MRav NLar SKHP SPer WCru WDin WPat |
| | - B&SWJ 9562 | WCru |
| | ***oiwakensis*** B&SWJ 3660 | WCru |
| | - B&SWJ 371 **new** | WCru |
| | ***pallida*** | EBee SKHP WPGP |
| | ***pinnata*** misapplied | see *M.* x *wagneri* 'Pinnacle' |
| | ***pinnata*** ambig. | EPfP EPla MBar |
| | ***pumila*** | WCru |
| | ***repens*** | EPla GCal NLar |
| | - 'Rotundifolia' | EPla |
| | x ***savilliana*** | EPla MBlu WPGP |
| | - 'Commissioner' | CWib |
| § | ***trifolia*** | GCal |
| | ***trifoliolata*** var. ***glauca*** | CEnd CPMA NLar |
| | x ***wagneri*** 'Fireflame' | EPla GCal |
| | - 'Hastings Elegant' | CPMA NLar |
| | - 'Moseri' | NLar SSpi WCot WPat |
| § | - 'Pinnacle' $\Psi^{H4}$ | ELan EPfP EPla LRHS MAsh MGos MLan SPer SPoG WDin |
| | - 'Sunset' | CPMA MBlu NLar |
| | - 'Undulata' | EPfP MBlu NLar SRms WHCG |

## *Maianthemum* (*Convallariaceae*)

| | |
|---|---|
| ***atropurpureum*** | EBee WCru |
| ***bicolor*** | CDes MBri SWat |

| | |
|---|---|
| ***bifolium*** | CBct CDes CHid EBee EBrs ECho EPot GBuc GCra LEdu MNrw MTho NBro NMen SRms WCru WPGP WPnP WTin |
| - from Yakushima | CStu |
| § - subsp. ***kamtschaticum*** | CBct CLAP CPom CRow CWsd EBee ECha EHrv NLar NRya WCot WTin |
| - - B&SWJ 4360 | WCru WPrP |
| - - CD&R 2300 **new** | WCru |
| * - - var. ***minimum*** | GCal GEdr WCru |
| ***canadense*** | CBct EBee EBrs ECho EPot GCal GGar GKir MNrw NBid NMen WCru WPnP |
| * ***chasmanthum*** | EBee EPPr LRHS |
| ***comaltepecense*** B&SWJ 10215 | WCru |
| ***dilatatum*** | see *M. bifolium* subsp. *kamtschaticum* |
| ***dulongense*** **new** | EBee |
| ***flexuosum*** B&SWJ 9026 **new** | WCru |
| - B&SWJ 9069 | WCru |
| - B&SWJ 9255 | WCru |
| ***formosanum*** | EBee EPPr WCot |
| - B&SWJ 349 | WCru |
| ***forrestii*** | EBee WCru |
| ***fuscum*** | GBin WCru |
| - var. ***cordatum*** **new** | WCru |
| ***gongshanense*** **new** | EBee |
| ***henryi*** | EBee ECho GEdr WCru |
| ***japonicum*** | EBee ECho WHil |
| - B&SWJ 1179 | WCru |
| - B&SWJ 4714 **new** | WCru |
| ***lichiangense*** | EBee |
| ***oleraceum*** | CBct EBee ECho GBin GEdr LEdu WCot |
| - B&SWJ 2148 | WCru |
| ***paniculatum*** B&SWJ 10305 **new** | WCru |
| ***purpureum*** | EBee |
| § ***racemosum*** 🏆$^{H4}$ | Widely available |
| - subsp. ***amplexicaule*** | GBin GCal WPrP |
| - - 'Emily Moody' | CFwr CPou ELan SKHP WPGP |
| - dwarf | ECho |
| - 'Wisley Spangles' | LRHS MBri |
| ***salvinii*** B&SWJ 9000 | WCru |
| - B&SWJ 9019 **new** | WCru |
| - B&SWJ 9086 **new** | WCru |
| ***stellatum*** | CBct CRow EBee EBrs ECha ECho EPPr EPla EPot GAuc GEdr LEdu LHop MLLN NChi NMyG WCru WPnP WTin |
| ***szechuanicum*** | EBee GEdr WCru |
| ***tatsiense*** | CAby ECho WCru |
| ***trifolium*** | ECho |
| * ***yunnanense*** **new** | EBee |

## *Maihuenia* (*Cactaceae*)

| | |
|---|---|
| ***poeppigii*** | SIng SPlb |
| - JCA 2.575.600 | WCot |

## *Maireana* (*Chenopodiaceae*)

| | |
|---|---|
| ***georgei*** | SPlb |

## *Malacothamnus* (*Malvaceae*)

| | |
|---|---|
| ***fremontii*** | MDKP |

## *Malus* ✿ (*Rosaceae*)

| | |
|---|---|
| § 'Adirondack' | CDoC CWSG EBee EMil EMui EPfP GKir LRHS MAsh MBri MGos MWat NLar SCoo SLim SPoG |
| 'Admiration' | see *M.* 'Adirondack' |
| x ***adstringens*** 'Almey' | ECrN |
| - 'Hopa' | CDul CLnd MAsh |
| - 'Simcoe' | CLnd CTho EHig LLHF |
| 'Aldenhamensis' | see *M.* x *purpurea* 'Aldenhamensis' |
| x ***arnoldiana*** **new** | LMaj |
| x ***atrosanguinea*** 'Gorgeous' | CCAT CDul CLnd CTho CWSG EBee ECrN GKir GTwe LRHS MAsh MGos MSwo NBlu NLar SCoo SKee SLim SPer SPoG WBod WDin WJas WOrn |
| ***baccata*** | CDul CMCN CTho GTwe NWea SCoo SEND |
| - 'Dolgo' | CCAT CDoC CTho SKee |
| - 'Gracilis' | SBLw |
| - 'Lady Northcliffe' | CLnd CTho |
| - var. ***mandshurica*** | CTho |
| - 'Street Parade' | LMaj |
| aff. ***baccata*** | NWea |
| - MF 96038 | SSpi |
| § ***bhutanica*** | CDul CLnd CTho EPfP GKir MAsh SCrf SPer |
| ***brevipes*** | CLnd CTho GKir MBri NLar SCoo SPoG |
| 'Butterball' | CDul CLnd CTho ECrN EMui EPfP GKir LMaj SCoo SLim SPer SPoG WDin WJas |
| 'Candymint Sargent' | CLnd |
| 'Cave Hill' | CLnd |
| * 'Cheal's Weeping' | ECrN LAst NBea |
| Coccinella = 'Courtarou' | WDin |
| 'Comtessa de Paris' | MAsh |
| 'Coralburst' | MAsh MBri |
| ***coronaria*** var. ***dasycalyx*** 'Charlottae' (d) | CDul CLnd EBee EPfP SMHT SPer SPur |
| - 'Elk River' | LRHS SCoo |
| 'Crimson Brilliant' | CLnd |
| 'Crittenden' | CLnd ECrN MAsh MRav SLim SMHT |
| * 'Directeur Moerlands' | CCVT CDoC EBee ECrN EMil EPfP GKir IArd MAsh MGos SPur WDin WJas |
| ***domestica*** (F) | ECrN WMou |
| - 'Acklam Russet' (D) | SKee |
| - 'Acme' (D) | ECrN MCoo SDea SKee |
| - 'Adams's Pearmain' (D) | CCAT CTho ECrN EMui GKir GTwe LRHS MAsh MCoo SDea SKee WJas WOrn |
| - 'Admiral' (D) | ECrN |
| - 'Akane' (D) | SDea |
| - 'Alfriston' (C) | CAgr SKee |
| § - 'Alkmene' (D) 🏆$^{H4}$ | CAgr ECrN SDea SKee |
| - 'All Doer' (D/C/Cider) | CTho |
| - 'Allen's Everlasting' (D) | GTwe SDea SKee |
| - 'Allington Pippin' (D) | CSBt CTho CTri ECrN SDea SKee WJas |
| - Ambassy = 'Dalil'$^{PBR}$ (D) | SLon |
| - 'American Mother' | see *M. domestica* 'Mother' |
| - 'Ananas Reinette' (D) | ECrN |
| - 'Anna Boelens' (D) | SDea |
| - 'Annie Elizabeth' (C) | CAgr CCAT CTho CWib ECrN GKir GTwe LAst MCoo SDea SKee SVic WJas |
| - 'Anniversary' (D) | SDea |
| - 'Api Rose' (D) | SKee WJas |
| - 'Ard Cairn Russet' (D) | ECrN GTwe SDea SKee WGwG |
| - 'Aromatic Russet' (D) | SKee |
| - 'Arthur Turner' (C) 🏆$^{H4}$ | CCAT CCVT CDoC CTri ECrN EMui GKir GTwe LBuc SCrf SDea SKee WJas |
| - 'Ashmead's Kernel' (D) 🏆$^{H4}$ | CAgr CCAT CSBt CTho CTri CWib ECrN EMui EPfP GKir GTwe LBuc LRHS MAsh MRav MWat NWea SCrf SDea SKee SVic WHar WJas WOrn |

| | |
|---|---|
| - 'Ashton Bitter' (Cider) | CCAT CTho GTwe |
| - 'Ashton Brown Jersey' (Cider) | CCAT |
| - 'Autumn Pearmain' (D) | SDea WJas |
| - 'Baker's Delicious' (D) | CCAT ECrN SDea SKee |
| - 'Ball's Bittersweet' (Cider) | CCAT CTho |
| - 'Ballyfatten' (C) | IFFs |
| - 'Ballyvaughan Seedling' (D) **new** | IFFs |
| - 'Balsam' | see *M. domestica* 'Green Balsam' |
| - 'Banana Pippin' | CEnd |
| - 'Banns' (D) | ECrN |
| - 'Bardsey' (D) | CAgr EMui LBuc WGwG |
| - 'Barnack Beauty' (D) | CTho SKee |
| - 'Barnack Orange' (D) | SKee |
| - 'Baxter's Pearmain' (D) | ECrN SDea SKee |
| - 'Beauty of Bath' (D) | CAgr CCAT CCVT CDoC CDul CTho CTri CWib ECrN EMui GKir GTwe LAst LBuc SDea SKee WJas |
| - 'Beauty of Hants' (D) | ECrN |
| - 'Beauty of Kent' (C) | SDea SKee |
| - 'Beauty of Moray' (C) | GKir GQui SKee |
| - 'Bedwyn Beauty' (C) | CTho |
| - 'Beeley Pippin' (D) | GTwe SDea SKee |
| - 'Bell Apple' (Cider/C) | CCAT CTho |
| - 'Belle de Boskoop' (C/D) ♀H4 | CAgr CCAT GTwe MCoo SDea SKee WGwG |
| - 'Belvoir Seedling' (D/C) | SKee |
| - 'Bembridge Beauty' (F) | SDea |
| - 'Ben's Red' (D) | CAgr CCAT CEnd CTho SKee |
| - 'Bess Pool' (D) | SDea SKee WJas |
| - 'Bewley Down Pippin' | see *M. domestica* 'Crimson King' |
| - 'Bickington Grey' (Cider) | CTho |
| - 'Billy Down Pippin' (F) | CTho |
| - 'Bismarck' (C) | CCAT ECrN SKee |
| - 'Black Dabinett' (Cider) | CCAT CEnd CTho |
| - 'Black Tom Putt' (C/D) | CTho |
| - 'Blenheim Orange' (C/D) ♀H4 | Widely available |
| - 'Blenheim Red' | see *M. domestica* 'Red Blenheim' |
| - 'Bloody Butcher' (C) | IFFs |
| - 'Bloody Ploughman' (D) | ECrN GKir GTwe LRHS SKee |
| - 'Blue Pearmain' (D) | SDea |
| - 'Blue Sweet' (Cider) | CTho |
| - Bolero = 'Tuscan'$^{PBR}$ (D/Ball) | ECrN LRHS MCoo SDea SKee |
| - 'Boston Russet' | see *M. domestica* 'Roxbury Russet' |
| - 'Bountiful' (C) | CAgr CCAT CCVT CDoC CSBt CTri CWib ECrN EMui GKir GTwe LBuc MAsh MBri SDea SKee SPoG WBVN WHar |
| - 'Braddick Nonpareil' (D) | SKee |
| - 'Braeburn' (D) | CAgr CCAT CSut ECrN EMui LAst LRHS MNHC SCrf SDea SKee WHar |
| - 'Braintree Seedling' (D) | ECrN |
| - 'Bramley's Seedling' (C) ♀H4 | Widely available |
| - 'Bramley's Seedling' clone 20 | CDoC EMui MBri NLar SCoo SDea SPoG WHar |
| - 'Bread Fruit' (C/D) | CEnd CTho |
| - 'Breakwell's Seedling' (Cider) | CCAT CTho |
| - 'Brenchley Pippin' (D) | SKee |
| - 'Bridgwater Pippin' (C) | CCAT CTho WJas |
| - 'Broad-eyed Pippin' (C) | SKee |
| - 'Broadholm Beauty' | EMui MAsh |
| - 'Brookes's' (D) **new** | WHar |
| - 'Brown Crofton' (D) | IFFs |
| - 'Brown Snout' (Cider) | CCAT CTho SKee |
| - 'Brownlees Russet' (D) | CAgr CCAT CTho CTri GTwe MCoo NWea SDea WGwG |
| - 'Brown's Apple' (Cider) | CCAT GTwe |
| - 'Broxwood Foxwhelp' (Cider) | CCAT |
| - 'Burn's Seedling' (D) | CTho |
| - 'Burr Knot' (C) | ECrN SKee |
| - 'Burrowhill Early' (Cider) | CTho |
| - 'Bushey Grove' (C) | SDea SKee |
| - 'Buttery Do' | CTho |
| - 'Cadbury' | CCAT |
| - 'Calville Blanc d'Hiver' (D) | SKee |
| - 'Cambusnethan Pippin' (D) | GQui SKee |
| - 'Camelot' (Cider/C) | CCAT |
| - 'Cap of Liberty' (Cider) | CCAT |
| - 'Captain Broad' (D/Cider) | CCAT CEnd CTho |
| - 'Captain Kidd' (D) | EMui |
| - 'Captain Smith' (F) | CEnd |
| - 'Carlisle Codlin' (C) | GKir GTwe NLar NWea SDea |
| - 'Caroline' (D) | ECrN |
| - 'Catherine' (C) | ECrN |
| - 'Catshead' (C) | CAgr CCAT ECrN GKir GQui SDea SKee WJas |
| - 'Cellini' (C/D) | SDea |
| - 'Charles Ross' (C/D) ♀H4 | Widely available |
| - 'Charlotte'$^{PBR}$ (C/Ball) | MGos SDea |
| - 'Chaxhill Red' (Cider/D) | CCAT CTho |
| - 'Cheddar Cross' (D) | CAgr CTri ECrN |
| - 'Chelmsford Wonder' (C) | ECrN SKee |
| - 'Chisel Jersey' (Cider) | CCAT CTri |
| - 'Chivers Delight' (D) | CAgr CCAT CSBt ECrN EMui GKir GTwe MCoo SDea SKee WJas |
| - 'Chorister Boy' (D) | CTho |
| - 'Christmas Pearmain' (D) | CTho ECrN GTwe SDea SKee |
| - 'Cider Lady's Finger' (Cider) | CCAT SKee |
| - 'Cissy' (D) **new** | WGwG |
| - 'Claygate Pearmain' (D) ♀H4 | CCAT CTho CTri ECrN GTwe MCoo SDea SKee SVic WJas |
| - 'Clopton Red' (D) | ECrN SKee |
| - 'Clydeside' | GKir GQui |
| - 'Coat Jersey' (Cider) | CCAT |
| - 'Cockle Pippin' (D) | CAgr CTho SDea |
| - 'Coeur de Boeuf' (C/D) | SKee |
| - 'Coleman's Seedling' (Cider) | CTho |
| - 'Collogett Pippin' (C/Cider) | CCAT CEnd CTho |
| - 'Colonel Vaughan' (C/D) | SKee |
| - 'Cooper's Seedling' (C) | SCrf |
| - 'Cornish Aromatic' (D) | CAgr CCAT CTho GTwe SCrf SDea SKee WGwG WJas |
| - 'Cornish Gilliflower' (D) | CAgr CCAT CTho ECrN EMui LRHS MCoo SDea SKee WJas WOrn |
| - 'Cornish Honeypin' (D) | CEnd CTho |
| - 'Cornish Longstem' (D) | CAgr CEnd CTho |
| - 'Cornish Mother' (D) | CEnd CTho |
| - 'Cornish Pine' (D) | CEnd CTho SDea SKee |
| - 'Coronation' (D) | SDea SKee |
| - 'Corse Hill' (D) | CCAT CTho |
| - 'Costard' (C) | GTwe SKee |
| - 'Cottenham Seedling' (C) | ECrN SKee |
| - 'Coul Blush' (D) | SKee |
| - 'Court of Wick' (D) | CAgr CCAT CTho ECrN GKir SKee SVic |
| - 'Court Pendu Plat' (D) | CAgr CCAT CTho GKir LBuc MWat NWea SDea SKee WJas WOrn |
| - 'Court Royal' (Cider) | CCAT |
| - 'Cow Apple' (C) | CCAT |
| - 'Cox Cymraeg' (D) | WGwG |
| - 'Cox's Orange Pippin' (D) | CBcs CCAT CCVT CDul CMac CSBt CTri CWib ECrN EMui GTwe LAst LRHS MAsh MWat NPri SCrf SDea SKee SPer WJas WOrn |

| | | |
|---|---|---|
| | - 'Cox's Pomona' (C/D) | SDea SKee WJas |
| | - 'Cox's Rouge de Flandres' (D) | SKee |
| | - 'Cox's Selfing' (D) | CDoC CTri CWSG CWib EMui EPfP GKir GTwe LBuc MAsh MBri MGan MGos MNHC SCrf SDea SKee SPoG WHar WJas |
| | - 'Craigflower Classic' **new** | GKir |
| | - 'Crawley Beauty' (C) | CAgr CCAT GTwe SDea SKee WJas |
| | - 'Crawley Reinette' (D) | SKee |
| | - 'Crimson Beauty of Bath' (D) | CAgr |
| | - 'Crimson Bramley' (C) | CCAT LAst |
| | - 'Crimson Cox' (D) | SDea |
| § | - 'Crimson King' (Cider/C) | CAgr CCAT |
| | - 'Crimson King' (D) | CAgr |
| | - 'Crimson Queening' (D) | SKee |
| | - 'Crimson Victoria' (Cider) | CTho |
| | - Crispin | see *M. domestica* 'Mutsu' |
| § | - 'Crowngold' (D) | EMui GTwe |
| | - 'Cutler Grieve' (D) | SDea |
| | - Cybèle = 'Delrouval' | LBuc |
| | - 'Dabinett' (Cider) | CCAT CTho CTri EMui GTwe SCrf SDea SKee WOrn |
| | - 'D'Arcy Spice' (D) | CAgr CCAT ECrN EMil EMui EPfP MCoo SDea SKee WGwG |
| | - 'Dawn' (D) | SKee |
| | - 'Deacon's Blushing Beauty' (C/D) | SDea |
| | - 'Deacon's Millennium' | SDea |
| | - 'Decio' (D) | SKee |
| | - 'Devon Crimson Queen' (D) | CTho |
| | - 'Devon Crisp' (D) **new** | CSut |
| | - 'Devonshire Buckland' (C) | CEnd CTho |
| | - 'Devonshire Crimson Queen' (D) | SDea |
| | - 'Devonshire Quarrenden' (D) | CAgr CCAT CEnd CTho ECrN GKir SDea SKee SVic WJas |
| | - 'Diamond' (D) **new** | WGwG |
| | - 'Discovery' (D) ♀$^{H4}$ | Widely available |
| | - 'Doctor Harvey' (C) | ECrN |
| | - 'Doctor Kidd's Orange Red' | see *M. domestica* 'Kidd's Orange Red' |
| | - 'Don's Delight' (C) | CTho |
| | - 'Dove' (Cider) | CCAT |
| | - 'Dredge's Fame' (D) | CTho |
| | - 'Duchess's Favourite' (D) | SKee |
| | - 'Dufflin' (Cider) | CCAT CTho |
| | - 'Duke of Cornwall' (C) | CTho |
| | - 'Duke of Devonshire' (D) | CTho CTri SDea SKee |
| N | - 'Dumeller's Seedling' | see *M. domestica* 'Dummellor's Seedling' |
| § | - 'Dummellor's Seedling' (C) ♀$^{H4}$ | CCAT SDea SKee |
| | - 'Dunkerton Late Sweet' (Cider) | CCAT CTho EMil |
| | - 'Dunn's Seedling' (D) | SDea |
| § | - 'Dutch Mignonne' (D) | ECrN SKee |
| | - 'Dymock Red' (Cider) | CCAT |
| | - 'Early Blenheim' (D/C) | CCAT CEnd CTho |
| | - 'Early Bower' (D) | CEnd |
| | - 'Early Julyan' (C) | GKir GQui SKee |
| | - 'Early Victoria' | see *M. domestica* 'Emneth Early' |
| | - Early Windsor = 'Alkmene' | see *M. domestica* 'Alkmene' |
| | - 'Early Worcester' | see *M. domestica* 'Tydeman's Early Worcester' |
| | - 'East Lothian Pippin' (C) | GQui SKee |
| | - 'Easter Orange' (D) | GTwe SKee |
| | - 'Ecklinville' (C) | SDea |
| | - 'Edith Hopwood' (D) | ECrN |
| | - 'Edward VII' (C) ♀$^{H4}$ | CCAT CDoC GKir GTwe SCrf SDea SKee |
| | - 'Egremont Russet' (D) ♀$^{H4}$ | Widely available |
| | - 'Ellis' Bitter' (Cider) | CCAT CTho GTwe SKee SVic |
| | - 'Ellison's Orange' (D) ♀$^{H4}$ | CAgr CCAT CDul CSBt CTri CWib ECrN EMui EPfP GKir GTwe LAst LBuc MAsh NWea SDea SKee SVic WHar WJas WOrn |
| | - 'Elstar' (D) ♀$^{H4}$ | CWib ECrN EMui GKir GTwe LAst MRav NBlu SDea SKee |
| | - 'Elton Beauty' (D) | SDea |
| § | - 'Emneth Early' (C) ♀$^{H4}$ | CAgr ECrN EMui GKir GTwe SDea SKee WJas WOrn |
| | - 'Empire' (D) | LAst SKee |
| | - 'Encore' (C) | SDea |
| | - 'Endsleigh Beauty' (D) **new** | CEnd |
| | - 'English Codlin' | CCAT CTho CTri |
| | - 'Epicure' | see *M. domestica* 'Laxton's Epicure' |
| | - 'Ernie's Russet' (D) | SDea |
| | - 'Eros' (D) | ECrN |
| | - 'Essex Pippin' (D) | ECrN |
| | - 'Evening Gold' (C) | SDea |
| | - 'Eve's Delight' (D) | SDea |
| | - 'Excelsior' (C) | ECrN |
| | - 'Exeter Cross' (D) | CCAT ECrN SDea |
| | - 'Eynsham Dumpling' (C) | MWat |
| | - 'Fair Maid of Devon' (Cider) | CAgr CCAT CEnd CTho |
| | - 'Fairfield' (D) | CTho |
| | - 'Falstaff'$^{PBR}$ (D) ♀$^{H4}$ | CAgr CCAT CCVT CDoC ECrN EMui EPfP GKir GTwe MGos SCoo SDea SKee WBVN WJas |
| | - 'Farmer's Glory' (D) | CAgr CTho |
| | - 'Fiesta'$^{PBR}$ (D) ♀$^{H4}$ | Widely available |
| | - 'Fillbarrel' (Cider) | CCAT |
| | - 'Firmgold' (D) | SDea |
| | - 'Flame' (D) | ECrN |
| | - 'Flamenco'$^{PBR}$ | see *M. domestica* 'Obelisk' |
| § | - 'Flower of Kent' (C) | CCAT SCrf SDea SKee |
| | - 'Flower of the Town' (D) | SKee |
| | - 'Forfar' | see *M. domestica* 'Dutch Mignonne' |
| | - 'Forge' (D) | CAgr SDea |
| | - 'Fortune' | see *M. domestica* 'Laxton's Fortune' |
| | - 'Foulden Pearmain' (D) | ECrN |
| | - 'Foxwhelp' (Cider) **new** | SKee |
| | - 'Francis' (D) | ECrN |
| | - 'Frederick' (Cider) | CCAT CTho |
| | - 'French Crab' (C) | SDea |
| | - 'Freyberg' (D) | SKee |
| | - 'Fuji' (D) | SDea SKee |
| | - 'Gala' (D) | CMac CSBt EMui GTwe LAst SCoo SCrf SDea SKee WHar |
| § | - 'Gala Mondial' (D) | WJas |
| | - 'Gala Royal' | see *M. domestica* 'Royal Gala' |
| | - 'Galloway Pippin' (C) | GKir GQui GTwe SKee |
| | - 'Garnet' (D) | ECrN |
| | - 'Gascoyne's Scarlet' (D) | CCAT GKir SDea SKee |
| | - 'Gavin' (D) | CAgr SDea SKee |
| | - 'Genesis II' (D/C) | SDea |
| | - 'Genet Moyle' (C/Cider) | CCAT CTri WJas |
| | - 'George Carpenter' (D) | SDea SKee |
| | - 'George Cave' (D) | CTho ECrN GTwe MCoo SDea SKee WJas |
| | - 'George Neal' (C) ♀$^{H4}$ | CAgr SDea |
| | - 'Gibbon's Russet' (D) **new** | IFFs |
| | - 'Gilliflower of Gloucester' (D) | CTho |
| | - 'Gin' (Cider) | CCAT |
| | - 'Gladstone' (D) | CAgr CTho SKee |
| § | - 'Glass Apple' (C/D) | CCAT CEnd CTho |
| | - 'Gloria Mundi' (C) | SDea SKee |

| | |
|---|---|
| - 'Gloster '69' (D) | NBlu SDea |
| - 'Gloucester Royal' (D) | CTho |
| - 'Gloucester Underleaf' | CTho |
| - 'Golden Ball' | CTho |
| - 'Golden Bittersweet' (D) | CAgr CTho |
| - 'Golden Delicious' (D) 𝕐H4 | CDul CSBt CSut CWib ECrN EMui EPfP LAst NBlu SCrf SDea SKee SPer SVic WHar WOrn |
| - 'Golden Glow' (C) | SDea |
| - 'Golden Harvey' (D) | CAgr CCAT |
| - 'Golden Jubilee' | CEnd |
| - 'Golden Knob' (D) | CCAT CTho |
| - 'Golden Noble' (C) 𝕐H4 | CAgr CCAT CDoC CTho CTri ECrN GKir GTwe MCoo SDea SKee WOrn |
| - 'Golden Nugget' (D) | CAgr |
| - 'Golden Pippin' (C) | CAgr CCAT SKee SVic |
| - 'Golden Reinette' (D) | GTwe SKee |
| - 'Golden Russet' (D) | CAgr ECrN GTwe SDea SKee |
| - 'Golden Spire' (C) | MCoo SDea SKee |
| - 'Gooseberry' (C) | SKee |
| - 'Goring' (Cider) | CTho |
| - 'Grand Sultan' (D) | CCAT |
| - 'Granny Smith' (D) | CDul CLnd CWib ECrN GTwe LAst SCrf SDea SKee SPer SVic WHar |
| - 'Gravenstein' (D) | CCAT GKir GQui SDea SKee |
| § - 'Green Balsam' (C) | CTri |
| - 'Green Kilpandy Pippin' (C) | GQui |
| - 'Green Roland' | ECrN |
| - 'Greensleeves' PBR (D) 𝕐H4 | CAgr CCAT CDoC CMac CSBt CTri CWSG CWib ECrN EMui GKir GTwe LAst MAsh MGan MGos SDea SKee SPoG WBVN WHar WJas WOrn |
| - 'Grenadier' (C) 𝕐H4 | CAgr CCAT CDoC CSBt CTri ECrN EMui GKir GTwe LRHS MGos SDea SKee SVic WJas WOrn |
| - 'Halstow Natural' (Cider) | CAgr CTho |
| - 'Hambledon Deux Ans' (C) | SDea |
| - 'Hangy Down' (Cider) | CCAT CTho |
| - 'Harbert's Reinette' (D) | SKee |
| § - 'Harry Master's Jersey' (Cider) | CCAT CTho CTri SDea SKee |
| - 'Harvester' (D) | CTho |
| - 'Harvey' (C) | SDea |
| - 'Hawthornden' (C) | GQui GTwe SKee |
| - 'Hereford Cross' (D) | SKee |
| - 'Herefordshire Beefing' (C) | WJas WOrn |
| - 'Herefordshire Russet' PBR | EMui LBuc LRHS MAsh MBri MCoo SKee WOrn |
| - 'Herring's Pippin' (D) | GTwe SDea |
| - 'High View Pippin' (D) | SKee |
| - 'Hoary Morning' (C) | CCAT CTho ECrN SDea SKee |
| - 'Hocking's Green' (C/D) | CAgr CCAT CEnd CTho |
| - 'Holland Pippin' (C) | SKee |
| - 'Hollow Core' (C) | CAgr CTho |
| - 'Holstein' (D) | CTho SDea SKee |
| - 'Honey Pippin' (D) | ECrN |
| - 'Horneburger Pfannkuchen' (C) | SKee |
| - 'Horsford Prolific' (D) | ECrN |
| - 'Howgate Wonder' (C) | CAgr CCAT CCVT CDoC CDul CSBt CWib ECrN EMui GKir GTwe LAst LBuc LRHS MAsh SCrf SDea SKee SPer SVic WBVN WHar WJas |
| - 'Hubbard's Pearmain' (D) | ECrN SKee |
| - 'Hunter's Majestic' (D/C) | ECrN |
| - 'Hunt's Duke of Gloucester' (D) | CTho |
| - 'Idared' (D) 𝕐H4 | CCAT CWib ECrN GKir SDea SKee SVic |

| | |
|---|---|
| - 'Improved Dove' (Cider) | CCAT |
| - 'Improved Keswick' (C/D) | CEnd CTho |
| - 'Improved Lambrook Pippin' (Cider) | CCAT CTho CTri |
| - 'Improved Redstreak' (Cider) | CTho |
| - 'Ingrid Marie' (D) | SDea SKee WJas |
| - 'Irish Peach' (D) | CAgr CCAT ECrN GKir GTwe IFFs MCoo SDea SKee WJas |
| - 'Isaac Newton's Tree' | see *M. domestica* 'Flower of Kent' |
| - 'Isle of Wight Pippin' (D) | SDea |
| - 'Isle of Wight Russet' (D) | SDea |
| - 'Jackson's' | see *M. domestica* 'Crimson King' |
| - 'James Grieve' (D) 𝕐H4 | Widely available |
| - 'James Lawson' (D) | SKee |
| - 'Jerseymac' (D) | SDea |
| - 'Jester' (D) | ECrN GTwe SDea SKee |
| - 'John Standish' (D) | CAgr CCAT CTri GTwe SCrf SDea |
| - 'John Toucher's' | see *M. domestica* 'Crimson King' |
| - 'Johnny Andrews' (Cider) | CAgr CCAT CTho |
| - 'Johnny Voun' (D) | CEnd CTho |
| - 'Jonagold' (D) 𝕐H4 | CTri CWib ECrN EMil EMui GTwe LAst MAsh SCrf SDea SKee SPer SVic WJas |
| - 'Jonagold Crowngold' | see *M. domestica* 'Crowngold' |
| § - 'Jonagored' PBR (D) | SDea SKee |
| - 'Jonared' (D) | GTwe |
| - 'Jonathan' (D) | SDea SKee |
| - 'Jordan's Weeping' (C) | GTwe SDea WJas |
| - 'Josephine' (D) | SDea |
| - 'Joybells' (D) | GKir |
| - 'Jubilee' | see *M. domestica* 'Royal Jubilee' |
| - 'Jumbo' | LBuc MAsh MBri MCoo SKee |
| - 'Jupiter' PBR (D) 𝕐H4 | CCAT CDul CSBt CTri CWib ECrN GKir GTwe LAst MAsh SDea SKee WJas WOrn |
| - 'Kandil Sinap' (D) | SKee |
| - 'Kapai Red Jonathan' (D) | SDea |
| - 'Karmijn de Sonnaville' (D) | SDea |
| § - 'Katja' (D) | CAgr CCAT CCVT CDoC CTri CWib ECrN EMui GKir GTwe LAst LBuc MAsh NLar SCoo SDea SKee SPer WHar WJas WOrn |
| - Katy see *M. domestica* 'Katja' | |
| - 'Kent' (D) | ECrN EMui GTwe MCoo NLar SCrf SDea SKee |
| - 'Kentish Fillbasket' (C) | SKee |
| - 'Kentish Pippin' (C/Cider/D) | SKee |
| - 'Kerry Pippin' (D) | IFFs SKee |
| - 'Keswick Codlin' (C) | CTho ECrN GKir GTwe MCoo NLar NWea SDea SKee WJas |
| § - 'Kidd's Orange Red' (D) 𝕐H4 | CAgr CCAT CTri ECrN EMui GQui GTwe LAst LBuc LRHS SCrf SDea SKee WJas |
| - 'Kilkenny Pearmain' (D) **new** | IFFs |
| - 'Kill Boy' | CTho |
| - 'Killerton Sharp' (Cider) | CTho |
| - 'Killerton Sweet' (Cider) | CTho |
| - 'King Byerd' (C/D) | CCAT CEnd CTho |
| - 'King Luscious' (D) | SDea |
| § - 'King of the Pippins' (D) 𝕐H4 | CCAT CTho CTri ECrN GTwe SCrf SDea SKee SVic WOrn |
| - 'King Russet' (D) 𝕐H4 | SDea |
| - 'King's Acre Pippin' (D) | CCAT SDea WJas |
| - 'Kingston Bitter' (Cider) | CTho |
| - 'Kingston Black' (Cider/C) | CCAT CEnd CTho CTri ECrN GTwe SDea SKee |
| - 'Kirton Fair' (D) | CTho |
| - 'Lady Henniker' (D) | CCAT CTho ECrN GTwe SDea SKee WJas |

| | | |
|---|---|---|
| | - 'Lady of the Wemyss' (C) | GKir GQui SKee |
| | - 'Lady Sudeley' (D) | CTho SDea SKee |
| | - 'Lady's Finger' (C/D) | CEnd GKir |
| | - 'Lady's Finger of Lancaster' (C/D) | SKee |
| | - 'Lady's Finger of Offaly' (D) | SDea |
| | - 'Lake's Kernel' (D) | CTho |
| | - 'Lamb Abbey Pearmain' (D) | SKee |
| | - 'Lane's Prince Albert' (C) ♀H4 | CAgr CCAT CSBt ECrN EMui GKir GTwe MGos MRav MWat NWea SCoo SCrf SDea SKee SVic WHar WJas WOrn |
| | - 'Langley Pippin' (D) | SDea |
| § | - 'Langworthy' (Cider) | CCAT CTho |
| | - 'Lass o' Gowrie' (C) | GKir GQui SKee |
| § | - 'Laxton's Epicure' (D) ♀H4 | CAgr CDul ECrN GTwe LAst SDea SKee WJas |
| § | - 'Laxton's Fortune' (D) ♀H4 | CCAT CDul CMac CSBt CTri CWib ECrN EMui GKir GTwe LAst SCrf SDea SKee WHar WJas |
| | - 'Laxton's Pearmain' (D) | MCoo |
| | - 'Laxton's Rearguard' (D) | WJas |
| | - 'Laxton's Royalty' (D) | SDea |
| § | - 'Laxton's Superb' (D) | CBcs CCAT CCVT CDoC CSBt CTri CWib ECrN EMui GKir GTwe LAst LBuc LRHS MCoo MGan NPri NWea SCrf SDea SKee SPer SVic WHar WJas WOrn |
| | - 'Leathercoat Russet' (D) | CAgr CCAT SKee |
| | - 'Lemon Pippin' (C) | CCAT ECrN SDea SKee |
| | - 'Lemon Pippin of Gloucestershire' (D) | CTho |
| | - 'Lewis's Incomparable' (C) | SKee |
| | - 'Liberty' (D) | GKir SDea |
| | - 'Limberland' (C) | CTho |
| | - 'Limelight' (D) | EMui LRHS MAsh MBri MCoo NLar SCoo SKee |
| | - 'Link Wonder' | CEnd |
| | - 'Lodgemore Nonpareil' (D) | SKee |
| | - 'Lodi' (C) | SDea |
| | - 'London Pearmain' (D) | ECrN |
| | - 'London Pippin' (C) | CAgr CTho |
| | - 'Longkeeper' (D) | CAgr CEnd CTho |
| | - 'Longstem' (Cider) | CTho |
| | - 'Lord Burghley' (D) | SDea |
| | - 'Lord Derby' (C) | CAgr CCAT CDul CMac CTho CWib ECrN EMui GKir GTwe LAst MBri SCrf SDea SKee SVic |
| | - 'Lord Hindlip' (D) | GTwe SDea |
| | - 'Lord Lambourne' (D) ♀H4 | CAgr CCAT CCVT CDoC CDul CMac CSBt CTri CWib ECrN EMui EPfP GKir GTwe LAst LRHS MAsh MCoo MWat SCrf SDea SKee SPer WBVN WHar WJas WOrn |
| | - 'Lord of the Isles' (F) | CAgr CCAT |
| | - 'Lord Stradbroke' (C) | ECrN SKee |
| | - 'Lord Suffield' (C) | CTri ECrN |
| | - 'Lough Tree of Wexford' (D) **new** | IFFs |
| | - 'Lucombe's Pine' (D) | CAgr CEnd CTho ECrN SVic WGwG |
| | - 'Lucombe's Seedling' (D) | CTho |
| | - 'Lynn's Pippin' (D) | ECrN |
| | - 'Mabbott's Pearmain' (D) | SDea |
| | - 'Maclean's Favourite' (D) | ECrN |
| | - 'Madresfield Court' (D) | SDea SKee WJas |
| | - 'Maggie Sinclair' (D) | GQui |
| | - 'Maid of Kent' **new** | CCAT |
| | - 'Major' (Cider) | CCAT |
| | - 'Maldon Wonder' (D) | ECrN |
| | - 'Malling Kent' (D) | EMui SDea |
| | - 'Maltster' (D) | SKee WJas |
| | - 'Manaccan Primrose' (C/D) | CEnd |
| | - 'Margil' (D) | CCAT SDea SKee |
| | - 'Maxton' (D) | ECrN |
| | - 'May Queen' (D) | SDea WJas |
| | - 'Maypole' PBR (D/Ball) | MAsh MGos SDea WJas |
| | - 'McIntosh' (D) | SKee |
| | - 'Médaille d'Or' (Cider) | SKee |
| | - 'Melba' (D) | SKee |
| | - 'Melon' (D) | SDea |
| | - 'Melrose' (D) | ECrN GTwe SVic |
| | - 'Merchant Apple' (D) | CCAT CTho CTri |
| | - 'Meridian' PBR (D) | CAgr CDoC ECrN EMil EMui SDea |
| | - 'Merton Knave' (D) | GTwe SDea |
| | - 'Merton Russet' (D) | SDea |
| | - 'Merton Worcester' (D) | ECrN SDea SKee |
| | - 'Michaelmas Red' (D) | GTwe SKee WJas |
| | - 'Michelin' (Cider) | CCAT CTri GTwe SDea SKee WOrn |
| | - 'Miller's Seedling' (D) | SKee |
| | - 'Millicent Barnes' (D) | SDea |
| | - 'Mollie's Delicious' (D) | SKee |
| | - 'Monarch' (C) | CAgr CCAT CTri ECrN GTwe SDea SKee |
| | - 'Mondial Gala' | see *M. domestica* 'Gala Mondial' |
| | - 'Monidel' PBR | ECrN |
| | - 'Montfort' (D) | ECrN |
| | - 'Morgan's Sweet' (C/Cider) | CCAT CEnd CTho CTri SDea SKee |
| | - 'Moss's Seedling' (D) | SDea |
| § | - 'Mother' (D) ♀H4 | CAgr CCAT CDoC CTri ECrN GTwe SCrf SDea SKee |
| § | - 'Mutsu' (D) | CCAT CTri ECrN SCrf SDea SKee |
| | - 'Nant Gwrtheyrn' (D) | WGwG |
| | - 'Nasona' (D) | SKee |
| | - 'Nettlestone Pippin' (D) | SDea |
| | - 'Newton Wonder' (D/C) ♀H4 | CAgr CCAT CCVT CDoC CMac CSBt CTho CTri CWib ECrN EMui GTwe LAst LBuc MCoo SCrf SDea SKee WJas WOrn |
| | - 'Newtown Pippin' (D) | SDea |
| | - 'Nine Square' (D) | CCAT CTho |
| | - 'Nittany Red' (D) | SDea |
| | - 'No Pip' (C) | CTho |
| | - 'Nolan Pippin' (D) | ECrN |
| | - 'Nonpareil' (D) | SKee |
| | - 'Norfolk Beauty' (C) | ECrN SKee |
| | - 'Norfolk Beefing' (C) | ECrN SDea SKee |
| | - 'Norfolk Royal' (D) | CDoC ECrN GTwe SDea SKee |
| | - 'Norfolk Royal Russet' (D) | ECrN |
| | - 'Norfolk Summer Broadend' (C) | SKee |
| | - 'Norfolk Winter Coleman' (C) | SKee |
| | - 'Northcott Superb' (D) | CTho |
| | - 'Northern Greening' (C) | SKee |
| § | - 'Northwood' (Cider) | CCAT CTho SKee |
| | - 'Nutmeg Pippin' (D) | CCAT ECrN SDea |
| | - Nuvar Freckles (D) | SKee |
| | - Nuvar Gold (D) | SKee |
| | - Nuvar Golden Elf | SKee |
| | - Nuvar Golden Hills (D) | SKee |
| | - Nuvar Home Farm (D) | SKee |
| | - Nuvar Long Harvest (D) | SKee |
| | - Nuvar Melody (D) | SKee |
| | - Nuvar Red Gloss (D) | SKee |
| | - 'Oaken Pin' (C) | CCAT CTho |
| § | - 'Obelisk' PBR (D) | MCoo NPri SDea |
| | - 'Old Pearmain' (D) | SDea SKee |
| | - 'Old Somerset Russet' (D) | CCAT CTho |

| | |
|---|---|
| - 'Opal'PBR (D) | ECrN |
| - 'Opalescent' (D) | SKee |
| - 'Orange Goff' (D) | SKee |
| - 'Orkney Apple' (F) | SKee |
| - 'Orleans Reinette' (D) | CAgr CCAT CTho CTri CWib ECrN GTwe LBuc LRHS MWat SCrf SDea SKee WJas |
| - 'Oslin' (D) | GKir SKee |
| - 'Otava'PBR **new** | SKee |
| - 'Owen Thomas' (D) | CTri |
| - 'Oxford Conquest' (D) | MWat |
| - 'Paignton Marigold' (Cider) | CTho |
| - 'Park Farm Pippin'PBR (F) | GKir |
| - 'Pascoe's Pippin' (D/C) | CTho |
| - 'Paulared' (D) | SKee |
| - 'Payhembury' (C/Cider) | CAgr CTho CTri |
| - 'Pear Apple' (D) | CAgr CEnd CTho |
| - 'Pearl' (D) | ECrN SDea |
| - 'Peasgood's Nonsuch' (C) 🏆H4 | CAgr CCAT CDoC ECrN GKir GTwe MAsh MGan SCrf SDea SKee SLon WOrn |
| - 'Pendragon' (D) | CTho |
| - 'Penhallow Pippin' (D) | CTho |
| - 'Peter Lock' (C/D) | CAgr CCAT CEnd CTho NWea |
| - 'Peter's Pippin' (D) | SDea |
| - 'Peter's Seedling' (D) | SDea |
| - 'Pethyre' (Cider) | CCAT |
| - 'Pig Aderyn' (C) **new** | WGwG |
| - 'Pig y Glomen' (C) **new** | WGwG |
| - 'Pig's Nose Pippin' (D) | CEnd |
| - 'Pig's Nose Pippin' Type III (D) | CAgr CTho |
| - 'Pig's Snout' (Cider/C/D) | CCAT CEnd CTho |
| - 'Pine Apple Russet' | CAgr |
| - 'Pine Golden Pippin' (D) | SKee |
| - 'Pinova' (D) | CAgr |
| - 'Pitmaston Pine Apple' (D) | CCAT CTho CTri ECrN LAst MAsh MCoo SCrf SDea SKee WOrn |
| - 'Pitmaston Russet Nonpareil' (D) | SKee |
| - 'Pixie' (D) 🏆H4 | CCAT CWib EMui GTwe LRHS SDea SKee WJas |
| - 'Plum Vite' (D) | CAgr CTho CTri |
| - 'Plympton Pippin' (C) | CEnd CTho CTri |
| - Polka = 'Trajan'PBR (D/Ball) | MGos SDea SKee |
| - 'Polly' (C/D) | CEnd |
| - 'Polly Whitehair' (C/D) | CCAT CTho SDea |
| - 'Poltimore Seedling' | CTho |
| - 'Pomeroy of Somerset' (D) | CCAT CTho CTri |
| - 'Ponsford' (C) | CAgr CCAT CTho |
| - 'Port Allen Russet' (C/D) | GKir GQui |
| - 'Port Wine' | see *M. domestica* 'Harry Master's Jersey' |
| - 'Porter's Perfection' (Cider) | CCAT |
| - 'Princesse' | ECrN EMui GKir SDea SKee |
| - 'Profit' | CTho |
| - 'Quarry Apple' (C) | CTho |
| - 'Queen' (C) | CAgr CTho ECrN SKee |
| - 'Queen Cox' (D) | CTri ECrN EMui SDea SKee SLon |
| - 'Queen Cox' self-fertile | CSut CWib EMui LCro SDea |
| - 'Queens' (D) | CTho |
| - 'Quench' (D/Cider) | CTho |
| - 'Radford Beauty' | MCoo |
| - 'Rajka' (D) | SKee |
| - 'Red Alkmene' (D) | MBri |
| - 'Red Belle de Boskoop' (D) | CAgr |
| § - 'Red Blenheim' (C/D) | SKee |
| - 'Red Bramley' (C) | CWib GKir |
| - 'Red Charles Ross' (C/D) | SDea |
| - 'Red Delicious' (D) | SCrf |
| - 'Red Devil' (D) | CAgr CTri CWSG ECrN EMui GKir GTwe LAst MBri MNHC NLar SCoo SDea SKee SPoG WHar WJas |
| - 'Red Ellison' (D) | CCAT CTho CTri GTwe SDea |
| - 'Red Elstar' (D) | SCrf |
| - 'Red Falstaff'PBR (D) | CAgr CCAT CCVT CDoC CMac ECrN EMui GKir LBuc LRHS MAsh MBri MCoo NLar SKee SPoG WBVN WHar |
| - 'Red Fuji' (D) | SDea |
| - 'Red James Grieve' | GKir |
| - 'Red Jersey' (Cider) | CCAT |
| - 'Red Joaneting' (D) | SKee |
| - 'Red Jonagold'PBR | see *M. domestica* 'Jonagored' |
| - 'Red Jonathan' (D) | SDea |
| - 'Red Miller's Seedling' (D) | ECrN SCrf SDea |
| - 'Red Rattler' (D) | CTho |
| - 'Red Roller' (D) | CTho |
| - 'Red Ruby' (F) | CTho |
| - 'Red Sauce' (C) | SKee |
| - 'Red Victoria' (C) | GTwe |
| - 'Red Windsor' | EMui GKir LRHS MAsh NLar SCoo SKee SPoG WHar |
| - 'Redcoat Grieve' (D) | GKir SDea |
| - 'Redsleeves' (D) | CAgr ECrN GTwe SDea SKee |
| - 'Redstrake' (Cider) | CCAT |
| - 'Reine des Reinettes' | see *M. domestica* 'King of the Pippins' |
| - 'Reinette Descardre' (D) **new** | SVic |
| - 'Reinette d'Obry' (Cider) | CCAT |
| - 'Reinette du Canada' (D) | SKee |
| - 'Reinette Rouge Etoilée' (D) | SDea |
| - 'Reverend Greeves' (C) | SDea |
| - 'Reverend McCormick' | CTho |
| - 'Reverend W. Wilks' (C) | CAgr CDoC CSBt CTri ECrN EMui GKir LAst LRHS MAsh MWat SCrf SDea SKee WJas WOrn |
| - 'Ribston Pippin' (D) 🏆H4 | CCAT CCVT CTho CTri CWib ECrN GTwe LRHS MCoo MWat SCrf SDea SKee WJas WOrn |
| - 'Rival' (D) | CAgr SDea WJas |
| - 'Robert Blatchford' (C) | ECrN |
| - 'Rome Beauty' (D) | SDea |
| - 'Rosemary Russet' (D) 🏆H4 | CAgr CCAT CTho GKir GTwe MCoo SCrf SDea SKee |
| - 'Ross Nonpareil' (D) | CAgr GTwe IFFs SDea SKee |
| - 'Rosy Blenheim' (D) | ECrN |
| - 'Rough Pippin' (D) | CCAT CEnd SKee |
| - 'Roundway Magnum Bonum' (D) | CAgr CTho SDea |
| § - 'Roxbury Russet' (D) | SKee |
| § - 'Royal Gala' (D) 🏆H4 | ECrN EMui LAst SDea SLon |
| § - 'Royal Jubilee' (C) | CCAT |
| - 'Royal Russet' (C) | CEnd ECrN SDea |
| - 'Royal Snow' (D) | SKee |
| - 'Royal Somerset' (C/Cider) | CCAT CTho CTri |
| - 'Rubinette' (D) | ECrN EMil MGos SDea |
| - 'Rubinola'PBR **new** | SKee |
| - 'Saint Albans Pippin' (D) | SKee |
| - 'Saint Augustine's Orange' (D) | SKee |
| - 'Saint Cecilia' (D) | SDea WGwG |
| § - 'Saint Edmund's Pippin' (D) 🏆H4 | CTho ECrN GTwe MCoo SCrf SDea SKee WGwG |
| - 'Saint Edmund's Russet' | see *M. domestica* 'Saint Edmund's Pippin' |
| - 'Saint Everard' (D) | SKee |

| | |
|---|---|
| – 'Sam Young' (D) | CAgr SKee |
| – 'Sandlands' (D) | SDea |
| – 'Sandringham' (C) | ECrN SKee |
| – 'Sanspareil' (D) | CAgr SKee |
| – 'Saturn' | CAgr CTri EMui GTwe SDea SKee |
| – 'Saw Pits' (F) | CAgr CEnd |
| – 'Scarlet Crofton' (D) | IFFs |
| – 'Scarlet Nonpareil' (D) | SDea SKee |
| – 'Scotch Bridget' (C) | GKir NBid SCoo SKee WOrn |
| – 'Scotch Dumpling' (C) | GKir GTwe MCoo |
| – 'Scrumptious'$^{PBR}$ (D) | CAgr CDoC CDul CMac EPfP GKir LBuc LRHS MAsh MBri MLan NLar NPri NWea SCoo SKee SPer SPoG WHar |
| – 'Seabrook's Red' (D) | ECrN |
| – 'Seaton House' (C) | GKir |
| – 'Sercombe's Natural' (Cider) | CTho |
| – 'Severn Bank' (C) | CCAT CTho |
| – 'Sheep's Nose' (C) | CCAT CTho SDea |
| – 'Shenandoah' (C) | SKee |
| – 'Sidney Strake' (C) | CAgr CEnd |
| – 'Sir Isaac Newton's' | see *M. domestica* 'Flower of Kent' |
| – 'Sir John Thornycroft' (D) | SDea |
| – 'Slack Ma Girdle' (Cider) | CCAT CTho |
| – 'Smart's Prince Arthur' (C) | SDea |
| – 'Snell's Glass Apple' | see *M. domestica* 'Glass Apple' |
| – 'Somerset Lasting' (C) | CCAT CTri |
| – 'Somerset Redstreak' (Cider) | CCAT CTho CTri GTwe |
| – 'Sops in Wine' (C/Cider) | CCAT CTho SKee |
| – 'Sour Bay' (Cider) | CAgr CTho |
| – 'Sour Natural' | see *M. domestica* 'Langworthy' |
| – 'Spartan' (D) | CCAT CCVT CDoC CMac CSBt CTri CWib ECrN EMui GKir GTwe LAst LRHS MGan MGos NPri SCrf SDea SKee SPer SVic WJas WOrn |
| – 'Spencer' (D) | CTri ECrN SKee |
| – 'Spotted Dick' (Cider) | CTho |
| – 'Stable Jersey' (Cider) | CCAT |
| – 'Stamford Pippin' (D) | SDea |
| – 'Stanway Seedling' (C) | ECrN |
| – 'Star of Devon' (D) | CCAT CEnd SDea SKee |
| – 'Stark' (D) | SDea |
| – 'Starking' (D) | ECrN |
| – 'Starkrimson' (D) | SKee |
| – 'Stark's Earliest' (D) | SVic |
| – 'Stembridge Cluster' (Cider) | CCAT |
| – 'Stembridge Jersey' (Cider) | CCAT |
| – 'Steyne Seedling' (D) | SDea |
| – 'Stirling Castle' (C) | CAgr GKir GQui GTwe SKee WGwG |
| – 'Stobo Castle' (C) | GKir GQui SKee |
| – 'Stockbearer' (C) | CTho |
| – 'Stoke Edith Pippin' (D) | WOrn |
| – 'Stoke Red' (Cider) | CCAT CTho |
| – 'Strawberry Pippin' (D) | CTho |
| – 'Striped Beefing' (C) | ECrN |
| – 'Sturmer Pippin' (D) | CCAT CDul CSBt CTri ECrN GTwe SCrf SDea SKee |
| * – 'Sugar Apple' | CTho |
| – 'Sugar Bush' (C/D) | CTho |
| – 'Sugar Loaf' | see *M. domestica* 'Sugar Apple' |
| – 'Summer Golden Pippin' (D) | SKee |
| – 'Summer Stubbard' (D) | CCAT |
| – 'Summerred' (D) | ECrN EMil NBlu |
| – 'Sunburn' (D) | ECrN |
| – 'Sunnydale' (D/C) | SDea |
| – 'Sunrise'$^{PBR}$ (D) | EMui SKee |
| – 'Sunset' (D) ♀H4 | Widely available |
| – 'Suntan' (D) ♀H4 | CCAT CWib ECrN EMil GTwe LAst MWat SDea SKee |
| – 'Superb' | see *M. domestica* 'Laxton's Superb' |
| – 'Surprise' (D) | GTwe |
| – 'Sweet Alford' (Cider) | CCAT CTho ECrN |
| – 'Sweet Bay' (Cider) | CAgr CTho |
| – 'Sweet Caroline' (D) | ECrN |
| – 'Sweet Cleave' (Cider) | CTho |
| – 'Sweet Coppin' (Cider) | CCAT CTho CTri |
| – 'Sweet Society' (D) | EMui LBuc LRHS MAsh MCoo WHar |
| – 'Tale Sweet' (Cider) | CCAT CTho |
| – 'Tamar Beauty' (F) | CEnd |
| – 'Tan Harvey' (Cider) | CCAT CEnd CTho |
| – 'Tare de Ghinda' | SKee |
| – 'Taunton Cross' (D) | CAgr |
| – 'Taunton Fair Maid' (Cider) | CCAT CTho |
| – 'Taylor's' (Cider) | CCAT SDea |
| – 'Ten Commandments' (D/Cider) | CCAT SDea |
| – Tentation = 'Delblush'$^{PBR}$ (D) | SLon |
| – 'Tewkesbury Baron' (D) | CTho |
| – 'The Rattler' (F) | CEnd |
| – 'Thomas Rivers' (C) | SDea |
| – 'Thorle Pippin' (D) | SKee |
| – 'Tidicombe Seedling' (D) | CTho |
| – 'Tom Putt' (C) | CAgr CCAT CCVT CTho CTri CWib ECrN GTwe LBuc MAsh SDea SKee WJas WOrn |
| – 'Tommy Knight' (D) | CAgr CCAT CEnd CTho |
| – 'Topaz' (D) | SKee |
| – 'Totnes Apple' (D) | CTho |
| – 'Tower of Glamis' (C) | GKir GQui GTwe SKee |
| – Town Farm Number 59 (Cider) | CTho |
| – 'Tregonna King' (C/D) | CCAT CEnd CTho |
| – 'Tremlett's Bitter' (Cider) | CCAT CTho SDea SKee SVic |
| – 'Trwyn Mochyn' (C) | WGwG |
| – 'Twenty Ounce' (C) | WJas |
| § – 'Tydeman's Early Worcester' (D) | CAgr CLnd CWib ECrN GTwe SDea SKee SVic WJas |
| – 'Tydeman's Late Orange' (D) | ECrN EMil EMui GTwe LAst LRHS MCoo SDea SKee WOrn |
| – 'Uncle John's Cooker' (C) **new** | IFFs |
| – 'Upton Pyne' (D) | CCAT CTho SCrf SDea |
| – 'Vallis Apple' (Cider) | CCAT CTho |
| – 'Veitch's Perfection' (C/D) | CTho |
| – 'Venus Pippin' (C/D) | CEnd |
| – 'Vicar of Beighton' (D) | ECrN |
| – 'Vicary's Late Keeper' | CTho |
| – 'Vickey's Delight' (D) | SDea |
| – 'Vileberie' (Cider) | CCAT |
| – 'Vista-bella' (D) | ECrN SDea |
| – 'Wagener' (D) | ECrN SDea SKee |
| – 'Waltham Abbey Seedling' (C) | ECrN |
| – Waltz = 'Telamon'$^{PBR}$ (D/Ball) | MGos SDea SKee |
| – 'Warner's King' (C) ♀H4 | CCAT CTho CTri SCrf SDea SKee WJas |
| – 'Warrior' | CTho |
| – 'Wealthy' (D) | SDea |
| – 'Wellington' (C) | see *M. domestica* 'Dummellor's Seedling' (C) |
| – 'Wellington' (Cider) | CAgr CTho |
| – 'Welsh Russet' (D) | SDea |
| – 'West View Seedling' (D) | ECrN |
| – 'White Alphington' (Cider) | CTho |

| | | |
|---|---|---|
| | - 'White Close Pippin' (Cider) | CTho |
| | - 'White Jersey' (Cider) | CCAT |
| | - 'White Joaneting' (D) | CCAT GTwe |
| | - 'White Melrose' (C) | GKir GTwe LRHS MCoo SDea |
| | - 'White Transparent' (C/D) | SDea SKee |
| | - 'Whitpot Sweet' (F) | CEnd |
| | - 'Wick White Styre' (Cider) | CTho |
| | - 'William Crump' (D) | CCAT CTho ECrN SDea SKee WJas |
| | - 'Winston' (D) 🏆H4 | CAgr CCAT CSBt CTri ECrN GTwe MAsh MCoo NBlu NWea SCrf SDea SVic |
| | - 'Winter Banana' (D) | ECrN SDea SKee SVic |
| | - 'Winter Gem' (D) | CAgr CCAT CDoC ECrN EMil EMui LBuc LRHS MGos SDea SKee WBVN WHar |
| | - 'Winter Lawrence' | CTho |
| | - 'Winter Lemon' (C/D) | GQui |
| | - 'Winter Majetin' (C) | ECrN |
| | - 'Winter Peach' (D/C) | CAgr CEnd CTho ECrN |
| | - 'Winter Quarrenden' (D) | SDea |
| | - 'Winter Queening' (D/C) | SDea |
| | - 'Winter Stubbard' (C) | CTho |
| | - 'Woodbine' | see *M. domestica* 'Northwood' |
| | - 'Woodford' (C) | ECrN |
| | - 'Woolbrook Pippin' (D) | CAgr CCAT CEnd CTho |
| | - 'Woolbrook Russet' (C) | CCAT CEnd CTho ECrN SKee |
| | - 'Worcester Pearmain' (D) 🏆H4 | Widely available |
| | - 'Wormsley Pippin' (D) | ECrN |
| | - 'Wyatt's Seedling' | see *M. domestica* 'Langworthy' |
| | - 'Wyken Pippin' (D) | CCAT ECrN GTwe SDea SKee WJas |
| | - 'Yarlington Mill' (Cider) | CCAT CTho CTri SDea SKee SVic |
| | - 'Yellow Ingestrie' (D) | MAsh SKee WHar WJas |
| | - 'Yellow Styre' (Cider) | CTho |
| | - 'Zabergäu Renette' (D) | SKee |
| | 'Donald Wyman' | CLnd NLar SCoo |
| | 'Echtermeyer' | see *M.* x *gloriosa* 'Oekonomierat Echtermeyer' |
| § | 'Evereste' 🏆H4 | Widely available |
| | ***florentina*** | CLnd CTho EBee EPfP LLHF SLon SSpi |
| | - 'Rosemoor' | EBee |
| | ***floribunda*** 🏆H4 | Widely available |
| | 'Fontana' | MGos |
| | 'Gardener's Gold' | CEnd CTho |
| § | x ***gloriosa*** 'Oekonomierat Echtermeyer' | CCAT GKir SDea WDin WJas |
| | 'Golden Gem' | CCAT EBee EMil EPfP GTwe LRHS SLim |
| | 'Golden Hornet' | see *M.* x *zumi* 'Golden Hornet' |
| | 'Harry Baker' | EMui LRHS MAsh MBlu MBri NLar SCoo SLim SPoG |
| | 'Hillieri' | see *M.* x *scheideckeri* 'Hillieri' |
| | ***hupehensis*** 🏆H4 | CCAT CDul CEnd CLnd CMCN CSBt CTho CTri EBee ECrN EHig EPfP GKir LRHS MBlu MGos MRav SCrf SHBN SLPl WMou WPGP WPat |
| | 'Hyde Hall Spire' | LRHS MAsh MGos SCoo SPoG |
| | 'John Downie' (C) 🏆H4 | Widely available |
| | 'Kaido' | see *M.* x *micromalus* |
| | ***kansuensis*** | CLnd EPfP MBri |
| | 'Laura' | CWSG ECrN EMil EMui EPfP GKir LRHS MAsh MGos NLar SCoo SKee SPoG |
| | 'Lisa' | CLnd |
| | x ***magdeburgensis*** | CCVT CDul CLnd CSBt |
| | 'Makamik' **new** | EWTr |
| | 'Marshal Ōyama' | CTho |
| | 'Mary Potter' | CLnd CTho |
| § | x ***micromalus*** | CBcs CLnd |
| | x ***moerlandsii*** | CLnd |
| | - 'Liset' | CDul CEnd CLnd CSBt CWib EBee ECrN EHig MBri SCoo SMHT SPer SPoG WFar |
| § | - 'Profusion' | CBcs CDul CLnd CTri CWSG EBee ECrN ELan LAst LCro LRHS MGos MRav MSwo NPri NWea SCrf SHBN SPer WBVN WDin WFar WJas |
| | - 'Profusion Improved' | CCAT CEnd CSBt CWSG GKir MWat NLar SCoo SKee WHar WOrn |
| | 'Mokum' **new** | LMaj |
| | 'Molten Lava' | CLnd |
| | ***niedzwetzkyana*** | see *M. pumila* 'Niedzwetzkyana' |
| | Nuvar Carnival | SKee |
| | Nuvar Dusty Red | SKee |
| | Nuvar Marble | SKee |
| | Nuvar Red Lantern | SKee |
| | ***orthocarpa*** | CLnd |
| | Perpetu | see *M.* 'Evereste' |
| | 'Pink Glow' | CLnd CSBt EMui LRHS MAsh MBlu NLar SCoo SLim SPoG WHar |
| | 'Pink Mushroom' | LRHS NLar SCoo |
| | 'Pink Perfection' | CDoC CEnd ECrN LRHS SHBN SPer |
| | Pom'Zaï = 'Courtabri' | CDoC |
| | 'Pond Red' | CLnd |
| | 'Prairie Fire' | MAsh MBri SCoo |
| | ***prattii*** | CTho EPfP |
| | 'Princeton Cardinal' | CLnd EBee GKir MAsh SCoo SPoG |
| | 'Professor Sprenger' | see *M.* x *zumi* 'Professor Sprenger' |
| | 'Profusion' | see *M.* x *moerlandsii* 'Profusion' |
| | ***prunifolia*** 'Pendula' | MGan |
| | ***pumila*** 'Cowichan' | CLnd ECrN GKir |
| | - 'Dartmouth' | CCAT CDul CLnd CSBt CSam CTri ECrN |
| | - 'Montreal Beauty' | CLnd GKir SCoo WJas WOrn |
| § | - 'Niedzwetzkyana' | CLnd |
| § | x ***purpurea*** 'Aldenhamensis' | CLnd SDea WDin WOrn |
| | - 'Eleyi' | CDul CLnd ECrN LAst NWea WDin |
| | - 'Lemoinei' | CLnd ECrN EWTr |
| | - 'Neville Copeman' | CCVT CDoC CDul CLnd EBee ECrN EWTr MBlu MGos SMHT SPur WJas |
| | - 'Pendula' | see *M.* x *gloriosa* 'Oekonomierat Echtermeyer' |
| | 'R.J. Fulcher' | CLnd CTho |
| | 'Ralph Shay' | CLnd |
| | 'Red Ace' | CDul |
| | 'Red Barron' | CLnd |
| | 'Red Glow' | CLnd EBee ECrN WJas |
| | 'Red Jade' | see *M.* x *scheideckeri* 'Red Jade' |
| | 'Red Obelisk' | LRHS MBri SCoo SPoG WBod |
| | 'Red Peacock' | CLnd |
| | 'Robinson' | CLnd SPoG |
| § | x ***robusta*** | CLnd CTri GTwe LRHS LSRN NWea SCrf SLon SMHT |
| | - 'Red Sentinel' 🏆H4 | Widely available |
| | - 'Red Siberian' | ECrN SDea SHBN SPer |
| | - 'Yellow Siberian' | CLnd SPer |
| | ***rockii*** | GAuc |
| | 'Royal Beauty' 🏆H4 | CDoC CDul CWib EBee EPfP GKir GTwe LAst LRHS MAsh MBri MGos MSwo SCoo SCrf SMHT SPer WBod WDin WHar WOrn |
| | 'Royalty' | Widely available |
| | 'Rudolph' | CCAT CCVT CDul CLnd EBee ECrN EWTr GKir LBuc LMaj LRHS MAsh MGos SCoo SLim SPer SPoG WJas WOrn |
| | 'Ruth Ann' | CLnd |
| | ***sargentii*** | see *M. toringo* subsp. *sargentii* |
| | 'Satin Cloud' | CLnd |
| § | x ***scheideckeri*** 'Hillieri' | CDul CLnd ECrN MAsh |
| § | - 'Red Jade' | CCAT CDul CMCN CTri CWib EBee ECrN ELan EPfP GKir GTwe LAst |

| | | |
|---|---|---|
| | | LRHS MBar MGos MRav MSwo MWat NBlu NPri NWea SCrf SHBN SPer WDin WFar WJas WOrn |
| | Siberian crab | see *M.* x *robusta* |
| | ***sieboldii*** | see *M. toringo* |
| | - 'Wooster' | CLnd |
| | ***sikkimensis*** | WHCr |
| | 'Silver Drift' | CLnd SCoo |
| | 'Snowcloud' | CCAT CDul CLnd EBee ECrN LRHS MAsh SLim SPer WOrn |
| | ***spectabilis*** | CLnd |
| | 'Street Parade' | CLnd SCoo |
| | 'Striped Beauty' | CLnd CTho |
| | x ***sublobata*** | CLnd |
| | 'Sun Rival' | CCAT CCVT CDoC CDul CEnd CLnd CSBt CWSG EMui EPfP GKir GTwe LRHS MAsh MBri MGos SCoo SLim SPoG WHar WJas WOrn |
| | ***sylvestris*** | CArn CCVT CDul CLnd CRWN CTri ECrN EMac EPfP GKir LBuc MMuc MRav NBee NWea WDin WMou |
| § | ***toringo*** | CCAT CLnd CTho ECrN EPfP LMaj MBri WSHC |
| I | - var. ***arborescens*** | CLnd CTho |
| | - 'Browers' **new** | LMaj |
| § | - subsp. ***sargentii*** | CDul CLnd CTho ECrN EWTr LAst MBri MGos MRav NWea SMHT SPer |
| | - - 'Tina' | CLnd MAsh SPoG |
| | - 'Scarlett' | IArd LRHS MAsh MBri NLar SCoo |
| | ***toringoides*** | see *M. bhutanica* |
| | - 'Mandarin' | GKir MBri NLar SCoo |
| | ***transitoria*** ♀H4 | CCAT CDoC CDul CEnd CLnd CTho EBee EHig ELan EMil EPfP GKir LRHS MAsh MBlu MBri NWea SCoo SPoG SSpi WPGP |
| | - 'Thornhayes Tansy' | CAbP CTho SPoG |
| | ***trilobata*** | CCAT CLnd CTho EBee EMil EPfP LMaj LRHS MBlu MBri MGos SCoo SEND SPoG |
| | - 'Guardsman' | GKir MAsh MBri NLar SCoo SPoG SSpi |
| | ***tschonoskii*** ♀H4 | Widely available |
| | 'Van Eseltine' | CCAT CDul CLnd CSBt CWSG CWib EBee ECrN EPfP GKir GTwe LRHS MAsh MWat SPer SPoG WHar WJas WPat |
| | 'Veitch's Scarlet' | CDul CLnd CSBt GKir GTwe |
| | 'Wedding Bouquet' **new** | MAsh |
| | Weeping Candied Apple = 'Weepcanzam' | CLnd |
| | 'White Star' | CCVT CDoC CDul CLnd CSBt CWSG ECrN SCoo SLim SPoG |
| | 'Winter Gold' | CDoC CDul CLnd LMaj SCrf SEND SPoG |
| | 'Wisley Crab' | CLnd EMil GTwe SDea SKee |
| | ***yunnanensis*** | EPfP GAuc GKir |
| | - var. ***veitchii*** | CTho |
| | x ***zumi*** var. ***calocarpa*** | CLnd CTho |
| § | - 'Golden Hornet' ♀H4 | Widely available |
| § | - 'Professor Sprenger' | CLnd CSam EPfP LMaj SCoo SPer |

## *Malva* (*Malvaceae*)

| | | |
|---|---|---|
| | ***alcea*** var. ***fastigiata*** | CSec ECGP EShb LRHS NBro NBur SPer SRms WFar WPer |
| | ***bicolor*** | see *Lavatera maritima* |
| | 'Gibbortello' | CSec |
| | ***moschata*** | CArn CBcs CHrt CPrp CRWN CSec CSev EBWF EBee ECtt ELan EPfP GJos MHer MNHC NMir SIde SPer SPlb SWat WGwG WHer WMoo |
| | - f. ***alba*** ♀H4 | Widely available |
| | - 'Pink Perfection' | EShb |
| | - 'Romney Marsh' | see *Althaea officinalis* 'Romney Marsh' |
| | - ***rosea*** | EPfP GMaP LAst NBlu NCot NPer SPoG SWvt |
| | ***pusilla*** | CCCN |
| | 'Sweet Sixteen' | EBee MBNS NLar |
| | ***sylvestris*** | CArn CSec EBWF MNHC NBro NSco SMad SWat WFar WHer WJek WMoo |
| | - 'Bardsey Blue' | WGwG |
| | - 'Blue Fountain' **new** | MBNS |
| | - 'Brave Heart' | CSec EShb GBri GJos NBur NLar SHGN SPav SWvt |
| I | - 'Magic Hollyhock' (d) | SGar |
| | - Marina = 'Dema'PBR | EBee ELan NLar WFar |
| | - subsp. ***mauritiana*** | GBri NPer WMoo |
| | - - 'Bibor Fehlo' | CSpe EBee MWhi NBur |
| | - 'Mystic Merlin' | EBee SPav |
| | - 'Perry's Blue' | NPer |
| | - 'Primley Blue' | CWCL EBee ECha ECtt ELan EPfP GBri GMaP MRav MSCN MTho NBPC NGdn NPer SMad SPer WFar |
| | - 'Zebrina' | EBee GBri LDai NBur NGdn NPer SEND SHGN SWvt WBrE WMoo WRha |

## *Malvastrum* (*Malvaceae*)

| | | |
|---|---|---|
| | x ***hypomadarum*** | see *Anisodontea* x *hypomadara* (Sprague) D.M. Bates |
| | ***lateritium*** | Widely available |

## *Malvaviscus* (*Malvaceae*)

| | | |
|---|---|---|
| | ***arboreus*** | CHll CKob LEdu |
| | - var. ***mexicanus*** | CKob |
| | - pink-flowered | CKob |

## mandarin see *Citrus reticulata*

## mandarin, Cleopatra see *Citrus reshni*

## *Mandevilla* (*Apocynaceae*)

| | | |
|---|---|---|
| § | x ***amabilis*** | CCCN |
| | - 'Alice du Pont' ♀H1 | CCCN CSpe ELan EShb MJnS SOWG SPer |
| | x ***amoena*** | see *M.* x *amabilis* |
| | ***boliviensis*** ♀H1 | CCCN CRHN ELan SOWG |
| § | ***laxa*** ♀H2 | CCCN CHEx CHll CSec CSpe ELan EShb SAga SOWG WCot WHrl WSHC |
| | ***sanderi*** | CCCN EShb LRHS MBri MJnS |
| | - 'Rosea' | NScw |
| | ***splendens*** ♀H1 | CCCN EPfP LRHS SOWG |
| | ***suaveolens*** | see *M. laxa* |

## *Mandragora* (*Solanaceae*)

| | | |
|---|---|---|
| | ***autumnalis*** | CFwr CWan GCal MSal NLar WCot |
| | ***caulescens*** | CFir EBee |
| § | ***officinarum*** | CArn EEls GCal GPoy LEdu MHer MSal NGHP SMad |

## *Manettia* (*Rubiaceae*)

| | | |
|---|---|---|
| | ***inflata*** | see *M. luteorubra* |
| § | ***luteorubra*** | CCCN ELan WCot |

## *Manfreda* see *Agave*

## *Mangifera* (*Anacardiaceae*)

| | | |
|---|---|---|
| | ***indica*** (F) | CCCN |

## mango see *Mangifera indica*

## *Manglietia* (*Magnoliaceae*)

| | | |
|---|---|---|
| | ***chevalieri*** HWJ 533 | WCru |
| | ***conifera*** | SSpi WPGP |
| | ***insignis*** | CBcs CHEx SKHP SSpi WPGP |
| | ***yuyuanensis*** | CBcs |

## *Maranta* (*Marantaceae*)

*leuconeura* var. *erythroneura* ♀H1 — EShb XBlo
- var. *kerchoveana* ♀H1 — CHal EShb LRHS MBri XBlo

## *Marattia* (*Marattiaceae*)

*salicina* new — WRic

## *Margyricarpus* (*Rosaceae*)

§ *pinnatus* — CFee GEdr GGar MMHG NWCA WPer
*setosus* — see *M. pinnatus*

## *Mariscus* see *Cyperus*

## marjoram, pot see *Origanum onites*

## marjoram, sweet see *Origanum majorana*

## marjoram, wild, or oregano see *Origanum vulgare*

## *Marrubium* (*Lamiaceae*)

sp new — SEND
§ *bourgaei* var. *bourgaei* 'All Hallow's Green' — CFee EAEE EBee ECha ECtt EGoo GBuc GKir LHop LRHS MRav SLon SPoG WOut WWlt
*candidissimum* — see *M. incanum*
* *cylleneum* 'Velvetissimum' — WCHb
§ *incanum* — EGoo
*libanoticum* — WPer
*pestalloziae* — EBee
*supinum* — CArn
*vulgare* — CArn CPrp ELau GBar GPoy MHer MNHC SIde WCHb WHer WLHH WPer
- 'Green Pompon' — ELau NLar

## *Marshallia* (*Asteraceae*)

*grandiflora* — CDes EBee SUsu
*mohrii* new — EBee
*trinerva* — ELon SUsu WHil

## *Marsilea* (*Marsileaceae*)

*quadrifolia* — MSKA
- variegated (v) new — LLWG

## *Marsippospermum* (*Juncaceae*)

*gracile* — ECou

## *Mascarena* see *Hyophorbe*

## *Massonia* (*Hyacinthaceae*)

*depressa* — CStu
*echinata* — CStu WCot
aff. *echinata* — CStu ECho
*jasminiflora* — WCot
*pustulata* — CStu WCot

## *Mathiasella* (*Apiaceae*)

*bupleuroides* — CAby EBee LSou
- 'Green Dream' — CBcs CBre EBee ECGP ECtt ELon GBin NDov SUsu WClo WCot WCra

## *Matricaria* (*Asteraceae*)

*chamomilla* — see *M. recutita*
*parthenium* — see *Tanacetum parthenium*
§ *recutita* — CArn GPoy MNHC

## *Matteuccia* (*Woodsiaceae*)

*intermedia* — see *Onoclea intermedia*
*orientalis* — CLAP EBee ERod GCal GGar NGby NLar NMyG NOrc SKHP WFar WMoo WRic
*pensylvanica* — CLAP EBee EMon ITim WRic
*struthiopteris* ♀H4 — Widely available
- 'Bedraggled Feathers' — EMon
* - 'Depauperata' — CLAP
- 'Erosa' — EMon
- 'Jumbo' — CCCN CLAP EBee

## *Matthiola* (*Brassicaceae*)

*fruticulosa* 'Alba' — CDes WPGP
- subsp. *perennis* — NWCA SEND WHal
*incana* — CHrt CSec EBee LRHS MArl NLar SBHP SPad WCFE WPer WRHF
- *alba* — ECha ELan GBBs LSou SPav WCot WPtf
- purple-flowered — LSou WCot
*sinuata* — GGar
white-flowered perennial — CArn CHrt CSev CSpe ECGP MLHP MSte NPer SEND SMeo SPhx WEas

## *Maurandella* (*Scrophulariaceae*)

§ *antirrhiniflora* — CSec EWld LRHS

## *Maurandya* (*Scrophulariaceae*)

§ *barclayana* — CDTJ CHll CSpe MBri SEND SGar WRos
- *alba* — CSpe
'Bridal Bouquet' — CCCN EBee LSou
*erubescens* — see *Lophospermum erubescens*
*lophantha* — see *Lophospermum scandens*
*lophospermum* — see *Lophospermum scandens*
'Pink Ice' — see *Lophospermum scandens* 'Pink Ice'
'Red Dragon' — see *Lophospermum* 'Red Dragon'
§ *scandens* new — CSec
§ 'Victoria Falls' — SOWG

## *Maytenus* (*Celastraceae*)

*boaria* — CMCN EPfP GBin GGal IArd IDee LEdu NLar SAPC SArc SEND WFar WPGP
*disticha* — LEdu
*magellanica* — WFar

## *Mazus* (*Scrophulariaceae*)

*miquelii* — EBee
*reptans* — EBee ECho EDAr EPfP GEdr NPer NWCA WBVN
- B&SWJ new — GEdr
- 'Albus' — EBee ECho EMFW GEdr LLWG SPlb
- 'Blue' — LLWG

## *Mecardonia* (*Scrophulariaceae*)

'Goldflake' — CCCN LSou NBlu
'Sundona Early Yellow' new — LAst

## *Meconopsis* ✿ (*Papaveraceae*)

*baileyi* — see *M. betonicifolia*
Ballyrogan form — GEdr IBlr
× *beamishii* — GBuc
§ *betonicifolia* ♀H4 — Widely available
- var. *alba* — CSec EBee ELan EPfP GBuc GCra GGGa GKev GKir GMaP MCot NBlu NChi NCob NLar NSum SRms
- cluster-headed new — ITim
- 'Glacier Blue' — GCra
- 'Hensol Violet' — EBee GBuc GCal GCra GGGa GKev NLar NSum
*cambrica* — CHrt CPLG CTri EBWF EBee EHrv ELan EPfP GGar NCot NHol NPri SGar SIng WBrk WFar WHer WPnP
- 'Anne Greenaway' (d) — WCot

| | | |
|---|---|---|
| | - var. ***aurantiaca*** | SBch WFar |
| | - ***flore-pleno*** (d) | GBuc MTho NBid WCot |
| | - - orange-flowered (d) | NBid NBir WCot |
| § | - 'Frances Perry' | EBee GBuc GCal IBlr WCot WFar WRos |
| | - 'Rubra' | see *M. cambrica* 'Frances Perry' |
| | ***chelidoniifolia*** | GCra GKir IBlr IGor NBid WCru WFar |
| | x ***cookei*** | GMac |
| | - 'Old Rose' | GMaP |
| | ***delavayi*** | GGGa |
| N | Fertile Blue Group | WFar |
| N | - 'Blue Ice' | see *M.* (Fertile Blue Group) 'Lingholm' |
| N | - 'Kingsbarns' | GGGa |
| N | - 'Lingholm' | Widely available |
| | George Sherriff Group | GBuc GCal GCra GEdr IBlr NBir |
| | - 'Ascreavie' | GMaP |
| | - 'Branklyn' ambig. | CGHE GBri IBlr WFar WPGP |
| | - 'Dalemain' | GMaP |
| | - 'Huntfield' | GMaP |
| | - 'Jimmy Bayne' | GBuc GEdr GGGa GKir GMaP |
| | - 'Spring Hill' | GBuc IBlr |
| | ***grandis*** misapplied | see *M.* George Sherriff Group |
| | ***grandis*** ambig. | CHar EGle GAbr GEdr ITim MNrw NSla SRms |
| | ***grandis*** Prain | EBee MCot |
| | - Balruddery form | GGGa |
| | - GS 600 | see *M.* George Sherriff Group |
| | ***horridula*** | CSec GGGa MTho NLar |
| | (Infertile Blue Group) 'Bobby Masterton' | GBuc GCra |
| | - 'Crarae' new | GGGa |
| | - 'Crewdson Hybrid' | GBuc GMaP NLar |
| | - 'Dawyck' | see *M.* (Infertile Blue Group) 'Slieve Donard' |
| | - 'Mrs Jebb' | GBuc GCra GMaP |
| | - 'Slieve Donard' AGM H4 | GBri GBuc GCal GCra GMaP IBlr ITim |
| | ***integrifolia*** | GGGa GGar GKev WFar |
| | ***lancifolia*** | ITim |
| | 'Lingholm' | see *M.* (Fertile Blue Group) 'Lingholm' |
| N | ***napaulensis*** misapplied | CSam CSec EBee GAbr GCra GEdr GGGa GGar GKev GKir LHop MDun NChi NHol NLar NSum WCAu WMoo |
| | - red-flowered | CBcs GBuc ITim MDun |
| | - pink-flowered | NGdn WPGP |
| | ***nudicaulis*** | see *Papaver nudicaule* |
| | 'Ormswell' ambig. | GBuc IBlr |
| | ***paniculata*** | GGGa ITim MDun MHar |
| | - from Bhutan new | GCra |
| | - from Ghunsa, Nepal | CLAP |
| | - ginger foliage | MDun |
| | ***pseudointegrifolia*** | EWld GCra GGGa |
| | ***punicea*** | GGGa GMaP GMac |
| | ***quintuplinervia*** AGM H4 | CLAP GCra GGGa GMaP IGor NBir NChi NSla NSum WHal |
| | - 'Kaye's Compact' | GBuc |
| N | ***regia*** misapplied | GAbr ITim LHop NLar WMoo |
| | x ***sarsonsii*** | NSum |
| | x ***sheldonii*** misapplied (fertile) | see *M.* Fertile Blue Group |
| | x ***sheldonii*** misapplied (sterile) | see *M.* Infertile Blue Group |
| | x ***sheldonii*** ambig. | CBcs CBow CHar CWCL EBee GAbr GBuc GKir ITim MBri MCot MDun NBPC NBir SRms WBod WCru WFar |
| | x ***sheldonii*** G.Taylor | NPer |
| | ***simplicifolia*** | GGGa GKev |
| | ***superba*** | GBuc GGGa |
| | ***villosa*** | EBee GBuc GCra GGGa GKev IBlr WCru WFar |
| | ***wallichii*** misapplied | see *M. wallichii* Hook. |
| § | ***wallichii*** Hook. | CMil GGGa NLar |
| | 'Willie Duncan' | CSec GKir GMaP ITim |

## *Medicago* (*Papilionaceae*)

| | | |
|---|---|---|
| | ***arborea*** | CArn SEND SPlb |
| | ***lupulina*** new | EBWF |
| | ***sativa*** | NLar WHer WSFF |

## *Medinilla* (*Melastomataceae*)

| | | |
|---|---|---|
| | ***magnifica*** AGM H1 | CCCN LRHS MBri |

## medlar see *Mespilus germanica*

## *Meehania* (*Lamiaceae*)

| | | |
|---|---|---|
| | ***cordata*** | CLAP EBee NLar |
| | ***fargesii*** | CDes CLAP |
| | ***urticifolia*** | EBee EPPr GCal MHar MSte WSHC |
| | - B&SWJ 1210 | WCru |
| | - 'Wandering Minstrel' (v) | CDes CLAP EBee WCot |

## *Megaskepasma* (*Acanthaceae*)

| | | |
|---|---|---|
| | ***erythrochlamys*** new | MJnS |

## *Melaleuca* (*Myrtaceae*)

| | | |
|---|---|---|
| | ***acerosa*** | SOWG |
| | ***acuminata*** | SPlb |
| | ***alternifolia*** | CArn CCCN ECou EOHP GPWP GPoy IDee LAst MHer MSal NTHB SOWG SPlb WHer |
| | ***armillaris*** | CBgR CCCN CDoC CStu IDee SEND SGar SOWG SPlb |
| | - pink-flowered | SOWG |
| | ***blaeriifolia*** | ECou |
| | ***bracteata*** | ECou |
| | ***citrina*** | SOWG |
| | ***coccinea*** | SOWG |
| | ***cuticularis*** | SPlb |
| | ***decora*** | SOWG |
| | ***decussata*** | ECou SOWG SPlb |
| § | ***diosmatifolia*** | CPLG |
| | ***elliptica*** | SOWG |
| | ***ericifolia*** | CTri SOWG SPlb |
| | ***erubescens*** | see *M. diosmatifolia* |
| | ***filifolia*** | SOWG |
| | ***fulgens*** | SOWG SPlb |
| | - apricot-flowered | SOWG |
| * | - 'Hot Pink' | SOWG |
| | - purple-flowered | SOWG |
| | ***gibbosa*** | CPLG EBee ECou IDee LSou SEND SKHP SOWG WSHC |
| | ***holosericea*** misapplied | see *M. smartiorum* |
| | ***huegelii*** | SOWG |
| | ***hypericifolia*** | CPLG CTrC ECou SOWG SPlb |
| | ***incana*** | EBee SOWG |
| | ***lateritia*** | ECou SOWG |
| | ***leucadendra*** | MSal |
| | ***linariifolia*** | CCCN ECou SPlb |
| | ***nesophila*** | ECou EShb IDee SOWG SPlb |
| | ***pentagona*** var. ***subulifolia*** | ECou |
| | ***platycalyx*** | SOWG |
| | ***pulchella*** | ECou SOWG |
| | ***pungens*** | SPlb |
| | ***pustulata*** | ECou EShb SOWG |
| | ***radula*** | SOWG |
| * | ***rosmarinifolia*** | SOWG |
| § | ***smartiorum*** | SOWG |
| | ***spathulata*** | SOWG |
| | ***squamea*** | EBee GGar SPlb WBrE |
| * | ***squarmania*** | SOWG |
| | ***squarrosa*** | CPLG CTrC ECou SOWG SPlb |

| | |
|---|---|
| ***thymifolia*** | ECou SOWG SPlb |
| ***viridiflora*** | GQui |
| ***wilsonii*** | ECou SOWG |

## *Melandrium* see *Vaccaria*

| | |
|---|---|
| ***rubrum*** | see *Silene dioica* |

## *Melanoselinum* (*Apiaceae*)

| | |
|---|---|
| § ***decipiens*** | CAbb CArn CHEx CHrt CSec CSpe EBee ERCP EWes LEdu SKHP SPhx WPGP |

## *Melasphaerula* (*Iridaceae*)

| | |
|---|---|
| ***graminea*** | see *M. ramosa* |
| § ***ramosa*** | CBre CStu ERos WPrP |

## *Melia* (*Meliaceae*)

| | |
|---|---|
| § ***azedarach*** | CArn CBcs CCCN EBee EShb GPoy IFFs WPGP |
| - B&SWJ 7039 | WCru |
| - var. ***japonica*** | see *M. azedarach* |

## *Melianthus* (*Melianthaceae*)

| | |
|---|---|
| ***comosus*** | EBee EHig EShb EWes LPio NLar SCoo SPlb WCot WGwG WOut |
| ***elongatus*** | CPne |
| ***major*** ♀H3 | Widely available |
| ***minor*** | CFir CHid LPio |
| ***villosus*** | CBod CBow CFir COlW EBee EWes LPio MCCP SPlb SPoG WOut |

## *Melica* (*Poaceae*)

| | |
|---|---|
| ***altissima*** 'Alba' | EHoe MLHP |
| - 'Atropurpurea' | Widely available |
| ***ciliata*** | COlW EBee EHoe GFor MMoz MWhi NLar SSvw WMnd |
| - subsp. ***taurica*** | EPPr |
| ***macra*** | EHoe EPPr SApp |
| ***nutans*** | CWCL EHoe EPPr EPla EShb EWsh GBin GFor NLar NWCA SBch WRos |
| ***penicillaris*** | EBee EPPr MAvo WPer |
| ***persica*** | EPPr |
| ***transsilvanica*** | EPPr GFor NBre |
| - 'Atropurpurea' | EBee SPer |
| - 'Red Spire' | CWib EHig EShb MBNS MWhi SHDw SMad WMoo |
| ***uniflora*** | GFor NOak |
| - f. ***albida*** | ECha EGoo EHoe EPPr MAvo MHar SLPl WCot |
| - 'Variegata' (v) | CBre CWsd ECha EHoe ELon EPPr EPla EShb LBMP MBri MMoz NGdn SEND WCot WMoo WTin |

## *Melicope* (*Rutaceae*)

| | |
|---|---|
| ***ternata*** | ECou |

## *Melicytus* (*Violaceae*)

| | |
|---|---|
| ***alpinus*** | ECou |
| ***angustifolius*** | ECou |
| ***crassifolius*** | ECou EPla WFar |
| ***obovatus*** | ECou NLar |
| ***ramiflorus*** | CHEx ECou |

## *Melilotus* (*Papilionaceae*)

| | |
|---|---|
| ***officinalis*** | CArn GPoy NSco SIde WHer |
| - subsp. ***albus*** | CArn |

## *Melinis* (*Poaceae*)

| | |
|---|---|
| sp. new | CSpe |
| ***nerviglumis*** | CKno LEdu |
| § - 'Savannah' | CSpe CWib |
| ***roseus*** | EHul |

## *Meliosma* (*Meliosmaceae*)

| | |
|---|---|
| ***cuneifolia*** | CBcs NLar |
| ***dilleniifolia*** subsp. ***tenuis*** new | CBcs CPLG |
| ***myriantha*** | SSpi |
| ***parviflora*** B&SWJ 8408 | WCru |

## *Melissa* (*Lamiaceae*)

| | |
|---|---|
| ***officinalis*** | CArn CHal CHrt CPbn CTri CWan ELau GJos GKir GMaP GPoy LCro MBar MBri MHer MNHC NBir SECG SIde SPlb SVic SWal WBrk WPer |
| - 'All Gold' | CArn CBre CPbn CPrp CSev ECha EGoo EHoe ELan ELau EOHP GBar NBid NVic SPer SPoG WMoo |
| § - 'Aurea' (v) | Widely available |
| * - 'Compacta' | CHFP CPbn GPoy MHer |
| - 'Lime Balm' | CPbn EOHP |
| - 'Quedlinburger Niederliegende' | CArn CPbn |
| N - 'Variegata' misapplied | see *M. officinalis* 'Aurea' |

## *Melittis* (*Lamiaceae*)

| | |
|---|---|
| ***melissophyllum*** | CArn CFir CLAP CPom CSpe EBee EMon LEdu LPio LSou MRav MSte MWea NChi NMen SMrm SRms SSvw SUsu WAbb WCAu WCra |
| - subsp. ***albida*** | EBee EMon LPio |
| - pink-flowered | CDes EMon SUsu |
| - 'Royal Velvet Distinction' PBR | EBee MRav |

## *Melliodendron* (*Styracaceae*)

| | |
|---|---|
| ***xylocarpum*** | IArd IDee |

## *Menispermum* (*Menispermaceae*)

| | |
|---|---|
| ***canadense*** | CTri GPoy MSal SHBN |
| ***davuricum*** | MSal NLar |

## *Menstruocalamus* (*Poaceae*)

| | |
|---|---|
| ***sichuanensis*** | WPGP |

## *Mentha* ✿ (*Lamiaceae*)

| | |
|---|---|
| ***angustifolia*** Corb. | see *M.* x *villosa* |
| ***angustifolia*** Host | see *M. arvensis* |
| ***angustifolia*** ambig. | CPbn SIde |
| ***aquatica*** | CArn CBen CPbn CRow CWat EBWF EHon ELau EMFW EPfP GPWP GPoy LPBA MHer MNHC NPer NSco SIde SPlb SVic SWal SWat WFar WHer WMAq WMoo WPnP WSFF |
| § - var. ***crispa*** | CPbn SIde |
| - krause minze | see *M. aquatica* var. *crispa* |
| - 'Mandeliensis' | CPbn |
| § ***arvensis*** | CArn CPbn ELau MHer MSal NSco SIde WJek |
| - 'Banana' | CPbn LSou MHer MNHC NGHP SIde WLHH |
| - var. ***piperascens*** | MHer MSal SIde |
| § - - 'Sayakaze' | CArn CPbn ELau |
| - var. ***villosa*** | CPbn |
| ***asiatica*** | CPbn ELau MHer SIde WHer |
| 'Betty's Slovakian' | CPbn |
| Bowles' mint | see *M.* x *villosa* var. *alopecuroides* Bowles mint |
| * ***brevifolia*** | CPbn SIde WHer |
| ***cervina*** | CBen CDWL CPbn CWat EHon EMFW LPBA MHer NLar SIde SWat WJek |
| * - ***alba*** | CDWL CPbn LPBA MHer NLar WMAq |

| | | |
|---|---|---|
| I | 'Chocolate Peppermint' | MNHC NBir WHer |
| | ***citrata*** | see *M.* x *piperita* f. *citrata* |
| | 'Clarissa's Millennium' | CPbn SIde |
| | ***cordifolia*** | see *M.* x *villosa* |
| | ***corsica*** | see *M. requienii* |
| | ***crispa*** L. (1753) | see *M. spicata* var. *crispa* |
| | ***crispa*** L. (1763) | see *M. aquatica* var. *crispa* |
| | ***crispa*** ambig. x (x ***piperita***) | CArn CPbn GBar |
| | 'Dionysus' | CPbn SIde |
| | x ***dumetorum*** | CPbn |
| | 'Eau de Cologne' | see *M.* x *piperita* f. *citrata* |
| | eucalyptus mint | CPbn ELau GBar GPWP MHer NGHP WGwG WRha |
| | ***gattefossei*** | CArn ELau |
| | x ***gentilis*** | see *M.* x *gracilis* |
| § | x ***gracilis*** | CArn CHby CPbn ELau GBar NGHP NPri SIde WJek |
| | - 'Aurea' | see *M.* x *gracilis* 'Variegata' |
| § | - 'Variegata' (v) | CHFP CHrt CPbn CPrp CSev CWan ECha ELau GGar GPoy ILis MBar MCot MHer MNHC NBlu NPri NVic SPlb WFar WHer WPer |
| | ***haplocalyx*** | CArn ELau MSal SIde |
| * | 'Hillary's Sweet Lemon' | CPbn ELau MHer SIde |
| | 'Julia's Sweet Citrus' | CPbn MHer SIde |
| * | ***lacerata*** | SIde |
| | lavender mint | CPrp ELau GBar GPWP GPoy MHer MNHC NGHP NTHB WJek WRha |
| § | ***longifolia*** | CPbn CPrp CWan ELau GBar SBch SIde SPlb WEas WHer WJek WPer |
| | - Buddleia Mint Group | CArn CPbn EBee ELau GGar GPWP MHer MRav NGHP SIde WLHH WRha |
| | - dwarf | CPbn |
| | - subsp. ***schimperi*** | CPbn MHer SIde WJek WLHH |
| | - silver-leaved | CArn CHFP CPbn ELau MHer MNHC NLar WOut |
| * | - 'Variegata' (v) | CPbn CPrp ELau WJek |
| | Nile Valley mint | CArn CPbn CPrp ELau SHDw SIde WCHb |
| | x ***piperita*** | CArn CHby CHrt CPbn CSev CWan ECha EHoe ELau GAuc GBar GGar GJos GPoy ILis LHop MBri MHer MNHC NGHP NPri NVic SPlb SWal WPer |
| | - 'Black Mitcham' | CArn CPbn GBar |
| | - black peppermint | CHby CPbn EPfP GKir GPWP MMuc MNHC NBir NGHP NHol NLar NTHB SBch SWal WGwG |
| § | - f. ***citrata*** | CArn CHby COIW CPbn CPrp CTri ECha ELau GBar GGar GJos GMaP GPWP GPoy MBar MBri MHer MNHC NBir NBlu NGHP SHDw SIde SPlb STre SVic WGwG WPer |
| | - - from Portugal **new** | CPbn |
| * | - - 'Basil' | CHrt CPbn CPrp CWan ELau GBar GPWP MHer MNHC MRav NGHP NHol NTHB SBch SHDw SIde WGwG WJek WLHH WRha |
| | - - 'Bergamot' | CPbn |
| | - - 'Chocolate' | CArn CPbn CPrp CWan ELau EOHP EPfP GBar GGar GJos GPWP ILis MHer MNHC NGHP NPri SHDw SIde WGwG WJek WMoo WPer |
| | - - 'Grapefruit' | CPbn CPrp CTca CWan GBar ILis LFol LSou NGHP SWal WGwG WJek WLHH |
| | - - 'Lemon' | CPbn CPrp CWan ELau GBar GKir GPWP GPoy MBri MHer MNHC NGHP SHDw SIde WCHb WGwG WJek WPer WRha |
| | - - 'Lime' | CHrt CPbn CPrp CWan GBar GPWP ILis LSou MHer NGHP NPri SHDw SIde SPlb WCHb WGwG WJek WLHH |
| | - - 'Orange' | CPbn GBar MHer MNHC NGHP WDyG WLHH |
| | - - 'Reverchonii' | CPbn SIde |
| | - - 'Swiss Ricola' | MHer SIde |
| | - 'Logee's' (v) | CPbn GBar MNHC NGHP NHol NPri NTHB SIde WCHb WHer WJek WRha |
| | - f. ***officinalis*** | CPbn ELau SIde |
| | - var. ***ouweneellii*** Belgian mint | CPbn SIde |
| | - 'Reine Rouge' | CPbn SIde |
| | - 'Swiss' | NGHP NLar |
| I | - Swiss mint | CArn CPbn CPrp GPWP WGwG WOut |
| | - white-flowered | CArn CPbn GBar MHer WGwG |
| | 'Polynesian Mint' **new** | CPbn |
| | ***pulegium*** | CArn CHby COIW CPbn CPrp CRWN CSev CTri CWan EBWF ELau EMFW GBar GPWP GPoy MHer MNHC NPri SIde SPlb SRms SVic SWal WCHb WHer WJek WPer |
| | - 'Upright' | CArn CBod CPbn GBar GPoy MHer NTHB SHDw SIde WCHb WJek WPer |
| § | ***requienii*** | Widely available |
| | ***rotundifolia*** misapplied | see *M. suaveolens* |
| | ***rotundifolia*** (L.) Hudson | see *M.* x *villosa* |
| | ***rubra*** var. ***raripila*** | see *M.* x *smithiana* |
| | 'Russian' curled leaf | CPbn |
| | 'Russian' plain leaf | CPbn |
| | 'Sayakarze' | see *M. arvensis* var. *piperascens* 'Sayakaze' |
| § | x ***smithiana*** | CArn CPbn CPrp CWan ELau GBar GPWP GPoy ILis MHer MNHC NBir NGHP NPri WHer WLHH WPer WRha |
| | - 'Capel Ulo' (v) | ELau WHer |
| | 'South of France' **new** | CPbn |
| § | ***spicata*** | Widely available |
| | - Algerian fruity | CPbn SIde |
| | - 'Austrian' | CPbn |
| * | - 'Brundall' | CPbn ELau ILis SIde |
| | - 'Canaries' | CPbn |
| * | - var. ***crispa*** | CArn CPbn CPrp CWan ECha ELau GBar GGar GPWP LEdu LHop MHer MNHC NGHP NHol NPri SIde SPlb WCHb WCot WPer WRha |
| | - - 'Moroccan' | CArn CHFP CPbn CPrp CSev ELau EOHP GAbr GBar GGar GJos GPWP GPoy LEdu MHer MNHC NGHP NPri NVic SBch SEND SHDw SIde STre WCHb WJek WLHH |
| | - - 'Persian' | CPbn |
| | - 'Guernsey' | CPbn SHDw SIde WLHH |
| | - 'Irish' | CPbn |
| | - 'Kentucky Colonel' | CPbn |
| | - 'Mexican' | CArn CPbn |
| | - 'Newbourne' | CPbn ELau SIde |
| | - 'Pharaoh' | CArn CPbn |
| | - 'Rhodos' | CPbn |
| | - 'Russian' | NGHP NHol NTHB SIde |
| | - 'Small Dole' (v) | SHDw |
| | - 'Spanish' **new** | GPWP |
| | - 'Spanish Furry' | CPbn MHer SIde |
| | - 'Spanish Pointed' | CPbn ELau SIde |
| | - 'Tashkent' | CArn CHby CPbn ELau EOHP GKir LEdu MHer MNHC NGHP SHDw SIde WCHb WGwG WJek WLHH |
| | - subsp. ***tomentosa*** | CPbn |
| * | - 'Variegata' (v) | CPbn SHDw WGwG |
| | - 'Verte Blanche' | CPbn |

| | | |
|---|---|---|
| § | ***suaveolens*** | CArn CHby CPbn CWan ELau GBar GJos GMaP GPWP GPoy ILis LCro MBri MHer MNHC NGHP NPri SIde SPlb SVic SWal WBrk WLHH WPer WSFF |
| * | - 'Grapefruit' | GPWP NGHP NPri |
| | - 'Jokka' | CPbn EBee |
| * | - 'Mobillei' | CPbn SIde WJek |
| * | - 'Pineapple' | GKir WGwG |
| | - subsp. ***timija*** | CPbn ELau SIde WJek |
| | - 'Variegata' (v) | Widely available |
| | 'Sweet Pear' | CPbn |
| | ***sylvestris*** L. | see *M. longifolia* |
| * | ***verona*** | CPbn |
| § | x ***villosa*** | CArn CPbn SIde |
| § | - var. ***alopecuroides*** Bowles' mint | CBre CHrt CPbn CPrp ELau GBar GGar GPWP GPoy ILis MHer MNHC NBir NGHP SIde STre SWat WGwG WHer WJek |
| | ***viridis*** | see *M. spicata* |

## *Mentzelia* (*Loasaceae*)

| | | |
|---|---|---|
| | ***decapetala*** | CSpe |

## *Menyanthes* (*Menyanthaceae*)

| | | |
|---|---|---|
| | ***trifoliata*** | CBen CRow CWat EHon ELau EMFW GBar GPoy LLWG LPBA MCCP MMuc MSKA NPer NSco NVic WBVN WFar WHal WMAq |

## *Menziesia* (*Ericaceae*)

| | | |
|---|---|---|
| | ***alba*** | see *Daboecia cantabrica* f. *alba* |
| | ***ciliicalyx lasiophylla*** | see *M. ciliicalyx* var. *purpurea* |
| | - var. ***multiflora*** | EPfP |
| § | - var. ***purpurea*** | GGGa |
| | ***ferruginea*** | SSta |
| | 'Spring Morning' | WAbe |
| | 'Ulva' | GGGa |

## *Mercurialis* (*Euphorbiaceae*)

| | | |
|---|---|---|
| | ***perennis*** | EBWF GPoy NSco WHer WShi |

## *Merendera* (*Colchicaceae*)

| | | |
|---|---|---|
| | ***attica*** | EBrs ECho |
| | ***eichleri*** | see *M. trigyna* |
| | ***filifolia*** | ECho |
| § | ***montana*** | EBrs ECho ERos GKev WIvy WThu |
| | ***pyrenaica*** | see *M. montana* |
| | ***raddeana*** | see *M. trigyna* |
| | ***sobolifera*** | WCot WFar |
| § | ***trigyna*** | EBrs ECho |

## *Merremia* (*Convolvulaceae*)

| | | |
|---|---|---|
| | ***pinnata*** | MSal |
| § | ***tuberosa*** | SOWG |

## *Mertensia* (*Boraginaceae*)

| | | |
|---|---|---|
| | ***ciliata*** | CMdw CPom GKir LRHS MNrw NBid SWat |
| | ***maritima*** | CSpe EWll GMaP GPoy MSal |
| | - subsp. ***asiatica*** | see *M. simplicissima* |
| | ***primuloides*** | GAuc |
| | ***pterocarpa*** | see *M. sibirica* |
| | ***pulmonarioides*** | see *M. virginica* |
| § | ***sibirica*** | CLAP CSpe EBee GKir NChi NLar SMrm SPhx SPlb |
| § | ***simplicissima*** | CMea ECho GKir MNrw NBir SMrm SPhx SPlb WFar WHoo |
| § | ***virginica*** ♀H4 | CArn CBro CLAP CPrp CSec CWCL EBee EBrs ECho ELan EPfP EPot EWTr GGar GKev GKir LAma NBid NBir NLar NPri NWCA SMrm SPoG SRms WCru WFar |
| | ***viridis*** | SPhx |

## *Merwilla* (*Hyacinthaceae*)

| | | |
|---|---|---|
| § | ***plumbea*** | WCot WHil |

## *Meryta* (*Araliaceae*)

| | | |
|---|---|---|
| | ***sinclairii*** | CHEx |

## *Mesembryanthemum* (*Aizoaceae*)

| | | |
|---|---|---|
| | 'Basutoland' | see *Delosperma nubigenum* |
| | ***brownii*** | see *Lampranthus brownii* |

## *Mespilus* (*Rosaceae*)

| | | |
|---|---|---|
| | ***germanica*** (F) | CBcs CDul CLnd CSBt CTri EBee ECrN ELan IDee LMaj MWat NLar NScw SBLw SDnm SHBN SLon WDin WFar WMou WOrn |
| | - 'Bredase Reus' (F) | SKee |
| | - 'Dutch' (F) | SDea SKee |
| | - 'Large Russian' (F) | CAgr |
| | - 'Macrocarpa' (F) | SKee |
| | - 'Monstrous' (F) | SDea |
| | - 'Nottingham' (F) | Widely available |
| | - 'Royal' (F) | CAgr MBri MCoo SCoo SKee |
| | - 'Westerveld' (F) | SKee |
| | ***germanicus*** 'Iranian' (F) new | SKee |

## *Metapanax* see *Pseudopanax*

## *Metaplexis* (*Asclepiadaceae*)

| | | |
|---|---|---|
| | ***japonica*** B&SWJ 8459 | WCru |

## *Metarungia* (*Acanthaceae*)

| | | |
|---|---|---|
| | ***longistrobus*** | GFai |

## *Metasequoia* ✿ (*Cupressaceae*)

| | | |
|---|---|---|
| | ***glyptostroboides*** ♀H4 | Widely available |
| | - 'Emerald Feathers' | ECho |
| | - 'Fastigiata' | see *M. glyptostroboides* 'National' |
| | - 'Gold Rush' | Widely available |
| | - 'Green Mantle' | ECho EHul |
| | - 'Matthaei Broom' | NLar SLim SPoG |
| | - 'Miss Grace' | NLar SLim |
| § | - 'National' | ECho MBlu |
| | - 'Sheridan Spire' | CEnd MBlu WPGP |
| | - 'Spring Cream' | ECho NLar |
| | - 'Waasland' | LRHS MBlu SLim |
| | - 'White Spot' (v) | ECho MBlu SLim |

## *Metrosideros* (*Myrtaceae*)

| | | |
|---|---|---|
| | ***carminea*** | CCCN CTrC CTsd |
| § | ***excelsa*** | CHEx CHll CTrC CTrG EBak ECou |
| | - 'Aurea' | ECou |
| | - 'Fire Mountain' | CTrC |
| | - 'Parnell' | CBcs CCCN |
| | - 'Scarlet Pimpernel' | SOWG |
| | - 'Spring Fire' | CBcs CCCN |
| | - 'Vibrance' | CTrC |
| | ***kermadecensis*** | ECou |
| | - 'Radiant' (v) | CBcs |
| | - 'Red and Gold' | CDoC CTrC |
| | - 'Twisty' (v) new | CBcs |
| | - 'Variegata' (v) | CBcs CDoC CTrC ECou MLan |
| | ***lucida*** | see *M. umbellata* |
| | 'Moon Maiden' | SOWG |
| | 'Pink Lady' | CTrC |
| | ***robusta*** | CBcs CCCN CHEx |
| | - ***aureovariegata*** | CCCN EShb |
| | x ***subtomentosa*** 'Mistral' | ECou |
| | 'Thomasii' | SOWG |
| | ***tomentosa*** | see *M. excelsa* |

§ ***umbellata*** CBcs CCCN CHEx CTrC EBee ECou EShb GGal GGar
***villosa*** SOWG
- 'Tahiti' CBcs

## *Meum* (*Apiaceae*)

***athamanticum*** CArn CSev CSpe CWsd EBee EBrs EDAr EGle EHrv GCal GPoy LRHS MAvo MRav MSal MTho NBid NChi NSti SGar WFar WHil WPer WPrP WTin

## *Michauxia* (*Campanulaceae*)

***campanuloides*** SPad
***laevigata*** WCot
***tchihatchewii*** CCCN CDTJ CSpe GKev NGBl WBor

## *Michelia* (*Magnoliaceae*)

'Allspice' SKHP
***champaca*** CCCN CSec
***chapensis*** CBcs SSpi
- HWJ 621 WCru
***compressa*** CCCN EPfP
***doltsopa*** CBcs CCCN CGHE CHEx EBee EMil EPfP SSpi SSta WPGP
- 'Silver Cloud' CBcs CDoC
***figo*** CAbb CBcs CCCN CDoC EBee EPfP EWTr MBri SKHP SSpi SSta WPGP
- var. ***crassipes*** SSpi
- var. ***figo*** SSpi
***foveolata*** CBcs SSpi
- var. ***cinerascens*** CWib WPGP
'Jack Fogg' SKHP
***macclurei*** CBcs SSpi WPGP
***maudiae*** CBcs CDoC CGHE CPLG EBee EPfP ISea NLar SKHP SSpi WPGP
***odora*** CWib
***sinensis*** see *M. wilsonii*
'Touch of Pink' **new** CBcs
§ ***wilsonii*** CWib
***yunnanensis*** CCCN SKHP SSpi WPGP

## *Microbiota* (*Cupressaceae*)

***decussata*** 🏆H4 CBcs CDoC CKen CMac CRob CSBt ECho EHul EMil EOrn EPla GKir LAst LBee LRHS MBar MGos MWat NHol NWea SEND SLim SPoG WCFE WFar
- 'Gold Spot' SLim
- 'Jakobsen' CDoC CKen
- 'Trompenburg' CKen

## *Microcachrys* (*Podocarpaceae*)

***tetragona*** CDoC ECho ECou EHul EOrn SCoo SIng WThu

## *Microcoelum* see *Lytocaryum*

***weddelianum*** see *Lytocaryum weddellianum*

## *Microlaena* see *Ehrharta*

## *Microlepia* (*Dennstaedtiaceae*)

***speluncae*** EShb MBri
***strigosa*** CCCN CLAP EBee LLHF LRHS WRic
- 'Crispa' **new** EBee

## *Micromeria* (*Lamiaceae*)

***chamissonis*** GPoy
***corsica*** see *Acinos corsicus*
***croatica*** NMen
***fruticosa*** CArn
***graeca*** CArn
***rupestris*** see *M. thymifolia*
§ ***thymifolia*** NMen SPlb
***viminea*** see *Satureja viminea*

## *Microseris* (*Asteraceae*)

***ringens*** hort. see *Leontodon rigens*

## *Microsorum* (*Polypodiaceae*)

***brachylepis*** 'Crispa' **new** EBee
***diversifolium*** see *Phymatosorus diversifolius*

## *Microstrobos* (*Podocarpaceae*)

***fitzgeraldii*** CKen
***niphophilus*** ECou

## *Microtropis* (*Celastraceae*)

***petelotii*** HWJ 719 WCru

## *Mikania* (*Asteraceae*)

***araucana*** LSou
§ ***dentata*** MBri
***ternata*** see *M. dentata*

## *Milium* (*Poaceae*)

***effusum*** COld GKir
- 'Aureum' 🏆H4 Widely available
- var. ***esthonicum*** EBee EPPr
- 'Yaffle' (v) CBre CFir CKno CNat EBee ECha EGle EPPr EShb GKir LEdu MCCP MWat SPoG SSvw SUsu WCot WLeb

## *Millettia* (*Papilionaceae*)

***japonica*** 'Hime Fuji' NLar
murasaki-natsu-fuji see *M. reticulata*
§ ***reticulata*** CPLG

## *Milligania* (*Asteliaceae*)

***densiflora*** IBlr

## *Millingtonia* (*Bignoniaceae*)

***hortensis*** **new** CSec

## *Mimosa* (*Mimosaceae*)

***pudica*** CCCN CDTJ LRHS

## *Mimulus* (*Scrophulariaceae*)

'A.T. Johnson' NVic
'Andean Nymph' see *M. naiandinus*
§ ***aurantiacus*** 🏆H2-3 CElw CHal CSpe CTri EBak EBee ECtt LHop NBir NPer SAga SDnm SGar SMrm SPet SPlb SPoG SUsu
§ - var. ***puniceus*** CSpe CTri EBee EDif LAst LHop LRHS LSou SAga SBHP SHom SMrm SRkn
- 'Pure Gold' EBee EDif
- 'Tangerine' EDif
x ***bartonianus*** see *M.* x *harrisonii*
***bifidus*** 'Tapestry' CSpe SAga
- 'Trish' CSpe SAga
- 'Verity Buff' EDif
§ - 'Verity Purple' EDif
- 'Wine' see *M. bifidus* 'Verity Purple'
x ***burnetii*** ECho LPBA SRms
***cardinalis*** 🏆H3 CDWL CSec EBee ELan EPfP LPBA MNrw MSKA MTho NBir SMrm SPer WBor WFar WHil WMoo WPer
- 'Dark Throat' SGar
- 'Red Dragon' SBHP
- yellow-flowered **new** CSec
***cupreus*** GKev
- 'Minor' ECho
- 'Whitecroft Scarlet' 🏆H4 ECho ECtt ELan EPfP LPBA LRHS LSou SRms WPer
***eastwoodiae*** CPBP

| | |
|---|---|
| 'Eleanor' | ECtt LSou SAga SGar SHom SMrm SUsu |
| 'Firedragon' new | GKir |
| ***glutinosus*** | see *M. aurantiacus* |
| - ***atrosanguineus*** | see *M. aurantiacus* var. *puniceus* |
| - ***luteus*** | see *M. aurantiacus* |
| § ***guttatus*** | CSec CWat EMFW NPer NSco SRms WMoo WPer WPnP |
| § - 'Richard Bish' (v) | CBow EShb MCCP |
| § x ***harrisonii*** | EBee EPfP EWes LSou SAga |
| 'Highland Gold' new | NBlu |
| 'Highland Orange' | ECho EPfP GKir SPlb SPoG WGor WPer |
| 'Highland Pink' | ECho EPfP NBlu SPlb SPoG WGor WPer |
| 'Highland Pink Rose' | WFar |
| 'Highland Red' ♀H4 | ECho ECtt EPfP GGar GKev GKir LPBA SPlb SPoG SRms WFar WPer |
| 'Highland Yellow' | ECho ECtt GKev GKir LPBA SPlb SPoG WFar WPer |
| hose-in-hose (d) | CDWL NPer |
| 'Inca Sunset' | EWes |
| ***langsdorffii*** | see *M. guttatus* |
| ***lewisii*** ♀H3 | CHll MTho SPav SPer SRms WRha |
| ***longiflorus*** subsp. ***calycinus*** | SKHP |
| - 'Santa Barbara' | MWte |
| ***luteus*** | CBen CSec CWat EHon EPfP LPBA NHol NPer SPlb WBrk WFar WMAq |
| § - 'Gaby' (v) | LPBA |
| - 'Variegatus' misapplied | see *M. guttatus* 'Richard Bish' |
| - 'Variegatus' | see *M. luteus* 'Gaby' |
| - 'Variegatus' ambig. (v) | NPer |
| 'Malibu Ivory' | MDKP |
| 'Malibu Orange' | EPfP |
| 'Malibu Red' | MDKP |
| ***minimus*** | CSec ECho |
| ***moschatus*** | EBee |
| § ***naiandinus*** ♀H3 | CMMP CSec LRHS SPlb SRms |
| - C&W 5257 | WRos |
| 'Orange Glow' | EPfP WHal |
| orange hose-in-hose (d) | NBir |
| 'Orkney Lemon' | NSti |
| ***pictus*** new | CSec |
| 'Popacatapetl' | CHll EDif LHop LSou MSte SAga SBHP SMrm |
| 'Prairie Caramel' new | EDif |
| 'Prairie Cerise' new | EDif |
| 'Prairie Citron' new | EDif |
| 'Prairie Coral' new | EDif |
| 'Prairie Lilac Frost' new | EDif |
| 'Prairie Peach' new | EDif |
| 'Prairie Sunshine' new | EDif |
| ***primuloides*** | ECho EWes SIng SPlb |
| 'Puck' | ECho ECtt GKir |
| 'Quetzalcoatl' | LSou SAga SMrm |
| ***ringens*** | CBen CSec CWat EBee EDif EHon EMFW EPfP GBri LPBA MSKA NBir NPer SPlb SRms WFar WHil WMAq WMoo WPer |
| 'Threave Variegated' (v) | EBee GBuc MRav NBir WFar |
| ***tilingii*** | CSec ECho EShb |
| 'Western Hills' | MLLN |
| 'Wine Red' | see *M. bifidus* 'Verity Purple' |
| 'Wisley Red' | ECho ECot SRms |
| 'Yellow Velvet' | ECho |

## *Mimusops* (*Sapotaceae*)

| | |
|---|---|
| ***elengi*** new | CSec |

## *Mina* see *Ipomoea*

## mint, apple see *Mentha suaveolens*

## mint, Bowles see *M.* x *villosa* var. *alopecuroides*

## mint, curly see *M. spicata* var. *crispa*

## mint, eau-de-Cologne see *M.* x *piperita f. citrata*

## mint, ginger see *M.* x *gracilis*

## mint, horse or long-leaved see *M. longifolia*

## mint, pennyroyal see *M. pulegium*

## mint (peppermint) see *M.* x *piperita*

## mint round-leaved see *M. suaveolens*

## mint, (spearmint) see *M. spicata*

## *Minuartia* (*Caryophyllaceae*)

| | |
|---|---|
| ***capillacea*** | ECho |
| ***caucasica*** | see *M. circassica* |
| § ***circassica*** | NWCA WPer |
| ***juniperina*** | GKir |
| ***laricifolia*** | GKir LRHS |
| ***parnassica*** | see *M. stellata* |
| § ***stellata*** | EAlp EPot NDlv NMen SIng |
| - NS 758 | NWCA |
| § ***verna*** | EAlp ECho EDAr NMen |
| - subsp. ***caespitosa*** | CTri ECho |
| - - 'Aurea' | see *Sagina subulata* var. *glabrata* 'Aurea' |

## *Mirabilis* (*Nyctaginaceae*)

| | |
|---|---|
| ***jalapa*** | CArn CPLG CSec EBrs EPfP EShb LAma LEdu LRHS MBri MSal SBod SEND SPad SRms WHil WTou |
| - 'Buttermilk' | CCCN |
| - red-flowered new | WTou |
| - white-flowered | CSpe WTou |
| ***viscosa*** new | CSec |

## *Miscanthus* ✿ (*Poaceae*)

| | |
|---|---|
| ***capensis*** | SPlb |
| ***chejuensis*** B&SWJ 8803 | WCru |
| ***flavidus*** B&SWJ 6749 | WCru |
| ***floridulus*** misapplied | see *M.* x *giganteus* |
| ***floridulus*** ambig. | EBee NLar NOak WFar WPrP |
| ***floridulus*** (Labill.) Warb. ex K. Schum. & Lauterb. HWJ 522 | WCru |
| § x ***giganteus*** | CHar CKno EAlp EBee EHoe ELon EPPr EUJe EWsh GAbr GCal GQue MAvo MCCP MMoz MMuc NBea NDov NOak NVic SApp SDix SEND SMad SPlb WCot WFar |
| - 'Gilt Edge' (v) | CBow CKno EPPr EWsh MAvo SApp |
| - 'Gotemba' (v) | EBee EPPr EWes EWsh SApp |
| 'Golden Bar' | EBrs GBuc |
| 'Gotemba Gold' | SApp |
| 'Mount Washington' | SApp |
| ***nepalensis*** | CBod CElw CEnt CHrt CKno CMil CPLG CWCL EAlp EBee ECre EHoe EPGN ERas EWes EWsh LEdu MAvo MNrw MWte SDix SMHy SMrm SUsu WTin |
| - B&SWJ 2302 | WCru |
| - 'Shikola' new | WCru |
| ***oligostachyus*** | NGdn SMrm |
| § - 'Afrika' | CHar CKno CPen EBee |
| I - 'Nanus Variegatus' (v) | CDes CKno CRow EBee EHoe EWes LEdu MAvo MMoz WCot WPGP |

| | | |
|---|---|---|
| | 'Pos' | SApp |
| § | 'Purpurascens' | CAby CKno CPrp CWCL ECha EHoe EHrv EHul EPla EShb EWsh LRHS LSRN MAvo MBrN MMoz MMuc MWhi NOak SApp SMrm SWal WBor WMoo WTin |
| | ***sacchariflorus*** misapplied | see *M.* x *giganteus* |
| | ***sacchariflorus*** ambig. | CAbb CBcs CDul CHEx CKno CRow EBee ECha EFul EHrv ELan EPfP EPla EShb LCro LPBA LRHS MBlu MBrN MLLN SPer SPla WFar WMoo |
| | ***sacchariflorus*** Hack. | EHoe EUJe MMuc MWhi SMrm |
| | - 'Robustus' | CHVG |
| | ***sinensis*** | CEnt CHEx CHrt CTri EBla GFor LEdu MMoz NGBl NLar NOak SVic WDin WMoo WRos |
| | - from Yakushima | GKir |
| | - 'Adagio' | CBod CHar CKno CPen EAEE EBee EBrs EGle EPPr GBin LEdu NBsh NDov SHDw SMHy WCot WPrP |
| | - 'Afrika' | see *M. oligostachyus* 'Afrika' |
| | - 'Andante' **new** | CKno |
| | - 'Arabesque' | EBee EPPr ERas MMoz NLar SApp |
| | - 'Augustfeder' | CHar CPen EBee EGle EPPr LEdu LRHS NBsh |
| | - 'Autumn Light' | CKno CPen EBrs EPPr |
| | - 'Ballerina' | CHar CPen |
| | - 'Blütenwunder' | CHar CKno CPen EBee EGle |
| | - 'China' | Widely available |
| | - var. ***condensatus*** | LSou |
| | - - 'Cabaret' (v) | Widely available |
| | - - 'Central Park' | see *M. sinensis* var. *condensatus* 'Cosmo Revert' |
| § | - - 'Cosmo Revert' | CPen EBee EWsh LEdu MMoz WDyG |
| | - - 'Cosmopolitan' (v) ♀H4 | Widely available |
| | - - 'Emerald Giant' | see *M. sinensis* var. *condensatus* 'Cosmo Revert' |
| | - 'David' | CPen EAEE EBee EPPr LEdu MBNS NBsh |
| | - 'Dixieland' (v) | CHar CKno EGle EHoe ELan EPPr EWsh LEdu MMoz SApp |
| | - 'Emmanuel Lepage' | CHar CKno CPen EPPr |
| | - 'Ferner Osten' | Widely available |
| | - 'Flamingo' ♀H4 | Widely available |
| | - 'Flammenmeer' | CHar CPen |
| | - 'Gaa' | SApp |
| | - 'Gearmella' | CBod EGle EWsh GKir LEdu LRHS |
| | - 'Gewitterwolke' ♀H4 | CHar CKno EGle EWes SMHy SMad |
| | - 'Ghana' ♀H4 | CHar CKno CPen EBee EGle ELon GBin SMHy |
| | - 'Giraffe' | CDTJ CDes CHar CKno CPen EBee EWes LEdu WPGP |
| | - 'Gnome' | CKno CPen EAEE EBee EPPr MMHG NDov |
| | - 'Gold Bar' (v) | CBow CChe CElw CKno CMHG CMea EBee ECtt EMil EPPr EUJe LEdu LSou MBNS NCGa NMoo SMad SPer SPoG SUsu WClo WCot WCra WGwG WMoo |
| | - 'Goldfeder' (v) | CPen EBee EHoe |
| | - 'Goliath' | CHar CPen EAEE EBee EHoe ELon EPPr ERas GBin IPot LBMP LEdu LRHS MBNS SMrm WFar WPnP WPrP |
| | - 'Gracillimus' | Widely available |
| | - 'Gracillimus Nanus' **new** | CKno |
| | - 'Graziella' | Widely available |
| | - 'Grosse Fontäne' ♀H4 | CWCL EBee EBla EHoe ELan EPGN EPPr EPla EWsh GKir LEdu LRHS NBsh SMHy WAul WMoo |
| | - 'Haiku' | CHar CPen EPPr GBin LEdu NDov SPhx WPrP |
| | - 'Helga Reich' | EBee SApp |
| | - 'Hercules' | CPen EPPr MAvo MMoz SApp |
| | - 'Hermann Müssel' | CHar CPen EAlp EBee EWes GBin LEdu NDov SMHy SPhx WPrP |
| | - 'Hinjo' (v) | CDes CElw CHar CKno CSpe EBee ECGP ECha ECtt EPPr EUJe EWsh GBin GCal GQue LBMP LEdu LSou SApp SPoG WCot WCra WFar WPGP WPrP |
| I | - 'Jubilaris' (v) | EWes |
| | - 'Juli' | CSsd EBrs ERas WPrP |
| | - 'Kaskade' ♀H4 | CHar CKno CWCL EBee EBrs EGle EHoe EPGN EPPr IPot LEdu LRHS MAvo MMoz MSte SApp SMeo SMrm WFar WMoo |
| | - 'Kirk Alexander' (v) | MAvo SApp |
| | - 'Kleine Fontäne' ♀H4 | Widely available |
| | - 'Kleine Silberspinne' ♀H4 | Widely available |
| | - 'Krater' | CHar CKno EBee EBrs EPPr LEdu MBrN SMeo SWat |
| | - 'Kupferberg' | CHar |
| § | - 'Little Kitten' | CDes CHar CKno CPen CSpe EBee EGle EPPr EPla EWsh LEdu MBar MSte SMad SPoG WMoo WPGP |
| | - 'Little Zebra' (v) | CKno EBee EPPr EPfP EShb LRHS LSRN MGos NOak SPoG |
| | - 'Malepartus' | Widely available |
| | - 'Morning Light' (v) ♀H4 | Widely available |
| | - 'Nippon' | CBow CElw CHrt CKno CPrp CWCL EAEE EBee EBla EHoe EPPr EPla EWsh GKir LEdu LHop LRHS MCCP MMoz NDov NGdn NOrc SDys SPer WPGP |
| | - 'Nishidake' | CHar CPen EBee |
| | - 'November Sunset' | EBrs EPPr ERas EWes IPot MMoz |
| | - 'Overdam' | GKir |
| | - 'Poseidon' | EPPr MAvo SDys |
| | - 'Positano' | CKno EBee EPPr MMoz WPGP |
| | - 'Professor Richard Hansen' | CHar CKno CPen GBin NDov SMHy WPrP |
| | - 'Pünktchen' (v) | CHar CKno CPen CWCL EAEE EBee ECha EGle EHoe EPPr EPla EUJe GBin LEdu MAvo MSte SApp SHDw SMHy SMad SMrm SPhx WFar WMoo WPnP WTin |
| | - var. ***purpurascens*** misapplied | see *M.* 'Purpurascens' |
| | - 'Rigoletto' (v) | EPPr SApp |
| | - 'Roland' | CHar CKno CPen EBee GBin SPhx |
| | - 'Roterpfeil' | CHar CPen SMHy SMeo |
| | - 'Rotfeder' | GKir |
| | - 'Rotfuchs' | CHar CPen EBee MGos MSte SAga WFar |
| | - 'Rotsilber' | Widely available |
| I | - 'Russianus' | EWsh |
| | - 'Samurai' | CHar EPPr GMaP GQue MAvo SMrm |
| | - 'Sarabande' | CHar CKno EBee EGle EHoe EHul ELan EPPr EWsh IPot LRHS MSte NDov SApp SMHy SMrm WFar WGwG WMoo |
| | - 'Septemberrot' ♀H4 | CHVG CHar CKno CPrp CWCL EBee LEdu SPoG |
| § | - 'Silberfeder' ♀H4 | Widely available |
| | - 'Silberpfeil' (v) | EHoe EWsh MSte |
| | - 'Silberspinne' | CMdw EBee EBla EGle EPla ERas LEdu MCCP MWat NDov NGdn SAga SApp SMHy SMeo SPlb WAul WDin |
| | - 'Silberturm' | CHar CKno EBee SPoG |
| | - Silver Feather | see *M. sinensis* 'Silberfeder' |
| | - 'Sioux' | CHar CKno EBee EBrs EGle EHoe EPPr EPla EShb GBin LEdu LRHS MMoz MSte SPer WOVN WTin |

| | | |
|---|---|---|
| | - 'Sirene' | CHar EAEE EBee EBrs ECGP EGle EHoe EPGN EPPr EPla LRHS MBNS MBlu NBsh WFar WPrP |
| | - 'Spätgrün' | CHar EPla |
| | - 'Strictus' (v) ♀$^{H4}$ | Widely available |
| | - 'Tiger Cub' (v) | CWCL EBee MAvo SApp |
| | - 'Undine' ♀$^{H4}$ | CHar CKno CMea CPrp CSam EAEE EBee EBla EBrs ECha EGle EHoe EHrv ELan EPGN EPla EWsh LEdu LRHS MLLN MMoz MSte NDov SPla WMoo WPrP |
| | - 'Variegatus' (v) | Widely available |
| | - 'Vorläufer' | CHar CKno CPen EBrs EHoe EWsh LEdu SAga |
| | - 'Wetterfahne' | CHar EGle LEdu |
| § | - 'Yaku-jima' | CHar CSam EBee ECha EGle MWhi SPoG |
| | - 'Yakushima Dwarf' | Widely available |
| | - 'Zebrinus' (v) ♀$^{H4}$ | Widely available |
| | - 'Zwergelefant' | CHar MMoz SMHy |
| I | 'Spartina' | SApp |
| | ***tinctorius*** 'Nanus Variegatus' misapplied | see *M. oligostachyus* 'Nanus Variegatus' |
| | ***transmorrisonensis*** | CHar CHid CKno EBee EHoe ELan GBin GFor MAvo MMoz NBsh NDov NNor NOak SAdn SApp SMHy SMad SWal WTin |
| | - B&SWJ 3697 | WCru |
| | ***yakushimensis*** | see *M. sinensis* 'Yaku-jima', *M. sinensis* 'Little Kitten' |

## *Mitchella* (*Rubiaceae*)

| | | |
|---|---|---|
| | ***repens*** | CBcs EBee GBin WCru |
| | ***undulata*** B&SWJ 10928 **new** | WCru |
| * | - f. ***quelpartensis*** B&SWJ 4402 **new** | WCru |

## *Mitella* (*Saxifragaceae*)

| | | |
|---|---|---|
| | ***breweri*** | CHid CSec ECha GCal GGar MRav MSte NHol NSti SBch SRms WEas WFar WMoo WTin |
| | ***caulescens*** | ECha NBro NHol WMoo WPrP |
| | ***diphylla*** | EPPr |
| | ***formosana*** | EPPr |
| | - B&SWJ 125 | WCru |
| | ***japonica*** B&SWJ 4971 | WCru |
| | ***kiusiana*** | CLAP |
| | - B&SWJ 5888 | WCru |
| | ***makinoi*** | CBct CLAP EBee |
| | - B&SWJ 4992 | WCru |
| | ***ovalis*** | EBee EPPr |
| | ***pauciflora*** B&SWJ 6361 | WCru |
| | ***pentandra*** | WMoo |
| | ***stylosa*** | LLHF |
| | - B&SWJ 5669 | WCru |
| | ***yoshinagae*** | GEdr SBch WMoo |
| | - B&SWJ 4893 | CHid WCru WPrP WPtf |

## *Mitraria* (*Gesneriaceae*)

| | | |
|---|---|---|
| | ***coccinea*** | CBcs CCCN CEnt CMac CStu CTrG CTsd CWib ECho ELan LBMP LSou MBlu MDun SArc SBod SLon SPer SSpi WPic |
| | - 'Bellamy's Orange' **new** | WBod |
| | - Clark's form | CSam CTrC EBee GGar LAst MDun NLar WBor |
| | - 'Lake Caburgua' | CSpe GCal GGal GGar IArd IDee NSti |
| | - 'Lake Puyehue' | CBcs CCCN CDoC CFee EBee EMil EPfP GAbr GQui LRHS MAsh MGos SWvt WAbe WCru WFar WPGP WSHC |

## *Moehringia* (*Caryophyllaceae*)

| | | |
|---|---|---|
| | ***muscosa*** | WCot |

## *Molinia* (*Poaceae*)

| | | |
|---|---|---|
| | ***altissima*** | see *M. caerulea* subsp. *arundinacea* |
| | ***caerulea*** | CRWN CWib EBWF EHul EPPr GFor GKir LAst LCro MBlu NChi NGBl |
| § | - subsp. ***arundinacea*** | CKno CWCL ECha EPPr GFor MBNS MMuc NLar SApp SLPl WPer |
| | - - 'Bergfreund' | CKno CSam EBee EHoe EPGN EPPr EWsh MAvo NDov SApp SMHy SPhx SUsu WDyG WMoo WPrP WTin |
| | - - 'Cordoba' | CKno EPPr GBin NDov SMHy SPhx |
| | - - 'Fontäne' | CPen CSam EBee EHoe EPPr EWsh GCal GQue LEdu MSte NDov NNor SApp SPhx |
| | - - 'Karl Foerster' | Widely available |
| | - - 'Poul Petersen' | CKno EPPr NDov SPhx |
| | - - 'Skyracer' | CChe CKno COIW CPrp CSam EBee EBla EHoe EPPr EWsh GBri GCal GQue MAvo MMoz MWhi NDov SMHy SMad SPhx SPoG SUsu WCot WFar WMoo |
| | - - 'Staefa' | EHoe |
| | - - 'Transparent' | Widely available |
| | - - 'Windsaule' | CKno EBee EPPr NDov SPhx |
| | - - 'Windspiel' | CKno CRow CSam EAEE EBee ECha EGle EHoe EMil EMon EPGN EPPr EWsh LEdu LRHS MAvo NDov SApp SPhx SPoG SWal WCAu WCot WMoo WPGP WTin |
| | - - 'Zuneigung' | CKno CSam EBrs EPPr MAvo NDov SApp SPhx |
| | - subsp. ***caerulea*** | CHar |
| | - - 'Carmarthen' (v) | EBee EHoe EPGN EPPr MAvo SApp WHal WPnP WPrP |
| | - - 'Claerwen' (v) | ECha EPPr GBuc GCal SMHy SPhx WMoo |
| | - - 'Coneyhill Gold' (v) | EPPr |
| | - - 'Dauerstrahl' | CKno EBee EPPr GBin GCal GQue MAvo NDov NHol |
| | - - 'Edith Dudszus' | CKno CWCL EAEE EBee ECha EGle EHoe EPPr EWsh GQue LEdu LRHS MAvo MBrN MBri MMoz MNFA NDov NGdn NHol SApp SMHy SPer WLeb WMoo WPGP |
| | - - 'Heidebraut' | CWsd EAEE EAlp EBee EBla EGle EHoe EHul EPGN EPPr GBin GQue LRHS NBro NDov SApp SPhx WFar WMoo WPnP |
| | - - 'Moorflamme' | CKno CSam EHoe EPPr MAvo SPhx |
| | - - 'Moorhexe' | Widely available |
| | - - 'Overdam' | NDov |
| | - - 'Strahlenquelle' | CKno CSam EBee EGle EHoe ELan EMon EPGN EPPr GCal LPla LRHS MAvo MMoz MSte NBro NDov NHol WPGP |
| | - - 'Variegata' (v) ♀$^{H4}$ | Widely available |
| | - 'Heiliger Hain' **new** | SMHy |
| | ***litoralis*** | see *M. caerulea* subsp. *arundinacea* |

## *Molopospermum* (*Apiaceae*)

| | | |
|---|---|---|
| | ***peloponnesiacum*** | CAby CSpe EBee ELon GCal LEdu MLLN NChi NLar NSti SPhx WCru WSHC |

## *Moltkia* (*Boraginaceae*)

| | | |
|---|---|---|
| § | ***doerfleri*** | NBir NChi |
| § | x ***intermedia*** ♀$^{H4}$ | CMea WAbe WFar |
| | ***petraea*** | LLHF WFar |

## *Moluccella* (*Lamiaceae*)

***laevis*** 'Pixie Bells' — CSpe

## *Momordica* (*Cucurbitaceae*)

***balsamina*** — MSal
***charantia*** — MSal

## *Monachosorum* (*Adiantaceae*)

***henryi*** — WRic

## *Monadenium* (*Euphorbiaceae*)

***lugardiae*** — MBri
'Variegatum' (v) — MBri

## *Monarda* (*Lamiaceae*)

'Adam' — EBee GCal LRHS LSRN MLLN MSte NBre NDov WCAu WSHC
'Amethyst' — EBee ECtt EWes SIde
'Aquarius' — EAEE EBee EPPr LRHS MSte NCob NDov NGHP NHol NPro NSti SPla WAul WCAu WCHb WFar WWlt
***austromontana*** — see *M. citriodora* subsp. *austromontana*
'Baby Spice' — EBee NCob
§ 'Balance' — CPrp CWCL EAEE EAro EBee ECtt EPfP GCal LBMP MCot MRav NBro NCGa NCob NDov NGHP NGdn NHol NSti SMeo SPhx SPla WCAu WCHb WFar WPGP WSHC WWlt
'Beauty of Cobham' $\Upsilon^{H4}$ — CHar CPrp EBee ECha ELan EPfP GKir GMaP LAst LCro LEdu LHop LRHS MBri MHer MSte NDov NGHP NHol NLar NPri SMad SPer SPhx WBor WCHb WWlt
'Blaukranz' — NBre
§ 'Blaustrumpf' — CElw EBee ECtt GBBs GBri MSte NCob NDov NLar SPer
Blue Stocking — see *M.* 'Blaustrumpf'
Bowman — see *M.* 'Sagittarius'
***bradburyana*** — EShb LLHF NBre NLar WCHb
'Cambridge Scarlet' $\Upsilon^{H4}$ — Widely available
'Capricorn' — GBuc LRHS MSte NBre WCHb
'Cherokee' — GBri NCob NHol SPhx WCHb WFar
***citriodora*** — CArn ECtt GPWP GPoy LRHS MNHC MSal NSti SIde SPlb SRms SWat WLHH
§ - subsp. ***austromontana*** — EAro NBir SBch SGar SIde SVic WFar WPer
- - 'Bee's Favourite' **new** — SPad
'Comanche' — EBee EHrv EWes NCob NDov WCHb WFar
'Croftway Pink' $\Upsilon^{H4}$ — Widely available
I 'Dark Ponticum' — NCob
***didyma*** — CArn CHar CWan EPfP GKir MSal NBro NGHP SWat WBrE WJek
- 'Coral Reef' **new** — EBrs LRHS
- 'Duddiscombe' — CPrp CSam CWCL
- 'Goldmelise' — NBre NGHP WMoo
'Earl Grey' **new** — WRHF
'Elsie's Lavender' — CAby EBee EGle GBri GBuc LPla NDov NLar SAga SPhx WAul WCHb
'Fireball'$^{PBR}$ — CWCL EBee ECtt GAbr LLHF NBPC NCob NLar SBig
§ 'Fishes' — CHVG EAEE EBee ECtt EHrv ELan EPPr EWes MCot MRav MSte NCob NDov NGHP NHol NLar SPla STes WCHb WFar WSHC WWlt
***fistulosa*** — CArn CWan GPoy MNHC MSal WJek WLHH WMoo WPer
'Gardenview Scarlet' $\Upsilon^{H4}$ — Widely available
Gemini — see *M.* 'Twins'
'Gewitterwolke' — CSam EBee GBin
'Hartswood Wine' — NHol SMad SMrm
'Heidelerche' — EPPr
'Jacob Cline' — CCVN GBin NBre NCob NDov SMrm STes
'Kardinal' — EBee EMil GBin NHol
'Lambada' — EBee SPav
Libra — see *M.* 'Balance'
'Lilac Queen' — NCob
'Loddon Crown' — CHar COlW EBee ECtt GQue LRHS MBri MDKP NCob NGHP NHol NLar SIde WCHb WFar WRha WSHC
'Mahogany' — EBee ELan EWTr GBri GMaP LRHS NCob NGHP NHol SMad SPer WCHb WSHC
'Marshall's Delight' $\Upsilon^{H4}$ — CElw CPrp EBee ECtt EWes LSou NCob NGHP NHol NLar SGar SMrm WCAu WFar WHil
'Melissa' — EBee EMil LSRN NBre
***menthifolia*** — CArn EAro EBee GCal GPWP LSou MCot SMrm
'Mohawk' — CPrp CWCL EAEE EBee ECtt EHrv EPPr LRHS MWat NChi NCob NDov NHol NOrc SPer WCAu WCHb WHil
'Mrs Perry' — EWes NGHP
'Neon' — NDov SPhx
'Night Rider' **new** — EWes
'On Parade' — EAEE EBee ECGP ECtt EWll MMHG MSte NCob NDov NHol
'Ou Charm' — CWCL EBee EWes GBri LCro LRHS MLLN MMHG MWat NDov NGHP NLar SMrm WCHb WFar
'Panorama' — EAro ECtt MSal NHol NLar SGar SPad SPet SPlb WMoo WPer
'Panorama Red Shades' (Panorama Series) — CWib EAro MNHC NGHP SPet
'Pawnee' — NDov WCHb
Petite Delight = 'Acpetdel' — CAbP CBcs EBee ECtt EHoe ELan EPfP GBin LHop LRHS MDun NCob NDov NGHP NHol NLar SMad SPla WFar
'Petite Pink Supreme' — EBee EPfP MLLN
'Pink Supreme'$^{PBR}$ — EPfP GAbr NCob NLar
'Pink Tourmaline' — EBee NDov NGby NHol SMad SMrm SPhx WCHb WFar
Pisces — see *M.* 'Fishes'
'Poyntzfield Pink' — GPoy
Prairie Night — see *M.* 'Prärienacht'
§ 'Prärienacht' — Widely available
***punctata*** — CArn CBod CWCL EAro EBee EDAr ELan LRHS MLLN MSal NGdn SDnm SPav SWat WCHb WFar WMoo
- 'Fantasy' — NGHP
'Purple Ann' — NDov
'Raspberry Wine' — ECtt GBri
'Ruby Glow' — CAby CWCL EAEE EBee EHrv IPot LRHS MArl MMHG NCGa NDov NHol SMad SMrm SPhx WCHb WFar
§ 'Sagittarius' — EAEE EBee LBMP LRHS MMHG NCGa NChi NCob NGdn NHol SPla SPur WCAu WCHb
'Sahin's Mildew-free' — WCHb
'Saxon Purple' — NDov NLar
§ 'Schneewittchen' — Widely available
'Scorpion' — CWCL EAro EBee ECtt EHrv ELan EPPr LBMP LEdu LRHS MRav MSte NBPC NBir NCob NDov NHol NOrc NPro SMrm SPhx SWvt WCAu WCHb WPGP WSHC
'Shelley' **new** — ECha
'Sioux' — EHrv EWes GBuc LRHS WCHb WFar WRha

| | | |
|---|---|---|
| | 'Snow Maiden' | see *M.* 'Schneewittchen' |
| | 'Snow Queen' | CSam EAEE EAro EBee ECtt EPPr LBMP LRHS MWat NCob NHol NLar NPro SHar SPla SPur STes |
| | Snow White | see *M.* 'Schneewittchen' |
| | 'Squaw' 🏆$^{H4}$ | Widely available |
| | 'Talud' 🏆$^{H4}$ | EBee NDov |
| § | 'Twins' | CMil CPrp CWCL EBee EPPr LRHS MLLN NDov NGHP NHol SWvt WCAu WCHb WSHC |
| | 'Velvet Queen' | LSou |
| | 'Vintage Wine' | CAby CWCL ECtt GBri NCob NDov WCHb WCot WFar |
| | 'Violacea' | NHol WCHb |
| | 'Violet Queen' 🏆$^{H4}$ | EAEE EAro EBee EBrs ECtt EWes LBMP LRHS NBre NCob NHol NPro SCoo SMrm WCAu WFar WHil |

## *Monardella* (*Lamiaceae*)

| | | |
|---|---|---|
| | ***macrantha*** | CPBP |
| | - subsp. ***hallii*** new | CPBP |
| | ***nana*** subsp. ***arida*** | CPBP |
| | - subsp. ***tenuiflora*** | CPBP |
| | ***odoratissima*** | CArn |

## *Monochoria* (*Pontederiaceae*)

| | | |
|---|---|---|
| § | ***hastata*** | CDWL LLWG MSKA |

## *Monopsis* (*Campanulaceae*)

| | | |
|---|---|---|
| | ***unidentata*** | CSec |

## *Monstera* (*Araceae*)

| | | |
|---|---|---|
| | ***deliciosa*** (F) 🏆$^{H1}$ | MBri SRms XBlo |
| | - 'Variegata' (v) 🏆$^{H1}$ | MBri SRms |

## *Montbretia* see *Crocosmia*

| | | |
|---|---|---|
| | x ***crocosmiiflora*** | see *Crocosmia* x *crocosmiiflora* |
| | ***pottsii*** | see *Crocosmia pottsii* |

## *Montia* (*Portulacaceae*)

| | | |
|---|---|---|
| | ***australasica*** | see *Neopaxia australasica* |
| | ***perfoliata*** | see *Claytonia perfoliata* |
| | ***sibirica*** | see *Claytonia sibirica* |

## *Moraea* (*Iridaceae*)

| | | |
|---|---|---|
| | ***alticola*** | CPne CWsd EBee EBrs ECho GGar SKHP WPGP |
| | ***atropunctata*** | ITim |
| § | ***bellendenii*** | EBee WCot |
| | ***comptonii*** | CPBP |
| | ***elegans*** | CPBP |
| | ***huttonii*** | CCCN CFir CPBP CSec CSpe CWsd EBee EDif EPPr GBBs SMad WBVN WCot WPic WSHC |
| | ***iridioides*** | see *Dietes iridioides* |
| | ***loubseri*** | EBee WCot |
| | ***lurida*** | WCot |
| | ***pavonia*** var. ***lutea*** | see *M. bellendenii* |
| | ***polyanthos*** | EBee |
| | ***polystachya*** | EBrs ECho LRHS |
| | ***robusta*** | GCal |
| | ***spathacea*** | see *M. spathulata* |
| § | ***spathulata*** | CBro CPLG EBee ERos GCal LEdu SKHP WCot |
| | ***tricolor*** | CPBP |
| | ***tulbaghensis*** | EBee WCot |
| | ***vegeta*** | CPBP WCot |
| | ***villosa*** | WCot |

## *Moricandia* (*Brassicaceae*)

| | | |
|---|---|---|
| | ***moricandioides*** | CSpe |

## *Morina* (*Morinaceae*)

| | | |
|---|---|---|
| * | ***afghanica*** | GAbr |
| | ***alba*** | GCra NChi |
| | ***longifolia*** | Widely available |
| | ***persica*** | EWes EWld GBuc LPio NLar WHoo |
| | ***polyphylla*** | GPoy |

## *Morisia* (*Brassicaceae*)

| | | |
|---|---|---|
| | ***hypogaea*** | see *M. monanthos* |
| § | ***monanthos*** | GMaP MBar NLAp NWCA SRot WFar |
| | - 'Fred Hemingway' | ECho ITim LRHS NDlv NMen NSla SIng WAbe WThu |

## *Morus* ✿ (*Moraceae*)

| | | |
|---|---|---|
| | ***alba*** | CAgr CArn CBcs CCVT CDul CLnd CMCN CMen CTho CWib ECrN ELan EPfP GTwe LBuc LMaj MGos SBLw SHBN WDin WFar |
| | - 'Macrophylla' | CMCN NLar |
| | - 'Pendula' | CBcs CDoC CDul CEnd CLnd CTho CTri ECrN ELan EMil GTwe LAst LPan LRHS MAsh MBlu MBri MLan NLar SBLw SCoo SHBN SLim SPer SPoG WDin WOrn |
| | - 'Platanifolia' | LMaj MBlu SBLw |
| | - var. ***tatarica*** | CAgr LEdu NLar |
| § | ***bombycis*** | IFFs LPan SBLw |
| | 'Capsrum' (F) | CAgr |
| | 'Carmen' (F) | CAgr |
| | 'Illinois Everbearing' (F) | CAgr ECrN |
| | 'Italian' (F) | CAgr |
| | 'Ivory' (F) | CAgr |
| | ***kagayamae*** | see *M. bombycis* |
| | ***latifolia*** 'Spirata' | NLar |
| | ***nigra*** (F) 🏆$^{H4}$ | Widely available |
| § | - 'Chelsea' (F) | CAgr CDul CEnd CTho CTri ECrN EMui EPfP GTwe LRHS MBri MGan MGos MLan NWea SCoo SKee SPer SPoG WHar WOrn WPGP |
| | - 'Jerusalem' | MAsh |
| | - 'King James' | see *M. nigra* 'Chelsea' |
| | - 'Large Black' (F) | EMui |
| | - 'Wellington' (F) | CEnd LPan |
| | ***rubra*** | NLar |
| | - 'Nana' | MBri |

## *Mosla* (*Lamiaceae*)

| | | |
|---|---|---|
| | ***dianthera*** | EBee EWld GCal MAvo MNrw WSHC |

## *Muehlenbeckia* (*Polygonaceae*)

| | | |
|---|---|---|
| | ***astonii*** | ECou |
| | ***australis*** | ECou |
| | ***axillaris*** misapplied | see *M. complexa* |
| § | ***axillaris*** Walp. | CBcs CTri ECou EPla GGar SBig |
| | - 'Mount Cook' (f) | ECou |
| | - 'Ohau' (m) | ECou |
| § | ***complexa*** | CBcs CDoC CHEx CSec CTrC CTri CWib EBee ECou EPfP EPla EShb LRHS MCCP NSti SAPC SArc SEND SLim SLon SWvt WCFE WPGP WSHC |
| | - (f) | ECou |
| | - 'Nana' | see *M. axillaris* Walp. |
| | - var. ***trilobata*** | CHEx CTrC EBee EPla GCal IBlr SSta WDyG |
| | - 'Ward' (m) | ECou |
| | ***ephedroides*** | ECou |
| | - 'Clarence Pass' | ECou |
| * | - var. ***muricatula*** | ECou |
| | ***gunnii*** | ECou |
| | ***platyclados*** | see *Homalocladium platycladum* |

## *Muhlenbergia* (*Poaceae*)

| | | |
|---|---|---|
| | ***capillaris*** | CKno SHDw |
| | ***dumosa*** | CKno |
| | ***japonica*** 'Cream Delight' (v) | CPen EBee EHoe LEdu SHDw |
| | ***mexicana*** | EBee GFor LEdu WPGP |
| | ***rigens*** | CKno SApp |

## *Mukdenia* (*Saxifragaceae*)

| | | |
|---|---|---|
| | ***acanthifolia*** | CLAP EBee WCru |
| | ***rossii*** | CDes CLAP EBee ELon EMon EPla GCal IFro LEdu MSte NLar NMyG SMad WCot WCru WHil WPGP WPrP WThu WTin |
| | - 'Crimson Fans' | see *M. rossii* 'Karasuba' |
| | - dwarf | CLAP GCal |
| § | - 'Karasuba' | CLAP GEdr NBhm NMyG |
| | - 'Ōgon' | CLAP EBee |
| | - 'Shishiba' **new** | GEdr |
| | - variegated (v) | EBee EMon |

## mulberry see *Morus*

## *Murraya* (*Rutaceae*)

| | | |
|---|---|---|
| * | ***elliptica*** | SOWG |
| | ***exotica*** | see *M. paniculata* |
| | ***koenigii*** | EOHP GPoy |
| § | ***paniculata*** | CArn EShb GPoy |

## *Musa* ✿ (*Musaceae*)

| | | |
|---|---|---|
| | sp. | WCot |
| | from Tibet | CKob |
| | from Yunnan, China | see *M. itinerans* 'Yunnan' |
| § | ***acuminata*** | MBri |
| | - 'Bordelon' | CKob |
| § | - 'Dwarf Cavendish' (AAA Group) (F) ♀$^{H1}$ | CKob EAmu ELan EPfP ISea LRHS MJnS NLar NScw SPer XBlo |
| | - 'Grand Nain' x ***acuminata*** 'Zebrina' | EAmu |
| | - 'Williams' (AAA Group) (F) | EAmu |
| | - 'Zebrina' ♀$^{H1+3}$ | CDTJ CKob EAmu LRHS MJnS XBlo |
| | ***balbisiana*** | CKob EAmu |
| | ***basjoo*** ♀$^{H3-4}$ | Widely available |
| I | - 'Rubra' | CCCN EAmu ESwi |
| | - 'Sakhalin' | CKob SAdn |
| | 'Burmese Blue' | CKob |
| | 'Cavendish Super Dwarf' | MJnS |
| | ***cavendishii*** | see *M. acuminata* 'Dwarf Cavendish' |
| § | ***coccinea*** ♀$^{H1}$ | XBlo |
| | ***ensete*** | see *Ensete ventricosum* |
| | 'Helen' | ETod MJnS |
| | ***hookeri*** | see *M. sikkimensis* |
| * | ***iterans glaucum*** | CDTJ |
| § | ***itinerans*** 'Yunnan' | CKob EAmu |
| § | ***lasiocarpa*** | CAbb CBct CDTJ CDWL CDoC CHEx CHll CKob CMHG CSec EAmu EShb ETod EUJe IDee LCro LRHS MBri MJnS NPal NScw SBig WCot WGwG |
| | ***laterita*** | CKob |
| | ***mannii*** | CKob |
| | ***nana*** misapplied | see *M. acuminata* 'Dwarf Cavendish' |
| | ***nana*** Lour. | see *M. acuminata* |
| | ***ornata*** ♀$^{H1}$ | CCCN LPal MJnS XBlo |
| | - 'African Red' | CKob |
| | - 'Macro' | CKob |
| | - 'Purple' | CKob |
| | x ***paradisiaca*** | CKob |
| | Goldfinger = 'Fhia-01' (AAAB Group) (F) | |
| | - 'Hajaré' (ABB Group) (F) | CKob |
| | - 'Malbhog' (AAB Group) (F) | CKob |
| | - 'Ney Poovan' (AB Group) (F) | CCCN EAmu |
| | - 'Orinoco' (ABB Group) (F) | CKob EAmu |
| | - 'Rajapuri' (AAB Group) (F) | CKob EAmu MJnS |
| | 'Royal Purple' (*ornata* hybrid) | CKob |
| § | ***sikkimensis*** | CDTJ CDoC CKob EAmu ELan ETod EUJe EWes LPJP LRHS MJnS SBig SChr WFar XBlo |
| | - 'Red Tiger' | CCCN CDoC CKob EAmu MREP |
| | 'Tandarra Red' **new** | CDoC LSou SVil |
| | 'Tropicana' | SSto XBlo |
| | ***uranoscopus*** misapplied | see *M. coccinea* |
| | ***velutina*** ♀$^{H1+3}$ | CCCN CDoC CKob EAmu ETod MJnS SBig |

## *Muscari* ✿ (*Hyacinthaceae*)

| | | |
|---|---|---|
| | PF | NWCA |
| | 'Aleyna' **new** | NMin |
| | ***ambrosiacum*** | see *M. muscarimi* |
| | ***anatolicum*** | EBrs ECho |
| | ***armeniacum*** ♀$^{H4}$ | CBro CTca CTri EBrs ECho EGoo EPfP ERos LRHS MBri MCot NChi SRms WCot WFar WShi |
| | - 'Argaei Album' | EBrs ECho EPot GAuc LAma |
| | - 'Atlantic' | EBrs ECho ERCP LRHS |
| | - 'Babies Breath' | see *M.* 'Jenny Robinson' |
| | - 'Blue Pearl' | EBrs ECho GKev LRHS |
| | - 'Blue Spike' (d) | CBro EBla EBrs ECho EPfP ERCP LAma LRHS MBri NBir NBlu SPer WCot WFar WGwG |
| | - 'Cantab' | EBrs ECho GKev |
| | - 'Christmas Pearl' ♀$^{H4}$ | EBrs ECho SPhx WCot |
| | - 'Dark Eyes' | CTca EBrs ECho EPfP LRHS SPer WFar WHil |
| | - 'Early Giant' | ECho |
| | - 'Fantasy Creation' | EBla EBrs ECho EPot |
| | - 'Heavenly Blue' | ECho |
| | - 'New Creation' | ECho |
| | - 'Peppermint' **new** | ERCP NMin |
| | - 'Saffier' ♀$^{H4}$ | CGrW EBrs ECho LAma SPhx WCot |
| | - 'Valerie Finnis' | Widely available |
| * | ***auchadra*** | ERos |
| | ***aucheri*** ♀$^{H4}$ | ECho ERos LAma MSte NRya |
| * | - var. ***bicolor*** | WCot |
| | - 'Blue Magic' | CBro EBrs ECho EPot |
| | - 'Mount Hood' | CMea CTca EBla EBrs ECho ERCP |
| | - 'Ocean Magic' **new** | ERCP |
| § | - 'Tubergenianum' | EBrs ECho |
| | - 'White Magic' **new** | ERCP WCot |
| § | ***azureum*** ♀$^{H4}$ | CAvo CBgR CBro CFFs CSec CTca EBrs ECho ELan EPfP ERos GMaP LAma LEdu NMen NWCA SPhx WCot |
| | - 'Album' | CBgR CBro CSsd CTca EBla EBrs ECho EGoo ERos LAma LRHS SPhx WCot |
| | 'Baby's Breath' | see *M.* 'Jenny Robinson' |
| | 'Blue Dream' | EBrs ECho |
| | 'Blue Eyes' | EBrs ECho WCot |
| | 'Blue Star' | EBrs ECho |
| | ***botryoides*** | EBrs ECho ERos LAma LEdu |
| | - 'Album' | CAvo CBro CFFs CMea CTca CTri EBla EBrs ECho EPfP EWTr LAma LBMP MBri NChi SMrm SPer SRms WBor WCot WShi |
| | ***caucasicum*** | ECho ERos WCot |
| | ***chalusicum*** | see *M. pseudomuscari* |
| § | ***comosum*** | CArn CBro EBrs ECho EPfP LEdu LRHS NWCA WRos |

| | | |
|---|---|---|
| * | - 'Album' | ECho |
| | - 'Monstrosum' | see *M. comosum* 'Plumosum' |
| | - 'Pinard' | EBrs ECho ERos |
| § | - 'Plumosum' | CAvo CTca EBla EBrs ECho EMon EPfP EPot LAma LEdu MBri SBch WAul WCot WHil |
| | ***dionysicum*** | EBrs ECho |
| | - HOA 8965 | WCot EBee |
| | ***grandifolium*** | ERos |
| | - JCA 689.450 | WCot |
| | - var. ***populeum*** | ERos |
| | ***inconstrictum*** | ECho |
| § | 'Jenny Robinson' ♀H4 | CMil CWsd EBla ECho EHrv SCnR SMad WCot |
| | ***latifolium*** ♀H4 | CBro CTca EBla EBrs ECho EPfP EPot ERCP GAuc GGar LAma LRHS MLLN NBPN NChi SBch SMrm SPer SPhx WBor WCot WTin |
| * | - 'Blue Angels' | NBir |
| § | ***macrocarpum*** | CAvo CBro CTca EBee EBrs ECha ECho EPot ERos GAuc LAma WAbe WCot |
| | - 'Golden Fragrance' PBR | CBgR CMil CPom EBrs ECho EPot ERCP LRHS WCot |
| | ***mirum*** | ECho |
| | ***moschatum*** | see *M. muscarimi* |
| § | ***muscarimi*** | CAvo CBgR CBro CStu EBrs ECho ERCP LAma LEdu NWCA WCot WHil |
| | - var. ***flavum*** | see *M. macrocarpum* |
| § | ***neglectum*** | CSWP CSec EBrs ECho ERos ITim LAma SEND WShi WWst |
| | ***pallens*** | EBrs ECho ERos LRHS NWCA WCot |
| | ***paradoxum*** | see *Bellevalia paradoxa* |
| | ***parviflorum*** | EBrs ECho ERos |
| § | ***pseudomuscari*** ♀H4 | EBrs ECho ERos WCot |
| | ***racemosum*** | see *M. neglectum* |
| | 'Sky Blue' | EBrs ECho WCot |
| § | ***spreitzenhoferi*** | EBrs ECho ERos |
| | 'Superstar' | EBrs ECho LEdu WCot |
| § | ***tenuiflorum*** | ECho WCot |
| | ***tubergenianum*** | see *M. aucheri* 'Tubergenianum' |
| | ***weissii*** | ERos |
| | 'White Beauty' | ECho |

## *Muscarimia* (*Hyacinthaceae*)

| | | |
|---|---|---|
| | ***ambrosiacum*** | see *Muscari muscarimi* |
| | ***macrocarpum*** | see *Muscari macrocarpum* |

## *Musella* see *Musa*

## *Mussaenda* (*Rubiaceae*)

| | | |
|---|---|---|
| | ***erythrophylla*** | MJnS |
| | 'Tropic Snow' **new** | CCCN |

## *Musschia* (*Campanulaceae*)

| | | |
|---|---|---|
| | ***wollastonii*** | CHEx ECre |

## *Mutisia* (*Asteraceae*)

| | | |
|---|---|---|
| | 'Glendoick' | GGGa |
| | ***ilicifolia*** | LRHS MTPN |
| | ***retusa*** | see *M. spinosa* var. *pulchella* |
| § | ***spinosa*** var. ***pulchella*** | EBee GGal GKev |

## *Myoporum* (*Myoporaceae*)

| | | |
|---|---|---|
| | ***debile*** | see *Eremophila debilis* |
| | ***laetum*** | CDoC CHEx CPLG CTrC |

## *Myosotidium* (*Boraginaceae*)

| | | |
|---|---|---|
| § | ***hortensia*** | Widely available |
| | - white-flowered | ITim |
| | ***nobile*** | see *M. hortensia* |

## *Myosotis* (*Boraginaceae*)

| | | |
|---|---|---|
| | from Eyre Mountains, New Zealand | NWCA |
| | ***alpestris*** 'Alba' **new** | GJos |
| | - 'Ruth Fischer' | NBir NMen |
| * | ***aquatica*** | NSco |
| | ***arvensis*** | SECG |
| | ***australis*** | NWCA |
| | ***capitata*** | ECou |
| | ***colensoi*** | ECou NMen NWCA |
| | ***explanata*** | NMen |
| | ***macrantha*** | GBin |
| | Masha strain **new** | CNat |
| | ***palustris*** | see *M. scorpioides* |
| | ***pulvinaris*** | CPBP ECou |
| | ***rakiura*** | EPPr SBch |
| § | ***scorpioides*** | CBen CRow CWat EBWF EHon EMFW EPfP LPBA MSKA SCoo SPer SPlb SRms SWat WBrk WMAq WMoo WPnP |
| | - 'Alba' | CDWL LPBA MSKA SPer |
| | - 'Ice Pearl' | CBen ECha |
| | - Maytime = 'Blaqua' (v) | CDWL NBir SPer |
| | - 'Mermaid' | CBen CRow CWat ECha EHon EMFW EPfP LLWG LPBA LRHS SBch SDix SWat WFar WPer WPnP |
| | - 'Pinkie' | CDWL CWat EMFW LPBA SWat |
| | - 'Snowflakes' | CWat EMFW SWat |
| | - variegated (v) **new** | MSKA |
| | ***sylvatica*** | CRWN EBWF NMir |
| | - 'Ultramarine' ♀H4 | GJos |
| | 'Unforgettable' (v) | CBow NBro NCob |

## *Myrceugenia* (*Myrtaceae*)

| | | |
|---|---|---|
| | ***ovata*** | CTrG |
| | ***planipes*** | CTrG |

## *Myrica* (*Myricaceae*)

| | | |
|---|---|---|
| | ***californica*** | CDul LEdu NLar WPGP |
| | ***cerifera*** | CArn NLar |
| | ***gale*** | CAgr CRWN EMil GPoy GQue MCoo MGos NLar SWat WDin WFar |
| | ***pensylvanica*** | EHig ELau GAuc LEdu NBlu NLar |

## *Myricaria* (*Tamaricaceae*)

| | | |
|---|---|---|
| | ***germanica*** | NLar |

## *Myriophyllum* (*Haloragaceae*)

| | | |
|---|---|---|
| | ***propinquum*** | EMFW |
| * | 'Red Stem' | LPBA |
| | ***spicatum*** | CDWL EHon EMFW NSco WMAq |
| | ***verticillatum*** | CWat EHon SCoo |

## *Myrrhidendron* (*Apiaceae*)

| | | |
|---|---|---|
| | ***donnellsmithii*** B&SWJ 10484 | WCru |
| | ***glaucescens*** B&SWJ 10699 **new** | WCru |

## *Myrrhis* (*Apiaceae*)

| | | |
|---|---|---|
| | ***odorata*** | Widely available |
| | - 'Forncett Chevron' | GCal LEdu |

## *Myrsine* (*Myrsinaceae*)

| | | |
|---|---|---|
| | ***africana*** | CWib SBLw |
| | ***aquilonia*** **new** | ECou |
| | ***divaricata*** | CTrC |
| | ***nummularia*** | GGar WThu |

## *Myrteola* (*Myrtaceae*)

| | | |
|---|---|---|
| § | ***nummularia*** | ISea NMen WThu |

## *Myrtus* (*Myrtaceae*)

| | | |
|---|---|---|
| | ***apiculata*** | see *Luma apiculata* |
| | ***bullata*** | see *Lophomyrtus bullata* |
| | ***chequen*** | see *Luma chequen* |
| | ***communis*** ♀H3 | Widely available |
| | - 'Flore Pleno' (d) | ELau EOHP |
| | - 'Jenny Reitenbach' | see *M. communis* subsp. *tarentina* |
| | - 'Microphylla' | see *M. communis* subsp. *tarentina* |
| | - 'Nana' | see *M. communis* subsp. *tarentina* |
| § | - subsp. ***tarentina*** ♀H3 | Widely available |
| | - - 'Compacta' | LBuc NLar |
| | - - 'Microphylla Variegata' (v) | CBcs GBar GQui MHer NGHP SPer STre WJek |
| I | - - 'Variegata' | EOHP EPla SBLw |
| | - 'Tricolor' | see *M. communis* 'Variegata' |
| § | - 'Variegata' (v) | Widely available |
| | ***dulcis*** | see *Austromyrtus dulcis* |
| | 'Glanleam Gold' | see *Luma apiculata* 'Glanleam Gold' |
| | ***lechleriana*** | see *Amomyrtus luma* |
| | ***luma*** | see *Luma apiculata* |
| | ***nummularia*** | see *Myrteola nummularia* |
| * | ***paraguayensis*** | CTrC |
| | x ***ralphii*** | see *Lophomyrtus* x *ralphii* |
| | 'Traversii' | see *Lophomyrtus* x *ralphii* 'Traversii' |
| | ***ugni*** | see *Ugni molinae* |
| * | ***variegata*** 'Penlee' (v) | CTrG |

# N

## *Nabalus* (*Asteraceae*)

| | |
|---|---|
| ***albus*** | see *Prenanthes alba* |

## *Nananthus* (*Aizoaceae*)

| | |
|---|---|
| ***vittatus*** | WAbe |

## *Nandina* (*Berberidaceae*)

| | | |
|---|---|---|
| | ***domestica*** ♀H3 | Widely available |
| | - B&SWJ 4923 | WCru |
| | - B&SWJ 11113 **new** | WCru |
| | - 'Fire Power' ♀H3 | Widely available |
| | - 'Harbor Dwarf' | LRHS SKHP SPoG WFar |
| | - var. ***leucocarpa*** | EPla MBlu NLar |
| | - 'Little Princess' | EPla |
| | - 'Nana' | see *N. domestica* 'Pygmaea' |
| | - 'Nana Purpurea' | EPla GCal |
| | - 'Orhime' | NLar |
| § | - 'Pygmaea' | CBct CMen WDin |
| | - 'Richmond' | CBcs CEnd CSBt EBee ELan EPfP LAst LRHS MAsh MGos NLar NVic SBod SHBN SLim SPer SPla SPoG SRkn SSto SWvt WCFE WFar |
| | - 'Wood's Dwarf' | MGos |

## *Nannorrhops* (*Arecaceae*)

| | |
|---|---|
| ***ritchieana*** | LPal |

## *Napaea* (*Malvaceae*)

| | |
|---|---|
| ***dioica*** | WCot |

## *Narcissus* ✿ (*Amaryllidaceae*)

| | | |
|---|---|---|
| | 'Abba' (4) | CQua |
| | 'Abstract' (11a) | CQua |
| | 'Accent' (2) ♀H4 | CQua LRHS WRos |
| | 'Accomplice' (3) **new** | IRhd |
| | 'Achduart' (3) | CQua |
| | 'Achentoul' (4) | CQua |
| | 'Achnasheen' (3) | CQua |
| | 'Acropolis' (4) | CQua EBrs EPfP IHer |
| | 'Actaea' (9) ♀H4 | CBro CQua CTca EBrs MBri |
| | 'Acumen' (2) | CQua |
| | 'Admiration' (8) | CQua |
| | 'Advocat' (3) | CQua |
| | 'African Sunset' (3) | IRhd |
| | 'Agnes Mace' (2) | IRhd |
| | 'Ahwahnee' (2) | CQua IRhd |
| | 'Ainley' (2) | CQua |
| | 'Aintree' (3) | CQua |
| | 'Aircastle' (3) | CQua |
| | 'Akepa' (5) | CQua |
| | 'Albatross' (3) | CQua WShi |
| I | ***albidus*** subsp. ***occidentalis*** (13) | ERos |
| | 'Albus Plenus Odoratus' | see *N. poeticus* 'Plenus' ambig. |
| | 'Alpine Winter' (1) | IRhd |
| | 'Alston' (2) | IRhd |
| | 'Alto' (2) | IRhd |
| | 'Altruist' (3) | CQua ERCP |
| | 'Altun Ha' (2) | CQua IRhd |
| | 'Amazing Grace' (2) | IRhd |
| | 'Amber Castle' (2) | CQua |
| | 'Ambergate' (2) | CQua EBrs LAma |
| | 'American Heritage' (1) | CQua IRhd |
| | 'American Robin' (6) | CQua |
| | 'American Shores' (1) | CQua IRhd |
| | 'Amstel' (4) | CQua |
| | 'Andalusia' (6) | ERos |
| | 'Angel' (3) | CQua |
| | 'Angel Eyes' (a) | EBrs |
| | 'Angel Face' (3) | CQua IRhd |
| | 'Angelito' (3) ♀H4 | IRhd |
| | Angel's Tears | see *N. triandrus* subsp. *triandrus* var. *triandrus* |
| | 'Angel's Wings' (2) | CQua |
| | 'Angkor' (4) | CQua |
| | 'An-gof' (7) | CQua |
| | 'Apotheose' (4) | CQua LRHS |
| | 'Applins' (2) | IRhd |
| | 'Apricot' (1) | CBro |
| | 'Apricot Blush' (2) | CQua |
| | 'April Love' (1) | CQua |
| | 'April Snow' (2) | CBro CQua |
| | 'April Tears' (5) ♀H4 | NMin |
| | 'Aranjuez' (2) | CQua |
| | 'Arctic Gem' (3) | CQua |
| | 'Arctic Gold' (1) ♀H4 | CQua LAma |
| | 'Ardress' (2) | CQua |
| | 'Ardview' (3) | IRhd |
| | 'Argosy' (1) | CQua |
| | 'Arid Plains' (3) | IRhd |
| | 'Arish Mell' (5) | CQua |
| | 'Arkle' (1) ♀H4 | CQua |
| | 'Arleston' (2) | IRhd |
| | 'Armidale' (3) | IRhd |
| | 'Armoury' (4) | CQua |
| | 'Arndilly' (2) | CQua |
| | 'Arpege' (2) | CQua |
| | 'Arran Isle' (2) | IRhd |
| | 'Arthurian' (1) | IRhd |
| | 'Articol' (11a) **new** | CQua |
| | 'Arwenack' (11a) | CQua |
| | 'Ashmore' (2) | CQua IRhd |
| | 'Ashton Wold' (2) | CQua |
| | 'Asila' (2) | IRhd |
| | 'Assertion' (2) | IRhd |
| § | ***assoanus*** (13) | CBro CQua EBrs ECho EPot ERos LAma MSSP NMen NMin |
| | 'Astropink' (11a) | CQua |
| § | ***asturiensis*** (13) ♀H3-4 | CSam ECho MNrw NMin |
| | ***asturiensis*** x ***cyclamineus*** | NMen |

| | |
|---|---|
| - 'Navarre' (I) | WCot |
| 'Atricilla' (11a) | IRhd |
| 'Auchrannie' (2) | IRhd |
| 'Audubon' (2) | CQua |
| 'Auntie Eileen' (2) | CQua |
| 'Auspicious' (2) | IRhd |
| 'Autumn Gold' (7) | EBrs |
| 'Avalanche' (8) ♀H3 | CQua EBrs NMin |
| 'Avalanche of Gold' (8) | CQua |
| 'Avalon' (2) | CQua |
| 'Azocor' (1) | IRhd |
| 'Baby Moon' (7) | CQua CTca EBrs EPot GEdr GKev LAma LEdu LRHS LSou MBrN MBri NHol NMin |
| 'Badanloch' (3) | CQua |
| 'Badbury Rings' (3) ♀H4 | CQua |
| 'Bala' (4) **new** | CQua |
| 'Balalaika' (2) | CQua |
| 'Baldock' (4) | CQua |
| 'Ballinamallard' (3) | IRhd |
| 'Ballydorn' (9) | IRhd |
| 'Ballygarvey' (1) | CQua |
| 'Ballygowan' (3) | IRhd |
| 'Ballyrobert' (1) | CQua |
| 'Baltic Shore' (3) | IRhd |
| 'Balvenie' (2) | CQua |
| 'Bambi' (1) | ERos |
| 'Bandesara' (3) | CQua IRhd |
| 'Bandit' (2) | CQua |
| 'Banker' (2) **new** | CQua |
| 'Banstead Village' (2) | CQua |
| 'Bantam' (2) ♀H4 | CBro CQua ERos |
| 'Barbary Gold' (2) **new** | CQua |
| 'Barlow' (6) | CQua |
| 'Barnesgold' (1) | IRhd |
| 'Barnham' (1) **new** | CQua |
| 'Barnsdale Wood' (2) | CQua |
| 'Barnum' (1) ♀H4 | IRhd |
| 'Barrett Browning' (3) | EBla EBrs LRHS |
| 'Barrii' (3) **new** | CQua |
| 'Bartley' (6) | CQua |
| 'Bath's Flame' (3) | CAvo CQua IHer WShi |
| 'Bear Springs' (4) | IRhd |
| 'Beautiful Dream' (3) **new** | CQua |
| 'Bebop' (7) | CBro |
| 'Bedruthan' (2) | CQua |
| 'Beersheba' (1) | CQua EBrs |
| 'Belbroughton' (2) | CQua |
| 'Belcanto' (11a) | CQua |
| 'Belfast Lough' (1) | IRhd |
| 'Bell Rock' (1) | CQua |
| 'Bell Song' (7) | CAvo CBro CFFs CMea CQua CTca EBrs EPfP ERCP ERos LRHS LSou NHol |
| 'Bella Vista' (2) | LRHS WRos |
| 'Belzone' (2) | CQua |
| 'Ben Aligin' (1) | CQua |
| 'Ben Hee' (2) ♀H4 | CQua |
| 'Berceuse' (2) | CQua IRhd |
| 'Bere Ferrers' (4) | CQua |
| 'Bergerac' (11a) | CQua |
| 'Berlin' (2) | ERos |
| 'Bernardino' (2) | CQua |
| 'Beryl' (6) | CAvo CBro CQua EBrs ERos LRHS NMin |
| 'Best Seller' (1) | SPer |
| 'Bethal' (3) | CQua |
| 'Betsy MacDonald' (6) | CQua |
| 'Biffo' (4) | CQua |
| 'Bikini Beach' (2) | IRhd |
| 'Bilbo' (6) | CBro CQua |
| 'Binkie' (2) | CBro CQua |
| 'Birchwood' (3) **new** | CQua |
| 'Birdsong' (3) | CQua |
| 'Birma' (3) | EFam LAma |
| 'Bishops Light' (2) | CQua |
| 'Blair Athol' (2) | CQua |
| 'Blarney' (3) | CQua |
| 'Blisland' (9) | CQua |
| 'Blossom' (4) | CQua |
| 'Blushing Lady' (7) | EBrs |
| 'Blushing Maiden' (4) | CQua |
| 'Bob Spotts' (2) | CQua |
| 'Bobbysoxer' (7) | CBro CQua ERos MTho |
| 'Bobolink' (2) | CQua |
| 'Bodelva' (2) | CQua |
| 'Bodwannick' (2) | CQua |
| 'Bold Prospect' (1) | CQua |
| 'Bolton' (7) | CBro |
| 'Bon Viveur' (11a) | IRhd |
| 'Bosbigal' (11a) | CQua |
| 'Boscastle' (7) | CQua |
| 'Boscoppa' (11a) | CQua |
| 'Boslowick' (11a) ♀H4 | CQua |
| 'Bosmeor' (2) | CQua |
| 'Bossa Nova' (3) | CQua |
| 'Bossiney' (11a) | CQua |
| 'Bosvale' (11a) | CQua |
| 'Bosvigo' (11a) **new** | CQua |
| 'Bouzouki' (2) | IRhd |
| 'Bowles Early Sulphur' (1) | CRow |
| 'Boyne Bridge' (1) | IRhd |
| 'Brandaris' (11a) | CQua |
| 'Bravoure' (1) ♀H4 | CQua |
| 'Brentswood' (8) | CQua |
| 'Bridal Crown' (4) ♀H4 | EBrs EPfP LAma SPer |
| 'Bright Flame' (2) | CQua |
| 'Bright Spot' (8) **new** | CQua |
| 'Brindaleena' (2) | IRhd |
| 'Brindle Pink' (2) | IRhd |
| 'Broadland' (2) | CQua |
| 'Broadway Star' (11b) | EBrs LAma |
| 'Brodick' (3) | CQua IRhd |
| 'Bronzewing' (1) **new** | IRhd |
| 'Brookdale' (1) | CQua |
| 'Brooke Ager' (2) ♀H4 **new** | IRhd |
| 'Broomhill' (2) ♀H4 | CQua |
| ***broussonetii*** (13) | EBrs ECho |
| 'Bryanston' (2) ♀H4 | CQua |
| 'Budock Bells' (5) | CQua |
| 'Budock Water' (2) | CQua |
| 'Bugle Major' (2) | CQua |
| ***bulbocodium*** (13) ♀H3-4 | CBro CStu EBrs ITim LBee LEdu LRHS NWCA SBch SPer SRms |
| - from Atlas Mountains, Morocco **new** | MSSP |
| § - subsp. ***bulbocodium*** (13) | CBro |
| § - - var. ***citrinus*** (13) | SSpi |
| - - var. ***conspicuus*** (13) | CArn CBro CHar CPMA CQua CTca EBrs ECho EPfP EPot ERCP ERos GEdr ITim LAma MSSP NMen NMin NRya SBch SGar WCot |
| * - - ***filifolius*** (13) | CBro |
| § - - var. ***graellsii*** (13) | NSla |
| - - var. ***nivalis*** (13) | EBrs ECho ERos |
| - - var. ***pallidus*** (13) | ERos GEdr |
| § - - var. ***tenuifolius*** (13) | CStu NMen |
| § - Golden Bells Group | CAvo CBro CFFs CMea CQua CSam CSsd CWCL EBrs ECho EPot GKir GMaP LRHS MBri SPer |
| - 'Ice Warrior' **new** | SKHP |
| - var. ***mesatlanticus*** | see *N. romieuxii* subsp. *romieuxii* var. *mesatlanticus* |
| - subsp. ***praecox*** (13) | ECho WCot |
| - - var. ***paucinervis*** (13) | EBrs ECho |

| | Name | Suppliers |
|---|---|---|
| | - subsp. ***romieuxii*** | see *N. romieuxii* |
| | - subsp. ***tananicus*** | see *N. cantabricus* subsp. *tananicus* |
| I | - subsp. ***viriditubus*** (13) | ERos |
| | - subsp. ***vulgaris*** | see *N. bulbocodium* subsp. *bulbocodium* |
| | ***bulbocodium* x *romieuxii*** **new** | WCot |
| | 'Bunchie' (5) | CQua |
| | 'Bunclody' (2) | CQua |
| | 'Bunting' (7) ♀$^{H4}$ | CQua |
| | 'Burning Bush' (3) | IRhd |
| | 'Burntollet' (1) | CQua |
| | 'Burravoe' (1) **new** | CQua |
| | 'Busselton' (3) | IRhd |
| | 'Butterscotch' (2) | CQua |
| | 'By George!' (2) | EBrs |
| | 'C.J. Backhouse' (2) | CQua |
| | 'Cabernet' (2) | IRhd |
| | 'Cacatua' (11a) | IRhd |
| | 'Cadgwith' (2) | CQua |
| | 'Cairntoul' (3) | CQua |
| | 'Calamansack' (2) | CQua |
| | ***calcicola*** (13) | CWoo ERos |
| I | - 'Idol' **new** | NMin |
| | 'California Rose' (4) | CQua IRhd |
| | 'Camellia' (4) | EFam |
| | 'Camelot' (2) ♀$^{H4}$ | CQua EPfP SPer |
| | 'Cameo Angel' (2) | CQua |
| | 'Cameo King' (2) | CQua |
| | 'Camoro' (10) | NMen |
| | 'Campernelli Plenus' | see *N.* x *odorus* 'Double Campernelle' |
| | 'Campion' (9) | CQua IRhd |
| | 'Canaliculatus' (8) | CArn CBro CQua CTca EBrs ECho EPfP ERos GKev LAma LRHS MBri SPer WGwG |
| | ***canaliculatus*** Gussone | see *N. tazetta* subsp. *lacticolor* |
| | 'Canary' (7) | CQua |
| | 'Canarybird' (8) | CQua WShi |
| | 'Canasta' (11a) | CQua |
| | 'Canisp' (2) | CQua |
| | 'Cantabile' (9) ♀$^{H4}$ | CBro CQua CTca |
| | ***cantabricus*** (13) | EBrs ECho EPot |
| | - subsp. ***cantabricus*** (13) | ERos |
| | - - var. ***foliosus*** (13) ♀$^{H2}$ | EBrs ECho GKev NMen SCnR WCot |
| § | - subsp. ***tananicus*** (13) | ECho |
| | 'Canticle' (9) | IRhd |
| | 'Capax Plenus' | see *N.* 'Eystettensis' |
| | 'Cape Cornwall' (2) | CQua |
| | 'Cape Helles' (3) | IRhd |
| | 'Cape Point' (2) | IRhd |
| | 'Capisco' (3) | CQua |
| | 'Caramba' (2) | CQua |
| | 'Carbineer' (2) | CQua EFam |
| | 'Carclew' (6) | CQua |
| | 'Cardiff' (2) | CQua |
| | 'Cardinham' (3) | CQua |
| | 'Cargreen' (9) | CQua |
| | 'Carib Gipsy' (2) ♀$^{H4}$ | CQua IRhd |
| | 'Caribbean Snow' (2) | CQua |
| | 'Carlton' (2) ♀$^{H4}$ | CQua EBrs EFam LAma |
| | 'Carnearny' (3) | CQua |
| | 'Carnkeeran' (2) | CQua |
| | 'Carnkief' (2) | CQua |
| | 'Carnyorth' (11a) | CQua |
| | 'Carole Lombard' (3) | CQua |
| | 'Carwinion' (2) | CQua |
| | 'Cassata' (11a) | EBrs EFam EPfP LAma NBir |
| | 'Castanets' (8) | IRhd |
| | 'Casterbridge' (2) | CQua IRhd |
| | 'Catalyst' (2) | IRhd |
| | 'Catistock' (2) | CQua |
| | 'Causeway Sunset' (2) | IRhd |
| | 'Cavalryman' (3) | IRhd |
| | 'Caye Chapel' (3) | CQua |
| | 'Cazique' (6) | CQua |
| | x ***cazorlanus*** (13) | ITim MSSP |
| | 'Ceasefire' (2) | IRhd |
| | 'Cedar Hills' (3) | CQua |
| | 'Cedric Morris' (1) | CBro CDes CElw CLAP ECha EHrv GBuc NDov |
| | 'Celestial Fire' (2) | CQua |
| | 'Celtic Gold' (2) | CQua |
| | 'Centannées' (11b) | EBrs |
| | 'Centrefold' (3) | CQua |
| | 'Cha-cha' (6) | CBro CQua |
| | 'Chanson' (1) | IRhd |
| | 'Chanterelle' (11a) | EBla LAma |
| | 'Chantilly' (2) **new** | CQua |
| | 'Chapman's Peak' (2) | IRhd |
| | 'Charity May' (6) ♀$^{H4}$ | CQua |
| | 'Charleston' (2) | CQua |
| | 'Chasseur' (2) | IRhd |
| | 'Chaste' (1) | CQua IRhd |
| | 'Chat' (7) | CQua |
| | 'Cheer Leader' (3) | CQua |
| | 'Cheerfulness' (4) ♀$^{H4}$ | CAvo CFFs CMea CQua EBrs LAma LRHS MBri |
| | 'Cheesewring' (3) | CQua |
| | 'Cheetah' (1) | CQua IRhd |
| | 'Chelsea Girl' (2) | CQua |
| | 'Cheltenham' (2) | CQua |
| | 'Chenoweth' (2) | CQua |
| | 'Chérie' (7) | CBro CQua |
| | 'Cherish' (2) | CQua |
| | 'Cherry Glow' (3) **new** | IRhd |
| | 'Cherrygardens' (2) | CQua IRhd |
| | 'Chesapeake Bay' (1) | CQua |
| | 'Chesterton' (9) ♀$^{H4}$ | CQua |
| | 'Chickadee' (6) | CBro CQua |
| | 'Chickerell' (3) | CQua |
| | 'Chief Inspector' (1) | IRhd |
| | 'Chiloquin' (1) | CQua |
| | 'China Doll' (2) | CQua |
| | 'Chinchilla' (2) | CQua IRhd |
| | 'Chingah' (1) | IRhd |
| | 'Chinita' (8) | CBro CQua |
| | 'Chipper' (5) | NMin |
| | 'Chit Chat' (7) ♀$^{H4}$ | CBro CQua EBrs EPot ERos LRHS NMin |
| | 'Chobe River' (1) | IRhd |
| | 'Chorus Line' (8) | IRhd |
| | 'Churston Ferrers' (4) | CQua |
| | 'Chy Noweth' (2) | CQua |
| | 'Chysauster' (2) | CQua |
| | 'Cisticola' (3) | IRhd |
| | ***citrinus*** | see *N. bulbocodium* subsp. *bulbocodium* var. *citrinus* |
| | 'Citron' (3) | CQua |
| | 'Citronita' (3) | CQua |
| | 'Clare' (7) | CBro CQua IRhd NMin |
| | 'Claverley' (2) | CQua |
| | 'Clearbrook' (2) | CQua |
| | 'Cloud Nine' (2) | CBro |
| | 'Clouded Yellow' (2) | CQua IRhd |
| | 'Clouds Rest' (2) | IRhd |
| | 'Codlins and Cream' | see *N.* 'Sulphur Phoenix' |
| | 'Coldbrook' (2) | CQua |
| | 'Colin's Joy' (2) | CQua |
| | 'Coliseum' (2) **new** | IRhd |
| | 'Colleen Bawn' | CQua EBrs |
| | 'Colley Gate' (3) | CQua |
| | 'Colliford' (2) | CQua |
| | 'Colorama' (11a) | CQua |
| | 'Colourful' (2) | IRhd |

| | | |
|---|---|---|
| | 'Columbus' (2) | CQua |
| | 'Colville' (9) | CQua |
| | 'Comal' (1) | CQua |
| | 'Compressus' | see *N.* x *intermedius* 'Compressus' |
| | 'Compton Court' (3) | IRhd |
| | ***concolor*** | see *N. triandrus* subsp. *triandrus* var. *concolor* |
| | 'Conestoga' (2) | CQua IRhd |
| | 'Confuoco' (2) | EFam |
| | 'Congress' (11a) | CQua |
| * | 'Connie Number 1' | CStu |
| | 'Conowingo' (11a) | CQua |
| | 'Conspicuus' ambig. | CQua LAma |
| | 'Content' (1) | CQua |
| | 'Cool Autumn' (2) | CQua |
| | 'Cool Crystal' (3) | CQua |
| | 'Cool Evening' (11a) | CQua IRhd |
| | 'Cool Pink' (2) | CQua |
| | 'Cool Shades' (2) | CQua |
| | 'Coolmaghery' (2) | IRhd |
| | 'Coombe Creek' (6) | CQua |
| | 'Copper Nob' (2) | IRhd |
| | 'Copper Rings' (3) | CQua |
| | 'Copperfield' (2) | CQua |
| | 'Cora Ann' (7) | CBro |
| | 'Coral Fair' (2) | CQua |
| | 'Corbiere' (1) | CQua IRhd |
| | ***cordubensis*** (13) | CBro EBrs ECho GEdr |
| | 'Cornet' (6) | CQua |
| | 'Cornish Chuckles' (12) | CBgR CBro CQua CTca |
| | 'Cornish Sun' (2) | CQua |
| | 'Cornish Vanguard' (2) | CQua |
| | 'Cornsilk' (11a) | CQua |
| | 'Coroboree' | IRhd |
| | 'Corofin' (3) | CQua |
| | 'Coromandel' (2) | IRhd |
| | 'Corozal' (3) | CQua |
| | 'Cosmic Dance' (3) | IRhd |
| | 'Cotinga' (6) | CQua EBrs NMin |
| | 'Countdown' (2) | CQua |
| | 'Coverack Glory' (2) | CQua |
| | 'Crackington' (4) ♀H4 | CQua IRhd |
| | 'Craig Stiel' (2) | CQua |
| | 'Creag Dubh' (2) | CQua |
| | 'Creed' (6) | CQua |
| | 'Crenver' (3) | CQua |
| | 'Crevenagh' (2) | IRhd |
| | 'Crewenna' (1) | CQua |
| | 'Crill' (7) | CQua |
| | 'Crimson Chalice' (3) | CQua IRhd |
| | 'Cristobal' (1) | CQua |
| | 'Crock of Gold' (1) | CQua |
| | 'Croesus' (2) | CQua |
| | 'Crofty' (6) | CQua |
| | 'Croila' (2) | CQua |
| | 'Crowndale' (4) | CQua IRhd |
| | 'Crugmeer' (11a) | CQua |
| | 'Cryptic' (1) | CQua IRhd |
| | 'Crystal Star' (2) | CQua |
| | ***cuatrecasasii*** (13) | ERos |
| | 'Cudden Point' (2) | CQua |
| | 'Cul Beag' (3) | CQua |
| | 'Culmination' (2) | CQua |
| | 'Cultured Pearl' (2) | CQua |
| | 'Curlew' (7) | CQua EBrs |
| | 'Curly' (2) | EBrs |
| | ***cyclamineus*** (13) ♀H4 | CBro CPom CWCL CWoo CWsd EPot MSSP SCnR SRms WAbe |
| | 'Cyclope' (1) | CQua |
| | ***cypri*** (8) | CQua |
| | 'Cyros' (1) | CQua |
| | 'Dailmanach' (2) | CQua IRhd |
| | 'Dailmystic' (2) | IRhd |

| | |
|---|---|
| 'Dallas' (3) | CQua |
| 'Dambuster' | IRhd |
| 'Damson' (2) | CQua |
| 'Dan du Plessis' (8) | CQua |
| 'Dancing Queen' (2) | IRhd |
| 'Dardanelles' (2) | IRhd |
| 'Dateline' (3) | CQua |
| 'David Alexander' (1) | CQua |
| 'David Mills' (2) | CQua |
| 'Dawn Call' (2) | IRhd |
| 'Dawn Run' (2) | IRhd |
| 'Dawn Sky' (2) | CQua |
| 'Daydream' (2) ♀H3 | CQua EBrs |
| 'Daymark' (8) | CQua |
| 'Dayton Lake' (2) | CQua |
| 'Debutante' (2) | CQua |
| 'December Bride' (11a) | CQua |
| 'Decision' (2) **new** | IRhd |
| 'Defence Corps' (1) **new** | IRhd |
| 'Delia' (6) | IRhd |
| 'Dell Chapel' (3) | CQua |
| 'Delnashaugh' (4) | CQua EBrs LAma LRHS NHol |
| 'Delos' (3) | CQua |
| 'Delphin Hill' (4) | IRhd |
| 'Delta Flight' (6) | IRhd |
| 'Demand' (2) | CQua |
| 'Demeanour' | IRhd |
| 'Demmo' (2) | CQua |
| 'Dena' (3) | IRhd |
| 'Denali' (1) | IRhd |
| 'Derryboy' (3) | IRhd |
| 'Descant' (1) | IRhd |
| 'Desdemona' (2) ♀H4 | CQua |
| 'Desert Bells' (7) | CQua |
| 'Desert Orchid' (2) | CQua |
| 'Dewy Dell' (3) **new** | IRhd |
| 'Dick Wilden' (4) | EBla EBrs |
| 'Dickcissel' (7) ♀H4 | CBro CQua EBrs ERos |
| 'Dimity' (3) | CQua |
| 'Dimple' (9) | CQua |
| 'Dinkie' (3) | CBro |
| 'Diversity' (11a) | IRhd |
| 'Doctor Hugh' (3) ♀H4 | CQua IRhd |
| 'Doctor Jazz' (2) | CQua |
| 'Dolly Mollinger' (11b) | EBla EBrs |
| 'Doombar' (1) | CQua |
| 'Dora Allum' (2) | CQua |
| 'Dorchester' (4) | CQua IRhd |
| 'Double Campernelle' | see *N.* x *odorus* 'Double Campernelle' |
| 'Double Fashion' (4) | EBrs |
| double pheasant eye | see *N. poeticus* 'Plenus' ambig. |
| double Roman | see *N.* 'Romanus' |
| 'Double White' (4) | CQua CTca |
| 'Doubleday' (4) | CQua IRhd |
| 'Doublet' (4) | CQua |
| 'Doubtful' (3) | CQua |
| 'Dove Wings' (6) ♀H4 | CQua |
| 'Dover Cliffs' (2) | CQua |
| 'Downlands' (3) | CQua |
| 'Downpatrick' (1) | CQua |
| 'Dragon Run' (2) | CQua |
| 'Drama Queen' (11a) | IRhd |
| 'Dream Catcher' (2) **new** | IRhd |
| 'Drumbeg' (2) | IRhd |
| 'Drumlin' (1) ♀H4 | IRhd |
| ***dubius*** (13) | CBro EBrs ECho EPot |
| 'Duiker' (6) | IRhd |
| 'Duke of Windsor' (2) | EFam |
| 'Dulcimer' (9) | CQua |
| 'Dunadry Inn' (4) | IRhd |
| 'Dunkeld' (2) | CQua |
| 'Dunkery' (4) | CQua IRhd |

| | |
|---|---|
| 'Dunley Hall' (3) | CQua IRhd |
| 'Dunmurry' (1) | CQua |
| 'Dunskey' (3) | CQua |
| 'Dupli Kate' (4) | IRhd |
| 'Dusky Lad' (2) | IRhd |
| 'Dusky Maiden' (2) | IRhd |
| 'Dutch Delight' (2) | IRhd |
| 'Dutch Master' (1) 𝕐$^{H4}$ | CQua EBrs LAma LRHS |
| 'Early Bride' (2) | CQua |
| 'Early Splendour' (8) | CQua |
| 'Earthlight' (3) | CQua |
| 'Easter Bonnet' (2) | EBla |
| 'Easter Moon' (2) | CQua |
| 'Eastern Dawn' (2) | CQua |
| 'Eastern Promise' (2) | CQua |
| 'Eaton Song' (12) 𝕐$^{H4}$ | CBro CQua |
| 'Eddy Canzony' (2) | CQua |
| 'Edenderry' (1) | IRhd |
| 'Edgbaston' (2) | CQua |
| 'Edge Grove' (2) | CQua |
| 'Edward Buxton' (3) | CQua LRHS |
| 'Egard' (11a) | CQua LRHS |
| 'Egmont King' (2) | CQua |
| 'Eland' (7) | CQua |
| 'Elburton' (2) | CQua |
| 'Electrus' (11a) | IRhd |
| ***elegans*** (13) | CAvo EBrs ECho |
| 'Elf' (2) | CBro CQua |
| 'Elfin Gold' (6) | CQua IRhd |
| 'Elizabeth Ann' (6) | CQua |
| 'Elka' (1) | CAvo CBgR CBro CQua NMin |
| 'Ella D' (2) | CQua |
| 'Ellen' (2) | LRHS |
| 'Elphin' (4) | CQua |
| 'Elrond' (2) | CQua |
| 'Elven Lady' (2) | CQua |
| 'Elvira' (8) | CBro CQua |
| 'Emcys' **new** | NMin |
| 'Emerald Pink' (3) | CQua |
| 'Emily' (2) | CQua |
| 'Eminent' (3) | CQua |
| 'Emperor' (1) **new** | CQua |
| 'Emperor's Waltz' (6) | CQua IRhd |
| 'Empress of Ireland' (1) 𝕐$^{H4}$ | CQua EBrs IHer IRhd |
| 'English Caye' (1) | CQua |
| 'Ensemble' (4) | CQua |
| 'Enterprise' (4) | CQua |
| 'Epona' (3) | CQua |
| 'Erlicheer' (4) | CQua EBrs |
| 'Escapee' (2) | IRhd |
| 'Estrella' (3) | CQua |
| 'Ethereal Beauty' (2) | IRhd |
| 'Ethos' (1) | IRhd |
| 'Etincelante' (11a) | EBrs NMin |
| 'Euryalus' (1) | CQua |
| 'Eve Robertson' (2) | CQua |
| 'Evening' (2) | CQua |
| 'Evesham' (3) | IRhd |
| 'Exotic Beauty' (4) | EBrs |
| 'Eyeglass' (3) | IRhd |
| 'Eyelet' (3) | IRhd |
| 'Eype' (4) | IRhd |
| 'Eyrie' (3) | IRhd |
| § 'Eystettensis' (4) | CBro ECha ERos IBlr |
| 'Fair Head' (9) | CQua |
| 'Fair Prospect' (2) | CQua |
| 'Fair William' (2) | CQua |
| 'Fairgreen' (3) | CQua |
| 'Fairlawns' (3) | CQua |
| 'Fairmile' (3) | CQua |
| 'Fairy Chimes' (5) | CBro CQua NMin |
| 'Fairy Footsteps' (3) | CQua IRhd |
| 'Fairy Island' (3) | CQua |
| 'Fairy Spell' (3) | IRhd |
| 'Fairy Tale' (3) | CQua |
| 'Falconet' (8) 𝕐$^{H4}$ | CBro CQua EBrs EPfP ERos |
| 'Falmouth Bay' (3) | CQua |
| 'Falstaff' (2) | CQua |
| 'Famecheck Giant' | EFam |
| 'Famecheck Luck' (2) | EFam |
| 'Famecheck Silver' (11b) | EFam |
| 'Fanline' (11a) **new** | CQua |
| 'Far Country' (2) | CQua |
| I 'Fashion' (11b) | CQua |
| 'Fashion Model' | IRhd |
| 'Fastidious' (2) | CQua |
| 'February Gold' (6) 𝕐$^{H4}$ | CAvo CBro CFFs EBrs EPfP EPot ERCP ERos LAma LRHS MBri NBir SGar SPer SPhx SRms WShi |
| 'February Silver' (6) | CBro EBrs EPot ERCP LAma SPhx |
| 'Felindre' (9) | CQua |
| 'Feline Queen' (1) | IRhd |
| 'Feock' (3) | CQua |
| ***fernandesii*** (13) | CBro EBrs ECho ERos NMin SCnR WCot WThu |
| 'Ferndown' (3) | CQua IRhd |
| 'ffitch's Folly' (2) | CQua |
| 'Fidelity' (1) | LRHS WRos |
| 'Filoli' (1) | CQua IRhd |
| 'Finchcocks' (2) | CQua |
| 'Fine Gold' (1) | CQua |
| 'Fine Romance' (2) | CQua |
| 'Finland' (2) | CQua |
| 'Fiona MacKillop' (2) | IRhd |
| 'Fire Tail' (3) | CQua IHer WShi |
| 'First Born' (6) | CQua |
| 'First Formal' (3) | CQua |
| 'Flambards Village' (4) | CQua |
| 'Flirt' (6) | CQua |
| 'Flomay' (7) | CBro |
| 'Florida Manor' (3) | IRhd |
| 'Flower Drift' (4) | EPfP |
| 'Flower Record' (2) | LAma LRHS |
| 'Flycatcher' (7) | CQua |
| 'Flying Colours' (4) | IRhd |
| 'Flying High' (3) | CQua |
| 'Foff's Way' (1) | CQua |
| 'Foresight' (1) | CQua EFam |
| 'Forge Mill' (2) | CQua |
| 'Fortissimo' (2) | EBrs |
| 'Fortune' (2) | CQua EFam LAma MBri |
| 'Fossie' (4) **new** | CQua |
| 'Foundling' (6) 𝕐$^{H4}$ | CBro CQua |
| 'Foxhunter' (2) | CQua |
| 'Fragrant Breeze' (2) | EBrs |
| 'Fragrant Rose' (2) | CQua EBrs IRhd |
| 'Francolin' (1) | IRhd |
| 'Frank' (9) | IRhd |
| 'Freedom Rings' (2) | CQua |
| 'Freedom Stars' (11a) | IRhd |
| 'Fresco' (11a) | IRhd |
| 'Fresh Lime' (1) | CQua |
| 'Fresno' (3) | IRhd |
| 'Frigid' (3) | CQua |
| 'Frogmore' (6) | CQua |
| 'Front Royal' (2) | CQua |
| 'Frosted Pink' (2) | IRhd |
| 'Frostkist' (6) | CBro CQua |
| 'Frou-frou' (4) | CQua |
| 'Frozen Jade' (1) | CQua |
| 'Fruit Cup' (7) | CQua EPfP |
| 'Fulwell' (4) | CQua |
| 'Furbelow' (4) | CQua |
| 'Furnace Creek' (2) | IRhd |
| 'Fynbos' (3) | IRhd |

| | |
|---|---|
| ***gaditanus*** (13) | CBro ERos |
| 'Galilee' (3) | EBrs |
| 'Gamebird' (1) | IRhd |
| 'Garden News' (3) | IRhd |
| 'Garden Princess' (6) | CBro EBrs LRHS |
| 'Garden Treasure' (2) **new** | IRhd |
| 'Gay Cavalier' (4) | CQua |
| 'Gay Kybo' (4) ♀H4 | CQua |
| 'Gay Song' (4) | CQua |
| § ***gayi*** (13) | CQua WShi |
| 'Geevor' (4) | CQua |
| 'Gellymill' (2) | CQua |
| 'Gemini Girl' (2) | CQua |
| 'George Leak' (2) | CQua |
| 'Georgie Girl' (6) | CQua |
| 'Geranium' (8) ♀H4 | CBro CQua EBrs EPfP LAma LRHS SMeo SPer |
| 'Gettysburg' (2) | CQua |
| 'Gillan' (11a) | CQua |
| 'Gin and Lime' (1) ♀H4 | CQua |
| 'Gipsy Moon' (2) | CQua |
| 'Gipsy Queen' (1) | CBgR CQua NMin |
| 'Gironde' (11) | CQua |
| 'Glacier' (1) | CQua |
| 'Glen Cassley' (3) | CQua |
| 'Glen Clova' (2) | CQua |
| 'Glendermott' (2) | CQua |
| 'Glenside' (2) | CQua |
| 'Glissando' (2) | CQua |
| 'Gloriosus' (8) | CQua |
| 'Glover's Reef' (1) | CQua |
| 'Glowing Pheonix' (4) | CQua WShi |
| 'Glowing Red' (4) | CQua |
| 'Goff's Caye' (2) | CQua IRhd |
| 'Golant' (2) | CQua |
| 'Gold Bond' (2) | CQua IRhd |
| 'Gold Charm' (2) | CQua |
| 'Gold Convention' (2) ♀H4 | CQua IRhd |
| 'Gold Ingot' (2) | IRhd |
| 'Gold Medallion' (1) | CQua |
| 'Gold Top' (2) | CQua |
| 'Golden Amber' (2) | CQua |
| 'Golden Aura' (2) ♀H4 | CQua |
| 'Golden Bear' (4) | CQua |
| 'Golden Bells' | see *N. bulbocodium* Golden Bells Group |
| 'Golden Cheer' (2) | CQua |
| 'Golden Cycle' (6) | CQua |
| 'Golden Dawn' (8) ♀H3 | CQua EBrs EPfP |
| 'Golden Ducat' (4) | CQua LAma MBri NBir |
| 'Golden Flute' (2) | IRhd |
| 'Golden Gamble' (11a) | IRhd |
| 'Golden Halo' (2) | CQua |
| 'Golden Harvest' (1) | CQua EBrs LAma |
| 'Golden Incense' (7) | CQua |
| 'Golden Jewel' (2) ♀H4 | CQua |
| 'Golden Joy' (2) | CQua |
| 'Golden Lady' (1) | LRHS |
| 'Golden Lion' (1) | CQua EPfP SPer |
| 'Golden Marvel' (1) | CQua |
| 'Golden Orbit' (4) | CQua |
| 'Golden Phoenix' (4) | CQua WShi |
| 'Golden Quince' (12) | CBro CQua |
| 'Golden Rain' (4) | CQua |
| 'Golden Rapture' (1) ♀H4 | CQua |
| 'Golden Sceptre' (7) | CBro |
| 'Golden Sheen' (2) | CQua |
| 'Golden Splash' (11a) | IRhd |
| 'Golden Spur' (1) | CQua LAma |
| 'Golden Torch' (2) | CQua |
| 'Golden Vale' (1) ♀H4 | CQua |
| 'Goldfinger' (1) ♀H4 | CQua IRhd NMin |
| 'Goldhanger' (2) | CQua |
| 'Goldsithney' (2) | CBro |
| 'Golitha Falls' (2) | CQua |
| 'Good Fella' (2) **new** | CQua |
| 'Good Measure' (2) | CQua |
| 'Goonbell' (2) | CQua |
| 'Gorran' (3) | CQua |
| 'Gossmoor' (4) | CQua |
| ***graellsii*** | see *N. bulbocodium* subsp. *bulbocodium* var. *graellsii* |
| 'Grand Monarque' | see *N. tazetta* subsp. *lacticolor* 'Grand Monarque' |
| 'Grand Opening' (4) | IRhd |
| 'Grand Primo Citronière' (8) | CBgR CQua |
| 'Grand Prospect' (2) | CQua |
| 'Grand Soleil d'Or' (8) | CQua EBrs LAma NHol |
| 'Great Expectations' (2) | CQua |
| 'Greatwood' (1) | CQua |
| 'Green Howard' (3) | EBrs ECho |
| 'Green Lodge' (9) | IRhd |
| 'Greenlet' (6) | CQua MSte |
| 'Greenodd' (3) | CQua |
| 'Greenpark' (9) | IRhd |
| 'Grenoble' (2) | CQua |
| 'Gresham' (4) | CQua IRhd |
| 'Gribben Head' (4) | CQua |
| 'Groundkeeper' (3) | IRhd |
| 'Grullemans Senior' (2) | EFam |
| 'Gulliver' (3) | CQua |
| 'Gunwalloe' (11a) | CQua |
| 'Guy Wilson' (2) | CQua |
| 'Gwennap' (1) | CQua |
| 'Gwinear' (2) | CQua |
| 'Hacienda' (1) | CQua |
| 'Half Moon Caye' (2) | CQua |
| 'Halley's Comet' (3) | CQua IRhd |
| 'Halloon' (3) | CQua |
| 'Halvose' (8) | CBro |
| 'Halzephron' (2) | CQua |
| 'Hambledon' (2) ♀H4 | CQua |
| 'Hampton Court' (2) | CQua |
| 'Happy Dreams' (2) | IRhd |
| 'Happy Fellow' (2) | CQua |
| 'Happy Valley' (2) | IRhd |
| 'Harbour View' (2) | IRhd |
| 'Harmony Bells' (5) | CQua |
| 'Harp Music' (2) | IRhd |
| 'Harpers Ferry' (1) | CQua |
| 'Hartlebury' (3) | CQua |
| 'Hawangi' (3) | IRhd |
| 'Hawera' (5) ♀H4 | CAvo CBro CFFs CMea CQua CTca EBrs ECGP EGoo EPfP EPot GKev LAma LEdu LRHS LSou MBri SPer SPhx WHal |
| 'Heamoor' (4) ♀H4 | CQua |
| ***hedraeanthus*** (13) | EBrs ECho EPot |
| - SG 13 | WCot |
| 'Helford Dawn' (2) | CQua |
| 'Helford Sunset' (2) | CQua |
| 'Helios' (2) | CQua |
| ***hellenicus*** | see *N. poeticus* var. *hellenicus* |
| ***henriquesii*** | see *N. jonquilla* var. *henriquesii* |
| 'Henry Irving' (1) | CQua |
| 'Hero' (1) | CQua |
| 'Hesla' (7) | CBro |
| 'Heslington' (3) | CQua |
| 'Hexameter' (9) | CQua |
| 'Hexworthy' (3) | CQua |
| 'Hibernian' (4) **new** | IRhd |
| 'Hicks Mill' (1) | CQua |
| 'High Society' (2) ♀H4 | CQua |
| 'Highfield Beauty' (8) ♀H4 | CQua |
| 'Highgrove' (1) | CQua |

| | | |
|---|---|---|
| | 'Highlite' (2) | CQua |
| | 'Hilda's Pink' (2) | CQua |
| | 'Hill Head' (9) | IRhd |
| | 'Hillstar' (7) 𝕐$^{H4}$ | CQua EBrs IRhd LRHS MSte |
| | ***hispanicus*** (13) | EBrs ECho |
| | 'Hocus Pocus' (3) | IRhd |
| | 'Hollypark' (3) | IRhd |
| | 'Holme Fen' (2) | CQua |
| | 'Home Fires' (2) | CQua |
| | 'Homestead' (2) 𝕐$^{H4}$ | IRhd |
| | 'Honey Pink' (2) | CQua |
| | 'Honeybird' (1) | CQua |
| | 'Honeyorange' (2) | IRhd |
| | 'Hoopoe' (8) 𝕐$^{H4}$ | CBro CQua EBrs LRHS |
| | 'Horace' (9) | CQua |
| | 'Horn of Plenty' (5) | CBgR CBro CQua EBrs |
| | 'Hornpipe' (1) | IRhd |
| | 'Hors d'Oeuvre' (8) | CBro |
| | 'Hospodar' (2) | CQua |
| | 'Hot Gossip' (2) | CQua |
| | 'Hotspur' (2) | CQua |
| | 'Hugh Town' (8) | CAvo CBgR CQua |
| | 'Hullabaloo' (2) | IRhd |
| | ***humilis*** misapplied | see *N. pseudonarcissus* subsp. *pseudonarcissus* var. *humilis* |
| | 'Hunting Caye' (2) | CQua |
| | 'Huntley Down' (1) | CQua |
| | 'Ice Chimes' (5) | CQua |
| | 'Ice Dancer' (2) | CQua |
| | 'Ice Diamond' (4) | CQua |
| | 'Ice Follies' (2) 𝕐$^{H4}$ | CQua EBrs EFam LAma MBri NBir SPer |
| | 'Ice King' (4) | EBla EBrs NBir SPer |
| | 'Ice Wings' (5) 𝕐$^{H4}$ | CAvo CBro CFFs CQua EBrs EPot ERos MSte NMin WShi |
| | 'Idless' (1) | CQua |
| | 'Immaculate' (2) | CQua |
| | 'Inara' (4) | CQua |
| | 'Inbal'$^{PBR}$ (8) | EBrs |
| | 'Inca' (6) | CQua |
| | 'Inchbonnie' (2) | CQua |
| | 'Independence Day' (4) | CQua |
| | 'Indian Chief' (4) | EFam |
| | 'Indian Maid' (7) 𝕐$^{H4}$ | CQua IRhd |
| | 'Indora' (4) | CQua |
| | 'Inner Glow' (2) | IRhd |
| | 'Innisidgen' (8) | CQua |
| | 'Innovator' (4) | IRhd |
| | 'Inny River' (1) | IRhd |
| | 'Interim' (2) | CQua |
| | x ***intermedius*** (13) | CBro CQua ERos WAbe WCot |
| § | - 'Compressus' (8) | CQua |
| | 'Intrigue' (7) 𝕐$^{H4}$ | CQua IRhd LRHS SPer |
| | 'Invercassley' (3) | CQua |
| | 'Ipi Tombi' (2) | EBrs ERos |
| | 'Ireland's Eye' (9) | CQua |
| | 'Irene Copeland' (4) | CQua |
| | 'Irish Fire' (2) | CQua |
| | 'Irish Light' (2) | CQua |
| | 'Irish Linen' (3) | CQua |
| | 'Irish Luck' (1) | CQua |
| | 'Irish Minstrel' (2) 𝕐$^{H4}$ | CQua |
| | 'Irish Wedding' (2) | CQua |
| | 'Isambard' (4) | CQua |
| | 'Islander' (4) | CQua |
| | 'Ita' (2) | IRhd |
| | 'Itzim' (6) 𝕐$^{H4}$ | CAvo CBro CFFs CQua EBrs ECho ERos LRHS |
| | 'Jack Snipe' (6) 𝕐$^{H4}$ | CAvo CBro CFFs CQua EBrs ECGP ECho EPfP EPot ERos LAma LRHS MBri MSte SPhx WShi |
| | 'Jack Wood' (11a) | CQua |
| | 'Jackadee' (2) | IRhd |
| | 'Jake' (3) | IRhd |
| | 'Jamage' (8) | CQua |
| | 'Jamaica Inn' (4) | CQua CTca |
| | 'Jambo' (2) | IRhd |
| | 'Jamboree' (2) | CQua |
| | 'Jamestown' (3) | IRhd |
| | 'Janelle' (2) | CQua |
| | 'Jantje' (11a) | CQua |
| | 'Javelin' (2) | IRhd |
| | 'Jeanine' (2) | CQua |
| | 'Jeanne Bicknell' (4) | CQua |
| | 'Jedna' (2) | CQua |
| | 'Jenny' (6) 𝕐$^{H4}$ | CBro CMea CQua CTca EBla EBrs EPot ERos LAma LEdu MCot NBir WShi |
| | 'Jersey Carlton' (2) | CQua |
| | 'Jersey Roundabout' (4) | CQua |
| | 'Jersey Torch' (4) | CQua |
| | 'Jetfire' (6) 𝕐$^{H4}$ | CBro CMea CQua CTca EBrs ECho EPfP EPot ERCP ERos LAma LRHS LSou NHol SPer WShi |
| | 'Jezebel' (3) | CBro |
| | 'Jimmy Noone' (1) | CQua |
| | 'Jim's Gold' (2) | CQua |
| | 'Jodi' (11b) | IRhd |
| | 'Jodi's Sister' (11a) | IRhd |
| | 'Johanna' (5) | CBro |
| | 'John Daniel' (4) | CQua |
| | 'John Lanyon' (3) | CQua |
| | 'John's Delight' (3) | CQua |
| | x ***johnstonii*** | CBro EBrs ECho EPot NMin |
| | - 'Queen of Spain' (10) | CAvo |
| | ***jonquilla*** (13) 𝕐$^{H4}$ | CAvo CBro CQua EBrs EPot ERos LAma LEdu LRHS NMin SPhx WShi |
| § | - var. ***henriquesii*** (13) | CQua EBrs ECho NMin SCnR SPhx |
| | 'Joppa' (7) | CQua |
| | 'Joy Bishop' | see *N. romieuxii* 'Joy Bishop' |
| | 'Joybell' (6) | CQua |
| | 'Juanita' (2) | EPfP LRHS |
| | 'Juano' (1) **new** | IRhd |
| | 'Jules Verne' (2) | CQua |
| | 'Julia Jane' | see *N. romieuxii* 'Julia Jane' |
| | 'Jumblie' (12) 𝕐$^{H4}$ | CBro CQua EBrs EPfP EPot ERos GGar LAma MBri SPer |
| | ***juncifolius*** | see *N. assoanus* |
| | 'June Lake' (2) | CQua IRhd |
| | 'Kabani' (9) | CQua |
| | 'Kalimna' (1) | CQua |
| | 'Kamau' (9) | IRhd |
| | 'Kamms' (1) | CQua |
| | 'Kamura' (2) | CQua |
| | 'Kanchenjunga' (1) | CQua |
| | 'Kathy's Clown' (6) | CQua |
| | 'Katie Heath' (5) | EBrs ECho ERCP LRHS |
| | 'Katrina Rea' (6) | CQua |
| | 'Kaydee' (6) 𝕐$^{H4}$ | CQua IRhd NMin SPhx |
| | 'Kea' (6) | CQua |
| | 'Keats' (4) | CBro CQua |
| | 'Kebaya' (2) | CQua |
| | 'Kehelland' (4) | CBro |
| | 'Kelly Bray' (1) | CQua |
| | 'Kenellis' (10) | CBgR CBro CQua EBrs EPot GEdr MSte |
| | 'Kernow' (2) | CQua |
| | 'Kidling' (7) | CQua EBrs ECho NMin |
| | 'Killara' (8) | CQua |
| | 'Killearnan' (9) | CQua |
| | 'Killigrew' (2) | CQua |
| | 'Killivose' (3) | CQua |
| | 'Kiltonga' (2) | IRhd |
| | 'Kilworth' (2) | CQua EFam |
| | 'Kimmeridge' (3) | CQua |
| | 'King Alfred' (1) | CQua EPfP GKir SPer |
| | 'King Size' (11a) | CQua LRHS |

| | |
|---|---|
| 'Kinglet' (7) | CQua |
| 'King's Grove' (1) ♀$^{H4}$ | CQua |
| 'Kings Pipe' (2) | CQua |
| 'Kingscourt' (1) ♀$^{H4}$ | CQua |
| 'Kingsleigh' (1) **new** | IRhd |
| 'Kissproof' (2) | EBla EBrs |
| 'Kit Hill' (7) | CQua CTca |
| 'Kitten' (6) | CQua |
| 'Kitty' (6) | CBro ERos |
| 'Kiwi Magic' (4) | CQua IRhd |
| 'Kiwi Solstice' (4) | CQua |
| 'Kiwi Sunset' (4) | CQua |
| 'Knocklayde' (3) | CQua |
| 'Knowing Look' (3) | IRhd |
| 'Kokopelli' (7) ♀$^{H4}$ | CBro CQua EBrs NMin |
| 'Korora Bay' (1) | IRhd |
| 'La Argentina' (2) | EFam |
| 'La Riante' (3) | CQua |
| 'Ladies' Choice' (7) | IRhd |
| 'Ladies' Favorite' (7) | IRhd |
| 'Lady Ann' (2) | IRhd |
| 'Lady Be Good' (2) | CQua |
| 'Lady Diana' (2) **new** | CQua |
| 'Lady Eve' (11a) | IRhd |
| 'Lady Margaret Boscawen' (2) | CQua |
| 'Lady Serena' (9) | CQua |
| 'Lake Tahoe' (2) | IRhd |
| 'Lalique' (3) | CQua |
| 'Lamanva' (2) | CQua |
| 'Lamlash' (2) | IRhd |
| 'Lanarth' (7) | CBro |
| 'Lancaster' (3) | CQua |
| 'Langarth' (11a) | CQua |
| 'Lapwing' (5) | CBro ERos IRhd |
| 'Larkelly' (6) | CBro ERos |
| 'Larkhill' (2) | CQua |
| 'Larkwhistle' (6) ♀$^{H4}$ | EBrs ERos LAma LRHS |
| 'Las Vegas' (1) | EBrs |
| 'Latchley' (2) | CQua CTca |
| 'Lauren' (3) | IRhd |
| 'Lavender Lass' (6) | CQua |
| 'Lavender Mist' (2) | CQua |
| 'Lazy River' (1) | CQua |
| 'Leading Light' (2) | CQua |
| 'Lee Moor' (1) | CQua CTca |
| 'Lemon Beauty' (11b) | CQua EBla |
| 'Lemon Drops' (5) ♀$^{H4}$ | CMea CQua EBrs ECho EPot ERCP EROs LRHS MSte SPhx |
| 'Lemon Grey' (3) | IRhd |
| 'Lemon Heart' (5) | CBro |
| 'Lemon Silk' (6) | CBro CMea CQua EBrs ECho NMin SPhx |
| 'Lemon Snow' (2) | IRhd |
| 'Lemonade' (3) | CQua |
| 'Lennymore' (2) | CQua IRhd |
| 'Lewis George' (1) | CQua |
| 'Libby' (2) | IRhd |
| 'Liberty Bells' (5) | CBro CQua EBrs ECho LAma MBri |
| 'Liebeslied' (3) | CQua |
| 'Life' (7) | CQua |
| 'Lighthouse' (3) | CQua |
| 'Lighthouse Reef' (1) | CQua IRhd |
| 'Lilac Charm' (6) | CQua IRhd |
| 'Lilac Hue' (6) | CBro |
| 'Lilac Mist' (2) | CQua |
| 'Lilliput' ambig. | CQua |
| 'Limbo' (2) | CQua IRhd |
| 'Limehurst' (2) | CQua |
| 'Limpopo' (3) | IRhd |
| 'Lindsay Joy' (2) | CQua |
| 'Lintie' (7) | CBro CQua EBrs ERos LEdu |
| 'Lisbarnett' (3) | IRhd |
| 'Lisnamulligan' (3) | IRhd |
| 'Lisnaruddy' (3) | IRhd |
| 'Little Beauty' (1) ♀$^{H4}$ | CBgR CBro CMea CQua EBrs ECho EPot ERos LAma MBrN NMin |
| 'Little Dancer' (1) | CBro CQua |
| 'Little Dorr' (4) **new** | IRhd |
| 'Little Gem' (1) ♀$^{H4}$ | CBgR CBro CMea CQua EBrs LAma LRHS SPer |
| 'Little Jewel' (3) | CQua |
| 'Little Karoo' (3) | IRhd |
| 'Little Rosie' (2) | IRhd |
| 'Little Rusky' (7) | CQua NMin |
| 'Little Sentry' (7) | CBro CQua |
| 'Little Soldier' (10) | CQua |
| 'Little Spell' (1) | CQua EBrs |
| 'Little Witch' (6) | CBro CQua EBrs ECho EPot ERos LAma WShi |
| 'Littlefield' (7) | CQua |
| 'Liverpool Festival' (2) | CQua |
| 'Lobularis' | see *N. pseudonarcissus* 'Lobularis' |
| ***lobularis*** misapplied | see *N. nanus* |
| ***lobularis*** Schultes | see *N. obvallaris* |
| 'Loch Alsh' (3) | CQua IRhd |
| 'Loch Assynt' (3) | CQua |
| 'Loch Brora' (2) | CQua |
| 'Loch Coire' (3) | CQua |
| 'Loch Fada' (2) | CQua |
| 'Loch Hope' (2) | CQua |
| 'Loch Leven' (2) | CQua |
| 'Loch Lundie' (2) | CQua |
| 'Loch Maberry' (2) | CQua |
| 'Loch Naver' (2) | CQua |
| 'Loch Owskeich' (2) ♀$^{H4}$ | CQua |
| 'Loch Stac' (2) | CQua |
| 'Logan Rock' (7) | CQua |
| 'Lordship' (1) | CQua |
| 'Lorikeet' (1) | CQua |
| 'Lothario' (2) | LAma MBri |
| 'Lough Gowna' (1) | IRhd |
| 'Loveny' (2) | CQua |
| 'Lubaantun' (1) | CQua |
| 'Lucifer' (2) | CQua |
| 'Lucky Chance' (11a) | IRhd |
| 'Lundy Light' (2) | CQua |
| 'Lynher' (2) | CQua |
| 'Lyrebird' (3) | CQua |
| 'Lyric' (9) | CQua |
| 'Lysander' (2) | CQua |
| x ***macleayi*** (13) | CQua NMin |
| 'Madam Speaker' (4) | CQua |
| 'Magician' (2) | IRhd |
| 'Magna Carta' (2) | CQua |
| 'Magnet' (1) | LAma |
| 'Magnificence' (1) | CQua |
| 'Mai's Family' (6) | CQua |
| 'Majarde' (2) | EFam |
| 'Majestic Star' (1) | CQua |
| 'Mallee' (11a) | IRhd |
| 'Malpas' (3) **new** | CQua |
| 'Malvern City' (1) | CQua LRHS |
| 'Mamma Mia' (4) | IRhd |
| 'Manaccan' (1) | CQua |
| 'Mangaweka' (6) | CQua |
| 'Manly' (4) ♀$^{H4}$ | CQua LRHS |
| 'Mantle' (2) | CQua |
| 'Maria Pia' (11a) **new** | IRhd |
| 'Marieke' (1) | EBrs |
| 'Marilyn Anne' (2) | CQua |
| 'Marjorie Hine' (2) | CQua |
| 'Marjorie Treveal' (4) | CQua |
| 'Marlborough' (2) | CQua |
| 'Marlborough Freya' (2) | CQua |
| 'Marshfire' (2) | CQua |

| | |
|---|---|
| 'Martha Washington' (8) | CBro CQua |
| 'Martinette' (8) | CQua CTca EBrs MBri |
| 'Martinsville' (8) | CQua |
| ***marvieri*** | see *N. rupicola* subsp. *marvieri* |
| 'Mary Copeland' (4) | CQua LAma |
| 'Mary Kate' (2) | CQua IRhd |
| 'Mary Lou' (6) | IRhd |
| 'Mary Veronica' (3) | CQua |
| 'Marzo' (7) | CQua IRhd |
| 'Matador' (8) | CQua IRhd |
| 'Mawla' (1) | CQua |
| 'Max' (11a) | CQua |
| 'Maximus' ambig. | CQua |
| 'Maya Dynasty' (2) | CQua |
| 'Mazzard' (4) | CQua |
| 'Media Girl' (2) | IRhd |
| x ***medioluteus*** (13) | CBro CQua NMin |
| 'Medusa' (8) | CBro |
| 'Melancholy' (1) | CQua |
| 'Melbury' (2) | CQua |
| 'Meldrum' (1) | CQua |
| 'Memento' (1) | CQua |
| 'Menabilly' (4) | CQua |
| 'Men-an-Tol' (2) | CQua |
| 'Menehay' (11a) ♀H4 | CQua IRhd |
| 'Merlin' (3) ♀H4 | CQua LAma NMin |
| 'Merry Bells' (5) | CQua |
| 'Merrymeet' (4) | CQua |
| 'Mersing' (3) | CQua |
| 'Merthan' (9) | CQua |
| 'Midas Touch' (1) | CQua |
| 'Midget' | CBgR CBro CQua ECho EPot ERos GKev LAma |
| 'Mike Pollock' (8) | CQua |
| 'Milan' (9) | CQua |
| 'Millennium Sunrise' (2) | CQua |
| 'Millennium Sunset' (2) | CQua |
| 'Millgreen' (1) | LRHS |
| 'Milly's Magic' (2) | CQua |
| 'Minicycla' (6) | CBro EBrs MSSP |
| ***minimus*** misapplied | see *N. asturiensis* |
| 'Minnow' (8) ♀H3 | CAvo CBro CFFs CMea CQua EBrs ECho EPfP ERCP ERos GKev LAma LRHS MBri NBir NBlu SPer |
| ***minor*** (13) ♀H4 | CBro CQua EBrs ECha ECho EPot LAma LRHS NMin WCot WShi |
| - 'Douglasbank' (1) | CBro |
| - var. ***pumilus*** 'Plenus' | see *N.* 'Rip van Winkle' |
| - Ulster form | IBlr MSSP |
| 'Mint Julep' (3) ♀H4 | EBrs LRHS SPhx |
| 'Minute Waltz' (6) | CQua |
| 'Miss Klein' | NMin |
| 'Miss Muffitt' (1) | CAvo CBgR CQua |
| 'Mission Bells' (5) ♀H4 | CQua IRhd |
| 'Mission Impossible' (11a) | CQua |
| 'Misty Glen' (2) ♀H4 | CQua |
| 'Misty Moon' (3) | CQua |
| 'Mite' (6) ♀H4 | CBro CMea CQua EPot ERos LAma NMin |
| 'Mithrel' (11a) | CQua |
| 'Mitylene' (2) | CQua |
| 'Mitzy' | NMin |
| 'Modern Art' (2) | EBrs |
| 'Mondragon' (11a) | CQua EBrs EFam |
| 'Mongleath' (2) | CQua |
| 'Monks Wood' (1) | CQua |
| 'Monksilver' (3) | CQua |
| 'Montclair' (2) | CQua |
| 'Montego' (3) | CQua |
| 'Moon Dream' (1) | CQua |
| 'Moon Ranger' (3) | CQua IRhd |
| 'Moon Rhythm' (4) | IRhd |
| 'Moon Shadow' (3) | CQua |
| 'Moon Tide' (3) | IRhd |
| 'Moon Valley' (2) | IRhd |
| 'Moonstruck' (1) | CQua |
| 'Morab' (1) | CQua |
| 'Moralee' (4) | IRhd |
| 'Morvah Lady' (5) | CQua |
| 'Morval' (2) **new** | CQua |
| § ***moschatus*** (13) ♀H4 | CBro CQua EBrs ECho EPot LAma LRHS NMin WCot WShi |
| - 'Cernuus Plenus' (4) | CQua |
| 'Mother Catherine Grullemans' (2) | EFam |
| 'Motmot' | CQua |
| 'Mount Fuji' (2) | CQua |
| 'Mount Hood' (1) ♀H4 | EBrs EPfP LAma LRHS NBir SPer |
| 'Mount Rainier' (1) | CQua |
| 'Movie Star' (2) | IRhd |
| 'Mowser' (7) | CQua |
| 'Mr Julian' (6) | CQua |
| 'Mrs Langtry' (3) | CQua WShi |
| 'Mrs R.O. Backhouse' (2) | CQua EBla WShi |
| 'Mullion' (3) | CQua |
| 'Mulroy Bay' (1) | CQua IRhd |
| 'Multnomah' (2) | LRHS |
| 'Murlough' (9) | CQua |
| 'Muscadet' (2) | CQua |
| 'My Sunshine' (2) | CQua |
| 'Mystic' (3) | CQua |
| 'Naivasha' (2) | IRhd |
| 'Namraj' (2) | CQua |
| 'Nancegollan' (7) | CBro CQua |
| 'Nangiles' (4) | CQua |
| 'Nanpee' (7) | CQua |
| 'Nansidwell' (2) | CQua |
| 'Nanstallon' (1) | CQua |
| § ***nanus*** | CMea CWCL |
| - 'Midget' (1) | EBrs ECho |
| 'Nederburg' (1) | IRhd |
| 'Nelly' ambig. | CQua |
| 'Nether Barr' (2) | IRhd |
| § ***nevadensis*** (13) | ERos |
| 'New Hope' (3) | CQua |
| 'New Life' (3) | CQua |
| 'New Penny' (3) | CQua IRhd |
| 'New-baby' (7) | CQua CTca EBrs EPfP LRHS NMin |
| 'Newcastle' (1) | CQua |
| 'Newcomer' (3) | CQua |
| 'Night Music' (4) | CQua |
| 'Nightcap' (1) | CQua |
| 'Nirvana' (7) | CBro |
| 'Niveth' (5) | CQua |
| § ***nobilis*** (13) **new** | EPot |
| - var. ***leonensis*** (13) **new** | ECho |
| - var. ***nobilis*** (13) | NMin |
| 'Nonchalant' (3) | CQua IRhd |
| 'Norma Jean' (2) | CQua |
| 'Nor-nor' (2) | CBro ERos |
| 'North Rim' (2) | CQua |
| 'Northern Sceptre' (2) | IRhd |
| 'Noss Mayo' (6) | CBro CQua |
| 'Notre Dame' (2) ♀H4 | CQua IRhd |
| 'Numen Rose' (2) | IRhd |
| Nylon Group (10) | CBro EBrs ECho EPot GEdr |
| - yellow (10) | ECho EPot |
| 'Oadby' (1) | CQua |
| 'Obdam' (4) | EBla EBrs LRHS |
| 'Obelisk' (11a) | CQua |
| ***obesus*** (13) | CWsd EBrs ECho ERos MSSP WCot |
| 'Obsession' (2) | CQua |
| § ***obvallaris*** (13) ♀H4 | CArn CAvo CBro CFFs CQua CTca EBrs ECho EPfP EPot ERCP ERos IHer LRHS SBch SGar SMeo SPer WHer WPtf WShi |

| | | |
|---|---|---|
| | 'Ocarino' (4) | CQua |
| | 'Ocean Blue' (2) | IRhd |
| | 'Odd Job' | CQua |
| | x ***odorus*** (13) | EBrs IHer LRHS WShi |
| § | - 'Double Campernelle' (4) | CQua ECho SPer WShi |
| | - 'Rugulosus' | see *N.* 'Rugulosus' |
| | 'Oecumene' (11a) | CQua |
| | old pheasant's eye | see *N. poeticus* var. *recurvus* |
| | 'Orange Monarch' (2) | EFam |
| | 'Orange Queen' (3) | EBrs LRHS |
| | 'Orange Walk' (3) | CQua IRhd |
| | 'Orangery' (11a) | EBla EBrs EFam LAma |
| | 'Orchard Place' (3) | CQua |
| | 'Oregon Pioneer' (2) | IRhd |
| | 'Orkney' (2) | CQua |
| | 'Ormeau' (2) ♀H4 | CQua |
| | 'Oryx' (7) ♀H4 | CQua IRhd |
| | 'Osmington' (2) | CQua |
| | 'Ouma' (1) | CQua |
| | 'Outline' (2) | IRhd |
| | 'Ouzel' (6) | CQua |
| | 'Oykel' (3) | CQua |
| | 'Oz' (12) | CBro CQua ERos NMin |
| | ***pachybolbus*** | EBrs NMin |
| | 'Pacific Coast' (8) ♀H4 | CQua ECho LAma NMin |
| | 'Pacific Mist' (11a) | CQua |
| | 'Pacific Rim' (2) | CQua IRhd |
| | 'Painted Desert' (3) | CQua |
| | 'Palace Pink' (2) **new** | IRhd |
| | 'Pale Sunlight' (2) | CQua |
| § | ***pallidiflorus*** (13) | ECha |
| | 'Palmares' (11a) | CQua LEdu |
| | 'Pamela Hubble' (2) | CQua |
| | 'Pampaluna' (11a) | CQua |
| | 'Panache' (1) | CQua |
| | 'Panorama Pink' (3) | IRhd |
| | 'Paper White' | see *N. papyraceus* |
| | 'Paper White Grandiflorus' (8) | CQua MBri SPer |
| | 'Papillon Blanc' (11b) | EBrs |
| | 'Papua' (4) ♀H4 | CQua |
| § | ***papyraceus*** (13) | CQua CStu LAma |
| | - subsp. ***panizzianus*** | CQua |
| | 'Paradigm' (4) | IRhd |
| | 'Paramour' (4) **new** | IRhd |
| | 'Parcpat' (7) | CBro |
| | 'Parisienne' (11a) | EBla |
| | 'Park Springs' (3) | CQua |
| | 'Parkdene' (2) | CQua |
| | 'Party Time' (2) | IRhd |
| | 'Passionale' (2) ♀H4 | CQua LAma NBir |
| | 'Pastiche' (2) | CQua |
| | 'Patabundy' (2) | CQua |
| | 'Pathos' (3) | IRhd |
| | 'Patois' (9) | CQua IRhd |
| | 'Patrick Hacket' (1) | CQua |
| | 'Paula Cottell' (3) | CBro |
| | 'Pay Day' (1) | CQua |
| | 'Peach Prince' (4) | CQua |
| | 'Pearl Wedding' (3) | CQua |
| | 'Pearlax' | see *N.* 'Perlax' |
| | 'Pearlshell' (11a) | CQua |
| | 'Peeping Tom' (6) ♀H4 | CBro EBrs ECho ERCP ERos LAma SRms |
| | 'Peggy's Gift' (3) | IRhd |
| | 'Pemboa' | CQua |
| | 'Pencrebar' (4) | CAvo CBro CMea CQua CTca EBrs EPot ERos LAma NMin WShi |
| | 'Pend Oreille' (3) | CQua |
| | 'Pengarth' (2) | CQua |
| | 'Penjerrick' (9) | CQua |
| | 'Penkivel' (2) ♀H4 | CQua |
| | 'Pennance Mill' (2) | CQua |
| | 'Pennine Way' (1) | CQua |
| | 'Pennyfield' (2) | CQua |
| | 'Penpol' (7) | CBro CQua |
| | 'Penril' (6) | CBgR CQua ERos |
| | 'Penstraze' (7) | CQua |
| | 'Pentewan' (2) | CQua LRHS |
| | 'Pentille' (1) | CQua |
| | 'Pentire' (11a) | CQua |
| | 'Penvale' | CQua |
| | 'Peppercorn' (6) | CQua |
| | 'Pequenita' (7) | CBro |
| | 'Percuil' (6) | CQua |
| | 'Perdredda' (3) | CQua |
| | 'Perimeter' (3) | CQua |
| | 'Peripheral Pink' (2) | CQua |
| § | 'Perlax' (11a) | CQua |
| | 'Permissive' (2) | IRhd |
| | 'Personable' (2) | CQua |
| | 'Petanca' | IRhd |
| | 'Petillant' (3) | EBrs |
| | 'Petit Four' (4) | EBla EBrs LAma |
| | 'Petrel' (5) | CBro CQua EBrs EPot LEdu MSte NMyG SPhx |
| | 'Phalarope' (6) | CQua |
| | 'Phantom' (11a) | CQua |
| | 'Phil's Gift' (1) | CQua |
| | 'Phinda' (2) | IRhd |
| | 'Phoenician' (2) | CQua |
| | 'Picoblanco' (2) | CBro CQua NMin |
| | 'Pigeon' (2) | CQua |
| | 'Pincambo' (2) | IRhd |
| | 'Pineapple Prince' (2) ♀H4 | CQua |
| | 'Pink Angel' (7) | CQua EBrs |
| | 'Pink Champagne' (4) | CQua EBrs |
| | 'Pink Charm' (2) | EBrs |
| | 'Pink Evening' (2) | CQua |
| | 'Pink Formal' (11a) | CQua |
| | 'Pink Gilt' (2) | IRhd |
| | 'Pink Glacier' (11a) | CQua |
| | 'Pink Holly' (11a) | CQua |
| | 'Pink Ice' (2) | CQua |
| | 'Pink Pageant' (4) | CQua IRhd |
| | 'Pink Paradise' (4) | CQua EBrs IRhd |
| | 'Pink Perry' (2) | IRhd |
| | 'Pink Sapphire' (2) | CQua |
| | 'Pink Silk' (1) | CQua IRhd |
| | 'Pink Smiles' (2) | SPer |
| | 'Pink Surprise' (2) | CQua |
| | 'Pink Tango' (11a) | CQua |
| | 'Pipe Major' (2) | CQua EPfP SPer |
| | 'Pipers Barn' (7) | CQua |
| | 'Piper's End' (3) | CQua |
| | 'Piper's Gold' (1) | CQua |
| | 'Pipestone' (2) | CQua |
| | 'Pipit' (7) ♀H4 | CAvo CBro CFFs CQua CTca EBrs ECho EPfP ERos LAma LEdu MBri MNrw NBir SPer SPhx WShi |
| | 'Piraeus' (4) | IRhd |
| | 'Pismo Beach' (2) | CQua |
| | 'Pistachio' (1) | EBrs |
| | 'Pitchroy' (2) | CQua |
| | 'Pitt's Diamond' (3) | CQua |
| | 'Pixie's Sister' (7) ♀H4 | CQua NMin |
| | ***poeticus*** (13) | CAvo LRHS WHer |
| § | - var. ***hellenicus*** (13) | CBro CQua |
| | - old pheasant's eye | see *N. poeticus* var. *recurvus* |
| | - var. ***physaloides*** (13) | CQua EBrs ECho SPhx |
| | - 'Plenus' ambig. (4) | CBro CQua EBrs EPot ERCP GKir GQui WShi |
| | - 'Praecox' (3) | CBro |
| § | - var. ***recurvus*** (13) ♀H4 | CArn CBro CFFs CMea CQua CTca EBrs ECGP ECho EPfP EPot ERCP IHer LAma NBir SMeo SPer WShi |

| | | |
|---|---|---|
| | 'Poet's Way' (9) | CQua |
| | 'Pol Crocan' (2) | CQua IRhd |
| | 'Pol Dornie' (2) | CQua |
| | 'Pol Voulin' (2) | CQua IRhd |
| | 'Polar Ice' (3) | CMea EBrs LAma |
| | 'Polglase' (8) | CBro |
| | 'Polgooth' (2) | CQua |
| | 'Polly's Pearl' (8) | CQua |
| | 'Polnesk' (7) | CBro |
| | 'Polruan' | CQua |
| | 'Poltreen' | CQua |
| | 'Polwheveral' (2) | CQua |
| | 'Pooka' (3) | IRhd |
| | 'Poppy's Choice' (4) | CQua |
| | 'Pops Legacy' (1) | CQua IRhd |
| | 'Porthchapel' (7) | CQua |
| | 'Portloe Bay' (3) | CQua |
| | 'Portrush' (3) | CQua |
| | 'Potential' (1) | CQua |
| | 'Powerstock' (2) | IRhd |
| | 'Prairie Fire' (3) | CQua IRhd |
| | 'Preamble' (1) | CQua |
| I | 'Precocious' (2) $\Upsilon^{H4}$ | CQua LRHS WRos |
| | 'Premiere' (2) | CQua |
| | 'Presidential Pink' (2) | CQua |
| | 'Pretty Baby' (3) | CQua |
| | 'Pride of Cornwall' (8) | CBro |
| | 'Primrose Beauty' (4) | CQua |
| | 'Princeps' (1) | CQua |
| | 'Princess Zaide' (3) | CQua |
| | 'Princeton' (3) | CQua |
| | 'Prism' (2) | CQua |
| | 'Problem Child' | IRhd |
| | 'Probus' (1) | CQua |
| | 'Professor Einstein' (2) | EBrs EPfP |
| | 'Prologue' (1) | CQua |
| | 'Prototype' (6) | IRhd |
| | 'Proud Fellow' (1) | IRhd |
| | 'Proverbial Pink' (2) **new** | IRhd |
| | 'Prussia Cove' (2) | CQua |
| | ***pseudonarcissus*** (13) $\Upsilon^{H4}$ | CBro CQua CRow CTca EBrs LAma SPhx WHer WShi |
| | - subsp. ***eugeniae*** (13) | EPot |
| | - subsp. ***gayi*** | see *N. gayi* |
| § | - 'Lobularis' | CArn CAvo CBro CFFs CQua EBrs ECho EPot ERos MBri SPer |
| | - subsp. ***moschatus*** | see *N. moschatus* |
| | - subsp. ***nevadensis*** | see *N. nevadensis* |
| | - subsp. ***nobilis*** | see *N. nobilis* |
| | - subsp. ***pallidiflorus*** | see *N. pallidiflorus* |
| § | - subsp. ***pseudonarcissus*** var. ***humilis*** (13) | EBrs ECho |
| | 'Pueblo' (7) | EBrs ERos LRHS WShi |
| | 'Pulsar' (2) | IRhd |
| | ***pumilus*** (13) | EBrs ECho EPot ERos LRHS NMin WShi |
| | 'Punchline' (7) $\Upsilon^{H4}$ | CQua NMin |
| | 'Puppet' (5) | CQua |
| | 'Purbeck' (3) $\Upsilon^{H4}$ | CQua IRhd |
| | 'Quail' (7) $\Upsilon^{H4}$ | CQua CTca EBrs EPfP ERos LAma LSou MBri SPer |
| | 'Quasar' (2) $\Upsilon^{H4}$ | CQua |
| | Queen Anne's double daffodil | see *N.* 'Eystettensis' |
| | 'Queen Juliana' (1) | CQua |
| | 'Queen Mum' (1) | CQua |
| | 'Queen's Guard' (1) | IRhd |
| | 'Quick Step' (7) | CQua IRhd |
| | 'Quiet Hero' (3) | IRhd |
| | 'Quiet Man' (1) | IRhd |
| | 'Quiet Waters' (1) | CQua |
| | 'Quince' (12) | CBro CQua LSou MSte |
| | 'Radiant Gem' (8) | CQua |
| | ***radiiflorus*** (13) | NMin |
| | - var. ***poetarum*** (13) | CBro CQua |
| | 'Radjel' (4) | CQua |
| | 'Rainbow' (2) $\Upsilon^{H4}$ | CQua |
| | 'Rame Head' (1) | CQua |
| | 'Rameses' (2) | CQua |
| | 'Rapture' (6) $\Upsilon^{H4}$ | CBro CQua EBrs IRhd NMin |
| | 'Rashee' (1) | CQua |
| | 'Raspberry Ring' (2) | CQua |
| | 'Rathowen Gold' (1) | CQua |
| | 'Ravenhill' (3) | CQua |
| | 'Rebekah' (4) | CQua |
| | 'Recital' (2) | CQua |
| | 'Red Coat' (2) **new** | CQua |
| | 'Red Devon' (2) $\Upsilon^{H4}$ | CQua |
| | 'Red Era' (3) | CQua |
| | 'Red Reed' (1) | IRhd |
| | 'Red Socks' (6) | CQua |
| | 'Refrain' (2) | CQua |
| | 'Regal Bliss' (2) | CQua |
| | 'Reggae' (6) $\Upsilon^{H4}$ | CBro CQua EBrs ERCP IRhd LRHS |
| | 'Rembrandt' (1) | CQua |
| | 'Rendezvous Caye' (2) | CQua |
| | 'Replete' (4) | CQua EBla EBrs LRHS |
| | 'Reprieve' (3) | CQua |
| | ***requienii*** | see *N. assoanus* |
| | 'Reverse Image' (11a) **new** | CQua |
| | 'Ribald' (2) | IRhd |
| | 'Ridgecrest' (3) | IRhd |
| | ***rifanus*** | see *N. romieuxii* subsp. *romieuxii* var. *rifanus* |
| * | 'Rijnveld's Early Bicolor' | CAvo |
| | 'Rijnveld's Early Sensation' (1) $\Upsilon^{H4}$ | CAvo CBro CFFs CMea CQua EBrs ECha ERos WCot |
| | 'Rikki' (7) | CBro CQua ERos NMin |
| | 'Rima' (1) | CQua |
| | 'Rimmon' (3) | CQua |
| | 'Ring Fence' (3) | IRhd |
| | 'Ringhaddy' (3) | IRhd |
| | 'Ringing Bells' (5) | CQua |
| | 'Ringleader' (2) | CQua |
| | 'Ringmaster' (2) | CQua |
| | 'Ringmer' (3) | CQua |
| | 'Rio Bravo' (2) | IRhd |
| | 'Rio Gusto' (2) | IRhd |
| | 'Rio Lobo' (2) | IRhd |
| | 'Rio Rondo' (2) | IRhd |
| | 'Rio Rouge' (2) | IRhd |
| § | 'Rip van Winkle' (4) | CAvo CBro CFFs CQua CSWP CTca CWCL EBla EBrs EPfP EPot ERCP ERos IHer LAma LRHS MBri NHol WHal WShi |
| | 'Rippling Waters' (5) $\Upsilon^{H4}$ | CBro CQua EBrs ECGP EPot ERos LAma |
| | 'Ristin' (1) | CQua |
| | 'Rival' (6) | CQua |
| | 'River Dance' (2) | IRhd |
| | 'River Queen' (2) | CQua IRhd |
| | 'Rockall' (3) | CQua |
| | 'Rockery White' (1) | NMin |
| | 'Roger' (6) | CBro CQua |
| | 'Romance' (2) $\Upsilon^{H4}$ | EBrs LAma |
| § | 'Romanus' (4) | CQua CTca |
| § | ***romieuxii*** (13) $\Upsilon^{H2-3}$ | CBro CPBP EPot ERos ITim LRHS SBch SChr SCnR WAbe WCot |
| | - JCA 805 | EPot |
| | - SF 370 | WCot |
| | - subsp. ***albidus*** (13) | ECho EPot WCot |
| § | - - var. ***zaianicus*** (13) | EBrs ECho GKev SPhx |
| | - - SB&L 82 | WCot |
| * | - - - f. ***lutescens*** (13) | GEdr |
| | - 'Atlas Gold' | GEdr SCnR |
| § | - 'Joy Bishop' (10) | EPot ERos SCnR |

| | |
|---|---|
| § - 'Julia Jane' (10) | EBrs ECho EPot ERos GEdr LRHS NMin SCnR SPhx WCot |
| * - 'Prolific' (10) | CLyd |
| - subsp. ***romieuxii*** | EBrs ECho SPhx WCot |
| § - - var. ***mesatlanticus*** (13) | ECho ERos |
| § - - var. ***rifanus*** (13) | EBrs ECho SPhx |
| - - - B 8929 | WCot |
| - 'Treble Chance' (10) | EPot GEdr |
| 'Rosannor Gold' (11a) | CQua |
| 'Roscarrick' (6) | CQua |
| 'Rose of May' (4) | CQua WShi |
| 'Rose of Tralee' (2) | CQua |
| 'Rose Royale' (2) | CQua |
| 'Rosedown' (5) | CBro |
| 'Rosemerryn' (2) | CQua |
| 'Rosemoor Gold' ♀$^{H4}$ | CBro CQua LRHS |
| 'Rosevine' (3) | CQua |
| 'Roseworthy' (2) | EBla ERos |
| 'Rosy Trumpet' (1) | CBro |
| 'Roxton' (4) | IRhd |
| 'Royal Armour' (1) | LRHS |
| 'Royal Ballet' (2) | CQua |
| 'Royal Connection' (8) | CQua |
| 'Royal Marine' (2) | CQua |
| 'Royal Princess' (3) | CQua |
| 'Royal Regiment' (2) | CQua |
| 'Rubh Mor' (2) | CQua |
| 'Ruby Rose' (4) | IRhd |
| 'Ruby Wedding' (2) | IRhd |
| 'Rubythroat' (2) | CQua |
| 'Ruddy Rascal' (2) | IRhd |
| § 'Rugulosus' (7) ♀$^{H4}$ | CBro CQua EBrs ECho ERos |
| * 'Rugulosus Flore Pleno' (d) | EBrs ECho LRHS |
| ***rupicola*** (13) | CBro CQua CWoo EBrs EPot ERos MSSP NMen NMin NSla NWCA SCnR |
| § - subsp. ***marvieri*** (13) ♀$^{H2}$ | EPot ERos |
| § - subsp. ***watieri*** (13) | CBro CQua CWsd ERos LLHF NMin |
| 'Rustom Pasha' (2) | CQua |
| 'Rytha' (2) | CQua |
| 'Saberwing' (5) | CQua |
| 'Sabine Hay' (3) | CQua |
| 'Sabrosa' (7) | CBro NMin |
| 'Sagana' (9) **new** | CQua |
| 'Sailboat' (7) ♀$^{H4}$ | CBro EBrs LRHS LSou NMin |
| 'Saint Agnes' (8) | CQua |
| 'Saint Budock' (1) | CQua |
| 'Saint Day' (5) | CQua |
| 'Saint Dilpe' (2) | CQua |
| 'Saint Keverne' (2) ♀$^{H4}$ | CQua EPfP |
| 'Saint Keyne' (8) | CQua |
| 'Saint Patrick's Day' (2) | CQua EBla LAma SPer |
| 'Saint Peter' (4) | CQua |
| 'Saint Petroc' (9) **new** | CQua |
| 'Saint Piran' (7) | CQua |
| 'Salakee' (2) | CQua |
| 'Salcey Forest' (1) | CQua |
| 'Salmon Trout' (2) | CQua |
| 'Salome' (2) ♀$^{H4}$ | CQua EBla EBrs EPfP LAma LRHS MCot NBir |
| 'Salute' (2) | CQua |
| 'Samantha' (4) | CQua |
| 'Samaria' (3) | CBro |
| 'Samba' (5) | ERos |
| 'Sancerre' (11a) | CQua |
| 'Sandycove' (2) | CQua |
| 'Santa Claus' (4) | CQua |
| 'Sargeant's Caye' (1) | CQua |
| 'Satchmo' (1) **new** | CQua |
| 'Satsuma' (1) | CQua |
| 'Saturn' (3) | CQua |
| 'Saturnalia' | IRhd |
| 'Savoir Faire' (2) | IRhd |
| ***scaberulus*** (13) | EPot ERos |
| 'Scarlet Chord' (2) | CQua |
| 'Scarlet Elegance' (2) | CQua |
| 'Scarlet Gem' (8) | NHol |
| 'Scarlett O'Hara' (2) | CQua |
| 'Scented Breeze' (2) | IRhd |
| 'Scilly Spring' (8) | CAvo |
| 'Scilly White' (8) | CQua |
| 'Scorrier' (2) | CQua |
| 'Scrumpy' (2) | CQua |
| 'Sea Dream' (3) | CQua |
| 'Sea Gift' (7) | CBro |
| 'Sea Green' (9) | CQua |
| 'Sea Legend' (2) | CQua |
| 'Sea Princess' (3) | CQua |
| 'Sea Shanty' (2) | IRhd |
| 'Seagull' (3) | CAvo CQua ECho LAma WShi |
| 'Sealing Wax' (2) | CQua |
| 'Segovia' (3) ♀$^{H4}$ | CBro CMea CQua EBla EBrs EPot ERos LAma LRHS NHol NMin SCnR SPer SPhx |
| 'Selma Lagerlöf' (2) | EFam |
| 'Sempre Avanti' (2) | LAma MBri |
| 'Sennocke' (5) | CBro |
| 'Seraglio' (3) | CQua |
| 'Serena Beach' (4) | IRhd |
| 'Serena Lodge' (4) ♀$^{H4}$ | CQua IRhd |
| ***serotinus*** (13) | EBrs ECho EPot WCot |
| 'Sextant' (6) | CQua |
| 'Shangani' (2) | IRhd |
| 'Sheelagh Rowan' (2) | CQua IRhd |
| 'Sheer Joy' (6) | IRhd |
| 'Sheleg' (8) | EBrs |
| 'Shepherd's Hey' (7) | CQua EPfP |
| 'Sherborne' (4) ♀$^{H4}$ | CQua |
| 'Sherpa' (1) | IRhd |
| 'Sheviock' (2) | CQua |
| 'Shindig' (2) | IRhd |
| 'Shining Light' (2) | CQua |
| 'Shortcake' (2) | CQua |
| 'Shrimp Boat' (11a) | IRhd |
| 'Siam' (2) | EFam |
| 'Sidhe' (5) **new** | CQua |
| 'Sidley' (3) | CQua IRhd |
| 'Signorina' (2) | IRhd |
| 'Silent Valley' (1) ♀$^{H4}$ | CQua |
| 'Silk Cut' (2) | CQua |
| 'Silkwood' (3) | CQua |
| 'Silver Bells' (5) | CQua |
| 'Silver Chimes' (8) | CAvo CBro CFFs CQua CTca EBrs ECho EPfP ERos LAma LEdu NBir |
| 'Silver Convention' (1) | CQua |
| 'Silver Crystal' (3) | IRhd |
| 'Silver Kiwi' (2) | CQua |
| 'Silver Minx' (1) | CQua |
| 'Silver Plate' (11a) | CQua |
| 'Silver Shell' (11a) | CQua |
| 'Silver Standard' (2) | CQua |
| 'Silver Surf' (2) | CQua IRhd |
| 'Silversmith' (2) | CQua |
| 'Silverthorne' (3) | CQua |
| 'Silverwood' (3) | CQua IRhd |
| 'Singing Pub' (3) | IRhd |
| 'Sinopel' (3) | EBrs LAma |
| 'Sir Samuel' (2) | CQua |
| 'Sir Watkin' (2) | CQua |
| 'Sir Winston Churchill' (4) ♀$^{H4}$ | CQua EPfP LAma SPer |
| 'Skerry' (2) | CQua |
| 'Skilliwidden' (2) ♀$^{H4}$ | CQua |
| 'Skookum' (3) **new** | CQua |

| | | |
|---|---|---|
| | 'Skywalker' (2) | IRhd |
| | 'Slieveboy' (1) | CQua |
| | 'Slipstream' (6) | IRhd |
| | 'Small Fry' (1) | CQua |
| | 'Small Talk' (1) | CQua NMin |
| | 'Smiling Maestro' (2) | CQua |
| | 'Smiling Twin' (11a) | EBrs |
| | 'Smokey Bear' (4) | CQua |
| | 'Smooth Sails' (3) | CQua |
| | 'Snipe' (6) | CQua NMin |
| | 'Snoopie' (6) | CQua |
| | 'Snow Bunting' (7) | CBro |
| | 'Snowcrest' (3) | CQua |
| | 'Snowshill' (2) | CQua |
| | 'Soft Focus' (2) | IRhd |
| | 'Solar System' (3) | IRhd |
| | 'Solar Tan' (3) | CQua |
| | 'Solera' (2) **new** | IRhd |
| | 'Solferique' (2) | CQua |
| | 'Soloist' (2) | IRhd |
| | 'Sonata' (9) | CQua |
| | 'Songket' (2) | CQua |
| | 'Soprano' (2) | CQua IRhd |
| | 'Sorcerer' (3) | CQua |
| | 'South Street' (2) | CQua |
| | 'Spaniards Inn' (4) | CQua CTca |
| | 'Sparkling Tarts' (8) | CQua |
| | 'Sparnon' (11a) | CQua |
| | 'Sparrow' (6) | CQua |
| | 'Special Envoy' (2) $\Upsilon^{H4}$ | CQua |
| | 'Speenogue' (1) | IRhd |
| | 'Spellbinder' (1) $\Upsilon^{H4}$ | CQua EFam MBri |
| | 'Spin Doctor' (3) | IRhd |
| | 'Spindletop' (3) $\Upsilon^{H4}$ | IRhd |
| | 'Spirit of Rame' (3) | CQua |
| | 'Split Image' (2) | IRhd |
| | 'Split Vote' (11a) | IRhd |
| | 'Sportsman' (2) | CQua |
| | 'Spring Dawn' (2) | EPfP LRHS LSou SPer |
| | 'Spring Joy' | ERos |
| | 'Spring Morn' (2) | IRhd |
| | 'Spring Pride' (2) | LRHS |
| | 'Spun Honey' (4) **new** | CQua |
| | 'Stainless' (2) | EBrs MSte SPhx |
| | 'Stann Creek' (1) | CQua |
| | 'Stanway' (3) | CQua IRhd |
| | 'Star Glow' (2) | CQua |
| | 'Star Quality' (3) | IRhd |
| | 'Starfire' (7) | CQua |
| | 'State Express' (2) | CQua |
| | 'Steenbok' (3) | IRhd |
| | 'Stella' (2) | WShi |
| | 'Stella Glow' (3) **new** | IRhd |
| | 'Stenalees' (6) | CQua |
| | 'Step Forward' (7) | ERos |
| | 'Stilton' (9) | CQua |
| | 'Stinger' (2) | CQua |
| | 'Stint' (5) $\Upsilon^{H4}$ | CBro CQua |
| | 'Stocken' (7) | CBro CPBP CQua ERos MSSP |
| | 'Stoke Charity' (2) | CQua |
| | 'Stoke Doyle' (2) | CQua |
| | 'Stormy Weather' (1) | CQua |
| | 'Stratosphere' (7) $\Upsilon^{H4}$ | CQua NMin |
| | 'Strines' (2) | CQua NMin |
| | 'Suave' (3) | CQua |
| | 'Subtle Shades' (2) **new** | IRhd |
| | 'Sugar and Spice' (3) | CQua |
| | 'Sugar Bird' (2) | IRhd |
| | 'Sugar Cups' (8) | CQua |
| | 'Sugar Loaf' (4) | CQua |
| | 'Sugarbush' (7) | CBro EBrs |
| | 'Suisgill' (4) | CQua |
| § | 'Sulphur Phoenix' (4) | CQua WShi |
| | 'Summer Solstice' (3) | IRhd |
| | 'Sun Disc' (7) $\Upsilon^{H4}$ | CBro CMea CQua EBrs ECho EPot ERos LAma LSou MBri NMin SPer |
| | 'Sunday Chimes' (5) | CQua |
| | 'Sundial' (7) | CBro CQua EBrs ECho EPot ERos LAma LRHS NMin |
| | 'Sunrise' (3) | CQua |
| | 'Sunstroke' (2) | CQua |
| | 'Suntory' (3) | CQua |
| | 'Suntrap' (2) | IRhd |
| | 'Surfside' (6) $\Upsilon^{H4}$ | CQua EBrs ERos LRHS |
| | 'Surprise Packet' | IRhd |
| | 'Surrey' (2) | CQua |
| | 'Suzie Dee' (6) | IRhd |
| | 'Suzie's Sister' (6) | IRhd |
| | 'Suzy' (7) $\Upsilon^{H4}$ | CBro LAma |
| | 'Swaledale' (2) | CQua |
| | 'Swallow' (6) | CQua |
| | 'Swallow Wing' (6) | IRhd |
| | 'Swanpool' (3) | CQua |
| | 'Swanvale' (1) | CQua |
| | 'Swedish Fjord' (2) | CQua |
| | 'Sweet Blanche' (7) | CQua |
| | 'Sweet Harmony' (2) | EBrs |
| | 'Sweet Lorraine' (2) | CQua |
| | 'Sweet Pepper' (7) | CBro |
| | 'Sweet Sue' (3) | CQua |
| | 'Sweetness' (7) $\Upsilon^{H4}$ | CAvo CBro CFFs CMea CQua EBrs LAma SPer WPtf WShi |
| | 'Swing Wing' (6) | CQua |
| | 'Sydling' (5) | CQua |
| I | 'Sylph' (1) | CQua |
| | 'Taffeta' (10) | CBro |
| | 'Tahiti' (4) $\Upsilon^{H4}$ | CQua EBrs EPfP LAma |
| | 'Talgarth' (2) **new** | CQua |
| | 'Tamar Fire' (4) $\Upsilon^{H4}$ | CQua CTca |
| | 'Tamar Lad' (2) | CQua CTca |
| | 'Tamar Lass' (3) | CQua CTca |
| | 'Tamar Snow' (2) | CQua |
| | 'Tamara' (2) | CQua SPer |
| | 'Tangent' (2) | CQua |
| | 'Tarlatan' (10) | CBro ERos |
| | 'Tasgem' (4) | CQua |
| | 'Taslass' (4) | CQua |
| | 'Tater-Du' (5) | CQua |
| | ***tazetta*** (13) | EBrs |
| § | - subsp. ***lacticolor*** (13) | CBgR CQua EBrs ERCP LRHS |
| § | - - 'Grand Monarque' (8) | CBro CQua |
| * | - var. ***odoratus*** | CQua |
| | - subsp. ***papyraceus*** | see *N. papyraceus* |
| | 'Teal' (1) | CQua |
| | 'Tehidy' (3) | CQua |
| § | 'Telamonius Plenus' (4) | CBro CQua IGor WCot WShi |
| | 'Temba' | IRhd |
| | 'Temple Cloud' (4) | IRhd |
| | ***tenuifolius*** | see *N. bulbocodium* subsp. *bulbocodium* var. *tenuifolius* |
| | 'Terracotta' (2) | CQua IRhd |
| | 'Terrapin' (3) | IRhd |
| | 'Tête-à-tête' (12) $\Upsilon^{H4}$ | CAvo CBro CFFs CHar CMea CQua CTca EBrs EPfP EPot ERCP ERos GKir LAma LRHS LSou MBri MNHC NBlu SPer WHal |
| I | 'Thalia' (5) | CAvo CBro CFFs CMea CQua CTca EBrs EPfP ERCP ERos LAma LEdu LRHS MBri MCot MSte NBir NHol SPer WShi |
| | 'The Alliance' (6) $\Upsilon^{H4}$ | CBro CQua |
| | 'The Grange' (1) | CQua |
| | 'The Knave' (6) | CQua |
| | 'Thistin' (1) | IRhd |
| | 'Thoresby' (3) | CQua |
| | 'Thoughtful' (5) | CBro CQua |

| | |
|---|---|
| 'Tibet' (2) | CQua |
| 'Tideford' (2) | CQua |
| 'Tidy Tippet' (2) **new** | IRhd |
| 'Tiercel' (1) | CQua |
| 'Tiffany Jade' (3) | CQua |
| 'Tiger Moth' (6) | CQua |
| 'Timolin' (3) | CQua |
| 'Tinderbox' (2) | IRhd |
| 'Tiritomba' (11a) | CQua |
| 'Tittle-tattle' (7) | CQua |
| 'Toby' (2) | CBro ERos |
| 'Toby the First' (6) | CAvo CQua EBrs |
| 'Tommora Gold' (2) | CQua |
| 'Tommy White' (2) | CQua |
| 'Top Hit' (11a) | CQua |
| 'Topolino' (1) ♀$^{H4}$ | CAvo CBro CFFs CQua EBrs EPot LAma SGar |
| 'Torianne' (2) | CQua |
| 'Torridon' (2) | CQua |
| 'Toscanini' (2) | EFam |
| 'Toto' (12) ♀$^{H4}$ | CBro CQua LRHS MBri |
| 'Tracey' (6) ♀$^{H4}$ | CQua EBrs LAma SPhx |
| 'Treasure Hunt' (2) **new** | IRhd |
| 'Trebah' (2) ♀$^{H4}$ | CQua |
| 'Treble Two' (7) | CQua |
| 'Trecara' (3) | CQua |
| 'Trefusis' (1) | CQua |
| 'Trehane' (6) | CQua |
| 'Trelawney Gold' (2) | CQua |
| 'Tremough Dale' (11a) | CQua |
| 'Trena' (6) ♀$^{H4}$ | CBro CQua EBrs ERCP NMin |
| 'Tresamble' (5) | CBro CQua EBrs LAma |
| 'Trevaunance' (6) | CQua |
| 'Treverva' (6) | CQua |
| 'Treviddo' (2) | CQua |
| 'Trevithian' (7) ♀$^{H4}$ | CBro CQua EBla EBrs GGar LAma |
| 'Trewarvas' (2) | CQua |
| 'Trewirgie' (6) | CBro CQua |
| 'Trewoon' (4) | CQua |
| ***triandrus*** var. ***albus*** | see *N. triandrus* subsp. *triandrus* var. *triandrus* |
| § - subsp. ***triandrus*** var. ***concolor*** (13) | CBro EBrs ECho |
| § - - var. ***triandrus*** (13) | CQua CWCL EBrs ECho |
| 'Tricollet' (11a) | EBrs NHol |
| 'Trident' (3) | CQua |
| 'Trielfin' (5) **new** | IRhd |
| 'Tripartite' (11a) ♀$^{H4}$ | CQua EBrs NMin |
| 'Triple Crown' (3) ♀$^{H4}$ | CQua IRhd |
| 'Tristram' (2) | CQua |
| 'Tropic Isle' (4) | CQua |
| 'Tropical Heat' (2) | IRhd |
| 'Trousseau' (1) | CQua |
| 'Troutbeck' (3) | CQua |
| 'Tru' (3) | CQua |
| 'Trueblood' (3) | IRhd |
| 'Trumpet Warrior' (1) ♀$^{H4}$ | CQua IRhd |
| 'Tryst' (2) | CQua |
| 'Tudor Minstrel' (2) | CQua |
| 'Tuesday's Child' (5) ♀$^{H4}$ | CQua ERos |
| 'Tullynagee' (3) | IRhd |
| 'Turncoat' (6) | CQua |
| 'Tutankhamun' (2) | CQua |
| 'Tweeny' (2) | CQua |
| 'Twink' (4) | CQua |
| 'Tyee' (2) | CQua |
| 'Tyrian Rose' (2) | CQua IRhd |
| 'Tyrone Gold' (1) ♀$^{H4}$ | CQua IRhd |
| 'Tyrree' (1) | IRhd |
| 'Tywara' (1) | CQua |
| 'Ulster Bank' (3) | CQua |
| 'Ulster Bride' (4) | CQua |
| 'Uncle Duncan' (1) | CQua IRhd |
| 'Unique' (4) ♀$^{H4}$ | CQua EBla LAma |
| 'Unsurpassable' (1) | CQua LAma |
| 'Upalong' (12) | CQua |
| 'Upshot' (3) | CQua |
| 'Urchin' (2) | IRhd |
| 'Utiku' (6) | CQua |
| 'Val d'Incles' (3) | CQua IRhd |
| 'Valdrome' (11a) | CQua EBla |
| 'Valinor' (2) | CQua |
| 'Van Sion' | see *N.* 'Telamonius Plenus' |
| 'Vanellus' (11a) | IRhd |
| 'Veneration' (1) | CQua |
| 'Verdin' (7) | CQua |
| 'Verger' (3) | LAma MBri |
| 'Vernal Prince' (3) ♀$^{H4}$ | CQua |
| 'Verona' (3) ♀$^{H4}$ | CQua |
| 'Verran Rose' (2) | IRhd |
| 'Vers Libre' (9) | CQua |
| 'Vice-President' (2) | CQua |
| 'Vickie Linn' (6) | IRhd |
| 'Victoria' (1) | CQua |
| 'Victorious' (2) | CQua |
| 'Vigil' (1) ♀$^{H4}$ | CQua |
| 'Viking' (1) ♀$^{H4}$ | CQua |
| 'Violetta' (2) | CQua |
| 'Virginia Waters' (3) | CQua |
| 'Volcanic Rim' | IRhd |
| 'Vulcan' (2) ♀$^{H4}$ | CQua |
| 'W.P. Milner' (1) | CAvo CBro CQua EBla EBrs EPfP EPot ERCP IHer LAma NMin WShi |
| 'Wadavers' (2) | CQua |
| 'Waif' (6) | CQua |
| 'Waldon Pond' (3) | CQua |
| 'Waldorf Astoria' (4) | CQua IRhd |
| 'Walton' (7) | CQua |
| 'War Dance' (3) | IRhd |
| 'Warbler' (6) | CQua LAma NMin |
| 'Warmington' (3) | CQua |
| 'Watamu' (3) | IRhd |
| 'Waterperry' (7) | CBro EBrs LAma |
| 'Watership Down' (2) | CQua |
| 'Watersmeet' (4) **new** | CQua |
| ***watieri*** | see *N. rupicola* subsp. *watieri* |
| 'Wavelength' (3) | IRhd |
| 'Waxwing' (5) | CQua |
| 'Wayward Lad' (3) | IRhd |
| 'Wee Bee' (1) | CQua |
| 'Weena' (2) | CQua |
| 'Welcome' (2) | CQua |
| 'West Post' **new** | IRhd |
| 'Westward' (4) | CQua |
| 'Whang-hi' (6) | CQua ERos |
| 'Wheal Bush' (4) | CQua |
| 'Wheal Coates' (7) ♀$^{H4}$ | CBgR CQua |
| 'Wheal Honey' (1) | CQua |
| 'Wheal Jane' (2) | CQua |
| 'Wheal Kitty' (7) | CBgR CQua ERos |
| 'Wheal Rose' (4) **new** | CQua |
| 'Wheatear' (6) | CQua IRhd NMin SPhx |
| 'Whetstone' (1) | CQua |
| 'Whisky Galore' (2) | CQua |
| 'Whisky Mac' (2) | CQua |
| 'White Emperor' (1) | CQua |
| 'White Empress' (1) | CQua |
| 'White Lady' (3) | CAvo CQua IHer LAma WShi |
| 'White Lion' (4) ♀$^{H4}$ | CQua EFam LAma LRHS NHol |
| 'White Majesty' (1) | CQua |
| 'White Marvel' (4) | CQua EBrs |
| 'White Medal' (4) | EBrs |
| 'White Nile' (2) | CQua |
| 'White Prince' (1) | CQua |

| | |
|---|---|
| 'White Star' (1) | CQua |
| 'White Tie' (3) **new** | CQua |
| 'Wicklow Hills' (3) | CQua |
| 'Widgeon' (2) | CQua |
| 'Wild Honey' (2) | CQua |
| 'Will Scarlett' (2) | CQua |
| ***willkommii*** (13) | CBro CPBP CQua EBrs ECho ERos MSSP NMin |
| 'Wind Song' (2) | CQua |
| 'Winged Victory' (6) | CQua |
| 'Winholm Jenni' (3) | CQua |
| 'Winifred van Graven' (3) | CQua |
| 'Winter Waltz' (6) | CQua |
| 'Witch Doctor' (3) | IRhd |
| 'Witch Hunt' (4) | IRhd |
| 'Wodan' (2) | EFam |
| 'Woodcock' (6) | CBro CQua |
| 'Woodland Prince' (3) | CQua |
| 'Woodland Star' (3) | CQua |
| 'Woodley Vale' (2) | CQua |
| 'Woolsthorpe' (2) | CQua |
| 'Xit' (3) | CAvo CBro CPBP CQua EBrs NMin SPhx |
| 'Xunantunich' (2) | CQua IRhd |
| 'Yellow Belles' (5) | IRhd |
| 'Yellow Cheerfulness' (4) ♀H4 | EBrs EPfP LAma LRHS MBri |
| 'Yellow Minnow' (8) | CQua |
| 'Yellow River' (1) | LAma |
| 'Yellow Wings' (6) | EBrs ECho |
| 'Yellow Xit' (3) | CQua NMin |
| 'Yoley's Pond' (2) | CQua |
| 'York Minster' (1) | CQua IRhd |
| 'Young American' (1) | CQua |
| 'Young Blood' (2) | CQua IRhd |
| 'Yum-Yum' (3) | IRhd |
| ***zaianicus*** | see *N. romieuxii* subsp. *albidus* var. *zaianicus* |
| - ***lutescens*** | see *N. romieuxii* subsp. *albidus* var. *zaianicus* f. *lutescens* |
| 'Zekiah' (1) | CQua |
| 'Zion Canyon' (2) | CQua |
| 'Ziva' (8) | CAvo CFFs EBrs NHol |
| 'Zwynner' **new** | IRhd |

## *Nardostachys* (*Valerianaceae*)

| | |
|---|---|
| ***grandiflora*** | GPoy |

## *Nardus* (*Poaceae*)

| | |
|---|---|
| ***stricta*** | CRWN EBWF |

## *Nassella* (*Poaceae*)

| | |
|---|---|
| ***formicarum*** (Delile) Barkworth **new** | EBee |
| ***tenuissima*** | see *Stipa tenuissima* |
| ***trichotoma*** | CChe CHrt CKno CMea CWsd EBee EHoe EMon EPPr EWsh LDai LRHS MCCP SLim SPoG WHal WPGP WRos |

## *Nasturtium* (*Brassicaceae*)

| | |
|---|---|
| 'Banana Split' | CCCN NPri |
| ***officinale*** | CPrp EMFW MSKA SVic SWat WHer |

## *Nauplius* (*Asteraceae*)

| | |
|---|---|
| ***sericeus*** | CSpe |

## *Nautilocalyx* (*Gesneriaceae*)

| | |
|---|---|
| ***pemphidius*** | WDib |

## *Navarretia* (*Polemoniaceae*)

| | |
|---|---|
| ***squarrosa*** **new** | CSec |

## nectarine see *Prunus persica* var. *nectarina*

## *Nectaroscordum* (*Alliaceae*)

| | |
|---|---|
| sp. | WFoF |
| ***bivalve*** | ERos |
| ***koelzii*** | EBee |
| § ***siculum*** | Widely available |
| § - subsp. ***bulgaricum*** | CSec CTca EBee EBrs ECha EPfP EPot ERos IBlr LBMP LRHS MDun MNrw NBid NGHP SPhx WAbb WBrE WCot WTin |
| ***tripedale*** | EBee |

## *Neillia* (*Rosaceae*)

| | |
|---|---|
| ***affinis*** | CDul EBee ECrN EPfP LAst LLHF MBri NBid NLar NPro SCoo SWvt WBVN WDin WHCG |
| ***longiracemosa*** | see *N. thibetica* |
| ***sinensis*** | MRav |
| § ***thibetica*** | CBcs CDul CPLG EBee ECrN ELan EMil EPfP EWTr GCra GKir IDee MBlu MLHP MRav NPri SLim SLon SMad SPer SSpi SSta SWvt WBod WBor WDin WFar |
| ***thyrsiflora*** var. ***tunkinensis*** HWJ 505 | WCru |

## *Nelumbo* (*Nelumbonaceae*)

| | |
|---|---|
| 'Baby Doll' | CDWL |
| 'Charles Thomas' **new** | CDWL |
| 'Chawan Basu' | CDWL |
| 'Debbie Gibson' | CDWL |
| 'Momo Botan' | CDWL |
| 'Mrs Perry D. Slocum' | CDWL |
| ***nucifera*** | XBlo |
| - 'Shiroman' | CDWL |

## *Nematanthus* (*Gesneriaceae*)

| | |
|---|---|
| 'Apres' | WDib |
| 'Black Magic' | CHal WDib |
| 'Christmas Holly' | WDib |
| 'Freckles' | WDib |
| § ***gregarius*** ♀H1 | CHal EBak WDib |
| § - 'Golden West' (v) | CHal WDib |
| - 'Variegatus' | see *N. gregarius* 'Golden West' |
| 'Lemon and Lime' | WDib |
| ***radicans*** | see *N. gregarius* |
| 'Tropicana' ♀H1 | CHal WDib |

## *Nemesia* (*Scrophulariaceae*)

| | |
|---|---|
| Amelie = 'Fleurame' PBR | GKir LRHS SPer SPoG |
| (Aromatica Series) | LSou |
| Aromatica Royal = 'Balaroyal' PBR **new** | |
| - Aromatica Compact White = 'Balarcomwit' PBR | NPri |
| - Aromatica True Blue = 'Balartublue' PBR | NPri |
| Berries and Cream = 'Fleurbac' **new** | SPoG SVil |
| 'Blue Button' **new** | LSou |
| 'Bluebird' | see *N.* Bluebird = 'Hubbird' |
| § Bluebird = 'Hubbird' PBR | CHll |
| Blue Lagoon = 'Pengoon' PBR (Maritana Series) | LAst LSRN SCoo WGor |
| Blushing Bride = 'Yablush' | LSou |
| § ***caerulea*** | ECtt WPer |
| N - 'Joan Wilder' (clonal) | ECtt |

| | | |
|---|---|---|
| | Candy Girl = 'Pencand' PBR (Maritana Series) | SCoo |
| | Celine = 'Fleurcel' | SPoG |
| | Claudette = 'Fleurcla' | SPoG |
| § | ***denticulata*** ♀H3-4 | CHal CHar CPrp ECtt EPfP LHop LRHS MArl MAvo SAga SCoo SGar SPer SPoG SRms WBrE WFar WFoF |
| | - 'Celebration' PBR | LRHS |
| | - 'Confetti' | see *N. denticulata* |
| | - 'Maggie' | LBuc |
| | 'Fleurie Blue' | LRHS SPoG |
| | ***foetens*** | see *N. caerulea* |
| | 'Fragrant Cloud' | CChe ELan EPfP LRHS LSou MCCP MNrw SPer SPla |
| | 'Fragrant Gem' | LSRN SHGN SPoG |
| | ***fruticans*** misapplied | see *N. caerulea* |
| | 'Golden Eye' | EPfP LBuc LSRN LSou |
| | Honey Girl = 'Penhon' PBR (Maritana Series) | LAst LSRN SCoo WGor |
| | Ice Pink = 'Fleuripi' | SPoG |
| | 'Innocence' ♀H3 | CHal CPrp EBee LAst MArl NBlu SCoo |
| | (Karoo Series) Karoo Blue = 'Innkablue' PBR | LSou SCoo |
| | - Karoo Pink = 'Innkapink' PBR | LSou |
| | - Karoo White = 'Innkarwhi' **new** | LSou |
| | 'Lemon Drop' | SVil |
| § | Melanie = 'Fleuron' ♀H3 | EPfP LRHS |
| | 'Orchard Blue' | EBee EPfP MAvo |
| | 'Pensky' | SCoo |
| | 'Pippa Manby' | ECtt |
| | Pure Lagoon = 'Penpur' **new** | LAst |
| | 'Rose Wings' | EPfP |
| | Sugar Girl = 'Pensug' PBR (Maritana Series) | EPfP LAst LSRN |
| | 'Sugar Plum' | EPfP LBuc SPoG |
| | (Sunsatia Series) Sunsatia Banana = 'Intraibana' PBR | LAst LHop |
| | - Sunsatia Blackberry = 'Inuppink' PBR | LHop SCoo |
| | - Sunsatia Cranberry = 'Intraired' PBR | LAst LSou SCoo |
| | - Sunsatia Lemon = 'Intraigold' PBR | LSou SCoo |
| | - Sunsatia Mango = 'Inupyel' PBR | LHop |
| | - Sunsatia Peach = 'Inupcream' PBR | LAst SCoo SVil |
| | ***sylvatica*** | CSpe |
| | 'Utopia Painted Face' (Utopia Series) **new** | ENor |
| | Vanilla Mist = 'Grega' PBR | EPfP LBuc LSou SPoG |
| | 'White Wings' PBR | EPfP |
| | 'Wisley Vanilla' | LRHS SPoG |

## *Nemophila* (*Hydrophyllaceae*)

| | | |
|---|---|---|
| | ***menziesii*** 'Penny Black' | CSpe |

## *Neodypsis* (*Arecaceae*)

| | | |
|---|---|---|
| | ***decaryi*** | CCCN EAmu LPal XBlo |

## *Neolitsea* (*Lauraceae*)

| | | |
|---|---|---|
| | ***glauca*** | see *N. sericea* |
| § | ***sericea*** | CBcs SSpi |

## *Neomarica* ✿ (*Iridaceae*)

| | | |
|---|---|---|
| | ***caerulea*** | CDes SKHP WCot |
| | ***gracilis*** | WPGP |

## *Neopanax* (*Araliaceae*)

| | | |
|---|---|---|
| § | ***arboreus*** | CAbb CBcs CDoC CHEx CTrC ECou LEdu SBig |
| | ***colensoi*** | CTrC |
| § | ***laetus*** | CAbb CBcs CDoC CHEx CTrC ECou LEdu SAPC SArc SBig |

## *Neopaxia* (*Portulacaceae*)

| | | |
|---|---|---|
| § | ***australasica*** | ECou EDAr |
| | - bronze-leaved | see *N. australasica* 'Ohau' |
| | - 'Lyndon' | ECou |
| § | - 'Ohau' | ECou EDAr |

## *Neoregelia* (*Bromeliaceae*)

| | | |
|---|---|---|
| | ***carolinae*** | MBri |
| § | - (Meyendorffii Group) 'Flandria' (v) | MBri |
| | - - 'Meyendorffii' | MBri XBlo |
| | - f. ***tricolor*** (v) ♀H1 | CHal MBri |
| | Claret Group | MBri |
| | 'Hojo Rojo' | XBlo |
| | 'Marconfos' | XBlo |

## *Neoshirakia* (*Euphorbiaceae*)

| | | |
|---|---|---|
| | ***japonica*** | MBri WPGP |
| | - B&SWJ 8744 | WCru |

## *Neottianthe* (*Orchidaceae*)

| | | |
|---|---|---|
| | ***cucullata*** | EFEx |

## *Nepenthes* (*Nepenthaceae*)

| | | |
|---|---|---|
| | ***alata*** | CSWC |
| | ***alata*** x ***ventricosa*** | SHmp |
| | ***ampullaria*** | CSWC |
| | ***bongso*** | SHmp |
| | x ***coccinea*** | MBri |
| | ***densiflora*** | SHmp |
| | ***diatas*** **new** | SHmp |
| | ***fusca*** | CSWC |
| | ***fusca*** x ***maxima*** | SHmp |
| | ***izumiae*** **new** | SHmp |
| | ***khasiana*** | SHmp |
| | ***lowii*** | SHmp |
| | ***maxima*** x ***mixta*** | SHmp |
| | ***mira*** **new** | SHmp |
| | ***peliolata*** **new** | SHmp |
| | ***rajah*** | SHmp |
| | 'Rebecca Soper' | SHmp |
| | ***sanguinea*** | SHmp |
| | ***sibuyanensis*** **new** | SHmp |
| | ***spectabilis*** | SHmp |
| | ***stenophylla*** | SHmp |
| | ***truncata*** highland form | SHmp |

## *Nepeta* ✿ (*Lamiaceae*)

| | | |
|---|---|---|
| | RCB AM -3 **new** | WCot |
| | RCB/TQ -H-6 **new** | WCot |
| | 'Blue Beauty' | see *N. sibirica* 'Souvenir d'André Chaudron' |
| | ***bucharica*** | GBuc |
| * | ***buddlejifolium*** | NBre NLar |
| * | - 'Gold Splash' | NBre |
| | ***camphorata*** | MLLN MSte NBre SAga SIde SMrm |
| | ***cataria*** | CArn CPrp CTri CWan EBWF ELau GBar GPoy MHer MNHC MSal NBro NGHP NPri NTHB SECG SIde SVic WMoo WPer |
| § | - 'Citriodora' | CArn CHar CPrp EAro EBee ELan ELau GBar GPWP GPoy MHer MNHC MSal NGHP SIde SUsu WCHb |
| | ***citriodora*** Dum. | see *N. cataria* 'Citriodora' |

| | | |
|---|---|---|
| | ***clarkei*** | EAro EBee EPPr EWTr LEdu MDKP MHar MMHG MSte NDov SBod SEND SIde SWat WMoo WPer |
| | 'Dropmore' | EBee |
| § | x ***faassenii*** ♀H4 | Widely available |
| | - 'Alba' | COIW EBee ECtt EPfP GBar LAst NBre NGHP NLar SHGN WFar |
| | - 'Blauknirps' | EBee NBre |
| | - 'Kit Cat' | CSpe EBee LCro LSRN MSte NDov NGby |
| | - 'Select' **new** | WPtf |
| | ***glechoma*** 'Variegata' | see *Glechoma hederacea* 'Variegata' |
| | ***govaniana*** | Widely available |
| | ***grandiflora*** | EBee MRav NBre SIde WFar WHer WOut |
| | - 'Blue Danube' | NDov SIde |
| | - 'Bramdean' | CElw CMea EBee ECtt EWes MBri MCot MHar MRav NDov SBch SPhx WKif |
| | - 'Dawn to Dusk' | Widely available |
| | - 'Pool Bank' | EBee ECtt EWes GCal LPla LSou MAvo NBre NGby SGar SIde SMrm |
| | - 'Wild Cat' | EBee EPfP LCro MBri MSte WFar |
| | ***hederacea*** 'Variegata' | see *Glechoma hederacea* 'Variegata' |
| | ***italica*** | EBee SHar SIde |
| | ***kubanica*** | LPla |
| | ***laevigata*** | EBee |
| | ***lanceolata*** | see *N. nepetella* |
| | ***latifolia*** | NBre SIde |
| | - 'Super Cat' | EBee |
| | 'Lilac Cloud' | NBir |
| * | ***longipes*** hort. | Widely available |
| | ***macrantha*** | see *N. sibirica* |
| | ***melissifolia*** | EBee SBch WCHb WPer |
| | ***mussinii*** misapplied | see *N.* x *faassenii* |
| | ***mussinii*** Spreng. | see *N. racemosa* |
| § | ***nepetella*** | EBee GBri LBMP NBir NChi WFar WPer |
| | ***nervosa*** | CHFP CKno CSec CSpe EBee ECha ELan EPfP GKir LAst MBri MCot MHer MNHC MSte NBro NPri NSti SPer SUsu WFar WMnd WSHC |
| | - 'Blue Carpet' | CSpe |
| | - 'Blue Moon' | EAEE EBee NBid SMrm WFar WHil |
| | - 'Forncett Select' | CSam MRav NBre SDys SMrm |
| | - 'Pink Cat' **new** | GKir MDKP SPhx |
| § | ***nuda*** | CSam CSec EAro EBee ECha ECtt MDKP MHar MLLN SIde WFar |
| | - 'Accent' **new** | GBin |
| | - subsp. ***albiflora*** | EBee ECha |
| * | - 'Anne's Choice' | EBee GBin MSte SIde |
| * | - 'Grandiflora' | NBre NLar WMoo |
| | - 'Isis' | EBee |
| | - 'Purple Cat' | GBin LLHF LSou MSte SIde WFar WOut WRHF |
| | - 'Snow Cat' | EBee GBin LSou MDKP MSte SIde SPhx WOut |
| | ***pannonica*** | see *N. nuda* |
| | ***parnassica*** | CDMG CElw CSec EBee ECtt GKev LRHS MWhi NBPC NLar SBod SIde SMad SMrm SPav SPoG SWal WFar WMnd WMoo |
| | ***phyllochlamys*** | CPBP EBee NCGa |
| | 'Porzellan' | EBee LAst LPla MSte SMrm |
| § | ***prattii*** | CSpe EBee MWat NCGa NLar NPro SBod SEND SIde SMrm SPla |
| § | ***racemosa*** ♀H4 | CArn CHby CPbn CSev CWan ELau EPfP GBar GKir LRHS MNHC MRav MSCN SIde WMoo WPtf |
| | - ***alba*** | WFar |
| | - 'Amelia' | WOut |

| | | |
|---|---|---|
| | - 'Blue Ice' | GBuc SIde |
| | - 'Grog' | EBee SIde |
| | - 'Leporello' (v) | EPPr |
| | - 'Little Titch' | CBod CPrp EAEE EBee ECtt EHig EPfP EShb LAst LRHS LSRN MCot MNFA MSte NCGa NLar NVic SAga SIde SMrm SPla SPoG SWat WFar |
| | - 'Snowflake' | CBcs CMea EAEE EBee ELan EPfP EShb EWTr GMaP LBMP MCot MHer MSte NBir SAga SIde SMrm SPer SPet SPla SPoG SWvt WCAu WClo WFar |
| | - 'Superba' | EMon GBuc NBre WFar |
| | - 'Walker's Low' | Widely available |
| * | 'Rae Crug' | ECtt EWes |
| | ***reichenbachiana*** | see *N. racemosa* |
| § | ***sibirica*** | COIW EBee ECha ELan EPfP GMac LBMP LEdu LRHS MHer MRav MSCN NBid NBro NDov NPri SBch SRkn WCot WFar WHal WPer WPtf |
| § | - 'Souvenir d'André Chaudron' | CSam CSpe CWCL EBee ECtt EHrv ELan EPfP EWTr GKir GMaP LAst LEdu LHop LRHS MBri MCot MLLN MNrw MRav NCob SMad SPer WCAu WCot WEas WFar WHoo |
| | ***sintenisii*** | NBre |
| | 'Six Hills Giant' | Widely available |
| | ***stewartiana*** | CSec EAro GBuc LDai LLHF MLLN NLar WMoo WOut |
| | - ACE 1611 | GBuc |
| | - BWJ 7999 | WCru |
| | ***subsessilis*** | Widely available |
| | - 'Candy Cat' | EBee EHrv MBri MDKP NBPC SBHP |
| | - 'Cool Cat' | EBee ECGP LCro LSRN MDKP MSte NLar NPro SIde SMrm SPhx WFar |
| | - Nimbus = 'Yanim' | CCVN EBee SPoG SRkn |
| | - pink-flowered | CAby ECha EGle MAvo MLLN MSte SMrm |
| | - 'Sweet Dreams' | CHar CKno EAEE EBee ECtt EMil GBri LBMP LEdu MBri MCot MDKP MRav NGby NLar NPro NSti SHar SPhx WCAu WFar WMnd |
| | - 'Washfield' **new** | LCro MSte |
| | ***tenuifolia*** | MSal |
| | ***transcaucasica*** 'Blue Infinity' | CSec NBre NLar WMnd WMoo |
| | ***troodii*** | MDKP SIde |
| | ***tuberosa*** | CBod CSpe EAro EBee ECha EDAr GBuc MAvo MCot MHer MRav SBch SIde SPav STes WCot WHoo WMnd WMoo |
| | 'Veluws Blauwtje' | EBee |
| | ***yunnanensis*** | CDes CMdw EBee EPPr GKev LEdu LPla SMrm SPhx SSvw WOut |

## *Nephrolepis* (*Oleandraceae*)

| | |
|---|---|
| ***cordifolia*** | MBri WRic |
| ***duffii*** | EShb WRic |
| ***exaltata*** 'Bostoniensis' | MBri |
| - 'Smithii' | MBri |
| - 'Smithii Linda' | MBri |
| - 'Teddy Junior' | MBri |
| ***falcata*** **new** | WRic |
| ***pendula*** **new** | WRic |

## *Nephrophyllidium* (*Menyanthaceae*)

| | |
|---|---|
| ***crista-galli*** | IBlr |

## *Nerine* ✿ (*Amaryllidaceae*)

| | |
|---|---|
| 'Afterglow' | ECho LAma SGar |
| 'Albivetta' | CBgR CFwr EBee EBrs ECho EPot LPio WCot |
| ***angustifolia*** | CPen |

| | |
|---|---|
| 'Aries' | WCot |
| 'Audrey' | WCot |
| 'Aurora' | WCot |
| 'Baghdad' | WCot |
| 'Belladonna' | WCot |
| 'Berlioz' | WCot |
| 'Blanchefleur' | WCot |
| ***bowdenii*** ♀H3-4 | Widely available |
| - 'Alba' | CBro CSec CStu EBee ECho ELan EPot ERCP GAbr LPio LRHS SCoo SMHy |
| - 'Codora' | CBgR CCCN CFwr CPen ECho LHop LSou SPer |
| - 'E.B.Anderson' | EBee WCot WVal |
| - Irish clone **new** | WCot |
| - 'Kinn McIntosh' | WCot WVal |
| - 'Manina' | CMdw MSte WCot WVal |
| - 'Marjorie' | EMal WCot |
| - 'Mark Fenwick' | CBcs CBro CDes EBee ECha ERas MSte WCot WOld WVal |
| - 'Marnie Rogerson' | CBro CPne EBee MSte SMHy WCot |
| § - 'Mollie Cowie' (v) | EBee EMon GCal IBlr MAvo WCot WCru WHil WSHC WVal |
| - 'Ostara' **new** | CFwr EBee |
| - pale pink, striped darker | CDes |
| - 'Pink Triumph' | CAbP CBcs EBee EBla EBrs ECho EHig EShb GBuc GQui IBlr LAma LRHS MSte NHol SChr SPer SPla WCot WHoo WVal |
| - 'Porlock' | EBee |
| - 'Quinton Wells' | SPhx |
| - 'Ted Allen's Early' **new** | EBla |
| - 'Variegata' | see *N. bowdenii* 'Mollie Cowie' |
| - Washfield form | SMHy |
| - 'Wellsii' | CDes CMil EBee MAvo WCot WVal |
| 'Canasta' | WCot |
| 'Catkin' | WCot |
| 'Corletta' **new** | WCot |
| ***corusca*** 'Major' | see *N. sarniensis* var. *corusca* |
| ***crispa*** | see *N. undulata* |
| 'Eve' | WCot |
| ***filamentosa*** | CBro EBrs ECho |
| ***filifolia*** | CPen CSpe ECho ERos GKev ITim MNrw MTho WAbe WCot WHil |
| ***flexuosa*** | CPne CWsd ECho MRav |
| - 'Alba' | CAvo CBgR CBro CDes CPen CWsd EBee EBrs ECha ECho EPot EWTr EWll LRHS MRav MSte SPhx WAbe WCot |
| 'Fucine' | CDes EBee WCot |
| 'Gloaming' | WCot |
| 'Hera' | CBro EMon MSte SPhx WVal |
| ***hesseoides*** | WCot |
| * ***hirsuta*** | EBee EBrs ECho |
| ***humilis*** | CStu CWsd EBee EBrs ECho |
| - Breachiae Group | CStu SBch |
| 'Jenny Wren' | WCot |
| 'Kasmir' | CDes WCot |
| 'King of the Belgians' | ECho LAma WCot WVal |
| 'Kodora' | CSec EBee EBrs ECho |
| ***krigei*** | CPen |
| 'Lady Cynthia Colville' | WVal |
| 'Lady Eleanor Keane' | WCot |
| 'Lady Havelock Allen' | CMil WCot |
| ***laticoma*** | WCot |
| 'Leila Hughes' | WCot |
| 'Lyndhurst Salmon' | WCot |
| 'Mansellii' | CBro IHer WCot |
| 'Maria' | WCot WVal |
| ***masoniorum*** | CBro CStu ERos MTho SBch WCot WThu |
| 'Miss Cator' | WCot WVal |
| 'Mrs Cooper' **new** | WCot |
| 'Mrs Dent Brocklehurst' **new** | WCot |
| 'Nikita' | CFwr CPen CTca EBee EBrs ECho EPot MSte |
| 'November Cheer' | ECho |
| 'Pantaloon' **new** | WVal |
| ***peersii*** | WCot WVal |
| 'Plymouth' | SChr |
| ***pudica*** | SBch |
| - pink-flowered | CBgR EBee WCot WVal |
| 'Purple Prince' | LRHS |
| 'Quest' **new** | WVal |
| 'Red Pimpernel' | ECho LAma |
| ***rehmannii*** | EBee EBrs |
| 'Rose Princess' | LRHS |
| 'Rushmere Star' | CBgR CDes EBee SChr WCot |
| 'Salmon Supreme' | LRHS |
| ***sarniensis*** ♀H2-3 | CBro CFwr CPne EBee EBrs ECha ECho EPot IHer LRHS MSte WCot WHil WVal |
| * - 'Alba' | LPio WCot |
| § - var. ***corusca*** | CStu LAma WVal |
| - - 'Major' | EBrs ECho SChr WCot |
| - var. ***curvifolia*** f. ***fothergillii*** | WCot |
| - late, dull red-flowered | CDes |
| 'Snowflake' | WCot |
| 'Stephanie' | CBro CCCN CFwr CTca EBee EBrs ECho EShb LAma LHop LRHS LSou SPer SWal WFar WHoo |
| § ***undulata*** | CBgR CBro CCCN CPne CSut CTca EBee EBrs ECha ECho ERos LAma LRHS LSou MSte SPer WCot WHil |
| * - 'Alba' | SPhx |
| 'Vicky' | WCot |
| 'Virgo' | CMdw ECho |
| 'White Swan' | ECho LAma |
| 'Zeal Candy Stripe' | CFir WVal |
| 'Zeal Giant' ♀H3-4 | CAvo CBro CFFs CFir CPne GCal WVal |
| 'Zeal Grilse' | CDes CPne |
| 'Zeal Salmon' | CPne |
| 'Zeal Silver Stripe' | CFir WVal |

## *Nerium* ✿ (*Apocynaceae*)

| | |
|---|---|
| ***oleander*** misapplied | see *N. oleander* 'Soeur Agnès' |
| ***oleander*** L. | CAbb CArn CHll CSec CTri EBak EBee EEls ELan EShb LRHS MJnS NLar SArc SChr SEND SPad SPer SPoG SRms SWal |
| - 'Album' | EEls |
| - 'Album Plenum' (d) | EEls |
| - 'Alsace' | EEls |
| - 'Altini' | EEls |
| - 'Angiolo Pucci' | EEls |
| - 'Bousquet d'Orb' | EEls |
| § - 'Carneum Plenum' (d) | EEls |
| - 'Cavalaire' (d) | EEls |
| * - 'Clare' | SOWG |
| - 'Cornouailles' | EEls |
| - 'Docteur Golfin' | EEls |
| - 'Emile Sahut' | EEls |
| - 'Emilie' | EEls |
| - 'Flavescens Plenum' (d) | CKob EEls EShb |
| - 'Géant des Batailles' (d) | EEls SOWG |
| - 'Hardy Red' | EEls |
| - 'Hawaii' | EEls |
| - 'Isle of Capri' | SOWG |
| - 'J.R.' | EEls |
| - 'Jannoch' | EEls |
| - 'Louis Pouget' (d) | EEls |
| - 'Madame Allen' (d) | EEls |
| - 'Maresciallo Graziani' | EEls |

- 'Margaritha' EEls
- 'Marie Gambetta' EEls
- 'Mont Blanc' (d) EEls
- 'Mrs Roeding' see *N. oleander* 'Carneum Plenum'
- 'Nana Rosso' EEls
- 'Oasis' (d) EEls
- subsp. ***oleander*** EEls
- 'Papa Gambetta' EEls
- 'Petite Pink' EEls MREP
- 'Petite Red' EEls MREP
- 'Petite Salmon' EEls SEND
- 'Professeur Granel' (d) EEls
- 'Provence' (d) EEls SOWG
- 'Rose des Borrels' (d) EEls
- 'Rosée du Ventoux' (d) EEls SOWG
- 'Roseum' EEls
- 'Roseum Plenum' (d) CRHN EEls
- 'Rosita' EEls
- salmon-flowered **new** SEND
- 'Sealy Pink' EEls

* - 'Snowflake' SOWG

§ - 'Soeur Agnès' EEls

- 'Soleil Levant' EEls
- 'Souvenir d'Emma Schneider' EEls
- 'Souvenir des Iles Canaries' EEls
- 'Splendens' (d) SOWG
- 'Splendens Giganteum' (d) EEls
- 'Splendens Giganteum Variegatum' (d/v) EEls
- 'Tito Poggi' EEls
- 'Vanilla Cream' CBcs MCot MWea SPoG
- 'Variegatum' (v) ♀H1+3 CHll CKob EShb
- 'Variegatum Plenum' (d/v) CBow WCot
- 'Villa Romaine' EEls
- 'Ville de Carpentras' (d) EEls

## *Nertera* (*Rubiaceae*)

***balfouriana*** ECou
***granadensis*** EShb MBri

## *Neviusia* (*Rosaceae*)

***alabamensis*** CBcs NLar

## *Nicandra* (*Solanaceae*)

***physalodes*** CArn CHby CSec ILis MSal NBir NVic SMrm WRos
- 'Splash of Cream' (v) CCCN
- 'Violacea' CSec CSpe SRms SWvt WTou

## *Nicotiana* (*Solanaceae*)

***alata*** CSec
***alata* x *mutabilis*** CSec
***glauca*** CHll CSpe EBee EShb LDai LFur MSte NLar SDnm SPav
'Hopleys' CSpe
***knightiana*** CSec CSpe EBee
***langsdorffii*** ♀H3 CSpe EBee EMon GBri LPio MCot SDnm SPav
- 'Cream Splash' (v) EBee LSou
'Lime Green' ♀H3 CSpe MCot
***mutabilis*** CHll CSec CSpe EBee LDai MWea SBch SPhx WPGP
- 'Marshmallow' **new** MCot
***rustica*** CSec WTou
***suaveolens*** CBre CSpe MSte
***sylvestris*** ♀H3 CDTJ CHEx CSec CSpe CWSG EBee ELan EPfP MCot SDnm SEND SPav SWvt
***tabacum*** CArn CSec SPav
- var. ***macrophylla*** CDTJ
'Tinkerbell' CSec CSpe MCot

## *Nidularium* (*Bromeliaceae*)

***flandria*** see *Neoregelia carolinae* (Meyendorffii Group) 'Flandria'
***innocentii*** XBlo

## x *Niduregelia* (*Bromeliaceae*)

§ 'Surprise' MBri

## *Nierembergia* (*Solanaceae*)

***caerulea*** see *N. linariifolia*
***hippomanica*** see *N. linariifolia*
§ ***linariifolia*** ♀H1 CAbP EBee EHrv
§ ***repens*** CStu ECho EDAr NLar
***rivularis*** see *N. repens*
***scoparia*** 'Mont Blanc' LRHS
- 'Purple Robe' LRHS

## *Nigella* (*Ranunculaceae*)

***hispanica*** L. **new** CSec
***papillosa*** 'African Bride' CSpe
- 'Midnight' CSpe

## *Nigritella* see *Gymnadenia*

## *Nipponanthemum* (*Asteraceae*)

§ ***nipponicum*** CAby CDes CWan EBee ECho GCal GMac LAst MNrw NSti SRms WBrk WCot
- B&SWJ 10872 **new** WCru

## *Noccaea* see *Thlaspi*

## *Nolina* (*Dracaenaceae*)

***bigelovii*** CBrP
***lindheimeriana*** **new** EBee
***longifolia*** EAmu WCot
***nelsonii*** EAmu WPGP
***parviflora*** NJM 05.010 **new** WPGP
***texana*** CTrC NWCA

## *Nomocharis* (*Liliaceae*)

***aperta*** CExc CFwr CWCL EBee EBrs ECho EHrv EPot GBBs GBuc GCra GEdr GGar GKir LAma MLul WCru
- ACE 2271 WWst
- CLD 229 GBuc WWst
- CLD 482 GEdr
- CLD 524 WWst
- KGB 777 GEdr
***farreri*** EBee EBrs ECho
x ***finlayorum*** EBee EBrs ECho GBuc GEdr WWst
***mairei*** see *N. pardanthina*
***meleagrina*** CFwr EBee EBrs ECho EPot GAuc GBuc GEdr LAma MLul WAbe WWst
***nana*** see *Lilium nanum*
***oxypetala*** see *Lilium oxypetalum*
§ ***pardanthina*** CWsd EBee GBuc GGGa GGar GMac NSla WAbe
- CLD 1490 EHrv WWst
- f. ***punctulata*** EBee GBuc GGGa WCru WWst

* ***pianma*** **new** EBee

***saluenensis*** EBee EBrs ECho GGGa WAbe WWst

## *Nonea* (*Boraginaceae*)

***lutea*** EHig LSou MHar MLLN NOrc NSti WCHb WHal WRos

## *Nothochelone* see *Penstemon*

## *Nothofagus* ✿ (*Fagaceae*)

| | |
|---|---|
| § ***alpina*** | CDul CMCN GBin NWea WDin WPGP |
| ***antarctica*** | Widely available |
| ***betuloides*** new | GBin |
| ***cunninghamii*** | CBcs IArd |
| ***dombeyi*** | CBcs CDoC CDul CLnd CTho EBee EPfP GBin IArd ISea LHyd NWea SAPC SArc SSpi STre WPGP |
| ***fusca*** | CBcs CDoC MGos |
| ***glauca*** new | CDul |
| ***menziesii*** | CBcs CDul CTrC |
| ***nervosa*** | see *N. alpina* |
| ***nitida*** | GBin IArd IDee |
| ***obliqua*** | CDoC CDul CLnd CMCN NWea STre WDin |
| ***procera*** misapplied | see *N. alpina* |
| ***procera*** Oerst. | see *N. alpina* |
| ***pumilio*** | GBin |

## *Notholaena* see *Cheilanthes*

## *Notholirion* (*Liliaceae*)

| | |
|---|---|
| ***bulbuliferum*** | EBee EBrs ECho EPot GBuc GCra GKev WAbe |
| - Cox 5074 new | WWst |
| ***campanulatum*** | EBee EBrs ECho WWst |
| - SDR 310 | GKev |
| ***macrophyllum*** | EBee EBrs ECho EPot GBuc WWst |
| ***thomsonianum*** | EBee EBrs ECho WWst |

## *Nothopanax* see *Polyscias*

## *Nothoscordum* (*Alliaceae*)

| | |
|---|---|
| sp new | GCal |
| ***gracile*** | CFir WPrP |
| ***neriniflorum*** | see *Caloscordum neriniflorum* |
| ***strictum*** | EBee ECho |

## *Nuphar* (*Nymphaeaceae*)

| | |
|---|---|
| ***advenum*** | LPBA |
| ***japonica*** | CDWL |
| - var. ***variegata*** (v) | CRow NLar |
| ***lutea*** | CRow EHon EMFW LPBA MMuc NSco SCoo SWat |
| - subsp. ***advena*** | EMFW |
| ***pumila*** | CDWL |

## *Nuxia* (*Buddlejaceae*)

| | |
|---|---|
| ***congesta*** | EShb |
| ***floribunda*** | EShb |

## *Nylandtia* (*Polygalaceae*)

| | |
|---|---|
| ***spinosa*** | SPlb |

## *Nymphaea* ✿ (*Nymphaeaceae*)

| | |
|---|---|
| 'Afterglow' (T/D) | CDWL |
| ***alba*** (H) | CBen CRWN CRow CWat EHon EMFW EPfP LCro LPBA MSKA NBir NSco SCoo SVic SWat WFar WMAq |
| 'Alba Plenissima' (H) | WPnP |
| 'Albatros' misapplied | see *N.* 'Hermine' |
| § 'Albatros' Latour-Marliac (H) | CDWL CWat LPBA MSKA NPer SWat WPnP |
| 'Albatross' | see *N.* 'Albatros' Latour-Marliac, *N.* 'Hermine' |
| 'Albert Greenberg' (T/D) | CDWL |
| * 'Albida' | CDWL WMAq XBlo |
| 'Almost Black' (H) | CBen CDWL MSKA |
| 'Amabilis' (H) | CBen CDWL CRow EMFW LPBA MSKA SWat WMAq |
| 'American Star' (H) | CBen CWat EMFW SWat WMAq |
| 'Andreana' (H) | CDWL CWat LLWG LPBA MSKA SWat |
| 'Anne Emmet' (T/D) | CDWL |
| 'Arabian Nights' (T/D) | CDWL |
| 'Arc-en-ciel' (H) | CBen CDWL LPBA SCoo SWat WMAq |
| 'Arethusa' (H) | LPBA |
| 'Atropurpurea' (H) | CBen CDWL EMFW LLWG LPBA MSKA NPer SWat WMAq |
| 'Attraction' (H) | CBen CDWL CRow EHon EMFW EPfP LPBA MSKA NPer SCoo SVic SWat WMAq XBlo |
| 'Aurora' (H) | CBen CDWL EMFW LCro LPBA SVic SWat WMAq WPnP |
| 'Barbara Davies' (H) | LLWG |
| 'Barbara Dobbins' (H) | CBen CDWL LLWG LPBA MSKA |
| 'Bateau' (H) | LLWG |
| 'Berit Strawn' (H) | LLWG |
| 'Bernice Ikins' (H) new | MSKA |
| 'Berthold' (H) | CBen |
| 'Black Princess' (H) | CDWL |
| 'Blue Horizon' (T/D) | CDWL |
| 'Brakeleyi Rosea' (H) | CBen LPBA MSKA WMAq |
| 'Burgundy Princess' (H) | CDWL CWat LLWG MSKA NPer |
| ***candida*** (H) | CBen EHon EMFW MSKA NPer WMAq |
| 'Candidissima' (H) | CDWL SWat |
| § ***capensis*** (T/D) | XBlo |
| 'Carolina Sunset' (H) | LLWG |
| 'Caroliniana' (H) | CDWL |
| 'Caroliniana Nivea' (H) | CBen CDWL EHon EMFW |
| 'Caroliniana Perfecta' (H) | CBen LPBA MSKA SWat |
| 'Celebration' (H) | LLWG MSKA |
| 'Charlene Strawn' (H) | CWat EMFW LLWG LPBA WMAq |
| 'Charles de Meurville' (H) | CBen CDWL CRow EMFW LPBA MSKA NPer SVic WMAq |
| 'Château le Rouge' (H) | LLWG |
| 'Clyde Ikins' (H) | MSKA |
| 'Colonel A.J. Welch' (H) | CBen EHon EMFW LCro LPBA MSKA NPer SCoo SWat WFar WMAq |
| 'Colorado' (H) | CBen CDWL LLWG MSKA NPer |
| ***colorata*** | see *N. capensis* |
| 'Colossea' (H) | CBen CWat EMFW LPBA MSKA NPer WPnP |
| 'Comanche' (H) | CBen EMFW MSKA NPer WMAq |
| 'Conqueror' (H) | CBen EMFW IArd LPBA MSKA NPer SCoo SVic SWat WFar |
| 'Dallas' (H) | EMFW |
| § 'Darwin' (H) | CBen CDWL CWat EMFW LPBA MSKA NPer SWat WMAq |
| 'David' (H) | CBen CWat LLWG |
| 'Denver' (H) | LLWG MSKA |
| 'Ellisiana' (H) | CBen CDWL EMFW LLWG LPBA MSKA NPer SWat |
| 'Escarboucle' (H) ♀H4 | CBen CDWL CRow CWat EHon EMFW LPBA MSKA NLar NPer SCoo SVic SWat WMAq WPnP XBlo |
| 'Esmeralda' (H) | SWat |
| 'Evelyn Randig' (T/D) | CDWL |
| 'Excalibur' | CDWL |
| § 'Fabiola' (H) | CBen CDWL CRow EHon EMFW EPfP LPBA MSKA NPer SCoo WFar WMAq |
| 'Fiesta' | MSKA |
| 'Fire Crest' (H) | CBen CDWL EHon EMFW LPBA MSKA NPer SCoo SVic SWat WFar WMAq |
| 'Fireball' (H) new | MSKA |
| 'Fritz Junge' (H) | CBen |
| 'Froebelii' (H) | CBen CDWL CRow CWat EHon EMFW LCro LPBA MSKA NPer SWat WFar WMAq WPnP |

| | | |
|---|---|---|
| | 'Fulva' (H) | LLWG |
| | 'Galatée' (H) | CBen CDWL MSKA |
| | 'Geisha Girl' | CDWL MSKA |
| | 'General Pershing' (T/D) | CDWL |
| | 'Georgia Peach' (H) | CDWL LLWG MSKA |
| | 'Gladstoneana' (H) ♀$^{H4}$ | CBen CRow CWat EHon EMFW LPBA MSKA NPer SCoo SWat WMAq |
| | 'Gloire du Temple-sur-Lot' (H) | CBen CDWL EHon EMFW NPer SWat WMAq |
| | 'Gloriosa' (H) | CBen CDWL LPBA NPer SCoo SWat WFar |
| | 'Gold Medal' (H) | CBen LLWG MSKA |
| | 'Golden West' (T/D) | CDWL |
| | 'Gonnère' (H) ♀$^{H4}$ | CBen CDWL CRow CWat EHon EMFW EPfP LCro LPBA MSKA NPer SWat WMAq WPnP |
| | 'Graziella' (H) | LPBA MSKA WMAq WPnP |
| | 'Green Smoke' (T/D) | CDWL |
| | 'Gypsy' (H) | LLWG |
| | 'H.C. Haarstick' (T/N) | CDWL |
| | 'Hal Miller' (H) | LLWG |
| | 'Hassell' (H) | LLWG |
| | 'Helen Fowler' (H) | CDWL EMFW SWat WMAq |
| | x ***helvola*** | see *N.* 'Pygmaea Helvola' |
| § | 'Hermine' (H) | CBen CDWL EMFW MSKA NPer SWat WMAq |
| | 'Highlight' | LLWG |
| | 'Hollandia' misapplied | see *N.* 'Darwin' |
| | 'Hollandia' Koster (H) | SWat |
| | 'Indiana' (H) | CBen CDWL EMFW LPBA MSKA NPer WMAq |
| | 'Inner Light' | LLWG MSKA |
| | 'James Brydon' (H) ♀$^{H4}$ | CBen CDWL CRow CWat EHon EMFW EPfP LPBA MSKA NLar NPer SCoo SVic SWat WFar WMAq WPnP |
| | 'Jean de Lamarsalle' (H) | LLWG |
| | 'Jerusalem Dawn' **new** | MSKA |
| § | 'Joanne Pring' (H) | SWat |
| | 'Joey Tomocik' (H) | CBen CDWL CWat EMFW LLWG LPBA MSKA SCoo WMAq |
| | 'June Alison' (T/D) | CDWL |
| | 'King of Siam' (T/D) | CDWL |
| | 'King of the Blues' (T/D) **new** | MSKA |
| | 'Lactea' (H) | CBen CDWL LLWG |
| | 'Laura Strawn' (H) | LLWG |
| | 'Laydekeri Alba' | CDWL |
| | 'Laydekeri Fulgens' (H) | CBen CDWL EMFW LPBA MSKA SWat WMAq |
| | 'Laydekeri Lilacea' (H) | CBen CDWL CRow LPBA SWat WMAq |
| | 'Laydekeri Purpurata' (H) | CDWL LPBA SWat |
| | 'Laydekeri Rosea' misapplied | see *N.* 'Laydekeri Rosea Prolifera' |
| § | 'Laydekeri Rosea Prolifera' (H) | CBen EMFW LPBA |
| | 'Lemon Chiffon' (H) | CBen CDWL MSKA |
| | 'Lemon Mist' | LLWG MSKA |
| | 'Lily Pons' (H) | CBen MSKA |
| | 'Limelight' | SWat |
| | 'Liou' (H) | CBen LLWG MSKA |
| | 'Little Sue' (H) | CDWL LLWG MSKA |
| | 'Livingstone' (H) | LLWG |
| | 'Luciana' | see *N.* 'Odorata Luciana' |
| | 'Lucida' (H) | CBen CDWL EMFW LPBA MSKA SWat WMAq |
| | 'Madame de Bonseigneur' (H) | CDWL |
| | 'Madame Wilfon Gonnère' (H) | CBen CDWL CWat EHon EMFW LPBA MSKA NPer SVic SWat WMAq |
| | 'Marliacea Albida' (H) | CBen CDWL CWat EHon EMFW LPBA MSKA NPer SWat WFar WMAq WPnP XBlo |
| | 'Marliacea Carnea' (H) | CBen CDWL CRow EHon EMFW EPfP LCro LPBA MSKA NPer SCoo SWat WFar WMAq |
| § | 'Marliacea Chromatella' (H) ♀$^{H4}$ | CBen CDWL CRow CWat EHon EMFW EPfP LPBA MSKA NLar SCoo SVic SWat WFar WMAq WPnP XBlo |
| | 'Marliacea Rosea' (H) | CBen EMFW MSKA SWat WMAq XBlo |
| | 'Marliacea Rubra Punctata' (H) | LPBA |
| | 'Maroon Beauty' (T/N) | CDWL |
| | 'Mary' (H) | LLWG |
| | 'Masaniello' (H) | CBen CDWL CRow EHon EMFW EPfP LPBA MSKA SWat WMAq |
| | 'Maurice Laydeker' (H) | CBen CDWL LLWG |
| | 'Maxima' | see *N.* 'Odorata Maxima' |
| | 'Mayla' | CBen LLWG LPBA MSKA NPer |
| § | 'Météor' (H) | CBen CWat EMFW LCro MSKA WMAq |
| | ***mexicana*** | MSKA |
| | 'Midnight' (T/D) | CDWL |
| | 'Millennium Pink' | CDWL MSKA |
| | 'Moorei' (H) | CBen CDWL EHon EMFW LPBA MSKA SWat WMAq |
| | 'Mrs George H. Pring' (T/D) | CDWL |
| | 'Mrs Martin E. Randig' (T/D) | CDWL |
| | 'Mrs Richmond' misapplied | see *N.* 'Fabiola' |
| | 'Mrs Richmond' Latour-Marliac (H) | SWat XBlo |
| | 'Neptune' (H) | LLWG |
| | 'Newchapel Beauty' | WMAq |
| | 'Newton' (H) | CBen CDWL LLWG MSKA SWat WMAq |
| | 'Nigel' (H) | CBen EMFW LLWG MSKA SWat |
| | 'Norma Gedye' (H) | CBen CWat LPBA MSKA SWat WMAq |
| | 'Odalisque' (H) | CBen EMFW |
| § | ***odorata*** (H) | CBen CRow EHon EMFW LPBA MSKA SCoo WMAq |
| § | - var. ***minor*** (H) | CBen CDWL CRow LPBA MSKA SWat WFar WMAq |
| | - 'Pumila' | see *N. odorata* var. *minor* |
| | - subsp. ***tuberosa*** (H) | CBen LPBA |
| | 'Odorata Alba' | see *N. odorata* |
| § | 'Odorata Luciana' (H) | EMFW |
| § | 'Odorata Maxima' (H) | WMAq |
| | 'Odorata Sulphurea' (H) | CBen CDWL EHon SWat WFar WPnP |
| § | 'Odorata Sulphurea Grandiflora' (H) | CBen CDWL CRow EMFW LPBA MSKA SCoo SWat XBlo |
| § | 'Odorata Turicensis' (H) | LPBA MSKA |
| | 'Odorata William B. Shaw' | see *N.* 'W.B. Shaw' |
| | 'Orange Commanche' | CDWL |
| | 'Pam Bennett' (H) | CBen LLWG |
| | 'Pamela' (T/D) | CDWL |
| | 'Panama Pacific' (T/D) | XBlo |
| | 'Patio Joe' | CDWL LLWG MSKA |
| | 'Paul Hariot' (H) | CDWL CWat EHon EMFW LPBA MSKA NPer SWat WMAq WPnP |
| | 'Peace Lily' | LLWG MSKA |
| | 'Peach Glow' | LLWG MSKA |
| | 'Peaches and Cream' (H) | CDWL MSKA |
| | Pearl of the Pool (H) | SWat |
| | 'Perry's Baby Red' (H) | CBen CDWL CWat EMFW LLWG MSKA NPer SCoo WMAq |
| | 'Perry's Crinkled Pink' (H) | CBen |
| | 'Perry's Double White' (H) | MSKA NPer |
| | 'Perry's Double Yellow' **new** | MSKA |
| | 'Perry's Dwarf Red' (H) | MSKA |
| | 'Perry's Fire Opal' (H) | CDWL MSKA NPer |
| | 'Perry's Orange Sunset' **new** | MSKA |

'Perry's Pink' (H) SWat WMAq
'Perry's Pink Bicolor' (H) LLWG
'Perry's Red Beauty' (H) CBen
'Perry's Red Bicolor' (H) LLWG
'Perry's Red Glow' (H) MSKA
'Perry's Red Wonder' (H) CBen
'Perry's Viviparous Pink' (H) CBen
'Perry's White Star' (H) LLWG
'Perry's Yellow Sensation' see *N.* 'Yellow Sensation'
'Peter Slocum' (H) CDWL SWat
'Phoebus' (H) CBen CDWL SWat
'Picciola' (H) LLWG
'Pink Domino' **new** CDWL MSKA
'Pink Grapefruit' (H) XBlo
pink hybrid CDWL
'Pink Opal' (H) CBen CDWL CWat EMFW LPBA
'Pink Peony' (H) MSKA
'Pink Pumpkin' (H) LLWG
'Pink Sensation' (H) CBen CDWL EMFW LLWG MSKA NPer SWat WMAq
'Pink Sparkle' (H) LLWG
'Pink Sunrise' (H) MSKA
'Pöstlingberg' (H) LLWG LPBA
'Princess Elizabeth' (H) CBen EHon LLWG LPBA
'Pygmaea Alba' see *N. tetragona*
§ 'Pygmaea Helvola' (H) ♀H4 CBen CDWL CRow CWat EHon EMFW LCro LPBA MSKA NLar NPer SCoo SVic SWat WMAq WPnP
'Pygmaea Rubis' (H) CRow EHon LPBA SWat WMAq
'Pygmaea Rubra' (H) CBen CDWL CWat EMFW LCro MSKA NLar NPer SCoo SVic WMAq WPnP
'Ray Davies' (H) CBen EMFW LLWG
'Red Paradise' (H) **new** MSKA
'Red Spider' (H) CWat EMFW LPBA MSKA NPer SVic
'Rembrandt' misapplied see *N.* 'Météor'
'Rembrandt' Koster (H) CDWL LPBA
'René Gérard' (H) CBen CDWL CWat EHon EMFW LPBA MSKA NPer SWat WFar WMAq WPnP
'Rosanna Supreme' (H) LLWG SWat
'Rose Arey' (H) CBen CDWL EHon EMFW LPBA MSKA NPer SCoo SVic SWat WMAq
'Rose Magnolia' (H) CDWL SWat
§ 'Rosea' (H) LPBA
'Rosennymphe' (H) CBen LCro LPBA MSKA NPer SWat WFar WMAq
'Rosy Morn' (H) CBen LLWG MSKA
'Saint Louis Gold' (T/D) CDWL
'Seignouretti' (H) EMFW
'Shady Lady' **new** MSKA
'Sioux' (H) CBen CDWL EHon EMFW LPBA MSKA NPer SVic WMAq XBlo
'Sirius' (H) CBen CDWL EMFW LLWG LPBA MSKA SWat
'Snow Princess' EMFW LPBA WPnP
'Solfatare' (H) LLWG
'Somptuosa' (H) EPfP
'Splendida' (H) WMAq
'Starbright' LLWG
'Starburst' (H) **new** MSKA
'Steven Strawn' (H) LLWG
'Sultan' (H) MSKA
'Sunny Pink' CDWL LLWG MSKA
'Sunrise' see *N.* 'Odorata Sulphurea Grandiflora'
§ ***tetragona*** (H) CBen CDWL CRow CWat EHon EMFW LPBA NPer WFar WMAq
- 'Alba' see *N. tetragona*
- 'Johann Pring' see *N.* 'Joanne Pring'
'Texas Dawn' (H) CBen CDWL EMFW LLWG MSKA WMAq
'Thomas O'Brian' LLWG
'Tina' (T/D) CDWL
'Tuberosa Flavescens' see *N.* 'Marliacea Chromatella'
'Tuberosa Richardsonii' (H) CBen EHon EMFW MSKA NPer WFar
***tuberosa*** 'Rosea' see *N.* 'Rosea'
'Turicensis' see *N.* 'Odorata Turicensis'
'Vésuve' (H) CDWL EMFW LLWG MSKA SWat
'Virginalis' (H) EMFW LLWG LPBA MSKA NPer SWat WMAq
'Virginia' (H) LLWG
§ 'W.B. Shaw' (H) CBen EHon EMFW LPBA MSKA NPer SWat WMAq
'Walter Pagels' (H) CBen CDWL EMFW LLWG WMAq
'Weymouth Red' (H) CBen
'White Delight' (T/D) CDWL
'White Sultan' (H) LLWG MSKA
'William Doogue' (H) MSKA
'William Falconer' (H) CBen CDWL CWat EMFW LPBA MSKA NPer SWat
'Wow' (H) CDWL MSKA
'Yellow Commanche' CDWL
'Yellow Dazzler' (T/D) CDWL
'Yellow Princess' (H) CDWL
'Yellow Queen' (H) MSKA
§ 'Yellow Sensation' (H) CBen
'Yul Ling' (H) EMFW LLWG MSKA SWat
'Zeus' CDWL MSKA

## *Nymphoides* (*Menyanthaceae*)

***peltata*** CWat EMFW EPfP MSKA NLar NPer NSco SCoo SVic WFar WMAq WPnP
§ - 'Bennettii' EHon LPBA

## *Nyssa* (*Cornaceae*)

***aquatica*** CTho SBir SSpi SSta
***sinensis*** ♀H4 CAbP CBcs CDoC CMCN CTho ELan EPfP GKir IDee LRHS MAsh MBlu SBir SReu SSpi SSta
- Nymans form EPfP LRHS SBir
***sylvatica*** ♀H4 Widely available
- 'Autumn Cascades' EPfP MBlu NLar WPGP
§ - 'Haymen's Red' **new** SSpi
- 'Isobel Grace' **new** SSpi
- 'Jermyns Flame' CAbP EPfP LRHS MAsh MBri SBir SPoG SSpi
- 'Miss Scarlet' (f) NLar
- Red Rage see *N. sylvatica* 'Haymen's Red'
- 'Red Red Wine' CGHE EPfP MBlu SBir WPGP
- 'Sheffield Park' CAbP EPfP LRHS MAsh SBir SSpi
- 'Windsor' EPfP LRHS MAsh SBir SSpi
- 'Wisley Bonfire' (m) CAbP CGHE EBee ECrN EPfP LRHS MBri NLar SBir SKHP SPoG SSpi WPGP

# O

## *Oakesiella* see *Uvularia*

## *Ochagavia* (*Bromeliaceae*)

§ sp. CHEx NPal SAPC SArc
***carnea*** WCot WGwG
- RCB RA S-2 **new** LSou
***elegans*** WPGP
§ ***litoralis*** **new** EBee
* ***rosea*** CHEx

## *Ochna* (*Ochnaceae*)

***serrulata*** CCCN

## *Ocimum* (*Lamiaceae*)

| | | |
|---|---|---|
| | 'African Blue' | CArn CBod ELau EOHP GPoy LSou MHer NGHP NPri NTHB SPoG |
| § | ***americanum*** | NGHP |
| | - 'Meng Luk' | see *O. americanum* |
| | - 'Spice' | see *O.* 'Spice' |
| | ***basilicum*** | CArn CSev GPoy LRHS NPri SIde SWat WPer |
| | - 'Anise' | see *O. basilicum* 'Horapha' |
| | - 'Ararat' | NGHP |
| | - ***camphorata*** | see *O. kilimandscharicum* |
| * | - 'Cinnamon' | LRHS MNHC MSal NGHP SHDw WJek |
| | - 'Cuban' new | GPoy |
| | - 'Genovese' | ELau MHer MNHC NGHP NVic |
| | - 'Glycyrrhiza' | see *O. basilicum* 'Horapha' |
| | - 'Green Globe' | MNHC NGHP |
| | - 'Green Ruffles' | EPfP LRHS MNHC WJek |
| | - 'Holy' | see *O. tenuiflorum* |
| § | - 'Horapha' | CArn MHer MNHC MSal NGHP SIde WJek |
| * | - 'Horapha Nanum' | NGHP WJek |
| | - 'Mrs Burns' | NGHP |
| | - 'Napolitano' | CBod NGHP SIde SWat WJek |
| | - var. ***purpurascens*** | CArn CSev SIde |
| | - - 'Dark Opal' | CBod MNHC NGHP NPri SHDw WJek |
| | - - 'Purple Ruffles' | CHFP EPfP MNHC SIde SWat WJek |
| | - - 'Red Rubin' | MHer MNHC WJek |
| | - var. ***purpurascens*** x ***kilimandscharicum*** | CSpe GPoy |
| | - 'Sweet Genovase' new | SVic |
| | - 'Thai' | see *O. basilicum* 'Horapha' |
| | ***canum*** | see *O. americanum* |
| | x ***citriodorum*** | CArn LRHS MNHC MSal NGHP SHDw SIde WJek |
| | - 'Lime' | MNHC NGHP WJek |
| | - 'Siam Queen' | LRHS MHer WJek |
| | 'Cypriot' new | GPoy |
| | ***gratissimum*** | ELau |
| § | ***kilimandscharicum*** | GPoy |
| | ***minimum*** | CArn CBod CSev ELau LRHS MHer MNHC NGHP SIde WJek WPer |
| | ***sanctum*** | see *O. tenuiflorum* |
| § | 'Spice' | NGHP |
| | 'Spicy Globe' | WJek |
| § | ***tenuiflorum*** | CArn CHFP GPoy LRHS MNHC MSal NGHP SHDw SIde WJek |

## *Odontonema* (*Acanthaceae*)

| | | |
|---|---|---|
| | ***schomburgkianum*** | CCCN |

## *Oemleria* (*Rosaceae*)

| | | |
|---|---|---|
| | ***cerasiformis*** | CBcs EPfP EPla NLar NWea SSpi WCot WEas WHCG WSHC |

## *Oenanthe* (*Apiaceae*)

| | | |
|---|---|---|
| | ***aquatica*** 'Variegata' (v) | EMFW |
| | ***crocata*** | EBWF |
| * | ***javanica*** 'Atropurpurea' | EHoe |
| | - 'Flamingo' (v) | CBen ELan EMon EPfP GCal GGar LEdu LPBA NBro SGar WFar WMAq WSHC |
| | ***lachenalii*** new | EBWF |

## *Oenothera* ✿ (*Onagraceae*)

| | | |
|---|---|---|
| | from South America | MTho |
| § | ***acaulis*** | CSpe MNrw SBch SBri SGar SPhx WRos |
| | - ***alba*** | MDKP WCot |
| § | - 'Aurea' | CSec |
| | - 'Lutea' | see *O. acaulis* 'Aurea' |
| | 'Apricot Delight' | CSec EBee EHoe MBNS NBur STes WMnd WMoo |
| § | ***biennis*** | CArn COld CSev CWan EBWF ELan GPoy LCro LEdu MDun MHer NBro NGHP SECG SGar SIde SPhx WBrk WEas WFar WHer WJek WPer WSFF |
| | ***caespitosa*** | CSec |
| | - subsp. ***caespitosa*** NNS 93-505 | NWCA |
| * | ***campylocalyx*** | CSec LDai |
| | ***childsii*** | see *O. speciosa* |
| | ***cinaeus*** | see *O. fruticosa* subsp. *glauca* |
| | 'Cold Crick' new | EBee |
| | 'Colin Porter' | CCge CSec CSsd EBur NBur NWCA WHrl WMoo WPer |
| | 'Copper Canyon' | CSam MBNS |
| | 'Crown Imperial' | CChe EBee LEdu MCCP NHol SHar SLon SPer SPoG SSto |
| | 'Crown of Gold' | ELan LLHF SPoG |
| | ***elata*** subsp. ***hirsutissima*** new | CSec |
| § | - subsp. ***hookeri*** | CSec EWes MHar NBre WPer |
| | ***erythrosepala*** | see *O. glazioviana* |
| | 'Finlay's Fancy' | WCru |
| § | ***fruticosa*** | CSec NLar SPlb |
| | - 'African Sun'[PBR] | EBee ECtt EWes SBod SRot |
| | - 'Camel' (v) | EGle LDai LHop MDKP NPro SMrm SUsu WHrl |
| | - Fireworks | see *O. fruticosa* 'Fyrverkeri' |
| § | - 'Fyrverkeri' ♀H4 | CBcs CMea EBee ECtt ELan EShb GKir LAst LCro LEdu LHop MRav MWat NBlu NGdn NHol NVic SBod SMrm SPer SPla SWvt WAul WBVN WCAu WMnd WRos |
| § | - subsp. ***glauca*** ♀H4 | CElw CEnt CHrt CSec EPfP MDKP MNrw MWhi SPer SRms WEas WPer |
| | - - 'Erica Robin' (v) | CBct CMea CPrp EBee ECtt EGle EHoe GBuc LAst LHop MRav NGdn SAga SMad SMrm SPla SPoG SRot SWvt WCAu WCot WHoo WPGP |
| | - - 'Frühlingsgold' (v) | CBct EShb SUsu |
| | - - Solstice | see *O. fruticosa* subsp. *glauca* 'Sonnenwende' |
| § | - - 'Sonnenwende' | CBre CElw CEnt CSec EBee EBrs MAvo MLLN NLar NPro SPad WMoo |
| | - - 'Sunspot' (v) | GBuc SGar |
| | - Highlight | see *O. fruticosa* 'Hoheslicht' |
| § | - 'Hoheslicht' | EBee |
| | - 'Lady Brookeborough' | MRav |
| | - 'Michelle Ploeger' | EGle NBre NCGa SUsu |
| | - 'Silberblatt' (v) | CBow EBee LSou WAul |
| | - 'W. Cuthbertson' | EBee |
| | - 'Yellow River' | CElw EBee LRHS |
| | - 'Youngii' | CSec CWan EPfP LEdu MCCP MLLN WPer |
| | ***glabra*** misapplied | ECha NSti SIng |
| | ***glabra*** Miller | see *O. biennis* |
| § | ***glazioviana*** | CSec CWan MNHC NBir SVic WFar WPer |
| | ***grandis*** | CSec |
| | ***hookeri*** | see *O. elata* subsp. *hookeri* |
| | ***kunthiana*** | CEnt CSec ECho MDKP MHer NWCA WMnd WMoo WPer |
| | - 'Glowing Magenta' | EBee SHGN |
| | ***lamarckiana*** | see *O. glazioviana* |
| | 'Lemon Sunset' | CSec CSsd EHig LSou NBur NGHP SPad WMoo |
| | ***linearis*** | see *O. fruticosa* |
| | 'Longest Day' | CSec LEdu LRHS MArl MBrN |
| § | ***macrocarpa*** ♀H4 | Widely available |
| | - subsp. ***fremontii*** 'Silver Wings' | ECtt LBMP |
| | - subsp. ***incana*** | CMea CSpe NBre SMad |

| | | |
|---|---|---|
| | ***macrosceles*** | NBre |
| * | ***minima*** | CSec MDKP |
| | ***missouriensis*** | see *O. macrocarpa* |
| | ***muricata*** | CSec NBre |
| | ***oakesiana*** | CSec EBee SPhx |
| | ***odorata*** misapplied | see *O. stricta* |
| | ***odorata*** Hook. & Arn. | see *O. biennis* |
| | ***odorata*** Jacquin | CArn |
| | - cream-flowered | CSpe WFar |
| | ***organensis*** | CDes EBee MLLN NBre WPGP |
| | ***pallida*** 'Innocence' | LRHS MBNS NBre |
| | ***parviflora*** | CSec |
| | 'Penelope Hobhouse' | CBct GBuc SUsu |
| § | ***perennis*** | CEnt CMea CSec EBee NBre NPro SRms WBVN WEas WPer |
| | ***pumila*** | see *O. perennis* |
| | ***rosea*** | CSec NBur |
| | 'Silky Orchid' | ELon SWal |
| § | ***speciosa*** | CMHG EBee EShb LAst NBre SEND SPer WFar WPer |
| * | - 'Alba' | EBee EWes |
| | - 'Ballerina' | LHop WCFE |
| | - var. ***childsii*** | see *O. speciosa* |
| | - 'Pink Petticoats' | ECha EShb NPer SWat |
| | - 'Rosea' | ECho LEdu SPlb SWat WPer |
| | - 'Siskiyou' | CHrt CSpe EAEE EBee ECtt EPfP GBuc GKir LBMP LEdu SCoo SGar SIng SMad SMrm SPer SRot SUsu |
| | - Twilight = 'Turner01'[PBR] (v) | SHar |
| | - 'Woodside White' | ELon SMrm |
| § | ***stricta*** | CHar CHrt CMea CSec ECGP EGoo GCal SIng WBrk WPer |
| * | - 'Moonlight' | SGar |
| § | - 'Sulphurea' | CHar CMHG CMea CMil CSec EGoo ELan EWld GCal IFro MNFA NPer SBch SGar SMrm SPhx SUsu WAbb WCot WPer |
| | 'Summer Sun' | EAEE EBee LBMP MSte NBre |
| | ***syrticola*** | NBre |
| | ***taraxacifolia*** | see *O. acaulis* |
| | ***tetragona*** | see *O. fruticosa* subsp. *glauca* |
| | - var. ***fraseri*** | see *O. fruticosa* subsp. *glauca* |
| | ***versicolor*** | WCFE |
| | - 'Sunset Boulevard' | CPom CSam CSec CSpe CWCL EBee EGoo GBuc LDai NGHP SBod SGar SMrm SPer SWal WFar WMoo |

## *Olea* (*Oleaceae*)

| | | |
|---|---|---|
| | ***europaea*** (F) | Widely available |
| | - subsp. ***africana*** | CTrC WPGP |
| | - 'Aglandau' (F) | CAgr |
| | - 'Bouteillan' (F) | CAgr |
| | - 'Cailletier' (F) | CAgr |
| | - 'Chelsea Physic Garden' (F) | CDoC WPGP |
| § | - 'Cipressino' (F) | ESwi LPan SBLw |
| | - 'El Greco' (F) | CBcs |
| | - 'Frantoio' (F) | CAgr |
| | - 'Pyramidalis' | see *O. europaea* 'Cipressino' |
| * | - 'Sativa' (F) | EMui |

## *Olearia* ✿ (*Asteraceae*)

| | | |
|---|---|---|
| | ***albida*** misapplied | see *O.* 'Talbot de Malahide' |
| | ***albida*** Hook. f. | GGar |
| | - var. ***angulata*** | CTrC CTsd |
| | ***algida*** | ECou GGar |
| | ***arborescens*** | GGar |
| | ***argophylla*** | CPLG ECou GGar |
| | ***avicenniifolia*** | CBcs CMac ECou GGar |
| | ***canescens*** | CPne |
| | x ***capillaris*** | CDoC EBee ECou GGar |
| | ***chathamica*** | GGar IFFs |
| § | ***cheesemanii*** | CBcs CDoC CMHG CPLG CTrC CWsd GGal GGar NLar SPer |
| | ***coriacea*** | ECou |
| | 'County Park' | ECou |
| | ***erubescens*** | CDoC CPLG |
| | ***floribunda*** | GGar |
| | ***frostii*** | CTsd GGar IDee |
| | ***furfuracea*** | ECou |
| | ***glandulosa*** | ECou GGar |
| | ***gunniana*** | see *O. phlogopappa* |
| | x ***haastii*** | Widely available |
| | - 'McKenzie' | ECou |
| | ***hectorii*** | ECou |
| § | 'Henry Travers' | CBcs CCCN CDoC CPLG EPfP GGar GQui IDee NMun |
| | ***ilicifolia*** | CDoC EBee EPfP GGar IFFs LRHS SPoG |
| § | ***ilicifolia*** x ***moschata*** | GGar WKif |
| | ***insignis*** | see *Pachystegia insignis* |
| | ***ledifolia*** | GGar |
| | ***lepidophylla*** | ECou |
| | - 'Silver Knight' **new** | EBee |
| | - silver-leaved | ECou |
| | ***lirata*** | ECou GGar |
| | ***macrodonta*** ♀H3 | Widely available |
| | - 'Intermedia' | GGar |
| | - 'Major' | CCCN GGal GGar SHBN |
| | - 'Minor' | CBcs CCCN CDoC CMac CTrC ELan EPfP GBin GGar GQui SPlb WFar |
| | x ***mollis*** misapplied | see *O. ilicifolia* x *O. moschata* |
| | x ***mollis*** (Kirk) Cockayne | EBee GQui |
| | - 'Zennorensis' ♀H3 | CBcs CCCN CDoC EPfP GGar IArd IDee IFFs SOWG WDin WEas WPGP |
| | ***moschata*** | GGar NLar |
| | ***moschata*** x ***nummularifolia*** var. ***cymbifolia*** | GGar |
| | ***myrsinoides*** | CPLG |
| | ***nummularifolia*** | CBcs CCCN CDoC CHll CTrC CTri EBee ECou EPfP EPla GGar ISea SEND SPer SSto STre SWvt WBod WDin WFar WKif |
| | - var. ***cymbifolia*** | ECou |
| | - 'Little Lou' | ECou |
| | ***odorata*** | CPLG ECou ISea NLar WFar WHCG |
| | ***oleifolia*** | see *O.* 'Waikariensis' |
| | ***paniculata*** | CBcs CDoC CMHG CTrC CTri EBee EPfP GGar IFFs ISea SLon |
| § | ***phlogopappa*** | CHrt CSBt CTri ECou GGar WBrE |
| | - 'Comber's Blue' | CBcs CCCN EBee EPfP GGar GKir LRHS LSRN SCoo SKHP SPer WBod |
| § | - 'Comber's Pink' | CBcs CCCN CDoC CPLG CWan EBee ELon EPfP GGar GKir ISea LRHS LSRN NPer SAga SCoo SPer WBod WEas WKif WLeb |
| | - pink-flowered | CTrG |
| | - 'Rosea' | see *O. phlogopappa* 'Comber's Pink' |
| | - 'Sawtooth' **new** | GGar |
| | - Splendens Group | WFar |
| I | - var. ***subrepanda*** (DC.) J.H. Willis | CTrC GGal GGar LEdu SEND |
| | - 'Tournaig Titch' **new** | GGar |
| | ***ramulosa*** | CCCN CDoC CPLG EBee |
| | - 'Blue Stars' | ECou GGar |
| | - var. ***ramulosa*** | ECou |
| | - 'White Stars' | ECou |
| | ***rani*** misapplied | see *O. cheesemanii* |
| | ***rani*** Druce | IFFs ISea |
| * | ***rossii*** | CTrC |

| | |
|---|---|
| x ***scilloniensis*** misapplied | see *O. stellulata* DC. |
| x ***scilloniensis*** ambig. | IFFs |
| x ***scilloniensis*** Dorrien-Smith ♀H3 | CCCN CChe CTsd GGar NBlu |
| - 'Master Michael' | CCCN CDoC ELon EPfP ERas LRHS MRav NPri SBod SOWG SPer SPoG SRGP WEas WKif WSHC |
| ***semidentata*** misapplied | see *O.* 'Henry Travers' |
| ***solandri*** | CCCN CDoC CHEx CMac CTsd EBee ECou EPla GGar IDee LRHS SDix SEND SPer STre |
| - 'Aurea' | CBcs GQui |
| ***stellulata*** misapplied | see *O. phlogopappa* |
| § ***stellulata*** DC. | CPLG CSBt CTrG CWSG CWib EBee ECou EPfP GGal ISea LRHS MWat NPri SCoo SDix SGar SOWG SPer SPla WDin WEas WFar WHCG WPic |
| - 'Michael's Pride' | CPLG |
| - var. ***rugosa*** | ECou |
| § 'Talbot de Malahide' | EHig GGar |
| ***traversii*** | CBcs CCCN CDoC CHrt CMHG CSBt CTrC CTsd EBee GGal GGar IFFs SEND WHer |
| - 'Tweedledum' (v) | CBow CCCN CDoC CTrC CWib ECou GGar SSto |
| - 'Variegata' (v) **new** | CTsd |
| ***virgata*** | CCCN CHEx ECou GBin GGar GQui LEdu MCot WCot |
| - var. ***laxiflora*** | CTrC WHer |
| - var. ***lineata*** | CDoC CPLG ECou GGar NLar SEND WDin WSHC |
| - - 'Dartonii' | CBcs CDoC EBee ECou GGar LRHS MBlu SBig SLPl |
| § 'Waikariensis' | CMHG CPLG CTrC CWsd EBee ECou GGar IDee LRHS MSCN SEND SLon WCFE WDin |

## *Oligoneuron* see *Solidago*

## *Oligostachyum* (*Poaceae*)

| | |
|---|---|
| ***lubricum*** | see *Semiarundinaria lubrica* |
| ***oedogonatum*** **new** | WPGP |

## olive see *Olea europaea*

## *Olsynium* (*Iridaceae*)

| | |
|---|---|
| § ***douglasii*** ♀H4 | CBro CMea EBee EPot GEdr GKev LLHF NMen NRya SIng WAbe WCot |
| - 'Album' | GAbr GBin GEdr NMen NRya NSla SIng WHal |
| - dwarf | GEdr |
| - var. ***inflatum*** | EWes |
| § ***filifolium*** | NWCA |
| § ***junceum*** | MDKP WPGP |
| - JCA 12289 | MTho |
| ***trinerve*** B&SWJ 10459 **new** | WCru |

## *Omphalodes* (*Boraginaceae*)

| | |
|---|---|
| ***cappadocica*** ♀H4 | CElw CEnt CHrt EAEE EBee EPot IFoB LBMP LEdu LRHS NBro NCob NPer NSum NWCA SGar SPer SRms SWat WBrk WFar |
| - 'Anthea Bloom' | GBuc IBlr |
| - 'Blueberries and Cream' (v) | WCot |
| - 'Cherry Ingram' ♀H4 | Widely available |
| - 'Lilac Mist' | CElw CLAP EBee LLWP MRav NCob SBch SRms SSvw SWat SWvt WGwG WTin |
| - 'Parisian Skies' | CLAP |
| - 'Starry Eyes' | Widely available |
| ***kuzinskyanae*** | CSec |
| § ***linifolia*** ♀H4 | CMea CSec CSpe MCot NMen SBch |
| - ***alba*** | see *O. linifolia* |
| ***luciliae*** | CLAP WThu |
| - var. ***cilicica*** **new** | WFar |
| ***nitida*** | CSpe EMon GGar NRya |
| ***verna*** | Widely available |
| - 'Alba' | Widely available |
| - 'Elfenauge' | CMil EGle EMon GBin NBir NCGa NRya SMrm SSvw WCot |
| - ***grandiflora*** | WCot |

## *Omphalogramma* (*Primulaceae*)

| | |
|---|---|
| ***delavayi*** SDR 5167 **new** | GKev |
| ***forrestii*** | CExc |

## *Oncostema* see *Scilla*

## onion see *Allium cepa*

## *Onixotis* (*Colchicaceae*)

| | |
|---|---|
| ***triquetra*** | WCot |

## *Onobrychis* (*Papilionaceae*)

| | |
|---|---|
| ***viciifolia*** | EBWF EBee MSal WSHC |

## *Onoclea* (*Woodsiaceae*)

| | |
|---|---|
| § ***intermedia*** | EMon |
| ***sensibilis*** ♀H4 | Widely available |
| - copper-leaved | CHEx CRow CWsd WPGP |
| - 'Rotstiel' **new** | EBee |

## *Ononis* (*Papilionaceae*)

| | |
|---|---|
| ***fruticosa*** | NLar |
| ***repens*** | CArn EBWF MSal NMir SEND |
| ***rotundifolia*** | CPom MSal |
| ***spinosa*** | EBWF EBee MHer MSal WFar WPer |

## *Onopordum* (*Asteraceae*)

| | |
|---|---|
| ***acanthium*** | CArn CBct CHrt CSec EBee EBrs ECha ELan EPfP GAbr GBar GKir GMaP MHer MWat NBid NVic SIde SPoG WCAu WCHb WCot WFar WHer WHil WMnd |
| ***arabicum*** | see *O. nervosum* |
| ***bracteatum*** | WPer |
| ***illyricum*** | WCot |
| § ***nervosum*** ♀H4 | CArn CSpe EBee NBur SAga SRms WFar |

## *Onosma* (*Boraginaceae*)

| | |
|---|---|
| ***alborosea*** | CMdw CSev EBee ECha EGoo GBri GCal GCra GEdr SAga SEND WEas WKif WPGP WSHC |
| ***echioides*** | GEdr |
| ***nana*** | GEdr |
| ***taurica*** ♀H4 | CMdw |

## *Onychium* (*Adiantaceae*)

| | |
|---|---|
| ***contiguum*** | WAbe |
| ***japonicum*** | EFer GQui SMad SRms WAbe |

## *Ophiopogon* ✿ (*Convallariaceae*)

| | |
|---|---|
| BWJ 8244 from Vietnam | WCru |
| from India **new** | GCal |
| 'Black Dragon' | see *O. planiscapus* 'Nigrescens' |
| ***bodinieri*** | CBct ECho ERos EWes LEdu |
| - B&L 12505 | CLAP EBee EPPr EPla |
| ***caulescens*** B&SWJ 8230 **new** | WCru |
| aff. ***caulescens*** HWJ 590 | WCru |
| ***chingii*** | EBee EPPr EPla GCal LEdu SCnR |
| ***formosanus*** | CPrp GBin SKHP |
| - B&SWJ 3659 | EBee WCru |

| | | |
|---|---|---|
| | 'Gin-ryu' | see *Liriope spicata* 'Gin-ryu' |
| | ***graminifolius*** | see *Liriope muscari* |
| | ***intermedius*** | CBct CStu EBee EPPr EPla ERos GGar MSte NLar SGar WCot WPGP |
| | - GWJ 9387 | WCru |
| § | - 'Argenteomarginatus' | EBee ECho ERos EWes WPGP |
| | - 'Variegatus' | see *O. intermedius* 'Argenteomarginatus' |
| § | ***jaburan*** | EBee ECho EShb LBMP LEdu MSte NHol WMoo |
| | - 'Variegatus' | see *O. jaburan* 'Vittatus' |
| § | - 'Vittatus' (v) | CMHG CSBt ECho EHoe ELan EMil EPfP EShb EWes LEdu MCCP MGos SAga WCot WFar |
| | ***japonicus*** | CBro ECho EPfP EPla EShb LEdu |
| | - B&SWJ 1871 **new** | WCru |
| | - 'Albus' | CLAP ECho NHol |
| | - 'Compactus' | CDoC EBee SKHP SPla WPGP |
| | - 'Kigimafukiduma' | CBgR CPen MRav SPad WCot |
| | - 'Kyoto' | EPPr NLAp |
| | - 'Minor' | CBct CEnd CKno CSBt EBee EPPr EPfP EPla NLar WPGP |
| | - 'Nanus Variegatus' (v) | CDes EBee EMon NChi WHil |
| | - 'Nippon' | CPrp EBee ECho EHoe EPPr GGar LAst LRHS |
| * | - 'Tama-ryu Number Two' | ECho EPPr |
| * | - 'Variegatus' (v) | CDTJ CKno CPrp ECho LEdu SLPl |
| | ***malcolmsonii*** B&SWJ 5264 | WCru |
| | ***parviflorus*** GWJ 9387 **new** | WCru |
| | - HWJK 2093 **new** | WCru |
| | ***planiscapus*** | CEnd CFee CKno CMHG CPLG CSWP CSam CSev EBee ECho EPPr EPla EShb GAbr MNHC MSte MTho MWat NBro SPad SPla STre WMoo |
| * | - 'Albovariegatus' | WFar |
| | - 'Green Dragon' | ELan |
| | - 'Kansu' **new** | LRHS |
| | - ***leucanthus*** | EPPr WCot |
| | - 'Little Tabby' (v) | CBow CDes CLAP CSpe CWsd EBee ECho EPla MDKP MMoz MWhi NPro WCot WDyG WHal WPGP WTin |
| * | - ***minimus*** | ECho ERos |
| § | - 'Nigrescens' ♀H4 | Widely available |
| | - 'Silver Ribbon' | ECho MDKP SGar |
| | ***scaber*** B&SWJ 1842 **new** | WCru |
| | 'Spring Gold' | CMil EMon |
| | 'Tama-hime-nishiki' (v) | EMon |

## *Ophrys* (*Orchidaceae*)

| | | |
|---|---|---|
| | ***apifera*** | CFir NLAp SHdy WHer |
| | - subsp. ***trollii*** | NLAp |
| | ***apifera*** x ***holoserica*** **new** | NLAp |
| | ***apifera*** x ***scolopax*** **new** | NLAp |
| | ***araneola*** **new** | NLAp |
| | ***bombyliflora*** | NLAp |
| | ***fuciflora*** | NLAp SHdy |
| | ***heldreichii*** **new** | NLAp |
| | ***holoserica*** | NLAp |
| | ***insectifera*** | SHdy |
| | ***speculum*** | NLAp |
| | ***sphegodes*** | NLAp SHdy |

## *Oplismenus* (*Poaceae*)

| | | |
|---|---|---|
| | ***africanus*** 'Variegatus' (v) | see *O. hirtellus* 'Variegatus' |
| § | ***hirtellus*** 'Variegatus' ♀H1 | CHal |
| | ***undulatifolius*** | EBee |

## *Opopanax* (*Apiaceae*)

| | | |
|---|---|---|
| | ***chironium*** | LEdu |

## *Opuntia* ✿ (*Cactaceae*)

| | | |
|---|---|---|
| | ***compressa*** | see *O. humifusa* |
| § | ***humifusa*** | CDTJ EAmu SChr SMad |
| | ***microdasys*** | SWal |
| | - var. ***albospina*** | SWal |
| § | ***polyacantha*** | LPJP SChr SPlb |
| | ***rhodantha*** | see *O. polyacantha* |

## orange, sour or Seville see *Citrus aurantium*

## orange, sweet see *Citrus sinensis*

## *Orbea* (*Asclepiadaceae*)

| | | |
|---|---|---|
| | ***caudata*** **new** | CFwr |
| § | ***variegata*** ♀H1 | CFwr EShb |
| | ***verrucosa*** **new** | CFwr |

## *Orchis* (*Orchidaceae*)

| | | |
|---|---|---|
| | ***anthropophora*** | EFEx |
| | ***elata*** | see *Dactylorhiza elata* |
| | ***foliosa*** | see *Dactylorhiza foliosa* |
| | ***fuchsii*** | see *Dactylorhiza fuchsii* |
| | ***italica*** | SHdy |
| | ***laxiflora*** | see *Anacamptis laxiflora* |
| | ***maculata*** | see *Dactylorhiza maculata* |
| | ***maderensis*** | see *Dactylorhiza foliosa* |
| | ***majalis*** | see *Dactylorhiza majalis* |
| § | ***mascula*** | NLAp SHdy WHer |
| | ***militaris*** | GAuc NLAp WHer |
| | ***morio*** | see *Anacamptis morio* |
| | ***purpurea*** | NLAp SHdy |
| | ***simia*** | NLAp SHdy |

## oregano see *Origanum vulgare*

## *Oreomyrrhis* (*Apiaceae*)

| | | |
|---|---|---|
| | ***argentea*** | CSec EHig NMen |

## *Oreopteris* (*Thelypteridaceae*)

| | | |
|---|---|---|
| § | ***limbosperma*** | SRms WRic |

## *Oreorchis* (*Orchidaceae*)

| | | |
|---|---|---|
| | ***patens*** **new** | WWst |

## *Oresitrophe* (*Saxifragaceae*)

| | | |
|---|---|---|
| | ***rupifraga*** | WCru |

## *Origanum* ✿ (*Lamiaceae*)

| | | |
|---|---|---|
| | ***acutidens*** | WCHb |
| | ***amanum*** ♀H2-3 | CPBP EBee ECho EWes MDKP NBir NMen WAbe WPat |
| | - var. ***album*** | EBee ECho LLHF NSla WAbe |
| | x ***applii*** | ELau |
| | 'Barbara Tingey' | CPBP CSpe CWCL EBee ECho ELan EWes ITim LBee MNrw MSte MTho NWCA SMeo SPhx SUsu WAbe WCFE |
| | 'Bristol Cross' | EBee ECha GBar MHer NGby |
| | 'Buckland' | EBee ECho ECtt EPot MHer MSte NMen NWCA SPhx WAbe WPat WSHC |
| | ***caespitosum*** | see *O. vulgare* 'Nanum' |
| § | ***calcaratum*** | EBee ECho LLHF MTho WAbe WPat |
| | 'Carols Delight' **new** | NGby |
| | ***creticum*** | see *O. vulgare* subsp. *hirtum* |
| | ***dictamnus*** | CArn CStu EBee ECho EEls EPot GPoy LLHF LRHS NWCA SHDw WAbe WJek |
| | 'Dingle Fairy' | CMMP EBee ECho EDAr EPot EWes GBar MCot MHer MLLN MNrw MTho NBir NWCA SBch SIde SIng SRot WGwG WMoo |

| | |
|---|---|
| 'Emma Stanley' | WAbe |
| 'Erntedank' | EBee |
| 'Frank Tingey' | EBee ECho LLHF SUsu |
| 'Gold Splash' | CPbn EPfP GBar SIde WMoo |
| ***heracleoticum*** L. | see *O. vulgare* subsp. *hirtum* |
| 'Hot and Spicy' | CPbn GBar NPri |
| 'Ingolstadt' | SAga SPhx |
| 'Kent Beauty' | Widely available |
| 'Kent Beauty Variegated' (v) | ECho |
| ***laevigatum*** 🏆H3 | CArn CMHG ECho ELan EPfP EPot MHar MHer NBro NMir NPer NWCA SGar SIde SUsu WMoo WPer WSHC |
| - 'Herrenhausen' 🏆H4 | Widely available |
| - 'Hopleys' | Widely available |
| - 'Purple Charm' | EBee EDAr MNHC NBre NBsh SIde |
| ***majorana*** | CArn CPbn CSev ELan ELau MHer MNHC MSal SIde SWal SWat WJek WPer |
| I - 'Aureum' | SWal |
| - Pagoda Bells = 'Lizbell'PBR | CWCL LHop SIde WHoo |
| 'Marchants Seedling' | SMHy |
| ***microphyllum*** | CFee CPbn EDAr GBar MTho NMen SIng SMeo |
| ***minutiflorum*** | EBee ECho LLHF |
| 'Norton Gold' | CBre EBee ECha ECtt EPot GBar GBuc MHer NBre NHol NPer SIde SMrm |
| 'Nymphenburg' | CFee CSam EBee LSou MHer MSte NCob SIde WCru WHer |
| ***onites*** | CArn CHby CPbn CWan ELau GBar ILis MHer MNHC MSal NBlu SIde SPlb WBrk WGwG WHer WJek WPer |
| 'Phoenix Seedling' | SPhx |
| 'Purple Cloud' | NBir |
| 'Rosenkuppel' | CMea CPbn EBee ECha ECtt ELan EPot GCal LHop MCot MHer MLHP MRav MSte NCGa NGHP SMad SMeo SPer SPhx SPla SPlb WMoo WPnn |
| 'Rotkugel' | CAby CMHG CWsd EBee EGle LSou MSte SMrm SPhx WCru |
| ***rotundifolium*** 🏆H4 | EBee ECho ELan LLHF MDKP MHer NBir SBch WAbe |
| - hybrid | MDKP |
| ***scabrum*** | CArn |
| - subsp. ***pulchrum*** | CStu |
| - - 'Newleaze' | LHop SBch WHoo |
| ***syriacum*** | CArn |
| 'Tinpenny Pink' | WTin |
| ***tournefortii*** | see *O. calcaratum* |
| ***tytthanthum*** | EMon |
| ***villosum*** | see *Thymus villosus* |
| ***virens*** | CArn GBar ILis MCCP |
| ***vulgare*** | Widely available |
| - from Israel | ELau |
| - 'Acorn Bank' | CArn CBod CHFP CPbn CPrp EBee EGoo EShb EWes GBar MNHC NHol NLar SAga SIde WCHb WGwG WHer WJek |
| - var. ***album*** | CElw WAlt |
| - 'Aureum' 🏆H4 | Widely available |
| - 'Aureum Crispum' | CPbn CPrp CWan ECha EGoo ELau GAbr GBar GPoy ILis NBid NBlu NGHP SBch SIde SWat WJek WRha |
| - 'Compactum' | Widely available |
| - 'Corinne Tremaine' (v) | NBir WHer |
| - 'Country Cream' (v) | Widely available |
| - ***formosanum*** B&SWJ 3180 | WCru |
| § - 'Gold Tip' (v) | CEnt CMea CPbn CSev EBee ELau GBar ILis MCot MHer MNHC NGHP NPri SIde SPlb SWat WCHb WFar WHer |
| - 'Golden Shine' | CMMP EBee EHoe EWes NGHP SIde WRha |
| § - subsp. ***hirtum*** | CArn CHby CPbn GPoy LEdu MSal SPlb WJek WPer |
| - - 'Greek' | CBod CEnt CPrp CWan ELau MHer MNHC NGHP WGwG |
| § - 'Nanum' | CHFP ECho GBar WJek |
| - 'Nyamba' | GPoy |
| - 'Pink Mist'PBR | EBee |
| - 'Polyphant' (v) | CPbn CSev EBee EGle GBar LSou MLLN NBir WBrE WCHb WJek |
| - subsp. ***prismaticum*** | GBar |
| - 'Thumble's Variety' | CElw CMea CPrp EAEE EBee ECha EGle EGoo EHoe EPot GBar GCal LHop MBri MHer MRav NCob NGHP NHol SIde SSvw SWat WEas WMnd WMoo |
| - 'Tomintoul' | GPoy |
| - 'Variegatum' | see *O. vulgare* 'Gold Tip' |
| - 'Webb's White' | GBar |
| - 'White Charm' | CPbn NHol SIde |
| 'Z'Attar' | MHer SIde |

## *Orixa* (*Rutaceae*)

| | |
|---|---|
| ***japonica*** | CPLG EPfP GAuc NLar WFar WPGP |
| - 'Variegata' (v) | EPfP LLHF NLar SPoG |

## *Orlaya* (*Apiaceae*)

| | |
|---|---|
| ***grandiflora*** | CAby CBre CFir CHFP CSec CSpe LPio MAvo MCot NChi SBch SUsu WCot WFar WHal |

## *Ornithogalum* (*Hyacinthaceae*)

| | |
|---|---|
| ***arabicum*** | CBro CHid CMea EBrs ECho EPfP LAma LRHS MBri MLLN SPhx WCot |
| ***arcuatum*** | WCot |
| ***arianum*** | EBee EBrs ECho |
| ***balansae*** | see *O. oligophyllum* |
| ***caudatum*** | see *O. longibracteatum* |
| ***chionophilum*** | EBee EBrs ECho |
| ***comosum*** | ECho |
| ***dubium*** 🏆H1 | EBrs ECho WCot |
| ***exscapum*** | CStu ECho |
| ***fimbriatum*** | EBee EBrs ECho |
| ***lanceolatum*** | WCot |
| § ***longibracteatum*** | CHEx CSec CStu EBee ECho GAuc SChr WGwG WPrP |
| ***magnum*** | CAvo CFFs CMea CSsd EBee EBrs ECho ERCP GAuc LRHS MNrw WCot WHil |
| - 'Saguramo' | EBrs |
| ***montanum*** | ECho |
| 'Mount Everest' | ECho |
| 'Mount Fuji' | EBrs ECho |
| ***nanum*** | see *O. sigmoideum* |
| ***narbonense*** | EBee EBrs ECho GAuc GBuc LRHS MMHG SPhx WCot |
| ***nutans*** 🏆H4 | CAvo CBro CFFs CHid CMea CStu EBee EBrs ECho EMon EPfP EPot GCal LAma LBMP MAvo MCot MLLN MNrw NBir NMen NWCA SMrm SPhx WAul WCot WFar |
| § ***oligophyllum*** | CStu EBee EBrs ECho EPfP EPot ERCP MMHG MNrw NWCA WCot |
| § ***orthophyllum*** | CStu EBrs WCot |
| - HOA 9405 new | EBee |
| ***platyphyllum*** | EBrs |
| ***ponticum*** | ECho ERos |
| ***pyramidale*** | CDes EBee EBrs ECho EPot GAuc LRHS MNrw WCot |

| | | |
|---|---|---|
| | - short **new** | SMHy |
| | ***pyrenaicum*** | CAvo CStu EBee ECha ERos WCot WShi |
| | - Flavescens Group | EBee |
| | ***reverchonii*** | CDes EBee EBrs ECho ERos WCot |
| | ***saundersiae*** | CHid CSec EBee EBrs ECho |
| | ***schmalhausenii*** | WWst |
| | ***sibthorpii*** | see *O. sigmoideum* |
| § | ***sigmoideum*** | CStu EBrs ECho |
| | ***sintenisii*** | EBee EBrs ECho LRHS |
| | ***sphaerocarpum*** | WCot |
| | ***tenuifolium*** | see *O. orthophyllum* |
| | - subsp. ***aridum*** | WWst |
| | ***thyrsoides*** ♀H1 | CCCN CSec EBrs ECho EPfP ERCP LAma |
| | ***ulophyllum*** | EBee EBrs ECho |
| | ***umbellatum*** | CAvo CBro CFFs CTri EBrs ECho ELan EMon EPfP EWTr GAbr GPoy LAma LHop LRHS MBri MNrw NMen SECG SPer SRms WBVN WFar WHil WPer WShi |
| | ***unifolium*** | ECho |

## *Orobanche* (*Scrophulariaceae*)

| | | |
|---|---|---|
| | sp. | SKHP |

## *Orontium* (*Araceae*)

| | | |
|---|---|---|
| | ***aquaticum*** | CBen CDWL CWat EHon EMFW LLWG LPBA MSKA NLar NPer SWat WMAq |

## *Orostachys* (*Crassulaceae*)

| | | |
|---|---|---|
| | ***furusei*** | EDAr WCot WFar |
| | - 'Grey Cloud' **new** | GKev |
| § | ***spinosa*** | EDAr EWes NMen WFar |

## *Oroxylum* (*Bignoniaceae*)

| | | |
|---|---|---|
| | ***indicum*** | CArn |

## *Orthrosanthus* (*Iridaceae*)

| | | |
|---|---|---|
| | ***chimboracensis*** | CDes CFir MDKP MGos MWea NLar WFar WPGP WPer |
| | - B&SWJ 10234 | WCru |
| | - JCA 13743 | CPou |
| | - RCB/Eq **new** | EBee |
| | ***laxus*** | CBgR CFir CHid CSec CWsd ECou EPau ERos GBuc GMac LLHF MAvo MCot SHom SMad WMoo WPrP |
| | ***multiflorus*** | CDes CSpe CWCL EBee WPGP |
| | ***polystachyus*** | CCVN CSec CSpe CTca CTsd EBee ERos MAvo MWea SMrm SSvw SUsu WMoo WSHC |

## *Orychophragmus* (*Brassicaceae*)

| | | |
|---|---|---|
| | ***violaceus*** **new** | CCCN |

## *Oryzopsis* (*Poaceae*)

| | | |
|---|---|---|
| | ***hymenoides*** | LDai LEdu |
| | ***lessoniana*** | see *Anemanthele lessoniana* |
| | ***miliacea*** | CHrt CKno CSpe EBee ECha EHoe EMon EPPr EWsh GFor GQue LDai NDov SMHy SUsu WCot WPGP |
| | ***paradoxa*** | EPPr |

## *Oscularia* (*Aizoaceae*)

| | | |
|---|---|---|
| § | ***deltoides*** ♀H1-2 | CCCN WCor WEas |

## *Osmanthus* (*Oleaceae*)

| | | |
|---|---|---|
| | ***armatus*** | CAbP CTri EPfP NLar WFar |
| § | × ***burkwoodii*** ♀H4 | Widely available |
| § | ***decorus*** | CBcs CTri EBee ELan EPfP EWTr GKir MGos MRav MWea NLar SPer SPla WBod WDin WFar |
| | ***delavayi*** ♀H4 | Widely available |
| | - 'Latifolius' | CPMA EPfP LRHS MAsh SLon SPoG WFar |
| | ***forrestii*** | see *O. yunnanensis* |
| | × ***fortunei*** | CPLG EPfP LLHF MGos SLPl WFar |
| | ***fragrans*** | EShb SLon |
| | - 'Latifolius' | CBcs |
| | - f. ***thunbergii*** | CBcs |
| § | ***heterophyllus*** | CBcs CDul EBee EPfP EWTr MBar MRav NLar SPer SReu SRms SSta WDin WFar |
| § | - all gold | CAbP CDoC EBee LAst MBlu SPer SPla |
| | - 'Argenteomarginatus' | see *O. heterophyllus* 'Variegatus' |
| § | - 'Aureomarginatus' (v) | CBcs CDoC CMHG CSBt CTsd EBee EHoe EPfP LRHS NWea SHBN SLon SPer SPoG |
| | - 'Aureus' misapplied | see *O. heterophyllus* all gold |
| | - 'Aureus' Rehder | see *O. heterophyllus* 'Aureomarginatus' |
| § | - 'Goshiki' (v) | Widely available |
| N | - 'Gulftide' ♀H4 | CDul EBee ECrN EPfP LRHS MGos NLar SCoo SPoG WFar |
| | - 'Kembu' (v) | NLar |
| | - 'Myrtifolius' | NLar |
| | - 'Ogon' | MBar |
| | - 'Purple Shaft' | CAbP ELan EPfP LRHS MAsh NHol |
| | - 'Purpureus' | CAbP CBcs CBgR CDoC CDul CMHG CSam CWib EBee ECrN EHoe EPfP LRHS MBri MGos MRav NHol SCoo SEND SLim SLon SPer SSpi WDin |
| | - 'Rotundifolius' | CBcs NLar |
| | - Tricolor | see *O. heterophyllus* 'Goshiki' |
| § | - 'Variegatus' (v) ♀H4 | Widely available |
| | ***ilicifolius*** | see *O. heterophyllus* |
| | ***rigidus*** | NLar |
| | ***serrulatus*** | NLar WPGP |
| | ***suavis*** | GKir LRHS NLar |
| § | ***yunnanensis*** | EBee EPfP LRHS MBlu NLar SAPC SArc SSpi WFar WPGP |

## × *Osmarea* see *Osmanthus*

## *Osmaronia* see *Oemleria*

## *Osmitopsis* (*Asteraceae*)

| | | |
|---|---|---|
| | ***asteriscoides*** | GFai |

## *Osmorhiza* (*Apiaceae*)

| | | |
|---|---|---|
| | ***aristata*** B&SWJ 1607 | WCru |

## *Osmunda* ✿ (*Osmundaceae*)

| | | |
|---|---|---|
| | sp. | CCCN |
| | ***cinnamomea*** ♀H4 | CCCN CFwr CLAP CMil CWCL EBee EWes GBin GCal MAsh NMyG WPGP WRic |
| | ***claytoniana*** ♀H4 | CLAP CMil EBee EFer GBin MAsh NHol NLar NMyG NVic WCru WPnP WRic |
| | ***japonica*** | CLAP EBee GBin |
| | ***regalis*** ♀H4 | Widely available |
| | - from southern USA **new** | CLAP |
| | - 'Cristata' ♀H4 | CFwr CLAP EBee ELan GBin MBri MRav NBid NHol NLar NMyG WFib WPGP WRic |
| | - 'Gracilis' **new** | EBee |
| | - 'Purpurascens' | Widely available |
| | - var. ***spectabilis*** | CCCN CLAP WRic |
| | - 'Undulata' | NHol WFib |

## *Osteomeles* (*Rosaceae*)

| | | |
|---|---|---|
| | ***subrotunda*** | MBri |

## *Osteospermum* (*Asteraceae*)

| | | |
|---|---|---|
| | 'African Queen' | see *O.* 'Nairobi Purple' |
| | 'Almach'PBR (Springstar Series) | LSou MBNS |
| | 'Arctur'PBR | LAst |
| | 'Arusha' (Cape Daisy Series) **new** | LSou |
| | Banana Symphony = 'Sekiin47' (Symphony Series) | CCCN CWCL LRHS LSou MBNS SMrm |
| | ***barberae*** misapplied | see *O. jucundum* |
| | 'Blackthorn Seedling' | see *O. jucundum* 'Blackthorn Seedling' |
| | 'Blue Streak' | CCCN |
| | 'Brickell's Hybrid' | see *O.* 'Chris Brickell' |
| | 'Buttermilk' ♀H1+3 | CCCN CHal CTsd ELan WCor WWlt |
| | 'Cannington John' | GCra |
| | 'Cannington Roy' | CBcs CCCN CHrt CMHG COIW CSam EBee ECtt EPfP GAbr LSRN SPoG |
| | 'Castor' | LAst |
| | ***caulescens*** misapplied | see *O.* 'White Pim' |
| § | 'Chris Brickell' | CHal GCal MSte |
| | Dodoma Light Purple = 'Akdolip' (Cape Daisy Series) **new** | WRHF |
| | ***ecklonis*** | CCCN CDTJ CHll CTri GGar GMaP IBlr ISea NBro NGdn WPer |
| | - var. ***prostratum*** | see *O.* 'White Pim' |
| | 'Edna Bond' | WEas |
| | 'Gemma'PBR (Springstar Series) | MBNS |
| | 'Giles Gilbey' (v) | CCCN CHal MBNS NBur |
| | 'Gold Sparkler' (v) | SMrm |
| | 'Gweek Variegated' (v) | CCCN |
| | 'Helen Dimond' | LBuc |
| | (Hip Hop Series) Hip Hop Orange = 'Sakost 013' **new** | LSou |
| | - Hip Hop Yellow = 'Sakost 12'PBR **new** | LSou WGor |
| | 'Hopleys' ♀H3-4 | MHer SEND |
| | 'Irish' | EPot GBuc IGor LSou SMrm |
| § | ***jucundum*** ♀H3-4 | CChe CEnt CMHG CMea CTri CWCL ECha EPfP LRHS LSRN MLHP MRav NBir NChi NGdn NHol NPer SEND SPlb SRms WBVN WBrk |
| § | - 'Blackthorn Seedling' ♀H3-4 | CMea GBuc MWte NGdn SAga SUsu |
| | - var. ***compactum*** | CHEx CLyd CPBP ELan EPfP EShb GCal GGar MBri MHar NPer SPoG SPur WAbe WHoo WPat |
| | - 'Jackarandum' | MDKP |
| § | - 'Killerton Pink' | WPer |
| § | - 'Langtrees' ♀H3-4 | LHop SMrm |
| | - 'Nanum' **new** | EDAr |
| | Kalanga Rosy = 'Aksinto'PBR (Cape Daisy Series) | LRHS |
| | 'Keia'PBR (Springstar Series) | CCCN LSou |
| | 'Killerton Pink' | see *O. jucundum* 'Killerton Pink' |
| § | 'Lady Leitrim' ♀H3-4 | CCCN CHEx CHrt ECha EPfP EShb GBri GCra GGar IBlr LHop LSRN NPer SAga SPoG SSvw WFar |
| | 'Langtrees' | see *O. jucundum* 'Langtrees' |
| | 'Lemon Symphony'PBR (Symphony Series) | CBcs LRHS MBNS SVil |
| | 'Malindi'PBR (Cape Daisy Series) | WGor WRHF |
| | Milk Symphony = 'Seiremi' (Symphony Series) | CCCN CWCL MBNS |
| | 'Mirach' (Springstar Series) | CWCL LSou MBNS |
| § | 'Nairobi Purple' | CCCN CFee CHEx CHal COIW ELan NBur WCor |
| | Nasinga Cream = 'Aknam'PBR (Cape Daisy Series) | CCCN |
| | Nasinga Purple = 'Aksullo'PBR (Cape Daisy Series) | EPfP LRHS |
| | ***oppositifolium*** | CCCN |
| | Orange Symphony = 'Seimora'PBR (Symphony Series) | CCCN CWCL LRHS LSou MBNS SMrm SVil |
| | 'Pale Face' | see *O.* 'Lady Leitrim' |
| | Peach Symphony = 'Seitope'PBR (Symphony Series) | CWCL LRHS SMrm |
| | 'Peggyi' | see *O.* 'Nairobi Purple' |
| I | 'Pink Superbum' | CHEx |
| | 'Pink Whirls' ♀H1+3 | CCCN |
| | 'Pollux'PBR (Springstar Series) | MBNS |
| | 'Port Wine' | see *O.* 'Nairobi Purple' |
| | 'Seaside'PBR (Side Series) | EPfP |
| | 'Serenity Cream' (Serenity Series) | SVil |
| | 'Silver Sparkler' (v) ♀H1+3 | CCCN CDTJ ELan EShb MBNS MHer NBur SSto WBrE |
| | Sonja = 'Sunny Sonja'PBR | EPfP |
| | 'Sparkler' | CCCN CHEx MSte |
| | Springstar Series | CBcs |
| | 'Stardust'PBR | LBuc LRHS NPer SCoo SPoG |
| | 'Sunny Alex'PBR | LRHS |
| | 'Sunny Amanda'PBR | LSou SRGP |
| | 'Sunny Amelia' | LAst SRGP |
| | 'Sunny Cecil'PBR | LRHS SRGP |
| | 'Sunny Dark Martha'PBR | EPfP LAst LRHS |
| | 'Sunny Flora'PBR | SRGP |
| | 'Sunny Martha'PBR | LAst |
| | 'Sunny Mary'PBR | LAst LSou SRGP |
| | 'Sunny Nathalie' | LAst SRGP |
| | 'Sunny Philip'PBR | SRGP |
| | 'Sunny Plum Serena'PBR | SRGP |
| | 'Sunny Serena'PBR | LAst LRHS SRGP |
| | 'Sunny Stephanie'PBR | LAst SRGP |
| | 'Sunny Zara'PBR | SRGP |
| * | 'Superbum' | CHEx |
| I | 'Superbum' x 'Lady Leitrim' | CHEx |
| | 'Tauranga' | see *O.* 'Whirlygig' |
| | 'Tresco Peggy' | see *O.* 'Nairobi Purple' |
| | 'Tresco Pink' | CCCN |
| | 'Tresco Purple' | see *O.* 'Nairobi Purple' |
| | 'Uranus' | SRGP |
| | 'Vega' | LAst |
| | Warembo Arwen = 'Sakcadwar' (Cape Daisy Series) **new** | LSou WGor |
| | 'Weetwood' ♀H3-4 | CCCN CMHG ECtt EPot EShb GCal LHop MBNS MHer MLHP MSte NLar SAga SPoG WEas WFar |
| § | 'Whirlygig' ♀H1+3 | CCCN MHer |
| § | 'White Pim' ♀H3-4 | CDTJ CHll CMHG ELan ELon GBuc LCro MBNS NPer SDix SMrm SPer SPhx SPoG SUsu |
| | 'Wine Purple' | see *O.* 'Nairobi Purple' |
| | 'Wisley Pink' | EPyc |
| | 'Zaurak'PBR (Springstar Series) | CCCN CWCL LAst LSou MBNS WGor |
| | 'Zulu'PBR (Cape Daisy Series) | CCCN |

## *Ostrowskia* (*Campanulaceae*)

| | | |
|---|---|---|
| | ***magnifica*** | MTho |

## *Ostrya* (*Corylaceae*)

| | |
|---|---|
| ***carpinifolia*** | CBcs CDul CLnd CMCN CTho CWib EBee ECrN EHig EMil EPfP EWTr GKir LRHS MBar MBlu MMuc NLar NWea SBLw |
| ***japonica*** | CDul CMCN NLar |
| ***virginiana*** | EPfP IArd |

## *Othonna* (*Asteraceae*)

| | |
|---|---|
| ***capensis*** | CHal |
| ***cheirifolia*** | CCCN CMea EGoo EHoe ELan EWes NBir SEND WBrk WEas WPer |

## *Othonnopsis* see *Othonna*

## *Ourisia* (*Scrophulariaceae*)

| | |
|---|---|
| x ***bitternensis*** 'Cliftonville Roset' | WAbe |
| ***caespitosa*** | EBee GGar GKev IBlr NMen |
| - var. ***gracilis*** | NMen |
| ***coccinea*** | EBee ELon GAbr GBuc GCra GEdr GGar GKev GKir GMac IBlr LRHS NBir NMen NRya NWCA |
| ***crosbyi*** | GEdr GGar IBlr |
| ***crosbyi*** x ***macrocarpa*** | IBlr |
| 'Loch Ewe' | CPLG GAbr GBuc GEdr GGar GKir IBlr MDun WCru WPGP |
| ***macrocarpa*** | IBlr |
| ***macrophylla*** | EBee GBin GBuc GGar IBlr IGor LLHF |
| - subsp. ***lactea*** | IBlr |
| ***macrophylla*** x ***modesta*** | IBlr |
| ***microphylla*** | WAbe |
| - f. ***alba*** | WAbe |
| ***polyantha*** F&W 8487 | CPBP WAbe |
| - 'Cliftonville Scarlet' | CPBP WAbe WFar |
| 'Snowflake' ΨH4 | GAbr GEdr IBlr MDun NBir NMen WAbe |

## *Oxalis* (*Oxalidaceae*)

| | |
|---|---|
| ***acetosella*** | CHid CRWN EBWF MHar MHer NSco SIng WHer WShi |
| - var. ***rosea*** <u>new</u> | SIng WAlt |
| - var. ***subpurpurascens*** | MMHG WCot |
| ***adenophylla*** ΨH4 | Widely available |
| - dark | MTho |
| ***adenophylla*** x ***enneaphylla*** | see *O.* 'Matthew Forrest' |
| ***anomala*** | EBrs ECho ERos WCot |
| ***arborescens*** | CHEx |
| § ***articulata*** | CArn GBuc MTho NPer SEND WCot |
| - 'Alba' | CSec LRHS WCot |
| - 'Aureoreticulata' | MTho |
| - 'Festival' | WCot |
| 'Beatrice Anderson' | LRHS MTho NMen |
| 'Black Velvet' (Xalis Series) <u>new</u> | MBNS |
| ***bowiei*** | CPBP CStu EBee EBrs ECho EPot |
| - 'Amarantha' PBR | EBee EBrs ECho |
| 'Bowles' White' | MTho |
| ***brasiliensis*** | CPBP CStu ECho EPot MTho NMen |
| brick-orange-flowered | WCot |
| 'Burgundy Wine' (Xalis Series) <u>new</u> | MBNS |
| ***chrysantha*** | WAbe |
| ***compacta*** F&W 8011 | CPBP |
| ***corniculata*** var. ***atropurpurea*** | MTho |
| ***deppei*** | see *O. tetraphylla* |
| § ***depressa*** | CStu CTri EBee EBrs ECho EPot EWes GEdr LLHF MTho NBir NLAp NMen NRya NSla SIng SRms WBrE WFar |
| - 'Irish Mist' | CStu EBee EBrs ECho WHil |
| * ***ecklonia*** var. ***sonderi*** | EBee EBrs ECho WCot |
| ***enneaphylla*** ΨH4 | CElw ECho EPot GGar GMaP LRHS MTho NMen NRya SBch WFar |
| - F&W 2715 | CPBP |
| - 'Alba' | CMea CPBP ECho ERos GBuc GEdr GGar NMen NSla NWCA WAbe WIvy |
| - 'Lady Elizabeth' | CPBP |
| - 'Minutifolia' | ERos LLHF LRHS MTho NMen NRya NSla |
| * - 'Minutifolia Rosea' | CGra |
| - 'Rosea' | CBgR EBrs ECho EPot ERos GKev MTho NRya NSla |
| - 'Ruth Tweedie' | CGra NSla |
| - 'Sheffield Swan' | CGra ECho GEdr LLHF NMen NSla WAbe |
| ***falcatula*** | WCot |
| 'Fanny' | CStu EBee EBrs ECho |
| ***flava*** | ECho |
| ***floribunda*** misapplied | see *O. articulata* |
| ***fourcadei*** | WCot |
| ***gigantea*** | CSpe |
| ***glabra*** | CPBP WAbe |
| 'Gwen McBride' | CGra CPBP WAbe |
| ***hedysaroides*** | CCCN |
| 'Hemswell Knight' | NMen |
| ***hirta*** | CPBP EPot MTho |
| - 'Gothenburg' | CPBP EBee ECho ERos MTho NMen SIng |
| ***imbricata*** | CPBP EBee ECho EPot LLHF |
| ***inops*** | see *O. depressa* |
| 'Ione Hecker' ΨH4 | CBgR CGra CLyd CPBP EBrs ECho EPot ERos GEdr GGar GKev GMaP ITim MTho NHar NLAp NMen NRya NSla WAbe WIvy |
| * ***karroica*** | EBee EBrs ECho NMen WCot |
| § ***laciniata*** | CGra ERos ITim MTho NHar NMen NSla WAbe |
| - hybrid seedlings | NHar |
| - 'Seven Bells' | WAbe |
| ***lactea*** double-flowered | see *O. magellanica* 'Nelson' |
| ***lasiandra*** | CCCN EBee EBrs ECho EPot ERos |
| § ***lobata*** | CBro CPBP CStu EBee EBrs ECho ERos EWes LHop LRHS MTho WAbe WFar |
| ***loricata*** | EBrs ECho NMen |
| ***magellanica*** | CRow CSpe CTri ECho EDAr GGar LBee MTho NPro SIng SPlb WFar WMoo WPer |
| - 'Flore Pleno' | see *O. magellanica* 'Nelson' |
| § - 'Nelson' (d) | CRow CSpe CStu EBee ECho EWes GBuc GCal GGar GMac LBee LRHS MTho NBir NPer WMoo WPer WPnP WPrP WPtf |
| ***massoniana*** | EBee EBrs ECho SIng WAbe |
| § 'Matthew Forrest' | NDlv NMen WAbe |
| ***megalorrhiza*** | SChr |
| § ***melanosticta*** | CBro CStu EBee EBrs ECho EPot LLHF SIng |
| ***monophylla*** | EBee EBrs ECho |
| ***namaquana*** | EBee ECho WCot |
| ***obtriangulata*** | EBrs ECho |
| ***obtusa*** | CBgR CLyd CStu EBee EBrs ECho MTho SCnR WCot |
| - apricot-flowered | WCot |
| ***oregana*** | CBgR CDes CHid CRow EBee ELon GBuc GGar WCot WCru WPGP WPrP WSHC |
| - f. ***smalliana*** | EWes WCru |
| ***palmifrons*** | CPBP ECho EPot LLHF MTho |
| ***patagonica*** | EBrs ECho EPot ERos GEdr NMen |
| ***perdicaria*** | see *O. lobata* |
| ***polyphylla*** | EBee EBrs ECho |

| | |
|---|---|
| - var. ***heptaphylla*** | SIng |
| - var. ***pentaphylla*** | EPot |
| § ***ptychoclada*** | CSpe |
| § ***purpurea*** | EBrs ECho MWea WAbe |
| - 'Ken Aslet' | see *O. melanosticta* |
| ***regnellii*** | see *O. triangularis* subsp. *papilionacea* |
| ***rosea*** misapplied | see *O. rubra* |
| § ***rubra*** | EBee EBrs WBrE |
| ***semiloba*** | EBee EBrs ECho GCal NCGa WCot |
| ***speciosa*** | see *O. purpurea* |
| ***squamata*** | LLHF NLAp WPat |
| ***squamosoradicosa*** | see *O. laciniata* |
| ***stipularis*** | LLHF |
| ***succulenta*** misapplied | see *O. ptychoclada* |
| ***succulenta*** ambig. | CHll |
| 'Sunny' | EBrs ECho |
| 'Sunset Velvet' | CHal LAst SVil WBor WCot |
| 'Superstar' | NMen WAbe |
| § ***tetraphylla*** | CAgr CMMP EBee EBrs ECho LAma LRHS MTho NPer WRha |
| * - ***alba*** | ECho |
| - 'Iron Cross' | CHEx CSec EBee EBrs ECho EPot LAma MMHG NBir WBVN WHil WPer |
| 'Tima' | CPBP |
| ***tortuosa*** | WCot |
| ***triangularis*** | CAgr CCCN CDow CHEx CHal CSec CTca ECho EOHP EShb LAma MAvo NBir NBlu NPer WBrE WFar |
| - 'Birgit' | EBee ECho |
| - 'Cupido' | EBee ECho GGar WPer |
| - 'Mijke' | EBee EBrs ECho |
| § - subsp. ***papilionacea*** $\mathbb{Y}^{H1}$ | EBee EBrs ECho LAma LRHS MMHG |
| - - 'Atropurpurea' | CSpe EBee LHop WBVN |
| * - - ***rosea*** | EBee WCot |
| - subsp. ***triangularis*** | EBee EBrs ECho EUJe LDai NCGa |
| ***truncatula*** | SIng |
| ***tuberosa*** | GGar GPoy ILis LEdu |
| 'Ute' | CGra CLyd CPBP GEdr NSla |
| ***valdiviensis*** | EDAr MDKP NBur |
| ***versicolor*** $\mathbb{Y}^{H1}$ | CPBP CStu EBee EBrs ECho EPot ERos MTho NBir NMen SCnR WAbe WCot WHil |
| - 'Clove Ball' | WPtf |
| ***vulcanicola*** | CCCN CStu LSou SDix WDyG |
| - 'Burgundy' | NPri |
| ***zeekoevleyensis*** | WCot |

## *Oxycoccus* see *Vaccinium*

## *Oxydendrum* (*Ericaceae*)

| | |
|---|---|
| ***arboreum*** | CAbP CBcs CDoC CEnd CMCN EBee EPfP IDee IFFs IMGH LRHS MBri MMuc NLar SCoo SSpi SSta WDin WFar WOrn WPGP |
| - 'Chameleon' | SPer SPoG SSpi SSta |

## *Oxylobium* (*Papilionaceae*)

| | |
|---|---|
| ***ellipticum*** | GGar |

## *Oxypetalum* (*Asclepiadaceae*)

| | |
|---|---|
| ***caeruleum*** | see *Tweedia caerulea* |
| ***solanoides*** | CSec CSpe EBee EHig |

## *Oxyria* (*Polygonaceae*)

| | |
|---|---|
| ***digyna*** | CSec GGar NLar |

## *Oxytropis* (*Papilionaceae*)

| | |
|---|---|
| ***borealis*** var. ***viscida*** | CPBP |
| ***oreophila*** var. ***juniperina*** | CPBP |
| ***purpurea*** | LLHF NWCA |
| ***shokanbetsuensis*** | LLHF |

## *Oziroë* (*Hyacinthaceae*)

| | |
|---|---|
| § ***biflora*** new | CSec |

## *Ozothamnus* (*Asteraceae*)

| | |
|---|---|
| § ***coralloides*** $\mathbb{Y}^{H2-3}$ | ECou NDlv NHar SIng WAbe |
| § 'County Park Silver' | EWes ITim MDKP NDlv NLAp NWCA WPat |
| § ***hookeri*** | CBcs CDoC EBee ECou GGar MBrN MRav NLar SPer WJek WPat |
| § ***ledifolius*** $\mathbb{Y}^{H4}$ | CBcs CDoC CMHG EBee ELan EPfP ERas GGar MBri NBir SLon SPer SPoG WDin WHCG WPat WSHC |
| § ***rosmarinifolius*** | CBcs CDoC CTrG CTsd EBee ELan EPfP GGar LRHS MSwo SPer WBod WDin WEas WFar WHCG |
| - 'Kiandra' | ECou |
| - 'Silver Jubilee' $\mathbb{Y}^{H3}$ | Widely available |
| ***scutellifolius*** | ECou |
| ***secundiflorus*** | GGar |
| § ***selago*** | ECou NDlv WCot WThu |
| § - var. ***tumidus*** | ITim SIng WThu |
| 'Sussex Silver' | GGar |
| 'Threave Seedling' | CDoC ELan GBin LRHS SKHP SPer |
| § ***thyrsoideus*** | WFar |

# P

## *Pachyphragma* (*Brassicaceae*)

| | |
|---|---|
| § ***macrophyllum*** | CPom CSev EBee ECGP ECha EGle EHrv ELan EMon GBuc GCal IBlr LRHS MNFA NLar NSti WCot WCru WMoo WPGP WSHC |

## *Pachyphytum* (*Crassulaceae*)

| | |
|---|---|
| ***oviferum*** | SChr SEND |

## *Pachypodium* (*Apocynaceae*)

| | |
|---|---|
| ***brevicaule*** | LToo |
| ***lamerei*** $\mathbb{Y}^{H1}$ | LToo |
| ***lealii*** subsp. ***saundersii*** | LToo |
| ***namaquanum*** | LToo |
| ***rosulatum*** var. ***gracilius*** | LToo |
| ***succulentum*** | LToo |

## *Pachysandra* (*Buxaceae*)

| | |
|---|---|
| ***axillaris*** | CLAP EBee GCal SKHP |
| - BWJ 8032 | WCru |
| - 'Crûg's Cover' new | WCru |
| ***procumbens*** | CLAP EBee EHrv EPla NLar SKHP WCot WCru |
| - 'Angola' (v) new | WCot |
| ***stylosa*** | EPla MRav NLar SMad |
| ***terminalis*** | Widely available |
| - 'Green Carpet' $\mathbb{Y}^{H4}$ | Widely available |
| - 'Green Sheen' | ECha MGos WFar |
| - 'Variegata' (v) $\mathbb{Y}^{H4}$ | Widely available |

## *Pachystachys* (*Acanthaceae*)

| | |
|---|---|
| ***lutea*** $\mathbb{Y}^{H1}$ | CHal EShb LRHS MJnS |

## *Pachystegia* (*Asteraceae*)

| | |
|---|---|
| § ***insignis*** | GGar IDee |

## *Pachystima* see *Paxistima*

## *Packera* (*Asteraceae*)

| | |
|---|---|
| § ***aurea*** | MSal SKHP |

# *Paederia* (Rubiaceae)

| | |
|---|---|
| ***scandens*** | WSHC |
| - HWJ 656 | WCru |
| - var. ***mairei*** B&SWJ 989 | WCru |

# *Paederota* (*Scrophulariaceae*)

| | |
|---|---|
| § ***bonarota*** | CLyd |
| ***lutea*** | NWCA |

# *Paeonia* ✿ (*Paeoniaceae*)

| | |
|---|---|
| 'Age of Gold' (S) | WCAu |
| ***albiflora*** | see *P. lactiflora* |
| 'Alley Cat' | WAul |
| 'America' | GBin MBri WCAu |
| 'Angelo Cobb Freeborn' | WCAu |
| ***anomala*** | CFir CSec EBee EGle GEdr MHom MPhe NLar NSla WCot |
| § - var. ***anomala*** | GBin |
| - var. ***intermedia*** | EBee EBrs EGle GCal |
| - subsp. ***veitchii*** | see *P. veitchii* |
| 'Argosy' | WCAu |
| ***arietina*** | see *P. mascula* subsp. *arietina* |
| 'Athena' | GBin |
| 'Auten's Red' | WCAu |
| 'Bai He Wo Xue' (S) **new** | SImb |
| 'Bai Xue Ta' (S) **new** | SImb |
| ***banatica*** | see *P. officinalis* subsp. *banatica* |
| 'Banquet' (S) | WCAu |
| § 'Bartzella' (d) **new** | GBin |
| ***beresovskii*** | EBee EBrs |
| 'Black Monarch' | WCAu |
| 'Black Panther' (S) | WCAu |
| 'Black Pirate' (S) | CKel WCAu |
| 'Blaze' | GMaP LRHS WCAu WCot |
| Blue and Purple Giant | see *P. suffruticosa* 'Zi Lan Kui' |
| 'Bolero' | CHFP |
| 'Border Charm' **new** | GBin |
| 'Bridal Icing' | WCAu |
| 'Bride's Dream' | GBin |
| ***broteroi*** | EBee EBrs SKHP |
| 'Buckeye Belle' | CKel EBee EPfP GBin LFur LPio MBri MHom MNrw MSte MWea NBPN NBrd SPoG SWat WAul WCAu |
| 'Burma Midnight' | GBin |
| 'Burma Ruby' | GBin WCAu |
| 'Cai Hui' (S) **new** | SImb |
| 'Callie's Memory' **new** | GBin |
| ***cambessedesii*** 🏆$^{H2-3}$ | CBro CSpe EBee EBrs EGle EPPr EPot GBin GKev LHop LRHS MSte MTho NBir NLar NMen NSla NWCA SSpi SUsu WAbe WCot |
| 'Canary Brilliant' PBR **new** | GBin |
| 'Cao Zhou Hong' (S) **new** | SImb |
| 'Cardinal's Robe' **new** | GBin |
| 'Carina' **new** | GBin |
| 'Carol' | WCAu |
| ***caucasica*** | see *P. mascula* subsp. *mascula* |
| 'Chalice' **new** | GBin |
| x ***chamaeleon*** | EBee EBrs |
| 'Cheddar Royal' | GBin |
| 'Cherry Ruffles' | WCAu |
| 'Chinese Dragon' (S) | CKel WCAu |
| 'Chocolate Soldier' | GBin |
| 'Chong Zhong Xiao' (S) **new** | SImb |
| 'Chu E Huang' (S) **new** | SImb |
| 'Chun Hong Jiao Yan' (S) **new** | SImb |
| 'Claire de Lune' | GBin LCro MBri SHar WCAu WCot |
| 'Claudia' | WCAu |
| 'Coral Charm' | GBin WCot |
| 'Coral Fay' | GBin MSte WCAu |
| 'Coral 'n' Gold' | WCAu |
| 'Coral Sunset' | GBin NBrd |
| 'Coral Supreme' | GBin WCot |
| ***corallina*** | see *P. mascula* subsp. *mascula* |
| ***coriacea*** **new** | EBee |
| - var. ***atlantica*** | CBro |
| Crimson Red | see *P. suffruticosa* 'Hu Hong' |
| 'Crusader' | WCAu |
| 'Cytherea' | MHom WCAu |
| 'Dancing Butterflies' | EBee GKir LSRN WCAu WHil |
| ***daurica*** | see *P. mascula* subsp. *triternata* |
| 'Dawn Glow' | WCAu |
| ***decomposita*** | GBin MPhe |
| ***decora*** | see *P. peregrina* |
| 'Defender' | WCAu |
| ***delavayi*** (S) 🏆$^{H4}$ | Widely available |
| - BWJ 7775 | WCru |
| - from China (S) | MPhe |
| - var. ***angustiloba*** f. ***alba*** | EBrs |
| § - - f. ***angustiloba*** (S) | SSpi |
| - - - 'Coffee Cream' | CKel |
| § - - f. ***trollioides*** (S) | EBrs WCAu |
| - var. ***atropurpurea*** | see *P. delavayi* var. *delavayi* f. *delavayi* |
| § - var. ***delavayi*** f. ***delavayi*** | WAbe |
| § - - f. ***lutea*** (S) | Widely available |
| - var. ***ludlowii*** | see *P. ludlowii* |
| - var. ***lutea*** | see *P. delavayi* var. *delavayi* f. *lutea* |
| - 'Mrs Colville' **new** | GCal |
| - 'Mrs Sarson' | CHid CSpe ELan GBin LFur MCCP NCGa NHol SWat |
| - Potaninii Group | see *P. delavayi* var. *angustiloba* f. *angustiloba* |
| - Trollioides Group | see *P. delavayi* var. *angustiloba* f. *trollioides* |
| ***delavayi*** x ***delavayi*** var. ***delavayi*** f. ***lutea*** | ELan |
| ***delavayi*** x ***suffruticosa*** | SSpi |
| 'Dou Lu' (S) **new** | SImb |
| Drizzling Rain Cloud | see *P. suffruticosa* 'Shiguregumo' |
| 'Early Glow' | GBin |
| 'Early Scout' | GBin MHom NCGa WAul WCAu WCot |
| 'Early Windflower' | EGle GBin WCAu |
| 'Eastgrove Ruby Lace' | WEas |
| 'Eden's Perfume' | GBin LRHS NLar SHBN WCot |
| 'Elizabeth Foster' | WCAu |
| 'Ellen Cowley' | GBin WCAu |
| ***emodi*** | CAvo EBrs LPio |
| 'F. Koppius' | CKel |
| 'Fairy Princess' | GBin WAul WCAu |
| 'Fen Er Qiao' (S) **new** | SImb |
| 'Fen He Piao Xiang' (S) **new** | SImb |
| 'Fen Zhong Guan' (S) **new** | SImb |
| 'Feng Dan Bai' (S) **new** | SImb |
| 'Firelight' | GBin WCAu |
| 'First Dutch Yellow' | see *P.* 'Garden Treasure' |
| 'Flame' | EBee EBrs GBin GKir MNrw MSte MWea SPer WAul WCAu WCot |
| Fragrance and Beauty | see *P. suffruticosa* 'Lan Tian Yu' |
| 'Fuchsia Cuddles' **new** | GBin |
| § Gansu Group (S) | CKel EBrs MHom MPhe |
| - 'Bai Bi Fen Xia' (S) | MPhe |
| - 'Bai Bi Lan Xia' (S) | MPhe |
| - 'Bing Shan Xue Lian' (S) | MPhe |
| - 'Cheng Xin' (S) | MPhe |
| - 'Fen He' (S) | MPhe |
| - 'Fen Jin Yu Zhu' (S) **new** | MPhe |
| - 'Feng Xian' (S) | MPhe |
| - 'He Hua Deng' (S) **new** | MPhe |
| - 'Hei Feng Die' (S) **new** | MPhe |
| - 'Hei Tian E' (S) **new** | MPhe |

| | |
|---|---|
| – 'Hei Xuan Feng' (S) | MPhe |
| – 'He Ping Lian' (S) | MPhe |
| – 'Hong Lian' (S) | MPhe |
| – 'Hong Xia Ying Xue' (S) **new** | MPhe |
| – 'Huang He' (S) | MPhe |
| – 'Hui He' (S) | MPhe |
| – 'Ju Hua Fen' (S) **new** | MPhe |
| – 'Lan Hai Yiu Bo' (S) | MPhe |
| – 'Lan He' (S) | MPhe |
| – 'Lan Tian Meng' (S) **new** | MPhe |
| – 'Li Xiang' (S) | MPhe |
| – 'Lian Chun' (S) | MPhe |
| – 'Mo Hai Yin Bo' (S) **new** | MPhe |
| – 'Mo Hai Yin Zhou' (S) **new** | MPhe |
| – 'Shu Sheng Peng Mo' (S) | MPhe |
| – 'Tao Hua Nu' (S) **new** | MPhe |
| – 'Tie Mian Wu Si' (S) **new** | MPhe |
| – 'Xue Hai Bing Xin' (S) | MPhe |
| – 'Xue Lian' (S) | MPhe SImb |
| – 'Ye Guang Bei' (S) **new** | MPhe |
| – 'Yu Ban Xiu Qiu' (S) **new** | MPhe |
| – 'Yu Lu Lian Dan' (S) **new** | MPhe |
| – 'Zi Die Ying Feng' (S) | MPhe |
| – 'Zong Ban Bai' (S) **new** | MPhe |
| Gansu Mudan Group | see *P.* Gansu Group |
| § 'Garden Treasure' **new** | GBin |
| 'Gaugin' (S) | WCAu |
| 'Gejinzi' (S) **new** | SImb |
| 'Gold Standard' | GBin WAul |
| 'Golden Bowl' | CKel |
| 'Golden Dream' | see *P.* 'Bartzella' |
| 'Golden Glow' | WCAu |
| 'Golden Isles' | CKel |
| 'Golden Thunder' | CKel |
| Green Dragon Lying on a Chinese Inkstone | see *P. suffruticosa* 'Qing Long Wo Mo Chi' |
| 'Hei Hua Kui' | see *P. suffruticosa* 'Hei Hua Kui' |
| 'Hesperus' (S) | WCAu |
| 'High Noon' (S) | CKel MPhe NBPC SPer SWat WCAu |
| 'Ho-gioku' | GBin |
| 'Hoki' | CKel |
| 'Hong Bao Shi' (S) **new** | SImb |
| 'Hong Zhu Nv' (S) **new** | SImb |
| 'Honor' | WCAu |
| 'Horizon' | GBin |
| 'Hua Er Qiao' (S) **new** | SImb |
| 'Huan Huai Kui' (S) **new** | SImb |
| § 'Huang Hua Kui' (S) | CKel |
| 'Huang Jin Chui' (S) **new** | SImb |
| ***humilis*** | see *P. officinalis* subsp. *microcarpa* |
| 'Huo Lian Jin Dan' (S) **new** | SImb |
| 'Illini Belle' | GBin |
| 'Illini Warrior' | WAul WCAu |
| 'Isani Gidui' | see *P. lactiflora* 'Isami-jishi' |
| ***japonica*** misapplied | see *P. lactiflora* |
| ***japonica*** ambig. | GEdr |
| ***japonica*** (Makino) Miyabe & Takeda | EBee |
| 'Jean E. Bockstoce' | WCAu |
| 'Jin Xiu Qiu' (S) **new** | SImb |
| 'Jin Yu Jiao Zhang' (S) | SImb |
| 'Jing Yu' (S) **new** | SImb |
| 'Joseph Rock' | see *P. rockii* |
| 'Joyce Ellen' | GBin WCAu |
| 'Juan Ye Hong' (S) **new** | SImb |
| 'Julia Rose' **new** | GBin |
| 'Jun Yan Hong' (S) **new** | SImb |
| 'Kamikaze' | CKel |
| ***kavachensis*** | EBee EBrs EGle GBin GCal MSte |
| 'Kinkaku' | see *P.* x *lemoinei* 'Souvenir de Maxime Cornu' |
| 'Kinko' | see *P.* x *lemoinei* 'Alice Harding' |
| 'Kinshi' | see *P.* x *lemoinei* 'Chromatella' |
| 'Kintei' | see *P.* x *lemoinei* 'L'Espérance' |
| 'Koikagura' | CKel |
| 'Kokamon' | CKel |
| 'Kun Shan Ye Guang' | CKel |
| § ***lactiflora*** | EBee EHrv LFur MPhe WWst |
| – 'A.F.W. Hayward' | CKel |
| – 'Abalone Pearl' | GBin |
| – 'Adolphe Rousseau' | CBcs EBee NBlu WCAu |
| * – 'Afterglow' | CKel |
| – 'Agida' | GBin MRav |
| – 'Agnes Mary Kelway' | CKel |
| – ***alba*** | CExc |
| – 'Albert Crousse' | CBcs CKel GBin NBir NBlu SWat WCAu |
| – 'Alexander Fleming' | CHFP EBee ECot MBNS MWea NBir SWat WBrE WCAu |
| – 'Algae Adamson' | CKel |
| – 'Alice Harding' | GBin WCAu |
| – 'Amibilis' | WCAu |
| – 'Amo-no-sode' | WCAu |
| – 'Angel Cheeks' | GBin WCAu |
| – 'Anna Pavlova' | CKel MRav |
| – 'Antwerpen' | MBri WCAu |
| – 'Arabian Prince' | CKel |
| – 'Argentine' | SHBN WCAu |
| – 'Asa Gray' | CKel |
| – 'Auguste Dessert' | CKel GBin MWea WCAu WCot |
| § – 'Augustin d'Hour' | CKel EBee |
| – 'Aureole' | CKel MRav |
| – 'Avalanche' | EBee EPfP GBin NBPC NLar SMrm |
| – 'Ballerina' | CKel MRav |
| – 'Barbara' | CKel WCAu |
| – 'Baroness Schröder' | EBee ELan GBin |
| – 'Barrington Belle' | EPfP GBin MBri MSte WAul |
| – 'Barrymore' | CHFP CKel |
| – 'Beacon' | CKel |
| – 'Beatrice Kelway' | CKel |
| – 'Belle Center' | GBin WCAu |
| – 'Best Man' | NGdn WCAu |
| – 'Bethcar' | CKel |
| – 'Better Times' | WCAu |
| – 'Bev' **new** | GBin |
| – 'Big Ben' | GBin WCAu |
| – 'Blaze of Beauty' | CKel |
| – 'Bluebird' | CKel |
| – 'Blush Queen' | ELan WCAu |
| – 'Border Gem' | MRav |
| – 'Bouchela' | EBee |
| – 'Boule de Neige' | EWll |
| – 'Bower of Roses' | CKel |
| – 'Bowl of Beauty' ♀H4 | Widely available |
| – 'Bowl of Cream' | EBee GBin SHBN SWat SWvt WCAu |
| – 'Bracken' | CKel |
| – 'Break o' Day' | WCAu |
| – 'Bridal Gown' | GBin WCAu |
| – 'Bridal Shower' **new** | MBNS |
| – 'Bridal Veil' | CKel |
| – 'Bridesmaid' | CKel MRav |
| – 'British Beauty' | CKel MRav |
| – 'Bunker Hill' | CKel EBee GBin MBri SPer SWvt WCAu |
| – 'Butter Bowl' | GBin MBri WCAu |
| – 'Canarie' | MBri |
| – 'Candeur' | CKel EBee |
| – 'Cang Long' | CKel |
| – 'Captivation' | CKel |
| – 'Carnival' | CKel |
| – 'Caroline Allain' | CKel |
| – 'Carrara' | GBin |

| | |
|---|---|
| – 'Cascade' | CKel |
| – 'Catherine Fontijn' | CHFP CKel GBin SHar WCAu |
| – 'Charles' White' | EBee EGle EPfP GBin NBPC WCAu |
| – 'Charm' | GBin WCAu |
| – 'Cheddar Charm' | WAul WCAu |
| – 'Cheddar Gold' ♀H4 | GKir |
| – 'Cheddar Supreme' **new** | GBin |
| – 'Cherry Hill' | WCAu |
| – 'Chestine Gowdy' | CKel |
| – 'Chief Wapello' | GBin |
| – 'Chun Xiao' | CKel |
| – 'Circus Circus' **new** | GBin |
| – 'Claire Dubois' | CKel GBin WCAu |
| – 'Cora Stubbs' | MBNS |
| – 'Cornelia Shaylor' | WCAu |
| – 'Couronne d'Or' | GBin WCAu |
| – 'Crimson Glory' | CKel |
| – 'Crinkles Linens' **new** | GBin |
| – 'Dandy Dan' | WCAu |
| – 'Dawn Crest' | CKel EBee |
| – 'Dayspring' | CKel |
| – 'Daystar' | MRav |
| – 'Decorative' | CKel |
| – 'Delachei' | CKel |
| – 'Denise' | MRav |
| – 'Dinner Plate' | GBin MBri SPer WCAu WCot |
| – 'Do Tell' | GBin NLar SPer WCAu |
| – 'Docteur H. Barnsby' | CKel |
| – 'Doctor Alexander Fleming' | CKel SWat SWvt |
| – 'Dominion' | CKel |
| – 'Don Juan' | CKel |
| – 'Doreen' | CFir EBee GBin MBri MRav SHBN SHar WCAu |
| – 'Doris Cooper' | WCAu |
| – 'Dorothy Welsh' | CKel |
| – 'Dragon' | CKel |
| – 'Dresden' | WCAu |
| – 'Duchesse de Nemours' ♀H4 | Widely available |
| – 'Duchesse d'Orléans' | WCAu |
| – 'Edouard Doriat' | WCAu |
| – 'Edulis Superba' | CKel EBee EGle ELan GBin MBNS NMoo NPer SHar SPer SPur WCAu |
| – 'Elizabeth Stone' | CKel |
| – 'Ella Christine Kelway' | CKel |
| – 'Elsa Sass' | WCAu |
| – 'Emma Klehm' | GBin WCAu |
| – 'Emperor of India' | CKel MRav |
| – 'Enchantment' | CKel |
| – 'English Princess' | CKel |
| – 'Ethereal' | CKel |
| – 'Evelyn Tibbets' | GBin |
| – 'Evening Glow' | CKel |
| – 'Evening World' | CKel |
| – 'Fairy's Petticoat' | WCAu |
| – 'Fashion Show' | CKel |
| – 'Félix Crousse' ♀H4 | CBcs CKel CTri ELan EPfP EWsh GMaP LAst MBNS MRav MSte NBir SMrm SRms SWat WCAu |
| – 'Felix Supreme' | GBin |
| – 'Fen Chi Jin Yu' | CKel |
| – 'Festiva Maxima' ♀H4 | CHFP CKel CSBt CTri CWCL EBee ECot ELan EPfP GBin GKir LRHS MSte NBir NLar SHBN SPer SPla SRms SRot SWat SWvt WAul WCAu WHoo |
| – 'Florence Ellis' | GBin |
| – 'France' | CKel |
| – 'Fuji-no-mine' | GBin |
| – 'Garden Lace' | GBin |
| – 'Gardenia' | EBee EBrs EPfP GBin SHBN |
| – 'Gay Paree' | GBin NLar SPer WCAu |
| – 'Gayborder June' | CKel WCAu |
| – 'Gene Wild' | GBin WCAu |
| – 'Général MacMahon' | see *P. lactiflora* 'Augustin d'Hour' |
| – 'General Wolfe' | CKel |
| – 'Germaine Bigot' | CKel WCAu |
| – 'Gertrude' | GBin |
| – 'Gilbert Barthelot' | WCAu |
| – 'Gladys McArthur' **new** | GBin |
| – 'Gleam of Light' | CKel |
| – 'Globe of Light' | GBin |
| – 'Gloriana' | WCAu |
| – 'Glory Hallelujah' | WCAu |
| – 'Glowing Candles' | WCAu |
| – 'Go-Daigo' | GBin |
| – 'Golden Fleece' | WCAu |
| – 'Green Lotus' | WAul |
| – 'Guidon' | WCAu |
| – 'Gypsy Girl' | CKel |
| – 'Hakodate' | CKel |
| – 'Heartbeat' | CKel |
| – 'Helen Hayes' | GBin WCAu |
| – 'Henri Potin' | GBin |
| – 'Henry Bockstoce' | GBin |
| – 'Her Grace' | CKel |
| – 'Herbert Oliver' | CKel |
| – 'Hermione' | CKel GBin |
| – 'Hiawatha' | WCAu |
| – 'Hit Parade' | WCAu |
| – 'Honey Gold' | ELan GBin GKir LPio NBrd SHBN SPoG WAul WCAu |
| – 'Huang Jin Lun' | CKel |
| – 'Hyperion' | CKel |
| – 'Immaculée' | EBee GBin LPio MBri SPoG |
| – 'Inspecteur Lavergne' | CKel EBee LAst LRHS MBri MWea SPer WAul WCAu WCot |
| – 'Instituteur Doriat' | CKel GBin MBri WCAu |
| § – 'Isami-jishi' | GBin |
| – 'Jacorma' | CFir GBin WHoo |
| – 'Jacques Doriat' | CKel |
| – 'Jadwigha' | EBee |
| – 'James Pillow' | WCAu |
| – 'Jan van Leeuwen' | EBee EPfP GBin MSte WCAu WCot |
| – 'Jappensha-Ikhu' | GBin |
| – 'Jeanne d'Arc' | CKel |
| – 'Jewel' | CKel |
| – 'Jin Chi Yu' | CKel |
| – 'John Howard Wigell' | WCAu |
| – 'Joseph Plagne' | CKel |
| – 'Joy of Life' | CKel |
| – 'June Morning' | CKel |
| – 'June Rose' | WCAu |
| – 'Kakoden' **new** | GBin |
| – 'Kansas' | CHFP EBee ELan EPfP ERas GBin GKir MBri NBir NGdn NMoo WCAu WCot WFar |
| – 'Karen Gray' | GBin WCAu |
| – 'Karl Rosenfield' | CKel CSBt EBee ECot EGle EPfP GKir LAst LCro LRHS MSte SPer SPla SPoG SRms STes SWvt WFar WHoo |
| – 'Kathleen Mavoureen' | CKel |
| – 'Kelway's Betty' | CKel |
| – 'Kelway's Brilliant' | CKel |
| – 'Kelway's Circe' | CKel |
| – 'Kelway's Daystar' | CKel |
| – 'Kelway's Exquisite' | CKel |
| – 'Kelway's Glorious' | CSam EBee EPfP GBin GKir LBMP LFur LPio MBNS NLar SMrm WCAu |
| – 'Kelway's Lovely' | CKel GBin |
| – 'Kelway's Lovely Lady' | CKel |
| – 'Kelway's Majestic' | CKel |
| – 'Kelway's Scented Rose' | CKel |
| – 'Kelway's Supreme' | CKel SWat |

| | | |
|---|---|---|
| | – 'King of England' | GBin |
| | – 'Knighthood' | CKel |
| | – 'Kocho-jishi' | CKel |
| | – 'Königswinter' **new** | GBin |
| § | – 'Koningin Wilhelmina' | GBin MNrw |
| | – 'Krinkled White' | EBee GBin MHom MRav NLar SHar SMeo SUsu WAul WCAu WCot |
| | – 'La Belle Hélène' | CKel |
| | – 'La France' | GBin |
| | – 'La Lorraine' | CKel |
| | – 'Lady Alexandra Duff' $\mathbb{Y}^{H4}$ | CKel EBee EPfP GBin GKir MRav MWea NBir SCoo SRms SWvt WCAu |
| | – 'Lady Kate' | WCAu |
| | – 'Lady Ley' | CKel |
| | – 'Lady Mayoress' | CKel |
| | – 'Lady Orchid' | EPfP NGdn WCAu |
| | – 'Lancaster Imp' | GBin WAul |
| | – 'Langport Triumph' | CKel |
| | – 'Laura Dessert' $\mathbb{Y}^{H4}$ | EBee EPfP GBin GKir MBri MWea SHBN SPer WCAu |
| | – 'Le Cygne' | GBin |
| | – 'L'Eclatante' | CKel EBee GBin |
| | – 'Legion of Honor' | CKel WCAu |
| | – 'Lemon Ice' | CKel |
| | – 'Lemon Queen' | GBin |
| | – 'L'Etincelante' | GBin LCro |
| | – 'Lights Out' | GBin |
| | – 'Lillian Wild' | EBee GBin WCAu |
| | – 'Little Medicineman' | CElw EBee GBin NBhm |
| | – 'Liukrecija' | GBin |
| | – 'Lois Kelsey' | WCAu |
| | – 'Longfellow' | CKel |
| | – 'Lora Dexheimer' | WCAu |
| | – 'Lord Calvin' | WCAu |
| | – 'Lord Kitchener' | CKel GBin |
| | – 'Lorna Doone' | CKel |
| | – 'Lotus Queen' | GBin NLar SHar WCAu |
| | – 'Louis Barthelot' | WCAu |
| | – 'Louis Joliet' | ELan MSte |
| | – 'Lowell Thomas' | WCAu |
| | – 'Lyric' | CKel |
| | – 'Madame Calot' | ERas SRms WCAu |
| | – 'Madame Claude Tain' | MBri |
| | – 'Madame de Verneville' | CKel WCAu |
| | – 'Madame Ducel' | CKel WCAu |
| | – 'Madame Emile Debatène' | CWCL EBee MBNS NMoo NOrc SHBN WCAu |
| | – 'Madame Gaudichau' **new** | MAvo |
| | – 'Madame Jules Dessert' | EBee WCAu |
| | – 'Madelon' | CKel WCAu |
| | – 'Maestro' | GBin |
| | – 'Magic Orb' | CKel |
| | – 'Margaret Truman' | CKel WCAu |
| | – 'Marguérite Gerard' | WCAu |
| | – 'Marie Crousse' | WCAu |
| | – 'Marie Lemoine' | CKel EBee GBin WCAu WCot |
| | – 'Marietta Sisson' | WCAu |
| | – 'Mary Brand' | WCAu |
| | – 'Masterpiece' | CKel |
| | – 'May Treat' **new** | GBin |
| | – 'Merry Mayshine' | GBin WCAu |
| | – 'Midnight Sun' | MBri WCAu |
| | – 'Minnie Shaylor' | WCAu |
| | – 'Mischief' | WCAu |
| | – 'Miss America' | EPfP GBin WCAu |
| | – 'Miss Eckhart' | CKel EBee GBin WCAu |
| | – 'Miss Mary' | EPfP LAst SHar |
| | – 'Mister Ed' | GBin WCAu |
| | – 'Mistral' | CHFP CKel MBri |
| | – 'Mo Zi Ling' | WCAu |
| | – 'Monsieur Jules Elie' $\mathbb{Y}^{H4}$ | CKel EBee EPfP GBin LAst LPio MBri MHom NBPC NCGa SPer SPla WAul WCAu WHoo |
| | – 'Monsieur Martin Cahuzac' | CFir EBee GBin WCAu |
| | – 'Moon of Nippon' | EBee |
| | – 'Moon River' | EPfP GBin SHBN |
| | – 'Moonglow' | WCAu |
| | – 'Mother's Choice' | GBin SHBN WCAu WCot |
| | – 'Mr G.F. Hemerik' | CKel EBee GBin MBri WCAu WCot |
| | – 'Mr Thim' | WCAu |
| | – 'Mrs Edward Harding' | WCAu |
| | – 'Mrs F.J. Hemerik' | WCAu |
| | – 'Mrs Franklin D. Roosevelt' | GBin WCAu |
| | – 'Mrs J.V. Edlund' | GBin WCAu |
| | – 'Mrs Livingston Farrand' | WCAu |
| | – 'My Pal Rudy' | GBin WCAu |
| | – 'Myrtle Gentry' | GBin |
| | – 'Nancy Nicholls' | WCAu |
| | – 'Nancy Nora' | SPer |
| | – 'Neomy Demay' **new** | GBin |
| | – 'Nice Gal' | WCAu |
| | – 'Nick Shaylor' | GBin WCAu |
| | – 'Nippon Beauty' | EBee EGle GBin NBPC NLar |
| | – 'Ornament' | CKel |
| | – 'Orpen' | CKel |
| | – 'Paola' | CKel |
| | – 'Paul Bunyan' | GBin |
| | – 'Paul M. Wild' | NLar WCAu |
| | – 'Peche' | EBee |
| * | – 'Pecher' | CWCL LPio NMoo NPer SMrm |
| | – 'Peregrine' | CKel |
| | – 'Peter Brand' | GBin NLar |
| | – 'Philippe Rivoire' | WCAu |
| | – 'Philomèle' | WCAu |
| | – 'Pico' | WCAu |
| | – 'Pillow Talk' | EBee ERas GBin WCAu |
| | – 'Pink Cameo' | EBee NBrd NLar SHBN WCAu WCot |
| | – 'Pink Giant' | WCAu |
| | – 'Pink Lemonade' | WCAu |
| | – 'Pink Parfait' | GBin LRHS SPer WCAu WCot |
| | – 'Pink Princess' | GBin MBri WCAu |
| | – 'Polar King' | WCAu |
| | – 'Port Royale' | CKel |
| | – 'President Franklin D. Roosevelt' | SWat WCAu |
| | – 'Président Poincaré' | CKel SWat |
| | – 'President Taft' | see *P. lactiflora* 'Reine Hortense' |
| | – 'Primevere' | EBee EPfP EWll GBin GKir LAst LPio MSte NBir NLar NMoo SHBN SHar SPer WCAu |
| | – 'Qi Hua Lu Shuang' | CKel |
| | – 'Qing Wen' | CKel |
| | – 'Queen of Sheba' | WCAu |
| | – 'Queen Victoria' | GBin |
| | – 'Queen Wilhelmina' | see *P. lactiflora* 'Koningin Wilhelmina' |
| | – 'Raoul Dessert' | WCAu |
| | – 'Raspberry Sundae' | ELan GBin MRav NBrd NLar SPer STes WCAu |
| | – 'Ray Payton' **new** | GBin |
| | – 'Red Dwarf' | CKel |
| | – 'Red Emperor' | WCAu |
| | – 'Red Rover' | CKel |
| | – 'Red Sarah Bernhardt' | ELan |
| § | – 'Reine Hortense' | CKel GBin MRav WCAu |
| | – 'Renato' | GBin NCGa |
| | – 'Richard Carvel' | WCAu |
| | – 'Ruth Cobb' | WCAu |
| | – 'Sante Fe' | EPfP SHBN WCAu |
| | – 'Sarah Bernhardt' $\mathbb{Y}^{H4}$ | Widely available |
| | – 'Scarlet O'Hara' | GBin |
| | – 'Schaffe' | GBin |
| | – 'Sea Shell' | GBin NLar SHar |
| | – 'Shawnee Chief' | WCAu |
| | – 'Shen Tao Hua' | CKel |

| | |
|---|---|
| – 'Shimmering Velvet' | CKel SAga |
| – 'Shi-pen Kue' | EBee |
| – 'Shirley Temple' | CHFP CKel CWCL EBee ELan GBin GKir GMaP LCro LFur MBNS MRav MSte NBir SPoG WCAu WCot |
| – 'Silver Flare' | CKel |
| – 'Soft Salmon Joy' | GBin |
| – 'Solange' | CKel EBee GBin LPio NLar STes WCAu |
| – 'Sorbet' | CWCL EBee EPfP GKir LPio MBNS NBPC NBir NLar NMoo NPer SMrm STes WBor WCAu |
| – 'Spellbinder' **new** | GBin |
| – 'Starlight' | WCAu |
| – 'Strephon' | CKel |
| – 'Sweet Melody' | GBin WCAu |
| – 'Sweet Sixteen' | WCAu |
| – 'Sword Dance' | EBee EGle EWll GBin SPoG |
| – 'Taff' | EBee |
| – 'Tamate-boko' | WCAu |
| – 'The Mighty Mo' | GBin |
| – 'The Nymph' | NBir |
| – 'Thérèse' | WCAu |
| – 'Tom Eckhardt' | GBin SPer |
| – 'Top Brass' | EBee GBin MRav NLar WCAu |
| – 'Topeka Garnet' **new** | GBin |
| – 'Toro-no-maki' | WCAu |
| – 'Translucient' | CKel |
| – 'Victoire de la Marne' | EBee |
| – 'Violet Dawson' | GBin |
| – 'Vogue' | EBee GBin SWvt WCAu |
| – 'Walter Faxon' | GBin |
| – 'West Elkton' | GBin |
| – 'Westerner' | GBin WCAu |
| – 'White Ivory' | WCAu |
| – 'White Rose of Sharon' | CKel |
| – 'White Wings' | CBcs CKel CTri EBee EGle ELan EPfP GBin GKir LCro LFur LPio MAvo MSte MWea NBPC NSti SPer SWat SWvt WAul WCAu WCot |
| – 'Whitleyi Major' ♀H4 | GKir MPhe WCot |
| – 'Wiesbaden' | WCAu |
| – 'Wilbur Wright' | GBin WCAu |
| – 'Wine Red' **new** | GBin |
| – 'Wladyslawa' | EBee EBrs GBin WCot |
| – 'Xue Feng' | CKel |
| – 'Yan Fei Chu Yu' | CKel |
| – 'Yan Zi Dian Yu' | CKel |
| – 'Zhong Sheng Feng' **new** | GBin |
| – 'Zhu Sha Dian Yu' | CKel |
| – 'Zuzu' | GBin WAul WCAu |
| x ***lagodechiana*** | EBrs |
| 'Late Windflower' | EBrs EGle GCra LPio MHom |
| x ***lemoinei*** (S) | GBin WHal |
| § – 'Alice Harding' (S) | CKel SPer WCAu |
| § – 'Chromatella' (S) | CKel LAma |
| § – 'L'Espérance' (S) | LAma WCAu |
| § – 'Souvenir de Maxime Cornu' (S) | CKel EMui EPfP LAma LRHS MGos WCAu |
| 'Lian Bao Shi' (S) **new** | SImb |
| 'Ling Hua Zhan Lu' (S) **new** | SImb |
| ***lithophila*** | see *P. tenuifolia* subsp. *lithophila* |
| ***lobata*** 'Fire King' | see *P. peregrina* |
| 'Lois Arleen' | WCAu |
| 'Lou Yan Hong' (S) **new** | SImb |
| 'Lu Fen' (S) **new** | SImb |
| 'Lu Xiang Qiu' (S) **new** | SImb |
| § ***ludlowii*** (S) ♀H4 | Widely available |
| ***lutea*** | see *P. delavayi* var. *delavayi* f. *lutea* |
| – var. ***ludlowii*** | see *P. ludlowii* |
| ***macrophylla*** | MPhe |
| 'Magenta Gem' | WAul |
| 'Mai Fleuri' | WCAu |

| | |
|---|---|
| ***mairei*** | CExc CFir MPhe WCot |
| 'Marchioness' (S) | CKel WCAu |
| ***mascula*** | CBro EBee EPfP LHop LLHF NBir NLar WCot |
| – from Sicily | MPhe |
| § – subsp. ***arietina*** | MWat WEas WKif |
| – – 'Northern Glory' | WCAu |
| – subsp. ***hellenica*** | EBrs MHom |
| – – from Sicily | MPhe |
| § – subsp. ***mascula*** | EBee EBrs EGle GBin MHom NLar WCot |
| – – from Georgia | MPhe WPGP |
| § – subsp. ***russoi*** | EBrs EGle GBin WCot WThu |
| – – from Sardinia | MPhe |
| – – 'Reverchoni' | EBee EBrs MHom |
| § – subsp. ***triternata*** | CLAP EBee EBrs EGle LFur MHom MPhe NLar WBor WCot |
| – – from Crimea | WPGP |
| 'Mei Gui Hong' (S) **new** | SImb |
| 'Mikuhino Akebono' | CKel |
| ***mlokosewitschii*** ♀H4 | Widely available |
| – 'Fedora' | EBrs |
| – hybrids **new** | GKev |
| – 'Pearl Rose' **new** | GBin |
| ***mollis*** | see *P. officinalis* subsp. *villosa* |
| 'Molouzhenghui' (S) **new** | SImb |
| 'Montezuma' | MBri WCAu |
| 'Moonrise' | WCAu |
| 'My Love' | GBin |
| 'Ni Hong Huan Cai' (S) **new** | SImb |
| 'Nymphe' | CKel EBee EPfP GKir LPio MRav NBrd WAul WCAu |
| ***obovata*** ♀H4 | CFir EBrs EGle GKir LFur MPhe MSal WCot |
| – var. ***alba*** ♀H4 | CExc EBrs GBin GEdr GKev NDlv WAbe WEas WThu |
| – 'Grandiflora' | GKir |
| – var. ***willmottiae*** | MPhe |
| ***officinalis*** | CMil EBee EGle EWsh GCra GPoy |
| – WM 9821 from Slovenia | MPhe |
| – 'Alba Plena' | CPou GKir GMaP MRav MSte SWvt WCAu |
| – 'Anemoniflora Rosea' ♀H4 | EBee EGle EPfP GBin GKir MBri MHom SWvt WCAu |
| § – subsp. ***banatica*** | EBee EBrs EPPr GKev MHom MPhe MSte WCAu WCot |
| – 'China Rose' | GBin WCAu |
| – subsp. ***humilis*** | see *P. officinalis* subsp. *microcarpa* |
| – 'Lize van Veen' | GBin WCAu |
| § – subsp. ***microcarpa*** | EBee |
| – 'Mutabilis Plena' | EBee IBlr WCAu |
| – 'Rosea Plena' ♀H4 | CKel EBee ECtt EPfP GBin GKir GMaP LAst LHop MRav SPer SWat SWvt WCAu WFar |
| – 'Rosea Superba Plena' | WCAu |
| – 'Rubra Plena' ♀H4 | CPou CTri CWCL EBee EBrs ECtt EPfP GAbr GBin GCra GKir GMaP LAst LHop MBri MHom MRav NGdn SHBN SPer SRms SWat SWvt WAul WCAu WCot WFar |
| § – subsp. ***villosa*** | CKel CMdw EBee EBrs ELan GAbr GBin GKev NLar SEND WCAu WFar |
| 'Oriental Gold' | CKel |
| ***ostii*** (S) | CExc CKel MPhe |
| § – 'Feng Dan Bai' (S) | CKel EBee GBin MPhe WCAu |
| 'Paladin' | GBin |
| ***papaveracea*** | see *P. suffruticosa* |
| ***paradoxa*** | see *P. officinalis* subsp. *microcarpa* |
| 'Paula Fay' | EBee EPfP GBin MRav NLar WCAu |
| 'Peachy Rose' | GBin |
| Peony with the Purple Roots | see *P. suffruticosa* 'Shou An Hong' |

| | | |
|---|---|---|
| § | ***peregrina*** | CAby CBro CHFP CWsd EBee EBrs ECho EPot GBin GEdr MPhe NLar NSla SSpi WAbe WCAu WCot |
| | - 'Fire King' | GBin |
| § | - 'Otto Froebel' ♀H4 | GBin MHar NLar WCAu WCot |
| | - 'Sunshine' | see *P. peregrina* 'Otto Froebel' |
| | 'Phoenix White' (S) | MBlu |
| | 'Pink Hawaiian Coral' | GBin SHar WCot |
| | 'Postilion' | GBin WCAu |
| | ***potaninii*** | see *P. delavayi* var. *angustiloba* f. *angustiloba* |
| | 'Prairie Charm' | GBin |
| | 'Prairie Moon' | GBin NBrd NLar |
| | 'Qing Xiang Bai' (S) **new** | SImb |
| | 'Qing Xin Hong' (S) **new** | SImb |
| | 'Red Charm' | EBrs GBin LPio MBNS MBri MHom SHBN WCAu WCot |
| | 'Red Glory' | GBin |
| | 'Red Magic' | EBee MBri NBPC NLar SMrm WFar |
| | 'Red Red Rose' | WCAu |
| | 'Renown' (S) | CKel |
| | 'Requiem' | GBin WCAu |
| | 'Robert W. Auten' | WCAu |
| § | ***rockii*** (S) | CBcs CKel CSpe EBee EPfP GAuc MPhe NLar WCot |
| | - hybrid | see *P.* Gansu Group |
| | - subsp. ***linyanshanii*** | MPhe |
| | 'Roman Gold' | CKel |
| | ***romanica*** | see *P. peregrina* |
| | 'Rose Garland' | GBin WCAu |
| | 'Roselette' | GBin WCAu |
| | Rouge Red | see *P. suffruticosa* 'Zhi Hong' |
| | 'Roy Pehrson's Best Yellow' | GBin |
| | ***ruprechtiana*** | EBrs WCot |
| | ***russoi*** | see *P. mascula* subsp. *russoi* |
| | 'Scarlett O'Hara' | GBin NBrd SHar SPer WCAu WCot |
| | 'Shan Hu Tai' (S) **new** | SImb |
| | Shandong Red Lotus | see *P. suffruticosa* 'Lu He Hong' |
| | 'Shao Nu Qun' (S) **new** | SImb |
| | 'Sheng Dan Lou' (S) **new** | SImb |
| | 'Sheng Ge Jin' (S) **new** | SImb |
| | 'Shi Ba Hao' (S) **new** | SImb |
| | 'Shimano-fuji' | CKel |
| | 'Showanohokori' | CKel |
| | 'Silver Dawn' | GBin |
| | ***sinensis*** | see *P. lactiflora* |
| | ***sinjianensis*** | see *P. anomala* var. *anomala* |
| | x ***smouthii*** | MBri |
| | 'Soshi' | GBin |
| | 'Stardust' | WCAu |
| | ***steveniana*** | EBee EBrs GBin MHom MPhe NLar |
| § | ***suffruticosa*** (S) | CWib ELan GBin MGos MPhe NBlu |
| | - 'Akashigata' (S) | CKel |
| | - 'Alice Palmer' (S) | CKel |
| | - 'Bai Yu' (S) | CBcs |
| | - 'Bai Yulan' (S) | LLHF |
| | - Bird of Rimpo | see *P. suffruticosa* 'Rimpo' |
| | - Black Dragon Brocade | see *P. suffruticosa* 'Kokuryū-nishiki' |
| | - Black Flower Chief | see *P. suffruticosa* 'Hei Hua Kui' |
| | - Brocade of the Naniwa | see *P. suffruticosa* 'Naniwa-nishiki' |
| | - 'Cardinal Vaughan' (S) | CKel |
| | - Charming Age | see *P. suffruticosa* 'Howki' |
| | - 'Chen Hong' (S) | SImb |
| | - 'Da Hu Hong' (S) | SImb |
| | - 'Dou Lu' (S) | CBcs CKel MPhe |
| | - Double Cherry | see *P. suffruticosa* 'Yae-zakura' |
| | - 'Duchess of Kent' (S) | CKel |
| | - 'Duchess of Marlborough' (S) | CKel |
| | - 'Er Qiao' (S) | CBcs CKel MPhe |
| | - Eternal Camellias | see *P. suffruticosa* 'Yachiyo-tsubaki' |
| | - 'Fen Qiao' (S) | CBcs |
| | - Flight of Cranes | see *P. suffruticosa* 'Renkaku' |
| | - Floral Rivalry | see *P. suffruticosa* 'Hana-kisoi' |
| | - 'Fuji Zome Goromo' (S) | CKel |
| * | - 'Glory of Huish' (S) | CKel |
| | - 'Godaishu' (S) | CKel LAma LRHS MPhe SPer |
| | - 'Guan Shi Mo Yu' (S) | MPhe SImb |
| § | - 'Hakuojisi' (S) | CKel EPfP WCAu |
| § | - 'Hana-daijin' (S) | LAma LRHS SPer WCAu |
| § | - 'Hana-kisoi' (S) | CKel GBin LAma MPhe WCAu |
| | - 'Haru-no-akebono' (S) | CKel |
| § | - 'Hei Hua Kui' (S) | MPhe SImb |
| § | - 'Higurashi' (S) | EPfP |
| § | - 'Howki' (S) | WCAu |
| § | - 'Hu Hong' (S) | EBee WCAu |
| | - Jewel in the Lotus | see *P. suffruticosa* 'Tama-fuyo' |
| | - Jewelled Screen | see *P. suffruticosa* 'Tama-sudare' |
| | - 'Jia Ge Jin Zi' (S) | CKel |
| | - 'Jitsugetsu-nishiki' (S) | CKel |
| | - 'Joseph Rock' | see *P. rockii* |
| | - Kamada Brocade | see *P. suffruticosa* 'Kamada-nishiki' |
| § | - 'Kamada-fuji' (S) | CKel LAma WCAu |
| § | - 'Kamada-nishiki' (S) | CKel |
| § | - 'Kaow' (S) | CKel WCAu |
| | - King of Flowers | see *P. suffruticosa* 'Kaow' |
| | - King of White Lions | see *P. suffruticosa* 'Hakuojisi' |
| * | - 'Kingdom of the Moon' (S) | LRHS |
| | - 'Kinkaku' | see *P.* x *lemoinei* 'Souvenir de Maxime Cornu' |
| | - 'Kinshi' | see *P.* x *lemoinei* 'Alice Harding' |
| | - 'Kokucho' (S) | CKel |
| § | - 'Kokuryū-nishiki' (S) | CKel GBin LAma SPer SPoG |
| | - 'Koshi-no-yuki' (S) | CKel |
| § | - 'Lan Tian Yu' (S) | SImb |
| § | - 'Lu He Hong' (S) | SImb WCAu |
| | - Magnificent Flower | see *P. suffruticosa* 'Hana-daijin' |
| | - 'Montrose' (S) | CKel |
| * | - 'Mrs Shirley Fry' (S) | CKel |
| | - 'Mrs William Kelway' (S) | CKel |
| § | - 'Naniwa-nishiki' (S) | CKel |
| | - 'Nigata Akashigata' (S) | CKel |
| | - Pride of Taisho | see *P. suffruticosa* 'Taisho-no-hokori' |
| § | - 'Qing Long Wo Mo Chi' (S) | CKel SImb WCAu |
| | - 'Reine Elisabeth' (S) | CKel |
| § | - 'Renkaku' (S) | CKel LRHS SPer WCAu |
| § | - 'Rimpo' (S) | CKel EPfP GBin LAma SPer |
| | - subsp. ***rockii*** | see *P. rockii* |
| | - 'Rou Fu Rong' (S) | EBee SImb WCAu |
| | - 'Sheng Hei Zi' (S) | CBcs |
| § | - 'Shiguregumo' (S) | CKel |
| | - 'Shimadaigin' (S) | CKel MPhe |
| | - 'Shimane-chojuraku' (S) | CKel |
| | - 'Shimane-hakugan' (S) | CKel |
| | - 'Shimane-seidai' (S) | CKel |
| | - 'Shimanishiki' (S) | CKel SPer |
| | - 'Shin Shima Kagayaki' (S) | CKel |
| | - 'Shintoyen' (S) | CKel |
| § | - 'Shou An Hong' (S) | SImb |
| | - 'Sumi-no-ichi' (S) | CKel |
| | - 'Superb' (S) | CKel |
| § | - 'Taisho-no-hokori' (S) | CKel LRHS WCAu |
| § | - 'Taiyo' (S) | CKel EPfP LAma LRHS MPhe SPer |
| § | - 'Tama-fuyo' (S) | CKel LAma |
| § | - 'Tama-sudare' (S) | CKel LCro WCAu |
| | - The Sun | see *P. suffruticosa* 'Taiyo' |
| | - Twilight | see *P. suffruticosa* 'Higurashi' |
| | - Wisteria at Kamada | see *P. suffruticosa* 'Kamada-fuji' |
| | - 'Wu Jin Yao Hui' (S) | CBcs SImb WCAu |
| | - 'Wu Long Peng Sheng' (S) | CKel GBin SImb WCAu |
| | - 'Xiao Tao Hong' (S) | CBcs |
| | - 'Xue Ta' (S) | CKel |
| § | - 'Yachiyo-tsubaki' (S) | CKel LAma NBlu WCAu |
| § | - 'Yae-zakura' (S) | LAma WCAu |

| | | |
|---|---|---|
| | - 'Yan Long Zi Zhu Pan' (S) | CKel |
| | - 'Yin Hong Qiao Dui' (S) | CKel SImb |
| | - 'Yomo-zakura' (S) | LRHS |
| | - 'Yoshinogawa' (S) | CKel EPfP LRHS |
| | - 'Yu Ban Bai' (S) | SImb |
| | - 'Zha Sha Lei' (S) | GBin |
| | - 'Zhao Fen' (S) | NBPC NPer SImb |
| § | - 'Zhi Hong' (S) | CKel SImb |
| | - 'Zhu Sha Lei' (S) | CKel EBee SImb |
| | - 'Zi Er Qiao' (S) | CKel |
| § | - 'Zi Lan Kui' (S) | CKel SImb |
| | 'Sunshine' | see *P. peregrina* 'Otto Froebel' |
| | 'Taiheko' | CKel |
| | 'Ten' i' | CKel |
| | ***tenuifolia*** | CLAP CSpe EBee EGle EPPr GAuc GBin GCal GKir LFur LPio MAvo MDun MHom MSte MWea NMen NSla SMad SPoG WBor WCAu WCot |
| | - subsp. ***carthalinica*** | MPhe |
| § | - subsp. ***lithophila*** | EBee MHom MPhe WWst |
| | - 'Plena' | EBrs EPot GEdr LFur NBhm NLar WWst |
| | - 'Rosea' | EBrs |
| | 'Thunderbolt' (S) | WCAu |
| | ***tomentosa*** | CMil MHom MPhe |
| | ***turcica*** | GBin |
| | 'Vanilla Twist' | WAul |
| § | ***veitchii*** | CAby EBee EBrs EPfP GAuc GBin GCal GEdr GKev GKir GMaP LPio MHom MTho NBid NDlv NLar NMen SSpi WCAu |
| | - from China | MPhe |
| | - 'Alba' | LPio SPhx |
| | - pale-flowered **new** | GCal |
| | - var. ***woodwardii*** | CAvo CMdw CMil EBee EBrs ECho EGle ERos GBin GCra GGar GKev GKir LPio MRav MTho NSla NWCA SSpi WCAu WCot WHoo WWst |
| I | - - 'Alba' | EBrs |
| | 'Vesuvian' | CKel WCAu |
| | 'Viking Full Moon' **new** | GBin |
| | 'Walter Mains' | WCAu |
| | White Phoenix | see *P. ostii* 'Feng Dan Bai' |
| | 'Wine Angel' | GBin |
| | ***wittmanniana*** | EBee EBrs GBin GCal NLar WCAu WCot |
| | 'Xiang Yu' (S) **new** | SImb |
| | 'Xiao Hu Die' (S) **new** | SImb |
| § | 'Yao Huang' (S) | CBcs MPhe SImb WCAu |
| | Yao's Yellow | see *P.* 'Yao Huang' |
| | 'Yellow Crown' | GBin SHar WCAu |
| | 'Yellow Dream' | GBin SCoo WCAu WCot |
| | 'Yellow Emperor' | GBin WCot |
| | Yellow Flower of Summer | see *P.* 'Huang Hua Kui' |
| | 'Yellow Gem' **new** | GBin |
| | 'Yian Long Zi Zhu Pan' (S) **new** | SImb |
| | 'Ying Ri Hong' (S) **new** | SImb |
| | 'Yu Lan Piao Xiang' (S) **new** | SImb |
| | 'Zhi Hu Die' (S) **new** | SImb |
| | 'Zhong Sheng Huang' (S) **new** | SImb |
| | 'Zhuang Yuan Hong' (S) **new** | SImb |

## *Paesia* (*Dennstaedtiaceae*)

| | | |
|---|---|---|
| | ***scaberula*** | CDes CLAP NBir SSpi WAbe |

## *Paliurus* (*Rhamnaceae*)

| | | |
|---|---|---|
| | ***spina-christi*** | CArn CBcs IDee NLar SLon |

## *Pallenis* (*Asteraceae*)

| | | |
|---|---|---|
| § | ***maritima*** | CCCN NWCA |
| | - 'Golden Dollar' | NPri |

## *Pamianthe* (*Amaryllidaceae*)

| | | |
|---|---|---|
| | ***peruviana*** **new** | WVal |

## *Panax* (*Araliaceae*)

| | | |
|---|---|---|
| | ***bipinnatifidus*** var. ***bipinnatifidus*** **new** | EBee |
| | ***ginseng*** | EBee GKev GPoy |
| | ***japonicus*** | GPoy WCru |
| | - BWJ 7932 | WCru |
| | ***quinquefolius*** | GPoy MMuc MSal |

## *Pancratium* (*Amaryllidaceae*)

| | | |
|---|---|---|
| | ***maritimum*** | CArn CSec CTca EBee EBrs ECho GKev LRHS |

## *Pandanus* (*Pandanaceae*)

| | | |
|---|---|---|
| | ***utilis*** | EAmu LPal |

## *Pandorea* (*Bignoniaceae*)

| | | |
|---|---|---|
| | ***jasminoides*** | CHal CHll CRHN CTri CTsd EBak EBee ECot EPfP EShb LRHS SOWG |
| | - 'Alba' | EShb |
| § | - 'Charisma' (v) | CBcs CBow CHll EBee EMil EPfP EShb LSou SOWG SPer WCot |
| | - 'Lady Di' | CHEx SOWG WCot |
| | - 'Rosea' | MJnS SMrm |
| | - 'Rosea Superba' ♀H1 | CBcs CHEx CRHN EBee SBod SPer |
| | - 'Variegata' | see *P. jasminoides* 'Charisma' |
| | ***lindleyana*** | see *Clytostoma calystegioides* |
| | ***pandorana*** | CRHN EBee IDee LRHS SAdn SLim |
| | - 'Golden Showers' | CBcs CCCN CRHN EBee EShb MRav SEND SLim SOWG SPoG |

## *Panicum* (*Poaceae*)

| | | |
|---|---|---|
| | ***amarum*** 'Dewey Blue' **new** | CKno |
| | ***bulbosum*** | CKno EHoe EPPr EPla |
| | ***clandestinum*** | EBee EHoe EPPr EPla EWes GFor MCCP NPro |
| | ***miliaceum*** 'Purple Majesty' | CWib WBor |
| | - 'Violaceum' | CKno CSpe |
| | 'Squaw' | EBla LRHS NOrc |
| | ***virgatum*** | CHFP CRWN CTri GFor LCro NBre WMnd WPer |
| | - 'Blue Tower' | CKno ELon EPPr SApp SPhx SUsu |
| | - 'Cloud Nine' | CKno CPen EBee EGle EPPr LCro LHop MAvo NDov NLar SApp SMHy SPhx SUsu WHal |
| | - 'Dallas Blues' | CKno CPen CPrp CSpe EAEE EBee EBla ECha EHoe EPPr EWes EWsh LCro LEdu MAvo MRav MSte NBsh NOak SApp SHDw SMHy SMeo SPer WFar WMoo |
| | - 'Farbende Auslese' **new** | EBee |
| | - 'Hänse Herms' | CKno EAlp EBee EGle EHoe LPio MAvo MSte SApp SPhx SPla WFar |
| | - 'Heavy Metal' | Widely available |
| | - 'Heiliger Hain' | CHar EBee MWea |
| I | - 'Kupferhirse' | CKno EBee EPPr |
| | - 'Northwind' | CKno CPen EBee EPPr MAvo NDov SApp SMHy SPhx WFar |
| | - 'Pathfinder' | SApp |
| | - 'Prairie Sky' | CKno CWCL EAEE EBee EGle EHoe ELon EPPr GBin LEdu LPio MAvo MBri NLar SApp SMHy SMeo SPhx SUsu WPGP |
| | - 'Red Cloud' | CKno EGle MSte |
| | - 'Red Metal' **new** | IPot |
| | - 'Rehbraun' | EBee EBrs EGle EHoe EPPr EWsh LEdu LPio NGdn NOak SAga SApp SMrm SPhx SWal WCAu WFar WTin |

| | | |
|---|---|---|
| | - 'Rotstrahlbusch' | CKno CPrp CWib EBee EBla EGle EHoe EPPr MAvo MBri MSte MWhi NBea NOrc SMrm SPer SWal WCot WMnd WMoo WPGP |
| | - 'Rubrum' | CKno EBee ECha ECot EHoe ELan EPPr EPfP LRHS MAvo MRav SApp SDix SHBN SPla WMoo WPrP |
| | - 'Shenandoah' | Widely available |
| | - 'Squaw' | Widely available |
| | - 'Strictum' | CSpe EBee EHoe EHul EMil EPPr EWes LEdu LPla NLar SApp SMHy SMeo SPhx SUsu WMoo |
| | - 'Warrior' | Widely available |

## *Papaver* ✿ (*Papaveraceae*)

| | | |
|---|---|---|
| | ***alboroseum*** | LRHS |
| | 'Alpha Centauri' (Super Poppy Series) | LLHF SWat WHoo |
| | ***alpinum*** L. | CSec CSpe ECho LRHS NBlu SIng SPet SRms SWat WFar |
| | - 'Famecheck Double Orange' (d) | EFam |
| | - 'Flore Pleno' (d) | NBir |
| | ***amurense*** | LEdu NLar SWat |
| | ***anomalum album*** | CSpe |
| | ***apokrinomenon*** | CSec ELan |
| | ***argemone*** | CSec |
| | ***atlanticum*** | EBee GKev LDai MLan NBre NBro SPlb |
| | - 'Flore Pleno' (d) | CSec CSpe IFro MCCP NBre NBro WFar |
| | 'Aurora' (Super Poppy Series) | SWat |
| | 'Beyond Red' (Super Poppy Series) | SWat |
| | ***bracteatum*** | see *P. orientale* var. *bracteatum* |
| | 'Bright Star' (Super Poppy Series) | SWat |
| | ***burseri*** | SRot |
| | 'Cathay' (Super Poppy Series) | SWat |
| | 'Celebration' (Super Poppy Series) | SWat |
| | ***commutatum*** 𝕐H4 | CSpe CWCL ELan LEdu SWat WEas |
| | ***corona-sancti-stephani*** | SWat |
| | 'Eccentric Silk' (Super Poppy Series) | SWat |
| | ***fauriei*** | GKev WRos |
| § | 'Fire Ball' (d) | ECha GCal IGor LHop MLLN MWat NBid NBre NBro NLar SHGN SWat WMnd WRHF |
| | ***glaucum*** **new** | CSec |
| | 'Harlequin' (Super Poppy Series) | SWat |
| | 'Heartbeat' PBR (Super Poppy Series) | SWat |
| | ***heldreichii*** | see *P. pilosum* subsp. *spicatum* |
| | ***hybridum*** 'Flore Pleno' (d) | NSti SWat |
| | ***involucratum*** | NWCA |
| | 'Jacinth' (Super Poppy Series) | CDes LLHF SWat WHoo |
| | ***lateritium*** | CHid CPou SRms |
| | - 'Fire Ball' | see *P.* 'Fire Ball' |
| | - 'Nanum Flore Pleno' | see *P.* 'Fire Ball' |
| | 'Lauffeuer' | SWat |
| | 'Matador' 𝕐H4 | WBor |
| | 'Medallion' (Super Poppy Series) | CDes LLHF SWat WHoo |
| § | ***miyabeanum*** | CSec CSpe ECho ELan LRHS NWCA WFar WPer |
| | - ***album*** | ECho |
| | - ***tatewakii*** | see *P. miyabeanum* |
| | ***nanum*** 'Flore Pleno' | see *P.* 'Fire Ball' |
| § | ***nudicaule*** | CSec ELan GKir |
| | - 'Aurora Borealis' | CSpe |
| | - Champagne Bubbles Group | NBlu NPri SWat WFar |
| * | - var. ***croceum*** 'Leder' **new** | CSec |
| | - Garden Gnome Group | see *P. nudicaule* Gartenzwerg Series |
| § | - Gartenzwerg Series | COlW CSpe EMil GAbr MBri MHav NLar SPlb WFar WGor |
| | - 'Illumination' | MBri |
| | - 'Pacino' | EMil EWll LRHS NLar SPet SPoG SRms WFar |
| | - 'Summer Breeze Orange' 𝕐H4 | MBri NPri |
| | - 'Summer Breeze Yellow' | NPri |
| | - Wonderland Series | EHrv SPet |
| | - - 'Wonderland Orange' | NPri |
| | - - 'Wonderland White' | NPri |
| | - - 'Wonderland Yellow' | NPri |
| N | ***orientale*** | CBcs EPfP LAst NBlu NNor SRms SWat WBor WBrE WFar WPer |
| | - 'Abu Hassan' | SWat |
| | - 'Aglaja' 𝕐H4 | CElw EBee ECtt GAbr GBBs GBin LAst LPio MSte NCGa NGdn NSti SAga SMrm SMrs SPhx SUsu SWat WCot WHoo |
| | - 'Aladin' | NBre SWat |
| | - 'Ali Baba' | NBre SWat |
| | - 'Alison' | SWat |
| | - 'Allegro' | CMea CSBt EAEE EBee ECtt GAbr GKir GMaP LAst LCro LRHS MBNS MBri MHer MRav NCGa NGdn NVic SPer SPlb SWat SWvt WBVN WCAu |
| | - 'Arwide' | CMil SWat |
| | - 'Aslahan' | ECha ELon MRav NBre SWat |
| | - 'Atrosanguineum' | NBre SWat |
| | - 'Avebury Crimson' | MWat SWat |
| | - 'Baby Kiss' PBR | EBee ECtt MAvo SWat |
| | - 'Ballkleid' | ECha SWat |
| | - 'Beauty Queen' | CCge EAEE EBee ECha ECot GMac LPio LRHS MRav NGdn SDix SWat |
| | - 'Bergermeister Rot' | SWat |
| | - 'Big Jim' | SPla SWat |
| | - 'Black and White' 𝕐H4 | CDes CSpe EBee ECha EGle EHrv ELan EPfP GMaP LBMP LRHS MRav MSte NBPC SApp SPla SWat WCAu |
| | - 'Blackberry Queen' | SWat |
| | - 'Blickfang' | NBre SWat |
| | - 'Blue Moon' | WHal |
| | - 'Bolero' | EBee ECtt NCGa NLar |
| | - 'Bonfire' | EAEE EHrv LRHS LSou NCob |
| | - 'Bonfire Red' | EBee SWat WCAu |
| § | - var. ***bracteatum*** 𝕐H4 | CWsd NBir NBur SMHy SMrm SWat WMoo WRHF |
| | - 'Brilliant' | EBee LRHS MWat NBre NBur NGdn NLar SWat WFar WMoo |
| | - 'Brooklyn' | CWCL EBee ECtt IPot LPio LSRN MAvo NBre SWat |
| | - 'Burning Heat' | EBee ECtt MSCN SPer |
| | - 'Carmen' | MNrw MSCN MSte NBPC NCGa NLar |
| * | - 'Carneum' | NBre NLar SPoG |
| | - 'Carnival' | CMil EBee NBre NLar SWat |
| | - 'Castagnette' | NLar |
| | - 'Catherina' | NBre SWat |
| | - 'Cedar Hill' | EAEE EBee ECtt EWes GCal GMac LRHS MRav NBre NBsh SMrm SWat |
| | - 'Cedric Morris' 𝕐H4 | CSpe ECha EGle ELan EPPr LPio MRav MSte SPhx SWat WCot WHoo WMnd |
| | - 'Central Park' | EBee WFar |
| I | - 'Charming' pink-flowered | CAby CCge EAEE EBee ECtt MNFA MWat NGdn SPhx SWat |

- 'Checkers' CTri MHav MLHP SEND
- 'China Boy' EBee SWat WHrl
- 'Choir Boy' CEnt ECtt EGle NBur NLar SGar STes SWat WHrl WMoo
- 'Clochard' CElw EBee SWat
- 'Coral Reef' EBee GBBs MHer MLHP NBur SAga SMeo SWat WHer WMoo
- 'Corrina' EBee NBre SWat
- 'Curlilocks' CPar EAEE EBee ECtt ELan ELon EPfP LRHS MRav MWat SAga SMrs SPer SPoG SRms SWat SWvt WCot WHoo
- 'Derwisch' ELon NBre SWat
- * - 'Diana' SWat
- 'Domino' GMac MWea NBPN NCGa STes
- 'Double Pleasure' EBee ECtt MSCN NBre NLar NMoo SWat WHrl
- 'Doubloon' (d) EBee NBre NGdn SWat
- 'Dwarf Allegro' WMnd
- 'Effendi' ♀H4 EBee IPot MAvo NBre SPhx SUsu SWat
- 'Elam Pink' EGle MLLN SWat WCot
- 'Erste Zuneigung' ECha ELon SPhx SUsu SWat
- 'Eskimo Pie' SWat
- 'Fancy Feathers' EBee ECtt IPot LAst MWea NBhm SWat
- 'Fatima' CDes CMil NBre SWat WHrl
- 'Feuerriese' SWat
- 'Feuerzwerg' SWat
- 'Fiesta' CAby GKir NBre SMeo SWat
- 'Flamenco' ECtt SWat
- 'Flamingo' EBee ELon SWat
- 'Forncett Summer' CPar EAEE EBee ECtt ELon GMac LPio MRav NBre NBsh NGby NGdn SMrs SPer STes SWat WCAu WCot WHoo
- 'Frosty' (v) SHar
- 'Fruit Punch' **new** EDAr
- 'Garden Glory' EAEE EBee ECtt ELon GCra GMac LRHS LSRN NBre SMrs SWat WCAu
- 'Garden Gnome' SPet
- 'Glowing Embers' CSpe LRHS SWat
- 'Glowing Rose' CAby ELon MDKP NBre SWat
- Goliath Group EAEE ECha ELan ELon LRHS MAvo MRav NBro NVic SAga SDix SRms SWat WFar WMnd
- - 'Beauty of Livermere' Widely available
- 'Graue Witwe' CAby EBee EGle SApp SMHy SWat WHrl WTin
- 'Halima' NBre SWat
- 'Harlem' CSpe CWCL EBee IPot MAvo NBPN NLar SMrm SWat WCAu WHrl
- 'Harvest Moon' (d) EBee ECtt LCro LRHS NPer SPad SPhx SWat WHal WHil
- 'Heidi' SWat
- 'Hewitt's Old Rose' NBre
- 'Hula Hula' ECha ELon SWat
- 'Indian Chief' CMHG CWCL EPfP GMac IPot LPio LRHS MAvo MSte NBPC NBro NMoo NPer NPri SMrm WBor WCAu WFar
- 'Joanne' NLar
- 'John III' ♀H4 CAby EBee LPio LPla SPhx SWat
- 'John Metcalf' EBee ECtt EPPr LPio LRHS MAvo MLLN MRav NBre NSti SMrs SWat WCAu WCot
- 'Juliane' EBee ECha ECtt EGle GMac MNFA MSte NSti SPhx SWat WCot WTin
- 'Karine' ♀H4 CDes CElw CSam CSpe EBee ECha EGle ELan EPPr EPfP GBBs GMaP GMac LCro LPio LRHS MWte NPri SMHy SPhx SWat WCAu WHoo WPtf WTin
- 'Khedive' (d) ♀H4 EBee SWat
- 'King George' SWat
- 'King Kong' IPot NBPC NLar
- 'Kleine Tänzerin' CMil CSam GBri GMac MLLN MRav MSte NBre NGdn NPri NSti SPad SWat WCAu WCot
- 'Kollebloem' NBre SWat
- 'Lady Frederick Moore' GMac LPio MLLN NBre SWat
- 'Lady Roscoe' NBre SWat
- 'Ladybird' LRHS MSte NBre
- 'Lambada' SWat
- 'Lauren's Lilac' CAby CMdw EAEE EBee ELon LPio NBre SMeo SMrs SPhx SWat
- 'Leuchtfeuer' ♀H4 CDes EBee ECha NBre SMHy SPhx SWat
- 'Lighthouse' ♀H4 EBee SWat
- 'Lilac Girl' CSpe EBee ECha ECtt EGle EWll GMaP GMac LHop LPio MSte NLar SApp SPhx STes SUsu SWat WHoo WHrl
- 'Louvre' EBee ECtt EHrv GBin MAvo NLar SMrm SMrs WFar
- 'Maiden's Blush' NBre NGby NSti SWat
- 'Mandarin' EBee NBhm NMoo
- 'Manhattan' Widely available
- 'Marcus Perry' EAEE EBee ECtt EPfP EWes GMaP LRHS SPoG SWat WCAu WFar
- 'Mary Finnan' CTca EAEE EBee NBre SWat
- 'Master Richard' SWat
- 'May Queen' (d) CBgR EWes IBlr LRHS MRav NBre NBro NSti SWat WCot WHrl WPnn
- 'May Sadler' EBee NBre SWat
- 'Midnight' ELon NBre SWat
- 'Miss Piggy' EBee IPot LLHF SPer
- 'Mrs H.G. Stobart' SWat
- 'Mrs Marrow's Plum' see *P. orientale* 'Patty's Plum'
- 'Mrs Perry' CMMP CMea CSBt CSam EBee ECtt ELan EPfP GMaP LRHS MRav MWat NGdn NPer NPri SPer SPla SRGP SRms SRot SWat WBrk WCAu WCot WFar WMnd WTin
- 'Nanum Flore Pleno' see *P.* 'Fire Ball'
- 'Noema' SWat
- 'Orange Glow' NBre NMoo NPri SWat WMoo
- 'Orangeade Maison' NBre SWat
- 'Oriana' LRHS NBre SWat
- 'Oriental' SWat
- 'Pale Face' SWat
- 'Papillion' PBR EBee GKir WFar WPtf
- § - 'Patty's Plum' Widely available
- 'Perry's White' Widely available
- 'Peter Pan' CAby MLLN NBre SWat
- 'Petticoat' ECtt ELan NBre SWat
- 'Picotée' EBee EBrs ECtt EHrv ELan EPfP GBBs LBMP LPio LRHS MRav NBPC NBro NCGa NCob NGdn NMoo SPer SPhx SPoG SWat SWvt WBrE WCAu WFar
- 'Pink Lassie' NBre SWat
- 'Pink Panda' SWat
- 'Pink Ruffles' PBR EBee SWat
- 'Pinnacle' CDes EBee ELon LRHS NGdn NPri SWat WFar
- 'Pizzicato' CEnt CMea CSec CWib EHrv GBBs MBri MNHC NPer SGar SPet SWal SWat WFar WMoo WRHF
- 'Pizzicato White' NBre
- 'Place Pigalle' EBee EHrv EPfP LHop LPio LSou MWea NBPC NGdn NOrc SMrm SPer WCra
- 'Polka' SWat
- 'Prince of Orange' SWat WHil
- Princess Victoria Louise see *P. orientale* 'Prinzessin Victoria Louise'

- 'Prinz Eugen' CMil EBee ELon NBre NBsh SWat
§ - 'Prinzessin Victoria Louise' CSWP EBee EGoo EPfP EShb GMaP LAst LRHS MBri MLLN NGdn NPri SSvw SWat WBVN WBrk WFar WPer
- 'Prospero' NBre
- 'Queen Alexandra' EHrv NGdn NLar
- 'Raspberry Queen' CDes CMea EBee ECtt EGle ELan GMaP GMac LRHS MArl MRav MSte NBPC NPri NSti SApp SMrm SPhx STes SWat WBor WCot WCra WFar WHal WHoo WMnd WTin
- 'Raspberry Ruffles' NBre SPhx SWat
- 'Rembrandt' ECot EHrv EMil MDKP NBre NMoo SMrm SWat WPer
- 'Rose Queen' NBre
- 'Rosenpokal' EAEE EBee LRHS NGdn SWat
- 'Roter Zwerg' ECha ELon SWat
- 'Royal Chocolate Distinction' CElw CSpe CWCL EBee ECtt ELon EPPr EPfP GBri LCro LPio MAvo MWea NBPC NBPN NLar NMoo NPri NSti SPoG SWat
- 'Royal Wedding' CCge CHFP CTri EAEE EBee EShb EWTr GKir LHop LRHS LSRN MBri MHer NGdn NLar SMad SPer SPla SPoG SSvw SWat WFar WMoo
- 'Ruffled Patty' **new** WHlf
* - 'Saffron' CAby CElw SWat
- 'Salmon Glow' (d) CBcs GKir SSvw SWat WFar WPer
- 'Salome' GKir SWat
- scarlet-flowered NCot
- 'Scarlet King' EAEE LRHS NBre NOrc SWat
- 'Scarlett O'Hara' (d) ECtt EPfP LLHF NPri SWat WFar
- 'Showgirl' EBee MLLN NBre SWat
* - 'Silberosa' SWat
- 'Sindbad' ECtt ELon GMac LRHS MAvo MRav SPhx SWat
- 'Snow Goose' CAby CMil LPla NBre SPhx SWat WHoo
- 'Spätzünder' NBre SWat
- 'Springtime' EWes GMac LAst LRHS MRav NGdn NLar SWat WCAu WTin
- 'Staten Island' EBee ECtt MNrw
- 'Stokesby Belle' NBre
- Stormtorch see *P. orientale* 'Sturmfackel'
§ - 'Sturmfackel' NBre SWat
- 'Suleika' NBre SWat
- 'Sultana' ECha ELon GMac MWat SMrs SWat WCAu
- 'The Promise' CAby NBre SWat
- 'Tiffany' CBow CMil CSpe EBee ECtt GAbr GMac LPio LSou MAvo NCGa NGdn NLar SMad SMrm SPer SPla SSvw STes SWat WClo WCot WCra
- 'Trinity' SWat
- 'Türkenlouis' CMHG CSpe EBee ECGP ECtt EPfP GCra GKir GMaP GMac LAst LBMP LSRN MSCN SMrm SPad SPer SPoG STes SWat WCAu WFar WTin WWlt
- 'Turkish Delight' CAby EBee ECtt ELon EPfP EShb GCra GKir GMac LSRN MLLN MRav MSte MWat NBid NBir NPri SPhx SPoG SRGP STes SWat SWvt WCAu WFar WMnd
- 'Tutu' SWat
- 'Victoria Dreyfuss' SWat
- 'Viola' SWat
- 'Violetta' SWat
- 'Walking Fire' MNrw
- 'Water Babies' SWat
- 'Watermelon' EBrs ECtt GBBs GKir IPot LRHS MLLN NBPC NPri NSti SMeo SMrm SPer STes SWat WBor WCAu WFar WHoo
- 'White Karine' GMac
- 'White King' NBre
- 'Wild Salmon' NBre
- 'Wisley Beacon' ELon NBre SWat
- 'Wunderkind' EBee ECtt GKir SWat WCAu

'Party Fun' CSpe SWal
***paucifoliatum*** CDes NBre SDix
***pilosum*** GCal SRms SWat WTin
§ - subsp. ***spicatum*** CMea CSpe ECGP ECha EGle EWTr GAbr LBMP LHop MHar MSte NBir NChi STes SUsu WCot WFar WMoo
***rhaeticum*** CSec GKev NBre
'Rhapsody in Red' (Super Poppy Series) SWat
***rhoeas*** CArn EBWF GPoy LCro WJek
- Angels' Choir Group (d) CSec SWat
- Mother of Pearl Group CSpe MCot SWat
***rupifragum*** CEnt CHrt CSec CSsd ECha LEdu MLLN NPol SGar SWal WCot WEas WFar WPer WPnn WRha
- 'Double Tangerine Gem' see *P. rupifragum* 'Flore Pleno'
§ - 'Flore Pleno' (d) CSWP CSpe LSou MBri NBre NChi WBrk WCFE WFar WHrl WMoo
- 'Tangerine Dream' MCCP SPet
'Serena' (Super Poppy Series) SWat
'Shasta' (Super Poppy Series) LLHF SWat WHoo
***somniferum*** CArn CWCL GPoy MSal SWat
- 'Black Beauty' (d) CSpe SWat
- 'Black Paeony' CWCL
- 'Flemish Antique' CWCL
- (Laciniatum Group) 'Swansdown' (d) CSpe
- var. ***paeoniiflorum*** (d) CWCL SWat
- 'Pink Chiffon' SWat WEas
- single white-flowered **new** CSpe
- 'White Cloud' (d) CWCL SWat
'Tequila Sunrise' (Super Poppy Series) CDes SWat
'The Cardinal' NBre
***triniifolium*** CSpe
- RCB AM -10 **new** WCot
'Vesuvius' (Super Poppy Series) SWat
'Viva' (Super Poppy Series) SWat

## papaya (paw paw) see *Carica papaya*

## *Parabenzoin* see *Lindera*

## *Parachampionella* see *Strobilanthes*

## *Paradisea* (*Asphodelaceae*)

***liliastrum*** ♀H4 CHid CSec EBee ECho EPPr ERos GCal GEdr GKir IGor SRms WBVN WHoo WSHC
- 'Major' ECho SPhx
***lusitanica*** CAvo CDes CHid CMHG CPom CPrp CSam CSpe CWsd EBee ECho ERos GCal GKev GMac IBlr IFro MCot SWal WBVN WCot WHoo WPGP WThu WTin

## *Parahebe* (*Scrophulariaceae*)

'Betty' GGar
x ***bidwillii*** GJos MHer NDlv NWCA SRms SRot
- 'Kea' CFee EBee ECou ECtt MDKP SRot WPer
***canescens*** ECou
§ ***catarractae*** CHar CMHG CPLG CTri CWib EBee ECho ECou EPfP GCra GGar MLHP MNrw MWat NBir NBro SPoG SUsu WBrE WFar WKif WMnd WPer

| | | |
|---|---|---|
| | – from Chatham Island | EWes |
| | – 'Baby Blue' | CAbP EPfP |
| | – blue-flowered | CDoC CHar GKir SPer |
| | – 'County Park' | ECou |
| | – 'Cuckoo' | ECou NHol |
| § | – 'Delight' ♀H3 | CPLG ECho ECou EWes GCal GGar GMaP GQue LHop LRHS MHer NHol NPer SDix SRot WFar |
| | – subsp. ***diffusa*** | ECho ECou ERas NPer NVic NWCA |
| | – – 'Annie' | ECou NHol |
| | – subsp. ***martinii*** | ECou |
| | – 'Miss Willmott' | ECho NPri NVic SBch SPer SPlb WBVN WBod WPer |
| | – 'Porlock Purple' | see *P. catarractae* 'Delight' |
| | – 'Rosea' | CEnt ECho SSto WFar |
| | – white-flowered | CSpe ECho LHop MLHP SUsu WPer |
| § | ***formosa*** | WHCG |
| | – 'Aspley White' new | ECou |
| | – erect | GGar |
| | 'Gillian' | SWal WPer |
| | 'Greencourt' | see *P. catarractae* 'Delight' |
| § | ***hookeriana*** | GGar |
| § | – var. ***olsenii*** | ECou GGar |
| | 'Jean' | GGar |
| | 'Joy' | ECou EWes |
| | 'Julia' | GGar |
| | ***linifolia*** | CTri |
| § | ***lyallii*** | EBee ECGP ECho ECou GJos GKir GMaP LAst MBar MHer MMuc MSwo MWat NDlv NHol NPol NWCA SPlb SRms WKif |
| | – 'Baby Pink' | EPfP |
| | – 'Clarence' | ECou |
| | – 'Glacier' | ECou |
| | – 'Julie-Anne' ♀H3 | CAbP EBee ECou EPfP GCal GMaP LRHS |
| | – 'Rosea' | CTri WPer |
| | – 'Summer Snow' | ECou |
| | 'Mervyn' | CTri ECho MDKP NDlv WPer |
| | ***olsenii*** | see *P. hookeriana* var. *olsenii* |
| § | ***perfoliata*** ♀H3-4 | CMHG CMea CPLG CSpe EBee ECha ECho EGle EGoo ELan EPPr EPfP GCal GCra GGar LEdu LHop NChi SBod SKHP SPer SPla SRms SUsu WCFE WPat WPer WWFP |
| | – dark blue-flowered | GBuc SMad |
| | – 'Pringle' | CAbP EPfP LRHS |
| | 'Snow Clouds' new | GKev SRot |
| | 'Snowcap' | CDoC EPfP LRHS SPlb |

## *Parajubaea* (*Arecaceae*)

| | | |
|---|---|---|
| | ***cocoides*** | LPal |

## *Parakmeria* see *Magnolia*

## *Paramongaia* (*Amaryllidaceae*)

| | | |
|---|---|---|
| | ***weberbaueri*** new | WVal |

## *Paraquilegia* (*Ranunculaceae*)

| | | |
|---|---|---|
| | ***adoxoides*** | see *Semiaquilegia adoxoides* |
| § | ***anemonoides*** | CPLG WAbe |
| | ***grandiflora*** | see *P. anemonoides* |

## *Paraserianthes* (*Mimosaceae*)

| | | |
|---|---|---|
| | ***distachya*** | see *P. lophantha* |
| § | ***lophantha*** ♀H1 | CDTJ CHEx CRHN EBak EShb IDee SAPC SArc SOWG |

## *Parasyringa* see *Ligustrum*

## *Parathelypteris* (*Thelypteridaceae*)

| | | |
|---|---|---|
| § | ***novae-boracensis*** new | EBee |

## x *Pardancanda* (*Iridaceae*)

| | | |
|---|---|---|
| | ***norrisii*** | CFir CPen EBee EWes LRHS |
| | – 'Dazzler' | CHFP |

## *Pardanthopsis* (*Iridaceae*)

| | | |
|---|---|---|
| | ***dichotoma*** | EBee EWes |

## *Parietaria* (*Urticaceae*)

| | | |
|---|---|---|
| | ***judaica*** | GPoy MSal WHer WSFF |

## *Paris* ✿ (*Trilliaceae*)

| | | |
|---|---|---|
| | Chen Yi 8 | WCot |
| | ***bashanensis*** | CExc |
| | ***chinensis*** | EBee WCru |
| | – B&SWJ 265 from Taiwan | WCru |
| | ***cronquistii*** | CLAP EBee GKev MLul |
| | ***daliensis*** | CExc |
| | ***delavayi*** | EBee WCru |
| | – var. ***delavayi*** | MLul |
| | – var. ***petiolata*** | EBee |
| | ***dulongensis*** new | EBee |
| | ***fargesii*** | CSec EBee GAuc LAma MLul WCru |
| | – var. ***brevipetalata*** | EBee WCru |
| | – var. ***petiolata*** | WCru |
| | ***forrestii*** | WCru |
| * | ***hubeiensis*** | CExc |
| | ***incompleta*** | CLAP EPot GCal SSpi WCru |
| | ***japonica*** | WCru |
| | ***lancifolia*** from Taiwan B&SWJ 3044 | WCru |
| | ***luquanensis*** | MLul |
| | ***mairei*** | WCru |
| | ***marmorata*** | CExc EBrs WCru |
| | ***polyphylla*** ♀ | CArn CBct CBro CFir CLAP CSec EBee EBrs ECho GAuc GEdr LAma MLul MNrw WAbe WCru WFar WPnP WSHC WShi WWst |
| | – B&SWJ 2125 | WCru |
| | – Forrest 5945 | GCal |
| | – HWJCM 475 | WCru |
| | – SDR 2828 new | GKev |
| | – var. ***alba*** | CFir GKev |
| | – var. ***stenophylla*** | CFir CLAP CSec EBee LAma MLul WCru |
| | ***quadrifolia*** | CFir CHFP CLAP CSec GGar GPoy NMen SPhx SSpi SUsu WCru WFar WHer WPGP WPnP WShi WTin |
| | ***tetraphylla*** | WCru |
| | ***thibetica*** | CFir CLAP WCru |
| | – var. ***apetala*** | WCru |
| | ***verticillata*** | CLAP GAuc LAma WCru |

## *Parochetus* (*Papilionaceae*)

| | | |
|---|---|---|
| § | ***africanus*** ♀H2 | CHid ELon |
| | ***communis*** misapplied | see *P. africanus* |
| | ***communis*** ambig. | CBcs CFee CPLG MSCN NPer WRha |
| | ***communis*** Buch.-Ham. ex D. Don CC 3660 | WRos |
| | – B&SWJ 7215 from Golden Triangle | WCru |
| | – HWJCM 526 from Himalaya | WCru |
| | – from Himalaya | EBee GCra |
| * | – 'Blue Gem' | CCCN |
| | – dark-flowered | GBuc GGar |

## *Paronychia* (*Illecebraceae*)

| | | |
|---|---|---|
| | ***argentea*** | WPat WPer |
| § | ***capitata*** | CLyd CTri EAlp SRms WPer |
| | ***kapela*** | SPlb WPer |
| | – 'Binsted Gold' (v) | CBow LRHS WPer |
| § | – subsp. ***serpyllifolia*** | GBin NRya |

***nivea*** see *P. capitata*
***serpyllifolia*** see *P. kapela* subsp. *serpyllifolia*

## *Parrotia* (*Hamamelidaceae*)

***persica*** ♀H4 Widely available
- 'Biltmore' CPMA
- 'Burgundy' CPMA NLar
- 'Felicie' CPMA EPfP NLar
- 'Jodrell Bank' CPMA MBlu MBri NLar
§ - 'Lamplighter' (v) CPMA
- 'Pendula' CMCN CPMA EPfP
- 'Vanessa' CBcs CDoC CMCN CPMA EWes MBlu MBri MGos NLar SLPl WDin WFar WMou WOrn WPat
- 'Variegata' see *P. persica* 'Lamplighter'

## *Parrotiopsis* (*Hamamelidaceae*)

***jacquemontiana*** CBcs CPMA MBlu NLar SSpi

## *Parrya* (*Brassicaceae*)

***menziesii*** see *Phoenicaulis cheiranthoides*

## parsley see *Petroselinum crispum*

## *Parsonsia* (*Apocynaceae*)

***capsularis*** ECou
***heterophylla*** ECou

## *Parthenium* (*Asteraceae*)

***integrifolium*** CArn GKir GPoy MSal
* ***virginicum*** SPhx

## *Parthenocissus* (*Vitaceae*)

TH CHEx
§ ***henryana*** ♀H4 Widely available
***himalayana*** CBcs
- CC 4519 EWld
- 'Purpurea' see *P. himalayana* var. *rubrifolia*
§ - var. ***rubrifolia*** CWCL EBee ELan LRHS MAsh NLar SLim SLon SPoG WCru WFar
***inserta*** CTsd NLar
***laetevirens*** NLar
§ ***quinquefolia*** ♀H4 Widely available
- var. ***engelmannii*** CBcs EBee LAst LBuc MGos NBlu SPer WCFE
- 'Guy's Garnet' WCru
- Star Showers = 'Monham' (v) EBee EPfP LRHS MGos
***semicordata*** B&SWJ 6551 WCru
***striata*** see *Cissus striata*
***thomsonii*** see *Cayratia thomsonii*
§ ***tricuspidata*** ♀H4 CCVT CDul CWib EBee ECtt EHoe EPfP GKir LAst MGos SPer SReu WDin WFar
- 'Beverley Brook' CMac EBee ERas LBuc MBri NLar SBod SPer SPla SRms WFar
- 'Crûg Compact' CGHE WCru
- 'Fenway Park' LBuc MBlu MGos
- 'Green Spring' CBcs EBee ERas IArd MGos NLar
- 'Lowii' CMac EBee ECot EPfP ERas LBuc LRHS MAsh MBlu MGos MRav NLar SLon
- 'Minutifolia' SPer
- 'Purpurea' MBlu MGos
- 'Robusta' CHEx EBee EPfP LCro LPan
§ - 'Veitchii' Widely available

## *Pasithea* (*Anthericaceae*)

***caerulea*** CAvo

## *Paspalum* (*Poaceae*)

***glaucifolium*** CElw LEdu
***quadrifarium*** CHrt CKno CMHG EHoe EMon EPPr LDai WCot WPrP
- RCB/Arg RA-5-5 EBee

## *Passerina* (*Thymelaeaceae*)

***montana*** NWCA

## *Passiflora* ✿ (*Passifloraceae*)

RCB/Arg R-7 WCot
***actinia*** CPas CRHN
***adenopoda*** CPas
'Adularia' CCCN CPas LRHS
***alata*** (F) ♀H1 CCCN CPas LRHS
- 'Shannon' (F) CPas
x ***alatocaerulea*** see *P.* x *belotii*
***allantophylla*** CPas
'Allardii' CCCN CPas EShb LRHS
***alnifolia*** new CPas
***amalocarpa*** CPas
***ambigua*** CPas
§ 'Amethyst' ♀H1 CCCN CPas CRHN CSBt CSPN EAmu EBee EMil LHop LRHS LSRN MAsh MRav SPad SPla SPoG WFar WPGP WPat
***amethystina*** misapplied see *P.* 'Amethyst'
§ ***amethystina*** Mikan CBcs CPas ECre LRHS
***ampullacea*** (F) CPas
'Anastasia' CCCN CPas
'Andy' CCCN
'Anemona' CPas
***anfracta*** CPas
'Angelo Blu' CCCN
***antioquiensis*** misapplied see *P.* x *exoniensis*
***antioquiensis*** ambig. CBcs CDoC CPas CRHN CTsd LRHS SOWG
***antioquiensis*** ambig. x ***exoniensis*** 'Hill House' CHll
***antioquiensis*** ambig. x ***mixta*** CTrC
***antioquiensis*** Karst ♀H2 CHll EBee ISea
***apetala*** CPas
***arbelaezii*** CPas
***arida*** var. ***pentaschista*** CPas
x ***atropurpurea*** CCCN CPas
§ ***aurantia*** CPas CTsd LRHS
***auriculata*** CPas
'Aurora' CPas
***banksii*** see *P. aurantia*
'Barborea' CPas
§ x ***belotii*** CCCN CPas EAmu EQua EShb LRHS
- 'Impératrice Eugénie' see *P.* x *belotii*
***biflora*** Lamarck CPas LRHS
'Blaumilch' CPas
'Blue Bird' CCCN
'Blue Moon' CCCN CPas
***boenderi*** CPas
***bogatensis*** CPas
***brevifila*** CPas
'Byron Beauty' CCCN CPas
'Cacita' CPas
§ ***caerulea*** ♀H3 Widely available
- 'Clear Sky' CPas
- 'Constance Elliott' Widely available
- ***rubra*** CSBt MGos WFar
x ***caeruleoracemosa*** see *P.* x *violacea*
***candollei*** new CPas
***capsularis*** CPas
***chinensis*** see *P. caerulea*
***cincinnata*** CPas
***cinnabarina*** CPas
***citrifolia*** CCCN CPas
***citrina*** CPas LRHS SOWG
***cobanensis*** CPas
***coccinea*** (F) CPas LRHS
***colinvauxii*** CPas
x ***colvillii*** CHll CPas

| | | |
|---|---|---|
| | ***complanata*** new | CPas |
| | ***conzattiana*** | CPas |
| | 'Coordination' | CCCN |
| § | ***coriacea*** | CPas LRHS |
| | ***costaricensis*** | CPas |
| | 'Crimson Tears' new | CPas |
| | 'Crimson Trees' | CCCN |
| § | ***cuneata*** 'Miguel Molinari' | CPas |
| | ***cuprea*** | CPas |
| I | 'Curiosa' | CPas LRHS |
| | ***cuspidifolia*** | CPas |
| § | ***cyanea*** | CPas |
| | 'Debby' | CPas |
| | x ***decaisneana*** (F) | CCCN CPas |
| | ***dioscoreifolia*** | CPas |
| | ***discophora*** | CPas |
| | 'Eclipse' | CPas |
| | 'Eden' | CCCN CPas EAmu LBuc LCro LRHS MBri NLar SCoo SLim SPoG SRkn |
| | ***edulis*** (F) | CAgr CCCN CPas LRHS MJnS SVic |
| | - f. ***flavicarpa*** (F) | CPas |
| | - 'Golden Nugget' (F) | CPas |
| | - 'Norfolk' (F) | CPas |
| | - 'Panama Gold' | CPas |
| | - 'Pink Cheek' | CPas |
| | - 'Possum Purple' | CPas |
| | ***eichleriana*** | CPas |
| | ***elegans*** | CPas |
| | 'Elizabeth' (F) | CPas |
| | 'Empress Eugenie' | see *P.* x *belotii* |
| | 'Excel' | CPas |
| § | x ***exoniensis*** ♀H1 | CHll CPas CRHN ECre LRHS |
| | 'Fairylights' | CCCN |
| | ***filipes*** | CPas |
| | 'Fledermouse' | CPas |
| | 'Flying V' | CCCN CPas |
| | ***foetida*** | CPas SOWG |
| | - var. ***galapagensis*** | CPas |
| | - var. ***hastata*** | CPas |
| | - var. ***hirsuta*** (F) | CPas |
| | - var. ***hirsutissima*** | CPas |
| | - var. ***vitacea*** new | CPas |
| I | ***gabrielliana*** | CPas |
| | ***garckei*** | CPas |
| | ***gibertii*** | CPas EShb |
| | ***gilbertiana*** | CPas WFar |
| | ***glandulosa*** | CPas |
| | ***gracilis*** | CPas |
| | ***gritensis*** | CPas |
| | ***guatemalensis*** | CPas |
| | ***haematostigma*** new | CPas |
| | ***hahnii*** | CPas EAmu |
| | ***helleri*** | CPas |
| | ***herbertiana*** (F) | CPas |
| | ***holosericea*** | CPas |
| | ***incana*** | see *P. seemannii* |
| | ***incarnata*** (F) | CAgr CArn CPas MSal SPlb |
| | 'Incense' (F) ♀H1 | CCCN CPas LRHS SPlb WFar |
| | ***indecora*** | CPas |
| | 'Inspiration' | CPas |
| | 'Inverleith' | CPas |
| | ***jatunsachensis*** | CPas |
| | 'Jeanette' | CPas |
| | 'Jelly Joker' | CCCN CPas |
| | ***jorullensis*** | CPas |
| | ***juliana*** | CPas |
| | ***kalbreyeri*** | CPas |
| | ***karwinskii*** | CPas |
| | 'Kate Adie' | CPas |
| | ***kermesina*** | CPas |
| | x ***kewensis*** | CCCN CPas |
| | - 'Déjà Vu' new | CPas |

| | | |
|---|---|---|
| | 'Lady Margaret' | CPas LRHS MJnS |
| | ***lancearia*** | CPas |
| | ***lancetellesis*** | CPas |
| | ***laurifolia*** (F) | CPas |
| § | ***ligularis*** (F) | CPas LRHS |
| | 'Lilac Lady' | see *P.* x *violacea* 'Tresederi' |
| | ***lindeniana*** | CPas |
| | ***lobata*** | CPas |
| | ***loefgrenii*** | CPas |
| | ***lourdesae*** | see *P. cuneata* 'Miguel Molinari' |
| | ***lowei*** | see *P. ligularis* |
| | ***lutea*** | CPas |
| | ***macrophylla*** | CPas |
| | ***maliformis*** (F) | CHll CPas |
| | ***manicata*** (F) | CPas |
| | 'Maria' | CCCN |
| | 'Mary Jane' | CCCN |
| | ***matthewsii*** | CPas |
| | 'Mavis Mastics' | see *P.* x *violacea* 'Tresederi' |
| | ***mayana*** | see *P. caerulea* |
| | ***membranacea*** (F) | CPas |
| | ***menispermifolia*** | see *P. pilosa* |
| | ***microstipula*** | CPas |
| | ***miersii*** | CPas |
| | 'Mini Lamb' new | CPas |
| | ***miniata*** new | CPas |
| | ***misera*** | CPas |
| | ***mixta*** (F) | CCCN EBee |
| | - B&SWJ 10756 | WCru |
| * | - var. ***pinanga*** | CPas |
| | ***mollissima*** misapplied (F) | see *P. tarminiana* |
| | ***mollissima*** ambig. (F) | CAgr CCCN CHll CPas CRHN CTsd EBee EShb LRHS SOWG SPlb |
| | ***moluccana*** | CPas |
| | ***mooreana*** | CPas |
| | ***morifolia*** | CPas EShb |
| | ***mucronata*** | CPas |
| | ***multiflora*** | CPas |
| | ***murucuja*** | CCCN CPas |
| | ***naviculata*** | CPas |
| | - RCB/Arg P-12 | WCot |
| | ***nephrodes*** | CPas |
| | 'New Incense' | CPas |
| | ***nigradenia*** | CPas |
| | ***obtusifolia*** | see *P. coriacea* |
| | ***oerstedii*** | CPas |
| | - var. ***choconiana*** | CPas |
| | ***onychina*** | see *P. amethystina* Mikan |
| | ***organensis*** | CPas |
| | 'Oriental Sunset' | CPas |
| | ***ornithoura*** | CPas |
| | ***pallida*** | CPas |
| I | ***pardifolia*** | CPas |
| | ***parritae*** | CPas |
| | 'Paulo' new | CPas |
| | ***penduliflora*** | CPas |
| | ***perfoliata*** | CPas |
| | 'Peter Lawerence' | CCCN |
| | ***phoenicea*** | CPas |
| § | ***pilosa*** | CPas |
| | ***pilosicorona*** | CPas |
| | 'Pink Jewel' | CPas |
| | 'Pink Polka Dot' | CPas |
| | x ***piresiae*** | CCCN CPas LRHS |
| | ***pittieri*** | CPas |
| | ***platyloba*** | CPas |
| | ***punctata*** | CPas |
| | 'Pura Vida' | LRHS |
| | 'Pura Vida 1' | CPas |
| | 'Pura Vida 2' | CPas |
| | 'Purple Haze' | CCCN CPas CRHN CWib EAmu EBee LRHS |

| | |
|---|---|
| 'Purple-heart' | CPas |
| ***quadrangularis*** (F) 🏆H1 | CCCN CHll CPas CWSG IDee LRHS MJnS |
| ***quadriglandulosa*** | CPas |
| ***quinquangularis*** | CBcs CPas |
| ***racemosa*** 🏆H2 | CPas CTsd EBee LAst LRHS MNHC SOWG |
| 'Red Inca' | CPas |
| ***reflexiflora*** | CPas |
| ***resticulata*** | CPas |
| ***retipetala*** | see *P. cyanea* |
| ***rovirosae*** | CPas LRHS |
| ***rubra*** | CCCN CPas SLim |
| ***sagasteguii*** | CPas |
| 'Saint Rule' | CPas |
| 'Sancap' | CPas |
| ***sanguinolenta*** | CPas LRHS |
| 'Sapphire' | CPas |
| 'Sarah Aimee' | CPas LRHS |
| § ***seemannii*** | CPas |
| ***serrata*** | see *P. serratodigitata* |
| ***serratifolia*** | CPas |
| § ***serratodigitata*** | CPas |
| ***sexflora*** | CPas |
| ***sexocellata*** | see *P. coriacea* |
| 'Simply Red' | CPas LRHS |
| 'Smythiana' | CPas EShb |
| ***sprucei*** | CPas |
| ***standleyi*** | CPas |
| 'Star of Bristol' 🏆H2 | CPas EAmu SLim |
| 'Star of Clevedon' | CPas |
| 'Star of Kingston' | CPas |
| 'Star of Surbiton' | CPas LRHS |
| ***suberosa*** | CPas CSec |
| ***sublanceolata*** | CPas |
| ***subpeltata*** | CPas LRHS |
| ***subrotunda*** | CPas |
| 'Sunburst' | CCCN CHEx CPas LRHS |
| 'Surprise' **new** | CPas |
| ***talamancensis*** | CPas |
| § ***tarminiana*** **new** | CPas |
| 'Temptation' **new** | CPas |
| ***tenuifila*** | CPas |
| ***tetrandra*** | CPLG CPas ECou |
| ***tiliifolia*** | CPas |
| 'Tinalandia' | CPas |
| x ***tresederi*** | see *P.* x *violacea* 'Tresederi' |
| ***trialata*** | CPas |
| ***tridactylites*** | CPas |
| ***trifasciata*** | CCCN CPas EShb |
| ***triloba*** | CPas |
| ***tripartita*** | CPas |
| ***tuberosa*** | CPas |
| ***tulae*** | CPas LRHS |
| ***umbilicata*** | CPas SKHP WCru |
| ***urbaniana*** | CPas |
| 'Val Bishop' **new** | CPas |
| ***vespertilio*** | CPas |
| § x ***violacea*** 🏆H1 | CBcs CPas CRHN SGar WFar |
| - 'Dedorina' | CPas |
| - 'Eynsford Gem' | CCCN CPas EAmu |
| - 'Lilac Lady' | see *P.* x *violacea* 'Tresederi' |
| § - 'Tresederi' | CPas CTsd WFar |
| - 'Victoria' | CPas CSBt EBee LRHS SLim |
| ***vitifolia*** (F) | CPas LRHS SOWG |
| - 'Scarlet Flame' (F) | CPas LRHS |
| 'White Lightning' | LBuc MAsh SPoG SWvt |
| 'White Star' **new** | CPas |
| ***xiikzodz*** | CPas |
| ***yucatanensis*** | CPas |
| ***zamorana*** | CPas |

## passion fruit see *Passiflora*

## passion fruit, banana see *Passiflora mollissima*

## *Pastinaca* (*Apiaceae*)

| | |
|---|---|
| ***sativa*** | EBWF |

## *Patersonia* (*Iridaceae*)

| | |
|---|---|
| ***occidentalis*** | SPlb |

## *Patrinia* (*Valerianaceae*)

| | |
|---|---|
| ***gibbosa*** | CSec EBee LRHS SEND WFar WMoo WPnP |
| - B&SWJ 874 | WCru |
| ***saniculifolia*** | CSec |
| ***scabiosifolia*** | Widely available |
| - B&SWJ 8740 | WCru |
| - 'Nagoya' | MNrw |
| ***triloba*** | ECho EDAr GBuc GCal GEdr GKir LSou SUsu WBVN WFar WMoo WPnP |
| * - 'Minor' | ECho |
| - var. ***palmata*** | EBee WDyG WFar WMoo WPnP |
| ***villosa*** | CPLG EBee NDov NGdn NLar SSvw |

## *Paulownia* (*Scrophulariaceae*)

| | |
|---|---|
| ***catalpifolia*** | EBee EGFP EPla LLHF NLar |
| ***elongata*** | CBcs EGFP LLHF NLar |
| ***fortunei*** | CBcs MBlu SEND SPlb WBVN WPat |
| - Fast Blue = 'Minfast' | EBee EMil EPfP ESwi LLHF LSRN MAsh SLon SPoG WPGP |
| ***kawakamii*** | WPGP |
| - B&SWJ 6784 | WCru |
| ***taiwaniana*** B&SWJ 7134 | WCru |
| ***tomentosa*** 🏆H3 | Widely available |
| - 'Coreana' | CHll |
| - - B&SWJ 8503 | WCru |

## *Pavonia* (*Malvaceae*)

| | |
|---|---|
| ***hastata*** | EShb |
| ***missionum*** | CSpe EShb |
| * ***volubilis*** | CCCN |

## paw paw (false banana) see *Asimina triloba*

## paw paw (papaya) see *Carica papaya*

## *Paxistima* (*Celastraceae*)

| | |
|---|---|
| ***canbyi*** | NLar WThu |

## peach see *Prunus persica*

## pear see *Pyrus communis*

## pear, Asian see *Pyrus pyrifolia*

## pecan see *Carya illinoinensis*

## *Pedicularis* (*Scrophulariaceae*)

| | |
|---|---|
| SDR 2931 **new** | GKev |
| SDR 4523 **new** | GKev |
| ***axillaris*** | EBee |
| - SDR 1745 | GKev |
| ***longiflora*** var. ***tubiformis*** | EBee |
| - - SDR 4606 **new** | GKev |
| ***rex*** | EBee |
| ***rhinanthoides*** subsp. ***tibetica*** | EBee |
| ***superba*** SDR 4248 **new** | GKev |

## *Peganum* (*Zygophyllaceae*)

| | |
|---|---|
| ***harmala*** | CArn MSal |

# *Pelargonium* ✿ (*Geraniaceae*)

| | | |
|---|---|---|
| | 'A Happy Thought' | see *P.* 'Happy Thought' |
| | 'A.M. Mayne' (Z/d) | WFib |
| | 'Abba' (Z/d) | WFib |
| | 'Abbie Hillier' (R) **new** | LDea |
| | 'Abel Carrière' (I/d) | SPet |
| | ***abrotanifolium*** (Sc) | CRHN LPio MBPg MHer SSea WFib WGwG |
| | 'Abundance' (Sc) | LDea MBPg |
| | ***acerifolium*** misapplied | see *P. vitifolium* |
| | ***acetosum*** | LPio MHer MSte SSea |
| * | - 'Variegatum' (v) | LPio MSte |
| | 'Acushla by Brian' (Sc) | MBPg |
| | 'Ada Green' (R) | LDea WFib |
| | 'Adam's Quilt' (Z/C) | WEas |
| | 'Adele' (Min/d) | ESul |
| | 'Ade's Elf' (Z/St) | NFir SSea |
| | 'Aerosol' (Min) | ESul |
| | 'Ailsa' (Min/d) | ESul |
| | 'Ainsdale Beauty' (Z) | SSea WFib |
| | 'Ainsdale Claret' (Z) | SSea |
| | 'Ainsdale Eyeful' (Z) | WFib |
| | 'Ainsdale Glasnost' (Z) | SSea |
| | 'Ainsdale Happiness' (Z/d) | SSea |
| | 'Akela' (Min) | ESul |
| | 'Alan West' (Z/St) | SSea |
| | ***alchemilloides*** | CRHN CSec LPio |
| | 'Alcyone' (Dw/d) | ESul WFib |
| | 'Alde' (Min) | NFir SSea WFib |
| | 'Aldenham' (Z) | WFib |
| | 'Aldham' (Min) | ESul WFib |
| | 'Aldwyck' (R) | ESul LDea WFib |
| | 'Alex Kitson' (Z) | WFib |
| | 'Alex Mary' (R) | ESul SSea |
| | 'Algenon' (Min/d) | ESul WFib |
| I | 'Alice' (Min) | WFib |
| | 'Alice Greenfield' (Z) | NFir SSea |
| | 'Alison' (Dw) | ESul |
| | 'All My Love' (R) | LDea |
| | 'Alma' (Dw/C) | ESul |
| | 'Almond' (Sc) | MBPg |
| | 'Altair' (Min/d) | ESul |
| | 'Amari' (R) | WFib |
| | 'Amazon' (R) | ESul |
| | 'Ambrose' (Min/d) | ESul LVER WFib |
| | Amelit = 'Pacameli'PBR (I/d) | LAst LSou WGor |
| | 'American Prince of Orange' (Sc) | MBPg |
| | 'Amethyst' (R) | ESul LDea NBur SCoo SPet WFib |
| § | Amethyst = 'Fisdel'PBR (I/d) ♀H1+3 | ECtt LDea LVER NPri |
| | 'Amour' (R) | ESul |
| I | 'Amy' (Dw) | WFib |
| | 'Andersonii' (Z/Sc) | MBPg |
| | 'Andrew Salvidge' (R) | LDea |
| | 'Androcles' (A) | LDea |
| | 'Angela' (R) | ESul LDea |
| | 'Angela Read' (Dw) | ESul |
| | 'Angela Thorogood' (R) | ESul |
| | 'Angela Woodberry' (Z) | WFib |
| | Angeleyes Series (A) | LAst LRHS SSea |
| | - Angeleyes Bicolor = 'Pacbicolor'PBR (A) | LAst NPri |
| | - Angeleyes Burgundy = 'Pacburg'PBR (A) | LAst SSea |
| | - Angeleyes Orange (A) **new** | LSou |
| | - Angeleyes Randy (A) | SSea |
| | - Angeleyes Velvet Duet (A) | LAst |
| | 'Angelique' (Dw/d) | ESul LVER NFir WFib |
| | 'Anglia' (Dw) | ESul |
| | 'Ann Field' (Dw/d) | ESul |
| | 'Ann Hoystead' (R) ♀H1+3 | ESul NFir WFib |
| | 'Ann Redington' (R) | ESul |
| | 'Anna' (Dw) | ESul |
| | 'Anna Scheen' (Min) | ESul |
| | 'Anne' (I/d) | WFib |
| | 'Annsbrook Aquarius' (St) | ESul NFir |
| | 'Annsbrook Beauty' (A/C) | ESul MBPg NFir WFib |
| | 'Annsbrook Capricorn' (St/d) | ESul |
| | 'Annsbrook Fruit Sundae' (A) | LDea |
| | 'Annsbrook Jupitor' (Z/St) | ESul NFir |
| | 'Annsbrook Mars' (St/C) | ESul |
| | 'Annsbrook Peaches' (Min) | ESul |
| | 'Annsbrook Pluto' (Z/St) | ESul |
| | 'Annsbrook Venus' (Z/St) | ESul |
| | 'Anthony Ayton' (R) | ESul |
| | Anthony = 'Pacan' (Z/d) | LAst |
| | (Antik Series) Antik Orange = 'Tikorg'PBR (Z) ♀H1+3 | LVER |
| | - Antik Pink = 'Tikpink'PBR (Z) | LVER |
| | - Antik Salmon = 'Tiksal'PBR (Z) | LVER |
| | - Antik Violet = 'Tikvio'PBR (Z) | LVER |
| | 'Antoine Crozy' (ZxI/d) | WFib |
| | 'Antoinette' (Min) | ESul |
| | 'Antonnia Scammell' (St/d) | ESul |
| | 'Apache' (Z/d) ♀H1+3 | CHal WFib |
| | 'Aphrodite' (Z) | ECtt |
| | 'Apollo' (R) | ESul |
| | ***appendiculatum*** | LPio |
| | 'Apple Betty' (Sc) | MBPg WFib |
| | 'Apple Blossom Rosebud' (Z/d) ♀H1+3 | CStu ECtt EShb ESul LAst LVER MBri MCot SSea WBrk WFib |
| | 'Appleblossom' (Angeleyes Series) **new** | LSou |
| | 'Appledram' (R) | LDea |
| | 'Apri Parmer' (Min) | ESul |
| | 'Apricot' (Z/St) | ESul LAst WGor |
| | 'Apricot Queen' (I/d) | LDea |
| | 'Apricot Star' | MSte SAga |
| | 'Aprika' **new** | WGor |
| | 'April Hamilton' (I) | LDea WFib |
| | 'April Showers' (A) | LDea WFib |
| | 'Aquarell' (R) | ESul |
| | Arcona 2000 = 'KleconaPBR | LSou |
| | 'Arctic Frost' | WFib |
| § | 'Arctic Star' (Z/St) | CSpe ESul LVER MCot NFir SSea WBrk WFib |
| | 'Ardens' | CSpe EBee ESul LHop LPio LSou MCot MHer MSte NCob NFir SMrm SSea SUsu SWvt WCot WFib WGwG |
| | 'Ardwick Cinnamon' (Sc) | ESul LDea MBPg NFir WFib |
| | ***aridum*** | LPio |
| | (Aristo Series) Aristo Apricot = 'Regapri' (R) | LAst WGor |
| | - Aristo Beauty = 'Regbeauty'PBR (R) | LAst LSou |
| | - Aristo Clara Schumann (R) | LAst |
| | - Aristo Claret = 'Regros'PBR (R) | LAst |
| | - Aristo Lavender = 'Reglav'PBR (R) | LAst WGor |
| | - Aristo Red Velvet = 'Regvel'PBR (R) | LAst |
| | - Aristo Schoko = 'Regschoko' (R) | LAst WGor |

| | | |
|---|---|---|
| | - Aristo Velvet (R) **new** | LSou |
| | - Aristo Violet = 'Regvio'[PBR] (R) | LAst |
| | 'Arnside Fringed Aztec' (R) | LDea WFib |
| | 'Aroma' (Sc) | MBPg |
| | 'Arthington Slam' (R) | LDea |
| | 'Ashby' (U/Sc) | CWCL LVER MBPg MHer NFir SSea |
| | 'Ashfield Jubilee' (Z/C) | NFir |
| | 'Ashfield Monarch' (Z/d) ♀H1+3 | NFir SSea |
| | 'Ashfield Serenade' (Z) ♀H1+3 | SSea WFib |
| | 'Ashley Stephenson' (R) | WFib |
| | 'Askham Fringed Aztec' (R) ♀H1+3 | ESul LDea SSea WFib |
| | 'Askham Slam' (R) | LDea |
| | ***asperum*** Ehr. ex Willd. | see *P.* 'Graveolens' |
| | 'Asperum' | MBPg |
| | 'Astrakan' (Z/d) | SSea |
| | 'Athabasca' (Min) | ESul |
| | 'Atlantic Burgundy' **new** | CWCL |
| § | 'Atomic Snowflake' (Sc/v) | CArn CHal ESul GBar LDea MBPg MCot MHer MNHC MSte SDnm SIde SPet SSea WFib |
| | 'Atrium' (U) | WFib |
| | 'Attar of Roses' (Sc) ♀H1+3 | CArn CHal CHrt CRHN CTca ESul GBar LDea LVER MBPg MCot MHer MSte NFir NPri SDnm SIde SSea WBrk WFib WGwG |
| | 'Attraction' (Z/Ca/d) | SSea |
| | 'Aubusson' (R) | ESul |
| | 'Auntie Billie' (A) | LDea |
| | 'Aurelia' (A) | LDea |
| | 'Aurora' (Z/d) | LAst LSou LVER SSea |
| | 'Aurore' (U) | see *P.* 'Unique Aurore' |
| | ***australe*** | CRHN LPio MCot SBch SChr WFib |
| | 'Australian Bute' (R) | ESul LSou LVER |
| | 'Australian Mystery' (R/Dec) | CSpe ESul LPio MSte NFir SAga WFib |
| | 'Autumn Colours' (Min) | ESul |
| | 'Autumn Haze' (R) | ESul |
| | 'Aztec' (R) ♀H1+3 | ESul LDea LVER MSte NBur NFir SSea WFib |
| | 'Baby Bird's Egg' (Min) | ESul WFib |
| | 'Baby Brocade' (Min/d) | ESul WFib |
| | 'Baby Harry' (Dw/v) | WFib |
| | 'Baby Helen' (Min) | ESul |
| | 'Baby James' (Min) | ESul |
| | 'Baby Snooks' (A) | ESul LDea |
| | 'Babylon' (R) | ESul |
| | 'Badley' (Dw) | ESul |
| | 'Balcon Lilas' | see *P.* 'Roi des Balcons Lilas' |
| | 'Balcon Rose' | see *P.* 'Hederinum' |
| I | 'Ballerina' (Min) | WFib |
| | 'Ballerina' (R) | see *P.* 'Carisbrooke' |
| | 'Bandit' (Min) | ESul |
| | 'Banstead Beacon' | LVER |
| | 'Banstead Beauty' | LVER |
| | 'Banstead Village' (Z) | LVER |
| | 'Bantam' (Min/d) | ESul WFib |
| | 'Barbara Houghton' (Dw/d) | WFib |
| § | 'Barbe Bleu' (I/d) | ECtt LDea LVER NFir SSea WFib |
| | 'Barcelona' (R) | ESul |
| | 'Barham' (Min/d) | ESul |
| | 'Barking' (Min/z) | ESul NFir |
| | 'Barnston Dale' (Dw/d) | ESul NFir |
| | 'Bath Beauty' (Dw) | CSpe WEas |
| | 'Baylham' (Min) | ESul |
| | Beach = 'Fisbea' (I/d) | NPri |
| | 'Beacon Hill' (Min) | ESul |
| | 'Beatrice Cottington' (I/d) | WFib |
| | 'Beatrix' (Z/d) | LVER |
| | 'Beau Geste' (R) | ESul |
| | 'Beauty of Diane' (I/d) | LDea |
| | 'Beauty of Eastbourne' misapplied | see *P.* 'Lachskönigin' |
| | 'Beidermeier' (R) | ESul |
| | 'Belinda Adams' (Min/d) ♀H1+3 | NFir |
| | Belladonna = 'Fisopa' (I/d) | ECtt SCoo |
| | 'Belvedere' (R) | ESul |
| | 'Bembridge' (Z/St/d) | SSea WFib |
| | 'Ben Franklin' (Z/d/v) ♀H1+3 | ESul NFir SSea |
| | 'Ben Matt' (R) | WFib |
| | 'Ben Nevis' (Dw/d) | ESul LVER |
| | 'Ben Picton' (Z/d) | WFib |
| | 'Bentley' (Dw) | ESul |
| | 'Berkswell Blush' (A) | LDea |
| | 'Berkswell Calypso' (A) **new** | LDea |
| | 'Berkswell Carnival' (A) | LDea |
| | 'Berkswell Champagne' (A) | LDea |
| | 'Berkswell Charm' (A) **new** | LDea |
| | 'Berkswell Dainty' (A) | LDea |
| | 'Berkswell Debonair' (A) | LDea |
| | 'Berkswell Gaiety' (A) | LDea |
| | 'Berkswell Jester' (A) **new** | LDea |
| | 'Berkswell Lace' (A) | LDea |
| | 'Berkswell Pixie' (A) | LDea |
| | 'Berkswell Rosette' (A) **new** | LDea |
| | 'Berkswell Sparkler' (A) | LDea |
| | 'Berkswell Windmill' (A) | LDea |
| | Bernardo = 'Guiber'[PBR] (I/d) | LAst |
| | 'Bernice Ladroot' | LDea |
| | 'Beromünster' (Dec) | ESul LDea MHer MSte NFir SAga WFib |
| | 'Bert Pearce' (R) | ESul LDea WFib |
| | 'Beryl Read' (Dw) | CWCL ESul |
| | 'Beryl Reid' (R) | ESul LDea WFib |
| | 'Berylette' (Min/d) | ESul |
| | 'Bess' (Z/d) | ESul |
| | 'Bette Shellard' (Z/d/v) | NFir |
| | 'Betty Merry' (R) | LDea |
| | 'Betty Read' (Dw) | ESul |
| | 'Betty West' (Min/d) | ESul |
| | ***betulinum*** | LPio SSea WFib |
| | 'Bianca' (Min/d) | ESul LVER |
| | 'Big Apple' (Sc) | MBPg |
| | 'Bildeston' (Dw/C) | ESul WFib |
| | 'Bill West' (I) | SSea WFib |
| | 'Billie Read' (Dw/d) | ESul |
| | 'Bingo' (Min) | ESul |
| | 'Bird Dancer' (Dw/St) ♀H1+3 | CHal ESul LVER MHer MSte NFir SAga SBch SSea SWal WBrk |
| | 'Birdbush Andy Pandy' (Sc) | MBPg |
| | 'Birdbush Bella' (Sc) | MBPg |
| | 'Birdbush Billy' (Sc) **new** | MBPg |
| | 'Birdbush Blush' (Sc) | MBPg |
| | 'Birdbush Bobby' (Sc) **new** | MBPg |
| | 'Birdbush Bold and Beautiful' (Sc) | MBPg |
| | 'Birdbush Bramley' (Sc) | MBPg |
| | 'Birdbush Chloe' (St) | MBPg |
| | 'Birdbush Claire Louise' (Sc) | MBPg |
| | 'Birdbush Dawndew' (Sc) | MBPg |
| | 'Birdbush Eleanor' (Z) | MBPg WFib |
| | 'Birdbush Julie Anne' (Sc) | MBPg |
| | 'Birdbush Kay Lye' (Sc) **new** | MBPg |
| | 'Birdbush Lemonside' (Sc) | MBPg |
| | 'Birdbush Linda Creasey' (Sc) | MBPg |

| | |
|---|---|
| 'Birdbush Matty' | MBPg |
| 'Birdbush Miriam' (Sc) | MBPg |
| 'Birdbush Nutty' (Sc) | MBPg |
| 'Birdbush Pinky and Perky' (U) | MBPg |
| 'Birdbush Sweetness' (Sc) | MBPg |
| 'Birdbush Too Too O' (Sc) | MBPg |
| 'Birdbush Velvet' (Sc) | MBPg |
| 'Birdbush Victoria' (Sc) **new** | MBPg |
| 'Birthday Girl' (R) | WFib |
| 'Bitter Lemon' (Sc) | ESul MBPg |
| 'Black Butterfly' | see *P.* 'Brown's Butterfly' |
| 'Black Knight' (R) | CSpe EShb LVER MSte SAga |
| 'Black Knight' Lea (Dw/d/C) | ESul MSte NFir |
| 'Black Magic' (R) | NPri |
| 'Black Night' (A) | ESul MBPg |
| 'Black Pearl' (Z/d) | LVER |
| 'Black Prince' (R/Dec) | NFir WFib |
| 'Black Top' (R) | ESul |
| 'Black Velvet' (R) | ESul LDea MCot |
| 'Black Vesuvius' | see *P.* 'Red Black Vesuvius' |
| 'Blackcurrant Yhu' (Dec) **new** | NFir |
| 'Blackdown Delight' (Z) | NFir |
| 'Blackdown Sensation' (Dw/Z) | NFir |
| 'Blakesdorf' (Dw) | ESul |
| Blanca = 'Penwei'$^{PBR}$ (Dark Line Series) (Z/d) | LAst LSou LVER |
| Blanche Roche = 'Guitoblanc' (I/d) | LAst LSou NBlu SCoo |
| § 'Blandfordianum' (Sc) | LDea LPio MHer MSte |
| 'Blandfordianum Roseum' (Sc) | LDea |
| 'Blaze Away' | SSea |
| 'Blazonry' (Z/v) | WFib |
| 'Blendworth' (R) | LDea |
| 'Blooming Gem' (Min/I/d) | LDea |
| 'Blue Beard' | see *P.* 'Barbe Bleu' |
| 'Blue Orchid' (R) | ESul |
| Blue Sybil = 'Pacblusy'$^{PBR}$ (I/d) | LAst LSou LVER |
| 'Blue Wine' | SAga |
| Blue Wonder = 'Pacbla'$^{PBR}$ (Z/d) | LAst LSou WGor |
| 'Bluebeard' | see *P.* 'Barbe Bleu' |
| Blue-Blizzard = 'Fisrain'$^{PBR}$ (I) | SCoo |
| 'Blush Petit Pierre' (Min) | ESul |
| 'Blushing Bride' (I/d) | LDea |
| 'Blushing Emma' (Dw/d) | ESul |
| 'Bob Hall' (St) | ESul |
| 'Bob Newing' (Min/St) | ESul WFib |
| 'Bobberstone' (Z/St) | LVER WFib |
| 'Bold Appleblossom' (Z) | SSea WFib |
| 'Bold Carmine' (Z/d) | NFir |
| 'Bold Carousel' (Z/d) | WFib |
| 'Bold Dawn' (Z) | NFir |
| 'Bold Flame' (Z/d) | WFib |
| 'Bold Limelight' (Z/d) | WFib |
| 'Bold Melody' (Z) **new** | SSea |
| 'Bold Pixie' (Dw/d) | WFib |
| 'Bold Sunrise' (Z/d) | LVER NFir |
| 'Bold Sunset' (Z/d) | LVER NFir WFib |
| 'Bold White' (Z) | NFir |
| 'Bolero' (U) 🏆$^{H1+3}$ | LVER MSte NFir SSea WFib |
| 'Bon Bon' (Min/St) | WFib |
| 'Bonito' (I/d) | LVER SSea |
| 'Bonnie Austin' (St) | ESul |
| 'Bonny' (Min/St) | ESul |
| 'Bosham' (R) | ESul LDea WFib |
| 'Both's Snowflake' (Sc/v) | GBar GGar MBPg |

| | |
|---|---|
| ***bowkeri*** | WFib |
| 'Brackenwood' (Dw/d) 🏆$^{H1+3}$ | ESul LVER NFir |
| 'Bramford' (Dw) | ESul |
| 'Braque' (R) | LDea |
| Bravo = 'Fisbravo'$^{PBR}$ (Z/d) | WFib |
| 'Break o' Day' (R) | LDea WEas |
| 'Bredon' (R) 🏆$^{H1+3}$ | ESul |
| 'Brenda' (Min/d) | ESul WFib |
| 'Brenda Hyatt' (Dw/d) | ESul WFib |
| 'Brenda Kitson' (Z/d) | LVER |
| 'Brettenham' (Min) | ESul |
| 'Brian West' (Min/St/C) **new** | ESul |
| 'Briarlyn Beauty' (A) | LDea MBPg |
| 'Briarlyn Moonglow' (A) | ESul LDea SSea |
| 'Bridesmaid' (Dw/d) | ESul LVER NFir WFib |
| 'Bright Eyes' ambig. (Dw) | WFib |
| 'Brightstone' (Z/d) | WFib |
| 'Brightwell' (Min/d) | ESul |
| 'Brilliant' (Dec) | MBPg WFib |
| 'Brilliantine' (Sc) | ESul MBPg MHer WFib |
| 'Bristol' (Z/v) | SSea |
| 'Britannia' (R) | LDea |
| 'Brixworth Pearl' (Z) | WFib |
| 'Brockbury Scarlet' (Ca) | WFib |
| 'Bronze Corinne' (Z/C/d) | SPet |
| 'Bronze Velvet' (R) | LDea |
| 'Brook's Purple' | see *P.* 'Royal Purple' |
| 'Brookside Betty' (Dw/C/d) | ESul |
| 'Brookside Bolero' (Z) | ESul |
| 'Brookside Candy' (Dw/d) | ESul |
| 'Brookside Champagne' (Min/d) | ESul |
| 'Brookside Fiesta' (Min/d) | ESul |
| 'Brookside Flamenco' (Dw/d) | ESul WFib |
| 'Brookside Free Spirit' (Min/D) **new** | ESul |
| 'Brookside Melody' (Min/D) **new** | ESul |
| 'Brookside Polka' (Dw/D) **new** | ESul |
| 'Brookside Primrose' (Min/C/d) | ESul NFir WFib |
| 'Brookside Rosita' (Min) | ESul |
| 'Brookside Serenade' (Dw) | ESul WFib |
| 'Brookside Spitfire' (Dw/d) | ESul |
| 'Brookside Tango' (Min/D) **new** | ESul |
| § 'Brown's Butterfly' (R) | ECtt EShb ESul LDea LPio NFir SSea WFib |
| 'Brunswick' (Sc) | ESul LDea MBPg MHer MSte WFib |
| 'Bucklesham' (Dw) | ESul |
| 'Bullfinch' (R) | ESul |
| 'Bumblebee' (Dw) | ESul |
| 'Burgenlandmädel' (Z/d) | LVER |
| 'Burns Country' (Dw) **new** | NFir |
| 'Burstall' (Min/d) | ESul |
| 'Bushfire' (R) 🏆$^{H1+3}$ | ESul LDea WFib |
| 'Butley' (Min) | ESul |
| 'Butterfly' (Min/v) | ECtt NPri |
| Butterfly = 'Fisam'$^{PBR}$ (I) | NFir SCoo |
| 'Button 'n' Bows' (I/d) | WFib |
| ***caffrum*** | LPio |
| 'Cal' | see *P.* 'Salmon Irene' |
| Calais = 'Paclai' | LAst |
| 'California Brilliant' (U) | MBPg MHer |
| 'Calignon' (Z/St) | SSea WFib |
| 'Camphor Rose' (Sc) | ESul GPWP LDea MBPg MHer NFir SSea |
| 'Can-can' (I/d) | WFib |
| 'Candy' (Min/d) | ESul |

| | | |
|---|---|---|
| | 'Candy Kisses' (D) | ESul |
| | Candy Rose = 'Pacdy' | LAst |
| | ***canescens*** | see *P.* 'Blandfordianum' |
| | 'Capel' (Dw/d) | ESul |
| | ***capitatum*** | LPio MBPg MHer MNHC WFib |
| | 'Capri' (Sc) | MBPg WFib |
| | 'Capricorn' (Min/d) | ESul |
| | 'Captain Starlight' (A) | CRHN ESul LDea LVER MBPg MHer NFir SSea WFib |
| | 'Caravan' (A) | LDea |
| | 'Cardinal' | see *P.* 'Kardinal' |
| | 'Cardington' (St/Dw) | ESul |
| | 'Carefree' (U) | LPio MSte NFir WFib |
| § | 'Carisbrooke' (R) ♀H1+3 | ESul LDea WEas WFib |
| | 'Carl Gaffney' | LDea |
| | 'Carmel' (Z) | WFib |
| | 'Carnival' (R) | see *P.* 'Marie Vogel' |
| | 'Carol' (R) | ESul |
| | 'Carol Gibbons' (Z/d) | LVER NFir WFib |
| | 'Carol Helyar' (Z/d) | WFib |
| | 'Carole Munroe' (Z/d) | LVER |
| | 'Caroline' (Dec) | ESul |
| | 'Caroline Plumridge' (Dw) | ESul |
| | 'Caroline Schmidt' (Z/d/v) | CHal LAst LVER MCot MSte NFir SSea WBrk WFib |
| | 'Carolyn' (Dw) | ESul |
| | 'Carolyn Hardy' (Z/d) | WFib |
| | Cascade Lilac | see *P.* 'Roi des Balcons Lilas' |
| | Cascade Pink | see *P.* 'Hederinum' |
| | Cascade Red | see *P.* 'Red Cascade' |
| | 'Catford Belle' (A) ♀H1+3 | CHal ESul LDea SSea |
| | 'Cathay' (Z/St) | ESul NFir SSea |
| | 'Catherine Wheels' (Z/St) | LVER |
| | 'Cathy' (R) | NFir |
| | ***caucalifolium*** subsp. ***caucalifolium*** | LPio |
| | - subsp. ***convolvulifolium*** | LPio WFib |
| | 'Celebration' (Z/d) | ESul |
| | 'Cerise' (I/d) **new** | SSea |
| | 'Cézanne' (R) | ESul LDea LVER MCot WFib |
| | 'Chantilly Claret' (R) | LDea |
| | 'Chantilly Lace' (R) | ESul LDea |
| | 'Charity' (Sc) ♀H1+3 | CHal EOHP ESul LDea MBPg MCot MHer MSte NFir SSea WBrk WFib |
| | 'Charlie Boy' (R) | LDea |
| | 'Charlotte Amy' (R) | LDea |
| | 'Charlotte Bidwell' (Min) | ESul |
| | 'Charlotte Bronte' (Dw/v) | WFib |
| | 'Charm' (Min) | ESul |
| | 'Charmay Adonis' | NFir |
| | 'Charmay Alf' (A) | LDea |
| | 'Charmay Aria' (A) | LDea |
| | 'Charmay Bagatelle' (A) | LDea |
| | 'Charmay Electra' (A) | LDea |
| | 'Charmay Marjorie' (A) | LDea |
| | 'Charmay Snowflake' (Sc/v) | ESul MBPg |
| | 'Chattisham' (Dw/C) | ESul NFir |
| | 'Chelmondiston' (Min/d) | ESul |
| | 'Chelsea Diane' (Min) | LVER |
| | 'Chelsea Gem' (Z/d/v) ♀H1+3 | LVER NFir WFib |
| | 'Chelsea Morning' (Z/d) | WFib |
| | 'Chelsea Star' (Z/d/v) | LVER |
| | 'Chelsworth' (Min/d) | ESul |
| | 'Chelvey' (R) | LDea |
| | 'Cherie' (R) | ESul LDea |
| | 'Cherie Bidwell' (Dw/d/v) | ESul |
| | 'Cherie Maid' (Z/v) | SSea |
| | 'Cherry' (Min) | WFib |
| | 'Cherry Baby' (Dec) | NFir |
| | 'Cherry Cocktail' (Z/d/v) | NFir |
| | 'Cherry Hazel Ruffled' (R) | ESul LDea |
| | 'Cherry Orchard' (R) | ESul LDea NBur SSea WFib |
| | 'Cherry Sundae' (Z/d/v) | ESul |
| | 'Cheryldene' (R) | LDea |
| | 'Chew Magna' (R) | WFib |
| | 'Chi-Chi' (Min) | ESul |
| | 'Chieko' (Min/d) | WFib |
| | 'Chime' (Min/d) | ESul |
| | 'China Doll' (Dw/d) | WFib |
| | 'Chinz' (R) | NFir SAga |
| | 'Chocolate Drops' (Z) | LVER |
| § | 'Chocolate Peppermint' (Sc) | CHal CHrt CRHN CSev EAro ESul LDea MBPg MCot MHer MNHC NBur NFir SIde SSea WBrk WFib |
| | 'Chocolate Tomentosum' | see *P.* 'Chocolate Peppermint' |
| | 'Chrissie' (R) | ESul WFib |
| | 'Christina Beere' (R) | LDea |
| | 'Christopher Ley' (Z) | LVER |
| | 'Chusan' (R) | SSea |
| | 'Cindy' (Dw/d) | ESul WFib |
| | 'Citriodorum' (Sc) ♀H1+3 | LDea MBPg MCot MHer WFib |
| | 'Citronella' (Sc) | CRHN LDea MBPg MHer MSte SSea WFib |
| | ***citronellum*** (Sc) | LPio MBPg |
| | 'City of Bath' **new** | CWCL |
| | 'Clara Read' (Dw) | ESul |
| | 'Claret Rock Unique' (U) | LDea MBPg MSte SSea WFib |
| | 'Clarissa' (Min) | ESul |
| | 'Clatterbridge' (Dw/d) | ESul LVER NFir |
| | 'Claude Read' (Dw) | ESul |
| | 'Claudette' (Min) | ESul |
| | 'Claudius' (Min) | ESul |
| | 'Claydon' (Dw/d) | ESul NFir |
| | 'Claydon Firebird' (R) | ESul SAga |
| | 'Clorinda' (U/Sc) | CHal CHrt CRHN EShb ESul GBar LVER MBPg MCot MHer MSte NBur SIde SSea WFib |
| | 'Clorinda Variegated' | see *P.* 'Variegated Clorinda' |
| | 'Clovelly Rose' **new** | CWCL |
| | 'Clown' (R) | ESul |
| | 'Coconut Ice' (Dw) | ESul LVER |
| | 'Coddenham' (Dw/d) | ESul LVER WFib |
| § | 'Colonel Baden-Powell' (I/d) | LDea WFib |
| | 'Colwell' (Min/d) | WFib |
| | 'Concolor Lace' | see *P.* 'Shottesham Pet' |
| | 'Confetti' (R) | ESul |
| | 'Contrast' (Z/C/v) | CWCL LAst LRHS MBri SCoo SPoG SSea WFib |
| | 'Cook's Peachblossom' | WFib |
| | 'Copdock' (Min/d) | ESul |
| | 'Copthorne' (U/Sc) ♀H1+3 | CRHN ESul LDea LVER MBPg MCot MHer MSte SAga SSea WFib |
| | 'Coral Frills' (Min/d) | ESul |
| | 'Coral Reef' (Z/d) | LVER |
| | ***cordifolium*** | CRHN WFib |
| | - var. ***rubrocinctum*** **new** | NFir |
| | ***coriandrifolium*** | see *P. myrrhifolium* var. *coriandrifolium* |
| | 'Cornell' (I/d) | ECtt WFib |
| | ***cortusifolium*** | MHer |
| | 'Corvina' (R) | WFib |
| | 'Cotta Lilac Queen' (I/d) | LVER |
| | 'Cottenham Beauty' (A) | ESul LDea NFir |
| | 'Cottenham Belle' (A) | ESul |
| | 'Cottenham Bliss' (A) | ESul |
| | 'Cottenham Charm' (A) | ESul LDea |
| | 'Cottenham Cheer' (A) **new** | ESul |
| | 'Cottenham Cynthia Haird' (A) | ESul |
| | 'Cottenham Delight' (A) | ESul LDea NFir |
| | 'Cottenham Gem' (A) | ESul |
| | 'Cottenham Glamour' (A) | ESul NFir |
| | 'Cottenham Harmony' (A) | ESul LDea |
| | 'Cottenham Jubilee' (A) | ESul LDea MHer |

| | | |
|---|---|---|
| | 'Cottenham Mervyn Haird' (A) | ESul |
| | 'Cottenham Star' (A) | ESul |
| | 'Cottenham Surprise' (A) | ESul LDea MBPg MSte NFir |
| | 'Cottenham Treasure' (A) | ESul LDea |
| | 'Cottenham Wonder' (A) | ESul |
| | 'Cotton Candy' (Min/d) | ESul |
| | 'Cottontail' (Min) | ESul WFib |
| | ***cotyledonis*** | WFib |
| | 'Countess di Pralormo' (Z/v) **new** | LVER |
| | 'Countess of Scarborough' | see *P.* 'Lady Scarborough' |
| | 'Country Girl' (R) | SPet |
| | 'Cover Girl' (Z/d) | WFib |
| | 'Cowes' (St/Min/d) | ESul |
| | 'Cramdon Red' (Dw) | WFib |
| | 'Crampel's Master' (Z) | LVER |
| | 'Cransley Blends' (R) | ESul LDea |
| | 'Cransley Star' (A) | LDea WFib |
| | 'Cream 'n' Green' (R/v) | ESul NFir |
| | 'Creamery' (d) | WFib |
| | 'Creamy Nutmeg' (Sc/v) | CArn CHal CHrt EShb ESul GBar LDea MHer NFir SSea |
| | 'Creeting St Mary' (Min) | ESul |
| | 'Creeting St Peter' (Min) | ESul |
| | 'Crescendo' (I/d) | ECtt |
| | 'Crimson Fire' (Z/d) | MBri |
| | 'Crimson Unique' (U) ♀H1+3 | CSpe MBPg MCot MHer SAga SSea WFib |
| § | ***crispum*** (Sc) | GBar GPoy LDea MBPg WRha |
| § | - 'Golden Well Sweep' (Sc/v) | MBPg WFib |
| | - 'Major' (Sc) | ESul MBPg MCot WFib |
| | - 'Minor' (Sc) | MBPg MHer |
| | - 'Peach Cream' (Sc/v) | CHal ESul MBPg WFib |
| | - 'Prince Rupert' (Sc) | MBPg |
| | - 'Variegatum' (Sc/v) ♀H1+3 | CHal CRHN GBar GGar GPoy LDea LVER MBPg MCot MHer NFir SIde SPet SSea WFib |
| | ***crithmifolium*** | MHer |
| | 'Crock O Day' (I/d) | LVER |
| | 'Crocketta' (I/d/v) | LVER NFir |
| | 'Crocodile' (I/C/d) | CDow ECtt EShb LDea LVER MHer NFir SSea SWal WBrk WFib |
| | 'Crowfield' (Min/d) | ESul WFib |
| | 'Crowfoot Rose' (Sc) | EAro GBar |
| | 'Crown Jewels' (R) | LDea |
| | 'Crystal Palace Gem' (Z/v) | LRHS LVER SSea WFib |
| | 'Crystal West' (Min/St) | ESul |
| | ***cucullatum*** | ESul LPio SSea WFib |
| | - 'Flore Plenum' | MHer WFib |
| | 'Culpho' (Min/C/d) | ESul |
| | 'Cupid' (Min/Dw/d) | WFib |
| | 'Cyril Read' (Dw) | ESul |
| § | 'Czar' (Z/C) | SCoo |
| | 'Dainty Lassie' (Dw/v) | ESul |
| | 'Dainty Maid' (Sc) | ESul GGar MBPg NFir SAga SSea |
| | 'Dale Queen' (Z) | WFib |
| | 'Dallimore' (Dw) | ESul |
| | 'Danielle Marie' (A) | LDea |
| | 'Danton' (Z/d) | WFib |
| | 'Dark Ascot' (Dec) | ESul |
| | 'Dark Lady' (Sc) | MBPg |
| | 'Dark Red Irene' (Z/d) | WFib |
| | 'Dark Secret' (R) | CSpe ESul LDea MSte WFib |
| | 'Dark Venus' (R) | ESul LDea WFib |
| | Dark-Red-Blizzard = 'Fisblizdark' (I) | CWCL NPri |
| | 'Darmsden' (A) ♀H1+3 | ESul LDea NFir SSea |
| | 'David John' (Dw/d) | ESul |
| | 'David Mitchell' (Min/Ca/d) | ESul |
| | 'Davina' (Min/d) | ESul WFib |
| | 'Dawn Star' (Z/St) | ESul NFir |
| | 'Deacon Arlon' (Dw/d) | ESul LVER |
| | 'Deacon Avalon' (Dw/d) | WFib |
| | 'Deacon Barbecue' (Z/d) | ESul WFib |
| | 'Deacon Birthday' (Z/d) | ESul LVER WFib |
| | 'Deacon Bonanza' (Z/d) | ESul LVER SSea WFib |
| | 'Deacon Clarion' (Z/d) | ESul WFib |
| | 'Deacon Constancy' (Z/d) | ESul |
| | 'Deacon Coral Reef' (Z/d) | ESul WFib |
| | 'Deacon Finale' (Z/d) | ESul LVER |
| | 'Deacon Fireball' (Z/d) | ESul LVER WFib |
| | 'Deacon Flamingo' (Z/d) | ESul WBrk |
| | 'Deacon Gala' (Z/d) | ESul WFib |
| | 'Deacon Golden Bonanza' (Z/C/d) | ESul WFib |
| | 'Deacon Golden Gala' (Z/C/d) | ESul |
| | 'Deacon Golden Lilac Mist' (Z/C/d) | ESul WFib |
| | 'Deacon Jubilant' (Z/d) | ESul |
| | 'Deacon Lilac Mist' (Z/d) | ESul LVER SSea WFib |
| | 'Deacon Mandarin' (Z/d) | ESul WFib |
| | 'Deacon Minuet' (Z/d) | ESul NFir WFib |
| | 'Deacon Moonlight' (Z/d) | ESul LVER |
| | 'Deacon Peacock' (Z/C/d) | ESul WFib |
| | 'Deacon Picotee' (Z/d) | ESul SSea WFib |
| | 'Deacon Regalia' (Z/d) | ESul MHer WFib |
| | 'Deacon Romance' (Z/d) | ESul SSea |
| § | 'Deacon Summertime' (Z/d) | ESul WFib |
| | 'Deacon Sunburst' (Z/d) | ESul LVER |
| | 'Deacon Suntan' (Z/d) | ESul |
| | 'Deacon Trousseau' (Z/d) | ESul LVER WFib |
| | 'Dean's Delight' (Sc) | LDea MBPg |
| | 'Debbie' (A) | LDea |
| | 'Debbie Parmer' (Dw/d) | ESul |
| | 'Debbie Thrower' (Dw) | ESul |
| | 'Deborah Miliken' (Z/d) | ESul NFir WFib |
| | 'Decora Impérial' (I) | LVER |
| | 'Decora Lavender' | see *P.* 'Decora Lilas' |
| § | 'Decora Lilas' (I) | ECtt LAst LVER SPet |
| | 'Decora Mauve' | see *P.* 'Decora Lilas' |
| | 'Decora Pink' | see *P.* 'Decora Rouge' |
| | 'Decora Red' | see *P.* 'Decora Rouge' |
| § | 'Decora Rose' (I) | ECtt LAst SPet |
| § | 'Decora Rouge' (I) | ECtt LAst SPet |
| | 'Deerwood Darling' (Min/v/d) | WFib |
| | 'Deerwood Lavender Lad' (Sc) | ESul LDea MBPg MHer SSea WFib |
| | 'Deerwood Lavender Lass' | ESul LDea LPio MBPg MHer |
| | 'Deerwood Pink Puff' (St/d) | WFib |
| | 'Delightful' (R) | WFib |
| | 'Delilah' (R) | LDea |
| | 'Delli' (R) | NFir NPer SMrm WFib |
| | 'Delta' (Min/d) | ESul |
| | 'Denebola' (Min/d) | ESul |
| | 'Dennis Hunt' (Z/C) | NFir |
| | ***denticulatum*** | GBar MHer SSea |
| § | - 'Filicifolium' (Sc) | CHal CRHN EShb ESul LDea LPio LVER MBPg MHer SSea WFib |
| | 'Diana Hull' | MBPg |
| | 'Diane' (Min/d) | ESul |
| | 'Diane Louise' (d) | SSea |
| | 'Dibbinsdale' (Z) | ESul LVER NFir |
| | ***dichondrifolium*** (Sc) | LPio LVER MBPg MHer NFir SSea WFib |
| | ***dichondrifolium*** x ***reniforme*** (Sc) | ESul NFir |
| | 'Dinky' (Min/d) | ESul |
| | 'Display' ambig. (Dw/v) | WFib |
| | 'Distinction' (Z) | LAst MHer NFir SPoG SSea WFib |
| | 'Doctor A. Chipault' (I/d) | LDea |

| | |
|---|---|
| 'Dollar Bute' (R) | ESul |
| 'Dolly Read' (Dw) | ESul |
| 'Dolly Varden' (Z/v) ♀H1+3 | ESul LDea LVER NFir SSea WFib |
| 'Don's Carosel' (Z/v) | SSea |
| 'Don's Helen Bainbridge' (Z/C) | NFir |
| 'Don's Mona Noble' (Z/C) | NFir SSea |
| 'Don's Richard A. Costain' (Z/C) | NFir |
| 'Don's Southport' (Z/v) | NFir |
| 'Don's Swanland Girl' (Min) | ESul |
| 'Don's Wensleydale' (Dw/C) new | ESul |
| 'Dorcas Brigham Lime' (Sc) | CSpe EAro SAga |
| 'Dorcus Bingham' (Sc) | GBar MBPg |
| 'Doris Frith' (R) | LDea |
| 'Doris Hancock' (R) | WFib |
| 'Doris Shaw' (R) | ESul |
| 'Dorothy May' (A) | LDea |
| 'Double Grace Wells' (Min/d) | ESul |
| 'Double New Life' (Z/d) | CHal |
| 'Double Pink' (R/d) | WFib |
| 'Dovedale' (Dw/C) | ESul WFib |
| 'Downlands' (Z/d) | SWal WFib |
| 'Dragon's Breath' (Z/St) | LVER |
| 'Dresden China' (R) | ESul LDea |
| 'Dresden White' (Dw) | WFib |
| Dresdner Apricot = 'Pacbriap'PBR (I/d) | LVER |
| 'Dubonnet' (R) | LDea SSea |
| 'Duchess of Devonshire' (U) | WFib |
| 'Duke of Edinburgh' | see *P.* 'Hederinum Variegatum' |
| 'Dulcie' (Min) | ESul |
| 'Dunkery Beacon' (R) | ESul WFib |
| 'Dusty Rose' (Min) | ESul |
| 'E. Dabner' (Z/d) | WFib |
| 'Earl of Chester' (Min/d) ♀H1+3 | WFib |
| 'Earliana' (Dec) | ESul LDea |
| 'Earlsfour' (R) | LDea MSte |
| 'East Sussex' (Dw/C) new | ESul |
| 'Easter Promise' (R) | ESul |
| ***echinatum*** | CSpe LPio MBPg MHer SSea |
| - 'Album' | LPio SSea WFib |
| - 'Miss Stapleton' | see *P.* 'Miss Stapleton' |
| 'Eden Gem' (Min/d) | WFib |
| 'Edith Stern' (Dw/d) | ESul |
| 'Edmond Lachenal' (Z/d) | WFib |
| 'Edwards Michael' (A) | LDea |
| 'Eileen' (Min/d) | ESul |
| 'Eileen Nancy' (Z) new | NFir |
| 'Eileen Postle' (R) ♀H1+3 | WFib |
| 'Eileen Stanley' (R) | LDea |
| 'Elaine' (R) | LDea |
| 'Elaine Thompson' (R) | LDea |
| Elbe Silver = 'Pensil' (I) | LAst NFir SCoo |
| 'Elizabeth Angus' (Z) | SSea WFib |
| 'Elizabeth Read' (Dw) | ESul |
| 'Ella Martin' (St) | ESul |
| 'Elmfield' (St/Min/d) | ESul |
| 'Elmsett' (Dw/C/d) | ESul LVER NFir SSea WFib |
| 'Elna' (Min) | ESul |
| ***elongatum*** | SSea |
| 'Els' (Dw/St) | ESul LVER WBrk |
| 'Elsi' (I x Z/d/v) | LVER WFib |
| 'Elsie Gillam' (St) | ESul LVER WFib |
| 'Elsie Hickman' (R) | ESul LDea NBur |
| 'Elsie Portas' (Z/C/d) | ESul |
| 'Embassy' (Min) | ESul WFib |
| Emilia = 'Pactina' | LAst LSou WGor |
| 'Emma Game' (Z/St) | WFib |
| 'Emma Hössle' | see *P.* 'Frau Emma Hössle' |
| 'Emma Jane Read' (Dw/d) | ESul NFir WFib |
| 'Emmy Sensation' (R) | LDea |
| 'Ena' (Min) | ESul |
| 'Encore' (Z/d/v) | LVER |
| ***endlicherianum*** | LPio NBhm WWFP |
| 'Endsleigh' (Sc) | MBPg SBch |
| 'Enid Brackley' (R) | ESul |
| 'Erwarton' (Min/d) | ESul NFir |
| 'Escapade' (Min/d) | ESul |
| 'Eskay Gold' (A) | WFib |
| 'Eskay Jewel' (A) | WFib |
| 'Eskay Sugar Candy' (A) | WFib |
| 'Eskay Verglo' (A) | WFib |
| 'Evelyn' (Min) | ESul |
| Evening Glow = 'Bergpalais'PBR | LVER |
| 'Evka'PBR (I/v) | CWCL LAst LVER SCoo SSea |
| 'Excalibur' (Z/Min/v) | LVER |
| 'Explosive' (I) | NPri |
| ***exstipulatum*** | EShb SSea WEas |
| 'Fabian Gane' (St) new | LVER SSea |
| 'Fair Dinkum' (Z/v) | ESul |
| 'Fair Ellen' (Sc) | ESul LDea MBPg MHer WFib |
| 'Fairlee' (DwI) | WFib |
| 'Fairy Lights' (Dw/St) | ESul NFir |
| 'Fairy Orchid' (A) | ESul LDea WFib |
| 'Fairy Queen' | LDea MHer |
| 'Falkenham' (Min) | ESul |
| 'Falkland Brother' (Z/C/v) | WFib |
| 'Falkland Hero' (Z/v) | NFir |
| 'Fallen Angel' (Z/St) | LVER |
| 'Fandango' (Z/St) | ESul NFir WFib |
| 'Fanny Eden' (R) | CWCL WFib |
| 'Fantasia' white-flowered (Dw/d) ♀H1+3 | ESul WFib |
| 'Fareham' (R) ♀H1+3 | LDea MSte WFib |
| 'Feneela' (Dw/d) | ESul |
| 'Fenland' (R) | ESul |
| 'Fenton Farm' (Dw/C) | ESul NFir WFib |
| 'Fern Mint' (Sc) | MBPg |
| 'Festal' (Min/d) | ESul |
| 'Fiat Queen' (Z/d) | WFib |
| 'Fiery Sunrise' (R) | ESul LDea |
| 'Fiesta' (I/d) | LDea |
| 'Fifth Avenue' (R) | CSpe ESul LPio MSte WFib |
| 'Filicifolium' | see *P. denticulatum* 'Filicifolium' |
| 'Fir Trees Audrey B' (St) | NFir |
| 'Fir Trees Big Show' (I/v) | NFir |
| 'Fir Trees Celebration' (Sc) new | NFir |
| 'Fir Trees Eileen' (St) | NFir |
| 'Fir Trees Ele' (A/v) | NFir |
| 'Fir Trees Fantail' (Min) new | NFir |
| 'Fir Trees Flamingo' (Dw) | NFir |
| 'Fir Trees Jack' (Z/Dw) | NFir |
| 'Fir Trees John Grainger' (Z/v) | NFir |
| 'Fir Trees Mark' (R/Dec/v) | NFir SAga |
| 'Fir Trees Nan' (R/Dec) | NFir |
| 'Fir Trees Ruby Wedding' (C) | NFir |
| 'Fir Trees Silver Wedding' (Z/C/d) | NFir |
| 'Fir Trees Sparkler' (Min/C) | NFir |
| 'Fire Dancer' (R) | ESul |
| 'Fire Dragon' (Z/St/d) | SSea |
| 'Fireball'PBR | LAst LSou |
| 'Firebrand' (Z/d) | LVER |
| 'Firefly' (Min/d) | ESul |
| 'Firestone' (Dw) | ESul |
| 'Fireworks' (Dw) new | SWal |

| | |
|---|---|
| (Fireworks Series) | LAst |
| Fireworks Cherry = 'Fiwocherry'PBR (Z) | |
| - Fireworks Cherry-white = 'Fiwocher'PBR (Z) | LAst SSea |
| - Fireworks Light Pink = 'Fiwopink'PBR (Z/St) | LAst |
| - Fireworks Red-white = 'Fiworewhi'PBR (Z) | LAst |
| - Fireworks Salmon = 'Fiwosal'PBR (Z) | LAst |
| - Fireworks Scarlet = 'Fiwoscarl'PBR (Z) | LAst |
| - Fireworks White = 'Fiwowit'PBR (Z) | LAst |
| 'First Blush' (R) | WFib |
| 'First Love' (Z) | NFir |
| 'Flakey' (I/d/v) ♀H1+3 | ESul LDea NFir |
| 'Flaming Katy' (Min) **new** | ESul |
| 'Flamingo' | LVER |
| 'Flarepath' (Z/C/v) | NFir |
| 'Flash' (Min) | ESul |
| 'Flecks' (Min/St) | ESul |
| 'Fleur-de-lys' (A) | LDea |
| 'Fleurette' (Min/d) | CHal ESul |
| 'Fleurisse' (Z) | WFib |
| 'Flirt' (Min) | WFib |
| 'Floral Cascade' (Fr/d) | SSea |
| 'Floria Moore' (Dec) | ESul NBur NFir SAga SSea |
| 'Flower Basket' (R/d) | ESul LDea NFir |
| Flower Fairy Berry = 'Sweberry' (Flower Fairy Series) **new** | WGor |
| 'Flower of Spring' (Z/v) ♀H1+3 | CHal SSea |
| 'Flowton' (Dw/d) | ESul |
| 'Foxhall' (Dw) | ESul |
| Foxy = 'Pacfox' (Z) | LAst LSou |
| ***fragrans*** | EAro |
| Fragrans Group (Sc) | CHal CRHN CSev ESul GBar GPoy LVER MBPg MCot MHer SDnm SPet SSea WFib WGwG |
| § - 'Fragrans Variegatum' (Sc/v) | CDow CSev ESul MBPg NFir SWal WBrk WFib |
| - 'Snowy Nutmeg' | see *P.* (Fragrans Group) 'Fragrans Variegatum' |
| 'Fraiche Beauté' (Z/d) | WFib |
| 'Francis Gibbon' (Z/d) | WFib |
| 'Francis James' (Z) | WFib |
| 'Francis Kelly' (R) | ESul |
| 'Francis Parrett' (Min/d) ♀H1+3 | ESul WFib |
| 'Francis Read' (Dw/d) | ESul |
| 'Frank Headley' (Z/v) ♀H1+3 | CHal EShb ESul LAst LRHS LVER MCot MSte NPer NVic SAga SCoo SDnm SIde SSea SWal WFib |
| § 'Frau Emma Hössle' (Dw/d) | ESul LVER WFib |
| 'Freak of Nature' (Z/v) | ESul MHer NFir SSea WFib |
| 'Frensham' (Sc) | ESul LDea MBPg MHer SSea WFib |
| 'Freshfields Suki' (Dw) | NFir |
| 'Freshwater' (St/C) | ESul SSea WFib |
| 'Freston' (Dw) | ESul |
| 'Friary Wood' (Z/C/d) | ESul NFir WFib |
| 'Friesdorf' (Dw/Fr) | ESul LVER MCot MHer NFir WBrk WFib |
| 'Frills' (Min/d) | ESul NFir |
| 'Fringed Angel' (A) | CFee |
| 'Fringed Apple' (Sc) | LDea MBPg NBur |
| 'Fringed Aztec' (R) ♀H1+3 | CWCL ESul LDea LVER NFir SPet SSea WFib |
| 'Fringed Jer'Ray' (A) | LDea |
| 'Fringed Rouletta' (I) | LDea |

| | |
|---|---|
| 'Frosty' misapplied | see *P.* 'Variegated Kleine Liebling' |
| 'Frosty Petit Pierre' | see *P.* 'Variegated Kleine Liebling' |
| 'Frou Frou' | LVER |
| 'Frühlingszauber Lila' (R) | ESul |
| 'Fruity' (Sc) | MBPg |
| ***frutetorum*** | MBPg |
| ***fruticosum*** | EShb LPio WFib |
| 'Fuji' (R) | NFir |
| ***fulgidum*** | CSpe EShb ESul LPio NFir WFib |
| 'Funny Girl' (R) | ESul |
| 'Fynn' (Dw) | ESul |
| 'Gabriel' (A) | ESul LDea |
| 'Galilee' (I/d) ♀H1+3 | LDea LVER |
| Galleria Sunrise = 'Sunrise' (R) | ESul LDea LVER WEas |
| 'Galway Girl' (Sc) | MBPg |
| 'Galway Star' (Sc/v) ♀H1+3 | MBPg MHer WBrk WFib |
| 'Garland' (Dw/d) | ESul |
| 'Garnet' (Z/d) | ESul |
| 'Garnet Rosebud' (Min/d) | ESul LVER NFir WFib |
| 'Gartendirektor Herman' (Dec) | ESul NBur NFir SSea WFib |
| 'Gatwig' **new** | LSou WGor |
| 'Gaudy' (Z) | WFib |
| 'Gay Baby' (DwI) | ESul LDea |
| 'Gay Baby Supreme' (DwI) | ESul |
| 'Gemini' (Z/St/d) | CWCL NFir SSea WFib |
| 'Gemma' (R) | ESul NFir SAga |
| 'Gemma Jewel' (R) ♀H1+3 | ESul |
| 'Gemma Rose' (R) | LDea |
| I 'Gemstone' (Min) | ESul |
| 'Gemstone' (Sc) ♀H1+3 | LDea MBPg MHer WBrk |
| 'Genie' (Z/d) | WFib |
| 'Gentle Georgia' (R) | WFib |
| 'Geofbar' (R) | ESul |
| 'Geoff May' (Min) | ESul |
| 'Georgia' (R) | WFib |
| 'Georgia Peach' (R) | ESul WFib |
| 'Georgie' (R) | LDea |
| 'Georgina Blythe' (R) ♀H1+3 | WFib |
| 'Gerald Portas' (Dw/C) | ESul |
| 'Gerald Wells' (Min) | ESul LVER |
| 'Geraldine' (Min) | ESul |
| 'Gesa' | LAst |
| 'Gess Portas' (Z/v) | ESul |
| 'Giant Butterfly' (R) | ESul |
| 'Giant Oak' (Sc) | ESul MBPg MSte |
| ***gibbosum*** | LPio MHer SSea WFib |
| 'Gilda' (R/v) | LDea |
| 'Gill' (Min/Ca) | ESul |
| 'Ginger Frost' (Sc/v) | WFib |
| 'Ginger Rogers' (Z) | NFir |
| 'Glacier Claret' (Z) | WFib |
| 'Glacis'PBR (Quality Series) (Z/d) | LAst LSou |
| 'Gladys Evelyn' (Z/d) | WFib |
| 'Gladys Stevens' (Min/d) | ESul |
| 'Gladys Weller' (Z/d) | WFib |
| ***glaucum*** | see *P. lanceolatum* |
| 'Gleam' (Z/d) | LVER |
| 'Glen Sheree' (R) | ESul |
| 'Gloria Pearce' (R) | ESul LDea SSea |
| 'Glowing Embers' (R) | ESul LDea SSea |
| § ***glutinosum*** | WFib |
| 'Goblin' (Min/d) | ESul LVER WFib |
| 'Godfreys Pride' (Sc) | MBPg |
| 'Godshill' (R) | LDea |
| 'Goesta' (Z/d) | LSou |
| Golden AngelPBR | see *P.* 'Sarah Don' |
| 'Golden Baby' (DwI/C) | ESul LDea NFir WFib |
| 'Golden Brilliantissimum' (Z/v) | ESul SSea WFib |

'Golden Butterfly' (Z/C) ESul
'Golden Chalice' (Min/v) ESul NFir WFib
'Golden Clorinda' (U/Sc/C) CRHN LDea MBPg NFir SSea
'Golden Ears' (Dw/St/C) ESul NFir NPer WFib
'Golden Edinburgh' (I/v) WFib
'Golden Everaarts' (Dw/C) ESul
'Golden Fleece' (Dw/C/d) ESul
'Golden Gates' (Z/C) ESul
'Golden Harry Hieover' (Z/C) ♀H1+3 ESul MBri MHer SSea
'Golden Lilac Gem' (I/d) WFib
'Golden Petit Pierre' (Min/C) ESul SSea
'Golden Princess' (Min/C) WFib
'Golden Princess' (R) SSea
'Golden Roc' (Min/C) ESul
'Golden Square' (Dw/St) WFib
'Golden Staphs' (Z/St/C) ESul MHer NFir SSea WFib
'Golden Stardust' (Z/St) ESul LVER
'Golden Wedding' (Z/d/v) NFir
'Golden Well Sweep' see *P. crispum* 'Golden Well Sweep'
'Goldilocks' (A) ESul
'Gooseberry Leaf' see *P. grossularioides*
'Gordano Midnight' (R) LDea
'Gordon Quale' (Z/d) WFib
'Gosbeck' (A) SSea WFib
'Gothenburg' (R) ESul
'Gottweig' (Z) ESul
'Grace' (A) LDea
'Grace Thomas' (Sc) ♀H1+3 LDea MBPg MHer WFib
'Grace Wells' (Min) ESul WFib
'Grand Duchess' (R) LDea
'Grand Slam' (R) CWCL ESul LDea LVER NFir WFib
'Grandad Mac' (Dw/St) ESul NFir SSea
***grandiflorum*** LPio MHer WFib
'Grandma Fischer' see *P.* 'Grossmutter Fischer'
'Grandma Ross' (R) ESul
'Grandma Thompson' (R) ESul
'Granny Hewitt' (Min/d) ESul
***graveolens*** *sensu* J.J.A. van der Walt LDea LPio SBch WFib
§ 'Graveolens' (Sc) CHal ESul GBar GPoy LVER MBPg MHer SSea WFib
'Great Bricett' (Dw/d) ESul
'Green Ears' (Z/St) ESul
'Green Eyes' (I/d) MHer
'Green Goddess' (I/d) LDea
'Green Gold Petit Pierre' (Min) ESul
'Green Lady' (Sc) MBPg
'Green Silver Galaxy' (St) ESul
'Green Woodpecker' (R) LDea SSea
§ 'Greengold Kleine Liebling' (Min/C/v) ESul
'Greengold Petit Pierre' see *P.* 'Greengold Kleine Liebling'
'Greetings' (Min/v) ESul MBri SSea WFib
'Grey Lady Plymouth' (Sc/v) ESul LDea MBPg MCot MHer NFir WFib
'Grey Sprite' (Min/v) ESul WFib
§ 'Grossmutter Fischer' (R) LDea
§ ***grossularioides*** CSec EOHP MBPg MHer
- 'Coconut' MBPg
'Grozser Garten' (Dw) ESul
'Grozser Garten Weiss' (Dw) ESul
'Guardsman' (Dw) ESul
'Guernsey Flair' (Z) **new** NFir
'Gwen' (Min/v) NFir
'Hadleigh' (Min) ESul
'Halo' (R) ESul
§ 'Hannaford Star' (Z/St) WFib
'Hannah West' (Z/C) **new** SSea
'Hansen's Pinkie' (R) LDea
'Hansen's Wild Spice' (Sc) GBar LPio MBPg SAga
'Happy Appleblossom' (Z/v/d) NFir
'Happy Birthday' (Z/T) LVER
(Happy Face Series) LAst
Happy Face Amethyst = 'Penrad'PBR (I)
- Happy Face Mex = 'Pacvet'PBR (I) LAst LSou LVER
- Happy Face Scarlet = 'Penhap'PBR (I) LAst
- Happy Face Velvet Red = 'Pachafvel' (I) LAst LSou
- Happy Face White = 'Pacfali' (I) LAst
§ 'Happy Thought' (Z/v) ♀H1+3 CHal ESul LVER MBri MCot NFir NVic SCoo SSea WFib
'Happy Valley' (R) ESul LVER
'Harbour Lights' (R) ESul LDea WFib
'Harewood Slam' (R) ESul LDea MSte WFib
'Harkstead' (Dw) ESul
'Harlequin' (Dw) ESul
'Harlequin Mahogany' (I/d) LDea LVER
'Harlequin Picotee' (I/d) LDea
'Harlequin Pretty Girl' (I x Z/d) LVER WFib
'Harlequin Rosie O'Day' (I) LDea WFib
'Harlequin Ted Day' (I/d) LDea
Harmony (Z/Dw) LVER
'Harvard' (I/d) WFib
'Havenstreet' (Dw/St) ESul
'Hazel' (R) WFib
'Hazel Anson' (R) LDea
'Hazel Barolo' (R) LDea
'Hazel Birkby' (R) LDea
'Hazel Burtoff' (R) ESul LDea
'Hazel Butterfly' (R) **new** NBur
'Hazel Candy' (R) ESul
'Hazel Carey' (R) LDea
'Hazel Cerise' (R) LDea
'Hazel Cherry' (R) CWCL ESul LDea MSte SSea WFib
'Hazel Chick' (R) ESul
'Hazel Choice' (R) ESul LDea NFir
'Hazel Claret' (R) **new** SSea
'Hazel Dean' (R) NFir
'Hazel Glory' (R) LDea
'Hazel Gowland' (R) LDea
'Hazel Gypsy' (R) ESul LDea NFir
'Hazel Harmony' (R) ESul LDea
'Hazel Henderson' (R) LDea
'Hazel Herald' (R) ESul LDea
'Hazel Orchid' (R) ESul
'Hazel Perfection' (R) NFir
'Hazel Ripple' (R) ESul
'Hazel Rose' (R) LDea NBur
'Hazel Satin' (R) LDea
'Hazel Star' (R) ESul WFib
'Hazel Stardust' (R) ESul LDea NFir
'Hazel Wright' (R) LDea SSea
§ 'Hederinum' (I) LSou
§ 'Hederinum Variegatum' (I/v) CDow CHal MCot NFir SPet SSea WFib
'Heidi' (Min/d) ESul
'Helen Bainbridge' (Z/C) **new** LVER
'Helen Christine' (Z/St) ESul LVER NFir WFib
'Helena' (I/d) LDea
'Hemingstone' (A) LDea
'Hemley' (Sc) LDea LVER MBPg
'Henhurst Gleam' (Dw/d) ESul
'Henley' (Min/d) ESul
'Henry Weller' (A) ESul MBPg NFir WFib
'Hermanus Show' (Sc) MBPg

| | |
|---|---|
| 'Hermione' (Z/d) | CHal WFib |
| 'High Fidelity' (R) | ESul |
| 'Highfields Appleblossom' (Z) | LVER |
| 'Highfields Attracta' (Z/d) | WFib |
| 'Highfields Ballerina' (Z/d) | LVER |
| 'Highfields Candy Floss' (Z/d) | LVER NFir |
| 'Highfields Charisma' (Z/d) | LVER |
| 'Highfields Contessa' (Z/d) | WFib |
| 'Highfields Delight' (Z) | WFib |
| 'Highfields Fancy' (Z/d) | LVER NFir |
| 'Highfields Festival' (Z/d) | NFir WFib |
| 'Highfields Flair' (Z/d) | LVER |
| 'Highfields Melody' (Z/d) | WFib |
| 'Highfields Pride' (Z) | WFib |
| 'Highfields Prima Donna' (Z/d) | LVER |
| 'Highfields Sugar Candy' (Z/d) | LVER WFib |
| 'Highfields Symphony' (Z) | LVER WFib |
| 'Highfields Vogue' (Z) | LVER |
| 'Hilbre Island' (Z/C/d) | NFir |
| 'Hildegard' (Z/d) | CHal |
| 'Hills of Snow' (Z/v) | CHal MBri MHer SSea WFib |
| 'Hillscheider Amethyst'$^{PBR}$ | see *P.* Amethyst = 'Fisdel' |
| 'Hindoo' (RxU) | CSpe LVER NFir SAga SSea WFib |
| 'Hindoo Rose' (U) | NFir |
| 'Hintlesham' (Min) | ESul |
| ***hirtum*** | LPio |
| ***hispidum*** | LPio MBPg MHer SSea |
| 'Hitcham' (Min/d) | ESul WFib |
| 'Holbrook' (Dw/C/d) | ESul NFir WFib |
| 'Hollywood Star' (Z) | EBrs |
| 'Honeywood Lindy' (R) | ESul LDea |
| 'Honeywood Lindy Variegated' (R/V) **new** | ESul |
| 'Honeywood Margaret' (R) | ESul |
| 'Honeywood Suzanne' (Min/Fr) | ESul LVER NFir |
| 'Honneas' (Dw) | ESul |
| 'Honnestolz' (Dw) | ESul |
| 'Hope Valley' (Dw/C/d) ♀$^{H1+3}$ | ESul NFir |
| 'Horace Parsons' (R) | ESul WFib |
| 'Horace Read' (Dw) | ESul |
| 'Horning Ferry' (Dw) | ESul |
| 'House and Garden' (R) | NFir |
| 'Hula' (U x R) | MHer |
| 'Hulda Conn' (Z/Ca/d) | WFib |
| 'Hulverstone' (Dw/St) | ESul |
| 'Hunter's Moon' (Z/C) | NFir |
| 'Hurdy-gurdy' (Z/d/v) | ESul |
| 'Ian Read' (Min/d) | ESul LVER |
| 'Ibiza' (Dw/C) **new** | ESul |
| 'Icing Sugar' (I/d) | ESul LDea WFib |
| ***ignescens*** | MBPg |
| 'Immaculatum' (Z) | WFib |
| 'Imperial'$^{PBR}$ (R) | LAst |
| 'Imperial Butterfly' (A/Sc) | CRHN ESul GGar LDea LVER MBPg MSte NFir WFib |
| 'Inca' (R) | ESul |
| Ingres = 'Guicerdan'$^{PBR}$ (I/d) ♀$^{H1+3}$ | LSou |
| 'Inspiration' (R) | ESul |
| ***ionidiflorum*** | CSpe EShb LPio MBPg MCot MHer SAga |
| 'Ipswich Town' (Dw/d) | ESul |
| 'Irene' (Z/d) ♀$^{H1+3}$ | WFib |
| 'Irene Collet' (R) | LDea |
| 'Irene Toyon' (Z) ♀$^{H1+3}$ | WFib |
| 'Isabell' (Quality Series) (Z/d) | LSou |

| | |
|---|---|
| 'Isidel' (I/d) ♀$^{H1+3}$ | WFib |
| 'Islington Peppermint' (Sc) | LPio MBPg WFib |
| 'Isobel Eden' (Sc) | LDea MBPg |
| 'Ivalo' (Z/d) | WFib |
| 'Ivory Snow' (Z/d/v) | ESul LVER NFir SSea WFib |
| 'Jacey' (Z/d) | LVER |
| 'Jack of Hearts' (I x Z/d) | WFib |
| 'Jack Simmons' (Z/d/Dw) | ESul |
| 'Jack Wood' (Z/d) | NFir WFib |
| § 'Jackie' (I/d) | EShb LVER MBri WFib |
| 'Jackie Gall' | see *P.* 'Jackie' |
| 'Jackpot Wild Rose' (Z/d) | WFib |
| 'Jacqui Caws' (Dw) | ESul |
| 'Jake Brougham' (St) | ESul |
| 'Jane Biggin' (Dw/C/d) | ESul |
| 'Janet Dean' (R) | LDea |
| 'Janet Hofman' (Z/d) | WFib |
| 'Janet Kerrigan' (Min/d) | ESul WFib |
| 'Jasmin' (R) | ESul LDea |
| 'Jaunty' (Min/d) | ESul |
| 'Jayne' (Min/d) | ESul |
| 'Jayne Eyre' (Min/d) | CHal ESul WFib |
| 'Jazzy' (Min/St) | ESul |
| 'Jean Bart' (I) | LVER SSea |
| 'Jean Caws' (Z/St) | WFib |
| 'Jeanetta' (R) | LDea |
| 'Jeanie Hunt' (Z/C/d) | NFir |
| 'Jeanne' (Z) **new** | WFib |
| § 'Jeanne d'Arc' (I/d) | WFib |
| 'Jenifer Read' (Dw) | ESul |
| 'Jennifer' (Min) | ESul |
| 'Jennifer Strange' (R) | ESul |
| 'Jericho' (Z/St/v) | ESul LVER |
| 'Jer'Ray' (A) | ESul LDea NFir SSea WFib |
| 'Jessel's Unique' (U) | LDea MHer MSte SPet SSea |
| 'Jessica' | LVER SAga |
| 'Jewel' (R) | ESul |
| 'Jill Brown' (Min/St/C) **new** | ESul |
| 'Jimbar' (R) | ESul |
| 'Jinny Reeves' (R) | LDea |
| 'Jip's Freda Burgess' (Z/C/d) | NFir |
| 'Jip's Nippy' (Dw) **new** | NFir |
| 'Jip's Rosy Glow' (Min/d) | ESul NFir |
| 'Jip's Twink' (Iv/v) **new** | NFir |
| 'Joan Cashmere' (Z/d) | ESul |
| 'Joan Fontaine' (Z) | WFib |
| 'Joan Hayward' (Min) | ESul |
| 'Joan Morf' (R) | ESul LDea NFir SSea WFib |
| 'Joan of Arc' | see *P.* 'Jeanne d'Arc' |
| 'Joan Sharman' (Min) | ESul |
| 'Joanna Pearce' (R) | LDea |
| 'John Thorp' (R) | LDea |
| 'John's Angela' | LVER |
| 'John's Pride' (Dw) | MBri NFir SSea |
| 'Joseph Haydn' (R) | ESul LDea MSte |
| 'Joseph Paul' (R) | SSea |
| 'Joseph Wheeler' (A) | ESul LDea |
| 'Joy' (R) ♀$^{H1+3}$ | ESul LDea LRHS LSou NFir WCot WFib |
| 'Joy' (I) | SAga SPet |
| I 'Joy' (Z/d) | LAst SSea |
| 'Joy Lucille' (Sc) | CSev ESul LDea MBPg |
| 'Joyful' (Min) | ESul |
| 'Jubilant' (R) | ESul |
| 'Judy Read' (Dw) | ESul |
| 'Julia' (R) ♀$^{H1+3}$ | LDea |
| 'Juliana' (R) | LAst LDea |
| 'Julie Bannister' (R) | ESul |
| 'Julie Smith' (R) | ESul LDea WFib |
| 'June Filbey' (R) | LDea |
| 'Jungle Night' (R) | ESul |
| 'Juniper' (Sc) | MBPg WFib |

| | | |
|---|---|---|
| | 'Jupiter' (R) | ESul |
| | 'Just Bella' (d) **new** | NFir |
| | 'Just Beth' (Z/C/d) | NFir |
| | 'Just Joss' (Dw/d) | NFir |
| | 'Just Rita' (A) | SSea |
| | 'Just William' (Min/C/d) | ESul WFib |
| | 'Kamahl' (R) | ESul WFib |
| | 'Kandi Waterman' (Z/St/C) **new** | LVER |
| § | 'Kardinal' (Z/d) | SPet |
| | 'Karl Hagele' (Z/d) | LVER WFib |
| | 'Karl Offenstein' (R) | ESul |
| | 'Karmin Ball' | WFib |
| | ***karrooense*** Knuth | MHer |
| | 'Karrooense' | see *P. quercifolium* |
| | 'Kathleen' (Min) | ESul |
| | 'Kathleen Gamble' (Z) | WFib |
| | 'Kathryn' (Min) | ESul |
| | 'Kathryn Portas' (Z/v) | ESul |
| | 'Kathy Kirby' (R) | ESul |
| | 'Katie' (R) | LDea |
| | 'Katie Hillier' (R) | LDea |
| | 'Katrine' | CWCL LAst LSou WGor |
| | 'Kayleigh Aitken' (R) | CWCL NFir |
| | 'Kayleigh West' (Min) | ESul SSea |
| | 'Keepsake' (Min/d) | ESul WFib |
| | 'Keith Vernon' (Z) | NFir |
| | 'Kelly Brougham' (St/dw) | ESul |
| | 'Ken Lea' (Z/v) | ESul |
| | 'Ken Salmon' (Dw/d) | ESul |
| | 'Kenny's Double' (Z/d) | WFib |
| | 'Kensington' (A) | LDea |
| | 'Kerensa' (Min/d) | ESul WFib |
| | 'Kershy' (Min) | ESul |
| | 'Kesgrave' (Min/d) | ESul LVER WFib |
| | 'Kettlebaston' (A) ♀$^{H1+3}$ | LDea WFib |
| | 'Kewense' (Z) | EShb |
| | 'Kimono' (R) | ESul NBur NFir |
| | 'Kinder Gaisha' (R) | NFir |
| | 'King Edmund' (R) | ESul LDea NFir |
| | 'King of Balcon' | see *P.* 'Hederinum' |
| | 'King of Denmark' (Z/d) | LVER WFib |
| | 'King Solomon' (R) | LDea WFib |
| | 'Kirton' (Min/d) | ESul |
| § | 'Kleine Liebling' (Min) | ESul WFib |
| | 'Knaves Bonfire' (R) | ESul |
| | 'Korcicum' (Sc) | MBPg |
| | 'Krista' (Min/d) | ESul WFib |
| | 'Kyoto' (R) | NFir |
| | 'Kyra' (Min/d) | ESul WFib |
| | 'La France' (I/d) ♀$^{H1+3}$ | LDea MCot WFib |
| | 'La Paloma' (R) | ESul WFib |
| | 'Laced Mini Rose Cascade' (I) | NFir |
| | Laced Red Mini Cascade = 'Achspen' (I) | NFir |
| § | 'Lachskönigin' (I/d) | LVER SPet WFib |
| | 'Lady Ilchester' (Z/d) | WFib |
| | 'Lady Love Song' (R) | ESul LSou NFir WFib |
| | 'Lady Mary' (Sc) | ESul MBPg MHer |
| | 'Lady Mavis Pilkington' (Z/d) | WFib |
| | 'Lady Plymouth' (Sc/v) ♀$^{H1+3}$ | CHal CHrt CRHN CSpe CTca CWan EPfP EShb ESul GBar GGar LDea LPio LRHS LVER MBPg MCot MHer MNHC MSte NFir SBch SPet SSea WFib |
| § | 'Lady Scarborough' (Sc) | ESul GBar LDea LPio MBPg MHer WFib |
| | 'Lady Scott' (Sc) | MBPg |
| | 'Lady Woods' (Z) | SSea |
| | ***laevigatum*** | MHer |
| | 'Lakeland' (I) | ESul SSea |
| | 'Lakis' (R) | LDea |
| | 'Lamorna' (R) | ESul LDea |
| | 'Lancastrian' (Z/d) | WFib |
| § | ***lanceolatum*** | LPio MHer |
| | 'Langley' (R) | ESul LDea |
| | 'Lanham Lane' (I) | LDea |
| | 'Lanham Royal' (Dw/d) | ESul |
| | 'Lara Aladin' (A) | LDea MBPg |
| | 'Lara Ballerina' | NFir |
| | 'Lara Candy Dancer' (Sc) ♀$^{H1+3}$ | CRHN ESul LDea MBPg SBch WBrk WFib |
| | 'Lara Jester' (Sc) | MBPg MHer WFib |
| | 'Lara Maid' (A) ♀$^{H1+3}$ | WFib |
| | 'Lara Nomad' (Sc) | LDea MBPg |
| | 'Lara Starshine' (Sc) ♀$^{H1+3}$ | EAro ESul LPio MBPg MHer NFir SSea WFib |
| | 'Lara Waltz' (R/d) | WFib |
| | 'Lark' (Min/d) | ESul |
| | 'Larkfield' (Z/v) | SSea |
| N | 'Lass o' Gowrie' (Z/v) | ESul LVER MSte NFir |
| | 'Latte Coffee' (R) | ESul |
| | 'Laura Parmer' (Dw/St) | ESul |
| | 'Laura Wheeler' (A) | ESul LDea |
| | 'Laurel Hayward' (R) | WFib |
| | 'Lauren Alexandra' (Z/d) | WFib |
| | Lauretta = 'Pacamla'$^{PBR}$ (Quality Series) (Z/d) | LAst LSou |
| | Lavenda = 'Penlava'$^{PBR}$ (Dark Line Series) (Z/d) | LAst LSou |
| | 'Lavender Grand Slam' (R) ♀$^{H1+3}$ | ESul LDea LVER NFir |
| | 'Lavender Harewood Slam' (R) | ESul LDea |
| | 'Lavender Mini Cascade'$^{PBR}$ | see *P.* Lilac Mini Cascade = 'Lilamica' |
| | 'Lavender Sensation' (R) | WFib |
| | 'Lavender Wings' (I) | LDea |
| | 'Lawrenceanum' | ESul LPio WFib |
| | 'Layham' (Dw/d) | ESul |
| | 'L'Elégante' (I/v) ♀$^{H1+3}$ | CHal LDea LVER MHer SSea SWal WEas WFib |
| | 'Lemon Air' (Sc) | ESul MBPg |
| | 'Lemon Crisp' | see *P. crispum* |
| | 'Lemon Fancy' (Sc) | LDea LVER MBPg MCot MHer NFir WFib |
| | 'Lemon Kiss' (Sc) | MBPg |
| | 'Lemon Meringue' (Sc) | MBPg |
| | 'Lemon Toby' (Sc) | MBPg |
| | 'Len Chandler' (Min) | ESul |
| | 'Lenore' (Min/d) | ESul |
| | 'Leo' (Min) | ESul |
| | 'Leonie Holbrow' (Min) | ESul |
| | 'Lesley Judd' (R) | ESul |
| | 'Lesmona' | LSou |
| | 'Lessland' | LVER |
| | 'Leywood Bonanza' **new** | CWCL |
| | Lila Compakt-Cascade | see *P.* 'Decora Lilas' |
| | Lilac Cascade | see *P.* 'Roi des Balcons Lilas' |
| | 'Lilac Domaine de Courson' (Sc) | MBPg |
| | 'Lilac Domino' | see *P.* 'Telston's Prima' |
| | 'Lilac Elaine' (R) | LDea |
| | 'Lilac Gem' (Min/I/d) | LDea MCot |
| | 'Lilac Gemma' (R) | ESul |
| | 'Lilac Jewel' (R) | ESul |
| | 'Lilac Joy' (R) | ESul LVER SSea |
| § | Lilac Mini Cascade = 'Lilamica'$^{PBR}$ (I) | ESul LAst LDea LVER NFir |
| | 'Lili Marlene' (I) | SPet |
| | 'Lilian' (Min) | ESul LSou |
| | 'Lilian Pottinger' (Sc) | CArn CHal CRHN ESul GBar LDea MBPg MHer NFir SSea |
| | 'Lilian Woodberry' (Z) | WFib |

| | | |
|---|---|---|
| | 'Limoneum' (Sc) | CSev LDea MBPg MHer NBur |
| | 'Linda' (R) | ESul |
| | 'Lindsey' (Min) | ESul |
| | 'Lipstick' (St) | WFib |
| | 'Lisa' (Min/C) | ESul WFib |
| | 'Lisa Jo' (St/v/Dw/d) | WFib |
| | 'Little Alice' (Dw/d) 🏆$^{H1+3}$ | ESul NFir WFib |
| | 'Little Blakenham' (A) | ESul LDea SSea |
| | 'Little Fi-fine' (Dw/C) | ESul |
| | 'Little Gem' (Sc) | LDea MBPg MHer SSea WFib |
| | 'Little Jim' (Min/d) | NFir |
| | 'Little Jip' (Z/d/v) | LVER NFir WFib |
| | 'Little Lisa' (Dw) **new** | ESul |
| | 'Little Margaret' (Min/v) | ESul |
| | 'Little Primular' (Min) | ESul |
| | 'Little Rascal' (A) | LDea |
| | 'Little Spikey' (St/Min/d) | ESul WFib |
| | 'Lively Lady' (Dw/C) | ESul |
| | 'Lizzie Hillier' (R) | LDea |
| | ***lobatum*** | LPio |
| | ***longicaule*** | LPio MBPg |
| | ***longifolium*** | LPio |
| | 'Lord Baden-Powell' | see *P.* 'Colonel Baden-Powell' |
| | 'Lord Bute' (R) 🏆$^{H1+3}$ | CSpe ECtt EShb ESul GGar LAst LDea LRHS LVER MCot MHer MSte NFir NPer SAga SBch SDnm SIde SMrm SPet SSea SUsu WEas WFib WPen |
| | 'Lord Constantine' (R) | LDea |
| | 'Lord de Ramsey' | see *P.* 'Tip Top Duet' |
| | 'Lord Roberts' (Z) | WFib |
| | Lorena = 'Pacdala'$^{PBR}$ (Dark Line Series) (Z/d) | LAst WGor |
| | 'Loretta' (Dw) | ESul |
| | 'Lorna' (Dw/d) | ESul |
| | 'Lorraine' (Dw) | ESul |
| | Lotus = 'Floscala' (Z/d) | LAst |
| | 'Lotusland' (Dw/St/C) | LSou NFir WFib |
| | 'Louise' (Min) | ESul |
| I | 'Louise' (R) | ESul NFir |
| | 'Louise Waddington' (Min/St) | ESul |
| | 'Love Song' (R/v) | ESul LDea LSou NFir SSea WFib |
| | 'Love Story' (Z/v) | ESul |
| | 'Loveliness' (Z) | WFib |
| * | 'Loverly' (Min/d) | ESul |
| | 'Lovesdown' (Dw/St) | ESul |
| | 'Lowood' (R) | ESul |
| | 'Lucie Caws' (St/d) | ESul |
| | 'Lucilla' (Min) | ESul |
| | 'Lucinda' (Min) | ESul |
| | 'Lucy' (Min) | ESul |
| | 'Lucy Gunnett' (Z/d/v) | ESul NFir |
| | 'Lucy Jane' (R) | ESul LDea |
| | 'Lulu' (I/d) | NPri |
| | Luna = 'Fisuna' (I/d) | NPri |
| | ***luridum*** | WCot |
| | 'Lustre' (R) | ESul |
| | 'Lyewood Bonanza' (R) | ESul LDea WFib |
| | 'Lynne Valerie' (A) | LDea |
| | 'Lyric' (Min/d) | ESul WFib |
| | 'Mabel Grey' (Sc) 🏆$^{H1+3}$ | CHal CRHN CSev CSpe EShb ESul LPio LVER MBPg MCot MHer MSte NBur NFir NPer SBch SIde SSea WFib |
| § | 'Madame Auguste Nonin' (U/Sc) | CDow CHrt ESul LVER MBPg MHer NFir SSea WFib |
| | 'Madame Butterfly' (Z/d/v) | ESul NFir |
| | 'Madame Crousse' (I/d) 🏆$^{H1+3}$ | WFib |
| | 'Madame Fournier' (Dw/C) | ESul |
| | 'Madame Layal' (A) | MHer MSte NFir SAga WFib |
| | 'Madame Margot' | see *P.* 'Hederinum Variegatum' |
| | 'Madame Salleron' (Min/v) 🏆$^{H1+3}$ | LAst LDea LRHS LSou LVER MSte SWal |
| | 'Madame Thibaut' (R) | LDea MSte |
| | 'Madge Taylor' (R) | NFir |
| | 'Magaluf' (I/C/d) | SSea |
| | 'Magda' (Z/d) | ESul |
| | ***magenteum*** | ESul |
| | 'Magic Lantern' (Z/C) | NFir |
| | 'Magic Moments' (R) | ESul |
| | 'Magnum' (R) | WFib |
| | 'Maid of Honour' (Min) | ESul |
| | 'Maiden Petticoat' | SAga |
| | 'Mairi' (A) | LDea WFib |
| | 'Majorca' (Dw/C) **new** | ESul |
| | 'Mandala' | LVER |
| | 'Mandarin' (R) | ESul |
| | 'Mangles' Variegated' (Z/v) | WFib |
| | 'Mantilla' (Min) | ESul |
| | 'Manx Maid' (A) | ESul LDea NFir |
| | 'Maple Leaf' (Sc) | MBPg |
| | 'Marble Sunset' | see *P.* 'Wood's Surprise' |
| | 'Marchioness of Bute' (R/Dec) | LDea LVER MSte NFir SSea WFib |
| | 'Maréchal MacMahon' (Z/C) | SSea |
| | 'Margaret Harris' (A) **new** | ESul |
| | 'Margaret Parmenter' (I/C) | ESul |
| | 'Margaret Pearce' (R) | LDea |
| | 'Margaret Salvidge' (R) | LDea |
| | 'Margaret Soley' (R) 🏆$^{H1+3}$ | LDea WFib |
| | 'Margaret Thorp' | LVER |
| | 'Margaret Waite' (R) | ESul WFib |
| | 'Margery Stimpson' (Min/d) | ESul WFib |
| | 'Maria Wilkes' (Z/d) | WFib |
| | 'Marie Rober' (R) | ESul |
| | 'Marie Rudlin' (R) | LVER SSea |
| | 'Marie Thomas' (Sc) | LDea MBPg SBch SSea |
| § | 'Marie Vogel' (R) | ESul MSte |
| | Marimba = 'Fisrimba'$^{PBR}$ | NPri SCoo |
| | 'Marion' (Min) | ESul |
| | 'Mariquita' (R) | WFib |
| | 'Marja' (R) | LDea |
| | 'Mark' (Dw/d) | WFib |
| | 'Marmalade' (Min/d) | ESul WFib |
| | 'Marquis of Bute' (R/v) | ESul LVER NFir |
| | 'Marquita' (R) | ESul |
| | 'Martha Parmer' (Min) | ESul |
| | 'Martin Parrett' (Min/d) | WFib |
| | 'Martin's Splendour' (Min) | ESul |
| | 'Martlesham' (Dw) | ESul |
| | 'Mary' (R) | ESul |
| | 'Mary Caws' (Dw/Z/d) | ESul |
| | 'Mary Ellen Tanner' (Min/d) | ESul |
| | 'Mary Harrison' (Z/d) | WFib |
| | 'Mary Read' (Min) | ESul |
| | 'Mary Webster' (Min) | ESul |
| | 'Masquerade' (R) | ESul SPet |
| | 'Masquerade' (Min) | ESul |
| | 'Master Paul' (Z/v) | ESul |
| | 'Maureen' (Min) | ESul LVER NFir |
| | 'Mauve Beauty' (I/d) | WFib |
| | Maxime = 'Fismaxi'$^{PBR}$ (I/d) | NPri |
| | 'Maxime Kovalevski' (Z) | WFib |
| | 'Maxine' (Z/C) | NFir |
| | 'May Day' (R) | LDea WFib |
| | 'May Magic' (R) | ESul NFir WFib |
| | 'Mayfield County Girl' (R) | ESul |
| | 'Mayor of Seville' (Z/d) | WFib |
| | 'Meadowside Dark and Dainty' (St) | NFir WFib |
| | 'Meadowside Fancy' (Z/d/C) | LVER |
| | 'Meadowside Harvest' (Z/St/C) | NFir WFib |

| | | |
|---|---|---|
| | 'Meadowside Julie Colley' (Dw) | NFir |
| | 'Meadowside Mahogany' (Z/C) | LVER |
| | 'Meadowside Midnight' (St/C) | MHer WFib |
| | 'Meadowside Orange' (Z/d) | LVER |
| | 'Medallion' (Z/C) | SSea |
| | 'Meditation' (Min) | ESul |
| | 'Medley' (Min/d) | WFib |
| | 'Megan Hannah' (Dw/c/d) | NFir |
| | 'Meike' (R) | ESul |
| | 'Melanie' (R) | ESul LDea |
| | 'Melanie' (Min) | ESul |
| * | 'Melissa' (Min) | ESul |
| | 'Melissa' (R) | ESul |
| | 'Melody'PBR (Tempo Series) (Z/d) | LAst |
| | Melosilver = 'Penber' (Tempo Series) (Z/d/v) | SPoG |
| | 'Memento' (Min/d) | ESul WFib |
| | 'Mendip' (R) | WFib |
| | 'Mendip Anne' (R) | NFir |
| | 'Mendip Barbie' (R) | NFir |
| | 'Mendip Blanche' (R) | NFir |
| | 'Mendip Candy Floss' (R) | ESul |
| | 'Mendip Lorraine' (R) | ESul |
| | 'Mendip Louise' (R) **new** | NFir |
| | 'Mendip Sarah' (R) **new** | NFir |
| | 'Menorca' (Dw/C/d) | ESul WFib |
| | 'Meon Maid' (R) | ESul LDea SMrm WFib |
| | 'Mere Casino' (Z) | WFib |
| | 'Mere Greeting' (Z/d) | WFib |
| | 'Mere Sunglow' (R) | LDea |
| | 'Merlin' (Sc) | MBPg |
| | 'Mexica Katrine' | LAst |
| | 'Mexica Tomcat' (I/d) | LAst |
| | 'Mexically Rose' (R) | ESul |
| | 'Mexican Beauty' (I) | CHal WFib |
| | 'Mexicana' | see *P.* 'Rouletta' |
| | 'Mexicanerin' | see *P.* 'Rouletta' |
| | 'Michael' (A) | ESul LDea MHer NFir |
| | 'Michelle' (Min/C) | LDea |
| | 'Michelle West' (Min) | ESul WFib |
| | 'Midas Touch' (Dw/C/d) | ESul |
| | 'Mikado' (R) | ESul |
| | 'Milden' (Dw/Z/C) | ESul NFir |
| | 'Millbern Clover' (Min/d) | ESul |
| | 'Millbern Sharna' (Min/d) | ESul |
| | Millennium Dawn (Dw) | LVER |
| | 'Millfield Gem' (I/d) | LVER WFib |
| | 'Millfield Rose' (I/d) | LVER |
| | 'Mimi' (Dw/C/d) | ESul |
| | 'Mina Lorenzen' (R) | ESul |
| | 'Minah's Cascade' (Z/d) | LVER |
| | 'Mini-Czech' (Min/St) | ESul LVER WBrk |
| | 'Minnie' (Z/d/St) | LVER WBrk |
| | 'Minstrel Boy' (R) | CSpe ESul LDea NFir SSea WFib |
| | 'Minuet' (Z/d) | SSea |
| | 'Minx' (Min/d) | WFib |
| | 'Miranda' (Dw) | ESul |
| | 'Miranda Deep Salmon' | WGor |
| | 'Miss Australia' (R/v) | LDea MBPg |
| | 'Miss Burdett Coutts' (Z/v) | ESul LVER MHer WFib |
| | 'Miss Liverbird' (I/d) | WBrk |
| | 'Miss McKinsey' (Z/St/d) | LVER NFir |
| | 'Miss Muffett' (Min/d) | WFib |
| § | 'Miss Stapleton' | LPio MHer WFib |
| | 'Miss Wackles' (Min/d) | ESul |
| | 'Misterioso' (R) | WFib |
| | 'Misty Morning' (R) | WFib |
| | 'Modesty' (Z/d) | WFib |
| | 'Mohawk' (R) | ESul LDea LVER NFir WFib |
| | 'Mole' | see *P.* 'The Mole' |
| | Molina = 'Fismoli' (I/d) | NPri |
| | 'Mollie' (R) | CSpe |
| | 'Mona Lisa'PBR | ESul |
| | 'Monarch' (Dw/v) | ESul |
| | 'Monica Bennett' (Dw) | ESul |
| | 'Monkwood Charm' (R) | ESul |
| | 'Monkwood Rhapsody' (R) | ESul |
| | 'Monkwood Rose' (A) | LDea NFir |
| | 'Monkwood Sprite' (R) | ESul LDea SMrm |
| | 'Monsal Dale' (Dw/C/d) | ESul |
| | 'Monsieur Ninon' misapplied | see *P.* 'Madame Auguste Nonin' |
| § | 'Monsieur Ninon' (U) | CRHN MSte WFib |
| | 'Mont Blanc' (Z/v) | ESul LVER WFib |
| | 'Montague Garabaldi Smith' (R) | WFib |
| | 'Moon Maiden' (A) | CSpe ESul LDea WFib |
| | 'Moor' (Min/d) | ESul |
| | 'Moppet' (Min/d) | ESul |
| | 'Morello'PBR (R) | ESul |
| | 'More's Victory' (U/Sc) | SSea |
| | 'Morning Cloud' (Min/d) | ESul |
| | 'Morval' (Dw/C/d) ♀H1+3 | ESul LVER WFib |
| | 'Morwenna' (R) | ESul LDea LPio MHer MSte NFir SMrm WFib |
| | 'Mosaic Gay Baby' (I/v/d) | WFib |
| | 'Mosaic Silky' (Z/C/d/v) | LVER |
| | 'Mountie' (Dw) | ESul |
| | 'Mozart' (R) | ESul |
| | 'Mr Everaarts' (Dw/d) | ESul |
| | 'Mr Henry Cox' (Z/v) ♀H1+3 | ESul LVER MHer NFir WFib |
| | 'Mr Wren' (Z) | CHal LVER SSea WFib |
| | 'Mrs Cannell' (Z) | WFib |
| | 'Mrs Dumbrill' (A) | ESul LDea LVER |
| | 'Mrs Farren' (Z/v) | MCot |
| | 'Mrs G.H. Smith' (A) | ESul LDea MBPg MSte NFir SSea WFib |
| | 'Mrs G. Morf' (R) | SSea |
| | 'Mrs Innes Rogers' (R) | ESul |
| | 'Mrs Kingsbury' (U) | WFib |
| | 'Mrs Langtry' (R) | LDea |
| | 'Mrs Martin' (I/d) | WFib |
| | 'Mrs McKenzie' (Z/St) | WFib |
| | 'Mrs Morf' (R) | LDea NFir |
| | 'Mrs Parker' (Z/d/v) | ESul LRHS LVER NFir WFib |
| | 'Mrs Pat' (Dw/St/C) | NFir SSea |
| | 'Mrs Pollock' (Z/v) | LAst LRHS LSou LVER MCot NVic SCoo SSea WBrk WFib |
| | 'Mrs Quilter' (Z/C) ♀H1+3 | LVER MBri MHer NVic SSea WBrk WFib |
| | 'Mrs Salter Bevis' (Z/Ca/d) | ESul WFib |
| | 'Mrs Strang' (Z/d/v) | LVER SSea |
| | 'Mrs Tarrant' (Z/d) | CHal |
| | 'Mrs Taylor' (Sc) | MBPg |
| | 'Mrs W.A.R. Clifton' (I/d) | LDea WFib |
| | ***multicaule*** | LPio |
| | - subsp. ***multicaule*** | EShb |
| | ***mutans*** | WFib |
| | 'Müttertag' (R) | MSte |
| § | 'Mutzel' (I/v) | LVER NFir |
| | 'My Chance' (Dec) | NFir SSea WFib |
| | 'My Choice' (R) | LDea |
| | ***myrrhifolium*** | LPio SAga |
| § | - var. ***coriandrifolium*** | LPio MHer WFib |
| | 'Mystery' (U) ♀H1+3 | CWCL LPio LVER MBPg NFir SAga SSea WFib |
| | 'Nacton' (Min) | ESul |
| | 'Nancy Grey' (Min) | ESul NFir |
| | 'Nancy Mac' (St) | ESul |
| | 'Narina' (I) | SCoo |
| | 'Natalie' (Dw) | ESul |

| | |
|---|---|
| 'Naughton' (Min) | ESul |
| 'Needham Market' (A) | ESul LDea MSte WFib |
| 'Neene' (Dw) | ESul |
| 'Neil Clemenson' (Sc) | WFib |
| 'Nell Smith' (Z/d) | WFib |
| 'Nellie' (R) | ESul LDea SSea |
| 'Nellie Green' (R) | LDea |
| 'Nellie Nuttall' (Z) | WFib |
| 'Nervosum' (Sc) | ESul MBPg |
| 'Nervous Mabel' (Sc) 𝕐$^{H1+3}$ | ESul LDea LPio MBPg MHer WBrk WFib |
| 'Nettlecombe' (Min/St) | ESul |
| 'Nettlestead' (Dw/d) | ESul LVER |
| 'Nettlestone' (Dw/d) | ESul |
| 'Nettlestone Star' (Min/St) | ESul |
| 'New Day' (A) | LDea |
| 'New Life' (Z) | ESul NFir |
| 'Newbridge' (St/Min/d) | ESul |
| 'Newton Rigg' (Sc) | MBPg |
| 'Newtown' (Min/St) | ESul |
| 'Nicola Buck' (R) | LDea NFir |
| 'Nicor Star' (Min) | ESul WFib |
| 'Nikki' (A) | LDea |
| 'Nimrod' (R) | LDea |
| 'Noche' (R) | ESul LDea SMrm |
| 'Noel' (Z/Ca/d) | WFib |
| 'Noele Gordon' (Z/d) | LVER WFib |
| 'Noir' (R) | SSea |
| 'Nono' (I) | WFib |
| 'Norrland' (Z/d) | LVER |
| 'Nostra' | LSou |
| ***oblongatum*** | LPio NFir |
| 'Occold Embers' (Dw/C) | ESul NFir |
| 'Occold Lagoon' (Dw/d) | ESul |
| 'Occold Orange Tip' (Min/d) | ESul |
| 'Occold Profusion' (Dw/d) | ESul NFir |
| 'Occold Shield' (Dw/C/d) | ESul LAst LRHS NFir SDnm WBrk WFib |
| 'Occold Tangerine' (Z) | WFib |
| 'Occold Volcano' (Dw/C/d) | WFib |
| ***odoratissimum*** (Sc) | CHal ESul GBar GPoy LDea MBPg MHer NFir SSea WFib |
| 'Odyssey' (Min) | WFib |
| 'Offton' (Dw) | ESul |
| 'Old Orchard' (A) | LDea |
| 'Old Rose' (Z/d) | WFib |
| 'Old Spice' (Sc/v) | ESul GBar LDea MBPg NFir SWal WFib |
| 'Oldbury Duet' (A/v) | ESul LDea LSou MBPg MHer NFir SSea |
| 'Olga Shipstone' (Sc) | MBPg |
| 'Oliver Welfare' (Dw/C) **new** | ESul |
| 'Olivia' (R) | CWCL WFib |
| 'Onalee' (Dw) | ESul WFib |
| 'Opera House' (R) | WFib |
| 'Orange' (Z/St) | MBPg |
| 'Orange Fizz' (Sc) | ESul MHer NFir SDnm WBrk |
| 'Orange Fizz' (Z/d) | LDea |
| 'Orange Imp' (Dw/d) | ESul |
| 'Orange Parfait' (R) | WFib |
| I 'Orange Princeanum' (Sc) | MBPg |
| 'Orange Ruffy' (Min) | ESul |
| 'Orangeade' (Dw/d) | LVER WFib |
| 'Orchid Clorinda' (Sc) | MBPg WFib |
| 'Orchid Paloma' (Dw/d) | ESul |
| 'Oregon Hostess' (Dw) | ESul |
| 'Oriental Delight' (R) | ESul |
| 'Orion' (Min/d) | ESul SSea WFib |
| 'Orsett' (Sc) 𝕐$^{H1+3}$ | LDea LVER MBPg |
| 'Otto's Red' (R) | NFir |
| 'Our Gynette' (Dec) | NFir SSea |

| | |
|---|---|
| 'Overchurch' (Dw) **new** | NFir |
| 'Oyster' (Dw) | ESul |
| PAC cultivars | see under selling name |
| 'Paddie' (Min) | ESul |
| 'Pagoda' (Z/St/d) | ESul LVER MHer MSte WFib |
| 'Paisley Red' (Z/d) | NFir WFib |
| 'Pam Craigie' (R) | LDea |
| 'Pamela' (R) | ESul |
| 'Pamela Vaughan' (Z/St) | WFib |
| 'Pampered Lady' (A) | LDea NFir |
| ***panduriforme*** | LPio MBPg WFib |
| ***papilionaceum*** | CHEx CRHN LPio MCot MHer SSea WEas WFib |
| 'Parisienne' (R) | ESul LDea WFib |
| 'Parmenter Pink' (Min) | ESul |
| 'Party Dress' (Z/d) | WFib |
| 'Pat Hannam' (St) | WFib |
| 'Paton's Unique' (U/Sc) 𝕐$^{H1+3}$ | CHal CRHN EShb LVER MBPg MCot MHer MSte NFir SPet SSea WFib |
| 'Patricia Andrea' (T) | ESul LVER NFir NPer WFib |
| 'Patricia O'Reilly' (R) **new** | LDea |
| 'Patricia Read' (Min) | ESul |
| 'Paul Crampel' (Z) | CHal MHer SSea WFib |
| 'Paul West' (Min/d) | ESul |
| 'Pauline' (Min/d) | ESul SSea |
| 'Pauline Harris' (R) | LDea |
| 'Pax' (R) | LDea |
| 'Peace' (Min/C) | ESul WFib |
| 'Peace Palace' (Dw) | ESul |
| 'Peach Princess' (R) | ESul NFir SSea |
| 'Peaches' (Z) | LSou |
| 'Peaches and Cream' (R) | MBPg |
| 'Peacock' | LDea |
| 'Pebbles' (Z/Min) | LVER |
| 'Peggy Clare' (Dw/St) | ESul |
| 'Peggy Sue' (R) | ESul LDea LVER |
| 'Peggy West' (Min/C/d) | SSea |
| PELFI cultivars | see under selling name |
| ***peltatum*** | LPio WFib |
| 'Penny' (Z/d) | WFib |
| 'Penny Dixon' (R) | NFir |
| 'Penny Lane' (Z) | WFib |
| 'Penny Serenade' (Dw/C) | ESul |
| 'Pensby' (Dw) | ESul NFir |
| 'Peppermint Lace' (Sc) | MBPg |
| 'Peppermint Scented Rose' (Sc) | MBPg |
| 'Peppermint Star' (Z/St) | ESul SSea |
| 'Perchance' (R) | SSea |
| 'Perfect' (Z) | WFib |
| Perlenkette Orange = 'Orangepen'$^{PBR}$ (Quality Series) (Z/d) | LAst LSou |
| Perlenkette Sabine (Quality Series) (Z/d) | LAst LSou |
| 'Pershore Princess' | WBrk |
| 'Persian King' (R) | LDea |
| 'Persian Ruler' (Min) | ESul |
| 'Persimmon' (Z/St) | WFib |
| 'Petals' (Z/v) | MSte |
| 'Peter Beard' (Dw/d) | ESul |
| 'Peter Godwin' (R) | ESul LDea WFib |
| 'Peter Read' (Dw/d) | ESul |
| 'Peter's Choice' (R) | ESul LDea SSea WFib |
| 'Peter's Luck' (Sc) 𝕐$^{H1+3}$ | ESul MBPg |
| 'Petit Pierre' | see *P.* 'Kleine Liebling' |
| 'Petite Blanche' (Dw/d) | SSea WFib |
| 'Philomel' (I/d) | SPet |
| 'Phlox New Life' (Z) | ESul |
| 'Phyllis' (Z) | LDea MCot |
| 'Phyllis' (U/v) | ESul LVER MBPg MHer NFir SAga SSea |

| | | |
|---|---|---|
| | 'Phyllis Brooks' (R) | ESul |
| | 'Phyllis Read' (Min) | ESul |
| | 'Phyllis Richardson' (R/d) | ESul LDea LVER |
| | 'Picotee' | SSea |
| | 'Pin Mill' (Min/d) | ESul |
| | 'Pink Aura' (Min/St) | ESul SSea |
| | 'Pink Aurore' (U) | MSte WFib |
| | 'Pink Blush' (Min/St) | ESul |
| | 'Pink Bonanza' (R) | ESul LDea NFir WFib |
| | 'Pink Bouquet' (R) | ESul |
| | 'Pink Capitatum' | see *P.* 'Pink Capricorn' |
| § | 'Pink Capricorn' (Sc) | CHrt CRHN ESul MBPg MHer SDnm WFib |
| | 'Pink Carnation' (I/d) | LDea |
| | 'Pink Cascade' | see *P.* 'Hederinum' |
| | 'Pink Champagne' (Sc) | CRHN ESul MBPg MCot MHer |
| | 'Pink Dolly Varden' (Z/v) | SSea WFib |
| | 'Pink Domaine de Courson' (Sc) | MBPg |
| | 'Pink Flamingo' (R) | LDea |
| | 'Pink Fondant' (Min/d) | ESul WFib |
| | 'Pink Fringed Aztec' (R) | SSea |
| | 'Pink Gay Baby' | see *P.* 'Sugar Baby' |
| | 'Pink Golden Ears' (Dw/St/C) | ESul |
| | 'Pink Golden Harry Hieover' (Z/C) | ESul |
| | 'Pink Happy Thought' (Z/v) | SDnm SSea WFib |
| | 'Pink Ice' (Min/d) | ESul NFir |
| | 'Pink Margaret Pearce' (R) | ESul |
| | 'Pink Mini Cascade' | see *P.* 'Rosa Mini-cascade' |
| | 'Pink Needles' (Min/St) | ESul WFib |
| | 'Pink Paradox' (Sc) | LDea MBPg |
| | 'Pink Rambler' (Z/d) | WFib |
| | 'Pink Raspail' (Z/d) | SSea |
| | 'Pink Rosebud' (Z/d) | SSea WFib |
| | 'Pink Snow' (Min/d) | ESul |
| | 'Pink Sparkler' (Dw/St/C) **new** | ESul |
| | 'Pink Spirit' (I) **new** | NPri |
| | 'Pink Splash' (Min/d) | ESul |
| | 'Pink Tiny Tim' (Min) | ESul |
| | Pink-Blizzard = 'Fispink' (I) | NPri |
| | 'Pippa' (Min/Dw) | ESul |
| | 'Pixie' (Min) | ESul |
| | 'Playmate' (Min/St) | ESul WFib |
| | 'Plum Rambler' (Z/d) | EShb SSea WFib |
| | 'Poetesse' (A) | LDea |
| | 'Polestar' (Min/St) | ESul |
| | 'Polka' (U) | ESul LVER MBPg MHer NFir SAga SSea WFib |
| | 'Pompeii' (R) | ESul LDea NFir SSea WFib |
| | 'Poquita' (Sc) | MBPg |
| | 'Porchfield' (Min/St) | ESul |
| | 'Portsmouth' (R) | ESul |
| | 'Potter Heigham' (Dw) | ESul |
| | 'Powder Puff' (Dw/d) | WFib |
| | 'Praeludium Scarlet' | WGor |
| | 'Presto' (Dw/St) | ESul |
| | 'Preston Park' (Z/C) | MCot WFib |
| | 'Pretty Girl' (I) | LDea MCot |
| | 'Pretty Petticoat' (Z/d) | WFib |
| | 'Pretty Polly' (Sc) | LDea MBPg WFib |
| | 'Pride of Exmouth' | CStu |
| | 'Prim' (Dw/St/d) | ESul WFib |
| | 'Prince Consort' (R) | LDea |
| | 'Prince of Orange' (Sc) | CArn CHrt CRHN CSev ESul GBar GPoy LDea LVER MBPg MCot MHer MSte NFir SIde SSea WFib |
| | 'Princeanum' (Sc) ♀H1+3 | MBPg MHer WFib |
| | 'Princess Alexandra' (Z/d/v) | ESul NFir |
| | 'Princess Anne' (Z) | MSte |
| | 'Princess Josephine' (R) | LDea MCot WFib |
| | 'Princess of Balcon' | see *P.* 'Roi des Balcons Lilas' |
| | 'Princess of Orange' (Sc/v) **new** | NFir |
| | 'Princess of Wales' (R) | ESul LDea LVER SSea WFib |
| | 'Princess Virginia' (R/v) | ESul LDea SSea WFib |
| | 'Priory Salmon' (St/d) | EShb ESul |
| | 'Priory Star' (St/Min/d) | ESul WFib |
| | 'Prosperity' (Sc) | LDea MBPg |
| | ***pseudoglutinosum*** | WFib |
| | 'Pungent Peppermint' (Sc) | MBPg |
| | 'Purple Emperor' (R) | ESul LDea WFib |
| | 'Purple Flare' (St) | ESul |
| | 'Purple Heart' (Dw/St/C) | ESul NFir |
| I | 'Purple Radula Rosea' (Sc) | MBPg |
| | 'Purple Rambler' (Z/d) | ESul |
| | 'Purple Rogue' (R) | WFib |
| | 'Purple Unique' (U/Sc) | CSpe EShb ESul LDea MCot MHer MSte NFir SSea WFib |
| | Purpurball 2 = 'Penbalu'PBR (Quality Series) (Z/d) | LAst LSou |
| | 'Pygmalion' (Z/d/v) | SSea WFib |
| | 'Quakeress' (R) | ESul |
| | 'Quakermaid' (Min) | ESul |
| | 'Quantock' (R) | ESul WFib |
| | 'Quantock Angelique' (A) **new** | NFir |
| | 'Quantock Beauty' (A) | ESul LDea |
| | 'Quantock Blonde' (A) | CWCL LDea |
| | 'Quantock Candy' (A) | NFir |
| | 'Quantock Classic' (A) | NFir |
| | 'Quantock Cobwebs' (A) | NFir |
| | 'Quantock Darren' (A) | NFir |
| | 'Quantock Jayne' (A) | ESul |
| | 'Quantock Kendy' (A) | CWCL ESul LDea NFir |
| | 'Quantock Kirsty' (A) | LDea NFir |
| | 'Quantock Louise' (A) | NFir |
| | 'Quantock Marjorie' (A) | CWCL ESul LDea MBPg NFir |
| | 'Quantock Matty' (A) | ESul LDea NFir |
| | 'Quantock May' (A) | LDea NFir |
| | 'Quantock Medoc' (A) | ESul LDea |
| | 'Quantock Millennium' (A) | CWCL ESul LDea NFir |
| | 'Quantock Mr Nunn' (A) | NFir |
| | 'Quantock Philip' (A) | ESul |
| | 'Quantock Rory' (A) | LDea |
| | 'Quantock Rose' (A) | CWCL ESul LDea MBPg |
| | 'Quantock Sapphire' (A) | LDea |
| | 'Quantock Sarah' (A) | ESul |
| | 'Quantock Shirley' (A) | ESul LDea |
| | 'Quantock Star' (A) | CWCL LDea MBPg NFir |
| | 'Quantock Star Gazer' (A/Sc) | NFir |
| | 'Quantock Ultimate' (A) | ESul MBPg NFir |
| | 'Quantock Variegated Matthew' (A/v) | NFir |
| | 'Quantock Victoria' (A) | ESul |
| | 'Queen of Denmark' (Z/d) | WFib |
| | 'Queen of Hearts' (I x Z/d) | LVER WFib |
| | 'Queen of Sheba' (R) | LDea |
| | 'Queen of the Lemons' | EAro |
| N | ***quercifolium*** (Sc) | CHal CRHN CSev GPoy LPio MBPg MHer NFir WFib |
| | – variegated (v) | MBPg MHer |
| | ***quinquelobatum*** | CSpe LPio |
| | 'R.A.Turner' (Z/d) | WFib |
| | 'Rachel' (Min) | ESul |
| | ***radens*** (Sc) | EPfP LPio WFib |
| | 'Rads Star' (Z/St) | ESul NFir SSea WFib |
| | 'Radula' (Sc) ♀H1+3 | CSev ESul GBar LDea MBPg MHer MNHC SSea WFib |
| | 'Radula Roseum' (Sc) | MBPg SSea WFib |
| | 'Ragamuffin' (Dw/d) | ESul |

| | | |
|---|---|---|
| | 'Rager's Pink' (Dw/d) | ESul |
| | 'Rager's Star' (Dw) | ESul |
| | 'Rager's Veri-Star' (Min/C) | ESul |
| | 'Ragtime' (St) | NPri |
| | 'Raphael' (A) | LDea |
| | 'Raspberry Parfait' (R) | LDea |
| | 'Raspberry Ripple' (A) | ESul LDea NFir SSea WFib |
| | 'Raspberry Surprise' (R) | ESul LVER SSea |
| | 'Raspberry Yhu' (R) | ESul |
| | 'Ray Bidwell' (Min) | ESul NFir WFib |
| | 'Raydon' (Min) | ESul |
| | 'Reba' **new** | ESul |
| | 'Rebecca' (Min/d) | ESul WFib |
| I | 'Rebecca' (Sc) | MBPg |
| | 'Red Admiral' (Min/d/v) | ESul |
| § | 'Red Black Vesuvius' (Min/C) | CHal ESul SSea WFib |
| | 'Red Cactus' (St) | NFir |
| | 'Red Capri' (Sc) | MBPg |
| § | 'Red Cascade' (I) ♀H1+3 | WFib |
| | 'Red Glitter' (Dw/St) | ESul |
| | 'Red Ice' (Min/d) | ESul NFir |
| | 'Red Pandora' (z) | LVER NFir WFib |
| | 'Red Pimpernella' | LVER |
| | 'Red Rambler' (Z/d) | CHal ESul LVER WBrk WFib |
| | 'Red Robin' (R) | WCot |
| | 'Red Silver Cascade' | see *P.* 'Mutzel' |
| | 'Red Spider' (Dw/Ca) | EShb ESul WFib |
| | 'Red Starstorm' (Dw/St) | ESul |
| | 'Red Startel' (Z/St/d) | WFib |
| | 'Red Susan Pearce' (R) | ESul WFib |
| | 'Red Sybil Holmes' (I) | LSou LVER |
| | Red Sybil = 'Pensyb'PBR (I/d) | LAst LSou NBlu |
| | 'Red Witch' (Dw/St/d) | ESul LVER SSea WBrk WFib |
| | Red-Blizzard = 'Fizzard'PBR (I) | MCot NPri SCoo |
| § | Red-Mini-Cascade = 'Rotemica' (I) | ESul LAst LDea LVER WFib |
| | 'Redondo' (Dw/d) | ESul LVER |
| | 'Reflections' (Z/d) | WFib |
| | 'Reg 'Q'' (Z/C) | NFir |
| | Reggae Bright Red = 'Fip 202' (I) | NPri |
| | 'Regina' (Z/d) | LVER NFir WFib |
| | 'Rembrandt' (R) | LDea LVER SSea WFib |
| | 'Renate Parsley' | EShb ESul LPio MBPg MHer NFir SSea WFib |
| | 'Rene Roué' (Dw/d/v) | ESul |
| | ***reniforme*** | GBar LPio MBPg MHer SAga SSea SUsu WFib |
| | 'Retah's Crystal' (Z/v) | ESul LVER |
| | 'Rhian Harris' (A) | LDea |
| | Rhodonit = 'Paccherry'PBR (I/d) | LAst LSou |
| | 'Richard Gibbs' (Sc) | GGar LDea MBPg MHer |
| | 'Richard Key' (Z/d/C) | WFib |
| | 'Ricky Cheerful' (A) **new** | LDea |
| | 'Ricky Promise' (A) | LDea |
| | 'Ricky Ruby' (A) | LDea |
| | 'Rietje van der Lee' (A) | ESul WFib |
| | 'Rigel' (Min/d) | ESul LVER NFir |
| | 'Rigi' (I/d) | MBri |
| | 'Rigoletto' (I) | LDea NFir SSea |
| | 'Rimey' (St) | NFir SSea |
| | 'Rimfire' (R) | CWCL ESul LDea LVER MHer NFir WFib |
| | 'Rimfire Dark' (R) **new** | ESul |
| | 'Rio Grande' (I/d) | LDea LVER MHer NFir SPet WFib |
| | 'Rising Sun' | NFir |
| | 'Rita Scheen' (A/v) | ESul LDea SSea |
| | 'Ritchie' (R) | ESul |
| | 'Robbie Hare' (R) | ESul |

| | | |
|---|---|---|
| | 'Robe'PBR (Quality Series) (Z/d) | LAst LVER |
| | 'Rober's Lemon Rose' (Sc) | CRHN CTca ESul GBar LDea MBPg MCot MHer SIde SSea WBrk |
| | 'Rober's Salmon Coral' (Dw/d) | ESul |
| | 'Robert Fish' (Z/C) | ESul LRHS SCoo |
| | 'Robert McElwain' (Z/d) | WFib |
| | 'Robin' (Sc) | LDea LVER MBPg |
| | 'Robin' (R) | LDea SSea |
| | 'Robin's Unique' (U) | NFir WFib |
| | 'Robyn Hannah' (St/d) | NFir |
| | ***rodneyanum*** | CDes |
| | 'Roger's Delight' (R/Sc) | MBPg |
| | 'Rogue' (R) | MSte WFib |
| | 'Roi des Balcons' | see *P.* 'Hederinum' |
| § | 'Roi des Balcons Lilas' (I) ♀H1+3 | LSou MBPg WFib |
| | 'Roi des Balcons Rose' | see *P.* 'Hederinum' |
| | 'Roller's Echo' (A) | ESul LDea WFib |
| | 'Roller's Pathfinder' (I/d/v) | LDea LVER |
| | 'Roller's Pioneer' (I/v) | LDea LVER SAga SSea |
| | 'Roller's Satinique' (U) ♀H1+3 | LPio MBPg MHer SSea |
| | 'Roller's Shadow' (A) | ESul LDea |
| | 'Rollisson's Unique' (U) | MBPg MHer MSte NBur SSea WFib |
| | 'Romeo' (R) | CSpe LVER |
| | Romy (I) | LDea |
| | 'Rookley' (St/d) | ESul |
| | 'Rosa Della Sera' (St) | LVER |
| § | 'Rosa Mini-cascade' (I) | ESul LAst LVER NFir |
| | 'Rosaleen' (Min) | ESul |
| | 'Rosalie' (R) | ESul |
| | 'Rose Bengal' (A) | CRHN ESul LDea WFib |
| | Rose Evka = 'Penevro'PBR (Dw/I/v) | LAst |
| | 'Rose Jewel' (R) | ESul |
| | 'Rose of Amsterdam' (Min/d) | ESul WFib |
| | 'Rose Paton's Unique' (U/Sc) | LDea |
| | 'Rose Silver Cascade' (I) | LDea LVER MCot |
| | 'Rosebud Supreme' (Z/d) | ESul WFib |
| | 'Rosecrystal'PBR (Sweetheart Series) (Z/d) | LVER |
| | 'Rosina Read' (Dw/d) | ESul |
| | 'Rosmaroy' (R) | ESul LDea LVER SSea WFib |
| | 'Rosy Dawn' (Min/d) | WFib |
| | 'Rosy Morn' (R) | NFir |
| | 'Rote Mini-cascade' | see *P.* Red-Mini-Cascade = 'Rotemica' |
| § | 'Rouletta' (I/d) | ECtt LAst LDea LVER NPri WFib |
| | 'Round Leaf Rose' (U) | MBPg |
| | 'Rousillon' (R) | LDea |
| | 'Royal Ascot' (R) | ESul LDea MSte NFir SAga SPet SSea |
| | 'Royal Carpet' (Min/d) | ESul |
| | 'Royal Celebration' (R) **new** | ESul |
| | 'Royal Court' (R) | LDea |
| | 'Royal Decree' (R) | LDea |
| | 'Royal Hussar' (R) **new** | ESul |
| | 'Royal Knight' (R) **new** | ESul |
| | 'Royal Magic' (R) | LDea |
| | 'Royal Majesty' (R) **new** | ESul |
| | 'Royal Norfolk' (Min/d) | ESul LVER NFir |
| | 'Royal Oak' (Sc) ♀H1+3 | CRHN CSev CTca EAro ESul GBar LDea LVER MBPg MCot MHer MNHC NBur SBch SGar SPet SSea WFib WRha |
| | 'Royal Opera' (R) | LDea |
| | 'Royal Pride' (R) | LDea |
| | 'Royal Prince' (R) **new** | ESul |
| | 'Royal Princess' (R) ♀H1+3 | LDea |
| § | 'Royal Purple' (Z/d) | CHal LVER WFib |

| | |
|---|---|
| 'Royal Sovereign' (Z/C/d) | LDea |
| 'Royal Star' (R) | LDea LVER |
| 'Royal Surprise' (R) | ESul LDea NFir |
| 'Royal Wedding' (R) | ESul |
| 'Royal Winner' (R) | LDea |
| 'Ruben' (d) | LAst LSou |
| 'Ruby' (Min/d) | ESul WFib |
| Ruby Dream = 'Fisruby'[PBR] (I) | NPri |
| 'Ruby Orchid' (A) | LDea |
| 'Ruby Wedding' (Z) | ESul |
| 'Ruffled Velvet' (R) | SSea |
| 'Rushmere' (Dw/d) | ESul WFib |
| 'Rusty' (Dw/C/d) | ESul |
| 'Sabine'[PBR] (Z/d) | LVER |
| 'Saint Elmo's Fire' (St/Min/d) | SSea WFib |
| 'Saint Helen's Favourite' (Min) | ESul SSea |
| Saint Malo = 'Guisaint'[PBR] (I) | NFir |
| 'Sally Munro' (R) | LDea SSea |
| 'Sally Read' (Dw/d) | ESul |
| 'Salmon Beauty' (Dw/d) | WFib |
| 'Salmon Black Vesuvius' (Min/C) | ESul |
| § 'Salmon Irene' (Z/d) | WFib |
| Salmon Princess = 'Pacsalpri' **new** | LSou |
| 'Salmon Queen' | see *P.* 'Lachskönigin' |
| ***salmoneum*** | SSea |
| 'Saltford' (R) | ESul |
| 'Samantha' (R) | ESul WFib |
| 'Samantha Stamp' (Dw/d/C) | WFib |
| Samelia = 'Pensam'[PBR] (Dark Line Series) (Z/d) | LAst |
| 'Sammi Caws' (St) | ESul |
| 'Sancho Panza' (Dec) 𝕐[H1+3] | CSpe ESul LDea LVER MBPg MHer MSte SSea WFib |
| 'Sandford' (Dw/St) | ESul |
| 'Sandown' (Dw/d) | ESul |
| 'Sandra Lorraine' (I/d) | WFib |
| 'Sanguineum' | CSpe |
| 'Santa Marie' (R) | LDea |
| 'Santa Paula' (I/d) | ECtt LDea |
| § 'Sarah Don'[PBR] (A/v) | LSou WFib |
| 'Sarah Hunt' (Min/d) | NFir |
| 'Sarah Jane' (Sc) | MBPg |
| 'Sassa'[PBR] (Quality Series) (Z/d) | LAst LSou |
| Satellite (Z/St) | SSea |
| 'Satsuki' (R) | ESul LDea NFir |
| ***scabrum*** | MBPg |
| 'Scarlet Gem' (Z/St) | WBrk WFib |
| 'Scarlet Nosegay' | CHal |
| I 'Scarlet O'Hara' (Z) | LVER |
| 'Scarlet Pet' (U) | CRHN ESul MBPg NFir SMrm |
| 'Scarlet Pimpernel' (Z/C/d) | ESul |
| 'Scarlet Rambler' (Z/d) | EShb SSea WFib |
| 'Scarlet Unique' (U) | CHrt CRHN LDea MSte SMHy SSea WFib |
| ***schizopetalum*** | WFib |
| § 'Schneekönigin' (I/d) | ECtt LDea LVER MSte |
| § 'Schottii' | LPio NFir WFib |
| x ***schottii*** | see *P.* 'Schottii' |
| 'Scottow Star' (Z/C) | WFib |
| 'Seale Star' (Dw/St/C) **new** | SSea |
| 'Seaview Silver' (Min/St) | WFib |
| 'Seaview Sparkler' (Z/St) | WFib |
| 'Secret Love' (Sc) | LDea MBPg |
| 'Seeley's Pansy' (A) | LDea MHer SAga WFib |
| 'Sefton' (R) 𝕐[H1+3] | ESul LDea WFib |

| | |
|---|---|
| 'Selecta Royal Blue' (I) | LSou |
| 'Selena' (Min) | LDea |
| 'Semer' (Min) | ESul |
| * 'Serre de la Madone' (Sc) | WEas |
| 'Shalfleet' (Min/St) | ESul |
| 'Shalimar' (St) | MSte NFir |
| 'Shanks' (Z) | NFir |
| 'Shannon' | WFib |
| 'Sharon' (Min/d) | ESul |
| 'Sheila' (Dw) | ESul |
| 'Shelley' (Dw) | ESul |
| 'Shimmer' (Z/d) | LVER |
| 'Shirley Ash' (A) | LDea WFib |
| 'Shirley Gillam' (Z/St/v) | ESul LVER |
| Shocking Pink = 'Pensho'[PBR] (Quality Series) (Z/d) | LAst |
| Shocking Violet = 'Pacshovi'[PBR] (Quality Series) (Z/d) | LAst LSou |
| 'Shogan' (R) | NFir |
| 'Shorwell' (Dw/C/d) | ESul |
| § 'Shottesham Pet' (Sc) | ESul MBPg MHer |
| 'Show Off' (Z) | LVER |
| 'Shrubland Pet' (U/Sc) | LPio SSea |
| 'Shrubland Rose' (Sc) | LPio SSea |
| 'Sid' (R) | LDea |
| ***sidoides*** | CDow CSpe EBee ESul LPio MBPg MCot MHer MWea NFir SAga SBch SPhx SSea WEas WFib WGwG |
| - black-flowered | CSpe SUsu |
| - 'Sloe Gin Fizz' | CSpe LPio |
| Sidonia = 'Pensid'[PBR] (Dark Line Series) (Z/d) | LAst LSou WGor |
| 'Sienna' (R) | ESul LDea NBur NFir |
| 'Sil Claudio'[PBR] (Z) | LAst |
| 'Sil Frauke'[PBR] (Z) | LAst LSou |
| 'Sil Friesia'[PBR] (Z) | LAst |
| 'Sil Gesa'[PBR] (Z) | LAst |
| 'Sil Liske'[PBR] (Z) | LAst LSou |
| 'Sil Pia'[PBR] (I) | LAst LSou WGor |
| 'Sil Raiko'[PBR] | LAst |
| 'Sil Renko'[PBR] (Z) | LAst |
| 'Sil Rumika'[PBR] | LAst |
| 'Sil Sören' | LAst LSou |
| 'Sil Tedo'[PBR] (Z) | LAst LSou |
| 'Sil Teske'[PBR] (I) | LAst |
| 'Sil Tomke'[PBR] (I) | LAst LSou |
| 'Silver Anne' (R/v) | ESul NFir |
| 'Silver Dawn' (Min/St) | ESul |
| 'Silver Delight' (v/d) | WFib |
| 'Silver Dusk' (Min/St) | ESul |
| 'Silver Glitter' (Dw/St) | ESul |
| 'Silver Kewense' (Dw/v) | ESul NFir WFib |
| 'Silver Leaf Rose' (Sc) | MBPg |
| 'Silver Rimfire' (R) | ESul |
| 'Silver Snow' (Min/St/d) | ESul WFib |
| 'Silver Wings' (Z/v) | ESul LVER NFir SSea |
| 'Silvia' (R) | ESul |
| 'Simon Read' (Dw) | ESul |
| 'Simplicity' (Z) | LVER |
| 'Sir Colin' (Z) | SSea |
| 'Skelly's Pride' (Z) | WFib |
| 'Skies of Italy' (Z/C/d) | MBri MHer SSea WFib |
| 'Small Fortune' (Min/d) | ESul |
| 'Smuggler' (R) | LDea |
| 'Snape' (Min) | ESul |
| 'Sneezy' (Min) | ESul NFir |
| 'Snow Cap' (MinI) | NFir |
| 'Snow Flurry' (Sc) | MBPg WBrk |
| Snow Queen | see *P.* 'Schneekönigin' |
| 'Snow White' (Min) | ESul |
| 'Snowbaby' (Min/d) | ESul |

| | | |
|---|---|---|
| | 'Snowberry' (R) | ESul |
| | 'Snowbright' (St/d) | ESul |
| | 'Snowdrift' (I/d) | LVER SSea WFib |
| | 'Snowflake' (Min) | see *P.* 'Atomic Snowflake' |
| | 'Snowstorm' (Z) | WFib |
| | 'Snowy Baby' (Min/d) | WFib |
| | 'Sofie' | see *P.* 'Decora Rose' |
| | 'Solent Waves' (R) | ESul LDea |
| | 'Solferino' (A) | ESul LDea |
| | Solidor (I/d) ♀H1+3 | LDea NFir |
| | Solo = 'Guillio' (Z/I) | LVER |
| | 'Somersham' (Min) | ESul WFib |
| | 'Something Else' (Z/St/d) | LVER |
| | 'Something Special' (Z/d) | LVER NFir WFib |
| | 'Sonata' (Dw/d) | ESul |
| | 'Sophie' (R) | ESul |
| | Sophie Casade | see *P.* 'Decora Rose' |
| | 'Sophie Caws' (St) | ESul |
| | 'Sophie Dumaresque' (Z/v) | LVER MBri NFir SSea WFib |
| | 'Sorcery' (Dw/C) | ESul |
| | 'Sound Appeal' (A) | ESul LDea MBPg |
| | 'South American Bronze' (R) ♀H1+3 | ESul LDea SMrm WFib |
| | 'South American Pink' (R) | ESul |
| | 'Southern Belle' (A) | LDea SSea |
| | 'Southern Belle' (Z/d) | WFib |
| | 'Southern Charm' (Z/v) | LVER NFir |
| | 'Southern Cherub' (A) | LDea |
| | 'Southern Damsel' (R) | ESul |
| | 'Southern Fairy' (A) **new** | ESul |
| | 'Southern Festival' (Dw) | ESul |
| | 'Southern Flamenco' (R) | ESul |
| | 'Southern Frills' (A) **new** | ESul |
| | 'Southern Galaxy' (Min/St) | ESul |
| | 'Southern Gem' (Min/d) | ESul |
| | 'Southern Michaela' (A) | ESul |
| | 'Southern Peach' (Min/d) | ESul |
| | 'Southern Posy' (Dw) | ESul |
| | 'Southern Purity' (Min) | ESul |
| | 'Southern Rosina' (Dw) | ESul |
| | 'Southern Siewigy' (Dec) | ESul |
| | 'Southern Starlight' (A) **new** | ESul |
| | 'Souvenir' (R) | ESul LDea SSea |
| | 'Sowoma Lavender' (Sc) | MBPg |
| | 'Spanish Angel' (A) ♀H1+3 | CWCL ESul LDea NFir SSea WFib |
| | 'Spanish Banks' (Z/St/v) | ESul LVER |
| | 'Sparkler' (Z) | LVER |
| | 'Spellbound' (R) | WFib |
| | 'Spital Dam' (Dw/d) | ESul NFir |
| | 'Spitfire' (Z/Ca/d/v) | ESul LVER WFib |
| | 'Spithead Cherry' (R) | LDea |
| § | 'Splendide' | CRHN CSpe EShb ESul LPio MBPg MHer MSCN NFir SSea SWvt WCot WEas WFib |
| | 'Splendide' white-flowered | LPio MBPg |
| | 'Spotlite Hotline' (I) | LDea |
| | 'Spotlite Winner' (I) | LDea |
| | 'Spot-on-bonanza' (R) | ESul LDea NFir SSea WFib |
| | 'Spring Bride' (R) | LDea |
| | 'Spring Park' (A) | ESul LVER MHer SSea WFib |
| I | 'Springfield Alba' (R) | ESul |
| | 'Springfield Black' (R) | ESul LDea LVER MCot SSea |
| | 'Springfield Joy' (R) | ESul |
| | 'Springfield Pearl' (R) | ESul LDea |
| | 'Springfield Purple' (R) | ESul |
| | 'Springfield Unique' (R) | ESul LDea |
| | 'Springtime' (Z/d) | WFib |
| I | 'Springtime' (R) | ESul |
| | 'Sproughton' (Dw) | ESul |
| | 'Stacey' (R) | ESul LDea |
| | 'Stadt Bern' (Z/C) | LAst LVER MBri MSte NFir |
| | 'Stan Shaw' (R) | LDea |
| | 'Stanley Park' (St) **new** | SSea |
| | x ***stapletoniae*** | see *P.* 'Miss Stapleton' |
| | 'Star Flair' (St/Min/d) | ESul |
| | 'Star Flecks' (St) | NFir |
| | 'Star of Persia' (Z/Ca/d) | WFib |
| | 'Star Storm' (St/d) | ESul |
| | 'Starflecks' (St) | LVER |
| | 'Starlet' (Ca) | WFib |
| | 'Starlight' (R) | WFib |
| | 'Starlight Magic' (A) ♀H1+3 | ESul LDea |
| | 'Starry Eyes' (Dw) | ESul |
| | 'Startel Salmon' (Z/St) | MHer |
| | 'Stella Marinella' **new** | LVER |
| | 'Stella Read' (Dw/d) | ESul |
| | 'Stella Vernante' **new** | LVER |
| | 'Stellar Arctic Star' | see *P.* 'Arctic Star' |
| | 'Stellar Hannaford Star' | see *P.* 'Hannaford Star' |
| | 'Stephen Read' (Min) | ESul |
| | 'Stewart Meehan' (R) | LDea |
| | 'Stolen Kisses' (Min/D) **new** | ESul |
| | 'Strawberries and Cream' (Z/St) | NFir |
| | 'Strawberry Fayre' (Dw/St) | LVER WFib |
| | 'Strawberry Sundae' (R) | ESul LDea MSte WFib |
| | 'Stringer's Delight' (Dw/v) | ESul LVER |
| | 'Stringer's Souvenir' (Dw/d/v) | SSea |
| | 'Stuart Mark' (R) | LDea |
| | 'Stutton' (Min) | ESul |
| | 'Suffolk Agate' (R) | ESul |
| | 'Suffolk Amethyst' (A) | ESul |
| | 'Suffolk Coral' (R) | ESul |
| | 'Suffolk Coral Salmon' (R) **new** | ESul |
| | 'Suffolk Emerald' (A) | ESul |
| | 'Suffolk Garnet' (Dec) | ESul |
| | 'Suffolk Jade' (Min) | ESul |
| | 'Suffolk Jet' (Min) | ESul |
| § | 'Sugar Baby' (DwI) | ECtt ESul LAst LDea MBri MCot WFib |
| | 'Summer Cloud' (Z/d) | WFib |
| | 'Summer Rose Lilac' (I) | NPri |
| | 'Summertime' (Z/d) | see *P.* 'Deacon Summertime' |
| | 'Sun Rocket' (Dw/d) | WFib |
| | 'Sundridge Moonlight' (Z/C) | WFib |
| | 'Sundridge Surprise' (Z) | WFib |
| | 'Sunraysia' (Z/St) | WFib |
| | 'Sunridge Moonlight' (Dw) | NFir |
| | 'Sunset Snow' (R) | ESul LVER NFir WFib |
| | 'Sunspot' (Min/C) | NFir |
| | 'Sunspot Kleine Liebling' (Min) | SSea WFib |
| | 'Sunspot Petit Pierre' (Min/v) | WFib |
| | 'Sunstar' (Min/d) | ESul WFib |
| | 'Super Rose' (I) | SPet |
| | 'Super Rupert' (Sc) | MBPg |
| | 'Supernova' (Z/St/d) | ESul WFib |
| | 'Surcouf' (I) | WFib |
| | 'Susan Hillier' (R) | LDea |
| | 'Susan Payne' (Dw/d) | ESul LVER MHer |
| | 'Susan Pearce' (R) | ESul LDea LVER |
| | 'Susan Read' (Dw) | ESul |
| | 'Susie 'Q'' (Z/C) | LVER SSea |
| | 'Sussex Delight' (Min) | SPet |
| | 'Sussex Gem' (Min/d) | ESul WFib |
| | 'Sussex Lace' | see *P.* 'White Mesh' |
| | 'Suzanne' (St) | LVER |
| | 'Swainham Mellow Yellow' (Z) | LVER |
| | 'Swanland Lace' (I/d/v) | WFib |
| | 'Swedish Angel' (A) | ESul LDea NFir SSea WFib |

| | |
|---|---|
| 'Sweet Lady Mary' (Sc) | LDea MBPg |
| 'Sweet Mimosa' (Sc) 🏆H1+3 | CHal CHrt CRHN CTca ESul GBar LVER MBPg MCot MHer MSte NFir SDnm SSea WBrk WFib |
| 'Sweet Miriam' (Sc) | GBar LDea MBPg |
| 'Sweet Rosina' (Sc) | MBPg |
| 'Sweet Sixteen' | WFib |
| 'Sweet Sue' (Min) | ESul |
| 'Swilland' (A) | LDea LVER WFib |
| 'Sybil Bradshaw' (R) | LDea |
| 'Sybil Holmes' (I/d) | ECtt LAst LVER MBri NBlu SPet SSea WFib |
| 'Sylbar' (R) | ESul |
| 'Sylvia' (R) | ESul |
| 'Sylvia Gale' (R) | ESul |
| 'Sylvia Marie' (d) | NFir |
| 'Taffety' (Min) | ESul WFib |
| 'Tamie' (Dw/d) | ESul NFir |
| 'Tammy' (Dw/d) | ESul |
| 'Tangerine' (Min/Ca/d) | ESul LVER SSea WFib |
| 'Tangerine Elf' (St) | WFib |
| 'Tanzy' (Min) | ESul |
| 'Tapriz' (R) | ESul |
| 'Tara Caws' (Z) <u>**new**</u> | ESul |
| 'Taspo' (R) | ESul |
| 'Tattingstone' (Min) | ESul |
| 'Tattoo' (Min) | ESul |
| 'Tavira' (I/d) | SPet |
| 'Tazi' (Dw) | ESul |
| 'Ted Dutton' (R) | ESul |
| 'Telstar' (Min/d) | ESul |
| § 'Telston's Prima' (R) | ESul LDea |
| 'Tenderly' (Dw/d) | ESul |
| 'Tenerife Magic' (MinI/d) | ESul |
| ***tetragonum*** | CRHN EShb MBPg MHer SSea WFib |
| 'The Axe' (A) | LDea |
| 'The Barle' (A) 🏆H1+3 | LDea WFib |
| 'The Boar' (Fr) 🏆H1+3 | EShb LDea MSte SRms WFib |
| 'The Bray' (A) | LDea |
| 'The Creedy' (A) | LDea |
| 'The Culm' (A) | ESul LDea MSte SSea WFib |
| 'The Czar' | see *P.* 'Czar' |
| 'The Dart' (A) | LDea |
| 'The Heddon' (A) | LDea |
| 'The Joker' (I/d) | WFib |
| 'The Kenn-Lad' (A) | LDea |
| 'The Lowman' (A) | LDea SSea |
| 'The Lyn' (A) | ESul LDea |
| § 'The Mole' (A) | ESul LDea LVER MBPg MHer MSte SSea WFib |
| 'The Okement' (A) | LDea MSte SSea |
| 'The Otter' (A) | ESul LDea SSea |
| 'The Tamar' (A) | CFee LDea SSea |
| 'The Tone' (A) 🏆H1+3 | LDea |
| 'The Yar' (Z/St) | WFib |
| 'Thomas' (Sc) | MBPg |
| 'Thomas Earle' (Z) | WFib |
| 'Thomas Gerald' (Dw/C) | ESul |
| 'Tilly' (Min) | CHal NFir |
| 'Tim' (Min) | ESul |
| 'Timothy Clifford' (Min/d) | ESul |
| 'Tinkerbell' (A) | LDea |
| § 'Tip Top Duet' (A) 🏆H1+3 | CHal ESul LDea LRHS LSou LVER MHer NFir SMrm SSea WFib |
| 'Tirley Garth' (A) | WFib |
| 'Tomcat'PBR (I/d) | LAst LVER SSea WGor |
| ***tomentosum*** (Sc) 🏆H1+3 | CArn CHEx CHal CRHN CSev CSpe CTca EAro EShb ESul GBar GPoy LDea LPio LVER MBPg MCot MHer MNHC NFir SBch SSea WFib |
| - 'Chocolate' | see *P.* 'Chocolate Peppermint' |
| Tomgirl = 'Pactomgi'PBR (IxZ/d) | LAst LVER SSea WGor |
| 'Tommay's Delight' (R) | LDea |
| 'Tony' (Min) | ESul |
| 'Topan' (R) | ESul |
| 'Topcliffe' (Dw/St) | ESul |
| 'Topscore' (Z/d) | WFib |
| 'Tornado' (R) | CWCL ESul NFir SAga WFib |
| 'Torrento' (Sc) | ESul GBar LDea MBPg MHer WFib |
| 'Tortoiseshell' (R) | WFib |
| 'Tracy' (Min/d) | ESul NFir |
| ***transvaalense*** | LPio NFir |
| 'Treasure Trove' (Z/v) | NFir |
| ***tricolor*** misapplied | see *P.* 'Splendide' |
| ***tricolor*** Curt. | NFir |
| ***tricuspidatum*** | CSpe LPio |
| ***trifidum*** | LPio MBPg SSea WFib |
| 'Trimley' (Dw/d) | ESul |
| 'Trinket' (Min/d) | WFib |
| 'Triomphe de Nancy' (Z/d) | WFib |
| ***triste*** | LFur LPio SSea SUsu WFib |
| 'Trixie' (R) | LDea |
| 'Trudie' (Dw/Fr) | ESul LVER MHer WBrk WFib |
| 'Tu Tone' (Dw/d) | ESul |
| 'Tuddenham' (Min/d) | ESul |
| 'Tuesday's Child' (Dw/C) | ESul |
| 'Tunias Perfecta' (R) | ESul |
| 'Turkish Coffee' (R) | CWCL ESul LVER NFir WFib |
| 'Turkish Delight' (Dw/C) | ESul NFir SSea WFib |
| 'Tuyo' (R) | WFib |
| 'Tweedle-Dum' (Dw) | ESul |
| 'Tweenaway' (Dw) | ESul |
| 'Twinkle' (Min/d) | ESul WFib |
| 'Two Dees' (Dw/d) <u>**new**</u> | NFir |
| 'Ullswater' (Dw/C) | ESul |
| § 'Unique Aurore' (U) | LVER MBPg MHer MSte |
| 'Unique Mons Ninon' | see *P.* 'Monsieur Ninon' |
| 'Unity' (Dw) | LVER |
| 'Urban White' (Dec) | CSpe SAga WFib |
| ***urbanum*** | EShb |
| 'Urchin' (Min/St) | ESul NFir WFib |
| 'Ursula Key' (Z/c) | WFib |
| 'Ursula's Choice' (A) | WFib |
| 'Val Merrick' (Dw/St) | WFib |
| 'Valencia' (R) | ESul |
| 'Valentina' (Min/d) | ESul |
| 'Valentine' (Z/C) | ESul WFib |
| 'Vancouver Centennial' (Dw/St/C) 🏆H1+3 | ESul GKir LAst LRHS LVER MBri MCot MHer NFir SAga SCoo SDnm SPoG SSea SWal WFib |
| 'Vandersea' | EAro |
| 'Variegated Attar of Roses' (Sc/v) | MBPg |
| § 'Variegated Clorinda' (Sc/v) | WFib |
| 'Variegated Fragrans' | see *P.* (Fragrans Group) 'Fragrans Variegatum' |
| 'Variegated Giroflée' (I/v) <u>**new**</u> | SSea |
| 'Variegated Joy Lucille' (Sc/v) | MBPg |
| § 'Variegated Kleine Liebling' (Min/v) | ESul SSea WFib |
| 'Variegated Madame Layal' (A/v) 🏆H1+3 | WFib |
| 'Variegated Petit Pierre' (Min/v) | WFib |
| 'Vasco da Gama' (Dw/d) | ESul |
| 'Vectis Allure' (Z/St) | LVER |
| 'Vectis Dream' (St) | ESul |
| 'Vectis Fanfare' (St/d) | ESul |
| 'Vectis Finery' (St/d) | ESul NFir |
| 'Vectis Glitter' (Z/St) | ESul LVER NFir SSea WBrk WFib |
| 'Vectis Pink' (Dw/St) | SSea WFib |
| 'Vectis Purple' (Z/d) | WFib |
| 'Vectis Sparkler' (Dw/St) | ESul NFir |

| | | |
|---|---|---|
| | 'Vectis Spider' (Dw/St) | ESul NFir |
| | 'Vectis Starbright' (Dw/St) | WFib |
| | 'Vectis Volcano' (Z/St) | WFib |
| | 'Velvet Duet' (A) ♀$^{H1+3}$ | CHal LDea LRHS LVER MBPg NFir SSea |
| | 'Venus' (Min/d) | ESul |
| | 'Vera Vernon' (Z/v) | SSea |
| | 'Verdale' (A) | GGar LDea WFib |
| | 'Verity Palace' (R) | ESul LDea WFib |
| | 'Verona' (Z/C) | CHal MBri SSea |
| | 'Verona Contreras' (A) | CWCL ESul LDea NFir WFib |
| | 'Vicki Town' (R) | WFib |
| | 'Vicky Claire' (R) | CSpe ESul LDea NFir WFib |
| | Vicky = 'Pacvicky'$^{PBR}$ (I) | LAst LSou |
| | 'Vickybar' (R) | ESul |
| | Victor = 'Pacvi'$^{PBR}$ (Quality Series) (Z/d) | LAst LSou |
| | 'Victoria' (Z/d) | LAst LSou |
| | 'Victoria Regina' (R) | ESul LDea |
| | 'Village Hill Oak' (Sc) | ESul LDea MBPg |
| | Ville de Dresden = 'Pendresd'$^{PBR}$ (I) | LAst |
| | 'Ville de Paris' | see *P.* 'Hederinum' |
| | 'Vina' (Dw/C/d) | WFib |
| | 'Vincent Gerris' (A) | ESul LDea |
| | Vinco = 'Guivin'$^{PBR}$ (I/d) | LAst LSou WGor |
| | ***violareum*** misapplied | see *P.* 'Splendide' |
| | 'Violet Lambton' (Z/v) | WFib |
| I | 'Violetta' (R) | LDea WFib |
| | 'Virginia' (R) | LDea SPet |
| | 'Viscossisimum' (Sc) | MHer |
| | ***viscosum*** | see *P. glutinosum* |
| § | ***vitifolium*** | MBPg |
| | 'Vivat Regina' (Z/d) | WFib |
| | 'Voo Doo' (Dec) | ESul |
| | 'Voodoo' (U) ♀$^{H1+3}$ | CSpe EShb LAst LPio LSou MBPg MHer MSte NFir SAga SSea WBrk WCot WFib |
| | 'Wallace Fairman' (R) | LDea |
| | 'Wallis Friesdorf' (Dw/C/d) | ESul |
| | 'Wantirna' (Z/v) | ECtt MHer NFir SSea |
| | 'Warrenorth Coral' (Z/C/d) | NFir WFib |
| | 'Warrenorth Thulite' | LVER |
| | 'Warrion' (Z/d) | LVER SSea |
| | 'Washbrook' (Min/d) | ESul NFir |
| | 'Watersmeet' (R) | LDea SSea |
| | 'Wattisham' (Dec) | LDea |
| | 'Waveney' (Min) | ESul |
| | 'Wayward Angel' (A) ♀$^{H1+3}$ | ESul LDea LVER SSea WFib |
| | 'Wedding Royale' (Dw/d) | ESul WFib |
| | 'Welcome' (Z/d) | WFib |
| | 'Welling' (Sc) | ESul GBar LDea LVER MBPg MHer NFir |
| | 'Wendy Jane' (Dw/d) | WFib |
| | 'Wendy Read' (Dw/d) | ESul WFib |
| | 'Wendy-O' (R) | LDea |
| | 'Wensum' (Min/d) | ESul |
| | 'Westdale Appleblossom' (Z/d/C) | ESul LVER SSea WBrk WFib |
| | 'Westerfield' (Min) | ESul |
| | 'Westside' (Z/d) | WFib |
| | 'Westwood' (Z/St) | WFib |
| | 'Wherstead' (Min) | ESul |
| | 'Whisper' (R) | WFib |
| | 'White Bird's Egg' (Z) | WFib |
| | 'White Boar' (Fr) | EShb MSte WFib |
| | 'White Bonanza' (R) | ESul WFib |
| | 'White Charm' (R) | ESul LDea |
| | 'White Chiffon' (R) | ESul LVER NBur |
| | 'White Christmas' (Min/St) **new** | ESul |
| | 'White Duet' (A) | LDea |
| | 'White Eggshell' (Min) | ESul LVER WFib |
| | 'White Feather' (Z/St) | MHer |
| | 'White Glory' (R) ♀$^{H1+3}$ | ESul NFir |
| | 'White Lively Lady' (Dw/C) | ESul |
| § | 'White Mesh' (I/v) | ECtt MBri |
| | 'White Prince of Orange' (Sc) | MBPg WBrk |
| | 'White Roc' (Min/d) | ESul |
| | 'White Unique' (U) | CHal CSpe LDea MBPg MHer MSte SPet SSea WFib |
| | 'White Velvet Duet' (A) | ESul |
| | White-Blizzard = 'Fisbliz'$^{PBR}$ | NPri SCoo |
| | 'Wickham Lad' (R) | LDea |
| | Wico = 'Guimongol'$^{PBR}$ (I/d) | LAst LSou WGor |
| | 'Wild Spice' (Sc) | LDea LVER |
| | 'Wildmalva' (Sc) | MBPg |
| | 'Wilf Vernon' (Min/d) | ESul |
| | 'Wilhelm Kolle' (Z) | WFib |
| | 'Wilhelm Langath' | SCoo SDnm |
| | 'Willa' (Dec) | WFib |
| | 'Winford Festival' | LVER |
| | 'Winnie Read' (Dw/d) | ESul |
| | 'Wirral Target' (Z/d/v) | ESul |
| | 'Wispy' (Dw/St/C) | ESul |
| | 'Witnesham' (Min/d) | ESul |
| | 'Wolverton' (Z) | WFib |
| § | 'Wood's Surprise' (Min/I/d/v) | EShb ESul LDea |
| | 'Wooton's Unique' | CSpe |
| | 'Wordsworth' | MBPg |
| | 'Wychwood' (A/Sc) | LDea MBPg |
| | 'Yale' (I/d) ♀$^{H1+3}$ | LDea MBri MSte WFib |
| | 'Yhu' (R) | ESul LDea NBur NFir SAga WFib |
| | 'Yolanda' (Dw/C) | ESul |
| | 'York Florist' (Z/d/v) | LVER |
| | 'Yvonne' (Z) | WFib |
| | 'Zama' (R) | NFir |
| | 'Zena' (Dw) | ESul |
| | 'Zinc' (Z/d) | WFib |
| | 'Zoe' (A) | LDea |
| | ***zonale*** | SSea WFib |
| | 'Zulu King' (R) | WFib |
| | 'Zulu Warrior' (R) | WFib |

## *Peliosanthes* (*Convallariaceae*)

| | | |
|---|---|---|
| | ***monticola*** B&SWJ 5183 | WCru |

## *Pellaea* (*Adiantaceae*)

| | | |
|---|---|---|
| | ***andromedifolia*** | WRic |
| | ***atropurpurea*** | CLAP WFib |
| § | ***calomelanos*** | WRic |
| | ***falcata*** | CLAP EShb MBri SEND WRic |
| | ***hastata*** | see *P. calomelanos* |
| | ***rotundifolia*** ♀$^{H2}$ | CHal CLAP EBee EShb LLHF LRHS MBri STre WRic |
| | ***viridis*** | WRic |
| | – var. ***macrophylla*** | WRic |

## *Pellionia* see *Elatostema*

## *Peltandra* (*Araceae*)

| | | |
|---|---|---|
| | ***alba*** | see *P. sagittifolia* |
| § | ***sagittifolia*** | CRow |
| | ***undulata*** | see *P. virginica* |
| § | ***virginica*** | CDWL CRow EBee EMFW LPBA NPer SWat |
| | – 'Snow Splash' (v) | CRow |

## *Peltaria* (*Brassicaceae*)

| | | |
|---|---|---|
| | ***alliacea*** | CSpe GBin LEdu SAga |
| | ***turkmena*** | CSec |

## ***Peltiphyllum*** see *Darmera*

## ***Peltoboykinia*** (*Saxifragaceae*)

| | | |
|---|---|---|
| § | ***tellimoides*** | CLAP CSec EBee GCal GEdr GKev GKir NBir WBVN WFar WMoo |
| | ***watanabei*** | CAby CDes CLAP CSec EBee GEdr LEdu NLar WCru WMoo WPGP |

## ***Pennantia*** (*Icacinaceae*)

| | | |
|---|---|---|
| | ***baylisiana*** | ECou |
| | ***corymbosa*** | ECou |
| | - 'Akoroa' | ECou |
| | - 'Woodside' | ECou |

## ***Pennellianthus*** see *Penstemon*

## ***Pennisetum*** ✿ (*Poaceae*)

| | | |
|---|---|---|
| § | ***alopecuroides*** | Widely available |
| | - Autumn Wizard | see *P. alopecuroides* 'Herbstzauber' |
| | - 'Black Beauty' | CSpe SMHy SPhx |
| | - 'Cassian's Choice' | CKno CSam EBee EHoe ELon SMrm |
| | - 'Caudatum' | CKno CPen EBee SApp |
| | - f. ***erythrochaetum*** **new** | EBee |
| | - - 'Ferris' | EBee WCru |
| | - 'Foxtrot' **new** | IPot |
| | - 'Gelbstiel' **new** | EBee |
| | - 'Hameln' | Widely available |
| § | - 'Herbstzauber' | CFir CKno CMdw CPen CPrp CSam EBee EGle EHoe EPfP LEdu LHop SPoG |
| | - 'Little Bunny' | CKno CPen CSpe CWib EBee EBrs EHoe ELan EMon EPPr EPfP EQua GCal LRHS NGdn SApp SWvt WBor WDin WFar |
| | - 'Little Honey' (v) | CKno EBee EHoe MAvo MBNS NLar SPla |
| | - 'Magic' | CPen EHoe MAvo MDKP |
| | - 'Moudry' | CKno CPen CSam EAlp EBee EHoe LBMP MAvo NSti SHDw WFar |
| | - 'National Arboretum' | EBee EHoe EPPr LEdu SApp SMad |
| | - var. ***purpurascens*** | NDov |
| | - f. ***viridescens*** | CKno COIW EBee ECha EGle EHoe ELan EPPr EPfP EShb EWsh GFor LEdu LRHS MLLN MMoz MWhi SApp SWal WPer |
| | - 'Weserbergland' | CKno CSam EBee EHoe SApp |
| | - 'Woodside' | CKno CSam CWCL EBee EHoe EPPr EQua LEdu MBNS SApp SMad SPla |
| | ***compressum*** | see *P. alopecuroides* |
| | ***flaccidum*** | CHrt CSam EBee EHul EPPr |
| | ***glaucum*** 'Purple Majesty' | CKno CSpe CWCL MNrw NGBl NPri SCoo SMad SUsu WBor WPrP |
| | ***incomptum*** | EHoe WHal |
| | - purple-flowered | EBee MMoz |
| | ***longistylum*** misapplied | see *P. villosum* |
| | ***macrostachyum*** 'Burgundy Giant' | MGos |
| | ***macrourum*** | Widely available |
| | ***massaicum*** | SIng |
| | - 'Red Buttons' | see *P. thunbergii* 'Red Buttons' |
| | ***orientale*** Ψ$^{H3}$ | Widely available |
| | - 'Karley Rose'[PBR] | CKno CPen EAlp EBee EGle EHoe EHrv EWes IPot LCro LEdu MAvo NDov SHDw SPhx SSvw SUsu |
| I | - 'Robustum' | CDes SApp |
| | - 'Shenandoah' | SApp |
| * | - 'Shogun' | CKno CPen EBee MAvo WCot |
| | - 'Tall Tails' | CHFP CHar CKno CPen EAlp EBee ECGP ECha EHoe EPPr EWes IPot LBMP LEdu MAvo NBHF NDov NSti SMad WCot |
| | 'Paul's Giant' | CKno SApp |
| | ***purpureum*** | LEdu |
| | ***rueppellii*** | see *P. setaceum* |
| § | ***setaceum*** Ψ$^{H3}$ | CKno CWib EHig EShb LBMP MNrw SHDw SIde |
| | - 'Eaton Canyon' | CKno EBee SPad |
| | - 'Emelia Mae' **new** | SHDw |
| | - 'Rubrum' Ψ$^{H4}$ | CAbb CBcs CKno CSpe CWCL EAlp EBee EShb GMaP LAst LHop LSRN MAvo MGos NPri SCoo SDix SGar SHDw SMad SMrm SPad SPoG SRkn SRot SUsu SWvt WCot |
| § | ***thunbergii*** 'Red Buttons' | CKno CPen EAlp EGle IPot LEdu MAvo MDKP SHDw SMHy SUsu |
| § | ***villosum*** Ψ$^{H3}$ | Widely available |

## **pennyroyal** see *Mentha pulegium*

## ***Penstemon*** ✿ (*Scrophulariaceae*)

| | | |
|---|---|---|
| | P&C 150 | CFee |
| | RCB/MO A-7 | WCot |
| | 'Abberley' | MBNS WPer |
| | 'Abbeydore' | SLon |
| | 'Abbotsmerry' | EPfP MBNS SAga SGar SLon SPhx |
| | 'Agnes Laing' | LPen MBNS SLon SPlb |
| | ***albertinus*** | see *P. humilis* |
| § | 'Alice Hindley' Ψ$^{H3}$ | Widely available |
| | ***alpinus*** | CSec EAro |
| § | 'Andenken an Friedrich Hahn' Ψ$^{H4}$ | Widely available |
| § | ***angustifolius*** | MNrw SRms |
| | - NNS 99-102 **new** | EBee |
| | 'Apple Blossom' misapplied | see *P.* 'Thorn' |
| | 'Apple Blossom' Ψ$^{H3-4}$ | Widely available |
| | ***arizonicus*** | see *P. whippleanus* |
| | 'Ashton' | CElw LPen MBNS SAga SLon SUsu |
| | ***attenuatus*** | EBee |
| | 'Audrey Cooper' | CChe MBNS SLon |
| | 'Axe Valley Jessica' | SAga |
| | 'Axe Valley Pixie' | CEnt SAga |
| | ***azureus*** | CFir EBee |
| | - subsp. ***angustissimus*** **new** | GKev |
| | - subsp. ***azureus*** | NLAp |
| | 'Baby Lips' | LLHF |
| | 'Barbara Barker' | see *P.* 'Beech Park' |
| § | ***barbatus*** | CAby CEnt CFee EHrv ELan EPfP MLan SPer SRms WFar |
| | - 'Cambridge Mixed' | LRHS NBlu |
| | - subsp. ***coccineus*** | CMea EAro EBee EMon LPen LRHS MBNS NChi NLar |
| | - 'Iron Maiden' | NBPC |
| | - 'Jingle Bells' | EAEE EPfP LPen NBPC SPav |
| | - orange-flowered | SMrm SPlb |
| | - 'Peter Catt' | LSou MDKP SMrm |
| | - var. ***praecox*** | EPfP MBNS WPer |
| | - - f. ***nanus*** | LRHS MSte SRms |
| | - - - 'Rondo' | MNFA NLar NWCA WBrE |
| | ***barrettiae*** | LLHF |
| | 'Beckford' | CPrp EBee EPfP EShb LLHF MBNS WCFE |
| § | 'Beech Park' Ψ$^{H3}$ | EBee ECtt ELan EWes IGor LPen MBNS NBir SAga WHCG |
| | 'Bisham Seedling' | see *P.* 'White Bedder' |
| | 'Blackbird' | Widely available |
| | 'Blue Spring' misapplied | see *P. heterophyllus* 'Blue Spring' |
| | 'Blueberry Fudge' (Ice Cream Series) **new** | WHlf |
| | 'Bodnant' | CHFP LLHF LSou MBNS WHoo WPer |
| | ***bradburii*** | see *P. grandiflorus* |
| | 'Bredon' | CElw MBNS NChi SAga WBrk |
| | ***bridgesii*** | see *P. rostriflorus* |

| | | |
|---|---|---|
| | 'Bubblegum' (Ice Cream Series) **new** | WHlf |
| | 'Burford Purple' | see *P.* 'Burgundy' |
| | 'Burford Seedling' | see *P.* 'Burgundy' |
| | 'Burford White' | see *P.* 'White Bedder' |
| § | 'Burgundy' | CHrt CSam CTca CWCL EBee ECtt GMaP GMac LLWP LPen LRHS MCot MRav NBir NPer NPri SAga SBch SGar SMrm WFar WHCG WPer |
| | ***caeruleus*** | see *P. angustifolius* |
| | ***californicus*** | CPBP WAbe WFar |
| | ***calycosus*** | EBee |
| § | ***campanulatus*** | CEnt CWCL EAro EBee ECtt EPfP EWes GEdr MHer MLLN NDlv NMen SAga SRms WFar WPer |
| | - PC&H 148 | EAro GBri SGar |
| | - ***pulchellus*** | see *P. campanulatus* |
| | - ***roseus*** misapplied | see *P. kunthii* |
| | 'Candy Pink' | see *P.* 'Old Candy Pink' |
| | ***cardwellii*** | EWes ITim SRms |
| | ***cardwellii*** x ***davidsonii*** | WAbe |
| | 'Carolyn Orr' (v) | CBow EBee ECtt LSou |
| | ***caryi*** | CSec |
| | 'Castle Forbes' | EPyc GMac LPen MBNS MLLN SAga WHCG WPer |
| | 'Catherine de la Mare' | see *P. heterophyllus* 'Catherine de la Mare' |
| * | 'Centra' | MBNS MLLN |
| | 'Charles Rudd' | CWCL EBee ECGP ECtt ELon LLWP LPen LSRN MBNS MLLN SAga SPav SRGP SWal SWvt WCot WHCG |
| § | 'Cherry' ♀H3 | GMac LPen MBNS MHer NBur SGar SHar SMrm SPla SPlb WHCG WPer |
| | 'Cherry Ripe' misapplied | see *P.* 'Cherry' |
| § | 'Chester Scarlet' ♀H3 | CWCL GMac LPen MBNS MNrw MRav MSte SDix SGar SLon WHCG WPer |
| | ***cinicola*** | LLHF |
| | 'Claret' **new** | SAga |
| | ***cobaea*** | EBee SUsu WPer |
| | ***comarrhenus cyaneus*** | see *P. cyaneus* |
| | 'Comberton' | MBNS SAga |
| | ***confertus*** | CEnt CSec CTri CWGN EAro EBee ECho EPot LPen MBNS NChi NLAp NMen NWCA SGar SRms WBVN WGwG WPer |
| | 'Connie's Pink' ♀H3 | ECtt LPen MBNS MSte NBur SGar SLon WHCG |
| * | 'Coral Pink' | SLon |
| | 'Cottage Garden Red' | see *P.* 'Windsor Red' |
| § | 'Countess of Dalkeith' | CBcs EBee ECtt ELan EWes LLWP LPen LRHS MLLN MNrw MRav SGar SMrm SPer SPlb SUsu SWvt WCAu WCot WFar WHCG |
| | ***crandallii*** | CPBP |
| § | - subsp. ***taosensis*** | NWCA |
| | ***cristatus*** | see *P. eriantherus* |
| § | ***cyaneus*** | EBee |
| | ***davidsonii*** | ECho EWes NLAp SRms WAbe WFar |
| | - var. ***davidsonii*** | CPBP |
| § | - var. ***menziesii*** ♀H4 | MDun SRms |
| | - - 'Broken Top Mountain' | CLyd |
| | - - 'Microphyllus' | LLHF WAbe |
| | - var. ***praeteritus*** | MDKP |
| | 'Dazzler' | CMMP CWCL LPen MBNS NChi SAga SMrm SWvt WPer |
| | 'Devonshire Cream' | CWCL LPen LRHS MBNS SAga WHCG |
| | ***diffusus*** | see *P. serrulatus* |
| | ***digitalis*** | CRWN ECha GCal LPen MBNS NWCA SHar WFar WHCG WPer |
| § | - 'Husker Red' | Widely available |
| | - 'Purpureus' | see *P. digitalis* 'Husker Red' |
| | - 'Ruby Tuesday' | CDes EBee EWes SUsu WPGP |
| | - white-flowered | SPhx SRms SWal |
| | ***discolor*** pale lavender-flowered | NBir WFar |
| § | 'Drinkstone Red' | ECtt EGoo EPfP LPen MBNS NChi SAga SDix WHCG WPer |
| | 'Drinkwater Red' | see *P.* 'Drinkstone Red' |
| | ***eatonii*** | NBPC |
| | 'Edithae' | CSec LPen MWte SRms WEas |
| | 'Ellwood Red Phoenix' **new** | MBNS |
| | 'Elmley' | EBee EPfP MBNS MLLN |
| § | ***eriantherus*** | CGra |
| | Etna = 'Yatna' | EAEE ECtt EMil EPfP GKev GKir LBMP LHop SAga SAll SMrm SPad WBor WHlf |
| | ***euglaucus*** | EBee GKev LLHF |
| § | 'Evelyn' ♀H4 | CTri ECha ELan EPfP GKir LAst LRHS MBNS MCot MHer MRav NBir SPer SPet SPla SPlb SPoG SRGP SRms SWvt WFar WHCG WKif WPtf WSHC |
| | 'Evelyn' x 'Papal Purple' | LPen |
| | 'Fanny's Blush' | CWGN SAga |
| | 'Firebird' | see *P.* 'Schoenholzeri' |
| | 'Flame' | LHop LPen LRHS MBNS NBur SAga SLon WHCG WPer |
| | 'Flamingo' | CPrp CWCL EBee ECtt ELon EPfP EWes LAst LPen LRHS LSRN MBNS MSte NBir NPri SAga SGar SMrm SPet SPoG STes SWal SWvt WCFE WFar |
| | ***frutescens*** | LHop |
| | ***fruticosus*** | EBee EDAr NWCA WAbe WFar |
| § | - var. ***scouleri*** ♀H4 | MAsh NLAp SRms WBVN |
| | - - f. ***albus*** ♀H4 | CSpe WAbe WKif |
| | - - 'Amethyst' | WAbe WBod |
| | - - f. ***ruber*** | NWCA |
| | - var. ***serratus*** 'Holly' | NMen SHGN |
| | Fujiyama = 'Yayama'PBR | ECtt EMil GKir LHop LRHS NScw SAll SGar SPad WFar WHlf |
| | 'Garden Red' | see *P.* 'Windsor Red' |
| | 'Garnet' | see *P.* 'Andenken an Friedrich Hahn' |
| | ***gentianoides*** | NBro |
| | - B&SWJ 10271 **new** | WCru |
| | 'Geoff Hamilton' | CElw CWGN EBee EPfP LHop LPen LSRN MBNS SAga SUsu |
| | 'George Elrick' | LPen |
| § | 'George Home' ♀H3 | CWCL ECtt EWes LPen LRHS MBNS MLLN MSte NBur SMrm WHCG |
| | 'Ghent Purple' | CFee |
| | 'Gilchrist' | LRHS SGar SLon SPhx |
| | ***glaber*** | CEnt CMea EAro EBee GMac LHop LLWP LPen LSRN SPlb WKif WPer |
| | - 'Roundway Snowflake' | CWGN MAvo SAga SHar SPhx |
| | - white-flowered | SGar |
| | ***globosus*** | EDAr |
| | 'Gloire des Quatre Rues' | MBNS |
| | ***gormanii*** | EAro SGar |
| | ***gracilis*** | WPer |
| § | ***grandiflorus*** | CSec EAro EBee EDAr EShb |
| | - 'Prairie Snow' | EBee |
| | 'Great Witley' | WPer |
| | ***grinnellii*** **new** | WFar |
| | ***hallii*** | CSec EWes |
| | ***harbourii*** **new** | CPBP |
| | ***hartwegii*** ♀H3-4 | CSec EPyc LPen WHCG WPer |
| | - 'Albus' | LHop LPen MSte SGar WHCG |
| | - 'Tubular Bells Rose' | ECGP NGBl SPad SPet |
| | 'Helenetti' | SDys |
| | ***heterodoxus*** | SGar |
| | - NNS 93-564 | NWCA |
| § | ***heterophyllus*** | CMea CWCL LCro LPen MNrw MSCN NBir NGBl NGdn SGar SPet SRkn SRms WEas WHCG WKif WPer |
| | - 'Blue Eye' | WBrk |

| | | |
|---|---|---|
| | - 'Blue Fountain' | CHar LPen MAvo |
| | - 'Blue Gem' | CElw CTri GKir LRHS SIng SPla |
| § | - 'Blue Spring' | EBee ECtt EPfP LPen LRHS MMHG MSte NBir NLar SAga SPoG SWal WAbe |
| § | - 'Catherine de la Mare' ♀H4 | CHar CPrp EBee ELan GKir LHop LPen LRHS LSRN MAvo MHer MMuc MWat NBir NBro SAga SBch SMrm SPer SPla SRGP SWal SWvt WEas WFar WKif |
| | - 'Electric Blue' | MCCP SGar |
| | - 'Heavenly Blue' | Widely available |
| | - 'Jeanette' | WCot WHoo |
| | - 'Les Holmes' | SAga |
| | - subsp. ***purdyi*** | EPyc WHCG |
| | - 'Roehrslev' | LPen |
| | - 'True Blue' | see *P. heterophyllus* |
| | - 'Züriblau' | EBee GMac LPen SPlb |
| § | 'Hewell Pink Bedder' ♀H3 | EAEE EBee ECtt EPfP GBri LPen LRHS MBNS MSte SGar SMad SMrm SWvt WFar WHCG WHil WHoo WMnd WPer |
| | 'Hewitt's Pink' | ECtt SLon |
| | 'Hidcote Pink' ♀H3-4 | Widely available |
| | 'Hidcote Purple' | CElw CMMP SAga SHar WHoo |
| * | 'Hidcote White' | GBri MHer SAga SWvt |
| | 'Hillview Pink' | SLon |
| | 'Hillview Red' | MBNS |
| § | ***hirsutus*** | CEnt CSec SGar WBVN WFar WPer |
| | - f. ***albiflorus*** | CEnt CSec NWCA |
| | - var. ***minimus*** | CSec |
| | - var. ***pygmaeus*** | CLyd EBee ECho EDAr EShb GKev MHer NMen NWCA SGar SPlb SRms WAbe WHoo WPer |
| | - - f. ***albus*** | CSec NWCA SHGN WPer |
| | - - 'Purpureus' | WAbe |
| | 'Hopleys Variegated' (v) | CBow CWGN MBNS MHer NBir SAga SPav SPoG SWvt |
| § | ***humilis*** | CSec MLLN SRms |
| | - 'Pulchellus' | NWCA |
| | ***isophyllus*** ♀H3-4 | EPfP LPen SAga SEND WFar WHCG WPer WPtf |
| | ***jamesii*** | CSec EBee WHrl |
| | Jean Grace = 'Penbow' | CHar LRHS |
| | 'Jessica' | CWGN SAga WCFE |
| | 'John Booth' | MBNS MSte WEas |
| | 'John Nash' misapplied | see *P.* 'Alice Hindley' |
| | 'John Nash' | CHFP MHer SAga SRkn |
| | 'John Spedan Lewis' | SLon |
| | 'Joy' | EPyc LPen MBNS MLLN MSte WPer |
| | 'Juicy Grape' (Ice Cream Series) **new** | WHlf |
| | 'June' | see *P.* 'Pennington Gem' |
| | 'Kate Gilchrist' | SLon |
| | Kilimanjaro = 'Yajaro' | EMil LRHS SAll SMrm WRHF |
| | 'King George V' | Widely available |
| | 'Knight's Purple' | LPen MBNS WHCG |
| | 'Knightwick' | LPen MBNS SGar WPer |
| § | ***kunthii*** | CSec EAro EBee EPPr GEdr LHop LLWP LPen MDKP NBur SAga WHrl WOut WPer |
| | - upright | SGar |
| | 'Lady Hamilton' **new** | MBNS |
| § | ***laetus*** subsp. ***roezlii*** | ECho EPot GGar LHop LRHS MAsh MDun NDlv NLAp NSla SRms |
| | ***laricifolius*** | CPBP |
| § | 'Le Phare' | LPen LRHS MBNS WHCG WPer |
| | ***leonensis*** | CSec EAro |
| | 'Lilac and Burgundy' | EBee LPen LRHS MBNS SAga SMrm SWvt WFar |
| | 'Lilac Frost' **new** | EBee LLHF |
| | 'Lilliput' | ENor EPfP GBin LHop LRHS MBNS NPri SIng SPet SPoG |
| | ***linarioides*** | LPen NLAp SAga WPat |
| | 'Little Witley' | LPen WHCG WPer |
| | 'Lord Home' | see *P.* 'George Home' |
| | 'Lucinda Gilchrist' | SLon |
| | ***lyallii*** | CSec EAro EHrv ELan LPen LSou MCCP MLLN SRms WPer WPtf |
| | 'Lynette' | LPen LRHS MBNS SPlb WHCG WPer |
| | 'Macpenny's Pink' | EBee EPyc LPen MBNS SAga |
| § | 'Madame Golding' | CWCL GMac LPen LRHS MBNS MNrw SGar SPlb SRkn WHCG WPer |
| | 'Malvern Springs' | MBNS |
| | 'Margery Fish' ♀H3 | CElw EBee EPyc EWes LPen LRHS MNrw MSte WPer |
| | 'Marilyn Ross' | MBNS SLon |
| | 'Maurice Gibbs' ♀H3 | CBcs CChe CMMP CWCL EAEE ECtt EPfP EPyc EWes LPen LSRN MBNS MLLN NBPC SAga SGar SPav SRGP WBrE WHCG WMnd |
| | 'Melting Candy' (Ice Cream Series) **new** | WHlf |
| | ***mensarum*** | GMac |
| | ***menziesii*** | see *P. davidsonii* var. *menziesii* |
| | Mexicali hybrids | EDAr LPen MLLN WFoF |
| | x ***mexicanus*** 'Sunburst Ruby' | EDAr GMac LRHS MAsh |
| | 'Midnight' | ELan EPfP GBri LLWP LPen MRav MSte SGar SWvt WCot WHCG WMnd WPer |
| | 'Mint Pink' | SAga |
| | 'Modesty' | EPfP LPen LRHS MBNS NBur SAga WHCG WPer |
| | 'Mother of Pearl' | Widely available |
| | 'Mrs Golding' | see *P.* 'Madame Golding' |
| | 'Mrs Miller' | ECtt LPen MBNS NBur |
| | 'Mrs Morse' | see *P.* 'Chester Scarlet' |
| | ***mucronatus*** | CSec |
| | ***multiflorus*** | CSec LPen |
| § | 'Myddelton Gem' | LPen LRHS MWat WCot WFoF WHCG |
| | 'Myddelton Red' | see *P.* 'Myddelton Gem' |
| | ***neotericus*** | NWCA |
| | ***newberryi*** ♀H4 | CGra MDKP SAga WBVN WKif |
| | - f. ***humilior*** | EPot |
| § | - subsp. ***sonomensis*** | GEdr WAbe WFar |
| * | 'Newbury Gem' | EBee LSRN MBNS MLLN SRGP SWvt WFar |
| | 'Oaklea Red' | ECtt EPyc |
| § | 'Old Candy Pink' | CFee LPen MBNS MSte SWvt WPer |
| | 'Osprey' ♀H3 | Widely available |
| | ***ovatus*** | CSpe CWsd EBee ELan LPen MLLN NDlv SGar SPhx SRms |
| | 'Overbury' | EBee LPen MBNS NChi SAga |
| | ***pallidus*** | EBee |
| | ***palmeri*** | EAro LEdu |
| | 'Papal Purple' | CChe CMea LLWP LPen LRHS MAsh MBNS MHer MSte NBir NChi SAga SLon SRms WFar WHCG |
| | 'Patio Bells Pink' | LPen MLHP MLLN |
| | 'Patio Bells Shell' | LRHS WHlf |
| | 'Patio Coral' | ECtt |
| | 'Patio Wine' | ECtt SLon |
| | 'Peace' | LPen LRHS MBNS MRav SLon WHCG |
| | 'Pearl' | EPyc |
| § | 'Pennington Gem' ♀H3 | CBcs ELan GMac LHop LLWP LPen LRHS MHer MNrw MSte NBir NGdn SPer SWvt WHCG WPer WWlt |
| | 'Pensham Amelia Jane' | ECtt EPfP LSRN LSou MWea SAga SAll SRGP WHlf |
| | 'Pensham Arctic Fox' | EBee ECtt LHop MWea SAga SLon |
| | 'Pensham Arctic Sunset' | SAga SLon WHrl |
| | 'Pensham Bilberry Ice' | ECtt EPyc MLLN SPav WMnd |

| | | |
|---|---|---|
| | 'Pensham Blackberry Ice' | CFir ECGP ECtt EPfP EPyc LSou MBri MWea SPav WMnd |
| | 'Pensham Blueberry Ice' | CWGN EBee EPyc LSou MBri MLLN SAll SPav WFar WMnd WWlt |
| | 'Pensham Bow Bells' | SAga |
| | 'Pensham Capricorn Moon' | ECtt SAga SLon SRGP |
| | 'Pensham Cassis Royale' | MLLN |
| | 'Pensham Claret' | WFar |
| | 'Pensham Czar' | CAby ECtt MWea SAga SAll |
| | 'Pensham Dorothy Wilson' | EBee EPyc SMrm SRGP |
| | 'Pensham Edith Biggs' | CWCL EBee ECtt EPfP SHGN SMrm WFar |
| | 'Pensham Eleanor Young' | ECtt LSou MWea SAll SRGP SWal |
| | 'Pensham Freshwater Pearl' | CElw SAga WHoo |
| | 'Pensham Great Expectations' | EBee MLLN SAga |
| | 'Pensham Just Jayne' | CElw EBee ECtt EPyc LSRN MLLN NPro SLon SRGP WMnd |
| | 'Pensham Kay Burton' | EPfP EPyc SMrm SRGP WMnd |
| | 'Pensham Laura' | CWGN EBee ECtt LSRN MBNS MBri MWea SAga SAll SRGP WHlf |
| | 'Pensham Loganberry Ice' | LSou MBri |
| | 'Pensham Marjorie Lewis' | SLon WMnd |
| | 'Pensham Miss Wilson' | SAga |
| | 'Pensham Petticoat' | EBee WWlt |
| | 'Pensham Plum Jerkum' | CWGN ECtt EPyc MBri MLLN MWea SAll SPoG SWal WMnd |
| | 'Pensham Raspberry Ice' | MBri MLLN SAga SPav WMnd |
| | 'Pensham Son of Raven' | SAga |
| | 'Pensham Tayberry Ice' | ECtt EPyc MLLN SAga SAll SGar WMnd |
| | 'Pensham Tiger Belle Coral' | EBee NChi SAga |
| | 'Pensham Tiger Belle Rose' | SAga SLon |
| | 'Pensham Victoria Plum' | CTca MHer SHar WHoo |
| | 'Pensham Wedding Bells' | EBee SPoG WFar |
| | 'Pensham Wedding Day' | LSRN LSou MBNS MBri SAga SAll SRGP WHlf |
| | ***perfoliatus*** | EBee |
| | 'Pershore Carnival' | NPro SAga |
| | 'Pershore Fanfare' | LPen SAga WHrl |
| | 'Pershore Pink Necklace' | CWCL LPen LRHS MLLN SMrm SWvt WCot WHCG |
| | 'Phare' | see *P.* 'Le Phare' |
| | 'Phyllis' | see *P.* 'Evelyn' |
| | ***pinifolius*** ♀H4 | CDMG CEnt CMea CTri ECho ECtt EDAr EPot GAbr GKev GKir GMaP LRHS NLAp SPoG SRms WFar WHoo WPat |
| | - dwarf | GKev |
| | - 'Mersea Yellow' | CMea EBee ECho ECtt EDAr EPfP EPot GAbr GEdr GKev GKir LHop LRHS NDlv NLAp NWCA SPlb SPoG WFar WPat WPer |
| | - 'Wisley Flame' ♀H4 | EAlp ECho EPfP EPot EWes GEdr GKir NRya NWCA |
| | 'Pink Bedder' | see *P.* 'Hewell Pink Bedder', 'Sutton's Pink Bedder' |
| | 'Pink Endurance' | CWsd LPen MBNS MSte SRkn WHCG WHal WPer |
| | 'Pink Profusion' | MRav |
| | 'Port Wine' ♀H3 | CMea CSam CTri CWCL ELon EPfP GMaP LPen LRHS LSRN MCot MLLN MWat NBPC NBir NChi SAga SMrm SPer SPla SPoG SWal WBrE WCot WHCG WKif WMnd WPer |
| | 'Powis Castle' | ECtt EWes MHar SAga WPer WWlt |
| | 'Prairie Dusk' | LPen |
| | 'Prairie Fire' | EBee LPen |
| * | 'Prairie Pride' | LPen |
| | 'Pretty Petticoat' **new** | IPot |
| | 'Primrose Thomas' | SAga |
| | 'Priory Purple' | MBNS SLon WHCG WHrl WPer |

| | | |
|---|---|---|
| | ***procerus*** | ECho EDAr GBri MLLN SRms WPer |
| § | - var. ***formosus*** | EPot NMen WAbe WFar |
| | - - NNS 01-345 | NWCA |
| | - 'Hawkeye' | CGra |
| § | - 'Roy Davidson' ♀H4 | CMea EPot LBee LHop LRHS NLAp NMen WAbe WFar |
| | - var. ***tolmiei*** | CElw CSec EPot GCal GEdr NMen |
| | ***pubescens*** | see *P. hirsutus* |
| | ***pulchellus*** Greene | see *P. procerus* var. *formosus* |
| | ***pulchellus*** Lindl. | see *P. campanulatus* |
| * | ***pulcherrimus*** | NBro |
| | ***pumilus*** | SRms |
| | 'Purple and White' | see *P.* 'Countess of Dalkeith' |
| | 'Purple Bedder' | CHar CHrt EBee EPfP LPen LSRN MLHP MLLN MNrw MWat NBir SAga SMrm SPav SPoG SRkn SWvt WCFE WFar WGor WHCG |
| | 'Purple Passion' | CElw EBee EBrs EHrv EPfP EWes LPen LRHS |
| | 'Purple Pixie' **new** | LLHF |
| | 'Purpureus Albus' | see *P.* 'Countess of Dalkeith' |
| | ***purpusii*** | LLHF WAbe |
| | 'Rajah' | LPen |
| | 'Raven' ♀H3 | Widely available |
| | 'Razzle Dazzle' | LPen LRHS MBNS SMrm SPlb SPoG WCot WPer |
| | 'Red Ace' | MNrw |
| | 'Red Emperor' | ECtt LPen MHar SPlb WHCG WPer |
| | 'Red Knight' | CWCL GCra LPen LRHS MBNS |
| | 'Rich Purple' | EPyc LRHS MBNS SPlb |
| | 'Rich Ruby' | CWCL CWGN EBee EBrs ECtt EHrv ELan EPfP EWes LHop LLWP LPen MCot MNrw NBir SAga SPlb SRGP SWvt WCot WHCG WPer |
| | ***richardsonii*** | CSec EShb MNrw NWCA SRms WPer |
| | - var. ***dentata*** | CGra |
| | 'Ridgeway Red' | MBNS WCFE |
| | ***roezlii*** Regel | see *P. laetus* subsp. *roezlii* |
| | 'Ron Sidwell' | SGar SLon |
| § | ***rostriflorus*** NNS 03-094 | NWCA |
| | 'Rosy Blush' | LPen MBNS SAga SPlb WHCG |
| | 'Roundhay' | CFee NChi |
| | 'Roy Davidson' | see *P. procerus* 'Roy Davidson' |
| | 'Royal White' | see *P.* 'White Bedder' |
| | 'Rubicundus' ♀H3 | CWCL CWGN EBee ECtt EHrv ELan ELon EPfP LHop LPen LRHS MBNS MWte SAga SMrm SPla SPoG SWvt WCot WFar WHCG WMnd |
| | 'Ruby' misapplied | see *P.* 'Schoenholzeri' |
| | 'Ruby Field' | EPyc WCFE WHCG |
| | 'Ruby Gem' | LPen |
| | ***rupicola*** ♀H4 | EPot LHop LRHS NSla WAbe |
| | - 'Albus' | LLHF NLAp NSla WAbe |
| | - 'Conwy Lilac' | WAbe |
| | - 'Conwy Rose' | WAbe |
| | 'Russian River' | EAEE EBee ECtt EPPr EPfP EPyc EWes LHop LPen LRHS LSRN SBch SGar SPlb WHCG WPer |
| | ***rydbergii*** | NLAp |
| * | Saskatoon hybrids | EBee |
| | Saskatoon hybrids rose | SLon |
| § | 'Schoenholzeri' ♀H4 | Widely available |
| | ***scouleri*** | see *P. fruticosus* var. *scouleri* |
| § | ***serrulatus*** | CSec EPot EWes LHop MSte SGar WBVN WHrl WKif |
| | 'Shell Pink' | LPen NChi WPer |
| * | 'Sherbourne Blue' | GBuc SAga SLon WCot WPer |
| | 'Shock Wave' | MCCP MSte SAga |
| * | 'Shrawley' | WPer |
| | 'Sissinghurst Pink' | see *P.* 'Evelyn' |
| | 'Six Hills' | GBri SRms WAbe WPat |
| | 'Skyline' | EAro EPfP |

| | | |
|---|---|---|
| | ***smallii*** | CEnt CMHG EAro EBee ECtt EDAr EPPr EShb EWes GMac LPen LSRN MAsh MCCP MMuc NBPC NWCA SGar SPhx WPGP WPer |
| | 'Snow Storm' | see *P.* 'White Bedder' |
| | 'Snowflake' | see *P.* 'White Bedder' |
| | 'Son of Raven' | SAga |
| | ***sonomensis*** | see *P. newberryi* subsp. *sonomensis* |
| | 'Sour Grapes' misapplied | see *P.* 'Stapleford Gem' |
| | 'Sour Grapes' ambig. | MCot |
| § | 'Sour Grapes' M. Fish ♀H3-4 | Widely available |
| | 'Southcombe Pink' | LPen MLLN WHCG |
| | 'Southgate Gem' | CWCL LCro LPen LRHS MBNS MNrw MWat SWvt WHCG |
| | 'Souvenir d'Adrian Regnier' | EBee LPen MBNS SGar |
| | 'Souvenir d'André Torres' misapplied | see *P.* 'Chester Scarlet' |
| | 'Souvenir d'André Torres' | LLWP LPen |
| § | 'Stapleford Gem' ♀H3 | Widely available |
| | 'Strawberries and Cream' (Ice Cream Series) **new** | WHlf |
| | 'Strawberry Fizz' | SLon |
| | ***strictus*** | CSec EAro EBee EGoo EPPr EShb EWTr LPen MBNS MCCP MLLN MNFA SGar SKHP SMrm SPoG SRms WPer |
| | - 'Bandera' | WFar |
| | Stromboli = 'Yaboli' | LBMP |
| § | 'Sutton's Pink Bedder' | MBNS SPlb |
| | 'Sylvia Buss' | LPen |
| | tall pink-flowered | see *P.* 'Welsh Dawn' |
| N | 'Taoensis' | EWes MBNS SGar |
| | ***taosensis*** | see *P. crandallii* subsp. *taosensis* |
| | ***tenuis* new** | CSec |
| | ***teucrioides*** | EPot NLAp NWCA |
| | - JCA 1717050 | CPBP |
| | 'The Juggler' | CChe EBee EPfP LPen LRHS MBNS MLLN SMrm SPav SPoG WFar WMnd |
| § | 'Thorn' | CSpe CWGN EBee ECtt ELan EShb LPen LRHS MLLN MNrw MSte MWat NBir SAga SMrm SPer SPhx SPla SPoG SWal SWvt WHCG |
| | 'Threave Pink' | CPrp CWCL LLWP MBNS MRav SEND SMrm SPer SPoG SWvt |
| | 'Thundercloud' | SAga |
| | 'Torquay Gem' | CHFP EBee GBuc LLHF LPen MBNS WCot WHCG WPer |
| | ***triphyllus* new** | CSec |
| | 'True Sour Grapes' | see *P.* 'Sour Grapes' M. Fish |
| | 'Tubular Bells Red' | NGBl |
| § | ***unilateralis*** | CSec |
| | ***utahensis*** | GBri SAga WKif WPer |
| | ***venustus*** | GBuc MHar MNrw NCob SRms WRos |
| | - 'Kuhn' **new** | CSec |
| | Vesuvius = 'Yasius' | EAEE ECtt EMil EPfP EPyc GKir SAga SMrm SPad WFar WHlf |
| | ***virens*** | CPBP WPer |
| | ***virgatus*** subsp. ***asa-grayi*** | see *P. unilateralis* |
| | - 'Blue Buckle' | CSpe EBee EShb NBir NLar SPlb WFar |
| | ***watsonii*** | CSec EBee ELan MLLN SRms |
| § | 'Welsh Dawn' | CEnt LPen MBNS |
| § | ***whippleanus*** | CSec EAro MWea SPhx WAbb |
| | - 'Chocolate Drop' | WRos |
| § | 'White Bedder' ♀H3 | Widely available |
| | 'Whitethroat' Sidwell | LPen MBNS SAga SLon WHCG |
| I | 'Whitethroat' purple-flowered | SMrm WPer |
| | ***wilcoxii*** | CSec EBee |
| | 'Willy's Purple' | MBNS SLon |
| § | 'Windsor Red' | CTri EBee ECtt EPfP LPen LRHS MBNS MSCN MSte NBPC SAga SGar SPoG SWal SWvt WCot WGor WHCG WHil |
| | ***wislizeni*** | CSec MLan SRms |
| | 'Woodpecker' | EBee SAga SGar SPer SPoG SWal WHil |

## *Pentachondra* (*Epacridaceae*)

| | | |
|---|---|---|
| | ***pumila*** | IBlr |

## *Pentaglottis* (*Boraginaceae*)

| | | |
|---|---|---|
| § | ***sempervirens*** | CArn EPfP MHer MSal WHil |

## *Pentagramma* (*Adiantaceae*)

| | | |
|---|---|---|
| | ***triangularis*** | WRic |

## *Pentapterygium* see *Agapetes*

## *Pentas* (*Rubiaceae*)

| | | |
|---|---|---|
| | ***lanceolata*** | CCCN CHal ELan EShb LRHS MBri |

## *Penthorum* (*Penthoraceae*)

| | | |
|---|---|---|
| | ***sedoides* new** | WPer |

## *Peperomia* (*Piperaceae*)

| | | |
|---|---|---|
| § | ***argyreia*** ♀H1 | MBri |
| | ***arifolia*** | CHal |
| | ***caperata*** | LRHS MBri |
| | ***clusiifolia*** | CHal |
| | - 'Variegata' (v) | CHal |
| | ***glabella*** | CHal |
| | - 'Variegata' (v) | CHal |
| | ***obtusifolia*** 'Jamaica' | MBri |
| | - (Magnoliifolia Group) 'Golden Gate' (v) | MBri |
| | - - 'Greengold' | CHal MBri |
| | - - 'USA' ♀H1 | MBri |
| | - 'Tricolor' (v) | MBri |
| | ***orba*** 'Pixie' | MBri |
| I | - 'Pixie Variegata' (v) | MBri |
| | ***pulchella*** | see *P. verticillata* |
| | ***rotundifolia* new** | EShb |
| | ***sandersii*** | see *P. argyreia* |
| | ***scandens*** ♀H1 | MBri |
| | - 'Variegata' (v) | CHal MBri |
| § | ***verticillata*** | CHal |

## pepino see *Solanum muricatum*

## peppermint see *Mentha* x *piperita*

## *Perezia* (*Asteraceae*)

| | | |
|---|---|---|
| | ***linearis*** | GBuc NLar |
| | ***recurvata*** | GKev NWCA |

## *Pericallis* (*Asteraceae*)

| | | |
|---|---|---|
| § | ***lanata*** (L'Hér.) B. Nord. | CHII EShb MBlu WPic |
| | - Kew form | CSpe SAga |
| | ***multiflora*** | LHop SAga |
| | Senetti Series | MGos NBlu NPer SECG |

## *Perilla* (*Lamiaceae*)

| | | |
|---|---|---|
| § | ***frutescens*** var. ***crispa*** ♀H2 | CArn CSpe |
| | - green-leaved | MNHC |
| | - var. ***japonica* new** | GPoy |
| | - var. ***nankinensis*** | see *P. frutescens* var. *crispa* |
| | - var. ***purpurascens*** | CArn EShb MNHC WJek |
| | - 'Shizo Green' | CSpe |

## *Periploca* (*Asclepiadaceae*)

| | | |
|---|---|---|
| | ***graeca*** | CArn CBcs CMac CRHN EBee SLon SPoG WCot WSHC WTou |

| | |
|---|---|
| ***purpurea*** | WSHC |
| - B&SWJ 7235 | WCru |
| ***sepium*** | CPLG |

## *Peristrophe* (*Acanthaceae*)

| | |
|---|---|
| ***speciosa*** | ECre |

## *Pernettya* see *Gaultheria*

## *Perovskia* (*Lamiaceae*)

| | |
|---|---|
| ***abrotanoides*** | WBod |
| ***atriplicifolia*** | CArn CBcs CMea MHer MNHC NSti SUsu WHCG WMnd WPer |
| - 'Little Spire'PBR | CBow CHFP CMac CSpe EMil EPfP EWes GBin LBuc MAsh NBrd NBsh NLar NPri SPad SPer SPoG WSHC |
| 'Blue Haze' | EBrs GCal SMHy |
| 'Blue Spire' ♀H4 | Widely available |
| 'Filigran' | EBee EGoo EMil GBuc LBMP LRHS MAsh NBsh SKHP SPoG WFar WPat |
| 'Hybrida' | EBee EMil LRHS |
| 'Longin' | LRHS |

## *Persea* (*Lauraceae*)

| | |
|---|---|
| ***americana*** new | CCCN |
| ***indica*** | CCCN WPGP |
| ***thunbergii*** | CHEx WPGP |

## *Persicaria* (*Polygonaceae*)

| | | |
|---|---|---|
| | SDR 4566 new | GKev |
| § | ***affinis*** | CBcs CBen CSBt EBee GAbr MBar MTho MWhi NBro NVic SWat WBrE WBrk WCFE WFar WMoo WRHF |
| § | - 'Darjeeling Red' ♀H4 | Widely available |
| | - 'Dimity' | see *P. affinis* 'Superba' |
| § | - 'Donald Lowndes' ♀H4 | Widely available |
| | - 'Kabouter' | EBee GBin |
| § | - 'Superba' ♀H4 | Widely available |
| | ***alata*** | see *P. nepalensis* |
| | ***alpina*** | CRow SBch |
| | ***amphibia*** | CRow MSKA NSco SWat |
| § | ***amplexicaulis*** | CBre CHVG CKno COld CPrp CRow CSpe EBee ELan EWes GKir GMaP MCot MHer MSte NChi NOrc SEND WBor WFar WGwG WMoo WRHF WTin |
| | - 'Alba' | CElw CHar CKno CRow EBee ECha EPPr EPla GBuc GCal LBMP LHop MCot MLLN MSte NDov SPhx SPoG SWat WCAu WFar WMnd WMoo WPnP WTin |
| | - 'Arun Gem' | see *P. amplexicaulis* var. *pendula* |
| | - 'Atrosanguinea' | CKno CRow CTri EBee ECha ELan EMFW EPla GGar LRHS MNFA MRav NBir NDov NVic SPer SRms SWat SWvt WCAu WFar WOld |
| | - 'Baron' | CRow |
| | - 'Betty Brandt' new | EBee |
| | - 'Blush Clent' | EBee WHoo WTin |
| | - 'Border Beauty' | EBee NDov |
| | - 'Clent Charm' | EBee NBsh |
| | - 'Cottesbrooke Gold' | CRow ECtt LSou |
| | - 'Dikke Floskes' | CRow EMon |
| | - 'Early Pink Lady' | EMon |
| | - 'Firedance' | CKno IPot NDov SMHy SMrm SPhx SWat WCot |
| | - 'Firetail' ♀H4 | Widely available |
| | - 'High Society' | EBee |
| | - 'Inverleith' | CBre CDes CHar CKno CRow EBee ECha ECtt EPPr EPla EWll GGar GQue LRHS MAvo NDov WCot WMoo WPGP WPnP |
| I | - 'Jo and Guido's Form' | EBee SUsu WFar |
| * | - var. ***pendula*** | CRow EBee NBir WFar WMoo |
| | - - HWJK 2255 new | WCru |
| | - 'Pink Lady' | CRow NLar |
| | - 'Rosea' | CElw CKno CRow CSam EBee ECha EGle ELan EPla GQue MCot MSte NBro NChi NDov NSti SDys SMeo SPhx SWat WCAu WDyG WFar WMoo WPGP |
| | - 'Rosy Clent' | EBee |
| | - 'Rowden Gem' | CRow EPla WMoo |
| | - 'Rowden Jewel' | CRow EPla |
| | - 'Rowden Rose Quartz' | CRow |
| | - 'Summer Dance' | EBee EMon NBre NDov NLar |
| | - Taurus = 'Blotau' | CElw CKno EBee EBrs ECha EGle EPla MBri MLLN NDov NLar NSti SMHy WCAu WFar WPGP WPnP WTin |
| § | ***bistorta*** | CArn CRow EBWF ELau GBar GPWP GPoy MHer MMuc MSal MWhi NBir NGHP NSco SRms SWat WDyG |
| | - subsp. ***carnea*** | CRow EBee EBla ECha GGar LLWG LRHS MMuc NBir NDov WFar WMoo |
| | - 'Hohe Tatra' | CDes CRow EBee NDov WFar WMoo |
| § | - 'Superba' ♀H4 | Widely available |
| | ***bistortoides*** | MSal |
| | ***campanulata*** | CElw CRow EBee ECha ECtt EHoe GAbr GBuc GGar GMaP MCot NBid NBro SPer WFar WMoo WOld WRHF |
| | - Alba Group | CElw EBee GCal GGar MCot NBro WHer WMoo |
| | - var. ***lichiangense*** | GBin |
| | - 'Madame Jigard' | CRow GBin |
| | - 'Rosenrot' | CBre CKno CRow GBuc NBir NHol NLar SWat WFar WOld |
| | - 'Southcombe White' | CRow EPla GBri WPer |
| § | ***capitata*** | CHal CRow SIng SRms WMoo |
| | - 'Pink Bubbles' | ECtt EHoe SPet SWvt |
| | ***conspicua*** | EBee NBre |
| * | ***elata*** | GBuc NBur |
| | ***emodi*** | CRow NBre |
| | ***hydropiper*** 'Fastigiata' | CArn |
| § | ***longiseta*** | MSal |
| * | ***macrophylla*** | CRow LDai WFar |
| I | - 'Cally Strain' new | GCal |
| | ***microcephala*** | CRow EWes |
| | - 'Red Dragon'PBR | Widely available |
| | - var. ***wallichii*** | CRow |
| * | ***milletii*** | CRow EBrs GBuc MTho NDov NLar WCAu WCru WFar |
| § | ***mollis*** | CRow EBee WDyG WPGP |
| * | ***nakaii*** | EBee |
| | ***neofiliformis*** | EBee |
| § | ***nepalensis*** | CRow EBee EPPr EShb |
| § | ***odorata*** | CArn ELau EOHP GPWP GPoy ILis MHer MNHC MSal NGHP NPri SHDw SIde WJek |
| | ***orientalis*** | MSal SMHy |
| * | ***polymorpha*** | Widely available |
| | ***polystachya*** | see *P. wallichii* |
| | 'Red Baron' new | EPPr |
| | ***regeliana*** | EBee LRHS |
| § | ***runcinata*** | CRow EBee GGar NBid NBir NCob NLar WFar WHer WMoo WPer WPtf |
| | - Needham's form | CRow NBid |
| | ***scoparia*** | see *Polygonum scoparium* |
| | ***sphaerostachya*** Meisn. | see *P. macrophylla* |
| | ***tenuicaulis*** | CBre CRow CSpe EBee ECho EHrv EMon EPla GGar NChi SBch WCot WCru WFar WMoo |

| | |
|---|---|
| § ***tinctoria*** | EOHP |
| § ***vacciniifolia*** ♀H4 | Widely available |
| - 'Ron McBeath' | CRow |
| § ***virginiana*** | CRow ECtt GCal MSal WMoo |
| - 'Batwings' **new** | LRHS |
| - Compton's form | CRow EBee ECha EPPr GCal LDai NCob WAul WCot |
| - 'Filiformis' | EBee ECtt GBin MHar SWvt WCot WDyG WRos |
| - 'Lance Corporal' | CMac CRow EBee EPPr EPla MAvo NBre NCob NLar SMrm WMnd WMoo |
| - 'Moorland Moss' | WMoo |
| - Variegata Group | CRow ECha EPla MBNS WCot WMoo WOld |
| - - 'Painter's Palette' (v) | Widely available |
| - white-flowered | EPPr NCob |
| ***vivipara*** | CRow NLar WCot |
| § ***wallichii*** | CRow EBee NBre NLar SDix SWat WCot WMoo WPtf |
| § ***weyrichii*** | EBee EMon GCal NBir NBro NLar WCot WFar WMoo |

## persimmon see *Diospyros virginiana*

## persimmon, Japanese see *Diospyros kaki*

## *Petamenes* see *Gladiolus*

## *Petasites* (*Asteraceae*)

| | |
|---|---|
| ***albus*** | EBee EMon GPoy MHer NBre NLar |
| ***formosanus*** | LEdu |
| - B&SWJ 3025 | WCru |
| ***fragrans*** | CNat EBee ELan EMon MHer NLar SWat WFar WHer |
| § ***frigidus*** var. ***palmatus*** | CRow EBee EPla LEdu NBre NLar WCru WPGP |
| - - JLS 86317CLOR | SMad |
| - var. ***palmatus*** 'Golden Palms' | CBow EHrv NBre |
| ***hybridus*** | EBee EMFW LEdu MSKA NSco SMad SWat WHer WMAq WSFF |
| ***japonicus*** | CBcs GPoy |
| - var. ***giganteus*** | CArn CHEx CRow ECha ELan EMon EPPr EPfP EUJe LEdu NVic SWat WMoo |
| § - - 'Nishiki-buki' (v) | CHEx CMCo CRow EBee EMon EPPr EPla MSKA NBir NSti SMad WBor WCHb WFar WPGP |
| - - 'Variegatus' | see *P. japonicus* var. *giganteus* 'Nishiki-buki' |
| - f. ***purpureus*** | CDes CMCo EPPr EWes WPGP |
| ***palmatus*** | see *P. frigidus* var. *palmatus* |
| ***paradoxus*** | CDes CLAP CMCo EMon EPPr EWes LEdu SMad WCot |

## *Petrea* (*Verbenaceae*)

| | |
|---|---|
| ***volubilis*** | CCCN CHII MJnS SOWG |

## *Petrocallis* (*Brassicaceae*)

| | |
|---|---|
| ***lagascae*** | see *P. pyrenaica* |
| § ***pyrenaica*** | NWCA |

## *Petrocoptis* (*Caryophyllaceae*)

| | |
|---|---|
| ***pyrenaica*** | EBur SRms |
| § - subsp. ***glaucifolia*** | CSec NBir NLar |

## *Petrocosmea* (*Gesneriaceae*)

| | |
|---|---|
| ***begoniifolia*** **new** | WAbe |
| ***grandiflora*** **new** | WAbe |
| ***iodioides*** **new** | WAbe |
| ***kerrii*** | WAbe |
| - 'Crème de Crûg' | WCru |
| aff. ***martini*** 'Crûg's Capricious' | WCru |
| ***minor*** | WAbe |
| ***rosettifolia*** | WAbe |
| ***sericea*** | WAbe |

## *Petrophytum* (*Rosaceae*)

| | |
|---|---|
| ***caespitosum*** | WAbe |
| ***cinerascens*** | WAbe |
| § ***hendersonii*** | NHol SIng WAbe |

## *Petrorhagia* (*Caryophyllaceae*)

| | |
|---|---|
| 'Pink Starlets' | CSec GBri LHop SHGN |
| ***prolifera*** **new** | CSec |
| ***saxifraga*** ♀H4 | CDMG CSpe EBur ECho EShb NPri SRms SWal WMoo WPer WPnn WPtf |
| - 'Rosette' | MTho |

## *Petroselinum* (*Apiaceae*)

| | |
|---|---|
| § ***crispum*** | CArn CSev GPoy ILis LCro MBar MNHC NBlu NGHP SIde SPoG SWal WLHH WPer |
| - 'Bravour' ♀H4 | ELau MHer |
| - 'Champion Moss Curled' | SVic |
| - 'Darki' | CSev NGHP NPri |
| - French | CArn ELau MHer MNHC NBlu NPri NVic SPoG WJek WLHH |
| - 'Hank' (v) **new** | CNat |
| - 'Italian' | see *P. crispum* var. *neapolitanum* |
| § - var. ***neapolitanum*** | ELau SIde SPoG SVic WLHH |
| - 'Super Moss Curled' | NVic SWal |
| § - var. ***tuberosum*** | MHer MNHC SIde SVic WHer |
| - variegated (v) | CNat |
| ***hortense*** | see *P. crispum* |
| ***tuberosum*** | see *P. crispum* var. *tuberosum* |

## *Petteria* (*Papilionaceae*)

| | |
|---|---|
| ***ramentacea*** | NLar WBVN |

## *Petunia* (*Solanaceae*)

| | |
|---|---|
| 'Bavarian Belle' | LAst |
| Blue Spark = 'Dancasblue'PBR (Cascadias Series) | LAst |
| Candyfloss = 'Kercan'PBR (Tumbelina Series) | LAst NPri |
| Cherry Ripple (Tumbelina Series) **new** | LAst NPri |
| (Conchita Series) | SVil |
| Conchita Blueberry Frost = 'Conblue'PBR ♀H3 | |
| - Conchita Pink Kiss = 'Mediopimo'PBR | SVil |
| - Conchita Strawberry Frost = 'Constraw'PBR ♀H3 | SVil WGor |
| (Conchita Doble Series) | SVil |
| Conchita Doble Lavender = 'Condost177'PBR (d) | |
| - Conchita Doble Pink = 'Condopink'PBR (d) | SVil |
| 'Fanfare Flame' | SVil |
| Julia = 'Kerjul'PBR (Tumbelina Series) | NPri |
| Katrina (Tumbelina Series) | LAst |
| Margarita = 'Kermar'PBR (Tumbelina Series) | LAst |
| ***patagonica*** | WAbe |
| Petini Pink Vein (Petini Series) **new** | NPri |

| | |
|---|---|
| Pink Spark = 'Dancaspink'PBR (Cascadias Series) | LAst |
| Priscilla = 'Kerpril'PBR (Tumbelina Series) | LAst LSou NPri |
| * 'Purple Surprise' | LAst |
| Queen (Tumbelina Series) | LAst |
| 'Ramblin' Red' | LAst |
| Sunray = 'Dancas110' | SVil |
| Supertunia Royal Magenta = 'Kakegawa S36'PBR (Supertunia Series) | SVil |
| (Surfinia Series) Surfinia Amethyst | LAst |
| - Surfinia Baby Pinkmorn = 'Sunbapimo'PBR | LAst |
| - Surfinia Blue = 'Sunblu' | LAst LSou NPri WGor |
| - Surfinia Blue Vein = 'Sunsolos'PBR | LAst NBlu WGor |
| - Surfinia Burgundy | LAst NBlu WGor |
| - Surfinia Crazy Pink = 'Sunrovein' | LAst NPri |
| - Surfinia Double Lilac (d) **new** | LAst |
| - Surfinia Double Purple = 'Keidopuel'PBR (d) | LAst |
| - Surfinia Double Red Celebration (d) **new** | LSou |
| - Surfinia Giant Purple = 'Sunlapur'PBR | LAst |
| - Surfinia Hot Pink = 'Marrose'PBR | LAst LSou WGor |
| - Surfinia Hot Red = 'Sunhore' **new** | LAst |
| - Surfinia Hot Salmon = 'Sunshore' **new** | NBlu |
| - Surfinia Lime = 'Keiyeul'PBR | LAst NBlu NPri WGor |
| - Surfinia Pastel 2000 = 'Sunpapi'PBR | LAst WGor |
| - Surfinia Patio Blue = 'Keipabukas'PBR | LAst |
| - Surfinia Patio Red = 'Sunremi' **new** | NBlu |
| - Surfinia Pink Ice = 'Hakice'PBR (v) | LAst NBlu NPri WGor |
| - Surfinia Pink Vein = 'Suntosol'PBR ♀H3 | WGor |
| - Surfinia Purple = 'Shihi Brilliant' ♀H3 | LSou NBlu NPri WGor |
| * - Surfinia Purple Sunrise | LAst |
| - Surfinia Red = 'Keirekul'PBR | LAst NPri WGor |
| - Surfinia Rose Vein = 'Sunrove'PBR | LAst NBlu WGor |
| - Surfinia Sky Blue = 'Keilavbu'PBR ♀H3 | LAst NPri WGor |
| - Surfinia Soft Pink | WGor |
| - Surfinia Vanilla = 'Sunvanilla'PBR | LSou |
| - Surfinia Velvet | LAst |
| - Surfinia Victorian Cream = 'Sunmilk' **new** | LAst |
| - Surfinia Victorian Lilac = 'Sunraspberry' **new** | LAst |
| - Surfinia Victorian Yellow = 'Sunpatiki' | LAst LSou NPri WGor |
| - Surfinia White = 'Kesupite' | LAst |
| Victoria = 'Kervic'PBR (Tumbelina Series) **new** | LAst |

## *Peucedanum* (*Apiaceae*)

| | |
|---|---|
| ***japonicum*** | CSpe |
| - B&SWJ 8816B | WCru |
| ***ostruthium*** | GPoy |
| - 'Daphnis' (v) | CDes CElw CSpe EBee EGle EMon EPPr LEdu LPla NChi NLar NPro WHrl |
| ***palustre*** | EBWF |
| ***praeruptorum*** **new** | CArn EBee |
| ***siamicum*** B&SWJ 264 | WCru |
| ***thodei*** **new** | SPlb |
| ***verticillare*** | CArn CSec CSpe EBee EBrs GQue MNFA NChi NDov NLar SDix SMad SMrm SPhx WFar WSHC |

## *Phacelia* (*Hydrophyllaceae*)

| | |
|---|---|
| ***bolanderi*** | LDai |

## *Phaedranassa* (*Amaryllidaceae*)

| | |
|---|---|
| BKBlount 2623 | WCot |
| ***carmiolii*** | WCot |
| ***cinerea*** | EBrs |
| ***dubia*** | ECho WCot |
| * ***montana*** | ECho |
| ***tunguraguae*** | EBrs ECho |
| ***viridiflora*** | EBrs ECho WCot |

## *Phaedranthus* see *Distictis*

## *Phaenocoma* (*Asteraceae*)

| | |
|---|---|
| ***prolifera*** | SPlb |

## *Phaenosperma* (*Poaceae*)

| | |
|---|---|
| ***globosa*** | CFwr CHrt CSam CSec CSpe EBee EGle EHig EHoe EPPr EWes EWsh LEdu MAvo SPhx SUsu WBor WPGP WPrP WTou |

## *Phagnalon* (*Asteraceae*)

| | |
|---|---|
| ***saxatile*** RCB RL -21 **new** | WCot |

## *Phaiophleps* see *Olsynium*

| | |
|---|---|
| ***nigricans*** | see *Sisyrinchium striatum* |

## *Phalaris* (*Poaceae*)

| | |
|---|---|
| ***arundinacea*** | EMFW EPla GFor MBNS MLan MMuc SPlb SVic SWat WTin |
| - 'Elegantissima' | see *P. arundinacea* var. *picta* 'Picta' |
| - var. ***picta*** | CBen CDul CHEx CTri CWCL CWib EMFW MMuc MSKA NBid NBir NBur NPer SApp SPoG WDin WFar |
| - - 'Aureovariegata' (v) | CBcs CSWP MRav NGdn NPer SWat WMoo |
| - - 'Feesey' (v) | Widely available |
| - - 'Luteopicta' (v) | EBee EGoo EHoe EPPr EPfP MMuc WTin |
| - - 'Luteovariegata' (v) | EShb NGdn |
| § - - 'Picta' (v) ♀H4 | COIW EBee ELan EPfP EPla GFor GKir LPBA MBar SPer SWal SWat WMoo |
| - - 'Streamlined' (v) | EPPr EPla EWsh SLPl WFar WMoo |
| - - 'Tricolor' (v) | CPen EBee EHoe EPla MBar |

## *Phanerophlebia* (*Dryopteridaceae*)

| | |
|---|---|
| ***caryotidea*** | see *Cyrtomium caryotideum* |
| ***falcata*** | see *Cyrtomium falcatum* |
| ***fortunei*** | see *Cyrtomium fortunei* |

## *Pharbitis* see *Ipomoea*

## *Phaseolus* (*Papilionaceae*)

| | |
|---|---|
| ***caracalla*** | see *Vigna caracalla* |
| ***vulgaris*** 'Yin Yang' | LSou |

## *Phedimus* see *Sedum*

## *Phegopteris* (*Thelypteridaceae*)

| | | |
|---|---|---|
| § | ***connectilis*** | EBee EFer EMon SRms WRic |
| | ***decursive-pinnata*** | CFwr CLAP EBee EMon GBri NHol NLar SPoG WFib WRic |

## *Phellodendron* (*Rutaceae*)

| | | |
|---|---|---|
| | ***amurense*** | CBcs CCCN CDul CMCN ELan EPfP GAuc IFFs LEdu NLar SBLw SEND WBor WDin WPGP |
| | - var. ***sachalinense*** | EGFP LRHS |
| | ***chinense*** | CMCN EGFP |
| | ***japonicum*** | EGFP |
| | - B&SWJ 11175 new | WCru |
| | ***lavalleei*** | EPfP |

## *Phenakospermum* (*Strelitziaceae*)

| | | |
|---|---|---|
| | ***guianense*** | XBlo |

## *Philadelphus* ✿ (*Hydrangeaceae*)

| | | |
|---|---|---|
| | F&M 152 | WPGP |
| | SDR 2823 new | GKev |
| | 'Albâtre' (d) | MBri |
| | ***argyrocalyx*** | GKir |
| | 'Avalanche' | CMHG CPLG EBee GKir LRHS NLar NPro SRms WDin WFar WHCG |
| | 'Beauclerk' $\Upsilon^{H4}$ | CDoC CDul CMHG CSBt CTri EBee ECrN EPfP GGal GKir GQui LRHS MBri MGos MRav NBro NHol NWea SPer SPoG SReu SRms SWvt WDin WHCG WKif |
| | 'Belle Etoile' $\Upsilon^{H4}$ | Widely available |
| | 'Bicolore' | EBee NLar |
| | 'Boule d'Argent' (d) | CMHG |
| | 'Bouquet Blanc' | EBee GKir GQui MRav NLar SPer SRms WPat |
| | ***brachybotrys*** | EPfP MRav WHCG |
| | 'Buckley's Quill' (d) | EBee ECrN EMil EPfP EQua EWes MRav SWvt |
| | 'Burfordensis' | EBee EPfP LAst MRav WPGP |
| | 'Burkwoodii' | LRHS |
| | aff. ***calvescens*** | MRav |
| | -BWJ 8005 | WCru |
| | ***caucasicus*** | WPGP |
| | ***coronarius*** | CBcs CDul CTri EPfP GKir LBuc MWhi NWea SGar SHBN SPer WDin |
| | - 'Aureus' $\Upsilon^{H4}$ | Widely available |
| | - 'Bowles' Variety' | see *P. coronarius* 'Variegatus' |
| § | - 'Variegatus' (v) $\Upsilon^{H4}$ | Widely available |
| | 'Coupe d'Argent' | MRav |
| | 'Dame Blanche' (d) | EBee GKir LBuc LRHS MAsh MRav |
| | ***delavayi*** | CGHE EPfP GGal GKir MBri NWea SChF SGar SKHP WHCG WPGP |
| | - var. ***calvescens*** | see *P. purpurascens* |
| | - var. ***melanocalyx*** | GCra GKir WPGP |
| | 'Enchantement' (d) | MRav SDix WBod |
| § | 'Erectus' | CSBt CWib EBee EPfP LEdu MGos MRav SPer SPla SPoG WDin WHCG WPat |
| | 'Etoile Rose' | GKir |
| | 'Frosty Morn' (d) | CBcs GKir MBri MGos MRav NBro SPer SPla SPoG WGwG |
| | ***hirsutus*** new | GKir |
| | ***incanus*** | GKir |
| | - B&SWJ 8616 | WCru |
| § | 'Innocence' (v) | CMac CPLG CWSG EBee ECrN EHoe ELan EPfP LAst LBMP LRHS MAsh MBri MGos MRav MSwo NBlu NPri NPro SAga SHBN SPer SPla SPoG SReu WFar WHCG |
| | 'Innocence Variegatus' | see *P.* 'Innocence' |
| § | ***insignis*** | MRav WBod |
| | x ***lemoinei*** | CDul CTri EHig EWTr MGos MWat SHBN WDin WFar |
| | - 'Erectus' | see *P.* 'Erectus' |
| I | - 'Lemoinei' | NWea |
| | ***lewisii*** | CPLG GKir |
| | - L 1896 | WPGP |
| | ***maculatus*** | GKir |
| | - 'Mexican Jewel' | EBee SKHP WPGP |
| | ***madrensis*** | LHop MRav |
| | 'Manteau d'Hermine' (d) $\Upsilon^{H4}$ | Widely available |
| | 'Marjorie' | EBee |
| | ***mexicanus*** | EBee MSte WSHC |
| | - B&SWJ 10253 new | WCru |
| | - 'Rose Syringa' | CGHE WPGP |
| | ***microphyllus*** | CDul CMHG CPSs EBee ELan EPfP GKir LAst LRHS MGos MRav MWhi NHol SLon SPer SReu SSpi WBVN WHCG WPat WSHC |
| | - var. ***occidentalis*** | NLar |
| | 'Miniature Snowflake' (d) | WPat |
| | 'Minnesota Snowflake' (d) | CBcs CMac EBee ECtt EQua EWes GKir LBuc LRHS LSRN MRav NHol NLar NPro SPur WDin WFar |
| | 'Mont Blanc' | CBcs EBee MRav WFar |
| | 'Mrs E.L. Robinson' (d) | CMac EBee ECtt GKir LAst LBuc LRHS NLar WBor WPat |
| | 'Natchez' (d) | CMac EBee ECtt WDin WPat |
| | 'Oeil de Pourpre' | MRav |
| | ***palmeri*** | WPGP |
| | ***pekinensis*** | CPLG |
| | 'Perryhill' | MRav |
| | 'Polar Star' | CBcs GBin NCGa WBod |
| § | ***purpurascens*** | EPfP EWes GQui MRav SLon WPGP WPat |
| | - BWJ 7540 | WCru |
| | x ***purpureomaculatus*** | GKir MRav WPat |
| | ***schrenkii*** | NLar WPGP |
| | - B&SWJ 8465 | WCru |
| § | 'Silberregen' | CDul CMac EBee ECtt EPfP GKir LAst MAsh MBar MBri MGos MMuc MRav NHol NPro SHBN SMad SPoG SRms SWvt WBod WFar WPat WRHF |
| | Silver Showers | see *P.* 'Silberregen' |
| | 'Snow Velvet' | EBee ECrN EPfP LRHS |
| | 'Snowbelle' (d) | EBee LBMP MAsh MBri MWea NBro NHol SWvt |
| | 'Snowflake' | CWSG GKir NMoo |
| | 'Souvenir de Billiard' | see *P. insignis* |
| | ***subcanus*** | CPLG MRav |
| | 'Sybille' $\Upsilon^{H4}$ | CDul CMHG ECrN EPfP GKir LRHS MRav MSwo SDix SPer SPoG SRms SSpi WHCG WKif WPat WSHC |
| | ***tenuifolius*** | CMCN NLar |
| | ***tomentosus*** | CPLG GKir WHCG WPGP |
| | - B&SWJ 2707 | WCru |
| | - GWJ 9215 | WCru |
| | 'Virginal' (d) | Widely available |
| | 'Voie Lactée' | MRav |
| | White Icicle = 'Biały Sopel' | CCCN WBrE |
| | White Rock = 'Pekphil' | CDoC CMac CPLG CWSG EBee EQua GKir LAst LLHF LRHS MRav NMoo SLim SPer SPoG WPat |
| | 'Yellow Cab' | MBri NLar SPoG |
| | 'Yellow Hill' | EMil LRHS SPoG |

## *Philesia* (*Philesiaceae*)

| | | |
|---|---|---|
| | ***buxifolia*** | see *P. magellanica* |
| § | ***magellanica*** | GGGa SSpi WBod WCru |
| | - 'Rosea' | CWib EPfP IBlr LRHS MAsh SPoG |

## *Phillyrea* (Oleaceae)

| | | |
|---|---|---|
| | ***angustifolia*** | CBcs CDul CGHE CMCN CSpe EBee ELan EPfP ERom IFFs MBri MGos SBig SEND SLPl SPer SSpi WDin WFar WSHC |
| | - f. ***rosmarinifolia*** | CCCN CPLG EBee ELan EPfP EPla LAst MBri NLar SLPl WFar WPGP |
| | ***decora*** | see *Osmanthus decorus* |
| § | ***latifolia*** | CSpe EBee EGFP ELan EPfP LRHS MWea NLar SAPC SArc SLPl SSpi WDin WFar WPGP |
| I | - 'Rodrigueziensis' | WCFE |
| | ***media*** | see *P. latifolia* |

## *Philodendron* (Araceae)

| | | |
|---|---|---|
| | ***epipremnum*** | see *Epipremnum pinnatum* |
| | ***erubescens*** 'Burgundy' ♀H1 | CHal LRHS |
| | - 'Red Emerald' | CHal |
| * | ***rubrum*** | XBlo |
| | ***scandens*** ♀H1 | CHal |
| | - 'Mica' | XBlo |
| | ***selloum*** | EAmu XBlo |
| | ***xanadu*** | XBlo |

## *Philotheca* (Rutaceae)

| | | |
|---|---|---|
| | ***buxifolia*** new | ECou |
| | - 'Cascade of Stars' | SOWG |

## *Phlebodium* (Polypodiaceae)

| | | |
|---|---|---|
| § | ***aureum*** ♀H1 | CSpe EShb WRic |
| | - 'Mandaianum' new | WRic |

## *Phleum* (Poaceae)

| | | |
|---|---|---|
| | ***bertolonii*** | CRWN EBWF |
| | ***pratense*** | EHoe GQue WSFF |

## *Phlomis* ✿ (Lamiaceae)

| | | |
|---|---|---|
| * | ***anatolica*** | NLar |
| * | - 'Lloyd's Variety' | CAbP CSam ELan LRHS MAsh MSte SPer WPen |
| | ***betonicoides*** B&L 12600 | EPPr |
| | ***bovei*** subsp. ***maroccana*** | IFro WHal |
| | ***cashmeriana*** | CBcs CHFP EBee ECha LCro LDai LSou MCot MNFA NChi NLar SEND SKHP WFar WPtf WWlt |
| | ***chrysophylla*** ♀H3 | CAbP EBee ECha ELan EPfP LRHS NLar SDix SPer WCFE |
| | ***crinita*** | EBee |
| | 'Edward Bowles' | CDul LSRN MRav NBid SKHP SLPl SLon SWvt |
| * | 'Elliot's Variety' | CPLG |
| | ***fruticosa*** ♀H4 | Widely available |
| | - white-flowered | ECrN |
| | ***grandiflora*** | SEND |
| | ***italica*** | Widely available |
| | ***lanata*** ♀H3-4 | CAbP EBee ELan EPfP LRHS MSte NPro SKHP SPer WEas WKif |
| | - 'Pygmy' | CHVG MGos NPro SLon |
| | ***leucophracta*** 'Golden Janissary' | WPGP |
| | ***longifolia*** | EBee EGoo EPfP LHop LRHS LSou MGos NLar SKHP SPer |
| | - var. ***bailanica*** | CSam EBee LRHS WFar |
| | ***lycia*** | LRHS |
| | ***macrophylla*** | SPhx |
| | ***pratensis*** | EBee |
| | ***purpurea*** | CAbP CArn CPLG CSam EBee ELan EPfP LRHS MAsh NBir WCot WOVN |
| | - ***alba*** | EBee EPfP LHop SKHP |
| | - subsp. ***almeriensis*** | CMdw CPom |
| § | ***russeliana*** ♀H4 | Widely available |
| | ***samia*** Boiss. | see *P. russeliana* |
| | ***samia*** L. | CEnt CPom EBee EBrs LDai LHop NBPC NCGa NChi NDov NGdn NLar SKHP WCot WFar WHal WPtf |
| | ***taurica*** | GAbr NChi SDix WHoo |
| | ***tuberosa*** | CBcs CFir CKno COIW CPou EBee EBrs EPPr EPfP EWTr GKir LAst LEdu LLWP LSRN NDov NGdn NLar SMrm SPet WCAu WCot WGwG WHoo WMnd WOVN WPGP |
| | - 'Amazone' | CFir CKno EBee ECha EHrv EPfP LCro LHop MAvo MRav NBid NCGa NDov NOrc NSti SAga SMad SMrm SUsu WCAu WFar WMnd |
| | - 'Bronze Flamingo' | CHFP CMac EBee ECGP EHrv EPfP ERCP LAst MAvo MLan MRav NBHF NDov NOrc SKHP SMrm WMnd WPer |
| | ***viscosa*** misapplied | see *P. russeliana* |

## *Phlox* ✿ (Polemoniaceae)

| | | |
|---|---|---|
| | ***adsurgens*** ♀H4 | ITim NCob |
| | - 'Mary Ellen' | ITim NHar |
| | - 'Oregon Blush' | NHar |
| | - 'Red Buttes' | CLyd ECho NHar |
| | - 'Wagon Wheel' | CWCL EBee ECho EPPr EWes GGar GKev GKir ITim LAst LRHS NSla SIng SMrm SPlb SRms SRot WCFE WFar |
| | ***amplifolia*** | EBee NBre WFar |
| | x ***arendsii*** 'Anja' | NDov WCot |
| | - 'Babyface' | NDov NGdn |
| | - 'Early Star' | EBee |
| | - 'Eyecatcher' | NBro NGdn |
| | - 'Lilac Girl' | NBre |
| | - 'Lilac Star' | CFir |
| | - 'Lisbeth' | SUsu WCot |
| | - 'Luc's Lilac' | CMHG CPrp ECtt GBin GBuc LLHF LRHS NBro NDov NGdn SMeo SMrm SMrs SPhx STes WAul WWlt |
| § | - 'Miss Jill' (Spring Pearl Series) | CMMP CSsd EBee MSCN NCob NDov NHol SPet WCot WHoo WTin |
| § | - 'Miss Jo-Ellen' (Spring Pearl Series) | GBri |
| § | - 'Miss Karen' (Spring Pearl Series) | NBro |
| § | - 'Miss Margie' (Spring Pearl Series) | GBri GMaP LEdu NBir |
| § | - 'Miss Mary' (Spring Pearl Series) | EBrs ECtt ELan GBri GMaP LAst MDKP NCGa NHol NPro |
| § | - 'Miss Wilma' (Spring Pearl Series) | GMaP |
| | - 'Paul' | WCot |
| | - 'Ping Pong' | EBee LDai NBPC NBre NBro NPro STes |
| | - 'Pink Attraction' | MNrw NBro NCGa |
| | - 'Purple Star' | CPrp EBee |
| | - 'Rosa Star' | CFir EBee NBre |
| | - 'Sabine' | CFir EBee |
| | - 'Suzanne' | EBee |
| | ***austromontana*** | EPot GKev NWCA |
| | 'Bavaria' | EAlp LLHF |
| | ***bifida*** | ECho |
| | - 'Alba' | ECho LLHF LSou WFar |
| | - blue-flowered | ECho LSou SUsu |
| | - 'Minima Colvin' | ECho ECtt EPot GKev |
| | - 'Petticoat' | CLyd CMea CPBP EPot MDKP SUsu WFar |
| | - 'Ralph Haywood' | CLyd CPBP CWCL EPot GBuc ITim |
| | - 'Starbrite' | CLyd LRHS WFar |
| | - 'Thefi' | EWes LLHF MNrw |
| | ***borealis*** | see *P. sibirica* subsp. *borealis* |
| * | - ***arctica*** | EAlp EPot |

| | | |
|---|---|---|
| | ***bryoides*** | see *P. hoodii* subsp. *muscoides* |
| | ***caespitosa*** | ECho EWes NDlv |
| | - subsp. ***condensata*** | see *P. condensata* |
| | ***canadensis*** | see *P. divaricata* |
| | ***carolina*** subsp. ***angusta*** | SUsu |
| | - 'Bill Baker' ♀H4 | Widely available |
| | - 'Magnificence' | CPrp EBee EGle EMon EWes GBuc GMac LRHS MDKP MHar MMuc MSte SMad STes WCot WSHC WTin |
| | - 'Miss Lingard' ♀H4 | CPrp CSam CWCL EBee ECtt EGle GBuc GMac LAst MAvo MSte NBid NBir NGdn NHol NLar NSti SAga SMrm SPla WAul WCot WFar |
| | 'Casablanca' | NDov SMrm |
| | 'Charles Ricardo' | EWes GBuc GMac SUsu WHoo |
| | 'Chattahoochee' | see *P. divaricata* subsp. *laphamii* 'Chattahoochee' |
| § | ***condensata*** | ECho WPat |
| | ***covillei*** | see *P. condensata* |
| | 'Daniel's Cushion' | see *P. subulata* 'McDaniel's Cushion' |
| | ***diffusa*** | WAbe |
| § | ***divaricata*** ♀H4 | GKir MSte SBod SHBN SPlb |
| | - 'Blue Dreams' | CFir ECtt EHrv GBuc LRHS MNrw MSte NCob SPla SUsu WFar WHal WPGP WSHC WWlt |
| | - 'Blue Perfume' | CMHG CPrp EBee ECtt LCro LSou NBro NCGa NLar SHGN SMrm WFar |
| | - 'Clouds of Perfume' | CMMP COlW CWCL EAEE EBee ECtt GBri GMaP LAst LRHS LSRN NCGa NCob NDov NLar SBod SMrm SPoG STes WFar |
| | - 'Dirigo Ice' | EAEE EBee EHrv GBri LHop MWte NLar SIng WFar WSHC |
| | - 'Eco Texas Purple' | EBee ECtt IPot NCGa NCob NPro SAga SPoG WFar WPGP WWlt |
| | - 'Fuller's White' | CWCL ECtt |
| | - subsp. ***laphamii*** | EGle EWes WFar |
| § | - - 'Chattahoochee' ♀H4 | Widely available |
| | - - 'Chattahoochee Variegated' (v) | LRHS SUsu |
| § | - 'Louisiana Purple' | WSHC |
| | - 'May Breeze' | EBee ECho EGle EHrv GKir GMaP LHop LRHS MNrw MSte NCGa NCob SIng SPla SUsu WFar WPGP WSHC WWlt |
| | - 'Plum Perfect' | EBee LLHF NBhm NBro NMyG WFar WPtf |
| * | - 'White Perfume' | CMHG CMMP CPrp CWCL EBee EWes GBri IPot LAst LSou MBrN MDKP NBro NCGa NCob NLar SHGN SMrm SPoG STes WFar |
| | ***douglasii*** | GKir NPol NWCA SRms |
| | - 'Alba' new | GJos |
| | - 'Apollo' | CTri ECho EPot LLHF LRHS NHar NMen WAbe |
| | - 'Boothman's Variety' ♀H4 | ECha ECho EDAr ELan EPfP EPot LRHS MLHP MWat NMen SRms WAbe |
| | - 'Crackerjack' ♀H4 | ECho ECtt EDAr ELan EPfP EPot GAbr GJos GKev GKir GMaP LRHS MHer MLHP NBir NMen SIng SPoG SRGP WAbe WFar |
| | - 'Eva' | CMMP CPBP ECho ECtt EDAr EPot GMaP LIMB LRHS LSRN NBir NMen NPri NWCA SRGP WAbe WFar |
| | - 'Galaxy' | ECho |
| | - 'Georg Arends' new | EPot |
| | - 'Ice Mountain' | CPBP ECho ELan EPot GMaP NWCA SIng SPoG SRot WFar |
| | - 'Iceberg' ♀H4 | ECho GJos NMen WAbe |
| | - 'Lilac Cloud' | EAlp ECtt EDAr GJos NPro SHGN WAbe |
| | - Lilac Queen | see *P. douglasii* 'Lilakönigin' |
| § | - 'Lilakönigin' | ECho |
| | - 'Napoleon' | CPBP ECho EPot LLHF NMen WAbe |
| | - 'Ochsenblut' | EAlp ECho EPot GEdr LLHF MHer MLHP NHar SIng WAbe |
| | - 'Red Admiral' ♀H4 | EAlp ECho ECtt EPfP EWes GEdr GKir GMaP MWat NMen WCFE WFar WRHF |
| | - 'Rose Cushion' | ECho EDAr EWes MHer NMen |
| | - 'Rose Queen' | CLyd ECho |
| | - 'Rosea' | ECho EDAr ELan GEdr GMaP NMen NPol WBVN WFar |
| | - 'Silver Rose' | ECho EPot GEdr MWat NWCA |
| | - 'Sprite' | SRms |
| | - 'Tycoon' | see *P. subulata* 'Tamaongalei' |
| | - 'Violet Queen' | ECho EWes WFar |
| | - 'Waterloo' | ECho EPot NMen |
| I | - 'White Admiral' | ECtt EPot LRHS LSRN NPro SIng |
| | ***drummondii*** 'Classic Cassis' new | SPoG |
| | 'Fancy Feelings' (Feelings Series) | NBro NCob |
| | ***glaberrima*** 'Morris Berd' | EBee WPGP |
| | ***hendersonii*** | CGra |
| | ***hoodii*** | CGra ECho |
| § | - subsp. ***muscoides*** | ECho |
| | ***idahoensis*** | CWsd |
| | ***jonesii*** new | GKev |
| | 'Kelly's Eye' ♀H4 | CMMP CPBP ECho ECtt EPot LRHS NBir NHar NHol NMen SPoG WBVN WFar |
| | ***kelseyi*** | ECho EPot NWCA WAbe |
| | - 'Lemhi Purple' | CGra CPBP |
| | - 'Rosette' | CLyd ECho LIMB LRHS MDKP NMen WFar WPer |
| | Light Pink Flame = 'Bareleven'PBR | SPoG |
| | Lilac Flame = 'Barten'PBR | SPoG |
| | ***longifolia*** subsp. ***brevifolia*** | CPBP GKev WAbe |
| | 'Louisiana' | see *P. divaricata* 'Louisiana Purple' |
| | ***maculata*** | NOrc WPer |
| | - 'Alpha' ♀H4 | Widely available |
| | - Avalanche | see *P. maculata* 'Schneelawine' |
| | - 'Delta' | CCVN CWCL EBee EPfP GBuc LSou NBPC NHol SMad SPer SWvt WBor WCAu WFar |
| | - 'Natascha' | Widely available |
| | - 'Omega' ♀H4 | CMHG CPLG CPrp CWCL EAEE EBee ECtt GBuc GGar GKir GMaP LRHS MMuc MRav MSte NBid NGdn NHol NLar SMad SPer SPla SWvt WAul WCAu WFar WSHC |
| | - 'Princess Sturdza' ♀H4 | SDix |
| | - 'Reine du Jour' | GMac LPla LSou MDKP MSte NDov SAga SMrm SPhx SUsu WSHC |
| | - 'Rosalinde' | CPrp EAEE EBee ECtt ELon GBuc LRHS MMuc MRav MSte NCob NHol NLar SPla SRGP STes SWvt WCAu WFar WHil WSHC |
| § | - 'Schneelawine' | GKir SPlb |
| | 'Matineus' | SPhx |
| | 'Millstream' | see *P.* x *procumbens* 'Millstream' |
| | 'Millstream Jupiter' | ECho |
| | 'Minnie Pearl' | SKHP |
| | ***muscoides*** | see *P. hoodii* subsp. *muscoides* |
| | ***nivalis*** | CPBP |
| | - 'Jill Alexander' | CMea SAga |
| | - 'Nivea' | EPot GJos LRHS LSou SIng WAbe |
| | ***paniculata*** | EMon GCra NBid NDov SDix SMeo SPhx WCot WTin |
| | - 'Aida' | EBee |
| | - var. ***alba*** | CMoH MAvo NDov SDix WCot WTin |

| | | |
|---|---|---|
| | – 'Alba Grandiflora' ♀H4 | EHrv GMaP MAvo NChi NCob WEas WHoo |
| | – 'Amethyst' misapplied | see *P. paniculata* 'Lilac Time' |
| | – 'Amethyst' Foerster | CFir CSam EBee EGle EHrv EWTr LCro NBir NLar NOrc NPri SPet SWat WCAu WFar |
| I | – 'Aureovariegata Undulata' (v) | WCot |
| | – 'Balmoral' | EBee ECtt EPfP GCra GKir LCro LRHS MLHP MRav MSte NCob NDov NSti SMrs SPoG SWat SWvt |
| | – 'Barnwell' | SWat |
| | – 'Becky Towe'[PBR] (v) | CBow EBee ECtt EGle ELon LHop LLHF LSou NLar SPoG WCot WRHF |
| | – 'Bill Green' | LRHS |
| | – 'Blue Boy' | EBee ECtt EGle GMaP LRHS MDKP MSCN NBir NBro NChi NGby NGdn NLar WBrE WClo WFar WHil WMnd |
| | – 'Blue Evening' | CAby LSou MCot NCob |
| | – 'Blue Ice' ♀H4 | CAby EBee ELan LRHS MCot MSCN NBro NCob SPhx SPla |
| | – 'Blue Paradise' | Widely available |
| | – 'Blushing Bride' | SRms |
| | – 'Border Gem' | CBcs EBee ECtt GKir MCot MRav MSte NChi NCob NHol NLar SDix SMrs SPur SWat SWvt WBrk |
| | – 'Branklyn' | EBrs GCra GKir LRHS |
| | – 'Brigadier' ♀H4 | CTri EBee ECtt ELan GMaP LRHS MCot MDKP MWat NCob NGdn NVic SMrm SPer SPla SPoG SRms WCAu WFar |
| | – 'Bright Eyes' ♀H4 | Widely available |
| | – 'Burgi' | SDix |
| | – 'Candy Floss' | LLHF NCob |
| | – 'Caroline van den Berg' | SRms |
| | – 'Cecil Hanbury' | NLar SRms |
| | – 'Chintz' | MRav SRms |
| | – 'Cinderella' | EBee |
| § | – 'Cool of the Evening' | EBee SPhx WKif |
| | – Count Zeppelin | see *P. paniculata* 'Graf Zeppelin' |
| | – 'Danielle' | CSBt EBee MSCN MWea |
| | – 'Darwin's Choice' | see *P. paniculata* 'Norah Leigh' |
| | – 'David' | Widely available |
| | – 'Delilah'[PBR] | EBee NCob NDov |
| | – 'Discovery' | EBee EHrv EWes IPot MCot NCob SPla STes SWat WCAu |
| | – 'Dodo Hanbury-Forbes' ♀H4 | GKir |
| | – 'Doghouse Pink' | SDix |
| | – 'Dresden China' | SWat |
| § | – 'Düsterlohe' | CSam EBee EGle GAbr GBuc GMac IPot MSCN NBir NDov NLar NSti STes SWat WCot WFar WHil WHoo |
| | – 'Eclaireur' misapplied | see *P. paniculata* 'Düsterlohe' |
| | – 'Eclaireur' Lemoine | NCob SWat |
| | – 'Eden's Crush' | CMMP NBre NVic |
| | – 'Eden's Flash' | EBee ECtt EGle |
| | – 'Eden's Glory' | EGle |
| | – 'Eden's Smile' | EBee MSCN |
| | – 'Elisabeth' (v) | EBee LSRN SRGP |
| | – 'Elizabeth Arden' | MRav MSte NLar SWat |
| | – 'Empty Feelings'[PBR] (Feelings Series) | EBee EGle GBin NBro NCob |
| | – 'Etoile de Paris' | see *P. paniculata* 'Toits de Paris' Symons-Jeune |
| | – 'Europa' | EBee ECtt ELan LRHS MCot NBir NCob NGdn NHol NLar SPer SPla SPoG WCAu WFar |
| | – 'Eva Cullum' | EAEE EBee ECtt EGle GCra GKir GMaP LRHS MArl MCot MRav NBPC NCGa NHol NLar NMoo SPer SPoG SWat WBor WCot WRHF |
| | – 'Eventide' ♀H4 | CSam CWCL EBee ECtt EPfP GKir LBMP LRHS MArl MCot MRav NCob SPer SPoG SPur SWat WCAu WCot |
| | – 'Excelsior' | MRav |
| | – 'Fairy's Petticoat' | MWat |
| | – 'Ferris Wheel' | NCob |
| | – 'Flamingo' | EBee LRHS MBrN NGby NLar SWvt |
| | – 'Fondant Fancy' **new** | SPoG |
| | – 'Franz Schubert' | CHrt CSam EBee ECtt EGle EPfP GCra GKir LCro LRHS MCot MLHP MRav NBir NGdn NLar NSti SPer SPhx STes SWat SWvt WCot WFar WKif |
| § | – 'Frau Alfred von Mauthner' | COIW ECtt GKev SMrm |
| | – 'Frosted Elegance' (v) | ECtt LSou |
| | – 'Fujiyama' | see *P. paniculata* 'Mount Fuji' |
| | – 'Giltmine' (v) | NCob |
| | – 'Glamis' | MWat |
| | – 'Goldmine'[PBR] (v) | ELan IBal MCCP MWea NBro NCob NSti SPoG WCot |
| § | – 'Graf Zeppelin' | ECtt ELan LBMP LRHS NGby SRms |
| | – 'Grenadine Dream' **new** | LLHF SPoG |
| | – 'Harlequin' (v) | CBcs CMil EBee ECha ECtt EHoe GBuc GMaP LAst MCCP MCot NBPC NBid NBro NCob NLar NSti SPer SPla SPoG WBVN WCAu WCot WFar WWlt |
| | – 'Hesperis' | CAby CMdw EBee GBin NDov SMeo SMrm SPhx WFar |
| | – 'Iris' | CDes CMoH GBuc SMrm SRms |
| | – 'Jubilee' | CMMP |
| | – 'Judy' | LSRN NBro |
| | – 'Jules Sandeau' | MBri NCob |
| § | – 'Juliglut' | MWea SWat WCot |
| | – July Glow | see *P. paniculata* 'Juliglut' |
| | – 'Katarina' | CElw ECtt NLar WBor |
| | – 'Katherine' | NLar |
| | – 'Kirchenfürst' | MBri NBir SMrm |
| | – 'Kirmesländler' | EBee ECtt GBin LRHS MLLN NCob NLar SWat |
| | – 'Lads Pink' **new** | SDix |
| | – 'Lady Clare' | SRms |
| | – 'Landhochzeit' | EBee GBin LRHS NCob WFar |
| * | – 'Laura' | CMMP EBee ECtt EGle EWTr IPot NBPC NBro NPri NVic SMrm SPet SPoG SRGP STes WBor WCot WFar WHoo WMnd WRHF |
| § | – 'Lavendelwolke' | CSam EBee GCal NBir NCob NLar SWat |
| | – Lavender Cloud | see *P. paniculata* 'Lavendelwolke' |
| | – 'Le Mahdi' ♀H4 | ELan MBrN MRav MWat SMeo SRms SWat |
| | – 'Lichtspel' | CAby NDov SAga SMeo SPhx |
| § | – 'Lilac Time' | CSBt EBee EHrv EWll LSRN MDKP MSte MWat NCob NLar NMoo SWat SWvt |
| | – 'Little Boy' | CElw EBrs ECtt LRHS LSou MDKP MNrw MSCN NLar WFar |
| | – 'Little Laura' | CElw CMHG EBee ECtt LRHS LSRN MAvo MCCP MWea NLar NOrc WBor |
| | – 'Little Princess' | ELon LLHF NLar SMrm SRGP WMnd |
| | – 'Lizzy'[PBR] | NLar |
| | – 'Manoir d'Hézèques' | WCot |
| | – 'Mary Christine' (v) | EBee NBid |
| | – 'Mary Fox' | CSam |
| | – 'Mia Ruys' | MArl MLHP MLLN |
| | – 'Midnight Feelings' (Feelings Series) | LLHF NBPN NBro NCob NLar SMrm WCot |
| | – 'Mies Copijn' | GMaP WFar |
| | – 'Milly van Hoboken' | WKif |

| | | |
|---|---|---|
| | - 'Miss Elie' | CMMP EGle LAst NGdn WFar WHoo WWlt |
| | - 'Miss Holland' | EGle LAst MSCN MWea NBPC NGdn SPet STes |
| | - 'Miss Jessica' | LAst NDov STes |
| | - 'Miss Jill' | see *P.* x *arendsii* 'Miss Jill' |
| | - 'Miss Jo-Ellen' | see *P.* x *arendsii* 'Miss Jo-Ellen' |
| | - 'Miss Karen' | see *P.* x *arendsii* 'Miss Karen' |
| | - 'Miss Kelly' | CMMP CMdw EBee LRHS MWea SRGP WHoo |
| | - 'Miss Margie' | see *P.* x *arendsii* 'Miss Margie' |
| | - 'Miss Mary' | see *P.* x *arendsii* 'Miss Mary' |
| | - 'Miss Pepper' | CWCL EBee MMuc NLar SMrm WBor WFar WHil WWlt |
| | - 'Miss Universe' | CMMP EGle MCCP WHil |
| | - 'Miss Wilma' | see *P.* x *arendsii* 'Miss Wilma' |
| | - 'Monica Lynden-Bell' | Widely available |
| | - 'Mother of Pearl' ♀H4 | EAEE EBee ELan IPot LRHS MWat NCob NHol NVic SPer SPoG SUsu WFar WWlt |
| § | - 'Mount Fuji' ♀H4 | Widely available |
| | - 'Mount Fujiyama' | see *P. paniculata* 'Mount Fuji' |
| | - 'Mrs A.E. Jeans' | SRms |
| | - 'Natural Feelings' PBR (Feelings Series) | CSpe ELan MCCP MWea NBro NCob NLar WCot WWlt |
| | - 'Newbird' | SRms WHal |
| | - 'Nicky' | see *P. paniculata* 'Düsterlohe' |
| § | - 'Norah Leigh' (v) | Widely available |
| | - 'Orange Perfection' | see *P. paniculata* 'Prince of Orange' |
| | - 'Othello' | CSam EBee EBrs ECtt GBuc GKir LRHS NCob NSti SUsu WFar WMnd WWlt |
| | - 'Otley Choice' | EAEE EBee ECtt LRHS MHer MRav MSte MWat NCob NHol NLar SCoo SWat |
| | - 'P.D. Williams' | WCot |
| | - 'Pastorale' | WCot |
| | - 'Pax' | CAby EMon SMeo SPhx |
| | - 'Peppermint Twist' **new** | MNrw MWea WHlf |
| | - 'Pink Posie' (v) | MBri WFar |
| | - 'Pinky Hill' | CElw |
| | - 'Pleasant Feelings' PBR (Feelings Series) | NBro NCob |
| | - 'Popeye' | ECtt MBri NLar |
| § | - 'Prince of Orange' ♀H4 | CBcs CSam EAEE EBee ECtt ELan EPfP GBuc LRHS LSRN MRav MWat NBlu NCGa NCob NHol NLar NPri SAga SPad SPer SPoG STes SWvt WAul WCot WMnd |
| | - 'Prospero' Foerster ♀H4 | CHar CSam EBee EHrv LBMP MCot MRav NBid SPer SWat |
| | - 'Rainbow' | EGle ELon |
| | - 'Red Feelings' PBR (Feelings Series) | NBro NCob SPoG |
| | - 'Red Indian' | MCot MWat |
| | - 'Red Riding Hood' | EBrs ECtt LAst MSCN NBPC SPet WRHF |
| I | - 'Reddish Hesperis' | NDov |
| | - 'Rembrandt' | CPLG GBri WCot |
| | - 'Rijnstroom' | CBcs EBee ECot ECtt GKir LRHS NLar SMrm WBrk WFar |
| | - 'Robert Poore' | GBin NCob |
| | - 'Rosa Pastell' | CAby CDes EGle EHrv ELon EMon GBri LPla LSou NCob SMrm SPhx SUsu |
| | - 'Rowie' | NBid NCob WBor |
| | - 'Rubymine' PBR (v) | LLHF NCob |
| | - 'San Antonio' | WFar |
| | - 'Sandringham' | EBee EHrv EPfP GKir LRHS MArl MLHP MNrw MRav MSte NBir NHol SPer SPoG SWvt WCAu WWlt |
| § | - 'Schneerausch' | LPla SPhx |
| | - 'Septemberglut' | NLar |
| | - 'Silvermine' (v) | CBow MCCP NBro SDnm |
| | - 'Sir Malcolm Campbell' | EBee |
| | - 'Skylight' | EBee EHrv LSRN MAvo NBre NBro NVic SDix SPer WAul |
| | - 'Snow White' | NBre NVic |
| | - Snowdrift | see *P. paniculata* 'Schneerausch' |
| | - 'Speed Limit 45' | WCot |
| | - 'Spitfire' | see *P. paniculata* 'Frau Alfred von Mauthner' |
| | - 'Starburst' | EBee NBro NGdn NLar STes WHil |
| | - 'Starfire' ♀H4 | Widely available |
| | - 'Steeple Bumpstead' | EBee LSou NCob WCot |
| | - 'Sternhimmel' | LPla |
| | - 'Tenor' | CDes CFir CHar CTri EAEE EBee ECtt EPfP LAst LRHS MCot MDKP MSte NCob NDov NGdn NHol NLar NPri SPla SPoG SWvt WBor WBrE WCAu WCot WFar WPGP |
| | - 'The King' | CElw EBee EGle GBri LRHS MAvo MDKP MSte NBro NGby NLar SWat WBor WSHC |
| | - 'Toits de Paris' misapplied | see *P. paniculata* 'Cool of the Evening' |
| | - 'Toits de Paris' ambig. | MAvo |
| § | - 'Toits de Paris' Symons-Jeune | SPhx WSHC |
| | - 'Uspekh' | COlW CSam EAEE EBee EBrs ECtt EPPr EShb EWes MDKP MSte NBro NCGa NCob NGdn NHol NOrc SAga SPer SPoG SUsu WFar |
| | - 'Utopia' | CDes CSam ELon LPla NLar SMrm SPhx SUsu |
| | - 'Van Gogh' | CMdw EHrv |
| | - 'Vintage Wine' | MSte |
| | - 'Violetta Gloriosa' | LPla MWte SMrm SPhx |
| | - 'Visions' | WHil |
| | - 'Wendy House' | LLHF MNrw NCob |
| | - 'Wenn Schon Denn Schon' | EBee GBin |
| | - 'White Admiral' ♀H4 | Widely available |
| | - White Flame = 'Bartwentynine' PBR | EBee EPPr |
| | - 'Wilhelm Kesselring' | EBee ELon NBre WBor |
| | - 'Windsor' ♀H4 | EBee ECtt ELon EPfP GBri GCal GKir LRHS MLLN NDov NHol NLar SCoo SPoG SRms SWvt WCAu WClo WFar |
| | ***pilosa*** | ECha NPro WFar |
| | Pink Flame = 'Bartwelve' PBR | EBee SPoG |
| | 'Pride of Rochester' **new** | GJos |
| § | x ***procumbens*** 'Millstream' ♀H4 | EPPr WClo |
| | - 'Variegata' (v) | EAlp ECha ECho EPot LRHS MDKP NPri SPlb SRot SUsu WFar |
| | Purple Flame = 'Barfourteen' PBR | EBee SPoG |
| | 'Sandra' | LRHS |
| | 'Scented Pillow' | LRHS |
| | 'Sherbet Cocktail' **new** | MWea |
| § | ***sibirica*** subsp. ***borealis*** | EDAr WAbe |
| | 'Sileniflora' | EPot |
| | ***stansburyi*** | CPBP |
| | - dwarf **new** | GKev |
| | ***stolonifera*** | MNrw |
| I | - 'Alba' | CBcs EBee EWll |
| | - 'Ariane' | CWCL ECha EPPr LSou WCFE WFar |
| | - 'Blue Ridge' ♀H4 | CPLG CWCL EBee ECha ECtt EPPr EPfP EShb GBuc GKir LSRN MRav SRms WFar |
| | - 'Bob's Motley' (v) | ECtt |
| | - compact | EPot |
| | - 'Compact Pink' | WFar |

| | | |
|---|---|---|
| | – 'Fran's Purple' | CWsd EBee ELon NBro WCFE WFar WPGP |
| | – 'Home Fires' | EBee ECtt ELon EPPr EPfP EWll LEdu MNrw NBro NLar SAga SMrm SPlb WFar |
| | – 'Mary Belle Frey' | CEnt EBee MSte WFar |
| | – 'Montrose Tricolor' (v) | EPPr LHop NBro |
| | – 'Pink Ridge' | EWll MNrw NBir WRos |
| | – 'Purpurea' | CWCL EBee EPPr EWll LEdu LSou MMuc |
| | – variegated (v) | GKir |
| | – 'Violet Vere' | GBuc WFar |
| | ***subulata*** | NWCA |
| | – 'Alexander's Surprise' | CMea EAlp ECho EDAr EPfP EPot LBee LRHS NBir SPlb SRGP |
| | – 'Amazing Grace' | CTri CWCL ECho EDAr EPfP EWes GKir LHop LIMB LRHS MHer NLar SIng SPoG WAbe |
| | – 'Apple Blossom' | EDAr NPro SPet SPoG SRms WFar |
| | – 'Atropurpurea' | EDAr LIMB SPoG |
| | – Beauty of Ronsdorf | see *P. subulata* 'Ronsdorfer Schöne' |
| | – 'Betty' | ECtt |
| | – 'Blue Eyes' | see *P. subulata* 'Oakington Blue Eyes' |
| | – 'Bonita' | CPBP EAlp ECho EPot GJos GKir LBee LRHS MMuc MWte WBor |
| | – 'Bressingham Blue Eyes' | see *P. subulata* 'Oakington Blue Eyes' |
| | – 'Brightness' | ECho |
| | – 'Brilliant' | ECho SIng |
| | – subsp. ***brittonii*** 'Rosea' | GEdr WFar |
| | – 'Candy Stripe' | see *P. subulata* 'Tamaongalei' |
| | – 'Cavaldes White' | SPoG |
| | – 'Christine Bishop' | LRHS |
| | – 'Coral Eye' | EAlp |
| | – 'Daisy Hill' | CPBP |
| | – 'Drumm' | see *P. subulata* 'Tamaongalei' |
| | – 'Emerald Cushion' | CSam CTri CWCL ECho ECtt EDAr GEdr GKev GKir LRHS MDKP MWat WBVN WRHF |
| | – 'Emerald Cushion Blue' | CPLG EAlp ECho EPfP GJos LIMB NBir NMen NPri NPro SGar SPlb SPoG WAbe WFar WPer |
| | – 'Fairy' | WPer |
| | – 'Fort Hill' | NHar |
| | – 'G.F. Wilson' | see *P. subulata* 'Lilacina' |
| * | – 'Holly' | EPot LLHF NMen |
| | – 'Jupiter' | ECho |
| | – 'Kimono' | see *P. subulata* 'Tamaongalei' |
| § | – 'Lilacina' | CMea ECho ECtt GEdr GMaP LRHS MWat NLar |
| § | – 'Maischnee' | CMea CTri ECho ECtt EPfP LRHS MWat NHol SIng SPlb WFar |
| | – 'Marjorie' | CLyd ECho ECtt GEdr GJos LBee MHer NBir NPri NWCA SIng SPoG SRGP WFar WRHF |
| | – May Snow | see *P. subulata* 'Maischnee' |
| § | – 'McDaniel's Cushion' ♀H4 | CPLG EAlp ECha ECho EDAr ELan ELon EPfP EPot GAbr GEdr GJos GKev GKir ITim LAst LBee LHop MLHP MMuc NHar NMen NWCA SPlb SPoG WAbe WCFE WFar |
| | – 'Mikado' | see *P. subulata* 'Tamaongalei' |
| | – 'Moonlight' | ECtt EDAr GJos |
| | – 'Nettleton Variation' (v) | EAlp ECho EDAr EPPr EPfP EPot EWes GKev GKir LHop LRHS MDKP MHer SIng SPlb SPoG SRot WBrE |
| § | – 'Oakington Blue Eyes' | GKir SRms |
| | – 'Pink Buttons' | LAst |
| | – 'Pink Pearl' | EWes |
| | – 'Purple Beauty' | CMea CWCL EPot GGar GJos LIMB LLHF MWte NHar SPoG WFar WSHC |
| | – 'Red Wings' ♀H4 | ECho ECtt EPfP GKir LRHS NMen SRms |
| § | – 'Ronsdorfer Schöne' | EPot LBee LLHF LRHS NBir |
| | – 'Samson' | LRHS LSRN MMuc |
| | – 'Sarah' **new** | LLHF |
| | – 'Scarlet Flame' | CMea CSam ECho EDAr EPfP EPot NHol NPri SRGP STes WFar |
| | – 'Schneewittchen' | GKir |
| | – 'Snow Queen' | see *P. subulata* 'Maischnee' |
| § | – 'Tamaongalei' | CMea CPBP CTri CWCL EAlp ECho EDAr EPfP EPot EWes GGar GJos GKev GKir GMaP MMuc NHol SCoo SIng SPet SPoG SRms STes WBor WCFE WFar |
| | – 'Temiskaming' | CTri ECho ECtt EDAr EWes GEdr LBee LRHS MLHP NMen SPoG SRms WAbe WSHC |
| | – 'Tschernobyl' | EPot |
| | – violet seedling | CLyd |
| | – 'White Delight' | EAlp ECho ECtt EDAr EPfP GJos LAst LBee LRHS NMen SPet SPoG WBor WFar |
| | – 'Winifred' | CMea |
| | – 'Zwergenteppich' **new** | LLHF |
| | 'Sweet William' | LRHS SRGP |

## *Phoebe* (*Lauraceae*)

| | | |
|---|---|---|
| | ***sheareri*** | WPGP |

## *Phoenicaulis* (*Brassicaceae*)

| | | |
|---|---|---|
| § | ***cheiranthoides*** | LLHF |

## *Phoenix* (*Arecaceae*)

| | | |
|---|---|---|
| | ***canariensis*** ♀H1+3 | Widely available |
| | ***dactylifera*** (F) | CDTJ EAmu ETod LPal SBig |
| | ***reclinata*** | CKob EAmu ETod LPJP NPal XBlo |
| | ***roebelenii*** ♀H1+3 | CBrP CDTJ CDoC CTsd LCro LPal MBri SBig |
| | – 'Multistem' | XBlo |
| | ***rupicola*** | EAmu LPal |
| | ***sylvestris*** | EAmu LPal |
| | ***theophrastii*** | CPHo EAmu LEdu LPJP LPal |

## *Phormium* ✿ (*Phormiaceae*)

| | | |
|---|---|---|
| § | 'Alison Blackman' PBR | CBcs CBct CDoC CSBt CTrC CWil EBee ESwi EWsh IBlr LHop LSRN MGos MREP NBlu NScw SCoo SPoG SSto |
| | 'Amazing Red' | CTrC CWil ESwi IBal IBlr |
| | 'Apricot Queen' (v) | Widely available |
| | Ballyrogan variegated (v) | IBlr |
| | 'Black Edge' | CWil IBlr MRav NPri |
| | 'Bronze Baby' | Widely available |
| | 'Buckland Ruby' | CBct CDoC CWil |
| | 'Carousel' | CTrC ESwi IBal |
| | 'Chocolate Fingers' **new** | CBcs |
| | ***colensoi*** | see *P. cookianum* |
| § | ***cookianum*** | CHEx CTrC CWil ECre EPfP GGar GKir IBlr MGos SAPC SArc SCoo SEND WFar |
| | – 'Alpinum Purpureum' | see *P. tenax* 'Nanum Purpureum' |
| | – dwarf | IBlr SLPl |
| | – 'Flamingo' | Widely available |
| | – 'Golden Wonder' | IBlr |
| | – subsp. ***hookeri*** 'Cream Delight' (v) ♀H3-4 | Widely available |
| | – – 'Tricolor' (v) ♀H3-4 | Widely available |
| | 'Copper Beauty' | NMoo WDyG |
| | 'Crimson Devil' | CBcs CTrC GGar IBal MREP NScw WFar |
| | 'Dark Delight' | CBcs CDoC IBlr MAsh SPoG |
| | 'Dazzler' (v) | CBcs CDoC GKir IBlr LAst LSou MGos SHBN WCot |

| | | |
|---|---|---|
| § | 'Duet' (v) ♀$^{H3}$ | CCCN CDoC CSBt CTrC CWib CWil EBee EHoe EPfP ESwi IBlr LRHS MGos MREP NLar SPla SWvt WFar |
| | 'Dusky Chief' | CSBt CTrC CWil ESwi IBal LRHS WPat |
| | 'Dusky Princess' | ESwi |
| | 'Emerald Isle' | CDoC CWil |
| | 'Evening Glow' (v) | CBcs CCCN CTrC EBee ELan EPfP ESwi ETod GKir IBlr LFCN LRHS MBri MGos MREP SPla SPoG SRkn SWvt WCot WFar WLeb WPat |
| | 'Firebird' | ESwi IBlr LSRN SAga SWvt |
| | 'Fortescue's Bronze' | CWil |
| | 'Glowing Embers' | CTrC ESwi IBal WLeb |
| | 'Gold Ray' | CTrC ESwi IBal IBlr MREP NLar |
| | 'Gold Sword' (v) | CBcs CCCN CDoC CMHG CSBt CTrC CWil EBee ESwi IBal IBlr LRHS MBri MGos SSto |
| | 'Golden Alison'$^{PBR}$ | see *P.* 'Alison Blackman' |
| | 'Green Sword' | CCCN |
| | 'Guardsman' (v) | IBlr |
| | 'Jack Spratt' (v) | CWil ECou EHoe ELan IBal IBlr MSwo SPoG SWvt WPrP |
| | 'Jester' (v) | Widely available |
| | 'Limelight' | CWil SWvt |
| | 'Mahogany' | CWil |
| § | 'Maori Chief' (v) | CSBt EBee ELan EPfP ESwi IBlr LRHS NMoo SHBN SWvt WFar WLeb WPat |
| § | 'Maori Maiden' (v) | CBcs CCCN CChe CDoC CDul CSBt CTrC CTri EBee ECre EHoe EPfP ESwi LAst LFCN LRHS MAsh MBri MGos MRav SRkn SSto SWvt WFar |
| § | 'Maori Queen' (v) | CBcs CCCN CChe CDTJ CDoC CSBt CTrC CWil EBee ELan EPfP ESwi IBlr LCro LRHS MBri MGos MSwo NMoo SCoo SEND SPer SRkn SSto SWvt WCot WFar WPGP |
| § | 'Maori Sunrise' (v) | Widely available |
| | 'Margaret Jones'$^{PBR}$ | CBcs CBct CCCN CTrC CWil EBee SLim WViv |
| | 'Merlot'$^{PBR}$ | CWil |
| | 'Pink Jester' | EMil |
| | 'Pink Panther' (v) | Widely available |
| | 'Pink Stripe' (v) | CBcs CDoC CSBt CWil EBee ECrN EQua ESwi IBlr LRHS MBri NPal SHBN SPoG SWvt WCot |
| | 'Platt's Black' | Widely available |
| | 'Rainbow Chief' | see *P.* 'Maori Chief' |
| | 'Rainbow Maiden' | see *P.* 'Maori Maiden' |
| | 'Rainbow Queen' | see *P.* 'Maori Queen' |
| | 'Rainbow Sunrise' | see *P.* 'Maori Sunrise' |
| | 'Red Sensation' | EPfP LRHS |
| I | 'Rubrum' | CTrC CWil ESwi GKir IBal |
| | 'Sea Jade' | CWil IBlr |
| | 'Stormy Dawn' | WCot |
| | 'Sundowner' (v) ♀$^{H3}$ | Widely available |
| | 'Sunset' (v) | CBcs CCCN CChe CSBt IBlr IFoB SWvt |
| | 'Surfer' (v) | CBcs CWil EHoe IBlr LHop MCCP WBod WLeb |
| | 'Surfer Boy' | CSBt CWil LAst |
| | 'Surfer Bronze' | CCCN CSBt CWil EBee ETod IBal LSou MGos SSto |
| | 'Surfer Green' | CCCN CTsd ESwi IBal MGos WHer |
| | ***tenax*** ♀$^{H4}$ | Widely available |
| | - 'Atropurpureum' | CHEx EUJe GKir LAst |
| | - 'Bronze' | CHEx CWil SWvt |
| | - 'Co-ordination' | CCCN CWil EBee EPfP IBlr ISea LRHS |
| | - 'Deep Purple' | CHEx |
| | - 'Duet' | see *P.* 'Duet' |
| * | - dwarf | IBlr SLPl |
| I | - 'Giganteum' | CHEx |
| * | - ***lineatum*** | SEND |
| § | - 'Nanum Purpureum' | EHoe IBlr MSte SEND |
| | - Purpureum Group ♀$^{H3-4}$ | Widely available |
| | - 'Radiance' (v) | CWil IBlr |
| | - 'Rainbow Queen' | see *P.* 'Maori Queen' |
| | - 'Rainbow Sunrise' | see *P.* 'Maori Sunrise' |
| | - Sweet Mist = 'Phos2' **new** | EBee |
| | - 'Variegatum' (v) ♀$^{H3-4}$ | CDTJ CSBt CTrC EBee ELon EPfP ETod IBal IBlr LPal LRHS MGos NMoo SAPC SArc SEND SPer SRms WBrE WFar WHoo |
| | - 'Veitchianum' (v) | CWil IBlr LRHS SPer |
| | 'Thumbelina' | CBcs CCCN ERas ESwi IFoB MSte NBPN SSto WPat |
| | 'Tom Thumb' | GGar WDin WPrP |
| | 'Wings of Gold' | ESwi ETod IBal MAsh SPoG |
| | 'Yellow Wave' (v) ♀$^{H3}$ | Widely available |

## *Photinia* ✿ (*Rosaceae*)

| | | |
|---|---|---|
| | ***arbutifolia*** | see *Heteromeles salicifolia* |
| | ***beauverdiana*** | CTho GKir SRms WFar |
| | - var. ***notabilis*** | EPfP MBri NLar |
| § | 'Branpara'$^{PBR}$ | CTrC EBee LSou WHar |
| | ***davidiana*** | CDul CSam CTri EBee ELan EPfP ISea MRav NLar SPer SRms WBod WDin WFar |
| | - 'Palette' (v) | Widely available |
| | - var. ***undulata*** | CMHG |
| | - - 'Fructu Luteo' | CAbP CMHG CSam CTrG EPfP EPla GGal NLar WFar |
| | - - 'Prostrata' | CMac CTri ELan EQua MRav NLar WFar |
| | x ***fraseri*** | CMCN |
| | - 'Allyn Sprite'$^{PBR}$ | LSou WHar |
| | - 'Birmingham' | CMac EBee EWes GKir SRms WDin |
| | - 'Canivily' | EMil EWes MGos NLar SPad SPoG |
| * | - 'Ilexifolium' **new** | ESwi |
| | - 'Purple Peter' | CEnd |
| | - 'Red Robin' ♀$^{H4}$ | Widely available |
| | - 'Red Select' | EQua NPri WPat |
| | - 'Robusta' | CMac CTrC EBee EPfP LRHS MAsh SWvt |
| I | - 'Robusta Compacta' | EMil MWea WFar |
| | ***glabra*** | SArc |
| | - B&SWJ 8903 | WCru |
| § | - 'Parfait' (v) | CAbP ELan ERas MAsh SHBN SPer SPla WFar |
| | - 'Pink Lady' | see *P. glabra* 'Parfait' |
| | - 'Rubens' | ELan EPfP LRHS MAsh MRav SLon SPer SPla SSta WPat |
| | - 'Variegata' | see *P. glabra* 'Parfait' |
| | ***glomerata*** misapplied | see *P. prionophylla* |
| | ***lasiogyna*** | CMCN |
| | ***microphylla*** HWJ 564 | WCru |
| | ***parvifolia*** | EPfP |
| § | ***prionophylla*** | CHEx GKir |
| | 'Redstart' | CAbP CMac EBee EPfP LRHS LSou MGos NPro SLon SPer SSta SWvt WMoo |
| § | ***serratifolia*** | CBcs CDul CHEx EBee EPfP GKir LRHS MBri NLar SAPC SArc SPer SPoG SSpi WFar WPGP |
| | - 'Jenny' **new** | LSou |
| | ***serrulata*** | see *P. serratifolia* |
| | - Curly Fantasy = 'Kolcurl' | EMil MGos NLar SPoG |
| | 'Super Hedge'$^{PBR}$ | see *P.* 'Branpara' |
| | 'Super Red' **new** | CSBt |
| | ***villosa*** ♀$^{H4}$ | CAbP CGHE CTho EBee GAuc GKir MBar NPal SPoG |
| | - B&SWJ 8877 | WCru |

| | |
|---|---|
| - var. ***laevis*** | CPLG EPfP |
| - f. ***maximowicziana*** | EPfP GAuc |

## *Phragmites* (*Poaceae*)

| | |
|---|---|
| from Sichuan, China | EPPr |
| § ***australis*** | CBen CDWL CRWN CWat EBWF EMFW GFor LPBA MSKA NMir SVic SWat WFar WMAq WPnP |
| - subsp. ***australis*** var. ***striatopictus*** | EMon EPPr |
| - - 'Variegatus' (v) | CBen CDWL CKno CNat CWCL CWat EBee ECGP EHoe EMFW EMon EPPr EPla EShb EWsh LLWG LPBA LRHS MMoz MWhi NBir SHBN SLPl SMad WFar WMoo |
| - subsp. ***pseudodonax*** | EMon EPPr |
| ***communis*** | see *P. australis* |
| ***karka*** | EPPr |
| - 'Candy Stripe' (v) | CBen CDWL EPPr MSKA |
| - 'Variegatus' (v) | NLar |

## *Phrynium* (*Marantaceae*)

| | |
|---|---|
| ***pubinerve*** | CKob |

## *Phuopsis* (*Rubiaceae*)

| | |
|---|---|
| § ***stylosa*** | CHrt CSev CTri EBee ECha ELan ELon EPfP GAbr GMaP IFoB LRHS MCot MHer MLHP NBid NBir NBro NChi SPoG SRms WCAu WFar WMoo WPer |
| - 'Purpurea' | CElw EBee MNrw MRav NChi |

## *Phygelius* ✿ (*Scrophulariaceae*)

| | |
|---|---|
| ***aequalis*** | CFee MNrw MRav SPla WMoo WPer |
| - ***albus*** | see *P. aequalis* 'Yellow Trumpet' |
| - 'Apricot Trumpet' | GKir |
| - 'Aureus' | see *P. aequalis* 'Yellow Trumpet' |
| - Cedric Morris form | SHom |
| - 'Cream Trumpet' | see *P. aequalis* 'Yellow Trumpet' |
| - 'Indian Chief' | see *P.* x *rectus* 'African Queen' |
| - 'Pink Trumpet' | EAro SCoo SMrm SPet |
| - 'Sani Pass' | CBcs CPom EBee ECtt ELon EPfP GBri GMaP LAst LRHS LSRN MBri MRav MSCN SCoo SHom SPer SPet SPoG SRms SWvt |
| - 'Trewidden Pink' ♀H4 | CChe CWib EBee ELan ELon EPfP LAst LHop MAsh MHer MSCN NGdn SHom SLim SWvt WFar WHoo WMnd WMoo WPGP |
| § - 'Yellow Trumpet' ♀H3-4 | Widely available |
| § ***capensis*** ♀H3-4 | CDul CWib ELan EPfP GCra GGal LCro MHer NLar SBch SGar SHom SPet SRms SUsu WFar WMnd WPer |
| - CD&R | EWes WHil |
| - ***coccineus*** | see *P. capensis* |
| - orange-flowered | LHop SHom |
| Cherry Ripe = 'Blacher'PBR | LSou MBri |
| 'Golden Gate' | see *P. aequalis* 'Yellow Trumpet' |
| Logan form | MCCP |
| 'Madame Aerts' | WSHC |
| New Sensation = 'Blaphy'PBR | EMil MAsh SPer SWvt |
| § x ***rectus*** 'African Queen' ♀H3-4 | CFee CHrt EBee ECrN ECtt ELan EPfP GKir MLHP MRav MSwo NBir NGdn NHol SHom SMad SPlb SWvt WFar WKif WMnd WMoo WPer |
| - 'Aylesham's Pride' | SHom |
| - 'Devil's Tears' ♀H4 | CBcs CFee EBee ELan EMil EPfP GKir LAst MAvo MCot NHol SHom SLim SPad SRot SWvt WBod WMnd WMoo WPGP WPer |
| - 'Ivory Twist'PBR | LBuc LRHS SHom SPer |
| - 'Jodie Southon' | LSou SHom SUsu |
| * - 'Logan's Pink' | LSRN |
| - 'Moonraker' | CHrt CTri EBee ECtt ELan EMil EPfP GBuc LAst LRHS MAsh MHer MRav MWat NGdn NLar SHom SMad SPlb SPoG SRms SRot WFar WHoo WKif WMoo WPGP |
| - 'Pink Elf' | ELan SHom |
| - 'Raspberry Swirl'PBR | EPfP LBuc MAsh SHom |
| - 'Salmon Leap' ♀H4 | CBcs CTri EBee ELan EPfP GKir LAst LBMP LSRN MAsh MBNS SHom SLim SPad SPlb SRot SWvt WFar WHoo WMnd WMoo WPer |
| - Somerford Funfair Apricot = 'Yapapr' | SWvt |
| - Somerford Funfair Coral = 'Yapcor'PBR | CDoC EAEE EBee GKev LHop LRHS LSou MBri NLar SIng SLim SPav SRkn SWvt WFar WGor |
| - Somerford Funfair Cream = 'Yapcre'PBR | CDoC EBee EPfP LBMP LHop LRHS LSou MBri NLar NPri SGar SIng SLim SPav SPoG SRkn SWvt WFar |
| - Somerford Funfair Orange = 'Yapor'PBR | EBee LBMP LHop LRHS MBri NLar NPri SIng SLim SPav SPoG SWvt WFar WGor |
| - Somerford Funfair Wine = 'Yapwin' | CBcs EBee ELan EPfP EShb GJos LHop LSou MAsh MBNS MBri NLar NPri SGar SIng SLim SMrm SPav SPoG SRkn SWvt WFar |
| - Somerford Funfair Yellow = 'Yapyel'PBR | EBee LRHS MHav SLim SWvt |
| - 'Sunshine' | EBee ELan LHop MDKP SHom SMrm |
| - 'Sweet Dreams'PBR | LBuc LRHS SHom |
| § - 'Winchester Fanfare' | CSBt EBee ECtt ELan EMil EPfP GKir GMaP LAst LBMP MRav MWat NGdn NHol NVic SHom SLim SMrm SPer SPla SWvt WFar WGwG WMoo WPer |
| - 'Winton Fanfare' | see *P.* x *rectus* 'Winchester Fanfare' |

## *Phyla* (*Verbenaceae*)

| | |
|---|---|
| ***lanceolata*** | LLWG |
| § ***nodiflora*** | CStu ECha EEls NWCA SEND SIng WPer |
| § - var. ***canescens*** | WHal |

## *Phylica* (*Rhamnaceae*)

| | |
|---|---|
| ***arborea*** 'Superba' | CBcs IDee |

## *Phyllagathis* (*Melastomataceae*)

| | |
|---|---|
| ***cavaleriei*** new | EBee |

## *Phyllanthus* (*Euphorbiaceae*)

| | |
|---|---|
| ***glaucus*** | MBri |

## x *Phylliopsis* (*Ericaceae*)

| | |
|---|---|
| 'Coppelia' ♀H4 | CWsd GEdr GKev ITim LLHF WPat |
| ***hillieri*** 'Askival' | LSou WAbe |
| - 'Pinocchio' | GKir ITim LRHS NLar WAbe WPat WThu |
| 'Hobgoblin' | WAbe |
| 'Mermaid' | ITim WThu |
| 'Sprite' | WPat |
| 'Sugar Plum' | CCCN CWSG EBee IDee ITim NDlv NLar SSta SWvt WThu |

## *Phyllocladus* (*Phyllocladaceae*)

| | |
|---|---|
| ***alpinus*** | CDoC CDul ECou NLar |
| ***aspleniifolius*** | IDee |

## *Phyllodoce* (*Ericaceae*)

| | |
|---|---|
| ***aleutica*** | ECho NMen SRms WThu |
| x ***alpina*** | GKir |

| | | |
|---|---|---|
| | ***caerulea*** ♀H4 | ECho NLar |
| | - ***japonica*** | see *P. nipponica* |
| * | - var. ***japonica*** | GKir WThu |
| | - 'W.M. Buchanan's Peach Seedling' **new** | GKir NHar |
| | ***empetriformis*** | ECho GKir MBar SRms WThu |
| | x ***intermedia*** 'Fred Stoker' | GKev GKir |
| § | ***nipponica*** ♀H4 | NMen |
| | - var. ***oblongo-ovata*** | NMen |
| | ***tsugifolia*** | NLar |

# *Phyllostachys* ✿ (*Poaceae*)

| | | |
|---|---|---|
| | ***angusta*** | EPla MWht SBig |
| | ***arcana*** | EPla GKir |
| | - 'Luteosulcata' | CEnt CGHE EBee EPla GBin MMoz MMuc MWht NLar NPal WPGP |
| § | ***atrovaginata*** | EPla ERod |
| | ***aurea*** ♀H4 | Widely available |
| | - 'Albovariegata' (v) | EBee EFul ENBC EPla MREP |
| | - 'Flavescens Inversa' | EPla ERod MWht |
| | - 'Holochrysa' | CBrP CDul EFul EPla ERod MWht WPGP |
| | - 'Koi' | CDTJ CGHE EFul EPla ERod LPal MMoz MWht NMoo NPal SBig SEND WPGP |
| | ***aureocaulis*** | see *P. aureosulcata* f. *aureocaulis*, *P. vivax* f. *aureocaulis* |
| | ***aureosulcata*** | CWib EBee EFul EMui EPfP EPla ERod GKir LEdu LRHS MAsh MMoz MWht NMoo SBLw WBVN WMoo |
| | - f. ***alata*** | see *P. aureosulcata* f. *pekinensis* |
| | - 'Argus' | EPla |
| § | - f. ***aureocaulis*** ♀H4 | Widely available |
| | - 'Harbin' | EPla ERod |
| | - 'Harbin Inversa' | CDTJ EPla ERod |
| | - 'Lama Tempel' | CDTJ EPla WPGP |
| § | - f. ***pekinensis*** | EPla MMoz NLar SBig SPer WPGP |
| | - f. ***spectabilis*** ♀H4 | Widely available |
| | ***bambusoides*** | CDTJ EPla GKir MLan SBig SDix |
| | - 'Albovariegata' (v) **new** | EPla |
| | - 'Allgold' | see *P. bambusoides* 'Holochrysa' |
| | - 'Castilloni Inversa' | CGHE EAmu EPla ERod ETod EWes LEdu LPal MMoz MWht WPGP |
| | - 'Castillonii' | CAbb CBcs EAmu EBee EFul ENBC EPla ERod EWes GKir LEdu LPal MMoz MWht NMoo NPal SBLw SBig SDix SEND WOrn WPGP |
| § | - 'Holochrysa' | CDTJ CDoC CEnt EPla ERod MGos MMoz MWht NMoo NPal SEND WPGP |
| | - 'Katashibo' | EPla |
| | - 'Kawadana' | EPla ERod |
| | - f. ***lacrima-deae*** | CAgr CDTJ CTrC EBee EPfP EPla ETod GBin MJnS |
| | - 'Marliacea' | EPla ERod LPJP SBig |
| | - 'Subvariegata' | EPla WPGP |
| | - 'Sulphurea' | see *P. bambusoides* 'Holochrysa' |
| | - 'Tanakae' | CDTJ ENBC MMoz NLar NMoo SBig WPGP |
| | - 'Violascens' | EPla NMoo SBig |
| | ***bissetii*** | Widely available |
| | ***circumpilis*** | EPla |
| | ***congesta*** misapplied | see *P. atrovaginata* |
| | ***decora*** | EBee ENBC EPla ERod MMoz MWht NLar NMoo NPal SEND WPGP |
| | ***dulcis*** | CEnt EPfP EPla ERod LEdu LPJP MWht SBig WDyG WPGP |
| § | ***edulis*** | CAgr CDTJ CTrC EFul EPla ERod MMoz MWht SBig WPGP |
| § | - 'Heterocycla' | XBlo |
| | - f. ***pubescens*** | see *P. edulis* |
| | ***fimbriligula*** **new** | EPla |
| | ***flexuosa*** | CEnt EFul EPfP EPla GKir IMGH MWht SEND WPGP |
| | ***glauca*** | CDTJ EPla ERod ETod LCro MMoz MWht NLar NMoo NPal SBig WDyG |
| | - f. ***yunzhu*** | EPla ERod MWht |
| | ***heteroclada*** | CAgr CDTJ CEnt NMoo |
| | - 'Solid Stem' misapplied | see *P. purpurata* 'Straight Stem' |
| | ***heterocycla*** | see *P. edulis* 'Heterocycla' |
| | - f. ***pubescens*** | see *P. edulis* |
| | ***humilis*** | CBcs CDul CEnt EBee ENBC EPla ERod MCCP MGos MMoz MWhi MWht NLar NMoo NPal SBig |
| | ***iridescens*** | EPla EUJe NLar SBig |
| | ***kwangsiensis*** **new** | EPla |
| | ***lithophila*** | EPla |
| | ***lofushanensis*** | EPla |
| | ***makinoi*** | ERod |
| | ***mannii*** | EPla MWht |
| | ***meyeri*** | EPla |
| | ***nidularia*** | EPla ERod MMoz SBig |
| | - f. ***farcta*** | EPla |
| § | - f. ***glabrovagina*** | EPla |
| | - smooth-sheathed | see *P. nidularia* f. *glabrovagina* |
| | ***nigella*** | EPla |
| | ***nigra*** ♀H4 | Widely available |
| | - 'Boryana' | CAbb CDoC CEnt CGHE EAmu EBee EFul EPfP EPla GKir MAsh MGos MLan MMoz MWht NMoo SArc SBig SEND SWvt WFar WMoo WPGP |
| | - 'Fulva' | EPla |
| | - 'Hale' | EPla MWht |
| | - f. ***henonis*** ♀H4 | EAmu EFul EMil ENBC EPla ERod EUJe LPal MJnS MLan MMoz MWht NBea NLar NMoo SBig SEND WDyG WPGP |
| | - 'Megurochiku' | EPla ERod MWht |
| | - f. ***nigra*** | EPla MLan SPer |
| | - f. ***punctata*** | CDoC EBee ENBC EPfP EPla ERod MAvo MLan MWht NGdn SEND WDyG WMoo WPGP |
| | - 'Tosaensis' | EPla |
| | - 'Wisley' | EPla |
| | ***nuda*** | EAmu EPla ERod EWsh GKir MMoz MWht NLar NPal |
| | - f. ***localis*** | EPla MWht |
| | ***parvifolia*** | CEnt EPla ERod MWht WPGP |
| | ***platyglossa*** | EPla ERod WPGP |
| | ***praecox*** | EPla ETod NMoo |
| | - f. ***notata*** | EPla |
| | - f. ***viridisulcata*** | EAmu EPla |
| | ***prominens*** **new** | EPla |
| | ***propinqua*** | CDoC CDul EBee ENBC EPla ERod GBin LEdu MMoz MMuc MWht NMoo |
| | - 'Li Yu Gan' | EPla |
| * | ***pubescens*** 'Mazel' | SPlb |
| § | ***purpurata*** 'Straight Stem' | EPla MWht |
| | ***rubicunda*** | EPla |
| | ***rubromarginata*** | CDTJ CEnt EPla ERod MWht NLar WPGP |
| | 'Shanghai 3' | EAmu ETod |
| | ***stimulosa*** | EPla ERod LPan MWht |
| | ***sulphurea*** | CDTJ GKir NMoo |
| | - 'Houzeau' | EPla ERod |
| § | - 'Mitis' **new** | LMaj |
| | - 'Robert Young' | EPla |
| § | - f. ***viridis*** | EPla ERod LPal MAsh MWht NMoo SBig SEND |
| | - var. ***viridis*** 'Mitis' | see *P. sulphurea* 'Mitis' |
| | ***varioauriculata*** **new** | EBee |
| | ***violascens*** | CBcs CEnt EFul EPla ERod MMoz MWht SBig WPGP |
| | ***virella*** | EPla |

- ***viridiglaucescens*** — CBcs CDTJ EFul EPfP EPla ETod GKir LPan MAvo MBrN MMoz MWht NLar SArc SBig SEND SPla
- ***viridis*** — see *P. sulphurea* f. *viridis*
- ***vivax*** — EFul EPfP EPla ERod EUJe GKir GQui LEdu MJnS MMoz MREP MWht NLar SBig
- § - f. ***aureocaulis*** ♀$^{H4}$ — Widely available
- - - 'Huanwenzii' — CDTJ CGHE CTrC EAmu EFul EMui ENBC EPla ERod ETod MGos MMoz MWht NMoo NScw
- - 'Katrin' — LEdu
- * - 'Sulphurea' — XBlo

## x *Phyllothamnus* (*Ericaceae*)

- ***erectus*** — WAbe WPat

## *Phymatosorus* (*Polypodiaceae*)

- § ***diversifolius*** — CGHE SKHP WPGP

## *Phymosia* (*Malvaceae*)

- § ***umbellata*** — CRHN SOWG

## *Phyodina* see *Callisia*

## *Physalis* (*Solanaceae*)

- SDR 2502 **new** — GKev
- ***alkekengi*** ♀$^{H4}$ — CSec CTri EBee EPfP GKir MLan NBir NLar SWvt WFar
- - var. ***franchetii*** — CArn CPrp CSBt EBee ECha ELan EPfP LCro LRHS MHer MWat NBir NBro NCGa NPri NVic SPer SPla SPoG SRms WCAu WFar WMnd WMoo WOld WPer WTin
- - - dwarf — NLar SPoG
- - - 'Gigantea' — ECGP GBuc MNHC NChi NGBl NLar SPad SPlb WHil
- - - 'Gnome' — EBee MBri STes WFar
- - - 'Variegata' (v) — ECtt EPla EWes LEdu MAvo NPro SEND WOld
- ***angulata*** B&SWJ 7016 — WCru
- ***campanula*** B&SWJ 10409 — WCru
- ***edulis*** — see *P. peruviana*
- § ***peruviana*** (F) — CBod CCCN SHDw SVic

## *Physocarpus* (*Rosaceae*)

- ***malvaceus*** — EWes
- ***monogynus*** — NLar
- ***opulifolius*** — CDul EWTr IFFs MSal
- - 'Dart's Gold' ♀$^{H4}$ — Widely available
- - 'Diablo d'Or' — CDoC EBee EHoe EMil LRHS MAsh
- - 'Diabolo'$^{PBR}$ ♀$^{H4}$ — Widely available
- - Lady in Red = 'Tuilad'$^{PBR}$ **new** — EWes LAst MWea SPoG
- § - 'Luteus' — CDoC CMHG CSam CWib EPfP IMGH ISea MBar MRav SPer SRms WBod WDin WFar WMoo WPat
- § - 'Seward' **new** — MGos NBPN SPoG
- - Summer Wine — see *P. opulifolius* 'Seward'
- - 'Tilden Park' — EBee
- ***ribesifolius*** 'Aureus' — see *P. opulifolius* 'Luteus'

## *Physochlaina* (*Solanaceae*)

- ***orientalis*** — MSal NLar WAul

## *Physoplexis* (*Campanulaceae*)

- § ***comosa*** ♀$^{H2-3}$ — ECho EPot ITim LRHS NMen NSla

## *Physostegia* (*Lamiaceae*)

- ***angustifolia*** — NBre
- § ***virginiana*** — CSBt CTri GBar GKir GMaP LAst MBNS SGar SPoG SWat WBrk WFar WRHF
- - 'Alba' — CEnt COIW CSBt CTri EBee EHrv ELon EPfP EShb GBar GBri GJos GMaP LEdu MSte NBPC NLar NOrc SPet SPlb WHrl WRha
- § - 'Crown of Snow' — CDWL CFir CMMP EBee ECtt GKir MBNS MHer MRav MWat NPri SPoG SWal SWvt WFar WHil WPer
- - 'Grandiflora' — CFir
- - 'Miss Manners' — EAEE EBee ECtt MCot MSte NCGa SPer SRGP SUsu WHil
- - 'Olympic Gold' (v) — MDKP MRav WFar
- - 'Red Beauty' — CFir EBee MDKP SPla
- - 'Rose Crown' **new** — LRHS
- - 'Rose Queen' — COIW CTri MHar MWat NBre WTin
- - 'Rosea' — CBcs EBee GJos IFoB MDKP MMuc NBPC NBre SPad SPoG SWal SWvt WFar WHrl WPer
- - Schneekrone — see *P. virginiana* 'Crown of Snow'
- - 'Snow Queen' — see *P. virginiana* 'Summer Snow'
- - var. ***speciosa*** — WFar
- § - - 'Bouquet Rose' — CDWL CPrp EBee ECha EHrv EPfP GKir LEdu MCot MHer MNFA MRav MSte NBir NHol SPer SWvt WAul WCAu WFar WGwG WMoo WRos
- - - Rose Bouquet — see *P. virginiana* var. *speciosa* 'Bouquet Rose'
- - - 'Variegata' (v) — Widely available
- § - 'Summer Snow' ♀$^{H4}$ — CBcs CPrp EBee ECha ELan EPfP GKir LHop MBri NCGa NHol SPla SRms SWat WBrk WCAu WFar WMnd
- - 'Summer Spire' — EBee EHrv ELan MSte NHol WFar
- - 'Vivid' ♀$^{H4}$ — CKno EBee ECha ELan EMon EPfP EShb MBri MCot MRav NCGa NHol SAga SDix SPer SPet SPla SPlb SRms WCAu WCot WHil WHoo WMnd WMoo WTin
- - 'Wassenhove' — EMon SMrm

## *Phyteuma* (*Campanulaceae*)

- ***balbisii*** — see *P. cordatum*
- ***comosum*** — see *Physoplexis comosa*
- § ***cordatum*** — GJos
- ***hemisphaericum*** — ECho
- ***humile*** — EDAr
- ***nigrum*** — EBee ECho LLHF MNrw NBid NChi WPGP
- ***orbiculare*** — CSec EBWF
- ***scheuchzeri*** — CEnt CSec CSpe EBee ECho EPfP GEdr NChi NOrc NPri NWCA SBch SGar SMad SRms WHoo
- ***sieberi*** — CPBP
- ***spicatum*** — CDes NBro

## *Phytolacca* (*Phytolaccaceae*)

- ***acinosa*** — EWld GPoy MSal NLar SWat WHil
- - HWJ 647 — WCru
- § ***americana*** — CArn CHEx COld CPom CSev EBee ELan EPfP GPoy MBNS MCot MHer MSal NLar SIde SMad SRms SWat WAbb WCru WFar WHil WJek WMnd WMoo
- - B&SWJ 8817A **new** — WCru
- - 'Silberstein' (v) — CBct EBee LDai MBNS MHer NLar SBHP WCot
- - 'Variegata' — NBir
- ***clavigera*** — see *P. polyandra*
- ***decandra*** — see *P. americana*
- ***dioica*** — CHEx CPLG LEdu
- ***esculenta*** — LEdu LHop
- ***icosandra*** — EWld
- - B&SWJ 8988 — WCru
- - B&SWJ 11251 **new** — WCru
- ***japonica*** B&SWJ 3005 **new** — NBid

| | |
|---|---|
| - B&SWJ 4897 | WCru |
| ***octandra*** B&SWJ 9514 | WCru |
| § ***polyandra*** | EWld NBid NBro NLar SRms WBor |
| ***rivinoides*** B&SWJ 10264 | WCru |
| ***rugosa*** B&SWJ 7132 new | WCru |

## *Piaranthus* (*Asclepiadaceae*)

| | |
|---|---|
| § ***decorus*** subsp. ***cornutus*** new | CFwr |
| ***geminatus*** new | CFwr |
| ***ruschii*** | see *P. decorus* subsp. *cornutus* |

## *Picea* (*Pinaceae*)

| | |
|---|---|
| § ***abies*** | CCVT CChe CDul CLnd CSBt CTri CWib EHul EMac EPfP GKir IFFs LAst LBuc LRHS MBar MBri MGos MMuc NWea SCoo SLim SPer SPoG WBVN WDin WMou |
| - 'Acrocona' | ECho EHul EOrn GKir MAsh MBar MBlu MBri MGos NLar SCoo |
| - 'Archer' | CKen |
| - 'Argenteospica' (v) | ECho NHol |
| - 'Aurea' | ECho EOrn IMGH MGos |
| - 'Capitata' | CKen MBar NLar |
| - 'Ceejay's Gem' | SCoo |
| - 'Clanbrassiliana' | CDoC CKen ECho IMGH MAsh MBar MGos NLar SCoo WFar |
| - Compacta Group | ECho LBee LRHS |
| I - 'Congesta' | CKen |
| - 'Crippsii' | CKen |
| I - 'Cruenta' | CKen |
| - 'Cupressina' | CKen |
| - 'Diffusa' | CKen MBar SCoo |
| - 'Dumpy' | CKen NLar |
| - 'Elegans' | MBar |
| - 'Ellwangeriana' | NLar |
| - 'Excelsa' | see *P. abies* |
| - 'Fahndrich' | CKen CMen |
| - 'Finedonensis' | MGos NHol NLar |
| - 'Formanek' | CDoC CKen CMen ECho NLar |
| - 'Four Winds' | CAbP CKen NLar |
| - 'Frohburg' | CKen ECho GKir MBar MGos |
| - 'Globosa' | ECho MBar |
| - 'Globosa Nana' | ECho LAst MGos |
| - 'Goblin' | NLar |
| - 'Goldstart' | MGos |
| - 'Gregoryana' | CKen CMac ECho IMGH MBar NDlv WAbe |
| - 'Hasin' | NLar |
| - 'Heartland Gem' | CKen |
| - 'Himfa' | NLar |
| - 'Horace Wilson' | CKen CMen |
| - 'Humilis' | CKen |
| - 'Hystrix' | CRob NLar |
| - 'Inversa' | CKen EBrs ECho EHul EOrn GKir MBar MBlu MGos SLim |
| - 'J.W. Daisy's White' | see *P. glauca* 'J.W. Daisy's White' |
| - 'Jana' | CKen |
| - 'Kral' | CKen |
| - 'Little Gem' ♀H4 | CDoC CFee CKen CMac CMen ECho EHul EOrn GEdr GKir IMGH LBee LRHS MAsh MBar NWea SCoo SLim SPer SPoG WFar |
| - 'Marcel' new | CKen |
| - 'Maxwellii' | EHul MBar |
| - 'Mikulasovice' | NLar |
| - 'Nana' | MBar |
| - 'Nana Compacta' | CKen CMen CRob EHul IMGH LAst LBee MBar WFar |
| - 'Nidiformis' ♀H4 | CDoC CKen CMac CMen CRob CSBt CTri ECho EHul EOrn GKir LAst MBar NBlu NHol NWea SCoo SLim SPer SPoG SRms WDin WFar |
| - 'Norrkoping' | CKen |
| - 'Ohlendorffii' | CKen ECho EHul MBar MGos NLar SCoo |
| - 'Pachyphylla' | CKen |
| - 'Pendula Major' | SHBN |
| - 'Procumbens' | MBar |
| - 'Pumila' | EOrn |
| - 'Pumila Nigra' | ECho EHul MBar MGos SLim SPoG |
| - 'Pusch' | CKen CMen NLar |
| - 'Pygmaea' | CKen ECho MBar MGos NLar |
| - 'Reflexa' | ECho EHul IMGH NHol |
| - 'Repens' | ECho MBar MBlu |
| - 'Rydal' | CBcs CDoC CKen MAsh MGos NLar |
| - 'Saint James' | CKen |
| - 'Saint Mary's Broom' | CMen |
| - 'Starý Smolivec' | NLar |
| - 'Tabuliformis' | MBar |
| - 'Tompa' new | EMil |
| - 'Tufty' | EOrn |
| - 'Vermont Gold' | CKen NLar SLim |
| - 'Waugh' | MBar |
| - Will's Dwarf | see *P. abies* 'Wills Zwerg' |
| § - 'Wills Zwerg' | EMil GKir MAsh SCoo |
| ***ajanensis*** | GAuc |
| § ***alcoquiana*** var. ***alcoquiana*** | GKir NWea |
| I - 'Prostrata' | MBar |
| - var. ***reflexa*** | MPkF |
| ***asperata*** | GKir NWea |
| ***bicolor*** | see *P. alcoquiana* var. *alcoquiana* |
| I - 'Prostrata' new | MGos |
| ***brachytyla*** | GKir |
| ***breweriana*** ♀H4 | Widely available |
| - 'Emerald Midget' | NLar |
| - 'Kohout's Dwarf' | CKen |
| ***engelmannii*** | CDul GKir NWea |
| - 'Compact' | EBrs GKir |
| - subsp. ***engelmannii*** | CKen GKir |
| - 'Jasper' | NLar |
| ***glauca*** | CDul CTri NWea |
| - Alberta Blue = 'Haal'PBR | CKen CRob ECho EOrn GKir LRHS MAsh SLim WFar |
| - var. ***albertiana*** 'Alberta Globe' | CDoC CRob CSBt ECho EHul EOrn GKir IMGH LBee MAsh MBar MBri MGos NDlv NHol SAga SCoo SLim SPoG WFar |
| - - 'Conica' | Widely available |
| - - 'Gnome' | CKen |
| - - 'Laurin' | CDoC CKen CRob ECho EOrn LBee MAsh MBar MGos |
| - - 'Tiny' | CKen EOrn MBar WBor WGor |
| - 'Arneson's Blue Variegated' (v) | CDoC CKen EMil MAsh SLim WFar WGor |
| - 'Blue Planet' | CKen MGos NLar |
| - 'Blue Wonder' | MBri |
| - 'Coerulea' | ECho GKir MBar |
| I - 'Coerulea Nana' | ECho NLar |
| - 'Cy's Wonder' | CKen |
| - 'Echiniformis' ♀H4 | CKen ECho LBee MBar MBri |
| - 'Goldilocks' | CKen |
| § - 'J.W. Daisy's White' | CBcs CKen CRob EBrs ECho EMil EOrn GKir LRHS MAsh MGos NLar NWea SCoo SLim SPer SPoG WBor WFar WGor |
| I - 'Julian Potts Monstrosa' | NLar |
| - 'Lilliput' | CKen ECho EHul EMil EOrn MBar MBri MGos NLar |
| § - 'Nana' | CKen |
| - 'Piccolo' | CBcs CKen ECho GKir LRHS MAsh NHol SLim |
| - 'Pixie' | CKen |

| | | |
|---|---|---|
| | - 'Rainbow's End' (v) | CKen ECho EMil MGos NLar SLim WFar |
| | - 'Sander's Blue' | CKen CRob ECho EOrn EPfP LAst LBee MBri MGos SLim SPoG WFar |
| | - 'Zuckerhut' | MBar MBri |
| | ***glehnii*** 'Sasanosei' | CKen |
| | - 'Shimezusei' | CKen |
| | ***jezoensis*** | CKen CMen GKir MGos |
| | - 'Chinese Marl' | NLar |
| | - subsp. ***hondoensis*** | CMen GKir |
| | - 'Marianbad' **new** | CKen |
| | - 'Yatsabusa' | CKen CMen |
| | ***koraiensis*** | GAuc GKir NWea |
| | ***kosteri*** 'Glauca' | see *P. pungens* 'Koster' |
| | ***koyamae*** | GKir NWea |
| | ***likiangensis*** | CDul EPfP ISea |
| | - var. ***balfouriana*** | see *P. likiangensis* var. *rubescens* |
| | - var. ***purpurea*** | see *P. purpurea* |
| § | - var. ***rubescens*** | GKir MGos NHol WOrn |
| | ***mariana*** | GGar GKir NWea |
| | - 'Aureovariegata' (v) | ECho WFar |
| | - 'Austria Broom' | CKen |
| | - 'Doumetii' | EOrn |
| | - 'Fastigiata' | CKen EOrn |
| | - 'Nana' ♀H4 | Widely available |
| I | - 'Pygmaea' | CKen |
| | x ***mariorika*** | MBar |
| | - 'Gnom' | MGos |
| | - 'Machala' | ECho |
| | ***meyeri*** | GKir |
| | ***morrisonicola*** | CKen GKir |
| | ***obovata*** | GAuc |
| | - var. ***coerulea*** | GAuc GKir NLar NWea |
| | ***omorika*** ♀H4 | CBcs CDul CMCN EMac EWTr GKir IFFs LBuc MBar MGos NWea SPer SPoG WCFE WDin WFar WMou WRHF |
| I | - 'Aurea' | ECho |
| | - 'Bruns' **new** | GKir |
| | - 'Frohnleiten' | CKen |
| | - 'Frondenberg' | CKen ECho |
| | - 'Karel' | CKen NLar |
| | - 'Minimax' | CKen ECho |
| | - 'Nana' ♀H4 | ECho EHul GKir MAsh MBar MGos SCoo SLim SPoG WFar |
| | - 'Pendula' ♀H4 | CDoC ECho GKir LRHS MBar MBlu NLar NPal SLim SPoG SSta |
| | - 'Pendula Bruns' **new** | SLim |
| | - 'Peve Tijn' | LRHS NLar SPoG |
| | - 'Pimoko' | CKen GKir MAsh MGos NLar SCoo |
| | - 'Pygmy' | CKen |
| | - 'Schneverdingen' | CKen |
| | - 'Tijn' | CKen SLim |
| | - 'Treblitsch' | CKen NLar |
| | ***orientalis*** ♀H4 | CDul GKir NWea WMou |
| | - 'Aurea' (v) ♀H4 | CMac ECho ECrN EHul ELan GKir LPan MBar MBri MGos MLan NHol NPri SCoo SHBN SLim WDin |
| | - 'Aureospicata' | CDoC CTho ECho MAsh MBlu SCoo |
| | - 'Bergman's Gem' | CKen |
| | - 'Early Gold' (v) | WFar |
| | - 'Golden Start' | NLar SLim |
| | - 'Gowdy' | MBar NLar |
| | - 'Jewel' | CKen NLar |
| | - 'Kenwith' | CKen ECho |
| | - 'Mount Vernon' | CKen |
| | - Nana Group | SCoo |
| | - Pendula Group | MGos |
| | - 'Professor Langner' | CKen SLim |
| | - 'Skylands' | CDoC CKen ECho ELan GKir MAsh MBri MGos NHol NLar SLim SPoG |
| | - 'Tom Thumb' | CKen NLar SLim |
| | - 'Wittboldt' | MAsh |
| | ***pungens*** | GKir MBar WDin |
| | - 'Baby Blueeyes' | ECho MPkF WFar |
| | - 'Blaukissen' | CKen |
| | - 'Blue Mountain' | ECho LAst MPkF NScw |
| | - 'Blue Pearl' | NLar |
| | - 'Blue Trinket' | GKir |
| | - 'Drayer' | ECho MPkF |
| | - 'Edith' | CKen EBrs GKir LRHS MPkF SLim WFar |
| | - 'Endtz' | EBrs ECho MPkF |
| | - 'Erich Frahm' | CTri ECho GKir LRHS MAsh MBar MGos MPkF SLim WFar |
| | - 'Fat Albert' | CDul CWib ECho GKir MGos NLar SLim SPoG WFar |
| | - 'Frieda' | NLar SLim |
| | - Glauca Group | CDul CLnd EMac EWTr GKir MBar NWea SCoo SPoG WBVN WDin WFar WMou WOrn |
| | - - 'Glauca Procumbens' | CMen NLar |
| § | - - 'Glauca Prostrata' | ECho EHul GKir MBar |
| | - 'Glauca Globosa' | see *P. pungens* 'Globosa' |
| | - 'Globe' | CKen CMen |
| I | - 'Globosa' ♀H4 | CBcs CDoC CKen CRob CSBt ECho EHul EOrn GKir LBee MAsh MBar MBri MGos NPri NWea SCoo SHBN SLim SPer SPoG SRms WFar |
| I | - 'Globosa Viridis' | ECho |
| | - 'Gloria' | CKen GKir |
| | - 'Hoopsii' ♀H4 | CDul CMac CRob CSBt ECho EHul EPfP GKir LAst LMaj LRHS MAsh MBar MGos NBlu NWea SHBN SLim SPoG SWvt WDin WFar |
| | - 'Hoto' | EHul EOrn GKir MBar MGos |
| | - 'Hunnewelliana' | EOrn |
| | - 'Iseli Fastigiate' | CRob ECho GKir MAsh MBri MGos SCoo SLim SPer SPoG |
| | - 'Iseli Foxtail' | NLar |
| § | - 'Koster' ♀H4 | CDoC CMac CRob CSBt ECho EHul EPfP GKir MBar MGos NScw NWea SLim SPoG SRms WDin WFar |
| | - 'Lucky Strike' | CDoC CKen ECho MGos NLar |
| | - 'Maigold' (v) | CKen EBrs ECho MAsh NLar SLim |
| | - 'Moerheimii' | ECho EHul MBar NLar |
| | - 'Montgomery' | CKen ECho GKir MBar NLar |
| | - 'Mrs Cesarini' | CKen |
| | - 'Nimety' | CKen NLar |
| | - 'Oldenburg' | GKir LAst MBar NLar NWea SLim |
| | - 'Procumbens' | CKen |
| | - 'Prostrata' | see *P. pungens* 'Glauca Prostrata' |
| | - 'Rovelli's Monument' | NLar |
| | - 'Saint Mary's Broom' | CKen NLar |
| | - 'Schovenhorst' | ECho EHul WFar |
| | - 'Snowkiss' | ECho MPkF WFar |
| | - 'Spek' | ECho GKir MGos MPkF |
| | - 'Thomsen' | ECho EHul GKir MAsh NScw |
| | - 'Thuem' | ECho EHul EPfP MGos NDlv NLar WFar |
| | - 'Waldbrunn' | CKen ECho MAsh SLim SPoG |
| | - 'Wendy' | CKen |
| § | ***purpurea*** | GKir |
| | ***retroflexa*** | NWea |
| | ***rubens*** | NLar NWea |
| | ***schrenkiana*** | CMCN GKir |
| | ***sitchensis*** | CDul GKir IFFs NWea WMou |
| | - 'Nana' | CDoC ECho |
| | - 'Papoose' | see *P. sitchensis* 'Tenas' |
| | - 'Silberzwerg' | CKen ECho NLar SLim SPoG |
| | - 'Strypemonde' | CKen |
| § | - 'Tenas' | CDoC CKen CRob EBrs ECho EOrn GKir MAsh NLar SLim SPoG |
| | ***smithiana*** | CDul CTho EPfP GKir ISea NLar NWea |

| | | |
|---|---|---|
| I | - 'Aurea' | MGos |
| | - 'Sunray' | SLim |
| | ***wilsonii*** | CKen GKir NLar |

## *Picrasma* (*Simaroubaceae*)

| | | |
|---|---|---|
| | ***ailanthoides*** | see *P. quassioides* |
| § | ***quassioides*** | EPfP MBri WPGP |

## *Picris* (*Asteraceae*)

| | | |
|---|---|---|
| | ***echioides*** | CArn WHer |

## *Picrorhiza* (*Scrophulariaceae*)

| | | |
|---|---|---|
| | ***kurrooa*** | GPoy |

## *Pieris* ✿ (*Ericaceae*)

| | | |
|---|---|---|
| | 'Bert Chandler' | LRHS MAsh SPoG SSpi |
| | 'Brouwer's Beauty' | SLim |
| | 'Firecrest' 𝕐H4 | CMHG CTrG MMuc SSpi |
| | 'Flaming Silver' (v) 𝕐H4 | Widely available |
| | ***floribunda*** | GKir |
| | 'Forest Flame' 𝕐H4 | Widely available |
| | ***formosa*** B&SWJ 2257 | WCru |
| | - var. ***forrestii*** | CDoC CWib ISea NWea |
| | - - 'Fota Pink' | WHar |
| | - - 'Jermyns' | MRav SHBN |
| | - - 'Wakehurst' 𝕐H3 | CAbP CDul CTrG CTri CWSG ELon EPfP ISea LHyd LRHS MAsh MGos MRav NWea SPer SSpi WBod WFar |
| | Havila = 'Mouwsvila' (v) | MGos NHol NLar WFar |
| | ***japonica*** | GGal GKir MGos SArc SReu WDin |
| | - 'Astrid' | MGos |
| | - 'Bisbee Dwarf' | MBar NHol |
| | - 'Blush' 𝕐H4 | GKir LRHS MBri MGos NHol SHBN |
| | - 'Bonfire' | CCCN CEnd EBee ELan EMil EQua ISea LBuc LRHS MBri MGos NLar SPoG |
| | - 'Brookside Miniature' | NHol |
| | - 'Carnaval' (v) | CCCN CDoC CEnd CSBt CWib EBee ELan ELon EMil ISea LBuc LRHS LSRN MAsh MGos NLar NPri SCoo SPer SPoG SWvt WFar |
| | - 'Cavatine' 𝕐H4 | CMHG GKir LRHS |
| § | - 'Christmas Cheer' | EMil EQua GKir LSou NLar SSto WFar WMoo |
| | - 'Cupido' | CDoC EMil GKir MAsh MBar MGos NHol NLar SPoG WBod WFar |
| | - 'Debutante' 𝕐H4 | CBcs CWSG CWib EBee ELan EMil EPfP GKir LRHS MAsh MBri MDun MGos NHol NLar NPri SCoo SPoG SSpi SWvt WFar |
| | - 'Don' | see *P. japonica* 'Pygmaea' |
| | - 'Dorothy Wyckoff' | CMHG CSBt CTrG CWSG GKir LRHS MDun NDlv NHol SHBN SPer SSta |
| | - 'Flaming Star' | ECot SWvt |
| | - 'Flamingo' | GKev LRHS MBar MGos NDlv NHol |
| | - 'Grayswood' 𝕐H4 | EPfP NHol WFar |
| I | - 'Katsura' | CBcs CDoC CMac CSBt EBee ELan EMil EPfP GKir LBuc LRHS MAsh MBlu MBri MGos NLar NPri SCoo SPer SPoG SRkn SSpi SSta WBod |
| | - 'Little Heath' (v) 𝕐H4 | Widely available |
| | - 'Little Heath Green' 𝕐H4 | CChe CDoC CSBt CTrG GKir LHyd MAsh MBar MGos MMuc NDlv NHol NPri SPer SPoG SSta SSto SWvt WFar WMoo |
| | - 'Minor' | GKev MBar NHol WThu |
| | - 'Mountain Fire' 𝕐H4 | Widely available |
| | - 'Passion' **new** | CEnd MGos |
| | - 'Pink Delight' 𝕐H4 | CAbP CDoC GKir LRHS LSRN LSou MBar MRav SHBN SPoG SRms SSto WGwG |
| | - 'Prelude' 𝕐H4 | CSBt CTrG CWSG EMil GKev GKir LRHS MAsh MRav NHol NLar NMen SPad SPoG WAbe WBod WFar |
| | - 'Purity' 𝕐H4 | CBcs CDoC CMHG CWSG EPfP GKir LRHS MBar MGos NHol SPer SReu SSta SSto SWvt WBod WDin WFar |
| § | - 'Pygmaea' | NHol SSta |
| | - 'Red Mill' | CEnd CSBt CWSG EPfP GKir MAsh MHav SPer SSpi WFar |
| | - 'Rosalinda' | NLar WFar |
| | - 'Rosea' | LHyd |
| | - 'Sarabande' 𝕐H4 | GKir MAsh MBar NLar SPoG SSta |
| | - 'Scarlett O'Hara' | CSBt GKir MGos NLar |
| | - 'Select' | MGos |
| | - 'Silver Mills' | MGos |
| | - Taiwanensis Group | CMHG EPfP GGar LRHS MBar MDun NLar NWea SRms SSta WFar |
| | - 'Temple Bells' | CSBt GKir MGos |
| | - 'Tickled Pink' | GKir |
| | - 'Valley Rose' | CGHE CSBt ELan ELon EPfP GKir LLHF MAsh MGos MHav NLar SMad SPoG SSpi WFar |
| | - 'Valley Valentine' 𝕐H4 | Widely available |
| | - 'Variegata' misapplied | see *P. japonica* 'White Rim' |
| | - 'Variegata' ambig. | MMuc |
| | - 'Variegata' (Carrière) Bean (v) | CMHG EPfP GKir LHyd MAsh MBar MGos NHol SHBN SPer SPoG SReu SSta WDin WFar WHar |
| | - 'Wada's Pink' | see *P. japonica* 'Christmas Cheer' |
| | - 'White Pearl' | CAbP MAsh MGos |
| § | - 'White Rim' (v) 𝕐H4 | CDul CSBt EPfP MAsh SPlb WBod WFar |
| | - 'William Buchanan' | MBar NHol WThu |
| | - var. ***yakushimensis*** | NLar |
| | ***koidzumiana*** | CWsd SSta |
| | ***nana*** | GKev GKir WThu |

## *Pilea* (*Urticaceae*)

| | | |
|---|---|---|
| * | 'Anette' | MBri |
| | ***cadierei*** 𝕐H1 | CHal MBri |
| | ***depressa*** | CHal |
| | ***involucrata*** 'Norfolk' 𝕐H1 | CHal |
| § | ***microphylla*** | CHal EBak EShb |
| | ***muscosa*** | see *P. microphylla* |
| | ***nummulariifolia*** | CHal |
| | ***peperomioides*** 𝕐H1 | CHal CSev |
| | ***repens*** | MBri |

## *Pileostegia* (*Hydrangeaceae*)

| | | |
|---|---|---|
| | sp **new** | GGal |
| | ***viburnoides*** 𝕐H4 | Widely available |
| | - B&SWJ 3565 | WCru |
| | - B&SWJ 7132 **new** | WCru |

## *Pilosella* (*Asteraceae*)

| | | |
|---|---|---|
| § | ***aurantiaca*** | CArn CHrt CMCo CRWN CSec CSsd EBWF ELan LEdu MHer NBid NOrc NPri SECG SIde WCAu WFar WHer WMoo WSFF |
| § | - subsp. ***carpathicola*** | GGar |
| § | ***officinarum*** | EBWF NBlu NRya |
| | x ***stoloniflora*** 'Phil Clark' **new** | WAlt |

## *Pilularia* (*Marsileaceae*)

| | | |
|---|---|---|
| | ***globulifera*** | CBgR |

## *Pimelea* (*Thymelaeaceae*)

| | | |
|---|---|---|
| | ***coarctata*** | see *P. prostrata* |
| | ***drupacea*** | ECou |
| | ***ferruginea*** | ECou |
| | - 'Magenta Mist' | SOWG |

| | | |
|---|---|---|
| | ***filiformis*** | ECou |
| | ***ligustrina*** | GGar |
| § | ***prostrata*** | CTri ECho ECou EPot LRHS MBar SRot WPer |
| | - f. ***parvifolia*** | ECou |
| | ***tomentosa*** | ECou LRHS |

## *Pimpinella* (*Apiaceae*)

| | | |
|---|---|---|
| | ***anisum*** | CArn MSal SIde SVic |
| | ***bicknellii*** | EBee WPGP |
| | ***flahaultii*** | EBee |
| | ***major*** new | EBWF |
| | - 'Rosea' | Widely available |
| | ***saxifraga*** | LEdu NBre |

## pineapple guava see *Acca sellowiana*

## pineapple see *Ananas comosus*

## *Pinellia* (*Araceae*)

| | | |
|---|---|---|
| | ***cordata*** | CPom CSec EBee LEdu MDKP MSte NMen SChF WCot WCru |
| | - pink-flowered new | GEdr |
| | ***pedatisecta*** | CDes CPom EBee GEdr LEdu LFur LPio MDKP SChF WCot |
| | ***pinnatisecta*** | see *P. tripartita* |
| | ***ternata*** | CSec CStu EBee EBrs GEdr LEdu MSal NMen WCot WPnP WWst |
| | - B&SWJ 3532 | WCru |
| § | ***tripartita*** | CFee CPLG CPom CStu EBee ECho LFur MDKP SChF WAbe WBVN WCot WPrP |
| | - B&SWJ 1102 | WCru |
| | - 'Dragon Tails' (v) new | SKHP |
| | - 'Purple Face' | WCru |
| | - 'Silver Dragon' new | GEdr |

## *Pinguicula* (*Lentibulariaceae*)

| | | |
|---|---|---|
| | ***acuminata*** | SHmp |
| | ***crassifolia*** | CHew |
| | ***crassifolia*** × ***emarginata*** | SHmp |
| | ***cyclosecta*** | CHew CSWC SHmp |
| | ***debbertiana*** new | SHmp |
| | ***ehlersiae*** | EFEx |
| | ***esseriana*** | CSWC EFEx |
| | ***grandiflora*** | CSWC EECP EFEx GCra LRHS MCCP NMen NRya NWCA WAbe |
| | ***hemiepiphytica*** | CHew |
| | ***heterophylla*** | CHew SHmp |
| | ***jaumavensis*** | CHew |
| | ***lauana*** | CHew SHmp |
| | ***leptoceras*** | CFir |
| | ***longifolia*** subsp. ***longifolia*** | EFEx |
| | ***macrophylla*** | CHew SHmp |
| | ***macrophylla*** × ***zecheri*** | SHmp |
| | ***moctezumae*** | SHmp |
| | ***moranensis*** var. ***caudata*** | EFEx |
| | - ***moreana*** | EFEx |
| | - ***superba*** | EFEx |
| * | ***pilosa*** | SHmp |
| | ***rotundiflora*** | CHew SHmp |
| | ***vulgaris*** | EFEx |
| | 'Weser' | CSWC |

## pinkcurrant see *Ribes rubrum* (P)

## *Pinus* ✿ (*Pinaceae*)

| | | |
|---|---|---|
| | ***albicaulis*** 'Flinck' | CKen |
| | - 'Nana' | see *P. albicaulis* 'Noble's Dwarf' |
| | - 'No. 3' | CKen |
| § | - 'Noble's Dwarf' | CKen |
| | ***aristata*** | CDul CLnd EHul EOrn GKir MAsh MBar MBlu MBri MGos SCoo WDin |
| | - 'Cecilia' | CKen |
| | - 'Kohout's Mini' | CKen |
| | - 'Sherwood Compact' | CKen GKir NLar |
| | - 'So Tight' | CKen |
| | ***armandii*** | CAgr CDoC CDul CTrC GKev GKir |
| | - 'Gold Tip' | CKen |
| | ***attenuata*** | GKir |
| | ***austriaca*** | see *P. nigra* subsp. *nigra* |
| N | ***ayacahuite*** | CKen GKir |
| | - F&M 100A | WPGP |
| | ***balfouriana*** 'Dwarf Form' J.W. Spingarn | CKen |
| | ***banksiana*** | CDul GKir SCoo |
| | - 'Arctis' | NLar |
| | - 'Chippewa' | CKen ECho |
| I | - 'Compacta' | CKen |
| | - 'H.J. Welch' | CKen |
| | - 'Manomet' | CKen |
| | - 'Neponset' | CKen |
| | - 'Schneverdingen' | CKen NLar |
| | - 'Schoodic' | ECho NLar SLim SPoG |
| | - 'Uncle Fogy' | ECho MGos NLar |
| | - 'Wisconsin' | CKen |
| | ***brutia*** | CDoC |
| | - var. ***eldarica*** | GAuc |
| | ***bungeana*** | CDoC CDul CLnd CMCN CTho EPfP GKir MBlu SLPl |
| | - 'Diamant' | CKen |
| | - 'June's Broom' new | CKen |
| | ***canariensis*** | EHul GGar IDee |
| | ***cembra*** | CAgr CDul CLnd EHul GKir MBar NLar NWea STre |
| | - 'Aurea' | see *P. cembra* 'Aureovariegata' |
| § | - 'Aureovariegata' (v) | ECho LRHS SCoo SPoG |
| | - 'Barnhourie' | CKen |
| | - 'Blue Mound' | CKen |
| | - 'Chalet' | CKen |
| | - 'Compacta Glauca' | ECho MBri |
| | - Glauca Group | SCoo |
| * | - 'Griffithii' | WDin |
| | - 'Inverleith' | CKen |
| | - 'Jermyns' | CKen |
| | - 'King's Dwarf' | CKen |
| | - 'Ortler' | CKen |
| | - 'Roughills' | CKen |
| | - 'Stricta' | CKen ECho |
| | - witches' broom | CKen |
| | ***contorta*** | CBcs CDoC CDul GKir IFFs MBar MGos NWea SPlb WDin WMou |
| | - 'Asher' | CKen ECho SCoo |
| I | - 'Compacta' | SCoo |
| | - 'Frisian Gold' | CKen SLim |
| | - var. ***latifolia*** | CDul CLnd GKir WDin |
| | - 'Spaan's Dwarf' | CKen ECho MBar MGos NLar SCoo SLim SPoG |
| | ***coulteri*** ♀H4 | CDul CMCN CTho ECho EPfP GKir SBig SCoo SKHP WThu |
| | ***densiflora*** | CDul CMCN GAuc LEdu |
| | - 'Alice Verkade' | CDoC CMen CRob ECho EHul GKir LRHS MAsh MBri NLar SCoo SLim WFar |
| | - 'Aurea' | MBar MGos NLar SLim |
| | - 'Golden Ghost' | NLar SLim |
| | - 'Jane Kluis' | CKen ECho EHul EOrn GKir LRHS MBri NHol NLar SCoo SLim WFar |
| | - 'Jim Cross' | CKen |
| | - 'Low Glow' | CKen ECho EOrn LRHS NLar NScw SLim |
| | - 'Oculus-draconis' (v) | ECho EOrn GKir MBar MGos NLar SLim WFar |

| | | |
|---|---|---|
| | - 'Pendula' | CKen ECho EOrn NLar SCoo SLim WFar |
| I | - 'Pygmaea' **new** | EOrn |
| * | - 'Pyramidalis' | ECho |
| | - 'Umbraculifera' | CDoC CMen ECho GKir IMGH MAsh MBar MGos NLar SCoo SSta WFar |
| I | - 'Umbraculifera Nana' | ECho |
| § | ***devoniana*** | CBrP CDoC LRHS SLim |
| | ***edulis*** | CAgr GAuc |
| | - 'Juno' | CKen |
| | ***elliottii*** | SBig |
| | ***engelmanii*** 'Glauca' | EBrs WFar |
| | ***fenzeliana*** **new** | CKen |
| | ***flexilis*** | CDul NWea |
| | - 'Firmament' | ECho SLim SPoG |
| | - 'Glenmore Dwarf' | CKen |
| | - 'Nana' | CKen |
| | - 'Tarryall' | CKen |
| | - 'Vanderwolf's Pyramid' | CRob MAsh NLar |
| | - WB No 1 | CKen |
| | - WB No 2 | CKen |
| | ***gerardiana*** | GAuc GKir |
| | ***greggii*** | EPfP IDee |
| | ***griffithii*** | see *P. wallichiana* |
| | ***halepensis*** | GAuc |
| § | ***hartwegii*** | CDul |
| § | ***heldreichii*** 🏆H4 | CDoC ECho GKir LPan MBar MGos SCoo WFar WHCr |
| | - 'Aureospicata' | MBar NLar |
| | - 'Compact Gem' | CDoC CKen EBrs ECho LBee LRHS MBar MBri MGos NLar SCoo SLim SSta |
| | - 'Dolce Dorme' | CKen NLar |
| | - 'Groen' | CKen |
| | - 'Kalous' | NLar |
| | - var. ***leucodermis*** | see *P. heldreichii* |
| | - - 'Irish Bell' | NLar |
| | - - 'Pirin 7' | NLar |
| | - 'Malink' | CKen ECho SLim |
| | - 'Ottocek' | CKen |
| | - 'Pygmy' | CKen ECho |
| | - 'Satellit' | CDoC CTri ECho EHul EMil EOrn GKir LRHS MAsh MGos NLar SCoo SLim SPoG |
| | - 'Schmidtii' | see *P. heldreichii* 'Smidtii' |
| § | - 'Smidtii' 🏆H4 | CDoC CKen CRob ECho GKir LRHS MAsh MBar MGos NLar SLim |
| | - 'Zwerg Schneverdingen' | CKen NLar |
| | ***jeffreyi*** 🏆H4 | CTho GAuc GKir ISea MBar NWea |
| | - 'Joppi' | CKen CRob NLar SLim |
| | ***koraiensis*** | GKir NWea SCoo SLim |
| | - 'Bergman' | CKen |
| | - 'Dragon Eye' | CKen |
| | - 'Jack Corbit' | CKen |
| | - 'Shibamichi' (v) | CKen |
| | - 'Silver Lining' | MAsh |
| | - 'Silveray' | MAsh NLar SLim |
| | - 'Silvergrey' | CKen |
| | - 'Winton' | CKen NLar SLim |
| | ***leucodermis*** | see *P. heldreichii* |
| | ***magnifica*** | see *P. devoniana* |
| * | ***meyerei*** **new** | GAuc |
| | ***monophylla*** | ECho |
| | ***montezumae*** misapplied | see *P. hartwegii* |
| | ***montezumae*** ambig. | SAPC SArc |
| | ***montezumae*** Lamb. | CDul SBig |
| | ***monticola*** | CDul |
| | - 'Pendula' | CKen MBar |
| | - 'Pygmy' | see *P. monticola* 'Raraflora' |
| § | - 'Raraflora' | CKen |
| | - 'Skyline' | MBar NLar |
| | - 'Windsor Dwarf' | CKen |
| | ***mugo*** | CArn CBcs CChe CDul CSBt CTri EHul GKir MBar MGos NWea WBrE WDin WFar |
| | - 'Allgau' | CKen |
| | - 'Amber Glow' **new** | NLar |
| | - 'Benjamin' | CKen ECho MGos NLar SCoo |
| | - 'Bisley Green' | ECho EMil |
| | - 'Brownie' | CKen |
| | - 'Carsten' | CKen ECho MGos SCoo SLim |
| | - 'Carsten's Wintergold' | EMil GKir MAsh MBri NLar SCoo SPoG |
| | - 'Chameleon' | NLar |
| | - 'Corley's Mat' | CKen ECho GKir LAst NHol NLar SCoo SLim |
| | - 'Dachstein 3' | NLar |
| | - 'Devon Gem' | ECho SPoG |
| | - 'Dezember Gold' | NLar SLim |
| | - 'Flanders Belle' | ECho SCoo SLim SPoG |
| | - 'Gnom' | CDul ECho EHul EOrn GKir IMGH LRHS MBar MBri MGos SCoo WDin WFar |
| | - 'Golden Glow' | CKen ECho MBri NLar SCoo SLim |
| | - 'Hesse' | ECho GKir SCoo |
| | - 'Hoersholm' | CKen ECho |
| | - 'Humpy' | CKen CMen CRob ECho EOrn GKir IMGH LBee LRHS MAsh MBar MBri MGos NLar SCoo SLim WFar |
| | - 'Ironsides' | CKen |
| | - 'Jacobsen' | CKen NLar |
| | - 'Janovsky' | CKen ECho EOrn SCoo |
| | - 'Kamila' | NLar |
| | - 'Kissen' | CKen ECho MGos NLar |
| | - 'Klosterkotter' | ECho MGos NLar SCoo WFar |
| | - 'Kobold' | ECho NHol WFar |
| | - 'Krauskopf' | CKen |
| | - 'Laarheide' | CRob ECho GKir SCoo |
| | - 'Laurin' | CKen ECho |
| | - 'Little Lady' | NLar |
| | - 'Marand' | ECho |
| | - 'March' | CKen ECho EHul |
| | - 'Mini Mops' | CKen ECho NLar |
| | - 'Minikin' | CKen EOrn MAsh |
| | - 'Mops' 🏆H4 | CDul CMen CRob ECho EHul EPfP GKir LBee LRHS MAsh MBar MBlu MBri MGos NHol NPri NWea SCoo SLim SPer SPoG SSta WDin WFar |
| | - 'Mops Midget' | CRob ECho EOrn MAsh |
| | - var. ***mughus*** | see *P. mugo* subsp. *mugo* |
| § | - subsp. ***mugo*** | EMac EOrn GAuc LPan MBar NBlu NWea WCFE WFar |
| | - 'Mumpitz' | CKen |
| | - 'Ophir' | CBcs CDoC CDul CKen CMen CRob ECho EHul EOrn EPfP GKir IMGH LAst LBee LRHS MBar MBri MGos NLar SCoo SLim SPer SPla SSta WDin WFar |
| | - 'Orange Sun' | MBri |
| | - 'Pal Maleter' (v) | CRob ECho GKir MAsh NLar SCoo SLim SPoG |
| | - 'Paradekissen' | NLar |
| | - 'Paul's Dwarf' | CKen NLar |
| | - 'Picobello' | LRHS NLar SLim |
| | - 'Piggelmee' | CKen ECho NLar |
| | - Pumilio Group 🏆H4 | CDoC CDul CLnd ECho ECrN EHul EOrn GBin IFFs MBar MGos NBlu NHol NWea SCoo SHBN STre WBVN WCFE WDin WFar WMoo |
| | - 'Pygmy' | ECho |
| | - var. ***rostrata*** | see *P. mugo* subsp. *uncinata* |
| | - 'Rushmore' | CKen |
| | - 'Schilderhaus' | NLar |
| | - 'Spaan' | CKen |
| | - 'Sunshine' (v) | CKen NLar |

| | | |
|---|---|---|
| | - 'Suzi' | CKen |
| | - 'Tuffet' | ECho MGos NLar |
| | - 'Uelzen' | CKen NLar |
| § | - subsp. ***uncinata*** | GAuc LMaj NWea SCoo SLim WFar |
| | - - 'Grüne Welle' | CKen ECho NLar SLim |
| | - - 'Paradekissen' | CKen NLar |
| | - 'Varella' | CKen LRHS NLar SCoo SLim |
| | - 'White Tip' | CKen ECho |
| | - 'Winter Gold' | CKen EBrs ECho EHul EOrn EPfP LAst LPan MGos NLar NWea SPoG SSta WFar |
| | - 'Winter Sun' | CRob ECho |
| | - 'Winzig' | CKen |
| | - 'Zundert' | CKen ECho EHul GKir MBar MGos NLar |
| | - 'Zwergkugel' | CKen |
| | ***muricata*** 𝕐H4 | CDoC CDul CLnd GKir MGos NWea |
| | ***nigra*** 𝕐H4 | CBcs CDul CLnd CSBt CTri ECrN GKir LMaj MBar MGos SAPC SArc SCoo SHBN WBrE WDin WMou |
| | - var. ***austriaca*** | see *P. nigra* subsp. *nigra* |
| | - 'Bambino' | CKen |
| | - 'Black Prince' | CKen EBrs ECho EOrn GKir IMGH LBee LRHS MAsh MGos NLar SCoo SLim SPoG WFar WGor |
| | - var. ***calabrica*** | see *P. nigra* subsp. *laricio* |
| | - var. ***caramanica*** | see *P. nigra* subsp. *pallasiana* |
| N | - 'Cebennensis Nana' | CKen |
| | - var. ***corsicana*** | see *P. nigra* subsp. *laricio* |
| * | - 'Fastigiata' | GKir |
| | - 'Frank' | CKen ECho NLar |
| | - 'Globosa' | ECho |
| | - 'Green Tower' | NLar |
| | - 'Hornibrookiana' | CKen ECho NLar SCoo |
| | - 'Komet' | NLar SCoo |
| § | - subsp. ***laricio*** 𝕐H4 | CCVT CDoC CDul CKen ECrN EMac LAst MBar MGos NWea SBLw WMou |
| | - - 'Bobby McGregor' | CKen ECho GKir |
| | - - 'Globosa Viridis' | ECho GKir IMGH NHol SLim |
| | - - 'Goldfingers' | CKen ECho NLar SLim |
| | - - 'Moseri' | CKen ECho EOrn SLim SSta |
| | - - 'Pygmaea' | CKen ECho EOrn WFar |
| | - - 'Spingarn' | CKen ECho |
| | - - 'Talland Bay' | CKen ECho |
| | - - 'Wurstle' | CKen |
| | - subsp. ***maritima*** | see *P. nigra* subsp. *laricio* |
| | - 'Molette' | GKir |
| | - 'Nana' | ECrN MBri |
| § | - subsp. ***nigra*** | CCVT CDoC CLnd CTho ECrN GKir IFFs LPan MGos NLar NWea SPer WFar |
| | - - 'Birte' | CKen |
| | - - 'Bright Eyes' | ECho EOrn GKir IMGH LBee LRHS MAsh SCoo SLim SPoG |
| | - - 'Helga' | CKen NLar SCoo |
| | - - 'Schovenhorst' | CKen ECho |
| | - - 'Skyborn' | CKen |
| | - - 'Strypemonde' | CKen |
| | - - 'Yaffle Hill' | CKen ECho |
| | - 'Obelisk' | CKen NLar SCoo |
| § | - subsp. ***pallasiana*** | CDul NLar |
| | - 'Richard' | CKen NLar |
| | - 'Rondello' | NLar |
| | - 'Spielberg' | NLar |
| | ***oocarpa*** | CDul |
| | ***palustris*** | CDoC CDul CLnd LRHS MAsh SBig SKHP SLim |
| | ***parviflora*** | CTri GKir SPlb WDin WThu |
| | - 'Adcock's Dwarf' 𝕐H4 | CDoC CKen ECho GKir MBar MGos NLar SCoo SLim SPoG |
| | - Aizu-goyo Group | ECho |
| | - 'Al Fordham' | CKen |
| | - 'Aoi' | CKen CMen |
| | - 'Ara-kawa' | CKen CMen |
| | - 'Atco-goyo' **<u>new</u>** | CKen |
| | - Azuma-goyo Group | CKen CMen |
| I | - 'Baasch's Form' | CKen MGos |
| | - 'Bergman' | CDoC ECho MAsh MBar NLar |
| | - 'Blauer Engel' | CDoC ECho MGos |
| | - 'Blue Giant' | ECho NLar |
| | - 'Bonnie Bergman' | CKen ECho GKir NLar |
| | - 'Brevifolia' | NLar |
| I | - 'Contorta' **<u>new</u>** | EOrn |
| | - 'Dai-ho' | CKen |
| | - 'Daisetsusan' | CKen |
| | - 'Doctor Landis Gold' | CKen ECho |
| | - 'Dougal' **<u>new</u>** | CKen |
| | - 'Fatsumo' | CKen |
| | - 'Fukai' (v) | CKen MGos NLar |
| | - 'Fukiju' | CKen |
| | - Fukushima-goyo Group | CKen CMen |
| | - 'Fuku-zu-mi' | CKen ECho |
| | - 'Fu-shiro' | CKen |
| | - 'Gin-sho-chuba' | CKen |
| | - Glauca Group | CDoC CMac CRob ECho EHul MBar MBlu MBri MGos NPal STre WFar |
| I | - 'Glauca Nana' | CKen |
| | - 'Goldilocks' | CKen ECho NLar |
| | - 'Gyok-ke-sen' | CKen |
| | - 'Gyo-ko-haku' | CKen |
| | - 'Gyokuei' | CKen |
| | - 'Gyokusen Sämling' | CKen NLar |
| | - 'Gyo-ku-sui' | CKen CMen ECho |
| | - 'H2' **<u>new</u>** | CKen |
| | - 'Hagaromo Seedling' | CKen CMen ECho MAsh NLar |
| | - 'Hakko' | CKen |
| | - 'Hatchichi' | CKen |
| | - 'Ibo-can' | CKen CMen |
| | - 'Ichi-no-se' | CKen |
| | - 'Iri-fune' | CKen |
| | - Ishizuchi-goyo Group | CKen |
| | - 'Ka-ho' | CKen ECho |
| | - 'Kanrico' | CKen |
| | - 'Kanzan' | CKen |
| | - 'Kiyomatsu' | CKen NLar |
| | - 'Kobe' | CKen ECho NLar |
| | - 'Kokonoe' | CKen CMen |
| | - 'Kokuho' | CKen NLar |
| | - 'Koraku' | CKen |
| | - 'Kusu-dama' | CKen |
| | - 'Meiko' | CKen CMen ECho |
| | - 'Michinoku' | CKen |
| | - 'Momo-yama' | CKen |
| | - 'Myo-jo' | CKen |
| | - Nasu-goyo Group | CKen |
| | - 'Negishi' | CDoC CKen CMen CRob GKir LPan MAsh NLar SCoo SLim |
| | - 'Nellie D.' | NLar |
| | - 'Ogon-janome' | CKen LRHS SLim SPoG |
| | - 'Ossorio Dwarf' | CKen |
| | - 'Regenhold' | CKen |
| | - 'Richard Lee' | CKen |
| | - 'Ryo-ku-ho' | CKen |
| | - 'Ryu-ju' | CKen NLar |
| | - 'Sa-dai-jin' | CKen |
| | - 'San-bo' | CKen ECho MBar MGos |
| § | - 'Saphir' | CKen ECho |
| | - 'Schoon's Bonsai' | CDoC NLar |
| | - 'Setsugekka' | CKen |
| | - 'Shika-shima' | CDoC CKen |
| | - 'Shimada' | CKen |
| | - Shiobara-goyo Group | CKen |
| | - 'Shirobana' | NLar |
| | - 'Shizukagoten' | CKen |

| | | |
|---|---|---|
| | - 'Shu-re' | CKen |
| | - 'Sieryoden' | CKen |
| | - 'Smout' **new** | CKen |
| | - 'Tani-mano-uki' | CKen |
| | - 'Tempelhof' | CTho GKir LMaj MAsh MBar NBlu NHol NLar |
| | - 'Templeflora' | MLan |
| | - 'Tenysu-kazu' | CKen |
| | - 'Tokyo Dwarf' | CKen |
| | - 'Tribune' | CDoC NLar |
| | - 'Venus' | EOrn |
| | - 'Walker's Dwarf' **new** | CKen |
| | - 'Watnong' | CKen |
| | - 'Zelkova' | CMen ECho |
| | - 'Zui-sho' | CKen |
| | ***patula*** 🏆$^{H2-3}$ | CBgR CCCN CDoC CDul CLnd GKir LAst NWea SAPC SArc SBig SBir SCoo SLim SPlb SPoG WPGP |
| | ***peuce*** | CDul GAuc GKir MBar NLar NWea |
| | - 'Arnold Dwarf' | CKen |
| | - 'Cesarini' | CKen |
| | - 'Thessaloniki Broom' | CKen |
| | ***pinaster*** 🏆$^{H4}$ | CBcs CDoC CDul CLnd EHul GKir IFFs MMuc |
| | ***pinea*** 🏆$^{H4}$ | CAgr CArn CCVT CDoC CKen CLnd CMac CTho ECrN ELau EPfP IFFs LEdu LMaj LPan LRHS MGos NPri NWea SAPC SArc SBLw SCoo SEND WPGP |
| | - 'Queensway' | CKen |
| | ***ponderosa*** 🏆$^{H4}$ | CDul CLnd GAuc GKir NWea |
| | - var. ***scopulorum*** | NWea |
| | ***pumila*** | CRob |
| | - 'Buchanan' | CKen ECho |
| | - 'Draijer's Dwarf' | ECho EOrn GKir SCoo SLim |
| | - 'Dwarf Blue' | ECho MAsh |
| | - 'Glauca' 🏆$^{H4}$ | CKen MBar |
| | - 'Globe' | CDoC ECho MAsh MBri NLar |
| | - 'Jeddeloh' | CKen |
| | - 'Knightshayes' | CKen |
| | - 'Säntis' | CKen ECho |
| | - 'Saphir' | see *P. parviflora* 'Saphir' |
| | ***radiata*** 🏆$^{H3-4}$ | CBcs CCVT CDoC CDul CLnd CSBt CTrC CTri ECrN ELan GKir IFFs LRHS NBee NWea SAPC SArc SCoo SHBN SPer STre WDin WFar |
| | - Aurea Group | CDoC CKen CTho ECho EOrn GKir LRHS MAsh MGos NScw SBir SCoo SLim SPoG WFar |
| | - 'Bodnant' | CKen |
| | - 'Isca' | CKen ECho |
| | - 'Marshwood' (v) | CKen ECho MGos SLim |
| | ***resinosa*** 'Don Smith' | CKen |
| | - 'Joel's Broom' | CKen |
| | - 'Quinobequin' | CKen |
| | ***roxburghii*** | CDoC CDul ISea SKHP WPGP |
| | ***sabineana*** | GAuc |
| | x ***schwerinii*** | CDoC ECho LRHS MAsh MBri |
| | - 'Wiethorst' | CKen IArd NLar SLim SPoG |
| | ***sibirica*** | GKev GKir |
| | - 'Mariko' | CKen |
| | ***strobiformis*** 'Coronado' | CKen |
| | - 'Loma Linda' | CKen |
| | ***strobus*** | CBcs CCVT CDul CLnd CMen GKir IFFs ISea LPan MBar MGos MMuc NWea SLim WDin WFar |
| § | - 'Alba' | MGos SLim |
| | - 'Amelia's Dwarf' | CKen |
| | - 'Anna Fiele' | CKen |
| | - 'Bergman's Mini' | CKen NLar |
| | - 'Bergman's Pendula Broom' | CKen |

| | | |
|---|---|---|
| I | - 'Bergman's Sport of Prostrata' | CKen |
| | - 'Bloomer's Dark Globe' | CKen |
| | - 'Blue Shag' | ECho EOrn GKir MBri MGos NLar SCoo SLim SPoG |
| | - 'Cesarini' | CKen |
| | - 'Densa' | CKen ECho MAsh |
| | - 'Dove's Dwarf' | CKen |
| | - 'Edel' | NLar |
| | - 'Ed's Broom' | CKen |
| | - 'Elkins Dwarf' | CKen |
| | - 'Fastigiata' | CKen ECho IMGH MBri |
| | - 'Green Curls' | CKen |
| | - 'Greg' | CKen ECho NLar |
| | - 'Hershey' | CKen |
| | - 'Hillside Gem' | CKen |
| | - 'Himmelblau' | IArd NLar SLim |
| | - 'Horsford' | CKen ECho LRHS NLar SLim |
| | - 'Jericho' | CKen EOrn |
| | - 'Julian Pott' | CKen |
| | - 'Julian's Dwarf' | CKen |
| | - 'Krügers Lilliput' | GKir LRHS NLar SLim |
| | - 'Louie' | CKen NLar SLim |
| | - 'Macopin' | ECho EMil NLar SCoo |
| | - 'Mary Butler' | CKen |
| | - 'Merrimack' | CKen ECho NLar |
| | - 'Minima' | CKen ECho EOrn LRHS MAsh MBar MBlu MBri MGos NLar NWea SCoo SLim SPoG WGor |
| | - 'Minuta' | CKen |
| | - 'Nana' | see *P. strobus* Nana Group |
| § | - Nana Group | MGos NPri |
| | - 'Nivea' | see *P. strobus* 'Alba' |
| | - 'Northway Broom' | CKen ECho SLim |
| | - 'Ontario' | MBlu |
| | - 'Pendula' | CKen IDee |
| I | - 'Pendula Broom' | CKen |
| | - 'Radiata' | CTri EHul EPla MBar NLar |
| | - 'Reinshaus' | CKen ECho |
| | - 'Sayville' | CKen |
| | - 'Sea Urchin' | CKen ECho NLar SLim SPoG |
| | - 'Secrest' | NLar |
| I | - 'Tortuosa' | NLar |
| | - 'Uncatena' | CKen |
| | - 'Verkade's Broom' | CKen |
| | - 'Wendy' | NLar |
| | ***sylvestris*** 🏆$^{H4}$ | Widely available |
| | - 'Abergeldie' | CKen |
| | - 'Alderly Edge' | CMen WFar |
| | - 'Andorra' | CKen MGos |
| § | - 'Argentea' | CMen ECho SLim |
| § | - Aurea Group 🏆$^{H4}$ | CDul CKen CMac CMen EBrs ECho EHul EMil EPfP GBin GKir IMGH LRHS MAsh MBar MBlu MBri NHol NLar NWea SCoo SHBN SLim SPer SSta WFar |
| | - 'Aurea' | see *P. sylvestris* Aurea Group |
| | - 'Avondene' | CKen ECho |
| | - 'Bergfield' | CMen ECho NLar |
| | - 'Beuvronensis' 🏆$^{H4}$ | CKen CLnd CMac CMen ECho EOrn GKir IMGH LRHS MGos NHol NLar SCoo SLim |
| | - 'Bonna' | CLnd GKir SCoo SLim |
| | - 'Brevifolia' | MBar MGos |
| | - 'Buchanan's Gold' | CKen |
| | - 'Burghfield' | CKen CMen ECho WFar |
| | - 'Chantry Blue' | CDoC CMen CRob ECho EHul EOrn GKir IMGH LAst LBee LRHS MAsh MBar MBri MGos NHol NLar SCoo SLim WFar |
| | - 'Clumber Blue' | CKen |
| | - 'Compressa' | SLim |
| | - 'Corley' | ECho |

| | | |
|---|---|---|
| | - 'Dereham' | CKen ECho |
| | - 'Doone Valley' | CKen ECho GKir MGos SCoo WFar |
| | - 'Edwin Hillier' | see *P. sylvestris* 'Argentea' |
| | - Fastigiata Group | CDoC CDul CEnd CKen CMen CRob ECho EMil EOrn GKir IMGH LBee LRHS MAsh MBar MGos SCoo SLim SPoG WFar |
| | - 'Frensham' | CKen ECho EOrn IMGH MAsh MGos NHol SCoo WFar |
| | - 'Globosa' | ECho GKir LRHS |
| | - 'Gold Coin' | CDoC CDul CKen CMen ECho EOrn EPfP GKir MAsh MGos NHol NLar SCoo SLim SPoG WFar |
| | - 'Gold Medal' | CKen ECho GKir SLim WFar |
| | - 'Grand Rapids' | CKen |
| | - 'Gwydyr Castle' | CKen |
| | - 'Hibernia' | CRob |
| | - 'Hillside Creeper' | CKen ECho GKir SCoo SLim SPoG |
| | - 'Humble Pie' | CKen |
| | - 'Inverleith' (v) | ECho EHul GKir MGos SCoo SLim SPoG WFar |
| | - 'Jeremy' | CKen ECho EOrn GKir NHol SCoo SLim SPoG |
| | - 'John Boy' | CMen ECho NLar |
| | - 'Kelpie' | ECho GKir LRHS SCoo SLim |
| | - 'Kenwith' | CKen ECho |
| | - 'Lakeside Dwarf' | CMen ECho |
| | - 'Lodge Hill' | CMen CRob ECho EOrn GKir IMGH LRHS MAsh SCoo SLim |
| | - 'Longmoor' | CKen ECho MGos NLar |
| | - 'Martham' | CKen CMen ECho |
| | - 'Mitsch Weeping' **new** | CKen |
| * | - 'Moseri' | CRob ECho EOrn GKir MAsh SPoG |
| | - 'Munches Blue' | CKen |
| | - 'Nana' misapplied | see *P. sylvestris* 'Watereri' |
| | - 'Nana Compacta' | CMen |
| § | - 'Nisbet's Gem' | CKen CMen ECho |
| | - 'Padworth' | CMen NLar |
| | - 'Peve Heiheks' | NLar |
| | - 'Peve Miba' | NLar |
| I | - 'Pine Glen' | CKen |
| | - 'Piskowitz' | CKen |
| | - 'Pixie' | CKen ECho MGos NLar |
| I | - 'Prostrata' | SCoo |
| | - 'Pulham' | ECho |
| | - 'Pygmaea' | SCoo SLim |
| | - 'Reedham' | ECho |
| | - 'Repens' | CKen |
| | - 'Saint George' | CKen |
| | - 'Sandringham' | ECho |
| | - 'Saxatilis' | CKen CMen ECho EOrn GKir MAsh |
| | - subsp. ***scotica*** | GQue NWea |
| | - 'Scott's Dwarf' | see *P. sylvestris* 'Nisbet's Gem' |
| | - 'Scrubby' | ECho NLar |
| | - 'Sentinel' | CKen ECho SLim |
| | - 'Skjak I' | CKen NLar |
| | - 'Skjak II' | CKen ECho SCoo |
| | - 'Skogbygdi' **new** | NLar |
| | - 'Slimkin' | CKen |
| | - 'Spaan's Slow Column' | CKen ECho GKir SCoo SLim |
| | - 'Tabuliformis' | ECho |
| | - 'Tage' | CKen ECho |
| | - 'Tanya' | CKen MAsh |
| | - 'Tilhead' | CKen ECho |
| | - 'Treasure' | CKen ECho |
| | - 'Trefrew Quarry' | CKen |
| | - 'Variegata' (v) | MGos |
| § | - 'Watereri' | CMac ECho EHul GKir IMGH LAst LBee LPan MAsh MBar MBri NHol NPri SCoo SLim SPer WDin WFar |
| | - 'Westonbirt' | CKen CMen ECho EHul |
| | - 'Wishmoor' | ECho |
| | - 'Wolf Gold' | CKen ECho |
| | - 'Xawrey 1' | NLar |
| * | - 'Yaff Hill' | ECho GKir |
| | ***tabuliformis*** | CDul NMun STre |
| | ***taeda*** | GAuc NWea WPGP |
| | ***taiwanensis*** | CDoC |
| | ***thunbergii*** | CDul CLnd CMen EHul ELan GAuc GKir IFFs MGos NWea STre |
| | - 'Akame' | CKen CMen |
| | - 'Akame Yatsabusa' | CMen |
| | - 'Aocha-matsu' (v) | CKen CMen NLar |
| | - 'Arakawa-sho' | CKen CMen |
| | - 'Awaji' **new** | EOrn |
| | - 'Banshosho' | CKen CMen ECho EOrn LRHS MGos NLar SLim |
| | - 'Beni-kujaku' | CKen CMen |
| | - 'Compacta' | CKen CMen |
| | - var. ***corticosa*** 'Fuji' | CMen |
| | - - 'Iihara' | CMen |
| | - 'Dainagon' | CKen CMen |
| | - 'Eechee-nee' | CKen |
| | - 'Hayabusa' | CMen |
| | - 'Iwai' | CMen |
| | - 'Janome' | CMen |
| | - 'Katsuga' | CMen |
| | - 'Kotobuki' | CKen CMen CRob EOrn GKir NLar WFar |
| | - 'Koyosho' | CMen |
| | - 'Kujaku' | CKen CMen |
| | - 'Kyokko' | CKen CMen |
| | - 'Kyushu' | CKen CMen EOrn |
| | - 'Maijima' **new** | NLar |
| | - 'Mikawa' **new** | CMen |
| | - 'Miyajuna' | CKen CMen |
| | - 'Nishiki-ne' | CKen CMen |
| | - 'Nishiki-tsusaka' | CMen ECho |
| | - 'Oculus-draconis' (v) | CMen ECho |
| | - 'Ogon' | CKen CMen GKir LRHS NLar SLim |
| | - 'Porky' | CKen CMen |
| § | - 'Sayonara' | CKen CMen ECho EOrn GKir MAsh NLar SCoo SLim SPoG |
| | - 'Senryu' | CKen CMen |
| | - 'Shinsho' | CKen CMen |
| | - 'Shio-guro' | CKen CMen EOrn MAsh |
| | - 'Suchiro' **new** | EOrn |
| | - 'Suchiro Yatabusa' | CKen CMen ECho |
| | - 'Sunsho' | CKen CMen ECho |
| | - 'Taihei' | CKen CMen |
| I | - 'Thunderhead' | CKen CMen LRHS MAsh NLar SLim |
| | - 'Yatsubusa' | see *P. thunbergii* 'Sayonara' |
| | - 'Ye-i-kan' | CKen |
| | - 'Yoshimura' | CMen |
| | - 'Yumaki' | CKen CMen ECho MGos SCoo |
| | ***torreyana*** **new** | GAuc |
| | ***uncinata*** | see *P. mugo* subsp. *uncinata* |
| | - 'Etschtal' | CKen |
| | - 'Jezek' | CKen SLim |
| | - 'Kostelnicek' | NLar |
| | - 'Leuco-like' | CKen |
| | - 'Offenpass' | CKen |
| | - 'Susse Perle' | CKen |
| | ***virginiana*** | GAuc |
| | - 'Wate's Golden' | CKen NLar |
| § | ***wallichiana*** ♀H4 | CDoC CDul CGHE CKen CMCN CRob CTho ECho ECrN EHul EPfP EPla GAuc MAsh MBar MBlu MGos MLan MMuc NHol NLar NWea SBir SLim SPoG STre WDin WFar WOrn WPGP |
| | - SF 00001 | ISea |
| | - 'Densa' | LPan NLar SLim |
| | - 'Densa Hill' **new** | LRHS |
| | - 'Nana' | CKen EHul MBar NLar SCoo SLim SPoG |

| | |
|---|---|
| - 'Umbraculifera' | LRHS |
| - 'Zebrina' (v) | MAsh MBar MBlu MGos NLar |
| ***yunnanensis*** | CDoC CDul CTho |

## *Piper* (*Piperaceae*)

| | |
|---|---|
| ***auritum*** | GPoy |
| ***betle*** | MSal |
| ***excelsum*** | see *Macropiper excelsum* |
| ***nigrum*** | MSal |

## *Piptanthus* (*Papilionaceae*)

| | |
|---|---|
| ***forrestii*** | see *P. nepalensis* |
| ***laburnifolius*** | see *P. nepalensis* |
| § ***nepalensis*** | CBcs CDul CSBt CSpe EBee ECrN ELan EMil EPau EPfP GGar GKir LRHS MGos MWhi NBid SGar SHBN SLon SOWG SPer SPoG SRms WBVN |
| - B&SWJ 2241 | WCru |
| ***tomentosus*** | MMHG WPGP |

## *Pistacia* (*Anacardiaceae*)

| | |
|---|---|
| ***chinensis*** | CMCN EPfP |
| ***lentiscus*** | CArn CBcs EAro MGos SEND |

## *Pistia* (*Araceae*)

| | |
|---|---|
| ***stratiotes*** | LPBA MSKA NPer SCoo |

## *Pitcairnia* (*Bromeliaceae*)

| | |
|---|---|
| ***bergii*** | CHll |
| ***heterophylla*** | WCot |

## *Pittosporum* ✿ (*Pittosporaceae*)

| | |
|---|---|
| ***anomalum*** | ECou |
| - (f) | ECou |
| - (m) | ECou |
| - 'Falcon' | ECou |
| - 'Raven' (f) | ECou |
| - 'Starling' (m) | ECou |
| 'Arundel Green' | CDoC CWSG EBee EJRN EMil EPfP LFCN LRHS MAsh NHol SLim SRms SWvt |
| ***bicolor*** | ECou EShb GGal GQui SAPC SArc WBor WPGP |
| - 'Cradle' (f) | ECou |
| - 'Mount Field' (f) | ECou |
| ***buchananii*** | SGar |
| ***colensoi*** | ECou |
| - 'Cobb' (f) | ECou |
| - 'Wanaka' (m) | ECou |
| ***crassifolium*** | CCCN CHEx ECou EHig GGal WBrE WPGP |
| - 'Havering Dwarf' (f) | ECou |
| - 'Napier' (f) | ECou |
| - 'Variegatum' (v) | EShb WPat |
| ***crassifolium*** x ***tenuifolium*** | CWib ECou SWvt |
| 'Craxten' (f) | CCCN ECou EJRN |
| 'Crinkles' (f) | ECou |
| ***daphniphylloides*** B&SWJ 6789 | WCru |
| - RWJ 9913 **new** | WCru |
| 'Dark Delight' (m) | ECou |
| ***divaricatum*** | ECou |
| 'Emerald Lake' | MGos |
| 'Essex' (f/v) | ECou EJRN |
| ***eugenioides*** | CHEx CMHG CTrG GGar |
| - 'Mini Green' | CPen NLar WBrE |
| - 'Platinum' (v) | CBcs CCCN MGos |
| - 'Variegatum' (v) ♀H3 | Widely available |
| 'Garnettii' (v) ♀H3 | Widely available |
| ***heterophyllum*** | CPen ECou EWes SHBN |
| - 'Ga Blanca' | CPen |
| - variegated (v) | ECou EWTr WSHC |
| 'Holbrook' (v) | CSam |
| 'Humpty Dumpty' | ECou EJRN |
| ***illicioides*** var. ***angustifolium*** B&SWJ 6771 | WCru |
| - - RWJ 9846 **new** | WCru |
| - var. ***illicioides*** B&SWJ 6712 | WCru |
| ***lineare*** | ECou |
| ***michiei*** | ECou |
| - (f) | ECou |
| - (m) | ECou |
| - 'Jack' (m) | ECou |
| - 'Jill' (f) | ECou |
| 'Nanum Variegatum' | see *P. tobira* 'Variegatum' |
| ***obcordatum*** | ECou |
| - var. ***kaitaiaense*** | ECou |
| 'Oliver Twist' | LFCN SCoo |
| ***omeiense*** | ECou ECre EWes SKHP |
| 'Peter Pan' | EJRN |
| ***pimeleoides*** var. ***reflexum*** (m) | ECou |
| 'Purple Princess' | ECou EJRN |
| ***ralphii*** | CCCN ECou WPGP |
| - 'Green Globe' | ECou SKHP |
| - 'Variegatum' (v) | CGHE EMil EPla SKHP SSpi WPGP |
| 'Saundersii' (v) | EQua LRHS SCoo |
| ***tenufolium*** 'Croxton' | CCCN |
| ***tenuifolium*** ♀H3 | Widely available |
| - 'Abbotsbury Gold' (f/v) | CAbb CBcs CCCN CDoC CMac CTri EBee ECou EHoe ELan EMil EWes GBri LAst LFCN LRHS MGos MREP SAga SEND SHBN SLim SPer SPla SSto WBod WGob WSHC |
| - 'County Park' | CCCN LRHS WFar |
| - 'County Park Dwarf' | CPen ECou EJRN EQua MAsh |
| - 'Deborah' (v) | ECou EJRN LSou SSto |
| - 'Dixie' | CPen ECou |
| § - 'Eila Keightley' (v) | CMHG EJRN SAga |
| - 'Elizabeth' (m/v) | CAbP CBcs CDoC CMac CTrC EBee ECou EJRN EMil IArd LAst LRHS LSRN MBri MGos MREP NHol NMun |
| - 'French Lace' | CBcs CCCN EBee ECou EJRN ELan EMil ERas GAbr GKev LFCN MAsh MREP NHol NLar SEND SHBN WFar |
| - 'Gold Star' | CDoC ECou LBMP LRHS MAsh MGos NHol NPal SCoo SLim SPer SPoG WFar WMoo |
| - 'Golden Cut' | NLar |
| - 'Golden King' | CCCN CDoC CMHG CMac CSBt EBee EJRN EPfP LRHS LSou MAsh NHol NScw SLim SPoG SRms SSto |
| - 'Golden Princess' (f) | ECou EJRN |
| - 'Golf Ball' **new** | CTrC |
| - 'Green Elf' | ECou EJRN |
| - 'Green Thumb' | CMac CWSG EBee ELan LRHS |
| - 'Irene Paterson' (m/v) ♀H3 | Widely available |
| - 'James Stirling' | CCCN CPMA ECou EPfP LRHS SSto |
| - 'John Flanagan' | see *P. tenuifolium* 'Margaret Turnbull' |
| - 'Limelight' (v) | CBcs CSBt CSPN CWGN LRHS MGos MREP NHol SPoG |
| - 'Loxhill Gold' | CAbP CCCN CPen EBee IArd LFCN LRHS LSou MGos NHol NScw SSto |
| § - 'Margaret Turnbull' (v) | CBcs CPen CTrC ECou EJRN EWes LSRN MBri MGos |
| - 'Marjory Channon' (v) | EPfP LRHS |
| - 'Mellow Yellow' | CAbP |
| - 'Moonlight' (v) | CBcs CTrC EBee LRHS SKHP WDin |
| - 'Mountain Green' | CMac LSou MGos |

- 'Nutty's Leprechaun' CCCN
- 'Pompom' CCCN SRms WPat
- 'Purpureum' (m) CCCN CMac CSBt CSam CTri EBee ECou EHoe EPfP ERas LAst LBMP LRHS LSRN MBri MREP SAga SCoo SHBN SPer SPla SPoG SRms SSto WSHC
- 'Silver Magic' (v) CBcs CPen CSBt EJRN MGos
- 'Silver 'n' Gold' LRHS
- 'Silver Princess' (f) ECou EJRN
- 'Silver Queen' (f/v) ♀H3 Widely available
- 'Silver Sheen' (m) CBcs CPen EBee ECou LRHS MGos
- 'Stevens Island' CBcs LRHS MGos
- 'Stirling Gold' (f/v) ECou EPfP EWes
- 'Sunburst' see *P. tenuifolium* 'Eila Keightley'
- 'Tandara Gold' (v) CBcs CCCN CDoC CDul CSBt CTrC EBee ECou EJRN EPfP ERas LBMP LRHS LSRN MAsh MGos MREP SLim SPla SPoG WBrE WFar WGob
- 'Tiki' (m) CBcs CCCN CDoC CTrC ECou LRHS
- 'Tom Thumb' ♀H3 Widely available
- 'Tresederi' (f/m) CCCN CMac CTrC CTsd EBee ECou LRHS WFar
- 'Variegatum' (m/v) CBcs CDoC CSBt EBee ECou EQua GBri GGar LAst LCro LRHS MAsh MGos SPoG SWvt
- 'Victoria' (v) CBcs CCCN CDoC CTrC EBee EMil MGos SPoG WFar
- 'Warnham Gold' (m) ♀H3 CDoC CMac CSBt CWib EBee ECou ECrN EJRN ELan EPfP GBri LAst LRHS MAsh MCCP MGos SLim SPer SPoG SSpi SSto WAbe
- 'Wendle Channon' (m/v) CCCN CMac CSBt CSam EBee ECot ECou EHoe EMil EPfP EQua ERas LRHS MAsh NCGa NHol SLim SSto WGob WSHC
- 'White Cloud' **new** CBcs
- 'Wrinkled Blue' CTrC LRHS MGos

***tobira*** ♀H3 Widely available
- B&SWJ 4362 WCru
* - 'Cuneatum' CCCN CDoC CWGN LHop SAga
* - 'Nanum' CBcs CCCN CDoC EBee ECou ELan EPfP ERom ETod LPan LRHS MAsh MGos MREP SAPC SArc SLim SPer SPla SPoG WDin WFar
§ - 'Variegatum' (v) ♀H2-3 CBcs CCCN CHll CMac CSam CWGN EBee ECou ECrN ELan EPfP GQui LHop LRHS MGos MREP SAga SBod SDnm SHBN SLim SLon SPer SPla SPoG SSta SSto WSHC

***truncatum*** ECre EWes
***undulatum*** CHEx ECou
***viridiflorum*** ECou EShb

## *Plagianthus* (*Malvaceae*)

***betulinus*** see *P. regius*
***divaricatus*** CBcs CTrC ECou ECre WPGP
***lyallii*** see *Hoberia lyallii*
§ ***regius*** CBcs SBig

## *Plagiorhegma* see *Jeffersonia*

## *Planera* (*Ulmaceae*)

***aquatica*** EGFP

## *Plantago* (*Plantaginaceae*)

***asiatica*** MSal
- 'Variegata' (v) CSec EBee GBuc NBro

***camtschatica*** CSec
***coronopus*** EBWF
***cynops*** MTho
***lanceolata*** EBWF NMir WSFF
- 'Bomi-noka' CNat
- 'Dent's Downs Link' (v) WCot
- 'Golden Spears' CBre EBee NSti
- 'Keer's Pride' (v) WCot
- 'Streaker' (v) WCot
- 'White Whiskers' CNat

***major*** 'Atropurpurea' see *P. major* 'Rubrifolia'
- 'Bowles' Variety' see *P. major* 'Rosularis'
- 'Frills' CNat EBee
- 'Rosenstolz' CRow
§ - 'Rosularis' CArn CNat CRow CSec CSpe CSsd EBee EDAr ILis LEdu MBNS MHer MTho NBro NChi SPav WCAu WHer
§ - 'Rubrifolia' CArn CHid CRow CSec CSpe EBee EShb LCro LDai MBNS MHer NBid NBro NChi NSti WCAu WHer WMoo WPer
- 'Subtle Streak' (v) WAlt
- 'Tony Lewis' CNat WAlt

***maritima*** EBWF WHer
***media*** CSec EBWF MHer
***psyllium*** L. CArn MSal
***rosea*** see *P. major* 'Rosularis'
***sempervirens*** CSec
***uniflora*** Hook. f. WCot

## *Platanthera* (*Orchidaceae*)

***bifolia*** NLAp SHdy
***ciliaris*** **new** NLAp
***hologlottis*** CSec EFEx
***metabifolia*** EFEx

## *Platanus* ✿ (*Platanaceae*)

x ***acerifolia*** see *P.* x *hispanica*
§ x ***hispanica*** ♀H4 CBcs CCVT CDul CLnd CMCN CTho EBee ECrN EMac EPfP EWTr LAst LBuc LMaj LPan MAsh MGos MMuc NWea SBLw SEND SHBN SPer WDin WFar WMou
- 'Alphen's Globe' **new** LPan
- 'Bloodgood' SBLw
- 'Dakvorm' SBLw
- 'Dortmund' SBLw
- 'Pyramidalis' CTho SBLw WOrn
- 'Suttneri' (v) CEnd CLnd CTho WMou

***mexicana*** F&M 065 **new** WPGP
***orientalis*** ♀H4 CCVT CLnd CMCN CTho EBee EPfP GKir LEdu NLar SBLw SLPl WDin WMou
- MSF 0028 from Sfendili, Crete WPGP
- 'Cuneata' IFFs
§ - f. ***digitata*** ♀H4 CDoC CDul CLnd CMCN CTho EPfP ERod GKir MBlu SBLw SLPl SPur WMou
- var. ***insularis*** CEnd WPGP
- 'Laciniata' see *P. orientalis* f. *digitata*
- 'Minaret' CDul WMou
- 'Mirkovec' CDoC GKir MBri SMad SPer WMou

## *Platycarya* (*Juglandaceae*)

***strobilacea*** CMCN EGFP EPfP NLar

## *Platycerium* (*Polypodiaceae*)

***alcicorne*** misapplied see *P. bifurcatum*
§ ***bifurcatum*** ♀H1 CCCN MBri WRic XBlo
'Lemoinei' **new** WRic

## *Platycladus* (*Cupressaceae*)

§ ***orientalis*** 'Aurea Nana' ♀H4 CDoC CKen CMac CSBt CWib ECho EHul EPfP GKir IMGH LAst LBee LPan LRHS MAsh MBar MBri

| | |
|---|---|
| | MGos NBlu NHol NWea SLim SPla SPoG WCFE WDin WEas WFar |
| - 'Autumn Glow' | CKen LRHS MAsh SCoo SPoG WGor |
| - 'Beverleyensis' | NLar |
| - 'Blue Cone' | MBar |
| - 'Caribbean Holiday' | MAsh |
| - 'Collen's Gold' | EHul EOrn MBar |
| - 'Conspicua' | CKen CWib ECho EHul EMil LBee MBar |
| § - 'Elegantissima' 🏆$^{H4}$ | CDoC CMac ECho EHul EOrn LBee LPan MBar |
| - 'Franky Boy' | CDoC EMil MGos NLar SLim SPoG |
| - 'Golden Pillar' | EOrn |
| - 'Golden Pygmy' | CKen EOrn MAsh |
| - 'Juniperoides' | EHul MBar NHol |
| - 'Kenwith' | CKen |
| - 'Lemon 'n' Lime' | SCoo |
| - 'Little Susie' | CRob |
| - 'Madurodam' | MBar |
| - 'Magnifica' | EHul |
| - 'Meldensis' | CDoC CTri EHul MBar |
| - 'Minima' | CRob EHul WGor |
| - 'Minima Glauca' | CKen MBar |
| - 'Purple King' | SCoo SLim |
| I - 'Pyramidalis Aurea' | LBee LRHS NHol SCoo |
| - 'Raffles' **new** | NHol |
| - 'Rosedalis' | CKen CMac CSBt ECho EHul EPfP LBee LRHS MAsh MBar SCoo SLim SPla WFar |
| - 'Sanderi' | MBar WCFE |
| § - 'Semperaurea' | CMac IMGH |
| - 'Shirley Chilcott' | LBee MAsh |
| - 'Sieboldii' | EHul |
| - 'Southport' | LBee LRHS MAsh |
| - 'Summer Cream' | CKen EHul MBar |
| - 'Westmont' (v) | CKen EOrn |

## *Platycodon* ✿ (*Campanulaceae*)

| | |
|---|---|
| ***grandiflorus*** 🏆$^{H4}$ | CArn CMea CTri EBee ECha EPot GKev GKir LHop MHer MNrw MSal NGBl SGar SIng SMrm SRms WHoo |
| - 'Albus' | CBro EBee ECho EPfP LHop SPer SPla SWvt WHoo WPer |
| - Apoyama Group 🏆$^{H4}$ | CLyd CSec ECho GKev NMen WHoo WPer |
| - - 'Fairy Snow' | CBgR CMdw EBee ECho ELan EShb GGar GKev ITim LBMP NBre WEas WHoo |
| - (Astra Series) 'Astra Blue' | CSpe ECho EPfP SPad WHoo |
| - - 'Astra Double Blue' (d) | CSpe |
| - - 'Astra Pink' | LRHS WHoo |
| - - 'Astra White' | WHoo |
| - 'Blaue Glocke' | NBre |
| - 'Blue Pearl' | WHoo |
| - 'Florist Rose' | WOut |
| - 'Fuji Blue' | EBee NLar SPur |
| - 'Fuji Pink' | CBro CPrp EAEE EBee ECho ELan EPfP LAst LHop MRav NLar SMrm SPad SPoG SPur SWvt WCAu |
| - 'Fuji White' | EBee ECho ELan LAst NLar SMrm SPur WCAu |
| - 'Hakone' | LAst LHop MRav SMrm WHoo |
| - 'Hakone Blue' | CBgR ECho EShb ITim NBre NLar SMrm |
| * - 'Hakone Double Blue' (d) | EAEE EBee ELan MBNS SPoG SRms WCAu |
| - 'Hakone White' | CBgR CMdw CPrp EBee ECho EPfP GKev ITim LAst MRav NGby NLar NMen SMad SMrm SPoG WHoo |
| - 'Mariesii' 🏆$^{H4}$ | CBgR CBro CSBt EAEE EBee ECho ECtt EPfP LAst NBir NMen SMrm SPer SPla SPlb SPoG SRms SWvt WEas WHoo WPer WSHC |
| - Mother of Pearl | see *P. grandiflorus* 'Perlmutterschale' |
| § - 'Perlmutterschale' | CBgR CMMP CPrp EAEE EBee ECho EPPr EPfP IPot LBMP WAul WHoo |
| - pink-flowered | GKev |
| - ***pumilus*** | GKev NChi NWCA WHoo |
| - ***roseus*** | GKev |
| - 'Sentimental Blue' | CWib EBee ECho EWll NLar SPet |
| - 'Shell Pink' | see *P. grandiflorus* 'Perlmutterschale' |
| - white-flowered, double | CBro |
| - 'Zwerg' | ECho EShb LBMP NBre |

## *Platycrater* (*Hydrangeaceae*)

| | |
|---|---|
| ***arguta*** | WCru |
| - B&SWJ 6266 | WCru |

## *Plectranthus* (*Lamiaceae*)

| | |
|---|---|
| sp. | LAst SPoG |
| from Puerto Rico | CArn |
| ***ambiguus*** | EOHP |
| - 'Manguzuku' | EOHP |
| - 'Umigoye' | EOHP |
| ***amboinicus*** | CArn CHal EOHP NTHB WDyG |
| * - 'Variegatus' (v) | EOHP |
| - 'Well Sweep Wedgewood' | EOHP |
| ***argentatus*** 🏆$^{H2}$ | CDMG CDoC CHal CMdw CPom CSam CSev CSpe EBee EOHP MCot MSte SDix SEND SGar SMrs SUsu WDyG WKif WWlt |
| - 'Hill House' (v) | CHll CPne EOHP |
| ***australis*** misapplied | see *P. verticillatus* |
| ***behrii*** | see *P. fruticosus* |
| Blue Angel = 'Edelblau' | EOHP |
| ***ciliatus*** | CPne EOHP SGar WWlt |
| - 'All Gold' | CPne |
| - 'Easy Gold' | CHal EOHP |
| - 'Sasha' | CCCN CDoC CHal CHll ECtt EOHP EShb SPet SUsu |
| ***coleoides*** 'Marginatus' | see *P. forsteri* 'Marginatus' |
| - 'Variegatus' | see *P. madagascariensis* 'Variegated Mintleaf' |
| Cuban oregano | EOHP |
| ***dolichopodus*** | EOHP |
| ***ecklonii*** | EOHP WDyG |
| - NJM 02.010 | WPGP |
| - 'Medley-Wood' | EOHP |
| ***ernstii*** | EOHP |
| ***excisus*** | EOHP |
| § ***forsteri*** 'Marginatus' | CHal EOHP SGar |
| § ***fruticosus*** | CHal CPne |
| - 'Frills' | EOHP |
| - 'James' | EOHP |
| ***hadiensis*** var. ***tomentosus*** 'Carnegie' | EOHP |
| - - green-leaved | EOHP |
| I - 'Variegata' | CPne |
| - var. ***woodii*** **new** | EOHP |
| ***hilliardiae*** | CPne |
| ***madagascariensis*** | CPne EOHP |
| - gold-leaved | EOHP |
| § - 'Variegated Mintleaf' (v) 🏆$^{H1}$ | CHal EOHP SPet SRms |
| 'Marble Ruffles' | EOHP |
| menthol-scented, large-leaved | EOHP |
| - small-leaved | EOHP MNHC |
| 'Nico' | CSpe EOHP |
| § ***oertendahlii*** 🏆$^{H1}$ | CHal EBak EOHP EShb |
| - silver-leaved | EOHP |
| - 'Uvongo' | CPne |

| | | |
|---|---|---|
| | ***ornatus*** | EOHP MCCP NScw |
| | - 'Pee Off' | EOHP |
| | ***purpuratus*** | EOHP |
| | ***rehmannii*** | EOHP |
| | ***saccatus*** | CPne GFai |
| | ***spicatus*** | EOHP |
| | - 'Nelspruit' | EOHP |
| | Swedish ivy | see *P. verticillatus*, *P. oertendahlii* |
| § | ***thyrsoideus*** | CHal ECre EOHP |
| § | ***verticillatus*** | CHal EOHP |
| | Vick's plant | EOHP |
| | ***zatarhendii*** | EOHP |
| | ***zuluensis*** | CDoC CFee CHal CMdw CPne CSpe EOHP EShb SBch SMrs WBor WOld |
| | - dark-leaved | EOHP |
| | - 'Symphony' | CFee |

## *Pleioblastus* ✿ (*Poaceae*)

| | | |
|---|---|---|
| | ***akebono*** | see *P. argenteostriatus* 'Akebono' |
| § | ***argenteostriatus*** 'Akebono' | CMCo |
| § | - 'Okinadake' (v) | EBee EPla |
| § | - f. ***pumilus*** | CDoC EBee EHoe EPfP GKir LPan LRHS MBlu MMoz MMuc MWht NHol SPla SPlb WFar WPer |
| | ***auricomus*** | see *P. viridistriatus* |
| | - 'Vagans' | see *Sasaella ramosa* |
| § | ***chino*** | EPla |
| | - var. ***argenteostriatus*** | see *P. argenteostriatus* 'Okinadake' |
| | - f. ***aureostriatus*** (v) | EPla LEdu MGos MMoz |
| | - f. ***elegantissimus*** | CDoC CEnd CEnt CFir CGHE EBee ENBC EPla ERod MGos MMoz MWhi NMoo SBig WMoo WPGP WPnP |
| | - var. ***hisauchii*** | EPla |
| | - 'Kimmei' | EPla |
| | ***fortunei*** | see *P. variegatus* 'Fortunei' |
| | 'Gauntlettii' | see *P. argenteostriatus* f. *pumilus* |
| | ***glaber*** 'Albostriatus' | see *Sasaella masamuneana* 'Albostriata' |
| | ***gramineus*** | EBee EPla |
| § | ***hindsii*** | EPla ERod GBin LPan MMoz NMoo SEND |
| § | ***humilis*** | ELan ENBC GKir LPan |
| | - var. ***pumilus*** | see *P. argenteostriatus* f. *pumilus* |
| | ***kongosanensis*** new | EBee |
| | - 'Aureostriatus' (v) | EPla |
| | ***linearis*** | CAbb CBcs CMCo EAmu EFul EPla ERod LPal MMoz MWht NMoo SBig WMoo WPGP |
| | ***longifimbriatus*** | see *Sinobambusa intermedia* |
| | ***oleosus*** | EPla |
| § | ***pygmaeus*** | Widely available |
| § | - 'Distichus' | CEnt EFul EHul ENBC EPPr EPla LCro LRHS MGos MMoz MMuc MWht NGdn NLar NMoo WMoo |
| § | - 'Mirrezuzume' | CPLG WFar |
| * | - var. ***pygmaeus*** 'Mini' | WCot |
| § | ***simonii*** | CMCo EBee EFul GBin LRHS MMoz MWhi MWht SPoG |
| | - 'Variegatus' (v) | EPla MBar NGdn SPer WPGP |
| § | ***variegatus*** (v) ♀H4 | Widely available |
| § | - 'Fortunei' (v) new | EBee MWhi |
| | - 'Tsuboii' (v) | CAbb CChe CDTJ CDoC CSBt EPPr EPla ERod GQui LAst LPal LRHS MAvo MBrN MBri MMoz MWhi MWht NMoo WFar WMoo WPGP WPnP |
| § | ***viridistriatus*** ♀H4 | Widely available |
| | - 'Chrysophyllus' | EPla MMoz |
| | - f. ***variegatus*** (v) | CHEx SAga SWvt WMoo |
| | ***yixingensis*** | EPla |

## *Pleione* ✿ (*Orchidaceae*)

| | | |
|---|---|---|
| | **Adams gx** | LBut |
| | ***albiflora*** | CFwr |
| | **Aldabra gx** new | NSpr |
| | **Alishan gx** 'Merlin' | LBut |
| | - 'Mother's Day' | LBut |
| | - 'Mount Fuji' | EPot LBut |
| | **Asama gx** 'Red Grouse' | LBut |
| | **Askia gx** | LBut |
| | ***aurita*** | CFwr LBut |
| | **Bandai-san gx** | EPot LBut |
| | - 'Sand Grouse' | LBut |
| | x ***barbarae*** | LBut |
| | **Barcena gx** | LBut |
| | **Berapi gx** 'Purple Sandpiper' | LBut |
| | **Betty Arnold gx** new | LBut |
| | **Brigadoon gx** | LBut NSpr |
| | - 'Stonechat' | LBut |
| | - 'Woodcock' | LBut |
| | **Britannia gx** | LBut |
| | - 'Doreen' | EPot LBut |
| § | ***bulbocodioides*** | CFwr ERos IHer LBut NSpr |
| | - Limprichtii Group | see *P. limprichtii* |
| | - 'New Forest' | NSpr |
| | - Pricei Group | see *P. formosana* Pricei Group |
| § | - 'Yunnan' | CFwr NSpr |
| | **Captain Hook gx** | EPot LBut |
| | ***chunii*** | EFEx LBut |
| | x ***confusa*** | EPot LBut |
| | **Danan gx** | EPot LBut |
| | **Deriba gx** | LBut |
| | **Egmont gx** 'Jay' | LBut |
| | **Eiger gx** | ERos LBut |
| | - cream | ERos LBut |
| | **El Pico gx** 'Goldcrest' | NSpr |
| | - 'Pheasant' | LBut NSpr |
| | **Erebus gx** 'Redpoll' new | LBut |
| | **Erh Hai gx** | NSpr |
| | **Etna gx** 'Bullfinch' | LBut |
| | **Follifoot gx** 'Princess Tiger' | NSpr |
| | ***formosana*** ♀H2 | CKob CTri EBrs ECho EFEx EPot GBuc LAma LEdu NCGa SAga SEND SIng WFar WPGP |
| | - Alba Group | CFwr CTri EBrs ECho WFar |
| | - - 'Claire' | EPot ERos LBut NSpr |
| | - - 'Snow Bunting' | LBut |
| | - 'Avalanche' | EPot |
| | - 'Blush of Dawn' | LBut |
| | - 'Cairngorm' | NSpr |
| | - 'Greenhill' | EPot LBut |
| | - 'Lucy Diamond' | NSpr |
| | - 'Pitlochry' | LBut |
| § | - Pricei Group | ERos SIng |
| | - - 'Oriental Grace' | LBut |
| | - - 'Oriental Splendour' | LBut |
| | - 'Red Spot' | EPot SIng |
| | - 'Snow White' | LBut |
| | ***forrestii*** | CFwr EBrs EFEx EPot LAma |
| | **Fu Manchu gx** | NSpr |
| | **Fuego gx** | EPot NSpr WAbe |
| | **Ganymede gx** | LBut |
| | **Gerry Mundey gx** | EPot NSpr |
| | - 'Tinney's Firs' new | LBut |
| § | ***grandiflora*** | CFwr EPot LBut |
| | **Harlequin gx** 'Norman' | LBut |
| | **Heathfield gx** | NSpr |
| | **Hekla gx** | ERos NSpr |
| | - 'Partridge' | LBut |
| | ***hookeriana*** | CFwr |
| | ***humilis*** | LBut NSpr |

| | |
|---|---|
| **Jorullo gx** | NSpr WAbe |
| - 'Long-tailed Tit' | LBut |
| **Keith Rattray gx** 'Kelty' | LBut |
| **Kenya gx** | LBut |
| - 'Bald Eagle' | LBut |
| **Kilauea gx** | LBut |
| - 'Curlew' | LBut |
| **Kohala gx** | LBut |
| **Krakatoa gx** | LBut NSpr |
| - 'Wheatear' new | LBut |
| **Kublai Khan gx** | NSpr |
| **Leda gx** | LBut |
| § ***limprichtii*** ♀H2 | CFwr EBrs EFEx EPot LBut NSpr |
| ***maculata*** | CFwr EFEx |
| **Marco Polo gx** | LBut NSpr |
| **Marion Johnson gx** | EPot LBut |
| **Masaya gx** | LBut |
| **Mauna Loa gx** new | LBut |
| **Mawenzi gx** | LBut |
| **Myojin gx** | LBut |
| **Novarupta gx** | LBut |
| **Orizaba gx** | LBut |
| **Paricutin gx** | LBut |
| ***pinkepankii*** | see *P. grandiflora* |
| **Piton gx** | EPot LBut |
| § ***pleionoides*** | EPot LBut |
| ***pogonioides*** misapplied | see *P. pleionoides* |
| ***pogonioides*** (Rolfe) Rolfe | see *P. bulbocodioides* |
| ***praecox*** | CFwr |
| **Quizapu gx** 'Peregrine' | LBut |
| **Rainier gx** | LBut |
| **Rakata gx** 'Blackbird' | LBut |
| - 'Redwing' | LBut |
| - 'Shot Silk' | LBut NSpr |
| - 'Skylark' | LBut |
| **San Salvador gx** | LBut |
| **Sangay gx** | LBut |
| **Santorini gx** | LBut |
| ***saxicola*** | CFwr LBut |
| ***scopulorum*** | EFEx |
| **Shantung gx** | CFir EPot LAma NSpr SIng |
| - R6.7 | NSpr |
| - R6.48 | NSpr |
| - 'Candyfloss' | NSpr |
| - 'Christine' | NSpr |
| - 'Ducat' | EPot LBut NSpr |
| - 'Gerry Mundey' | LBut NSpr |
| - 'Golden Jubilee' | NSpr |
| - 'Golden Plover' | LBut |
| - 'Mikki' | NSpr |
| - 'Muriel Harberd' ♀H2 | NSpr |
| - 'Pixie' | NSpr |
| - 'Ridgeway' | LBut NSpr |
| - 'Silver Anniversary' | LBut |
| **Shepherd's Warning gx** 'Gillian Clare' | NSpr |
| - 'Mary Buchanan' | NSpr |
| **Sorea gx** | LBut |
| **Soufrière gx** | LBut |
| - 'Sunrise' | NSpr |
| ***speciosa*** Ames & Schltr. | see *P. pleionoides* |
| **Starbotton gx** | NSpr |
| **Stromboli gx** | NSpr |
| - 'Fireball' | EPot NSpr |
| **Surtsey gx** | EPot |
| **Swaledale gx** | NSpr |
| **Taal gx** 'Red-tailed Hawk' | LBut |
| x ***taliensis*** | LBut |
| **Tarawera gx** | LBut |
| **Tolima gx** | NSpr |
| - 'Moorhen' | LBut LEdu |
| **Tongariro gx** | CPBP EPot ERos NSpr SIng |
| - 'Jackdaw' | NSpr |
| **Versailles gx** | EPot ERos |
| - 'Bucklebury' ♀H2 | LBut |
| - 'Heron' | LBut |
| **Vesuvius gx** | EBrs EPot NSpr WAbe |
| - 'Grey Wagtail' | LBut |
| - 'Leopard' | LBut NSpr |
| - 'Phoenix' | EPot LBut NSpr |
| - 'Tawny Owl' | LBut |
| **Vicky gx** | NSpr |
| **Volcanello gx** | EPot NSpr |
| - 'Honey Buzzard' | LBut |
| - 'Song Thrush' | LBut |
| 'Wharfedale Pine Warbler' | LBut |
| ***yunnanensis*** misapplied | see *P. bulbocodioides* 'Yunnan' |
| ***yunnanensis*** (Rolfe) Rolfe | LBut |
| **Zeus Weinstein gx** | LBut |
| - 'Desert Sands' | LBut |

## *Pleomele* see *Dracaena*

## *Pleurospermum* (*Apiaceae*)

| | |
|---|---|
| HWJK 2329 from Nepal | WCru |
| aff. ***amabile*** BWJ 7886 | WCru |
| ***benthamii*** B&SWJ 2988 | WCru |
| ***brunonis*** | NChi |
| ***calcareum*** B&SWJ 8008 | WCru |

## plum see *Prunus domestica*

## *Plumbago* (*Plumbaginaceae*)

| | |
|---|---|
| § ***auriculata*** ♀H1-2 | CBcs CCCN CHEx CRHN CSBt CTri CWSG EBak EBee ELan EPfP EShb ISea LRHS MBri MLan NPal SMrm SOWG SPer SRms SVic |
| - var. ***alba*** ♀H1-2 | CBcs CHal CRHN CSev EBak EBee EMil EPfP EShb MLan SOWG |
| - 'Crystal Waters' | CCCN CDoC ELan EShb |
| - dark blue-flowered | CSpe MJnS |
| ***caerulea*** | CSpe |
| ***capensis*** | see *P. auriculata* |
| § ***indica*** ♀H1 | CCCN CHal EShb MJnS SOWG |
| - ***rosea*** | see *P. indica* |
| ***larpentiae*** | see *Ceratostigma plumbaginoides* |

## *Plumeria* (*Apocynaceae*)

| | |
|---|---|
| sp. | MJnS |
| ***rubra*** ♀H1 | CCCN EShb SOWG XBlo |
| - f. ***acutifolia*** | SOWG |

## *Pneumatopteris* (*Thelypteridaceae*)

| | |
|---|---|
| ***pennigera*** | WRic |

## *Poa* (*Poaceae*)

| | |
|---|---|
| ***alpina*** | NGdn NLar |
| ***chaixii*** | EHoe EPPr EPla GFor NLar SLPl |
| ***cita*** | GFor GMaP WPnP |
| ***colensoi*** | CKno EBee EHoe EPPr GKev MAvo WPnP |
| x ***jemtlandica*** | EHoe EPPr |
| ***labillardierei*** | CKno CWCL EBee EBrs ECha EHoe EMon EPPr EWsh GGar GQue MAvo MSte SEND SPer SPoG SUsu WDyG WMoo WPrP |
| ***trivialis*** | CRWN EBWF |
| I 'Variegata' | SApp |

## *Podalyria* (*Papilionaceae*)

| | |
|---|---|
| ***calyptrata*** | SPlb |
| ***sericea*** | SPlb |

## *Podocarpus* (*Podocarpaceae*)

| | |
|---|---|
| ***acutifolius*** | CBcs CDoC ECou EPla GGar GKir MBar STre |

| | |
|---|---|
| - (f) | ECou |
| - (m) | ECou |
| ***alpinus*** R. Br. ex Hook. f. | NHol |
| ***andinus*** | see *Prumnopitys andina* |
| 'Autumn Shades' (m) | ECou |
| 'Blaze' (f) | CBcs CDoC CRob ECou EMil NHol NLar SCoo SLim SPoG |
| ***chilinus*** | see *P. salignus* |
| 'Chocolate Box' (f) | ECou |
| 'County Park Fire'$^{PBR}$ (f) | CBcs CDoC CKen CRob CWSG ECho ECou EMil EOrn EPfP MAsh MGos NHol SCoo SLim SPoG SWvt WFar WGor |
| 'County Park Treasure' | ECou |
| ***cunninghamii*** | CBcs ECou |
| - 'Kiwi' (f) | ECou MGos |
| - 'Roro' (m) | CBcs CDoC ECou |
| ***cunninghamii*** x ***nivalis*** (f) | ECou |
| ***dacrydioides*** | see *Dacrycarpus dacrydioides* |
| ***elongatus*** | CTrC IDee |
| - 'Blue Chip' **new** | CBcs |
| 'Flame' | CDoC ECho ECou EPla SCoo |
| 'Havering' (f) | CDoC ECou MGos |
| ***henkelii*** | CTrC EShb GGar |
| 'Jill' (f) | ECou |
| ***latifolius*** | CAbb ECou EShb IDee |
| ***lawrencei*** | EHul GGar WThu |
| - (f) | ECou MBar |
| - 'Alpine Lass' (f) | ECou |
| - 'Blue Gem' (f) | CDoC CRob ECou EOrn EPla IArd IDee LRHS MAsh MBar MBri MGos MMuc NHol SCoo SLim WFar |
| - 'Kiandra' | ECou |
| - 'Kosciuszko' **new** | ECou |
| - 'Pine Lake' **new** | ECou |
| - 'Red Tip' | CDoC CRob EMil LRHS MAsh SCoo SLim STre WGor |
| 'Lucky Lad' **new** | ECou |
| 'Macho' (m) | ECou |
| ***macrophyllus*** | CHEx EOrn NLar SAPC SArc SMad STre WFar |
| - (m) | ECou WFar |
| - 'Aureus' | CBcs |
| 'Maori Prince' (m) | CDoC ECou EPla MGos |
| ***nivalis*** | CBcs CDul CMac CTrC ECou EOrn EPla GCal GGar GKir MBar SCoo SRms STre |
| - 'Arthur' (m) | ECou |
| - 'Bronze' | CDoC ECou EPla MGos |
| - 'Christmas Lights' (f) | CKen ECou |
| - 'Clarence' (m) | ECou |
| - 'Cover Girl' | CRob SPoG |
| - 'Green Queen' (f) | ECou |
| - 'Hikurangi' | CDoC |
| - 'Jack's Pass' (m) | ECou SCoo |
| - 'Kaweka' (m) | ECou |
| - 'Kilworth Cream' (v) | CBcs CDoC CRob ECho ECou EMil EPla MAsh MGos NHol NLar SCoo SLim SWvt WGor |
| - 'Little Lady' (f) | ECou |
| - 'Livingstone' (f) | ECou |
| - 'Lodestone' (m) | ECou |
| - 'Moffat' (f) | CBcs CDoC ECou |
| - 'Otari' (m) | ECou NLar |
| - 'Park Cover' | ECou |
| - 'Princess' (f) | ECou |
| - 'Ruapehu' (m) | CDoC ECou EPla |
| - 'Trompenburg' | NLar |
| ***nubigenus*** | CBcs |
| 'Orangeade' (f) | CBcs MGos NLar |
| 'Red Embers' | CDoC ECho ECou SCoo |
| * 'Redtip' | SLim |
| § ***salignus*** 🏆$^{H3}$ | CBcs CBrd CDoC CDul CHEx CPLG EPfP EPla GGal IDee IFFs ISea LRHS SAPC SArc SLim WFar WPic WSHC |
| - (f) | ECou WFar |
| - (m) | ECou |
| 'Soldier Boy' **new** | ECou |
| ***spicatus*** | see *Prumnopitys taxifolia* |
| 'Spring Sunshine' (f) | CBcs CDoC ECou EPla MGos NLar |
| ***totara*** | CBcs CTrC ECou GGar LEdu WFar |
| - 'Albany Gold' | CTrC |
| - 'Aureus' | CBcs CDoC ECou EPla MBar SCoo SHBN WFar |
| - 'Pendulus' | CDoC ECou |
| 'Young Rusty' (f) | CBcs CDoC ECou EPla MAsh MGos |

## *Podophyllum* (*Berberidaceae*)

| | |
|---|---|
| ***aurantiocaule*** | EBee GGGa |
| § ***delavayi*** | CAby CBct CFir CLAP EBee EBla EBrs ECho GEdr MDun NLar WCot WCru |
| ***difforme*** | CBct CLAP EBee GEdr SKHP WCru |
| ***emodi*** | see *P. hexandrum* |
| - var. ***chinense*** | see *P. hexandrum* var. *chinense* |
| § ***hexandrum*** | Widely available |
| § - var. ***chinense*** | CBro CLAP CRow EBee EBla ECho GBuc GCal GEdr GKev IBlr ITim LEdu SMad WCru |
| - - BWJ 7908 | WCru |
| - - SDR 4409 **new** | GKev |
| - 'Chinese White' | WCot |
| - 'Majus' | CFir CLAP EBee EBrs MSte SMad WHal |
| 'Kaleidoscope' (v) | CBow NBhm SKHP |
| ***peltatum*** | CArn CBct CBro CHid CLAP COld CRow CSec EBee EBla EBrs ECho EWld GBBs GEdr GPoy LAma LEdu NMyG NSti SPhx WCru WFar WPGP WPnP |
| - var. ***peltatum*** f. ***deamii*** **new** | EBee |
| ***pleianthum*** | CAby CBct CLAP EBee GEdr WCot WCru |
| - B&SWJ 282 from Taiwan | WCru |
| - short | WCru |
| 'Spotty Dotty' **new** | CBct CWCL EBee GEdr GQue NSti |
| * ***tsayuensis*** | CBct |
| ***veitchii*** | see *P. delavayi* |
| ***versipelle*** | CLAP EBee SKHP WCru |

## *Podranea* (*Bignoniaceae*)

| | |
|---|---|
| ***brycei*** | CRHN EShb |
| § ***ricasoliana*** | CHEx CRHN EShb SOWG |

## *Pogonatherum* (*Poaceae*)

| | |
|---|---|
| § ***paniceum*** | MBri |
| ***saccharoideum*** | see *P. paniceum* |

## *Pogostemon* (*Lamiaceae*)

| | |
|---|---|
| from An Veleniki Herb Farm, Pennsylvania | CArn |
| § ***cablin*** | GPoy MSal |
| ***patchouly*** | see *P. cablin* |

## *Polemonium* ✿ (*Polemoniaceae*)

| | |
|---|---|
| ***acutiflorum*** | see *P. caeruleum* subsp. *villosum* |
| ***acutifolium*** var. ***nipponicum*** | see *P. caeruleum* var. *nipponicum* |
| ***ambervicsii*** | see *P. pauciflorum* subsp. *hinckleyi* |
| 'Apricot Beauty' | see *P. carneum* 'Apricot Delight' |
| N ***archibaldiae*** 🏆$^{H4}$ | EBee NBir SRms |
| § ***boreale*** | CSec EBee ECho GKir NPol SWvt WFar WMoo |
| - 'Heavenly Habit' | EBee MWhi NVic SHGN |

| | | |
|---|---|---|
| | 'Blue Pearl' | CElw CMea EBee ELan EPfP EShb LHop MBri MLLN MNrw NBro NCob NGdn NPol NPri SGar SPer SPla WFar |
| | ***brandegeei*** misapplied | see *P. pauciflorum* |
| § | ***brandegeei*** Greene | SHGN WPer |
| | - subsp. ***mellitum*** | see *P. brandegeei* Greene |
| § | ***caeruleum*** | Widely available |
| | - 'Bambino Blue' | EBee GKir NBre SWvt WPer |
| | - Brise d'Anjou = 'Blanjou'PBR (v) | CHid CMMP EBee EBrs ECrN EHrv ELan EPfP EWes GAbr GKir GMaP LAst LRHS MBri MSte NBir NCGa NCob NPol SPer SPla SWvt WCot WFar |
| | - subsp. ***caeruleum*** | GKev |
| | - - f. ***album*** | Widely available |
| I | - f. ***dissectum*** | NPol |
| | - 'Golden Showers' (v) | NPro |
| | - var. ***grandiflorum*** | see *P. caeruleum* subsp. *himalayanum* |
| § | - subsp. ***himalayanum*** | CSec GAbr MCot MHar NBur WFar WMoo WPer WPtf |
| | - 'Humile' | see *P.* 'Northern Lights' |
| | - 'Idylle' | NCot |
| § | - var. ***nipponicum*** | CSec NPol WPer |
| | - 'Pam' (v) | CBow EBee NPol WCot |
| | - 'Snow and Sapphires' (v) | LAst MBri MCCP NPer SPav SPoG SRkn SWvt |
| § | - subsp. ***villosum*** | NPol |
| | - subsp. ***vulgare*** | NPol |
| | - white-flowered **new** | GJos |
| | ***californicum*** | NPol |
| | ***carneum*** | CTri CWan ECGP ECha EGle GKir GMaP MCCP MNFA MNrw MTho NPol SPad SPhx WAul WCAu WFar WMoo WPer |
| § | - 'Apricot Delight' | EBee EHig GBri GJos GMac MCCP MNrw NBir NGdn NPol SGar SIde SPoG STes WBVN WFar WHer WPer WPnP WPtf |
| | ***cashmerianum*** | see *P. caeruleum* subsp. *himalayanum* |
| | ***chartaceum*** | LLHF |
| | 'Churchills' | CBre EBee WPGP WPrP WSHC |
| | 'Dawn Flight' | WFar |
| | ***delicatum*** | see *P. pulcherrimum* Hook. subsp. *delicatum* |
| | 'Eastbury Purple' | CElw CWCL |
| | 'Elworthy Amethyst' | CElw EBee MAvo NPol WPGP |
| | ***eximium*** | EBee LLHF |
| | ***flavum*** | see *P. foliosissimum* var. *flavum* |
| | ***foliosissimum*** misapplied | see *P. archibaldiae* |
| | ***foliosissimum*** A. Gray | CSec EBee IGor MNrw WPer |
| | - var. ***albiflorum*** | see *P. foliosissimum* var. *alpinum* |
| § | - var. ***alpinum*** | NBir NPol |
| | - 'Cottage Cream' | CBre CDes NPol |
| § | - var. ***flavum*** | NPol |
| | - var. ***foliosissimum*** | EWes NPol |
| | - 'White Spirit' | NPol |
| | 'Glebe Cottage Lilac' | CElw CHar EBee GCra NBir SBch WPGP |
| | ***grandiflorum*** | NPol |
| | 'Hannah Billcliffe' | CDes CElw ECtt EWes MBrN NChi NCot NPol WPGP |
| | 'Heavenly Blue' | ECtt |
| § | 'Hopleys' | GBar GBri GCal NChi NCot WFar |
| | x ***jacobaea*** | CDes EBee WCot WPGP WTin |
| | 'Katie Daley' | see *P.* 'Hopleys' |
| | 'Lace Towers' | NSti |
| | 'Lambrook Mauve' ♀H4 | Widely available |
| | ***liniflorum*** | CSec |
| | 'Mary Mottram' | NPol |
| | ***mellitum*** | see *P. brandegeei* Greene |
| | 'North Tyne' | NChi NPol |
| § | 'Northern Lights' | CDes CSev CWCL EBee EGle ELon EMon EPPr EWes GBri LCro MNrw NCot NDov NPol NSti SBch SSvw SUsu WCot WFar WMoo WPGP |
| | 'Norwell Mauve' | MNrw |
| | ***occidentale*** subsp. ***occidentale*** | NPol |
| § | ***pauciflorum*** | CEnt CStu EBee ECtt EHrv EPfP IFro MNFA MNrw MTho NBir NHol SPer SUsu WCAu WFar WMoo WPer |
| § | - subsp. ***hinckleyi*** | CSec NCot NPol SGar |
| § | - subsp. ***pauciflorum*** | NPol SGar SPav |
| | - silver-leaved | see *P. pauciflorum* subsp. *pauciflorum* |
| | - 'Sulphur Trumpets' | ECtt SPav SWvt WFar |
| | - subsp. ***typicum*** | see *P. pauciflorum* subsp. *pauciflorum* |
| | 'Pink Beauty' | CBre EBee ELan EPPr EPfP MLLN NBre NCob NCot NGdn NPol SPla |
| | ***pulchellum*** Salisb. | see *P. reptans* |
| | ***pulchellum*** Turcz. | see *P. caeruleum* |
| | ***pulcherrimum*** misapplied | see *P. boreale* |
| | - 'Tricolor' | see *P. boreale* |
| | ***pulcherrimum*** Hook. | GCal NBro SPoG WPer |
| | - ***album*** | CGra GKev |
| § | - subsp. ***delicatum*** | MTho NPol |
| | - subsp. ***pulcherrimum*** | LLHF NPol |
| § | ***reptans*** | CArn GBar GBri GPoy MHer MSal NBro NPol WAul WFar WMoo WPer WPtf |
| | - 'Album' | see *P. reptans* 'Virginia White' |
| | - 'Blue Ice' | NPol |
| | - 'Firmament' | EBee WPGP |
| * | - 'Sky Blue' | NBro |
| | - 'Stairway to Heaven'PBR (v) | Widely available |
| | - 'Touch of Class' **new** | EBee |
| § | - 'Virginia White' | CBre CDes CElw CMea CSev EBee MAvo NChi NPol SUsu WFar |
| | - 'White Pearl' | EHig EShb NPri |
| | 'Ribby' | NPol |
| | ***richardsonii*** misapplied | see *P.* 'Northern Lights' |
| | ***richardsonii*** Graham | see *P. boreale* |
| | 'Sapphire' | CBre ELan EMon MBrN NPol |
| | ***scopulinum*** | see *P. pulcherrimum* Hook. subsp. *delicatum* |
| | 'Sonia's Bluebell' | CDes CElw CWCL EBee ECtt EWes LPio MAvo MDKP MNrw MSte NCot NDov NPol NSti SUsu WPGP |
| | 'Theddingworth' | MAvo NPol WFar |
| | ***vanbruntiae*** | NPol |
| | ***viscosum*** | GBuc NPol SGar |
| | - f. ***leucanthum*** | NPol |
| | ***yezoense*** | CBre CSec GBri MNrw NBre NCot NPol SPhx WFar |
| | - var. ***hidakanum*** | NPol |
| | - - Bressingham Purple = 'Polbress' | CBow EAEE EBee EBrs EWes GBin MBNS MBri NBsh NCGa NDov NOrc SMad SPer WFar |
| | - - 'Purple Rain' | Widely available |
| | - 'Midnight Rain' | CSpe |

## *Polianthes* (*Agavaceae*)

| | | |
|---|---|---|
| § | ***geminiflora*** | EBrs |
| | ***nelsonii*** | CFir |
| | ***tuberosa*** ♀H1-2 | CBcs CCCN CSpe CStu EBrs ECho IHer LRHS |
| | - 'The Pearl' (d) | CDes CSec EBrs ECho LAma WHil WPGP |

## *Poliomintha* (*Lamiaceae*)

| | | |
|---|---|---|
| | ***bustamanta*** | NBir SPhx |
| | ***maderensis*** F&M 195 | WPGP |

## *Poliothyrsis* (*Flacourtiaceae*)

| | |
|---|---|
| ***sinensis*** ♀H4 | CAbP CTho EBee EPfP LRHS MBri NLar WPGP WPat |

## *Polygala* (*Polygalaceae*)

| | |
|---|---|
| ***calcarea*** | ECho LLHF WPat |
| - Bulley's form | EPot |
| - 'Lillet' ♀H4 | ECho EPot EWes LHop LLHF LRHS NLAp NLar NMen NSla WFar WPat |
| ***chamaebuxus*** ♀H4 | CBcs ECho GKev GKir LSou MDKP MGos NDlv NLar NSla NWCA SKHP SRms WSHC |
| I - ***alba*** | LBee LSou NLar SChF WAbe |
| § - var. ***grandiflora*** ♀H4 | CBcs CFir ECho EMil EPfP EPot GEdr GGar GKir LBee MAsh MBar MDun MGos MWat NLAp NMen NSla SChF SIng SPoG WAbe WBod WFar WPat WSHC |
| - 'Kamniski' | ECho NLar |
| - 'Loibl' | EPot MAsh |
| - 'Purpurea' | see *P. chamaebuxus* var. *grandiflora* |
| - 'Rhodoptera' | see *P. chamaebuxus* var. *grandiflora* |
| § x ***dalmaisiana*** ♀H1 | CAbb CCCN CHEx CHll CRHN CSpe EBee MWea SAga SGar WAbe WCFE |
| ***myrtifolia*** | CCCN CTrC EMil GFai MGos MREP SGar SMrm SPlb |
| - 'Grandiflora' | see *P.* x *dalmaisiana* |
| 'Rhubarb Rock' **new** | GKir |
| ***tenuifolia*** | CArn |
| ***vayredae*** | NLar |
| ***virgata*** | EBee EShb WBod |

## *Polygonatum* ✿ (*Convallariaceae*)

| | |
|---|---|
| ***acuminatifolium*** | EBla |
| ***altelobatum*** | EBla |
| - B&SWJ 286 | WCru |
| - B&SWJ 1886 **new** | WCru |
| ***arisanense*** B&SWJ 3839 **new** | WCru |
| § ***biflorum*** | Widely available |
| - dwarf | EBla EPla |
| ***canaliculatum*** | see *P. biflorum* |
| ***cirrhifolium*** | CDes CFir CLAP CMdw CPom EBee EBla ELan EPot GBin GEdr GKir WCot WCru WPGP WPrP |
| - red-flowered | WCot |
| ***commutatum*** | see *P. biflorum* |
| 'Corsley' | CPou |
| ***cryptanthum*** | EBla EPot WCru |
| ***curvistylum*** | CAvo CBct CHFP CLAP CPom CStu EBee EBla ECha EGle EHrv EPPr GEdr IFoB MNFA NLar NRya SPhx WAbe WCru WFar |
| - CLD 761 | GEdr |
| ***cyrtonema*** misapplied | see *Disporopsis pernyi* |
| ***cyrtonema*** Hua | CLAP EBee |
| - B&SWJ 271 | MPoH WCru |
| * ***desoulavyi*** var. ***yezoense*** B&SWJ 764 | MPoH WCru |
| ***falcatum*** misapplied | see *P. humile* |
| ***falcatum*** A. Gray | CLyd EBee EBla EGle EPot WHer WThu |
| - B&SWJ 1077 | WCru |
| - silver-striped | CLAP EPot GEdr |
| - - B&SWJ 5101 | WCru |
| - 'Variegatum' | see *P. odoratum* var. *pluriflorum* 'Variegatum' |
| 'Falcon' | see *P. humile* |
| ***filipes*** | EBee WCru |
| ***franchetii*** | CExc GEdr |
| ***fuscum*** | WCru |
| ***geminiflorum*** | CBct CLAP CPom EBla WCot WFar |
| - McB 2448 | GEdr |
| ***giganteum*** | see *P. biflorum* |
| ***glaberrimum*** | CAvo CBct EBee EBla WCot |
| § ***graminifolium*** | CBct CLAP CPom EBee EBla EBrs ECho EPot ERos GEdr MSte NMen SCnR WCot WCru |
| - G-W&P 803 | IPot |
| § ***hirtum*** | CBct CLAP CPom EBla EBrs ECho EMon EPPr EPla IFoB LEdu WCru WFar WTin |
| - BM 7012 | EBee MPoH |
| - dwarf | WCot |
| ***hookeri*** | Widely available |
| - McB 1413 | GEdr |
| § ***humile*** | CBct CLAP EBee EBla EBrs ECho EHrv EMon EPPr EPfP ERos GBri GCal GGar GKir IBal LAst NMen NMyG SUsu WAul WCot WCru WFar WHil |
| § x ***hybridum*** ♀H4 | Widely available |
| - 'Betberg' | CBct CLAP CRow EBla ECha EHrv EPPr NBir WCot |
| - 'Flore Pleno' (d) | CBct EBla WHer |
| - 'Nanum' | CBct CHid EBla |
| - 'Purple Katie' **new** | MPoH |
| § - 'Striatum' (v) | Widely available |
| - 'Variegatum' | see *P.* x *hybridum* 'Striatum' |
| - 'Wakehurst' | EBla EHrv |
| - 'Weihenstephan' | EBee EBla GCal |
| - 'Welsh Gold' (v) **new** | CAvo |
| ***inflatum*** | EBla ECho WCru |
| - B&SWJ 922 | WCru |
| ***involucratum*** | ECho WCru |
| - B&SWJ 4285 | WCru |
| ***japonicum*** | see *P. odoratum* |
| - 'Aureum' | see *P. odoratum* golden |
| ***kingianum*** | CExc EBee |
| - yellow-flowered B&SWJ 6545 **new** | WCru |
| - - B&SWJ 6562 | WCru |
| 'Langthorns Variegated' (v) | ELan |
| ***lasianthum*** | WCru |
| - B&SWJ 671 | WCru |
| ***latifolium*** | see *P. hirtum* |
| ***leptophyllum*** KEKE 844 | GEdr |
| ***macropodum*** **new** | EBee |
| ***maximowiczii*** | CPom EBee EPPr GCal WCru |
| 'Multifide' **new** | EBee |
| ***multiflorum*** misapplied | see *P.* x *hybridum* |
| ***multiflorum*** L. | Widely available |
| - ***giganteum*** hort. | see *P. biflorum* |
| * - 'Ramosissima' **new** | EBla |
| * ***nanum*** 'Variegatum' (v) | CBcs CWCL ECho |
| ***nodosum*** | EBee EBla WCru |
| ***obtusifolium*** | EBee EBla |
| § ***odoratum*** ♀H4 | CAby CAvo CBct CBro CPom CRow CSWP EBee EBla EBrs ECho EHrv EPfP EPla GMaP IBlr MSal NBid NLar NRya WCru WFar WHil WPnP |
| § - dwarf | ECho EMon IBlr LEdu |
| - 'Flore Pleno' (d) ♀H4 | CDes CLAP CPom CRow EBee EBla EBrs ECha ECho EHrv EPla EPot LEdu SCnR SMHy WCot WHoo WPGP WPnP WPrP WTin |
| § - golden-flowered | CBct |
| - 'Grace Barker' | see *P.* x *hybridum* 'Striatum' |
| - Kew form | EPot |
| - var. ***pluriflorum*** | EBee GBuc IBlr |
| § - - 'Variegatum' (v) ♀H4 | Widely available |

| | | |
|---|---|---|
| | - 'Red Stem' | MPoH WCru |
| | - 'Silver Wings' (v) | CBct CLAP EBla ECha EHrv NBir |
| | ***officinale*** | see *P. odoratum* |
| | ***oppositifolium*** | EBee EBla WFar |
| | - B&SWJ 2537 | WCru |
| § | ***orientale*** | CBct CHid CLAP EBee EBla EBrs ECho WCot |
| | ***pluriflorum*** | see *P. graminifolium* |
| | ***polyanthemum*** | see *P. orientale* |
| | ***prattii*** | EBee EBla |
| | - CLD 325 | GEdr |
| | ***pubescens*** | CBct EBee WCru WThu |
| | ***pumilum*** | see *P. odoratum* dwarf |
| | ***punctatum*** | EBee LEdu WFar |
| | - B&SWJ 2395 | CBct EBla WCru |
| | ***roseum*** | CDes CLAP CPom EPPr GEdr GKev WHer WPGP |
| | - SBQE 310 **new** | MPoH |
| | ***sewerzowii*** | EBee EBla EPla |
| | ***sibiricum*** | CAvo CBct CPom EBla GEdr IBlr WCot WCru |
| | - DJHC 600 | CDes |
| | ***stenophyllum*** | CAvo EBla WCru |
| | ***stewartianum*** | CLAP CPom EBee EPPr IBlr |
| | ***tessellatum*** **new** | EBee |
| | aff. ***tessellatum*** B&SWJ 9752 **new** | WCru |
| | ***tonkinense*** HWJ 551 | MPoH WCru |
| | - HWJ 861 **new** | WCru |
| | ***verticillatum*** | Widely available |
| | - 'Giant One' **new** | EBee |
| | - 'Himalayan Giant' | CHid EBee EBla ECho IPot |
| * | - 'Roseum' **new** | GKir |
| * | - 'Rubrum' | CArn CBct CLAP CRow CSec EBee EBla EGle EHrv EPPr EPla GEdr IBlr IPot LEdu LFur MAvo MSte MTho NBid NGby SPhx WCot WHil WPrP |
| | - 'Serbian Dwarf' | CBct CHid EBee EBla ECho IPot |
| | aff. ***verticillatum*** | CSpe EMon |
| | aff. ***wardii*** B&SWJ 6599 | WCru |
| | ***zanlanscianense*** | CBct EBee EBla WCru WFar |

## *Polygonum* ✿ (*Polygonaceae*)

| | | |
|---|---|---|
| | ***affine*** | see *Persicaria affinis* |
| | - 'Darjeeling Red' | see *Persicaria affinis* 'Darjeeling Red' |
| | - 'Donald Lowndes' | see *Persicaria affinis* 'Donald Lowndes' |
| | - 'Superbum' | see *Persicaria affinis* 'Superba' |
| | ***amplexicaule*** | see *Persicaria amplexicaulis* |
| | ***aubertii*** | see *Fallopia baldschuanica* |
| | ***aviculare*** | CArn |
| | ***baldschuanicum*** | see *Fallopia baldschuanica* |
| | ***bistorta*** | see *Persicaria bistorta* |
| | - 'Superbum' | see *Persicaria bistorta* 'Superba' |
| | ***capitatum*** | see *Persicaria capitata* |
| | ***compactum*** | see *Fallopia japonica* var. *compacta* |
| | ***equisetiforme*** misapplied | see *P. scoparium* |
| | ***filiforme*** | see *Persicaria virginiana* |
| | ***forrestii*** | EBee |
| | ***longisetum*** | see *Persicaria longiseta* |
| | ***molle*** | see *Persicaria mollis* |
| | ***multiflorum*** | see *Fallopia multiflora* |
| | ***odoratum*** | see *Persicaria odorata* |
| | ***polystachyum*** | see *Persicaria wallichii* |
| | ***runciforme*** | see *Persicaria runcinata* |
| § | ***scoparium*** | CBcs CRow EPPr EPla SDys SIng WFar WOld WTin |
| | ***tinctorium*** | see *Persicaria tinctoria* |
| | ***vacciniifolium*** | see *Persicaria vacciniifolia* |
| | ***weyrichii*** | see *Persicaria weyrichii* |

## *Polylepis* (*Rosaceae*)

| | | |
|---|---|---|
| | ***australis*** | EBee EPla LEdu MBri SMad WCot WCru WPGP |
| | - tall **new** | WPGP |
| | ***pauta*** | WPGP |

## *Polymnia* (*Asteraceae*)

| | | |
|---|---|---|
| | ***sonchifolia*** | LEdu MSal |
| | ***uvedalia*** | see *Smallanthus uvedalius* |

## *Polypodium* ✿ (*Polypodiaceae*)

| | | |
|---|---|---|
| | ***aureum*** | see *Phlebodium aureum* |
| | - 'Glaucum' | CSpe WCot |
| | ***australe*** | see *P. cambricum* |
| | ***californicum*** 'Sarah Lyman' | SKHP |
| § | ***cambricum*** | EBee EFer WCot WFib WRic WTin |
| | - 'Barrowii' | CBgR CLAP WAbe WFib |
| I | - 'Cambricum' 🏆H4 | CBgR CLAP GCal WAbe WRic |
| | - 'Cristatum' | CLAP WFib |
| | - (Cristatum Group) 'Grandiceps Forster' | CLAP |
| | - - 'Grandiceps Fox' 🏆H4 | WFib |
| | - 'Hornet' | GBin WFib |
| | - 'Macrostachyon' | CLAP EFer GBin WFib |
| | - 'Oakleyae' | SMHy |
| | - 'Omnilacerum Oxford' | CLAP |
| | - 'Prestonii' | CBgR EBee WAbe WCot WFib |
| | - Pulcherrimum Group | CLAP WAbe WRic |
| | - - 'Pulcherrimum Addison' | GBin WAbe WFib |
| | - - 'Pulchritudine' | CLAP WAbe |
| | - 'Richard Kayse' | CDes CLAP EBee WAbe WCot WFib WPGP |
| | - Semilacerum Group | WRic |
| | - - 'Carew Lane' | WFib |
| | - - 'Robustum' | WFib |
| | - 'Whilharris' 🏆H4 | CLAP CWsd SMHy WAbe |
| I | x ***coughlinii*** bifid | WFib |
| | ***formosanum*** | WRic |
| | ***glycyrrhiza*** | CLAP GPoy WFib |
| | - bifid | see *P.* x *coughlinii* bifid |
| | - 'Longicaudatum' 🏆H4 | CLAP EBee EMon GBin WAbe WCot WFib |
| | - 'Malahatense' | CLAP |
| | - 'Malahatense' (sterile) | WAbe |
| | ***interjectum*** | CBgR CLAP CWCL EBee EBrs EFer MAsh MMoz NVic WPnP WRic |
| | - 'Cornubiense' 🏆H4 | CBgR CDes CLAP EBee EMon GEdr MMoz NBid NBir NHol NVic WAbe WTin |
| | - 'Glomeratum Mullins' | WFib |
| | x ***mantoniae*** | WFib WIvy |
| | - 'Bifidograndiceps' | NBid WFib WRic |
| | ***scouleri*** | CLAP NBro |
| | ***subauriculatum*** 'Knightii' | see *Goniophlebium subauriculatum* 'Knightiae' |
| | ***virginianum*** **new** | EBee |
| | ***vulgare*** | Widely available |
| | - 'Bifidocristatum' | see *P. vulgare* 'Bifidomultifidum' |
| § | - 'Bifidomultifidum' | CBgR CLAP CWCL EMon EWTr GBin GCal GEdr LLWP LRHS MAsh MCCP MGos NHol NLar SEND SPla STes WCot |
| * | - 'Congestum Cristatum' | SRms |
| | - 'Cornubiense Grandiceps' | GCal SRms WIvy WRic |
| * | - 'Cornubiense Multifidum' | EBee WCot |
| | - 'Elegantissimum' | WFib |
| | - 'Parsley' **new** | WCot |
| | - 'Ramosum Hillman' | EBee |
| | - 'Trichomanoides Backhouse' | CLAP GCal WAbe WFib |

## *Polypogon* (*Poaceae*)

| | |
|---|---|
| ***monspeliensis*** | CSec |

## *Polypompholyx* see *Utricularia*

## *Polyscias* (*Araliaceae*)

| | |
|---|---|
| ***elegans*** | MBri |
| ***fruticosa*** | MBri |
| ***scutellaria*** 'Pennockii' (v) | MBri |

## *Polystichum* ✿ (*Dryopteridaceae*)

| | |
|---|---|
| BWJ 8182 from China | WCru |
| ***acrostichoides*** | CDes CFwr CLAP CMHG EBee EPPr ERod GEdr GQui LRHS MBri NLar NMyG WPGP WRic |
| ***aculeatum*** ♀H4 | Widely available |
| I - Densum Group | EFer |
| - Grandiceps Group | EFer |
| - 'Portia' | WFib |
| ***altum*** | CExc |
| ***andersonii*** | CLAP CWCL EBee NHol WRic |
| ***bissectum*** | CExc CFwr |
| ***braunii*** | CBcs CMHG CPrp CWCL EBee EGol EQua GBin GMaP LRHS MMoz MMuc NHol NLar WFib WPnP WRic |
| ***caryotideum*** | see *Cyrtomium caryotideum* |
| ***deltodon*** | CExc EBee |
| ***dracomontanum*** | WRic |
| x ***dycei*** | WRic |
| ***falcatum*** | see *Cyrtomium falcatum* |
| ***fortunei*** | see *Cyrtomium fortunei* |
| ***imbricans*** | CLAP SArc |
| ***interjectum*** | MRav |
| ***makinoi*** | CCCN CLAP EBee NHol WFib WRic |
| ***munitum*** ♀H4 | Widely available |
| ***neolobatum*** | NVic WFib |
| - BWJ 8182 **new** | WCru |
| ***polyblepharum*** ♀H4 | Widely available |
| ***proliferum*** ambig. | EPot EWTr WPtf |
| ***proliferum*** (R. Br.) C. Presl | CLAP GCal SBig WFib WRic |
| * - ***plumosum*** | CFwr LAst |
| ***richardii*** | EUJe GBin SBig WRic |
| ***rigens*** | CFwr CLAP CPrp EBee LRHS LSou MAsh MMuc NDlv NHol NLar SRms SRot WCru WFib WRic |
| ***setiferum*** ♀H4 | Widely available |
| § - Acutilobum Group | CBgR CFwr CLAP CMHG CPrp CWCL EBee ECha EPla GMaP LRHS NHol SDix SMad SPer SRms STes WMoo WPGP WPnP WPrP |
| - Congestum Group | CBgR CPrp GBin MMoz NCGa NHol SPer SRms WFib WRic |
| - 'Congestum' | CFwr CLAP CWCL EBee ELan EMil EPfP ERod LRHS MAsh MDun MRav NBir NHol NMyG NSti SPla SPoG SSto WBor WCot WGor WMoo WPrP |
| - 'Congestum Cristatum' | LAst |
| - 'Cristatopinnulum' | CFwr CGHE CLAP EBee EPla WPGP |
| - Cristatum Group | CLAP EHrv SRms |
| - Cruciatum Group | CLAP |
| - Divisilobum Group | CBcs CFee CLAP CMHG CRow EFer ELan EMon EWsh LPBA MGos MLHP MMoz NHol NVic SPla SRms STre WAbe WAul WFar WFib WHoo WIvy WPGP WRic WTin |
| - - 'Caernarvon' **new** | CLAP |
| - - 'Dahlem' | CDoC CFwr CLAP EBee ECha EFer ELan EMon EPfP EWsh GKir GMaP LRHS MCot MDun MMoz MSte NHol NMoo SPoG SSto WAbe WBor WFib WMoo WPnP WRic |
| - - 'Divisilobum Densum' ♀H4 | CBgR CLAP EHrv EPfP LRHS NBir NOrc |
| - - 'Herrenhausen' | Widely available |
| - - 'Divisilobum Iveryanum' ♀H4 | CLAP EFer NHol SRms WFib |
| - - 'Divisilobum Laxum' | CLAP |
| - - 'Madame Patti' | MMoz |
| - - 'Mrs Goffey' | CGHE WFib WPGP |
| - 'Foliosum' | CLAP |
| - Foliosum Group | EFer |
| - 'Gracile' | MRav NBir |
| - 'Grandiceps' | CGHE CLAP EBee EFer ELan WPGP |
| - 'Hamlet' | WFib |
| - 'Helena' | WFib |
| - 'Hirondelle' | SRms |
| - Lineare Group | GKir WFib |
| - Multilobum Group | CLAP SRms WFib |
| - 'Othello' | WFib |
| - Perserratum Group | GBin NBid WFib |
| - 'Plumo-Densum' | see *P. setiferum* 'Plumosomultilobum' |
| - 'Plumosodensum' | see *P. setiferum* 'Plumosomultilobum' |
| - Plumosodivisilobum Group | CLAP CRow ECha EGol GBin LSou NBid SPla WAbe WFib |
| - - 'Baldwinii' | CLAP WFib |
| - - 'Bland' | WFib |
| I - 'Plumosomultilobum' | Widely available |
| - Plumosum Group | CBgR CGHE CLAP CMHG CSpe EBee EFer NOrc SAPC SArc SRot |
| - - dwarf | CSBt |
| * - ***plumosum grande*** 'Moly' | SRms |
| - 'Portmeirion' | CLAP |
| - Proliferum Group | see *P. setiferum* Acutilobum Group |
| * - 'Proliferum Wollaston' | CBcs CFwr CPrp CWCL EBee EMil MMoz SSto |
| - 'Pulcherrimum Bevis' ♀H4 | CLAP CWsd EBee ECGP GBin MRav NBid NMyG SDix SUsu WCot WFib WPGP WPnP WRic |
| * - 'Ramopinnatum' | CLAP |
| - Rotundatum Group | CLAP EBee |
| - - 'Cristatum' | CLAP |
| - - 'Rotundatum Ramosum' | CLAP |
| - 'Smith's Cruciate' | CFwr CLAP GBin WFib |
| - 'Wakeleyanum' | EFer SRms |
| - 'Wollaston' | CFwr CLAP ETod GBin MAsh MRav NBid NHol NLar WAbe |
| ***silvaticum*** | EFer |
| ***tripteron*** | EBee |
| ***tsussimense*** ♀H4 | Widely available |
| ***vestitum*** | CLAP CTrC EUJe GBin MMoz SBig WRic |

## *Polyxena* (*Hyacinthaceae*)

| | |
|---|---|
| ***corymbosa*** | CStu ECho |
| § ***ensifolia*** | EBrs ECho ERos LLHF |
| ***longituba*** | ECho EDif |
| ***odorata*** | CLyd CStu EBrs ECho |
| ***pygmaea*** | see *P. ensifolia* |

## *Pomaderris* (*Rhamnaceae*)

| | |
|---|---|
| ***apetala*** | CPLG |
| ***elliptica*** | CPLG ECou |
| ***kumeraho*** **new** | CCCN |

## pomegranate see *Punica granatum*

## *Poncirus* (*Rutaceae*)

| | |
|---|---|
| § ***trifoliata*** | CAgr CArn CBcs CCCN CDoC CTri EBee ELan EPfP IMGH LEdu LRHS |

| | |
|---|---|
| | MBlu MJnS MRav NWea SMad SPer SPlb SPoG WBVN WDin WFar WPGP WPat WSHC |
| - 'Flying Dragon' | SMad |

## *Ponerorchis* (*Orchidaceae*)

| | |
|---|---|
| ***graminifolia*** | CBct EBee LAma WWst |

## *Pontederia* (*Pontederiaceae*)

| | |
|---|---|
| ***cordata*** $\Upsilon^{H4}$ | CBen CDWL CHEx CRow CWat EHon ELan EMFW EPfP ILad LPBA MCCP MMuc MSKA NPer SCoo SPlb SWat WFar WMAq WPnP |
| - f. ***albiflora*** | CDWL CRow CWat EPfP LPBA MCCP NLar WMAq |
| - 'Blue Spires' | CDWL MSKA SPer |
| § - var. ***lancifolia*** | CBen CRow EMFW EPfP LPBA MCCP MSKA NPer SWat WTin |
| - 'Pink Pons' | CDWL CRow MSKA NLar |
| ***dilatata*** | see *Monochoria hastata* |
| ***lanceolata*** | see *P. cordata* var. *lancifolia* |

## *Populus* ✿ (*Salicaceae*)

| | |
|---|---|
| x ***acuminata*** | WMou |
| ***alba*** | CCVT CDoC CDul CLnd CSBt CTho CTri CWib ECrN EMac GKir LBuc MBar NBee NWea SBLw SHBN SPer WDin WMou WOrn |
| - 'Bolleana' | see *P. alba* f. *pyramidalis* |
| - 'Nivea' | SBLw |
| § - f. ***pyramidalis*** | SRms WMou |
| § - 'Raket' | CCVT CLnd CTho ECrN ELan SBLw SPer |
| - 'Richardii' | CLnd ECrN GKir MAsh MBar SPer WCot WFar WMou |
| - Rocket | see *P. alba* 'Raket' |
| ***alba*** x ***grandidentata*** | WMou |
| § 'Balsam Spire' (f) $\Upsilon^{H4}$ | CDoC CDul CLnd CTho EMac GKir NWea WDin WMou |
| § ***balsamifera*** | CCVT CDoC CSBt CTho CTri ECrN EMac GKir MGos NWea SBLw SHBN SPer SRms WCot WDin WFar |
| - 'Vita Sackville West' | MBlu |
| x ***berolinensis*** | CDoC |
| x ***canadensis*** | ECrN SBLw |
| § - 'Aurea' $\Upsilon^{H4}$ | CDoC CDul CLnd CTho CWib EBee EMac LCro LRHS MGos MRav NWea SPer WDin WFar WMou |
| - 'Aurea' x ***jackii*** 'Aurora' | WDin |
| - 'Robusta' (m) | CDoC CDul CLnd CTri EMil LBuc NWea WDin WMou |
| - 'Serotina' (m) | CCVT CDoC CDul ECrN WDin WMou |
| x ***candicans*** misapplied | see *P.* x *jackii* |
| x ***canescens*** | CDoC CDul CLnd ECrN MMuc NWea SBLw WDin WMou |
| - 'De Moffart' (m) | SBLw |
| - 'Tower' | WMou |
| x ***generosa*** 'Beaupré' | WDin WMou |
| § x ***jackii*** (f) | WDin |
| - 'Aurora' (f/v) | CBcs CDul CLnd CSBt CTrG EBee ELan GKir LBuc MBar MBri MGos MMuc MRav NBee NBlu NPri NWea SBLw SHBN SPer SRms WDin WFar WHar WJas |
| ***lasiocarpa*** $\Upsilon^{H4}$ | CDoC CEnd CGHE CMCN CPLG CSdC CTho EBee ELan EMil EPfP EPla IArd MBlu MRav SBLw SLPl WMou WPGP |
| ***maximowiczii*** | WMou |
| ***nigra*** | CDul CLnd CTho EMac EPfP NWea WDin |
| - (f) | ECrN SLPl |
| - (m) | SLPl |
| - subsp. ***betulifolia*** | CCVT CDul CLnd CWan NWea WDin WMou |
| - - (f) | ECrN WMou |
| - - (m) | ECrN WMou |
| - 'Italica' (m) $\Upsilon^{H4}$ | CCVT CDoC CDul CLnd CSBt CTho CTri CWib ECrN ELan EMac GKir LBuc MGos NBee NWea SBLw SHBN SPer SRms WDin WOrn |
| - 'Italica Aurea' | see *P. nigra* 'Lombardy Gold' |
| § - 'Lombardy Gold' (m) | CEnd ECrN MBlu |
| - 'Pyramidalis' | see *P. nigra* 'Italica' |
| 'Serotina Aurea' | see *P.* x *canadensis* 'Aurea' |
| ***simonii*** 'Fastigiata' | WMou |
| - 'Obtusata' | WMou |
| ***szechuanica*** | WMou |
| § - var. ***tibetica*** | WMou |
| ***tacamahaca*** | see *P. balsamifera* |
| 'Tacatricho 32' | see *P.* 'Balsam Spire' |
| ***tomentosa*** | WMou |
| ***tremula*** $\Upsilon^{H4}$ | CCVT CDoC CDul CLnd CRWN CSBt CTho CTri CWib EBee ECrN ELan EMac EWTr GKir LBuc LRHS NBee NWea SBLw SHBN SPer WDin WHar WMou WOrn |
| § - 'Erecta' | CDul CEnd CLnd CTho EBee LMaj MBlu MBri MMuc SMad WFar WMou |
| - 'Fastigiata' | see *P. tremula* 'Erecta' |
| - 'Pendula' (m) | CEnd CLnd CTho EBee ECrN GKir SBLw WCFE WDin WMou |
| ***trichocarpa*** | CDul CTho ECrN LMaj NWea SPer |
| - 'Fritzi Pauley' (f) | CDul CTho WMou |
| ***violascens*** | see *P. szechuanica* var. *tibetica* |
| ***yunnanensis*** | WMou |

## *Porophyllum* (*Asteraceae*)

| | |
|---|---|
| ***ruderale*** | MSal |

## *Portulaca* (*Portulacaceae*)

| | |
|---|---|
| 'Firegold' | SVil |
| ***grandiflora*** | MBri |
| ***oleracea*** | CArn MHer MNHC SIde SVic WJek |
| - var. ***aurea*** (hort.) G. Don | MNHC WJek |

## *Portulacaria* (*Portulacaceae*)

| | |
|---|---|
| ***afra*** 'Variegata' | EShb |

## *Potamogeton* (*Potamogetonaceae*)

| | |
|---|---|
| ***crispus*** | CDWL CWat EHon EMFW MSKA NSco WMAq |
| ***natans*** | EMFW NSco SEND |
| ***pectinatus*** | CWat |

## *Potentilla* ✿ (*Rosaceae*)

| | |
|---|---|
| SDR 2916 **new** | GKev |
| ***alba*** | CTri EBee ECha ECho ELan GBuc GGar GMac MLHP MRav MWat NChi SPer SUsu WAul WPer |
| ***alchemilloides*** | CMac WPer |
| ***alpicola*** | WPer |
| ***ambigua*** | see *P. cuneata* |
| ***andicola*** | EBee NBre |
| ***anserina*** | CArn EBWF EGoo GBar MHer WHer |
| - 'Golden Treasure' (v) | EBee MLLN NBre WHer |
| ***anserinoides*** | EGoo GCal WMoo WPer |
| ***arbuscula*** misapplied | see *P. fruticosa* 'Elizabeth' |
| - 'Beesii' | see *P. fruticosa* 'Beesii' |
| 'Arc-en-ciel' | CHid CKno EBee ECtt GBuc GMac LAst LSRN MAvo MBNS MBri MLHP NBPC NCGa NLar NPro SHar SPoG STes SUsu WBor WCAu WFar WMoo WPnP WWFP |

| | | |
|---|---|---|
| | ***argentea*** | CRWN EBWF GKir MBNS SPlb WFar |
| | ***arguta*** | EBee NBre |
| | ***argyrophylla*** | see *P. atrosanguinea* var. *argyrophylla* |
| * | - ***insignis rubra*** | NWCA |
| | ***atrosanguinea*** | Widely available |
| § | - var. ***argyrophylla*** | COlW CSam CWCL EBee ECha EHig ELan EPPr EPfP GCal LHop LRHS MNFA MRav MWat NBir NBro SRms WClo WFar WHil WMoo WPer |
| | - - SS&W 7768 | MSte |
| | - 'Fireball' (d) **new** | GJos WPer |
| | - var. ***leucochroa*** | see *P. atrosanguinea* var. *argyrophylla* |
| * | - 'Sundermannii' **new** | LLHF |
| | ***aurea*** | CSec EBee ECho ECtt EPfP MTho NBlu NLAp NMir NNor NWCA WBrk WPat |
| | - 'Aurantiaca' | EWes NLar SRot |
| § | - subsp. ***chrysocraspeda*** | NMen |
| § | - 'Goldklumpen' | EAEE ECtt MRav NPro |
| | - 'Plena' (d) | SRot |
| | 'Blazeaway' | CMHG EBee ECGP ECtt LBMP LRHS LSou MBNS NBsh NGdn NPro WCAu WFar |
| * | ***boraea*** | CSec |
| | ***brevifolia*** | NWCA |
| | ***calabra*** | EBee ECha EWes WHer |
| § | ***cinerea*** | CTri ECho LBee LLHF |
| | ***collina*** | CSec EHig LLHF |
| § | ***crantzii*** | CMea EBee MBar MSte SRms |
| | - 'Nana' | see *P. crantzii* 'Pygmaea' |
| § | - 'Pygmaea' | ECho ECtt EPfP NBir NMen |
| § | ***cuneata*** $\Upsilon^{H4}$ | CSec ECho GAbr MMuc MTho NWCA SIng WPer |
| | - CC 5287 **new** | GKev |
| | ***davurica*** 'Abbotswood' | see *P. fruticosa* 'Abbotswood' |
| | ***delavayi*** | MNrw |
| | ***detommasii*** | LLHF WAbe |
| | - MESE 400 | EBee |
| | ***dickinsii*** | NMen |
| | 'Emilie' | CSpe EBee ECtt EGle GCal MBNS MBri NLar NPro SUsu SWvt WBor WFar WHal |
| § | ***erecta*** | CArn CRWN CWan EBWF GBar GPoy MSal |
| | ***eriocarpa*** | EBee ECho ECtt EPau GEdr MWat NLAp NMen SPer WAbe WPat |
| | - var. ***tsarongensis*** CC 4627 | EWld |
| | 'Esta Ann' | EBee ECtt EPPr MBNS NCGa SRGP |
| | 'Etna' | CEnt CHFP CHar CKno EBee ECtt ELan GMac LPio MLHP MNFA MNrw NBir NChi SBri WCAu WMoo WPGP WPer |
| | 'Everest' | see *P. fruticosa* 'Mount Everest' |
| | 'Fireflame' | ECha NBre NLar WMoo |
| | ***fissa*** | CSec EBee MNrw MSte NBir NBre SPhx |
| | 'Flambeau' (d) | EBee ECtt GCal LDai LHop MNFA MRav NBre NCob NGdn NLar NPro WMoo |
| | 'Flamenco' | CSam CTri ECtt GKir GMac MArl MBNS MBri MLHP MNrw MRav NBir NChi SAga WAbb WFar |
| | ***fragariiformis*** | see *P. megalantha* |
| | ***fruticosa*** | LBuc MGan NWea |
| § | - 'Abbotswood' $\Upsilon^{H4}$ | Widely available |
| | - 'Abbotswood Silver' (v) | LAst MSwo SLim WFar WMoo |
| | - 'Annette' | CMac NPro |
| | - 'Apple Blossom' | CWib |
| | - var. ***arbuscula*** hort. | see *P. fruticosa* 'Elizabeth' |
| | - 'Argentea Nana' | see *P. fruticosa* 'Beesii' |
| | - 'Baby Bethan'$^{PBR}$ (d) **new** | CBgR LLHF NHol |
| § | - 'Beesii' | ELan EPfP ERas MBar SPla |
| | - 'Bewerley Surprise' | NBir WHCG |
| | - 'Cascade' | LHop |
| | - 'Chelsea Star' $\Upsilon^{H4}$ | CMac LSRN MAsh MGos |
| | - 'Chilo' (v) | MGos WMoo |
| | - 'Clotted Cream' | MBar |
| | - var. ***dahurica*** W 1213 | WPGP |
| | - - 'Farrer's White' | WFar |
| | - - 'Hersii' | see *P. fruticosa* 'Snowflake' |
| | - - 'Rhodocalyx' | WFar |
| | - 'Dart's Cream' | LRHS MGan |
| | - 'Dart's Golddigger' | CTri SEND |
| | - 'Daydawn' | Widely available |
| § | - 'Elizabeth' | Widely available |
| | - 'Farreri' | see *P. fruticosa* 'Gold Drop' |
| | - 'Floppy Disc' | ELan EPfP LRHS MGos NHol SHBN SPla |
| | - 'Glenroy Pinkie' | CSam EPfP MRav NLar SCoo SLon |
| § | - 'Gold Drop' | CMac |
| | - 'Golden Dwarf' | MGos |
| | - 'Golden Spreader' | GKir |
| | - 'Goldfinger' | CCVT CChe CDoC CSBt EBee ELan EPfP GKir LHop LRHS MAsh MGos MRav MSwo MWat NHol NPri SCoo SLim SPer SPlb SPoG WAbe WDin |
| | - Goldkugel | see *P. fruticosa* 'Gold Drop' |
| | - 'Goldstar' | CDul EQua GKir IArd LRHS MBri MGos NHol SCoo SLon WFar WHCG |
| | - 'Goldteppich' | LBuc MBar NBlu SHBN |
| | - 'Goscote' | MGos |
| | - 'Grace Darling' | CAbP ELan EPfP EWes GGar NBir NHol SPoG SWvt WBVN WBrE WHCG WMoo |
| | - 'Groneland' $\Upsilon^{H4}$ | EPfP MAsh |
| | - 'Haytor's Orange' | CWib |
| | - 'Hopleys Little Joker' | WFar |
| | - 'Hopleys Orange' $\Upsilon^{H4}$ | CChe CDoC CEnt CHar EPfP EWes GKir LHop LRHS MRav MWat NHol NPri SCoo WFar WGor WMoo |
| | - 'Hurstbourne' | NPro |
| | - 'Jackman's Variety' $\Upsilon^{H4}$ | CSam CWib MAsh SPer SRms WRHF |
| | - 'Katherine Dykes' | CDoC CDul CTri CWib EBee EPfP GKir LBMP LRHS LSRN MBar MRav NPri NWea SCoo SLim SLon SPer SPoG SRms WBVN WDin WFar WHar WMoo |
| * | - 'King Cup' $\Upsilon^{H4}$ | MAsh |
| § | - 'Klondike' | CBcs CSBt EPfP GKir MGan NWea WHil |
| | - 'Kobold' | MBar |
| * | - 'Lemon and Lime' | MBlu NBir NPro |
| | - 'Limelight' $\Upsilon^{H4}$ | CSBt EBee ELan EPfP LRHS LSou MAsh MRav MSwo NHol SPla SPoG WFar WHCG |
| | - 'Longacre Variety' | CMac CTri EQua MBar MSwo NWea SLPl WFar |
| | - 'Lovely Pink'$^{PBR}$ | see *P. fruticosa* 'Pink Beauty' |
| § | - 'Maanelys' | ELan EQua MGan MWat NHol NWea SPer SRms WDin WFar WHCG WMoo |
| § | - 'Manchu' | CDoC CMac MBar MRav MWat SHBN SLPl SPer SRms WCFE |
| | - Mango Tango = 'Uman'$^{PBR}$ | CDoC LBuc |
| § | - Marian Red Robin = 'Marrob'$^{PBR}$ $\Upsilon^{H4}$ | CDoC CDul CSBt CWib EBee ELan EPfP GKir LAst LCro LRHS MAsh MBri MRav MSwo MWat NCGa NHol NPri NWea SCoo SLim SLon SPer SPoG SWvt WDin |

| | | |
|---|---|---|
| | - 'Medicine Wheel Mountain' ♀H4 | ELan EWes LRHS MAsh MGos MRav NHol NLar NPro SCoo SLim SPer WHCG |
| | - Moonlight | see *P. fruticosa* 'Maanelys' |
| § | - 'Mount Everest' | EQua NWea SLon SRms WBod |
| | - 'Nana Argentea' | see *P. fruticosa* 'Beesii' |
| | - 'New Dawn' | CDoC LRHS MBri WFar |
| | - 'Orangeade' | LRHS MAsh NLar |
| | - 'Peaches and Cream' | WEas |
| * | - 'Peachy Proud' | NPro |
| § | - 'Pink Beauty' PBR ♀H4 | CDoC CSBt EBee ELan EPfP LRHS LSRN MAsh MBrN MRav NCGa NHol NPri SCoo SPer SPoG SWvt WMoo |
| | - 'Pink Pearl' | WMoo |
| | - 'Pink Whisper' | NPro |
| | - 'Pretty Polly' | CWSG ELan EPfP LAst LRHS MAsh MBar MGos MSwo NHol SHBN SPla SSta WBor WDin WFar WMoo |
| | - 'Primrose Beauty' ♀H4 | CDoC CDul EBee ECrN ELan EPfP GKir LAst LBMP LRHS MAsh MBar MRav MSwo NHol NPri SCoo SEND SLim SPer SPlb SPoG WBod WDin WFar WMoo |
| § | - Princess = 'Blink' | CBcs CDul CWSG ELan GKir LBMP LRHS MAsh MBar MRav MSwo SCoo SLim SPer SReu SRms WBVN WDin WFar |
| | - var. ***pumila*** | GKev |
| | - 'Red Ace' | Widely available |
| | - Red Robin PBR | see *P. fruticosa* Marian Red Robin = 'Marrob' |
| | - var. ***rigida*** CC 3685 | WRos |
| | - 'Royal Flush' | MBar NHol |
| | - 'Snowbird' | EBee EPfP LRHS MGos NPro SLim WFar |
| § | - 'Snowflake' | CBcs WMoo |
| | - 'Sommerflor' ♀H4 | EPfP EQua MAsh MRav |
| | - 'Sophie's Blush' | CChe MRav NHol NWea WDin WHCG WSHC |
| | - 'Summer Sorbet' | NPri |
| | - 'Sunset' | CBcs CSam CWSG CWib EBee ECrN ELan EPfP GKir LRHS MBar MGos MRav NBir NHol NWea SCoo SLim SPer SRms SSta WBVN WFar WMoo |
| | - 'Super Ace' | MGos |
| | - 'Tangerine' | Widely available |
| | - 'Tilford Cream' | Widely available |
| | - 'Tom Conway' | CMac NLar WHCG |
| | - var. ***veitchii*** | CSBt SHBN SSto |
| | - 'Vilmoriniana' | CTri ELan EPfP GCal LRHS MLHP MRav SPer SPoG SSpi WAbe WCFE WHCG WSHC |
| | - 'Wessex Silver' | CHar WHCG |
| | - 'Whirligig' | CMac WHCG |
| | - 'Wickwar Beauty' | CWib |
| | - 'William Purdom' | WHCG |
| | - 'Yellow Bird' ♀H4 | LRHS MAsh MGos SPoG |
| | 'Gibson's Scarlet' ♀H4 | Widely available |
| | ***glandulosa*** | MNrw NBre WBrk |
| | 'Gloire de Nancy' (d) | CTca CWCL IGor LBMP LHop MRav NBir NChi WPrP |
| | 'Gold Clogs' | see *P. aurea* 'Goldklumpen' |
| | ***gracilis*** | CSec |
| | ***grandiflora*** | CSec |
| | 'Hamlet' **new** | EBrs |
| | 'Helen Jane' | GBuc GJos GKir LEdu LPio MHer NBir NGdn NLar NPro SAga STes WFar WMnd WPer |
| | ***heptaphylla*** | NBre |
| | 'Herzblut' | EBee GBuc MNrw NLar |
| | x ***hopwoodiana*** | Widely available |
| * | x ***hybrida*** 'Jean Jabber' | EBee EWll GBuc GMac MRav NBur NLar NPro |
| | ***hyparctica*** | MDKP |
| | - ***nana*** | LBee |
| | 'Jack Elliot' | NPro |
| | 'Light My Fire' | EBee LLHF MAvo MBNS NMoo |
| | 'Mandshurica' | see *P. fruticosa* 'Manchu' |
| | 'Maynard's' | NDov |
| § | ***megalantha*** ♀H4 | Widely available |
| | - 'Gold Sovereign' | EBee EPfP NPro SPoG |
| | 'Melton' | EBee MNrw NBir |
| * | 'Melton Fire' | CEnt CWan ECtt EShb GJos GKir LAst LEdu MNHC NBir NBur SBri WFar WMnd WMoo |
| | 'Monarch's Velvet' | see *P. thurberi* 'Monarch's Velvet' |
| | 'Monsieur Rouillard' (d) | CSam CTca CWCL EBee ECtt GCra GKir IPot MCot MNrw MRav MWat NCGa NGdn SPoG WHal WHoo WMnd |
| | 'Mont d'Or' | MRav |
| | ***montana*** | WHer WPer |
| | ***nepalensis*** | CEnt CSec EBee EHoe LAst MLHP NBro NChi NPro SBri |
| | - 'Flammenspiel' | WFar |
| | - 'Master Floris' | GCal SAga WFar WHal |
| § | - 'Miss Willmott' ♀H4 | Widely available |
| | - 'Ron McBeath' | Widely available |
| | - 'Roxana' | CTca EBee ECGP ELan GBuc MRav NBro SRGP WAbb WFar WMoo WPer |
| | - 'Shogran' | COIW EBee EWTr GBuc GJos GMac LAst NHol NLar NPro NVic SPad WHil WPtf |
| § | ***neumanniana*** | EBWF NBir NPri |
| | - 'Goldrausch' | LEdu |
| § | - 'Nana' | ECho EPot LBee MHer MMuc MWat NLAp NLar NMen NRya SPlb SRms WEas WFar WMoo WPat |
| | - white-flowered | LAst |
| | ***nevadensis*** | CLyd CTri ECho GEdr SRms WPer |
| | ***nitida*** | GEdr GKev NMen SRms WAbe |
| | - 'Alba' | ECho EPot NLAp NMen WAbe |
| | - 'Rubra' | CFir ECho EDAr NBir NLAp NWCA SRms WAbe WFar WPat |
| | ***nivalis*** | ECho |
| * | 'Olympic Mountains' | WPer |
| | ***palustris*** | CWat EBWF EBee NLar WMoo |
| | ***parvifolia*** 'Klondike' | see *P. fruticosa* 'Klondike' |
| | ***pedata*** | LLWP NChi |
| | ***pensylvanica*** | CSec LLHF |
| | 'Pink Panther' | see *P. fruticosa* Princess = 'Blink' |
| | aff. ***polyphylla*** | GKev |
| | ***pulvinaris*** **new** | EPot |
| | ***recta*** | COIW CSec EBWF MNHC NPri WRos |
| | - 'Alba' | CEnt EGoo GMaP LAst LDai NBre NBur WPer WPtf |
| | - 'Citrina' | see *P. recta* var. *sulphurea* |
| | - 'Macrantha' | see *P. recta* 'Warrenii' |
| § | - var. ***sulphurea*** | CEnt CSec CSsd EBee EGoo GMac IGor LAst MHer MLHP MNrw NBir NBre SIng SPhx WCAu WFar WHal WHoo WMnd WMoo WPer WPtf WTin |
| § | - 'Warrenii' | CSBt CSec EBee EPla GKir GMaP LAst LRHS MBNS MRav NBir SIng SPad SPer SRms WCAu WFar WHal WMoo WPer |
| | ***reptans*** | CRWN EBWF |
| | - 'Pleniflora' (d) | WAlt |
| | 'Roxanne' (d) | MHer |
| | ***rupestris*** | CSec EBWF ECha MLLN MNrw NDlv NSti SBri SGar WCAu WFar WHal WMoo WPer WPtf |
| | ***simplex*** | EBee NBre |

| | | |
|---|---|---|
| | ***speciosa*** | EWes IGor WMoo |
| | ***sterilis*** | CHid EBWF WSFF |
| | 'Sungold' | ECho WHCG |
| | ***tabernaemontani*** | see *P. neumanniana* |
| | ***ternata*** | see *P. aurea* subsp. *chrysocraspeda* |
| | ***thurberi*** | CAby EBee EGle MCot MMHG MNrw NBHF NLar NMoo SHGN SPhx WMoo WSHC |
| § | - 'Monarch's Velvet' | Widely available |
| | - 'Pirate's Gold' | NPro |
| | ***tommasiniana*** | see *P. cinerea* |
| | x ***tonguei*** ♀$^{H4}$ | Widely available |
| | ***tormentilla*** | see *P. erecta* |
| | 'Twinkling Star' | EBee ECtt MBNS NCGa |
| | ***uniflora*** | GKev |
| | ***verna*** | see *P. neumanniana* |
| | - 'Pygmaea' | see *P. neumanniana* 'Nana' |
| | ***villosa*** | see *P. crantzii* |
| | 'Volcan' | CMea EBee EWes MBri NChi NDov NPro SAga SMHy SUsu WAbb WFar WHal WPGP |
| | 'White Queen' | EBee GMac MNrw NBre NBur NCob SHar SPoG |
| | 'William Rollison' ♀$^{H4}$ | Widely available |
| | ***willmottiae*** | see *P. nepalensis* 'Miss Willmott' |
| | 'Yellow Queen' | CBcs CTri EMil EPfP GMaP LHop MBNS MNrw MRav NHol SPer WCAu WFar |

## *Poterium* see *Sanguisorba*

| | | |
|---|---|---|
| | ***sanguisorba*** | see *Sanguisorba minor* |

## *Prasium* (*Lamiaceae*)

| | | |
|---|---|---|
| | ***majus*** | CSpe |

## *Pratia* (*Campanulaceae*)

| | | |
|---|---|---|
| | ***angulata*** 'Jack's Pass' | ECho |
| § | - 'Treadwellii' | EAlp ECha ECho EDAr GEdr GGar LRHS SPlb WHal |
| | - 'Woodside' | ECho ECou EDAr |
| | ***angulata*** x ***pedunculata*** | GGar |
| | 'Celestial Spice' | EDAr |
| § | ***pedunculata*** | CPLG CTca CTri ECha ECho ECou ECtt EDAr ELan EPfP GGar GKir LBee LLWG LRHS MBar NBlu NChi SIng SPet SPlb SPoG SRms WFar WMoo WPer WPtf |
| | - 'Blue Stars' | EDAr |
| | - 'County Park' | CEnt CSpe CTri EAlp ECha ECho ECou EDAr ELan EPfP GAbr GGar GKev GKir MBar SIng SPlb SPoG SRms WHoo WMoo WPer |
| | - 'Kiandra' | ECou |
| | - 'Tom Stone' | MBNS |
| | - 'White Stars' | SIng |
| § | ***perpusilla*** | ECou EDAr |
| | - 'Fragrant Carpet' | ECou EDAr |
| | - 'Summer Meadows' | ECou |

## *Premna* (*Verbenaceae*)

| | | |
|---|---|---|
| * | ***vanrensburgii*** new | CCCN |

## *Prenanthes* (*Asteraceae*)

| | | |
|---|---|---|
| § | ***alba*** | EBee |

## *Preslia* see *Mentha*

## *Primula* ✿ (*Primulaceae*)

| | | |
|---|---|---|
| | Lismore 79-26 | NHol |
| | ***acaulis*** | see *P. vulgaris* |
| | 'Adrian Jones' (Au) | IPen ITim NHol WAbe |
| | 'Alan Robb' (Pr/Prim/d) | CWCL ECtt EPfP NCGa NGHP NHol SPer SRGP WFar |
| | 'Alexina' (*allionii* hybrid) (Au) | GKev NHar |
| | ***algida*** (Al) | ECho |
| | 'Alice Collins' | CGra |
| § | ***allionii*** (Au) ♀$^{H2}$ | IPen LRHS NSum WAbe |
| | - GFS 1984 (Au) | CGra |
| | - Hartside 383/3 | NHol |
| | - HNG 12 | ITim |
| | - 'A.K. Wells' (Au) | WAbe |
| | - 'Agnes' (Au) | CGra NMen |
| | - 'Aire Waves' | see *P.* x *loiseleurii* 'Aire Waves' |
| * | - 'Alexander' (Au) | CGra |
| | - 'Andrew' (Au) | CGra |
| | - 'Anna Griffith' (Au) | IPen LRHS NRya NWCA WAbe |
| | - 'Anne' (Au) | IPen NDlv |
| | - 'Aphrodite' (Au) | NHar |
| | - 'Apple Blossom' (Au) | GAbr GKev |
| | - 'Archer' (Au) | IPen ITim NDlv NHol |
| | - 'Ares' (Au) | NHar |
| | - 'Aries Violet' (Au) | NHar |
| | - 'Austen' (Au) | NDlv |
| | - 'Avalanche' (Au) | IPen ITim WAbe |
| | - 'Bill Martin' (Au) | IPen ITim |
| | - 'Bishop' (Au) new | CGra |
| | - 'Blood Flake' | IPen |
| | - 'Cherry' (Au) | CGra |
| | - 'Chivalry' (Au) | CGra |
| | - 'Circes Flute' (Au) | NHar |
| | - 'Crowsley Variety' (Au) | LRHS NMen NWCA WAbe |
| | - 'Crusader' (Au) | ITim WThu |
| | - 'Duncan' (Au) | ITim |
| § | - 'Edinburgh' (Au) | GKev IPen ITim NHol |
| | - 'Edrom' (Au) | IPen ITim |
| | - 'Eliza' (Au) new | CGra |
| | - 'Elizabeth Baker' (Au) | IPen ITim WAbe |
| | - 'Elizabeth Earle' (Au) | ITim WAbe |
| | - 'Elliott's Large' | see *P. allionii* 'Edinburgh' |
| | - 'Elliott's Variety' | see *P. allionii* 'Edinburgh' |
| | - 'Eureka' (Au) | CGra |
| | - 'Fanfare' (Au) | IPen LRHS NHar |
| | - 'Frank Barker' (Au) | NHol |
| | - 'Gavin Brown' (Au) | CGra IPen ITim |
| | - 'Gilderdale Glow' (Au) | CGra GKev NRya |
| | - 'Giuseppi's Form' | see *P. allionii* 'Mrs Dyas' |
| | - 'Grandiflora' (Au) | GKev ITim |
| | - 'Hartside 12' (Au) | IPen |
| | - 'Hartside 12' x 'Appleblossom' (Au) | CGra |
| | - 'Hartside 6' (Au) | IPen NHar |
| | - 'Hemswell' (Au) | NHol |
| | - 'Hocker Edge' (Au) | GKev NHol |
| | - 'Io 2' (Au) | NHar |
| | - 'Ions Amethyst' (Au) | NHar |
| | - 'Jenny' (Au) | CGra |
| | - 'Joe Elliott' (Au) | IPen |
| | - 'Joseph Collins' (Au) | CGra |
| | - 'Julia' (Au) | CGra |
| | - K R W | see *P. allionii* 'Ken's Seedling' |
| § | - 'Kath Dryden' (Au) | IPen LLHF |
| § | - 'Ken's Seedling' (Au) | IPen |
| | - 'Lacewing' (Au) | CGra |
| | - 'Laura Louise' (Au) | CGra |
| | - 'Little O' (Au) | WAbe |
| | - 'Lucy' (Au) | NHar |
| | - 'Malcolm' (Au) | CGra |
| | - 'Margaret Earle' (Au) | WAbe |
| | - 'Marjorie Wooster' (Au) | IPen ITim NWCA |
| | - 'Martin' (Au) | IPen ITim |
| | - 'Mary Berry' (Au) | CPBP IPen WAbe |
| | - 'Maurice Dryden' (Au) | CGra |
| | - 'Mentors' (Au) | CGra |
| | - 'Molly' (Au) | IPen |
| § | - 'Mrs Dyas' (Au) | IPen NHol WAbe |

| | | |
|---|---|---|
| | - 'Neptunes Wave' (Au) | NHar |
| | - 'New Dawn' (Au) | NHar |
| I | - 'Norma' (Au) | WAbe |
| | - 'Peggy Wilson' (Au) | GKev NLar |
| | - 'Perkie' (Au) | IPen |
| | - 'Picton's Variety' (Au) | NDlv |
| | - 'Pink Ice' (Au) | GCai ITim NHol |
| | - 'Pinkie' (Au) | CGra |
| | - 'Praecox' (Au) | CGra IPen |
| | - 'Raymond Wooster' (Au) | LRHS NHol |
| | - 'Robert' (Au) | CGra |
| | - 'Scimitar' (Au) | CGra NHol |
| | - 'Snowflake' (Au) | CGra GKev IPen ITim LRHS NWCA WAbe |
| | - 'Stanton House' (Au) | NDlv |
| | - 'Tranquillity' (Au) | ITim NHar NHol WAbe |
| | - 'Travellers' (Au) | IPen |
| | - 'William Earle' (Au) | GKev ITim LRHS NDlv NHol WAbe |
| | ***allionii*** x ***auricula*** 'Blairside Yellow' (Au) | ECho IPen NSum |
| | ***allionii*** x ***auricula*** 'Old Red Dusty Miller' (Au) | ECho |
| | ***allionii*** x ***clusiana*** (Au) | ECho |
| | ***allionii*** x ***hirsuta*** (Au) | ITim NHol NLAp SIng |
| | ***allionii*** x 'Lismore Treasure' (Au) | CPBP NWCA |
| | ***allionii*** x ***pubescens*** (Au) | ECho |
| | ***allionii*** x ***pubescens*** 'Harlow Car' (Au) | CLyd |
| | ***allionii*** x 'Snow Ruffles' (Au) | ITim |
| | ***allionii*** x 'White Linda Pope' (Au) | IPen NHar |
| | ***alpicola*** (Si) 𝕐H4 | CBod CFee CRow CSWP CWCL EBee EPfP EShb GAbr GAuc GEdr GGar GKev IPen LPBA NBHF NBid NBro NDlv NGdn NHol NLAp NSum NWCA SPer WBVN |
| | - var. ***alba*** (Si) | CDWL CRow CSWP EBee GAuc GBuc GEdr GGar GKev IPen MNrw NBid |
| | - - AC 5478 **new** | GKev |
| § | - var. ***alpicola*** (Si) | CLAP CSWP EBee GBuc GCra GEdr GKev GKir IPen MNrw WHil |
| | - hybrids (Si) | STes |
| | - 'Kevock Sky' (Si) | EBee GKev |
| | - 'La Luna' (Si) **new** | MMuc |
| | - var. ***luna*** | see *P. alpicola* var. *alpicola* |
| | - var. ***violacea*** (Si) | CAby CDWL CLAP CRow CSWP EBee GCra GGar GKev IPen LRHS MMuc MNrw NBid NHol NLAp WFar WPer |
| | 'Altaica' | see *P. elatior* subsp. *meyeri* |
| | ***altaica grandiflora*** | see *P. elatior* subsp. *meyeri* |
| | 'Amethyst' (Pr/Poly) | WSHC |
| | ***amethystina*** (Am) | WAbe |
| | - SDR 3244 **new** | GKev |
| | - SDR 4745 | GKev |
| | - subsp. ***brevifolia*** (Am) **new** | GKev |
| | ***amoena*** | see *P. elatior* subsp. *meyeri* |
| | ***angustifolia*** (Pa) | WAbe |
| | ***anisodora*** | see *P. wilsonii* var. *anisodora* |
| | 'Annemijne' | EMon |
| | x ***arctotis*** | see *P.* x *pubescens* |
| | ***aurantiaca*** (Pf) | CFir EBee GBuc GCai GEdr GKev GKir IPen SRms |
| | ***aureata*** (Pe) | GKev WAbe |
| | ***auricula*** L. (Au) 𝕐H4 | EDAr IPen LRHS MHer NBro NSla SPer SPet SPlb SPoG WAbe |
| | - var. ***albocincta*** (Au) | EBee NWCA |
| | - subsp. ***bauhinii*** (Au) | GAuc |
| | ***auricula*** ambig. (Au) | CTsd GKev WRHF |

| | |
|---|---|
| ***auricula*** misapplied '2nd Vic' (Au) | SPop WFar WHil |
| - A74 (Au) | NCob NPri STre |
| - 'A.E. Matthews' (Au) **new** | NHol |
| - 'Abrigde' (Au/d) | WAln |
| - 'Achates' (Au/A) | WAln |
| - 'Admiral' (Au/A) | WAln |
| - 'Adrian' (Au/A) | IPen NBro NDro SPop WHil |
| - 'Adrienne Ruan' (Au/A) | MOne |
| - 'Aga Khan' (Au/A) | WAln |
| - 'Agamemnon' (Au/A) | WAln WCre |
| - 'Alamo' (Au/A) | SPop WCre |
| - 'Alan Ball' (Au) | WCre |
| - 'Alan Ravenscroft' (Au/A) | SPop WAln WFar |
| - 'Alansford' (Au/A) | WAln |
| - 'Albert Bailey' (Au/d) | GAbr GCai IPen ITim NDro SPop WAln WCre |
| - 'Alexandra Georgina' (Au/A) | WAln |
| - 'Alf' (Au/A) | SPop WAln |
| - 'Alfred Charles' (Au/A) | WAln |
| - 'Alfred Niblett' (Au/S) | IPen |
| - 'Alice Haysom' (Au/S) | CWCL ELan GAbr GCai IPen ITim MAsh MOne NDro SDnm SPav SPop WCre WFar |
| - 'Alicia' (Au/A) | NDro NHol SDnm SPop WCre |
| - 'Alison Jane' (Au/A) | WCre WHil |
| - 'Alison Telford' (Au/A) | WHil |
| - 'Allensford' (Au/A) | WCre |
| - 'Alloway' (Au/d) | WAln |
| - 'Almand' (Au/d) | WAln |
| - alpine mixed (Au/A) | EPfP GKir NBlu SRms |
| - 'Amicable' (Au/A) | NDro NHol SPop WCre |
| - 'Ancient Order' (Au/A) | WAln |
| - 'Ancient Society' (Au/A) | GAbr IPen NDro SPop |
| - 'Andrea Julie' (Au/A) | IPen ITim MOne SPop WCre WHil |
| - 'Andrew Hunter' (Au/A) | NDro SPop WAln |
| - 'Andy Cole' (Au/A) | SPop WAln |
| - 'Angel Eyes' (Au/St) **new** | SPop |
| - 'Angela Gould' (Au) **new** | GAbr |
| - 'Angie' (Au/d) | WAln |
| - 'Angostura' (Au/d) **new** | SPop |
| - 'Ann Taylor' (Au/A) | IPen |
| - 'Anne Hyatt' (Au/d) | GAbr WAln |
| - 'Anne Swithinbank' (Au/d) | WAln |
| - 'Antoc' (Au/S) | SPop |
| - 'Anwar Sadat' (Au/A) | GAbr NDro SPop WCre WFar |
| - 'Applecross' (Au/A) | CWCL IPen ITim NDro SPop WCre |
| - 'April Moon' (Au/S) | NDro SPop WAln |
| - 'April Tiger' (Au/St) | WAln |
| - 'Arabian Night' (Au/A) | WAln |
| - 'Arctic Fox' | SPop WAln |
| - 'Argus' (Au/A) | GAbr NDro NHol SPop WCre WHil |
| - 'Arlene' (Au/A) | WAln |
| - 'Arthur Delbridge' (Au/A) | NDro WFar |
| - 'Arundel Cross' (Au) **new** | IPen |
| - 'Arundell' (Au/S/St) | EBee GAbr GCai ITim MAsh MOne NDro NHol SPop WCre WFar WHil |
| - 'Ashcliffe Gem' (Au/A) | WAln |
| - 'Ashcliffe Gold' (Au/A) | WAln |
| - 'Astolat' (Au/S) | CWCL EBee GAbr GKev IPen ITim MAsh NDro NRya SDnm SPav SPop WCre |
| - 'Athene' (Au/S) | IPen MOne NDro SPop WAln |
| - 'Atlantic' (Au/S) **new** | NDro |
| - 'Audacity' (Au/d) | WAln |
| - 'Aurora' (Au/A) | EDAr WCre |
| - 'Austin' (Au/A) | IPen WAln WCre |
| - 'Avon Citronella' (Au) | SPop |
| - 'Avril' (Au/A) | SPop WAln |
| - 'Avril Hunter' (Au/A) | IPen ITim NDro NHol SPop WCre |
| - 'Aztec' (Au/d) | WAln |

| | |
|---|---|
| - 'Bacchante' (Au/d) | WAln |
| - 'Bacchus' (Au/A) | NDro |
| - 'Baggage' (Au) | SPop |
| - 'Balbithan' (Au/B) | GAbr |
| - 'Baltic Amber' (Au) | SPop |
| - 'Barbara Mason' | WAln |
| - 'Barbarella' (Au/S) | NDro SPop |
| - Barnhaven doubles (Au/d) | CSWP GAbr NSum |
| - 'Barnhaven Gold' (Au) new | IPen |
| - 'Basilio' (Au/S) | WAln |
| - 'Basuto' (Au/A) | IPen ITim NDro SPop WCre WHil |
| - 'Beatrice' (Au/A) | CTri EShb GAbr GCai IPen NDro NHol SPop WCre WFar WHil |
| - 'Beauty of Bath' (Au/S) | WAln |
| - 'Bedford Lad' (Au/A) | WCre |
| - 'Beechen Green' (Au/S) | GAbr GCai ITim MAsh NDro SPop WCre |
| - 'Behold' (Au) | WCre |
| - 'Bellamy Pride' (Au/B) | GAbr IPen MAsh NDro SPop |
| - 'Belle Zana' (Au/S) | MAsh NDro SPop WAln |
| - 'Bellezana' | IPen |
| - 'Ben Lawers' (Au/S) | SPop |
| - 'Ben Wyves' (Au/S) | NHol SPop WCre |
| - 'Bendigo' (Au/S) | SPop WAln |
| - 'Bewitched' (Au/A) | NDro NHol WAln |
| - 'Big Ben' (Au/S) | ECho |
| - 'Bilbo Baggins' (Au/A) | WAln |
| - 'Bill Bailey' (Au) | MOne NDro SPop WCre |
| - 'Bizarre' (Au) | WCre |
| - 'Black Ice' (Au/S) | WAln |
| - 'Black Jack'PBR (Au/d) | EBee MWea |
| - 'Black Knight' (Au/d) | WAln |
| - 'Blackfield' (Au/S) | SPop |
| - 'Blackpool Rock' (Au/St) | WAln |
| - 'Blairside Yellow' (Au/B) | ECho EWes LLHF NLAp NSla |
| - 'Blakeney' (Au/d) | GCai WAln |
| - 'Blossom' (Au/A) | GAbr WFar |
| - 'Blue Bonnet' (Au/A/d) | NDro WAln |
| - 'Blue Bonnet' (Au/A/d) | GAbr SPop WCre |
| - 'Blue Chips' (Au/S) | NDro SPop WAln |
| - 'Blue Cliffs' (Au/S) | WAln |
| - 'Blue Denim' (Au/S) | WAln |
| - 'Blue Frills' (Au) | WAln |
| - 'Blue Heaven' | MOne NDro SPop WCre |
| - 'Blue Jean' (Au/S) | GAbr IPen SPop |
| - 'Blue Moon' (Au/S) | WAln |
| - 'Blue Nile' (Au/S) | SPop WCre |
| - 'Blue Skies' (Au/St) new | SPop |
| - 'Blue Velvet' (Au/B) | GAbr GKir IPen LLHF NBro WCre WHil |
| - 'Blue Yodeler' (Au/A) | SPop |
| - 'Blush Baby' (Au/St) | SPop |
| - 'Blushing Timpany' (Au) new | ITim |
| - 'Bob Dingley' (Au/A) | WCre |
| - 'Bob Lancashire' (Au/S) | IPen ITim MOne NDro NHol SPop WCre |
| - 'Bold Tartan' (Au/St) | WAln |
| - 'Bollin Tiger' (Au/St) | WAln |
| - 'Bonafide' (Au/d) | WAln |
| - 'Bonanza' (Au/S) | WAln |
| - 'Bookham Firefly' (Au/A) | GAbr IPen NHol NRya SPop WCre WFar |
| - 'Boortree Bush' (Au) new | WCre |
| - 'Boromir' (Au/A) | WAln |
| - 'Bradford City' (Au/A) | EBee NDro SDnm SPav |
| - 'Bradmore Bluebell' (Au) new | GAbr |
| - 'Bran' (Au/B) new | NDro |
| - 'Branno' (Au/S) | WAln |
| - 'Brasso' (Au) | WAln |
| - 'Brazen Hussy' (Au/d) | WAln |
| - 'Brazil' (Au/S) | EBee GAbr IPen ITim LRHS MOne NDro NHol SPav SPop WCre WHil |
| - 'Brazos River' (Au/A) | WAln |
| - 'Brenda's Choice' (Au/A) | IPen NDro SPop WCre WFar |
| - 'Brentford Bees' (Au/St) | WAln |
| - 'Bright Eyes' (Au/A) | IPen WCre |
| - 'Broad Gold' (Au/A) | MOne SPop WAln WCre |
| - 'Broadwell Gold' (Au/B) | EBee GAbr MAsh NDro NLar SPop |
| - 'Brocade' (Au/St) | NDro |
| - 'Brompton' (Au/S) | WAln |
| - 'Brookfield' (Au/S) | IPen ITim MAsh NDro SPop WCre |
| - 'Broughton' (Au/S) | SPop |
| - 'Brown Ben' (Au) | SPop |
| - 'Brown Bess' (Au/A) | GAbr GCai IPen ITim MAsh MOne SPop WCre |
| - 'Brownie' (Au/B) | CWCL NBir SDnm SPav |
| - 'Buccaneer' | ECho WAln |
| - 'Bucks Green' (Au/S) | GAbr SPop |
| - 'Butterwick' (Au/A) | GAbr GMaP IPen LRHS NDro SPav SPop |
| - 'C.G. Haysom' (Au/S) | GAbr NDro NRya SPop WCre |
| - 'C.W. Needham' (Au/A) | CWCL IPen SPop WCre |
| - 'Calypso' (Au/d) | SPop WAln |
| - 'Cambodunum' (Au/A) | IPen SPop WCre |
| - 'Camelot' (Au/d) | EBee ECho ELan GCai GKev MOne NBro NDro NHol SPop WCre WFar WHil |
| - 'Cameo' (Au/A) | WCre |
| - 'Cameo Beauty' (Au/d) | SPop |
| - 'Camilla' (Au/A) | WAln |
| - 'Candida' (Au/d) | IPen NDro SPop WAln WCre |
| - 'Caramel' (Au/A) | IPen WAln |
| - 'Cardinal Red' (Au/d) new | SPop |
| - 'Carioca' (Au/A) | WAln |
| - 'Carole' (Au/A) | WFar |
| - 'Carzon' (Au/A) new | NDro |
| - 'Catherine Redding' (Au/d) | WAln |
| - 'Catherine Wheel' (Au/St) | WAln |
| - 'Chaffinch' (Au/S) | GAbr IPen MOne NDro SPop |
| - 'Chamois' (Au/B) | GAbr IPen WHil |
| - 'Channel' (Au/S) | WAln |
| - 'Chantilly Cream' (Au/d) | WAln |
| - 'Charles Bronson' (Au/d) | NDro WAln |
| - 'Charles Rennie' (Au/B) | NDro SPop WAln |
| - 'Charlie's Aunt' (Au/A) | WAln |
| - 'Checkmate' (Au) | SPop WAln |
| - 'Chelsea Bridge' (Au/A) | IPen MOne SPop WCre |
| - 'Chelsea Girl' (Au/d) | MOne |
| - 'Cheops' | NDro |
| - 'Cheops' (Au/A) new | NDro |
| - 'Cherry' (Au/S) | GAbr IPen NDro |
| - 'Cherry Picker' (Au/A) | NDro SPop WCre WFar |
| - 'Cheyenne' (Au/S) | GAbr MAsh WCre |
| - 'Chiffon' (Au/S) | IPen NDro SPop WAln |
| - 'Chiquita' (Au/d) new | SPop |
| - 'Chloë' (Au/S) | MOne NDro |
| - 'Chloris' (Au/S) | WAln |
| - 'Chorister' (Au/S) | EBee ECho GAbr GCai IPen ITim MOne NDro NHol WHil |
| - 'Cicero' (Au/A) | SPop WAln |
| - 'Cindy' (Au/A) | ECho |
| - 'Cinnamon' (Au/d) | ITim MAsh NDro SPop WCre |
| - 'Ciribiribin' (Au/A) | WAln |
| - 'Clare' (Au/S) | GAbr IPen MAsh NDro SPop |
| - 'Clatter-Ha' (Au/d) | WHil |
| - 'Claudia Taylor' (Au) | SPop |
| - 'Clouded Yellow' (Au/S) | SPop WAln |
| - 'Cloudy Bay' (Au) | CHFP CWCL MBNS WCot WCra |
| - 'Cloverdale' (Au/d) | WAln |
| - 'Clunie' (Au/S) | IPen NDro WCre |
| - 'Clunie II' (Au/S) | IPen ITim WFar |

- 'Cobden Meadows' (Au/A) WAln WCre
- 'Coffee' (Au/S) IPen MAsh NDro NRya WCre WFar
- 'Colbury' (Au/S) NDro SPop WCre
- 'Colonel Champney' (Au/S) NDro SPop
- 'Comet' (Au/S) IPen NDro
- 'Connaught Court' (Au/A) EBee WAln WCre
- 'Conservative' (Au/S) GAbr IPen
- 'Consett' (Au/S) IPen WHil
- 'Coppi' (Au/A) IPen SPop WAln
- 'Coral Sea' (Au/S) MAsh WAln
- 'Cornmeal' (Au/S) NDro WAln WHil
- 'Corntime' (Au/S) WAln
- 'Corporal Jones' (Au/S) **new** SPop
- 'Corporal Kate' (Au/St) WAln
- 'Corrie Files' (Au/d) WAln
- 'Cortez Silver' (Au/S) WAln
- 'Cortina' (Au/S) ECho GAbr GCai IPen ITim MOne NDro NRya SDnm SPav SPop WCre WFar
- 'County Park Red' (Au/B) ECou NDro
- 'Crackley Tagetes' (Au/d) ECho
- 'Craig Dhu' (Au/B) **new** SPop
- 'Craig Vaughan' (Au/A) NHol SPop
- 'Crecy' (Au/A) SPop WAln
- 'Crimson Glow' (Au/d) NDro SPop WAln
- 'Cuckoo Fair' GAbr IPen SPop WCre
- 'Cuckoo Fare' (Au/S) WAln
- 'Cuddles' (Au/A) WAln
- 'Curry Blend' (Au/B) GAbr NDro
- 'Daftie Green' (Au/S) GAbr IPen MOne NDro WCre
- 'Dales Red' (Au/B) GAbr ITim NDro SDnm SPop WAln WHil
- 'Dan Tiger' (Au/St) WAln
- 'Daniel' (Au/A) NDro WAln
- 'Daphnis' (Au/S) GAbr WAln
- 'Dark Eyes' (Au/d) NDro SPop WAln
- 'Dark Lady' (Au/A) WAln
- 'Dark Red' (Au/S) IPen
- 'David Beckham' (Au/d) WAln
- 'Decaff' (Au/St) WAln
- 'Deckchair' (Au) SPop
- 'Dedham' (Au/d) WAln
- 'Delilah' (Au/d) GAbr ITim MOne NDro SPop
- 'Denise' (Au/S) WAln
- 'Denna Snuffer' (Au/d) GAbr
- 'Devon Cream' (Au/d) ECho SPop WFar
- 'Diane' (Au/A) MOne
- 'Digby' (Au/d) NDro WAln
- 'Digit' (Au/d) WAln

* - 'Dill' (Au/A) WAln
- 'Dilly Dilly' (Au/A) SPop WAln
- 'Divint Dunch' (Au/A) IPen NDro SPop WCre WFar
- 'Doctor Duthie' (Au/S) SPop WAln
- 'Doctor Lennon's White' (Au/B) GAbr IPen SPop WHil
- 'Dolly Viney' (Au/d) GAbr WAln
- 'Donhead' (Au/A) NDro SPop WCre WFar
- 'Donna Clancy' (Au/S) SPop
- 'Dorado' (Au/d) WAln
- 'Doreen Stephens' (Au/A) WAln WFar
- 'Dorothy' (Au/S) WAln
- 'Doublet' (Au/d) ECho GAbr GCai IPen NDro NHol SPop WCre WFar WHil
- 'Doubloon' (Au/d) ECho
- 'Doublure' (Au/d) GAbr NDro SPop WHil
- 'Douglas Bader' (Au/A) NDro SPop WCre
- 'Douglas Black' (Au/S) GAbr NDro SPop WCre
- 'Douglas Blue' (Au/S) WAln
- 'Douglas Green' (Au/S) CWCL IPen SPop
- 'Douglas White' (Au/S) SPop
- 'Dovedale' (Au/S) NDro WAln
- 'Doyen' (Au/d) MAsh WAln
- 'Drax' (Au/A) WAln
- 'Dubarii' (Au/A) WAln
- 'Duchess of Malfi' (Au/S) SPop
- 'Duchess of York' (Au) GBuc LLWP
- 'Dusky Girl' (Au/A) WAln
- 'Dusky Maiden' (Au/A) GAbr GCai NDro SPop WCre WHil
- 'Dusky Yellow' (Au/B) ECho
- 'Dusty Miller' (Au/B) EBee ECho MRav NBir NHol
- 'Eastern Promise' (Au/A) GCai NDro SPop WFar
- 'Ed Spivey' (Au/A) WCre
- 'Eddy Gordon' (Au/A) WAln
- 'Eden Alexander' (Au/B) **new** NDro
- 'Eden David' (Au/B) SPop WHil
- 'Edith Allen' (Au/A) WAln
- 'Edward Sweeney' (Au/S) WAln
- 'Eglinton' WCre
- 'Elf Star' (Au/A) **new** SPop
- 'Eli Jenkins' (Au) WAln
- 'Elizabeth Ann' (Au/A) GAbr NDro SPop
- 'Ellen Thompson' (Au/A) NDro SPop WCre WFar
- 'Ellsinore' (Au) **new** IPen
- 'Elsie' (Au/A) WCre
- 'Elsie May' (Au/A) ITim MAsh MOne NDro SPop WCre
- 'Elsinore' (Au/S) MAsh WCre
- 'Emberglow' (Au/d) WAln
- 'Embley' (Au/S) ITim SPop
- 'Emery Down' (Au/S) NDro SPop
- 'Emily' (Au/d) **new** SIng
- 'Emmett Smith' (Au/A) NDro WAln
- 'Enigma' (Au/S) WAln
- 'Envy' (Au/S) NHol WAln
- 'Erica' (Au/A) IPen NDro SPop WCre WHil
- 'Erjon' (Au/S) NDro SPop WAln
- 'Error' (Au/S) WAln
- 'Esso' (Au/S) **new** NDro
- 'Etna' (Au/S) WAln
- 'Ettrick' (Au/S) WAln
- 'Eve Guest' (Au/A) NDro
- 'Eventide' (Au/S) EBee MAsh SPop
- 'Everest Blue' (Au/S) MAsh SPop WCre
- 'Excalibur' (Au/d) NDro SPop WAln
- 'Exhibition Blau' (Exhibition Series) (Au/B) WHil
- 'Eyeopener' (Au/A) SPop WAln WCre
- 'Fairy' (Au/A) WAln
- 'Fairy Moon' (Au/S) IPen WAln
- 'Falaraki' (Au/A) SPop WAln
- 'Faloonside' (Au) **new** WCre
- 'Falstaff' (Au/d) WAln
- 'Fanciful' (Au/S) NDro
- 'Fancy Free' (Au) SPop
- 'Fandancer' (Au/A) WAln
- 'Fanfare' (Au/S) NDro SPop WAln
- 'Fanny Meerbeck' (Au/S) GAbr GCai IPen MOne NDro SPop WFar
- 'Faro' (Au/S) MAsh WAln WCre
- 'Favourite' (Au/S) GAbr IPen ITim MOne NDro NHol SPop WCre WFar WHil
- 'Fen Tiger' (Au/St) SPop
- 'Fennay' (Au/S) WAln
- 'Ferrybridge' (Au/A) IPen
- 'Fiddler's Green' (Au) GAbr NDro SPop
- 'Figaro' (Au/S) GAbr MAsh NDro SPop WAln
- 'Finchfield' (Au/A) IPen NDro NHol
- 'Firecracker' (Au) WAln
- 'Firenze' (Au/A) SPop
- 'Firsby' (Au/d) GKev MAsh SPop WAln WCre
- 'First Lady' (Au/A) WAln
- 'Fishtoft' (Au/d) WAln
- 'Fitzroy' (Au/d) SPop

- 'Fleminghouse' (Au/S) GAbr MAsh NDro SPop
- 'Florence Brown' (Au/S) ITim
- 'Forest Lemon' (Au/d) new SPop
- 'Forest Pines' (Au/S) WAln
- 'Fradley' (Au/A) IPen WAln
- 'Frank Bailey' (Au/d) MAsh SPop WAln
- 'Frank Crosland' (Au/A) NDro WCre
- 'Frank Faulkner' (Au/A) WAln
- 'Frank Jenning' (Au/A) NDro WAln
- 'Fred Booley' (Au/d) GAbr IPen ITim MAsh NDro NHol SPop WCre WHil
- 'Fred Livesley' (Au/A) WAln
- 'Fresco' (Au/A) SPop
- 'Friskney' (Au/d) WAln
- 'Frittenden Yellow' (Au/B) GAbr SPop
- 'Frosty' (Au/S) NDro
- 'Fuller's Red' (Au/S) SPop WCre WFar
- 'Funny Valentine' (Au/d) IPen MAsh SPop
- 'Fuzzy' (Au/St) WAln
- 'G.L.Taylor' (Au/A) IPen
- 'Gaia' (Au/d) SPop WAln
- 'Galatea' (Au/S) WAln
- 'Galen' (Au/A) WFar
- 'Ganymede' (Au/d) WAln
- 'Gary Pallister' (Au/A) MAsh WAln
- 'Gavin Ward' (Au/S) WAln
- 'Gay Crusader' (Au/A) GAbr ITim NDro SPop WCre WFar
- 'Gazza' (Au/A) WAln
- 'Gee Cross' (Au/A) GAbr IPen
- 'Geldersome Green' (Au/S) GCai MAsh NDro SPop WCre
- 'Gemini' (Au/S) new NDro
- 'General Champney' (Au) new WCre
- 'Generosity' (Au/A) SPop
- 'Geordie' (Au/A) WAln
- 'George Harrison' (Au/B) NDro SPop
- 'George Jennings' (Au/A) NDro WAln
- 'George Swinford's Leathercoat' (Au/B) NDro WHil
- 'Geronimo' (Au/S) GAbr IPen MAsh SPop
- 'Ghost Grey' (Au) WCre
- 'Girl Guide' (Au/S) WAln
- 'Gizabroon' (Au/S) CWCL EBee GAbr GCai NDro SDnm SPav SPop WCre
- 'Glasnost' (Au/S) WAln
- 'Gleam' (Au/S) ECho EDAr GCai GKev ITim LLHF NDro SPop WCre WFar WHil
- 'Glencoe' (Au/S) ECho
- 'Gleneagles' (Au/S) EShb GCai IPen NDro SPop WAln WCre
- 'Glenelg' (Au/S) GAbr ITim MAsh NDro SPop WCre WHil
- 'Glenluce' (Au/S) SPop
- 'Glenna Goodwin' (Au/d) WAln
- 'Gnome' (Au/B) GAbr IPen NHol
- 'Gold Seam' (Au/A) WAln
- 'Golden Boy' (Au/A) WAln
- 'Golden Chartreuse' (Au/d) GAbr
- 'Golden Eye' (Au/S) WAln
- 'Golden Fleece' (Au/S) GAbr GCai SPop
- 'Golden Hill' (Au/S) SPop
- 'Golden Hind' (Au/d) NBro NDro SPop WCre
- 'Golden Splendour' (Au/d) IPen MAsh NDro SPop WCre WFar
- 'Golden Wedding' (Au/A) IPen SPop WAln
- 'Goldie' (Au/S) new NDro
- 'Goldthorn' (Au/A) WCre
- 'Goldwin' (Au/A) WAln
- 'Gollum' (Au/A) WAln
- 'Good Report' (Au/A) NDro SPop WFar
- 'Grabley' (Au/S) SPop WAln
- 'Grandad's Favourite' (Au/B) SPop
- 'Green Elg' (Au) new NHol
- 'Green Finger' (Au/S) SPop
- 'Green Frill' (Au) ITim
- 'Green Goddess' (Au/St) WAln
- 'Green Isle' (Au/S) GAbr IPen MAsh MOne NDro SPop WCre WFar
- 'Green Jacket' (Au/S) IPen WCre
- 'Green Magic' (Au/S) WAln
- 'Green Meadows' (Au/S) SPop WAln
- 'Green Parrot' (Au/S) GAbr SPop WCre
- 'Green Shank' (Au/S) IPen ITim NDro SPop
- 'Greenfield's Fancy' (Au) EBee
- 'Greenfinger' (Au/S) MOne WAln
- 'Greenheart' (Au/S) SPop
- 'Greenpeace' (Au/S) LRHS NDro SPop
- 'Greensleeves' (Au/S) SPop
- 'Greenways' (Au/S) WAln
- 'Greta' (Au/S) EBee ECho GAbr IPen ITim NDro NHol SPop WCre WFar WHil
- 'Gretna Green' (Au/S) SPop
- 'Grey Dawn' (Au/S) SPop WAln
- 'Grey Edge' ECho
- 'Grey Friar' (Au/S) WAln
- 'Grey Hawk' (Au/S) IPen NDro SPop
- 'Grey Lady' (Au/S) WAln
- 'Grey Lag' (Au/S) WHil
- 'Grey Monarch' (Au/S) GAbr GCai ITim MAsh NDro SPop
- 'Grey Owl' (Au/S) WAln
- 'Grizedale' (Au/S) WAln
- 'Grüner Veltliner' (Au/S) NDro SPop
- 'Guinea' (Au/S) GAbr IPen SPop
- 'Gwen' (Au/A) MOne NDro SPop WAln WCre
- 'Gwen Baker' (Au/d) SPop WCre
- 'Gwenda' (Au/A) SPop WAln WHil
- 'Gypsy Rose Lee' (Au/A) WAln
- 'Habanera' (Au/A) NDro SPop WCre WFar
- 'Hadrian's Shooting Star' (Au/d) WAln
- 'Haffner' (Au/S) MAsh SPop
- 'Hallmark' (Au/A) WAln
- 'Handsome Lass' (Au/St) new SPop
- 'Hardley' (Au/S) WAln
- 'Harmony' (Au/B) NBro NDro NHol
- 'Harry Hotspur' (Au/A) IPen NDro SPop WFar WHil
- 'Harry 'O'' (Au/S) NDro SPop WCre
- 'Harvest Glow' (Au/S) IPen SPop WHil
- 'Hawkwood' (Au/S) CWCL GAbr IPen ITim MAsh NDro SDnm SPav SPop WFar
- 'Hawkwood Fancy' (Au/S) WCre
- * 'Hazel' (Au/A) IPen MOne NDro SPop WCre
- 'Headdress' (Au/S) SPop WCre
- 'Heady' (Au/A) SPop WHil
- 'Heart of Gold' (Au/A) MAsh SPop WAln
- 'Hebers' (Au) SPop WAln
- 'Helen' (Au/S) GAbr IPen NDro SPop WHil
- 'Helen Barter' (Au/S) NDro SPop
- 'Helen Ruane' (Au/d) EBee GKev SPop WAln WCre
- 'Helena' (Au/S) IPen MAsh NDro SPop WFar
- 'Helena Dean' (Au/d) MAsh WAln
- 'Hetty Woolf' (Au/S) ECho GAbr ITim NDro NHol WCre
- 'Hew Dalrymple' (Au/S) ITim SPop
- 'High Hopes' (Au) WAln
- 'Hinton Admiral' (Au/S) IPen NDro SPop WAln
- 'Hinton Fields' (Au/S) CWCL EBee EShb GAbr GCai IPen MAsh MOne NDro SDnm SPav SPop WCre WFar WHil
- 'Hobby Horse' (Au) NDro

| | |
|---|---|
| - 'Hoghton Gem' (Au/d) | WAln |
| - 'Holyrood' (Au/S) | GAbr IPen ITim SPop |
| - 'Honey' (Au/d) | NBro NDro SPop WAln |
| - 'Honeymoon' (Au/S) | WAln |
| - 'Hopleys Coffee' (Au/d) | GAbr GCai NDro SPop WAln WCre |
| - 'Iago' (Au/S) | MAsh WAln |
| - 'Ian Greville' (Au/A) | IPen SPop WAln |
| - 'Ibis' (Au/S) | GAbr WAln WCre |
| - 'Ice Maiden' (Au) | MOne NDro SPop WAln |
| - 'Idmiston' (Au/S) | ECho MAsh NDro SPop WCre WFar |
| - 'Immaculate' (Au/A) | SPop WAln |
| - 'Impassioned' (Au/A) | SPop WAln WFar |
| - 'Impeccable' (Au/A) | WAln |
| - 'Imperturbable' (Au/A) | NDro SPop WAln |
| - 'Indian Love Call' (Au/A) | IPen ITim NDro SPop WCre WFar WHil |
| - 'Iris Scott' (Au/A) **new** | NDro |
| - 'Isabel' (Au/S) | WAln |
| - 'Isabella' (Au) | WAln |
| - 'Jack Dean' (Au/A) | NHol SPop WAln WCre WFar WHil |
| - 'James Arnot' (Au/S) | GAbr IPen NRya SPop |
| - 'Jane' (Au/S) | WAln |
| - 'Jane Myers' (Au/d) | WAln WHil |
| - 'Janet' (Au) | ECho GEdr |
| - 'Janie Hill' (Au/A) | MOne SPop WCre |
| - 'Jean Fielder' (Au/A) | SPop |
| - 'Jean Jacques' (Au/A) | WAln |
| - 'Jean Walker' (Au/B) **new** | SPop |
| - 'Jeannie Telford' (Au/A) | SPop WCre |
| - 'Jenny' (Au/A) | EBee ECho GEdr IPen ITim NDro SPop WCre WFar |
| - 'Jersey Bounce' (Au/A) | NDro WAln |
| - 'Jesmond' (Au/S) | WAln |
| - 'Jessie' (Au/d) | WAln |
| - 'Joan Elliott' (Au/A) | GAbr |
| - 'Joanne' (Au/A) | WCre |
| - 'Joe Perks' (Au/A) | IPen NDro SPop WAln WFar |
| - 'Joel' (Au/S) | IPen NDro SPop WAln WCre |
| - 'John Stewart' (Au/A) | SPop |
| - 'John Wayne' (Au/A) | MAsh NDro WCre |
| - 'John Woolf' (Au/S) | ECho NDro |
| - 'Jonathon' (Au/A) | WAln |
| - 'Jorvic' (Au/S) **new** | NDro |
| - 'Joy' (Au/A) | CWCL ECho IPen LLHF MAsh NDro SPop WCre WHil |
| - 'Joyce' (Au/A) | GAbr IPen SPop WCre |
| - 'Judith' (Au/B) **new** | NDro |
| - 'Julia' (Au/S) | WAln |
| - 'June' (Au/A) | NDro WAln |
| - 'Jungfrau' (Au/d) | WAln |
| - 'Jupiter' (Au/S) | NDro WAln |
| - 'Just Steven' (Au/A) | WAln |
| - K85 (Au/S) **new** | SPop |
| - 'Karen Cordrey' (Au/S) | EBee ECho GAbr GKev IPen ITim MAsh NDro NHol SDnm SPav SPop WCre WFar WHil |
| - 'Karen McDonald' (Au/A) | SPop |
| - 'Kath Dryden' | see *P. allionii* 'Kath Dryden' |
| - 'Ken Chilton' (Au/A) | WAln WFar WHil |
| - 'Kentucky Blues' (Au/d) | SPop |
| - 'Kercup' (Au/A) | SPop WCre |
| - 'Kevin Keegan' (Au/A) | SPop WHil |
| - 'Key West' (Au/A) | SPop WAln |
| - 'Khachaturian' (Au/A) | NDro WAln |
| - 'Kim' (Au/A) | IPen MOne NDro |
| - 'Kingcup' (Au/A) | SPop WCre |
| - 'Kingfisher' (Au/A) | ITim NDro SPop WHil |
| - 'Kiowa' (Au/S) | SPop |
| - 'Kirklands' (Au/d) | ITim SPop |
| - 'Klondyke' (Au/A) | WAln |
| - 'Königin der Nacht' (Au/St) | NDro WAln WHil |
| - 'Lady Daresbury' (Au/A) | GAbr SPop WFar |
| - 'Lady Day' (Au/d) **new** | SPop |
| - 'Lady Diana' (Au/S) | WAln |
| - 'Lady Emma Monson' (Au/S) | ITim |
| - 'Lady Joyful' (Au/S) | WCre |
| - 'Lady of the Vale' (Au/A) | WAln |
| - 'Lady Penelope' (Au/S) | WAln |
| - 'Lady Zoë' (Au/S) | NDro NHol SPop WAln WCre |
| - 'Lambert's Gold' (Au) | GAbr SPop |
| - 'Lamplugh' (Au/d) | IPen MOne |
| - 'Lancelot' (Au/d) | SPop WAln |
| - 'Landy' (Au/A) | NDro SPop WCre |
| - 'Langley Park' (Au/A) | EShb IPen NDro SPop WHil |
| - 'Lara' (Au/A) | WAln |
| - 'Laredo' (Au/A) | WAln |
| - 'Larry' (Au/A) | NDro SPop WAln WCre WFar |
| - 'Last Chance' (Au/St) **new** | SPop |
| - 'Lavender Lady' (Au/B) | IPen NDro SPav |
| - 'Lavenham' (Au/S) | WAln |
| - 'Laverock' (Au/S) | NBir NBro NHol WCre |
| - 'Laverock Fancy' (Au/S) | GCai IPen ITim NDro NHol |
| - 'Lazy River' (Au/A) | WAln |
| - 'Leather Jacket' (Au) | GAbr |
| - 'Lechistan' (Au/S) | ECho GAbr IPen ITim MAsh NDro SPop WCre |
| - 'Lee' (Au/A) | IPen WAln WCre |
| - 'Lee Clark' (Au/A) | WAln |
| - 'Lee Paul' (Au/A) | GAbr GCai IPen MAsh MOne NDro NHol SPop WCre WHil |
| - 'Lee Sharpe' (Au/A) | IPen SPop WAln |
| - 'Lemmy Getatem' (Au/d) | SPop |
| - 'Lemon Drop' (Au/S) | ITim NBro NDro SPop |
| - 'Lemon Sherbet' (Au/B) | SPop WHil |
| - 'Lepton Jubilee' (Au/S) | GAbr WAln |
| - 'Leroy Brown' (Au/A) | WAln |
| - 'Lester' (Au/d) **new** | SPop |
| - 'Letty' (Au/S) | WAln |
| - 'Leverton' (Au/d) | WAln |
| - 'Lichfield' (Au/A/d) | IPen SPop WAln WCre |
| - 'Light Music' (Au/d) | WAln |
| - 'Lila' (Au/S) | NDro WAln |
| - 'Lilac Domino' (Au/S) | GAbr IPen ITim NDro SPop WAln WFar WHil |
| - 'Lillian Hill' (Au/A) | WAln |
| - 'Lima' (Au/d) | WAln |
| - 'Limelight' (Au/A) | SPop WAln |
| - 'Limelight' (Au/S) | IPen WAln |
| - 'Lincoln Charm' (Au) | GAbr |
| - 'Lincoln Chestnut' (Au/d) **new** | SPop |
| - 'Lincoln Imp' (Au/d) | SPop |
| - 'Lindsey Moreno' (Au/S) | WAln |
| - 'Ling' (Au/A) | NDro SPop WCre |
| - 'Linnet' (Au/B) **new** | NDro |
| - 'Lintz' (Au) | MAsh NDro |
| - 'Lisa' (Au/A) | IPen ITim SPop WCre WFar WHil |
| - 'Lisa Clara' (Au/S) | EBee GCai IPen ITim MAsh NDro SPop WFar |
| - 'Lisa's Smile' (Au/S) | GCai ITim MOne NDro SPop WHil |
| - 'Little Rosetta' (Au/d) | ITim NDro WAln WCre WHil |
| - 'Lord Saye and Sele' (Au/St) | GAbr GCai IPen ITim NDro SPop WCre WHil |
| - 'Lorenzo' (Au/S) **new** | NDro |
| - 'Lothlorien' (Au/A) | WAln |
| - 'Louisa Woolhead' (Au/d) | SPop |
| - 'Lovebird' (Au/S) | CWCL GAbr ITim MAsh NDro SPop |
| - 'Lucky Strike' (Au) | WAln |
| - 'Lucy Locket' (Au/B) | CWCL EBee IPen MOne NDro NHol WCre |
| - 'Ludlow' (Au/S) | GAbr WAln |
| - 'Lupy Minstrel' (Au/S) | NDro |
| - 'Lynn' (Au/A) | WAln |

- 'MacWatt's Blue' GAbr IGor IPen MOne NDro SPop
- 'Madelaine Palmer' (Au/d) **new** SPop
- 'Maggie' (Au/S) GAbr NDro SPop WCre
- 'Magnolia' (Au/B) WCre WHil
- 'Maid Marion' (Au/d) WCre
- 'Maizie' (Au/S) WAln
- 'Mandarin' (Au/A) NDro SPop WCre WFar
- 'Mansell's Green' (Au/S) ITim WAln
- 'Mara Cordrey' (Au) MOne
- 'Margaret' (Au/S) GAbr
- 'Margaret Dee' (Au/d) WAln
- 'Margaret Faulkner' (Au/A) GAbr GCai WCre
- 'Margaret Irene' (Au/A) IPen SPop WAln WCre
- 'Margaret Martin' (Au/S) IPen NDro SPop WAln
- 'Margot Fonteyn' (Au/A) SPop WAln WHil
- 'Marie Crousse' (Au/d) CMea CPBP CSsd GMaP NDro NHol SPop WCre WFar
- 'Marigold' (Au/d) WFar
- 'Marion Howard Spring' (Au/A) WAln WCre
- 'Marion Tiger' (Au/St) WAln
- 'Mark' (Au/A) IPen MAsh NBro SPop WCre
- 'Marmion' (Au/S) IPen ITim NDro SPop WAln WFar WHil
- 'Martha Livesley' (Au/A) WAln
- 'Martha's Choice' (Au/A) WAln
- 'Martin Fish' (Au) WCre
- 'Martin Luther King' (Au/S) CWCL
- 'Mary' (Au/d) GAbr SPop
- 'Mary Taylor' (Au/S) WAln
- 'Mary Zach' (Au/S) WHil
- 'Matthew Yates' (Au/d) CWCL EBee GAbr GCai IPen ITim MAsh MOne NDro NHol NPri SDnm SPav SPop WCot WCre WHil WRha
- 'Maureen Millward' (Au/A) IPen NDro SPop WCre
- 'May' (Au/A) WAln WCre
- 'Mazetta Stripe' (Au/S/St) GAbr ITim NDro NLar SPop
- 'Meadowlark' (Au/A) ITim SPop WAln WCre
- 'Mease Tiger' (Au/St) GAbr WAln
- 'Megan' (Au/d) WAln
- 'Mellifluous' (Au) WAln WCre
- 'Melody' (Au/S) IPen SPop
- 'Mere Green' (Au/S) WAln
- 'Merlin' (Au/A) EBee IPen
- 'Merlin' (Au/S) WAln
- 'Merlin Stripe' (Au/St) IPen MOne NDro SPop WCre WHil
- 'Mermaid' (Au/d) NDro
- 'Merridale' (Au/A) GAbr WCre WHil
- 'Mersey Tiger' (Au/S) GAbr ITim SPop WCre WHil
- 'Metha' (Au/A) WAln
- 'Mexicano' (Au/A) WAln
- 'Michael' (Au/S) SPop WAln
- 'Michael Watham' (Au/S) WAln
- 'Michael Wattam' (Au/S) WAln
- 'Mick' (Au/A) MAsh WAln
- 'Midnight' (Au/A) WAln
- 'Mikado' (Au/S) IPen MAsh SPop
- 'Milkmaid' (Au/A) WMAq
- 'Millicent' (Au/A) WAln WFar
- 'Mink' (Au/A) WFar
- 'Minley' (Au/S) GAbr GCai ITim NBir NBro NDro NHol SPop WCre WHil
- 'Minstrel' (Au/S) NDro
- 'Mipsie Miranda' (Au/d) SPop
- 'Mirabella Bay' (Au/A) WAln
- 'Mirandinha' (Au/A) WAln
- 'Miriam' (Au/A) SPop WAln
- 'Mish Mish' (Au/d) NDro WHil
- 'Miss Bluey' (Au/d) SPop WAln
- 'Miss Newman' (Au/A) SPop WAln
- 'Miss Pinky' SPop
- 'Mojave' (Au/S) CWCL GAbr IPen ITim NDro NHol NRya SPop WCre WHil
- 'Mollie Langford' (Au/A) SPop WAln WHil
- 'Monet' (Au/S) WAln
- 'Moneymoon' (Au/S) IPen NDro WCre WHil
- 'Monk' (Au/S) ITim NDro
- 'Monk's Eleigh' (Au/A) WAln
- 'Moonglow' (Au/S) MAsh
- 'Moonlight' (Au/S) GAbr WAln
- 'Moonrise' (Au/S) NDro
- 'Moonriver' (Au/A) ITim NHol SPop WAln WCre WFar
- 'Moonshadow' (Au/d) WAln
- 'Moselle' (Au/S) NDro WAln
- 'Mr A' (Au/S) SPop
- 'Mr Greenfingers' (Au) WCre
- 'Mrs J.H. Watson' (Au) **new** WCre
- 'Mrs L. Hearn' (Au/A) IPen ITim NDro SPop
- 'Mrs R. Bolton' (Au/A) WFar
- 'Murray Lanes' (Au/A) WAln
- 'My Fair Lady' (Au/A) WAln
- 'Nankenan' (Au/S) ITim WAln WHil
- 'Neat and Tidy' (Au/S) ECho GAbr LRHS MAsh NDro NRya SPop WCre WFar
- 'Nefertiti' (Au/A) IPen NDro SPop WAln
- 'Nessun Dorma' (Au) SPop
- 'Nessundorma' (Au/A) WAln
- 'Neville Telford' (Au/S) GAbr IPen MAsh
- 'Nickity' (Au/A) GAbr IPen ITim NDro SPop WFar
- 'Nicola Jane' (Au/A) SPop WAln
- 'Nigel' (Au/d) GAbr
- 'Nightwink' (Au/S) WAln
- 'Nina' (Au/A) WAln
- 'Nita' (Au/d) WAln
- 'Nitelford' (Au) MOne
- 'Nocturne' (Au/S) IPen MAsh NBro NDro NHol SPop
- 'Noelle' (Au/S) ITim
- 'Nona' (Au/d) NDro SPop
- 'Nonchalance' (Au/A) NDro SPop WHil
- 'Notability' (Au/A) WAln
- 'Notable' (Au/A) WAln
- 'Nymph' (Au/d) SPop WHil
- 'Oakie' (Au/S) WAln
- 'Oban' (Au/S) ITim SPop
- 'Oikos' (Au/B) SPop
- 'Ol' Blue Eyes' (Au/St) WAln
- 'Old Black Isle Dusty Miller' (Au/B) **new** NDro
- 'Old Clove' MOne
- 'Old Clove Red' (Au/B) GAbr NDro
- 'Old Cottage Blue' (Au/B) **new** NDro
- 'Old England' (Au/S) SPop
- 'Old Gold' (Au/S) CWsd GAbr IPen NDro NHol WFar
- 'Old Irish Blue' (Au/B) ECho IGor
- 'Old Irish Green' (Au/B) **new** NDro
- 'Old Irish Scented' (Au/B) GAbr IGor IPen NBro NDro WHil
- 'Old Mustard' (Au/B) NDro SMHy
- 'Old Pink Dusty Miller' (Au/B) GAbr IPen
- § - 'Old Purple Dusty Miller' (Au/B) GAbr
- 'Old Red Dusty Miller' (Au/B) LLHF MSte SPop WHil
- 'Old Red Elvet' (Au/S) SPop WAln
- 'Old Smokey' (Au/A) NDro SPop WAln WHil
- 'Old Suffolk Bronze' (Au/B) GAbr NDro WHil
- 'Old Yellow Dusty Miller' (Au/B) EWes GAbr GCai IPen MSte NBro NDro NHol NRya WHil

| | |
|---|---|
| - 'Olivia' (Au/d) | SPop |
| - 'Olton' (Au/A) | IPen |
| - 'Optimist' (Au/St) | SPop |
| - 'Opus One' (Au/A) | WAln |
| - 'Orb' (Au/S) | GAbr IPen ITim MAsh NDro SPop WCre |
| - 'Ordvic' (Au/S) | WAln |
| - 'Orlando' (Au/S) | NDro SPop WAln |
| - 'Orwell Tiger' (Au/St) | IPen SPop |
| - 'Osbourne Green' (Au/B) | GAbr GCai NDro SPop WCre WHil |
| - 'Otto Dix' (Au/A) | WAln |
| - 'Overdale' (Au/A) | WAln |
| - 'Paddlin Madeleine' (Au/A) | WAln |
| - 'Pagoda Belle' (Au/A) | WAln |
| - 'Paleface' (Au/A) | IPen ITim NDro WAln WCre |
| - 'Pam Tiger' (Au/St) | WAln |
| - 'Panache' (Au/S) | WAln |
| - 'Papageno' (Au/St) | WAln |
| - 'Paphos' (Au/d) | SPop |
| - 'Paradise Yellow' (Au/B) | GEdr NDro SPop |
| - 'Paragon' (Au/A) | ITim WHil |
| - 'Party Time' (Au/S) | IPen WAln |
| - 'Pastiche' (Au/A) | NDro WCre |
| - 'Pat' (Au/S) | SPop |
| - 'Pat Barnard' (Au) | IPen |
| - 'Patience' (Au/S) | NDro SPop WHil |
| - 'Patricia Barras' (Au/S) | WAln |
| - 'Pauline Taylor' (Au/d) | WAln |
| - 'Pegasus' (Au/d) | SPop WAln |
| - 'Peggy' (Au/A) | GAbr WHil |
| - 'Peggy's Lad' (Au/A) | WAln |
| - 'Pequod' (Au/A) | SPop WAln |
| - 'Peter Beardsley' (Au/A) | WAln |
| - 'Peter Hall' (Au/d) | WAln |
| - 'Phantom' (Au) | WAln |
| - 'Pharaoh' (Au/A) | EShb NDro SPop WAln WFar |
| - 'Phyllis Douglas' (Au/A) | IPen ITim NDro SPop WCre WHil |
| - 'Pierot' (Au/A) | IPen NDro SPop WCre WHil |
| - 'Piers Telford' (Au/A) | CWCL EBee GAbr GCai IPen NDro SBch SDnm SPav SPop WCre |
| - 'Piglet' (Au) | GAbr |
| - 'Pink Fondant' (Au/d) | WAln |
| - 'Pink Hint' (Au/B) **new** | NDro |
| - 'Pink Lady' (Au/A) | NBro SPop |
| - 'Pink Panther' (Au/S) | WAln |
| - 'Pinkie' (Au/A) | WAln WHil |
| - 'Pinkie Dawn' (Au) **new** | NDro |
| - 'Pinstripe' | IPen MOne SPop WCre WHil |
| - 'Pioneer Stripe' (Au/S) | IPen WHil |
| - 'Pippin' (Au/A) | GAbr IPen NBro NDro SPop WCre WFar WHil |
| - 'Pixie' (Au/A) | IPen WAln |
| - 'Playboy' (Au/A) | WAln |
| - 'Plush Royal' (Au/S) | WAln |
| - 'Polestar' (Au/A) | SPop WCre WFar |
| - 'Pop's Blue' (Au/S/d) | SPop |
| - 'Portree' (Au/S) | GAbr SPop |
| - 'Pot o' Gold' (Au/S) | EBee ECho IPen ITim MAsh NDro SPop WCre WHil |
| - 'Prague' (Au/S) | IPen NBir NDro NHol SPop |
| - 'Pretender' (Au/A) | SPop WAln |
| - 'Prince Bishop' (Au/S) | NDro WAln |
| - 'Prince Charming' (Au/S) | IPen ITim MOne SPop |
| - 'Prince John' (Au/A) | CWCL ITim NBro NDro NHol SPop WCre WHil |
| - 'Proctor's Yellow' (Au/B) **new** | NDro |
| - 'Prometheus' (Au/d) | MAsh NRya SPop WAln WCre |
| - 'Purple Dusty Miller' | see *P. auricula* 'Old Purple Dusty Miller' |
| - 'Purple Glow' (Au/d) | WAln |
| - 'Purple Haze' | SPop |
| - 'Purple Sage' (Au/S) | GCai NHol |
| - 'Purple Velvet' (Au/S) | CWCL IPen NDro NHol SPop |
| - 'Quatro' (Au/d) | SPop WAln |
| - 'Queen Alexandra' (Au/B) | GAbr NDro |
| - 'Queen Bee' (Au/S) | GAbr NDro WFar |
| - 'Queen of Sheba' (Au/S) | WAln |
| - 'Queen's Bower' (Au/S) | SPop |
| - 'Quintessence' (Au/A) | WAln WCre |
| - 'R.L. Bowes' (Au/A) **new** | NDro |
| - 'Rab C. Nesbitt' (Au/A) | WAln |
| - 'Rabley Heath' (Au/A) | GCai NDro SPop WCre |
| - 'Rachel' (Au/A) | GAbr WAln |
| - 'Rajah' (Au/S) | CWCL EBee ECho GAbr IPen ITim MOne NDro NHol SPop WCre WFar WHil |
| - 'Raleigh Stripe' (Au/St) | IPen NDro WAln |
| - 'Ralenzano' (Au/A) | WAln |
| - 'Rameses' (Au/A) | IPen WAln WCre |
| - 'Rebecca Hyatt' (Au/d) | WAln |
| - 'Red Admiral' (Au) | WAln |
| - 'Red Arrows' (Au) | WAln |
| - 'Red Embers' (Au/S) | WAln |
| - 'Red Gauntlet' (Au/S) | EDAr GAbr GCai IPen ITim MRav MSte NDro NHol SPop WFar WHil |
| - 'Red Mark' (Au/A) | WHil |
| - 'Red Rum' (Au/S) | GAbr |
| - 'Red Vulcan' (Au) | WCre |
| - 'Red Wire' | SPop |
| - 'Redcar' (Au/A) | GAbr WAln WCre |
| - 'Redstart' (Au/S) | IPen ITim WHil |
| - 'Regency' (Au/A) | WAln |
| - 'Remus' (Au/S) | CWCL ECho ELan GAbr GCai IPen ITim LLHF MAsh NDro NHol SPop WCre WHil |
| - 'Rene' (Au/A) | GAbr IPen WCre |
| - 'Respectable' (Au/A) | WAln |
| - 'Reverie' (Au/d) | WAln |
| - 'Riatty' (Au/d) | GAbr WAln |
| - 'Richard Shaw' (Au/A) | IPen MOne |
| - 'Ring of Bells' (Au/S) | WAln |
| - 'Risdene' (Au) **new** | IPen |
| - 'Rita' (Au/S) | WAln |
| - 'Robbo' (Au/B) **new** | NDro |
| - 'Robert Lee' (Au/A) | WAln |
| - 'Roberto' (Au/S) | MAsh WAln |
| - 'Robin Hood Stripe' (Au/St) **new** | SPop |
| - 'Robinette' (Au/d) | SPop |
| - 'Rock Sand' (Au/S) | ECho GCai NDro WHil |
| - 'Rodeo' (Au/A) | GAbr IPen SPop WPat |
| - 'Rolts' (Au/S) | CWCL EBee ECho EShb GAbr GKev IPen ITim NBro NDro NHol SDnm SPav SPop WCre WFar |
| - 'Ronnie Johnson' (Au) | WAln |
| - 'Ronny Simpson' | WCre |
| - 'Rosalie' (Au) | SPop |
| - 'Rosalie Edwards' (Au/S) | SPop |
| - 'Rose Conjou' (Au/d) | GAbr IPen NDro SPop WAln |
| - 'Rose Kaye' (Au/A) | IPen SPop |
| - 'Rose Three' (Au) | WCre |
| - 'Rosebud' (Au/S) | GAbr NDro |
| - 'Rosemary' (Au/S) | ITim NDro SPop WCre WHil |
| - 'Rosie' (Au/S) **new** | NDro |
| - 'Rothesay Robin' (Au/A) | WAln |
| - 'Rowena' (Au/A) | GCai IPen NBro NDro SDnm SPav SPop WCre WHil |
| - 'Roxborough' (Au/A) | CWCL IPen WAln |
| - 'Roxburgh' (Au/A) | NDro SPop WCre |
| - 'Roy Keane' (Au/A) | IPen SPop |
| - 'Royal Mail' (Au/S) | SPop WAln |
| - 'Royal Marine' (Au/S) | WAln |
| - 'Royal Velvet' (Au/S) | GAbr IPen NHol WHil |

| | |
|---|---|
| - 'Rusty Dusty' (Au) | IGor |
| - 'Ryecroft' (Au/A) | WAln |
| - 'Sabrina' (Au/A) | WAln |
| - 'Saginaw' (Au/A) | WAln |
| - 'Sailor Boy' (Au/S) | NDro SPop |
| - 'Saint Boswells' (Au/S) | GAbr NRya SPop WAln |
| - 'Saint Quentin' (Au/S) | WAln |
| - 'Salad' (Au/S) | GAbr |
| - 'Sally' (Au/A) | WAln |
| - 'Sam Gamgee' (Au/A) | WAln |
| - 'Sam Hunter' (Au/A) | NDro SPop WAln |
| - 'Samantha' (Au/A) | WAln |
| - 'Sandhills' (Au/A) | MAsh WAln |
| - 'Sandra' (Au/A) | ECho ELan GAbr IPen NDro SPop WCre WHil |
| - 'Sandra's Lass' (Au/A) | SPop WAln |
| - 'Sandwood Bay' (Au/A) | EShb GAbr GCai LRHS MAsh MOne NBro NDro NHol SPop WCre |
| - 'Sarah Gisby' (Au/d) | SPop |
| - 'Sarah Lodge' (Au/d) | CWCL GAbr IPen MAsh NDro SPop WCre |
| - 'Satin Doll' (Au/d) **new** | SPop |
| - 'Scipio' (Au/S) | NDro WAln |
| - 'Scorcher' (Au/S) | IPen NDro SPop WAln |
| - 'Searchlight' (Au) **new** | WCre |
| - 'Second Victory' (Au) | NDro WCre |
| - 'Serenity' (Au/S) | NDro NHol WCre |
| - 'Sergeant Wilson' (Au) | SPop WAln |
| - 'Shalford' (Au/d) | NDro SPop WCre |
| - 'Sharman's Cross' (Au/S) | WAln |
| - 'Sharon Louise' (Au/S) | IPen MAsh WCre |
| - 'Sheila' (Au/S) | ECho GAbr ITim MAsh NDro SPop WCre WHil |
| - 'Shere' (Au/S) | SPop WCre |
| - 'Shergold' (Au/A) | WCre |
| - 'Sherwood' (Au/S) | GCai IPen MAsh NDro SPop WHil |
| - 'Shirley' (Au/S) | SPop WAln |
| - 'Shotley' (Au/A) | SPop |
| - 'Showman' (Au/S) | WAln |
| - 'Showtime' (Au/S) **new** | NDro |
| - 'Sibsey' (Au/d) | CWCL MAsh SPop WAln |
| - 'Sidney' (Au/A) | WAln |
| - 'Silas' (Au/B) | SPav |
| - 'Silmaril' (Au) | SPop WAln |
| - 'Silverway' (Au/S) | ITim SPop WCre WHil |
| - 'Simply Red' (Au) | IPen NDro SPop WAln |
| - 'Sir John' (Au/A) | MAsh |
| - 'Sir Robert' (Au/d) | WAln |
| - 'Sirbol' (Au/A) | IPen NDro SPop WCre WFar |
| - 'Sirius' (Au/A) | CWCL GAbr IPen ITim LRHS MOne NDro NHol NRya SPop WCre WFar WHil |
| - 'Skipper' (Au/d) | SPop |
| - 'Skylark' (Au/A) | GAbr IPen ITim SPop WAln WCre WHil |
| - 'Skyliner' (Au/A) | NDro |
| - 'Slioch' (Au/S) | ECho GAbr IPen ITim NDro NHol SPop WCre |
| - 'Slip Anchor' (Au/A) | WAln |
| - 'Smart Tar' (Au/S) | WAln |
| - 'Snooty Fox' (Au/A) | GAbr IPen MOne SPop |
| - 'Snowy Owl' (Au/S) | GAbr NDro SPop WCre |
| - 'Somersby' (Au/d) | SPop WAln |
| - 'Soncy Face' (Au/A) | MAsh WAln |
| - 'Sonny Boy' (Au/A) | WAln |
| - 'Sophie' (Au/d) | SPop WAln |
| - 'South Barrow' (Au/d) | GAbr SPop WCre WHil |
| - 'Sparky' (Au/A) | WAln |
| - 'Spartan' (Au) | WAln |
| - 'Spokey' (Au) **new** | IPen |
| - 'Spring Meadows' (Au/S) | GAbr MAsh MOne NDro NHol SPop |
| - 'Springtime' (Au/A) | SPop WAln |
| - 'Standish' (Au/d) | GAbr |
| - 'Stant's Blue' (Au/S) | EShb GCai IPen NBro NDro |
| - 'Star Wars' (Au/S) | GAbr MAsh NDro NHol SPop WAln |
| - 'Starburst' (Au/S) | WAln |
| - 'Starling' (Au/B) | GAbr IPen NDro SPop |
| - 'Starry' (Au/S) | MOne WCre |
| - 'Stella Coop' (Au/d) | NDro WAln |
| - 'Stoke Poges' (Au/A) | WAln |
| - 'Stoney Cross' (Au/S) | SPop |
| - 'Stonnal' (Au/A) | SPop WHil |
| - 'Stormin Norman' (Au/A) | NDro SPop WAln |
| - 'Striped Ace' (Au/St) **new** | NDro |
| - 'Stripey' (Au/d) | IPen NHol WAln |
| - 'Stromboli' (Au/d) | SPop |
| - 'Subliminal' (Au/A) | WAln |
| - 'Sue' (Au/A) | WCre WFar |
| - 'Sugar Plum Fairy' (Au/S) | GAbr NDro WHil |
| - 'Sultan' (Au/A) | WAln |
| - 'Summer Sky' (Au/A) | SPop WCre |
| - 'Sumo' (Au/A) | GAbr SPop WAln WCre WHil |
| - 'Sunflower' (Au/A/S) | EShb GAbr ITim MAsh SPop WCre |
| - 'Sunsplash' (Au) **new** | WCre |
| - 'Sunstar' (Au/S) | NDro |
| - 'Super Para' (Au/S) | GAbr IPen NDro SPop WHil |
| - 'Superb' (Au/S) | WAln |
| - 'Susan' (Au/A) | ITim NDro WCre |
| - 'Susannah' (Au/d) | CWCL GAbr GCai GMaP IPen LRHS MOne NDro NHol NPri SDnm SPav SPop WCre WFar WHil |
| * - 'Sweet Chestnut' (Au/S) | WAln |
| - 'Sweet Georgia Brown' (Au/A) | SPop WAln |
| - 'Sweet Pastures' (Au/S) | ECho GAbr IPen NDro NHol SPop WCre |
| - 'Sword' (Au/d) | CWCL ECho GAbr IPen MAsh MOne NDro NHol SPop WAln WCre WFar WHil |
| - 'Symphony' (Au/A) | ITim MOne NDro SPop WFar WHil |
| - 'T.A. Hadfield' (Au/A) | SPop WFar WHil |
| - 'Taffeta' (Au/S) | CWCL EBee NDro SDnm SPav WAln |
| - 'Tall Purple Dusty Miller' (Au/B) | SPop |
| - 'Tally-ho' (Au/A) | WAln |
| - 'Tamino' (Au/S) | NDro WAln |
| - 'Tandem' (Au/St) | WAln |
| - 'Tarantella' (Au/A) | NDro SPop |
| - 'Tawny Owl' (Au/B) | NBro |
| - 'Tay Tiger' (Au/St) | GAbr SPop |
| - 'Teawell Pride' (Au/d) | SPop |
| - 'Ted Gibbs' (Au/A) | MOne NDro WAln WCre |
| - 'Ted Roberts' (Au/A) | EShb NDro SPop WCre WFar |
| - 'Teem' (Au/S) | GAbr IPen MAsh NDro NRya SPop WCre |
| - 'Temeraire' (Au/A) | WAln |
| - 'Tenby Grey' (Au/S) | WCre |
| - 'Tender Trap' (Au/A) | WAln |
| - 'Terpo' (Au/A) | WAln |
| - 'The Baron' (Au/S) | GCai IPen ITim MOne NDro SPop WCre WFar |
| - 'The Bishop' (Au/S) | IPen SPop WHil |
| - 'The Cardinal' (Au/d) | WAln |
| - 'The Egyptian' (Au/A) | IPen SPop WAln WHil |
| - 'The Hobbit' (Au/A) | WAln |
| - 'The Raven' (Au/S) | ITim MAsh SPop |
| - 'The Sneep' (Au/A) | IPen NDro SPop WCre |
| - 'The Snods' (Au/S) | EBee IPen NDro SPop |
| - 'The Wrekin' (Au/S) | WAln |
| - 'Thetis' (Au/A) | SPop WCre WFar |
| - 'Thirlmere' (Au/d) | WAln |
| - 'Three Way Stripe' (St) | WCre WHil |
| - 'Thutmoses' (Au/A) | WAln |
| - 'Tiger Tim' (Au/St) | WAln |
| - 'Tim' (Au) **new** | IPen |

| | |
|---|---|
| - 'Tinker' (Au/S) | WAln |
| - 'Tinkerbell' (Au/S) | IPen SPop WCre |
| - 'Titania' (Au) | SPop |
| - 'Toffee Crisp' (Au/A) | IPen WAln |
| - 'Tom Farmer' (Au) | WCre |
| - 'Tomboy' (Au/S) | IPen MAsh NDro SDnm SPop |
| - 'Toolyn' (Au/S) | NDro WAln |
| - 'Tosca' (Au/S) | EBee GCai IPen ITim MAsh NDro NRya SPop WCre WFar WHil |
| - 'Trish' | GAbr |
| - 'Trojan' (Au/S) | MAsh |
| - 'Trouble' (Au/d) | EBee GAbr GMaP IPen LRHS MAsh NDro NRya SPop WCre WHil |
| - 'Troy Aykman' (Au/A) | SPop WAln |
| - 'Trudy' (Au/S) | GAbr GCai IPen ITim MOne NDro SPop WCre WHil |
| - 'True Briton' (Au/S) | IPen SPop WCre |
| - 'Trumpet Blue' (Au/S) | SPop WFar |
| - 'Tummel' | NDro SPop WAln WHil |
| - 'Twiggy' (Au/S) | GCai NDro NRya SPop WAln |
| - 'Tye Lea' (Au/S) | WAln |
| - 'Typhoon' (Au/A) | IPen SPop WCre |
| - 'Uncle Arthur' (Au/A) | WAln |
| - 'Unforgettable' (Au/A) | WAln |
| - 'Upton Belle' (Au/S) | IPen MAsh SPop WAln |
| - 'Valerie' (Au/A) | IPen ITim SPop |
| - 'Valerie Clare' | WAln |
| - 'Vee Too' (Au/A) | GAbr SPop WCre WHil |
| - 'Vega' (Au/A) | SPop WAln |
| - 'Vein' (Au/St) | WAln |
| - 'Velvet Moon' (Au/A) | WAln WFar |
| - 'Venetian' (Au/A) | NDro SPop WAln WFar |
| - 'Venus' (Au/A) | WAln |
| - 'Vera' (Au/A) | SPop |
| - 'Verdi' (Au/A) | WAln |
| - 'Vesuvius' (Au/d) **new** | IPen SPop |
| - 'Victoria' (Au/S) | WAln |
| - 'Victoria de Wemyss' (Au/A) | WCre |
| - 'Victoria Park' (Au/A) | WAln |
| - 'Virginia Belle' (Au/St) | WAln |
| - 'Vivian' (Au/S) | WAln |
| - 'Vulcan' (Au/A) | ECho NBro SPop |
| - 'Walter Lomas' (Au/S) | WAln |
| - 'Walton' (Au/A) | CWCL GAbr MAsh NDro SPop WCre WFar WHil |
| - 'Walton Heath' (Au/d) | ECho IPen MAsh NDro SPop WCre WFar |
| - 'Wanda's Moonlight' (Au/d) | WAln |
| - 'Warpaint' (Au/St) **new** | NDro |
| - 'Watchett' (Au/S) | WAln |
| - 'Wayward' (Au/S) | WCre |
| - 'Wedding Day' (Au/S) | ITim WAln |
| - 'Wentworth' (Au/A) | IPen WAln |
| - 'Whistle Jacket' (Au/S) | NDro SPop WAln |
| - 'White Ensign' (Au/S) | ECho GAbr IPen ITim NDro SPop WCre WFar |
| - 'White Water' (Au/A) | SPop WAln |
| - 'White Wings' (Au/S) | GCai ITim NDro SPop |
| - 'Whitecap' (Au/S) | WAln |
| - 'Whoopee' (Au/A) | WAln |
| - 'Wichita Falls' (Au/A) | WAln |
| - 'Wilf Booth' (Au/A) | SPop WAln WFar |
| - 'William Telford' (Au) | MOne |
| - 'Wincha' (Au/S) | EShb GCai NDro SPop WCre |
| - 'Windways Mystery' (Au/B) | GAbr NDro |
| - 'Windways Pisces' (Au/d) | WAln |
| - 'Winifrid' (Au/A) | EShb GAbr LRHS NDro NHol SPop WCre WFar |
| - 'Witchcraft' (Au) | SPop |
| - 'Woodmill' (Au/A) | IPen SPop WAln |
| - 'Wycliffe Midnight' (Au) | GAbr NDro |
| - 'Wye Hen' (Au/St) | WAln |
| - 'Wye Lemon' (Au/S) **new** | SPop |
| - 'X2' (Au) **new** | WHil |
| - 'Yellow Hammer' (Au/S) | WAln |
| - 'Yellow Isle' (Au/S) | WAln |
| - 'Yitzhak Rabin' (Au/A) | WAln WHil |
| - 'Yorkshire Grey' (Au/S) | IPen NBro |
| - 'Zambia' (Au/d) | ECho GAbr NDro SPop WCre |
| - 'Zircon' (Au/S) | WAln |
| - 'Zodiac' (Au/S) | WAln |
| - 'Zoe' (Au/A) | WAln |
| - 'Zoe Ann' (Au/S) | WAln |
| - 'Zorro' (Au/St) | WAln |
| ***auriculata*** (Or) | EBee GKev |
| 'Barbara Barker' (Au) | GEdr NMen |
| 'Barbara Midwinter' (Pr) | CDes GAbr SHar WAbe |
| Barnhaven Blues Group (Pr/Prim) $\Upsilon^{H4}$ | CSWP EBla GAbr |
| Barnhaven doubles (Pr/Prim/d) | CSWP |
| Barnhaven Gold-laced Group | see *P.* Gold-laced Group Barnhaven |
| Barnhaven hybrids | NSum |
| Barnhaven Traditional Group (Pr) | CSWP |
| 'Beatrice Wooster' (Au) | CLyd GKev GKir IPen ITim NDlv NLAp NWCA |
| 'Beeches' Pink' | GAbr NHar |
| ***beesiana*** (Pf) | Widely available |
| (Belarina Series) 'Belarina Butter Yellow' (Pr/Prim/d) | CWCL EPfP NLar SIng SMrm SVil WHil |
| - 'Belarina Cobalt Blue' (Pr/Prim/d) **new** | CWCL SIng SMrm WHil |
| - 'Belarina Cream' (Pr/Prim/d) | CHVG CWCL LLHF SIng SVil WHil |
| - 'Belarina Pink Ice' (Pr/Prim/d) | CWCL LHop SIng SMrm SVil WHil |
| - 'Belarina Rosette Nectarine' (Pr/Prim/d) | CWCL LAst SIng SVil WHil |
| 'Belinda' | ITim |
| ***bellidifolia*** (Mu) | EBee GEdr GKev IPen |
| § - subsp. ***hyacinthina*** (Mu) | WAbe |
| aff. ***bellidifolia*** (Mu) SDR 1868 **new** | GKev |
| ***beluensis*** | see *P.* x *pubescens* 'Freedom' |
| § x ***berninae*** 'Windrush' (Au) | WAbe |
| 'Bewerley White' | see *P.* x *pubescens* 'Bewerley White' |
| ***bhutanica*** | see *P. whitei* 'Sherriff's Variety' |
| 'Big Red Giant' (Pr/Prim/d) | CWCL ECtt NGHP |
| ***bileckii*** | see *P.* x *forsteri* 'Bileckii' |
| 'Blue Riband' (Pr/Prim) | CDes CWsd EBee LLHF WFar |
| 'Blue Sapphire' (Pr/Prim/d) | CWsd GAbr NCGa NGHP SPer |
| 'Blutenkissen' (Pr/Prim) | GAbr |
| 'Bon Accord Cerise' (Pr/Poly/d) | GAbr |
| 'Bon Accord Lilac' (Pr/Poly/d) | GAbr |
| 'Bon Accord Purple' (Pr/Poly/d) | WFar |
| ***boothii*** (Pe) | NHar NSum |
| - EN 82 **new** | NHar |
| - EN 382 | NHar WThu |
| - ***alba*** (Pe) | LLHF NHar |
| - subsp. ***repens*** (Pe) | CEnt MNrw |
| 'Boothman's Ruby' | see *P.* x *pubescens* 'Boothman's Variety' |
| § ***bracteosa*** (Pe) | GKev ITim |
| Bressingham (Pf) | WFar |
| ***brevicaula*** | see *P. brevicula* |

| | |
|---|---|
| § ***brevicula*** (Cy) SDR 4770 **new** | GKev |
| 'Broadwell Milkmaid' | WAbe |
| 'Broadwell Pink' (Au) | WAbe |
| 'Broadwell Ruby' (Au) | WAbe |
| 'Bronwyn' (Pr/Prim) | WCot |
| 'Broxbourne' | ITim NHol NLAp |
| 'Buckland Wine' (Pr/Prim) | CElw |
| x ***bulleesiana*** (Pf) | CMMP CWCL EBee EMFW EPfP EWTr GKev LBMP LRHS MBri NBro NChi NGdn NHol NLar SMrm SPad SPer SPet SRms SWat WBrE WFar WHil WMnd WMoo WPer WPnP |
| - Moerheim hybrids (Pf) | WFar |
| ***bulleyana*** (Pf) ♀H4 | Widely available |
| - ACE 2484 | WAbe |
| - SDR 4261 **new** | GKev |
| ***burmanica*** (Pf) | CSec EBee GAbr GBuc GEdr GGar GKir IPen MMuc SRms SWat WFar WMoo |
| 'Butter's Bronze' (Pr/Prim) | WOut |
| 'Butterscotch' (Pr/Prim) | CSWP |
| 'Caerulea Plena' (Pr/Prim) | GCal NBid |
| ***calliantha*** (Cy) **new** | GKev |
| Candelabra hybrids (Pf) | CBre CBro CHar COlW CWCL ECho GAbr GGar GKir ITim LSou MNHC NBir NCob NGdn SMrm SPet SWal SWat WCra WFar WRos |
| Candy Pinks Group (Pr/Prim) | CSWP |
| ***capitata*** (Ca) | CMMP CSWP CSpe EBee ECho EDAr EPfP GAbr GKev IPen NWCA SPer SPoG WAbe WFar WGwG WWFP |
| - subsp. ***mooreana*** (Ca) | CFir CSec CTsd EAlp EWTr IPen LBMP NDlv NGdn NLAp NSum SPet SPlb SRot WFar WHil WHrl WPtf |
| 'Captain Blood' (Pr/Prim/d) | ECtt EPfP MSte SIng WFar WRha |
| Casquet mixture (Pr/Prim) | CSWP |
| ***cernua*** (Mu) | GKev IPen |
| Chartreuse Group (Pr/Poly) | CSWP WRha |
| § ***chionantha*** (Cy) ♀H4 | CLAP CSec CWCL EBee EPfP GAbr GAuc GCra GGar GKev GKir LRHS NBir NCob NGdn NHol NMyG SPer WAbe WFar WGwG WPtf |
| - SDR 4610 **new** | GKev |
| - subsp. ***chionantha*** (Cy) | EBee IPen |
| § - subsp. ***melanops*** (Cy) | EBee GAuc LRHS |
| § - subsp. ***sinopurpurea*** (Cy) | CLAP CWCL EBee GGar GKev GKir IPen MDKP NCGa NLar NSum SPer WAbe WBVN WFar WHil WPer |
| - - SDR 2747 **new** | GKev |
| - - SDR 2861 | GKev |
| - - SDR 4418 **new** | GKev |
| ***chungensis*** (Pf) | CBcs CLAP CSec CWCL EBee EDAr GBuc GCra GEdr GGar GKev GKir IPen MLLN NBPC NDlv NGdn NHol NSti SRms STes SWvt WAbe WMoo |
| § ***chungensis*** x ***pulverulenta*** (Pf) | CHid CLAP CWCL EBee GBuc GCai GEdr GKir NBPC NHol NLar WAbe WFar WMnd |
| x ***chunglenta*** | see *P. chungensis* x *P. pulverulenta* |
| 'Clarence Elliott' (Au) | CDes CGra CLyd CMea CPBP GKev IPen ITim MAsh NHar WAbe WFar |
| ***clarkei*** (Or) | CLyd GEdr WAbe |
| ***clusiana*** (Au) | WAbe WFar |
| - 'Murray-Lyon' (Au) | NMen |
| ***cockburniana*** (Pf) ♀H4 | CBcs EBee EBla EDAr GAuc GEdr GGar GKev GQui IPen MDKP NGdn SRms SWat WAbe WFar |
| - SDR 1967 | GKev |
| - hybrids (Pf) | SWat |
| - yellow-flowered (Pf) | EBee GEdr GKev GMac IPen |
| ***concholoba*** (Mu) | GKev NLAp |
| 'Corporal Baxter' (Pr/Prim/d) | EPfP LLHF NGHP NLar WRha |
| ***cortusoides*** (Co) | CLAP CMil CSec CWsd EBee EDAr GAbr GCra GKev GKir IPen LSou NLar SRms |
| - SDR 2831 | GKev |
| Cowichan Amethyst Group (Pr/Poly) | CDes CHFP CSWP EBee NCGa |
| Cowichan Blue Group (Pr/Poly) | CHFP CSWP NCGa |
| Cowichan Garnet Group (Pr/Poly) | CDes CHFP CSWP GBuc NCGa WPGP |
| Cowichan Red Group (Pr/Poly) | WFar |
| Cowichan Venetian Group (Pr/Poly) | CDes CSWP NCGa WFar |
| Cowichan Yellow Group (Pr/Poly) | CHFP NCGa WCot |
| 'Coy' | CGra WAbe |
| 'Craven Gem' (Pr/Poly) | GBuc |
| Crescendo Series (Pr/Poly) | GAbr WHil |
| 'Crimson Velvet' (Au) | GAbr IPen ITim NLAp |
| ***crispa*** | see *P. glomerata* |
| ***cuneifolia*** (Cu) | GKev |
| ***darialica*** (Al) | EBee GKev LLHF |
| 'Dark Rosaleen' (Pr/Poly) | GAbr NDov WCra |
| 'David Valentine' (Pr) | EBla EMon GAbr GBuc |
| 'Dawn Ansell' (Pr/Prim/d) | CDes CHrt CRow CWCL EBla EPfP GAbr LRHS MSte NBir NCGa NDov NGHP SPer SRGP WCot WFar WHer WHil |
| Daybreak Group (Pr/Poly) | CSWP NCGa |
| ***deflexa*** (Mu) | IPen LRHS |
| ***denticulata*** (De) ♀H4 | Widely available |
| - var. ***alba*** (De) | CBcs CSam CTri CWat EBee ECha ECho EPfP GAbr GCra GGar LRHS MBri NBid NCob NHol NOrc NPri SPer SPoG WBrE WCAu WMoo WPer |
| - blue-flowered (De) | ECho GAbr GKir MWat NLar NPri WFar |
| - 'Glenroy Crimson' (De) | CLAP EBee SRms SWvt |
| - 'Karryann' (De/v) | CBow EBee EMon SUsu WCot |
| - lilac-flowered (De) | ECho EHon MWat NCob NPri SPoG |
| - 'Prichard's Ruby' (De) | NCob |
| - purple-flowered (De) | ECho WMoo |
| - red-flowered (De) | ECho GGar GKir NOrc WMoo |
| - 'Robinson's Red' (De) | GBuc |
| - 'Ronsdorf' (De) | LRHS NBPC |
| - rose-flowered (De) | GKir |
| - 'Rubin' (De) | CDWL CHrt ECho EHon GAbr MBrN MBri MLHP NCob SPer SPoG SRms WPer |
| - 'Rubinball' (De) | EBee NHol |
| x ***deschmannii*** | see *P.* x *vochinensis* |
| 'Desert Sunset' (Pr/Poly) | CSWP NCGa |
| 'Devon Cream' (Pr/Prim) | CWsd WFar |
| 'Dianne' | see *P.* x *forsteri* 'Dianne' |
| 'Discovering Stripes' (Pr/Poly) | WHil |
| 'Don Keefe' | ECtt GBin GEdr GMac LSou MBNS NDov NLar WCot WCra |
| 'Dorothy' (Pr/Poly) | MRav |
| 'Double Lilac' | see *P. vulgaris* 'Lilacina Plena' |
| 'Duckyls Red' (Pr/Prim) | EMon GBuc WHal |
| 'Dusky Lady' | MBri WFar |
| 'Early Bird' (*allionii* hybrid) (Au) | IPen |

| | | |
|---|---|---|
| | 'Easter Bonnet' (Pr/Prim) | LRHS NBid WCot |
| | ***edgeworthii*** | see *P. nana* |
| § | ***elatior*** (Pr) ♀H4 | Widely available |
| | - hose-in-hose (Pr/d) | NBid |
| | - hybrids (Pr) | CSec GAbr |
| I | - 'Jessica' | WFar WHil |
| | - subsp. ***leucophylla*** (Pr) | EBee ECho SBch |
| § | - subsp. ***meyeri*** (Pr) | EBee GKev GKir |
| I | - 'Mrs Statham's Oxslip' (Pr) | CWsd |
| | 'Elizabeth Killelay'PBR (Pr/Poly/d) | Widely available |
| | 'Ethel Barker' (Au) | IPen ITim LRHS NDlv NHol NLAp SIng |
| | 'Eugénie' (Pr/Prim/d) | NGHP NLar SRGP |
| | 'Fairy Rose' (Au) | IPen ITim NHol WAbe |
| | ***farinosa*** (Al) | CEnt EBee EDAr GKir IPen NGdn NLAp NSum SPoG WFar |
| | ***fasciculata*** (Ar) | GCai GEdr NWCA |
| | - CLD 345 | WAbe |
| | 'Fife Yellow' (Pr/Prim/d) | GBuc |
| | 'Fire Opal' | EBrs |
| | Firefly Group (Pr/Poly) | NCGa WCot |
| § | ***firmipes*** (Si) | EWes IPen |
| § | ***flaccida*** (Mu) | GAuc GEdr GGGa GKev IPen NLAp WAbe |
| | Flamingo Group (Pr/Poly) | CSWP NCGa |
| | ***florida*** (Y) | NCob |
| | ***florindae*** (Si) ♀H4 | Widely available |
| | - bronze-flowered (Si) | CSec GKir GQui NBir SWat |
| | - buff-flowered **new** | GAuc |
| | - hybrids (Si) | CDWL EHrv GAbr GEdr GKir GMaP ITim LBMP NCob NHol WHil |
| | - Keillour hybrids (Si) | NGdn WPtf |
| | - magenta-flowered (Si) | MDKP |
| | - 'Muadh' (Si) **new** | MMuc |
| | - orange-flowered (Si) | CSam GCal GMac IPen LLWG MDKP MNrw WFar WMoo |
| | - peach-flowered (Si) | MDKP |
| | - 'Ray's Ruby' (Si) | CHar CLAP EBee GBuc MDKP MNrw NBir NGdn SWat WRos WWFP |
| | - red-flowered (Si) | CDWL GBin GBuc GGar GKev IPen NBid NLar NSum WFar |
| | - terracotta-flowered (Si) | CSWP NGdn |
| | Footlight Parade Group (Pr/Prim) | CSWP |
| | ***forbesii*** (Mo) CC 4084 | CPLG |
| | ***forrestii*** (Bu) | EBee GAuc GKev IPen WAbe |
| § | x ***forsteri*** 'Bileckii' (Au) | LRHS NBir NLAp NWCA SRms WAbe |
| § | - 'Dianne' (Au) | EDAr GAbr GBuc GKev NBro NHol NRya WAbe |
| | 'Francisca' (Pr/Poly) | CBgR CElw CHFP CHid CMHG CSpe CWCL EBee EBla ECtt GAbr LLHF LSou MBNS MNrw NChi NCot NDov NGdn NMyG NSti SUsu WCot WCra WGwG WHil WKif |
| | 'Freckles' (Pr/Prim/d) | CWCL SWat |
| | 'Freedom' | see *P.* x *pubescens* 'Freedom' |
| | ***frondosa*** (Al) ♀H4 | CWCL ECho GCra IPen MDKP NLAp NMen NWCA WAbe |
| | ***gambeliana*** (Cf) | GKev |
| | - AC 5467 | GKev |
| | 'Garryard Guinevere' | see *P.* 'Guinevere' |
| | 'Garryarde Crimson' | LLHF |
| | ***gaubana*** (Sp) | GKev NLAp |
| | ***geraniifolia*** (Co) | GEdr |
| § | 'Gigha' (Pr/Prim) | CSWP CSpe EBee |
| | ***glaucescens*** (Au) | GKev NSum WFar |
| § | ***glomerata*** (Ca) | ECho GBuc IPen |
| | - CC 3843 | GKev |
| | - GWJ 9213 | WCru |
| | - SDR 3924 **new** | GKev |
| | 'Glowing Embers' (Pf) | GKev LRHS NBir |
| | ***glutinosa*** All. | see *P. allionii* |
| | Gold-laced Group (Pr/Poly) | Widely available |
| § | - Barnhaven (Pr/Poly) | EBla GAbr GKir NBir |
| | - Beeches strain (Pr/Poly) ♀H4 | NCob |
| | 'Gordon' | MOne |
| | ***gracilipes*** (Pe) | CDes CLAP CWsd MDKP NHol NLAp SRms WAbe |
| | - L&S 1166 | WAbe |
| | - early-flowering (Pe) | GCra WAbe |
| | - 'Major' | see *P. bracteosa* |
| | - 'Minor' | see *P. petiolaris* |
| | ***graminifolia*** | see *P. chionantha* |
| | ***grandis*** (Sr) | IPen |
| | 'Green Lace' (Pr/Poly) | NBhm WCot |
| | 'Groenekan's Glorie' (Pr/Prim) | GAbr GEdr LRHS MRav NBir NSum WFar |
| § | 'Guinevere' (Pr/Poly) ♀H4 | Widely available |
| | 'Hall Barn Blue' | CBgR EAlp GAbr GEdr NBPC NHar NHol NMyG |
| § | ***halleri*** (Al) | EBee GKev IPen MDKP NDlv NLAp NSum WAbe |
| | - DJHC 0083 | WCru |
| | - 'Longiflora' | see *P. halleri* |
| | Harbinger Group (Pr/Prim) | CSWP |
| | Harbour Lights mixture (Pr/Poly) | CSWP NCGa |
| | Harlow Carr hybrids (Pf) | CSWP GCai GQui LRHS MLLN NDlv NSla SPoG WMoo |
| | Harvest Yellows Group (Pr/Poly) | NCGa WCot |
| | 'Helmswell Abbey' (Au) | GKev |
| | ***helodoxa*** | see *P. prolifera* |
| | 'Hemswell Blush' (Au) | CSpe GCai GKev ITim MOne NLAp NLar WCre |
| | 'Hemswell Ember' (Au) | CPBP GCai MOne NDlv NHol NLAp NRya |
| | ***heucherifolia*** (Co) | GAuc GKev IPen |
| | - SDR 3224 **new** | GKev |
| | ***hidakana*** (R) | GEdr |
| | ***hirsuta*** (Au) | GEdr IPen |
| | - 'Lismore Snow' (Au) | NHar WAbe |
| | - ***nivea*** (Au) | GKev |
| | - red-flowered (Au) | GKev NLAp |
| | ***hoi*** (Cy) **new** | GKev |
| | hose-in-hose (Pr/Poly/d) | CSWP MNrw |
| | hose-in-hose, Barnhaven (Pr/Poly) | WFar |
| | 'Hyacinthia' (Au) | CLyd IPen NLar |
| | ***hyacinthina*** | see *P. bellidifolia* subsp. *hyacinthina* |
| | ***ianthina*** | see *P. prolifera* |
| | ***incana*** (Al) | EBee GKev |
| | Indian Reds Group (Pr/Poly) | CSWP |
| | 'Ingram's Blue' (Pr/Poly) | CBgR LRHS WPen |
| | Inshriach hybrids (Pf) | CMHG CSWP NSum WFar |
| | ***integrifolia*** (Au) | GBuc GEdr WAbe |
| | - SDR 1318 **new** | GKev |
| | - SDR 1338 **new** | GKev |
| | ***integrifolia*** x ***minima*** 'Kilchuimin' (Au) | GEdr |
| § | 'Inverewe' (Pf) ♀H4 | CRow GBin GCra GKev GQui NBir NBre NChi NMun SUsu |
| | ***involucrata*** | see *P. munroi* |
| | ***ioessa*** (Si) | EWes GCra GQui NGdn |
| | - var. ***hopeana*** (Si) | EBee GKev NSum |
| | - hybrids (Si) | NLAp |
| | 'Iris Mainwaring' (Pr/Prim) | GAbr GCra GEdr NHol NWCA WCot |
| | ***irregularis*** (Pe) | WAbe |

| | | |
|---|---|---|
| | Jack in the Green Group (Pr/Poly) | CDMG CSWP MNrw MRa v WBor WFar WRha |
| | - Barnhaven (Pr/Poly) | EBla |
| | Jackanapes Group (Pr/Poly) | EBla |
| | ***japonica*** (Pf) | CMHG CRow CSam ECha GAuc GGar GQui IPen ITim LPBA LRHS MNHC NBid NBro NGdn NHol SUsu SWat WAbe WBrE WFar WMoo WPer |
| | - 'Alba' (Pf) | CPrp CTri EBee ECho EHrv EPfP EWTr GAuc GEdr GGar GKir IPen NBid NDlv NGdn NMyG NPri SPer WAbe WCAu WFar WHil |
| | - 'Apple Blossom' (Pf) | CCVN CFir CMHG COIW CWCL EBee GBri GCai GEdr GKev GKir GMac IPen LBMP MBNS MBri NBHF NGdn NHol NPri SWvt WFar WHoo WPnP |
| * | - 'Carminea' (Pf) | CMil COIW CWCL EBee GBuc GEdr GKev GKir IPen NBro NGdn NLar WFar |
| | - 'Fuji' (Pf) | CSWP NBro |
| | - 'Fuji' hybrids (Pf) | NLar |
| | - hybrids (Pf) | GCra GKir |
| | - 'Jim Saunders' (Pf) **new** | SLon |
| | - 'Merve's Red' (Pf) | CAby CDes EBee WPGP |
| | - 'Miller's Crimson' (Pf) $\mathbb{Y}^{H4}$ | Widely available |
| | - 'Oriental Sunrise' (Pf) | CMil CSWP EBee GKev |
| | - pale pink-flowered (Pf) | NSum |
| | - 'Peninsula Pink' (Pf) | IPen |
| | - 'Pinkie' (Pf) | IPen |
| | - 'Postford White' (Pf) $\mathbb{Y}^{H4}$ | Widely available |
| | - Redfield strain (Pf) | IPen WHil |
| | - red-flowered (Pf) | IPen WAbe |
| | - 'Splendens' (Pf) | IPen |
| | - 'Valley Red' (Pf) | GBuc GCai IPen |
| | ***jesoana*** (Co) | CSec EWld GGar LLHF WHil |
| | - B&SWJ 618 | WCru |
| | - var. ***pubescens*** (Co) **new** | EBee |
| | 'Joan Hughes' (*allionii* hybrid) (Au) | CLyd WAbe |
| | 'Joanna' | ECou MHer |
| | 'Johanna' (Pu) | GAbr GBuc GEdr GKev NGdn NHar NHol NSum NWCA WAbe |
| | 'John Fielding' (Sr x Pr) | CBgR CBro CElw GAbr GEdr MCot |
| | 'Jo-Jo' (Au) | CLyd WAbe |
| | ***juliae*** (Pr) | ECho EDAr GEdr GKev LRHS NBid NSum NWCA SPlb WAbe WCot |
| I | - 'Millicent' (Pr) | WCot |
| | - white-flowered (Pr) | NSum |
| | 'Kate Haywood' | CLyd |
| | 'Ken Dearman' (Pr/Prim/d) | CWCL ECtt EPfP MBNS MSte NBir NGHP SIng SPer SRGP WFar |
| | ***kewensis*** (Sp) $\mathbb{Y}^{H2}$ | EShb GKev |
| | 'Kinlough Beauty' (Pr/Poly) | EMon GAbr GEdr LLHF NRya NSti NWCA WEas |
| § | ***kisoana*** (Co) | CLAP CWsd EBla GCai GKev IPen LLHF WCru |
| | - var. ***alba*** (Co) | CLAP EBee |
| | - var. ***shikokiana*** | see *P. kisoana* |
| | - 'Velvet' (Co) | GEdr |
| | 'Kusum Krishna' **new** | GEdr NHar |
| | 'Lady Greer' (Pr/Poly) $\mathbb{Y}^{H4}$ | CSam EBee EDAr EPfP GAbr GBuc GEdr GKev LLWP MCot MHer NChi NGdn NHar NLAp NRya NSti NWCA SAga SIng WFar WHer |
| | ***latifolia*** f. ***pyrenaica*** (Au) **new** | GKev |
| | ***latisecta*** (Co) | GEdr IPen |
| § | ***laurentiana*** (Al) | CSec CTsd EBee GAuc NMen |
| | 'Lea Gardens' (*allionii* hybrid) (Au) | IPen ITim NHol |
| | 'Lee Myers' (*allionii* hybrid) (Au) | IPen ITim NDlv |
| | ***leucophylla*** | see *P. elatior* |
| | 'Lilac Domino' (Au) | IPen |
| | 'Lilian Harvey' (Pr/Prim/d) | CElw CHrt EPfP WRHF |
| | 'Lindum Moonlight' | ITim |
| | 'Lindum Serenade' (Au) | WThu |
| | 'Lingwood Beauty' (Pr/Prim) | GAbr |
| | 'Lismore Bay' (Au) **new** | GKev |
| | 'Lismore Jewel' (Au) | WAbe |
| | 'Lismore Sunshine' | NHar |
| | 'Lismore Treasure' (Au) | CGra WAbe |
| | 'Lismore Yellow' (Au) | GKev NHar WAbe |
| | 'Little Egypt' (Pr/Poly) | NCGa |
| | ***littoniana*** | see *P. vialii* |
| | x ***loiseleurii*** 'Aire Mist' (Au) | CGra CLyd CPBP GCai IPen ITim MAsh MOne NHar NHol NLAp NMen NRya NSum SIng WAbe WHil |
| § | - 'Aire Waves' (Au) | CLyd GCai ITim NHar NHol NLAp NMen |
| | - 'Pink Aire Mist' (Au) **new** | WHil |
| | - 'White Waves' (Au) | IPen |
| | ***longiflora*** | see *P. halleri* |
| | ***luteola*** (Or) | EBee ECho EWTr GGar GKev GKir LLHF NGdn NLar NSum WFar WPer |
| | ***macrocalyx*** | see *P. veris* |
| | ***macrophylla*** (Cy) | EBee GKev |
| | 'MacWatt's Claret' | GAbr LLWP |
| | 'MacWatt's Cream' | CSWP EBee EBla EWTr GAbr GCra GEdr GKir LHop LRHS SIng WCot |
| | ***magellanica*** (Al) | EBee GKev NGdn WAbe |
| | ***malacoides*** (Mo) | GKev MBri |
| | mandarin red-flowered (Pf) | CSWP |
| | ***marginata*** (Au) $\mathbb{Y}^{H4}$ | CPne ECho GEdr GKir IPen LFox LHop LRHS NDlv NHol NLAp NSum SBch SIng WAbe WFar |
| | - from the Dolomites (Au) | NHol |
| | - 'Adrian Evans' (Au) | ITim |
| | - ***alba*** (Au) | NBro NDlv NHol NLAp WFar |
| | - 'Baldock's Purple' (Au) | IPen |
| | - 'Barbara Clough' (Au) | CLyd GEdr IPen ITim WFar |
| | - 'Beamish' (Au) $\mathbb{Y}^{H4}$ | CLyd NBro NHol NRya |
| | - 'Beatrice Lascaris' (Au) | MOne NRya WAbe |
| | - 'Beverley Reid' (Au) | ITim |
| | - 'Boothman's Variety' (Au) | CTri ECho NLAp |
| | - 'Caerulea' (Au) | CLyd GKev MOne NLAp WAbe |
| | - 'Clear's Variety' (Au) | IPen ITim |
| | - 'Correvon's Variety' (Au) | CLyd WAbe |
| | - cut-leaved (Au) | NHol |
| | - 'Doctor Jenkins' (Au) | IPen ITim NHol NLar NRya |
| | - 'Drake's Form' (Au) | IPen NLAp NLar NRya |
| | - dwarf (Au) | LRHS |
| | - 'Earl L. Bolton' | see *P. marginata* 'El Bolton' |
| § | - 'El Bolton' (Au) | IPen NHol WAbe |
| | - 'Elizabeth Fry' (Au) | CLyd IPen LFox |
| | - 'F.W. Millard' (Au) | NRya |
| | - 'Grandiflora' (Au) | IPen NHol |
| | - 'Highland Twilight' (Au) | IPen NSla WAbe |
| | - 'Holden Variety' (Au) | IPen ITim NDlv NHol NRya WAbe |
| | - 'Ivy Agee' (Au) | CLyd IPen ITim NLAp NRya |
| | - 'Janet' (Au) | CLyd NLAp |
| | - 'Jenkins Variety' (Au) | CLyd ECho |
| | - 'Kesselring's Variety' (Au) | CLyd CMMP CMea ECho GCai GEdr IPen MOne NDlv NLAp WAbe WFar WTin |
| | - 'Laciniata' (Au) | IPen LRHS |
| | - lilac-flowered (Au) | IPen LFox |
| | - 'Linda Pope' (Au) $\mathbb{Y}^{H4}$ | CLyd GCai GKev IPen ITim NBir NDlv NHar NHol NLAp NSla NSum WAbe |
| | - maritime form (Au) | IPen |

| | |
|---|---|
| - 'Millard's Variety' (Au) | CLyd IPen ITim |
| - 'Miss Fell' (Au) | IPen |
| - 'Mrs Gatenby' (Au) | NWCA |
| - 'Nancy Lucy' (Au) | WAbe |
| - 'Napoleon' (Au) | GEdr IPen ITim MSCN NLAp |
| - 'Prichard's Variety' (Au) ♀$^{H4}$ | CLyd ECho GEdr IPen ITim LFox NCob NDlv NLAp NMyG NRya NWCA WAbe WFar |
| - 'Rosea' (Au) | IPen |
| - 'Sheila Denby' (Au) | IPen ITim NLAp |
| - 'Snowhite' (Au) | NHar |
| - 'The President' (Au) | ITim |
| - violet-flowered (Au) | ECho |
| - 'Waithman's Variety' (Au) | IPen NLAp NRya |
| - wild-collected (Au) | NHol |
| 'Marianne Davey' (Pr/Prim/d) | MRav |
| 'Marie Crousse' (Pr/Prim/d) | CWCL EPfP GAbr NWCA SRGP WCot WFar WHal WRha |
| Marine Blues Group (Pr/Poly) | CSWP NCGa |
| 'Maris Tabbard' (Au) | IPen NLar WAbe |
| 'Mars' (*allionii* hybrid) (Au) | NDlv NHol NRya |
| 'Marven' (Au) | CLyd GCai GEdr IPen |
| 'Mary Anne' | GAbr |
| 'Mauve Mist' (Au) | MAsh |
| Mauve Victorians Group (Pr/Poly) | CSWP |
| ***maximowiczii*** (Cy) | GBuc GKev NLAp |
| ***megaseifolia*** (Pr) | GKev |
| ***melanops*** | see *P. chionantha* subsp. *melanops* |
| x ***meridiana*** (Au) | NHol |
| § - 'Miniera' (Au) | IPen ITim SIng WAbe |
| 'Mexico' | LLHF WCot |
| Midnight Group | CSWP NCGa |
| 'Miniera' | see *P.* x *meridiana* 'Miniera' |
| ***minima*** (Au) | NBro NLar NSla WAbe |
| - var. ***alba*** (Au) | NRya |
| ***minima*** x ***wulfeniana*** | see *P.* x *vochinensis* |
| 'Miss Indigo' (Pr/Prim/d) | CDes CHrt CWCL ECtt EPfP GMaP MBNS MRav MSte NGHP SGar SPer WCAu WCot WFar WHil |
| ***mistassinica*** var. ***macropoda*** | see *P. laurentiana* |
| ***miyabeana*** (Pf) | IPen |
| - B&SWJ 3407 | WCru |
| ***modesta*** (Al) | CSec |
| - var. ***faurieae*** (Al) | GAuc IPen NWCA |
| - - f. ***leucantha*** (Al) | GKev |
| - 'Nemuro-koza-kura' (Al/v) | CBow EMon |
| ***mollis*** (Co) | EBee GKev |
| ***moupinensis*** | CLAP EBee GGGa WAbe WCot |
| * 'Mrs Eagland' | GAbr |
| 'Mrs Frank Neave' (Pr/Prim) | IPen |
| 'Mrs McGillivray' (Pr/Prim) | GAbr |
| § ***munroi*** (Ar) | CDes EBee GEdr GKev IPen WAbe WRos |
| § - subsp. ***yargongensis*** (Al) | GAbr GAuc GGar GKev IPen LRHS WAbe WFar |
| - - SDR 3096 | GKev |
| ***muscarioides*** (Mu) | EBee IPen |
| Muted Victorians Group (Pr/Poly) | CHFP CSWP NCGa |
| § ***nana*** (Pe) | GKev IPen |
| - 'Alba' (Pe) | WAbe |
| - blue-flowered (Pe) | GKev |
| 'Netherall Castlederg' **new** | CWsd |
| 'Netta Dennis' (Pe) | NHar |
| New Pinks Group (Pr/Poly) | CSWP NCGa |
| 'Nightingale' | ITim NHol |
| ***nipponica*** (Su) | GEdr |
| ***nivalis*** Pallas | see *P. chionantha* |
| § ***nivalis*** (Fed.) Halda subsp. ***xanthobasis*** (Cy) | EBee |
| ***nutans*** Delavay ex Franch. | see *P. flaccida* |
| ***obconica*** (Ob) | LRHS MBri |
| ***obtusifolia*** (Cy) | EBee GKev |
| 'Old Port' (Pr/Poly) | CBgR CElw EBee GKev LLWP NMen WCot |
| Old Rose Victorians Group (Pr/Poly) | CSWP |
| ***orbicularis*** (Cy) | GKev |
| 'Oriental Sunset' | MDKP |
| Osiered Amber Group (Pr/Prim) | CSWP |
| 'Our Pat' (Pr/Poly/d) | GAbr |
| pale blue-flowered (Poly) | SSth |
| ***palinuri*** (Au) | IPen |
| ***palmata*** (Co) | GEdr |
| Paloma Series **new** | LRHS |
| 'Pamilata' **new** | EBee GKev |
| 'Paris '90' (Pr/Poly) | CHFP CSWP NCGa |
| ***parryi*** (Pa) | EBee GKev NLAp WFar |
| 'Peardrop' (Au) | GAbr NHol |
| ***pedemontana*** (Au) | GKev MSte WAbe |
| - 'Alba' (Au) | CGra WPat |
| 'Perle von Bottrop' (Pr/Prim) | GAbr |
| 'Peter Klein' (Or) | GBuc GEdr LLHF NHol WAbe WTin |
| ***petiolaris*** misapplied | see *P.* 'Redpoll' |
| § ***petiolaris*** Wall. (Pe) | GCra MDun NHar NSum NWCA WAbe |
| - Sherriff's form | see *P.* 'Redpoll' |
| 'Petticoat' | NCGa NLar SPer |
| 'Pincushion' **new** | GEdr |
| 'Pink Aire' (Au) | ITim NMen NRya |
| 'Pink Fairy' (Au) | IPen ITim |
| 'Pink Ice' (*allionii* hybrid) (Au) | CGra CHVG CLyd CPBP GKev ITim NHol NRya |
| ***poissonii*** (Pf) | CDWL CTri EBee ELan GAuc GCra GEdr GGar GKev GKir GQui IBal IPen LPBA NGby NGdn NHol SPad WAbe WGwG WShi |
| - ACE 2030 | EPot |
| - B&SWJ 7525 | WCru |
| - SDR 3201 | GKev |
| polyanthus (Pr/Poly) | WFar |
| ***polyneura*** (Co) | EBee EDAr GEdr GGar GKev IGor IPen NBid NGdn SRms WCot |
| 'Port Wine' (Pr) | EBla GAbr |
| ***prenantha*** (Pf) | EBee GKev LLHF WAbe |
| - SDR 3909 **new** | GKev |
| ***primulina*** (Mi) SDR 3940 **new** | GKev |
| § ***prolifera*** (Pf) ♀$^{H4}$ | Widely available |
| § x ***pubescens*** (Au) ♀$^{H4}$ | EAlp IPen LFox NGdn NLAp WPer |
| - 'Alison Gibbs' (Au) | MOne |
| - 'Apple Blossom' (Au) | CLyd IPen |
| - 'Balfouriana' (Au) | LFox NHol |
| - 'Bewerley White' (Au) | EBee ECho EPfP IPen MOne NDlv NHol NLAp NMyG WCre |
| - 'Blue Wave' (Au) | IPen |
| § - 'Boothman's Variety' (Au) | CLyd CTri EAlp ECho EDAr EPfP GKev ITim LRHS MSte NDlv NLAp NMyG WFar WHoo WTin |
| - 'Carmen' | see *P.* x *pubescens* 'Boothman's Variety' |
| - 'Christine' (Au) | CDes CLyd CMea GKev IPen ITim NBir NDlv NSum WCot |
| - 'Cream Viscosa' (Au) | NDlv NLAp |
| - 'Faldonside' (Au) | CLyd IPen NDlv NSum |
| § - 'Freedom' (Au) | CLyd CTri ECho GAbr GKev IPen ITim LRHS MAsh NBir NDlv NHol NLAp NLar SRms WEas |

| | | |
|---|---|---|
| | - 'Harlow Car' | CLyd CMea CPBP GMac GQui IPen NDlv NSum NWCA WFar WTin |
| | - 'Hazel's White' (Au) **new** | GKev |
| | - 'Henry Hall' (Au) | CLyd EWes MOne |
| | - 'Joan Danger' (Au) | CLyd IPen ITim |
| | - 'Joan Gibbs' (Au) | CLyd ECho GCai IPen ITim MOne NLAp |
| | - 'Lilac Fairy' (Au) | IPen ITim NDlv NHol SIng |
| | - 'Mrs J.H. Wilson' (Au) | CGra CLyd GEdr NDlv NHol NRya |
| | - 'Pat Barwick' (Au) | GKir IPen ITim LFox NLAp WTin |
| | - 'Peggy Fell' (Au) | WHil |
| | - 'Rufus' (Au) | CLyd ECho EWes GAbr WCot WTin |
| | - 'S.E. Matthews' (Au) | NHol |
| | - 'Sid Skelton' (Au) | IPen |
| | - 'Snowcap' (Au) | CGra CPBP IPen |
| | - 'Sonya' (Au) | IPen |
| | - 'The General' (Au) | CLyd CTri IPen ITim MOne SPop |
| § | - 'Wedgwood' (Au) | GCai IPen |
| | - 'Winifred' (Au) | NDro NHol SPop |
| | - yellow-flowered (Au) | IPen |
| | ***pulchella*** (Pu) | GKev |
| | ***pulverulenta*** (Pf) $\Psi^{H4}$ | Widely available |
| | - Bartley hybrids (Pf) $\Psi^{H4}$ | CDWL CDes CWCL GBuc GMac LSou NBre |
| | - 'Bartley Pink' (Pf) | GBuc |
| | 'Quaker's Bonnet' | see *P. vulgaris* 'Lilacina Plena' |
| | 'Rachel Kinnen' (Au) | IPen ITim SIng WFar |
| | 'Ravenglass Vermilion' | see *P.* 'Inverewe' |
| | 'Red Velvet' (Pr/Prim/d) | CWCL MSte NGHP |
| § | 'Redpoll' (Pe) | CLAP MDKP NHar WAbe |
| | ***reidii*** (So) | GEdr NSla |
| | - CC 4624 | GKev |
| | - var. ***williamsii*** (So) | GKev IPen LLHF |
| * | - - ***alba*** (So) | WAbe |
| | 'Reverie' (Pr/Poly) | CSWP NCGa |
| | 'Rheniana' (Au) | IPen ITim SIng |
| | 'Romeo' (Pr/Prim) | WCot |
| | ***rosea*** (Or) $\Psi^{H4}$ | CAby CRow EBee ECho EDAr EMFW EPfP GAuc GEdr IPen LRHS MMuc NBid NBir NLAp NRya NVic WFar |
| | - 'Delight' | see *P. rosea* 'Micia Visser-de Geer' |
| | - 'Gigas' (Or) | GBuc NHol WFar |
| | - 'Grandiflora' (Or) | CPrp EAlp ECho EHon EPfP GGar GKev LPBA MRav MWat NDlv NWCA SIng SPoG SRms SWal SWat WFar WHil WPer |
| § | - 'Micia Visser-de Geer' (Or) | LRHS WTin |
| § | ***rotundifolia*** (Cf) | IPen |
| | 'Rowallane Rose' (Pf) | CBro GBuc IGor |
| I | 'Rowena' | GCra LLHF WCot |
| | ***roxburghii*** | see *P. rotundifolia* |
| | 'Roy Cope' (Pr/Prim/d) | CWCL EPfP GAbr NBir SGar SRGP WFar |
| | 'Roydon Ruby' | WCot |
| | ***rubra*** | see *P. firmipes* |
| | ***rupicola*** (Y) | GKev |
| | ***rusbyi*** (Pa) | CGra EBee GKev NWCA |
| | - subsp. ***ellisiae*** (Pe) | CGra IPen |
| | ***saxatilis*** (Co) | WFar |
| | ***scandinavica*** (Al) | EBee GAuc |
| | x ***scapeosa*** (Pe) | GKev |
| § | 'Schneekissen' (Pr/Prim) | CBre GAbr GCra GEdr IPen MBri MHer NBro NCGa NChi NGHP NMyG NPro WHil |
| | ***scotica*** (Al) | EDAr GAuc GPoy LFox NSla WAbe |
| | ***secundiflora*** (Pf) | CDWL CLAP CWCL EBee EDAr ELan GCra GEdr GGGa GGar GKev GKir LPBA NLAp SPlb SRms SWat WFar WGwG WMoo |
| | - B&SWJ 7547 | WCru |
| | - SDR 4435 **new** | GKev |
| | x ***serrata*** | see *P.* x *vochinensis* |
| | ***serratifolia*** (Pf) | GGGa |
| | - SDR 5165 **new** | GKev |
| | ***sibthorpii*** | see *P. vulgaris* subsp. *sibthorpii* |
| | ***sieboldii*** (Co) $\Psi^{H4}$ | CEnt CGra CRow ECho GCai GKev ITim LFox MLHP MNrw NMen NRya NWCA SRms WAbe WFar |
| | - 'Bide-a-Wee Blue' (Co) | NBid |
| | - 'Blacksmith's Blue' (Co) **new** | EBla |
| I | - 'Blue Lagoon' (Co) | EBee EBrs GKir MMHG |
| | - 'Blue Shades' (Co) | IPen |
| | - blue-flowered (Co) | CLAP CWCL ECho GEdr NMen |
| | - 'Blush' (Co) | CLAP GEdr |
| | - 'Carefree' (Co) | CLAP IPen LLHF NBro NLar NMen |
| | - 'Cherubim' (Co) | EBee GCra GKir MMHG |
| | - 'Dancing Ladies' (Co) | CLAP CMil CSWP EBla IPen NBro WFar |
| | - 'Duane's Choice' (Co) | CDes |
| | - 'Frilly Blue' (Co) | EBrs |
| | - 'Galaxy' (Co) | NBro NRya |
| | - 'Geisha Girl' (Co) | CFir CLAP CSpe EBla EBrs GKir MRav NLar WAbe WFar |
| | - f. ***lactiflora*** (Co) | CDes CLAP EBee GMac IPen NBro NDov NMen SMHy SRot WFar WPGP WTin |
| | - 'Lilac Sunbonnet' (Co) | EPfP LLHF LRHS NWCA WFar |
| | - 'Manakoora' (Co) | CLAP CSWP EBee IPen NBro NSum WFar |
| | - 'Mikado' (Co) | CLAP EBee EBrs GCra GKir IPen MRav WFar |
| | - 'Pago-Pago' (Co) | CDes CLAP EBee IPen NBro WFar |
| | - 'Purple Back' (Co) | EBee |
| | - 'Seraphim' (Co) | CLAP EBee EBrs GKir MMHG |
| | - 'Snowflake' (Co) | CLAP EBrs MMHG NLar NSla WAbe |
| | - 'Tah-ni' (Co) | CMil NBro NSum |
| | - 'Winter Dreams' (Co) | CLAP CSWP NBid NBro NSum WFar |
| | ***sikkimensis*** (Si) $\Psi^{H4}$ | CEnt CRow CWCL ECho EDAr EPot EWTr GAuc GEdr GGGa GGar GKev GKir IPen LPBA MNrw NGdn NSum SPoG WBVN WFar WHil WPnP |
| | - ACE 1422 | GBuc |
| | - ACE 2234 | GKev |
| | - B&SWJ 4808 | WCru |
| | - CC&McK 1022 | GQui |
| | - SDR 1717 | GKev |
| | - SDR 3099 **new** | GKev |
| | - SDR 4528 from high altitude **new** | GKev |
| | - SDR 4763 **new** | GKev |
| | - from Bhutan **new** | GCra |
| | - var. ***pseudosikkimensis*** (Si) | IPen |
| | - var. ***pudibunda*** (Si) | EBee GEdr GKev |
| | - 'Tilman Number 2' (Si) | CWCL GAbr |
| | aff. ***sikkimensis*** (Si) | GKir ITim |
| | - ACE 2176 | GBuc |
| | Silver-laced Group (Pr/Poly) | SWvt WCot WFar WPtf |
| | - 'Silver Lining' (Pr/Poly) | LRHS |
| | 'Silverwells' (Pf) | GEdr |
| | ***simensis*** (Sp) | GKev |
| | ***sinopurpurea*** | see *P. chionantha* subsp. *sinopurpurea* |
| | 'Sir Bedivere' (Pr/Prim) | CDes GAbr GBuc NLar |
| | ***smithiana*** | see *P. prolifera* |
| | 'Snow Carpet' | see *P.* 'Schneekissen' |
| | 'Snow Cushion' | see *P.* 'Schneekissen' |
| | 'Snow White' (Pr/Poly) | GEdr MRav |
| | Snowcushion | see *P.* 'Schneekissen' |
| | 'Snowruffles' | ITim |

| | |
|---|---|
| ***sonchifolia*** (Pe) | CFir CLAP GGGa MDun WCot |
| - SDR 2560 | GKev |
| - from Tibet (Pe) | MDun |
| aff. ***soongii*** (Cy) SDR 4849 **new** | EBee GKev |
| ***sorachiana*** | see *P. yuparensis* |
| ***souliei*** (Y) SDR 1855 | GKev |
| 'Sparkling Eyes' | WCot |
| ***spectabilis*** (Au) | EBee GEdr GKev |
| ***specuicola*** (Al) | GKev |
| Spice Shades Group (Pr/Poly) | CSWP GKir NCGa WCot |
| ***stenocalyx*** (Pu) | WAbe |
| 'Stradbrook Charm' (Au) | CPBP NHol WFar WThu |
| 'Stradbrook Dainty' (Au) | WFar |
| 'Stradbrook Dream' (Au) | ITim NLAp WFar |
| 'Stradbrook Gem' (Au) | WAbe |
| 'Stradbrook Lucy' (Au) | IPen ITim NHol NLAp WAbe WFar |
| Striped Victorians Group (Pr/Poly) | CHFP CSWP NCGa |
| 'Sue Jervis' (Pr/Prim/d) | CWCL NBir NCGa NGHP NLar NSti NSum SPer WGwG WHal WPrP WRha |
| ***suffrutescens*** (Su) | WAbe |
| 'Sunshine Susie' (Pr/Prim/d) | CHrt CWCL EPfP MBNS MRav MSte NCGa NGHP SIng SPer SRGP WCot WHil |
| ***szechuanica*** (Cy) SSSE 292 **new** | EBee |
| ***takedana*** (Bu) | LLHF |
| 'Tantallon' (Pe) | GGGa ITim |
| Tartan Reds Group (Pr/Prim) | CSWP |
| 'Tawny Port' (Pr/Poly) | GAbr GBuc NBro SRms |
| 'Tie Dye' (Pr/Prim) | CBgR CDes CElw CHFP EBla ECGP GAbr GBin GBri GEdr LRHS MNrw NBPC NBhm NCGa NCot NLar SPoG WCot WFar |
| 'Tipperary Purple' (Pr/Prim) | GAbr GEdr |
| 'Tomato Red' (Pr/Prim) | CBgR |
| 'Tony' (Au) | CGra CPBP IPen WAbe |
| 'Top Affair' (Au/d) | IPen WAln |
| 'Tournaig Pink' (Pf) | GGar |
| 'Val Horncastle' (Pr/Prim/d) | CWCL ECtt EPfP GAbr GMaP LRHS MBNS MDKP MNrw MSte NCGa NGHP NLar SIng WClo WCot WFar |
| § ***veris*** (Pr) ♀H4 | Widely available |
| - subsp. ***columnae*** (Pr) | EBee |
| - feather-petalled (Pr) | WCot |
| - hybrids (Pr) | SGar |
| - 'Katy McSparron' (Pr/d) | CMea CSsd EBee GCra GKir WBor WCot |
| - subsp. ***macrocalyx*** (Pr) | EBee GKev NWCA WHil |
| - orange-flowered (Pr) | CSec MHer WMoo |
| - red-flowered (Pr) | NBid NGdn SPer WMoo |
| - 'Sunset Shades' (Pr) | CAby NGHP NLar WFar WPer |
| ***vernalis*** | see *P. vulgaris* |
| ***verticillata*** (Sp) | GKev IPen |
| § ***vialii*** (So) ♀H4 | Widely available |
| Violet Victorians Group (Pr/Poly) | CSWP |
| § x ***vochinensis*** (Au) | CFee GKev NWCA |
| § ***vulgaris*** (Pr/Prim) ♀H4 | Widely available |
| - var. ***alba*** (Pr/Prim) | CRow CWsd NSla WAbe WBrk |
| - 'Alba Plena' (Pr/Prim) | CRow GBuc GCal GGar IGor MBri NSum |
| - 'Alex Brenton' (Pr/d) | LHop |
| - green-flowered | see *P. vulgaris* 'Viridis' |
| § - 'Lilacina Plena' (Pr/Prim/d) | CDes CWCL EPfP GCal GMaP MBNS MRav NCGa NGHP NSum SPer WFar |
| § - subsp. ***sibthorpii*** (Pr/Prim) ♀H4 | CMHG CSam EBee EBla EBrs ECho GAbr GBuc IPen ITim LFox LLWP LRHS MHer MLHP MRav NBro NChi NGHP NHol NMyG SRms WEas WHil |
| § - 'Viridis' (Pr/Prim/d) | CDes CRow EBla |
| ***waltonii*** (Si) | CMil EBee GBuc GCai GEdr GKev IPen MDKP MNrw |
| 'Wanda' (Pr/Prim) ♀H4 | CBcs CTri EBla ECho GAbr GCra LBMP LLWP LRHS NBid NSti NVic SRGP SRms WBrk WCFE WCot WEas WFar WHil WTin |
| Wanda Group (Pr/Prim) | ECho |
| 'Wanda Hose-in-hose' (Pr/Prim/d) | EBla EMon GAbr GCra LLWP MMHG NBir NChi SSvw WCot WHer WHil |
| 'Wanda Jack in the Green' (Pr/Prim) | CBgR CRow MLLN WCot WFar |
| ***wardii*** | see *P. munroi* |
| ***warshenewskiana*** (Or) | EBee ECtt GEdr GGar GKev MNrw NCob NHol NLAp NMen NRya NWCA WAbe WFar WGwG WPat |
| ***watsonii*** (Mu) | CSec EBee GAbr GKev NLAp SWat |
| - ACE 1402 | IPen |
| - SDR 1626 **new** | GKev |
| - SDR 1673 **new** | GKev |
| 'Wedgwood' | see *P.* x *pubescens* 'Wedgwood' |
| 'Welsh Blue' **new** | CSpe |
| 'Wharfedale Bluebell' (Au) | CLyd NBir NRya |
| 'Wharfedale Buttercup' (Au) | NHar |
| 'Wharfedale Butterfly' (Au) | ITim NHol |
| 'Wharfedale Crusader' (Au) | ITim |
| 'Wharfedale Gem' (*allionii* hybrid) (Au) | GCai ITim NLAp NRya WAbe |
| 'Wharfedale Ling' (*allionii* hybrid) (Au) | CGra CPBP GCai GKev NLar NRya |
| 'Wharfedale Sunshine' (Au) | GKev ITim |
| 'Wharfedale Superb' (*allionii* hybrid) (Au) | ITim NLAp |
| 'Wharfedale Village' (Au) | CLyd ITim NLAp WThu |
| 'White Linda Pope' (Au) | CLyd NMen |
| 'White Wanda' (Pr/Prim) | GAbr NDov WHil |
| ***whitei*** (Pe) | CWsd |
| § - 'Sherriff's Variety' (Pe) | CLAP |
| ***wigramiana*** (So) CC 4940 **new** | GKev |
| - CC 4941 **new** | GKev |
| 'William Genders' (Pr/Poly) | GAbr |
| ***wilsonii*** (Pf) | CDWL CSec CTri CTsd GBuc GKev GKir LDai MDKP MOne NDlv SWat WBVN WFar WGwG WHil WHoo |
| § - var. ***anisodora*** (Pf) | CLAP EBee GKev GKir GQui IPen NGdn WHrl |
| 'Windrush' | see *P.* x *berninae* 'Windrush' |
| 'Winter White' | see *P.* 'Gigha' |
| 'Wisley Crimson' | see *P.* 'Wisley Red' |
| § 'Wisley Red' (Pr/Prim) | CElw |
| ***wulfeniana*** (Au) | EDAr GEdr GKev WAbe |
| ***xanthobasis*** | see *P. nivalis* (Fed.) Halda subsp. *xanthobasis* |
| ***yargongensis*** | see *P. munroi* subsp. *yargongensis* |
| ***yunnanensis*** (Y) | GKev |
| § ***yuparensis*** (Al) | EBee IPen NWCA |
| ***zambalensis*** (Ar) | GKev IPen WAbe |

## *Prinsepia* (*Rosaceae*)

| | |
|---|---|
| ***sinensis*** | CArn CBcs CFee CMCN MBlu NLar SLon WSHC |
| ***utilis*** | CTrG |

## *Prionosciadium* (*Apiaceae*)

| | |
|---|---|
| ***thapsoides*** B&SWJ 10345 | WCru |

## *Pritchardia* (*Arecaceae*)

| | | |
|---|---|---|
| | ***affinis*** | XBlo |

## *Pritzelago* (*Brassicaceae*)

| | | |
|---|---|---|
| | ***alpina*** | GEdr NPro |

## *Prostanthera* (*Lamiaceae*)

| | | |
|---|---|---|
| | ***aspalathoides*** | ECou EWes SOWG |
| | 'Badja Peak' | CTrC MAsh WAbe WBod |
| | ***baxteri*** | ECou |
| | ***chlorantha*** | SOWG |
| | ***cuneata*** ♀H4 | Widely available |
| | - 'Alpine Gold' | CMHG CWSG LAst NMun WBrE WFar |
| | - Kew form | WPGP |
| * | ***digitiformis*** | ECou SOWG |
| | ***incisa*** | CTsd SHDw SPla |
| | - 'Rosea' | EOHP SBod |
| | ***lasianthos*** | CBcs CDoC CHll CTsd ECou EWes SAga SHDw SOWG |
| | - 'Kallista Pink' | SOWG |
| | - var. ***subcoriacea*** | CPLG CRHN |
| | ***magnifica*** | SOWG |
| | 'Mauve Mantle' | ECou SOWG |
| | ***melissifolia*** | CArn CTsd ECre EShb LHop |
| § | - var. ***parvifolia*** | CBcs CTsd EBee ECre WAbe |
| | 'Mint Delight' | LRHS |
| | 'Mint Royale' | LBuc |
| | 'Mint-Ice' | LBuc LRHS |
| | ***nivea*** | ECou |
| | ***ovalifolia*** ♀H2 | CTca ECou SAga SOWG |
| I | - 'Variegata' | ECou SOWG |
| | 'Poorinda Ballerina' | CDoC CTsd CWSG EBee ECou EOHP EShb LHop MGos MNHC SOWG SPer SPoG WFar WLeb |
| | ***rotundifolia*** ♀H2 | CDul CHEx CSBt CSev CTrG CTri CWSG EBee ECho EOHP MNHC MSCN NGHP SEND SOWG SPer WBod WLeb |
| | - 'Chelsea Girl' | see *P. rotundifolia* 'Rosea' |
| § | - 'Rosea' ♀H2 | CDoC CSBt CTrC CTrG CTsd EBee ECou GGar MMuc NHol SPoG |
| * | ***scheelii*** | SOWG |
| | ***scutellarioides*** 'Lavender Lady' | ECou |
| | ***sericea*** **new** | LRHS |
| | ***sieberi*** misapplied | see *P. melissifolia* var. *parvifolia* |
| | ***walteri*** | EBee ECou SKHP SOWG |

## *Protea* (*Proteaceae*)

| | | |
|---|---|---|
| | ***aurea*** | SPlb |
| | ***burchellii*** | SPlb |
| | 'Christine' **new** | CTrC |
| | ***coronata*** | SPlb |
| | ***cynaroides*** | CBcs CCCN CHEx CTrC CTsd IDee LRHS SBig SOWG SPlb WBor |
| | ***dracomontana*** | SPlb |
| | ***effusa*** | SPlb |
| | ***eximia*** | CBcs LRHS SPlb WBor |
| | ***grandiceps*** | CBcs CCCN LRHS SPlb |
| | ***lacticolor*** | SPlb |
| | ***laurifolia*** | SPlb |
| | ***nana*** | SPlb |
| | ***neriifolia*** | CCCN SPlb |
| | - 'Alba' **new** | CTrC |
| | - 'Ruby' **new** | CTrC |
| | - 'Snowcrest' | CTrC |
| | ***obtusifolia*** | SPlb |
| | 'Pink Ice' | CTrC |
| | ***repens*** | SPlb WBor |
| | ***subvestita*** | CTrC SPlb |
| | ***susannae*** | SPlb |
| | ***venusta*** | CTrC |

## *Prumnopitys* (*Podocarpaceae*)

| | | |
|---|---|---|
| § | ***andina*** | GKir WFar WThu |
| | ***elegans*** | see *P. andina* |
| § | ***taxifolia*** | CTrC ECou |

## *Prunella* (*Lamiaceae*)

| | | |
|---|---|---|
| § | ***grandiflora*** | CArn CHby CPrp CSec ECha GBar GKir MHav SPad SWat WCHb WFar WMoo WPGP |
| | - 'Alba' | CHFP CSBt EBee ECha EPfP GMaP NGHP NGdn NLar SPer SPla WCAu WCHb WFar |
| | - 'Bella Deep Rose' | WFar |
| | - 'Blue Loveliness' | GKir WCHb |
| | - 'Carminea' | EBee ECtt NGby SPer |
| | - light blue-flowered | GBar NLar WFar WMoo |
| | - 'Loveliness' ♀H4 | CDoC EBee ECha ECtt GKir GMaP MNFA MRav NBro NGdn NSti NVic SPer SPla SPlb SRGP WCAu WFar WTin |
| | - 'Pagoda' | CEnt CSpe NBre NLar WCHb |
| | - 'Pink Loveliness' | CPrp LRHS SRms WCHb |
| | - 'Rosea' | CElw CSBt EBee EPfP WOut |
| | - 'Rubra' | EBee GAbr NGHP NLar WMoo WPer |
| | - 'White Loveliness' | CPrp LRHS WPer |
| | ***incisa*** | see *P. vulgaris* |
| * | 'Inshriach Ruby' | GBin |
| | ***laciniata*** | EBee EShb WCHb WMoo |
| § | ***vulgaris*** | CArn CRWN CSec EBWF GBar GPoy MHer MNHC MSal NLan NMir NPri NSco SECG WCHb WHer WMoo |
| | - f. ***leucantha*** | GBar WAlt WHer |
| | - 'Marbled White' (v) | WAlt |
| | - var. ***rubrifolia*** | WRha |
| | - 'Ruth Wainwright' (v) | WCHb |
| | - variegated (v) **new** | WAlt |
| | - 'Voile' | LAst WAlt |
| | x ***webbiana*** | see *P. grandiflora* |
| | - 'Gruss Aus Isernhagen' | EBee |

## *Prunus* ✿ (*Rosaceae*)

| | | |
|---|---|---|
| | 'Accolade' ♀H4 | Widely available |
| § | 'Amanogawa' ♀H4 | Widely available |
| | ***americana*** | EMui |
| | ***amygdalus*** | see *P. dulcis* |
| | ***armeniaca*** 'Alfred' (F) | EMui GTwe SDea SKee SPer |
| | - 'Bredase' (F) | CWib EMil SDea |
| | - 'Early Moorpark' (F) | CAgr CWib ECrN EPfP GTwe LAst MBri SDea SLon WOrn |
| | - 'Farmingdale' (F) | SDea |
| | - Flavorcot = 'Bayoto'PBR (F) | CAgr CSut SPer |
| | - 'Garden Aprigold' (F) | EMui MGos NPri SPoG |
| | - 'Goldcot' (F) | CAgr EPfP LRHS MBri MCoo SDea SKee WHar WOrn |
| | - 'Golden Glow' (F) | CAgr ECrN EMil EMui GTwe LRHS MCoo SKee |
| | - 'Goldrich' (F) | CAgr |
| | - 'Hargrand' (F) | CAgr SVic |
| | - 'Harogem' (F) | CAgr |
| | - 'Hemskirke' (F) | SKee |
| | - 'Hongaarse' (F) | SDea |
| | - 'Isabella' (F) | CAgr ECrN LRHS MBri MCoo SPoG |
| | - 'Moorpark' (F) ♀H3 | CEnd CSBt CTri CWib EMui GKir GTwe LAst LBuc MAsh MGos SDea SHBN SKee SPer |
| | - 'New Large Early' (F) | EMui GTwe SDea SEND SKee |
| | - 'Petit Muscat' (F) **new** | CSut |
| | - 'Tomcot' (F) | CAgr CTho ECrN EMui LBuc LRHS MCoo SKee SPoG |

| | Name | Suppliers |
|---|---|---|
| | - 'Tross Orange' (F) | CWib SDea |
| | ***avium*** ♀$^{H4}$ | CBcs CCVT CDul CLnd CRWN CSBt CTri CWib ECrN EMac EPfP GKir LBuc LMaj MBar MGos MMuc MRav MSwo NBee NWea SHBN SPer WDin WHar WMoo WMou WOrn |
| | - 'Amber Heart' (F) | SKee |
| | - 'August Heart' (F) | SKee |
| | - 'Bigarreau de Schrecken' | SKee |
| | - 'Bigarreau Gaucher' (F) | SHBN SKee |
| § | - 'Bigarreau Napoléon' (F) | GTwe SCrf SHBN SKee SVic |
| | - 'Birchenhayes' | see *P. avium* 'Early Birchenhayes' |
| | - 'Black Eagle' (F) | CTho SKee |
| | - 'Black Elton' (F) | SKee |
| | - 'Black Glory' (F) | SKee |
| | - 'Black Heart' (F) | CWib |
| | - 'Black Tartarian' (F) | SKee |
| | - 'Bottlers' | see *P. avium* 'Preserving' |
| | - 'Bradbourne Black' (F) | ECrN SCrf SKee |
| | - 'Bullion' (F) | CEnd CTho |
| | - 'Burcombe' (F) | CEnd CTho |
| | - Celeste = 'Sumpaca'$^{PBR}$ (D) | CTri EMil EMui GTwe MBri NLar SDea SKee SPoG WOrn |
| | - 'Cherokee' | see *P. avium* 'Lapins' |
| | - 'Colney' (F) ♀$^{H4}$ | GTwe NLar SKee WJas |
| | - 'Crown Morello' (F) | CSut |
| | - 'Dun' (F) | CTho |
| § | - 'Early Birchenhayes' (F) | CEnd CTho |
| | - 'Early Rivers' (F) | CSBt CWib ECrN GTwe NLar SDea SHBN SKee |
| | - 'Elton Heart' (F) | CTho SKee |
| | - 'Emperor Francis' (F) | ECrN |
| | - 'Erianne' (F) | SKee |
| | - 'Fice' (F) | CEnd CTho |
| | - 'Florence' (F) | SKee |
| | - 'Governor Wood' (F) | GTwe SKee |
| | - 'Grandiflora' | see *P. avium* 'Plena' |
| | - 'Greenstem Black' (F) | CTho |
| | - 'Hannaford' (D/C) | CTho |
| | - 'Hertford' (F) ♀$^{H4}$ | SKee |
| | - 'Inga' (F) | SKee |
| | - 'Kentish Red' (F) | CTho SKee |
| § | - 'Lapins' (F) | CAgr CDul CTho CTri ECrN EMui GTwe LAst LRHS NLar SDea SKee SPoG WHar WJas WOrn |
| | - 'May Duke' | see *P.* x *gondouinii* 'May Duke' |
| | - 'Merchant' (F) ♀$^{H4}$ | ECrN GTwe SKee |
| | - 'Merton Crane' (F) | SKee |
| | - 'Merton Favourite' (F) | SKee |
| | - 'Merton Glory' (F) | CSBt ECrN EMui GTwe MGos SCrf SKee WOrn |
| | - 'Merton Late' (F) | SKee |
| | - 'Merton Marvel' (F) | SKee |
| | - 'Merton Premier' (F) | SKee SVic |
| | - 'Merton Reward' | see *P.* x *gondouinii* 'Merton Reward' |
| | - 'Nabella' (F) | MAsh WJas |
| | - 'Napoléon' | see *P. avium* 'Bigarreau Napoléon' |
| | - 'Newstar' (F) | EMui |
| | - 'Noble' (F) | SKee |
| | - 'Noir de Guben' (F) | ECrN GTwe SKee |
| | - 'Noir de Meched' (D) | SKee |
| | - 'Nutberry Black' (F) | SKee |
| | - 'Old Black Heart' (F) | SKee |
| | - 'Penny' (F) | EMui SKee |
| § | - 'Plena' (d) ♀$^{H4}$ | Widely available |
| § | - 'Preserving' (F) | CTho |
| | - 'Regina' (F) | CSut |
| | - 'Ronald's Heart' (F) | SKee |
| | - 'Roundel Heart' (F) | SKee |
| | - 'Schauenburger' (F) | SKee |
| | - 'Small Black' (F) | CTho |

| | Name | Suppliers |
|---|---|---|
| | - 'Starkrimson' (F) | ECrN |
| | - 'Stella' (F) ♀$^{H4}$ | Widely available |
| | - 'Stella Compact' (F) | CWib ECrN LAst MBri SDea WHar |
| | - 'Summer Sun' (D) ♀$^{H4}$ | CAgr CSut CTho CTri EMil EMui GTwe LBuc LRHS MAsh MBri MCoo NLar SCoo SDea SKee SPoG WHar |
| | - 'Summit' (F) | SHBN SKee |
| | - 'Sunburst' (F) | CAgr CCVT CEnd CMac CTho CTri CWib ECrN EMil EMui GTwe LAst LBuc LRHS MBri SCoo SDea SKee SPer SPoG SVic WHar WJas WOrn |
| | - 'Sweetheart' (F) | CAgr EMui GTwe MBri SKee SPoG |
| | - 'Sylvia' (F) | CAgr |
| | - 'Turkish Black' (F) | SKee |
| | - 'Van' (F) | CSBt ECrN GTwe SKee |
| | - 'Vega' (F) | CAgr GTwe LBuc SKee WJas |
| | - 'Waterloo' (F) | CTho SKee |
| | - 'Werdersche Braune' (F) | SKee |
| | - 'White Heart' (F) | CTho CWib ECrN SKee |
| | - 'Zweitfrühe' (F) | GKir |
| | 'Beni-yutaka' | CEnd CTho GKir LRHS MAsh SCoo SLim |
| | ***besseyi*** | CAgr GAuc |
| | 'Blaze' | see *P. cerasifera* 'Nigra' |
| | x ***blireana*** (d) ♀$^{H4}$ | CDoC CDul CEnd CTri EPfP LAst LCro LRHS MBar MBri MGos MRav MWat NLar NWea SBLw SCoo SPer SPoG WFar WHar |
| | - 'Moseri' (d) | SBLw |
| | 'Blushing Bride' | see *P.* 'Shōgetsu' |
| | 'Candy Floss' | see *P.* 'Matsumae-beni-murasaki' |
| | ***cerasifera*** | CDul CRWN CTri ECrN EMac GKir LBuc MAsh NWea SEND SPer SVic WDin |
| | - 'Cherry Plum' (F) | CTri ECrN SDea SKee |
| | - 'Crimson Dwarf' | SCoo SWvt |
| | - 'First' (F) | CAgr |
| | - 'Golden Sphere' (F) | CAgr CTho EMui WOrn |
| | - 'Gypsy' (F) | CAgr CTho EMui WOrn |
| | - 'Hessei' (v) | CBow CEnd EBee LRHS MBlu MBri MGos MRav SCoo SPoG |
| § | - Myrobalan Group (F) | ECrN EMui MRav SDea |
| | - - 'Magda Jensen' (C) | CAgr |
| § | - 'Nigra' ♀$^{H4}$ | Widely available |
| | - 'Pendula' | CTho ECrN WFar |
| § | - 'Pissardii' | CDul CWib ECrN GKir LAst LMaj MBar MRav NBea NWea SCoo SLim WFar WJas |
| * | - 'Princess' | CEnd CWSG EMui |
| | - 'Spring Glow' | CCVT CEnd EBee EPfP LRHS SCoo SLim SPoG WOrn |
| | - 'Woodii' | SBLw |
| | ***cerasus*** 'Montmorency' (F) | SKee |
| | - 'Morello' (C) ♀$^{H4}$ | Widely available |
| | - 'Nabella' (F) | SKee |
| | - 'Rhexii' (d) | CDul CLnd ECrN MAsh MBri MGos SPer SPoG |
| | 'Champagne Dream' | SCoo |
| | 'Cheal's Weeping' | see *P.* 'Kiku-shidare-zakura' |
| | 'Chocolate Ice' | see *P.* 'Matsumae-fuki' |
| § | x ***cistena*** ♀$^{H4}$ | CCVT CDul CSBt CWSG EBee ELan EPfP LAst MDun MGan MGos SBLw SCoo SHBN SPla SPlb SPoG WDin |
| | - 'Crimson Dwarf' | see *P.* x *cistena* |
| | 'Collingwood Ingram' | GKir MBri MGos SPoG |
| | ***conradinae*** | see *P. hirtipes* |
| | 'Daikoku' | GKir |
| | ***davidiana*** | SPlb |
| | ***domestica*** 'Angelina Burdett' (D) | GTwe SDea SKee |
| | - 'Anna Späth' (C/D) | SKee |

| | | |
|---|---|---|
| | - 'Ariel' (C/D) | SDea SKee |
| | - 'Autumn Compote' (C) | SKee |
| | - 'Avalon' (D) | CAgr CCVT ECrN GTwe SDea SKee |
| | - 'Belgian Purple' (C) | SKee |
| | - 'Belle de Louvain' (C) | CDul CTho CTri ECrN EMil GTwe SDea SKee |
| | - 'Birchenhayes' (F) | CEnd |
| | - 'Black Diamond' | see *P. salicina* 'Black Diamond' |
| | - 'Blaisdon Red' (C) | CTho |
| | - 'Blue Rock' (C/D) ♀H4 | MCoo SKee |
| | - 'Blue Tit' (C/D) ♀H4 | CAgr CTho EMui GTwe SDea SKee |
| | - 'Bonne de Bry' (D) | SKee |
| | - 'Brandy Gage' (C/D) | SKee |
| | - 'Brassai Szilvaja' (F) | SKee |
| | - 'Bryanston Gage' (D) | CTho SKee |
| | - 'Burbank's Giant' | see *P. domestica* 'Giant Prune' |
| | - 'Burcombe' (F) | CEnd |
| | - 'Cambridge Gage' (D) ♀H4 | CAgr CCVT CDoC CDul CTri CWib ECrN EMui EPfP GKir GTwe LAst LCro LRHS MAsh MBri MGan MWat NPri SCoo SCrf SDea SHBN SKee SPer SPoG WJas WOrn |
| | - 'Chrislin' (F) | CAgr CTho |
| | - 'Coe's Golden Drop' (D) | CCAT ECrN EMui GTwe LAst MGos MRav SDea SKee SPer |
| | - 'Count Althann's Gage' (D) | ECrN GTwe SDea SKee |
| | - 'Cox's Emperor' (C) | SKee |
| | - 'Crimson Drop' (D) | SKee |
| | - 'Cropper' | see *P. domestica* 'Laxton's Cropper' |
| | - 'Curlew' (C) | SDea SKee |
| | - 'Czar' (C) ♀H4 | CAgr CCAT CCVT CDoC CDul CSBt CTri CWib ECrN EMui EPfP GKir GTwe LAst LBuc MAsh MGos NPri NWea SDea SKee SPer SPoG SVic WHar WOrn |
| | - 'Denbigh Plum' (D) **new** | WGwG |
| | - 'Denniston's Superb' | see *P. domestica* 'Imperial Gage' |
| | - 'Diamond' (C) | SKee |
| | - 'Dittisham Black' (C) | CAgr CTho |
| | - 'Dittisham Ploughman' (C) | CTho SKee |
| | - 'Drap d'Or d'Esperen' (D) | SKee |
| | - 'Dunster Plum' (F) | CAgr CTho CTri CWib |
| | - 'Early Laxton' (C/D) ♀H4 | ECrN GTwe LAst SDea SKee |
| | - 'Early Prolific' | see *P. domestica* 'Rivers's Early Prolific' |
| | - 'Early Rivers' | see *P. domestica* 'Rivers's Early Prolific' |
| | - 'Early Transparent Gage' (C/D) | CCAT CSBt CTho ECrN EMil EMui GTwe LAst LBuc MCoo SCoo SDea SKee |
| | - 'Early Victoria' (C/D) | SDea |
| | - 'Edwards' (C/D) ♀H4 | CTri CWib ECrN GTwe SDea SKee |
| | - 'Excalibur' (D) | CAgr ECrN GTwe SDea SKee |
| § | - German Prune Group (C) | MCoo SKee |
| § | - 'Giant Prune' (C) | CCAT ECrN GTwe SDea SKee |
| I | - 'Godshill Big Sloe' (F) | SDea |
| | - 'Godshill Blue' (C) | SDea |
| | - 'Godshill Minigage' (F) | SDea |
| | - 'Golden Transparent' (D) | CTho GTwe MCoo SKee |
| | - 'Goldfinch' (D) | GTwe MCoo SKee |
| | - Green Gage Group | see *P. domestica* Reine-Claude Group |
| | - - 'Lindsey Gage' (F) | SKee WBVN |
| | - 'Grey Plum' (F) | CAgr CTho |
| | - 'Grove's Late Victoria' (C/D) | CCAT SKee |
| | - 'Guthrie's Late Green' (D) | SKee |
| | - 'Hackman' (F) | SKee |
| | - 'Herman' (C/D) | CAgr ECrN EMil GKir GTwe LAst LRHS MBri SDea SKee SPoG |
| | - 'Heron' (F) | ECrN GTwe SKee |
| | - 'Impérial Epineuse' (D) | SKee |
| § | - 'Imperial Gage' (C/D) ♀H4 | CAgr CCAT CSBt CTho CTri ECrN EMui GTwe MAsh NLar SDea SKee WOrn |
| | - 'Italian Prune' (F) **new** | MCoo |
| | - subsp. ***italica*** | EMui |
| | - 'Jan James' (F) | CEnd |
| | - 'Jefferson' (D) ♀H4 | CAgr ECrN EMui GTwe LAst NLar SDea SKee SVic |
| * | - 'Jubilaeum' (D) | CAgr EMui GTwe SCoo SKee |
| | - 'Kea' (C) | CAgr CTho SKee |
| | - 'Kirke's' (D) | CCAT CTho CTri ECrN GTwe SDea SKee WOrn |
| | - 'Landkey Yellow' (F) | CAgr CTho |
| | - 'Langley Gage' (F) | CAgr ECrN SDea |
| | - 'Late Muscatelle' (D) | SKee |
| § | - 'Laxton's Cropper' (C) | CTri GTwe MCoo SKee |
| | - 'Laxton's Delight' (D) ♀H4 | GTwe |
| | - 'Laxton's Gage' (D) | SDea SKee |
| | - 'Mallard' (D) ♀H4 | SKee |
| | - 'Manaccan' (C) | CAgr CTho |
| | - 'Marjorie's Seedling' (C) ♀H4 | Widely available |
| | - 'McLaughlin' (D) | SKee |
| | - 'Merton Gage' (D) | SKee |
| | - 'Merton Gem' (C/D) | GTwe SKee |
| | - 'Monarch' (C) | GTwe SKee |
| | - 'Newark' (F) | SKee |
| | - 'Olympia' (C/D) | SKee |
| | - 'Ontario' (C/D) | ECrN SKee |
| | - 'Opal' (D) ♀H4 | CAgr CCAT CCVT CDoC CDul CMac CWSG CWib ECrN EMui GTwe LBuc MAsh MBri MGos MLan MWat NBlu NWea SCoo SCrf SDea SEND SKee SPoG WOrn |
| | - 'Orleans' (C) | SKee |
| | - 'Oullins Gage' (C/D) ♀H4 | CAgr CCAT CCVT CDoC CDul CSBt CTri CWib ECrN EMui EPfP GTwe LAst LBuc MBri MGan MRav NBlu SDea SEND SKee SPer SPoG SVic WJas WOrn |
| | - 'Pershore' (C) ♀H4 | CAgr CCAT CDul CTho CWib ECrN GTwe LAst MAsh MBri SDea SKee WHar WOrn |
| | - 'Pond's Seedling' (C) | CSBt SDea SKee |
| | - 'President' (C/D) | SDea |
| | - 'Priory Plum' (D) | SDea |
| | - 'Purple Pershore' (C) | CAgr CCAT CTri CWib ECrN GTwe SDea SKee WOrn |
| | - 'Quetsche d'Alsace' | see *P. domestica* German Prune Group |
| | - 'Reeves' (C) ♀H4 | GTwe MCoo SKee |
| | - 'Reine-Claude Dorée' | see *P. domestica* Reine-Claude Group |
| § | - Reine-Claude Group (C/D) | ECrN EMui GKir GTwe MGos SDea SKee SPer |
| | - - 'Old Green Gage' | see *P. domestica* (Reine-Claude Group) 'Reine-Claude Vraie' |
| | - - 'Reine Claude de Brahy' (D) | SKee |
| | - - 'Reine-Claude de Bavais' (D) | CCAT CTho CTri GTwe SDea SKee |
| | - - 'Reine-Claude de Vars' (D) | SVic |
| | - - 'Reine-Claude Violette' (D) | ECrN SKee |
| § | - - 'Reine-Claude Vraie' (C/D) | CAgr CCAT CCVT CSBt CWib ECrN EMui EPfP GKir LAst SPoG WJas WOrn |
| § | - - 'Willingham Gage' (C/D) | GTwe LRHS MAsh MLan SKee |

| | | |
|---|---|---|
| § | - 'Rivers's Early Prolific' (C) | CAgr CSBt CTho CTri ECrN EPfP GTwe MCoo NWea SCoo SDea SHBN SKee WHar |
| | - 'Royale de Vilvoorde' (D) | SKee |
| | - 'Sanctus Hubertus' (D) ♀H4 | CTri ECrN EPfP GTwe SDea SKee |
| | - 'Severn Cross' (D) | GTwe SKee |
| | - 'Stanley' (C/D) | SVic |
| | - 'Stella' | CCVT CDul LAst NPri |
| | - 'Stint' (C/D) | SKee |
| | - 'Swan' (C) | ECrN GTwe SKee |
| | - 'Syston White' | CTho MGos |
| | - 'Thames Cross' (D) | SKee |
| | - 'Transparent Gage' (D) | ECrN |
| | - 'Upright' (F) | CEnd |
| | - 'Utility' (D) | SKee |
| | - 'Valor' (C/D) ♀H4 | ECrN |
| | - 'Victoria' (C/D) ♀H4 | Widely available |
| | - 'Violetta'PBR (C/D) | EMui GTwe SKee |
| | - 'Warwickshire Drooper' (C) | CAgr CTho CWib GTwe LAst SCoo SDea SKee WBVN WOrn |
| | - 'Washington' (D) | SDea SKee |
| | - 'White Magnum Bonum' (C) | SDea |
| | - 'Willingham' | see *P. domestica* (Reine-Claude Group) 'Willingham Gage' |
| | - 'Wyedale' (C) | GTwe |
| § | ***dulcis*** | CDul CLnd CTri CWSG CWib ECrN EMui EPfP EWTr LAst LRHS MREP MWat NBea NWea SBLw SCoo SCrf SDea SEND SVic WBVN WDin WOrn |
| | - 'Ai' (F) | CAgr |
| | - 'Ardechoise' (F) | CAgr |
| | - 'Ferraduel' (F) | CAgr |
| | - 'Ferragnes' (F) | CAgr |
| | - 'Lauranne' (F) | CAgr |
| | - 'Macrocarpa' (F) | ECrN |
| | - 'Mandaline' (F) | CAgr |
| * | - 'Phoebe' (F) | CAgr |
| | - 'Princesse' (F) **new** | EMil |
| | - 'Supernova' (F) | CCCN |
| | - 'Titan' (F) | ECrN |
| | - 'Tuono' (F) | CCCN |
| | Easter Bonnet = 'Comet'PBR | CTri EPfP LBuc LRHS NPri |
| | x ***eminens*** 'Umbraculifera' | SBLw |
| | Fragrant Cloud = 'Shizuka' | CWSG CWib EMil GKir LRHS MAsh MBri SCoo SLim SPer SPoG WOrn |
| | ***fruticosa*** 'Globosa' | LPan NHol |
| | 'Fugenzō' | CSBt GKir |
| | ***glandulosa*** 'Alba Plena' (d) | CEnd CSBt EBee ECrN LRHS NBea SBLw SHBN SPlb SPoG SRms SWvt WBod WCFE WDin |
| | - 'Rosea Plena' | see *P. glandulosa* 'Sinensis' |
| § | - 'Sinensis' (d) | CEnd CPLG CSBt EBee LRHS SBLw SHBN SPoG SRms WDin |
| § | x ***gondouinii*** 'May Duke' (F) | CTho SKee SVic |
| § | - 'Merton Reward' (F) | SKee |
| | - 'Schnee' | SBLw |
| | 'Gyoikō' | CEnd CTho GKir |
| | 'Hally Jolivette' | CEnd ELan GKir LRHS MAsh NWea SBLw WDin |
| | 'Hillieri' | ECrN MBar MGos |
| | 'Hillieri Spire' | see *P.* 'Spire' |
| | 'Hilling's Weeping' | EBee |
| | ***himalaica*** **new** | EHig |
| § | ***hirtipes*** | CLnd CTho |
| | 'Hokusai' | GKir |
| | Hollywood | see *P.* 'Trailblazer' |

| | | |
|---|---|---|
| | 'Horinji' | GKir MBri SCoo |
| | 'Ichiyo' (d) ♀H4 | ECrN EPfP GKir LAst MBri SCoo SCrf SPer |
| | ***incisa*** | CTri NBea NWea SPer |
| | - 'Ariane' **new** | LMaj |
| | - 'Beniomi' | MRav |
| | - 'February Pink' | CAbP CPMA MRav SBLw WDin |
| | - 'Fujima' | CSBt EBee LAst |
| | - 'Kojo-no-mai' | Widely available |
| | - 'Mikinori' | CSBt GKir MBlu NLar SCoo WFar |
| | - 'Oshidori' | CSBt GKir LRHS MBri MGos MRav NLar SLim SRms WFar |
| * | - 'Otome' | WFar |
| | - 'Paean' | NLar |
| | - 'Pendula' | CPMA GKir SCoo |
| | - 'Praecox' ♀H4 | CSBt CTho CWSG EPfP LRHS MWat SCoo |
| | - 'The Bride' | CDul CEnd CWSG GKir LRHS MAsh MBri SCoo |
| § | - f. ***yamadae*** | CPMA LBMP MBri NLar |
| | ***insititia*** (F) | CRWN |
| | - 'Abergwyngregin' (C) **new** | WGwG |
| | - 'Black Bullace' (F) | EMui |
| § | - 'Bradley's King Damson' (C) | ECrN GTwe SKee |
| | - bullace (C) | NWea SDea |
| | - 'Countess' (F) **new** | CTri |
| | - 'Dittisham Damson' (C) | CTho |
| | - 'Farleigh Damson' (C) ♀H4 | CAgr CWib ECrN EMil GKir GTwe LBuc NWea SDea SEND SKee SPer SPoG SVic WJas |
| | - 'Godshill Damson' (C) | SDea |
| | - 'Golden Bullace' | see *P. insititia* 'White Bullace' |
| | - 'King of Damsons' | see *P. insititia* 'Bradley's King Damson' |
| | - 'Langley Bullace' (C) | CAgr CTho ECrN EMui GTwe NLar SKee |
| | - 'Lisna' (F) **new** | CTri |
| | - 'Merryweather Damson' (C) | Widely available |
| | - 'Mirabelle de Nancy' (C) | CAgr CTho CTri GTwe LAst LMaj SDea SKee |
| | - 'Mirabelle de Nancy (Red)' (C) | SDea |
| § | - 'Prune Damson' (C) ♀H4 | CAgr CDoC CTho CTri CWSG ECrN EMui GTwe LAst LBuc MAsh MBri NLar SDea SKee SPer WHar WJas WOrn |
| | - 'Shepherd's Bullace' (C) | CAgr CTho SKee |
| | - 'Shropshire Damson' | see *P. insititia* 'Prune Damson' |
| | - 'Small Bullace' (C) | CAgr SKee |
| § | - 'White Bullace' (C) | CAgr SKee |
| | - 'Yellow Apricot' (C) | SKee |
| § | ***jamasakura*** | CDul |
| | 'Jō-nioi' | CDul CEnd CTho MBri SBLw |
| § | 'Kanzan' ♀H4 | Widely available |
| § | 'Kiku-shidare-zakura' ♀H4 | Widely available |
| | Korean hill cherry | see *P. verecunda* |
| | 'Kulilensis Ruby' | GKir SLPl |
| | 'Kursar' ♀H4 | CDul CLnd CSBt CTho CTri EBee EMui EPfP GKir LRHS MAsh MBri NLar NWea SCoo SCrf SLim WOrn |
| | ***laurocerasus*** ♀H4 | CBcs CCVT CChe CDul CPMA CTrG CWSG EBee ECrN ELan EMac EPfP GKir LAst MGos MRav MWat NBea NWea SEND SPer SPoG SReu WBVN WFar WMoo WMou |
| | - 'Angustifolia' | WDin |
| | - 'Aureovariegata' | see *P. laurocerasus* 'Taff's Golden Gleam' |
| | - 'Camelliifolia' | CTri EPla EQua MBlu WCFE WDin WHCG |

| | | |
|---|---|---|
| N | - 'Castlewellan' (v) | CDoC CDul CTri EPfP EPla LAst LHop MBar MGos MSwo NBea NHol NPro SDix SLim SPer SPoG SSta WDin WFar WHar WLeb WMoo |
| | - 'Caucasica' | CEnd LPan MGos |
| | - 'Cherry Brandy' | GKir MRav SLPl SPer WDin |
| | - Dart's Lowgreen | see *P. laurocerasus* Low 'n' Green = 'Interlo' |
| | - Etna = 'Anbri' PBR | EBee EPfP IFFs LBuc LRHS LSou MBri MGos NPri SWvt |
| | - 'Gajo' | SPer WBor |
| | - 'Green Marble' (v) | CPMA CTri EBee EHoe |
| | - 'Herbergii' | IFFs NLar |
| § | - 'Latifolia' | CHEx EPla EQua SLPl |
| § | - Low 'n' Green = 'Interlo' | MRav |
| | - 'Magnoliifolia' | see *P. laurocerasus* 'Latifolia' |
| | - 'Mano' | MGos NLar |
| | - 'Marbled White' | see *P. laurocerasus* 'Castlewellan' |
| | - 'Miky' | CPMA |
| | - 'Mischeana' | SLPl |
| | - 'Mount Vernon' | MBar MBlu MGos WDin |
| | - 'Novita' | EMil |
| | - 'Otinii' | CHEx |
| | - 'Otto Luyken' ♀H4 | Widely available |
| | - Renault Ace = 'Renlau' | MGos |
| | - 'Reynvaanii' | CPMA MBri |
| | - 'Rotundifolia' | Widely available |
| | - 'Schipkaensis' | SLPl SPer |
| § | - 'Taff's Golden Gleam' (v) | CBow CPMA |
| | - 'Van Nes' | CPMA EBee IFFs NLar WDin |
| | - 'Variegata' misapplied | see *P. laurocerasus* 'Castlewellan' |
| | - 'Variegata' ambig. (v) | CWib EPla SRms |
| | - 'Whitespot' **new** | MMuc |
| | - 'Zabeliana' | CDul CTri EBee ECrN EPfP GKir MBar MGos MSwo NHol NWea SHBN SPer SRms WDin WFar |
| | ***litigiosa*** | GKir LRHS MBri NLar SCoo SPoG |
| | 'Little Pink Perfection' | MBri SCoo |
| | ***lusitanica*** ♀H4 | Widely available |
| | - subsp. ***azorica*** | CDoC CPLG EQua MRav WFar WPGP |
| | - 'Myrtifolia' | CTri EBee ECrN EPfP EPla EQua GKir LRHS MBri MLLN MRav SLon SWvt WCFE WDin WMoo |
| | - 'Variegata' (v) | CBcs CDul CTri CWib EBee EHoe ELan EPla LAst LHop LRHS MGos MLHP MRav MSwo NHol NSti SDix SHBN SLim SPer SPla SPoG SSta WDin WFar WMoo |
| | ***maackii*** | EPfP MMuc SBLw SEND SSpi WDin |
| | - 'Amber Beauty' | CDoC CDul CEnd EBee EPfP GBin GKir LMaj MRav SBLw SCoo WDin WFar |
| | 'Mahogany Lustre' | see *P. serrula* 'Mahogany Lustre' |
| | ***mandshurica*** | GKir |
| | ***maritima*** **new** | GAuc |
| § | 'Matsumae-beni-murasaki' | GKir SCoo |
| | 'Matsumae-beni-tamanishiki' | GKir |
| § | 'Matsumae-fuki' | GKir MBri MLan NWea SPoG |
| | 'Matsumae-hana-gasa' | GKir MBri |
| § | 'Matsumae-hanagasa' | EBee GKir LRHS MBri NLar SPoG |
| | 'Mount Fuji' | see *P.* 'Shirotae' |
| | ***mume*** | CMCN CMen WDin |
| § | - 'Beni-chidori' | CEnd CWib EBee ECrN EPfP LBuc LRHS MBlu MBri MGos NBea NLar SCoo SHBN SLim SPoG WJas WOrn WPGP |
| | - 'Beni-shidori' | see *P. mume* 'Beni-chidori' |
| § | - 'Omoi-no-mama' (d) | CEnd CMen |
| | - 'Omoi-no-wac' | see *P. mume* 'Omoi-no-mama' |
| | - 'Pendula' | ECrN |
| | ***myrobalana*** | see *P. cerasifera* Myrobalan Group |
| | ***nipponica*** var. ***kurilensis*** 'Brilliant' | CBcs GKir MBri MGos NLar SCrf WOrn |
| | - - 'Ruby' | CBcs CDul CEnd GKir MBri MGos NBlu WFar |
| | 'Okame' ♀H4 | CChe CDul CLnd CSam CTho EBee ECrN ELon EPfP GKir LAst LCro LRHS MAsh MGos MRav NWea SCoo SCrf SLPl SLim SPer SPoG WFar WOrn |
| * | 'Okame Harlequin' (v) | SLim SPoG |
| | 'Okumiyako' misapplied | see *P.* 'Shōgetsu' |
| | ***padus*** | CCVT CDul CLnd CRWN CSBt CTri ECrN EMac GKir LBuc MGos MSwo NBea NBee NBlu NWea SBLw WDin WMou WOrn |
| | - 'Albertii' | CCVT CTho GKir MMuc SCoo WJas |
| | - 'Colorata' ♀H4 | CBcs CDoC CDul CEnd CSam CTho ECrN ELan EMil EWTr GKir LBuc LMaj MAsh MGos NBee SBLw SCoo SHBN SPer WCot WDin WFar WJas |
| | - 'Grandiflora' | see *P. padus* 'Watereri' |
| | - 'Plena' (d) | CTho |
| | - 'Purple Queen' | CEnd CTho ECrN SCoo |
| | - 'Red Ball' **new** | LPan |
| § | - 'Watereri' ♀H4 | CCVT CDoC CDul CEnd CLnd CMCN CTho CWib EBee ECrN ELan EPfP EWTr LMaj NWea SBLw SCoo SHBN SLim SPer WDin WJas WOrn |
| | 'Pandora' ♀H4 | CDul CLnd EBee ECrN EPfP GKir LAst LCro LRHS MAsh MBri MGos MRav MSwo NBea NBee NWea SBLw SCoo SCrf SEND SHBN SPer SPoG WFar WOrn |
| | ***pendula*** | SCrf |
| | - var. ***ascendens*** 'Rosea' | EBee |
| § | - 'Pendula Rosea' ♀H4 | CDoC CDul CEnd CSBt CTri CWib EPfP GKir LAst LPan SBLw SCrf SPer SPoG WFar WJas WOrn |
| § | - 'Pendula Rubra' ♀H4 | CDoC CLnd CSBt CWib EBee ECrN EPfP GKir LAst LRHS MAsh MBri MGos MSwo SCoo SHBN SLim SPer SPoG WOrn WPat |
| § | - 'Stellata' | MBri SPer |
| | ***pensylvanica*** | LMaj |
| | ***persica*** 'Amsden June' (F) | CWib GTwe LRHS SDea SKee |
| | - 'Bellegarde' (F) | GTwe SDea |
| | - 'Bonanza' (F) | EMui LCro |
| | - 'Clara Meyer' | CTri |
| | - 'Darling' (F) **new** | SVic |
| | - 'Dixi Red' (F) | CAgr LPan |
| | - 'Doctor Hogg' (F) | SDea |
| | - 'Duke of York' (F) ♀H3 | CTri GTwe SDea SKee WOrn |
| | - 'Foliis Rubris' (F) | CDul WPGP |
| | - 'Francis' (F) | SKee |
| | - 'Garden Lady' (F) | GTwe SKee SPoG |
| | - 'Hale's Early' (F) | GTwe LRHS SEND SKee SPer WOrn |
| | - 'Hylands' (F) | SDea |
| | - 'Kestrel' (F) | SKee |
| | - 'Melred' (F) | MGos |
| | - 'Melred Weeping' (F) | SBLw |
| | - 'Mesembrine' PBR (F) | EMui |
| | - 'Natalia' (F) | SDea |
| | - var. ***nectarina*** Crimson Gold (F) | SDea |
| | - - 'Early Gem' (F) | SDea |
| | - - 'Early Rivers' (F) ♀H3 | GTwe SDea SPer |
| | - - 'Elruge' (F) | GTwe SDea |
| | - - 'Fantasia' (F) | SDea |
| | - - 'Fire Gold' (F) | SDea |
| | - - 'Garden Beauty' (F/d) | EMui SPoG |
| | - - 'Humboldt' (F) | GTwe SDea SKee |
| | - - 'John Rivers' (F) | GTwe SDea |

| | | |
|---|---|---|
| | - - 'Lord Napier' (F) ♀H3 | CAgr CDoC CSBt CTri CWSG CWib EMui EPfP GKir LAst LBuc LRHS MAsh MGos SDea SKee SPer SPoG SVic WHar WOrn |
| | - - 'Nectared' (F) | CWib |
| | - - 'Nectarella' (F) | EMui LCro SKee |
| | - - 'Pineapple' (F) | CAgr CTri GTwe LRHS SDea SKee SPoG |
| | - - 'Ruby Gold' (F) | SDea |
| | - - 'Terrace Ruby' (F) | CDul MGos SPoG |
| | - 'Peregrine' (F) ♀H3 | CAgr CDul CSBt CTri CWSG CWib EMui EPfP GKir GTwe LAst LBuc LRHS MAsh MBri MGan MGos MLan SDea SHBN SKee SPer SPoG WJas |
| | - 'Pink Peachy' (F) | NLar |
| | - 'Purpurea' | EBee |
| | - 'Red Haven' (F) | CAgr CWib GTwe SDea SKee SVic |
| | - 'Redwing' (F) **new** | CAgr |
| | - 'Reliance' (F) | SDea |
| | - 'Robin Redbreast' (F) | SDea |
| | - 'Rochester' (F) ♀H3 | CAgr CSBt CWSG CWib EMui GTwe LAst LRHS MBri SDea SKee SPer SPoG WOrn |
| | - 'Royal George' (F) | GTwe |
| | - 'Sanguine de Savoie' (F) **new** | EMui |
| | - 'Saturne' (F) | EMui SPoG |
| | - 'Springtime' (F) | SDea |
| | - 'Terrace Amber' (F) | EMui MGos SPoG |
| | - 'Terrace Diamond' (F) | MGos SPoG |
| | - 'Terrace Garnet' (F) | MGos NBPN SPoG |
| | - 'White Peachy' (F) | NLar |
| | x ***persicoides*** 'Angélique' | EMil GKir |
| | - 'Ingrid' (F) | CAgr LBuc MCoo SCoo |
| | - 'Pollardii' | MAsh NWea WJas |
| | - 'Robijn' (F) | CAgr ECrN LBuc |
| | - 'Spring Glow' | CDoC MBri MWea NWea WJas |
| | 'Petite Noir' | MAsh |
| | 'Pink Parasol' | see *P.* 'Matsumae-hanagasa' |
| | 'Pink Perfection' ♀H4 | CBcs CDul CLnd CSBt CWSG CWib EBee ECrN EPfP GKir LAst LRHS MAsh MBri MGos MWat NBee NLar SCrf SHBN SPer WDin WFar WHar WJas WOrn |
| | 'Pink Shell' ♀H4 | CLnd EBee ECrN EPfP GKir MBri SPur WOrn |
| | ***pissardii*** | see *P. cerasifera* 'Pissardii' |
| | 'Pissardii Nigra' | see *P. cerasifera* 'Nigra' |
| | ***prostrata*** | GAuc |
| * | - 'Anita Kistler' | ECho |
| * | - var. ***discolor*** | NLar |
| | ***pseudocerasus*** 'Cantabrigiensis' | ECrN |
| | ***pumila*** var. ***depressa*** | EMil MBlu MMHG MRav NLar NPro |
| | 'Royal Burgundy' (d) | CCVT CDul CEnd CLnd CWSG EBee ECrN EMil GKir LRHS LSRN MAsh MBri MDun MGos MWat NBee SCoo SLim SPer SPoG SPur WFar WHar WOrn |
| | ***rufa*** | CPMA CTho EBee SSpi |
| § | ***salicina*** 'Black Diamond' (F) | SDea |
| | ***sargentii*** ♀H4 | Widely available |
| | - 'Charles Sargent' | GKir |
| | - 'Columnaris' | GKir |
| | - 'Rancho' | CLnd SCoo WFar WOrn |
| | x ***schmittii*** | CLnd ECrN SCoo SPer WJas |
| | 'Sekiyama' | see *P.* 'Kanzan' |
| | ***serotina*** | CDul NLar SBLw |
| § | ***serrula*** ♀H4 | Widely available |
| | - Dorothy Clive form | EBee LRHS |
| § | - 'Mahogany Lustre' | WFar WPat |
| | - var. ***tibetica*** | see *P. serrula* |
| | ***serrula*** x ***serrulata*** | CBcs CTho |
| | ***serrulata*** (d) | MGos |
| | - 'Erecta' | see *P.* 'Amanogawa' |
| | - 'Grandiflora' | see *P.* 'Ukon' |
| | - 'Longipes' | see *P.* 'Shōgetsu' |
| | - 'Miyako' misapplied | see *P.* 'Shōgetsu' |
| N | - var. ***pubescens*** | see *P. verecunda* |
| | - 'Rosea' | see *P.* 'Kiku-shidare-zakura' |
| | - var. ***spontanea*** | see *P. jamasakura* |
| | 'Shidare-zakura' | see *P.* 'Kiku-shidare-zakura' |
| | 'Shimizu-zakura' | see *P.* 'Shōgetsu' |
| | 'Shirofugen' ♀H4 | Widely available |
| § | 'Shirotae' ♀H4 | Widely available |
| § | 'Shōgetsu' ♀H4 | CBcs CDul CEnd CLnd CSBt CTho CWSG EBee ECrN ELan EPfP GKir LAst LMaj LRHS MAsh MBri NBlu SCrf SHBN SLim SPer SPoG WDin |
| | 'Shosar' | CEnd CWib ECrN EHig GKir LAst LRHS SCoo SPer SPoG |
| | x ***sieboldii*** 'Caespitosa' | GKir |
| | 'Snow Goose' | CDoC EBee GKir LAst LMaj LRHS SCoo WFar |
| | 'Snow Showers' | CEnd CWSG EBee EMil EMui GKir LRHS MAsh MBri MNHC MWat NWea SPer SPoG |
| | ***spinosa*** | CCVT CDoC CDul CRWN CTri ECrN EMac EPfP GKir LBuc LRHS MAsh MBar MBlu NWea SPer SVic WDin WFar WMou |
| | - 'Plena' (d) | CEnd CTho MBlu |
| | - 'Purpurea' | MBlu MBri NHol WDin WHCG WMou WPat |
| § | 'Spire' ♀H4 | CCVT CDoC CDul CLnd CMCN CSBt CTho CWib EBee ECrN EHig EPfP GKir LAst LBuc LRHS MGos MSwo NBlu NWea SCoo SHBN SPer SPoG WDin WFar WJas WOrn |
| | x ***subhirtella*** | LAst |
| | - var. ***ascendens*** | see *P. pendula* var. ***ascendens*** |
| | - 'Autumnalis' ♀H4 | Widely available |
| | - 'Autumnalis Rosea' ♀H4 | Widely available |
| | - 'Fukubana' | CLnd EBee ECrN EPfP GKir SBLw |
| | - 'Pendula' misapplied | see *P. pendula* 'Pendula Rosea' |
| | - 'Pendula Plena Rosea' (d) | LAst LPan SBLw |
| | - 'Pendula Rosea' | see *P. pendula* 'Pendula Rosea' |
| | - 'Pendula Rubra' | see *P. pendula* 'Pendula Rubra' |
| N | - 'Rosea' | CLnd MRav WBVN |
| | - 'Stellata' | see *P. pendula* 'Stellata' |
| | 'Sunset Boulevard' | GKir |
| | 'Taihaku' ♀H4 | Widely available |
| | 'Taki-nioi' | ECrN |
| | 'Taoyame' | GKir |
| | ***tenella*** | CAgr ECrN ELan WCot |
| | - 'Fire Hill' | CPMA CSBt CWib ECho ELan EPfP LRHS MGos MRav MWea NHol SBLw SHBN SPer SSpi WBod WCFE WCot WDin WJas WOrn |
| | ***tibetica*** | see *P. serrula* |
| | ***tomentosa*** | CAgr ECrN LLHF MAsh WBVN |
| § | 'Trailblazer' (C/D) | CEnd CLnd CSBt CTho ECrN EWTr LAst SBLw SPer WOrn |
| | ***triloba*** | CBcs CSBt CWib ECrN LBuc LRHS NBee NHol NPri NWea SBLw SHBN WDin |
| | - 'Multiplex' (d) | ECho MGos MRav SPer SRms WJas |
| | - Rosemund = 'Korros' | SCrf |
| § | 'Ukon' ♀H4 | Widely available |
| | 'Umineko' | CDoC CLnd CWib ECrN GKir GQue LPan MGos SCoo SLPl SPer WDin WHar |
| § | ***verecunda*** | CLnd NWea WJas |
| | - 'Autumn Glory' | CTho NBea |

| | |
|---|---|
| ***virginiana*** 'Schubert' | CDul CLnd EBee ECrN SBLw SCoo WFar WJas WOrn WPat |
| 'White Cloud' | CDul |
| ***yamadae*** | see *P. incisa* f. *yamadae* |
| x ***yedoensis*** | LMaj |
| - 'Ivensii' | CBcs CDul CSBt CWib EBee GKir LMaj LPan NBee NWea SCoo SHBN SPer WDin |
| - 'Moerheimii' | GKir |
| - 'Pendula' | see *P.* x *yedoensis* 'Shidare-yoshino' |
| - 'Perpendens' | see *P.* x *yedoensis* 'Shidare-yoshino' |
| § - 'Shidare-yoshino' | CCVT CEnd CLnd CSBt EBee ECrN EPfP GKir LPan LRHS MBar MBri MGos MRav MSwo MWat NWea SBLw SLim SPoG WOrn |
| § - 'Somei-Yoshino' ♀H4 | CCVT CDul CLnd CMCN CSBt CTho CTri CWSG EBee ECrN EPfP GKir LAst MAsh MBri NWea SBLw SLim SPer WDin WHar WJas WOrn |
| 'Yoshino' | see *P.* x *yedoensis* 'Somei-Yoshino' |
| 'Yoshino Pendula' | see *P.* x *yedoensis* 'Shidare-yoshino' |

## *Pseuderanthemum* (*Acanthaceae*)

| | |
|---|---|
| ***atropurpureum*** | see *P. carruthersii* var. *atropurpureum* |
| ***carruthersii*** var. ***atropurpureum*** 'Rubrum' new | CSpe LSou WHil |
| - - 'Variegatum' (v) new | WHil |
| ***laxiflorum*** | CCCN |
| ***reticulatum*** orange-flowered | CCCN |

## *Pseudocydonia* (*Rosaceae*)

| | |
|---|---|
| § ***sinensis*** | CAgr CBcs CMen NLar |

## *Pseudofumaria* see *Corydalis*

| | |
|---|---|
| ***alba*** | see *Corydalis ochroleuca* |
| ***lutea*** | see *Corydalis lutea* |

## *Pseudogynoxys* (*Asteraceae*)

| | |
|---|---|
| ***chenopodioides*** | ELan SOWG |

## *Pseudolarix* (*Pinaceae*)

| | |
|---|---|
| § ***amabilis*** ♀H4 | CDoC CMCN CTho ECrN EHul EPfP GKir MBar MBlu MBri MPkF NHol NWea SLim SPoG SSpi WPGP |
| ***kaempferi*** | see *P. amabilis* |

## *Pseudolithos* (*Asclepiadaceae*)

| | |
|---|---|
| ***caput-viperae*** | LToo |

## *Pseudomuscari* see *Muscari*

| | |
|---|---|
| ***azureum*** | see *Muscari azureum* |

## *Pseudopanax* (*Araliaceae*)

| | |
|---|---|
| (Adiantifolius Group) | CBcs CDoC CHEx CTrC ESwi |
| 'Adiantifolius' | GQui |
| - 'Cyril Watson' ♀H1 | CBcs CDoC CHEx EBee ELan SBig SEND |
| ***arboreus*** | see *Neopanax arboreus* |
| ***chathamicus*** | CDoC CHEx SAPC SArc |
| ***crassifolius*** | CAbb CBcs CBrP CHEx CTrC EAmu EBee ESwi EUJe GBin SAPC SArc SBig SKHP |
| - var. ***trifoliolatus*** | CHEx |
| ***davidii*** | SLon |
| ***discolor*** | ECou LEdu |
| ***ferox*** | CAbb CBcs CBrP EAmu EUJe GBin IDee SAPC SArc SBig SKHP SMad |
| ***laetus*** | see *Neopanax laetus* |
| ***lessonii*** | CBcs CHEx ECou |
| - 'Gold Splash' (v) ♀H1 | CBcs CDoC CDul CHEx CTrC EBee SBig SEND |
| - 'Nigra' | CTrC |
| - 'Rangitira' | CBcs CTrC SBig |
| 'Linearifolius' | CHEx CTrC LEdu |
| 'Purpureus' ♀H1 | CDoC CHEx CTrC ESwi |
| 'Sabre' | CHEx CTrC |
| 'Trident' | CDoC CHEx CTrC ECou LEdu SKHP |

## *Pseudophegopteris* (*Thelypteridaceae*)

| | |
|---|---|
| ***levingei*** | EMon |

## *Pseudophoenix* (*Arecaceae*)

| | |
|---|---|
| * ***nativo*** | MBri |

## *Pseudosasa* (*Poaceae*)

| | |
|---|---|
| ***amabilis*** misapplied | see *Arundinaria gigantea* |
| § ***amabilis*** (McClure) Keng f. | EPla WFar |
| § ***japonica*** ♀H4 | Widely available |
| § - 'Akebonosuji' (v) | CEnt CGHE EFul EPla MMoz MWht NMoo WPGP |
| I - var. ***pleioblastoides*** | EPla MWht |
| - 'Tsutsumiana' | CHEx CMCo EBee ELon EPla ERod MMoz MWht NLar NMoo SBig |
| - 'Variegata' | see *P. japonica* 'Akebonosuji' |
| ***orthotropa*** | see *Sinobambusa orthotropa* |
| ***usawai*** | EPla |
| ***viridula*** | MWht NMoo |

## *Pseudostellaria* (*Caryophyllaceae*)

| | |
|---|---|
| ***heterophylla*** new | EBee |

## *Pseudotsuga* (*Pinaceae*)

| | |
|---|---|
| § ***menziesii*** ♀H4 | CBcs CDul CLnd ECrN EMac EPfP GKir IFFs LRHS MBar MBlu MMuc NWea WDin WFar WMou |
| - 'Bhiela Lhota' | CKen |
| - 'Blue Wonder' | CKen |
| - 'Densa' | CKen |
| - 'Fastigiata' | CKen |
| - 'Fletcheri' | CKen MBar |
| - var. ***glauca*** | GKir MBar |
| - 'Glauca Pendula' | MBar MBlu MGos |
| I - 'Gotelli's Pendula' | CKen |
| - 'Graceful Grace' | CKen |
| - 'Idaho Gem' | CKen |
| - 'Julie' | CKen |
| - 'Knaphill' | GKir NLar |
| - 'Little Jamie' | CKen MBar |
| - 'Lohbrunner' | CKen |
| - 'McKenzie' | CKen |
| - 'Nana' | CKen |
| - 'Oudemansii' new | GKir |
| - 'Stairii' | CKen |
| ***taxifolia*** | see *P. menziesii* |

## *Pseudowintera* (*Winteraceae*)

| | |
|---|---|
| § ***colorata*** | CBcs CDoC CMac CPLG CWib EBee GCal GGar GKir IDee IMGH ISea LBuc NHol WCru WFar WFoF |
| I - 'Elliot's form' | CWsd |
| - 'Mount Congreve' | CBcs IArd LBuc MBri NLar SSpi |
| - 'Red Leopard' new | LRHS |

## *Psidium* (*Myrtaceae*)

| | |
|---|---|
| ***cattleyanum*** | see *P. littorale* var. *longipes* |
| ***guajava*** (F) | CCCN XBlo |
| § ***littorale*** var. ***longipes*** (F) | CCCN XBlo |

## *Psilotum* (*Psilotaceae*)

| | |
|---|---|
| ***nudum*** | ECou |

## *Psoralea* (*Papilionaceae*)

| | |
|---|---|
| ***glabra*** | SPlb |
| ***glandulosa*** | CArn CMdw WSHC |
| ***oligophylla*** | SPlb |
| ***pinnata*** | CPLG CTrC CTrG IDee SEND |

## *Psychotria* (*Rubiaceae*)

| | |
|---|---|
| ***capensis*** | CPLG EShb |

## *Ptelea* (*Rutaceae*)

| | |
|---|---|
| ***trifoliata*** | CArn CBcs CDul CLnd CTho CWib EBee ECrN EMil EPfP EWTr IMGH MBlu MBri SBLw SPer SRms WDin WOrn WPGP |
| - 'Aurea' ♀H4 | CAbP CBcs CCVT CEnd CLnd CPLG CPMA EBee ELan EMil EPfP GBin GKir LRHS MAsh MBlu MBri MGos SBLw SHBN SMad SPer SPoG SSpi WDin WPat |
| - 'Fastigiata' | CDul EPfP |

## *Pteracanthus* see *Strobilanthes*

## *Pteridophyllum* (*Papaveraceae*)

| | |
|---|---|
| ***racemosum*** | CWsd EBee EFEx EPot GEdr WCru |

## *Pteris* (*Pteridaceae*)

| | |
|---|---|
| from Yunnan | CLAP |
| ***angustipinna*** B&SWJ 6738 | WCru |
| ***argyraea*** | MBri |
| ***biaurita*** new | EShb |
| ***cretica*** ♀H1+3 | CHEx EShb MBri SAPC SArc |
| - var. ***albolineata*** ♀H1 | EShb GQui MBri SRms XBlo |
| - 'Cristata' | MBri |
| - 'Gautheri' | MBri |
| - 'Parkeri' | EShb MBri |
| - 'Rivertoniana' | MBri |
| - 'Rowei' | MBri XBlo |
| - 'Wimsettii' | MBri |
| ***dentata*** | WRic |
| ***ensiformis*** | MBri |
| * - 'Arguta' | MBri |
| - 'Victoriae' | EShb MBri |
| ***gallinopes*** | CLAP |
| ***nipponica*** | WRic |
| * ***staminea*** new | XBlo |
| ***tremula*** | CHEx EShb GQui MBri SRms WRic |
| ***umbrosa*** | MBri WRic |
| ***vittata*** | SRms |
| ***wallichiana*** | CDTJ CGHE CHEx CLAP WPGP |

## *Pterocarya* (*Juglandaceae*)

| | |
|---|---|
| ***fraxinifolia*** ♀H4 | CBcs CDul CLnd CMCN CTrG ECrN EGFP EPfP LMaj MBlu MMuc NWea SBLw WDin WPat |
| - IDS 02 new | WHCr |
| x ***rehderiana*** | CTho MBlu WMou |
| ***rhoifolia*** | MBri |
| ***stenoptera*** | CDTJ CDul CMCN CTho EGFP |
| - 'Fern Leaf' | EPfP MBlu SMad WMou WPGP |

## *Pterocephalus* (*Dipsacaceae*)

| | |
|---|---|
| ***depressus*** | CPBP WPat |
| ***parnassi*** | see *P. perennis* |
| § ***perennis*** | CMea ECho LRHS MHer NBir NMen NRya NWCA SRms WEas WHoo |
| - subsp. ***perennis*** | EBee EGoo WHrl |
| ***pinardii*** | NWCA |

## *Pterodiscus* (*Pedaliaceae*)

| | |
|---|---|
| ***ngamicus*** | LToo |
| ***speciosus*** | LToo |

## *Pterostylis* (*Orchidaceae*)

| | |
|---|---|
| ***coccinea*** | ECho |
| ***curta*** | CStu ECho SCnR SKHP |

## *Pterostyrax* (*Styracaceae*)

| | |
|---|---|
| ***corymbosa*** | CMCN CPMA IArd IDee MBlu NLar SSpi WFar |
| ***hispida*** ♀H4 | CAbP CBcs CDoC CDul CEnd CMCN CPMA CWib EBee EPfP EPla IArd IDee LAst LRHS MBlu MBri MGos MRav NLar SSpi SSta WDin WFar WPGP |

## *Ptilostemon* (*Asteraceae*)

| | |
|---|---|
| ***afer*** | CMdw EGoo EHrv NChi SMrm |
| § ***diacantha*** | CSam EBee IFoB LHop NBPC NPri WOut |
| ***echinocephalus*** | EBee GKir MDKP NBhm NBre |

## *Ptilotrichum* see *Alyssum*

| | |
|---|---|
| ***spinosum*** 'Roseum' | see *Alyssum spinosum* 'Roseum' |

## *Puccinellia* (*Poaceae*)

| | |
|---|---|
| ***distans*** | EBWF |

## *Pueraria* (*Papilionaceae*)

| | |
|---|---|
| ***montana*** var. ***lobata*** | CAgr CArn MSal |

## *Pulicaria* (*Asteraceae*)

| | |
|---|---|
| § ***dysenterica*** | CArn EBWF MHer MSal NMir SIde WCHb WSFF |

## *Pulmonaria* (*Boraginaceae*)

| | |
|---|---|
| ***affinis*** 'Margaret' | NCob |
| ***angustifolia*** ♀H4 | EBee EPfP EWTr GKev GKir GMaP LRHS MNrw MSal NOrc SRms WCru WEas WFar WTin |
| * - ***alba*** | IFoB |
| - 'Azurea' | CBro CElw EBee ELan EMon EPPr EPfP GAbr GMaP IBlr LAst LRHS MBNS MNHC MRav NBro NCGa SMrm SPer SPla SRms WCAu WCFE WFar WMnd |
| - 'Blaues Meer' | CFir CSBt CSam EBee EPfP GAbr GBuc GKir LCro WCru |
| - 'Munstead Blue' | CElw CLAP CMac ECha EGle EHrv LCro LRHS MRav MTho NCob NHol NRya NSti SRms WCru |
| - 'Rubra' | see *P. rubra* |
| 'Apple Frost' | CLAP EBee NBhm NLar NSti |
| 'Barfield Regalia' | CMHG EBee EMon IGor NSti SDys WCru |
| 'Benediction' | CDes NSti SPhx |
| § 'Beth's Blue' | EMon WCAu WCru |
| 'Beth's Pink' | ECha GAbr WCru WFar |
| 'Blauer Hügel' | CElw EMon NSti |
| 'Blauhimmel' | EMon GCra |
| 'Blue Buttons' | CBow CFir EBee ECtt EQua GQue NSti |
| 'Blue Crown' | CElw CLAP CSev EBee EHrv EWes GBuc LRHS WCAu WEas |
| 'Blue Ensign' | Widely available |
| 'Blue Moon' | see *P. officinalis* 'Blue Mist' |
| 'Blue Pearl' | NSti |
| 'Blueberry Muffin' | CSpe |
| 'Bonnie' | CMea SAga |
| 'Botanic Hybrid' | WCru |
| 'British Sterling' | EBee |
| Cally hybrid | CElw CLAP EMon GCal NBre NSti WCru |
| 'Cedric Morris' | CElw |
| 'Chintz' | CLAP CSam GBuc SMrm |

| | | |
|---|---|---|
| | 'Cleeton Red' | NSti |
| | 'Coral Springs' | GKir MAvo NSti |
| | 'Corsage' | ECtt |
| | 'Cotton Cool' | CElw CGHE CLAP CMac CPrp EAEE EBee ECha ECtt EHoe EMon EShb GBuc MAvo MBNS MCot MNFA NCGa NOrc NSti SPer SUsu WCAu WCru WMoo WPGP |
| | 'De Vroomen's Pride' (v) | MSte WMnd |
| | 'Diana Clare' | Widely available |
| | 'Elworthy Rubies' | CElw EPPr |
| | 'Emerald Isles' | NSti |
| | 'Excalibur' | EBee EHrv EPPr GBuc NLar |
| | 'Fiona' | MAvo WCAu |
| | 'Glacier' | CBro CElw CMoH CTca EBee EMon EPfP LRHS MSte NSti WCru |
| | 'Hazel Kaye's Red' | LLWP NSti |
| | 'Highdown' | see *P.* 'Lewis Palmer' |
| | 'Ice Ballet' (Classic Series) | EBee LRHS |
| | 'Joan's Red' | CElw WTin |
| § | 'Lewis Palmer' ♀H4 | CBro CMHG CMea CSam EBee ECtt EPla GCal GKir GMaP IBlr LRHS MAvo NBid NBir NHol SRGP WBrk WCFE WCot WCru WHoo WTin |
| | 'Lime Close' | SAga |
| | 'Linford Blue' | WCru |
| | 'Little Star' | EBee EMon GBuc NBre NSti SRGP SUsu WCru |
| | ***longifolia*** | CArn CBro CFee CHar CPrp EAEE EBee ECha EHoe ELan EPfP GAbr LCro LLWP MSal NBir NGdn NOrc NSti WBrk WEas WFar |
| § | - 'Ankum' | CElw CLAP CSam EGle EPfP EPla GBuc GKir LRHS MBrN MRav MSte NBir NSti WCot WMoo WWlt |
| | - 'Ballyrogan Blue' | IBlr |
| | - 'Bertram Anderson' | CBgR CPrp CSsd CTca EBee ECtt GKir GMaP LCro LRHS MLLN NBir NVic SPer SRGP SWvt WBrk WCAu WCot WFar WMnd |
| | - subsp. ***cevennensis*** | CHar CLAP EBee EBrs EPfP GKir MBNS MBri MLLN MSte NCGa NSti WCAu WPtf |
| | - 'Coen Jansen' | see *P. longifolia* 'Ankum' |
| | - 'Coral Spring' | GKir NBre SHGN WCAu |
| | - 'Dordogne' | CLAP GBuc GKir MLLN MRav NBir NLar WCAu WCru |
| | - 'Howard Eggins' | EBee |
| | 'Lovell Blue' | NCot |
| | 'Majesté' | Widely available |
| | 'Margery Fish' ♀H4 | CBro CHar CLAP CSam EBee ECGP EPfP GKir LRHS MLLN SPer WMnd |
| | 'Mary Mottram' | CElw ECtt ELan MLLN NBir NPol NSti SAga SMrm WCru WMnd WMoo |
| | 'Matese Blue' | CLAP |
| | 'Mawson's Blue' | CLAP ECha EMon EWes GKir LRHS MRav MWat MWea NBir NChi SWvt WBrk WCru WEas WMoo WRHF WSHC |
| | 'May Bouquet'PBR | NSti |
| | 'Melancholia' | IBlr |
| | 'Merlin' | CLAP EMon LRHS |
| § | 'Milchstrasse' | CLAP |
| | Milky Way | see *P.* 'Milchstrasse' |
| | ***mollis*** | CLAP CSWP EBee ECGP EGoo EMon GCal IBlr LRHS MNrw NSti SBch WCru |
| | - 'Royal Blue' | MRav |
| | - 'Samobor' | CLAP |
| | 'Moonshine'PBR | NSti |
| | 'Moonstone' | CLAP |
| | 'Mountain Magic'PBR | CHVG ECtt EWll NSti SIde |
| | 'Mournful Purple' | EHrv |
| | 'Mrs Kittle' | CElw CMMP EAEE EBee EPPr GBri GBuc IFoB MLLN MRav NBir NSti SDys WBrk WCru WFar WMnd |
| | 'Mystique' **new** | EBee |
| | 'Netta Statham' | ECha NSti |
| | 'Northern Lights'PBR | SHar |
| | 'Nürnberg' | EMon |
| | ***officinalis*** | CArn CBro CHby EHon GBar GPoy IFoB MHer MLHP NVic SIde WBrk WCru WFar |
| | - 'Alba' | ELan WBrk |
| § | - 'Blue Mist' | CBro CElw CLAP EBee ECha ELan GBri GBuc GMaP NBir WAbb WBrk WCot WHoo WMnd WMoo WTin |
| | - 'Bowles' Blue' | see *P. officinalis* 'Blue Mist' |
| | - Cambridge Blue Group | CPrp EBee EMon GMaP LRHS MBNS MRav MWat NBir NLar WCAu WCot WCru WPtf |
| * | - 'Frühlingslied' **new** | EBee |
| | - ***rubra*** | see *P. rubra* |
| | - 'Stillingfleet Gran' | NSti |
| | - 'White Wings' | CElw CLAP EBee EPla GKir LRHS MRav NLar NPri SIde SPoG WFar WMoo |
| | - 'Wuppertal' | EBee |
| | 'Oliver Wyatt's White' | CLAP EBee SRGP |
| | Opal = 'Ocupol' | Widely available |
| | 'Polar Splash' | EBee GBin GKir SIde SMrm SPoG SRot WFar |
| | 'Raspberry Splash'PBR | CBct CLAP CPom EBee GKev LHop NLar NSti SHar SIde SMrm SPoG |
| | 'Richard Nutt' | EMon |
| * | 'Rowlatt Choules' | MAvo |
| | 'Roy Davidson' | CLAP CSam EBee ECtt EHrv EMon EPPr GKir LHop LRHS NBir NCGa NChi NSti SRGP SWvt WCot WFar WPtf |
| § | ***rubra*** ♀H4 | CBcs CElw CPom CSWP ECha ELan EShb GAbr GKir LLWP MLHP MMuc MWte NBid NCob NOrc NSti SRms WCAu WFar WTin |
| | - var. ***alba*** | see *P. rubra* var. *albocorollata* |
| § | - var. ***albocorollata*** | CBre CElw CMHG EBee ECha EGle EHrv EMon GAbr MSte NBid SHar WBrk WFar |
| | - 'Ann' | CElw CLAP NMoo SMrm WCru WFar WTin |
| | - 'Barfield Pink' | CBro ELan GBar GCal GKir LRHS MLLN NBir NLar WRHF |
| | - 'Barfield Ruby' | EMon GBuc MAvo |
| | - 'Bowles' Red' | CPrp EBee ECtt EHrv EPfP GKir IFoB LAst MRav MWat NBir NGdn SIde SPer STes WFar WMnd |
| | - 'David Ward' (v) | Widely available |
| | - 'Rachel Vernie' (v) | CLAP CPom CPou MAvo MHar WBrk WCot |
| | - 'Redstart' | Widely available |
| § | ***saccharata*** | ECha EHrv ELan GMaP IFro SIde SRms WCAu WFar |
| | - 'Alba' | CBro CElw ECha GBuc MMuc SRms |
| | - Argentea Group ♀H4 | CBro CSev CTri EBee ELan EPfP GMaP LBMP LRHS MRav MTho NGdn WCAu |
| | - 'Brentor' | EBee WCru |
| | - 'Clent Skysilver' | EBee |
| | - 'Dora Bielefeld' | Widely available |
| | - 'Frühlingshimmel' | CBro CElw EBee ECtt GKir MRav WCAu WFar |
| | - 'Glebe Cottage Blue' | CElw WCru |
| | - 'Jill Richardson' | ELan |
| | - 'Lady Lou's Pink' | WCru |

| | |
|---|---|
| - 'Leopard' | CElw CEnt CLAP CMac CMea COlW CSam EBee ECtt GBuc GMaP LRHS MLLN NBir NBre SApp SRGP SRot WBrk WClo WCot WFar WHoo |
| - 'Mrs Moon' | CTri CWib EBee ECtt EPfP GMaP LAst LBMP LCro MBNS MHer NOrc NPri SPer SRGP SWvt WMnd |
| - 'Old Rectory Silver' | CLAP NBir |
| - 'Picta' | see *P. saccharata* |
| - 'Pink Dawn' | CMHG WMnd |
| - pink-flowered | WCru |
| - 'Reginald Kaye' | CElw ECha EWes MAvo MNrw SHBN |
| - 'Silverado'PBR | EBee ECtt GKir MHer NOrc |
| - 'Stanhoe' | EBee EWes |
| - 'White Barn' | see *P.* 'Beth's Blue' |
| 'Saint Ann's' | CElw EMon NBre NSti WCru |
| 'Samurai' | EBee GBin MBNS NSti WPtf |
| 'Silver Lance' | GKir |
| 'Silver Maid' | WCAu |
| 'Silver Sabre' | IBlr |
| 'Silver Shimmers'PBR | SHar |
| 'Silver Surprise' | WCot |
| 'Sissinghurst White' ♀H4 | Widely available |
| 'Smoky Blue' | CLAP CSBt EBee ECtt EMon EPfP LBMP MRav NBPC NMoo SMrm SWat WCru WFar WMnd |
| 'Spilled Milk' | EBee NBre NLar |
| 'Stillingfleet Meg' | CLAP EAEE EBee ECGP ECtt LAst MAvo MBNS MCot MLLN NCob NHol NSti SPla SRGP |
| 'Tim's Silver' | EBee |
| 'Trevi Fountain' | CBct CLAP COlW EBee EShb GJos GKev GKir LHop NBre NSti SIde SMrm SPoG SRot WCot |
| 'Vera May' ♀H4 | NSti |
| 'Victorian Brooch'PBR | CBct CLAP COlW EBee GAbr GKev GKir GQue LRHS LSou MBri NLar NSti SIde WFar WPtf |
| 'Weetwood Blue' | CBre CLAP EBee EPfP EPla MNrw MSte WCru |
| 'Wendy Perry' | CElw |
| 'Wisley White' | CElw |

## *Pulsatilla* (*Ranunculaceae*)

| | |
|---|---|
| ***alba*** | CBro NWCA |
| ***albana*** | CBro LHop LRHS |
| - 'Lutea' | EBee GKev |
| ***alpina*** | ECho SRms WPat |
| § - subsp. ***apiifolia*** ♀H4 | EBee ELan NRya |
| - subsp. ***sulphurea*** | see *P. alpina* subsp. *apiifolia* |
| ***ambigua*** | GKev LLHF |
| ***bungeana*** | EBee GKev |
| ***cernua*** | CBro EBee GBuc LHop |
| ***dahurica*** | CSec |
| x ***gayeri*** | ECho LLHF NBir |
| ***georgica*** | WAbe |
| ***halleri*** ♀H4 | EBee ECho GKev |
| - pale blue-flowered | CSec |
| - subsp. ***slavica*** ♀H4 | EBee LRHS NWCA |
| - subsp. ***taurica*** | MSte |
| ***lutea*** | see *P. alpina* subsp. *apiifolia* |
| ***montana*** | GBuc NMen SPlb WFar |
| ***multifida*** | GBuc |
| ***occidentalis*** | EBee |
| § ***patens*** | LLHF NBHF |
| ***pratensis*** | CSec GPoy SRms |
| - subsp. ***nigricans*** | CSec LHop LRHS WFar |
| ***rubra*** | ECho GKev NGHP SRot |
| ***turczaninovii*** | GBuc LLHF |
| § ***vernalis*** ♀H2 | ECho EPot GBuc NSla WAbe |
| § ***vulgaris*** ♀H4 | Widely available |
| - 'Alba' ♀H4 | Widely available |
| - 'Barton's Pink' | CBro EWes GKir LHop LRHS SIng |
| - 'Blaue Glocke' | EWll GEdr MCot NLar NPri SMrm SWvt WFar WHil WRHF |
| - double, fringed (d) | WFar |
| - 'Eva Constance' | CBro EAEE GKev LHop LRHS SIng |
| - 'Gotlandica' | CLyd |
| - subsp. ***grandis*** | CSec NMen |
| - - 'Papageno' | CPBP CSpe EAEE EAlp EBee ECho GMaP LAst LBMP LHop MAvo NHol NLar NWCA SMrm SRot WCra WFar WHil |
| - Heiler hybrids | CPrp EAEE EBee LBMP NGdn WCra WFar WHal |
| - Red Clock | see *P. vulgaris* 'Röde Klokke' |
| § - 'Röde Klokke' | EBee ECtt GEdr GKev ITim MAvo MCot MWat MWhi NBPC NHol NLar NPri SMrm SPad SWvt WFar WHil |
| - ***rosea*** | GAbr |
| - Rote Glocke | see *P. vulgaris* 'Röde Klokke' |
| - var. ***rubra*** | Widely available |
| § - 'Weisse Schwan' | ECho GEdr GKir GMaP NHol NMen |
| - White Swan | see *P. vulgaris* 'Weisse Schwan' |
| ***zimmermannii*** | NWCA |

## pummelo see *Citrus maxima*

## *Punica* (*Lythraceae*)

| | |
|---|---|
| ***granatum*** | CBcs CHEx CMen CTsd EPfP ERom LPan MGos MREP SBLw SDnm SLim SOWG STre SVic WBVN WSHC |
| - 'André le Roi' (F) | SLPl |
| - 'Chico' | CBcs SEND |
| - 'Legrelleae' (d) | SEND SLPl |
| - 'Maxima Rubra' | IFFs |
| - var. ***nana*** ♀H3 | CAgr CArn CCCN CMen EPfP EShb LPan MREP SMrm SPer SRms WPat |
| - f. ***plena*** (d) | CBcs EMil MRav WCFE |
| * - 'Striata' | SOWG |

## *Purshia* (*Rosaceae*)

| | |
|---|---|
| ***mexicana*** F&M 092 new | WPGP |
| aff. ***mexicana*** B&SWJ 9040 | WCru |

## *Puschkinia* (*Hyacinthaceae*)

| | |
|---|---|
| ***scilloides*** | CMil EBrs ECho LRHS NBir |
| - 'Aragat's Gem' | EBrs ECho |
| § - var. ***libanotica*** | CBro CTca EBrs ECho ELon EPfP EPot IHer LAma LHop LRHS SPer SPhx WCot WRHF WShi |
| - - 'Alba' | EBrs ECho EPot LAma LRHS SPer SPhx |

## *Puya* (*Bromeliaceae*)

| | |
|---|---|
| RCB/Arg L-3 | WCot |
| RCB/Arg L-5 | WCot |
| RCB/Arg S-2 | WCot |
| ***alpestris*** | CBrP CCCN CHEx CTrC EAmu EBee EShb LRHS SAPC SBig SChr WCot WPGP |
| ***berteroana*** | CCCN CDTJ EBee EShb SPlb |
| ***castellanosii*** CDPR 3109 | WPGP |
| ***chilensis*** | CAbb CBcs CCCN CDTJ CDoC CHEx CKob CTrG EAmu EBee LRHS SAPC SArc SPlb |
| ***coerulea*** | CCCN CDTJ CFir EAmu EBee ELon LEdu SMad |
| ***gilmartiniae*** | WCot |
| ***laxa*** | SChr |
| ***mirabilis*** | CDTJ CHEx CKob CTrC EBee ESwi |
| ***venusta*** | CCCN CDTJ EBee SPlb |
| ***weberbaueri*** | CHEx |

## *Pycnanthemum* (*Lamiaceae*)

| | |
|---|---|
| ***pilosum*** | CArn EBee ELau MHer MSal NBre NLar NPri SBch SIde SWal |
| ***tenuifolium*** | NBre |
| ***virginianum*** | GCal |

## *Pycnostachys* (*Lamiaceae*)

| | |
|---|---|
| ***reticulata*** | EOHP EShb |
| ***urticifolia*** | ECre EOHP EWes |

## *Pygmea* see *Chionohebe*

## *Pyracantha* (*Rosaceae*)

| | |
|---|---|
| Alexander Pendula = 'Renolex' | LHop MRav MSwo SRms WFar |
| ***angustifolia*** | WCFE |
| § ***atalantioides*** | CMac SPlb WCFE |
| § - 'Aurea' | ERas WFar |
| 'Brilliant' | EBee EPfP SCoo |
| 'Buttercup' | EPla |
| ***coccinea*** | EBee |
| § - 'Lalandei' | GKir LAst |
| - 'Red Column' | Widely available |
| - 'Red Cushion' | MGos MRav SRms |
| ***crenulata*** | WCFE |
| Dart's Red = 'Interrada' | CSBt EBee GKir LRHS SLim SPoG |
| 'Fiery Cascade' | SPoG SRms |
| ***gibbsii*** | see *P. atalantioides* |
| - 'Flava' | see *P. atalantioides* 'Aurea' |
| 'Golden Charmer' ♀H4 | EBee ECtt EPfP GKir LRHS MAsh MGan MGos MRav MSwo NBlu NLar NPri NWea SCoo SHBN SPer SPoG SRms SWvt WBod WDin WFar WRHF |
| 'Golden Dome' | LRHS |
| 'Golden Glow' | LRHS |
| 'Golden Sun' | see *P.* 'Soleil d'Or' |
| 'Harlequin' (v) | SHBN WFar |
| 'John Stedman' | see *P.* 'Stedman's' |
| 'Knap Hill Lemon' | CChe MBlu |
| ***koidzumii*** 'Victory' | EBee MGos |
| 'Mohave' | CChe CMac EBee ECrN ELan GKir LRHS MAsh MBar MGan MNHC MWat NPri NWea SCoo SHBN SLim SPer SRms SWvt WBod WDin |
| 'Mohave Silver' (v) | CWSG ELan LAst LRHS MWat |
| 'Monrovia' | see *P. coccinea* 'Lalandei' |
| 'Mozart' | EBee |
| 'Navaho' | EPfP GKir SCoo SPoG |
| 'Orange Charmer' | CTri EBee ELan EPfP GKir LHop MGan MGos MRav MWat NBlu NWea SHBN SPer SPlb WBod WFar |
| 'Orange Glow' ♀H4 | Widely available |
| * 'Red Pillar' | GKir |
| 'Renault d'Or' | SLPl |
| ***rogersiana*** ♀H4 | EBee ECrN EPfP MRav WFar |
| - 'Flava' ♀H4 | CSBt EBee ECrN EPfP ERas LAst MBar MRav NMun NWea SPoG |
| 'Rosedale' | EBee |
| Saphyr Jaune = 'Cadaune'PBR | CBcs CCVT CDoC CEnd CSBt CWSG EBee EMil EPfP ERas GKir LBMP LCro MGos MRav SCoo SPer WBod |
| Saphyr Orange = 'Cadange'PBR ♀H4 | CBcs CCVT CDoC CEnd CSBt CWSG EBee EMil EPfP EPla ERas GKir LCro LRHS MBri MGos MRav NCGa SCoo SPer |
| Saphyr Panache = 'Cadvar'PBR (v) | EBee |
| Saphyr Rouge = 'Cadrou'PBR ♀H4 | CBcs CCVT CDoC CEnd CSBt CWSG EBee EMil EPfP ERas GKir LCro LRHS MBri MGos MRav NCGa NPri SCoo SPer WBod WFar |
| 'Shawnee' | CSBt CWib EBee ECot MSwo MWat |
| § 'Soleil d'Or' | Widely available |
| 'Sparkler' (v) | CMac CSBt EHoe EMil LAst LPan MGos WFar |
| § 'Stedman's' | NLar |
| 'Teton' ♀H4 | CMac CWSG EBee ECrN ELan EPfP EPla GKir LAst LHop LPan LRHS MAsh MBar MBri MSwo MWat SPoG SRms WDin WFar |
| 'Ventoux Red' | SCoo |
| 'Watereri' | NWea SLPl SPer WFar |
| 'Yellow Sun' | see *P.* 'Soleil d'Or' |

## *Pyrenaria* (*Theaceae*)

| | |
|---|---|
| ***spectabilis*** | see *Tutcheria spectabilis* |

## *Pyrethropsis* see *Rhodanthemum*

| | |
|---|---|
| ***hosmariense*** | see *Rhodanthemum hosmariense* |

## *Pyrethrum* see *Tanacetum*

## *Pyrola* (*Ericaceae*)

| | |
|---|---|
| ***minor*** | NMen |
| ***rotundifolia*** | WHer |

## *Pyrostegia* (*Bignoniaceae*)

| | |
|---|---|
| ***venusta*** | CCCN SOWG |

## *Pyrrocoma* (*Asteraceae*)

| | |
|---|---|
| ***clementis*** | EBee |

## *Pyrrosia* (*Polypodiaceae*)

| | |
|---|---|
| ***lingua*** | WRic |
| ***polydactyla*** new | EBee |

## *Pyrus* ✿ (*Rosaceae*)

| | |
|---|---|
| ***amygdaliformis*** | CTho |
| - var. ***cuneifolia*** | CLnd |
| ***betulifolia*** | CMCN EHig WJas |
| ***calleryana*** 'Bradford' | CLnd |
| - 'Capital' new | LMaj |
| - 'Chanticleer' ♀H4 | Widely available |
| - 'Chanticleer' variegated (v) | CLnd |
| ***communis*** (F) | CCVT CDul CTri EMac LBuc SBLw SPer SPlb WMou |
| - 'Abbé Fétel' (D) | SKee |
| - 'Barnet' (Perry) | CTho |
| - 'Baronne de Mello' (D) | CTho SKee |
| - 'Beech Hill' (F) | CDul CLnd EBee ECrN EPfP SBLw SPer |
| - 'Belle Guérandaise' (D) | SKee |
| - 'Belle Julie' (D) | SKee |
| - 'Beth' (D) ♀H4 | CAgr CDoC CMac CSBt CTri CWib ECrN EMil EMui EPfP GKir GTwe LAst LBuc MAsh MBri NPri SDea SKee SPer WHar WOrn |
| - 'Beurré Alexandre Lucas' (D) | SKee |
| - 'Beurré Bedford' (D) | SKee |
| - 'Beurré d'Amanlis' (D) | SKee |
| - 'Beurré d'Avalon' (D) | SKee |
| - 'Beurré de Naghin' (C/D) | SKee |
| - 'Beurré Diel' (D) | SKee |
| - 'Beurré Dumont' (D) | CAgr |
| - 'Beurré Giffard' (D) | CAgr |
| - 'Beurré Hardy' (D) ♀H4 | CAgr CCAT CCVT CDoC CDul CMac CSBt CTho CTri CWib ECrN EMui GKir GTwe LAst LPan LRHS MBri MGan MWat SDea SKee SPer WOrn |
| - 'Beurré Jean van Geert' (D) | GKir |
| - 'Beurré Mortillet' (D) | SKee |
| - 'Beurré Rance' (F) | SKee |

| | | |
|---|---|---|
| | - 'Beurré Six' (D) | SKee |
| | - 'Beurré Superfin' (D) ♀H4 | ECrN GTwe MCoo SKee |
| | - 'Bianchettone' (D) | SKee |
| | - 'Bishop's Thumb' (D) | SDea |
| | - 'Black Worcester' (C) | GTwe MAsh SDea SKee WJas WOrn |
| | - 'Blakeney Red' (Perry) | CTho SDea |
| | - 'Blickling' (D) | SKee |
| | - 'Brandy' (Perry) | CTho SDea SKee |
| | - 'Bristol Cross' (D) | CAgr GTwe SKee |
| § | - 'Butirra Precoce Morettini' (D) | SDea |
| | - 'Cannock' (F) **new** | CCAT |
| | - 'Catillac' (C) ♀H4 | CAgr CTho GTwe SKee |
| | - 'Chalk' | see *P. communis* 'Crawford' |
| | - 'Charneaux' (F) **new** | SVic |
| | - 'Chaumontel' (D) | SKee |
| | - 'Clapp's Favourite' (D) | CTho ECrN SKee SVic |
| | - 'Comte de Lamy' (D) | SKee |
| | - 'Concorde'PBR (D) ♀H4 | Widely available |
| | - 'Conference' (D) ♀H4 | Widely available |
| § | - 'Crawford' (D) | SKee |
| | - 'Deacon's Pear' (D) | SDea |
| | - 'Devoe' (D) | SDea |
| | - 'Docteur Jules Guyot' (D) | CAgr ECrN SDea SKee |
| | - 'Doyenné du Comice' (D) ♀H4 | Widely available |
| | - 'Duchesse d'Angoulême' (D) | SKee |
| | - 'Durondeau' (D) | GTwe SDea SKee |
| | - 'Emile d'Heyst' (D) | GTwe MCoo |
| | - 'Eva Baltet' (D) | SKee |
| | - 'Fertility' (D) | CLnd SKee |
| | - 'Fertility Improved' | see *P. communis* 'Improved Fertility' |
| | - 'Fondante d'Automne' (D) | CAgr CTho SKee |
| | - 'Forelle' (D) | SKee |
| | - 'Glou Morceau' (D) | CAgr ECrN EMui GTwe MCoo MWat SDea SKee |
| | - 'Gorham' (D) ♀H4 | CAgr CTho ECrN GTwe MCoo SKee |
| | - 'Gratiole de Jersey' (D) | CTho |
| | - 'Green Pear of Yair' (D) | SKee |
| | - 'Hacon's Imcomparable' (D) | SKee |
| | - 'Harrow Delight' (D) | SDea |
| | - 'Harvest Queen' (D/C) | SDea |
| | - 'Hendre Huffcap' (Perry) | CCAT |
| | - 'Hessle' (D) | CAgr GTwe MCoo NWea SDea SKee |
| § | - 'Improved Fertility' (D) | CAgr CDoC GTwe SDea SKee |
| | - Invincible = 'Delwinor' (D/C) | CAgr CDul EMui LBuc LRHS MCoo SPoG |
| | - 'Jargonelle' (D) | CAgr CTho ECrN GTwe SDea SKee |
| | - 'Jeanne d'Arc' (D) **new** | SVic |
| | - 'Joséphine de Malines' (D) ♀H4 | CAgr GTwe SDea SKee WOrn |
| | - 'Kieffer' (C) | CAgr |
| | - 'Laxton's Foremost' (D) | CAgr SKee |
| | - 'Légipont' (F) **new** | CAgr |
| | - 'Louise Bonne of Jersey' (D) ♀H4 | CAgr CDoC CMac CTri ECrN EMui GTwe LAst MGos SDea SKee |
| | - 'Marguérite Marillat' (D) | SDea SKee |
| | - 'Marie-Louise' (D) | SKee |
| | - 'Max Red Bartlett' | MCoo |
| | - 'Merton Pride' (D) | CAgr CTho CTri ECrN GTwe MCoo MWat SDea SKee |
| | - 'Moonglow' (D/C) | CAgr MCoo SDea |
| | - 'Moorcroft' (Perry) | SKee |
| | - 'Morettini' | see *P. communis* 'Butirra Precoce Morettini' |
| | - 'Nouveau Poiteau' (C/D) | CAgr CTho ECrN GTwe SKee |
| | - 'Nye Russet Bartlett' (F) | CAgr |
| | - 'Olivier de Serres' (D) | SKee |
| | - 'Onward' (D) ♀H4 | CAgr CCAT CDul CLnd CTri CWib ECrN EMil EMui GTwe MAsh MBri NWea SDea SKee SPoG WHar WOrn |
| | - 'Ovid' (D) | CAgr |
| § | - 'Packham's Triumph' (D) | CAgr CDoC CTri CWib ECrN GTwe SDea SKee SVic |
| | - 'Passe Crassane' (D) | SKee |
| | - 'Pear Apple' (D) | SDea |
| | - 'Pitmaston Duchess' (C/D) ♀H4 | ECrN GTwe MCoo SDea SKee |
| | - 'Red Comice' (D/C) | GTwe SKee |
| | - 'Red Sensation Bartlett' (D/C) | EMui GTwe LBuc MAsh SKee |
| | - 'Robin' (C/D) | SDea SKee |
| | - 'Roosevelt' (D) | SKee |
| | - 'Santa Claus' (D) | SDea SKee |
| | - 'Seckel' (D) | SKee |
| | - 'Sierra' (D) | CAgr |
| | - 'Snowdon Queen' (D) **new** | WGwG |
| | - 'Souvenir du Congrès' (D) | CAgr |
| | - 'Terrace Pearl' | EMui SPoG |
| | - 'Thompson's' (D) | GTwe SKee |
| | - 'Triumph' | see *P. communis* 'Packham's Triumph' |
| | - 'Uvedale's St Germain' (C) | SKee |
| | - 'Verbelu' | SKee |
| | - 'Verdi' (F) **new** | MBri |
| | - 'Vicar of Winkfield' (C/D) | GTwe SDea SKee |
| | - 'Williams' Bon Chrétien' (D/C) ♀H4 | Widely available |
| | - 'Williams Red' (D/C) | CSut EMui GTwe SKee |
| | - 'Winter Nelis' (D) | CAgr CTri CWib ECrN GKir GTwe LRHS SDea SKee |
| | ***cordata*** | CDul CTho |
| | ***elaeagnifolia*** var. ***kotschyana*** | CDul CEnd GKir SLim WOrn |
| | - 'Silver Sails' | CLnd EMil GKir LRHS MAsh MBlu MGos NLar SCoo SPur SSpi |
| | ***nivalis*** | CDul CLnd CTho EBee ECrN EPfP LMaj MBri MRav SBLw SCoo SPer |
| | - 'Catalia' | MBri NLar SCoo SPoG |
| | ***pyraster*** | CDul |
| | ***pyrifolia*** **new** | GAuc |
| | - '20th Century' | see *P. pyrifolia* 'Nijisseiki' |
| | - 'Hosui' (F) | SVic |
| | - 'Kosui' (F) **new** | SVic |
| | - 'Kumoi' (F) | SDea |
| § | - 'Nijisseiki' (F) | SVic |
| | - 'Shinseiki' (F) | CAgr CLnd EMui LRHS SDea SKee |
| | - 'Shinsui' (F) | SDea SKee |
| * | ***salicifolia*** var. ***orientalis*** | CTho |
| | - 'Pendula' ♀H4 | Widely available |
| | ***ussuriensis*** | CTho GAuc |

# Q

## *Qiongzhuea* see *Chimonobambusa*

## *Quercus* ✿ (*Fagaceae*)

| | | |
|---|---|---|
| | ***acerifolia*** | EPfP |
| § | ***acuta*** | CBcs IArd |
| | ***acutifolia*** | SBir |
| | ***acutifolia*** x ***mexicana*** | SBir |
| | ***acutissima*** | CBcs CLnd CMCN EPfP MBlu MBri SBir |
| | - 'Gobbler' **new** | SBir |

| | | |
|---|---|---|
| | ***aegilops*** | see *Q. ithaburensis* subsp. *macrolepis* |
| | ***afares*** new | SBir |
| | ***affinis*** | SBir |
| | ***agrifolia*** | CDul CMCN SBir WPGP |
| | ***alba*** | CMCN SBir WDin WPGP |
| | ***aliena*** | CDul CMCN SBir |
| | ***alnifolia*** | CDul |
| | ***arkansana*** | SBir |
| | ***austrina*** | CMCN SBir |
| | x ***beadlei*** | see *Q.* x *saulii* |
| | ***berberidifolia*** new | SBir |
| | ***bicolor*** | CDul CMCN EPfP MBri SBir WDin |
| | ***borealis*** | see *Q. rubra* |
| | ***breweri*** | see *Q. garryana* var. *breweri* |
| | ***buckleyi*** | CMCN MBri |
| | x ***bushii*** | CMCN EPfP MBlu MBri SBir |
| | ***canariensis*** ♀H4 | CBcs CLnd CMCN CTho CTrG EPfP GKir |
| | ***canariensis*** x ***faginea*** NJM 03.001 | WPGP |
| | ***castaneifolia*** | CDul CMCN EPfP SBLw SBir WDin |
| | - 'Green Spire' ♀H4 | CDoC CMCN CTho EPfP GKir IArd MBlu SEND SMad SPer |
| | ***cerris*** | CBcs CCVT CDoC CDul CLnd CMCN EBee ECrN EMac EMil EPfP GKir LAst LMaj LPan MGos MLan NWea SBLw SBir SEND SPer STre WDin WFar WMou |
| | - 'Afyon Lace' new | MBlu |
| § | - 'Argenteovariegata' (v) | CDul CEnd CMCN CTho EBee ELan EMil EPfP GKir LRHS MAsh MBlu MBri MGos NLar SBir SMad SPoG WOrn WPGP WPat |
| * | - 'Marmorata' | SBir |
| | - 'Variegata' | see *Q. cerris* 'Argenteovariegata' |
| | - 'Wodan' | CMCN EPfP GKir MBlu |
| | ***chapmanii*** | SBir |
| | ***chrysolepis*** | CMCN EPfP |
| | ***coccifera*** | CDul CGHE CMCN EPla SKHP SSpi WDin WPGP |
| | - subsp. ***calliprinos*** | WPGP |
| | ***coccinea*** | CBcs CDul CMCN CTho CTri ECrN EPfP GKir MMuc NBea NWea SBLw SBir SLim SPer SPoG WDin |
| | - 'Splendens' ♀H4 | CDoC CDul CEnd CHll CMCN CPMA CTri ELan EPfP LPan MAsh MBlu MBri SBLw SHBN SPer WDin WOrn WPat |
| | ***conspersa*** | SBir |
| | ***crassipes*** | SBir |
| | x ***deamii*** | SBir |
| | ***dentata*** | CMCN EPfP WDin |
| | - 'Carl Ferris Miller' | CBcs CMCN EPfP GKir MBlu MBri SBir WPat |
| | - 'Pinnatifida' | CMCN EPfP GKir IDee MBlu SBir SMad WPat |
| | - 'Sir Harold Hillier' | MBlu SMad |
| | ***douglasii*** | CMCN |
| | ***dumosa*** | CMCN SBir |
| | ***elliotii*** new | SBir |
| | ***ellipsoidalis*** | CDul CMCN MBri SBir |
| | - 'Hemelrijk' | CDoC EPfP MBlu MBri |
| | ***emoryi*** | CDul CMCN SBir |
| | ***engleriana*** | CExc |
| | ***fabrei*** | SBir |
| | ***falcata*** | CDul CMCN EPfP SBir |
| | - var. ***pagodifolia*** | see *Q. pagoda* |
| | x ***fernaldii*** | CMCN MBlu |
| | ***frainetto*** | CCVT CDoC CDul CLnd CMCN CTho EBee ECrN EPfP GKir ISea LMaj LPan MLan NWea SBLw SBir SEND SPer WDin WMou |
| | - 'Hungarian Crown' ♀H4 | CMCN EPfP GKir MBlu SBir SMad |
| | - 'Trotworth' | MBri |
| | - 'Trump' | CLnd CMCN MBlu |
| | ***gambelii*** | CMCN |
| | ***garryana*** | CMCN |
| § | - var. ***breweri*** | SBir |
| | - var. ***fruticosa*** | see *Q. garryana* var. *breweri* |
| | ***georgiana*** | CMCN EPfP SBir |
| | ***gilva*** | CDul CMCN |
| | ***glabra*** | see *Lithocarpus glaber* |
| | ***glandulifera*** | see *Q. serrata* |
| § | ***glauca*** | CDul CMCN EPfP SAPC SArc SBir WPGP |
| | ***gravesii*** | CMCN EPfP SBir |
| | ***grisea*** | CDul CMCN SBir |
| | x ***hastingsii*** | CMCN SBir |
| | x ***hawkinsiae*** new | SBir |
| | ***hemisphaerica*** | CDul CMCN EPfP SBir |
| | x ***heterophylla*** | CMCN EPfP SBir |
| | x ***hickelii*** | CMCN EPfP SBir |
| | - 'Gieszelhorst' | MBlu |
| | ***hinckleyi*** | WDin |
| § | x ***hispanica*** | CLnd GKir |
| | - 'Ambrozyana' | CDul CMCN SMad WDin |
| | - 'Diversifolia' | CMCN EPfP MBlu |
| | - 'Fulhamensis' | CMCN GKir MBlu SBir SEND |
| § | - 'Lucombeana' ♀H4 | CBcs CDul CMCN CSBt CTho EPfP IDee MBlu SBir SPer |
| § | - 'Pseudoturneri' | CBcs CDul EBee EPfP GKir LPan MBlu |
| | - 'Suberosa' | CTho |
| | - 'Waasland' | MBri SBir |
| | - 'Wageningen' | CMCN EPfP MBri SBir |
| | ***hypoleucoides*** | EPfP MBri |
| | ***ilex*** ♀H4 | Widely available |
| | ***ilicifolia*** | CMCN SBir |
| | ***imbricaria*** | CDul CMCN EPfP MBlu SBir WDin |
| § | ***incana*** Bartram | SBir |
| | ***incana*** Roxb. | see *Q. leucotrichophora* |
| | x ***introgressa*** | SBir |
| | ***ithaburensis*** | EPfP |
| § | - subsp. ***macrolepis*** | CMCN LEdu SBir |
| | - - 'Hemelrijk Silver' | SBir |
| | x ***jackiana*** | EPfP |
| | ***kelloggii*** | CBcs CMCN |
| | x ***kewensis*** | CDul CMCN LMaj SBir |
| | ***laevigata*** | see *Q. acuta* |
| | ***laevis*** | CDul CMCN EPfP SBir |
| | ***lanata*** new | SBir |
| | 'Langtry' new | SBir |
| § | ***laurifolia*** | CDul CMCN |
| | ***laurina*** | SBir |
| § | ***leucotrichophora*** | CDul CMCN GKir WCFE |
| | ***liaotungensis*** | see *Q. wutaishanica* |
| | x ***libanerris*** | SBir |
| | - 'Rotterdam' | CDul CMCN |
| | ***libani*** | CMCN EPfP WDin |
| | ***lobata*** | CMCN LEdu |
| | x ***lucombeana*** | see *Q.* x *hispanica* |
| | - 'William Lucombe' | see *Q.* x *hispanica* 'Lucombeana' |
| | x ***ludoviciana*** | CMCN EPfP GKir MBri SBir |
| | ***lyrata*** | CMCN |
| | 'Macon' | GKir LPan |
| | ***macranthera*** | CLnd CMCN EPfP SBir |
| | ***macrocarpa*** | CDul CMCN EPfP MBri SBir SMad WDin |
| | - var. ***macrocarpa*** new | SBir |
| | ***macrolepis*** | see *Q. ithaburensis* subsp. *macrolepis* |
| | ***marilandica*** | CBcs CEnd CMCN EPfP GKir MBlu SBir WPGP |
| | 'Mauri' | MBri |
| | ***mexicana*** | CDul CMCN SBir |

| | | |
|---|---|---|
| | ***michauxii*** | CDul CMCN GKir SBir |
| | ***mongolica*** | GKir MBlu SBir |
| | - subsp. ***crispula*** var. ***grosseserrata*** | CMCN WPGP |
| | ***muhlenbergii*** | CDul CMCN MBlu SBir |
| | x ***mutabilis*** **new** | SBir |
| | ***myrsinifolia*** | see *Q. glauca* |
| | ***myrtifolia*** | EPfP |
| | ***nigra*** | CMCN SBir |
| | ***nuttallii*** | see *Q. texana* |
| | ***obtusa*** | see *Q. laurifolia* |
| | ***oglethorpensis*** | SBir |
| § | ***pagoda*** | CMCN MBlu SBir |
| | ***palustris*** ♀H4 | CCVT CDoC CDul CLnd CMCN CTho ECrN EMac EPfP EWTr GKir IArd LMaj LPan MAsh MBlu MLan MMuc NWea SBLw SBir SPer STre WDin WOrn |
| * | - 'Compacta' | EPfP |
| | - 'Green Dwarf' | CMCN MBlu |
| | - 'Pendula' | CEnd CMCN |
| | - 'Swamp Pygmy' | CMCN EPfP MBlu |
| * | ***parusca*** | SBir |
| | ***pedunculata*** | see *Q. robur* |
| | ***pedunculiflora*** | see *Q. robur* subsp. *pedunculiflora* |
| § | ***petraea*** ♀H4 | CDoC CDul CLnd ECrN EMac EPfP GKir IMGH LBuc MBlu NBee NLar NWea SBLw SPer WDin WFar WMou |
| | - 'Acutiloba' | SBir |
| § | - 'Insecata' | CDoC CDul CEnd CMCN |
| | - 'Laciniata' | see *Q. petraea* 'Insecata' |
| § | - 'Purpurea' | CDul CMCN GKir MBlu |
| | - 'Rubicunda' | see *Q. petraea* 'Purpurea' |
| § | ***phellos*** | CDul CLnd CMCN ECrN EPfP LRHS MBlu MBri SBir SLPl SPoG WDin |
| | - var. ***latifolia*** | see *Q. incana* Bartram |
| | ***phillyreoides*** | CBcs CDul CMCN EPfP IDee SBir SLPl WDin |
| | ***polymorpha*** | CDul CMCN |
| | 'Pondaim' | CMCN GKir MBri SBir |
| | ***pontica*** | CDul CMCN EPfP GKir MBlu NWea WPat |
| | ***prinoides*** | CMCN |
| | ***prinus*** misapplied | see *Q. michauxii*. |
| | ***prinus*** L. | CMCN EPfP SBir |
| | ***pubescens*** | CMCN EMac SBir |
| | ***pumila*** Michx. | see *Q. prinus* L. |
| | ***pumila*** Walt. | see *Q. phellos* |
| | ***pumila*** ambig. | SBir |
| | ***pyrenaica*** | CDul CMCN CTho MBri |
| | - 'Pendula' | CMCN EPfP WDin |
| | ***rhysophylla*** | EPfP GKir MBlu SBir |
| | x ***riparia*** | SBir |
| § | ***robur*** ♀H4 | Widely available |
| | - 'Argenteomarginata' (v) | CDul CMCN MBlu SMad |
| | - 'Atropurpurea' | EBee MGos WDin |
| * | - 'Compacta' | MBlu |
| | - 'Concordia' | CDoC CDul CEnd CLnd CMCN EBee ELan EPfP GKir LRHS MAsh MBlu NLar NWea SMad WDin |
| | - 'Contorta' | CMCN |
| | - 'Cristata' | CMCN |
| * | - ***dissecta*** | CMCN |
| | - 'Facrist' | CDul SBir |
| | - f. ***fastigiata*** | CDoC CDul CLnd CTho EBee ECrN EPfP GKir IMGH MBar MGos NBee NWea SBLw SBir SCoo SLPl SLim SPer SPoG WDin WFar WOrn |
| | - - 'Koster' ♀H4 | CDoC CDul CMCN CTri EPfP LMaj LPan MBlu NWea SPoG |
| | - 'Filicifolia' misapplied | see *Q. robur* 'Pectinata' |
| | - 'Filicifolia' | see *Q.* x *rosacea* 'Filicifolia' |
| | - var. ***haas*** | CDul |
| | - 'Irtha' | EPfP |
| | - 'Menhir' **new** | MBlu |
| § | - 'Pectinata' | EPfP GKir MBlu WDin |
| § | - subsp. ***pedunculiflora*** | CMCN SBir |
| | - 'Pendula' | CEnd CMCN MBlu MGos |
| | - 'Purpurascens' | CEnd CMCN MBlu |
| | - 'Purpurea' **new** | MBlu |
| * | - 'Pyramidalis Punctata' **new** | IArd |
| | - 'Raba' | CMCN |
| | - 'Rita's Gold' **new** | MBlu |
| | - 'Salicifolia' | MBlu |
| | - Sherwood oak clone | SMad |
| | - 'Strypemonde' | CMCN |
| | - f. ***variegata*** (v) | CPMA MGos |
| | - - 'Fürst Schwarzenburg' (v) | MBlu |
| § | x ***rosacea*** 'Filicifolia' | CEnd GKir NLar WPat |
| | ***rotundifolia*** NJM 03.009 | WPGP |
| § | ***rubra*** ♀H4 | Widely available |
| | - 'Aurea' | CDul CEnd CMCN CPMA EBee EPfP MBlu SPer WPGP |
| | - 'Boltes Gold' | MBlu |
| | - 'Cyrille' **new** | SBir |
| | - 'Magic Fire' | CDul EPfP MBlu MBri SMad |
| * | - 'Sunshine' | CMCN MBlu MBri |
| | ***rugosa*** | CDul CMCN SBir |
| | x ***runcinata*** | SBir |
| | ***sadleriana*** | CDul CMCN GKir |
| | ***salicina*** | WPGP |
| | ***sartorii*** | SBir |
| § | x ***saulii*** | CMCN SBir |
| | x ***schochiana*** | EPfP |
| | x ***schuettei*** | SBir |
| § | ***serrata*** | CDoC CMCN MBri SBir |
| | ***sessiliflora*** | see *Q. petraea* |
| | ***shumardii*** | CDul CMCN EPfP MBlu MBri SBir WDin WPGP |
| | ***stellata*** | CMCN EPfP SBir |
| | ***suber*** | CBcs CCVT CDoC CDul CLnd CMCN CTho ELan EPfP EPla GGal IArd ISea LEdu LMaj LPan LRHS MGos MREP SAPC SArc SEND WDin WPGP |
| | - 'Sopron' **new** | MBlu |
| § | ***texana*** | CDul CMCN EPfP SBir |
| | - 'New Madrid' | MBri |
| | ***trojana*** | CMCN SBir |
| | x ***turneri*** | CDoC CLnd CMCN CTho EPfP MBri SBLw WDin |
| | - 'Pseudoturneri' | see *Q.* x *hispanica* 'Pseudoturneri' |
| | ***variabilis*** | CMCN EPfP SBir |
| | ***velutina*** | CDul CLnd CMCN CPMA CTho EPfP IDee SBir WPGP |
| | - 'Albertsii' | MBlu |
| | - 'Oakridge Walker' **new** | MBri |
| | - 'Rubrifolia' | CMCN EPfP |
| | 'Vilmoriana' | GKir IArd |
| | ***virginiana*** | CDul CMCN |
| | x ***warburgii*** | EPfP |
| | x ***warei*** 'Windcandle' **new** | MBlu |
| | ***wislizeni*** | CBcs CDul CMCN EGFP SBir |
| § | ***wutaishanica*** | CDul CMCN |

## *Quillaja* (*Rosaceae*)

| | | |
|---|---|---|
| | ***saponaria*** | CArn CCCN CTrG |

## quince see *Cydonia oblonga*

## *Quisqualis* (*Combretaceae*)

| | | |
|---|---|---|
| | ***indica*** | CCCN SOWG |

# R

## *Rabdosia* see *Isodon*

## *Racosperma* see *Acacia*

## *Radermachera* (*Bignoniaceae*)

| | |
|---|---|
| ***sinica*** ♀H1 new | EShb |

## *Ramonda* (*Gesneriaceae*)

| | |
|---|---|
| § ***myconi*** ♀H4 | CLAP CPBP ECho EWes GEdr GKev ITim LLHF LSou NLAp NLar NMen NSla SChF SIng SRms WAbe |
| - var. ***alba*** | CLAP ECho MTho WKif WThu |
| - 'Jim's Shadow' | WAbe |
| - 'Rosea' | CLAP |
| ***nathaliae*** ♀H4 | CLAP CSec WAbe WThu |
| - 'Alba' | CLAP NSla |
| ***pyrenaica*** | see *R. myconi* |
| ***serbica*** | ECho WThu |

## *Randia* (*Rubiaceae*)

| | |
|---|---|
| ***formosa*** new | CCCN |

## *Ranunculus* ✿ (*Ranunculaceae*)

| | |
|---|---|
| ***abnormis*** | WAbe |
| ***aconitifolius*** | CSpe EBee ECha ECho GCra GKir GMaP NLar SHar SWat WHal WMnd WSHC |
| - 'Flore Pleno' (d) ♀H4 | Widely available |
| ***acris*** | CSec EBWF NBir NLan NPer |
| * - 'Citrinus' | CElw CEnt EGle MCot MHar MSte NCGa NRya SHar WHal WMoo WRha |
| - 'Cricket' (v) | WAlt |
| - 'Farrer's Yellow' | CRow |
| - 'Flore Pleno' (d) ♀H4 | CDes CElw CFee CFir CRow EBee ECha ECho EGle EHrv ELan EPPr EPfP GBuc GQue MCot MRav MSte NBid NBro NCGa NDov NGdn NRya NSti SPoG SRms WCAu WHil WMoo |
| - 'Hedgehog' | EBee ECho EPPr LSou NDov WPrP |
| - 'Stevenii' | CFee CRow EPPr IGor SDix WHal WSHC |
| - 'Sulphureus' | CBre EBee ECha WEas WFar WHal |
| ***alpestris*** | ECho GEdr NMen NRya |
| ***amplexicaulis*** | ERos GMaP NHar NMen WAbe |
| ***aquatilis*** | CWat EHon EMFW MSKA NSco SWat WPnP |
| x ***arendsii*** 'Moonlight' | CWsd SRot SUsu |
| ***asiaticus*** | EBrs WCot |
| ***baurii*** | ECho |
| ***bilobus*** | NMen |
| ***bulbosus*** | NSco |
| § - 'F.M. Burton' | EBee EGle EHrv NRya WCot |
| - ***farreri*** | see *R. bulbosus* 'F.M. Burton' |
| - 'Speciosus Plenus' | see *R. constantinopolitanus* 'Plenus' |
| ***calandrinioides*** ♀H2-3 | CBgR EBee ECho EWes NBir SIng WAbe WCot |
| - SF 137 | WCot |
| § ***constantinopolitanus*** 'Plenus' (d) | CElw CRow ECha MBri MLLN MRav NBid NBro NRya SUsu WCot WEas WFar WMoo |
| ***cortusifolius*** | SWat |
| ***crenatus*** | ECho GAuc GEdr NMen NRya WAbe |
| ***creticus*** | ECho SPoG |
| ***extorris*** 'Flore Pleno' | CDes |
| ***ficaria*** | CArn CNat CRow CTri EBWF GBar MHer MSal NChi NMir NSco WFar WHer WShi |
| - 'Aglow in the Dark' | CHid EBee |
| - var. ***albus*** | CHid CRow ELon EMon ERos LEdu NRya SIng SPoG WAlt WOut |
| - anemone-centred | see *R. ficaria* 'Collarette' |
| - 'Ashen Primrose' | CRow EBee |
| § - var. ***aurantiacus*** | CBgR CRow CStu ECha ECho EMon ERos MRav NLar NRya SIng SPhx SPoG SRms WAbe WFar WOut |
| - 'Bantam Egg' | CRow |
| - 'Blackadder' | CRow |
| - 'Bowles' Double' | see *R. ficaria* 'Double Bronze', 'Picton's Double' |
| - 'Brambling' | CBre CHid CLAP CRow ECho EMon LEdu MRav SBch SIng SSvw WAlt WPrP |
| - 'Brazen Child' | CRow EBee MDKP |
| - 'Brazen Daughter' | CRow |
| - 'Brazen Hussy' | Widely available |
| - 'Bregover White' | CRow |
| - 'Budgerigar' | CRow |
| - subsp. ***bulbilifer*** 'Chedglow' | CRow MDKP |
| - 'Bunch' (d) | CRow |
| - 'Cartwheel' (d) | CRow EBee |
| - 'Champernowne Giant' | CRow |
| - 'Chocolate Cream' | CRow |
| § - subsp. ***chrysocephalus*** | CRow ECha EMon NRya SBch SIng WCot WFar |
| - 'Clouded Yellow' (v) | CRow |
| - 'Coffee Cream' | CRow EBee |
| - 'Coker Cream' | CRow |
| § - 'Collarette' (d) | CHid CRow CStu EBee ECho ELon EMon EPot ERos GBar GBuc LEdu MAvo MTho NBir NMen NRya SIng SPoG WAbe WFar |
| - 'Coppernob' | CBre CHid CRow CWsd EBee ECha ECho ELon MAvo MDKP SBch SIng WCot WFar WOut WPnP |
| - 'Corinne Tremaine' | WHer |
| - 'Crawshay Cream' | CRow EBee |
| - 'Cupreus' | see *R. ficaria* var. *aurantiacus* |
| - 'Damerham' (d) | CHid CRow EMon |
| - 'Dappled Grey' | GKir WAlt |
| - 'Deborah Jope' | CRow SUsu |
| - 'Diane Rowe' | EMon |
| - 'Dimpsey' | CRow |
| § - 'Double Bronze' (d) | CBgR CHid CRow CStu EBee ECho EMon ERos GBuc LEdu MDKP MTho NBir NLar NRya SIng |
| - double cream-flowered | see *R. ficaria* 'Double Mud' |
| § - 'Double Mud' (d) | CBgR CBow CHid CLAP CRow CSpe CStu EMon ERos EWsh GBuc LEdu MTho NRya SIng SPoG WAbe WFar WHal WSHC |
| - double yellow-flowered | see *R. ficaria flore-pleno* |
| - double, green-eyed (d) | CHid CRow GKir LEdu |
| - 'Dusky Maiden' | CRow EMon NLar SBch SIng WFar |
| - 'E.A. Bowles' | see *R. ficaria* 'Collarette' |
| - 'Elan' (d) | CDes CRow EBee |
| - subsp. ***ficariiformis*** | EBee EMon |
| § - ***flore-pleno*** (d) | CBgR CFee CHid CRow CStu CTri EBee ECha ECho ELan ELon EMon EPPr ERos NRya NSti SBch SIng SRms WAbe WCot WFar |
| - 'Fried Egg' | CRow |
| - 'Granby Cream' | EMon |
| - 'Green Petal' | CHid CRow CStu EBee ECho EMon EPPr EPot GBuc GKir LEdu MDKP MHer MTho NBir NLar NRya SIng SPhx WHal WHer WOut |

| | | |
|---|---|---|
| | - 'Greencourt Gold' (d) | CRow |
| | - 'Holly' | see *R. ficaria* 'Holly Green' |
| | - 'Holly Bronze' | CRow |
| § | - 'Holly Green' | CRow ECho |
| | - 'Hoskin's Miniature' | CRow |
| | - 'Hoskin's Variegated' (v) | CRow |
| | - 'Hyde Hall' | EMon NLar SBch SIng WFar WPrP |
| | - 'Jake Perry' | CDes CHid EBee |
| | - 'Jane's Dress' | CHid CRow |
| | - 'Ken Aslet Double' (d) | CDes CRow EBee EMon LEdu WHal WOut |
| | - 'Lambrook Black' | WHer |
| | - 'Lambrook Variegated' (v) **new** | EMon |
| | - 'Laysh On' (d) | CRow |
| | - 'Lemon Queen' | CHid |
| | - 'Leo' | EMon MDKP |
| | - 'Limelight' | CRow |
| | - 'Little Southey' | CRow |
| | - subsp. ***major*** | see *R. ficaria* subsp. *chrysocephalus* |
| | - 'Melanie Jope' **new** | EBee |
| | - 'Mimsey' (d) | CRow EBee |
| | - 'Mobled Jade' | CHid CRow EBee |
| | - 'Mud' | MDKP |
| | - 'Newton Abbot' | CBre CRow |
| I | - 'Nigrifolia' | EBee MDKP |
| | - 'Oakenden Cream' | CRow |
| | - 'Old Master' | CBow EBee MAvo NCGa WCot |
| | - 'Orange Sorbet' | CRow EBee EMon LEdu NLar |
| § | - 'Picton's Double' (d) | CRow CStu GBar MTho NRya WAbe |
| | - 'Primrose' | CHid CRow EMon MTho NLar NRya SIng |
| | - 'Primrose Brassy' | EMon |
| | - 'Primrose Elf' | CRow EBee |
| | - 'Quantock Brown' | CBgR |
| | - 'Quillet' (d) | CRow EMon |
| | - 'Ragamuffin' (d) | CDes CRow EBee EMon LEdu WPrP |
| | - 'Randall's White' | CBgR CRow CSWP CStu EBee MRav MTho SHar WFar WPtf WSHC |
| | - 'Rowden Magna' | CRow |
| | - 'Salad Bowl' (d) | CRow |
| | - 'Salmon's White' | CBre CRow EBee ECho ELan EPPr MRav NBir NCGa NLar NRya SIng WFar WHal WHer WHrl WPtf |
| | - 'Samidor' | CRow |
| | - 'Sheldon' | CRow |
| | - 'Sheldon Silver' | CHid CRow |
| | - 'Silver Collar' | EMon LEdu |
| | - 'Single Cream' | EMon |
| | - 'Snow Bunting' **new** | EMon |
| | - 'Suffusion' | CRow |
| | - 'Sutherland's Double' (d) | CRow |
| | - 'Sweet Chocolate' | CRow |
| | - 'Torquay Elf' | CRow EBee |
| | - 'Tortoiseshell' | CHid CRow EBee EMon MAvo MDKP WFar WPtf |
| | - 'Trenwheal' (d) | CRow |
| | - 'Tubby' **new** | WAlt |
| | - 'Undercurrent' (v) | WAlt |
| | - 'Winkworth' | EMon |
| | - 'Wisley Double' | see *R. ficaria* 'Double Bronze' |
| | - 'Wisley White' | NSti |
| | - 'Witchampton' | CDes |
| | - 'Yaffle' | CBre CHid CRow EBee EMon MDKP MRav SIng |
| | ***flammula*** | CBen CDWL CRow CWat EBWF EHon EMFW LPBA MSKA NSco SWat WPnP |
| | - subsp. ***minimus*** | CRow |
| | ***gouanii*** | NRya |
| | ***gramineus*** ♀H4 | CSec CWCL CWsd EBee ECho EDAr EPot ERos GBuc GKir GMaP LBee LRHS MNrw MTho MWat NMen NRya SPhx SPoG SRms SUsu WCAu WFar WHil WPer |
| | - 'Pardal' | CWsd SCnR WFar |
| * | ***guttatus*** | NMen |
| | ***illyricus*** | CDes EBee ECha EDAr EPPr NRya WHal |
| | ***kochii*** | EBee ECho EPot |
| | ***lanuginosus*** | EPPr |
| | ***lingua*** | CFir COld EBWF EMFW MCCP NSco SPlb WSFF |
| | - 'Grandiflorus' | CBen CRow EHon LPBA MMuc MSKA NPer SWat WHal WMAq WPnP |
| | ***lyallii*** | GGar WAbe |
| | ***macrophyllus*** | CSec |
| | ***millefoliatus*** | EBee ECho ERos GBuc MTho NMen WPGP |
| | ***montanus*** double-flowered (d) | EBee EBrs SHar WCot |
| | - 'Molten Gold' ♀H4 | CStu ECho ECtt GMaP MRav MTho NRya WAbe |
| | ***nivicola*** | NWCA |
| | ***parnassiifolius*** | NMen WAbe |
| | ***platanifolius*** | EBrs SMHy SPhx |
| | ***pyrenaeus*** | NMen |
| | ***repens*** 'Boraston O.S.' (v) | WCHb |
| | - 'Broken Egg' (v) | WAlt |
| | - 'Buttered Popcorn' (v) | CBow CRow EBee NLar WMoo |
| | - 'Cat's Eyes' (v) | CDes EBee MAvo WAlt |
| | - 'Creeping Beauty' | WAlt |
| | - 'Dinah Myte' (v) | WAlt |
| | - 'Gloria Spale' | CBre CRow WAlt |
| | - 'In Vein' (v) | WAlt |
| | - 'Joe's Golden' | WAlt |
| | - 'Orkney Chocolate' **new** | WAlt |
| | - 'Orkney Lemon' **new** | WAlt |
| | - var. ***pleniflorus*** (d) | CBre CRow EBee GGar SPhx WAlt WEas WFar |
| | - semi-double (d) | WAlt |
| | - 'Snowdrift' (v) | EMon EPPr LEdu WAlt WCot |
| | - 'Time Bomb' (v) | WAlt |
| | - 'Timothy Clark' (d) | CBre EMon WAlt WSHC |
| | ***sardous*** **new** | EBWF |
| | ***sceleratus*** | EBWF WHer |
| | ***seguieri*** | WAbe |
| | ***serbicus*** | EPPr |
| | ***speciosus*** 'Flore Pleno' | see *R. constantinopolitanus* 'Plenus' |

## *Ranzania* (*Berberidaceae*)

| | | |
|---|---|---|
| | ***japonica*** | WCru |

## *Raoulia* (*Asteraceae*)

| | | |
|---|---|---|
| | ***australis*** misapplied | see *R. hookeri* |
| | ***australis*** Hook.f. ex Raoul | EDAr GEdr GKir ITim MBar MWat NRya NWCA SIng WHoo |
| § | - Lutescens Group | ECha ECho EPot |
| | ***haastii*** | ECho ECou ITim |
| § | ***hookeri*** | ECha ECho ECou EDAr GEdr ITim MWat NWCA SPlb SRms WAbe WFar WPat |
| | - var. ***laxa*** | EWes |
| | x ***loganii*** | see x *Leucoraoulia loganii* |
| | ***lutescens*** | see *R. australis* Lutescens Group |
| | ***monroi*** | ITim |
| | ***petriensis*** | ECho |
| | ***subsericea*** | ECho ECou EWes NMen NWCA |
| | ***tenuicaulis*** | ECha ECou SPlb |

## *Raoulia* x *Leucoraoulia* see x *Leucoraoulia*

## raspberry see *Rubus idaeus*

## *Ratibida* (*Asteraceae*)

| | |
|---|---|
| ***columnifera*** | CMea CRWN EBee EPfP LRHS LSou MSCN NBre SPav SPet |
| - 'Cheyenne Yellow' | EBrs |
| - f. ***pulcherrima*** | CMea CSpe EBee LHop LSou NBre SPav SPet WCAu |
| - red-flowered | SPav |
| - 'Red Midget' | EBrs SPav SUsu |
| ***pinnata*** | CEnt CRWN CSam CSec EBee LSRN MSCN NBre SMad SMrs SPav SPet SPhx SPlb WCAu WHal WMnd |
| ***tagetes*** | SPav |

## *Ravenala* (*Strelitziaceae*)

| | |
|---|---|
| ***madagascariensis*** | EAmu LPal MJnS XBlo |

## *Ravenea* (*Arecaceae*)

| | |
|---|---|
| ***rivularis*** | CCCN EAmu LPal XBlo |

## *Rechsteineria* see *Sinningia*

## redcurrant see *Ribes rubrum* (R)

## *Rehderodendron* (*Styracaceae*)

| | |
|---|---|
| ***macrocarpum*** | CBcs CTrG |

## *Rehmannia* (*Scrophulariaceae*)

| | |
|---|---|
| ***angulata*** misapplied | see *R. elata* |
| § ***elata*** ♀H2 | Widely availablet |
| - 'White Dragon' | CSpe LPio |
| ***glutinosa*** ♀H3 | EWTr |

## *Reineckea* (*Convallariaceae*)

| | |
|---|---|
| § ***carnea*** | CDes CFee CHid CPLG CStu EBee ECha ELan EPPr EPla ERos GEdr GGar LEdu MAvo MHar NSti SDys SPlb SUsu WCru WPGP WPtf WTin |
| - B&SWJ 4808 | WCru |
| - SDR 330 | GKev |
| - 'Variegata' (v) | WCot WCru |
| aff. ***carnea*** BWJ 8096 from Sichuan **new** | WCru |

## *Reinwardtia* (*Linaceae*)

| | |
|---|---|
| § ***indica*** | CCCN CHll CPLG EShb SAdn SMrm |
| ***trigyna*** | see *R. indica* |

## *Remusatia* (*Araceae*)

| | |
|---|---|
| ***hookeriana*** | CKob EAmu |
| ***pumila*** | CKob EAmu EUJe |
| ***vivipara*** | CKob EUJe |

## *Reseda* (*Resedaceae*)

| | |
|---|---|
| ***alba*** | MHer |
| ***lutea*** | CBod MSal SECG SIde |
| ***luteola*** | CHby EBWF GBar GPoy MHer MSal NSco SECG WCHb WHer WLHH WSFF |

## *Restio* (*Restionaceae*)

| | |
|---|---|
| ***brunneus*** | EBee WPGP |
| ***dispar*** **new** | CTrC |
| ***festuciformis*** | EAmu EHoe |
| ***quadratus*** | WPGP |
| ***subverticillatus*** | see *Ischyrolepis subverticillata* |
| ***tetraphyllus*** | CBcs CBct CFir CPen CTrC EBee EHoe GCal LAst LHop WCot WDyG WPGP |

## *Retama* (*Papilionaceae*)

| | |
|---|---|
| § ***monosperma*** | EShb |

## *Reynoutria* see *Fallopia*

## *Rhamnella* (*Rhamnaceae*)

| | |
|---|---|
| ***franguloides*** | CMCN |

## *Rhamnus* (*Rhamnaceae*)

| | |
|---|---|
| ***alaternus*** var. ***angustifolia*** | WFar WPGP |
| § - 'Argenteovariegata' (v) ♀H4 | Widely available |
| - 'Variegata' | see *R. alaternus* 'Argenteovariegata' |
| ***californica*** | NLar |
| ***cathartica*** | CCVT CDul CLnd CTri ECrN EMac EPfP LBuc NLar NWea WDin WMou WSFF |
| ***frangula*** | see *Frangula alnus* |
| ***imeretina*** | CGHE WPGP |
| ***pallasii*** | NLar |
| ***pumila*** | NLar |
| ***purshiana*** | MSal |
| ***taquetii*** | NLar |

## *Rhaphiolepis* (*Rosaceae*)

| | |
|---|---|
| x ***delacourii*** | CMHG CMac CWSG CWib EBee ELan EPfP LRHS MBri MWea SRms WBod WHCG WPic |
| - 'Coates' Crimson' | CDoC EBee ELan EMil EPfP LAst LHop MBri SHBN SLon SOWG WPat WSHC |
| - Enchantress = 'Moness' | CMHG CSam CTsd EBee ELan EPfP ERas LRHS |
| - 'Pink Cloud' **new** | MBri |
| - 'Spring Song' | SLon |
| ***indica*** | ERom |
| - B&SWJ 8405 | WCru |
| - 'Coppertone' | EMil LRHS |
| - Springtime = 'Monme' | SEND SPer WDin |
| ***umbellata*** ♀H2-3 | CBcs CHEx CSam CTri CWib EBee ELan EPfP GKir LAst LHop LRHS MBri MRav SEND SLon SOWG WFar WHCG WPat WSHC |
| - f. ***ovata*** B&SWJ 4706 | WCru |

## *Rhaphithamnus* (*Verbenaceae*)

| | |
|---|---|
| ***cyanocarpus*** | see *R. spinosus* |
| § ***spinosus*** | EBee EPfP GBin GGar GKir IArd IDee MBri WBod |

## *Rhapidophyllum* (*Arecaceae*)

| | |
|---|---|
| ***hystrix*** | CBrP LPal NPal WCot |

## *Rhapis* ✿ (*Arecaceae*)

| | |
|---|---|
| § ***excelsa*** ♀H1 | EAmu LPal NPal XBlo |
| ***multifida*** | LPal |

## *Rhazya* (*Apocynaceae*)

| | |
|---|---|
| ***orientalis*** | see *Amsonia orientalis* |

## *Rheum* ✿ (*Polygonaceae*)

| | |
|---|---|
| CC 4612 | WCot |
| CC 4613 | WCot |
| CC 4768 | WCot |
| CC 4845 | WCot |
| CC 5243 **new** | EWld |
| GWJ 9329 from Sikkim | WCru |
| HWJK 2354 from Nepal **new** | WCru |
| § 'Ace of Hearts' | Widely available |
| 'Ace of Spades' | see *R.* 'Ace of Hearts' |
| ***acuminatum*** | EBee WPGP |
| - HWJCM 252 | WCru |
| ***alexandrae*** | CFir EBee EWes GCal GCra LPio NChi WCot |

| | |
|---|---|
| - BWJ 7670 | WCru |
| - SDR 2924 | GKev |
| - SDR 4602 **new** | GKev |
| - SDR 4757 **new** | GKev |
| ***altaicum*** | LEdu |
| 'Andrew's Red' | GTwe |
| § ***australe*** | CAgr CArn CFir CRow EBee GCal LEdu LPBA LPio LRHS MLLN NBro NLar WCot WFar WHoo WMnd |
| N x ***cultorum*** | see *R.* x *hybridum* |
| ***delavayi*** | EBee GCal GKev |
| - BWJ 7592 | WCru |
| ***emodi*** | see *R. australe* |
| ***forrestii*** | GAuc |
| § x ***hybridum*** | SEND |
| - 'Appleton's Forcing' | GTwe |
| - 'Baker's All Season' | GTwe |
| - 'Brandy Carr Scarlet' | NGHP |
| - 'Canada Red' | GTwe |
| - 'Cawood Delight' | GKir GTwe LRHS MMuc NGHP SEND |
| - 'Champagne' | CAgr EMil GTwe |
| - 'Daw's Champion' | GTwe |
| - 'Early Cherry' | GTwe |
| - 'Fenton's Special' | CTri GTwe MCoo NGHP |
| - 'Glaskin's Perpetual' | CAgr CWib LBuc MAsh |
| - 'Grandad's Favorite' 🏆$^{H4}$ | EBrs |
| - 'Greengage' | GTwe |
| - 'Hadspen Crimson' | CBct WCot |
| - 'Hammond's Early' | GTwe SEND |
| - 'Harbinger' | GTwe |
| - 'Hawke's Champagne' 🏆$^{H4}$ | GTwe |
| - 'Holsteiner Blut' | ECho |
| - 'Livingstone'$^{PBR}$ | EPfP LRHS |
| - 'Mac Red' 🏆$^{H4}$ | GTwe |
| - 'Prince Albert' | GTwe NGHP |
| - 'Red Champagne' | NGHP |
| - 'Red Prolific' | GTwe |
| - 'Reed's Early Superb' 🏆$^{H4}$ | GTwe |
| - 'Stein's Champagne' 🏆$^{H4}$ | GTwe |
| - 'Stockbridge Arrow' | CSut CTri GTwe NGHP |
| - 'Stockbridge Bingo' | GTwe |
| - 'Stockbridge Emerald' | GTwe |
| - 'Stockbridge Guardsman' | GTwe |
| - 'Strawberry' | EMil EMui GTwe NBir |
| - 'Strawberry Red' | LRHS |
| - 'Strawberry Surprise' | GTwe |
| - 'Sutton's Cherry Red' | GTwe |
| - 'The Sutton' | CWib GTwe |
| - 'Timperley Early' 🏆$^{H4}$ | CDoC CMac CSBt CTri CWib EMui EPfP GKir GTwe LRHS MAsh MGos MMuc NBlu NGHP NPri SCoo SDea SKee SPer SPoG |
| - 'Tingley Cherry' | GTwe |
| - 'Valentine' | MAsh |
| - 'Victoria' | CAgr CDoC CTri CWib ELau GTwe LBuc LRHS MAsh MCoo MHer MMuc MNHC NGHP SPoG SVic WHar |
| - 'Zwolle Seedling' | GTwe |
| ***kialense*** | CBct CDes GCal NBid NSti WPGP WPnP |
| ***moorcroftianum*** | EBee |
| ***nobile*** | EBee |
| - SDR 4750 **new** | GKev |
| ***officinale*** | CArn CBct CHEx GCal LRHS MBri SIde SWat |
| ***palmatum*** | CArn CBcs CDWL CSec CWat EBee ECha ELan EMFW EPfP GCra GMaP LAst LPBA LRHS MCot MNHC MRav MSal NGdn SPer SWat WCAu WFar |
| - 'Atropurpureum' | see *R. palmatum* 'Atrosanguineum' |
| § - 'Atrosanguineum' 🏆$^{H4}$ | CBct CMea CRow EBee ECha ELan EPfP EPla GBuc GCal GKir IFro LBMP LPBA LRHS MBri MMuc MRav NBid NBro SPer SPlb SPoG SWat WCot WCru WMnd |
| - 'Bowles' Crimson' | CBct GKir LBuc MBri NBid |
| - 'Red Herald' | CBct GKir LBuc WCot |
| - 'Rubrum' | EBee GKir LRHS MCCP NBir NCGa NChi NHol WFar |
| - 'Savill' | GKir LBuc LRHS MBri MRav |
| - var. ***tanguticum*** | Widely available |
| - - 'Rosa Auslese' | WHil |
| ***rhaponticum*** | NLar |
| ***ribes*** | EBee GBin WCot |
| ***subacaule*** | NLar |
| ***tataricum*** | EBee LEdu |

## *Rhinanthus* (*Scrophulariaceae*)

| | |
|---|---|
| ***minor*** | CSec NSco |

## *Rhodanthe* (*Asteraceae*)

| | |
|---|---|
| § ***anthemoides*** | ECou SEND |
| § - 'Paper Cascade' | LRHS |
| ***charsleyae*** **new** | CSec |
| § ***chlorocephala*** subsp. ***rosea*** 'Blanche' **new** | CSec |

## *Rhodanthemum* (*Asteraceae*)

| | |
|---|---|
| from High Atlas, Morocco | SIng |
| 'African Eyes' | EBee ECho EPfP GGar LBuc LRHS MGos NBhm NPri SPoG SRot SUsu |
| § ***atlanticum*** | ECho EWes |
| § ***catananche*** | CCCN CPBP ECho EWes LSou MBNS SRot |
| § - 'Tizi-n-Test' | ECho LRHS WKif |
| - 'Tizi-n-Tichka' | CPBP ECho EWes LRHS SUsu |
| § ***gayanum*** | CCCN EBee ECho EShb EWes LRHS WCot |
| - 'Flamingo' | see *R. gayanum* |
| § ***hosmariense*** 🏆$^{H4}$ | Widely available |

## *Rhodiola* (*Crassulaceae*)

| | |
|---|---|
| SDR 4759 **new** | GKev |
| SDR 4909 **new** | GKev |
| ***amablis*** **new** | GAuc |
| ***bupleuroides*** CLD 1196 | EMon |
| ***crassipes*** | see *R. wallichiana* |
| ***cretinii*** HWJK 2283 | WCru |
| § ***fastigiata*** | EBee EMon GCal GKev NMen NWCA |
| § ***heterodonta*** | CSam ECha EGle ELan EMon MRav WCot |
| ***himalensis*** misapplied | see *R.* 'Keston' |
| ***himalensis*** (D. Don) Fu | CTri EBee EMon GKev |
| - HWJK 2258 | WCru |
| § ***ishidae*** | CTri |
| § 'Keston' | CTri |
| § ***kirilovii*** | EMon |
| - var. ***rubra*** | WFar |
| ***linearifolia*** | EMon |
| § ***pachyclados*** | EAlp EBur ECho ECtt EDAr GKir GMaP LBee MBar MHer NBir NHol NRya SEND SPlb SRot WAbe WEas WFar WHoo WPer |
| aff. ***purpureoviridis*** | WFar |
| - BWJ 7544 | WCru |
| § ***rosea*** | Widely available |
| ***semenovii*** | EBee MHar NLar |
| ***sinuata*** HWJK 2318 | WCru |
| - HWJK 2326 | WCru |
| § ***trollii*** | WAbe |

| | | |
|---|---|---|
| § | ***wallichiana*** | EMon MLHP NBid WCot |
| | - GWJ 9263 | WCru |
| | - HWJK 2352 | WCru |

## *Rhodochiton* (*Scrophulariaceae*)

| | | |
|---|---|---|
| § | ***atrosanguineus*** ♀H1-2 | CBcs CCCN CEnd CHEx CSec CSpe ELan EPfP ERas EShb GGar GKev ITim LRHS MAsh SGar SOWG SPer SPoG WBor |
| | ***volubilis*** | see *R. atrosanguineus* |

## *Rhodocoma* (*Restionaceae*)

| | | |
|---|---|---|
| | ***arida*** | CBct CCCN WPGP |
| | ***capensis*** | CAbb CBcs CBct CCCN CFir CPen CSpe CTrC CTsd EAmu EBee WPGP |
| | ***fruticosa*** | CTrC |
| | ***gigantea*** | CBcs CCCN CPen CTrC EBee ESwi WPGP |

## *Rhododendron* ✿ (*Ericaceae*)

| | | |
|---|---|---|
| | FH134 | SLdr |
| | SDR 1804 | GKev |
| | SDR 1815 **new** | GKev |
| | SDR 1883 | GKev |
| | 'A. Gilbert' | SHea |
| | 'A.J. Ivens' | see *R.* 'Arthur J. Ivens' |
| | 'Abegail' | MGos SLdr |
| | 'Abendsonne' **new** | MDun |
| | ***aberconwayi*** | LMil SLdr SReu WBod |
| | - 'His Lordship' | GGGa LHyd LMil WBod |
| | ***acrophilum*** (V) Argent 2768 | GGGa |
| | 'Ada Brunieres' (K) | CSdC |
| | 'Addy Wery' (EA) ♀H3-4 | CDoC ECho MBar MGos SLdr SPoG |
| | ***adenogynum*** | GGGa LMil SLdr |
| | - Cox 6502 | GGGa |
| § | - Adenophorum Group | EMui |
| | - - F 20444 | SLdr |
| | ***adenophorum*** | see *R. adenogynum* Adenophorum Group |
| | ***adenopodum*** | GGGa SLdr |
| | ***adenosum*** | NHol |
| | - R 18228 | GGGa |
| | 'Admiral Piet Hein' | SReu |
| | 'Adonis' (EA/d) | CMac EMil LMil LRHS MBar NLar NMun SLdr |
| | 'Adriaan Koster' (M) | SLdr |
| | 'Adriaan Koster' (hybrid) | SHea |
| | 'Advance' (O) | SLdr |
| | ***aeruginosum*** | see *R. campanulatum* subsp. *aeruginosum* |
| | ***aganniphum*** | GGGa LMil |
| § | - var. ***aganniphum*** Doshongense Group | GGGa |
| | - - - KR 4979 | LMil |
| | - - Glaucopeplum Group | GGGa |
| | - - Schizopeplum Group | GGGa |
| | - var. ***flavorufum*** | GGGa MDun |
| | - - EGM 160 | LMil |
| | - pink-flowered, KR 3528 from Pe, Doshang La | LMil |
| | x ***agastum*** PW 98 | LMil |
| | 'Ahren's Favourite' | MAsh |
| | 'Aida' (R/d) | CSBt SReu |
| | 'Aksel Olsen' | CTri GEdr GKir LRHS MAsh MBar MDun |
| | 'Aladdin' (EA) | ECho SLdr WBod WBrE WFar |
| | Aladdin Group | SReu |
| | 'Aladdin' (*auriculatum* hybrid) | GGGa |
| | 'Albatross' **new** | LHyd |
| | Albatross Group | IDee LMil SLdr SReu |
| | 'Albatross Townhill Pink' | LMil |
| | 'Albert Schweitzer' ♀H4 | CDoC CWri EMil GGGa GKir LMil MBar MDun SLdr SPoG WBod WFar |
| | ***albrechtii*** (A) | GGGa LMil SReu |
| | - Whitney form (A) | LMil |
| | 'Alena' | GGGa LMil |
| | 'Alex Hill' | CBcs |
| | 'Alexander' (EA) ♀H4 | LMil LRHS LSRN MAsh MGos SHBN SReu |
| | 'Alfred' | CWri LMil LRHS MAsh NMun |
| | 'Alice' (EA) | LHyd SLdr |
| | 'Alice' (hybrid) ♀H4 | CSBt LHyd LMil SHea SLdr SReu |
| | 'Alice de Stuers' (M) | SLdr |
| | Alison Johnstone Group | CBcs GGGa GGar MDun SLdr SReu WPic |
| | 'Aloha' | MBar NDlv SHBN |
| | Alpine Gem Group | GQui SLdr |
| | 'Alpine Gem' | LHyd |
| | ***alutaceum*** var. ***alutaceum*** | GGGa |
| § | - - Globigerum Group R 11100 | GGGa |
| § | - var. ***iodes*** | GGGa |
| § | - var. ***russotinctum*** | GGGa MDun |
| | - - R 158 | SLdr |
| § | - - Triplonaevium Group USDAPI 59442/R10923 | GGGa |
| | ***amagianum*** (A) | GGGa LMil |
| | ***ambiguum*** | LMil SLdr SReu WBod |
| I | - 'Crosswater' | LMil |
| | - dwarf | CBcs |
| | - 'Golden Summit' | GGGa |
| | - 'Jane Banks' | LMil |
| | 'Ambrosia' (EA) | CSBt |
| | 'America' | CBcs MAsh MBar MDun SHea WFar |
| | 'Amity' | CSBt CWri ECho LMil MAsh MBri MLea SLdr WFar WGwG |
| § | 'Amoenum' (EA/d) | CBcs CDoC CMac CSBt CTrG ECho LHyd LMil MBar MGos SLdr SPer WBod WFar WPic |
| | 'Amoenum Coccineum' (EA/d) | GKev SReu |
| | Amor Group | LHyd SHea |
| | 'Amoretto' **new** | MDun |
| | 'Anah Kruschke' | GGGa LCro MAsh SLdr SPoG |
| | 'Analin' | see *R.* 'Anuschka' |
| | 'Anchorite' (EA) | LMil SLdr |
| * | 'Andrae' | SReu |
| | 'Angelo' | LHyd LMil |
| | Angelo Group | CWri LHyd LMil SLdr SReu |
| | Anita Group | SHea |
| | 'Anita Dunstan' | MLea |
| | 'Ann Aberconway' **new** | WBod |
| | 'Ann Callingham' (K) | CSdC |
| | 'Ann Lindsay' | NLar SReu |
| | 'Anna Baldsiefen' | ELon LMil MGos NLar SPoG SReu WBVN WBod |
| | 'Anna H. Hall' | MAsh |
| | 'Anna Rose Whitney' | CBcs CTri CWri GKir LHyd LPan LRHS MAsh MBar MDun MGos NPri SHBN |
| | 'Annabella' (K) ♀H4 | CSdC LMil MDun SLdr |
| | ***annae*** | GGGa LMil |
| | aff. ***annae*** C&H 7185 | LMil |
| | 'Anne Frank' (EA) | MGos WBod WFar |
| | 'Anne George' | LHyd |
| | 'Anne Teese' | GGGa IDee LMil SLdr |
| | 'Annegret Hansmann' | GGGa |
| | 'Anneke' (A) | LMil MBar MDun SLdr SReu SSta WBod WFar |
| | 'Anouk' (EA) **new** | NMun |
| | ***anthopogon*** | LMil |
| | - 'Betty Graham' | GGGa |
| I | - 'Crosswater' | LMil |

| | | |
|---|---|---|
| | - subsp. ***hypenanthum*** | LMil MDun |
| | - - 'Annapurna' | GGGa WAbe |
| § | ***anthosphaerum*** | GGGa SLdr SReu |
| | 'Antilope' (Vs) | CWri ECho ISea LMil MDun MGos MLea NHol NLar SLdr SPer SReu SSta WBVN |
| | 'Antonio' | LMil |
| § | 'Anuschka' | EMil GKir LMil LRHS MAsh MDun MMuc |
| § | ***anwheiense*** | CWri LHyd LMil SHea |
| | ***aperantum*** F 27022 | GGGa |
| | ***apodectum*** | see *R. dichroanthum* subsp. *apodectum* |
| | 'Apotrophia' | SLdr |
| N | 'Appleblossom' (EA) | see *R.* 'Ho-o' |
| | 'Apple Blossom' ambig. | CMac |
| | 'Apple Blossom' Wezelenburg (M) | NBlu NHol SLdr |
| | 'Apricot Blaze' (A) | MDun NHol |
| | 'Apricot Fantasy' | LMil MDun |
| | 'Apricot Surprise' | CTri LMil LRHS MAsh |
| | 'Apricot Top Garden' | SLdr |
| | 'April Dawn' | GGGa |
| | 'April Glow' | LHyd |
| | 'April Showers' (A) | LMil |
| I | 'Arabella' | MAsh |
| | 'Arabesk' (EA) | EMil MBri SLdr WFar |
| | ***araiophyllum*** KR 4029 | LMil |
| | ***arborescens*** (A) | GGGa LMil SLdr |
| | - pink-flowered (A) | LMil |
| | ***arboreum*** | CDoC CHEx CWri GGGa LMil LRHS MDun SLdr SReu WPic |
| | - B&SWJ 2244 | WCru |
| | - 'Blood Red' | SLdr |
| | - subsp. ***cinnamomeum*** | CDoC GGGa GGar IDee LMil SLdr SReu |
| | - - var. ***album*** | LHyd SLdr SReu |
| | - - var. ***cinnamomeum*** Campbelliae Group | NLar SLdr |
| | - - var. ***roseum*** | GGGa |
| * | - - - ***crispum*** | SLdr |
| | - - - 'Tony Schilling' | LHyd LMil SLdr SReu |
| | - subsp. ***delavayi*** | GGGa LMil SLdr |
| | - - C&H 7178 | GGGa |
| | - - EGM 360 | LMil |
| | - 'Heligan' | CWri SReu |
| | - mid-pink-flowered | SLdr |
| § | - subsp. ***nilagiricum*** | GGGa SLdr |
| | - var. ***roseum*** | SHea SLdr |
| § | - subsp. ***zeylanicum*** | SLdr |
| | ***arboreum*** x ***grande*** | SLdr |
| | 'Arctic Fox' (EA) | GGGa |
| § | 'Arctic Glow' | GKir |
| | 'Arctic Regent' (K) | CSdC GQui SLdr |
| | 'Arctic Tern' | see x *Ledodendron* 'Arctic Tern' |
| § | ***argipeplum*** | GGGa SLdr |
| | 'Argosy' ♀H4 | LMil SLdr SReu |
| | ***argyrophyllum*** | CWri GKir SLdr |
| | - subsp. ***argyrophyllum*** | SLdr |
| | - - W/A 1210 | SLdr |
| § | - subsp. ***hypoglaucum*** | GGGa |
| | - - JN **new** | GGGa |
| § | - - 'Heane Wood' | GGGa |
| | - subsp. ***nankingense*** | GGGa LMil |
| | - - 'Chinese Silver' ♀H4 | CDoC IDee LHyd LMil MDun SReu |
| § | ***arizelum*** | CDoC GGGa GKir LMil LRHS MDun SLdr |
| | - BASEX 9580 | GGGa |
| | - R 25 | GGGa |
| | - subsp. ***arizelum*** Rubicosum Group | LMil MDun |
| | ***armitii*** (V) Woods 2518 | GGGa |

| | | |
|---|---|---|
| | 'Arneson Gem' (M) | CBcs CDoC CSam GGGa ISea LMil LRHS MAsh NLar SLdr |
| | 'Arneson Pink' | ISea NLar |
| | 'Arpege' (Vs) | LMil MDun NLar SReu |
| | 'Arthur Bedford' | CBcs CSBt SLdr SReu |
| § | 'Arthur J. Ivens' | SLdr |
| | 'Arthur Osborn' | GGGa SSpi |
| | 'Arthur Stevens' | SLdr |
| | 'Asa-gasumi' (EA) | LHyd SLdr |
| | 'Ascot Brilliant' | SLdr |
| | ***asterochnoum*** | LMil |
| | - C&H 7051 | GGGa |
| | - EGM 314 | LMil |
| | Asteroid Group | SLdr |
| | 'Astrid' | CDoC LMil LSRN |
| | ***atlanticum*** (A) | GGGa GKev LMil |
| | - 'Seaboard' (A) | IDee LMil SLdr |
| | ***atlanticum*** x ***canescens*** | GKev |
| | Augfast Group | ISea SLdr WBod |
| | 'August Lamken' | MDun |
| | ***augustinii*** | CTrG CWri GGGa LHyd LMil MLea SLdr SSpi SSta WBod |
| | - subsp. ***augustinii*** C&H 7048 | GGGa |
| § | - subsp. ***chasmanthum*** | GGGa LMil MDun WBod |
| | - - white-flowered C&Cu 9407 | GGGa |
| | - compact EGM 293 | LMil |
| § | - Electra Group | CDoC GGGa IDee LHyd LMil MDun SLdr SPer |
| | - Exbury best form | LHyd LMil MDun SReu |
| § | - subsp. ***hardyi*** | GGGa |
| | - pale lilac-flowered | SLdr |
| | - 'Picton Blue' | WPic |
| § | - subsp. ***rubrum*** | GGGa |
| * | - 'Trewithen' | LMil |
| I | - 'Werrington' | SLdr SReu |
| | - white-flowered **new** | LHyd |
| § | ***aureum*** | GGGa LMil SLdr |
| | ***auriculatum*** | CBcs GGGa GKir IDee LHyd LMil MDun NLar SLdr SReu SSpi SSta WBVN |
| | - PW 50 | GGGa |
| | - Reuthe's form | SReu |
| | ***auriculatum*** x ***hemsleyanum*** | GGGa |
| | ***auritum*** | GGGa SLdr WPic |
| | 'Aurora' (K) | SLdr |
| | 'Aurore de Royghem' | SLdr |
| | ***austrinum*** (A) | IDee LMil |
| | - yellow-flowered (A) | LMil |
| | 'Autumn Glow' (EA) | LMil |
| | 'Autumn Gold' | SLdr |
| | 'Avalanche' ♀H4 | LMil SLdr SReu |
| | Avocet Group | LMil SLdr |
| | 'Award' | LMil |
| | 'Aya-kammuri' (EA) | LHyd SLdr |
| | Azamia Group | LHyd |
| | Azor Group | LHyd SHea SReu |
| | Azrie Group | SLdr |
| § | 'Azuma-kagami' (EA) | ISea LCro LHyd LMil SLdr WBod WFar |
| | 'Azurika' | SPoG |
| | 'Azurro' | CDoC GGGa LMil NLar |
| | 'Azurwolke' | LMil |
| | 'B. de Bruin' | SHea |
| | 'Babette' | see *R.* (Volker Group) 'Babette' |
| | 'Babuschka' | LMil |
| | 'Bad Eilsen' | MAsh |
| | 'Baden-Baden' | CTri ECho GEdr GKir LHyd MAsh MBar MDun MGos NHol NMun SHBN SLdr SPoG WBod WFar |

| | |
|---|---|
| 'Bagshot Ruby' | SHea SLdr SReu |
| ***baileyi*** | GGGa SLdr |
| ***bainbridgeanum*** | LMil SLdr |
| * 'Baker's Lavender' (EA) **new** | CTrh |
| 'Balalaika' | MDun NLar |
| ***balangense*** EN 3530 | GGGa |
| ***balfourianum*** | GGGa SLdr |
| 'Balsaminiflorum' | see *R. indicum* 'Balsaminiflorum' |
| 'Baltic Amber' (A) | GGGa |
| 'Balzac' (K) | CDoC CSam ECho LMil MAsh MGos MLea SLdr SPer SPur WBVN |
| 'Bambi' | SLdr SReu |
| 'Bandoola' | SReu |
| 'Barbara Coates' (EA) | SLdr |
| 'Barbarella' **new** | MDun |
| ***barbatum*** | CDoC CHEx CWri GGGa GGar IDee LHyd LMil MDun SLdr WPic |
| - B&SWJ 2237 | WCru |
| - B&SWJ 2624 **new** | WCru |
| 'Barbecue' (K) | LMil |
| Barclayi Group | LHyd SLdr |
| 'Bariton' | LMil |
| ***barkamense*** | LMil |
| 'Barmstedt' | CWri MAsh |
| 'Barnaby Sunset' | GGGa LMil LRHS |
| 'Bashful' ♀H4 | CSBt ECho EMui EPfP MGos SLdr SReu |
| § ***basilicum*** | CDoC GGGa GKir IDee LMil LRHS SLdr |
| x ***bathyphyllum*** Cox 6542 | GGGa |
| ***bauhiniiflorum*** | see *R. triflorum* var. *bauhiniiflorum* |
| ***beanianum*** | GGGa |
| - KC 122 | GGGa |
| - compact | see *R. piercei* |
| 'Beatrice Keir' | LMil MDun SReu |
| 'Beattie' (EA) | LMil |
| Beau Brummel Group | LMil SHea |
| 'Beaulieu Manor' | GQui |
| 'Beauty of Littleworth' | LHyd SHea SReu |
| 'Beaver' (EA) | LMil |
| 'Beefeater' | SLdr |
| 'Beefeater' x ***yakushimanum*** | SLdr |
| ***beesianum*** | GGGa LMil SLdr |
| - KR 4150 | LMil |
| 'Beethoven' (EA) ♀H3-4 | CTrG LHyd SLdr SReu WBod WPic |
| 'Belkanto' | CDoC MDun NBlu SPoG |
| 'Belle Heller' | SLdr |
| 'Bellini' **new** | EMil |
| 'Bengal' | ECho GEdr GKir LRHS MBar MDun NDlv NHol SReu |
| 'Bengal Beauty' (EA) | GQui SLdr |
| 'Bengal Fire' (EA) | CMac SLdr |
| 'Bergensiana' | SReu |
| 'Bergie Larson' | CBcs ECho LMil MAsh MDun MLea MMuc SLdr |
| ***bergii*** | see *R. augustinii* subsp. *rubrum* |
| 'Berg's 10' **new** | MLea |
| 'Berg's Yellow' | CWri ECho ISea LMil MAsh MDun MLea WBVN WFar |
| 'Berlinale' **new** | MDun |
| 'Bernstein' | MAsh SPoG WFar |
| 'Berryrose' (K) ♀H4 | CBcs CSBt CTri CWri ECho EPfP GKir LHyd LMil MAsh MBar MGos MLea NLar SLdr SPer WBVN WBod WFar |
| Berryrose Group | CDoC MDun |
| 'Bert's Own' | SLdr |
| 'Beryl Taylor' | GGGa |
| 'Betty' (EA) | CTrG LHyd |
| 'Betty Anne Voss' (EA) | ECho GKir LHyd LRHS LSRN MAsh MGos NPri SCoo SLdr SReu |
| 'Betty Wormald' | CSBt ECho GKir LHyd LMil MBri MGos MLea MMuc SHBN SHea SLdr SPer WBVN |
| ***bhutanense*** | LMil |
| - CH&M | GGGa |
| Bibiani Group | SHea SLdr |
| 'Big Punkin' | LMil |
| 'Bijou de Ledeberg' (EA) | CMac |
| 'Billy Budd' | SLdr |
| 'Birthday Girl' | ECho LMil LSRN MAsh MDun MLea SBod SPoG |
| Biskra Group | GGGa LMil |
| 'Blaauw's Pink' (EA) ♀H3-4 | CDoC CDul CMac CSBt CTrh ECho EPfP GKir GQui LCro LHyd LMil MAsh MBar MBri MGos SLdr SPer SPlb SPoG SReu SRms WFar |
| 'Black Hawk' (EA) | CBcs CTrG |
| 'Black Knight' (A) | SLdr |
| 'Black Magic' | CDoC CWri LMil |
| 'Black Sport' | MLea |
| Blaue Donau | see *R.* 'Blue Danube' |
| 'Blazecheck' | MGos SCoo |
| 'Blewbury' ♀H4 | LHyd LMil MDun SLdr SReu SSta |
| 'Blue Beard' | SLdr |
| 'Blue Bell' | SHea |
| 'Blue Boy' | CDoC LMil MDun |
| 'Blue Chip' | LHyd SLdr |
| § 'Blue Danube' (EA) ♀H3-4 | CDoC CDul CMac CSBt CTrG CTri ECho EMil EPfP GKir LHyd LMil LRHS MAsh MBar MBri MDun MGos NBlu NPri SLdr SPer SPoG SReu SSta WBod WFar WPic |
| Blue Diamond Group | CBcs CMHG ECho EPfP LCro LRHS MAsh MBar MDun MGos NHol SHBN SLdr SReu SRms |
| 'Blue Diamond' | CSBt ECho ELon GKir LHyd LSRN MLea SPer SPoG WBod WGwG |
| 'Blue Haze' | LHyd |
| 'Blue Monday' | WBod |
| 'Blue Moon' | LMil |
| 'Blue Peter' ♀H4 | CSBt CWri ECho EMil EPfP GGGa LCro LHyd LMil MAsh MBar MDun MGos MLea SBod SHBN SLdr SPer SPoG SReu SSta |
| 'Blue Pool' | LMil MBar |
| Blue Ribbon Group | CMHG SLdr |
| 'Blue Star' | GGar LHyd MDun MLea NMen |
| 'Blue Steel' | see *R. fastigiatum* 'Blue Steel' |
| Blue Tit Group | CBcs CDoC CSBt CTrG EPfP GKev GKir LHyd LRHS MAsh MBar MDun NHol SHBN SLdr SReu SSta STre WBod |
| Bluebird Group | CSBt MAsh MBar MDun MGos NHol NWCA SLdr SPoG SRms WBod |
| Bluestone Group | WBod |
| 'Bluette' | MDun MLea NDlv |
| 'Blurettia' | CDoC CWri LMil MAsh MMuc NLar |
| 'Blutopia' | LMil |
| 'Bob Bovee' | NLar |
| 'Bob's Blue' | MDun |
| 'Boddaertianum' | LHyd SHea SLdr SReu |
| ***bodinieri*** | WBod |
| 'Bodnant Yellow' | LMil WBod |
| 'Bonfire' | SHea SLdr SReu |
| ***boothii*** | GGGa |
| 'Bo-peep' | GQui LHyd LMil SReu |
| Bo-peep Group | CBcs SLdr |
| 'Borde Hill' (R) **new** | SHea |
| 'Boskoop Ostara' | CBcs LMil MGos |
| 'Boule de Neige' | MDun |

| | |
|---|---|
| 'Bouquet de Flore' (G) ♀H4 | CDoC CSdC EPfP LMil MBar SLdr SReu |
| Bow Bells Group | CSam ISea LHyd MAsh MBar MDun MGos MLea SHBN |
| 'Bow Bells' ♀H4 | ECho EPfP GEdr GKir LMil LRHS NHol NLar NPri SHea SLdr WBod WFar |
| ***brachyanthum*** | GGGa |
| - subsp. ***hypolepidotum*** | GGGa LMil |
| ***brachycarpum*** | GGGa SLdr |
| - subsp. ***brachycarpum*** Tigerstedtii Group | LMil |
| - 'Roseum Dwarf' | GGGa |
| 'Brambling' | GGGa |
| 'Brazier' (EA) | LHyd SLdr |
| 'Brazil' (K) | CSBt EMil |
| 'Bremen' | LMil |
| 'Brianna' | GGGa |
| Bric-à-brac Group | CBcs SLdr |
| 'Bric-à-brac' | LHyd MDun WThu |
| 'Bridesmaid' (O) | EPfP SLdr SPoG |
| 'Bright Forecast' (K) | CWri NLar SLdr |
| 'Brigitte' | CDoC CWri GGGa LMil LRHS LSRN MAsh MDun NPri SLdr |
| 'Brilliant' (EA) | MGos |
| 'Brilliant' (hybrid) | MGos NHol WFar |
| 'Brilliant Blue' (EA) | MAsh |
| 'Brilliant Crimson' (EA) | SLdr |
| 'Britannia' | CBcs CSBt CSam CWri EPfP GKir LHyd MAsh MBar SHBN SHea SPer SReu WFar |
| 'Britannia' x ***griersonianum*** | SLdr |
| 'Brocade' | CSam LHyd LMil MDun SHea SLdr |
| 'Bronze Fire' (A) | NHol SLdr SReu WBod |
| 'Brown Eyes' | ECho ISea MAsh MDun MLea SLdr WFar |
| 'Bruce Brechtbill' ♀H4 | CDoC CWri ECho GGGa LMil MAsh MBri MDun MGos MMuc NHol NLar SLdr SReu SSta |
| 'Bruce Hancock' (Ad) | ECho WBVN |
| § 'Bruns Gloria' | LMil MDun |
| 'Bruns Schneewitchen' | SReu |
| 'Buccaneer' (EA) | LHyd |
| 'Bud Flanagan' | MDun |
| 'Buketta' | GGGa MDun |
| ***bullatum*** | see *R. edgeworthii* |
| 'Bulstrode' (EA) | SHea |
| ***bulu*** C&V 9503 | GGGa |
| 'Bungo-nishiki' (EA/d) | CMac |
| ***bureavii*** ♀H4 | CDoC GGGa GKir IDee LHyd LMil MDun MGos SLdr SReu SSta |
| - SEH 211 | LMil |
| - SF 517 | ISea |
| - 'Ardrishaig' | GGGa |
| ***bureavii*** x Elizabeth Group | SReu |
| ***bureavii*** x ***yakushimanum*** | SReu |
| ***bureavioides*** | GKir LMil SReu |
| - Cox 5076 | GGGa |
| 'Burletta' | GGGa |
| ***burmanicum*** | GGGa LMil MDun WBod |
| 'Busuki' **new** | LMil |
| 'Butter Brickle' | LMil MDun MLea WBVN WFar |
| 'Butter Yellow' | ECho MDun WBod |
| 'Butterball' | GGGa |
| 'Buttercup' (K) | MBar |
| 'Butterfly' | MDun SHea SLdr |
| 'Buttermint' | CDoC CWri ECho GQui MDun MGos MLea SBod SHBN WBVN WFar |
| 'Buttons and Bows' (K) | GGGa |
| 'Buzzard' (K) | CSdC LMil |
| 'Byron' (A/d) | LMil SLdr |
| 'Caerhays Lavender' | CBcs |
| ***caesium*** | SLdr |
| ***calendulaceum*** (A) | GKev LMil |
| - red-flowered (A) | LMil |
| - yellow-flowered (A) | IDee LMil |
| Calfort Group | SLdr |
| 'Calico' (K) | CSdC |
| ***caliginis*** (V) | GGGa |
| ***callimorphum*** | GGGa LMil |
| - var. ***myiagrum*** F 21821a | SLdr |
| ***calophytum*** ♀H4 | GGGa GKir IDee LMil LRHS SLdr |
| - EGM 343 | LMil |
| - var. ***openshawianum*** C&H 7055 | GGGa |
| ***calostrotum*** | CWri WAbe |
| - SF 357 | ISea |
| - 'Gigha' ♀H4 | GGGa LLHF LMil LRHS MAsh MDun MGos SLdr WAbe |
| § - subsp. ***keleticum*** ♀H4 | CDoC CTrG GEdr MBar MDun MGos WAbe WFar |
| - - F 21756 | SLdr |
| - - R 58 | LMil |
| § - - Radicans Group | GEdr MBar MDun MLea NHol WAbe WBod WThu |
| - - - USDAPI 59182/R11188 | MLea |
| - subsp. ***riparium*** SF 95089 | ISea |
| - - Calciphilum Group | GGGa MDun WThu |
| § - - Nitens Group | CDoC GBin GGGa IDee MAsh NDlv NMen WAbe |
| § - - Rock's form R178 | GGGa |
| ***caloxanthum*** | see *R. campylocarpum* subsp. *caloxanthum* |
| Calrose Group **new** | WBod |
| 'Calsap' | GGGa NLar |
| Calstocker Group | LMil |
| ***camelliiflorum*** | GGGa MDun |
| 'Campanile' **new** | MDun |
| ***campanulatum*** | LMil MDun SLdr SReu WAbe |
| - HWJCM 195 | WCru |
| § - subsp. ***aeruginosum*** | GGGa LMil MDun NLar SLdr SReu |
| - ***album*** | SLdr |
| § 'Campfire' (EA) | SLdr WBod |
| Campirr Group | LHyd |
| ***campylocarpum*** | GGGa IDee LHyd LMil MDun SLdr SReu |
| - B&SWJ 2462 | WCru |
| - from East Nepal | MDun |
| § - subsp. ***caloxanthum*** | GGGa LMil MDun SLdr |
| - - KR 6152 | LMil |
| ***campylogynum*** ♀H4 | LMil MLea NMen SSpi WAbe |
| - SF 95181 | ISea |
| - 'Album' | see *R.* 'Leucanthum' |
| - 'Bramble' | MDun |
| - Charopoeum Group | GGGa MBar MDun WBod WThu |
| - - 'Patricia' | ECho MDun WThu |
| - claret-flowered | GGGa MDun WBod |
| § - Cremastum Group | CTrG GGGa LHyd |
| - - 'Bodnant Red' | GGGa LHyd MDun WBod |
| - 'Crushed Strawberry' **new** | WBod |
| - var. ***leucanthum*** | see *R.* 'Leucanthum' |
| - Myrtilloides Group | CDoC ECho GGGa GQui LHyd LMil MDun MGos NMen NWCA SLdr SReu WAbe WBod |
| - - Farrer 1046 | GGGa |
| - pink-flowered | MBar WAbe |
| - salmon pink-flowered | ECho GEdr MDun WBod |
| ***camtschaticum*** | GAuc GGGa LMil MBri |
| - from Hokkaido, Japan | NMen |

| | |
|---|---|
| - var. ***albiflorum*** | GGGa NMen |
| - red-flowered | GGGa |
| ***canadense*** (A) | GGGa SLdr |
| - f. ***albiflorum*** (A) | GGGa LMil |
| - dark-flowered (A) | LMil |
| - 'Deer Lake' (A) | SReu |
| 'Canary' | SReu |
| ***canescens*** (A) | LMil |
| 'Cannon's Double' (K/d) ♀H4 | CWri GGGa ISea LHyd LMil MAsh MBri MDun MGos MLea NLar SLdr SPer |
| 'Canzonetta' (EA) ♀H4 | ECho GGGa LMil LRHS MAsh MGos NMun WBrE |
| 'Capistrano' | GGGa |
| ***capitatum*** | GGGa |
| 'Caprice' (EA) | SReu |
| 'Captain Jack' | GGGa SLdr |
| 'Caractacus' | MBar WFar |
| 'Carat' (A) | SLdr SReu |
| ***cardiobasis*** | see *R. orbiculare* subsp. *cardiobasis* |
| Carita Group | SHea SReu |
| 'Carita Charm' | SLdr |
| 'Carita Golden Dream' | LMil |
| 'Carita Inchmery' | LHyd SHea SLdr |
| 'Carmen' | CWri ECho GEdr GGGa GKir ISea LHyd LMil MAsh MBar MDun MGos MLea NHol NMen SHBN SLdr SReu SRms WBVN |
| ***carneum*** | GGGa LMil |
| 'Carnival' (EA) | CBcs |
| 'Caroline' | EMui |
| 'Caroline Allbrook' ♀H4 | CWri ECho EMil EPfP GGGa LHyd LMil MAsh MBri MDun MGos MLea NHol NLar SLdr SPoG WBVN |
| 'Caroline de Zoete' | LHyd SHea |
| ***carolinianum*** | see *R. minus* var. *minus* Carolinianum Group, *R. minus* var. *minus* |
| 'Cary Ann' | CBcs CTri CWri GKir LRHS MAsh SLdr SReu WFar |
| 'Casablanca' (EA) | SLdr |
| 'Cassata' | LMil MDun |
| 'Cassley' (Vs) | LMil SLdr |
| 'Castle of Mey' | SLdr |
| ***catacosmum*** | GGGa |
| ***catawbiense*** | GGGa LHyd SLdr |
| 'Catawbiense Album' | CTri CWri GGGa GKir MAsh WFar |
| 'Catawbiense Boursault' | SLdr WFar |
| 'Catawbiense Grandiflorum' | CDoC EMil GKir LMil NMun WFar |
| 'Catherine Hopwood' | SLdr |
| § ***caucasicum*** 'Cunningham's Sulphur' | MDun |
| 'Caucasicum Pictum' | GGGa LHyd LMil MBar SLdr |
| 'Cavalcade' | GKir |
| Cavalier Group | MDun |
| 'Cecile' (K) ♀H4 | CBcs CDoC CSam CWri ECho EMil GKir LHyd LMil MAsh MBar MBri MDun MGos NBlu SBod SLdr SPer SReu WBVN |
| 'Celestial' (EA) | CMac |
| 'Centennial' | see *R.* 'Washington State Centennial' |
| ***cephalanthum*** | GGGa LMil |
| - subsp. ***cephalanthum*** SBEC 0751 | WAbe |
| - - Crebreflorum Group | GGGa LMil WAbe |
| - - Nmaiense Group C&V 9513 | GGGa |
| - subsp. ***platyphyllum*** | GGGa |
| ***cerasinum*** | GGGa ISea LMil |
| - C&V 9504 | GGGa |
| - SF 95067 | ISea |
| - 'Cherry Brandy' | LHyd |
| 'Cetewayo' ♀H4 | CWri LMil SReu |
| ***chaetomallum*** | see *R. haematodes* subsp. *chaetomallum* |
| ***chamaethomsonii*** | GGGa LMil |
| - CCH&H 8195 | GGGa |
| - SF 95084 | ISea |
| - var. ***chamaethauma*** KW 5847 | LMil |
| - - KR 3506 from Pe, Doshang La | LMil |
| ***chameunum*** | see *R. saluenense* subsp. *chameunum* |
| § 'Champagne' ♀H3-4 | CSBt EPfP GKir LHyd LMil LRHS MAsh MDun SHea SLdr SReu |
| ***championiae*** | GGGa |
| 'Chanel' (Vs) | MDun SReu SSta |
| ***changii*** | GGGa |
| 'Chanticleer' (EA) | SLdr SReu |
| ***chapaense*** | see *R. maddenii* subsp. *crassum* |
| 'Chapeau' | LMil |
| ***charitopes*** | GGGa LMil |
| § - subsp. ***tsangpoense*** | GGGa GQui NHol |
| 'Charlemagne' (G) | SLdr |
| * 'Charles Puddle' | WBod |
| Charmaine Group | GGGa NHol WBod |
| 'Charme La' | GGGa |
| ***chasmanthum*** | see *R. augustinii* subsp. *chasmanthum* |
| 'Cheer' | CWri MAsh MBar MMuc SLdr SReu WFar |
| 'Cheerful Giant' (K) | MGos |
| 'Chelsea Reach' (K/d) | CSdC |
| 'Chelsea Seventy' | MAsh NLar SLdr |
| 'Cherokee' | SLdr |
| 'Cherries and Cream' | LMil |
| 'Chetco' (K) | LMil SLdr |
| 'Chevalier Félix de Sauvage' ♀H4 | LMil SHea SReu |
| 'Cheyenne' | SLdr |
| 'Chiffchaff' | LHyd NMen WAbe |
| 'Chikor' | CBcs CSBt CTrG ECho GEdr GGGa GKir MAsh MBar MBri MDun MGos NHol SLdr WBod WFar |
| China Group | SReu |
| 'China A' | SLdr |
| 'Chinchilla' (EA) | GQui |
| 'Chink' | CBcs MBar MDun SLdr |
| 'Chionoides' | GGGa NBlu SLdr WBod |
| 'Chipmunk' (EA/d) | GKir LRHS |
| 'Chippewa' (EA) | CTri GGGa LMil |
| 'Chocolate Ice' (K/d) | SLdr |
| 'Chopin' (EA) | WBod |
| 'Choremia' ♀H3 | LHyd LMil MLea SHea SLdr SReu WBod |
| 'Chorus Line' **new** | MDun |
| 'Chris' (EA) | SLdr |
| ***christi*** (V) | GGGa |
| 'Christina' (EA/d) | CMac LMil NHol NLar SLdr SReu WBod |
| 'Christmas Cheer' (EA/d) | see *R.* 'Ima-shojo' |
| 'Christmas Cheer' (hybrid) | CBcs CDoC CMac CSBt CWri EMil GGGa GGal GKir ISea LHyd LMil MAsh MGos MLea NBlu NLar SHBN SLdr SPer SPoG SReu WPic |
| 'Chromatella' | SLdr |
| ***chrysanthum*** | see *R. aureum* |
| ***chryseum*** | see *R. rupicola* var. *chryseum* |
| ***chrysodoron*** | GGGa LMil |
| ***ciliatum*** | CBcs CTrG GGGa IDee LHyd SLdr |
| ***ciliicalyx*** subsp. ***lyi*** | see *R. lyi* |
| Cilpinense Group | CBcs MAsh MBar MDun MMuc SLdr SPer WFar |

| | |
|---|---|
| 'Cilpinense' ♀H3-4 | CMac CSBt CWri ECho EPfP GGGa LHyd LMil LRHS NPri SHea SPoG SReu WBVN WBod WBrE WPic |
| ***cinnabarinum*** | LMil MDun SLdr |
| - subsp. ***cinnabarinum*** | MDun SLdr |
| - - BL&M 234 | LMil |
| - - 'Aestivale' | LMil |
| - - Blandfordiiflorum Group | GGGa LMil SLdr |
| § - - 'Conroy' | GGGa LMil MDun MLea SReu |
| - - 'Nepal' | LHyd LMil |
| - - Roylei Group | GGGa LHyd LMil MDun SLdr WPic |
| - - - 'Magnificum' | MDun |
| - - - 'Vin Rosé' | LMil MDun |
| § - subsp. ***tamaense*** | GGGa |
| - - KW 21021 | GGGa |
| § - subsp. ***xanthocodon*** | IDee LMil MDun SLdr |
| § - - Concatenans Group | GGGa LHyd LMil MDun SLdr WPic |
| - - - C&V 9523 | GGGa |
| - - - KW 5874 | LMil |
| - - - 'Amber' | MDun |
| - - - 'Copper' | SLdr |
| - - 'Daffodilly' | LHyd |
| - - Purpurellum Group | GGGa MDun SLdr WBod |
| Cinnkeys Group | GGGa MDun |
| Cinzan Group | LMil SReu |
| 'Circus' **new** | MDun |
| ***citriniflorum*** | LMil |
| - R 108 | GGGa LMil |
| - Brodick form | LMil |
| - var. ***citriniflorum*** | LMil |
| - var. ***horaeum*** | SLdr |
| - - F 21850* | GGGa |
| 'Citronella' | SLdr |
| 'Claydian Variegated' (v) | GGGa |
| ***clementinae*** | GGGa GKev MDun |
| - F 25705 | LMil |
| - JN 729 | GGGa |
| - SDR 3230 **new** | GKev |
| 'Cliff Garland' | GQui LMil |
| 'Coccineum Speciosum' (G) ♀H4 | CDoC CSBt CSdC GGGa IDee LMil LRHS MBar |
| ***coelicum*** F 25625 | GGGa |
| ***coeloneuron*** | GGGa LMil MDun |
| - EGM 334 | LMil |
| 'Colin Kenrick' (K/d) | CSdC SLdr |
| ***collettianum*** H&W 8975 | GGGa |
| 'Colonel Coen' | CWri GKir LMil MBri MGos MLea SHBN WBVN |
| Colonel Rogers Group | LHyd SLdr SReu |
| (Comely Group) 'Golden Orfe' | SLdr |
| ***complexum*** F 15392 | GGGa |
| 'Comte de Gomer' (hybrid) | CBcs |
| ***concatenans*** | see *R. cinnabarinum* subsp. *xanthocodon* Concatenans Group |
| ***concinnum*** | CWri LHyd MDun SLdr |
| - Pseudoyanthinum Group | GGGa GQui LMil MDun SLdr WPic |
| 'Conroy' | see *R. cinnabarinum* subsp. *cinnabarinum* 'Conroy' |
| 'Constable' | LHyd |
| 'Contina' | GGGa |
| ***cookeanum*** | see *R. sikangense* var. *sikangense* Cookeanum Group |
| 'Coral Mist' | GGGa LMil MDun |
| 'Coral Reef' | SLdr SReu |
| 'Coral Sea' (EA) | MDun SLdr SReu |
| 'Corany' (A) | SLdr |
| ***coriaceum*** | GGGa LMil SLdr |
| 'Corneille' (G/d) ♀H4 | CSBt LMil SLdr |

| | |
|---|---|
| 'Cornish Cracker' | SLdr |
| Cornish Cross Group | LHyd SLdr SReu |
| Cornish Early Red Group | see *R.* Smithii Group |
| 'Cornish Red' | see *R.* Smithii Group |
| Cornubia Group | SLdr |
| 'Corona' | SHea |
| 'Coronation Day' | SHea SLdr SReu |
| 'Corry Koster' | SHea |
| ***coryanum*** | GGGa |
| - KR 5775 | LMil |
| - 'Chelsea Chimes' | LMil SLdr |
| 'Cosmopolitan' | CWri LCro LMil LRHS MAsh MBar MDun MGos MMuc SLdr SPoG SReu |
| Cote Group (A) | SLdr |
| 'Countess of Athlone' | SLdr |
| 'Countess of Derby' | MDun SHea SReu |
| 'Countess of Haddington' ♀H2 | CBcs LMil MDun SLdr |
| 'Countess of Stair' | WFar WPic |
| ***cowanianum*** | GGGa WAbe |
| Cowslip Group | CSam CTri CWri LMil LRHS MAsh MBar MDun MGos MLea NPri SHBN SLdr SReu WBod |
| ***coxianum*** C&H 475B | GGGa |
| 'Cranbourne' | LHyd SReu |
| 'Crane' ♀H4 | EPfP GGGa GKir GQui LLHF LMil LRHS MAsh MDun NPri |
| ***crassum*** | see *R. maddenii* subsp. *crassum* |
| 'Cream Crest' | GQui MDun SHBN WFar |
| 'Cream Glory' | LHyd |
| 'Creamy Chiffon' | CWri ECho LHyd MDun MGos MLea WBVN |
| § 'Creeping Jenny' | ECho GGGa GGal GGar LHyd MBar MDun SLdr WBod |
| ***cremastum*** | see *R. campylogynum* Cremastum Group |
| 'Crème Brûlée' **new** | LMil |
| 'Crest' ♀H3-4 | GGGa LHyd LMil MAsh MDun MGos SHBN SLdr WBod |
| 'Crete' ♀H4 | LMil MDun |
| 'Crimson Pippin' | LMil |
| ***crinigerum*** | GGGa IDee LHyd LMil MDun |
| - JN 756 | GGGa |
| 'Crinoline' (K) | SLdr SReu |
| 'Croceum Tricolor' (G) | CSdC |
| Crossbill Group | CBcs |
| * ***crossium*** | SReu |
| 'Crosswater Belle' | LMil |
| 'Crosswater Red' (K) | LMil |
| 'Crown Jewel' (EA/d) | WBod |
| ***cubittii*** | see *R. veitchianum* Cubittii Group |
| ***cucullatum*** | see *R. roxieanum* var. *cucullatum* |
| ***cumberlandense*** (A) | GGGa IDee LMil |
| - 'Sunlight' (A) | LMil MBri |
| ***cuneatum*** | GGGa |
| 'Cunningham's Blush' | GGGa SHBN |
| 'Cunningham's Sulphur' | see *R. caucasicum* 'Cunningham's Sulphur' |
| 'Cunningham's White' | CBcs CSBt CSam CTri CWri ELan EMil EPfP GGGa GKir LCro LMil LRHS MAsh MBar MDun MGos MMuc SLdr SPer SPoG SReu WBod WFar |
| 'Cupcake' | see *R.* 'Delp's Cupcake' |
| 'Cupreum Ardens' (G) | CSdC |
| 'Curlew' ♀H4 | CSBt EPfP GEdr GGGa GKev GKir ISea LMil LRHS MAsh MBar MBri MDun MGos NHol NMen SHBN SLdr SReu SSpi WBVN WBod WFar |
| ***cyanocarpum*** | GGGa LMil |
| - Bu 294 | GGGa |

| | | |
|---|---|---|
| | 'Cynthia' ♀H4 | CBcs CSBt CSam CWri ECho EPfP GGGa GKir ISea LHyd LMil LSRN MBar MBri MDun MGos SHBN SLdr SPer SReu SSta WBVN WBod |
| | 'Daimio' (EA) | LHyd |
| | 'Dairymaid' | SReu |
| | ***dalhousieae*** | GGGa SLdr |
| § | - var. ***rhabdotum*** | GGGa SLdr |
| | Damaris Group | SLdr |
| | 'Damaris Logan' | see *R.* 'Logan Damaris' |
| | 'Damozel' | SHea SLdr |
| | 'Daphne Daffarn' | SHea |
| | 'Daphne Millais' | SHea SLdr |
| | 'Dartmoor Blush' | SReu |
| | 'Dartmoor Pixie' | SReu |
| | 'Dartmoor Rose' | SReu |
| | ***dasypetalum*** | MBar MDun NDlv |
| | ***dauricum*** | WBod |
| | - 'Arctic Pearl' | GGGa |
| | - 'Midwinter' ♀H4 | GGGa LHyd SLdr |
| * | 'Dauricum Splendens' | WBod |
| | 'David' ♀H4 | LHyd SHea SLdr SReu |
| | ***davidii*** | GGGa LMil SLdr |
| | - AC 4100 | LMil |
| | - EN 4213 | GGGa |
| | ***davidsonianum*** ♀H3-4 | GGGa LMil SLdr SSpi WPic |
| | - Bodnant form | LMil MDun WBod |
| | - 'Caerhays Blotched' | SLdr |
| | - 'Caerhays Pink' | GGGa SLdr |
| | - 'Ruth Lyons' | LMil |
| | 'Daviesii' (G) ♀H4 | Widely available |
| | 'Dawn's Delight' | SLdr |
| * | 'Day Dawn' | GKir SReu |
| | 'Day Dream' | SHea SReu |
| N | 'Daybreak' (EA/d) | see *R.* 'Kirin' |
| | 'Daybreak' (K) | GQui |
| | 'Dear Grandad' (EA) | CTri LMil LRHS NPri SCoo |
| | 'Dear Grandma' **new** | LMil |
| | 'Dearest' (EA) | LRHS NPri |
| | 'Debutante' | NHol WBod |
| | ***decorum*** ♀H4 | CDoC GGGa GKev ISea LMil MDun SLdr SReu WPic |
| | - Bu 286 | NHol |
| | - C&H 7023 | GGGa |
| | - 'Cox's Uranium Green' | SReu |
| § | - subsp. ***diaprepes*** | LHyd |
| | - - 'Gargantua' | SReu |
| | - late-flowering | LMil |
| | - pink-flowered | SLdr |
| | ***decorum* x *yakushimanum*** | SLdr SReu |
| | ***degronianum*** | GGGa |
| § | - subsp. ***degronianum*** | LMil SLdr |
| | - - 'Gerald Loder' | LHyd |
| § | - subsp. ***heptamerum*** | GGGa MDun |
| | - - 'Ho Emma' | LMil MDun |
| | - - 'Oki Island' | LMil |
| | - 'Rae's Delight' | LMil |
| | - subsp. ***yakushimanum*** | see *R. yakushimanum* |
| | ***dekatanum*** | GGGa |
| | ***deleiense*** | see *R. tephropeplum* |
| | 'Delicatissimum' (O) | CBcs CDoC CWri ECho GGGa GQui MAsh MLea MMuc NLar SBod SLdr SPer WBVN WBrE WGwG |
| § | 'Delp's Cupcake' | NLar |
| | 'Delta' | NBlu |
| | ***dendricola*** | SLdr |
| | - KW 20981 | GGGa |
| | ***dendrocharis*** | GGGa |
| | - CC&H 4012 | GGGa |
| | - Cox 5016 | GGGa NHol WAbe |
| | - 'Glendoick Gem' | GGGa |
| * | 'Denny's Rose' (A) | LMil MDun SReu |
| | 'Denny's Scarlet' | MDun SReu |
| | 'Denny's White' | LMil MDun NHol SLdr SReu WBod |
| | ***denudatum*** C&H 70102 | GGGa |
| | - C&H 7118 | GGGa |
| | - EGM 294 | LMil |
| | - SEH 334 | LMil |
| | ***desquamatum*** | see *R. rubiginosum* Desquamatum Group |
| | x ***detonsum*** F 13784 | SLdr |
| | 'Devisiperbile' (EA) | SLdr |
| | (Diamant Group) 'Diamant Enzianblau' (EA) | LMil |
| | - 'Diamant Purpur' | see *R.* Diamant Group purple-flowered |
| | - 'Diamant Rot' | see *R.* Diamant Group red-flowered |
| | - lilac-flowered (EA) | ECho LMil MLea |
| | - pink-flowered (EA) | ECho LMil MDun MGos MLea SLdr |
| § | - purple-flowered (EA) | ECho LMil MDun MGos MLea SLdr WBod |
| § | - red-flowered (EA) | ECho LMil MDun MLea SLdr WBod |
| | - rosy red-flowered (EA) | ECho |
| | - salmon pink-flowered (EA) | LMil |
| | - white-flowered (EA) | ECho MDun MLea SLdr |
| | 'Diana Pearson' | LHyd |
| | ***diaprepes*** | see *R. decorum* subsp. *diaprepes* |
| | ***dichroanthum*** | GGGa LMil MDun SLdr SReu |
| § | - subsp. ***apodectum*** | GGGa LMil |
| | - subsp. ***dichroanthum*** SBEC 545 | GGGa |
| § | - subsp. ***scyphocalyx*** | LMil SLdr |
| | - - F 24546 | GGGa |
| | - subsp. ***septentrionale*** JN 575 | GGGa |
| | ***didymum*** | see *R. sanguineum* subsp. *didymum* |
| | 'Dietrich' | WFar |
| | ***dignabile*** C&V 9569 | GGGa |
| | - KR 5385 | LMil |
| | ***dilatatum*** | LMil |
| | ***dimitrum*** | MDun |
| | 'Diny Dee' | MGos |
| | 'Diorama' (Vs) | SReu SSta |
| | 'Directeur Charles Baumann' | SLdr |
| § | 'Directeur Moerlands' (M) | SLdr |
| | ***discolor*** | see *R. fortunei* subsp. *discolor* |
| | 'Doc' | EPfP GKir MAsh MBar MDun MGos NDlv SLdr SReu WFar |
| | 'Doctor A. Blok' | SLdr |
| | 'Doctor Ernst Schäle' | GGGa |
| | 'Doctor H.C. Dresselhuys' | EMil MBar SHBN |
| | 'Doctor M. Oosthoek' (M) ♀H4 | CSBt SLdr SReu |
| | 'Doctor V.H. Rutgers' | MBar MDun WFar |
| | 'Don Giovanni' | NLar |
| | 'Don Quixote' (K) | CSdC MAsh |
| | 'Doncaster' | GKir MBar MGos SHBN SHea WFar |
| | 'Dopey' ♀H4 | CBcs CSBt CWri ECho EMui EPfP GGGa GGar GKir LHyd LMil LRHS MAsh MBar MBri MDun MGos MLea NDlv NHol SHBN SLdr SPoG SReu WBVN |
| | 'Dora Amateis' ♀H4 | CBcs CDoC ECho GGGa GKir LMil LRHS MAsh MBar MGos NHol NPri SLdr SPer SReu WPic |
| | Dormouse Group | CBcs ECho LMil SHea SLdr SReu WBVN WFar |
| | 'Dorothea' | SLdr |
| | 'Dorset Sandy' (EA) | LMil |
| | 'Dörte Reich' | GGGa |
| | ***doshongense*** | see *R. aganniphum* var. *aganniphum* Doshongense Group |
| | 'Double Beauty' (EA/d) | SReu SSta |

| | |
|---|---|
| 'Double Damask' (K/d) ♀H4 | SLdr |
| 'Double Date' (d) | SLdr |
| double yellow | SLdr |
| 'Douglas McEwan' | MDun SLdr |
| 'Dracula' (K) | GGGa |
| Dragonfly Group | SReu |
| Dragonfly Group x ***serotinum*** | SLdr |
| 'Drake's Mountain' | MBar MDun MLea |
| 'Drapa' (EA) | GGGa |
| 'Dreamland' ♀H4 | CBcs CDoC CSBt CWri ECho EMil GKir LMil LRHS MAsh MDun MGos MLea NLar SLdr SReu WBod WFar |
| 'Driven Snow' (EA) | SLdr |
| ***drumonium*** | see *R. telmateium* |
| 'Drury Lane' (K) | GQui LMil |
| ***dryophyllum*** misapplied | see *R. phaeochrysum* var. *levistratum* |
| 'Duchess of Teck' | SReu |
| 'Dusky Dawn' | SLdr |
| 'Dusky Orange' | MDun SReu |
| 'Dusty' | MDun |
| 'Dusty Miller' | GKir LHyd LRHS MAsh MBar MDun MGos NDlv NLar SHBN SLdr WBod |
| 'Earl of Athlone' | SHea SReu |
| 'Earl of Donoughmore' | MDun SReu SSta |
| 'Early Beni' (EA) | LHyd |
| 'Ebony Pearl' | CBcs ECho GBin GGGa MGos WBVN WGwG |
| ***eclecteum*** | LMil MDun SLdr |
| - Cox 6054 | GGGa |
| - 'Rowallane Yellow' | SLdr |
| § ***edgeworthii*** ♀H2-3 | GGGa ISea SLdr WAbe |
| - KC 0106 | GGGa |
| 'Edith Bosley' | GGGa |
| Edmondii Group | LHyd |
| 'Edna Bee' (EA) | LMil |
| 'Effner' | LMil LRHS |
| 'Egret' ♀H4 | ECho GEdr GGGa LMil MAsh MBar MDun MGos MLea NLar SLdr WAbe WThu |
| 'Ehrengold' | LMil |
| 'Eider' | GGGa MAsh SLdr SReu |
| 'Eileen' | LMil |
| 'El Camino' | ECho ISea LMil SHBN SLdr |
| 'El Greco' | SLdr |
| Eldorado Group | GQui |
| 'Eleanor' (EA) | WBod |
| Electra Group | see *R. augustinii* Electra Group |
| ***elegantulum*** | GGGa LMil MDun |
| 'Elfin Gold' | SReu |
| 'Elisabeth Hobbie' ♀H4 | ECho GEdr GGGa GKir LMil MAsh MBar MDun |
| Elizabeth Group | CBcs GGGa LHyd LMil LRHS MAsh MBar SBod SHBN SLdr SPer SReu WFar |
| N 'Elizabeth' (EA) | CSBt EPfP MGos NWCA SLdr |
| 'Elizabeth' | CTri CWri ECho GKir LSRN MGos NHol NPri SHea WBod |
| 'Elizabeth de Rothschild' | MDun SLdr |
| 'Elizabeth Jenny' | see *R.* 'Creeping Jenny' |
| 'Elizabeth Lockhart' | ECho GEdr GQui MBar MDun MGos WBod |
| 'Elizabeth of Glamis' | GGGa |
| 'Elizabeth Red Foliage' | CTri GGGa GKir LHyd LMil LRHS MAsh MDun SPer SReu |
| ***elliottii*** | GGGa |
| Elsae Group | SLdr |
| 'Else Frye' | GGGa |
| 'Elsie Lee' (EA/d) ♀H3-4 | CTrh ECho GGGa LHyd LMil MAsh SLdr |
| 'Elsie Pratt' (A) | MBar NHol |
| 'Elsie Straver' | MDun NHol SHBN SLdr SReu |
| 'Elsie Watson' | GGGa |
| 'Elspeth' | LHyd |
| 'Emasculum' | LMil SLdr SReu |
| Emerald Isle Group | SReu |
| 'Endsleigh Pink' | LMil WBod |
| 'English Roseum' | SLdr |
| 'Erato' | GGGa |
| ***eriocarpum*** 'Jitsugetsuse' (EA) | LHyd |
| ***eriogynum*** | see *R. facetum* |
| ***eritimum*** | see *R. anthosphaerum* |
| 'Ernest Inman' | LHyd LMil SLdr |
| ***erosum*** | GGGa SLdr |
| 'Esmeralda' | CMac CTrG |
| Ethel Group | SLdr |
| 'Etna' (EA) | SLdr |
| 'Etta Burrows' | CWri GGGa MDun |
| 'Euan Cox' | GGGa NMen |
| ***eudoxum*** | GGGa |
| 'Eunice Updike' (EA) | LHyd |
| 'Europa' | SReu |
| ***eurysiphon*** Arduaine form | GGGa |
| 'Evelyn Hyde' (EA) | LMil |
| 'Evening Fragrance' (A) | SReu |
| 'Everbloom' (EA) | SLdr |
| 'Everest' (EA) | LHyd LMil MAsh NLar SLdr WBod |
| 'Everestianum' | GGGa MBar SHea SLdr |
| 'Everitt Hershey' (A) | SLdr |
| § 'Everlasting' | SReu |
| Everred = '851C' | GGGa |
| 'Evita' (EA) | GGGa |
| ***exasperatum*** KC 0116 | GGGa |
| - KC 0126 | GGGa |
| - KW 8250 | GGGa |
| 'Exbury Calstocker' | LMil |
| 'Exbury Naomi' | LHyd LMil SLdr |
| 'Exbury White' (K) | GQui |
| ***excellens*** | LMil |
| - AC 146 | GGGa |
| - KR 7616 **new** | ISea |
| - SF 92074 | ISea |
| - SF 92079 | ISea |
| ***eximium*** | see *R. falconeri* subsp. *eximium* |
| 'Exquisitum' (O) ♀H4 | CDoC CWri ECho EPfP GGGa LMil MBri MLea NLar SLdr WBVN WBrE |
| ***exquisitum*** | see *R. oreotrephes* Exquisitum Group |
| ***faberi*** | GGGa LMil SLdr |
| - subsp. ***prattii*** | see *R. prattii* |
| 'Fabia' ♀H3 | CBcs CMac GGGa LMil MAsh MDun SHea |
| Fabia Group | MDun SLdr |
| 'Fabia Roman Pottery' | MDun |
| § 'Fabia Tangerine' | MDun MLea SReu WBod |
| 'Fabia Waterer' | LMil SLdr |
| § ***facetum*** | GGGa LMil MDun |
| - AC 3049 | LMil |
| 'Faggetter's Favourite' ♀H4 | LMil MDun SHea SReu SSta |
| Fairy Light Group | LMil SLdr |
| 'Falcon' | see *R.* (Hawk Group) 'Hawk Falcon' |
| ***falconeri*** ♀H3-4 | CDoC CHEx CWri GGGa ISea LMil MDun MGos SLdr |
| - from East Nepal | MDun |
| § - subsp. ***eximium*** | CDoC GGGa LMil MDun |
| 'Falling Snow' **new** | MDun |
| 'Fanny' | see *R.* 'Pucella' |
| 'Fantastica' ♀H4 | CDoC ELan EMil EPfP GGGa LHyd LMil LRHS MAsh MBri MDun MLea NLar WBod |
| ***fargesii*** | see *R. oreodoxa* var. *fargesii* |
| 'Fashion' | CTrG SLdr |

| | | |
|---|---|---|
| | ***fastigiatum*** | GEdr ISea LMil MBar MLea |
| | - C&H 7159 | GGGa |
| | - SBEC 804/4869 | GGGa MDun WThu |
| § | - 'Blue Steel' ♀H4 | CBcs CTri CWri ECho GKir LMil MAsh MDun MGos SPlb SPoG SReu WPat |
| | 'Fastuosum Flore Pleno' (d) ♀H4 | CBcs CSBt CWri EPfP GBin GGGa GKir ISea LHyd LMil MBar MDun MGos MLea SHea SLdr SPer SPoG SReu SSta WFar |
| | 'Fatima' **new** | LMil |
| | ***faucium*** | GGGa ISea LMil |
| | - KR 5024 | GGGa |
| | - KR 5040 | LMil |
| | - KR 6229 | LMil |
| | 'Favorite' (EA) | LHyd NMun SLdr |
| | 'Fedora' (EA) | CBcs SLdr |
| | 'Fénelon' (G) | SLdr |
| | ***ferrugineum*** | GGGa LHyd LMil MBar MGos WBod |
| | - 'Plenum' (d) | MDun |
| | 'Festivo' **new** | MDun |
| | 'Feuerwerk' (K) | EMil SLdr |
| | ***fictolacteum*** | see *R. rex* subsp. *fictolacteum* |
| | Fine Feathers Group | WBod |
| | Fire Bird Group | SHea SLdr |
| | 'Fire Rim' | GGGa |
| | 'Fireball' (K) ♀H4 | CBcs CDoC CSam CTri CWri GGGa GKir LHyd LMil MAsh MBri MGos MLea NDlv NMun SBod SLdr SPer WBrE WMoo |
| | 'Fireball' (hybrid) | SLdr |
| | Firedrake Group | SReu |
| | 'Firefly' (EA) | see *R.* 'Hexe' |
| | 'Fireglow' | CSBt CSdC LMil SLdr WFar |
| I | 'Firelight' (hybrid) | LMil |
| | 'Fireman Jeff' | SLdr |
| | 'Firetail' | SHea |
| | 'Flaming Bronze' | SReu |
| | 'Flaming Gold' | GGGa MAsh |
| | Flamingo Group | SLdr |
| § | ***flammeum*** (A) | LMil |
| | ***flammeum* x *atlanticum*** (A) **new** | GKev |
| | 'Flanagan's Daughter' | GKir LMil LRHS |
| | 'Flautando' | LMil MDun |
| | Flava Group | see *R.* Volker Group |
| | ***flavidum*** | CBcs GGGa SLdr |
| | - Cox 6143 | GGGa |
| | - 'Album' | SLdr WBod WThu |
| | ***fletcherianum*** 'Yellow Bunting' | GGGa |
| § | ***flinckii*** | ECho GGGa LHyd LMil MDun |
| | - CH&M 3080 | GGGa |
| | ***floccigerum*** | GGGa LMil SLdr |
| | 'Floradora' (M) | SReu |
| | 'Floriade' | LHyd |
| | 'Floriade' x ***yakushimanum*** | SLdr |
| | ***floribundum*** | LMil SLdr |
| | - EGM 294 | LMil |
| | - 'Swinhoe' | SLdr |
| | 'Florida' (EA/d) ♀H3-4 | CMac LMil MAsh SLdr SReu WBod WFar WMoo |
| | 'Flower Arranger' (EA) | LMil LRHS NPri SCoo |
| I | 'Fluidum' **new** | MDun |
| | ***formosum*** | CBcs GGGa GQui SLdr |
| § | - var. ***formosum*** Iteaphyllum Group | GGGa WBod |
| | - - 'Khasia' | GGGa |
| | - var. ***inaequale*** C&H 301 | GGGa |
| | ***forrestii*** | GGGa |
| | - KR 6113 | LMil |
| | - subsp. ***forrestii*** | LMil |

| | | |
|---|---|---|
| | - - Repens Group | GGGa GKev LMil SLdr |
| | - - - 'Seinghku' | GGGa WThu |
| | - Tumescens Group | GGGa WThu |
| | - - C&V 9517 | GGGa |
| | 'Fortune' | LHyd |
| | Fortune Group | SLdr |
| | ***fortunei*** | GGGa LHyd LMil LRHS MDun SLdr |
| § | - subsp. ***discolor*** ♀H4 | GGGa LMil MDun SLdr |
| | - - PW 34 | GGGa |
| | - - (Houlstonii Group) 'John R. Elcock' | IDee LMil |
| | - subsp. ***discolor*** x 'Lodauric Iceberg' | SLdr |
| | - 'Foxy' | SLdr |
| | - 'Lu-Shan' | MDun |
| | - 'Mrs Butler' | see *R. fortunei* 'Sir Charles Butler' |
| § | - 'Sir Charles Butler' | LMil MDun SLdr |
| | 'Fox Hunter' | SLdr |
| | ***fragariiflorum*** | ISea |
| | - C&V 9519 | GGGa |
| | - LS&E 15828 | GGGa |
| | 'Fragrans' | SLdr |
| | 'Fragrant Star' (A) | GGGa SLdr |
| | 'Fragrantissimum' ♀H2-3 | CBcs CTrG CWri GGGa GGar ISea LHyd LMil MDun MRav NLar SKHP SLdr WBod WPic |
| | 'Francesca' | GGGa |
| | Francis Hanger (Reuthe's) Group | SLdr SReu |
| | 'Frank Baum' | SReu |
| | 'Frank Galsworthy' ♀H4 | LMil SReu |
| | 'Frans van der Bom' (M) | SLdr |
| | 'Fraseri' (M) | SLdr |
| | 'Fred Hamilton' | CWri |
| | 'Fred Nutbeam' (EA) | LMil |
| | 'Fred Peste' | CDoC ECho GKir LMil MAsh MBri MDun MGos MLea SReu |
| | 'Fred Wynniatt' | LHyd SLdr |
| | 'Fred Wynniatt Stanway' | see *R.* 'Stanway' |
| | 'Frere Organ' (G) | SLdr |
| | 'Freya' (R/d) | LMil SLdr |
| | 'Frieda' (EA) | SLdr |
| | 'Frigata' (A) | SLdr |
| | 'Frilled Petticoats' | SReu |
| | 'Frilly Lemon' (K/d) | MDun NLar SLdr |
| | 'Frosted Orange' (EA) | LMil MAsh SLdr |
| | 'Frosthexe' | GGGa WAbe |
| | 'Fulbrook' | LMil |
| | ***fulgens*** | GGGa LMil MDun |
| | ***fulvum*** ♀H4 | CDoC GGGa IDee LHyd LMil MDun SLdr SReu SSta |
| | - AC 3083 | LMil |
| | - subsp. ***fulvoides*** | LMil |
| | - - Cox 6532 | GGGa |
| § | 'Fumiko' (EA) | CSBt LRHS MAsh MBar MDun MGos MLea NMun WFar |
| | 'Furnivall's Daughter' ♀H4 | CSBt CWri ECho EPfP GGGa GKir LHyd LMil MBar MDun MGos MLea MMuc NLar SHea SLdr SPer SReu SSta WFar |
| | 'Fusilier' | SHea SReu |
| | 'Gabrielle Hill' (EA) | CDoC MAsh MGos SLdr |
| | 'Gaiety' (EA) | LMil SReu |
| | 'Galactic' | SLdr |
| | ***galactinum*** | LMil MDun |
| | - EN 3537 | GGGa |
| | 'Gandy Dancer' | CWri MDun SLdr |
| | 'Garden State Glow' (EA/d) | SLdr |
| | 'Garibaldi' | SHea |
| | 'Gartendirektor Glocker' | CWri ECho GGGa MAsh MDun SLdr |
| | 'Gartendirektor Rieger' ♀H4 | CWri GGGa LMil MAsh MDun SHea SReu |

| | | |
|---|---|---|
| | 'Gauche' (A) | GQui SLdr |
| | 'Gaugin' | GQui |
| | Gaul Group | SLdr |
| | 'Gay Lady' | SLdr |
| | 'Geisha' (EA) | GKir MBar |
| | 'Geisha Lilac' | see *R.* 'Hanako' |
| | 'Geisha Orange' | see *R.* 'Satschiko' |
| | 'Geisha Pink' | see *R.* 'Momoko' |
| | 'Geisha Purple' | see *R.* 'Fumiko' |
| | 'Geisha Red' (EA) | see *R.* 'Kazuko' |
| | 'Geisha White' | see *R.* 'Hisako' |
| | 'Gena Mae' (A/d) | GGGa SLdr |
| | 'General Eisenhower' | CSBt SHea SReu |
| | 'General Eric Harrison' | SLdr |
| | 'General Practitioner' | SLdr |
| | 'General Sir John du Cane' | SHea |
| | 'General Wavell' (EA) | CMac SLdr |
| | 'Gene's Favourite' | SReu |
| | ***genestierianum*** CC&H 8080 | GGGa |
| | 'Geoffrey Millais' | LMil |
| | 'Georg Arends' (Ad) | GKir LRHS NPri SLdr |
| | 'George Haslam' | SLdr |
| | 'George Hyde' (EA) | LMil LRHS LSRN MGos SCoo |
| | 'George Reynolds' (K) | MLea SLdr |
| | 'George's Delight' | GGGa MAsh |
| | 'Georgette' | LHyd SLdr |
| § | x ***geraldii*** | SLdr |
| | 'Germania' | EMil LMil LRHS MAsh MBar SPoG SReu WBod |
| | Gertrud Schäle Group | CDoC CTri GEdr MBar MDun SHea SReu |
| | Gibraltar Group | CTri |
| | 'Gibraltar' (K) ♀H4 | CBcs CDoC CSBt CTri CWri EMil EPfP GGGa GKir LMil MAsh MBar MBri MDun MGos MLea NBlu NPri SBod SLdr SPer SReu SSta WBod WFar WMoo |
| | ***giganteum*** | see *R. protistum* var. *giganteum* |
| | 'Gilbert Mullie' (EA) | LMil NBlu |
| I | 'Gill's Arboreum' | SLdr |
| | 'Gill's Crimson' | SHea SLdr SReu |
| | 'Ginger' (K) | CSBt CWri LMil SLdr |
| | 'Ginny Gee' ♀H4 | CDoC CSBt CWri ECho EPfP GEdr GGGa GGar GKev GKir LHyd LMil LRHS MAsh MBar MDun MGos MLea NHol NMen SLdr SReu SSta WBod WFar |
| | 'Gipsy King' | SHea SLdr |
| § | 'Girard's Hot Shot' (EA) | ECho GQui ISea LRHS MAsh MGos SLdr SReu WBVN WFar |
| | 'Girard's Hot Shot' variegated (EA/v) | ECho GGGa MAsh NMun |
| | 'Glacier' (EA) | MGos SLdr |
| | ***glanduliferum*** C&H 7131 | GGGa |
| | - EGM 347 | LMil |
| | - PW 044 from Miao Miao Shan | LMil |
| | 'Glanzblatt' **new** | MDun |
| | ***glaucophyllum*** | GGGa LMil MDun SLdr WAbe WBod |
| | - var. ***album*** | GGGa |
| | - Borde Hill form | LMil |
| | 'Glendoick Butterscotch' | GGGa |
| | 'Glendoick Dream' (EA) | GGGa |
| | 'Glendoick Ermine' (EA) | GGGa |
| | 'Glendoick Frolic' | GGGa |
| | 'Glendoick Garnet' (EA) | GGGa |
| | 'Glendoick Glacier' | GGGa |
| | 'Glendoick Goblin' (EA) | GGGa |
| | 'Glendoick Gold' | GGGa |
| | 'Glendoick Honeydew' | GGGa |
| | 'Glendoick Ice Cream' **new** | GGGa |
| | 'Glendoick Mystique' | GGGa |
| | 'Glendoick Petticoats' | GGGa |
| | 'Glendoick Ruby' | GGGa |
| | 'Glendoick Silver' | GGGa |
| | 'Glendoick Vanilla' | GGGa |
| | 'Glendoick Velvet' | GGGa |
| | 'Gletschernacht' | CWri LMil |
| | ***glischrum*** | GGGa |
| | - subsp. ***glischroides*** | GGGa LMil |
| | - subsp. ***glischrum*** | GGGa |
| § | - subsp. ***rude*** | GGGa |
| | - - C&V 9524 | GGGa |
| | ***globigerum*** | see *R. alutaceum* var. *alutaceum* Globigerum Group |
| | ***glomerulatum*** | see *R. yungningense* Glomerulatum Group |
| | 'Gloria' | see *R.* 'Bruns Gloria' |
| | 'Gloria Mundi' (G) | SHea |
| | 'Gloriana' | WBod |
| | 'Glory of Littleworth' (Ad) | LMil |
| | 'Glowing Embers' (K) | CDoC CSam CTri CWri ECho EMil GKir LMil LRHS MAsh MBri MDun MLea NHol NPri SLdr SPur SReu WBVN |
| | Goblin Group | SLdr |
| | 'Gog' (K) | CSBt |
| | 'Gold Mohur' | SLdr SReu |
| § | 'Goldbukett' | GGGa LHyd NLar |
| | 'Golden Bee' | GGGa NHol |
| | 'Golden Belle' | CWri |
| | Golden Bouquet | see *R.* 'Goldbukett' |
| | 'Golden Clipper' | LHyd |
| | 'Golden Coach' | CWri ECho ISea MDun MGos SBod SLdr SPer WBVN |
| | 'Golden Eagle' (K) | CDoC ECho GGar ISea LMil LRHS MAsh MDun MGos SLdr WBVN |
| | 'Golden Flare' (K) | CBcs CDoC CSam CWri ECho MAsh MBri MLea MMuc NBlu NDlv NMun SLdr WBrE WMoo |
| | 'Golden Fleece' | SReu |
| | 'Golden Gate' | CDoC CSBt ECho MDun SReu WFar |
| | 'Golden Horn' (K) | GQui |
| | 'Golden Lights' (A) | CDoC CWri ECho LMil MBri MDun MGos SBod SLdr WBVN WGwG |
| | 'Golden Melodie' **new** | MDun |
| | 'Golden Orfe' | LHyd |
| | Golden Oriole Group | NHol |
| § | - 'Talavera' | SSpi |
| | 'Golden Princess' | LMil MDun NHol |
| | 'Golden Ruby' | ECho MGos SPer |
| | 'Golden Splendour' | LMil |
| | 'Golden Sunlight' | see *R.* 'Directeur Moerlands' |
| | 'Golden Sunset' (K) | CSdC ECho LMil MAsh MBar MDun MLea NHol NLar SLdr SPoG SPur |
| | 'Golden Torch' ♀H4 | Widely available |
| | 'Golden Wedding' | CBcs CSBt CWri ECho LHyd LMil LSRN MDun MGos MLea NDlv NLar SBod SLdr SPoG WBVN |
| | 'Golden Wit' | MDun MMuc |
| | 'Goldfinger' | MDun MGos |
| | 'Goldflamme' | SLdr |
| | 'Goldflimmer' (v) | CDoC EMil GGGa LMil LRHS MAsh MGos MLan MLea NBlu NPri SLdr SPoG SReu WFar |
| | 'Goldfort' | SReu |
| | 'Goldika' | LMil |
| | 'Goldkollier' **new** | MDun |
| | 'Goldkrone' ♀H4 | CWri EPfP GGGa LHyd LMil MAsh MDun MGos MLea NLar SLdr SPer SReu |
| | Goldschatz = 'Goldprinz' | EMil GGGa LMil |
| | 'Goldstrike' | CDoC LMil SLdr |
| | 'Goldsworth Crimson' | LHyd |

| | |
|---|---|
| 'Goldsworth Orange' | CSBt CWri ECho GGGa MAsh MGos SBod SLdr SReu |
| 'Goldsworth Pink' | SReu |
| 'Goldsworth Yellow' | CSBt MGos SReu |
| 'Goldtopas' (K) | LMil |
| 'Goldzwerg' **new** | MDun |
| 'Golfer' | CWri GGGa LMil MLea |
| 'Gomer Waterer' ♀H4 | Widely available |
| ***gongshanense*** | GGGa |
| 'Gordian' **new** | MDun |
| 'Govenianum' (Ad) | SLdr |
| 'Grace Seabrook' | CSBt CSam CTri CWri ECho GGGa GKir LHyd MDun MGos MMuc SBod SLdr SPer SReu WBVN |
| ***gracilentum*** (V) | GGGa |
| 'Graciosum' (O) | SReu |
| 'Graf Lennart' | LMil MDun |
| 'Graffito' **new** | LMil MDun |
| 'Graham Thomas' | LMil SReu |
| 'Grand Slam' | ECho ISea MDun MLea WBVN |
| ***grande*** | GGGa LMil SLdr |
| 'Grandeur Triomphante' (G) | CSdC |
| ***gratum*** | see *R. basilicum* |
| 'Graziella' | GGGa LMil MDun |
| 'Greensleeves' | LMil LRHS |
| 'Greenway' (EA) | CBcs SLdr |
| 'Grenadier' | SHea |
| 'Greta' (EA) | LHyd |
| 'Gretzel' | NLar SReu |
| ***griersonianum*** | GGGa LHyd LMil MDun WPic |
| ***griersonianum*** x ***yakushimanum*** | SLdr |
| ***griffithianum*** | GGGa SLdr |
| 'Gristede' ♀H4 | ECho LMil LRHS MAsh MDun NHol SLdr SReu |
| ***groenlandicum*** | see *Ledum groenlandicum* |
| 'Grosclaude' | CMac SHea |
| 'Grouse' x ***keiskei*** var. ***ozawae*** 'Yaku Fairy' | ECho |
| 'Grumpy' | CBcs CSBt CWri ECho EMil EMui GGGa GKir LHyd LMil LRHS MAsh MBar MGos NDlv SBod SHBN SLdr SReu WBod |
| 'Gudrun' **new** | MDun |
| 'Guelder Rose' | SLdr |
| 'Gumpo' (EA) | CBcs CMac SLdr WBod |
| 'Gumpo Pink' (EA) | SLdr WBod |
| 'Gumpo White' (EA) | LCro LRHS MAsh MGos NLar WBod |
| 'Gundula' | LMil |
| 'Gwenda' (EA) | CTri LHyd SLdr |
| 'Gwillt-king' | CBcs |
| 'H.H. Hume' (EA) | SLdr |
| ***habrotrichum*** | GGGa LMil |
| 'Hachmann's Anastasia' | LMil MDun |
| 'Hachmann's Brasilia' | EMil LMil LRHS MDun SReu |
| 'Hachmann's Charmant' | EMil GGGa LMil MDun |
| 'Hachmann's Constanze' | EMil LMil |
| 'Hachmann's Diadem' | LMil LRHS |
| 'Hachmann's Eskimo' | LMil LRHS |
| 'Hachmann's Feuerschein' | LMil NBlu NLar |
| 'Hachmann's Junifeuer' **new** | LMil MDun |
| 'Hachmann's Kabarett' | LMil MDun |
| 'Hachmann's Marianne' | LMil |
| 'Hachmann's Marlis' ♀H4 | EMil LHyd LMil MAsh SReu |
| § 'Hachmann's Polaris' ♀H4 | CDoC LHyd LMil MBri MDun WBod |
| 'Hachmann's Porzellan' ♀H4 | EMil LMil NLar |
| § 'Hachmann's Rokoko' (EA) | GGGa LMil |
| ***haematodes*** | GGGa LHyd LMil MDun SRms |
| - CLD 1283 | LMil |
| - 'Blood Red' | SLdr |
| § - subsp. ***chaetomallum*** | GGGa LMil SLdr |
| - - JN 493 | GGGa |
| - subsp. ***haematodes*** | LMil |
| - - SBEC 585 | GGGa |
| 'Haida Gold' | SLdr SReu |
| 'Halfdan Lem' | CBcs CDoC CDul ECho GGGa LHyd MAsh MBri MDun MGos MLea SHBN SLdr SPer SReu SSta WBVN |
| 'Hallelujah' | MAsh |
| 'Halopeanum' | SHea SLdr |
| 'Hamlet' (M) | LMil |
| 'Hampshire Belle' **new** | LMil |
| 'Hana-asobi' (EA) | LHyd SLdr WBod |
| § 'Hanako' (EA) | GEdr GKir LRHS MBar MDun MGos MLea NDlv WBod |
| ***hanceanum*** 'Canton Consul' | GGGa LHyd |
| - Nanum Group | GGGa WBod |
| 'Hansel' | CDoC ECho GQui LMil MAsh MDun NLar WFar |
| ***haofui*** Guiz 75 | GGGa |
| Happy Group | ECho SHBN |
| 'Hardijzer Beauty' (Ad) | SLdr |
| ***hardyi*** | see *R. augustinii* subsp. *hardyi* |
| 'Harkwood Premiere' | GGGa |
| 'Harkwood Red' (EA) | SLdr |
| Harmony Group | SLdr |
| 'Harry Tagg' | CTrG SLdr WAbe |
| 'Harumiji' (EA) | SLdr |
| 'Harvest Moon' (K) | GKir MDun SCoo SLdr SReu |
| 'Harvest Moon' (hybrid) | CSBt MBar SReu |
| 'Hatsugiri' (EA) | CMac LHyd LMil MBar SLdr SReu |
| (Hawk Group) 'Hawk Buzzard' | SLdr |
| § - 'Hawk Falcon' | SReu |
| 'Heather Macleod' (EA) | SLdr |
| ***heatheriae*** | IDee LMil |
| - KR 6150 | GGGa |
| - KR 6158 | GGGa |
| - KR 6176 | LMil |
| ***heftii*** | SLdr |
| 'Helen Close' (EA) | SLdr |
| 'Helen Curtis' (EA) | MAsh SReu |
| 'Helene Schiffner' ♀H4 | GGGa LMil SReu |
| ***heliolepis*** | GGGa LMil WPic |
| - SF 489 | ISea |
| - SF 516 | ISea |
| - var. ***fumidum*** | see *R. heliolepis* var. *heliolepis* |
| § - var. ***heliolepis*** | LMil |
| - - CN&W 1038 | ISea |
| ***hemidartum*** | see *R. pocophorum* var. *hemidartum* |
| ***hemitrichotum*** | WThu |
| ***hemsleyanum*** | GGGa IDee LMil MDun SLdr |
| ***heptamerum*** | see *R. degronianum* subsp. *heptamerum* |
| 'Herbert' (EA) | CMac |
| 'Heureuse Surprise' (G) | SLdr |
| § 'Hexe' (EA) | CTrh WBod |
| 'High Summer' | LMil |
| 'Hilda Margaret' | SReu |
| 'Hilda Niblett' (EA) | MGos |
| 'Hille' | LMil |
| 'Hinamayo' | see *R.* 'Hinomayo' |
| 'Hino-crimson' (EA) ♀H3-4 | CBcs CDoC CMac CSBt CTrG CTri LMil LRHS MAsh MBar MBri MGos NHol SLdr SPer SPoG SReu SSta WFar |
| 'Hinode-giri' (EA) | CBcs CMac CSBt LHyd MAsh SLdr SReu WBod WFar WPic |
| 'Hinode-no-taka' (EA) | LHyd |

| | | |
|---|---|---|
| N | 'Hinomayo' (EA) ♀$^{H3-4}$ | CMac CTrG CTri EPfP GKir GQui LHyd LMil MBar SLdr SReu SSta WBod WPic |
| | 'Hino-scarlet' | see *R.* 'Campfire' |
| | 'Hino-tsukasa' (EA) | SLdr |
| | ***hippophaeoides*** | GKev LAst LMil MDun NMen SLdr WAbe WFar WGwG |
| | - F 22197a | SLdr |
| | - Yu 13845 | GGGa LMil MDun |
| | - 'Bei-ma-shan' | see *R. hippophaeoides* 'Haba Shan' |
| | - 'Blue Silver' | GGGa LMil LRHS MAsh NLar NMun |
| | - 'Glendoick Iceberg' | GGGa |
| § | - 'Haba Shan' ♀$^{H4}$ | GGGa LMil MDun |
| | ***hirsutum*** | GGGa LHyd LMil WBod |
| | - f. ***albiflorum*** | GGGa SReu |
| | - 'Flore Pleno' (d) | ECho GEdr GGar GKev MBar MDun |
| | ***hirtipes*** | GGGa LMil |
| | - C&V 9546 | GGGa |
| | - KR 5059 | LMil |
| | - KR 5219 | LMil |
| § | 'Hisako' (EA) | GEdr MDun NDlv |
| | ***hodgsonii*** | CDoC GGGa GKir IDee LMil MDun NHol SLdr |
| | - B&SWJ 2656 | WCru |
| | - TSS 9 | SLdr |
| | - TSS 42A | SLdr |
| | 'Holden' | WFar |
| | 'Hollandia' (hybrid) | SHBN |
| | 'Homebush' (K/d) ♀$^{H4}$ | CBcs CDoC CTri CWri EPfP GGGa GKev LCro LHyd LMil LRHS MAsh MBar MBri MDun MGos SLdr SPer SPoG SSta WBVN |
| | 'Honey Butter' | LMil |
| | 'Honeysuckle' (K) | MBar NHol SLdr SReu WBod |
| | 'Hong Kong' | MAsh |
| | ***hongkongense*** | GGGa |
| § | 'Ho-o' (EA) | CBcs NLar SLdr |
| | ***hookeri*** | CTrG SReu |
| | - Tigh-na-Rudha form | GGGa |
| | 'Hope Findlay' | LHyd |
| | 'Hoppy' | CBcs CSBt CWri GKir LMil MAsh MDun MGos MLea NMun SLdr SPoG WBVN |
| | 'Horizon Monarch' ♀$^{H3-4}$ | CDoC CWri EMil GGGa LHyd LMil LRHS MDun WBod |
| | ***horlickianum*** | GGGa |
| | 'Hortulanus H. Witte' (M) | CSBt SLdr SReu WFar |
| | 'Hot Shot' | see *R.* 'Girard's Hot Shot' |
| | 'Hot Shot Variegated' (EA/V) | CDoC |
| | 'Hotei' ♀$^{H4}$ | CBcs CDoC CSBt CWri ECho EPfP GEdr GGGa GKir LHyd LMil LRHS MAsh MBar MDun MGos NPri SHBN SHea SReu WBVN WBod WFar |
| | Hotspur Group (K) | LHyd |
| | 'Hotspur' (K) | CSBt CSam CWri ECho GBin MGos NLar SLdr SPer WBVN |
| | 'Hotspur Red' (K) ♀$^{H4}$ | CDoC CDul GKev LMil MAsh SReu |
| | 'Hotspur Yellow' (K) | SReu |
| | ***huanum*** | LMil |
| | - C&H 7073 | GGGa |
| | - EGM 316 | LMil |
| | 'Hugh Koster' | CSBt MGos SLdr |
| | aff. ***huidongense*** KR 7315 **new** | LMil |
| | 'Hullaballoo' | LMil |
| | 'Humboldt' | LMil WFar |
| | Humming Bird Group | CMHG GEdr GGGa GGar GKev LHyd MBar MDun NHol SHBN SLdr SRms WBod |
| | 'Hussar' | CWri |
| | 'Hyde and Seek' | GQui |
| | 'Hydie' (EA/d) | LMil LRHS MGos |
| | 'Hydon Amethyst' | LHyd |
| | 'Hydon Ben' | LHyd |
| | 'Hydon Comet' | LHyd |
| | 'Hydon Dawn' ♀$^{H4}$ | CDoC CWri GGGa GKir LHyd LMil MAsh MDun MGos MLea NDlv NLar SHea SReu SSta |
| | 'Hydon Glow' | LHyd |
| | 'Hydon Gold' | LHyd |
| | 'Hydon Haley' | LHyd |
| | 'Hydon Hunter' ♀$^{H4}$ | LHyd LMil MLea NDlv SHea SLdr SReu SSta |
| | 'Hydon Juliet' | LHyd |
| | 'Hydon Mist' | LHyd |
| | 'Hydon Pearl' | LHyd |
| | 'Hydon Pink' | SHea |
| | 'Hydon Rodney' | LHyd |
| | 'Hydon Salmon' | LHyd |
| | 'Hydon Velvet' | LHyd LMil SReu |
| | ***hylaeum*** BASEX 9659 | GGGa |
| | Hyperion Group | SReu SSta WFar |
| | ***hyperythrum*** | GGGa LHyd MDun SLdr |
| | - ETOT 196 | MDun |
| | ***hypoglaucum*** | see *R. argyrophyllum* subsp. *hypoglaucum* |
| | - 'Heane Wood' | see *R. argyrophyllum* subsp. *hypoglaucum* 'Heane Wood' |
| | 'Ice Cube' | ECho MBri MDun MMuc NLar SBod WFar |
| | 'Iceberg' | see *R.* 'Lodauric Iceberg' |
| | 'Idealist' | CWri LMil SReu |
| | 'Ightham Gold' | SReu |
| | 'Ightham Peach' | SReu |
| | 'Ightham Purple' | SReu |
| | 'Ightham Yellow' | MDun SHea SLdr SReu |
| | 'Igneum Novum' (G) | SReu |
| | 'Il Tasso' (R/d) | SLdr |
| § | 'Ilam Melford Lemon' (A) | LMil |
| § | 'Ilam Ming' (A) | LMil |
| | 'Ilam Violet' | LHyd LMil |
| | 'Imago' (K/d) | CSdC SLdr |
| § | 'Ima-shojo' (EA/d) | CSBt LHyd LMil LRHS SLdr WBod |
| | ***impeditum*** | CBcs CSBt CWib ECho GGGa GKev GQui LAst LHyd LRHS MAsh MBar MDun MGos MLea NMen SLdr SPer SPoG SReu SSta WBVN WBrE WFar |
| | - F 29268 | GGGa |
| | - 'Blue Steel' | see *R. fastigiatum* 'Blue Steel' |
| | - 'Indigo' | LLHF MDun WAbe |
| | - 'Pygmaeum' | GEdr WAbe WThu |
| | - Reuthe's form | SReu |
| | - 'Williams' | SLdr |
| | ***imperator*** | see *R. uniflorum* var. *imperator* |
| | 'Impi' | SReu |
| | Impi Group | MDun NLar |
| | 'Inamorata' | SLdr |
| | ***indicum*** (EA) | WBVN |
| § | - 'Balsaminiflorum' (EA/d) | CMac SLdr |
| § | - 'Macranthum' (EA) | LHyd SLdr WBod |
| | x ***inopinum*** | GGGa |
| | ***insigne*** ♀$^{H4}$ | GGGa IDee LMil MDun |
| | - Reuthe's form | SReu |
| | ***insigne*** x ***yakushimanum*** | SReu |
| | x ***intermedium*** white-flowered | GGGa |
| | Intrepid Group | SReu |
| | ***intricatum*** | GGGa |
| | Intrifast Group | GGGa LHyd NMen |
| | ***iodes*** | see *R. alutaceum* var. *iodes* |
| | 'Irene Koster' (O) ♀$^{H4}$ | CDoC CSBt CWri EPfP GGGa LHyd LMil MAsh MBri MDun MLea NLar SBod SLdr WBrE WCFE |

| | |
|---|---|
| 'Irish Mist' | GGGa |
| 'Irohayama' (EA) ♀H3-4 | CMac GQui LHyd LMil SLdr |
| ***irroratum*** | LMil SLdr |
| - subsp. ***irroratum*** C&H 7100 | GGGa |
| * - subsp. ***kontumense*** var. ***ningyuenense*** EGM 339 | LMil SLdr |
| - 'Langbianense' KR 3295 | LMil |
| - 'Polka Dot' | GGGa LHyd LMil SLdr |
| 'Isabel Pierce' | CWri LMil |
| Isabella Group | MAsh SLdr WFar |
| 'Isabella Mangles' | LHyd |
| 'Isola Bella' | GGGa |
| 'Issho-no-haru' (EA) | WBod |
| ***iteaphyllum*** | see *R. formosum* var. *formosum* Iteaphyllum Group |
| 'Ivery's Scarlet' | GKir |
| 'Ivette' (EA) | CMac LHyd |
| Iviza Group | SReu |
| 'Izayoi' (EA) | WBod |
| 'J.C. Williams' | CBcs |
| 'J.G. Millais' | SLdr |
| 'J.J. de Vink' | SHea |
| 'J.M. de Montague' | see *R.* 'The Hon. Jean Marie de Montague' |
| 'J.R.R. Tolkien' | SLdr |
| 'Jabberwocky' | LHyd |
| 'Jack Skilton' | LHyd SLdr |
| 'Jacksonii' | ISea MBar SHea SLdr |
| Jalisco Group | SLdr |
| 'Jalisco Elect' | LMil SLdr |
| 'Jalisco Emblem' | SLdr |
| 'Jalisco Goshawk' | SHea SLdr |
| 'Jalisco Janet' | SHea SLdr |
| 'James Barto' | LHyd SLdr |
| 'James Burchett' ♀H4 | LMil SLdr SReu |
| 'James Gable' (EA) | MAsh SLdr |
| 'Jan Bee' | SLdr |
| 'Jan Dekens' | SReu |
| 'Jan Steen' (M) | SLdr |
| 'Janet Blair' | CWri MDun SLdr WBVN |
| 'Janet Ward' | LHyd SReu |
| 'Janine Alexandre Debray' | SLdr |
| ***japonicum*** (A. Gray) Valcken | see *R. molle* subsp. *japonicum* |
| - Schneider var. ***japonicum*** | see *R. degronianum* subsp. *heptamerum* |
| - var. ***pentamerum*** | see *R. degronianum* subsp. *degronianum* |
| 'Jason' | SLdr |
| ***javanicum*** (V) | GGGa |
| 'Jean Marie Montague' | see *R.* 'The Hon. Jean Marie de Montague' |
| 'Jeff Hill' (EA) | ECho MMuc NLar SReu WBVN |
| 'Jenny' | see *R.* 'Creeping Jenny' |
| 'Jeremy Davies' | SReu |
| 'Jervis Bay' | SReu |
| 'Jingle Bells' | GGGa NLar |
| 'Joan Paton' (A) | SLdr |
| 'Jock' | SLdr |
| Jock Group | CBcs CMHG |
| 'Jock Brydon' (O) | GGGa LMil SLdr |
| 'Jock Coutts' (K) | CSdC |
| 'Johann Sebastian Bach' (EA) | WBod |
| 'Johann Strauss' (EA) | GKir WBod |
| 'Johanna' (EA) ♀H4 | CBcs CDoC CTri GGGa GKir LMil LRHS MAsh MBar MMHG NHol NLar SLdr SPer SReu WBod |
| 'John Barr Stevenson' | LHyd |
| 'John Cairns' (EA) | CMac LHyd MBar SLdr WBod WPic |
| 'John Walter' | MBar SHea SLdr |
| 'John Waterer' | CSBt SHea WFar |
| 'Johnny Bender' | SLdr |
| ***johnstoneanum*** | CBcs GGGa LMil SLdr WBod |
| - KW 7732 | SLdr |
| - 'Double Diamond' (d) | LMil |
| 'Jolie Madame' (Vs) | CSam CWri ECho EMil LMil LRHS MAsh MBri MLea NLar NPri SLdr SPur SReu |
| 'Josefa Blue' | GGGa |
| 'Joseph Baumann' (G) | CSdC SLdr |
| 'Joseph Hill' (EA) | ECho NHol SReu |
| 'Josephine Klinger' (G) | CSdC SReu |
| 'Jubilant' | SHea |
| 'Jubilee' | SLdr |
| Jubilee Queen Group | SLdr |
| 'June Fire' (A) | MDun SReu |
| 'Jungfrau' | CWri |
| 'Junifee' **new** | MDun |
| ***kaempferi*** (EA) | CBcs LHyd LMil SLdr |
| - 'Damio' | see *R. kaempferi* 'Mikado' |
| - 'Firefly' | see *R.* 'Hexe' |
| § - 'Mikado' (EA) | LMil SReu |
| - orange-flowered (EA) | CMac |
| 'Kakiemon' (EA) | LHyd |
| 'Kalinka' | EMil LHyd LMil LRHS MDun NHol SPoG |
| 'Kaponga' | CDoC MGos |
| 'Karen Triplett' | LMil |
| 'Karin' | MDun SHBN SLdr |
| 'Karin Seleger' | GGGa |
| 'Kasane-kagaribi' (EA) | LHyd |
| ***kasoense*** HECC 10009 | GGGa |
| - HECC 10040 | GGGa |
| 'Kate Waterer' ♀H4 | CWri MBar MDun MGos MLan SReu WFar |
| N 'Kathleen' (A) | SLdr |
| 'Kathleen' van Nes (EA) | LHyd |
| 'Katisha' (EA) | LHyd SLdr |
| 'Katsura-no-hana' (EA) **new** | WBod |
| 'Katy Watson' | SReu |
| ***kawakamii*** (V) | GGGa |
| § 'Kazuko' (EA) | GEdr LCro LRHS MBar MDun MGos MLea NDlv WBod WFar |
| ***keiskei*** | LHyd LLHF |
| - compact | GKev SLdr |
| - var. ***ozawae*** 'Yaku Fairy' ♀H4 | GGGa ITim LMil MDun WAbe WThu |
| ***keleticum*** | see *R. calostrotum* subsp. *keleticum* |
| 'Ken Janeck' ♀H4 | GGGa MDun NLar |
| § ***kendrickii*** | GGGa MDun |
| 'Kentucky Colonel' | SLdr |
| 'Kentucky Minstrel' (K) | SLdr |
| 'Kermesinum' (EA) | CTri LMil MBar MGos NMun SLdr SPlb SReu |
| I 'Kermesinum Album' (EA) | LMil MBar MGos SLdr SReu |
| I 'Kermesinum Rosé' (EA) | CSBt ECho GGGa LMil MAsh MBar MDun MGos MLea SLdr SReu |
| ***kesangiae*** | ISea MDun SLdr |
| - CH&M 3058 | GGGa |
| - CH&M 3099 | GGGa |
| - var. ***album*** KCSH 0362 **new** | GGGa |
| Kewense Group | LHyd |
| ***keysii*** | GGGa LHyd LMil MDun SLdr |
| - EGM 064 | LMil |
| - KC 0115 | GGGa |
| 'Kilimanjaro' | GGGa LHyd LMil SHea SReu |
| 'Kimbeth' | GGGa |
| 'Kimigayo' (EA) | LHyd |
| 'King George' Loder | see *R.* 'Loderi King George' |
| 'King George' van Nes | SReu |
| 'King of Shrubs' | NLar |
| ***kingianum*** | see *R. arboreum* subsp. *zeylanicum* |
| 'Kings Ride' | LHyd |

| | | |
|---|---|---|
| | 'Kingston' | MDun |
| § | 'Kirin' (EA/d) | CBcs CMac CSBt LHyd SLdr WBod |
| | 'Kirishima' (EA) | SRms |
| | 'Kiritsubo' (EA) | LHyd |
| | 'Kitty Cole' | SLdr |
| | ***kiusianum*** (EA) 🏆$^{H4}$ | GGGa LHyd LMil SReu SRms WAbe |
| | - 'Album' (EA) | LHyd LMil SReu WAbe |
| | - 'Hillier's Pink' (EA) | LMil |
| | 'Kiwi Majic' | LMil MDun |
| | 'Klondyke' (K) 🏆$^{H4}$ | CBcs CSBt CTri EMil EPfP GGGa GKir LCro LMil LRHS MAsh MDun MGos NPri SBod SLdr SPoG SReu |
| | 'Kluis Sensation' 🏆$^{H4}$ | CSBt LHyd MDun NHol SHBN SHea SLdr SReu |
| | 'Kluis Triumph' | SLdr SReu |
| | 'Knap Hill Apricot' (K) | CSdC LMil |
| | 'Knap Hill Red' (K) | CDoC LMil WMoo |
| | 'Knap Hill White' (K) | CSdC |
| | 'Kobold' (EA) | SLdr |
| | 'Koche-ne-mo' | WBod |
| | 'Koichiro Wada' | see *R. yakushimanum* 'Koichiro Wada' |
| | 'Kokardia' | EMil LMil |
| | ***kongboense*** | GGGa |
| | - C&V 9540 | GGGa |
| | 'Königstein' (EA) | LMil |
| § | 'Koningin Emma' (M) | LMil NLar SLdr |
| § | 'Koningin Wilhelmina' (M) | SLdr WBod |
| | ***konori*** var. ***phaeopeplum*** (V) | GGGa |
| | 'Koromo-shikibu' (EA) | GGGa GKir |
| | 'Koromo-shikibu White' (EA) | GGGa |
| | 'Koster's Brilliant Red' (M) | CSBt EPfP LMil MGos SReu |
| | ***kotschyi*** | see *R. myrtifolium* |
| | 'Kralingen' | NLar |
| | 'Kupferberg' | GGGa |
| § | 'Kure-no-yuki' (EA/d) | CSBt CTrG EPfP LHyd LMil SLdr |
| | 'Lackblatt' | see *R.* (Volker Group) 'Lackblatt' |
| | ***lacteum*** | LMil MDun SLdr |
| | - SBEC 345 | GGGa |
| | 'Lady Alice Fitzwilliam' 🏆$^{H2-3}$ | CBcs CEnd CMHG CTrG GGGa IDee ISea LHyd LMil |
| | 'Lady Armstrong' | CSBt |
| | Lady Bessborough Group | SLdr |
| | 'Lady Bowes Lyon' | SLdr |
| | Lady Chamberlain Group | GGGa SLdr |
| | 'Lady Chamberlain Salmon Trout' | see *R.* 'Salmon Trout' |
| | 'Lady Clementine Mitford' 🏆$^{H4}$ | CSBt CWri ECho EPfP GGGa GQui LHyd LMil MAsh MBri MDun MGos MLea MMuc NLar SHBN SHea SLdr SPer SPoG SReu |
| | 'Lady Digby' | CWri |
| | 'Lady Eleanor Cathcart' | SHea SLdr |
| | 'Lady Grey Egerton' | SHea |
| | 'Lady Longman' | LHyd SHea |
| | 'Lady Louise' (EA) | SLdr |
| | 'Lady Primrose' | SReu |
| | 'Lady Robin' (EA) | SLdr |
| | 'Lady Romsey' 🏆$^{H4}$ | LMil SLdr |
| | 'Lady Rosebery' (K) | CSdC MDun |
| | Ladybird Group | SReu |
| | ***laetum*** (V) | GGGa |
| | Lamellen Group | LHyd SLdr |
| | 'Lampion' | GGGa |
| | 'Lamplighter' | SHea SLdr SReu |
| | ***lanatoides*** | LMil |
| | - C&C 7548 | GGGa |
| | - C&C 7574 | GGGa |
| | - C&C 7577 | GGGa |
| | - KR 6385 | LMil |
| | ***lanatum*** | GGGa LMil |
| | - dwarf, cream-flowered | GGGa |
| | - Flinckii Group | see *R. flinckii* |
| | ***lanatum*** x ***yakushimanum*** | GGGa |
| | 'Langworth' | CWri ECho GQui ISea LMil MAsh MDun MGos MLea SLdr SReu |
| | ***lanigerum*** | LMil MDun SReu |
| | - C&V 9530 | GGGa |
| | - KW 8251 | GGGa |
| | ***lapponicum*** Confertissimum Group | GGGa |
| | - Parvifolium Group from Siberia | GGGa WAbe |
| | 'Lapwing' (K) | SLdr |
| | 'Laramie' | GGGa |
| | 'Lascaux' | SReu |
| | 'Late Inverue' (EA) | MAsh |
| | 'Late Love' (EA) | CDoC MGos |
| | late pink, from Inverewe | WBVN |
| § | ***latoucheae*** (EA) PW 86 | GGGa |
| | ***laudandum*** var. ***temoense*** | GGGa |
| | Laura Aberconway Group | SHea SLdr WBod |
| | 'Laura Morland' (EA) | LHyd |
| | 'Lava Flow' | LHyd |
| | 'Lavender Girl' 🏆$^{H4}$ | GGGa LHyd LMil NLar SHea SLdr SReu SSta |
| | 'Lavender Lady' (EA) | CTrG |
| | 'Lavendula' | GGGa |
| | 'Le Progrès' | CDoC LMil MAsh |
| | 'Lea Rainbow' | MLea |
| | 'Ledifolium' | see *R.* x *mucronatum* |
| | 'Ledifolium Album' | see *R.* x *mucronatum* |
| | 'Lee's Dark Purple' | CSBt CWri LMil MBar MDun WFar |
| | 'Lee's Scarlet' | LMil |
| | 'Lem' | NLar SReu |
| | 'Lemon Dream' | LMil |
| * | 'Lemon Drop' (A) | GGGa |
| | 'Lemonora' (M) | LRHS MBri SLdr |
| | 'Lem's 45' | CWri ECho ISea MDun SLdr |
| | 'Lem's Cameo' 🏆$^{H3}$ | GGGa LHyd LMil MDun SReu SSta |
| | 'Lem's Monarch' 🏆$^{H4}$ | CBcs CDoC CDul CWri GGGa GKir LHyd LMil MBri MDun MGos MLea SReu SSta |
| | 'Lem's Tangerine' | CDoC LMil |
| | 'Lemur' (EA) | ECho GEdr GGGa MAsh MDun MLea NHol NLar SReu WBod WThu |
| | 'Leny' (EA) | NHol |
| | 'Leo' (EA) | GQui LHyd SLdr |
| | 'Leo' (hybrid) | EPfP |
| | 'Leonardslee Giles' | SLdr |
| | 'Leonardslee Primrose' | SLdr |
| | Leonore Group | SReu |
| | ***lepidostylum*** | CBcs CWri GGGa LHyd LMil MBar MDun NHol SLdr SReu WFar |
| | ***lepidotum*** | GGGa LMil MDun WAbe |
| | - Elaeagnoides Group | GGGa |
| | - yellow-flowered McB 110 | WThu |
| § | ***leptocarpum*** | GGGa |
| | ***leptothrium*** | GGGa |
| | Letty Edwards Group | CSBt SLdr SReu |
| § | 'Leucanthum' | GGGa WThu |
| | ***leucaspis*** | GGGa LHyd MDun SLdr SReu |
| | ***levinei*** | GGGa |
| | 'Lewis Monarch' | GQui |
| | 'Libretto' | NLar |
| | 'Lila Pedigo' | CWri ECho MAsh MBri MDun MLea SPer WBVN WFar |
| | 'Lilac Time' (EA) | MBar SLdr |
| | 'Lilacinum' (EA) | WPic |
| | ***liliiflorum*** Guiz 163 | GGGa |
| | 'Lilliput' (EA) | MAsh |
| | 'Lily Marleen' (EA) | CTri LRHS SCoo SReu |

| | | |
|---|---|---|
| | 'Linda' 🏆H4 | CBcs CSam CTri ECho EPfP GGGa LMil LRHS LSRN MAsh MBar MDun MGos SLdr |
| | 'Linda Lee' | SLdr |
| | ***lindleyi*** | GQui LHyd |
| | - L&S | GGGa |
| | - 'Dame Edith Sitwell' | LMil |
| | 'Linearifolium' | see *R. stenopetalum* 'Linearifolium' |
| | Lionel's Triumph Group | LMil SLdr |
| | 'Little Beauty' (EA) | SLdr |
| | 'Little Ben' | ECho GEdr MBar MDun |
| | 'Loch Awe' | GGGa |
| | 'Loch Earn' | GGGa |
| | 'Loch Laggan' | GGGa |
| | 'Loch Leven' | GGGa |
| | 'Loch Lomond' | GGGa |
| | 'Loch Morar' | GGGa |
| | 'Loch o' the Lowes' | GGGa MBri MDun MGos WFar |
| | 'Loch Rannoch' | GGGa MGos WBVN WFar |
| | 'Loch Tummel' | GGGa |
| | ***lochiae*** (V) | GGGa |
| | 'Lochinch Spinbur' | GQui |
| | x ***lochmium*** | GGGa |
| | Lodauric Group | SLdr SReu |
| § | 'Lodauric Iceberg' 🏆H3-4 | LMil SLdr SReu |
| | 'Lodbrit' | SReu |
| | Loderi Group | SLdr |
| | 'Loderi Fairy Queen' | SLdr |
| | 'Loderi Fairyland' | LHyd |
| | 'Loderi Game Chick' 🏆H3-4 | LHyd MDun SLdr SReu |
| | 'Loderi Georgette' | SLdr |
| | 'Loderi Helen' | SLdr |
| § | 'Loderi King George' 🏆H3-4 | CBcs CDoC CDul CSBt CWri ECho GGGa IDee ISea LHyd LMil MDun MGos MLea SLdr SPer SReu SSta WBVN WBod |
| | 'Loderi Kunoo' **new** | WBod |
| | 'Loderi Patience' | SLdr |
| | 'Loderi Pink Coral' | LMil SLdr |
| | 'Loderi Pink Diamond' 🏆H3-4 | CDoC CWri LMil MDun SLdr WBod |
| | 'Loderi Pink Topaz' 🏆H3-4 | LHyd SLdr |
| | 'Loderi Pretty Polly' | CWri SLdr |
| | 'Loderi Princess Marina' | SLdr |
| | 'Loderi Sir Edmund' | LHyd SLdr |
| | 'Loderi Sir Joseph Hooker' | LHyd SLdr WBod |
| | 'Loderi Titan' | SLdr SReu |
| | 'Loderi Venus' 🏆H3-4 | CWri GGGa LHyd MDun SLdr SReu SSta WBVN |
| | 'Loderi White Diamond' | LHyd SLdr WBod |
| | 'Loder's White' 🏆H3-4 | CWri GGGa LHyd LMil MDun MLea SHea SLdr SReu SSta |
| § | 'Logan Damaris' | LHyd SLdr SReu |
| | ***longesquamatum*** | GGGa LMil SLdr |
| | ***longipes*** | LMil SLdr |
| | - EGM 336 | LMil |
| | - var. ***longipes*** C&H 7072 | GGGa |
| | - - C&H 7113 | GGGa |
| | ***longistylum*** | GGGa |
| | 'Looking Glass' | MDun |
| | 'Lord Roberts' 🏆H4 | CBcs CDoC CSBt CTri CWri ECho EPfP GGGa GKir LCro LMil MAsh MBar MGos MLea SHBN SHea SLdr SReu WBVN WBod WFar WMoo |
| | 'Lord Swaythling' | LHyd SLdr |
| | 'Loreley' | NLar |
| | 'Lori Eichelser' | GEdr MDun |
| | 'Lorna' (EA) | GQui LMil WBod |
| | 'Louis Aimée van Houtte' (G) | SLdr |
| | 'Louis Hellebuyck' (G) | SLdr |
| | 'Louis Pasteur' | SReu |
| | 'Louisa' (EA) | MAsh |
| | 'Louisa Hill' (EA) | MGos |
| | 'Louise' (EA) | SLdr |
| | 'Louise Dowdle' (EA) | SLdr |
| | 'Love Poem' | GGGa |
| | 'Lovely William' | CMac LMil SLdr |
| | ***lowndesii*** | WAbe |
| | ***luciferum*** CER 9935 | GGGa |
| | 'Lucinda' **new** | MDun |
| | 'Lucy' (A) **new** | NMun |
| | 'Lucy Lou' | GGGa |
| | ***ludlowii*** | GGGa |
| | ***ludwigianum*** | GGGa |
| | 'Lugano' | NLar |
| | 'Lullaby' (EA) | GKir SLdr |
| | 'Lumina' | NLar |
| | 'Lunar Queen' | LHyd SLdr |
| | Luscombei Group | SLdr |
| | ***luteiflorum*** | LMil |
| | - KW 21556 | GGGa |
| | ***lutescens*** | CBcs ISea LMil MDun SHea SLdr SReu SSta WAbe |
| | - C&H 7124 | GGGa |
| | - 'Bagshot Sands' 🏆H3-4 | GGGa LHyd LMil |
| | ***luteum*** (A) 🏆H4 | Widely available |
| | - 'Golden Comet' (A) | GGGa |
| § | ***lyi*** KR 2962 | GGGa |
| | ***maccabeanum*** 🏆H3-4 | CBcs CDoC CWri GGGa GKir IDee ISea LHyd LMil LRHS MBri MDun MLea SLdr SPer SReu SSpi SSta WFar WHer |
| | - SEH 27 | GGGa |
| | - SEH 52 | GGGa |
| | - deep cream-flowered | SLdr |
| | - Embley form | SLdr |
| | - Reuthe's form | SReu |
| | - Tower Court form | SLdr |
| | ***maccabeanum*** x ***sinogrande*** | SReu |
| | ***macgregoriae*** (V) Woods 2646 | GGGa |
| | ***macranthum*** | see *R. indicum* 'Macranthum' |
| | 'Macranthum Roseum' (EA) | MMHG |
| | ***macrophyllum*** | GGGa |
| | ***macrosmithii*** | see ***R. argipeplum*** |
| | 'Macrostemon' | see *R.* (Obtusum Group) 'Macrostemon' |
| | ***maculiferum*** | GGGa SLdr |
| | - subsp. ***anwheiense*** | see ***R. anwheiense*** |
| | 'Madame Galle' | NBlu |
| | 'Madame Knutz' (A) | SLdr |
| | 'Madame Masson' | CDoC CTri CWri ECho EMil GGGa GKir ISea LMil LRHS MAsh MBri MDun MGos MLea NPri SBod SHBN SLdr SPer SPoG SReu SSta WBVN WBod WFar |
| | 'Madame van Hecke' (EA) | CTri GKir LMil LRHS MBri SLdr WFar |
| | ***maddenii*** | CDoC LMil SLdr WPic |
| § | - subsp. ***crassum*** | CBcs GGGa LMil SKHP SLdr WPic |
| | - - SDR 3335 **new** | GKev |
| § | - subsp. ***maddenii*** Polyandrum Group | CBcs GGal GQui ISea SLdr |
| | 'Madeline's Yellow' | SLdr |
| | 'Mademoiselle Masson' | WFar |
| | 'Magic Flute' (EA) | LRHS MGos WBod |
| I | 'Magic Flute' (V) | LMil NPri SCoo |
| | 'Magnificum' (O) | SLdr |
| | ***magnificum*** | SReu |
| | 'Maharani' | GGGa MDun |
| | 'Maja' (G) | SLdr |
| § | ***makinoi*** 🏆H4 | GGGa GKir LHyd LLHF LMil MDun NLar NMen SLdr SReu SSpi SSta |

| | |
|---|---|
| - 'Fuju-kaku-no-matsu' | MGos NLar |
| ***mallotum*** | GGGa IDee LHyd LMil MDun SLdr SReu |
| - BASEX 9672 | GGGa |
| - Farrer 815 | GGGa |
| 'Malvaticum' (EA) | WBod |
| 'Malwine' **new** | MDun |
| Mandalay Group | LHyd SHea |
| 'Mandarin Lights' (A) | LMil LRHS MBri |
| ***maoerense*** | GGGa |
| 'Marcel Ménard' | CDoC EMil LMil NBlu NLar SReu WBod WFar |
| 'Marchioness of Lansdowne' | CSBt SHea |
| 'Marcia' | SLdr |
| 'Mardi Gras' | CDoC GGGa LMil MLea |
| Margaret Dunn Group | CWri |
| 'Margaret Falmouth' | SReu |
| 'Margaret George' (EA) | LHyd |
| 'Maricee' | GGGa |
| 'Marie Curie' | LMil SReu |
| 'Marie Verschaffelt' (G) | SLdr |
| 'Marilee' (EA) | CDoC ECho LRHS MAsh MGos NLar SLdr |
| Mariloo Group | SLdr |
| 'Marinus Koster' | MDun SLdr |
| 'Marion Street' ♀H4 | LHyd LMil SLdr SReu |
| 'Markeeta's Flame' | MDun |
| 'Markeeta's Prize' ♀H4 | CDoC CWri ECho EPfP GGGa LMil LRHS MAsh MBri MDun MGos MLea NPri SBod SHea SLdr SReu WBVN |
| 'Marley Hedges' | GGGa LMil |
| 'Marlies' (A) | SLdr |
| 'Marmot' (EA) | ECho MBar MDun MLea NLar WBod |
| 'Mars' | GGGa SLdr SReu |
| 'Martha Hitchcock' (EA) | SRms |
| 'Martha Isaacson' (Ad) ♀H4 | LMil MGos SReu |
| 'Martine' (Ad) | MGos |
| ***martinianum*** | LMil SLdr |
| aff. ***martinianum*** KW 21557 | GGGa |
| 'Maruschka' (EA) | LMil NMun |
| 'Mary Fleming' | MAsh MDun SBod SLdr |
| 'Mary Helen' (EA) | LHyd LMil LRHS MAsh NPri SCoo WBod |
| 'Mary Meredith' (EA) | LHyd |
| 'Mary Poppins' (K) | CTri LCro LMil LRHS SCoo SPoG |
| 'Maryke' | LMil |
| 'Master of Elphinstone' (EA) | SLdr |
| Matador Group | SLdr SReu |
| 'Matador' | LHyd LMil SHea WBod |
| ***maximum*** | GGGa |
| - SDR 2205 | GKev |
| - SDR 2302 **new** | GKev |
| § 'Maxwellii' (EA) | CMac SLdr |
| 'May Day' ♀H3-4 | CMac NLar SHea WBod |
| May Day Group | CBcs CWri ISea MDun MGos SHBN SLdr |
| 'May Glow' | MGos |
| May Morn Group | SReu |
| 'Mayor Johnstone' | CTri MAsh NPri |
| ***meddianum*** | GGGa |
| - var. ***atrokermesinum*** KW 2100a | GGGa |
| Medea Group | SLdr |
| Medusa Group | GGGa SHea SLdr SReu |
| ***megacalyx*** | GGGa ISea |
| 'Megan' (EA) | ECho GGGa MAsh MMuc NLar WGwG |
| ***megaphyllum*** | see *R. basilicum* |
| ***megeratum*** | GGGa SLdr SReu |
| - 'Bodnant' | WAbe WBod |
| ***mekongense*** | GGGa |
| - KR 5044 | LMil |
| - var. ***mekongense*** | SReu |
| § - var. ***melinanthum*** | SReu |
| - var. ***rubrolineatum*** | LMil |
| 'Melford Lemon' | see *R.* 'Ilam Melford Lemon' |
| 'Melidioso' | LMil MDun |
| 'Melina' (EA/d) | GGGa LMil |
| ***melinanthum*** | see *R. mekongense* var. *melinanthum* |
| 'Merganser' ♀H4 | GEdr GGGa LMil MDun MLea NDlv NHol SReu WAbe WBod WThu |
| 'Merlin' (EA) | SLdr |
| 'Meteor' elepidote **new** | SHea |
| Metis Group | WBod |
| ***metternichii*** | see *R. degronianum* subsp. *heptamerum* |
| - var. ***pentamerum*** | see *R. degronianum* subsp. *degronianum* |
| 'Mi Amor' | LMil |
| 'Miami' (A) | SLdr |
| 'Michael Hill' (EA) | CDoC LHyd MAsh |
| 'Michael Waterer' | MDun SLdr |
| 'Michael's Pride' | GQui |
| ***micranthum*** | GGGa MDun SLdr |
| ***microgynum*** | LMil |
| - F 14242 | GGGa |
| ***microleucum*** | see *R. orthocladum* var. *microleucum* |
| ***micromeres*** | see *R. leptocarpum* |
| 'Midnight Mystique' | GGGa MDun |
| 'Midsummer' | CWri SHea SLdr |
| 'Mikado' (EA) | see *R. kaempferi* 'Mikado' |
| 'Mikado' (hybrid) | SLdr |
| 'Milton' (R) | LMil SLdr |
| § ***mimetes*** var. ***simulans*** F 20428 | GGGa |
| 'Mimi' (EA) | CMac LHyd |
| 'Mimra' | SLdr |
| 'Mina van Houtte' (G) | SLdr |
| 'Mindy's Love' | LMil |
| 'Ming' | see *R.* 'Ilam Ming' |
| 'Minterne Cinnkeys' | MDun |
| ***minus*** | GQui |
| - SDR 2228 | GKev |
| § - var. ***minus*** | SLdr |
| § - - Carolinianum Group | LMil |
| - - - 'Epoch' | LMil |
| § - - Punctatum Group | MBar |
| 'Miss Muffet' (EA) | SLdr |
| 'Moerheim' ♀H4 | CBcs CWri ECho EMil LRHS MAsh MBar MGos NHol SReu WBVN WBrE |
| § 'Moerheim's Pink' | LHyd LMil MDun NHol SLdr |
| 'Moidart' (Vs) | LMil |
| 'Moira Salmon' (EA) | LHyd |
| § ***molle*** subsp. ***japonicum*** (A) | GGGa LMil SLdr |
| - - JR 871 | GGGa |
| - subsp. ***molle*** (A) | LMil |
| - - C&H 7181 | GGGa |
| ***mollicomum*** F 30940 | SLdr |
| 'Mollie Coker' | CWri SLdr |
| Mollis orange-flowered (M) | MBar SRms |
| - pink-flowered (M) | GGGa MBar NBlu SRms |
| - red-flowered (M) | MBar NBlu SRms |
| - salmon-flowered (M) | GGGa GQui |
| - yellow-flowered (M) | GQui MBar NBlu SRms |
| 'Molly Ann' | ECho GGGa MDun MGos SLdr |
| 'Molten Gold' (v) | LMil LRHS MAsh |
| § 'Momoko' (EA) | GKir LRHS |
| ***monanthum*** CCH&H 8133 | GGGa |

| | | |
|---|---|---|
| | ***monosematum*** | see *R. pachytrichum* var. *monosematum* |
| | ***montroseanum*** | CDoC IDee ISea LMil MDun SLdr SSpi WCru |
| * | - 'Baravalla' | GGGa |
| | - white-flowered | SLdr |
| | 'Moon Maiden' (EA) | ECho GQui NLar SLdr |
| | Moonshine Group | SLdr |
| | 'Moonshine' | SReu |
| | 'Moonshine Bright' | LHyd MDun |
| | Moonstone Group | CWri MBar MDun MLea SLdr WBod |
| | - pink-tipped | GEdr |
| | 'Moonwax' | CWri SLdr |
| § | 'Morgenrot' | EMil EMui GGGa MAsh MGos SReu WFar |
| | ***morii*** | GGGa LHyd LMil MDun |
| | 'Morning Cloud' ♀H4 | CAbP ECho EPfP LHyd LMil LRHS MAsh MBar NDlv NHol NPri SReu |
| | 'Morning Magic' | LHyd SLdr |
| | Morning Red | see *R.* 'Morgenrot' |
| | 'Moser's Maroon' | CWri ECho MGos MLea NLar SLdr SPoG WBVN |
| | 'Motet' (K/d) | CSdC SLdr |
| | 'Mother of Pearl' | SHea SLdr SReu |
| | 'Mother's Day' (EA) ♀H4 | Widely available |
| | Moulten Gold = 'Blattgold' | GGGa |
| | 'Mount Everest' | GGGa LHyd LMil SReu SSta |
| | 'Mount Rainier' (K) | SLdr SReu |
| | 'Mount Saint Helens' | GGGa LMil SLdr |
| | 'Mount Seven Star' | see *R. nakaharae* 'Mount Seven Star' |
| | 'Mountain Star' | SLdr |
| | ***moupinense*** | GGGa IDee LHyd LMil SLdr SReu |
| | 'Möwe' (K) | LMil |
| | 'Mozart' (EA) | WBod |
| | 'Mrs A.C. Kenrick' | SHea SLdr |
| | 'Mrs A.T. de la Mare' ♀H4 | CSBt GGGa LHyd LMil MDun NHol SHea SLdr SReu SSta |
| | 'Mrs Betty Robertson' | ECho LMil MAsh MDun MGos SLdr SReu |
| | 'Mrs C.B. van Nes' | SReu |
| | Mrs C. Whitner Group | SLdr |
| | 'Mrs C. Whitner' x Tally Ho Group | SLdr |
| | 'Mrs Charles E. Pearson' ♀H4 | CSBt LMil SHBN SHea SLdr SReu |
| | 'Mrs Davies Evans' ♀H4 | CWri LHyd MBar SReu SSta |
| | 'Mrs Dick Thompson' | SReu |
| | 'Mrs Donald Graham' | SReu |
| | 'Mrs E.C. Stirling' | SRms |
| | 'Mrs Emil Hager' (EA) | LHyd SLdr |
| | 'Mrs Furnivall' ♀H4 | CBcs CDoC CWri ECho EPfP GGGa GKir LHyd LMil LRHS MDun MGos MLea MMuc SHea SLdr SReu |
| | 'Mrs G.W. Leak' | CSBt CSam CWri EPfP GGGa GKir LHyd LMil MDun MLea SHBN SHea SLdr SReu |
| | 'Mrs Henry Agnew' | SLdr |
| | 'Mrs J.C. Williams' ♀H4 | LMil |
| | 'Mrs J.G. Millais' | LMil MDun SHea |
| | 'Mrs James Horlick' | CWri |
| | 'Mrs John Kelk' | LMil |
| | 'Mrs Kingsmill' | SLdr |
| | 'Mrs Lionel de Rothschild' ♀H4 | MDun SReu |
| | 'Mrs P.D. Williams' | SReu |
| | 'Mrs Peter Koster' (M) | SLdr WFar |
| | 'Mrs R.S. Holford' ♀H4 | SHea SLdr |
| | 'Mrs T.H. Lowinsky' ♀H4 | CDoC CSBt ECho EPfP GGGa GKir LMil MAsh MDun MGos MLea SHea SLdr SPer SReu SSta WBVN |
| | 'Mrs W.C. Slocock' | GKir MDun SLdr |
| | 'Mucronatum' | see *R.* x *mucronatum* |
| § | x ***mucronatum*** (EA) | CBcs LHyd SRms WBod WPic |
| | ***mucronulatum*** | CBcs GGGa WBod |
| | - var. ***chejuense*** | see *R. mucronulatum* var. *taquetii* |
| | - 'Cornell Pink' ♀H4 | GGGa LHyd WFar |
| | - pink-flowered | WPGP |
| § | - var. ***taquetii*** | GGGa |
| | 'Muncaster Hybrid' | NMun |
| | 'Muncaster Mist' | LHyd |
| § | ***myrtifolium*** | LMil |
| | ***nakaharae*** (EA) | SLdr SReu |
| § | - 'Mariko' (EA) | LHyd MBar NHol SLdr WThu |
| § | - 'Mount Seven Star' (EA) ♀H4 | ECho GGGa LHyd LMil MGos NHol SLdr WAbe WBVN |
| § | - orange-flowered (EA) | ECho LMil LRHS MAsh MGos MMuc NDlv NPri SHBN SReu |
| | - pink-flowered (EA) | ECho ELon LMil MAsh MGos NDlv NLar SLdr SPer SReu SSta |
| | - red-flowered (EA) | ECho MGos |
| | 'Nakahari Orange' | see *R. nakaharae* orange-flowered |
| | 'Nakahari-mariko' | see *R. nakaharae* 'Mariko' |
| | 'Nancy Buchanan' (K) | SLdr |
| | 'Nancy Evans' ♀H3-4 | CDoC CSBt CWri ECho EPfP GGGa GKir LHyd LMil LRHS MAsh MDun MLea NPri SLdr SReu SSpi WFar |
| | 'Nancy of Robinhill' (EA) | SReu |
| | 'Nancy Waterer' (G) ♀H4 | EPfP LMil NLar SReu |
| | 'Nanki Poo' (EA) | LHyd SLdr |
| | Naomi Group | CWri LHyd SHea SLdr |
| | 'Naomi' (EA) | GQui SHBN SLdr WPic |
| | 'Naomi Astarte' | MDun SLdr |
| | 'Naomi Hope' | SLdr |
| | 'Naomi Nautilus' | LMil |
| | 'Naomi Stella Maris' | LHyd |
| | 'Narcissiflorum' (G/d) ♀H4 | CDoC CSBt CTri EPfP IDee LHyd LMil NLar |
| | 'Naselle' | GGGa LMil SReu |
| | 'Nassau' (EA/d) | MAsh |
| | ***neriiflorum*** | GGGa MDun SReu |
| | - subsp. ***neriiflorum*** | GKir |
| | - - L&S 1352 | GGGa |
| § | - subsp. ***phaedropum*** | MDun |
| | - - CCH&H 8125 | GGGa |
| | ***nervulosum*** Sleumer (V) | GGGa |
| | 'Nestor' | SReu |
| | 'New Comet' | LHyd SLdr |
| | 'New Moon' | SReu |
| | 'Newcomb's Sweetheart' | LMil MDun |
| | 'Niagara' (EA) ♀H3-4 | CTrh EPfP LHyd LMil MGos NMen SLdr SPoG WBod |
| | 'Nichola' (EA) | SReu |
| | 'Nico' (EA) | CMac LRHS WBod |
| | 'Nicoletta' | LMil |
| | 'Night Sky' | CDoC ECho GGGa LHyd LMil LRHS MAsh MDun MGos MLea NLar SBod SLdr WBVN |
| | 'Nightingale' | LMil SReu |
| | ***nigroglandulosum*** | GGGa |
| | ***nilagiricum*** | see *R. arboreum* subsp. *nilagiricum* |
| | 'Nimbus' | LMil SLdr |
| | Nimrod Group | SLdr |
| | 'Nippon' | SLdr |
| | ***nipponicum*** | SReu |
| | 'Nishiki' (EA) | CMac |
| | ***nitens*** | see *R. calostrotum* subsp. *riparium* |
| | ***nitidulum*** var. ***omeiense*** KR 185 | GGGa |
| | ***nivale*** subsp. ***boreale*** | WPic |
| | - - Ramosissimum Group | GGGa |
| | ***niveum*** ♀H4 | GGGa IDee LMil LRHS MDun SLdr SReu |
| | - B&SWJ 2611 **new** | WCru |

| | | |
|---|---|---|
| | – B&SWJ 2659 **new** | WCru |
| | – B&SWJ 2675 | WCru |
| | – 'Nepal' | LHyd |
| | ***nobleanum*** | see *R.* Nobleanum Group |
| § | Nobleanum Group | GGGa LHyd LMil SLdr SSta |
| | 'Nobleanum Album' | GGGa GGal LHyd LMil SReu SSta |
| | 'Nobleanum Coccineum' | GGal ISea SLdr SReu |
| | 'Nobleanum Lamellen' | SLdr |
| | 'Nobleanum Venustum' | CSBt LHyd LMil SReu SSta WBod |
| | 'Nofretete' | GGGa |
| | 'Nora' | WPic |
| | 'Nordlicht' (EA) | SLdr |
| | 'Norfolk Candy' **new** | LMil MDun |
| N | 'Norma' (R/d) ♀$^{H4}$ | SReu |
| | Norman Shaw Group | LHyd |
| | 'Northern Hi-Lights' (A) | LMil LRHS MAsh SLdr |
| | 'Northern Lights' | see *R.* 'Arctic Glow' |
| | 'Northern Star' | LHyd |
| | 'Nova Zembla' | CDoC CTri ECho EMil EPfP GGGa GKir LMil LRHS MAsh MBar MGos NPri SHBN SLdr SPer SPoG SReu SSta WBVN WBod WBrE |
| | ***nudiflorum*** | see *R. periclymenoides* |
| | ***nudipes*** | LMil |
| | ***nuttallii*** | GGGa LMil SLdr |
| | 'Oban' | GEdr ITim LMil MDun NMen WAbe WThu |
| | ***obtusum*** f. ***amoenum*** | see *R.* 'Amoenum' |
| | Obtusum Group (EA) | LHyd SLdr |
| § | – 'Macrostemon' (EA) | WBod |
| | ***occidentale*** (A) ♀$^{H4}$ | GGGa GGal IDee LMil MDun SLdr SSpi |
| | ***ochraceum*** | LMil |
| | – C&H 7052 | GGGa |
| | – EGM 312 | LMil |
| | 'Odee Wright' | CTri CWri GGGa LRHS MAsh MDun NLar NPri SLdr SReu |
| | 'Odoratum' (Ad) | MLea |
| | 'Oh! Kitty' | CWri ECho MLea |
| | 'Oi-no-mezame' (EA) | LHyd SLdr |
| | 'Old Copper' | CWri SLdr |
| | 'Old Gold' (K) | ECho ISea SLdr SReu |
| | 'Old Port' ♀$^{H4}$ | CWri GGGa LHyd LMil SHBN SHea |
| | 'Olga' ♀$^{H4}$ | CBcs LHyd LMil MDun SHea SLdr SReu SSta |
| | 'Olga Niblett' (EA) | LMil LRHS MGos SReu |
| | ***oligocarpum*** Guiz 148* | GGGa |
| | 'Olin O. Dobbs' | SReu |
| | 'Olive' | LHyd LMil |
| | 'Olympic Flame' (EA) | LMil |
| | Olympic Lady Group | LHyd MLea SLdr |
| | Omar Group | MBar |
| § | 'One Thousand Butterflies' | GGGa MDun SLdr |
| | 'Ophelia' | SLdr |
| | 'Oporto' | SLdr |
| | 'Orange Beauty' (EA) ♀$^{H3-4}$ | CBcs CDoC CMac CSBt CTrh ECho GGGa GKir LHyd LMil MAsh MBar MGos SLdr SReu WBVN WBod WFar |
| | 'Orange King' (EA) | LMil MGos |
| | 'Orange Scout' | SLdr |
| | 'Orange Sunset' | MDun |
| | 'Orangengold' | MDun |
| | ***orbiculare*** ♀$^{H3-4}$ | GGGa LMil MDun SLdr |
| | – C&K 230 | GGGa |
| § | – subsp. ***cardiobasis*** | MDun SLdr |
| | – Sandling Park form | SReu |
| | 'Orchid Lights' | GKir LRHS MAsh |
| | 'Oregon' (EA) | SLdr |
| | ***oreodoxa*** | LMil |
| § | – var. ***fargesii*** ♀$^{H4}$ | GGGa LHyd LMil SLdr |
| | – var. ***oreodoxa*** | LMil |
| | – – EN 4212 | GGGa |
| | ***oreotrephes*** | IDee LHyd LMil MDun SHea SLdr SReu WBod |
| | – 'Bluecalyptus' | GGGa |
| § | – Exquisitum Group | CBcs SLdr SReu |
| | – 'Pentland' | GGGa LMil |
| | Orestes Group | SLdr |
| | ***orthocladum*** | LMil |
| § | – var. ***microleucum*** | GGGa WThu |
| | – var. ***orthocladum*** F 20488 | GGGa |
| | 'Oryx' (O) | CSdC |
| | 'Osaraku Seedling' (EA) | EPfP GKir |
| | 'Osmar' ♀$^{H4}$ | GGGa MGos SReu |
| | 'Ostara' | MDun MGos |
| | 'Ostergold' | LMil LRHS |
| | 'Oudijk's Sensation' | CBcs CWri ECho GQui MAsh MDun MGos MMuc SLdr WBVN WBrE |
| | ***ovatum*** CN&W 548 | ISea |
| | 'Oxydol' (K) | MBri MMuc SLdr |
| § | ***pachypodum*** | GGGa |
| | – KR 4053 | LMil |
| | ***pachysanthum*** ♀$^{H4}$ | CDoC LHyd LMil MDun SLdr SReu SSpi |
| | – RV 72/001 | GGGa SLdr |
| | – 'Crosswater' | IDee LMil MDun |
| | ***pachysanthum*** × ***yakushimanum*** | GGGa SReu |
| | ***pachytrichum*** | GGGa SLdr |
| | – W 1435 | SLdr |
| § | – var. ***monosematum*** | SLdr SReu |
| | – – CN&W 953 | LMil |
| | – var. ***pachytrichum*** 'Sesame' | LMil |
| | 'Palestrina' (EA) ♀$^{H3-4}$ | CBcs CMac CSBt CTrh ECho EPfP GKir LHyd LMil MAsh MGos NHol SLdr SPer SReu SSta WBod WFar |
| | 'Pallas' (G) | SReu |
| | 'Palma' | see *R. parmulatum* 'Palma' |
| | 'Pamela Miles' (EA) | LHyd |
| | 'Pamela Robinson' | LHyd |
| | 'Pamela-Louise' | LHyd |
| | 'Pancake' | CMac |
| | 'Panda' (EA) ♀$^{H4}$ | CDoC CSBt CTri ECho EPfP GGGa GKir LHyd LMil LRHS MBar MDun MLea NDlv NLar SReu WBod |
| | 'Papaya Punch' | LMil MDun |
| | 'Paprika Spiced' | CWri ECho ISea LMil MAsh MDun MGos MLea NLar SBod WBVN WFar |
| | 'Paris' | LHyd |
| | 'Parkfeuer' (A) | LMil LRHS SLdr |
| | ***parmulatum*** | LMil MDun WBod |
| | – 'Ocelot' | GGGa LHyd MDun |
| § | – 'Palma' | WBod |
| | ***parryae*** | GGGa |
| | 'Patty Bee' ♀$^{H4}$ | Widely available |
| | ***patulum*** | see *R. pemakoense* Patulum Group |
| | 'Peace' | GGGa WAbe WBod |
| | 'Peach Blossom' | see *R.* 'Saotome' |
| | 'Peach Lady' | SLdr |
| | 'Peep-bo' (EA) | LHyd SLdr |
| | 'Peeping Tom' | MDun SReu |
| | ***pemakoense*** | CSBt CTrG GGGa IDee MBar MDun NHol SLdr SReu WAbe WBod |
| § | – Patulum Group | MBar SLdr |
| | 'Pemakofairy' | WAbe WThu |
| | ***pendulum*** LS&T 6660 | GGGa |
| | Penelope Group | SReu |
| | 'Penheale Blue' ♀$^{H4}$ | CWri GGGa LMil MDun NLar |
| | 'Penjerrick Cream' | SLdr |
| | 'Pennsylvannia' (A) | GGGa |
| | 'Penny' | SReu |
| | ***pentaphyllum*** (A) | LMil |

| | | |
|---|---|---|
| | 'Peppina' | GGGa |
| | 'Percy Wiseman' ♀H4 | CBcs CDoC CSBt CSam CWri ECho EPfP GGGa GGar GKir ISea LHyd LMil LRHS MAsh MBar MBri MDun MGos MLea NDlv NPri SLdr SPer SPoG SReu SSta WFar |
| | 'Perfect Lady' | LMil |
| § | ***periclymenoides*** (A) | GGGa GKev LMil |
| | 'Persil' (K) ♀H4 | CBcs CSBt CWri ECho EPfP GGGa GKir LCro LHyd LMil LRHS MAsh MBar MBri MDun MGos MLea NBlu SCoo SLdr SPer SReu WBVN WBod WBrE |
| | 'Peter Bee' | GGGa |
| | 'Peter Berg' | MGos |
| | 'Peter John Mezitt' | see *R.* (PJM Group) 'Peter John Mezitt' |
| | 'Peter Koster' (M) | SHea WFar |
| | 'Peter Koster' (hybrid) | CWri SHBN SLdr WFar |
| | ***petrocharis*** Guiz 120 | GGGa |
| | 'Petrouchka' (K) | MDun |
| | 'Pfauenauge' | LMil MDun |
| | ***phaedropum*** | see *R. neriiflorum* subsp. *phaedropum* |
| | ***phaeochrysum*** | GGGa LMil SLdr |
| | - var. ***agglutinatum*** | GGGa |
| § | - var. ***levistratum*** | SLdr SReu |
| | 'Phalarope' | GEdr MBar SLdr SReu WBod |
| | 'Phoebe' (R/d) | SLdr SReu |
| | 'Phyllis Korn' | CDul CWri LHyd MDun NLar SLdr |
| | 'Piccolo' (K/d) | CSdC |
| § | ***piercei*** | LMil MDun |
| | - KW 11040 | GGGa |
| | Pilgrim Group | LMil |
| | ***pingianum*** | LMil SLdr |
| | - EGM 304 | LMil |
| | - KR 184 | GGGa |
| | 'Pink Bride' | SLdr |
| | 'Pink Cameo' | CWri |
| | 'Pink Cherub' ♀H4 | ECho EMui MAsh MBar MDun SLdr SReu |
| | 'Pink Delight' | GQui NLar |
| I | 'Pink Delight' (A) | MAsh MGos SLdr |
| | 'Pink Drift' | CSBt ECho LMil LRHS MBar MDun MGos NHol SHBN SLdr SPer WBod WBrE |
| | 'Pink Gin' | LMil MDun |
| | 'Pink Glory' | SLdr |
| | 'Pink Lady' ambig. (A) | SReu |
| | 'Pink Leopard' | LMil SLdr |
| | 'Pink Mimosa' (Vs) | SLdr |
| | 'Pink Pancake' (EA) ♀H4 | ECho EPfP GKir GQui LMil LRHS MGos NLar NPri SLdr |
| | 'Pink Pearl' (EA) | see *R.* 'Azuma-kagami' |
| | 'Pink Pearl' (hybrid) | CBcs CSBt CTri CWri ECho EPfP GGGa GKir LMil LRHS MAsh MBar MBri MDun MGos MMuc NPri SHea SLdr SPer SPoG SReu SSta WBVN WBod WFar |
| | 'Pink Pebble' ♀H3-4 | LHyd MDun MLea WBod |
| | 'Pink Perfection' | MBar MGos SHea SLdr SReu WFar |
| | 'Pink Photo' | SLdr |
| | 'Pink Polar Bear' | LMil |
| | 'Pink Ruffles' | SLdr WBod |
| | 'Pink Sensation' | MDun |
| | 'Pintail' | GGGa IDee LMil |
| | 'Pipit' | GGGa |
| | 'Pippa' (EA) | CMac CTrG |
| | PJM Group | MDun |
| § | - 'Peter John Mezitt' ♀H4 | LHyd MAsh SLdr |
| | 'PJM Elite' | LHyd NLar |
| | ***planetum*** | LMil |
| | ***platypodum*** | GGGa |

| | | |
|---|---|---|
| | 'Pleasant White' (EA) | LMil NMun |
| | 'Plover' | GGGa |
| | ***pocophorum*** | GGGa SLdr |
| | - 'Cecil Nice' | LHyd |
| § | - var. ***hemidartum*** | GGGa |
| | - var. ***pocophorum*** | SLdr |
| | 'Point Defiance' | CWri ECho GGGa ISea LMil MDun NLar SLdr SPer |
| | 'Polar Bear' (EA) | MBar MDun SLdr |
| | 'Polar Bear' ♀H3-4 | CBcs CSBt CSam IDee ISea LHyd LMil MGos MLan SReu WBVN |
| | Polar Bear Group | CWri ECho GGGa LMil MLea SLdr |
| | 'Polaris' | see *R.* 'Hachmann's Polaris' |
| | 'Polaris' (EA) | SReu |
| | 'Polarnacht' | CDoC EMil LMil MDun |
| § | ***poluninii*** | GGGa |
| | ***polyandrum*** | see *R. maddenii* subsp. *maddenii* Polyandrum Group |
| § | ***polycladum*** Scintillans Group | LHyd MBar MDun MLea NHol SLdr WPic |
| | - - 'Policy' ♀H4 | GGGa SReu |
| | ***polylepis*** | GGGa |
| | - C&K 284 | GGGa |
| | ***ponticum*** | CBcs CDul CSBt CTri MBar MGos SPer SReu WBod WFar |
| | - AC&H 205 | GGGa |
| | - 'Foliis Purpureis' | SReu |
| § | - 'Variegatum' (v) | CBcs CSBt CTri EMil EPfP GGGa LMil LRHS MAsh MBar MDun MGos MLea NPri SLdr SPer SPoG SReu SRms SSta WBod WFar |
| | 'Pooh-Bah' (EA) | LHyd |
| | 'Pook' | LHyd |
| | 'Popocatapetl' | SReu |
| | Portia Group **new** | WBod |
| | 'Potlatch' | GGGa |
| | ***poukhanense*** | see *R. yedoense* var. *poukhanense* |
| | 'Praecox' ♀H4 | CBcs CDul CSBt ECho EPfP GGGa ISea LHyd LMil LRHS MAsh MBar MDun MGos MMuc NBlu NHol NPri SHBN SLdr SPer SPoG SReu SSta WBod WFar |
| | ***praestans*** | GGGa LMil MDun SLdr |
| | ***praevernum*** | GGGa LMil |
| § | ***prattii*** | SLdr |
| | - 'Perry Wood' | LMil |
| | 'Prawn' | SReu |
| | Prelude Group | SLdr |
| | ***preptum*** | GGGa SLdr |
| | 'President Roosevelt' (v) | CSBt EPfP GKir LMil LRHS MAsh MDun MGos MLea NPri SHBN SPer SPoG SReu WBod WFar |
| | 'Pretty Woman' | LMil |
| | 'Pride of Leonardslee' | SLdr |
| | 'Pridenjoy' | LMil |
| | 'Prima Donna' | LMil SPoG |
| | ***primuliflorum*** | GGGa WAbe |
| | - 'Doker-La' | LMil WAbe |
| | - white-flowered | WAbe |
| | 'Prince Camille de Rohan' | LMil SHea |
| | 'Prince Henri de Pays Bas' (G) | CSdC SLdr |
| | 'Princess Alice' | CBcs LHyd WAbe WBod WPic |
| | 'Princess Anne' ♀H4 | CMHG CSam ECho EPfP GEdr GGGa LHyd LMil MAsh MBar MDun MGos MLea SHBN SLdr SPer SPoG SReu SSta WBod |
| | 'Princess Galadriel' | SLdr |
| | 'Princess Ida' (EA) | LHyd |
| | 'Princess Juliana' | ECho ISea MLea WBod WMoo |
| | 'Princess Margaret of Windsor' (K) | GQui LMil |
| | 'Princess Margaret Toth' | CSdC |

| | | |
|---|---|---|
| | ***principis*** | LMil SLdr |
| | - C&V 9547 | GGGa |
| | - SF 95085 | ISea |
| | - 'Lost Horizon' | CDoC LMil MDun |
| § | - Vellereum Group | SLdr |
| | - - SF 99093 | ISea |
| § | ***prinophyllum*** (A) | IDee LMil |
| | 'Prins Bernhard' (EA) | MAsh SLdr |
| | 'Prinses Juliana' (EA) | MMuc SLdr SReu WFar |
| | 'Professor Hugo de Vries' ♀H4 | SHea SLdr SReu |
| | 'Professor J.H. Zaayer' | MGos |
| | ***pronum*** | GGGa |
| | - R.B. Cooke form | GGGa |
| | - Towercourt form | GGGa |
| | 'Prostigiatum' | SLdr |
| | ***prostratum*** | see *R. saluenense* subsp. *chameunum* Prostratum Group |
| | ***proteoides*** | GGGa |
| * | - 'Ascreavie' | GGGa |
| | ***proteoides* x *tsariense*** | GGGa |
| | ***proteoides* x *yakushimanum*** | GGGa |
| | ***protistum*** | SLdr |
| | - KR 1986 | GGGa |
| § | - var. ***giganteum*** | SReu |
| | ***pruniflorum*** | GGGa |
| | ***prunifolium*** (A) | GGGa LMil SLdr |
| | ***przewalskii*** | GGGa |
| | - subsp. ***dabanshanense*** | GGGa |
| | ***pseudochrysanthum*** ♀H4 | GGGa LHyd LMil NLar SLdr SReu SSta |
| | ***pseudociliipes*** | GGGa |
| | Psyche Group | see *R.* Wega Group |
| | 'Psyche' (EA) | MDun |
| | 'Ptarmigan' ♀H3-4 | CBcs ECho EPfP GEdr GGGa IDee LHyd LMil MBar MGos MLea NHol NMen SLdr SPoG SReu SSta WBVN WFar |
| | ***pubicostatum*** | LMil |
| | - AC 2051 | LMil |
| | - CN&W 906 | ISea |
| § | 'Pucella' (G) ♀H4 | CSBt CWri NLar SLdr SReu |
| | ***pudorosum*** L&S 2752 | GGGa |
| | 'Pulchrum Maxwellii' | see *R.* 'Maxwellii' |
| | ***pumilum*** | GGGa GKev LLHF MDun NMen WAbe WThu |
| | 'Puncta' | SLdr |
| | ***punctatum*** | see *R. minus* var. *minus* Punctatum Group |
| | 'Purple Diamond' | see *R.* Diamant Group purple-flowered |
| | purple Glenn Dale (EA) | SLdr |
| | 'Purple Heart' | LMil SPoG |
| | 'Purple Queen' (EA/d) | MAsh |
| | 'Purple Splendor' (EA) | CMac SLdr |
| | 'Purple Splendour' ♀H4 | CBcs CSBt CWri ECho EPfP IDee LHyd LMil MAsh MBar MDun MGos MLea MMuc SHBN SPer SReu SSta WBVN WBod WFar WMoo |
| | 'Purple Triumph' (EA) ♀H3 | LMil LRHS SLdr SReu SSta WBod |
| | 'Purpurkissen' (EA) | LMil |
| | 'Purpurtraum' (EA) ♀H4 | GGGa LMil |
| | 'Quail' | GGGa |
| | Quaver Group | SRms |
| | 'Queen Alice' | CDoC MDun |
| | 'Queen Elizabeth II' ♀H4 | LHyd |
| | Queen Emma | see *R.* 'Koningin Emma' |
| | 'Queen Mary' | MBar MDun SHea |
| | 'Queen Mother' | see *R.* 'The Queen Mother' |
| | 'Queen of England' (G) | CSdC |
| | 'Queen of Hearts' | LHyd LMil SHea SLdr SReu |
| | 'Queen Souriya' | SLdr SReu |
| | Queen Wilhelmina | see *R.* 'Koningin Wilhelmina' |
| | 'Queenswood Centenary' | LMil |
| | 'Quentin Metsys' (R) | SLdr |
| | ***quinquefolium*** (A) | GGGa LMil SLdr |
| | 'Raby' (A) **new** | LMil |
| | ***racemosum*** ♀H4 | ISea LMil MBar MDun SLdr SSpi WAbe |
| | - SDR 3336 **new** | GKev |
| | - SSNY 47 | GGGa |
| | - 'Rock Rose' ♀H3-4 | CWri GGGa LHyd LMil |
| | ***racemosum* x *tephropeplum*** | MBar |
| | 'Racil' | MBar MDun MGos |
| | 'Racine' (G) | SLdr |
| | 'Racoon' (EA) ♀H4 | GGGa GKir |
| | 'Radiant' (M) | SLdr |
| | ***radicans*** | see *R. calostrotum* subsp. *keleticum* Radicans Group |
| | 'Rainbow' | SLdr |
| | 'Ramapo' ♀H4 | CDoC ECho GGGa LMil LRHS MAsh MBar MDun MGos NHol NMen NPri SPer SReu WBVN WBod |
| | ***ramsdenianum*** | GGGa LMil SLdr |
| | 'Raphael de Smet' (G/d) | SReu |
| | 'Rashomon' (EA) | LHyd SLdr |
| | 'Raspberry Ripple' | SReu |
| | 'Raymond Burfield' | SLdr |
| | 'Razorbill' ♀H4 | CDoC ECho GGGa LMil MGos WBod |
| | 'Recital' **new** | GGGa |
| | ***recurvoides*** | GGGa LHyd LMil MDun SLdr SReu WBod |
| | - Keillour form | GGGa |
| | 'Red and Gold' **new** | GGGa |
| | 'Red Arrow' | LHyd |
| | 'Red Carpet' | LMil SLdr |
| | 'Red Dawn' | LRHS |
| | 'Red Delicious' | CWri GGGa LMil WBVN |
| | 'Red Diamond' | see *R.* Diamant Group red-flowered |
| | 'Red Fountain' (EA) | ECho MAsh MGos SLdr WPat |
| | 'Red Glow' | LHyd |
| | 'Red Glow' x ***yakushimanum*** | SLdr |
| | 'Red Jack' | CWri GGGa LMil MAsh WBod |
| | 'Red Panda' (EA) | GGGa |
| | 'Red Pimpernel' (EA) | SLdr |
| | 'Red Sunset' (EA/d) | SLdr |
| | 'Red Wood' | GGGa |
| | 'Redwing' (EA) | CDoC MAsh SLdr WBod |
| | 'Reich's Charmant' | GGGa |
| | 'Rendezvous' ♀H4 | LMil SLdr SReu |
| | 'Rennie' (A) | ECho MGos MLea |
| | 'Renoir' ♀H4 | CSBt LHyd LMil SLdr SReu |
| | 'Replique' (Vs) | SLdr |
| | ***reticulatum*** (A) | CBcs GGGa LMil SLdr SReu |
| * | - ***leucanthum*** (A) | GGGa |
| | - 'Sea King' (A) | LHyd |
| | ***retusum*** (V) | GGGa |
| | 'Reuthe's Purple' | LHyd NHol SReu WAbe WThu |
| | 'Rêve d'Amour' (Vs) | MDun SLdr SReu SSta |
| | Review Order Group | WPic |
| | 'Rex' (EA) | MAsh SLdr WFar |
| | ***rex*** | CDoC GGGa IDee LMil LRHS MDun SLdr |
| | - EGM 295 | LMil |
| | - subsp. ***arizelum*** | see *R. arizelum* |
| § | - subsp. ***fictolacteum*** ♀H3-4 | CDoC GGGa LMil MDun SLdr SReu |
| | - - SDR 3268 **new** | GKev |
| | - - SF 649 | ISea |
| | - - Miniforme Group | MDun |
| | - subsp. ***gratum*** | LMil |

| | | |
|---|---|---|
| | - yellow-flowered AC 901 | MDun |
| | - - AC 2079 | LMil |
| | ***rex* x *yakushimanum*** | SReu |
| | ***rhabdotum*** | see *R. dalhousieae* var. *rhabdotum* |
| | 'Ria Hardijzer' | LMil |
| | ***rigidum*** | ISea |
| * | - ***album*** | LMil WBod |
| | 'Ring of Fire' | CWri ECho LMil MDun MGos MLea SLdr WBVN |
| | 'Ripe Corn' | SLdr SReu |
| | ***ripense*** (EA) | LHyd |
| | 'Riplet' | MDun NDlv NLar WBod |
| | 'Ripples' (EA) | CTrh |
| | ***ririei*** | GGGa LHyd LMil SLdr SReu |
| | - AC 2036 | LMil |
| | 'Robert Croux' | SLdr |
| | 'Robert Keir' | SLdr |
| | 'Robert Korn' | CDoC LMil MDun |
| | 'Robert Seleger' | GGGa LMil LRHS MAsh SReu |
| | 'Robert Whelan' (A) | MDun NHol NLar SReu |
| | 'Robin Hill Frosty' (EA) | SLdr |
| | 'Robinette' | CBcs CWri ECho LMil MAsh SLdr |
| | 'Rocket' | CDoC CTri ECho MAsh MDun MGos MLea NBlu SLdr WBVN |
| | 'Rokoko' | see *R.* 'Hachmann's Rokoko' |
| | Romany Chai Group | LHyd |
| | 'Romany Chal' | SHea |
| | 'Rosa Mundi' | CSBt |
| | 'Rosata' (Vs) ♀$^{H4}$ | MDun SReu SSta |
| | 'Rose Bud' | CBcs CSBt CTri MDun |
| | 'Rose de Flandre' (G) | SLdr |
| | 'Rose Elf' | MDun NDlv WThu |
| | 'Rose Glow' (A) | GKir MDun SReu |
| | 'Rose Gown' | SReu |
| | 'Rose Greeley' (EA) | CDoC ECho GQui NLar SLdr SReu WBod WFar WGwG |
| | 'Rose Haze' (A) | MDun SReu |
| | 'Rose Torch' (A) | MDun SReu |
| | ***roseatum*** F 17227 | GGGa |
| | 'Rosebud' (EA/d) ♀$^{H3-4}$ | CBcs CMac CTrh LHyd MBar MGos NHol SLdr SReu WBod |
| | 'Rosemary Hyde' (EA) | LMil SLdr |
| | ***roseotinctum*** | see *R. sanguineum* subsp. *sanguineum* var. *didymoides* Roseotinctum Group |
| | ***roseum*** | see *R. prinophyllum* |
| | 'Roseum Elegans' | CDoC EMil MBar NMun NPri WFar |
| | 'Rosiflorum' | see *R. indicum* 'Balsaminiflorum' |
| | 'Rosy Dream' | CAbP CWri ECho MAsh MDun MMuc |
| | 'Rosy Fire' (A) | NHol SReu |
| | 'Rosy Lea' | MLea |
| | 'Rosy Lights' (A) | CTri LMil SBod |
| | 'Rothenburg' | CSam LHyd MDun SLdr |
| | ***rothschildii*** | CDoC GGGa LMil |
| | - C&Cu 9312 | GGGa |
| | 'Rouge' | SHea |
| | ***rousei*** (V) | GGGa |
| | ***roxieanum*** | IDee LMil SReu |
| § | - var. ***cucullatum*** | GKir ISea MDun |
| | - - CN&W 695 | LMil |
| | - - SBEC 350 | GGGa |
| | - var. ***oreonastes*** ♀$^{H4}$ | GGGa LMil MDun SSta |
| | - - USDAPI 59222/R11312 | GGGa |
| | - - Nymans form | SReu |
| | - var. ***parvum*** | GGGa |
| | 'Royal Blood' | SLdr |
| | 'Royal Command' (K) | CWri LMil MBar MDun SLdr |
| | Royal Flush Group | CBcs |
| | 'Royal Lodge' (K) | SLdr |
| | 'Royal Mail' | SHea |
| | 'Royal Ruby' (K) | CWri ECho MGos MLea SLdr |
| | 'Roza Stevenson' | LHyd LMil SLdr WBod |

| | | |
|---|---|---|
| | 'Rubicon' | CWri ECho GQui MDun MMuc SLdr |
| | ***rubiginosum*** | CBcs GGGa LHyd LMil |
| § | - Desquamatum Group | CBcs LHyd SLdr |
| | - pink-flowered | LMil |
| | - white-flowered | LMil |
| | ***rubineiflorum*** | GGGa |
| | 'Rubinetta' (EA) | LMil WFar |
| | 'Ruby F. Bowman' | CBcs SReu |
| | 'Ruby Hart' | GGGa LSRN MDun NHol SReu |
| | Ruddigore Group | WBod |
| | ***rude*** | see *R. glischrum* subsp. *rude* |
| | 'Ruffles and Frills' | MDun |
| | ***rufum*** | GGGa SLdr |
| | ***rupicola*** | NMen SLdr |
| § | - var. ***chryseum*** | GGGa LHyd |
| | - var. ***muliense*** Yu 14042 | GGGa |
| | ***russatum*** ♀$^{H4}$ | EPfP GGGa LMil MDun SLdr WAbe WFar |
| | - blue-black-flowered | LMil |
| | - 'Purple Pillow' | CSBt |
| | ***russotinctum*** | see *R. alutaceum* var. *russotinctum* |
| | 'Sacko' | CWri GGGa LLHF LMil MAsh MDun NHol NLar WBVN |
| | 'Saffrano' | NLar |
| | 'Saffron Queen' | CBcs CTrG ISea LMil SLdr WBod WPic |
| | 'Sahara' (K) | CSdC LMil SLdr |
| | 'Saint Breward' | CTrG GQui LHyd MDun MLea SLdr WBod |
| | 'Saint Kew' | SLdr |
| | 'Saint Merryn' ♀$^{H4}$ | CTrG ECho GEdr GGGa LHyd MDun NLar SLdr WBod |
| | 'Saint Minver' | SLdr |
| | 'Saint Tudy' | EPfP LHyd MDun SLdr WAbe |
| | 'Sakata Red' (EA) | WBod |
| | 'Salmon Queen' (M) | WFar |
| | 'Salmon Sander' (EA) | SLdr |
| § | 'Salmon Trout' | LMil |
| | 'Salmon's Leap' (EA/v) | CSBt GKir GQui LHyd LMil LRHS MAsh NPri SHBN SLdr SReu WAbe WFar |
| | ***saluenense*** | GGGa LMil SLdr WThu |
| | - JN 260 | GGGa |
| § | - subsp. ***chameunum*** | GGGa LMil SLdr |
| § | - - Prostratum Group | GGGa WAbe |
| | - subsp. ***riparioides*** | see *R. calostrotum* subsp. *riparium* Rock's form R178 |
| | 'Sammetglut' | CWri SReu |
| | 'Samuel Taylor Coleridge' (M) | NLar |
| | 'Sanderling' | GGGa |
| | 'Sang de Gentbrugge' (G) | CSdC SReu |
| | ***sanguineum*** | GGGa LMil MDun SLdr |
| § | - subsp. ***didymum*** | GGGa MDun |
| § | - subsp. ***sanguineum*** var. ***didymoides*** Roseotinctum Group USDAPI 59038/R10903 | GGGa |
| | - - var. ***haemaleum*** | CWri GGGa LMil |
| | - - var. ***sanguineum*** F 25521 | LMil |
| | 'Santa Maria' | ECho MAsh SLdr SReu SSta WBrE |
| | 'Santorina' **new** | MDun |
| § | 'Saotome' (EA) | LHyd SLdr |
| | 'Sapphire' | CSBt CTrG GEdr MAsh MBar MDun NDlv SLdr SRms WThu |
| | 'Sappho' | CBcs CDul CSBt CWri ECho EPfP GBin GGGa GKir ISea LHyd LMil MBar MBri MDun MGos MLea SHBN SLdr SPer SReu SSta WBVN WFar |
| | 'Sapporo' | LMil |

| | |
|---|---|
| 'Sarah Boscawen' | SReu |
| ***sargentianum*** | GGGa LMil NMen WAbe WThu |
| - 'Whitebait' | GGGa WAbe |
| 'Sarita Loder' | LHyd |
| 'Sarled' 🏆$^{H4}$ | GGGa LMil NMen SHea WThu |
| Sarled Group | SRms WAbe |
| 'Sarsen' (K) | CSdC |
| 'Satan' (K) 🏆$^{H4}$ | CSBt SKHP SReu |
| § 'Satschiko' (EA) 🏆$^{H4}$ | CBcs CSBt EPfP GEdr GGGa GKir LRHS MAsh MBar MDun MGos MLea NDlv NMun SLdr WBod |
| Satsuki type (EA) | ECho |
| 'Saturne' (G) | SLdr |
| 'Saturnus' (M) | LRHS |
| ***scabrifolium*** | CTrG |
| § - var. ***spiciferum*** | GGGa NMun SLdr WAbe WPic |
| - - SF 502 | ISea |
| 'Scandinavia' | LHyd SHea |
| 'Scarlet Wonder' 🏆$^{H4}$ | CBcs CDoC CMHG CSBt CWri ECho EPfP GEdr GGGa GKir IDee LMil LRHS MAsh MBar MBri MDun MGos NHol NPri SHea SLdr SPer SPoG SReu WBod WFar WMoo |
| 'Schlaraffia' | NLar |
| ***schlippenbachii*** (A) | CBcs CTrG GGGa LMil SLdr SSpi WBod WPic |
| - 'Sid's Royal Pink' (A) | LMil MDun |
| 'Schneekrone' 🏆$^{H4}$ | EMil GGGa LMil MAsh MDun |
| 'Schneeperle' (EA) | LMil |
| 'Schneespiegel' | MDun |
| 'Schneewolke' | LMil |
| 'Schubert' (EA) | MBar WBod |
| ***scintillans*** | see *R. polycladum* Scintillans Group |
| 'Scintillation' | CWri GGGa ISea LMil MAsh MBar MDun MLea SHBN SLdr |
| ***scopulorum*** | SLdr |
| - C&C 7571 | GGGa |
| - KW 6354 | GGGa |
| - SF 99032 **new** | ISea |
| 'Scotian Bells' | GGGa |
| ***scottianum*** | see *R. pachypodum* |
| 'Scout' (EA) | NMun SLdr |
| ***scyphocalyx*** | see *R. dichroanthum* subsp. *scyphocalyx* |
| Seagull Group | SLdr |
| ***searsiae*** | SLdr |
| 'Seaview Sunset' | GGGa |
| 'Seb' | SLdr |
| 'Second Honeymoon' | CBcs CWri ECho LMil MAsh MLea NLar SReu WFar |
| ***seinghkuense*** | GGGa |
| CCH&H 8106 | |
| - KW 9254 | GGGa |
| ***selense*** | GGGa |
| - subsp. ***jucundum*** | GGGa MDun |
| ***semnoides*** | GGGa LMil SLdr |
| 'Senator Henry Jackson' | GGGa MLea |
| 'Sennocke' | LHyd |
| 'September Song' | CBcs CSBt CWri ECho GGGa LMil MAsh MBri MDun MGos MLea MMuc NHol NLar SLdr WBVN WFar WPic |
| ***serotinum*** | LHyd LMil SLdr SReu |
| - C&H 7189 | GGGa |
| ***serpyllifolium*** (A) | CBcs SLdr |
| 'Sesostris' (G) | CSdC |
| 'Sesterianum' | CMHG SLdr |
| Seta Group | CBcs SLdr SReu |
| 'Seta' | CAbP LHyd SHea WBod WPic WThu |
| ***setosum*** | GGGa MDun |
| 'Seven Stars' | CSBt |

| | |
|---|---|
| 'Shamrock' | CDoC EPfP GEdr GKir ISea LRHS MAsh MBar MDun MGos MLea NMun SLdr SPoG SReu WBod WFar |
| 'Sheila' (EA) | CSBt LRHS NPri |
| ***shepherdii*** | see *R. kendrickii* |
| ***sherriffii*** | GGGa MDun |
| 'Shiko' (EA) | MAsh |
| 'Shiko Lavender' (A) | LMil SPoG |
| Shilsonii Group | SLdr SReu |
| 'Shi-no-noe' (EA) | SLdr |
| 'Shin-seikai' (EA/d) | SLdr |
| 'Shintoki-no-hagasane' (EA) | LHyd WBod |
| Shot Silk Group | SLdr |
| 'Shrimp Girl' | GKir LHyd MAsh MDun SLdr SReu |
| ***sichotense*** | GAuc GGGa |
| ***sidereum*** | GGGa LMil SLdr |
| ***siderophyllum*** | SLdr |
| ***sikangense*** | SLdr |
| - EGM 108 | LMil |
| - var. ***exquisitum*** | GGGa ISea MDun |
| - - EGM 349 from Wumenshan | LMil |
| - var. ***sikangense*** | LMil |
| § - - Cookeanum Group | SLdr |
| § 'Silberwolke' 🏆$^{H4}$ | LMil MAsh SReu |
| 'Silver Anniversary' | MGos |
| Silver Cloud | see *R.* 'Silberwolke' |
| 'Silver Edge' | see *R. ponticum* 'Variegatum' |
| 'Silver Fountain' (EA) | LMil |
| 'Silver Glow' (EA) | CMac |
| 'Silver Jubilee' 🏆$^{H4}$ | CBcs LHyd LMil |
| 'Silver Moon' (EA) | SLdr |
| 'Silver Queen' (A) | ECho EMil MGos |
| 'Silver Sixpence' | CBcs CSBt ECho EPfP GKir ISea LRHS MAsh MBar MDun MGos SHBN SLdr SPoG SReu |
| 'Silver Skies' | LMil |
| 'Silver Slipper' (K) 🏆$^{H4}$ | GKir LHyd LMil MAsh MBar MBri MDun MLea NHol NLar SLdr SPoG SReu SSta WFar |
| 'Silver Thimbles' (V) | GGGa |
| 'Silverwood' (K) | LMil |
| 'Silvester' (EA) | MAsh MBri SLdr |
| 'Simona' | MDun SReu |
| ***simsii*** (EA) | CMac LMil SLdr |
| ***simulans*** | see *R. mimetes* var. *simulans* |
| ***sinofalconeri*** | IDee LMil LRHS SLdr |
| - C&H 7183 | GGGa |
| - SEH 229 | LMil |
| ***sinogrande*** 🏆$^{H3}$ | CBcs CDoC CHEx CWri GGGa IDee LHyd LMil LRHS MBri MDun SLdr WFar |
| - KR 4027 | LMil |
| 'Sir Charles Lemon' 🏆$^{H3-4}$ | CDoC CWri ECho GGar GKir LHyd LMil MAsh MDun MGos MLea NLar SHea SKHP SLdr SPer SReu |
| 'Sir Robert' (EA) | LRHS |
| 'Sir William Lawrence' (EA) | SReu |
| 'Skookum' | MBri MDun MGos WBVN |
| 'Sleepy' | CBcs CSBt ECho MAsh MGos NDlv |
| ***smirnowii*** | GGGa LMil SHea SReu |
| ***smithii*** | see *R. argipeplum* |
| - Argipeplum Group | see *R. argipeplum* |
| § Smithii Group | CWri SReu |
| 'Sneezy' | CBcs CSBt CWri ECho EPfP GGGa GKir LHyd LRHS MAsh MBar MGos NHol SBod SLdr WBod WFar |
| 'Snipe' | CBcs CTri ECho GEdr ISea LMil LRHS MAsh MBar MDun MGos NHol NPri SLdr SPoG SReu WBod |
| 'Snow' (EA) | CSBt MBar SLdr |
| 'Snow Hill' (EA) | GQui LHyd LMil LRHS |

| | |
|---|---|
| 'Snow Lady' | CBcs ECho EPfP GEdr GGar GQui MAsh MBar MDun MGos SLdr SPoG SReu WBVN |
| 'Snow Queen' | LMil |
| Snow Queen Group | LMil SReu |
| Snow White Group | LMil |
| 'Snowbird' (A) | GGal LMil MAsh NLar |
| 'Snowflake' (EA/d) | see *R.* 'Kure-no-yuki' |
| 'Snowy River' **new** | WBod |
| 'Soho' (EA) | CSdC GQui |
| 'Soir de Paris' (Vs) | GGGa LHyd LMil MAsh MBar MBri MDun MLea NDlv NHol NLar SBod SLdr SReu SSta WBVN WBod WBrE WFar |
| 'Soldier Sam' | SReu |
| 'Solidarity' | ECho MAsh MBri MDun MGos MLea WBVN |
| 'Solway' (Vs) | CSdC LMil |
| 'Son de Paris' (A) | GQui |
| 'Sonata' | CWri GGGa MDun SReu WBod |
| 'Songbird' | LHyd LMil MBar MDun SLdr SReu WBod |
| ***sororium*** (V) KR 3080 | GGGa |
| - KR 3085 | LMil |
| Souldis Group | MDun SLdr |
| ***souliei*** | GKir LMil MDun SLdr |
| - deep pink-flowered | GGGa |
| - white-flowered | GGGa |
| 'Southern Cross' | SLdr |
| 'Souvenir de D.A. Koster' | SLdr |
| 'Souvenir de Doctor S. Endtz' 🏆$^{H4}$ | CSBt MBar SHea SLdr |
| 'Souvenir du Président Carnot' (G/d) | SLdr |
| 'Souvenir of Anthony Waterer' 🏆$^{H4}$ | MDun SHea SReu |
| 'Souvenir of W.C. Slocock' | SHBN SLdr SReu |
| 'Sparkler' (Vs) | GGGa |
| ***speciosum*** | see *R. flammeum* |
| 'Spek's Orange' (M) 🏆$^{H4}$ | MGos |
| ***sperabile*** var. ***weihsiense*** | GGGa SLdr |
| ***sperabiloides*** | GGGa |
| ***sphaeranthum*** | see *R. trichostomum* |
| ***sphaeroblastum*** | GGGa SLdr |
| - var. ***wumengense*** | ISea MDun |
| - - CN&W 968 | GGGa |
| ***spiciferum*** | see *R. scabrifolium* var. *spiciferum* |
| ***spilotum*** | GGGa SLdr |
| 'Spinner's Glory' | MAsh |
| ***spinuliferum*** | GGGa WBod |
| - SF 247 | ISea |
| 'Spitfire' | MDun NHol SReu |
| 'Splendens' (G) | CSdC |
| 'Spring Beauty' (EA) | CMac SLdr SReu |
| 'Spring Magic' | SLdr |
| 'Spring Pearl' | see *R.* 'Moerheim's Pink' |
| 'Spring Rose' | SLdr |
| 'Spring Sunshine' | LMil |
| 'Springbok' | LHyd |
| 'Squirrel' (EA) 🏆$^{H4}$ | CDoC ECho GEdr GGGa GKir LHyd LMil MAsh MDun MGos MLea NDlv NHol NLar SLdr SReu WBod |
| 'Squirrel' tall (EA) | SLdr |
| Stadt Essen Group | LMil SLdr |
| 'Stadt Westerstede' | LMil |
| ***stamineum*** | GGGa |
| 'Standishii' | SLdr |
| 'Stanley Rivlin' | LHyd |
| § 'Stanway' | SLdr |
| 'Starbright Champagne' | LMil |
| 'Starcross' | LHyd |
| 'Starfish' | SReu |
| 'Statuette' **new** | MDun |

| | |
|---|---|
| § ***stenopetalum*** 'Linearifolium' (A) | CMac LHyd LMil SLdr WAbe |
| ***stenophyllum*** | see *R. makinoi* |
| ***stewartianum*** | GGGa LMil MDun SLdr |
| 'Stewartstonian' (EA) | CMac CTrh LHyd MBar NHol SPoG SReu SSta WBod WFar WPic |
| 'Stoat' (EA) | GQui MDun |
| 'Stopham Girl' (A) | LMil |
| 'Stopham Lad' (A) | LMil |
| 'Stranraer' | MDun |
| 'Strategist' | SHea SLdr |
| 'Strawberry Cream' | GGGa |
| 'Strawberry Ice' (K) 🏆$^{H4}$ | CBcs CDoC CSBt CWri ECho EPfP GGGa GKir ISea LMil LRHS MAsh MBar MBri MDun MGos MMHG NLar SLdr SPer SReu WMoo |
| 'Strawberry Sundae' **new** | MLea |
| ***strigillosum*** | GGGa LMil MDun SLdr |
| - C&H 7035 | GGGa |
| - EGM 305 | LMil |
| - EGM 338 | LMil |
| - Reuthe's form | SReu |
| 'Suave' | WBod |
| ***subansiriense*** C&H 418 | GGGa |
| ***suberosum*** | see *R. yunnanense* Suberosum Group |
| ***succothii*** | MDun SLdr |
| - LS&H 21295 | SLdr |
| 'Suede' | MDun |
| 'Sui-yohi' (EA) | LHyd |
| ***sulfureum*** SBEC 249 | GGGa |
| 'Sulphamer' | SLdr |
| 'Sulphur Queen' **new** | WBod |
| 'Summer Blaze' (A) | SReu |
| 'Summer Flame' | SReu |
| 'Summer Fragrance' (O) 🏆$^{H4}$ | LMil MDun NHol SReu SSta |
| 'Summer Snow' **new** | MDun |
| 'Sun Chariot' (K) | CBcs CSam LMil MAsh MLea MMHG SLdr SReu |
| 'Sun of Austerlitz' | SHea |
| 'Sunbeam' (hybrid) | SReu |
| 'Sunny' (V) | GGGa |
| (Sunrise Group) 'Sunrise' | SLdr |
| 'Sunset Pink' (K) | SLdr |
| 'Sunte Nectarine' (K) 🏆$^{H4}$ | ECho GQui LHyd LMil MBri MDun MLea NLar SLdr |
| ***superbum*** (V) | GGGa |
| 'Superbum' (O) | SLdr |
| 'Surprise' (EA) | CDoC CTrh CTri EPfP SLdr |
| 'Surrey Heath' | CBcs CDoC CWri ECho EMil EPfP GKir LMil LRHS MAsh MBar MDun MGos MMuc NDlv NMun SLdr WBod |
| 'Susan' 🏆$^{H4}$ | CSBt CWri GGGa LHyd LMil MDun SLdr SPer SPoG SReu |
| 'Susannah Hill' (EA) | CBcs CDoC MAsh MGos SLdr |
| 'Sussex Bonfire' | SLdr |
| ***sutchuenense*** | CDoC GGGa IDee LMil MDun SLdr |
| - var. ***geraldii*** | see *R.* x *geraldii* |
| 'Swamp Beauty' | CWri ECho GGar LMil MAsh MDun MLea MMuc NLar WBVN WGwG |
| 'Swansong' (EA) | CMac |
| 'Sweet Simplicity' | CSBt CWri SHea |
| 'Sweet Sue' | SLdr SReu |
| 'Swift' | ECho GGGa GQui LLHF LMil MAsh NHol NPri SReu WBVN |
| 'Sword of State' (K) | CWri |
| 'Sylphides' (K) | MDun |
| 'Sylvester' | CTri LMil LRHS MGos NMen NMun NPri SReu |
| 'T.S. Black' (EA) | SLdr |
| ***taggianum*** 'Cliff Hanger' | LMil |

| | | |
|---|---|---|
| | 'Taka-no-tsukasa' (EA) | SLdr |
| | 'Takasago' (EA/d) | CBcs LHyd |
| | 'Talavera' | see *R.* (Golden Oriole Group) 'Talavera' |
| | ***taliense*** | GGGa LHyd LMil MDun |
| | - KR 4056 from Cangshan | LMil |
| | Tally Ho Group | SHea SLdr |
| | ***tamaense*** | see *R. cinnabarinum* subsp. *tamaense* |
| | 'Tama-no-utena' (EA) | LHyd SLdr |
| | 'Tamarindos' | LMil |
| | 'Tanager' (EA) | CTrh SLdr |
| | 'Tangerine' | see *R.* 'Fabia Tangerine' |
| | 'Tarantella' | LMil NBlu |
| | ***tashiroi*** (EA) | SLdr |
| | 'Taurus' 𝕐$^{H4}$ | CDoC CWri ECho GGGa ISea LMil MAsh MDun MGos MLea SLdr WBVN |
| | ***taxifolium*** (v) | GGGa |
| | 'Tay' (K) | SLdr |
| | 'Teal' | ECho GEdr MBar MDun MGos MLea NHol |
| | 'Teddy Bear' | CWri GGGa GGar LMil MDun MLea SLdr |
| § | ***telmateium*** | SLdr |
| | ***temenium*** | MDun |
| | - var. ***gilvum*** 'Cruachan' | GGGa |
| | 'Temple Belle' | CWri ECho GKev MDun WBod |
| | Temple Belle Group | CSam LHyd NDlv SLdr |
| | 'Tender Heart' (K) | SLdr |
| § | ***tephropeplum*** | GGGa MDun |
| | - USDAPQ 3914/R18408 | GGGa |
| | - Deleiense Group | see *R. tephropeplum* |
| | 'Tequila Sunrise' | LHyd LMil |
| | 'Terra-cotta' | LMil |
| | 'Terra-cotta Beauty' (EA) | CTrG |
| | 'Tessa' | CBcs ECho MAsh MMuc WBrE |
| | Tessa Group | LMil MGos |
| | 'Tessa Bianca' | GGGa |
| | 'Tessa Roza' (EA) 𝕐$^{H4}$ | GGGa GQui LHyd |
| | ***thayerianum*** | GGGa |
| | 'The Dowager' | SLdr |
| | 'The Freak' | SLdr |
| § | 'The Hon. Jean Marie de Montague' 𝕐$^{H4}$ | CSam CWri EPfP GKir LMil MAsh MBri MDun MGos MLea SHea SLdr SReu WBVN |
| | 'The Master' 𝕐$^{H4}$ | LHyd LMil SLdr SReu |
| | 'The Moor' **new** | WBod |
| § | 'The Queen Mother' | LHyd |
| | ***thomsonii*** | CDoC GGGa IDee LHyd LMil MDun NHol SLdr SReu |
| | - B&SWJ 2638 | WCru |
| | - subsp. ***lopsangianum*** | GGGa |
| | - subsp. ***thomsonii*** L&S 2847 | GGGa |
| | 'Thor' | GGGa MDun SReu |
| | 'Thousand Butterflies' | see *R.* 'One Thousand Butterflies' |
| | 'Thunderstorm' | LHyd SReu |
| | ***thymifolium*** | GGGa |
| | 'Tibet' 𝕐$^{H3-4}$ | GQui LMil MBar MDun SHBN SLdr |
| | 'Tidbit' 𝕐$^{H4}$ | GGGa LMil MGos MLea SLdr |
| | 'Timothy James' | GKir MAsh |
| | 'Tina Heinje' **new** | EMil |
| | 'Tinkerbird' | GGGa |
| | 'Tinsmith' (K) | SLdr |
| | 'Tit Willow' (EA) | GKir LHyd LRHS NPri SCoo SLdr |
| | 'Titian Beauty' | CBcs CDoC CSBt CWri ECho EPfP GGGa ISea LHyd LMil LRHS MAsh MDun MGos NDlv NPri SBod SLdr SPer SPoG WBVN WBrE WFar |
| | 'Titipu' (EA) | LHyd SLdr |
| | 'Titness Delight' | SLdr |
| | 'Tolkien' | SReu |
| | 'Tom Hyde' (EA) | LMil |
| | 'Top Banana' | MDun SLdr |
| | 'Topsvoort Pearl' | SReu |
| | 'Torchlight' (EA) **new** | LMil |
| | 'Toreador' (EA) | CTrG SLdr |
| | 'Torero' | GGGa |
| | 'Tornado' | MAsh WFar |
| | 'Torridon' (Vs) | LMil |
| | 'Tortoiseshell Champagne' | see *R.* 'Champagne' |
| | 'Tortoiseshell Orange' 𝕐$^{H3-4}$ | CSBt EMil LHyd LMil MDun SHBN SHea SLdr SPoG SReu SSta |
| | 'Tortoiseshell Salome' | SHea SLdr SReu |
| | 'Tortoiseshell Scarlet' | MDun SReu |
| | 'Tortoiseshell Wonder' 𝕐$^{H3-4}$ | CSBt EPfP LMil LRHS MAsh NPri SHea SLdr SReu |
| | 'Totally Awesome' (K) | MBri SLdr |
| | 'Toucan' (K) | CSBt MDun SLdr |
| | 'Tower Beauty' (A) | LHyd |
| | 'Tower Dainty' (A) | LHyd |
| | 'Tower Daring' (A) | LHyd SLdr |
| | 'Tower Dexter' (A) | LHyd |
| | 'Tower Dragon' (A) | LHyd LMil SLdr |
| | 'Trail Blazer' | GGGa |
| | ***traillianum*** | GGGa LMil SLdr |
| | - SDR 2599 | GKev |
| | Treasure Group | SLdr |
| | 'Treecreeper' | GGGa |
| | 'Tregedna Red' | SReu |
| | 'Trelawny' | SLdr |
| | 'Trewithen Orange' | MBar MDun SHBN SLdr |
| | ***trichanthum*** | GGGa LMil |
| | - 'Honey Wood' | LMil SLdr |
| | - white-flowered | LMil |
| | ***trichocladum*** | ISea |
| § | ***trichostomum*** | GGGa SSpi WAbe WBod |
| | - Ledoides Group | LMil |
| | - - 'Collingwood Ingram' (EA) 𝕐$^{H4}$ | LMil SLdr |
| | ***triflorum*** | GGGa ISea LMil MDun |
| | - C&V 9573 | GGGa |
| | - SF 95149 | ISea |
| § | - var. ***bauhiniiflorum*** | CBcs GGGa SLdr |
| | 'Trilby' | SReu |
| | ***trilectorum*** | GGGa |
| | 'Trill' (EA) | SLdr |
| | 'Trinidad' | MDun |
| | ***triplonaevium*** | see *R. alutaceum* var. *russotinctum* Triplonaevium Group |
| | 'Troll' (EA) | SLdr |
| | 'Tromba' | LMil |
| | 'Trude Webster' | GGGa |
| | ***tsangpoense*** | see *R. charitopes* subsp. *tsangpoense* |
| | ***tsariense*** | GGGa LMil |
| | - Poluninii Group | see *R. poluninii* |
| | - var. ***trimoense*** | GGGa IDee LMil MDun |
| | - - KW 8288 | LMil |
| | - 'Yum Yum' | GGGa SLdr |
| § | ***tsusiophyllum*** | GGGa |
| | 'Tsuta-momiji' (EA) | LHyd SLdr |
| | 'Tuffet' | SLdr SReu |
| | 'Tunis' (K) | LHyd |
| | 'Turacao' | GGGa |
| | 'Twilight Pink' | SLdr |
| | 'Twilight Sky' (A) | SLdr |
| | 'Ukamuse' (EA/d) | LHyd SLdr |
| | 'Ulrike Jost' **new** | MDun |
| | 'Umpqua Queen' (K) | MBri |
| | ***ungernii*** | GGGa LMil SLdr |
| § | ***uniflorum*** var. ***imperator*** | LMil |
| | - - KW 6884 | GGGa |

| | |
|---|---|
| 'Unique' (G) | CSBt ECho EPfP ISea MGos MMuc NHol SLdr SPer |
| 'Unique' (*campylocarpum* hybrid) ♀H4 | CBcs CSam GGGa LHyd MAsh MBri MDun SHBN SHea SLdr SReu SSta |
| 'Unique Marmalade' | ECho LMil MBri SLdr WBVN |
| ***uvariifolium*** | GGGa ISea SLdr |
| - Cox 6519 | GGGa |
| - KR 4158 from Zhongdian, Napa Hai | LMil |
| - SDR 2857 **new** | GKev |
| - var. ***griseum*** | IDee LMil SLdr |
| - - C&C 7506 | GGGa |
| - - KR 3423 | LMil |
| - - KR 3428 | LMil |
| - - KR 3774 | LMil |
| - - KR 3782 | LMil |
| - 'Reginald Childs' | LMil SLdr |
| - 'Yangtze Bend' | GGGa |
| ***vaccinioides*** (V) CCH&H 8051 | GGGa |
| 'Valentine' (EA) | GGGa |
| ***valentinianum*** | CBcs GGGa SLdr WAbe |
| - var. ***oblongilobatum*** C&H 7186 | LMil |
| 'Van' | CDoC LMil |
| 'Van Houttei Flore Pleno' | SLdr |
| 'Van Nes Sensation' | LMil |
| 'Van Weerden Poelman' | NLar |
| Vanessa Group | GGal LMil SReu WBod |
| 'Vanessa Pastel' ♀H3-4 | CMac GGGa LHyd LMil MDun SReu WBod |
| Vanity Fair Group | WBod |
| Varna Group **new** | WBod |
| ***vaseyi*** (A) ♀H3-4 | GGGa GKev LMil SLdr |
| - 'White Find' | GGGa |
| - white-flowered (A) | LMil |
| 'Vayo' (A) | SLdr |
| ***veitchianum*** | GGGa |
| § - Cubittii Group | GGGa SLdr |
| - - 'Ashcombe' | LHyd |
| - KNE Cox 9001 | GGGa |
| 'Veldtstar' | LHyd |
| ***vellereum*** | see *R. principis* Vellereum Group |
| ***venator*** | GGGa MDun |
| 'Venetian Chimes' | CSBt ECho ISea MDun NLar SLdr SReu |
| ***vernicosum*** | GGGa LMil |
| - JN 180 | GGGa |
| - SDR 3018 **new** | GKev |
| - SF 415 | ISea |
| 'Veryan Bay' | CBcs |
| 'Vespers' (EA) | MAsh |
| ***vialii*** (A) | GGGa |
| 'Victoria Hallett' | SLdr SReu |
| 'Vida Brown' (EA/d) | CMac SLdr SReu WThu |
| 'Viking' (EA) | LHyd |
| 'Viking Silver' | GGGa |
| 'Vinecourt Dong' **new** | ISea |
| 'Vinecourt Duke' (R/d) | CWri ECho LRHS MAsh MDun MLea MMuc NLar SBod SLdr WBVN |
| 'Vinecourt Troubador' (K/d) | CWri LMil MAsh MDun SBod WBVN |
| 'Vineland Dream' (K/d) | CWri ECho MAsh SLdr |
| 'Vineland Fragrance' | MDun SLdr |
| 'Vintage Rosé' ♀H4 | LMil MLea SLdr SPoG SReu |
| 'Violet Longhurst' (EA) | LHyd |
| 'Violetta' (EA) | NMen SLdr |
| Virginia Richards Group | CWri LRHS MAsh MGos SLdr SReu |
| ***viridescens*** 'Doshong La' | GGGa LMil |
| ***viscidifolium*** | GGGa |
| 'Viscosepalum' (G) | CSdC |
| ***viscosum*** (A) ♀H4 | GGGa GQui IDee LMil MDun MLea SLdr SReu SSpi WBVN WBrE WPic |
| - SDR 2312 | GKev |
| - 'Grey Leaf' (Vs) | LMil |
| - var. ***montanum*** (A) | IBlr |
| - f. ***rhodanthum*** (A) | LMil |
| - 'Roseum' (Vs) | LMil |
| 'Viscount Powerscourt' | SLdr |
| 'Viscy' ♀H4 | CDul CSBt CWri ECho EPfP GGGa GQui LHyd LMil MBri MDun MGos NLar WBVN WBod WBrE |
| § Volker Group | CWri LMil LRHS MAsh MBar MDun SReu SSta WFar |
| § - 'Babette' | LMil |
| § - 'Lackblatt' | LMil MBri SLdr |
| 'Vulcan' ♀H4 | EPfP GGGa LMil MLea SHBN |
| 'Vulcan' x ***yakushimanum*** | SReu |
| 'Vuyk's Rosyred' (EA) ♀H4 | CBcs CDoC CMac CSBt CTri GKir GQui LHyd LMil LRHS MAsh MBar MGos NHol SLdr SPer SPoG SReu WBod WFar |
| 'Vuyk's Scarlet' (EA) ♀H4 | CBcs CDoC CDul CMac CSBt CTrh CTri EPfP GKir GQui LHyd LMil LRHS MAsh MBar MDun MGos NHol NPri SLdr SPer SPlb SReu SSta WBod WFar |
| 'W.E. Gumbleton' (M) | SReu |
| 'W.F.H.' ♀H4 | CWri LMil MDun SLdr |
| ***wadanum*** var. ***leucanthum*** | LMil |
| 'Wagtail' | WAbe |
| 'Walküre' **new** | LMil |
| ***wallichii*** | GGGa LHyd MDun SLdr |
| - B&SWJ 2480 **new** | WCru |
| - DM 21 | LMil |
| Walloper Group | SReu |
| 'Wallowa Red' (K) | ECho GBin MLea SLdr |
| 'Wally Miller' | ECho ISea MAsh MDun SReu WFar |
| aff. ***walongense*** C&H 373 | GGGa |
| ***wardii*** | CBcs GGGa GKir IDee ISea LHyd LMil MDun SHea SLdr |
| - KR 4913 | LMil |
| - KR 5268 | LMil |
| - L&S | SReu |
| - var. ***puralbum*** | GGGa |
| - var. ***wardii*** | LMil |
| - - Litiense Group | SLdr |
| - - - CN&W 1079 | ISea |
| 'Ward's Ruby' (EA) | CTrh |
| § 'Washington State Centennial' (A) | GGGa MBri |
| ***wasonii*** | CDoC GGGa LHyd LMil |
| - f. ***rhododactylum*** KW 1876 | GGGa |
| - var. ***wenchuanense*** C 5046 | GGGa |
| 'Waterfall' | SLdr WBod |
| ***watsonii*** | GGGa |
| - Cox 5075 | GGGa |
| ***wattii*** | GGGa |
| 'Waxbill' | GGGa |
| ***websterianum*** | SLdr |
| - Cox 5123 | GGGa |
| 'Wee Bee' ♀H4 | CDoC CSBt ECho GEdr GGGa GGar GKir LLHF LMil MAsh MDun MLea NDlv NHol NLar SLdr SPoG SReu WBod |
| § Wega Group | LHyd |
| 'Welkin' | WBod |
| 'Wendy' | MAsh SPoG |
| 'Western Lights' (A) | LMil LRHS MAsh |
| 'Westminster' (O) | LMil |
| 'Weston's Pink Diamond' (d) | GGGa LMil |
| 'Weybridge' | SLdr |
| ***weyrichii*** (A) | GGGa LMil |

| | |
|---|---|
| 'Wheatear' | GGGa |
| 'Whidbey Island' | LMil |
| 'Whisperingrose' | LMil MDun NDlv |
| 'White Bird' | ISea |
| 'White Frills' (EA) | ECho SLdr |
| White Glory Group | SLdr |
| 'White Gold' | GGGa MDun |
| 'White Grandeur' (EA) | CTrh |
| 'White Jade' (EA) | SLdr |
| 'White Lady' (EA) | LMil MBar SLdr |
| 'White Lights' (A) ♀H4 | EPfP GKir LMil LRHS MAsh NPri SLdr |
| 'White Perfume' | MDun SReu |
| 'White Rosebud' (EA) | SReu WFar |
| 'White Swan' (K) | MGos |
| 'White Swan' (hybrid) | SReu |
| 'White Wings' | GQui LHyd SLdr |
| 'Whitethroat' (K/d) ♀H4 | CSdC CWri ECho EPfP GQui ISea LMil MAsh MDun MLea MMHG SLdr SPer WBVN |
| 'Whitney's Dwarf Red' | SLdr |
| 'Wigeon' | GGGa LMil NHol |
| ***wightii*** | GGGa MDun SLdr |
| - B&SWJ 2431 **new** | WCru |
| 'Wild Affair' | MDun |
| 'Wilgen's Ruby' | CDoC CSBt GKir LMil MBar MGos NBlu NHol SHBN SHea SLdr SPoG WBod WFar |
| 'Willbrit' | CBcs CWri ECho LHyd MAsh MGos SLdr WBVN WBrE |
| 'William III' (G) | SLdr |
| ***williamsianum*** ♀H4 | CBcs CTrG CWri ECho GBin GEdr LMil LRHS MBar MDun MLea SLdr SReu SRms SSpi WBod WFar |
| - Caerhays form | LMil MDun |
| - 'Special' | GGGa |
| 'Willy' (EA) | SLdr |
| ***wilsoniae*** | see *R. latoucheae* |
| Wilsonii Group | CTrG |
| ***wiltonii*** ♀H4 | GGGa IDee LHyd LMil MDun SLdr |
| - CC&H 3906 | GGGa |
| 'Windlesham Scarlet' | LHyd SLdr |
| 'Windsor Hawk' | CWri |
| 'Windsor Lad' | SHea SReu |
| 'Windsor Sunbeam' (K) | CWri |
| Wine and Roses = 'Pinkros' | GGGa |
| 'Winsome' (hybrid) ♀H3 | CBcs GGGa LHyd NPri SHea SReu |
| Winsome Group | CWri LRHS MAsh MBar MDun SLdr SSta |
| 'Winston Churchill' (M) | MBar NHol SReu |
| 'Wintergreen' (EA) | GKir MMuc |
| 'Wishmoor' | SLdr SReu |
| 'Wisley Blush' | LMil LRHS |
| 'Witch Doctor' | LMil MDun |
| 'Witchery' | GGGa |
| 'Wombat' (EA) ♀H4 | CTri EPfP GGGa GKir LHyd LMil LRHS MGos NHol NLar NPri SLdr SReu |
| ***wongii*** | GGGa GQui SLdr |
| 'Woodcock' | SHea WBod |
| 'Wren' | ECho GEdr GGGa LMil MAsh MBar MDun MGos MLea SReu WBVN WBod |
| 'Wryneck' (K) | CSdC SLdr SReu |
| 'Wye' (K) | SLdr |
| ***xanthocodon*** | see *R. cinnabarinum* subsp. *xanthocodon* |
| ***xanthostephanum*** | WAbe |
| - CCH&H 8070 | GGGa |
| - KR 3095 | LMil |
| - KR 4462 | LMil |
| 'Yaku Angel' | MDun |

| | |
|---|---|
| 'Yaku Incense' | ECho MAsh MBri MDun MLea MMuc |
| 'Yaku Prince' | ECho MAsh MDun MGos SLdr WFar |
| § ***yakushimanum*** | CBcs CDoC CMHG CSam CWri ECho EPfP GGGa GKev GKir IDee ISea LHyd LMil MAsh MBar MBri MDun MGos MLea MMuc NHol SLdr SPer SReu SSta WFar |
| - 'Berg' | MDun |
| - Exbury form | SReu |
| - Exbury form x ***roxieanum*** var. ***oreonastes*** | SReu |
| - FCC form | see *R. yakushimanum* 'Koichiro Wada' |
| § - 'Koichiro Wada' ♀H4 | EPfP GGGa GGar GKir LHyd LMil LRHS MAsh MDun MGos NHol SLdr SReu |
| - subsp. ***makinoi*** | see *R. makinoi* |
| - 'Mist Maiden' | GGar |
| - 'Snow Mountain' | SReu |
| 'Yamato-no-hikari' | WBod |
| * 'Yaya' | SLdr |
| 'Yaye-hiryu' (EA) | LHyd |
| § ***yedoense*** var. ***poukhanense*** | SLdr SReu |
| 'Yellow Cloud' (K) | ECho LMil MDun MLea SBod |
| 'Yellow Cloud' (A) **new** | SBod |
| 'Yellow Hammer' ♀H4 | CBcs CTrG ECho EMil EPfP ISea LHyd LMil MDun WBod WBrE WFar |
| Yellow Hammer Group | CWri GGGa LAst MGos SHBN SLdr SPer SReu SSta |
| 'Yellow Rolls Royce' | MDun |
| 'Yol' | SLdr |
| 'Youthful Sin' | ISea |
| ***yuefengense*** | GGGa |
| ***yungningense*** | MDun |
| § - Glomerulatum Group | SLdr |
| ***yunnanense*** | GGGa GGal GKev IDee ISea LHyd LMil MDun SLdr SSpi |
| - AC 751 | MDun |
| - C&H 7145 | GGGa |
| - SF 379 | ISea |
| - SF 400 | ISea |
| - SF 96102 | ISea |
| - 'Openwood' ♀H3-4 | LMil LRHS |
| - pink-flowered | GGGa |
| - 'Red Throat' | SLdr |
| - red-blotched | LMil |
| § - Suberosum Group | SLdr |
| - white-flowered | GGGa LMil |
| ***zaleucum*** | LMil MDun |
| - AC 685 | MDun |
| - F 15688 | GGGa |
| - KR 2687 | GGGa |
| - KR 3979 | LMil |
| - SF 347 | ISea |
| - SF 578 | ISea |
| 'Zanna' | SHea |
| Zelia Plumecocq Group | SReu |
| ***zeylanicum*** | see *R. arboreum* subsp. *zeylanicum* |
| Zuiderzee Group | SLdr |

## *Rhodohypoxis* (*Hypoxidaceae*)

| | |
|---|---|
| 'Albrighton' | CWsd ECho ERos EWes GEdr IBal ITim LAma NHol NMen SIng WAbe WPat |
| 'Andromeda' | EWes |
| 'Appleblossom' | CFwr CPen CSec CTca EBrs ECho EPot ERos EWes IBal LBee MSte NHol NLar NMen SCnR SIng WAbe WFar |

| | |
|---|---|
| ***baurii*** 🏆H4 | CAvo CMea CPBP CTca ECho GEdr IBal ITim LRHS MTho NBir NMen NSla NWCA SPoG SRms WAbe WFar |
| - 'Abigail' **new** | EWes |
| - 'Alba' | CMea ECho IBal NMen NWCA |
| - var. ***baurii*** | EWes LBee SIng |
| - 'Bridal Bouquet' (d) | EWes NHol WAbe WFar |
| - 'Coconut Ice' | EPot EWes |
| - var. ***confecta*** | CPen CWsd ECho EWes ITim NHol SIng |
| - 'Daphne Mary' | EWes |
| - 'David Scott' | EWes |
| - 'Douglas' | CPen CTca EBrs ECho EPfP EWes GEdr IBal ITim LAma NHol NMen SIng WAbe WFar |
| - 'Dulcie' | CPen EBrs ECho EWes GEdr ITim SCnR SUsu WAbe WFar |
| - 'Goliath' | EWes |
| - 'Lily Jean' (d) | CFwr CSec CStu EBrs ECho EPfP EWes GEdr IBal LRHS NCGa NLar SIng WCot |
| - 'Mars' | EWes NHol |
| - 'Pearl' | ECho ITim NLar |
| - 'Perle' | ECho ERos EWes GEdr NHol SCnR WAbe |
| - 'Pictus' | ECho IBal ITim |
| - 'Pink Pearl' | EPot EWes IBal NHol WAbe |
| - pink-flowered | CWsd EBrs ITim NLAp WCru |
| - var. ***platypetala*** | CSec CStu EBrs ECho EPfP EPot EWes GEdr IBal ITim NHol NMen WAbe |
| - var. ***platypetala*** × ***milloides*** | IBal LLHF NHol WAbe |
| - - - Burtt 6981 | EWes |
| - 'Rebecca' | ECho EWes |
| - 'Red King' | EWes IBal |
| - red-flowered | EBrs ECho NLAp SPlb |
| - 'Susan Garnett-Botfield' | CWsd ECho EPot EWes GEdr IBal NMen WAbe WFar |
| - 'The Bride' | EWes |
| - white-flowered | CWsd EBrs ECho EPot NLAp NMen |
| 'Betsy Carmine' | CPen GEdr IBal WAbe |
| 'Bright Eyes' (d) | EWes |
| 'Burgundy' | NHol SIng |
| 'Candy Stripe' | ECho EWes GEdr SIng |
| 'Carina' | EWes |
| 'Confusion' | EWes NHol WAbe WFar |
| 'Dainty Dee' (d) | EWes |
| 'Dawn' | CPen CTca CWsd EBrs ECho EPot EWes GEdr IBal LAma NLar NMen SIng WAbe |
| ***deflexa*** | CGra CLyd CPBP CPen CWsd ECho EWes GEdr GKev IBal ITim MSte NHol SCnR SIng WAbe WFar |
| 'Donald Mann' | ECho EWes LLHF NHol NMen WAbe |
| double, red-flowered (d) | CStu |
| 'Dusky' | CFwr EBrs EWes GEdr |
| 'E.A. Bowles' | CPen ECho EWes IBal ITim NMen WAbe WFar |
| 'Ellicks' | IBal |
| 'Emily Peel' | CFwr EBrs ECho EWes LLHF NHol WAbe |
| 'Eva-Kate' | ECho ERos EWes ITim LAma NHol SIng WAbe WFar WPat |
| 'Fred Broome' | CTca CWsd EBrs ECho EWes GEdr LAma NHol NMen SIng WAbe WFar WPat |
| 'Garnett' | ECho EDAr EWes IBal NMen WAbe |
| 'Goya' (d) **new** | NHol |
| 'Great Scot' | ECho ERos EWes GEdr IBal ITim WAbe WFar |
| 'Harlequin' | ECho EPot EWes GEdr IBal ITim LAma NHol NMen SIng WAbe WFar |
| 'Hebron Farm Biscuit' | see *Hypoxis parvula* var. *albiflora* 'Hebron Farm Biscuit' |
| 'Hebron Farm Cerise' | see × *Rhodoxis* 'Hebron Farm Cerise' |
| 'Hebron Farm Pink' | see × *Rhodoxis hybrida* 'Hebron Farm Pink' |
| § 'Helen' | ECho EWes GEdr IBal SIng WAbe WFar |
| 'Hinky Pinky' | CFwr GEdr |
| 'Holden Rose' | ECho NHol |
| hybrids | CWCL ELan |
| 'Jupiter' | GEdr NHol |
| 'Kiwi Joy' (d) | CFwr CStu EWes LLHF NHol WFar |
| 'Knockdolian Red' | NHol |
| 'Margaret Rose' | CTca CWsd ECho EWes IBal ITim LLHF NHol NMen WAbe WFar |
| 'Midori' | EWes GEdr SUsu |
| ***milloides*** | CTca CWsd EBrs ECho EPot EWes GEdr GGar IBal ITim LBee NHol NLAp NMen NWCA SIng WAbe WFar |
| - 'Claret' | CEnt CSam CStu CWsd ECho EWes IBal ITim LLHF NHol SAga SIng SUsu WAbe WFar WPat |
| - 'Damask' | CStu CWsd EWes SAga |
| - 'Drakensberg Snow' | EWes |
| - giant | ECho |
| 'Monty' | ECho EWes GEdr SIng WAbe |
| 'Mystery' | EWes NHol WAbe |
| 'Naomi' | EWes |
| 'New Look' | EBrs ECho ERos EWes GEdr IBal LLHF NMen SIng WAbe WFar WGor |
| 'Pearl White' | ECho IBal |
| 'Picta' (v) | ECho EPot EWes GEdr IBal LAma LBee NHol WAbe |
| 'Pink Ice' | GEdr IBal |
| 'Pinkeen' | CWsd ECho EPot EWes GEdr IBal ITim LLHF SIng WAbe WFar |
| 'Pinkie' | IBal |
| 'Pintado' | CWsd EWes |
| 'Raspberry Ice' **new** | NHol |
| 'Rosie Lee' | EWes WAbe |
| 'Ruth' | EBrs ECho EWes IBal LAma MSte NHol WAbe WFar |
| 'Shell Pink' | EWes IBal ITim NHol WAbe |
| 'Snow' | EWes |
| 'Snow White' | EWes NHol |
| 'Starlett' | EWes NHol |
| 'Starry Eyes' (d) | CStu ECho EWes |
| 'Stella' | EBrs ECho EPot ERos EWes GEdr IBal MSte NHol NMen SIng WAbe |
| 'Tetra Pink' | ECho EWes IBal NHol SIng WAbe |
| 'Tetra Red' | CTca EBrs ECho EPot EWes IBal NHol NMen SIng WAbe WFar |
| 'Tetra Rose' | GEdr |
| 'Tetra White' | see *R.* 'Helen' |
| ***thodiana*** | CGra CStu CWsd ECho ERos EWes GEdr IBal NHol NMen SCnR SIng WAbe WFar |
| 'Twinkle Star Mixed' | LBuc |
| 'Two Tone' | EWes |
| 'Venetia' | CMea ECho IBal NHol WAbe |
| 'Westacre Picotee' | EWes |
| 'White Prince' | IBal |
| 'Wild Cherry Blossom' | CFwr ECho EWes SIng |

## *Rhodohypoxis* × *Hypoxis* see × *Rhodoxis*

| | |
|---|---|
| ***R. baurii*** × ***H. parvula*** | see × *Rhodoxis hybrida* |

## *Rhodophiala* (*Amaryllidaceae*)

| | |
|---|---|
| WAL 7443 | WCot |
| WAL 9561 | WCot |
| § ***advena*** | EPot WCot |

| | | |
|---|---|---|
| | ***bagnoldii*** F&W 8695 | WCot |
| § | ***bifida*** | SCnR WCot |
| | ***chilensis*** | WCot |
| | ***elwesii*** | WCot |
| | ***fulgens*** | WCot |
| | 'Harry Hay' | WCot |
| | ***montana*** | CFee |
| | ***pratensis*** | EBee |
| | ***rhodolirion*** | WCot |

## *Rhodora* see *Rhododendron*

## *Rhodothamnus* (*Ericaceae*)

| | | |
|---|---|---|
| | ***chamaecistus*** | WAbe |
| | ***sessilifolius*** new | WThu |

## *Rhodotypos* (*Rosaceae*)

| | | |
|---|---|---|
| | ***kerrioides*** | see *R. scandens* |
| § | ***scandens*** | CPLG CSec CTri CWib EBee EMil EPfP EPla EShb EWTr IMGH MBri MMHG MWea NLar SEND SLon SSpi WCru WPat WSHC |

## x *Rhodoxis* (*Hypoxidaceae*)

| | | |
|---|---|---|
| | 'Aurora' | EWes |
| | 'Bloodstone' | EWes NHol |
| | 'Hebron Farm Biscuit' | see *Hypoxis parvula* var. *albiflora* 'Hebron Farm Biscuit' |
| § | 'Hebron Farm Cerise' | ERos EWes GEdr NMen |
| | 'Hebron Farm Rose' | LLHF |
| § | ***hybrida*** | CPen CPne CSec EBrs ECho EWes IBal ITim NMen SIng WAbe |
| | - 'Aya San' | EWes SIng |
| § | - 'Hebron Farm Pink' | CBro CWsd ECho ERos EWes GEdr IBal NHol NMen SCnR SIng WAbe WFar |
| | - 'Hebron Farm Red Eye' | EWes GEdr SCnR SIng WAbe WFar |
| | - 'Pink Stars' new | SIng |
| | - 'Ruby Giant' new | SIng |
| | - 'White Knight' new | SIng |
| | - 'White Stars' new | SIng |
| | 'Little Pink Pet' | EWes |
| | 'Samson' new | EWes |

## *Rhoeo* see *Tradescantia*

## *Rhopalostylis* (*Arecaceae*)

| | | |
|---|---|---|
| | ***baueri*** | CBrP LPal |
| | ***sapida*** | CBrP CKob CTrC LPal |
| | - 'Chatham Island' | CBrP |
| | - 'East Cape' | SBig |

## rhubarb see *Rheum* x *hybridum*

## *Rhus* (*Anacardiaceae*)

| | | |
|---|---|---|
| | ***ambigua*** | EPfP |
| | - B&SWJ 3656 | WCru |
| | - large-leaved B&SWJ 10884 new | WCru |
| § | ***aromatica*** | CAgr CArn EBee ELan EPfP NLar |
| | ***chinensis*** | CDoC CMCN EPfP NLar |
| | ***copallina*** | EBee ELan EPfP LRHS |
| | ***coriaria*** | CArn EPfP NLar |
| | ***cotinus*** | see *Cotinus coggygria* |
| | ***glabra*** | CArn CBcs CDoC EPfP MGos SPer WDin |
| | - 'Laciniata' misapplied | see *R.* x *pulvinata* Autumn Lace Group |
| | - 'Laciniata' Carrière | NLar |
| | ***glauca*** | EShb |
| N | ***hirta*** | see *R. typhina* |
| | ***incisa*** | SPlb |
| | ***integrifolia*** | CArn |
| | ***magalismontana*** | EShb |
| | ***potaninii*** | EPfP GKir LRHS MAsh |
| § | x ***pulvinata*** Autumn Lace Group | EBee EPfP MGos SHBN WPat |
| | - - 'Red Autumn Lace' $\Upsilon^{H4}$ | GKir LRHS MBlu MBri MRav SPer |
| § | ***radicans*** | CArn COld GPoy WHer |
| | ***succedanea*** | CDTJ |
| | ***toxicodendron*** | see *R. radicans* |
| | ***trichocarpa*** | EPfP SSpi |
| | ***trilobata*** | see *R. aromatica* |
| N | ***typhina*** $\Upsilon^{H4}$ | CBcs CDoC CDul CHEx CLnd CTrG CTri EBee ECrN ELan EPfP GKir LRHS MAsh MBar MGos MRav NBea NBlu NPri NWea SHBN SPer SPoG SSta WBrE WDin WFar |
| § | - 'Dissecta' $\Upsilon^{H4}$ | CBcs CDoC CDul CLnd CSBt EBee ECrN ELan EPfP GKir LPan MAsh MBar MBri MGan MGos MRav MWat NBea NBlu NPri SEND SPer SPoG WDin WFar WOrn |
| | - 'Laciniata' hort. | see *R. typhina* 'Dissecta' |
| | - 'Radiance' new | MAsh |
| | - Tiger Eyes = 'Bailtiger'$^{PBR}$ | EBee ELan EPfP LBuc LRHS MAsh MBlu MBri MGos SCoo SPoG |
| § | ***verniciflua*** | CLnd EGFP NLar SSpi |

## *Rhynchelytrum* see *Melinis*

| | | |
|---|---|---|
| | ***nerviglume*** 'Savannah' | see *Melinis nerviglumis* 'Savannah' |

## *Rhynchospora* (*Cyperaceae*)

| | | |
|---|---|---|
| | ***colorata*** | CKno CRow NPer SGar SHom WHal |
| | ***latifolia*** | CKno SHDw WCot |

## *Ribes* ✿ (*Grossulariaceae*)

| | | |
|---|---|---|
| | ***alpinum*** | CPLG EMac MRav MWht NSti NWea SPer SRms WDin WGwG |
| | - 'Aureum' | CAbP EHoe WCot WDin |
| | - 'Schmidt' | EBee |
| | ***americanum*** 'Variegatum' (v) | EHoe ELan EPla MRav NHol SPer WPat |
| | ***aureum*** new | EHig |
| | - hort. | see *R. odoratum* |
| * | - 'Roxby Red' | MCoo |
| | 'Ben Hope'$^{PBR}$ (B) | CAgr CSBt EMui MAsh |
| | 'Black Velvet' (D) | CAgr MCoo |
| § | x ***culverwellii*** (F) | CAgr CWib EMil EMui GTwe LBuc LEdu MAsh SDea SPoG SVic |
| | ***divaricatum*** | CAgr LEdu |
| | ***gayanum*** | CPMA NLar |
| | x ***gordonianum*** | Widely available |
| | ***himalense*** GWJ 9331 | WCru |
| | jostaberry | see *R.* x *culverwellii* |
| | ***laurifolium*** | CBcs CDoC CDul CPLG EBee ELan EQua ERas EWTr GKir LAst MBri MRav NLar SPer WDin WFar WHCG WSHC |
| | - (f) | CMac EPfP |
| | - (m) | CHar CMac EPfP WPat |
| | - 'Mrs Amy Doncaster' | EPla WCot |
| | - Rosemoor form | CDoC CSam EPfP SKHP SPoG SSpi WCot WHCG WPGP |
| | ***malvifolium*** new | SEND |
| | ***menziesii*** | CHll EWes WCot |
| | ***nigrum*** | SEND |
| | - 'Baldwin' (B) | CDoC CTri EPfP LRHS MAsh NLar SDea SKee SPer SPoG |
| | - 'Barchatnaja' (B) | CAgr |
| | - 'Ben Alder'$^{PBR}$ (B) | CAgr CWib GKir LRHS MAsh SDea |
| | - 'Ben Connan'$^{PBR}$ (B) $\Upsilon^{H4}$ | CAgr CSBt CWib EMil EMui EPfP GKir GTwe LRHS MAsh MBri MGos NLar SCoo SDea SKee SPer SPoG |
| | - 'Ben Gairn'$^{PBR}$ (B) | CAgr |

| | | |
|---|---|---|
| | - 'Ben Lomond'PBR (B) ♀H4 | CAgr CSBt CTri CWib EMil EMui GTwe LAst LBuc LRHS MAsh MGos MRav SDea SKee SPer SVic |
| | - 'Ben More' (B) | CAgr CWib MBri SDea |
| | - 'Ben Nevis' (B) | CAgr CTri CWib GTwe SDea SKee |
| | - 'Ben Sarek'PBR (B) ♀H4 | CAgr CDoC CSBt CSut CTri CWib EMil EMui GTwe LBuc LRHS MAsh MGos MNHC MRav NLar SDea SKee SPer SPoG WOrn |
| | - 'Ben Tirran'PBR (B) | CAgr CDoC CSBt CWib EMil GKir LBuc LRHS MAsh MBri MGos NLar SKee SPoG WOrn |
| | - 'Black Reward' (B) | CAgr MCoo |
| | - 'Boskoop Giant' (B) | CAgr CTri GTwe MGan SPer |
| * | - 'Byelorussian Sweet' (B) | CAgr |
| | - 'Consort' (B) | CAgr |
| * | - 'Hystawneznaya' (B) | CAgr |
| | - 'Jet' (B) | CAgr EMil GTwe SPer |
| * | - 'Kosmicheskaya' (B) | CAgr |
| | - 'Pilot Alexander Mamkin' (B) | CAgr |
| | - 'Seabrook's' (B) | CAgr MGan |
| | - 'Titania' (B) | EMui LRHS |
| | - 'Tsema' (B) | MCoo |
| | - 'Wellington XXX' (B) | CAgr CTri GTwe LBuc MGan NBlu SPer |
| | - 'Westwick Choice' (B) | GTwe |
| § | ***odoratum*** | Widely available |
| | - 'Crandall' | CAgr LEdu |
| | ***praecox*** | CBcs SEND |
| | 'Redwing' (R) | LRHS |
| | ***rubrum*** 'Blanka' (W) | CSut EMil |
| | - 'Cascade' (R) | CAgr |
| | - 'Cherry' (R) | CAgr MCoo |
| | - 'Fay's New Prolific' (R) | GTwe |
| | - 'Hollande Rose' (P) | GTwe |
| | - 'Jonkheer van Tets' (R) ♀H4 | CAgr CSBt CWib EMil EMui EPfP GTwe IArd LRHS MAsh MCoo NLar SDea SEND SKee SPer |
| | - 'Junifer' (R) | CAgr EMil EMui GTwe LRHS SKee |
| | - 'Laxton's Number One' (R) | CAgr CTri EMui GTwe MAsh MGan MRav SDea SPer SPoG |
| | - 'Laxton's Perfection' (R) | MCoo |
| | - 'October Currant' (P) | GTwe |
| | - 'Raby Castle' (R) | GTwe |
| | - 'Red Lake' (R) ♀H4 | CAgr CTri CWib EPfP GTwe LBuc LCro LRHS MGan MGos MNHC NBlu NLar SDea SKee SPer SPoG WOrn |
| | - 'Redpoll' (R) | LRHS |
| | - 'Redstart' (R) | CAgr CSBt CTri CWib GKir GTwe LBuc MAsh NLar SDea SKee SPoG |
| | - 'Rondom' (R) | CAgr SDea SVic |
| | - 'Rosetta' (R) | MCoo |
| | - 'Rovada' (R) | CAgr CSBt CSut CWib EMil EMui GKir GTwe LRHS MAsh SKee |
| | - 'Stanza' (R) ♀H4 | CAgr EMil GTwe MCoo SDea SEND |
| | - 'Transparent' (W) | GTwe |
| § | - 'Versailles Blanche' (W) | CAgr CMac CSBt CTri CWib EMui EPfP GTwe LBuc MAsh MBri MGan MGos SDea SEND SKee SPer SPoG WOrn |
| | - 'White Dutch' (W) | MCoo |
| | - 'White Grape' (W) ♀H4 | GTwe |
| | - 'White Pearl' (W) | MCoo SDea SVic |
| | - White Versailles | see *R. rubrum* 'Versailles Blanche' |
| | - 'Wilson's Long Bunch' (R) | GTwe |
| | ***sanguineum*** | CDul EMac MBar WBVN WFar WMoo |
| I | - 'Atrorubens Select' | MBri |
| | - 'Brocklebankii' | CAbP CMac CPLG EBee ELan EMil EPfP LRHS MGos MRav NHol SHBN SLim SPer SPla WCFE WPat WPen WSHC |
| | - 'King Edward VII' | Widely available |
| | - 'Koja' | EBee GBin LBuc LRHS LSRN MBri MGos NPri SPoG WPat |
| | - 'Lombartsii' | MRav |
| | - 'Poky's Pink' | CMac EWTr MBri MGos MRav WOVN |
| | - 'Pulborough Scarlet' ♀H4 | Widely available |
| | - 'Red Bross' **new** | MAsh |
| | - 'Red Pimpernel' | CSBt EBee LBMP LSRN MBNS NCGa SCoo SPoG SWvt WFar |
| | - 'Splendens' | EBee |
| | - 'Taff's Kim' (v) | EPla |
| | - 'Tydeman's White' | CChe CDul CPLG CSBt ELan EPfP MBar NLar NPri SDnm SGar SSpi WPat WSHC |
| | - var. ***variegata*** | CMac WFar |
| | - White Icicle = 'Ubric' ♀H4 | Widely available |
| | ***speciosum*** ♀H3 | Widely available |
| | ***uva-crispa*** 'Achilles' (D) | GTwe |
| | - 'Admiral Beattie' (F) | GTwe |
| | - 'Annelii' | CAgr SDea |
| | - 'Bedford Red' (C/D) | GTwe |
| | - 'Bedford Yellow' (C/D) | GTwe |
| | - 'Beech Tree Nestling' (D) | GTwe |
| | - 'Blucher' (D) | GTwe |
| | - 'Bright Venus' (D) | GTwe |
| | - 'Broom Girl' (D) | GTwe |
| | - 'Captivator' (C) | GTwe SDea |
| | - 'Careless' (D) ♀H4 | CMac CSBt EMil EMui GKir GTwe LRHS MAsh MGan MGos SDea SKee SPer |
| | - 'Catherine' | SDea |
| | - 'Cook's Eagle' (C) | GTwe |
| | - 'Cousen's Seedling' (D) | GTwe |
| | - 'Criterion' (D) | GTwe |
| | - 'Crown Bob' (C/D) | GTwe MGan |
| | - 'Dan's Mistake' (D) | GTwe |
| | - 'Drill' (D) | GTwe |
| | - 'Early Sulphur' (D) | GTwe SDea |
| | - 'Firbob' (D) | GTwe |
| | - 'Forester' (D) | GTwe |
| | - 'Freedom' (C) | GTwe |
| | - 'Gipsy Queen' (D) | GTwe |
| | - 'Glenton Green' (D) | GTwe |
| | - 'Golden Ball' (D) | SDea |
| | - 'Golden Drop' (D) | GTwe |
| | - 'Green Gem' (C/D) | GTwe |
| | - 'Green Ocean' (D) | GTwe |
| | - 'Greenfinch' (C) ♀H4 | CAgr EMui GTwe SDea |
| | - 'Guido' (F) | GTwe |
| | - 'Gunner' (C/D) | GTwe |
| | - 'Heart of Oak' (F) | GTwe |
| | - 'Hebburn Prolific' (D) | GTwe |
| | - 'Hedgehog' (D) | GTwe |
| | - 'Hero of the Nile' (D) | GTwe |
| | - 'High Sheriff' (D) | GTwe |
| | - 'Hinnonmäki' (F) | CAgr CSBt LBuc MAsh |
| | - 'Hinnonmäki Grön' **new** | NBlu |
| | - 'Hinnonmäki Gul' (D) | CAgr CSut EMil GKir LBuc MAsh MGos SDea SPoG |
| | - 'Hinnonmäki Röd' (C/D) | CAgr EMil GTwe LBuc MAsh MBri MCoo SDea SPoG SVic |
| | - 'Howard's Lancer' (C/D) | GTwe SDea |
| | - 'Invicta' (C) ♀H4 | CAgr CDoC CMac CSBt CSut CTri CWSG EMil EMui EPfP GKir LBuc LRHS MAsh MBri MGan MGos MNHC MRav SCoo SDea SKee SPer SPoG WBVN WOrn |
| | - 'Ironmonger' (D) | GTwe |
| | - 'Jubilee' (C/D) | LBuc MGos |
| | - 'Keen's Seedling' (D) | GTwe |
| | - 'Keepsake' (C/D) | GTwe SDea WBVN |
| | - 'King of Trumps' (F) | GTwe |

| | |
|---|---|
| - 'Lancashire Lad' (C/D) | GTwe |
| - 'Langley Gage' (D) | GTwe MCoo |
| - 'Laxton's Amber' (D) | GTwe |
| - 'Leveller' (D) ♀H4 | CMac CTri EMui GKir GTwe LAst LBuc LRHS MAsh MCoo MGan MGos SDea SKee SPer |
| - 'London' (C/D) | GTwe |
| - 'Lord Derby' (C/D) | GTwe |
| - 'Martlet' (F) | CAgr GTwe LBuc MAsh MCoo SPoG |
| - 'May Duke' (C/D) | SDea |
| - 'Mitre' (D) | GTwe |
| - 'Pax'PBR (D) | CAgr CDoC CSBt CSut EMil EMui EPfP GKir GTwe LBuc LRHS MAsh SDea SKee WOrn |
| - 'Peru' (D) | GTwe |
| - 'Pitmaston Green Gage' (D) | GTwe |
| - 'Plunder' | GTwe |
| - 'Queen of Trumps' (D) | GTwe |
| - var. ***reclinatum*** 'Aston Red' | see *R. uva-crispa* 'Warrington' |
| - 'Red Champagne' | GTwe |
| - 'Remarka' (C/D) | EMui |
| - 'Rifleman' (D) | GTwe |
| - 'Rokula'PBR (C/D) | CDoC EMui GTwe SDea SKee |
| - 'Rosebery' (D) | GTwe |
| - 'Scotch Red Rough' (D) | GTwe |
| - 'Scottish Chieftan' (D) | GTwe |
| - 'Snow' (F) | EPfP SCoo |
| - 'Snowdrop' (D) | GTwe |
| - 'Spinefree' (C) | GTwe |
| - 'Surprise' (D) | GTwe |
| - 'Telegraph' (F) | GTwe |
| - 'Tom Joiner' (F) | GTwe |
| - 'Victoria' (C/D) | GTwe |
| § - 'Warrington' | GTwe |
| - 'Whinham's Industry' (C/D) ♀H4 | CMac CSBt CTri EMil EMui GKir GTwe LAst LBuc LRHS MAsh MGos MRav SDea SPer SPoG WBVN |
| - 'White Lion' (C/D) | GTwe |
| - 'White Transparent' (C) | GTwe |
| - 'Whitesmith' (C/D) | CTri GTwe MCoo MGan SDea |
| - 'Woodpecker' (D) | GTwe |
| - 'Yellow Champagne' (D) | GTwe |
| ***valdivianum*** | WCot |
| ***viburnifolium*** | CBcs LEdu NLar |
| 'Worcesterberry' (C) | EMui MGos SDea SPer |

## *Richea* (*Epacridaceae*)

| | |
|---|---|
| ***dracophylla*** | GGar SAPC |

## *Ricinocarpos* (*Euphorbiaceae*)

| | |
|---|---|
| ***pinifolius*** | ECou |

## *Ricinus* (*Euphorbiaceae*)

| | |
|---|---|
| ***communis*** | CDTJ |
| - 'Carmencita' ♀H3 | SGar |
| - 'Carmencita Pink' | CDTJ |
| - 'Carmencita Red' | CDTJ EUJe MJnS SWal |
| - 'Dominican Republic' **new** | CDTJ |
| - 'Gibsonii' | CDTJ |
| - 'Impala' | CDTJ CSpe |
| - 'New Zealand Black' **new** | CDTJ MJnS |
| - 'Zanzibariensis' | CDTJ EShb MJnS |

## *Riocreuxia* (*Asclepiadaceae*)

| | |
|---|---|
| ***torulosa*** | CCCN SPlb |

## *Robinia* (*Papilionaceae*)

| | |
|---|---|
| x ***ambigua*** | SSpi |
| § ***boyntonii*** | EMil LSRN SLon |
| § ***hispida*** | CDul CEnd CLnd CWib ECrN ELan EPfP EWTr MAsh MBlu SBLw SHBN SPer SPoG SSpi WDin WJas WOrn |
| - 'Macrophylla' | CEnd |
| - 'Rosea' misapplied | see *R. boyntonii*, *R. hispida* |
| - 'Rosea' ambig. | CBcs EBee SBLw |
| ***kelseyi*** | CDul EBee EHig EWes SPer |
| x ***margaretta*** Casque Rouge | see *R.* x *margaretta* 'Pink Cascade' |
| § - 'Pink Cascade' | CCVT CDoC CDul CEnd CLnd EBee ECrN EPfP LAst LMaj LPan LRHS MAsh MBlu MGos MREP SBLw SBod SCoo SCrf SEND SHBN SLim SLon SPer WDin WFoF WPGP |
| ***pseudoacacia*** | CCVT CDul CLnd EBee ECrN ELan EMac EWTr LBuc LPan MCoo SBLw SPlb WBVN WDin WFar |
| - 'Bessoniana' | CDul EBee ECrN EHig LAst LMaj SBLw SCoo |
| - 'Fastigiata' | see *R. pseudoacacia* 'Pyramidalis' |
| - 'Frisia' ♀H4 | Widely available |
| - 'Inermis' hort. | see *R. pseudoacacia* 'Umbraculifera' |
| § - 'Lace Lady'PBR | CWSG EBee ELan EPfP LPan LRHS MAsh MBri MGos MRav NLar SCoo SLim SPoG |
| - 'Myrtifolia' | SBLw |
| § - 'Pyramidalis' | EBee SBLw |
| - 'Rozynskiana' | CDul |
| - 'Tortuosa' | CDul CEnd EBee ECrN EHig ELan EMil LAst LPan LRHS MBlu MGos SBLw SPer WPGP |
| - 'Twisty Baby'PBR | see *R. pseudoacacia* 'Lace Lady' |
| § - 'Umbraculifera' | CDul CLnd ECrN EMac EMil LMaj LPan MBri MGos SBLw SCoo |
| - 'Unifoliola' | LMaj SBLw |
| x ***slavinii*** 'Hillieri' ♀H4 | CDoC CDul CEnd CLnd EBee ECrN EHig ELan EPfP EWTr LRHS LSRN MAsh MBlu MBri MGos SCrf SEND SPer SPoG WOrn WPGP |

## *Rochea* see *Crassula*

## *Rodgersia* ✿ (*Saxifragaceae*)

| | |
|---|---|
| ACE 2303 | GBuc |
| CLD 1329 | NHol |
| CLD 1432 | NHol |
| from Tibet | CWsd |
| ***aesculifolia*** ♀H4 | Widely available |
| - green bud | IBlr |
| - var. ***henrici*** | CBct CLAP CRow LPio NBro NMyG SWat WMoo |
| - - hybrid | EBee GBuc ITim NHol NLar WAul WHil |
| - pink-flowered | SSpi |
| - 'Red Dawn' | EBee IBlr |
| - 'Red Leaf' **new** | GCal |
| aff. ***aesculifolia*** petaloid | IBlr |
| 'Blickfang' | IBlr |
| 'Borodin' **new** | EBee |
| Cally strain | EDAr GCal |
| 'Die Anmutige' | CLAP CRow |
| 'Die Schöne' | CLAP EBee GBin NLar |
| 'Die Stolze' | EBee GBin |
| 'Elfenbeinturm' | EBee IBlr |
| 'Herkules' | CBct CSam EBee ECha ECtt EGle EHoe GBin GCal GMaP LSou MBNS NBhm NLar SSpi WCot WGwG WPnP |
| 'Ideal' | WCot |
| 'Irish Bronze' ♀H4 | CLAP EBee EBrs ELon GBin GKir LPio LRHS WCAu WFar WMoo WPnP |
| 'Koriata' | IBlr |

| | |
|---|---|
| 'Kupfermond' | CRow IBlr |
| 'La Blanche' | EBee ECtt ELon EWTr SPoG WCot WGwG WPnP |
| 'Maigrün' | IBlr |
| ***nepalensis*** | CLAP IBlr MDun |
| 'Panache' | GBin IBlr |
| 'Parasol' | CBct CLAP CWsd GBin GBuc IBlr NHol SSpi WPGP |
| ***pinnata*** | Widely available |
| - B&SWJ 7741A | WCru |
| - L 1670 | CLAP SSpi |
| - SDR 3301 | GKev |
| - from Himalaya **new** | GCal |
| - from SW China | GCal |
| - 'Alba' | EBee GCal IBlr MLLN NHol WMAq |
| - 'Buckland Beauty' | CDes CWsd IBlr SSpi WPGP |
| - 'Cally Salmon' | EGle EWes GCal IBlr |
| - 'Chocolate Wing' | CLAP EBee EPPr EPfP ESwi GBin IPot LPio MAvo MBNS NBPN NBhm NLar NMoo SPoG WBor WFar WMoo |
| - 'Crûg Cardinal' | GCal WCru |
| - 'Elegans' | CBct CDes EBee EHoe ELan EMFW EPfP EPla GKir GMaP IBlr LCro LRHS MRav NHol NMyG NOrc SMad SPer SWvt WAul WCot WHil WPnP |
| - 'Fireworks' | CFir CLAP EBee ELan GBin IPot MSte SPer WFar |
| - 'Jade Dragon Mountain' | IBlr |
| - 'Maurice Mason' | CLAP CMoH EBee EGle IBlr SMHy |
| - 'Mont Blanc' | IBlr |
| - Mount Stewart form | IBlr |
| - 'Perthshire Bronze' | IBlr |
| - pink-flowered | WCru |
| - 'Rosea' | IBlr |
| - 'Superba' ♀H4 | Widely available |
| - white-flowered | GAbr WCru |
| ***pinnata* x *sambucifolia*** | IBlr |
| ***podophylla*** ♀H4 | Widely available |
| - SDR 5158 **new** | GKev |
| - 'Braunlaub' | CLAP EBee MBNS NBPN NBro SMad WFar WMoo WPnP |
| - 'Bronceblad' | IBlr |
| - Donard form | GBin IBlr MBri WPGP |
| - 'Rotlaub' | CDes CLAP CRow EBee EGle GBin IBlr LRHS WCot WMoo WPGP |
| - 'Smaragd' | CDes CLAP CRow EGle GBin GCal IBlr LRHS NLar |
| ***purdomii*** hort. | CLAP EBrs GCal GKir LRHS WCot WPGP |
| 'Reinecke Fuchs' | IBlr |
| 'Rosenlicht' | CRow |
| 'Rosenzipfel' | IBlr |
| ***sambucifolia*** | CBcs CDWL CLAP CRow EBee EMFW GCal GKev GKir ITim LEdu MLHP NLar NSti SPer WCAu WFar WMoo WPnP |
| - B&SWJ 7899 | WCru |
| - dwarf pink-flowered | IBlr |
| - dwarf white-flowered | IBlr |
| - 'Mountain Select' | EBee GCal WCot WFar |
| - white-flowered | ITim |
| ***tabularis*** | see *Astilboides tabularis* |

## *Rohdea* (*Convallariaceae*)

| | |
|---|---|
| ***japonica*** | CHEx EBee WCot WPGP |
| - B&SWJ 4853 | WCru |
| - 'Godaishu' (v) | WCot |
| - 'Gunjaku' (v) | EMon WCot |
| - 'Lance Leaf' | EPla |
| - long-leaved | WCot WFar |
| - 'Miyakonojo' (v) | EBee WCot |
| - 'Talbot Manor' (v) | CBct EBee EBla EPla WCot |
| - 'Tama-jishi' (v) | WCot |
| - 'Tuneshige Rokujo' (v) | WCot |
| ***watanabei*** B&SWJ 1911 | WCru |

## *Romanzoffia* (*Hydrophyllaceae*)

| | |
|---|---|
| ***californica*** | EBee GKev |
| § ***sitchensis*** | CTri EPPr MAvo |
| ***suksdorfii*** E. Greene | see *R. sitchensis* |
| ***tracyi*** | CDes CLAP EBee GGar GKev NRya WPrP |
| ***unalaschcensis*** | CLAP CSec EBee GKev GKir NWCA SRms WPer WPtf |

## *Romneya* (*Papaveraceae*)

| | |
|---|---|
| ***coulteri*** ♀H4 | Widely available |
| § - var. ***trichocalyx*** | CBct CFir CGHE EBee SKHP WPGP |
| § - 'White Cloud' ♀H4 | CBct EBee ELan EPla SKHP SSpi WPGP |
| x ***hybrida*** | see *R. coulteri* 'White Cloud' |
| ***trichocalyx*** | see *R. coulteri* var. *trichocalyx* |

## *Romulea* (*Iridaceae*)

| | |
|---|---|
| ***amoena*** 'Nieuwoudtville' | ECho |
| ***autumnalis*** | ECho |
| ***barkerae*** 'Paternoster' | ECho |
| ***battandieri*** | EBrs ECho |
| ***bulbocodium*** | CBro CSec ECho WAbe |
| - var. ***clusiana*** | EBrs ECho |
| - var. ***crocea*** | CStu EBrs ECho |
| * - 'Knightshayes' | SCnR |
| ***campanuloides*** | CSec EDif WAbe |
| ***columnae*** | EBrs ECho |
| ***dichotoma*** | ECho |
| ***gigantea*** | CStu |
| ***kamisensis*** | ECho |
| ***leipoldtii*** | ECho |
| ***linaresii*** | ECho GKev |
| ***longituba*** | see *R. macowanii* |
| * ***luteoflora*** var. ***sanguinea*** | EBee ECho NMen |
| § ***macowanii*** | EBrs ECho |
| - var. ***alticola*** | WAbe |
| ***namaquensis*** | ECho |
| ***nivalis*** | EBrs ECho |
| ***obscura*** var. ***blanda*** | ECho |
| - var. ***obscura*** | ECho |
| - var. ***subtestacea*** | ECho |
| ***ramiflora*** | CPBP CPLG EBrs ECho |
| ***requienii*** | NMen |
| ***tempskyana*** | CPBP EBrs ECho |
| * ***zahnii*** | CSec GKev |

## *Rondeletia* (*Rubiaceae*)

| | |
|---|---|
| ***amoena*** | SOWG |

## *Rorippa* (*Brassicaceae*)

| | |
|---|---|
| ***amphibia*** **new** | MSKA |
| ***nasturtium-aquaticum*** | EMFW WMAq |

## *Rosa* ✿ (*Rosaceae*)

| | |
|---|---|
| ACE 241 | CFee |
| UNK 22 from East Himalaya **new** | GCal |
| UNK 229 from East Himalaya **new** | GCal |
| A Shropshire Lad = 'Ausled'PBR (S) | CSRo LRHS LStr MAus MJon SSea SWCr |
| A Whiter Shade of Pale = 'Peafanfare'PBR (HT) **new** | ESty SMrm SWCr |
| Abbeyfield Rose = 'Cocbrose'PBR (HT) ♀H4 | GCoc MGan MRav SPer |

| | |
| --- | --- |
| § 'Abbotswood' (*canina* hybrid) | MAus |
| Abigaile = 'Tanelaigib' (F) | MJon |
| Abraham Darby = 'Auscot'PBR (S) | CGro EBee ELon EPfP LAst LCro LRHS LStr MAus MJon MRav NLar SEND SMrm SPer SSea SWCr WAct WHCG |
| Absent Friends = 'Dicemblem'PBR (F) | IDic |
| ***acicularis*** | GAuc |
| 'Adam Messerich' (Bb) | MAus SLon SWCr WHCG |
| 'Adélaïde d'Orléans' (Ra) ♀H4 | CRHN CSRo LRHS MAsh MAus MRav SPer SWCr WAct WHCG |
| Admirable = 'Searodney' (Min) | MJon |
| 'Admiral Rodney' (HT) | MGan MJon |
| Agatha Christie = 'Kormeita'PBR (ClF) | MGos MRav SWCr |
| 'Aglaia' (Ra) | MAus WHCG |
| 'Agnes' (Ru) ♀H4 | CGro ECnt EPfP EWTr GCoc IArd LRHS MAus MGan MRav NLar SMrm SPer SPoG SSea SWCr WAct WHCG WOVN |
| 'Agnès Schilliger' | MRav |
| 'Aimée Vibert' (N) | CSam MAus MRav NLar SMrm SPer SWCr WAct WHCG |
| 'Alain Blanchard' (G) | MAus MGan SWCr WHCG |
| Alan Titchmarsh = 'Ausjive' (S) | ESty LRHS LStr MAus SCoo SMrm SPer SWCr |
| § x ***alba*** 'Alba Maxima' (A) | CBgR GCoc LRHS MAus MGan MRav NLar SPer SSea SWCr WAct WHCG |
| § - 'Alba Semiplena' (A) ♀H4 | LRHS MAus MGan SPer SWCr WAct WHCG |
| - Celestial | see *R.* 'Céleste' |
| - 'Maxima' | see *R.* x *alba* 'Alba Maxima' |
| Alba Meidiland = 'Meiflopan'PBR (S/GC) | WOVN |
| 'Albéric Barbier' (Ra) ♀H4 | CRHN CSBt CSam EBee ECnt ELan EPfP EWTr LCro LRHS LStr MAus MBri MGan MJon MRav NBir NPri NWea SMrm SPer SPoG SSea SWCr WAct WHCG |
| 'Albertine' (Ra) ♀H4 | Widely available |
| 'Alchymist' (S/Cl) | CPou EBee EPfP LRHS MAus MGan MRav NLar SPer SWCr WAct WHCG |
| Alec's Red = 'Cored' (HT) | CBcs CGro CSBt CTri CWSG GCoc LAst LCro LRHS LSRN LStr MAsh MAus MGan MJon MRav NPri SMrm SPer SPoG SWCr |
| Alexander = 'Harlex' (HT) ♀H4 | CGro CSBt GCoc LGod LStr MAus MGan MJon MRav SPer SSea SWCr |
| 'Alexander von Humboldt' (Cl) | MGan NLar |
| 'Alexandre Girault' (Ra) | CRHN LRHS MAus MLan NLar SPer SWCr WHCG |
| 'Alfred de Dalmas' misapplied | see *R.* 'Mousseline' |
| 'Alfresco'PBR (ClHT) | CSBt LGod MAsh MJon SSea SWCr |
| 'Alida Lovett' (Ra) | MAus |
| Alison = 'Coclibee'PBR (F) | GCoc |
| § 'Alister Stella Gray' (N) | LRHS MAsh MAus MCot MGan NLar SLon SMrm SPer SSea SWCr WAct WHCG |
| 'Allen Chandler' (ClHT) | MAus |
| 'Allgold' (F) | CBcs CGro GKir MGan SWCr |
| Alnwick Castle = 'Ausgrab'PBR (S) | EPfP MAsh MAus MBri SCoo SWCr |
| 'Aloha' (ClHT) ♀H4 | CBcs CGro CTri EBee EPfP ESty LAst LCro LRHS LStr MAsh MAus MBri MCot MGan MJon MRav NLar SPer SPoG SSea SWCr WAct |
| ***alpina*** | see *R. pendulina* |

| | |
| --- | --- |
| 'Alpine Sunset' (HT) | CTri ELon ESty MAsh MRav SPer SPoG SWCr |
| ***altaica*** misapplied | see *R. spinosissima* 'Grandiflora' |
| ***altaica*** Willd. | see *R. spinosissima* |
| Altissimo = 'Delmur' (Cl) | EBee MAus MGan SPer SSea SWCr WAct |
| 'Amadis' (Bs) | MAus WHCG |
| Amanda = 'Beesian' (F) | ESty |
| 'Amazing Grace' (HT) | SWCr |
| Amber Abundance = 'Harfizz'PBR (Abundance Series) (S) | ESty MRav SWCr |
| Amber Cover = 'Poulbambe'PBR (Towne & Country Series) (GC) | EBee SWCr |
| Amber Nectar = 'Mehamber'PBR (F) | MAsh MJon SWCr |
| Amber Queen = 'Harroony'PBR (F) ♀H4 | CGro CSBt CTri EPfP ESty GCoc IArd LGod LStr MAsh MAus MBri MGan MJon MRav NPri SMrm SPer SPoG SWCr |
| Amber Star = 'Manstar' (Min) | MJon |
| Amber Sunset = 'Manamsun' (Min) | MJon |
| Ambridge Rose = 'Auswonder' (S) | LRHS MAus MJon SPer |
| 'Amélia' | see *R.* 'Celsiana' |
| Amelia = 'Poulen011'PBR (Renaissance Series) (S) | ECnt SWCr |
| 'American Pillar' (Ra) | CGro CRHN CSBt CSam CTri CWSG EBee ECnt ELan LCro LRHS LStr MAsh MAus MGan MRav SPer SPoG SSea SWCr WKif |
| 'Amy Robsart' (RH) | MAus MGan |
| 'Anaïs Ségalas' (G) | MAus |
| § 'Andersonii' (*canina* hybrid) | MAus WAct |
| 'Andrea' (ClMin) | MJon |
| § 'Anemone' (Cl) | MAus |
| ***anemoniflora*** | see *R.* x *beanii* |
| ***anemonoides*** | see *R.* 'Anemone' |
| - 'Ramona' | see *R.* 'Ramona' |
| 'Angel Gates' (Ra) | WAct |
| Angela Rippon = 'Ocaru' (Min) | CSBt MJon SPer SWCr |
| 'Angela's Choice' (F) | MGan SWCr |
| Anisley Dickson = 'Dickimono'PBR (F) ♀H4 | IDic LGod MGan SPer |
| 'Ann Aberconway' (F) | WBod |
| Ann = 'Ausfete'PBR (S) | LRHS MAus |
| Anna Ford = 'Harpiccolo' (Min/Patio) ♀H4 | CWSG LStr MAus MGan SPer SWCr |
| Anna Livia = 'Kormetter'PBR (F) ♀H4 | EBls ECnt MJon |
| Anne Boleyn = 'Ausecret'PBR (S) | LRHS MAus SCoo SWCr |
| 'Anne Cocker' (F) | GCoc |
| 'Anne Dakin' (ClHT) | MAus |
| Anne Harkness = 'Harkaramel' (F) | MAus MGan SPer |
| 'Anne of Geierstein' (RH) | MAus MGan NHaw |
| Antique '89 = 'Kordalen'PBR (ClF) | MGos MJon |
| Aperitif = 'Macwaira'PBR (HT) | EBee ECnt ESty MJon |
| apothecary's rose | see *R. gallica* var. *officinalis* |
| 'Apple Blossom' (Ra) | MGan SSea WHCG |
| Apricot Abundance = 'Harfracas' **new** | SWCr |
| 'Apricot Nectar' (F) | MAus MGan NHaw SPer |
| 'Apricot Silk' (HT) | CBcs CTri MAus MGan MRav SPer SWCr |
| Apricot Summer = 'Korpapiro' (Patio) | MBri |

Apricot Sunblaze = 'Savamark' (Min) — CSBt
'Archiduc Joseph' misapplied — see *R.* 'Général Schablikine'
Ards Beauty = 'Dicjoy' (F) — SPer
'Arethusa' (Ch) — EBee SLon SPla SWCr
'Arizona Sunset' (Min) — MJon
§ ***arkansana*** var. ***suffulta*** — WHCG
Armada = 'Haruseful' (S) — SSea
'Arrillaga' (HP) — MAus
'Arthur Bell' (F) ♀H4 — CSBt EPfP ESty GKir IArd LCro LRHS LStr MAsh MAus MGan MRav NPri SMrm SPer SPoG SSea SWCr
'Arthur de Sansal' (DPo) — MAus WHCG
***arvensis*** — CCVT CRWN LBuc MAus NHaw NWea WAct
'Assemblage des Beautés' (G) — MAus
'Astra Desmond' (Ra) — WTin
Atlantic Star = 'Fryworld'PBR (F) — SWCr
Audrey Wilcox = 'Frywilrey' (HT) — CSBt
'Auguste Gervais' (Ra) — LRHS MAus SPer WHCG
Austrian copper rose — see *R. foetida* 'Bicolor'
Austrian yellow — see *R. foetida*
Autumn Colours = 'Poulfl003'PBR (F) **new** — ECnt
'Autumn Delight' (HM) — MAus WHCG
Autumn Fire — see *R.* 'Herbstfeuer'
'Autumn Sunlight' (ClF) — MGan SPer
'Autumn Sunset' (S/Cl) — MJon
'Autumnalis' — see *R.* 'Princesse de Nassau'
'Aviateur Blériot' (Ra) — MAus
'Avignon' (F) — ECnt
Avon = 'Poulmulti'PBR (GC) ♀H4 — EBee ELan GCoc MJon MRav SPer SWCr WHCG
Awakening = 'Probuzení' (Cl) — EBee MGan NLar SWCr WHCG WOVN
'Ayrshire Splendens' — see *R.* 'Splendens'
'Baby Bio' (F/Patio) — CBcs
'Baby Darling' (Min) — MGan SWCr
'Baby Faurax' (Poly) — MAus
Baby Gold Star (Min) — see *R.* 'Estrellita de Oro'
Baby Love = 'Scrivluv'PBR (yellow) (Min/Patio) ♀H4 — CTri LGod MAus
Baby Masquerade = 'Tanba' (Min) — MGan MJon MRav SMrm SPer SWCr
Babyface = 'Rawril'PBR (Min) — ESty
'Ballerina' (HM/Poly) ♀H4 — CBcs CGro CSBt EBee ECnt ELan EPfP ESty GCoc LGod LRHS LStr MAsh MAus MBri MGan MJon MLan MRav NPri SPer SSea SWCr WAct WHCG WKif
Ballindalloch Castle = 'Cocneel'PBR (F) — GCoc
'Baltimore Belle' (Ra) — CRHN MAus WAct WHCG
***banksiae*** (Ra) — CPou GQui SRms
- SF 96051 — ISea
- ***alba*** — see *R. banksiae* var. *banksiae*
§ - var. ***banksiae*** (Ra/d) — CDul CPou CSBt CTri EBee ELan EPfP LPan LStr MAus SEND SPer
- 'Lutea' (Ra/d) ♀H3 — Widely available
- var. ***normalis*** (Ra) — CSBt LRHS MAus NSti SLon SWCr WCot WHer
I - 'Rosea' — NLar
'Bantry Bay' (ClHT) — CSBt EBee ELan LStr MGan NBlu SLon SPer SPla SSea SWCr
Barbara Austin = 'Austop'PBR (S) — LRHS MAus
Barkarole = 'Tanelorak'PBR (HT) — CSBt ESty LStr
'Baron de Wassenaer' (CeMo) — MGan
'Baron Girod de l'Ain' (HP) — EBee ELon ESty LAst MAus MCot MGan MRav NHaw NLar SMrm SPla SWCr WAct WHCG
'Baroness Rothschild' (HP) — see *R.* 'Baronne Adolph de Rothschild'
'Baroness Rothschild' (HT) — see *R.* Baronne Edmond de Rothschild
'Baroness Rothschild', ambig — see *R.* Baronne Edmond de Rothschild, Baronne Edmond de Rothschild, Climbing
§ 'Baronne Adolph de Rothschild' (HP) — MGan MRav
§ Baronne Edmond de Rothschild = 'Meigriso' (HT) — MAus MGan WAct
§ Baronne Edmond de Rothschild, Climbing = 'Meigrisosar' (Cl/HT) — CSBt
'Baronne Prévost' (HP) — MAus WAct WHCG
Baroque Floorshow = 'Harbaroque'PBR (S) — CGro MRav
§ x ***beanii*** (Ra) — EPla SMad
'Beau Narcisse' (G) — MAus
'Beauté' (HT) — MGan
Beautiful Britain = 'Dicfire'PBR (F) — CWSG IDic LStr MGan MHav MRav SLon SWCr
Beautiful Sunrise = 'Bostimebide'PBR (ClPatio) — MAsh MJon SWCr
Behold = 'Savahold' (Min) — MJon
'Bel Ange' (HT) — MGan SWCr
§ Bella = 'Pouljill'PBR (Renaissance Series) (S) — CPou EPfP
'Belle Amour' (AxD) — MAus SWCr WAct WHCG
Belle Blonde = 'Menap' (HT) — MGan SPer
'Belle de Crécy' (G) ♀H4 — CPou CSam EBee GKir LRHS LStr MAsh MAus SPer SWCr WAct WHCG
'Belle des Jardins' misapplied — see *R.* x *centifolia* 'Unique Panachée'
Belle Epoque = 'Fryyaboo'PBR (HT) — GCoc LStr MGan MJon SWCr
'Belle Isis' (G) — MAus MRav SPer
'Belle Portugaise' (ClT) — MAus
§ 'Belvedere' (Ra) — MAus MGan SWCr WAct WHCG
Benita = 'Dicquarrel' (HT) — IDic
Benjamin Britten = 'Ausencart'PBR (S) — CSBt EPfP LRHS MAsh MAus MJon SWCr
§ 'Bennett's Seedling' (Ra) — SSea
Benson and Hedges Gold = 'Macgem' (HT) — CWSG
Benson and Hedges Special = 'Macshana'PBR (Min) — MJon
Berkshire = 'Korpinka'PBR (GC) ♀H4 — LStr MGan SWCr
Best of Friends = 'Pouldunk'PBR (HT) — ECnt LSRN SWCr
Best Wishes = 'Chessnut'PBR (Cl/v) — CSBt EBls LSRN MGan SWCr
Bettina = 'Mepal' (HT) — MGan
Betty Boop = 'Wekplapic'PBR (F) — MJon SWCr
Betty Driver = 'Gandri'PBR (F) — MGan SPer
Betty Harkness = 'Harette'PBR (F) — LStr
'Betty Prior' (F) — GCoc MGan
§ Bewitched = 'Poulbella'PBR (Castle Series) (F) — ECnt EPfP SWCr

| | | |
|---|---|---|
| | Bianco = 'Cocblanco'PBR (Patio/Min) | GCoc MAus MRav |
| § | 'Big Chief' (HT) | MJon |
| | Big Purple = 'Stebigpu'PBR (HT) | ECnt ESty MJon SWCr |
| | Birthday Boy = 'Tan97607'PBR (HT) | CGro ESty LStr |
| | Birthday Girl = 'Meilasso'PBR (F) | ESty LStr MJon MRav SMrm SSea SWCr |
| | Birthday Wishes = 'Guesdelay' (HT) | CTri LRHS MAsh SWCr |
| | Bishop Elphinstone = 'Cocjolly' (F) | GCoc |
| | Black Baccara = 'Meidebenne'PBR | ESty MBri SWCr |
| | Black Beauty = 'Korfleur' (HT) | MAus MJon |
| | 'Black Ice' (F) | CGro MGan SWCr |
| | 'Black Jack' (Ce) | see *R.* 'Tour de Malakoff' |
| | Black Jade = 'Benblack' (Min/Patio) | MJon |
| | 'Blairii Number Two' (ClBb) ♀H4 | LRHS MAus MRav NLar SPer SWCr WAct WHCG WKif |
| | 'Blanche de Vibert' (DPo) | EBee MAus |
| | 'Blanche Double de Coubert' (Ru) ♀H4 | CDul CSam CTri EBee ECnt ELan EPfP GCoc LBuc LCro LSRN LStr MAus MGan MJon SPer SSea SWCr WAct WEas WHCG WOVN |
| | 'Blanche Moreau' (CeMo) | MAus MGan NHaw NLar SLon SPer WAct |
| | 'Blanchefleur' (CexG) | EBee MAus MRav |
| | 'Blesma Soul' (HT) **new** | CSBt |
| | 'Blessings' (HT) ♀H4 | CBcs CGro CSBt LCro LSRN LStr MAsh MAus MGan MGos MJon MLan MRav NBlu SMrm SPer SWCr |
| | 'Bleu Magenta' (Ra) ♀H4 | EBee IArd MAus MRav NLar SWCr WAct WHCG WKif |
| | 'Bloomfield Abundance' (Poly) | CPou EPfP MAus MGan MRav SPer SWCr WAct WHCG WHer |
| | 'Blossomtime' (Cl) | SMad SPer |
| | 'Blue Diamond' (HT) | SWCr |
| | Blue for You = 'Pejamblu' (F) **new** | ECnt ESty LStr |
| | Blue Moon = 'Tannacht' (HT) | CGro CTri ELan GCoc LAst MGan MHav MJon MRav NPri SPer SPoG SSea SWCr |
| | Blue Peter = 'Ruiblun'PBR (Min) | ESty MJon |
| | 'Blush Damask' (D) | WHCG |
| | 'Blush Hip' (A) | MAus |
| | 'Blush Noisette' | see *R.* 'Noisette Carnée' |
| | 'Blush Rambler' (Ra) | CSBt EBee MAus MGan SPer SPla SSea SWCr WAct WHCG |
| | 'Blushing Lucy' (Ra) | MTPN SMrm WAct WHCG |
| | Blythe Spirit = 'Auschool'PBR (S) | LCro LStr MAus MBNS |
| | 'Bobbie James' (Ra) ♀H4 | CSRo EBee EPfP LRHS LStr MAus MGan MJon MRav NLar SEND SPer SSea SWCr WAct WBVN WHCG |
| | Bonica = 'Meidomonac'PBR (GC) ♀H4 | Widely available |
| § | Bonita = 'Poulen009'PBR (Renaissance Series) (S) | EBee ECnt LRHS |
| | 'Bonn' (HM/S) | CBcs |
| | 'Bonnie Scotland' (HT) | MGan SWCr |
| | Boogie-Woogie = 'Poulyc006'PBR (Courtyard Series) (Cl) | ECnt LRHS MAsh SWCr |
| | 'Boule de Neige' (Bb) | CBcs CBgR CGro EBee ECnt ELan ELon EPfP GCoc LCro LRHS LStr MAus MGan MRav SPer SPla SWCr WAct WHCG WOVN |
| | 'Bouquet d'Or' (N) | MAus SMrm SWCr |
| | 'Bouquet Tout Fait' misapplied | see *R.* 'Nastarana' |
| | 'Bouquet Tout Fait' (N) | WHCG |
| | 'Bourbon Queen' (Bb) | MAus SWCr |
| | Bow Bells = 'Ausbells' (S) | MAus |
| | Bowled Over = 'Tandolgnil'PBR (F) | ESty SWCr |
| | Boy O Boy = 'Dicuniform' (GC) | IDic |
| § | ***bracteata*** | CHll CRHN EWes GQui MAus WHCG |
| | Brass Ring | see *R.* Peek-a-boo |
| | Brave Heart = 'Horbondsmile' (F) | MAus MBri MRav SPoG SWCr |
| | Breath of Life = 'Harquanne'PBR (ClHT) | CGro CSBt CTri CWSG ELan EPfP LGod LStr MAus MGan MJon MRav SMrm SPer SPoG SWCr |
| | Breathtaking = 'Hargalore'PBR (HT) | ESty SWCr |
| | Bredon = 'Ausbred' (S) | MAus |
| § | 'Brenda Colvin' (Ra) | ISea MAus |
| | 'Brian's Star' (F) **new** | MGan |
| | Bride = 'Fryyearn'PBR (HT) | ESty GCoc LStr MGan MRav SMrm SWCr |
| | Bridge of Sighs = 'Harglowing'PBR (Cl) | ECnt ESty LStr MAsh MBri MJon NPri SPoG SWCr |
| | Bright Day = 'Chewvermillion'PBR (ClMin) | MAsh SSea SWCr |
| | Bright Fire = 'Peaxi'PBR (Cl) | MBri SPer SSea |
| | Bright Smile = 'Dicdance' (F/Patio) | IDic MAus MGan MRav |
| | Brilliant Pink Iceberg = 'Probril' (F) | EBee LStr SWCr |
| | 'Brindis' (ClF) | MGan SWCr |
| | Britannia = 'Frycalm'PBR (HT) | ECnt ESty LRHS MAsh MJon SWCr |
| | Broadlands = 'Tanmirsch'PBR (GC) | MGan NLar SLon SWCr |
| | Brother Cadfael = 'Ausglobe'PBR (S) | LRHS LStr MAsh MAus MBri NLar SCoo SPer SSea SWCr |
| | Brown Velvet = 'Maccultra'PBR (F) | ESty MJon SMrm SWCr |
| § | ***brunonii*** (Ra) | CPLG EWes MAus WCot |
| | - CC 4515 | GKev |
| | - CC 5142 **new** | GKev |
| | - 'Betty Sherriff' (Ra) | GGar |
| § | - 'La Mortola' (Ra) | EBee MAus MRav SPer SWCr |
| | Brush-strokes = 'Guescolour' (F) | ESty SWCr |
| | 'Buff Beauty' (HM) ♀H4 | Widely available |
| | 'Bullata' | see *R.* x *centifolia* 'Bullata' |
| § | 'Burgundiaca' (G) | MAus SSea WAct |
| | Burgundian rose | see *R.* 'Burgundiaca' |
| | Burgundy Ice = 'Prose'PBR (F) | CGro CSBt EBls ECnt ESty LGod LStr MGan SMrm SWCr |
| | 'Burma Star' (F) | MGan SWCr |
| | burnet, double pink | see *R. spinosissima* double pink |
| | burnet, double white | see *R. spinosissima* double white |
| | Bush Baby = 'Peanob'PBR (Min) | LGod LStr SWCr |
| | Buttercup = 'Ausband'PBR (S) | LRHS MAus |
| | Buxom Beauty = 'Korbilant'PBR (HT) | ECnt ESty GCoc LRHS MGos MJon NPri SCoo SWCr |
| | 'C.F. Meyer' | see *R.* 'Conrad Ferdinand Meyer' |
| | 'Café' (F) | SWCr |
| | ***californica*** (S) | GAuc MAus |
| | - 'Plena' | see *R. nutkana* 'Plena' |
| | 'Callisto' (HM) | MAus SWCr WHCG |
| § | Calypso = 'Poulclimb'PBR | ECnt SSea SWCr |

| | | |
|---|---|---|
| | 'Camayeux' (G) | CPou EBee ECnt MAus NLar SPer SWCr WAct WHCG |
| | Cambridgeshire = 'Korhaugen'PBR (GC) | LStr MAus NPri SPer SSea SWCr |
| | 'Camélia Rose' (Ch) | WHCG |
| | 'Cameo' (Poly) | MAus MGan |
| | Camille Pisarro = 'Destricol' (F) | MRav SPoG |
| | 'Canary Bird' | see *R. xanthina* 'Canary Bird' |
| | Candle in the Wind = 'Mackincat' (S) | MJon |
| | Candy Rose = 'Meiranovi' (S) | MBri |
| | ***canina*** (S) | CArn CCVT CDul CGro CLnd CRWN CTri EMac EPfP GKir LBuc MAus MRav NWea WFar WMou |
| | - 'Abbotswood' | see *R.* 'Abbotswood' |
| | - 'Andersonii' | see *R.* 'Andersonii' |
| | 'Cantabrigiensis' (S) ♀H4 | CSam EBee EPfP MAus NLar SLon SPer SSea SWCr WAct WFar WHCG |
| | Canterbury = 'Ausbury' (S) | MAus |
| | 'Capitaine Basroger' (CeMo) | MAus |
| | 'Capitaine John Ingram' (CeMo) ♀H4 | MAus SLon SPer SSea SWCr WHCG |
| | 'Captain Christy' (ClHT) | see *R.* 'Climbing Captain Christy' |
| | Caramella = 'Korkinteral'PBR (HT) | MGos |
| | 'Cardinal de Richelieu' (G) ♀H4 | CPou CSam CTri ELon EPfP EWTr GCoc GKir LAst LCro LRHS LStr MAsh MAus MCot MGan MRav NLar SPer SPoG SWCr WAct WHCG |
| | Cardinal Hume = 'Harregale' (S) | MGan NHaw SPer |
| | Carefree Days = 'Meirivouri' (Patio) | EPfP LRHS MAsh SPoG SWCr |
| | Carefree Wonder = 'Meipitac' (S) | LAst |
| | 'Caring' (Patio) | SWCr |
| | Caring for You ambig. | LSRN |
| | Caring for You = 'Coclust'PBR (HT) | GCoc |
| | 'Carmenetta' (S) | MAus NHaw WAct |
| | 'Carol' (Gn) | see *R.* 'Carol Amling' |
| § | 'Carol Amling' (Gn) | MJon |
| | ***carolina*** | LHop NHaw SLPl WHCG |
| | 'Caroline Testout' | see *R.* 'Madame Caroline Testout' |
| | Cascade = 'Poulskab'PBR (ClMin) | EBee ECnt |
| § | Casino = 'Macca' (ClHT) | CTri LAst MAsh MGan MHav MJon MRav SPer SPoG SWCr |
| | 'Castle Apricot'PBR | see *R.* Lazy Days |
| | 'Castle Cream' | see *R.* Perfect Day |
| | 'Castle Fuchsia Pink'PBR | see *R.* Bewitched = 'Poulbella' |
| | 'Castle Lilac'PBR | see *R.* Lambert Castle |
| | Castle of Mey = 'Coclucid' (F) | GCoc |
| | 'Castle Red'PBR | see *R.* Krönberg |
| | 'Castle Shrimp Pink'PBR | see *R.* Fascination = 'Poulmax' |
| | 'Castle Yellow'PBR | see *R.* Summer Gold |
| | 'Catherine Mermet' (T) | MAus |
| § | 'Cécile Brünner' (Poly) ♀H4 | CTri EBee ECnt ELan GCoc LStr MAus MGan MLan NLar SMad SMrm SPer SPla SSea SWCr WAct WHCG |
| | 'Cécile Brünner, White' | see *R.* 'White Cécile Brünner' |
| | Celebration 2000 = 'Horcoffitup'PBR (S) | MAus |
| § | 'Céleste' (A) ♀H4 | EPfP GCoc LRHS LStr MRav NLar SPer SSea SWCr WAct WHCG WOVN |
| | 'Célina' (CeMo) | MGan |
| | 'Céline Forestier' (N) ♀H3 | CPou MAus MRav SPer SWCr WHCG |
| § | 'Celsiana' (D) | CSam LRHS MAus MLan SPer SSea SWCr WAct WHCG |
| | Centenaire de Lourdes = 'Delge' (F) | LCro |
| | Centenary = 'Koreledas'PBR (F) ♀H4 | MGos SPer |
| § | x ***centifolia*** (Ce) | LRHS MAus MRav SMad SWCr WAct WHCG |
| § | - 'Bullata' (Ce) | MAus |
| § | - 'Cristata' (Ce) ♀H4 | ECnt EPfP LStr NLar SPer SSea SWCr WAct WHCG |
| § | - 'De Meaux' (Ce) | MAus MRav NLar SPer SPla WAct WHCG |
| § | - 'Muscosa' (CeMo) | GCoc LStr MAus MGan MRav SEND SPoG SWCr WAct |
| | - 'Parvifolia' | see *R.* 'Burgundiaca' |
| § | - 'Shailer's White Moss' (CeMo) | LRHS MAus MGan SSea WHCG |
| | - 'Spong' (Ce) | EWTr MAus SWCr |
| § | - 'Unique' (Ce) | MAus SWCr |
| § | - 'Unique Panachée' (Ce) | MAus MGan SWCr |
| | 'Centifolia Variegata' | see *R.* x *centifolia* 'Unique Panachée' |
| | Centre Stage = 'Chewcreepy'PBR (S/GC) | MJon |
| | 'Cerise Bouquet' (S) ♀H4 | LRHS MAus MGan MRav SPer SWCr WAct WHCG WKif |
| | Champagne Cocktail = 'Horflash'PBR (F) ♀H4 | SPer |
| | 'Champagne Dream' (Patio) | LRHS SWCr |
| | Champagne Moments = 'Korvanaber'PBR (F) | CGro CSBt EBee EBls ECnt ELan EPfP ESty GCoc LGod LRHS LStr MAsh MBri MGan MGos MJon MRav NPri SMrm SPer SPoG SWCr |
| | 'Champneys Pink Cluster' (China hybrid) | MAus |
| | Chandos Beauty = 'Harmisty' (HT) | ECnt ESty GCoc LStr SWCr |
| | 'Chanelle' (F) | MGan SDix SPer SWCr |
| | Chantal Merieux = 'Masmaric' (Generosa Series) (S) | MRav |
| | Chapeau de Napoléon | see *R.* x *centifolia* 'Cristata' |
| | 'Chaplin's Pink Climber' (Cl) | MGan SWCr |
| | Charity = 'Auschar' (S) | MAus |
| | Charles Austin = 'Ausles' (S) | MAus MRav WAct WHCG |
| | Charles Darwin = 'Auspeet'PBR (S) | MAus SCoo SPer |
| | Charles de Gaulle | see *R.* Katherine Mansfield |
| | 'Charles de Mills' (G) ♀H4 | CSRo CSam ECnt ELan ELon EPfP EWTr LCro LRHS LStr MAsh MAus MGan MRav NLar SPer SSea SWCr WAct WHCG |
| | Charles Rennie Mackintosh = 'Ausren'PBR (S) | CSBt LRHS LStr MAus SWCr |
| | Charlie's Rose = 'Tanellepa' (HT) | ESty MBri SWCr |
| | Charlotte = 'Auspoly'PBR (S) ♀H4 | EPfP ESty LRHS LSRN LStr MAus MBri MJon SCoo SPer SSea SWCr |
| | Charmian = 'Ausmian' (S) | MAus |
| | Charming Cover = 'Poulharmu'PBR (Towne & Country Series) (GC/S) | SWCr |
| | Chartreuse de Parme = 'Delviola' (S) | LCro MRav |
| | 'Château de Clos-Vougeot' (HT) | IArd |
| | Chatsworth = 'Tanotax'PBR (Patio/F) | MHav MRav SPer SSea SWCr |

| | |
|---|---|
| Chaucer = 'Auscer' (S) | MAus |
| § Cheek to Cheek = 'Poulslas'PBR (Courtyard Series) (ClMin) | MAsh SWCr |
| Cheerful Charlie = 'Cocquimmer'PBR (F) | GCoc MRav SWCr |
| Chelsea Belle = 'Talchelsea' (Min) | MJon |
| Cherry Brandy '85 = 'Tanryrandy'PBR (HT) | CSBt MGan |
| Cheshire = 'Fryelise'PBR (HT) | GCoc MJon |
| Cheshire = 'Korkonopi'PBR (County Rose Series) (S) | MAus |
| 'Cheshire Life' (HT) | MAus MJon |
| Chester Cathedral = 'Franshine' (HT) | MJon |
| 'Chevy Chase' (Ra) | WAct |
| Chianti = 'Auswine' (S) | MAus MGan NLar WAct WHCG |
| Chicago Peace = 'Johnago' (HT) | MGan SWCr |
| Child of AchievementPBR | see *R.* Bella = 'Pouljill' |
| Childhood Memories = 'Ferho' (HM/Cl) | SPla SWCr |
| Chilterns = 'Kortemma'PBR (GC) | SWCr |
| 'Chinatown' (F/S) ♀H4 | CBcs CGro CSBt LStr MAsh MAus MGan MJon MRav SPer SPoG SWCr |
| ***chinensis*** misapplied | see *R.* x *odorata* |
| - 'Old Blush' | see *R.* x *odorata* 'Pallida' |
| Chloe = 'Poulen003'PBR (Renaissance Series) (S) | CPou ECnt SLon SWCr |
| 'Chloris' (A) | CPou |
| Chris = 'Kirsan'PBR (Cl) | EBee ECnt ESty MGan MJon SMrm SWCr WGor |
| Christian Dior = 'Meilie' (HT) | SWCr |
| 'Christine Gandy' (F) | MGan |
| Christopher = 'Cocopher' (HT) | GCoc |
| Christopher Columbus = 'Meinronsse' (HT) | IArd |
| Christopher Marlowe = 'Ausjump'PBR (S) | MAus SCoo SWCr |
| Cider Cup = 'Dicladida'PBR (Min/Patio) ♀H4 | CTri ESty IDic LStr MAus SWCr |
| 'Cinderella' ambig. (Cl) | MGos SWCr |
| 'Cinderella' (Min) | CSBt MGan |
| Citron-fraise = 'Delcifra' (S) | SWCr |
| City Lights = 'Poulgan'PBR (Patio) | CSBt |
| 'City of Cardiff' (HT) | MGan |
| 'City of Leeds' (F) | CWSG MAsh MGan |
| City of London = 'Harukfore'PBR (F) | CSBt MJon SPer SWCr |
| 'City of Portsmouth' (F) | CBcs |
| City of York = 'Direktör Benschop' (Cl) | MCot |
| Clair Matin = 'Meimont' (ClS) | MAus SPer SWCr WAct |
| 'Claire Jacquier' (N) | MAus SPer SWCr WHCG |
| Claire Rayner = 'Macpandem' (F/Patio) | MJon |
| Claire Rose = 'Auslight'PBR (S) | CGro LRHS MAus MJon MRav SMrm SPer SPoG |
| Claire's Dream = 'Guesideal' **new** | SWCr |
| Claret = 'Frykrisfal' (HT) **new** | ESty GCoc LStr SWCr |
| Clarinda = 'Cocsummery'PBR (F) | GCoc |
| Claude Monet = 'Jacdesa' (HT) | MRav SPoG |
| Cleo = 'Beebop' (HT) | MJon |
| 'Cliff Richard' (F) | ESty SWCr |
| 'Climbing Alec's Red' (ClHT) | SWCr |
| 'Climbing Allgold' (ClF) | SLon SWCr |
| 'Climbing Arthur Bell' (ClF) ♀H4 | CSBt CTri ESty GCoc LAst LGod MAsh SPer SPoG SSea SWCr |
| 'Climbing Ballerina' (Ra) | CSBt MGan SWCr |
| 'Climbing Blue Moon' (ClHT) | LAst MGan MHav SWCr |
| § 'Climbing Captain Christy' (ClHT) | MAus |
| 'Climbing Cécile Brünner' (ClPoly) ♀H4 | CSBt CTri EBee ECnt EPfP LRHS LStr MAus MGan MRav NLar SPer SSea SWCr WAct WHCG |
| 'Climbing Château de Clos-Vougeot' (ClHT) | MAus |
| 'Climbing Christine' (ClHT) | MAus |
| § 'Climbing Columbia' (ClHT) | SPer WHCG |
| 'Climbing Crimson Glory' (ClHT) | CPou MAus MGan SWCr WAct |
| § 'Climbing Devoniensis' (ClT) | CPou |
| 'Climbing Ena Harkness' (ClHT) | CBcs CTri GCoc LRHS MAus MBNS MGan MRav SEND SPer SPla SPoG SWCr |
| 'Climbing Etoile de Hollande' (ClHT) ♀H4 | CSBt CSam CTri CWSG EPfP GCoc LCro LRHS LStr MAsh MAus MGan MJon MRav SMad SPer SPoG SSea SWCr |
| Climbing Fragrant Cloud = 'Colfragrasar' (ClHT) | CBcs ELan MGan SWCr |
| Climbing Gold Bunny = 'Meigro-Nurisar' (ClF) | MJon |
| 'Climbing Iceberg' (ClF) ♀H4 | CGro CSBt EBee ELan EPfP ESty EWTr IArd LCro LRHS LStr MAsh MAus MGan MJon MRav SPer SPla SPoG SSea SWCr WAct WHCG |
| 'Climbing Jazz'PBR | see *R.* That's Jazz |
| 'Climbing Josephine Bruce' (ClHT) | LRHS MGan SWCr |
| 'Climbing la France' (ClHT) | MAus MRav |
| § 'Climbing Lady Hillingdon' (ClT) ♀H3 | ECGP ELon EPfP LRHS MAus MGan MRav NLar SPer SSea SWCr WAct WHCG |
| 'Climbing Lady Sylvia' (ClHT) | CSBt EBee EPfP LRHS MAus MGan SPer SWCr |
| 'Climbing Little White Pet' | see *R.* 'Félicité Perpétue' |
| 'Climbing Madame Abel Chatenay' (ClHT) | MAus |
| 'Climbing Madame Butterfly' (ClHT) | LRHS MAus MGan NLar SPer SWCr |
| 'Climbing Madame Caroline Testout' (ClHT) | CPou CTri EBee MAsh MAus NPri SPer SWCr |
| § 'Climbing Madame Edouard Herriot' (ClHT) | MAus SWCr |
| 'Climbing Madame Henri Guillot' (ClHT) | MAus |
| 'Climbing Maman Cochet' (ClT) | MAus |
| 'Climbing Masquerade' (ClF) | MAus MGan MHav MJon MRav SPer SSea SWCr |
| § 'Climbing Mevrouw G.A. van Rossem' (ClHT) | MAus |
| 'Climbing Mrs Aaron Ward' (ClHT) | MAus |
| 'Climbing Mrs G.A. van Rossem' | see *R.* 'Climbing Mevrouw G.A. van Rossem' |
| 'Climbing Mrs Herbert Stevens' (ClHT) | EBee LRHS MAus MRav SPer SWCr WHCG |

| | Name | Suppliers |
|---|---|---|
| | 'Climbing Mrs Sam McGredy' (ClHT) 𝕐H4 | CSBt CSam MAus MGan SWCr |
| | 'Climbing Niphetos' (ClT) | MAus |
| | 'Climbing Ophelia' (ClHT) | CPou MAus SPer SWCr |
| | Climbing Orange Sunblaze = 'Meiji Katarsar'PBR (ClMin) | SPer |
| | 'Climbing Pascali' (ClHT) | MGan |
| § | 'Climbing Paul Lédé' (ClT) | EBee LRHS MAus SWCr |
| | 'Climbing Peace' (ClHT) | CSBt SPer SWCr |
| | 'Climbing Picture' (ClHT) | MAus |
| § | 'Climbing Pompon de Paris' (ClMinCh) | CTri LHop LRHS MAus MGan MRav SEND SLPl SMrm SPer WHCG |
| | 'Climbing Ruby Wedding' | SPoG |
| | 'Climbing Shot Silk' (ClHT) 𝕐H4 | CSBt EBee MGan SPer SWCr |
| § | 'Climbing Souvenir de la Malmaison' (ClBb) | CPou EBee MAus MCot SPer SWCr WAct WHCG |
| | 'Climbing Sterling Silver' (ClHT) | MGan |
| | Climbing Super Star = 'Tangostar' (ClHT) | MAus |
| | 'Climbing Sutter's Gold' (ClHT) | MGan |
| | 'Climbing The Queen Elizabeth' (ClF) | SWCr |
| | 'Climbing White Cloud'PBR | see *R.* White Cloud = 'Korstacha' |
| | Clodagh McGredy = 'Macswanle'PBR (F) | MJon |
| | Cloud Nine = 'Fryextra'PBR (HT) | EBee ECnt ESty GCoc LGod SMrm SWCr |
| | Cocktail = 'Meimick' (S) | MGan |
| | 'Coconut Ice' (HT) | SWCr |
| | 'Colby School' (F) **new** | EBls |
| | Colchester Beauty = 'Cansend' (F) | ECnt |
| | Colchester Castle = 'Poulcs008'PBR | ECnt |
| | Colibri = 'Meimal' (Min) | SPer |
| § | 'Colonel Fabvier' | MAus |
| | colonial white | see *R.* 'Sombreuil' |
| | 'Columbian' | see *R.* 'Climbing Columbia' |
| | 'Commandant Beaurepaire' (Bb) | LRHS MAus SWCr WKif |
| | common moss | see *R.* x *centifolia* 'Muscosa' |
| | Commonwealth Glory = 'Harclue'PBR (HT) | SWCr |
| | 'Compassion' (ClHT) 𝕐H4 | Widely available |
| * | 'Compassionate' (F) | MRav |
| | 'Complicata' (G) 𝕐H4 | CTri ECGP EPfP EWTr LRHS LStr MAus MCot MGan MRav SMrm SPer SSea SWCr WAct WHCG WOVN |
| | 'Comte de Chambord' misapplied | see *R.* 'Madame Knorr' |
| | Comtes de Champagne = 'Ausufo'PBR (S) | MAus SCoo |
| | 'Comtesse Cécile de Chabrillant' (HP) | MAus SWCr |
| | 'Comtesse de Lacépède' misapplied | see *R.* 'Du Maître d'Ecole' |
| § | 'Comtesse de Murinais' (DMo) | MAus |
| | Comtesse de Ségur = 'Deltendre' (S) | MRav |
| § | 'Comtesse du Caÿla' (Ch) | MAus SSea |
| | 'Comtesse Vandal' (HT) | WAct |
| | ConcertPBR (Cl) | see *R.* Calypso |
| | 'Conditorum' (G) | WAct |
| | Congratulations = 'Korlift' (HT) | CSBt ECnt GCoc IArd LCro LSRN LStr MAus MGan MGos MJon MRav NPri SMrm SPer SSea SWCr |
| | Connie = 'Boselftay'PBR (F) | SWCr |
| § | 'Conrad Ferdinand Meyer' (Ru) | CSBt MAus MGan NHaw SPer |
| | Conservation = 'Cocdimple'PBR (Min/Patio) | GCoc LAst SWCr |
| | Constance Finn = 'Hareden'PBR (F) | MRav |
| | 'Constance Spry' 𝕐H4 | EBee ELan EPfP EWTr LCro LRHS LStr MAus MGan MJon MRav NLar NPri SMrm SPer WCr WAct WHCG |
| § | 'Cooperi' (Ra) | CAbP CWib GGal MAus MCot SPer SSea SWCr WAct WHCG WKif WPGP |
| | Cooper's Burmese | see *R.* 'Cooperi' |
| | 'Copenhagen' (ClHT) | MAus |
| | Copper Pot = 'Dicpe' (F) | SPer |
| | 'Coral Cluster' (Poly) | MAus MGan |
| | Coral Reef = 'Cocdarlee'PBR (Min/Patio) | SWCr |
| | 'Coral Satin' (Cl) | MGan |
| | Cordelia = 'Ausbottle'PBR (S) | MAus MBri |
| | 'Cornelia' (HM) 𝕐H4 | CBcs CSBt CSam CTri EBee EPfP IArd LAst LRHS LStr MAsh MAus MCot MGan MJon MRav NPri SMrm SPer SSea SWCr WAct WHCG WOVN |
| | Coronation Street = 'Wekswetrup' (F) | MJon |
| | 'Coronet' (F) | WAct WHCG |
| | Corvedale = 'Ausnetting'PBR (S) | MAus |
| | cottage maid | see *R.* x *centifolia* 'Unique Panachée' |
| | Cottage Rose = 'Ausglisten'PBR (S) | CGro MAus MRav SWCr |
| | Countess of Wessex = 'Beacream' (S) | MBri SWCr |
| | 'Coupe d'Hébé' (Bb) | MAus |
| | Courage = 'Poulduf'PBR (HT) | ECnt |
| | Courvoisier = 'Macsee' (F) | CSBt |
| | 'Cramoisi Picotée' (G) | MAus |
| | 'Cramoisi Supérieur' (Ch) | MAus |
| | Crathes Castle = 'Cocathes' (F) | GCoc |
| | Crazy for You = 'Wekroalt'PBR (F) | ESty LGod LSRN MAsh MJon SSea SWCr |
| | Cream Abundance = 'Harflax'PBR (Abundance Series) (F) | ESty LStr SWCr |
| | Crème Anglaise = 'Ganang'PBR (Cl) | EBee ECnt MGan |
| | Crème Brûlée = 'Ganbru'PBR (Cl) | MGan |
| | Crème de la Crème = 'Gancre'PBR (Cl) | CSBt EBee ECnt ESty GCoc MBri MGan MJon MRav SMrm SPer SWCr WAct |
| | 'Crépuscule' (N) | EBee SWCr WHCG |
| | Cressida = 'Auscress' (S) | MAus |
| | crested moss | see *R.* x *centifolia* 'Cristata' |
| | Cricri = 'Meicri' (Min) | MAus MGan |
| | Crimson Cascade = 'Fryclimbdown'PBR (Cl) | ESty LRHS MAsh MAus MBri MGan MRav SSea SWCr WHCG |
| | crimson damask | see *R. gallica* var. *officinalis* |
| | 'Crimson Descant' (Cl) | ECnt |
| | 'Crimson Globe' (Mo) | MGan |
| | 'Crimson Glory' (HT) | EBee MGan NWea SWCr |
| | 'Crimson Shower' (Ra) 𝕐H4 | CSRo CSam LRHS MAus MGan MJon MRav SMrm SPer SWCr WAct WHCG WHer |
| | 'Cristata' | see *R.* x *centifolia* 'Cristata' |

| | | |
|---|---|---|
| | Crocus Rose = 'Ausquest'PBR (S) | ELon EPfP LCro LRHS MAus MBri MRav SWCr |
| | Crown Princess Margareta = 'Auswinter'PBR (S) | EBee ECnt EPfP LCro LRHS MAsh MAus MBri MJon SCoo SPer SSea SWCr |
| | cuisse de nymphe | see *R.* 'Great Maiden's Blush' |
| | 'Cupid' (ClHT) | EWTr MAus SPer SWCr |
| I | 'Cutie' (Patio) | SWCr |
| | Cymbeline = 'Auslean' (S) | SPer |
| | Dacapo = 'Poulcy012' (Courtyard Series) (ClPatio) | ECnt |
| | 'D'Aguesseau' (G) | EBee MAus SWCr |
| | 'Daily Mail' | see *R.* 'Climbing Madame Edouard Herriot' |
| | 'Dainty Bess' (HT) | EBee EWTr MAus SSea SWCr |
| | 'Dainty Maid' (F) | MAus SWCr |
| | x ***damascena*** var. ***bifera*** | see *R.* x *damascena* var. *semperflorens* |
| § | - var. ***semperflorens*** (D) | CBgR MAus MRav NLar SWCr WAct WHCG WKif |
| | - 'Trigintipetala' misapplied | see *R.* 'Professeur Emile Perrot' |
| § | - var. ***versicolor*** (D) | MGan SEND SPer SSea SWCr WAct |
| | 'Dame de Coeur' (HT) | NBlu SWCr |
| | Dame Wendy = 'Canson' (F) | MAus MGan |
| | Dames de Chenonceau = 'Delpabra' (S) | LCro MRav |
| | 'Danaë' (HM) | CSam MAus SWCr WHCG |
| | Dancing Pink = 'Hendan' (F) | MJon |
| | Dancing Queen = 'Fryfeston' (ClHT) | ECnt GCoc LGod SWCr |
| | Danny Boy = 'Dicxcon'PBR (Patio) | IDic MJon SWCr WGor |
| | 'Danse du Feu' (Cl) | CBcs CGro CSBt CTri CWSG EBee ELan GKir LGod LRHS LStr MAsh MAus MGan MJon MRav NPri SMrm SPer SPoG SWCr WBVN |
| | 'Daphne Gandy' (F) | MGan |
| | Dapple Dawn = 'Ausapple' (S) | MAus SPer |
| | Darling Flame = 'Meilucca' (Min) | MRav SWCr |
| | 'Dart's Defender' (Ru) | SLPl |
| | David Whitfield = 'Gana'PBR (F) | MGan SWCr |
| | ***davidii*** | MAus |
| | Dawn Chorus = 'Dicquasar'PBR (HT) ♀H4 | CGro CSBt CWSG ECnt EPfP ESty IDic LGod LRHS LStr MAsh MAus MBri MGan MRav SPer SPoG SWCr |
| | 'Daybreak' (HM) | CTri MAus SWCr WAct WHCG |
| | Dazzling Delight = 'Cocuseful'PBR (F) | GCoc |
| | 'De la Grifferaie' **new** | WAct |
| | 'De Meaux' | see *R.* x *centifolia* 'De Meaux' |
| | 'De Meaux, White' | see *R.* 'White de Meaux' |
| § | 'De Resht' ♀H4 | CBgR CPou CTri EBee ECnt EPfP GKir LCro LRHS MAsh MAus MCot MGan MJon MRav NLar SPer SPla SSea SWCr WAct WHCG WKif |
| | 'Dearest' (F) | CBcs CSBt MGan MHav MRav SPer SWCr |
| | 'Debbie Thomas' (HT) | MJon |
| | Deb's Delight = 'Legsweet'PBR (F) | MJon |
| | 'Debutante' (Ra) | CSam EBee EWTr LRHS MAus SWCr WHCG |
| | 'Deep Secret' (HT) ♀H4 | CGro CSBt CTri CWSG EBee ECnt EPfP ESty GCoc LRHS LStr MAsh MGan MJon MRav NPri SPer SPoG SSea SWCr |
| | 'Delambre' (DPo) | MAus |
| | 'Delicata' (Ru) | MAus |
| | Dentelle de Malines = 'Lenfro' (S) | LRHS MAus WAct |
| | Desert Island = 'Dicfizz'PBR (F) | GCoc IDic SWCr |
| | 'Designer Sunset' (Patio) | SWCr |
| § | 'Desprez à Fleurs Jaunes' (N) | EBee IArd LRHS MAus MRav NLar SPer SWCr WHCG |
| | 'Devon Maid' (ClHT) | SWCr |
| | 'Devoniensis' (ClT) | see *R.* 'Climbing Devoniensis' |
| | Diamond Border = 'Pouldiram'PBR (Towne & Country Series) (S) | EBee |
| | 'Diamond Jubilee' (HT) | CSBt MGan SWCr |
| | Diamond = 'Korgazell'PBR (Patio) | ESty GCoc LStr MGos MJon |
| | 'Diamond Wishes'PBR (HT) | see *R.* Misty Hit |
| | Dick's Delight = 'Dicwhistle' (GC) | ESty IDic MJon SWCr |
| | Die Welt = 'Diekor' (HT) | MJon |
| | 'Dioressence' **new** | LCro |
| | 'Directeur Alphand' (HP) | WHCG |
| | Dizzy Heights = 'Fryblissful'PBR (Cl) | EBee ECnt GCoc MAsh MGan SWCr |
| | 'Docteur Grill' (T) | MAus |
| | Doctor Goldberg = 'Gandol' (HT) | MGan |
| | Doctor Jackson = 'Ausdoctor' (S) | MAus |
| | Doctor Jo = 'Fryatlanta'PBR (F) | SWCr |
| | 'Doctor John Snow' (HT) | MGan |
| | 'Doctor W. Van Fleet' (Ra/Cl) | MAus |
| | 'Don Juan' (ClHT) | MGan SWCr |
| | 'Doris Tysterman' (HT) | CGro CTri LStr MAus MGan SMrm SPer SWCr |
| | Dorothy = 'Cocrocket'PBR (F) | GCoc MRav |
| | 'Dorothy Perkins' (Ra) | CGro CSBt CTri GCoc LRHS MAus MGan MJon MRav NLar NPer SPer SSea SWCr WHCG |
| | 'Dorothy Wheatcroft' (F) | MGan |
| | 'Dortmund' (ClHScB) ♀H4 | LGod LRHS MAus MGan NHaw SPer SWCr WAct WHCG |
| | Double Delight = 'Andeli' (HT) | CGro ESty GCoc MGan MJon SPer SWCr |
| | 'Dream Girl' (Cl) | MAus |
| | Dream Lover = 'Peayetti'PBR (Patio) | ESty MJon SWCr |
| | 'Dreaming Spires' (Cl) | CSBt SPer SSea SWCr |
| | Drummer Boy = 'Harvacity'PBR (F/Patio) | MGan SPer SWCr |
| § | 'Du Maître d'Ecole' (G) | EBee ELon MAus MRav SWCr WHCG WHer |
| | Dublin Bay = 'Macdub' (Cl) ♀H4 | CSBt CTri EBee ECnt ELan EPfP ESty GKir IArd LAst LGod LRHS LStr MAsh MBri MGan MJon MRav SMrm SPer SPoG SSea SWCr WAct |
| | 'Duc de Guiche' (G) ♀H4 | CSam EWTr MAus SLon SPer SWCr WAct WHCG WHer |
| | Duchess of Cornwall = 'Tan97157' (HT) | SWCr |
| | 'Duchess of Portland' | see *R.* 'Portlandica' |
| | Duchess of YorkPBR | see *R.* Sunseeker |
| | 'Duchesse d'Angoulême' (G x Ce) | MAus |
| | 'Duchesse de Buccleugh' (G) | MAus MRav WAct |
| § | 'Duchesse de Montebello' (G) ♀H4 | MAus NLar SLon SPer SWCr WAct WHCG |
| | 'Duchesse de Verneuil' (CeMo) | MAus |

| | |
|---|---|
| 'Duke of Edinburgh' (HP) | MAus |
| 'Duke of Wellington' (HP) | EBee SWCr WHCG |
| 'Duke of Windsor' (HT) | MGan MHav SPer SWCr |
| 'Dundee Rambler' (Ra) | MAus |
| § 'Duplex' (S) | LRHS MAus MRav WAct WHCG |
| 'Dupontii' (S) | MAus MGan NLar SPer WAct WOVN |
| 'Dupuy Jamain' (HP) | WHCG |
| 'Dusky Maiden' (F) | MAus MCot SWCr WHCG |
| Dusty Springfield = 'Horluvdust' (F) | MGan SWCr |
| 'Dutch Gold' (HT) | CWSG MAus MGan MHav SPer SWCr |
| 'E.H. Morse' | see *R.* 'Ernest H. Morse' |
| 'Easlea's Golden Rambler' (Ra) ♀H4 | CSBt EBee ELon EPfP LRHS MAus MRav SLon SWCr WAct WHCG |
| 'Easter Morning' (Min) | SPer |
| Easy Cover = 'Pouleas'PBR (Towne & Country Series) (GC) | SWCr |
| Easy Going = 'Harflow'PBR (F) | IArd MAsh MRav SWCr |
| 'Eblouissant' (Poly) | MGan |
| ***ecae*** | MAus |
| 'Eddie's Jewel' (*moyesii* hybrid) | MAus MGan SWCr |
| 'Eden Rose' (HT) | MGan SMrm |
| Eden Rose '88 = 'Meiviolin'PBR (ClHT) | MJon SPer SWCr |
| Edith Holden = 'Chewlegacy'PBR (F) | ESty |
| 'Edward Hyams' | MAus |
| ***eglanteria*** | see *R. rubiginosa* |
| Eglantyne = 'Ausmak'PBR (S) ♀H4 | CSBt EPfP ESty GCoc LCro LRHS LStr MAus MBri MJon MRav SMrm SPer SPoG SSea SWCr |
| 'Eleanor' (Patio) | SLon |
| Eleanor = 'Poulberin'PBR (S) | ECnt SLon SWCr |
| 'Elegance' (ClHT) | MAus |
| § ***elegantula*** 'Persetosa' (S) | MAus NLar SPer SWCr WAct WHCG |
| Elfe = 'Tanelfe' (HT) | NHaw |
| § Elina = 'Dicjana'PBR (HT) ♀H4 | CSBt EBee ECnt IDic LGod LStr MAus MGan MGos MJon MRav SPer SPoG SWCr |
| Elizabeth = 'Coctail'PBR (F) | GCoc |
| 'Elizabeth Harkness' (HT) | CWSG MAus MGan SPer SWCr |
| Elizabeth of Glamis = 'Macel' (F) | CGro CTri CWSG GCoc MGan MHav SPer SWCr |
| Elizabeth Stuart = 'Maselstu' (Generosa Series) (S) | MRav |
| Elle = 'Meibderos'PBR (HT) | ESty |
| Ellen = 'Auscup' (S) | MAus |
| 'Ellen Poulsen' (Poly) | MGan |
| 'Ellen Willmott' (HT) | EBee MAus MCot SPer SWCr |
| 'Elmshorn' (S) | CBcs MGan WHCG |
| 'Else Poulsen' (F) | WHCG |
| Emanuel = 'Ausuel' (S) | MAus |
| Emilien Guillot = 'Masemgui' (Generosa Series) (S) | MRav |
| 'Emily Gray' (Ra) | CGro CSBt CTri EBee ECnt ELon GKir LRHS LStr MAsh MAus MGan MRav NPri SPer SPoG SWCr WAct WHCG |
| 'Emma Wright' (HT) | MAus |
| 'Emotion' (F) | SWCr |
| 'Empereur du Maroc' (HP) | MAus MRav WHCG |
| Empress Michiko = 'Dicnifty'PBR (HT) | ESty IDic |
| 'Ena Harkness' (HT) | CTri ELan LRHS MGan SWCr |
| § 'Enfant de France' (HP) | MCot |
| § England's Rose = 'Ausrace'PBR (S) | MAus |
| English Elegance = 'Ausleaf' (S) | MAus |
| English Garden = 'Ausbuff'PBR (S) | CGro EBee EPfP LRHS LStr MAus MRav SMrm SPer SWCr |
| 'English Miss' (F) ♀H4 | CSBt CTri EBee ECnt EPfP ESty LAst LStr MAsh MAus MGan MJon MRav SPer SPoG SWCr |
| 'Erfurt' (HM) | MAus MGan SPer SWCr WHCG |
| § 'Erinnerung an Brod' (S) | WHCG |
| § 'Ernest H. Morse' (HT) | CSBt CTri CWSG GCoc LAst MGan MJon MRav SPer SPoG SSea SWCr |
| 'Ernest May' (HT) | SSea |
| Escapade = 'Harpade' (F) ♀H4 | MAus SWCr |
| Especially for You = 'Fryworthy'PBR (HT) | CSBt CTri ESty GCoc LGod LRHS LSRN LStr MAsh NPri SCoo SSea SWCr |
| Essex = 'Poulnoz'PBR (GC) | MRav SPer SWCr |
| § 'Estrellita de Oro' (Min) | SPer SWCr |
| 'Etain' (Ra) | ECnt |
| § 'Etendard' (Cl) | MGan MRav SMrm SPer SPla SWCr WAct |
| Eternal Flame = 'Korassenet'PBR (F) | MGos SWCr |
| Eternally Yours = 'Macspeego'PBR (HT) | ECnt MJon |
| 'Ethel' (Ra) | CPou EBee SWCr |
| 'Etoile de Hollande' (HT) | CSBt EBee ELan GKir LRHS NLar NPri SLon SMrm WAct |
| 'Eugénie Guinoisseau' (Mo) | WHCG |
| Euphoria = 'Intereup'PBR (GC/S) | GCoc IDic SWCr |
| Euphrates = 'Harunique' (*persica* hybrid) | MAus WAct |
| 'Europeana' (F) | MGan |
| 'Evangeline' (Ra) | MAus |
| Evelyn = 'Aussaucer'PBR (S) ♀H4 | CSBt EBee EPfP ESty GCoc LRHS LStr MAsh MAus MGan MJon MRav SMrm SPer SPla SWCr |
| § Evelyn Fison = 'Macev' (F) | CSBt CTri ELan MAus MGan MRav SPer SWCr |
| Evening Light = 'Chewpechette'PBR (ClMin) | MAsh SWCr |
| Evening Light = 'Tarde Gris' (ClMin) | MBri SSea |
| 'Excelsa' (Ra) | CSBt CTri EPfP GKir IArd LGod MAsh MGan MRav NWea SWCr |
| Eye Paint = 'Maceye' (F) | MAus SMrm SWCr |
| 'Eyecatcher' (F) | EBee ECnt |
| 'F.E. Lester' | see *R.* 'Francis E. Lester' |
| § 'F.J. Grootendorst' (Ru) | EBee LRHS MAus MGan SSea WAct |
| Fab = 'Bosconpea'PBR (F) | SWCr |
| 'Fabvier' | see *R.* 'Colonel Fabvier' |
| Fairhope = 'Talfairhope' (Min) | MJon |
| Fairy Prince = 'Harnougette' (GC) | ESty |
| Fairy Queen = 'Sperien' (Poly/GC) | IDic MAsh SWCr |
| 'Fairy Rose' | see *R.* 'The Fairy' |
| Fairyland = 'Harlayalong' (Poly) | MGan |
| Faithful = 'Haressay'PBR (F) | SWCr |
| Falstaff = 'Ausverse'PBR (S) | CSBt CSRo ECnt EPfP LCro LRHS LStr MAsh MAus MBNS MJon MRav SSea SWCr |
| 'Fantin-Latour' (*centifolia* hybrid) ♀H4 | CTri EBee ECnt ELan EPfP EWTr GCoc LAst LCro LRHS LStr MAus MCot MGan MRav SMad SMrm SPer SSea SWCr WAct WHCG WKif |
| ***farreri*** var. ***persetosa*** | see *R. elegantula* 'Persetosa' |

| | | |
|---|---|---|
| | Fascination = 'Jacoyel' (Castle Series) (HT) | LStr MBri SCoo |
| § | Fascination = 'Poulmax'PBR (F) $\Upsilon^{H4}$ | CSBt EBee ECnt EPfP GCoc LRHS MAsh MGan MRav SPer SWCr |
| | Favourite Hit = 'Poululv'PBR (Patio) | MAsh |
| | ***fedtschenkoana*** misapplied | MAus SPer WAct WHCG |
| | ***fedtschenkoana*** Regel | SLPl |
| | Fée des Neiges | see *R.* Iceberg |
| | 'Felicia' (HM) $\Upsilon^{H4}$ | CSBt CSam CTri EBee ECnt ELan EPfP GCoc GKir LCro LGod LRHS LStr MAsh MAus MCot MGan MJon MRav SMrm SPer SPoG SWCr WAct WHCG WKif WOVN |
| | 'Félicité Parmentier' (AxD) $\Upsilon^{H4}$ | EBee LRHS MAus MGan MRav NLar SPer SWCr WAct WHCG |
| § | 'Félicité Perpétue' (Ra) $\Upsilon^{H4}$ | CBcs CSBt CSRo EBee ELan EPfP GCoc GKir ISea LRHS LStr MAsh MAus MGan MRav SEND SPer SPoG SWCr WAct WHCG |
| | Felicity Kendal = 'Lanken' (HT) | MHav MJon |
| | 'Fellemberg' (ClCh) | MAus WHCG |
| | Fellowship = 'Harwelcome'PBR (F) $\Upsilon^{H4}$ | ECnt ESty LGod LStr MAus MGan MJon MRav SCoo SSea SWCr |
| | Feminine Hit = 'Poulhi015'PBR **new** | MAsh |
| | 'Ferdinand Pichard' (Bb) $\Upsilon^{H4}$ | CBgR CPou CSBt ECnt ELon EPfP ESty EWTr LAst LCro LRHS MAsh MAus MBri MCot MGan MJon MRav SPer SPoG SSea SWCr WAct WFoF WHCG WKif WOVN |
| | Ferdy = 'Keitoli'PBR (GC) | MRav SPer SWCr |
| | Fergie = 'Ganfer'PBR (F/Patio) | MGan SWCr |
| I | 'Fern's Rose' (F) **new** | SWCr |
| | ***ferruginea*** | see *R. glauca* Pourr. |
| | Festival = 'Kordialo'PBR (Patio) | ESty LStr MRav SMrm SPer SWCr |
| | Fetzer Syrah Rosé = 'Harextra'PBR | ESty |
| | Fiery Hit = 'Poulfiry'PBR (PatioHit Series) (Min) | ECnt MAsh |
| | Fiery Sunblaze = 'Meineyta'PBR (Min) | SWCr |
| | Fiesta = 'Macfirinlin' (Patio) | MJon |
| | ***filipes*** | GAuc |
| | - 'Brenda Colvin' | see *R.* 'Brenda Colvin' |
| § | - 'Kiftsgate' (Ra) $\Upsilon^{H4}$ | Widely available |
| § | 'Fimbriata' (Ru) | CPou MAus NLar SMrm SPer SSea SWCr WAct |
| | Financial Times Centenary = 'Ausfin' (S) | MAus |
| | Fiona = 'Meibeluxen'PBR (S/GC) | LSRN MLan SWCr |
| | 'First Great Western' (HT) **new** | ESty LStr |
| | 'First Love' (HT) | MGan SWCr |
| | 'Fisher and Holmes' (HP) | MAus WAct WHCG |
| | Fisherman's Friend = 'Auschild'PBR (S) | MAus SPer |
| | Flashdance = 'Poulyc004'PBR (ClMin) | ECnt |
| | 'Flora McIvor' (RH) | MAus MGan NHaw |
| | 'Flore' (Ra) | CRHN MAus |
| | 'Florence Mary Morse' (S) | SDix |
| | Florence Nightingale = 'Ganflor'PBR (F) | MGan SWCr |
| | 'Flower Carpet Coral'PBR (GC) | CGro ECnt GCoc LRHS MAsh MBri NPri SCoo SWCr |
| | Flower Carpet Gold = 'Noalesa'PBR (GC) | ECnt EPfP GCoc LRHS MAsh MBri NPri SPoG SWCr |
| | Flower Carpet PinkPBR | see *R.* Pink Flower Carpet |
| | Flower Carpet Red Velvet = 'Noare'PBR (GC) | CGro ECnt ELan EPfP GCoc LRHS LStr MAsh MGan NPri SCoo SPer SPoG SWCr |
| § | Flower Carpet Sunshine = 'Noason'PBR (GC) | CGro CTri ELan EPfP GCoc LRHS LStr SCoo SPer SWCr |
| | Flower Carpet White = 'Noaschnee'PBR (GC) $\Upsilon^{H4}$ | CGro CTri ELan EPfP GCoc LRHS LStr MAsh MGan NPri SCoo SPer SPoG SWCr |
| | Flower Power = 'Frycassia'PBR (Patio) | CSBt ECnt ESty GCoc LStr MAsh MAus MJon MRav NPri SMrm SPoG SWCr |
| § | ***foetida*** (S) | MAus NHaw |
| § | - 'Bicolor' (S) | LRHS MAus NHaw NLar SPer WAct |
| § | - 'Persiana' (S) | MAus MGan NHaw SPer |
| | ***foliolosa*** | SLPl WHCG |
| | Fond Memories = 'Kirfelix'PBR (Patio) | ESty LStr MJon SMrm SWCr |
| | For You With Love = 'Fryjangle' (Patio) | MGan SWCr |
| | Forever Royal = 'Franmite' (F) | ESty |
| | Forever Young = 'Jacimgol'PBR (F) | IDic |
| | ***forrestiana*** | MAus WHCG |
| | x ***fortuneana*** (Ra) | WFar |
| | Fortune's double yellow | see *R.* x *odorata* 'Pseudindica' |
| | 'Fountain' (HT/S) | MAus MGan SPer SWCr |
| | Fragrant Cloud = 'Tanellis' (HT) | CGro CTri CWSG ECnt EPfP ESty GCoc LAst LRHS LStr MAsh MAus MBri MCot MGan MJon MLan MRav NPri SMrm SPer SPoG SSea SWCr |
| | 'Fragrant Delight' (F) $\Upsilon^{H4}$ | CSBt ELan ELon GCoc LAst LStr MAus MGan MJon MRav SPer SWCr |
| | Fragrant Dream = 'Dicodour'PBR (HT) | CGro ESty IDic LStr MGan MRav SWCr |
| | Fragrant Memories = 'Korpastato'PBR (HT/S) | GCoc LRHS MGos SCoo SWCr |
| | Fragrant Plum = 'Aroplumi' (HT) **new** | SSea |
| | 'Francesca' (HM) | CPou LRHS MAus MGan SPer SWCr WAct WHCG |
| | Francine Austin = 'Ausram'PBR (S/GC) | LRHS MAus MJon SPer SWCr WAct |
| § | 'Francis E. Lester' (HM/Ra) $\Upsilon^{H4}$ | CRHN CSRo CSam EBee EPfP EWTr LRHS MAus MBri MJon NLar SMrm SPer SSea SWCr WAct WHCG |
| | x ***francofurtana*** misapplied | see *R.* 'Impératrice Joséphine' |
| | - 'Empress Josephine' | see *R.* 'Impératrice Joséphine' |
| | 'François Juranville' (Ra) $\Upsilon^{H4}$ | CPou CRHN CSBt EPfP EWTr GGal LAst LRHS LStr MAsh MAus MBri MCot MGan MRav NLar SLon SMad SMrm SPer SWCr WAct |
| | 'Frau Dagmar Hartopp' | see *R.* 'Fru Dagmar Hastrup' |
| § | 'Frau Karl Druschki' (HP) | MAus WAct |
| | 'Fred Loads' (F/S) $\Upsilon^{H4}$ | MAus MGan MRav |
| | Freddie Mercury = 'Batmercury' (HT) | MJon |
| | Free as Air = 'Mehbronze' (Patio) | MBri |
| | Freedom = 'Dicjem'PBR (HT) $\Upsilon^{H4}$ | CGro CTri EBls ECnt GCoc IDic LGod LStr MAus MGan MGos MRav SPer SWCr |
| | 'Frensham' (F) | CBcs LStr MGan SSea SWCr |
| | Fresh Pink (Min/Poly) | MGan |
| | Friend for Life = 'Cocnanne'PBR (F) $\Upsilon^{H4}$ | GCoc LSRN MJon MRav SMrm SWCr |
| | 'Fritz Nobis' (S) $\Upsilon^{H4}$ | LRHS LStr MAus MGan MRav NHaw NLar SPer SWCr WAct WKif |

| | | |
|---|---|---|
| | Frothy = 'Macfrothy'PBR (Patio) | ECnt MJon |
| § | 'Fru Dagmar Hastrup' (Ru) 🏆H4 | CDul CSBt EBee ECnt ELan EPfP GCoc LBuc LRHS LStr MAus MGan MJon NLar SMad SPer SWCr WAct WHCG WOVN |
| | 'Frühlingsanfang' (PiH) | CTri MAus WAct |
| | 'Frühlingsduft' (PiH) | WAct |
| | 'Frühlingsgold' (PiH) 🏆H4 | CBcs ELan EPfP EWTr GCoc LRHS LStr MAus MGan MRav NLar NWea SPer SPoG SWCr WAct WHCG WKif WOVN |
| | 'Frühlingsmorgen' (PiH) | EWTr GCoc LStr MAus MGan MRav NPri SLon SPer SSea SWCr WHCG WKif WOVN |
| | Fulton Mackay = 'Cocdana'PBR (HT) | GCoc MGan |
| | Fyvie Castle = 'Cocbamber' (HT) | GCoc |
| | 'Gail Borden' (HT) | MGan SWCr |
| § | ***gallica*** (G) | WAct |
| § | - var. ***officinalis*** (G) 🏆H4 | CAbP CSam CTri GCoc GPoy LRHS MAsh MAus MGan MJon MRav NLar SPer SSea SWCr WAct WHCG |
| § | - 'Versicolor' (G) 🏆H4 | Widely available |
| | Galway Bay = 'Macba' (ClHT) | EBee ELon LRHS MAsh MGan MRav SPer SWCr |
| § | Garden News = 'Poulrim'PBR (HT) | ECnt SWCr |
| | 'Gardenia' (Ra) | CPou EBee MAus SPer SWCr WHCG |
| | 'Gardiner's Pink' (Ra) | MCot WHCG |
| | 'Garnette Carol' | see *R.* 'Carol Amling' |
| | 'Garnette Pink' | see *R.* 'Carol Amling' |
| | 'Gaujard' | see *R.* Rose Gaujard |
| | 'Gelbe Dagmar Hastrup'PBR | see *R.* Yellow Dagmar Hastrup |
| | 'Général Jacqueminot' (HP) | MAus |
| | 'Général Kléber' (CeMo) | MAus MRav SPer SSea WAct |
| § | 'Général Schablikine' (T) | MAus SWCr WAct |
| | Genesis = 'Fryjuicy' (Patio) | ECnt SWCr |
| N | ***gentiliana*** H. Lév. & Variot | see *R. multiflora* var. *cathayensis* |
| | Gentle Hermione = 'Ausrumba' | MAus SWCr |
| | Gentle Touch = 'Diclulu'PBR (Min/Patio) | CSBt CWSG IDic LAst MRav SPer SPla SWCr |
| | Geoff Hamilton = 'Ausham'PBR (S) | CSBt ESty LRHS LStr MAsh MAus MBNS SCoo SPer SSea SWCr |
| | 'Georg Arends' (HP) | MAus |
| | George Best = 'Dichimanher' (Patio) **new** | IDic |
| | 'George Dickson' (HT) | MAus |
| | 'Georges Vibert' (G) | MAus |
| | Geraldine = 'Peahaze' (F) | MHav |
| | 'Geranium' (*moyesii* hybrid) 🏆H4 | CBcs CDul CSam EBee ELan EPfP GCoc GKir IArd LCro LGod LRHS LStr MAsh MAus MBri MGan MJon MRav NBlu NScw SEND SPer SSea SWCr WAct WHCG WOVN |
| | Gerbe d'Or | see *R.* Casino |
| | 'Gerbe Rose' (Ra) | MAus |
| | Gertrude Jekyll = 'Ausbord'PBR (S) 🏆H4 | Widely available |
| | 'Ghislaine de Féligonde' (Ra/S) | CPou CSam EBee LStr MGan NLar SMrm SPer SSea SWCr WHCG WPen |
| | Ghita = 'Poulren013'PBR (S) | see *R.* Millie |
| | ***gigantea*** 'Cooperi' | see *R.* 'Cooperi' |
| | Giggles = 'Kingig' (Min) | MJon |
| | Ginger Syllabub = 'Harjolina'PBR (Cl) | ESty GCoc MBri MRav SWCr |
| | Gingernut = 'Coccrazy'PBR (Patio) | SWCr |
| | Gipsy Boy | see *R.* 'Zigeunerknabe' |
| | Glad Tidings = 'Tantide'PBR (F) | CSBt CWSG LAst MBri MGan MRav SPer SWCr |
| | Glamis Castle = 'Auslevel'PBR (S) | CBcs CTri LCro LRHS LStr MAsh MAus MBri SCoo SMrm SPer SWCr |
| | ***glauca*** ambig. | EMac LCro |
| § | ***glauca*** Pourr. (S) 🏆H4 | Widely available |
| | 'Glenfiddich' (F) | CSBt CTri CWSG GCoc LStr MAus MBri MRav NPri NWea SPer SWCr |
| | 'Glenn Dale' (Cl) | EBee |
| | Glenshane = 'Dicvood' (GC/S) | IDic MRav |
| | Global Beauty = 'Tan 94448' (HT) | SMrm SWCr |
| | 'Gloire de Bruxelles' (HP) | MRav |
| | 'Gloire de Dijon' (ClT) | Widely available |
| | 'Gloire de Ducher' (HP) | MAus MGan NHaw WAct WHCG |
| | 'Gloire de France' (G) | MAus MRav WHer |
| | 'Gloire de Guilan' (D) | MAus SWCr WAct |
| | 'Gloire des Mousseuses' (CeMo) | EBee EWTr WHCG |
| | 'Gloire du Midi' (Poly) | MAus |
| | 'Gloire Lyonnaise' (HP) | EBee SLon WHCG |
| | 'Gloria Mundi' (Poly) | EWTr SWCr |
| | Gloriana = 'Chewpope'PBR (ClMin) | CGro ESty LRHS MAsh MAus MBri MJon MRav SCoo SMrm SPer SSea SWCr |
| | Glorious = 'Interictira'PBR (HT) | ESty IDic MBri MJon SWCr |
| | 'Glory of Seale' (S) **new** | SSea |
| | Glowing Amber = 'Manglow' (Min) | ESty MJon |
| | Goddess of Love = 'Horradhe' (S) **new** | SWCr |
| | Gold Symphonie = 'Macfraba' (Min) | MAsh |
| | 'Goldbusch' (RH) | MGan WAct |
| | 'Golden Anniversary' (Patio) | LStr MAsh SPer SWCr |
| | Golden Beauty = 'Korberbeni'PBR (F) | ESty MGos |
| | Golden Beryl = 'Manberyl' (Min) | MJon |
| | Golden Celebration = 'Ausgold'PBR (S) 🏆H4 | CGro CSBt CWSG EBee ECnt EPfP ESty GCoc LGod LRHS LSRN LStr MAsh MAus MBri MJon MRav NLar SMad SMrm SPer SPoG SSea SWCr |
| | 'Golden Chersonese' (S) | MAus |
| | Golden Future = 'Horanymoll'PBR (Cl) | MJon SWCr |
| | Golden Gate = 'Korgolgat' (ClHT) | ESty LStr MBri MGos SWCr |
| | Golden Jewel = 'Tanledolg'PBR (F/Patio) | ESty MAsh MBri SPoG SWCr |
| | Golden Jubilee = 'Cocagold' (HT) | CTri GCoc MRav SWCr |
| | Golden Kiss = 'Dicalways'PBR (HT) | GCoc IDic SWCr |
| | Golden Memories = 'Korholesea'PBR (F) | CGro CSBt EBls ESty GCoc LGod LRHS LStr MAsh MGos MJon MRav NPri SCoo SPer SPoG SWCr |
| § | Golden Penny = 'Rugul' (Min) | MGan |
| | 'Golden Rambler' | see *R.* 'Alister Stella Gray' |
| | 'Golden Salmon' (Poly) | MGan |
| | 'Golden Showers' (Cl) 🏆H4 | Widely available |
| | 'Golden Slippers' (F) | CBcs |
| | Golden Symphonie = 'Meitoleil' (Min/Patio) | SWCr |
| | Golden Tribute = 'Horannfree' (F) | MGan |
| | Golden Trust = 'Hardish'PBR (Patio) | LStr |

| | |
|---|---|
| Golden Wedding = 'Arokris'PBR (F/HT) | Widely available |
| 'Golden Wedding Celebration' (F) | CGro ESty SWCr |
| 'Golden Wings' (S) ♀H4 | CTri ELan EPfP GCoc LRHS LStr MAsh MAus MGan MJon MRav NLar SEND SMrm SPer SSea SWCr WAct WHCG |
| Golden Years = 'Harween'PBR (F) | SMrm |
| 'Goldfinch' (Ra) | CSRo EBee ELan EPfP LRHS LStr MAsh MAus MRav NLar SPer SWCr WAct WHCG |
| Goldstar = 'Candide' (HT) | ECnt MGan |
| Good as Gold = 'Chewsunbeam'PBR (ClMin) | CSBt ECnt ESty LStr MBri MJon SPer SWCr |
| Good Life = 'Cococircus'PBR (HT) | GCoc SCoo SPer SPoG SWCr |
| Good Luck = 'Burspec' (F/Patio) | GCoc SWCr |
| Good News 95 = 'Chespink'PBR | SWCr |
| Gordon Snell = 'Dicwriter' (F) | IDic |
| Gordon's College = 'Cocjabby'PBR (F) ♀H4 | ESty GCoc MJon |
| Grace = 'Auskeppy'PBR (S) | CSBt EPfP ESty MAus MBri MJon SSea SWCr |
| Gracious Queen = 'Bedqueen' (HT) | GCoc |
| Graham Thomas = 'Ausmas'PBR (S) ♀H4 | Widely available |
| Grande Amore = 'Korcoluma'PBR (HT) | GCoc MGos SWCr |
| Grand-mère Jenny = 'Grem' (HT) | MGan |
| 'Grandpa Dickson' (HT) | CSBt CWSG LAst LBMP LGod MAsh MAus MGan MJon MRav NPri SPer SWCr |
| Granny's Favourite (Patio/F) | LSRN SWCr |
| Great Expectations = 'Jacdal' (F) | EBee SPoG |
| Great Expectations = 'Lanican' (HT) | CBcs |
| Great Expectations = 'Mackalves'PBR (F) | CSBt ECnt EPfP ESty GCoc IArd LGod LRHS LStr MAsh MJon MRav SCoo SPer SWCr |
| § 'Great Maiden's Blush' (A) | GCoc MRav NLar WAct |
| 'Great News' (F) | MAus |
| Greenall's Glory = 'Kirmac'PBR (F/Patio) | MAus MJon MRav |
| 'Greenmantle' (RH) | MAus |
| Greensleeves = 'Harlenten' (F) | SPer SWCr |
| Greetings = 'Jacdreco'PBR (F) | IDic MAsh MRav SWCr |
| Grenadine = 'Poulgrena'PBR (HT) | ECnt |
| 'Grootendorst' | see *R.* 'F.J. Grootendorst' |
| 'Grootendorst Supreme' (Ru) | MAus SPer |
| N 'Gros Chou de Hollande' (Bb) | WHCG |
| Grouse = 'Korimro'PBR (S/GC) ♀H4 | GCoc LRHS MAus NLar SPer SWCr WAct WOVN |
| 'Gruss an Aachen' (Poly) | EPfP LStr MAus MGan NLar SPer SWCr WAct WHCG |
| 'Gruss an Teplitz' (China hybrid) | MAus SPer WHCG |
| Guardian Angel <u>**new**</u> | SWCr |
| 'Guinée' (ClHT) | CSBt EBee ECnt ELan ELon EPfP ESty GKir LAst LCro LRHS LStr MAsh MAus MGan MRav NPri SMrm SPer SPla SPoG SSea SWCr WHCG |
| Guletta | see *R.* Golden Penny |
| 'Gustav Grünerwald' (HT) | MAus |
| Guy Savoy = 'Delstrimen'PBR (F) | MRav SPoG |
| Gwen Mayor = 'Cocover'PBR (HT) | GCoc |
| Gwent = 'Poulurt'PBR (GC) | CSBt ELan GCoc LSRN LStr SEND SPer SWCr WAct WOVN |
| § ***gymnocarpa*** var. ***willmottiae*** | MGan SPer SSea WAct WHCG |
| Gypsy Boy | see *R.* 'Zigeunerknabe' |
| 'Hakuun' (F/Patio) ♀H4 | MAus MGan MHav SWCr |
| 'Hamburger Phönix' (Ra) | CGro MGan SPer WAct |
| Hampshire = 'Korhamp'PBR (GC) | MAus MGan |
| Hand in Hand = 'Haraztec'PBR (Patio/Min) | MAsh SPoG SWCr |
| Handel = 'Macha' (Cl) ♀H4 | CGro CSBt CTri CWSG ELan ELon EPfP ESty LAst LRHS LStr MAsh MGan MJon MRav SMrm SPer SPoG SSea SWCr WBVN |
| Hanky Panky = 'Wektorcent'PBR | EBls ESty GCoc MJon SWCr |
| Hannah Gordon = 'Korweiso'PBR (F) | EBls ECnt MGan MHav SWCr |
| 'Hansa' (Ru) | EMil GCoc LBuc MAus MGan SPer SWCr WHCG WOVN |
| Happy Anniversary = 'Bedfranc'PBR | ESty MJon NPri SMrm SWCr |
| Happy Anniversary = 'Delpre' (F) | CGro CTri LCro LRHS LStr MAsh MRav SPoG SSea |
| Happy Anniversary ambig. | LSRN |
| 'Happy Birthday' (Min/Patio) | CWSG ESty LCro LStr SPoG SWCr |
| Happy Child = 'Auscomp'PBR (S) | CWSG LRHS MAus MJon MLan SPer SWCr |
| Happy Retirement = 'Tantoras'PBR (F) | CGro ESty GCoc LRHS LSRN LStr MAsh MGan MRav SCoo SMrm SPoG SSea SWCr |
| 'Happy Thought' (Min) | CWSG |
| Happy Times = 'Bedone'PBR (Patio/Min) | LRHS MAsh SPoG SWCr |
| § x ***harisonii*** 'Harison's Yellow' (PiH) | MAus |
| § - 'Williams Double Yellow' (PiH) | GCoc MAus MGan WAct |
| Harlow Carr = 'Aushouse'PBR | LRHS MAus SCoo SWCr |
| 'Harry Edland' (F) | SSea SWCr |
| 'Harry Wheatcroft' (HT) | CBcs CGro MAus MGan SPer SWCr |
| Harvest Fayre = 'Dicnorth'PBR (F) | CGro CTri IDic MGan SPer |
| Havana Hit = 'Poulpah032' <u>**new**</u> | MAsh |
| 'Headleyensis' (S) | MAus SLon WHCG |
| Heart of Gold = 'Coctarlotte'PBR (HT) | EBee ECnt GCoc MRav SWCr |
| Heartbeat '97 = 'Cocorona'PBR (F) | SWCr |
| Heartbreaker = 'Weksibyl' (Min) | MJon |
| Heather Austin = 'Auscook'PBR (S) | LRHS MAus |
| Heather Honey = 'Horsilbee' (HT) | SWCr |
| 'Heather Muir' (*sericea* hybrid) (S) | MAus |
| 'Heaven Scent' (F) | MJon |

| | | |
|---|---|---|
| | Heavenly Rosalind = 'Ausmash'PBR (S) | LRHS MAus |
| § | 'Hebe's Lip' (DSwB) | MAus MGan WAct |
| | 'Helen Knight' (*ecae* hybrid) (S) | MAsh MAus SSea WHCG |
| | Helena = 'Poulna'PBR (Renaissance Series) (S) | LRHS |
| | ***helenae*** | CTri EBee MAus MGan NLar SPer SWCr |
| | - hybrid | SWCr WHCG |
| | Hello = 'Cochello' (Min/Patio) | SWCr |
| | ***hemisphaerica*** (S) | MAus WAct |
| § | 'Henri Martin' (CeMo) | MAus MGan NLar SLon SMrm SPer SWCr WAct WHCG |
| | Henri Matisse = 'Delstrobla' (HT) | MRav SPoG |
| | 'Henry Nevard' (HP) | MAus |
| | Her Majesty = 'Dicxotic'PBR (F) | IDic |
| § | 'Herbstfeuer' (RH) | MAus SPer SWCr |
| | Heritage = 'Ausblush'PBR (S) | CGro EBee ELan ELon EPfP GCoc LGod LRHS LStr MAus MRav SLon SMrm SPer SPla SWCr WHCG WOVN |
| | 'Hermosa' (Ch) | CBgR LAst LRHS MAus MRav SPla SWCr WAct WHCG |
| | Hero = 'Aushero' (S) | MAus |
| | Hertfordshire = 'Kortenay'PBR (GC) ♀H4 | ELan MAus MRav NPri SPer SWCr |
| | 'Hiawatha' (Ra) | SWCr |
| | 'Hidcote Gold' (S) | MAus |
| § | 'Hidcote Yellow' (Cl) | EBee LRHS MAus SPer SWCr |
| | Hide and Seek = 'Diczodiac'PBR (F) | IDic |
| | High Flier = 'Fryfandango'PBR (Cl) | SWCr |
| | High Hopes = 'Haryup'PBR (Cl) ♀H4 | CSBt EBee ECnt EPfP LRHS LStr MAsh MAus MGan MJon SPer SPla SPoG SSea SWCr WHCG |
| | 'Highdownensis' (*moyesii* hybrid) (S) | ELan MAus SPer |
| | Highfield = 'Harcomp' (Cl) | CSBt MAus SPer SWCr |
| | Hilda Murrell = 'Ausmurr' (S) | MAus |
| | 'Hillieri' (*moyesii* hybrid) | MAus |
| | 'Hippolyte' (G) | MAus |
| | Hole-in-one = 'Horeagle' (F) | SWCr |
| | holy rose | see *R.* x *richardii* |
| | 'Homère' (T) | MAus |
| | Honey Bunch = 'Cocglen'PBR (F) | GCoc LStr MRav SPer SWCr |
| | Honeybun = 'Tan98264'PBR (Patio) **new** | ESty |
| | Honeymoon | see *R.* 'Honigmond' |
| | Honeywood = 'Fryfixit'PBR (F) | GCoc |
| § | 'Honigmond' (F) | CWSG SWCr |
| | 'Honorine de Brabant' (Bb) | CPou EBee MAus SPer SPla SWCr WHCG WKif |
| | Hospitality = 'Horcoff'PBR (F) | ESty |
| | Hot Chocolate = 'Wekpaltez' (F) | ECnt ELan EPfP ESty GCoc LGod LRHS LStr MAsh MGan MJon MRav NPri SCoo SMrm SPoG SWCr |
| | Hot Stuff = 'Maclarayspo' (Min) | MJon SWCr |
| | Hot Tamale = 'Jacpoy' (Min) | MJon |
| | House Beautiful = 'Harbingo'PBR (Patio) | MRav |
| | 'Hugh Dickson' (HP) | MAus NLar SWCr |
| | ***hugonis*** | see *R. xanthina* f. *hugonis* |
| | - 'Plenissima' | see *R. xanthina* f. *hugonis* |
| | Humanity = 'Harcross'PBR (F) | MRav |
| | 'Hunter' (Ru) | WAct |
| | Hyde Hall = 'Ausbosky'PBR | LRHS MAsh MAus SCoo SWCr |
| | I Love You = 'Geelove' (HT) | SWCr |
| | Ice Cream = 'Korzuri'PBR (HT) ♀H4 | CWSG ECnt GCoc LCro LStr MAus MGan MGos MJon MRav SMrm SWCr |
| | Ice Meidiland = 'Meivahyn'PBR (S/GC) **new** | SWCr |
| § | Iceberg = 'Korbin' (F) ♀H4 | Widely available |
| | 'Iced Ginger' (F) | MGan SPer |
| | 'Illusion' (Cl/F) | SWCr |
| § | 'Impératrice Joséphine' ♀H4 | CSam LRHS MAus MRav NLar SWCr WAct WHCG |
| | In Memory Of **new** | SWCr |
| | In the Pink = 'Peaverity' (F) | SWCr |
| | Incognito = 'Briincog' (Min) | MJon |
| | Indian Summer = 'Peaperfume'PBR (HT) ♀H4 | CSBt CWSG ESty GCoc LGod MHav MRav SMrm SPoG SWCr |
| | 'Indigo' (DPo) | CPou MAus SWCr WHCG |
| | Ingrid Bergman = 'Poulman'PBR (HT) ♀H4 | CTri ECnt LStr MAus MBri MGan MGos MJon MLan MRav SMrm SPoG SWCr |
| | Innocence = 'Cocoray'PBR (Patio) | GCoc |
| | Intrigue = 'Korlech'PBR (F) | CSBt LStr MJon SWCr |
| | Invincible = 'Runatru'PBR (F) | MGan |
| | 'Ipsilanté' (G) | MAus WAct |
| | 'Irène Watts' (Ch) | CPou EBee ECre EPfP MAus NLar SPla SSea SWCr WAct WHCG |
| | Iris = 'Ferecha' (HT) | GCoc |
| | Iris Webb = 'Chewell' (F) | SWCr |
| | Irish Eyes = 'Dicwitness'PBR (F) | CWSG ECnt EPfP ESty IArd IDic LGod LRHS LStr MAsh MBri MGan MJon MRav NPri SCoo SMrm SPer SSea SWCr |
| | Irish Hope = 'Harexclaim'PBR (F) | SWCr |
| | Irish Wonder | see *R.* Evelyn Fison |
| | Irresistible = 'Tinresist' (Min/Patio) | MJon |
| | Isabella = 'Poulisab'PBR (Renaissance Series) (S) | CPou CTri ECnt EPfP LRHS SWCr |
| | IsisPBR (HT) | see *R.* Silver Anniversary = 'Poulari' |
| | 'Ispahan' (D) ♀H4 | CFee CSRo EPfP LRHS MAsh MAus NLar SLPl SLon SPer SWCr WAct WHCG |
| | Jack's Wish = 'Kirsil' (HT) | MJon |
| § | x ***jacksonii*** 'Max Graf' (GC/Ru) | EPfP LRHS MAus MGan MRav WAct WFar |
| | - Red Max GrafPBR | see *R.* Rote Max Graf |
| § | - White Max Graf = 'Korgram'PBR (GC/Ru) | MRav WAct |
| | Jacobite rose | see *R.* x *alba* 'Alba Maxima' |
| | 'Jacpico' | see *R.* 'Pristine' |
| | Jacqueline du Pré = 'Harwanna'PBR (S) ♀H4 | CSBt ECnt EPfP ESty EWTr GCoc LRHS MAus MCot MGan MJon MRav NLar SMrm SPer SWCr WAct WHCG |
| | Jacquenetta = 'Ausjac' (S) | MAus |
| N | 'Jacques Cartier' misapplied | see *R.* 'Marchesa Boccella' |
| | James Galway = 'Auscrystal'PBR (S) | CSBt CWSG ELon LRHS LStr MAus MBri MJon SCoo SSea SWCr |
| | 'James Mason' (G) | CSam MAus |
| | 'James Mitchell' (CeMo) | MAus WHCG |

| | | |
|---|---|---|
| | 'James Veitch' (DPoMo) | MAus WHCG |
| | Jane Asher = 'Peapet' (Min/Patio) | SWCr |
| | Janet = 'Auspishus'$^{PBR}$ (S) | CSBt LRHS MAus SWCr |
| | 'Janet's Pride' (RH) | MAus |
| § | 'Japonica' (CeMo) | MAus SWCr |
| § | Jardins de Bagatelle = 'Meimafris' (HT) | MJon MRav |
| | Jasmina = 'Korcentex' (Cl) | ESty MGos SWCr |
| | 'Jaune Desprez' | see *R.* 'Desprez à Fleurs Jaunes' |
| | Jayne Austin = 'Ausbreak'$^{PBR}$ (S) | CSBt CWSG MAus SPer SWCr |
| | Jazz$^{PBR}$ (Cl) | see *R.* That's Jazz |
| | Jean = 'Cocupland'$^{PBR}$ (Patio) | GCoc |
| | Jean Kenneally = 'Tineally' (Min) | MJon |
| | 'Jean Mermoz' (Poly) | MAus SWCr |
| | 'Jeanie Deans' (RH) | MAus |
| | 'Jeanne de Montfort' (CeMo) | MAus |
| | 'Jenny Duval' misapplied | see *R.* 'Président de Sèze' |
| | 'Jenny Wren' (F) | MAus |
| | 'Jenny's Dream' (HT) | LGod |
| | Jenny's Rose = 'Cansit' (F) | EBee ECnt MGan SWCr |
| | 'Jens Munk' (Ru) | NHaw WAct |
| | Jillian McGredy = 'Macarnhe' (F) | MJon |
| | Jill's Rose = 'Ganjil'$^{PBR}$ (F) | MGan SWCr |
| | 'Jimmy Greaves' (HT) | MGan |
| | 'Joanne' (HT) | MJon |
| | Joëlle Marouani = 'Masjoma' (Generosa Series) (S) | MRav |
| | 'John Cabot' (S) | SSea |
| | John Clare = 'Auscent'$^{PBR}$ (S) | LRHS MAus SWCr |
| | John Gibb = 'Coczorose' (F) | GCoc |
| | 'John Hopper' (HP) | MAus SWCr |
| | Johnnie Walker = 'Frygran'$^{PBR}$ (HT) | SWCr |
| | 'Jolly Roger' (F) **new** | SWCr |
| | 'Josephine Bruce' (HT) | CBcs CSBt LGod LRHS MGan SWCr |
| | 'Joseph's Coat' (S/Cl) | IArd LGod LStr MGan SSea SWCr |
| | 'Journey's End' (HT) | MGan SWCr |
| | 'Jubilee Celebration' (F) | EPfP |
| | Jubilee Celebration = 'Aushunter'$^{PBR}$ (S) | CSBt EPfP ESty LRHS MAus SWCr |
| | Jude the Obscure = 'Ausjo'$^{PBR}$ (S) | ELon ESty LRHS MAus MBri MJon SWCr |
| | 'Julia's Rose' (HT) | CGro LStr MAus MGan MJon SPer SWCr |
| | 'Juno' (Ce) | MAus SWCr WHCG |
| | 'Just for You' (F) | SWCr |
| | Just for You = 'Moryou' (Min) **new** | LSRN |
| | 'Just Jenny' (Min) | MJon |
| | 'Just Joey' (HT) ♀$^{H4}$ | CGro CSBt CWSG ECnt ELan EPfP GCoc IArd LGod LRHS LStr MAsh MAus MBri MGan MJon MRav NPri SMrm SPer SPoG SSea SWCr |
| | Just Married | SPoG SWCr |
| | 'Karlsruhe' (Cl) **new** | SSea |
| | 'Katharina Zeimet' (Poly) | CPou CTri MAus MGan NLar SMad SWCr WAct WHCG |
| § | Katherine Mansfield = 'Meilanein' (HT) | CSBt |
| | 'Kathleen Ferrier' (F) | MGan |
| | 'Kathleen Harrop' (Bb) | EBee LRHS LStr MAus NLar SMrm SPer SSea SWCr WAct WHCG |
| | Kathleen's Rose = 'Kirkitt' (F) | MJon |

| | | |
|---|---|---|
| | Kathryn McGredy = 'Macauclad' (HT) | ESty MJon |
| § | Kathryn Morley = 'Ausclub'$^{PBR}$ (F) | LRHS MAus |
| | 'Katie' (ClF) | MGan SWCr |
| N | 'Kazanlik' misapplied | see *R.* 'Professeur Emile Perrot' |
| | Keep Smiling = 'Fryflorida' (HT) | GCoc LGod LStr MAsh SMrm SWCr |
| | Keepsake = 'Kormalda' (HT) | MGan MJon |
| § | Kent = 'Poulcov'$^{PBR}$ (Towne & Country Series) (S/GC) ♀$^{H4}$ | CSBt ECnt ELan EPfP ESty GCoc LCro LStr MGan MJon MRav NPri SMrm SPer SPla SPoG SWCr WAct WHCG |
| | 'Kew Rambler' (Ra) | CRHN CSam EBee LCro MAus MRav SEND SPer WHCG |
| | 'Kiese' (*canina* hybrid) | NHaw |
| | 'Kiftsgate' | see *R. filipes* 'Kiftsgate' |
| | 'Kilworth Gold' (HT) | MGan |
| | Kind Regards = 'Peatiger' (F) | SWCr |
| | King's Macc = 'Frydisco'$^{PBR}$ (HT) | ESty MAus SWCr |
| | 'King's Ransom' (HT) | CBcs CSBt MGan MHav MRav SPer SPoG SWCr |
| | Kirsch Cover = 'Poultc004' **new** | SWCr |
| | Knock Out = 'Dadler' (F) | MAsh SWCr |
| § | 'Königin von Dänemark' (A) ♀$^{H4}$ | CSRo CSam EBee ECnt ELon EPfP GCoc LCro LRHS MAus MRav NLar SPer SSea SWCr WAct WHCG |
| § | 'Kordes' Magenta' (S/F) | MAus |
| | 'Kordes' Robusta' | see *R.* Robusta |
| | Korona = 'Kornita' (F) | SPer |
| | 'Korresia' (F) | CSBt CTri EBee ECnt EPfP ESty GCoc LAst LGod LStr MAsh MAus MBri MGan MJon MRav SPer SPoG SWCr |
| | Kristin = 'Benmagic' (Min) | MJon |
| § | Krönberg = 'Poultry'$^{PBR}$ (Castle Series) (F) | EPfP |
| | 'Kronprinzessin Viktoria von Preussen' (Bb) | MAus WHCG |
| | L.D. Braithwaite = 'Auscrim'$^{PBR}$ (S) ♀$^{H4}$ | CGro ELan ELon EPfP GCoc LAst LCro LGod LRHS LStr MAus MGan MJon MRav NLar NPri SEND SPer SWCr WAct WHCG |
| | 'La Belle Distinguée' (RH) | MAus WHCG |
| | 'La Belle Sultane' | see *R.* 'Violacea' |
| | 'La France' (HT) | MAus |
| | 'La Mortola' | see *R. brunonii* 'La Mortola' |
| | 'La Perle' (Ra) | CRHN MAus |
| | 'La Reine Victoria' | see *R.* 'Reine Victoria' |
| | 'La Rubanée' | see *R.* x *centifolia* 'Unique Panachée' |
| | La Sévillana = 'Meigekanu' (F/GC) | EBee SPer SWCr WAct WOVN |
| | 'La Ville de Bruxelles' (D) ♀$^{H4}$ | LRHS MAus SLon SPer WAct WHCG |
| | 'Lady Curzon' (Ru) | MAus |
| | Lady Emma Hamilton = 'Ausbrother' (S) | LRHS MAus SCoo |
| | 'Lady Gay' (Ra) | SWCr WHCG WOVN |
| | 'Lady Godiva' (Ra) | MAus |
| | 'Lady Hillingdon' (T) | MAus |
| | 'Lady Hillingdon' (ClT) | see *R.* 'Climbing Lady Hillingdon' |
| | 'Lady Iliffe' (HT) | MGan SWCr |
| | Lady in Red = 'Sealady' (Min) | MJon |
| | 'Lady Love '95' (Patio) | SWCr |
| | Lady MacRobert = 'Coclent' (F) | GCoc |
| § | Lady Meillandina = 'Meilarco' (Min) | CSBt |

| | |
|---|---|
| Lady Mitchell = 'Haryearn' (HT) | SWCr |
| Lady Penelope = 'Chewdor'PBR (ClHT) | CSBt ELon MAsh MJon SSea SWCr |
| § 'Lady Penzance' (RH) 🏆H4 | CBcs MAus MGan SPer SWCr WAct |
| Lady Rachel = 'Candoodle' (F) | ECnt |
| Lady Rose = 'Korlady' (HT) | MAsh SWCr |
| Lady Sunblaze | see *R.* Lady Meillandina |
| 'Lady Sylvia' (HT) | EWTr LRHS MAus MGan SPer SWCr |
| 'Lady Waterlow' (ClHT) | EWTr MAus NLar SPer SWCr WHCG |
| ***laevigata*** (Ra) | MAus NLar |
| - 'Anemonoides' | see *R.* 'Anemone' |
| Laguna = 'Koradigel' (Cl) | MGos |
| L'Aimant = 'Harzola'PBR (F) 🏆H4 | CSBt ESty GCoc LGod LStr MAus MGan MRav SWCr |
| 'Lamarque' (N) | CPou EBee MAus SWCr |
| § Lambert Castle = 'Poulcs006'PBR (F) | SWCr |
| Lancashire = 'Korstesgli'PBR (GC) 🏆H4 | ECnt ESty GCoc LGod LSRN LStr MAus MGan MRav SMrm SWCr |
| Laura Anne = 'Cocclarion' (HT) | GCoc |
| Laura Ashley = 'Chewharla' (GC/ClMin) | MAus SWCr |
| Laura Ford = 'Chewarvel'PBR (ClMin) 🏆H4 | CGro CSBt CTri LRHS LStr MAsh MAus MGos MHav MJon MRav NPri SMrm SPer SSea SWCr |
| 'Laure Davoust' (Ra) | CPou EBee |
| 'Lavender Jewel' (Min) | MAus |
| 'Lavender Lassie' (HM) 🏆H4 | CSam EBee MAus MGan SMrm SPer SSea SWCr WHCG |
| 'Lavender Pinocchio' (F) | MAus |
| Lavender Symphonies **new** | SWCr |
| LaviniaPBR | see *R.* Lawinia |
| § Lawinia = 'Tanklewi'PBR (ClHT) 🏆H4 | CSBt EPfP LStr MAsh MRav NPri SPer SWCr |
| 'Lawrence Johnston' | see *R.* 'Hidcote Yellow' |
| § Lazy Days = 'Poulkalm'PBR (F) | EBee ECnt EPfP SWCr |
| 'Le Rêve' (Cl) | MAus SWCr |
| 'Le Vésuve' (Ch) | MAus |
| Leander = 'Auslea' (S) | MAus |
| Leaping Salmon = 'Peamight'PBR (ClHT) | CGro CSBt EBee ELan ELon ESty GCoc LAst LGod LStr MAus MGan MRav SPer SWCr |
| 'Leda' (D) | MAus NLar SPer SSea SWCr WAct |
| 'Lemon Pillar' | see *R.* 'Paul's Lemon Pillar' |
| Léonardo de Vinci = 'Meideauri'PBR (F) | CSBt |
| 'Léontine Gervais' (Ra) | CAbP CRHN EBee LRHS MAus MBri MRav NLar SWCr WAct |
| 'Leo's Eye' | EPfP SWCr |
| Leslie's Dream = 'Dicjoon' (HT) | IDic |
| 'Leverkusen' (Cl) 🏆H4 | EBee EWTr LRHS MAus MCot MGan MJon MRav SMrm SPer SPla SPoG SWCr WAct WHCG |
| 'Ley's Perpetual' (ClT) | EBee SWCr |
| x ***lheritieriana*** (Bs) | SWCr |
| Lichfield Angel = 'Ausrelate' (S) **new** | SCoo |
| Lichtkönigin Lucia = 'Korlillub' (S) | SSea |
| Life Begins at 40! = 'Horhohoho' (F) | LSRN SWCr |
| Light Fantastic = 'Dicgottago' (F) **new** | GCoc IDic |
| 'Lilac Charm' (F) | SWCr |
| 'Lilac Dream' (F) | SWCr |
| Lilac Rose = 'Auslilac' (S) | MAus |
| Lilian Austin = 'Ausli' (S) | MAus |
| Liliana = 'Poulsyng'PBR (S) | ECnt LRHS SPla SWCr |
| Lilli Marlene = 'Korlima' (F) | CSBt CWSG MGan MHav SPer SWCr |
| Lincoln Cathedral = 'Glanlin'PBR (HT) | MJon SPer SWCr |
| Lincolnshire Yellow Belly **new** | SWCr |
| 'Lionheart' (HT) | SWCr |
| Lisa = 'Kirdisco' (F) | MJon |
| Little Bo-peep = 'Poullen'PBR (Min/Patio) 🏆H4 | MJon |
| 'Little Buckaroo' (Min) | LGod SPer SWCr |
| Little Cherub = 'Tan00814' (Patio) **new** | ESty SWCr |
| 'Little Flirt' (Min) | MAus MGan SWCr |
| 'Little Gem' (DPMo) | MAus MGan |
| Little Jackie = 'Savor' (Min) | MJon |
| Little Muff = 'Horluisbond' (Min) | MJon |
| Little Rambler = 'Chewramb'PBR (MinRa) 🏆H4 | CSBt ECnt LRHS LStr MAus MBri MGan MGos MJon SCoo SPer SSea SWCr |
| 'Little White Pet' | see *R.* 'White Pet' |
| Little Woman = 'Diclittle' PBR (Patio) | IDic LStr |
| 'Little Wonder' (F) | SWCr |
| Lochinvar = 'Ausbilda' PBR (S) | MAus |
| 'Long John Silver' (Cl) | MAus SSea |
| ***longicuspis*** misapplied | see *R. **mulliganii*** |
| ***longicuspis*** Bertol. (Ra) | SPla |
| - AC 2097 | GGar |
| § - var. ***sinowilsonii*** (Ra) | GCal GGar MAus SWCr |
| aff. ***longicuspis*** AC 1808 | GGar |
| Lord Byron = 'Meitosier' (ClHT) | LStr SSea SWCr |
| 'Lord Penzance' (RH) | CGro MGan MRav NHaw SPer WAct |
| Lorna = 'Cocringer' (F) | GCoc |
| 'L'Ouche' misapplied | see *R.* 'Louise Odier' |
| 'Louis Gimard' (CeMo) | MAus WAct |
| 'Louis XIV' (Ch) | WHCG |
| § 'Louise Odier' (Bb) | CBgR EBee ECnt ELon EPfP IArd LRHS LStr MAus MCot MGan MJon MLan MRav NLar SPer SPla SSea SWCr WAct WHCG WKif WOVN |
| Love & Peace = 'Baipeace'PBR (HT) | ELan ESty SWCr |
| Love Knot = 'Chewglorious'PBR (ClMin) | CSBt ECnt ESty MAsh MBri MJon MRav SCoo SMrm SSea SWCr WGor |
| § Lovely Bride = 'Meiratcan'PBR (Patio) | MAsh SWCr |
| Lovely Fairy = 'Spevu'PBR (Poly/GC) | IDic WAct |
| Lovely Lady = 'Dicjubell'PBR (HT) 🏆H4 | CSBt EBee EBls ECnt ESty IDic LStr MGan MJon MRav SMrm SSea SWCr |
| Lovely Meidiland | see *R.* Lovely Bride |
| 'Lovers' Meeting' (HT) | MGan MRav SPer SSea SWCr |
| Loving Memory = 'Korgund'PBR (HT) | CGro CSBt CWSG ECnt ESty GCoc IArd LSRN LStr MGan MGos MJon MRav NPri SMrm SPer SPoG SWCr |
| Lucetta = 'Ausemi' (S) | MAus |
| ***luciae*** var. ***onoei*** | CLyd |
| 'Lucy Ashton' (RH) | MAus |
| Lucy = 'Kirlis' (F) | MJon |
| Ludlow CastlePBR | see *R.* England's Rose |
| 'Lykkefund' (Ra) | MAus WHCG |
| 'Mabel Morrison' (HP) | MAus |
| Macartney rose | see *R. bracteata, R.* The McCartney Rose |

| | Name | Suppliers |
|---|---|---|
| | Macmillan Nurse = 'Beamac' (S) | ESty MCot |
| | 'Macrantha' (Gallica hybrid) | LRHS MAus SPer WAct |
| | ***macrophylla*** | MAus WAct |
| | - B&SWJ 2603 | WCru |
| § | - 'Master Hugh' ♀H4 | MAus |
| | 'Macyou'PBR | see *R.* Regensberg |
| | 'Madame Abel Chatenay' (HT) | MAus |
| | 'Madame Alfred Carrière' (N) ♀H4 | Widely available |
| | 'Madame Alice Garnier' (Ra) | CPou EBee SPer SWCr |
| | 'Madame Bravy' (T) | MAus |
| | 'Madame Butterfly' (HT) | MAus MGan MLan SPer SSea SWCr |
| § | 'Madame Caroline Testout' (HT) | GKir LRHS MGan MRav SPoG |
| | 'Madame de la Roche-Lambert' (DPMo) | CPou EBee MAus WAct WHCG |
| | 'Madame de Sancy de Parabère' (Bs) | EWTr IArd MAus SWCr |
| | 'Madame Driout' (ClT) | WHCG |
| | 'Madame Ernest Calvat' (Bb) | CPou MAus SWCr |
| | 'Madame Eugène Résal' misapplied | see *R.* 'Comtesse du Cayla' |
| | Madame Figaro = 'Delrona' (S) | MRav SMrm |
| | 'Madame Georges Bruant' (Ru) | MAus |
| § | 'Madame Grégoire Staechelin' (ClHT) ♀H4 | CWSG ECnt ELan ELon EPfP EWTr LAst LCro LRHS LStr MAsh MAus MBri MGan MJon MRav SMad SMrm SPer SPoG SWCr WAct WHCG |
| | 'Madame Hardy' (ClD) ♀H4 | CPou CSBt ECnt ELon EPfP EWTr GCoc LGod LRHS LStr MAus MGan MJon MRav NLar SMrm SPer SSea SWCr WAct WHCG WOVN |
| | 'Madame Isaac Pereire' (ClBb) ♀H4 | CSBt CTri EBee ECnt ELon EPfP ESty GCoc GKir LRHS LStr MAsh MAus MBri MGan MJon MRav SMad SMrm SPer SPoG SSea SWCr WAct WHCG |
| | 'Madame Jules Gravereaux' (ClT) | MAus |
| | 'Madame Jules Thibaud' (Poly) | MAus |
| § | 'Madame Knorr' (DPo) ♀H4 | CBgR CPou EBee ECnt EPfP GKir LRHS MAsh MRav NLar SEND SPer SSea SWCr WAct WHCG WOVN |
| | 'Madame Laurette Messimy' (Ch) | MAus WHCG |
| | 'Madame Lauriol de Barny' (Bb) | MAus MGan MRav NHaw NLar SLon SWCr WHCG |
| | 'Madame Legras de Saint Germain' (AxN) | CPou EBee MAus NLar SPer SWCr WAct WHCG |
| | 'Madame Louis Laperrière' (HT) | MAus |
| | 'Madame Louis Lévêque' (DPMo) | NLar SWCr WAct WHCG |
| | 'Madame Pierre Oger' (Bb) | EBee ECnt LRHS LStr MAus MGan MRav SPer SWCr WAct |
| | 'Madame Plantier' (AxN) | CPou LRHS MAus MRav NHaw NLar SPer SWCr WHCG WOVN |
| | 'Madame Scipion Cochet' (T) | SWCr WHCG |
| | 'Madame Zöetmans' (D) | MAus |
| | 'Madeleine Seltzer' (Ra) | ECGP MGan |
| | 'Madge' (HM) | SDix |
| | 'Magenta' (S/F) | see *R.* 'Kordes' Magenta' |
| | Magic Carpet = 'Jaclover'PBR (S/GC) ♀H4 | CWSG EBee ECnt ELan GCoc IDic MAus MGan MRav SMrm SPer SSea SWCr |
| | Magic Hit = 'Poulhi004'PBR (Min) | SWCr |
| | 'Magnifica' (RH) | MAus MGan |
| | 'Maid of Kent'PBR (Cl) | CSBt MJon SCoo SPer SWCr |
| | 'Maiden's Blush' (A) ♀H4 | CTri ELan GKir LRHS MAsh MAus MGan SPer SSea SWCr WHCG |
| | 'Maiden's Blush, Great' | see *R.* 'Great Maiden's Blush' |
| | 'Maigold' (ClPiH) ♀H4 | CBcs CGro CSam CTri CWSG EBee ECnt ELan EPfP EWTr GCoc GKir LCro LGod LRHS LStr MAsh MAus MGan MJon MRav SMad SPer SPoG SWCr WAct WHCG |
| | Majestic = 'Poulpm001'PBR (Paramount Series) (HT) | EBee |
| | Make a Wish = 'Mehpat'PBR (Min/Patio) | ESty LStr |
| | Maltese rose | see *R.* 'Cécile Brünner' |
| | Malvern Hills = 'Auscanary'PBR (Ra) | CSBt LRHS MAus MBri MGan MJon SSea SWCr WAct |
| | Mandarin = 'Korcelin'PBR (Min) | ESty LStr MJon MRav |
| | 'Manning's Blush' (RH) | MAus WAct |
| | Manou Meilland = 'Meitulimon' (HT) | SSea |
| | Many Happy Returns = 'Harwanted'PBR (S/F) ♀H4 | CGro CSBt CWSG EBee ECnt ELan EPfP GCoc LGod LRHS LSRN LStr MAsh MGan MGos MJon MRav NPri SMrm SPer SPoG SSea SVic SWCr |
| | 'Marbrée' (DPo) | MAus |
| | 'Märchenland' (F/S) | MAus |
| § | 'Marchesa Boccella' (DPo) ♀H4 | CPou CSam CTri EBee ELon EPfP GKir LRHS MAsh MAus MGan NLar NPri SPer SPla SSea SWCr WAct WHCG |
| | 'Marcia Gandy' (HT) | MGan |
| | 'Maréchal Davoust' (CeMo) | MAus WAct |
| | 'Maréchal Niel' (N) | EShb EWTr MAus SPer SWCr WHCG |
| | 'Margaret' (HT) | MGan SWCr |
| | Margaret Merril = 'Harkuly' (F) ♀H4 | Widely available |
| | Margaret's World = 'Kirbill' (F) | MJon |
| | 'Margo Koster' (Poly) | MAus |
| | 'Marguerite Hilling' (S) ♀H4 | CTri EBee EPfP MAus MGan MRav NLar SPer SSea SWCr WAct WHCG WOVN |
| | Maria McGredy = 'Macturangu'PBR (HT) | MJon |
| | 'Mariae-Graebnerae' | MAus SLPl |
| | 'Marie Louise' (D) | MAus WAct WHCG |
| | 'Marie Pavič' (Poly) | MAus WHCG |
| | 'Marie van Houtte' (T) | MAus |
| | 'Marie-Jeanne' (Poly) | MAus |
| | Marilyn Monroe = 'Weksunspat' (HT) | MJon |
| | Marinette = 'Auscam'PBR (S) | MAus |
| | Marjorie Fair = 'Harhero' (Poly/S) ♀H4 | EPfP ESty MAsh MAus MGan MRav SWCr |
| | Marjorie Marshall = 'Hardenier'PBR | MRav |
| | 'Marlena' (F/Patio) | GCoc MAus |
| | Marry Me = 'Dicwonder'PBR (Patio) ♀H4 | IDic |
| | 'Martha' (Bb) | MAus |
| | 'Martian Glow' (F/S) | MGan NLar |
| | 'Martin Frobisher' (Ru) | MAus NHaw SSea |
| I | 'Mary' (Poly) | LStr |
| | Mary Magdalene = 'Ausjolly'PBR (S) | LRHS LStr MAus SWCr |

| | | |
|---|---|---|
| | 'Mary Manners' (Ru) | NLar SPer |
| | Mary Rose = 'Ausmary'[PBR] (S) ♀H4 | CGro CSBt CWSG EBee ELan ELon EPfP EWTr GCoc LGod LRHS LStr MAsh MAus MBri MGan MJon MRav NPri SMrm SPer SPoG SSea SWCr WKif |
| | 'Mary Wallace' (Cl) | MAus |
| | Mary Webb = 'Auswebb' (S) | MAus |
| | Marylin = 'Meiguitan' | CWGr |
| | 'Masquerade' (F) | CBcs CGro CWSG ELan MGan MRav SMrm SPer SSea SWCr |
| | 'Master Hugh' | see *R. macrophylla* 'Master Hugh' |
| | Matangi = 'Macman' (F) ♀H4 | MGan SWCr |
| | Matawhero Magic[PBR] | see *R.* Simply the Best |
| | 'Max Graf' | see *R.* x *jacksonii* 'Max Graf' |
| | 'Maxima' | see *R.* x *alba* 'Alba Maxima' |
| | 'May Queen' (Ra) | CPou EBee EWTr LRHS MAus MGan MRav NLar SPer SWCr WHCG |
| | Mayor of Casterbridge = 'Ausbrid'[PBR] (S) | LRHS MAus |
| | 'McCartney Rose'[PBR] | see *R.* The McCartney Rose |
| | 'Meg' (ClHT) | EBee LRHS MAus MGan SMrm SPer SSea SWCr WAct WHCG |
| | 'Meg Merrilies' (RH) | MAus MGan NLar SSea WAct |
| | 'Megiddo' (F) | MGan SWCr |
| | 'Meicobuis'[PBR] | see *R.* Terracotta |
| | Meillandina = 'Meirov' (Min) | MLan |
| | Mellow Yellow = 'Wekosomit' (HT) | GCoc |
| | Melody Maker = 'Dicqueen'[PBR] (F) | CWSG IDic MHav SWCr |
| | Memento = 'Dicbar' (F) ♀H4 | MGan SWCr |
| | 'Memoriam' (HT) | MGan SWCr |
| | 'Memories Are Made of This' (F) **new** | MGan |
| | Memory Lane = 'Peavoodoo'[PBR] (F) | SWCr |
| | 'Mermaid' (Cl) ♀H3-4 | CBcs CDul CGro CSBt CTri EBee ECnt ELon EPfP LHop LRHS LStr MAus MGan MJon SMad SMrm SPer SPla SPoG SSea SWCr WAct WHCG |
| § | Message = 'Meban' (HT) | SWCr |
| | 'Meteor' (F/Patio) | MGan |
| § | 'Mevrouw Nathalie Nypels' (Poly) ♀H4 | LRHS LStr MAus MRav SPer SWCr WHCG WKif WOVN |
| | Michael Crawford = 'Poulvue'[PBR] (HT) | ECnt |
| | 'Michèle Meilland' (HT) | MAus |
| | Michelle Chetcuti = 'Kirchief' (HT) | MJon |
| | x ***micrugosa*** | MAus |
| | - 'Alba' | MAus |
| § | Millie = 'Poulren013'[PBR] (Renaissance Series) | ECnt SWCr |
| | 'Mills and Boon' (F) | MGan |
| | 'Minnehaha' (Ra) | LGod MAus SSea SWCr |
| | Minnie Pearl = 'Savahowdy' (Min) | MJon |
| | ***mirifica stellata*** | see *R. stellata* var. *mirifica* |
| | Mischief = 'Macmi' (HT) | MGan SPer SWCr |
| | Miss Alice = 'Ausjake'[PBR] (S) | CSRo LRHS MAus |
| | Miss Dior = 'Harencens'[PBR] (S) | MRav |
| | 'Miss Edith Cavell' (Poly) | MAus |
| | Miss Flippins = 'Tuckflip' (Min) | MJon |
| | Missing You = 'Horcakebread' (F) | MGan SWCr |
| § | 'Mister Lincoln' (HT) | ESty LGod MGan SPer SSea SWCr |
| | Mistress Quickly = 'Ausky'[PBR] (S) | LRHS MAus |
| § | Misty Hit = 'Poulhi011'[PBR] (PatioHit Series) (Patio) | ECnt LRHS LSRN MAsh SWCr |
| | 'Mojave' (HT) | MGan SWCr |
| | 'Moje Hammarberg' (Ru) | MJon WAct |
| | Molineux = 'Ausmol'[PBR] (S) ♀H4 | CSBt CTri ECnt EPfP LRHS MAsh MAus MBri SMrm SSea SWCr |
| | 'Monique' (HT) | MGan SWCr |
| | Moonbeam = 'Ausbeam' (S) | MAus |
| | 'Moonlight' (HM) | CTri ELan EWTr LRHS MAus MGan MRav SPer SWCr WAct WHCG |
| | 'Morgengruss' (Cl) | MGan SWCr |
| | Moriah = 'Ganhol'[PBR] (HT) | MGan |
| | 'Morletii' (Bs) | MRav SWCr WHCG |
| | 'Morning Jewel' (ClF) ♀H4 | GCoc MGan SPer |
| | Morning Mist = 'Ausfire' (S) | LRHS MAus SSea |
| § | 'Morsdag' (Poly/F) | LAst LStr MJon SWCr |
| | Mortimer Sackler = 'Ausorts'[PBR] (S) | LCro LRHS MAus MBri MJon SCoo SWCr |
| | ***moschata*** (Ra) | MAus MRav SSea SWCr WAct WHCG |
| | - 'Autumnalis' | see *R.* 'Princesse de Nassau' |
| | - var. ***nepalensis*** | see *R. brunonii* |
| | Mother's Day | see *R.* 'Morsdag' |
| | Mother's Joy = 'Horsiltrop' (F) | LSRN SWCr |
| | Mountain Snow = 'Aussnow' (Ra) | CSRo LRHS MAus SWCr |
| | Mountbatten = 'Harmantelle' (F) ♀H4 | CBcs CGro CWSG ELan EPfP LBMP LGod LRHS LStr MAsh MAus MGan MJon MRav NPri SPer SPoG SSea SWCr |
| § | 'Mousseline' (DPoMo) | CPou EBee MAus MRav NLar SMrm SPer SWCr WAct WHCG |
| | 'Mousseuse du Japon' | see *R.* 'Japonica' |
| | ***moyesii*** (S) | CTri ELan GCra GKev GKir ISea MAus MGan NWea SPer WAct WOVN |
| | - 'Evesbatch' (S) | WAct |
| | 'Mozart' (HM) | SWCr WHCG |
| | 'Mr Bluebird' (MinCh) | MAus MGan SMrm SWCr |
| | 'Mr Lincoln' | see *R.* 'Mister Lincoln' |
| | 'Mrs Anthony Waterer' (Ru) | MAus SPer SWCr WAct WHCG |
| | 'Mrs Arthur Curtiss James' (ClHT) | EBee SWCr |
| | Mrs Doreen Pike = 'Ausdor'[PBR] (Ru) | MAus |
| | 'Mrs Eveline Gandy' (HT) | MGan |
| | 'Mrs Honey Dyson' (Ra) | WHCG |
| | 'Mrs John Laing' (HP) | EBee ELon EPfP LRHS MAus MRav NLar SLon SPer SWCr |
| | 'Mrs Oakley Fisher' (HT) | EWTr MAus SDix SMrm SPer SWCr WAct |
| | 'Mrs Paul' (Bb) | MAus |
| | 'Mrs Sam McGredy' (HT) | MAus MGan SSea SWCr |
| | 'Mullard Jubilee' (HT) | MGan NBlu SWCr |
| § | ***mulliganii*** (Ra) ♀H4 | EBee EPfP MAus SPer SWCr WAct WHCG |
| | ***multibracteata*** (S) | MAus WHCG |
| | ***multiflora*** (Ra) | LBuc MAus NHaw NWea WAct |
| § | - var. ***cathayensis*** (Ra) | MAus WBor WHCG |
| § | - 'Grevillei' (Ra) | CPou EBee MAus SPer SWCr |
| | - 'Platyphylla' | see *R. multiflora* 'Grevillei' |
| | 'Mum in a Million' **new** | NPri |
| | Mummy[PBR] | see *R.* Newly Wed |
| | ***mundi*** | see *R. gallica* 'Versicolor' |
| | - 'Versicolor' | see *R. gallica* 'Versicolor' |
| | 'Mutabilis' | see *R.* x *odorata* 'Mutabilis' |

| | | |
|---|---|---|
| | 'My Choice' (HT) | MGan SWCr |
| | My Everything = 'Coccastle' (F) | ESty GCoc |
| | My Love = 'Cogamo' (HT) | MJon |
| | My Mum = 'Webmorrow'$^{PBR}$ | ESty SMrm SWCr |
| | My Valentine = 'Mormyval' (HT) **new** | ESty LStr |
| | Myriam = 'Cocgrand' (HT) | GCoc |
| | Mystique = 'Kirmyst' (F) | EBls MJon |
| | Nahéma = 'Deléri' (Cl) | LCro MRav SWCr |
| | 'Nan of Painswick' | WAct |
| | Nancy = 'Poulninga'$^{PBR}$ (Renaissance Series) | SWCr |
| | 'Narrow Water' (Ra) | CPou EBee NLar SWCr WAct WHCG |
| § | 'Nastarana' (N) | EBee SWCr |
| | 'Nathalie Nypels' | see *R.* 'Mevrouw Nathalie Nypels' |
| | 'National Trust' (HT) | IArd MGan MJon SMrm SPer SWCr |
| | 'Nelson's Pride' (F) **new** | EBls |
| | 'Nestor' (G) | MAus SWCr |
| | 'Nevada' (S) $\mathbb{Y}^{H4}$ | CSBt CTri EBee ECnt ELan EPfP GCoc IArd LAst LGod LStr MAus MCot MGan MLan MRav NWea SPer SSea SWCr WAct WHCG WOVN |
| | Never Forgotten = 'Gregart' (HT) | SWCr |
| | New Age = 'Wekbipuhit'$^{PBR}$ (F) | ESty GCoc MJon SWCr |
| | 'New Arrival' (Patio/Min) | MGan SWCr |
| § | 'New Dawn' (Cl) $\mathbb{Y}^{H4}$ | Widely available |
| | 'New Look' (F) | MGan SWCr |
| | New Zealand = 'Macgenev'$^{PBR}$ (HT) | MJon SWCr |
| § | Newly Wed = 'Dicwhynot'$^{PBR}$ (Patio) | IDic LStr MJon |
| | News = 'Legnews' (F) | MAus MGan |
| | Nice Day = 'Chewsea'$^{PBR}$ (ClMin) $\mathbb{Y}^{H4}$ | CGro CSBt CWSG EPfP ESty LGod LRHS LStr MAsh MJon MRav SMrm SPer SPoG SSea SWCr |
| | 'Nice 'n' Easy' (Patio) | SWCr |
| | 'Nicola' (F) | MGan SWCr |
| | Nigel Hawthorne = 'Harquibbler' (S) | WAct |
| | Night Light = 'Poullight'$^{PBR}$ (Courtyard Series) (Cl) | ECnt MBri MGan MRav SWCr |
| | Night Sky = 'Dicetch'$^{PBR}$ (F) | IDic SSea |
| | Nina = 'Mehnina'$^{PBR}$ (S) | SWCr |
| | Nina = 'Poulren018' (S) **new** | ECnt |
| | Nina Nadine = 'Kirhand' (F) | MJon |
| | 'Nina Weibull' (F) | NBlu SWCr |
| | ***nitida*** | EMac MAus MGan NHaw NWea SEND SPer SSea SWCr WAct WHCG WHer WOVN |
| | Noble Antony = 'Ausway'$^{PBR}$ (S) | LRHS LStr MAus MJon SWCr |
| § | 'Noisette Carnée' (N) | CSRo CSam EBee EPfP GCra LRHS LStr MAus MBNS MGan MJon MLan MRav NLar SLPl SPer SSea SWCr WAct |
| | Norfolk = 'Poulfolk'$^{PBR}$ (GC) | SPer SPla SWCr |
| | 'Norma Major' (HT) | MJon |
| | Northamptonshire = 'Mattdor'$^{PBR}$ (GC) | MGan |
| | 'Northern Lights' (HT) | GCoc |
| | 'Norwich Pink' (Cl) | MAus |
| | 'Norwich Salmon' (Cl) | MAus |
| | 'Norwich Union' (F) | MBri |
| | Nostalgia = 'Savarita' (Min) | CGro MAsh MGan |
| | Nostalgie = 'Taneiglat'$^{PBR}$ (HT) | EBee EBls ECnt ESty LStr MBri MJon MRav SPoG SSea SWCr |
| | 'Nottingham Millennium' (F) | MGan |
| | 'Nova Zembla' (Ru) | MAus |
| | 'Nozomi' (ClMin/GC) $\mathbb{Y}^{H4}$ | CGro CLyd CTri ELan ESty GCoc MAus MGan MJon MRav SMad SMrm SPer SWCr WAct WHCG WOVN |
| | 'Nuits de Young' (CeMo) $\mathbb{Y}^{H4}$ | GCoc MAus SSea SWCr WAct WHCG |
| | 'Nur Mahal' (HM) | MAus SWCr WHCG |
| | ***nutkana*** (S) | MAus |
| § | - 'Plena' (S) $\mathbb{Y}^{H4}$ | EPfP MAus MGan NLar SWCr WAct WHCG |
| | 'Nymphenburg' (HM) | MAus SPer SWCr |
| | 'Nyveldt's White' (Ru) | MAus |
| | Octavia Hill = 'Harzeal'$^{PBR}$ (F/S) | CSBt EWTr MRav NPri SPer |
| § | x ***odorata*** | SVic |
| | - 'Fortune's Double Yellow' | see *R.* x *odorata* 'Pseudindica' |
| § | - 'Mutabilis' (Ch) $\mathbb{Y}^{H3-4}$ | CRHN EBee ECre EPfP EWTr GCoc GGal LCro LRHS MAus MBri MCot MGan MRav SMad SMrm SPer SPoG SSea SWCr WAct WCFE WCot WHCG WKif WOVN |
| § | - 'Pallida' (Ch) | CBgR EPfP GCoc MAus MCot MRav SPer SPla SSea WAct WHCG |
| § | - 'Pseudindica' (ClCh) | MAus |
| § | - Sanguinea Group (Ch) | WHCG |
| | - - 'Bengal Crimson' (Ch) | LRHS WCot |
| § | - 'Viridiflora' (Ch) | EBee MAus SLon SMad SPer SSea SWCr WHCG |
| | Odyssey = 'Franski'$^{PBR}$ (F) | ESty |
| | 'Oeillet Flamand' | see *R.* 'Oeillet Parfait' |
| | 'Oeillet Panaché' (Mo) | WAct |
| § | 'Oeillet Parfait' (G) | MAus |
| | ***officinalis*** | see *R. gallica* var. *officinalis* |
| | 'Oklahoma' (HT) | MGan SWCr |
| | old blush China | see *R.* x *odorata* 'Pallida' |
| | old cabbage | see *R.* x *centifolia* |
| | Old John = 'Dicwillynilly' (F) | IDic |
| | old pink moss rose | see *R.* x *centifolia* 'Muscosa' |
| | Old Port = 'Mackati'$^{PBR}$ (F) | IArd MJon SWCr |
| | old red moss | see *R.* 'Henri Martin' |
| | old velvet moss | see *R.* 'William Lobb' |
| | old yellow Scotch (PiH) | see *R.* x *harisonii* 'Williams Double Yellow' |
| | Olympic Palace = 'Poulymp'$^{PBR}$ (Palace Series) (F) | EBee ECnt |
| | 'Omar Khayyám' (D) | MAus MRav SWCr |
| | ***omeiensis*** | see *R. sericea* subsp. *omeiensis* |
| | 'One Another' (F) **new** | MGan |
| | Open Arms = 'Chewpixcel'$^{PBR}$ (ClMin) $\mathbb{Y}^{H4}$ | ESty MAus MBri MJon SPer SSea SWCr |
| | 'Ophelia' (HT) | MAus MGan SWCr |
| | 'Orange Sensation' (F) | CTri CWSG MAus MGan MHav MLan |
| § | Orange Sunblaze = 'Meijikatar'$^{PBR}$ (Min) | CSBt MGan SPer |
| | Orangeade (F) | SWCr |
| | Oranges and Lemons = 'Macoranlem'$^{PBR}$ (S/F) | CGro CSBt EBls ECnt ELan ESty LGod LStr MAsh MAus MGan MJon SPoG SSea SWCr |
| | 'Orient Express' (HT) | CWSG |
| | 'Osiana' **new** | SWCr |
| | Othello = 'Auslo'$^{PBR}$ (S) | MAus SPer SWCr WAct |
| | 'Our Beth' (S) **new** | EBls |

| | |
|---|---|
| 'Our Dream' (Patio) | MAsh |
| Our George = 'Kirrush' (Patio) | MJon |
| Our Jubilee = 'Coccages' (HT) | ESty SVic |
| Our Love = 'Andour' (HT) | CWSG |
| Our Molly = 'Dicreason' (GC/S) | IDic MGan MJon SWCr |
| Oxfordshire = 'Korfullwind'PBR (GC) ♀H4 | LStr MRav SWCr |
| Paddy McGredy = 'Macpa' (F) | MGan |
| Paddy Stephens = 'Macclack'PBR (HT) | MJon SWCr |
| Painted Moon = 'Dicpaint' (HT) | ESty |
| Panache = 'Poultop'PBR (Patio) | ECnt LStr MAsh SMrm SWCr |
| 'Papa Gontier' (T) | MAus |
| Papa Meilland = 'Meisar' (HT) | CGro CSBt MAus MGan MHav MJon SPer SWCr |
| Paper Anniversary (Patio) | LSRN SWCr |
| Papi Delbard = 'Delaby' (Cl) | MRav |
| § 'Para Ti' | MAus MGan MJon SPer SWCr |
| 'Parade' (Cl) ♀H4 | MAus MRav SWCr WHCG |
| 'Paradise' (Patio) | SPoG SWCr |
| Paradise = 'Wezip' (HT) | MGan |
| 'Parkdirektor Riggers' (Cl) | EBee LStr MAus MBri MGan MLan NLar SPer SWCr WHCG |
| 'Parkjuwel' (CeMo) | MGan |
| Parson's pink China | see *R.* x *odorata* 'Pallida' |
| Partridge = 'Korweirim'PBR (GC) | MAus MGan SPer SWCr WAct WOVN |
| 'Party Girl' (Min) | MJon |
| ***parvifolia*** | see *R.* 'Burgundiaca' |
| Pas de Deux = 'Poulhult'PBR (Courtyard Series) (ClF) | LRHS MAsh SWCr |
| Pascali = 'Lenip' (HT) | CTri GCoc MAus MGan MJon MRav NBlu NPri SMrm SPer SSea SWCr |
| Pat Austin = 'Ausmum'PBR (S) ♀H4 | CSBt EBee ECnt EPfP LRHS LStr MAus MBNS MBri MRav NLar SWCr |
| Pathfinder = 'Chewpobey' (GC) | MJon SSea |
| Patricia = 'Korpatri' (F) | SWCr |
| 'Paul Crampel' (Poly) | MAus MGan WAct |
| 'Paul Lédé' (ClT) | see *R.* 'Climbing Paul Lédé' |
| Paul McCartneyPBR (HT) | see *R.* The McCartney Rose = 'Meizeli' |
| 'Paul Neyron' (HP) | MAus SPer SWCr |
| 'Paul Ricault' (CexHP) | MAus |
| Paul Shirville = 'Harqueterwife'PBR (HT) ♀H4 | ELan MAus MGan MLan MRav SPer SWCr |
| 'Paul Transon' (Ra) ♀H4 | CPou CRHN EBee EPfP LRHS MAus NLar SMrm SPer WHer |
| § 'Paulii' (Ru/GC) | MAus SWCr WAct WOVN |
| 'Paulii Alba' | see *R.* 'Paulii' |
| 'Paulii Rosea' (Ru/GC) | MAus MGan WAct |
| 'Paul's Himalayan Musk' (Ra) ♀H3-4 | Widely available |
| § 'Paul's Lemon Pillar' (ClHT) | EBee LAst LRHS MAus NLar SMrm SPer SSea SWCr |
| 'Paul's Scarlet Climber' (Cl/Ra) | CGro CSBt ELan EPfP GKir LAst LCro LGod LStr MAsh MAus MGan MJon MRav NBlu NPri SEND SPer SWCr |
| 'Paul's Single White Perpetual' (Ra) | WHCG |
| 'Pax' (HM) | CPou MAus SWCr WAct WHCG WKif |
| Peace = 'Madame A. Meilland' (HT) ♀H4 | CGro CSBt ECnt ELan EPfP ESty GCoc LCro LGod LRHS LStr MAsh MAus MBri MGan MJon MRav NBlu NPri SMrm SPer SPoG SSea SWCr |
| Peace Sunblaze (Min) | see *R.* Lady Meillandina |
| Peacekeeper = 'Harbella'PBR (F) | CSBt MRav SWCr |
| Peach Blossom = 'Ausblossom' (S) | MAus |
| Peach Clementine = 'Tan94475'PBR (Min) **new** | MAsh |
| 'Peach Grootendorst' (Ru) **new** | SWCr |
| § Pearl Abundance = 'Harfrisky'PBR (F) | ESty SWCr |
| § Pearl Anniversary = 'Whitston'PBR (Min/Patio) | CSBt ESty LCro LSRN LStr MRav SMrm SWCr |
| Pearl Drift = 'Leggab' (S) | MAus MJon SMrm SPer SWCr WHCG |
| Pearl Meidiland **new** | SWCr |
| PeaudoucePBR | see *R.* Elina |
| § Peek-a-boo = 'Dicgrow' (Min/Patio) | IDic MGan MRav SPer |
| Peer Gynt = 'Korol' (HT) | MGan NBlu SWCr |
| Pegasus = 'Ausmoon'PBR (S) | LRHS LStr MAus SSea |
| § ***pendulina*** | LBuc MAus NHaw |
| - 'Nana' | NHol |
| 'Penelope' (HM) ♀H4 | CSBt CSam CTri EBee ECnt ELan EPfP GCoc LCro LRHS LStr MAsh MAus MBri MCot MGan MJon MLan MRav SPer SSea SWCr WAct WHCG WKif WOVN |
| Penny Lane = 'Hardwell'PBR (Cl) ♀H4 | CSBt EBee ECnt EPfP ESty GCoc LAst LBMP LGod LRHS LStr MAsh MAus MBri MGan MGos MJon MRav NPri SCoo SMrm SPer SPoG SSea SWCr |
| Pensioner's Voice = 'Fryrelax'PBR (F) | MGan SWCr |
| x ***penzanceana*** | see *R.* 'Lady Penzance' |
| Peppermint Ice = 'Bosgreen' (F) | SWCr |
| Perception = 'Harzippee'PBR (HT) | SWCr |
| Perdita = 'Ausperd' (S) | ESty LRHS MAus MJon MLan MRav SPer |
| Perennial Blue = 'Mehblue' | EBee ECnt ESty SMad SSea SWCr |
| § Perfect Day = 'Poulrem' (F) | ECnt |
| Perfecta = 'Koralu' (HT) | MGan |
| 'Perle des Jardins' (T) | MAus |
| § 'Perle d'Or' (Poly) ♀H4 | EBee ECGP ECnt EPfP MAus MGan NLar SDix SLon SMad SPer SWCr WAct WHCG |
| Perpetually Yours = 'Harfable'PBR (Cl) | CGro LStr MRav SCoo SWCr |
| Persian yellow | see *R. foetida* 'Persiana' |
| Peter Pan = 'Chewpan'PBR (Min) | MAsh MAus MJon SWCr |
| Peter Pan = 'Sunpete' (Patio) | LRHS NPri SPoG |
| 'Petite de Hollande' (Ce) | MAus NLar SPer WAct WHCG |
| 'Petite Lisette' (CexD) | MAus NLar |
| Phab Gold = 'Frybountiful'PBR (F) | ESty GCoc MAsh |
| Pheasant = 'Kordapt'PBR (GC) | GCoc MAus MGan MJon SPer SWCr WAct WOVN |
| Phillipa = 'Poulheart'PBR (S) | ECnt SWCr |

| | |
|---|---|
| Phoebe (Ru) | see *R.* 'Fimbriata' (Ru) |
| 'Phyllis Bide' (Ra) ♀H4 | CAbP CSRo EBee EPfP IArd LRHS LStr MAus MGan MJon NLar SPer SSea SWCr WAct WHCG WKif |
| Picasso = 'Macpic' (F) | MGan NHaw SWCr |
| Piccadilly = 'Macar' (HT) | CGro CSBt CTri MGan MJon MRav SPer SSea SWCr |
| Piccolo = 'Tanolokip' PBR (F/Patio) | CGro ESty LStr MBri MJon MRav SWCr |
| 'Picture' (HT) | MGan SPer SWCr |
| Pigalle '84 = 'Meicloux' (F) | SWCr |
| 'Pilgrim' PBR | see *R.* The Pilgrim |
| ***pimpinellifolia*** | see *R. spinosissima* |
| - 'Altaica' | see *R. spinosissima* 'Grandiflora' |
| - double yellow | see *R.* x *harisonii* 'Williams Double Yellow' |
| - 'Harisonii' | see *R.* x *harisonii* 'Harison's Yellow' |
| Pink Abundance = 'Harfrothy' PBR (Abundance Series) (F) | ESty LStr SWCr |
| Pink Bells = 'Poulbells' PBR (GC) | GCoc MAus SPer |
| 'Pink Bouquet' (Ra) | CRHN |
| 'Pink Favorite' (HT) | CSBt MGan SPer SWCr |
| Pink Fizz = 'Poulycool' (ClPatio) | ECnt LRHS MAsh |
| § Pink Flower Carpet = 'Noatraum' PBR | (GC) ♀H4 CGro CSBt CTri ECnt ELan EPfP GCoc LRHS LStr MAsh MAus MBri MGan NPri SCoo SPer SPoG SWCr |
| 'Pink Garnette' | see *R.* 'Carol Amling' |
| 'Pink Grootendorst' (Ru) ♀H4 | EBee EPfP LRHS MAus MGan NLar SPer SSea SWCr WAct WHCG |
| § Pink Hit = 'Poultipe' PBR (Min/Patio) | ECnt LRHS MAsh SWCr |
| Pink La Sevillana = 'Meigeroka' PBR (F/GC) | SWCr WAct |
| 'Pink Medley' (F) **new** | MAsh |
| pink moss | see *R.* x *centifolia* 'Muscosa' |
| 'Pink Parfait' (F) | MAus MGan SPer |
| Pink Peace = 'Meibil' (HT) | MRav SWCr |
| 'Pink Perpétué' (Cl) | CBcs CGro CSBt CTri ECnt ELan ELon EPfP GCoc GKir LAst LRHS LStr MAsh MAus MGan MJon MRav SPer SPoG SSea SWCr WAct |
| 'Pink Prosperity' (HM) | MAus |
| 'Pink Showers' (ClHT) | WAct |
| Pink Skyliner = 'Franwekpink' PBR (ClPatio) | EBls MJon |
| Pink Surprise = 'Lenbrac' (Ru) | MAus |
| Pirouette = 'Poulyc003' PBR (Cl) | ECnt LRHS MAsh |
| 'Playboy' (F) | GCoc |
| Playtime = 'Morplati' (F) | MAus |
| Pleine de Grâce = 'Lengra' (S) | MAus |
| Poetry in Motion = 'Harelan' PBR (HT) | EBls MJon SWCr |
| Polar Star = 'Tanlarpost' PBR (HT) | CSBt EBee ECnt LCro LGod LStr MAsh MGan MRav SPer SWCr |
| x ***polliniana*** | SLPl |
| 'Polly' (HT) | MGan SWCr |
| ***pomifera*** | see *R. villosa* L. |
| - 'Duplex' | see *R.* 'Duplex' |
| 'Pompon Blanc Parfait' (A) | MAus |
| 'Pompon de Bourgogne' | see *R.* 'Burgundiaca' |
| 'Pompon de Paris' (ClMinCh) | see *R.* 'Climbing Pompon de Paris' |
| 'Pompon Panaché' (G) | MAus |
| Portland rose | see *R.* 'Portlandica' |
| 'Portland Trailblazer' | see *R.* 'Big Chief' |
| § 'Portlandica' (Po) | CTri GKir LRHS MAsh MAus SPer WAct WHCG |
| Portmeirion = 'Ausguard' PBR (S) | MAus SCoo |
| Pot o' Gold = 'Dicdivine' (HT) | SPer SWCr |
| Pour Toi (Min) | see *R.* 'Para Ti' |
| prairie rose | see *R. setigera* |
| 'Precious Memories' (Min) **new** | SWCr |
| Precious Moments = 'Lyopr' | SWCr |
| 'Precious Platinum' (HT) | LGod MJon SPer SWCr |
| Preservation = 'Bosiljurika' PBR (S/F) | SWCr |
| § 'Président de Sèze' (G) ♀H4 | MAus NLar SPer SWCr WAct WHCG |
| 'President Herbert Hoover' (HT) | ESty |
| Pretty in Pink = 'Dicumpteen' PBR (GC) | EBee ECnt IDic MJon SWCr |
| Pretty Jessica = 'Ausjess' (S) | CGro LRHS MAus MJon MLan MRav SMrm SPer |
| Pretty Lady = 'Scrivo' PBR (F) ♀H4 | LStr MAus MJon SSea |
| Pretty Polly = 'Meitonje' PBR (Min) ♀H4 | CGro EPfP ESty LAst LRHS LStr MAsh MBri MGan MRav SPer SPoG SWCr |
| Pride of England = 'Harencore' PBR (HT) | EBls GCoc MJon SWCr |
| Pride of Scotland = 'Macwhitba' (HT) | GCoc MJon |
| 'Prima Ballerina' (HT) | CGro CSBt CTri CWSG GCoc LRHS LStr MAsh MGan MJon SPer SSea SWCr |
| ***primula*** (S) ♀H3-4 | MAus MGan MJon NLar SSea SWCr WAct WHCG |
| 'Prince Camille de Rohan' (HP) | MAus SWCr WHCG |
| 'Prince Charles' (Bb) | MAus SWCr WKif |
| Prince Palace = 'Poulzin' PBR (Palace Series) (F) | ECnt |
| Prince Regent = 'Genpen' (S) | SSea |
| Princess Alexandra = 'Pouldra' PBR (Renaissance Series) (S) | CTri ECnt EPfP LRHS SWCr |
| Princess Alice = 'Hartanna' (F) | MGan SWCr |
| Princess Nobuko = 'Coclistine' PBR (HT) | GCoc |
| 'Princess of Wales' (HP) | EPfP |
| Princess of Wales = 'Hardinkum' PBR (F) ♀H4 | CGro CSBt EPfP LRHS LStr MAsh MBri MGan MRav NPri SCoo SPer SWCr |
| Princess Royal = 'Dicroyal' PBR (HT) | IDic |
| § 'Princesse de Nassau' (Ra) | MAus WAct WHCG |
| 'Princesse Louise' (Ra) | CRHN MAus |
| 'Princesse Marie' misapplied | see *R.* 'Belvedere' |
| § 'Pristine' (HT) | MAus SPer |
| § 'Professeur Emile Perrot' (D) | SWCr WAct |
| 'Prolifera de Redouté' misapplied | see *R.* 'Duchesse de Montebello' |
| 'Prosperity' (HM) ♀H4 | CBcs CSam CTri EPfP GCoc LRHS MAus MCot MGan MJon MRav SPer SWCr WAct WHCG WOVN |
| Prospero = 'Auspero' (S) | MAus NLar |
| 'Pure Abundance' (F) | SWCr |

| | |
|---|---|
| Pure Bliss = 'Dictator'PBR (HT) | EBee ECnt ESty IDic MGan SWCr |
| 'Purezza' (Ra) | NLar |
| 'Purity' (Cl) | EBee SWCr |
| 'Purple Beauty' (HT) | MGan SWCr |
| Purple Skyliner = 'Franwekpurp'PBR (ClS) | ESty MJon |
| Purple Tiger = 'Jacpurr'PBR (F) | ESty IDic LStr SMrm SWCr |
| 'Purpurtraum' (Ru) | WHCG |
| Quaker Star = 'Dicperhaps' (F) | IDic |
| quatre saisons | see *R.* x *damascena* var. *semperflorens* |
| 'Quatre Saisons Blanche Mousseuse' (DMo) | SWCr WAct |
| Queen Elizabeth | see *R.* 'The Queen Elizabeth' |
| Queen Margarethe = 'Poulskov'PBR (F) | ECnt |
| Queen Mother = 'Korquemu'PBR (Patio) ♀H4 | CSBt ELan EPfP GCoc LGod LStr MAus MGan MRav NPri SMrm SPer SPoG SWCr |
| Queen of Denmark | see *R.* 'Königin von Dänemark' |
| Queen of Sweden = 'Austiger'PBR | ECnt LRHS MAus SWCr |
| Queen's Palace = 'Poulelap'PBR (F) | ECnt |
| 'Rachel' (HT) **new** | EBls |
| 'Rachel' ambig. | GCoc |
| Rachel = 'Tangust'PBR (HT) | CSBt ESty LStr MJon MRav SPoG SWCr |
| Racy Lady = 'Dicwaffle'PBR (HT) | IDic MJon SWCr |
| Radio Times = 'Aussal'PBR (S) | ESty MAus |
| Rainbow Magic = 'Dicxplosion'PBR (Patio) | ESty IDic |
| 'Ralph Tizzard' (F) | SSea |
| 'Rambling Rector' (Ra) ♀H4 | Widely available |
| Rambling Rosie = 'Horjasper' (Ra) | ECnt ESty LGod MAsh MJon SWCr |
| § 'Ramona' (Ra) | MAus SWCr |
| 'Raubritter' ('Macrantha' hybrid) | CAbP ECGP LRHS MAus SPer SSea SWCr WAct WHCG |
| Ray of Hope = 'Cocnilly'PBR (F) | GCoc LGod SWCr |
| Ray of Sunshine = 'Cocclare'PBR (Patio) | GCoc |
| Raymond Blanc = 'Delnado' (HT) | SWCr |
| 'Raymond Chenault' (Cl) | CGro MGan |
| Rebecca (Patio) | ESty |
| 'Rebecca Claire' (HT) | SWCr |
| Reconciliation = 'Hartillery'PBR (HT) | SWCr |
| Red AbundancePBR | see *R.* Songs of Praise |
| Red Bells = 'Poulred'PBR (Min/GC) | MAus WOVN |
| Red Blanket = 'Intercell' (S/GC) | GCoc MAus SPer WAct WFar WOVN |
| Red Caviar = 'Poulfl001'PBR (HT) | EBee ECnt |
| Red Coat = 'Auscoat' (F) | MAus |
| Red Devil = 'Dicam' (HT) | MAsh MGan MJon MRav SCoo SWCr |
| Red Eden Rose = 'Meidrason'PBR (Cl) | ESty SSea SWCr |
| 'Red Facade' (Cl) | MAsh |
| Red Finesse = 'Korvillade'PBR | MAsh MGos |
| 'Red Grootendorst' | see *R.* 'F.J. Grootendorst' |
| Red Hot = 'Macbigma' (Patio) | MJon |
| 'Red Max Graf'PBR | see *R.* Rote Max Graf |
| Red Meidiland = 'Meineble'PBR (GC) | SWCr |
| red moss | see *R.* 'Henri Martin' |
| Red New Dawn | see *R.* 'Etendard' |
| Red Rascal = 'Jacbed'PBR (S/Patio) | CSBt IDic |
| red rose of Lancaster | see *R. gallica* var. *officinalis* |
| 'Red Wing' (S) | MAus |
| Redouté = 'Auspale'PBR (S) | LRHS MAus SPer SWCr |
| Reflections = 'Simref' (F) **new** | SWCr |
| § Regensberg = 'Macyoumis'PBR (F/Patio) | MAus MBri MGan MJon MRav SPer SWCr |
| 'Reine des Violettes' (HP) | CGro CPou ELon EPfP GKir IArd LRHS LStr MAsh MAus MCot MGan MRav NLar SPer SPoG SWCr WAct WHCG |
| § 'Reine Victoria' (Bb) | EBee EPfP LRHS LStr MAus MCot MGan MRav SPer SPla SWCr WAct |
| § Remember = 'Poulht001'PBR (HT) | ECnt EPfP MAsh SWCr |
| Remember Me = 'Cocdestin'PBR (HT) ♀H4 | CSBt CWSG ECnt ESty GCoc IArd LCro LGod LSRN LStr MAus MBri MGan MGos MJon MRav NPri SMrm SPer SPoG SSea SWCr |
| Remembrance = 'Harxampton'PBR (F) ♀H4 | CTri EBls ESty LGod LRHS LSRN LStr MAsh MGan MJon MRav NPri SMrm SPer SPoG SWCr |
| Renaissance = 'Harzart'PBR (HT) | CSBt GCoc LStr SWCr |
| 'René André' (Ra) | CPou CRHN MAus SWCr |
| 'René d'Anjou' (CeMo) | MAus |
| 'Rescht' | see *R.* 'De Resht' |
| Rest in Peace = 'Bedswap' (Patio/F) | SWCr |
| 'Rêve d'Or' (N) | CSam MAus SLon SPer SWCr |
| 'Réveil Dijonnais' (ClHT) | MAus |
| Rhapsody in Blue = 'Frantasia'PBR (S) | CGro CSBt EBee ECnt ELan EPfP ESty GCoc LCro LGod LRHS LStr MAsh MAus MGan MGos MJon MLan MRav NPri SCoo SMad SMrm SPer SSea SWCr |
| § x ***richardii*** | MAus MGan MRav WAct WHCG |
| Rick Stein = 'Tan96205'PBR (HT) | LStr SWCr |
| 'Rival de Paestum' (T) | MAus |
| 'River Gardens' | NPer |
| Rob Roy = 'Cocrob' (F) | GCoc MGan SPer SWCr |
| Robbie Burns = 'Ausburn' (PiH) | MAus WAct |
| 'Robert le Diable' (Ce x G) | CPou MAus NLar SPer SWCr WAct |
| 'Robin Hood' (HM) | SWCr |
| § Robusta = 'Korgosa' (Ru) | EBee ECnt MAus MGan SSea SWCr |
| Rockabye Baby = 'Dicdwarf' (Patio) | ESty GCoc IDic SMrm SWCr |
| 'Roger Lambelin' (HP) | MAus |
| Romance = 'Tanezamor'PBR (S) | MRav |
| Romantic Palace = 'Poulmanti'PBR (F) | ECnt |
| 'Rosa Mundi' | see *R. gallica* 'Versicolor' |
| Rosabell = 'Cocceleste'PBR (F/Patio) | ESty GCoc |
| Rosarium Uetersen = 'Kortersen' (ClHT) | MJon |
| § 'Rose d'Amour' (S) ♀H4 | CFee MAus SWCr |
| 'Rose de Meaux' | see *R.* x *centifolia* 'De Meaux' |
| 'Rose de Meaux White' | see *R.* 'White de Meaux' |
| 'Rose de Rescht' | see *R.* 'De Resht' |
| 'Rose du Maître d'Ecole' | see *R.* 'Du Maître d'Ecole' |
| 'Rose du Roi' (HP/DPo) | MAus WAct WHCG |

| | | |
|---|---|---|
| | 'Rose du Roi à Fleurs Pourpres' (HP) | MAus |
| § | Rose Gaujard = 'Gaumo' (HT) | LGod MAsh MGan SWCr |
| | Rose of Picardy = 'Ausfudge' | LRHS MAus SSea SWCr |
| * | 'Rose of Yunnan' | WAct |
| | Rose Pearl = 'Korterschi'PBR (S) | MGan |
| | Rose-Marie = 'Ausome'PBR (S) | MAus SWCr |
| | 'Rose-Marie Viaud' (Ra) | CFee CPou CSam EBee MAus SWCr WHCG |
| | 'Rosemary Gandy' (F) | MGan |
| | Rosemary Harkness = 'Harrowbond'PBR (HT) | ESty LStr MRav SPer |
| | 'Rosemary Rose' (F) | SPer |
| | Rosemoor = 'Austough'PBR | CSBt LRHS MAsh MAus SWCr |
| | Rosendal = 'Pouldahle'PBR (F) | EBee |
| | Rosenprofessor SieberPBR | see *R.* The Halcyon Days Rose |
| | 'Roseraie de l'Haÿ' (Ru) ♀H4 | Widely available |
| | Rosy Cushion = 'Interall' (S/GC) ♀H4 | CSam LRHS MAus MGan MLan SPer SWCr WAct WHCG WOVN |
| | Rosy Future = 'Harwaderox' (F/Patio) | CSBt SMrm SWCr |
| | 'Rosy Mantle' (Cl) | CBcs CSBt MGan SPer SWCr |
| § | Rotary Sunrise = 'Fryglitzy' (HT) | CSBt MBri |
| § | Rote Max Graf = 'Kormax'PBR (GC/Ru) | MRav WAct |
| | 'Roundelay' (HT) | MAus |
| | ***roxburghii*** (S) | EPfP LEdu MGan SWCr WAct WHCG |
| | - f. ***normalis*** (S) | CFee |
| | - 'Plena' | see *R. roxburghii* f. *roxburghii* |
| § | - f. ***roxburghii*** (d/S) | MAus |
| | 'Royal Albert Hall' (HT) | GCoc |
| | Royal Celebration = 'Wekbiphitsou' (F) | MJon |
| | Royal CopenhagenPBR (HT) | see *R.* Remember = 'Poulht001' |
| | 'Royal Gold' (ClHT) | MGan |
| | 'Royal Occasion' (F) | SPer SWCr |
| | Royal Parks = 'Harlyric'PBR (HT) | GCoc |
| | Royal William = 'Korzaun'PBR (HT) ♀H4 | CSBt ELan ESty GCoc LBMP LCro LGod LRHS LStr MAsh MAus MBri MGan MGos MJon MRav NBlu NPri SPer SWCr |
| § | ***rubiginosa*** | CArn CCVT CDul CRWN EMac EPfP GPoy IFro ILis LBuc MAus MHer MJon MRav NWea SPer SWCr WAct WMou |
| | ***rubra*** | see *R. gallica* |
| | ***rubrifolia*** | see *R. glauca* Pourr. |
| | 'Rubrotincta' | see *R.* 'Hebe's Lip' |
| | ***rubus*** (Ra) | MAus |
| | - SF 96062 | ISea |
| § | - var. ***glandulifera*** | WAct |
| | - ***velutescens*** | see *R. rubus* var. *glandulifera* |
| | Ruby Anniversary = 'Harbonny'PBR (Patio) | CSBt CWSG ESty LCro LStr MAsh MHav MRav SCoo SMrm SPoG SVic SWCr |
| | Ruby Celebration = 'Peawinner'PBR (F) | CWSG EBls ESty MJon SMrm SWCr |
| | 'Ruby Pendant' (Min) | MJon |
| | Ruby Ruby = 'Weksactrumi' (Min) **new** | MAsh |
| | 'Ruby Wedding' (HT) | Widely available |
| | 'Ruga' (Ra) | SMrm |
| | ***rugosa*** (Ru) | CDul CLnd CTri EMac EPfP GGar GKir LBuc MAsh MAus MBri MHer MRav NWea SPlb SVic SWCr WBVN |
| | - 'Alba' (Ru) ♀H4 | Widely available |
| | - 'Rubra' (Ru) ♀H4 | CBcs CCVT CTri CWib EPfP GKir LAst LBuc LCro LStr MGan SMrm SPer SPoG SVic WAct |
| | - Sakhalin form | MCCP |
| | - 'Scabrosa' | see *R.* 'Scabrosa' |
| | 'Rugosa Atropurpurea' (Ru) | GKir |
| | 'Rugspin' (Ru) | WAct |
| | 'Rumba' (F) | NBlu SWCr |
| | 'Rural England' (Ra) **new** | EBls |
| | Rush = 'Lenmobri' (S) | MAus |
| | Rushing Stream = 'Austream' (GC) | CSRo MAus |
| | 'Ruskin' (HP×Ru) | MAus |
| | 'Russelliana' (Ra) | MAus SWCr WAct WKif WRha |
| | Safe Haven = 'Jacreraz'PBR (F) | ECnt IDic MGan |
| | Saint Alban = 'Auschesnut'PBR (S) | CSBt MAus SWCr |
| | Saint Boniface = 'Kormatt' (F/Patio) | CSBt |
| | 'Saint Catherine' (Ra) | CFee |
| | Saint Cecilia = 'Ausmit'PBR (S) | LRHS MAus SMrm SWCr |
| | Saint Dunstan's Rose = 'Kirshru' (S) | MJon |
| | Saint Edmunds RosePBR | see *R.* Bonita |
| | Saint John = 'Harbilbo'PBR (F) | CSBt MRav |
| | Saint John's rose | see *R.* × *richardii* |
| | Saint Mark's rose | see *R.* 'Rose d'Amour' |
| | 'Saint Nicholas' (D) | CAbP MAus |
| | Saint Swithun = 'Auswith'PBR (S) | EBee ECnt LCro LRHS MAsh MAus MJon SSea SWCr |
| | 'Salet' (DPMo) | MAus WHCG |
| | 'Sally Holmes' (S) ♀H4 | EBee ECnt GCoc MAus MGan MJon MRav SMrm SPer SSea SWCr WAct WHCG |
| | Sally's Rose = 'Canrem' (HT) | EBee ECnt SWCr |
| | SalsaPBR | see *R.* Cheek to Cheek |
| | Salvation = 'Harlark'PBR **new** | ECnt ESty |
| | Samaritan = 'Harverag'PBR (HT) | CSBt ESty MRav SWCr |
| | ***sancta*** | see *R.* × *richardii* |
| | 'Sander's White Rambler' (Ra) ♀H4 | CRHN CSam CTri EBee EPfP LRHS LStr MAus MGan MJon MRav NLar SMad SPer SSea SWCr WAct WHCG |
| | Sandra = 'Carsandra' | EPfP SLon |
| | Sandra = 'Poulen055'PBR (Renaissance Series) (S) | LRHS SWCr |
| | 'Sanguinea' | see *R.* × *odorata* Sanguinea Group |
| | Sarah (HT) | see *R.* Jardins de Bagatelle |
| | 'Sarah van Fleet' (Ru) | CTri EBee ELon EPfP GCoc IArd LRHS LStr MAus MCot MGan MRav NLar SMad SPer SPla SWCr WAct WOVN |
| | Sarah, Duchess of YorkPBR | see *R.* Sunseeker |
| | Satin Abundance **new** | SWCr |
| | Savoy Hotel = 'Harvintage'PBR (HT) ♀H4 | CGro CSBt ECnt LStr MAus MGan MRav SMrm SPer SWCr |
| § | 'Scabrosa' (Ru) ♀H4 | EBee ECnt GCoc GKir LAst LRHS MAsh MAus MGan MJon NLar SLon SPer SPoG SSea SWCr WAct WHCG WOVN |
| | Scarborough Fair = 'Ausoran' (S) | MAus SWCr |

| | | |
|---|---|---|
| | Scarlet Fire | see *R.* 'Scharlachglut' |
| | Scarlet Glow | see *R.* 'Scharlachglut' |
| | Scarlet Hit = 'Poulmo'$^{PBR}$ (PatioHit Series) (P) | ECnt MAsh SWCr |
| | Scarlet Patio = 'Kortingle'$^{PBR}$ (Patio) | ESty LRHS MAsh SPoG SWCr |
| | Scarlet Queen Elizabeth = 'Dicel' (F) | CBcs MRav |
| | 'Scented Abundance' (F) | SWCr |
| | 'Scented Air' (F) | MGan |
| | Scented Carpet = 'Chewground'$^{PBR}$ (GC) | ECnt SMrm SWCr |
| | Scented Memory = 'Poulht002'$^{PBR}$ (HT) | ECnt |
| | Scentimental = 'Wekplapep'$^{PBR}$ (F) | ESty MAsh SCoo SSea SWCr |
| | 'Scentsation' (Min) | SMrm |
| | Scent-sation = 'Fryromeo'$^{PBR}$ (HT) | CWSG GCoc LGod LRHS MAsh MGan MRav NPri SCoo SPoG SWCr |
| | Scepter'd Isle = 'Ausland'$^{PBR}$ (S) ♀$^{H4}$ | CSBt EBee ECnt LRHS LStr MAsh MAus SCoo SPer SSea SWCr |
| § | 'Scharlachglut' (ClS) ♀$^{H4}$ | CPou EWTr LRHS MAus MCot MGan MRav SPer SWCr WAct WHCG WOVN |
| * | ***schmidtiana*** | CFee |
| | 'Schneelicht' (Ru) | MAus |
| | Schneewittchen | see *R.* Iceberg |
| § | 'Schneezwerg' (Ru) ♀$^{H4}$ | CGro EBee GCoc MAus MGan MJon MRav NLar SPer SPla SSea SWCr WAct WHCG |
| | 'Schoolgirl' (Cl) | CBcs CGro CSBt CTri EBee ELan EPfP GCoc GKir LAst LRHS LStr MAsh MGan MJon MRav NPri SMad SPer SPoG SSea SWCr |
| | 'Scintillation' (S/GC) | MAus |
| | Scotch pink (PiH) | WAct |
| | Scotch rose | see *R. spinosissima* |
| | Scotch yellow (PiH) | see *R.* x *harisonii* 'Williams Double Yellow' |
| | 'Seagull' (Ra) ♀$^{H4}$ | CGro CTri CWSG ECnt EPfP ESty LAst LGod LRHS LStr MAsh MGan MJon MRav NPri NWea SLon SMrm SPer SPla SPoG SSea SWCr WHCG WHer |
| | 'Seale Pink Diamond' (S) **new** | SSea |
| | 'Sealing Wax' (*moyesii* hybrid) | NLar WAct |
| | Selfridges = 'Korpriwa' (HT) | MJon |
| | 'Semiplena' | see *R.* x *alba* 'Alba Semiplena' |
| | ***sericea*** (S) | CFee GBin MAus WHCG |
| | - CC 3306 | WRos |
| | - SDR 3969 **new** | GKev |
| | - var. ***morrisonensis*** B&SWJ 7139 | WCru |
| § | - subsp. ***omeiensis*** BWJ 7550 | WCru |
| | - - f. ***pteracantha*** (S) | ELan EPfP EWTr GGar MAus MGan MRav NLar NWea SMad SPer SPoG SSea SWCr WAct WOVN |
| | - - - 'Atrosanguinea' (S) | CArn |
| | ***sertata*** | GAuc |
| § | ***setigera*** | MAus |
| | ***setipoda*** (S) | MAus WAct WFar WHCG |
| | seven sisters rose | see *R. multiflora* 'Grevillei' |
| | Seventh Heaven = 'Fryfantasy'$^{PBR}$ (HT) | GCoc SWCr |
| | Sexy Rexy = 'Macrexy'$^{PBR}$ (F) ♀$^{H4}$ | CGro CSBt EPfP ESty GCoc LAst LBMP LRHS LSRN LStr MAsh MAus MBri MGan MJon MLan MRav SMrm SPer SWCr |
| | 'Shailer's White Moss' | see *R.* x *centifolia* 'Shailer's White Moss' |
| | Sharifa Asma = 'Ausreef'$^{PBR}$ (S) | CSBt EBee ELan ELon LCro LRHS LStr MAus MBNS MRav SLon SMrm SPer SWCr WAct |
| | Sheila's Perfume = 'Harsherry'$^{PBR}$ (HT/F) | EBee ECnt ESty GCoc LStr MGan MJon MRav SPer SWCr |
| | Shine On = 'Dictalent'$^{PBR}$ (Patio) ♀$^{H4}$ | CSBt ECnt ESty IDic MAsh MRav SPoG SWCr |
| | Shining Light = 'Cocshimmer'$^{PBR}$ (Patio) | GCoc SCoo SWCr |
| | Shocking Blue = 'Korblue' (F) | CSBt MGan MJon SPer SWCr |
| | Shona = 'Dicdrum' (F) | IDic |
| | 'Shot Silk' (HT) | CSBt MGan SWCr |
| | Showtime = 'Baitime' **new** | MAsh SWCr |
| | Shrimp Hit = 'Poulshrimp'$^{PBR}$ (Patio) | ECnt MAsh |
| | 'Shropshire Lass' (S) | LRHS MAus |
| § | Silver Anniversary = 'Poulari'$^{PBR}$ (HT) ♀$^{H4}$ | CGro CSBt CTri EBee ECnt ELan GCoc LAst LCro LGod LRHS LStr MAsh MAus MGan MGos MJon MRav NPri SCoo SPer SPoG SSea SWCr |
| | Silver Anniversary ambig. | LSRN |
| | Silver Ghost = 'Kormifari' (S) | MGos |
| | 'Silver Jubilee' (HT) ♀$^{H4}$ | CBcs CGro CSBt EBee EPfP ESty GCoc IArd LBMP LGod LRHS LStr MAsh MAus MGan MJon MLan MRav SPer SVic SWCr |
| | 'Silver Lining' (HT) | SWCr |
| | 'Silver Moon' (Cl) | CRHN |
| | 'Silver Wedding' (HT) | CWSG ELan GCoc IArd LAst MAus MHav MLan MRav NBir NWea SMrm SPer SVic SWCr |
| | 'Silver Wedding Celebration' (F) | CTri ESty |
| | Silver Wishes$^{PBR}$ | see *R.* Pink Hit |
| | Simba = 'Korbelma' (HT) | MGan |
| | 'Simplex Multiflora' | CWib |
| | Simply Heaven = 'Diczombie'$^{PBR}$ (HT) | ESty GCoc IDic SWCr |
| § | Simply the Best = 'Macamster'$^{PBR}$ (HT) | CGro CSBt EBls ECnt ELan ESty GCoc LGod LRHS LStr MAsh MAus MGos MJon MRav NPri SCoo SMrm SPer SPoG SWCr |
| § | Singin' in the Rain = 'Macivy' (F) | MJon |
| | ***sinowilsonii*** | see *R. longicuspis* var. *sinowilsonii* |
| | 'Sir Cedric Morris' (Ra) | EBee SSea SWCr WAct |
| | Sir Clough = 'Ausclough' (S) | MAus |
| | Sir Edward Elgar = 'Ausprima'$^{PBR}$ (S) | LStr MAus |
| I | 'Sir Galahad' white-flowered (F) | MRav |
| | 'Sir Joseph Paxton' (Bb) | CAbP MAus |
| | 'Sir Paul Smith' (Cl) **new** | EBls |
| | Sir Walter Raleigh = 'Ausspry' (S) | MAus MRav SMrm |
| | Sister Elizabeth = 'Auspalette' (S) **new** | MAsh SCoo SWCr |
| | 'Skyrocket' | see *R.* 'Wilhelm' |
| | Smarty = 'Intersmart' (S/GC) | CAbP MAus SPer WAct |
| | 'Smooth Angel' (HT) | MGan |
| | Smooth Lady = 'Hadlady' (HT) | MGan |
| | Smooth Melody = 'Hadmelody' (F) | LAst |
| | Smooth Prince = 'Hadprince' (HT) | LAst |

| | |
|---|---|
| 'Smooth Velvet' (HT) | LAst |
| Snow Carpet = 'Maccarpe' (Min/GC) | ELan MAus MJon SSea |
| 'Snow Dwarf' | see *R.* 'Schneezwerg' |
| Snow Goose = 'Auspom'PBR (Cl/S) | CSBt CSRo LRHS MAus MBri SSea SWCr |
| Snow Hit = 'Poulsnows'PBR (Min/Patio) | ECnt LRHS SWCr |
| 'Snow Queen' | see *R.* 'Frau Karl Druschki' |
| Snow Sunblaze = 'Meigovin' (Min) | CSBt MRav SPer SPoG |
| Snowball = 'Macangeli' (Min/GC) | MJon |
| Snowcap = 'Harfleet'PBR (Patio) | ESty SPoG |
| 'Snowdon' (Ru) | LRHS MAus |
| 'Snowdrift' W.R. Smith (Ra) | WHCG |
| 'Snowflake' (Ra) | WHCG |
| 'Soldier Boy' (Cl) | SWCr WHCG |
| Solitaire = 'Macyefre'PBR (HT) | MJon |
| § Solo Mio = 'Poulen002'PBR (Renaissance Series) (S) | CTri ECnt LRHS SPla SWCr |
| § 'Sombreuil' (ClT) | EBee EPfP IArd LRHS MAsh MAus MRav NLar SPer SPla SSea SWCr WAct WHCG |
| Something Special = 'Macwyo'PBR (HT) | EBee ECnt ESty GCoc MJon SWCr |
| Song and Dance (HT) **new** | ESty GCoc |
| § Songs of Praise = 'Harkimono'PBR (Abundance Series) (F) | ESty SWCr |
| Sonia | see *R.* Sweet Promise |
| 'Sophia'PBR | see *R.* Solo Mio |
| 'Sophie's Perpetual' (ClCh) | CPou LRHS MAus MGan SLon SPer SWCr WAct WHCG |
| Sophy's Rose = 'Auslot'PBR (S) | ESty LRHS LStr MAus MBri MJon SPer SSea SWCr |
| ***soulieana*** (Ra/S) ♀H3-4 | MAus WAct WKif |
| 'Soupert et Notting' (DPoMo) | LRHS MAus MRav SPer SWCr WAct |
| 'Southampton' (F) ♀H4 | EPfP LStr MAsh MAus MRav SPer SSea SWCr |
| 'Souvenir d'Alphonse Lavallée' (ClHP) | WHCG |
| 'Souvenir de Brod' | see *R.* 'Erinnerung an Brod' |
| 'Souvenir de Claudius Denoyel' (ClHT) | MAus MGan SPer WAct |
| 'Souvenir de la Malmaison' (ClBb) | see *R.* 'Climbing Souvenir de la Malmaison' |
| 'Souvenir de la Malmaison' (Bb) | GCoc MAus MGan MRav NLar SPer SWCr WAct |
| Souvenir de Louis Amade = 'Delilac' (S) | MRav |
| 'Souvenir de Madame Léonie Viennot' (ClT) | CPou EBee MAus MRav SPoG SWCr |
| 'Souvenir de Saint Anne's' (Bb) | EWTr MAus SWCr WAct WHCG |
| 'Souvenir di Castagneto' (HP) | MRav |
| 'Souvenir du Docteur Jamain' (ClHP) | CPou EBee ELan ELon ESty EWTr LStr MAus MGan MRav NLar SMrm SPer SPoG SSea SWCr WAct WHCG WKif |
| Spangles = 'Ganspa'PBR (F) | MGan NHaw |
| 'Spanish Beauty' | see *R.* 'Madame Grégoire Staechelin' |
| Sparkling Scarlet = 'Meihati' (ClF) | ELan MAsh |
| Sparkling Yellow = 'Poulgode'PBR (GC/S) | SWCr |
| Special Anniversary = 'Whastiluc'PBR (HT) | CGro EPfP ESty GCoc LRHS MAsh MBri NPri SCoo SMrm SPoG SWCr |
| Special Child = 'Tanaripsa' | LStr SWCr |
| Special Friend = 'Kirspec'PBR (Patio) | ESty GCoc LStr MJon |
| Special Occasion = 'Fryyoung'PBR (HT) | ESty GCoc MGos MRav SMrm SWCr |
| 'Spectabilis' (Ra) | EWTr WHCG |
| Spek's Centennial (F) | see *R.* Singin' in the Rain |
| SpellboundPBR | see *R.* Garden News |
| 'Spencer' misapplied | see *R.* 'Enfant de France' |
| Spice of Life = 'Diccheeky'PBR (F/Patio) | IDic |
| § ***spinosissima*** | CDul EBee EMac GKir LBuc LRHS MAus MGan NHaw NWea SPer SSea WAct WHCG WOVN |
| - 'Andrewsii' ♀H4 | MAus MRav WAct |
| § - double pink-flowered | WBor |
| § - double white-flowered | CNat ECha GCoc IGor MAus WAct |
| - 'Dunwich Rose' | EBee EPfP LRHS MAus MCot MGan MJon SPer SWCr WAct WHCG |
| - 'Falkland' | ECha GCra MAus |
| - 'Glory of Edzell' | MAus |
| § - 'Grandiflora' | MAus |
| - 'Marbled Pink' | MAus |
| - 'Mary, Queen of Scots' | MAus MGan SRms WAct |
| - 'Mrs Colville' | MAus |
| - 'Ormiston Roy' | MAus |
| - 'Robbie' | WAct |
| - 'Single Cherry' | MAus SSea |
| - 'Variegata' (v) | CArn |
| - 'William III' | EWes GCra MAus SLPl |
| Spirit of Freedom = 'Ausbite'PBR (S) | ESty LRHS MAsh MAus SSea SWCr |
| § 'Splendens' (Ra) | EBee SLPl SWCr WAct |
| Saint Helena = 'Canlish' (F) | ECnt |
| 'Stanwell Perpetual' (PiH) | CSam EBee EPfP GCoc LStr MCot MRav NLar SEND SMrm SPer SSea SWCr WAct WHCG WOVN |
| 'Star of Waltham' (HP) | SWCr WHCG |
| 'Star Performer'PBR (ClPatio) | CSBt EBee ECnt ESty MAsh MJon SSea SWCr |
| Stardust = 'Peavandyke'PBR (Patio/F) | ESty MJon SWCr |
| Starina = 'Megabi' (Min) | MGan SWCr |
| Starlight Express = 'Trobstar'PBR (Cl) | MAsh SCoo SPer SPoG SWCr |
| Starry Eyed = 'Horcoexist' (Patio) | MGan SWCr |
| 'Stars 'n' Stripes' (Min) | LGod MAus |
| Stella (HT) | MGan SWCr |
| ***stellata*** | MAus |
| § - var. ***mirifica*** | EBee MAus MGan SSea SWCr |
| 'Sterling Silver' (HT) | MGan SWCr |
| Sting = 'Meimater'PBR | SWCr |
| Strawberries and Cream = 'Geestraw' (Min/Patio) | ELan ESty |
| Strawberry Fayre = 'Arowillip'PBR (Min/Patio) | ESty MRav SPoG |
| Strawberry Hill = 'Ausrimini' (S) **new** | MAsh SCoo SWCr |
| § Sue Hipkin = 'Harzazz'PBR (HT) | ESty MRav SWCr |
| Suffolk = 'Kormixal'PBR (S/GC) | CGro CSBt ELan GCoc LStr MAus MGan MRav SPer SSea SWCr WAct |
| ***suffulta*** | see *R. arkansana* var. *suffulta* |
| Sugar and Spice = 'Peaallure'PBR (Patio) | SPoG |
| Sugar Baby = 'Tanabagus'PBR (Patio) | ESty SWCr |

| | | |
|---|---|---|
| | Sugar 'n' Spice = 'Tinspice' (Min) | MRav |
| | Suma = 'Harsuma' (GC) | ESty MJon SMrm SWCr WAct |
| | Summer Breeze = 'Korelasting'PBR (Cl) | MGos |
| | Summer Dream = 'Frymaxicot'PBR (F) | CSBt |
| | Summer Fever = 'Tan99106' (Patio) | SWCr |
| | Summer Fragrance = 'Tanfudermos'PBR (HT) | CSBt ESty GCoc SWCr |
| § | Summer Gold = 'Poulreb'PBR (F) | ECnt EPfP SWCr |
| | 'Summer Holiday' (HT) | SPer SWCr |
| | Summer Memories = 'Koruteli' (Palace Series) (F) | MGos |
| | Summer Palace = 'Poulcape'PBR (F/Patio) | ECnt |
| | Summer Snow = 'Weopop' (Patio) | MJon |
| | Summer Song = 'Austango' (S) | LRHS MAus |
| | Summer Wine = 'Korizont'PBR (Cl) ♀H4 | CSBt EBee ECnt GKir LRHS MAsh MGan MGos MJon NPri SCoo SPer SPoG SWCr |
| | Summertime = 'Chewlarmoll'PBR (Patio/Cl) | CGro CSBt EBee ECnt ELan GCoc LGod LRHS LStr MAsh MGan MGos MJon MRav NPri SCoo SMrm SPer SPoG SWCr |
| | Sun Hit = 'Poulsun'PBR (PatioHit Series) (Patio) | CSBt ECnt MAsh MRav SWCr |
| | 'Sunblaze'PBR | see *R.* Orange Sunblaze = 'Meijikatar' |
| | Sunblest = 'Landora' (HT) | LRHS MAsh MRav SPoG SWCr |
| | 'Sunny Abundance' | SWCr |
| | Sunrise = 'Kormarter'PBR (Cl) | ESty MBri SWCr |
| § | Sunseeker = 'Dicracer'PBR (F/Patio) | EPfP IDic LRHS MAsh MRav SPoG SWCr |
| § | Sunset Boulevard = 'Harbabble'PBR (F) ♀H4 | CSBt EBee ECnt LGod LStr MAsh MAus MBri MGan MRav SCoo SPer SWCr |
| | Sunset CelebrationPBR | see *R.* Warm Wishes = 'Fryxotic' |
| | 'Sunshine' (Poly) | MGan |
| | 'Sunsilk' (F) | SWCr |
| | Sunsplash = 'Cocweaver'PBR (F) | GCoc MRav SMrm SWCr |
| | Super Dorothy = 'Heldoro' (Ra) | MAus MJon SSea SWCr |
| | Super Elfin = 'Helkleger'PBR (Ra) ♀H4 | LStr MGan MJon MRav SMrm SPer SSea SWCr |
| | Super Excelsa = 'Helexa' (Ra) | ESty LStr MAus MGan MJon SSea SWCr |
| | Super Fairy = 'Helsufair'PBR (Ra) | EBee ECnt LStr MAus MGan MJon MRav SPer SSea SWCr |
| § | Super Sparkle = 'Helfels'PBR (Ra) | ECnt LStr SSea SWCr |
| § | Super Star = 'Tanorstar' (HT) | LStr MGan MJon MRav SWCr |
| | 'Surpasse Tout' (G) | MAus SWCr |
| § | 'Surpassing Beauty of Woolverstone' (ClHP) | WHCG |
| | Surprise = 'Presur'PBR (Fs/HT) | SWCr |
| | Surrey = 'Korlanum'PBR (GC) ♀H4 | CSBt ECnt ELan ESty LCro LGod LStr MAus MGan MRav NLar SMrm SPer SPla SPoG SSea SWCr WAct |
| | Susan = 'Poulsue' (S) | ECnt SWCr |
| | Sussex = 'Poulave'PBR (GC) | CSBt GCoc LStr MGan MRav NPri SPer SPoG SWCr |
| | 'Sutter's Gold' (HT) | MAus MGan |
| | Swan = 'Auswhite' (S) | MAus |

| | | |
|---|---|---|
| | Swan Lake = 'Macmed' (Cl) | ECnt ELan EPfP LGod LStr MGan MHav MRav NPri SPer SWCr |
| | Swany = 'Meiburenac' (Min/GC) ♀H4 | ESty LSRN MAus MGan SPer SWCr WHCG |
| | Sweet Cover = 'Poulweeto'PBR (Towne & Country Series) | SWCr |
| | Sweet Dream = 'Fryminicot'PBR (Patio) ♀H4 | CGro CSBt CTri ECnt ELan EPfP ESty GCoc LAst LGod LRHS LStr MAsh MAus MBri MGan MJon MRav NPri SMrm SPer SPla SPoG SSea SWCr |
| | 'Sweet Fairy' (Min) | CSBt |
| | Sweet Haze = 'Tan97274'PBR **new** | CSBt ESty LGod LStr MGan |
| | Sweet Juliet = 'Ausleap'PBR (S) | CSBt CSRo CWSG ESty LGod LRHS MAus MCot MJon SMrm SPer SWCr |
| * | 'Sweet Lemon Dream' (Patio) | CTri |
| | Sweet Magic = 'Dicmagic'PBR (Min/Patio) ♀H4 | CGro CSBt CTri EPfP IDic LRHS LStr MAsh MBri MGan MJon MRav NPri SMrm SPla SPoG SWCr |
| | Sweet Memories = 'Whamemo' (Patio) | CTri ECnt EPfP ESty GCoc LGod LRHS LStr MAsh MJon MRav NPri SCoo SMrm SPer SPla SPoG SWCr |
| § | Sweet Promise = 'Meihelvet' (GC) | MGan SPer |
| | Sweet Remembrance = 'Kirr' (HT) | LStr MJon SWCr |
| | 'Sweet Repose' (F) | MGan |
| | 'Sweet Revelation'PBR | see *R.* Sue Hipkin = 'Harzazz' |
| | Sweet Symphonie = 'Meibarke'PBR (Patio) | SWCr |
| | 'Sweet Velvet' (F) | MGan |
| | 'Sweet Wonder' (Patio) | EPfP MAsh SMrm SPoG SWCr |
| N | Sweetheart = 'Cocapeer' (HT) | GCoc MBri |
| | 'Sweetie' (Patio) | SWCr |
| | ***sweginzowii*** | GAuc MAus |
| | 'Sydonie' (HP) | SWCr WHCG |
| | 'Sympathie' (ClHT) | MGan MGos SMrm SPer SSea |
| | Tall Story = 'Dickooky'PBR (F) ♀H4 | IDic MJon SWCr WHCG WOVN |
| | Tamora = 'Austamora' (S) | MAus |
| | Tango = 'Macfirwal' (F) | MJon |
| | Tango = 'Poulyc005'PBR (Cl/Patio) | SWCr |
| | Tango Showground = 'Chewpattens' (GC) **new** | SSea |
| | Tapis Jaune | see *R.* Golden Penny |
| | Tatoo = 'Poulyc002'PBR (Cl/Patio) | ECnt SWCr |
| | Tatton = 'Fryentice'PBR (F) | EBls ESty MAus MJon SWCr |
| | Tawny Tiger = 'Frygolly'PBR (F) | ESty GCoc |
| | Tea Clipper = 'Ausrover' (S) **new** | MAsh SCoo |
| | Tear Drop = 'Dicomo'PBR (Min/Patio) | IDic LStr MGan SWCr |
| | Teasing Georgia = 'Ausbaker'PBR (S) | EBee ECnt EPfP ESty LCro LRHS MAus MBri MJon SCoo SMrm SSea SWCr |
| | 'Telstar' (F) | MGan |
| | Temptress = 'Korramalu'PBR (Cl) | MAsh MGos MJon |
| | Tenacious = 'Macblackpo'PBR (F) | ESty LStr |
| | Tequila Sunrise = 'Dicobey'PBR (HT) ♀H4 | CGro CTri ECnt ELan EPfP ESty IDic LRHS LStr MAsh MAus MGan MJon MRav SMrm SPer SPoG SWCr |
| § | Terracotta = 'Meicobuis'PBR (HT) | ESty SMrm SWCr |

| | | |
|---|---|---|
| | Tess of the d'Urbervilles = 'Ausmove'$^{PBR}$ (S) | LCro LRHS LStr MAus MBri SCoo SWCr |
| | 'Tessa' (F) | MGan SWCr |
| | Thank You = 'Chesdeep'$^{PBR}$ (Patio) | ESty LStr MGan SWCr |
| § | That's Jazz = 'Poulnorm'$^{PBR}$ (Courtyard Series) (ClF) | EBee ECnt LRHS MAsh MJon SMrm SWCr |
| | The Alexandra Rose = 'Ausday'$^{PBR}$ (S) | LRHS MAus SMrm |
| | The Attenborough Rose = 'Dicelope'$^{PBR}$ (F) | IDic SWCr |
| | 'The Bishop' (CexG) | MAus |
| | 'The Bishop of Bradford' (ClPiH) | ECnt |
| | The Care Rose = 'Horapsunmolbabe' (Patio) | SWCr |
| | The Compass Rose = 'Korwisco'$^{PBR}$ (S) | MGos SPer |
| | The Countryman = 'Ausman'$^{PBR}$ (S) | ELon LRHS MAus SSea SWCr |
| | The Dark Lady = 'Ausbloom'$^{PBR}$ (S) | LRHS MAus SPer SWCr |
| | 'The Doctor' (HT) | MGan |
| | The Dove = 'Tanamola'$^{PBR}$ (F) | MGan |
| | 'The Ednaston Rose' (Cl) | WHCG |
| § | 'The Fairy' (Poly) $\Upsilon^{H4}$ | CSBt CTri EBee ECnt ELan EPfP EWTr LAst LBMP LGod LStr MAsh MAus MGan MJon MRav SMrm SPer SPla SSea SWCr WAct WCFE WHCG WOVN |
| | 'The Garland' (Ra) $\Upsilon^{H4}$ | CRHN EBee EWTr LRHS MAsh MAus NLar SPer SWCr WHCG |
| | The Generous Gardener = 'Ausdrawn'$^{PBR}$ (S) | CSRo EPfP LCro LRHS MAsh MAus SCoo SWCr |
| | The Gold Award Rose = 'Poulac008' (Palace Series) (Patio) | ECnt |
| § | The Halcyon Days Rose = 'Korparesni'$^{PBR}$ (F) | MGos |
| | The Herbalist = 'Aussemi' (S) | LRHS MAus SSea |
| | The Ingenious Mr Fairchild = 'Austijus'$^{PBR}$ (S) | LCro MAus SCoo SWCr |
| | The Jubilee Rose = 'Poulbrido'$^{PBR}$ (F) | ECnt SCoo |
| | 'The Lister Rose' (F) | MGan |
| | The Maidstone Rose = 'Kordauerpa' | SCoo |
| | 'The Margaret Coppola Rose'$^{PBR}$ | see *R.* White Gold = 'Cocquiriam' |
| | The Mayflower = 'Austilly'$^{PBR}$ (S) | CSBt CSRo LCro LRHS MAsh MAus MBri MJon SSea SWCr |
| § | The McCartney Rose = 'Meizeli'$^{PBR}$ (HT) | LStr MHav MJon SDix SPer SWCr |
| | 'The New Dawn' | see *R.* 'New Dawn' |
| | The Nun = 'Ausnun' (S) | MAus |
| | The Painter = 'Mactemaik'$^{PBR}$ (F) | LStr MJon SSea |
| § | The Pilgrim = 'Auswalker'$^{PBR}$ (S) | CSBt CSam EPfP ESty LRHS LStr MAus MBri MJon SMrm SPer SPla SSea SWCr WHCG |
| | The Prince = 'Ausvelvet'$^{PBR}$ (S) | LRHS LStr MAus MBNS NLar SPer SSea |
| | The Prince's Trust = 'Harholding'$^{PBR}$ (Cl) | LStr MBri MJon |
| | 'The Prioress' (S) | MAus |
| § | 'The Queen Elizabeth' (F) | CBcs CGro CSBt CTri CWSG ECnt GCoc LGod LStr MAsh MBri MGan MJon MRav NPri SEND SPer SPoG SWCr |
| | The Reeve = 'Ausreeve' (S) | MAus |
| | The Rotarian | see *R.* Rotary Sunrise |
| I | 'The Rugby Rose' (HT) | MGan SWCr |
| | The Scotsman = 'Poulscots'$^{PBR}$ (HT) | GCoc SWCr |
| | The Shepherdess = 'Austwist' | MAus SSea |
| | The Soham Rose$^{PBR}$ | see *R.* Pearl Abundance |
| | The Soroptimist Rose = 'Benstar' (Patio) | MJon |
| | The Squire = 'Ausquire' (S) | MAus |
| | The Times Rose = 'Korpeahn'$^{PBR}$ (F) $\Upsilon^{H4}$ | EBee ECnt LGod LStr MAus MGan MJon MRav SPer |
| | 'Thelma' (Ra) | MAus |
| | 'Thérèse Bugnet' (Ru) | MAus NHaw |
| | Thinking of You =) 'Frydandy'$^{PBR}$ (HT | ESty GCoc LGod LRHS LStr MAsh MGan NPri SWCr |
| | 'Thisbe' (HM) | MAus SPer WAct WHCG |
| | Thomas Barton = 'Meihirvin' (HT) | LStr SWCr |
| | 'Thoresbyana' | see *R.* 'Bennett's Seedling' |
| | 'Thoughts of You' (Patio) | SWCr |
| | 'Threave' (B) | EBee SWCr WHCG |
| | Three Cheers = 'Dicdomino'$^{PBR}$ (F) | IDic |
| | threepenny bit rose | see *R. elegantula* 'Persetosa' |
| | Thumbs Up = 'Hornothing' (S) **new** | EBls |
| | ***tibetica*** | GAuc |
| | Tickled Pink = 'Fryhunky' (F) | CGro CSBt EBee EBls ECnt ESty GCoc LGod MAsh MGan NPri SCoo SMrm SPer SPoG SWCr |
| | Tigris = 'Harprier' (*persica* hybrid) (S) | WAct |
| | Times Past = 'Harhilt'$^{PBR}$ (Cl) | ESty GCoc LStr MGan MJon MRav SPoG SWCr |
| | 'Tina Turner' (HT) | MJon |
| | Tintinara = 'Dicuptight'$^{PBR}$ (HT) | ECnt IDic |
| | Tip Top = 'Tanope' (F/Patio) | CBcs MGan SPer |
| | 'Tipo Ideale' | see *R.* x *odorata* 'Mutabilis' |
| | Titanic = 'Macdako'$^{PBR}$ (F) | MJon |
| | 'Toby Tristam' (Ra) | CRHN |
| | Together Forever = 'Dicecho'$^{PBR}$ (F) | GCoc IDic |
| | 'Tom Foster' (HT) | MJon |
| | 'Tom Marshall' | WHCG |
| | 'Tom Tom' (F) **new** | NBlu |
| | ***tomentosa*** | CSec |
| | Too Hot to Handle = 'Macloupri' (S/Cl) | MJon SSea |
| | Top Marks = 'Fryministar'$^{PBR}$ (Min/Patio) | CGro CSBt CTri GCoc LGod LStr MGan MJon MRav NPri SCoo SPer SWCr |
| | Topaz Jewel$^{PBR}$ | see *R.* Yellow Dagmar Hastrup = 'Moryelrug' |
| | Topkapi Palace = 'Poulthe'$^{PBR}$ (Palace Series) (F) | ECnt |
| | Toprose = 'Cocgold'$^{PBR}$ (F) | GCoc MAsh |
| | 'Topsi' (F/Patio) | SPer |
| § | 'Tour de Malakoff' (Ce) | CPou CSBt LRHS MAus MRav NLar SPer SWCr WAct WHCG WKif |
| | Tournament of Roses = 'Jacient' (HT) | MJon |
| | Tower Bridge = 'Haravis' (HT) | ESty |
| | 'Trade Winds' (HT) | MGan SWCr |
| | Tradescant = 'Ausdir'$^{PBR}$ (S) | LRHS MAus |
| | Tradition$^{PBR}$ | see *R.* Tradition '95 |

| | | |
|---|---|---|
| § | Tradition '95 = 'Korkeltin'[PBR] (Cl) ♀H4 | MGos |
| | 'Treasure Trove' (Ra) | CRHN LRHS MAus MGan MJon NLar SMrm SWCr WAct |
| | Trevor Griffiths = 'Ausold'[PBR] (S) | MAus |
| | 'Tricolore de Flandre' (G) | MAus |
| | 'Trier' (Ra) | CPou MAus SWCr WHCG |
| | 'Trigintipetala' misapplied | see *R.* 'Professeur Emile Perrot' |
| | 'Triomphe de l'Exposition' (HP) | MAus |
| | 'Triomphe du Luxembourg' (T) | MAus |
| | ***triphylla*** | see *R.* x *beanii* |
| | Troika = 'Poumidor' (HT) ♀H4 | CSBt ELan LRHS LStr MAsh MAus MGan MRav NBlu SPer SPoG SWCr |
| | Troilus = 'Ausoil' (S) | MAus |
| | 'Tropicana' | see *R.* Super Star |
| | Trumpeter = 'Mactru' (F) ♀H4 | CSBt EBee ECnt IArd LRHS LStr MAsh MAus MBri MGan MJon MRav SPer SPoG SWCr |
| | 'Tuscany' (G) | GCoc MAus SPer WAct WHCG |
| | 'Tuscany Superb' (G) ♀H4 | CPou CSBt CSam EBee EPfP EWTr ISea LAst LCro LRHS MAus MCot MGan MRav NLar SEND SMrm SPer SSea SWCr WAct WHCG WKif |
| | Twenty-one Again! = 'Meinimo'[PBR] (HT) | SWCr |
| | Twice in a Blue Moon = 'Tan96138'[PBR] (HT) | EBee EBls ECnt ESty LGod LRHS MAsh MJon MRav SCoo SMrm SWCr |
| | Twist = 'Poulstri'[PBR] (Courtyard Series) (ClPatio) | CGro ECnt ESty MAsh |
| | Tynwald = 'Mattwyt' (HT) | LStr MGos MJon SPer |
| | 'Ulrich Brünner Fils' (HP) | MAus |
| | Uncle Walter = 'Macon' (HT) | SMrm SWCr |
| | UNICEF = 'Cocjojo'[PBR] (F) | GCoc |
| | 'Unique Blanche' | see *R.* x *centifolia* 'Unique' |
| | Valencia = 'Koreklia'[PBR] (HT) ♀H4 | CSBt ECnt MAus |
| | Valentine Heart = 'Dicogle'[PBR] (F) ♀H4 | CSBt ESty IArd IDic LRHS MAsh MAus MBri MRav SWCr |
| | Valiant Heart = 'Poulberg' (F) | ECnt |
| | Vanilla Twist = 'Dicghost' (F) **new** | IDic |
| | 'Vanity' (HM) | MAus |
| | 'Variegata di Bologna' (Bb) | EPfP EWTr LRHS MAus MRav SLon SSea SWCr WAct |
| | Variety Club = 'Haredge' (Patio) | LGod |
| | 'Veilchenblau' (Ra) ♀H4 | CRHN CSBt EBee ECnt ELan EPfP EWTr LAst LCro LGod LRHS LStr MAus MGan MRav NLar NPri SMrm SPer SPoG SSea SWCr WAct WHCG WKif |
| | Velvet Abundance (F) **new** | SPoG |
| | Velvet Fragrance = 'Fryperdee'[PBR] (HT) | CSBt EBee ECnt ESty GCoc LRHS LStr MAus MBri MGan MJon MRav SMrm SWCr |
| | 'Venusta Pendula' (Ra) | MAus |
| | 'Verschuren' (HT/v) | MJon |
| | ***versicolor*** | see *R. gallica* 'Versicolor' |
| | Versigny = 'Masversi' (Generosa Series) (S) | MRav |
| | 'Vick's Caprice' (HP) | MAus SWCr |
| | 'Vicomtesse Pierre du Fou' (ClHT) | MAus |
| | 'Victor Madeley' (F) | MGan |
| | Vidal Sassoon = 'Macjuliat'[PBR] (HT) | MGan MJon SWCr |
| | 'Village Maid' | see *R.* x *centifolia* 'Unique Panachée' |
| § | ***villosa*** L. | CArn MAus WAct |
| | - 'Duplex' | see *R.* 'Duplex' |
| § | 'Violacea' (G) | EBee LRHS MAus WAct WHCG |
| | 'Violette' (Ra) | CPou CRHN EBee EWTr MAus SPer SWCr WAct WHCG |
| | ***virginiana*** ♀H4 | CFee GAuc GCal MAus MGan MSte NHaw NWea SPer SWCr WAct WHCG |
| | - 'Harvest Song' | NHaw |
| | - 'Plena' | see *R.* 'Rose d'Amour' |
| | 'Viridiflora' | see *R.* x *odorata* 'Viridiflora' |
| | Waltz = 'Poulkrid'[PBR] (Courtyard Series) (ClPatio) | ECnt LRHS MAsh SWCr |
| | 'Waltz Time' (HT) **new** | NBlu |
| | Wandering Minstrel = 'Harquince' (F) | SWCr |
| | ***wardii*** var. ***culta*** | MAus |
| | Warm Welcome = 'Chewizz'[PBR] (ClMin) ♀H4 | CGro ECnt EPfP ESty LCro LGod LRHS LStr MAsh MAus MBri MGan MGos MJon MRav SMad SMrm SPer SPoG SSea SWCr |
| § | Warm Wishes = 'Fryxotic'[PBR] (HT) ♀H4 | CSBt EBee ECnt ESty GCoc LGod LRHS LSRN LStr MAsh MAus MGan MGos MHav MJon MRav NPri SMrm SPoG SWCr |
| | 'Warrior' (F) | MGan SPer |
| | Warwick Castle = 'Auslian'[PBR] (S) | MAus |
| | Warwickshire = 'Korkandel'[PBR] (GC) | SPer SWCr |
| | ***webbiana*** | MAus WHCG |
| | Wedding Celebration = 'Poulht006' (HT) | ECnt |
| | 'Wedding Day' (Ra) | Widely available |
| | Wee Cracker = 'Cocmarris'[PBR] (Patio) | GCoc LGod |
| | Wee Jock = 'Cocabest' (F/Patio) | GCoc SWCr |
| | 'Weetwood' (Ra) | CRHN SPer |
| | Weisse Wolcke[PBR] | see *R.* White Cloud = 'Korstacha' |
| | Welcome Home = 'Koraubala'[PBR] (F) | MGos |
| | 'Well Done' (Patio) | SPoG SWCr |
| | Well-Being = 'Harjangle'[PBR] (S) | ESty MJon SWCr |
| | 'Wendy Cussons' (HT) | CBcs CGro CTri CWSG GCoc MGan MJon MRav SPer SWCr |
| | Wenlock = 'Auswen' (S) | MAus SPer |
| | 'West Country Millennium' (F) | MGan |
| | Westerland = 'Korwest' (F/S) ♀H4 | MGan MJon SWCr WAct |
| | Where the Heart Is = 'Cocoplan'[PBR] (HT) | ESty GCoc |
| | 'Whisky Gill' (HT) | MGan |
| | Whisky Mac = 'Tanky' (HT) | CBcs CGro CSBt CTri CWSG ELan GCoc MGan MHav MJon MRav NPri SMrm SPer SPoG |
| | 'White Bath' | see *R.* x *centifolia* 'Shailer's White Moss' |
| | White Bells = 'Poulwhite'[PBR] (Min/GC) | MRav SPer |
| § | 'White Cécile Brünner' (Poly) | MAus WHCG |
| | 'White Christmas' (HT) | MGan SWCr |
| § | White Cloud = 'Korstacha'[PBR] (S/ClHT) ♀H4 | CSBt EBee ECnt EPfP ESty LGod LRHS MGos MJon SWCr WHCG |
| | White Cloud = 'Savacloud' (Min) | MBri |
| | 'White Cockade' (Cl) | EBee GCoc MGan SMrm SPer SWCr |
| | White Cover[PBR] | see *R.* Kent |

| | | |
|---|---|---|
| § | 'White de Meaux' (Ce) | MAus |
| | White Diamond = 'Interamon'PBR (S) | EBee ECnt IDic SWCr |
| § | White Gold = 'Cocquiriam'PBR (F) | GCoc MRav SMrm SPoG SWCr |
| | 'White Grootendorst' (Ru) | MAus SSea WAct |
| | White Knight (HT) | see *R.* Message = 'Meban' |
| | White Max GrafPBR | see *R.* x *jacksonii* White Max Graf = 'Korgram' |
| | white moss | see *R.* 'Comtesse de Murinais', *R.* x *centifolia* 'Shailer's White Moss' |
| § | 'White Pet' (Poly) 🏆H4 | CSBt EBee ECnt EPfP GCoc LGod LStr MAus MBri MCot MGan MJon MRav SEND SMrm SPer SPla SWCr WAct WKif |
| | white Provence | see *R.* x *centifolia* 'Unique' |
| | 'White Queen Elizabeth' (F) | SWCr |
| | white rose of York | see *R.* x *alba* 'Alba Semiplena' |
| | White Skyliner = 'Franwekwhit'PBR (ClS) | EBls MJon |
| | 'White Tausendschön' (Ra) | MAus |
| | 'White Wings' (HT) | EWTr MAus MGan SPer SWCr WAct WHCG WKif |
| | 'Whitson'PBR | see *R.* Pearl Anniversary = 'Whitston' |
| N | ***wichurana*** (Ra) | MAus MGan SWCr WHCG |
| | - 'Variegata' (Ra/v) | CBow CSWP |
| * | - 'Variegata Nana' (Ra/v) | MRav |
| | 'Wickwar' (Ra) | CSWP GCal GGal MSte WAct WHCG |
| | Wife of Bath = 'Ausbath' (S) | MAus |
| | Wild Edric = 'Aushedge' (Ru) | LRHS MAus SCoo SWCr |
| | Wild Rover **new** | ESty LStr |
| | Wild Thing = 'Dichirap' (S) **new** | IDic |
| | Wildeve = 'Ausbonny'PBR (S) | CSRo LCro LRHS MAus MBri SWCr |
| | Wildfire = 'Fryessex' (Patio) | ECnt ESty LGod LRHS MAsh MAus SWCr |
| § | 'Wilhelm' (HM) | MAus MRav SPer WHCG |
| | 'Will Scarlet' (HM) | MAus SSea |
| | 'William Allen Richardson' (N) | MAus WHCG |
| | 'William Cobbett' (F) | SSea |
| § | 'William Lobb' (CeMo) 🏆H4 | CPou CRHN CSBt EBee EPfP EWTr LCro LRHS LStr MAsh MAus MCot MGan MRav SPer SSea SWCr WAct WHCG WKif |
| | William Morris = 'Auswill'PBR (S) | CSBt EBee LCro LRHS MAus MJon SWCr |
| | William Shakespeare = 'Ausroyal'PBR (S) | CSRo LRHS MAsh MBNS MCot SPer |
| | William Shakespeare 2000 = 'Ausromeo'PBR (S) | CSBt ECnt EPfP ESty LCro LGod MAus MBNS MBri SCoo SSea SWCr |
| | 'William Tyndale' (Ra) | MJon WHCG WOVN |
| | 'Williams' Double Yellow' | see *R.* x *harisonii* 'Williams Double Yellow' |
| | ***willmottiae*** | see *R. gymnocarpa* var. *willmottiae* |
| | Wilton = 'Eurosa' | SWCr |
| | Wiltshire = 'Kormuse'PBR (S/GC) 🏆H4 | CSBt ECnt ESty LSRN LStr MJon MRav NPri SMrm SWCr |
| | Winchester Cathedral = 'Auscat'PBR (S) | CGro CSBt CSRo EBee ECnt ELon EPfP ESty LCro LGod LRHS LStr MAsh MAus MBri MJon MRav NLar NPri SMrm SPer SPoG SSea SWCr |
| | Windflower = 'Auscross' (S) | LRHS MAus |
| | Windrush = 'Ausrush' (S) | MAus MJon SPer SWCr WAct WHCG |
| | Wine and Dine = 'Dicuncle' (GC) | IDic |
| | Winter Magic = 'Foumagic' (Min) | MJon |
| | 'Wintoniensis' (*moyesii* hybrid) | WAct WHCG |
| | Wise Portia = 'Ausport' (S) | MAus |
| | Wishing = 'Dickerfuffle'PBR (F/Patio) | IDic MAus MGan SWCr |
| | Wisley = 'Ausintense'PBR (S) | CSBt LRHS MAsh MAus SCoo SSea SWCr |
| | With All My Love = 'Coczodiac'PBR (HT) | CSBt ESty GCoc LStr |
| | With Love = 'Andwit' (HT) | SWCr |
| | With Thanks = 'Fransmoov'PBR (HT) | ESty SWCr |
| | 'Woburn Abbey' (F) | CWSG SSea |
| | 'Wolley-Dod' | see *R.* 'Duplex' |
| | Woman o'th' North | see *R.* Woman o'th' North = 'Kirlon' |
| § | Woman o'th' North = 'Kirlon' (F/Patio) | MJon |
| | Wonderful News = 'Jonone'PBR (Patio) | ESty MJon |
| | Wonderful = 'Poulpmt005' (HT) | EBee ECnt SWCr |
| § | ***woodsii*** | MAus WHCG |
| | - var. ***fendleri*** | see *R. woodsii* |
| | 'Woolverstone Church Rose' | see *R.* 'Surpassing Beauty of Woolverstone' |
| | Worcestershire = 'Korlalon'PBR (GC) | CSBt GCoc MAus MGan MMHG MRav SPer SSea SWCr WAct |
| § | ***xanthina*** 'Canary Bird' (S) 🏆H4 | Widely available |
| § | - f. ***hugonis*** 🏆H4 | MAus MGan NHaw SPer SWCr WAct |
| | X-rated = 'Tinx' (Min) | MJon |
| | Yellow Button = 'Auslow' (S) | WAct |
| | 'Yellow Cécile Brünner' | see *R.* 'Perle d'Or' |
| | Yellow Charles Austin = 'Ausyel' (S) | MAus |
| § | Yellow Dagmar Hastrup = 'Moryelrug'PBR (Ru) | MGan MJon SPer SPla SWCr WAct WOVN |
| | 'Yellow Doll' (Min) | MAus SWCr |
| * | 'Yellow Dream' (Patio) | SPoG |
| | Yellow Floorshow = 'Harfully'PBR (GC) | MRav |
| | Yellow Flower CarpetPBR | see *R.* Flower Carpet Sunshine |
| | 'Yellow Patio' (Min/Patio) | LRHS LStr MAsh SPoG SWCr |
| | yellow Scotch | see *R.* x *harisonii* 'Williams Double Yellow' (PiH) |
| | Yellow Sunblaze = 'Meitrisical' (Min) | CSBt |
| | 'Yesterday' (Poly/F/S) 🏆H4 | EBee EWTr MAsh MAus MGan SWCr |
| | York and Lancaster | see *R.* x *damascena* var. *versicolor* |
| | Yorkshire = 'Korbarkeit'PBR (GC) | GCoc LGod LStr MRav |
| | 'Yorkshire Lady' (HT) | MJon |
| | 'Yvonne Rabier' (Poly) 🏆H4 | LStr MAus MGan MRav SPer WAct WHCG WKif |
| | Zambra = 'Meicurbos' (F) | CBcs |
| | 'Zéphirine Drouhin' (Bb) | Widely available |
| § | 'Zigeunerknabe' (S) | EBee ECnt ELan MAus MGan MRav NLar SPer SPoG SWCr WAct WHCG |
| | Zorba = 'Poulyc008'PBR (Patio/Cl) | ECnt |
| | 'Zweibrücken' (Cl) | MGan |

## *Roscoea* ✿ (*Zingiberaceae*)

| | | |
|---|---|---|
| | ACE 2539 | GEdr |
| | ***alpina*** | CBro CLAP CPLG CPrp EBee EBrs ECho EHrv EPPr EPot ERos GBuc GEdr GKir ITim MTho NGdn NLAp NMen NWCA SRms WCru |

| | |
|---|---|
| - CC 1820 | IBlr |
| - CC 3667 | GEdr WRos |
| - pink-flowered | IBlr LFur |
| - purple-flowered | IBlr |
| - short | WCru |
| § ***auriculata*** | Widely available |
| - early-flowering | IBlr NCot WCru |
| - 'Floriade' | CLAP EBee GBuc GMac IBlr SKHP |
| - late-flowering | WCru |
| - 'Special' | CLAP |
| - 'White Cap' new | EBee |
| ***auriculata*** x ***australis*** | IBlr |
| ***auriculata*** x ***cautleyoides*** var. ***pubescens*** brown-stemmed new | IBlr |
| ***auriculata*** x ***cautleyoides*** var. ***pubescens*** green-stemmed new | IBlr |
| ***australis*** | CFir GBuc GEdr MNrw WCru |
| - pink-flowered | NCot |
| - - KW 22124 | IBlr |
| - purple-flowered KW 22124 | IBlr |
| 'Ballyrogan Lavender' | IBlr |
| 'Beesiana' | Widely available |
| 'Beesiana' dark-flowered | ERos IBlr |
| 'Beesiana' pale-flowered | ECho ERos EWld LEdu WCru |
| 'Beesiana' white-flowered | CBct CDes CFwr CLAP EBee EBrs EHrv ELon EPfP EPot GEdr IBlr MMHG NBir NGdn NMyG WPGP |
| ***brandisii*** | CBct EBee EBrs ECho |
| ***capitata*** | CLAP |
| ***cautleyoides*** ♀H4 | Widely available |
| I - 'Alba' | EUJe NGdn NLAp WCot |
| - var. ***cautleyoides*** | CDWL |
| - - red-flowered | CFir |
| - - white-flowered | CFir |
| - 'Early Purple' | CDes CLAP ECho WPGP |
| - 'Early Yellow' new | EBee |
| - hybrid | ECho MLLN |
| - 'Jeffrey Thomas' | CBct CFwr CLAP CSam EBee EBrs ECha ECho EPPr EPot GBuc GCal GEdr IBlr MLHP NBhm NMyG SKHP SRGP WCot |
| - 'Kew Beauty' ♀H4 | CDes CFir CLAP CMea CWsd EAEE EBee GCal GEdr GKir MTho SMHy SRms WCot WPGP |
| - 'Kew Beauty' seedlings | EGle |
| - late, lavender-flowered | IBlr |
| - late, yellow-flowered | IBlr |
| - 'Paars' | NBhm |
| - plum-flowered | IBlr |
| - var. ***pubescens*** new | IBlr |
| - 'Purple Giant' | CLAP WCot |
| - purple-flowered | CWsd GBuc IBlr NHar |
| - 'Reinier' | CLAP EBee GBuc GCal SKHP WCot |
| - 'Vanilla' new | EBee |
| - 'Vanilla Ice' new | SKHP |
| - 'Washfield Purple' | IBlr |
| ***cautleyoides*** x ***humeana*** | CLAP IBlr |
| ***cautleyoides*** x ***scillifolia*** dark-flowered | IBlr |
| ***debilis*** var. ***debilis*** | EPot IBlr |
| ***forrestii*** purple-flowered new | IBlr |
| - yellow-flowered new | IBlr |
| 'Gestreept' | CLAP |
| 'Himalaya' | CLAP EBee |
| ***humeana*** ♀H4 | CBct CBro CFee CLAP CSam EBrs ECho EPot ERos GEdr GMac LAma LRHS WCFE WCot WThu |
| - ACE 2539 | IBlr |
| - 'Alba' new | IBlr |
| - Forrest's form | IBlr |
| - lavender-flowered | IBlr |
| - 'Long Acre Sunrise' | CLAP |
| - f. ***lutea*** | CLAP IBlr |
| - pink-flowered | IBlr |
| - 'Purple Streaker' | CBct CDes CLAP EBee WPGP |
| - 'Rosemoor Plum' | CLAP GEdr |
| - 'Snowy Owl' | CLAP WCot |
| - f. ***tyria*** | IBlr |
| - - 'Inkling' | GBuc WWst |
| 'Monique' | CDes CLAP EBee IBlr NHar WPGP |
| ***praecox*** new | IBlr |
| ***procera*** misapplied | see *R. auriculata* |
| ***procera*** Wall. | see *R. purpurea* |
| 'Purple King' new | EBee |
| § ***purpurea*** | Widely available |
| - CC 3628 | WCot |
| - HWJK 2020 new | WCru |
| - HWJK 2169 new | WCru |
| - HWJK 2175 new | WCru |
| - HWJK 2400 | WCru |
| - HWJK 2401 new | WCru |
| - HWJK 2407 new | WCru |
| - KW 13755 | IBlr |
| - MECC 2 | IBlr |
| - MECC 10 | IBlr |
| - 'Brown Peacock' | CDes CLAP IBlr SKHP WCot WPGP |
| - var. ***gigantea*** | CLAP IBlr |
| - - CC 1757 | MNrw |
| - lilac-flowered | CDWL |
| - 'Nico' | CLAP EBee ELan WCot |
| - 'Niedrig' | EBee |
| - pale-flowered | EBla |
| - 'Peacock' | CLAP EBee IBlr WFar |
| - 'Peacock Eye' | CLAP IBlr WCot |
| - var. ***procera*** | see *R. purpurea* |
| - 'Red Gurkha' | CDes CLAP |
| - Rosemoor form | CLAP WWst |
| - short | CLAP IBlr |
| - tall | CLAP NLAp WPGP |
| - 'Wisley Amethyst' | CLAP CPrp GEdr IBlr NCot |
| ***schneideriana*** | IBlr MLul WThu |
| ***scillifolia*** | CBro CDes CFir CPBP ECho ERos GBuc GEdr GKev GKir LAma LHop LRHS MAvo MTho NBir NGdn NMen WPrP |
| - dark-flowered | CPom CStu EBee EHrv IBlr WCru WPGP WThu |
| - pink-flowered | EBee ECho EHrv ERos GEdr IBlr IFoB NMen NMyG WAbe WCot WHil WPrP |
| ***tibetica*** | CFir CLAP EBee GEdr GKev IBlr WCru WThu |
| - ACE 2538 | IBlr |
| - SDR 467 new | GKev |
| aff. ***tibetica*** new | IBlr |
| ***tumjensis*** | CLAP EBee EWes IBlr |
| 'Vincent' | EBee SKHP WCot |
| ***wardii*** | IBlr |
| 'Yeti' | CLAP EBee |

## rosemary see *Rosmarinus officinalis*

## *Rosmarinus* ✿ (*Lamiaceae*)

| | |
|---|---|
| ***corsicus*** 'Prostratus' | see *R. officinalis* Prostratus Group |
| ***lavandulaceus*** misapplied | see *R. officinalis* Prostratus Group |
| ***officinalis*** | Widely available |
| - SDR 5234 new | GKev |
| - var. ***albiflorus*** | CArn CPrp CSev ELau EOHP EPfP GBar GPoy LRHS MBar MHer MNHC SDow SHDw SLim SPer SPlb STre WCHb WGwG |

| | | |
|---|---|---|
| | - - 'Lady in White' | CSBt EBee ELan EPfP GBar LRHS MHer NGHP SDow SEND SPer SPoG WGwG WJek |
| | - 'Alderney' | GBar MHer SDow |
| § | - var. ***angustissimus*** 'Benenden Blue' ♀H4 | CSBt CWan CWib EAro EBee EGoo ELau EOHP EPfP EShb GBar GPoy LHop LRHS SDix SEND SPer SPlb STre SUsu WGwG |
| | - - 'Corsican Blue' | CArn EBee ELan EPfP GBar GPoy MHer MNHC NGHP SDow SHDw SIde SPer WBrE WPer |
| | - - 'Corsicus Prostratus' | ELau |
| * | - 'Argenteovariegatus' | WPGP |
| | - 'Aureovariegatus' | see *R. officinalis* 'Aureus' |
| § | - 'Aureus' (v) | CBow CTca GBar WCHb WEas WJek |
| | - 'Baby P.J.' **new** | EOHP |
| | - 'Baie d'Audierne' | EMil |
| | - 'Barbecue' PBR | ELau MHer NGHP SIde |
| | - 'Blue Lagoon' | EBee ELau EOHP MHer MNHC NGHP SIde WCHb WGwG WJek |
| | - 'Blue Rain' | CBod EAro GPWP LAst MHer NGHP SIde |
| | - 'Boule' | CArn CBod CPrp MHer SDow WCHb WGwG WJek |
| | - 'Bowles' | ELau |
| | - 'Capercaillie' | SDow |
| | - 'Collingwood Ingram' | see *R. officinalis* var. *angustissimus* 'Benenden Blue' |
| | - 'Cottage White' | WGwG |
| | - dwarf, blue-flowered | ELau GBar |
| | - dwarf, white-flowered | WCHb |
| | - 'Farinole' | CArn CBod CPrp ELau GBar MNHC |
| | - 'Fastigiatus' | see *R. officinalis* 'Miss Jessopp's Upright' |
| | - 'Fota Blue' | CArn CBod CBow CPrp CTsd CWib EAro ELau GBar IArd MHer MNHC NGHP SAga SDow SHDw SIde SPoG WCHb WFar WGwG WJek |
| | - 'Frimley Blue' | see *R. officinalis* 'Primley Blue' |
| | - 'Genges Gold' (v) | ECtt SPoG |
| | - 'Golden Rain' | see *R. officinalis* 'Joyce DeBaggio' |
| | - 'Gorizia' | CBcs GBar SDow WGwG |
| | - 'Green Ginger' | CBod CHFP CPrp ELan EOHP EPfP GBar GBin LHop LRHS MAsh MHer MRav MSCN NGHP NPer SDow SPer SPoG WCHb WGwG WMnd |
| | - 'Guilded' | see *R. officinalis* 'Aureus' |
| | - 'Gunnel's Upright' | GBar WRha |
| | - 'Haifa' | CBod EBee ECtt ELau GGar NGHP SIde WCHb |
| | - 'Heavenly Blue' | GBar |
| | - 'Henfield Blue' | SHDw |
| | - 'Iden Blue' | SIde |
| | - 'Iden Blue Boy' | SIde |
| | - 'Iden Pillar' | SIde |
| § | - 'Joyce DeBaggio' (v) | MHer SDow WGwG |
| | - 'Ken Taylor' | SPhx |
| | - 'Lady in Blue' | WGwG |
| | - ***lavandulaceus*** | see *R. officinalis* Prostratus Group |
| | - 'Lilies Blue' | GPoy |
| | - 'Lockwood Variety' | see *R. officinalis* (Prostratus Group) 'Lockwood de Forest' |
| | - 'Majorca Pink' | CChe CSBt CSpe CTca CWan EGoo ELau GBar GGar MHer MNHC NPri SDow SIde SPer SPoG SRms SSto WCHb WGwG |
| | - 'Maltese White' | WCot |
| | - 'Marenca' | ELau MNHC WCHb |
| | - 'Mason's Finest' | SDow |
| | - 'McConnell's Blue' ♀H4 | CArn CDoC CHFP CPrp EBee ELan ELau EShb GBar LHop LRHS MAsh MGos MNHC SDow SHDw SPla WCHb WFar WGwG WHoo WPGP |
| * | - 'Miss Jessopp's Prostrate' | GKir |
| § | - 'Miss Jessopp's Upright' ♀H4 | Widely available |
| | - 'Mrs Harding' | CBod MHer |
| | - 'Pointe du Raz' | CAbP EBee ELan EMil EPfP MAsh SChF SPoG |
| § | - 'Primley Blue' | CArn CMea CPrp CSam CSev CTsd CWSG EBee ECtt ELau GBar LRHS LSou MHer MNHC MRav NGHP SIde SPoG WCHb WFar WPer |
| § | - Prostratus Group | Widely available |
| | - - 'Capri' | CAbP CDul CSBt ECtt LRHS MAsh MBrN MHer NGHP SPoG |
| | - - 'Gethsemane' | SIde |
| | - - 'Jackman's Prostrate' | CBcs ECtt |
| § | - - 'Lockwood de Forest' | GBar LSou WGwG |
| | - f. ***pyramidalis*** | see *R. officinalis* 'Miss Jessopp's Upright' |
| | - ***repens*** | see *R. officinalis* Prostratus Group |
| | - 'Rex' | CBod ELau |
| | - 'Roman Beauty' | CBcs LAst LRHS LSRN NPri SPoG |
| | - 'Roseus' | CArn CEnt CPrp CSBt CWib EBee ELan ELau EMil EPfP GPoy LHop LRHS MAsh MHer MNHC SDow SLim SPoG SUsu WAbe WGwG WHer WMnd WPer |
| | - 'Russell's Blue' | WFar |
| | - 'Salem' | CBod MHer |
| | - 'Sea Level' | CBod ELau MHer WCHb WGwG |
| | - 'Severn Sea' ♀H4 | Widely available |
| | - 'Shimmering Stars' | SDow |
| | - 'Silver Sparkler' | WPat |
| | - Silver Spires = 'Wolros' | MNHC WFar |
| | - 'Sissinghurst Blue' ♀H4 | CArn CDul CSev CWan EBee ECha ECrN ELan ELau EMil EPfP GBar LRHS MHer MLHP MNHC MRav NGHP SDow SIde SLim SPer SPlb SRms WCHb WClo WGwG |
| | - 'Sissinghurst White' | WGwG |
| | - 'South Downs Blue' | SHDw |
| | - 'Spanish Snow' | WGwG |
| | - 'Sudbury Blue' | EAro EBee ELau EMil EPfP GBar MHer MNHC NGHP SDow SHDw WEas WFar WJek |
| | - 'Trusty' | CWan GBar LRHS |
| | - 'Tuscan Blue' | Widely available |
| | - 'Variegatus' | see *R. officinalis* 'Aureus' |
| | ***repens*** | see *R. officinalis* Prostratus Group |

# *Rostrinucula* (*Lamiaceae*)

| | | |
|---|---|---|
| | ***dependens*** | EMil EWes MBri NLar |
| | ***sinensis*** | CPLG |

# *Rosularia* ✿ (*Crassulaceae*)

| | | |
|---|---|---|
| | sp. **new** | MWat |
| | from Sandras Dag | CWil LBee |
| | ***alba*** | see *R. sedoides* var. *alba* |
| | ***alpestris*** from Rhotang Pass | WThu |
| § | ***chrysantha*** | EBur EDAr EPot LRHS NMen SFgr SIng SPlb |
| | - number 1 | CWil |
| | ***crassipes*** | see *Rhodiola wallichiana* |
| | ***lineata*** RCB RL -20 **new** | WCot |
| § | ***muratdaghensis*** | EBur |
| | ***pallida*** A. Berger | see *R. chrysantha* |
| | ***pallida*** ambig. | SFgr |
| | ***platyphylla*** misapplied | see *R. muratdaghensis* |
| | ***sedoides*** | CWil LRHS MBar SIng |
| § | - var. ***alba*** | ECho EDAr EPot GGar WTin |
| | ***sempervivum*** | CWil ECho EWes NMen |

| | |
|---|---|
| § - subsp. ***glaucophylla*** | CWil WAbe WThu |
| ***spatulata*** hort. | see *R. sempervivum* subsp. *glaucophylla* |

## *Rothmannia* (*Rubiaceae*)

| | |
|---|---|
| ***capensis*** | EShb SOWG |

## *Rubia* (*Rubiaceae*)

| | |
|---|---|
| ***peregrina*** | CArn GPoy MSal |
| ***tinctorum*** | CArn CBod CHby EOHP GBar GPoy MSal SWat WCHb WSFF |

## *Rubus* ✿ (*Rosaceae*)

| | |
|---|---|
| RCB/Eq C-1 | WCot |
| ***alceifolius*** Poir. | CFee MBlu SDys |
| ***arcticus*** | EBee ECtt EPPr GAuc GGar MCCP NLAp NLar SHar SRms SRot WCru WPat |
| - subsp. ***stellatus*** **new** | GAuc |
| x ***barkeri*** | ECou |
| § 'Benenden' ♀H4 | Widely available |
| 'Betty Ashburner' | CAgr CBcs CDoC CDul EBee ECrN EPfP EWTr GQui LAst LBuc MGos MRav MWhi NHol SLPl SPer WDin WMoo WTin |
| ***biflorus*** ♀H4 | EMon EPfP EWes LEdu MBlu WPGP |
| 'Black Butte' | CSut EMil EMui LRHS SDea SVic |
| 'Boatsberry' | SDea |
| 'Boysenberry, Thornless' (F) | EMil EMui GTwe LBuc LRHS MGan SDea SPer |
| ***buergeri*** B&SWJ 5555 **new** | WCru |
| ***calophyllus*** | CDul WPGP |
| ***calycinoides*** Hayata | see *R. rolfei* |
| ***chamaemorus*** | GAuc GPoy |
| 'Chesapeake' (F) **new** | EMil |
| ***cissoides*** | WCot |
| ***cockburnianus*** (F) | CArn CBcs CTri CWib EBee ELan EPfP EWTr GCra GKir IFoB LBuc LRHS MBlu MRav MSwo NHol NSti NWea SPer SPlb SRms WDin WEas WFar |
| - 'Goldenvale' ♀H4 | Widely available |
| ***crataegifolius*** | CPom CWan MRav WPat |
| ***deliciosus*** | WFar |
| ***discolor*** Himalayan berry (F) | NWea |
| 'Emerald Spreader' | GKir SBod WMoo |
| ***flagelliflorus*** | MBar |
| ***fockeanus*** misapplied | see *R. rolfei* |
| ***formosensis*** B&SWJ 1798 | WCru |
| N ***fruticosus*** agg. | WSFF |
| - 'Adrienne' (F) | CAgr CSBt EMui MAsh |
| - 'Ashton Cross' (F) | CDoC GTwe LBuc |
| - 'Bedford Giant' (F) | CSBt ECrN GTwe LBuc MAsh MGan MGos SEND SPoG |
| - 'Black Satin' (F) | CAgr LRHS NLar SDea SVic |
| - 'Chester' (F) | EMil SKee |
| - 'Fantasia'PBR (F) ♀H4 | EMui |
| - 'Godshill Goliath' (F) | SDea |
| - 'Helen' (F) | CAgr CSut EMil EMui MAsh SDea |
| - 'Himalayan Giant' (F) | GTwe MGan MRav NLar SDea SPer |
| - 'John Innes' (F) | MCoo |
| - 'Kotata' (F) | EMil MRav |
| - 'Loch Ness'PBR (F) ♀H4 | CAgr CWib EMil EMui GKir GTwe IArd LBuc LRHS MCoo SCoo SDea SKee |
| - 'Merton Thornless' (F) | CSBt CWib GTwe MAsh MGan MGos |
| - 'No Thorn' (F) | SDea |
| - 'Oregon Thornless' (F) | CAgr CCVT CDoC CSBt CWib ECrN EMui EPfP GTwe LCro LRHS MAsh MRav NLar SCoo SDea SPoG SRms WOrn |
| - 'Parsley Leaved' (F) | SDea |
| * - 'Sylvan' (F) | EMil MCoo MGos SPer |
| - 'Thornfree' (F) | CAgr CDoC CTri NLar SDea |
| - 'Variegatus' (v) | MBlu SMad WCot |
| - 'Veronique' (F) | EMui |
| - 'Waldo' (F) | CAgr CSBt CWib ECrN EMui LBuc MAsh MBri MGos SDea |
| aff. ***gachetensis*** B&SWJ 10603 **new** | WCru |
| 'Golden Showers' | CWib |
| ***henryi*** | EPla MRav NLar NSti SLon SPoG WCot |
| - var. ***bambusarum*** | CMCN EBee EPla MCCP MRav NVic WCru |
| ***hupehensis*** | SLPl |
| ***ichangensis*** | CBcs EPla LEdu |
| ***idaeus*** | GPoy |
| - 'All Gold' (F) | CSut EMil MAsh SVic |
| - 'Aureus' (F) | ECha ELan EPla EWes MRav NBid NBre WCot WFar WMoo |
| - 'Autumn Bliss'PBR (F) ♀H4 | CAgr CSBt CTri CWSG CWib ECrN EMui EPfP GKir GTwe LBuc LCro LEdu LRHS MAsh MBri MGan MGos MNHC MRav SCoo SDea SKee SPer SPoG SVic WOrn |
| - 'Fallgold' (F) | CAgr CWib EMui EPfP LRHS MCoo MMuc SKee SPer SPoG |
| - 'Galante'PBR (F) | EMui |
| - 'Glen Ample'PBR (F) ♀H4 | CAgr CSBt CSut CTri CWSG CWib ECrN EMil EMui EPfP GTwe LBuc LEdu LRHS MAsh MBri MCoo SCoo SDea SKee SPer SPoG SVic WOrn |
| - 'Glen Clova' (F) | CAgr CSBt CTri CWib ECrN GKir GTwe LCro LRHS MAsh MGan MGos MNHC MRav NBlu SKee SPer SPoG SVic WOrn |
| - 'Glen Lyon'PBR (F) | CWib EMui GTwe LBuc MAsh MBri SCoo |
| - 'Glen Magna'PBR (F) | CSBt CWSG CWib EMui GTwe LBuc LRHS MAsh MBri MRav SCoo SDea SKee SPoG |
| - 'Glen Moy'PBR (F) ♀H4 | CAgr CSBt CTri CWib ECrN EMil EMui EPfP GTwe MAsh MGos SCoo SDea SKee |
| - 'Glen Prosen'PBR (F) ♀H4 | CAgr CSBt CWib ECrN EMui GKir GTwe LCro MAsh MBri MGos SCoo SDea SKee SPer |
| - 'Heritage' (F) | CWib MAsh MGos SCoo |
| - 'Joan J'PBR (F) | CSut EMil |
| - 'Joan Squire'PBR (F) | SKee |
| - 'Julia' (F) | CAgr GTwe LCro MCoo |
| - 'Leo'PBR (F) ♀H4 | CAgr CSBt CTri CWib EMui GTwe MAsh MGos SCoo SKee SPer |
| - 'Malling Admiral' (F) ♀H4 | CSBt CTri CWib EMui GKir GTwe MAsh SCoo SKee SPer |
| - 'Malling Delight' (F) | CSBt CWib MAsh SCoo |
| - 'Malling Jewel' (F) ♀H4 | CSBt CWib EMui GKir GTwe LBuc MAsh MGan SDea SKee SPer |
| - 'Malling Promise' (F) | CWib |
| - 'Octavia' (F) | CSBt CSut EMil EMui MAsh MCoo SPoG |
| - 'Polka'PBR (F) | ECrN SKee SVic |
| - 'Redsetter' (F) | EMui |
| - 'Summer Gold' (F) | GTwe |
| - 'Tulameen' (F) | CAgr CSBt CWib EMil EMui LRHS MAsh MBri SCoo SKee SPoG SVic |
| - 'Valentina' (F) **new** | EMil |
| - 'Zeva Herbsternte' (F) | CWib MAsh |
| ***irenaeus*** | EBla |
| Japanese wineberry | see *R. phoenicolasius* |
| 'Karaka Black'PBR **new** | EMil |
| 'Kenneth Ashburner' | CDoC NLar SLPl WFar WTin |
| 'King's Acre Berry' (F) | EMui |

| | |
|---|---|
| ***laciniatus*** | EPla |
| ***leucodermis*** NNS 00-663 | EPPr |
| ***lineatus*** | CDoC CMCo CWib EPfP EWes LRHS MCot NSti SDix SMad WCru WDin WPGP WPat |
| - B&SWJ 11261 from Sumatra new | WCru |
| - HWJ 892 from Vietnam | WCru |
| - HWJK 2045 from Nepal | WCru |
| - from Nepal | GCra |
| x ***loganobaccus*** 'Brandywine' | SDea |
| - 'Ly 59' (F) 🏆$^{H4}$ | ECrN EMui EPfP GTwe MRav SDea SKee SPer SRms |
| - 'Ly 654' (F) 🏆$^{H4}$ | CSBt GTwe LBuc MBri MGos SDea SPer |
| - thornless (F) | CAgr CTri CWSG CWib ECot GTwe MAsh MGan SDea SPoG SVic |
| 'Malling Minerva' (F) new | CSut |
| 'Margaret Gordon' | MRav |
| ***microphyllus*** 'Variegatus' (v) | MRav WPat |
| § ***nepalensis*** | CAgr CDoC GCra LEdu |
| - from Nepal new | GCra |
| ***nutans*** | see *R. nepalensis* |
| ***odoratus*** | CPLG CSec EBee ELan EPPr EPfP EWTr LEdu MBlu MRav NBid NPal SPer WBor WCot WFar WHCG WTin |
| ***parviflorus*** | CArn |
| - double (d) | EPPr WCru |
| - 'Sunshine Spreader' | EHoe WPat |
| ***pectinellus*** var. ***trilobus*** | CFee EWld LEdu NLar |
| - - B&SWJ 1669B | WCru |
| ***peltatus*** | CGHE NLar WPGP |
| ***pentalobus*** | see *R. rolfei* |
| § ***phoenicolasius*** | CAgr CCCN EMui EPfP GTwe LEdu LHop MBlu MCoo MGan MRav NSti SDea SPer SPoG SVic WAbb WHCG WPGP |
| § ***rolfei*** | CTri EPPr MBar NMyG WFar |
| - 'Emerald Carpet' | CAgr NLar SBod |
| - B&SWJ 3546 from Taiwan | WCru |
| - B&SWJ 3878 from the Philippines | WCru |
| ***rosifolius*** | CSpe |
| - 'Coronarius' (d) | CFee CHar CSpe ECrN ELan GAbr LSou MRav NPro WCot WFar |
| ***sachalinensis*** | GAuc |
| ***sanctus*** | CNat |
| ***setchuenensis*** | CMCN CSWP EWes |
| 'Silvan' (F) 🏆$^{H4}$ | EMui GTwe SEND |
| ***spectabilis*** | CBcs CSev CWib ELan EPPr EPla EWTr LEdu MMuc MRav WFar WRha WSHC WWFP |
| - 'Flore Pleno' | see *R. spectabilis* 'Olympic Double' |
| § - 'Olympic Double' (d) | Widely available |
| ***splendidissimus*** B&SWJ 2361 | WCru |
| ***squarrosus*** | ECou EHig |
| * ***stelleri*** new | GAuc |
| 'Sunberry' (F) | CCCN GTwe SDea |
| ***swinhoei*** B&SWJ 1735 | WCru |
| ***taiwanicola*** | EBla EDAr GEdr |
| - B&SWJ 317 | GBin WCru |
| Tayberry Group (F) 🏆$^{H4}$ | CSBt CTri ECrN EMui GTwe MAsh MGan MGos NLar SPer SRms SVic |
| - 'Buckingham' (F) | CSut EMil EMui GTwe LBuc MAsh SPoG SVic |
| - 'Medana Tayberry' (F) | CAgr EMui EPfP LRHS SDea SKee SPoG |
| § ***thibetanus*** 🏆$^{H4}$ | Widely available |
| - 'Silver Fern' | see *R. thibetanus* |
| ***treutleri*** B&SWJ 2139 new | WCru |
| ***tricolor*** | CAgr CBcs CDul CSBt CTri CWib EBee ECrN EPfP GBri GKir MBlu MMuc MRav MSwo NHol SDix SHBN SPer WDin WHCG WMoo |
| - 'Dart's Evergreen' | SLPl |
| - 'Ness' | SLPl |
| ***tridel*** 'Benenden' | see *R.* 'Benenden' |
| ***trilobus*** B&SWJ 9096 | WCru |
| - 'Tummelberry' new | MCoo |
| 'Tummelberry' (F) | EMil GTwe SEND |
| ***ulmifolius*** 'Bellidiflorus' (d) | GCal MBlu MRav MSwo NSti SDix WAbb WEas WHrl |
| ***ursinus*** | LEdu |
| 'Veitchberry' (F) | GTwe |
| ***xanthocarpus*** | NLar |
| 'Youngberry' (F) | SDea |

## *Rudbeckia* ✿ (*Asteraceae*)

| | |
|---|---|
| Autumn Sun | see *R. laciniata* 'Herbstsonne' |
| ***californica*** | WPer |
| - var. ***intermedia*** from Anthony Brooks | WCot |
| ***deamii*** | see *R. fulgida* var. *deamii* |
| ***echinacea purpurea*** | see *Echinacea purpurea* |
| ***fulgida*** | GKir NNor |
| § - var. ***deamii*** 🏆$^{H4}$ | Widely available |
| - var. ***fulgida*** | EBee SMad SMrm |
| § - var. ***speciosa*** 🏆$^{H4}$ | CKno CMMP CSam EBee ECha ECtt ELan EPfP GAbr LAst MHar MMuc NBPC SBch SPlb SRms WEas WFar WMoo WPer WPtf WTin |
| - var. ***sullivantii*** 'Goldsturm' 🏆$^{H4}$ | Widely available |
| - Viette's Little Suzy = 'Blovi' | EBee EBrs GKir LRHS |
| ***gloriosa*** | see *R. hirta* |
| 'Golden Jubilee' | LRHS |
| ***grandiflora*** var. ***alismifolia*** new | EBee |
| § ***hirta*** | CHar CHrt NBir |
| - 'Autumn Colours' (mixed) | CMea |
| - 'Cherokee Sunset' (d) new | CSpe |
| - 'Chim Chiminee' | LBMP |
| - 'Indian Summer' 🏆$^{H3}$ | SPav |
| - 'Irish Eyes' | SPav |
| - 'Marmalade' | LBMP NGBl |
| - 'Prairie Sun' | LBMP NGBl |
| - var. ***pulcherrima*** | SMHy |
| - 'Sonora' | SPoG WHal |
| - 'Toto' 🏆$^{H3}$ | LBMP SPav SWvt |
| - 'Toto Gold' | LBMP |
| - 'Toto Rustic' | LBMP |
| July Gold | see *R. laciniata* 'Juligold' |
| ***laciniata*** | CElw CHFP CKno CMac CSam EBee EBrs ELan EMon EPPr GCal GKir GQue LEdu MDKP MHar NLar NOrc NSti SMHy SPhx WMoo WOld |
| - 'Golden Glow' | see *R. laciniata* 'Hortensia' |
| - 'Goldquelle' (d) 🏆$^{H4}$ | Widely available |
| § - 'Herbstsonne' 🏆$^{H4}$ | Widely available |
| § - 'Hortensia' (d) | EBee EMon GQue MAvo MLLN WHoo WOld |
| § - 'Juligold' | CPrp EBee IPot LBMP MAvo MBNS NBre NGdn SMrm SPla SPoG WCAu WFar |
| - 'Starcadia Razzle Dazzle' | EBee WCot |
| ***maxima*** | CDes CKno COIW CSpe EBee ECha EDAr GCal GMac IFoB LEdu LRHS MAvo MBri MCCP NCGa NLar NPri NSti SDix SMad SMrm SPhx SPlb SUsu WCot WFar |
| ***missouriensis*** | NBre SUsu |

| | |
|---|---|
| ***mollis*** | EBee NBre |
| ***newmannii*** | see *R. fulgida* var. *speciosa* |
| ***nitida*** | EShb |
| ***occidentalis*** | GKev MLLN NBre NVic WFar WPer |
| - 'Black Beauty'PBR | EBee EHrv EPfP GKir NBPN NBhm NMoo NSti SBig WMnd |
| - 'Green Wizard' | Widely available |
| * ***paniculata*** | EBee LLHF NBre SPhx WCot |
| ***purpurea*** | see *Echinacea purpurea* |
| ***speciosa*** | see *R. fulgida* var. *speciosa* |
| ***subtomentosa*** | CDes CSam EBee EMon EWes GCal MAvo MDKP MNFA NBre NSti SMHy WCAu WOld |
| - 'Loofahsa Wheaten Gold' | WCot |
| 'Takao' | CWCL EBee LSou MAvo MDKP MLLN MNrw MWea NBsh NLar SPoG SUsu WBor WWFP |
| ***triloba*** | CDes CEnt CHFP CMea CSam EBee ECha EPfP EShb MNrw NBPC NGdn SMad SMrs SPet WCAu WFar WMoo WPGP WTin |

**rue** see *Ruta graveolens*

## *Ruellia* (*Acanthaceae*)

| | |
|---|---|
| ***amoena*** | see *R. brevifolia* |
| § ***brevifolia*** | CSpe ECre |
| ***humilis*** | EBee EShb NLar WHil |
| ***macrantha*** | CCCN EShb MJnS |
| ***makoyana*** ♀H1 | CHal CSev EShb MBri |
| 'Mr Foster' | CHal |
| ***tweediana*** | EShb MJnS |

## *Rumex* (*Polygonaceae*)

| | |
|---|---|
| ***acetosa*** | CArn CHby CSev CWan EBWF ELau GBar GPoy LRHS MCoo MHer MNHC NBir NGHP NPri NSco SEND SIde WHer WLHH WSFF |
| - 'Abundance' | ELau |
| - subsp. ***acetosa*** 'Saucy' (v) | WAlt WCot |
| - 'De Belleville' | CPrp NPri |
| - 'Profusion' | GPoy |
| - subsp. ***vinealis*** | EBee WCot |
| ***acetosella*** | CArn EBWF MNHC MSal NMir WSFF |
| ***alpinus*** | EBee LEdu SPhx WCot |
| ***flexuosus*** | EBee MDKP NLar WJek |
| ***hydrolapathum*** | CArn EBWF EMFW LPBA MMuc MSKA SPlb WSFF |
| ***patientia*** | CArn |
| ***sanguineus*** | CTri EPfP EShb LBMP LPBA MSKA NCob NLar SWal WBrk WFar WMAq |
| - var. ***sanguineus*** | CArn CBgR CElw CRow CSev EBee ELan EPla IFoB LRHS MHer MNrw MTho NBro NHol WHer WLHH |
| 'Schavel' | LEdu WOut |
| ***scutatus*** | CArn CHby CPrp CSev ELau GPoy MNHC SIde SPlb WHer WJek WLHH WOut |
| - 'Silver Shield' | CBod CRow ELau MHer SIde WCHb WJek WLHH |
| ***venosus*** | MSal |

## *Rumohra* (*Davalliaceae*)

| | |
|---|---|
| sp <u>new</u> | SEND |
| ***adiantiformis*** ♀H1 | CCCN EBee LRHS SEND WFib WRic |
| - RCB/Arg D-2 | WCot |

## *Ruscus* ✿ (*Ruscaceae*)

| | |
|---|---|
| ***aculeatus*** | Widely available |
| - (f) | WFar WMou |
| - (m) | WCFE WMou |
| - hermaphrodite | EPfP EPla EWes GCal MBri SMad WPGP WPat WThu |
| - var. ***aculeatus*** 'Lanceolatus' (f) | GCal |
| - var. ***angustifolius***. | EPla |
| - - (f) | EPla |
| - 'Christmas Berry' | ELan EPfP NLar |
| - 'John Redmond'PBR | CBgR CSBt CSpe EBee ELan ELon EWes LAst LLHF LRHS MAsh MWea NHol NMun SLon SPer SPoG WBor WCot WPGP |
| * - 'Wheeler's Variety' (f/m) | CPMA MRav |
| ***hypoglossum*** | SEND WPGP WRHF |
| x ***microglossum*** (f) | CDul |
| ***racemosus*** | see *Danae racemosa* |

## *Ruspolia* (*Acanthaceae*)

| | |
|---|---|
| ***seticalyx*** | EShb |

## *Russelia* (*Scrophulariaceae*)

| | |
|---|---|
| § ***equisetiformis*** ♀H1 | CHll EShb MJnS SOWG |
| - 'Lemon Falls' | EShb SOWG |
| ***juncea*** | see *R. equisetiformis* |

## *Ruta* (*Rutaceae*)

| | |
|---|---|
| ***chalepensis*** | CArn EBee |
| ***corsica*** | CArn |
| ***graveolens*** | CArn CWan EPfP GBar GPoy MNHC NPri SECG SIde WJek WLHH WPer |
| - 'Jackman's Blue' | CBcs CDul CPrp CSev CTri EBee EHoe ELan EOHP EPfP GKir GMaP GPoy LAst MGos MHer MRav MSwo SLim SPer SRms WMnd |
| - 'Variegata' (v) | CBow CWan ELan GBar MNHC NPer WJek |

## x *Ruttyruspolia* (*Acanthaceae*)

| | |
|---|---|
| 'Phyllis van Heerden' | GFai SOWG |

# S

## *Sabal* (*Arecaceae*)

| | |
|---|---|
| § ***bermudana*** | EAmu |
| ***causiarum*** | EAmu |
| ***etonia*** | LPal |
| § ***mexicana*** | EAmu |
| ***minor*** | CBrP CDTJ CHEx CPHo EAmu ETod LPal MREP NPal SBig |
| ***palmetto*** | CDoC EAmu LPal |
| ***princeps*** | see *S. bermudana* |
| ***rosei*** | LPal |
| ***texana*** | see *S. mexicana* |
| ***uresana*** | LPal |

## *Saccharum* (*Poaceae*)

| | |
|---|---|
| ***arundinaceum*** | CKno EPPr |
| § ***baldwinii*** | GFor |
| ***officinarum*** | MJnS |
| - var. ***violaceum*** | MJnS |
| ***ravennae*** | CBod EBee GCal GFor MSte MWhi SApp SEND SMad SPlb WFar |
| ***strictum*** (Baldwin) Nutt. | see *S. baldwinii* |

## *Sadleria* (*Blechnaceae*)

| | |
|---|---|
| ***cyatheoides*** | WRic |

**sage** see *Salvia officinalis*

**sage, annual clary** see *Salvia viridis*

## sage, biennial clary see *Salvia sclarea*

## sage, pineapple see *Salvia elegans*

## *Sageretia* (*Rhamnaceae*)

| | | |
|---|---|---|
| § | ***thea*** | CMen STre |
| | ***theezans*** | see *S. thea* |

## *Sagina* (*Caryophyllaceae*)

| | | |
|---|---|---|
| | ***boydii*** | ECho |
| | ***subulata*** | ECho EDAr SVic |
| § | - var. ***glabrata*** 'Aurea' | CMea CTri EAlp ECha ECho ECtt EDAr GKir GMaP SIng SPoG SRms WEas WFar WPer |

## *Sagittaria* (*Alismataceae*)

| | | |
|---|---|---|
| | 'Bloomin Babe' | CRow |
| | ***graminea*** 'Crushed Ice' (v) | CRow |
| | ***japonica*** | see *S. sagittifolia* |
| | ***latifolia*** | COld LPBA NPer SMad |
| * | ***leucopetala*** 'Flore Pleno' (d) | NLar NPer |
| § | ***sagittifolia*** | CBen CDWL CRow CWat EHon EMFW EPfP LLWG LPBA MSKA NSco WMAq WPnP |
| | - 'Flore Pleno' (d) | CBen CDWL CRow CWat EMFW LPBA WMAq |
| | - var. ***leucopetala*** | WMAq |

## *Saintpaulia* (*Gesneriaceae*)

| | |
|---|---|
| 'Arctic Frost' **new** | WDib |
| 'Bangle Blue' | WDib |
| 'Beatrice Trail' | WDib |
| 'Betty Stoehr' | WDib |
| 'Blue Dragon' | WDib |
| 'Bob Serbin' (d) | WDib |
| 'Bohemian Sunset' | WDib |
| 'Buffalo Hunt' | WDib |
| 'Centenary' | WDib |
| 'Cherries 'n' Cream' | WDib |
| 'Chiffon Fiesta' | WDib |
| 'Chiffon Mist' (d) | WDib |
| 'Chiffon Moonmoth' | WDib |
| 'Chiffon Stardust' | WDib |
| 'Chiffon Vesper' | WDib |
| 'Coroloir' | WDib |
| 'Delft' (d) | WDib |
| 'Electric Dreams' | WDib |
| 'Gillian' **new** | WDib |
| 'Golden Glow' (d) | WDib |
| 'Halo' (Ultra Violet Series) | WDib |
| 'Halo's Aglitter' | WDib |
| 'Irish Flirt' (d) | WDib |
| 'Lemon Drop' (d) | WDib |
| 'Lemon Whip' (d) | WDib |
| 'Love Spots' | WDib |
| 'Lucky Lee Ann' (d) | WDib |
| 'Ma Mars' **new** | WDib |
| 'Marching Band' | WDib |
| 'Mermaid' (d) | WDib |
| 'Midget Lillian' (v) | WDib |
| 'Midnight Flame' | WDib |
| 'Midnight Waltz' | WDib |
| 'Ness' Crinkle Blue' **new** | WDib |
| 'Nubian Winter' | WDib |
| 'Otoe' | WDib |
| 'Powder Keg' (d) | WDib |
| 'Powwow' (d/v) | WDib |
| 'Rainbow Limelight' **new** | WDib |
| 'Ramblin' Magic' (d) | WDib |
| 'Rapid Transit' (d) | WDib |
| 'Rhapsodie Clementine' **new** | WDib |
| 'Rob's Bamboozle' | WDib |
| 'Rob's Calypso Beat' **new** | WDib |
| 'Rob's Cloudy Skies' (d) | WDib |
| 'Rob's Dandy Lion' | WDib |
| 'Rob's Denim Demon' | WDib |
| 'Rob's Dust Storm' (d) | WDib |
| 'Rob's Firebrand' | WDib |
| 'Rob's Gundaroo' (d) | WDib |
| 'Rob's Heat Wave' (d) | WDib |
| 'Rob's Hopscotch' | WDib |
| 'Rob's Ice Ripples' (d) | WDib |
| 'Rob's June Bug' | WDib |
| 'Rob's Loose Goose' | WDib |
| 'Rob's Love Bite' | WDib |
| 'Rob's Macho Devil' | WDib |
| 'Rob's Mad Cat' (d) | WDib |
| 'Rob's Red Bug' (d/r) | WDib |
| 'Rob's Rinky Dink' (d) | WDib |
| 'Rob's Sarsparilla' (d) | WDib |
| 'Rob's Seduction' | WDib |
| 'Rob's Shadow Magic' (d) | WDib |
| 'Rob's Smarty Pants' | WDib |
| 'Rob's Sticky Wicket' | WDib |
| 'Rob's Toorooka' (d) | WDib |
| 'Rob's Twinkle Pink' | WDib |
| ***shumensis*** | WDib |
| 'Sky Bandit' (d) | WDib |
| 'Sky Bells' (v) | WDib |
| 'The Madam' | WDib |
| 'Tippy Toe' (d) | WDib |

## *Salix* ✿ (*Salicaceae*)

| | | |
|---|---|---|
| | ***acutifolia*** | EBee ELan EQua IFFs SPla WDin |
| | - 'Blue Streak' (m) 🏆$^{H4}$ | CDul CEnd CWiW CWon EPfP EPla EWes MAsh MBlu MRav NBir NHol NLar SMHy SWat WFar |
| | - 'Lady Aldenham No 2' | EPla |
| | - 'Pendulifolia' (m) | SBLw WPat |
| | ***aegyptiaca*** | CDoC CWon ECrN MBlu NWea WMou |
| | ***alba*** | CCVT CDul CLnd CWiW ECrN EMac GGal IFFs LBuc LMaj NWea SBLw WDin WMou WOrn |
| | - f. ***argentea*** | see *S. alba* var. *sericea* |
| | - 'Aurea' | CLnd CTho CWon MRav WIvy WMou |
| | - 'Belders' (m) | SBLw |
| | - var. ***caerulea*** | CDul CLnd CWon NWea WMou |
| | - - 'Wantage Hall' (f) | CWiW CWon |
| | - 'Cardinalis' (f) | CWiW CWon GQue ISea SWat |
| | - 'Chermesina' hort. | see *S. alba* var. *vitellina* 'Britzensis' |
| | - 'Dart's Snake' | CTho ELan EPfP EPla MAsh MBrN MRav NLar NScw SCoo |
| | - 'Golden Ness' | MBlu |
| | - 'Hutchinson's Yellow' | CDoC CTho CWon ECrN EQua MGos NLar NWea SCoo SLim WDin |
| | - 'Liempde' (m) | MRav NWea SBLw |
| | - 'Raesfeld' (m) | CWiW CWon |
| | - 'Saint Oedendrode' | CWon |
| § | - var. ***sericea*** 🏆$^{H4}$ | CBcs CDoC CDul CLnd CTho CWon EPfP MBlu MRav NWea SBLw SHBN SPer WDin WIvy WMou |
| | - 'Splendens' | see *S. alba* var. *sericea* |
| | - 'Tristis' misapplied | see *S.* x *sepulcralis* var. *chrysocoma* |
| § | - 'Tristis' ambig. | CCVT CLnd CTri ELan GKir LRHS MBri MGos MSwo NLar NWea SBLw SLim SRms SWat WDin WFar WHar |
| | - 'Tristis' Gaud. | MMuc |

| | | |
|---|---|---|
| | - var. ***vitellina*** ♀H4 | CDul CTri CWon EMac EPfP GQue LBuc LPan MBNS MBrN NWea SLon SWat WDin WIvy WJas WMoo |
| § | - - 'Britzensis' (m) ♀H4 | Widely available |
| | - - 'Nova' **new** | SWat |
| § | - - 'Yelverton' | CWon SWat |
| | - 'Vitellina Pendula' | see *S. alba* 'Tristis' ambig. |
| | - 'Vitellina Tristis' | see *S. alba* 'Tristis' ambig. |
| § | ***alpina*** | ECho NBir NHar |
| | 'Americana' | CWiW |
| | ***amplexicaulis*** 'Pescara' (m) | CWiW |
| | ***amygdaloides*** | CWiW CWon |
| | 'Aokautere' | see *S.* x *sepulcralis* 'Aokautere' |
| | ***apennina*** 'Cisa Pass' | CWon |
| | ***apoda*** | CWon |
| | - (m) | ECho WPer |
| § | ***arbuscula*** | CWon ECho GAuc NWCA WDin |
| | ***arctica*** var. ***petraea*** | CWon NLAp WPat |
| | ***arenaria*** | see *S. repens* var. *argentea* |
| | ***aurita*** | GAuc NLar NWea |
| | ***babylonica*** | CEnd CTrG CWon LPan SBLw SHBN WMou |
| | - 'Annularis' | see *S. babylonica* 'Crispa' |
| | - 'Bijdorp' | MBri NLar |
| § | - 'Crispa' | CDul CWon ELan EPla LHop MBri MTPN NPro SMad SPla WFar |
| | - 'Pan Chih-kang' | CWiW NLar |
| | - var. ***pekinensis*** | CWon |
| | - - 'Snake' | CWon |
| § | - - 'Tortuosa' ♀H4 | Widely available |
| * | - 'Tortuosa Aurea' | LPan MCCP SWvt |
| | x ***balfourii*** | CWon |
| | ***bebbiana*** | CWon |
| | 'Blackskin' (f) | CWiW |
| | x ***blanda*** | CWon |
| | ***bockii*** | EBee LLHF LRHS MBar MMuc SKHP WFar |
| § | 'Bowles' Hybrid' | MRav WMou |
| | 'Boydii' (f) ♀H4 | CFee CWon EBee ECho EPfP EPot GAbr GEdr GKir ITim LEdu MGos NBir NHol NLAp NMen NRya NSla SIng SPoG SRms WAbe WFar WPat |
| § | 'Boyd's Pendulous' (m) | CLyd CWib MBar |
| | ***breviserrata*** | CLyd NWCA |
| | ***burjatica*** | CWon |
| | - 'Germany' **new** | CWon |
| | - 'Korso' **new** | CWon |
| | ***caesia*** | EMac NWCA WIvy |
| | x ***calodendron*** (f) | CWon |
| | ***candida*** | CWon GAuc |
| | ***cantabrica*** | CWon |
| | ***caprea*** | CBcs CCVT CDul CLnd CTri CWon ECrN EMac EPfP IFFs LBuc LMaj NWea SBLw SPer WDin WMou WSFF |
| | - 'Black Stem' | CDul |
| | - 'Curlilocks' | MBar MSwo |
| § | - 'Kilmarnock' (m) | Widely available |
| | - var. ***pendula*** (m) | see *S. caprea* 'Kilmarnock' (m) |
| | - 'Pendula' | see *S. caprea* 'Kilmarnock' |
| | - 'Silberglanz' | CWon |
| | ***caprea*** x ***lanata*** **new** | CWon |
| | x ***capreola*** | CWon |
| | ***cashmiriana*** | CLyd CWon GAuc GEdr WPat |
| | ***caspica*** | CWon |
| * | - ***rubra nana*** | SWat |
| | x ***cernua*** | NWCA |
| | ***chaenomeloides*** | EBrs |
| | 'Chrysocoma' | see *S.* x *sepulcralis* var. *chrysocoma* |
| | ***cinerea*** | CBcs CDoC CWon ECrN EMac GKir IFFs LBuc NWea SBLw WDin |
| | - 'Bude' **new** | CWon |
| | - subsp. ***oleifolia*** x ***hibernica*** **new** | CWon |
| | - 'Tricolor' (v) | CArn NPro |
| | - 'Variegata' (v) | WBod |
| | ***cordata*** | CWon ECrN SLPl WDin |
| | - 'Purpurescens' **new** | CWon |
| | x ***cottetii*** | GAuc MBar WDin |
| | ***daphnoides*** | CCVT CDoC CDul CLnd EBee EHig EMac EPfP GKir MBrN MGos MSwo NWea SBLw SEND SPer SPla SRms STre SWat WDin WFar WJas WMou WSFF |
| | - 'Aglaia' (m) | CBcs CWon ECrN MGos WIvy |
| | - 'Continental Purple' | CWon |
| | - 'Lady Aldenham' **new** | CWon |
| | - 'Meikle' (f) | CWiW SWat |
| | - 'Netta Statham' (m) | CWiW CWon |
| | - 'Ovaro Udine' (m) | CWiW |
| | - 'Oxford Violet' (m) | CWon ECrN NWea WIvy |
| | - 'Pendulifolia' **new** | CWon |
| | - 'Purple Heart' **new** | CWon |
| | - 'Sinker' | WIvy |
| | - 'Stewartstown' | CWiW |
| | - 'Wynter Bloom' | CWon |
| | x ***dasyclados*** | CWon |
| | - 'Grandis' | NWea |
| | ***discolor*** | CWon |
| § | x ***doniana*** 'Kumeti' | CWiW |
| | 'E.A. Bowles' | see *S.* 'Bowles' Hybrid' |
| | x ***ehrhartiana*** | CNat CWon |
| § | ***elaeagnos*** | CCVT CDoC CLnd CTho CTri ECrN EPfP GKir MBlu MBrN MRav SLon SWat WDin WFar WMou |
| § | - subsp. ***angustifolia*** ♀H4 | CDul CWon EBee EHig ELan EMil EPfP GKir GQue IFFs MAsh MBar MRav MSwo NLar NWea SEND SRms STre WIvy |
| | 'Elegantissima' | see *S.* x *pendulina* var. *elegantissima* |
| | x ***erdingeri*** | EPla |
| | ***eriocephala*** 'American Mackay' (m) | CWiW |
| | - 'Green USA' | CWon |
| | - 'Kerksii' (m) | CWiW CWon |
| | - 'Mawdesley' (m) | CWiW |
| | - 'Russelliana' (f) | CWiW CWon |
| § | 'Erythroflexuosa' | CBcs CDoC CEnd CWon EBee ELan EPfP EPla LAst LBMP LHop LRHS MAsh MBar MGos MRav NScw NWea SLim SPer SPla SPoG SWat WDin WFar WHer WPat |
| | ***exigua*** | Widely available |
| | ***fargesii*** | CDoC CEnd CFee CWon EBee ELan EPfP GKir LEdu LHop LRHS MAsh MBlu MGos MRav NBid NHol SDix SMad SPoG SSpi WCru WFar WPGP WPat |
| | ***fargesii*** x ***magnifica*** | WPGP |
| § | x ***finnmarchica*** | GAuc GEdr NWCA |
| | x ***forbyana*** **new** | CWon |
| | ***formosa*** | see *S. arbuscula* |
| | ***fragilis*** | CCVT CDul CLnd ECrN EMac IFFs LMaj MRav NWea SBLw WDin WMou |
| § | - var. ***furcata*** | CTri CWon GBin GKev NWCA WPat |
| | - 'Legomey' | WIvy |
| | x ***friesiana*** | CWon |
| | x ***fruticosa*** 'McElroy' (f) | CWiW |
| | ***fruticulosa*** | see *S. fragilis* var. *furcata* |
| | 'Fuiri-koriyanagi' | see *S. integra* 'Hakuro-nishiki' |
| | ***furcata*** | see *S. fragilis* var. *furcata* |

| | | |
|---|---|---|
| | ***glabra*** **new** | CWon |
| | ***glauca*** | CNat |
| | ***glaucophylloides*** | CWon |
| | ***glaucosericea*** | EPla |
| | 'Golden Curls' | see *S.* 'Erythroflexuosa' |
| | ***gracilistyla*** | CTho CWon ECrN NWea SCoo SLPl WMou |
| § | - 'Melanostachys' (m) | Widely available |
| | x ***greyi*** | EPla NPro NWCA |
| | ***hastata*** (f) | SWat |
| | - 'Wehrhahnii' (m) ♀H4 | CBcs CMea CWib CWon EBee ECho ELan EPfP GCra GKir LEdu LRHS MBar MBlu MRav MSwo MWhi NBir NWea SHBN SPer SWat WCFE WDin WFar WPat WPer |
| | ***helvetica*** ♀H4 | CBcs EBee ECho ELan EPfP MBar MBlu MRav NBir NWCA NWea SHBN SPer WAbe WDin WFar WPat |
| | ***herbacea*** | ECho GAuc GEdr NMen |
| | ***hibernica*** | see *S. phylicifolia* |
| I | ***himalayas*** | CWon |
| | x ***hirtei*** 'Delamere' **new** | CWon |
| | - 'Rosewarne' | CWon |
| | ***hookeriana*** | CDul CLnd CTho CWon EBee ELan EPla MBlu MBrN MRav SLPl WCFE WIvy WMou WPGP WTin |
| | ***humilis*** var. ***microphylla*** | CWon |
| | x ***hungarica*** | CWon |
| | ***incana*** | see *S. elaeagnos* |
| | ***integra*** | CWon |
| | - 'Albomaculata' | see *S. integra* 'Hakuro-nishiki' |
| | - 'Flamingo'PBR | SPoG |
| § | - 'Hakuro-nishiki' (v) | Widely available |
| | - 'Pendula' (f) | CEnd MAsh MBri |
| | ***irrorata*** | CDul CLnd CTho CWon EBee ECrN EPfP GKir IFFs MBlu MRav MSwo SWat |
| | 'Jacquinii' | see *S. alpina* |
| | ***kinuyanagi*** (m) | CWon ELan EPla WIvy |
| § | ***koriyanagi*** | CWiW CWon |
| | 'Kumeti' | see *S.* x *doniana* 'Kumeti' |
| | 'Kuro-me' | see *S. gracilistyla* 'Melanostachys' |
| | x ***laestadiana*** | GAuc |
| | ***laggeri*** **new** | CWon |
| | ***lanata*** ♀H4 | Widely available |
| | - 'Drake's Hybrid' | NMen |
| | - 'Mrs Mac' (m) | CWon |
| | ***lapponum*** | GAuc GEdr GKir NWea SRms |
| | ***lasiandra*** **new** | CWon |
| | x ***laurina*** (f) | CWon |
| § | ***lindleyana*** | CDul GKir |
| | ***linearistipularis*** **new** | CWon |
| | ***lucida*** | CWon ECrN |
| | ***mackenzieana*** | CWon |
| | ***magnifica*** ♀H4 | CDul CEnd CGHE CLnd CMCN CTho CWon EBee EHig ELan EMil EPfP EPla GKir IArd IDee LEdu MSte NWea SMad SPoG SSpi SWat WDin WFar WMou WPGP |
| | 'Mark Postill' (f) | CDoC CWon EBee EMil GBin GKir LRHS MBNS MMuc SPla SPoG SPur |
| | ***matsudana*** 'Tortuosa' | see *S. babylonica* var. *pekinensis* 'Tortuosa' |
| | - 'Tortuosa Aureopendula' | see *S.* 'Erythroflexuosa' |
| | 'Melanostachys' | see *S. gracilistyla* 'Melanostachys' |
| | x ***meyeriana*** | CWon WIvy |
| | - 'Lumley' (f) | CWiW |
| | ***mielichhoferi*** **new** | CWon |
| | x ***mollissima*** var. ***hippophaifolia*** 'Jefferies' (m) | CWiW |
| | - - 'Notts Spaniard' (m) | CWiW |
| | - - 'Stinchcombe' | WIvy |
| | - - 'Trustworthy' (m) | CWiW |
| | - var. ***undulata*** 'Kottenheider Weide' (f) | CWiW |
| | ***moupinensis*** | CWon EPfP IArd IDee MBri NLar WAbe |
| | - EDHCH 97.319 | WPGP |
| | aff. ***moupinensis*** from Vietnam **new** | WPGP |
| § | ***myrsinifolia*** | EBee EPla MBlu MMuc |
| | - subsp. ***alpicola*** | CWon |
| | ***myrsinites*** var. ***jacquiniana*** | see *S. alpina* |
| | ***myrtilloides*** | CLyd |
| | - 'Pink Tassels' (m) | ECho GEdr NWCA SIng |
| | ***myrtilloides*** x ***repens*** | see *S.* x *finnmarchica* |
| | ***nakamurana*** var. ***yezoalpina*** | CEnd CFee CWon EBee EMil EPot EWes GEdr MBlu MRav NHar NHol NPro NWCA SKHP WAbe WFar WIvy WPat |
| | ***nepalensis*** | see *S. lindleyana* |
| | ***nigra*** **new** | CWon |
| | ***nigricans*** | see *S. myrsinifolia* |
| | ***nivalis*** | see *S. reticulata* subsp. *nivalis* |
| | 'Onusta' (m) | EWTr |
| | x ***ovata*** | NMen |
| § | x ***pendulina*** var. ***elegantissima*** | CTho CWon SWat |
| | ***pentandra*** | CDul CLnd ECrN GKir IFFs NWea WDin WFar WMou |
| | - 'Patent Lumley' | CWiW CWon |
| | ***petiolaris*** **new** | CWon |
| | 'Philip's Fancy' | NWCA |
| § | ***phylicifolia*** | ECrN GKir NWea WMou |
| | - 'Malham' (m) | CWiW CWon |
| § | ***purpurea*** | CCVT CDul EMac GKir IFFs NWea SRms WDin WGwG WMou |
| | - 'Brittany Green' (f) | CWiW CWon |
| | - 'Continental Reeks' | CWiW WIvy |
| | - 'Dark Dicks' (f) | CWiW CWon NLar WIvy |
| | - 'Dicky Meadows' (m) | CWiW CWon WIvy |
| | - 'Goldstones' | CWiW NLar WIvy |
| | - f. ***gracilis*** | see *S. purpurea* 'Nana' |
| | - 'Green Dicks' | CWiW CWon WIvy |
| | - 'Helix' | see *S. purpurea* |
| | - 'Howki' (m) | CWon WMou |
| | - 'Irette' (m) | CWiW |
| | - 'Jagiellonka' (f) | CWiW WIvy |
| | - var. ***japonica*** | see *S. koriyanagi* |
| | - subsp. ***lambertiana*** | CWiW WIvy |
| | - 'Lancashire Dicks' (m) | CWiW |
| | - 'Leicestershire Dicks' (m) | CWiW |
| | - 'Light Dicks' | CWiW CWon |
| | - 'Lincolnshire Dutch' (f) | CWiW |
| § | - 'Nana' | EMac EPfP IFFs MMuc NLar NWea SLPl SLon SPer SPur STre WFar WMoo |
| | - 'Nancy Saunders' (f) | CTho CWiW CWon EHoe EPla GBuc GCal MBNS MBlu MBrN MBri MRav MSte NLar NPro NSti SCoo SMHy SUsu WCot WIvy |
| I | - 'Nicholsonii Purpurascens' | CWon |
| | - 'Pendula' ♀H4 | CCVT CEnd CWib CWon EBee ECrN EMil LAst LRHS MAsh MBar MBri MGos MRav MSwo NBlu NWea SPer WDin |
| | - 'Read' (f) | CWiW |
| | - 'Reeks' (f) | CWiW CWon |
| | - 'Richartii' (f) | CWiW CWon |
| | - 'Uralensis' (f) | CWiW CWon |
| | ***pyrenaica*** | EWes NWCA |
| | ***pyrenaica*** x ***retusa*** | ECho |

| | | |
|---|---|---|
| | ***pyrifolia*** | CWon |
| | ***rehderiana*** | CWon |
| | ***reinii*** new | CWon |
| | ***repens*** | ECho EMac GAuc NWea SRms STre SWat WDin WGwG |
| § | - var. ***argentea*** | CWon EPfP EQua EWes GAuc MMuc MRav NWCA NWea SPer STre WDin WFar |
| | - 'Armando'PBR | MGos |
| | - 'Iona' (m) | CLyd MBar |
| | - ***pendula*** | see *S.* 'Boyd's Pendulous' (m) |
| | - 'Voorthuizen' (f) | CWib ECho LAst MBar MGos WDin |
| | ***reticulata*** ♀H4 | ECho EPot GKir NBir NLAp NMen NRya WAbe |
| § | - subsp. ***nivalis*** | NWCA |
| | ***retusa*** | CTri ECho GAuc NBir NLAp |
| | ***retusa*** x ***serpyllifolia*** | EPot NWCA |
| | 'Robin Redbreast' new | CWon |
| | ***rosmarinifolia*** misapplied | see *S. elaeagnos* subsp. *angustifolia* |
| § | x ***rubens*** var. ***basfordiana*** | GKir |
| | - 'Basfordiana' (m) | CDoC CDul CLnd CTho CWiW CWon EPla EWes MBNS MRav SWat WMou |
| | - 'Bouton Aigu' | CWiW |
| | - 'Farndon' | CWiW |
| | - 'Farndon Red' new | CWon |
| | - 'Flanders Red' (f) | CWiW CWon |
| | - 'Fransgeel Rood' (m) | CWiW CWon |
| | - 'Glaucescens' (m) | CWiW |
| | - 'Golden Willow' | CWiW CWon |
| | - 'Hutchinson's Brown' | CWon |
| | - 'Jaune de Falaise' | CWiW CWon |
| | - 'Jaune Hâtive' | CWiW |
| | - 'Laurina' | CWiW |
| | - 'Natural Red' (f) | CWiW CWon |
| | - 'Parsons' | CWiW |
| | - 'Rouge Ardennais' | CWiW CWon |
| | - 'Rouge Folle' | CWiW |
| | - 'Russet' (f) | CWiW |
| | x ***rubra*** | CWiW |
| | - 'Abbey's Harrison' (f) | CWiW |
| | - 'Continental Osier' (f) | CWiW CWon |
| | - 'Eugenei' (m) | CDul ECrN EPla GQui MBlu SWat WIvy WMou |
| | - 'Fidkin' (f) | CWiW |
| | - 'Harrison's' (f) | CWiW |
| | - 'Harrison's Seedling A' (f) | CWiW |
| | - 'Mawdesley' | CWiW |
| | - 'Mawdesley Seedling A' (f) | CWiW |
| | - 'Pyramidalis' | CWiW |
| | ***sachalinensis*** 'Kioryo' | CWon |
| | ***salvaefolia*** new | CWon |
| | x ***sanguinea*** | see *S.* x *rubens* var. *basfordiana* |
| | x ***savensis*** new | CWon |
| | Scarlet Curls = 'Scarcuzam' | CWon WPat |
| | ***schwerinii*** | CWon |
| | - 'Hilliers' new | CWon |
| | ***scouleriana*** new | CWon |
| | x ***sepulcralis*** | NWea |
| § | - 'Aokautere' | CWiW |
| | - 'Caradoc' | CWiW NScw |
| § | - var. ***chrysocoma*** | Widely available |
| | x ***sericans*** | CWon |
| | ***serissaefolia*** new | CWon |
| | ***serpyllifolia*** | CLyd CTri NHar NMen WAbe WPat |
| | ***serpyllum*** | see *S. fragilis* var. *furcata* |
| | 'Setsuka' | see *S. udensis* 'Sekka' |
| | ***silesiaca*** new | CWon |
| | x ***simulatrix*** | EPot GAuc MBar NWCA |
| | x ***smithiana*** | CLnd CWon GKir NWea |
| | ***songarica*** new | GKir |
| | x ***stipularis*** (f) | NWea |
| | 'Stuartii' | MBar NMen NWCA SRms |
| | ***subopposita*** | CDul EBee ELan EWes MBar MMuc NPro SLon STre WGwG |
| | ***thomasii*** | GAuc |
| | ***triandra*** | CWon WMou |
| | - 'Black German' (m) | CWiW |
| | - 'Black Hollander' (m) | CWiW NLar WIvy |
| | - 'Black Maul' | CWiW |
| | - 'Brilliant' new | CWon |
| | - 'Champion B' new | CWon |
| | - 'Grisette de Falaise' | CWiW |
| | - 'Grisette Droda' (f) | CWiW |
| | - 'Houghton's Black' new | CWon |
| | - 'Light French' new | CWon |
| | - 'Long Bud' | CWiW |
| | - 'Noir de Challans' | CWiW |
| | - 'Noir de Touraine' | CWiW CWon |
| | - 'Noir de Villaines' (m) | CWiW CWon WIvy |
| | - 'Oliveacea' new | CWon |
| | - 'Rouge d'Orléans' | CWon |
| | - 'Sarda d'Anjou' | CWiW |
| | - 'Semperflorens' (m) | CNat CWon NLar |
| | - 'Whissander' | CWiW WIvy |
| | - 'Zwarre Driebast' new | CWon |
| | x ***tsugaluensis*** 'Ginme' (f) | CWon IFFs SLPl WPat |
| § | ***udensis*** 'Sekka' (m) | CWon EBee ECtt ELan EPfP IFFs MBlu NBir NWea STre SWat WFar WIvy WMou |
| | ***uva-ursi*** | CLyd |
| | ***viminalis*** | CCVT CDul CLnd CWon ECrN EMac IFFs LBuc NWea SVic WDin WMou |
| | - 'Black Satin' | CWon |
| | - 'Brown Merrin' | WIvy |
| | - 'Gigantea' (m) new | CWon |
| | - 'Green Gotz' | CWiW WIvy |
| | - 'Reader's Red' (m) | WIvy |
| | - 'Regalis' new | CWon |
| | - 'Riefenweide' | WIvy |
| | - 'Romanin' | CWon |
| | - 'Yellow Osier' | WIvy |
| | ***vitellina*** 'Pendula' | see *S. alba* 'Tristis' ambig. |
| | ***waldsteiniana*** | GAuc MBar NWCA |
| | x ***wimmeriana*** | SRms |
| | 'Yelverton' | see *S. alba* var. *vitellina* 'Yelverton' |
| * | ***zatungensis*** new | CWon |

## Salsola (*Chenopodiaceae*)

| | |
|---|---|
| ***soda*** | CArn |

## Salvia ✿ (*Lamiaceae*)

| | | |
|---|---|---|
| | ACE 2172 | SPin |
| | CD&R 1162 | CAby SPin |
| | CD&R 1458 | SPin |
| | CD&R 1495 | SHGN SPin |
| | CD&R 3071 | SPin |
| | DJH 93T | SPin |
| | PC&H 226 | SPin |
| | ***acetabulosa*** | see *S. multicaulis* |
| | ***adenophora*** new | SPin |
| | ***aerea*** | CPom |
| | ***aethiopis*** | EAro EWes SDnm SPav SPin WOut |
| § | ***africana*** | GGar SPin WDyG WOut |
| | ***africana-caerulea*** | see *S. africana* |
| | ***africana-lutea*** | see *S. aurea* |
| | ***agnes*** | SPin |
| | ***albimaculata*** | CPBP SPin |
| | ***algeriensis*** | CSec CSpe SBch SPin |
| | ***amarissima*** | SPin |
| | 'Amber' | SPin SUsu |
| | ***ambigens*** | see *S. guaranitica* 'Blue Enigma' |

| | |
|---|---|
| ***ampelophylla*** B&SWJ 10751 | WCru |
| § ***amplexicaulis*** | EAro EPyc LSou MWea NLar SBch SMrm SPin WPer |
| ***amplifrons*** new | EWld SPin |
| ***angustifolia*** Cav. | see *S. reptans* |
| ***angustifolia*** Mich. | see *S. azurea* |
| 'Anthony Parker' | MAJR SAga SDys SPin WOut |
| ***apiana*** | CArn EAro EOHP EPyc MDKP MHer MSal SAga SGar SPin |
| ***argentea*** ♀H3 | Widely available |
| ***arizonica*** | CPom EAro GCal MHom MLLN MSte SDys SPin |
| ***aspera*** new | SPin |
| ***atrocyanea*** | CSpe EBee EPyc LPio MAJR MAsh MLLN SDys SGar SPin WHal WKif WWlt |
| ***aucheri*** | GBar |
| § ***aurea*** | CHal CHll CSec CSev EShb GBar LHop LPio MSte SAga SGar SPin |
| - 'Kirstenbosch' | CDes CSev EAro EBee ECtt EWld MLLN SDys SPin WGwG WHer WKif WOut WPGP WPer |
| ***aurita*** | SPin |
| - var. ***galpinii*** | SPin |
| ***austriaca*** | SPin |
| § ***azurea*** | CRWN CSpe MSte SAga SBod SMrm SPin |
| - var. ***grandiflora*** | SPin WWlt |
| ***bacheriana*** | see *S. buchananii* |
| § ***barrelieri*** | SPin SUsu |
| 'Belhaven' | GCal SPin WDyG |
| ***bertolonii*** | see *S. pratensis* Bertolonii Group |
| ***bicolor*** Des. | see *S. barrelieri* |
| 'Black Knight' | MAvo SDys SPin SUsu |
| ***blancoana*** | ECha ELau GBar MHer MLLN MSte SAga SBch SDys SPin |
| ***blepharophylla*** | CSpe EAro EBee ECtt EPyc EShb LHop LPio MCot MHer MSCN MSte NGHP SAga SDnm SPav SPin SRkn |
| - 'Diablo' | ECtt SAga SDys SKHP SPin |
| - 'Painted Lady' | MAsh SDys SPin WOut WWlt |
| 'Blue Chiquita' | SDys SPin |
| 'Blue Sky' | EWld SDys |
| 'Blue Vein' | NPri |
| ***bowleyana*** new | EBee |
| ***bracteata*** new | SPin |
| ***brandegeei*** | SPin |
| ***broussonetii*** | SPin WOut |
| § ***buchananii*** ♀H1+3 | CHal CHll CPom CSWP CSam CSpe EAro EBee ECtt EPfP EPyc EShb EWld GQui LHop LPio MAsh MHer MLLN NGHP SAga SPav SPin SPoG SRkn SWal WFar |
| ***bulleyana*** misapplied | see *S. flava* var. *megalantha* |
| ***bulleyana*** Diels | CHFP CSev EBee EDAr EWes EWld GKev LEdu MDKP MLLN MMHG NChi NGHP NLar SDnm SPav WCru WFar |
| ***cacaliifolia*** ♀H1+3 | CDMG CPLG CRHN CSpe ECtt EPyc EWld GBar MAsh MHer MLLN MNrw MSte NGHP SAga SBch SDnm SGar SPer SPin SRkn SUsu WFar WPic WSHC WWlt |
| ***cadmica*** | SPin |
| ***caerulea*** misapplied | see *S. guaranitica* 'Black and Blue' |
| ***caerulea*** L. | see *S. africana* |
| ***caespitosa*** | NMen NWCA SPin |
| ***campanulata*** | CPom EWld SPhx SPin |
| - CC&McK 1071 | CFir |
| - DJHC C394 new | SPin |
| - GWJ 9294 | WCru |
| ***canariensis*** | CSpe EAro EShb IGor MLLN SPin WOut |
| ***candelabrum*** ♀H3-4 | CAbP CArn CMea CSpe ECtt EWld MHer MLLN MSte SAga SBch SPav SPhx SPin WCHb WEas WKif WSHC WWlt |
| ***candidissima*** | SPin |
| ***canescens*** | EAro |
| ***cardinalis*** | see *S. fulgens* |
| ***carduacea*** | CSec SPin |
| ***carnea*** new | EWld |
| - from Valle de Bravo, Mexico new | SDys |
| ***castanea*** | SPin |
| ***caudata*** new | SPin |
| ***cavalerieri*** var. ***simplicifolia*** new | EBee |
| ***cedrosensis*** | SDys |
| § ***chamaedryoides*** | CSev CWGN EBee EPyc MHom NGHP SDnm SDys SGar SPet SPhx SPin |
| - var. ***isochroma*** | EAro MAsh SDys SPin |
| - 'Marine Blue' | MAsh MCot SDys SPin |
| - silver-leaved | CSpe MSte SAga SPhx SPin |
| aff. ***chamaedryoides*** B&SWJ 9032 from Guatemala | SPin WCru |
| ***chamaedryoides*** x ***microphylla*** | EAro |
| ***chamelaeagnea*** | EBee GFai LHop SDys SHar SPin WPrP |
| ***chapalensis*** | SAga SPin |
| ***cheinii*** new | SPin |
| ***chiapensis*** | CSpe MAJR MAsh MLLN SAga SDys SPin WWlt |
| ***chinensis*** | see *S. japonica* |
| 'Christine Yeo' | CDes EBee ECtt EPPr EPyc EWld GGar MAsh MDKP MHer MSte NGHP SAga SBch SDys SGar SMeo SPav SPin SWal WDyG WMnd WPGP WSHC |
| ***cinnabarina*** | SPin |
| ***cleistogama*** misapplied | see *S. glutinosa* |
| ***clevelandii*** | CDow EAro EWes MAJR MHer SPav WJek |
| - 'Winnifred Gilman' | CWGN EAro MSte SBHP SDys |
| ***clinopodioides*** | SPin |
| ***coahuilensis*** misapplied | see *S. greggii* x *serpyllifolia* |
| ***coahuilensis*** ambig. | CAby LSou MAsh SAga SGar SMeo SMrm SPin SRkn WSHC |
| ***coahuilensis*** Fernald | EAro WHil |
| ***coccinea*** | SPin |
| - 'Brenthurst' | SDys SPin |
| - 'Forest Fire' new | SDys SUsu |
| - (Nymph Series) 'Coral Nymph' | ECtt EPyc LDai LRHS SDnm SDys SMrm SPav SPin SUsu |
| - - 'Lady in Red' ♀H3 | ECtt SDys SPav |
| * - - 'Snow Nymph' | ECtt SUsu |
| ***columbariae*** | SPin |
| ***concolor*** misapplied | see *S. guaranitica* |
| ***concolor*** Lamb. ex Benth. | CDes EWld GCal MHom SPin WDyG WPGP WSHC |
| ***confertiflora*** | Widely available |
| ***corrugata*** | CBcs CDes CFee CPne CSam CSpe EBee EPyc EShb EWld GCal IDee LHop MAsh MAvo MHer MLLN NBsh NGHP SDys SPin SRkn SUsu WPGP WPic WWlt |
| 'Crème Caramel' | EPyc MAsh SDys |
| ***cruickshanksii*** new | SPin |
| ***cyanescens*** | CPBP EPot EWld SPin |
| ***cyanicalyx*** new | SDys |
| ***daghestanica*** | SDys SPin |

| | |
|---|---|
| I ***dangitalis*** SDR 4332 new | EBee GKev |
| ***darcyi*** misapplied | see *S. roemeriana* |
| ***darcyi*** J. Compton | CAby CDTJ CHll CPom CSpe EBee EPyc EWes EWld LPio MCot MSte SAga SDys SKHP SPin WEas WHil WSHC WWlt |
| ***davidsonii*** | SPin |
| ***dentata*** | SDys SPin |
| ***desoleana*** | EAro SPin |
| ***digitaloides*** BWJ 7777 | SPin WCru |
| ***discolor*** ♀H1 | Widely available |
| * - ***nigra*** | CArn CMdw |
| ***disermas*** | SDys SPin SPlb |
| ***disjuncta*** | SPin |
| - 'Chimbango' new | SDys |
| ***divinorum*** | EOHP GPoy MSal NGHP |
| ***dolichantha*** | CDMG CHFP CSpe EAro EPyc MAvo MDKP SBch SBod SEND SGar SPin WMoo WPtf |
| ***dolomitica*** | SPav SPin |
| ***dombeyi*** | CHll CPne EAro EWld SDys SPin |
| ***dominica*** | SAga SPin |
| ***dorisiana*** | CFee CPne CSpe EAro ELan EOHP MAsh MLLN SDys SPin |
| ***eigii*** | SPin |
| ***elegans*** | CSev CTca ELau EWes GCra MAJR MHom MSte SAga SMad SPoG WFar |
| - 'Honey Melon' | CAby EOHP MAsh NGHP SDys SUsu |
| § - 'Scarlet Pineapple' | Widely available |
| - 'Sonoran Red' | EAro SDys |
| - 'Tangerine' | CArn CPrp CWan ELau EOHP EPyc GBar LAst LFol LSou MHer MNHC NGHP SDnm SPin WGwG WLHH |
| ***evansiana*** BWJ 8013 | SPin |
| 'Eveline' new | EBee |
| ***excelsa*** new | SPin |
| ***fallax*** | MHar SPin |
| ***farinacea*** | SPin |
| - 'Rhea' | LRHS |
| - 'Strata' | LRHS MNHC SDys |
| - 'Victoria' ♀H3 | ELau MCot SDys |
| § ***flava*** var. ***megalantha*** | CDes EBee EBla ELan LEdu LRHS LSRN NGdn SPin WFar WPer |
| - - BWJ 7974 | WCru |
| ***florida*** new | SPin |
| ***forreri*** | CDes EAro EBee EPyc MAsh SAga SBHP SDys SPin WPGP |
| - 'Karen Dyson' | SDys |
| § ***forsskaolii*** | Widely available |
| - white-flowered new | SPin |
| 'Frieda Dixon' | EOHP |
| § ***fruticosa*** | CArn EAro ELau EPyc LRHS SIde SPin |
| § ***fulgens*** ♀H3 | EWld GBar ILis MAsh MHom NGHP SAga SBHP SBch SGar SPin SRkn WFar WOut WRha WWlt |
| ***gesneriiflora*** | CAby ECtt EWld MSte SAga SDys SPin WOut |
| - 'Tequila' | MAJR SPin |
| ***gilliesii*** | SPin |
| ***glabrescens*** new | SPin |
| - B&SWJ 10919 new | WCru |
| - 'Momobana' new | EBee |
| - 'Shi-ho' new | EBee |
| ***glechomifolia*** | SPin |
| 'Gloomy' new | SPin |
| § ***glutinosa*** | CArn CHFP CSec CSpe EAro EBee ECtt EPPr EPyc EWld GCal LDai MCot MNrw NBro SAga SPav SPin SWal WCAu WGwG WPer |
| ***graciliramulosa*** new | SPin |
| ***gracilis*** | SPin |

| | |
|---|---|
| ***grahamii*** | see *S. microphylla* var. *microphylla* |
| ***gravida*** new | SPin |
| ***greggii*** | CDMG ECtt EWes EWld MHer MSte NGHP SBod WKif WPer |
| - CD&R 1148 | EAro MCot SDys |
| - 'Alba' | CHal EBee LPio MAsh NGHP SAga SDys SPin |
| - 'Blush Pink' | see *S. microphylla* 'Pink Blush' |
| - 'Caramba' (v) | CBow CDow EAro EBee EPyc MLLN NGHP SAga SDnm SHGN SPav SPoG |
| - 'Devon Cream' | see *S. greggii* 'Sungold' |
| - 'Diane' new | MAsh |
| - 'Magenta' | MDKP WHil |
| - 'Magnet' new | SPin |
| - (Navajo Series) 'Navajo Bright Red' new | EPyc |
| * - - 'Navajo Cream' | EAro EPyc SAga WFar |
| * - - 'Navajo Dark Purple' | EAro EPyc SAga WFar |
| - - Navajo Pink = 'Rrds019' | SGar |
| - - Navajo Rose = 'Rfds018' | WFar |
| - - Navajo Salmon Red = 'Rfds016' | EPyc WFar |
| * - - 'Navajo White' | EPyc WFar |
| - 'Peach' misapplied | see *S.* x *jamensis* 'Pat Vlasto' |
| - 'Peach' | CDes CSpe CWGN EBee ELau EPfP EPyc LHop LRHS MAsh MCot MHar MHer MLLN MSte NGHP SAga SDnm SGar SPav SPin WMnd WPGP WWlt |
| - salmon-flowered new | EPyc |
| - 'Sierra San Antonio' | see *S.* x *jamensis* 'Sierra San Antonio' |
| - 'Sparkler' (v) | EPfP MAsh SBch |
| - 'Stormy Pink' | CAby CDes CHll CMdw CSpe CWGN EBee EPyc MCot SAga WIvy WPGP WSHC WWlt |
| § - 'Sungold' | CWGN EAro EBee ECtt EPfP EPyc LHop LRHS MAsh MHom MLLN MWte NGHP SAga SBch SDys SHGN SPin WMnd |
| - variegated (v) | EHoe |
| - yellow-flowered | LRHS |
| ***greggii*** x ***lycioides*** | see *S. greggii* x *serpyllifolia* |
| § ***greggii*** x ***serpyllifolia*** | CAbP CSpe EPyc MCot SAga SDys SGar SPin WPGP |
| ***grewiifolia*** new | SPin |
| § ***guaranitica*** | CBcs CEnt CHEx CPne ECtt EPyc EShb GCra MCot SAga SDnm SDys SPav SPer SPin SRkn WCHb WKif WPGP WWlt |
| - 'Argentine Skies' | EBee ECtt EPPr EPyc MAvo MSte SAga SDys SMrm SPin WPGP WWlt |
| § - 'Black and Blue' | CPne CRHN CSWP CSev CWCL EBee ECtt EPPr EPyc GCal LPio MAvo MCot MSte NBsh NGHP SAga SBch SDnm SGar SPav SPhx SPin SUsu WPGP WPer WPrP WSHC |
| § - 'Blue Enigma' ♀H3-4 | Widely available |
| - 'Indigo Blue' | ECtt EPfP MAsh MLLN SPin WWlt |
| - 'Purple Splendor' | CPne EShb |
| - purple-flowered | CSam |
| ***haematodes*** | see *S. pratensis* Haematodes Group |
| ***haenkei*** | SPin |
| - 'Prawn Chorus' | CSpe SAga |
| ***heerii*** new | SPin |
| ***heldreichiana*** | SPin |
| ***henryi*** | SPin |
| ***hians*** | CPom EAro EBee GBar GCra MDKP MLLN MNrw SAga SDnm SGar SPav SPin SRms WPer |
| - CC 1787 | SPin |

| | |
|---|---|
| ***hierosolymitana*** | SPin |
| ***hirtella*** | SPin |
| ***hispanica*** misapplied | see *S. lavandulifolia* |
| ***hispanica*** L. | CSam SPin |
| ***holwayi*** | SPin |
| - B&SWJ 8995 **new** | WCru |
| ***horminum*** | see *S. viridis* var. *comata* |
| ***huberi*** | SPin |
| ***hypargeia*** | SPin |
| ***indica*** | SPin |
| 'Indigo Spires' | CHll CMHG CSpe CWGN EBee ECtt EPPr EShb EWld GCal LPio MAsh MCot MHar MHom MLLN NDov SAga SDys SMrm SPhx SPin WDyG WPen WSHC WWlt |
| ***interrupta*** | EWes SAga SPin WKif WPen |
| ***involucrata*** ♀H3 | CFir CPom CSev EWld GCra GQui MCot MHom NBro NBur SBch SDys SPin WSHC |
| - 'Bethellii' ♀H3-4 | Widely available |
| - 'Boutin' ♀H3 | MAJR MAsh MHom MLLN SAga SDys |
| § - 'Hadspen' | CHll CRHN CSam CSpe GCal MAJR MSte SPin WKif |
| - 'Joan' | SDys SPin |
| - 'Mrs Pope' | see *S. involucrata* 'Hadspen' |
| * - var. ***puberula*** | MAJR SDys SPin |
| ***iodantha*** | SAga SDys SPin |
| - 'Louis Saso' | SPin |
| ***iodochroa*** | CDes |
| - B&SWJ 10252 | CHFP SPin WCru |
| x ***jamensis*** | CAby CSpe CWGN EAro EBee ECtt ELon EPfP EPyc EWes EWld LBuc LRHS MAsh MAvo MBri MWea NGHP NPri SAga SDys SGar SPin SUsu WOut WWlt |
| - 'Cherry Queen' | CSpe EAro EBee EPyc MAsh SAga SDys SPin WFar WWlt |
| - 'Dark Dancer' | CWGN MAsh SDys WWlt |
| - 'Desert Blaze' (v) | CAbP CBow CDes EAro EBee ECtt EPyc MCot MHar MHer NCGa NGHP SDys SMrm SPin WHer WLeb WPGP |
| - 'Devantville' | CAby |
| - 'Dysons' Orangy Pink' | CAby CSpe SAga |
| - 'James Compton' | EAro EPyc MHom MSte SDys SGar |
| - 'La Luna' | CEnt CPom CSam CTri CWGN EAro ECtt EPfP EPyc EShb EWld GGar LHop LPio MCot MHar MHer MHom MSte SDys SEND SGar SHGN SPin WFar WMnd WPGP WSHC |
| - 'La Siesta' | EAro EBee NGHP SDys |
| - 'La Tarde' | CAby CEnt CTri MAsh MHom MSte NGHP SBch SDys |
| - 'Lemon Sorbet' | SDys |
| - 'Los Lirios' ♀H3-4 | CPom CSpe CTri EAro EPyc MSte SAga SDys SMrm SPin |
| - 'Maraschino' | CAbP EAro EBee EPfP EPyc LPio MAsh SDys SMrm SPin WMnd WWlt |
| * - 'Mauve' | EPyc SAga SDys |
| - 'Moonlight Over Ashwood' (v) | EAro EPyc MAsh SBHP SDys SPin WWlt |
| - 'Moonlight Serenade' | CAby EAro EBee EPyc MAsh MWea SAga SBch SDys SHGN WHoo |
| § - 'Pat Vlasto' | EAro EBee EPyc MHom MWea NGHP SDys SPin |
| - 'Peter Vidgeon' **new** | SDys |
| - 'Pleasant Pink' | CSev EBee EPyc MAsh SAga SDys SPin |
| - 'Plum Wine' | MAsh |
| - 'Raspberry Royale' ♀H3-4 | CDes CPom CSev CWGN EAro EBee ECtt EPfP EPyc GBar LHop MAsh MCot MHer MLLN MSte NGHP SDnm SGar SMrm SPav SPin WHoo WMnd WSHC |
| - 'Red Velvet' | CAby ECtt MAsh MHer MHom NGHP SUsu WEas WSHC WWlt |
| - 'Señorita Leah' | EPyc SDys SUsu |
| § - 'Sierra San Antonio' | CSev EAro ECtt EPfP MAsh MHom MWea SAga SBHP SDys SMrm SUsu |
| § - 'Trebah' | CDes CPom CSpe ECre EPyc MAsh MCot MHom MSte MWea SAga SDys SGar SPav SPin SPoG SRot WIvy WPGP |
| - 'Trenance' | CAby ECre EPyc MHom MSte SDys SGar SPav SPin SRot WSHC |
| - white-flowered | SPin |
| § ***japonica*** | SPin |
| - 'Alba' **new** | SPin |
| 'Jean's Purple Passion' **new** | SPin |
| ***judaica*** | SPin |
| ***jurisicii*** | CArn CFir CWib EAro EBee EPyc SPav SPin WJek |
| - pink-flowered | CSpe SPin |
| ***karwinskyi*** | SPin |
| - B&SWJ 9081 | WCru |
| ***keerlii*** | SPin |
| ***koyamae*** | SPin |
| 'Lady Strybing' **new** | SPin |
| ***lanceolata*** | EAro SPin |
| ***lanigera*** | SPin |
| ***lasiantha*** **new** | SPin |
| § ***lavandulifolia*** | Widely available |
| ***lavanduloides*** | SPin |
| - B&SWJ 9053 | WCru |
| ***lemmonii*** | see *S. microphylla* var. *wislizeni* |
| ***leptophylla*** | see *S. reptans* |
| ***leucantha*** ♀H1 | Widely available |
| - 'Eder' (v) | MAJR SDys SPin |
| - 'Midnight' | IFoB |
| - 'Purple Velvet' | EBee MAJR MAsh MHom MSte NGHP SDix SDys SPin WOut WWlt |
| - 'San Marcos Lavender' | SPin |
| - 'Santa Barbara' | CHll SDys |
| ***leucocephala*** **new** | SPin |
| ***leucophylla*** NNS 01-375 | SPin |
| ***littae*** | SPin |
| ***longispicata*** | SPin |
| ***longistyla*** | SPin |
| ***lycioides*** misapplied | see *S. greggii* x *serpyllifolia* |
| ***lycioides*** A. Gray | CAbP CHll LPio SDys SPhx SPin SRkn WDyG |
| ***lyrata*** | CSec EOHP MDKP MSal SGar SPin WOut |
| - 'Burgundy Bliss' | see *S. lyrata* 'Purple Knockout' |
| § - 'Purple Knockout' | CBod CBow CKno EAro EBee EHoe EMil EPPr EPfP EPyc EShb GKev LAst LHop NBPN NGHP SBod SGar SHGN SPav SPhx SPin SWal |
| - 'Purple Vulcano' | see *S. lyrata* 'Purple Knockout' |
| ***macellaria*** misapplied | see *S. microphylla* |
| ***macellaria*** Epling | CSam |
| ***macrophylla*** **new** | GCal SPin |
| ***madrensis*** | MAJR SPin |
| - 'Dunham' | GCal SDys |
| ***marocana*** | IFro |
| ***melissodora*** | SDys SPin |
| ***mellifera*** | CArn SPin |
| ***merjamie*** | EBee SPin |
| - 'Mint-sauce' | CHFP EAro GBar WFar WHer WPer |
| ***mexicana*** | CSam SPin |
| - B&SWJ 10288 **new** | WCru |
| - T&K 550 | CArn |
| - 'Lollie Jackson' | MAJR |
| - var. ***minor*** | EWld MAJR SPin |

| | | |
|---|---|---|
| | - 'Snowflake' | MAJR |
| | - 'Tula' | SDys SPin |
| | ***meyeri*** | EWld MAJR MHom SPin WWlt |
| § | ***microphylla*** | CArn CHrt CMHG CPom CPrp CWan EAro ELau EOHP EWes GBar GGar LAst LFol LHop MHer MSCN NSti SPet WHCG WPer |
| | - CD&R 1141 | SPin |
| | - 'Belize' | EAro MAsh NGHP WWlt |
| | - 'Cerro Potosi' | CMdw CPom CSev CSpe EBee ELon EPyc MAsh MLLN MSte NGHP SAga SDys SGar SMrm SPin SUsu WDyG WPen WWlt |
| | - 'Dieciocho de Marzo' | SDys |
| | - 'Hot Lips' | see *S.* x *jamensis* |
| | - 'Huntington' | EOHP SPin |
| | - hybrid, purple-flowered | CPom |
| | - 'Kew Red' ♀H3-4 | CFir CHVG CSpe CWGN EBee MNrw MWea NGHP SBch SPin WHoo WPen |
| | - 'La Trinidad' | SDys |
| I | - 'Lutea' **new** | MAsh |
| | - 'Maroon' **new** | SDys |
| § | - var. ***microphylla*** | CFee CHal CRHN CSev CSpe CTri CWib EBee ECtt ELan EOHP EPfP MCot MHer MNHC NGHP SGar SOWG SPav SPin SRkn WCFE WFar WPer WSHC |
| | - - 'La Foux' | ECtt MCot MWea SBch SDys SMeo SMrm SPhx |
| | - - 'Newby Hall' ♀H3-4 | CAby CDes EBee ECtt EPyc EWes MSte NGHP SDys SPhx SPoG WPGP |
| N | - var. ***neurepia*** | see *S. microphylla* var. *microphylla* |
| | - 'Orange Door' | EPyc SDys SUsu |
| | - 'Oregon Peach' | EPfP LRHS |
| | - 'Oxford' | NGHP SDys SPin |
| § | - 'Pink Blush' ♀H3-4 | CAby EAro EBee ECtt ELan EPfP EPyc GBri LAst LRHS MAsh MCot MHer MHom MLLN MSte NGHP SMrm SPin WHil WKif WPGP WSHC |
| | - 'Pleasant View' ♀H3-4 | CAby EPyc MAsh |
| | - 'Robin's Pride' **new** | SDys |
| | - 'Rosy Cheeks' | WOut |
| § | - 'Ruth Stungo' (v) | ECre |
| | - 'San Carlos Festival' | CDes CPom CSev EAro ECtt EPyc MAsh NGHP SBch SDys SPin WPGP WWlt |
| | - 'Trelawny Rose Pink' | see *S.* 'Trelawney' |
| | - 'Trelissick Creamy Yellow' | see *S.* 'Trelissick' |
| | - 'Trewithen Cerise' | see *S.* 'Trewithen' |
| | - 'Variegata' splashed | see *S. microphylla* 'Ruth Stungo' |
| | - 'Wild Watermelon' | EAro EPyc MAsh SAga SDys |
| § | - var. ***wislizeni*** | EPyc SDys SPin |
| | - 'Zaragoza' | SPin |
| | ***miltiorhiza*** | CArn EBee MSal SPin |
| | ***miniata*** | CSev CSpe MAJR SBHP SDys SPin |
| | ***misella*** | CMdw CSpe SPin |
| | ***mohavensis*** | SPin |
| | ***moorcroftiana*** | SDnm SPin |
| | ***muelleri*** misapplied | see *S. greggii* x *serpyllifolia* |
| | ***muelleri*** Epling | EAro EBee EPyc SAga |
| | ***muirii*** | SHar SPin |
| | 'Mulberry Jam' | CDes CHll CMdw CSev CSpe CWGN EAro EBee ECtt EPyc EWes EWld GBri GCal MAJR MAsh MHom SAga SDys SPin SUsu WKif WPGP WWlt |
| § | ***multicaulis*** ♀H4 | EBee EPyc GBri MSte SPin WCot WEas |
| | ***munzii*** | CFir SPin |
| * | ***murrayi*** | CAbP SPin |
| | ***namaensis*** | EAro SDys SPin |
| | ***nana*** B&SWJ 10272 | SPin WCru |
| | ***napifolia*** | EBee NBHF SAga SBod SDnm SPav SPhx SPin WGwG WPer |
| | 'Nazareth' | EAro |
| | ***nemorosa*** | CSec EPyc SPin SRms |
| | - 'Amethyst' ♀H4 | CPrp EBee EGle ELon EPPr EPfP LAst LRHS MBri MLLN MRav MSte NDov NMoo NPri SDys SHBN SMHy SPhx WCAu WCot WKif WWlt |
| | - Blue Mound | see *S.* x *sylvestris* 'Blauhügel' |
| | - 'Caradonna' | Widely available |
| | - East Friesland | see *S. nemorosa* 'Ostfriesland' |
| | - 'Lubecca' ♀H4 | CPrp EBee EBrs ECGP ECtt EGle EHrv EPfP EPla EShb LHop LRHS MBri MCot MLLN NDov NLar SMrm SPer WCAu WFar WMnd |
| | - Marcus = 'Haeumanarc'PBR | CKno CPrp CSpe EBee ECtt EGle ELan EPfP EPyc LAst LHop LLWG LRHS LSRN MBNS MBri MLLN NLar SDys SPla WCot WFar WSHC |
| | - 'Midsummer' | EWld |
| § | - 'Ostfriesland' ♀H4 | Widely available |
| | - 'Phoenix Pink' | SPhx |
| | - 'Pink Friesland' **new** | EBee EPPr LRHS |
| | - 'Plumosa' | see *S. nemorosa* 'Pusztaflamme' |
| | - 'Porzellan' ♀H4 | ECtt |
| § | - 'Pusztaflamme' ♀H4 | CPrp CWGN EBee ECha ECtt EPfP NBsh NOrc SMrm SUsu WCAu |
| | - 'Rose Queen' | ECtt EPPr GKir LBMP MCot MWat NBir SDys SPer SPla SWat WFar |
| | - 'Rosenwein' | CSam EAro EBee GBuc LDai MAvo MDKP MNrw NBPC NGdn SMrm SPhx |
| | - 'Royal Distinction' | EBee ECtt NBsh SUsu |
| | - 'Schwellenburg' | EBee EGle EPfP LBuc LHop MAvo NBPC NBsh NMoo SPoG SUsu WCot |
| | - 'Sensation Rose' | EBrs GBin |
| § | - subsp. ***tesquicola*** | CSec ECGP ECha EPyc LSRN MWhi NGdn NLar SMrm SPhx WFar WOut |
| | - 'Wesuwe' | EBee ELon EPPr NBsh NDov NGby |
| | ***neurepia*** | see *S. microphylla* var. *microphylla* |
| | ***nilotica*** | CSec EAro EBee EHig SPin SWal |
| | ***nipponica*** B&SWJ 5829 | SPin WCru |
| | - 'Fuji Snow' (v) | CBow EBee EPyc LSou MLLN |
| | - var. ***trisecta*** **new** | SPin |
| | ***nubicola*** | CPLG EBee EPPr EWld GKev GPoy LDai SPin WOut |
| | ***nutans*** | SPin |
| | ***oblongifolia*** B&SWJ 10315 **new** | WCru |
| | ***officinalis*** | Widely available |
| | - 'Alba' | see *S. officinalis* 'Albiflora' |
| § | - 'Albiflora' | CArn CBod ECtt EOHP GBar MSte SBch SPin WCHb WJek WPer |
| N | - 'Aurea' ambig. | CWib ECho GKir GPoy MBar |
| | - 'Berggarten' | CArn CPrp EBee ECha ELau EPfP GBar GCal LHop LPio MBri MHer MRav SDix SPhx SPin WCFE WHer WMnd |
| | - 'Blackcurrant' | CHal LSou |
| § | - broad-leaved | CSWP ELau MHer SWat WJek |
| | - 'Crispa' | EOHP SPin WCHb |
| | - 'Extrakta' | SPhx |
| | - 'Grandiflora' | EAro |
| | - 'Grete Stolze' | EBee LPla |
| | - 'Herrenhausen' | MSte |
| § | - 'Icterina' (v) ♀H4 | Widely available |
| | - 'Kew Gold' | MRav |
| | - ***latifolia*** | see *S. officinalis* broad-leaved |
| | - narrow-leaved | see *S. lavandulifolia* |
| | - 'Nazareth'PBR | EBee |

| | | |
|---|---|---|
| * | - 'Pink Splash' (v) | CBow WCHb |
| | - ***prostrata*** | see *S. lavandulifolia* |
| | - 'Purpurascens' ♀H4 | Widely available |
| | - 'Purpurascens Variegata' (v) | WEas |
| | - 'Robin Hill' | CHFP GBar |
| | - 'Rosea' | CArn EOHP WCHb |
| | - Tomentosa Group | CArn |
| | - 'Tricolor' (v) | Widely available |
| | - 'Variegata' | see *S. officinalis* 'Icterina' |
| | - variegated (v) | ECho |
| | ***omeiana*** | EWld |
| | - BWJ 8062 | WCru |
| | - 'Crûg Thundercloud' | WCru |
| | ***oppositiflora*** misapplied | see *S. tubiflora* |
| | ***oppositiflora*** ambig. | MAJR SAga SDys SPin |
| | ***orbignaei*** | SPin |
| | ***oxyphora*** | SDys SPin |
| | ***pachyphylla*** | SPin |
| | ***pachystachya*** | SPin |
| | pale blue, B&SWJ 8985 from Guatemala | WCru |
| § | ***patens*** ♀H3 | Widely available |
| | - 'Alba' misapplied | see *S. patens* 'White Trophy' |
| | - 'Blue Angel' | EAro EWes IFoB |
| | - 'Cambridge Blue' ♀H3 | Widely available |
| | - 'Chilcombe' | CSam EBee ECtt EPyc MAsh MCot MLLN MSte SAga SDys SPin WHil WOut WWlt |
| | - 'Guanajuato' | CBcs CSam CSpe EBee EPyc EShb EWes GMaP IFoB LAst LPio MAsh MHar MHer MSCN MSte NGHP SAga SDnm SDys SMad SMrm SPin SRkn SRot SUsu WHoo WSHC |
| | - 'Guanajuato Lavender' | LPio MHar |
| | - tall **new** | SUsu |
| | - lavender-flowered **new** | SBch |
| | - 'Oxford Blue' | see *S. patens* |
| | - 'Royal Blue' | see *S. patens* |
| § | - 'White Trophy' | CBcs CHFP EBee ELan EPyc EShb EWld GCal LHop LRHS MBNS MCot MHer MSte NGHP NPri SDnm SDys SGar SMrm SPer SPin SWal WFar |
| | ***pauciserrata*** | SPin |
| | ***penstemonoides*** | SDys SPin |
| | ***personata*** **new** | SPin |
| | 'Peru Blue' | CSpe SDys |
| | ***phlomoides*** | CSec |
| | 'Phyllis' Fancy' | MAsh |
| | ***pinguifolia*** | SPin |
| | 'Pink Ice' | CPom |
| | ***pisidica*** | SPin |
| | ***platystoma*** **new** | SPin |
| | ***plectranthoides*** | SPin |
| | ***pogonochila*** | CPom |
| | ***polystachya*** | SPin |
| * | 'Powis Castle' **new** | MHom |
| | ***praeclara*** **new** | SPin |
| | ***pratensis*** | CAby CArn CSec CWib EBWF EBee ELan EPyc GJos MNHC MSal NChi SECG SGar SPin WOut WPer |
| | - 'Albiflora' | CDes |
| § | - Bertolonii Group | EPyc SPin |
| § | - Haematodes Group ♀H4 | ECha ELan EPyc LDai MNrw NLar SBch SDnm SPav SPin SRms WPer |
| | - 'Indigo' ♀H4 | CDes CPrp EBee ECGP ECtt EPPr EPfP LRHS MCot MRav NDov NLar SPhx SPin SUsu WMnd WPGP |
| | - 'Lapis Lazuli' | CDes EAro EBee EMon EWes LCro NBre NBsh SPhx SPin WKif |
| | - 'Pink Delight'PBR | EBee MSte |
| | - 'Rose Rhapsody' | CAby EAro EDAr LDai WFar WHil |
| | - 'Rosea' | EBee ECha SPhx SPin |
| | - 'Swan Lake' | CBod CMHG EAro NBHF NCGa NChi NHol SAga SPhx SPlb WHil WPer |
| | - 'White Swan' | CAby SPlb |
| | ***pratensis*** × ***transylvanica*** **new** | GJos |
| | ***prostrata*** | EOHP |
| | ***prunelloides*** | SPin |
| | ***przewalskii*** | CHFP CPom EAro EWld GBar MCCP MCot MSal SAga SDnm SGar SPhx SPin WPer |
| | - ACE 1157 | EBee |
| | - BWJ 7920 | SPin WCru |
| | ***pulchella*** | MAJR SPin |
| | 'Purple Majesty' | CHll CPne CSev CSpe EBee EPPr EShb LHop LPio MAvo MLLN MSte SAga SDys SMrm SPhx SPin SRkn SUsu WKif WWlt |
| | 'Purple Queen' | MBri SDys SPoG WOut WWlt |
| | ***purpurea*** | LSRN SPin |
| | ***ranzaniana*** **new** | SPin |
| | ***recognita*** | NBHF SPin WKif WSHC |
| | ***recurva*** **new** | SPin |
| | ***reflexa*** | SPin |
| | ***regeliana*** misapplied | see *S. virgata* Jacq. |
| | ***regeliana*** Trautv. | MLLN NBir SPin |
| | ***regla*** | MAJR MAsh NGHP SDys SPin WHil |
| | - 'Jame' | SPin |
| | - 'Mount Emory' | SPin |
| | - 'Royal' **new** | SPin |
| | ***repens*** | CDMG CSec EAro EBee EPyc IGor SDys SPhx SPin WOut |
| | - var. ***repens*** | SGar |
| § | ***reptans*** | CSam CSpe LHop SPin WPer |
| | - from Mexico | SDys |
| | - from Western Texas | SDys |
| | ***retinervia*** **new** | SPin |
| | ***ringens*** | EAro NBHF SBHP SDys SPin |
| | ***riparia*** misapplied | see *S. rypara* |
| | ***roborowskii*** | SPin |
| § | ***roemeriana*** ♀H3 | CSec CSpe EBee EPyc IFoB MHom NWCA SAga SDnm SDys SPhx SPin SUsu WPGP |
| | ***roscida*** **new** | SPin |
| | 'Rose Queen' ambig. | LLWG |
| | ***rubescens*** | SDys SPin |
| | ***rubiginosa*** | SDys SPin |
| | ***runcinata*** | EAro EPyc SPhx SPin |
| | ***rutilans*** | see *S. elegans* 'Scarlet Pineapple' |
| § | ***rypara*** | CPom EAro SDys SPin |
| | ***sagittata*** | MAJR SDys SPin WOut WWlt |
| * | ***sauntia*** | SPin |
| | ***scabiosifolia*** | SPin |
| | ***scabra*** | CFir CSec EBee MSte NBsh SDys SPin WOut |
| | ***sclarea*** | CArn CHby ECtt ELau GPoy MHer MNHC NChi NGHP NGdn SECG SIde SPin WCHb WLHH WPer WRHF |
| | - var. ***sclarea*** | CKno EBee EBla ECtt |
| | - var. ***turkestanica*** hort. | Widely available |
| § | - 'Vatican White' | EAro EBee EBrs LDai LHop MBri NChi SBch SDnm SPav WMnd WPer WSHC |
| | - white-bracted | CBod CWib NDlv NGHP NLar SBod SPin SWvt |
| * | ***scordifolia*** | SPin |
| | ***scutellarioides*** | SPin |
| | ***semiatrata*** misapplied | see *S. chamaedryoides* |
| | ***semiatrata*** ambig. | CMdw IFoB LPio |
| | ***semiatrata*** Zucc. | CDes CPom CSpe EBee EWld SAga SDys SPin |

| | | |
|---|---|---|
| | 'Serenade' **new** | NDov |
| | ***serpyllifolia*** | SDys SPin |
| | - white-flowered **new** | WOut |
| | ***sessei*** | SPin |
| | ***setulosa*** **new** | SPin |
| | 'Silas Dyson' | EPyc EWld SAga SBch SDys |
| | 'Silke's Dream' | CWGN EAro EBee ECtt EPyc EWld MAsh MWea SBHP SDys SPin SUsu WPen WWlt |
| | ***sinaloensis*** | EBee EPyc MAsh SBch SDys SPin WFar |
| | ***somalensis*** | SDys SHar SPin WPen |
| | ***spathacea*** ♀H3-4 | EShb MDKP SDys SPhx SPin |
| | ***spendens*** 'Uli' **new** | SUsu |
| | ***splendens*** | SPin |
| | - 'Dancing Flame' (v) | EBee EPyc |
| | - 'Helen Dillon' **new** | SDys |
| | - 'Peach' | SDys SPin SUsu |
| | - 'Salsa Burgundy' (Salsa Series) **new** | WWlt |
| § | - 'Van-Houttei' ♀H3 | CSpe ECre EPyc GCal MLLN SDys SPin WWlt |
| | ***sprucei*** | SPin |
| | ***squalens*** | SPin |
| | ***stachydifolia*** **new** | SPin |
| § | ***staminea*** | CSec SDys SPhx SPin |
| | ***stenophylla*** | CSec EAro SPin WOut WPer |
| | 'Stephanie' **new** | SDys |
| | ***stepposa*** | SPin |
| | ***striata*** **new** | SPin |
| | ***styphelus*** **new** | SPin |
| * | ***suberecta*** **new** | WHil |
| | ***subrotunda*** **new** | SDys SPin |
| | 'Sue Templeton' **new** | SPin |
| | x ***superba*** ♀H4 | CPrp CSBt EBee ECtt ELan EPfP EPyc LAst LEdu LRHS MBri MHer MWat SDix SHBN SHar SPer SRms SSvw WHoo |
| | - 'Adrian' | CMHG CPrp EBee ECtt LRHS NBsh |
| | - 'Dear Anja' | EBee EGle LHop NDov SAga SPhx |
| | - 'Merleau' | EPyc |
| | - 'Merleau Rose' | EBee |
| | - 'Rubin' ♀H4 | EBee ECtt NBre NDov SMrm SPhx |
| I | - 'Superba' | CSev ECha ECtt EHrv MRav SPhx SRkn WCAu |
| | x ***sylvestris*** | CSec LAst SPin |
| § | - 'Blauhügel' ♀H4 | CPrp EBee ECha ECtt ELan ELon EPfP EShb LRHS MArl MLLN MSte NDov NPri SBch SGar SMrm SPhx WCAu WPer |
| § | - 'Blaukönigin' | EBee EPfP GMaP LRHS MNHC MWat NLar NMir NVic SPet SPhx SPlb SPoG SWal SWvt WFar WHil WPer |
| | - Blue Queen | see *S.* x *sylvestris* 'Blaukönigin' |
| | - 'Lye End' | ECtt MRav NDov |
| § | - 'Mainacht' ♀H4 | Widely available |
| | - May Night | see *S.* x *sylvestris* 'Mainacht' |
| | - 'Negrito' | EBee EWll NDov SMrm |
| | - 'Rhapsody in Blue' PBR | EBee EMil LBuc LRHS NDov NLar WCot |
| | - 'Rose Queen' | EBee ECha ECtt ELan EPfP EShb GMaP LCro LHop LRHS MNHC MSte NDov NOrc SCoo SHBN SPet SPhx SPoG SWal SWvt WPer |
| | - 'Rügen' | EBee EGle EPyc MBri |
| | - 'Schneehügel' | EBee ECha EGle ELan ELon EPPr EPfP GMaP LAst LRHS MBNS MBri NBre NCob NMoo NPri NPro SMrm SPer WCAu WMnd |
| | - 'Tänzerin' ♀H4 | EBee ELon EPPr EPyc NDov SDys SMrm SUsu WCot |
| | - 'Viola Klose' | CHar CMHG CPrp CWGN EBee EBrs ECha ECtt EGle EShb GBuc LCro LHop LRHS LSRN MBri MCot NBsh NGdn NLar WCAu |
| | - 'Wissalink' | SMad |
| | ***tachiei*** hort. | see *S. forsskaolii* |
| | 'Tammy' | SPin |
| | ***taraxacifolia*** | SDys SPin SUsu WOut |
| | ***tesquicola*** | see *S. nemorosa* subsp. *tesquicola* |
| | ***tianschanica*** **new** | SPin |
| | ***tiliifolia*** | CArn CSec EAro SEND SPav SPin SRms |
| | ***tingitana*** | SDys SPin WOut |
| | ***tomentosa*** | SPin |
| | ***transcaucasica*** | see *S. staminea* |
| | ***transsylvanica*** | CSec EPPr LDai SDnm SMrm SPav SPhx SPin STes WCAu WPer |
| | - 'Blue Spire' | EBee ECtt EHig MCot MWhi SPav SPur |
| | 'Trebah Lilac White' | see *S.* x *jamensis* 'Trebah' |
| § | 'Trelawney' | EPyc MHar MHom MSte SDys SPav SPin SRot WOut |
| § | 'Trelissick' | CHFP ECre EPyc LAst LHop MAsh MHom MSte SDys SPav SPin SRot WWlt |
| § | 'Trewithen' | CPom ECre EPyc LAst MSte SPav SPin SPoG SRot |
| | ***trijuga*** | SPin |
| | ***triloba*** | see *S. fruticosa* |
| | ***tubifera*** | MAsh SAga SPin |
| § | ***tubiflora*** ♀H1+3 | EPyc MAJR SPin WWlt |
| | ***uliginosa*** ♀H3-4 | Widely available |
| | - 'African Skies' | CChe EBee MNrw SPin WDyG |
| | ***urica*** | CSpe EWld MAJR SDys SPav SPin |
| | - short | CMdw CSpe SDys |
| | 'Valerie' | SDys |
| | 'Van-Houttei' | see *S. splendens* 'Van-Houttei' |
| | 'Vatican City' | see *S. sclarea* 'Vatican White' |
| | ***verbenaca*** | CArn EBWF EPyc MHer MSal NMir NSco SPin WOut WPer |
| | - pink | CSec GQue SPhx |
| | ***verticillata*** | CArn EBee EGoo EHrv EPyc LEdu NSti SDys SEND SPin WCAu WFar WPer |
| § | - 'Alba' | CAbP CSec EBee ECtt EPPr EPfP EShb GJos LBMP LLWG MCot MRav NGdn SPer SPin WCAu WPer |
| | - subsp. ***amasiaca*** | SGar |
| | - 'Purple Rain' | Widely available |
| | - 'Smouldering Torches' | LPla NDov SPhx |
| | - 'White Rain' | see *S. verticillata* 'Alba' |
| | ***villicaulis*** | see *S. amplexicaulis* |
| | ***villosa*** | SPin |
| § | ***virgata*** Jacq. | SGar SPin WOut |
| | ***viridis*** | CSec MNHC SPin |
| § | - var. ***comata*** | MCot NGHP SIde WJek |
| | - var. ***viridis*** | SBod WHrl |
| | ***viscosa*** ambig. | EPyc |
| | ***viscosa*** Jacq. | SPin WOut |
| | - 'Framboise' **new** | EBee MCot |
| | ***wagneriana*** | MAJR MHar SPin |
| | 'Watermelon' **new** | CWGN |
| | 'Waverly' | CDes CHll CSpe EBee EWld MAJR MAsh MCot MSte SAga SDix SDys SUsu WOut WWlt |
| | ***xalapensis*** | MAJR SPin |
| | ***yunnanensis*** | SKHP |
| | - BWJ 7874 | WCru |
| | aff. ***yunnanensis*** | SPin |

## *Salvinia* (*Salviniaceae*)

| | |
|---|---|
| sp. | LPBA |
| ***natans*** | MSKA |

## *Sambucus* ✿ (*Caprifoliaceae*)

| | | |
|---|---|---|
| | ***adnata*** | SDix WFar |
| | - B&SWJ 2252 | WCru |
| | ***caerulea*** | see *S. nigra* subsp. *caerulea* |
| | ***callicarpa*** | NLar |
| | ***chinensis*** B&SWJ 6542 | WCru |
| | ***coraensis*** | see *S. williamsii* subsp. *coreana* |
| | ***ebulus*** | EBee GKir LEdu NLar SMad |
| | - DJHC 0107 | WCru |
| | ***formosana*** | LEdu |
| | - B&SWJ 1543 | WCru |
| § | ***javanica*** B&SWJ 4047 | WCru |
| | ***kamtschatica*** | WBVN |
| | ***mexicana*** B&SWJ 10349 **new** | WCru |
| | ***miquelii*** | NLar |
| | ***nigra*** | CArn CBcs CCVT CDul CRWN EMac GKir GPoy NWea SIde WDin WFar WMou WSFF |
| | - 'Albomarginata' | see *S. nigra* 'Marginata' |
| | - 'Albovariegata' (v) | CDoC EBee LSou SEND WMoo |
| * | - 'Ardwall' | CAgr GCal |
| N | - 'Aurea' ♀H4 | CBcs CDul CLnd CSBt CWan ELan EMac EPfP GKir MBar MRav NWea SPer WDin WFar WMoo WSHC |
| | - 'Aureomarginata' (v) | CBgR EBee ECrN ELan EPPr EPfP ISea MRav NLar NSti SHBN WCFE WFar |
| | - 'Bradet' | CAgr |
| | - 'Cae Rhos Lligwy' | CAgr WHer |
| § | - subsp. ***caerulea*** | EPfP SMad |
| | - subsp. ***canadensis*** 'Aurea' | CWib MBar NWea WHar |
| | - - 'Goldfinch' | LRHS NHol |
| | - - 'John's' | CAgr |
| | - - 'Maxima' | EPfP EWes SMad SMrm WCot |
| | - - 'York' (F) | CAgr |
| | - 'Donau' | CAgr |
| § | - 'Eva'PBR | Widely available |
| | - 'Frances' (v) | EPPr WCot |
| | - 'Franzi' | CAgr |
| | - 'Fructu Luteo' | NLar |
| § | - 'Gerda'PBR ♀H4 | Widely available |
| | - 'Godshill' (F) | CAgr SDea |
| | - 'Haschberg' | CAgr |
| | - 'Heterophylla' | see *S. nigra* 'Linearis' |
| | - 'Ina' | CAgr |
| | - 'Körsör' (F) | NLar |
| | - f. ***laciniata*** ♀H4 | CBgR CDul CPLG EBee ELan EPPr EPfP EPla GCal GKir MBlu MLLN MMuc MRav NBea NGHP NSti NWea SDix SLon WCFE WCot WDin WFar WPGP |
| § | - 'Linearis' | CPMA ELan EPla MRav NLar |
| | - 'Long Tooth' | CDul CNat |
| | - 'Madonna' (v) | CBgR EBee EPla LRHS LSou MBlu MGos MLLN MRav NLar SPer SPla WBrE WCot |
| § | - 'Marginata' (v) | CBcs CDul CWan CWib EHoe GKir MBar MHer MLLN MRav SDix SLon SPer SPoG WBod WCot WDin WFar WHar |
| | - 'Marion Bull' (v) | CDul CNat |
| I | - 'Marmorata' | NLar |
| I | - 'Monstrosa' | NLar SMad |
| | - 'Nana' | EMon |
| | - 'Plaque' (v) | CNat |
| | - 'Plena' (d) | EPla WCot |
| | - f. ***porphyrophylla*** 'Black Beauty'PBR | see *S. nigra* 'Gerda' |
| | - - 'Black Lace'PBR | see *S. nigra* 'Eva' |
| § | - - 'Guincho Purple' | CBcs CDoC CDul CTri CWib EBee ECrN EHoe ELan EPPr EPfP GKir MBar MCCP MHer MRav NBlu NHol WCot WDin WFar WMoo |
| | - - 'Purple Pete' | CDul CNat |
| | - - 'Thundercloud' | CBcs CDul CMHG EWes LBMP MAsh MBri NChi NLar NPro WCFE WCot WFar WPat |
| | - 'Pulverulenta' (v) | CBgR CBow CDoC CWib EPla GCal GKir LHop MLLN MRav NLar SPer WCot |
| | - 'Purpurea' | see *S. nigra* f. *porphyrophylla* 'Guincho Purple' |
| | - 'Pyramidalis' | CPMA EPla MBlu NLar SMad |
| | - 'Sambu' (F) | CAgr |
| | - 'Samdal' (F) | CAgr |
| | - 'Samidan' (F) | CAgr |
| | - 'Samnor' (F) | CAgr |
| | - 'Sampo' (F) | CAgr |
| | - 'Samyl' (F) | CAgr |
| * | - 'Tenuifolia' | MRav |
| | - 'Urban Lace' | CAgr |
| | - 'Variegata' | see *S. nigra* 'Marginata' |
| | - f. ***viridis*** | CAgr CBgR CNat EMon |
| | ***racemosa*** | EPfP NWea WRha |
| | - 'Aurea' | EHoe |
| | - 'Chedglow' | CNat |
| | - 'Crûg Lace' | WCru |
| | - 'Goldenlocks' | EWes LRHS MAsh MGos MSwo NLar SPer |
| | - 'Plumosa Aurea' | Widely available |
| | - 'Sutherland Gold' ♀H4 | Widely available |
| | - 'Tenuifolia' | CPMA CSWP ELan EPfP ERas LRHS NLar SMad WPGP |
| | ***tigranii*** | NLar |
| | ***wightiana*** | see *S. javanica* |
| § | ***williamsii*** subsp. ***coreana*** | CMCN WFar |

## *Samolus* (*Primulaceae*)

| | | |
|---|---|---|
| | ***repens*** | CPBP ECou LLHF |
| | ***valerandi*** **new** | EBWF |

## *Sanchezia* (*Acanthaceae*)

| | | |
|---|---|---|
| | ***nobilis*** misapplied | see *S. speciosa* |
| § | ***speciosa*** | CHal |

## *Sandersonia* (*Colchicaceae*)

| | | |
|---|---|---|
| | ***aurantiaca*** | CFFs CPne EBrs ECho EPot LAma LRHS |

## *Sanguinaria* (*Papaveraceae*)

| | | |
|---|---|---|
| | ***canadensis*** | Widely available |
| | - f. ***multiplex*** (d) | CDes CLAP EBrs ECho EMon EPot ERos GEdr GKir LRHS NBir |
| | - - 'Plena' (d) ♀H4 | CBct CBro CLyd CSpe CWCL EBee ECho GCra GKev GPoy LAma NDov NHol NMen NRya SIng SPer SPoG WAbe WBVN WEas WFar WPGP WTin |

## *Sanguisorba* ✿ (*Rosaceae*)

| | | |
|---|---|---|
| | DJHC 535 from Korea | SMHy |
| § | ***albiflora*** | CCVN CDes CHar CKno CRow EBee EBla EGle ELan EMon GBuc LCro LPla MAvo MRav NDov NGdn NLar NPro SPhx SWat WCAu WFar WMoo WPGP |
| | ***armena*** | CElw EBee EBla EWes MNrw NDov SSvw WTin |
| | ***benthamiana*** | CHEx |
| | 'Blacksmiths Burgundy' | EBla |
| | 'Blackthorn' **new** | NDov |
| | 'Burr Blanc' **new** | SMHy |

| | | |
|---|---|---|
| | ***canadensis*** | CDes CKno CRow EBee EBla ECha EPPr GCal GMaP GPoy LPio MAvo MSte NBir NDov NVic SMeo SPhx SWat WAul WCAu WCot WFar WMoo WOld WTin |
| | - 'Twisty' **new** | LPla |
| * | ***caucasica*** | EBee EPPr EWes LEdu LPla NBre NDov SMeo SPhx |
| | 'Chocolate Tip' | EBee EBla IPot NBro |
| | 'Dark Knight' **new** | WCHb |
| | ***dodecandra*** | CSec |
| | ***hakusanensis*** | CDes CHar CKno EBee EBla EPPr IFro LEdu MAvo MNrw NBir NBre NBro NChi NDov NPro SMeo WCot WFar WPGP WTin |
| | - B&SWJ 8709 | WCru |
| | 'John Coke' | NLar |
| | 'Korean Snow' | NDov SPhx SUsu |
| | ***magnifica*** | CDes CFir EWes GCal LEdu WPGP |
| | - ***alba*** | see *S. albiflora* |
| | ***menziesii*** | Widely available |
| | - 'Dali Marble' (v) **new** | CBow CCVN EBee |
| § | ***minor*** | CArn CHby CPrp EBee EBla ELau GBar GKir GPoy MDun MHer MNHC NBro NGHP NMir SIde SPlb WBrk WCHb WGwG WHer WMoo |
| | - subsp. ***minor*** **new** | EBWF |
| | ***obtusa*** | Widely available |
| | - var. ***albiflora*** | see *S. albiflora* |
| | - 'Chatto' **new** | EBee |
| | - white-flowered **new** | CDes |
| | ***officinalis*** | CArn CKno CSam CWan EBWF EBee EBla EDAr EGle EHrv EPPr GBar GQue LEdu MHer MNFA NMir NPro SPer SPhx SWat WCAu WFar WMoo |
| | - CDC 262 | CAby NDov |
| | - CDC 282 | SPhx |
| | - 'Arnhem' | CKno CMdw EBla EGle EPPr LEdu NDov SMHy SMeo SMrm SPhx SUsu WCot WTin |
| | - 'False Tanna' | CWib WFar |
| | - 'Lemon Splash' (v) | CBow EBee EBla WCot |
| | - 'Martin's Mulberry' | EGle EWes |
| | - 'Pink Tanna' | CDes CElw CKno EBee EBla EGle EMon EPPr GBBs LEdu MAvo MDKP MSte NBhm NBid NBre NBro NDov NGHP NSti SMHy SMrm SPhx SPoG SUsu WCot WMoo WTin |
| | - 'Red Thunder' | EBee EPPr IPot LCro NCGa NDov NLar |
| | - 'Shiro-fukurin' (v) | CDes EBee EMon WCot |
| | ***parviflora*** | see *S. tenuifolia* var. *parviflora* |
| | ***pimpinella*** | see *S. minor* |
| | 'Pink Brushes' | EBla NDov NLar SPhx |
| | ***riishirensis*** | EBee |
| | ***sitchensis*** | see *S. stipulata* |
| § | ***stipulata*** | EBee EGle GCal GKir MNrw NDov NGby |
| | 'Tanna' | Widely available |
| | 'Tanna' seedling | EPPr EShb |
| | ***tenuifolia*** | CEnt EBla EGle GBBs GCal GKir IFro MCot NDov NLar NPro SBHP SMrm SPhx WMoo |
| | - 'Alba' | CDes CKno EBee EBla EGle EMon EWes GBuc GCal GQue MAvo MSte NDov NPro SMad SPhx WCot WFar WOld |
| | - 'Big Pink' | GCal MNrw |
| § | - var. ***parviflora*** | CDes EBee LEdu MAvo MNrw NCob NLar SMHy SMeo WPGP WTin |
| | - - white-flowered | EBla |
| | - 'Pink Elephant' | CDes CKno EBee EBla ECtt EPPr GBin LDai LEdu NDov NLar SMad WPGP WTin |
| | - 'Purpurea' | CDes CKno EBee EBla EPPr LEdu MAvo NDov NLar WFar WPGP |
| | - 'Stand Up Comedian' | EBee NLar |
| | - 'White Elephant' | EBla |
| | 'Touch of Green' | EBla |

# *Sanicula* (*Apiaceae*)

| | |
|---|---|
| ***coerulescens*** | NBhm WCot |
| ***europaea*** | EBWF EBee GBar GPoy NSco WHer WTin |

# *Sansevieria* (*Dracaenaceae*)

| | |
|---|---|
| ***trifasciata*** 'Golden Hahnii' (v) ♀H1 | EShb MBri |
| - 'Hahnii' ♀H1 **new** | EShb |
| - var. ***laurentii*** (v) ♀H1 | MBri |
| - 'Moonshine' ♀H1 **new** | EShb |
| ***zeylanica*** **new** | EShb |

# *Santolina* (*Asteraceae*)

| | | |
|---|---|---|
| | ***benthamiana*** | EAro |
| § | ***chamaecyparissus*** ♀H4 | Widely available |
| | - var. ***corsica*** | see *S. chamaecyparissus* var. *nana* |
| | - 'Double Lemon' (d) | EBee EPfP SPla WCot |
| | - 'Lambrook Silver' | CArn CDoC EBee EGoo EOHP EPfP LRHS MAsh MBNS SCoo SLim SPla SPoG |
| | - 'Lemon Queen' | CArn CDoC EBee EGoo ELau EPfP GBar LRHS MAsh MGos MNHC MSwo NBir NPri SIde SPla SWat WCHb WFar WGwG WPer |
| | - subsp. ***magonica*** | GKir |
| § | - var. ***nana*** ♀H4 | CPrp EBee ECho EPfP LRHS MAsh MBar MHer MRav MSwo SPoG SRms SWat WClo WLeb WPer |
| | - - 'Weston' | ECho |
| | - 'Pretty Carol' | CAbP EBee ELan EMil EPfP GBar GGar LRHS LSRN LSou MAsh MBri NGHP SIde SMeo SPla WFar |
| | - 'Small-Ness' | CMea EBee ECho EGoo ELan EPfP EWes GBar GEdr LRHS MAsh MHer MSte NLAp SIng SPer SPoG STre SWvt WAbe WFar WPer |
| | ***elegans*** | WAbe |
| | ***incana*** | see *S. chamaecyparissus* |
| | ***pectinata*** | see *S. rosmarinifolia* subsp. *canescens* |
| | ***pinnata*** | CArn CSev MHer WPer |
| § | - subsp. ***neapolitana*** ♀H4 | CArn CHFP CSBt CSev CWib EBee ECha ECho ECrN ELan EPfP GBar MBri MNHC NCob NPri SDix SIde WEas WHCG WMnd WTin |
| | - - cream | see *S. pinnata* subsp. *neapolitana* 'Edward Bowles' |
| § | - - 'Edward Bowles' | Widely available |
| | - - 'Sulphurea' | CArn CMea EBee ECGP ECrN EGoo EPfP LRHS MAsh NCob NGHP SPer SPhx WKif WPer |
| | ***rosmarinifolia*** | CArn CDoC CDul CWan EBee ECrN ELau MRav NGHP SLon SPlb SRms STre WCHb |
| § | - subsp. ***canescens*** | EBee EPfP WPer |
| | - 'Lemon Fizz' **new** | LSou NPri SPoG |
| § | - subsp. ***rosmarinifolia*** | CPrp CSev ECha ECrN EGoo ELan EPfP GBar LRHS MHer MRav SDix SIde SPer SPoG SWvt WBrE WCHb WDin WFar WGwG WHoo |
| | - - 'Primrose Gem' ♀H4 | CBcs CDoC CPrp CSBt CSam CTri EBee ECha ECho ECrN ELau EMil |

| | |
|---|---|
| | EPfP GBar LHop LRHS MAsh MSwo MWat NCob NPri SPer SPla SWvt WPer |
| - - white-flowered | SSvw |
| ***tomentosa*** | see *S. pinnata* subsp. *neapolitana* |
| ***virens*** | see *S. rosmarinifolia* subsp. *rosmarinifolia* |
| ***viridis*** | see *S. rosmarinifolia* subsp. *rosmarinifolia* |

## *Sanvitalia* (*Asteraceae*)

| | |
|---|---|
| Aztekengold = 'Starbini' | LAst NBlu WGor |
| 'Little Sun' | LRHS SPet |
| ***procumbens*** 'Irish Eyes' **new** | CSpe |
| 'Sunbini'PBR | CSpe LSou NPri SVil WGor |

## *Sapindus* (*Sapindaceae*)

| | |
|---|---|
| ***mukorossi*** | CBcs |

## *Saponaria* (*Caryophyllaceae*)

| | |
|---|---|
| x ***boissieri*** | GKev |
| 'Bressingham' ♀H4 | EAlp ECho ECtt EDAr EPfP EPot LBee LRHS NLAp NMen SIng SPoG WAbe WPat |
| ***caespitosa*** | ECho EWes |
| x ***lempergii*** 'Max Frei' | CAbP CSam EBee ELon GBuc LRHS LSou MRav MSte NCob NDov SAga SDix SHar SPhx WCot WOld WSHC |
| ***lutea*** | GKev |
| ***ocymoides*** ♀H4 | CMea EBee ECha ECho ECtt EDAr EHon EPfP GAbr GBar LRHS MLHP MNHC NBlu NMen NPri NVic SPer SPlb SPoG SRms SWal WBor WCFE WFar WPer |
| - 'Alba' | ECha ECho WFar |
| - 'Rubra Compacta' ♀H4 | LRHS WAbe |
| - 'Snow Tip' | EBee ECho ECtt EPfP NGdn NLar SBch |
| - 'Splendens' | ECho |
| ***officinalis*** | CArn CBre CHby CHrt CPbn CSec CWan EBWF GBar GPoy LEdu MHer MLHP MSal NGHP NPri SIde SPlb WBrk WFar WHer WMoo WPer |
| - 'Alba Plena' (d) | CBre EBee EBrs ECha EWTr GBar NLar SHar WCHb WFar WHer WPer WPtf WRha WTin |
| - 'Betty Arnold' (d) | EBee ECtt EWes GMac WCot WFar WTin |
| § - 'Dazzler' (v) | GBar WCHb WHer |
| - 'Rosea Plena' (d) | Widely available |
| - 'Rubra Plena' (d) | CBre ELan EWes MWhi NBre NGHP SHar WCHb WHer WRha WTin |
| - 'Variegata' | see *S. officinalis* 'Dazzler' |
| x ***olivana*** ♀H4 | EAlp ECho EPot GAbr MTho NLAp NMen WAbe WPat |
| ***pamphylica*** | MNrw |
| ***persica*** | GKev |
| ***pulvinaris*** | see *S. pumilio* Boiss. |
| ***pumila*** | NGdn SPlb |
| § ***pumilio*** Boiss. **new** | CSec EDAr |
| 'Rosenteppich' | ECtt WPat |
| ***zawadskii*** | see *Silene zawadskii* |

## *Saposhnikovia* (*Apiaceae*)

| | |
|---|---|
| ***divaricata*** | CArn MSal |

## *Sarcocapnos* (*Papaveraceae*)

| | |
|---|---|
| ***enneaphylla*** | LSRN |

## *Sarcococca* ✿ (*Buxaceae*)

| | |
|---|---|
| ***confusa*** ♀H4 | Widely available |
| ***hookeriana*** ♀H4 | CTrG ECot EPfP IFoB LAst LSRN MAsh MBlu MDun MSwo NBlu NPri WFar WPGP |
| - B&SWJ 2585 | WCru |
| - HWJK 2393 | WCru |
| - Sch 1160 | CGHE |
| - Sch 2396 | EPla |
| - var. ***digyna*** ♀H4 | Widely available |
| - - 'Purple Stem' | CHar CTri EPfP EPla ERas MGos MRav NBPN NLar SCoo SPoG WCru WDin |
| I - - 'Schillingii' | CPMA WCru |
| - var. ***hookeriana*** | CPMA |
| - - GWJ 9369 | WCru |
| - var. ***humilis*** | Widely available |
| ***orientalis*** | CAbP CMCN CPMA ELan EPfP EPla LBuc LRHS MAsh MGos SKHP SPla SPoG SSpi WFar WPGP |
| 'Roy Lancaster' | see *S. ruscifolia* 'Dragon Gate' |
| ***ruscifolia*** | CBcs CBgR CDul CMCN CPMA CSBt EBee ECrN ELan EPfP EPla ERas GKir LRHS MAsh MGos MRav NPri SLim SLon SPer SPoG SRms SSpi WCru WFar |
| - var. ***chinensis*** ♀H4 | CPMA CSam EPfP EPla SKHP SLon WCru WFar WGwG WPGP |
| - - L 713 | EPla |
| § - 'Dragon Gate' | CDoC CGHE CPMA EBee ELan EPfP EPla EWTr LLHF LRHS MAsh MBlu SKHP SLon SPoG SReu SSta WCot WPGP WPat |
| ***saligna*** | CBcs CPMA EBee EPfP NLar SKHP SLon WCru |
| ***vagans*** B&SWJ 7285 | WCru |
| ***wallichii*** | CGHE EBee MBlu SKHP WPGP |
| - B&SWJ 2291 | WCru |
| - GWJ 9427 | WCru |

## *Sarcostemma* (*Asclepiadaceae*)

| | |
|---|---|
| ***viminale*** | EShb |

## *Sarmienta* (*Gesneriaceae*)

| | |
|---|---|
| ***repens*** ♀H2 | CGHE SKHP WAbe WCru WPGP |

## *Sarothamnus* see *Cytisus*

## *Sarracenia* ✿ (*Sarraceniaceae*)

| | |
|---|---|
| x ***ahlesii*** | CHew |
| ***alata*** | CFwr CHew CSWC EECP MCCP SHmp WSSs |
| - all green **new** | SHmp |
| - 'Black Tube' | WSSs |
| - heavily-veined | SHmp WSSs |
| - pubescent | CSWC EECP WSSs |
| - 'Red Lid' | CSWC EECP WSSs |
| - wavy lid | SHmp WSSs |
| - white-flowered | WSSs |
| ***alata*** x ***flava*** var. ***maxima*** | CSWC |
| x ***areolata*** | CHew CSWC WSSs |
| x ***catesbyi*** ♀H1 | CHew CSWC SHmp WSSs |
| x ***courtii*** | CSWC |
| 'Dixie Lace' | CSWC |
| 'Evendine' | CSWC |
| x ***excellens*** ♀H1 | CSWC WSSs |
| x ***exornata*** | CSWC |
| ***flava*** ♀H1 | CFwr CSWC CSec MCCP WSSs |
| - all green giant | see *S. flava* var. *maxima* |
| - var. ***atropurpurea*** | EECP WSSs |
| - 'Burgundy' | MYeo WSSs |
| - var. ***cuprea*** | CSWC WSSs |
| - var. ***flava*** | CHew EECP WSSs |
| § - var. ***maxima*** | CHew CSWC EECP WSSs |
| - var. ***ornata*** | CHew CSWC EECP SHmp WSSs |

| | | |
|---|---|---|
| | - var. ***rubricorpora*** | CHew EECP SHmp WSSs |
| | - var. ***rugelii*** | CHew EECP MYeo SHmp WSSs |
| | - veinless | CSWC |
| | x ***harperi*** | CSWC |
| | 'Juthatip Soper' | SHmp WSSs |
| | 'Ladies in Waiting' | CSWC |
| | ***leucophylla*** ♀H1 | CFwr CHew CSWC SHmp WSSs |
| | - from Okaloosa Co., Florida **new** | SHmp |
| | - 'Deer Park Alabama' **new** | SHmp |
| | - green | WSSs |
| | - ***popei*** | EECP |
| | - pubescent | WSSs |
| | - 'Schnell's Ghost' | WSSs |
| | ***leucophylla*** x ***oreophila*** | CSWC EECP |
| | 'Lynda Butt' | SHmp WSSs |
| | x ***miniata*** | EECP SHmp |
| | ***minor*** | CSWC EECP SHmp WSSs |
| | - var. ***minor*** **new** | CHew |
| § | - 'Okee Giant' | CSWC MYeo WSSs |
| | - var. ***okeefenokeensis*** **new** | CHew |
| | - 'Okefenokee Giant' | see *S. minor* 'Okee Giant' |
| | ***minor*** x ***oreophila*** | CSWC |
| | x ***mitchelliana*** ♀H1 | CFwr WSSs |
| | x ***moorei*** | CHew WSSs |
| | - 'Brook's Hybrid' | CHew CSWC EECP WSSs |
| | x ***moorei*** x (***leucophylla*** x ***moorei***) | EECP |
| | ***oreophila*** | CHew CSWC MYeo SHmp WSSs |
| | ***oreophila*** x ***purpurea*** subsp. ***venosa*** | CSWC |
| | x ***popei*** | CSWC |
| | ***psittacina*** | CHew CSWC EECP SHmp WSSs |
| * | - f. ***heterophylla*** | CSWC MYeo |
| | ***purpurea*** | NWCA WFar |
| | - subsp. ***purpurea*** | CFwr CHew CSWC MCCP SHmp WSSs |
| | - - f. ***heterophylla*** | CSWC MYeo WSSs |
| | - subsp. ***venosa*** | CHew CSWC SHmp WSSs |
| | - - var. ***burkii*** | CSWC WSSs |
| | x ***readii*** | SHmp WSSs |
| | - 'Farnhamii' | CSWC EECP |
| | x ***readii*** x (***leucophylla*** x ***readii***) | EECP |
| | x ***rehderi*** | SHmp |
| | ***rubra*** | CSWC EECP WSSs |
| | - subsp. ***alabamensis*** | CHew CSWC SHmp WSSs |
| | - subsp. ***gulfensis*** | CHew CSWC SHmp WSSs |
| * | - - f. ***heterophylla*** | CSWC WSSs |
| | - subsp. ***jonesii*** | CSWC EECP WSSs |
| * | - - f. ***heterophylla*** | CSWC WSSs |
| | - subsp. ***rubra*** | CHew CSWC WSSs |
| | - subsp. ***wherryi*** | CHew CSWC EECP WSSs |
| | - - giant | WSSs |
| | - - yellow-flowered | CSWC WSSs |
| | 'Umlanftiana' **new** | CSWC |

## *Saruma* (*Aristolochiaceae*)

| | | |
|---|---|---|
| | ***henryi*** | CAby CDes CExc CLAP CMea CPom EBee LSou SKHP SUsu WCot WCru WPGP WSHC |

## *Sasa* ✿ (*Poaceae*)

| | | |
|---|---|---|
| | ***chrysantha*** misapplied | see *Pleioblastus chino* |
| | ***disticha*** 'Mirrezuzume' | see *Pleioblastus pygmaeus* 'Mirrezuzume' |
| | ***glabra*** f. ***albostriata*** | see *Sasaella masamuneana* 'Albostriata' |
| | ***kagamiana*** | EBee NLar |
| | ***kurilensis*** | CMCo EBee EPla LPal MWhi MWht NMoo WFar |
| § | - 'Shima-shimofuri' (v) | CMCo EPPr EPfP EPla ERod MMoz MWht |
| | - 'Shimofuri' | see *S. kurilensis* 'Shima-shimofuri' |
| | - short | EPla |
| | ***nana*** | see *S. veitchii* f. *minor* |
| | ***oshidensis*** | EPla |
| § | ***palmata*** | CAbb CDul COld CTrG CWib EBee EHoe LCro MCCP MMuc MWhi SEND WDin WFar WHer WPnP |
| | - f. ***nebulosa*** | CBcs CBct CDoC CFir CHEx EFul EHul ENBC EPfP EPla EWes MBrN MMoz MWht NMoo SAPC SArc SSto WDyG WFar WMoo WPnP |
| | ***quelpaertensis*** | EPla MWht |
| | ***tessellata*** | see *Indocalamus tessellatus* |
| | ***tsuboiana*** | CDoC EBee ENBC EPla GQui LPal MMoz MNHC MWht NGdn NLar SBig WDyG WFar WMoo |
| § | ***veitchii*** | CAbb CBcs CKno CTrC CTrG EBee ECha EHoe ENBC EPfP EPla GKir LEdu MMoz MMuc MREP NMoo SPer SPla WBor WDin WFar WMoo |
| § | - f. ***minor*** | EBee MCCP MMoz WMoo |

## *Sasaella* (*Poaceae*)

| | | |
|---|---|---|
| | ***glabra*** | see *S. masamuneana* |
| § | ***masamuneana*** | CDul ENBC EPla |
| § | - 'Albostriata' (v) | CDoC CEnt CMCo CWib EBee ENBC EPPr EPla ERod GAbr LEdu LPal MBar MCCP MMoz MWht NGdn NMoo SBig SSto WDyG WFar WMoo WPGP |
| | - f. ***aureostriata*** (v) | EPla MMoz NPal |
| § | ***ramosa*** | CHEx CTca EBee EPla LEdu MCCP MMoz MWht NMoo WDin |

## *Sassafras* (*Lauraceae*)

| | | |
|---|---|---|
| | ***albidum*** | CArn CBcs CCCN CMCN CTho EBee EPfP LEdu MBri SKHP SSpi WPGP |
| | ***tzumu*** | CGHE WPGP |

## satsuma see *Citrus unshiu*

## *Satureja* ✿ (*Lamiaceae*)

| | | |
|---|---|---|
| § | ***coerulea*** ♀H4 | CWan ECho EWes NBir NLAp |
| | ***douglasii*** | EOHP GBar MNHC SHDw WJek |
| | - 'Indian Mint' PBR | MHer NGHP |
| | ***hortensis*** | CBod GPoy ILis MHer MNHC SIde WJek WLHH |
| | - 'Selektion' | LLWP |
| | ***montana*** | CArn CHby CPrp CWan ECho ELau GKev GPoy ILis LLWP MBri MHer MNHC NGHP NMen SDix SEND SHGN SIde SRms SVic WCHb WHer WPer |
| * | - ***citriodora*** | GPoy MHer WJek |
| | - 'Coerulea' | see *S. coerulea* |
| § | - subsp. ***illyrica*** | WJek WPer |
| | - prostrate white | NGHP |
| | - 'Purple Mountain' | CHFP GPoy LLWP MHer |
| | - ***subspicata*** | see *S. montana* subsp. *illyrica* |
| | ***parnassica*** | LLWP WPer |
| | ***repanda*** | see *S. spicigera* |
| § | ***spicigera*** | CArn CBod CPBP CPrp EBee ECho ELau EPot GBar GEdr LEdu LFol LLWP MHer NBir NMen SHGN SIde WCHb WJek WLHH WPer |
| | ***thymbra*** | CArn EOHP SHDw |
| § | ***viminea*** | EOHP |

## *Saurauia* (*Actinidiaceae*)

| | | |
|---|---|---|
| | TH **new** | CHEx |
| | ***subspinosa*** | CHEx |

## *Sauromatum* (*Araceae*)

| | |
|---|---|
| ***guttatum*** | see *S. venosum* |
| § ***venosum*** | CHEx CKob CMea CSec CStu EAmu EBee EBrs ECho EShb GCal LAma LEdu LFur LRHS SBig SHaC WCot WCru WPGP WRos |

## *Saururus* (*Saururaceae*)

| | |
|---|---|
| ***cernuus*** | CBen CDWL CHEx CRow CWat EHon ELan EMFW EPfP LPBA SRms SWat WMAq |
| ***chinensis*** | CRow EBee |

## *Saussurea* (*Asteraceae*)

| | |
|---|---|
| ***albescens*** | EBee WCot |
| ***costus*** **new** | CArn |
| ***obvallata*** HWJK 2272 | WCru |
| ***uniflora*** GWJ 9269 | WCru |

## savory, summer see *Satureja hortensis*

## savory, winter see *Satureja montana*

## *Saxegothaea* (*Podocarpaceae*)

| | |
|---|---|
| ***conspicua*** | CDoC ECou GBin IDee |

## *Saxifraga* ✿ (*Saxifragaceae*)

| | |
|---|---|
| McB 1377 | CLyd |
| McB 1397 from Nepal | CLyd |
| SEP 22 | CLyd |
| SEP 45 | CLyd |
| 'Ada' (x *petraschii*) (7) | NMen |
| 'Aemula' (x *borisii*) (7) | NMen |
| § 'Afrodite' (*sempervivum*) (7) | CLyd |
| ***aizoides*** (9) | ECho GKev |
| - var. ***atrorubens*** (9) | CSec ECho |
| ***aizoon*** | see *S. paniculata* |
| 'Aladdin' (x *borisii*) (7) | NMen |
| 'Alan Hayhurst' (8) | WAbe WFar |
| 'Alan Martin' (x *boydilacina*) (7) | CLyd ECho EPot MHer NMen |
| 'Alba' (*oppositifolia*) (7) | CLyd ECho ELan EWes ITim NDlv NLAp NWCA WAbe |
| 'Alba' (x *apiculata*) (7) | ECho EDAr EPot LFox LRHS MHer NLAp NMen NRya SPlb WAbe WPat |
| 'Alba' (x *arco-valleyi*) | see *S.* 'Ophelia' |
| 'Albert Einstein' (x *apiculata*) (7) | NMen |
| 'Albertii' (*callosa*) | see *S.* 'Albida' |
| § 'Albida' (*callosa*) (8) | ECho WAbe |
| 'Aldebaran' (x *borisii*) (7) | NMen |
| 'Aldo Bacci' (Milford Group) (7) | NMen |
| 'Alfons Mucha' (7) | CLyd EPot NMen WAbe |
| 'Allendale Acclaim' (x *lismorensis*) (7) | NDlv NMen |
| 'Allendale Accord' (*diapensioides* x *lilacina*) (7) | NDlv NMen |
| 'Allendale Allure' (7) | NMen |
| 'Allendale Amber' (7) | NMen |
| 'Allendale Andante' (x *arco-valleyi*) (7) | CLyd NMen |
| 'Allendale Angel' (x *kepleri*) (7) | CLyd NMen WAbe |
| 'Allendale Argonaut' (7) | CLyd NDlv NMen WAbe |
| 'Allendale Ballad' (7) | NMen WAbe |
| 'Allendale Ballet' (7) | CLyd NMen |
| 'Allendale Bamby' (x *lismorensis*) (7) | NMen |
| 'Allendale Banshee' (7) | CLyd NMen |
| 'Allendale Beau' (x *lismorensis*) (7) | CPBP NMen |
| 'Allendale Beauty' (7) | CLyd NMen |
| 'Allendale Betty' (x *lismorensis*) (7) | CLyd NMen |
| 'Allendale Billows' (7) | NMen |
| 'Allendale Blossom' (x *limorensis*) (7) | CLyd NMen |
| 'Allendale Bonny' (7) | EPot NMen WAbe |
| 'Allendale Boon' (x *izari*) (7) | CLyd NMen |
| 'Allendale Bounty' (7) | CLyd NMen |
| 'Allendale Bravo' (x *lismorensis*) (7) | CLyd NMen WAbe |
| 'Allendale Cabal' (7) | CLyd NMen |
| 'Allendale Carol' (7) **new** | CLyd |
| 'Allendale Celt' (x *novacastelensis*) (7) | CLyd NMen |
| 'Allendale Charm' (Swing Group) (7) | CLyd CPBP NMen WAbe |
| 'Allendale Chick' (7) | NHar NMen |
| 'Allendale Comet' (7) | NMen |
| 'Allendale Dance' (7) | NMen |
| 'Allendale Desire' (7) **new** | CLyd WAbe |
| 'Allendale Divine' (7) | WAbe |
| 'Allendale Dream' (7) | EPot NMen |
| 'Allendale Duo' (7) | NMen WAbe |
| 'Allendale Elegance' (7) | CLyd NMen |
| 'Allendale Elf' (7) | CLyd NMen |
| 'Allendale Elite' (7) | CLyd NMen |
| 'Allendale Enchantment' (7) | NMen |
| 'Allendale Envoy' (7) | EPot NMen WAbe |
| 'Allendale Epic' (7) | NHar NMen WAbe |
| 'Allendale Fairy' (7) | NHar NMen |
| 'Allendale Fame' (7) | NMen |
| 'Allendale Frost' (7) | NMen |
| 'Allendale Garnet' (7) | CLyd NMen |
| 'Allendale Ghost' (7) | NMen |
| 'Allendale Goblin' (7) | NHar NMen NWCA WAbe |
| 'Allendale Grace' (7) | CLyd NMen WAbe |
| 'Allendale Gremlin' (7) | NMen |
| 'Allendale Harvest' (7) | NMen WAbe |
| 'Allendale Hobbit' (7) | NHar NMen WAbe |
| 'Allendale Host' (7) | NMen WAbe |
| 'Allendale Icon' (x *polulacina*) (7) **new** | WAbe |
| 'Allendale Imp' (7) **new** | WAbe |
| 'Allendale Ina' (7) | NHar NMen WAbe |
| 'Allendale Joy' (x *wendelacina*) (7) | NMen |
| 'Allendale Pearl' (x *novacastelensis*) (7) | CLyd NMen |
| 'Allendale Ruby' (7) | CLyd NMen |
| 'Allendale Snow' (x *rayei*) (7) | NMen |
| 'Alpenglow' (7) | NMen |
| ***alpigena*** (7) | CLyd EPot WAbe |
| 'Amitie' (x *gloriana*) (7) | CFee NMen |
| ***andersonii*** (7) | CLyd NDlv NMen NRya WAbe |
| 'Andrea Cesalpino' (Renaissance Group) (7) | WAbe |
| x ***andrewsii*** (8x11) | MTho |
| ***angustifolia*** Haw. | see *S. hypnoides* |
| 'Anna' (x *fontanae*) (7) | NMen |
| 'Anne Beddall' (x *goringiana*) (7) | CLyd NMen WAbe |
| 'Antonio Vivaldi' (7) | NMen WAbe |
| 'Aphrodite' (*sempervivum*) | see *S.* 'Afrodite' |
| x ***apiculata*** *sensu stricto* hort. | see *S.* 'Gregor Mendel' |
| 'Apple Blossom' (15) | ECtt GKev NPro NRya SPoG WGor WHoo |

| | | |
|---|---|---|
| | 'Arabella' (x *edithae*) (7) | ECho |
| | 'Archdale' (*paniculata*) (8) | EAlp |
| § | 'Arco' (x *arco-valleyi*) (7) | NMen |
| | x ***arco-valleyi*** *sensu stricto* hort. | see *S.* 'Arco' |
| | x ***arendsii*** purple-flowered (15) | NNor |
| § | 'Aretiastrum' (x *boydii*) (7) | CLyd LFox NDlv NMen |
| | ***aretioides*** (7) | NMen |
| | 'Ariel' (x *hornibrookii*) (7) | CLyd LFox NMen |
| | 'Arthur' (x *anglica*) (7) | NMen |
| | 'Assimilis' (x *petraschii*) (7) | CLyd NMen |
| | 'August Hayek' (x *leyboldii*) (7) | NMen |
| | 'Aurea Maculata' (*cuneifolia*) | see *S.* 'Aureopunctata' |
| | 'Aurea' (*umbrosa*) | see *S.* 'Aureopunctata' |
| § | 'Aureopunctata' (x *urbium*) (11/v) | CTri ECha ECho EDAr GAbr GBuc GKev GKir LBMP MHer MRav NHol SPer SPlb SRms WMoo |
| | 'Autumn Tribute' (*fortunei*) (5) | CLAP WAbe WFar |
| | 'Balcana' (*paniculata*) (8) | WAbe |
| | 'Baldensis' | see *S. paniculata* var. *minutifolia* |
| | 'Ballawley Guardsman' (15) | ELon LFox SIng |
| § | 'Beatrix Stanley' (7) | CLyd LFox MHer NDlv NHol NLAp NMen NRya WGor |
| | 'Becky Foster' (x *borisii*) (7) | NMen |
| | 'Bellisant' (x *hornibrookii*) (7) | CLyd NMen |
| | 'Berenika' (x *bertolonii*) (7) | NMen |
| | 'Beryl' (x *anglica*) (7) | NMen |
| | 'Bettina' (x *paulinae*) (7) | NMen |
| | x ***biasolettoi*** *sensu stricto* hort. | see *S.* 'Phoenix' |
| | x ***bilekii*** (7) | CLyd ECho NMen |
| | 'Black Beauty' (15) | CMea MHer SIng |
| | 'Black Ruby' (*fortunei*) (5) | Widely available |
| | 'Blackberry and Apple Pie' (*fortunei*) (5) | CBct CBod CElw CLAP EBee ECtt GEdr IBal MBrN MLHP MNrw MSte NBro NHol NMen NMyG SWvt WAul WCot WFar |
| | 'Blaník' (x *borisii*) (7) | CLyd NMen |
| | 'Blanka' (x *borisii*) (7) | NMen |
| | 'Bob Hawkins' (15/v) | CLyd EAlp EDAr LFox NHol |
| § | 'Bodensee' (x *hofmannii*) (7) | EPot NDlv WPat |
| | 'Bohdalec' (x *megaseiflora*) (7) | NMen |
| | 'Bohemia' (7) | CLyd ECho ITim NMen NSla WAbe |
| | x ***borisii*** *sensu stricto* hort. | see *S.* 'Sofia' |
| | 'Bornmuelleri' (7) | NMen |
| | 'Boston Spa' (x *elisabethae*) (7) | CLyd ECho ECtt LRHS MHer NDlv NLAp NMen SPlb WPat |
| | 'Brailes' (x *poluanglica*) (7) | CLyd NMen |
| | 'Bridget' (x *edithae*) (7) | CLyd CMea ECho LFox LRHS NDlv NMen SIng WAbe |
| | 'Brno' (x *elisabethae*) (7) | NMen |
| | ***bronchialis*** (10) | CLyd |
| | 'Brookside' (*burseriana*) (7) | NMen |
| | ***brunoniana*** | see *S. brunonis* |
| § | ***brunonis*** (1) | LFox WCru |
| | - CC&McK 108 | NWCA |
| | 'Bryn Llwyd' **new** | WAbe |
| | ***bryoides*** (10) | CLyd ECho NRya |
| * | 'Buckland' (*fortunei*) (5) | CWsd |
| | x ***burnatii*** (8) | CLyd LFox LRHS NDlv NMen NPro WGor |
| | ***burseriana*** (7) | ECho NLAp WAbe WGor |
| | 'Buster' (x *hardingii*) (7) | NMen |
| | 'Buttercup' (x *kayei*) (7) | CLyd EPot NLAp NMen WHoo |
| | x ***byam-groundsii*** (7) | CLyd |
| | ***caesia*** misapplied (x *fritschiana*) | see *S.* 'Krain' |
| | ***caesia*** L. (8) | SRms |
| § | ***callosa*** (8) 🏆H4 | ECho EDAr GEdr MDKP MHer MLHP MWat NHol NLAp WAbe WEas WFar WPat WTin |
| | - subsp. ***callosa*** (8) | ECho |
| § | - - var. ***australis*** (8) | NBro NHol NMen |
| | - var. ***lantoscana*** | see *S. callosa* subsp. *callosa* var. *australis* |
| | - ***lingulata*** | see *S. callosa* |
| | ***callosa*** x ***cochlearis*** | see *S.* Silver Farreri Group |
| | 'Cambridge Seedling' (7) | NDlv NMen |
| | 'Camyra' (7) | WAbe |
| | x ***canis-dalmatica*** | see *S.* 'Canis-dalmatica' |
| § | 'Canis-dalmatica' (x *gaudinii*) (8) 🏆H4 | CLyd CSsd ECho ECtt EGoo EPot GEdr GGar LRHS NDlv NHar NHol NMen NWCA WGor WPer |
| § | 'Carmen' (x *elisabethae*) (7) | NDlv NLAp NMen WAbe |
| § | 'Carniolica' (*paniculata*) (8) | CLyd GKir LFox MBar NBro NHol NMen NWCA |
| | 'Carniolica' (x *pectinata*) (8) | WAbe |
| | ***carolinica*** | see *S.* 'Carniolica' (*paniculata*) |
| | ***cartilaginea*** | see *S. paniculata* subsp. *cartilaginea* |
| | 'Castor' (x *bilekii*) (7) | NMen |
| | 'Caterhamensis' (*cotyledon*) (8) | NHar |
| | 'Cathy Reed' (x *polulacina*) (7) | NMen |
| | ***caucasica*** (7) | ECho |
| | - var. ***desoulavyi*** | see *S. desoulavyi* |
| | ***cebennensis*** (15) 🏆H2 | CLyd EPot LFox NMen NRya |
| | - dwarf (15) | WAbe |
| | ***cespitosa*** (15) | WAbe |
| | 'Chambers' Pink Pride' | see *S.* 'Miss Chambers' |
| | 'Charlecote' (x *poluanglica*) (7) | CLyd |
| | 'Charles Chaplin' (7) | CLyd CPBP ECho NHar NMen WAbe |
| | 'Cheap Confections' (*fortunei*) (4) | CBct CBod CHEx CLAP EBee ECtt EWll GAbr GEdr LLHF MSte NHol NMen SPla WBor WCot WFar WMoo WOld WPGP |
| § | ***cherlerioides*** (10) | ECtt NRya NVic WFar |
| | 'Cherry Pie' (*fortunei*) (5) | CBct CLAP EBee GAbr LHop LLHF MBNS MNrw NBir NHar NMyG WCot WGwG |
| | 'Cherrytrees' (x *boydii*) (7) | NMen WAbe |
| * | 'Chetwynd' (*marginata*) (7) | CLyd NMen WAbe |
| | 'Chez Nous' (x *gloriana*) (7/v) | CLyd NMen |
| | 'Chodov' (7) | EPot NMen |
| | 'Christine' (x *anglica*) (7) | CLyd ECho LFox NDlv NHol NLAp NMen |
| | ***cinerea*** (7) | NMen WAbe |
| | 'Cio-Cio-San' (Vanessa Group) (7) | NMen |
| | 'Citronella' (7) | ECho WAbe |
| | 'Claire Felstead' (*cinerea* x *poluniniana*) (7) | NMen |
| | 'Clare' (x *anglica*) (7) | NMen |
| | 'Clare Island' (*rosacea*) (15) | SIng |
| § | 'Clarence Elliott' (*umbrosa*) (11) 🏆H4 | CLyd CMea CTri EBee ECho EWes GCal GJos GKev MDKP MHar MHer NHol NRya NVic WFar WHoo WPat |
| | 'Claude Monet' (7) **new** | CPBP WAbe |
| | 'Claudia' (x *borisii*) (7) | NMen |
| | 'Cleo' (x *boydii*) (7) | NMen |

| | |
|---|---|
| 'Cloth of Gold' (*exarata* subsp. *moschata*) (15) | CLyd EAlp ECha ECho ECtt ELan GMaP LAst LRHS MBar MHer NHol NMen NRya SIng SPer SPlb SPoG SRms WAbe WBVN WFar |
| ***cochlearis*** (8) | CTri GEdr LBee LRHS MWat NBro NDlv NMen SBch WAbe WPer |
| 'Cockscomb' (*paniculata*) (8) | EAlp ECho NHol NMen NRya WAbe |
| ***columnaris*** (7) | NMen WAbe |
| 'Combrook' (x *poluanglica*) (7) | CLyd NMen |
| 'Coningsby Queen' (x *hornibrookii*) (7) | NMen |
| ***continentalis*** (15) | NWCA |
| 'Conwy Snow' (*fortunei*) (5) | CLAP NHar WAbe WFar |
| 'Conwy Star' (*fortunei*) (5) | CLAP NHar WAbe WFar |
| 'Coolock Gem' (7) | CLyd NMen WAbe |
| 'Coolock Kate' (7) | CLyd CStu NMen WAbe |
| 'Cordata' (*burseriana*) (7) | NMen |
| 'Corona' (x *boydii*) (7) | LFox NMen |
| 'Correnie Claret' (15) | EWes |
| 'Correvoniana' Farrer (*paniculata*) (8) | EDAr MHer WFar |
| ***cortusifolia*** (5) | CLAP ECho |
| - B&SWJ 5879 | WCru |
| - var. ***fortunei*** | see *S. fortunei* |
| - var. ***stolonifera*** (5) | ECho GCal |
| - - B&SWJ 6205 | WCru |
| 'Cotton Crochet' (*fortunei*) (5/d) | CBct EBee ECtt GEdr LAst MBNS MLLN NMyG WBor WCot WFar WOld |
| ***cotyledon*** (8) | ECho NHol WEas WPer |
| § 'Cranbourne' (x *anglica*) (7) 🏆$^{H4}$ | CLyd CMea ECho LFox LRHS NHol NLAp NMen WPat |
| 'Cream' (*paniculata*) (8) | ECho |
| 'Cream Seedling' (x *elisabethae*) (7) | ECho NDlv NLAp NMen |
| 'Crenata' (*burseriana*) (7) | CLyd LFox NDlv NMen WAbe WHoo |
| 'Crimson Rose' (*paniculata*) | see *S.* 'Rosea' (*paniculata*) |
| § ***crustata*** (8) | EAlp ECho MDKP NMen WThu |
| - var. ***vochinensis*** | see *S. crustata* |
| 'Crystal Pink' (*fortunei*) (5/v) | CBct CMil EBee ECtt EHrv GAbr GEdr GKev LAst LHop LRHS MNrw NBro NHar NMen NMyG WCot WFar WGwG WOld |
| 'Crystalie' (x *biasolettoi*) (7) | NDlv NMen NRya WPat |
| 'Cultrata' (*paniculata*) (8) | NBro |
| 'Cumulus' (*iranica* hybrid) (7) 🏆$^{H4}$ | CLyd EDAr EPot NMen WAbe |
| § ***cuneifolia*** (11) | ECho GGar GKir LBee LRHS MHer MWat NDlv NSti NWCA WFar WPer WRos |
| - var. ***capillipes*** | see *S. cuneifolia* subsp. *cuneifolia* |
| § - subsp. ***cuneifolia*** (11) | ECtt |
| * - var. ***subintegra*** (11) | ECho |
| ***cuscutiformis*** | see *S.* 'Cuscutiformis' |
| § 'Cuscutiformis' (*stolonifera*) (5) | CElw CHid EBee EBla EWld GEdr SBch SIng SRms WCru WPGP |
| ***cymbalaria*** (2) | EBur SIng |
| 'Cyril Mortimor Pritchard' (x *hardingii*) (7) | CLyd |
| ***dahurica*** | see *S. cuneifolia* |
| 'Dainty Dame' (x *arco-valleyi*) (7) | CLyd LFox NDlv NMen |
| 'Dana' (x *megaseiflora*) (7) | CLyd NHol NMen |
| 'Dartington Double' (15/d) | EWes WFar |
| 'Dartington Double White' (15/d) | NHol |
| 'David' (7) | NMen WAbe |
| 'Dawn Frost' (7) | CLyd EPot NDlv NLAp NMen WAbe |
| 'Delia' (x *hornibrookii*) (7) | CLyd NMen |
| § 'Denisa' (x *pseudokotschyi*) (7) | NMen |
| ***densa*** | see *S. cherlerioides* |
| 'Densa' (*hypnoides*) (15) | EAlp |
| 'Dentata' (x *geum*) | see *S.* 'Dentata' (x *polita*) |
| § 'Dentata' (x *polita*) (11) | CMea CSpe ECha ECho GGar NVic WMoo |
| 'Dentata' (x *urbium*) | see *S.* 'Dentata' (x *polita*) |
| § ***desoulavyi*** (7) | NMen |
| ***diapensioides*** (7) | CLyd WAbe |
| ***dinnikii*** (7) | NMen WAbe |
| x ***dinninaris*** (7) | NMen |
| 'Dobruška' (x *irvingii*) (7) | NMen |
| 'Doctor Clay' (*paniculata*) (8) | EAlp GKev NHar NMen NRya WAbe |
| 'Doctor Ramsey' (8) | ECtt EWes GEdr LBee LRHS NBro NDlv NHol NLar NMen WAbe WGor WPnn |
| 'Don Giovanni' (7) | WAbe |
| 'Donald Mann' (15) | EWes |
| 'Dorothy Milne' (7) | NMen |
| 'Drakula' (*ferdinandi-coburgi*) (7) | CLyd LRHS NDlv NMen SIng |
| 'Dubarry' (15) | EWes NRya WPnn |
| 'Dulcimer' (x *petraschii*) (7) | NMen |
| 'Duncan Lowe' (*andersonii*) (7) 🏆$^{H4}$ | CLyd |
| 'Dwight Ripley' (7) | LFox |
| 'Edgar Irmscher' (7) | CLyd LFox NDlv NMen |
| 'Edith' (x *edithae*) (7) | ECho LRHS SIng |
| 'Edward Elgar' (x *megaseiflora*) (7) | NHol NMen |
| 'Elf' (7) | see *S.* 'Beatrix Stanley' |
| 'Eliot Hodgkin' (x *millstreamiana*) (7) | LFox NMen |
| x ***elisabethae*** Sünd. (7) | EDAr |
| - *sensu stricto* hort. | see *S.* 'Carmen' |
| 'Elizabeth Sinclair' (x *elisabethae*) (7) | CLyd EPot GKev ITim NMen |
| 'Ellie Brinckerhoff' (x *hornibrookii*) (7) | NMen |
| 'Elliott's Variety' | see *S.* 'Clarence Elliott' (*umbrosa*) |
| x ***engleri*** (8) | CLyd |
| § 'Ernst Heinrich' (x *heinrichii*) (7) | CLyd NMen |
| 'Esther' (x *burnatii*) (8) | CMea GEdr GKev LRHS NHol NMen NWCA SRGP WAbe WPnn |
| § 'Eulenspiegel' (x *geuderi*) (7) | CLyd EPot NHol NMen |
| 'Eva Hanzliková' (x *izari*) (7) | CLyd NMen WAbe |
| ***exarata*** (15) | LFox NMen WAbe |
| - subsp. ***moschata*** 'Elf' (15) | ECtt EPfP LRHS NHol NMen SRms WGor |
| fair maids of France | see *S.* 'Flore Pleno' |
| 'Fairy' (*exarata* subsp. *moschata*) (15) | CMea ECtt ELan EPot GKir |
| 'Faldonside' (x *boydii*) (7) 🏆$^{H4}$ | CLyd LFox NDlv NLAp NMen NRya WAbe WHoo WPat |
| 'Falstaff' (*burseriana*) (7) | CLyd LFox NDlv NHol NRya WAbe |
| x ***farreri*** (15) | GEdr |
| § 'Faust' (x *borisii*) (7) | NMen WAbe |
| 'Favorit' (x *bilekii*) (7) | NMen |
| § ***federici-augusti*** subsp. ***grisebachii*** (7) 🏆$^{H2-3}$ | CLyd ECho EPot GKev NSla WAbe WFar |
| 'Ferdinand' (x *hofmannii*) (7) | NMen |
| ***ferdinandi-coburgi*** (7) 🏆$^{H4}$ | CLyd ECtt EPot LFox LRHS NDlv NRya WAbe WBrE |
| § - subsp. ***chrysospleniifolia*** var. ***rhodopea*** (7) | CLyd EPot LRHS NDlv NMen SIng |

| | |
|---|---|
| - var. ***pravislavii*** | see *S. ferdinandi-coburgi* subsp. *chrysospleniifolia* var. *rhodopea* |
| - var. ***radoslavoffii*** | see *S. ferdinandi-coburgi* subsp. *chrysospleniifolia* var. *rhodopea* |
| 'Findling' (15) | EPot NHol NMen SPoG WAbe |
| 'Firebrand' (x *kochii*) (7) | NMen WAbe |
| 'Five Color' (*fortunei*) | see *S.* 'Go-nishiki' (5) |
| § ***flagellaris*** (1) | NMen WAbe |
| 'Flavescens' misapplied | see *S.* 'Lutea' (*paniculata*) (8) |
| x ***fleischeri*** (7) | NMen |
| § 'Flore Pleno' (*granulata*) (15/d) | CFir EBee EWes LFox MAvo NBir SIng SUsu WAbe WCot WFar |
| 'Florissa' (*oppositifolia*) (7) | CLyd |
| 'Flowers of Sulphur' | see *S.* 'Schwefelblüte' |
| 'Flush' (x *petraschii*) (7) | WAbe |
| § ***fortunei*** (5) ♀H4 | CHEx CLAP ECho EWTr GKir GMaP IFro NBir NLAp SRms WAbe WCru WMoo |
| - B&SWJ 6346 | WCru |
| - f. ***alpina*** (5) | CLAP |
| - - from Hokkaido (5) | CLAP WCru |
| - var. ***koraiensis*** (5) B&SWJ 8688 | WCru |
| - 'Musgrove Pink' **new** | CLAP |
| - var. ***obtusocuneata*** (5) | CLAP EBee ECho LLHF NMen WAbe |
| - f. ***partita*** (5) | CLAP GEdr WCru |
| - var. ***pilosissima*** (5) B&SWJ 8557 | WCru |
| - pink-flowered (5) | CLAP WAbe WFar |
| - var. ***suwoensis*** (5) | CLAP |
| 'Foster's Gold' (x *elisabethae*) (7) | CLyd NMen WAbe |
| 'Four Winds' (15) | EWes SPoG |
| 'Francesco Redi' (7) | NMen WAbe |
| 'Francis Cade' (8) | GAbr WAbe |
| 'Frank Sinatra' (x *poluanglica*) (7) | CLyd NMen |
| 'Franz Liszt' (7) | WAbe |
| 'Franzii' (x *paulinae*) (7) | NMen |
| 'Freckles' | GKev |
| 'Frederik Chopin' (7) | EPot WAbe |
| 'Friar Tuck' (x *boydii*) (7) | NMen WAbe |
| 'Friesei' (x *salmonica*) (7) | CLyd EPot NMen |
| x ***fritschiana*** (8) | GEdr NMen |
| 'Fumiko' (*fortunei*) (5) | CLAP WAbe WCru |
| 'Funkii' (x *petraschii*) (7) | NMen |
| 'Gaertneri' (x *mariae-theresiae*) (7) | NMen |
| 'Gaiety' (15) | EAlp GKir SPoG WFar |
| 'Galaxie' (x *megaseiflora*) (7) | CLyd LFox NDlv NMen |
| 'Ganymede' (*burseriana*) (7) | NMen |
| 'Gelber Findling' (7) | EPot WAbe |
| 'Gem' (x *irvingii*) (7) | NDlv NMen |
| 'General Joffre' (15) | see *S.* 'Maréchal Joffre' |
| 'Geoff Wilson' (x biasolettoi) | NMen |
| ***georgei*** (7) | CLyd NMen WAbe |
| ***georgei*** x 'Winifred' (7) | CLyd |
| 'Gertie Pritchard' (x *megaseiflora*) | see *S.* 'Mrs Gertie Prichard' |
| x ***geuderi*** *sensu stricto* hort. | see *S.* 'Eulenspiegel' |
| § x ***geum*** (11) | CHid MLHP MRav WFar WMoo |
| - Dixter form (11) | ECha SUsu |
| 'Gleborg' (15) | EAlp EWes SPoG |
| 'Gloria' (*burseriana*) (7) ♀H4 | CLyd LFox LRHS NMen NSla SIng WPat |
| x ***gloriana*** *sensu stricto* hort. (7) | see *S.* 'Godiva' |
| 'Gloriana' | see *S.* 'Godiva' |
| 'Gloriosa' (x *gloriana*) (7) | see *S.* 'Godiva' |
| § 'Godiva' (x *gloriana*) (7) | CLyd NMen WAbe |
| 'Goeblii' (7) | NDlv |
| 'Gold Dust' (x *eudoxiana*) (7) | CLyd ECho LFox NLAp NMen NRya |
| 'Golden Falls' (15/v) | EAlp EWes LAst NHol SPlb SPoG |
| Golden Prague (x *pragensis*) | see *S.* 'Zlatá Praha' |
| § 'Go-nishiki' (*fortunei*) (5) | EBee LLHF |
| 'Goring White' (7) | NMen WAbe |
| 'Gothenburg' (7) | CLyd NMen WAbe |
| 'Grace Farwell' (x *anglica*) (7) | ECho MBar NDlv NHol NMen NRya NWCA WAbe WHoo |
| 'Grace' (x *arendsii*) (15/v) | see *S.* 'Seaspray' |
| ***granulata*** (15) | CRWN EBWF ECho EDAr GJos NSco WAbe WFar |
| 'Gratoides' (x *grata*) (7) | NMen |
| § 'Gregor Mendel' (x *apiculata*) (7) ♀H4 | CLyd CMea CSam ECho ECtt EPot LRHS NDlv NHol NLAp NMen SRms WAbe WFar WHoo |
| ***grisebachii*** | see *S. federici-augusti* subsp. *grisebachii* |
| 'Haagii' (x *eudoxiana*) (7) | CTri ECho ELan NDlv NLAp NMen |
| 'Harbinger' (7) | CLyd WAbe WGor |
| 'Hare Knoll Beauty' (8) | ECho GKev ITim NHar NLAp NMen NRya WAbe |
| 'Harlow Car' (7) | CLyd LFox NMen NSla |
| 'Harry Marshall' (x *irvingii*) (7) | CLyd NDlv NHol NMen |
| 'Harry Smith' (x *cimganii*) (7) **new** | WAbe |
| 'Hartside Pink' (*umbrosa*) (11) | CLyd |
| 'Hartswood White' (15) | MWat |
| 'Harvest Moon' (*stolonifera*) (5) | CBow CHEx |
| 'Hedwig' (x *malbyana*) (7) | NMen |
| x ***heinreichii*** *sensu stricto* hort. | see *S.* 'Ernst Heinrich' |
| 'Hi-Ace' (15/v) | CLyd ECtt EDAr LFox MHer NLAp SPlb |
| 'Highdownensis' (*cotyledon*) (8) | NDlv |
| 'Hime' (*stolonifera*) (5) | WCru WHil |
| 'Hindhead Seedling' (x *boydii*) (7) | CLyd LRHS NDlv NMen SIng WAbe |
| ***hirsuta*** (11) | EBla EWld GGar IFro MMuc WCru |
| 'Hirsuta' (x *geum*) | see *S.* x *geum* |
| 'Hirtella' Ingwersen (*paniculata*) (8) | EPot |
| 'His Majesty' (x *irvingii*) (7) | LFox NMen |
| 'Hocker Edge' (x *arco-valleyi*) (7) | CLyd ITim LFox NDlv NMen |
| 'Holden Seedling' (15) | ECtt EWes |
| x ***hornibrookii*** (7) | WPat |
| ***hostii*** (8) | CLyd ECho EDAr GKev LBee NHol NLAp WTin |
| - subsp. ***hostii*** (8) | GAuc GEdr |
| - - var. ***altissima*** (8) | STre |
| - subsp. ***rhaetica*** (8) | GBin NBro NDlv NMen WAbe |
| 'Hradčany' (x *megaseiflora*) (7) | NMen |
| 'Hsitou Silver' (*stolonifera*) (5) | CFee EBee EPPr MDKP WCru |
| 'Hunscote' (x *poluanglica*) (7) | NMen |
| hybrid JB 11 | NMen |
| § ***hypnoides*** (15) | SPoG WAbe |
| 'Iceland' (*oppositifolia*) (7) | WAbe |
| 'Icicle' (x *elisabethae*) (7) | NMen |
| 'Ignaz Dörfler' (x *doerfleri*) (7) | NMen WAbe |
| ***imparilis*** (5) | CLAP EHrv GEdr WCru |

| | | |
|---|---|---|
| | 'Ingeborg' (15) | ECha SIng |
| | ***iranica*** (7) | CLyd NMen |
| | - pink (7) | CPBP |
| | 'Irene Bacci' (x *baccii*) (7) | CLyd NMen |
| | 'Iris Prichard' (x *hardingii*) (7) | CLyd WAbe |
| | x ***irvingii*** (7) | ECho NDlv |
| | - *sensu stricto* hort. | see *S.* 'Walter Irving' |
| | 'Isobel Young' (7) | WAbe |
| | 'Ivana' (x *caroliquarti*) (7) | CPBP NMen WAbe |
| | ***jacquemontiana*** (1) | WAbe |
| | 'James' (7) | NSla |
| | 'James Bremner' (15) | GMaP NBlu |
| | 'Jan Neruda' (x *megaseiflora*) (7) | NMen |
| | 'Jan Palach' (x *krausii*) (7) | CMea EPot NMen |
| | 'Jason' (x *elisabethae*) (7) | NMen |
| | 'Jenkinsiae' (x *irvingii*) (7) 🏆H4 | CFee CLyd CStu ECho EDAr EPot GMaP LRHS NDlv NLAp NMen NRya WAbe WPat |
| | 'Joachim Barrande' (x *siluris*) (7) | WAbe |
| § | 'Johann Kellerer' (x *kellereri*) (7) | CFee LFox NDlv WAbe |
| | 'John Tomlinson' (*burseriana*) (7) | CLyd NMen |
| | 'Josef Čapek' (x *megaseiflora*) (7) | CLyd EPot NMen |
| | 'Josef Mánes' (x *borisii*) (7) | NMen |
| | 'Joy' | see *S.* 'Kaspar Maria Sternberg' |
| | 'Judith Shackleton' (x *abingdonensis*) (7) | CLyd NDlv NHol NMen WAbe |
| | 'Juliet' | see *S.* 'Riverslea' |
| § | ***juniperifolia*** (7) | CMea ECho ECtt EDAr LRHS MHer NDlv NLAp NWCA SRms |
| | - subsp. ***sancta*** | see *S. sancta* |
| | 'Jupiter' (x *megaseiflora*) (7) | CLyd NDlv NLAp NMen WAbe |
| | 'Kampa' (7) | CLyd NMen |
| § | ***karadzicensis*** (7) | NMen |
| | 'Karasin' (7) | CLyd NMen |
| | 'Karel Čapek' (x *megaseiflora*) (7) | CLyd EPot NDlv NRya NSla WAbe |
| | 'Karel Stivín' (x *edithae*) (7) | CLyd NMen |
| | 'Karlštejn' (x *borisii*) (7) | NDlv |
| § | 'Kaspar Maria Sternberg' (x *petraschii*) (7) | CLyd LFox NMen WPat |
| | 'Kath Dryden' (7) | ECho ECtt GKev NHol WAbe |
| | 'Kathleen Pinsent' (8) 🏆H4 | CLyd ECho NWCA WAbe |
| | 'Kathleen' (x *polulacina*) (7) | CLyd NLAp WAbe |
| | x ***kellereri*** *sensu stricto* hort. | see *S.* 'Johann Kellerer' |
| | 'Kew Gem' (x *petraschii*) (7) | ECho NMen |
| | 'Kewensis' (x *kellereri*) (7) | NDlv NMen WAbe |
| | 'Kineton' (x *poluanglica*) (7) | NMen |
| | 'King Lear' (x *bursiculata*) (7) | CLyd EPot LFox LRHS NMen |
| | 'Kinki Purple' (*stolonifera*) (5) | EBee EHrv EPPr EWld GGar WCru |
| | 'Klondike' (x *boydii*) (7) | WAbe |
| | 'Knapton Pink' (15) | ECtt EDAr EPfP NPro NRya SIng SPoG WAbe WFar |
| | 'Knapton White' (15) | SPoG |
| | 'Knebworth' (8) | ECho |
| * | 'Koigokora' (*fortunei*) (5) | WOld |
| | 'Kokaku' (*fortunei*) **new** | LLHF |
| § | 'Kolbiana' (x *paulinae*) (7) | CLyd |
| | 'Kon Tiki' (7) | WAbe |
| * | 'Kosumosu' (*fortunei*) (5) | WOld |
| § | 'Krain' (x *fritschiana*) (8) | ECho |
| | 'Krákatit' (x *megaseiflora*) (7) | NMen |
| | 'Krasava' (x *megaseiflora*) (7) | CLyd EPot NMen |
| | 'Kyrilli' (x *borisii*) (7) | CLyd NMen |
| | 'Labe' (x *arco-valleyi*) (7) | CLyd NMen WAbe |
| | 'Ladislav Čelakovský' (7) | NMen WAbe |
| | 'Lady Beatrix Stanley' | see *S.* 'Beatrix Stanley' |
| | 'Lagraveana' (*paniculata*) (8) 🏆H4 | ECtt EDAr MMuc NDlv NRya WGor |
| | x ***landaueri*** *sensu stricto* hort. | see *S.* 'Leonore' |
| | 'Lantoscana Superba' (*callosa* subsp. *australis*) (8) | EPot |
| | 'Latonica' (*callosa*) (8) | EAlp EPot |
| | 'Lemon Hybrid' (x *boydii*) (7) | NMen |
| | 'Lemon Spires' (7) | NMen WAbe |
| | 'Lenka' (x *byam-groundsii*) (7) | NMen NSla WAbe |
| | 'Leo Gordon Godseff' (x *elisabethae*) (7) | LRHS NDlv NMen |
| § | 'Leonore' (x *landaueri*) (7) | LRHS |
| | 'Letchworth Gem' (x *urbium*) (11) | ECho GCal |
| | 'Lidice' (7) | CLyd NDlv NMen WHoo |
| | 'Lilac Time' (x *youngiana*) (7) | NMen WAbe |
| | ***lilacina*** (7) | CLyd NMen |
| | 'Lindau' (7) | NMen |
| | ***lingulata*** | see *S. callosa* |
| | 'Lismore Carmine' (x *lismorensis*) (7) | CLyd NDlv NMen NWCA |
| | 'Lismore Cherry' (7) | CLyd |
| | 'Lismore Gem' (x *lismorensis*) (7) | ECho ITim NMen |
| | 'Lismore Mist' (x *lismorensis*) (7) | CLyd CPBP NMen |
| | 'Lismore Pink' (x *lismorensis*) (7) | CLyd EPot NDlv NMen NWCA |
| | 'Lissadell' (*callosa*) **new** | GKev |
| * | 'Little Piggy' (*epiphylla*) (5) | WCru |
| | 'Lohengrin' (x *hoerhammeri*) (7) | EPot NMen |
| | 'Long Acre Pink' (*fortunei*) (5) | CLAP |
| | ***longifolia*** (8) | CSec ECho EPot GKev NSla WGor |
| | 'Louis Armstrong' (Blues Group) (7) | CPBP |
| | Love Me | see *S.* 'Miluj Mne' |
| | ***lowndesii*** (7) | WAbe |
| | 'Loxley' (*poluanglica*) (7) | GEdr |
| | 'Ludmila Šubrová' (x *bertolonii*) (7) | CLyd NMen |
| | 'Lusanna' (x *irvingii*) (7) | CLyd |
| | 'Lutea' (*aizoon*) | see *S.* 'Lutea' (*paniculata*) |
| | 'Lutea' (*diapensioides*) | see *S.* 'Wilhelm Tell', 'Primulina' |
| | 'Lutea' (*marginata*) | see *S.* 'Faust' |
| § | 'Lutea' (*paniculata*) (8) 🏆H4 | EAlp ECho EDAr EHoe EPot GEdr GMaP NBro NDlv NHol |
| § | 'Luteola' (x *boydii*) (7) 🏆H4 | NDlv WAbe |
| | 'Lužníce' (x *poluluteopurpurea*) (7) | NMen |
| | ***macedonica*** | see *S. juniperifolia* |
| | ***maderensis*** (15) | GKev |
| | 'Magdalena' (x *thomasiana*) (7) | NMen |
| | 'Major' (*cochlearis*) (8) 🏆H4 | LRHS WGor |
| | 'Major Lutea' | see *S.* 'Luteola' |
| | 'Maly Trpaslik' (7) | WAbe |
| | 'Marc Chagall' (Decora Group) (7) **new** | WAbe |

| | | |
|---|---|---|
| § | 'Maréchal Joffre' (15) | GAbr GMaP LAst NPri |
| | 'Margarete' (x *borisii*) (7) | CLyd NMen |
| | ***marginata*** (7) | CLyd LFox WAbe |
| | - var. ***balcanica*** | see *S. marginata* subsp. *marginata* var. *rocheliana* |
| | - var. ***karadzicensis*** | see *S. karadzicensis* |
| | - subsp. ***marginata*** var. ***boryi*** (7) | CLyd NMen WAbe |
| | - - var. ***coriophylla*** (7) | EPot NMen NWCA WAbe |
| § | - - var. ***rocheliana*** (7) | CLyd EPot NDlv NMen SAga |
| | - - - 'Balkan' (7) | CLyd |
| | 'Maria Callas' (x *poluanglica*) (7) | CLyd WGor |
| | 'Maria Luisa' (x *salmonica*) (7) | CFee LFox NDlv NMen NWCA WAbe |
| | 'Marianna' (x *borisii*) (7) | CLyd CMea NDlv NHol NMen NRya |
| | 'Maroon Beauty' (*stolonifera*) (5) | ECtt EPPr MDKP NBre WCot |
| | 'Mars' (x *elisabethae*) (7) | NMen |
| | 'Marshal Joffre' (15) | see *S.* 'Maréchal Joffre' (15) |
| § | 'Martha' (x *semmleri*) (7) | CLyd NMen |
| | 'Mary Golds' (Swing Group) (7) | CLyd EDAr WGor |
| | ***matta-florida*** (7) | NMen |
| | 'May Queen' (7) | NMen |
| | x ***megaseiflora*** *sensu stricto* hort. | see *S.* 'Robin Hood' |
| | 'Melrose' (x *salmonica*) (7) | NMen |
| | ***mertensiana*** (6) | GEdr NBir WCru |
| | 'Meteor' (7) | NDlv NRya |
| | ***micranthidifolia*** (4) | CLAP EBee WPGP |
| | 'Mikuláš Koperník' (x *zenittensis*) (7) | WAbe |
| | 'Millstream' (8) | NWCA |
| | 'Millstream Cream' (x *elisabethae*) (7) | CLyd ECho ITim NMen |
| § | 'Miluj Mne' (x *poluanglica*) (7) | ECho LFox NDlv NHol NMen WAbe |
| | 'Minnehaha' (x *elisabethae*) (7) | WAbe |
| | 'Minor' (*cochlearis*) (8) 🏆H4 | EAlp GKev LFox LRHS NHol NMen NWCA SIng WGor WPat |
| § | 'Miss Chambers' (x *urbium*) (11) | SMHy SUsu WCot WMoo WPen WSHC |
| | 'Mona Lisa' (x *borisii*) (7) | CLyd NMen WAbe |
| | 'Monarch' (8) 🏆H4 | WAbe |
| | 'Moonlight' (x *boydii*) | see *S.* 'Sulphurea' |
| | 'Morava' (7) | NMen |
| * | 'Mossy Pink' | NBlu SPoG |
| | 'Mossy Red' | SPoG |
| | 'Mossy Triumph' | see *S.* 'Triumph' (x *arendsii*) |
| | 'Mother of Pearl' (x *irvingii*) (7) | CLyd ECho NDlv NLAp NMen WAbe |
| | 'Mother Queen' (x *irvingii*) (7) | CLyd NLAp NMen WPat |
| | 'Mount Nachi' (*fortunei*) (5) | Widely available |
| § | 'Mrs Gertie Prichard' (x *megaseiflora*) (7) | LFox NMen WAbe |
| | 'Mrs Helen Terry' (x *salmonica*) (7) | CLyd NDlv NMen |
| | 'Mrs Leng' (x *elisabethae*) (7) | MDKP NMen |
| | 'Myra Cambria' (x *anglica*) (7) | NDlv NHol NMen WAbe |
| | 'Myra' (x *anglica*) (7) | CLyd ECho LFox NHol NMen NWCA WHoo WPat |
| | 'Myriad' (7) | CLyd NMen |
| | 'Nancye' (x *goringiana*) (7) | CLyd ITim NDlv NMen WAbe |
| § | ***nelsoniana*** (4) | NHol |
| | 'Nimbus' (*iranica*) (7) | CLyd NMen WAbe |
| | 'Niobe' (x *pulvilacina*) (7) | CLyd NMen |
| | 'Notata' (*paniculata*) (8) | NLAp |
| | 'Nottingham Gold' (x *boydii*) (7) | CLyd EAlp NMen |
| | 'Obristii' (x *salmonica*) (7) | NDlv NMen NRya |
| § | ***obtusa*** (7) | EPot MHer NMen |
| | 'Ochroleuca' (x *elisabethae*) (7) | NMen |
| | 'Odysseus' (*sancta*) (7) | NMen |
| | 'Olymp' (*scardica*) (7) | NMen |
| | 'Opalescent' (7) | CLyd LFox NMen |
| § | 'Ophelia' (x *arco-valleyi*) (7) | NMen |
| | ***oppositifolia*** (7) | ECho GKir MHer NLAp NSla SPlb SRms WAbe WFar |
| | - subsp. ***oppositifolia*** var. ***latina*** (7) | CLyd ECho EPot NLAp |
| | 'Oriole' (x *boydii*) (7) | NMen |
| | 'Orjen' (*paniculata* var. *orientalis*) (8) | GEdr |
| | 'Ottone Rosai' (Toscana Group) (7) | NMen |
| | 'Oxhill' (7) | ITim NMen |
| § | ***paniculata*** (8) | ECho EDAr EHoe GGar GKev GMaP LRHS MDKP MWat NDlv NLAp NSla SPlb SRms WAbe WFar WHoo WRHF |
| § | - subsp. ***cartilaginea*** (8) | NHol WAbe |
| | - subsp. ***kolenatiana*** | see *S. paniculata* subsp. *cartilaginea* |
| § | - var. ***minutifolia*** (8) | CLyd CPBP CTri ECho LFox LRHS MBar MWat NBro NDlv NHol NLAp NMen NRya NWCA SPlb WAbe |
| | ***paradoxa*** (15) | EPot GEdr LRHS NHol WGor |
| | 'Parcevalis' (x *finnisiae*) (7x9) | CLyd WAbe |
| | 'Parsee' (x *margoxiana*) (7) | NDlv NMen |
| | 'Paula' (x *paulinae*) (7) | NMen |
| | 'Peach Blossom' (7) | CLyd NDlv NMen NRya |
| | 'Peach Melba' (7) | CLyd CStu EAlp EPot NMen WAbe WFar |
| * | 'Peachy Head' | NMen |
| | 'Pearl Rose' (x *anglica*) (7) | LFox |
| | 'Pearly Gates' (x *irvingii*) (7) | CLyd NDlv NMen |
| | 'Pearly Gold' (15) | NRya WFar |
| | 'Pearly King' (15) | GKev GMaP WAbe WFar |
| | x ***pectinata*** Schott, Nyman & Kotschy | see *S.* 'Krain' |
| | 'Penelope' (x *boydilacina*) (7) | CLyd CMea CStu ECho NMen WAbe WHoo WPat |
| | ***pensylvanica*** (4) | GCal GCra |
| | 'Perikles' (7) | NMen |
| | 'Peter Burrow' (x *poluanglica*) (7) 🏆H4 | CLyd CPBP ECho NMen WAbe |
| | 'Peter Pan' (15) | EAlp EDAr EPfP EPot GJos GMaP LFox MHer NHol NMen NPro NRya SIng SPoG WFar WPnn |
| | 'Petra' (7) | CLyd EPot NMen WAbe WFar |
| | x ***petraschii*** (7) | CLyd |
| § | 'Phoenix' (x *biasolettoi*) (7) | LRHS WThu |
| | 'Pilatus' (x *boydii*) (7) | NMen |
| | 'Pink Cloud' (*fortunei*) (5) | CLAP NHar WAbe WFar |
| | 'Pink Haze' (*fortunei*) (5) | CLAP NHar WAbe |
| | 'Pink Mist' (*fortunei*) (5) | CLAP NHar WAbe WFar |
| | 'Pink Pagoda' (*nipponica*) (5) | CDes CLAP EBee GEdr WCot WCru WPGP |
| | 'Pink Pearl' (7) | CMea NMen |
| | 'Pixie' (15) | CTri ECtt NHol NMen SIng SPoG SRms |
| | 'Pixie Alba' | see *S.* 'White Pixie' |
| | 'Plena' (*granulata*) | see *S.* 'Flore Pleno' |
| | 'Pollux' (x *boydii*) (7) | ITim NMen |
| | ***poluniniana*** (7) | CLyd LFox WAbe |

| | Name | Suppliers |
|---|---|---|
| | ***poluniniana*** x 'Winifred' (x *poluanglica*) (7) | CLyd ECho EPot |
| | 'Pompadour' (15) | NPro |
| | 'Popelka' (subsp. *marginata* var. *rocheliana*) (7) | CLyd NMen |
| | ***porophylla*** (7) | NMen |
| | - var. ***thessalica*** | see *S. sempervivum* f. *stenophylla* |
| | aff. ***porophylla*** (7) | NWCA |
| | 'Precious Piggy' (*epiphylla*) (5) | WCru |
| | 'Primrose Bee' (x *apiculata*) (7) | ITim |
| | 'Primrose Dame' (x *elisabethae*) (7) | ECho ITim MDKP NMen WAbe |
| | 'Primulaize' (9x11) | CLyd MHer MWat NMen |
| | 'Primulaize Salmon' (9x11) | NDlv NHol WHoo WPer |
| § | 'Primulina' (x *malbyana*) (7) | LFox NMen |
| | ***primuloides*** | see *S.* 'Primuloides' |
| § | 'Primuloides' (*umbrosa*) (11) 🏆$^{H4}$ | ECho EDAr GKir LFox MMuc NMen NPri SPoG SRms SWvt WEas WFar |
| | 'Prince Hal' (*burseriana*) (7) | CLyd EAlp ECho EDAr LRHS NDlv NMen |
| | 'Princess' (*burseriana*) (7) | CLyd EDAr LRHS NMen |
| | 'Probynii' (*cochlearis*) (8) | MWat NDlv NMen WAbe |
| | 'Prometheus' (x *prossenii*) (7) | CLyd |
| | 'Prospero' (x *petraschii*) (7) | NMen |
| | x ***prossenii*** *sensu stricto* hort. | see *S.* 'Regina' |
| | 'Pseudofranzii' (x *paulinae*) (7) | NWCA |
| | x ***pseudokotschyi*** *sensu stricto* hort | see *S.* 'Denisa' |
| | 'Pseudopungens' (x *apiculata*) (7) | EPot |
| | 'Pseudoscardica' (x *wehrhahnii*) (7) | NMen |
| | 'Pseudovaldensis' (*cochlearis*) (8) | NHar WAbe |
| | ***pubescens*** (15) | WAbe |
| | - subsp. ***iratiana*** (15) | EPot NLAp |
| | ***punctata*** (4) | see *S. nelsoniana* |
| | 'Pungens' (x *apiculata*) (7) | NDlv NMen |
| | 'Purple Piggy' (*epiphylla*) (5) | CFee CLAP EBee WCru |
| | 'Purpurea' (*fortunei*) | see *S.* 'Rubrifolia' |
| § | 'Pygmalion' (x *webrii*) (7) | CLyd WGor |
| | 'Pyramidalis' (*cotyledon*) (8) | EPfP SRms |
| | 'Pyrenaica' (*oppositifolia*) (7) | ECho NMen |
| | 'Quarry Wood' (x *anglica*) (7) | CLyd NHol NMen |
| | 'Rainsley Seedling' (8) | GKev ITim NBro NMen |
| | ***ramulosa*** (7) | NMen |
| | 'Red Poll' (x *poluanglica*) (7) | CLyd CPBP ITim NDlv NMen NRya NWCA WAbe |
| * | 'Regent' | WAbe |
| § | 'Regina' (x *prossenii*) (7) | CLyd MHer NMen |
| | ***retusa*** (7) | CLyd NMen WAbe |
| § | 'Riverslea' (x *hornibrookii*) (7) | LFox LRHS NMen WAbe |
| § | 'Robin Hood' (x *megaseiflora*) (7) | CFee CLyd CPBP LFox NMen WHoo WPat |
| | 'Rokujō' (*fortunei*) (5) | CLAP EBee NLar NPro WFar |
| | 'Romeo' (x *hornibrookii*) (7) | CLyd NMen |
| | 'Rosa Tubbs' **new** | GKev |
| | 'Rosea' (*cortusifolia*) (5) | CLAP CWsd NHar |
| § | 'Rosea' (*paniculata*) (8) 🏆$^{H4}$ | GMaP LBMP LBee NBro NDlv NHol NSla SRms WFar |
| | 'Rosea' (x *stuartii*) (7) | NDlv NMen |
| | 'Rosemarie' (7) | CLyd ECho NMen |
| | 'Rosenzwerg' (15) | WFar |
| | 'Rosina Sündermann' (x *rosinae*) (7) | EPot NDlv NMen |
| | ***rotundifolia*** (12) | CLyd EBee MDKP NHol |
| | - subsp. ***chrysospleniifolia*** var. ***rhodopea*** (12) | WCru |
| | 'Roy Clutterbuck' (7) | NMen |
| | 'Rubella' (x *irvingii*) (7) | CLyd |
| | 'Rubra' (*aizoon*) | see *S.* 'Rosea' (*paniculata*) |
| § | 'Rubrifolia' (*fortunei*) (5) | CLAP CSpe EBee ECha ECtt EHoe GAbr GEdr IBal LAst MBri MCot NMen NMyG SAga SMad SPet SWvt WAbe WBor WClo WCot WCru WFar |
| * | 'Ruby Red' | NPro |
| * | 'Ruby Wedding' (cortusifolia) (5) | WCru |
| | ***rufescens*** (5) | EHrv GEdr |
| | - BWJ 7510 | WCru |
| | - BWJ 7684 | WCru |
| | 'Rusalka' (x *borisii*) (7) | CLyd NMen |
| | 'Russell Vincent Prichard' (x *irvingii*) (7) | NMen |
| | 'Ruth Draper' (*oppositifolia*) (7) | WAbe WFar |
| | 'Ruth McConnell' (15) | CMea |
| | 'Sabrina' (x *fallsvillagensis*) (7) | CLyd |
| | 'Saint John's' (8) | EBur ECho GEdr WAbe |
| | 'Saint Kilda' (*oppositifolia*) (7) | ITim |
| | x ***salmonica*** *sensu stricto* hort. | see *S.* 'Salomonii' |
| § | 'Salomonii' (x *salmonica*) (7) | CLyd NDlv NMen SRms |
| | 'Samo' (x *bertolonii*) (7) | CLyd NMen |
| § | ***sancta*** (7) | CLyd ECho LFox LRHS NMen SRms WAbe |
| | - subsp. ***pseudosancta*** (7) | see *S. juniperifolia* |
| | - - var. ***macedonica*** | see *S. juniperifolia* |
| | 'Sandpiper' (7) | NMen |
| | 'Sanguinea Superba' (x *arendsii*) (15) 🏆$^{H4}$ | SIng |
| | 'Sara Sinclair' (x *arco-valleyi*) (7) | CMea |
| | 'Šárka' (7) | NMen |
| | ***sarmentosa*** | see *S. stolonifera* |
| | 'Sartorii' | see *S.* 'Pygmalion' |
| | 'Saturn' (x *megaseiflora*) (7) | NMen WAbe |
| | 'Sázava' (x *poluluteopurpurea*) (7) | CLyd NMen WAbe |
| | ***scardica*** (7) | NBro NMen |
| | - var. ***dalmatica*** | see *S. obtusa* |
| | - var. ***obtusa*** | see *S. obtusa* |
| § | 'Schelleri' (x *petraschii*) (7) | NMen |
| § | 'Schwefelblüte' (15) | GMaP NPri NWCA SPoG WPat |
| | ***scleropoda*** (7) | EPot NMen |
| § | 'Seaspray' (x *arendsii*) (15/v) | EWes |
| | 'Seissera' (*burseriana*) (7) | NMen |
| | 'Semafor' (x *megaseiflora*) (7) | NMen |
| | x ***semmleri*** *sensu stricto* hort. | see *S.* 'Martha' |
| | ***sempervivum*** (7) | CLyd LFox NGdn NMen NSla NWCA WTin |
| § | - f. ***stenophylla*** (7) | ECho MHer |
| | ***sendaica*** (5) | CLAP EBee WCru |

| | | |
|---|---|---|
| | - B&SWJ 7448 (5) | GEdr |
| § | 'Silver Cushion' (15/v) | CMea CTri EDAr ELan GGar GKir LAst LRHS MBar NBlu NPri NPro SBch SPer SPlb SPoG WAbe WFar |
| | 'Silver Edge' (x *arco-valleyi*) (7) | NMen WAbe |
| | 'Silver Maid' (x *engleri*) | NMen |
| | 'Silver Mound' | see *S.* 'Silver Cushion' |
| | 'Silver Velvet' (*fortunei*) (5) | CBct CLAP ECtt GEdr LRHS MBNS NMyG WCot |
| | 'Sir Douglas Haig' (15) | SIng |
| | 'Sissi' (7) **new** | CPBP |
| | 'Slack's Ruby Southside' (Southside Seedling Group) ♀H4 | MDKP NLAp NSla WAbe WFar |
| | 'Snowcap' (*pubescens*) (15) | NWCA |
| | 'Snowdon' (*burseriana*) (7) | NMen |
| § | 'Snowflake' (8) (Silver Farreri Group) ♀H4 | NDlv WAbe |
| § | 'Sofia' (x *borisii*) (7) | EPot LFox NMen WFar |
| | 'Sorrento' (*marginata*) (7) | NMen |
| | Southside Seedling Group ♀H4 | Widely available |
| | - 'Southside Star' ♀H4 | WAbe WFar |
| | 'Spartakus' (x *apiculata*) (7) | NDlv |
| | ***spathularis*** (11) | CEnt EBee MHar WCot WEas |
| | 'Speciosa' (*burseriana*) (7) | NDlv |
| | 'Splendens' (*oppositifolia*) (7) ♀H4 | ECho EPfP LFox NDlv NHol NLAp SRms WAbe WPat |
| | 'Spotted Dog' | see *S.* 'Canis-dalmatica' (x *gaudinii*) |
| | 'Sprite' (15) | LRHS SPoG |
| | ***spruneri*** (7) | NMen |
| | - var. ***deorum*** (7) | NMen |
| | 'Stansfieldii' (*rosacea*) (15) | EAlp NMen SPlb SPoG WFar |
| | ***stenophylla*** subsp. ***stenophylla*** | see *S. flagellaris* |
| | ***stolitzkae*** (7) | NMen WAbe |
| § | ***stolonifera*** (5) ♀H2 | CArn CCVN CEnt CHEx CHal CSpe ECho EWTr GBin LDai MHar NBro SDix SIng SWvt WFar WMoo WPnn |
| | ***stribrnyi*** (7) | NMen |
| | - JCA 861-400 | NWCA |
| | 'Sturmiana' (*paniculata*) (8) | NMen SRms |
| | 'Sue Drew' (*fortunei*) **new** | LLHF |
| | 'Suendermannii Major' (x *kellereri*) (7) | CLyd LRHS NRya |
| | 'Suendermannii' (x *kellereri*) (7) | NDlv SIng |
| | 'Sugar Plum Fairy' (*fortunei*) (5) | CBct EBee EHrv LFur MBNS SPer WCot WGwG |
| § | 'Sulphurea' (x *boydii*) (7) | LFox LRHS NMen SIng WAbe WHoo WPat |
| | 'Swan' (x *fallsvillagensis*) (7) | NMen |
| | 'Sylva' (x *elisabethae*) (7) | NMen |
| | 'Symons-Jeunei' (8) | WAbe |
| | 'Tábor' (x *schottii*) (7) | NMen |
| | 'Tamayura' (*fortunei*) (5) | LSou |
| | 'Theoden' (*oppositifolia*) (7) ♀H4 | CLyd ECho EWes NLAp NWCA WAbe |
| | 'Theresia' (x *mariae-theresiae*) (7) | NDlv NMen |
| | 'Thorpei' (x *gusmusii*) (7) | NMen |
| | 'Timmy Foster' (x *irvingii*) (7) | CLyd NHol NMen |
| | ***tombeanensis*** (7) | CLyd EPot NMen |
| | 'Tricolor' (*stolonifera*) (5) ♀H2 | CBow EBak WFar |
| | ***trifurcata*** (15) | GGar |
| | 'Tristan' (*stribrnyi*) **new** | GKev |
| § | 'Triumph' (x *arendsii*) (15) | ECtt GMaP NPri SPoG WBVN |

| | | |
|---|---|---|
| | 'Tully' (x *elisabethae*) (7) | NLAp WGor WPat |
| | 'Tumbling Waters' (8) ♀H4 | EAlp ECho EPot GAbr GKev LHop LRHS NHol NMen NSla SIng WAbe WFar WGor WPat |
| § | 'Tvoje Píseň' (x *poluanglica*) (7) | CLyd ECho NDlv NMen |
| § | 'Tvůj Den' (x *poluanglica*) (7) | ECho NDlv NMen |
| § | 'Tvůj Polibek' (x *poluanglica*) (7) | ECho MDKP NDlv NMen |
| § | 'Tvůj Přítel' (x *poluanglica*) (7) | ECho NDlv |
| § | 'Tvůj Úsměv' (x *poluanglica*) (7) | CLyd ECho NDlv NMen |
| § | 'Tvůj Úspěch' (x *poluanglica*) (7) | CLyd ECho EPot NDlv NHol NMen WAbe |
| | 'Tycho Brahe' (x *doerfleri*) (7) | CLyd NDlv NMen WAbe |
| | 'Tysoe' (7) | CLyd NMen |
| | ***umbrosa*** (11) | CSec CTri EBee ECho EDAr GKir LAst LEdu LRHS MMuc MRav SPer SPlb SRms SWvt WBor WCAu WFar WMoo |
| | - var. ***primuloides*** | see *S.* 'Primuloides' |
| | 'Unique' | see *S.* 'Bodensee' |
| | x ***urbium*** (11) ♀H4 | CHEx CTri EBee ECho ELan EPfP EWTr LAst LEdu NSti SIng SRms WBrk WFar WPer |
| | 'Vaccariana' (*oppositifolia*) (7) | ECho NHol |
| | 'Václav Hollar' (x *gusmusii*) (7) | NMen |
| | 'Vahlii' (x *smithii*) (7) | NMen |
| | 'Valborg' | see *S.* 'Cranbourne' |
| | 'Valentine' | see *S.* 'Cranbourne' |
| | 'Valerie Finnis' | see *S.* 'Aretiastrum' |
| | 'Valerie Keevil' (x *anglica*) (7) | NMen |
| | ***vandellii*** (7) **new** | EPot |
| I | 'Variegata' (*cuneifolia*) (11/v) | ECho ECtt EPfP GGar MBar NBlu NHol NVic SPet SPlb SPoG WFar WMoo WPer |
| | 'Variegata' (*umbrosa*) | see *S.* 'Aureopunctata' |
| I | 'Variegata' (x *urbium*) (11/v) | EBee ECho EPfP GGar LAst NLar NSti NVic SRms SSto WEas WFar |
| | ***vayredana*** (15) | NWCA WAbe |
| | ***veitchiana*** (5) | EBee GEdr NBro |
| | 'Vesna' (x *borisii*) (7) | CLyd NMen |
| | 'Vincent van Gogh' (x *borisii*) (7) | CLyd NMen |
| | 'Vladana' (x *megaseiflora*) (7) | CLyd EPot NMen SIng |
| | 'Vlasta' (7) | CLyd NMen |
| | 'Vltava' (7) | CLyd NMen |
| | 'Volgeri' (x *hofmannii*) (7) | CLyd NMen |
| | 'Vreny' (8) | GKev |
| | 'Wada' (*fortunei*) (5) | CAbP CBct CDes CLAP CSam EAEE EBee ECtt GBuc GEdr GKev LAst LFur LRHS MSte NBir NMyG NPri SPer WBor WCot WFar WOld WPGP |
| | 'Wallacei' (15) | NMen |
| | 'Walpole's Variety' (8) | WPer |
| | 'Walter Ingwersen' (*umbrosa*) (11) | SIng SRms |
| § | 'Walter Irving' (x *irvingii*) (7) | CLyd NHol NMen WAbe |
| | 'Weisser Zwerg' (15) | WAbe |
| | 'Wellesbourne' (x *abingdonensis*) (7) | CLyd |
| | 'Welsh Dragon' (15) | WAbe |
| | 'Welsh Red' (15) | WAbe WFar |
| | 'Welsh Rose' (15) | WAbe |
| | ***wendelboi*** (7) | CLyd LFox NMen |

| | | |
|---|---|---|
| | 'Wendrush' (x *wendelacina*) (7) | CLyd NMen WAbe |
| | 'Wendy' (x *wendelacina*) (7) | NMen WAbe |
| | 'Wetterhorn' (*oppositifolia*) (7) | CLyd |
| | 'Wheatley Gem' (7) | NMen |
| | 'Wheatley Lion' (x *borisii*) (7) | NMen |
| | 'Wheatley Rose' (7) | CLyd LRHS |
| | 'White Cap' (x *boydii*) (7) | NMen |
| | 'White Craggs' **new** | NHol |
| | 'White Imp' (7) | NMen |
| § | 'White Pixie' (15) | CLyd EAlp ECtt EDAr EPfP GMaP LFox MHer NHol NPri NPro NRya SIng SPer SPlb SPoG SRms WFar |
| | 'White Star' (x *petraschii*) | see *S.* 'Schelleri' |
| | 'Whitehill' (8) 🏆H4 | CLyd CMea EAlp ECho ECtt ELan GEdr GJos GKir GMaP ITim LBee LFox LRHS MDKP NBro NHol NMen SPet WFar WHoo WPat WPer WTin |
| § | 'Wilhelm Tell' (x *malbyana*) (7) | NMen |
| | 'William Boyd' (x *boydii*) (7) | NSla WAbe |
| | 'Winifred Bevington' (8x11) 🏆H4 | CLyd EAlp ECho EDAr GKev LRHS MMuc NBro NDlv NHol NLAp NMen NRya SAga SMad WFar WHoo WPer WPnn |
| | 'Winifred' (x *anglica*) (7) | CLyd ECho EPot LFox NLAp NMen WAbe |
| | 'Winston Churchill' (15) | CTri EPfP LRHS NHol NPri SIng |
| I | 'Winston Churchill Variegata' | EAlp NHol |
| | 'Winton' (x *paulinae*) (7) | CLyd NMen WAbe |
| | 'Wisley' (*federici-augusti* subsp. *grisebachii*) (7) 🏆H2-3 | NLAp NMen WPat |
| | 'Wisley Primrose' | see *S.* 'Kolbiana' |
| | 'Woodside Ross' (15) | ECtt |
| | 'Yellow Rock' (7) | NDlv NMen NRya |
| | Your Day | see *S.* 'Tvůj Den' |
| | Your Friend | see *S.* 'Tvůj Přítel' |
| | Your Good Fortune | see *S.* 'Tvůj Úspech' |
| | Your Kiss | see *S.* 'Tvůj Polibek' |
| | Your Smile | see *S.* 'Tvůj Úsměv' |
| | Your Song | see *S.* 'Tvoje Píseň' |
| | Your Success | see *S.* 'Tvůj Úspěch' |
| | 'Yuinagi' (*fortunei*) (5) | WOld |
| | x ***zimmeteri*** (8x11) | CLyd ECho NMen |
| § | 'Zlatá Praha' (x *pragensis*) (7) | CLyd NDlv NMen NRya WAbe |
| | 'Zlin' (x *leyboldii*) (7) | NMen |

## *Scabiosa* (*Dipsacaceae*)

| | | |
|---|---|---|
| | ***africana*** | CElw EWes LSou SHar |
| | ***alpina*** L. | see *Cephalaria alpina* |
| | ***argentea*** | EBee EWes LEdu SMHy SUsu WPGP |
| | ***atropurpurea*** | CEnt EGoo LEdu SPav WFar |
| | - 'Ace of Spades' | CSpe CWCL EBee LCro SMad SPav WPGP |
| § | - 'Chile Black' | Widely available |
| § | - 'Chilli Pepper' | CWCL EPfP LHop MGos NLar NPri SAga SPoG SRGP |
| § | - 'Chilli Red' | SAga |
| § | - 'Chilli Sauce' | CWCL EPfP LHop MGos NLar NPri SPoG |
| | - dark-flowered | SPav |
| | - 'Nona' | LLHF |
| | - 'Peter Ray' | CElw ECtt SPav WWlt |
| | - 'Salmon Queen' | NBre |
| | ***banatica*** | see *S. columbaria* |
| | 'Blue Diamonds' | CKno WHil |
| | 'Burgundy Bonnets' | EBee LRHS |
| § | 'Butterfly Blue' | CMHG EBee ECtt EPfP LCro LFur LRHS LSRN MBri NBPC NLar NMoo SCoo SHBN SMrm SPer SPla SPoG SWvt WAul WCAu WCot WFar |
| | ***caucasica*** | CEnt EPfP GKir LAst LEdu NBlu SPhx WFar WHoo |
| | - var. ***alba*** | CBcs CKno EBee EHrv EPfP GKir WFar WHal WHoo |
| | - 'Blausiegel' | CSam EBee ECtt LAst LBMP MLHP NBre NGdn SPet SPla |
| | - 'Clive Greaves' 🏆H4 | CHar CTri EBee ECha ECtt EHrv ELan EPfP GKir LCro LHop MBri MCot MRav NCob SPad SPer SPet SPla SRms SWvt WEas WFar WHlf |
| | - 'Deep Waters' | CSpe |
| | - 'Fama' | CMdw CSpe CWCL CWib EBee EShb LCro LHop NBir NLar SMrm SPlb SPoG SRms WFar WHil WPtf |
| | - 'Goldingensis' | CWCL GJos MHer NBre NGdn NPri WBVN WPer |
| | - House's hybrids | CSBt GJos NGdn SRms |
| | - 'Isaac House' | EBee NLar |
| | - 'Kompliment' | MWhi NBre NLar SMrm |
| | - 'Lavender Blue' | NBPC WFar |
| | - 'Miss Willmott' 🏆H4 | CMMP CSam EBee ECha ECtt ELan EPfP LAst LBMP LHop LRHS MBri MCot MHer MLHP MRav NCGa NCob SPer SPet SPla SWvt WCAu WFar WMnd |
| | - 'Moerheim Blue' | EBee |
| | - 'Moonstone' | EBee |
| | - Perfecta Series | CSpe CWib EBee LAst LRHS MMHG NGdn NLar SWat |
| | - - 'Perfecta Alba' | CEnt COIW CSpe CWib EBee ECtt GJos GKir GMaP GMac LAst MWat NChi NLar NOrc NPri SHGN SMrm SPad SPer STes SWat WPtf |
| | - - 'Perfecta Lilac Blue' | CWib GMaP GMac STes WRHF |
| | - 'Stäfa' | CKno CMMP EBee ECha EShb EWTr MRav NCGa NLar SPer SPla SUsu WFar WMnd |
| | 'Chile Black' | see *S. atropurpurea* 'Chile Black' |
| | 'Chile Pepper'PBR | see *S. atropurpurea* 'Chilli Pepper' |
| | 'Chile Red' | see *S. atropurpurea* 'Chilli Red' |
| | 'Chile Sauce'PBR | see *S. atropurpurea* 'Chilli Sauce' |
| | 'Chile Spice' | WHlf |
| | ***cinerea*** | SPhx |
| § | ***columbaria*** | CSec EBWF EBee ECGP MLLN MMuc NBre NLan NMir NSco NWCA SECG WHer WJek WSFF |
| * | - ***alpina*** | CSec GKev |
| | - 'Flower Power' | EBee EWll |
| | - 'Misty Butterflies' | EDAr EShb GBri LSou NBHF NGdn NLar NMoo SPad STes SVil WBrE WFar |
| | - 'Nana' | CMdw CSec EBee EGoo EShb GEdr NBir NGdn NLar NMen NPri SBch WCFE WFar WGwG WHil WHrl |
| § | - subsp. ***ochroleuca*** | CKno CSec CSpe ECha EDAr EGoo EHrv EShb GCal LEdu LLWP MCot MLLN NBir NDov NLar NPri SMad SPhx SRms WCAu WFar WHoo WPGP WTin |
| | - - MESE 344 | EBee |
| | - - 'Moon Dance' **new** | EDAr |
| | - 'Pincushion Pink' | NBHF NGdn NPri WFar WHil |
| | ***cretica*** | CSpe |
| | ***drakensbergensis*** | CDMG EBee EWes LSou MTPN SPav WHrl |
| | ***farinosa*** | CDes EBee ECtt LEdu LSou SAga SGar WFar WPer |
| | ***gigantea*** | see *Cephalaria gigantea* |

| | |
|---|---|
| ***graminifolia*** | CSec EBrs ECho EGoo GBuc GKev MDKP NBir NMen NWCA SBch SRms |
| - JM 990 **new** | EBee |
| - ***rosea*** | EWes |
| 'Grand Stone' | GBri |
| 'Helen Dillon' | CFir EBee ECtt EWes LSou |
| ***incisa*** | CSec |
| 'Irish Perpetual Flowering' | ECtt NDov WCot |
| ***japonica*** | WPer |
| - var. ***acutiloba*** | SPhx |
| - var. ***alpina*** | CEnt CPrp CSec EBee GAbr GBuc IBal MLLN NGdn NHol SHGN SPet SPhx WAbe WHoo WTin |
| ***lachnophylla*** | GCal |
| 'Little Emily' | NDov SUsu |
| ***lucida*** | EAEE EBee ECho ECtt EPfP EShb LRHS MRav NLAp NPri WCAu WPGP WPer |
| 'Midnight' | CMea CSpe |
| 'Miss Havisham' | EBee ECtt EWes LEdu LSou WPGP |
| 'Monita Pink' **new** | CMoH |
| ***montana*** (Bieb.) DC. | see *Knautia tatarica* |
| ***montana*** Mill. | see *Knautia arvensis* |
| ***ochroleuca*** | see *S. columbaria* subsp. *ochroleuca* |
| ***parnassi*** | see *Pterocephalus perennis* |
| 'Peggotty' | EBee ECtt |
| 'Perpetual Flowering' | see *S.* 'Butterfly Blue' |
| Pink Buttons = 'Walminipink' | CFir EBee LRHS SPla |
| 'Pink Mist'PBR | EBee ECtt EPfP EWll LRHS MBri NBir NLar SCoo SHBN SMrm SPer SPoG SRms WCAu |
| ***prolifera*** | CSec |
| ***pterocephala*** | see *Pterocephalus perennis* |
| ***rhodopensis*** | EBee |
| 'Rosie's Pink' | ECtt |
| ***rumelica*** | see *Knautia macedonica* |
| 'Satchmo' | see *S. atropurpurea* 'Chile Black' |
| ***silenifolia*** | EBee |
| ***succisa*** | see *Succisa pratensis* |
| ***tatarica*** | see *Cephalaria gigantea* |
| ***tenuis*** | CSpe LPio SHar SPhx |
| ***triandra*** | CSpe EBee LEdu LHop |
| ***ucranica*** | EShb GJos |
| ***vestina*** | CSec |

## *Scadoxus* ✿ (*Amaryllidaceae*)

| | |
|---|---|
| ***multiflorus*** | EBrs LAma LRHS MBri WCot |
| § - subsp. ***katherinae*** 𝕐H1 | ECho |

## *Scaevola* (*Goodeniaceae*)

| | |
|---|---|
| ***aemula*** 'Blue Fan'PBR | see *S. aemula* 'Blue Wonder' |
| § - 'Blue Wonder'PBR | LSou NPer SWvt |
| - New Wonder = 'Newon'PBR | LAst |
| - 'Petite Wonder' | CHal |
| - Whirlwind Blue = 'Scablhatis'PBR **new** | NBlu |
| - 'White Fan' **new** | LAst |
| - 'Zig Zag'PBR | CCCN LSou NPri |
| Blauer Facher = 'Saphira'PBR | CCCN |
| 'Brillant'PBR **new** | LSou |
| ***crassifolia*** | CSec SPlb |
| 'Diamond' | LAst LSou |
| 'Mini Blue' | CCCN |
| ***saligna*** Blue Yonder = 'Scabushy' | LSou |

## *Scandix* (*Apiaceae*)

| | |
|---|---|
| ***pecten-veneris*** | MSal |

## *Schefflera* (*Araliaceae*)

| | |
|---|---|
| ***actinophylla*** 𝕐H1 | SRms |
| ***alpina*** B&SWJ 8247 | WCru |
| - HWJ 585 **new** | WCru |
| - HWJ 936 **new** | WCru |
| ***arboricola*** 𝕐H1 | CHEx SEND XBlo |
| - 'Benzon' **new** | LRHS |
| - 'Charlotte' (v) **new** | LRHS |
| - 'Compacta' | MBri |
| - 'Gold Capella' 𝕐H1 | MBri SEND XBlo |
| - 'Kalahari' **new** | XBlo |
| - 'Melanie' (v) **new** | LRHS |
| - 'Trinetta' | LRHS MBri |
| ***brevipedicellata*** HWJ 870 | WCru |
| ***chapana*** HWJ 983 **new** | WCru |
| ***delavayi*** | CExc CHEx |
| § ***elegantissima*** 𝕐H1 | EShb SEND |
| - 'Castor' | EShb |
| - 'Castor Variegata' (v) | EShb |
| ***enneaphylla*** HWJ 1018 **new** | WCru |
| ***fantsipanensis*** B&SWJ 8228 | WCru |
| ***gracilis*** HWJ 622 | WCru |
| ***kornasii*** HWJ 918 | WCru |
| ***microphylla*** B&SWJ 3872 | WCru |
| ***petelotii*** B&SWJ 8210 **new** | WCru |
| ***rhododendrifolia*** | CHEx |
| - GWJ 9375 | WCru |
| ***taiwaniana*** | CHEx |
| - B&SWJ 7096 | WCru |
| - RWJ 10000 **new** | WCru |
| - RWJ 10016 **new** | WCru |

## *Schima* (*Theaceae*)

| | |
|---|---|
| ***argentea*** | see *S. wallichii* subsp. *noronhae* var. *superba* |
| ***wallichii*** subsp. ***liukiuensis*** | CBcs |
| § - subsp. ***noronhae*** var. ***superba*** | CCCN EPfP |
| - subsp. ***wallichii*** var. ***khasiana*** | ISea |
| ***yunnanensis*** | see *S. argentea* |

## *Schinus* (*Anacardiaceae*)

| | |
|---|---|
| ***molle*** | IDee |
| ***polygamus*** | CBcs |

## *Schisandra* (*Schisandraceae*)

| | |
|---|---|
| TH | CHEx |
| ***arisanensis*** B&SWJ 3050 | WCru |
| aff. ***bicolor*** BWJ 8151 | WCru |
| ***chinensis*** | CAgr CArn CBcs EBee EBrs GPoy LEdu MSwo WBVN |
| - B&SWJ 4204 | WCru |
| ***grandiflora*** | CDoC EBee ECot ELan EPfP LRHS MBlu NLar SCoo WGwG |
| - B&SWJ 2245 | WCru |
| - var. ***cathayensis*** | see *S. sphaerandra* |
| - 'Jamu' (m) **new** | WCru |
| - 'Lahlu' (f/F) **new** | WCru |
| ***grandiflora*** x ***rubriflora*** | WCru |
| ***henryi*** subsp. ***yunnanensis*** B&SWJ 6546 | WCru |
| aff. ***neglecta*** BWJ 7739 | WCru |
| ***nigra*** B&SWJ 5897 | WCru |

| | | |
|---|---|---|
| | ***propinqua*** var. ***sinensis*** | CBcs CMac CSPN LEdu MBlu NLar WSHC |
| | - - BWJ 8148 | WCru |
| | ***rubriflora*** | CHEx CSPN CTri CWSG EBee EPfP GKir LRHS MBlu MGos NSti SHBN SPer SSpi |
| | - (f) | CBcs ELan EMil MGos WSHC |
| | - (m) | NHol |
| | - BWJ 7557 **new** | WCru |
| § | ***sphaerandra*** BWJ 7898 **new** | WCru |
| | ***sphenanthera*** | EBee ELan EMil EPfP IMGH LRHS NLar WSHC |
| | ***verrucosa*** HWJ 664 | WCru |

## *Schivereckia* (*Brassicaceae*)

| | | |
|---|---|---|
| | ***doerfleri*** | CSec MWat |

## *Schizachyrium* (*Poaceae*)

| | | |
|---|---|---|
| § | ***scoparium*** | CKno CSpe EBee EHoe EPPr EPau GCal IFoB LBMP LRHS MWhi NSti SUsu |
| | - 'Cairo' **new** | EBee |

## *Schizanthus* (*Solanaceae*)

| | | |
|---|---|---|
| | ***hookeri*** | CSec |
| | ***porrigens*** | CSpe |

## *Schizocodon* see *Shortia*

## *Schizolobium* (*Caesalpiniaceae*)

| | | |
|---|---|---|
| | ***excelsum*** | SBig |

## *Schizopetalon* (*Brassicaceae*)

| | | |
|---|---|---|
| | ***walkeri*** | CSpe |

## *Schizophragma* (*Hydrangeaceae*)

| | | |
|---|---|---|
| | ***corylifolium*** | CBcs GCal NLar |
| | ***hydrangeoides*** | CBcs CDoC EBee ELan EPfP EWTr GKir LRHS MBlu MGos NPal NPri SHBN SLim SLon SPer SPoG SSpi SSta SWvt WDin |
| | - B&SWJ 5489 **new** | WCru |
| | - B&SWJ 5732 **new** | WCru |
| | - B&SWJ 5954 | WCru |
| | - 'Brookside Littleleaf' | see *Hydrangea anomala* subsp. *petiolaris* var. *cordifolia* 'Brookside Littleleaf' |
| | - B&SWJ 6119 from Yakushima, Japan | WCru |
| | - B&SWJ 8505 from Korea | WCru |
| | - B&SWJ 8522 from Ullüngdõ, Korea **new** | WCru |
| | - from Korea | MBri |
| | - 'Iwa Garami' | MBri NLar |
| | - 'Moonlight' | Widely available |
| * | - f. ***quelpartensis*** B&SWJ 1160 | WCru |
| | - 'Roseum' ΥH4 | Widely available |
| | ***integrifolium*** ΥH4 | CBcs CMac EBee ELan EPfP LCro NLar SDix SHBN SSpi WPGP WSHC |
| | - var. ***fauriei*** | NLar WSHC |
| | - - B&SWJ 1701 | WCru |
| | aff. ***megalocarpum*** BWJ 8150 | WCru |

## *Schizostachyum* (*Poaceae*)

| | | |
|---|---|---|
| § | ***funghomii*** | EPla MMoz SEND WPGP |

## *Schizostylis* ✿ (*Iridaceae*)

| | | |
|---|---|---|
| § | ***coccinea*** | Widely available |
| | - f. ***alba*** | Widely available |
| | - 'Anne' | WHoo |
| | - 'Ballyrogan Giant' | CFir CTca EBee ECho GBuc IBlr MAvo NCot NHol WPGP WSHC |
| | - 'Big Moma' | NCot |
| | - 'Cardinal' | NHol WFar |
| | - 'Caroline' | NCot |
| | - 'Cindy Towe' | EBee EGle GBuc |
| | - 'Countesse de Vere' | EBee NCot |
| | - 'Elburton Glow' | NCot WFar WHoo |
| | - 'Fenland Daybreak' | Widely available |
| | - 'Gigantea' | see *S. coccinea* 'Major' |
| | - 'Good White' | EBee EGle MAvo NBir |
| | - 'Grandiflora' | see *S. coccinea* 'Major' |
| | - 'Hilary Gould' | CPrp GBuc MAvo NCGa NCot WFar WHal |
| | - 'Hint of Pink' | MDKP |
| | - 'Jack Frost' | EBee GMac MAvo WMoo |
| | - 'Jennifer' ΥH4 | Widely available |
| | - 'Maiden's Blush' | CPrp EBrs ECGP ECtt EGle EHrv GBuc GKir LRHS MAvo MCot MDKP MSte NCot NHol NLar SPet WFar |
| § | - 'Major' ΥH4 | Widely available |
| * | - 'Marietta' | MAvo NCot |
| | - 'Mollie Gould' | CTca EAEE EBee EBla ECtt EGle EHrv ELon EShb GCra GMac LAst LBMP LPio MAvo MBNS MMHG NBre NCGa NCot NHol NLar SCoo SRGP WFar WPrP WTin |
| | - 'Mrs Hegarty' | Widely available |
| | - 'November Cheer' | CPrp CTca EBrs ECot IBlr LRHS MSte NBir NCot NLar WFar |
| | - 'Oregon Sunset' | EBee GBuc MDKP |
| | - 'Pallida' | CMil CPom CSam ECha ECtt EHrv ELan GBuc MLHP MRav MWea NBir NCot NLar WFar |
| | - 'Pink Marg' | NCot |
| | - 'Professor Barnard' | CCCN CFee CHar CPrp CSpe CTca EBee ECho ELon EShb GAbr IBlr LAst MBNS MSte NBir NCot SApp SMrm SPla WFar WHil WMoo WOld WPnn |
| | - 'Red Dragon' | GBuc GMac NCot NHol WFar WHoo |
| | - 'Salmon Charm' | EBrs GBin GBuc LRHS WFar |
| | - salmon-flowered **new** | NCot |
| | - 'Salome' | NCot |
| | - 'Silver Pink' | IBlr |
| | - 'Snow Maiden' | CAbP CBgR CElw ECtt GBuc GMac MAvo NCot SPav |
| | - 'Strawberry' | NCot SPav |
| | - 'Strawberry Fair' | SMrm |
| § | - 'Sunrise' ΥH4 | Widely available |
| | - 'Sunset' | see *S. coccinea* 'Sunrise' |
| | - 'Tambara' | CMHG CMdw CPou CSam EBee EHrv GAbr GBuc MAvo MWea NCot NLar SApp SMrm WFar |
| | - 'Vera' | NCot |
| | - 'Viscountess Byng' | CAby CBro CTca CTri EBee ECho EGle ELon EPau GAbr IBlr IGor LAst MSCN NBir NCot NLar SMrm SPav SPer WFar WPer |
| | - 'Wilfred H. Bryant' | CBro CKno CMea CPen CSpe EAEE EBee ECtt EShb GCal GKev LAst LBMP LEdu LPio MBNS MBri MCot MDKP NCGa NCot NHol NSti SPoG SRot STes SUsu |
| | - 'Zeal Salmon' | CAby CBro CFee CFir CPou CPrp ECha GAbr LHop MAvo NBir NCot NHol SApp SMHy WFar WMoo |
| * | ***rosea*** | CChe EBrs |

## *Schoenoplectus* (*Cyperaceae*)

| | |
|---|---|
| § ***lacustris*** | EBWF EMFW GFor MSKA SVic |
| § - subsp. ***tabernaemontani*** | EBWF |
| - - 'Albescens' (v) | CBen CDWL CKno CWat EBee EMFW LPBA MSKA SWal SWat WHal WPrP |
| - - 'Zebrinus' (v) | CBen CDWL CKno CWat EAlp EHon ELan EMFW EPfP LPBA MMuc MSKA NScw SPlb SWat WFar WHal WMAq WPrP |

## *Schoenus* (*Cyperaceae*)

| | |
|---|---|
| ***pauciflorus*** | CWCL EBee ECou EHoe EPPr EWes NOak WMoo WPGP WPrP |

## *Schotia* (*Caesalpiniaceae*)

| | |
|---|---|
| ***afra*** | CKob |
| ***brachypetala*** | CKob |

## *Sciadopitys* (*Sciadopityaceae*)

| | |
|---|---|
| ***verticillata*** ♀H4 | CBcs CDoC CDul CKen CSBt CTho EHul GKir IDee LBee LPan LRHS MAsh MBar MBlu MBri MDun MGos NWea SCoo SLim SPoG SSpi SWvt WDin WFar WOrn |
| - 'Firework' | CKen |
| - 'Globe' | CKen |
| - 'Gold Star' | CKen |
| - 'Goldammer' | NLar |
| - 'Golden Rush' | CKen ECho MAsh MGos NLar |
| - 'Goldmahne' | CKen |
| - 'Grüne Kugel' | CKen ECho NLar SLim |
| - 'Jeddeloh Compact' | CKen |
| - 'Kupferschirm' | CKen ECho NLar |
| - 'Mecki' | CKen ECho |
| - 'Megaschirm' | CKen |
| - 'Ossorio Gold' | CKen ECho |
| - 'Picola' | CKen ECho NLar |
| - 'Pygmy' | CKen |
| - 'Richie's Cushion' | CKen ECho NLar |
| - 'Shorty' | CKen |
| - 'Speerspitze' | CKen |
| - 'Starburst' | CKen |
| - 'Sternschnuppe' | CKen ECho NLar SLim |
| - 'Wintergreen' new | CKen |

## *Scilla* (*Hyacinthaceae*)

| | |
|---|---|
| ***adlamii*** | see *Ledebouria cooperi* |
| x ***allenii*** | see x *Chionoscilla allenii* |
| ***amethystina*** | see *S. litardierei* |
| ***amoena*** | EBrs ECho WCot |
| ***aristidis*** | EBrs ECho |
| - from Algeria | ECho |
| ***autumnalis*** | CAvo CDes CPom CStu CTca EBWF EBrs ECho EPot ERos LAma WCot WShi WThu |
| - from Crete | ECho |
| - subsp. ***fallax*** | CTca EBrs ECho |
| ***bifolia*** ♀H4 | CAvo CBro CFFs CPom CStu EBrs ECho EPot LAma LLWP LRHS SPhx WCot WShi |
| - RS 156/83 new | ECho |
| - 'Alba' | EBrs ECho LRHS SPhx |
| - 'Norman Stevens' | SCnR |
| - 'Rosea' | EBrs ECho EPot LAma LLWP LRHS WShi |
| ***bithynica*** ♀H4 | WShi |
| ***campanulata*** | see *Hyacinthoides hispanica* |
| ***chinensis*** | see *S. scilloides* |
| ***cilicica*** | CStu ERos SPhx |
| ***greilhuberi*** | CStu EBrs ECho ERos WAbe WCot WWst |
| ***haemorrhoidalis*** new | WCot |
| ***hohenackeri*** | ERos SPhx WThu |
| - BSBE 811 | WCot |
| ***hughii*** | EBrs ECho |
| ***hyacinthoides*** | EBrs ECho ERos WBVN WCot |
| ***ingridiae*** | ECho ERos WWst |
| ***italica*** | see *Hyacinthoides italica* |
| ***japonica*** | see *S. scilloides* |
| ***latifolia*** from Morocco | ECho |
| ***libanotica*** | see *Puschkinia scilloides* var. *libanotica* |
| ***liliohyacinthus*** | CBro CRow EBrs ECho IBlr MMHG SSvw WSHC WShi WWst |
| - 'Alba' | ERos |
| ***lingulata*** | CStu ECho ERos WCot |
| - var. ***ciliolata*** | CBro CGra EBrs ECho EPot ERos |
| § ***litardierei*** ♀H4 | CBgR CMea CPom CStu EBrs ECho EPPr EPot ERos LAma LRHS MBri NMen SPhx WShi |
| - ***hoogiana*** | ERos |
| - 'Orjen' | EBrs ECho |
| ***lutea*** hort. | see *Ledebouria socialis* |
| ***melaina*** | WCot |
| ***messeniaca*** | CPom |
| - MS 38 from Greece | WCot |
| ***mischtschenkoana*** ♀H4 | CAvo CBro CHid ECho EPot LAma MBri SPer WBVN |
| - 'Armenia' | EBrs |
| § - 'Tubergeniana' ♀H4 | CBgR CFFs CMea EBee EBrs ECho GKev SPhx WCot |
| - 'Zwanenburg' | ECho |
| ***monophyllos*** | CStu ECho |
| - var. ***tingitana*** | ERos |
| ***morrisii*** | CWsd ERos |
| ***natalensis*** | see *Merwilla plumbea* |
| ***non-scripta*** | see *Hyacinthoides non-scripta* |
| ***numidica*** | EBrs ECho |
| ***nutans*** | see *Hyacinthoides non-scripta* |
| ***obtusifolia*** | EBrs ECho WCot |
| - subsp. ***intermedia*** new | ECho |
| ***persica*** ♀H4 | CAvo CPom EBrs ECho ERos WCot |
| - JCA 0.876.501 | WCot |
| ***peruviana*** | Widely available |
| - S&L 285 | WCot |
| - SB&L 20/1 | WCot |
| - 'Alba' | CBro CFwr CSWP CSpe CStu ECho LPio MTho SMrm WCot |
| * - var. ***ciliata*** | WCot |
| - 'Grand Bleu' | CFwr |
| - var. ***ifniensis*** | WCot |
| - var. ***venusta*** S&L 311/2 | WCot |
| ***pratensis*** | see *S. litardierei* |
| ***puschkinioides*** | ECho WCot |
| ***ramburei*** | EBrs ECho |
| ***reverchonii*** | EBrs ECho ERos WWst |
| ***rosenii*** | EBrs ECho |
| § ***scilloides*** | EBrs ECho ERos SCnR |
| ***siberica*** ♀H4 | CAvo CFFs CTca EBrs ECho EPfP IHer LAma LRHS MWat SBch SMrm SPer SPhx WRHF WShi |
| - 'Alba' | CBro CTca EBrs ECho EPfP EPot LAma LHop LRHS SBch WShi |
| - subsp. ***armena*** | ECho |
| - 'Spring Beauty' | CBro CMdw CMea EBrs ECho EPot GKev LAma LHop LRHS MBri SPhx SRms |
| - var. ***taurica*** | ECho ERos |
| 'Tubergeniana' | see *S. mischtschenkoana* 'Tubergeniana' |
| ***verna*** | CDes EBWF EBrs ECho ERos WHer WShi WThu |
| ***vicentina*** | see *Hyacinthoides vicentina* |
| ***violacea*** | see *Ledebouria socialis* |

## *Scindapsus* (*Araceae*)

| | |
|---|---|
| ***aureus*** | see *Epipremnum aureum* |
| ***pictus*** (v) | LRHS MBri |

## *Scirpoides* (*Cyperaceae*)

| | |
|---|---|
| § ***holoschoenus*** | CRWN EBWF EBee |

## *Scirpus* (*Cyperaceae*)

| | |
|---|---|
| ***cernuus*** | see *Isolepis cernua* |
| ***holoschoenus*** | see *Scirpoides holoschoenus* |
| ***lacustris*** | see *Schoenoplectus lacustris* |
| - 'Spiralis' | see *Juncus effusus* f. *spiralis* |
| ***maritimus*** | see *Bolboschoenus maritimus* |
| ***tabernaemontani*** | see *Schoenoplectus lacustris* subsp. *tabernaemontani* |

## *Scleranthus* (*Illecebraceae*)

| | |
|---|---|
| ***biflorus*** | CTrC ECho EDAr EWes NDlv NWCA SPlb WPer |
| ***perennis*** | ECho |
| ***uniflorus*** | CLyd CTrC ECho EShb NHol SMad SPlb WPrP |

## *Sclerochiton* (*Acanthaceae*)

| | |
|---|---|
| ***harveyanus*** | EShb |

## *Scoliopus* (*Trilliaceae*)

| | |
|---|---|
| ***bigelowii*** | SCnR WHal WWst |
| ***hallii*** | EBee EBrs GEdr NMen SCnR WCot WCru WWst |

## *Scolopendrium* see *Asplenium*

## *Scopolia* (*Solanaceae*)

| | |
|---|---|
| ***anomala*** | CArn |
| ***carniolica*** | CArn CFir CHFP COld EBee EGle ELan EMon GKir GPoy IBlr LEdu MBlu MCot MHar MPhe MSal MSte NChi NLar NSti SPhx SPlb WCru WPGP WSHC |
| § - var. ***brevifolia*** | EHrv EPPr GBin LEdu SDys SPhx WHil WTin |
| - - WM 9811 | MPhe |
| - from Poland | LEdu |
| - subsp. ***hladnikiana*** | see *S. carniolica* var. *brevifolia* |
| - 'Zwanenburg' | CHFP EBrs EHrv EPPr EPot EWes LEdu NBPN SPhx WCot |
| ***lurida*** | see *Anisodus luridus* |
| ***physaloides*** | MSal |
| ***sinensis*** | see *Atropanthe sinensis* |
| ***stramoniifolia*** | MHar |

## *Scrophularia* (*Scrophulariaceae*)

| | |
|---|---|
| ***aquatica*** | see *S. auriculata* |
| § ***auriculata*** | EBWF EPfP LPBA MHer MSal NMir NPer WHer |
| § - 'Variegata' (v) | CArn CBcs EBee ECha ECtt EHoe ELan EPfP GCal GKir LPBA LRHS MAvo MBri MDun MHer NBid NSti SDnm SPer SPoG SRms WFar WSHC |
| ***buergeriana*** | MSal |
| - 'Lemon and Lime' misapplied | see *Teucrium viscidum* 'Lemon and Lime' |
| ***callianttha*** | MDKP |
| ***fargesii*** | CExc |
| ***grandiflora*** | EWld NBre WFar |
| ***nodosa*** | CArn CRWN CSec EBWF EBee GPoy MSal NMir NSco WHer |
| - ***tracheliodes*** | CNat |
| - ***variegata*** | see *S. auriculata* 'Variegata' |
| ***scopolii*** | EBee |

## *Scutellaria* ✿ (*Lamiaceae*)

| | |
|---|---|
| § ***alpina*** | CPBP CSec ECho GEdr GJos SPlb SRms SRot WGor WPer |
| - 'Arcobaleno' | CEnt LLHF SUsu |
| - 'Greencourt' | WPat |
| - 'Moonbeam' | GEdr SHGN SMrm |
| ***altissima*** | CArn CDMG CHFP CSec ECha ELan ELon GBuc GKir MMuc MSal NBro NCGa SBod SMrm SPlb WCHb WPtf |
| 'Amazing Grace' | EWes |
| ***baicalensis*** | CArn EBee GJos GPoy IBlr MSal MWhi SBHP SMrm WPer WPtf |
| ***barbata*** | MSal |
| ***canescens*** | see *S. incana* |
| ***columnae*** | EBee |
| ***costaricana*** new | EShb |
| ***diffusa*** | ECtt WPer |
| ***formosana*** 'China Blue' | EPfP |
| ***galericulata*** | CSec CWan EBWF GPoy MHer MNHC MSal NVic WCHb WHer |
| ***hastata*** | see *S. hastifolia* |
| § ***hastifolia*** | CTri ECho ECot ECtt WPer |
| § ***incana*** | CBct CHFP CPom CSam EBee ECGP EHrv ELan ELon EMon EPPr LHop LPla LRHS MWea NDov SMHy SMrm SUsu WCot WOut |
| ***indica*** | WCFE WPat |
| - var. ***japonica*** | see *S. indica* var. *parvifolia* |
| § - var. ***parvifolia*** | CPBP EBee EBur ECho EWes GEdr SRot |
| - - 'Alba' | CPBP ECho LLHF LRHS |
| ***lateriflora*** | CArn CBod CSec GBar GPoy MSal NCGa WCHb WHer WJek |
| ***maekawae*** | CSpe WPGP |
| - B&SWJ 557a | WCru |
| ***novae-zelandiae*** | ECou LRHS |
| ***orientalis*** | CMdw ECtt GCal GEdr LRHS SBch WAbe WPat |
| - subsp. ***bicolor*** | ECtt NWCA |
| - 'Eastern Sun' | EBee |
| - subsp. ***pectinata*** | ITim |
| - subsp. ***pinnatifida*** | GEdr NWCA |
| ***pontica*** | CPBP GEdr SBch SMrm WFoF |
| ***prostrata*** | LLHF WPat |
| ***scordiifolia*** | CEnt CLyd CMea CMil CSam EBee ECha ECho EDAr GEdr GMaP NRya NWCA SBHP SMrm SRms WFar WHal WHoo WTin |
| - 'Seoul Sapphire' | CSpe EWes LSou WBVN WPtf |
| ***strigillosa*** new | EBee |
| ***suffrutescens*** 'Texas Rose' | CSpe EBee EMon LLHF MWea SIng SRot |
| ***supina*** | see *S. alpina* |
| ***tournefortii*** | ECtt LLWP WPtf |
| * ***zhongdianensis*** | WPtf |

## seakale see *Crambe maritima*

## *Sebaea* (*Gentianaceae*)

| | |
|---|---|
| ***thomasii*** | WAbe |

## *Securigera* see *Coronilla*

## *Sedastrum* see *Sedum*

## *Sedum* ✿ (*Crassulaceae*)

| | |
|---|---|
| § B&SWJ 737 | EGoo |
| NS 622 | NWCA |
| § 'Abbeydore' | EBee EBrs EGle EGoo EMon EWsh LPla NBsh NGby WAbb WPGP |
| ***acre*** | CTri EBWF ECho ECot GPoy LEdu MBar MHer MNHC NBlu SEND SPlb |

| | | |
|---|---|---|
| | - 'Aureum' | ECho EDAr EHoe EPfP LAst MBar NLar NPri SPer SPoG WFar WPat |
| | - 'Elegans' | ECtt GKir |
| | - 'Golden Queen' | EAlp SPlb SPoG |
| | - 'Minus' | ECho EDAr |
| § | - subsp. ***neglectum*** var. ***majus*** | CChe EBee EGle EPfP GBin IPot LSou NBPN NLar SMad WCFE |
| | - 'Oktoberfest' | EAlp WFar |
| | ***adolphi*** | EPfP |
| | ***aizoon*** | CSec EAro ECho GCal GKir LAst NBre SIde SPlb WBVN WFar |
| | - 'Aurantiacum' | see *S. aizoon* 'Euphorbioides' |
| § | - 'Euphorbioides' | EBee ECha ECtt EGoo ELan LDai LRHS MHer MRav NLar SAga SGar SPer SPlb WFar WTin |
| | ***albescens*** | see *S. forsterianum* f. *purpureum* |
| | ***alboroseum*** | see *S. erythrostictum* |
| § | ***album*** | CHal EAlp EBWF NBro WPer |
| | - 'Coral Carpet' | EAlp ECho ECtt EDAr EPfP EPot GKev MBar MRav MWat NRya SFgr SPoG WCot WFar |
| | - subsp. ***gypsicola*** | see *S. gypsicola* |
| | - subsp. ***teretifolium*** var. ***murale*** | CTri MBar STre |
| | ***altissimum*** | see *S. sediforme* |
| | ***altum*** | EMon NBre WCot WFar |
| | ***amplexicaule*** | see *S. amplexicaule* subsp. *tenuifolium* |
| § | - subsp. ***tenuifolium*** | EBur |
| | ***anacampseros*** | EGoo NHol SEND SUsu WFar WPer |
| | - B&SWJ 723 | WCru |
| | ***anglicum*** | EBWF |
| | ***athoum*** | see *S. album* |
| | ***atlanticum*** | see *S. dasyphyllum* subsp. *dasyphyllum* var. *mesatlanticum* |
| | 'Autumn Charm' | see *S.* 'Lajos' |
| | 'Autumn Fire' | EBee |
| | Autumn Joy | see *S.* 'Herbstfreude' |
| | ***balfourii*** HWJ 824 **new** | WCru |
| | 'Bertram Anderson' ΨH4 | Widely available |
| | ***beyrichianum*** misapplied | see *S. glaucophyllum* |
| | ***bithynicum*** 'Aureum' | see *S. hispanicum* var. *minus* 'Aureum' |
| | 'Blade Runner' **new** | EBee MBNS |
| | ***brevifolium*** | GGar |
| | ***caeruleum*** | CSec EGle SIng |
| | 'Carl' | Widely available |
| | ***caucasicum*** | WAbb WCot WEas |
| | ***cauticola*** ΨH4 | CLyd CSpe ECho EDAr GBuc GCal GEdr MBrN MHar MHer MRav NBre SRms SRot WAbe |
| | - from Lida | ECho |
| | - 'Coca-Cola' | CBct CCVN EAlp ECtt EHoe LAst NPri SPoG WFar |
| | - 'Lidakense' ΨH4 | CHEx CMea ECho ECtt EGle EPfP GKir LRHS MBar MBri MLHP NSla SBch SIng SPer SPlb SRot WFar |
| | - 'Purpurine' | ECho GCal |
| | - 'Robustum' | see *S.* 'Ruby Glow' |
| | 'Chocolate' | EBee EPPr MBNS |
| | ***compressum*** | see *S. palmeri* subsp. *palmeri* tetraploid |
| | ***confusum*** Hemsl. | SChr SEND WFar |
| | ***crassipes*** | see *Rhodiola wallichiana* |
| | ***crassularia*** | see *Crassula setulosa* 'Milfordiae' |
| | 'Crazy Ruffles' | WCot |
| | ***cryptomerioides*** B&SWJ 054 | WCru |
| | ***cyaneum*** Rudolph | WAbe |
| | ***dasyphyllum*** | ECho EDAr MBar MWat NRya SPlb SRms |
| | - subsp. ***dasyphyllum*** | CHal |
| § | - - var. ***mesatlanticum*** | GKev NBir |
| | - ***mucronatis*** | see *S. dasyphyllum* subsp. *dasyphyllum* var. *mesatlanticum* |
| | 'Diamond Edge' (v) **new** | EBee |
| | ***divergens*** | SMad |
| | ***douglasii*** | see *S. stenopetalum* 'Douglasii' |
| | ***drymarioides*** | NBre |
| | 'Dudley Field' | MHer |
| | 'Eleanor Fisher' | see *S. telephium* subsp. *ruprechtii* |
| | ***ellacombeanum*** | see *S. kamtschaticum* var. *ellacombeanum* |
| § | ***erythrostictum*** | CWan MTho WAbb |
| | - 'Frosty Morn' (v) | Widely available |
| § | - 'Mediovariegatum' (v) | CChe COlW EAEE EBee EGle EGoo ELan EMon EPfP EShb EWsh LBMP LRHS MHer MNrw MRav SHBN SPad SWvt WBor WFar WMnd WMoo WPer |
| | 'Evening Cloud' | EBee ECha |
| | ***ewersii*** | CHEx EBee ECho ECtt EDAr GMaP LRHS NBro NLar SPlb WAbe |
| | - var. ***homophyllum*** 'Rosenteppich' | LBuc LRHS MBrN SWvt |
| | ***fabaria*** | see *S. telephium* subsp. *fabaria* |
| | ***fastigiatum*** | see *Rhodiola fastigiata* |
| | ***forsterianum*** subsp. ***elegans*** | SPlb |
| § | - f. ***purpureum*** | NRya |
| | ***frutescens*** | STre |
| | ***furfuraceum*** | CStu NMen WAbe |
| | Garnet Brocade = 'Garbro'$^{PBR}$ | CCVN |
| § | ***glaucophyllum*** | WFar WPer |
| | 'Gold Mound' | EPfP LAst MGos MHar NLar SVil |
| * | 'Green Expectations' | ECtt EGle EShb LRHS MRav MSte NBre NBsh |
| § | ***gypsicola*** | EBee WPer |
| | 'Harvest Moon' | EBur |
| § | 'Herbstfreude' ΨH4 | Widely available |
| | ***heterodontum*** | see *Rhodiola heterodonta* |
| | ***hidakanum*** | ECtt EHoe GGar GMaP NBro NHol NMen WHoo WPat WTin |
| | ***himalense*** misapplied | see *Rhodiola* 'Keston' |
| | ***hispanicum*** | EAlp ECho EDAr MHer NBre SPlb |
| | - ***glaucum*** | see *S. hispanicum* var. *minus* |
| § | - var. ***minus*** | ECho ECtt MBar SEND SIng SPlb |
| § | - - 'Aureum' | ECha ECho EDAr MBar NHol SPoG |
| | - 'Pewter' | see *S.* 'Pewter' |
| | ***humifusum*** | EBur EPot NWCA SIng |
| § | ***hybridum*** | WEas |
| | - 'Czar's Gold' | EAlp |
| | 'Indian Chief' | CMMP CPrp CTca EAEE EBee ECtt EGle GCra GKir GMaP LAst LRHS MBrN MRav MSte SCoo SMrm SPoG WFar WMnd WMoo |
| | ***ishidae*** | see *Rhodiola ishidae* |
| | 'Jaws'$^{PBR}$ | CAby CKno EBee ECGP ECtt EGle LSou SMrm SPoG WCot WRHF |
| | 'José Aubergine' **new** | EBee MSte |
| | 'Joyce Henderson' | COlW EBee EBrs ECtt EGle GKir GQue LHop MCot MRav NCob NLar SMrm SPer SRGP SUsu WBrk WCot WEas WMoo WTin |
| | ***kamtschaticum*** ΨH4 | EAlp ECho GAuc GJos MBar WFar |
| | - B&SWJ 10870 **new** | WCru |
| § | - var. ***ellacombeanum*** ΨH4 | EDAr EGoo NMen SEND WCot |
| | - - B&SWJ 8853 | WCru |
| § | - var. ***floriferum*** 'Weihenstephaner Gold' | CEnt CTri ECho ECtt EDAr EGoo EPfP GAbr GEdr GGar GKir GMaP LRHS MBar MHer MRav MWat NBir NMen NPri NVic SIng SPlb SPoG SRms WFar WPat |

| | | |
|---|---|---|
| | - var. ***kamtschaticum*** 'Variegatum' (v) ♀H4 | CLyd CMea EAlp EBee ECho ECtt EDAr EHoe EPfP GKir LAst LBMP MHer MMuc MWat SIng SPoG SRms SRot SWvt WEas |
| | - var. ***middendorffianum*** | see *S. middendorffianum* |
| | ***kirilovii*** | see *Rhodiola kirilovii* |
| § | 'Lajos' (v) | EBee NSti |
| | ***lanceolatum*** | WPer |
| | ***laxum*** subsp. ***heckneri*** | WAbe |
| | - subsp. ***laxum*** NNS 01-378 **new** | NWCA |
| | ***lineare*** | CHEx LAst SSto |
| | ***litorale*** | CSec |
| | 'Little Gem' | see x *Cremnosedum* 'Little Gem' |
| § | ***lydium*** | CTri ECho GKir MBar MHer SFgr SPlb |
| | - 'Aureum' | see *S. hispanicum* var. *minus* 'Aureum' |
| | - 'Bronze Queen' | see *S. lydium* |
| | ***makinoi*** 'Ōgon' | EBee |
| I | 'Marchants Best Red' ♀H4 | SMHy SUsu |
| | 'Matrona' ♀H4 | Widely available |
| | ***maweanum*** | see *S. acre* subsp. *neglectum* var. *majus* |
| § | ***middendorffianum*** | CLyd CSec ECho EDAr EGoo GKev MBrN MHer MWat NMen SPoG SRms SRot WFar |
| | 'Moonglow' | ECtt NMen |
| | ***moranense*** | CHal SEND |
| | ***morganianum*** ♀H1 | CHal EBak |
| N | ***nevii*** hort. | EGle SPlb |
| | ***nicaeense*** | see *S. sediforme* |
| | ***obcordatum*** | NMen |
| | ***obtusatum*** misapplied | see *S. oreganum* |
| § | ***obtusatum*** A. Gray | EAlp ECtt EDAr GGar GKev NBro NSla STre WFar WPnn |
| | - subsp. ***boreale*** NNS 01-123 **new** | NWCA |
| | ***oppositifolium*** | see *S. spurium* 'Album' |
| § | ***oreganum*** | ECha ECho EDAr GAbr GMaP MBar MHer MWat NMen SPlb SRms SRot STre |
| | - 'Procumbens' | see *S. oreganum* subsp. *tenue* |
| § | - subsp. ***tenue*** | LEdu NHol NRya WPat |
| § | ***oregonense*** | EBur NMen |
| * | ***oryzifolium*** 'Minus' | EAlp EBur |
| | ***oxypetalum*** | STre |
| | ***pachyclados*** | see *Rhodiola pachyclados* |
| | ***pachyphyllum*** | EPfP |
| | ***palmeri*** | CHEx CSpe LSou MRav NBir SChr SSvw |
| § | - subsp. ***palmeri*** tetraploid | EDAr SEND |
| § | 'Pewter' | ECho |
| | ***pilosum*** | NMen NWCA |
| | 'Pink Chablis'PBR (v) | EBee MLLN NBhm WCot |
| § | ***pluricaule*** | ECho SPlb SRms |
| | ***populifolium*** | EBee ECha GCal MHer STre WPer |
| | 'Postman's Pride'PBR | EBee IPot LBuc WCot WMoo |
| | ***praealtum*** | CSec GGar SChr SEND STre WCot |
| | ***pulchellum*** | SPlb |
| | 'Red Cauli' ♀H4 | CKno EBee EGle GBin IPot LPio MBNS MBri NCGa NPro SMHy SPhx SUsu WFar |
| | 'Red Rum' | LRHS SMeo |
| | ***reflexum*** L. | see *S. rupestre* L. |
| | ***reptans*** | ECho |
| | ***rhodiola*** | see *Rhodiola rosea* |
| | ***rosea*** | see *Rhodiola rosea* |
| | ***rubroglaucum*** misapplied | see *S. oregonense* |
| | ***rubroglaucum*** Praeger | see *S. obtusatum* A. Gray |
| | x ***rubrotinctum*** | CHEx CHal EBee SChr |
| | - 'Aurora' | SChr |
| § | 'Ruby Glow' ♀H4 | Widely available |
| | 'Ruby Port' | CSpe |
| § | ***rupestre*** L. | EAlp EBWF ECho GGar MBNS MBar MWat NBlu SPlb SPoG WFar WHer |
| | - 'Angelina' | EBee EPPr EWes MAvo MGos NBir NHol NPro SRGP SUsu WCot |
| | - 'Monstrosum Cristatum' | NBir SMad WAlt |
| | ***ruprechtii*** | see *S. telephium* subsp. *ruprechtii* |
| | 'Samuel Oliphant' | EBee WCot |
| | ***sarcocaule*** hort. | see *Crassula sarcocaulis* |
| | ***sarmentosum*** | ECho |
| § | ***sediforme*** | CArn CTca EDAr |
| | - ***nicaeense*** | see *S. sediforme* |
| | ***selskianum*** | EBee GGar NBre |
| | ***sempervivoides*** | CSec ECho |
| | ***sexangulare*** | EAlp ECho EDAr GGar MBar MHer NRya SEND SFgr SPlb SRms STre WFar WPer |
| | ***sibiricum*** | see *S. hybridum* |
| | ***sieboldii*** | EBee ECho GJos |
| | - 'Mediovariegatum' (v) ♀H2-3 | CHEx COIW EAlp ECho EWll LAst MHer NPri SPlb WFar |
| | 'Silvermoon' | EBur ECtt NHol |
| | ***spathulifolium*** | CTri ECha ECho EPot MDKP WEas |
| | - 'Aureum' | EBur ECho ECtt GKev MWat NRya WAbe |
| | - 'Cape Blanco' ♀H4 | Widely available |
| | - 'Purpureum' ♀H4 | Widely available |
| | ***spectabile*** ♀H4 | CArn CChe CHEx CPrp CTri EBee ELan EPfP GJos GMaP LRHS MCot MHer MRav NGdn SGar SPlb SRms WBVN WBor WBrk WCAu WFar WSFF WTin |
| | - 'Abendrot' | EMon |
| | - 'Album' | CHEx |
| | - 'Brilliant' ♀H4 | Widely available |
| | - 'Carmen' | EBee WMoo |
| | - 'Hot Stuff' **new** | NBhm |
| | - 'Iceberg' | Widely available |
| | - 'Lisa' | EMon GBin MTPN NLar |
| | - 'Meteor' | EBee MBNS MLLN MSte MWat NLar SMrm WCAu WPer |
| * | - 'Mini' | ELan MRav |
| | - 'Neon' | EBee LRHS NDov |
| | - 'Pink Fairy' | WHil |
| | - 'Rosenteller' | EBee EGle EMon NBre SMrm |
| | - September Glow | see *S. spectabile* 'Septemberglut' |
| § | - 'Septemberglut' | EBee EGoo EMon NBre NSti WCot |
| | - 'Stardust' | CKno CPrp CTri EBee EBrs EGle EMil EPfP GKev GMaP LCro MBNS MHer MRav NCGa NOrc SMrm SPer SPet SPoG WCAu WFar WGor |
| | - 'Steven Ward' | EBee EWes SRGP |
| | - 'Variegatum' | see *S. erythrostictum* 'Mediovariegatum' |
| | ***spinosum*** | see *Orostachys spinosa* |
| | ***spurium*** | CHEx ECho EGoo GJos NHol NPro SEND SGar SPoG SRms STre |
| § | - 'Album' | EGoo NRya |
| | - 'Atropurpureum' | ECha SMrm WMoo |
| | - 'Coccineum' | EAlp ECho MBar MNHC WBVN |
| | - Dragon's Blood | see *S. spurium* 'Schorbuser Blut' |
| | - 'Erdblut' | NMen |
| | - 'Fuldaglut' | CHal CTri EBee ECho EDAr EHoe GBuc GMaP GQue NRya SIng SMrm SPer WFar WMoo WPer WPnn |
| | - 'Green Mantle' | EBee ECha ECho EPfP SSto |
| | - Purple Carpet | see *S. spurium* 'Purpurteppich' |
| | - 'Purpureum' | EGoo SRms |
| § | - 'Purpurteppich' | EBee ECho ECtt MRav NBPN NBro NHol NLar SRms |
| | - 'Roseum' | EWll SRms |

| | |
|---|---|
| - 'Ruby Mantle' | EWll GKev GKir SBch SPoG SWvt WBVN |
| § - 'Schorbuser Blut' ♀H4 | CMea EBee ECho ECtt EPau EPfP EPot GKev GKir MCot MLHP MWat NBir NRya NVic SPlb SRGP SRms WEas WFar WHoo WTin |
| - 'Summer Glory' | EAlp NLar |
| § - 'Tricolor' | CHEx CTri EAlp EBee ECha ECho EDAr EGoo EHoe GGar LAst LBMP MBar MHer MLHP MRav NHol NPri NRya SBod SIng SPlb SPoG STre WFar WMoo |
| - 'Variegatum' (v) | see *S. spurium* 'Tricolor' |
| - 'Voodoo' | CChe EAlp EBee ECtt EWes MHar MHer |
| ***stenopetalum*** | SPlb |
| § - 'Douglasii' | MHer SRms |
| 'Stewed Rhubarb Mountain' | CPrp EAEE EBee EBla ECtt EGle LBMP LDai LHop LSou MBNS MCot MRav MSte NBro NBsh NOrc SMrm WCot WFar WMoo WPGP |
| ***stoloniferum*** | ECho |
| 'Strawberries and Cream' | Widely available |
| 'Sunset Cloud' | CHEx CMHG CSam EBee ECtt EGle EWes GCal IPot LPla LRHS NBre NCob |
| ***takesimense*** B&SWJ 8518 | WCru |
| ***tatarinowii*** | EDAr |
| ***telephium*** | CArn CMea CSec NBir SRms |
| - 'Abbeydore' | see *S.* 'Abbeydore' |
| - 'Arthur Branch' | EBee EPPr GBin GBuc MNrw MSte MTho |
| - 'Black Emperor' | EBee |
| - 'Black Jack' | EBee IPot LBuc MAsh MGos NBPN NBsh NDov SPoG WCot |
| - 'Bon Bon' | EBee EGle MBNS NBPN WPtf |
| - 'Bronco'PBR **new** | EBee |
| - 'El Cid' | EBee EGle EWes |
| - Emperor's Waves Group | EDAr GQue NGdn WRHF |
| § - subsp. ***fabaria*** | EWsh WAbb WCot WFar |
| - - var. ***borderei*** | CElw EGle EMon LHop LPla LRHS SBch SPhx SUsu |
| * - 'Hester' | EBee |
| - 'Jennifer' | WCot |
| - 'Karfunkelstein' | GBin NDov SPhx SUsu |
| - 'Leonore Zuuntz' | EBee NBre |
| - 'Lynda Windsor'PBR | CBct CBow CWCL EBee ECtt EGle EHrv EPfP LAst LHop MBNS NBPN NBhm NLar NMoo SPoG SRGP SWvt |
| - subsp. ***maximum*** | MGos SMrm |
| - - 'Atropurpureum' ♀H4 | CMea COlW EBee EGle ELan EPfP MRav SGar SWvt WCot WEas |
| - - 'Bressingham Purple' | EBrs |
| - - 'Gooseberry Fool' | COlW EBee ECGP EGle EGoo EMon GMaP LCro NSti SBch SPhx WCot WFar |
| - 'Möhrchen' | CPrp EBee EGle EHrv EWsh GMaP LRHS MHar MLLN MRav NGdn NLar SMrm SPla SPoG WCAu WFar WMnd WMoo |
| - 'Munstead Red' | Widely available |
| - 'Picolette' | EBee MBNS NBPN |
| § - 'Purple Emperor' ♀H4 | Widely available |
| - 'Ringmore Ruby' | EBee MHar WCot |
| § - subsp. ***ruprechtii*** | COlW CPrp EBee ECha ECtt EGle EGoo EMon EPPr EPfP GAuc GMaP LHop LRHS MCot MNFA MRav NSti SMeo SPer SPet SPhx WBVN WEas WFar WMoo WPer |
| - - 'Citrus Twist' | EBee EBla ECtt LBMP LRHS LSou MBNS NBhm NBsh NPro WPtf |
| - - 'Hab Gray' | CBgR CSpe EBee ECtt EGle EWes GBin GQue LAst MSte NLar SUsu WCot WGwG |
| - - 'Pink Dome' **new** | ECha |
| - subsp. ***telephium*** 'Lynda et Rodney' | CKno EGle EGoo EMon EWes MSte WCot |
| - - var. ***purpureum*** | GCra |
| - 'Variegatum' (v) | LRHS MDKP WHal |
| - 'Xenox'PBR | EBee ECtt EPfP EWll GBin IPot LRHS MBNS NBsh WCot |
| ***tenuifolium*** | see *S. amplexicaule* subsp. *tenuifolium* |
| - subsp. ***ibericum*** | see *S. amplexicaule* subsp. *tenuifolium* |
| ***ternatum*** | SBch WFar |
| ***trollii*** | see *Rhodiola trollii* |
| ***urvillei*** Sartorianum Group | MHer |
| ***ussuriense*** | EBee EMon SUsu WOut |
| 'Vera Jameson' ♀H4 | Widely available |
| ***viviparum*** B&SWJ 8662 | WCru |
| 'Wallaceum' | EAlp |
| 'Washfield Purple' | see *S. telephium* 'Purple Emperor' |
| 'Weihenstephaner Gold' | see *S. kamtschaticum* var. *floriferum* 'Weihenstephaner Gold' |
| ***weinbergii*** | see *Graptopetalum paraguayense* |
| ***yezoense*** | see *S. pluricaule* |

## *Seemannia* see *Gloxinia*

## *Selaginella* ✿ (*Selaginellaceae*)

| | |
|---|---|
| ***apoda*** | MBri |
| ***braunii*** | CLAP SKHP WCot |
| ***helvetica*** | CKob CStu |
| ***kraussiana*** ♀H1 | CHal CKob CLAP EDAr GGar LRHS MBri NHol WRic |
| - 'Aurea' | CCCN CHal CLAP SMad WRic |
| - 'Brownii' ♀H1 | CCCN CLAP LRHS |
| - 'Gold Tips' | CCCN CLAP LRHS |
| ***lepidophylla*** | EBrs SVic |
| ***martensii*** ♀H1 | CKob |
| ***moellendorfii*** | WRic |
| ***sanguinolenta*** | CKob CStu SIng |
| ***uncinata*** ♀H1 | CExc CLAP WRic |

## *Selago* (*Scrophulariaceae*)

| | |
|---|---|
| ***myrtifolia*** | GFai |

## *Selinum* (*Apiaceae*)

| | |
|---|---|
| ***carvifolium*** | CSec EBee LDai NLar |
| ***tenuifolium*** | see *S. wallichianum* |
| § ***wallichianum*** | CDes CRow CSpe CWsd EBrs ECGP EDAr EGoo ELan EWTr GBuc GCal GCra GKir MWat NBPC NBid NCGa NDov SKHP SMHy SMeo SPer SPhx SUsu WCot WFar WHal WHil WPGP |
| - EMAK 886 | EBee GPoy NSti SDix |
| - HWJK 2224 | WCru |
| - HWJK 2347 | WCru |

## *Selliera* (*Goodeniaceae*)

| | |
|---|---|
| ***radicans*** | ECou EDAr GGar |
| - 'Lake Ellerman' | NHol |

## *Semele* (*Ruscaceae*)

| | |
|---|---|
| ***androgyna*** | CHEx CRHN |

## *Semiaquilegia* (*Ranunculaceae*)

| | |
|---|---|
| § ***adoxoides*** | CPom CSec SHar |
| 'Early Dwarf' | EDif NLar |
| § ***ecalcarata*** | CDes CMea CPom CSec ECho GBBs GBuc GGar GKir LDai MAvo NLar |

| | | |
|---|---|---|
| | | SBch SMrs SRms SSvw WCru WFar WHal WPGP WPer |
| * | - f. ***bicolor*** | CPom WCru |
| | - 'Snowbell' **new** | WCru |
| | ***simulatrix*** | see *S. ecalcarata* |

## *Semiarundinaria* (*Poaceae*)

| | | |
|---|---|---|
| | from Korea | EPla |
| § | ***fastuosa*** ♀H4 | CDoC CEnt CHEx EAmu EBee EFul ENBC EPfP EPla ERod LMaj LPal MBri MMoz MWht NMoo NVic SAPC SArc SEND SPlb |
| | - var. ***viridis*** | CEnt EBee EPla ERod LPJP MWht SBig WCru |
| | ***kagamiana*** | CDoC CMCo EBee ENBC EPla MMoz MMuc MWhi MWht NMoo SBig |
| § | ***lubrica*** | MWht |
| | ***makinoi*** | CGHE EAmu EPla MWht WPGP |
| | ***nitida*** | see *Fargesia nitida* |
| § | ***okuboi*** | CEnt ENBC EPla ERod LPal MMoz MWht |
| | ***villosa*** | see *S. okuboi* |
| | ***yamadorii*** | EPla ERod MMoz MWht |
| | - 'Brimscombe' | EPla |
| | ***yashadake*** | EPla ERod |
| | - 'Gimmei' | EPla |
| | - f. ***kimmei*** | CAbb CDoC CDul ENBC EPla ERod LCro MAsh MGos MMoz MMuc MREP MWht NMoo SBLw SBig SEND WDyG WFar WMoo WPGP |

## *Semnanthe* see *Erepsia*

## *Sempervivella* see *Rosularia*

## *Sempervivum* ✿ (*Crassulaceae*)

| | | |
|---|---|---|
| | from Andorra | NHol |
| | from Sierra Nova | NDlv |
| | 'Abba' | CMea MOne WHal WPer |
| | ***acuminatum*** | see *S. tectorum* var. *glaucum* |
| | 'Adelaar' | CWil NMen |
| | 'Adelmoed' | CWil SFgr |
| | 'Adeltruid' | NHol |
| | 'Adlerhorst' | NHol |
| | 'Aglow' | MHom MOne NMen |
| | 'Aladdin' | CWil MOne NMen SRms |
| | 'Albernelli' | NHol SFgr |
| | 'Alchimist' | MOne |
| | 'Alcithoë' | MOne |
| | 'Aldo Moro' | CWil ECha EDAr GAbr LBee LRHS MHom MOne MWat NMen SFgr WIvy |
| | 'Alidae' | MOne |
| | ***allionii*** | see *Jovibarba allionii* |
| | 'Alluring' | GAbr MOne |
| | 'Alpha' | CTca EBee LBee LRHS MOne NHol NMen SFgr SIng SRms STre WHal WPer WTin |
| | ***altum*** | CWil MHom NMen SIng |
| | 'Amanda' | CWil ECha MOne NMen SIng SRms WHoo WPer WTin |
| | 'Ambergreen' | NMen |
| | ***andreanum*** | see *S. tectorum* var. *alpinum* |
| | 'Apache' Payne | see *Jovibarba heuffelii* 'Apache' |
| | 'Apache' Haberer | MOne MWat NMen |
| | 'Apollo' | NHol SFgr |
| | 'Apple Blossom' | CMea ECha MOne NMen SIng |
| | ***arachnoideum*** ♀H4 | Widely available |
| | - from Cascade Piste 7 | MOne |
| | - from the Abruzzi, Italy | SIng |
| | - 'Ararat' | SDys |
| | - 'Boria' | MOne |
| | - var. ***bryoides*** | CWil MBrN NMen WAbe WIvy WPer |
| | - 'Cebennense' **new** | GKev |
| | - 'Clärchen' | EPot NHol NMen NSla SFgr |
| | - cristate | CWil |
| * | - ***densum*** | EDAr MBrN NRya WAbe WFar |
| | - subsp. ***doellianum*** | see *S. arachnoideum* subsp. *tomentosum* var. *glabrescens* |
| | - form No 1 | ECho |
| | - 'Laggeri' | see *S. arachnoideum* L. subsp. *tomentosum* (C.B. Lehm. & Schnittsp.) Schinz & Thell. |
| | - 'Opitz' | WPer |
| | - 'Peña Prieta' | NHol |
| | - red | NMen |
| | - 'Red Wings' | ECha MOne NMen SRms |
| | - 'Rubrum' | CHEx CTca EDAr GGar GKir GMaP LRHS MOne |
| | - 'Sultan' | MOne |
| | - subsp. ***tomentosum*** misapplied | see *S.* x *barbulatum* 'Hookeri' |
| § | - subsp. ***tomentosum*** (C.B. Lehm. & Schnittsp.) Schinz & Thell. ♀H4 | CHEx CHal CWil MHer NHol NMen NPer SFgr SIng SPlb SRms WAbe WGor WPer |
| | - - GDJ 92.04 | CWil |
| § | - subsp. ***tomentosum*** var. ***glabrescens*** | NMen SDys WPat |
| | - - 'Minus' | NHol NMen SIng |
| § | - - 'Stansfieldii' | GAbr NMen SDys SIng STre WHal |
| § | - 'White Christmas' | CTca CWil MHer |
| | ***arachnoideum*** x ***calcareum*** | CWil NHol NMen WIvy WTin |
| | ***arachnoideum*** x ***montanum*** | see *S.* x *barbulatum* |
| | ***arachnoideum*** x ***nevadense*** | CWil SDys |
| | ***arachnoideum*** x ***pittonii*** | CWil NHol NMen WAbe |
| | ***arenarium*** | see *Jovibarba arenaria* |
| | ***armenum*** | MOne NMen |
| | - var. ***insigne*** | MOne |
| | 'Arondina' | CWil |
| | 'Aross' | CMea GAbr NMen |
| | 'Arrowheads Red' | MOne MWat |
| | 'Artist' | CWil MOne NMen SFgr |
| | ***arvernense*** | see *S. tectorum* |
| | 'Ashes of Roses' | CTca EGoo EPot ITim MHom MOne NMen WAbe WGor WPer |
| | 'Asteroid' | CWil MOne NMen |
| | 'Astrid' | CWil |
| | ***atlanticum*** | MHom NDlv NMen NSla SRot |
| | - from Atlas Mountains, Morocco | CWil MOne |
| | - from Oukaïmeden, Morocco | CWil GAbr MOne NHol NMen WTin |
| | - 'Edward Balls' | CWil MOne SDys SFgr |
| | 'Atlantis' ambig. | NHol |
| | 'Atropurpureum' ambig. | CHEx CWil EDAr GAbr MBrN MOne NMen SRms WGor WIvy WPer |
| | 'Averil' | CWil |
| | 'Averley' | MOne |
| | 'Aymon Correvon' | MOne |
| | ***balcanicum*** | CWil EDAr MOne NMen WIvy |
| | ***ballsii*** | NMen |
| | - from Kambeecho, Greece | MHom |
| | - from Smólikas, Greece | CWil MHom MOne NMen |
| | - from Tschumba Petzi, Greece | CWil MHom MOne SDys SIng |
| | 'Banderi' | MOne MWat |
| | 'Banjo' | MOne |

| | | |
|---|---|---|
| | 'Banyan' | MTPN |
| | 'Barbarosa' | CWil MOne |
| § | x ***barbulatum*** | NMen SDys WPer |
| § | - 'Hookeri' | CTri CWil EPot MOne NLar NMen SFgr SIng WAbe WPer |
| | 'Bascour Zilver' | CMea CWil ECha LBee MOne SFgr SIng WHal |
| | 'Beaute' | MOne |
| | 'Bedivere' | CPBP CWil LBee MOne NMen SRms |
| | 'Bedivere Crested' | CWil |
| * | 'Bedley Hi' | MHom MOne |
| | 'Bella Donna' | MHom MOne NHol NMen WPer |
| | 'Bella Meade' | CWil MOne NMen SFgr SRms WPer |
| | 'Bellotts Pourpre' | CWil NHol |
| | 'Bennerbroek' | MOne |
| | 'Benny Hill' | CWil MOne |
| | 'Bernstein' | CWil MHer MOne SFgr SIng WHal |
| | 'Beta' | MHom MOne NHol NMen WAbe WPer WTin |
| | 'Bethany' | CWil MOne NHol NMen WHal |
| | 'Bicolor' ambig. | EPfP |
| | 'Big Mal' | NHol |
| | 'Big Slipper' | MOne NHol |
| | 'Binstead' | MOne NHol |
| | 'Birchmaier' | NMen SFgr |
| | 'Black Beauty' | EPot |
| | 'Black Cap' | MOne |
| | 'Black Claret' | NHol |
| | 'Black Knight' | CTca LBee LRHS MHer SRms WHal |
| | 'Black Mini' | CTca CWil EPot GAbr MDKP NBir NMen SRms WAbe |
| | 'Black Mountain' | CHEx CWil LBee MOne MWat SIng |
| | 'Black Prince' | CTca ECha SPer |
| | 'Black Velvet' | WIvy WPer |
| | 'Blackie' new | GKev |
| | 'Bladon' | WPer |
| | 'Blari' | MOne |
| | 'Blood Sucker' | WGor |
| | 'Blood Tip' | CHEx CHal CMea CWil EBee ECha GAbr GCra LBee LRHS MHer NHol NMen NRya SPoG SRms WFar WGor WHal WPer |
| | 'Blue Boy' | CTca CWil ECha EPot GAbr LBee LRHS MOne MSte NHol NMen SFgr SRms WPer |
| | 'Blue Moon' | MOne NMen |
| | 'Blue Time' | CTca MOne SFgr WHoo WTin |
| | 'Blush' | CTca EDAr MOne |
| | 'Boissieri' | see *S. tectorum* subsp. *tectorum* 'Boissieri' |
| | 'Bold Chick' | MOne |
| | 'Booth's Red' | CHEx MOne NMen SIng WGor |
| | 'Boreale' | see *Jovibarba hirta* subsp. *borealis* |
| | ***borisii*** | see *S. ciliosum* var. *borisii* |
| | ***borissovae*** | CWil MHom NMen SDys |
| | 'Boromir' | CWil MOne |
| | 'Boule de Neige' | NMen |
| | 'Bowles's Variety' | WPer |
| | ***brevipilum*** from Turkey | MOne |
| | 'Bright Eyes' | MOne |
| | 'Britta' | MOne SDys |
| | 'Brock' | CWil ECha MHer MHom NHol WPer |
| | 'Bronco' | CTca CWil EBee ECho GAbr LBee MHom MOne NMen SRms WCot WFar |
| | 'Bronze Beauty' new | WRos |
| | 'Bronze Pastel' | CTca CWil ECha MHom MOne NMen NSla SFgr SRms SRot WGor WTin |
| | 'Bronze Tower' | NHol |
| | 'Brown Owl' | CWil ECho MOne MWat NHol SRms WFar |
| | 'Brownii' | GAbr MOne NMen WPer WTin |
| | 'Brunette' | ECho GAbr |
| | 'Burgundy' | ECha MOne |
| | 'Burgundy Velvet' | MOne |
| | 'Burnatii' | see *S. montanum* subsp. *burnatii* |
| | 'Burning Desire' | CTca WGor |
| | 'Butterfly' | MOne |
| | 'Café' | CWil EGoo MWat NHol NMen SFgr SRms WIvy WPer |
| | x ***calcaratum*** | SRms |
| | ***calcareum*** | CMea CSam CTca CWil EPot GKir LRHS MOne NBro NMen SPlb SPoG SRms SRot WFar WHoo WPer |
| | - from Alps, France | CWil MOne |
| | - from Calde la Vanoise, France | CWil MOne NMen |
| | - from Ceüze, France | CWil MOne WIvy |
| | - from Cherion | MOne |
| | - from Col Bayard, France | CWil GAbr MOne NMen |
| | - from Colle St Michel, France | CWil MOne NMen SFgr |
| | - from Cleizé, France | see *S. calcareum* 'Limelight' |
| | - from Gorges supérieures du Cians, France | CWil MOne NMen |
| | - from Guillaumes, Mont Ventoux, France | CWil MOne NMen SFgr SRot WHoo |
| | - from La Mata de la Riba, Spain | MOne |
| | - from Mont Ventoux, France | CWil MOne |
| | - from Petite Ceüse, France | SRot |
| | - - GDJ 92.15 | CWil |
| | - - GDJ 92.16 | CWil |
| | - from Queyras, France | CWil MOne NMen |
| | - from Route d'Annôt, France | CWil MOne NMen |
| | - from Triora, Italy | CWil MOne NHol NMen |
| | - 'Benz' | SDys |
| | - 'Cristatum' | CStu |
| | - 'Extra' | CHEx CWil GAbr SFgr SRot |
| | - 'Greenii' | CTca CWil LRHS MOne NDlv NHol NMen SIng SPlb |
| § | - 'Grigg's Surprise' | CWil MHer MOne NMen |
| § | - 'Limelight' | CMea CTca CWil MOne NHol NMen SPoG WHal WIvy WPer WTin |
| | - 'Monstrosum' | see *S. calcareum* 'Grigg's Surprise' |
| | - 'Mrs Giuseppi' | CTca CWil EBee ECho ETod GAbr LBee LRHS MOne MSte NMen SFgr SRms STre WAbe WFar WPer |
| | - 'Pink Pearl' | CWil MOne NMen SDys SFgr WIvy WTin |
| | - 'Sir William Lawrence' | CMea CPBP CWil ECho EDAr NMen SFgr WAbe WHal WHoo WIvy WPer WThu WTin |
| | 'Caldera' | NHol |
| | ***californicum*** | SIng |
| * | ***callosum barnesii*** | GAbr |
| * | ***calopticum*** x ***nevadense*** | WTin |
| | 'Cameo' | see *Jovibarba heuffelii* var. *glabra* 'Cameo' |
| | 'Canada Kate' | CWil NHol WPer |
| | 'Cancer' | MOne |
| | 'Candy Floss' | CTca CWil MOne NMen SIng WGor |
| | ***cantabricum*** | CWil EDAr NMen SIng WThu |
| | - from Cuengas Piedras | MOne |
| | - from Cuevas del Sil, Spain | CWil MOne |
| | - from Navafria, Spain | CWil MOne NHol SIng WTin |
| | - from Peña Prieta, Spain | MOne NMen |
| | - from Piedrafita, Spain | MOne |

| | | |
|---|---|---|
| | - from Riaño, Spain | CWil GAbr |
| | - from San Glorio, Spain | CWil GAbr MOne NMen |
| | - from Santander, Spain | NHol |
| | - from Ticeros | MOne NMen |
| | - from Tizneros, Spain | CWil |
| | - from Valvarnera, Spain | MOne NMen |
| | - subsp. ***cantabricum*** from Leitariegos, Spain | CWil GAbr MHom MOne NMen |
| | - - from Peña de Llesba, Spain GDJ 93.13 | CWil |
| | - - from Pico del Lobo, Spain | CWil |
| | - subsp. ***guadarramense*** | see *S. vicentei* subsp. *paui* |
| | - - from Pico del Lobo, Spain, No 1 | MOne SRot |
| | - - from Pico del Lobo, Spain, No 2 | MOne |
| | - - from Valvanera, Spain, No 1 | CWil NMen |
| | - subsp. ***urbionense*** | CWil |
| | - - from El Gatón, Spain | CWil |
| | - - from Picos de Urbión, Spain | CWil MOne NMen |
| | ***cantabricum*** x ***montanum*** subsp. ***stiriacum*** | WEas WTin |
| | ***cantabricum*** x ***montanum*** subsp. ***stiriacum*** 'Lloyd Praeger' | CWil |
| | 'Canth' | MWat NHol |
| | 'Caramel' | MOne |
| * | x ***carlsii*** | MOne |
| | 'Carluke' | MOne |
| | 'Carmen' | CHal GAbr MOne SFgr |
| | 'Carneum' | MOne NHol |
| | 'Carnival' | CHal MOne NMen WPer |
| | ***caucasicum*** | CWil GKir MHom MOne NMen SIng SPoG |
| | 'Cauticola' | MOne |
| | 'Cavo Doro' | CWil MOne SFgr |
| | 'Celon' | MOne |
| | 'Centennial' | MOne |
| | 'Chalon' | MOne |
| | ***charadzeae*** | CWil LBee LRHS MOne NHol |
| | 'Cherry Frost' | ECho MOne NDlv NMen SFgr |
| | 'Cherry Glow' | see *Jovibarba heuffelii* 'Cherry Glow' |
| | 'Chivalry' | MOne |
| | 'Chocolate' | MOne NHol SIng WPer |
| § | x ***christii*** | MOne NHol NMen |
| | 'Christmas Time' | MOne NHol SFgr |
| | ***ciliosum*** ♀H4 | CMea CPBP CWil ECho GMaP NMen NRya |
| § | - var. ***borisii*** | CWil EPfP GCal GKev NDlv NMen NRya WAbe WHal |
| | - from Alí Butús, Bulgaria | SDys |
| | - var. ***galicicum*** from Mali Hat, Albania | NMen WPer |
| | ***ciliosum*** x ***ciliosum*** var. ***borisii*** | CHal CTri NMen |
| | ***ciliosum*** x ***grandiflorum*** | CWil MOne NMen |
| | ***ciliosum*** x ***marmoreum*** | NMen |
| | ***ciliosum*** x ***tectorum*** | WTin |
| | 'Cindy' | MOne SRms |
| | 'Circlet' | CWil MOne NMen |
| | 'Cistaceum' | WEas |
| | 'Clara Noyes' | MOne WFar WPer |
| | 'Clare' | MHer MOne |
| | 'Claudine' | MOne |
| | 'Clemanum' | MOne |
| | 'Cleveland Morgan' | ECha LRHS MHom MOne NBro NMen |
| | 'Climax' ambig. | CTca EBee ECho MHom MOne NMen SSto WFar |
| | 'Clisette' | CTca |
| | 'Cobweb Capers' | MHom MOne |
| | 'Cobweb Centres' | MOne NMen |
| | 'Cochise' | MOne |
| | 'Collage' | MOne NHol WPer |
| | 'Collecteur Anchisi' | MOne NHol SDys SFgr |
| | 'Commander Hay' ♀H4 | CHEx COlW CTca CWil EDAr EPfP ETod EWes GAbr GCra GKev MBNS MHom MOne MWat NDov NMen NPer SRGP SRms STre WEas WHal WIvy WPer |
| | 'Comte de Congae' | MOne NMen |
| | 'Congo' | MOne NMen SFgr |
| | 'Conran' | NHol |
| | 'Corio' | MOne |
| | 'Cornstone' | ECha NHol |
| | 'Corona' | CWil MOne MWat NHol SFgr SRms WPer |
| | 'Corsair' | CWil ECha EDAr GKev MBrN MOne NMen SFgr SIng WGor WIvy WPer WTin |
| | 'Cranberry' | MOne |
| | 'Cresta' | MOne |
| | 'Crimson King' | SFgr |
| | 'Crimson Velvet' | CHEx CMea EDAr LBee LRHS MOne NHol SFgr WPer |
| § | 'Crispyn' | CWil EPot LBee MHer MHom MOne NHol NMen SFgr SIng WEas WPer |
| | 'Croky' | MOne |
| | 'Croton' | WPer |
| | 'Cupream' | CWil NDlv SRms WPer |
| | 'Czakor' | NHol |
| | 'Dakota' | CWil MOne NHol NMen SFgr |
| | 'Dallas' | CWil MOne NHol NMen SRms |
| | 'Damask' | CWil LBee MOne NMen SFgr WPer |
| | 'Dame Arsac' | MOne |
| | 'Dancer's Veil' | MOne |
| | 'Darjeeling' | CWil |
| | 'Dark Beauty' | CMea CWil ECha MOne NMen WAbe WCot WGor WHal WPer WRos |
| | 'Dark Cloud' | CWil LBee LRHS MOne WHoo WIvy WPer |
| | 'Dark Point' | CWil MHom MOne NMen SFgr SIng |
| | 'Darkie' | CWil SFgr WPer |
| | ***davisii*** | ECha |
| | 'Deep Fire' | CWil MOne NHol NMen SRms WAbe WIvy WTin |
| | x ***degenianum*** | GAbr MOne NMen SFgr WPer |
| | 'Delta' | NMen WHoo WTin |
| | ***densum*** | see *S. tectorum* |
| | 'Devon Glow' | CTca |
| | 'Devon Jewel' | CTca WGor |
| | 'Diamant' | MOne |
| | 'Diane' | CWil SFgr |
| | 'Director Jacobs' | CWil EDAr MOne NHol NMen SFgr WEas WPer WTin |
| | 'Doctor Roberts' | NHol |
| | ***dolomiticum*** | NMen |
| | - from Rif Sennes, Italy | MOne |
| | ***dolomiticum*** x ***montanum*** | CWil GKev MOne NBro NMen SFgr WTin |
| | 'Donarrose' | NHol SFgr SIng |
| | 'Downland Queen' | CWil MOne NHol |
| | 'Dragoness' | MOne |
| | 'Duke of Windsor' | MOne NMen SFgr |
| | 'Dusky' | MOne |

| | |
|---|---|
| 'Dyke' | CTri CWil GAbr MOne NHol NMen SFgr WHal |
| ***dzhavachischvilii*** | MOne NMen |
| 'Edge of Night' | CWil NHol SRms |
| 'Eefje' | CWil |
| EKB 1727 | MOne |
| 'El Greco' | MOne |
| 'El Toro' | ECha MHom |
| 'Elene' | MOne |
| 'Elgar' | MOne SIng WIvy WPer |
| 'Elizabeth' | WPer |
| 'Elvis' | CWil GAbr NMen SFgr |
| 'Emerald Giant' | CWil MOne NHol SFgr SRms WPer WTin |
| 'Emerson's Giant' | CWil MOne NMen |
| 'Emma Jane' | MOne |
| 'Emmchen' | CWil |
| 'Engle's' | CMea CTca CTri EBee ECha GKev LRHS MHer MOne NMen SRms WHal WPer |
| 'Engle's 13-2' | MOne NBro NHol NMen |
| 'Engle's Rubrum' | CPBP EPot LBee NHol NMen |
| ***erythraeum*** | CMea MHom NHol NMen WFar WHal |
| - from Pirin, Bulgaria | MOne NMen SIng |
| - from Rila, Bulgaria | NMen |
| - 'Red Velvet' | MOne |
| 'Excalibur' | MOne NMen WIvy |
| 'Exhibita' | CWil MOne SDys SRms |
| 'Exorna' | CTca CWil ECha MHom MOne NMen SFgr SIng WEas WIvy WPer |
| 'Fabienne' | CWil |
| 'Fair Lady' | CWil MHom MOne NMen |
| 'Fairy' **new** | EPot |
| 'Fame' | MOne NHol |
| 'Fat Jack' | CWil MWat |
| x ***fauconnettii*** | CWil EDAr NHol NMen SFgr SIng |
| § - f. ***flavipilum*** | WFar |
| - 'Thompsonii' | CWil MOne NHol NMen SIng |
| 'Feldmaier' | MOne WFar |
| 'Festival' | MOne NMen |
| 'Feu de Printemps' | MOne |
| 'Fiery Furness' | MOne |
| 'Fiesta' | WHal |
| ***fimbriatum*** | see *S.* x *barbulatum* |
| 'Finerpointe' | MOne |
| 'Fire Glint' | CWil MOne NHol SIng SRms WIvy |
| 'Firebird' | MOne NMen SFgr |
| 'Firefly' | MOne |
| 'First Try' | MOne |
| 'Flaming Heart' | CTca CWil EDAr MBrN MOne NMen WGor WPer |
| 'Flamingo' | ECha MOne NMen |
| 'Flamme' | MOne |
| 'Flanders Passion' | CTca ECha EPot ITim LBee LRHS NMen SRms WPer |
| 'Flasher' | WPer |
| 'Flavipilum' | see *S.* x *fauconnettii* f. *flavipilum* |
| 'Fluweel' | MOne |
| 'Fontanae' | MOne |
| 'Forden' | CHEx MOne SFgr WGor |
| 'Ford's Amiability' | SDys |
| 'Ford's Shadows' | SDys |
| 'Ford's Spring' | CWil MOne NHol NMen WIvy WPer |
| 'Freckles' | MOne |
| 'Freeland' | WPer |
| 'Frigidum' | NDlv |
| 'Frolic' | MOne SIng |
| 'Fronika' | CWil |
| 'Frost and Flame' | NHol |
| 'Frosty' | CWil MOne SFgr SRms |
| 'Fuego' | CWil MHom MOne SFgr |

| | |
|---|---|
| x ***funckii*** | CHEx CTca CWil EDAr MBrN MOne NHol NMen SDys SIng WPer WTin |
| 'Furryness' | MOne |
| 'Fuzzy Wuzzy' | MOne |
| 'Gallivarda' | CWil |
| 'Gambol' | NHol |
| 'Gamma' | CHEx CWil LBee LRHS NHol NMen SDys SIng SRms WEas WTin |
| 'Garnet' | ECho WIvy WPer |
| 'Gay Jester' | CTca CTri CWil MOne SFgr WHoo WTin |
| 'Gazelle' | WIvy WPer |
| 'Genevione' | CWil |
| 'Georgette' | CWil ECha NMen WPer |
| 'Ginger' | MOne |
| 'Ginnie's Delight' | CWil NMen |
| 'Gipsy' | CWil MOne MWat |
| ***giuseppii*** | LBee MHer NHol NMen SIng WPer |
| - GDJ 93.04 from Cumbre de Cebolleda | CWil |
| - GDJ 93.17 from Coriscao, Spain | CWil |
| - from Peña Espigüete, Spain | CWil MOne NMen SDys |
| - from Peña Prieta, Spain | CWil MOne NMen |
| 'Gizmo' | CWil SFgr |
| 'Glaucum' | see *S. tectorum* var. *glaucum* |
| 'Gleam' | MOne |
| 'Gloriosum' ambig. | SFgr WPer |
| 'Glowing Embers' | CWil MHom MOne NMen WHal WPer |
| 'Godaert' | CTca |
| 'Goldie' | MOne |
| 'Gollum' | MOne |
| 'Granada' | NMen |
| 'Granat' | CWil MHer MOne NMen SRms WIvy WPer |
| 'Granby' | CWil ECho LBee MOne NMen SDys |
| ***grandiflorum*** | CWil NMen SIng WPer |
| - from Valpine | MOne NMen |
| - 'Fasciatum' | CWil MOne NMen |
| - 'Keston' | MOne |
| ***grandiflorum*** x ***montanum*** | see *S.* x *christii* |
| ***grandiflorum*** x ***tectorum*** | see *S.* x *hayekii* |
| 'Grannie's Favourite' | MOne |
| 'Grape Idol' | CWil |
| 'Grapetone' | MHom NMen SDys WHal |
| 'Graupurpur' | CWil |
| 'Gray Dawn' | MHom |
| 'Green Apple' | CWil GAbr MHom NMen SDys |
| 'Green Gables' | WPer |
| 'Green Giant' | MTPN |
| 'Green Ice' **new** | CWil |
| 'Greenwich Time' | NMen |
| * ***greigii*** | GKir |
| 'Grenadier' | MOne |
| 'Grey Ghost' | NMen WIvy WPer |
| 'Grey Green' | CWil NHol |
| 'Grey Lady' | CMea CWil |
| 'Grey Owl' | CTca GMaP LRHS |
| 'Grey Velvet' | CWil |
| 'Greyfriars' | CMea CTca EPot EWll LBee LRHS NMen SFgr WGor WPer |
| 'Greyolla' | CWil WPer |
| 'Gruaud Larose' | NHol |
| 'Grünrand' | MOne |
| 'Grünschnabel' | MOne |
| 'Grünspecht' | MOne |
| x ***guiseppe*** | WRos |
| 'Gulle Dame' | CTca CWil SFgr |

| | | |
|---|---|---|
| | 'Halemaumau' | CWil MOne |
| I | 'Hall's Hybrid' | CTca CWil GAbr NBro SRms STre |
| | 'Hall's Seedling' | GKir |
| | 'Happy' | CWil MOne NMen SFgr SRms WGor WIvy WPer WThu |
| | 'Hart' | CTca CWil NHol SRms WTin |
| | 'Hartside' | MOne |
| * | 'Haubyi' | CTca |
| | 'Haullauer's Seedling' | MOne |
| | 'Havana' | NMen |
| § | x ***hayekii*** | MOne |
| | 'Hayling' | EDAr LRHS MOne NHol NMen SIng SRms WPer |
| | 'Heavenly Joy' | NHol |
| | 'Heigham Red' | CTca CWil LBee LRHS MOne NHol NMen WPer |
| | 'Heliotroop' | MOne SDys SRot |
| | ***helveticum*** | see *S. montanum* |
| | 'Hester' | CHEx CTca CWil ECho GAbr MBrN MWat NBro NMen SIng SRms WFar |
| | 'Hey-hey' | CTca EPot LBee LRHS MBrN NMen SPlb SRms WPer |
| | 'Hidde' | CWil SFgr WIvy WPer |
| | 'Hidde's Roosje' | MOne NMen |
| | 'Hirsutum' | see *Jovibarba allionii* |
| | ***hirtum*** | see *Jovibarba hirta* |
| | 'Hispidulum' | MOne |
| | 'Hookeri' | see *S.* x *barbulatum* 'Hookeri' |
| | 'Hopi' | CWil MOne NHol SRms |
| | 'Hortulanus Smit' | NMen |
| | 'Hugo' **new** | SIng |
| | 'Hullabaloo' | MOne |
| | 'Hurricane' | CWil MOne WIvy WPer |
| | 'Icicle' | CHEx CMea CTca LRHS NBro NHol NMen SIng SRms WAbe WGor |
| | ***imbricatum*** | see *S.* x *barbulatum* |
| | 'Imperial' | CWil MHom |
| | 'Infinity' | CTca |
| | ***ingwersenii*** | MHom MOne SIng |
| | ***ingwersenii*** x ***pumilum*** | CWil |
| | ***ingwersenii*** x ***pumilum*** from Spain | MOne NMen |
| | 'Interlace' | MOne |
| | 'Iophon' | LBee MOne |
| | 'Irazu' | CWil GAbr MOne NMen SDys SFgr SRms WPer |
| | 'Isaac Dyson' | SDys SRot |
| | ***italicum*** | MHom NMen |
| | 'Itchen' | MOne NMen |
| | 'Iwo' | CHEx NMen SFgr WIvy |
| | 'Jack Frost' | CWil MOne NBro NMen SFgr |
| | 'Jacquette' | CWil |
| | 'Jade' ambig. | MOne |
| | 'Jamie's Pride' | WGor |
| | 'Jane' | MOne |
| | 'Jelly Bean' | CWil MOne MWat NMen SFgr |
| | 'Jet Stream' | CWil EPPr NMen SDys WGor |
| | 'Jewel Case' | CWil LRHS MOne NMen SRms |
| | 'John T.' | MOne WEas |
| | 'Jolly Green Giant' | MHom MOne |
| | 'Jo's Spark' | NSla |
| | 'Jubilee' | CMea CTca CWil ECho EDAr ELan EPot GKev MHer NHol NMen SRms STre WGor WPer |
| | 'Jubilee Tricolor' | NHol NMen SFgr WAbe |
| | 'Jungle Fires' | CTca CWil EPot ITim NHol SDys SRms WHoo |
| | 'Jungle Shadows' | EDAr MWat |
| | 'Jurato' | NHol |
| | 'Justine's Choice' | CWil SRms |
| | 'Kalinda' | MHom NMen |
| | 'Kansas Gorge' | CTca |
| | 'Kappa' | CTri MOne NBro NHol NMen SDys SRot WPer |
| | 'Katmai' | CWil NHol |
| | 'Kelly Jo' | CWil EBee EWll ITim NBro NMen WFar WTin |
| | 'Kelut' | MOne |
| | 'Kermit' | MHom NMen |
| | 'Kerneri' | NHol |
| | 'Kibo' | MOne WIvy |
| | 'Kimble' | WPer |
| | ***kindingeri*** | CWil MHom NMen NWCA |
| | 'King George' | CHal CTri CWil ECha GKev GKir ITim LBee LRHS MOne NMen SFgr SRms STre WGor WHal WHoo WPer WTin |
| | 'Kip' | CMea ECha NMen SIng WGor WIvy WPer |
| | 'Kismet' | MWat NMen |
| | 'Koko Flanel' | CWil SFgr |
| | 'Kolagas Mayfair' | MOne |
| | 'Korspel Glory 4' | CWil |
| | 'Korspelsegietje' | CWil GAbr |
| | ***kosaninii*** | MOne NHol NMen SFgr SIng WPer WTin |
| | - from Koprivnik, Slovenia | MOne NMen SDys WAbe |
| * | - from Visitor | CWil MOne |
| | - 'Hepworth' | NHol |
| | 'Krakeling' | MOne |
| | 'Kramer's Purpur' | NMen |
| | 'Kramer's Spinrad' | CHEx CMea CTca CWil ECha GAbr LBee LEdu LRHS MOne NMen NWCA SDys SFgr SIng STre WEas WHoo WIvy WTin |
| | 'La Serenissima' | MOne |
| | 'Lady Kelly' | CMea MOne NMen WIvy |
| | 'Launcelot' | ECha WPer |
| | 'Lavender and Old Lace' | CHEx CWil GAbr LRHS NMen SFgr WPer |
| | 'Laysan' | CWil NHol |
| | Le Clair's hybrid No 4 | NMen |
| | 'Lennik's Glory' | see *S.* 'Crispyn' |
| | 'Leocadia's Nephew' | MOne NMen |
| | 'Leocadia's Niece' | MOne |
| | 'Leon Smits' | CWil |
| | 'Les Yielding' | MOne |
| | 'Lilac Time' | CWil GAbr LRHS MHer MOne MWat NMen SFgr SRms WHal WIvy WPer |
| | 'Limbo' | CWil |
| | 'Linaria' | MTPN |
| | 'Lion King' **new** | CWil |
| | 'Lipari' | ECha EPot NMen SRms |
| | 'Lipstick' | NMen |
| | 'Lively Bug' | CWil LBee LRHS SDys SIng WGor WPer |
| | 'Lloyd Praeger' | see *S. montanum* subsp. *stiriacum* 'Lloyd Praeger' |
| | 'Lonzo' | CWil SRms |
| | 'Lustrous' | MOne |
| | 'Lynn's Choice' | CWil GAbr MOne SFgr WHal WIvy WPer |
| | ***macedonicum*** | EDAr NDlv NMen WTin |
| | - from Ljuboten, Macedonia/Kosovo | CWil MOne NMen |
| | 'Madeleine' | CWil |
| | 'Magic Spell' | CWil MOne NMen |
| | 'Magical' | CWil |
| | 'Magnificum' | CWil NMen WGor |
| | 'Mahogany' | CHEx CTca CTri CWil ECho EDAr LBee LRHS MHer MOne NHol NMen NWCA SFgr SRms SWal WEas WGor WHal WIvy |
| | 'Maigret' | CWil WPer |

| | | |
|---|---|---|
| | 'Majestic' | CWil LBee NMen |
| | 'Major White' | CHEx |
| | 'Malby's Hybrid' | see *S.* 'Reginald Malby' |
| | 'Marella' | WPer |
| | 'Maria Laach' | CWil MWat |
| | 'Marijntje' | CWil MWat NHol NMen WPer |
| | 'Marjorie Newton' | CWil WPer |
| § | ***marmoreum*** | CTca ECho EPot GKev LBee LRHS NMen SRms STre WHal WPer |
| | - from Kanzan Gorge, Bulgaria | EPot MOne NHol NMen SIng |
| | - from Monte Tirone, Italy | SDys |
| | - from Okol, Albania | MOne NMen |
| | - var. ***angustissimum*** | CTca |
| | - 'Brunneifolium' | CWil EGoo GAbr LBee LRHS MOne NHol NMen SIng WIvy WPer |
| | - subsp. ***marmoreum*** var. ***dinaricum*** | MHer NMen |
| | 'Marshall' | MWat |
| | 'Matador' | MOne |
| | 'Mate' | NMen |
| | 'Maubi' | CHEx |
| | 'Mauna Kea' | WPer |
| | 'Mauvine' | MOne NHol |
| | 'Mayfair Imp' | MOne |
| | 'Medallion' | MOne SFgr |
| | 'Meisse' | ECho MOne |
| | 'Melanie' | CWil MBrN NMen WIvy |
| | 'Mercury' | CTca CWil GAbr LRHS NBro NHol NMen SRms |
| | 'Merkur' | MOne |
| | 'Merlin' | MWat |
| | 'Midas' | CTca CWil ECha SFgr |
| | 'Milá' | CWil |
| | 'Minaret' | MOne |
| | 'Mini Frost' | CWil NMen SIng WPer |
| | 'Missouri Rose' | NHol |
| | 'Mixed Spice' | CWil |
| | 'Moerkerk's Merit' | CWil NHol NMen |
| | 'Monases' | MWat |
| | 'Mondstein' | CWil GMaP MOne SFgr SRms WIvy WPer |
| | 'Monique' **new** | WPer |
| | 'Montage' | CWil |
| § | ***montanum*** | LEdu LRHS NMen WPer |
| | - from Arbizion | CWil MOne |
| | - from Monte Tirone **new** | LBee |
| | - from Monte Tonale, Italy | CWil |
| | - from Windachtal, Germany | CWil NMen |
| § | - subsp. ***burnatii*** | CWil MHom MOne MWat NMen WIvy |
| | - subsp. ***carpaticum*** | CWil |
| | - - 'Cmiral's Yellow' | CSec EPot NMen SFgr WAbe WIvy |
| * | - Fragell form | SFgr |
| | - subsp. ***montanum*** | CWil |
| | - 'Rubrum' | see *S.* 'Red Mountain' |
| | - subsp. ***stiriacum*** | CTca CWil MOne NMen SFgr SIng |
| § | - - 'Lloyd Praeger' | CWil LBee LRHS MOne NMen SDys SFgr WIvy WPer |
| | ***montanum*** x ***tectorum*** var. ***boutignyanum*** GDJ 94.15 | CWil |
| | 'Moondrops' | CWil |
| | 'More Honey' | CWil NMen SFgr SRms |
| | 'Morning Glow' | CMea WGor WHal WPer |
| | 'Mount Hood' | LRHS MWat SRms WHal |
| | 'Mrs Elliott' | MOne |
| | 'Mulberry Wine' | CWil LBee LRHS MWat NHol |
| | 'Mystic' | CWil MBrN MWat NMen WPer |
| | 'Neon' | CWil |
| | 'Neptune' | MWat |
| | ***nevadense*** | CWil EPot MOne NMen SFgr SRms |

| | | |
|---|---|---|
| | - GDJ 96A-07 from Calar de Santa Barbara, Spain | CWil |
| | - from Puerto de San Francisco | CWil MOne |
| | - var. ***hirtellum*** | CWil NMen SIng |
| | 'Nico' | CWil MWat SRms |
| | 'Night Raven' | CMea WIvy WPer |
| | 'Nigrum' | see *S. tectorum* 'Nigrum' |
| | 'Niobe' | MOne SFgr WHal |
| | 'Noir' | CWil EDAr NBPN NBro NMen WAbe WRos |
| | 'Norbert' | CWil EDAr SRms WIvy WPer |
| | 'Norne' | MOne |
| | 'Nörtofts Beauty' | MOne |
| | 'Nouveau Pastel' | CMea CWil MOne NMen WHal WPer |
| | 'Novak' | CWil |
| | 'Octet' | CWil MOne NMen SIng |
| | ***octopodes*** | EDAr NBir SIde |
| | - var. ***apetalum*** | CWil GAbr MOne NMen SIng SRms WIvy WOut |
| | 'Oddity' | CPBP CTca CWil ECha MBrN MHer NMen WCot WHal WPer |
| | 'Ohio Burgundy' | ECha LRHS MOne NDlv NMen WPer WTin |
| | 'Old Rose' | MOne |
| | 'Olivette' | ECha NMen WPer WTin |
| | 'Omega' | MOne WPer |
| | 'Ornatum' | EPot MHer MHom MOne NMen SRms WAbe WEas WHal WIvy WPer |
| | ***ossetiense*** | CWil GAbr GKev MOne NMen |
| | 'Othello' | CHEx CHal CTca CTri EBee EPfP GCra GKev NBPN NBir STre WCot WPer WTin |
| | 'Pacific Blue Ice' | SIng |
| | 'Pacific Feather Power' | NMen |
| | 'Pacific Purple Shadows' | CWil |
| | 'Packardian' | CWil GKev MOne NHol NMen SFgr WIvy |
| | 'Painted Lady' | CWil |
| | 'Palissander' | EDAr GAbr GKev MOne NMen SFgr WPer |
| | 'Pam Wain' | MHom NMen |
| | 'Panola Fire' | WFar |
| | 'Parade' | MOne |
| | 'Paricutin' | SDys |
| | 'Passionata' | CWil SFgr |
| | 'Pastel' | CTca CWil NMen SIng |
| | ***patens*** | see *Jovibarba heuffelii* |
| | 'Patrician' | CWil LBee LRHS SRms |
| | 'Peggy' | CTca CWil WGor |
| | 'Pekinese' | CTca CWil EDAr EPot GKev ITim LBee LRHS MSte NBro NHol NMen SIng SRms WCot WEas WGor WPer |
| | 'Penny Jo' | CTca |
| | 'Peterson's Ornatum' | MOne SDys |
| | 'Petsy' | CWil SRms |
| | 'Pilatus' | ECha EWes GKev LBMP SRms WFar WPer |
| | x ***piliferum*** 'Hausmannii' | MOne |
| | 'Pink Astrid' | CWil |
| | 'Pink Button' **new** | CWil |
| | 'Pink Cloud' | CWil MWat NMen SRms |
| | 'Pink Dawn' | MOne |
| | 'Pink Delight' | MOne |
| | 'Pink Flamingoes' | MOne SRot |
| | 'Pink Lemonade' | CWil MHom |
| | 'Pink Mist' | WPer |
| | 'Pink Puff' | CWil MHom MOne NMen SRms |
| | 'Pink Stirling' | CTca |
| | 'Pippin' | CMea CWil SRms WPer |
| | 'Piran' | CWil MOne |

| | | |
|---|---|---|
| | ***pittonii*** | CHal CMea CWil EPot GAbr NMen WHal |
| | 'Pixie' | CWil GKev MOne NDlv NMen SFgr WIvy WPer |
| | 'Plum Frosting' | WGor |
| | 'Plum Mist' | NHol |
| | 'Plumb Rose' | CWil MOne NMen WIvy WPer |
| | 'Pluto' | CWil LBee NHol |
| | 'Polaris' | CWil MHom |
| | 'Poldark' | MOne |
| | 'Pompeon' | MOne |
| | 'Ponderosa' | CWil |
| | 'Pottsii' | CWil MOne |
| I | 'Powellii' | MOne SIng |
| | 'Procton' | MOne |
| | 'Proud Zelda' | GAbr MOne NMen |
| | 'Průhonice' | CWil MOne SRms WFar |
| | 'Pseudo-ornatum' | LBee LRHS SRms |
| | 'Pumaros' | NMen SDys |
| | ***pumilum*** | CWil LRHS MBar NMen |
| | - from Adyl-Su, Chechnya, Russia, No 1 | CWil |
| | - from Armkhi | SDys |
| | - from El'brus, Russia, No 1 | CWil |
| | - from Techensis | CWil NMen |
| | - 'Sopa' | CWil MOne NMen |
| | 'Purdy' | MHom WAbe |
| | 'Purdy's 50-6' | CWil GAbr |
| | 'Purdy's 70-40' | MOne |
| | 'Purple Beauty' | EDAr EPot MOne |
| | 'Purple King' | MHom SDys |
| | 'Purple Queen' | CWil EDAr SIng |
| | 'Pygmalion' | CWil SIng |
| | 'Queen Amalia' | see *S. reginae-amaliae* |
| | 'Quintessence' | CWil NHol SFgr SRms |
| | 'Racey' | CWil |
| | 'Ragtime' | MOne MWat |
| | 'Ramses' | MOne MWat SDys |
| | 'Raspberry Ice' | CMea ITim LBee NBro NHol NMen WPer |
| | 'Rauer Kulm' | CWil |
| * | 'Rauheit' | MOne WFar |
| | 'Rauhreif' | WFar |
| | 'Red Ace' | CWil ECha GAbr MWat NBro NMen SFgr SRms WFar WPer |
| | 'Red Beam' | CWil MOne |
| | 'Red Birch' **new** | SIng |
| | 'Red Chips' | MHom |
| | 'Red Cross' | MOne |
| | 'Red Delta' | CWil MOne NBir NMen SFgr WCot |
| | 'Red Devil' | CWil EBee ECha MOne NHol NMen SFgr WHoo WPer WTin |
| | 'Red King' | MOne |
| | 'Red Lion' | CWil SFgr |
| | 'Red Lynn' | CWil |
| § | 'Red Mountain' | CHal CWil LBee LRHS MOne SRms |
| | 'Red Pink' | CWil MOne |
| | 'Red Robin' | GMaP LRHS MOne SIng |
| | 'Red Rum' | MWat WPer |
| | 'Red Shadows' | LBee WPer WTin |
| | 'Red Spider' | CWil MHom NBro NMen |
| | 'Red Summer' | MOne |
| | 'Regal' | MOne NMen |
| | 'Regina' | NMen |
| | ***reginae*** | see *S. reginae-amaliae* |
| § | ***reginae-amaliae*** | CWil EPot NHol NMen |
| | - from Kambeecho, Greece, No 2 | NMen SDys |
| | - from Mavri Petri | CWil MOne SDys |
| | - from Sarpun, Turkey | CWil NMen SDys WTin |
| | - from Vardusa, Serbia | CWil SDys |
| § | 'Reginald Malby' | CTri ECho GMaP LRHS NMen SFgr SRms WIvy |
| | 'Reinhardt' | CMea CTca CWil ECha EDAr EPot LRHS MBrN MHer MOne NMen SIng SRms WCot WFar WHal WHoo WIvy WPer |
| | 'Remus' | CWil ECha MOne NMen SDys SFgr SRms WGor |
| | 'Rex' | MWat NMen |
| | 'Rhône' | CWil LBee MOne |
| * | ***richardii*** | MBar |
| | 'Risque' | CWil LBee WPer |
| | 'Rita Jane' | CTca CWil ECha MHom MOne NMen SFgr WTin |
| | 'Robin' | ITim LBee LRHS NBro NHol SRms WTin |
| | 'Ronny' | CWil |
| | 'Rose Splendour' | NHol |
| | x ***roseum*** | MOne |
| | - 'Fimbriatum' | CWil GAbr LBee LRHS NDlv NHol SFgr WEas |
| | 'Rosie' | CMea CPBP CTca CWil EPot GAbr ITim LBee LRHS MOne NHol NMen SIng SRms WHal WHoo WPer WTin |
| | 'Rotkopf' | CTca CWil MOne NHol NMen SFgr SRms |
| | 'Rotmantel' | SDys WTin |
| | 'Rotsandsteinriese' | MOne SIng |
| | 'Rotund' | CWil |
| | 'Rouge' | NMen |
| | 'Royal Mail' | MOne |
| | 'Royal Opera' | CWil EDAr MOne NMen |
| | 'Royal Ruby' | CTca ECha LBee LRHS NMen SRms WIvy |
| | 'Rubellum' | CWil MOne |
| | 'Rubellum Mahogany' | SFgr |
| | 'Rubikon Improved' | MOne |
| | 'Rubin' | CMea CTri ECha EGoo EPPr EPfP GGar MSte MWat NBir NBlu NMen NWCA SGar SPoG SRms WAbe WEas WPer |
| I | 'Rubra Ash' | CWil MOne NMen WAbe WTin |
| | 'Rubrum Ray' | CWil MOne SRms |
| * | 'Ruby Glow' | EDAr |
| | 'Russian River' | WHoo WTin |
| | 'Rusty' | CWil SFgr |
| | ***ruthenicum*** | EDAr LRHS MHom |
| | - 'Regis-Fernandii' | ECho |
| | 'Safara' | CWil |
| | 'Saffron' | MOne NMen |
| | 'Saga' | MHom MOne |
| | 'Sanford's Hybrid' | MOne |
| | 'Sarah' | MOne NMen |
| | 'Sarotte' | CWil |
| | 'Sassy Frass' | CTca NMen |
| | 'Saturn' | MOne MWat NMen |
| | ***schlehanii*** | see *S. marmoreum* |
| | ***schnittspahnii*** | MOne |
| | x ***schottii*** | MOne |
| | 'Seminole' | CWil MOne |
| | 'Serena' | MOne |
| | 'Sha-Na' | CWil |
| | 'Sharon's Pencil' | CWil |
| | 'Sheila' | GAbr |
| | 'Shirley Moore' | CWil MOne SFgr WTin |
| | 'Shirley's Joy' | CHal NMen WTin |
| | 'Sideshow' | CWil MOne |
| | 'Sigma' | MOne |
| | 'Silbering' | EBee |
| | 'Silberkarneol' misapplied | see *S.* 'Silver Jubilee' |
| | 'Silberspitz' | CTca CWil MHer MHom NBro NMen WOut WPer |
| | 'Silver Cup' | CWil SFgr WIvy |
| § | 'Silver Jubilee' | CMea CTca CWil ECha EDAr GAbr MWat NBro NDlv SPlb SRms WGor |

| | | |
|---|---|---|
| | 'Silver Queen' | CWil SFgr |
| | 'Silver Shadow' | CTca WGor |
| | 'Silver Thaw' | CWil ECha EDAr NMen SFgr SIng |
| | 'Silverine' | CWil |
| | 'Silvertone' | CWil |
| | 'Simonkaianum' | see *Jovibarba hirta* |
| | 'Sioux' | CPBP CTca CWil GAbr LBee LRHS MBrN NMen SIng WFar WHal WIvy WPer WTin |
| | 'Skrocki's Bronze' | GAbr WPer |
| | 'Slabber's Seedling' | CTca CWil |
| | 'Small Wonder' | CWil |
| | 'Smaragd' | CWil ECha LBee WFar |
| | 'Smokey Jet' | SFgr |
| | 'Snowberger' | CMea CTca CWil EPot LRHS MOne NMen SFgr SRms WGor WHal WPer |
| | 'Soarte' | MOne |
| | ***soboliferum*** | see *Jovibarba sobolifera* |
| | 'Soothsayer' | CTca CWil MOne NMen |
| | ***sosnowskyi*** | CWil MOne NMen |
| | 'Spanish Dancer' | NMen |
| | 'Sparkler' | CTca |
| | 'Speciosum' | MOne |
| | 'Spherette' | CTca CWil MBrN NMen WAbe WPer |
| | 'Spice' | MOne |
| | 'Spider's Lair' | SIng |
| | 'Spinellii' | MOne WThu WTin |
| | 'Spiver's Velvet' | MOne |
| | 'Sponnier' | MOne |
| | 'Springmist' | CMea CTca CWil EPot GAbr GMaP MBrN MOne SFgr SRms WGor WPer WRos WTin |
| | 'Sprite' | CWil MOne NMen SDys WIvy WTin |
| | 'Squib' **new** | CWil |
| | ***stansfieldii*** | see *S. arachnoideum* subsp. *tomentosum* 'Stansfieldii' |
| | 'Starion' | CWil MOne |
| | 'Starshine' | MHer NHol NMen SFgr |
| | 'State Fair' | CTca CWil MWat NHol NMen SIng WIvy WPer |
| | 'Strawberry Fields' | MOne MWat |
| | 'Strider' | CWil GAbr WTin |
| | 'Stuffed Olive' | CWil MOne MWat SDys SRot |
| I | 'Subanum' | MOne |
| | 'Sun Waves' | CWil MOne NHol SDys SFgr |
| | 'Sunray Magic' | CTca WGor |
| | 'Sunrise' | MOne |
| | 'Super Dome' | CWil |
| | 'Supernova' | MOne |
| | 'Syston Flame' | CWil NMen |
| | 'Tambimuttu' | MOne |
| | 'Tarantula' | CTca |
| | 'Tarita' | CWil |
| | 'Tarn Hows' | MOne |
| § | ***tectorum*** ♀H4 | CArn CHby CSam CTri CWil ECho EDAr ELan EPfP GKev GKir GPoy LBee LRHS MBar MHer MNHC NBlu NMen SIde SPlb STre WFar WJek |
| | - from Eporn | CWil MOne NMen |
| § | - var. ***alpinum*** | CWil LRHS MHom MOne NBro NHol NMen |
| | - - from Sierra del Cadi, Spain | MOne NHol |
| | - var. ***andreanum*** | CWil |
| | - 'Atropurpureum' | ECho ELan NHol NMen WTin |
| | - 'Atrorubens' | NHol |
| | - 'Atroviolaceum' | EDAr NHol NLar NMen WFar WIvy WTin |
| * | - 'Aureum' | SFgr |
| | - var. ***boutignyanum*** GDJ 94.02 from Sant Joan de Caselles, Andorra | CWil |
| | - - GDJ 94.03 from Sant Joan de Caselles, Andorra | CWil |
| | - - GDJ 94.04 from Route de Tuixén, Spain | CWil |
| | - var. ***calcareum*** | ECho MOne |
| | - subsp. ***cantalicum*** | SRms |
| § | - var. ***glaucum*** | MOne NDlv |
| § | - 'Nigrum' | LBee LRHS MHer MOne NBro NHol NMen SDys SRms WGor WTin |
| | - 'Red Flush' | CTca CWil EDAr GKir MBrN NMen SDys SFgr SPoG WFar WPer |
| | - 'Royanum' | GAbr |
| * | - subsp. ***sanguineum*** | EDAr |
| | - 'Sunset' | CMea EDAr NMen SDys SFgr SIng WHal |
| | - subsp. ***tectorum*** | CTca MOne |
| § | - - 'Boissieri' | CWil NMen SRms WIvy |
| | - - 'Triste' | CHEx CWil LBee LRHS MOne NMen SRms WAbe WFar |
| | - 'Violaceum' | MHom SIng SRms STre WGor |
| | ***tectorum* x *zeleborii*** | WTin |
| | 'Tederheid' | LBMP MOne |
| | 'Telfan' | MOne NMen |
| | 'Tenburg' | CTca MOne |
| | 'Terracotta Baby' | CTca CWil SFgr SIng |
| | 'Thayne' | NMen |
| | 'The Platters' | CWil |
| | 'The Rocket' | CWil |
| | x ***thompsonianum*** | CWil NHol NMen SFgr |
| | 'Thunder' | CWil |
| | 'Tiffany' | NHol WPer |
| | 'Tiger Bay' | NHol |
| | 'Tina' | WPer |
| | 'Tip Top' | CTca CWil SFgr |
| | 'Titania' | CWil MWat NBro NMen WHal WTin |
| | 'Tombago' | MOne |
| | 'Topaz' | CWil ECha LBee LRHS MOne NMen SFgr SRms |
| | 'Tordeur's Memory' | CWil LBee LRHS MOne NMen |
| | 'Toy Enamel' | CTca |
| | 'Trail Walker' | CWil LBee LRHS MOne SRms |
| | ***transcaucasicum*** | CWil |
| | 'Tree Beard' | CWil |
| | 'Tristesse' | CWil EDAr GAbr MOne NMen SFgr WGor |
| | 'Truva' | CWil MOne NMen SFgr SIng |
| | 'Tumpty' | WGor |
| | 'Twilight Blues' | CWil SFgr |
| | 'Undine' | CWil SFgr |
| | x ***vaccarii*** | CWil NMen |
| | 'Vanbaelen' | CWil GAbr NMen SDys |
| | 'Vanessa' | CWil |
| | x ***versicolor*** | NHol |
| | 'Veuchelen' | CWil MOne |
| | ***vicentei*** | CTca MHom NMen WFar WTin |
| | - from Gaton | LBee LRHS MOne NMen WFar |
| § | - subsp. ***paui*** | NSla |
| | 'Victorian' | MOne |
| | 'Video' | CWil MHom MWat NMen SFgr |
| | 'Virgil' | CTca CWil GAbr MBrN NMen SDys SIng WAbe WCot WGor WPer WRos WTin |
| I | 'Virginius' | CWil GAbr |
| | 'Warners Pink' | MDKP |
| | 'Watermelon Rind' | MOne MWat |
| | ***webbianum*** | see *S. arachnoideum* L. subsp. *tomentosum* (C.B. Lehm. & Schnittsp.) Schinz & Thell. |
| | 'Webby Flame' | CWil |
| | 'Webby Ola' | NMen |
| | 'Wega' | NMen |
| | 'Weirdo' | CTca CWil |

| | | |
|---|---|---|
| | 'Wendy' | MOne MWat NMen |
| | 'Westerlin' | CWil ECha MOne NMen SIng |
| | 'White Christmas' | see *S. arachnoideum* 'White Christmas' |
| | 'White Eyes' | NMen |
| | 'Whitening' | GAbr NMen |
| I | 'Woolcott's Variety' | CTca CWil EBee ECho LRHS MDKP MOne NBir NMen SFgr WFar WPer WTin |
| | ***wulfenii*** | CWil NMen |
| * | **- *roseum*** | EDAr |
| | 'Xaviera' | CWil |
| | ***zeleborii*** | CHal SDys WHal |
| | 'Zenith' | CWil GAbr SFgr SRms |
| | 'Zenobia' | MHom |
| | 'Zenocrate' | WHal |
| | 'Zepherin' | CWil |
| | 'Zilver Moon' | CWil NMen |
| | 'Zircon' | NMen |
| | 'Zone' | CHEx NMen |
| | 'Zorba' | NMen |
| | 'Zulu' | ECha SFgr |

## *Senecio* (*Asteraceae*)

| | | |
|---|---|---|
| | B&SWJ 9115 from Guatemala | WCru |
| | B&SWJ 10361 from Guatemala | WCru |
| | B&SWJ 10703 from Colombia | WCru |
| § | ***articulatus*** | CHal EShb SGar |
| | ***aureus*** | see *Packera aurea* |
| | ***bicolor*** subsp. ***cineraria*** | see *S. cineraria* |
| | ***bidwillii*** | see *Brachyglottis bidwillii* |
| | ***buchananii*** | see *Brachyglottis buchananii* |
| | ***candicans*** | see *S. cineraria* |
| | ***cannabifolius*** | CSec |
| | ***chrysanthemoides*** | see *Euryops chrysanthemoides* |
| | ***chrysocoma*** | CSec |
| § | ***cineraria*** | NBlu |
| | - 'Ramparts' | EBee |
| | - 'Silver Dust' 𝕐$^{H3}$ | EPfP LRHS SBch |
| | - 'White Diamond' | ECha |
| * | ***coccinilifera*** | SBch |
| | ***compactus*** | see *Brachyglottis compacta* |
| | ***crassissimus*** | EShb |
| | ***doria*** | LRHS WCot WFar WHrl |
| | ***doronicum*** | EBee |
| | ***elegans*** | CSec |
| | ***fistulosus*** | LEdu |
| | ***formosoides*** B&SWJ 10736 new | WCru |
| | ***formosus*** B&SWJ 10700 | WCru |
| | - B&SWJ 10746 new | WCru |
| | 'Goldplate' | NLar |
| | 'Gregynog Gold' | see *Ligularia* 'Gregynog Gold' |
| | ***greyi*** misapplied | see *Brachyglottis* (Dunedin Group) 'Sunshine' |
| | ***greyi*** Hook. | see *Brachyglottis greyi* (Hook. f.) B. Nord. |
| | ***heritieri*** DC. | see *Pericallis lanata* (L'Hér.) B. Nord. |
| | ***hoffmannii*** | EShb |
| | ***kleiniiformis*** | EShb |
| | ***laxifolius*** hort. | see *Brachyglottis* (Dunedin Group) 'Sunshine' |
| | ***leucophyllus*** | WAbe |
| | ***leucostachys*** | see *S. viravira* |
| | ***macroglossus*** | CHll EShb |
| | - 'Variegatus' (v) 𝕐$^{H1}$ | CHal EShb |
| | ***maritimus*** | see *S. cineraria* |
| | ***monroi*** | see *Brachyglottis monroi* |
| | ***niveoaureus*** B&SWJ 714 | WCru |
| | ***petasitis*** | CHEx |
| | ***polyodon*** | CCCN CSpe EBla EShb GBin GBri ILad MAvo MNrw MWea NCGa NDov NLar SPhx WMoo WPGP |
| | - S&SH 29 | CFir EBee SAga |
| | - subsp. ***subglaber*** | EBee EMon EWes |
| | ***przewalskii*** | see *Ligularia przewalskii* |
| | ***pulcher*** | CDTJ CDes CGHE CSam EBee GBri LEdu LSou MNrw MTho SHar SMrm SUsu WCot WPGP |
| | ***reinholdii*** | see *Brachyglottis rotundifolia* |
| | ***rowleyanus*** | EBak EShb |
| | ***scandens*** | CBre CCCN CMac CPLG EShb MNrw WPGP |
| | ***scaposus*** | WCot |
| | ***seminiveus*** | EBee |
| § | ***serpens*** | CHal CStu EShb SEND |
| § | ***smithii*** | CHid CRow ELan LLWG NBid WCot WCru WFar |
| | ***spedenii*** | see *Brachyglottis spedenii* |
| | ***squalidus*** | WHer |
| | 'Sunshine' | see *Brachyglottis* (Dunedin Group) 'Sunshine' |
| | ***talinoides*** subsp. ***cylindricus*** 'Himalaya' | EShb |
| | ***tanguticus*** | see *Sinacalia tangutica* |
| § | ***viravira*** 𝕐$^{H3-4}$ | CWan EBee EGoo EPfP ERas EShb MCot SMad SMrm SPer WEas WSHC |

## *Senna* (*Caesalpiniaceae*)

| | | |
|---|---|---|
| | ***alata*** B&SWJ 9772 | WCru |
| | ***alexandrina*** | CCCN EBee EShb SKHP WPGP |
| | ***artemisioides*** 𝕐$^{H1}$ | SOWG |
| § | ***corymbosa*** | CBcs CCCN CHEx CRHN CSec CSpe CTri LRHS SOWG |
| | ***didymobotrya*** | SOWG |
| | x ***floribunda*** | EMil |
| § | ***marilandica*** | CArn EBee ELan EWes WCot WHil |
| § | ***obtusifolia*** | EBee MSal |
| | ***retusa*** | CHEx |
| | ***septemtrionalis*** | CCCN EBee WPGP |
| | ***spectabilis*** | CSec |

## *Sequoia* (*Cupressaceae*)

| | | |
|---|---|---|
| | ***sempervirens*** 𝕐$^{H4}$ | CBcs CDoC CDul CLnd CMCN CMen CTho CTrG ECrN EHul EPfP ERom ISea LMaj MBar MLan MMuc SBLw SPoG WDin WMou |
| | - 'Adpressa' | CDoC CDul CMac CRob CSli CTho EHul EOrn EPla IDee MAsh MBar MGos NHol NWea SCoo SLim WFar |
| | - 'Cantab' | CDul SLim |
| | - 'Prostrata' | CDoC CSli EMil EOrn LRHS MAsh MMuc SLim WFar |

## *Sequoiadendron* (*Cupressaceae*)

| | | |
|---|---|---|
| | ***giganteum*** 𝕐$^{H4}$ | Widely available |
| | - 'Bajojeka' | NLar |
| | - 'Barabits Requiem' | GKir IDee LRHS MBlu NLar SLim SMad |
| | - 'Blauer Eichzwerg' | NLar SLim |
| | - 'Blue Iceberg' | CKen |
| | - 'Bultinck Yellow' | NLar SMad |
| | - 'Conrad Appel' | NLar |
| | - 'French Beauty' | NLar |
| | - 'Glaucum' | CDoC CTho EMil LPan LRHS MAsh MBlu MBri NLar SLim SMad SPoG |
| | - 'Greenpeace' | MBlu NLar |
| | - 'Hazel Smith' | IArd IDee SMad |
| | - 'Little Stan' | CKen NLar |
| | - 'Pendulum' | CDoC CKen EMil ERod GKir LPan MBlu MGos NLar SLim SMad SWvt |
| | - 'Peve Bonsai' | NLar |

| | |
|---|---|
| - 'Philip Curtis' | NLar |
| - 'Powdered Blue' | NLar |
| - 'Type Wittbold Muller' | NLar |
| - 'Variegatum' (v) | GKir MAsh MGos |
| - 'Von Martin' | NLar |

## *Serapias* (*Orchidaceae*)

| | |
|---|---|
| ***lingua*** | SCnR |
| ***parviflora*** | WHer |

## *Serenoa* (*Arecaceae*)

| | |
|---|---|
| ***repens*** | CBrP EAmu LPal |

## *Seriphidium* (*Asteraceae*)

| | |
|---|---|
| ***caerulescens*** var. ***gallicum*** | EEls |
| § ***canum*** | EEls MHer |
| § ***ferganense*** | EEls |
| § ***fragrans*** | EEls |
| § ***maritimum*** | CArn GGar GPWP ILis MHer NSti |
| - var. ***maritimum*** | EEls |
| § ***nutans*** | EEls MCot MRav |
| § ***tridentatum*** | CArn EBee |
| - subsp. ***tridentatum*** | EEls |
| - subsp. ***wyomingense*** | EEls |
| ***tripartitum*** var. ***rupicola*** | EEls |
| § ***vallesiacum*** ΨH4 | EBee EEls SUsu WEas |
| ***vaseyanaum*** | EEls |

## *Serissa* (*Rubiaceae*)

| | |
|---|---|
| ***foetida*** | see *S. japonica* |
| § ***japonica*** | STre |
| - 'Pink Mystic' | EMil |
| - ***rosea*** | STre |
| - 'Variegata' (v) | STre |
| - 'White Snow' new | MGos |

## *Serratula* (*Asteraceae*)

| | |
|---|---|
| ***coronata*** | EBee |
| - subsp. ***insularis*** f. ***alba*** new | EBee |
| § ***seoanei*** | CKno CMea CPom CWsd EBee ECha EDAr EMon LHop MCot MHer MLHP MWat SAga SBch SDix SPhx SRms SUsu WCot WEas WFar WMoo WPGP WPat WPrP WTin |
| ***shawii*** | see *S. seoanei* |
| ***tinctoria*** | CArn EBee GBar MSal NLar NMir SPhx WOut |
| - subsp. ***macrocephala*** | EBee EBrs LRHS SHGN |
| ***wolffii*** | EBee |

## *Serruria* (*Proteaceae*)

| | |
|---|---|
| ***florida*** | SPlb |

## *Sesamum* (*Pedaliaceae*)

| | |
|---|---|
| ***indicum*** | CArn |

## *Sesbania* (*Papilionaceae*)

| | |
|---|---|
| ***punicea*** | CCCN CSpe SOWG |

## *Seseli* (*Apiaceae*)

| | |
|---|---|
| ***elatum*** | CSpe LPio |
| - subsp. ***osseum*** | EBee LPio |
| ***globiferum*** | LPio SPhx |
| ***gummiferum*** | CArn CSpe EBee LDai LPio SDix SEND SKHP SPhx |
| ***hippomarathrum*** | LPio SMHy SPhx SUsu WCot WHoo WHrl WPGP |
| ***libanotis*** | CSpe EBee LEdu LPio LPla MLLN NDov NLar SAga SBch SPhx |
| ***montanum*** | CDes CSpe EBee WPGP |
| ***rigidum*** | EBee |

## *Sesleria* (*Poaceae*)

| | |
|---|---|
| ***autumnalis*** | EBee EMon LEdu LPla SPhx |
| ***caerulea*** | CSam EAlp EBee EHig EHoe ELan EMil GFor LEdu MBar MLLN MMoz MWhi NLar WPtf |
| - 'Malvern Mop' | EBee WHrl WPGP |
| * ***candida*** | EPPr |
| ***glauca*** | EHoe NLar NOak NPro WPer |
| ***heufleriana*** | CElw CWCL EBee EHoe EPPr EPla GFor NLar SLPl SPlb |
| ***insularis*** | EMon EPPr EShb |
| 'Morning Dew' | EBee GCal |
| ***nitida*** | CKno EBee EHoe EMon GFor LBMP LEdu MMoz SApp SPhx WPGP |
| ***rigida*** | EHoe |
| ***sadleriana*** | EBee EPPr EWes EWsh GFor |

## *Setaria* (*Poaceae*)

| | |
|---|---|
| RCB/Arg BB-2 | WCot |
| ***italica*** new | WTou |
| ***macrostachya*** ΨH3 | CKno GFor LLWP SBch SPhx SUsu |
| ***palmifolia*** | CHEx CHll CKno CKob EPPr SDix WCot WDyG |
| - BWJ 8132 | WCru |
| ***viridis*** | CHrt CSpe NSti WCot WTin |

## *Setcreasea* see *Tradescantia*

## shaddock see *Citrus maxima*

## Sharon fruit see *Diospyros kaki*

## *Shepherdia* (*Elaeagnaceae*)

| | |
|---|---|
| ***argentea*** | CBcs NLar |

## *Sherardia* (*Rubiaceae*)

| | |
|---|---|
| ***arvensis*** | MSal |

## *Shibataea* (*Poaceae*)

| | |
|---|---|
| ***chinensis*** | EBee |
| ***kumasaca*** | CAbb CBcs CDoC CEnt CHEx EBee ENBC EPfP EPla ERod IBal LEdu LPal MBrN MCCP MMoz MWht NMoo NVic SBig SLPl WPGP |
| - 'Aureostriata' | EPla |
| ***lancifolia*** | CMCo EPla |

## *Shortia* (*Diapensiaceae*)

| | |
|---|---|
| ***galacifolia*** | IBlr |
| - var. ***brevistyla*** | IBlr |
| ***soldanelloides*** | IBlr |
| - var. ***ilicifolia*** | IBlr |
| - 'Kuju' new | EBee |
| - var. ***magna*** | IBlr |
| ***uniflora*** | IBlr NHar |
| - var. ***orbicularis*** 'Grandiflora' | CMac CWsd IBlr |

## *Sibbaldia* (*Rosaceae*)

| | |
|---|---|
| ***procumbens*** | CSec GAuc GKir |

## *Sibbaldiopsis* (*Rosaceae*)

| | |
|---|---|
| ***tridentata*** 'Lemon Mac' | MAsh SIng |
| - 'Nuuk' | LRHS MAsh MBar NHol |

## *Sibthorpia* (*Scrophulariaceae*)

| | |
|---|---|
| ***europaea*** | CGHE CHEx CPLG |

## *Sida* (*Malvaceae*)

| | |
|---|---|
| ***hermaphrodita*** | EBee |

## *Sidalcea* (*Malvaceae*)

| | | |
|---|---|---|
| | 'Brilliant' | CBcs EBee EPfP LAst LRHS MDKP MNrw NBPC NBir NSti SPer SRkn WFar WMoo WWFP |
| | ***candida*** | CBgR CSam CSec CTca EBee ECtt ELan EPfP GGar GMaP LAst LEdu LHop LRHS MBNS MRav MSte NGdn NSti SMrm SPer SPla SPoG SUsu WCAu WCot WFar |
| | - 'Bianca' | CMea EBee EHrv EShb MSte NLar NPri WFar WHal WMoo WPer |
| | 'Candy Girl' | EBee WBor |
| | 'Crimson King' | WFar |
| | 'Croftway Red' | CBgR CFir CTca EBee ELan EPfP GCra GGar LRHS MAvo MCot MRav NBro NCob NGdn NHol SAga SMrm SPet SPoG SWvt WAul WCAu WFar WMoo |
| | ***cusickii*** | WOut |
| | 'Elsie Heugh' ♀H4 | Widely available |
| * | ***grandiflora*** | EBee |
| | ***hendersonii*** | EBee |
| | ***hickmanii*** subsp. ***anomala*** | EBee |
| | ***hirtipes*** | EBee |
| | 'Little Princess'PBR | CElw CFir EBee EWes GBri GKir LBuc MBNS NDov NLar SPoG WFar |
| | 'Loveliness' | CMMP EBee ECtt ELan EShb LHop LSou MAvo MRav NBro NChi NCob NGdn NHol NLar SAga SBch |
| | ***malviflora*** | NBre SEND SRms WBVN |
| | - 'Alba' | WFar |
| | 'Monarch' | MDKP WFar |
| | 'Moorland Rose Coronet' | WMoo |
| | 'Mr Lindbergh' | EBee EPfP MAvo NHol SAga WFar |
| | 'Mrs Borrodaile' | CBgR CMMP CMac CTca EBee ECtt GBuc GMac LAst MBNS MBri MLHP MRav NBro NCob NGdn NHol NPro SMrm WCAu WFar WMoo |
| | 'Mrs Galloway' | WFar |
| | 'Mrs T. Alderson' | WFar WMoo |
| | 'My Love' | ECha NDov |
| | ***neomexicana*** | SMrm |
| | 'Oberon' | EBee GBuc WFar |
| | ***oregana*** | NBid NGdn |
| | - subsp. ***spicata*** | WFar WMoo |
| | 'Party Girl' | Widely available |
| | 'Präriebrand' | LSou SAga |
| | 'Purpetta' | CBgR COlW EBee EWTr MDKP NGBl NLar NPro STes WPer |
| | 'Reverend Page Roberts' | MRav WCot WFar |
| | 'Rosaly' | CEnt CMdw EBee GAbr IFoB LBMP NLar STes WFar WGor WHal WPer |
| | 'Rosanna' | EBee GAbr GMaP NLar SPhx WHal WPer |
| | 'Rose Bud' | CElw EBee |
| | 'Rose Queen' | CKno CTca EBee ECha LHop LRHS MAvo MBNS MCot MRav NBro NCob NHol SPer SRms WCAu WFar |
| | 'Rosy Gem' | EBee ECtt LCro NBre WFar |
| | Stark's hybrids | SRms |
| | 'Sussex Beauty' | CMCo CPrp CSam EBee MArl MAvo MBri MLHP MLLN MRav MSte NCGa NDov NGdn SMrm SPer WAul WFar WMoo |
| | 'Sweet Joy' | SMrm |
| | 'The Duchess' | WFar |
| | 'William Smith' ♀H4 | CPrp CSam EBee ECha ECtt EPfP EWes GKir LAst MBri MLLN MRav NCGa NChi NCob NGdn NOrc SGar SMrm SPer SPhx SPla WBVN WCAu WFar WMoo |
| | 'Wine Red' | CFir CKno CMHG EBee EShb IPot LAst MAvo MCot MDKP MSte NCob NGdn SBch SWvt WCAu WCra WFar |

## *Sideritis* (*Lamiaceae*)

| | | |
|---|---|---|
| | ***hyssopifolia*** | EBee |
| | ***scordioides*** | EBee |
| | ***syriaca*** | CArn EBee EOHP SGar |

## *Sieversia* (*Rosaceae*)

| | | |
|---|---|---|
| § | ***pentapetala*** | GEdr WAbe WFar |
| | ***reptans*** | see *Geum reptans* |

## *Silaum* (*Apiaceae*)

| | | |
|---|---|---|
| | ***silaus*** | NMir |

## *Silene* (*Caryophyllaceae*)

| | | |
|---|---|---|
| | SDR 4329 new | GKev |
| | ***acaulis*** | EAlp ECho EDAr MTho NLAp NLar NMen SRms WAbe |
| § | - subsp. ***acaulis*** | ECho SPlb SRms |
| | - 'Alba' | ECho EWes NLan NMen WAbe WPat |
| | - 'Blush' | NLAp NMen WAbe WRos |
| | - subsp. ***elongata*** | see *S. acaulis* subsp. *acaulis* |
| | - 'Frances' | EPot GMaP NHar NLAp NMen NRya NSla WAbe |
| | - 'Francis Copeland' | ECho NMen |
| | - 'Helen's Double' (d) | ECho |
| * | - ***minima*** | EPot |
| | - 'Mount Snowdon' | ECho ELan EPfP EWes GKir GMaP LBee NLAp NLar NMen NRya NWCA SPlb SPoG SRms SRot WHoo WPat |
| | - 'Pedunculata' | see *S. acaulis* subsp. *acaulis* |
| | ***alba*** | see *S. latifolia* |
| § | ***alpestris*** | CSec EBee MBar MTho SRms SRot WFar WMoo WThu |
| | - 'Flore Pleno' (d) ♀H4 | EDAr EWes LBee NSla WAbe WPat |
| | ***araratica*** | WAbe |
| | ***argaea*** | WAbe |
| | x ***arkwrightii*** | see *Lychnis* x *arkwrightii* |
| | ***armeria*** | CSec WHer |
| | - 'Electra' | CSpe |
| | ***asterias*** | CSec GBuc GCal GCra IGor MNrw NBid NBre NSti WPer |
| | - MESE 429 | GBin |
| | ***atropurpurea*** | see *Lychnis viscaria* subsp. *atropurpurea* |
| | ***bellidioides*** | WPGP |
| | ***brahuica*** | CSec |
| | ***californica*** | NWCA SKHP |
| | ***caroliniana*** | CHrt |
| | - subsp. ***wherryi*** | CSec WFar |
| | ***chungtienensis*** | EBee |
| § | ***compacta*** | CSec NLar WKif |
| § | ***davidii*** | EBee |
| | ***dinarica*** | CSec |
| § | ***dioica*** | CArn CHrt CRWN CSec EBWF EGoo LEdu MHer MNHC NLan NLar NMir NVic SECG SWat WMoo WRos WSFF WShi |
| | - 'Clifford Moor' (v) | ECtt EHoe NSti SCoo |
| | - 'Compacta' | see *S. dioica* 'Minikin' |
| § | - 'Flore Pleno' (d) | GCra MCot MRav MTho NBid NBro NGdn SMrm WEas WFar WHoo WTin |
| § | - 'Graham's Delight' (v) | MSCN WCHb |
| | - 'Inane' | CDes CWsd EBee EPPr WAlt WPGP |
| | - f. ***lactea*** | MHer |
| | - lilac-flowered | WCot |
| § | - 'Minikin' | ECha EGoo EMon WAlt WTin |

- 'Pat Clissold' (v) — WCHb
- 'Pembrokeshire Pastel' (v) — WAlt
- 'Richmond' (d) — EBee GBuc NBre SHar
- 'Rosea Plena' (d) — CBre MTho NCob
- 'Rubra Plena' — see *S. dioica* 'Flore Pleno'
- 'Thelma Kay' (d/v) — CFee CSev EBee ECtt EWes GBuc MDun NBid NBre NLar WMoo WPGP WWFP
- 'Underdine' — EBee EWes
- 'Valley High' (v) — EWes
- 'Variegata' — see *S. dioica* 'Graham's Delight'

***elisabethae*** — EPot GKir
§ ***fimbriata*** — CFir CSpe EBee EHrv ELan EPyc EShb GMaP LEdu MCot MMHG MNFA MRav NChi NSti SAga SBri SMrm WAbb WCot WKif WMoo WPGP WPen WPtf WRHF WSHC WTin
***foliosa*** new — CSec
***gallica*** var. ***quinquevulnera*** — CSec
***hookeri*** Ingramii Group — EBee GKev
- subsp. ***pulverulenta*** new — CGra
***inflata*** — see *S. vulgaris*
***kantzeensis*** — see *S. davidii*
***keiskei*** — CSec
- var. ***akaisialpina*** — ITim
- var. ***minor*** — CPBP EWes LRHS MTho WAbe
***laciniata*** 'Jack Flash' — EHig WHrl
§ ***latifolia*** — CArn CSec EBWF NMir NSco
- subsp. ***alba*** — SECG
***maritima*** — see *S. uniflora*
***maroccana*** — CRWN
***mexicana*** — CSec
***moorcroftiana*** — EBee GKev
***multifida*** — see *S. fimbriata*
***nigrescens*** HWJK 2287 — WCru
***noctiflora*** — CSec EBWF
***nutans*** — EBWF SRms WHer WSFF
***orientalis*** — see *S. compacta*
***parishii*** var. ***latifolia*** NNS 03-556 — NWCA
***pusilla*** — EDAr NLar
***quadridentata*** misapplied — see *S. alpestris*
***regia*** — MNrw NBre SKHP WPGP
'Rolley's Favourite' — EBee
***rubra*** — see *S. dioica*
***rupestris*** — GKev
***schafta*** ♀H4 — CHal CHrt CTri EAlp ECha ECho ECtt EPfP GKev LRHS NBid NCob NPri NWCA SRms WAbe WFar WHoo WPer WWlt
- 'Abbotswood' — see *Lychnis* x *walkeri* 'Abbotswood Rose'
- 'Persian Carpet' new — WRHF
- 'Robusta' — WAbe
- 'Shell Pink' — ECha EWes GJos LBee LRHS LSou NCob NDov NLar NWCA WHoo
***sieboldii*** — see *Lychnis coronata* var. *sieboldii*
***suksdorfii*** — CSec EPot
* ***tenuis*** — GBuc
- ACE 2429 — GBuc
§ ***uniflora*** — CHrt EBWF ECho ECtt EPfP GGar GKev MCot MNHC MWat NBid NBlu NBro SBch SPlb SRms SWal WFar WMoo
- 'Alba Plena' — see *S. uniflora* 'Robin Whitebreast'
I - 'Compacta' — CEnt ECho EDAr EPPr NDlv WMoo
§ - 'Druett's Variegated' (v) — Widely available
- 'Flore Pleno' — see *S. uniflora* 'Robin Whitebreast'
§ - 'Robin Whitebreast' (d) — CHar EBee ECha ECho ECtt EPfP GCal MBar MTho MWat NBid NBro NPri SRms SRot WMoo WPer WSHC
- 'Rosea' — EBee ECtt EPfP GGar GKev GKir MMuc MRav SPlb SRot WFar WOut WPer
- 'Silver Lining' (v) — GBuc
- 'Variegata' — see *S. uniflora* 'Druett's Variegated'
- Weisskehlchen — see *S. uniflora* 'Robin Whitebreast'
- 'White Bells' — CTri ECtt NBlu WHoo WKif WSHC
***virginica*** — CDes SKHP
§ ***vulgaris*** — CRWN CSec EBWF LEdu MHer NLan NMir NSco SECG
- SDR 1761 — GKev
- subsp. ***maritima*** — see *S. uniflora*
***wallichiana*** — see *S. vulgaris*
'Wisley Pink' — ECtt
***yunnanensis*** — SPhx WSHC
§ ***zawadskii*** — CSec GBuc MDKP NHol SWal WTin

## *Silphium* (*Asteraceae*)

***integrifolium*** — EBee NBre NDov SAga SMad WCot WOld
***laciniatum*** — CArn EBee NBre NDov SMad SMrm SPhx WCot
***perfoliatum*** ♀H4 — CArn COld EBee ELon GPoy NBre NDov NLar SMrm SPhx SUsu WCot WFar WOld
***terebinthinaceum*** — EPPr NDov SMad SPhx WCot

## *Silybum* (*Asteraceae*)

***marianum*** — CArn CSec CSpe EBee ELan EPfP GAbr GPWP GPoy MNHC MSCN MSal NGHP SECG SIde SPav WFar WHer WTou
- 'Adriana' — SPav

## *Simmondsia* (*Simmondsiaceae*)

***chinensis*** — CArn EOHP MSal

## *Sinacalia* (*Asteraceae*)

§ ***tangutica*** — CSam EBee ECha EPPr GGar MAvo MBNS MWhi NBid NBro NCGa NDov SDix WAbb WCru

## *Sinarundinaria* (*Poaceae*)

***anceps*** — see *Yushania anceps*
***jaunsarensis*** — see *Yushania anceps*
***maling*** — see *Yushania maling*
***murielae*** — see *Fargesia murielae*
***nitida*** — see *Fargesia nitida*

## *Sinningia* (*Gesneriaceae*)

'Blue Wonder' — MBri
* ***caerulea*** — WDib
***canescens*** ♀H1 — WDib
§ ***cardinalis*** — CHal CSpe EBak WDib
- 'Innocent' — WDib
§ x ***cardosa*** — MBri
'Diego Rose' — MBri
'Duchess of York' — CSut
'Duke of York' — CSut
'Kaiser Wilhelm' — MBri
***nivalis*** — WDib
***speciosa*** 'Etoile de Feu' — MBri
- 'Kaiser Friedrich' — MBri
- 'Mont Blanc' — MBri
- 'Violacea' — MBri
***tubiflora*** — CSpe

## *Sinobambusa* (*Poaceae*)

§ ***intermedia*** — EBee EPla
* ***orthotropa*** — EPla WPGP

| | | |
|---|---|---|
| | ***rubroligula*** | EPla NMoo WPGP |
| | ***tootsik*** | EPla |
| § | - 'Albostriata' (v) | EBee EPla LPJP |
| | - 'Variegata' | see *S. tootsik* 'Albostriata' |

## x *Sinocalycalycanthus* (*Calycanthaceae*)

| | |
|---|---|
| ***raulstonii*** 'Hartlage Wine' | CPMA EPfP MBri SSpi |
| 'Venus' **new** | SSpi |

## *Sinocalycanthus* (*Calycanthaceae*)

| | |
|---|---|
| ***chinensis*** | CBcs CMCN CPMA EBee ELan EPfP IArd IDee IMGH MBlu MBri NLar SSpi WBVN WPGP |

## *Sinofranchetia* (*Lardizabalaceae*)

| | |
|---|---|
| sp. | CBcs WCru |

## *Sinojackia* (*Styracaceae*)

| | |
|---|---|
| ***xylocarpa*** | CBcs EPfP MBlu MBri NLar WFar |

## *Sinowilsonia* (*Hamamelidaceae*)

| | |
|---|---|
| ***henryi*** | NLar |

## *Siphocampylus* (*Campanulaceae*)

| | |
|---|---|
| ***foliosus*** CDPR 3240 | WPGP |

## *Siphocranion* (*Lamiaceae*)

| | | |
|---|---|---|
| § | ***macranthum*** | CDes EWes MHar WPGP |

## *Sisymbrium* (*Brassicaceae*)

| | | |
|---|---|---|
| § | ***luteum*** | WHil |

## *Sisyrinchium* ✿ (*Iridaceae*)

| | | |
|---|---|---|
| | from Ecuador **new** | GCal |
| | x ***anceps*** | see *S. angustifolium* |
| § | ***angustifolium*** | CMHG CSec EAlp EBur ECha ECho LPBA MBNS MBar MCot MNFA MSal NBir NLAp NLar SChF SPlb SRms WBrk WPer WPtf |
| | - ***album*** | ECho MCot NLar |
| | - 'Lucerne' **new** | EBee |
| § | ***arenarium*** | CMea CPBP EBur |
| | ***atlanticum*** | NBro SUsu WPer |
| | ***bellum*** hort. | see *S. idahoense* var. *bellum* |
| | - dwarf | EBee |
| | ***bermudianum*** | see *S. angustifolium* |
| | - 'Album' | see *S. graminoides* 'Album' |
| | 'Biscutella' | Widely available |
| | 'Blue France' **new** | EPot |
| | 'Blue Ice' | CMea CPBP CWCL EAlp EBee EBur EDAr MAvo NDov NLAp WAbe WHoo WMoo WPat WPer WRHF WRos |
| | ***boreale*** | see *S. californicum* |
| | ***brachypus*** | see *S. californicum* Brachypus Group |
| | 'Californian Skies' | Widely available |
| § | ***californicum*** | CBen CSec EBur ECho EHon EMFW EPfP LPBA MBar NBro NHol SMrm WFar WMAq WPer |
| § | - Brachypus Group | EAlp EBee ECho ECtt EDAr EPfP GKir MBNS MMuc NBir NBlu NLAp NLar NPri NVic SGar SPad SPlb SPoG SWal SWvt WMoo |
| * | ***capsicum*** | CPLG CSec |
| § | ***chilense*** | ERos |
| | ***coeleste*** | EBur |
| | ***commutatum*** | ECho MNrw SGar |
| | ***convolutum*** | GGar NDov |
| | - B&SWJ 9117 | WCru |
| | ***cuspidatum*** | see *S. arenarium* |
| | 'Deep Seas' | SUsu |
| | ***demissum*** | EBur |
| | ***depauperatum*** | CLyd CSec EBur EDAr MNrw WHer WPer |
| | 'Devon Blue' | ECho |
| | 'Devon Skies' | CHid CMCo CMHG CTca CWCL EBur ECho MDKP MWea NMen SBch SIng SWvt WAbe WFar WRos |
| | ***douglasii*** | see *Olsynium douglasii* |
| | 'Dragon's Eye' | CElw CMea CPBP EBur EWes MAvo MBrN SIng SMHy SMrm SRot WPer |
| | 'E.K. Balls' | Widely available |
| | ***elmeri*** | EBur |
| | 'Emmeline' | EBee EBur |
| | ***filifolium*** | see *Olsynium filifolium* |
| | ***graminoides*** | CSec EBur EDAr IFoB NBro WPer |
| § | - 'Album' | EBur GGar LRHS NBro WPer |
| | ***grandiflorum*** | see *Olsynium douglasii* |
| | 'Hemswell Sky' | CLyd EBur ECho EHoe NRya |
| | 'Iceberg' | EAro EBee EBur EDAr EShb SBch SUsu |
| | ***idahoense*** | CSec ECha ECho EDAr GEdr GKev LSou MHer NRya SPlb SRms |
| | - 'Album' | see *S. idahoense* var. *macounii* 'Album' |
| § | - var. ***bellum*** | CKno EBee EBur ECho EPfP GGar IFro MBNS NPri NWCA SGar SPet SRms SSto WMoo WPat WPer |
| | - - pale-flowered | CKno NDov SMHy SUsu |
| | - - 'Rocky Point' | CElw CLyd CMCo CSpe EAro EBee EBur EWes GJos MMuc NLAp SPoG SRot WFar WHoo WPat |
| | - var. ***macounii*** | EBee GEdr WFar |
| § | - - 'Album' ♀H4 | CMea CSec CSsd EAlp EBur ECho EDAr EMFW ERos GAbr GKev MTho MWat NLAp SAga SPet WAbe WFar WPat WPer |
| | ***iridifolium*** | see *S. micranthum* |
| | ***junceum*** | see *Olsynium junceum* |
| | ***littorale*** | CPLG CSec EBur NLar WPer |
| | ***macrocarpon*** ♀H2-3 | CFee CLyd CPBP CSsd EBur ECho ERos LRHS MDKP NMen SWal WPer |
| | 'Marie' | EBee EBur |
| | 'Marion' | CElw CKno CMea CPBP MAvo MBrN NDov NLar SBch SMHy SMrm SPet SRot WPer |
| | 'May Snow' | see *S. idahoense* var. *macounii* 'Album' |
| | 'Miami' | EBur |
| § | ***micranthum*** | CBro CSec EBur ECho WRos |
| | ***montanum*** | ECho ERos |
| | 'Mrs Spivey' | EBee EBur ECho ECtt MBar MHer NBir |
| | 'North Star' | see *S.* 'Pole Star' |
| | ***nudicaule*** x ***montanum*** | CFee EBur ECho GAbr MNrw NLAp NRya SRot WPer |
| | ***palmifolium*** | CBod CDes CSpe CSsd EBee MAvo MDKP MHar MHer MLLN MNrw MWea NCGa SGar WCot |
| | - JCA 2.880.010 | SKHP WPGP |
| | ***patagonicum*** | CPLG CSec EBur EDAr ERos GBuc WPer |
| § | 'Pole Star' | CFee CLyd CSpe EBee EBur ECho LSou WFar WPer WRos |
| | 'Quaint and Queer' | CPLG CWCL EBee EBur ECha ECho ECtt EHoe EPot EShb MBrN MLHP MNFA MSCN MTho NBir NBro NChi NLAp SHBN SWvt WMnd WMoo WPer WSHC |
| | 'Raspberry' | CMea CSpe EBee EBur WRos |
| | 'Sapphire' | NPri WFar |
| | ***scabrum*** | see *S. chilense* |
| | 'Sisland Blue' | EBur EWes |

| | | |
|---|---|---|
| § | ***striatum*** | Widely available |
| § | - 'Aunt May' (v) | Widely available |
| | - 'Variegatum' | see *S. striatum* 'Aunt May' |

## *Sium* (*Apiaceae*)

| | | |
|---|---|---|
| | ***sisarum*** | ELau GPoy MHer MSal |

## *Skimmia* ✿ (*Rutaceae*)

| | | |
|---|---|---|
| | ***anquetilia*** | CMac MBar |
| | ***arborescens*** GWJ 9374 | WCru |
| | - subsp. ***nitida*** B&SWJ 8239 | WCru |
| | ***arisanensis*** B&SWJ 7114 | WCru |
| | x ***confusa*** | WFar |
| | - 'Kew Green' (m) $\Upsilon^{H4}$ | Widely available |
| | ***japonica*** | CDul CMHG CMac CWib GQui MGan MGos NBlu NScw SReu SSta WDin WFar WHCG |
| | - B&SWJ 5053 | WCru |
| | - (f) | CMac CTrG CTri ELan EPfP GGal SRms |
| | - (m) **new** | GGal |
| | - 'Alba' | see *S. japonica* 'Wakehurst White' |
| | - 'Bowles' Dwarf Female' (f) | CMHG EPla MAsh MBar MBri MGos MRav MWht NHol SLim SLon |
| | - 'Bowles' Dwarf Male' (m) | CMHG EPla MAsh MBar NHol SLim |
| | - 'Bronze Knight' (m) | CMac EBee EQua MAsh MBar MBri MRav NHol SLim WFar |
| | - 'Cecilia Brown' (f) | WFar |
| | - 'Chameleon' | MAsh NHol |
| * | - 'Claries Repens' | EPla |
| | - compact (f) **new** | GGal |
| | - 'Dad's Red Dragon' | NHol |
| | - 'Emerald King' (m) | MBar MBri WFar |
| N | - 'Foremanii' | see *S. japonica* 'Veitchii' |
| § | - 'Fragrans' (m) $\Upsilon^{H4}$ | CDoC CMac CSBt CTri CWib EBee ECrN EPfP GKir LRHS MBar MBri MGos MRav NHol NPri SHBN SLim SPer SPoG SWvt WBod WFar WGob WGwG |
| | - 'Fragrant Cloud' | see *S. japonica* 'Fragrans' |
| | - 'Fragrantissima' (m) | WBod WFar |
| | - 'Fructu Albo' | see *S. japonica* 'Wakehurst White' |
| | - 'Godrie's Dwarf' (m) | CWSG EBee EMil EPfP IArd LRHS WFar |
| | - 'Highgrove Redbud' (f) | MBar MGos WBod |
| | - var. ***intermedia*** f. ***repens*** | WFar |
| | - - B&SWJ 5560 | WCru |
| | - 'Keessen' (f) | WFar |
| | - 'Kew White' (f) | CAbP CDoC CWib EBee EPfP EQua GKir IArd LRHS MAsh MBlu MGos MLan NHol NPal SHBN SLon SPer SRms SWvt WCFE WDin WFar WHCG |
| | - Luwian = 'Wanto'$^{PBR}$ | EBee NHol WCFE WFar |
| | - 'Marlot' (m) | EBee EPfP NLar SPoG |
| | - 'Nymans' (f) $\Upsilon^{H4}$ | CDoC CEnd CSam EBee ELan EPfP GKir LBMP LCro LRHS MAsh MBar MBri MRav NDlv SHBN SLim SPer SPla SPoG SReu SRms SSpi SSta WFar WGob |
| | - 'Obovata' (f) | EPla |
| | - 'Pigmy' (f) | CPLG |
| | - 'Red Dragon' (f) | CMac |
| | - 'Red Princess' (f) | EPla LAst WFar |
| * | - 'Red Riding Hood' | LBMP NHol SLon |
| | - 'Redruth' (f) | CBcs CDoC CMac CSBt CSam EBee EQua GKir LAst LHop LRHS MAsh MBar MGos MWat NHol SSta SSto WFar |
| § | - subsp. ***reevesiana*** | Widely available |
| | - - B&SWJ 3763 | WCru |
| | - - 'Chilan Choice' (f/m) | EPfP SLim SPla SSta |
| | - - 'Fata Morgana' (m) | MGos |
| | - - var. ***reevesiana*** | LCro |
| | - - - B&SWJ 3544 | WCru |
| | - - 'Robert Fortune' (f/m) | MBar |
| § | - Rogersii Group | CMac CTri MBar |
| | - - 'Dunwood' | MBar |
| | - - 'George Gardner' | EBee EMil MBar |
| | - - 'Helen Goodall' (f) | MBar |
| | - - 'Nana Mascula' (m) | CTri MGos |
| | - - 'Rockyfield Green' | MBar |
| | - - 'Snow Dwarf' (m) | MBar WFar |
| | - 'Rubella' (m) $\Upsilon^{H4}$ | Widely available |
| | - 'Rubinetta' (m) | EPfP GKir IArd LSRN MAsh MBar MGos NHol SLim WFar |
| | - 'Ruby Dome' (m) | MAsh MBar NHol WFar |
| | - 'Ruby King' (m) | CDoC CSBt ECrN EQua IArd LSRN MBar MHav NHol NLar |
| | - 'Scarlet Dwarf' (f) | EBee MAsh MBar NHol |
| | - 'Scarlet Queen' (f) | CWib |
| | - 'Tansley Gem' (f) | EPfP LRHS MAsh MBri MWht SPoG SSta WFar |
| | - 'Thelma King' | GKir WFar |
| § | - 'Veitchii' (f) | CBcs CDul CMac CSBt CTri CWSG EBee ELan EPfP GKir IArd IMGH LRHS MAsh MBar MGos MRav MWat NHol SEND SHBN SLim SPer SPoG SWvt WBod WDin |
| § | - 'Wakehurst White' (f) | CMHG CMac CSBt CTri EPfP GKir MBar MRav SLim SLon SReu SSpi WBod WFar |
| | - 'White Gerpa' | MGos |
| | - 'Winifred Crook' (f) | EPla GKir MBar MBri WFar |
| | - 'Winnie's Dwarf' | MGos |
| | - 'Wisley Female' (f) | CTri ECtt NHol WFar |
| | ***laureola*** | CDoC CPLG CSam EBee ECot MRav NHol SRms WFar WSHC |
| | - GWJ 9364 | WCru |
| | - 'Borde Hill' (f) | NPri |
| | - subsp. ***multinervia*** B&SWJ 8259 | WCru |
| * | ***mica*** | ISea |
| | 'Olympic Flame' | CWSG GKir MBlu MGos SHBN WFar |
| | ***reevesiana*** | see *S. japonica* subsp. *reevesiana* |
| | ***rogersii*** | see *S. japonica* Rogersii Group |

## *Smallanthus* (*Asteraceae*)

| | | |
|---|---|---|
| § | ***uvedalius*** | MSal |

## *Smilacina* see *Maianthemum*

## *Smilax* (*Smilacaceae*)

| | | |
|---|---|---|
| | B&SWJ 6628 from Thailand | WCru |
| | F&M 051 **new** | WPGP |
| | from Thailand | LEdu |
| | ***asparagoides*** 'Nanus' | see *Asparagus asparagoides* 'Myrtifolius' |
| | ***aspera*** | EBee EPla EShb LEdu WCru WPGP |
| | ***china*** B&SWJ 4427 | WCru |
| | ***discotis*** | CBcs SEND |
| | ***glaucophylla*** B&SWJ 2971 | WCru |
| | ***nipponica*** B&SWJ 4331 | WCru |
| | ***rotundifolia*** | LEdu |
| | ***sieboldii*** | LEdu MRav |
| | - B&SWJ 744 | WCru |

## *Smithiantha* (*Gesneriaceae*)

| | | |
|---|---|---|
| | 'Bigots Rule' **new** | EABi |
| | ***cinnabarina*** **new** | EABi |
| | 'Extra Sassy' | EABi |
| | 'Little One' | EOHP WDib |
| | 'Multiflora' | EABi WDib |
| I | 'Temple Bells' | EABi |

## *Smyrnium* (*Apiaceae*)

| | |
|---|---|
| ***olusatrum*** | CArn CSev CSpe EBWF EBee GBar GPWP MHer MNHC MSal SIde STre SWat WHer |
| ***perfoliatum*** | CHid CSec CSpe EBee EHrv ELan ELon EWes LPio NBir NChi SDix SMrm WCot WEas WFar WHal WSHC |
| ***rotundifolium*** | LPio WCot |

## *Solandra* (*Solanaceae*)

| | |
|---|---|
| ***grandiflora*** misapplied | see *S. maxima* |
| ***hartwegii*** | see *S. maxima* |
| § ***maxima*** | CCCN CHII EShb MJnS |

## *Solanum* (*Solanaceae*)

| | |
|---|---|
| B&SWJ 10395 from Guatemala **new** | WCru |
| ***atropurpureum*** | CDTJ CSpe |
| ***conchifolium*** hort. | see *S. linearifolium* |
| ***crispum*** | NBir SGar WDin |
| - 'Autumnale' | see *S. crispum* 'Glasnevin' |
| - 'Elizabeth Jane Dunn' (v) | WCot |
| § - 'Glasnevin' ♀H3 | Widely available |
| - 'Variegatum' (v) | WGwG |
| ***dulcamara*** | CArn EBWF GPoy |
| - 'Hullavington' (v) | CNat |
| - 'Lucia' (v) | CNat |
| - 'Variegatum' (v) | CMac CWan EBee ECrN EHoe EPfP NSti SPoG WFar WSHC |
| ***hispidum*** | CHEx |
| ***jasminoides*** | see *S. laxum* |
| ***laciniatum*** | CArn CCCN CDTJ CHEx CPLG CSec CSev CSpe EShb EWes GGal GGar LHop MCot SAPC SArc SBig SGar SPav WKif WWlt |
| § ***laxum*** | EBee EShb GGal LRHS MSwo NSti SPer SPoG SRms SWvt WDin WFar WSHC |
| - 'Album' ♀H3 | Widely available |
| - 'Album Variegatum' (v) | CWib ELan LRHS NBlu NSti WSHC |
| * - 'Aureovariegatum' (v) | CBcs CSBt EBee EPfP EShb LBMP MGos MNHC SCoo SLim SPer SPla SPlb |
| - 'Coldham' **new** | SMad |
| § ***linearifolium*** | EBee LBMP WPGP |
| ***mammosum*** | CDTJ |
| ***muricatum*** (F) | CCCN EShb |
| ***pseudocapsicum*** | MBri |
| - 'Ballon' | MBri |
| - variegated (v) | EShb WCot |
| ***pyracanthum*** **new** | SMad |
| ***quitoense*** (F) | CDTJ CHEx SBig |
| § ***rantonnetii*** | CCCN CHII ELan EShb IDee LCro MCot MJnS SOWG |
| - 'Royal Robe' | CBcs CRHN CTri |
| - 'Variegatum' (v) | CSpe EShb MSCN WCot |
| ***salicifolium*** | EShb |
| ***seaforthianum*** | EShb SOWG |
| § ***sessiliflorum*** (F) | MJnS |
| ***sisymbriifolium*** | CSec WWlt |
| aff. ***stenophyllum*** B&SWJ 10744 | WCru |
| ***topiro*** | see *S. sessiliflorum* |
| ***wendlandii*** | CHII |

## *Solaria* (*Alliaceae*)

| | |
|---|---|
| sp. | GCal |

## *Soldanella* (*Primulaceae*)

| | |
|---|---|
| ***alpina*** | EBee ECho GCra GKev GKir LBMP MTho NMen SIng SRms WAbe |
| - SDR 3537 **new** | GKev |
| I - 'Alba' | ECho WAbe |
| ***carpatica*** | EBee ECho GKev LLHF NHol WAbe |
| - 'Alba' | ECho GKev MDKP NHar NSla WAbe |
| ***carpatica* x *pusilla*** | CPBP ECho NHar NRya |
| ***carpatica* x *villosa*** | ECho MDKP |
| ***cyanaster*** | ECho GEdr GJos NRya WAbe |
| ***dimoniei*** | CFee EBee ECho GKev ITim NMen NSla WAbe |
| § ***hungarica*** | CLyd ECho MTho WAbe WFar |
| ***minima*** | ECho GJos NDlv NMen NRya NSla WAbe |
| - 'Alba' | WAbe |
| ***minima* x *pusilla*** | NHol |
| ***montana*** | CLAP CLyd ECho GJos GKev LLHF MDun MTho NLar NMen WRha |
| - subsp. ***hungarica*** | see *S. hungarica* |
| ***pindicola*** | ECho EWes GBuc NDlv NMen NWCA WAbe WFar |
| ***pusilla*** | GBin ITim |
| * - ***alba*** | ECho |
| 'Sudden Spring' | WAbe |
| ***villosa*** | CBgR CDes CLAP EBee ECho GGar GKev LEdu LRHS MTho NHol NRya SBch WAbe WFar WSHC |

## *Soleirolia* (*Urticaceae*)

| | |
|---|---|
| ***soleirolii*** | CHEx CHal CKob CTri LPBA LRHS MBri MCCP MWhi SIng SPer STre WHer |
| - 'Argentea' | see *S. soleirolii* 'Variegata' |
| § - 'Aurea' | CHal CKob CTri SIng STre |
| - 'Golden Queen' | see *S. soleirolii* 'Aurea' |
| - 'Silver Queen' | see *S. soleirolii* 'Variegata' |
| § - 'Variegata' (v) | CHal CKob LPBA WHer |

## *Solenomelus* (*Iridaceae*)

| | |
|---|---|
| ***chilensis*** | see *S. pedunculatus* |
| § ***pedunculatus*** | CFee CSec WPGP |
| ***sisyrinchium*** | ERos |

## *Solenopsis* (*Campanulaceae*)

| | |
|---|---|
| ***axillaris*** | see *Isotoma axillaris* |

## *Solenostemon* ✿ (*Lamiaceae*)

| | |
|---|---|
| 'Autumn Rainbow' | EShb WDib |
| 'Beauty' (v) | CHal WDib |
| 'Beauty of Lyons' | CHal |
| 'Beckwith's Gem' | CHal |
| 'Bizarre Croton' (v) | CHal |
| 'Black Dragon' | CHal |
| 'Black Heart' | WDib |
| 'Black Prince' | CHal EShb WDib |
| 'Brilliant' (v) | WDib |
| 'Buttercup' | CHal WDib |
| 'Buttermilk' (v) ♀H1 | CHal |
| 'Carnival' (v) | CHal WDib |
| 'Chamaeleon' (v) | WDib |
| 'City of Liverpool' | CHal |
| 'Combat' (v) | CHal SVil WDib |
| 'Copper Sprite' | CHal |
| 'Crimson Ruffles' (v) ♀H1 | CHal WDib |
| 'Crimson Velvet' | CHal |
| 'Dairy Maid' (v) | CHal |
| 'Dazzler' (v) | CHal |
| 'Display' | CHal WDib |
| 'Dracula' | CHal |
| 'Etna' (v) | CHal |
| 'Firefly' | CHal |
| 'Flamestitch' | CSpe |
| 'Freckles' (v) | CHal WDib |
| 'Funfair' (v) | CHal |

| | | |
|---|---|---|
| | 'Gloriosus' | CHal |
| | 'Glory of Luxembourg' (v) ♀H1 | CHal |
| | 'Goldie' (v) | CHal |
| | 'Inky Fingers' (v) | EShb WDib |
| | 'Juliet Quartermain' | CHal WDib |
| | 'Jupiter' | CHal |
| | 'Kentish Fire' (v) | CHal |
| | 'Kiwi Fern' (v) | CHal WDib |
| | 'Klondike' | CHal |
| | Kong Series | LRHS SPoG |
| | - 'Kong Rose' | NPri |
| | 'Laing's Croton' (v) | CHal WDib |
| | 'Lemondrop' | CHal |
| | 'Lord Falmouth' ♀H1 | CHal WDib |
| | 'Melody' (v) | CHal WDib |
| | 'Midas' | CHal |
| | 'Midnight' | EShb |
| | 'Mission Gem' (v) | CHal SVil |
| | 'Muriel Pedley' (v) | CHal |
| | 'Ottoman' | CHal |
| | 'Paisley Shawl' (v) ♀H1 | CHal EShb WDib |
| | 'Palisandra' | CSpe |
| | ***pentheri*** | CHal |
| | 'Peter Wonder' (v) | CHal SVil WDib |
| | 'Picturatus' (v) ♀H1 | CHal WDib |
| | 'Pineapple Beauty' (v) ♀H1 | CHal EShb WDib |
| | 'Pineapplette' ♀H1 | CHal WDib |
| | 'Purple Oak' | CHal |
| | 'Raspberry Ripple' | CHal |
| | 'Red Angel' | WDib |
| | 'Red Croton' (v) | WDib |
| | 'Red Mars' | WDib |
| | 'Red Nettie' (v) | CHal WDib |
| | 'Red Rosie' | CHal EShb WDib |
| | 'Red Stinger' | CHal |
| | 'Red Velvet' | CHal |
| | 'Rose Blush' (v) | CHal WDib |
| | 'Roy Pedley' | CHal WDib |
| | 'Royal Scot' (v) ♀H1 | CHal WDib |
| | 'Salmon Plumes' (v) | CHal |
| | 'Scarlet Ribbons' | CHal |
| | 'Speckles' (v) | CHal |
| | 'Strawberry Jam' | CHal |
| | ***thyrsoideus*** | see *Plectranthus thyrsoideus* |
| | 'Treales' (v) | CHal WDib |
| | 'Vesuvius' | CHal |
| | 'Walter Turner' (v) ♀H1 | CHal SVil WDib |
| | 'White Gem' (v) | CHal |
| | 'White Pheasant' (v) | CHal |
| | 'Winsome' (v) | CHal WDib |
| | 'Winter Sun' (v) | CHal |
| | 'Wisley Flame' | WDib |
| | 'Wisley Tapestry' (v) ♀H1 | CHal WDib |

## *Solidago* (*Asteraceae*)

| | | |
|---|---|---|
| | Babygold | see *S.* 'Goldkind' |
| | ***brachystachys*** | see *S. cutleri* |
| | ***caesia*** | EBee ECha EMon EShb EWes MSte NBir SMHy WFar WMoo WOld WTin |
| | ***canadensis*** | CTri ELan NBre SEND SPlb WFar WHer |
| | - var. ***scabra*** | WOld WTin |
| | 'Cloth of Gold' | CBcs EBee ECho GKir NPro SWvt WMnd WOld |
| § | 'Crown of Rays' | CPrp ECtt MRav WFar WMnd |
| § | ***cutleri*** | EBee ECho ELan GEdr MBar MTho MWat NLar SPlb SRms WFar WTin |
| I | - ***nana*** | ECho EWes WAbe WBor |
| | 'Ducky' **new** | EBee |
| | 'Dzintra' | EBee |
| | 'Early Bird' | WFar |
| § | ***flexicaulis*** | GMaP |
| | - 'Variegata' (v) | CWan EBee ELan EMon EPfP EWsh GKir GMaP MHar NLar NSti WFar WHer WOld WPer |
| | 'Gardone' ♀H4 | WFar |
| | ***gigantea*** | EMon WFar WPer |
| | ***glomerata*** | EMon EShb NBre NLar NNor SMrm WPer |
| | Golden Baby | see *S.* 'Goldkind' |
| § | 'Golden Dwarf' | LRHS MBri |
| | 'Golden Fleece' | see *S. sphacelata* 'Golden Fleece' |
| | 'Golden Thumb' | see *S.* 'Queenie' |
| | 'Golden Wings' | CBre |
| | 'Goldenmosa' ♀H4 | CAby CSBt EBee EPfP EWes GMaP LRHS MRav SPer SPoG WCot WFar WOld |
| | 'Goldilocks' | NPri SRms |
| § | 'Goldkind' | CHrt CMMP CSBt CTri EBee ECho ECtt EPfP EShb GKir MNHC MWhi NBPC NNor NOrc SEND SPoG SWal SWvt WBrk WFar |
| | Goldzwerg | see *S.* 'Golden Dwarf' |
| | 'Harvest Gold' | CElw |
| | ***hispida*** | EMon |
| | ***hybrida*** | see x *Solidaster luteus* |
| | ***latifolia*** | see *S. flexicaulis* |
| | 'Laurin' | EBee EMil EPfP MBri NLar WTin |
| | 'Ledsham' | EBee LEdu LRHS MCot NBre SPoG WMnd |
| | 'Lemore' | see x *Solidaster luteus* 'Lemore' |
| | 'Leraft' | EBee |
| | 'Linner Gold' | NBre |
| | ***odora*** | MSal |
| | ***ohioensis*** | EBee |
| * | 'Peter Pan' | LHop WFar |
| § | 'Queenie' | ECha ECho MHer MLHP NBre NPro NVic SRms |
| | ***rigida*** | NBre SMrm WCot WPer |
| | - JLS 88002WI | EMon |
| | ***roanensis*** | NBre |
| | ***rugosa*** | ECha NBre SEND SPhx WCot |
| | - subsp. ***aspera*** | EMon |
| | - 'Fireworks' | CBgR CBre CHVG CMHG CPrp CSam EBee EBrs ECtt ELon EPPr GQue MAvo MBNS MHar MNFA MSte NBPC NDov SPoG SUsu WCot WFar WHoo WOld WTin WWlt |
| | ***sciaphila*** | EBee NBre |
| | ***sempervirens*** | WCot WFar |
| | - 'Goldene Wellen' **new** | EBee |
| | ***simplex*** subsp. ***simplex*** var. ***nana*** | NWCA WPer |
| | 'Sonnenschein' | NBre |
| | ***speciosa*** | NBre WPer |
| | ***spectabilis*** var. ***confinis*** | EBee |
| § | ***sphacelata*** 'Golden Fleece' | EBee LHop LRHS NBre WFar WHoo WMnd |
| | ***spiraeifolia*** | NBre |
| | Strahlenkrone | see *S.* 'Crown of Rays' |
| | Sweety = 'Barseven'PBR | EBee MBri |
| | 'Tom Thumb' | MRav SRms WEas |
| | ***uliginosa*** | EShb NBre |
| | ***ulmifolia*** | EBee NBre |
| | ***virgaurea*** | CArn CSam EBWF EBee GPoy MHer MNHC NBre NLar NSco SMrm WHer WPer |
| | - subsp. ***alpestris*** var. ***minutissima*** | CLyd NBre WPat |
| | - var. ***cambrica*** | see *S. virgaurea* subsp. *minuta* |
| § | - subsp. ***minuta*** | EDAr GBin |
| § | - 'Variegata' (v) | EHoe NPro WAlt |
| | ***vulgaris*** 'Variegata' | see *S. virgaurea* 'Variegata' |

## x *Solidaster* (Asteraceae)

| | | |
|---|---|---|
| | ***hybridus*** | see x *S. luteus* |
| § | ***luteus*** | CBgR EBee GBri MBri MHar SRms WEas WFar |
| § | - 'Lemore' ♀H4 | CHrt CMea CPrp EBee ELan EPfP EWsh GMac LAst LDai MWat NCGa NPri NSti NVic SMrm SPer WCot WFar |
| | 'Super' | WCot WFar |

## *Sollya* (Pittosporaceae)

| | | |
|---|---|---|
| | ***fusiformis*** | see *S. heterophylla* |
| § | ***heterophylla*** ♀H1 | Widely available |
| | - 'Alba' | CBcs CCCN EBee ELan EPfP LRHS SPoG SWvt |
| | - mauve-flowered | ECou |
| | - 'Pink Charmer' | EBee ELan LRHS SPer SPoG WSHC |
| | - pink-flowered | CCCN CSPN EPfP LBMP SEND SPad SWvt |

## *Sonchus* (Asteraceae)

| | | |
|---|---|---|
| | ***fruticosus*** | CHEx CSec |
| | ***giganteus*** | CHII |
| | ***palustris*** | EMon |
| | ***pinnatus*** | SPlb |

## *Sophora* (Papilionaceae)

| | | |
|---|---|---|
| § | ***davidii*** | CGHE CWib EBee EPfP EWTr MBlu MGos MWea SKHP SOWG WPGP WSHC |
| | ***flavescens*** | NLar |
| | ***japonica*** ♀H4 | CAbP CBcs CDul CLnd CSBt CWib EPfP LMaj MGos SBLw SHBN SPlb WBod WDin WOrn |
| | - 'Pendula' | ELan EMil LMaj LRHS MBlu MGos NPal SBLw |
| | - Princeton Upright = 'Fleright' | EMil |
| § | 'Little Baby' | CAbP CWib EBee EPfP LAst LBuc LSRN MCCP MGos MWea SDix SPoG SWvt WPGP WPat |
| | ***macrocarpa*** | GQui WBod |
| | ***microphylla*** | CHEx CTri EBee ECou EPfP IFro LHop SEND WBVN WHer WPGP |
| | - 'Dragon's Gold' | CBcs EBee ECou ELan EPfP LBuc LRHS MAsh SCoo SPoG SSpi SSta WDin |
| | - 'Early Gold' | GQui |
| | - var. ***fulvida*** | ECou |
| | - var. ***longicarinata*** | ECou |
| | ***molloyi*** | ECou |
| | ***prostrata*** misapplied | see *S.* 'Little Baby' |
| | ***prostrata*** ambig. | CBcs CGHE |
| | ***prostrata*** Buch. | ECou |
| | - Pukaki form | ECou |
| | Sun King = 'Hilsop'PBR ♀H4 | CBcs CCVT CWGN EBee ELan EMui EPfP EWes GKir LCro LRHS LSRN MBlu MGos MLan MWea NCGa NLar NPri SCoo SLon SPoG |
| | ***tetraptera*** ♀H3 | CAbP CBcs CDul CMac CTsd EBee ECou EPfP GGal GQui ISea MLan SEND SRms WBVN WBor WPGP WPic |
| | ***viciifolia*** | see *S. davidii* |

## *Sorbaria* (Rosaceae)

| | | |
|---|---|---|
| | SF 95205 | ISea |
| | ***aitchisonii*** | see *S. tomentosa* var. *angustifolia* |
| | ***arborea*** | see *S. kirilowii* |
| | aff. ***assurgens*** BWJ 8185 | WCru |
| § | ***kirilowii*** | CPLG MRav NLar SLon SMad SPer WBVN WDyG WOut |
| | ***lindleyana*** | see *S. tomentosa* |
| | ***rhoifolia*** | EPfP |
| | ***sorbifolia*** | CAbP CBcs EBee ECrN EMil EWTr GAuc GKir LRHS MBar MLHP NPro SEND SPer SPlb SPoG WDin WFar |
| | - 'Sem'PBR | CBgR EBee ELan EMil EPfP GBin LBuc LRHS MAsh MGos MLan MWea NCGa NHol NLar NPal NPri SPoG WBor WHar WMoo |
| | - var. ***stellipila*** | SLPl |
| | - - B&SWJ 776 | WCru |
| § | ***tomentosa*** | CAbP SHBN WHCG |
| § | - var. ***angustifolia*** ♀H4 | CBcs CDul CTri CWan EBee ELan EPfP EWTr GAuc GKir MRav NHol NPro SEND SLon SPer WEas WFar WHer |

## x *Sorbocrataegus* see x *Crataegosorbus*

## x *Sorbopyrus* (Rosaceae)

| | | |
|---|---|---|
| | ***auricularis*** | CTho |

## *Sorbus* ✿ (Rosaceae)

| | | |
|---|---|---|
| | CLD 1437 new | GAuc |
| | Guiz 119 new | GKir |
| | SDR 5114 new | GKev |
| | ***alnifolia*** | CLnd CMCN EBee EPfP MBlu MBri SLPl |
| | - B&SWJ 10948 new | WCru |
| | ***americana*** | CLnd NWea |
| | - 'Belmonte' | GKir SBLw |
| | - ***erecta*** | see *S. decora* (Sarg.) C.K. Schneid. |
| | ***amoena*** new | GKir |
| | - CLD 311 new | GKir |
| | aff. ***amurensis*** B&SWJ 8665 | WCru |
| | ***anglica*** | CDul CNat GKir |
| | ***apiculata*** new | GKir |
| | - CLD 310 new | GAuc GKir |
| | 'Apricot' | CEnd GKir |
| | 'Apricot Lady' | MAsh MGos |
| | 'Apricot Queen' | CLnd EBee ECrN EMil LAst SBLw WFar |
| | ***aria*** | CCVT CDul CLnd CSBt CTri ECrN EMac EPfP GAuc GKir LBuc MBar MGan MGos NBee NWea WDin WMou WOrn |
| | - 'Aurea' | CLnd MBlu MGos WFar |
| | - 'Chrysophylla' | CDul CSBt EBee ECrN GKir IMGH MGos NWea SLim SPer |
| | - 'Decaisneana' | see *S. aria* 'Majestica' |
| | - 'Lutescens' ♀H4 | Widely available |
| | - 'Magnifica' | CDoC CDul CTho ECrN ELan LMaj LPan SBLw SCoo WDin WJas |
| § | - 'Majestica' ♀H4 | CCVT CDoC CDul CLnd CTho EBee ECrN EHig GKir LPan NWea SBLw SCoo SPer SPoG WHar WJas WOrn |
| | - 'Mitchellii' | see *S. thibetica* 'John Mitchell' |
| | - 'Orange Parade' | SBLw |
| | x ***arnoldiana*** 'Cerise Queen' | GKir |
| | - 'Golden Wonder' | see *S.* 'Lombarts Golden Wonder' |
| | ***aronioides*** misapplied | see *S. caloneura* |
| | ***arranensis*** | CDul CNat GKir |
| § | ***aucuparia*** | Widely available |
| | - 'Aspleniifolia' | CBcs CCVT CDul CLnd CMCN CSBt CWSG EBee ECrN GKir LAst LPan LRHS MAsh MGos MWat NWea SBLw SLim SPer SPoG WDin WFar WJas WOrn |
| I | - 'Aurea' | SBLw SKHP |
| | - 'Beauty of Banff' new | GKir |

| | | |
|---|---|---|
| § | - 'Beissneri' | CDul CLnd EPfP GBin GKir MBri MGos NLar NWea SCoo SLon |
| | - Cardinal Royal = 'Michred' | CCVT CDoC ECrN GKir GQui LRHS SCoo WJas |
| | - 'Crème Lace' | CDul GKir SCoo |
| | - 'Dirkenii' | CDul CWSG GBin GKir MAsh WDin WJas |
| § | - var. ***edulis*** (F) | CDul CLnd CTho ECrN LBuc LMaj LPan MGos SBLw SCoo WDin |
| | - - 'Rossica' misapplied | see *S. aucuparia* var. *edulis* 'Rossica Major' |
| § | - - 'Rossica Major' | CDul ECrN GQui MMuc SBLw SCoo WFar |
| | - 'Ember Glow' | GKir |
| § | - 'Fastigiata' | CEnd CLnd CTri ECrN EPfP GKir LAst LMaj MGos NBee SBLw WDin WFar |
| | - 'Hilling's Spire' | CTho GKir MAsh MLan |
| | - 'Pendula' | CDul EBee SBLw |
| | - ***pluripinnata*** | see *S. scalaris* Koehne |
| | - var. ***rossica*** Koehne | see *S. aucuparia* var. *edulis* |
| | - 'Rossica Major' | see *S. aucuparia* var. *edulis* 'Rossica Major' |
| | - 'Scarlet King' | see *S.* x *thuringiaca* 'Scarlet King' |
| | - 'Sheerwater Seedling' ♀H4 | CCVT CDoC CDul CLnd CMCN CSBt EBee ECrN ELan EPfP GKir LAst LMaj LRHS MGos MLan MMuc MRav MSwo NBlu NPri SLim SPer SSta WDin WFar WOrn |
| | - 'Wettra' | SBLw |
| | - 'Winterdown' | CNat |
| | - 'Xanthocarpa' | see *S. aucuparia* var. *xanthocarpa* |
| § | - var. ***xanthocarpa*** ♀H4 | CLnd ECrN EPfP EWTr LMaj SBLw WDin |
| | Autumn Spire = 'Flanrock' | CDoC CLnd CWSG GKir LRHS MAsh MBri MGos MLan NLar SCoo SPoG WHar |
| | 'Bellona' | WPat |
| | ***bissetii*** new | GKir |
| | 'Boyne Bay' new | GKir |
| | 'Brilliant Yellow' | GKir |
| | ***bristoliensis*** | GAuc GKir |
| | 'Burka' | see *Aronia* x *Sorbus* 'Burka' |
| | ***californica*** new | GKir |
| § | ***caloneura*** | CBcs EPfP GKir MBlu SSpi WPGP |
| | 'Carpet of Gold' | CLnd GKir |
| | ***cashmiriana*** Hedl. ♀H4 | Widely available |
| | ***chamaemespilus*** | GAuc WPat |
| | 'Chamois Glow' | GKir WJas |
| | 'Chinese Lace' | Widely available |
| § | ***commixta*** | Widely available |
| | - 'Embley' ♀H4 | CBcs CCVT CDul CMCN CSBt CSam CTho CTri ECrN ELan EPfP EWTr GKir GQue LCro MBar MBlu MGos MMuc MRav NWea SMHT SPer SPoG SSta WDin WFar WOrn |
| | - 'Jermyns' | GKir |
| | - var. ***rufoferruginea*** | GKir GQui |
| | - - B&SWJ 6078 | WCru |
| | ***conradinae*** misapplied | see *S. pohuashanensis* (Hance) Hedlund |
| | ***conradinae*** Koehne | see *S. esserteauana* |
| | 'Copper Kettle' | GKir MAsh MBri NLar SCoo SPoG |
| | 'Coral Beauty' | CDul CLnd |
| | 'Covert Gold' | CEnd CLnd |
| | ***croceocarpa*** | CDul GKir |
| | ***cuspidata*** | see *S. vestita* |
| § | ***decora*** (Sarg.) C.K. Schneid. | NBlu SBLw |
| * | - 'Grootendorst' | CDul |
| | - var. ***nana*** | see *S. aucuparia* 'Fastigiata' |
| | ***devoniensis*** | CDul CNat CTho GKir |
| | - 'Devon Beauty' | CAgr |
| | ***discolor*** misapplied | see *S. commixta* |

| | | |
|---|---|---|
| | ***discolor*** (Maxim.) Maxim. | CLnd EBee GAuc GKir MBlu NWea WJas |
| | - MF 96172 new | GKir |
| | ***domestica*** | CDul EPfP WDin |
| | - 'Rosie' | CAgr |
| | 'Eastern Promise' | CSam CWSG EBee ECrN GKir LCro LRHS MAsh MBlu MBri MLan MWat NLar NWea SCoo SLim SMHT WDin WJas WOrn |
| § | ***eburnea*** Harry Smith 12799 new | GKir GQui |
| | ***eminens*** | CDul CNat |
| | ***epidendron*** | GKir |
| § | ***esserteauana*** | CTho EPfP |
| | - 'Flava' | GKir |
| | 'Fastigiata' | see *S. aucuparia* 'Fastigiata', *S.* x *thuringiaca* 'Fastigiata' |
| | ***folgneri*** | CEnd |
| | - 'Emiel' | EPfP MBlu MBri |
| | - 'Lemon Drop' | CDul CEnd CLnd CPMA CWSG EPfP GKir MAsh MBlu MLan NLar SCoo SMad SSpi |
| § | ***foliolosa*** | CLnd EPfP GKir NWea SCoo |
| | ***forrestii*** | EPfP GKir NBea NLar SLPl SMHT |
| * | ***fortunei*** | CLnd |
| I | ***fruticosa*** McAllister | CEnd CLnd EBee EPfP GAuc GKev GKir NWea SSta WJas |
| | - 'Koehneana' | see *S. koehneana* C.K. Schneid. |
| | 'Ghose' | CEnd CLnd GKir MBlu SCoo SPer SSpi |
| | 'Glendoick Gleam' | GGGa |
| | 'Glendoick Glory' | GGGa |
| | 'Glendoick Ivory' | GGGa |
| | 'Glendoick Pearl' | GGGa |
| | 'Glendoick Ruby' | GGGa |
| | 'Glendoick Spire' | GGGa |
| | 'Glendoick White Baby' | GGGa |
| | ***glomerulata*** | LLHF |
| | 'Golden Wonder' | see *S.* 'Lombarts Golden Wonder' |
| | ***gonggashanica*** | GKir |
| * | ***gorrodini*** | CLnd |
| § | ***graeca*** | CMCN GAuc GKir SEND |
| | 'Granatnaja' | see x *Crataegosorbus* 'Granatnaja' |
| | ***granulosa*** HWJ 1041 new | WCru |
| | ***harrowiana*** | GKir WPat |
| | 'Harvest Moon' | GQui |
| | ***hedlundii*** | GBin GKir MGos NLar WOrn WPGP |
| | ***helenae*** | GKir |
| | ***hemsleyi*** | CDul CLnd GKir WPGP |
| | - 'John Bond' | GKir MBri |
| | x ***hostii*** | CLnd MRav SPer |
| | ***hupehensis*** C.K. Schneid. ♀H4 | Widely available |
| | - 'November Pink' | see *S. hupehensis* 'Pink Pagoda' |
| § | - var. ***obtusa*** ♀H4 | CBrd CCVT CDoC CDul CLnd CMCN EPfP EWTr GKev GKir SSpi WDin |
| § | - 'Pink Pagoda' | CDoC CDul CLnd CWSG EBee ECrN EMui EPfP GKir IArd IMGH LRHS LSRN MBlu MDun MGos MRav MWat NWea SCoo SLim SLon SPer SPoG WDin WFar |
| | - red-berried new | GGal |
| | - 'Rosea' | see *S. hupehensis* var. *obtusa* |
| | ***hybrida*** misapplied | see *S.* x *thuringiaca* |
| | ***hybrida*** L. | ECrN |
| | - 'Gibbsii' ♀H4 | CDoC CLnd EBee EHig ELan EPfP EWTr GAuc GKir MAsh MBri MLan SPur WHar |
| | ***insignis*** | CDoC EPfP WPat |
| | ***intermedia*** | CCVT CDul CLnd CSBt CTho CTri CWib ECrN GKir MGos NBee NBlu NWea SBLw SEND WDin WHar WMou |

| | | |
|---|---|---|
| | - 'Brouwers' | ELan LMaj LPan SBLw |
| | ***japonica*** B&SWJ 10813 **new** | WCru |
| | - B&SWJ 11048 **new** | WCru |
| | 'Joseph Rock' | Widely available |
| § | x ***kewensis*** | CDul CLnd NWea SMHT SPlb |
| | 'Kirsten Pink' | CDul CLnd CWib EBee ECrN GKir MMuc SMHT SPer WFar |
| | ***koehneana*** hort. | see *S. fruticosa* McAllister |
| § | ***koehneana*** C.K. Schneid. ♀H4 | CBcs CLnd CMCN ECrN EHig EWTr GGGa GKev GKir GQui IDee NMen NWea SCoo WPat WTin |
| | aff. ***koehneana*** | see *S. eburnea* |
| | 'Kukula' | GKir |
| | ***kurzii*** | GKir |
| | - KR 1501 | GKir |
| | ***lanata*** misapplied | see *S. vestita* |
| | ***lancastriensis*** | CDul CNat GKir |
| | ***latifolia*** | CLnd ECrN NWea SBLw WDin |
| | - 'Henk Vink' **new** | LMaj |
| | 'Leonard Messel' | GKir MAsh MBri SCoo SPoG |
| | 'Leonard Springer' | ECrN EPfP GKir GQui SSta |
| | ***leptophylla*** | CDul CNat GKir |
| | ***leyana*** | WMou |
| | ***ligustrifolia*** HWJ 984 **new** | WCru |
| | 'Likjornaja' **new** | EPfP |
| § | 'Lombarts Golden Wonder' | CBcs CDoC CDul CLnd MBlu NWea SBLw WJas |
| | 'Maidenblush' | SBLw |
| | ***matsumurana*** misapplied | see *S. commixta* |
| | ***matsumurana*** (Makino) Koehne | GKir |
| | ***megalocarpa*** | CDoC CPMA EPfP SSpi WPGP WPat |
| | ***microphylla*** GWJ 9252 | WCru |
| | ***minima*** | GKir |
| | 'Molly Sanderson' | SSta |
| | ***monbeigii*** (Card.) Yü | GAuc GKir |
| | ***moravica*** 'Laciniata' | see *S. aucuparia* 'Beissneri' |
| | ***mougeotii*** | GKir |
| § | ***munda*** | CMCN GBin GKir SCoo |
| | nova CLD 1437 **new** | GAuc |
| | 'Peachi-Ness' | CLnd |
| | 'Pearly King' | CSam CTho MAsh NBea WJas |
| | ***pekinensis*** | see *S. reticulata* subsp. *pekinensis* |
| § | 'Pink Pearl' | CDul GKir |
| | 'Pink-Ness' | EBee GKir NLar SCoo SPoG |
| | ***pogonopetala*** Koehne | GAuc GKir |
| | ***pohuashanensis*** misapplied | see *S.* x *kewensis* |
| § | ***pohuashanensis*** (Hance) Hedlund | GKir |
| | ***porrigentiformis*** | CDul CNat |
| | ***poteriifolia*** | GAuc GGGa GKev GKir NHar WPat |
| | ***prattii*** misapplied | see *S. munda* |
| | ***prattii*** Koehne | GKev GKir |
| | - var. ***subarachnoidea*** | see *S. munda* |
| * | ***pseudobalsomnensis*** | CBcs |
| | ***pseudofennica*** | GKir |
| | ***pseudovilmorinii*** | EWTr GBin GKir |
| | - MF 93044 | SSpi |
| | ***randaiensis*** | GQui SPlb |
| | - B&SWJ 3202 | NHol SSpi WCru |
| | 'Ravensbill' | GKir MAsh |
| | 'Red Tip' | CDul MWat |
| | ***reducta*** ♀H4 | CBcs CEnd CSWP CSec EBee EHig EPfP GAuc GBin GKev GKir GQui ISea LRHS MBlu NHar NHol NWea SCoo SPer SPoG WDin WFar |
| | ***reflexipetala*** misapplied | see *S. commixta* |
| | ***rehderiana*** misapplied | see *S. aucuparia* |
| | ***rehderiana*** Koehne | CLnd GKir |
| § | ***reticulata*** subsp. ***pekinensis*** | GKir |
| | ***rosea*** | CSBt EMui GKir LRHS |
| | - 'Rosiness' | CLnd EHig EPfP GKir MBri MLan SCoo SLim |
| | 'Rowancroft Coral Pink' | CDul EBee MBar MGos |
| | ***rufopilosa*** | GKir WPat |
| | 'Salmon Queen' | CLnd |
| | ***sargentiana*** ♀H4 | Widely available |
| | ***scalaris*** ambig. | EMil GAuc MGos |
| § | ***scalaris*** Koehne | CBcs CCVT CEnd CTho CTri EBee EPfP GKir LRHS MAsh MBlu MGos SCoo SPer SPoG SSpi WDin WJas WOrn |
| | 'Schouten' | ECrN SBLw |
| | ***scopulina*** misapplied | see *S. aucuparia* 'Fastigiata' |
| | ***setschwanensis*** | CMCN GGGa GKir |
| | 'Signalman' | GKir |
| | ***subcuneata*** **new** | CNat |
| | 'Sunshine' | CCVT CDoC CDul GKir MAsh MGos MMuc NLar WJas |
| | ***thibetica*** | WPGP |
| § | - 'John Mitchell' ♀H4 | CAgr CDul CEnd CLnd CMCN CWib ECrN EPfP GKir GQui LRHS MAsh MBlu MBri MGos MRav NBea NLar NWea SBir SLim SMHT SPer SPoG WFar WJas WOrn |
| | aff. ***thibetica*** BWJ 7757a | WCru |
| | ***thomsonii*** GWJ 9363 | WCru |
| § | x ***thuringiaca*** | GAuc LBuc NBea WMou |
| § | - 'Fastigiata' | CBcs CDul CLnd CSBt EPfP LPan MAsh MGos MMuc NBee SBLw SCoo WDin WJas |
| § | - 'Scarlet King' | EBee |
| | ***torminalis*** | CCVT CDul CLnd CTho CTri EBee ECrN EMac EPfP GKir LRHS MBlu MBri MRav NWea SBLw SCoo SEND SPer SPoG WDin WFar WHar WMou WOrn |
| | ***umbellata*** | CMCN GKir |
| | - var. ***cretica*** | see *S. graeca* |
| | ***ursina*** | see *S. foliolosa* |
| | x ***vagensis*** | CLnd GKir WMou |
| | ***verrucosa*** var. ***subulata*** HWJ 579 | WCru |
| | - - HWJ 925 **new** | WCru |
| § | ***vestita*** | CLnd CMCN CTho GKir MBlu |
| | ***vexans*** | CDul CNat GBin |
| | ***vilmorinii*** ♀H4 | Widely available |
| | - 'Robusta' | see *S.* 'Pink Pearl' |
| | ***wardii*** | CBcs CLnd CTho EPfP GKir MBlu |
| | 'White Wax' | CDul CWSG EPfP GKir GQue LAst MGos MMuc SBLw SPer SPoG WDin WPat |
| | 'Wilfrid Fox' | CLnd EHig SHBN SLPl |
| | ***wilmottiana*** | CDul GKir |
| | ***wilsoniana*** | CLnd GKir GQui |
| | - C 5018 **new** | GKir |
| | - C&H 7122 **new** | GKir |
| | 'Wisley Gold' | CWSG LRHS MAsh MGos NLar SCoo SLim SPoG WHCr |

## *Sorghastrum* (*Poaceae*)

| | | |
|---|---|---|
| | ***avenaceum*** | see *S. nutans* |
| § | ***nutans*** | CKno CRWN CWCL GFor LEdu SMad |
| | - 'Indian Steel' | CSam EBee ECha GFor GQue MSte NBsh |

## *Sorghum* (*Poaceae*)

| | | |
|---|---|---|
| | ***halepense*** | MSte |

## sorrel, common see *Rumex acetosa*

## sorrel, French see *Rumex scutatus*

## *Souliea* see *Actaea*

## soursop see *Annona muricata*

## *Sparaxis* (*Iridaceae*)

**bulbifera** EСho
**grandiflora** subsp. **grandiflora** CGrW ECho WCot
hybrids LAma
**parviflora** ECho
**tricolor** EBrs ECho WHil
**variegata** subsp. **metelerkampiae** (v) CDes
**villosa** ECho

## *Sparganium* (*Sparganiaceae*)

§ **erectum** CRow CSec EHon EMFW LPBA NPer NSco SWat WMAq WSFF
**ramosum** see *S. erectum*

## *Sparrmannia* (*Tiliaceae*)

**africana** ♀H1 CBcs CHEx CHll CKob CTrG EAmu EShb MBri SDnm SPav WBod
**palmata** see *S. ricinocarpa*
§ **ricinocarpa** CKob

## *Spathipappus* see *Tanacetum*

## *Spartina* (*Poaceae*)

'Dafken' new EBee
**patens** EPPr
**pectinata** CHEx CHar GFor
- 'Aureomarginata' (v) Widely available

## *Spartium* (*Papilionaceae*)

**junceum** ♀H4 CArn CBcs CDoC CDul CEnd CTri EBee ECrN ELan EMil EPfP LAst LRHS MGos NBlu NSti SArc SDix SGar SHBN SPer SPoG SRms WBod WDin
- 'Brockhill Compact' CDoC EBee EMil LRHS

## *Spartocytisus* see *Cytisus*

## *Spathantheum* (*Araceae*)

**orbignyanum** EBee LFur WCot

## *Spathiphyllum* (*Araceae*)

'Viscount' MBri
**wallisii** CHal LRHS MBri

## spearmint see *Mentha spicata*

## *Speirantha* (*Convallariaceae*)

§ **convallarioides** CDes CGHE CLAP CPom CStu EBee ECho EHrv ELon EPPr ERos LEdu WCot WCru WPGP WPrP
**gardenii** see *S. convallarioides*

## *Spergularia* (*Caryophyllaceae*)

**purpurea** ECho
**rupicola** CSec EBWF ECho

## *Sphacele* see *Lepechinia*

## *Sphaeralcea* (*Malvaceae*)

sp new SAga
**ambigua** ELan
'Childerley' CSpe EBee LHop SAga SMrm SMrs
**coccinea** SPlb
**fendleri** CHll
'Hopleys Lavender' EBee EPPr LAst LHop LSou NLar SAga SWvt
'Hyde Hall' EBee EPPr WBor
**incana** CSpe SAga
**malviflora** CDTJ WPer
**miniata** CHll ELan SAga SMrm
**munroana** CDMG CDTJ CPom CSev EBee ECGP ELan LHop SAga SRkn
- 'Dixieland Pink' EBee
- 'Manor Nursery' (v) LHop
- pale pink-flowered ECtt
* - 'Shell Pink' CSpe ECGP
'Newleaze Coral' CSpe EBee LHop LSou NLar SAga SMrs SPoG SUsu SWvt
'Newleaze Pink' LHop SAga SRkn
**obtusiloba** CSpe
**remota** CPLG SPlb
**umbellata** see *Phymosia umbellata*

## *Sphaeromeria* (*Asteraceae*)

§ **capitata** NWCA

## *Spigelia* (*Loganiaceae*)

**marilandica** CDes
- 'Wisley Jester' GKir LBuc LRHS MBri SCoo SKHP SMrm

## *Spilanthes* (*Asteraceae*)

**acmella** misapplied see *Acmella oleracea*
**oleracea** see *Acmella oleracea*

## *Spiraea* (*Rosaceae*)

'Abigail' CDoC
**albiflora** see *S. japonica* var. *albiflora*
**arborea** see *Sorbaria kirilowii*
**arcuata** EMac
§ 'Arguta' ♀H4 Widely available
x **arguta** 'Bridal Wreath' see *S.* 'Arguta'
**bella** SLon WTin
**betulifolia** CDul MRav NHol WDin WHCG
- var. **aemiliana** CWSG EBee ECtt LBMP MAsh MGos SLPl WFar
x **billardii** misapplied see *S.* x *pseudosalicifolia*
x **bumalda** see *S. japonica* 'Bumalda'
- 'Wulfenii' see *S. japonica* 'Walluf'
**callosa** 'Alba' see *S. japonica* var. *albiflora*
**canescens** CPLG GKev
§ **cantoniensis** 'Flore Pleno' (d) SLon
- 'Lanceata' see *S. cantoniensis* 'Flore Pleno'
x **cinerea** 'Grefsheim' ♀H4 CDoC CSBt EBee ECtt MBri MMuc SLim SPer SPlb WCFE WDin WFar
**crispifolia** see *S. japonica* 'Bullata'
**douglasii** CMac GAuc MBar
**formosana** WCru
- B&SWJ 1597 CPLG
§ x **foxii** SLPl
**fritschiana** CMac SLPl SLon
**hayatana** SLon
- RWJ 10014 WCru
**hendersonii** see *Petrophytum hendersonii*
**japonica** GKir SBod WFar
§ - var. **albiflora** CMac CSBt CTri CWib ELan EPfP GKir LAst LBMP LRHS MBar MGos MRav MSwo MWat NHol NPri SEND SHBN SLim SPer SPla SRms SWvt WDin WFar WHCG WMoo
- 'Alpina' see *S. japonica* 'Nana'
- 'Alpine Gold' GBin NPro
- 'Anthony Waterer' (v) Widely available
- 'Barkby Gold' MGos
- 'Blenheim' SRms

| | | |
|---|---|---|
| § | - 'Bullata' | CFee CMac EBee EPfP GEdr MBar NWCA SPer SRms WAbe |
| § | - 'Bumalda' | WFar |
| | - 'Candlelight' ℽ$^{H4}$ | CAbP CSBt CWSG EBee EPfP GKir LAst LRHS MAsh MBri MGos NHol NPri SCoo SHBN SLim SPer SPla SPoG SWvt WMoo |
| | - 'Coccinea' **new** | ELon |
| | - 'Crispa' | EMil EPfP LRHS MBar NPro WBod WFar WLeb WMoo |
| | - 'Dart's Red' ℽ$^{H4}$ | GKir NPri WFar |
| | - 'Firelight' | CAbP CSBt EBee EHoe ELan EPfP GKir LAst LHop LRHS MAsh MBri MGos MSwo NHol NPri SCoo SLim SPer SPla SPoG SSta SWvt WDin WFar |
| § | - 'Genpei' | CChe CMac MAsh NBlu SPer |
| | - 'Glenroy Gold' | SLon |
| | - 'Gold Mound' | CChe CMac CPLG CWSG CWib EBee ECrN EHoe ELan EPfP GKir LBMP LRHS MAsh MBar MGos MRav MSwo NHol NPri SCoo SPer SPlb SRms WDin WFar WHar |
| | - Golden Princess = 'Lisp'$^{PBR}$ ℽ$^{H4}$ | CMac CTri CWSG EPfP GKir LBuc LRHS MAsh MBar MGos NPri SCoo SReu SRms SSta WCFE WDin WFar |
| | - 'Goldflame' | Widely available |
| | - 'Little Princess' | CBcs CDul CMac CWSG CWib EBee ECrN EMil GKir LRHS MAsh MBar MRav MSwo NHol NPri SCoo SLim SPer SRGP SRms SSta SWvt WBVN WDin WFar WHar WMoo |
| | - 'Macrophylla' | CEnt |
| | - Magic Carpet = 'Walbuma'$^{PBR}$ (v) ℽ$^{H4}$ | EBee EBrs GKir LRHS MAsh NLar SCoo SPoG |
| | - 'Magnifica' | WHCG WPat |
| § | - 'Nana' ℽ$^{H4}$ | CMac CSBt ECho MAsh MBar MRav SRms WEas WPer |
| | - 'Nyewoods' | see *S. japonica* 'Nana' |
| | - 'Shiburi' | see *S. japonica* var. *albiflora* |
| N | - 'Shirobana' misapplied | see *S. japonica* 'Genpei' |
| N | - 'Shirobana' | see *S. japonica* var. *albiflora* |
| | - 'Snow Cap' | CWib |
| § | - 'Walluf' | CMac CPLG CTri CWib |
| | - 'White Cloud' | ELan |
| | - 'White Gold'$^{PBR}$ | CAbP CSBt EBee ELan EPfP LAst LRHS MAsh MBri NPro SCoo SPer SPoG SWvt WHar WMoo WOVN |
| | 'Margaritae' | SPer SWvt |
| | ***micrantha*** | CPLG |
| | ***nipponica*** | CBcs GKir LAst MBar |
| | - 'Halward's Silver' | EMil LBuc MGos MRav NHol NPro SLPl |
| | - 'June Bride' | NBlu |
| § | - 'Snowmound' ℽ$^{H4}$ | Widely available |
| | - var. ***tosaensis*** misapplied | see *S. nipponica* 'Snowmound' |
| | - var. ***tosaensis*** (Yatabe) Makino | LHop SReu |
| | ***palmata*** 'Elegans' | see *Filipendula purpurea* 'Elegans' |
| § | ***prunifolia*** (d) | CMac ECrN ELan MBlu MRav SLon SPer SPoG WBod WDin WPat |
| | x ***pseudosalicifolia*** 'Triumphans' | MMuc |
| | ***salicifolia*** | WFar |
| | ***stevenii*** | SPer |
| | 'Summersnow' | SLPl |
| | 'Superba' | see *S.* x *foxii* |
| | ***tarokoensis*** | GAuc |
| | ***thunbergii*** ℽ$^{H4}$ | CDul CSBt CTri CWib EBee ECrN EPfP MRav NWea SCoo SLim SPer SRms WDin WGwG WHCG |
| | - 'Fujino Pink' | WDin |
| | - 'Mellow Yellow' | see *S. thunbergii* 'Ogon' |
| | - 'Mount Fuji' | CAbP CMac CWib EHoe MGos MRav NPro WFar |
| § | - 'Ōgon' | WFar WPen |
| | ***ulmaria*** | see *Filipendula ulmaria* |
| | x ***vanhouttei*** | CBcs CSBt CTri EBee EMil EPfP MBar MRav MSwo SHBN SLim SPer SPla SRms WDin WFar |
| | - 'Gold Fountain' | GBin NHol SPoG WFar |
| | - 'Pink Ice' (v) | CAbP CDoC CMHG CWib EHoe EPfP LAst LBMP LHop LRHS MAsh MGos NHol SHBN SPer SPlb SPoG SWvt WDin WFar |
| | ***veitchii*** | MRav |
| | ***venusta*** 'Magnifica' | see *Filipendula rubra* 'Venusta' |

## *Spiranthes* (*Orchidaceae*)

| | | |
|---|---|---|
| | ***cernua*** | NLAp |
| | - var. ***odorata*** | LSou |
| | - - 'Chadd's Ford' | Widely available |
| | ***spiralis*** | WHer |

## *Spirodela* (*Lemnaceae*)

| | | |
|---|---|---|
| § | ***polyrhiza*** | CWat EMFW |

## *Spodiopogon* (*Poaceae*)

| | | |
|---|---|---|
| | ***sibiricus*** | CKno EBee EHoe EMon EPPr GFor LDai LEdu MSte MWhi SMad |

## *Sporobolus* (*Poaceae*)

| | | |
|---|---|---|
| | ***airoides*** | CKno EBee EHig EHoe EPPr GCal LPio MWea |
| | ***heterolepis*** | CKno EBee EHoe EShb GCal LPio MSte MWhi NDov SMad |
| | 'Heterolepis Cloud' | GBin |
| | ***wrightii*** | EBee |

## *Spraguea* (*Portulacaceae*)

| | | |
|---|---|---|
| | 'Powder Puff' | LRHS |
| § | ***umbellata*** | EDAr |

## *Sprekelia* (*Amaryllidaceae*)

| | | |
|---|---|---|
| | ***formosissima*** | CFir CSpe CStu EBrs ECho LAma LEdu LRHS SPav |

## *Stachys* ✿ (*Lamiaceae*)

| | | |
|---|---|---|
| | B&SWJ 10427 from Guatemala | WCru |
| | ***aethiopica*** 'Danielle' | see *S. thunbergii* 'Danielle' |
| § | ***affinis*** | CAgr CArn CFir ELau GPoy LEdu SVic |
| | ***albens*** | CSec EBla IFro |
| | ***albotomentosa*** | EBee EBla GBri LHop LSou MDKP SHar WCHb WCot WWlt |
| | ***alpina*** | CNat EBee |
| | x ***ambigua*** | EBWF |
| | ***bacanica*** | CDes EBee |
| | - MESE | WPGP |
| | ***betonica*** | see *S. officinalis* |
| § | ***byzantina*** | Widely available |
| § | - 'Big Ears' | CAby CBow EBee ECha EPfP EWTr GMaP LAst LCro LHop MBri MRav MWat NDov SBch SEND SMrm SPhx SPoG WBor WCAu WCFE WCot WFar WHoo WMnd WMoo |
| § | - 'Cotton Boll' | COlW EBee ECha GCal MHar SBch SPer WFar |
| | - 'Countess Helen von Stein' | see *S. byzantina* 'Big Ears' |
| | - gold-leaved | see *S. byzantina* 'Primrose Heron' |
| | - large-leaved | see *S. byzantina* 'Big Ears' |
| | - 'Limelight' | WCot |
| § | - 'Primrose Heron' | CMoH EBee ECha ECot GKev LRHS MRav NBid NLar NOrc SMrm SWvt WFar WOut |

| | | |
|---|---|---|
| | - 'Sheila McQueen' | see *S. byzantina* 'Cotton Boll' |
| | - 'Silky Fleece' | EBee ECha EDAr EShb GKir LBMP |
| | - 'Silver Carpet' | Widely available |
| § | - 'Striped Phantom' (v) | CBow EBla WCAu WCHb WEas |
| | - 'Variegata' | see *S. byzantina* 'Striped Phantom' |
| | ***candida*** | WAbe |
| | ***chrysantha*** | SPhx |
| | ***citrina*** | CMea EBee GCal SPhx |
| | ***coccinea*** | CHFP EBee ECtt EHrv EShb GBBs MCot MHer SBch SDnm SPav SRkn SWal WCHb WCot WFar WMoo WRos |
| | - B&SWJ 10418 | WCru |
| | ***corsica*** | WPGP |
| | ***cretica*** | WWlt |
| | ***densiflora*** | see *S. monieri* (Gouan) P.W. Ball |
| § | ***discolor*** | CMea EBee GBri MDKP MLLN NLar SBch SPhx WCot WOut WPer |
| | ***germanica*** | CPom EBee GPWP NBre |
| | ***glutinosa*** | MDKP |
| | ***grandiflora*** | see *S. macrantha* |
| | 'Hidalgo' | CSpe SAga |
| | ***iva*** | SPhx |
| | ***lanata*** | see *S. byzantina* |
| | ***lavandulifolia*** | WAbe |
| § | ***macrantha*** | Widely available |
| * | - 'Alba' | EBee ECha WMoo |
| | - 'Cally Splash' (v) | GCal |
| | - 'Hummelo' | see *S. officinalis* 'Hummelo' |
| * | - 'Nivea' | CSam EHrv ELan MMHG NBir |
| | - 'Robusta' ♀H4 | CDes ELan GCal NBro NGdn SMrm WCAu WCot WRHF |
| | - 'Rosea' | CElw CMHG EBee ELan GMaP LLWP MArl MAvo MLHP SPlb SWat WCFE WEas WPer WRha |
| | - 'Superba' | CSpe EBee EBla ECtt EPfP GCra GMaP LAst LBMP LRHS MBri MMHG MRav MWhi NBPC SPer SWvt WBor WCHb WCot WFar WMnd WMoo |
| | - 'Violacea' | EBee MAvo MBrN NChi WCot WPGP |
| | ***mexicana*** misapplied | see *S. thunbergii* |
| | ***monieri*** misapplied | see *S. officinalis* |
| | ***monieri*** ambig. | CAbP CMMP EBee EGle EShb GKev LBMP MAvo NLar SWal WPer |
| § | ***monieri*** (Gouan) P.W. Ball | CEnt GBin LBMP LEdu MAvo WOut |
| * | - 'Rosea' | EBee NBre NLar WOut |
| | - 'Saharan Pink' | see *S. officinalis* 'Saharan Pink' |
| | ***nivea*** | see *S. discolor* |
| | ***obliqua*** | NBre WOut |
| § | ***officinalis*** | CArn CEnt CPrp CRWN CSev CWan EBWF EBee GBar GPoy LEdu MHer MNHC MSal NLan NMir NPri WHer |
| | - SDR 3554 | GKev |
| | - 'Alba' | CArn CPrp EBee LEdu NBro STes WCAu WCHb WFar WHer WOut WRha WTin |
| | - dwarf, white | GCal |
| § | - 'Hummelo' | EBee ECtt EGle ELon EMon EPPr EPfP GAbr GQue LDai LHop LPla LSou MDKP MSte NBPC NDov NLar SAga SMrm SPhx SPoG SUsu WCAu WFar |
| | - mauve-flowered | WTin |
| | - 'Powder Puff' | EBee |
| | - 'Rosea' | CMea GCal NBro STes WCot WFar WSHC WTin |
| | - 'Rosea Superba' | EBee ECha MDKP NBre SIng WCAu WCot WFar WMoo |
| § | - 'Saharan Pink' | EBee EPfP LSou MHer WMoo WOut |
| | - 'Spitzenberg' | EMon SUsu |
| | - 'Wisley White' | EBee WCot |
| | ***olympica*** | see *S. byzantina* |
| | ***ossetica*** | CDes EBee |
| | ***palustris*** | CArn EBWF LPBA NLan NMir NSco WFar |
| | - albino **new** | WOut |
| | ***recta*** | CEnt NBHF SPhx |
| | ***scardica*** MESE 362 | MDKP |
| | ***setifera*** | EBee EBla NBre |
| | ***spicata*** | see *S. macrantha* |
| | ***sylvatica*** | CArn EBWF NLan NMir NSco WHer |
| | - 'Hoskin's Variegated' (v) | WCHb |
| | - 'Huskers' (v) | LSou NBre |
| | - 'Shade of Pale' | WAlt |
| § | ***thunbergii*** | CDes EShb LEdu MBrN MDKP MSte MWhi SBch SMeo SPhx SSvw SUsu WOut WPGP WPrP |
| § | - 'Danielle' | CBow CHFP EAro EBee ECtt LAst MHer NBre SPoG SRGP SRkn WMoo WOVN |
| | ***tuberifera*** | see *S. affinis* |

## *Stachytarpheta* (*Verbenaceae*)

| | | |
|---|---|---|
| | ***mutabilis*** | SBig |

## *Stachyurus* (*Stachyuraceae*)

| | | |
|---|---|---|
| | ***chinensis*** | CBcs CMCN CPMA CTri CWib IArd IDee IMGH LRHS MGos NLar SPoG |
| | - 'Celina' | CPMA EMil MBlu MBri MGos NLar |
| | - 'Goldbeater' | NLar |
| | - 'Joy Forever' (v) | CBcs CDoC CDul CEnd CMCN EBee EMil EPfP IArd IDee LLHF LSRN MBlu MBri MGos NLar SPoG SSpi SSta SWvt |
| | ***himalaicus*** | NLar |
| | - HWJCM 009 | WCru |
| | - HWJK 2035 | WCru |
| | ***leucotrichus*** | CPMA |
| | 'Magpie' (v) | CPMA EPfP MGos NLar SAga WCru |
| | ***praecox*** ♀H4 | Widely available |
| | - B&SWJ 8898 | WCru |
| | - var. ***matsuzakii*** | CPMA NBhm |
| | - - B&SWJ 2817 | WCru |
| | - - 'Scherzo' (v) | WCru |
| * | - 'Rubriflorus' | CPMA ELan EPfP LRHS MAsh MBri NLar SPoG WFar |
| | ***salicifolius*** | CGHE CPMA IDee MBri NLar SKHP SSpi WPGP |
| * | ***sigeyosii*** B&SWJ 6915 | WCru |
| | aff. ***szechuanensis*** BWJ 8153 | WCru |
| | ***yunnanensis*** | WSHC |

## *Stapelia* (*Asclepiadaceae*)

| | | |
|---|---|---|
| | ***asterias*** **new** | CFwr |
| | ***gettliffei*** | CFwr EShb |
| | ***gigantea*** ♀H1 **new** | CFwr |
| | ***grandiflora*** | CFwr EShb |
| | - 'Flavirostris' **new** | CFwr |
| | ***hirsuta*** **new** | CFwr EShb |
| | ***leendertziae*** **new** | CFwr |
| | ***macowanii*** **new** | CFwr |
| | ***marmoratum*** | see *Orbea variegata* |
| | ***mutabilis*** **new** | CFwr |
| | ***variegata*** | see *Orbea variegata* |

## *Staphylea* (*Staphyleaceae*)

| | | |
|---|---|---|
| | ***bolanderi*** | CBcs NLar |
| | ***bumalda*** | CBcs CPMA EPfP NLar |
| | - B&SWJ 11053 **new** | WCru |
| | ***colchica*** | CBcs EBee ELan EPfP EWTr MGos NLar NPal SMad SPer WDin WSHC |
| | x ***coulombieri*** **new** | CBcs |

| | |
|---|---|
| ***holocarpa*** | CBcs CPMA EPfP LHop MRav WFar |
| - 'Innocence' | CBcs CDul NLar |
| N - var. ***rosea*** | CPMA EPfP MBri SMad |
| N - 'Rosea' | CBcs CPMA MBlu NLar SKHP SSpi WSHC |
| ***pinnata*** | CAgr CBcs CEnd CPMA EBee EPfP LEdu SEND SMad WHCr WPat |
| ***trifolia*** | CAgr CBcs |

## *Statice* see *Limonium*

## *Stauntonia* (*Lardizabalaceae*)

| | |
|---|---|
| ***hexaphylla*** | CBcs CDoC CHEx CSam CTri EBee EPfP LRHS MAsh MBri SAdn SBig SPer SPoG SReu SRkn SSpi SSta WBrE WSHC |
| - B&SWJ 4858 | WCru |
| ***obovatifoliola*** B&SWJ 3685 | WCru |
| ***purpurea*** | NLar |
| - B&SWJ 3690 | WCru |
| ***yaoshanensis*** HWJ 1024 **new** | WCru |

## *Stegnogramma* (*Thelypteridaceae*)

| | |
|---|---|
| ***pozoi*** | EFer |

## *Stellaria* (*Caryophyllaceae*)

| | |
|---|---|
| ***graminea*** | EBWF |
| ***holostea*** | CArn CRWN EBWF NMir NSco WPtf WShi |

## *Stellera* (*Thymelaeaceae*)

| | |
|---|---|
| ***chamaejasme*** | CExc |

## *Stemmacantha* (*Asteraceae*)

| | |
|---|---|
| ***carthamoides*** | CArn MSal |
| § ***centaureoides*** | EBee ECGP ECha EGle GBin GCal GQue NBid NBre SMeo SPhx SUsu WCAu WCot |
| § ***rhapontica*** | NBre |

## *Stenanthium* (*Melanthiaceae*)

| | |
|---|---|
| ***robustum*** | WPGP |

## *Stenocarpus* (*Proteaceae*)

| | |
|---|---|
| ***sinuatus*** | EShb |

## *Stenochlaena* (*Blechnaceae*)

| | |
|---|---|
| ***palustris*** | MBri |

## *Stenomesson* (*Amaryllidaceae*)

| | |
|---|---|
| § ***miniatum*** | CStu WCot |
| ***pearcei*** | WCot WPrP |
| ***variegatum*** | WCot |

## *Stenotaphrum* (*Poaceae*)

| | |
|---|---|
| ***secundatum*** | EShb |
| - 'Variegatum' (v) ♀H1 | CHal EShb LSou WDyG |

## *Stephanandra* (*Rosaceae*)

| | |
|---|---|
| ***chinensis*** | SLon |
| ***incisa*** | CBcs CPLG GKev WHCG |
| § - 'Crispa' | CDoC CDul CTri EBee ECrN ELan EMil EPfP EWTr LAst LHop MBar MBlu MRav NHol SHBN SPer SPla SPoG WCFE WDin WFar WHCG WMoo |
| - 'Dart's Horizon' | SLPl |
| - 'Prostrata' | see *S. incisa* 'Crispa' |
| ***tanakae*** | CBcs CDoC CDul CPLG CTri EBee ELan EPfP EWTr IMGH LAst MBar MBlu MRav SHBN SLPl SLon SPer SPla SPoG WDin WFar WHCG |

## *Stephania* (*Menispermaceae*)

| | |
|---|---|
| ***japonica*** B&SWJ 2396 | WCru |

## *Stephanotis* (*Asclepiadaceae*)

| | |
|---|---|
| ***floribunda*** ♀H1 | CBcs CCCN EBak LRHS MBri SOWG |

## *Sterculia* (*Sterculiaceae*)

| | |
|---|---|
| ***rupestris*** | see *Brachychiton rupestris* |

## *Sternbergia* (*Amaryllidaceae*)

| | |
|---|---|
| 'Autumn Gold' | EBee EBrs ECho GKev LAma |
| ***candida*** | CBro EBrs ECho |
| § ***clusiana*** | EBrs ECho WWst |
| ***colchiciflora*** | CPBP EBrs ECho |
| ***fischeriana*** | CBro EBrs ECho |
| ***greuteriana*** | EBrs ECho EPot |
| ***lutea*** | CAvo CBro CPBP CStu EBrs ECho EPot ERCP EWes LAma LRHS NWCA SDix SPhx WEas WRHF WTin |
| - Angustifolia Group | CBro CDes CMea EBee EBrs ECho EMon WCot |
| ***macrantha*** | see *S. clusiana* |
| ***sicula*** | CBro CMea CStu EBrs ECho EPot WCot |
| - var. ***graeca*** | EBrs ECho |
| - - from Crete | ECho |
| - 'John Marr' | WThu |

## *Stevia* (*Asteraceae*)

| | |
|---|---|
| ***rebaudiana*** | CArn EBee EOHP GPoy MSal WCot |

## *Stewartia* ✿ (*Theaceae*)

| | |
|---|---|
| ***gemmata*** | see *S. sinensis* |
| 'Korean Splendor' | see *S. pseudocamellia* Koreana Group |
| ***koreana*** | see *S. pseudocamellia* Koreana Group |
| ***malacodendron*** ♀H4 | EPfP LRHS SSpi |
| ***monadelpha*** | CMen LLHF SSpi |
| ***ovata*** | CMen SSpi |
| N - var. ***grandiflora*** | LRHS |
| ***pseudocamellia*** ♀H4 | Widely available |
| § - Koreana Group ♀H4 | CBcs CDul CEnd CMCN CTho ECrN EPfP LRHS MBri MDun NLar SSpi WDin WFar WPGP |
| ***pteropetiolata*** | WPGP |
| ***rostrata*** | CBcs CPMA IArd IDee MBlu MBri NLar SSpi WFar |
| ***serrata*** | CMen IArd IDee NBhm SSpi |
| § ***sinensis*** ♀H4 | CPMA EPfP LPan MBlu NLar SSpi SSta |

## *Stigmaphyllon* (*Malpighiaceae*)

| | |
|---|---|
| ***ciliatum*** | CCCN |
| ***littorale*** | CCCN |

## *Stipa* (*Poaceae*)

| | |
|---|---|
| F&M 32 **new** | WPGP |
| ***arundinacea*** | see *Anemanthele lessoniana* |
| ***barbata*** | CKno CSpe EBee ECha EGle EHoe EPPr EWes LBMP LRHS MAvo SApp SPer SUsu WCot WKif WPGP |
| - 'Silver Feather' | EWsh SLim |
| * ***boysterica*** | CFee |
| ***brachytricha*** | see *Calamagrostis brachytricha* |
| § ***calamagrostis*** | Widely available |
| - 'Algau' **new** | GBin |
| - 'Lemperg' | EPPr |
| ***canescens*** **new** | SPhx |

| | |
|---|---|
| ***capillata*** | CAby CKno CWsd EAlp EBee EGle EHoe EPPr GCal GFor NCGa SMad SWal WOVN WPGP |
| - 'Brautschleier' | CHrt CWib NBre SWal WPtf |
| ***caudata*** **new** | EBee |
| ***chrysophylla*** F&W 9321 | WPGP |
| ***columbiana*** | MLLN |
| ***comata*** | EBee |
| ***elegantissima*** | CKno EHoe GFor |
| ***extremiorientalis*** | CKno ECha EPPr GFor SLPl SMad |
| * ***gerardi*** | SApp |
| ***gigantea*** ♀H4 | Widely available |
| - 'Gold Fontaene' | CDes CFir CKno EBee ECha EPPr EWes MAvo MMoz MNrw NDov SBch SMad SPhx WCot WMoo WPGP WPrP |
| - 'Pixie' | ELon EWsh SApp SPhx |
| ***grandis*** | CKno ECha EPPr GBin GFor WHal WMoo WPer |
| ***ichu*** | CKno SDix |
| ***joannis*** | GCal |
| ***lasiagrostis*** | see *S. calamagrostis* |
| ***lessingiana*** | CHrt CPLG CSam EAlp EBee EHul NLar SEND WMoo WPGP |
| ***offneri*** | EBee EPPr EWes |
| ***pekinense*** | EBee |
| ***pennata*** | CBcs CKno CMea GFor WFar |
| ***pontica*** **new** | SPhx |
| ***pseudoichu*** RCB/Arg Y-1 | WCot |
| ***pulcherrima*** | CBow EPPr GCal LBMP LRHS MAvo |
| - subsp. ***pulcherrima*** **new** | SPhx |
| - 'Windfeder' | CFir LBMP SLPl SMad SMrm |
| ***ramosissima*** | CKno |
| ***robusta*** | EBee EPPr |
| ***splendens*** misapplied | see *S. calamagrostis* |
| ***splendens*** Trin. | CSam WFoF |
| ***stenophylla*** | see *S. tirsa* |
| ***stipoides*** | GGar |
| ***tenacissima*** | EBee ECha EHul GFor NCob NPri SUsu WDin WMoo |
| ***tenuifolia*** misapplied | see *S. tenuissima* |
| ***tenuifolia*** Steud. | CHar CMea CMil EBee EHul EPfP LCro LRHS MBri MRav NBir NBro NHol NOak NSti NVic SIng SPer WCAu WHal WMoo |
| § ***tenuissima*** | Widely available |
| § ***tirsa*** | GBin NDov SPhx |
| ***turkestanica*** | EBee GBin NDov SHDw SUsu SWat WHal |
| ***ucrainica*** | GAbr GFor |
| ***verticillata*** | CKno |

## *Stokesia* (*Asteraceae*)

| | |
|---|---|
| ***cyanea*** | see *S. laevis* |
| § ***laevis*** | CMea CPrp EBee ECGP ECha EGle EPfP GAbr GKir GMac NBro NLar SMrm SPet SPlb WBrE WCAu WFar WMoo WPGP WPer |
| - 'Alba' | CMMP CPrp CTca EBee ECha EGle EHrv ELan EPfP GKir LAst MMuc MRav SPad SPer SPhx STes WCAu |
| - 'Blue Star' | Widely available |
| - 'Klaus Jelitto' | CFwr EBee LEdu SHar |
| - 'Mary Gregory' | Widely available |
| - mixed | CPou MLan |
| - 'Omega Skyrocket' | CMHG CPou EBee ELon LRHS MLLN NHol SMrm SPad SPoG SUsu WBor WCAu WFar |
| - 'Peach Melba' | EBee ECtt NCGa WMoo |
| - 'Purple Parasols' | CMMP COIW CTca CWGN EBee EBrs ECtt EGle EPfP EShb GMac LAst LHop LLWG NCGa NSti SMrm SPhx SPoG STes SUsu SWvt WAul WFar WMoo |
| - 'Silver Moon' | CMHG COIW EAEE EBee ECtt EGle EPfP EShb LAst MTPN NBir NHol SAga WBor WCot WFar |
| - 'Träumerei' | CWGN EAEE EBee EGle GMac LAst LRHS NHol SMrm SPet WMnd WMoo |

## *Stranvaesia* see *Photinia*

## x *Stranvinia* see *Photinia*

## *Stratiotes* (*Hydrocharitaceae*)

| | |
|---|---|
| ***aloides*** | CDWL CWat EHon EMFW LPBA NPer NSco SVic SWat WMAq WPnP |

## strawberry see *Fragaria*

## *Strelitzia* (*Strelitziaceae*)

| | |
|---|---|
| ***alba*** | CCCN EAmu |
| ***juncea*** | XBlo |
| ***nicolai*** | CAbb CDTJ CFwr CKob EAmu EShb EUJe LPal LPan MJnS NPer SBig XBlo |
| ***reginae*** ♀H1 | CAbb CBcs CKob ELan EShb EUJe LPal LPan LRHS MJnS MREP NPal NPer NScw SAPC SArc SBig SChr SEND SPlb SRms XBlo |
| - 'Kirstenbosch Gold' | NPal XBlo |

## *Streptocarpella* see *Streptocarpus*

## *Streptocarpus* ✿ (*Gesneriaceae*)

| | |
|---|---|
| 'Albatross' ♀H1 | SBrm SDnm SPav WDib |
| 'Alice' | SBrm WDib |
| 'Amanda' Dibley ♀H1 | SBrm WDib |
| 'Amanda'PBR Fleischle (Marleen Series) | WDib |
| 'Anne' | CSpe MCot SBrm WDib |
| 'Athena' | CSpe SBrm WDib |
| ***baudertii*** | WDib |
| 'Beryl' | WDib |
| 'Bethan' ♀H1 | SBrm WDib |
| 'Black Gardenia' | NBPN WDib |
| 'Black Panther' | NBPN WDib |
| 'Blue Bird' | SBrm |
| 'Blue Gem' | WDib |
| 'Blue Heaven' | SBrm WDib |
| 'Blue Moon' | CHal WDib |
| 'Blue Nymph' | WDib |
| § 'Blue Upstart' | SBrm |
| 'Blushing Bride' (d) | SDnm SPav WDib |
| * 'Boysenberry Delight' | WDib |
| 'Branwen' | SBrm SDnm SPav WDib |
| 'Brimstone' | SBrm |
| 'Bristol's Black Bird' | NBPN SBrm WDib |
| 'Bristol's Ice Castle' | SBrm WDib |
| 'Bristol's Red Typhoon' **new** | SBrm |
| 'Bristol's Very Best' | WDib |
| 'Buttons' | SBrm |
| ***caeruleus*** | WDib |
| 'Caitlin' | WDib |
| ***candidus*** | WDib |
| 'Carol' | SBrm WDib |
| 'Carys' ♀H1 | WDib |
| 'Catania' (Marleen Series) | WDib |
| 'Catrin' ♀H1 | SBrm WDib |
| ***caulescens*** | CHal WDib |
| * - 'Compactus' | CHal |
| - var. ***pallescens*** | EOHP WDib |
| 'Charlotte' | SBrm WDib |
| 'Chloe' **new** | WDib |
| 'Chorus Line' ♀H1 | SDnm SPav WDib |
| 'Clare' | WDib |

| | | |
|---|---|---|
| | 'Clouds' | CSpe SBrm |
| | 'Concord Blue' | WDib |
| | 'Constant Nymph' | SBrm WDib |
| | 'Coral Flair' | WDib |
| | 'Cranberry Velvet' **new** | SBrm |
| | 'Crystal Beauty' PBR | WDib |
| | 'Crystal Blush' PBR | WDib |
| | 'Crystal Charm' PBR | WDib |
| | 'Crystal Dawn' PBR | WDib |
| | 'Crystal Ice' PBR ♀H1 | WDib |
| | 'Crystal Snow' PBR | WDib |
| | 'Crystal Wonder' PBR | WDib |
| | ***cyaneus*** | WDib |
| | - subsp. ***polackii*** | WDib |
| | 'Cynthia' ♀H1 | SBrm WDib |
| | 'Dainty Lady' | SBrm |
| | 'Daphne' ♀H1 | WDib |
| | 'Demeter' | SBrm |
| | 'Diana' | SBrm WDib |
| | 'Dinas' **new** | WDib |
| | ***dunnii*** | SGar WDib |
| | 'Eira' | WDib |
| | 'Elegance' | SBrm |
| | 'Ella' | SBrm |
| | 'Ellie' **new** | WDib |
| | 'Elsi' | SBrm SDnm SPav WDib |
| | 'Emily' | SBrm WDib |
| | 'Emma' | SBrm WDib |
| | 'Falling Stars' ♀H1 | CSpe SBrm WDib |
| | 'Festival Wales' | SBrm WDib |
| | 'Fiona' | SBrm WDib |
| | ***floribundus*** hort. | WDib |
| | 'Franken Alison' **new** | SBrm |
| | 'Franken Jenny' **new** | SBrm |
| | 'Franken Kelly' **new** | SBrm |
| | 'Franken Misty Blue' **new** | SBrm |
| | 'Franken Texas Sunset' **new** | SBrm |
| | 'Frosty Diamond' **new** | SBrm |
| | ***gardenii*** | WDib |
| | 'Gillian' | SBrm |
| | ***glandulosissimus*** ♀H1 | CHal EOHP WDib |
| | 'Gloria' ♀H1 | CSpe SBrm WDib |
| | 'Gower Midnight' | SBrm |
| | 'Grape Slush' | WDib |
| | 'Gwen' | SBrm WDib |
| | 'Hannah Ellis' | SBrm |
| | 'Happy Snappy' ♀H1 | SBrm SDnm SPav WDib |
| | 'Heidi' ♀H1 | SDnm SPav WDib |
| | 'Helen' ♀H1 | SBrm WDib |
| | 'Huge White' | CSpe |
| | 'Ida' | SBrm |
| | 'Inky Fingers' | SBrm |
| | 'Izzy' | SBrm |
| | 'Jaco's Gem' | WDib |
| | 'Jacquie' **new** | WDib |
| | 'Jane Elizabeth' | SBrm |
| | 'Jennifer' ♀H1 | SBrm SDnm SPav WDib |
| | 'Joanna' | SBrm WDib |
| | ***johannis*** | WDib |
| | 'Josie' | SBrm |
| | 'Judith' | SBrm |
| | 'Julie' | WDib |
| | 'Karen' | SBrm SDnm SPav WDib |
| | ***kentaniensis*** | WDib |
| | 'Kim' ♀H1 | CSpe EShb MCot NBPN SBrm SDnm SPav WDib |
| | ***kirkii*** | WDib |
| | 'Lady Lavender' **new** | SBrm |
| | 'Largesse' | SBrm |
| | 'Laura' ♀H1 | SBrm WDib |
| | 'Lemon Ice' | SBrm |
| | 'Lisa' ♀H1 | SBrm |
| | 'Little Gem' | CSpe |
| | 'Louise' | SBrm WDib |
| | 'Lynette' | SBrm |
| | 'Lynne' | SBrm WDib |
| | 'Maassen's White' ♀H1 | SBrm WDib |
| | 'Mandy' | SDnm SPav WDib |
| | 'Margaret' | SBrm WDib |
| | 'Marie' | WDib |
| | 'Mary' | SBrm |
| | 'Megan' | SBrm WDib |
| | 'Melanie' Dibley ♀H1 | SBrm WDib |
| I | 'Melanie' Fleischle (Marleen Series) | WDib |
| | ***meyeri*** | WDib |
| | 'Midnight Flame' | EShb SBrm WDib |
| | 'Mini Nymph' | CSpe WDib |
| | 'Misty Pink' | SBrm |
| | ***modestus*** | WDib |
| | 'Molly' | SBrm |
| | 'Moonlight' | SBrm WDib |
| | 'Neptune' | SBrm WDib |
| | 'Nerys' PBR | SBrm WDib |
| | 'Nia' | CSpe WDib |
| | 'Nicola' | SBrm WDib |
| | 'Olga' | WDib |
| | 'Olwen' | WDib |
| | 'Padarn' **new** | WDib |
| | 'Pale Rider' | SBrm |
| | 'Party Doll' | SBrm WDib |
| | 'Passion Pink' | SBrm WDib |
| | 'Patricia' | SBrm |
| | 'Paula' ♀H1 | SBrm WDib |
| | ***pentherianus*** | WDib |
| | 'Pink Fondant' | CSpe |
| | 'Pink Souffle' | SBrm SDnm SPav WDib |
| | 'Plum Crazy' | SBrm |
| | ***polyanthus*** subsp. ***dracomontanus*** | WDib |
| | ***primulifolius*** | WDib |
| | - subsp. ***formosus*** | WDib |
| | 'Princesse' (Marleen Series) | WDib |
| | ***prolixus*** | WDib |
| * | 'Purple Passion' | SBrm |
| | ***rexii*** | WDib |
| | 'Rhiannon' | CSpe SBrm SDnm SPav WDib |
| | 'Rosebud' | SBrm WDib |
| | 'Rosemary' (d) | SPav WDib |
| | 'Ruby' ♀H1 | SBrm WDib |
| | 'Ruby Anniversary' | SBrm |
| | 'Ruffled Lilac' | CSpe SBrm |
| | 'Ruffles' | SBrm |
| | 'Sally' | SBrm WDib |
| | 'Sandra' | SBrm SDnm SPav WDib |
| | 'Sarah' | SBrm SPav WDib |
| | ***saxorum*** ♀H1 | CCCN CHal EOHP EShb LSou MBri SRms WDib WFar |
| | - compact | CCCN EOHP WDib |
| | 'Seren' **new** | WDib |
| | 'Sian' | SBrm SDnm SPav WDib |
| | ***silvaticus*** | WDib |
| | 'Snow White' ♀H1 | CSpe SDnm SPav WDib |
| | 'Something Special' | SBrm SDnm WDib |
| | 'Sophie' | WDib |
| | 'Southshore' | SBrm WDib |
| | 'Stacey' | SBrm |
| | 'Stella' ♀H1 | SBrm WDib |
| | 'Stephanie' | CSpe MCot WDib |
| | ***stomandrus*** | WDib |
| | 'Stormy' | SBrm |
| | 'Strawberry Fondant' | SBrm |
| | 'Sugar Almond' | CSpe SBrm |
| | 'Susan' ♀H1 | WDib |
| | 'Swaybelle' | SBrm |
| | 'Tanga' | SBrm |

| | |
|---|---|
| 'Tatan Blue' | SBrm |
| 'Terracotta' | SBrm |
| 'Texas Hot Chili' | SBrm WDib |
| ***thompsonii*** | WDib |
| 'Tina' ♀H1 | SBrm SDnm SPav WDib |
| 'Tracey' | SBrm WDib |
| 'Turbulent Tide' | SBrm |
| 'Upstart' | see *S.* 'Blue Upstart' |
| ***variabilis*** | WDib |
| 'Velvet Underground' | SBrm |
| 'Vera' | SBrm |
| 'Violet Lace' | CSpe SBrm |
| 'Watermelon Wine' new | WDib |
| ***wendlandii*** | WDib |
| 'Wendy' | SBrm SPav WDib |
| 'White Wings' | SBrm |
| 'Wiesmoor Red' | WDib |
| 'Winifred' | SBrm WDib |

## *Streptopus* (*Convallariaceae*)

| | |
|---|---|
| ***amplexifolius*** | EBee EBrs ECho GBuc NMen WCru |
| ***parviflorus*** new | EBee |
| ***roseus*** | EBee ECho |
| ***simplex*** | EBee |
| ***streptopoides*** new | EBee |

## *Streptosolen* (*Solanaceae*)

| | |
|---|---|
| ***jamesonii*** ♀H1 | CHal CHll CSev CSpe EBak ELan EShb SAga |

## *Strobilanthes* (*Acanthaceae*)

| | |
|---|---|
| CC 4071 | CPLG |
| CC 4573 | CPLG |
| ***anisophylla*** | EShb MBNS |
| ***atropurpurea*** misapplied | see *S. attenuata* |
| ***atropurpurea*** Nees | see *S. wallichii* |
| § ***attenuata*** | ECha ECtt ELan EPfP EWll GCal GCra GKev GKir LHop LLWP MRav NCGa NSti SGar WCAu WCot WCru WFar WMoo WPer WPic WWlt |
| - subsp. ***nepalensis*** | CHll CLAP WPrP WRHF |
| - 'Out of the Ocean' | WOut |
| - 'Pieter' | EMon |
| ***dyeriana*** ♀H1 | CAbP CHal CSpe EBak ECtt ELan EShb LSou MJnS SGar WCot WHil WRha |
| ***flexicaulis*** | CDes WPGP WPrP |
| - B&SWJ 354 | WCru |
| - clone 2 | LSou |
| ***nutans*** | CDes CLAP CPom CPou CSpe EBee LSou MHar WHil WPrP |
| ***rankanensis*** | CDes CLAP EBee NGby SDys SKHP SMHy WHil WPrP |
| - B&SWJ 1771 | WCru |
| 'Silver Star' | EShb |
| ***violacea*** | CPrp WPer |
| § ***wallichii*** | CDes CLAP EBee EPPr EWes EWld LSou MHar NSti SUsu WCru WFar WPrP WSHC |

## *Stromanthe* (*Marantaceae*)

| | |
|---|---|
| ***amabilis*** | see *Ctenanthe amabilis* |
| ***sanguinea*** | CHal MBri |
| - 'Triostar'PBR (v) | XBlo |
| 'Stripestar' | MBri |

## *Strongylodon* (*Papilionaceae*)

| | |
|---|---|
| ***macrobotrys*** | SOWG |

## *Strophanthus* (*Apocynaceae*)

| | |
|---|---|
| ***speciosus*** | CCCN CHll EShb |

## *Struthiopteris* (*Blechnaceae*)

| | |
|---|---|
| ***niponica*** | see *Blechnum niponicum* |

## *Stuartia* see *Stewartia*

## *Stylidium* (*Stylidiaceae*)

| | |
|---|---|
| ***affine*** | SPlb |
| ***graminifolium*** | GGar SPlb |
| - 'Little Sapphire' | EBee NBsh NOak |
| - 'Tiny Trina' | EBee LRHS NBsh NCGa NOak SUsu |

## *Stylomecon* (*Papaveraceae*)

| | |
|---|---|
| ***heterophylla*** | CSec |

## *Stylophorum* (*Papaveraceae*)

| | |
|---|---|
| ***diphyllum*** | CFwr CPBP CPou EBee ECha EWld GBri GEdr MRav MSal NMen WCru WFar WPnP |
| ***lasiocarpum*** | CPLG CPom CSec CSpe EWes EWld LFur MWhi NBid SGar WCru WPrP WRos |

## *Styphelia* (*Epacridaceae*)

| | |
|---|---|
| ***colensoi*** | see *Leucopogon colensoi* |

## *Styrax* (*Styracaceae*)

| | |
|---|---|
| from Yunnan | CExc |
| ***americanus*** | CBcs GAuc NLar |
| ***faberi*** | CExc |
| ***formosanus*** | CGHE CTho EBee |
| - var. ***formosanus*** | EPfP WPGP |
| - - B&SWJ 3803 | WCru |
| - var. ***hayatiana*** B&SWJ 6823 | WCru |
| ***hemsleyanus*** ♀H4 | CAbP CBcs CTho ECrN EPfP GKir IArd IDee IMGH LRHS MBlu MDun MMuc NLar SPer SSpi WFar WPGP |
| ***japonicus*** ♀H4 | Widely available |
| - B&SWJ 4405 | WCru |
| § - Benibana Group ♀H4 | SSta |
| - - 'Pink Chimes' | CAbP CBcs CMCN CPLG CPMA EBee ELan EPfP LRHS MAsh MBlu MBri NLar SCoo SKHP SPer SPoG SSpi SSta |
| - 'Carillon' | CPMA |
| - 'Emerald Pagoda' new | SSpi |
| - 'Fargesii' | CBcs CDoC CDul CPMA CTho ECrN EPfP IDee IMGH LRHS MDun SCoo SSpi WFar |
| - 'Purple Dress' | NLar |
| - 'Roseus' | see *S. japonicus* Benibana Group |
| - 'Sohuksan' | WPGP |
| ***obassia*** ♀H4 | CBcs CDul CMCN CPne CTho EPfP GKir IArd IDee LRHS MBlu MBri MDun NLar SPer SSpi |
| - B&SWJ 6023 | WCru |
| ***odoratissimus*** | CExc WPGP |
| ***wuyuanensis*** | CBcs |

## *Succisa* (*Dipsacaceae*)

| | |
|---|---|
| § ***pratensis*** | CArn EBWF EBee MHer MWea NDov NLan NLar NMen NSco NWCA SBch SMHy SPhx SUsu WHer WRHF WSFF WTin |
| - ***alba*** | EWes MDKP |
| - 'Buttermilk' | SKHP |
| - 'Derby Purple' new | CSpe |
| - dwarf | NRya |
| - 'Peddar's Pink' | EBee EWes SPhx WAlt |

## *Succisella* (*Dipsacaceae*)

***inflexa*** CSec EBee SPhx
- 'Frosted Pearls' EBee EDAr LLWP MWat WHil

## sunberry see *Rubus* 'Sunberry'

## *Sutera* (*Scrophulariaceae*)

(Abunda Series) Abunda Blue Improved = 'Balabimblu' NPri
- Abunda White Improved = 'Balabwhiti'PBR **new** NPri
Cabana Trailing White = 'Sutcatrwhi'PBR WGor
Candy Floss = 'Yasflos' LAst
Copia Series Copia Dark Pink = 'Dancop19' (Copia Series) NPri
- Copia Golden Leaves LAst NPri
- Copia Great Purple **new** LAst LSou
- Copia Gulliver Lilac **new** LSou
- Copia Gulliver Lavender = 'Dangul16' (Copia Series) **new** NPri
- Copia Gulliver White = 'Dangul14' (Copia Series) LAst LSou
- Copia Pink Touch LAst
***cordata*** 'Blizzard' LAst LSou WGor
- Blue Showers = 'Bacoble'PBR LAst NBlu
- Lavender Showers = 'Sunlav'PBR NPri
- 'Olympic Gold' (v) ECtt LAst NBlu SCoo SPoG
- 'Pink Domino' ECtt SPet
§ - 'Snowflake' ECtt LAst MLan NBlu NPer SCoo SPet SPoG
***microphylla*** CPBP
***neglecta*** SPlb WPGP
Sea Mist = 'Yagemil'PBR NPri
(Suteranova Series) Suteranova Big Pink = 'Danova912' **new** NPri
- Suteranova Pink = 'Mogoto' LAst

## *Sutherlandia* (*Papilionaceae*)

***frutescens*** CArn CBod CSpe SPlb WOut
- 'Prostrata' MBri WPat

## *Swainsona* (*Papilionaceae*)

***galegifolia*** CHll
- 'Albiflora' CSpe EBee SOWG WWlt

## sweet cicely see *Myrrhis odorata*

## *Swertia* (*Gentianaceae*)

***bimaculata*** EBee

## *Syagrus* (*Arecaceae*)

***botryophora*** **new** XBlo
§ ***romanzoffiana*** CBrP EAmu LPJP LPal
***weddeliana*** see *Lytocaryum weddellianum*

## x *Sycoparrotia* (*Hamamelidaceae*)

***semidecidua*** CBcs CPMA MBlu NLar SLPl WPGP
- 'Purple Haze' **new** NLar

## *Sycopsis* (*Hamamelidaceae*)

***sinensis*** CAbP CMCN CWib EBee EMil EPfP LRHS MBlu NLar SDnm SSpi WBod WDin WFar WPGP WSHC

## *Symphoricarpos* (*Caprifoliaceae*)

***albus*** CDul ECrN EMac GKir MSwo NWea SPoG WDin
- 'Constance Spry' SRms
§ - var. ***laevigatus*** EPfP LBuc MBar
§ - 'Taff's White' (v) WMoo
- 'Variegatus' see *S. albus* 'Taff's White'
x ***chenaultii*** 'Hancock' CMac EBee ECrN ELan EMac EMil EPfP MBar MGos MMuc MRav MSwo NPro SLim SPer WDin
x ***doorenbosii*** 'Magic Berry' EMil MBar MRav NWea
- 'Mother of Pearl' ELan EMac EPfP GKir MBar MGos MMuc MRav NBlu NWea SPer
- 'White Hedge' CSBt ELan LBuc MMuc MRav NWea SPer SPlb SPoG
***guatemalensis*** B&SWJ 1016 **new** WCru
***orbiculatus*** IMGH SLon
- 'Albovariegatus' see *S. orbiculatus* 'Taff's Silver Edge'
- 'Argenteovariegatus' see *S. orbiculatus* 'Taff's Silver Edge'
- 'Bowles' Golden Variegated' see *S. orbiculatus* 'Foliis Variegatis'
§ - 'Foliis Variegatis' (v) CTri EBee ECrN EHoe ELan EPfP MGos MRav NPro SPer WDin WEas WFar WHCG WSHC
§ - 'Taff's Silver Edge' (v) EHoe MBar
- 'Variegatus' see *S. orbiculatus* 'Foliis Variegatis'
***rivularis*** see *S. albus* var. *laevigatus*

## *Symphyandra* see *Campanula*

***asiatica*** see *Hanabusaya asiatica*

## *Symphyotrichum* see *Aster*

## *Symphytum* (*Boraginaceae*)

***asperum*** EBee ECha ELan EMon MRav MSal NLar WCHb WMoo
* ***azureum*** EBee ELan MSte NLar WCAu WCHb WFar WMnd
'Belsay' GBuc NChi
'Belsay Gold' SDix
***caucasicum*** ♀H4 CElw CMHG EBee ECha GBar GPoy IFro LEdu LRHS SBch SEND SIde SSvw WCHb WHer WHil WMoo WRha WWlt
- 'Eminence' EGoo WCHb
- 'Norwich Sky' CKno CPLG EBee EWld WCHb
- pale blue-flowered SSvw
***cordatum*** EBee EMon EPPr
'Denford Variegated' (v) NBid
§ 'Goldsmith' (v) Widely available
***grandiflorum*** CArn CTri CWan EBee GKev GPoy LEdu STes WGwG
* - 'Sky-blue-pink' NCot
'Hidcote Blue' CBct CBre CPrp CTri EBee ECha ECtt EPfP EPla GBar ILis LBMP LCro LRHS MSte NBro NCGa NGHP NHol SLPl SPer SPoG WCAu WCru WMnd WMoo
§ 'Hidcote Pink' CBct CPom CPrp EBee ECha EPla EWsh LBMP LCro LRHS MSte NBir SBch SLPl SPer SPoG WCAu WFar WMnd WMoo WPnP
'Hidcote Variegated' (v) WCHb
***ibericum*** CArn CSam EBee ECha EHrv EPfP EPla GBar GMaP GPoy LRHS NSti SGar SRms WBor WCAu WCHb WMoo
- 'All Gold' CArn EBrs ECha ECtt EWsh WCAu WMoo

| | |
|---|---|
| - 'Blaueglocken' | CSev EBee ECha WMoo WPrP |
| - dwarf | CPrp WMoo |
| - 'Gold in Spring' | EGoo NLar WCHb WFar |
| - 'Jubilee' | see *S.* 'Goldsmith' |
| - 'Lilacinum' | WHer |
| - 'Pink Robins' | WCHb |
| - 'Variegatum' | see *S.* 'Goldsmith' |
| - 'Wisley Blue' | CBcs EBee EPfP NLar WFar WMnd WMoo |
| 'Lambrook Sunrise' | CLAP EAEE EBee LAst LEdu LHop LRHS MBri MHar NBro NBsh SPla WCot WMoo |
| 'Langthorns Pink' | CPom ELan GBri GBuc GCal WCHb |
| 'Mereworth' | see *S.* x *uplandicum* 'Mereworth' |
| ***officinale*** | CArn COld CSev CWan EBee GBar GJos GPoy MHer MNHC MNrw MSal NGHP NMir NPer NPri NSco SIde SPoG SRms WBrk WHer |
| - 'Boraston White' | MHer WCHb |
| - var. ***ochroleucum*** | WHer |
| ***orientale*** | CPom EMon GCal WCHb |
| ***peregrinum*** | see *S.* x *uplandicum* |
| 'Roseum' | see *S.* 'Hidcote Pink' |
| 'Rubrum' | CDes CEnt EAEE EBee ECot EHrv ELan EPPr EPfP EWes LAst LBMP LEdu LRHS MAvo MHer NCGa NGHP NOrc SBch WCAu WCot WFar WGwG WPGP |
| ***tuberosum*** | CArn CBre CElw CEnt COld CPom CSam EPPr GPoy LEdu MHer MSte NHol SEND WBor WCHb WFar WHer WRha |
| § x ***uplandicum*** | CSev CTri EBee ELan GBar GCra GPoy MHer MSal SIde SVic WCHb WJek |
| - 'Axminster Gold' (v) | CBct CDes CEnt CLAP CMea IBlr LHop SPhx SUsu WPGP |
| - 'Bocking 14' | CAgr CBod CEnt CHby CPbn CPrp EBee EOHP GAbr GBar SIde WLHH |
| - 'Droitwich' (v) | WCot |
| § - 'Mereworth' (v) | CBct EBrs SEND SMad WCHb |
| - 'Moorland Heather' | MAvo WMoo |
| - 'Variegatum' (v) ♀H4 | CLAP EBee ECtt ELan EPfP EWes GBuc GMaP GPoy LAst LBMP MBri MTho NBir NGHP NGdn NSti SDix WCAu WCHb WCot WFar WMoo |

## *Symplocarpus* (*Araceae*)

| | |
|---|---|
| ***foetidus*** | ECho WCot |

## *Symplocos* (*Symplocaceae*)

| | |
|---|---|
| ***paniculata*** | see *S. sawafutagi* |
| § ***sawafutagi*** | CBcs EPla MBri NLar WPGP WPat |

## *Syncarpha* (*Asteraceae*)

| | |
|---|---|
| ***argyropsis*** | GFai |
| ***eximia*** | SPlb |

## *Syneilesis* (*Asteraceae*)

| | |
|---|---|
| ***aconitifolia*** | CDes CFwr CLAP EBee GEdr WCot WPGP |
| - B&SWJ 879 | WCru |
| ***palmata*** | CDes CLAP GEdr LEdu WCot |
| - B&SWJ 1003 | WCru |
| ***subglabrata*** | CLAP LEdu |
| - B&SWJ 298 | WCru |
| aff. ***tagawae*** B&SWJ 11191 new | WCru |

## *Syngonium* (*Araceae*)

| | |
|---|---|
| 'Maya Red' | MBri |
| ***podophyllum*** ♀H1 | XBlo |
| - 'Emerald Gem' | CHal |
| - 'Silver Knight' | MBri |
| - 'Variegatum' (v) | MBri |
| 'White Butterfly' | CHal MBri |

## *Synnotia* see *Sparaxis*

## *Synthyris* (*Scrophulariaceae*)

| | |
|---|---|
| ***missurica*** | CDes CLAP EBrs EPPr GBuc SKHP |
| - var. ***stellata*** | CLAP EBee EHrv EWsh LEdu NGby NHol WFar WHal WPGP |
| ***pinnatifida*** | GBuc NBir |
| ***reniformis*** | CLAP GBuc WPGP |

## *Synurus* (*Asteraceae*)

| | |
|---|---|
| ***pungens*** B&SWJ 10997 new | WCru |

## *Syringa* ✿ (*Oleaceae*)

| | |
|---|---|
| ***afghanica*** misapplied | see *S. protolaciniata* |
| ***afghanica*** C.K. Schneid. new | IArd |
| 'Alexander's Pink' | WGob |
| x ***chinensis*** 'Alba' | see *S.* 'Correlata' |
| - 'Persian Lilac' | ECrN WDin WFar WGob |
| - 'Saugeana' | EMil IDee NLar SPer |
| § 'Correlata' | SLon |
| ***emodi*** | WHCG |
| - 'Aurea' | IArd IDee MGos NLar |
| - 'Aureovariegata' | see *S. emodi* 'Elegantissima' |
| § - 'Elegantissima' (v) | CBcs CDoC CEnd CWGN EMil EPfP LLHF LRHS MAsh MDun SKHP SPoG SSpi WDin |
| 'Hagny' | WGob |
| x ***hyacinthiflora*** 'Clarke's Giant' | IDee |
| - 'Esther Staley' ♀H4 | EPfP MRav SBLw WGob |
| - 'Excel' new | WGob |
| - 'Maiden's Blush' | WGob |
| Josée = 'Morjos 060f' | CDoC EMil EPfP EQua LBMP MAsh NLar SCoo SPoG SWvt WFar WGob WPat |
| x ***josiflexa*** | CPLG |
| - 'Agnes Smith' | LAst NLar WGob |
| - 'Anna Amhoff' | GBin NLar |
| - 'Bellicent' ♀H4 | CEnd CLnd EBee ELan EPfP GKir ISea LAst MBar MRav NLar NPri NSti SCoo SHBN SMad SPer SPlb SPoG SRms SSpi SWvt WDin WGob WHCG WPat WPen |
| - 'James MacFarlane' | EBee NLar WGob |
| - 'Lynette' | EPla NPro |
| - 'Redwine' | EBee MGos NLar |
| § - 'Royalty' | EBee EMil MAsh NLar WGob |
| ***josikaea*** | CSBt EBee MBar NLar SCoo SPer WGob WHCG |
| 'Kim' | GKir MRav NLar |
| ***komarowii*** | NLar |
| - L 490 | GGGa |
| § - subsp. ***reflexa*** | CDul EPfP LLHF MBar MGos WDin WFar WGob |
| § x ***laciniata*** Mill. | CPMA EBee EHig EPfP LAst LRHS MGos MRav MWea NLar SCoo SEND SPer SSpi WGor WHCG WKif WPGP WRHF |
| § ***meyeri*** 'Palibin' ♀H4 | Widely available |
| ***microphylla*** | see *S. pubescens* subsp. *microphylla* |
| 'Minuet' | MGos NLar WGob |
| 'Miss Canada' | GKir MBri NLar WGob |
| ***palibiniana*** | see *S. meyeri* 'Palibin' |
| ***patula*** misapplied | see *S. meyeri* 'Palibin' |
| ***patula*** (Palibin) Nakai | see *S. pubescens* subsp. *patula* |
| ***pekinensis*** | see *S. reticulata* subsp. *pekinensis* |

| | |
|---|---|
| x ***persica*** ♀H4 | CPLG CPMA CSam CTri EPfP EWTr GKir MGos MRav NBea NLar NPal SLon SPer |
| - 'Alba' ♀H4 | CPMA EBee GQui MRav WFar WHCG WPat |
| - var. ***laciniata*** | see *S.* x *laciniata* Mill. |
| ***pinnatifolia*** | CBcs GKir IArd IDee MBri WHCG |
| x ***prestoniae*** 'Audrey' | WGob |
| - 'Coral' | WFar |
| - 'Desdemona' | SKHP SSta |
| - 'Donald Wyman' | MBri WGob |
| - 'Elinor' ♀H4 | CMHG EPfP MRav NSti SKHP SPer |
| - 'Helen' **new** | MAsh |
| - 'Hiawatha' | MGos |
| - 'Isabella' | MGos SCoo |
| - 'Nocturne' | MGos WFar WGob |
| - 'Royalty' | see *S.* x *josiflexa* 'Royalty' |
| § ***protolaciniata*** | LBMP MAsh MGos NLar SKHP WFar |
| - 'Kabul' | EPfP NLar |
| § ***pubescens*** subsp. ***microphylla*** | CFwr EWTr GKir |
| - - 'Superba' ♀H4 | Widely available |
| § - subsp. ***patula*** | CMac ECho EPfP MRav NWea SEND SLon SPla SPoG WFar |
| - - 'Miss Kim' ♀H4 | CDoC CSBt CWSG EBee ELan EMil IArd LAst LRHS LSRN MAsh MBri MGos MRav MSwo NBea NBlu NLar SCoo SHBN SLim SPoG SSta WDin WFar WGob WHCG WPat |
| 'Red Pixie' | CBgR EMil LBuc LRHS MBri MGos SCoo WGob |
| 'Red Prince' **new** | LRHS MAsh |
| ***reflexa*** | see *S. komarowii* subsp. *reflexa* |
| ***reticulata*** | WDin |
| - 'City of Toronto' | EBee |
| - 'Ivory Silk' | CWSG EPfP LLHF NLar WGob |
| § - subsp. ***pekinensis*** | CMCN GBin IDee WBVN |
| - - 'Pendula' | IArd IDee |
| - - 'Yellow Fragrance' | MBri |
| x ***swegiflexa*** | CDul CPLG NLar |
| ***sweginzowii*** | NLar SPer WFar |
| - 'Superba' | LAst WMoo |
| ***tomentella*** | NWea SRms |
| ***velutina*** | see *S. pubescens* subsp. *patula* |
| ***villosa*** | SPlb WBVN WDin WGob |
| ***vulgaris*** | ECrN EMac LBuc MBar NWea |
| - var. ***alba*** | MBar |
| - 'Albert F. Holden' | WGob |
| § - 'Andenken an Ludwig Späth' ♀H4 | Widely available |
| - 'Aurea' | EQua LBuc MRav NPro WFar |
| - Beauty of Moscow | see *S. vulgaris* 'Krasavitsa Moskvy' |
| - 'Belle de Nancy' (d) | CCCN CDul CWib EBee ELan ELon LAst MRav SBLw SEND SHBN SWvt WDin |
| - Burgundy Queen = 'Lecburg' | WGob |
| - 'Charles Joly' (d) ♀H4 | Widely available |
| - 'Comtesse d'Harcourt' | EMil EQua |
| - 'Congo' | GKir MRav NMoo SEND SPer WGob |
| - 'Edward J. Gardner' (d) | ECrN ELon SCoo |
| - 'Firmament' ♀H4 | EBee ELan EPfP MRav SCoo SEND SHBN SPer WGob |
| - 'G. J. Baardse' | SBLw |
| - 'Général Pershing' (d) | SBLw |
| - 'Katherine Havemeyer' (d) ♀H4 | Widely available |
| - Kindy Rose = 'Gaby' | EMil MAsh |
| § - 'Krasavitsa Moskvy' (d) | EWes GKir MBri |
| - 'La Tour d'Auvergne' | SBLw |
| - 'Lee Jewett Walker' **new** | WGob |
| - 'Lucie Baltet' | MBri |
| - 'Madame Florent Stepman' | CMac NLar SPer |
| - 'Madame Lemoine' (d) ♀H4 | Widely available |
| - 'Masséna' | EBee MRav SPer |
| - 'Maud Notcutt' | EWes |
| - 'Michel Buchner' (d) | CBcs CDul CWib EBee ELan GKir LAst MBar MGan MRav NLar NPri SBLw SCoo SLim SPer WBVN WGob |
| - 'Miss Ellen Willmott' (d) | MBri MRav SBLw |
| - 'Mont Blanc' | SBLw |
| - 'Mrs Edward Harding' (d) ♀H4 | EBee ECrN EPfP EQua LAst LBuc MGos MRav NLar NWea SCoo SPer SRGP |
| - 'Nadezhda' (d) | WGob |
| - 'Olivier de Serres' (d) | MBri SBLw |
| - 'P.P. Konchalovskii' | EMil |
| - 'Pat Pesata' **new** | WGob |
| - 'Paul Deschanel' (d) | EBee NLar |
| - 'Président Fallières' (d) | EBee |
| - 'Président Grévy' (d) | CDoC CLnd CMac EBee MMuc SBLw SPer |
| - 'President Lincoln' | SBLw |
| - 'Primrose' | CBcs CCCN CDul CMac CSBt CWib EBee ELan ELon EPfP GBin GKir IArd LAst LRHS MBri MGos MRav NLar NPri SCoo SEND SPer SPoG WDin WFar WGob |
| - 'Prince Wolkonsky' (d) | EBee EMil EPfP EQua WFar WGob |
| - 'Princesse Sturdza' | EMil |
| - 'Ruhm von Horstenstein' | EBee |
| - 'Sarah Sands' | WGob |
| - 'Sensation' | CDoC CSBt CWSG EBee ECrN ELon EPfP GKir IArd IMGH LAst LRHS LSRN MAsh MGos MRav MSwo NLar NPri NWea SCoo SEND SHBN SLim SPer SPoG WGob |
| - 'Silver King' | WGob |
| - 'Souvenir d'Alice Harding' (d) | LRHS |
| - 'Souvenir de Louis Spaeth' | see *S. vulgaris* 'Andenken an Ludwig Späth' |
| - 'Sweetheart' (d) | GKir |
| - variegated (v) | EWes MGos |
| - variegated double (d/v) | WCot |
| - 'Vestale' ♀H4 | EWes MRav |
| - 'Viviand-Morel' (d) | LLHF WGob |
| - 'Znamya Lenina' | MBri |
| ***wolfii*** | CArn WBVN |
| ***yunnanensis*** | CPLG GGGa LLHF WBod |
| - 'Prophecy' | WGob |
| - 'Rosea' | WGob |

## *Syzygium* (*Myrtaceae*)

| | |
|---|---|
| sp. **new** | CMen |
| ***australe*** | ERom EShb IDee |
| ***jambos*** | EShb |
| ***paniculatum*** | CMen CPLG EShb IDee |

# T

## *Tabernaemontana* (*Apocynaceae*)

| | |
|---|---|
| ***coronaria*** | see *T. divaricata* |
| § ***divaricata*** | CCCN SOWG |

## *Tacca* (*Taccaceae*)

| | |
|---|---|
| ***chantrieri*** | CCCN CSec EAmu EBrs ECho WVal |
| - 'Nivea' | WVal |
| 'Greenbay' **new** | WVal |
| ***integrifolia*** | CSec EAmu EBrs ECho WVal |

## *Tacitus* see *Graptopetalum*

## *Tagetes* (*Asteraceae*)

| | |
|---|---|
| ***lemmonii*** | SHDw SMad |
| ***lucida*** | CArn CBod EOHP MSal WJek |
| ***tenuifolia*** | CArn |

## *Taiwania* (*Cupressaceae*)

| | |
|---|---|
| ***cryptomerioides*** | CDul |

## *Talbotia* (*Velloziaceae*)

| | |
|---|---|
| § ***elegans*** | CSpe WFar |

## *Talinum* (*Portulacaceae*)

| | |
|---|---|
| ***calycinum*** | EAlp |
| 'Kingwood Gold' | CBow |
| ***okanoganense*** | CCCN CSec |
| ***paniculatum*** | CCCN CSec |
| 'Zoe' | CPBP |

## tamarillo see *Cyphomandra betacea*

## tamarind see *Tamarindus indica*

## *Tamarindus* (*Caesalpiniaceae*)

| | |
|---|---|
| ***indica*** (F) | SPlb |

## *Tamarix* (*Tamaricaceae*)

| | |
|---|---|
| ***africana*** | EBee EMil |
| ***chinensis*** new | CSBt |
| ***gallica*** | CMen CSBt NWea SAPC SArc WSHC |
| ***hampeana*** new | SEND |
| § ***parviflora*** | EBee EMil LRHS MGos |
| ***pentandra*** | see *T. ramosissima* |
| § ***ramosissima*** | CCCN CTri ECrN ELan EPfP MBar MBrN MWhi SEND SLim SRms SSta WDin WSHC |
| - 'Pink Cascade' | CBcs CCCN CDul CSBt EBee EMil EPfP GKir LCro LPan LRHS MBri MGos MREP MRav NBlu SPer SPoG SWvt WBod WDin |
| - 'Rosea' | CBcs MGan SLon |
| § - 'Rubra' ♀H4 | CChe CDoC CWSG EBee EMil EPfP GKir LRHS MBlu MGos NLar SEND SLon SMad SPer WDin |
| - 'Summer Glow' | see *T. ramosissima* 'Rubra' |
| ***tetrandra*** ♀H4 | Widely available |
| - 'Africance' | ERom |
| - var. ***purpurea*** | see *T. parviflora* |

## *Tamus* (*Dioscoreaceae*)

| | |
|---|---|
| ***communis*** | CArn MSal |

## *Tanacetum* ✿ (*Asteraceae*)

| | |
|---|---|
| sp. | EDAr WFar |
| § ***argenteum*** | ECho MRav SIde |
| - subsp. ***canum*** | ECho EWes |
| § ***balsamita*** | CArn COld CPrp EAro EBee ELan ELau GPWP GPoy LEdu MBri MHer MNHC MSal SHGN SWal WJek WLHH WPer WTin |
| § - subsp. ***balsamita*** | CBod GPoy MSal SIde |
| § - subsp. ***balsamitoides*** | CBod CHby CPrp GBar MHer WJek WLHH |
| - var. ***tanacetoides*** | see *T. balsamita* subsp. *balsamita* |
| - ***tomentosum*** | see *T. balsamita* subsp. *balsamitoides* |
| ***capitatum*** | see *Sphaeromeria capitata* |
| § ***cinerariifolium*** | CArn CBod CPrp CWan GBar GPoy MNHC |
| § ***coccineum*** | GPoy MSal NBPC SRms WFar |
| - 'Alfred' | EBee |
| - 'Aphrodite' (d) | EBee ECtt WCAu |
| - 'Beauty of Stapleford' | EBee NOrc WCAu WHil |
| - 'Bees' Pink Delight' | EBee SPoG |
| - 'Brenda' | EBee EPfP LHop MRav |
| - 'Duro' | CEnt GBuc |
| - 'Eileen May Robinson' ♀H4 | EBee ECot EPfP EShb LHop LSRN NBre NGdn WCAu |
| - 'Evenglow' | ECtt EPfP WCAu |
| - 'James Kelway' ♀H4 | EBee ECot ECtt ELan EPfP EShb GGar GKir MRav NBir SPoG SRms WCAu |
| - 'King Size' | SGar WFar |
| - 'Madeleine' (d) | LBMP |
| - 'Mont Blanc' new | EBee |
| - Robinson's giant-flowered | GJos SRms |
| - 'Robinson's Pink' | CMdw EBee ELan EPfP GKir GMaP NBre SRms |
| - 'Robinson's Red' | CSBt EBee GKir GMaP MBNS NPri NVic SMrs SPur SRms SWvt |
| - 'Robinson's Rose' | MBNS |
| - 'Scarlet Glow' | EBee |
| - 'Snow Cloud' | ELan NBre SPoG WCAu |
| § ***corymbosum*** | EBee GCal |
| - 'Festtafel' | EBee LPla |
| ***densum*** | ECho WCFE |
| - subsp. ***amani*** | EBee ECha ECho GBar GMaP MHer MWat NWCA SEND SPoG SRms |
| 'H.M. Pike' | NOrc |
| § ***haradjanii*** | CMea ECho ECtt ELan SBch WHer |
| ***herderi*** | see *Hippolytia herderi* |
| ***huronense*** | EBee |
| ***macrophyllum*** misapplied | see *Achillea grandifolia* Friv. |
| § ***macrophyllum*** (Waldst. & Kit.) Sch.Bip. | CTca ECtt EMon EPPr LPla SPhx WCot WPer |
| ***niveum*** | CArn EAro ECha MSal WCot |
| - 'Jackpot' | CSpe CWan CWib EAro EBee EDAr EPfP EWes MBri SHar SSvw |
| § ***parthenium*** | CArn CBod CHby CPbn CWan EBWF ELau GPoy MHer MNHC NPer SIde SPoG SRms SVic WHer |
| - 'Aureum' | CEnt CHid CPbn CPrp CRow CWan EBee ECha ELan ELau EWes GBar GPoy MBri MHer MNHC NGHP SIng SMad SPer SPlb SRms WCot WEas WFar WHer WMoo WPer |
| - double white-flowered (d) | CSWP GBar MNHC NPer SEND SRms |
| - 'Malmesbury' | CNat |
| - 'Plenum' (d) | EHrv SBch SIng |
| § - 'Rowallane' (d) | EBee ELan GBuc GMac MAvo MBri WCot |
| - 'Sissinghurst White' | see *T. parthenium* 'Rowallane' |
| - 'Snowball' (d) | IFro |
| - 'White Bonnet' (d) | WEas |
| ***poteriifolium*** | EBee EBrs |
| ***ptarmiciflorum*** 'Silver Feather' | MNHC WJek |
| Robinson's giant single mix strain new | GJos |
| ***vulgare*** | CArn CHby CSev EBWF ECtt ELau GPoy MHar MHer MNHC MSal NSco SIde SVic WLHH WMoo WSFF |
| - var. ***crispum*** | CBod CHby CPrp CWan EBee ELau GBar GPoy MHer SIde SMad WFar WJek WRha |
| - 'Isla Gold' (v) | CBow EBee EPPr EWes GBar GMaP LDai LHop MHar MRav NBid NBre NSti SEND SMrm WCHb WCot WFar WMoo WRha |
| - 'Silver Lace' (v) | CBow EBee GBar GBri NBid NGHP WCHb WFar WHer WMoo WOut |

## *Tanakaea* (*Saxifragaceae*)

| | |
|---|---|
| ***radicans*** | EBee WCru |

## tangelo see *Citrus* x *tangelo*

## tangerine see *Citrus reticulata*

## tangor see *Citrus* x *nobilis* Tangor Group

## *Tapiscia* (*Staphyleaceae*)

| | |
|---|---|
| ***sinensis*** | CExc |

## *Taraxacum* (*Asteraceae*)

| | |
|---|---|
| ***albidum*** | CSec |
| - DJH 452 | CHid |
| ***coreanum*** | WPrP |
| ***faeroense*** | EPPr WCot |
| ***officinale*** agg. | CArn |
| - variegated (v) | WCot |
| ***pseudoroseum*** | CNat |
| ***rubrifolium*** | CSpe EPPr |

## *Tarchonanthus* (*Asteraceae*)

| | |
|---|---|
| ***camphoratus*** | CTrC |

## tarragon see *Artemisia dracunculus*

## *Tasmannia* see *Drimys*

## *Taxodium* (*Cupressaceae*)

| | |
|---|---|
| ***ascendens*** 'Nutans' | see *T. distichum* var. *imbricatum* 'Nutans' |
| ***distichum*** 🏆H4 | Widely available |
| - 'Cascade Falls'PBR | CDul EMil MBlu MBri MGos NLar SLim |
| - 'Hursley Park' | SLim |
| - var. ***imbricatum*** | CGHE CMCN EPfP WPGP |
| § - - 'Nutans' 🏆H4 | CBcs CEnd CTho EMil GKir LPan LRHS MAsh MBlu SCoo SLim SMad |
| - 'Little Twister' | NLar |
| - 'Minaret' | MBlu |
| - 'Peve Minaret' | CDoC CMen LRHS MAsh MBri MGos NLar SLim |
| - 'Peve Yellow' | MBlu NLar |
| - 'Schloss Herten' | SLim |
| - 'Secrest' | CBcs LRHS MAsh MBlu MBri SLim |
| - Shawnee Brave = 'Mickelson' | MBlu NLar |
| ***mucronatum*** | CDoC |
| - F&M 198 | WPGP |

## *Taxus* ✿ (*Taxaceae*)

| | |
|---|---|
| ***baccata*** 🏆H4 | Widely available |
| - 'Adpressa' (f) | ECho |
| - 'Adpressa Aurea' (v) | CKen ECho EPla GKir SCoo |
| - 'Adpressa Variegata' (m/v) 🏆H4 | CDoC ECho EHul |
| - 'Aldenham Gold' | CKen |
| - 'Amersfoort' | CDoC EOrn NLar SCoo SLim SPoG |
| - 'Argentea Minor' | see *T. baccata* 'Dwarf White' |
| - Aurea Group | CDul NHol SRms STre |
| I - 'Aurea Pendula' | ECho EOrn GKir |
| I - 'Aureomarginata' (v) | CBcs CBow CSBt ECho EOrn MAsh SWvt |
| - 'Autumn Shades' | CBcs |
| - 'Bridget's Gold' | CKen |
| - 'Cavendishii' (f) | ECho |
| - 'Compacta' | EOrn EPla |
| - 'Corleys Coppertip' | CKen CRob ECho EHul EPot GKir MAsh MBar NHol NLar SCoo SLim WFar |
| - 'Cristata' | CKen NLar |
| - 'David' | IArd MBri NLar SCoo SPoG |
| - 'Dovastoniana' (f) 🏆H4 | CMac MBar NLar NWea SCoo WMou |
| - 'Dovastonii Aurea' (m/v) 🏆H4 | CMac ECho EHul EOrn EPfP EPla GKir MAsh MBar MBlu MBri MGos NLar NPri NWea SCoo SLim WCFE WDin WFar |
| - 'Drinkstone Gold' (v) | EHul |
| § - 'Dwarf White' (v) | ECho EOrn EPla SCoo WGor |
| - 'Elegantissima' (f/v) | CTho ECho EHul EPfP LRHS NWea SCoo WFar |
| - 'Erecta' (f) | EHul SHBN |
| § - 'Fastigiata' (f) 🏆H4 | Widely available |
| - Fastigiata Aurea Group | CDul CLnd CWib ECho EHul EPfP GKev GKir IArd LBuc LMaj MAsh MGan MGos NGHP NHol NPri SRms STre WBrE WFar WHar |
| - 'Fastigiata Aureomarginata' (m/v) 🏆H4 | Widely available |
| - 'Fastigiata Robusta' (f) | CDoC CRob ECho EPfP EPla GKir MBar MBri NHol SCoo SLim WFar |
| - 'Goud Elsje' | CKen NLar |
| - 'Green Column' | CKen |
| - 'Green Diamond' | CKen NLar |
| - 'Green Rocket' **new** | EMil |
| - 'Hibernica' | see *T. baccata* 'Fastigiata' |
| - 'Icicle' | CBcs ECho EPla MAsh MGos NLar |
| - 'Itsy Bitsy' | CKen |
| - 'Ivory Tower' | CBcs CDoC CKen ECho ELan EMil LBee LRHS MAsh MGos NLar SLim SPoG WFar WGor |
| - 'Klitzeklein' | CKen |
| - 'Laurie' | SCoo |
| - 'Melfard' | CDoC EHul |
| - 'Nutans' | CDoC CKen CRob ECho EOrn GKir IMGH MBar SCoo |
| - 'Overeynderi' | EHul |
| - 'Pendula' | MRav |
| - 'Prostrata' | CMac WFar |
| - 'Pygmaea' | CKen |
| - 'Repandens' (f) 🏆H4 | EHul IArd MBar NWea SHBN WCFE WDin WFar |
| I - 'Repens Aurea' (v) 🏆H4 | CDoC CKen CRob ECho ECrN EHul EOrn EPfP GKir LRHS MAsh MBar MGos SCoo WFar |
| - 'Semperaurea' (m) 🏆H4 | CAgr CBcs CDoC CMac ECho EHul EOrn GKir LBuc LRHS MAsh MBar MGan MGos NHol NWea SCoo SLim SPla WCFE WDin WFar |
| - 'Silver Spire' (v) | CKen MDKP |
| - 'Standishii' (f) 🏆H4 | Widely available |
| - 'Stove Pipe' | CKen |
| - 'Summergold' (v) | CRob ECho EHul ELan EPfP LRHS MAsh MBar MBri MGos MRav NBir NBlu NHol NLar SCoo SLim WDin WFar |
| - 'Washingtonii' (v) | IArd MBar SHBN |
| - 'White Icicle' | EOrn MGos WGor |
| ***brevifolia*** | EPla |
| ***cuspidata*** | CMen ECho GKir |
| - 'Aurescens' (v) | CKen EPla SRms |
| - 'Minuet' **new** | CKen |
| - var. ***nana*** hort. ex Rehder | EHul EOrn MBar |
| - 'Robusta' | EHul |
| - 'Straight Hedge' | CDoC EHul EMil LRHS SLim |
| x ***media*** 'Brownii' | LBuc |
| - 'Hicksii' (f) 🏆H4 | CDul GKir LBuc LMaj LRHS MBar MGan MGos NBlu NWea SCoo SLim WFar |
| - 'Hillii' | MBar SCoo |
| - 'Lodi' | LBee LRHS |
| - 'Strait Hedge' (f) | CAgr |

## Tayberry see *Rubus* Tayberry Group

## *Tecoma* (*Bignoniaceae*)

| | |
|---|---|
| x ***alata*** | SOWG |
| ***capensis*** ♀H1 | CHEx CSec CSev LRHS SOWG |
| - 'Aurea' | CSev EShb SOWG |
| - 'Coccinea' | EShb |
| - 'Lutea' | EShb LRHS |
| ***cochabambensis*** RCB/Arg L-8 | WCot |
| ***garrocha*** | EShb |
| 'Orange Glow' | SOWG |
| ***ricasoliana*** | see *Podranea ricasoliana* |
| ***stans*** | CSec SOWG |

## *Tecomanthe* (*Bignoniaceae*)

| | |
|---|---|
| ***speciosa*** | CHEx ECou SOWG |

## *Tecomaria* see *Tecoma*

## *Tecophilaea* (*Tecophilaeaceae*)

| | |
|---|---|
| ***cyanocrocus*** ♀H2 | CAvo CBro EBrs ECho EPot IHer LAma LRHS NMin WCot |
| - 'Leichtlinii' ♀H2 | CBro EBrs ECho EPot IHer LAma LRHS NMin SCnR |
| - 'Purpurea' | see *T. cyanocrocus* 'Violacea' |
| - Storm Cloud Group | CBro ECho |
| § - 'Violacea' | CAvo CBro EBrs ECho IHer LRHS NMin |
| ***violiflora*** | EBrs ECho LAma |

## *Tectaria* (*Dryopteridaceae*)

| | |
|---|---|
| ***gemmifera*** | GQui |

## *Telanthophora* (*Asteraceae*)

| | |
|---|---|
| ***grandifolia*** | CHEx SAPC SArc |

## *Telekia* (*Asteraceae*)

| | |
|---|---|
| § ***speciosa*** | CHar CHrt COIW CSam CSec CSpe EBee EBrs ELan EPfP GAbr GKir ITim MCCP NBro NChi SDix SLPl SPlb WCFE WFar WHer WHoo WMoo WPer |

## *Telesonix* see *Boykinia*

## *Teline* see *Genista*

## *Tellima* (*Saxifragaceae*)

| | |
|---|---|
| ***grandiflora*** | Widely available |
| - 'Bob's Choice' | WCot |
| - 'Delphine' (v) | CBow EBee EPPr SAga WCot WOut |
| - 'Forest Frost' | CBct CBow CMHG EBee EPPr GCai LBMP LHop NBre NGdn NHol NLar NSti WCot WMoo WOut |
| - Odorata Group | CBre EBee ECha LBMP MRav NSti WCot WMoo |
| - - 'Howells' **new** | WOut |
| - 'Purpurea' | see *T. grandiflora* Rubra Group |
| - 'Purpurteppich' | EBee EBrs ECha EHig EHrv EPPr GAbr LAst LRHS MRav NDov NGdn WCot WMnd WMoo WPnP |
| § - Rubra Group | Widely available |
| - 'Silver Select' | EPPr |

## *Telopea* (*Proteaceae*)

| | |
|---|---|
| 'Dawn Fire' | CTrC |
| ***oreades*** | GGal |
| ***speciosissima*** | CBcs CCCN CTrC SOWG SPlb |
| - 'Red Embers' | CTrC |
| ***truncata*** | CBcs CCCN GGal WCru |

## *Templetonia* (*Papilionaceae*)

| | |
|---|---|
| ***retusa*** | ECou |

## *Temu* see *Blepharocalyx*

## *Tephroseris* (*Asteraceae*)

| | |
|---|---|
| ***integrifolia*** | WHer |

## *Tephrosia* (*Papilionaceae*)

| | |
|---|---|
| ***vogelii*** | CArn |

## *Tetracentron* (*Tetracentraceae*)

| | |
|---|---|
| ***sinense*** | CBcs EPfP IArd IFFs LRHS NLar WPGP |

## *Tetradenia* (*Lamiaceae*)

| | |
|---|---|
| ***riparia*** | EOHP |

## *Tetradium* (*Rutaceae*)

| | |
|---|---|
| § ***daniellii*** | CBcs CCVT CMCN EPfP IArd IDee NLar SSpi WPGP WPat |
| * - ***henryi*** | NLar |
| § - Hupehense Group | CMCN GBin GKir MBri SEND WDin WOrn |
| - 'Moonlight' | MBri |
| ***glabrifolium*** | WPGP |
| - B&SWJ 3541 | WCru |
| ***ruticarpum*** | WPGP |
| - B&SWJ 6882 | WCru |
| * ***velutinum*** | NLar |

## *Tetragonia* (*Tetragoniaceae*)

| | |
|---|---|
| ***tetragonoides*** | CArn |

## *Tetragonolobus* see *Lotus*

## *Tetraneuris* (*Asteraceae*)

| | |
|---|---|
| § ***grandiflora*** | GAbr MAvo |
| § ***scaposa*** | EPot LRHS |

## *Tetrapanax* (*Araliaceae*)

| | |
|---|---|
| § ***papyrifer*** ♀H2-3 | CBrP CDTJ CHEx MBri NLar SAPC SArc SBig XBlo |
| - B&SWJ 7135 | WCru |
| - 'Empress' | WCru |
| - 'Rex' | CDTJ CGHE CHEx CPLG EAmu EGFP EUJe WCot WCru WPGP |

## *Tetrapathaea* see *Passiflora*

## *Tetrastigma* (*Vitaceae*)

| | |
|---|---|
| ***obtectum*** | CCCN CTsd ECre EWes MTPN |
| ***voinierianum*** ♀H1 | EShb MBri SAPC SArc WCot |

## *Tetratheca* (*Tremandraceae*)

| | |
|---|---|
| ***ciliata*** var. ***alba*** | SOWG |
| ***thymifolia*** | ECou |
| - pink-flowered | SOWG |

## *Teucridium* (*Verbenaceae*)

| | |
|---|---|
| ***parvifolium*** | ECou |

## *Teucrium* (*Lamiaceae*)

| | |
|---|---|
| * ***ackermannii*** | CLyd CMea ECho LBee LRHS NMen NWCA WAbe WEas WHoo WPat WTin |
| ***arduinoi*** | SEND |
| ***aroanium*** | ECho EPot GEdr LRHS MWat NMen NWCA |
| ***asiaticum*** | EGoo |
| ***bicolor*** | EBee |
| ***botrys*** | EDAr MHer MSal |

| | | |
|---|---|---|
| | ***canadense*** | MSal |
| | ***chamaedrys*** misapplied | see *T.* x *lucidrys* |
| | ***chamaedrys*** L. | CHal CPom CPrp CSam CWan CWib ECho EGoo GAbr GBar LEdu LRHS LSRN MSwo NGHP NPri NWCA SLim SRms STre WBrk WJek WTin |
| | - 'Nanum' | ECho NChi |
| | - 'Rose Carpet' | EGoo |
| | - 'Summer Sunshine' | LBuc LRHS MAsh |
| | - 'Variegatum' (v) | GBar WCHb WPer WRha |
| | aff. ***chamaedrys*** | MNHC |
| § | ***creticum*** | ECho |
| | ***divaricatum*** NS 614 | NWCA |
| | ***dunense*** | EAro |
| | ***flavum*** | CArn EBee EDAr EGoo NBre SGar WCHb |
| | ***fruticans*** | Widely available |
| | - 'Azureum' $\Psi^{H3}$ | CBcs CMMP COlW CWSG EBee ELan EPfP LAst LRHS LSou SMad SPer WEas |
| | - 'Compactum' | CChe CDoC COlW EBee ELan ELon EWTr LAst LSou MCCP MGos SLon SPer SPla SPoG WCFE WPGP |
| | - 'Drysdale' | CDoC EBee |
| | ***hircanicum*** | Widely available |
| | - 'Paradise Delight' | EBee ECtt MAvo MBNS NBPC NBid NOrc NPro WWlt |
| | - 'Purple Tails' | COlW CPrp CSpe CWib LSou MCot NBir NCob SPoG SWal WHal |
| | ***lamiifolium*** | EBee |
| § | x ***lucidrys*** | CArn CMea CPom CSev CSpe CWan EBee ECha ECho EGoo ELan ELau EPfP GPoy LAst LRHS MHer MRav MWat NGHP SGar SIde SPer SPoG WCFE WEas WHoo |
| | ***marum*** | CArn CMea CTri MSal NGHP NMen SHGN WJek |
| | ***massiliense*** misapplied | see *T.* x *lucidrys* |
| | ***massiliense*** L. | EAro EBee |
| | ***montanum*** | EGoo EShb GBar SHGN |
| | ***nivale*** | EBee |
| | ***polium*** | CPLG EBee ECho MWat NLAp WJek WPat WThu |
| | - subsp. ***aureum*** | NWCA |
| | ***pyrenaicum*** | CMea CPBP CPom EBee ECho EPot EWes GEdr MSte NWCA WPat |
| | ***rosmarinifolium*** | see *T. creticum* |
| | ***scordium*** | CNat MCot |
| | ***scorodonia*** | CArn COld CRWN CSec CSev EBWF EGoo ELau GBar GPoy MHer MNHC MSal NMir WHer WJek |
| | - 'Binsted Gold' | EBee EGoo EMon EPPr LDai LSou MHar NSti WAlt |
| | - 'Crispum' | CHFP CWan GBar GKir LBMP MHar MHer MLLN MMuc NBro NCob SBch SPer WBrE WCHb WGwG WHoo WJek WKif WMnd WMoo WPer |
| | - 'Crispum Marginatum' (v) | COlW EBee ECGP ECha EGoo EHoe EHrv EPPr EPfP GBar IBlr ILis LHop LRHS MNrw MRav NHol NSti WEas WFar WTin |
| | - 'Spring Morn' | EBee |
| | - 'Winterdown' (v) | CBow EBee EGoo EPPr NPro SAga SBch WCHb |
| | ***subspinosum*** | ECho LBee LRHS MWat NLAp NMen WHoo WPat |
| § | ***viscidum*** 'Lemon and Lime' (v) | EBee ECtt LHop LSou MHar NSti SDnm |
| | ***webbianum*** | EBee ECho |
| | 'Winterdown' | GBri WDyG |

## *Thalia* (*Marantaceae*)

| | |
|---|---|
| ***dealbata*** | CBen CDWL CHEx CMdw EAmu EMFW EUJe LLWG LPBA MSKA NLar SBig SDix WMAq |
| ***geniculata*** | CDWL MSKA |

## *Thalictrum* (*Ranunculaceae*)

| | | |
|---|---|---|
| | CC 4576 | CPLG GKev WCot |
| | CC 4577 | WCot |
| | SDR 2706 **new** | GKev |
| | from Afghanistan | see *T. isopyroides* |
| | ***actaeifolium*** | CLAP CWib GMac |
| | - B&SWJ 4664 | WCru |
| | - var. ***brevistylum*** | EBee LSou |
| | - - B&SWJ 8819 | WCru |
| | - - 'Twinkling Star' | EBee ELon GMac NCob NCot NDov WCot WCra WWlt |
| | - 'Perfume Star' **new** | NBrd |
| | ***adiantifolium*** | see *T. minus* 'Adiantifolium' |
| | ***alpinum*** | EBWF EDAr EPPr SBch |
| | ***angustifolium*** | see *T. lucidum* |
| | ***aquilegiifolium*** | Widely available |
| | - var. ***album*** | CMea CMil COlW EBee ECha EGle ELan EPfP GCra LAst LBMP LHop MSte NBid SPhx SPla WCAu WHil WMnd WPer |
| * | - 'Hybridum' | GBBs WFar WMoo WPer |
| | - 'Purple Cloud' | see *T. aquilegiifolium* 'Thundercloud' |
| | - 'Purpureum' | CPom CSev LBMP NLar SPla WCAu WHoo |
| * | - var. ***sibiricum*** B&SWJ 11007 **new** | WCru |
| | - 'Small Thundercloud' **new** | GCal |
| | - 'Sparkler' | GCai |
| § | - 'Thundercloud' $\Psi^{H4}$ | Widely available |
| | ***baicalense*** | CPom EBee |
| | 'Black Stockings' | CKno EBee MAvo MBNS SPoG |
| | ***chelidonii*** | CWsd GMaP MHar |
| | - GWJ 9349 | WCru |
| | - HWJK 2216 | WCru |
| | ***clavatum*** | CLAP EBee WPGP |
| | ***contortum*** | EBee SDys |
| | ***coreanum*** | see *T. ichangense* |
| | ***cultratum*** | CDes CWCL WPGP |
| | - HWJCM 367 | EBee NLar WCru |
| | ***dasycarpum*** | GMac MLLN NLar WFar WPnP |
| § | ***delavayi*** $\Psi^{H4}$ | Widely available |
| | - BWJ 7903 | WCru |
| | - DJHC 473 | WCru |
| | - var. ***acuminatum*** BWJ 7535 | WCru |
| | - - BWJ 7971 | WCru |
| | - 'Album' | Widely available |
| | - 'Ankum' | EBee |
| | - var. ***decorum*** | CElw CFwr CLAP CWCL EPPr GEdr GMac LPio MCot NBPC NCGa NCob NHol SPhx WCot WCru WSHC |
| | - - CD&R 2135 | CAby |
| | - 'Hewitt's Double' (d) $\Psi^{H4}$ | Widely available |
| | - var. ***mucronatum*** | WCru |
| | - purple-stemmed BWJ 7748 | WCru |
| | ***diffusiflorum*** | CEnt CLAP GBri GBuc GEdr GMac SUsu WCru WSHC |
| | ***dioicum*** | WPnP |
| | ***dipterocarpum*** misapplied | see *T. delavayi* |
| | ***dipterocarpum*** Franch. | EBee GKir MSCN NHol WMnd |
| | - ACE 4.878.280 | CMil |
| | ***elegans*** HWJK 2271 | WCru |
| | 'Elin' | Widely available |

| | | |
|---|---|---|
| | ***faberi*** **new** | EBee |
| | ***fendleri*** | GBin GBuc |
| | - var. ***polycarpum*** | WOut |
| | ***filamentosum*** | EBee |
| | - B&SWJ 777 | WCru |
| | - B&SWJ 4145 **new** | WCru |
| | - var. ***tenerum*** **new** | EBee |
| | - var. ***yakusimense*** B&SWJ 6094 | WCru |
| | ***finetii*** | CLAP EBee |
| | aff. ***finetii*** | CLAP |
| | ***flavum*** | CHar CWan EBWF ECtt NBro SMrm SPhx SWat WBrE WShi |
| | - 'Chollerton' | see *T. isopyroides* |
| § | - subsp. ***glaucum*** ♀H4 | Widely available |
| | - - dwarf **new** | CDes |
| | - - 'True Blue' | MSte |
| | - 'Illuminator' | CDes CKno CTri EBee EGle ELon EPPr EPfP GBri GKir LPio LRHS MArl MHer MRav SMad SMrm SPoG WCAu WCot WFar WPnP WPrP |
| | ***flexuosum*** | see *T. minus* subsp. *minus* |
| | ***foetidum*** | NBre |
| | - BWJ 7558 | WCru |
| | ***foliolosum*** B&SWJ 2705 | WCru |
| | - HWJK 2181 | WCru |
| | - S&SH 382 | GBri |
| | ***grandiflorum*** | NCob |
| | ***honanense*** | EBee |
| § | ***ichangense*** | EBee GBri |
| | - B&SWJ 8203 **new** | WCru |
| * | - var. ***minus*** | WCru |
| | - - 'Chinese Chintz' **new** | WCru |
| § | ***isopyroides*** | CFir CPom CSev EAEE EBee EBrs EPla GBin GBuc GCal GKev LAst LLWG LPio LRHS MCot MNFA MRav NChi NGdn NMen WCot WDyG WTin |
| | ***javanicum*** | EBee LEdu |
| | - B&SWJ 9506 | WCru |
| | - var. ***puberulum*** | GMac |
| | - - B&SWJ 6770 | WCru |
| | ***johnstonii*** B&SWJ 9127 | WCru |
| | ***kiusianum*** | Widely available |
| | - Kew form | GBuc WSHC |
| | ***koreanum*** | see *T. ichangense* |
| § | ***lucidum*** | CAby CKno CPou CSec CSpe EBee ELan EShb GMac ILad LPio MLLN MRav NBre NDov NLar NSti SGar SHar SMHy SPhx WCot WFar |
| | ***minus*** | CMHG CSec EBWF EBee ECGP ELan EMon GBuc GKir LPio MLLN NBre SEND |
| § | - 'Adiantifolium' | EBee GBuc MLLN MRav NBre NCob NGdn NLar SHar SRms WFar WPer |
| | - var. ***hypoleucum*** B&SWJ 8634 | WCru |
| | - subsp. ***kemense*** | EBee |
| § | - subsp. ***minus*** | NBre |
| § | - subsp. ***olympicum*** | WPer |
| | - subsp. ***saxatile*** | see *T. minus* subsp. *olympicum* |
| | - var. ***sipellatum*** B&SWJ 5051 | WCru |
| | ***morisonii*** | NBid |
| | ***occidentale*** JLS 86255 | MNrw |
| | ***omeiense*** | CDes EBee WPGP |
| | - BWJ 8049 | WCru |
| | ***orientale*** | EWes |
| | ***osmundifolium*** | WCru |
| | ***platycarpum*** B&SWJ 2261 | WCru |
| | ***polygamum*** | see *T. pubescens* |
| | ***przewalskii*** | WCru |
| § | ***pubescens*** | CAby ECha GAuc GBin GBri GMaP MSal NBre NDov SHar SUsu WPrP |
| | ***punctatum*** | CLAP LPio WCot |
| | - B&SWJ 1272 | WCru |
| | ***ramosum*** | EBee |
| | ***reniforme*** | CExc CFir GBuc GMac MHar WCot |
| | - B&SWJ 2610 | WCru |
| | - GWJ 9311 **new** | WCru |
| | - HWJK 2152 | WCru |
| | ***reticulatum*** | WCru |
| | - BWJ 7407 **new** | WCru |
| | ***rochebruneanum*** | Widely available |
| | ***rubescens*** **new** | EBee |
| | ***sachalinense*** | CDes EBee MCCP NCGa WOut WPGP |
| | - RBS 0279 | MHar WCot |
| | ***shensiense*** | GEdr |
| | ***simplex*** | EBee MLLN |
| | - var. ***brevipes*** B&SWJ 4794 | WCru |
| | ***speciosissimum*** | see *T. flavum* subsp. *glaucum* |
| * | ***sphaerostachyum*** | CPom GKir GMac ILad MWhi SMrm WCot WHal |
| | ***squarrosum*** | CDes EBee |
| | ***tenuisubulatum*** BWJ 7929 | WCru |
| | ***tuberosum*** | CDes CElw CMea CPom CWsd EBee EPot GBuc LLHF MLLN NDov NLAp WPGP WPat |
| | ***uchiyamae*** | CDes CFwr EBee EGle GBin GBri LBMP WCot WPGP |
| | ***virgatum*** B&SWJ 2964 | WCru |
| | ***yunnanense*** | WCru |

## *Thamnocalamus* (*Poaceae*)

| | | |
|---|---|---|
| | ***aristatus*** | CGHE EPfP EPla WDyG WPGP |
| | ***crassinodus*** | EPla SBig |
| | - dwarf | EPla |
| | - 'Gosainkund' | EPla |
| | - 'Kew Beauty' | CAbb CDTJ CDoC CEnt CGHE EFul EPfP EPla ERod MBrN MBri MMoz MWht NPal SBig WCot WDyG WPGP |
| | - 'Lang Tang' | CGHE EFul EPla ERod MMoz WPGP |
| | - 'Merlyn' | CDoC CEnt EPfP EPla ERod MMoz MWht WPGP |
| | - 'Pitt White' | MBri |
| | ***falcatus*** | see *Drepanostachyum falcatum* |
| | ***falconeri*** | see *Himalayacalamus falconeri* |
| | ***funghomii*** | see *Schizostachyum funghomii* |
| | ***khasianus*** | see *Drepanostachyum khasianum* |
| | ***maling*** | see *Yushania maling* |
| | ***spathaceus*** misapplied | see *Fargesia murielae* |
| § | ***spathiflorus*** | CEnt EFul EPla |
| | - subsp. ***nepalensis*** | EPla MMoz SBig WPGP |
| § | ***tessellatus*** | EFul ENBC EPla MMoz SEND WDyG |

## *Thamnochortus* (*Restionaceae*)

| | |
|---|---|
| ***bachmannii*** | CBcs CTrC |
| ***cinereus*** | CTrC EAmu WPGP |
| ***insignis*** | CBcs CHEx SPlb WPrP |
| ***lucens*** | CTrC |
| ***rigidus*** | CCCN CTrC |
| ***spicigerus*** | CTrC IDee |

## *Thapsia* (*Apiaceae*)

| | |
|---|---|
| ***decipiens*** | see *Melanoselinum decipiens* |
| ***garganica*** | CArn |

## *Thea* see *Camellia*

## *Thelypteris* (*Thelypteridaceae*)

| | |
|---|---|
| ***kunthii*** | EBee WRic |
| ***limbosperma*** | see *Oreopteris limbosperma* |
| ***nevadensis*** NNS 00-725 | WCot |
| ***noveboracensis*** | see *Parathelypteris novae-boracensis* |
| ***palustris*** | CRWN EBee EMon EWsh LPBA NHol NVic SRms WFib WPnP WRic |
| ***phegopteris*** | see *Phegopteris connectilis* |

## *Themeda* (*Poaceae*)

| | |
|---|---|
| ***japonica*** | EPPr |
| ***triandra*** | SMad |

## *Theobroma* (*Sterculiaceae*)

| | |
|---|---|
| ***cacao*** new | MJnS |

## *Thermopsis* (*Papilionaceae*)

| | |
|---|---|
| ***barbata*** ACE 2298 | EBee |
| ***caroliniana*** | see *T. villosa* |
| ***chinensis*** new | SPhx |
| ***fabacea*** | see *T. lupinoides* |
| ***lanceolata*** | CTri EBee EDAr EPfP GBin MBri MLLN NBPC NCGa NPri NSti SAga SMrm SPhx WAul WCAu WFar WHrl WPer |
| § ***lupinoides*** | CSec ECha EHrv EWTr EWld MHar MHer NBre WFar WPer |
| ***macrophylla*** | EBee |
| - 'Agnina' | WCot |
| ***mollis*** | CPLG NBid |
| ***montana*** | see *T. rhombifolia* var. *montana* |
| § ***rhombifolia*** var. ***montana*** | Widely available |
| § ***villosa*** | CPom CWCL EBee MLLN MRav MSte NBre NDov NGdn WCot WHoo WPGP |

## *Therorhodion* see *Rhododendron*

## *Thevetia* (*Apocynaceae*)

| | |
|---|---|
| ***neriifolia*** | CCCN |
| ***peruviana*** | LRHS MSal |

## *Thladiantha* (*Cucurbitaceae*)

| | |
|---|---|
| ***dubia*** | SDix |
| ***oliveri*** (f) | MSCN |

## *Thlaspi* (*Brassicaceae*)

| | |
|---|---|
| ***biebersteinii*** | see *Pachyphragma macrophyllum* |
| ***capaeifolium*** subsp. ***rotundifolium*** | GKev |
| white-flowered new | |
| ***fendleri*** | MNrw |
| ***montanum*** | CSec WBVN |

## *Thryptomene* (*Myrtaceae*)

| | |
|---|---|
| ***baeckeacea*** | CCCN |
| ***saxicola*** | ECou |
| - 'F.C. Payne' | CBcs |

## *Thuja* ✿ (*Cupressaceae*)

| | |
|---|---|
| 'Extra Gold' | see *T. plicata* 'Irish Gold' |
| 'Gnome' | IBal |
| 'Green Giant' | SLim |
| § ***koraiensis*** | GKir IDee LRHS MBar SCoo |
| ***occidentalis*** | EMac IFFs NWea |
| - 'Amber Glow' | CDoC CKen CRob CSBt ECho LRHS MAsh MGos NHol NLar SCoo SLim SPoG WBor |
| - Aurea Group | MBar |
| - 'Aureospicata' | EHul |
| - 'Bateman Broom' | CKen |
| - 'Beaufort' (v) | CKen EHul MBar |
| - 'Brabant' | CDul LMaj LPan NLar SCoo SLim |
| - 'Brobecks Tower' | CKen NLar SLim |
| - 'Caespitosa' | CFee CKen ECho NHol NLar SCoo WGor |
| - 'Cristata Aurea' | CKen |
| - 'Danica' ♀H4 | CMac CRob ECho EHul EOrn GKir MAsh MBar MMuc NWea SCoo SLim SPoG SRms WCFE WFar |
| - 'Degroot's Spire' | CKen SLim |
| - 'Dicksonii' | EHul |
| - 'Douglasii Aurea' (v) | CKen |
| - 'Ellwangeriana Aurea' | MGos |
| - Emerald | see *T. occidentalis* 'Smaragd' |
| - 'Ericoides' | CDoC CTri EHul LRHS MBar MGos SRms |
| - 'Europa Gold' | CDoC CDul EHul MBar MGos NHol NLar SLim |
| - 'Fastigiata' | MBar |
| - 'Filiformis' | CKen EPla |
| - 'Globosa' | CMac MBar WRHF |
| I - 'Globosa Variegata' (v) | CKen MBar |
| - 'Gold Drop' | CKen |
| - 'Golden Globe' | CDoC EHul EOrn LPan MBar MGos NHol SCoo SLim SPla WDin WRHF |
| - 'Golden Minaret' | EHul |
| - 'Golden Tuffet' | CDoC ECho MGos SCoo SLim |
| - 'Hetz Midget' | CKen ECho EHul IMGH MBar NHol NLar SCoo SLim SPlb WDin WFar |
| - 'Holmstrup' ♀H4 | CDoC CMac CRob CSBt CTri CWib EHul EOrn GKir LRHS MAsh MBar SCoo SHaC SLim SPoG SRms WDin WFar |
| - 'Holmstrup's Yellow' | EHul NHol SLim SPoG |
| - 'Hoveyi' | CMac CTri EHul |
| - 'Linesville' | CKen |
| - 'Little Champion' | EHul LBMP NLar |
| - 'Little Gem' | EHul MGos NHol NLar SRms WDin |
| - 'Lutea Nana' ♀H4 | CMac EHul EOrn MBar NDlv WCFE WRHF |
| - 'Marrisen's Sulphur' | EHul NLar SCoo SLim SPla |
| - 'Meineke's Zwerg' (v) | CKen NLar |
| - 'Miky' | CKen |
| - 'Mr Bowling Ball' | SCoo SLim |
| - 'Ohlendorffii' | CDoC CKen EHul EOrn MBar NHol |
| - 'Orientalis Semperaurescens' | see *Platycladus orientalis* 'Semperaurea' |
| - 'Perk Vlaanderen' (v) | EMon |
| I - 'Pumila Sudworth' | NHol |
| I - 'Pygmaea' | CKen MBar |
| - 'Pyramidalis Aurea' | MGos NHol |
| - 'Pyramidalis Compacta' | EHul WGor |
| - 'Recurva Nana' | EHul MBar NHol |
| - 'Rheingold' ♀H4 | Widely available |
| § - 'Smaragd' ♀H4 | Widely available |
| * - 'Smaragd Variegated' (v) | CKen |
| - 'Smokey' | CKen |
| - 'Southport' | CKen |
| - 'Spaethii' | EHul EOrn |
| - 'Spiralis' | EHul IMGH MBar NLar WCFE |
| § - 'Stolwijk' (v) | EHul EOrn MBar MGos SCoo |
| - 'Sunkist' | CKen CRob CSBt CSli CTri CWib ECho EHul EOrn GKir LAst LPan MAsh MBar MGos NHol SCoo SLim SPla SPoG WFar |
| - 'Teddy' | CDoC CRob ECho LBee LRHS MAsh NHol NLar SCoo SLim SPoG WFar |
| - 'Tiny Tim' | CDoC CMac CRob CSBt CWib ECho EHul GKir IMGH MBar MGos NHol SCoo WFar WGor |

| | | |
|---|---|---|
| | – 'Trompenburg' | CRob CSBt ECho EHul EOrn MAsh NLar SCoo |
| | – 'Wansdyke Silver' (v) | EHul EOrn LRHS MBar SCoo SLim SPoG WRHF |
| | – 'Wareana' | CMac |
| | – 'Wareana Aurea' | see *T. occidentalis* 'Wareana Lutescens' |
| § | – 'Wareana Lutescens' | CWib EHul EOrn MBar MGos NHol |
| | – 'Woodwardii' | EHul MBar |
| | – 'Yellow Ribbon' | CKen CSBt EHul GKir LRHS MBar NLar SCoo SLim SPla SPoG WFar |
| | ***orientalis*** | see *Platycladus orientalis* |
| | – 'Miller's Gold' | see *Platycladus orientalis* 'Aurea Nana' |
| | ***plicata*** | CCVT CChe CDul CMac CSBt EHul EMac EPfP IFFs MBar MGos NWea SLim SPer WDin WMou |
| | – 'Atrovirens' ♀H4 | CDul CTri ECrN LBee LBuc LMaj LPan LRHS MAsh MBar MBri MGos SBLw SCoo SHaC SLim SRms WDin WHar |
| * | – 'Atrovirens Aurea' | SLim |
| | – 'Aurea' ♀H4 | EHul LBee LRHS MAsh SLim SRms |
| | – 'Brooks Gold' | CKen |
| | – 'Can-can' (v) | CRob ECho LAst NLar SCoo |
| I | – 'Cole's Variety' | CWib MBar MGos SLim |
| | – 'Collyer's Gold' | CDul CTri EHul NHol NLar SHaC SRms |
| | – 'Copper Kettle' | CKen ECho EHul MAsh MBar NDlv NLar SCoo SLim WGor WRHF |
| | – 'Cuprea' | CKen EHul MBar |
| | – 'Doone Valley' | CKen CSli EHul EOrn MBar NDlv WFar |
| | – 'Excelsa' **new** | CDul LMaj |
| | – 'Fastigiata' ♀H4 | CDul CMac LRHS |
| | – 'Gelderland' | CTho ECho EHul NLar SCoo SLim WFar |
| | – Goldy = '4Ever'PBR **new** | MBri |
| | – 'Gracilis Aurea' | EHul |
| | – 'Grüne Kugel' | CDoC |
| | – 'Hillieri' | CDoC CDul MBar |
| § | – 'Irish Gold' (v) ♀H4 | CDul CMac LRHS |
| | – 'Rogersii' | CDoC CFee CKen CMac CTri ECho EHul EOrn EPfP GKir MAsh MBar MGos NHol SCoo SPoG SRms WFar |
| | – 'Stolwijk's Gold' | see *T. occidentalis* 'Stolwijk' |
| | – 'Stoneham Gold' ♀H4 | CDoC CFee CMac ECho EHul EOrn GKir LBee MAsh MBar MGos MMuc NHol SLim SPer SPoG SRms |
| | – 'Sunshine' | CKen |
| | – Verigold = 'Courtapli' **new** | SEND |
| | – 'Whipcord' | CBcs ECho EMil LRHS SCoo SLim |
| * | – 'Windsor Gold' | EHul |
| | – 'Winter Pink' (v) | CKen NLar |
| | – 'Zebrina' (v) | CBcs CDoC CDul CMac CSBt CSli CTri CWib ECho EHul ELan EOrn EPfP GKir LRHS MAsh MBar MGos NWea SCoo SHaC SLim SPer SPoG SWvt WDin WFar WHar |

## *Thujopsis* (*Cupressaceae*)

| | | |
|---|---|---|
| | ***dolabrata*** ♀H4 | CBcs CDul CTrG EHul GKir IFFs LRHS MBar NLar NWea SEND SHBN WBrE WDin WFar WPGP |
| | – 'Aurea' (v) | CDoC CKen EHul EOrn LRHS MBar MGos NLar SCoo SHBN SLim |
| | – 'Laetevirens' | see *T. dolabrata* 'Nana' |
| | – 'Melbourne Gold' | NLar |
| § | – 'Nana' | CDoC CKen CMac EHul EOrn IFFs MBar MGos NLar SCoo SLim SRms STre WFar |
| | – 'Variegata' (v) | CDul CFee EHul EMil EOrn LRHS MBar NLar SCoo SLim SPoG WDin WFar |
| | ***koraiensis*** (Nakai) hort. | see *Thuja koraiensis* |

## *Thunbergia* (*Acanthaceae*)

| | | |
|---|---|---|
| | ***alata*** | LBMP MBri SPoG |
| | – 'African Sunset' | CSpe EShb WHil |
| | – 'Alba' **new** | WHil |
| | – 'Lemon' **new** | WHil |
| | – 'Orange Beauty' **new** | WHil |
| | ***battiscombeii*** | CCCN EShb MJnS SOWG |
| | ***coccinea*** | CCCN EShb MJnS |
| | ***erecta*** | CCCN SOWG |
| | ***fragrans*** | EShb WHil |
| | ***grandiflora*** ♀H1 | CCCN CHll CTrG ELan EPfP EShb MJnS SOWG |
| | – 'Alba' | CCCN CHll EShb WHil |
| | ***gregorii*** ♀H1+3 | CCCN CHll CSpe EShb SOWG |
| | ***mysorensis*** ♀H1 | CCCN MJnS SOWG |
| | ***natalensis*** | CCCN EShb |

## thyme, caraway see *Thymus herba-barona*

## thyme, garden see *Thymus vulgaris*

## thyme, lemon see *Thymus citriodorus*

## thyme, wild see *Thymus serpyllum*

## *Thymus* ✿ (*Lamiaceae*)

| | | |
|---|---|---|
| | from Albania | CArn |
| | from Turkey | ECho EWes LLWP SHDw |
| § | 'Alan Bloom' | LLWP |
| | 'Anderson's Gold' | see *T. pulegioides* 'Bertram Anderson' |
| | ***azoricus*** | see *T. caespititius* |
| | 'Caborn Lilac Gem' | LLWP SHDw |
| | 'Caborn Pink Carpet' | LLWP |
| | 'Caborn Rosanne' | LLWP |
| § | ***caespititius*** | CArn ECho EDAr ELau GBar GMaP GPoy MHer NMen NRya SPlb SRot WAbe WCHb WPer |
| | ***caespitosus*** | CTri GKir LLWP |
| | ***camphoratus*** | CArn CBod CMea ELau EPot EWes GBar MHer MNHC NGHP NMen SHDw WAbe WJek |
| | – 'A Touch of Frost' | SHDw |
| | – 'Derry' | CSpe |
| | ***capitatus*** | CArn |
| | ***carnosus*** misapplied | see *T. vulgaris* 'Erectus' |
| | ***carnosus*** Boiss. | STre |
| | 'Carol Ann' (v) | ECho ELau EWes GBar LLWP MNHC |
| | 'Caroline' | SHDw |
| | 'Carshalton' | CWan |
| | ***cephalotos*** | WAbe |
| | ***ciliatus*** | LLWP WPer |
| | ***cilicicus*** misapplied | see *T. caespititius* |
| | ***cilicicus*** ambig. | MNHC NMen WCHb |
| | ***cilicicus*** Boiss. & Bail. | EWes GBar WAbe |
| | ***citriodorus*** | CArn CHby CHrt CWan ECho EDAr ELau GAbr GBar GKev GKir GPoy LLWP MBrN MHer MNHC MWat NGHP NPri SWal WBrE WJek WPer |
| | – 'Archer's Gold' | see *T. pulegioides* 'Archer's Gold' |
| | – 'Aureus' | see *T. pulegioides* 'Aureus' |
| | – 'Bertram Anderson' | see *T. pulegioides* 'Bertram Anderson' |
| § | – 'Golden King' (v) | CWan ECha ECho EDAr ELan GBar LHop LLWP LRHS MBar MBri MHer NGHP WCHb WHoo WPer |
| | – 'Golden Lemon' misapplied | see *T. pulegioides* 'Aureus' |

| | | |
|---|---|---|
| | - 'Golden Lemon' (v) | CArn GPoy LLWP WJek |
| | - 'Golden Queen' (v) | ECho EDAr GGar MHer MWat NBlu NGHP NPri SHDw SPer SPet SRms WFar |
| | - 'Lemon Supreme' | LLWP |
| | - 'Lime' | LLWP |
| | - ***repandus*** | see *T.* 'Rosemary's Lemon Carpet' |
| | - 'Silver King' (v) | ECho GKev LLWP |
| | - 'Silver Posie' | see *T. vulgaris* 'Silver Posie' |
| | - 'Silver Queen' (v) ♀H4 | CBcs CSam CWan EAlp ECha ECho EDAr ELan EPfP GBar GGar GKev GMaP LAst LRHS MBar MHer MNHC NBlu NGHP SPlb WFar |
| | - 'Variegatus' misapplied | see *T. citriodorus* 'Golden King' |
| * | - 'Variegatus' (v) | GBar LHop LSRN MBri NGHP |
| | 'Coccineus' | see *T.* Coccineus Group |
| N | Coccineus Group ♀H4 | CArn CPrp CTri ECha ECho ECtt ELan ELau GKir GMaP LCro LLWP LRHS MBar MBri MHer MNHC NGHP NHol NPri SIng SPer SRms SRot WAbe WHoo WPat WRHF |
| § | - 'Atropurpureus' misapplied | LLWP SHDw |
| | - 'Bethany' | LLWP SGar |
| § | - 'Hardstoft Red' (v) | GBar |
| § | - 'Purple Beauty' | LLWP MHer NGHP |
| § | - 'Purpurteppich' | LLWP |
| § | - 'Red Elf' | ECho GBar MHer NGHP SHDw WJek |
| | 'Coccineus Major' | CMea CWan ECho EDAr LRHS MHer MNHC SIde WJek |
| | ***comosus*** misapplied | SHDw WEas WPer |
| | 'Cow Green' | LLWP SHDw |
| | 'Creeping Lemon' | ELau GBar LLWP MHer NGHP SHDw WJek |
| | 'Dark Eyes' | SHDw |
| | 'Dartmoor' | GBar LLWP SHDw SIng |
| | 'Desboro' | GBar LLWP MBNS MHer NHol |
| | ***doerfleri*** | CLyd ECha LLWP |
| | - 'Bressingham' | CArn CMea CPrp CTri CWan ECho ECtt EDAr ELau GBar GKir LBee LLWP LRHS MHer MNHC NGHP NHol NPri SPlb SRms SWal WFar WPat WPer |
| | 'Doone Valley' (v) | Widely available |
| | ***drucei*** | see *T. polytrichus* subsp. *britannicus* |
| | 'E.B.Anderson' | see *T. pulegioides* 'Bertram Anderson' |
| | 'Eastgrove Pink' | LLWP SHDw |
| | 'Elf' | NWCA |
| | 'Emma's Pink' | LLWP |
| | ***erectus*** | see *T. vulgaris* 'Erectus' |
| * | ***ericoides*** | EPot |
| | 'Fragrantissimus' | CArn CEnt CHrt CMea CWan ELau GBar GPoy LLWP MHer MNHC MWat NGHP NPri SIde SPlb WFar WJek WPer |
| | 'Gibson's Cave' | LLWP |
| | 'Glenridding' | LLWP |
| | 'Gowbarrow' | LLWP |
| | 'Gratian' | LLWP SHDw |
| | 'Hans Stam' | LLWP |
| | 'Hardstoft Red' | see *T.* (Coccineus Group) 'Hardstoft Red' |
| § | 'Hartington Silver' (v) | CMea EAlp ECha ECho ECtt EPot EWes GBar GBuc GKev GKir GPoy LAst LBee LHop LRHS MHer MNHC NChi NGHP NHol NRya SIng SPlb WAbe WFar WHoo WPer |
| | ***herba-barona*** | CArn CHrt CMea CPrp CTri CWan ECha ELau GBar GPoy LEdu LLWP MHer MNHC MWat NGHP NHol NRya SIde SRms WPer |
| | - 'Bob Flowerdew' | LLWP |
| | - ***citrata*** | see *T. herba-barona* 'Lemon-scented' |
| § | - 'Lemon-scented' | ECha ELau GBar GPoy LLWP MHer SHDw SIde WCHb |
| | 'Highdown' | ECtt SHDw |
| | 'Highdown Adus' | SHDw |
| | 'Highdown Lemon' | SHDw |
| | 'Highdown Red' | SHDw |
| | 'Highdown Stretham' | SHDw |
| | 'Highland Cream' | see *T.* 'Hartington Silver' |
| | ***hirsutus*** | NBir |
| | 'Kurt' | LLWP SHDw |
| | 'Lake District' | LLWP |
| I | 'Lantanii' | LLWP SHDw |
| | ***lanuginosus*** misapplied | see *T. pseudolanuginosus* |
| | 'Lavender Sea' | ELau EWes LLWP |
| | 'Lemon Caraway' | see *T. herba-barona* 'Lemon-scented' |
| | 'Lemon Sorbet' | SHDw |
| * | 'Lemon Variegated' (v) | EDAr ELau EPfP GBar MNHC SPer SPoG |
| | ***leucotrichus*** | WPat |
| | 'Lilac Time' | EWes GBar LLWP MHer NGHP NTHB SHDw SIde SPlb WCHb WJek |
| | ***longicaulis*** | CArn CLyd ECha ELau GBar LLWP MHer WJek |
| | 'Low Force' | LLWP |
| | 'Marjorie' **new** | LLWP |
| | ***marschallianus*** | see *T. pannonicus* |
| | ***mastichina*** | CArn GBar |
| | - 'Didi' | MHer |
| | ***membranaceus*** | CPBP WAbe |
| | ***micans*** | see *T. caespititius* |
| | ***minus*** | see *Calamintha nepeta* |
| | ***montanus*** Waldst. & Kit. | see *T. pulegioides* |
| | 'Mountain Select' | LLWP SHDw |
| | ***neiceffii*** | CLyd ECha ELau GBar LLWP |
| | 'New Hall' | SHDw |
| | ***nummularius*** misapplied | see *T.* 'Pat Milne' |
| | ***odoratissimus*** | see *T. pallasianus* subsp. *pallasianus* |
| | 'Orange Balsam' | LLWP NHol |
| | 'Orange Spice' | LLWP SHDw SPoG |
| | ***pallasianus*** | ELau SHDw |
| § | - subsp. ***pallasianus*** | GBar |
| § | ***pannonicus*** | LLWP MHer WPer |
| § | 'Pat Milne' | ELau |
| | 'Peter Davis' | CArn CHFP GBar LHop LSRN MBNS MHer MNHC NBir NGHP NHol SIde WAbe WJek WRHF |
| | 'Pink Ripple' | CBod CMea EAlp EDAr ELau EWes GBar LLWP MHer NGHP SBch SHDw SIde SIng WCHb WHal WHoo WJek |
| | ***polytrichus*** misapplied | see *T. praecox* |
| § | ***polytrichus*** A. Kern. ex Borbás subsp. ***britannicus*** | CArn ECho GPoy LLWP LSou SHDw SPlb WAbe WJek WPer |
| | - - 'Minor' | ECho EPot LLWP WPer |
| | - - 'Orkney White' **new** | WAlt |
| § | - - 'Thomas's White' ♀H4 | CTri ECho LLWP |
| | - - 'Timothy's White' | CEnt |
| | 'Porlock' | CMea CPrp CTri CWan ECho ELau EPfP GBar GKir GMaP GPoy LLWP MHer MNHC NChi NGHP NRya SIde SRms WAbe WHoo WJek WPer |
| § | ***praecox*** | EBWF GBar LLWP MHer NLan NSco |
| | - subsp. ***arcticus*** | see *T. polytrichus* subsp. *britannicus* |
| | - - 'Albus' | see *T. polytrichus* subsp. *britannicus* 'Thomas's White' |

| | | |
|---|---|---|
| | 'Provence' | LLWP |
| § | ***pseudolanuginosus*** | CArn CTri CWan EAlp ECha ECho EDAr ELau EPot GBar GMaP LBee LCro LLWP LRHS MBNS MBri MHer MLHP MNHC NBir NChi NGHP NHol SPlb SRms WHoo WPer |
| | - 'Hall's Variety' | ELau GBar |
| § | ***pulegioides*** | CArn CBod CHby CHrt ELau GBar GGar GPoy LLWP MBri MHer MNHC NPri SBch SHDw SIde WJek WPer |
| § | - 'Archer's Gold' | Widely available |
| § | - 'Aureus' ♀H4 | GBar GGar GKev GKir GMaP LAst LCro LLWP LRHS MBar MBri MHer NBlu NWCA SGar SPer SPla SPlb WFar WHoo |
| § | - 'Bertram Anderson' ♀H4 | Widely available |
| | - 'Foxley' (v) | CBod CBow CWan ECho EHoe ELau EPfP GBar LLWP LSou MHer MNHC NGHP NHol NPro NTHB SHDw SIde SPlb WCHb WJek |
| | - 'Golden Dwarf' | LLWP |
| § | - 'Goldentime' | GBar LLWP LRHS NGHP |
| | - 'Sir John Lawes' | LLWP MHer SHDw |
| | - 'Sundon Hills' | LLWP |
| | - 'Tabor' | GBar GMaP MNHC NGHP NTHB SHDw WOut |
| | 'Rasta' (v) | EAlp EDAr LLWP |
| | 'Redstart' | ECha ELau GBar LBee LLWP LRHS MHer NGHP SBch SHDw SIde WCHb |
| | ***richardii*** subsp. ***nitidus*** misapplied | see *T. vulgaris* 'Suditin' |
| | - - 'Compactus Albus' | see *T. vulgaris* 'Snow White' |
| | 'Rosa Ceeping' | SHDw |
| | 'Rosalicht' | LLWP |
| | 'Rosalind' | SHDw |
| | 'Rosedrift' | LLWP SHDw |
| § | 'Rosemary's Lemon Carpet' | CArn LLWP |
| | ***rotundifolius*** misapplied | see *T. vulgaris* 'Elsbeth' |
| | 'Ruby Glow' | CEnt CHrt ELau EWes MHer SHDw WFar |
| | ***serpyllum*** misapplied | see *T. polytrichus* A. Kern. ex Borbás |
| | ***serpyllum*** ambig. | CArn ELau MBri NGHP SIde SPet SPlb SRms WJek WPer |
| | ***serpyllum*** L. | EAro LCro LLWP WBVN |
| | - var. ***albus*** | CPrp ECha ECho ELau GBar GPoy LAst LLWP MNHC NGHP NHol NPri SIde SPer SRms WHoo |
| | - 'Albus Variegatus' | see *T.* 'Hartington Silver' |
| N | - 'Annie Hall' | CWan ECho EDAr ELau EPfP EPot GAbr GBar GGar LAst LLWP LRHS MHer NGHP NPri SIde SPer STre WCFE WPer |
| | - 'Atropurpureus' | see *T.* (Coccineus Group) 'Atropurpureus' misapplied |
| | - 'August Moon' | LLWP |
| | - 'Barwinnock Snowdrift' (v) | GBar |
| | - ***coccineus*** 'Minor' misapplied | see *T.* Coccineus Group |
| | - - 'Minor' Bloom | see *T.* 'Alan Bloom' |
| | - 'Conwy Rose' | LLWP WAbe |
| N | - 'East Lodge' | LLWP MNHC |
| | - 'Elfin' | CLyd ECho EDAr EWes GKev LBee MBri SHDw SIng SPlb WAbe |
| N | - 'Fulney Red' | EWes |
| | - 'Goldstream' (v) | CLyd CMea ECho ELau EPfP GBar LHop LLWP LRHS MBar MBri MHer NGHP NHol NRya SPlb SRms WCHb WHoo WPer |
| | - 'Lemon Curd' | CWan ELau GBar LLWP MHer MNHC NGHP NHol SHDw SIde SPlb SPoG WCHb WFar WJek WRha |
| § | - 'Minimalist' | CArn CMea CWan ECha ELau GBar LLWP MBri MHer MLHP MNHC NHol NRya SBch SIde SPer SPet SPlb SRot WBVN WCHb WHoo WPat WPer |
| | - 'Minimus' | see *T. serpyllum* 'Minimalist' |
| § | - 'Minor' | CEnt CPrp CTri ECho ECtt GBar LLWP NMen NSla SHDw WAbe |
| N | - 'Minor Albus' | ECho GBar |
| | - 'Minus' | see *T. serpyllum* 'Minor' |
| | - 'Petite' | EPot EWes LLWP |
| N | - 'Pink Chintz' ♀H4 | Widely available |
| | - 'Posh Pinky' | EDAr EPot LLWP NMen |
| | - subsp. ***pulchellus*** | LLWP |
| | - 'Purple Beauty' | see *T.* (Coccineus Group) 'Purple Beauty' |
| | - 'Purpurteppich' | see *T.* (Coccineus Group) 'Purpurteppich' |
| | - 'Pygmaeus' | LLWP |
| | - 'Rainbow Falls' (v) | CBod EPfP GBar LLWP MNHC NGHP NHol SHDw SIde |
| | - 'Red Elf' | see *T.* (Coccineus Group) 'Red Elf' |
| | - 'Roger's Snowdrift' | LLWP |
| N | - 'Roseus' | GBar SIde |
| N | - 'Russetings' | CLyd CPrp EAlp ECtt ELau EPfP EPot GBar LLWP MBar MHer MNHC NGHP NHol SBch SIde SPer SRms WFar WHoo |
| N | - 'September' | LLWP MHer |
| | - 'Snowcarpet' | LLWP |
| N | - 'Snowdrift' | CArn CMea CWan ECho ECtt EDAr ELau EPfP EPot GBar GKev MBar MHer MNHC MWat NHol NMen NRya SBch SIde SPlb WCFE WFar WJek WPat WPer |
| N | - 'Splendens' | LLWP |
| | - subsp. ***tanaensis*** | CArn |
| | - 'Variegatus' | see *T.* 'Hartington Silver' |
| | - 'Vey' | ECho EWes GBar GMaP LLWP MHer NTHB SHDw SIng WCHb |
| | ***sibthorpii*** | CArn |
| N | 'Silver Posie' | see *T. vulgaris* 'Silver Posie' |
| | 'Snowdonia Idris' | LLWP |
| | 'Snowdonia Ifor' | LLWP |
| | 'Snowdonia Imperial Beauty' | LLWP |
| | 'Snowdonia Iorwerth' | LLWP |
| | 'Snowdonia Isolde' | LLWP |
| | 'Snowdonia Istyn' | LLWP |
| | 'Snowdonia Lass' | LLWP SHDw |
| | 'Snowdonia Pedr' | LLWP |
| | 'Snowdonia Pink Gem' | LLWP |
| | 'Snowdonia Pryderi' | LLWP |
| | 'Snowdonia Pwyll' | LLWP |
| | 'Snowdonia Rosie' | LLWP |
| | 'Snowdonia Rowena' | LLWP |
| | 'Snowman' | SHDw |
| | 'Swaledale' | LLWP |
| * | ***valesiacus*** | LLWP SHDw |
| § | ***villosus*** | ECho |
| | ***vulgaris*** | Widely available |
| | - ***albus*** | ECho GBar |
| | - 'Aureus' hort. | see *T. pulegioides* 'Goldentime' |
| | - 'Boule' | LLWP |
| * | - 'Compactus' | CHFP GPoy LLWP MAvo MNHC |
| | - 'Deutsche Auslese' | LAst LLWP |
| | - 'Diamantis' | LLWP |
| | - 'Dorcas White' | LLWP MHer WPer |
| § | - 'Elsbeth' | ECho ELau LLWP SHDw |
| | - 'English Winter' | GBar MNHC SIde |

| | |
|---|---|
| § – 'Erectus' | CArn CLyd GBar MHer WPer |
| – French | ELau LLWP MHer SHDw SPlb |
| – French, summer | SIde |
| – 'Golden Pins' | GBar MHer |
| – 'Lemon Queen' | ECho ELau |
| – 'Lucy' | CPrp GBar LLWP MHer MNHC |
| – 'Pinewood' | EAlp LLWP MHer SIde |
| – 'Silver Pearl' (v) | ECho |
| § – 'Silver Posie' | Widely available |
| § – 'Snow White' | ELau EWes LLWP SHDw |
| § – 'Suditin' | STre |
| 'Widecombe' (v) | LLWP MHer SHDw |
| ***zygis*** | CArn |

## *Tiarella* (*Saxifragaceae*)

| | |
|---|---|
| 'Black Snowflake'PBR | EBee |
| 'Black Velvet'PBR | GCai MLLN NCGa NLar SPer WFar |
| 'Braveheart' **new** | EBee SPoG |
| ***collina*** | see *T. wherryi* |
| ***cordifolia*** ♀H4 | Widely available |
| – 'Glossy' | CBct GBuc WPGP |
| – 'Oakleaf' | CLAP CMoH EBee NBre NBro WCAu |
| – 'Rosalie' | see x *Heucherella alba* 'Rosalie' |
| – 'Running Tapestry' | CLAP EBee WMoo |
| – 'Slick Rock' | EBee EPPr |
| 'Cygnet'PBR | CBct CLAP EBee ECtt EPPr GCai LHop MLLN SIng SPer SPoG SRot WFar |
| 'Dark Star' | ECtt NBre |
| 'Dunvegan' | EBee MLLN WFar WMoo |
| 'Elizabeth Oliver' | CLAP EBee |
| 'Freckles' | MRav |
| 'Hidden Carpet' | CHid |
| 'Inkblot' | EBee ELan MLLN NBro WCAu WFar WMoo |
| 'Iron Butterfly'PBR | CBct CChe CLAP CWCL EBee ECGP ECtt EPfP GBin GKev GMaP LAst LSRN MLLN MRav MSte NBro NCGa SPer SRot STes WFar WPGP |
| 'Jeepers Creepers'PBR | NCob NHol SHar |
| * 'Laciniate Runner' | CLAP |
| 'Martha Oliver' | CLAP EBee GBuc NBre SBch WPGP WTin |
| 'Mint Chocolate'PBR | CHFP CLAP CWCL EBee ECha ECtt EHoe EHrv ELan EMil EPfP GMaP MLLN MRav MSte NCob NGdn NLar SMrm SPer SPla SWvt WAul WCra WFar WPGP |
| Morning Star = 'Tntia042'PBR | EWll LAst MBri SRot |
| 'Neon Lights'PBR | CBow CHar EWes NBPC NBro NCob SPoG SWvt |
| § 'Ninja'PBR | CHid CWCL EBee EBrs ECha ECtt EHrv ELan ELon GMaP LAst LFur MAvo MDun MLLN MRav NLar NSti SPer SRot SWvt WFar WHoo |
| 'Petite Pink Bouquet' | ECtt |
| 'Pink Bouquet' | CAbP CBow CLAP EAEE EBee EBrs ECha ECtt EHrv GJos LBMP LRHS MBri MLLN NHol SPla WFar WGor WMoo WPnP |
| 'Pink Brushes' | EBee WPnP |
| 'Pink Skyrocket'PBR | CWGN EBee ECtt ELon GCai LLHF NCob NHol SHar SMrm WCra |
| 'Pinwheel' | EBee EBrs MRav NBre |
| 'Pirate's Patch'PBR | GCai LLHF NHol |
| ***polyphylla*** | CBow CSsd EBee ELan GAbr GBin MLLN NBre NLar SBch SWal WFar WMoo |
| – 'Baoxing Pink' | EBee WCru |
| – 'Filigran' | EBee EHig NHol NLar |
| – 'Moorgrün' | GCal WFar |
| – pink-flowered | CLAP CMoH CSec EHrv GBin |
| – – BWJ 8088 | WCru |
| 'Running Tiger' | EBee |
| 'Sea Foam' | EBee NHol |
| 'Simsalabim' **new** | EBee |
| 'Skeleton Key' | EBee |
| 'Skid's Variegated' (v) | CBow EBee ECtt EShb MBNS NSti SWvt WCot |
| 'Spanish Cross'PBR | NHol |
| 'Spring Symphony'PBR | CLAP CWCL EBee ECtt EShb GBin GCai LSou MBri NCGa NHol NLar NPer SHar SIng SMrm SPoG WFar |
| Starburst = 'Tntia041'PBR | LAst SIng |
| 'Starfish' | GMaP MLLN NBPC NBre NCob WPrP |
| 'Sugar and Spice' **new** | LSou NHol |
| 'Tiger Stripe' | EBee EPfP MRav NBro SPer WFar WMoo WPnP |
| ***trifoliata*** | MRav NBre WFar |
| ***unifoliata*** | MSal |
| 'Viking Ship'PBR | see x *Heucherella* 'Viking Ship' |
| § ***wherryi*** ♀H4 | CBcs CHrt CRow CWCL EBee ECtt EHig EHrv ELan EPfP GKir GMaP LAst LBMP NBir NBlu NBro NHol NOrc NPri SBch SPer SPla SPlb SRot SWvt WFar WMoo WPer WPnP |
| – 'Bronze Beauty' | CBct CLAP GBuc MRav NDov NPro SBch SPla WAbe WBrk WFar WMoo WPGP |
| – 'Green Velvet' | ECha |
| – 'Heronswood Mist' (v) | CAbP CBct CBow CFir EBee ECtt GEdr GQue LSou MLLN NBro SWvt WCot |
| – 'Montrose' | NBre WPGP |

## *Tibouchina* (*Melastomataceae*)

| | |
|---|---|
| ***grandifolia*** | CRHN WBod |
| ***granulosa*** | SOWG |
| ***heteromalla*** **new** | CCCN |
| 'Jules' | SOWG |
| * ***laxa*** 'Skylab' | SOWG |
| ***organensis*** | CHll SOWG WPGP |
| ***paratropica*** | CRHN WSHC |
| ***semidecandra*** hort. | see *T. urvilleana* |
| § ***urvilleana*** ♀H1 | Widely available |
| – 'Compacta' **new** | CCCN |
| – 'Edwardsii' | LSou MLan SAdn SMrm SUsu |
| – 'Rich Blue Sun' | CSpe |
| – variegated (v) | CCCN LSou WCot |

## *Tigridia* ✿ (*Iridaceae*)

| | |
|---|---|
| B&SWJ 10393 from Guatemala | WCru |
| ***lutea*** | ECho |
| ***pavonia*** | CPLG CSec CTca EBrs ECho EDif EWll IGor LAma MBri |
| – B&SWJ 10244 from Mexico | WCru |
| – 'Alba' | CFwr CHFP EBrs EDif WHil |
| – 'Alba Grandiflora' | EBee ERCP EWll |
| – 'Aurea' | CFwr EBee WHil |
| – 'Canariensis' | CHFP EBee EBrs WHil |
| – 'Lilacea' | CFwr CHFP EBee EBrs ECho ERCP EWll WHil |
| – 'Speciosa' | CFwr CHFP EBee WHil |

## *Tilia* ✿ (*Tiliaceae*)

| | |
|---|---|
| ***americana*** | CLnd CMCN GKir NWea SCoo |
| – 'Dentata' | CDul |
| – 'Nova' | CDoC SBLw |
| ***amurensis*** | CMCN GKir |
| – subsp. ***taquetii*** | GKir |
| ***argentea*** | see *T. tomentosa* |
| ***begoniifolia*** | see *T. dasystyla* |
| ***chenmoui*** | CMCN GKir MBlu MBri WPGP |

| | |
|---|---|
| ***chinensis*** | CMCN GKir |
| ***chingiana*** | CDul CMCN GKir MBlu SBir SLon |
| ***cordata*** ♀H4 | CBcs CCVT CDul CLnd CSBt CTho CTri EBee ECrN ELan EMac EPfP GKir LBuc LCro LMaj MAsh MSwo NBee NWea SBLw SCoo SHBN SPer WDin WMou WOrn |
| § - 'Böhlje' | CDul LPan SBLw SLPl WMoo |
| - 'Dainty Leaf' | CDul |
| - 'Erecta' | see *T. cordata* 'Böhlje' |
| - 'Greenspire' ♀H4 | CCVT CDoC CDul CLnd CWib EBee ECrN LMaj LPan LRHS NBee SBLw WOrn |
| - 'Len Parvin' | WPGP |
| - 'Lico' | CMen LMaj WMou |
| - 'Monto' | CMen |
| - 'Plymtree Gold' | CDul |
| - 'Roelvo' | CDul |
| - 'Swedish Upright' | CDul CLnd CTho |
| - 'Winter Orange' | CDul CEnd EBee ECrN GKir LAst LRHS MBlu MBri SBir SCoo |
| § ***dasystyla*** | CMCN WPGP |
| x ***euchlora*** ♀H4 | CBcs CCVT CDul CLnd CMCN EBee ECrN EPfP GKir LAst LMaj LPan NWea SBLw SPer SSta WDin WFar WOrn |
| § x ***europaea*** | CBcs CDul CLnd CRWN ELan EWTr NWea SBLw WMou |
| - 'Koningslinde' **new** | CDul |
| - 'Pallida' | CDul CLnd CTho LMaj MBlu NWea SBLw WMou |
| - 'Wratislaviensis' ♀H4 | CDoC CDul CLnd EPfP GKir LRHS MAsh MBlu NWea |
| x ***flavescens*** 'Glenleven' | CDul SBLw |
| § 'Harold Hillier' | MBlu |
| ***henryana*** | CDoC CDul CEnd CLnd CMCN CTho CWib EBee ECrN EMil EPfP ERod GKir IArd IDee MBlu MBri MMuc SBir WDin WPGP |
| § ***heterophylla*** | CMCN CTho WPGP |
| - var. ***michauxii*** | CLnd GKir |
| 'Hillieri' | see *T.* 'Harold Hillier' |
| ***insularis*** | CMCN GKir MBlu |
| ***japonica*** | CDul CMCN GKir WMou WPGP |
| ***kiusiana*** | CMCN GKir MBri WPGP |
| ***mandshurica*** | CMCN WPGP |
| ***maximowicziana*** | GKir WPGP |
| ***mexicana*** | WPGP |
| ***miqueliana*** | CMCN |
| 'Moltkei' | CLnd CMCN WPGP |
| ***mongolica*** | CDoC CDul CLnd CMCN CTho EBee EPfP GKir MBlu MMuc SCoo SMHT WPGP |
| ***monticola*** | see *T. heterophylla* |
| ***oliveri*** | CDul CMCN GKir MBlu NWea SBir WPGP |
| 'Petiolaris' ♀H4 | CCVT CDoC CDul CEnd CLnd CMCN EBee ECrN ELan EPfP GKir LRHS MBlu MSwo NBee NWea SBLw SHBN SPer SSta WDin |
| ***platyphyllos*** | CCVT CDul CLnd CMCN CSBt CTho CTri EBee ECrN EMac EMil EPfP EWTr GKir LAst LBuc NBee NWea SBLw SCoo SPer WDin WMou |
| - 'Aurea' | CDul CLnd CTho ECrN MBlu |
| - 'Corallina' | see *T. platyphyllos* 'Rubra' |
| - 'Dakvorm' | SBLw |
| - 'Delft' | SBLw |
| - 'Erecta' | see *T. platyphyllos* 'Fastigiata' |
| § - 'Fastigiata' | CDul CTho ECrN SBLw SLPl |
| - 'Laciniata' | CDul CMCN CTho EBee GKir LMaj MBlu |
| * - 'Pendula' | CTho |
| § - 'Rubra' ♀H4 | CDoC CLnd CTho ECrN EPfP GKir LBuc MGos NBee NWea SBLw WDin WFar |
| - 'Tortuosa' | MBlu |
| § ***tomentosa*** | CDul CLnd CMCN CTho ECrN ELan EMil GKir LMaj MMuc NWea SBLw SCoo SEND WDin WMou |
| - 'Brabant' ♀H4 | CDoC EPfP EWTr LMaj SBLw WFar |
| ***tuan*** | CMCN |
| x ***vulgaris*** | see *T.* x *europaea* |

## *Tilingia* (*Apiaceae*)

| | |
|---|---|
| ***ajanensis*** B&SWJ 11202 **new** | WCru |

## *Tillaea* see *Crassula*

## *Tillandsia* (*Bromeliaceae*)

| | |
|---|---|
| ***aeranthos*** | SChr |
| ***argentea*** ♀H1 | MBri |
| ***cyanea*** ♀H1 | LRHS MBri |
| ***usneoides*** | CHal SHmp |

## *Tinantia* (*Commelinaceae*)

| | |
|---|---|
| ***pringlei*** | CDes EBee LEdu SKHP WPGP WSHC |
| - AIM 77 | WCot |

## *Titanopsis* (*Aizoaceae*)

| | |
|---|---|
| ***calcarea*** ♀H1 | CCCN EPfP |

## *Tithonia* (*Asteraceae*)

| | |
|---|---|
| ***rotundifolia*** **new** | CSec CSpe |
| - 'Torch' | SMrm SUsu |

## *Todea* (*Osmundaceae*)

| | |
|---|---|
| ***barbara*** | WRic |

## *Tofieldia* (*Melanthiaceae*)

| | |
|---|---|
| ***calyculata*** | NHol |
| ***coccinea*** | EBee |
| ***pusilla*** | ERos |

## *Tolmiea* (*Saxifragaceae*)

| | |
|---|---|
| ***menziesii*** | EBee EWld MBri MCot NHol SPer SWal |
| - 'Goldsplash' | see *T. menziesii* 'Taff's Gold' |
| - 'Maculata' | see *T. menziesii* 'Taff's Gold' |
| § - 'Taff's Gold' (v) ♀H4 | CWan EBee EHoe EOHP EShb GAbr GMaP MHer NBid NGdn NVic SPlb WEas WHoo WTin |
| - 'Variegata' | see *T. menziesii* 'Taff's Gold' |

## *Tolpis* (*Asteraceae*)

| | |
|---|---|
| ***barbata*** | CSpe |

## *Tonestus* (*Asteraceae*)

| | |
|---|---|
| § ***lyallii*** | WPer |

## *Toona* (*Meliaceae*)

| | |
|---|---|
| § ***sinensis*** | CArn CDul CEnd CGHE CLnd CMCN CTho CWib ELan EPfP SPoG WBVN WFar WPGP |
| - 'Flamingo' (v) | CBcs EBee EPfP IDee LRHS MAsh MGos NLar SBig SMad SPoG SSta WCot |

## *Torenia* (*Scrophulariaceae*)

| | |
|---|---|
| (Moon Series) Pink Moon = 'Dantopkmn' | LAst |
| - Purple Moon = 'Dantopur'PBR | LAst LSou SVil |

| | |
|---|---|
| - Violet Moon | LAst |
| - White Moon = 'Dantorwhite'PBR | LAst |
| - Yellow Moon = 'Danmoon20' **new** | LAst LSou |
| Summer Wave Series | CCCN LSou SCoo |
| - 'Summer Wave Violet' | LSou |

## *Torilis* (*Apiaceae*)

| | |
|---|---|
| ***japonica*** | CBre EBWF |

## *Torreya* (*Taxaceae*)

| | |
|---|---|
| ***grandis*** | EGFP |

## *Townsendia* (*Asteraceae*)

| | |
|---|---|
| § ***alpigena*** var. ***alpigena*** | CGra CPBP |
| ***formosa*** | ECho |
| ***hookeri*** | CGra |
| ***incana*** | CPBP |
| ***leptotes*** | CPBP |
| ***montana*** | see *T. alpigena* var. *alpigena* |
| ***parryi*** | CSec GKev |
| § ***rothrockii*** | CGra GKev NMen |
| ***spathulata*** | CPBP |
| ***wilcoxiana*** misapplied | see *T. rothrockii* |

## *Toxicodendron* (*Anacardiaceae*)

| | |
|---|---|
| ***vernicifluum*** | see *Rhus verniciflua* |

## *Trachelium* (*Campanulaceae*)

| | |
|---|---|
| § ***asperuloides*** | WAbe |
| ***caerulem*** 'Black Knight' | CSpe |
| ***caeruleum*** ♀H1 | SGar |
| - 'Purple Umbrella' | CPLG NBre |
| ***jacquinii*** subsp. ***rumelianum*** | CGra CPBP NWCA WPat |

## *Trachelospermum* ✿ (*Apocynaceae*)

| | |
|---|---|
| from Nanking, China | EShb |
| § ***asiaticum*** ♀H2-3 | Widely available |
| - B&SWJ 4814 | WCru |
| - 'Golden Memories' | CWGN EMil EPfP LRHS MAsh MGos SKHP SLon SPoG SSpi SSta WPat |
| - 'Goshiki' (v) | CBow EShb GQui MGos WPat |
| - var. ***intermedium*** | NPal WPGP |
| - - B&SWJ 8733 | WCru |
| - 'Kulu Chiriman' | WCot |
| - 'Nagaba' (v) | SKHP |
| - 'Ogon Nishiki' (v) **new** | SKHP |
| - 'Theta' | SKHP |
| 'Chameleon' | NPal |
| ***jasminoides*** ♀H3-4 | Widely available |
| - B&SWJ 5117 | WCru |
| § - 'Japonicum' | CSPN LRHS SLon SPla WSHC |
| - 'Major' | CSPN CTrG EBee SSpi |
| * - 'Oblanceolatum' | GCal |
| - 'Tricolor' | CBcs SKHP SWvt WHil |
| - 'Variegatum' (v) ♀H3-4 | Widely available |
| - 'Waterwheel' | CWGN EBee EMil LRHS SKHP SSpi WPGP WSHC |
| - 'Wilsonii' | CDul CMac CSPN CSam EBee ELan EMil EPfP EShb GCal LHop LRHS MCCP SAPC SArc SBod SLim SPer SPoG SWvt WCru WHar WPGP WPat |
| ***majus*** misapplied | see *T. jasminoides* 'Japonicum' |
| ***majus*** Nakai | see *T. asiaticum* |

## *Trachycarpus* (*Arecaceae*)

| | |
|---|---|
| from Manipur | EAmu MJnS |
| § ***fortunei*** ♀H3-4 | Widely available |
| ***latisectus*** | CBrP CKob EAmu LPJP LPal NPal SBig |
| ***martianus*** | CKob CTrC EAmu LPJP LPal SBig SChr |
| ***nanus*** | CKob LPal |
| ***oreophilus*** | LPal |
| ***princeps*** | LPal |
| - from Meeldijk | CKob |
| ***takil*** | CBrP CKob EAmu EPla LPJP LPal MJnS NPal |
| ***wagnerianus*** | CBrP CDTJ CGHE CHid CPHo CTrC EAmu EBee EPla ETod EUJe LPJP LPal MJnS NPal SChr SMad WPGP |

## *Trachymene* (*Apiaceae*)

| | |
|---|---|
| ***coerulea*** | CSpe |

## *Trachystemon* (*Boraginaceae*)

| | |
|---|---|
| ***orientalis*** | CBre CHEx CPLG CSev EBee ECha EGol ELan EPfP LEdu MAvo MHar MRav NBid SBig SDnm WBor WCAu WCru WDyG WFar WHer WMoo WPnP |

## *Tradescantia* ✿ (*Commelinaceae*)

| | |
|---|---|
| ***albiflora*** | see *T. fluminensis* |
| x ***andersoniana*** W. Ludwig & Rohw. | see *T.* Andersoniana Group |
| § Andersoniana Group | CWan CWib MSal SPet WPer |
| - 'Baby Doll' | GKir |
| - 'Bilberry Ice' | Widely available |
| - 'Blue and Gold' | CBct COIW CSpe EBee ECtt ELon EMon EPPr EPfP GBuc LAst LBMP LHop LRHS MNFA MRav NPri NSti SPla SPoG WCAu WCot WFar |
| - 'Blue Stone' | CMdw CMea CSBt EBee ECha ECtt MRav NDov NPri SRms WFar WHoo WTin |
| - 'Bridal Veil' | CHll |
| - 'Caerulea Plena' | see *T. virginiana* 'Caerulea Plena' |
| - Carmine Glow | see *T.* (Andersoniana Group) 'Karminglut' |
| - 'Charlotte' | EBee EBrs ECGP ECha EMFW LSRN MCot NBre NBro NGdn SRGP WCAu WMnd |
| - 'Chedglow' | LHop |
| - 'Concord Grape' | Widely available |
| - 'Danielle' | EBee EPfP GMac |
| - 'Domaine de Courson' | EBee |
| - 'In the Navy' | LDai NBre NLar |
| - 'Innocence' | CMHG COIW CSBt CTri EBee ECha ECtt ELan EMFW EPfP GJos GMaP LHop LRHS NBPC NBir NCGa NGdn NOrc NPri NSti SPer SPla SPoG STes WFar WMnd |
| - 'Iris Prichard' | CPrp CTca EBee ELan EPfP GCra GMaP LAst LHop NBre NCGa NLar SRGP WFar |
| - 'Isis' ♀H4 | CBcs CHar CPrp CTri EBee ECGP ECtt ELan EPfP GCra GKir LCro LRHS MRav NBir NCGa NGdn NOrc SEND SPer SPla WMnd WTin |
| - 'J.C. Weguelin' ♀H4 | EBee EMil EPfP GKir LBMP NBir NBre SRms WCAu WMnd |
| § - 'Karminglut' | EBee ECtt ELan EPfP GKir GMaP LAst MNrw NBir NGdn NOrc NVic SPad WCAu WHil WHoo |
| - 'Leonora' | COIW CWan EBee EPfP NLar |
| - 'Little Doll' | CWCL ECtt EWTr GBri LAst MDKP MLLN MNFA NBro NPri WFar |
| - 'Little White Doll' | CPrp CWCL EBee ECtt GMac LAst MBNS MDKP MNFA MSte NBre WFar |
| - 'Mac's Double' (d) | EBee |
| - 'Mariella' | EBee GMac LAst |

- 'Mrs Loewer' EMon
- 'Navajo Princess' EBee
- 'Osprey' ♀H4 Widely available
- 'Pauline' CHar EBee ECtt EPla GKir LAst MNrw MRav NBir NLar WFar WHil WHoo WTin
- 'Perinne's Pink' CWCL EBee EBrs EPfP MBri NBPC NDov NLar NSti SUsu
- 'Pink Chablis'PBR CWCL EBee MNFA NBro NLar NMoo
- 'Purewell Giant' CMac CMoH CTri EBee ECot EMil LHop NBro NLar WGor WKif WMnd
- 'Purple Dome' CHar CMac CSsd EBee ECtt EMFW EPla GKir GMaP LAst MRav NBir NBro NCGa NGdn SEND SPla SPoG STes WCAu WMnd WTin
- 'Red Grape' COIW EBee ECtt MWhi NPro NSti WBor WCAu
- 'Rosi' EBee
- 'Rubra' CPrp EBee EPfP NOrc SBod SRms
- 'Satin Doll'PBR COIW EBee ECtt
- 'Snowbank' **new** EBee
- 'Sweet Kate' CBct CHar CWCL EBee LFur LSRN MBNS MCCP NBro SRGP WBor
- 'Sylvana' EBee EGle GMac SApp WCAu
- 'Temptation' **new** EBee
- 'Valour' CSBt EBee WFar
- 'Zwanenburg Blue' EBee ECha ECtt EHrv ELan GKir GMac LAst LBMP MLHP NCGa SPlb WMnd

'Angel Eyes' MDKP
'Baerbel' EBee
***blossfeldiana*** see *T. cerinthoides*
***canaliculata*** see *T. ohiensis*
§ ***cerinthoides*** CHal
§ ***fluminensis*** SChr
- 'Albovittata' CHal
§ - 'Aurea' ♀H1 CHal
- 'Laekenensis' (v) CHal MBri
- 'Maiden's Blush' (v) CHal CSpe EShb SGar SRms WFoF
- 'Quicksilver' (v) ♀H1 CHal EShb MBri
- 'Tricolor Minima' ♀H1 CHal
- 'Variegata' see *T. fluminensis* 'Aurea'
***longipes*** EBee
***multiflora*** see *Tripogandra multiflora*
***navicularis*** see *Callisia navicularis*
§ ***ohiensis*** CFee EBee LPBA MAvo
***pallida*** ♀H2-3 CHal EOHP
§ - 'Purpurea' ♀H2-3 EShb
***pendula*** see *T. zebrina*
'Purple Sabre' LAst SDys SMrm
***purpurea*** see *T. pallida* 'Purpurea'
***sillamontana*** ♀H1 CHal EOHP MBri
***spathacea*** CHal EShb
§ - 'Vittata' ♀H1 CHal
***tricolor*** see *T. zebrina*
***virginiana*** CMoH MWhi SGar
- 'Alba' GCal WPer
* - 'Brevicaulis' EBee ECha EPla ERos GBuc NBre NBro
§ - 'Caerulea Plena' (d) CHFP CHar CMHG EBee ELan EPfP EPla MRav NBPC NCGa SRms STes WFar WTin
- 'Rubra' ECGP SPlb
§ ***zebrina*** ♀H1 CHal EShb
- ***discolor*** CHal
- ***pendula*** see *T. zebrina*
- 'Purpusii' ♀H1 CHal SRms
- 'Quadricolor' (v) ♀H1 CHal

## *Tragopogon* (*Asteraceae*)

***crocifolius*** CSpe EBee SPhx WCot
***porrifolius*** CSec EBWF ILis SECG WGwG
***pratensis*** CArn EBWF NMir

## *Trautvetteria* (*Ranunculaceae*)

***carolinensis*** var. ***japonica*** CLAP GEdr WCru WPrP
- var. ***occidentalis*** CBct GEdr WCru

## *Trevesia* (*Araliaceae*)

***palmata*** CKob

## *Triadica* (*Euphorbiaceae*)

***sebifera*** SKHP

## *Trichopetalum* (*Anthericaceae*)

§ ***plumosum*** CBro ECho

## *Tricuspidaria* see *Crinodendron*

## *Tricyrtis* ✿ (*Convallariaceae*)

B&SWJ 3229 from Taiwan WCru
from Taiwan WFar
'Adbane' CBct CChe CLAP EBee ELan EPPr EWes GBuc GKev LRHS NLar SMrm WFar WGwG WRha
***affinis*** CLAP GAbr GBBs GBin GBuc GGar NLar
- B&SWJ 2804 WCru
- B&SWJ 5640 WCru
- B&SWJ 5847 WCru
- B&SWJ 6182 WCru
- B&SWJ 11169 **new** WCru
- 'Early Bird' LEdu WCru
- 'Meigetsu' (v) **new** EBee
- 'Sansyoku' **new** EBee GEdr
- 'Variegata' see *T.* 'Variegata'
'Amanagowa' CLAP WFar
***bakeri*** see *T. latifolia*
'Blue Wonder' EBee LCro MBNS NGdn NPro
***dilatata*** see *T. macropoda*
'Empress' CBct CHFP COIW CSam EBee EBla ELon EPfP EWes GCai IBal LEdu LSou MAvo MCCP NBPC NCob NHol SMrm SMrs SPet SPoG WFar
***flava*** EBee WCru
- 'Soshin' **new** EBee
***formosana*** ♀H4 Widely available
- B&SWJ 306 CLAP EBla MNrw WCot WFar
- B&SWJ 355 WCru WFar
- B&SWJ 3073 WCru
- B&SWJ 3616 WCru
- B&SWJ 3712 WCru WFar
- B&SWJ 6705 CLAP WCru WPrP
- B&SWJ 6741 WCru
- B&SWJ 6970 WCru
- B&SWJ 7071 WFar
- RWJ 10109 **new** WCru
- f. ***glandosa*** aff. 'Blu-Shing Toad' WCru
- 'Autumn Glow' (v) **new** EBee
- dark GAbr LBMP NCGa WFar
- 'Dark Beauty' CDes CEnt CLAP CPom CWCL EBee EHrv EWTr GBuc LCro MBri MCCP MCot MHer MSCN NBPC NPri NPro SMad SMrm SMrs SPad SPur SUsu WFar WPGP WWFP
- 'Emperor' (v) **new** EBee
- 'Gilt Edge' (v) CBct COIW CPLG CWCL EBee EPfP IBal LAst LSou MAvo MBNS MCCP

| | | |
|---|---|---|
| | | MDKP MRav NBPC NBid NBro NGdn NMoo NMyG NPri NSti SMrm SPoG WBrE WFar WPrP |
| | - f. ***glandosa*** | WFar |
| | - - B&SWJ 7084 | WCru |
| | - var. ***grandiflora*** B&SWJ 6905 | WCru WFar |
| | - pale | CBct WFar |
| | - 'Purple Beauty' | CBct CTca EBee MDKP MSte NMyG |
| | - 'Samurai' (v) | CLAP CMil CWCL EPPr EWes NCGa NMoo WCot WFar |
| | - 'Seiryu' | EBee |
| | - 'Shelley's' | CBct CLAP NBro WFar WPrP |
| | - 'Small Wonder' | WCru |
| | - 'Spotted Toad' **new** | WCru |
| § | - Stolonifera Group | CBcs CBro CMHG CMMP EBee EHrv ELan EPfP LEdu LHop LRHS MCot NGdn NHol SDix SPoG WFar WMnd |
| | - - B&SWJ 7046 | WCru WFar |
| | - 'Taroko Toad' | WCru WPrP |
| | - 'Tiny Toad' | WCru WFar |
| | - 'Variegata' (v) | CBct CBro CWan GBBs LEdu MMHG NBir NLar WBor WCru WFar |
| | - 'Velvet Toad' **new** | WCru |
| | 'Golden Leopard' **new** | EBee EPfP NSti |
| | 'Harlequin' | LEdu NLar WFar |
| § | ***hirta*** | Widely available |
| | - B&SWJ 2827 | WCru |
| | - B&SWJ 5971 **new** | WCru |
| | - B&SWJ 11182 **new** | WCru |
| | - B&SWJ 11227 **new** | WCru |
| | - 'Alba' | CMac EHrv MAvo SBch WFar WThu |
| * | - 'Albomarginata' (v) | CMac CPrp EAEE EBee EPPr EPfP EShb GCra LBMP MAvo MCCP MCot MHar NHol NLar NMyG NSti SBch SPoG SWvt WFar WPGP |
| | - 'Golden Gleam' | WCot WFar |
| | - 'Kinkazan' | EBee |
| | - 'Makinoi Gold' | WFar |
| | - var. ***masamunei*** 'Minazuki' **new** | EBee |
| | - 'Matsukaze' | CLAP CPom MAvo SUsu WFar |
| | - 'Miyazaki' | CBct CFir CLAP EGle GBuc LBMP MHer MMuc MNrw NCGa NLar WFar |
| | - 'Taiwan Atrianne' | CSam EAEE EBee ECGP GAbr LDai MDKP NBsh NCob NHol |
| | - 'Variegata' (v) | CBct CTca CTri EBrs ELon EWes GBuc LHop NLar WCot WCru WFar WHrl |
| N | Hototogisu | CBct CBro CLAP CPom EAEE EBee EBla EGle ELan EWTr GAbr GMac LHop LRHS MCCP MCot MTho NBir NHol NMyG SDnm SMrs SPav WFar WHil WMnd |
| | ***ishiiana*** | CDes CLAP CWsd EBla WCot WCru WFar WPGP |
| | - var. ***surugensis*** | EBla LEdu WCru WFar |
| | 'Ivory Queen' | WFar |
| | ***japonica*** | see *T. hirta* |
| | 'Kohaku' | CBct CLAP CPom CWsd EBee EBla ELan EPPr EWes NPro SPav WCot WCru WFar WPGP |
| | ***lasiocarpa*** | CBct CLAP GBin GQue LEdu MAvo NMyG WFar |
| | - B&SWJ 3635 | CLAP EBla WCru WFar |
| | - B&SWJ 6861 | WCru |
| | - B&SWJ 7013 | WCru WPrP |
| | - B&SWJ 7014 | WCru |
| | - B&SWJ 7103 | WCru |
| § | ***latifolia*** | CBct CTca CWsd EBee ELan EPPr GAbr GGar GKev GMaP LEdu MNrw NGdn NLar SPoG WBVN WCru WFar |
| | - B&SWJ 10996 from Japan **new** | WCru |
| | - from Japan | WFar |
| | - 'Yellow Sunrise' **new** | EBee |
| | 'Lemon Lime' (v) | CBct CBro CWsd MDKP NPro SPav |
| | 'Lightning Strike' (v) | CBct EBee ECtt EWes GBuc LEdu LSou MDKP NBPC NCob NHol NMyG SMrs SPoG WCot WFar |
| | 'Lilac Towers' | CBct EBrs ELan WCru WFar |
| | ***macrantha*** | CMil GBBs GGar WCru |
| § | - subsp. ***macranthopsis*** | CBct CLAP CWsd EBla EPot GBuc GEdr MDKP WCot WCru WFar |
| | - - 'Juro' (d) | WCru |
| | ***macranthopsis*** | see *T. macrantha* subsp. *macranthopsis* |
| * | ***macrocarpa*** | WFar |
| N | ***macropoda*** | CBct CFwr EBee EBla ELan EPfP GAbr GBuc GMaP LEdu MAvo MCCP NGdn NWCA SMad WFar WMnd |
| | - B&SWJ 1271 from Korea **new** | CBct EBla WCru |
| | - B&SWJ 2804 from Japan | WCru |
| | - B&SWJ 5013 | WCru |
| | - B&SWJ 5556 | WCru |
| | - B&SWJ 5847 | WCru |
| | - B&SWJ 6209 | WCru |
| | - B&SWJ 8700 | WCru |
| | - B&SWJ 8829 | WCru |
| | - from Yungi Temple, China | CLAP EBla EPPr MDKP WCot WFar |
| | - 'Tricolor' | WCot |
| | - variegated (v) | CBow |
| | ***maculata*** | WFar |
| | - HWJCM 470 | WCru |
| | - HWJK 2010 | WCru |
| | - HWJK 2411 | WCru |
| | 'Mine-no-yuki' **new** | EBee |
| | 'Moonlight Treasure' | CLAP EBee NHol |
| | ***nana*** | CLAP WCru |
| | - 'Karasuba' | EBee |
| | - 'Raven's Back' | WCru |
| | 'Niitaka' | EBee |
| | ***ohsumiensis*** | CBct CDes CLAP CPom CWsd EBee EBla ECha GBuc GEdr LEdu MDKP MHar MTho NMyG SBch SUsu WCru WFar WPGP |
| | - 'Lunar Eclipse' **new** | EBee GEdr |
| | - 'Nakatsugawa' (v) **new** | EBee |
| | ***perfoliata*** | CLAP CWsd LEdu WCru WFar |
| | - 'Spring Shine' (v) **new** | WCru |
| | 'Raspberry Mousse' | CDes CHFP CLAP CWCL EBee EHrv IPot LFur MBNS MWea NBPN NMoo NMyG NSti |
| | ***setouchiensis*** | WCru |
| | 'Shimone' | CHid CLAP EBee ECha ELan GBuc SBch WFar WKif |
| | 'Shining Light' | EBee |
| | 'Sinonome' | EBee GBin |
| | ***stolonifera*** | see *T. formosana* Stolonifera Group |
| | ***suzukii*** RWJ 10111 | WCru |
| | 'Taipei Silk' **new** | EBee |
| | 'Tojen' | Widely available |
| | 'Tresahor White' | CBct WFar |
| § | 'Variegata' (*affinis* hybrid) (v) | WFar |
| | 'Washfields' | CBct WFar WPGP |

| | |
|---|---|
| 'White Towers' | CBct CBro CHid CLAP CWCL EBee EBla ECha EHrv EPPr EPfP GBuc GKir LRHS MCot MRav NCGa NCob NHol NSti SPer SPet SRms WAul WCAu WFar |
| 'White Towers' spotted | WBrE |

## *Trifolium* (*Papilionaceae*)

| | |
|---|---|
| ***angustifolium*** | CArn |
| ***badium*** | CSec |
| ***fragiferum*** **new** | EBWF |
| ***incarnatum*** | CSec CSpe MHer |
| - 'Crimson Cones' **new** | MCot |
| ***medium*** | EBWF |
| ***ochroleucon*** | CElw CFwr CHFP EBWF EBee EDAr EHrv EPPr GBri GMaP LBMP MCCP MCot MNFA NSti SBch SSvw SWal WAul WCot WFar WMoo |
| ***pannonicum*** | CBgR CFir CMea EHrv EMon GCal MLLN MSte NBre NCot SUsu WFar WPGP WSHC WTin |
| ***pratense*** | EBWF GPoy MHer NSco SECG WSFF |
| - 'Dolly North' | see *T. pratense* 'Susan Smith' |
| - 'Ice Cool' | see *T. repens* 'Green Ice' |
| - 'Nina' | EBee WAlt |
| - 'Speech House' (v) | WAlt |
| - 'Splash' **new** | WAlt |
| § - 'Susan Smith' (v) | CBre CCCN EBee ECGP EHoe EWes GBuc GCal MNrw NGHP SIng WFar |
| ***repens*** | COld EBWF EHrv NSco SVic WCAu WSFF |
| - 'Douglas Dawson' | LDai |
| - 'Dragon's Blood' | EBee NPro SIng SVil WFar |
| - 'Gold Net' | see *T. pratense* 'Susan Smith' |
| - 'Good Luck' | MTho |
| § - 'Green Ice' | CBre EAEE EBee EHoe LRHS MBNS MTho NBir NCob NSti WAlt WCHb WFar WHal |
| - 'Harlequin' (v) | CNat EBee EHoe GGar MAvo MHer MTho WAlt WCot WFar WMoo WOut WPer |
| - 'Hiccups' (v) | WAlt |
| - pale pink-flowered | WAlt |
| - 'Pentaphyllum' | see *T. repens* 'Quinquefolium' |
| - 'Purpurascens' | CArn CBre CEnt EAEE ECGP EPfP GGar GMac ILis LRHS MAvo MBNS MHer NSti SPoG WKif |
| § - 'Purpurascens Quadrifolium' | CMea CSpe CWan EBee ECha ECho EHoe EPau EWes LBMP MCot NBid NGHP NMir NPer NPri SIng SPer SPlb WAlt WCHb WFar |
| - 'Quadrifolium' | EDAr |
| § - 'Quinquefolium' | EBee |
| - 'Saint Patrick' | CNat |
| - 'Stephanie' **new** | CNat |
| - 'Tetraphyllum Purpureum' | see *T. repens* 'Purpurascens Quadrifolium' |
| - 'Wheatfen' | CBow CBre CNat CRow EBee EHoe GBuc NDov NPer WCot |
| - 'William' | CBow CBre EBee EGoo LCro LEdu SPur WAlt WCot |
| ***rubens*** | Widely available |
| - 'Drama' **new** | SUsu |
| - 'Peach Pink' | CFwr CSpe EBee EMon EShb LHop LSou MLLN MMHG NCob SPhx SUsu WCot |
| - 'Red Feathers' | ECGP MCot MWea |
| * ***weedlii*** **new** | EBee |

## *Triglochin* (*Juncaginaceae*)

| | |
|---|---|
| ***maritimum*** | CRWN EBWF |
| ***palustre*** | CRWN |

## *Trigonella* (*Papilionaceae*)

| | |
|---|---|
| ***foenum-graecum*** | CArn MSal SIde |

## *Trillidium* see *Trillium*

## *Trillium* ✿ (*Trilliaceae*)

| | |
|---|---|
| ***albidum*** | CAby CLAP CWCL EBee EBrs ECho EPot GBuc GGar GMaP NMen SKHP SSpi SUsu WCru WHal |
| ***angustipetalum*** | CLAP EBrs SKHP |
| - hybrid | SKHP |
| ***apetalon*** | GEdr LAma WCru |
| ***camschatcense*** | CLAP EBee EBrs GBuc GEdr LAma LFur WCru |
| - from Japan | WWst |
| § ***catesbyi*** | CBro CLAP CSec CWCL EBee EBrs ECho EHrv EPot GEdr GGar IBal LAma NHol NMyG WCru WWst |
| ***cernuum*** | CLAP CWsd ECho GCra IBal MSte NMyG WCru WShi |
| ***chloropetalum*** | CBro EBee GBBs SSpi SUsu WCru WFar WKif WPGP |
| - var. ***chloropetalum*** x ***parviflorum*** | SKHP |
| § - var. ***giganteum*** ♀H4 | CLAP GBuc GEdr GKev GKir NMen SKHP SSpi WCru WWst |
| - var. ***rubrum*** | see *T. chloropetalum* var. *giganteum* |
| - white-flowered | CLAP ECha IBal |
| ***cuneatum*** | Widely available |
| - 'Bobby Masterson' **new** | EBee |
| ***decipiens*** | SKHP WWst |
| ***decumbens*** | SKHP WWst |
| ***discolor*** **new** | SKHP |
| ***erectum*** ♀H4 | Widely available |
| - f. ***albiflorum*** | CFir CLAP CWsd EBee EBrs ECho GBuc GEdr GGar LAma NHol NMyG SKHP SSpi WCru |
| - 'Beige' | CLAP GKev IBal |
| - f. ***luteum*** | CBct CLAP EPfP WWst |
| - purple-flowered | IBal |
| - red-flowered | IBal |
| ***erectum*** x ***flexipes*** | CAby CLAP EBee ECho EHrv GBuc GEdr GGar GKev MNrw NMen SKHP SSpi WWst |
| ***flexipes*** | CLAP CSec CWsd EBee EBrs ECho EHrv EPot GAuc GEdr GKev IBal LAma LRHS NMen SKHP SPhx SSpi WCru |
| - erect | NMen |
| - 'Harvington Selection' **new** | WWst |
| ***foetidissimum*** | SKHP WWst |
| ***govanianum*** | EBee WCru |
| ***grandiflorum*** ♀H4 | Widely available |
| - dwarf | NHar |
| - 'Flore Pleno' (d) | CLAP CWsd ECha ECho GBuc MTho SCnR SPhx WWst |
| - 'Kath's Dwarf' | GEdr |
| - 'Quicksilver' | SKHP |
| - f. ***roseum*** | CLAP EBrs WWst |
| - 'Snowbunting' (d) | EBrs EWes GKir LRHS MMHG NHar WThu |
| ***kurabayashii*** | CAby CBct CFir CFwr CLAP CPLG EBee EBrs ECho EPot GBuc GGar MNrw SKHP SSpi SUsu WCot WPGP WWst |
| ***lancifolium*** | SKHP WWst |
| ***ludovicianum*** | SKHP WWst |
| ***luteum*** ♀H4 | Widely available |
| ***maculatum*** | SKHP WWst |
| ***nivale*** | EBee WWst |

| | |
|---|---|
| ***ovatum*** | CLAP CWCL EBee GBuc GGar NMen SKHP SSpi SUsu WHal |
| - from Oregon | CLAP |
| - f. ***hibbersonii*** | CBro GBuc GCra NMen |
| - 'Roy Elliott' | EPot |
| ***parviflorum*** | CLAP ECho GEdr NMen SKHP SSpi |
| ***pusillum*** | CLAP EBee ECho ELan EPot GAuc GBBs GEdr GGar IBal NHol SKHP WAbe WWst |
| * - var. ***alabamicum*** | SKHP |
| - var. ***ozarkanum*** | SKHP |
| - var. ***pusillum*** | MSte |
| - var. ***virginianum*** | CLAP EBrs LAma WCru |
| ***recurvatum*** | CBcs CLAP CSec EBee EBrs ECho EHrv EPot GAbr GBBs GEdr GGar GKev IBal LAma NHol NMen NMyG SKHP WCru WFar WPnP |
| ***reliquum*** | SKHP WWst |
| ***rivale*** ♀H3 | CBro CElw CLAP ECho EHrv GBuc GKev ITim NMen SKHP WAbe WFar WWst |
| - pink-flowered | CWsd GEdr NMen |
| - 'Purple Heart' | CLAP GEdr SKHP |
| ***rugelii*** | CAby CBro CLAP EBee EBrs ECho EHrv EWes GAuc GBuc GMaP LAma NMen SKHP SSpi WCru WWst |
| - Askival hybrids | CLAP EBee EBrs ECho GBuc MNrw NMen SKHP SSpi WWst |
| ***rugelii*** x ***vaseyi*** | EBee EHrv EWes GBuc NMen SKHP SSpi WWst |
| ***sessile*** | CFwr CLAP EBee EBrs ECho GBBs GBuc GKev GKir IBal LAma LRHS MAvo NBir NMen NMyG SGar SKHP SMrm WCAu WFar WKif WPnP WSHC WShi |
| - 'Rubrum' | see *T. chloropetalum* var. *giganteum* |
| ***simile*** | CLAP CWsd EBee EBrs ECho EPot SKHP SSpi WWst |
| ***smallii*** | EBee LFur WWst |
| ***stamineum*** | CLAP ECho GEdr GGar IBal NMyG SKHP WWst |
| ***stylosum*** | see *T. catesbyi* |
| ***sulcatum*** | CBro CLAP CWCL EBee EBrs ECho EHrv EPot GAuc GBuc GEdr GGar GMaP IBal NMen SKHP SPhx SSpi WCru WFar |
| ***texanum*** | SKHP |
| ***tschonoskii*** | CLAP EBee EBrs ECho GBuc GEdr LAma WCru |
| - var. ***himalaicum*** | WCru |
| ***underwoodii*** | SKHP WWst |
| ***undulatum*** | CLAP EBee ECho GGar IBal LAma NHol NMen NMyG WCru WWst |
| ***vaseyi*** | CBro CLAP EBee EBrs ECho EHrv EPot EWes GAuc GBBs GBuc GEdr GGar LAma NMen SKHP SSpi WCru WWst |
| ***viride*** | CLAP EBla EPot GBBs IBal NGby WFar WPnP |
| ***viridescens*** | CLAP EBee EBrs ECho GEdr LAma NMyG WFar WWst |

## *Trinia* (*Apiaceae*)

| | |
|---|---|
| ***glauca*** | CSec |

## *Triosteum* (*Caprifoliaceae*)

| | |
|---|---|
| ***himalayanum*** | CLAP EBee GCal GKev |
| - BWJ 7907 | WCru |
| ***pinnatifidum*** | CLAP CPom GCal |

## *Tripetaleia* (*Ericaceae*)

| | |
|---|---|
| § ***bracteata*** | GAuc NLar |

## *Tripogandra* (*Commelinaceae*)

| | |
|---|---|
| § ***multiflora*** | CHal |

## *Tripsacum* (*Poaceae*)

| | |
|---|---|
| ***dactyloides*** | EPPr |

## *Tripterospermum* (*Gentianaceae*)

| | |
|---|---|
| ***affine*** new | EBee |
| * aff. ***chevalieri*** B&SWJ 8359 | WCru |
| ***cordifolium*** B&SWJ 081 | WCru |
| ***fasciculatum*** B&SWJ 7197 | WCru |
| aff. ***hirticalyx*** B&SWJ 8264 | WCru |
| ***japonicum*** | LLHF WAbe WBor |
| - B&SWJ 1168 | WCru |
| ***lanceolatum*** B&SWJ 085 | WCru |
| ***taiwanense*** B&SWJ 1205 | WCru |

## *Tripterygium* (*Celastraceae*)

| | |
|---|---|
| ***regelii*** | CBcs NLar WPGP |
| - B&SWJ 5453 | WCru |
| - B&SWJ 10921 new | WCru |
| ***wilfordii*** | WCru |

## *Trisetum* (*Poaceae*)

| | |
|---|---|
| ***flavescens*** | GFor NBre |

## *Tristagma* (*Alliaceae*)

| | |
|---|---|
| WAL 9450 | WCot |
| ***nivale*** new | EBee |
| - f. ***nivale*** F&W 9612 | WCot |

## *Triteleia* (*Alliaceae*)

| | |
|---|---|
| '4 U' new | CMea EBee ECho |
| ***bridgesii*** | WCot |
| ***californica*** | see *Brodiaea californica* |
| § 'Corrina' | CAvo CFFs CMdw EBee EBrs ECho EPot MNrw SMeo WHil |
| ***grandiflora*** | ECho WCot |
| ***hendersonii*** NNS 00-738 | WCot |
| ***hyacinthina*** | EBee EBrs ECho ERos WCot |
| - white-flowered new | CStu |
| ***ixioides*** | EBee ECho ERos |
| - var. ***scabra*** | WCot |
| - 'Splendens' | EBee EBrs ECho |
| - 'Starlight' | CAvo CFFs CSpe CSsd CTri EBee EBrs ECho EPot ERCP SBch SPhx WHil |
| § ***laxa*** | CSec ECho WBVN WCot |
| - 'Allure' | EBee EBrs ECho IPot |
| § - 'Koningin Fabiola' | CMea CPrp CTri EBee EBrs ECho EPfP EPot IPot LAma LHop LRHS MBri NBir SBch SEND SMeo SMrm SPer SPhx WBrE WCot WHoo |
| - Queen Fabiola | see *T. laxa* 'Koningin Fabiola' |
| ***lilacina*** NNS 00-745 | WCot |
| § ***peduncularis*** | CHFP EBee EBrs ECho SPhx WCot |
| - NNS 95-499 | WCot |
| 'Rudy' new | CAvo CMea EBee |
| x ***tubergenii*** | EBee EBrs ECho |
| ***uniflora*** | see *Ipheion uniflorum* |

## *Trithrinax* (*Arecaceae*)

| | |
|---|---|
| ***acanthocoma*** | CBrP EAmu LPJP LPal SBig |
| ***campestris*** | CBrP EAmu ETod LMaj LPal SBig |

## *Tritoma* see *Kniphofia*

## *Tritonia* (*Iridaceae*)

| | |
|---|---|
| ***crocata*** ♀H2-3 | CPou EBrs SBch |

| | |
|---|---|
| - 'Baby Doll' | CDes CPrp EBee EBrs LEdu WHil WPGP |
| - 'Bridal Veil' | EBrs EPot |
| - 'Pink Sensation' | CDes EBee EBrs ECho EPot WCot WHil WPGP |
| - 'Plymouth Pastel' | CDes |
| - 'Prince of Orange' | CPou WPGP |
| - 'Princess Beatrix' | CDes WCot WPGP |
| - 'Serendipity' | CDes CPrp CTca EBee EBrs |
| - 'Tangerine' | CTca EBrs EPot WPGP |
| § ***disticha*** subsp. ***rubrolucens*** | Widely available |
| ***hyalina*** | CPou EBee |
| ***laxifolia*** | CPne CTca EBee EBrs ECho LEdu |
| ***lineata*** | CDes CPou EBee EBrs ECho WPGP WPrP |
| - 'Parvifolia' | EBee |
| ***pallida*** | SPlb |
| ***rosea*** | see *T. disticha* subsp. *rubrolucens* |

## *Trochetiopsis* (*Sterculiaceae*)

| | |
|---|---|
| § ***ebenus*** | EShb WPGP |
| ***melanoxylon*** misapplied | see *T. ebenus* |

## *Trochocarpa* (*Epacridaceae*)

| | |
|---|---|
| ***clarkei*** | WThu |
| ***thymifolia*** red-flowered | WThu |
| - white-flowered | WAbe |

## *Trochodendron* (*Trochodendraceae*)

| | |
|---|---|
| ***aralioides*** | CBcs CDoC CHEx CTho CWib EBee ECrN EPfP ERas LRHS MBri MGos MMuc SAPC SArc SDix SKHP SLPl SLon SPer SReu SSpi SSta WCot WDin WPGP WSHC |
| - B&SWJ 1651 from Taiwan **new** | WCru |
| - B&SWJ 6727 from Taiwan | WCru |

## *Trollius* (*Ranunculaceae*)

| | |
|---|---|
| ACE 1187 | GEdr |
| SDR 2713 **new** | GKev |
| SDR 4816 **new** | GKev |
| ***acaulis*** | EBee ECho EGle EWes GAbr MTho WFar WPat |
| ***altaicus*** | EBee |
| ***asiaticus*** | EBee ECho GBuc WFar |
| aff. ***buddae*** BWJ 7958 | WCru |
| § ***chinensis*** | ECha EWld GCal GKev GKir NChi SRms SWat |
| - 'Golden Queen' ♀H4 | Widely available |
| - orange-flowered **new** | GKev |
| x ***cultorum*** 'Alabaster' | CDes CFir CLAP CMea CSam EBee ELan GBuc GKir LAst MCot MRav MSte NBPC NLar NSti SMad SMeo SPer SUsu WCFE WCot WFar WPGP WPnP WTin |
| - 'Baudirektor Linne' | MRav NGdn WFar |
| - Bressingham hybrids | WFar |
| - 'Byrne's Giant' | EBee WFar WPnP |
| - 'Canary Bird' | ELan EPfP GBri GCal NGdn SRms |
| - 'Cheddar' | CElw EBee EBla ECGP EPfP GCal GKir MBNS MBri MCCP MMHG MRav NBPC NBro NLar NOrc NPri NPro SHar WCra WFar |
| - 'Commander-in-chief' | CDes EBee WFar WPGP WPnP |
| - 'Earliest of All' | CDWL CPrp CSam EBee EGle GKir LRHS MSte NGby NGdn SPer SRms WFar WSHC |
| - 'Etna' | CDWL EBee EGle WFar WPnP |
| § - 'Feuertroll' | CDWL CMea CPrp EBee ECha GCal GKir LBMP MRav MSCN NBPC NCob NGby NPro SPoG SUsu WFar |
| - Fireglobe | see *T.* x *cultorum* 'Feuertroll' |
| - 'Glory of Leiden' | EBee |
| - 'Golden Cup' | ECot NBir NGdn |
| - 'Golden Monarch' | WFar |
| - 'Goldquelle' ♀H4 | EHon GKir |
| - 'Goliath' | EWes NCob SMad WFar |
| - 'Helios' | CSam ECha |
| - 'Lemon Queen' | CDWL CWat EBee EHrv EPfP GMaP LBMP LPBA LRHS MBri MNFA MRav NBPC NBlu SPer SPoG SWat WCAu WFar |
| - 'Meteor' | WFar |
| - **new** hybrids | WFar |
| - 'Orange Crest' | CElw EBee EGle GCal GKir WCFE WFar WHal |
| - 'Orange Globe' | EBee ELon GAbr LBMP NBPC NCob NGby SMrm WFar |
| - 'Orange Glow' | SMad |
| - 'Orange Princess' ♀H4 | CDWL CElw CWat EBee EPfP GKir GMaP LBMP LCro LRHS MCCP MSte NBro NLar NPri SPer SRms |
| - 'Orange Queen' | SWvt |
| - 'Prichard's Giant' | CDWL CMHG EBee EBla ELan GBri LAst NBro NGby WCAu WFar |
| § - 'Superbus' ♀H4 | CDes CPSs EBee ECho EGle ELan EPfP GKir GMaP LAst MBNS NGdn SPer WBrE WFar WMoo |
| - 'T. Smith' | EBee GMac NBro NGby WCot WFar |
| * - 'Taleggio' | EMon SPhx |
| - 'Yellow Beauty' | WFar |
| ***dschungaricus*** | EBee |
| ***europaeus*** | Widely available |
| - 'Superbus' | see *T.* x *cultorum* 'Superbus' |
| ***hondoensis*** | EBee GBin GCal NBur NLar NPro |
| ***ircuticus*** | EBee |
| ***laxus*** | EWes |
| - 'Albiflorus' | NWCA |
| ***ledebourii*** misapplied | see *T. chinensis* |
| ***pumilus*** | EBee ECha ECho ELan EWld GBri GCal GKir GMaP LRHS MHer NWCA SPer WAbe WFar WPer |
| - ACE 1818 | GBuc WCot |
| ***stenopetalus*** | CDes EBee ECha EWes GKir MBri MNrw MRav NMyG WFar WPGP |
| ***yunnanensis*** | EBee GBuc GKev NBid WFar WPnP |
| - CD&R 2097 | WCru |
| - f. ***eupetalus*** BWJ 7614 | WCru |
| - orange-flowered **new** | EBee GKev |

## *Tropaeolum* ✿ (*Tropaeolaceae*)

| | |
|---|---|
| ***azureum*** | CCCN |
| ***beuthii*** | EBee |
| ***brachyceras*** | CAvo CCCN CSec EBee WCot |
| ***ciliatum*** ♀H1 | CAvo CBro CCCN CFir CGHE CSam CStu EBee EBrs ECho ELan EPot MTho NBid WCot WCru WFar WHer WPGP |
| ***hookerianum*** subsp. ***austropurpureum*** | ERos |
| - subsp. ***hookerianum*** F&W 9467 | WPGP |
| ***incisum*** | CCCN EBee |
| ***nubigenum*** x ***polyphyllum*** **new** | CWsd |
| ***pentaphyllum*** | CAvo CSpe CWsd EBee ECho ELan EWes GCal GGar LFur LLHF MTho WCot |
| ***peregrinum*** | CSpe |
| ***polyphyllum*** | CCCN CWsd EBee ECha EPfP GBuc NBir SCnR SKHP SMHy WAbe WPGP |
| ***sessilifolium*** | EBee |
| ***speciosum*** ♀H4 | Widely available |

***sylvestre*** EWld NVic WCru
***tricolor*** ♀H1 CAvo CCCN EBee EBrs ECho ELan EPot GCal GGar MTho WBor
***tuberosum*** CEnd CSec EBrs ECho GPoy IHer
– var. ***lineamaculatum*** 'Ken Aslet' ♀H3 CBro CCCN CSec CSpe EBee EBrs ECha ECho ELan EPfP ERos GAbr GGar IHer LAma LRHS MCot MTho SPoG WCru WFar WPGP WPtf
– var. ***piliferum*** 'Sidney' IBlr WCru

## *Tsuga* ✿ (*Pinaceae*)

***canadensis*** CDul EHul LPan MBar NBlu NWea WDin WMou
– 'Abbott's Dwarf' CKen EOrn MGos
§ – 'Abbott's Pygmy' CKen
– 'Albospica' (v) EOrn WFar WGor
– 'Arnold Gold Weeper' CKen
– 'Aurea' (v) MBar NLar
– 'Bacon Cristate' CKen
– 'Baldwin Dwarf Pyramid' MBar
– 'Beehive' ECho WGor
– 'Bennett' MBar
– 'Betty Rose' (v) CKen
– 'Brandley' CKen
§ – 'Branklyn' CKen
– 'Cappy's Choice' CKen
– 'Cinnamonea' CKen
– 'Coffin' CKen
– 'Cole's Prostrate' CKen EOrn MAsh MBar NHol NLar
– 'Coryhill' ECho SCoo
– 'Creamey' (v) CKen
– 'Curley' CKen
– 'Curtis Ideal' CKen
– 'Essex' NLar
* – 'Everitt's Dense Leaf' CKen
– 'Everitt's Golden' CKen
– 'Fantana' CRob ECho EHul LBee LRHS MAsh MBar NHol NLar SCoo SLim
– 'Gentsch White' (v) MGos NLar
– 'Gracilis' new WThu
– 'Horsford' CKen NLar
– 'Horstmann' No 1 CKen
– 'Hussii' CKen NLar
– 'Jacqueline Verkade' CKen NLar
– 'Jeddeloh' ♀H4 CDoC CRob ECho EHul EOrn IMGH LRHS MAsh MBar MGos NHol SCoo SLim SPoG WDin
– 'Jervis' CKen NHol NLar
– 'Julianne' CKen
– 'Kingsville Spreader' CKen
– 'Little Joe' CKen
– 'Little Snow' CKen
I – 'Lutea' CKen
– 'Many Cones' CKen
– 'Minima' CKen
– 'Minuta' CDoC CKen ECho EHul EOrn LBee MBar MGos NLar SCoo SLon SPoG WGor
– 'Nana' EHul WDin
– 'Palomino' CKen
– 'Pendula' ♀H4 CDoC CKen ECho EHul EOrn EPfP LRHS MAsh MBar SLim SPoG WDin WFar
– 'Pincushion' CKen
– 'Popeleski' NLar
– 'Prostrata' see *T. canadensis* 'Branklyn'
– 'Pygmaea' see *T. canadensis* 'Abbott's Pygmy'
– 'Rugg's Washington Dwarf' CKen SCoo
– 'Snowflake' CKen MGos
– 'Stewart's Gem' CKen
– 'Verkade Petite' CKen
– 'Verkade Recurved' CKen MBar NLar
– 'Von Helms' Dwarf' CKen
– 'Warnham' CKen ECho EOrn LBee MAsh SCoo
***caroliniana*** 'La Bar Weeping' CKen NLar
***diversifolia*** 'Gotelli' CKen
***heterophylla*** ♀H4 CDoC CDul CLnd EPfP IFFs LBuc LRHS MBar NWea SHBN SPer STre WDin WFar
– 'Iron Springs' CKen EOrn
– 'Laursen's Column' CKen
– 'Thorsens Weeping' CKen
***menziesii*** see *Pseudotsuga menziesii*
***mertensiana*** 'Blue Star' CKen NLar
– 'Elizabeth' CDoC CKen
– 'Glauca' CKen NLar
I – 'Glauca Nana' CKen
I – 'Horstmann' CKen
– 'Quartz Mountain' CKen
***sieboldii*** B&SWJ 8520 new WHCr
– 'Baldwin' CKen
– 'Green Ball' CKen NLar
– 'Honeywell Estate' CKen
– 'Nana' CKen

## *Tsusiophyllum* (*Ericaceae*)

***tanakae*** see *Rhododendron tsusiophyllum*

## *Tuberaria* (*Cistaceae*)

***lignosa*** CStu WAbe

## *Tulbaghia* ✿ (*Alliaceae*)

sp. IHer
***acutiloba*** CPen ERos MHom WPrP
***alliacea*** CAvo EBla ECho ERos EShb NHoy WCot
***alliacea* × *violacea*** ECho
***capensis*** CPou LPio MHom
***cepacea*** ERos NBir WCot WHil
***cepacea* × *natalensis*** ERos
***cernua*** hybrid NHoy WPrP
aff. ***cernua*** CD&R 199 new CDes
***cernua* × *violacea*** WPrP
§ ***coddii*** CDes EBee MHom WCot WPrP
***coddii* × *violacea*** WPrP
***cominsii*** CPLG EDif SBch SCnR
***cominsii* × *violacea*** CAvo CPLG CTca EBee ERos MHom WPrP
'Cosmic' CPou WPrP
***dregeana*** ERos WCot
'Fairy Star' CDes EBee ERos EShb WCot WOut WPGP WPrP
***fragrans*** see *T. simmleri*
– 'Alba' EBrs
***galpinii*** CPen ERos NWCA WPrP
'Hazel' WPrP
'John May's Special' CDes CKno EBee EShb MSte SMrm SUsu WCot WPGP WPrP
***leucantha*** EBee ERos NHoy NWCA WPrP
– H&B 11996 CDes WPrP
– from Sentinel Park, South Africa WPrP
***maritima*** see *T. violacea* var. *maritima*
Marwood seedling EBee MHom MTPN
***montana*** CDes EBee WCot WPGP WPrP
***natalensis*** CPou EBee ECho WHoo
– B&V 421 CDes
– – clone 1 white new WPrP
– – clone 2 pink new WPrP
– CD&R 84 WPrP
– pink-flowered ECho ERos MHom WCot WPrP
***natalensis* × *verdoorniae*** new WPrP

***natalensis* x *verdoorniae* VOS 1966 new** WPrP
***natalensis* x *violacea*** NWCA
***poetica*** see *T. coddii*
§ ***simmleri*** CPou EBee EBla EBrs ECho EHrv EPot EPyc ERos EShb EWes GKev LAma LEdu LPio NHoy WCot
- 'Cheryl Renshaw' **new** CDes
- pink-flowered CPen CTca
- white-flowered CPen CPou CTca EPot
***verdoorniae*** ERos EShb WCot
***violacea*** Widely available
* - 'Alba' EBee EBla EPPr ERos GCal LPio NHoy NLAp SWat WFar WHoo WTin
- 'Dissect White' **new** WPrP
- RBGE form **new** MHom
I - 'Fine Form' SMHy
* - ***grandiflora*** CAvo
- 'John Rider' NWCA WPer
* - var. ***maritima*** EBee EDif ERos EShb GGar MHom NHoy NWCA WCot WPrP
- var. ***obtusa*** WPrP
- 'Pallida' CAvo CBro CDes CMdw CPne CPou CTca ECho LEdu LPio MSte NHoy NWCA WPGP WPrP
- 'Pearl' CPou WPrP
- 'Peppermint Garlic' **new** CDes
- var. ***robustior*** CPou CTca EBee EBla EWes NHoy WPrP
§ - 'Silver Lace' (v) Widely available
- 'Variegata' see *T. violacea* 'Silver Lace'
- var. ***violacea*** WPrP
- 'White Goddess' **new** CPou
- 'White Star' **new** EBee

## *Tulipa* ✿ (*Liliaceae*)

'Abba' (2) LRHS
'Absalon' (9) LAma
'Abu Hassan' (3) CAvo CFFs CMea EBrs LAma MBri SPhx
***acuminata*** (15) CAvo CBro CFFs CTca EBrs ECho ERCP LAma LEdu LRHS NMin SPhx
'Ad Rem' (4) MBri
'Addis' (14) ♀H4 LAma
'African Queen' (3) LAma
***agenensis*** EBrs
***aitchisonii*** see *T. clusiana*
'Aladdin' (6) LAma LRHS
'Aladdin's Record' (6) EBrs
***albertii*** (15) EBrs ECho LAma NMin WWst
'Alfred Cortot' (12) ♀H4 LAma
'Ali Baba' (14) ♀H4 LRHS
'Allegretto' (11) MBri
***altaica*** (15) ♀H4 EBrs ECho EPot LAma SBch
***amabilis*** see *T. hoogiana*
'American Eagle' (7) ERCP
'Ancilla' (12) ♀H4 CBro LAma
'Angélique' (11) ♀H4 CAvo CFFs CMea CTca EBrs EPfP ERCP LAma LRHS MCot NBir SMeo SPer
'Annie Schilder' (3) LRHS
'Antoinette'[PBR] (5) **new** SPer
'Apeldoorn' (4) EBrs LAma MBri SPer
'Apeldoorn's Elite' (4) ♀H4 LAma MBri
'Apricot Beauty' (1) ♀H4 CTca EBrs EPfP LAma LRHS MBri MCot MMHG NBir SPer SPhx
'Apricot Jewel' see *T. linifolia* (Batalinii Group) 'Apricot Jewel'
'Apricot Parrot' (10) ♀H4 CAvo CFFs EPfP LAma MBri SPer
'Arabian Mystery' (3) CAvo CFFs EBrs ERCP LAma
'Artist' (8) ♀H4 EBrs LAma MNFA
'Attila' (3) EBrs LAma
***aucheriana*** (15) ♀H4 CBro EBrs ECho EPot ERos LAma LLHF NMin SPhx
***australis*** (15) ECho
***aximensis*** (15) EBrs ECho LRHS
'Bacchus' (7) LAma
***bakeri*** see *T. saxatilis* Bakeri Group
'Ballade' (6) ♀H4 CAvo CFFs EBrs ERCP LAma MSte
'Ballerina' (6) ♀H4 CAvo CBro CFFs CMea CTca EBrs ERCP LAma LRHS MBri MMHG SMeo SPer SPhx
'Banja Luka' (4) EBrs
***batalinii*** see *T. linifolia* Batalinii Group
'Beauty of Apeldoorn' (4) LAma MBri
'Beauty Queen' (1) EBrs
'Bellflower' (7) LAma
***biebersteiniana*** (15) EBrs ECho SPhx
§ ***biflora*** (15) CBro CGrW CTca EBrs ECho EPot GKev LAma LLHF LRHS SMeo SPhx
***bifloriformis*** (15) EBrs ECho LRHS SPhx
I - 'Maxima' (15) EBrs NMin SPhx
- 'Starlight' (15) EBrs ECho IPot SPhx
'Big Chief' (4) ♀H4 LAma
'Big Smile' (5) LRHS
'Bird of Paradise' (10) EBrs
'Black Hero' (11) CAvo CFFs EBrs ERCP LAma LRHS MCot NBPN SMeo SPer
'Black Horse' (5) LAma
'Black Jewel' (7) ERCP
'Black Parrot' (10) ♀H4 CAvo CFFs CHid EBrs EPfP ERCP LAma LRHS MBri MCot MSte NBPN SMeo SPer SPhx
'Black Stallion' (11) LAma
'Blenda' (3) EBrs
'Bleu Aimable' (5) CAvo CFFs EBrs ERCP LAma MSte
'Blue Diamond' (11) CAvo CFFs ERCP LRHS SPer
'Blue Heron' (7) ♀H4 CAvo EBrs ERCP LAma MCot
'Blue Parrot' (10) CAvo CFFs EBrs EPfP ERCP LAma LRHS MSte
'Blue Ribbon' (3) CAvo CFFs
Blueberry Ripple see *T.* 'Zurel'
'Boutade' (14) NPer
'Bridesmaid' (5) LAma
'Burgundy' (6) CAvo EBrs ERCP LAma SMeo
'Burgundy Lace' (7) EBrs LAma SBch
'Café Noir' (5) ERCP
'Cairo'[PBR] **new** ERCP
'Calibra' (7) LRHS
'Calypso' (14) ♀H4 EBrs
'Candela' (13) ♀H4 LAma LRHS
'Candy Club' (5) EBrs LAma LRHS SPer
'Cantata' (13) CBro LAma
'Cape Cod' (14) EPfP LAma LRHS
'Cardinal Mindszenty' (2) **new** ERCP
'Carnaval de Nice' (11/v) ♀H4 CAvo CBro CFFs CTca EBrs ERCP LAma LRHS MBri SPer
'Carrousel' (7) EBrs
'Casablanca' (11) CMea EBrs
'Cassini' (3) LAma
§ ***celsiana*** (15) EBrs ECho LAma LRHS SPhx WWst
'China Pink' (6) ♀H4 CAvo CFFs CMea CTca EBrs EPfP ERCP LAma MBri MSte
'China Town' (8) ♀H4 EBrs ERCP LAma LRHS MBri
'Christmas Marvel' (1) EBrs LAma
***chrysantha*** Boiss. ex Baker see *T. montana*
'Claudia' (6) EPfP ERCP
'Cloud Nine' (5) LAma
§ ***clusiana*** (15) CBro CHFP EBrs ERCP IHer LAma MSSP MSte NMin SPhx WHer
- var. ***chrysantha*** (15) ♀H4 CAvo CFFs CGrW CMea EBrs ECho LAma LRHS SBch SPhx WHoo WShi
- - 'Tubergen's Gem' (15) CBro EBrs EPot LAma LRHS MBri SPhx

| | | |
|---|---|---|
| | - 'Cynthia' (15) $\Upsilon^{H4}$ | CHFP CTca EBrs ECGP EPot ERCP LAma LRHS MSte NMin SBch SMeo SPhx |
| | - 'Sheila' (15) | EBrs NMin SPhx |
| § | - var. ***stellata*** (15) | SPhx |
| | 'Colour Spectacle'$^{PBR}$ (5) | LSou |
| | 'Columbine' (5) | LAma |
| | 'Compostella' (14) | LRHS |
| | 'Concerto' (13) | CBro EBrs MBri NPer |
| | 'Corona' (12) | EBrs |
| | 'Couleur Cardinal' (3) | CBro EBrs LAma |
| | 'Creme Upstar' (11) | LRHS |
| | ***cretica*** (15) | EBrs ECho EPot NMin SPhx WWst |
| | 'Cummins' (7) **new** | ERCP |
| | 'Curly Sue' (7) | CAvo CFFs ERCP |
| | 'Czaar Peter' $\Upsilon^{H4}$ | CAvo CFFs LRHS MBri NPer |
| | 'Dancing Show' (8) | CAvo CFFs LAma |
| | ***dasystemon*** (15) | EBrs ECho EPot LAma LLHF SBch SPhx |
| | ***dasystemonoides*** (15) | EBrs ECho |
| | 'Davenport' (7) | LRHS |
| | 'David Teniers' (2) **new** | ERCP |
| | 'Daydream' (4) $\Upsilon^{H4}$ | SPer |
| | 'Daylight' (12) | EBrs |
| | 'Deirdre' (8) | LRHS |
| | ***didieri*** | see *T. passeriniana* |
| | 'Doll's Minuet' (8) | ERCP LAma SPer |
| | 'Don Quichotte' (3) $\Upsilon^{H4}$ | LRHS MBri |
| | 'Donna Bella' (14) $\Upsilon^{H4}$ | EPfP |
| | 'Dordogne' (5) | LRHS |
| | 'Double Price' (2) **new** | ERCP |
| | 'Douglas Bader' (5) | CAvo CFFs CMea |
| | 'Dreamboat' (14) | MBri SBch |
| | 'Dreaming Maid' (3) | LAma |
| | 'Dreamland' (5) $\Upsilon^{H4}$ | MBri |
| | 'Duc van Tol' (1) | IHer IPot |
| | 'Duc van Tol Aurora' **new** | IHer |
| | 'Duc van Tol Red and Yellow' (I) **new** | WHer |
| | 'Duc van Tol Rose' (1) | IHer LAma |
| | 'Duc van Tol Salmon' (1) | LAma |
| | 'Dynasty' (3) | LRHS |
| | 'Early Harvest' (12) $\Upsilon^{H4}$ | CAvo CFFs |
| | 'Easter Surprise' (14) $\Upsilon^{H4}$ | MBri |
| | ***eichleri*** | see *T. undulatifolia* |
| | 'Electra' (5) | LAma MBri |
| | 'Elegant Lady' (6) | CAvo CFFs EBrs EPfP LAma LRHS SPer |
| | 'Erna Lindgreen' (10) **new** | ERCP |
| | 'Esperanto' (8/v) $\Upsilon^{H4}$ | LAma |
| | 'Estella Rijnveld' (10) | EBrs LAma LRHS MBri MSte |
| | 'Esther' (5) | ERCP |
| | 'Eternal Flame' (2) | LAma |
| | 'Exotic Emperor' | LAma |
| | 'Eye Catcher' (8) | LRHS |
| | 'Fancy Frills' (7) $\Upsilon^{H4}$ | EBrs LAma LRHS |
| | 'Fantasy' (10) $\Upsilon^{H4}$ | LAma LRHS |
| | 'Fashion' (12) | EPfP |
| | 'Fats Domino' (3) | EBrs |
| | ***ferganica*** (15) | EBrs ECho EPot LAma NMin |
| | 'Finola' (11) | ERCP |
| | 'Fire Queen' (3) $\Upsilon^{H4}$ | EBrs LAma |
| | 'First Impression' (14) | LRHS |
| | 'Flair' (1) | LAma |
| | 'Flaming Parrot' (10) | CAvo CFFs EBrs LAma LRHS MBri |
| I | 'Flaming Purissima' (13) | CAvo CFFs |
| | 'Florosa' (8) **new** | ERCP |
| | 'Flowerdale' (14) | CAvo CFFs EBrs |
| | 'Fontainebleau' (3) | LRHS |
| | 'Freeman' (11) | LRHS |
| | 'Fringed Beauty' (7) $\Upsilon^{H4}$ | ERCP |
| | 'Fritz Kreisler' (12) | LAma |
| | 'Frosta' (7) | ERCP |
| | 'Fulgens' (6) | EBrs |
| | 'Gabriella' (3) | LRHS |
| | 'Garden Party' (3) $\Upsilon^{H4}$ | LAma |
| | 'Gavota' (3) | CAvo CFFs EBrs EPfP ERCP LAma LRHS SPer |
| | 'Generaal de Wet' (1) | EBrs IHer LAma MBri |
| | 'Georgette' (5) | LAma LRHS LSou MBri |
| | 'Gerbrand Kieft' (11) $\Upsilon^{H4}$ | EBrs ERCP |
| | 'Giuseppe Verdi' (12) | LAma MBri |
| | 'Glück' (12) $\Upsilon^{H4}$ | LRHS |
| | 'Golden Apeldoorn' (4) | LAma MBri SPer |
| | 'Golden Artist' (8) | EBrs EPfP LAma LRHS |
| | 'Golden Emperor' (13) | EBrs EPfP LAma SPer |
| | 'Golden Melody' (3) | EBrs LAma LRHS MCot |
| | 'Golden Nizza' (11) | LRHS |
| | 'Golden Oxford' (4) | LAma |
| | 'Golden Parade' (4) | LAma |
| | 'Goudstuk' (12) | LAma |
| | 'Green Wave' (10) | ERCP LAma |
| | ***greigii*** (14) | CBro |
| | ***grengiolensis*** (15) | EBrs ECho LAma LRHS WWst |
| | 'Groenland' (8) | CAvo CBro CFFs ERCP LAma LRHS MBri MCot MNFA SPer |
| | 'Gudoshnik' (4) | LAma |
| | 'Guus Papendrecht' (3) | LRHS |
| | ***hageri*** (15) | EBrs ECho LAma LRHS MBri SPhx |
| | - 'Splendens' (15) | EBrs LAma SMeo SPhx |
| | 'Hamilton' (7) $\Upsilon^{H4}$ | LAma |
| | 'Hans Dietrich Genscher' (3) | EBrs |
| | 'Happy Family' (3) | LAma LRHS |
| | 'Happy Generation' (3) | LAma LRHS MBri |
| | 'Happy Hour' (7) | ERCP |
| | 'Havran' (5) | CAvo CFFs ERCP LAma SBch |
| | 'Heart's Delight' (12) | CBro EBrs LAma MBri SBch |
| | 'Helmar' (3) | CAvo CFFs |
| | 'Hermitage' (3) | LAma |
| | ***heweri*** (15) | EBrs ECho NMin |
| | 'Hit Parade' (13) | LAma |
| | 'Hollandia' (3) | LRHS |
| | 'Hollywood' (8) | LAma |
| § | ***hoogiana*** (15) | EBrs ECho |
| § | ***humilis*** (15) | CBro CGrW ECho LAma LRHS MBri SPhx WShi |
| | - 'China Carol' (15) **new** | ERCP |
| | - 'Eastern Spice' **new** | NMin |
| | - 'Eastern Star' (15) | CSam CTca EBrs ECho GKev LAma LRHS MBri SPhx |
| § | - 'Lilliput' (15) | CBro CMea EBrs ECho EPot GKev LRHS NMin SPhx |
| | - 'Magenta Queen' (15) | EBrs SPhx |
| | - 'Odalisque' (15) | CMea EBrs EPot ERCP GKev LAma LRHS SPhx |
| | - 'Pegasus' (15) | EBrs NMin |
| | - 'Persian Pearl' (15) | CMea EBrs ECho EPfP EPot ERCP LAma LRHS MBri NMin SBch SPer SPhx WWFP |
| * | - 'Pink Charm' (15) | EBrs |
| | - var. ***pulchella*** Albocaerulea Oculata Group (15) | CMea CPou CTca EBrs EPot ERCP LAma LLHF LRHS MSte NMin WWst |
| | - 'Rosea' (15) | EBrs LRHS NMin |
| § | - Violacea Group (15) | CMea CPrp ECho LAma MBri |
| | - - black base (15) | CBro EBrs EPot GKev LRHS MBri NMin |
| | - - yellow base (15) | EBrs EPot GKev LAma LRHS |
| | - 'Zephyr' (15) | NMin |
| | 'Humming Bird' (8) | LAma |
| | 'Ile de France' (5) | LAma SPer |
| | ***iliensis*** (15) | EBrs ECho EPot NMin WWst |
| | ***ingens*** (15) | EBrs ECho LAma SPhx WWst |
| | 'Insulinde' (9) | LAma |
| | 'Inzell' (3) | EBrs EPfP LAma |

| | | |
|---|---|---|
| | 'Ivory Floradale' (4) ΨH4 | EBrs LAma |
| | 'Jackpot' (3) | ERCP |
| | 'Jeantine' (12) ΨH4 | EPfP |
| | 'Jewel of Spring' (4) ΨH4 | LAma |
| | 'Joffre' (1) | MBri |
| | 'Johann Strauss' (12) | CBro CTca LAma LRHS MBri |
| | 'Juan' (13) ΨH4 | LRHS MBri |
| | ***julia*** (15) | ECho NMin |
| | 'Karel Doorman' (10) | LAma |
| | ***kaufmanniana*** (12) | CAvo CFFs EBrs ECho EPot SBch WShi |
| | - 'Ugam' | LRHS |
| § | 'Kees Nelis' (3) | LRHS MBri |
| | 'Keizerskroon' (1) ΨH4 | IHer LAma |
| | ***kolpakowskiana*** (15) ΨH4 | EBrs ECho EPfP ERCP LAma LRHS MBri SBch SPhx |
| | ***kurdica*** (15) | EBrs ECho LAma LRHS SPhx WWst |
| | - purple-flowered (15) | ECho WWst |
| | - red-flowered (15) | WWst |
| | 'La Courtine' (5) | LRHS |
| | 'Lac van Rijn' (1) | IHer IPot |
| * | 'Lady Diana' (14) | MBri |
| | 'Lady Jane' (15) | CAvo CFFs CHFP CMea EBrs ERCP NMin SBch SPer SPhx |
| | 'Lambada' (7) ΨH4 | LRHS |
| | ***lanata*** (15) | EBrs ECho |
| | 'Latvian Gold' (15) | EBrs NMin |
| | 'Leen van der Mark' (3) | LAma MBri |
| | 'Libretto Parrot' (10) | LAma |
| | 'Lilac Perfection' (11) | CTca EBrs ERCP MBri |
| | 'Lilac Wonder' | see *T. saxatilis* (Bakeri Group) 'Lilac Wonder' |
| | 'Lilliput' | see *T. humilis* 'Lilliput' |
| | 'Lilyrosa' (6) | EBrs |
| | ***linifolia*** (15) ΨH4 | CAvo CFFs EBrs ECho EPfP EPot GKev LAma LRHS MBri SBch SPhx WShi |
| § | - Batalinii Group (15) ΨH4 | CBro EBrs ECho LAma MBri SPhx |
| § | - - 'Apricot Jewel' (15) | CBro CGrW EBrs ECho EPot GKev MSte SPhx |
| | - - 'Bright Gem' (15) ΨH4 | CAvo CBro CSam CTca EBrs ECho EPot GKev LAma LRHS MBri SBch SPer SPhx WCot |
| | - - 'Bronze Charm' (15) | CAvo CBro CFFs CMea EBrs ECGP ECho EPot IPot LAma MBri MSte NMin SPhx |
| | - - 'Honky Tonk' (15) | CMea EBrs ECho NMin SPhx |
| | - - 'Red Gem' (15) | EBrs ECho GKev LAma SPhx |
| | - - 'Red Hunter' (15) ΨH4 | SPer |
| | - - 'Red Jewel' (15) | MSte SBch |
| | - - 'Yellow Jewel' (15) | EBrs ECho LAma SPhx |
| § | - Maximowiczii Group (15) | CBro EBrs ECho EPot LAma SPhx |
| | 'Little Beauty' (15) ΨH4 | CAvo CFFs CMea CSam EBrs ECho EGoo GKev LAma LRHS MBri SBch SMeo WHoo |
| | 'Little Princess' (15) | CAvo CFFs CSam EBrs ECho EPfP LAma LRHS SMeo |
| | 'Lovely Surprise' (14) | EBrs |
| | 'Lucifer' (5) | ERCP |
| | 'Lucky Strike' (3) | MBri |
| | 'Mabel' (9) | LAma |
| § | 'Madame Lefeber' (13) | CBro EBrs LRHS MBri |
| | 'Magier' (5) | MBri |
| | 'Maja' (7) | CAvo CFFs MBri |
| | 'March of Time' (14) | MBri |
| | 'Mariette' (6) | CBro LAma LRHS MBri |
| | 'Marilyn' (6) | CAvo CFFs CMea EBrs LAma LRHS |
| | ***marjolletii*** (15) | CAvo CBro CFFs EBrs ECho ERos LAma SPhx |
| | 'Mary Ann' (14) | EBrs LAma |
| | 'Mascotte' (7) | ERCP |
| | 'Maureen' (5) ΨH4 | EBrs LAma LRHS |
| | ***mauritiana*** 'Cindy' (15) | EBrs ECho |
| | ***maximowiczii*** | see *T. linifolia* Maximowiczii Group |
| | 'Maytime' (6) | CAvo CFFs CMea LAma LRHS MBri |
| | 'Maywonder' (11) ΨH4 | MBri |
| | 'Menton' (5) | EBrs LAma LRHS |
| | 'Mickey Mouse' (1) | MBri |
| | 'Miss Holland' (3) | MBri |
| | 'Mona Lisa' (6) | CMea EBrs LAma LRHS |
| | 'Monsella' (2) | EBrs |
| § | ***montana*** (15) | CTca EBrs ECho EPfP EPot GKev LAma LRHS NMin SPhx |
| | - yellow-flowered | EBrs ECho WWst |
| | 'Monte Carlo' (2) ΨH4 | LAma LRHS MBri |
| | 'Montreux' (2) | ECho LAma |
| | 'Moonshine' (6) | LRHS |
| | 'Mount Tacoma' (11) | CAvo CBro CFFs EBrs EPfP ERCP LAma LRHS MBri MCot SMeo SPer |
| | 'Mr Van der Hoef' (2) | LAma MBri |
| | 'Mrs John T. Scheepers' (5) ΨH4 | LAma SBch |
| | 'Negrita' (3) | ERCP LAma LRHS MBri MCot SPer |
| | ***neustruevae*** (15) | CBro EBrs ECho EPot NMin SPhx WRos |
| | 'New Dawn' | SPer |
| | 'New Design' (3/v) | EBrs ERCP LAma MBri SPer |
| | 'New Look' (7) | EBrs |
| | 'Ollioules' (4) ΨH4 | EBrs LRHS |
| | 'Orange Bouquet' (3) ΨH4 | LAma LRHS MBri |
| | 'Orange Breeze' (13) | LRHS |
| | 'Orange Elite' (14) | LRHS MBri |
| | 'Orange Emperor' (13) ΨH4 | CAvo CFFs LAma LRHS MBri MCot SPer SPhx WCot |
| | 'Orange Favourite' (10) | CAvo CFFs LAma LRHS |
| | 'Orange Princess' (11) ΨH4 | CTca ERCP LRHS |
| | 'Orange Triumph' (11) | MBri |
| | 'Oranje Nassau' (2) ΨH4 | LAma MBri |
| | 'Oratorio' (14) ΨH4 | LRHS MBri |
| | ***orphanidea*** (15) | CGrW EBrs ECho LAma LRHS NMin SCnR SPhx |
| | - 'Flava' (15) | EBrs ECGP ECho EPot ERCP LAma SPhx |
| § | - Whittallii Group (15) ΨH4 | CAvo CFFs CHFP EBrs ECho EPot ERCP IPot LAma LRHS NMin SMeo SPhx WCot |
| | ***ostrowskiana*** (15) | EBrs ECho LAma NMin |
| | 'Oxford' (4) ΨH4 | LAma LRHS |
| | 'Oxford's Elite' (4) | LAma |
| | 'Paeony Gold' (11) **new** | IPot |
| | 'Page Polka' (3) | EBrs LRHS MBri |
| | 'Pandour' (14) | MBri |
| | 'Papillon' (9) | LAma |
| | 'Parade' (4) ΨH4 | MBri |
| § | ***passeriniana*** (15) | EBrs ECho LRHS |
| | 'Passionale' (3) | EPfP LRHS |
| | 'Paul Scherer' (3) | ERCP |
| | 'Peach Blossom' (2) | EBrs ERCP LAma LRHS MBri SPer |
| * | 'Peaches and Cream' | SPer |
| | 'Perestroyka' (5) | MBri |
| | ***persica*** | see *T. celsiana* |
| | 'Philippe de Comines' (5) | ERCP LAma |
| | 'Picture' (5) ΨH4 | EBrs ERCP LAma |
| | 'Pieter de Leur' (6) | EPfP LAma MBri SPer |
| | 'Pimpernel' (8/v) | LAma LRHS |
| | 'Pink Impression' (4) ΨH4 | EBrs LAma MBri SPer |
| | 'Pinocchio' (14) | LRHS MBri |
| | 'Plaisir' (14) ΨH4 | CAvo CFFs LAma MBri |
| | ***planifolia*** (15) | LRHS |
| | ***platystigma*** (15) | EBrs ECho LAma NMin SPhx |
| | ***polychroma*** | see *T. biflora* |
| | ***praestans*** (15) | EBrs ECho LAma SPer |

| | |
|---|---|
| - 'Fusilier' (15) ♀H4 | CBro EBrs ECGP EPfP EPot LAma LRHS MBri NBir SBch SPhx |
| - 'Unicum' (15/v) | EBrs ERCP LAma MBri NMin SBch |
| - 'Van Tubergen's Variety' (15) | EBrs LAma SPhx |
| - 'Zwanenburg Variety' (15) | EBrs |
| 'Prince of Sanseviero' (2) **new** | ERCP |
| 'Princeps' (13) | CBro LAma MBri |
| 'Princesse Charmante' (14) ♀H4 | EBrs MBri |
| 'Prinses Irene' (3) ♀H4 | CAvo CMea CTca EBrs EPfP ERCP LAma LRHS MBri NBir SBch SPer |
| 'Professor Röntgen' (10) | LAma |
| ***pulchella humilis*** | see *T. humilis* |
| § 'Purissima' (13) ♀H4 | CAvo CBro CFFs EBrs LAma LRHS MBri MCot MSte SPhx |
| 'Purple Prince' (5) | EPfP |
| 'Queen of Night' (5) | CAvo CBro CFFs CMea CTca EBrs EPfP ERCP LAma LRHS MBri MCot MSte NBPN SBch SPer SPhx WRos |
| 'Queen of Sheba' (6) ♀H4 | LAma |
| 'Recreado' (5) | CFFs EBrs ERCP SPhx |
| 'Red Bouquet' (3) | LRHS |
| 'Red Emperor' | see *T.* 'Madame Lefeber' |
| 'Red Georgette' (5) ♀H4 | LAma LSou MBri NBir |
| 'Red Impression'PBR (4) ♀H4 | LRHS |
| 'Red Paradise' (1) ♀H4 | LRHS |
| 'Red Riding Hood' (14) ♀H4 | CAvo CBro CFFs EBrs EPfP LAma LRHS MBri NBir SPer SPhx |
| 'Red Shine' (6) ♀H4 | CBro LAma LRHS MBri |
| 'Red Springgreen' (8) | LAma |
| Rembrandt mix | MBri |
| 'Renown Unique' (11) | ERCP LAma |
| ***rhodopea*** | see *T. urumoffii* |
| 'Ringo' | see *T.* 'Kees Nelis' |
| 'Robassa' (13) | EBrs |
| 'Rockery Master' (14) | EBrs |
| 'Rococo' (10) | ERCP LRHS MBri |
| 'Royal Virgin' (3) | CAvo CFFs |
| 'Salmon Jewel' (3) **new** | IPot |
| 'Sapporro' (6) | LAma |
| ***saracenica*** | EBrs |
| ***saxatilis*** (15) | CBro EBrs ECho EPfP LAma MBri MCot SMeo |
| § - Bakeri Group (15) | CPou EBrs ECho IPot |
| § - - 'Lilac Wonder' (15) ♀H4 | CAvo CBro CFFs CSam EBrs ECho EPot ERCP GGar GKev LAma LRHS MBri SBch SMeo SPhx |
| 'Scarlet Baby' (12) | EPfP LRHS MBri |
| 'Schoonoord' (2) | LAma MBri MCot |
| ***schrenkii*** (15) | EBrs ECho EPot ERCP IHer LAma NMin WWst |
| 'Shakespeare' (12) | CBro EBrs LAma |
| 'Shirley' (3) | CAvo CFFs CTca EBrs EPfP ERCP LAma LRHS MBri MCot WRos |
| 'Showwinner' (12) ♀H4 | CAvo CBro CFFs EBrs LAma MBri |
| 'Silver Standard' (1) **new** | IHer |
| 'Silverstream' (4) | LAma |
| 'Snow Parrot' (10) | CAvo CFFs |
| ***sogdiana*** (15) | EBrs ECho GAuc LAma NMin WWst |
| 'Sonnet' (6) | ERCP |
| 'Sorbet' (5) ♀H4 | EBrs LAma LRHS |
| ***sosnowskyi*** (15) | EBrs ECho |
| ***sprengeri*** (15) ♀H4 | CAvo CBro CLAP CMea CTca ECGP ECha ERCP ERas IPot LAma SCnR SUsu WHal WIvy WShi WTou |
| - Trotter's form (15) | WCot |
| 'Spring Green' (8) ♀H4 | CAvo CBro CFFs EBrs EPfP ERCP LAma LRHS MBri MCot MMHG MNFA MSte SBch SPer SPhx |
| ***stapfii*** (15) | EBrs ECho GAuc NMin WWst |
| ***stellata*** | see *T. clusiana* var. *stellata* |
| 'Stockholm' (2) ♀H4 | LAma |
| 'Stresa' (12) ♀H4 | CAvo CBro CFFs EBrs LAma LRHS |
| ***subpraestans*** (15) | EBrs ECho EPot LAma |
| 'Sunwing' | LSou |
| 'Super Parrot' (10) | LAma |
| 'Swan Wings' (7) | EBrs ERCP LAma LRHS SPer |
| 'Sweet Desire' (2) | EBrs |
| 'Sweet Harmony' (5) ♀H4 | LAma MBri |
| 'Sweetheart' (13) | CBro EBrs LRHS MBri SPer |
| ***sylvestris*** (15) | CBro CMea CTca EBrs ECho EPfP ERCP LAma LRHS MBri NMin SMeo SPhx WCot WHer WShi |
| 'Synaeda King' (6) ♀H4 | LRHS |
| ***systola*** (15) | WWst |
| ***tarda*** (15) ♀H4 | CAvo CBro CFFs EBla EBrs ECho EPfP GGar GKev LAma LSou MBri SBch SPhx WRos |
| - 'Kazakhstan' (15) | EBrs |
| 'Temple of Beauty' (5) ♀H4 | EBrs |
| ***tetraphylla*** (15) | EBrs ECho |
| 'Texas Flame' (10) | EBrs LAma LRHS MBri |
| 'Texas Gold' (10) | CFFs EBrs LAma |
| 'The First' (12) | GAvo CBro CFFs EBrs |
| 'The Lizard' (9) | LAma |
| 'Tinka' (15) | CMdw CMea CSam EBrs LSou NMin SPhx |
| 'Toplips' (11) | LRHS |
| 'Toronto' (14) ♀H4 | LAma LRHS LSou MBri |
| 'Toulon' (13) ♀H4 | MBri |
| 'Très Chic' (6) | CTca EBrs |
| 'Trinket' (14) ♀H4 | LAma |
| ***tschimganica*** (15) | EBrs ECho GAuc LAma LRHS WWst |
| ***tubergeniana*** (15) | EBrs ECho |
| - 'Keukenhof' (15) | EBrs |
| ***turkestanica*** (15) ♀H4 | CBro CSWP CTca EBrs ECho EGoo EPfP EPot ERCP EWTr LAma MBri NSla SBch SPhx WHoo |
| 'Turkish Delight' (14) | NPer |
| 'Typhoon' (3) | EBrs MSte |
| 'Uncle Tom' (11) | EPfP ERCP LAma MBri NBPN SBch |
| § ***undulatifolia*** (15) | EBrs ECho LAma |
| - 'Clare Benedict' (15) | EBrs |
| - 'Excelsa' (15) | EBrs SPhx |
| 'Union Jack' (5) ♀H4 | LAma |
| 'United States' (14) | EBrs NPer |
| 'Upstar' (11) | EBrs |
| ***urumiensis*** (15) ♀H4 | CAvo CBro CFFs EBrs ECho EPot GKev LAma MBri SBch SPhx WHoo |
| § ***urumoffii*** (15) | ECho GAuc LAma |
| 'Valentine' (3) ♀H4 | LRHS |
| 'Valery Gergiev' (7) | ERCP |
| 'Verona' (2) | EBrs LRHS |
| ***violacea*** | see *T. humilis* Violacea Group |
| 'Viridiflora' (8) | EBrs |
| ***vvedenskyi*** (15) | EBrs ECho EPot LAma SPhx WWst |
| - 'Tangerine Beauty' (15) ♀H4 | EBrs ECho LRHS MBri SBch SMeo SPhx |
| 'Washington' (3) | EBrs ERCP LRHS |
| 'Weber's Parrot' (10) | MBri |
| 'Weisse Berliner' (3) | CBro EBrs EPfP LAma LRHS |
| 'West Point' (6) ♀H4 | CAvo CBro CFFs EBrs ERCP LAma MBri MSte SPhx |
| 'White Dream' (3) | EBrs EPfP LAma MBri |
| 'White Elegance' (6) | SPer |
| 'White Emperor' | see *T.* 'Purissima' |
| 'White Parrot' (10) | CAvo CFFs EBrs ERCP LAma LRHS MSte SPhx |
| 'White Triumphator' (6) ♀H4 | CAvo CBro CFFs CMea EBrs ERCP LAma LRHS MCot MSte NBir SPhx |
| ***whittallii*** | see *T. orphanidea* Whittallii Group |

| | |
|---|---|
| 'Willemsoord' (2) | LAma MBri |
| ***wilsoniana*** | see *T. montana* |
| 'Wirosa' (11) ♀H4 | LRHS |
| 'World's Favourite' (4) | LRHS |
| 'Yellow Dawn' (14) | LRHS |
| 'Yellow Emperor' (5) | MBri |
| 'Yellow Flight' (3) | LAma LRHS |
| 'Yellow Pompenette'PBR (11) | ERCP |
| I 'Yellow Purissima' (13) ♀H4 | EPfP LRHS |
| 'Yokohama' (3) | EBrs LAma LRHS |
| 'Zampa' (14) ♀H4 | MBri |
| 'Zombie' (13) | LAma |
| 'Zomerschoon' (5) | EBrs LAma |
| § 'Zurel' (3) | CAvo EBrs EPfP ERCP LAma LRHS SPer |

## tummelberry see *Rubus* 'Tummelberry'

## *Tunica* see *Petrorhagia*

## *Tupistra* (*Convallariaceae*)

| | |
|---|---|
| ***aurantiaca*** | GEdr WCot |
| - B&SWJ 2267 | WCru WPrP |
| - B&SWJ 2401 new | WCru |
| ***chinensis*** | EBee |
| - 'Eco China Ruffles' | WCot |
| ***emeiensis*** new | EBee |
| ***fimbriata*** new | EBee |
| ***grandistigma*** | EBee |
| ***liangshanensis*** new | EBee |
| ***nutans*** | CKob |
| ***tui*** new | EBee |
| ***wattii*** B&SWJ 8297 | WCru |

## *Turnera* (*Turneraceae*)

| | |
|---|---|
| ***ulmifolia*** | MSal |

## *Turraea* (*Meliaceae*)

| | |
|---|---|
| ***obtusifolia*** | EShb |

## *Tussilago* (*Asteraceae*)

| | |
|---|---|
| ***farfara*** | CArn CNat EBWF GBar GPoy MHer MSal NMir NSco WHer WSFF |

## *Tutcheria* (*Theaceae*)

| | |
|---|---|
| § ***spectabilis*** | CExc EPfP |

## *Tweedia* (*Asclepiadaceae*)

| | |
|---|---|
| § ***caerulea*** ♀H2 | CBcs CDTJ CSpe EBee EMil SAga SBch SGar SKHP SPad WCot WOut |
| - pink-flowered | SPad |

## *Tylecodon* (*Crassulaceae*)

| | |
|---|---|
| ***paniculatus*** | LToo |

## *Typha* (*Typhaceae*)

| | |
|---|---|
| ***angustifolia*** | CBen CKno CRow CWat EHon EMFW GFor LPBA MMuc NPer NSco SPlb SWat WFar WPnP |
| ***gracilis*** | CBen EMFW LLWG |
| ***latifolia*** | CBen CRow CWat EHon EMFW GFor LPBA MSKA NBir NLan NPer NSco SWat WDyG WFar WHer WMAq WPnP |
| - 'Variegata' (v) | CBen CDWL CKno CRow CWat ELan EMFW LLWG LPBA MSKA NScw WCot WMAq |
| § ***laxmannii*** | CBen CDWL CRow EMFW GFor LPBA MSKA NLan WPnP |
| ***minima*** | CBen CDWL CRow CSsd CStu CWat EHoe EHon ELan EMFW EPfP LPBA MMuc MSKA NPer SCoo SMad SWat WFar WMAq WPnP WRos |
| ***shuttleworthii*** | CRow |
| ***stenophylla*** | see *T. laxmannii* |

## *Typhonium* (*Araceae*)

| | |
|---|---|
| ***alpinum*** | EBee |
| ***diversifolium*** | EBee |
| ***giganteum*** | SKHP WCot |
| ***kunmingense*** | EBee |
| ***roxburghii*** new | EBee |
| * ***trifoliatum yunnanense*** | EBee |

## *Typhonodorum* (*Araceae*)

| | |
|---|---|
| ***lindleyanum*** | XBlo |

# U

## ugli see *Citrus* x *tangelo* 'Ugli'

## *Ugni* (*Myrtaceae*)

| | |
|---|---|
| § ***molinae*** | CBcs CDul CFir CPrp CSBt CTrC EBee ELon GGal GGar GKev IDee LEdu MCCP MHer SAdn SKHP SLPl SOWG SWvt WCHb WDin WFar WJek WMoo WPic WSHC |
| - 'Flambeau' | CAgr EBee EMil LEdu LRHS MGos NLar SKHP SWvt WPic |

## *Ulex* (*Papilionaceae*)

| | |
|---|---|
| ***europaeus*** | CArn CCVT CDoC CDul CRWN ECrN ELan EPfP GPoy LBuc MCoo MGos MMuc NWea SCoo WDin WHar WMou |
| § - 'Flore Pleno' (d) ♀H4 | CBcs CBgR CDoC CDul CSBt EBee EMon EPfP EPla GAbr GGar IArd MBlu MGos NLar NWea SHBN SPer SPoG WFar |
| - 'Plenus' | see *U. europaeus* 'Flore Pleno' |
| ***gallii*** | WDin |
| - 'Mizen Head' | GGGa GGar MBlu MWhi SLon |
| § ***minor*** | EPla |
| ***nanus*** | see *U. minor* |

## *Ulmus* ✿ (*Ulmaceae*)

| | |
|---|---|
| ***alata*** | EGFP |
| ***americana*** 'Princeton' | CKno |
| 'Dodoens' | IArd MGos SBLw SCoo |
| § ***glabra*** | CDul CRWN ECrN EMac IFFs NWea SBLw SCoo WDin |
| - 'Camperdownii' | CDoC EBee ECrN ELan GKir LAst NBee SBLw |
| - 'Exoniensis' | CTho SBLw |
| - 'Gittisham' | CTho |
| - 'Horizontalis' | see *U. glabra* 'Pendula' |
| - 'Lutescens' | CDoC CEnd CTho CTri LRHS NWea SBLw SCoo SLim |
| § - 'Pendula' | CDul EMil SBLw |
| x ***hollandica*** 'Commelin' | SBLw |
| - 'Dampieri' | SBLw |
| § - 'Dampieri Aurea' | CDul CEnd EBee ECrN ELan EPfP GKir LBuc LRHS MAsh MBar MBlu MGos MRav NBee NBlu NHol SBLw SHBN SPer SPoG WDin WOrn WPat |
| - 'Groeneveld' | SBLw |
| - 'Jacqueline Hillier' | CDul CSpe ECho ELan EPfP EPla IMGH LAst LMaj MBar MGos SBLw SEND SLon SSto STre WAbe WCFE WDin WFar WPat |
| - 'Lobel' | CDul MGos SBLw |

| | |
|---|---|
| - 'Wredei' | see *U.* x *hollandica* 'Dampieri Aurea' |
| ***laevis*** | CDul ECrN |
| Lutèce = 'Nanguen' | CDoC |
| ***minor*** | EMac SBLw |
| - 'Dampieri Aurea' | see *U.* x *hollandica* 'Dampieri Aurea' |
| - subsp. ***sarniensis*** | SBLw |
| - 'Silvery Gem' (v) | LRHS |
| - 'Variegata' (v) | EBee SCoo |
| ***montana*** | see *U. glabra* |
| 'Morton Glossy' **new** | CDul |
| ***parvifolia*** | CMCN CMen NWea SMad STre WPGP |
| - 'Frosty' (v) | ECho |
| - 'Geisha' (v) | ECho ELan MAsh MGos MRav WBod WPat |
| § - 'Hokkaido' | CMen LLHF NLAp WAbe WPat WThu |
| - 'Pygmaea' | see *U. parvifolia* 'Hokkaido' |
| - 'Yatsubusa' | CLyd ECho EWes LLHF MAsh MRav NLar SIng STre WPat |
| 'Plantijn' | SBLw |
| ***procera*** | CTho ECrN LBuc MCoo MGos SMad WDin WSFF |
| - 'Argenteovariegata' (v) | CDul MGos SMad |
| - clone 2 **new** | SMad |
| ***pumila*** | EBee NWea |
| ***rubra*** | CArn EGFP MSal |
| 'Sapporo Autumn Gold' | CDoC LBuc LMaj WDin |
| x ***vegeta*** | SBLw |

## *Umbellularia* (*Lauraceae*)

| | |
|---|---|
| ***californica*** | CArn CPne EPfP GKir SAPC SArc SSpi WSHC |

## *Umbilicus* (*Crassulaceae*)

| | |
|---|---|
| ***rupestris*** | CArn CHrt CRWN CSec EBWF NWCA SChr WAbe WHer WShi |

## *Uncinia* (*Cyperaceae*)

| | |
|---|---|
| from Chile | GCal |
| * ***cyparissias*** from Chile | NBir |
| ***divaricata*** | ECou |
| ***egmontiana*** | CHFP EBee EBla EHoe EPPr EPau EPfP EShb EWsh GFor LBMP MNrw NLar SHGN WCot WFar WFoF WHrl WLeb WMnd WPtf |
| ***lechleriana*** | GBin |
| N ***rubra*** | Widely available |
| ***uncinata*** | CBcs CMMP ECha GFor LHop NCob NHol SDix |
| * - ***rubra*** | CFir CKno COIW CTri CWCL ECot EHrv IFro LAst LRHS MMHG MNrw NCob NGdn NPri SLim SMrm SPad SUsu SWvt WPGP |

## *Uniola* (*Poaceae*)

| | |
|---|---|
| ***latifolia*** | see *Chasmanthium latifolium* |
| ***paniculata*** | SApp |

## *Urceolina* (*Amaryllidaceae*)

| | |
|---|---|
| ***miniata*** | see *Stenomesson miniatum* |
| ***peruviana*** | see *Stenomesson miniatum* |

## *Urginea* (*Hyacinthaceae*)

| | |
|---|---|
| ***fugax*** | EBee |
| ***maritima*** | CArn CPou EBee EBrs ECho ERCP LAma LRHS MNrw MSal WCot |
| ***ollivieri*** | EBrs ECho |

## *Urospermum* (*Asteraceae*)

| | |
|---|---|
| ***dalechampii*** | CDes CSam CSec ECha LLWP SGar SUsu |

## *Ursinia* (*Asteraceae*)

| | |
|---|---|
| ***alpina*** | CPBP |
| ***montana*** | NWCA |
| ***nana*** | WFar |

## *Urtica* (*Urticaceae*)

| | |
|---|---|
| ***dioica*** 'Brightstone Bitch' (v) | CNat WAlt |
| - 'Chedglow 2' (v) | CNat |
| - 'Danae Johnston' (v) | WAlt |
| - 'Dayglo Delight' **new** | WAlt |
| - 'Dog Trap Lane' | CNat |
| - 'Dusting' (v) | WAlt |
| - 'Fearnvale Tigertooth' (v) | WAlt |
| - 'Good as Gold' | CNat WAlt |
| - subsp. ***gracilis*** var. ***procera*** | CNat |
| - OGG mutant | WAlt |
| - 'Spring Fever' | WAlt |
| - 'Worn Gilding' (v) | WAlt |
| ***galeopsifolia*** | CNat |

## *Utricularia* (*Lentibulariaceae*)

| | |
|---|---|
| sp. **new** | EECP |
| ***alpina*** | CSWC SHmp |
| ***australis*** | EFEx |
| ***biloba*** | CHew |
| ***bisquamata*** | CSWC SHmp |
| - 'Betty's Bay' **new** | CHew |
| ***blancheti*** | CSWC |
| ***calycifida*** | CSWC SHmp |
| ***dichotoma*** | CHew CSWC EFEx |
| ***exoleta*** R. Brown | see *U. gibba* |
| § ***gibba*** | EFEx |
| ***heterosepala*** | CHew |
| ***intermedia*** | EFEx |
| ***lateriflora*** | CHew EFEx |
| ***livida*** | CHew CSWC EECP EFEx SHmp |
| ***longifolia*** | CSWC SHmp |
| ***macrorhiza*** | CSWC |
| ***menziesii*** | EFEx |
| ***microcalyx*** | CHew SHmp |
| ***monanthos*** | CHew EFEx |
| ***nephrophylla*** | CHew SHmp |
| ***novae-zelandiae*** | CHew |
| ***ochroleuca*** | EFEx |
| ***paulineae*** | CHew |
| ***praelonga*** | CHew CSWC SHmp |
| ***prehensilis*** | CHew |
| ***pubescens*** | CSWC SHmp |
| ***reniformis*** | EFEx SHmp |
| - ***nana*** | EFEx |
| ***sandersonii*** | CHew CSWC EECP SHmp |
| - blue-flowered | CSWC EECP |
| ***simplex*** | CHew |
| ***subulata*** | EFEx |
| ***tricolor*** | CHew CSWC SHmp |
| ***uniflora*** | CHew |
| ***vulgaris*** | CDWL EFEx |
| ***warburgii*** **new** | CHew |
| ***welwitschii*** | CHew |

## *Uvularia* (*Convallariaceae*)

| | |
|---|---|
| § ***caroliniana*** | ECho |
| ***disporum*** | ECho |
| ***grandiflora*** ♀H4 | Widely available |
| - dwarf | ECho IBlr |
| - golden-leaved | WWst |
| - var. ***pallida*** | CBct CLAP CPom CStu CWsd EBee ECha ECho EGle EHrv EPPr EPot GBri GBuc GCal GEdr IBlr LEdu |

| | |
|---|---|
| | MRav NCGa SMHy SPhx SUsu WAbe WCru WFar WPGP WPnP |
| - 'Susie Lewis' | WCru |
| ***grandiflora* x *perfoliata*** | ECho IBlr NBir |
| ***perfoliata*** | CDes CLAP CWsd EBee ECha ECho EDAr EGle EPPr EPfP EPla EPot EWTr GBri GGar IBlr LAma LEdu MRav NChi SIng WAbe WBrE WCru WPGP WPnP |
| ***pudica*** | see *U. caroliniana* |
| ***sessilifolia*** | CBct CLAP EBee ECho EPot GEdr IBlr LAma LEdu NLar NMen SSvw WCru |

# V

## *Vaccaria* (*Caryophyllaceae*)

| | |
|---|---|
| § ***hispanica*** | MSal |
| ***segetalis*** | see *V. hispanica* |

## *Vaccinium* ✿ (*Ericaceae*)

| | |
|---|---|
| ***arctostaphylos*** | NLar SReu SWvt |
| 'Berkeley' (F) | CAgr CCCN CWib ECrN GTwe LBuc LRHS LSRN MAsh MBlu NLar NScw SDea SPoG |
| 'Bluejay' (F) | CWib GKir LRHS MAsh NLar SCoo SLon |
| 'Blueray' (F) | CWib |
| ***corymbosum*** (F) ♀H4 | CBcs EPfP MBar MGos MNHC NBlu SCoo SReu SSta WBVN WDin |
| - 'Blauweiss-goldtraube' (F) | CSBt CWSG CWib LSRN MBlu MGos NLar SDea SPer SPoG SVic WBVN WFar |
| - 'Blue Duke' (F) new | SLon |
| - 'Bluecrop' (F) | Widely available |
| - 'Bluegold' (F) | EMil LRHS MAsh MGos SLon |
| - 'Bluetta' (F) | CAgr CTri CWib EMui GKir GTwe LRHS MBri SCoo WFar |
| - 'Brigitta' (F) | EMil GTwe |
| - 'Chandler' (F) | CAgr CMac ECrN EMil LRHS MBri SPoG |
| - 'Coville' (F) | CWib EMui |
| - 'Darrow' (F) | CAgr CTrh GTwe LBuc LRHS SPoG |
| - 'Dixie' (F) new | NScw |
| - 'Elliott' (F) | EMil SKee |
| - 'Grover' (F) | LRHS SPer |
| - 'Herbert' (F) | CMac CTrh ECrN EMil EMui GTwe LBuc MGos |
| - 'Jersey' (F) | CWib EPfP LRHS MAsh MCoo MGos NLar SCoo SDea SPer SPoG SVic |
| - 'Legacy' (F) | EMil |
| - 'Nelson' (F) | SCoo |
| - 'Nui' (F) | SKee |
| - 'Pioneer' (F) | MBar |
| - 'Polaris' (F) | LRHS SPoG |
| - 'Stanley' | ELan LRHS MAsh |
| - 'Toro' (F) | CTrh ECrN EMil GTwe LBuc LRHS MAsh MGos |
| - 'Weymouth' (F) | SDea |
| ***crassifolium*** subsp. ***sempervirens*** 'Well's Delight' (F) | LRHS MAsh |
| ***cylindraceum*** ♀H4 | EPfP NLar WBod WFar WPat |
| - 'Tinkerbell' | WAbe |
| ***delavayi*** | ECho LRHS MAsh MBar NMen SReu SSta WAbe WFar WThu |
| 'Duke' (F) ♀H4 | CTrh CWib ELan EMil EPfP LRHS MAsh MGos SPoG |
| ***dunalianum*** | MMuc |
| - var. ***caudatifolium*** B&SWJ 1716 | WCru |
| - var. ***megaphyllum*** HWJ 515 new | WCru |
| 'Earliblue' (F) | CAgr CSBt EMil EMui LRHS MBri MGos SDea WFar |
| ***floribundum*** | CBcs CDoC CMHG ECho GGar GKir IDee LRHS MAsh NLar SPoG SSpi WPGP WPic |
| ***glaucoalbum*** ♀H3-4 | CAbP CDoC CWsd EPfP GGGa GKir LRHS MAsh MBar MRav SMad SPoG SSpi WBod WDin |
| * ***grandiflorum*** | ECho |
| ***griffithianum*** | SReu SSta |
| 'Groover' | LSRN |
| ***macrocarpon*** (F) | ECho ELan EMil EMui GKir GTwe LRHS MAsh MBar MMuc NWCA SDea SPoG SRms |
| - 'CN' (F) | CAgr MGos NLar |
| - 'Early Black' (F) | EMui MGos |
| - 'Franklin' (F) | CAgr |
| - 'Hamilton' (F) | GEdr LLHF NLAp NMen WThu |
| - 'Langlois' (F) new | NLar |
| - 'McFarlin' (F) | EMui |
| - 'Olson's Honkers' (F) | CAgr NLar |
| - 'Pilgrim' (F) | CAgr MAsh |
| - 'Red Star' (F) | EMui MCCP |
| 'Misty' (F) | CAgr SPoG |
| ***mortinia*** | NMen |
| ***moupinense*** | CDoC ECho GKir LRHS MAsh NMen WThu |
| - 'Variegatum' (v) | LLHF |
| ***myrsinites*** | ECho |
| ***myrtillus*** | GPoy MBar NWea WDin WSFF |
| 'Nimo Pink' | MBar |
| 'Northland' (F) | CSBt CWib GTwe MBri NLar NScw SCoo SDea SPoG |
| ***nummularia*** | EBee ECho GEdr MMuc NHar NLar NMen SSpi WAbe WThu |
| ***ovalifolium*** | GAuc |
| ***ovatum*** | CBcs CMHG IDee LRHS MBar SSta |
| - 'Thundercloud' | CAbP LRHS MAsh |
| § ***oxycoccos*** (F) | CArn GPoy MCoo MGos |
| ***padifolium*** | WPGP |
| ***pallidum*** | IBlr |
| ***palustre*** | see *V. oxycoccos* |
| 'Patriot' (F) | CAgr CSBt CTrh CWib EMil GTwe LBuc LRHS MGos NScw SCoo SPoG |
| ***praestans*** | CStu NHol WThu |
| ***retusum*** | WBod WDin WPic |
| ***sikkimense*** | GGGa |
| 'Spartan' ♀H4 | CWib EMil GTwe LRHS SCoo |
| 'Sunrise' (F) | GTwe LRHS |
| 'Sunshine Blue' (F) | CAgr EMui LBuc LRHS SKee |
| 'Tophat' (F) | CCCN EMui |
| ***uliginosum*** | CSec |
| ***vitis-idaea*** | CStu ECho EPfP EWes GGar GPoy MBar MGos SPoG SRot SVic WFar |
| - 'Autumn Beauty' | NLar |
| - 'Compactum' | EBee EWes LLHF LSou |
| - Koralle Group ♀H4 | CAgr EPfP MBar MBri NBlu NHol WPat |
| - subsp. ***minus*** | NLar NMen WAbe |
| - - 'Betsy Sinclair' | CStu |
| - 'Red Pearl' | CAgr CSBt EPfP LRHS MAsh MGos |
| * - 'Variegatum' (v) | EWes NLAp |
| ***wrightii*** var. ***formosanum*** | ECho |

## *Vagaria* (*Amaryllidaceae*)

| | |
|---|---|
| ***ollivieri*** | ECho |

## *Valeriana* (*Valerianaceae*)

'Alba' — see *Centranthus ruber* 'Albus'
***alliariifolia*** — EBee EMon GCal NBro WCot
***arizonica*** — MSte
'Coccinea' — see *Centranthus ruber*
***coreana*** — CFee WMoo
***dioica*** — EBWF
***hardwickii*** — EBee
***jatamansii*** — CArn EBee GPoy
***montana*** — NBro NRya SRms SWat WMoo
***officinalis*** — Widely available
- subsp. ***sambucifolia*** — CFee EPPr GCal NDov SHar WCAu WHil WOut
* - 'Variegata' (v) — WCHb
***phu*** 'Aurea' — Widely available
***pyrenaica*** — ECha EHrv EPPr GCal MMHG SPhx WCot WHil WMoo
***saxatilis*** — NLar NRya
***supina*** — NWCA
***wallrothii*** — CDes EBee WCot

## *Valerianella* (*Valerianaceae*)

§ ***locusta*** — CArn GPoy
***olitoria*** — see *V. locusta*

## *Vallea* (*Elaeocarpaceae*)

***stipularis*** — CDoC CHll CTsd

## *Vallota* see *Cyrtanthus*

## *Vancouveria* (*Berberidaceae*)

***chrysantha*** — CDes CFir CLAP CPom EBee ECha ERos GBuc MNrw MRav NLar NRya NWCA WCru WMoo
***hexandra*** — CBct CFir CGHE CLAP CPom EBee EHrv EPPr EPfP EPla ERos GBuc GEdr GKir LEdu NRya NSti NWCA SEND WCot WCru WMoo WPGP
***planipetala*** — CLAP WCru
I - 'Bellevue Strain' — WCot

## *Vania* see *Thlaspi*

## veitchberry see *Rubus* 'Veitchberry'

## *Vellozia* (*Velloziaceae*)

***elegans*** — see *Talbotia elegans*

## *Veltheimia* ✿ (*Hyacinthaceae*)

§ ***bracteata*** ♀H1 — CAbb CHal CHll CMdw CPou EBak EBrs ECho IBlr LToo NPal WCot
§ ***capensis*** ♀H1 — CSev
***viridifolia*** misapplied — see *V. capensis*
***viridifolia*** Jacq. — see *V. bracteata*

## x *Venidioarctotis* see *Arctotis*

## *Venidium* see *Arctotis*

## *Veratrum* ✿ (*Melanthiaceae*)

***album*** ♀H4 — CPne EBee EBrs ECha ECho GBuc GCal GPoy LEdu LRHS MRav NChi SMad WBrE WCot WCru WFar WHil WSHC
- var. ***flavum*** — CAby SPhx WCru
- var. ***oxysepalum*** — EBee WCru
***californicum*** — CBct CHid EBee GCal IBlr LBMP MNrw WCot WHil WSHC
- compact — MNrw
***dolichopetalum*** B&SWJ 4195 — WCru
***formosanum*** — CDes MNrw
- B&SWJ 1575 — WCru
- RWJ 9806 new — WCru
***grandiflorum*** B&SWJ 4416 — WCru
***longebracteatum*** new — WCru
***maackii*** — CWsd EBee GEdr
- var. ***japonicum*** — see *V. schindleri*
- var. ***maackii*** B&SWJ 5831 — WCru
- var. ***parviflorum*** new — GCal
***mengtzeanum*** — CBct EBee WCot
***nigrum*** ♀H4 — Widely available
- B&SWJ 4450 — WCru
§ ***schindleri*** — EBee LFur WCru
- B&SWJ 4068 — WCru
***stamineum*** — EBee WCru
***stenophyllum*** new — EBee
- var. ***taronense*** new — EBee
***viride*** — CHid ECha EWes GCal IBlr NMyG

## *Verbascum* ✿ (*Scrophulariaceae*)

***adzharicum*** — NBur WHoo
Allestree hybrids — EHrv
'Annie May' — CDes EBee EBla EPfP LPio LRHS LSRN NCob NOrc SPhx
'Apricot Sunset' — CDes EBee NCob SMeo SMrs SPhx WPGP
'Arctic Summer' — see *V. bombyciferum* 'Polarsommer'
***arcturus*** — CFee
'Aurora' — SJoh SMeo SPhx
'Aztec Gold' — CDes EBee MAvo SJoh SPhx WPGP
* ***bakerianum*** — EBla ECtt
'Bill Bishop' — ECho NHar
***blattaria*** — CSec EBWF EBee EHrv NBPC NBir SPav SWat WFar WHer
- f. ***albiflorum*** — CSec CSpe EBee LCro LHop LLWP MNFA NChi NDov NSti SGar SPhx SPlb WHer WMoo WTin
- 'Pink White Blush' — LSou
- pink-flowered — SPav
- yellow-flowered — SPav SWat
'Blushing Bride' — CMea EBee LLHF LSou NBhm WCot
§ ***bombyciferum*** — CBre CSev EBee ECha GJos GMaP SRms WCot
- BSSS 232 — WCru
* - 'Arctic Snow' — SPav
§ - 'Polarsommer' — CHrt CSpe EBee EPfP GKir MBri NBir NBlu NVic SPav SPer SPet SPoG SRms SWal SWat
- 'Silver Lining' — GJos NBur NLar NPer SDnm SPav SPhx
'Brookside' — MSte SPhx
'Broussa' — see *V. bombyciferum*
'Buttercup' — EBee WFar
'Caribbean Crush' — EBee ECtt ELan EPfP GKir LAst LSou NBPC NCGa NLar NMoo SMrm SPav SPer SPhx
***chaixii*** — CSam CSec ECha ECtt EHrv GAbr GBuc GKir MMHG NBir WFar WMoo WPer
- 'Album' ♀H4 — Widely available
- 'Blackberry Crush' new — MDKP
- 'Helene Bowles' — CHar
- 'Sixteen Candles' — NBHF NChi WHal WHil WPtf
***chaixii*** x 'Wendy's Choice' — MDKP
'Charles Harper' — MSte SPhx
'Charlotte' — MAvo SJoh
'Cherokee' — SJoh SPhx
'Cherry Helen' PBR — EBee EPfP LAst LCro MBri NLar NMoo SMrm SPer WHlf WOVN
'Claire' — MAvo SJoh SPhx
'Clementine' — SJoh SPhx

| | |
|---|---|
| (Cotswold Group) 'Cotswold Beauty' ♀H4 | CSam EAEE EBee EBla ECtt EPfP GKir LAst LRHS MRav MWat NDov NGdn SPer SPhx SPla WCAu WMnd WPGP |
| - 'Cotswold Queen' | CBcs CMMP EAEE EBee EBla ECtt ELan EPfP LBMP LCro MRav MWat NGdn SPer SPhx SWvt WCAu WMnd |
| - 'Gainsborough' ♀H4 | Widely available |
| - 'Mont Blanc' | EAEE EBee EBla ECot EHrv GMaP LAst LPio LRHS MRav MSte SWat |
| - 'Pink Domino' ♀H4 | CPrp EBee ECtt EHrv ELan EPPr EPfP GKir GMaP LCro LHop MDun MLHP MRav SDnm SPer SPet SPhx SPla SWvt WAul WCAu WFar WMnd |
| - 'Royal Highland' | CPrp EAEE EBee ECot ECtt EHrv ELan EPfP LPio NGdn NLar SDnm SPav SWvt WFar WWlt |
| - 'White Domino' | EBee GKir SPer SPla WCAu |
| 'Cotswold King' | see *V. creticum* |
| § ***creticum*** | CSpe MDKP SDnm SGar SPav SPla SUsu WCot WPGP |
| 'Daisy Alice' | LPio MSte SPhx |
| § ***densiflorum*** | CArn CSec EBee MBri SPer WFar |
| 'Dijon' | EBee ECtt EWes |
| ***dumulosum*** ♀H2-3 | EPot GCal NHol WAbe |
| 'Dusky Maiden' | NWCA |
| 'Ebenezer Howard' | LPio |
| 'Elektra' | MAvo SJoh |
| 'Ellenbank Jewel' | GMac |
| ***epixanthinum*** | GKev LSou MCCP MDKP NLar SPhx WOut |
| - MESE 552 | EBee |
| 'Gold Nugget' | MMHG |
| 'Golden Wings' ♀H2-3 | ECtt ITim NMen WAbe |
| Harptree smokey hybrids | CHar |
| 'Helen Johnson' | CBcs CMMP EBee EBla ECot ECtt EPfP GKir LAst LCro LHop LRHS LSRN MDun MRav NLar NPri SCoo SPav SPer SPla SRkn SWvt WCAu WCot WFar |
| 'Hiawatha' | MAvo SJoh SMeo SPhx |
| 'High Noon' | SJoh SPhx |
| x ***hybridum*** 'Banana Custard' | EAEE EBee ECtt GKir LSou NGBl |
| - 'Copper Rose' | ECtt EPfP MBri MHer |
| - 'Snow Maiden' | ECtt MHer MWte SDnm |
| - 'Wega' | NLar WHil |
| 'Hyde Hall Sunrise' | EPfP LBuc MGos SPoG |
| 'Innocence' | MDKP |
| 'Jackie' | CBcs CHar CMea COlW EBee ECtt EHrv ELan GKir LAst LHop LRHS LSRN MBri NPri SCoo SPav SPer SPoG SRGP WCot WFar WKif |
| 'Jackie in Pink' | EWes GKir LBuc LRHS NMoo WFar |
| 'Jackie in Yellow' | LLHF NMoo |
| 'Jolly Eyes' | EBee ECtt MBri |
| 'June Johnson' | EAEE EBee NBsh SHar |
| 'Kalypso' | MAvo SJoh SPhx |
| 'Klondike' | SJoh SPhx |
| 'Kynaston' | EBee EBla NGdn SHar |
| 'Lavender Lass' | EBee ECtt NGdn NSti WCot |
| 'Letitia' ♀H3 | CBcs CHar CMea EBee ECho ECtt ELan EPot EWes GCal LAst LRHS MTho NMen NWCA SIng SPav SRot SWvt WAbe WKif |
| ***longifolium*** | LRHS WFar |
| - var. ***pannosum*** | see *V. olympicum* |
| * ***luridifolium*** | EBee EPot SPhx WPGP |
| ***lychnitis*** | CArn CSec GJos SPhx WHer WKif |
| 'Megan's Mauve' | EAEE EBee EBla ECot EWll SPer SWvt |
| 'Merlin' **new** | SJoh |
| 'Monster' | SPhx WPGP |
| 'Moonlight' **new** | EBee |
| 'Moonshadow' | SJoh SPhx |
| 'Mystery Blonde' | MAvo SJoh SPhx |
| ***nigrum*** | CArn EBWF EBee ECtt EPfP GAbr NGHP NLar SEND WBrE WFar WMnd WMoo WPer |
| - var. ***album*** | ERCP NChi NGHP NLar WMoo |
| 'Norfolk Dawn' | CDes EBee EBla ECtt EPfP LAst MAvo MSte NCob NGdn SMeo SMrs SPhx WPGP |
| § ***olympicum*** | CHrt CKno CSam CWan EBee ECtt ELan EPfP GJos GKir MWat NGBl SDix SEND SMrm SPoG WBrE WCAu WCot WFar WPer |
| 'Pandora' | EBrs |
| 'Patricia' | CDes EBee EBla MSte NCob SPhx WPGP |
| 'Petra' | CDes SJoh SPhx WPGP |
| ***phlomoides*** | GJos SPhx |
| ***phoeniceum*** | CArn CEnt ELan EPfP GJos LRHS MNHC NBlu NBro SGar SPet SPlb SWal WBrE WEas WMoo WPer |
| * - 'Album' | CSpe |
| - 'Flush of Pink' | ECtt |
| - 'Flush of White' | EBee ECtt EPPr LAst LBMP LRHS MCot MWat NChi NGBl SDnm SPad SPav SSvw WGor WHil WMoo |
| - hybrids | CSpe CTri ECtt EGoo GMaP LBMP NGdn SRms SWat WFar WGor WPer |
| - 'Rosetta' | EShb GBri MCot MWat NGBl SPad WHil |
| - 'Violetta' | CSpe EBee EPPr EShb EWll LAst LBMP LCro LHop MCot NChi NGdn NSti NVic SPav SPer SPhx SPla STes WCAu WCFE WCot WFar WGor WHil WHrl WMoo |
| 'Phoenix' | CDes CTsd EBee SPhx WPGP |
| 'Pink Glow' | LRHS |
| 'Pink Ice' | EPPr MAvo MDKP MHar |
| 'Pink Kisses' | EBee LBuc LCro LLHF LRHS LSou NBPC SPer |
| 'Pink Petticoats' | LBuc LRHS MGos SPoG |
| (Pixie Series) 'Pixie Apricot' **new** | WHlf |
| - 'Pixie Blue' **new** | WHlf |
| - 'Pixie Pink' **new** | WHlf |
| - 'Pixie White' **new** | WHlf |
| 'Plum Smokey' PBR | CMea EBee ECtt ELon LLHF WCot |
| 'Primrose Cottage' | MBri SPhx |
| 'Primrose Path' | CBct LRHS SHar SRot |
| ***pulverulentum*** | EBWF |
| 'Purple Prince' | ECtt |
| ***pyramidatum*** | SPhx |
| 'Raspberry Ripple' | EAEE EBee ECtt ELan LAst LBMP LLHF NDov NMoo SPav SPer SPet WCot |
| ***roripifolium*** | EBee SPhx |
| 'Rosie' | EBee EBrs |
| 'Sierra Sunset' **new** | WWlt |
| 'South Country' **new** | SJoh |
| 'Southern Charm' | CChe EBee ECtt EGoo EWll GKir GMaP LBMP LRHS MBri MCCP NChi NGHP SPad SPav SPoG STes WFar WHil WPtf |
| 'Spica' | LCro NLar SPhx |
| ***spicatum*** | WFar |
| 'Sugar Plum' PBR | EBee ECtt LLHF |
| 'Summer Sorbet' | EBee ECtt ELan EPfP GKir LSou SPer SPoG WCot |
| ***thapsiforme*** | see *V. densiflorum* |
| ***thapsus*** | CBgR COld CSev EBWF GPoy MHer MNHC NMir NSco SECG SEND |
| 'Tropic Blush' | MAvo SJoh |

| | |
|---|---|
| 'Tropic Dawn' | MAvo SJoh |
| 'Tropic Moon' **new** | SJoh |
| 'Tropic Rose' | MAvo SJoh |
| 'Tropic Spice' | MAvo SJoh |
| 'Tropic Sun' | MAvo SJoh |
| 'Twilight' | EBrs |
| 'Valerie Grace' | MSte SPhx |
| 'Virginia' | SJoh SPhx |
| ***wiedemannianum*** | EBee |

## *Verbena* (*Verbenaceae*)

| | |
|---|---|
| (Aztec Series) Aztec Cherry Red = 'Balazcherd'$^{PBR}$ (G) | NPri |
| - Aztec Coral = 'Balazcoral' (G) | NPri |
| - Aztec Pearl = 'Balazpearl' (G) | SCoo |
| - Aztec Plum Magic = 'Balazplum'$^{PBR}$ (G) | NPri |
| - Aztec Silver Magic = 'Balazsilma'$^{PBR}$ (G) | NPri SCoo |
| - Aztec Red = 'Balazred' (G) | SCoo |
| 'Betty Lee' (G) | ECtt |
| 'Blue Prince' (G) | CSpe MAsh |
| § ***bonariensis*** 🏆$^{H3-4}$ | Widely available |
| 'Boon' (G) | ECtt |
| 'Booty' (G) | ECtt LSou |
| 'Boughton House' (G) | MSte |
| ***brasiliensis*** misapplied | see *V. bonariensis* |
| ***canadensis*** 'Perfecta' (G) | CSpe SHGN |
| - 'Snowflurry' (G) | CFir |
| 'Candy Carousel' (G) | SPet |
| ***chamaedrifolia*** | see *V. peruviana* |
| § 'Claret' (G) 🏆 | CAby CElw CSam CSpe EBee ECtt EPfP EShb GBri LCro LRHS LSRN LSou MCot MWea SAga SCoo SMHy SMeo SMrm SPhx SPoG SUsu |
| (Corsage Series) 'Corsage Peach' (G/d) | SMrm |
| - 'Corsage Red' (G/d) | LAst |
| ***corymbosa*** | CEnt CHid CHll CMMP CSec CWCL EBee ECGP ECha EPPr LHop MDKP NLar SAga SBod SPer WPer WPtf |
| - 'Gravetye' | CHrt EBee GBuc NChi NCob WFar |
| 'Diamond Butterfly' (G) | SAga |
| 'Diamond Merci' (G) | EShb SAga WHoo |
| Donalena Crimson Twinkle **new** | LAst |
| 'Edith Eddleman' (G) | EBee ECtt EPfP MNrw |
| Escapade Bright Eye = 'Esca Bright Eye' (Escapade Series) (G) | LAst |
| * 'Foxhunter' (G) | ECtt |
| 'Hammerstein Pink' | EBee EPfP |
| ***hastata*** | Widely available |
| * - 'Alba' | CEnt CHar CSec EBee EMon EPyc GBar GBuc GCal LDai MCot MDKP MLLN MRav SMrm SPoG WMoo WPer |
| - f. ***rosea*** | Widely available |
| - - 'Pink Spires' | LCro SPad |
| 'Hidcote Purple' (G) | MSte |
| 'Homestead Purple' (G) | CChe CSam CSev EBee ECtt ENor EPfP EShb LDai LRHS LSRN SAga SMrm SPer SPoG SUsu SWvt |
| ***incompta*** | see *V. bonariensis* |
| 'Jenny's Wine' | see *V.* 'Claret' |
| 'La France' (G) | CAby CSam EBee ECha ECtt EPfP EShb EWTr LSou SAga SDix SMHy SMeo SMrm SPhx SUsu WHoo WMnd |

| | |
|---|---|
| (Lanai Series) Lanai Blush White = 'Lan Bulewhit' $^{PBR}$ (G) **new** | LAst |
| - Lanai Burgundy = 'Lan Burg'$^{PBR}$ (G) | ECtt |
| - Lanai Lavender Star = 'Lan Lav Star' (G) | ECtt |
| - Lanai Peach = 'Lan Peachy'$^{PBR}$ (G) | ECtt LAst LSou |
| ***lasiostachys*** | EBee |
| ***litoralis*** | EBee LHop |
| 'Lois' Ruby' | see *V.* 'Claret' |
| ***macdougalii*** | CSec EGoo MDKP SPhx |
| ***officinalis*** | CArn CRWN CWan EBWF GBar GJos GPWP GPoy MHer MNHC MSal SIde WHer WJek WLHH WPer |
| ***patagonica*** | see *V. bonariensis* |
| § ***peruviana*** (G) | EBee EPfP EShb LBMP LRHS MAsh SAga SDix SIng SRms |
| 'Pink Bouquet' | see *V.* 'Silver Anne' |
| 'Pink Parfait' (G) | CHal EPfP LAst LHop SAga |
| 'Pink Pearl' (G) | ECtt |
| ***platensis*** (G) | GCal |
| 'Red Cascade' | SPet |
| § ***rigida*** 🏆$^{H3}$ | Widely available |
| - f. ***lilacina*** | EWTr |
| - - 'Lilac Haze' | EBee LRHS NSti SPoG SRkn |
| - - 'Polaris' | CHar EBee ELon EPfP EShb GMac LHop LSou MAvo MRav NDov SHar SMHy SMrm SPhx SUsu |
| - 'Santos' **new** | NPro |
| 'Seabrook's Lavender' **new** | LRHS MAsh |
| § 'Silver Anne' (G) 🏆$^{H3}$ | CHal CHrt CSam EBee ECtt LDai LSou MCot SDix SMrm SUsu |
| § 'Sissinghurst' (G) 🏆$^{H2-3}$ | CSam ECtt MAsh NPri SAga SIng SMrm SRms |
| ***stricta*** | CWCL MDKP NLar |
| Superbena Bushy Merlot = 'Usbena5002' (Superbena Series) (G) | NPri |
| (Tapien Series) Tapien Pink = 'Sunver'$^{PBR}$ (G) | LAst |
| - Tapien Salmon = 'Suntapiro'$^{PBR}$ (G) | LAst LSou NBlu WGor |
| - Tapien Sky Blue (G) | LAst LSou |
| - Tapien Violet = 'Sunvop'$^{PBR}$ (G) | LAst LSou NBlu |
| - Tapien White Dream = 'Suntapiwhid' (G) **new** | NBlu |
| - Tapien White = 'Suntapipurew'$^{PBR}$ (G) | LAst |
| (Temari Series) Temari Blue = 'Sunmariribu' $^{PBR}$ (G) | LAst |
| - Temari Burgundy = 'Sunmariwaba' (G) | LAst WGor |
| - Temari Coral Pink 2003 = 'Sunmariripi'$^{PBR}$ (G) | LAst |
| - Temari Neon Red = 'Sunmarineopi'$^{PBR}$ (G) | LAst |
| - Temari Violet = 'Sunmariba'$^{PBR}$ (G) | WGor |
| 'Tenerife' | see *V.* 'Sissinghurst' |
| 'Tonic Pink Splash' **new** | LSou |
| ***venosa*** | see *V. rigida* |
| Waterfall Blue = 'Dofall' | SMrm |
| 'White Sissinghurst' (G) | LAst |

## *Verbesina* (*Asteraceae*)

| | |
|---|---|
| ***alternifolia*** | CArn |
| - 'Goldstrahl' | EPPr NDov WPer |
| ***encelioides*** | CSec |
| ***helianthoides*** | CSec EWll LSou MHar WGwG WHil |

## *Vernonia* (*Asteraceae*)

| | |
|---|---|
| ***baldwinii*** new | EBee |
| ***crinita*** | CAby CSec ECha EWes LCro MCot NLar SMad SMrm SPhx WBor |
| - 'Betty Blindeman' | EBee |
| - 'Mammuth' | CDes EBee EWes LHop NCob NDov SMrm SPhx WCot |
| ***fasciculata*** | EShb EWes LPla LRHS MNFA NLar SMrm WCot |
| ***gigantea*** | EBee EWes MMuc NLar SBHP WHrl |
| ***missurica*** | EBee |
| ***noveboracensis*** | EBee NLar SMrm WPer |
| - 'Albiflora' | EBee EWes WPer |

## *Veronica* (*Scrophulariaceae*)

| | | |
|---|---|---|
| | ***amethystina*** | see *V. spuria* L. |
| | ***anagallis-aquatica*** | EBWF NSco |
| | 'Anna'PBR | NDov |
| | ***armena*** | CMea EBee ECho EWes MDKP MHer MSte MWat NMen NWCA SBch SRot WAbe WFar |
| | ***arvensis*** 'Chedglow' new | CNat |
| § | ***austriaca*** | MLLN NBre NChi WFar WMoo |
| | - var. ***dubia*** | see *V. prostrata* |
| | - 'Ionian Skies' | CMea CPBP CTri EBee ECha ECtt EGoo EPPr EWes GBuc GKir LBee LRHS MNrw SEND SGar SMrm SPer WAbe WFar WKif WPat WPer WSHC |
| | - 'Jacqueline' | NBre |
| § | - subsp. ***teucrium*** | CArn CSam CSec CTri EBee ECho MHav NDlv SRms WBrk WFar WPer |
| | - - 'Crater Lake Blue' ♀H4 | EAEE EBee ECtt ELan EShb GKir LAst LCro LEdu LHop LRHS MAvo MCot MRav NBid NBre NVic SMrm SPhx SPla SPlb SRms WCot WEas WFar WMnd WPer |
| | - - 'Kapitän' | ECha GBuc MNrw NPro WFar WPer |
| | - - 'Knallblau' | EBee EMil MBri NGby SMrm SSvw WFar |
| | - - 'Royal Blue' ♀H4 | EAEE EBee ECot EPfP EShb GBuc GMaP LAst LCro LRHS MNFA MWhi NSti SBch SRms WFar WMnd |
| | - subsp. ***vahlii*** MESE 124 | EBee |
| | 'Baby Doll' | IBal MBri NBhm NLar |
| | ***bachofenii*** | WTin |
| | ***beccabunga*** | CArn CBen CWat EBWF EHon EMFW EPfP GPoy LPBA MSKA NMir NPer NSco SWat WFar WHer WMAq WPnP WSFF |
| | - var. ***limosa*** | WAlt |
| | 'Bergen's Blue' | GMac NLar SHGN SHar |
| | Blue Bouquet | see *V. longifolia* 'Blaubündel' |
| | 'Blue Indigo' | EBee ELan IBal NBre NCGa NGdn |
| | 'Blue Spire' | SWat WPer |
| | ***bombycina*** | ECho |
| | - subsp. ***bolkardaghensis*** | NMen |
| | ***bonarota*** | see *Paederota bonarota* |
| | ***caespitosa*** | CPBP |
| | - subsp. ***caespitosa*** | CLyd NMen WAbe |
| | ***candida*** | see *V. spicata* subsp. *incana* |
| | x ***cantiana*** 'Kentish Pink' | GBuc MHer SPla WDyG WFar WMoo WPer |
| | ***caucasica*** | MWat |
| | ***chamaedrys*** | EBWF ECho NMir |
| § | - 'Miffy Brute' (v) | EBee NBir NPro |
| | - 'Pam' (v) | CBow ECtt WCHb |
| | - 'Variegata' | see *V. chamaedrys* 'Miffy Brute' |
| | - 'Waterrow' | WAlt |
| | - 'Yorkley Wood' | WAlt |
| | ***cinerea*** ♀H4 | CLyd CMea GMaP MHar MLHP SAga WEas WHoo |
| | ***dabneyi*** | CDes EBee WPGP |
| | 'Dark Martje' | EBee GBin WCot |
| | 'Darwin's Blue'PBR | CMHG CSec GAbr LRHS MBNS NLar NMoo NOrc WCot WHrl |
| | 'Ellen Mae' | EBee ECtt EWes WCAu WMnd |
| | 'Eveline'PBR | EBee ECtt EPfP LSou NLar WCot |
| | ***exaltata*** | CMdw EBee GBuc MSte NBur NChi NDov SMrm WCot WPer |
| | 'Fairytale' | CSpe EBee GBri GMac IPot NBsh NSti SMrm WBor |
| | 'Fantasy' | NDov |
| | ***filiformis*** 'Fairyland' (v) | EWes WCHb WFar |
| | ***formosa*** | see *Parahebe formosa* |
| § | ***fruticans*** | ECho NMen |
| | ***fruticulosa*** | NWCA |
| | ***gentianoides*** ♀H4 | Widely available |
| | - 'Alba' | CMea LAst NBid NBre NChi NGby NSti |
| | - 'Barbara Sherwood' | EBee EBrs GBin GKir GMac MLLN NBre |
| | - 'Blue Streak' | EWll NDlv WRHF |
| | - 'Lilacina' | EBee |
| | - 'Nana' | CEnt EBee EPfP SRGP |
| | - 'Pallida' | EBee EPfP GAbr MBrN MRav NMoo SEND SPlb WBor WFar |
| | - 'Robusta' | CHrt EBee ECGP EHrv GMac LHop NCGa NCob WMnd |
| | - 'Tissington White' | Widely available |
| | - 'Variegata' (v) | Widely available |
| | ***grandis*** | CDMG CSec EBee GAbr LEdu MAvo MDKP MMuc MWhi NBur NChi NLar SWal WFar WHrl WMoo |
| | x ***guthrieana*** | CAbP NMen SRms WFar |
| | ***hendersonii*** | see *V. subsessilis hendersonii* |
| | 'Heraud' | WCAu |
| | ***incana*** | see *V. spicata* subsp. *incana* |
| * | - 'Candidissima' | GCal |
| | 'Inspiration' | CMdw MLLN NBre NDov SMrm |
| | ***kellereri*** | see *V. spicata* |
| | ***kiusiana*** | CMHG EBee MWhi NBPC NLar SPhx WHrl WOut |
| * | - var. ***maxima*** | CSec EHig GQue SGar WBVN |
| | ***liwanensis*** | ECho NMen |
| | - Mac&W 5936 | MDKP |
| | ***longifolia*** | CHar CMea CSBt ECha ELan GCra MAvo MLHP NSti NVic WClo WFar WMoo |
| | - 'Alba' | EBee EGoo ELan LBMP MMuc NGby NLar STes WCAu WMoo |
| § | - 'Blaubündel' | CMdw EBee NDlv NGdn |
| | - 'Blauer Sommer' | EAEE EBee MCot NGdn SPer |
| § | - 'Blauriesin' | CTri EBee ECtt EMil EPfP GMaP MBri NBre SPer SSvw WFar |
| | - Blue Giantess | see *V. longifolia* 'Blauriesin' |
| | - 'Blue John' | EBee GMac NBre WCAu |
| | - 'Fascination' | EBee LAst NGdn NPro |
| | - 'Foerster's Blue' | see *V. longifolia* 'Blauriesin' |
| | - 'Joseph's Coat' (v) | CBow EBee NBre |
| | - 'Lila Karina' | EBee WPer |
| | - 'Lilac Fantasy' | CMMP CSec EBee ECtt GMac LAst MSCN NGdn NSti WCAu |
| | - 'Oxford Blue' | EBee SPoG WHoo WRHF |
| | - pink-flowered | EShb STes |
| | - 'Rose Tone' | ECha EGoo GJos MWea NLar SBHP WHal WHrl WMoo |
| | - 'Rosea' | WPer |

| | |
|---|---|
| - 'Schneeriesin' | CHar CPrp EAEE EBee ECha EHrv GMaP LRHS MRav NBir NLar SPer SPoG |
| ***lyallii*** | see *Parahebe lyallii* |
| 'Martje' | SMrm |
| ***montana*** | EBWF |
| - 'Corinne Tremaine' (v) | CBow EBee LSou NBir NLar SPoG SRms WHer |
| ***nipponica*** | CSec |
| ***nummularia*** | NBur |
| ***officinalis*** | CArn EBWF |
| - 'Cream Crackers' (v) **new** | WAlt |
| - 'Pathlight' **new** | WAlt |
| ***oltensis*** | CLyd CPBP ECho EDAr EPot EWes LLHF MHer NMen WAbe WPat |
| ***orchidea*** | EBee SRms |
| ***orientalis*** subsp. ***orientalis*** | NMen |
| ***ornata*** | EGoo WPer |
| 'Pacific Ocean' | EBee |
| ***pectinata*** | ECtt |
| - 'Rosea' | ECho ECtt EWes WPer |
| ***peduncularis*** 'Oxford Blue' | see *V. umbrosa* 'Georgia Blue' |
| ***perfoliata*** | see *Parahebe perfoliata* |
| ***petraea*** 'Madame Mercier' | SMrm SRot |
| 'Pink Damask' | CHar CSpe CWCL EAEE EBee ECtt ELan EPfP GMaP LRHS MBri MCot NCob NDov NLar NSti SMrm SUsu WFar WHoo WMnd WTin WWlt |
| ***pinnata*** 'Blue Eyes' | LBee LHop |
| - 'Blue Feathers' | CEnt EBee SMad SPhx |
| ***porphyriana*** | CSpe EBee EPPr EWTr SMad WClo WHil |
| ***prenja*** | see *V. austriaca* |
| 'Prince of Wales Feathers' | NCGa |
| § ***prostrata*** ♀H4 | CEnt CLyd CMea CSam CSec CTri ECho ECtt EDAr EPfP GJos GKev LAst LBee LRHS MLHP NHol SPoG SRms WEas WFar WHoo WMoo |
| - 'Alba' | MLHP MWat WFar WHoo |
| - 'Aztec Gold'PBR | NBro NLar NPro |
| § - 'Blauspiegel' | CPBP |
| - 'Blue Ice' | SMrm |
| - Blue Mirror | see *V. prostrata* 'Blauspiegel' |
| - 'Blue Sheen' | ECho ECtt GEdr NBir SIng WAbe WFar WMoo WPer |
| - 'Goldwell' **new** | EBee |
| - 'Lilac Time' | GKev GMaP NBir NLar SIng SPoG SRms |
| - 'Loddon Blue' | ECho LRHS NVic SRms WPer |
| - 'Miss Willmott' | see *V. prostrata* 'Warley Blue' |
| - 'Mrs Holt' | CLyd ECho ECtt GEdr LRHS MSCN NBir NHol NMen SIng SRGP SRms WAbe WBrk WFar |
| - 'Nana' | ECho ECtt EWes MWat NMen WAbe |
| - 'Nestor' | CTri ECGP EGoo GJos LIMB NDlv WMoo |
| - 'Rosea' | ECho MWat WPer |
| - 'Shirley Holt' | GKir NBir |
| - 'Spode Blue' ♀H4 | ECho ECtt GAbr GMaP LAst LHop LRHS NWCA SIng SPoG SRms WBVN WFar WMoo |
| - 'Trehane' | CEnt EBee ECho ECtt EDAr LAst LBee LHop LRHS MHer MWat NPri NRya SPlb SPoG SRms SRot WBVN WFar WMoo |
| § - 'Warley Blue' | ECho |
| * ***pseudolysimachion*** | MHer WMoo |
| 'Purpleicious' | EBee LRHS MAvo MBri SMrm SPoG |
| ***repens*** | ECho GJos NPro SPlb SPoG WPer |
| 'Rosalinde' | GBuc WPer |
| 'Royal Pink' | LAst MSCN NCGa NLar STes |

| | |
|---|---|
| ***rupestris*** | see *V. prostrata* |
| ***saturejoides*** | SRms WPer |
| ***saxatilis*** | see *V. fruticans* |
| ***schmidtiana*** | EShb WPer |
| - 'Nana' | GKev |
| ***selleri*** | see *V. wormskjoldii* |
| 'Shirley Blue' ♀H4 | CPrp CWib EBee ELan EPfP GKir LCro LSRN MHer MMuc MWat SPer SPoG SRGP SRms WCFE WPer |
| § ***spicata*** | EBee ELan EPfP GJos LEdu LRHS MBNS MDun NBid NBlu SECG SRms WBrk WCAu WFar WMoo WPer WTou |
| - 'Alba' | EBee EMil GJos MBNS MRav MWat NGby NLar WPer WTin |
| - 'Barcarolle' | EBee ELan EPfP MLLN NGby |
| § - 'Blaufuchs' | CSam ECtt |
| - 'Blue Bouquet' | NBre NLar |
| - Blue Fox | see *V. spicata* 'Blaufuchs' |
| § - 'Erika' | ECha ECtt EPfP GBuc IPot LCro MLLN MWat NBir NBre SUsu |
| § - 'Glory'PBR | EBee ECtt EPfP GBri GKir LAst LBuc LCro LSou MAvo MGos MSte NBre NMoo SPad SPer WBrE WCot WCra |
| - 'Heidekind' | Widely available |
| - 'High Five' | EBee IBal NBhm SPoG WWlt |
| - subsp. ***hybrida*** | WCot WHer |
| § - 'Icicle' | CDes EBee MBrN MSte NBre SUsu WHlf WRHF |
| § - subsp. ***incana*** | CMea CWan EBee ECho EHoe ELan EPfP EShb LBMP SPlb SRms SWat WCFE WFar WMoo WPer WTin |
| - - 'Nana' | ECha MLHP NBir SRms |
| - - 'Silbersee' | MLHP WHil |
| - - 'Silver Carpet' | EBee LAst LBMP LRHS LSou MRav NBre NSti SPer SPla WMnd |
| - - 'Wendy' | GCal LPla |
| - 'Nana Blauteppich' | NBre NLar NVic WFar |
| - 'Noah Williams' (v) | ECtt GBuc NPro |
| - 'Pink Goblin' | NBre WPer |
| - 'Pink Panther' | EBee NBhm WWlt |
| - Red Fox | see *V. spicata* 'Rotfuchs' |
| - 'Romiley Purple' | EBee MLLN MRav MSte NBre SPer WFar |
| - 'Rosalind' | NLar |
| - ***rosea*** | see *V. spicata* 'Erika' |
| - 'Rosenrot' | ECho |
| § - 'Rotfuchs' | CMHG CPrp EBee ECtt EHoe ELan EPfP GKir MAvo MRav NBPC NBir NMoo NOrc SPer SPoG SRms WBVN WCot WFar WPer WSHC |
| - 'Royal Candles'PBR | see *V. spicata* 'Glory' |
| - 'Sightseeing' | CWib GJos NBir NBre SPet SRms SWal WFar |
| - 'Twilight' | MBri |
| - 'Ulster Blue Dwarf' **new** | WPtf |
| - ***variegata*** (v) | MLLN NBir |
| § ***spuria*** L. | NBur WPer |
| ***stelleri*** | see *V. wormskjoldii* |
| ***subsessilis*** | WPer |
| - 'Blaue Pyramide' | NBre WPtf |
| * - ***hendersonii*** | NBre NGby |
| 'Sunny Border Blue' | EAEE EBee EPfP GBuc NBre NLar WCot WFar WRHF |
| ***telephiifolia*** | ECho ECtt EWes MDKP NMen NWCA WAbe |
| ***teucrium*** | see *V. austriaca* subsp. *teucrium* |
| ***thessalica*** | ECho |
| ***thymoides*** subsp. ***pseudocinerea*** | NWCA |
| ***umbrosa*** | LRHS WEas |
| I - 'Alba' | WPer |

| | |
|---|---|
| § – 'Georgia Blue' | Widely available |
| ***virginica*** | see *Veronicastrum virginicum* |
| 'Waterperry Blue' | LRHS WFar WPer |
| ***wherryi*** | WPer |
| 'White Icicle' | see *V. spicata* 'Icicle' |
| 'White Jolanda' | EBee ECtt EPfP MSCN NBsh NLar NPro NSti SMrm SPer |
| ***whitleyi*** | MMuc |
| § ***wormskjoldii*** | EBee ECho ECtt EDAr GAuc MAvo MBrN NCGa NLar NMen NWCA SRms WFar WPer |
| – 'Alba' | EBee MLHP WPer |

## *Veronicastrum* (*Scrophulariaceae*)

| | |
|---|---|
| ***axillare*** new | EBee |
| ***brunonianum*** | GCal |
| ***japonicum*** | CSec SGar |
| – var. ***australe*** B&SWJ 11009 new | WCru |
| ***latifolium*** | EBee GCal LPio WCot WSHC |
| – BWJ 8158 | WCru |
| ***sibiricum*** | CSec EBee ECha EShb GCal GQue LEdu NBid NBre NHol WCot WMoo |
| – BWJ 6352 | WCru |
| – 'Red Arrows' new | NDov |
| – var. ***yezoense*** | CSec MDKP |
| – – RBS 0290 | NPro WBVN |
| ***villosulum*** | CPom EBee EWes NBid NBro NLar SMrm WCot WCru WSHC |
| § ***virginicum*** | CArn CEnt CKno CTca EBee ECtt EHrv GBBs GCra GPoy LBMP MCot MLHP MMuc NBir SRms WMoo WPer |
| – 'Alboroseum' | WTin |
| – 'Album' | Widely available |
| – 'Apollo' | CBre EBee EBla ECtt EGle EPfP GAbr GMaP LAst LHop LPio MBri MCot MLLN NBro NLar NOrc NSti SMrm WAul WCAu WHrl |
| – 'Diane' | EGle GMaP NBre NDov |
| – 'Erica' | CCVN EBee EGle EPfP GBin GMac GQue LCro LPio NBPC NChi NDov NMoo NSti SMHy SMrm SPoG SPur |
| – 'Fascination' | Widely available |
| – var. ***incarnatum*** | see *V. virginicum* f. *roseum* |
| – 'Lavendelturm' | CAby CDes CSam EBee ECha EGle EMil GMaP IPot LCro MBri MCot MLLN NDov NLar NSti SMad SMrm SPer SPhx WAul WCot |
| – 'Pointed Finger' | GCal GMaP GMac LEdu NBre SMrm WWlt |
| § – f. ***roseum*** | EBee EBla ECha ELan GMaP LCro MCot MRav NBro NDov SMHy SPhx SPoG WFar WKif WMoo WSHC |
| – – 'Pink Glow' | CKno CTca EBee EBla EBrs ECtt EHoe ELan EPfP GAbr GMac LBMP LCro LHop MMuc MRav NDov NGdn NSti SMrm SPer SPhx SPla STes WCAu WFar WMnd |
| – 'Spring Dew' | CBre EBee ECtt EGle EPfP LPla MLLN NBid NBro NLar NPro SPhx WMnd |
| – 'Temptation' | EBee EGle GBin GMaP LCro MLLN NBre NBro NLar NPro SMHy SPhx SPoG SUsu WCAu |
| 'White Jolan' | CFir |

## *Verschaffeltia* (*Arecaceae*)

| | |
|---|---|
| ***splendida*** | XBlo |

## *Verticordia* (*Myrtaceae*)

| | |
|---|---|
| ***chrysantha*** | SOWG |
| ***longistylis*** | SOWG |
| ***minutiflora*** | SOWG |
| ***plumosa*** purple-flowered | SOWG |

## *Vestia* (*Solanaceae*)

| | |
|---|---|
| § ***foetida*** ♀H1 | CBcs CCCN CHll CPLG CPom CSec CSpe CWib EBee ELan ELon EMil EPfP MNrw NLar SBig SDnm SGar SOWG WKif WPGP WPer WSHC |
| ***lycioides*** | see *V. foetida* |

## *Vetiveria* (*Poaceae*)

| | |
|---|---|
| ***zizanioides*** | MSal |

## *Viburnum* ✿ (*Caprifoliaceae*)

| | |
|---|---|
| B&SWJ 10290 from Mexico new | WCru |
| ***acerifolium*** | LLHF WBod WFar WHCG WPat |
| ***alnifolium*** | see *V. lantanoides* |
| ***annamensis*** B&SWJ 8302 | WCru |
| ***atrocyaneum*** | CGHE CPLG EBee NLar WFar WHCG WPGP WPat |
| – B&SWJ 7272 | WCru |
| ***awabuki*** | CHEx EPfP MBlu MBri MGos NLar WPGP |
| – B&SWJ 3397 | WCru |
| – B&SWJ 6913 | WCru |
| – B&SWJ 8404 | WCru |
| § – 'Emerald Lustre' | CDoC CHEx WPat |
| ***betulifolium*** | CAbP CBcs CMCN CPLG CPMA EBee EPfP EPla EQua NHol NLar WBod WFar WHCG |
| – B&SWJ 1619 | WCru |
| – 'Hohuanshan' | WCru |
| ***bitchiuense*** | CPMA ELan WPat |
| x ***bodnantense*** | CMac CTri CWSG EBee LMaj MRav SAga WHar |
| – 'Charles Lamont' ♀H4 | Widely available |
| – 'Dawn' ♀H4 | Widely available |
| – 'Deben' ♀H4 | CMac EBee EPfP EQua GKir MRav SPer WBod WDin WFar WPat |
| ***bracteatum*** | NLar |
| ***buddlejifolium*** | CMac EPfP EWes GKir LHop WCru WFar WHCG WPGP |
| x ***burkwoodii*** | Widely available |
| – 'Anika' | NLar |
| – 'Anne Russell' ♀H4 | Widely available |
| – 'Chenaultii' | WCru WDin |
| – 'Compact Beauty' | CPMA EPfP WPat |
| – 'Conoy' | CPMA WPat |
| – 'Fulbrook' ♀H4 | CAbP CMHG EPfP GKir LRHS MAsh MGos WBod WDin WFar WPat |
| – 'Mohawk' | CAbP CDoC CEnd CPMA EBee ELan EMil EPfP IDee LRHS MAsh MBri NHol NLar SCoo SPla SPoG SWvt WFar WPGP WPat |
| – 'Park Farm Hybrid' ♀H4 | Widely available |
| x ***carlcephalum*** ♀H4 | Widely available |
| – 'Cayuga' | NLar WPat |
| * – 'Variegatum' (v) | CPMA |
| ***carlesii*** | CBcs CMac CTri CWib EBee EPfP GKir LAst LRHS MBlu MGan MRav MSwo NPri SBLw SCoo SLim SPer |
| – B&SWJ 8838 | WCru |
| – 'Aurora' ♀H4 | Widely available |
| – 'Charis' | CMac CPMA CSBt GKir LRHS NLar WBod |
| – 'Compactum' | CPMA MAsh NHol |

| | | |
|---|---|---|
| | - 'Diana' | CDoC CEnd CMHG CMac CPMA EPfP GKir LRHS MAsh MRav NLar SPer WBod WCFE WPGP WPat |
| | - 'Marlou' | CPMA NLar WPat |
| | ***cassinoides*** | EPfP GBin GKir WFar WPat |
| | - 'Sear Charm' | WPat |
| | 'Chesapeake' | CDoC CPMA EWes SEND WDin |
| | ***chingii*** | CGHE CPMA EBee SLon WPGP |
| | ***cinnamomifolium*** ♀H3 | CAbP CBcs CHEx CMac CPLG EBee EPfP GKir LRHS MAsh SAPC SArc SCoo SEND SLon SPer SPoG SSpi WBod WFar WHCG WPGP WSHC |
| * | 'Cornubia' **new** | GGal |
| | ***cotinifolium*** | CPLG GKev NLar WCot |
| | ***cylindricum*** | CGHE EBee EPfP GCal GKir LHop SKHP SSpi WCru WPGP |
| | - B&SWJ 6479 from Thailand | WCru |
| | - B&SWJ 7239 | WCru |
| | - B&SWJ 9719 from Vietnam **new** | WCru |
| | - BWJ 7778 from China | WCru |
| | - HWJCM 434 from Nepal | WCru |
| | ***dasyanthum*** | EPfP IArd NLar |
| | ***davidii*** ♀H4 | Widely available |
| | - (f) | CBcs CDoC CSBt ELan EPfP LAst MAsh MGos SHBN SPer SPla SPoG SReu SRms SSta WPat |
| | - (m) | CBcs CDoC CSBt CWSG ELan EPfP GKir MAsh MGos MRav SPer SPla SPoG SReu SRms SSta WPat |
| | - 'Angustifolium' | EBee EMil WFar |
| | ***dentatum*** | EPfP |
| | - 'Moon Glo' | NLar |
| | - 'White and Blue' | NLar |
| | ***dilatatum*** | CPne |
| | - B&SWJ 4456 | WCru |
| | - B&SWJ 8734 **new** | WCru |
| | - 'Erie' | EPfP |
| | - 'Iroquois' | EPfP |
| | - 'Michael Dodge' | EPfP NLar |
| | - 'Sealing Wax' | NLar |
| | ***erosum*** B&SWJ 3585 | WCru |
| | ***erubescens*** | CAbP CPMA GKir IDee WFar WPic |
| | - B&SWJ 8281 | WCru |
| | - var. ***gracilipes*** | CPMA EPfP ERas WPat |
| | - 'Lloyd Kenyon' **new** | NLar |
| | - 'Ward van Teylingen' **new** | EPfP |
| | 'Eskimo' | CAbP CBcs CMac CWSG EBee ECrN EPfP GKir LAst LRHS LSRN MAsh MBNS MBlu MGos MRav NMoo SLim SPoG SWvt WDin WFar WHCG |
| § | ***farreri*** ♀H4 | Widely available |
| | - 'Album' | see *V. farreri* 'Candidissimum' |
| § | - 'Candidissimum' | CDul CMac EBee ELan EPfP GKir IArd LHop LRHS MRav NLar SPer SPoG SSpi WBod |
| | - 'December Dwarf' | CPMA |
| | - 'Farrer's Pink' | CAbP CPMA NHol WBod |
| | - 'Fioretta' | NLar |
| | - 'Nanum' | CMac CPMA EBee EPfP LRHS MBar MBrN MRav MWat NHol NLar WFar WHCG WPat |
| | ***foetens*** | see *V. grandiflorum* f. *foetens* |
| | ***foetidum*** var. ***ceanothoides*** | NLar |
| | - var. ***rectangulatum*** B&SWJ 1888 **new** | WCru |
| | - - B&SWJ 3451 **new** | WCru |
| | - - B&SWJ 3637 | WCru |
| | 'Forrerican Didissimum' **new** | WBod |

| | | |
|---|---|---|
| | ***fragrans*** Bunge | see *V. farreri* |
| | 'Fragrant Cloud' | ECrN |
| | ***furcatum*** ♀H4 | EPfP IArd MBri NLar SSpi WBod WPat |
| | - B&SWJ 5939 | WCru |
| | x ***globosum*** 'Jermyns Globe' | CAbP CDoC CEnd CMHG EBee EMil EPfP GKir LAst MBar MGos MRav SLon SPoG WCru WDin WFar WHCG WPGP |
| | ***grandiflorum*** | CPMA EPfP NLar WDin |
| | - HWJK 2163 | WCru |
| § | - f. ***foetens*** | CPMA EPfP WBod |
| | ***harryanum*** | CAbP CMHG EBee EPfP MBNS NLar SOWG WCru WFar |
| | ***henryi*** | CAbP CPMA ECrN EPfP IDee NLar WDin WPat |
| | x ***hillieri*** | GBin MWhi WFar WHCG WKif |
| | - 'Winton' ♀H4 | CAbP CDoC CEnd CPMA CWib EBee EMil EPfP EPla GKir LHop LRHS LSRN MBri MGos NPal SLon SOWG SPoG SSpi WBod WCru WDin WFar WPGP |
| | 'Huron' | MGos WPat |
| | ***ichangense*** | CPMA NLar |
| | ***japonicum*** | CMac CPLG EBee EPfP NLar SHBN SLon WFar |
| | - B&SWJ 5968 | WCru |
| | x ***juddii*** ♀H4 | Widely available |
| | ***koreanum*** | WBod |
| | - B&SWJ 4231 | WCru |
| | ***lantana*** | CCVT CDul CLnd CRWN CTri CWib ECrN EMac GKir LAst LBuc NLar NWea SCoo SPer SPoG SVic WDin WFar WMou |
| | - 'Aureum' | EBee ECtt EHoe MAsh MBlu NLar SCoo |
| | - 'Candy' | NLar |
| | - var. ***discolor*** | NLar |
| | - 'Mohican' | EBee NLar |
| | - 'Variefolium' (v) | CPMA |
| § | ***lantanoides*** | EPfP GKir NLar SSpi |
| | ***lentago*** | CAbP NLar |
| | ***lobophyllum*** | EPfP NLar |
| | ***luzonicum*** B&SWJ 3930 | WCru |
| * | - var. ***floribundum*** B&SWJ 8281 | WCru |
| | - var. ***oblongum*** B&SWJ 3549 | WCru |
| | ***macrocephalum*** | CPMA SLon WDin WPat |
| | - f. ***keteleeri*** | CEnd CPMA |
| | ***mariesii*** | see *V. plicatum* f. *tomentosum* 'Mariesii' |
| | ***mongolicum*** | NLar |
| | ***nervosum*** B&SWJ 2251a | WCru |
| | ***nudum*** | EBee ECrN EPfP NLar |
| | - 'Pink Beauty' | CGHE CPMA CWSG EBee EMil LRHS NLar WFar WPGP WPat |
| | - 'Winterthur' | CPMA NLar |
| | ***odoratissimum*** misapplied | CBcs CHEx CPLG CSam EBee EMil EPfP ERas EWTr IArd MWea SEND SHBN SMad SSpi WSHC |
| | - 'Emerald Lustre' | see *V. awabuki* 'Emerald Lustre' |
| | ***odoratissimum*** Ker Gawl. RWJ 10046 | WCru |
| | 'Oneida' | NLar WDin WPat |
| | ***opulus*** | Widely available |
| | - var. ***americanum*** 'Bailey's Compact' | WPat |
| | - - 'Hans' | NLar |
| | - - 'Phillips' | CAgr |
| | - - 'Wentworth' | CAgr |
| | - 'Apricot' | NLar |
| | - 'Aureum' | Widely available |

| | |
|---|---|
| - 'Compactum' 🏆H4 | Widely available |
| * - 'Harvest Gold' | EBee GKir SCoo SLim SPoG |
| - 'Nanum' | CAbP CBcs EBee ELan ELon EPfP EPla EShb GKir LAst MBar MRav NHol NLar NMen NPro WDin WFar WHCG WPat |
| - 'Notcutt's Variety' 🏆H4 | EBee EPfP GKir MBlu MGos SHBN SRms WPat |
| - 'Park Harvest' | CDul EBee EPfP GKir LRHS NLar NSti SLPl WPat |
| § - 'Roseum' 🏆H4 | Widely available |
| - 'Sterile' | see *V. opulus* 'Roseum' |
| * - 'Sterile Compactum' | IMGH LAst SWvt WFar |
| - 'Sunshine' | MBri |
| N - 'Xanthocarpum' 🏆H4 | Widely available |
| ***parvifolium*** | NLar |
| ***pichinchense*** B&SWJ 10660 **new** | WCru |
| N ***plicatum*** | CTri CWib MBar WDin |
| - 'Janny' | MBlu |
| - 'Mary Milton' | NLar |
| - 'Nanum' | see *V. plicatum* f. *tomentosum* 'Nanum Semperflorens' |
| - 'Pink Sensation' | CPMA |
| § - f. ***plicatum*** | GKir |
| - 'Popcorn' | CAbP CPMA EBee EHig EMil EWTr LRHS LSRN MAsh MBri MRav SPoG SReu SSta WHCG WPat |
| - 'Rosace' | MBlu MBri NLar SSpi |
| - 'Roseum' | NBlu |
| - 'Shoshoni' | NLar |
| N - 'Sterile' | see *V. plicatum* f. *plicatum* |
| - f. ***tomentosum*** | EPfP WDin |
| - - 'Cascade' | EBee EWTr NLar SHBN SSpi |
| - - 'Dart's Red Robin' | ECtt LLHF NLar WPat |
| - - 'Elizabeth Bullivant' **new** | LLHF LRHS MAsh SLon SPoG |
| - - 'Grandiflorum' | CAbP CDoC EPfP GKir LRHS MBar MBri NLar SPer WHCG WMoo |
| - - 'Lanarth' | Widely available |
| § - - 'Mariesii' 🏆H4 | Widely available |
| - - 'Molly Schroeder' | MBri NLar |
| § - - 'Nanum Semperflorens' | CDoC CMac CWSG ECrN ECtt IArd MBlu MGos NBlu NHol SLPl SPer SPoG WFar WHCG WPat |
| - - 'Pink Beauty' 🏆H4 | Widely available |
| - - 'Rotundifolium' | MRav NLar SHBN WPat |
| - - 'Rowallane' | EPfP MBri WPat |
| - - 'Shasta' | CDoC CMCN EPfP MBri NLar WDin WFar |
| - - 'Summer Snowflake' | CDoC CEnd CWGN CWSG EBee ECrN EPfP LRHS MAsh MSwo NHol NPri SHBN SPer SPoG WDin WFar WHCG |
| - 'Watanabe' | see *V. plicatum* f. *tomentosum* 'Nanum Semperflorens' |
| 'Pragense' 🏆H4 | CAbP CBcs CDul CMCN EBee EPfP EQua GKir MBar MGos MMuc NBlu NHol SLon SPer WBod WDin WFar WHCG WPat |
| ***propinquum*** | CAbP NLar WFar |
| - B&SWJ 4009 | WCru |
| ***prunifolium*** | NLar |
| - 'Mrs Henry's Large' | NLar |
| ***punctatum*** B&SWJ 9532 | WCru |
| * 'Regenteum' | CWib |
| x ***rhytidophylloides*** | GKir WFar |
| - 'Alleghany' | EBee NLar WFar |
| - Dart's Duke = 'Interduke' | SLPl |
| - 'Willowwood' | EBee LRHS MAsh NLar SMad SPer SPoG WPat |
| ***rhytidophyllum*** | CBcs CDul CHEx CMac CTri EBee ECrN EPfP GKir LHop LPan MBar MGos MRav MSwo SBLw SCoo SHBN SPer SReu SRms WCFE WDin WFar WMoo |
| - 'Aldenham' **new** | GCal |
| - 'Roseum' | CPLG SLPl SWvt |
| - 'Variegatum' (v) | CPMA NLar |
| - 'Wisley Pink' **new** | LRHS |
| 'Royal Guard' | NLar WPat |
| ***sargentii*** | EPfP |
| - B&SWJ 8695 **new** | WCru |
| - f. ***flavum*** | NLar |
| - 'Onondaga' 🏆H4 | Widely available |
| - 'Susquehanna' | EPfP |
| ***semperflorens*** | see *V. plicatum* f. *tomentosum* 'Nanum Semperflorens' |
| § ***setigerum*** | EPfP IArd IDee NLar SKHP SLPl WPat |
| - 'Aurantiacum' | EPfP NLar |
| ***sieboldii*** B&SWJ 2837 | WCru |
| - 'Seneca' | EPfP NLar |
| ***subalpinum*** | GKir NLar |
| ***taiwanianum*** B&SWJ 3009 | WCru |
| ***theiferum*** | see *V. setigerum* |
| ***tinoides*** B&SWJ 10757 | WCru |
| ***tinus*** | Widely available |
| - 'Bewley's Variegated' (v) | CBcs EBee ECrN MGos MRav SPer SWvt |
| I - 'Compactum' | |
| - 'Eve Price' 🏆H4 | Widely available |
| - 'French White' 🏆H4 | CDoC CDul CMac CWSG EBee ELan ELon EPfP EPla LCro LRHS MGos MRav SCoo SLim SPoG SWvt WFar |
| - 'Gwenllian' 🏆H4 | Widely available |
| - 'Israel' | MBNS SPer SPla WFar |
| - 'Little Bognor' | NLar |
| - 'Lucidum' | CBcs CPMA CSam NLar SHBN WCFE WDin WFar |
| - 'Lucidum Variegatum' (v) | CMac CPMA SLim |
| * - 'Macrophyllum' | EBee SPoG SWvt WFar |
| - 'Purpureum' | CDul CSBt EBee ECrN EHoe ELon EPfP EPla GKir LRHS MAsh MGos MRav MSwo NHol SCoo SHBN SLPl SLim SPer SPoG WBrE WDin WFar WMoo WPat |
| - Spirit = 'Anvi'PBR | CAbP EBee LAst LSou MAsh MBri MGos NLar SCoo SPoG |
| - 'Spring Bouquet' | MAsh MGos NHol NLar |
| - 'Variegatum' (v) | Widely available |
| ***tomentosum*** | see *V. plicatum* |
| ***urceolatum*** B&SWJ 6988 | WCru |
| ***utile*** | EPfP NLar WFar WHCG WThu |
| aff. ***venustum*** B&SWJ 10477 **new** | WCru |
| ***wilsonii*** **new** | IArd |
| ***wrightii*** | EPfP MRav NLar WHCG WPat |
| - B&SWJ 8780 | WCru |
| - 'Hessei' | WPat |
| - var. ***stipellatum*** B&SWJ 5844 | WCru |

## *Vicia* (*Papilionaceae*)

| | |
|---|---|
| ***cracca*** | CSec EBWF NLan NMir NSco WSFF |
| ***sativa*** | EBWF NSco |
| ***sepium*** | NSco |
| ***sylvatica*** | CBgR CPom CSec EWes |
| ***unijuga*** | CPom |

## *Vigna* (*Papilionaceae*)

| | |
|---|---|
| § ***caracalla*** | CCCN MJnS |

## *Viguiera* (*Asteraceae*)

| | |
|---|---|
| ***multiflora*** | SEND |

## *Villarsia* (*Menyanthaceae*)

| | |
|---|---|
| ***bennettii*** | see *Nymphoides peltata* 'Bennettii' |

## *Vinca* (*Apocynaceae*)

| | |
|---|---|
| ***difformis*** ♀H3-4 | CBgR CHar CPom CTri CWan EBee ECha LLWP LRHS MGos NCGa NPri SBri SDix WHer WPic |
| * - 'Alba' | CPom GKir SBch |
| - subsp. ***difformis*** | EMon WBrE |
| - Greystone form | EPPr EPfP LHop MBNS NHol NLar SEND WCAu WGwG WRHF |
| - 'Jenny Pym' | CBgR COlW CTca EBee EPPr EWes GBuc GGar LHop LRHS MAvo MBNS MSte NHol SBch SEND SMad SPoG WFar |
| - 'Ruby Baker' | EBee LRHS NChi NPri WHrl |
| - 'Snowmound' | CWan EBee LRHS MRav SPoG |
| 'Hidcote Purple' | see *V. major* var. *oxyloba* |
| ***major*** | CBcs CDul CSBt CWib EBee ELan EPfP GKir GPoy LBuc LCro LRHS MGan MGos MSwo NPri NWea SHBN SPer SRms WDin WFar WGwG WMoo |
| - 'Alba' | CWib GBuc WEas |
| - 'Caucasian Blue' | WPGP |
| - 'Elegantissima' | see *V. major* 'Variegata' |
| - var. ***hirsuta*** hort. | see *V. major* var. *oxyloba* |
| § - subsp. ***hirsuta*** (Boiss.) Stearn | EMon WBod |
| - 'Honeydew' (v) | EMon |
| - 'Jason Hill' | EMon |
| § - 'Maculata' (v) | CDoC COlW CSBt EBee EHoe EMon LRHS LSou MBar MGos MSwo NBPC NHol NPri SEND SLim SPer SPoG SWvt WDin WMoo |
| § - var. ***oxyloba*** | CBgR CMac COlW COld CTri EBee ECtt ELan EMon EPla LHop MRav SLPl SPoG SRms WFar WHer WPic |
| - var. ***pubescens*** | see *V. major* subsp. *hirsuta* (Boiss.) Stearn |
| - 'Reticulata' (v) | ELan EMon |
| - 'Surrey Marble' | see *V. major* 'Maculata' |
| § - 'Variegata' (v) ♀H4 | Widely available |
| - Westwood form | CFee |
| - 'Wojo's Jem' (v) | CMac EBee EWes LBuc LRHS MAsh MAvo MBri MGos NPri SPoG SWvt WCot |
| ***minor*** | CBgR CDoC CDul ECrN ELan EPfP GAbr GKir GPoy LCro MAsh MBar MGos NBlu NPri NWea SVic WBrE WDin WFar |
| - f. ***alba*** ♀H4 | CBcs CDoC EBee ECha EGoo EPfP GBar LBMP LRHS MAsh MBar MGos NBlu NPri SHBN SPer STre WCot WFar WPtf |
| - 'Alba Aureovariegata' | see *V. minor* 'Alba Variegata' |
| - f. ***alba*** 'Gertrude Jekyll' ♀H4 | CBgR CDoC CSBt EBee ELan EPfP GKir ILis LCro LRHS LSRN MAsh MBri MGos MRav MWat NHol NPri SBod SCoo SEND SLim SPer SPla SPoG WBor WDin WMoo |
| § - 'Alba Variegata' (v) | CBgR CPLG EHoe EPla GAbr GGar GKir MBar MGos NGHP NHol NPro SRms STre WEas WFar WHoo |
| § - 'Argenteovariegata' (v) ♀H4 | Widely available |
| § - 'Atropurpurea' ♀H4 | Widely available |
| - 'Aurea' | SPla WFar |
| § - 'Aureovariegata' (v) | CBcs CDul EBee GAbr LRHS MBar MGos MRav NBlu NHol SPer SPlb SPoG WFar |
| - 'Azurea' | CHid |
| § - 'Azurea Flore Pleno' (d) ♀H4 | Widely available |
| * - 'Blue and Gold' | EAEE ECGP EGoo EMon MAvo |
| - 'Blue Drift' | EWes MSwo |
| - 'Blue Moon' | ECtt SPla |
| - 'Bowles' Blue' | see *V. minor* 'La Grave' |
| - 'Bowles' Variety' | see *V. minor* 'La Grave' |
| - 'Burgundy' | CFee SRms |
| - 'Caerulea Plena' | see *V. minor* 'Azurea Flore Pleno' |
| - 'Dartington Star' | see *V. major* var. *oxyloba* |
| - 'Double Burgundy' | see *V. minor* 'Multiplex' |
| - Green Carpet | see *V. minor* 'Grüner Teppich' |
| § - 'Grüner Teppich' | EMon WFar |
| - 'Illumination' (v) | Widely available |
| § - 'La Grave' ♀H4 | Widely available |
| - 'Marie' | MGos |
| § - 'Multiplex' (d) | CTca EBee ECtt EPPr EPla GBar MBar NChi NHol SRms WCFE WHrl |
| - 'Persian Carpet' (v) | EMon |
| - 'Purpurea' | see *V. minor* 'Atropurpurea' |
| - 'Ralph Shugert' | CMac EBee EPPr EWes LRHS MAsh NLar SPoG |
| - 'Rubra' | see *V. minor* 'Atropurpurea' |
| - 'Sabinka' | CHid EGoo EMon EPPr |
| - 'Silver Service' (d/v) | CFee CHid CWan EBee EMon GBuc MRav NHol WCot WHoo |
| - 'Variegata' | see *V. minor* 'Argenteovariegata' |
| - 'Variegata Aurea' | see *V. minor* 'Aureovariegata' |
| - 'White Gold' | EBee NHol NPro |
| ***sardoa*** | EBee EMon EPPr EWes |

## *Vincetoxicum* (*Asclepiadaceae*)

| | |
|---|---|
| ***forrestii*** | CPLG |
| ***fuscum*** **new** | EBee |
| § ***hirundinaria*** | EBee EPPr GPoy LEdu WGwG |
| ***nigrum*** | GCal NChi WCot WTin |
| ***officinale*** | see *V. hirundinaria* |
| ***scandens*** | CRHN |

## *Viola* ✿ (*Violaceae*)

| | |
|---|---|
| B&SWJ 8301 from Vietnam | WCru |
| 'Ada Segre' (Vt) **new** | CGro |
| 'Admiral Avellan' | see *V.* 'Amiral Avellan' |
| 'Admiration' (Va) | WBou |
| ***adunca*** | NWCA |
| - var. ***minor*** | see *V. labradorica* ambig. |
| § ***alba*** | EWes NMen |
| 'Alba Plena de Chevreuse' (dVt) **new** | CGro |
| 'Alethia' (Va) | GMac WBou |
| 'Alice' (Vt) | CGro |
| 'Alice Kate' | CAby WBou |
| 'Alice Witter' (Vt) | CBre CGro EBee ECha NChi |
| * 'Alison' (Va) | GMaP WBou |
| 'Amelia' (Va) | GKir WBou |
| 'Amethyst' (C) | EBee |
| I 'Amethyst' (Vt) **new** | CGro |
| § 'Amiral Avellan' (Vt) | CGro |
| 'Annaleisia' (Vt) **new** | CGro |
| I 'Annie' (Vt) | CBre CGro EBee LLHF |
| 'Arabella' (Va) | WBou |
| 'Ardross Gem' (Va) | CAby CCge ECho ECtt GAbr GKir GMac WBou WEas |
| ***arenaria*** | see *V. rupestris* |
| 'Arkwright's Ruby' (Va) | SRms |
| 'Ashvale Blue' (PVt) | CGro |
| 'Aspasia' (Va) ♀H4 | CAby GMac NCob WBou |
| 'Avril' (Va) | NCob |
| 'Avril Lawson' (Va) | GKev GQue SHar WBou |
| 'Baby Franjo' | NVic |
| 'Baby Lucia' (Va) | EWTr NVic SRms |
| 'Barbara' (Va) | WBou |
| 'Baroness de Rothschild' misapplied | see *V.* 'Baronne Alice de Rothschild' |

| | | |
|---|---|---|
| | 'Baroness de Rothschild' ambig. (Vt) | CGro |
| § | 'Baronne Alice de Rothschild' (Vt) | GMaP SHar |
| | 'Beatrice' (Vtta) | WBou |
| | 'Becky Groves' (Vt) | CGro |
| | 'Beechy's Double White' (d) | CGro |
| * | ***bella*** | WEas |
| § | 'Belmont Blue' (C) | CCge CEnt CSam CSpe EAlp EBee ECtt EWes GCal GCra GMaP GMac LCro LHop MHer MMuc MRav MSCN NBir NDov SPer SRkn SRms WBou WFar |
| § | ***bertolonii*** | WBou |
| | 'Beshlie' (Va) 𝕐H4 | EBee ECtt GMac WBou WEas WTin |
| * | ***betonicifolia albescens*** | EBee |
| | - var. ***oblongosagittata*** | CGro |
| | ***biflora*** | CMHG MTho NChi |
| | 'Black Bun' | WPGP |
| | 'Blue Butterfly' (C) | GMac |
| | 'Blue Moon' (C) | WBou WTin |
| | 'Blue Moonlight' (C) | CAby CElw EBee GBuc GMac LRHS MMuc |
| | 'Boughton Blue' | see *V.* 'Belmont Blue' |
| | 'Bournemouth Gem' (Vt) | CBre CGro |
| § | 'Bowles' Black' (T) | CArn CSWP CSpe EPfP GCal LBMP LEdu LRHS MMuc NBro NGHP NVic SPla SRGP SRms WEas WTou |
| | 'Boy Blue' (Vtta) | ECtt |
| | 'Bruneau' (dVt) | WCot |
| * | 'Bryony' (Vtta) | WBou |
| | 'Bullion' (Va) | EBee WBou |
| | 'Burncoose Yellow' | WBou |
| | 'Buttercup' (Vtta) | COlW EBee ECtt GKir GMaP GMac LSRN NCob SPoG WBou |
| | 'Butterpat' (C) | GMac |
| | 'Buxton Blue' (Va) | GBuc |
| | ***calcarata*** | EBee |
| | 'Candy' (Vt) | CGro |
| | ***canina*** | NBro NMir |
| * | - ***alba*** | CBre |
| | 'Carmine Witch' (Vt) **new** | CGro |
| | 'Carol' (Vt) **new** | CGro |
| | 'Carol Loxton' (Vt) **new** | CGro |
| | 'Catalina' | CGro |
| * | 'Catforth Gold' | NCob |
| | 'Catforth Suzanne' | NCob |
| | 'Cat's Whiskers' | CElw |
| | ***cazorlensis*** | WAbe |
| | ***chaerophylloides*** 'Beni-zuru' **new** | EBee |
| | - var. ***chaerophylloides*** | CGro |
| § | - var. ***sieboldiana*** | CPMA |
| | 'Charles William Groves' (Vt) | CGro EBee |
| | 'Charlotte' | WBou |
| | 'Christmas' (Vt) | CGro |
| | 'Cinders' (Vtta) | CAby GMac |
| | 'Citrina' (Va) | CSec |
| | 'Citron' (Va) | NCob |
| | 'Clementina' (Va) 𝕐H4 | MRav WBou |
| | 'Cleo' (Va) | EBee WBou |
| | 'Clive Farrell' (Vt) **new** | CGro |
| | 'Clive Groves' (Vt) | CGro CHid |
| | 'Coeur d'Alsace' (Vt) | CBre CGro EBee NCGa NLar WCot WEas WHal |
| | 'Colette' (Va) | WBou |
| | 'Colombine' (Vt) | CGro NSti SPad |
| | 'Columbine' (Va) | EBee ECtt EPfP GKir GMaP GMac LAst LCro LRHS MHer NBir NPri SIng SPer SPoG SSto WBou WFar |
| | 'Comte de Chambord' (dVt) | SHar WFar WRha |
| | 'Connigar' | CSam |
| § | 'Conte di Brazza' (dPVt) | CGro EHrv EShb SHar WFar WHer WRha |
| | 'Cordelia' (Va) | WFar |
| | 'Cordelia' (Vt) | CGro |
| | ***cornuta*** 𝕐H4 | CAby CElw CMea ECho GGar GKev GKir MLHP MWat NBir NBro NChi NCob SBch SPoG SRms WBou WFar WHoo WRos WTou |
| | - Alba Group 𝕐H4 | Widely available |
| § | - 'Alba Minor' | CAby CEnt CSsd EBee ECho EPfP EShb EWes GBuc GCal GMac IGor MWat NBro NChi SHGN WAbe WFar |
| | - blue-flowered | ECho MHer MLHP NCob SHGN WFar WMoo |
| | - 'Cleopatra' (C) | CAby GAbr GMac |
| | - 'Clouded Yellow' | CAby GMac |
| | - 'Gypsy Moth' (C) | CAby GMac |
| | - 'Icy But Spicy' | EBee EHrv WBou |
| | - Lilacina Group (C) | ECha MRav MSte NChi SWat WFar WMnd WPtf |
| | - 'Maiden's Blush' | CAby GMac NChi |
| | - 'Minor' 𝕐H4 | CAby CSam GMac NBro WAbe WBou |
| | - 'Minor Alba' | see *V. cornuta* 'Alba Minor' |
| | - 'Netta Statham' | CAby WBou |
| | - 'Pale Apollo' (C) | GMac |
| | - 'Purple Gem' | CAby |
| | - Purpurea Group | CMea ECha GBuc GCal NCob WMnd |
| | - 'Rosea' | ECha |
| | - 'Spider' | CAby GMac |
| | - 'Victoria's Blush' (C) | CAby CCge CSpe EBee ECtt GBuc GMaP GMac MMuc MSte NBir NChi NDov WBou |
| | - 'Violacea' | GMac |
| | - 'Yellow King' | EHrv |
| | ***corsica*** | CEnt CSpe EBee NChi SHGN |
| | 'Crepuscle' (Vt) | CGro |
| § | ***cucullata*** 𝕐H4 | ECho SRms WFar |
| § | - 'Alba' (Vt) | CBro CGro EBee ECho LLWP NBir NChi NSti SRms WEas |
| | - ***rosea*** | EWes |
| * | - 'Striata Alba' | NBre NBro |
| | 'Czar' | see *V.* 'The Czar' |
| | 'Daisy Smith' (Va) | CAby NChi WBou |
| | 'Dancing Geisha' (Vt) | EBee EHrv EPfP WAul |
| | 'Danielle Molly' **new** | WBou |
| | 'Dawn' (Vtta) | CAby EBee ECtt GKir GMaP NPri SIng SPer SPoG SRGP WBou |
| | 'Delia' (Va) | CAby |
| | 'Delicia' (Vtta) | NChi WBou |
| | ***delphinantha*** | WAbe |
| | 'Delphine' (Va) | MSte NChi |
| | 'Des Charentes' (Vt) | CGro |
| | 'Desdemona' (Va) | GMac WBou |
| | 'Devon Cream' (Va) | CAby GMac WBou |
| | 'Diana Groves' (Vt) | CGro |
| | 'Dick o' the Hills' (Vt) **new** | CGro |
| | ***dissecta*** | WCot |
| | - var. ***sieboldiana*** | see *V. chaerophylloides* var. *sieboldiana* |
| | 'Donau' (Vt) | CBre CGro |
| | 'Donna' (Vt) **new** | CGro |
| | 'Doreen' (Vt) | CGro |
| | 'Double White' (dVt) | CGro |
| | ***douglasii*** | CGro |
| | ***dubyana*** | GBuc NChi |
| | 'Duchesse de Parme' (dPVt) | CGro EBee EShb IFro NWCA SHar SRms |

| | | |
|---|---|---|
| | 'D'Udine' (dPVt) | CGro |
| | 'Dusk' | WBou |
| | 'E.A. Bowles' | see *V.* 'Bowles' Black' |
| | 'Eastgrove Blue Scented' (C) | GMaP GMac NCob WBou WEas WOut WPtf WWFP |
| | 'Eastgrove Ice Blue' (C) | WBou WEas |
| | 'Eastgrove Twinkle' (C) | NCob WEas |
| | ***eizanensis*** | MTho |
| | 'Elaine Quin' | EBee NPri SPer SPoG SRGP WBou |
| § | ***elatior*** | CEnt CSWP CSec EBee EBla EMon EPPr EWTr GBri GBuc LRHS MNrw NChi WPer WPtf WSHC |
| | 'Elizabeth' (Va) | EBee ECtt GKir WBou |
| | 'Elizabeth Bailes' (Vt) | CGro |
| | 'Elliot Adam' (Va) | WBou |
| | 'Elsie Coombs' (Vt) | CGro |
| | 'Emma' (Va) | CAby |
| | 'Emperor Blue Vein' | EBee EPfP LSou |
| | 'Emperor Magenta Red' | GJos LSou |
| | 'Emperor White' | LSou |
| | ***erecta*** | see *V. elatior* |
| | 'Eris' (Va) | NChi WBou |
| | 'Etain' (Va) | CCge COlW EAlp EBee ECho ECtt ELan EWes GBuc GMaP LAst LRHS MSte NCob NDov NPri SMrm SPhx SPoG WBou WEas |
| | 'Fabiola' (Vtta) | CAby GMac NBir |
| | 'Famecheck Apricot' | CPom EFam NChi |
| * | 'Fantasy' | CAby WBou |
| | ***fargesii*** B&SWJ 6728 **new** | WCru |
| | 'Fee Jalucine' (PVt) **new** | CGro |
| | 'Fiona' (Va) | CAby EBee GMaP GMac MCot MSte NChi NCob WBou |
| | 'Fiona Lawrenson' (Va) | WBou |
| | ***flettii*** | NChi |
| | 'Florence' (Va) | CAby NChi WBou |
| | 'Foxbrook Cream' (C) | CAby GBuc WBou |
| | 'Freckles' | see *V. sororia* 'Freckles' |
| | ***glabella*** | SKHP |
| | 'Gladys Findlay' (Va) | WBou |
| * | 'Glenda' | WBou |
| | 'Glenholme' | CAby GAbr GMac |
| | 'Gloire de Verdun' (PVt) | CGro NWCA SBch |
| | 'Gloriole' (Vt) | CGro |
| | 'Governor Herrick' (Vt) | CCge CGro |
| § | ***gracilis*** | NBir WFar |
| | - 'Lutea' | CSam |
| | - 'Major' | WBou |
| | 'Granddad's Violet' (Vt) | CGro |
| | 'Green Goddess'PBR | CSec EBee MWea NPri SPoG WFar |
| | 'Green Jade' (v) | NBir |
| | 'Grey Owl' (Va) | LRHS WBou WPGP |
| | 'Grovemount Blue' (C) | CMea |
| § | ***grypoceras*** var. ***exilis*** | EBee GBri NGdn |
| | - var. ***exilis*** 'Sylettas' | CBow GGar MMuc NBPC |
| | - f. ***variegata*** (v) | NBir |
| | 'Gustav Wermig' (C) | NDov WBou |
| | 'Hansa' (C) | GBin NChi |
| | 'Haslemere' | see *V.* 'Nellie Britton' |
| * | 'Heaselands' | SMHy SMrm |
| § | ***hederacea*** | CHFP CMHG CTsd EBee ECho ECou GQui IFoB NBro SAga SRms WFar |
| | - blue-flowered | SIng |
| | - 'Putty Road' (Vt) | CGro |
| | 'Helen' (Va) | ECtt |
| | 'Helena' (Va) | WBou |
| | 'Hespera' (Va) | WBou |
| | ***heterophylla*** subsp. ***epirota*** | see *V. bertolonii* |
| * | 'Hetty Gatenby' | WBou |
| | ***hirsutula*** | EBla EHrv |
| I | - 'Alba' | EBla |
| I | - 'Purpurea' | EBla |
| | 'Hudsons Blue' | CElw WEas |
| | 'Huntercombe Purple' (Va) ♀H4 | LHop MCot MWat NBir SRms WBou WHal WKif |
| | 'Iden Gem' (Va) | WBou |
| | 'Inverurie Beauty' (Va) ♀H4 | GMaP GMac NChi NDov WBou |
| | 'Irish Elegance' | see *V.* 'Sulfurea' |
| | 'Irish Molly' (Va) | CSpe EBee ECho ECtt ELan EPfP GGar GKev GKir GMaP GMac LRHS MHer MRav NPri SIng SMrm SPer SPoG SRGP SRms WBou WEas WFar WWlt |
| | 'Isabel' | WBou |
| | 'Isabella' (Vt) **new** | CGro |
| | 'Ivory Queen' (Va) | EBee GMac MRav WBou |
| | 'Jack Sampson' (Vt) | CGro |
| | 'Jackanapes' (Va) ♀H4 | CHVG EBee ECho ECtt ELan EPfP GKir LRHS NPri SIng SPer SPoG SRms WBou WFar |
| | 'Janet' (Va) | CHVG ECtt NPri SMrm SPoG SRGP |
| | ***japonica*** | GGar |
| | 'Jeannie Bellew' (Va) | ECtt NCob SPer SRms WBou WFar |
| | 'Jennifer Andrews' (Va) | WBou |
| | 'Jessie East' | WEas |
| | 'Joanna' (Va) | WBou |
| | 'John Raddenbury' (Vt) | CGro GMaP SHar |
| | ***jooi*** | CEnt CPBP CSec EBee ECho EWTr GKev MWea NBir NChi NMen SPhx SRms WPat WRha |
| | 'Josephine' (Vt) | CGro |
| | 'Josie' (Va) | WBou |
| | 'Joyce Gray' (Va) | CAby WBou |
| | 'Judy Goring' (Va) | GMac |
| | 'Julia' (Va) | WBou |
| | 'Julian' (Va) | CAby EBee GMac SRms WBou |
| | 'Juno' (Va) | GMac |
| | 'Jupiter' (Va) | EBee |
| | ***keiskei*** | CSec |
| | 'Kerry Girl' (Vt) | CGro |
| | 'Kitten' | CAby GMac MSte NChi NDov WBou |
| I | 'Kitty' | CCge |
| | 'Kitty White' (Va) | GMac |
| § | 'Königin Charlotte' (Vt) | CCge CGro COlW EBee EPfP GMac MHer NChi NWCA SSto WCot WFar WHil WMoo |
| | ***koreana*** | see *V. grypoceras* var. *exilis* |
| N | ***labradorica*** misapplied | see *V. riviniana* Purpurea Group |
| N | - ***purpurea*** misapplied | see *V. riviniana* Purpurea Group |
| § | ***labradorica*** ambig. | CHar ECho EMil EWTr LRHS MRav NPri WCra WFar |
| | ***lactiflora*** | EBee |
| | 'Lady Hume Campbell' (PVt) | CGro NWCA WHer |
| | 'Lady Jane' (Vt) | CGro |
| | 'Lady Saville' | see *V.* 'Sissinghurst' |
| | 'Laura' (C) | GBuc NCob |
| | 'Laura Cawthorne' | EBee |
| | 'Lavender Lady' (Vt) | CBre CGro |
| | 'Lavinia' (Va) | LRHS WBou |
| | 'Lees Peachy Pink' (Vt) | CGro |
| | 'Lemon Sorbet' | GBuc |
| | 'Letitia' (Va) | EBee GMaP NDov SRms WBou WFar |
| | 'Lianne' (Vt) | CDes CGro LLHF |
| | 'Lindsay' | WBou |
| | 'Little David' (Vtta) ♀H4 | CAby CSam CTri GMac SRms WBou WPGP |
| | 'Lord Nelson' (Va) | EBee |
| | 'Lord Plunket' (Va) | WBou |
| | 'Lorna Cawthorne' (C) | CAby MSte WBou |
| | 'Louisa' (Va) | GMac WBou |

| | | |
|---|---|---|
| § | ***lutea*** | NChi WBou |
| | – subsp. ***elegans*** | see *V. lutea* |
| | 'Luxonne' (Vt) | CBre CGro EBee |
| | 'Lydia Groves' (Vt) | CGro |
| | 'Lydia's Legacy' (Vt) | CGro SBch |
| | 'Madame Armandine Pagès' (Vt) | CBre CGro EBee |
| | 'Maggie Mott' (Va) ♀$^{H4}$ | ECha ECho ECtt GAbr GBuc GMac LHop LRHS NChi NDov NPri SPer SRGP WBou WFar WKif WWFP |
| | 'Magic' | CAby EBee GBuc GMaP GMac WBou |
| | 'Magnifico' | LAst LRHS |
| | ***mandshurica*** | NWCA |
| | – 'Fuji Dawn' (v) | CBow WCot WPtf |
| | – f. ***hasegawae*** | EPPr |
| | 'Margaret' (Va) | WBou |
| | 'Marie Rose' (Vt) | CGro |
| | 'Marie-Louise' (dPVt) | CDes CGro EBee EShb GMaP SHar SRGP |
| I | 'Mars' | ECtt GBin LSRN LSou WBor WFar |
| | 'Mars' (Va) | EBee ECtt MCCP SBch SHGN SMrm SRGP |
| | 'Martin' (Va) ♀$^{H4}$ | CAby COIW EBee ECha ECtt GMaP LHop LSRN MHer NDov SPer SPoG SRGP SSto WBou WFar |
| | 'Mary Mouse' | WBou |
| | 'Mauve Haze' (Va) | MSte WBou |
| | 'Mauve Radiance' (Va) | NVic WBou |
| | 'May Mott' (Va) | GMaP WBou |
| | 'Mayfly' (Va) | CAby MSte WBou |
| | 'Melinda' (Vtta) | NDov WBou |
| | 'Melting Moments' (Va) | EBee LAst SIng SMrm |
| | 'Mercury' (Va) | SHGN WBou |
| | 'Milkmaid' (Va) | CAby EBee NBir |
| | ***minor*** pale purple-flowered | EBee |
| | 'Miss Brookes' (Va) | WBou |
| | 'Mistress Mallory' (Vt) **new** | CGro |
| | 'Misty Guy' (Vtta) | NChi NDov WBou |
| | 'Molly Sanderson' (Va) ♀$^{H4}$ | CEnt COIW CSpe EAlp EBee ECha ECho ECtt ELan EPfP GGar GKir LAst LCro LHop LRHS MHer MMuc MRav NPri SIng SPer SPlb SPoG SRGP WBor WBou WFar |
| | 'Moonlight' (Va) ♀$^{H4}$ | CAby ECha ECho ELan GKir LHop MHer MMuc WBou |
| | 'Moonraker' | GMaP NBir |
| | 'Morwenna' (Va) | CAby WBou |
| | 'Mrs Cotterell' | GBuc |
| | 'Mrs David Lloyd George' (dVt) | CGro |
| | 'Mrs Lancaster' (Va) | CAby EBee GMaP GMac LHop LSRN NBir NChi NPri SPoG SRGP SRms WBou |
| | 'Mrs Pinehurst' (Vt) | CGro |
| | 'Mrs R. Barton' (Vt) | CGro SHar |
| | 'Mulberry' (Vt) **new** | CGro |
| | 'Myfawnny' (Va) | CAby CMea ECho ECtt ELan EWes GKir GMac LRHS SRms WBou WFar |
| | 'Neapolitan' | see *V.* 'Pallida Plena' |
| § | 'Nellie Britton' (Va) ♀$^{H4}$ | ECho ECtt SRms |
| | 'Netta Statham' | see *V.* 'Belmont Blue' |
| | 'Nora' | WBou |
| | 'Norah Church' (Vt) | CGro SSvw |
| | 'Norah Leigh' (Va) | EOHP WBou |
| | ***obliqua*** | see *V. cucullata* |
| | ***odorata*** (Vt) | CArn CBcs CBod CGro CRWN CSWP EBee EGoo EPfP GBar GMac GPoy LCro LRHS MRav NCob NPri NSco SIde SIng SPer SRms SVic WBor |

| | | |
|---|---|---|
| | – 'Alba' (Vt) | CBre CGro CPom CSWP CWan EBee ECho ELan EPfP EShb GBar ILis LAst MHer NCob NPri SRms WMoo |
| | – 'Alba Plena' (dVt) | EHrv WHer |
| | – 'Albiflora' | CEnt |
| | – apricot-flowered | see *V.* 'Sulfurea' |
| | – blue, double-flowered (d) | LHop |
| | – 'Dawnie' (Vt) **new** | CGro |
| | – var. ***dumetorum*** | see *V. alba* |
| | – 'Katy' | CPom |
| | – 'King of Violets' (dVt) | EBee SHar WCot WFar |
| | – pink-flowered | see *V. odorata* Rosea Group |
| | – 'Red Devil' | WCot WFar |
| | – ***rosea*** | see *V. odorata* Rosea Group |
| § | – Rosea Group (Vt) | CDes CEnt CPom EBee GBar GMac IFoB MRav SIde SIng WCot |
| * | – subsp. ***subcarnea*** (Vt) | SEND |
| | – 'Sulphurea' | see *V.* 'Sulfurea' |
| | – 'Weimar' | GBin |
| | 'Opéra' (Vt) | CGro LLHF |
| | 'Orchid Pink' (Vt) | CGro EBee GMaP SHar |
| § | 'Pallida Plena' (dPVt) | CBre CGro |
| | ***palmata*** | NPro |
| | 'Palmer's White' (Va) | WBou |
| | ***palustris*** | CRWN WHer WSFF WShi |
| | 'Pamela Zambra' (Vt) | GMaP SHar WPrP |
| | ***papilionacea*** | see *V. sororia* |
| * | 'Paradise Blue' (Vt) | CGro |
| | 'Parchment' (Vt) **new** | CGro |
| | 'Parme de Toulouse' (dPVt) | CGro |
| | 'Pasha' (Va) | GMac |
| | 'Pat Creasy' (Va) | CAby WBou |
| | 'Pat Kavanagh' (C) | CAby GAbr NChi NDov WBou |
| | 'Patience' | WBou |
| | ***pedata*** | CBro EBee EPot SKHP WAbe WHil WPer |
| | – f. ***alba*** **new** | IFoB |
| | – 'Bicolor' | WAbe |
| | ***pedatifida*** | CElw EBee MTho |
| | ***pensylvanica*** | see *V. pubescens* var. *eriocarpa* |
| | 'Peppered-palms' | EHrv |
| | 'Perle Rose' (Vt) | CGro EHrv EShb SHar |
| | x ***permixta*** | EMon |
| | 'Petra' (Vtta) | CAby GMac |
| | 'Phyl Dove' (Vt) | CGro |
| | 'Pickering Blue' (Va) | WBou |
| | 'Primrose Dame' (Va) | WBou |
| | 'Primrose Pixie' (Va) | WBou |
| | 'Prince Henry' (T) | MNHC |
| | 'Prince John' (T) | MNHC |
| | 'Princess Mab' (Vtta) | WBou |
| | 'Princess of Prussia' (Vt) | CBre CGro |
| | 'Princess of Wales' | see *V.* 'Princesse de Galles' |
| § | 'Princesse de Galles' (Vt) | CGro CTri NSti WHal |
| | 'Pritchard's Russian' (Vt) | CGro |
| | 'Prolific' (Vt) **new** | CGro |
| § | ***pubescens*** var. ***eriocarpa*** | SRms |
| | 'Purple Wings' (Va) | WBou |
| | 'Putty' | ECou |
| | Queen Charlotte | see *V.* 'Königin Charlotte' |
| | 'Queen Victoria' | see *V.* 'Victoria Regina' |
| | 'Raven' | GMac WBou |
| | 'Rawson's White' (Vt) | CGro |
| | 'Rebecca' (Vtta) | Widely available |
| | 'Rebecca Cawthorne' (C) | EBee |
| | 'Red Charm' (Vt) | EBee |
| | 'Red Giant' (Vt) | CGro CPrp EBla EHrv MRav |
| | 'Red Lion' (Vt) | CGro |
| | 'Red Queen' (Vt) | CGro NSti |
| | ***reichei*** | CRWN |
| | ***reichenbachiana*** | EBWF |
| | 'Reine des Blanches' (dVt) | EBee WCot |

'Reine des Neiges' (Vt) **new** CGro
***reniforme*** see *V. hederacea*
'Richard Staples' **new** SRGP
'Richard's Yellow' (Va) NCob
***riviniana*** CArn CRWN CSec EBWF MHer NSco SEND WHer WJek WSFF WShi
- dark pink-flowered **new** WAlt
- 'Ed's Variegated' (v) CBow EPPr WCot
§ - Purpurea Group Widely available
- white-flowered EBee EWes WAlt
'Rodney Davey' (Vt/v) NBir
'Rodney Marsh' NBir
'Rosanna' (Vt) NCob
'Roscastle Black' CMea EBee ECtt GMaP GMac LRHS NDov SMrm SPoG WBou WCot WPGP
'Rose Madder' (Vt) CGro
'Rosine' (Vt) CGro
'Royal Elk' (Vt) CGro
'Royal Robe' (Vt) CGro
'Rubra' (Vt) CGro WPer WPtf
§ ***rupestris*** CTri CWan ECho
* ***- rosea*** CEnt CPom CSsd EBee EDAr EPfP EShb IFro LLWP MHer NChi NWCA SBch STre WEas WOut
'Saint Helena' (Vt) CGro
***schariensis*** EWes
***selkirkii*** NBro NWCA
- 'Variegata' (v) GBuc NBir
***sempervirens*** SKHP
***septentrionalis*** see *V. sororia*
***- alba*** see *V. sororia* 'Albiflora'
- 'Rubra' CSec
'Serena' (Va) WBou
'Sherbet Dip' WBou
'Shirobana' NBir WCru
'Sidborough Poppet' CStu EWes
§ 'Sissinghurst' (Va) MHer NBir
'Sisters' (Vt) CGro
'Smugglers' Moon' CAby WBou
'Sophie' (Vtta) WBou
§ ***sororia*** EAEE EBee ECho EPPr LRHS MLHP MNrw NBir NBro WBrE WPen
* - 'Albiflora' ♀H4 CBre CGro CHFP CHid CMMP CSWP CWCL EBee EBrs ECho EMil EPfP GGar LEdu LRHS NWCA SPhx WCAu WCFE WFar WJek WPer
§ - 'Freckles' Widely available
- 'Freckles' dark EBee ECho LHop NWCA SPhx
- 'Priceana' CBre CCge CDes CElw CMMP EAEE EBee ECGP ECha EPyc EWTr NBir NChi SMrm WCot WPGP
- 'Red Sister' MHer
- 'Speckles' (v) CBow CPrp EBla EMon
* 'Spencer's Cottage' WBou
'Steyning' (Va) WBou
***stojanowii*** CEnt CSpe EBee ECho
***striata*** WRos
§ 'Sulfurea' (Vt) CEnt CGro CPBP CPMA EBee ECho EShb GMaP LLWP MHar MMHG NRya NWCA WCot WEas WFar WPer
- lemon-flowered (Vt) CGro
'Susan Chilcott' (Vt) **new** CGro
'Susanne Lucas' (Vt) **new** CGro
'Susie' (Va) WBou
'Swanley White' see *V.* 'Conte di Brazza'
'Sybil' (SP) WBou
'Sylvia Hart' MTho
'Tanith' (Vt) EBee
§ 'The Czar' (Vt) CBre CCge ILis NChi
'Tiger Eyes' (Va) EBee MWea SPoG
'Tina' (Va) EBee
'Titania' (Va) CGro
'Tom Tit' (Va) WBou
'Tony Venison' (C/v) EBee MTho SPoG SRGP WBou WFar WHer
***tricolor*** CPrp EBWF ECho EPfP GBar GPoy MHer MNHC NGHP NPri NSco SBch SECG SIde WJek
***vaginata*** **new** EBee
'Vanessa' (Va) GMac
***velutina*** see *V. gracilis*
***verecunda*** CLAP WSHC
- B&SWJ 604a WCru
'Victoria Cawthorne' (C) CAby CElw GBuc GMaP MCot MHer MSte MWat NChi NDov SHGN WBou WEas
§ 'Victoria Regina' (Vt) CBre CGro
'Virginia' (Va) WBou
'Vita' (Va) CAby GAbr GBuc GMac NDov SRms WBou
'Wasp' (Va) CAby GMac
'White Ladies' see *V. cucullata* 'Alba'
'White Pearl' (Va) SPhx WBou
'White Perfection' (C) LRHS
'White Swan' (Va) NChi
'William' (Va) NDov
'Winifred Jones' (Va) WBou
'Winona Cawthorne' (C) CAby EBee GAbr GMac NChi NDov
'Wisley White' EBee EWes WFar
'Woodlands Cream' (Va) GMac MHer NCob WBou
'Woodlands Lilac' (Va) WBou
'Yellow Prince' **new** EAlp
***yezoensis*** CSec
'Zara' (Va) WBou
'Zoe' (Vtta) EBee ECtt NPri SPer SPoG SRGP WBou WFar

## *Viscaria* (*Caryophyllaceae*)

***vulgaris*** see *Lychnis viscaria*

## *Vitaliana* (*Primulaceae*)

§ ***primuliflora*** ECho GKev NLAp NMen NRya NSla
- subsp. ***cinerea*** GKev
- subsp. ***praetutiana*** NHol NMen NWCA WPat
- subsp. ***tridentata*** NMen

## *Vitex* (*Verbenaceae*)

***agnus-castus*** CAgr CArn CBcs CDul COld EBee EOHP EShb GPoy LEdu LRHS MCCP MHer MNrw SLon SPer WDin WFar WHer WSHC
- 'Alba' CWib EBee EPfP
- var. ***latifolia*** CWib EBee ELan EPfP LRHS LSRN NLar NScw SPoG WPGP
I - 'Rosea' NLar
- 'Silver Spire' EBee ELan LRHS SPoG WPGP
***incisa*** see *V. negundo* var. *heterophylla*
***lucens*** CHEx
***negundo*** CArn EOHP
§ - var. ***heterophylla*** EWes

## *Vitis* ✿ (*Vitaceae*)

'Abundante' (F) WSuV
'Alden' (O/B) WSuV
'Amandin' (G/W) WSuV
***amurensis*** EBee EPfP LRHS MBri NLar
- B&SWJ 4138 WCru
'Atlantis' (O/W) WSuV
'Aurore' (W) WSuV
'Baco Noir' (O/B) GTwe SDea WSuV
'Bianca' (O/W) MCoo WSuV
Black Hamburgh see *V. vinifera* 'Schiava Grossa'
* 'Black Strawberry' (B) WSuV

| | | |
|---|---|---|
| § | 'Boskoop Glory' (O/B) $\Upsilon^{H4}$ | CMac EMil LBuc MAsh MCoo NBlu NPal SCoo SDea SEND WSuV |
| | 'Brant' (O/B) $\Upsilon^{H4}$ | Widely available |
| | 'Brilliant' (B) | WSuV |
| | 'Buffalo' (B) | WSuV |
| | 'Canadice' (O/R/S) | SDea WSuV |
| | 'Cascade' | see *V.* Seibel 13053 |
| | Castel 19637 (B) | WSuV |
| | 'Chambourcin' (B) | WSuV |
| | ***coignetiae*** $\Upsilon^{H4}$ | Widely available |
| | - B&SWJ 4550 from Korea | WCru |
| | - B&SWJ 4744 | WCru |
| | - B&SWJ 10882 from Japan new | WCru |
| | - Claret Cloak = 'Frovit'$^{PBR}$ | CBcs EBee ELan EPfP GKir LRHS LSRN MAsh MRav NLar SCoo SPer SPoG SSpi WPGP WPat |
| | - var. ***glabrescens*** B&SWJ 8537 | WCru |
| | 'Dalkauer' (W) | WSuV |
| I | 'Diamond' (B) | WSuV |
| | 'Dutch Black' (O/B) | WSuV |
| | 'Edwards No 1' (O/W) | WSuV |
| | 'Eger Csillaga' (O/W) | WSuV |
| | 'Einset' (B/S) | WSuV |
| | ***ficifolia*** | see *V. thunbergii* |
| | ***flexuosa*** B&SWJ 5568 | WCru |
| | - var. ***choii*** B&SWJ 4101 | WCru |
| § | 'Fragola' (O/R) | CAgr CMac CTri EBee EMil EPfP GTwe LCro LRHS MAsh MRav SDea SPer SRms WSuV |
| | 'Gagarin Blue' (O/B) | CAgr EMui GTwe SDea WSuV |
| | 'Glenora' (F/B/S) | WSuV |
| | 'Hecker' (O/W) | WSuV |
| | ***henryana*** | see *Parthenocissus henryana* |
| | 'Himrod' (O/W/S) | CCCN GTwe NPal SDea WSuV |
| | 'Horizon' (O/W) | WSuV |
| | ***inconstans*** | see *Parthenocissus tricuspidata* |
| | 'Interlaken' (O/W/S) | WSuV |
| | 'Kempsey Black' (O/B) | WSuV |
| | 'Kozmapalme Muscatoly' (O/W) | WSuV |
| | 'Kuibishevski' (O/R) | WSuV |
| | Landot 244 (O/B) | WSuV |
| | 'Léon Millot' (O/G/B) | CAgr CSBt EMui LRHS LSRN SDea WSuV |
| | 'Maréchal Foch' (O/B) | WSuV |
| | 'Maréchal Joffre' (O/B) | GTwe WSuV |
| | 'Mars' (O/B/S) | WSuV |
| | 'Merzling' (O/W) new | WSuV |
| | 'Munson R.W.' (O/R) new | WSuV |
| | 'Muscat Bleu' (O/B) | CCCN EMui WSuV |
| | 'Nero'$^{PBR}$ | CAgr |
| | 'New York Muscat' (O/B) $\Upsilon^{H4}$ | WSuV |
| | 'New York Seedless' (O/W/S) | WSuV |
| | 'Niagara' (O/W) | WSuV |
| | 'Niederother Monschrebe' (O/R) | WSuV |
| | Oberlin 595 (O/B) | WSuV |
| | 'Orion' (O/W) | EMui WSuV |
| | 'Paletina' (O/W) | WSuV |
| | parsley-leaved | see *V. vinifera* 'Ciotat' |
| | ***parvifolia*** | WPat |
| | 'Perdin' (O/W) | WSuV |
| | 'Phönix' (O/W) | CAgr EMil EMui GTwe MBri MGos NLar SKee SLim SPoG SVic WSuV |
| | ***piasezkii*** B&SWJ 5236 | WCru |
| * | 'Pink Strawberry' (O) | WSuV |
| | 'Pirovano 14' (O/B) | GTwe SDea WSuV |
| § | 'Plantet' (O/B) | WSuV |
| * | 'Poloske Muscat' (W) | EMui GTwe WSuV |

| | | |
|---|---|---|
| | ***pseudoreticulata*** | WPGP |
| | ***purpurea*** 'Spetchley Park' (O/B) | WSuV |
| | ***quinquefolia*** | see *Parthenocissus quinquefolia* |
| | 'Ramdas' (O/W) | WSuV |
| | Ravat 51 (O/W) | WSuV |
| | 'Rayon d'Or' (O/W) | WSuV |
| | 'Regent'$^{PBR}$ | CAgr CWSG EMui GTwe MBri MCoo MGos NLar SKee SLim SPoG WOrn WSuV |
| | 'Reliance' (O/R/S) | WSuV |
| | 'Rembrant' (R) | NPal WSuV |
| | ***riparia*** | NLar WCru |
| | 'Romulus' (O/G/W/S) new | WSuV |
| | 'Rondo' (O/B) | EMui |
| | - EM 6494-5 | WSuV |
| | 'Saturn' (O/R/S) | WSuV |
| | 'Schuyler' (O/B) | WSuV |
| | Seibel (F) | GTwe SDea |
| | Seibel 5279 | see *V.* 'Aurora' |
| | Seibel 5409 (W) | WSuV |
| | Seibel 5455 | see *V.* 'Plantet' |
| | Seibel 7053 | WSuV |
| | Seibel 9549 | WSuV |
| § | Seibel 13053 (O/B) | LRHS MAsh SDea WSuV |
| | Seibel 138315 (R) | WSuV |
| | 'Seneca' (W) | WSuV |
| | 'Serena' (O/W) | WSuV |
| § | 'Seyval Blanc' (O/W) | CAgr GTwe SDea WSuV |
| | Seyve Villard | NPer |
| | Seyve Villard 12.375 | see *V.* 'Villard Blanc' |
| | Seyve Villard 20.473 (F) | LRHS MAsh NPer |
| | Seyve Villard 5276 | see *V.* 'Seyval Blanc' |
| | 'Solaris' (O/W) new | WSuV |
| | 'Stauffer' (O/W) new | WSuV |
| | 'Suffolk Seedless' (B/S) | WSuV |
| | 'Tereshkova' (O/B) | CAgr SDea WSuV |
| | 'Thornton' (O/S) | WSuV |
| § | ***thunbergii*** B&SWJ 4702 | WCru |
| | 'Triomphe d'Alsace' (O/B) | CAgr CSBt EMui LRHS NPer SDea WSuV |
| | 'Trollinger' | see *V. vinifera* 'Schiava Grossa' |
| | 'Vanessa' (O/R/S) | SDea WSuV |
| § | 'Villard Blanc' (O/W) | WSuV |
| | ***vinifera*** | GKir MGos STrG |
| | - EM 323158B | WSuV |
| | - 'Abouriou' (O/B) | WSuV |
| | - 'Acolon' (O/B) | WSuV |
| | - 'Adelheidtraube' (O/W) | WSuV |
| | - 'Albalonga' (W) | WSuV |
| § | - 'Alicante' (G/B) | GTwe NPal SDea WSuV |
| | - 'Apiifolia' | see *V. vinifera* 'Ciotat' |
| | - 'Augusta Louise' (O/W) | WSuV |
| | - 'Auxerrois' (O/W) | WSuV |
| | - 'Bacchus' (O/W) | MBri NLar SDea SVic WSuV |
| | - 'Baresana' (G/W) | WSuV |
| | - 'Beauty' | CAgr |
| | - 'Black Alicante' | see *V. vinifera* 'Alicante' |
| | - 'Black Frontignan' (G/O/B) | WSuV |
| | - Black Hamburgh | see *V. vinifera* 'Schiava Grossa' |
| | - 'Black Monukka' (G/B/S) | WSuV |
| | - 'Black Prince' (G/B) | WSuV |
| | - 'Blue Portuguese' | see *V. vinifera* 'Portugieser' |
| § | - 'Bouvier' (W) | WSuV |
| | - 'Bouviertraube' | see *V. vinifera* 'Bouvier' |
| | - 'Buckland Sweetwater' (G/W) | GTwe MGos SDea WSuV |
| | - 'Cabernet Sauvignon' (O/B) | LRHS MAsh MGos NPer SDea WSuV |
| | - 'Cardinal' (O/R) | EMil WSuV |
| | - 'Carla' (O/R) new | WSuV |
| | - 'Centennial' (O/N/S) new | WSuV |

| | |
|---|---|
| - 'Chardonnay' (O/W) | CCCN EMui LRHS MAsh NPer SDea SVic WSuV |
| § - 'Chasselas' (G/O/W) | LRHS MAsh SDea WSuV |
| - 'Chasselas Blanc' (O/W) **new** | SVic |
| - 'Chasselas de Fontainebleau' (F) | CCCN EMil |
| - 'Chasselas de Tramontaner' (F) | EMil |
| - 'Chasselas d'Or' | see *V. vinifera* 'Chasselas' |
| - 'Chasselas Rosé' (G/R) | SVic WSuV |
| - 'Chasselas Rosé Royal' (O/R) | CCCN |
| - 'Chasselas Vibert' (G/W) | WSuV |
| - 'Chenin Blanc' (O/W) | WSuV |
| § - 'Ciotat' (F) | SDea WSuV |
| - 'Cot Précoce de Tours' (O/B) | WSuV |
| - 'Crimson Seedless' (R/S) | WSuV |
| - 'Csabyongye' (O/W) | WSuV |
| - 'Dattier de Beyrouth' (G/W) | EMil WSuV |
| - 'Dattier Saint Vallier' (O/W) | SVic WSuV |
| - 'Dolcetto' (O/B) | WSuV |
| - 'Dornfelder' (O/R) | CCCN CSut NLar SPoG WSuV |
| - 'Dunkelfelder' (O/R) | WSuV |
| - 'Early Van der Laan' (F) | NBlu |
| - 'Ehrenfelser' (O/W) | WSuV |
| - 'Elbling' (O/W) | WSuV |
| - 'Exalta' (G/W/S) **new** | CCCN WSuV |
| - 'Excelsior' (W) | WSuV |
| - 'Faber' (O/W) | WSuV |
| - 'Fiesta' (W/S) | WSuV |
| - 'Findling' (W) | WSuV |
| - 'Flame' | CAgr EMui |
| - 'Flame Red' (O/D) | CCCN |
| - 'Flame Seedless' (G/O/R/S) | EMui SPoG WSuV |
| - 'Forta' (O/W) | WSuV |
| - 'Foster's Seedling' (G/W) | GTwe SDea SVic WSuV |
| - 'Freisamer' (O/W) **new** | WSuV |
| - 'Frühburgunder' (O/B) | WSuV |
| - 'Gamay Hâtif des Vosges' | WSuV |
| - 'Gamay Noir' (O/B) | WSuV |
| - Gamay Teinturier Group (O/B) | WSuV |
| - 'Gewürztraminer' (O/R) | LRHS MAsh SDea WSuV |
| - 'Glory of Boskoop' | see *V.* 'Boskoop Glory' |
| - 'Golden Chasselas' | see *V. vinifera* 'Chasselas' |
| - 'Goldriesling' (O/W) | WSuV |
| - 'Gros Colmar' (G/B) | WSuV |
| - 'Grüner Veltliner' (O/W) | WSuV |
| - 'Gutenborner' (O/W) | WSuV |
| - 'Helfensteiner' (O/R) | WSuV |
| - 'Huxelrebe' (O/W) | WSuV |
| - 'Incana' (O/B) | EBee EPfP GCal MRav WCFE WCot WSHC |
| - 'Juliaumsrebe' (O/W) | WSuV |
| - 'Kanzler' (O/W) | WSuV |
| - 'Kerner' (O/W) | WSuV |
| - 'Kernling' (F) | WSuV |
| - 'King's Ruby' (F/S) | WSuV |
| - 'Lakemont' (O/W/S) | CAgr CCCN EMil EMui GTwe LRHS MBri SKee WSuV |
| - 'Lival' (O/B) | WSuV |
| - 'Madeleine Angevine' (O/W) | CAgr CDul EMui GTwe LRHS LSRN MAsh MGos NPer SDea WSuV |
| - 'Madeleine Celine' (B) | WSuV |
| - 'Madeleine Royale' (G/W) | WSuV |
| - 'Madeleine Silvaner' (O/W) | CSBt EMui GTwe LRHS MAsh MGos NPer SDea SPer WBVN WSuV |
| - 'Madresfield Court' (G/B) | GTwe WSuV |

| | |
|---|---|
| - 'Merlot' (G/B) | SDea WSuV |
| § - 'Meunier' (B) | WSuV |
| - 'Mireille' (F) | GTwe SDea WSuV |
| - 'Morio Muscat' (O/W) | WSuV |
| - 'Muscat Blanc à Petits Grains' (O/W) | SWvt WSuV |
| § - 'Müller-Thurgau' (O/W) | EMui GTwe LRHS LSRN MAsh MGos NPri SDea SPer SVic WSuV |
| - 'Muscat de Lierval' (O/B) | WSuV |
| - 'Muscat de Saumur' (O/W) | WSuV |
| - 'Muscat Hamburg' (G/B) | EMil EMui LRHS LSRN MAsh MGos NScw SDea SWvt WSuV |
| - 'Muscat of Alexandria' (G/W) | CBcs CCCN CMac EMui MRav NPal SDea SPer SVic |
| - 'Muscat Ottonel' (O/W) | WSuV |
| - 'Muscat Saint Laurent' (W) | WSuV |
| - 'Nebbiolo' (O/B) | WSuV |
| - 'No 69' (W) | WSuV |
| - 'Noir Hâtif de Marseille' (O/B) | WSuV |
| - 'Olive Blanche' (O/W) | WSuV |
| - 'Oliver Irsay' (O/W) | WSuV |
| - 'Optima' (O/W) | WSuV |
| - 'Ora' (O/W/S) | WSuV |
| - 'Ortega' (O/W) | CCCN WSuV |
| - 'Perle' (O/W) | WSuV |
| - 'Perle de Czaba' (G/O/W) | EMil WSuV |
| - 'Perlette' (O/W/S) | CCCN CSut EMui LRHS MAsh NPri WSuV |
| - 'Petit Rouge' (R) | WSuV |
| - 'Pinot Blanc' (O/W) | CCCN LRHS MAsh SVic WSuV |
| - 'Pinot Gris' (O/B) | SDea WSuV |
| - 'Pinot Noir' (O/B) | CCCN LRHS NPal SVic WSuV |
| § - 'Portugieser' (O/B) | WSuV |
| - 'Précoce de Bousquet' (O/W) | WSuV |
| - 'Précoce de Malingre' (O/W) | SDea |
| - 'Prima' (O/B) | WSuV |
| - 'Primavis Frontignan' (G/W) | WSuV |
| - 'Purpurea' (O/B) 🏆$^{H4}$ | Widely available |
| - 'Queen of Esther' (B) | GTwe MBri NLar SKee SLim SPoG WSuV |
| - 'Regner' (O/W) | WSuV |
| - 'Reichensteiner' (O/G/W) | SDea WSuV |
| - 'Riesling' (O/W) | CCCN LRHS MAsh SVic WSuV |
| - Riesling-Silvaner | see *V. vinifera* 'Müller-Thurgau' |
| - 'Rotberger' (O/G/B) **new** | WSuV |
| - 'Royal Muscadine' (G/O/W) | WSuV |
| - 'Saint Laurent' (G/O/W) | SVic WSuV |
| - 'Sauvignon Blanc' (O/W) | CCCN WSuV |
| - 'Scheurebe' (O/W) | WSuV |
| § - 'Schiava Grossa' (G/B/D) | Widely available |
| - 'Schönburger' (O/W) | SDea WSuV |
| - 'Schwarzriesling' | see *V. vinifera* 'Meunier' |
| - 'Sémillon' | LRHS MAsh |
| - 'Senator' (O/W) **new** | WSuV |
| - 'Septimer' (O/W) | WSuV |
| - 'Shiraz' (B) | WSuV |
| - 'Siegerrebe' (O/W/D) | CAgr EMui GTwe LRHS MAsh NPer SDea WSuV |
| - 'Silvaner' (O/W) | EMui WSuV |
| - 'Spetchley Red' | WCot WCru WPGP WPat |
| - strawberry grape | see *V.* 'Fragola' |
| § - 'Sultana' (W/S) | CAgr CCCN EMui GTwe SDea WSuV |

| | | |
|---|---|---|
| | - 'Theresa' | MBri SPoG WOrn WSuV |
| | - 'Thompson Seedless' | see *V. vinifera* 'Sultana' |
| * | - 'Triomphe' (O/B) | EMui |
| | - 'Triomphrebe' (W) | WSuV |
| | - 'Vitalis Gold' | MGos |
| | - 'Vitalis Ruby' | MGos |
| | - 'Wrotham Pinot' (O/B) | SDea WSuV |
| | - 'Würzer' (O/W) | WSuV |
| | - 'Zweigeltrebe' (O/B) | WSuV |
| * | 'White Strawberry' (O/W) | WSuV |
| | 'Zalagyöngye' (W) | WSuV |

## *Vriesea* (*Bromeliaceae*)

| | | |
|---|---|---|
| | ***carinata*** | MBri |
| | ***hieroglyphica*** | MBri |
| | x ***poelmanii*** | MBri |
| | x ***polonia*** | MBri |
| | ***saundersii*** ♀H1 | MBri |
| | ***splendens*** ♀H1 | MBri XBlo |
| | 'Vulkana' | MBri |

# W

## *Wachendorfia* (*Haemodoraceae*)

| | | |
|---|---|---|
| | ***brachyandra*** | GCal GGar |
| | ***thyrsiflora*** | CAbb CDes CFir CHEx CMCo CPLG CPen CPne CTsd EBee IGor LEdu WFar WPGP WPic |

## *Wahlenbergia* (*Campanulaceae*)

| | | |
|---|---|---|
| | sp. | ECou |
| | ***albomarginata*** | ECho ECou GGar GKev LRHS NWCA |
| | - 'Blue Mist' | ECho ECou |
| | ***ceracea*** | NLAp |
| | ***congesta*** | ECho LRHS |
| | ***cuspidata*** | GKev |
| | ***gloriosa*** | ECho ECou LRHS NLAp WAbe WFar |
| | ***pumilio*** | see *Edraianthus pumilio* |
| | ***rivularis*** | CSec |
| § | ***saxicola*** | CRow ECho GKev NWCA |
| | ***serpyllifolia*** | see *Edraianthus serpyllifolius* |
| | ***stricta*** | ECou GKev |
| | ***tasmanica*** | see *W. saxicola* |
| | ***undulata*** | CSec CSpe |

## *Waldsteinia* (*Rosaceae*)

| | | |
|---|---|---|
| | ***fragarioides*** | CSec |
| | ***geoides*** | EBee EPPr EPfP LAst NBre NLar NPro SPer |
| | ***ternata*** | Widely available |
| § | - 'Mozaick' (v) | EBee EWes NBid NBir NBre NPro |
| | - 'Variegata' | see *W. ternata* 'Mozaick' |

## walnut, black see *Juglans nigra*

## walnut, common see *Juglans regia*

## *Wallichia* (*Arecaceae*)

| | | |
|---|---|---|
| | ***densiflora*** | LPal |
| | ***disticha*** | LPal |

## *Wasabia* (*Brassicaceae*)

| | | |
|---|---|---|
| | ***wasabi*** | CArn GPoy LEdu |

## *Washingtonia* (*Arecaceae*)

| | | |
|---|---|---|
| | ***filifera*** ♀H1 | CAbb CCCN CDoC CPHo EAmu EShb ETod EUJe LPal MBri NMyG SAPC SArc SBig SEND SPlb WBrE |
| | ***robusta*** | CTrC EAmu LPal NPal SChr SPlb |

## *Watsonia* (*Iridaceae*)

| | | |
|---|---|---|
| | ***aletroides*** | CDes CPen CTca EBee EBrs ECho ERCP GCal LPio NCGa SKHP WCot WPGP |
| | ***angusta*** | CDes CGHE CPen CPne CPrp EBee IBlr WPGP |
| | - JCA 3.950.409 | WCot |
| | ***ardernei*** | see *W. borbonica* subsp. *ardernei* 'Arderne's White' |
| | ***beatricis*** | see *W. pillansii* |
| I | 'Best Red' | LPio WCot |
| § | ***borbonica*** | CAbb CPne CPou CPrp EShb NCot WCot |
| | - subsp. ***ardernei*** misapplied | see *W. borbonica* subsp. *ardernei* (Sander) Goldblatt 'Arderne's White' |
| | - subsp. ***ardernei*** (Sander) Goldblatt | EShb |
| § | - - 'Arderne's White' | CBre CDes CFul CGHE CPen CPne CPrp CTca CWsd EBee EBrs ECho ERos EShb GGar IBlr LPio MSte WPGP WPic |
| | - subsp. ***borbonica*** | CDes CWsd EBee IBlr WPGP |
| | ***brevifolia*** | see *W. laccata* |
| | ***coccinea*** Baker | see *W. spectabilis* |
| | ***coccinea*** Herb. ex Baker | CPBP WCot WPGP |
| | ***densiflora*** | CPou EShb IBlr IDee MSte WCot |
| | ***distans*** | EBee |
| | 'Flame' | NCGa |
| | ***fourcadei*** | CPne EBee EShb WPGP |
| | ***fulgens*** | CPne LEdu MSte |
| | ***galpinii*** | CFir EBee IBlr NCot WPGP |
| | - pink-flowered | CPrp |
| | ***gladioloides*** | WPGP |
| § | ***humilis*** | CDes CPBP CPou CPrp EBee WPGP |
| | ***knysnana*** | CDes CPou CPrp EShb IBlr WCot WPGP |
| § | ***laccata*** | CDes CFir CPBP CPne CPou CPrp EBee EShb ITim WCot WHil WPGP |
| | ***lepida*** | CPou EBee IBlr SKHP |
| | x ***longifolia*** | WCot |
| | ***marginata*** | CDes CPou SKHP WCot WHil WPGP |
| | - 'Star Spike' | WCot |
| | ***meriania*** | CPen CPou EBee ERCP IBlr NCGa WCot WHil |
| | - var. ***bulbillifera*** | CGHE CPrp CTca EBee EBrs ECho GAbr GCra GGal GGar GMac IBlr LPio NCot WPGP |
| * | 'Mount Congreve' | CTca |
| | 'Peachy Pink Orphan' **new** | CDes |
| § | ***pillansii*** | CAbb CGHE CHEx CPLG CPen CPne CPou CPrp CTca EBee ERos EShb IBlr LRHS SMrm WFar WMnd |
| | - pink-flowered | CPen CPrp |
| | - red-flowered | GBin |
| | - salmon-flowered | CPen |
| | pink-flowered | CDes EBee |
| | ***pyramidata*** | see *W. borbonica* |
| | ***roseoalba*** | see *W. humilis* |
| | ***schlechteri*** | WPGP |
| § | ***spectabilis*** | CPne WFar WPGP |
| | 'Stanford Scarlet' | CDes CPne CPou CPrp CWsd ELon GGar IBlr SChr SHom WPGP WSHC |
| | ***stenosiphon*** | IBlr |
| | ***strubeniae*** | IBlr |
| | ***tabularis*** | CAbb IBlr WCot |
| | ***transvaalensis*** | EBee |
| | 'Tresco Dwarf Pink' | CDes CPrp CSam IBlr LEdu WCot WPGP |

| | |
|---|---|
| Tresco hybrids | CAbb CHll CPen CPne CSsd GGal LRHS WCFE |
| ***vanderspuyae*** | CPLG CPne CPou CPrp IBlr NCot WCot WPGP |
| 'White Dazzler' | SApp |
| ***wilmaniae*** | CPne CPou CPrp EBee IBlr WPGP |
| - JCA 3.955200 | SKHP |
| - 'Ice Angel' | SKHP |
| ***zeyheri*** | WHil |

## *Wattakaka* see *Dregea*

## *Weigela* ✿ (*Caprifoliaceae*)

| | |
|---|---|
| CC 1231 | CPLG |
| 'Abel Carrière' | CMac CTri EBee ECtt EPfP EWes NWea SEND WCFE WFar |
| 'Anne Marie' | MGos |
| 'Avalanche' misapplied | see *W.* 'Candida' |
| 'Avalanche' Lemoine | see *W. praecox* 'Avalanche' |
| 'Boskoop Glory' | GQui SPer |
| § Briant Rubidor = 'Olympiade' (v) | CDoC CSBt CWSG EBee ECtt EHoe EMil EPfP GKir LAst LRHS MAsh MBNS MBar MGos MRav NCGa NHol NVic SEND SLim SPer SPlb SPoG WBod WFar |
| 'Bristol Ruby' | Widely available |
| § 'Candida' | CTri ELan EMil EWes MBar MRav NBlu NHol NLar SPer |
| 'Cappuccino' | EMil NLar SPoG |
| Carnaval = 'Courtalor'PBR | CBcs CWib EBee EMil EQua GKir LRHS LSou NHol NLar |
| 'Conquête' | GKir SLon |
| ***coraeensis*** | CHll MBlu MMHG WPat |
| - 'Alba' | SPer |
| ***decora*** | GQui |
| 'Eva Rathke' | CTri GKir NBir NLar NWea SCoo |
| 'Evita' | MBar MGos WFar |
| Feline = 'Courtamon' | MBri |
| ***florida*** | CDul EPfP MBar MGos SPad WGwG |
| - B&SWJ 8439 | WCru |
| - f. ***alba*** | CBcs WFar |
| * - 'Albovariegata' (v) | CPLG LAst WBVN |
| - 'Bicolor' | CMac ELan |
| - 'Bristol Snowflake' | CDul EBee EPfP GKir MBar MHer MSwo NBir NHol NLar SLon WBod |
| - 'Foliis Purpureis' 🏆H4 | Widely available |
| - Minor Black = 'Verweig 3' | MBri NLar NMun WCot |
| - Monet = 'Verweig'PBR (v) | EMil EPfP LAst LBuc LRHS MAsh MBri MCCP MGos MPkF NCGa NLar NMun NPri SLim SPoG WCot |
| - Moulin Rouge = 'Brigela'PBR | CBcs CDoC CSBt EPfP LBuc LRHS MBri MGos SPoG |
| - 'Pink Princess' | LRHS MSwo |
| - Rubigold | see *W.* Briant Rubidor |
| - 'Samabor' | WFar |
| - 'Sunny Princess' | EQua MBNS NHol NMun |
| - 'Suzanne' (v) | EBee MGos NPro |
| - 'Tango' | CPMA EBee ECtt LRHS MAsh NHol NPro |
| 'Florida Variegata' (v) 🏆H4 | Widely available |
| ***florida*** 'Versicolor' | CMHG CMac CPLG CWib GQui SLon SMrm WFar WGor |
| - Wine and Roses = 'Alexandra' | CAbP CBcs CDoC EBee EHoe ELan EMil EPfP GKir LAst LRHS LSRN MAsh MBri MGos MRav MWat NCGa NLar NPri SPoG SRGP SWvt WFar WLeb |
| 'Gold Rush' | EHoe NHol NLar |
| 'Golden Candy' | NPro |
| 'Gustave Malet' | CMCN GQui |
| ***hortensis*** | CPLG |
| ***japonica*** 'Dart's Colourdream' | EBee ECtt EWes GKir LAst LSou MRav NHol SCoo SLim |
| 'Jean's Gold' | ELan MGos MRav |
| 'Kosteriana Variegata' (v) | CSBt EBee EWTr LRHS MAsh SLon WFar |
| 'Looymansii Aurea' | CMHG CPLG CTri EBee ELan EPfP GKir LAst MRav SLon SPer WBod WDin WFar WHar |
| Lucifer = 'Courtared'PBR | CBcs CDoC NHol |
| ***maximowiczii*** | CPLG EBee GQui |
| § ***middendorffiana*** | Widely available |
| 'Minuet' | EBee EPfP MBar MGos MRav MSwo NPro SLPl |
| 'Mont Blanc' | MMHG |
| Nain Rouge = 'Courtanin'PBR | CBcs EBee GGar LRHS MBri NHol |
| 'Nana Variegata' (v) | CPLG ECrN ELon EPfP LRHS MBar MBri MHav SLPl WGwG |
| Naomi Campbell = 'Bokrashine'PBR | CBow GBin GGar GKir MGos MMHG MWea NLar SCoo WFar WHar WMoo |
| 'Newport Red' | EBee GKir MBNS MRav MWat NWea WFar |
| 'Pink Poppet' | CAbP CSBt EBee EMil LAst LBMP LRHS LSRN LSou MAsh NHol NLar NPro SCoo SPoG SWvt |
| ***praecox*** | ECrN |
| § - 'Avalanche' | ECtt MRav SGar |
| 'Praecox Variegata' (v) 🏆H4 | CChe CMac CTri EBee ELan EPfP GKir LAst LRHS MAsh MRav NBir SDix SPer SPla SPoG SReu SRms WCFE WFar WHCG |
| 'Red Prince' 🏆H4 | EBee ECrN ELan LAst LRHS MGos MSwo NCGa NHol NLar SPoG WBod |
| Rubidor | see *W.* Briant Rubidor |
| Rubigold | see *W.* Briant Rubidor |
| 'Ruby Queen'PBR | EPfP |
| 'Rumba' | CMac MRav NPro |
| ***sessilifolia*** | see *Diervilla sessilifolia* |
| 'Snowflake' | CChe ECrN ECtt EWTr GKir MBNS NPro SRms WDin WFar |
| ***subsessilis*** B&SWJ 1056 | WCru |
| 'Victoria' | CDul CWib EBee ECrN ECtt EHoe ELan EPfP LAst LBMP LRHS MAsh MGos MSwo NBir NHol SCoo SPer SPla SPoG WBrE WFar WGor WHar WMoo |
| 'Wessex Gold' (v) | WHCG |

## *Weinmannia* (*Cunoniaceae*)

| | |
|---|---|
| ***racemosa*** 'Kamahi' | CTrC |
| ***trichosperma*** | IArd IDee SAPC SArc |

## *Weldenia* (*Commelinaceae*)

| | |
|---|---|
| ***candida*** | EBla ECho IBlr LLHF NMen SIng WAbe |

## *Westringia* (*Lamiaceae*)

| | |
|---|---|
| ***angustifolia*** | ECou |
| ***brevifolia*** | ECou |
| - var. ***raleighii*** | ECou |
| § ***fruticosa*** 🏆H1 | CArn CBcs CCCN ECou EShb WJek |
| - 'Smokie' | ECou |
| - 'Variegata' (v) | GQui LHop MNHC WJek |
| ***longifolia*** | CCCN ECou |
| ***rosmariniformis*** | see *W. fruticosa* |
| 'Smokie' | CCCN SOWG |
| 'Wynyabbie Gem' | EBee LHop SEND |

## whitecurrant see *Ribes rubrum* (W)

## *Widdringtonia* (*Cupressaceae*)

| | | |
|---|---|---|
| | ***cedarbergensis*** | CPne GGar |
| | ***cupressoides*** | see *W. nodiflora* |
| § | ***nodiflora*** | GGar |
| | ***schwarzii*** | CBcs GGar |

## *Wigandia* (*Hydrophyllaceae*)

| | | |
|---|---|---|
| | ***caracasana*** | CHll CKob |

## wineberry see *Rubus phoenicolasius*

## *Wikstroemia* (*Thymelaeaceae*)

| | | |
|---|---|---|
| | ***gemmata*** | SCoo SSta |
| | ***kudoi*** | WCru |

## *Wisteria* ✿ (*Papilionaceae*)

| | | |
|---|---|---|
| § | ***brachybotrys*** | SLau SLim |
| § | - Murasaki-kapitan | CEnd CTri |
| | - 'Pink Chiffon' | LRHS MAsh |
| | - 'Shiro-beni' | CTri LRHS MGos |
| § | - 'Shiro-kapitan' | CEnd CSPN CTri CWGN EBee EPfP LPan LRHS MBri MDun MGos MRav NHol SCoo SHBN SLau SPer WBod WPGP WPat |
| * | - 'White Silk' | CBcs CEnd LRHS LSRN MGos |
| § | 'Burford' | CEnd CSPN CWGN EMui ERas LAst LRHS LSRN MAsh MBri MDun MGan MWat NHol SCoo SLau SLim WHar WPGP |
| | 'Caroline' | CBcs CCCN CDoC CEnd CSBt CSPN CSam CWGN EBee EPfP ERas GKir LRHS LSRN MAsh MGos MLan NPri SBLw SHBN SLau SPer SPur SSpi WPGP WSHC |
| | ***floribunda*** | CBcs CRHN CWib ELan EPfP GGal LCro LRHS SBLw SHBN WDin WFar |
| § | - 'Alba' ♀H4 | Widely available |
| | - 'Black Dragon' | see *W. floribunda* 'Yae-kokuryū' |
| | - 'Burford' | see *W.* 'Burford' |
| * | - 'Cascade' | MGos |
| § | - 'Domino' | CEnd CMac CTri EBee ELon EPfP IArd LHop LPan LRHS LSRN MAsh MBar MGan MGos MRav NHol SBLw SCoo SLau SLim SPer SSta WFar |
| | - 'Fragrantissima' | see *W. sinensis* 'Jako' |
| | - 'Geisha' | CBcs CEnd MLan SBLw |
| | - 'Golden Dragon' | SLim |
| | - 'Hagoromo Nishiki' (V) | MGos |
| * | - 'Harlequin' | CBcs CSPN EBee ECrN ELon GCal LRHS MAsh MGos NLar WFar |
| | - 'Hocker Edge' | SLau |
| | - 'Hon-beni' | see *W. floribunda* 'Rosea' |
| | - 'Honey Bee Pink' | see *W. floribunda* 'Rosea' |
| | - 'Honko' | see *W. floribunda* 'Rosea' |
| | - 'Issai' | LRHS |
| | - 'Issai Perfect' | LPan LRHS LSRN MAsh NLar SCoo |
| | - 'Jakohn-fuji' | see *W. sinensis* 'Jako' |
| § | - 'Kuchi-beni' | CBcs CEnd CSBt CSPN EBee ELan LAst LHop LRHS LSRN MAsh MGos NHol NLar SCoo SLau SPer SPoG |
| | - 'Lawrence' | CEnd CSPN LRHS MBri NLar SLau |
| | - 'Lipstick' | see *W. floribunda* 'Kuchi-beni' |
| | - 'Longissima' | see *W. floribunda* 'Multijuga' |
| | - 'Longissima Alba' | see *W. floribunda* 'Alba' |
| | - 'Macrobotrys' | see *W. floribunda* 'Multijuga' |
| | - 'Magenta' | CBcs LRHS |
| § | - 'Multijuga' ♀H4 | Widely available |
| | - Murasaki-naga | see *W. floribunda* 'Purple Patches' |
| | - 'Murasaki-noda' | EWTr |
| | - 'Nana Richin's Purple' | CEnd LRHS SLau |
| | - 'Peaches and Cream' | see *W. floribunda* 'Kuchi-beni' |
| | - 'Pink Ice' | see *W. floribunda* 'Rosea' |
| § | - 'Purple Patches' | LRHS MGos NPri |
| | - Reindeer | see *W. sinensis* 'Jako' |
| § | - 'Rosea' ♀H4 | Widely available |
| | - 'Royal Purple' | LRHS MBri NLar SLau SPoG WFar WGor |
| | - 'Russelliana' | CBcs EBee |
| | - 'Shiro-naga' | see *W. floribunda* 'Alba' |
| | - 'Shiro-nagi' | see *W. floribunda* 'Alba' |
| | - 'Shiro-noda' | see *W. floribunda* 'Alba' |
| | - 'Snow Showers' | see *W. floribunda* 'Alba' |
| N | - 'Violacea Plena' (d) | CBcs CDoC CDul CMac ECrN EPfP EQua LPan LRHS MGos NBlu NPri SHBN SPur SSto SWvt WDin WFar |
| N | - 'Yae-kokuryū' (d) | Widely available |
| | x ***formosa*** | MGan SLau SLim |
| | - 'Black Dragon' | see *W. floribunda* 'Yae-kokuryū' (d) |
| | - 'Domino' | see *W. floribunda* 'Domino' |
| | - 'Issai' Wada pro parte | see *W. floribunda* 'Domino' |
| | - 'Kokuryū' | see *W. floribunda* 'Yae-kokuryū' (d) |
| | - 'Yae-kokuryū' | see *W. floribunda* 'Yae-kokuryū' |
| | ***frutescens*** | EBee MAsh SBLw SLim WFar |
| | - 'Amethyst Falls' PBR | CEnd CWGN IArd LRHS SCoo |
| | - 'Magnifica' | see *W. macrostachya* 'Magnifica' |
| | Kapitan-fuji | see *W. brachybotrys* |
| | 'Lavender Lace' | CDul EBee EPfP LRHS LSRN MAsh NLar SLau SPoG WFar |
| | ***macrostachya*** 'Clara Mack' | IArd |
| § | - 'Magnifica' | LRHS |
| | ***multijuga*** 'Alba' | see *W. floribunda* 'Alba' |
| | 'Showa-beni' | CEnd CWGN EBee LHop LRHS MAsh MGos SCoo SLau SLim SPoG WPGP |
| | ***sinensis*** ♀H4 | Widely available |
| | - 'Alba' ♀H4 | Widely available |
| | - 'Amethyst' | CBcs CEnd CSBt CSPN EBee EPfP LRHS LSRN MAsh MBri MDun MGos MRav NSti SBLw SLau SPla SPoG SReu |
| | - 'Blue Sapphire' | CBcs CSPN EBee LRHS LSRN SLau SPur |
| * | - 'Caerulea' **new** | GAuc |
| | - 'Consequa' | see *W. sinensis* 'Prolific' |
| § | - 'Jako' | CEnd MGos |
| | - 'Oosthoek's Variety' | see *W. sinensis* 'Prolific' |
| I | - 'Pink Ice' | EWTr MAsh |
| | - 'Prematura' | see *W. floribunda* 'Domino' |
| | - 'Prematura Alba' | see *W. brachybotrys* 'Shiro-kapitan' |
| § | - 'Prolific' | Widely available |
| | - 'Rosea' | LSRN MGos SPur SWvt |
| | - 'Shiro-capital' | see *W. brachybotrys* 'Shiro-kapitan' |
| | 'Tiverton' | CBcs EBee |
| | ***venusta*** | see *W. brachybotrys* 'Shiro-kapitan' |
| | - 'Alba' | see *W. brachybotrys* 'Shiro-kapitan' |
| | - var. ***violacea*** | see *W. brachybotrys* Murasaki-kapitan |

## *Withania* (*Solanaceae*)

| | | |
|---|---|---|
| | ***somnifera*** | CArn EOHP GPoy MSal |

## *Wittsteinia* (*Alseuosmiaceae*)

| | | |
|---|---|---|
| | ***vacciniacea*** | WCru |

## *Wodyetia* (*Arecaceae*)

| | | |
|---|---|---|
| | ***bifurcata*** | EAmu LPal XBlo |

## *Wollemia* (*Araucariaceae*)

| | | |
|---|---|---|
| | ***nobilis*** **new** | WMou |

## *Woodsia* (*Woodsiaceae*)

| | |
|---|---|
| ***alpina*** new | EBee |
| ***ilvensis*** | EBee |
| ***obtusa*** | CLAP CWCL EBee EFer GMaP LAst LRHS NHol NLar NMyG SRot WPnP WRic |
| ***polystichoides*** ♀H4 | GQui SRms |

## *Woodwardia* (*Blechnaceae*)

| | |
|---|---|
| from Emei Shan, China | CLAP |
| ***areolata*** | SKHP |
| ***fimbriata*** | CBod CCCN CDes CHid CLAP CWCL EBee ERod GCal LRHS MAvo MGos NBPC NHol NMyG NWCA SBig WFib WMoo WPGP WRic |
| ***orientalis*** | WCot WFib |
| - var. ***formosana*** | CLAP |
| - - B&SWJ 6865 | WCru |
| ***radicans*** ♀H3 | CAbb CHEx CHid CLAP EWes EWld GQui ISea SAPC SArc WFib WPic WRic |
| ***unigemmata*** | CHEx CLAP EWes EWld SAPC SArc WAbe WFib WHal WRic |
| ***virginica*** | CLAP |

## Worcesterberry see *Ribes* 'Worcesterberry'

## *Worsleya* (*Amaryllidaceae*)

| | |
|---|---|
| ***raineri*** new | WVal |

## *Wulfenia* (*Scrophulariaceae*)

| | |
|---|---|
| ***carinthiaca*** | EBee ECho GEdr GKev NBir NHol NLar SBHP WPer |
| x ***schwarzii*** | CDes EBee |

## *Wurmbea* (*Colchicaceae*)

| | |
|---|---|
| ***recurva*** | CStu |

# X

## *Xanthium* (*Asteraceae*)

| | |
|---|---|
| ***sibiricum*** | CArn |

## *Xanthoceras* (*Sapindaceae*)

| | |
|---|---|
| ***sorbifolium*** ♀H3-4 | CArn CBcs CLnd CMCN CWib ECrN ELan EPfP GKir IDee LEdu MBlu MBri SCoo SMad SSpi WDin WFar WPat |

## *Xanthocyparis* see *Chamaecyparis*

## *Xanthorhiza* (*Ranunculaceae*)

| | |
|---|---|
| ***simplicissima*** | CArn CBcs CGHE CRow EPfP GCal LEdu MBri NLar SDys SPer SSpi WPGP |

## *Xanthorrhoea* (*Xanthorrhoeaceae*)

| | |
|---|---|
| ***australis*** | SPlb |
| ***glauca*** | CCCN |

## *Xanthosoma* (*Araceae*)

| | |
|---|---|
| ***sagittifolium*** | CDTJ CKob EAmu EUJe |
| ***violaceum*** | CDTJ CDWL CKob EAmu |

## *Xerochrysum* (*Asteraceae*)

| | |
|---|---|
| § ***bracteatum*** 'Coco' | CMHG CSpe MAJR WWlt |
| § - 'Dargan Hill Monarch' | CHll CMHG CSev CSpe MAJR SRms WWlt |
| § - 'Skynet' | MAJR WWlt |
| - 'Wollerton' | WWlt |

## *Xeronema* (*Phormiaceae*)

| | |
|---|---|
| ***callistemon*** | CTrC |

## *Xerophyllum* (*Melanthiaceae*)

| | |
|---|---|
| ***tenax*** | GBin GGar NMen |

## *Xylorhiza* see *Machaeranthera*

## *Xyris* (*Xyridaceae*)

| | |
|---|---|
| ***torta*** | WPGP |

# Y

## Youngberry see *Rubus* 'Youngberry'

## *Ypsilandra* (*Melanthiaceae*)

| | |
|---|---|
| ***cavaleriei*** | CExc GEdr SKHP |
| ***thibetica*** | CDes CExc CGHE CSpe EBee EBla GEdr LAma LEdu SKHP WCot WCru WPGP WSHC |

## *Yucca* ✿ (*Agavaceae*)

| | |
|---|---|
| SDR 3701 | GKev |
| ***aloifolia*** | CCCN CDoC CHEx EAmu ISea LRHS MGos MREP SAPC SArc SBig SChr SEND SMad SPlb |
| § - f. ***marginata*** (v) | EAmu LPal MREP SAPC SArc SBig |
| - 'Purpurea' | MAga SPlb |
| - 'Tricolor' (v) | MREP |
| - 'Variegata' | see *Y. aloifolia* f. *marginata* |
| ***angustifolia*** | see *Y. glauca* |
| ***angustissima*** NNS 99-509 | WCot |
| ***arizonica*** | CBrP |
| ***baccata*** | CCCN CTrC LEdu |
| - NNS 99-510 | WCot |
| ***carnerosana*** | CTrC EAmu |
| § ***elata*** | CCCN CTrC ETod |
| § ***elephantipes*** ♀H1 | EAmu ETod LRHS MBri SEND |
| - 'Jewel' (v) | EAmu SEND |
| ***faxoniana*** | MAga |
| ***faxoniana*** x ***glauca*** | MAga |
| ***filamentosa*** ♀H4 | Widely available |
| - 'Antwerp' new | GCal |
| - 'Bright Edge' (v) ♀H3 | Widely available |
| - 'Color Guard' (v) | CDul CTrC LAst MBri NLar WCot WFar |
| - 'Garland's Gold' (v) | CBcs CCCN CDoC GQui LRHS MAsh MGos SBig WCot WFar |
| - 'Variegata' (v) ♀H3 | CBcs EPfP LRHS MGos SRms WDin WFar |
| ***filifera*** | EAmu |
| ***flaccida*** | CBcs MGos NBlu SDix SEND SPoG |
| - 'Golden Sword' (v) ♀H3 | CBcs CDoC CHVG CSBt CTrC CWSG EBee ECrN ELan EPfP GKir LAst LRHS MAsh MCCP MGos MSCN MSwo NMoo NScw SLim SPer SPoG SSto SWvt WCot |
| - 'Ivory' ♀H3-4 | CBcs CDoC CEnd CHar EBee ECtt ELan EPfP GCal GKir LEdu LRHS LSRN MBlu MBri MGos MRav SPer SRms SSta SSto STre WMoo WPic |
| x ***floribunda*** | SAPC SArc |
| § ***glauca*** | CBrP EBee EPfP LEdu LRHS MBri MREP NPal SAPC SPoG |
| * - var. ***radiosa*** | CTrC |
| ***gloriosa*** ♀H4 | CBcs CDoC CHEx CTri EAmu EPfP EPla EUJe LRHS MGos MREP NPal NScw SAPC SArc SEND SHBN SPer SPlb SPoG SWvt WBrE WBrk |

| | | |
|---|---|---|
| | - 'Aureovariegata' | see *Y. gloriosa* 'Variegata' |
| | - 'Moon Frost' | WCot |
| § | - 'Variegata' (v) ♀$^{H4}$ | Widely available |
| | ***guatemalensis*** | see *Y. elephantipes* |
| | ***linearis*** | see *Y. thompsoniana* |
| | ***navajoa*** | GCal |
| | 'Nobilis' | CHEx SDix |
| | ***radiosa*** | see *Y. elata* |
| | ***recurvifolia*** ♀$^{H4}$ | CHEx EAmu EPfP GCal MGos NPal SAPC SArc |
| | - 'Variegata' (v) | WCot |
| | ***rigida*** | CBrP EAmu |
| | ***rostrata*** | CAbb CBrP CCCN CDTJ CTrC EAmu ETod LPal MREP SAPC SArc SChr |
| | 'Sapphire Star' **new** | CBow |
| | ***schidigera*** | WCot |
| | - NNS 03-597 | WCot |
| | ***schottii*** | CAbb CBrP CTrC MAga |
| § | ***thompsoniana*** | CTrC EAmu LPal |
| | - blue-leaved **new** | EAmu |
| | ***torreyi*** | CTrC SChr |
| | ***treculeana*** | EAmu MAga |
| | 'Vittorio Emanuele II' | SMad |
| | ***whipplei*** | CAbb CBcs CBrP CCCN CDoC CTsd EBee ELan IGor LEdu LRHS MAga MREP NPal SAPC SBig SSpi WPGP |
| | - SDR 3710 | GKev |
| | - subsp. ***caespitosa*** | GAuc WCot |
| | - subsp. ***intermedia*** | WCot |
| | - subsp. ***parishii*** | WCot |
| | - subsp. ***percursa*** | WCot |

## *Yushania* (*Poaceae*)

| | | |
|---|---|---|
| § | ***anceps*** | CBcs CDoC CEnt CHEx CPLG EBee EFul ENBC EPfP EPla GBin MBar MGos MMoz MWht NVic SAPC SArc SBig SEND WFar WMoo WPGP |
| | - 'Pitt White' | CEnt CGHE EBee EPla MWht WPGP |
| | - 'Pitt White Rejuvenated' | EPla ERod WPGP |
| | ***brevipaniculata*** | EPla |
| | ***chungii*** | EPla WPGP |
| | ***maculata*** | CEnt CMCo EPla ERod MMoz MWht SBig |
| § | ***maling*** | EPfP EPla ERod MMoz |
| | Yunnan 5 | EPla WPGP |

# Z

## *Zaluzianskya* (*Scrophulariaceae*)

| | |
|---|---|
| sp. | NMen |
| JCA 15665 | WAbe |
| ***capensis*** | CSec LPio |
| 'Katherine' | SIng SRot |
| ***microsiphon*** | SPlb |
| 'Orange Eye' | LHop LPio NPro NSla WAbe |
| ***ovata*** | CPBP EDAr EPot GBri GKev LHop LPio MTho NBur NSla NWCA SAga SIng SPoG WAbe |
| ***pulvinata*** | SPlb WAbe |
| 'Semonkong' | CMdw GCal LPio LSou MNrw MSte |

## *Zamia* (*Zamiaceae*)

| | |
|---|---|
| ***furfuracea*** | CBrP CKob LPal |
| ***muricata*** | LPal |
| ***skinneri*** | LPal |

## *Zamioculcas* (*Araceae*)

| | |
|---|---|
| ***zamiifolia*** | CCCN |

## *Zantedeschia* (*Araceae*)

| | | |
|---|---|---|
| § | ***aethiopica*** ♀$^{H3}$ | Widely available |
| | - B&SWJ 3959 | WCru |
| | - 'Apple Court Babe' | CElw CRow CStu GCal MAvo MNrw SMrm WDyG WPic |
| | - 'Caerwent' | CPen |
| | - 'Childsiana' | SApp |
| I | - 'Childsiana Lisa' | EBrs |
| | - 'Crowborough' ♀$^{H3}$ | Widely available |
| | - 'Gigantea' | CHEx |
| | - 'Glow' | CBct CBgR EBee LAst LSou MAvo MNrw NCGa NGdn SPer WCot WGwG |
| | - 'Green Goddess' ♀$^{H3}$ | Widely available |
| | - 'Little Gem' | SMad WFar |
| | - 'Luzon Lovely' **new** | WCru |
| * | - 'Marshmallow' | EAEE EBee EBla ELan EShb LRHS NCGa |
| | - 'Mr Martin' | CBct CCCN CDes CHid CStu CTrC EBee ELon EUJe EWll LAst LFur MNrw NCGa SBig SMad SPoG SWvt WCot WPGP |
| | - 'Pershore Fantasia' (v) | CBct EBee MAvo MNrw MSKA WCot WFar |
| | - pink-flowered | CHEx |
| | - 'Tiny Tim' | SChr |
| | - 'Whipped Cream' | MDKP MNrw |
| | - 'White Gnome' | CDes WFar WPGP |
| | - 'White Mischief' | EBee |
| | - 'White Sail' | CBct CPrp EAEE EBee EBla GCal LRHS MNrw MRav NGdn SPoG SWat |
| | ***albomaculata*** | CPLG CSec EBrs EPfP EPot LAma MNrw SGar SPlb |
| | 'Anneke' | CCCN EBrs ECho EPfP GGar SPer WBrE WFar |
| | 'Apricot Glow' | CHll |
| | 'Best Gold' | see *Z.* 'Florex Gold' |
| | 'Black Crusader'$^{PBR}$ | NBPN |
| | 'Black Eyed Beauty' | CSec EBrs LAma |
| | 'Black Magic' | CCCN EBrs ECho EPfP SPer WFar |
| | 'Black Pearl' | LAma |
| | 'Black Star' | see *Z.* 'Edge of Night' |
| | black-flowered | CSut |
| | 'Cameo' | CCCN EBrs ECho LAma WFar |
| | 'Carmine Red' | WBrE |
| | 'Celeste' | EBrs |
| | 'Crystal Blush' | LAma |
| § | 'Edge of Night' | CCCN EUJe LCro NBPN |
| | ***elliottiana*** ♀$^{H1}$ | CFir CHEx CHal CTri EBrs EPfP EUJe GQui LAma MNrw |
| | 'Flame' | EBrs |
| § | 'Florex Gold' | EPot |
| | 'Galaxy' | EBrs |
| | 'Harvest Moon' | EBrs LAma |
| | 'Kiwi Blush' | Widely available |
| | 'Lime Lady' | CBct ECha |
| | 'Majestic Red' | EBrs |
| | 'Mango' | EBrs EWll LAma MNrw WCot |
| | 'Pink Mist' | CBct EBrs ERCP EShb LAma SWal WPnP |
| | 'Pink Persuasion' | EBrs LAma MNrw WFar |
| | ***rehmannii*** ♀$^{H1}$ | EBrs EPfP EPot GQui LAma MNrw NLar SGar SRms |
| | 'Schwarzwalder'$^{PBR}$ | CSec EBrs ERCP EUJe LRHS |
| | 'Sensation' | EBrs |
| | 'Silver Lining' | LAma |
| | 'Solfatare' | EBrs ECho |
| | 'Sunshine' | EWll |
| | 'Treasure' | EBrs |
| | 'White Pixie' | EPfP SAga SPoG WViv |

## *Zanthorhiza* see *Xanthorhiza*

## *Zanthoxylum* (*Rutaceae*)

| | |
|---|---|
| ***acanthopodium*** B&SWJ 7237 | WCru |
| ***ailanthoides*** | EPfP |
| - B&SWJ 8535 | WCru |
| - RWJ 10048 new | WCru |
| ***americanum*** | CAgr ELan IArd IFFs LEdu |
| ***armatum*** | CAgr |
| ***bungeanum*** HWJK 2131 | WCru |
| ***fauriei*** B&SWJ 11080 new | WCru |
| ***oxyphyllum*** | WPGP |
| ***piperitum*** | CAgr EBee GPoy IArd IFFs SEND WBor WPGP |
| - B&SWJ 8593 | WCru |
| ***schinifolium*** | CAgr LEdu |
| - B&SWJ 1245 | WCru |
| ***simulans*** | CArn CBcs CDul CLnd CPLG EBee GBin LEdu MBlu NLar WPGP |

## *Zauschneria* (*Onagraceae*)

| | |
|---|---|
| ***arizonica*** | see *Z. californica* subsp. *latifolia* |
| § ***californica*** | CHll CSam CSec CTri EBee ECGP ECho EDAr EPfP LAst MBrN MWat NMen SGar SLon SWat WBod WHrl WPnn |
| § - subsp. ***cana*** | ECha MHar SWat |
| - - 'Sir Cedric Morris' | EPfP LRHS MAsh |
| § - 'Dublin' ♀H3 | CBcs EBee ECha ECho ECtt EDAr EPfP EPot LHop LRHS MAsh MHer MWat NWCA SAga SIng SPer SPoG SRkn SRot SUsu WAbe WCot WFar WHoo WKif WPat WSHC |
| - 'Ed Carman' | EBee ECtt LSou |
| § - subsp. ***garrettii*** | ECho NWCA SDys SWat |
| - 'Glasnevin' | see *Z. californica* 'Dublin' |
| § - subsp. ***latifolia*** | CWCL |
| - - 'Sally Walker' | EWes |
| § - subsp. ***mexicana*** | EPot MHer SRms |
| - 'Olbrich Silver' | EBee ECha ECtt EShb EWes LHop NMen NWCA SUsu WAbe WFar WHoo WPat |
| - 'Sierra Salmon' | WAbe WPat |
| - 'Solidarity Pink' | ECha MTho NMen NWCA WAbe WPat |
| - 'Western Hills' ♀H4 | CFir CLyd CSpe CTri EBee ECha ECho ECtt EDAr EPfP LHop LSou MRav NWCA SAga SEND SIng SPhx WAbe WHoo WPat |
| ***cana villosa*** | see *Z. californica* subsp. *mexicana* |
| I 'Pumilio' | EPot NMen WAbe |
| § ***septentrionalis*** | WAbe |

## *Zebrina* see *Tradescantia*

## *Zelkova* ✿ (*Ulmaceae*)

| | |
|---|---|
| ***carpinifolia*** | CDoC CDul CMCN CMen CTho LRHS MAsh NHol SBLw SPlb WDin |
| 'Kiwi Sunset' | EBee MAsh |
| ***schneideriana*** | CMen EGFP |
| ***serrata*** ♀H4 | CDul CLnd CMCN CMen CTho EBee ECrN EHig ELan EPfP GKir ISea LMaj MBar MBri NBea NHol NWea SBLw SBir SEND SPer STre WDin WFar WHCr |
| - B&SWJ 8491 from Korea | WCru |
| - 'Goblin' | CLnd MAsh WPat |
| - 'Green Vase' | LMaj LPan LRHS |
| - 'Urban Ruby' | MGos |
| - 'Variegata' (v) | CPMA MBlu MGos |
| - 'Yatsubusa' | STre |
| ***sinica*** | CMCN CMen |

## *Zenobia* (*Ericaceae*)

| | |
|---|---|
| ***pulverulenta*** | Widely available |
| - 'Blue Sky' | CAbP CMCN EPfP MAsh MBlu MBri NLar SPoG SSpi SSta WPGP |
| - 'Misty Blue' | GGGa LRHS |
| - 'Raspberry Ripple' | MBlu MBri NLar SSta |
| - 'Viridis' | NLar |

## *Zephyranthes* ✿ (*Amaryllidaceae*)

| | |
|---|---|
| ***atamasca*** | CStu ERos SKHP |
| ***candida*** | CAvo CBro CFFs CPBP CSec CSpe CStu EBee EBrs ECho EMon EPot ERos EShb ITim LAma LRHS SDix WHil |
| ***citrina*** | CGrW CPLG CSec EBee EBrs ECho EPot ERos LAma WCot |
| ***drummondii*** | CStu ECho WCot |
| ***flavissima*** | CBro EBrs ECho WCot WHil WPGP |
| ***grandiflora*** ♀H2-3 | ECho |
| 'Grandjax' | EBee WCot |
| 'La Buffa Rose' | CStu SKHP WCot |
| ***lindleyana*** | WCot |
| ***mexicana*** | ERos |
| ***minima*** | CStu ECho LLHF |
| ***robusta*** | see *Habranthus robustus* |
| ***rosea*** | CGrW CSec EBee EBrs EPot |
| ***verecunda*** | CStu SIng |

## *Zieria* (*Rutaceae*)

| | |
|---|---|
| ***cytisoides*** | ECou |

## *Zigadenus* (*Melanthiaceae*)

| | |
|---|---|
| ***elegans*** | EBee ECGP ECha EDAr ERos GAbr GCal LRHS SMad SUsu WSHC WTin |
| ***fremontii*** | EBla WCot |
| ***nuttallii*** | EBee EBrs ECho ERos LHop MDKP SPhx WCot |
| ***venenosus*** | WCot |
| ***virescens*** | EBrs |

## *Zingiber* (*Zingiberaceae*)

| | |
|---|---|
| ***chrysanthum*** | CKob |
| ***clarkei*** | CKob |
| ***malaysianum*** | CKob |
| ***mioga*** | CKob EBee GPoy LEdu MSal WDyG WPGP |
| - B&SWJ 4379 new | WCru |
| - 'Dancing Crane' (v) | CKob EBee IFro |
| ***officinale*** | CKob MSal |
| ***purpureum*** | CKob |
| ***rubens*** | CKob |
| 'Yellow Delight' | CKob |
| ***zerumbet*** | CKob |
| - 'Darceyi' (v) | CKob |

## *Zinnia* (*Asteraceae*)

| | |
|---|---|
| 'Red Spider' | CSpe |

## *Zizia* (*Apiaceae*)

| | |
|---|---|
| ***aptera*** | CDes EBee SPhx WPGP |
| ***aurea*** | SDix SPhx WSHC WTin |

## *Ziziphus* (*Rhamnaceae*)

| | |
|---|---|
| § ***jujuba*** (F) | CAgr |
| - 'Li' (F) | LPan |
| - var. ***spinosa*** | CArn |
| ***sativa*** | see *Z. jujuba* |

# Bibliography

This is by no means exhaustive but lists some of the more useful works used in the preparation of the *RHS Plant Finder*. The websites of raisers of new plants (not listed here) are also an invaluable source of information.

## General


African Botany Supplementary Vol. No. 13. Kirstenbosch, South Africa: National Botanic Gardens.

Allan, H.H., et al. 2000. *Flora of New Zealand.* Wellington. (5 vols).

Ball Colegrave. *Plant Listing 2006*. 2005. West Adderbury, Oxon: Ball Colegrave.

Ball Colegrave. *Seed Listing 2005/6*. 2005. West Adderbury, Oxon: Ball Colegrave.

Bean, W.J. 1988. *Trees and Shrubs Hardy in the British Isles.* (8th ed. edited by Sir George Taylor & D.L. Clarke & Supp. ed. D.L. Clarke). London: John Murray.

Beckett, K. (ed.). 1994. *Alpine Garden Society Encyclopaedia of Alpines.* Pershore, Worcs.: Alpine Garden Society.

Boufford, D.E., et al. (eds). 2003. *Flora of Taiwan Checklist.* A checklist of the vascular plants of Taiwan. Taipei, Taiwan: NTU. http://tai2.ntu.edu.tw/fot/v6/v6checklist.pdf

Bramwell, D. & Bramwell, Z.I. 2001. *Wild Flowers of the Canary Islands.* (2nd ed.). Madrid: Editorial Rueda, S.L.

Brickell, C. (ed.). 2003. *The Royal Horticultural Society A-Z Encyclopedia of Garden Plants.* (2nd ed.) London: Dorling Kindersley.

Brickell, C.D. et al (eds.). 2004. *International Code of Nomenclature for Cultivated Plants* (7th ed.). ISHS.

Brummitt, R.K. (comp.). 1992. *Vascular Plant Families and Genera.* Kew: Royal Botanic Gardens. www.kew.org/data/vascplnt.html

Castroviejo, S., Laínz, M., López González, G., Montserrat, P., Munoz Garmendia, F., Paiva, J. & Villar, L. (eds). *Flora Iberica.* 1987-2001. (Vols 1-8, 14). Madrid: Real Jardín Botánico, C.S.I.C.

Cave, Y. & Paddison, V. 1999. *The Gardener's Encyclopaedia of New Zealand Native Plants.* Auckland: Godwit.

Cooke, I. 1998. *The Plantfinder's Guide to Tender Perennials.* Newton Abbot, Devon: David & Charles.

Cronquist, A., Holmgren, A.H., Holmgren, N.H., Reveal, J.L. & Holmgren, P.H. et al. (eds). *Intermountain Flora: Vascular Plants of the Intermountain West, USA.* (1986-97). (Vols 1, 3-6). New York: New York Botanical Garden.

Davis, P.H., Mill, R.R. & Tan, K. (eds). 1965-88. *Flora of Turkey and the East Aegean Island.* (Vols 1-10). Edinburgh University Press.

Goldblatt, P. & Manning, J. 2000. *Cape Plants. A Conspectus of the Cape Flora of South Africa.* South Africa/USA: National Botanical Institute of South Africa/Missouri Botanical Garden.

Graf, A.B. 1963. *Exotica 3. Pictorial Cyclopedia of Exotic Plants.* (3rd ed.). New Jersey, USA: Roehrs.

Greuter, W., et al. (eds). 2000. *International Code of Botanical Nomenclature (Saint Louis Code).* Königstein, Germany: Koeltz Scientific Books.

Greuter, W., Brummitt, R.K., Farr, E., Kilian, N., Kirk, P.M. & Silva, P.C. (comps). 1993. *NCU-3.*

Grierson, A.J.C., Long, D.G. & Noltie, H.J. et al. (eds). 2001. *Flora of Bhutan.* Edinburgh: Royal Botanic Garden.

Güner, A., Özhatay, N., Ekîm, T., Baser, K.H.C. & Hedge, I.C. 2000. *Flora of Turkey and the East Aegean Islands.* Supp. 2. Vol. 11. Edinburgh: Edinburgh University Press.

Harkness, M.G. 1993. *The Bernard E. Harkness Seedlist Handbook.* (2nd ed.). London: Batsford.

Hickman, J.C. (ed.). 1993. *The Jepson Manual. Higher Plants of California.* Berkeley & Los Angeles: University of California Press.

Hillier, J. & Coombes, A. (eds). 2002. *The Hillier Manual of Trees & Shrubs.* (7th ed.). Newton Abbot, Devon: David & Charles.

Hirose, Y. & Yokoi, M. 1998. *Variegated Plants in Colour.* Iwakuni, Japan: Varie Nine.

Hirose, Y. & Yokoi, M. 2001. *Variegated Plants in Colour.* Vol. 2. Iwakuni, Japan: Varie Nine.

Hoffman, M. (ed.). 2005. *List of Woody Plants. International Standard ENA 2005-2010.* Netherlands: Applied Plant Research.

Huxley, A., Griffiths, M. & Levy, M. (eds). 1992. *The New RHS Dictionary of Gardening.* London: Macmillan.

Iwatsuki, K., et al. 1995. *Flora of Japan.* Vols I-IIIb. Tokyo, Japan: Kodansha Ltd.

Jelitto, L. & Schacht, W. 1990. *Hardy Herbaceous Perennials.* Portland, Oregon: Timber Press. (2 vols).

Krüssmann, G. & Epp, M.E. (trans.). 1986. *Manual of Cultivated Broad-leaved Trees and Shrubs.* London: Batsford (3 vols).

Leslie, A.C. (trans.). *New Cultivars of Herbaceous Perennial Plants 1985-1990.* Hardy Plant Society.

Mabberley, D.J. 1997. *The Plant-Book. A Portable Dictionary of the Vascular Plants.* (2nd ed.). Cambridge: Cambridge University Press.

Metcalf, L.J. 1987. *The Cultivation of New Zealand Trees and Shrubs.* Auckland: Reed Methuen.
Munz, P. 1973. *A Californian Flora and Supplement.* London: University of California Press.
Nelson, E.C. 2000. *A Heritage of Beauty: The Garden Plants of Ireland: An Illustrated Encyclopaedia.* Dublin: Irish Garden Plant Society.
Ohwi, J. 1965. *Flora of Japan.* Washington DC: Smithsonian Institution.
Phillips, R. & Rix, M. 1997. *Conservatory and Indoor Plants.* London: Macmillan. (2 vols).
Platt, K. (comp.). 2002. *The Seed Search.* (5th ed.). Sheffield: Karen Platt.
Polunin, O. & Stainton, A.. 1984. *Flowers of the Himalaya.* Oxford: Oxford University Press.
Press, J.R. & Short, M.J. (eds). 1994. *Flora of Madeira.* London: Natural History Museum/ HMSO.
Rehder, A. 1940. *Manual of Cultivated Trees and Shrubs Hardy in North America.* (2nd ed.). New York: Macmillan.
Rice, G. (ed.), 2006. *Encyclopedia of Perennials.* London: Dorling Kindersley.
Stace, C. 1997. *New Flora of the British Isles.* (2nd ed.). Cambridge: Cambridge University Press.
Stainton, A. 1988. *Flowers of the Himalaya. A Supplement.* Oxford University Press.
Stearn, W.T. 1992. *Botanical Latin.* (4th ed.). Newton Abbot, Devon: David & Charles.
Stearn, W.T. 1996. *Stearn's Dictionary of Plant Names for Gardeners.* London: Cassell.
Thomas, G.S. 1990. *Perennial Garden Plants. A Modern Florilegium.* (3rd ed.). London: Dent.
Trehane, P. (comp.). 1989. *Index Hortensis. Vol. 1: Perennials.* Wimborne: Quarterjack
Tutin, T.G., et al. (ed.). 1993. *Flora Europaea. Vol. 1. Psilotaceae to Platanaceae.* (2nd ed.). Cambridge University Press.
Tutin, T.G., et al. 1964. *Flora Europaea.* Cambridge University Press. Vols 1-5.
Walter, K.S. & Gillett, H.J. (eds). 1998. *1997 IUCN Red List of Threatened Plants.* Gland, Switzerland and Cambridge, UK: IUCN.
Walters, S.M. & Cullen, J. et al. (eds). 2000. *The European Garden Flora.* Cambridge: Cambridge University Press. (6 vols).

## GENERAL PERIODICALS

*Dendroflora*
*New, Rare and Unusual Plants.*
The Hardy Plant Society. *The Hardy Plant.*
The Hardy Plant Society. *The Sport.*
Internationale Stauden-Union. *ISU Yearbook.*
Royal Horticultural Society. *Hanburyana.*
Royal Horticultural Society. *The Garden.*
Royal Horticultural Society. *The Plantsman.*
Royal Horticultural Society. *The New Plantsman.*

## GENERAL WEBSITES

Annotated Checklist of the Flowering Plants of Nepal. www.efloras.org/flora_page.aspx?flora_id-110
Australian Biological Resources Study Flora Online. http://www.deh.gov.au/biodiversity/abrs/online-resources/flora/
Australian Cultivar Registration Authority. Dec 2006. www.anbg.gov.au/acra
Australian Plant Breeders Rights – Database Search. May 2006. http://pbr.ipaustralia.optus.com.au
Australian Plant Names Index. Australian National Botanic Gardens (comp.). Mar 2006. www.anbg.gov.au/anbg/names.html
Bolivia Checklist. www.efloras.org/flora_page.aspx?flora_id=40
Botanical Expedition in Myanmar Checklist http://persoon.si.edu/myarmar/
Canadian Ornamental Plant Foundation. Jan 2006. www.copf.org/plants_list.asp
Canadian Plant Breeders' Rights Office: Canadian Food Inspection Agency. Nov 2006. www.inspection.gc.ca/english/plaveg/pbrpov/pbrpove.shtml
Catálogo de las Plantas Vasculares de las República Argentina. Jan 2006. www.darwin.edu.ar/Publicaciones/CatalogoVascII/CatalogoVascII.asp
Darwin Checklist of Moroccan Vascular Plants http://www.herbarium.rdg.ac.uk/maroccanplants/checklist.asp
DEFRA Plant Varieties and Seeds Gazette. Dec 2006. www.defra.gov.uk/planth/pvs/gaz.htm
Fischer France. www.pelfi.fr
Flora Himalaya Checklist http://bauges.univ-savoie.fr/web/test/form.php
Flora Mesoamericana Internet Version (W3FM). Oct 2006. Missouri Botanical Garden. www.mobot.org/mobot/fm
Flora of Chile. www.efloras.org/flora_page.aspx?flora_id=60
Flora of China Checklist. Jan 2007. http://flora.huh.harvard.edu/china
Flora of North America Website. Jan 2006. Morin, N.R., et al. www.efloras.org/flora_page.aspx?flora_id=1
GRIN (Germplasm Resources Information Network) Taxonomy. Jul 2006. www.ars-grin.gov/cgi-bin/npgs/html/index.pl
Index Synonymique de la Flore de France. Oct 1999. www.dijon.inra.fr/flore-france/consult.htm
International Plant Names Index. Feb 2006. www.ipni.org
International Plant Names Index: Author Query. Oct 2006. www.ipni.org/ipni/authorsearchpage.do
IOPI Provisional Global Plant Checklist. Feb 2005. www.bgbm.fu-berlin.de/iopi/gpc/query.asp
Manaaki Whenua: Landcare Research in New Zealand Plants Database http://nzflora.landcareresearch.co.nz/

Manual de plantas de Costa Rica. Apr 2001. www.mobot.org/manual.plantas/lista.html
Plants Database. Jan 2007. USDA, NRCS. http://plants.usda.gov
Plants of Southern Africa: an Online Checklist http://posa.sanbi.org/searchspp.php
New Zealand Plant Variety Rights Office www.pvr.goct.nz/
Synonymized Checklist of the Vascular Flora of the United States, Puerto Rico and the Virgin Isles. BIOTA of North America Program. Jul 1998. www.csdl.tamu.edu/FLORA/b98/check98.htm
US Patent Full-Text Database. US Patent and Trademark Office, (comp.). Jan 2007. www.uspto.gov/patft/index.html
VAST TROPICOS. Jan 2004. http://mobot.mobot.org/W3T/Search/vast.html
World Checklist of Selected Families. 2007. www.kew.org/wcsp/home.do

## GENERA AND OTHER PLANT GROUPINGS

***Acacia***
Simmons, M.H. 1987. *Acacias of Australia.* (2nd ed.). Melbourne: Nelson.
***Acer***
Harris, J.G.S. 2000. *The Gardener's Guide to Growing Maples.* Newton Abbot, Devon: David & Charles.
Van Gelderen, C.J. & Van Gelderen, D.M. 1999. *Maples for Gardens.* A Color Encyclopedia. Portland, Oregon: Timber Press.
Vertrees, J.D. 2001. *Japanese Maples.* Momiji and Kaede. (3rd ed.). Portland, Oregon: Timber Press.
***Actaea***
Compton, J.A. & Culham, A. 2000. The Name is the Game. *The Garden* (RHS) 125(1):48-52.
Compton, J.A., Culham, A. & Jury, S.L. 1998. Reclassification of *Actaea* to Include *Cimicifuga* and *Souliea* (*Ranunculaceae). Taxon* 47:593-634.
***Adiantum***
Goudey, C.J. 1985. *Maidenhair Ferns in Cultivation.* Melbourne: Lothian.
***Agapanthus***
Snoeijer, W. 2004. *Agapanthus. A Revision of the Genus.* Portland, Oregon: Timber Press.
***Agavaceae***
Irish, M. & Irish, G. 2000. *Agaves, Yuccas and Related Plants.* A Gardener's Guide. Portland, Oregon: Timber Press.
***Aizoaceae***
Burgoyne, P. et al. 1998. *Mesembs of the World. Illustrated Guide to a Remarkable Succulent Group.* South Africa: Briza Publications.
***Allium***
Davies, D. 1992. *Alliums. The Ornamental Onions.* London: Batsford
Gregory, M., et al. 1998. *Nomenclator Alliorum.* Kew: Royal Botanic Gardens.
Mathew, B. 1996. *A Review of Allium Section Allium.* Kew: Royal Botanic Gardens.
***Androsace***
Smith, G. & Lowe, D. 1997. *The Genus Androsace.* Pershore, Worcs.: Alpine Garden Society.
***Anemone,*** Japanese
McKendrick, M. 1990. Autumn Flowering Anemones. *The Plantsman* 12(3):140-151.
McKendrick, M. 1998. Japanese Anemones. *The Garden* (RHS) 123(9):628-633.
***Anthemis***
Leslie, A. 1997. Focus on Plants: *Anthemis tinctoria. The Garden* (RHS) 122(8):552-555.
***Apiaceae***
Pimenov, M.G. & Leonov, M.V. 1993. *The Genera of the Umbelliferae.* Kew: Royal Botanic Gardens.
***Aquilegia***
Munz, P.A. 1946. *Aquilegia:* the Cultivated and Wild Columbines. *Gentes Herb.* 7(1):1-150.
***Araceae***
Govaerts, R. & Frodin, D.G. 2002. *World Checklist and Bibliography of Araceae (and Acoraceae).* Kew: Royal Botanic Gardens
***Araliaceae***
Frodin, D.G. & Govaerts, R. 2003. *World Checklist and Bibliography of Araliaceae.* Kew:Royal Botanic Gardens
***Arecaceae*** (***Palmae,*** palms)
Jones, D.L. 1995. *Palms Throughout the World.* Chatswood, NSW: Reed Books.
Uhl, N.W. & Dransfield, J. 1987. *Genera Palmarum.* A Classification of Palms Based on the Work of Harold E. Moore Jr. Lawrence, Kansas: Allen Press.
***Argyranthemum***
Humphries, C.J. 1976. A Revision of the Macaronesian Genus *Argyranthemum. Bull. Brit. Mus. (Nat. Hist.) Bot.* 5(4):145-240.
***Arisaema***
Gusman, G. & Gusman, L. 2002. *The Genus Arisaema: A Monograph for Botanists and Nature Lovers.* Ruggell, Leichtenstein: A.R. Gantner Verlag Kommanditgesellschaft.
Pradhan, U.C. 1997. *Himalayan Cobra Lilies* (Arisaema). Their Botany and Culture. (2nd ed.). Kalimpong, West Bengal, India: Primulaceae Books.
***Arum***
Bown, D. 2000. *Plants of the Arum Family.* (2nd ed.). Portland, Oregon: Timber Press.
Boyce, P. 1993. *The Genus Arum.* London: HMSO.
***Asclepiadaceae***
Eggli, U. (ed.). 2002. *Illustrated Handbook of Succulent Plants: Asclepiadaceae.* Heidelberg, Germany: Springer-Verlag.
***Aster***
Picton, P. 1999. *The Gardener's Guide to Growing Asters.* Newton Abbot: David & Charles.

***Asteraceae***

Bremer, K. et al. 1994. *Asteraceae: Cladistics and Classification*. Portland, Oregon: Timber Press.

Cubey, J. & Grant, M. 2004. *Perennial Yellow Daisies: RHS Bulletin No 6*. Wisley, Surrey: RHS. www.rhs.org.uk/plants/documents/yellowdaisies04.pdf

***Astilbe***

Noblett, H. 2001. *Astilbe. A Guide to the Identification of Cultivars and Common Species*. Cumbria: Henry Noblett.

***Aubrieta***

1975. *International Registration Authority Checklist*. Weihenstephan, Germany: (Unpublished).

**Bamboos**

Ohrnberger, D. 1999. *The Bamboos of the World*. Amsterdam: Elsevier.

***Begonia***

American Begonia Society Astro Branch Begonia Data Base. Jan 2000. http://absastro.tripod.com/data.htm

Ingles, J. 1990. *American Begonia Society Listing of Begonia Cultivars*. Revised Edition Buxton Checklist. American Begonia Society.

Tebbitt, M.C. 2005. *Begonias: Cultivation, Identification and Natural History*. Portland, Oregon: Timber Press.

Thompson, M.L. & Thompson, E.J. 1981. *Begonias*. The Complete Reference Guide. New York: Times Books.

***Berberidaceae***

Stearn, W.T. & Shaw, J.M.H. 2002. *The Genus Epimedium and Other Herbaceous Berberidaceae including the Genus Podophyllum*. Kew: Royal Botanic Gardens.

***Betula***

Ashburner, K. & Schilling. T. 1985. *Betula utilis* and its Varieties. *The Plantsman* 7(2):116-125.

Ashburner, K.B. 1980. *Betula* – a Survey. *The Plantsman* 2(1):31-53.

Hunt, D. (ed.). 1993. *Betula: Proceedings of the IDS Betula Symposium 1992*. Richmond, Surrey: International Dendrology Society.

***Boraginaceae***

Bennett, M. 2003. *Pulmonarias and the Borage Family*. London: Batsford.

***Bougainvillea***

Gillis, W.T. 1976. Bougainvilleas of Cultivation (*Nyctaginaceae*). *Baileya* 20(1):34-41.

Iredell, J. 1990. *The Bougainvillea Grower's Handbook*. Brookvale, Australia: Simon & Schuster.

Iredell, J. 1994. *Growing Bougainvilleas*. London: Cassell.

MacDaniels, L.H. 1981. A Study of Cultivars in *Bougainvillea* (*Nyctaginaceae*). *Baileya* 21(2): 77-100.

Singh, B., Panwar, R.S., Voleti, S.R., Sharma, V.K. & Thakur, S. 1999. *The New International Bougainvillea Check List*. (2nd ed.). New Delhi: Indian Agricultural Research Institute.

***Bromeliaceae***

Beadle, D.A. 1991. *A Preliminary Listing of all the Known Cultivar and Grex Names for the Bromeliaceae*. Corpus Christi, Texas: Bromeliad Society.

Bromeliad Cultivar Registry Online Databases. Jan 2007. Bromeliad Society International www.bsi.org/brom_info/cultivar/

***Brugmansia***

Haik, M. (comp.). Jan 2005. Brugmansia Database. American Brugmansia and Datura Society. www.abads.net/Registry

***Buddleja***

Stuart, D.D. 2006. *Buddlejas: Royal Horticultural Society Collector Guide*. Portland, Oregon: Timber Press.

**Bulbs**

Leeds, R. 2000. *The Plantfinder's Guide to Early Bulbs*. Newton Abbot, Devon: David & Charles.

KAVB Online registration pages http://kavb.back2p.soft-orange.com/kavb/kavbSG.nsf/plants-registered?OpenView&Count=18.

***Buxus***

Batdorf, L.R. 1995. *Boxwood Handbook. A Practical Guide to Knowing and Growing Boxwood*. Boyce, VA, USA: The American Boxwood Society.

***Camellia***

Trujillo, D. J. (ed.). 2002. *Camellia Nomenclature*. (24th revd ed.). Southern California Camellia Society.

Savige, T.J. (comp.). 1993. *The International Camellia Register*. The International Camellia Society. (2 vols).

Savige, T.J. (comp.). 1997. *The International Camellia Register*. Supp. to vols 1 and 2. The International Camellia Society.

***Campanula***

Lewis, P. & Lynch, M. 1998. *Campanulas*. A Gardeners Guide. (2nd ed.). London: Batsford.

Lewis, P 2002. *Campanulas in the Garden*. Pershore, Worcs.: Hardy Plant Society.

***Canna***

Cooke, I. 2001. *The Gardener's Guide to Growing Cannas*. Newton Abbot, Devon: David & Charles.

Gray, J. & Grant, M. 2003. *Canna: RHS Bulletin No 3*. Wisley, Surrey: RHS. www.rhs.org.uk/plants/documents/canna03.pdf

Hayward, K. Jan 2007. http://www.hartcanna.com

**Carnivorous Plants**

Schlauer, J. (comp.). Aug 2006. Carnivorous Plant Database. www.omnisterra.com/bot/cp_home.cgi

***Cercidiphyllum***

Dosmann, M.S. 1999. Katsura: a Review of *Cercidiphyllum* in Cultivation and in the Wild. *The New Plantsman* 6(1):52-62.

Dosmann, M., Andrews, S., Del Tredici, P. & Li, J. 2003. Classification and Nomenclature of Weeping Katsuras. *The Plantsman* 2(1):21-27.

***Chaenomeles***

Weber, C. 1963. Cultivars in the Genus *Chaenomeles. Arnoldia (Jamaica Plain)* 23(3):17-75.

***Chrysanthemum* (*Dendranthema*)**

Brummitt, D. 1997. *Chrysanthemum* Once Again. *The Garden* (RHS) 122(9):662-663.

Gosling, S.G. (ed.). 1964. *British National Register of Chrysanthemums.* Whetstone, London: National Chrysanthemum Society.

National Chrysanthemum Society. 2000. *British National Register of Names of Chrysanthemums Amalgamated Edition 1964-1999.* Tamworth, Staffordshire: The National Chrysanthemum Society.

National Chrysanthemum Society UK Cultivar Database. Oct 2004. www.nationalchrysanthemumsociety.org.uk/Register/index.html

***Cistus***

Demoly, J.-P. 2005. The identity of *Cistus* 'Grayswood Pink' and related plants. *The Plantsman* 4(2):76-80.

Page, R.G. Oct 2006. Cistus and Halimium Website. www.cistuspage.org.uk

***Citrus***

Davies, F.S. & Albrigo, L.G. 1994. *Citrus.* Wallingford, Oxon: Cab International.

Saunt, J. 1990. *Citrus Varieties of the World.* An Illustrated Guide. Norwich: Sinclair

***Clematis***

Clematis on the Web. Jan 2007. www.clematis.hull.ac.uk

Grey-Wilson, C. 2000. *Clematis: the Genus.* London: Batsford

HelpMeFind Clematis. Nov 2006. www.helpmefind.com/clematis

Johnson, M. 2001. *The Genus Clematis.* Södertälje, Sweden: Magnus Johnsons Plantskola AB & Bengt Sundström.

Matthews, V. (comp.). 2002. *The International Clematis Register and Checklist 2002.* London: RHS.

Supps 1 (2004) & 2 (2006). http://www.rhs.org.uk/learning/publications/registers/plantregisters.asp

Toomey, M. & Leeds, E. 2001. *An Illustrated Encyclopedia of Clematis.* Portland, Oregon: Timber Press.

**Conifers**

den Ouden, P. & Boom, B.K. 1965. *Manual of Cultivated Conifers.* The Hague: Martinus Nijhof.

Farjon, A. 1998. *World Checklist and Bibliography of Conifers.* Kew: Royal Botanic Gardens.

Knees, S. Feb 2005. Complete List of Conifer Taxa Accepted for Registration. RHS. www.rhs.org.uk/research/registration_conifers_accepted.asp

Krüssmann, G. & Epp, M.E. (trans.). 1985. *Manual of Cultivated Conifers.* London: Batsford.

Lewis, J. & Leslie, A.C. 1987. *The International Conifer Register. Pt 1. Abies* to *Austrotaxus.* London: RHS.

Lewis, J. & Leslie, A.C. 1989. *The International Conifer Register. Pt 2. Belis* to *Pherosphaera,* excluding the Cypresses. London: RHS.

Lewis, J. & Leslie, A.C. 1992. *The International Conifer Register. Pt 3. The Cypresses.* London: RHS.

Lewis, J. & Leslie, A.C. 1998. *The International Conifer Register. Pt 4. Juniperus.* London: RHS.

Welch, H.J. 1979. *Manual of Dwarf Conifers.* New York: Theophrastus.

Welch, H.J. 1991. *The Conifer Manual.* Vol. 1. Dordrecht, Netherlands: Kluwer Academic Publishers.

Welch, H.J. 1993. *The World Checklist of Conifers.* Bromyard, Herefordshire: Landsman's Bookshops Ltd.

***Cornus***

Cappiello, P. & Shadow, D. 2005. *Dogwoods.* Portland, Oregon: Timber Press.

Howard, R.A. 1961. Registration Lists of Cultivar Names in *Cornus L. Arnoldia (Jamaica Plain)* 21(2):9-18.

***Corydalis***

Lidén, M. & Zetterlund, H. 1997. *Corydalis. A Gardener's Guide and a Monograph of the Tuberous Species.* Pershore, Worcs.: Alpine Garden Society Publications Ltd.

***Corylus***

Crawford, M. 1995. *Hazelnuts: Production and Culture.* Dartington, Devon: Agroforestry Research Trust.

***Cotoneaster***

Fryer, J. & Hylmö, B. 1998. Seven New Species of *Cotoneaster* in Cultivation. *The New Plantsman* 5(3):132-144.

Fryer, J. & Hylmö, B. 2001. Captivating Cotoneasters. *The New Plantsman* 8(4):227-238.

Fryer, J. 1996. Undervalued Versatility. *Cotoneaster. The Garden* (RHS) 121(11):709-715.

***Crassulaceae***

Rowley, G. 2003. *Crassula: A Grower's Guide.* Venegono superiore, Italy: Cactus & Co.

Eggli, U. (ed.) 2003. *Illustrated Handbook of Succulent Plants.* Springer.

***Crocosmia***

Goldblatt, P., Manning, J.C. & Dunlop, G. 2004. *Crocosmia and Chasmanthe.* Portland, Oregon: Timber Press.

***Crocus***

Jacobsen, N., van Scheepen, J. & Ørgaard, M. 1997. The *Crocus chrysanthus – biflorus* Cultivars. *The New Plantsman* 4(1):6-38.

Mathew, B. 1982. *The Crocus. A Review of the Genus Crocus* (*Iridaceae*). London: Batsford.

Mathew, B. 2002. *Crocus* Up-date. *The Plantsman* 1(1):44-56.

***Cyclamen***

Clennett, C. Jan. 2003. Register of Cultivar Names. www.cyclamen.org/registrar_set.html

Grey-Wilson, C. 2003. *Cyclamen. A Guide for Gardeners, Horticulturists & Botanists.* London: Batsford.

Grey-Wilson, C. 2002 Sprenger's Alpine Cyclamen. *The Plantsman* 1(3):173-177.

***Cypripedium***

Cribb, P. 1997. *The Genus Cypripedium.* Portland, Oregon: Timber Press.

***Dahlia***

American Dahlia Society website. 2006. www.dahlia.org

Bates, D. Dahlia Plant Finder 2007. Jan 2007. www.dahliaworld.co.uk/availuk.htm

National Dahlia Society. 2005. *Classified Directory and Judging Rules.* (28th ed.) Aldershot, Hants: National Dahlia Society.

RHS & Hedge, R. (comps). 1969. *Tentative Classified List and International Register of Dahlia Names 1969.* (& Supps 1-13). London: RHS. Supps 13-17. 2002-06. http://www.rhs.org.uk/learning/publications/registers/plantregisters.asp

Winchester Growers Ltd English National Dahlia Collection website. Jan 2007. www.wgltd.co.uk

***Daphne***

Brickell, C. & White, R. 2000. A Quartet of New Daphnes. *The New Plantsman* 7(1):6-18.

Brickell, C. 2000. *Daphne.* Pt 2: Henderson's Daphne. *The New Plantsman* 7(2):114-122.

Brickell, C.D. & Mathew, B. 1976. *Daphne. The Genus in the Wild and in Cultivation.* Woking, Surrey: Alpine Garden Society.

Grey-Wilson, C. (ed.). 2001. *The Smaller Daphnes. The Proceedings of 'Daphne 2000', a Conference held at the Royal Horticultural Society.* Pershore, Worcs.: Alpine Garden Society.

***Delphinium***

1949. *A Tentative Check-list of Delphinium Names.* London: RHS.

1970. *A Tentative Check-list of Delphinium Names.* Addendum to the 1949 tentative check-list of *Delphinium* names. London: RHS.

Bassett,D. & Wesley, W. 2004. *Delphinium: RHS Bulletin No 5.* Wisley, Surrey: RHS. www.rhs.org.uk/plants/documents/delph04.pdf

Leslie, A.C. 1996. *The International Delphinium Register Cumulative Supp. 1970-1995.* London: RHS.

Leslie, A.C. 1996-2005. The International Delphinium Register Supp. 1994-99. *The Delphinium Society Year Book 1996-2005.* London: RHS.

***Dianthus***

Galbally, J. & Galbally, E. 1997. *Carnations and Pinks for Garden and Greenhouse.* Portland, Oregon: Timber Press.

Leslie, A.C. *The International Dianthus Register.* 1983-2002. (2nd ed. & Supps 1-19). London: RHS.

Supps 19-23. 2002-06. http://www.rhs.org.uk/learning/publications/registers/plantregisters.asp

***Dierama***

Hilliard, O.M. & Burtt, B.L. 1991. *Dierama. The Harebells of Africa.* Johannesburg; London: Acorn Books.

***Dionysia***

Grey-Wilson, C. 1989. *The Genus Dionysia.* Woking, Surrey: Alpine Garden Society.

***Douglasia***

Mitchell, B. 1999. Celebrating the Bicentenary of David Douglas: a Review of *Douglasia* in Cultivation. *The New Plantsman* 6(2):101-108.

***Dracaena***

Bos, J.J., Graven, P., Hetterscheid, W.L.A. & van de Wege, J.J. 1992. Wild and cultivated *Dracaena fragrans. Edinburgh J. Bot.* 49(3):311-331.

***Episcia***

Dates, J.D. 1993. *The Gesneriad Register 1993.* Check List of Names with Descriptions of Cultivated Plants in the Genera *Episcia* & *Alsobia.* Galesburg, Illinois: American Gloxinia & Gesneriad Society, Inc.

***Erica*** (see also Heathers)

Baker, H.A. & Oliver, E.G.H. 1967. *Heathers in Southern Africa.* Cape Town: Purnell.

Schumann, D., Kirsten, G. & Oliver, E.G.H. 1992. *Ericas of South Africa.* Vlaeberg, South Africa: Fernwood Press.

***Erodium***

Clifton, R. 1994. *Geranium Family Species Checklist. Pt 1 Erodium.* (4th ed.). The Geraniaceae Group.

Leslie, A.C. 1980. The Hybrid of *Erodium corsicum* with *Erodium reichardii. The Plantsman* 2:117-126.

Toomey, N., Cubey, J. & Culham, A. 2002. *Erodium × variabile. The Plantsman* 1(3): 166-172

Victor, D.X. (comp.). 2000. *Erodium: Register of Cultivar Names.* The Geraniaceae Group.

***Erythronium***

Mathew, B. 1992. A Taxonomic and Horticultural Review of *Erythronium* L. (*Liliaceae*). *J. Linn. Soc., Bot.* 109:453-471.

Mathew, B. 1998. The Genus *Erythronium. Bull. Alpine Gard. Soc. Gr. Brit.* 66(3):308-321.

***Eupatorium*** sensu lato

Hind, D.J.N. 2006. Splitting *Eupatorium. The Plantsman* (n.s.) 5(2):185-189.

***Euonymus***

Brown, N. 1996. Notes on Cultivated Species of *Euonymus. The New Plantsman* 3(4):238-243.

Lancaster, C.R. 1981. An Account of *Euonymus* in Cultivation and its Availability in Commerce. *The Plantsman* 3(3):133-166.

Lancaster, C.R. 1982. *Euonymus* in Cultivation – Addendum. *The Plantsman* 4:61-64, 253-254.

***Euphorbia***

Govaerts, R., Frodin, D.G. & Radcliffe-Smith, A. 2000. *World Checklist and Bibliography of Euphorbiaceae.* Kew: Royal Botanic Gardens.

Turner, R. 1995. *Euphorbias. A Gardeners Guide.* London: Batsford.

Witton, D. 2000. *Euphorbias.* Pershore, Worcs.: Hardy Plant Society.

***Fagales***

World Checklist and Bibliography Series: About the *Fagales.* Jan 2002. www.rbgkew.org.uk/wcb/aboutfag.html

***Fagus***

Dönig, G. 1994. *Die Park-und Gartenformen der Rotbuche Fagus sylvatica L.* Erlangen, Germany: Verlag Gartenbild Heinz Hansmann.

Wyman, D. 1964. Registration List of Cultivar Names of *Fagus* L. *J. Arnold Arbor.* 24(1):1-8.

***Fascicularia***

Nelson, E.C. & Zizka, G. 1997. *Fascicularia* (*Bromeliaceae*): Which Species are Cultivated and Naturalized in Northwestern Europe. *The New Plantsman* 4(4):232-239.

Nelson, E.C., Zizka, G., Horres, R. & Weising, K. 1999. Revision of the Genus *Fascicularia* Mez (*Bromeliaceae*). *Botanical Journal of the Linnean Society* 129(4):315-332.

**Ferns**

Checklist of World Ferns. March 2003. http://homepages.caverock.net.nz/~bj/fern

Johns, R.J. 1996. *Index Filicum.* Supplementum Sextum pro annis 1976-1990. Kew:Royal Botanic Gardens.

Johns, R.J. 1997. *Index Filicum.* Supplementum Septimum pro annis 1991-1995. Kew:Royal Botanic Gardens.

Jones, D.L. 1987. *Encyclopaedia of Ferns.* Melbourne, Australia: Lothian.

Kaye, R. 1968. *Hardy Ferns.* London: Faber & Faber

Rickard, M.H. 2000. *The Plantfinder's Guide to Garden Ferns.* Newton Abbot, Devon: David & Charles.

Rush, R. 1984. *A Guide to Hardy Ferns.* London: British Pteridological Society.

***Forsythia***

INRA Forsythia website. Dec 2000. www.angers.inra.fr/forsy/indexeng.html

***Fragaria***

Day, D. (ed.). 1993. *Grower Digest 3: Strawberries.* (Revd ed.). London: Nexus Business Communications.

***Fritillaria***

Clark, T. & Grey-Wilson, C. 2003. Crown Imperials. *The Plantsman* 2(1):33-47.

Mathew, B., et al. 2000. *Fritillaria* Issue. *Bot. Mag.* 17(3):145-185.

Pratt, K. & Jefferson-Brown, M. 1997. *The Gardener's Guide to Growing Fritillaries.* Newton Abbot: David & Charles.

Turrill, W.B. & Sealy, J.R. 1980. *Studies in the Genus Fritillaria (Liliaceae).* Hooker's Icones Plantarum Vol. 39 (1 & 2). Kew:Royal Botanic Gardens.

**Fruit**

Brogdale Horticultural Trust National Fruit Collection. Jan 2007. http://www.brogdale.org.uk/nfc_home.php

Bowling, B.L. 2000. *The Berry Grower's Companion.* Portland, Oregon: Timber Press.

Hogg, R. 1884. *The Fruit Manual.* (5th ed.). London: Journal of Horticulture Office.

***Fuchsia***

American Fuchsia Society Registration Database. Nov 2006. www.americanfuchsiasociety.org/linktoregistrationdatabase.html

Bartlett, G. 1996. *Fuchsias – A Colour Guide.* Marlborough, Wilts: Crowood Press.

Boullemier, Leo.B. (comp.). 1991. *The Checklist of Species, Hybrids and Cultivars of the Genus Fuchsia.* London, New York, Sydney: Blandford Press.

Boullemier, Leo.B. (comp.). 1995. *Addendum No 1 to the 1991 Checklist of Species, Hybrids and Cultivars of the Genus Fuchsia.* Dyfed, Wales: The British Fuchsia Society.

Goulding, E. 1995. *Fuchsias: The Complete Guide.* London: Batsford.

Johns, E.A. 1997. *Fuchsias of the 19th and Early 20th Century.* An Historical Checklist of Fuchsia Species & Cultivars, pre-1939. Kidderminster, Worcs.: British Fuchsia Society

Jones,L. & Miller, D.M. 2005. *Delphinium: RHS Bulletin No 12.* Wisley, Surrey: RHS. www.rhs.org.uk/plants/documents/fuchsia05.pdf

Stevens, R. Jan 2007. Find That Fuchsia. www.findthatfuchsia.info

Van Veen, G. Gelderse Fuchsia Info-site. www.geldersefuchsia.info

***Galanthus***

Bishop, M., Davis, A. & Grimshaw, J. 2001. *Snowdrops. A monograph of cultivated Galanthus.* Maidenhead: Griffin Press.

Davis, A.P., Mathew, B. (ed.) & King, C. (ill.). 1999. *The Genus Galanthus. A Botanical Magazine Monograph.* Oregon: Timber Press.

***Gentiana***

Bartlett, M. 1975. *Gentians.* Dorset: Blandford Press.

Halda, J.J. 1996. *The Genus Gentiana.* Dobré, Czech Republic: Sen.

Wilkie, D. 1950. *Gentians.* (2nd ed. revised). London: Country Life.

***Geranium***

Armitage, J. 2005. *Hardy Geraniums – Stage 1: RHS Bulletin No 10.* Wisley, Surrey: RHS. www.rhs.org.uk/plants/documents/geranium05.pdf

Armitage, J. 2006. *Hardy Geraniums – Stage 2: RHS Bulletin No 14.* Wisley, Surrey: RHS. www.rhs.org.uk/plants/documents/geranium06.pdf

Bath, T. & Jones, J. 1994. *The Gardener's Guide to Growing Hardy Geraniums.* Newton Abbot, Devon: David & Charles.

Bendtsen, B.H. 2005. *Gardening with Hardy Geraniums.* Portland, Oregon: Timber Press.

Clifton, R.T.F. 1995. *Geranium Family Species Check List Pt 2.* Geranium. (4th ed. issue 2). Dover: The Geraniaceae Group.

Jones, J., et al. 2001. *Hardy Geraniums for the Garden.* (3rd ed.). Pershore, Worcs.: Hardy Plant Society.

Victor, D.X. 2004. *Register of Geranium Cultivar Names.* (2nd ed.). The Geraniaceae Group. www.hardygeraniums.com/register_of_cultivar_names.htm

Yeo, P.F. 2002. *Hardy Geraniums.* (3rd ed.). Kent: Croom Helm.

***Gesneriaceae***

American Gloxinia and Gesneriad Society. Listing of registered gesneriads. 2005. www.aggs.org/ir_ges

Dates, J.D. 1986-1990. *The Gesneriad Register 1986-1987 & 1990.* Galesburg, Illinois: American Gloxinia & Gesneriad Society, Inc.

***Gladiolus***

British Gladiolus Society List of Cultivars Classified for Show Purposes 1994. Mayfield, Derbyshire: British Gladiolus Society.

1997-1998. British Gladiolus Society List of European, New Zealand & North American Cultivars Classified for Exhibition Purposes 1997 & 1998. Mayfield, Derbyshire: British Gladiolus Society.

Goldblatt, P. & Manning, J. 1998. *Gladiolus in Southern Africa.* Vlaeberg, South Africa: Fernwood Press.

Goldblatt, P. 1996. *Gladiolus in Tropical Africa.* Systematics Biology and Evolution. Oregon: Timber Press.

Lewis, G.J., Obermeyer, A.A. & Barnard, T.T. 1972. A Revision of the South African Species of *Gladiolus. J. S. African Bot.* (Supp. Vol. 10)

***Gleditsia***

Santamour, F.S. & McArdle, A.J. 1983. Checklist of Cultivars of Honeylocust (*Gleditsia triacanthos* L.). *J. Arboric.* 9:271-276.

***Grevillea***

Olde, P. & Marriott, N. 1995. *The Grevillea Book.* (3). Kenthurst, NSW: Kangaroo Press.

***Haemanthus***

Snijman, D. 1984. A Revision of the Genus *Haemanthus. J. S. African Bot.* (Supp. Vol. 12).

***Hamamelis***

Lane, C. 2005. *Witch Hazels.* Portland, Oregon: Timber Press.

**Heathers**

Nelson, E.C. Aug 2005. International Cultivar Registration Authority for Heathers. www.heathersociety.org.uk/registration.html

***Hebe***

Chalk, D. 1988. *Hebes and Parahebes.* Bromley, Kent: Christopher Helm (Publishers) Ltd.

Hutchins, G. 1997. *Hebes: Here and There. A Monograph on the Genus Hebe.* Caversham, Berks: Hutchins & Davies.

Metcalf, L.J. 2001. *International Register of Hebe Cultivars.* Canterbury, New Zealand: Royal New Zealand Institute of Horticulture (Inc.).

Metcalf, L.J. 2006. *Hebes: A Guide to Species, Hybrids and Allied Genera.* Portland, Oregon: Timber Press.

***Hedera***

Jury, S. et al. 2006. *Hedera algeriensis*, a Fine Species of Ivy. *Sibbaldia* 4: 93-108.

McAllister, H. 1988. Canary and Algerian Ivies. *The Plantsman* 10(1):27-29.

McAllister, H.A. & Rutherford, A. 1990. *Hedera helix and H. hibernica* in the British Isles. *Watsonia* 18:7-15.

Rose, P.Q. 1996. *The Gardener's Guide to Growing Ivies.* Newton Abbot, Devon: David & Charles.

Rutherford, A., McAllister, H. & Mill, R.R. 1993. New Ivies from the Mediterranean Area and Macaronesia. *The Plantsman* 15(2):115-128.

***Heliconia***

Berry, F. & Kress, W.J. 1991. *Heliconia. An Identification Guide.* Washington: Smithsonian Institution Press.

***Helleborus***

Burrell, C.C. & Tyler, J.K. 2006. *Hellebores: A Comprehensive Guide.* Portland, Oregon: Timber Press.

Mathew, B. 1989. *Hellebores.* Woking: Alpine Garden Society.

Rice, G. & Strangman, E. 1993. *The Gardener's Guide to Growing Hellebores.* Newton Abbot, Devon: David & Charles.

***Hemerocallis***

AHS – Registered Daylily Database. Nov 2006. http://database.tinkersgardens.com

Baxter, G.J. (comp.). 2003. *Hemerocallis Cultivar Registrations 1890-2002.* (CD-ROM Version 2003a.) Jackson, Tennessee: American Hemerocallis Society.

Kitchingman, R.M. 1985. Some Species and Cultivars of *Hemerocallis. The Plantsman* 7(2):68-89.

**Herbs**

Page, M. & Stearn, W. *Culinary Herbs: A Wisley Handbook.* London: RHS.

Phillips, R. & Foy, N. 1990. *Herbs.* London: Pan Books Ltd.

***Heuchera*** and × ***Heucherella***

Heims, D. & Ware, G. 2005. *Heucheras and Heucherellas: Coral Bells and Foamy Bells.* Portland, Oregon: Timber Press.

***Hibiscus***

Noble, C. Sep 2006. Australian Hibiscus Society Database Register. http://www.australianhibiscus.com/Database/database_register.htm

***Hippeastrum***

*Alfabetische Lijst van de in Nederland in Cultuur Zijnde Amaryllis (Hippeastrum) Cultivars.* 1980.

Hillegom, Netherlands: Koninklijke Algemeene Vereeniging Voor Bloembollencultur (KAVB).

Read, V.M. 2004. *Hippeastrum*. Portland, Oregon: RHS/Timber Press

***Hosta***

Hammelman, T. 2002. Giboshi.com Hosta Database. www.giboshi.com

Hosta Library. Aug 2006. www.hostalibrary.org

Grenfell, D. & Shadrack, M. 2004. *The Color Encyclopedia of Hostas*. Portland, Oregon: Timber Press.

Schmid, W.G. 1991. *The Genus Hosta*. London: Batsford.

***Hyacinthaceae***

Dashwood, M. & Mathew, B. 2006. *Hyacinthaceae – little blue bulbs: RHS Bulletin No 11*. Wisley, Surrey: RHS. www.rhs.org.uk/plants/documents/hyacinthaceae05.pdf

Mathew, B. 2005. *Hardy Hyacinthaceae* Pt 1: *Muscari. The Plantsman* 4(1):40-53.

Mathew, B. 2005. *Hardy Hyacinthaceae* Pt 2: *Scilla, Chionodoxa* and × *Chinoscilla. The Plantsman* 4(2):110-121.

***Hyacinthus***

Clark, T. 2000. Focus on Plants: Treasures of the East (Hyacinths). *The Garden* (RHS) 125(9):672-675.

Stebbings, G. 1996. Heaven Scent. *The Garden* (RHS) 121(2):68-72.

***Hydrangea***

Dirr, M.A. 2004. *Hydrangeas for American Gardens*. Portland, Oregon: Timber Press.

Haworth-Booth, M. 1975. *The Hydrangeas*. London: Garden Book Club.

Van Gelderen, C.J. & Van Gelderen, D.M. 2004. *Encyclopedia of Hydrangeas*. Portland, Oregon: Timber Press.

***Hypericum***

Lancaster, R. & Robson, N. 1997. Focus on Plants: Bowls of Beauty. *The Garden* (RHS) 122(8): 566-571.

***Ilex***

Andrews, S. 1983. Notes on Some *Ilex* × *altaclerensis* Clones. *The Plantsman* 5(2):65-81.

Andrews, S. 1984. More Notes on Clones of *Ilex* × *altaclerensis. The Plantsman* 6(3):157-166. Erratum vol.6 p.256.

Andrews, S. 1985. Holly Berries of a Varied Hue. *The Garden* (RHS) 110(11):518-522.

Andrews, S. 1994. Hollies with a Difference. *The Garden* (RHS) 119(12):580-583.

Dudley, T.R. & Eisenbeiss, G.K. 1973 & 1992. *International Checklist of Cultivated Ilex*. Pt 1 *Ilex opaca* (1973), Pt 2 *Ilex crenata* (1992). Washington DC: United States Dept of Agriculture.

Galle, F.C. 1997. *Hollies: the Genus Ilex*. Portland, Oregon: Timber Press.

***Iris***

Hoog, M.H. 1980. Bulbous Irises . *The Plantsman* 2(3):141-64.

Keppel, K. (ed.) 2001. *Iris Check List of Registered Cultivar Names 1990-1999*. Hannibal, New York: the American Iris Society.

Mathew, B. 1981. *The Iris*. London: Batsford.

Mathew, B. 1993. The Spuria Irises. *The Plantsman* 15(1):14-25.

Service, N. 1990. *Iris unguicularis. The Plantsman* 12(1):1-9.

Stebbings, G. 1997. *The Gardener's Guide to Growing Iris*. Newton Abbot: David & Charles.

The Species Group of the British Iris Society, (ed.). 1997. *A Guide to Species Irises*. Their Identification and Cultivation. Cambridge: Cambridge University Press.

***Jovibarba*** see under ***Sempervivum***

***Kalmia***

Jaynes, R.A. 1997. *Kalmia. Mountain Laurel and Related Species*. Portland, Oregon: Timber Press.

***Kniphofia***

Grant-Downton, R. 1997. Notes on *Kniphofia thomsonii* in Cultivation and in the Wild. *The New Plantsman* 4(3):148-156.

Taylor, J. 1985. *Kniphofia* – a Survey. *The Plantsman* 7(3):129-160.

***Kohleria***

Dates, J.D. (ed.) & Batcheller, F.N. (comp.). 1985 *The Gesneriad Register 1985. Check List of Names with Descriptions of Cultivated Plants in the Genus Kohleria*. Lincoln Acres, California: American Gloxinia and Gesneriad Society, Inc.

***Lachenalia***

Duncan, G.D. 1988. *The Lachenalia Hand Book*. Kirstenbosch, South Africa: National Botanic Gardens.

***Lantana***

Howard, R.A. 1969. A Check List of Names Used in the Genus *Lantana. J. Arnold Arbor.* 29(11): 73-109.

***Lathyrus***

Norton, S. 1996. *Lathyrus. Cousins of Sweet Pea*. Surrey: NCCPG.

***Lavandula***

Upson, T. & Andrews, S. 2004. *The Genus Lavandula*. Kew: Royal Botanic Garden.

**Legumes**

ILDIS. International Legume Database and Information Service. Nov 2005. Version 10.01. www.ildis.org/LegumeWeb

***Leptospermum***

Check List of *Leptospermum* Cultivars. 1963. *J. Roy. New Zealand Inst. Hort.* 5(5): 224-30.

Dawson, M. 1997. A History of *Leptospermum scoparium* in Cultivation – Discoveries from the Wild. *The New Plantsman* 4(1):51-59.

Dawson, M. 1997. A History of *Leptospermum scoparium* in Cultivation – Garden Selections. *The New Plantsman* 4(2):67-78.

***Lewisia***

Davidson, B.L.R. 2000. *Lewisias.* Portland, Oregon: Timber Press.

Elliott, R. 1978. *Lewisias.* Woking: Alpine Garden Society.

Mathew, B. 1989. *The Genus Lewisia.* Bromley, Kent: Christopher Helm.

***Liliaceae*** **sensu lato**

Mathew, B. 1989. Splitting the *Liliaceae. The Plantsman* 11(2):89-105.

***Lilium***

Leslie, A.C. *The International Lily Register 1982-2002.* (3rd ed. & supps 1-20). London: RHS.

Supps 20-23. 2002-06. http://www.rhs.org.uk/learning/publications/registers/plantregisters.asp

Online Lily Register. Dec 2006. www.lilyregister.com

***Lonicera***

Blahník, Z. 2006. *Lonicera* Cultivar Names: The First World List. *Acta Pruhoniciana* 81:59-64.

***Magnolia***

Callaway, D.J. Sep 2001. Magnolia Cultivar Checklist. www.magnoliasociety.org/index.html

Frodin, D.G. & Govaerts, R. 1996. *World Checklist and Bibliography of Magnoliaceae.* Kew: Royal Botanic Garden.

***Maianthemum***

Cubey, J.J. 2005. The Incorporation of *Smilacina* within *Maianthemum. The Plantsman* N.S.4(4).

***Malus***

Crawford, M. 1994. *Directory of Apple Cultivars.* Devon: Agroforestry Research Trust.

Fiala, J.L. 1994. *Flowering Crabapples.* The genus *Malus.* Portland, Oregon: Timber Press.

Rouèche, A. Nov 2006. Les Crets Fruits et Pomologie. www.pomologie.com

Smith, M.W.G. 1971. *National Apple Register of the United Kingdom.* London: MAFF

Spiers, V. 1996. *Burcombes, Queenies and Colloggetts.* St Dominic, Cornwall: West Brendon.

***Meconopsis***

Grey-Wilson, C. 1992. A Survey of the Genus *Meconopsis* in Cultivation. *The Plantsman* 14(1): 1-33.

Grey-Wilson, C. 2002. The True Identity of *Meconopsis napaulensis. Bot. Mag.* 23(2):176-209.

Meconopsis Group website www.meconopsis.org/

Stevens, E. & Brickell, C. 2001. Problems with the Big Perennial Poppies. *The New Plantsman* 8(1):48-61.

Stevens, E. 2001. Further Observations on the Big Perennial Blue Poppies. *The New Plantsman* 8(2):105-111.

***Miscanthus***

Jones, L. 2004. *Miscanthus: RHS Bulletin No 7.* Wisley, Surrey: RHS. www.rhs.org.uk/plant/documents/miscanthus04.pdf

***Moraea***

Goldblatt, P. 1986. *The Moraeas of Southern Africa.* Kirstenbosch, South Africa: National Botanic Gardens.

***Musa***

INIBAP *Musa* Germplasm Information System. Dec 2006. http//195.220.148.3:8013/mgis_2/homepage.htm

Musalogue 2: Diversity in the Genus *Musa.* 2001. http://bananas.bioversityinternational.org/files/files/pdf/publications/musalogue2.pdf

***Narcissus***

Blanchard, J.W. 1990. *Narcissus – A Guide to Wild Daffodils.* Woking, Surrey: Alpine Garden Society.

Kington, S. (comp.). 1998. *The International Daffodil Register and Classified List 1998* (3rd ed. & Supps 1-5, 1998-2002). London: RHS. www.rhs.org.uk/research/registerpages/intro.asp

Supps 6-9. 2002-06. http://www.rhs.org.uk/learning/publications/registers/plantregisters.asp

***Nematanthus***

Arnold, P. 1978. *The Gesneriad Register 1978.* Check List of *Nematanthus.* American Gloxinia and Gesneriad Society, Inc.

***Nerium***

Pagen, F.J.J. 1987. *Oleanders. Nerium L. and the Oleander Cultivars.* Wageningen, The Netherlands: Agricultural University Wageningen.

***Nymphaea***

International Water Lily Society. 1993. *Identification of Hardy Nymphaea.* Stapeley Water Gardens Ltd.

Swindells, P. 1983. *Waterlilies.* London: Croom Helm.

***Orchidaceae***

Shaw, J.M.H. Dec 2006. The International Orchid Register. www.rhs.org.uk/plants/registration_orchids.asp

***Origanum***

Paton, A. 1994. Three Membranous-bracted Species of *Origanum. Kew Mag.* 11(3):109-117.

White, S. 1998. *Origanum. The Herb Marjoram and its Relatives.* Surrey: NCCPG.

***Paeonia***

HelpMeFind Peonies. Jan 2007. www.helpmefind.com/peony/index.html

Kessenich, G.M. 1976. *Peonies.* (Variety Check List Pts 1-3). American Peony Society.

Osti, G.L. 1999. *The Book of Tree Peonies.* Turin: Umberto Allemandi.

Page, M. 1997. *The Gardener's Guide to Growing Peonies.* Newton Abbott: David & Charles.

Rogers, A. 1995. *Peonies.* Portland, Oregon: Timber Press.

Wang, L., et al. 1998. *Chinese Tree Peony.* Beijing: China Forestry Publishing House.

***Papaver***

Grey-Wilson, C. 1998. Oriental Glories. *The Garden* (RHS) 123(5):320-325.

Grey-Wilson, C. 2000. *Poppies. The Poppy Family in the Wild and in Cultivation.* London: Batsford.

***Passiflora***

Vanderplank, J. 2000. *Passiflora* Cultivars List (3rd draft, April 2001). *Passiflora* 10 (3/4): 23-39.

Vanderplank, J. 2002. *Passion Flowers.* (3rd ed.). London, England: Cassell.

***Pelargonium***

Abbott, P.G. 1994. *A Guide to Scented Geraniaceae.* Angmering, West Sussex: Hill Publicity Services.

Anon. 1978. *A Checklist and Register of Pelargonium Cultivar Names.* Pt 1 A-B. Australian Pelargonium Society.

Anon. 1985. *A Checklist and Register of Pelargonium Cultivar Names.* Pt 2: C-F. Australian Pelargonium Society.

Bagust, H. 1988. *Miniature and Dwarf Geraniums.* London: Christopher Helm.

Clifford, D. 1958. *Pelargoniums.* London: Blandford Press.

Clifton, R. 1999. *Geranium Family Species Checklist, Pt 4: Pelargonium.* The Geraniaceae Group.

Complete Copy of the Spalding Pelargonium Checklist. (Unpublished). USA.

Key, H. 2000. *1001 Pelargoniums.* London: Batsford.

Miller, D. 1996. *Pelargonium. A Gardener's Guide to the Species and Cultivars and Hybrids.* London: Batsford.

Pelargonium Palette: The Geranium and Pelargonium Society of Sydney Incorporated. Varieties – Alphabetical List. July 2000. www.elj.com/geranium/var/alphaind.htm

Van der Walt, J.J.A., et al. 1977. *Pelargoniums of South Africa.* (1-3). Kirstenbosch, South Africa: National Botanic Gardens.

***Penstemon***

Lindgren, D.T. & Davenport, B. 1992. List and description of named cultivars in the genus *Penstemon* (1992). University of Nebraska.

Nold, R. 1999. *Penstemons.* Portland, Oregon: Timber Press.

Way, D. & James, P. 1998. *The Gardener's Guide to Growing Penstemons.* Newton Abbott, Devon: David & Charles.

Way, D. 2006. *Penstemons.* Pershore, Worcs.: Hardy Plant Society.

***Phlomis***

Mann Taylor, J. 1998. *Phlomis: The Neglected Genus.* Wisley: NCCPG.

***Phlox***

Harmer, J. & Elliott, J. 2001. *Phlox.* Pershore, Worcs.: Hardy Plant Society.

Stebbings, G. 1999. Simply Charming. *The Garden* (RHS) 124(7):518-521.

Wherry, E.T. 1955. *The Genus Phlox.* Philadelphia, Pennsylvania: Morris Arboretum.

***Phormium***

Heenan, P.B. 1991. *Checklist of Phormium Cultivars.* Royal New Zealand Institute of Horticulture.

McBride-Whitehead, V. 1998. Phormiums of the Future. *The Garden* (RHS) 123(1):42-45.

***Pieris***

Bond, J. 1982. *Pieris* – a Survey. *The Plantsman* 4(2):65-75.

Wagenknecht, B.L. 1961. Registration Lists of Cultivar Names in the Genus *Pieris* D. Don. *Arnoldia (Jamaica Plain)* 21(8):47-50.

***Pittosporum***

Miller, D.M. 2006. RHS Plant Assessments: *Pittosporum tenuifolium* hybrids & cultivars. www.rhs.org.uk/plants/documents/pittosporum06HI.pdf.

***Plectranthus***

Miller, D. & Morgan, N. 2000. Focus on Plants: A New Leaf. *The Garden* (RHS) 125(11):842-845.

Shaw, J.M.H. 1999. Notes on the Identity of Swedish Ivy and Other Cultivated *Plectranthus. The New Plantsman* 6(2):71-74.

***Pleione***

Cribb, P. & Butterfield, I. 1999. *The Genus Pleione.* (2nd ed.). Kew: Royal Botanic Gardens.

Shaw, J.M.H. (comp.). Oct 2002. Provisional List of *Pleione* Cultivars. RHS. www.rhs.org.uk/plants/registerpages/Pleione_cv.PDF

***Poaceae* (*Gramineae*, grasses)**

Clayton, W.D., Harman, K.T. & Williamson, H. Mar 2006. World Grass Species Synonymy. www.kew.org/data/grasses-syn/download.htm

Clayton, W.D. & Renvoize, S.A. 1986. *Genera Graminum.* Grasses of the World. London: HMSO.

Darke, R. 1999. *The Colour Encyclopedia of Ornamental Grasses.* Sedges, Rushes, Restios, Cat-tails and Selected Bamboos. London: Weidenfeld & Nicolson.

Grounds, R. 1998. *The Plantfinder's Guide to Ornamental Grasses.* Newton Abott, Devon: David & Charles.

Wood, T. 2002. *Garden Grasses, Rushes and Sedges.* (3rd ed.). Abingdon, Oxon: John Wood.

***Polemonium***

Nichol-Brown, D. 2000. *Polemonium.* Wisley: NCCPG.

***Potentilla***

Davidson, C.G., Enns, R.J. & Gobin, S. 1994. *A Checklist of Potentilla fruticosa: the Shrubby Potentillas.* Morden, Manitoba: Agriculture & Agri-Food Canada Research Centre. Data also on Plant Finder Reference Library professional version CD-ROM 1999/2000.

Miller, D.M. 2002. *Shrubby Potentilla: RHS Bulletin No 1.* Wisley, Surrey: RHS. www.rhs.org.uk/plants/documents/potentilla_report.pdf

***Primula***

Richards, J. 2002 (2nd ed.). *Primula.* London: Batsford.

***Primula allionii***

Archdale, B. & Richards, D. 1997. *Primula allionii Forms and Hybrids.* National Auricula & Primula Society, Midland & West Section.

***Primula auricula*** hort.

Baker, G. *Double Auriculas.* National Auricula & Primula Society, Midland & West Section.

Baker, G. & Ward, P. 1995. *Auriculas.* London: Batsford.

Hawkes, A. 1995. Striped Auriculas. National Auricula & Primula Society, Midland & West Section.

Nicholle, G. 1996. *Border Auriculas.* National Auricula & Primula Society, Midland & West Section.

Robinson, M.A. 2000. *Auriculas for Everyone.* How to Grow and Show Perfect Plants. Lewes, Sussex: Guild of Master Craftsmen Publications.

Telford, D. 1993. *Alpine Auriculas.* National Auricula & Primula Society, Midland & West Section.

Ward, P. 1991. *Show Auriculas.* National Auricula & Primula Society, Midland & West Section.

***Proteaceae***

International *Proteaceae Register.* July 2002. (7th ed.). http://www.nda.agric.za/docs/Protea2002/proteaceae_register.htm

Rebelo, T. 1995. *Proteas. A Field Guide to the Proteas of Southern Africa.* Vlaeberg: Fernwood Press/National Botanical Institute.

***Prunus***

Crawford, M. 1996. *Plums.* Dartington, Devon: Agroforestry Research Trust.

Crawford, M. 1997. *Cherries: Production and Culture.* Dartington, Devon: Agroforestry Research Trust.

Jacobsen, A.L. 1992. *Purpleleaf Plums.* Portland, Oregon: Timber Press.

Jefferson, R.M. & Wain, K.K. 1984. *The Nomenclature of Cultivated Flowering Cherries (Prunus).* The Sato-Zakura Group. Washington DC: USDA.

Kuitert, W. 1999. *Japanese Flowering Cherries.* Portland, Oregon: Timber Press.

***Pulmonaria***

Bennett, M. 2003. *Pulmonarias and the borage family.* London: B.T. Batsford.

Hewitt, J. 1994. *Pulmonarias.* Pershore, Worcs.: Hardy Plant Society.

Hewitt, J. 1999. Well Spotted. *The Garden* (RHS) 124(2):98-103.

***Pyracantha***

Egolf, D.R. & Andrick, A.O. 1995. *A Checklist of Pyracantha Cultivars.* Washington DC: Agricultural Research Service.

***Pyrus***

Crawford, M. 1996. *Directory of Pear Cultivars.* Totnes, Devon: Agroforestry Research Institute.

Smith, M.W.G. 1976. *Catalogue of the British Pear.* Faversham, Kent: MAFF.

***Quercus***

Miller, H.A. & Lamb, S.H. 1985. *Oaks of North America.* Happy Camp, California: Naturegraph Publishers.

Mitchell, A. 1994. The Lucombe Oaks. *The Plantsman* 15(4):216-224.

***Rhododendron***

Argent, G., Fairweather, C. & Walter, K. 1996. *Accepted Names in Rhododendron section Vireya.* Edinburgh: Royal Botanic Garden.

Argent, G., Bond, J., Chamberlain, D., Cox, P. & Hardy, A. 1997. *The Rhododendron Handbook 1998.* Rhododendron Species in Cultivation. London: RHS.

Chamberlain, D.F. & Rae, S.J. 1990. A Revision of *Rhododendron* IV. Subgenus *Tsutsusi. Edinburgh J. Bot.* 47(2).

Chamberlain, D.F. 1982. A Revision of *Rhododendron* II. Subgenus *Hymenanthes. Notes Roy. Bot. Gard. Edinburgh* 39(2).

Chamberlain, D., Hyam, R., Argent, G., Fairweather, G. & Walter, K.S. 1996. *The Genus Rhododendron.* Edinburgh:Royal Botanic Garden.

Cullen, J. 1980. A Revision of *Rhododendron* I. Subgenus *Rhododendron* sections *Rhododendron* and *Pogonanthum. Notes Roy. Bot. Gard. Edinburgh* 39(1).

Davidian, H.H. 1982-1992 *The Rhododendron Species* (Vols 1-4). London: Batsford.

Galle, F.C. 1985. *Azaleas.* Portland, Oregon: Timber Press.

Leslie, A. C. (comp.). 1980. *The Rhododendron Handbook 1980.* London: RHS.

Leslie, A.C. (comp.) 2004. *The International Rhododendron Register and Checklist* (2nd ed.). London: RHS. 1st Supp. 2006. http://www.rhs.org.uk/learning/publications/registers/plantregisters.asp

Tamura, T. (ed.). 1989. *Azaleas in Kurume.* Kurume, Japan: International Azalea Festival '89.

***Ribes***

Crawford, M. 1997. *Currants and Gooseberries: Production and Culture.* Dartington, Devon: Agroforestry Research Trust.

***Rosa***

Beales, P., Cairns, T., et al. 1998. *Botanica's Rose: The Encyclopedia of Roses.* Hoo, Kent: Grange Books.

Cairns, T. (ed.). 2000. *Modern Roses XI. The World Encyclopedia of Roses.* London: Academic Press.

Dickerson, B.C. 1999. *The Old Rose Advisor.* Portland, Oregon: Timber Press.

Haw, S.G. 1996. Notes on Some Chinese and Himalayan Rose Species of Section *Pimpinellifoliae. The New Plantsman* 3(3):143-146.

HelpMeFind Roses. Nov 2006. www.helpmefind.com/rose/index.html

McCann, S. 1985. *Miniature Roses.* Newton Abbot, Devon: David & Charles.

Quest-Ritson, C. 2003. *Climbing Roses of the World.* Portland, Oregon: Timber Press.

Quest-Ritson, C. & Quest-Ritson, B. 2003. *The Royal Horticultural Society Encyclopedia of Roses: The Definitive A-Z Guide.* London: Dorling Kindersley.

Thomas, G.S. 1995. *The Graham Stuart Thomas Rose Book.* London: John Murray.

Verrier, S. 1996. *Rosa Gallica.* Balmain, Australia: Florilegium.

***Rosularia***

Eggli, U. 1988. A Monographic Study of the Genus *Rosularia. Bradleya* (Supp.) 6:1-118.

***Rubiaceae***

Govaerts, R. et al. 2005. *World Checklist & Bibliography of Rubiaceae (Draft Version).* www.kew.org/data/rubiaceae/index.htm

***Saintpaulia***

Goodship, G. 1987. *Saintpaulia Variety List* (Supp.). Slough, Bucks: Saintpaulia & Houseplant Society.

Moore, H.E. 1957. *African Violets, Gloxinias and Their Relatives.* A Guide to the Cultivated Gesneriads. New York: Macmillan.

***Salix***

Newsholme, C. 1992. *Willows.* The Genus *Salix.* London: Batsford.

Stott, K.G. 1971 *Willows for Amenity, Windbreaks and Other Uses.* Checklist of the Long Ashton Collection of Willows, with Notes on their Suitability for Various Purposes. Long Ashton Research Station: University of Bristol.

***Salvia***

Clebsch, B. 2003. *A Book of Salvias.* (2nd ed.). Portland, Oregon: Timber Press.

Compton, J. 1994. Mexican Salvias in Cultivation. *The Plantsman* 15(4):193-215.

***Saxifraga***

Bland, B. 2000. *Silver Saxifrages.* Pershore, Worcs.: Alpine Garden Society.

Dashwood, M. & Bland, B. 2005. *Silver Saxifrages: RHS Bulletin No 9.* Wisley, Surrey: RHS. www.rhs.org.uk/plants/documents/saxifraga05.pdf

McGregor, M. Jan 2006. Saxbase. Saxifrage Society. www.saxifraga.org/plants/saxbase/default.asp

McGregor, M. 1995. *Saxifrages: The Complete Cultivars & Hybrids: International Register of Saxifrages.* (2nd ed.). Driffield, E. Yorks: Saxifrage Society.

Webb, D.A. & Gornall, R.J. 1989. *Saxifrages of Europe.* Bromley, Kent: Christopher Helm.

***Sedum***

Evans, R.L. 1983. *Handbook of Cultivated Sedums.* Motcombe, Dorset: Ivory Head Press.

Lord, T. 2006. *Sedum* up for assessment. *The Plantsman* 5(4):244-252.

Stephenson, R. 1994. *Sedum. The Cultivated Stonecrops.* Portland, Oregon: Timber Press.

***Sempervivum***

Diehm, H. Jan 2006. www.semperhorst.de

Miklánek, M. 2002. *The List of Cultivars: Sempervivum and Jovibarba v. 7.01.* Pieštany, Slovakia: M. Miklánek (private distribution).

Miklánek, M. 2000. *List of Cultivars: Sempervivum and Jovibarba* v. 15.1. http://miklanek.tripod.com/MCS/cv.html

***Sinningia***

Dates, J.D. 1988. *The Gesneriad Register 1988. Check List of Names with Descriptions of Cultivated Plants in the Genus Sinningia.* Galesburg, Illinois: American Gloxinia and Gesneriad Society, Inc.

***Solenostemon***

Pedley, W.K. & Pedley, R. 1974. *Coleus – A Guide to Cultivation and Identification.* Edinburgh: Bartholemew.

***Sorbus***

McAllister, H. 2005. *The Genus Sorbus: Mountain Ash and Other Rowans.* Kew: Royal Botanical Gardens.

Snyers d'Attenhoven, C. 1999. *Sorbus* Lombarts hybrids *Belgische Dendrologie*: 76-81. Belgium.

Wright, D. 1981. Sorbus – a Gardener's Evaluation. *The Plantsman* 3(2):65-98.

***Spiraea***

Miller, D.M. 2003. *Spiraea japonica with coloured leaves: RHS Bulletin No 4.* Wisley, Surrey: Royal Horticultural Society. www.rhs.org.uk/plants/documents/spiraea03.pdf

***Streptocarpus***

Arnold, P. 1979. *The Gesneriad Register 1979: Check List of Streptocarpus.* Binghamton, New York: American Gloxinia & Gesneriad.

Dibleys Nurseries Online Catalogue. Oct 2005. www.dibleys.com.

**Succulents**

Eggli, U. (ed.) 2002. *Illustrated Handbook of Succulent Plants.* Heidelberg, Germany: Springer-Verlag.

Eggli, U. & Taylor, N. 1994. *List of Names of Succulent Plants other than Cacti Published 1950-92.* Kew: Royal Botanic Gardens.

Grantham, K. & Klaassen, P. 1999. *The Plantfinder's Guide to Cacti and Other Succulents.* Newton Abbot, Devon: David & Charles.

Jacobsen, H. 1973. *Lexicon of Succulent Plants.* London: Blandford.

***Syringa***

Vrugtman, F. 2000. *International Register of Cultivar Names in the Genus Syringa L. (Oleaceae).* (Contribution No 91). Hamilton, Canada: Royal Botanic Gardens.

***Tiliaceae***

Wild, H. 1984. *Flora of Southern Africa 21 (1: Tiliaceae).* Pretoria: Botanical Research Institute, Dept of Agriculture.

***Tillandsia***

Kiff, L.F. 1991. *A Distributional Checklist of the Genus Tillandsia.* Encino, California: Botanical Diversions.

***Trillium***
Case, F.W.J. & Case, R.B. 1997. *Trilliums*. Portland, Oregon: Timber Press.
Jacobs, D.L. & Jacobs, R.L. 1997. *American Treasures.* Trilliums in Woodland Garden. Decatur, Georgia: Eco-Gardens.
***Tulipa***
Bodegom, S. & van Scheepen, J. (eds). 2005. *Supplement 2005 Classified List and International Register of Tulip Names*. Hillegom, The Netherlands: Koninklijke Algemeene Vereeniging Voor Bloembollencultuur.
van Scheepen, J. (ed.). 1996. *Classified List and International Register of Tulip Names*. Hillegom, The Netherlands: Koninklijke Algemeene Vereeniging Voor Bloembollencultuur.
***Ulmus***
Green, P.S. 1964. Registratration of Cultivar Names in *Ulmus. Arnoldia (Jamaica Plain)* 24:41-80.
***Vaccinium***
Trehane, J. 2004. *Blueberries, Cranberries and Other Vacciniums*. Portland, Oregon: Timber Press.
**Vegetables**
Official Journal of the European Communities. Common catalogue of varieties of vegetable species. (24th ed.). Nov 2005. http://europa.eu.int/eur-lex/lex/JOHtml.do?uri=OJ:C:2005:275A:SOM:EN:HTML
Supps are also given on this website. http://europa.eu.int/eur-lex/lex/JOIndex.do
***Viola***
Coombes, R.E. 2003. *Violets.* (2nd ed.). London: Batsford.
Fuller, R. 1990. *Pansies, Violas & Violettas.* The Complete Guide. Marlborough: The Crowood Press.
Perfect, E.J. 1996. *Armand Millet and his Violets.* High Wycombe: Park Farm Press.
Robinson, P.M. & Snocken, J. 2003. Checklist of the Cultivated Forms of the Genus *Viola* including the Register of Cultivars. American Violet Society. http://americanvioletsociety.org/Registry/
Zambra, G.L. 1950. *Violets for Garden and Market.* (2nd ed.). London: Collingridge.
***Vitis***
Pearkes, G. 1989. *Vine Growing in Britain.* London: Dent.
Robinson, J. 1989. *Vines, Grapes and Wines.* London: Mitchell Beazley.
***Watsonia***
Goldblatt, P. 1989. *The Genus Watsonia.* A Systematic Monograph. South Africa: National Botanic Gardens.
***Weigela***
Howard, R.A. 1965. A Checklist of Cultivar Names in *Weigela. Arnoldia (Jamaica Plain)* 25:49-69.
***Wisteria***
Valder, P. 1995. *Wisterias.* A Comprehensive Guide. Balmain, Australia: Florilegium.
***Yucca***
Smith, C. 2004. *Yuccas: Giants among the Lilies.* NCCPG.
***Zauschneria***
Raven, P.H. 1977. Generic and Sectional Delimitation in *Onagraceae,* Tribe *Epilobieae. Ann. Missouri Bot. Gard.* 63(2):326-340.
Robinson, A. 2000. Focus on Plants: Piping Hot (*Zauschneria* Cultivars). *The Garden* (RHS) 125(9):698-699.

# INTERNATIONAL PLANT FINDERS

## UNITED KINGDOM

Pawsey, Angela (ed). (25th ed.). *Find That Rose!* Pub. May 2007. Celebrating the 25th Edition of *Find That Rose!* Lists approximately 3,450 varieties available in the UK together with basic type, colour and fragrance. New varieties are highlighted and cross-referenced, where applicable, to alternative selling names. Gives full details of around 50 growers/outlets, many offering mail order. Includes useful information on how to find a rose with a particular Christian name, or to celebrate a special event and where to see roses in bloom. For further information send sae to 303 Mile End Road, Colchester, Essex CO4 5EA. To order a copy send a cheque for £3.50 made out to *Find That Rose!* to the above address.
Visit the website on www.findthatrose.net.

# NURSERIES

THE FOLLOWING NURSERIES BETWEEN THEM STOCK AN UNRIVALLED CHOICE OF PLANTS. BEFORE MAKING A VISIT, PLEASE REMEMBER TO CHECK WITH THE NURSERY THAT THE PLANT YOU SEEK IS CURRENTLY AVAILABLE.

# Nursery Codes and Symbols

The first letter of each nursery code represents the area of the country in which the nursery is situated.

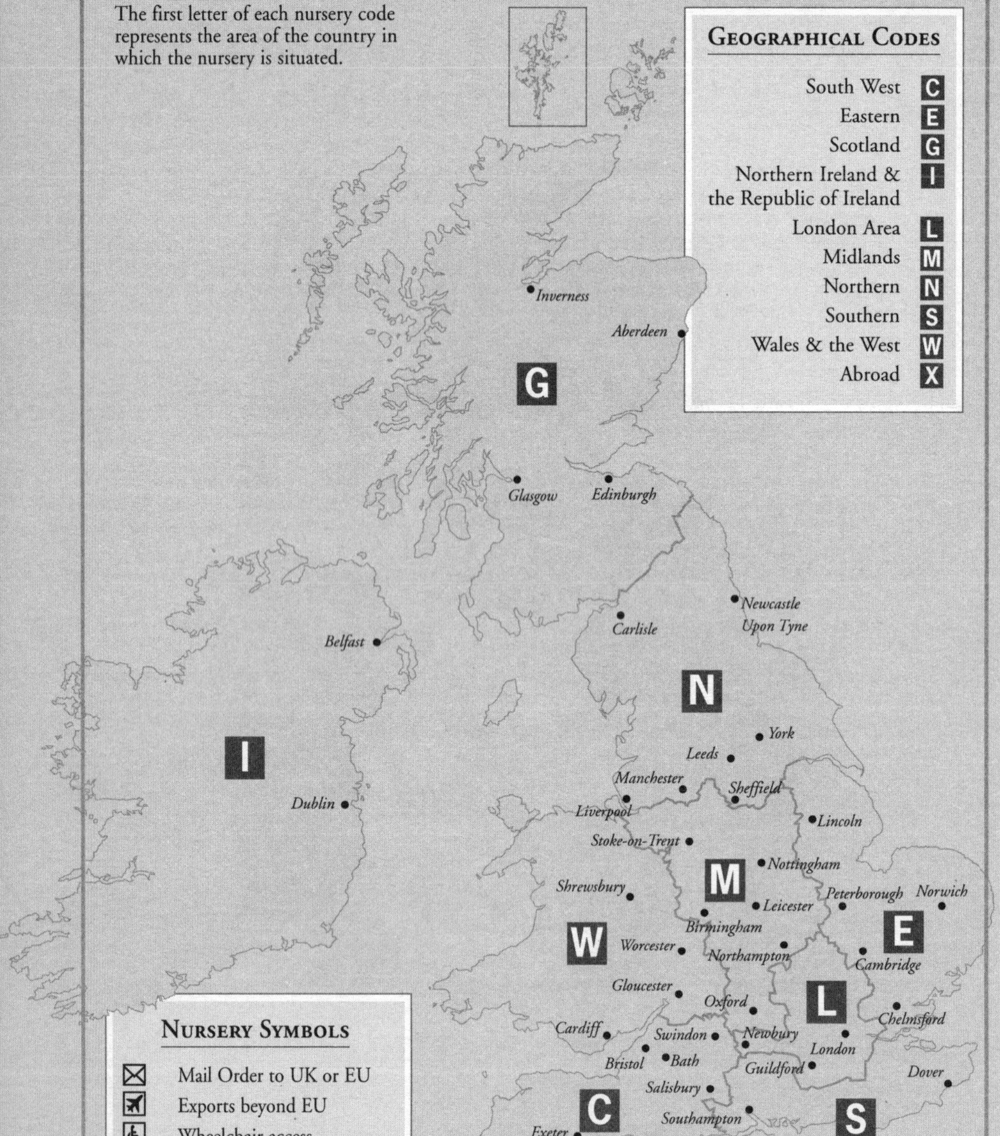


## Geographical Codes

| | |
|---|---|
| South West | C |
| Eastern | E |
| Scotland | G |
| Northern Ireland & the Republic of Ireland | I |
| London Area | L |
| Midlands | M |
| Northern | N |
| Southern | S |
| Wales & the West | W |
| Abroad | X |

## Nursery Symbols

- ☒ Mail Order to UK or EU
- ✈ Exports beyond EU
- ♿ Wheelchair access
- ∩ Delivers to shows
- ◆ See Display advertisement
- € Euro accepted

# USING THE THREE NURSERY LISTINGS

Your main reference from the Plant Directory is the Nursery Details by Code listing, which includes all relevant information for each nursery in order of nursery code. The Nursery Index by Name is an alphabetical list for those who know a nursery's name but not its code and wish to check its details in the main list. The Specialist Nurseries index is to aid those searching for a particular plant group.

## 1 NURSERY DETAILS BY CODE

Once you have found your plant in the Plant Directory, turn to this list to find out the name, address, opening times and other details of the nurseries whose codes accompany the plant.

KEY
- ⊠ Mail order to UK or EU
- Exports beyond EU
- Wheelchair access
- Delivers to shows
- € Euro accepted
- ◆ See Display advertisement

WHil **HILLVIEW HARDY PLANTS** ⊠ € ◆
(off B4176), Worfield, Nr Bridgnorth, Shropshire, WV15 5NT
Ⓣ (01746) 716454
Ⓕ (01746) 716454
Ⓔ hillview@onetel.net
Ⓦ www.hillviewhardyplants.com
**Contact:** Ingrid, John & Sarah Millington
**Opening Times:** 0900-1700 Mon-Sat Mar-mid-Oct. At other times, please phone first.
**Min Mail Order UK:** £15.00 + p&p
**Min Mail Order EU:** £15.00 + p&p
**Cat. Cost:** 5 × 2nd class.
**Credit Cards:** All major credit/debit cards
**Specialities:** Choice herbaceous perennials incl. *Aquilegia, Astrantia, Auricula, Primula, Crocosmia, Eucomis, Ixia, Phlox, Schizostylis, Verbascum, Acanthus.* Nat Collection of *Acanthus.*
**Notes:** Also sells wholesale.
**Map Ref:** W, B4 **OS Grid Ref:** SO772969

*A geographical code is followed by three letters reflecting the nursery's name*

*Refer to the box at the base of each right-hand page for a key to the symbols*

*Other information about the nursery*

*A brief summary of the plants available*

*The map letter is followed by the map square in which the nursery is located*

*The Ordnance Survey national grid reference for use with OS maps*

## 2 NURSERY INDEX BY NAME

If you seek a particular nursery, look it up in this alphabetical index. Note its code and turn to the Nursery Details by Code list for full information.

| | |
|---|---|
| Highfield Hollies | SHHo |
| Hill Garth Nursery | SHGN |
| Hill House Nursery & Gardens | CHll |
| Hillview Hardy Plants | WHil |
| **The Himalayan Garden Co.** | **NHim** |
| Holden Clough Nursery | NHol |
| Holly Gate Cactus Nursery | SHol |
| **Home Farm Plants** | **CHFP** |

## 3 SPECIALIST NURSERIES

A list of 32 categories under which nurseries have classified themselves if they exclusively, or predominantly, supply this range of plants.

### DROUGHT TOLERANT

CKno, CPne, EAlp, ECha, EFam, EGln, EGoo, EHoe, ETod, LLWG, LLWP, LPal, MAga, MHrb, NHoy, SAft, SDow, SIde, SIoW, SJoh, SKHP, SPhx, SUsu, WCor, WHil, WJek , WPnn

# How to Use the Nursery Listings

The details given for each nursery have been compiled from information supplied to us in answer to a questionnaire. In some cases, because of constraints of space, the entries have been slightly abbreviated.

**Nurseries are not charged for their entries and inclusion in no way implies a value judgement.**

## Nursery Details by Code (*page 816*)

Each nursery is allocated a code, for example GPoy. The first letter of each code indicates the main area of the country in which the nursery is situated. In this example, G=Scotland. The remaining three letters reflect the nursery's name, in this case Poyntzfield Herb Nursery.

In this main listing the nurseries are given in alphabetical order of codes for quick reference from the Plant Directory. All of the nurseries' details, such as address, opening times, mail order service etc., will be found here.

## Opening Times

Although opening times have been published as submitted and where applicable, **it is always advisable, especially if travelling a long distance, to check with the nursery first**. The initials NGS indicate that the nursery is open under the National Gardens Scheme.

## Mail Order ⊠

Many nurseries provide a mail order service. **This is, however, often restricted to certain times of the year or to particular genera**. Please check the **Notes** section of each nursery's entry for any restrictions or special conditions.

In some cases, the mail order service extends to all members of the European Union. Where this is offered, the minimum charge to the EU will be noted in the Nursery entry.

Where **'No minimum charge'** (Nmc) is shown, please note that to send even one plant may involve the nursery in substantial postage and packing costs. Some nurseries may not be prepared to send tender or bulky plants.

Where a nursery offers a **mail order only** service, this will be noted under **Opening Times** in the nursery entry.

## Export ✈

Export refers to mail order beyond the European Union. Nurseries that are prepared to consider exporting are indicated. However, there is usually a substantial minimum charge and, in addition, all the costs of Phytosanitary Certificates and Customs have to be met by the purchaser.

## Catalogue Cost

Some nurseries offer their catalogue free, or for a few stamps, but a large (at least A5) stamped addressed envelope is always appreciated as well. Overseas customers should use an equivalent number of International Reply Coupons (IRCs) in place of stamps.

Increasingly, nurseries are finding it more cost effective to produce catalogues on the Internet rather than printing them. Many nurseries also offer an online mail order facility.

## Wheelchair Access ♿

Nurseries are asked to indicate if their premises are suitable for wheelchair users. Where only partial access is indicated, this is noted in the Notes field and the nursery is not marked with the symbol.

The assessment of ease-of-access is entirely the responsibility of the individual nursery.

## Specialities

Nurseries list here the plants or genera that they supply and any National Collections of plants they may hold. Please note that some nurseries may charge an entry fee to visit a National Collection. Always enquire before visiting.

Nurseries will also note here if they only have small quantities of individual plants available for sale or if they will propagate to order.

## Notes

In this section, you will find notes on any restrictions to mail order or export; on limited wheelchair access; or the nursery site address, if this differs from the office address; together with any other non-horticultural information.

## Delivery to Shows

Many nurseries will deliver pre-ordered plants to flower shows for collection by customers. These are indicated by a marquee symbol. Contact the nursery for details of shows they attend.

## Payment in Euros €

A number of UK nurseries have indicated that they will accept payment in Euros. You should, however, check with the nursery concerned before making such a payment, as some will only accept cash and some only cheques, whilst others will expect the purchaser to pay bank charges.

## Maps

If you wish to visit any of the nurseries you can find its approximate location on the relevant map (following p.935), unless the nursery has requested this is not shown. Nurseries are also encouraged to provide their Ordnance Survey national grid reference for use with OS publications such as the Land Ranger series.

## Nursery Index by Name

For convenience, an alphabetical index of nurseries is included on p.926. This gives the names of all nurseries listed in the book in alphabetical order of nursery name together with their code.

## Specialist Nurseries (*page 933*)

This list of nurseries is intended to help those with an interest in finding specialist categories of plant. Nurseries have been asked to classify themselves under one or more headings where this represents the type of plant they *predominantly* or *exclusively* have in stock. For example, if you wish to find a nursery specialising in ornamental grasses, look up 'Grasses' in the listing where you will find a list of nursery codes. Then turn to the Nursery Details by Code, for details of the nurseries.

Please note that not all nurseries shown here will have plants listed in the Plant Directory. This may be their choice or because the *RHS Plant Finder* does not list seeds or annuals and only terrestrial orchids and hardy cacti. For space reasons, it is rare to find a nursery's full catalogue listed in the Plant Directory.

**In all cases, please ensure you ring to confirm the range available before embarking on a journey to the nursery.**
The specialist plant groups listed in this edition are:

Acid-loving
Alpines/rock
Aquatics/marginals
Bamboos
British wild flowers
Bulbous plants
Cacti & succulents
Carnivorous
Chalk-loving
Climbers
Coastal
Conifers
Conservatory
Drought-tolerant
Ferns
Fruit
Grasses
Hedging
Herbs
Marginal/bog plants
Orchids
Organic
Ornamental trees
Peat-free
Period plants
Propagate to order
Roses
Seeds
Specimen-sized plants
Topiary
Tropical plants

Perennials and shrubs have been omitted as these are considered to be too general and serviced by a great proportion of the nurseries.

## Deleted Nurseries

Every year some nurseries ask to be removed from the book. This may be a temporary measure because they are moving, or it may be permanent due to closure, sale, retirement, or a change in the way in they trade. Occasionally, nurseries are unable to meet the closing date and will re-enter the book in the following edition. Some nurseries simply do not reply and, as we have no current information on them, they are deleted.

*Please, never use an old edition*

# Nursery Details by Code

Please note that all these nurseries are listed in alphabetical order by their code. All nurseries are listed in alphabetical order by their name in the **Nursery Index by Name** on page 926.

## South West

**CAbb** **Abbotsbury Sub-Tropical Gardens** ⊠ ♿
Abbotsbury, Nr Weymouth, Dorset,
DT3 4LA
Ⓣ (01305) 871344
Ⓕ (01305) 871344
Ⓔ info@abbotsburygardens.co.uk
Ⓦ www.abbotsburyplantsales.co.uk
**Contact:** David Sutton
**Opening Times:** 1000-1800 daily mid Mar-1st Nov. 1000-1500 Nov-mid Mar.
**Min Mail Order UK:** £10.00 + p&p
**Cat. Cost:** £2.00 + A4 sae + 42p stamp
**Credit Cards:** Access Visa MasterCard Switch
**Specialities:** Less common & tender shrubs incl. palms, tree ferns, bamboos & plants from Australia, New Zealand & S. Africa.

**CAbP** **Abbey Plants** ⊠ ♿
Chaffeymoor, Bourton, Gillingham, Dorset,
SP8 5BY
Ⓣ (01747) 840841
**Contact:** K Potts
**Opening Times:** 1000-1300 & 1400-1700 Wed-Sat Mar-Nov. Dec-Feb by appt.
**Min Mail Order UK:** Nmc
**Cat. Cost:** 2 × 2nd class
**Credit Cards:** None
**Specialities:** Flowering trees & shrubs. Shrub roses incl. many unusual varieties. Limited stock.
**Map Ref:** C, B4 OS **Grid Ref:** ST762304

**CAbx** **Abraxas Gardens** ⊠ ♿
7 Little Keyford Lane, Frome, Somerset,
BA11 5BB
Ⓣ (01373) 472879
**Contact:** Duncan Skene
**Opening Times:** Not open, except by appt. Mail order only.
**Min Mail Order UK:** £20.00
**Cat. Cost:** Free. New list annually in Jan.
**Credit Cards:** None
**Specialities:** *Crocosmia*, *Iris sibirica*, *Hemerocallis* (spiders, spider variants & unusual forms). Many recent introductions available only in small numbers.
**Notes:** Plants despatched in Apr/May only.
**Map Ref:** C, B5 **OS Grid Ref:** ST775465

**CAby** **The Abbey Nursery** ♿
Forde Abbey, Chard, Somerset,
TA20 4LU
Ⓣ (01460) 220088
Ⓕ (01460) 220088
Ⓔ TheAbbeyNursery@btconnect.com
**Contact:** Peter Sims
**Opening Times:** 1000-1700 7 days, 1st Mar-31st Oct. Please phone first to check opening times in Mar.
**Cat. Cost:** None issued.
**Credit Cards:** All major credit/debit cards
**Specialities:** Hardy herbaceous perennials.
**Map Ref:** C, C4 **OS Grid Ref:** ST359052

**CAgr** **Agroforestry Research Trust** ⊠
46 Hunters Moon, Dartington,
Totnes, Devon,
TQ9 6JT
Ⓣ (01803) 840776
Ⓕ (01803) 840776
Ⓔ mail@agroforestry.co.uk
Ⓦ www.agroforestry.co.uk
**Contact:** Martin Crawford
**Opening Times:** Not open. Mail order only.
**Min Mail Order UK:** Nmc
**Min Mail Order EU:** Nmc
**Cat. Cost:** 4 × 1st class
**Credit Cards:** All major credit/debit cards
**Specialities:** Top & soft fruit, nut trees including *Castanea*, *Corylus*, *Juglans*, *Pinus*. Also seeds. Some plants in small quantities only.

C

CAni **ANITA ALLEN** ⊠
Shapcott Barton Estate, East Knowstone, South Molton, Devon, EX36 4EE
Ⓣ (01398) 341664
Ⓕ (01398) 341664
**Contact:** Anita Allen
**Opening Times:** By appt. only. Garden open under NGS.
**Min Mail Order UK:** Nmc.
**Cat. Cost:** 5 × 1st class & state which catalogue, Shasta daisies or *Buddleja*.
**Credit Cards:** None
**Specialities:** National Collections of *Leucanthemum* × *superbum* & *Buddleja davidii* & hybrids, 70+ cvs. 80+ accurately named Shasta daisies, a few in very short supply. Also many hardy perennials.
**Map Ref:** C, B3 **OS Grid Ref:** SS846235

CArn **ARNE HERBS** ⊠ ✈ € ♿
Limeburn Nurseries, Limeburn Hill, Chew Magna, Bristol, BS40 8QW
Ⓣ (01275) 333399
Ⓔ lyman@lyman-dixon.freeserve.co.uk
Ⓦ www.arneherbs.co.uk
**Contact:** A Lyman-Dixon & Jenny Thomas
**Opening Times:** 1000-1600 most weekdays, Sat mid-Mar-end Jun. Other times by telephone appt. only.
**Min Mail Order UK:** Nmc
**Min Mail Order EU:** Nmc
**Cat. Cost:** £3.75 UK, 10 × IRC, or A4 sae for free nondescriptive plantlist. Also online.
**Credit Cards:** None
**Specialities:** Herbs, some very rare. North American, Mediterranean & UK wild flowers. Also plants for reseach, conservation projects & historical recreations.
**Notes:** Will deliver to Farmers' Markets. Also sells wholesale.
**Map Ref:** C, A5 **OS Grid Ref:** ST563638

CAvo **AVON BULBS** ⊠ ⌂
Burnt House Farm, Mid-Lambrook, South Petherton, Somerset, TA13 5HE
Ⓣ (01460) 242177
Ⓕ (01460) 249025
Ⓔ info@avonbulbs.co.uk
Ⓦ www.avonbulbs.co.uk
**Contact:** C Ireland-Jones
**Opening Times:** Mail order only. Open Thu, Fri, Sat, mid-Sep-end Oct & mid Feb-end Mar for collection of pre-booked orders.
**Min Mail Order UK:** £10.00 + p&p
**Min Mail Order EU:** £20.00 + p&p
**Cat. Cost:** 4 × 2nd class
**Credit Cards:** Visa Access Switch MasterCard
**Specialities:** Some special snowdrops are only available in small quantities.
**Notes:** £1.00 handling charge for delivering plants to shows.
**Map Ref:** C, B5

CBcs **BURNCOOSE NURSERIES** ⊠ ✈ ⌂ ♿
Gwennap, Redruth, Cornwall, TR16 6BJ
Ⓣ (01209) 860316
Ⓕ (01209) 860011
Ⓔ burncoose@eclipse.co.uk
Ⓦ www.burncoose.co.uk
**Contact:** C H Williams
**Opening Times:** 0830-1700 Mon-Sat & 1100-1700 Sun.
**Min Mail Order UK:** Nmc
**Min Mail Order EU:** Individual quotations for EU sales.
**Cat. Cost:** £1.50 incl. p&p
**Credit Cards:** Visa Access Switch
**Specialities:** Extensive range of over 3500 ornamental trees & shrubs and herbaceous. Rare & unusual *Magnolia*, *Rhododendron*. Conservatory plants. 30 acre garden.
**Notes:** Also sells wholesale.
**Map Ref:** C, D1 **OS Grid Ref:** SW742395

CBct **BARRACOTT PLANTS** ⊠ ⌂ € ♿
Old Orchard, Calstock Road, Gunnislake, Cornwall, PL18 9AA
Ⓣ (01822) 832234
Ⓔ GEOFF@geoff63.freeserve.co.uk
Ⓦ www.barracottplants.co.uk
**Contact:** Geoff & Thelma Turner
**Opening Times:** 0900-1700 Thu-Sat, Mar-end Sep. Other times by appt.
**Min Mail Order UK:** Nmc
**Cat. Cost:** 2 × 1st class
**Credit Cards:** None
**Specialities:** Herbaceous plants: shade-loving, foliage & form. *Acanthus*, *Aspidistra*, *Astrantia*, *Bergenia*, *Convallaria*, *Disporum*, *Liriope*, *Polygonatum*, *Roscoea*, *Smilacina*, *Trillium*, *Tricyrtis* & *Uvularia*.
**Notes:** Also sells wholesale.
**Map Ref:** C, C3 **OS Grid Ref:** SX436702

CBdn **BOWDEN HOSTAS** ⊠ ✈ ♿
Sticklepath, Okehampton, Devon, EX20 2NL
Ⓣ (01837) 840989
Ⓕ (01837) 849180
Ⓔ info@bowdenhostas.com
Ⓦ www.bowdenhostas.com

KEY
⊠ Mail order to UK or EU ⌂ Delivers to shows
✈ Exports beyond EU € Euro accepted
♿ Accessible by wheelchair ◆ See Display advertisement

C

**Contact:** Tim Penrose
**Opening Times:** 1000-1600 Mon-Sat (1000-1500 Wed), 1st Mar to 30th Sep 2007.
**Min Mail Order UK:** Nmc
**Min Mail Order EU:** Nmc
**Cat. Cost:** Free.
**Credit Cards:** Visa Access EuroCard, Switch
**Specialities:** *Hosta* only. Nat. Collection of modern hybrid *Hosta*.
**Notes:** Also sells wholesale.
**Map Ref:** C, C3 **OS Grid Ref:** SX640940

**CBdw** BODWEN NURSERY ⊠
Pothole, St Austell, Cornwall, PL26 7DW
Ⓣ (01726) 883855
Ⓔ sales@bodwen-nursery.co.uk
Ⓦ www.bodwen-nursery.co.uk
**Contact:** John Geraghty
**Opening Times:** Not open. Mail order only.
**Min Mail Order UK:** Nmc
**Cat. Cost:** 2 × 2nd class
**Credit Cards:** None
**Specialities:** Japanese maples. Some rarer cultivars available in small quantities only.
**Notes:** Also sells wholesale.

**CBen** BENNETTS WATER GARDENS ⊠ ♿
Putton Lane, Chickerell, Weymouth, Dorset, DT3 4AF
Ⓣ (01305) 785150
Ⓔ enquiries@waterlily.co.uk
Ⓦ www.waterlily.co.uk
**Contact:** J Bennett
**Opening Times:** 1000-1700 Apr-Sep. Closed Mon & Sat.
**Min Mail Order UK:** Nmc
**Cat. Cost:** Sae for price list
**Credit Cards:** Visa Access MasterCard Switch
**Specialities:** Aquatic plants. Bog Plants. Nat. Collection of Water Lilies.
**Notes:** Mail order Mar-Sep only.
**Map Ref:** C, C5 **OS Grid Ref:** SY651797

**CBgR** BEGGAR'S ROOST PLANTS ⊠ € ♿
Lilstock, Bridgwater, Somerset, TA5 1SU
Ⓣ (01278) 741519
Ⓕ (01278) 741519
Ⓔ ro@beggarsroostplants.co.uk
Ⓦ www.beggarsroostplants.co.uk
**Contact:** Rosemary FitzGerald
**Opening Times:** By appt. only.
**Min Mail Order UK:** Nmc
**Min Mail Order EU:** Nmc
**Credit Cards:** None
**Specialities:** Garden-worthy bulbs & herbaceous, emphasising species. Classic perennials, incl. *Crocosmia* & *Hemerocallis*. Winter interest plants. Small quantities only.
**Map Ref:** C, B4 **OS Grid Ref:** ST168450

**CBnk** M.T. BENNALLACK ⊠
(Office) Aintree, Green Park Way, Chillington, Kingsbridge, Devon, TQ7 2HY
Ⓜ 07814 303363
**Contact:** M T Bennallack
**Opening Times:** By appt only Aug & Sept.
**Min Mail Order UK:** Nmc
**Cat. Cost:** 3 × 1st class.
**Credit Cards:** None
**Specialities:** Nat. Collection of *Aster novi-belgii*. Propagate to order in spring.
**Notes:** Mail order Apr & May only. Nursery not at this address.

**CBod** BODMIN PLANT AND HERB NURSERY ♿
Laveddon Mill, Laninval Hill, Bodmin, Cornwall, PL30 5JU
Ⓣ (01208) 72837
Ⓕ (01208) 76491
Ⓔ bodminnursery@aol.com
**Contact:** Mark Lawlor
**Opening Times:** 0900-1700 Mon-Sat Nov-Mar, 0900-1800 Mon-Sat Apr-Oct. 1000-1600 Sun.
**Credit Cards:** All major credit/debit cards
**Specialities:** Herbs, herbaceous & grasses, hardy geraniums & coastal plants. Interesting shrubs, fruit & ornamental trees.
**Map Ref:** C, C2 **OS Grid Ref:** SX053659

**CBow** BOWLEY PLANTS ⊠
Church Farm, North End, Ashton Keynes, Nr Swindon, Wiltshire, SN6 6QR
Ⓣ (01285) 640352
Ⓜ 07855 524929
Ⓦ www.bowleyplants.co.uk
**Contact:** Piers Bowley
**Opening Times:** Some Sat, Mar-Oct. Please phone first.
**Min Mail Order UK:** Nmc
**Cat. Cost:** 2 × 1st class
**Credit Cards:** None
**Specialities:** Variegated plants & coloured foliage. Alpines, perennials. shrubs, ferns, grasses & herbs. Some varieties in small numbers.
**Notes:** Also sells wholesale.
**Map Ref:** C, A6 **OS Grid Ref:** SU043945

**CBrd** BROADLEAS GARDENS LTD
Broadleas, Devizes, Wiltshire, SN10 5JQ
Ⓣ (01380) 722035
Ⓕ (01380) 722970

Ⓔ broadleasgardens@btinternet.com
**Contact:** Lady Anne Cowdray
**Opening Times:** 1400-1800 Wed, Thu & Sun Apr-Oct.
**Cat. Cost:** 1 × 1st class
**Credit Cards:** None
**Specialities:** General range.

CBre **Bregover Plants** ⊠ ⌂
Hillbrooke, Middlewood, North Hill, Nr Launceston, Cornwall, PL15 7NN
Ⓣ (01566) 782661
**Contact:** Jennifer Bousfield
**Opening Times:** 1100-1700 Wed, Mar-mid Oct and by appt.
**Min Mail Order UK:** Nmc
**Min Mail Order EU:** Nmc
**Cat. Cost:** 3 × 1st class
**Credit Cards:** None
**Specialities:** Unusual hardy perennials grown in small garden nursery. Available in small quantities only.
**Notes:** Mail order Oct-Mar only.
**Map Ref:** C, C2 **OS Grid Ref:** SX273752

CBro **Broadleigh Gardens** ⊠ ⌂ ♿
Bishops Hull, Taunton, Somerset, TA4 1AE
Ⓣ (01823) 286231
Ⓕ (01823) 323646
Ⓔ info@broadleighbulbs.co.uk
Ⓦ www.broadleighbulbs.co.uk
**Contact:** Lady Skelmersdale
**Opening Times:** 0900-1600 Mon-Fri for viewing only. Orders collected if notice given.
**Min Mail Order UK:** Nmc
**Min Mail Order EU:** Nmc
**Cat. Cost:** 2 × 1st class
**Credit Cards:** Switch MasterCard Maestro
**Specialities:** Jan catalogue: bulbs in growth (*Galanthus*, *Cyclamen* etc.) & herbaceous woodland plants (trilliums, hellebores etc). Extensive list of *Agapanthus*. June catalogue: dwarf & unusual bulbs, *Iris* (DB & PC). Nat. Collection of Alec Grey hybrid daffodils.
**Map Ref:** C, B4 **OS Grid Ref:** ST195251

CBrP **Brooklands Plants** ⊠
25 Treves Road, Dorchester, Dorset, DT1 2HE
Ⓣ (01305) 265846
Ⓔ Ian@cycads.fsnet.co.uk
**Contact:** Ian Watt
**Opening Times:** By appt. for collection of plants only.
**Min Mail Order UK:** £25.00 + p&p
**Min Mail Order EU:** £25.00 + p&p
**Cat. Cost:** 2 × 2nd class
**Credit Cards:** None
**Specialities:** Cycad nursery specialising in the more cold-tolerant species of *Encephalartos*, *Dioon*, *Macrozamia* & *Cycas*. Also hardy palms, *Agave*, *Yucca*, *Dasylirion* & bamboos. Some species available in small quantities only.
**Map Ref:** C, C5 **OS Grid Ref:** SY682897

CBur **Burnham Nurseries** ⊠ ✈ ⌂ ♿
Forches Cross, Newton Abbot, Devon, TQ12 6PZ
Ⓣ (01626) 352233
Ⓕ (01626) 362167
Ⓔ mail@orchids.uk.com
Ⓦ www.orchids.uk.com
**Contact:** Any member of staff
**Opening Times:** 1000-1600 Mon-Sun.
**Min Mail Order UK:** Nmc
**Min Mail Order EU:** £100.00 + p&p
**Cat. Cost:** A4 sae + 55p stamp
**Credit Cards:** Visa American Express MasterCard Maestro
**Specialities:** All types of orchid except British native types.
**Notes:** Please ask for details on export beyond EU.
**Map Ref:** C, C4 **OS Grid Ref:** SX841732

CCAT **Cider Apple Trees** ⊠ €
Kerian, Corkscrew Lane, Woolston, Nr North Cadbury, Somerset, BA22 7BP
Ⓣ (01963) 441101
Ⓦ www.ciderappletrees.co.uk
**Contact:** Mr J Dennis
**Opening Times:** By appt. only.
**Min Mail Order UK:** £9.50
**Min Mail Order EU:** £9.50
**Cat. Cost:** Free
**Credit Cards:** None
**Specialities:** *Malus* (speciality standard trees).
**Notes:** Also sells wholesale.
**Map Ref:** C, B5

CCCN **Cross Common Nursery** ⊠ ◆
The Lizard, Helston, Cornwall, TR12 7PD
Ⓣ (01326) 290722/290668
Ⓔ info@crosscommonnursery.co.uk
Ⓦ www.crosscommonnursery.co.uk
**Contact:** Suzy Bosustow
**Opening Times:** 1000-1700 7 days, Apr, May & Jun. Please phone for opening hours at other times.
**Min Mail Order UK:** Nmc

KEY
⊠ Mail order to UK or EU ⌂ Delivers to shows
✈ Exports beyond EU € Euro accepted
♿ Accessible by wheelchair ◆ See Display advertisement

C

**Cat. Cost:** Online only.
**Credit Cards:** All major credit/debit cards accepted for online sales only.
**Specialities:** Tropical/sub-tropical, coastal plants & conservatory plants. Wide range of grapevines and *Citrus* trees. Some plants available in small quantities only.
**Map Ref:** C,D1 **OS Grid Ref:** SW704116

**CCge** **COTTAGE GARDEN PLANTS AND HERBS** ⌂
4 Lundy View, Northam,
Bideford, Devon,
EX39 1BE
Ⓣ (01237) 470370
**Contact:** Shirley Bennett
**Opening Times:** Ring for private visit.
**Cat. Cost:** None issued
**Credit Cards:** None
**Specialities:** Cottage garden plants, herbs and esp. hardy geraniums (200+ varieties available).
**Notes:** Lectures given on 'Hardy Geraniums' & 'Cottage Garden Plants and Gardens'. Sells at Devon NCCPG, plant sales & other markets.

**CCha** **CHAPEL FARM HOUSE NURSERY** € ♿
Halwill Junction, Beaworthy, Devon,
EX21 5UF
Ⓣ (01409) 221594
Ⓕ (01409) 221594
**Contact:** Robin or Toshie Hull
**Opening Times:** 0900-1700 Tue-Sat, 1000-1600 Sun & B/hol Mons.
**Cat. Cost:** None issued.
**Credit Cards:** None
**Specialities:** Plants from Japan. Also herbaceous. Japanese garden design service offered.
**Map Ref:** C, C3

**CChe** **CHERRY TREE NURSERY** ♿
(Sheltered Work Opportunities), off New Road Roundabout, Northbourne,
Bournemouth, Dorset, BH10 7DA
Ⓣ (01202) 593537 (01202) 590840
Ⓕ (01202) 590626
**Contact:** Stephen Jailler
**Opening Times:** 0830-1530 Mon-Fri, 0900-1200 most Sats.
**Cat. Cost:** A4 sae + 66p stamps
**Credit Cards:** None
**Specialities:** Hardy shrubs, perennials, climbers, grasses.
**Notes:** Also sells wholesale.
**Map Ref:** C, C6

**CCVN** **CULM VIEW NURSERY** ⌂
Waterloo Farm, Clayhidon, Devon,
EX15 3TN
Ⓣ (01823) 680698
Ⓔ plants@culmviewnursery.co.uk
Ⓦ www.culmviewnursery.co.uk
**Contact:** Brian & Alison Jacobs
**Opening Times:** By appt. only for collection.
**Credit Cards:** None
**Specialities:** Hebaceous perennials grown in peat-free compost.

**CCVT** **CHEW VALLEY TREES** ⊠
Winford Road, Chew Magna, Bristol,
BS40 8QE
Ⓣ (01275) 333752
Ⓕ (01275) 333746
Ⓔ info@chewvalleytrees.co.uk
Ⓦ www.chewvalleytrees.co.uk
**Contact:** J Scarth
**Opening Times:** 0800-1700 Mon-Fri all year. 0900-1600 Sat, Sep-Jun. Closed Sun & B/hols.
**Min Mail Order UK:** Nmc
**Cat. Cost:** Free
**Credit Cards:** All major credit/debit cards
**Specialities:** Native British & ornamental trees, shrubs, apple trees & hedging.
**Notes:** Partial wheelchair access. Max. plant height for mail order 2m incl. roots. Also sells wholesale.
**Map Ref:** C, A5 **OS Grid Ref:** ST558635

**CDes** **DESIRABLE PLANTS** ⊠ ⌂
(Office) Pentamar, Crosspark, Totnes, Devon,
TQ9 5BQ
Ⓣ (01803) 864489 evenings
Ⓔ sutton.totnes@lineone.net
Ⓦ www.desirableplants.com
**Contact:** Dr J J & Mrs S A Sutton
**Opening Times:** Not open. Mail order only.
**Min Mail Order UK:** £15.00
**Cat. Cost:** 5 × 1st class.
**Credit Cards:** None
**Specialities:** Eclectic range of choice & interesting herbaceous plants by mail order.
**Notes:** Nursery not at this address.

**CDMG** **DOCTON MILL GARDENS** € ♿
Lyme Bridge, Hartland, Devon,
EX39 6EA
Ⓣ (01237) 441369
Ⓕ (01237) 441369
Ⓔ john@doctonmill.freeserve.co.uk
Ⓦ www.doctonmill.co.uk
**Contact:** John or Lana Borrett
**Opening Times:** 1000-1800 7 days, 1st Mar-31st Oct.

**Credit Cards:** All major credit/debit cards
**Specialities:** Most plants available in small quantities only.
**Map Ref:** C, B2

**CDob** **Samuel Dobie & Son** ⊠
Long Road, Paignton, Devon,
TQ4 7SX
Ⓣ 0870 112 3623
Ⓕ 0870 112 3624
Ⓦ www.dobies.co.uk
**Contact:** Customer Services
**Opening Times:** Not open. Mail order only. Phone line open 0830-1700 Mon-Fri (office). Also answerphone.
**Min Mail Order UK:** Nmc
**Cat. Cost:** Free
**Credit Cards:** Visa MasterCard Switch Delta
**Specialities:** Wide selection of popular flower & vegetable seeds. Also includes young plants, summer-flowering bulbs & garden sundries.
**Notes:** Mail order to UK & Rep. of Ireland only.

**CDoC** **Duchy of Cornwall** ⊠ ◆
Cott Road, Lostwithiel, Cornwall,
PL22 0HW
Ⓣ (01208) 872668
Ⓕ (01208) 872835
Ⓔ sales@duchyofcornwallnursery.co.uk
Ⓦ www.duchyofcornwallnursery.co.uk
**Contact:** Tracy Wilson
**Opening Times:** 0900-1700 Mon-Sat, 1000-1700 Sun & B/hols.
**Min Mail Order UK:** £14.00
**Cat. Cost:** None issued.
**Credit Cards:** All major credit/debit cards
**Specialities:** *Camellia*, *Fuchsia*, conifers & *Magnolia*. Also a huge range of garden plants incl. trees, shrubs, roses, perennials, fruit & conservatory plants.
**Notes:** Nursery partially available for wheelchair users.
**Map Ref:** C, C2 **OS Grid Ref:** SX112614

**CDow** **Downside Nurseries** ♿
Upper Westwood, Bradford-on-Avon,
Wiltshire, BA15 2DE
Ⓣ (01225) 862392
Ⓕ (01255) 866902
**Contact:** Lorraine Young
**Opening Times:** 0900-1700, 7 days.
**Cat. Cost:** Not available.
**Credit Cards:** All major credit/debit cards
**Specialities:** Herbaceous perennials, also shrubs, roses, trees & seasonal bedding.
**Notes:** Follow brown signs from B3109.
**Map Ref:** C, A5 **OS Grid Ref:** ST80591048

**CDTJ** **Desert to Jungle** ⊠ ⌂ ♿
Henlade Garden Nursery, Lower Henlade,
Taunton, Somerset, TA3 5NB
Ⓣ (01823) 443701
Ⓔ plants@deserttojungle.com
Ⓦ www.deserttojungle.com
**Contact:** Rob Gudge, Dave Root
**Opening Times:** 1000-1700 Mon-Sun, 1st Mar-31st Oct. Thu, Fri & Sat only Nov-Feb, or phone first.
**Min Mail Order UK:** Nmc
**Cat. Cost:** 1 × 1st class sae.
**Credit Cards:** All major credit/debit cards
**Specialities:** Exotic-looking plants giving a desert or jungle effect in the garden. Incl. *Canna*, aroids, succulents, tree ferns & bamboos.
**Notes:** Nursery shares drive with Mount Somerset Hotel. Also sells wholesale.
**Map Ref:** C, B4 **OS Grid Ref:** ST273232

**CDul** **Dulford Nurseries** ⊠ ♿
Cullompton, Devon, EX15 2DG
Ⓣ (01884) 266361
Ⓕ (01884) 266663
Ⓔ dulford.nurseries@virgin.net
Ⓦ www.dulford-nurseries.co.uk
**Contact:** Paul & Mary Ann Rawlings
**Opening Times:** 0730-1630 Mon-Fri.
**Min Mail Order UK:** Nmc
**Min Mail Order EU:** Nmc
**Cat. Cost:** Free.
**Credit Cards:** All major credit/debit cards
**Specialities:** Native, ornamental & unusual trees & shrubs incl. oaks, maples, beech, birch, chestnut, ash, lime, *Sorbus* & pines.
**Notes:** Also sells wholesale.
**Map Ref:** C, C4 **OS Grid Ref:** SY062062

**CDWL** **Dorset Water Lilies** ⌂ ♿
Yeovil Road, Halstock, Yeovil, Somerset,
BA22 9RR
Ⓣ (01935) 891668
Ⓕ (01935) 891946
Ⓔ dorsetwaterlily@tiscali.co.uk
Ⓦ www.dorsetwaterlily.co.uk
**Contact:** Richard Gallehawk
**Opening Times:** 0900-1600 Mon & Fri only, plus Sat in summer.
**Cat. Cost:** Free.
**Credit Cards:** None
**Specialities:** Hardy & tropical water lilies, lotus, marginal & bogside plants.

| KEY | | |
|---|---|---|
| | ⊠ Mail order to UK or EU | ⌂ Delivers to shows |
| | ✈ Exports beyond EU | € Euro accepted |
| | ♿ Accessible by wheelchair | ◆ See Display advertisement |

C

**Notes:** Pond design & construction service. Also sells wholesale.
**Map Ref:** C, C5 **OS Grid Ref:** ST543083

CElw **ELWORTHY COTTAGE PLANTS** ♿
Elworthy Cottage, Elworthy,
Nr Lydeard St Lawrence, Taunton,
Somerset, TA4 3PX
Ⓣ (01984) 656427
Ⓔ mike@elworthy-cottage.co.uk
Ⓦ www.elworthy-cottage.co.uk
**Contact:** Mrs J M Spiller
**Opening Times:** 1000-1630 Thu, late Mar-end Jul. Also by appt. Feb-Nov.
**Cat. Cost:** 3 × 2nd class
**Credit Cards:** None
**Specialities:** *Clematis* & unusual herbaceous plants esp. hardy *Geranium*, *Geum*, grasses, *Campanula*, *Crocosmia*, *Pulmonaria*, *Astrantia*, *Viola* & *Galanthus*. Some varieties only available in in small quantities.
**Notes:** Nursery on B3188, 5 miles north of Wiveliscombe, in centre of Elworthy village.
**Map Ref:** C, B4 **OS Grid Ref:** ST084349

CEnd **ENDSLEIGH GARDENS** ⊠ ♿ ◆
Milton Abbot, Tavistock, Devon,
PL19 0PG
Ⓣ (01822) 870235
Ⓕ (01822) 870513
Ⓔ Treemail@endsleigh-gardens.com
Ⓦ www.endsleigh-gardens.com
**Contact:** Michael Taylor
**Opening Times:** 0800-1700 Mon-Sat. 1000-1700 Sun.
**Min Mail Order UK:** Nmc
**Cat. Cost:** 2 × 1st class
**Credit Cards:** Visa Access Switch MasterCard
**Specialities:** Choice & unusual trees & shrubs incl. *Acer* & *Cornus* cvs. Old apples & cherries. *Wisteria*. Grafting service.
**Map Ref:** C, C3

CEnt **ENTWOOD FARM PLANTS**
Harcombe, Lyme Regis, Dorset,
DT7 3RN
Ⓣ (01297) 444034
**Contact:** Jenny & Ivan Harding
**Opening Times:** 1000-1700 Wed-Sat, Apr-end Sep. Sat only Mar & Oct. Other times, please phone first.
**Cat. Cost:** 3 × 1st class.
**Credit Cards:** None
**Specialities:** Perennials & bamboos. Selection of shrubs, grasses, herbs & bulbs. All stock propagated & grown at nursery, some in small quantities.
**Map Ref:** C,C4 **OS Grid Ref:** SY335953

CExc **EXCLUSIVE PLANTS** ⊠ €
Tretawn, High Cross, Constantine, Falmouth, Cornwall, TR11 5RE
Ⓜ 07775 811385
Ⓔ Pbonavia@lycos.co.uk
Ⓦ www.exclusiveplants.co.uk
**Contact:** Paul Bonavia
**Opening Times:** Not open. Mail order only.
**Min Mail Order UK:** Nmc
**Min Mail Order EU:** £20 + p&p
**Cat. Cost:** 2 × 1st class
**Credit Cards:** None
**Specialities:** Woodland plants.

CFee **FEEBERS HARDY PLANTS** ⊠ ♿ ◆
1 Feeber Cottage, Westwood, Broadclyst,
Nr Exeter, Devon, EX5 3DQ
Ⓣ (01404) 822118
Ⓔ Feebers@onetel.com
**Contact:** Mrs E Squires
**Opening Times:** Open at any reasonable time by prior telephone arrangement.
**Min Mail Order UK:** Nmc
**Min Mail Order EU:** Nmc
**Cat. Cost:** Sae + 36p stamp.
**Credit Cards:** None
**Specialities:** Plants for wet clay soils, alpines & hardy perennials incl. those raised by Amos Perry. Small quantities of plants held unless grown from seed.
**Notes:** Mail order limited. Nursery accessible for wheelchairs in dry weather only.
**Map Ref:** C, C4

CFFs **FLORAL FIREWORKS** ⊠
Burnt House Farm, Mid Lambrook,
South Petherton, Somerset,
TA13 5HE
Ⓣ (01460) 249060
Ⓕ (01460) 249025
Ⓔ info@floralfireworks.co.uk
Ⓦ www.floralfireworks.co.uk
**Contact:** Carol Atkins
**Opening Times:** Not open. Mail order only. Orders can be collected by prior arrangement.
**Min Mail Order UK:** £10.00 + p&p
**Min Mail Order EU:** £20.00 + p&p
**Cat. Cost:** 4 × 2nd class.
**Credit Cards:** All major credit/debit cards
**Specialities:** Bulbs.

CFir **FIR TREE FARM NURSERY** ⊠ € ♿
Tresahor, Constantine, Falmouth, Cornwall,
TR11 5PL
Ⓣ (01326) 340593
Ⓔ plants@cornwallgardens.com
Ⓦ www.cornwallgardens.com
**Contact:** Glynn Wrapson & Sorcha Hitchcox

**Opening Times:** 1000-1700 Mon-Sat & 1100-1600 Sun, Feb-Oct. By appt. Nov-Jan.
**Min Mail Order UK:** £25.00 + p&p
**Min Mail Order EU:** £40.00 + p&p
**Cat. Cost:** 6 × 1st class
**Credit Cards:** Visa Access Delta Switch
**Specialities:** Over 4000 varieties of cottage garden & rare perennials with many specialities. Also 80 varieties of *Clematis*. Some rare varieties available in small quantities only.
**Map Ref:** C, D1

**CFul** **THE RODNEY FULLER HELIANTHEMUM COLLECTION**
Coachman's Cottage, Higher Bratton Seymour, Wincanton, Somerset, BA9 8DA
Ⓣ (01963) 34480
Ⓔ coachmans@tinyworld.co.uk
**Contact:** Rodney Fuller
**Opening Times:** Open by appt. only.
**Cat. Cost:** 2 × 1st class
**Credit Cards:** None
**Specialities:** *Helianthemum*. Nat. Collection holder. Stock available in very small quantities only.

**CFwr** **THE FLOWER BOWER** ⊠
Woodlands, Shurton, Stogursey, Nr Bridgwater, Somerset, TA5 1QE
Ⓣ (01278) 732134
Ⓔ theflowerbower@yahoo.co.uk
**Contact:** Sheila Tucker
**Opening Times:** By appt. only.
**Min Mail Order UK:** Nmc
**Min Mail Order EU:** Nmc
**Cat. Cost:** 2 × 1st class
**Credit Cards:** None
**Specialities:** Unusual perennials, hardy geraniums, *Asclepiad*, *Clivia*, *Epiphyllum* & ferns.
**Notes:** Mail order Mar onwards.
**Map Ref:** C, B4 **OS Grid Ref:** ST203442

**CGHE** **GARDEN HOUSE ENTERPRISES** ♿
The Garden House, Buckland Monachorum, Yelverton, Devon, PL20 7LQ
Ⓕ (01822) 855358
Ⓦ www.thegardenhouse.org.uk
**Contact:** Ms Selman
**Opening Times:** 1030-1700 7 days 1st Mar-31st Oct.
**Cat. Cost:** 4 × 1st class
**Credit Cards:** All major credit/debit cards
**Specialities:** Fortescue & Buckland plants. South African plants.
**Map Ref:** C, C3 **OS Grid Ref:** SX496683

**CGra** **GRAHAM'S HARDY PLANTS** ⊠ ⛺ €
"Southcroft", North Road, Timsbury, Bath, BA2 0JN
Ⓣ (01761) 472187
Ⓔ graplant@aol.com
Ⓦ www.members.aol.com/graplant
**Contact:** Graham Nicholls
**Opening Times:** Not open to the public. Mail order and show sales only.
**Min Mail Order UK:** £2.00 + p&p
**Min Mail Order EU:** £5.00 + p&p
**Cat. Cost:** 2 × 1st class or 2 × IRC
**Credit Cards:** None
**Specialities:** North American alpines esp. *Lewisia*, *Eriogonum*, *Penstemon*, *Campanula*, *Kelseya*, *Phlox*.

**CGro** **C W GROVES & SON LTD** ⊠ ♿
West Bay Road, Bridport, Dorset, DT6 4BA
Ⓣ (01308) 422654
Ⓕ (01308) 420888
Ⓔ violets@grovesnurseries.co.uk
Ⓦ www.grovesnurseries.co.uk
**Contact:** Clive Groves
**Opening Times:** 0830-1700 Mon-Sat, 1030-1630 Sun.
**Min Mail Order UK:** Nmc
**Min Mail Order EU:** £15.00 + p&p
**Cat. Cost:** 2 × 1st class
**Credit Cards:** Visa Switch MasterCard
**Specialities:** Nursery & garden centre specialising in Parma & hardy *Viola*. Nat. Collection of *Viola odorata* cvs & Parma Violets. Main display at nursery in Feb, Mar & Apr.
**Notes:** Mainly violets by mail order.
**Map Ref:** C, C5 **OS Grid Ref:** SY466918

**CGrW** **THE GREAT WESTERN GLADIOLUS NURSERY** ⊠ €
17 Valley View, Clutton, Bristol, BS39 5SN
Ⓣ (01761) 452036
Ⓕ (01761) 452036
Ⓔ clutton.glads@btinternet.com
Ⓦ www.greatwesterngladiolus.co.uk
**Contact:** G F & J C Hazell
**Opening Times:** Mail order only. Open by appt. only.
**Min Mail Order UK:** Nmc
**Min Mail Order EU:** Nmc
**Cat. Cost:** 4 × 1st class (2 catalogues).
**Credit Cards:** None

KEY
⊠ Mail order to UK or EU ⛺ Delivers to shows
✈ Exports beyond EU € Euro accepted
♿ Accessible by wheelchair ◆ See Display advertisement

C

**Specialities:** *Gladiolus* species & hybrids, corms & seeds. Other South African bulbous plants.
**Notes:** Also sells wholesale.

**CHal** **Halsway Nursery** ⊠
Halsway, Nr Crowcombe, Taunton, Somerset, TA4 4BB
Ⓣ (01984) 618243
**Contact:** T A & D J Bushen
**Opening Times:** Most days, please phone first.
**Min Mail Order UK:** £2.00 + p&p
**Cat. Cost:** 2 × 1st class for *Coleus* & *Begonia* list only.
**Credit Cards:** None
**Specialities:** *Coleus* & *Begonia* (excl. tuberous & winter-flowering). Good range of greenhouse & garden plants.
**Map Ref:** C, B4 **OS Grid Ref:** ST125383

**CHar** **West Harptree Nursery** ⊠ € 
Bristol Road, West Harptree, Bath, Somerset, BS40 6HG
Ⓣ (01761) 221370
Ⓕ (01761) 221989
Ⓔ bryn@harptreenursery.co.uk
Ⓦ www.harptreenursery.co.uk
**Contact:** Bryn & Helene Bowles
**Opening Times:** From 1000 Mon-Sun 7 days, 1st Mar-31st Oct.
**Min Mail Order UK:** Nmc
**Min Mail Order EU:** Nmc
**Cat. Cost:** Large sae for free names list.
**Credit Cards:** MasterCard Visa Maestro Paypal
**Specialities:** Unusual herbaceous perennials & shrubs. Bulbs & grasses. Many AGM plants.
**Notes:** Also sells wholesale.
**Map Ref:** C, B5

**CHby** **The Herbary** ⊠ €
161 Chapel Street, Horningsham, Warminster, Wiltshire, BA12 7LU
Ⓣ (01985) 844442
Ⓔ info@beansandherbs.co.uk
Ⓦ www.beansandherbs.co.uk
**Contact:** Pippa Rosen
**Opening Times:** May-Sep by appt. only.
**Min Mail Order UK:** Nmc
**Min Mail Order EU:** Nmc
**Cat. Cost:** 4 × 1st class
**Credit Cards:** None
**Specialities:** Culinary, medicinal & aromatic herbs organically grown.
**Notes:** Mail order all year for organic vegetable seed & large variety of organic bean & herb seed.
**Map Ref:** C, B5 **OS Grid Ref:** ST812414

**CHew** **Hewitt-Cooper Carnivorous Plants** ⊠ €
The Homestead, Glastonbury Road, West Pennard, Somerset, BA6 8NN
Ⓣ (01458) 832844
Ⓕ (01458) 832712
Ⓔ sales@hccarnivorousplants.co.uk
Ⓦ www.hccarnivorousplants.co.uk
**Contact:** Nigel Hewitt-Cooper
**Opening Times:** By appt.
**Min Mail Order UK:** £10.00 + p&p
**Min Mail Order EU:** £30.00
**Cat. Cost:** 1 × 1st class/1 × IRC.
**Credit Cards:** None
**Specialities:** Carnivorous plants.
**Notes:** Mail order May-Nov.
**Map Ref:** C, B5

**CHEx** **Hardy Exotics** ⊠
Gilly Lane, Whitecross, Penzance, Cornwall, TR20 8BZ
Ⓣ (01736) 740660
Ⓕ (01736) 741101
Ⓔ contact@hardyexotics.co.uk
Ⓦ www.hardyexotics.co.uk
**Contact:** C Shilton/J Smith
**Opening Times:** 1000-1700 7 days Mar-Oct, 1000-1700 Mon-Sat Nov-Feb. Please phone first in winter months if travelling a long way.
**Min Mail Order UK:** £40 + carriage.
**Cat. Cost:** 4 × 1st class (no cheques).
**Credit Cards:** All major credit/debit cards
**Specialities:** Largest selection in the UK of trees, shrubs & herbaceous plants for tropical & desert effects. Hardy & half-hardy plants for gardens, patios & conservatories.
**Map Ref:** C, D1 **OS Grid Ref:** SW524345

**CHFP** **Home Farm Plants**
Devonshire Traditional Breed Centre, Downes, Crediton, Devon, EX17 3PL
Ⓣ (01363) 772430
Ⓕ (01363) 772462
Ⓔ info@homefarmplants.co.uk
Ⓦ www.homefarmplants.co.uk
**Contact:** Hazel Brandreth
**Opening Times:** 0930-1700 Tue-Sat, 1030-1630 Sun & B/hols. Closed Mon except B/hols.
**Cat. Cost:** 3 × 1st class.
**Credit Cards:** All major credit/debit cards
**Specialities:** Hardy & unusual herbaceous perennials & herbs. Some stock in small quantities, phone to check.
**Notes:** The nursery is part of the Devonshire Traditional Breed Centre. Café.
**Map Ref:** C, C3 **OS Grid Ref:** SX848998

**CHid** **HIDDEN VALLEY NURSERY** ⌂ €
Umberleigh, Devon, EX37 9BU
Ⓣ (01769) 560567
Ⓜ 07899 788789
Ⓔ lindleypla@tiscali.co.uk
**Contact:** Linda & Peter Lindley
**Opening Times:** Daylight hours, but please phone first.
**Cat. Cost:** 2 × 1st class
**Credit Cards:** None
**Specialities:** Hardy perennials esp. shade lovers & Chatham Island forget-me-nots (*Myosotidium hortensia*.)
**Map Ref:** C, B3 **OS Grid Ref:** SS567205

**CHll** **HILL HOUSE NURSERY & GARDENS** € ♿
Landscove, Nr Ashburton, Devon, TQ13 7LY
Ⓜ 05601 158218
Ⓕ (01803) 762716
Ⓔ sacha@garden.506.fsnet.co.uk
Ⓦ www.hillhousenursery.co.uk
**Contact:** Raymond, Sacha & Matthew Hubbard
**Opening Times:** 1100-1700 7 days, all year. Open all B/hols incl. Easter Sun. Tearoom open 1st Mar-30th Sep.
**Cat. Cost:** None issued.
**Credit Cards:** Delta MasterCard Switch Visa
**Specialities:** 3000+ varieties of plants, most propagated on premises, many rare or unusual. The garden, open to the public, was laid out by Edward Hyams.
**Notes:** Pioneers of glasshouse pests control by beneficial insects.
**Map Ref:** C, C3 **OS Grid Ref:** SX774664

**CHrt** **HORTUS NURSERY** ⊠ ♿
Shrubbery Bungalow, School Lane, Rousdon, Lyme Regis, Dorset, DT7 3XW
Ⓣ (01297) 444019
Ⓜ 07747 043997
Ⓕ (01297) 444019
Ⓔ plants@hortusnursery.com
Ⓦ www.hortusnursery.com
**Contact:** Marie-Elaine Houghton
**Opening Times:** 1000-1700 Wed-Sat, Mar-Oct. Other times by appt. Garden open as nursery.
**Min Mail Order UK:** £15.00 + p&p
**Cat. Cost:** 3 × 1st class
**Credit Cards:** None
**Specialities:** Ornamental grasses & perennials, particularly plants suitable for coastal gardens. Garden design & planting service.
**Map Ref:** C, C4 **OS Grid Ref:** SY296914

**CHVG** **HIDDEN VALLEY GARDENS** ♿
Treesmill, Nr Par, Cornwall, PL24 2TU
Ⓣ (01208) 873225
Ⓔ hiddenvalleygardens@yahoo.co.uk
Ⓦ www.hiddenvalleygardens.co.uk
**Contact:** Mrs P Howard
**Opening Times:** 1000-1800 7 days, 20th Mar-end Oct. Please phone for directions. Garden open as nursery.
**Cat. Cost:** None issued.
**Credit Cards:** None
**Specialities:** Cottage garden plants, *Crocosmia*, *Iris sibirica* & many unusual perennials which can be seen growing in the garden. Some stock available in small quantities. Display garden.
**Map Ref:** C, D2 **OS Grid Ref:** SX094567

**CIri** **THE IRIS GARDEN** ⊠ €
Yard House, Pilsdon, Bridport, Dorset, DT6 5PA
Ⓣ (01308) 868797
Ⓕ (01308) 868797
Ⓔ theirisgarden@aol.com
Ⓦ www.theirisgarden.co.uk
**Contact:** Clive Russell
**Opening Times:** Show garden open by appt. Please email or phone for details.
**Min Mail Order UK:** £15.00 + p&p
**Min Mail Order EU:** £25.00 + p&p
**Cat. Cost:** 8 × 1st class.
**Credit Cards:** All major credit/debit cards
**Specialities:** Modern bearded & beardless *Iris* from breeders in UK, USA, France, Italy & Australia. Nat. Collection of "Space Age" *Iris* applied for.
**Notes:** Orders for bearded iris & sibiricas must be received by end Jun & by end Aug for spurias.
**Map Ref:** C, C5 **OS Grid Ref:** SY421988

**CJas** **JASMINE COTTAGE GARDENS** ♿
26 Channel Road, Walton St Mary, Clevedon, Somerset, BS21 7BY
Ⓣ (01275) 871850
Ⓔ margaret@bologrew.demon.co.uk
Ⓦ www.bologrew.pwp.blueyonder.co.uk
**Contact:** Mr & Mrs M Redgrave
**Opening Times:** May to Sep, daily by appt. Garden open at the same times.
**Cat. Cost:** None issued.
**Credit Cards:** None

KEY
⊠ Mail order to UK or EU ⌂ Delivers to shows
✈ Exports beyond EU € Euro accepted
♿ Accessible by wheelchair ◆ See Display advertisement

C

**Specialities:** *Rhodochiton*, *Lophospermum*, Maurandya, *Dicentra macrocapnos*, *Salvia*, *Isotoma*, half-hardy geraniums.
**Map Ref:** C, A4 **OS Grid Ref:** ST405725

CKel **KELWAYS LTD** ⊠ ♠ € ♿
Langport, Somerset, TA10 9EZ
Ⓣ (01458) 250521
Ⓕ (01458) 253351
Ⓔ sales@kelways.co.uk
Ⓦ www.kelways.co.uk
**Contact:** David Root
**Opening Times:** 0900-1700 Mon-Fri, 1000-1700 Sat, 1000-1600 Sun.
**Min Mail Order UK:** £4.00 + p&p
**Min Mail Order EU:** £8.00 + p&p
**Cat. Cost:** Free.
**Credit Cards:** All major credit/debit cards
**Specialities:** *Paeonia*, *Iris*, *Hemerocallis* & herbaceous perennials. Nat. Collection of *Paeonia lactiflora*. Wide range of trees, shrubs & herbaceous.
**Notes:** Mail order for *Paeonia* & *Iris* only. Also sells wholesale.
**Map Ref:** C, B5 **OS Grid Ref:** ST434273

CKen **KENWITH NURSERY (GORDON HADDOW)** ⊠ ✈ € ♿ ◆
Blinsham, Nr Torrington, Beaford, Winkleigh, Devon, EX19 8NT
Ⓣ (01805) 603274
Ⓕ (01805) 603663
Ⓔ conifers@kenwith63.freeserve.co.uk
Ⓦ www.kenwithnursery.co.uk
**Contact:** Gordon Haddow
**Opening Times:** 1000-1630 Tue-Sat all year. Closed all B/hols.
**Min Mail Order UK:** £15.00 + p&p
**Min Mail Order EU:** £50.00 + p&p
**Cat. Cost:** 3 × 1st class
**Credit Cards:** Visa MasterCard
**Specialities:** All conifer genera. Grafting a speciality. Many new introductions to UK. Nat. Collection of Dwarf Conifers.
**Map Ref:** C, B3 **OS Grid Ref:** SS518160

CKno **KNOLL GARDENS** ⊠ ♠ ♿
Hampreston, Stapehill, Nr Wimborne, Dorset, BH21 7ND
Ⓣ (01202) 873931
Ⓕ (01202) 870842
Ⓔ enquiries@knollgardens.co.uk
Ⓦ www.knollgardens.co.uk
**Contact:** N R Lucas
**Opening Times:** 1000-1700 (or dusk if earlier) Wed-Sun. Open B/hol Mon & also Tue May-Oct. Closed from 16th Dec 2007, re-opening 1st Feb 2008.
**Min Mail Order UK:** Nmc
**Min Mail Order EU:** Nmc
**Cat. Cost:** 9 × 2nd class or order online
**Credit Cards:** Visa MasterCard
**Specialities:** Grasses (main specialism). Select perennials. Nat. Collections of *Pennisetum*, *Phygelius* & deciduous *Ceanothus*.
**Notes:** Also sells wholesale.
**Map Ref:** C, C6

CKob **KOBAKOBA** ⊠ ✈ €
2 High Street, Ashcott, Bridgwater, Somerset, TA7 9PL
Ⓣ (01458) 210700
Ⓜ 07870 624969
Ⓔ plants@kobakoba.co.uk
Ⓦ www.kobakoba.co.uk
**Contact:** Christine Smithee & David Constantine
**Opening Times:** Please phone for opening times.
**Min Mail Order UK:** Nmc
**Min Mail Order EU:** Nmc
**Cat. Cost:** 1 × 1st class for plant list or £4.50 for catalogue.
**Credit Cards:** Paypal
**Specialities:** Plants for tropical effect incl. *Ensete*, *Musa*, *Hedychium*, *Curcuma* & other *Zingiberaceae*. Conservatory & greenhouse plants.
**Map Ref:** C, B5 **OS Grid Ref:** ST434370

CLAP **LONG ACRE PLANTS** ⊠ ♠ ♿
South Marsh, Charlton Musgrove, Nr Wincanton, Somerset, BA9 8EX
Ⓣ (01963) 32802
Ⓕ (01963) 32802
Ⓔ info@longacreplants.co.uk
Ⓦ www.plantsforshade.co.uk
**Contact:** Nigel & Michelle Rowland
**Opening Times:** 1000-1300 & 1400-1700 Thu-Fri, 100-1300 Sat, Feb-Jun, Sep & Oct.
**Min Mail Order UK:** £25.00 + p&p
**Min Mail Order EU:** £50.00 + p&p
**Cat. Cost:** 3 × 1st class
**Credit Cards:** Switch MasterCard Visa Maestro
**Specialities:** Ferns, woodland bulbs & perennials. Nat. Collection of *Asarum*.
**Notes:** Lilies only outside EU.
**Map Ref:** C, B5

CLnd **LANDFORD TREES** ⊠ €
Landford Lodge, Landford, Salisbury, Wiltshire, SP5 2EH
Ⓣ (01794) 390808
Ⓕ (01794) 390037
Ⓔ sales@landfordtrees.co.uk

Ⓦ www.landfordtrees.co.uk
**Contact:** C D Pilkington
**Opening Times:** 0800-1700 Mon-Fri.
**Min Mail Order UK:** Please enquire.
**Min Mail Order EU:** Please enquire.
**Cat. Cost:** Free
**Credit Cards:** None
**Specialities:** Deciduous ornamental trees.
**Notes:** Mail order maximum size 120cms. Also sells wholesale.
**Map Ref:** C, B6 **OS Grid Ref:** SU247201

CLoc **C S Lockyer (Fuchsias)** ✉ ✈ ⛟ € ◆
Lansbury, 70 Henfield Road, Coalpit Heath, Bristol, BS36 2UZ
Ⓣ (01454) 772219
Ⓕ (01454) 772219
Ⓔ sales@lockyerfuchsias.co.uk
Ⓦ www.lockyerfuchsias.co.uk
**Contact:** C S Lockyer
**Opening Times:** 1000-1300, 1430-1700 most days, please ring.
**Min Mail Order UK:** 6 plants + p&p
**Min Mail Order EU:** £12.00 + p&p
**Cat. Cost:** 4 × 1st class
**Credit Cards:** None
**Specialities:** *Fuchsia.*
**Notes:** Many open days & coach parties. Limited wheelchair access. Also sells wholesale.
**Map Ref:** C, A5

CLyd **Lydford Alpine Nursery** ✉
2 Southern Cottages, Lydford, Okehampton, Devon, EX20 4BL
Ⓣ (01822) 820398
**Contact:** Julie & David Hatchett
**Opening Times:** By appt. only. Please ring for directions.
**Min Mail Order UK:** £10.00 + p&p
**Cat. Cost:** Sae for saxifrage list.
**Credit Cards:** None
**Specialities:** *Saxifraga*. Very wide range of choice & unusual alpines in small quantities.
**Notes:** Mail order *Saxifraga* only.
**Map Ref:** C, C3 **OS Grid Ref:** SX504830

CMac **Macpennys Nurseries** ✉
154 Burley Road, Bransgore, Christchurch, Dorset, BH23 8DB
Ⓣ (01425) 672348
Ⓕ (01425) 673917
Ⓔ office@macpennys.co.uk
Ⓦ www.macpennys.co.uk
**Contact:** T & V Lowndes
**Opening Times:** 0900-1700 Mon-Sat, 1100-1700 Sun. Closed Xmas & New Year.
**Min Mail Order UK:** Nmc
**Cat. Cost:** A4 sae with 4 × 1st class
**Credit Cards:** All major credit/debit cards
**Specialities:** General. Plants available in small quantities only.
**Notes:** Mail order available Sep-Mar, UK only. Nursery partially accessible for wheelchairs.
**Map Ref:** C, C6

CMCN **Mallet Court Nursery** ✉ ✈ ⛟ € ♿
Curry Mallet, Taunton, Somerset, TA3 6SY
Ⓣ (01823) 481493
Ⓕ (01823) 481493
Ⓔ malletcourtnursery@btinternet.com
Ⓦ www.malletcourt.co.uk
**Contact:** J G S & P M E Harris F.L.S.
**Opening Times:** 0930-1700 Mon-Fri summer, 0930-1600 winter. Sat & Sun by appt.
**Min Mail Order UK:** Nmc
**Min Mail Order EU:** Nmc
**Cat. Cost:** £1.50
**Credit Cards:** All major credit/debit cards
**Specialities:** Maples, oaks, *Magnolia*, hollies & other rare and unusual plants including those from China & South Korea.
**Notes:** Mail order Oct-Mar only. Also sells wholesale.
**Map Ref:** C, B4

CMCo **Meadow Cottage Plants** ⛟ € ♿
Pitt Hill, Ivybridge, Devon, PL21 0JJ
Ⓣ (01752) 894532
Ⓔ phil@pitthill.fsworld.co.uk
**Contact:** Mrs L P Hunt
**Opening Times:** By appt. only.
**Cat. Cost:** None issued.
**Credit Cards:** None
**Specialities:** Hardy geraniums, other hardy perennials, large ornamental grasses and bamboos. Some varieties available in small numbers only. All plants grown in peat-free compost.
**Notes:** Also sells wholesale.
**Map Ref:** C, D3

CMdw **Meadows Nursery** ✉
5 Rectory Cottages, Mells, Frome, Somerset, BA11 3PN
Ⓣ (01373) 812268
Ⓔ plants@meadowsnurserymells.co.uk
**Contact:** Sue Lees & Eddie Wheatley
**Opening Times:** 1000-1800 Wed-Sun 1st Feb-14th Oct & B/hols.

| KEY | | |
|---|---|---|
| | ✉ Mail order to UK or EU | ⛟ Delivers to shows |
| | ✈ Exports beyond EU | € Euro accepted |
| | ♿ Accessible by wheelchair | ◆ See Display advertisement |

C

**Min Mail Order UK:** Nmc
**Cat. Cost:** 3 × 1st class.
**Credit Cards:** None
**Specialities:** Hardy perennials, shrubs & some conservatory plants. *Kniphofia*.
**Map Ref:** C, B5 **OS Grid Ref:** ST729492

**CMea** THE MEAD NURSERY
Brokerswood, Nr Westbury, Wiltshire, BA13 4EG
Ⓣ (01373) 859990
Ⓦ www.themeadnursery.co.uk
**Contact:** Steve & Emma Lewis-Dale
**Opening Times:** 0900-1700 Wed-Sat & B/hols, 1200-1700 Sun, 1st Feb-10th Oct. Closed Easter Sun.
**Cat. Cost:** 5 × 1st class
**Credit Cards:** All major credit/debit cards
**Specialities:** Perennials, alpines, pot-grown bulbs and grasses.
**Map Ref:** C, B5 **OS Grid Ref:** ST833517

**CMen** MENDIP BONSAI STUDIO
Byways, Back Lane, Downside, Shepton Mallet, Somerset, BA4 4JR
Ⓣ (01749) 344274
Ⓕ (01749) 344274
Ⓔ jr.trott@ukonline.co.uk
Ⓦ www.mendipbonsai.co.uk
**Contact:** John Trott
**Opening Times:** Private nursery. Visits by appt. only.
**Cat. Cost:** Large sae for plant & workshop lists
**Credit Cards:** All major credit/debit cards
**Specialities:** Bonsai, Potensai, accent plants & garden stock. Acers, conifers, incl. many *Pinus thunbergii* species. *Stewartia*. Many plants available in small numbers only.
**Notes:** Education classes, lectures, demonstrations & club talks on bonsai. Stockist of most bonsai sundries.
**Map Ref:** C, B5

**CMHG** MARWOOD HILL GARDENS
Barnstaple, Devon, EX31 4EB
Ⓣ (01271) 342528
Ⓔ malcolmpharoah@supanet.com
Ⓦ www.marwoodhillgarden.co.uk
**Contact:** Malcolm Pharoah
**Opening Times:** 1100-1630, 7 days.
**Cat. Cost:** 3 × 1st class
**Credit Cards:** Visa Delta MasterCard Switch Solo
**Specialities:** Large range of unusual trees & shrubs. *Eucalyptus*, alpines, *Camellia*, *Astilbe*, bog plants & perennials. Nat. Collections of *Astilbe*, *Tulbaghia* & *Iris ensata*.
**Map Ref:** C, B3 **OS Grid Ref:** SS545375

**CMil** MILL COTTAGE PLANTS ⊠
The Mill, Henley Lane, Wookey, Somerset, BA5 1AP
Ⓣ (01749) 676966
Ⓔ millcottageplants@tiscali.co.uk
Ⓦ www.millcottageplants.co.uk
**Contact:** Sally Gregson
**Opening Times:** 1000-1800 Wed Mar-Sep or by appt. Phone for directions.
**Min Mail Order UK:** Nmc.
**Min Mail Order EU:** £20.00 + p&p
**Cat. Cost:** 4 × 1st class.
**Credit Cards:** All major credit/debit cards
**Specialities:** Rare *Hydrangea serrata* cvs, *H. aspera* cvs. Also *Papaver orientale*, *Arisaema*, *Tricyrtis*, *Epimedium*, ferns & grasses.
**Map Ref:** C, B5

**CMMP** M & M PLANTS
Lloret, Chittlehamholt, Umberleigh, Devon, EX37 9PD
Ⓣ (01769) 540448
Ⓕ (01769) 540448
Ⓔ MMPlants@Chittlehamholt.freeserve.co.uk
**Contact:** Mr M Thorne
**Opening Times:** 0930-1730 Tue-Sat, Apr-Oct & 1000-1600 Tue-Fri, Nov-Mar. Sat by appt. Aug.
**Cat. Cost:** 3 × 1st class.
**Credit Cards:** None
**Specialities:** Perennials. We also carry a good range of alpines, shrubs, trees & roses.
**Map Ref:** C, B3

**CMoH** MONITA HOUSE GARDEN ⊠
Eggesford, Chulmleigh, Devon, EX18 7JZ
Ⓣ (01769) 580081
Ⓜ 07748 563032
Ⓔ monitahouse@tiscali.co.uk
**Contact:** David Mitchell
**Opening Times:** 1000-1700, Sun & B/hols, 1st Apr-30th Oct. Please ring first.
**Min Mail Order UK:** Nmc
**Cat. Cost:** 4 × 1st class
**Credit Cards:** None
**Specialities:** Small nursery specialising in herbaceous perennials, many available in small quantities only.
**Map Ref:** C, B3 **OS Grid Ref:** SS681119

**CNat** NATURAL SELECTION ⊠ €
1 Station Cottages, Hullavington, Chippenham, Wiltshire, SN14 6ET
Ⓣ (01666) 837369
Ⓔ martin@worldmutation.demon.co.uk
Ⓦ www.worldmutation.demon.co.uk
**Contact:** Martin Cragg-Barber
**Opening Times:** Please phone first.

C

**Min Mail Order UK:** £9.00 + p&p
**Cat. Cost:** £1.00 or 5 × 2nd class
**Credit Cards:** None
**Specialities:** Unusual British natives & others. Also seed. Only available in small quantities.
**Map Ref:** C, A5 **OS Grid Ref:** ST898828

**CNMi** **Newport Mills Nursery** ⊠
Wrantage, Taunton, Somerset, TA3 6DJ
Ⓣ (01823) 490231
Ⓜ 07950 035668
Ⓕ (01823) 490231
**Contact:** John Barrington, Rachel Pettitt
**Opening Times:** By appt. only.
**Min Mail Order UK:** Nmc
**Min Mail Order EU:** Nmc
**Cat. Cost:** Free.
**Credit Cards:** None
**Specialities:** *Delphinium*. English scented varieties of perpetual flowering carnations. Some varieties only available in small quantities & propagated to order.
**Notes:** Mail order Apr-Sep for young delphiniums in 7cm pots. Dormant plants can be sent out in autumn/winter if requested.

**COld** **The Old Mill Herbary**
Helland Bridge, Bodmin, Cornwall, PL30 4QR
Ⓣ (01208) 841206
Ⓔ oldmillherbary@aol.com
Ⓦ www.oldmillherbary.co.uk
**Contact:** Mrs B Whurr
**Opening Times:** 1000-1700 Thu-Tue 25th Mar-30th Sep. Closed Wed.
**Cat. Cost:** 6 × 1st class
**Credit Cards:** None
**Specialities:** Culinary, medicinal & aromatic herbs.
**Notes:** Limited sales of medicinal herbs. Historical site in Area of Outstanding Natural Beauty. SSSI, SAC & AONB.
**Map Ref:** C, C2 **OS Grid Ref:** SX065717

**COlW** **The Old Withy Garden Nursery** ⊠
Grange Fruit Farm, Gweek, Helston, Cornwall, TR12 6BE
Ⓣ (01326) 221171
Ⓔ WithyNursery@fsbdial.co.uk
Ⓦ www.theoldwithygardennursery.co.uk
**Contact:** Sheila Chandler or Nick Chandler
**Opening Times:** 1000-1700 Wed-Mon, Feb-end Oct. 1000-1730 7 days, Apr-Sep.
**Min Mail Order UK:** £15.00
**Cat. Cost:** 4 × 1st class
**Credit Cards:** Maestro MasterCard Visa Delta
**Specialities:** Cottage garden plants, perennials, some biennials & grasses. Some varieties in small quantities only.
**Notes:** Partially accessible for wheelchairs (gravel paths). Also sells wholesale.
**Map Ref:** C, D1 **OS Grid Ref:** SW688255

**CPar** **Parks Perennials** ⌂
242 Wallisdown Road, Wallisdown, Bournemouth, Dorset, BH10 4HZ
Ⓣ (01202) 524464
Ⓔ parks.perennials@ntlworld.com
**Contact:** S. Parks
**Opening Times:** Apr-Oct most days, please phone first.
**Cat. Cost:** None issued.
**Credit Cards:** None
**Specialities:** Hardy herbaceous perennials.
**Map Ref:** C, C6

**CPas** **Passiflora (National Collection)** €
Lampley Road, Kingston Seymour, Clevedon, Somerset, BS21 6XS
Ⓣ (01934) 838895
Ⓜ 0776 834 0881
Ⓔ johnvanderplank@yahoo.co.uk
**Contact:** John Vanderplank
**Opening Times:** 0900-1700 7 days, 1st Aug-31st Aug. By appt. only remainder of year.
**Cat. Cost:** 3 × 1st class.
**Credit Cards:** None
**Specialities:** *Passiflora*. Nat. Collection of over 250 species & cultivars. Scientific status. Brickell Award 2004.
**Notes:** Mail order seed only. Plants must be collected from nursery. Pre-ordered plants may be picked up from the nursery at any time. Also sells wholesale.
**Map Ref:** C, A4

**CPbn** **Penborn Goat Farm** ♿
Penborn, Bounds Cross, Holsworthy, Devon, EX22 6LH
Ⓣ (01288) 381569
**Contact:** P R Oldfield
**Opening Times:** By appt. only.
**Credit Cards:** None
**Specialities:** *Mentha*, *Lavandula*, *Melissa*. Available in small quantities only.
**Map Ref:** C, C2

**CPBP** **Parham Bungalow Plants** ⊠ ⌂ €
Parham Lane, Market Lavington, Devizes, Wiltshire, SN10 4QA
Ⓣ (01380) 812605

KEY
⊠ Mail order to UK or EU ⌂ Delivers to shows
✈ Exports beyond EU € Euro accepted
♿ Accessible by wheelchair ◆ See Display advertisement

C

Ⓔ jjs@pbplants.freeserve.co.uk
**Contact:** Mrs D E Sample
**Opening Times:** Please ring first.
**Min Mail Order UK:** Nmc
**Min Mail Order EU:** Nmc
**Cat. Cost:** Sae.
**Credit Cards:** None
**Specialities:** Alpines & dwarf shrubs.
**Map Ref:** C, B6

**CPen** **Pennard Plants** ⊠ ✈ € 
3 The Gardens, East Pennard, Shepton Mallet, Somerset, BA4 6TU
Ⓣ (01749) 860039
Ⓕ 07043 017270
Ⓔ sales@pennardplants.com
Ⓦ www.pennardplants.com
**Contact:** Chris Smith
**Opening Times:** 1000-1500 Tue & Wed, 1st Mar-31st Oct.
**Min Mail Order UK:** Nmc
**Min Mail Order EU:** Nmc
**Cat. Cost:** 3 × 1st class
**Credit Cards:** All major credit/debit cards
**Specialities:** Ornamental grasses, *Agapanthus*, *Crocosmia*, *Dierama* & South African bulbous plants.
**Notes:** Nursery at The Walled Garden at East Pennard.
**Map Ref:** C, B5

**CPhi** **Alan Phipps Cacti** ⊠ €
62 Samuel White Road, Hanham, Bristol, BS15 3LX
Ⓣ (0117) 9607591
Ⓦ www.cactus-mall.com/alan-phipps/index.html
**Contact:** A Phipps
**Opening Times:** 10.00-1700 but prior phone call essential to ensure a greeting.
**Min Mail Order UK:** £5.00 + p&p
**Min Mail Order EU:** £20.00 + p&p
**Cat. Cost:** Sae or 2 × IRC (EC only)
**Credit Cards:** None
**Specialities:** *Mammillaria*, *Astrophytum* & *Ariocarpus*. Species & varieties will change with times. Ample quantities exist in spring. Limited range of *Agave*.
**Notes:** Euro accepted as cash only.
**Map Ref:** C, A5 **OS Grid Ref:** ST644717

**CPHo** **The Palm House** ⊠
8 North Street, Ottery St Mary, Devon, EX11 1DR
Ⓣ (01404) 815450
Ⓜ 07815 673397
Ⓔ george@thepalmhouse.co.uk
Ⓦ www.thepalmhouse.co.uk
**Contact:** George Gregory
**Opening Times:** Mail order only. Open by appt. only.
**Min Mail Order UK:** £15.00
**Cat. Cost:** 2 × 1st class
**Credit Cards:** All major credit/debit cards
**Specialities:** Palms.
**Notes:** Also sells wholesale.
**Map Ref:** C, C4 **OS Grid Ref:** SY098955

**CPLG** **Pine Lodge Gardens & Nursery** ♿
Cuddra, Holmbush, St Austell, Cornwall, PL25 3RQ
Ⓣ (01726) 73500
Ⓕ (01726) 77370
Ⓔ gardens@pine-lodge.co.uk
Ⓦ www.pine-lodge.co.uk
**Contact:** Ray & Shirley Clemo
**Opening Times:** 1000-1700 7 days all year, except 24th/25th/26th Dec.
**Cat. Cost:** 6 × 2nd class.
**Credit Cards:** None
**Specialities:** Rare & unusual shrubs & herbaceous, some from seed collected on plant expeditions each year. Nat. Collection of *Grevillea*. All plants available in small quantities only.
**Map Ref:** C, D2 **OS Grid Ref:** SX045527

**CPMA** **P M A Plant Specialities** ⊠ ✈
Junker's Nursery Ltd., Lower Mead, West Hatch, Taunton, Somerset, TA3 5RN
Ⓣ (01823) 480774
Ⓔ karan@junker.co.uk
Ⓦ www.junker.co.uk
**Contact:** Karan or Nick Junker
**Opening Times:** Strictly by appt. only.
**Min Mail Order UK:** Nmc
**Min Mail Order EU:** Nmc
**Cat. Cost:** 6 × 2nd class.
**Credit Cards:** None
**Specialities:** Choice & unusual shrubs incl. grafted *Acer palmatum*, *Cornus*, *Magnolia* & a wide range of *Daphne*. Small quantities of some hard to propagate plants, esp. daphnes. Reserve orders accepted. Lots of planted areas to see how the plants actually look growing in "real world" conditions.
**Notes:** Partial wheelchair access. Also sells wholesale.
**Map Ref:** C, B4 **OS Grid Ref:** ST280203

**CPne** **Pine Cottage Plants** ⊠ €
Pine Cottage, Fourways, Eggesford, Chulmleigh, Devon, EX18 7QZ
Ⓣ (01769) 580076
Ⓔ pcplants@supanet.com
Ⓦ www.pcplants.co.uk

C

Contact: Dick Fulcher
**Opening Times:** Special open weeks for *Agapanthus*, 1000-1900 daily, excl. Sun, 9th-17th Jul, 23rd Jul-18th Aug 2007. Other times by appt. only.
**Min Mail Order UK:** £20.00 + p&p
**Min Mail Order EU:** £20.00 + p&p
**Cat. Cost:** 4 × 1st class.
**Credit Cards:** Maestro MasterCard Visa
**Specialities:** Nat. Collection of *Agapanthus*. 150+ cvs available.
**Notes:** Mail order *Agapanthus* from Oct-Jun. Also sells wholesale.
**Map Ref:** C, B3 **OS Grid Ref:** SS683099

**CPom** **Pomeroy Plants**
Tower House, Pomeroy Lane, Wingfield, Trowbridge, Wiltshire, BA14 9LJ
Ⓣ (01225) 769551
Ⓜ 07895 096564
Ⓔ drsimonyoung@yahoo.co.uk
**Contact:** Simon Young
**Opening Times:** Mar-Nov. Please phone first.
**Cat. Cost:** 2 × 1st class.
**Credit Cards:** None
**Specialities:** Hardy, mainly species, herbaceous perennials. Many unusual and often small numbers. Specialities *Allium*, *Salvia* & shade-lovers, esp. *Epimedium*.
**Map Ref:** C, B5 **OS Grid Ref:** ST817569

**CPou** **Pounsley Plants** ⊠ € ♿
Pounsley Combe, Spriddlestone, Brixton, Plymouth, Devon, PL9 0DW
Ⓣ (01752) 402873
Ⓕ (01752) 402873
Ⓔ pou599@aol.com
Ⓦ www.pounsleyplants.com
**Contact:** Mrs Jane Hollow
**Opening Times:** Normally 1000-1700 Mon-Sat but please phone first.
**Min Mail Order UK:** £10.00 + p&p
**Min Mail Order EU:** £20.00 + p&p
**Cat. Cost:** 2 × 1st class
**Credit Cards:** None
**Specialities:** Unusual herbaceous perennials & cottage plants. Selection of *Clematis* & old roses. Large selection of South African monocots.
**Notes:** Mail order Nov-Feb only. Also sells wholesale.
**Map Ref:** C, D3 **OS Grid Ref:** SX521538

**CPrp** **Properplants.com** ⊠ ✈ ⛺
Penknight, Edgcumbe Road, Lostwithiel, Cornwall, PL22 0JD
Ⓣ (01208) 872291
Ⓕ (01208) 872291
Ⓔ info@Properplants.com
Ⓦ www.ProperPlants.com
**Contact:** Sarah Wilks
**Opening Times:** 1000-1800 or dusk if earlier, Tue & B/hols mid-Mar to end-Sep & by appt.
**Min Mail Order UK:** Nmc
**Min Mail Order EU:** Nmc
**Cat. Cost:** 4 × 1st class
**Credit Cards:** All major credit/debit cards
**Specialities:** Wide range of unusual & easy herbaceous perennials, esp. of South African origin. Ferns & grasses. Less common herbs.
**Notes:** Partially accessible for wheelchair users.
**Map Ref:** C, C2 **OS Grid Ref:** SX093596

**CPSs** **Plants for the Senses** ⊠
Corner Cottage, North Street, Dolton, Winkleigh, Devon, EX19 8QQ
Ⓣ (01805) 804467
Ⓔ michaelross@freenetname.co.uk
**Contact:** Michael Ross
**Opening Times:** Not open. Mail order only.
**Min Mail Order UK:** Nmc
**Cat. Cost:** 1 × 1st class.
**Credit Cards:** None
**Specialities:** Some emphasis on scented plants. Some stock in small quantities only.

**CPuk** **Pukka Plants** ⊠ € ♿
Count House Farm, Treglisson, Wheal Alfred Road, Hayle, Cornwall, TR27 5JT
Ⓣ (01872) 271129
Ⓕ (01872) 271129
Ⓔ sktrevena@gmail.com
Ⓦ www.pukkaplants.co.uk
**Contact:** Colin Young
**Opening Times:** 0900-1700, Mon-Sat, closed Sun.
**Min Mail Order UK:** £5.00
**Credit Cards:** All major credit/debit cards
**Specialities:** Grasses.
**Notes:** Also sells wholesale.
**Map Ref:** C, D1 **OS Grid Ref:** SW369578

**CQua** **Quality Daffodils** ⊠ ✈ € ◆
14 Roscarrack Close, Falmouth, Cornwall, TR11 4PJ
Ⓣ (01326) 317959
Ⓕ (01326) 317959
Ⓔ rascamp@daffodils.uk.com
Ⓦ www.qualitydaffodils.com
**Contact:** R A Scamp
**Opening Times:** Not open. Mail order only.

KEY
⊠ Mail order to UK or EU ⛺ Delivers to shows
✈ Exports beyond EU € Euro accepted
♿ Accessible by wheelchair ◆ See Display advertisement

C

**Min Mail Order UK:** Nmc
**Min Mail Order EU:** Nmc
**Cat. Cost:** 3 × 1st class
**Credit Cards:** All major credit/debit cards
**Specialities:** *Narcissus* hybrids & species. Some stocks are less than 100 bulbs.
**Notes:** Also sells wholesale.
**Map Ref:** C, D1

**CRea** **REALLY WILD FLOWERS** ⊠
H V Horticulture Ltd, Spring Mead, Bedchester, Shaftesbury, Dorset, SP7 0JU
Ⓣ (01747) 811778
Ⓕ 0845 009 1778
Ⓔ info@reallywildflowers.co.uk
Ⓦ www.reallywildflowers.co.uk
**Contact:** Grahame Dixie
**Opening Times:** Not open. Mail order only.
**Min Mail Order UK:** £40.00 + p&p
**Cat. Cost:** 3 × 1st class.
**Credit Cards:** None
**Specialities:** Native wild flowers for grasslands, woodlands & wetlands. Seeds, orchids & bulbs. Advisory & soil analysis services.
**Notes:** Also sells wholesale.

**CRHN** **ROSELAND HOUSE NURSERY** ⊠ ⌂
Chacewater, Truro, Cornwall, TR4 8QB
Ⓣ (01872) 560451
Ⓔ clematis@roselandhouse.co.uk
Ⓦ www.roselandhouse.co.uk
**Contact:** C R Pridham
**Opening Times:** 1300-1800 Tue & Wed, Apr-Sep. Other times by appt. Garden open to the public.
**Min Mail Order UK:** Nmc
**Cat. Cost:** Online only.
**Credit Cards:** None
**Specialities:** Climbing & conservatory plants. National Collections of *Clematis*
**Map Ref:** C, D1 **OS Grid Ref:** SW752445

**CRob** **ROBERTS NURSERIES** ⊠
East Allington, Totnes, Devon, TQ9 7QE
Ⓣ (01548) 521412
Ⓜ 07757 612965
Ⓕ (01548) 521533
Ⓔ info@conifersdirect.com
Ⓦ www.conifersdirect.com
**Contact:** W R Bartoszyn
**Opening Times:** By appt. only.
**Min Mail Order UK:** Nmc
**Cat. Cost:** 2 × 1st class.
**Credit Cards:** All major credit/debit cards
**Specialities:** Extensive range of hardy dwarf, ornamental conifers incl. old favourites, choice varieties & new introductions. A selected range of specimen shrubs & conifers in patio planters.
**Notes:** Also sells wholesale.
**Map Ref:** C, D3 **OS Grid Ref:** SX763495

**CRow** **ROWDEN GARDENS** ⊠ ✈ ♿
Brentor, Nr Tavistock, Devon, PL19 0NG
Ⓣ (01822) 810275
Ⓕ (01822) 810275
Ⓔ rowdengardens@btopenworld.com
Ⓦ www.rowdengardens.com
**Contact:** John R L Carter
**Opening Times:** By appt only.
**Min Mail Order UK:** Nmc
**Min Mail Order EU:** Nmc
**Cat. Cost:** 6 × 1st class
**Credit Cards:** None
**Specialities:** Aquatics, damp loving & associated plants incl. rare & unusual varieties. Nat. Coll. of *Caltha* & Water *Iris*. Some stock available in small quantities only.
**Notes:** Also sells wholesale
**Map Ref:** C, C3

**CRWN** **THE REALLY WILD NURSERY** ⊠ ✈ €
19 Hoopers Way, Torrington, Devon, EX38 7NS
Ⓣ (01805) 624739
Ⓕ (01805) 624739
Ⓔ thereallywildnursery@yahoo.co.uk
Ⓦ www.thereallywildnursery.co.uk
**Contact:** Kathryn Moore
**Opening Times:** Not open. Mail order only.
**Min Mail Order UK:** £10.00 + p&p
**Min Mail Order EU:** £20.00 + p&p
**Cat. Cost:** 3 × 1st class.
**Credit Cards:** Paypal
**Specialities:** Wildflowers, bulbs & seeds.
**Notes:** Mail order all year round, grown to order (plants in pots or plugs). Also sells wholesale.

**CSam** **SAMPFORD SHRUBS** ⊠ € ♿
Sampford Peverell, Tiverton, Devon, EX16 7EN
Ⓣ (01884) 821164
Ⓔ via website
Ⓦ www.samshrub.co.uk
**Contact:** M Hughes-Jones & S Proud
**Opening Times:** 0900-1700 Mon-Sat, 1000-1600 Sun, Feb-Jun. 0900-1700 Tue-Sat, Jul-Oct.
**Cat. Cost:** A5 sae 35p stamps.
**Credit Cards:** All major credit/debit cards
**Specialities:** Large displays of *Pulmonaria* & *Crocosmia*. Nat. Collection of *Helenium*.

**Notes:** Mail order available via website only for selected list. Despatched Mar.
**Map Ref:** C, B4 **OS Grid Ref:** ST043153

CSBt **St Bridget Nurseries Ltd** ⊠ ⌂ ♿
Old Rydon Lane, Exeter, Devon,
EX2 7JY
Ⓣ (01392) 873672
Ⓕ (01392) 876710
Ⓔ info@stbridgetnurseries.co.uk
Ⓦ www.stbridgetnurseries.co.uk
**Contact:** Garden Centre Plant Advice
**Opening Times:** 0800-1700 Mon-Sat, 1030-1630 Sun, 0900-1700 B/hols. Closed Xmas Day, Boxing Day, New Year's Day & Easter Sun.
**Min Mail Order UK:** Nmc
**Cat. Cost:** Free.
**Credit Cards:** All major credit/debit cards
**Specialities:** Large general nursery, with two garden centres.
**Notes:** Mail order available between Nov & Mar.
**Map Ref:** C, C4 **OS Grid Ref:** SX955905

CSdC **Sherwood Cottage** €
Newton St Cyres, Exeter, Devon,
EX5 5BT
Ⓣ (01392) 851589
Ⓔ vaughan.gallavan@connectfree.co.uk
**Contact:** Vaughan Gallavan
**Opening Times:** 1400-1700 Sun with Sherwood Gardens or by appt.
**Cat. Cost:** 2 × 1st class.
**Credit Cards:** None
**Specialities:** Magnolias, trees & shrubs. Nat. Coll. of Knap Hill azaleas. Ghent & species deciduous azaleas. Sherwood Garden new Nat. Collection of *Magnolia*. Stock available in small quantities only.
**Map Ref:** C, C3 **OS Grid Ref:** SX863967

CSec **Secret Seeds** ⊠ ✈ ⌂ € ♿
Cove, Tiverton, Devon, EX16 7RU
Ⓣ (01398) 331946
Ⓜ 07870 389889
Ⓕ (01398) 331946
Ⓔ mike@secretseeds.com
Ⓦ www.secretseeds.com
**Contact:** Mike Burgess
**Opening Times:** 1000-1730 7 days. Closed Xmas.
**Min Mail Order UK:** Nmc
**Min Mail Order EU:** Nmc
**Cat. Cost:** 2 × 1st class
**Credit Cards:** All major credit/debit cards
**Specialities:** *Echium*. Garden open.
**Notes:** Also sells wholesale

CSev **Lower Severalls Nursery** ⊠ ♿
Crewkerne, Somerset,
TA18 7NX
Ⓣ (01460) 73234
Ⓔ mary@lowerseveralls.co.uk
Ⓦ www.lowerseveralls.co.uk
**Contact:** Mary R Pring
**Opening Times:** 1000-1700 Tue, Wed, Fri, Sat, Mar-end Sep. Closed Aug.
**Min Mail Order UK:** £20.00
**Cat. Cost:** 4 × 1st class
**Credit Cards:** None
**Specialities:** Herbs, herbaceous.
**Notes:** Mail order perennials only.
**Map Ref:** C, B5 **OS Grid Ref:** ST457111

CSil **Silver Dale Nurseries** ⌂ €
Shute Lane, Combe Martin, Devon,
EX34 0HT
Ⓣ (01271) 882539
Ⓔ silverdale.nurseries@virgin.net
**Contact:** Roger Gilbert
**Opening Times:** 1000-1800 7 days. Closed Nov-Jan.
**Cat. Cost:** 4 × 1st class
**Credit Cards:** Visa MasterCard EuroCard
**Specialities:** Nat. Collection of *Fuchsia*. Hardy fuchsias (cultivars and species).
**Map Ref:** C, B3

CSim **Simpson's Seeds Ltd** ⊠ ♿
The Walled Garden Nursery,
Horningsham, Warminster, Wiltshire,
BA12 7NT
Ⓣ (01985) 845004
Ⓕ (01985) 845052
Ⓔ sales@simpsonsseeds.co.uk
Ⓦ www.simpsonsseeds.co.uk
**Contact:** Matthew Simpson
**Opening Times:** 1000-1700 Wed-Sun, Apr-May. 1000-1700 Tue-Fri & 1000-1300 Sat, rest of the year.
**Min Mail Order UK:** Nmc
**Min Mail Order EU:** Nmc
**Credit Cards:** Visa MasterCard Switch Maestro
**Specialities:** Large range of hardy perennials, limited quantities of each. Large range of seeds & vegetable plants. Specialities tomato & pepper.
**Notes:** Mail order catalogue currently only for seed & veg plants.
**Map Ref:** C, B5

KEY
⊠ Mail order to UK or EU ⌂ Delivers to shows
✈ Exports beyond EU € Euro accepted
♿ Accessible by wheelchair ◆ See Display advertisement

C

**CSli** **SLIPPS GARDEN CENTRE**
Butts Hill, Frome, Somerset, BA11 1HR
Ⓣ (01373) 467013
Ⓕ (01373) 467013
**Contact:** James Hall
**Opening Times:** 0900-1730 Mon-Sat, 1000-1630 Sun.
**Cat. Cost:** None issued
**Credit Cards:** Visa Access MasterCard Delta Switch
**Specialities:** *Achillea*.
**Notes:** Also sells wholesale.
**Map Ref:** C, B5

**CSna** **SNAPE COTTAGE** ⊠
Chaffeymoor, Bourton, Dorset, SP8 5BZ
Ⓣ (01747) 840330 (evenings only).
Ⓔ ianandangela@snapecottagegarden.co.uk
Ⓦ www.snapestakes.com
**Contact:** Mrs Angela Whinfield
**Opening Times:** 1030-1700, last 2 Suns in each month Feb-Aug incl. & every Thu May-Aug.
**Min Mail Order UK:** Nmc
**Cat. Cost:** Sae.
**Credit Cards:** None
**Specialities:** Old forms of many popular garden plants. Plantsman's garden open same time as nursery. Stock available in small quantities.
**Notes:** Mail order *Galanthus* only. List issued in Feb.
**Map Ref:** C, B5 **OS Grid Ref:** ST762303

**CSNP** **SECOND NATURE PLANT NURSERY**
Croft House, Aller, Somerset, TA10 0RA
Ⓣ (01458) 259190
Ⓔ allernursery@aol.com
**Contact:** Sarah Adamson
**Opening Times:** 0900-1700 Tue-Sat (closed Mon), 1000-1600 Sun. Closed Nov-Jan.
**Credit Cards:** None
**Specialities:** Hardy perennials.
**Map Ref:** C, B4

**CSpe** **SPECIAL PLANTS** ⊠ €
Hill Farm Barn, Greenways Lane, Cold Ashton, Chippenham, Wiltshire, SN14 8LA
Ⓣ (01225) 891686
Ⓔ derry@specialplants.net
Ⓦ www.specialplants.net
**Contact:** Derry Watkins
**Opening Times:** 1000-1700 7 days Mar-Oct. Other times please ring first to check.
**Min Mail Order UK:** £10.00 + p&p
**Min Mail Order EU:** £20.00 + p&p
**Cat. Cost:** 5 × 1st class (A5 sae only for seed list).
**Credit Cards:** All major credit/debit cards
**Specialities:** Tender perennials, *Pelargonium*, *Salvia*, *Streptocarpus*, hardy geraniums, *Anemone*, *Erysimum*, *Papaver*, *Viola* & grasses. Many varieties prop. in small numbers only. New introductions of S. African plants.
**Notes:** Mail order Sep-Mar only.
**Map Ref:** C, A5 **OS Grid Ref:** ST749726

**CSPN** **SHERSTON PARVA NURSERY** ⊠ €
Malmesbury Road, Sherston, Wiltshire, SN16 0NX
Ⓣ (01666) 840348
Ⓜ 07887 814843
Ⓕ (01666) 840059
Ⓔ sherstonparva@aol.com
Ⓦ www.sherstonparva.com
**Contact:** Martin Rea
**Opening Times:** 1000-1700 7 days 1st Feb-31th Dec. Closed Jan.
**Min Mail Order UK:** Nmc
**Min Mail Order EU:** Nmc
**Cat. Cost:** Free.
**Credit Cards:** MasterCard Delta Visa Switch
**Specialities:** *Clematis*, wall shrubs & climbers.
**Map Ref:** C, A5

**CSRo** **SCENTED ROSES** ⊠ €
Little Silver House, Romansleigh, South Molton, North Devon, EX36 4JL
Ⓣ (01769) 550485
Ⓕ (01769) 550485
**Contact:** Iain Billot
**Opening Times:** By appt. only.
**Min Mail Order UK:** Nmc
**Cat. Cost:** Free.
**Credit Cards:** None
**Specialities:** Roses. Carefully selected to survive North Devon climate. Ramblers & climbers a speciality.
**Notes:** Also sells wholesale.
**Map Ref:** N, B1 **OS Grid Ref:** SS728214

**CSsd** **SUNNYSIDE PLANTS** ⊠
Sunnyside, Leigh Road, Bradford-on-Avon, Wiltshire, BA15 2RQ
Ⓣ (01225) 862096
Ⓔ Filoman@fsmail.net
**Contact:** James Tracey
**Opening Times:** By prior arrangement only.
**Min Mail Order UK:** £6.00
**Credit Cards:** None
**Specialities:** Dry & lime-tolerant hardy plants. Smaller quantities of choice plants for damp or humus-rich conditions. Some plants available in small quantities only.
**Notes:** Mail order pre-arranged by phone.
**Map Ref:** C, A5 **OS Grid Ref:** ST832621

**CSto** **STONE LANE GARDENS** ⊠
Stone Farm, Chagford, Devon, TQ13 8JU
Ⓣ (01647) 231311
Ⓔ orders@mythicgarden.eclipse.co.uk
Ⓦ www.mythicgarden.eclipse.co.uk
**Contact:** Kenneth Ashburner
**Opening Times:** Please phone for opening times.
**Min Mail Order UK:** Nmc
**Cat. Cost:** £2.00 or 6 × 1st class for descriptive catalogue.
**Credit Cards:** None
**Specialities:** Wide range of wild provenance *Betula* & *Alnus*. Nat. Collection of Birch & Alder. Arboretum open all year with summer sculpture exhibition (charges apply).
**Notes:** Planting service available in West Country, details on request. Also sells wholesale.
**Map Ref:** C, C3 **OS Grid Ref:** SX708908

**CStu** **STUCKEY'S ALPINES** ⌂
38 Phillipps Avenue, Exmouth, Devon, EX8 3HZ
Ⓣ (01395) 273636
Ⓔ stuckeysalpines@aol.com
**Contact:** Roger & Brenda Stuckey
**Opening Times:** As NGS dates or by appt.
**Cat. Cost:** None issued.
**Credit Cards:** None
**Specialities:** Alpines in general. Hardy & half-hardy bulbs. Extensive choice of plants, many available only in small quantities.
**Map Ref:** C, C4

**CSut** **SUTTONS SEEDS** ⊠
Woodview Road, Paignton, Devon, TQ4 7NG
Ⓣ 0870 220 2899
Ⓕ 0870 220 2265
Ⓦ www.suttons-seeds.co.uk
**Contact:** Customer Services
**Opening Times:** (Office) 0830-1700 Mon-Fri. Also answerphone.
**Min Mail Order UK:** Nmc
**Min Mail Order EU:** £5.00
**Cat. Cost:** Free.
**Credit Cards:** Visa MasterCard Switch Delta
**Specialities:** Over 1,000 varieties of flower & vegetable seed, bulbs, plants & sundries.

**CSWC** **SOUTH WEST CARNIVOROUS PLANTS** ⊠ ✈ ⌂
Blackwater Nursery, Blackwater Road, Culmstock, Cullompton, Devon, EX15 3HP
Ⓣ (01823) 681669
Ⓕ 0870 705 3083
Ⓔ flytraps@littleshopofhorrors.co.uk
Ⓦ www.littleshopofhorrors.co.uk
**Contact:** Jenny Pearce & Alistair Pearce
**Opening Times:** By appt.
**Min Mail Order UK:** Nmc
**Min Mail Order EU:** Nmc
**Cat. Cost:** 2 × 2nd class
**Credit Cards:** All major credit/debit cards
**Specialities:** *Cephalotus*, *Nepenthes*, *Dionea*, *Drosera*, *Darlingtonia*, *Sarracenia*, *Pinguicula* & *Utricularia*. Specialists in hardy carnivorous plants & *Dionea muscipula* cvs.
**Map Ref:** C, B4

**CSWP** **SONIA WRIGHT PLANTS** ⊠ ⌂ ♿
Buckerfields Nursery, Ogbourne St George, Marlborough, Wiltshire, SN8 1SG
Ⓣ (01672) 841065
Ⓕ (01672) 541047
**Contact:** Sonia Wright & Alison Duxbury
**Opening Times:** 1000-1800 Tue-Sat.
**Min Mail Order UK:** £15.00 primulas only
**Min Mail Order EU:** £15.00 primulas only
**Cat. Cost:** 4 × 1st class.
**Credit Cards:** All major credit/debit cards. Not accepted over the phone.
**Specialities:** Barnhaven polyanthus & primroses. Grasses, grey-leaved plants, *Iris*, *Euphorbia*, *Penstemon*, old roses.
**Notes:** Mail order primroses only despatched autumn.
**Map Ref:** C, A6

**CTca** **TRECANNA NURSERY** ⊠ ⌂
Rose Farm, Latchley, Nr Gunnislake, Cornwall, PL18 9AX
Ⓣ (01822) 834680
Ⓕ (01822) 834680
Ⓔ mark@trecanna.com
Ⓦ www.trecanna.com
**Contact:** Mark Wash
**Opening Times:** 1000-1700 Wed-Sat & B/hols all year. Closed Xmas Day & Boxing Day.
**Min Mail Order UK:** £15.00
**Min Mail Order EU:** £20.00
**Cat. Cost:** £1.00
**Credit Cards:** All major credit/debit cards
**Specialities:** Hardy South African bulbs & plants. Extensive collections of less usual bulbs & perennials. *Crocosmia*, *Eucomis*, *Schizostylis* & *Sempervivum*.
**Notes:** Talks to garden societies, tours of the nursery. Partial wheelchair access.
**Map Ref:** C, C3 **OS Grid Ref:** SX247733

KEY
⊠ Mail order to UK or EU ⌂ Delivers to shows
✈ Exports beyond EU € Euro accepted
♿ Accessible by wheelchair ◆ See Display advertisement

C

CTgr **Tregrehan Garden** ♿
Tregrehan Garden Cottages & Nursery, Par, Cornwall, PL24 2SJ
Ⓣ (01726) 812438
Ⓕ (01726) 814389
Ⓔ info@tregrehan.org
Ⓦ www.tregrehan.org
**Contact:** Tom Hudson
**Opening Times:** 1030-1700 Wed-Sun, mid-Mar-end May. 1400-1700 Wed only, Jun-Aug.
**Credit Cards:** None
**Specialities:** *Camellia*, *Rhododendron*, *Nothofagus*, *Myosotidium*, tender trees & shrubs.
**Notes:** Also sells wholesale.
**Map Ref:** C, D2 **OS Grid Ref:** SX0553

CTho **Thornhayes Nursery** ⊠ €
St Andrews Wood, Dulford, Cullompton, Devon, EX15 2DF
Ⓣ (01884) 266746
Ⓕ (01884) 266739
Ⓔ trees@thornhayes-nursery.co.uk
Ⓦ www.thornhayes-nursery.co.uk
**Contact:** K D Croucher
**Opening Times:** 0800-1600 Mon-Fri. 0930-1400 Sat (Sep-Apr).
**Min Mail Order UK:** £100
**Min Mail Order EU:** Nmc
**Credit Cards:** None
**Specialities:** A broad range of forms of ornamental, amenity & fruit trees incl. West Country apple varieties.
**Notes:** Also sells wholesale.
**Map Ref:** C, C4

CTrC **Trevena Cross Nurseries** ⊠ € ♿
Breage, Helston, Cornwall, TR13 9PS
Ⓣ (01736) 763880
Ⓕ (01736) 762828
Ⓔ sales@trevenacross.co.uk
Ⓦ www.trevenacross.co.uk
**Contact:** Graham Jeffery, John Eddy
**Opening Times:** 0900-1700 Mon-Sat, 1030-1630 Sun.
**Min Mail Order UK:** Nmc
**Cat. Cost:** Online only.
**Credit Cards:** Access Visa Switch
**Specialities:** South African, Australian & New Zealand plants, incl. *Aloe*, *Protea*, tree ferns, palms, *Restio*, hardy succulents & wide range of other exotics.
**Map Ref:** C, D1 **OS Grid Ref:** SW614284

CTrG **Tregothnan Nursery** ⊠ ✈ € ♿
Estate Office, Tregothnan, Truro, Cornwall, TR2 4AN
Ⓣ (01872) 520000
Ⓕ (01872) 520583
Ⓔ bigplants@tregothnan.co.uk
Ⓦ www.tregothnan.com
**Contact:** Jonathon Jones
**Opening Times:** By appt. for collection only.
**Min Mail Order UK:** £25.00
**Min Mail Order EU:** £50.00
**Cat. Cost:** Online only.
**Credit Cards:** MasterCard Visa Delta EuroCard
**Specialities:** Unusual & rare plants from own stock. Extra large specimens available for instant effect. Known wild origin plants.
**Notes:** English tea production & marketing. Also sells wholesale.
**Map Ref:** C, D2 **OS Grid Ref:** SW859421

CTrh **Trehane Camellia Nursery** ⊠ ñ € ♿
J Trehane & Sons Ltd, Stapehill Road, Hampreston, Wimborne, Dorset, BH21 7ND
Ⓣ (01202) 873490
Ⓕ (01202) 873490
Ⓔ camellias@trehanenursery.co.uk
Ⓦ www.trehanenursery.co.uk
**Contact:** Lorraine or Jeanette
**Opening Times:** 0900-1630 Mon-Fri all year (excl. Xmas & New Year). 1000-1600 Sat-Sun in spring & by special appt.
**Min Mail Order UK:** Nmc
**Cat. Cost:** £1.90 cat./book.
**Credit Cards:** All major credit/debit cards
**Specialities:** Extensive range of *Camellia* species, cvs & hybrids. Many new introductions. Evergreen azaleas, *Pieris*, *Magnolia* & blueberries.
**Notes:** Also sells wholesale.
**Map Ref:** C, C6

CTri **Triscombe Nurseries** ⊠ ♿ ◆
West Bagborough, Nr Taunton, Somerset, TA4 3HG
Ⓣ (01984) 618267
Ⓔ triscombe.nurseries2000@virgin.net
Ⓦ www.triscombenurseries.co.uk
**Contact:** S Parkman
**Opening Times:** 0900-1300 & 1400-1730 Mon-Sat. 1400-1730 Sun & B/hols.
**Min Mail Order UK:** Nmc
**Cat. Cost:** 2 × 1st class
**Credit Cards:** None
**Specialities:** Trees, shrubs, roses, fruit, *Clematis*, herbaceous & rock plants.
**Map Ref:** C, B4

CTsd **Treseders** ⊠ ♿
Wallcottage Nursery, Lockengate, St. Austell, Cornwall, PL26 8RU
Ⓣ (01208) 832234
Ⓔ Treseders@btconnect.com

**Contact:** James Treseder
**Opening Times:** 1000-1700 Mon-Sat, 1000-1600 Sun.
**Min Mail Order UK:** Nmc
**Cat. Cost:** 60p
**Credit Cards:** All major credit/debit cards
**Specialities:** A wide range of choice & unusual plants grown in peat-free compost, incl. 200+ *Fuchsia* varieties.
**Notes:** Also sells wholesale
**Map Ref:** C, C2 **OS Grid Ref:** SX034620

CTuc **EDWIN TUCKER & SONS** ⊠ ♿
Brewery Meadow, Stonepark, Ashburton, Newton Abbot, Devon, TQ13 7DG
Ⓣ (01364) 652233
Ⓕ (01364) 654211
Ⓔ seeds@edwintucker.com
Ⓦ www.edwintucker.com
**Contact:** Geoff Penton
**Opening Times:** 0800-1700 Mon-Fri, 0800-1600 Sat.
**Min Mail Order UK:** Nmc
**Min Mail Order EU:** Nmc
**Cat. Cost:** Free
**Credit Cards:** Visa MasterCard Switch
**Specialities:** Nearly 120 varieties of seed potatoes, incl. 50 organic varieties. Wide range of vegetables, flowers, green manures & sprouting seeds in packets. All not treated. Nearly 200 varieties of organically produced seeds.

CWan **WANBOROUGH HERB NURSERY** ⛺ ♿
Callas Hill, Wanborough, Swindon, Wiltshire, SN4 0AG
Ⓣ (01793) 790327 (answering machine)
Ⓔ Biggs@wanbherbnursery.fsnet.co.uk
**Contact:** Peter Biggs
**Opening Times:** 1000-1700 Tue-Fri, w/ends 1000-1600, Mar-Oct. Other times by appt.
**Cat. Cost:** £1.00
**Credit Cards:** None
**Specialities:** Herbs, herbaceous, esp. culinary. Available in small quantities only.
**Map Ref:** C, A6 **OS Grid Ref:** SU217828

CWat **THE WATER GARDEN** ⊠ ♿
Hinton Parva, Swindon, Wiltshire, SN4 0DH
Ⓣ (01793) 790558
Ⓕ (01793) 791298
Ⓔ mike@thewatergarden.co.uk
Ⓦ www.thewatergarden.co.uk
**Contact:** Mike & Anne Newman
**Opening Times:** 1000-1700 Wed-Sun.
**Min Mail Order UK:** £10.00 + p&p
**Cat. Cost:** 4 × 1st class
**Credit Cards:** Visa Access Switch
**Specialities:** Water lilies, marginal & moisture plants, oxygenators & alpines.
**Map Ref:** C, A6

CWCL **WESTCOUNTRY NURSERIES (INC. WESTCOUNTRY LUPINS)** ⊠ ⛺ ♿ ◆
Donkey Meadow, Woolsery, Devon, EX39 5QH
Ⓣ (01237) 431111
Ⓕ (01237) 431111
Ⓔ info@westcountry-nurseries.co.uk
Ⓦ www.westcountry-nurseries.co.uk
**Contact:** Sarah Conibear
**Opening Times:** 1000-1600 7 days.
**Min Mail Order UK:** Nmc
**Min Mail Order EU:** Nmc
**Cat. Cost:** 2 × 1st class + A5 sae for full colour cat.
**Credit Cards:** All major credit/debit cards, Nochex payment accepted online.
**Specialities:** *Lupinus*, *Lewisia*, *Hellebore*, *Clematis*, cyclamen, acers, lavender, select perennials, grasses, ferns & climbers. Nat. Collection of Lupins.
**Map Ref:** C, B2 **OS Grid Ref:** SS351219

CWGN **WALLED GARDEN NURSERY** ⊠ ♿
Brinkworth House, Brinkworth, Nr Malmesbury, Wiltshire, SN16 9DQ
Ⓣ (01666) 826637
Ⓔ f.wescott@btinternet.com
Ⓦ www.clematis-nursery.co.uk
**Contact:** Fraser Wescott
**Opening Times:** 1000-1700, 7 days Mar-Oct. 1000-dusk, Mon-Fri Nov & Feb. Closed Dec & Jan.
**Min Mail Order UK:** £8.50
**Cat. Cost:** 3 × 1st class.
**Credit Cards:** All major credit/debit cards
**Specialities:** *Clematis* & climbers, with a selection of unusual perennials & shrubs.
**Map Ref:** C, A6 **OS Grid Ref:** SU002849

CWGr **WINCHESTER GROWERS LTD** ⊠ ✈ ♿
Varfell Farm, Long Rock, Penzance, Cornwall, TR20 8AQ
Ⓣ (01736) 335851
Ⓕ (01736) 851033
Ⓔ dahlias@wgltd.co.uk
Ⓦ www.national-dahlia-collection.co.uk
**Contact:** Michael Mann

KEY
⊠ Mail order to UK or EU ⛺ Delivers to shows
✈ Exports beyond EU € Euro accepted
♿ Accessible by wheelchair ◆ See Display advertisement

C

**Opening Times:** 1300-1630 Thu, Fri & Sat, 27th Jul-25th Aug 2007 incl. Open day 1000-1600 Sun 19th Aug 2007.
**Min Mail Order UK:** Nmc
**Min Mail Order EU:** Nmc
**Cat. Cost:** Free
**Credit Cards:** Visa Delta MasterCard Switch
**Specialities:** Nat. Collection of *Dahlia*. Due to large number of varieties, some stock available in small quantities only.
**Notes:** Also sells wholesale.
**Map Ref:** C, D1

**CWib** **WIBBLE FARM NURSERIES** ⊠ ⊠ ♿
Wibble Farm, West Quantoxhead,
Nr Taunton, Somerset, TA4 4DD
Ⓣ (01984) 632303
Ⓕ (01984) 633168
Ⓔ sales@wibblefarmnurseries.co.uk
Ⓦ www.wibblefarmnurseries.co.uk
**Contact:** Mrs M L Francis
**Opening Times:** 0800-1700 Mon-Fri, 1000-1600 Sat. All year excl. B/hols.
**Min Mail Order UK:** Nmc
**Min Mail Order EU:** Nmc
**Cat. Cost:** 3 × 1st class
**Credit Cards:** All major credit/debit cards
**Specialities:** Growers of a wide range of hardy plants, many rare & unusual.
**Notes:** Also sells wholesale.
**Map Ref:** C, B4

**CWil** **FERNWOOD NURSERY** ⊠ ⊠ ⌂ € ♿
Peters Marland, Torrington, Devon, EX38 8QG
Ⓣ (01805) 601446
Ⓔ hw@fernwood-nursery.co.uk
Ⓦ www.fernwood-nursery.co.uk
**Contact:** Howard Wills & Sally Wills
**Opening Times:** Any time by appt. Please phone first.
**Min Mail Order UK:** Nmc
**Min Mail Order EU:** Nmc
**Cat. Cost:** Sae for list.
**Credit Cards:** None
**Specialities:** Nat. Collection of *Sempervivum*, *Jovibarba*, *Rosularia* & *Phormium*.
**Notes:** Mail order for *Sempervivum*, *Jovibarba* & *Rosularia* only. 5 miles from RHS Rosemoor.
**Map Ref:** C, C3 **OS Grid Ref:** SS479133

**CWiW** **WINDRUSH WILLOW** ⊠ €
Higher Barn, Sidmouth Road, Aylesbeare,
Exeter, Devon, EX5 2JJ
Ⓣ (01395) 233669
Ⓕ (01395) 233669
Ⓔ windrushw@aol.com
Ⓦ www.windrushwillow.com
**Contact:** Richard Kerwood
**Opening Times:** Mail order only. Open by appt.
**Min Mail Order UK:** Nmc
**Min Mail Order EU:** Nmc
**Cat. Cost:** 2 × 1st class
**Credit Cards:** None
**Specialities:** *Salix*. Unrooted cuttings available Dec-Mar.
**Notes:** Also sells wholesale.

**CWon** **THE WONDER TREE** ⊠
35 Beaconsfield Road, Knowle, Bristol,
BS4 2JE
Ⓣ 0117 908 9057
Ⓜ 07989 333507
Ⓔ Kevin@wondertree.org.uk
Ⓦ www.wondertree.org.uk
**Contact:** Kevin Lindegaard
**Opening Times:** Not open. Mail order only.
**Min Mail Order UK:** £8.00
**Cat. Cost:** 2 × 1st class.
**Credit Cards:** None
**Specialities:** *Salix.*
**Notes:** Also sells wholesale.

**CWoo** **IAN AND ROSEMARY WOOD** ⊠
Newlands, 28 Furland Road, Crewkerne,
Somerset, TA18 8DD
Ⓣ (01460) 74630
Ⓔ eryth@wood31.waitrose.com
**Contact:** Ian and Rosemary Wood
**Opening Times:** By appt. only. Primarily mail order service. Enquiries welcomed to collect growing plants in season.
**Min Mail Order UK:** Nmc
**Cat. Cost:** 2 × 2nd class.
**Credit Cards:** None
**Specialities:** *Erythronium*, *Cyclamen* species & dwarf *Narcissus* species. Some species available in small quantities only, see catalogue.
**Map Ref:** C, B5

**CWri** **NIGEL WRIGHT RHODODENDRONS** ♿
The Old Glebe, Eggesford,
Chulmleigh, Devon,
EX18 7QU
Ⓣ (01769) 580632
Ⓔ wrightrhodos@aol.com
**Contact:** Nigel Wright
**Opening Times:** By appt. only. 7 days.
**Cat. Cost:** 2 × 1st class.
**Credit Cards:** None
**Specialities:** *Rhododendron* & deciduous azaleas. 200 varieties field grown, root-balled, some potted. For collection only. Specialist grower. Free advice & planting plans.
**Notes:** Also sells wholesale.
**Map Ref:** C, B3 **OS Grid Ref:** SS684106

CWsd **WILDSIDE NURSERY** ✉ ♿
Green Lane, Buckland Monachorum,
Nr Yelverton, Devon, PL20 7NP
Ⓣ (01822) 855755
Ⓔ wildside.plants@virgin.net
**Contact:** Keith & Ros Wiley
**Opening Times:** 1000-1700 Thu only, Mar-Oct.
**Min Mail Order UK:** Nmc
**Min Mail Order EU:** £30.00
**Cat. Cost:** 2 × 1st class.
**Credit Cards:** All major credit/debit cards
**Specialities:** *Anemone nemorosa, Erythronium, Epimedium, Trillium, Rhodohypoxis* & unusual woodland plants.
**Map Ref:** C,C3 **OS Grid Ref:** SX480679

CWSG **WEST SOMERSET GARDEN CENTRE** ✉ ♿
Mart Road, Minehead, Somerset, TA24 5BJ
Ⓣ (01643) 703812
Ⓕ (01643) 706476
Ⓔ wsgc@btconnect.com
Ⓦ www.westsomersetgardencentre.co.uk
**Contact:** Mrs J K Shoulders
**Opening Times:** 0800-1700 Mon-Sat, 1000-1600 Sun.
**Min Mail Order UK:** Nmc
**Cat. Cost:** None issued.
**Credit Cards:** Access Visa Switch Solo
**Specialities:** Wide general range. *Ceanothus.*
**Map Ref:** C, B4

CWVF **WHITE VEIL FUCHSIAS** ✉ ♿
Verwood Road, Three Legged Cross,
Wimborne, Dorset, BH21 6RP
Ⓣ (01202) 813998
**Contact:** A. C. Holloway
**Opening Times:** 0900-1300 & 1400-1700 Mon-Fri Jan-Dec, & Sat Jan-Aug. 0900-1300 Sun Jan-Jul, closed Sun Aug, closed Sat & Sun Sep-Dec.
**Min Mail Order UK:** 8 plants of your choice.
**Cat. Cost:** 4 × 1st class
**Credit Cards:** None
**Specialities:** Fuchsias. Small plants grown from Jan-Apr. Available in small quantities only.
**Map Ref:** C,C6

## EASTERN

EABi **ALISON BILVERSTONE** ✉
22 Kings Street, Swaffham, Norfolk,
PE37 7BU
Ⓣ (01760) 725026
Ⓔ lucybilverstone@hotmail.co.uk
**Contact:** Alison Bilverstone
**Opening Times:** Not open. Mail order only.
**Min Mail Order UK:** Nmc
**Cat. Cost:** Large sae.
**Credit Cards:** None
**Specialities:** *Achemene, Kohleria* & *Smithiantha* rhizomes, available Dec to mid-Apr. Stocked in small quantities.

EAEE **AEE** ✉
38 Church Close, Roydon, Diss, Norfolk,
IP22 5RQ
Ⓣ (01379) 651230
Ⓕ (01379) 651230
Ⓔ aeeloverofplants@fsmail.net
Ⓦ www.aeesupplyingplantlovers.com
**Contact:** Anne Etheridge
**Opening Times:** Not open. Mail order only.
**Min Mail Order UK:** Nmc.
**Min Mail Order EU:** Nmc.
**Cat. Cost:** 3 × 1st class.
**Credit Cards:** Paypal
**Specialities:** Perennials & grasses plus a few enticing alpines & shrubs. Alpines & shrubs available in small quantities only.
**Notes:** Garden maintenance, spring & autumn pruning. Talks available.

EAlp **THE ALPINE AND GRASS NURSERY** ✉ 
Northgate, Pinchbeck, Spalding, Lincolnshire,
PE11 3TB
Ⓣ (01775) 640935
Ⓔ info@alpinesandgrasses.co.uk
Ⓦ www.alpinesandgrasses.co.uk
**Contact:** Hayley Merrison
**Opening Times:** Please telephone.
**Min Mail Order UK:** 15 plants.
**Cat. Cost:** Online only.
**Credit Cards:** Paypal
**Specialities:** Alpines, rockery plants & ornamental grasses.
**Notes:** Also sells wholesale.
**Map Ref:** E, B1 **OS Grid Ref:** TF211262

EAmu **AMULREE EXOTICS** ✉ ♿
The Turnpike, Norwich Road (B1113),
Fundenhall, Norwich, Norfolk, NR16 1EL
Ⓣ (01508) 488101
Ⓕ (01508) 488101
Ⓔ SDG@exotica.fsbusiness.co.uk
Ⓦ www.turn-it-tropical.co.uk
**Contact:** S Gridley
**Opening Times:** 0930-1730 7 days spring-autumn, 1000-1630 7 days autumn-spring.

KEY
✉ Mail order to UK or EU — Delivers to shows
Exports beyond EU — € Euro accepted
♿ Accessible by wheelchair — ◆ See Display advertisement

E

**Min Mail Order UK:** Nmc
**Cat. Cost:** 2 × 1st class
**Credit Cards:** Visa MasterCard Electron Solo Switch
**Specialities:** Hardy & half-hardy plants for home, garden & conservatory. Palms, bamboos, bananas, tree ferns, cannas, gingers & much more.
**Notes:** Also sells wholesale.
**Map Ref:** E, B3 **OS Grid Ref:** DX123740

**EAro** **Aromafolia** ⊠ ♿
Barbers Farm, Leys Lane, Old Buckenham, Norfolk, NR17 1NT
Ⓣ (01953) 887713
Ⓔ enquiries@aromafolia.co.uk
Ⓦ www.aromafolia.co.uk
**Contact:** John Holden
**Opening Times:** 1000-1700 Fri, Sat, Sun & B/hols, Apr-Oct. Other times by appt.
**Min Mail Order UK:** £15.00
**Cat. Cost:** 3 × !st class.
**Credit Cards:** None
**Specialities:** Wide range of plants with aromatic foliage, incl. *Salvia*, *Monarda*, *Agastache*, *Nepeta*. All plants grown in peat-free compost. Some varieties only available in small quantities.
**Map Ref:** E,C3 **OS Grid Ref:** TM042913

**EBak** **B & H M Baker**
Bourne Brook Nurseries, Greenstead Green, Halstead, Essex, CO9 1RJ
Ⓣ (01787) 476369/472900
**Contact:** B, HM and C Baker
**Opening Times:** 0800-1630 Mon-Fri, 0900-1200 & 1400-1630 Sat & Sun, Mar-30th Jun.
**Cat. Cost:** 2 × 1st class + 33p
**Credit Cards:** MasterCard Delta Visa Switch
**Specialities:** *Fuchsia* & conservatory plants.
**Notes:** Also sells wholesale.
**Map Ref:** E, C2

**EBee** **Beeches Nursery** ⊠ ♿
Village Centre, Ashdon, Saffron Walden, Essex, CB10 2HB
Ⓣ (01799) 584362
Ⓕ (01799) 584421
Ⓦ www.beechesnursery.co.uk
**Contact:** Alan Bidwell/Kevin Marsh
**Opening Times:** 0830-1700 Mon-Sat, 1000-1700 Sun & B/hols.
**Min Mail Order UK:** £10.00
**Min Mail Order EU:** £20.00
**Cat. Cost:** 6 × 2nd class herbaceous list
**Credit Cards:** Visa Access MasterCard EuroCard, Switch
**Specialities:** Herbaceous specialists & extensive range of other garden plants.
**Notes:** Mail order generally from Oct-Feb, Mar-Sep where conditions permit. Trees not available by mail order.
**Map Ref:** E, C2 **OS Grid Ref:** TL586420

**EBla** **Blacksmiths Cottage Nursery** ⊠ ♿ € ♿
Langmere Road, Langmere, Dickleburgh, Nr Diss, Norfolk, IP21 4QA
Ⓣ (01379) 741136
Ⓕ (01379) 741917
Ⓔ Blackcottnursery@aol.com
Ⓦ www.blackcottnursery.co.uk
**Contact:** Ben or Jill Potterton
**Opening Times:** 1000-1700 Thu-Sun, Mar-Oct & 1000-1700 Fri & Sat, Nov-Feb.
**Min Mail Order UK:** Nmc
**Min Mail Order EU:** Nmc
**Cat. Cost:** 3 × 1st class
**Credit Cards:** All major credit/debit cards
**Specialities:** Over 2000 species grown. Large selection of shade plants. Large new display gardens.
**Notes:** Toilets & refreshments. Also sells wholesale.
**Map Ref:** E, C3

**EBls** **Peter Beales Roses** ⊠ ✈ ♿
London Road, Attleborough, Norfolk, NR17 1AY
Ⓣ (01953) 454707
Ⓕ (01953) 456845
Ⓔ info@peterbealesroses.co.uk
Ⓦ www.peterbealesroses.co.uk
**Contact:** Customer Advisers
**Opening Times:** 0900-1700 Mon-Sat, 1000-1600 Sun & B/hols.
**Min Mail Order UK:** Nmc
**Min Mail Order EU:** Nmc
**Cat. Cost:** Free to UK. Outside UK £5.00.
**Credit Cards:** All major credit/debit cards except American Express.
**Specialities:** Old fashioned roses & classic roses. Nat. Collection of Species Roses. Some stock available in small quantities only. Other plants on site.
**Notes:** Shop & bistro.
**Map Ref:** E, C3 **OS Grid Ref:** TM026929

**EBrs** **Bressingham Gardens (incorp. Van Tubergen UK)** ⊠ ♿
Bressingham, Diss, Norfolk, IP22 2AG
Ⓣ (01379) 688282
Ⓕ (01379) 687227
Ⓔ info@bressinghamgardens.com
Ⓦ www.bressinghamgardens.com
**Contact:** Fiona-Louise Tilden

**Opening Times:** Mail order 0900-1700 Mon-Fri. Gardens open daily 1030-1730 1st Apr-31st Oct.
**Min Mail Order UK:** Nmc
**Min Mail Order EU:** £100
**Cat. Cost:** None issued.
**Credit Cards:** Maestro Visa Access MasterCard
**Specialities:** Bulbs, grafted conifers, grasses & perennials. Nat. Collection of *Miscanthus*.
**Notes:** Also sells wholesale.
**Map Ref:** E, C3 **OS Grid Ref:** TM071807

**EBur** **JENNY BURGESS** ♿
Alpine Nursery, Sisland, Norwich, Norfolk, NR14 6EF
Ⓣ (01508) 520724
**Contact:** Jenny Burgess
**Opening Times:** Any time by appt.
**Credit Cards:** None
**Specialities:** Alpines, *Sisyrinchium* & *Campanula*. Nat. Collection of *Sisyrinchium*.
**Map Ref:** E, B3

**EBWF** **BRITISH WILD FLOWER PLANTS** ⊠ ♿
Burlingham Gardens, 31 Main Road, North Burlingham, Norfolk, NR13 4TA
Ⓣ (01603) 716615
Ⓕ (01603) 716615
Ⓔ office@wildflowers.co.uk
Ⓦ www.wildflowers.co.uk
**Contact:** Helen Tweed
**Opening Times:** 1000-1600 Mon-Fri. Weekends by appt.
**Min Mail Order UK:** Nmc
**Min Mail Order EU:** Nmc
**Cat. Cost:** £2.00 + p&p
**Credit Cards:** All major credit/debit cards
**Specialities:** Native wild flowers. 400 species. Quantities vary from 1 to 50,000.
**Notes:** Also sells wholesale.
**Map Ref:** E, B3 **OS Grid Ref:** TG371101

**ECGP** **CAMBRIDGE GARDEN PLANTS** ♿
The Lodge, Clayhithe Road, Horningsea, Cambridgeshire, CB25 9JD
Ⓣ (01223) 861370
**Contact:** Mrs Nancy Buchdahl
**Opening Times:** 1100-1730 Thu-Sun mid Mar-31st Oct. Other times by appt.
**Cat. Cost:** 4 × 1st class
**Credit Cards:** None
**Specialities:** Hardy perennials incl. wide range of *Geranium*, *Allium*, *Euphorbia*, *Penstemon*, *Digitalis*. Some shrubs, roses & *Clematis*.
**Map Ref:** E, C2 **OS Grid Ref:** TL497637

**ECha** **THE BETH CHATTO GARDENS LTD** ⊠ ♿
Elmstead Market, Colchester, Essex, CO7 7DB
Ⓣ (01206) 822007
Ⓕ (01206) 825933
Ⓔ info@bethchatto.fsnet.co.uk
Ⓦ www.bethchatto.co.uk
**Contact:** Beth Chatto
**Opening Times:** 0900-1700 Mon-Sat 1st Mar-31st Oct. 0900-1600 Mon-Fri 1st Nov-1st Mar. Closed Sun.
**Min Mail Order UK:** £20.00
**Min Mail Order EU:** Ask for details
**Cat. Cost:** £3.00 incl. p&p
**Credit Cards:** Visa Switch MasterCard
**Specialities:** Predominantly herbaceous. Many unusual for special situations.
**Map Ref:** E, D3 **OS Grid Ref:** TM069238

**ECho** **CHOICE LANDSCAPES** ⊠ ✈ € ♿
Priory Farm, 101 Salts Road, West Walton, Wisbech, Cambridgeshire, PE14 7EF
Ⓣ (01945) 585051
Ⓕ (01945) 580053
Ⓔ info@choicelandscapes.org
Ⓦ www.choicelandscapes.org
**Contact:** Michael Agg & Jillian Agg
**Opening Times:** 1000-1700 Tue-Sat 20th Feb-27th Oct 2007. Not open on show dates, please phone. Other times by appt.
**Min Mail Order UK:** £10.00
**Min Mail Order EU:** £10.00 + p&p
**Cat. Cost:** 6 × 1st class or 6 IRC
**Credit Cards:** Maestro Visa MasterCard Solo
**Specialities:** Dwarf conifers, alpines, acers, rhododendrons, bulbs, pines & lilies.
**Map Ref:** E, B1

**ECnt** **CANTS OF COLCHESTER** ⊠ ✈
Nayland Road, Mile End, Colchester, Essex, CO4 5EB
Ⓣ (01206) 844008
Ⓕ (01206) 855371
Ⓔ finder@cantsroses.co.uk
Ⓦ www.cantsroses.co.uk
**Contact:** Angela Pawsey
**Opening Times:** 0900-1300, 1400-1630 Mon-Fri. Sat varied, please phone first. Sun closed.
**Min Mail Order UK:** Nmc
**Min Mail Order EU:** Nmc
**Cat. Cost:** Free

KEY
⊠ Mail order to UK or EU — Delivers to shows
✈ Exports beyond EU — € Euro accepted
♿ Accessible by wheelchair — ◆ See Display advertisement

E

E

**Credit Cards:** Visa MasterCard Delta Solo Switch
**Specialities:** Roses. Unstaffed rose field can be viewed dawn-dusk every day from end Jun-end Sep.
**Notes:** Bare-root mail order end Oct-end Mar, containers Apr-Aug. Partial wheelchair access.
**Map Ref:** E, C3

**ECot** **THE COTTAGE GARDEN** € ♿
Langham Road, Boxted, Colchester, Essex, CO4 5HU
Ⓣ (01206) 272269
Ⓔ enquiries@thecottage-garden.co.uk
Ⓦ www.thecottage-garden.co.uk
**Contact:** Alison Smith
**Opening Times:** 0800-1700 7 days spring & summer. 0800-1700 Thu-Mon autumn/winter.
**Cat. Cost:** Free leaflet
**Credit Cards:** Visa Access Connect, Switch Delta
**Specialities:** 400 varieties of shrubs, 500 varieties of herbaceous. Huge range of trees, grasses, alpines, herbs, hedging, all home grown. Garden antiques.
**Map Ref:** E, C3 **OS Grid Ref:** TM003299

**ECou** **COUNTY PARK NURSERY**
Essex Gardens, Hornchurch, Essex, RM11 3BU
Ⓣ (01708) 445205
Ⓦ www.countyparknursery.co.uk
**Contact:** G Hutchins
**Opening Times:** 1000-1700 Mon-Sat excl. Wed, 1000-1700 Sun Mar-Oct. Nov-Feb by appt. only.
**Cat. Cost:** 3 × 1st class
**Credit Cards:** None
**Specialities:** Alpines & rare and unusual plants from New Zealand, Tasmania & the Falklands. Nat. Collection of *Coprosma*. Many plants in small quantities only.
**Map Ref:** E, D2

**ECre** **CREAKE PLANT CENTRE** ♿
Nursery View, Leicester Road, South Creake, Fakenham, Norfolk, NR21 9PW
Ⓣ (01328) 823018
**Contact:** Mr T Harrison
**Opening Times:** 1000-1300 & 1400-1730 7 days excl. Xmas.
**Cat. Cost:** None issued
**Credit Cards:** All major credit/debit cards
**Specialities:** Unusual shrubs, herbaceous, conservatory plants, old roses.
**Map Ref:** E, B1 **OS Grid Ref:** TF864353

**ECrN** **CROWN NURSERY** ⊠ ♿
High Street, Ufford, Woodbridge, Suffolk, IP13 6EL
Ⓣ (01394) 460755
Ⓕ (01394) 460142
Ⓔ enquiries@crown-nursery.co.uk
Ⓦ www.crown-nursery.co.uk
**Contact:** Anne Raymond
**Opening Times:** 0900-1700 (1600 in winter) Mon-Sat.
**Min Mail Order UK:** Nmc
**Cat. Cost:** 2 × 1st class
**Credit Cards:** All major credit/debit cards
**Specialities:** Mature & semi-mature native, ornamental & fruit trees. Heritage fruit varieties.
**Notes:** Mail order for small/young stock only. Also sells wholesale.
**Map Ref:** E, C3 **OS Grid Ref:** TM292528

**ECtt** **COTTAGE NURSERIES** ⊠ ♿
Thoresthorpe, Alford, Lincolnshire, LN13 0HX
Ⓣ (01507) 466968
Ⓕ (01507) 463409
Ⓔ bill@cottagenurseries.net
Ⓦ www.cottagenurseries.net
**Contact:** W H Denbigh
**Opening Times:** 0900-1700 7 days 1st Mar-31st Oct, 1000-1600 w/ends only Nov-Feb.
**Min Mail Order UK:** Nmc
**Cat. Cost:** 3 × 1st class
**Credit Cards:** Visa MasterCard Maestro
**Specialities:** Hardy perennials. Wide general range.
**Map Ref:** E, A2 **OS Grid Ref:** TF423716

**EDAr** **D'ARCY & EVEREST** ⊠ € ♿
(Office) PO Box 78, St Ives, Huntingdon, Cambridgeshire, PE27 4UQ
Ⓣ (01480) 497672
Ⓜ 07715 374440/1
Ⓕ (01480) 466042
Ⓔ angela@darcyeverest.co.uk
Ⓦ www.darcyeverest.co.uk
**Contact:** Angela Whiting, Richard Oliver
**Opening Times:** By appt. only. Coach parties welcome by appt.
**Min Mail Order UK:** £10.00 + p&p
**Min Mail Order EU:** £10.00 + p&p
**Cat. Cost:** 6 × 1st class
**Credit Cards:** None
**Specialities:** Alpines & selected perennials.
**Notes:** Nursery is at Pidley Sheep Lane (B1040), Somersham, Huntingdon, Cambs.
**Map Ref:** E, C2 **OS Grid Ref:** TL533276

E

**EDif** **DIFFERENT PLANTS** ⛺ ♿
The Mellis Stud, Gate Farm,
Cranley Green, Eye, Suffolk,
IP23 7NX
Ⓣ (01379) 870291
**Contact:** Fleur Waters
**Opening Times:** Sat-Thu by appt. only, closed Fri. Plant stall Eye market Fri 0900-1200.
**Cat. Cost:** 4 × 1st class
**Credit Cards:** None
**Specialities:** *Mimulus aurantiacus* & hybrids, half-hardy bulbous/cormous perennials incl. *Dietes*, *Aristea*, *Cypella*, *Tigridia* & *Anomatheca laxa*. Bulbs may be available in small quantities only.
**Map Ref:** E, C3

**EECP** **ESSEX CARNIVOROUS PLANTS** ☒
12 Strangman Avenue,
Thundersley, Essex,
SS7 1RB
Ⓣ (01702) 551467
Ⓔ Markecp@aol.com
Ⓦ www.essexcarnivorousplants.com
**Contact:** Mark Haslett
**Opening Times:** By appt. only.
**Min Mail Order UK:** Nmc
**Min Mail Order EU:** Nmc
**Cat. Cost:** Online or 2 × 1st class.
**Credit Cards:** None
**Specialities:** Good range of carnivorous plants. *Sarracenia*, *Drosera*. Nat. Collection of *Dionaea* forms & cvs. Some stock available in small quantities only.
**Notes:** Also sells wholesale
**Map Ref:** E, D2 **OS Grid Ref:** TQ797875

**EEls** **ELSWORTH HERBS** ☒ ♿
Avenue Farm Cottage, 31 Smith Street,
Elsworth, Cambridgeshire,
CB3 8HY
Ⓣ (01954) 267414
Ⓕ (01954) 267414
Ⓔ john.twibell@btinternet.com
**Contact:** Drs J D & J M Twibell
**Opening Times:** By appt. only.
**Min Mail Order UK:** £10.00
**Cat. Cost:** 3 × 1st class
**Credit Cards:** None
**Specialities:** Nat. Collections of *Artemisia* (incl. *Seriphidium*) & *Nerium oleander*. Wide range of *Artemisia* & *Seriphidium*, *Nerium oleander*. Stock available in small quantities only. Orders may require propagation from Collection material, for which we are the primary reference source.
**Map Ref:** E, C2

**EExo** **THE EXOTIC GARDEN COMPANY** ♿
Saxmundham Road, Aldeburgh, Suffolk,
IP15 5JD
Ⓣ (01728) 454456
Ⓦ www.theexoticgardenco.co.uk
**Contact:** Matthew Couchy
**Opening Times:** 1000-1700 Mon-Sat, 1000-1600 Sun.
**Min Mail Order UK:** Nmc
**Cat. Cost:** A4 sae
**Credit Cards:** All major credit/debit cards
**Specialities:** Palms (hardy & half-hardy), bamboos, tree ferns & other exotics. Extensive range of other garden plants, incl. specimens.
**Map Ref:** E, C3

**EFam** **FAMECHECK REBLOOMING IRIS** ☒ ✈ € ♿
Hilltrees, Wandlebury Hill (A1307),
Cambridge, Cambridgeshire, CB2 4AD
Ⓣ (01223) 243734 repeat ring after dark or leave phone number (not mobile).
**Contact:** Miss F Cook N.D.H.
**Opening Times:** 1030-1300, 7 days, but please phone first. Open Days Sats May & June.
**Min Mail Order UK:** £5.00
**Min Mail Order EU:** £5.00
**Cat. Cost:** 6 × 1st class for list.
**Credit Cards:** None
**Specialities:** Daffodils, long-lasting & weatherproof cut-flower varieties. Bearded *Iris* & orange violets. Space Age & Reblooming Bearded *Iris*. Some only available in small quantities. About 1000 modern varieties, mostly imported. NCH status applied for daffodils & *Iris*.
**Notes:** Nursery between Cambridge Botanic Garden & Wandlebury Wildlife Park, next to Gogmagog Golf Course on A1307.
**Map Ref:** E, C2

**EFer** **THE FERN NURSERY** ☒ ♿
Grimsby Road, Binbrook, Lincolnshire,
LN8 6DH
Ⓣ (01472) 398092
Ⓔ richard@timm984.fsnet.co.uk
Ⓦ www.fernnursery.co.uk
**Contact:** R N Timm
**Opening Times:** 0900-1700 Fri, Sat & Sun Apr-Oct or by appt.
**Min Mail Order UK:** Nmc
**Min Mail Order EU:** Nmc
**Cat. Cost:** 2 × 1st class

| KEY | | |
|---|---|---|
| | ☒ Mail order to UK or EU | ⛺ Delivers to shows |
| | ✈ Exports beyond EU | € Euro accepted |
| | ♿ Accessible by wheelchair | ◆ See Display advertisement |

E

**Credit Cards:** None
**Specialities:** Ferns.
**Notes:** Only plants listed in the mail order part of the catalogue will be sent mail order. Also sells wholesale.
**Map Ref:** E, A1 **OS Grid Ref:** TF212942

**EFEx** **Flora Exotica** ⊠ ✈ €
Pasadena, South-Green, Fingringhoe, Colchester, Essex, CO5 7DR
Ⓣ (01206) 729414
**Contact:** J Beddoes
**Opening Times:** Not open. Mail order only.
**Min Mail Order UK:** Nmc
**Min Mail Order EU:** Nmc
**Cat. Cost:** 4 × 1st class
**Credit Cards:** None
**Specialities:** Exotica flora incl. orchids.

**EFul** **Fulbrooke Nursery** ⊠ €
Home Farm, Westley Waterless, Newmarket, Suffolk, CB8 0RG
Ⓣ (01638) 507124
Ⓕ (01638) 507124
Ⓔ bamboo@fulbrooke.co.uk
Ⓦ www.fulbrooke.co.uk
**Contact:** Paul Lazard
**Opening Times:** By appt. most times incl. w/ends.
**Min Mail Order UK:** £5.50 + p&p
**Min Mail Order EU:** £6.00 + p&p
**Cat. Cost:** 3 × 1st class
**Credit Cards:** None
**Specialities:** Bamboos & grasses.
**Map Ref:** E, C2

**EGFP** **Grange Farm Plants** ⊠ ♿
Grange Farm, 38 Fishergate Road, Sutton St James, Spalding, Lincolnshire, PE12 0EZ
Ⓣ (01945) 440240
Ⓜ 07742 138760
Ⓕ (01945) 440355
Ⓔ ellis.family@tinyonline.co.uk
**Contact:** M C Ellis
**Opening Times:** Mail order only. Open by appt. only.
**Min Mail Order UK:** Nmc
**Cat. Cost:** 1 × 1st class
**Credit Cards:** None
**Specialities:** Rare trees & shrubs, esp. *Juglans*, *Fraxinus*. Some species available in small quantities only.
**Map Ref:** E, B2 **OS Grid Ref:** TF382186

**EGHG** **Goltho House Gardens & Nursery** ♿
Lincoln Road, Goltho, Market Rasen, Lincolnshire, LN8 5NF
Ⓣ (01673) 857768
Ⓔ s.hollingworth@homecall.co.uk
Ⓦ www.golthogardens.com
**Contact:** Debbie Hollingworth
**Opening Times:** 1000-1600 Sun & Wed only.
**Credit Cards:** None
**Specialities:** Hardy herbaceous perennials.
**Map Ref:** E, A1 **OS Grid Ref:** TF116783

**EGle** **Glen Chantry** €
Ishams Chase, Wickham Bishops, Essex, CM8 3LG
Ⓣ (01621) 891342
Ⓕ (01621) 891342
Ⓦ www.glenchantry.demon.co.uk
**Contact:** Sue Staines & Wol Staines
**Opening Times:** 1000-1600 Fri & Sat from 6th Apr-1st Sep. Sae for details.
**Cat. Cost:** 5 × 1st class
**Credit Cards:** None
**Specialities:** A wide & increasing range of perennials, many unusual.
**Notes:** Wheelchair access with care.
**Map Ref:** E, D2 **OS Grid Ref:** TM834133

**EGln** **Glenhirst Cactus Nursery** ⊠
Station Road, Swineshead, Nr Boston, Lincolnshire, PE20 3NX
Ⓣ (01205) 820314
Ⓕ (01205) 820614
Ⓔ info@cacti4u.co.uk
Ⓦ www.cacti4u.co.uk
**Contact:** N C & S A Bell
**Opening Times:** Visitors welcome, but by telephone appt. only.
**Min Mail Order UK:** £5.00
**Min Mail Order EU:** €15.00
**Cat. Cost:** 2 × 1st class
**Credit Cards:** Maestro Visa MasterCard Switch
**Specialities:** Extensive range of cacti & succulent plants, incl. Christmas cacti & orchid cacti. Hardy & half-hardy desert plants. Display gardens.
**Notes:** Will accept payment in euros online only.
**Map Ref:** E, B1 **OS Grid Ref:** TF245408

**EGol** **Goldbrook Plants** ⊠ ✈
Hoxne, Eye, Suffolk, IP21 5AN
Ⓣ (01379) 668770
Ⓕ (01379) 668770
**Contact:** Sandra Bond
**Opening Times:** 1000-1700 or dusk if earlier, Thu-Sun Apr-Sep, Sat & Sun Oct-Mar or by appt. Closed during Jan & Hampton Court Flower Show.
**Min Mail Order UK:** £15.00 + p&p

**Min Mail Order EU:** £100.00 + p&p
**Cat. Cost:** 4 × 1st class
**Credit Cards:** None
**Specialities:** Very large range of *Hosta* (1100+), *Hemerocallis*.
**Map Ref:** E, C3

**EGoo** **Elisabeth Goodwin Nurseries** ⊠ ♦ ♿
Elm Tree Farm, 1 Beeches Road, West Row, Bury St Edmunds, Suffolk, IP28 8NP
Ⓣ (01638) 713050
Ⓕ 0870 7053256
Ⓔ mail@e-g-n.co.uk
Ⓦ www.e-g-n.co.uk
**Contact:** Elisabeth Goodwin
**Opening Times:** By appt.
**Min Mail Order UK:** Nmc
**Cat. Cost:** Online only.
**Credit Cards:** None
**Specialities:** Drought tolerant plants for both sun & shade esp. *Helianthemum*, *Sedum*, *Teucrium*, *Vinca*, grasses, *Aquilegia*, *Achillea*, *Agastache* & *Onosma*. Some plants grown in ltd. quantities.
**Notes:** Also sells wholesale.
**Map Ref:** E, C2

**EHea** **The Heather Society** ⊠ €
Denbeigh, All Saints Road, Creeting St. Mary, Ipswich, Suffolk, IP6 8PJ
Ⓣ (01449) 711220
Ⓕ (01449) 711220
Ⓔ heathers@zetnet.co.uk
Ⓦ www.heathersociety.org.uk
**Contact:** David & Anne Small
**Opening Times:** Not open.
**Min Mail Order UK:** Nmc members, £11.50 non-members.
**Min Mail Order EU:** Nmc members, £12.50 non-members.
**Cat. Cost:** 1 × 1st class
**Credit Cards:** Visa MasterCard
**Specialities:** Heathers.
**Notes:** Mail order for Heather Society members within the EU, Apr only. Annual membership: UK £10.00; EC £11.00.

**EHig** **High Kelling Nursery** ⊠ € ♿
Selbrigg Road, High Kelling, Holt, Norfolk, NR25 6RJ
Ⓣ (01263) 712629
Ⓕ (01263) 711314
Ⓔ enquiries@highkellingnursery.co.uk
**Contact:** John & Paula Pierrepont
**Opening Times:** 1000-1800 Tue-Sat, 1000-1600 Sun, closed Mon.
**Min Mail Order UK:** Nmc
**Cat. Cost:** None.
**Credit Cards:** All major credit/debit cards
**Specialities:** Some stock available in small quantities only.
**Notes:** Also sells wholesale.
**Map Ref:** E, B3 **OS Grid Ref:** TG1039

**EHoe** **Hoecroft Plants** ⊠ € ♿
Severals Grange, Holt Road, Wood Norton, Dereham, Norfolk, NR20 5BL
Ⓣ (01362) 684206
Ⓔ hoecroft@acedial.co.uk
Ⓦ www.hoecroft.co.uk
**Contact:** Jane Lister
**Opening Times:** 1000-1600 Thu-Sun 1st Apr-14th Oct or by appt.
**Min Mail Order UK:** Nmc
**Min Mail Order EU:** Nmc
**Cat. Cost:** 5 × 2nd class/£1coin
**Credit Cards:** None
**Specialities:** 270 varieties of variegated and 350 varieties of coloured-leaved plants in all species. 250 grasses. Free entry to display gardens.
**Notes:** Nursery 2 miles north of Guist on B1110.
**Map Ref:** E, B3 **OS Grid Ref:** TG008289

**EHon** **Honeysome Aquatic Nursery** ⊠
The Row, Sutton, Nr Ely, Cambridgeshire, CB6 2PB
Ⓣ (01353) 778889
Ⓕ (01353) 777291
**Contact:** Mrs L S Bond
**Opening Times:** At all times by appt. only.
**Min Mail Order UK:** Nmc
**Cat. Cost:** 2 × 1st class
**Credit Cards:** None
**Specialities:** Hardy aquatic, bog & marginal.
**Notes:** Also sells wholesale.
**Map Ref:** E, C2

**EHrv** **Harveys Garden Plants** ⊠ ✈ ♦ € ♿
Great Green, Thurston, Bury St Edmunds, Suffolk, IP31 3SJ
Ⓣ (01359) 233363
Ⓕ (01359) 233363 & answerphone
Ⓔ admin@harveysgardenplants.co.uk
Ⓦ www.harveysgardenplants.co.uk
**Contact:** Roger Harvey
**Opening Times:** 0930-1630 Tue-Sat, 9th Jan-22rd Dec.

KEY
⊠ Mail order to UK or EU | ♦ Delivers to shows
✈ Exports beyond EU | € Euro accepted
♿ Accessible by wheelchair | ◆ See Display advertisement

E

**E**

**Min Mail Order UK:** 6 plants + p&p
**Min Mail Order EU:** Please enquire
**Cat. Cost:** 8 × 2nd class
**Credit Cards:** All major credit/debit cards
**Specialities:** *Helleborus*, *Anemone*, *Epimedium*, *Euphorbia*, *Eryngium*, *Galanthus*, *Astrantia*, *Pulmonaria* & other herbaceous perennials. Woodland plants. Nat. Collections of *Helenium* & *Chrysanthemum*.
**Map Ref:** E, C2 **OS Grid Ref:** 660939

**EHul** **HULL FARM** ⊠ ♿
Spring Valley Lane, Ardleigh, Colchester, Essex, CO7 7SA
Ⓣ (01206) 230045
Ⓕ (01206) 230820
**Contact:** J Fryer & Sons
**Opening Times:** 1000-1600 Mon-Sat, excl. Xmas.
**Min Mail Order UK:** £40.00 + p&p
**Cat. Cost:** 5 × 2nd class
**Credit Cards:** MasterCard Visa
**Specialities:** Conifers, grasses.
**Notes:** Also sells wholesale.
**Map Ref:** E, C3 **OS Grid Ref:** GR043274

**EJRN** **JOHN RAY NURSERY** € ♿
36 Station Road, Braintree, Essex, CM7 3QJ
Ⓜ 07866 296531
Ⓕ (01376) 322484
Ⓔ johnraynursery@talktalk.net
**Opening Times:** 0900-1730 Sat, 1030-1630 Sun & B/Hol.
**Cat. Cost:** None issued.
**Credit Cards:** None
**Specialities:** *Pittosporum*.
**Notes:** Also sells wholesale.

**EJWh** **JILL WHITE** ⊠ ⌂ ♿
78 Hurst Green, Brightlingsea, Essex, CO7 0NJ
Ⓣ (01206) 303547
**Contact:** Jill White
**Opening Times:** By appt. only.
**Min Mail Order UK:** Nmc
**Min Mail Order EU:** Nmc
**Cat. Cost:** Sae
**Credit Cards:** None
**Specialities:** *Cyclamen* species esp. *Cyclamen parviflorum*. *Cyclamen elegans*. Also seed.
**Notes:** Also sells wholesale.
**Map Ref:** E, D3 **OS Grid Ref:** TM088171

**EKMF** **KATHLEEN MUNCASTER FUCHSIAS** ♿
18 Field Lane, Morton, Gainsborough, Lincolnshire, DN21 3BY
Ⓣ (01427) 612329
Ⓔ jim@smuncaster.freeserve.co.uk
Ⓦ www.kathleenmuncasterfuchsias.co.uk
**Contact:** Kathleen Muncaster
**Opening Times:** 1000-dusk Thu-Tue. After mid-Jun please phone to check.
**Cat. Cost:** 2 × 1st class
**Credit Cards:** None
**Specialities:** *Fuchsia*. Nat. Collection of Hardy *Fuchsia* (full status).
**Map Ref:** E, A1

**ELan** **LANGTHORNS PLANTERY** ⊠ ♿
High Cross Lane West, Little Canfield, Dunmow, Essex, CM6 1TD
Ⓣ (01371) 872611
Ⓕ 0871 661 4093
Ⓔ info@langthorns.com
Ⓦ www.langthorns.com
**Contact:** E Cannon
**Opening Times:** 1000-1700 or dusk (if earlier) 7 days excl. Xmas fortnight.
**Min Mail Order UK:** £10.00
**Cat. Cost:** £1.50
**Credit Cards:** Visa Access Switch MasterCard Delta
**Specialities:** Wide general range with many unusual plants.
**Notes:** Mail order anything under 5ft tall.
**Map Ref:** E, D2 **OS Grid Ref:** TL592204

**ELar** **LARKSPUR NURSERY** ⊠
Fourways, Dog Drove South, Holbeach Drove, Spalding, Lincolnshire, PE12 0SD
Ⓣ (01406) 330830
Ⓔ info@larkspur-nursery.co.uk
Ⓦ www.larkspur-nursery.co.uk
**Contact:** Ashley Ramsbottom
**Opening Times:** Mail order only. Open by prior arrangement only.
**Min Mail Order UK:** Nmc
**Cat. Cost:** 2 × 1st class.
**Credit Cards:** None
**Specialities:** Delphiniums. Some varieties in small quantities. Order early to avoid disappointment.
**Notes:** Plants despatched from end April in 7 or 8cm pots. See website for details.

**ELau** **LAUREL FARM HERBS** ⊠ ♿
Main Road, Kelsale, Saxmundham, Suffolk, IP13 2RG
Ⓣ (01728) 668223
Ⓔ chris@laurelfarmherbs.co.uk
Ⓦ www.laurelfarmherbs.co.uk
**Contact:** Chris Seagon
**Opening Times:** 1000-1700 Wed-Mon 1st Mar-31st Oct. 1000-1500 Wed-Fri, 15th Nov-28th Feb. All other times, please phone first.

**Min Mail Order UK:** 6 plants + p&p
**Min Mail Order EU:** 12 plants
**Cat. Cost:** Online only.
**Credit Cards:** Visa MasterCard Switch Delta
**Specialities:** Herbs esp. rosemary, thyme, mint & sage.
**Notes:** Mail orders accepted by email, phone or post.
**Map Ref:** E, C3

**ELon** LONG HOUSE PLANTS ♿
The Long House, Church Road, Noak Hill, Romford, Essex, RM4 1LD
Ⓣ (01708) 371719
Ⓕ (01708) 346649
Ⓔ jeanlonghouse@uwclub.net
**Contact:** Tim Carter
**Opening Times:** 1000-1700 Fri, Sat & B/hols, 1000-1600 Sun, Mar-Oct.
**Cat. Cost:** Not available.
**Credit Cards:** All major credit/debit cards
**Specialities:** Interesting range of choice shrubs, grasses & herbaceous perennials. Many unusual varieties.
**Map Ref:** E, D2 **OS Grid Ref:** TQ554194

**EMac** FIRECREST (TREES & SHRUBS NURSERY) ⊠ € ♿
Hall Road, Little Bealings, Woodbridge, Suffolk, IP13 6LU
Ⓣ (01473) 625937
Ⓕ (01473) 625937
Ⓔ mac@firecrest.org.uk
Ⓦ www.firecrest.org.uk
**Contact:** Mac McGregor
**Opening Times:** 0830-1630 Mon-Fri, 1230 Sat.
**Min Mail Order UK:** Nmc
**Cat. Cost:** 2 × 1st class (bare root only).
**Credit Cards:** None
**Specialities:** Trees & shrubs.
**Notes:** Also sells wholesale.

**EMal** MARSHALL'S MALMAISON ⊠ ✈ €
Hullwood Barn, Shelley, Ipswich, Suffolk, IP7 5RE
Ⓣ (01473) 822400
Ⓔ jim@malmaisons.plus.com
**Contact:** J M Marshall/Sarah Cook
**Opening Times:** By appt. only.
**Min Mail Order UK:** £24.00 incl. p&p
**Min Mail Order EU:** £35.00 incl. p&p
**Cat. Cost:** 1st class sae.
**Credit Cards:** None
**Specialities:** Nat. Collections of Malmaison Carnations & Cedric Morris Irises.
**Notes:** Also sells wholesale.
**Map Ref:** E,C3 **OS Grid Ref:** TM006394

**EMar** LESLEY MARSHALL ⊠ ♿
Islington Lodge Cottage, Tilney All Saints, King's Lynn, Norfolk, PE34 4SF
Ⓣ (01553) 765103
Ⓔ daylilies@tiscali.co.uk
**Contact:** Lesley Marshall
**Opening Times:** 0930-1800 Mon, Wed, Fri-Sun May-Sep.
**Min Mail Order UK:** Nmc
**Cat. Cost:** 3 × 1st class.
**Credit Cards:** None
**Specialities:** *Hemerocallis* only, new & old varieties.
**Notes:** Nursery on A47 east of Tilney All Saints.
**Map Ref:** E, B1

**EMcA** S M MCARD (SEEDS) ⊠
39 West Road, Pointon, Sleaford, Lincolnshire, NG34 0NA
Ⓣ (01529) 240765
Ⓕ (01529) 240765
Ⓔ seeds@smmcard.com
Ⓦ www.smmcard.com
**Contact:** Susan McArd
**Opening Times:** Not open. Mail order only.
**Min Mail Order UK:** Nmc
**Min Mail Order EU:** Nmc
**Cat. Cost:** 2 × 2nd class
**Credit Cards:** None
**Specialities:** Unusual & giant vegetables esp. tree (Egyptian) onion. Seeds & plants.
**Notes:** Also sells wholesale.

**EMFW** MICKFIELD WATERGARDEN CENTRE LTD ⊠ € ♿
Debenham Road, Mickfield, Stowmarket, Suffolk, IP14 5LP
Ⓣ (01449) 711336
Ⓕ (01449) 711018
Ⓔ mike@mickfield.co.uk
Ⓦ www.watergardenshop.co.uk
**Contact:** Mike Burch
**Opening Times:** 0930-1700 7 days.
**Min Mail Order UK:** Nmc
**Min Mail Order EU:** £25.00 + p&p
**Cat. Cost:** Free.
**Credit Cards:** All major credit/debit cards
**Specialities:** Hardy aquatics, *Nymphaea* & moisture lovers.
**Notes:** Also sells wholesale.
**Map Ref:** E, C3 **OS Grid Ref:** TM141616

KEY
⊠ Mail order to UK or EU — Delivers to shows
✈ Exports beyond EU — € Euro accepted
♿ Accessible by wheelchair — ◆ See Display advertisement

E

**EMic** **Mickfield Hostas** ⊠ ⌂ € ♿
The Poplars, Mickfield,
Stowmarket, Suffolk,
IP14 5LH
Ⓣ (01449) 711576
Ⓕ (01449) 711576
Ⓔ mickfieldhostas@btconnect.com
Ⓦ www.mickfieldhostas.co.uk
**Contact:** Mr & Mrs R L C Milton
**Opening Times:** For specified dates see catalogue or website.
**Min Mail Order UK:** Nmc
**Min Mail Order EU:** Nmc
**Cat. Cost:** 4 × 1st class
**Credit Cards:** Visa MasterCard
**Specialities:** *Hosta*, over 1000 varieties (some subject to availability) mostly from USA. New varieties become available during the season. Waiting list option for rarities.
**Map Ref:** E, C3

**EMil** **Mill Race Garden Centre** ⊠ ♿
New Road, Aldham,
Colchester, Essex,
CO6 3QT
Ⓣ (01206) 242521
Ⓕ (01206) 242073
Ⓔ admin@millracegardencentre.co.uk
Ⓦ www.millracegardencentre.co.uk
**Contact:** Steve Canham
**Opening Times:** 0900-1730 7 days.
**Min Mail Order UK:** Nmc
**Credit Cards:** All major credit/debit cards
**Specialities:** Around 4000 varieties of plants always in stock.
**Map Ref:** E, C2 **OS Grid Ref:** TL918268

**EMon** **Monksilver Nursery** ⊠ €
Oakington Road, Cottenham,
Cambridgeshire,
CB24 8TW
Ⓣ (01954) 251555
Ⓕ (01223) 309119
Ⓔ plants@monksilver.com
Ⓦ www.monksilver.com
**Contact:** Joe Sharman & Alan Leslie
**Opening Times:** 1000-1600 Fri & Sat 1st Mar-30th Jun, 23rd Sep & Fri & Sat Oct.
**Min Mail Order UK:** £15.00 + p&p
**Min Mail Order EU:** £30.00 + p&p
**Cat. Cost:** 8 × 1st class
**Credit Cards:** None
**Specialities:** Herbaceous plants, grasses, *Anthemis*, *Arum*, *Helianthus*, *Lamium*, *Nepeta*, *Monarda*, *Salvia*, *Vinca*, sedges & variegated plants. Many NCCPG 'Pink Sheet' plants. Ferns.
**Map Ref:** E, C2 **OS Grid Ref:** TQ437665

**EMui** **Ken Muir Ltd** ⊠
Honeypot Farm, Rectory Road, Weeley Heath, Essex, CO16 9BJ
Ⓣ 0870 7479111
Ⓕ (01255) 831534
Ⓔ info@kenmuir.co.uk
Ⓦ www.kenmuir.co.uk
**Contact:** Ming Yang, Claire Higgins
**Opening Times:** 1000-1600.
**Min Mail Order UK:** Nmc
**Cat. Cost:** Free
**Credit Cards:** Visa Access Switch
**Specialities:** Fruit.
**Notes:** Also sells wholesale.
**Map Ref:** E, D3

**ENBC** **Norfolk Bamboo Company** ⊠
Vine Cottage, The Drift, Ingoldisthorpe, King's Lynn, Norfolk, PE31 6NW
Ⓣ (01485) 543935
Ⓕ (01485) 543314
Ⓔ Lewdyer@hotmail.com
Ⓦ www.norfolkbamboo.co.uk
**Contact:** Lewis Dyer
**Opening Times:** 1000-1700 Fri, Apr-Sep, or by appt.
**Min Mail Order UK:** £12.00 + p&p
**Cat. Cost:** 1 × 1st class sae for price list
**Credit Cards:** None
**Specialities:** Bamboos.
**Map Ref:** E, B2 **OS Grid Ref:** TF683333

**ENor** **Norfolk Lavender** ⊠ ♿
Caley Mill, Heacham, King's Lynn, Norfolk, PE31 7JE
Ⓣ (01485) 570384
Ⓕ (01485) 571176
Ⓔ admin@norfolk-lavender.co.uk
Ⓦ www.norfolk-lavender.co.uk
**Contact:** Henry Head
**Opening Times:** 0930-1700 7 days, Apr-Oct. 0930-1600 7 days, Nov-Mar.
**Min Mail Order UK:** Nmc
**Cat. Cost:** Free
**Credit Cards:** All major credit/debit cards
**Specialities:** Nat. Collection of *Lavandula*.
**Map Ref:** E, B2 **OS Grid Ref:** TF685368

**EOHP** **Old Hall Plants** ⊠ €
1 The Old Hall, Barsham, Beccles, Suffolk, NR34 8HB
Ⓣ (01502) 717475
Ⓔ info@oldhallplants.co.uk
Ⓦ www.oldhallplants.co.uk
**Contact:** Janet Elliott
**Opening Times:** By appt. only. Please phone first.
**Min Mail Order UK:** Nmc

**Min Mail Order EU:** Nmc
**Cat. Cost:** 4 × 1st class
**Credit Cards:** None
**Specialities:** A variety of rare herbs, house plants, *Plectranthus* & *Streptocarpus*.
**Notes:** Partial wheelchair access.
**Map Ref:** E, C3 **OS Grid Ref:** TM395904

**EOrn** **ORNAMENTAL CONIFERS** ◆
22 Chapel Road, Terrington St Clement, King's Lynn, Norfolk, PE34 4ND
Ⓣ (01553) 828874
Ⓕ (01553) 828874
Ⓦ www.japanesegardenplants.co.uk/
**Contact:** Peter Rotchell
**Opening Times:** 0930-1700 Thu-Tue, closed Wed. Closed 20th Dec-2nd Feb.
**Credit Cards:** None
**Specialities:** Conifers.
**Map Ref:** E, B1

**EPau** **PAUGERS PLANTS** ♿
Bury Road, Depden, Bury St Edmunds, Suffolk, IP29 4BU
Ⓣ (01284) 850527
Ⓦ www.paugersplants.co.uk
**Contact:** Geraldine Arnold
**Opening Times:** 0900-1730 Wed-Sat, 1000-1700 Sun & B/hols, 1st Mar-30th Nov.
**Cat. Cost:** None issued
**Credit Cards:** None
**Specialities:** Hardy shrubs & perennials in large or small quantities.
**Notes:** Also sells wholesale.
**Map Ref:** E, C2 **OS Grid Ref:** TL783568

**EPfP** **THE PLACE FOR PLANTS** ⌂ € ♿
East Bergholt Place, East Bergholt, Suffolk, CO7 6UP
Ⓣ (01206) 299224
Ⓕ (01206) 299224
Ⓔ sales@placeforplants.co.uk
**Contact:** Rupert & Sara Eley
**Opening Times:** 1000-1700 (or dusk if earlier) 7 days. Closed Easter Sun. Garden open Mar-Oct.
**Cat. Cost:** 2 × 1st class
**Credit Cards:** All major credit/debit cards
**Specialities:** Wide range of specialist & popular plants. National Coll. of Deciduous *Euonymus*. 15 acre mature garden with free access to RHS members during season.
**Map Ref:** E, C3

**EPGN** **PARK GREEN NURSERIES** ⊠ ✈ ⌂
Wetheringsett, Stowmarket, Suffolk, IP14 5QH
Ⓣ (01728) 860139
Ⓕ (01728) 861277
Ⓔ nurseries@parkgreen.fsnet.co.uk
Ⓦ www.parkgreen.co.uk
**Contact:** Richard & Mary Ford
**Opening Times:** 1000-1600 Mon-Sat, 1 Mar-30 Sep.
**Min Mail Order UK:** Nmc
**Min Mail Order EU:** Nmc
**Cat. Cost:** 4 × 1st class
**Credit Cards:** Visa MasterCard Delta Switch
**Specialities:** *Hosta*, ornamental grasses & herbaceous.
**Notes:** Mail order *Hosta* only.
**Map Ref:** E, C3 **OS Grid Ref:** TM136644

**EPla** **P W PLANTS** ⊠ ⌂ ♿
Sunnyside, Heath Road, Kenninghall, Norfolk, NR16 2DS
Ⓣ (01953) 888212
Ⓔ pw@hardybamboo.com
Ⓦ www.hardybamboo.com
**Contact:** Paul Whittaker
**Opening Times:** Every Fri & last Sat in every month, plus all Sats Apr-Sep.
**Min Mail Order UK:** Nmc
**Min Mail Order EU:** Nmc
**Cat. Cost:** 5 × 1st class
**Credit Cards:** All major credit/debit cards
**Specialities:** Bamboos, grasses, choice shrubs & perennials.
**Notes:** Does not deliver to Chelsea Show.
**Map Ref:** E, C3 **OS Grid Ref:** TM036846

**EPot** **POTTERTONS NURSERY** ⊠ ✈ ⌂ € ♿
Moortown Road, Nettleton, Caistor, Lincolnshire, LN7 6HX
Ⓣ (01472) 851714
Ⓕ (01472) 852580
Ⓔ sales@pottertons.co.uk
Ⓦ www.pottertons.co.uk
**Contact:** Robert Potterton
**Opening Times:** 0900-1600 7 days.
**Min Mail Order UK:** Nmc
**Min Mail Order EU:** Nmc
**Cat. Cost:** £2.00 in stamps
**Credit Cards:** Maestro MasterCard Visa
**Specialities:** Alpines, dwarf bulbs & woodland plants. Hardy orchids & *Pleione*.
**Notes:** Talks & tours by arrangement.
**Map Ref:** E, A1 **OS Grid Ref:** TA091001

**EPPr** **THE PLANTSMAN'S PREFERENCE** ⊠ ⌂ ♿
(Office) Lynwood, Hopton Road, Garboldisham, Diss, Norfolk, IP22 2QN

| KEY | | |
|---|---|---|
| | ⊠ Mail order to UK or EU | ⌂ Delivers to shows |
| | ✈ Exports beyond EU | € Euro accepted |
| | ♿ Accessible by wheelchair | ◆ See Display advertisement |

E

Ⓣ (01953) 681439 (office)
Ⓜ (07799) 855559 (nursery)
Ⓔ tim@plantpref.co.uk
Ⓦ www.plantpref.co.uk
**Contact:** Jenny & Tim Fuller
**Opening Times:** 0930-1700 Fri, Sat & Sun Mar-Oct. Other times by appt.
**Min Mail Order UK:** £15.00
**Min Mail Order EU:** £30.00
**Cat. Cost:** 5 × 1st class/IRCs or online.
**Credit Cards:** All major credit/debit cards
**Specialities:** Hardy geraniums (450), grasses & sedges (600+). Unusual & interesting perennials. Nat. Collection of *Molinia*.
**Notes:** Nursery is at Hall Farm, Church Road, South Lopham, Diss.
**Map Ref:** E, C3 **OS Grid Ref:** TM041819

**EPts** **Potash Nursery** ⊠ ♿
Cow Green, Bacton, Stowmarket, Suffolk, IP14 4HJ
Ⓣ (01449) 781671
Ⓔ enquiries@potashnursery.co.uk
Ⓦ www.potashnursery.co.uk
**Contact:** M W Clare
**Opening Times:** Pre-ordered plants can be collected by appt. only.
**Min Mail Order UK:** £12.00
**Cat. Cost:** 4 × 1st class
**Credit Cards:** Visa Delta MasterCard
**Specialities:** *Fuchsia*.
**Map Ref:** E, C3 **OS Grid Ref:** TM0565NE

**EPyc** **Pennycross Plants** ⊠
Earith Road, Colne, Huntingdon, Cambridgeshire, PE28 3NL
Ⓣ (01487) 841520
Ⓔ plants4u@tiscali.co.uk
**Contact:** Janet M Buist
**Opening Times:** 1000-1600 Mon-Fri, 1st Mar-31st Oct by appt.
**Min Mail Order UK:** Nmc
**Cat. Cost:** 1 × 2nd class for *Salvia* list only.
**Credit Cards:** None
**Specialities:** Hardy perennials. Salvias. Some plants available in ltd. quantities only.
**Notes:** Mail order for small *Salvia* plants only.
**Map Ref:** E, C2 **OS Grid Ref:** TL378759

**EQua** **Quaymount Nursery** ⊠ ♿
The Row, Wereham, Kings Lynn, Norfolk, PE33 9AY
Ⓣ (01366) 500691
Ⓕ (01366) 500611
Ⓔ info@quaymountplants.co.uk
Ⓦ www.quaymountplants.co.uk
**Contact:** Paul Markwell
**Opening Times:** 0900-1700 (or dusk if earlier) Mon-Fri, 1000-1600 Sat & Sun. Closed Sun Dec & Jan.
**Min Mail Order UK:** Nmc
**Cat. Cost:** 2 × 1st class
**Credit Cards:** All major credit/debit cards
**Specialities:** Wide range of specialist & popular plants. *Hydrangea*.
**Notes:** Specimen plants collection only. Also sells wholesale.
**Map Ref:** E, B2 **OS Grid Ref:** TF679006

**ERas** **Rasell's Nurseries** ♿
Little Bytham, Grantham, Lincolnshire, NG33 4QY
Ⓣ (01780) 410345
Ⓕ (01780) 410475
Ⓔ rasells.nurseries@virgin.net
**Contact:** Carole Wilson
**Opening Times:** 0900-1700 Mon-Sat, 1000-1600 Sun.
**Cat. Cost:** None issued.
**Credit Cards:** All major credit/debit cards
**Map Ref:** E, B1 **OS Grid Ref:** TF016178

**ERCP** **Rose Cottage Plants** ⊠
Bay Tree Farm, Epping Green, Essex, CM16 6PU
Ⓣ (01992) 573775
Ⓕ (01992) 561198
Ⓔ anne@rosecottageplants.co.uk
Ⓦ www.rosecottageplants.co.uk
**Contact:** Anne & Jack Barnard
**Opening Times:** 1400-2000 (or dusk if earlier) Wed, Mar-Oct, or by appt. Closed 4th Apr 2007.
**Min Mail Order UK:** Nmc
**Min Mail Order EU:** £20.00
**Cat. Cost:** Online, or A5 sae for bulb list.
**Credit Cards:** All major credit/debit cards
**Specialities:** Bulbs.
**Notes:** Mail order bulbs only. Separate mail order catalogue available online from Mar-Dec.
**Map Ref:** E, B1 **OS Grid Ref:** TL435053

**ERhR** **Rhodes & Rockliffe** ⊠ ✈ €
2 Nursery Road, Nazeing, Essex, EN9 2JE
Ⓣ (01992) 451598 (office hours)
Ⓕ (01992) 440673
Ⓔ RRBegonias@aol.com
**Contact:** David Rhodes or John Rockliffe
**Opening Times:** By appt.
**Min Mail Order UK:** £2.50 + p&p
**Min Mail Order EU:** £5.00 + p&p
**Cat. Cost:** 2 × 1st class
**Credit Cards:** None

**Specialities:** *Begonia* species & hybrids. Nat. Collection of *Begonia*. Plants propagated to order.
**Notes:** Mail order Apr-Sep only.
**Map Ref:** E, D2

**ERod** **THE RODINGS PLANTERY** ⊠ ✈ ⌂ €
Anchor Lane, Abbess Roding, Essex, CM5 0JW
Ⓣ (01279) 876421
Ⓕ (01279) 876421
Ⓔ janeandandy@therodingsplantery.co.uk
**Contact:** Jane & Andy Mogridge
**Opening Times:** By appt. only. Occasional open days, please phone for details.
**Min Mail Order UK:** £15.00 + p&p
**Min Mail Order EU:** £500.00 + p&p
**Cat. Cost:** 3 × 1st class
**Credit Cards:** None
**Specialities:** *Bamboo*. Rare & unusual trees.
**Map Ref:** E, D2

**ERom** **THE ROMANTIC GARDEN** ⊠ ✈ € ♿ ◆
Swannington, Norwich, Norfolk, NR9 5NW
Ⓣ (01603) 261488
Ⓕ (01603) 864231
Ⓔ enquiries@romantic-garden-nursery.co.uk
Ⓦ www.romantic-garden-nursery.co.uk
**Contact:** John Powles/John Carrick
**Opening Times:** 1000-1700 Wed, Fri & Sat all year, plus B/Hol Mondays.
**Min Mail Order UK:** £5.00 + p&p
**Min Mail Order EU:** £30.00 + p&p
**Cat. Cost:** 4 × 1st class
**Credit Cards:** All major credit/debit cards
**Specialities:** Conservatory. *Buxus* topiary, ornamental standards, large specimens. Hedging. Topiary
**Notes:** Also sells wholesale.
**Map Ref:** E, B3

**ERos** **ROSEHOLME NURSERY** ⊠ ✈ ♿
Roseholme Farm, Howsham, Market Rasen, Lincolnshire, LN7 6JZ
Ⓣ (01652) 678661
Ⓕ (01472) 852450
Ⓔ Pbcenterpr@aol.com
**Contact:** P B Clayton
**Opening Times:** Mail order only. By appt. for collection of orders.
**Min Mail Order UK:** Nmc
**Min Mail Order EU:** Nmc
**Cat. Cost:** 2 × 2nd class
**Credit Cards:** None
**Specialities:** Underground lines – bulbs, corms, rhizomes & tubers (esp. *Crocus*, *Iris*).
**Notes:** Also sells wholesale.
**Map Ref:** E, A1 **OS Grid Ref:** TA042048

**ESCh** **SHEILA CHAPMAN CLEMATIS** ⊠ ⌂ ♿
c/o Coveney Nurseries Ltd, 160 Ongar Road, Abridge, Romford, Essex, RM4 1AA
Ⓣ (01708) 688090
Ⓕ (01708) 688090
Ⓔ sheilachapman@hotmail.co.uk
Ⓦ www.sheilachapman.com
**Contact:** Sheila Chapman
**Opening Times:** 0930-1700 (or dusk in winter) all year excl. Xmas week.
**Min Mail Order UK:** Nmc
**Cat. Cost:** 4 × 1st class
**Credit Cards:** All major credit/debit cards
**Specialities:** Over 700 varieties of *Clematis*.
**Map Ref:** E, D2 **OS Grid Ref:** TQ483969

**ESgI** **SEAGATE IRISES** ⊠ ✈ € ♿
A17 Long Sutton By-Pass, Long Sutton, Lincolnshire, PE12 9RX
Ⓣ (01406) 365138
Ⓕ (01406) 365447
Ⓔ Sales@irises.co.uk
Ⓦ www.irises.co.uk
**Contact:** Julian Browse or Wendy Browse
**Opening Times:** 1000-1700 daily Apr-Sep. Please phone for appt. Oct-Mar.
**Min Mail Order UK:** Nmc
**Min Mail Order EU:** Nmc. Carriage at cost.
**Cat. Cost:** £3.00 or €8.00
**Credit Cards:** Maestro Visa MasterCard
**Specialities:** Different types of *Iris*, bearded, beardless & species hybrids with about 1000 varieties in all, both historic & modern. Some only available in small quantities. Many container-grown available to callers.
**Notes:** Also sells wholesale.
**Map Ref:** E, B1 **OS Grid Ref:** TF437218

**EShb** **SHRUBLAND PARK NURSERIES** ⊠ ⌂ €
Coddenham, Ipswich, Suffolk, IP6 9QJ
Ⓣ (01473) 833187
Ⓜ 07890 527744
Ⓕ (01473) 832838
Ⓔ gill@shrublandparknurseries.co.uk
Ⓦ www.shrublandparknurseries.co.uk
**Contact:** Gill Stitt
**Opening Times:** 1000-1700 Wed-Sun, Easter-30th Sep. Oct-Feb, please ring first.
**Min Mail Order UK:** £15.00
**Min Mail Order EU:** £25.00
**Cat. Cost:** 5 × 1st class, free by email
**Credit Cards:** All major credit/debit cards, Nochex, Paypal.

KEY
⊠ Mail order to UK or EU ⌂ Delivers to shows
✈ Exports beyond EU € Euro accepted
♿ Accessible by wheelchair ◆ See Display advertisement

**Specialities:** Hardy perennials. Tender perennials, climbers, ferns, conservatory plants, houseplants & succulents. Display beds in glasshouse & walled garden.
**Notes:** For directions phone, email or see website. Partial wheelchair access. Groups welcome.
**Map Ref:** E, C3 **OS Grid Ref:** TM128524

**EStC** **ST CLARE NURSERY** ⊠
Chapel Drove, Holbeach Drove, Lincolnshire,
PE12 0PT
Ⓣ (01406) 330233
Ⓔ stclarenursery@aol.com
**Contact:** Carlos Zeferino
**Opening Times:** Not open. Mail order only.
**Min Mail Order UK:** Nmc
**Cat. Cost:** £1.00
**Credit Cards:** All major credit/debit cards
**Specialities:** Small family-run nursery providing good quality plants.

**ESty** **STYLE ROSES** ⊠ € 
10 Meridian Walk, Holbeach, Spalding, Lincolnshire, PE12 7NR
Ⓣ (01406) 424089
Ⓜ 07932 044093 or 07780 860415
Ⓕ (01406) 424089
Ⓔ styleroses@aol.com
Ⓦ www.styleroses.co.uk
**Contact:** Chris Styles, Margaret Styles
**Opening Times:** Vary, please phone.
**Min Mail Order UK:** Nmc
**Min Mail Order EU:** Nmc
**Cat. Cost:** Free
**Credit Cards:** All major credit/debit cards
**Specialities:** Standard & bush roses.
**Notes:** Export subject to countries' plant health requirements, carriage & export certificates where required charged at cost. Also sells wholesale.
**Map Ref:** E, B1

**ESul** **BRIAN & PEARL SULMAN** ⊠
54 Kingsway, Mildenhall, Bury St Edmunds, Suffolk, IP28 7HR
Ⓣ (01638) 712297
Ⓕ (01638) 712297
Ⓔ pearl@sulmanspelargoniums.co.uk
Ⓦ www.sulmanspelargoniums.co.uk
**Contact:** Pearl Sulman
**Opening Times:** Mail order only. Not open except for Open Days 5th/6th May & 2nd/3rd Jun 2007. Phone for information about 2008 dates.
**Min Mail Order UK:** £23.00
**Cat. Cost:** 4 × 1st class
**Credit Cards:** Visa MasterCard
**Specialities:** *Pelargonium*. Some varieties only available in small quantities.
**Map Ref:** E, C2 **OS Grid Ref:** TL715747

**ESwi** **SWINES MEADOW GARDEN CENTRE**
€ ◆
47 Towngate East, Market Deeping, Peterborough, PE6 8LQ
Ⓣ 01778 343340
Ⓔ info@swinesmeadowgardencentre.co.uk
Ⓦ www.swinesmeadowgardencentre.co.uk
**Contact:** Colin Ward
**Specialities:** Hardy exotics, tree ferns, bamboos & phormiums.
**Map Ref:** E, B1 **OS Grid Ref:** TF150113

**ETho** **THORNCROFT CLEMATIS NURSERY** ⊠
The Lings, Reymerston, Norwich, Norfolk,
NR9 4QG
Ⓣ (01953) 850407
Ⓕ (01953) 851788
Ⓔ sales@thorncroft.co.uk
Ⓦ www.thorncroft.co.uk
**Contact:** Ruth P Gooch
**Opening Times:** 1000-1600 Tue-Sat all year, closed Sun & Mon. Open B/hol Mon.
**Min Mail Order UK:** Nmc
**Min Mail Order EU:** Nmc
**Cat. Cost:** 6 × 2nd class
**Credit Cards:** Maestro MasterCard Solo Visa Delta
**Specialities:** *Clematis*.
**Notes:** Does not export to USA, Canada or Australia.
**Map Ref:** E, B3 **OS Grid Ref:** TG039062

**ETod** **TODD'S BOTANICS** ⊠
West Street, Coggeshall, Colchester, Essex,
CO6 1NT
Ⓣ (01376) 561212
Ⓜ 07970 643711
Ⓕ (01376) 561212
Ⓔ info@toddsbotanics.co.uk
Ⓦ www.toddsbotanics.co.uk
**Contact:** Emma Macdonald
**Opening Times:** 0900-1700 Tue-Sun.
**Min Mail Order UK:** £20.00
**Cat. Cost:** 2 × 1st class
**Credit Cards:** All major credit/debit cards
**Specialities:** Hardy exotics, herbaceous. Bamboos, olives, palms, ferns, grasses, *Canna* & *Hedychium*.
**Notes:** Also sells wholesale.
**Map Ref:** E, D2 **OS Grid Ref:** TL843224

**EUJe** **Urban Jungle** ⊠
The Nurseries, Ringland Lane, Old Costessey, Norwich, Norfolk, NR8 5BG
Ⓣ (01603) 744997
Ⓕ (0709) 2366869
Ⓔ lizzy@urbanjungle.uk.com
Ⓦ www.urbanjungle.uk.com
**Contact:** Liz Browne
**Opening Times:** 1000-1700 Tue-Sun, closed Mon, Mar-Oct, 1000-1600 Fri-Sun, Nov-Feb. Open B/Hols except Xmas Day & Boxing Day.
**Min Mail Order UK:** £20.00
**Min Mail Order EU:** £20.00
**Cat. Cost:** 2 × 1st class
**Credit Cards:** All major credit/debit cards
**Specialities:** Exotic plants, gingers, bananas and aroids.

**EWes** **West Acre Gardens** ⛫ ♿
West Acre, King's Lynn, Norfolk, PE32 1UJ
Ⓣ (01760) 755562
**Contact:** J J Tuite
**Opening Times:** 1000-1700 7 days 1st Feb-30th Nov. Other times by appt.
**Cat. Cost:** None issued.
**Credit Cards:** Visa MasterCard Delta Switch
**Specialities:** Very wide selection of herbaceous & other garden plants incl. *Rhodohypoxis* & *Primula auricula*.
**Map Ref:** E, B1 **OS Grid Ref:** TF792182

**EWld** **Woodlands**
Peppin Lane, Fotherby, Louth, Lincolnshire, LN11 0UW
Ⓣ (01507) 603586
Ⓜ 07866 161864
Ⓔ annbobarmstrong@uwclub.net
**Contact:** Ann Armstrong
**Opening Times:** Flexible, but please phone or email to avoid disappointment.
**Cat. Cost:** None issued.
**Credit Cards:** None
**Specialities:** Small but interesting range of unusual plants, especially woodland and *Salvia*, all grown on the nursery in limited quantity.
**Notes:** Mature garden, art gallery & refreshments.
**Map Ref:** E, A2 **OS Grid Ref:** TF322918

**EWll** **The Walled Garden** ♿ ◆
Park Road, Benhall, Saxmundham, Suffolk, IP17 1JB
Ⓣ (01728) 602510
Ⓕ (01728) 602510
Ⓔ jim@thewalledgarden.co.uk
Ⓦ www.thewalledgarden.co.uk
**Contact:** Jim Mountain
**Opening Times:** 0930-1700 Tue-Sun Mar-Oct, Tue-Sat Nov-Feb.
**Cat. Cost:** 2 × 1st class
**Credit Cards:** All major credit/debit cards
**Specialities:** Tender & hardy perennials, over 1000 varieties, & wall shrubs.
**Map Ref:** E, C3 **OS Grid Ref:** TM371613

**EWsh** **Westshores Nurseries** ⊠
82 West Street, Winterton, Lincolnshire, DN15 9QF
Ⓣ (01724) 733940
Ⓔ westshnur@aol.com
Ⓦ www.westshores.co.uk
**Contact:** Gail & John Summerfield
**Opening Times:** 0930-1800 (or dusk) w/ends & B/hols, 1st Mar-31st Oct. Other times by appt.
**Min Mail Order UK:** £15.00
**Credit Cards:** All major credit/debit cards
**Specialities:** Ornamental grasses & herbaceous perennials.
**Map Ref:** E, A1 **OS Grid Ref:** SE927187

**EWTr** **Walnut Tree Garden Nursery** ⊠ €
Flymoor Lane, Rocklands, Attleborough, Norfolk, NR17 1BP
Ⓣ (01953) 488163
Ⓔ info@wtgn.co.uk
Ⓦ www.wtgn.co.uk
**Contact:** Jim Paine & Clare Billington
**Opening Times:** 0900-1800 Tue-Sun Feb-Nov & B/hols.
**Min Mail Order UK:** Nmc
**Cat. Cost:** 4 × 1st class
**Credit Cards:** All major credit/debit cards
**Map Ref:** E, B1 **OS Grid Ref:** TL978973

## Scotland

**GAbr** **Abriachan Nurseries** ⊠ ⛫ ♿
Loch Ness Side, Inverness, Inverness-shire, IV3 8LA
Ⓣ (01463) 861232
Ⓕ (01463) 861232
Ⓔ info@lochnessgarden.com
Ⓦ www.lochnessgarden.com
**Contact:** Mr & Mrs D Davidson
**Opening Times:** 0900-1900 daily (dusk if earlier) Feb-Nov.
**Min Mail Order UK:** Nmc
**Min Mail Order EU:** Nmc

KEY
⊠ Mail order to UK or EU ⛫ Delivers to shows
✈ Exports beyond EU € Euro accepted
♿ Accessible by wheelchair ◆ See Display advertisement

G

**Cat. Cost:** 4 × 1st class
**Credit Cards:** None
**Specialities:** Herbaceous, *Primula*, *Helianthemum*, hardy geraniums, *Sempervivum* & *Primula auricula*.
**Notes:** Wheelchair access to nursery only.
**Map Ref:** G, B2 **OS Grid Ref:** NH571347

G

**GAuc** **AUCHGOURISH GARDENS** ⊠
Street of Kincardine, by Boat of Garten, Inverness-shire, PH24 3BY
Ⓣ (01479) 831464
Ⓜ 07746 122775 or 07737 914292
Ⓕ (01479) 831672
Ⓔ auchgourishgardens@falsyde.sol.co.uk
Ⓦ www.thebotanicalnursery.com
**Contact:** Iain Brodie of Falsyde
**Opening Times:** 1000-1700 Mon-Fri, closed Sat, 1100-1700 Sun, 1st Apr-31st Oct.
**Min Mail Order UK:** £25.00
**Min Mail Order EU:** £40.00 + p&p at cost
**Cat. Cost:** Online only.
**Credit Cards:** Only accepted online not at Garden.
**Specialities:** Botanical species. *Betulaceae*, *Rosaceae*, *Ericaceae*, *Iridaceae*, *Liliaceae* & *Primulaceae*. Nursery is at Auchgourish Garden which is open Apr-Sep.
**Notes:** Mail order despatch Sep-Apr incl. subject to weather. No despatch May-Aug but plants can be uplifted any time by prior arrangement.
**Map Ref:** G, B2

**GBar** **BARWINNOCK HERBS** ⊠ €
Barrhill, by Girvan, Ayrshire, KA26 0RB
Ⓣ (01465) 821338
Ⓔ herbs@barwinnock.com
Ⓦ www.barwinnock.com
**Contact:** Dave & Mon Holtom
**Opening Times:** 1000-1700 Easter to end Sep. Closed Wed.
**Min Mail Order UK:** Nmc
**Min Mail Order EU:** Nmc
**Cat. Cost:** UK free, EU 2 × IRC.
**Credit Cards:** All major credit/debit cards
**Specialities:** Culinary, medicinal, fragrant-leaved plants & wildflowers organically grown.
**Map Ref:** G, D2 **OS Grid Ref:** NX309772

**GBBs** **BORDER BELLES** ⊠ ♠ ♿ ◆
Old Branxton Cottages, Innerwick, Nr Dunbar, East Lothian, EH42 1QT
Ⓣ (01368) 840325
Ⓕ (01368) 840325
Ⓔ mail@borderbelles.com
Ⓦ www.borderbelles.com
**Contact:** Gillian Moynihan
**Opening Times:** Please phone before visiting.
**Min Mail Order UK:** Nmc
**Min Mail Order EU:** On request
**Cat. Cost:** 3 × 1st class
**Credit Cards:** None
**Specialities:** *Anemone*, *Allium*, *Campanula*, *Diplarrhena*, hardy geraniums, *Hosta*, *Trillium*, *Tricyrtis*, woodland plants incl. *Actaea*, *Mertensia* & *Mitchella*.
**Notes:** Mail order Oct-Mar only. Also sells wholesale.

**GBin** **BINNY PLANTS** ⊠ ♠ € ♿
West Lodge, Binny Estate, Ecclesmachen Road, Nr Broxbourn, West Lothian, EH52 6NL
Ⓣ (01506) 858931
Ⓕ (01506) 858155
Ⓔ binnyplants@aol.com
Ⓦ www.binnyplants.co.uk
**Contact:** Billy Carruthers
**Opening Times:** 1000-1700 7 days. Closed mid-Dec to mid-Jan.
**Min Mail Order UK:** £25.00
**Min Mail Order EU:** £25.00
**Cat. Cost:** £2.50 refundable on ordering.
**Credit Cards:** Visa MasterCard Switch EuroCard
**Specialities:** Perennials incl. *Astilbe*, *Geranium*, *Hosta*, *Paeonia* & *Iris*. Plus large selection of grasses & ferns.
**Notes:** Mail order Sep-Apr only. Also sells wholesale.
**Map Ref:** G, C3

**GBri** **BRIDGE END NURSERIES** ♠ ♿
Gretna Green, Dumfriesshire, DG16 5HN
Ⓣ (01461) 800612
Ⓕ (01461) 800612
Ⓔ robinbird1@btconnect.com
Ⓦ www.bridgendnurseries.co.uk
**Contact:** R Bird
**Opening Times:** 0930-1700 all year. Evenings by appt.
**Cat. Cost:** None issued
**Credit Cards:** All major credit/debit cards
**Specialities:** Hardy cottage garden perennials. Many unusual & interesting varieties.

**GBuc** **BUCKLAND PLANTS** ⊠ € ♿
Whinnieliggate, Kirkcudbright, Kirkcudbrightshire, DG6 4XP
Ⓣ (01557) 331323
Ⓕ (01557) 331323
Ⓦ www.bucklandplants.co.uk
**Contact:** Rob or Dina Asbridge
**Opening Times:** 1000-1700 Thu-Sun 1st Mar-1st Nov & B/hols.

**Min Mail Order UK:** £20.00 + p&p
**Min Mail Order EU:** £50.00 + p&p
**Cat. Cost:** 3 × 1st class
**Credit Cards:** All major credit/debit cards
**Specialities:** A very wide range of scarce herbaceous & woodland plants incl. *Anemone*, *Cardamine*, *Crocosmia*, *Erythronium*, *Helleborus*, *Lilium*, *Meconopsis*, *Primula*, *Tricyrtis* & *Trillium*.
**Map Ref:** G, D2 **OS Grid Ref:** NX719524

GCai **Cairnsmore Nursery** ⊠ ⌂ ♿
Chapmanton Road, Castle Douglas, Kirkcudbrightshire, DG7 2NU
Ⓣ (01556) 504819
Ⓜ 07980 176458
Ⓔ cairnsmorenursery@hotmail.com
Ⓦ www.cairnsmorenursery.co.uk
**Contact:** Valerie Smith
**Opening Times:** 1000-1700, Tue-Sat, Mar-Oct.
**Min Mail Order UK:** Nmc
**Cat. Cost:** 4 × 1st class
**Credit Cards:** Visa MasterCard
**Specialities:** Primulas for the garden and cold greenhouse, incl. auriculas. Heucheras and *Tiarella*s.
**Map Ref:** G, D2 **OS Grid Ref:** NX756637

GCal **Cally Gardens** ⊠ ♿
Gatehouse of Fleet, Castle Douglas, Kirkcudbrightshire, DG7 2DJ
Ⓣ (01557) 815029 recorded information only.
Ⓔ cally.gardens@virgin.net
Ⓦ www.callygardens.co.uk
**Contact:** Michael Wickenden
**Opening Times:** 1000-1730 Sat-Sun, 1400-1730 Tue-Fri. Easter Sat-last Sun in Sept.
**Min Mail Order UK:** £15.00 + p&p
**Cat. Cost:** 3 × 1st class
**Credit Cards:** None
**Specialities:** Unusual perennials. *Agapanthus*, *Crocosmia*, *Eryngium*, hardy *Geranium* & grasses. Some rare shrubs, climbers & conservatory plants. 3500 varieties growing in an C18th walled garden.
**Notes:** Also sells wholesale
**Map Ref:** G, D2

GCoc **James Cocker & Sons** ⊠ ♿
Whitemyres, Lang Stracht, Aberdeen, Aberdeenshire, AB15 6XH
Ⓣ (01224) 313261
Ⓕ (01224) 312531
Ⓔ sales@roses.uk.com
Ⓦ www.roses.uk.com
**Contact:** Alec Cocker
**Opening Times:** 0900-1730 7 days.
**Min Mail Order UK:** Nmc
**Min Mail Order EU:** £5.40 + p&p
**Cat. Cost:** Free
**Credit Cards:** Visa MasterCard Delta Maestro
**Specialities:** Roses.
**Notes:** Also sells wholesale.
**Map Ref:** G, B3

GCra **Craigieburn Garden** ⌂ ♿
Craigieburn House, by Moffat, Dumfriesshire, DG10 9LF
Ⓣ (01683) 221250
Ⓕ (01683) 221250
**Contact:** Janet & Andrew Wheatcroft
**Opening Times:** 1030-1800 Fri, Sat, Sun, Easter-17 Oct 2004. Plus all English & Scottish public holidays. Other times by appt.
**Cat. Cost:** £1.00
**Credit Cards:** None
**Specialities:** *Meconopsis* plants for damp gardens, herbaceous perennials.
**Map Ref:** G, D3

GEdr **Edrom Nurseries** ⊠ ⌂ ♿
Coldingham, Eyemouth, Berwickshire, TD14 5TZ
Ⓣ (01890) 771386
Ⓕ (01890) 71387
Ⓔ info@edromnurseries.co.uk
Ⓦ www.edromnurseries.co.uk
**Contact:** Mr Terry Hunt
**Opening Times:** 0900-1700 Mon-Sun, 1 Mar-30 Sep. Other times by appt.
**Min Mail Order UK:** Nmc
**Min Mail Order EU:** £20.00
**Cat. Cost:** 3 × 2nd class. More plants listed online than in printed catalogue.
**Credit Cards:** All major credit/debit cards
**Specialities:** *Trillium*, *Arisaema*, *Primula*, *Gentiana*, *Meconopsis*, *Anemone* & other alpines. *Fritillaria*, hardy orchids.
**Map Ref:** G, C3 **OS Grid Ref:** NT873663

GFai **Fairholm Plants** ⊠
Fairholm, Larkhall, Lanarkshire, ML9 2UQ
Ⓣ (01698) 881671
Ⓕ (01698) 888135
Ⓔ fairholm.plants@stevenson-hamilton.co.uk
**Contact:** Mrs J M Hamilton
**Opening Times:** Apr-Oct by appt.
**Min Mail Order UK:** Nmc
**Cat. Cost:** 1 × 2nd class for descriptive list.

KEY
⊠ Mail order to UK or EU ⌂ Delivers to shows
✈ Exports beyond EU € Euro accepted
♿ Accessible by wheelchair ◆ See Display advertisement

**Credit Cards:** None
**Specialities:** *Abutilon* & unusual half-hardy perennials esp. South African. Nat. Collection of *Abutilon* cvs.
**Notes:** Mail order for young/small plants.
**Map Ref:** G, C2 **OS Grid Ref:** NS754515

G

**GFor** **Fordmouth Croft Ornamental Grass Nursery** ⊠ ♿
Fordmouth Croft, Meikle Wartle,
Inverurie, Aberdeenshire,
AB51 5BE
Ⓣ (01467) 671519
Ⓔ Ann-Marie@fmcornamentalgrasses.co.uk
Ⓦ www.fmcornamentalgrasses.co.uk
**Contact:** Robert & Ann-Marie Grant
**Opening Times:** Mail order only. Open strictly by appt. only.
**Min Mail Order UK:** Nmc
**Cat. Cost:** 2 × 1st class
**Credit Cards:** None
**Specialities:** Grasses, sedges, rushes. Small orders available.
**Notes:** Also sells wholesale.
**Map Ref:** G, B3 **OS Grid Ref:** NJ718302

**GGal** **Galloway Plant Company** ⊠ ♿
Claymoddie, Whithorn,
Newton Stewart, Dumfries & Galloway,
DG8 8LX
Ⓣ (01988) 500422
Ⓕ (01988) 500422
Ⓔ NICM567@aol.com
**Contact:** Robin & Mary Nicholson
**Opening Times:** By appt. only.
**Min Mail Order UK:** Nmc
**Cat. Cost:** 2 × 1st class.
**Credit Cards:** None
**Specialities:** Southern hemisphere *Hydrangea*. Available in small quantities only.
**Map Ref:** G, D2 **OS Grid Ref:** NX450377

**GGar** **Garden Cottage Nursery** ⊠ ♿
Tournaig, Poolewe, Achnasheen, Ross-shire,
IV22 2LH
Ⓣ (01445) 781777
Ⓔ sales@gcnursery.co.uk
Ⓦ www.gcnursery.co.uk
**Contact:** Ben Rushbrooke
**Opening Times:** 1030-1800 Mon-Sat mid Mar-mid Oct or by appt.
**Min Mail Order UK:** Nmc
**Cat. Cost:** 4 × 2nd class
**Credit Cards:** Visa Switch MasterCard
**Specialities:** A wide range of plants esp. those from the southern hemisphere, Asiatic primulas & plants for coastal gardens.
**Map Ref:** G, A2 **OS Grid Ref:** NG878835

**GGGa** **Glendoick Gardens Ltd** ⊠ ✈
Glencarse, Perth, Perthshire,
PH2 7NS
Ⓣ (01738) 860205
Ⓕ (01738) 860630
Ⓔ sales@glendoick.com
Ⓦ www.glendoick.com
**Contact:** P A, E P & K N E Cox
**Opening Times:** 1000-1600 Mon-Fri only, mid-Apr to mid-Jun, otherwise by appt. 1400-1700 1st & 3rd Sun in May. Garden centre open 7 days.
**Min Mail Order UK:** £40.00 + p&p
**Min Mail Order EU:** £100.00 + p&p
**Cat. Cost:** £2.00 or £1.50 stamps
**Credit Cards:** Visa MasterCard Delta Switch JCB
**Specialities:** Rhododendrons, azaleas and ericaceous, *Primula* & *Meconopsis*. Plants from wild seed. Many catalogue plants available at garden centre. 3 National Collections.
**Notes:** Wheelchair access to Garden Centre. Also sells wholesale.
**Map Ref:** G, C3

**GJos** **Jo's Garden Enterprise** ♿
Easter Balmungle Farm, Eathie Road, by Rosemarkie, Ross-shire, IV10 8SL
Ⓣ (01381) 621006
Ⓔ anne.chance@ukonline.co.uk
**Contact:** Joanna Chance
**Opening Times:** 1000 to dusk, 7 days.
**Cat. Cost:** None
**Credit Cards:** None
**Specialities:** Alpines & herbaceous perennials.
**Map Ref:** G, B2 **OS Grid Ref:** NH600742

**GKev** **Kevock Garden Plants & Flowers** ⊠ ✈ ⌂ €
16 Kevock Road, Lasswade, Midlothian,
EH18 1HT
Ⓣ 0131 454 0660
Ⓜ 07811 321585
Ⓕ 0131 454 0660
Ⓔ info@kevockgarden.co.uk
Ⓦ www.kevockgarden.co.uk
**Contact:** Stella Rankin
**Opening Times:** Not open. Mail order only.
**Min Mail Order UK:** £20.00
**Min Mail Order EU:** £20.00
**Cat. Cost:** 4 × 1st class
**Credit Cards:** Visa MasterCard Switch
**Specialities:** Chinese & Himalayan plants. *Androsace*, *Primula*, *Meconopsis*, *Iris*, woodland plants.
**Notes:** Also sells wholesale.

G

**GKir** **KIRKDALE NURSERY** ⊠ € ♿
Daviot, Nr Inverurie, Aberdeenshire, AB51 0JL
Ⓣ (01467) 671264
Ⓕ (01467) 671282
Ⓔ kirkdalenursery@btconnect.com
Ⓦ www.kirkdalenursery.co.uk
**Contact:** Geoff or Alistair
**Opening Times:** 1000-1700 7 days (summer), 1000-1600 7 days (winter).
**Min Mail Order UK:** £30.00 + p&p
**Min Mail Order EU:** £50.00 + p&p
**Cat. Cost:** None issued
**Credit Cards:** Visa Access Switch
**Specialities:** Trees, herbaceous, conifers. Some plants available in small quantities only.
**Notes:** Mail order strictly mid-Oct to mid-Mar, carriage at cost.
**Map Ref:** G, B3

**GLld** **LOCHLANDS (HRB LTD)** ⊠ ♿
Dundee Road, Forfar, Angus, DD8 1XF
Ⓣ (01307) 463621
Ⓕ (01307) 469665
Ⓔ vandelft@btinternet.com
Ⓦ lochlands@btinternet.com
**Contact:** John van Delft
**Opening Times:** 0830-1730 Mon-Sat, 1030-1630 Sun.
**Min Mail Order UK:** £25.00
**Cat. Cost:** Free.
**Credit Cards:** All major credit/debit cards
**Specialities:** Camellias.
**Notes:** Also sells wholesale.
**Map Ref:** G, C3 **OS Grid Ref:** NO444478

**GMac** **ELIZABETH MACGREGOR** ⊠ ♿
Ellenbank, Tongland Road, Kirkcudbright, Dumfries & Galloway, DG6 4UU
Ⓣ (01557) 330620
Ⓕ (01557) 330620
Ⓔ elizabeth.violas@btinternet.com
**Contact:** Elizabeth MacGregor
**Opening Times:** 1000-1700 Mon, Fri & Sat May-Sep, or please phone.
**Min Mail Order UK:** 6 plants £16.80 + p&p
**Min Mail Order EU:** £50.00 + p&p
**Cat. Cost:** 4 × 1st class or 5 × 2nd class
**Credit Cards:** All major credit/debit cards
**Specialities:** Violets, violas & violettas, old and new varieties. *Campanula*, *Geranium*, *Eryngium*, *Penstemon*, *Aster*, *Primula*, *Iris* & other unusual herbaceous.
**Map Ref:** G, D2 **OS Grid Ref:** NX692525

**GMaP** **MACPLANTS** ⌂
Berrybank Nursery, 5 Boggs Holdings, Pencaitland, East Lothian, EH34 5BA
Ⓣ (01875) 341179
Ⓕ (01875) 340842
Ⓔ sales@macplants.co.uk
Ⓦ www.macplants.co.uk
**Contact:** Claire McNaughton
**Opening Times:** 1030-1700, 7 days, Mar-end Sep.
**Cat. Cost:** 4 × 2nd class
**Credit Cards:** MasterCard Switch Visa
**Specialities:** Herbaceous perennials, alpines, hardy ferns, violas & grasses.
**Notes:** Nursery partially accessible to wheelchairs. Also sells wholesale.
**Map Ref:** G, C3 **OS Grid Ref:** NT447703

**GPoy** **POYNTZFIELD HERB NURSERY** ⊠ ✈ ♿
Nr Balblair, Black Isle,
Dingwall, Ross-shire,
IV7 8LX
Ⓣ (01381) 610352
Ⓕ (01381) 610352
Ⓔ info@poyntzfieldherbs.co.uk
Ⓦ www.poyntzfieldherbs.co.uk
**Contact:** Duncan Ross
**Opening Times:** 1300-1700 Mon-Sat 1st Mar-30th Sep, 1300-1700 Sun May-Aug.
**Min Mail Order UK:** £10.00 + p&p
**Min Mail Order EU:** £10.00 + p&p
**Credit Cards:** All major credit/debit cards
**Specialities:** Over 400 popular, unusual & rare herbs esp. medicinal. Also seeds.
**Notes:** Phone between 1200-1300 & 1800-1900 only.
**Map Ref:** G, B2 **OS Grid Ref:** NH711642

**GPWP** **PLANTS WITH PURPOSE** ⊠ ⌂
Middlebank Cottage, Smith's Brae,
Bankfoot, Perthshire,
PH1 4AH
Ⓣ (01738) 787278
Ⓜ 07871 451579
Ⓔ info@plantswithpurpose.co.uk
Ⓦ www.plantswithpurpose.co.uk
**Contact:** Margaret Lear
**Opening Times:** Sun, Tue & Wed, Apr-end Sep. Other times by appt.
**Min Mail Order UK:** £12.00
**Min Mail Order EU:** £12.00
**Cat. Cost:** Online or 3 × 1st class.
**Credit Cards:** All major credit/debit cards accepted online only.
**Specialities:** Herbs, esp. *Mentha* & *Artemisia*.
**Notes:** Partial wheelchair access.
**Map Ref:** G, C3 **OS Grid Ref:** NO067356

KEY
⊠ Mail order to UK or EU ⌂ Delivers to shows
✈ Exports beyond EU € Euro accepted
♿ Accessible by wheelchair ◆ See Display advertisement

G

**GQue** **Quercus Garden Plants** ♿
Rankeilour Gardens, Rankeilour Estate, Springfield, Fife, KY15 5RE
Ⓣ (01337) 810444
Ⓕ (01337) 810444
Ⓔ colin@quercus.uk.net
**Contact:** Colin McBeath
**Opening Times:** 1000-1700 Thu-Sun, end Mar-mid Oct. 1000-1400 Sat or by appt., Nov-Mar.
**Cat. Cost:** 4 × 1st class.
**Credit Cards:** All major credit/debit cards
**Specialities:** Easy & unusual plants for contemporary Scottish gardens.
**Notes:** Delivery service available on large orders at nursery's discretion. Also sells wholesale.
**Map Ref:** G, C3 **OS Grid Ref:** NO330118

**GQui** **Quinish Garden Nursery** ⊠
Dervaig, Isle of Mull, Argyll, PA75 6QL
Ⓣ (01688) 400344
Ⓕ (01688) 400344
Ⓔ quinishplants@aol.com
Ⓦ www.Q-gardens.org
**Contact:** Nicholas Reed
**Opening Times:** By appt. only.
**Min Mail Order UK:** Nmc
**Min Mail Order EU:** Nmc
**Cat. Cost:** 2 × 1st class
**Credit Cards:** None
**Specialities:** Choice garden shrubs & conservatory plants.
**Map Ref:** G, C1

**GSec** **The Secret Garden** ⊠
10 Pilmuir Road West, Forres, Moray, IV36 2HL
Ⓣ (01309) 674634
Ⓔ fixandig@aol.com
**Contact:** Mrs L. Dingwall
**Opening Times:** Mail order only. Open by appt. only.
**Min Mail Order UK:** Nmc
**Cat. Cost:** 84p
**Credit Cards:** None
**Specialities:** *Hosta.*

**GTwe** **J Tweedie Fruit Trees** ⊠
Maryfield Road Nursery, Nr Terregles, Dumfriesshire, DG2 9TH
Ⓣ (01387) 720880
**Contact:** John Tweedie
**Opening Times:** Please ring for times. Collections by appt.
**Min Mail Order UK:** Nmc
**Cat. Cost:** Sae
**Credit Cards:** None
**Specialities:** Fruit trees & bushes. A wide range of old & new varieties.
**Map Ref:** G, D2

**GUzu** **Uzumara Orchids** ⊠ €
9 Port Henderson, Gairloch, Ross-shire, IV21 2AS
Ⓣ (01445) 741228
Ⓕ (01445) 741228
Ⓔ i.la_croix@virgin.net
Ⓦ www.uzumaraorchids.com
**Contact:** Mrs I F La Croix
**Opening Times:** Mail order only. Open by appt only.
**Min Mail Order UK:** Nmc
**Min Mail Order EU:** Nmc
**Cat. Cost:** Sae
**Credit Cards:** None
**Specialities:** African & Madagascan orchids.

## N. Ireland & Republic

**IArd** **Ardcarne Garden Centre** € ♿
Ardcarne, Boyle, Co. Roscommon, Ireland
Ⓣ 00 353 (0)7196 67091
Ⓕ 00 353 (0)7196 67341
Ⓔ ardcarne@indigo.ie
Ⓦ www.ardcarnegc.com
**Contact:** James Wickham, Mary Frances Dwyer, Kirsty Ainge
**Opening Times:** 0900-1800 Mon-Sat, 1300-1800 Sun & B/hols.
**Credit Cards:** Access Visa American Express
**Specialities:** Coastal plants, native & unusual trees, specimen plants & semi-mature trees. Wide general range.
**Map Ref:** I, B1

**IBal** **Bali-hai Mail Order Nursery** ⊠ ☒ ⌂ € ♿
42 Largy Road, Carnlough, Ballymena, Co. Antrim, N. Ireland, BT44 0EZ
Ⓣ 028 2888 5289
Ⓕ 028 2888 5976
Ⓔ ianwscroggy@btopenworld.com
Ⓦ www.mailorderplants4me.com
**Contact:** Mrs M E Scroggy
**Opening Times:** Mon-Sat by appt. only.
**Min Mail Order UK:** Nmc
**Min Mail Order EU:** Nmc
**Cat. Cost:** £3.00 cheque, made payable to Mrs M.E. Scroggy.
**Credit Cards:** None
**Specialities:** *Hosta*, *Phormium*, *Rhodohypoxis* & other perennials. Tree ferns.
**Notes:** Exports beyond EU restricted to bare root perennials, no grasses. Also sells wholesale.
**Map Ref:** I, A3 **OS Grid Ref:** D287184

IBlr **Ballyrogan Nurseries** ⊠ € ♿
The Grange, Ballyrogan, Newtownards, Co. Down, N. Ireland, BT23 4SD
Ⓣ (028) 9181 0451 (evenings)
Ⓔ gary.dunlop@btinternet.com
**Contact:** Gary Dunlop
**Opening Times:** Only open by appt.
**Min Mail Order UK:** £10.00 + p&p
**Min Mail Order EU:** £20.00 + p&p
**Cat. Cost:** 2 × 1st class
**Credit Cards:** None
**Specialities:** Choice herbaceous. *Agapanthus, Celmisia, Crocosmia, Euphorbia, Meconopsis, Rodgersia, Iris, Dierama, Erythronium, Roscoea* & *Phormium*.
**Notes:** Also sells wholesale.
**Map Ref:** I, B3

ICro **Crocknafeola Nursery** €
Killybegs, Co. Donegal, Ireland
Ⓣ 00 353 (0)74 97 51018
Ⓕ 00 353 (0)74 97 51095
Ⓔ crocknafeola@hotmail.com
**Contact:** Fionn McKenna
**Opening Times:** 0900-1800 Mon, Tue, Thu-Sat, closed Wed. 1200-1800 Sun.
**Cat. Cost:** None issued
**Credit Cards:** None
**Specialities:** Bedding plants, herbaceous perennials, rhododendrons, plants for containers, roses, plus shrubs & hedging for coastal areas.
**Notes:** Also sells wholesale.
**Map Ref:** I, D2

IDee **Deelish Garden Centre** ⊠ €
Skibbereen, Co. Cork, Ireland
Ⓣ 00 353 (0)28 21374
Ⓕ 00 353 (0)28 21374
Ⓔ deel@eircom.net
Ⓦ www.deelish.ie
**Contact:** Bill & Rain Chase
**Opening Times:** 1000-1800 Mon-Sat, 1400-1800 Sun.
**Min Mail Order EU:** €50 (Ireland only).
**Cat. Cost:** Sae
**Credit Cards:** Visa Access
**Specialities:** Unusual plants for the mild coastal climate of Ireland. Conservatory plants. Sole Irish agents for Chase Organic Seeds.
**Notes:** No mail order outside Ireland.
**Map Ref:** I, D1

IDic **Dickson Nurseries Ltd** ⊠ ✈
Milecross Road, Newtownards, Co. Down, N. Ireland, BT23 4SS
Ⓣ (028) 9181 2206
Ⓕ (028) 9181 3366
Ⓔ mail@dickson-roses.co.uk
Ⓦ www.dickson-roses.co.uk
**Contact:** Linda Stewart
**Opening Times:** 0800-1230 & 1300-1700 Mon-Thu. 0800-1230 Fri. Closes at 1600 Mon-Thu Dec-Jan.
**Min Mail Order UK:** Nmc
**Min Mail Order EU:** £25.00 + p&p
**Cat. Cost:** Free
**Credit Cards:** None
**Specialities:** Roses esp. modern Dickson varieties. Most varieties are available in small quantities only.
**Notes:** Also sells wholesale.
**Map Ref:** I, B3

IFFs **Future Forests** ⊠ € ♿
Kealkil, Bantry, Co. Cork, Ireland
Ⓣ 00 353 (0) 27 66176
Ⓕ 00 353 (0) 27 66939
Ⓔ futureforests@eircom.net
Ⓦ www.futureforests.net
**Contact:** Nick Lain
**Opening Times:** 1000-1800 Mon-Sat (incl. B/hols), 1430-1800 Sun.
**Min Mail Order UK:** Nmc
**Min Mail Order EU:** Nmc
**Cat. Cost:** Free.
**Credit Cards:** Laser, MasterCard Visa
**Specialities:** Trees, shrubs, hedging, climbers, roses. Fruit trees. Ferns, grasses & perennials.
**Notes:** Mail order throughout Ireland & UK. Also sells wholesale.
**Map Ref:** I, D1 **OS Grid Ref:** W 083587

IFoB **Field of Blooms** ⊠ € ♿
Ballymackey, Lisnamoe, Nenagh, Co. Tipperary, Ireland
Ⓣ 00 353 (0) 67 29974
Ⓜ 08764 06044
Ⓔ guy2002@eircom.ie
Ⓦ www.nenagh.net/main/fieldofblooms.htm
**Contact:** Guy de Schrijver
**Opening Times:** Strictly by appt.
**Min Mail Order UK:** Nmc
**Min Mail Order EU:** Nmc
**Cat. Cost:** Free
**Credit Cards:** None
**Specialities:** Hellebores, herbaceous, hardy perennials, ornamental grasses & woodland plants.
**Map Ref:** I, C2

KEY
⊠ Mail order to UK or EU — Delivers to shows
✈ Exports beyond EU — € Euro accepted
♿ Accessible by wheelchair — ◆ See Display advertisement

**IFro** **FROGSWELL NURSERY €**
Clooncorlon, Straide,
Foxford, Co. Mayo,
Ireland
Ⓣ 00 353 (0)94 903 1420
Ⓕ 00 353 (0)94 903 1420
Ⓔ frogswell@gmail.com
Ⓦ www.frogswell.net
**Contact:** Celia Graebner
**Opening Times:** Feb-Oct by appt. Please phone first. Also Garden Open Days, see website for details.
**Cat. Cost:** Online only.
**Credit Cards:** None
**Specialities:** A small nursery specialising in shade & woodland plants & unusual perennials for the Irish climate, raised on site, some in small quantities. Garden visits by arrangement.
**Notes:** See website for location details.
**Map Ref:** I, B1 **OS Grid Ref:** M2497

**IGor** **GORTKELLY CASTLE NURSERY ⊠ €**
Upperchurch, Thurles, Co. Tipperary,
Ireland
Ⓣ 00 353 (0) 504 54441
**Contact:** Clare Beumer
**Opening Times:** Mail order only. Not open to the public.
**Min Mail Order UK:** £50.00
**Min Mail Order EU:** €50
**Cat. Cost:** 5 × 1st class (UK), 5 × 48c (Rep. of Ireland)
**Credit Cards:** None
**Specialities:** Choice perennials.
**Map Ref:** I, C2

**IHer** **HERITAGE BULBS ⊠ € ◆**
Tullynally Castle,
Castlepollard, Co. Westmeath,
Ireland
Ⓣ 00 353 (0) 44 96 62744
Ⓕ 00 353 (0) 44 96 62746
Ⓔ info@heritagebulbs.com
Ⓦ www.heritagebulbs.com
**Contact:** Alex Chisholm
**Opening Times:** Not open. Mail order only. Tullynally Castle Gardens open afternoons in Jun, Jul & Aug.
**Min Mail Order UK:** Nmc
**Min Mail Order EU:** Nmc
**Cat. Cost:** Free
**Credit Cards:** MasterCard Visa
**Specialities:** Rare & historic bulbs (www.heritagebulbs.com) & native bulbs for naturalising (www.wildaboutbulbs.com).
**Notes:** Also sells wholesale.
**Map Ref:** I, B2

**ILad** **LADYBIRD GARDEN NURSERY ⊠ ♠**
32 Ballykeigle Road, off Moss Road,
Nr Ballygowan, County Down,
BT23 5SD
Ⓣ (028) 9752 8025
Ⓔ millarjoyce@hotmail.com
Ⓦ www.ladybirdgarden.co.uk
**Contact:** Joyce Millar
**Opening Times:** Afternoons, Apr-Sep (not Wed or Sun). Other times (incl. evenings) by appt. Garden open to groups by appt. Please phone first if travelling a distance.
**Min Mail Order UK:** Nmc
**Cat. Cost:** 2 × 1st class or free by email.
**Credit Cards:** None
**Specialities:** Over 200 varieties of herbaceous perennials & grasses, beneficial for wildlife ranges. Some in small quantities only.
**Notes:** Partial wheelchair access. Also sells wholesale.
**Map Ref:** I, B3 **OS Grid Ref:** J453633

**ILis** **LISDOONAN HERBS ⊠ € ♿**
98 Belfast Road, Saintfield, Co. Down,
N. Ireland, BT24 7HF
Ⓣ (028) 9081 3624
Ⓔ b.pilcher@lisdoonanherbs.co.uk
Ⓦ www.lisdoonanherbs.co.uk
**Contact:** Barbara Pilcher
**Opening Times:** Wed & Fri am. For other times, please phone to check.
**Min Mail Order UK:** Nmc
**Min Mail Order EU:** Nmc
**Cat. Cost:** 2 × 1st class
**Credit Cards:** None
**Specialities:** Aromatics, herbs, kitchen garden plants, period plants, some native species. Freshly cut herbs & salads. Some stock available in limited quantities only. All peat-free.
**Map Ref:** I, B3 **OS Grid Ref:** J390624

**IMGH** **M G H NURSERIES € ♿**
50 Tullyhenan Road, Banbridge, Co. Down,
N. Ireland, BT32 4EY
Ⓣ (028) 4062 2795
**Contact:** Miss M G Heslip
**Opening Times:** By appt. only.
**Cat. Cost:** 3 × 1st class
**Credit Cards:** None
**Specialities:** Grafted conifers, holly, maples, box, ornamental trees & flowering shrubs.
**Map Ref:** I, B3

**IPen** **PENINSULA PRIMULAS ⊠ ♠ €**
72 Ballyeasborough Road, Kircubbin,
Co. Down, N. Ireland, BT22 1AD
Ⓣ 028 4277 2193

Ⓔ Peninsula.Primulas@btinternet.com
**Contact:** Philip Bankhead
**Opening Times:** Mail order only. Not open.
**Min Mail Order UK:** Nmc
**Min Mail Order EU:** Nmc
**Cat. Cost:** Free
**Credit Cards:** None
**Specialities:** Extensive selection of *Primula* species, plus auriculas.
**Map Ref:** I, B3

IPot **The Potting Shed** ⊠ ⌂ €
Bolinaspick, Camolin,
Enniscorthy, Co. Wexford,
Ireland
Ⓣ 00 353 (0)5393 83629
Ⓕ 00 353 (0)5393 83663
Ⓔ sricher@iol.ie
Ⓦ www.camolinpottingshed.com
**Contact:** Susan Carrick
**Opening Times:** 1300-1800, Thu-Sun (incl.), Mar-Sep 2007. Other times by appt.
**Min Mail Order UK:** Nmc
**Min Mail Order EU:** Nmc
**Cat. Cost:** 3 × 1st class
**Credit Cards:** MasterCard Visa
**Specialities:** Herbaceous & ornamental grasses.
**Map Ref:** I, C3

IRhd **Ringhaddy Daffodils** ⊠ ✈ €
Ringhaddy Road, Killinchy,
Newtownards, Co. Down, N. Ireland,
BT23 6TU
Ⓣ (028) 9754 1007
Ⓕ (028) 9754 2276
Ⓔ ringdaff@nireland.com
**Contact:** Nial Watson
**Opening Times:** Mail order only. Not open.
**Min Mail Order UK:** £20.00 + p&p
**Min Mail Order EU:** £50.00 + p&p
**Cat. Cost:** £2.50 redeemable on order.
**Credit Cards:** None
**Specialities:** New daffodil varieties for exhibitors and hybridisers. Small stock of some varieties.

ISea **Seaforde Gardens** ⊠ ✈ ⌂ € ♿
Seaforde, Co. Down, N. Ireland,
BT30 8PG
Ⓣ (028) 4481 1225
Ⓕ (028) 4481 1370
Ⓔ plants@seafordegardens.com
Ⓦ www.seafordegardens.com
**Contact:** P Forde
**Opening Times:** 1000-1700 Mon-Fri all year. 1000-1700 Sat & 1300-1800 Sun mid Feb-end Oct.
**Min Mail Order UK:** Nmc
**Min Mail Order EU:** Nmc
**Cat. Cost:** Free
**Credit Cards:** None
**Specialities:** Over 600 varieties of self-propagated trees & shrubs. Nat. Collection of *Eucryphia*.
**Notes:** Also sells wholesale.
**Map Ref:** I, B3

ISsi **Seaside Nursery** ⊠ € ♿
Claddaghduff, Co. Galway, Ireland
Ⓣ 00 353 (0)95 44687
Ⓕ 00 353 (0)95 44761
Ⓔ seaside@anu.ie
Ⓦ www.anu.ie/seaside/
**Contact:** Tom Dyck
**Opening Times:** 1000-1300 & 1400-1800 Mon-Sat, 1400-1800 Sun. Closed Sun 1 Nov-31 Mar.
**Min Mail Order UK:** Nmc
**Min Mail Order EU:** Nmc
**Cat. Cost:** €.50
**Credit Cards:** Visa MasterCard
**Specialities:** Plants & hedging suitable for seaside locations. Rare plants originating from Australia & New Zealand esp. *Phormium*, *Astelia*.
**Notes:** Also sells wholesale.
**Map Ref:** I, B1

ITim **Timpany Nurseries & Gardens** ⊠ ⌂ ♿
77 Magheratimpany Road, Ballynahinch,
Co. Down, N. Ireland,
BT24 8PA
Ⓣ (028) 9756 2812
Ⓕ (028) 9756 2812
Ⓔ timpany@alpines.freeserve.co.uk
Ⓦ www.alpines.freeserve.co.uk
**Contact:** Susan Tindall
**Opening Times:** 1000-1730 Tue-Sat, Sun by appt.
**Min Mail Order UK:** Nmc
**Min Mail Order EU:** £30.00 + p&p
**Cat. Cost:** £1.50
**Credit Cards:** Visa MasterCard
**Specialities:** *Celmisia*, *Androsace*, *Primula*, *Saxifraga*, *Helichrysum*, *Dianthus*, *Meconopsis*, *Cassiope*, *Rhodohypoxis*, *Cyclamen* & *Primula auricula*.
**Notes:** Also sells wholesale.
**Map Ref:** I, B3

KEY
⊠ Mail order to UK or EU ⌂ Delivers to shows
✈ Exports beyond EU € Euro accepted
♿ Accessible by wheelchair ◆ See Display advertisement

## LONDON AREA

**LAma** **JACQUES AMAND INTERNATIONAL** ☒ ✈ € ♿
The Nurseries, 145 Clamp Hill, Stanmore, Middlesex, HA7 3JS
Ⓣ (020) 8420 7110
Ⓕ (020) 8954 6784
Ⓔ bulbs@jacquesamand.co.uk
Ⓦ www.jacquesamand.com
**Contact:** John Amand & Stuart Chapman
**Opening Times:** 0900-1700 Mon-Fri, 1000-1400 Sat. Ltd. Sun opening in Dec & Jan.
**Min Mail Order UK:** Nmc
**Min Mail Order EU:** Nmc
**Cat. Cost:** 1 × 1st class
**Credit Cards:** All major credit/debit cards
**Specialities:** Rare and unusual species bulbs esp. *Arisaema*, *Trillium*, *Fritillaria*, tulips.
**Notes:** Also sells wholesale.
**Map Ref:** L, B3

**LAst** **ASTERBY & CHALKCROFT NURSERIES** ♿
The Ridgeway, Blunham, Bedfordshire, MK44 3PH
Ⓣ (01767) 640148
Ⓕ (01767) 640667
Ⓔ sales@asterbyplants.co.uk
Ⓦ www.asterbyplants.co.uk
**Contact:** Simon & Eva Aldridge
**Opening Times:** 1000-1700 7 days. Closed Xmas & Jan.
**Cat. Cost:** 2 × 1st class
**Credit Cards:** Visa MasterCard Switch
**Specialities:** Hardy shrubs, herbaceous & trees.
**Map Ref:** L, A3 **OS Grid Ref:** TL151497

**LBee** **BEECHCROFT NURSERY** ♿
127 Reigate Road, Ewell, Surrey, KT17 3DE
Ⓣ (020) 8393 4265
Ⓕ (020) 8393 4265
**Contact:** C Kimber
**Opening Times:** 1000-1600 Mon-Sat, 1000-1400 Sun and B/hols. Closed Xmas-New Year week.
**Cat. Cost:** None issued
**Credit Cards:** All major credit/debit cards
**Specialities:** Conifers & alpines.
**Notes:** Also sells wholesale.
**Map Ref:** L, C3

**LBMP** **BLOOMING MARVELLOUS PLANTS** ⌂
Korketts Farm, Aylesbury Road, Shipton, Winslow, Buckinghamshire, MK18 3JL
Ⓜ 07963 747305
Ⓔ alex@bmplants.co.uk
Ⓦ www.bmplants.co.uk
**Contact:** Alexia Ballance
**Opening Times:** 0900-1700 Mon-Sat, 1000-1600 Sun, 1st Mar-30th Sep. 1000-1600 Sat & Sun only, Oct. By appt. only Nov-Feb.
**Credit Cards:** All major credit/debit cards
**Specialities:** A mixture of unusual and familiar perennials, shrubs, grasses, ferns & bedding plants, most in more generous sizes than usually found in nurseries.
**Notes:** Located on the A413 just outside Winslow (if heading towards Aylesbury). Partial wheelchair access.
**Map Ref:** L, A2 **OS Grid Ref:** SP777271

**LBuc** **BUCKINGHAM NURSERIES** ☒ ✈ € ♿ ◆
14 Tingewick Road, Buckingham, MK18 4AE
Ⓣ (01280) 822133
Ⓕ (01280) 815491
Ⓔ enquiries@buckingham-nurseries.co.uk
Ⓦ www.buckingham-nurseries.co.uk
**Contact:** R J & P L Brown
**Opening Times:** 0830-1730 (1800 in summer) Mon-Sat, 1030-1630 Sun.
**Min Mail Order UK:** Nmc
**Min Mail Order EU:** Nmc
**Cat. Cost:** Free
**Credit Cards:** Visa MasterCard Switch
**Specialities:** Bare rooted and container grown hedging. Trees, shrubs, herbaceous perennials, alpines, grasses & ferns.
**Map Ref:** L, A2 **OS Grid Ref:** SP675333

**LBut** **YAFFLES** ☒ ♿
Harvest Hill, Bourne End, Buckinghamshire, SL8 5JJ
Ⓣ (01628) 525455
**Contact:** I Butterfield
**Opening Times:** 0900-1300 & 1400-1700. Please phone beforehand in case we are attending shows.
**Min Mail Order UK:** Nmc
**Min Mail Order EU:** £30.00 + p&p
**Cat. Cost:** 2 × 2nd class
**Credit Cards:** None
**Specialities:** Nat. Collection of *Pleione*. *Dahlia* for collection. Scientific Award 1999.
**Notes:** Only *Pleione* by mail order.
**Map Ref:** L, B3

**LCla** **CLAY LANE NURSERY** ☒ ⌂
3 Clay Lane, South Nutfield, Nr Redhill, Surrey, RH1 4EG
Ⓣ (01737) 823307
Ⓔ claylane.nursery@btinternet.com
Ⓦ www.claylane-fuchsias.co.uk
**Contact:** K W Belton
**Opening Times:** 1000-1700 Tue-Sun 1st Feb-

30th Jun. Other times by appt. Please phone before travelling.
**Min Mail Order UK:** £6.00
**Cat. Cost:** 4 × 2nd class
**Credit Cards:** None
**Specialities:** *Fuchsia*. Many varieties in small quantities only.
**Notes:** Mail order by telephone pre-arangement only.
**Map Ref:** L, C4

LCro **CROCUS.CO.UK** ⊠
Nursery Court, London Road, Windlesham, Surrey, GU20 6LQ
Ⓣ 0870 787 1414 (order line)
Ⓕ 0870 787 1412
Ⓔ customerservices@crocus.co.uk
Ⓦ www.crocus.co.uk
**Contact:** Peter Clay
**Opening Times:** Not open. Mail order only. Order lines open 24hrs, 7 days.
**Min Mail Order UK:** Nmc
**Cat. Cost:** Free.
**Credit Cards:** Visa MasterCard Solo Switch Delta

LCtg **COTTAGE GARDEN NURSERY** ◆
Barnet Road, Arkley, Barnet, Hertfordshire, EN5 3JX
Ⓣ (020) 8441 8829
Ⓕ (020) 8531 3178
Ⓔ nurseryinfo@cottagegardennursery-barnet.co.uk
Ⓦ www.cottagegardennursery-barnet.co.uk
**Contact:** David and Wendy Spicer
**Opening Times:** 0930-1700 Tue-Sat Mar-Oct, 0930-1600 Tue-Sat Nov-Feb, 1000-1600 Sun & B/hol Mon all year.
**Cat. Cost:** None issued.
**Credit Cards:** All major credit/debit cards
**Specialities:** General range of hardy shrubs, trees & perennials. Architectural & exotics, *Fuchsia*, seasonal bedding, patio plants.
**Map Ref:** L, B3 **OS Grid Ref:** TQ226958

LDai **DAISY ROOTS** ⊠ ⛫
(office) 8 Gosselin Road, Bengeo, Hertford, Hertfordshire, SG14 3LG
Ⓣ (01992) 582401
Ⓕ (01992) 582401
Ⓔ anne@daisyroots.com
Ⓦ www.daisyroots.com
**Contact:** Anne Godfrey
**Opening Times:** 1000-1600 Fri & Sat Mar-Oct, or by appt.
**Min Mail Order UK:** Nmc
**Cat. Cost:** 4 × 1st class
**Credit Cards:** None
**Specialities:** Ever-increasing range of choice & unusual perennials, particularly *Agastache*, *Anthemis*, *Centaurea*, *Digitalis*, *Erysimum*, *Salvia* & *Sedum*.
**Notes:** Also sells wholesale. Nursery is at Jenningsbury, London Road, Hertford Heath.
**Map Ref:** L, B4

LDea **DEREK LLOYD DEAN** ⊠ ✈ ⛫
8 Lynwood Close, South Harrow, Middlesex, HA2 9PR
Ⓣ (020) 8864 0899
Ⓔ lloyddeancbtinternet.com
Ⓦ www.dereklloyddean.com
**Contact:** Derek Lloyd Dean
**Opening Times:** Not open. Mail order only.
**Min Mail Order UK:** £2.50 + p&p
**Min Mail Order EU:** £2.50 + p&p
**Cat. Cost:** 2 × 1st class
**Credit Cards:** None
**Specialities:** Regal, angel, ivy & scented leaf *Pelargonium*. Nat. Collection of Angel *Pelargonium*.

LEdu **EDULIS** ⊠ ⛫ € ♿
(office) 1 Flowers Piece, Ashampstead, Berkshire, RG8 8SG
Ⓣ (01635) 578113
Ⓕ (01635) 578113
Ⓔ edulis.nursery@virgin.net
Ⓦ www.edulis.co.uk
**Contact:** Paul Barney
**Opening Times:** By appt. only.
**Min Mail Order UK:** £10.00 + p&p
**Min Mail Order EU:** £50.00 + p&p
**Cat. Cost:** 6 × 1st class
**Credit Cards:** None
**Specialities:** Unusual edibles, architectural plants, permaculture plants.
**Notes:** Nursery is at Bere Court Farm, Tidmarsh Lane, Pangbourne, RG8 8HT. Also sells wholesale.
**Map Ref:** L, B2 **OS Grid Ref:** SU615747

LFCN **FARNHAM COMMON NURSERIES LTD** ⛫ ♿
Crown Lane, Farnham Royal, Nr Slough, Buckinghamshire, SL2 3SF
Ⓣ (01753) 643108
Ⓕ (01753) 646818
Ⓔ sales@fcn.co.uk
Ⓦ www.fcn.co.uk
**Contact:** Elizabeth Apedaile

KEY
⊠ Mail order to UK or EU ⛫ Delivers to shows
✈ Exports beyond EU € Euro accepted
♿ Accessible by wheelchair ◆ See Display advertisement

L

**Opening Times:** 0800-1700 Mon-Fri, 0900-1700 Sat, 1000-1600 Sun (w/end retail only).
**Credit Cards:** All major credit/debit cards
**Specialities:** Good selection of ornamental trees, shrubs & herbaceous perennials, esp. *Pittosporum*, *Phormium*, *Iris* & *Heuchera*.
**Notes:** Also sells wholesale.
**Map Ref:** L, B3 **OS Grid Ref:** SU955832

LFol **FOLIAGE SCENTED & HERB PLANTS** ♿
Walton Poor, Crocknorth Road, Ranmore Common, Dorking, Surrey,
RH5 6SX
Ⓣ (01483) 282273
Ⓕ (01483) 282273
**Contact:** Mrs Prudence Calvert
**Opening Times:** Open during Apr-Sep, please phone for appt. if possible.
**Cat. Cost:** 3 × 2nd class
**Credit Cards:** None
**Specialities:** Herbs, aromatic & scented plants.
**Map Ref:** L, C3

LFox **FOXGROVE PLANTS** ⊠ ♿
Foxgrove, Enborne, Nr Newbury, Berkshire,
RG14 6RE
Ⓣ (01635) 40554
Ⓕ (01635) 30555
**Contact:** Mrs Louise Peters
**Opening Times:** 1000-1300 & 1400-1600 Thu, Fri, Sat, mid-Jan to end-Oct. Other times by appt. only.
**Min Mail Order UK:** Nmc
**Min Mail Order EU:** Nmc
**Cat. Cost:** £1.00
**Credit Cards:** None
**Specialities:** Hardy & unusual plants, incl. *Galanthus*, hellebores, grasses, *Penstemon*, alpines.
**Notes:** Mail order for *Galanthus* & grasses only.
**Map Ref:** L, C2

LFur **FURZE PARK NURSERY** ⊠
Furze Park Farm, Bycell Road, Maids Moreton, Buckingham, Buckinghamshire,
MK18 5AA
Ⓣ (01280) 821999
Ⓕ (01280) 821999
Ⓔ lucyhyde@btinternet.com
**Contact:** Lucy Hyde
**Opening Times:** 1000-1700 Thu & Fri. Other days by appt. Closed 1st Nov-1st Mar.
**Min Mail Order UK:** Nmc
**Cat. Cost:** None issued.
**Credit Cards:** None

**Specialities:** Friendly & helpful nursery specialising in new & unusual hardy perennials, many woodlanders incl. Himalayan & Japanese *Arisaema*.

LGod **GODLY'S ROSES** ⊠ ♿
Redbourn, St Albans, Hertfordshire,
AL3 7PS
Ⓣ (01582) 792255
Ⓕ (01582) 794267
**Contact:** Colin Godly
**Opening Times:** 0900-1700 summer, 7 days. 0900-dusk winter, 7 days. Closed Xmas to New Year's Day.
**Min Mail Order UK:** Nmc
**Cat. Cost:** Free
**Credit Cards:** Visa American Express Switch MasterCard
**Specialities:** Roses.
**Notes:** Standard roses not sent mail order. Also sells wholesale.
**Map Ref:** L, B3 **OS Grid Ref:** TL096137

LHop **HOPLEYS PLANTS LTD** ⊠ ♿ ◆
High Street, Much Hadham, Hertfordshire,
SG10 6BU
Ⓣ (01279) 842509
Ⓕ (01279) 843784
Ⓔ sales@hopleys.co.uk
Ⓦ www.hopleys.co.uk
**Contact:** Aubrey Barker
**Opening Times:** 0900-1700 Mon & Wed-Sat, 1400-1700 Sun. Closed Nov-Feb except by appt.
**Min Mail Order UK:** Nmc
**Cat. Cost:** 5 × 1st class
**Credit Cards:** Visa Access Switch
**Specialities:** Wide range of hardy & half-hardy shrubs & perennials.
**Notes:** £2.00 charge for delivery to shows. Also sells wholesale.
**Map Ref:** L, A4 **OS Grid Ref:** TL428196

LHyd **HYDON NURSERIES** ⊠ € ◆
Clock Barn Lane, Hydon Heath, Godalming, Surrey, GU8 4AZ
Ⓣ (01483) 860252
Ⓕ (01483) 419937
**Contact:** A F George, Rodney Longhurst & Mrs A M George
**Opening Times:** 0930-1700 Mon-Sat (closed for lunch 12.45-1400), Feb-mid Jun & Oct-mid Nov. Other months 0930-1600 Mon-Fri, 0930-1300 Sat. Sun by appt.
**Min Mail Order UK:** Nmc
**Min Mail Order EU:** £25.00 + p&p
**Cat. Cost:** £2.00 or 7 × 1st class or 10 × 2nd class

**Credit Cards:** None
**Specialities:** Large and dwarf *Rhododendron*, *yakushimanum* hybrids, azaleas (deciduous & evergreen), *Camellia* & other trees & shrubs. Specimen *Rhododendron*. Conservatory: scented tender rhododendrons & camellias.
**Notes:** Also sells wholesale.
**Map Ref:** L, C3

LIMB **I.M.B. Plants** ✉
2 Ashdown Close, Giffard Park, Milton Keynes, Buckinghamshire, MK14 5PX
Ⓣ (01908) 618911
Ⓔ imbrazier@btinternet.com
**Contact:** Ian Brazier
**Opening Times:** Not open. Mail order only.
**Min Mail Order UK:** Nmc
**Credit Cards:** None
**Specialities:** *Helianthemum*. All plants propagated in small quantities.

LLHF **Little Heath Farm (UK) (formerly Two Jays Alpines)**
Little Heath Lane, Potten End, Berkhamsted, Hertfordshire, HP4 2RY
Ⓣ (01442) 864951
Ⓕ (01442) 864951
Ⓔ john.spokes@talk21.com
**Contact:** John Spokes
**Opening Times:** 1000-1700 or dusk if earlier, 7 days.
**Cat. Cost:** Online only.
**Credit Cards:** Visa MasterCard
**Specialities:** Large range of alpines, herbaceous, shrubs, many available in small quantities only.
**Map Ref:** L, A3

LLWG **Lilies Water Gardens** ✉ ⛺ ♿
Broad Lane, Newdigate, Surrey, RH5 5AT
Ⓣ (01306) 631064
Ⓕ (01306) 631693
Ⓔ mail@plilieswatergardens.co.uk
Ⓦ www.lilieswatergardens.co.uk
**Contact:** Simon Harman
**Opening Times:** 0900-1700 Tues-Sat, 1st Mar-end Sep.
**Min Mail Order UK:** Nmc, but flat rate £10.00 delivery charge.
**Cat. Cost:** Online only.
**Credit Cards:** All major credit/debit cards
**Specialities:** Waterlilies, moist herbaceous. Astilbes, primulas, marginal plants. Tropical & semi-tropical frost-tender marginal & bog-garden plants. Dry-loving plants, attractive to bees & butterflies. Ferns, Shrubs.
**Map Ref:** L, C3

LLWP **L W Plants** ✉ ⛺
23 Wroxham Way, Harpenden, Hertfordshire, AL5 4PP
Ⓣ (01582) 768467
Ⓔ lwplants@waitrose.com
Ⓦ www.thymus.co.uk
**Contact:** Mrs M Easter
**Opening Times:** 1000-1700 most days, but please phone first.
**Min Mail Order UK:** Nmc
**Cat. Cost:** A5 sae + 5 × 2nd class (loose)
**Credit Cards:** None
**Specialities:** Plants from a plantsman's garden, esp. *Geranium*, grasses, *Penstemon* & *Thymus*. Nat. Collections. of *Thymus* (Scientific), *Hyssopus* & *Satureja*.
**Notes:** Mail order *Thymus* only.
**Map Ref:** L, B3 **OS Grid Ref:** TL141153

LMaj **Majestic Trees**
Chequers Meadow, Chequers Hill, Flamstead, St Albans, Hertfordshire, AL3 8ET
Ⓣ (01582) 843881
Ⓕ (01582) 843882
Ⓔ info@majesticgroup.co.uk
Ⓦ www.majestictrees.co.uk
**Contact:** Sarah Shynn
**Opening Times:** 0830-1700 Mon-Fri. 1000-1600 (1700 Mar-Oct) Sat. Closed Sun, B/hols & Xmas/New Year.
**Cat. Cost:** 6 × 1st class.
**Credit Cards:** MasterCard Visa Switch Maestro
**Specialities:** Semi-mature & mature containerised trees grown in airpot from 50ltr to 5000 ltr.
**Notes:** Also sells wholesale
**Map Ref:** L, B3 **OS Grid Ref:** TL08140815

LMil **Millais Nurseries** ✉ ♿
Crosswater Lane, Churt, Farnham, Surrey, GU10 2JN
Ⓣ (01252) 792698
Ⓕ (01252) 792526
Ⓔ sales@rhododendrons.co.uk
Ⓦ www.rhododendrons.co.uk
**Contact:** David Millais
**Opening Times:** 1000-1300 & 1400-1700 Mon-Fri. Sat spring & autumn. Daily in May and early Jun.
**Min Mail Order UK:** £30.00 + p&p
**Min Mail Order EU:** £60.00 + p&p
**Cat. Cost:** 4 × 1st class

KEY
✉ Mail order to UK or EU ⛺ Delivers to shows
✈ Exports beyond EU € Euro accepted
♿ Accessible by wheelchair ◆ See Display advertisement

**Credit Cards:** All major credit/debit cards
**Specialities:** Rhododendrons, azaleas, magnolias & acers.
**Notes:** Mail order Oct-Mar only. Also sells wholesale.
**Map Ref:** L, C3 **OS Grid Ref:** SU856397

**LMor** **Morehavens** ⊠ ♿
Sandpit Hill, Buckland Common, Tring, Hertfordshire, HP23 6NG
Ⓣ (01494) 758642
Ⓦ www.camomilelawns.co.uk
**Contact:** B Farmer
**Opening Times:** Mail order only. Open only for collection.
**Min Mail Order UK:** £18.00
**Min Mail Order EU:** £18.00 + p&p
**Cat. Cost:** Free
**Credit Cards:** None
**Specialities:** *Camomile* 'Treneague'.
**Notes:** Also sells wholesale.

**LPal** **The Palm Centre** ⊠ € ♿
Ham Central Nursery, opposite Riverside Drive, Ham Street, Ham, Richmond, Surrey, TW10 7HA
Ⓣ (020) 8255 6191
Ⓕ (020) 8255 6192
Ⓔ mail@thepalmcentre.co.uk
Ⓦ www.thepalmcentre.co.uk
**Contact:** Martin Gibbons
**Opening Times:** 0900-1700 (dusk in winter) 7 days. Admin & Order Dept. 0900-1700 Mon-Fri.
**Min Mail Order UK:** £10.00 + p&p
**Min Mail Order EU:** £10.00 + p&p
**Cat. Cost:** Free
**Credit Cards:** Visa MasterCard Switch
**Specialities:** Palms & cycads, exotic & sub-tropical, hardy, half-hardy & tropical. Seedlings to mature trees. Also bamboo, tree ferns & other exotics.
**Notes:** Also sells wholesale.

**LPan** **Pantiles Garden Centre** ⊠ ♿
Almners Road, Lyne, Chertsey, Surrey, KT16 0BJ
Ⓣ (01932) 872195
Ⓕ (01932) 874030
Ⓔ sales@pantiles-nurseries.co.uk
Ⓦ www.pantiles-nurseries.co.uk
**Contact:** Plant Area Manager
**Opening Times:** 0900-1800 Mon-Sat (summer), 0900-1700 Mon-Sat (winter), 1030-1630 Sun.
**Min Mail Order UK:** Nmc
**Min Mail Order EU:** £100.00 + p&p
**Cat. Cost:** Free
**Credit Cards:** Visa Switch MasterCard
**Specialities:** Large trees, shrubs, conifers & climbers in containers. Screening, architectural & unusual plants.
**Notes:** Also sells wholesale.
**Map Ref:** L, C3 **OS Grid Ref:** TQ017663

**LPBA** **Paul Bromfield – Aquatics** ⊠ € ♿
Maydencroft Lane, Gosmore, Hitchin, Hertfordshire, SG4 7QD
Ⓣ (01462) 457399
Ⓔ info@bromfieldaquatics.co.uk
Ⓦ www.bromfieldaquatics.co.uk
**Contact:** Debbie Edwards
**Opening Times:** Mail order only. Order online at website. Office open 1000-1700 Mon-Sat, Feb-Oct. Visitors please ring for appt.
**Min Mail Order UK:** £25.00 incl.
**Min Mail Order EU:** £100.00 incl.
**Cat. Cost:** Online only.
**Credit Cards:** Visa MasterCard Delta JCB Switch
**Specialities:** Water lilies, marginals & bog.
**Notes:** Also sells wholesale.

**LPen** **Penstemons by Colour** ⊠ €
Peterley Manor, Peterley, Prestwood, Great Missenden, Buckinghamshire, HP16 0HH
Ⓣ (01494) 866420
Ⓕ (01494) 866420
Ⓔ debra.hughes1@virgin.net
**Contact:** Debra Hughes
**Opening Times:** Any time by appt.
**Min Mail Order UK:** Nmc
**Min Mail Order EU:** Nmc
**Cat. Cost:** Free
**Credit Cards:** None
**Specialities:** *Penstemon*.
**Map Ref:** L, B3 **OS Grid Ref:** SU880994

**LPio** **Pioneer Nursery** ⊠ € ♿
Baldock Lane, Willian, Letchworth, Hertfordshire, SG6 2AE
Ⓣ (01462) 675858
Ⓔ milly@pioneerplants.com
Ⓦ www.pioneerplants.com
**Contact:** Nick Downing
**Opening Times:** 0900-1700 Tue-Sat 1000-1600 Sun, Mar-Oct, 1000-1600 Tue-Sat Nov, Dec & Feb.
**Min Mail Order UK:** £15.00 + p&p
**Min Mail Order EU:** €30
**Cat. Cost:** Online only.
**Credit Cards:** MasterCard Visa
**Specialities:** *Salvia*, tender perennials. Wide range of hard-to-find perennials & bulbs. Species *Pelargonium*.

**Notes:** Mail order via internet only. Also sells wholesale.
**Map Ref:** L, A3 **OS Grid Ref:** TL224307

LPJP **PJ's Palms and Exotics** ⊠ €
41 Salcombe Road, Ashford,
Middlesex,
TW15 3BS
Ⓣ (01784) 250181
**Contact:** Peter Jenkins
**Opening Times:** Mail order only 1st Mar-30th Nov. Visits by arrangement.
**Min Mail Order UK:** Nmc
**Min Mail Order EU:** Nmc
**Cat. Cost:** 2 × 1st class
**Credit Cards:** None
**Specialities:** Palms, bananas & other exotic foliage plants, hardy & half-hardy. *Trachycarpus wagnerianus* seeds available. Plants available in small quantities.
**Notes:** Also sells wholesale.
**Map Ref:** L, B3

LPla **The Plant Specialist**
7 Whitefield Lane, Great Missenden,
Buckinghamshire,
HP16 0BH
Ⓣ (01494) 866650
Ⓕ (01494) 866650
Ⓔ enquire@theplantspecialist.co.uk
Ⓦ www.theplantspecialist.co.uk
**Contact:** Sean Walter
**Opening Times:** 1000-1800 Thu, Fri, Sat, Apr-Oct.
**Cat. Cost:** £1.00
**Credit Cards:** All major credit/debit cards
**Specialities:** Herbaceous perennials, grasses, tender perennials, bulbs.
**Notes:** Also sells wholesale.

LRHS **Wisley Plant Centre (RHS)** ♿
RHS Garden, Wisley, Woking, Surrey,
GU23 6QB
Ⓣ (01483) 211113
Ⓕ (01483) 212372
Ⓔ wisleyplantcentre@rhs.org.uk
Ⓦ www.rhs.org.uk/wisleyplantcentre
**Opening Times:** 0930-1700 Mon-Sat, Oct-Mar. 0930-1800 Mon-Sat, Apr-Sep. 1030-1630 Sun all year.
**Cat. Cost:** None issued
**Credit Cards:** All major credit/debit cards
**Specialities:** Very wide range, many rare & unusual.
**Notes:** Programme of free special events throughout the year. Ring or check website for details.
**Map Ref:** L, C3

LSee **Seeds by Size** ⊠ ✈ €
45 Crouchfield, Boxmoor, Hemel Hempstead,
Hertfordshire, HP1 1PA
Ⓣ (01442) 251458
Ⓔ john-robert-size@seeds-by-size.co.uk
Ⓦ www.seeds-by-size.co.uk
**Contact:** John Robert Size
**Opening Times:** Not open. Mail order only.
**Min Mail Order UK:** Nmc
**Min Mail Order EU:** Nmc
**Cat. Cost:** Online only.
**Credit Cards:** Paypal
**Specialities:** Seeds. 12,000 varieties of flower, vegetable & herb seeds, including sweet peas, pansies, petunias, *Impatiens*, marigolds, ornamental grasses, cabbages, tomatoes, cauliflowers, herbs & onions. Oriental vegetables, hot peppers & sweet peppers.
**Notes:** Cash only euro payments. Also sells wholesale.

LSou **Southon Plants** ⊠ ♿ ◆
Mutton Hill, Dormansland, Lingfield, Surrey,
RH7 6NP
Ⓣ (01342) 870150
Ⓔ info@southonplants.com
Ⓦ www.southonplants.com
**Contact:** Mr Southon
**Opening Times:** 0900-1700 Mar-Oct, closed Wed in Nov. Dec & Jan please phone first.
**Min Mail Order UK:** Nmc
**Cat. Cost:** £2.00 or free online.
**Credit Cards:** All major credit/debit cards
**Specialities:** New & unusual hardy & tender perennials. Also hardy ferns, alpines, grasses, shrubs & climbers incl. many variegated plants.
**Notes:** Mail order. Please phone/email for details.
**Map Ref:** L, C4

LSRN **Spring Reach Nursery** ⊠ ♿
Long Reach, Ockham, Guildford, Surrey,
GU23 6PG
Ⓣ (01483) 284769
Ⓜ 07884 432666
Ⓕ (01483) 284769
Ⓔ n.hourhan@btopenworld.com
Ⓦ www.giftaplant.co.uk
**Contact:** Nick Hourhan
**Opening Times:** 7 days. Mon-Sat 1000-1700, Sun 1030-1630.
**Min Mail Order UK:** Nmc

KEY
⊠ Mail order to UK or EU — Delivers to shows
✈ Exports beyond EU — € Euro accepted
♿ Accessible by wheelchair — ◆ See Display advertisement

**Cat. Cost:** 3 × 1st class
**Credit Cards:** All major credit/debit cards
**Specialities:** Shrubs, grasses, bamboos, climbers, perennials, trees & *Clematis*, chalk-loving plants, hedging, specimen plants, acid-loving plants, soft fruit & top fruit.
**Notes:** Also sells wholesale.
**Map Ref:** L, C3

**LStr** **Henry Street Nursery** ⊠ ♿
Swallowfield Road, Arborfield,
Reading, Berkshire,
RG2 9JY
Ⓣ (0118) 9761223
Ⓕ (0118) 9761417
Ⓔ info@henrystreet.co.uk
Ⓦ www.henrystreet.co.uk
**Contact:** Mr M C Goold
**Opening Times:** 0900-1730 Mon-Sat, 1030-1630 Sun.
**Min Mail Order UK:** Nmc
**Min Mail Order EU:** Nmc
**Cat. Cost:** Free
**Credit Cards:** Visa Access Switch
**Specialities:** Roses.
**Notes:** Also sells wholesale.
**Map Ref:** L, C3

**LToo** **Toobees Exotics** ⊠ ✈ €
(Office) 20 Inglewood, St Johns, Woking,
Surrey, GU21 3HX
Ⓣ (01483) 722600
Ⓕ (01483) 751995
Ⓔ bbpotter@woking.plus.com
Ⓦ www.toobees-exotics.com
**Contact:** Bob Potter
**Opening Times:** Not open. Mail order & online shop only. Visits by appt. only.
**Min Mail Order UK:** Nmc
**Min Mail Order EU:** Nmc
**Cat. Cost:** Sae
**Specialities:** South African & Madagascan succulents, many rare & unusual species, plus air plants, *Euphorbia* & *Pachypodium*. Stock varies constantly.

**LVER** **The Vernon Geranium Nursery** ⊠ ♿
Cuddington Way, Cheam, Sutton, Surrey,
SM2 7JB
Ⓣ (020) 8393 7616
Ⓕ (020) 8786 7437
Ⓔ mrgeranium@aol.com
Ⓦ www.geraniumsuk.com
**Contact:** Philip James & Liz Sims
**Opening Times:** 0930-1730 Mon-Sat, 1000-1600 Sun, 1st Mar-30th Jun.
**Min Mail Order UK:** Nmc
**Min Mail Order EU:** Nmc
**Cat. Cost:** £2.00 UK, £2.50 EU
**Credit Cards:** All major credit/debit cards
**Specialities:** *Pelargonium* & *Fuchsia*.
**Map Ref:** L, C3 **OS Grid Ref:** TQ237615

## Midlands

**MACG** **Ashdale Cottage Garden Plants** ♿
204 Lambley Lane, Gedling,
Nottinghamshire, NG4 4PB
Ⓣ (0115) 966 6060
Ⓕ (0115) 966 6060
**Contact:** Stephen Mills
**Opening Times:** 0900-1700 Wed-Sun, Mar-Oct. Closed Nov-Feb.
**Cat. Cost:** None issued.
**Credit Cards:** All major credit/debit cards
**Specialities:** Wide range of rare and unusual herbaceous perennials.
**Map Ref:** M, B3

**MAga** **Agave Nursery** ⊠ ✈ ⌂ €
15 Sleetmoor Lane, Somercotes, Derbyshire,
DE55 1RB
Ⓜ 01773 605843/07814 787555/07791 627358
Ⓔ jon@agavenursery.wanadoo.co.uk
Ⓦ www.cactus-mall.com/agave
**Contact:** Jon & Sue Dudek
**Opening Times:** Mail order only. Open by appt. only.
**Min Mail Order UK:** Nmc
**Min Mail Order EU:** Nmc
**Cat. Cost:** Free
**Credit Cards:** None
**Specialities:** *Agave*, *Furcraea*, *Manfreda* & *Yucca*.
**Notes:** Also sells wholesale.
**Map Ref:** M, B2

**MAJR** **A J Robinson** ⊠
Sycamore Farm, Foston, Derbyshire,
DE65 5PW
Ⓣ (01283) 815635
Ⓕ (01283) 815635
**Contact:** A J Robinson
**Opening Times:** By appt. for collection of plants only.
**Min Mail Order UK:** £13.00
**Cat. Cost:** 2 × 1st class for list.
**Credit Cards:** None
**Specialities:** Extensive collection of tender perennials. *Salvias*. Nat. Collection of *Argyranthemum*.
**Notes:** Mail order argyranthemums only.
**Map Ref:** M, B2

**MArl** **ARLEY HALL NURSERY** ♿
Arley Hall Nursery,
Northwich, Cheshire,
CW9 6NA
Ⓣ (01565) 777479/777231
Ⓕ (01565) 777465
Ⓦ www.arleyhallandgardens.com
**Contact:** Jane Foster
**Opening Times:** 1100-1730 Tue-Sun Easter-end Sep. Also B/hol Mons.
**Cat. Cost:** 4 × 1st class
**Credit Cards:** All major credit/debit cards
**Specialities:** Wide range of herbaceous incl. many unusual varieties. Wide range of unusual pelargoniums.
**Notes:** Nursery is beside car park at Arley Hall Gardens.
**Map Ref:** M, A1 **OS Grid Ref:** SJ673808

**MAsh** **ASHWOOD NURSERIES LTD** ⊠ ♿
Ashwood Lower Lane, Ashwood,
Kingswinford, West Midlands,
DY6 0AE
Ⓣ (01384) 401996
Ⓕ (01384) 401108
Ⓔ ashwoodnurs@btconnect.com
Ⓦ www.ashwood-nurseries.co.uk
**Contact:** Mark Warburton & Philip Baulk
**Opening Times:** 0900-1700 Mon-Sat & 0930-1700 Sun excl. Xmas & Boxing Day.
**Min Mail Order UK:** Nmc
**Cat. Cost:** 6 × 1st class
**Credit Cards:** Visa Access MasterCard
**Specialities:** Large range of hardy plants, shrubs & dwarf conifers. Also specialise in *Cyclamen*. Hellebores, *Hepatica*, *Hydrangea* & *Salvia*. Nat. Collections of *Lewisia*
**Map Ref:** M, C2 **OS Grid Ref:** SO865879

**MAus** **DAVID AUSTIN ROSES LTD** ⊠ ✈ € ♿
Bowling Green Lane,
Albrighton, Wolverhampton,
WV7 3HB
Ⓣ (01902) 376300
Ⓕ (01902) 372142
Ⓔ retail@davidaustinroses.co.uk
Ⓦ www.davidaustinroses.com
**Contact:** Retail Dept
**Opening Times:** 0900-1700, 7 days.
**Min Mail Order UK:** Nmc
**Min Mail Order EU:** Nmc
**Cat. Cost:** Free
**Credit Cards:** Switch Visa MasterCard Maestro Access
**Specialities:** Roses. Nat. Collection of English Roses.
**Notes:** Also sells wholesale.
**Map Ref:** M, B1

**MAvo** **AVONDALE NURSERY** 🚚 ♿
(Office) 3 Avondale Road, Earlsdon,
Coventry, Warwickshire,
CV5 6DZ
Ⓣ (024) 766 73662
Ⓜ 07979 093096
Ⓕ (024) 766 73662
Ⓔ enquiries@avondalenursery.co.uk
Ⓦ www.avondalenursery.co.uk
**Contact:** Brian Ellis
**Opening Times:** 1000-1230, 1400-1700 Tue-Sun, Mar-Sep. Other times by appt.
**Cat. Cost:** 4 × 1st class
**Credit Cards:** None
**Specialities:** Rare & unusual perennials esp. *Aster*, *Eryngium*, *Leucanthemum*, *Geum*, *Crocosmia* & grasses. Display garden now open.
**Notes:** Nursery is at Russell's Nursery, Mill Hill, Baginton, Nr Coventry.
**Map Ref:** M, C2 **OS Grid Ref:** SP339751

**MBar** **BARNCROFT NURSERIES** ♿
Dunwood Lane, Longsdon, Nr Leek, Stoke-on-Trent, Staffordshire, ST9 9QW
Ⓣ (01538) 384310
Ⓕ (01538) 384310
Ⓦ www.barncroftnurseries.com
**Contact:** S Warner
**Opening Times:** 0930-1730 or dusk if earlier Fri-Sun all year. Closed Xmas to New Year.
**Cat. Cost:** Online only.
**Credit Cards:** None
**Specialities:** Extensive range of over 2000 heathers, conifers, shrubs, trees, climbers, dwarf grasses & rhododendrons. Display garden containing 400 heather cvs.
**Map Ref:** M, B1 **OS Grid Ref:** SJ948552

**MBec** **BEECHCROFT NURSERIES & GARDEN CENTRE** ♿ ◆
Madeley Road, Madeley Heath, Belbroughton, Stourbridge, West Midlands, DY9 9XA
Ⓣ (01562) 710358
Ⓕ (01562) 710507
Ⓔ mail@beechcroft.com
Ⓦ www.beechcroft.com
**Contact:** Paul Billingham
**Opening Times:** 0900-1730 Mon-Sat, 1100-1700 Sun. Close half-hour earlier in winter.
**Cat. Cost:** Free.
**Credit Cards:** All major credit/debit cards except American Express

KEY
⊠ Mail order to UK or EU — 🚚 Delivers to shows
✈ Exports beyond EU — € Euro accepted
♿ Accessible by wheelchair — ◆ See Display advertisement

M

**Specialities:** Shrubs, conifers, rhododendrons, azaleas, heathers, alpine & rockery plants, climbers & *Clematis*, outdoor ferns, wild flowers & trees. Large range of herbaceous perennials & roses.
**Notes:** Set in beautiful countryside just minutes from the centre of Birmingham & M5 Jct. 4.
**Map Ref:** M, C2 **OS Grid Ref:** SO951772

**MBlu** **BLUEBELL ARBORETUM & NURSERY** ⊠ ⌂ € ♿
Annwell Lane, Smisby, Nr Ashby de la Zouch, Derbyshire, LE65 2TA
Ⓣ (01530) 413700
Ⓕ (01530) 417600
Ⓔ sales@bluebellnursery.co.uk
Ⓦ www.bluebellnursery.co.uk
**Contact:** Robert & Suzette Vernon
**Opening Times:** 0900-1700 Mon-Sat & 1030-1630 Sun Mar-Oct, 0900-1600 Mon-Sat (not Sun) Nov-Feb. Closed 24th Dec-4th Jan & Easter Sun.
**Min Mail Order UK:** Nmc
**Min Mail Order EU:** Nmc
**Cat. Cost:** £1.50 + 3 × 1st class
**Credit Cards:** Visa Access Switch MasterCard
**Specialities:** Uncommon trees & shrubs. Woody climbers. Display garden & arboretum.
**Map Ref:** M, B1 **OS Grid Ref:** SK344187

**MBNS** **BARNSDALE GARDENS** ⊠ ⌂ ♿ ◆
Exton Avenue, Exton, Oakham, Rutland, LE15 8AH
Ⓣ (01572) 813200
Ⓕ (01572) 813346
Ⓔ office@barnsdalegardens.co.uk
Ⓦ www.barnsdalegardens.co.uk
**Contact:** Nick or Sue Hamilton
**Opening Times:** 0900-1700 Mar-May & Sep-Oct, 0900-1900 Jun-Aug, 1000-1600 Nov-Feb, 7 days. Closed 24th & 25th Dec.
**Min Mail Order UK:** Nmc
**Min Mail Order EU:** Nmc
**Cat. Cost:** A5 + 5 × 1st class
**Credit Cards:** All major credit/debit cards
**Specialities:** Wide range of choice & unusual garden plants. Over 160 varieties of *Penstemon*, over 250 varieties of *Hemerocallis*.
**Map Ref:** M, B3

**MBPg** **BARNFIELD PELARGONIUMS** ⊠
Barnfield, Off Wilnecote Lane, Belgrave, Tamworth, Staffordshire, B77 2LF
Ⓣ (01827) 250123
Ⓕ (01827) 250123
Ⓔ brianandjenniewhite@hotmail.com
**Contact:** Jennie & Brian White
**Opening Times:** Open by appt. only.
**Min Mail Order UK:** £4.00
**Min Mail Order EU:** £6.50
**Cat. Cost:** 4 × 2nd class
**Credit Cards:** None
**Specialities:** Over 200 varieties of scented leaf pelargoniums.

**MBri** **BRIDGEMERE NURSERIES** € ♿ ◆
Bridgemere, Nr Nantwich, Cheshire, CW5 7QB
Ⓣ (01270) 521100
Ⓕ (01270) 520215
Ⓔ info@bridgemere.co.uk
Ⓦ www.bridgemere.co.uk
**Contact:** Keith Atkey, Roger Pierce
**Opening Times:** 0900-1900 7 days, summer. 0900-1800 winter. Closed 25th & 26th Dec.
**Cat. Cost:** None issued
**Credit Cards:** Visa Access MasterCard Switch
**Specialities:** Huge range outdoor & indoor plants, many rare & unusual. Specimen shrubs.
**Map Ref:** M, B1 **OS Grid Ref:** SJ727435

**MBrN** **BRIDGE NURSERY** € ♿
Tomlow Road, Napton-on-the-Hill, Nr Rugby, Warwickshire, CV47 8HX
Ⓣ (01926) 812737
Ⓔ pmartino@beeb.net
Ⓦ www.Bridge-Nursery.co.uk
**Contact:** Christine Dakin & Philip Martino
**Opening Times:** 1000-1600 Mon-Sun 1st Feb-mid Dec. Other times by appt.
**Cat. Cost:** 4 × 1st class
**Credit Cards:** None
**Specialities:** Ornamental grasses, sedges & bamboos. Also range of shrubs & perennials. Display garden.
**Notes:** Also sells wholesale.
**Map Ref:** M, C2 **OS Grid Ref:** SP463625

**MCCP** **COLLECTORS CORNER PLANTS** ⊠ ⌂
33 Rugby Road, Clifton-upon-Dunsmore, Rugby, Warwickshire, CV23 0DE
Ⓣ (01788) 571881
**Contact:** Pat Neesam
**Opening Times:** By appt. only.
**Min Mail Order UK:** £20.00
**Cat. Cost:** 6 × 1st class
**Credit Cards:** None
**Specialities:** General range of choice herbaceous perennials, grasses, shrubs, palms, ferns & bamboos.
**Map Ref:** M, C3

**M**Coo **COOL TEMPERATE** ⊠ ✈
(office) 45 Stamford Street,
Awsworth, Nottinghamshire,
NG16 2QL
Ⓣ (0115) 916 2673
Ⓕ (0115) 916 2673
Ⓔ phil.corbett@cooltemperate.co.uk
Ⓦ www.cooltemperate.co.uk
**Contact:** Phil Corbett
**Opening Times:** 0900-1700, 7 days. Please ring/write first.
**Min Mail Order UK:** Nmc
**Min Mail Order EU:** Nmc
**Cat. Cost:** 3 × 1st class
**Credit Cards:** None
**Specialities:** Tree fruit, soft fruit, nitrogen-fixers, hedging, own-root fruit trees. Many species available in small quantities only.
**Notes:** Nursery at Trinity Farm, Awsworth Lane, Cossall, Notts. Also sells wholesale.
**Map Ref:** M, B2 **OS Grid Ref:** SK482435

**M**Cot **COTON MANOR GARDEN**
Guilsborough, Northampton,
Northamptonshire, NN6 8RQ
Ⓣ (01604) 740219
Ⓕ (01604) 740838
Ⓔ pasleytyler@cotonmanor.fsnet.co.uk
Ⓦ www.cotonmanor.co.uk
**Contact:** Caroline Tait
**Opening Times:** 1200-1730 Tue-Sat, 1st April (or Easter if earlier) to 30th Sep. Also Sun Apr, May & B/hol w/ends. Other times in working hours by appt.
**Cat. Cost:** None issued.
**Credit Cards:** MasterCard Visa
**Specialities:** Wide-range of herbaceous perennials (3000+ varieties), some available in small quantities only. Also tender perennials & selected shrubs.
**Notes:** Garden open. Tea rooms. Garden School. Partial wheelchair access.
**Map Ref:** M, C3 **OS Grid Ref:** SP675715

**M**Cri **CRIN GARDENS** ⊠
79 Partons Road, Kings Heath, Birmingham,
B14 6TD
Ⓣ 0121 443 3815
Ⓕ 0121 443 3815
Ⓔ cringardens@tiscali.co.uk
**Contact:** M Milinkovic
**Opening Times:** Not open. Mail order only.
**Min Mail Order UK:** Nmc
**Min Mail Order EU:** Nmc
**Cat. Cost:** 2 × 1st class
**Credit Cards:** None
**Specialities:** Lilies. Limited stock available on first come, first served, basis.

**M**DKP **D K PLANTS** ⌂
(Office) 19 Harbourne Road, Cheadle, Stoke on Trent, Staffordshire, ST10 1JU
Ⓣ (01538) 754460 (office)
Ⓜ 07779 545015 (nursery)
Ⓔ davidknoxc@aol.com
**Contact:** Dave Knox
**Opening Times:** 0900-2000 (or dusk if earlier) Mon-Tue & Thu-Fri. Other times by appt.
**Cat. Cost:** 4 × 1st class A4 sae plus 44p 1st or 37p 2nd class.
**Credit Cards:** None
**Specialities:** Unusual hardy alpines & perennials. All grown on the nursery.
**Notes:** Nursery is at new roundabout across from Queen's Arms pub, Freehay Crossroads, Freehay, Cheadle, ST10 1TR.
**Map Ref:** M, B1

**M**Dun **DUNGE VALLEY GARDENS** € ♿
Windgather Rocks, Kettleshulme, High Peak,
Cheshire, SK23 7RF
Ⓣ (01663) 733787
Ⓕ (01663) 733787
Ⓔ david@dungevalley.co.uk
Ⓦ www.dungevalley.co.uk
**Contact:** David Ketley
**Opening Times:** 1030-1700 Thu-Sun Mar & Apr, Tue-Sun May, Thu-Sun Jun, Jul & Aug. Open B/hols. Otherwise by appt.
**Cat. Cost:** 2 × 1st class
**Credit Cards:** All major credit/debit cards
**Specialities:** *Rhododendron* species & hybrids. Magnolias, acers, *Meconopsis*, trilliums, trees, shrubs & perennials, some rare & wild collected.
**Notes:** Also sells wholesale.
**Map Ref:** M, A2 **OS Grid Ref:** SJ989777

**M**Gan **GANDY'S (ROSES) LTD** ⊠
North Kilworth, Nr Lutterworth,
Leicestershire, LE17 6HZ
Ⓣ (01858) 880398
Ⓕ (01858) 880433
Ⓔ sales@gandys-roses.co.uk
Ⓦ www.gandys-roses.co.uk
**Contact:** Miss R D Gandy
**Opening Times:** 0900-1700 Mon-Sat.
**Min Mail Order UK:** Nmc
**Min Mail Order EU:** £25.00 + p&p
**Cat. Cost:** Free
**Credit Cards:** All major credit/debit cards

KEY
⊠ Mail order to UK or EU ⌂ Delivers to shows
✈ Exports beyond EU € Euro accepted
♿ Accessible by wheelchair ◆ See Display advertisement

M

**Specialities:** Wide range of rose varieties, hardy nursery stock & fruit.
**Notes:** Also sells wholesale.

**MGos** **Goscote Nurseries Ltd** ♿ ◆
Syston Road, Cossington, Leicestershire, LE7 4UZ
Ⓣ (01509) 812121
Ⓕ (01509) 814231
Ⓔ sales@goscote.co.uk
Ⓦ www.goscote.co.uk
**Contact:** James Toone, Brian Phipps
**Opening Times:** 7 days, year round, apart from between Xmas & New Year.
**Cat. Cost:** Online only.
**Credit Cards:** Visa Access MasterCard Delta Switch
**Specialities:** Japanese maples, rhododendrons & azaleas, *Magnolia*, *Camellia*, *Pieris* & other *Ericaceae*. Ornamental trees & shrubs, conifers, fruit, heathers, alpines, roses, *Clematis* & unusual climbers. Show Garden to visit.
**Notes:** Design & landscaping service available. Also sells wholesale.
**Map Ref:** M, B3 **OS Grid Ref:** SK602130

**MHar** **Harts Green Nursery**
89 Harts Green Road, Harborne, Birmingham, B17 9TZ
Ⓣ (0121) 427 5200
**Contact:** B Richardson
**Opening Times:** By appt. or NGS days, 1400-1700, 18th Apr, 16th May, 20th Jun, 18th Jul, 5 Sep 2007.
**Cat. Cost:** None issued.
**Credit Cards:** None
**Specialities:** Hardy perennials. Some in small quantities only.
**Map Ref:** M, C2 **OS Grid Ref:** SP030845

**MHav** **Haven Nurseries Ltd.** ⊠ ♿
Crab Lane, Bobbington, Nr Stourbridge, West Midlands, DY7 5DZ
Ⓣ (01384) 221543
Ⓕ (01384) 221320
Ⓔ info@havennurseries.co.uk
Ⓦ www.havennurseries.co.uk
**Contact:** Lynda Brettell
**Opening Times:** 0900-1730 Mon-Sat, 1000-1700 Sun, Mar-Oct. 0900-1630 Mon-Sat, 1030-1600 Sun, Nov-Feb.
**Min Mail Order UK:** Nmc
**Cat. Cost:** 4 × 1st class.
**Credit Cards:** All major credit/debit cards except American Express
**Specialities:** *Fuchsia*, *Geranium*, roses. Wide range of shrubs, conifers, home-grown bedding & many unusual cottage garden plants.
**Notes:** Also sells wholesale. Mail order bare-root roses only.
**Map Ref:** M, C2

**MHer** **The Herb Nursery** ♿
Thistleton, Oakham, Rutland, LE15 7RE
Ⓣ (01572) 767658
Ⓕ (01572) 768021
Ⓦ www.herbnursery.co.uk
**Contact:** Peter Bench
**Opening Times:** 0900-1800 (or dusk) 7 days excl. Xmas-New Year.
**Cat. Cost:** A5 sae.
**Credit Cards:** None
**Specialities:** Herbs, wild flowers, cottage garden plants, scented-leaf pelargoniums. Especially *Thymus*, *Mentha*, *Lavandula*.
**Map Ref:** M, B3

**MHom** **Homestead Plants** ⊠
The Homestead, Normanton, Bottesford, Nottingham, NG13 0EP
Ⓣ (01949) 842745
Ⓕ (01949) 842745
**Contact:** Mrs S Palmer
**Opening Times:** By appt.
**Min Mail Order UK:** Nmc
**Cat. Cost:** 4 × 2nd class
**Credit Cards:** None
**Specialities:** Unusual hardy & half-hardy perennials, especially *Paeonia* species. *Hosta*, *Jovibarba*, *Salvia*, *Sempervivum* & *Heliotrope*. Drought-tolerant asters. Most available only in small quantities. Nat. Collection of *Heliotropium* cultivars.
**Map Ref:** M, B3 **OS Grid Ref:** SK812407

**MHrb** **The Herb Garden** ⊠ ♿
Kingston House Estate, Race Farm Lane, Kingston Bagpuize, Oxfordshire, OX13 5AU
Ⓣ (01865) 823101
Ⓕ (01865) 820159
Ⓔ vcjw37@yahoo.com
Ⓦ www.KingstonHerbGarden.co.uk
**Contact:** Val Williams
**Opening Times:** Phone for appt. or check website for details.
**Min Mail Order UK:** Nmc
**Cat. Cost:** 2 × 1st class
**Credit Cards:** None
**Specialities:** Small nursery specialising in the more unusual lavenders, herbs, dye plants, olive & *Citrus* fruit trees according to season, displayed in a walled garden setting.
**Map Ref:** M, D2

**MIDC** **Ian and Deborah Coppack** ⊠ ♿
Woodside, Langley Road, Langley,
Macclesfield, Cheshire, SK11 0DG
Ⓣ (01260) 253308
Ⓕ (01260) 253308
Ⓔ ian.coppack_home@dslconnect.co.uk
**Contact:** Ian & Deborah Coppack
**Opening Times:** 0900-1700 Mar-Sep.
**Min Mail Order UK:** Nmc
**Cat. Cost:** 2 × 1st class
**Credit Cards:** None
**Specialities:** *Hosta*.
**Notes:** Also sells wholesale.
**Map Ref:** M, A2 **OS Grid Ref:** SJ938715

**MJac** **Jackson's Nurseries**
Clifton Campville, Nr Tamworth,
Staffordshire, B79 0AP
Ⓣ (01827) 373307
**Contact:** N Jackson
**Opening Times:** 0900-1800 Mon Wed-Sat, 1000-1700 Sun.
**Cat. Cost:** 2 × 1st class
**Credit Cards:** None
**Specialities:** *Fuchsia*.
**Notes:** Also sells wholesale.
**Map Ref:** M, B1

**MJnS** **Jungle Seeds and Gardens** ⊠
PO Box 45, Watlington SPDO, Oxfordshire,
OX49 5YR
Ⓣ (01491) 614765
Ⓕ (01491) 614765
Ⓔ enquiry@junglegardens.co.uk
Ⓦ www.junglegardens.co.uk
**Contact:** Penny White
**Opening Times:** Mail order only. Open by appt. only to collect plants.
**Min Mail Order UK:** £11.99 plants. One plant only, £7.85.
**Cat. Cost:** 2 × 1st class
**Credit Cards:** All major credit/debit cards
**Specialities:** Hardy, semi-hardy & conservatory exotics. Some items ltd. availability.

**MJon** **C & K Jones** ⊠ ✈ ⛺ € ♿
Golden Fields Nurseries, Barrow Lane, Tarvin,
Cheshire, CH3 8JF
Ⓣ (01829) 740663
Ⓕ (01829) 741877
Ⓔ keith@ckjones.freeserve.co.uk
Ⓦ www.jonestherose.co.uk
**Contact:** Keith Jones
**Opening Times:** Office hours 0930-1600 Fri-Mon. 1st w/end in each month only & the Fri & Mon either side. Closed Jan & Feb.
**Min Mail Order UK:** 1 plant + p&p
**Min Mail Order EU:** Nmc.
**Cat. Cost:** £1.00
**Credit Cards:** MasterCard Visa Maestro Electron Solo
**Specialities:** Roses.
**Notes:** Also sells wholesale.
**Map Ref:** M, B1

**MKay** **Kayes Garden Nursery** ♿
1700 Melton Road, Rearsby, Leicestershire,
LE7 4YR
Ⓣ (01664) 424578
Ⓔ hazelkaye.kgn@nascr.net
**Contact:** Hazel Kaye
**Opening Times:** 1000-1700 Tue-Sat & B/hols 1000-1200 Sun Mar-Oct. By appt. Nov, Dec & Feb. Closed Jan.
**Cat. Cost:** 2 × 1st class
**Credit Cards:** None
**Specialities:** Herbaceous, climbers & aquatic plants. Grasses. Nat. Collection of *Tradescantia* Andersoniana Group.
**Map Ref:** M, B3 **OS Grid Ref:** SK648140

**MLan** **Lane End Nursery** ♿
Old Cherry Lane, Lymm, Cheshire,
WA13 0TA
Ⓣ (01925) 752618
Ⓔ rsawyer@onetel.net
Ⓦ www.laneendnursery.co.uk
**Contact:** I Sawyer
**Opening Times:** 0930-1730 Thu-Tue Feb-Dec.
**Cat. Cost:** None issued
**Credit Cards:** None
**Specialities:** AGM plants with a wide range of choice & unusual shrubs, trees, perennials & ferns.
**Notes:** Nursery mostly accessible for wheelchair users.
**Map Ref:** M, A1 **OS Grid Ref:** SJ664850

**MLBr** **Leatherbritches Kitchen Garden & Nursery** ♿
(Office) 6 Sycamore Cottages,
Parwich, Ashbourne, Derbyshire,
DE6 1QL
Ⓣ (01335) 390571 answerphone
Ⓜ 07713 743295
**Contact:** Bill Whitfield
**Opening Times:** 1000-1700, 7 days (times vary in winter & poor weather).
**Credit Cards:** None

M

| KEY | | |
|---|---|---|
| | ⊠ Mail order to UK or EU | ⛺ Delivers to shows |
| | ✈ Exports beyond EU | € Euro accepted |
| | ♿ Accessible by wheelchair | ◆ See Display advertisement |

**Specialities:** Herbaceous, shrubs, alpines, bedding.
**Notes:** Nursery is situated opposite the Bentley Brook Inn, Bakewell Rd (A5056), Fenny Bentley, Ashbourne, DE6 1LF.
**Map Ref:** M, A2 **OS Grid Ref:** SK185503

**MLea** **Lea Rhododendron Gardens Ltd** ⊠ ✈ ♿
Lea, Matlock, Derbyshire, DE4 5GH
Ⓣ (01629) 534380/534260
Ⓕ (01629) 534260
Ⓦ www.leagarden.co.uk
**Contact:** Peter Tye
**Opening Times:** 1000-1730 7 days 20 Mar-30 Jun. Out of season by appt.
**Min Mail Order UK:** £15.00 + p&p
**Min Mail Order EU:** £15.00 + p&p
**Cat. Cost:** 30p + Sae
**Credit Cards:** All major credit/debit cards
**Specialities:** Rhododendrons & azaleas.
**Map Ref:** M, B1 **OS Grid Ref:** SK324571

M

**MLHP** **Longstone Hardy Plants Nursery** ⊠ ♿
(office) Stancil House, Barn Furlong, Great Longstone, Nr Bakewell, Derbyshire, DE45 1TR
Ⓣ (01629) 640136
Ⓜ 07762 083674
Ⓔ lucyinlongstone@hotmail.com
Ⓦ www.longstonehardyplants.co.uk
**Contact:** Lucy Wright
**Opening Times:** 1300-1700 Tue-Sat & B/hols, 1st Apr-30th Sep. 1300-1700 Sat, Mar-Oct. Other times by appt.
**Min Mail Order UK:** Nmc
**Cat. Cost:** 2 × 1st class
**Credit Cards:** None
**Specialities:** Specialist peat-free nursery displaying all our own hardy perennials, ornamental grasses, herbs & shrubs, incl. many unusual varieties. Some stock available in small quantities only. Can propagate to order.
**Notes:** Nursery at Station Road 150 yds on right after turning onto it at the village green.
**Map Ref:** M, A2 **OS Grid Ref:** SK198717

**MLLN** **Lodge Lane Nursery & Gardens** ⊠ ♿
Lodge Lane, Dutton, Nr Warrington, Cheshire, WA4 4HP
Ⓣ (01928) 713718
Ⓕ (01928) 713718
Ⓔ info@lodgelanenursery.co.uk
Ⓦ www.lodgelanenursery.co.uk
**Contact:** Jack Stewart
**Opening Times:** 1000-1700 Tue-Sun & B/hols, mid Mar-mid Sep. By appt. outside these dates.
**Min Mail Order UK:** Nmc
**Cat. Cost:** 3 × 1st class
**Credit Cards:** All major credit/debit cards
**Specialities:** Unusual perennials & shrubs incl. *Achillea*, *Allium*, *Astrantia*, *Campanula*, *Digitalis*, *Penstemon*, *Euphorbia*, *Geranium*, *Heuchera*, *Inula*, *Kniphofia*, *Nepeta*, *Papaver*, *Penstemon*, *Salvia* & ornamental grasses.
**Map Ref:** M, A1 **OS Grid Ref:** SJ586779

**MLod** **Lodge Farm Plants & Wildflowers** ⊠ 🏠 € ♿
Case Lane, Fiveways, Hatton, Warwickshire, CV35 7JD
Ⓣ (01926) 484649
Ⓜ 07977 631368
Ⓕ (01926) 484649
Ⓔ lodgefarmplants@btinternet.com
Ⓦ www.lodgefarmplants.com
**Contact:** Janet Cook & Nick Cook
**Opening Times:** Open 7 days all year, except Xmas Day & Boxing Day.
**Min Mail Order UK:** Nmc
**Cat. Cost:** Online only.
**Credit Cards:** None
**Specialities:** Wildflowers. Vegetable plants, soft fruit, topiary. Native trees & hedging. Wildflower seeds. Fruit trees, espalier, fan, stepovers & cordons.
**Notes:** Also sells wholesale.
**Map Ref:** M, C2 **OS Grid Ref:** SP223700

**MLul** **Lulworth Plants** ♿
28 Gladstone Street, Wigston Magna, Leicestershire, LE18 1AE
Ⓜ 07814 042889
**Contact:** Chris Huscroft
**Opening Times:** By appt. only.
**Cat. Cost:** Sae
**Credit Cards:** None
**Specialities:** *Arisaema*, plus small selection of shade-loving plants, small quantities only.
**Map Ref:** M, B3

**MMHG** **Morton Hall Gardens** ⊠ 🏠 ♿
Morton Hall, Ranby, Retford, Nottinghamshire, DN22 8HW
Ⓣ (01777) 702530
Ⓔ gill@mortonhall.fsbusiness.co.uk
Ⓦ www.morton-nurseries.co.uk
**Contact:** Gill McMaster
**Opening Times:** By appt.only

**Min Mail Order UK:** £5.00 + p&p
**Cat. Cost:** 3 × 1st class
**Credit Cards:** None
**Specialities:** Shrubs & perennials.
**Map Ref:** M, A3

**MMiN** **MILLFIELD NURSERIES** ⊠ € ♿
Mill Lane, South Leverton, Nr Retford, Nottinghamshire, DN22 0DA
Ⓣ (01427) 880422
Ⓕ (01427) 880422
**Contact:** Mr S G Clark
**Opening Times:** By appt. only.
**Min Mail Order UK:** Nmc
**Min Mail Order EU:** Nmc
**Cat. Cost:** 4 × 1st class.
**Credit Cards:** None
**Specialities:** *Hosta*. Some available in small quantities only.
**Map Ref:** M, A3 **OS Grid Ref:** SK789813

**MMoz** **MOZART HOUSE NURSERY GARDEN**
84 Central Avenue, Wigston, Leicestershire, LE18 2AA
Ⓣ (0116) 288 9548
**Contact:** Des Martin
**Opening Times:** By appt. only.
**Cat. Cost:** 5 × 1st class
**Credit Cards:** None
**Specialities:** *Bamboo*, ornamental grasses, rushes & sedges, ferns. Some stock available in small quantities.
**Map Ref:** M, C3

**MMuc** **MUCKLESTONE NURSERIES** ⊠ ◆
Church Farm, Rock Lane, Mucklestone, Nr Market Drayton, Shropshire, TF9 4DN
Ⓜ 07985 425829
Ⓔ enquiries@botanyplants.com
Ⓦ www.botanyplants.com
**Contact:** Brian Watkins
**Opening Times:** 0900-1700 Wed-Sat, Apr-Sep. 1000-1700 Sun, Apr-Jun. Other times by appt.
**Min Mail Order UK:** Nmc
**Cat. Cost:** Online only.
**Credit Cards:** None
**Specialities:** Trees, shrubs, grasses & perennials for acid & damp soils of the north & west UK.
**Map Ref:** M, B2 **OS Grid Ref:** SJ728373

**MNew** **NEWINGTON NURSERIES** € ♿
Newington, Wallingford, Oxfordshire, OX10 7AW
Ⓣ (01865) 400533
Ⓔ plants@newington-nurseries.co.uk
Ⓦ www.newington-nurseries.co.uk
**Contact:** Mrs A T Hendry
**Opening Times:** 1000-1700 Tues-Sun Mar-Oct, 1000-1600 Tues-Sun Nov-Feb.
**Cat. Cost:** 2 × 1st class
**Credit Cards:** Access MasterCard Visa Switch
**Specialities:** Unusual cottage garden plants, alpines, hardy exotics, conservatory plants & herbs. Nat. Collection of *Alocasia* (*Araceae*).
**Notes:** Also sells wholesale.
**Map Ref:** M, D3

**MNFA** **THE NURSERY FURTHER AFIELD** ⊠ ♿
Evenley Road, Mixbury, Nr Brackley, Northamptonshire, NN13 5YR
Ⓣ (01280) 848808
Ⓔ sinclair@nurseryfurtherafield.co.uk
Ⓦ www.nurseryfurtherafield.co.uk
**Contact:** Gerald & Mary Sinclair
**Opening Times:** 1000-1700 Wed-Sat, mid-Mar-end Sep. Other times by appt.
**Min Mail Order UK:** £15.00
**Cat. Cost:** 2 × 1st class
**Credit Cards:** None
**Specialities:** Worthwhile hardy perennials, many unusual. Large selection of *Geranium* & *Hemerocallis*. Nat. Collection of *Hemerocallis*.
**Notes:** Mail order for *Hemerocallis* only.
**Map Ref:** M, C3 **OS Grid Ref:** SP608344

**MNHC** **THE NATIONAL HERB CENTRE** ⊠ ♿
Banbury Road, Warmington, Nr Banbury, Oxfordshire, OX17 1DF
Ⓣ (01295) 690999
Ⓕ (01295) 690034
Ⓦ www.herbcentre.co.uk
**Contact:** Plant Centre Staff
**Opening Times:** 0900-1730 Mon-Sat, 1030-1700 Sun.
**Min Mail Order UK:** Nmc
**Credit Cards:** All major credit/debit cards
**Specialities:** Herbs, culinary & medicinal. Extensive selection of rosemary, thyme & lavender, in particular.
**Notes:** Min. carriage charge of £25 up to 10kg. Next day delivery. UK mainland only.
**Map Ref:** M, C2 **OS Grid Ref:** SP413471

**MNrw** **NORWELL NURSERIES** ⊠ ♿ ◆
Woodhouse Road, Norwell, Newark, Nottinghamshire, NG23 6JX
Ⓣ (01636) 636337
Ⓔ wardha@aol.com
**Contact:** Dr Andrew Ward

KEY
⊠ Mail order to UK or EU — Delivers to shows
Exports beyond EU — € Euro accepted
♿ Accessible by wheelchair — ◆ See Display advertisement

**Opening Times:** 1000-1700 Mon, Wed-Fri & Sun (Wed-Mon May & Jun). By appt. Aug & 20th Oct-1st Mar.
**Min Mail Order UK:** £12.00 + p&p
**Cat. Cost:** 3 × 1st class
**Credit Cards:** None
**Specialities:** A large collection of unusual & choice herbaceous perennials & alpines esp., hardy geraniums, *Geum*, cottage garden plants, *Hemerocallis*, grasses, salvias & woodland plants. Gardens open.
**Notes:** Also sells wholesale.
**Map Ref:** M, B3 **OS Grid Ref:** SK767616

M

**MOne** ONE HOUSE NURSERY ⊠ ♿
Buxton New Road, Macclesfield, Cheshire, SK11 0AD
Ⓣ (01625) 427087
Ⓔ louisebaylis@supanet.com
Ⓦ www.onehousenursery.co.uk
**Contact:** Miss J L Baylis
**Opening Times:** Only open weekend nearest to 1st of each month, Mar-Oct, 1000-1700, or ring for appt.
**Min Mail Order UK:** Nmc
**Credit Cards:** None
**Specialities:** Alpines & perennials. Good range of *Primula auricula*, *Sempervivum* & *Erodium*.
**Notes:** Mail order for *Sempervivum*, *Erodium* & auriculas only.
**Map Ref:** M, A2 **OS Grid Ref:** SJ943741

**MPet** PETER GRAYSON (SWEET PEA SEEDSMAN) ⊠ ✈
34 Glenthorne Close, Brampton, Chesterfield, Derbyshire, S40 3AR
Ⓣ (01246) 278503
Ⓕ (01246) 278503
**Contact:** Peter Grayson
**Opening Times:** Not open. Mail order only.
**Min Mail Order UK:** Nmc
**Min Mail Order EU:** Nmc
**Cat. Cost:** C5 sae, 1 × 2nd class
**Credit Cards:** None
**Specialities:** *Lathyrus* species & cvs. Large collection of old-fashioned sweet peas & over 100 Spencer sweet peas incl. own cvs and collection of old-fashioned cottage garden annuals & perennials.
**Notes:** Also sells wholesale.

**MPhe** PHEDAR NURSERY ⊠ ✈ €
Bunkers Hill, Romiley, Stockport, Cheshire, SK6 3DS
Ⓣ (0161) 430 3772
Ⓕ (0161) 430 3772
Ⓔ mclewin@phedar.com
Ⓦ www.phedar.com
**Contact:** Will McLewin
**Opening Times:** Frequent esp. in spring but very irregular. Please phone to arrange appt.
**Min Mail Order UK:** Nmc
**Min Mail Order EU:** Nmc
**Cat. Cost:** 2 × A5 envelopes or address labels + 4 × 1st class
**Credit Cards:** None
**Specialities:** *Helleborus*, *Paeonia*. Limited stock of some rare items.
**Notes:** Non-EU exports subject to destination & on an ad hoc basis only. Please contact nursery for details. Also sells wholesale.
**Map Ref:** M, A2 **OS Grid Ref:** SJ936897

**MPkF** PACKHORSE FARM NURSERY ⌂ ♿
Sandyford House, Lant Lane, Tansley, Matlock, Derbyshire, DE4 5FW
Ⓣ (01629) 57206
Ⓜ 07974 095752
Ⓕ (01629) 57206
**Contact:** Hilton W Haynes
**Opening Times:** 1000-1700 Tues & Wed, 1st Mar-31st Oct.. Any other time by appt. only.
**Cat. Cost:** 2 × 1st class for plant list.
**Credit Cards:** None
**Specialities:** *Acer*, rare stock is ltd. in supply. Other more unusual hardy shrubs, trees & conifers.
**Map Ref:** M, B2 **OS Grid Ref:** SK322617

**MPoH** POPPY HEADS LTD ⊠
Alcombe, 7 Bosden Fold Road, Hazel Grove, Stockport, Cheshire, SK7 4LQ
Ⓣ 0161 456 9009
Ⓔ kevinpratt@supanet.com
Ⓦ www.poppyheadltd.co.uk
**Contact:** Kevin & Suzanne Pratt
**Opening Times:** Not open. Mail order only.
**Min Mail Order UK:** £5.00
**Cat. Cost:** 30p or 1 × 1st class.
**Credit Cards:** None
**Specialities:** Large collection of cottage poppies. *Fritillaria*, *Polygonatum*, *Allium*. Large collection of *Eucomis* specialist bulbs.

**MRav** RAVENSTHORPE NURSERY ⊠ ♿
6 East Haddon Road, Ravensthorpe, Northamptonshire, NN6 8ES
Ⓣ (01604) 770548
Ⓕ (01604) 770548
Ⓔ ravensthorpenursery@hotmail.com
**Contact:** Jean & Richard Wiseman
**Opening Times:** 1000-1800 (dusk if earlier) Tue-Sun. Also B/hol Mons.
**Min Mail Order UK:** Nmc
**Min Mail Order EU:** Nmc

**Cat. Cost:** None issued.
**Credit Cards:** Visa MasterCard
**Specialities:** Over 2,600 different trees, shrubs & perennials with many unusual varieties.
**Notes:** Search & delivery service for large orders, winter months only.
**Map Ref:** M, C3 **OS Grid Ref:** SP665699

MREP **Rare and Exotic Plants (formerly Plants for All Reasons)** ⊠ ♿
Woodshoot Nurseries, King's Bromley, Burton-upon-Trent, Staffordshire, DE13 7HN
Ⓣ (01543) 472233
Ⓕ (01543) 472115
Ⓔ sales@rareandexoticplants.com
Ⓦ www.rareandexoticplants.com
**Contact:** Richard Flint
**Opening Times:** 0900-1700, 7 days.
**Min Mail Order UK:** £20.00 + p&p
**Cat. Cost:** 1 × 1st class
**Credit Cards:** All major credit/debit cards
**Specialities:** *Agave*, *Acacia*, *Bamboo*, *Citrus*, *Cordyline*, *Dicksonia*, *Nerium*, *Phormium*, *Pittosporum*, palms, olives & *Yucca*. Topiary.
**Notes:** Also sells wholesale.
**Map Ref:** M, B2 **OS Grid Ref:** SK127164

MSal **Salley Gardens** ⊠ ✈ € ♿
32 Lansdowne Drive, West Bridgford, Nottinghamshire, NG2 7FJ
Ⓣ (0115) 9233878 evenings
Ⓜ 07811 703982
Ⓔ richienothavens@hotmail.com
Ⓦ www.thesalleygardens.co.uk
**Contact:** Richard Lewin
**Opening Times:** 0900-1700 Sun only, 1st Apr-30th Sep and by appt. Please phone before visiting.
**Min Mail Order UK:** Nmc
**Min Mail Order EU:** Nmc
**Cat. Cost:** Sae
**Credit Cards:** None
**Specialities:** Medicinal plants esp. from North America & China. Dye plants, herbs, spices, seeds. Some species available in small quantities only.
**Notes:** Nursery is at Simkins Farm, Adbolton Lane, West Bridgford, Notts.
**Map Ref:** M, B3

MSCN **Stonyford Cottage Nursery** ⊠ ⌂ ♿
Stonyford Lane, Cuddington, Northwich, Cheshire, CW8 2TF
Ⓣ (01606) 888128
Ⓕ (01606) 888312
Ⓔ stonyfordplants@yahoo.co.uk
Ⓦ www.gardenchoice.co.uk
**Contact:** F A Overland
**Opening Times:** 1000-1730 Tue-Sun & B/hol Mons 1 Mar-31 Oct.
**Min Mail Order UK:** Nmc
**Min Mail Order EU:** Nmc
**Cat. Cost:** Not available this year
**Credit Cards:** All major credit/debit cards
**Specialities:** Wide range of herbaceous perennials, *Iris*, *Salvia*, hardy *Geranium* & grasses.
**Notes:** Also sells wholesale.
**Map Ref:** M, A1

MSGs **Showglads** ⊠ €
105 Derby Road, Bramcote, Nottingham, NG9 3GZ
Ⓣ (0115) 925 5498
Ⓔ rogerbb@lineone.net
Ⓦ www.showglads.com
**Contact:** Roger Braithwaite
**Opening Times:** Not open. Mail order only.
**Min Mail Order UK:** £4.00
**Cat. Cost:** 3 × 1st class
**Credit Cards:** None
**Specialities:** *Gladiolus*.

MSHN **Station House Nurseries** ⊠ ✈ ⌂ ♿
Station Road, Burton, South Wirral, Cheshire, CH64 5SD
Ⓣ 0151 353 0022
Ⓔ sion@eurodahlia.com
Ⓦ www.eurodahlia.com
**Contact:** Sion Jones
**Opening Times:** 0900-1700, 7 days. Closed Xmas to New Year.
**Min Mail Order UK:** Nmc
**Min Mail Order EU:** Nmc
**Cat. Cost:** 2 × 1st class.
**Credit Cards:** All major credit/debit cards
**Specialities:** *Dahlia*.
**Notes:** Also sells wholesale.
**Map Ref:** M, A1 **OS Grid Ref:** SJ304745

MSKA **Sweet Knowle Aquatics** ⊠ ♿
Wimpstone-Ilmington Road, Stratford-upon-Avon, Warwickshire, CV37 8NR
Ⓣ (01789) 450036
Ⓕ (01789) 450036
Ⓔ sweetknowleaquatics@hotmail.com
Ⓦ www.sweetknowleaquatics.co.uk
**Contact:** Zoe Harding
**Opening Times:** 0930-1700 Sun-Fri, closed Sat. Open B/hols.

KEY
⊠ Mail order to UK or EU ⌂ Delivers to shows
✈ Exports beyond EU € Euro accepted
♿ Accessible by wheelchair ◆ See Display advertisement

**Min Mail Order UK:** Nmc
**Cat. Cost:** By email only.
**Credit Cards:** All major credit/debit cards
**Specialities:** Aquatics. Hardy & tropical water lilies, marginals & oxygenators. 2 acres display garden open to the public (no charge).
**Map Ref:** M, C2 **OS Grid Ref:** SP207480

**MSmi** JOHN SMITH & SON ⊠ ♿
*Fuchsia* Centre, Thornton Nurseries, Thornton, Leicestershire, LE67 1AN
Ⓣ (01530) 230331
Ⓕ (01530) 230331
Ⓔ john@fuchsias.fsbusiness.co.uk
Ⓦ www.fuchsiaplants.co.uk
**Contact:** J Smith
**Opening Times:** 0800-1730 Mon-Sat all year & 7 days a week during Apr & May.
**Min Mail Order UK:** Nmc
**Cat. Cost:** Sae
**Credit Cards:** None
**Specialities:** Hardy, Half-hardy & large American *Fuchsia*.
**Notes:** Also sells wholesale.
**Map Ref:** M, B2

M

**MSSP** S & S PERENNIALS ⊠
24 Main Street, Normanton Le Heath, Leicestershire, LE67 2TB
Ⓣ (01530) 262250
**Contact:** Shirley Pierce
**Opening Times:** Afternoons only, otherwise please phone.
**Min Mail Order UK:** Nmc
**Cat. Cost:** 2 × 1st class
**Credit Cards:** None
**Specialities:** *Erythronium*, *Fritillaria*, hardy *Cyclamen*, dwarf *Narcissus* & *Anemone*. Stock available in small quantities only.
**Map Ref:** M, B1

**MSte** STEVENTON ROAD NURSERIES € ♿
Steventon Road, East Hanney, Wantage, Oxfordshire, OX12 0HS
Ⓣ (01235) 868828
Ⓕ (01235) 763670
Ⓔ johngraham.steventonroadnursery@virgin.net
Ⓦ www.steventonroadnurseries.co.uk
**Contact:** John Graham
**Opening Times:** 0900-1700 Mon-Fri, 1000-1700 Sat Mar-Nov. Winter by appt. Closed Sun.
**Cat. Cost:** 4 × 1st class
**Credit Cards:** None
**Specialities:** Tender & hardy perennials.
**Map Ref:** M, D2

**MSwo** SWALLOWS NURSERY ⊠ ♿
Mixbury, Brackley, Northamptonshire, NN13 5RR
Ⓣ (01280) 847721
Ⓕ (01280) 848611
Ⓔ enq@swallowsnursery.co.uk
Ⓦ www.swallowsnursery.co.uk
**Contact:** Chris Swallow
**Opening Times:** 0900-1300 & 1400-1700 (earlier in winter) Mon-Fri, 0900-1300 Sat.
**Min Mail Order UK:** £15.00
**Cat. Cost:** 3 × 1st class (plus phone number)
**Credit Cards:** Visa MasterCard Switch
**Specialities:** Growing a wide range, particularly shrubs, trees, roses and heathers.
**Notes:** Trees not for mail order unless part of larger order. Nursery transport used where possible, esp. for trees. Also sells wholesale.
**Map Ref:** M, C3 **OS Grid Ref:** SP607336

**MTho** A & A THORP
Bungalow No 5, Main Street, Theddingworth, Leicestershire, LE17 6QZ
Ⓣ (01858) 880496
**Contact:** Anita & Andrew Thorp
**Opening Times:** 1000-1700.
**Cat. Cost:** 4 × 1st class
**Credit Cards:** None
**Specialities:** Unusual plants or those in short supply.
**Map Ref:** M, C3

**MTis** TISSINGTON NURSERY ♿
(office) 7 Bensley Close, Chellaston, Derbyshire, DE73 6TL
Ⓣ (01335) 390650
Ⓜ 07929 720284
Ⓔ info@tissingtonnursery.co.uk
Ⓦ www.tissingtonnursery.co.uk
**Contact:** Mairi Longdon
**Opening Times:** 1000-1700 daily, 3rd Mar-end Oct.
**Cat. Cost:** 4 × 1st class
**Credit Cards:** None
**Specialities:** Choice & unusual perennials esp. *Achillea*, *Geranium*, *Geum*, *Helenium*, *Heuchera*, *Pulmonaria*, grasses & ferns.
**Notes:** Nursery is at The Old Kitchen Gardens, Tissington, Ashbourne, Derbyshire, DE6 1RA
**Map Ref:** M, B1 **OS Grid Ref:** SK176521

**MTPN** SMART PLANTS ⊠ ♿
Sandy Hill Lane, Off Overstone Road, Moulton, Northampton, NN3 7JB
Ⓣ (01604) 454106
**Contact:** Stuart Smart

**Opening Times:** 1000-1500 Thu & Fri, 1000-1700 Sat. Other times by appt.
**Min Mail Order UK:** Nmc
**Cat. Cost:** 3 × 1st class
**Credit Cards:** None
**Specialities:** Wide range of herbaceous, alpines, shrubs, grasses, hardy *Geranium*, *Sempervivum* & succulents.
**Map Ref:** M, C3

**MWar** **WARD FUCHSIAS** ⊠
5 Pollen Close, Sale, Cheshire, M33 3LS
Ⓣ (0161) 282 7434
**Contact:** K Ward
**Opening Times:** 0930-1700 Tue-Sun Feb-Jun incl. B/hols.
**Min Mail Order UK:** Nmc
**Cat. Cost:** Free
**Credit Cards:** None
**Specialities:** *Fuchsia*. Available in small quantities.
**Map Ref:** M, A2

**MWat** **WATERPERRY GARDENS LTD** ♿
Waterperry, Nr Wheatley, Oxfordshire, OX33 1JZ
Ⓣ (01844) 339226/254
Ⓕ (01844) 339883
Ⓔ office@waterperrygardens.co.uk
Ⓦ www.waterperrygardens.co.uk
**Contact:** Mr R Jacobs
**Opening Times:** 1000-1730 summer. 1000-1700 winter.
**Min Mail Order UK:** Nmc
**Cat. Cost:** Online only.
**Credit Cards:** All major credit/debit cards
**Specialities:** General, plus Nat. Collection of *Saxifraga* (subsect. *Kabschia* & *Engleria*).
**Map Ref:** M, D3 **OS Grid Ref:** SP630064

**MWea** **WEAR'S NURSERY** ♿
(office) 84 Wantage Road, Wallingford, Oxfordshire, OX10 0LY
Ⓜ 07790 425284
Ⓕ (01491) 837803
Ⓦ www.wearsnursery.co.uk
**Contact:** David Wear
**Opening Times:** 1000-1700 Mon-Sat, Feb-Oct. 1000-1600 Sun (closed Sun in Aug). 1000-1600 Mon-Sat, Nov-Jan, please telephone first as may be closed on some days in winter.
**Cat. Cost:** Plant list online.
**Credit Cards:** None
**Specialities:** Unusual herbaceous varieties & shrubs. Large selection of *Geranium*. Some plants only available in small numbers.
**Notes:** Nursery sited at High Road, Brightwell cum Sotwell, Wallingford.
**Map Ref:** M, D3 **OS Grid Ref:** SU590910

**MWhi** **WHITEHILL FARM NURSERY** ⊠ € ♿
Whitehill Farm, Burford, Oxfordshire, OX18 4DT
Ⓣ (01993) 823218
Ⓕ (01993) 822894
Ⓔ a.youngson@virgin.net
Ⓦ www.whitehillfarmnursery.co.uk
**Contact:** P J M Youngson
**Opening Times:** 0900-1800 (or dusk if earlier) 7 days.
**Min Mail Order UK:** £5.00 + p&p
**Min Mail Order EU:** £5.00 + p&p
**Cat. Cost:** 4 × 1st class
**Credit Cards:** All major credit/debit cards
**Specialities:** Grasses & bamboos, less common shrubs & perennials.
**Notes:** £1.00 of catalogue cost refunded on 1st order.
**Map Ref:** M, D2 **OS Grid Ref:** SP268113

**MWht** **WHITELEA NURSERY** ⊠ ♿
Whitelea Lane, Tansley, Matlock, Derbyshire, DE4 5FL
Ⓣ (01629) 55010
Ⓔ sales@uk-bamboos.co.uk
Ⓦ www.uk-bamboos.co.uk
**Contact:** David Wilson
**Opening Times:** By appt.
**Min Mail Order UK:** Nmc
**Cat. Cost:** Online only. Price list available 2 × 1st.
**Credit Cards:** None
**Specialities:** *Bamboo*, ivies. Substantial quantities of 45 cvs & species of bamboo, remainder stocked in small numbers only.
**Notes:** Also sells wholesale.
**Map Ref:** M, B1 **OS Grid Ref:** SK325603

**MWte** **THE WHITE HOUSE** ⊠
(office) Nicker Hill, Keyworth, Nottinghamshire, NG12 5EA
Ⓣ 0115 937 2049
Ⓜ 07804 865607
Ⓔ gillyhill@aol.com
Ⓦ www.rare-plants-by-post.co.uk
**Contact:** Gillian Hill
**Min Mail Order UK:** £10.00 + p&p
**Cat. Cost:** Online only.
**Credit Cards:** Paypal

KEY
⊠ Mail order to UK or EU — Delivers to shows
✈ Exports beyond EU — € Euro accepted
♿ Accessible by wheelchair — ◆ See Display advertisement

M

**Specialities:** *Agapanthus, Aster, Euphorbia, Geranium, Iris, Kniphofia, Miscanthus, Papaver orientale, Penstemon* & *Phlox.*

**MYeo** **Yeomans' Exotics** ⊠ ♿
2 Carrington Lane, Calverton, Nottingham, NG14 6HQ
Ⓣ 0115 965 4350
Ⓦ www.yeomansexotics.co.uk
**Contact:** Chris Yeomans
**Opening Times:** By appt. only Feb-Dec.
**Min Mail Order UK:** Nmc
**Min Mail Order EU:** Nmc
**Cat. Cost:** 1 × 1st class
**Credit Cards:** None
**Specialities:** Carnivorous plants.
**Notes:** Mail order seeds only. Also sells wholesale.

M

## Northern

**NBea** **Beamish Clematis Nursery** € ♿
Burntwood Cottage, Stoney Lane, Beamish, Co. Durham, DH9 0SJ
Ⓣ (0191) 370 0202
Ⓕ (0191) 370 0202
Ⓦ www.beamishclematisnursery.co.uk
**Contact:** Colin Brown or Jan Wilson
**Opening Times:** 0900-1700 Wed-Mon, closed Tue. Closed Easter Sun & Xmas week.
**Cat. Cost:** Online only.
**Credit Cards:** None
**Specialities:** *Clematis*, climbers, shrubs & ornamental trees.
**Map Ref:** N, B2 **OS Grid Ref:** NZ231535

**NBee** **Beechcroft Just Trees** ⊠ ♿
Bongate, Appleby-in-Westmorland, Cumbria, CA16 6UE
Ⓣ (01768) 351201
Ⓕ (01768) 351201
Ⓔ souribrown4@hotmail.com
**Contact:** Roger Brown
**Opening Times:** 0900-1700 Tue-Sun, closed Mon.
**Min Mail Order UK:** Nmc
**Cat. Cost:** Sae for tree list.
**Credit Cards:** None
**Specialities:** Hardy field-grown trees.
**Notes:** Mail order trees Nov-Mar only.
**Map Ref:** N, C1

**NBHF** **Boundary House Farm** ♿
Holmeswood, Rufford, West Lancashire, L40 1UA
Ⓣ (01704) 821333
Ⓕ (01704) 821333
Ⓔ gbirchal@gotadsl.co.uk
Ⓦ www.holmeswoodplants.co.uk
**Contact:** Linda Birchall
**Opening Times:** 1000-1700 Wed-Sat & Sun, Apr-Sep. Phone first.
**Credit Cards:** None
**Specialities:** *Achillea*. Grasses.
**Map Ref:** N, D1 **OS Grid Ref:** SD4217SE

**NBhm** **Beetham Nurseries** ♿
Pool Darkin Lane, Beetham, Nr Milnthorpe, Cumbria, LA7 7AP
Ⓣ (01539) 563630
Ⓕ (01539) 564487
**Contact:** S & L Abbit
**Opening Times:** 0900-1730 summer, 0900-1730 winter.
**Cat. Cost:** None issued
**Credit Cards:** Visa American Express Switch
**Specialities:** Comprehensive range of Trees, Shrubs & Herbaceous Plants. Many unusual varieties.
**Map Ref:** N, C1

**NBid** **Bide-A-Wee Cottage Gardens** ⊠ ♿
Stanton, Netherwitton, Morpeth, Northumberland, NE65 8PR
Ⓣ (01670) 772238
Ⓕ (01670) 772238
Ⓔ bideaweecg@aol.com
Ⓦ www.bideawee.co.uk
**Contact:** Mark Robson
**Opening Times:** 1330-1700 Sat & Wed, 21st Apr-29th Aug 2007.
**Min Mail Order UK:** £20.00
**Cat. Cost:** 3 × 1st class
**Credit Cards:** All major credit/debit cards
**Specialities:** Unusual herbaceous perennials, *Primula*, ferns, grasses. Nat. Collection of *Centaurea*.
**Map Ref:** N, B2 **OS Grid Ref:** NZ132900

**NBir** **Birkheads Secret Gardens & Nursery** ⊠ ♿
Nr Causey Arch, Sunniside, Newcastle-upon-Tyne, NE16 5EL
Ⓣ (01207) 232262
Ⓜ 07778 447920
Ⓕ (01207) 232262
Ⓔ birkheads.nursery@virgin.net
Ⓦ www.birkheadsnursery.co.uk
**Contact:** Mrs Christine Liddle
**Opening Times:** 1000-1700 daily (except Mon) Mar-Oct. Groups by appt.
**Min Mail Order UK:** Nmc
**Cat. Cost:** None issued
**Credit Cards:** All major credit/debit cards

**Specialities:** Hardy herbaceous perennials, grasses, bulbs & herbs. *Allium*, *Campanula*, *Digitalis*, *Euphorbia*, *Geranium*, *Primula*. Max. 30 of any plant propagated each year.
**Notes:** Mail order Nov-Feb only. Orders taken all year for winter deliveries.
**Map Ref:** N, B2 **OS Grid Ref:** NZ220569

**NBlu** BLUNDELL'S NURSERIES ♿
68 Southport New Road, Tarleton, Preston, Lancashire, PR4 6HY
Ⓣ (01772) 815442
Ⓕ (01772) 613917
Ⓔ jerplusjeff@aol.com
**Contact:** Any member of staff
**Opening Times:** 0900-1700 daily. Closed Dec-Jan.
**Cat. Cost:** None issued
**Credit Cards:** All major credit/debit cards
**Specialities:** Trees, shrubs, incl. topiary & large specimens, conifers. Perennials, alpines, ferns, heathers, herbs, hanging basket/bedding/conservatory plants, hedging, roses. Garden design service available.
**Notes:** Also sells wholesale.
**Map Ref:** N, D1

**NBPC** THE BARN PLANT CENTRE & GIFT SHOP ♿
The Square, Scorton, Preston, Lancashire, PR3 1AU
Ⓣ (01524) 793533
Ⓕ (01524) 793533
Ⓔ sales@plantsandgifts.co.uk
Ⓦ www.plantsandgifts.co.uk
**Contact:** Neil Anderton
**Opening Times:** 0900-1700 Mon-Sat, 1000-1800 Sun.
**Cat. Cost:** 2 1st class
**Credit Cards:** All major credit/debit cards
**Specialities:** 600 varieties of perennials.
**Map Ref:** N, C1 **OS Grid Ref:** GR501487

**NBPN** BLACK PLANTS NURSERY ⊠
35 Longfield Road, Crookes, Sheffield, S10 1QW
Ⓣ (0114) 268 1700
Ⓔ k@karenplatt.co.uk
Ⓦ www.blackplants.co.uk
**Contact:** Karen Platt
**Opening Times:** Not open. Mail order only.
**Min Mail Order UK:** 10 plants
**Min Mail Order EU:** 10 plants
**Cat. Cost:** 3 × 1st class
**Credit Cards:** Paypal
**Specialities:** All black or dark flowered & foliage plants. Over 2,750 plants.

**NBrd** BROADBENT LANDSCAPES ⊠ ♦
Field Cottage, 40 Etherley Lane, Bishop Auckland, County Durham, DL14 7QZ
Ⓣ (01388) 604189
Ⓜ 07974 996883
Ⓔ broadscapes@teesdaleonline.co.uk
**Contact:** Alison Broadbent
**Min Mail Order UK:** Nmc
**Cat. Cost:** Sae or email for list.
**Credit Cards:** None
**Specialities:** Eclectic mixture of perennials, shrubs, conifers, bulbs, grasses & ferns. Most available in small quantities. Garden design service.
**Map Ref:** N, C2 **OS Grid Ref:** NZ203294

**NBre** BREEZY KNEES NURSERIES ♿
Common Lane, Warthill, York, YO19 5XS
Ⓣ (01904) 488800
Ⓦ www.breezyknees.co.uk
**Contact:** Any member of staff
**Opening Times:** 0930-1700 7 days, 1st Apr-30th Sep.
**Credit Cards:** All major credit/debit cards
**Specialities:** Very wide range of perennials from popular favourites to something decidedly different.
**Map Ref:** N, C3 **OS Grid Ref:** SE675565

**NBro** BROWNTHWAITE HARDY PLANTS ⊠ ♿
Fell Yeat, Casterton, Kirkby Lonsdale, Lancashire, LA6 2JW
Ⓣ (015242) 71340 (after 1800).
**Contact:** Chris Benson
**Opening Times:** Tue-Sun 1st Apr-30th Sep.
**Min Mail Order UK:** Nmc
**Cat. Cost:** 4 × 1st class sae for catalogue. 2 × 2nd class for *Hydrangea* list. Sae for auricula list.
**Credit Cards:** None
**Specialities:** Herbaceous perennials incl. *Geranium*, *Hosta*, *Iris*, especially *I. ensata* & *I. sibirica*, also *Tiarella*, *Heucherella* & *Primula auricula*. Mail order for *Hydrangea*. Nat. Collection of *Ligularia*.
**Notes:** Follow brown signs from A65 between Kirkby Lonsdale & Cowan Bridge.
**Map Ref:** N, C1 **OS Grid Ref:** SD632794

**NBsh** BEAMISH COTTAGE GARDENS ♿ ♦
Planetree Farm, Beamish Burn, Stanley, Co. Durham, DH9 0RL
Ⓣ (01207) 284142

KEY
⊠ Mail order to UK or EU — Delivers to shows
Exports beyond EU — € Euro accepted
♿ Accessible by wheelchair — ♦ See Display advertisement

N

Ⓔ Wardenplanetree@aol.com
Ⓦ www.beamishcottagegardens.co.uk
**Contact:** David & Kim Warden
**Opening Times:** 1030-1730 Thu-Sun, plus B/hols.
**Credit Cards:** None
**Specialities:** Hardy perennials. Ornamental grasses, salvias, heleniums and hardy geraniums.

**NBur** **Burton Agnes Hall Nursery** ♿ ◆
Burton Agnes Hall Preservation Trust Ltd, Estate Office, Burton Agnes, Driffield, East Yorkshire, YO25 0ND
Ⓣ (01262) 490324
Ⓕ (01262) 490513
Ⓔ burton.agnes@farmline.com
Ⓦ www.burton-agnes.com
**Contact:** Mrs S Cunliffe-Lister
**Opening Times:** 1100-1700 Apr-Oct.
**Cat. Cost:** 4 × 1st class
**Credit Cards:** None
**Specialities:** Large range perennials & alpines. Many unusual varieties esp. *Penstemon*, *Osteospermum*, *Digitalis*, *Anemone*, *Geranium*. Nat. Coll. of *Campanula*.
**Notes:** Mail order Nov-Mar only.
**Map Ref:** N, C3

**NCGa** **Cath's Garden Plants** ✉ ♿
The Walled Garden, Heaves Hotel, Levens, Nr Kendal, Cumbria, LA8 8EF
Ⓣ (01539) 561126
Ⓕ (01539) 561126
Ⓔ cath@cathsgardenplants.fsbusiness.co.uk
Ⓦ www.cathsgardenplants.co.uk
**Contact:** Bob Sanderson
**Opening Times:** 1030-1630 Mon-Fri all year, except Xmas & New Year weeks. 1030-1700 Sat & Sun, Mar-Oct.
**Min Mail Order UK:** £15.00 + p&p
**Min Mail Order EU:** £25.00
**Cat. Cost:** 6 × 1st class
**Credit Cards:** All major credit/debit cards
**Specialities:** Wide variety of perennials, incl. uncommon varieties & selections of grasses, ferns, shrubs & climbing plants.
**Notes:** On A590 not in Levens village. Also sells wholesale.
**Map Ref:** N, C1 **OS Grid Ref:** SD497867

**NChi** **Chipchase Castle Nursery** ✉ ♿
Chipchase Castle, Wark, Hexham, Northumberland, NE48 3NT
Ⓣ (01434) 230083
Ⓔ info@chipchaseplants.co.uk
Ⓦ www.chipchaseplants.co.uk
**Contact:** Joyce Hunt & Alison Jones
**Opening Times:** 1000-1700 Thu-Sun & B/hol Mons Easter (or 1st Apr)-mid Oct.
**Min Mail Order UK:** Nmc
**Min Mail Order EU:** Nmc
**Cat. Cost:** A5 sae for list
**Credit Cards:** All major credit/debit cards
**Specialities:** Unusual herbaceous esp. *Eryngium*, *Geranium*, *Penstemon* & *Viola*. Some plants only available in small quantities.
**Notes:** Suitable for accompanied wheelchair users.
**Map Ref:** N, B2 **OS Grid Ref:** NY880758

**NChl** **Chiltern Seeds** ✉ €
Bortree Stile, Ulverston, Cumbria, LA12 7PB
Ⓣ (01229) 581137 (24 hrs)
Ⓕ (01229) 584549
Ⓔ info@chilternseeds.co.uk
Ⓦ www.chilternseeds.co.uk
**Opening Times:** Mail order only. Normal office hours, Mon-Fri.
**Min Mail Order UK:** Nmc
**Min Mail Order EU:** Nmc
**Cat. Cost:** 3 × 2nd class
**Credit Cards:** All major credit/debit cards
**Specialities:** Over 4,500 items of all kinds – wild flowers, trees, shrubs, cacti, annuals, houseplants, vegetables & herbs.

**NCob** **Cobble Hey Gardens** ♿
Off Hobbs Lane, Claughton-on-Brock, Garstang, Nr Preston, Lancashire, PR3 0QN
Ⓣ (01995) 602643
Ⓕ (01995) 602643
Ⓔ cobblehey@aol.com
Ⓦ www.cobblehey.co.uk
**Contact:** Edwina Miller
**Opening Times:** 1030-1630 Thu-Mon 1st Feb-24th Dec 2007
**Credit Cards:** All major credit/debit cards
**Specialities:** Wide range of unusual plants grown on hill farm at over 600ft. Specialises in *Phlox paniculata* & geraniums (Nat. Collection status applied for).
**Map Ref:** N, C1

**NCot** **Cottage Garden Plants** ✉
1 Sycamore Close, Whitehaven, Cumbria, CA28 6LE
Ⓣ (01946) 695831
Ⓔ expressplants@aol.com
Ⓦ www.cottagegardenplants.com
**Contact:** Mrs J Purkiss
**Opening Times:** Open by appt. For garden, consult local press & radio for charity openings.
**Min Mail Order UK:** Nmc

**Min Mail Order EU:** Nmc
**Cat. Cost:** 3 × 1st class sae
**Credit Cards:** Paypal
**Specialities:** Hardy perennials incl. *Crocosmia*, *Geranium*, *Primula*, *Schizostylis* & bog plants. Small quantities only.
**Map Ref:** N, C1

NCro **Croston Cactus** ⊠ ⛫ € ♿
43 Southport Road, Eccleston, Chorley, Lancashire, PR7 6ET
Ⓣ (01257) 452555
Ⓔ sales@croston-cactus.co.uk
Ⓦ www.croston-cactus.co.uk
**Contact:** John Henshaw
**Opening Times:** 0930-1700 by appt. only.
**Min Mail Order UK:** £5.00 + p&p
**Min Mail Order EU:** £10.00 + p&p
**Cat. Cost:** 2 × 1st or 2 × IRCs
**Credit Cards:** None
**Specialities:** Mexican cacti, *Echeveria* hybrids & some bromeliads & *Tillandsia*. Some items held in small quantities only. See catalogue.
**Map Ref:** N, D1

NDlv **Dalesview Nursery** ⊠ ♿
24 Braithwaite Edge Road, Keighley, West Yorkshire, BD22 6RA
Ⓣ (01535) 606531
Ⓔ nursery@dalesviewnursery.co.uk
Ⓦ www.dalesviewnursery.co.uk
**Contact:** David Ellis & Eileen Morgan
**Opening Times:** 1000-1700 Thu-Sun, Mar-Sep. Oct-Feb by appt., please telephone.
**Min Mail Order UK:** Nmc
**Min Mail Order EU:** Nmc
**Cat. Cost:** Plant list online.
**Credit Cards:** None
**Specialities:** Dwarf *Hebe*, *Saxifraga*, *Primula*, *Rhododendron*, *Fuchsia* & conifers.
**Notes:** Also sells wholesale.
**Map Ref:** N, C2

NDov **Dove Cottage Nursery & Garden** ♿
23 Shibden Hall Road, Halifax, West Yorkshire, HX3 9XA
Ⓣ (01422) 203553
Ⓔ info@dovecottagenursery.co.uk
Ⓦ www.dovecottagenursery.co.uk
**Contact:** Stephen & Kim Rogers
**Opening Times:** 1000-1700 Wed-Sun & B/hols Mar-Oct.
**Cat. Cost:** 6 × 2nd class.
**Credit Cards:** All major credit/debit cards
**Specialities:** Mainly selected perennials & grasses for naturalistic planting.
**Map Ref:** N, D2 **OS Grid Ref:** SE115256

NDro **Drointon Nurseries** ⊠ ✈ ⛫ ◆
Plaster Pitts, Norton Conyers, Ripon, North Yorkshire, HG4 5EF
Ⓣ (01765) 641849
Ⓜ 07909 971529
Ⓕ (01765) 640888
Ⓔ info@auricula-plants.co.uk
Ⓦ www.auricula-plants.co.uk
**Contact:** Robin & Annabel Graham
**Opening Times:** By appt. only.
**Min Mail Order UK:** Nmc
**Min Mail Order EU:** Nmc
**Cat. Cost:** 4 × 1st class.
**Credit Cards:** All major credit/debit cards
**Specialities:** *Primula auricula.* More than 500 cvs of show, alpine, double & border auriculas. Ltd. stocks of any one variety.

NEqu **Equatorial Plant Co.** ⊠ ✈ ⛫ €
7 Gray Lane, Barnard Castle, Co. Durham, DL12 8PD
Ⓣ (01833) 690519
Ⓕ (01833) 690519
Ⓔ equatorialplants@teesdaleonline.co.uk
Ⓦ www.equatorialplants.com
**Contact:** Dr Richard Warren
**Opening Times:** By appt. only.
**Min Mail Order UK:** Nmc
**Min Mail Order EU:** Nmc
**Cat. Cost:** Free
**Credit Cards:** Visa Access
**Specialities:** Laboratory-raised orchids only.
**Notes:** Also sells wholesale.

NFir **Fir Trees Pelargonium Nursery** ⊠ ⛫ ♿
Stokesley, Middlesbrough, Cleveland, TS9 5LD
Ⓣ (01642) 713066
Ⓕ (01642) 713066
Ⓔ mark@firtreespelargoniums.co.uk
Ⓦ www.firtreespelargoniums.co.uk
**Contact:** Helen Bainbridge
**Opening Times:** 1000-1600 7 days 1st Apr-31st Aug, 1000-1600 Mon-Fri 1st Sep-31st Mar.
**Min Mail Order UK:** £3.50 + p&p
**Cat. Cost:** 4 × 1st class or £1.00 coin
**Credit Cards:** MasterCard Visa Switch
**Specialities:** All types of *Pelargonium* – fancy leaf, regal, decorative regal, oriental regal,

KEY
⊠ Mail order to UK or EU ⛫ Delivers to shows
✈ Exports beyond EU € Euro accepted
♿ Accessible by wheelchair ◆ See Display advertisement

N

angel, miniature, zonal, ivy leaf, stellar, scented, dwarf, unique, golden stellar & species. Also dieramas.
**Map Ref:** N, C2

**NGBl** **Garden Blooms**
(office) The Ridings, Netherfield Drive, Guiseley, West Yorkshire, LS20 9DF
Ⓣ 0845 904937
Ⓕ 0870 0528148
Ⓔ info@gardenblooms.co.uk
Ⓦ www.gardenblooms.co.uk
**Contact:** Liz Webster
**Opening Times:** 1200-1600 Sat, Sun & B/hols end Mar-end Aug, but please check before travelling. Up-to-date details on website.
**Cat. Cost:** Online or A5 sae.
**Credit Cards:** None
**Specialities:** Hardy perennials. Available in small quantities only.
**Notes:** Nursery at Carlton Lane, East Carlton, Yeadon, LS19 7BE.
**Map Ref:** N, D2 **OS Grid Ref:** SE213430

**NGby** **Gilbey's Plants** ⊠ € ♿
The Walled Garden, Cemetery Road, Thirsk, North Yorkshire, YO7 4DA
Ⓣ (01765) 689927:(01845) 525285
Ⓕ (01765) 688272
Ⓔ gilbeyplants@aol.com
**Contact:** Giles N Gilbey
**Opening Times:** 1000-1700 Mon-Sat (closed Sun) 1st Mar-1st Oct. Winter by appt. only.
**Min Mail Order UK:** Nmc
**Min Mail Order EU:** Nmc
**Cat. Cost:** 4 × 1st class
**Credit Cards:** All major credit/debit cards
**Specialities:** Unusual hardy perennials & ferns.
**Notes:** Mail order Oct-Mar only. Also sells wholesale.
**Map Ref:** N, C2

**NGdn** **Garden House Nursery** ♿
The Square, Dalston, Carlisle, Cumbria, CA5 7LL
Ⓣ (01228) 710297
Ⓔ stephickso@hotmail.com
Ⓦ www.gardenhousenursery.co.uk
**Contact:** Stephen Hickson
**Opening Times:** 0900-1700 7 days Mar-Oct.
**Cat. Cost:** Plant list online only.
**Credit Cards:** None
**Specialities:** *Geranium*, *Hosta*, *Hemerocallis*, *Iris*, grasses & bamboos.
**Notes:** Also sells wholesale.
**Map Ref:** N, B1 **OS Grid Ref:** NY369503

**NGHP** **Green Garden Herbs** ⊠ ♿
13 West Bank, Carlton, North Yorkshire, DN14 9PZ
Ⓣ (01405) 860708
Ⓔ info@greengardenherbs.co.uk
Ⓦ www.greengardenherbs.co.uk
**Contact:** Sarah Clark
**Opening Times:** 1000-1700 Wed-Mon, Mar-Sep. Other times by appt.
**Min Mail Order UK:** £10.00
**Min Mail Order EU:** £10.00
**Cat. Cost:** Free with sae or online.
**Credit Cards:** All major credit/debit cards
**Specialities:** Herbs, aromatic, culinary, medicinal & ornamental, incl. *Salvia*, *Monarda*, *Thymus* & wide selection of *Lavandula*. Plants & seed available.
**Notes:** Also sells wholesale.
**Map Ref:** N, D3 **OS Grid Ref:** SE626242

**NHal** **Halls of Heddon** ⊠ ♿
(Office) West Heddon Nurseries, Heddon-on-the-Wall, Northumberland, NE15 0JS
Ⓣ (01661) 852445
Ⓕ (01661) 852398
Ⓔ orders@hallsofheddon.co.uk
Ⓦ www.hallsofheddon.co.uk
**Contact:** David Hall
**Opening Times:** 0900-1700 Mon-Sat 1000-1700 Sun.
**Min Mail Order UK:** Nmc
**Min Mail Order EU:** £25.00 + p&p
**Cat. Cost:** 3 × 2nd class
**Credit Cards:** MasterCard Visa Switch Delta
**Specialities:** *Chrysanthemum* & *Dahlia*. Wide range of herbaceous.
**Notes:** Mail order *Dahlia* & *Chrysanthemum* only. EU & export *Dahlia* tubers only. Also sells wholesale.
**Map Ref:** N, B2

**NHar** **Hartside Nursery Garden** ⊠
Nr Alston, Cumbria, CA9 3BL
Ⓣ (01434) 381372
Ⓕ (01434) 381372
Ⓔ Hartside@macunlimited.net
Ⓦ www.hartsidenursery.co.uk
**Contact:** S L & N Huntley
**Opening Times:** 1130-1630 Mon-Fri, 1230-1600 Sat, Sun & B/hols, mid Mar-31st Oct. All other times & winter by appt.
**Min Mail Order UK:** Nmc
**Min Mail Order EU:** £50.00 + p&p
**Cat. Cost:** 4 × 1st class or 3 × IRC
**Credit Cards:** All major credit/debit cards

**Specialities:** Alpines grown at altitude of 1100 feet in Pennines. *Primula*, ferns, *Gentian* & *Meconopsis*.
**Map Ref:** N, B1 **OS Grid Ref:** NY708447

**NHaw** THE HAWTHORNES NURSERY ⊠ ♿
Marsh Road, Hesketh Bank, Nr Preston, Lancashire, PR4 6XT
Ⓣ (01772) 812379
Ⓔ richardhaw@talktalk.net
Ⓦ www.hawthornes-nursery.co.uk
**Contact:** Irene & Richard Hodson
**Opening Times:** 0900-1800 7 days 1st Mar-30th Jun, Thu-Sun July-Oct. Gardens open for NGS.
**Min Mail Order UK:** £10.00
**Cat. Cost:** 5 × 1st class
**Credit Cards:** None
**Specialities:** *Clematis*, honeysuckle, choice selection of shrub & climbing roses, extensive range of perennials, mostly on display in the garden. Nat. Collection *Clematis viticella*.
**Map Ref:** N, D1

**NHer** HERTERTON HOUSE GARDEN NURSERY
Hartington, Cambo, Morpeth, Northumberland, NE61 4BN
Ⓣ (01670) 774278
**Contact:** Mrs M Lawley & Mr Frank Lawley
**Opening Times:** 1330-1730 Mon Wed Fri-Sun 1st Apr-end Sep. (Earlier or later in the year weather permitting.)
**Cat. Cost:** None issued
**Credit Cards:** None
**Specialities:** Country garden flowers.
**Map Ref:** N, B2 **OS Grid Ref:** NZ022880

**NHim** THE HIMALAYAN GARDEN CO. ⊠ ⌂ € ♿
The Hutts, Grewelthorpe, Ripon, Yorkshire, HG4 3DA
Ⓣ (01765) 658009
Ⓕ (01765) 658912
Ⓔ info@himalayangarden.com
Ⓦ www.himalayangarden.com
**Contact:** Peter Roberts
**Opening Times:** 1000-1600, Tues-Sun & B/hol Mon, mid Apr-mid Jun. During the rest of the year by appt. only.
**Min Mail Order UK:** £20.00
**Min Mail Order EU:** £50.00
**Cat. Cost:** Free.
**Credit Cards:** All major credit/debit cards
**Specialities:** Rare and unusual species & hybrid rhododendrons, azaleas, magnolias & *Cornus*, as well as other Himalayan plants.
**Notes:** Also sells wholesale.
**Map Ref:** N, C2 **OS Grid Ref:** SE218769

**NHol** HOLDEN CLOUGH NURSERY ⊠ ✈ ⌂ ♿ ◆
Holden, Bolton-by-Bowland, Clitheroe, Lancashire, BB7 4PF
Ⓣ (01200) 447615
Ⓕ (01200) 447197
Ⓔ enquiries@holdencloughnursery.co.uk
Ⓦ www.holdencloughnursery.co.uk
**Contact:** P J Foley
**Opening Times:** 0900-1630 Mon-Fri Mar-Oct & B/hol Mons, 0900-1630 Sat all year. Closed 25th Dec-1st Jan 2007 & Good Fri. Other times by appt. only.
**Min Mail Order UK:** Nmc
**Min Mail Order EU:** Nmc
**Cat. Cost:** 5 × 1st class
**Credit Cards:** MasterCard Visa Delta
**Specialities:** Large general list incl. *Crocosmia*, *Primula*, *Saxifraga*, *Sempervivum*, *Jovibarba*, *Astilbe*, grasses, *Hosta*, heathers & *Rhododendron*.
**Notes:** Seasonal mail order on some items. Also sells wholesale.
**Map Ref:** N, C2 **OS Grid Ref:** SD773496

**NHoy** HOYLAND PLANT CENTRE ⊠ ✈ ⌂ € ♿
54 Greenside Lane, Hoyland, Barnsley, Yorkshire, S74 9PZ
Ⓣ (01226) 744466
Ⓜ 07717 182169
Ⓕ (01226) 744466
Ⓔ hickman@hoyland13.freeserve.co.uk
Ⓦ www.somethingforthegarden.co.uk
**Contact:** Steven Hickman
**Opening Times:** All year round by appt. only.
**Min Mail Order UK:** Nmc
**Min Mail Order EU:** Nmc
**Cat. Cost:** 4 × 1st class.
**Credit Cards:** None
**Specialities:** *Agapanthus* & *Tulbaghia*. 400+ cvs. Nat. Collection status applied for. Some cvs available in small numbers only.
**Notes:** Also sells wholesale.
**Map Ref:** N, D2 **OS Grid Ref:** SE372010

**NLan** LANDLIFE WILDFLOWERS LTD ⊠ ♿
National Wildflower Centre, Court Hey Park, Liverpool, L16 3NA
Ⓣ (0151) 737 1819
Ⓕ (0151) 737 1820
Ⓔ gill@landlife.org.uk
Ⓦ www.wildflower.org.uk
**Contact:** Gillian Watson

| KEY | | |
|---|---|---|
| | ⊠ Mail order to UK or EU | ⌂ Delivers to shows |
| | ✈ Exports beyond EU | € Euro accepted |
| | ♿ Accessible by wheelchair | ◆ See Display advertisement |

N

**Opening Times:** 1000-1700, 7 days, 1st Mar-31st Aug.
**Min Mail Order UK:** £30.00 (plants), no min. for seeds.
**Cat. Cost:** Sae + 2 × 2nd class
**Credit Cards:** Visa Delta Access Switch Solo
**Specialities:** Wild herbaceous plants & seeds.
**Notes:** Cafe & shop. Admission charge to visitor centre. Also sells wholesale.
**Map Ref:** N, D1

**NLAp** **LANESIDE ALPINES** ⊠ ⌂ € ♿
74 Croston Road, Garstang, Preston, Lancashire, PR3 1HR
Ⓣ (01995) 605537
Ⓜ 0794 6659661
Ⓔ jcrhutch@aol.com
Ⓦ www.lanesidealpines.com
**Contact:** Jeff Hutchings
**Opening Times:** Thu-Sun, 1st Mar-30th Sep, but please phone first to check, as nursery closed when attending major shows.
**Min Mail Order UK:** £25.00
**Min Mail Order EU:** £25.00
**Cat. Cost:** Sae
**Credit Cards:** None
**Specialities:** Large selection of hardy terrestrial orchids plus composts & cultivation notes. Wide rane of alpines.
**Notes:** Mail order for orchids only during the winter. Also tufa, Seramis & Shap grit from the nursery.
**Map Ref:** N, D1

**NLar** **LARCH COTTAGE NURSERIES** ⊠ € ♿ ◆
Melkinthorpe, Penrith, Cumbria, CA10 2DR
Ⓣ (01931) 712404
Ⓕ (01931) 712727
Ⓔ plants@larchcottage.co.uk
Ⓦ www.larchcottage.co.uk
**Contact:** Joanne McCullock/Peter Stott
**Opening Times:** Daily from 1000-1730.
**Min Mail Order UK:** Nmc
**Min Mail Order EU:** Nmc
**Cat. Cost:** £3.50
**Credit Cards:** All major credit/debit cards except American Express
**Specialities:** Unusual & old-fashioned perennials. Rare & dwarf conifers. Unusual shrubs & trees.
**Notes:** Terraced restaurant & art gallery.
**Map Ref:** N, C1 **OS Grid Ref:** NY315602

**NLLv** **LEEDS LAVENDER** ⊠
at Greenscapes Nursery, Brandon Crescent, Shadwell, Leeds, LS17 9JH
Ⓣ (0113) 2892922
Ⓦ www.leedslavender.co.uk
**Contact:** Ruth Dorrington
**Opening Times:** 1000-1700, Mon-Sun, Feb-Nov. 1200-1600 Mon-Sun, Nov/Dec/Jan.
**Min Mail Order UK:** Nmc
**Cat. Cost:** 2 × 1st class
**Credit Cards:** None
**Specialities:** *Lavandula*. Limited numbers of particular varieties available at certain times, especially at end of summer.
**Notes:** Wheelchair access difficult in some areas. Large quantities of plants bigger than plug size. Ltd. mail order.
**Map Ref:** N, D2

**NMen** **MENDLE NURSERY** ⊠ ⌂ ♿
Holme, Scunthorpe, Lincolnshire, DN16 3RF
Ⓣ (01724) 850864
Ⓔ annearnshaw@lineone.net
Ⓦ www.mendlenursery.com
**Contact:** Mrs A Earnshaw
**Opening Times:** 1000-1600 Tue-Sun.
**Min Mail Order UK:** Nmc
**Min Mail Order EU:** Nmc
**Cat. Cost:** 3 × 1st class
**Credit Cards:** All major credit/debit cards
**Specialities:** Many unusual alpines esp. *Saxifraga* & *Sempervivum*.
**Map Ref:** N, D3 **OS Grid Ref:** SE925070

**NMin** **MINIATURE BULBS – THE WARREN ESTATE** ⊠ ⌂ €
9 Greengate Drive, Knaresborough, North Yorkshire, HG5 9EN
Ⓣ (01423) 542819
Ⓕ (01423) 542819
Ⓦ www.miniaturebulbs.co.uk
**Contact:** Ivor Fox
**Opening Times:** Not open. Mail order only.
**Min Mail Order UK:** £10.00
**Min Mail Order EU:** £10.00
**Cat. Cost:** 1 × 1st class.
**Credit Cards:** All major credit/debit cards, accepted online only.
**Specialities:** Rare & unusual miniature bulbs, incl. *Narcissus*, *Tulipa*, *Iris*, *Crocus*, *Fritillaria* & others. Spring bulb list sent out in April. Some stock in small quantities.
**Map Ref:** N, C2 **OS Grid Ref:** SE350584

**NMir** **MIRES BECK NURSERY** ⊠ ♿
Low Mill Lane, North Cave, Brough, East Riding, Yorkshire, HU15 2NR
Ⓣ (01430) 421543
Ⓔ admin@miresbeck.co.uk
Ⓦ www.miresbeck.co.uk

**Contact:** Judy Burrow & Martin Rowland
**Opening Times:** 1000-1600 Wed-Sat 1st Mar-30th Sep. 1000-1500 Wed-Fri 1st Oct-30th Nov & by appt.
**Min Mail Order UK:** Nmc
**Min Mail Order EU:** Nmc
**Cat. Cost:** 3 × 1st class
**Credit Cards:** None
**Specialities:** Wildflower plants of Yorkshire provenance.
**Notes:** Mail order for wildflower plants, plugs & seeds only. Also sells wholesale.
**Map Ref:** N, D3 **OS Grid Ref:** SE889316

**NMoo** MOOR MONKTON NURSERIES ⊠ ♿
Moor Monkton, York Road, Nr York, Yorkshire, YO26 8JJ
Ⓣ (01904) 738770
Ⓕ (01904) 738770
Ⓔ sales@bamboo-uk.co.uk
Ⓦ www.bamboo-uk.co.uk
**Contact:** Peter Owen
**Opening Times:** 0900-1700.
**Min Mail Order UK:** Nmc
**Cat. Cost:** 5 × 2nd class or email for details.
**Credit Cards:** All major credit/debit cards
**Specialities:** Bamboos, palms, ferns, unusual trees, shrubs & perennials.
**Notes:** Mail order for bamboo only. Also sells wholesale.
**Map Ref:** N, C2

**NMun** MUNCASTER CASTLE ⊠ ♿
Ravenglass, Cumbria, CA18 1RQ
Ⓣ (01229) 717614
Ⓕ (01229) 717010
Ⓔ info@muncasterplantcentre.co.uk
Ⓦ www.muncasterplantcentre.co.uk
**Contact:** Jason Haine
**Opening Times:** 1030-1700, 7 days, 10th Feb-5th Nov. Other times by appt.
**Min Mail Order UK:** Nmc
**Cat. Cost:** 2 × 1st class.
**Credit Cards:** All major credit/debit cards
**Specialities:** Hardy plants. *Rhododendron*, *Camellia*, *Magnolia*. Some rarer varieties may be in limited supply.
**Notes:** Mail order Oct-Apr only.
**Map Ref:** N, C1 **OS Grid Ref:** SD103964

**NMyG** MARY GREEN ⊠ ⛺ ♿
The Walled Garden, Hornby, Lancaster, Lancashire, LA2 8LD
Ⓣ (01524) 221989
Ⓜ 07778 910348
Ⓕ (01524) 221989
Ⓔ Marygreenplants@aol.com
**Contact:** Mary Green
**Opening Times:** By appt. only.
**Min Mail Order UK:** £10.00
**Cat. Cost:** 4 × 1st class
**Credit Cards:** None
**Specialities:** Hostas, astilbes, ferns & other shade-loving perennials.
**Map Ref:** N, C1 **OS Grid Ref:** SD588688

**NNor** NORCROFT NURSERIES ⊠ ♿
Roadends, Intack, Southwaite, Carlisle, Cumbria, CA4 0LH
Ⓣ (016974) 73933
Ⓜ 07789 050633
Ⓕ (016974) 73969
Ⓔ stellaandkeithbell@sbell44.fsnet.co.uk
**Contact:** Keith Bell
**Opening Times:** Every afternoon excl. Mon (open B/hol), Mar-Oct, or ring for appt.
**Min Mail Order UK:** Nmc
**Cat. Cost:** 2 × 2nd class
**Credit Cards:** None
**Specialities:** Hardy herbaceous, hostas, *Lilium*, *Hemerocallis*, *Penstemon*.
**Notes:** Also sells wholesale.
**Map Ref:** N, B1 **OS Grid Ref:** NY474433

**NOaD** OAK DENE NURSERIES ⊠ ⛺
10 Back Lane West, Royston, Barnsley, South Yorkshire, S71 4SB
Ⓣ (01226) 722253
**Contact:** J Foster or G Foster
**Opening Times:** 0900-1800 1st Apr-30th Sep, 1000-1600 1st Oct-31st Mar. (Closed 1230-1330.)
**Min Mail Order UK:** Phone for details.
**Min Mail Order EU:** Phone for details.
**Cat. Cost:** None issued.
**Credit Cards:** None
**Specialities:** Cacti, succulents (*Lithops*) & South African *Lachenalia* bulbs.
**Notes:** Also sells wholesale.
**Map Ref:** N, D2

**NOak** OAK TREE NURSERY ⊠ ⛺ ♿
Mill Lane, Barlow, Selby, North Yorkshire, YO8 8EY
Ⓣ (01757) 618409
Ⓔ gill.plowes@tesco.net
Ⓦ www.oaktreenursery.com
**Contact:** Gill Plowes
**Opening Times:** By appt. only.
**Min Mail Order UK:** £10.00 + p&p
**Cat. Cost:** 2 × 1st class

KEY
⊠ Mail order to UK or EU ⛺ Delivers to shows
✈ Exports beyond EU € Euro accepted
♿ Accessible by wheelchair ◆ See Display advertisement

N

**Credit Cards:** None
**Specialities:** Ornamental grasses & grass-like plants.
**Map Ref:** N, D3 **OS Grid Ref:** SE640285

**NOrc** **Orchard House Nursery**
Orchard House, Wormald Green, Nr Harrogate, North Yorkshire, HG3 3NQ
Ⓣ (01765) 677541
Ⓕ (01765) 677541
**Contact:** Mr B M Corner
**Opening Times:** 0800-1630 Mon-Fri.
**Cat. Cost:** Retail catalogue available at nursery.
**Credit Cards:** None
**Specialities:** Herbaceous perennials, ferns, grasses, water plants & unusual cottage garden plants.
**Notes:** Also sells wholesale.
**Map Ref:** N, C2

N

**NPal** **The Palm Farm** ⊠ € ♿
Thornton Hall Gardens, Station Road, Thornton Curtis, Nr Ulceby, Humberside, DN39 6XF
Ⓣ (01469) 531232
Ⓕ (01469) 531232
Ⓔ bill@palmfarm.fsbusiness.co.uk
Ⓦ www.thepalmfarm.com
**Contact:** W W Spink
**Opening Times:** 1400-1700 7 days.
**Min Mail Order UK:** £11.00 + p&p
**Min Mail Order EU:** £25.00 + p&p
**Cat. Cost:** 1 × 2nd class
**Credit Cards:** None
**Specialities:** Hardy & half-hardy palms, unusual trees, shrubs & conservatory plants. Some plants available only in small quantities.
**Notes:** Euro payment accepted only if purchaser pays bank commission. Mail order only if small enough to go by post (min. charge £12.50 p&p) or large enough to go by Palletline (min. charge £35.00 p&p). Also sells wholesale.
**Map Ref:** N, D3 **OS Grid Ref:** TA100183

**NPer** **Perry's Plants** € ♿
The River Garden, Sleights, Whitby, North Yorkshire, YO21 1RR
Ⓣ (01947) 810329
Ⓔ perry@rivergardens.fsnet.co.uk
Ⓦ www.perrysplants.co.uk
**Contact:** Pat & Richard Perry
**Opening Times:** 1000-1700 mid-March to Oct.
**Cat. Cost:** Large (A4) sae
**Credit Cards:** None
**Specialities:** *Lavatera*, *Malva*, *Erysimum*, *Euphorbia*, *Anthemis*, *Osteospermum* & *Hebe*. Uncommon hardy & container plants & aquatic plants.
**Map Ref:** N, C3 **OS Grid Ref:** NZ869082

**NPol** **Polemonium Plantery** ⊠ ⌂ ♿
28 Sunnyside Terrace, Trimdon Grange, Trimdon Station, Co. Durham, TS29 6HF
Ⓣ (01429) 881529
Ⓔ dandd@Polemonium.co.uk
Ⓦ www.Polemonium.co.uk
**Contact:** David or Dianne Nichol-Brown
**Opening Times:** By appt. only.
**Min Mail Order UK:** £10.00
**Cat. Cost:** Sae for list
**Credit Cards:** None
**Specialities:** Nat. Collection of *Polemonium* & related genera, plus some rare North American plants. The Collection holds Scientific Status.
**Notes:** Also sells wholesale.
**Map Ref:** N, B2 **OS Grid Ref:** NZ369353

**NPri** **Primrose Cottage Nursery** ♿ ◆
Ringway Road, Moss Nook, Wythenshawe, Manchester, M22 5WF
Ⓣ (0161) 437 1557
Ⓕ (0161) 499 9932
Ⓔ info@primrosecottagenursery.co.uk
Ⓦ www.primrosecottagenursery.co.uk
**Contact:** Caroline Dumville
**Opening Times:** 0900-1730 Mon-Sat, 0930-1730 Sun (summer). 0900-1700 Mon-Sat, 0930-1700 Sun (winter).
**Cat. Cost:** 1 × 37p stamp
**Credit Cards:** All major credit/debit cards
**Specialities:** Hardy herbaceous perennials, alpines, herbs, roses, patio & hanging basket plants. Shrubs.
**Notes:** Coffee shop open daily.
**Map Ref:** N, D2

**NPro** **ProudPlants** ⌂ ♿
East of Eden Nurseries, Ainstable, Carlisle, Cumbria, CA4 9QN
Ⓣ (01768) 896604
Ⓕ (01768) 896604
Ⓔ rogereastofeden@hotmail.com
**Contact:** Roger Proud
**Opening Times:** 0900-1800 7 days Mar-Nov. Other times by appt.
**Cat. Cost:** None issued
**Credit Cards:** None
**Specialities:** Interesting & unusual shrubs, perennials & alpines, esp. dwarf & ground cover plants.
**Map Ref:** N, B1 **OS Grid Ref:** HA1336186

**NRar** **Rarer Plants** ♿
Ashfield House, Austfield Lane, Monk Fryston, Leeds, LS25 5EH
Ⓣ (01977) 682263
**Contact:** Anne Watson
**Opening Times:** Feb, Mar. By appt. only.
**Cat. Cost:** Sae
**Credit Cards:** None
**Specialities:** *Helleborus.*
**Map Ref:** N, D2

**NRib** **Ribblesdale Nurseries** ♿
Newsham Hall Lane, Woodplumpton, Preston, Lancashire, PR4 0AS
Ⓣ (01772) 863081
Ⓕ (01772) 861884
Ⓔ angela@psadunnett.freeserve.co.uk
Ⓦ www.ribblesdalenurseries.co.uk
**Contact:** Mr & Mrs Dunnett
**Opening Times:** 0900-1800 Mon-Sat Apr-Sep, 0900-1700 Mon-Sat Oct-Mar. 1030-1630 Sun.
**Credit Cards:** Visa MasterCard Delta Switch
**Specialities:** Trees, shrubs & perennials. Conifers, hedging, alpines, fruit, climbers, herbs, aquatics, ferns & wildflowers.
**Map Ref:** N, D1 **OS Grid Ref:** SD515351

**NRob** **W Robinson & Sons Ltd** ⊠ ✈ € ♿
Sunny Bank, Forton, Nr Preston, Lancashire, PR3 0BN
Ⓣ (01524) 791210
Ⓕ (01524) 791933
Ⓔ info@mammothonion.co.uk
Ⓦ www.mammothonion.co.uk
**Contact:** Miss Robinson
**Opening Times:** 0900-1700 7 days Mar-Jun, 0800-1700 Mon-Fri Jul-Feb.
**Min Mail Order UK:** Nmc
**Min Mail Order EU:** Nmc
**Cat. Cost:** Free
**Credit Cards:** Visa Access American Express Switch
**Specialities:** Mammoth vegetable seed. Onions, leeks, tomatoes & beans. Range of vegetable plants in the spring.
**Notes:** Also sells wholesale.

**NRya** **Ryal Nursery** ⛫ ♿
East Farm Cottage, Ryal, Northumberland, NE20 0SA
Ⓣ (01661) 886562
Ⓕ (01661) 886918
Ⓔ alpines@ryal.freeserve.co.uk
**Contact:** R F Hadden
**Opening Times:** 1000-1600 Sun Mar-Jul & other times by appt.
**Cat. Cost:** Sae
**Credit Cards:** None
**Specialities:** Alpine & woodland plants. Mainly available in small quantities only. Nat. Collection of *Primula marginata.*
**Notes:** Also sells wholesale.
**Map Ref:** N, B2 **OS Grid Ref:** NZ015744

**NSco** **Scott's Wildflowers** ⊠ ♿
Swallow Hill Barn, 31 Common Side, Distington, Workington, Cumbria, CA14 4PU
Ⓣ (01946) 830486
Ⓔ scotts.wildflowers@virgin.net
Ⓦ www.scottswildflowers.co.uk
**Contact:** Ted Scott
**Opening Times:** 1000-1600 Mar-Oct, 1130-1500 Nov-Feb, 7 days.
**Min Mail Order UK:** £10.40 + £4.50 p&p
**Cat. Cost:** 3 × 1st class
**Credit Cards:** None
**Specialities:** Native British wildflowers, including aquatics.
**Notes:** Also sells wholesale.
**Map Ref:** N, C1

**NScw** **Scawsby Hall Nurseries** ⊠ ♿
Barnsley Road, Scawsby, Doncaster, South Yorkshire, DN5 7UB
Ⓣ (01302) 782585
Ⓕ (01302) 783434
Ⓔ mail@scawsbyhallnurseries.co.uk
Ⓦ www.the-plant-directory.com
**Contact:** David Lawson
**Opening Times:** 0930-1700 Mon-Sat 1100-1700 Sun.
**Min Mail Order UK:** Nmc
**Cat. Cost:** None issued
**Credit Cards:** Maestro Visa MasterCard Solo
**Specialities:** A wide range of herbaceous perennials, hardy trees, shrubs & indoor plants. Some indoor & aquatic plants in small quantities only.
**Map Ref:** N, D3 **OS Grid Ref:** SE542049

**NShi** **Shirley Tasker** ⊠ ⛫
6 Sandheys Drive, Churchtown, Southport, Merseyside, PR9 9PQ
Ⓣ (01704) 213048
Ⓜ 07951 834066
Ⓔ shirley@shirleysplants.fsnet.co.uk
Ⓦ www.stbegonias.com
**Contact:** Shirley & Terry Tasker
**Opening Times:** By appt. only.

KEY
⊠ Mail order to UK or EU ⛫ Delivers to shows
✈ Exports beyond EU € Euro accepted
♿ Accessible by wheelchair ◆ See Display advertisement

N

**Min Mail Order UK:** Nmc
**Cat. Cost:** 2 × 1st class
**Credit Cards:** None
**Specialities:** Nat. Collection of *Begonia* species & hybrids.
**Map Ref:** N, D1 **OS Grid Ref:** SD355183

**NSla** **Slack Top Nurseries** ⊠ ⌂ €
Hebden Bridge, West Yorkshire,
HX7 7HA
Ⓣ (01422) 845348
Ⓔ enquiries@slacktopnurseries.co.uk
Ⓦ www.slacktopnurseries.co.uk
**Contact:** M R or R Mitchell
**Opening Times:** 1000-1700 Fri-Sun 1st Mar-30th Sep & B/hol Mons 1st Mar-30th Sep.
**Min Mail Order UK:** £30.00
**Cat. Cost:** Sae
**Credit Cards:** None
**Specialities:** Alpine & rockery plants. *Celmisia semi-cordata, Gentiana, Saxifraga, Primula, Hepatica, Paeonia* & *Pulsatilla. Anemone nemorosa* cvs.
**Notes:** Suitable for wheelchairs but 2 steps at entrance. Also sells wholesale.
**Map Ref:** N, D2 **OS Grid Ref:** SD977286

**NSpr** **Springwood Pleiones** ⊠ ✈ € ♿
8 Tredgold Avenue, Leeds, LS16 9BU
Ⓣ (0113) 230 1158
Ⓔ simon@pleiones.com
Ⓦ www.pleiones.com
**Contact:** Simon Redshaw
**Opening Times:** By appt. only.
**Min Mail Order UK:** £4.00 + p&p
**Min Mail Order EU:** £4.00 + p&p
**Cat. Cost:** 1 × 1st class
**Credit Cards:** None
**Specialities:** *Pleione.*
**Map Ref:** N, D2 **OS Grid Ref:** SE256429

**NSti** **Stillingfleet Lodge Nurseries** ♿
Stillingfleet, North Yorkshire,
YO19 6HP
Ⓣ (01904) 728506
Ⓕ (01904) 728506
Ⓔ vanessa.cook@still-lodge.freeserve.co.uk
Ⓦ www.stillingfleetlodgenurseries.co.uk
**Contact:** Vanessa Cook
**Opening Times:** 1000-1600 Tue Wed Fri & Sat 1st Apr-18th Oct. Closed Sat in Aug.
**Cat. Cost:** 10 × 2nd class
**Credit Cards:** None
**Specialities:** Foliage & unusual perennials. Hardy geraniums, *Pulmonaria*, variegated plants & grasses. Nat. Collection of *Pulmonaria.*
**Map Ref:** N, C2

**NSum** **Summerdale Garden Nursery** ⊠
Summerdale House, Cow Brow, Lupton, Carnforth, Lancashire, LA6 1PE
Ⓣ (01539) 567210
Ⓔ summerdalenursery@btinternet.com
Ⓦ www.summerdalegardenplants.co.uk
**Contact:** Abi Sheals
**Opening Times:** 0930-1630 Thu, Fri & Sat, 1st Feb-31st Oct. Other times by appt. only.
**Min Mail Order UK:** £15.00
**Cat. Cost:** 4 × 1st class
**Credit Cards:** None
**Specialities:** Wide variety of pernnials, large collection of *Primula.* Many moist and shade-loving plants incl. *Meconopsis* & hellebores.
**Map Ref:** N, C1 **OS Grid Ref:** SD545819

**NTay** **Taylors Clematis Nursery** ⊠ ⌂ ♿ ◆
Sutton Road, Sutton, Nr Askern, Doncaster, South Yorkshire, DN6 9JZ
Ⓣ (01302) 700716
Ⓕ (01302) 708415
Ⓔ info@taylorsclematis.co.uk
Ⓦ www.taylorsclematis.co.uk
**Contact:** Chris & Suzy Cocks
**Opening Times:** Open by appt. only. Please ring for details.
**Min Mail Order UK:** Nmc
**Cat. Cost:** free
**Credit Cards:** All major credit/debit cards
**Specialities:** *Clematis* (over 300 varieties).
**Notes:** Also sells wholesale

**NTHB** **Tavistock Herb Nursery** ⊠ ⌂
Tavistock, Preston Old Road, Clifton, Lancashire, PR4 0ZA
Ⓣ (01772) 683505
Ⓕ (01772) 683505
Ⓔ tavistockherbs@themail.co.uk
**Contact:** Mrs C Jones
**Opening Times:** By appt. only.
**Min Mail Order UK:** Nmc
**Cat. Cost:** 3 × 1st class stamps
**Credit Cards:** None
**Specialities:** Herbs & wildflowers.
**Notes:** Main nursery at Garstang Road, Barton, near Preston, Lancs. Also sells wholesale.
**Map Ref:** N, D1

**NVic** **The Vicarage Garden** ⊠ ♿
Carrington, Manchester, M31 4AG
Ⓣ (0161) 775 2750
Ⓔ info@vicaragebotanicalgardens.co.uk
Ⓦ www.vicaragebotanicalgardens.co.uk
**Contact:** Paul Haine
**Opening Times:** 0900-1700 Mon-Sat, closed Thu. 1000-1630 Sun all year.
**Min Mail Order UK:** Nmc

**Cat. Cost:** 2 × 2nd class for list
**Credit Cards:** All major credit/debit cards
**Specialities:** Herbaceous, alpines, grasses, ferns.
**Notes:** Free admission to 7 acre gardens with coffee shop & mini zoo.
**Map Ref:** N, D2 **OS Grid Ref:** SJ729926

NWCA **WHITE COTTAGE ALPINES** ⊠ ◆
Sunnyside Nurseries, Hornsea Road, Sigglesthorne, East Yorkshire, HU11 5QL
Ⓣ (01964) 542692
Ⓕ (01964) 542692
Ⓔ plants@whitecottagealpines.co.uk
Ⓦ www.whitecottagealpines.co.uk
**Contact:** Sally E Cummins
**Opening Times:** 1000-1700 (or dusk) Thu-Sun & B/hol Mon 1 Mar-30 Sep. If travelling far, please phone first. In winter by appt. only.
**Min Mail Order UK:** Nmc.
**Min Mail Order EU:** £15.00 + p&p by card only.
**Cat. Cost:** 4 × 1st class
**Credit Cards:** Visa MasterCard Switch
**Specialities:** Alpines & rock plants. 500+ species incl. American, dwarf *Salix* & *Helichrysum*, also increasing range of *Penstemon*.
**Notes:** Euro payments by card only.
**Map Ref:** N, C3

NWea **WEASDALE NURSERIES LTD.** ⊠
Newbiggin-on-Lune, Kirkby Stephen, Cumbria, CA17 4LX
Ⓣ (01539) 623246
Ⓕ (01539) 623277
Ⓔ sales@weasdale.com
Ⓦ www.weasdale.com
**Contact:** Andrew Forsyth
**Opening Times:** 0830-1730 Mon-Fri. Closed w/ends, B/hols, Xmas through to the New Year.
**Min Mail Order UK:** Nmc
**Min Mail Order EU:** Nmc
**Cat. Cost:** £2.00 or 7 × 1st class. £2.00 by debit card, £2.50 by credit card.
**Credit Cards:** All major credit/debit cards
**Specialities:** Hardy forest trees, hedging, broadleaved & conifers. Specimen trees & shrubs grown at 850 feet (260 metre) elevation.
**Notes:** Mail order a speciality. Mail order Nov-Apr only. Also sells wholesale.

NWit **D S WITTON** ⊠
26 Casson Drive, Harthill, Sheffield, Yorkshire, S26 7WA
Ⓣ (01909) 771366
Ⓕ (01909) 771366
Ⓔ donshardyeuphorbias@btopenworld.com
Ⓦ www.euphorbias.co.uk
**Contact:** Don Witton
**Opening Times:** By appt. only.
**Min Mail Order UK:** Nmc
**Cat. Cost:** 1 × 1st class + sae
**Credit Cards:** None
**Specialities:** Nat. Collection of Hardy *Euphorbia*. Over 130 varieties.
**Notes:** Mail order plants, Oct-Feb. Mail order seed Oct-June.
**Map Ref:** N, D2 **OS Grid Ref:** SK494812

## SOUTHERN

SAdn **ASHDOWN FOREST GARDEN CENTRE & NURSERY**
Duddleswell, Ashdown Forest, Nr Uckfield, East Sussex, TN22 3JP
Ⓣ (01825) 712300
Ⓦ www.ashdownforestgardencentre.co.uk
**Contact:** Victoria Falletti
**Opening Times:** 0900-1730 winter, 0900-1800 summer.
**Credit Cards:** All major credit/debit cards
**Specialities:** Ornamental grasses, *Lavandula*, fuchsias.
**Notes:** Also sells wholesale.
**Map Ref:** S, C4 **OS Grid Ref:** TQ468283

SAft **AFTON PARK NURSERY**
Newport Road, Afton, Freshwater, Isle of Wight, PO40 9XR
Ⓣ (01983) 755774
Ⓕ (01983) 755774
Ⓔ paul@aftonpark.co.uk
Ⓦ www.aftonpark.co.uk
**Contact:** Paul Heathcote
**Opening Times:** 0900-1700 summer. 1000-1600 winter. Open all year except Xmas period.
**Cat. Cost:** 4 × 1st class
**Credit Cards:** Visa MasterCard
**Specialities:** Wide general range, emphasis on unusual perennials, grasses, coastal shrubs & plants for Mediterranean gardens.
**Map Ref:** S, D2 **OS Grid Ref:** SZ349864

SAga **BLUEBELL COTTAGE NURSERY (FORMERLY AGAR'S)** ⊠ €
Agars Lane, Hordle, Lymington, Hampshire, SO41 0FL
Ⓣ (01590) 683703
**Contact:** Diana Tombs, Debbie Ursell

KEY
⊠ Mail order to UK or EU — Delivers to shows
Exports beyond EU — € Euro accepted
Accessible by wheelchair — ◆ See Display advertisement

S

**Opening Times:** 1000-1700 Fri-Wed (closed Thu) Mar-Sep, 1000-1600 Fri-Mon (closed Tue-Thu) Feb & Oct-Dec, or by appt.
**Min Mail Order UK:** £15.00 + p&p
**Cat. Cost:** 4 × 1st class sae (list only).
**Credit Cards:** None
**Specialities:** *Penstemon* & *Salvia*. Also wide range of hardy plants incl. hardy & tender shrubs, climbers & herbaceous.
**Map Ref:** S, D2 **OS Grid Ref:** SZ275960

**SAll** **ALLWOOD BROS** ⊠ ♠ ♿
London Road, Hassocks, West Sussex, BN6 9NB
Ⓣ (01273) 844229
Ⓕ (01273) 846022
Ⓔ info@allwoods.net
Ⓦ www.allwoods.net
**Contact:** David & Emma James
**Opening Times:** Office 0900-1630 Mon-Fri. Answer machine all other times. Nursery 7 days, 1st Mar-30th Jun.
**Min Mail Order UK:** Nmc
**Min Mail Order EU:** Nmc
**Cat. Cost:** 2 × 1st class
**Credit Cards:** Access Visa MasterCard Switch
**Specialities:** *Dianthus* incl. hardy border carnations, pinks, perpetual & *D. allwoodii*, some available as seed. Certain lavender varieties. Penstemons.
**Notes:** Exports seed only.
**Map Ref:** S, D4 **OS Grid Ref:** TQ303170

S

**SAPC** **ARCHITECTURAL PLANTS (CHICHESTER) LTD** ⊠ ♠ € ♿ ◆
Lidsey Road Nursery, Westergate, Nr Chichester, West Sussex, PO20 6SU
Ⓣ (01243) 545008
Ⓕ (01243) 545009
Ⓔ chichester@architecturalplants.com
Ⓦ www.architecturalplants.com
**Contact:** Christine Shaw
**Opening Times:** 1000-1600 Sun-Fri all year. Closed Sat & B/hol Mons. Open Good Fri.
**Min Mail Order UK:** Nmc
**Cat. Cost:** Free
**Credit Cards:** All major credit/debit cards
**Specialities:** Architectural plants & hardy exotics esp. rare evergreen broadleaved trees & seaside exotics, spiky plants, yuccas/agaves.
**Notes:** Second nursery near Horsham, Code SArc. Also sells wholesale.
**Map Ref:** S, D3

**SApp** **APPLE COURT** ⊠ €
Hordle Lane, Hordle, Lymington, Hampshire, S041 0HU
Ⓣ (01590) 642130
Ⓕ (01590) 644220
Ⓔ applecourt@btinternet.com
Ⓦ www.applecourt.com
**Contact:** Angela & Charles Meads
**Opening Times:** 1000-1700 Fri, Sat, Sun & B/hol 1st Mar-31st Oct. Closed Nov-Feb.
**Min Mail Order UK:** Nmc
**Min Mail Order EU:** Nmc
**Cat. Cost:** 4 × 1st class
**Credit Cards:** All major credit/debit cards
**Specialities:** *Hemerocallis*, *Hosta*, grasses & ferns.
**Map Ref:** S, D2 **OS Grid Ref:** SZ270941

**SArc** **ARCHITECTURAL PLANTS** ⊠ ♠ € ♿ ◆
Cooks Farm, Nuthurst, Horsham, West Sussex, RH13 6LH
Ⓣ (01403) 891772
Ⓕ (01403) 891056
Ⓔ enquiries@architecturalplants.com
Ⓦ www.architecturalplants.com
**Contact:** Sarah Chandler
**Opening Times:** 0900-1700 Mon-Sat, closed Sun.
**Min Mail Order UK:** Nmc
**Cat. Cost:** Free
**Credit Cards:** All major credit/debit cards
**Specialities:** Architectural plants & hardy exotics & rare broadleaved trees, bamboos, spiky plants & ferns.
**Notes:** Second nursery near Chichester, code SAPC. Also sells wholesale.
**Map Ref:** S, C3

**SBch** **BIRCHWOOD PLANTS**
(office) 10 Westering, Romsey, Hampshire, SO51 7LY
Ⓣ (01794) 502192 or 02380 814345
Ⓔ lesleybaker@lycos.co.uk
Ⓦ www.birchwoodplants.co.uk
**Contact:** Lesley Baker
**Opening Times:** By appt. at nursery only for collection of plants. Plants available at Mottisfont Abbey (NT) but ring first to check availability.
**Cat. Cost:** Online only. A5 sae for plant list.
**Credit Cards:** None
**Specialities:** Wide range of plants, mainly herbaceous, many unusual. Good selection of salvias, geraniums, grasses & herbs, also good range for bees & butterflies & drought-tolerant plants. Some stock available in small quantities only.
**Notes:** Nursery at Gardener's Lane, Nr Romsey, SO51 6AD. Mottisfont accessible for wheelchairs.
**Map Ref:** S, D2 **OS Grid Ref:** SU333190

**SBHP** **BLEAK HILL PLANTS** ♿
Braemoor, Bleak Hill, Harbridge, Ringwood, Hampshire, BH24 3PX
Ⓣ (01425) 652983
Ⓔ tracey_netherway@btopenworld.com
**Contact:** Tracy Netherway
**Opening Times:** 0900-1800, Mon, Tue, Fri, Sat & 1000-1600 Sun, Mar-Oct. Closed Wed & Thu.
**Cat. Cost:** 2 x1st class
**Credit Cards:** None
**Specialities:** Hardy & half-hardy herbaceous perennials. Stock available in small quantities.
**Map Ref:** S, D1 **OS Grid Ref:** SU132111

**SBig** **BIG PLANT NURSERY** ✉ ♿
Hole Street, Ashington, West Sussex, RH20 3DE
Ⓣ (01903) 891466
Ⓕ (01903) 892829
Ⓔ info@bigplantnursery.co.uk
Ⓦ www.bigplantnursery.co.uk
**Contact:** Bruce Jordan
**Opening Times:** 0900-1700 Mon-Sat, 1000-1600 Sun & B/hols.
**Min Mail Order UK:** Please phone for further info.
**Cat. Cost:** A5 sae with 2 × 1st class
**Credit Cards:** All major credit/debit cards
**Specialities:** Bamboos, hardy exotics & palms, *Ginkgo*, *Betula*.
**Notes:** Also sells wholesale
**Map Ref:** S, D3 **OS Grid Ref:** TQ132153

**SBir** **BIRCHFLEET NURSERIES** ◆
Nyewood, Petersfield, Hampshire, GU31 5JQ
Ⓣ (01730) 821636
Ⓕ (01730) 821636
Ⓔ gammoak@aol.com
Ⓦ www.birchfleetnurseries.co.uk
**Contact:** John & *Daphne* Gammon
**Opening Times:** By appt. only. Please phone.
**Cat. Cost:** 2 × 1st class
**Credit Cards:** None
**Specialities:** Oaks. Beech. *Carpinus*. Nat. Collection of *Liquidambar*.
**Notes:** Nursery accessible for wheelchairs in dry weather. Also sells wholesale
**Map Ref:** S, C3

**SBLw** **BRIAN LEWINGTON** ✉ ♿
(office) April Cottage, Hendall Manor Farm, Heron's Ghyll, Uckfield, East Sussex, TN22 4BT
Ⓣ (01825) 731911
Ⓕ (01825) 731911
Ⓔ BHLewington@aol.com
Ⓦ www.treesandhedges.co.uk
**Contact:** Brian Lewington
**Opening Times:** 0800-1700 Sat. Other times by appt. only.
**Min Mail Order UK:** Nmc
**Specialities:** Larger size trees and hedging.
**Notes:** Nursery is at Leverett Farm, Dallington, Nr Heathfield, Sussex. Also sells wholesale.
**Map Ref:** S, D4 **OS Grid Ref:** TQ578172

**SBmr** **BLACKMOOR NURSERIES** ✉ ♿
Blackmoor Estate, Blackmoor, Liss, Hampshire, GU33 6BS
Ⓣ (01420) 473576
Ⓕ (01420) 487813
Ⓔ jonmunday@blackmoor.co.uk
Ⓦ www.blackmoor.co.uk
**Contact:** Jon Munday
**Opening Times:** 0730-1600.
**Min Mail Order UK:** Nmc
**Cat. Cost:** None issued.
**Credit Cards:** All major credit/debit cards
**Specialities:** Fruit trees, soft fruit & ornamental trees.
**Notes:** Also sells wholesale.
**Map Ref:** S, C3

**SBod** **BODIAM NURSERY** ♿
Bodiam, Robertsbridge, East Sussex, TN32 5RA
Ⓣ (01580) 830811
Ⓔ contact@bodiamnursery.com
Ⓦ www.bodiamnursery.co.uk
**Contact:** Anna-Marie Sapsted
**Opening Times:** 1000-1700 7 days. Closed Mon & Fri Dec & Jan.
**Cat. Cost:** None issued.
**Credit Cards:** Visa MasterCard Solo JCB
**Specialities:** Herbaceous perennials, grasses, conifers, *Camellia* & climbers. Acers. Shrubs, trees.
**Map Ref:** S, C5

**SBri** **BRICKWALL COTTAGE NURSERY** ♿
1 Brickwall Cottages, Frittenden, Cranbrook, Kent, TN17 2DH
Ⓣ (01580) 852425
Ⓔ sue.martin@talktalk.net
**Contact:** Sue Martin
**Opening Times:** By appt. only.
**Credit Cards:** None

KEY
✉ Mail order to UK or EU — Delivers to shows
Exports beyond EU — € Euro accepted
♿ Accessible by wheelchair — ◆ See Display advertisement

**Specialities:** Hardy perennials. Stock available in small quantities only. *Geum*. Nat. Collection (provisional) of *Geum*.
**Map Ref:** S, C5 **OS Grid Ref:** TQ815410

SBrm **Brambly Hedge** ⊠
Mill Lane, Sway, Hampshire, SO41 8LN
Ⓣ (01590) 683570
**Contact:** Kim Williams
**Opening Times:** By appt. only.
**Min Mail Order UK:** Nmc
**Cat. Cost:** 9"× 7" sae
**Credit Cards:** None
**Specialities:** National Collection of *Streptocarpus*. Available in small quantities only.
**Notes:** Mail order Mar-Sep, small quantities only available.
**Map Ref:** S, D2 **OS Grid Ref:** SZ294973

S

SCac **Cacti & Succulents** ⊠
Hammerfield, Crockham Hill, Edenbridge, Kent, TN8 6RR
Ⓣ (01732) 866295
**Contact:** Geoff Southon
**Opening Times:** Flexible. Please phone first.
**Min Mail Order UK:** Nmc.
**Cat. Cost:** None issued.
**Credit Cards:** None
**Specialities:** *Echeveria* & related genera & hybrids. *Agave*, haworthias, aloes, gasterias, crassulas. Large range of plants available in small quantities.

SCam **Camellia Grove Nursery** ⊠ ✈ ⌂ € ♿
Market Garden, Lower Beeding, West Sussex, RH13 6PP
Ⓣ (01403) 891412
Ⓔ sales@camellia-grove.com
Ⓦ www.camellia-grove.com
**Contact:** Chris Loder
**Opening Times:** 1000-1600 Mon-Sat, please phone first so we can give you our undivided attention.
**Min Mail Order UK:** Nmc
**Min Mail Order EU:** £100.00 + p&p
**Cat. Cost:** 2 × 1st class
**Credit Cards:** Switch MasterCard Visa
**Specialities:** Camellias & azaleas.
**Notes:** Also sells wholesale.
**Map Ref:** S, C3

SChF **Charleshurst Farm Nursery** ⊠ ⌂ €
Loxwood Road, Plaistow, Billingshurst, West Sussex, RH14 0NY
Ⓣ (01403) 752273
Ⓜ 07736 522788
Ⓔ Charleshurstfarm@aol.com
Ⓦ www.charleshurstplants.co.uk
**Contact:** Clive Mellor
**Opening Times:** Normally 0800-1700 Fri, Sat, Sun, Feb-Oct, but please ring first before travelling.
**Min Mail Order UK:** Nmc
**Min Mail Order EU:** Nmc
**Cat. Cost:** 2 × 1st class.
**Credit Cards:** None
**Specialities:** Shrubs including some more unusual species. Good range of daphnes & Japanese maples.
**Map Ref:** S, C3 **OS Grid Ref:** TQ015308

SChr **John Churcher** ⊠ ✈
47 Grove Avenue, Portchester, Fareham, Hampshire, PO16 9EZ
Ⓣ (023) 9232 6740
Ⓕ (023) 9232 6740
Ⓔ churchers.47@tiscali.co.uk
**Contact:** John Churcher
**Opening Times:** By appt. only. Please phone or email.
**Min Mail Order UK:** Nmc
**Min Mail Order EU:** Nmc
**Cat. Cost:** None issued.
**Credit Cards:** None
**Specialities:** Hardy *Opuntia*, *Aeonium*, *Agave*, *Aloe*, *Canna*, *Hedychium*, plus hardy bananas, palms, tree ferns & echiums for the exotic Mediterranean garden.
**Map Ref:** S, D2 **OS Grid Ref:** SU614047

SCmr **Cromar Nursery** ⊠ ♿
39 Livesey Street, North Pole, Wateringbury, Maidstone, Kent, ME18 5BQ
Ⓣ (01622) 812380
Ⓔ CromarNursery@aol.com
Ⓦ www.cromarnursery.co.uk
**Contact:** Debra & Martin Cronk
**Opening Times:** 0930-1700 daily except Wed.
**Min Mail Order UK:** Nmc
**Min Mail Order EU:** Nmc
**Cat. Cost:** 2 × 1st class
**Credit Cards:** All major credit/debit cards
**Specialities:** Ornamental & fruit trees.
**Map Ref:** S, C4 **OS Grid Ref:** TQ697547

SCnR **Colin Roberts** ⊠
Tragumna, Morgay Wood Lane, Three Oaks, Guestling, East Sussex, TN35 4NF
Ⓜ 07718 029909
**Contact:** Colin Roberts
**Opening Times:** Not open. Mail order only.
**Min Mail Order UK:** £20.00

**Cat. Cost:** 2 × 1st class
**Credit Cards:** None
**Specialities:** Dwarf bulbs & woodland plants incl. many rare & unusual, in small numbers.

SCog **Coghurst Camellias** ⊠ ⌂ € ♿
Ivy House Lane, Near Three Oaks, Hastings, East Sussex, TN35 4NP
Ⓣ (01424) 756228
Ⓔ rotherview@btinternet.com
Ⓦ www.rotherview.com
**Contact:** R Bates & W Bates
**Opening Times:** 0930-1600 7 days.
**Min Mail Order UK:** Nmc
**Min Mail Order EU:** Nmc
**Cat. Cost:** 4 × 1st class
**Credit Cards:** All major credit/debit cards
**Specialities:** *Camellia.*
**Notes:** Nursery is on the same site as Rotherview Nursery. Also sells wholesale.
**Map Ref:** S, D5

SCoo **Cooling's Nurseries Ltd** ♿
Rushmore Hill, Knockholt, Sevenoaks, Kent, TN14 7NN
Ⓣ (01959) 532269
Ⓕ (01959) 534092
Ⓔ Plantfinder@coolings.co.uk
Ⓦ www.coolings.co.uk
**Contact:** Mark Reeve & Dan Short
**Opening Times:** 0900-1700 Mon-Sat & 1000-1630 Sun.
**Cat. Cost:** None issued
**Credit Cards:** All major credit/debit cards, except American Express.
**Specialities:** Third generation family business offering large range of perennials, conifers & bedding plants. Many unusual shrubs & trees. Display garden.
**Notes:** Coffee shop.
**Map Ref:** S, C4 **OS Grid Ref:** TK477610

SCrf **Crofters Nurseries** € ♿
Church Hill, Charing Heath, Near Ashford, Kent, TN27 0BU
Ⓣ (01233) 712798
Ⓕ (01233) 712798
Ⓔ crofters.nursery1@virgin.net
**Contact:** John & Sue Webb
**Opening Times:** 1000-1700. Closed Sun-Tue. Please check first.
**Cat. Cost:** 3 × 1st class
**Credit Cards:** None
**Specialities:** Fruit, ornamental trees & conifers. Old apple varieties. Small number of *Prunus serrula* with grafted ornamental heads.
**Map Ref:** S, C5 **OS Grid Ref:** TQ923493

SDea **Deacon's Nursery** ⊠ ✈ € ◆
Moor View, Godshill, Isle of Wight, PO38 3HW
Ⓣ (01983) 840750 (24 hrs) or (01983) 522243
Ⓕ (01983) 523575
Ⓔ info@deaconsnurseryfruits.co.uk
Ⓦ www.deaconsnurseryfruits.co.uk
**Contact:** G D & B H W Deacon
**Opening Times:** 0800-1600 Mon-Fri May-Sep, 0800-1700 Mon-Fri 0800-1200 Sat Oct-Apr.
**Min Mail Order UK:** Nmc
**Min Mail Order EU:** Nmc
**Cat. Cost:** Free
**Credit Cards:** All major credit/debit cards
**Specialities:** Over 300 varieties of apple, old & new, pears, plums, gages, damsons, cherries. Modern soft fruit, grapes, hops, nuts & family trees.
**Notes:** Also sells wholesale.
**Map Ref:** S, D2

SDix **Great Dixter Nurseries** ⊠ ♿
Northiam, Rye, East Sussex, TN31 6PH
Ⓣ (01797) 253107
Ⓕ (01797) 252879
Ⓔ nursery@greatdixter.co.uk
Ⓦ www.greatdixter.co.uk
**Contact:** K Leighton
**Opening Times:** 0900-1230 & 1330-1700 Mon-Fri, 0900-1200 Sat all year. Also 1400-1700 Sat, Sun & B/hols Apr-Oct.
**Min Mail Order UK:** Nmc
**Min Mail Order EU:** Nmc
**Cat. Cost:** 4 × 1st class
**Credit Cards:** All major credit/debit cards
**Specialities:** *Clematis*, shrubs and plants. Gardens open.
**Notes:** Plants dispatched Sep-Mar only.
**Map Ref:** S, C5

SDnm **Denmans Garden, (John Brookes Ltd)** ♿
Denmans Lane, Fontwell, West Sussex, BN18 0SU
Ⓣ (01243) 542808
Ⓕ (01243) 544064
Ⓔ denmans@denmans-garden.co.uk
Ⓦ www.denmans-garden.co.uk
**Contact:** Claudia Murphy
**Opening Times:** 0900-1700 (dusk in winter) 7 days all year, except 25th & 26th Dec & 1st Jan.

KEY
⊠ Mail order to UK or EU ⌂ Delivers to shows
✈ Exports beyond EU € Euro accepted
♿ Accessible by wheelchair ◆ See Display advertisement

**Cat. Cost:** None issued
**Credit Cards:** Visa MasterCard
**Specialities:** Rare and unusual plants.
**Map Ref:** S, D3 **OS Grid Ref:** SU944070

**SDow** **Downderry Nursery** ⊠ ✈ € ♿
Pillar Box Lane, Hadlow,
Nr Tonbridge, Kent,
TN11 9SW
Ⓣ (01732) 810081
Ⓕ (01732) 811398
Ⓔ info@downderry-nursery.co.uk
Ⓦ www.downderry-nursery.co.uk
**Contact:** Dr S J Charlesworth
**Opening Times:** 1000-1700 Tue-Sun 1st May-31st Oct & B/Hols. Other times by appt.
**Min Mail Order UK:** Nmc
**Min Mail Order EU:** Nmc
**Cat. Cost:** 3 × 1st class
**Credit Cards:** Delta MasterCard Maestro Visa
**Specialities:** Nat. Collections of *Lavandula* and *Rosmarinus*.
**Map Ref:** S, C4 **OS Grid Ref:** TQ625521

S

**SDys** **Dysons Nurseries** ⊠ ♿
Great Comp Garden, Platt, Sevenoaks, Kent, TN15 8QS
Ⓣ (01732) 886154
Ⓔ dysonsnurseries@aol.com
Ⓦ www.dysons-salvias.co.uk
**Contact:** William T Dyson
**Opening Times:** 1100-1700 7 days 1st Apr-31st Oct. Other times by appt.
**Min Mail Order UK:** £18.00 + p&p
**Cat. Cost:** 2 × 1st class
**Credit Cards:** None
**Specialities:** *Salvias*, especially New World species and cultivars.
**Map Ref:** S, C4

**SECG** **The English Cottage Garden Nursery** ⊠ ⌂
Eggarton Cottages, Eggarton Lane,
Godmersham, Kent,
CT4 7DY
Ⓣ (01227) 730242
Ⓕ (01227) 730242
Ⓔ enquiries@englishplants.co.uk
Ⓦ www.englishplants.co.uk
**Contact:** Teresa Sinclair
**Opening Times:** 7 days, please phone first.
**Min Mail Order UK:** £10.00
**Cat. Cost:** Free
**Credit Cards:** MasterCard Visa Solo Electron Switch
**Specialities:** Small nursery offering variety of traditional cottage garden plants, wildflowers & herbs. Some wildflowers available in small quantities only. Also native hedging, meadow & wildflower seed.
**Notes:** Plants can be ordered & paid for online. Availability regularly updated on website. Also sells wholesale.
**Map Ref:** S, C5

**SEND** **East Northdown Farm** ⊠ € ♿ ◆
Margate, Kent, CT9 3TS
Ⓣ (01843) 862060
Ⓕ (01843) 860206
Ⓔ friend.northdown@ukonline.co.uk
Ⓦ www.botanyplants.com
**Contact:** Louise & William Friend
**Opening Times:** 0900-1700 Mon-Sat, 1000-1700 Sun all year. Closed Xmas week & Easter Sun.
**Min Mail Order UK:** Nmc
**Cat. Cost:** Online only.
**Credit Cards:** Visa Switch MasterCard
**Specialities:** Chalk & coast-loving plants.
**Map Ref:** S, B6

**SEWo** **English Woodlands** ⊠ ⌂
Burrow Nursery, Cross in Hand,
Heathfield, East Sussex,
TN21 0UG
Ⓣ (01435) 862992
Ⓕ (01435) 867742
Ⓔ michael@ewburrownursery.co.uk
Ⓦ www.ewburrownursery.co.uk
**Contact:** Michael Hardcastle
**Opening Times:** 8000-1700 Mon-Sat. Closed Sun.
**Min Mail Order UK:** £25.00
**Cat. Cost:** 4 × 1st class
**Credit Cards:** All major credit/debit cards
**Specialities:** Trees, large & small.
**Notes:** Also sells wholesale.
**Map Ref:** S, C4 **OS Grid Ref:** TQ557122

**SFgr** **Firgrove Plants** ⊠
24 Wykeham Field, Wickham,
Fareham, Hampshire,
PO17 5AB
Ⓣ (01329) 835206 after 1900 hours.
Ⓔ jenny@firgroveplants.demon.co.uk
Ⓦ www.firgroveplants.demon.co.uk
**Contact:** Jenny MacKinnon
**Opening Times:** Not open. Mail order only.
**Min Mail Order UK:** £7.00
**Cat. Cost:** Sae
**Specialities:** Wide range of houseleeks & smaller range of other alpines in small quantities.
**Notes:** Houseleeks by mail order Apr-mid Oct.

**SGar** **GARDEN PLANTS** ⊠ ⌂
Windy Ridge, Victory Road, St Margarets-at-Cliffe, Dover, Kent, CT15 6HF
Ⓣ (01304) 853225
Ⓔ GardenPlants@GardenPlants-nursery.co.uk
Ⓦ www.GardenPlants-nursery.co.uk
**Contact:** Teresa Ryder & David Ryder
**Opening Times:** 1000-1730 summer, 1000-1700 winter. Closed Tues.
**Min Mail Order UK:** Nmc
**Cat. Cost:** 2 × 1st class + A5 sae
**Credit Cards:** None
**Specialities:** Unusual perennials, *Penstemon* & *Salvia*.
**Notes:** Plantsman's garden open to view. Map essential for first visit. Also sells wholesale.
**Map Ref:** S, C6 **OS Grid Ref:** TR358464

**SHaC** **HART CANNA** ⊠ € ♿
27 Guildford Road West, Farnborough, Hampshire, GU14 6PS
Ⓣ (01252) 514421
Ⓕ (01252) 378821
Ⓔ plants@hartcanna.com
Ⓦ www.hartcanna.com
**Contact:** Keith Hayward
**Opening Times:** Visitors by arrangement.
**Min Mail Order UK:** Nmc
**Min Mail Order EU:** Nmc
**Cat. Cost:** Free.
**Credit Cards:** All major credit/debit cards
**Specialities:** *Canna*. National Collection of *Canna*.
**Notes:** Also sells wholesale.
**Map Ref:** S, C3

**SHar** **HARDY'S COTTAGE GARDEN PLANTS** ⊠ ♿
Priory Lane Nursery, Freefolk Priors, Whitchurch, Hampshire, RG28 7NJ
Ⓣ (01256) 896533
Ⓕ (01256) 896572
Ⓔ info@hardys-plants.co.uk
Ⓦ www.hardys-plants.co.uk
**Contact:** Rosy Hardy
**Opening Times:** 1000-1700 7 days, 1st Mar-31st Oct. 1000-1500 Mon-Fri, 1st Nov-28th Feb.
**Min Mail Order UK:** Nmc
**Cat. Cost:** 10 × 1st class.
**Credit Cards:** Visa Access Electron Switch Solo
**Specialities:** Wide range of herbaceous perennials incl. *Heuchera*, *Penstemon*, *Salvia*, *Verbascum* & *Viola*.
**Notes:** A charge of £2.00 is made for delivery of pre-ordered plants to shows. Offers trade discount. Also sells wholesale
**Map Ref:** S, C2

**SHBN** **HIGH BANKS NURSERIES LTD** ♿
Cranbrook Road, Gills Green, Hawkhurst, Kent, TN18 5EW
Ⓣ (01580) 754492
Ⓕ (01580) 754450
**Contact:** Peter Russell
**Opening Times:** 0800-1700 (1630 in winter) daily.
**Cat. Cost:** £1.50 (stamps) + A4 sae
**Credit Cards:** All major credit/debit cards
**Specialities:** Wide general range with many unusual plants. Minimum of 250,000 plants on site at any one time. Open ground stock limited between Nov and Feb.
**Notes:** Also sells wholesale.
**Map Ref:** S, C5

**SHDw** **HIGHDOWN NURSERY** ⊠ ✈ ⌂ €
New Hall Lane, Small Dole, Nr Henfield, West Sussex, BN5 9YH
Ⓣ (01273) 492976
Ⓕ (01273) 492976
Ⓔ highdown.herbs@btopenworld.com
**Contact:** A G & J H Shearing
**Opening Times:** 0900-1700 7 days.
**Min Mail Order UK:** £10.00 + p&p
**Min Mail Order EU:** £10.00 + p&p
**Cat. Cost:** 3 × 1st class
**Credit Cards:** None
**Specialities:** Herbs. Grasses.
**Notes:** Partial wheelchair access. Also sells wholesale.
**Map Ref:** S, D3

**SHdy** **HARDY ORCHIDS** ⊠ ⌂
Pitcot Lane, Owslebury, Winchester, Hampshire, SO21 1LR
Ⓣ (01962) 777372
Ⓕ (01962) 777664
Ⓔ orchids@hardyorchids.co.uk
Ⓦ www.hardyorchids.co.uk
**Contact:** Claudia Whales
**Opening Times:** Mail order only. Open by appt. only.
**Min Mail Order UK:** £15.00 + p&p
**Min Mail Order EU:** £15.00 + p&p
**Cat. Cost:** 2 × 1st class
**Credit Cards:** All major credit/debit cards
**Specialities:** Hardy orchids. *Dactylorhiza*, *Pleione*, *Anacamptis*, *Orchis*, *Ophrys*,

KEY
⊠ Mail order to UK or EU ⌂ Delivers to shows
✈ Exports beyond EU € Euro accepted
♿ Accessible by wheelchair ◆ See Display advertisement

S

*Epipactis, Cypripedium, Bletilla, Gymnadenia, Himantoglossum, Platanthera* & *Spiranthes.*
**Notes:** Also sells wholesale.

**SHea** **HEASELANDS GARDEN NURSERY** ⊠ €
The Old Lodge, Isaacs Lane,
Haywards Heath, West Sussex,
RH16 4SA
Ⓣ (01444) 458084
Ⓕ (01444) 458084
Ⓔ headgardener@heaselands.wanadoo.co.uk
Ⓦ www.heaselandsnursery.co.uk
**Contact:** Stephen Harding
**Opening Times:** 0800-1700, Mon-Fri, but please phone first. W/ends by appt. only.
**Min Mail Order UK:** £8.00
**Min Mail Order EU:** £8.00
**Cat. Cost:** Online. Monthly availability lists.
**Credit Cards:** None
**Specialities:** *Rhododendron* hybrids and deciduous azaleas, home-produced from cuttings. Some in small quantities. Nat. Collection of Mollis Azaleas & Knaphill/ Exbury Azaleas.
**Notes:** Also sells wholesale.
**Map Ref:** S, C4 **OS Grid Ref:** TQ314230

S

**SHGN** **HILL GARTH NURSERY** ♿
Woodgreen Road, Godshill,
Fordingbridge, Hampshire,
SP6 2LP
Ⓣ (01425) 657619
Ⓕ (01425) 657619
**Contact:** Mrs S J Giddins
**Opening Times:** 0930-1700 Thu & Sun, Mar-end Oct.
**Cat. Cost:** None issued
**Credit Cards:** None
**Specialities:** Small nursery offering a range of rare, unusual & traditional hardy perennials, shrubs & trees. Some stock may be limited.
**Map Ref:** S, D1

**SHHo** **HIGHFIELD HOLLIES** ⊠ ◆
Highfield Farm, Hatch Lane,
Liss, Hampshire,
GU33 7NH
Ⓣ (01730) 892372
Ⓕ (01730) 894853
Ⓔ louise@highfieldhollies.com
Ⓦ www.highfieldhollies.com
**Contact:** Mrs Louise Bendall Duck
**Opening Times:** By appt.
**Min Mail Order UK:** £60.00
**Cat. Cost:** £3.50 for illustrated cat.
**Credit Cards:** None
**Specialities:** 150+ species & cultivars *Ilex* incl. specimen trees, hedging & topiary. Some in short supply.
**Map Ref:** S, C3 **OS Grid Ref:** SU787276

**SHmp** **HAMPSHIRE CARNIVOROUS PLANTS** ⊠ ✈ ⌂ €
Ya-Mayla, Allington Lane,
West End, Southampton, Hampshire,
SO30 3HQ
Ⓣ (023) 8047 3314
Ⓜ 07703 258296
Ⓕ (023) 466080
Ⓔ matthew@msoper.freesave.co.uk
Ⓦ www.hantsflytrap.com
**Contact:** Matthew Soper
**Opening Times:** Mail order only. Open by appt. only.
**Min Mail Order UK:** Nmc
**Min Mail Order EU:** £50.00 + p&p
**Cat. Cost:** 2 × 2nd class
**Credit Cards:** Visa MasterCard
**Specialities:** Carnivorous plants esp. *Nepenthes, Heliamphora, Sarracenia Pinguicula* & *Utricularia.*
**Notes:** Also sells wholesale.

**SHom** **HOME PLANTS**
52 Dorman Ave North, Aylesham,
Canterbury, Kent, CT3 3BW
Ⓣ (01304) 841746
Ⓔ homeplants@supanet.com
**Contact:** Stuart & Sue Roycroft
**Opening Times:** By appt. only, please phone first.
**Cat. Cost:** Sae for list
**Credit Cards:** None
**Specialities:** *Phygelius* & unusual South African hardy plants. Limited stock, please phone first.

**SHyH** **HYDRANGEA HAVEN** ⊠ ✈ ⌂ € ♿
Market Garden, Lower Beeding, West Sussex,
RH13 6PP
Ⓣ (01403) 891412
Ⓔ sales@hydrangea-haven.com
Ⓦ www.hydrangea-haven.com
**Contact:** Chris Loder
**Opening Times:** 1000-1600 Mon-Sat, please phone first, so we can give you our undivided attention.
**Min Mail Order UK:** Nmc
**Min Mail Order EU:** £100.00 + p&p
**Cat. Cost:** 2 × 1st class
**Credit Cards:** Switch MasterCard Visa
**Specialities:** *Hydrangea.*
**Notes:** Also sells wholesale.
**Map Ref:** S, C3

SIde **Iden Croft Herbs** ⊠ ♿ ◆
Frittenden Road, Staplehurst, Kent,
TN12 0DH
Ⓣ (01580) 891432
Ⓕ (01580) 892416
Ⓔ idencroftherbs@yahoo.co.uk
Ⓦ www.herbs-uk.com
**Contact:** Tracey Pearman
**Opening Times:** 0900-1700 Mon-Sat & 1100-1700 Sun & B/hols, Mar-Sep. 0900-1600 Oct-Feb, closed w/ends.
**Min Mail Order UK:** £10.00
**Min Mail Order EU:** £25.00
**Cat. Cost:** 4 × 1st class.
**Credit Cards:** All major credit/debit cards
**Specialities:** Herbs, aromatic & wildflower plants & plants for bees & butterflies. Nat. Collections of *Mentha*, *Nepeta* & *Origanum*.
**Notes:** Wheelchairs available at nursery.
**Map Ref:** S, C5

SImb **Imberhorne Lane Nursery** ⊠ €
Imberhorne Lane, East Grinstead,
West Sussex, RH19 1TZ
Ⓣ (01342) 321175
Ⓕ (01342) 317477
Ⓔ gardenexpert@btinternet.com
Ⓦ www.camelliasonline.co.uk
**Contact:** Michael Dongray
**Opening Times:** 0900-1645, 7 days.
**Min Mail Order UK:** Nmc
**Min Mail Order EU:** Nmc
**Cat. Cost:** 3 × 1st class.
**Credit Cards:** All major credit/debit cards
**Specialities:** 300 varieties of *Camellia* plus extensive range of shrubs & herbaceous. 66 varieties of Chinese tree peony (*Paeonia suffruticosa*). 200 varieties of *Rhododendron* & azaleas. 40 varieties of *Acer*.
**Map Ref:** S, C4 **OS Grid Ref:** TQ377373

SIng **W E Th. Ingwersen Ltd** ⌂
Birch Farm Nursery, Gravetye,
East Grinstead, West Sussex,
RH19 4LE
Ⓣ (01342) 810236
Ⓔ info@ingwersen.co.uk
Ⓦ www.ingwersen.co.uk
**Contact:** M P & M R Ingwersen
**Opening Times:** 0900-1600 daily excl. Sun & B/hols, Mar-Sep. 0900-1600 Mon-Fri Oct-Feb.
**Cat. Cost:** 2 × 1st class
**Credit Cards:** None
**Specialities:** Very wide range of hardy plants, mostly alpines. Also seed.
**Notes:** Wheelchair-accessible with assistance.
**Map Ref:** S, C4

SIoW **Isle of Wight Lavender** ⊠ € ♿
Staplehurst Grange, Newport, Isle of Wight,
PO30 2NQ
Ⓣ (01983) 825272
Ⓕ (01983) 825272
Ⓔ sales@lavender.co.uk
Ⓦ www.lavender.co.uk
**Contact:** Paul Abbott
**Opening Times:** 1000-1800 daily, except closed Wed Oct-Mar. Closed Xmas week.
**Min Mail Order UK:** Nmc
**Cat. Cost:** 1st class sae
**Credit Cards:** All major credit/debit cards
**Specialities:** Lavender.
**Map Ref:** S, D2

SIri **Iris of Sissinghurst** ⊠ ⌂ € ◆
Roughlands Farm, Goudhurst Road,
Marden, Kent,
TN12 9NH
Ⓣ (01622) 831511
Ⓔ orders@irisofsissinghurst.com
Ⓦ www.irisofsissinghurst.com
**Contact:** Sue Marshall
**Opening Times:** Contact nursery or see website for opening times.
**Min Mail Order UK:** Nmc
**Min Mail Order EU:** Nmc
**Cat. Cost:** 2 × 1st class
**Credit Cards:** None
**Specialities:** *Iris*, short, intermediate & tall bearded, *ensata*, *sibirica* & many species.
**Map Ref:** S, C5 **OS Grid Ref:** TQ735437

SJoh **Vic Johnstone and Claire Wilson** €
43 Winchester Street, Whitchurch,
Hampshire, RG28 7AJ
Ⓣ (01256) 893144
**Contact:** Vic Johnstone, Claire Wilson
**Opening Times:** By appt. Please telephone first.
**Cat. Cost:** 2 × 1st class
**Credit Cards:** None
**Specialities:** National Collection of *Verbascum*. *Verbascum* only. Stock available in small quantities.

SKee **Keepers Nursery** ⊠
Gallants Court, Gallants Lane,
East Farleigh, Maidstone, Kent,
ME15 0LE
Ⓣ (01622) 726465

KEY
⊠ Mail order to UK or EU ⌂ Delivers to shows
✈ Exports beyond EU € Euro accepted
♿ Accessible by wheelchair ◆ See Display advertisement

Ⓕ 0870 705 2145
Ⓔ info@keepers-nursery.co.uk
Ⓦ www.keepers-nursery.co.uk
**Contact:** Hamid Habibi
**Opening Times:** All reasonable hours by appt.
**Min Mail Order UK:** Nmc
**Cat. Cost:** Online only.
**Credit Cards:** Visa MasterCard Switch Maestro
**Specialities:** Old & unusual top fruit varieties. Top fruit propagated to order.
**Map Ref:** S, C4

**SKHP** **KEVIN HUGHES PLANTS** ⊠ ✈ ♠ €
Heale House, Middle Woodford,
Salisbury, Wiltshire,
SP4 6NT
Ⓜ 07720 718671
Ⓕ (01590) 679506
Ⓔ kevin@kevinhughesplants.com
Ⓦ www.kevinhughesplants.com
**Contact:** Kevin Hughes
**Opening Times:** 1000-1700 Wed-Sat, 1st Mar-31st Oct. Other times by appt. only.
**Min Mail Order UK:** £10.00
**Min Mail Order EU:** £20.00
**Cat. Cost:** 3 × 1st class
**Credit Cards:** None
**Specialities:** Choice & desirable shrubs, herbaceous, ferns. Specialities incl. legumes, *Magnolia*, *Trillium* (Nat. Collection status applied for), Mediterranean & deer-resistant plants.
**Notes:** Mail order only between Oct & Feb.
**Map Ref:** S, D2 **OS Grid Ref:** SZ310980

**SLan** **LANGLEY BOXWOOD NURSERY LTD** ⊠ ✈ € ♿ ◆
Langley Lane, Rake, Nr Liss,
Hampshire,
GU33 7JN
Ⓣ (01730) 894467
Ⓕ (01730) 894703
Ⓔ sales@boxwood.co.uk
Ⓦ www.boxwood.co.uk
**Contact:** Russell Coates
**Opening Times:** 0800-1630 Mon-Fri, 1000-1600 Sat. Please phone for directions.
**Min Mail Order UK:** Nmc
**Min Mail Order EU:** Nmc
**Cat. Cost:** 4 × 1st class
**Credit Cards:** All major credit/debit cards
**Specialities:** *Buxus* species, cultivars & hedging. Good range of topiary, *Taxus*, and 'character-pruned' specimens. Nat. Collection of *Buxus*. Evergreen topiary & hedging.
**Notes:** Also sells wholesale.
**Map Ref:** S, C3 **OS Grid Ref:** SU812290

**SLau** **THE LAURELS NURSERY** ⊠ €
Benenden, Cranbrook, Kent, TN17 4JU
Ⓣ (01580) 240463
Ⓕ (01580) 240463
Ⓦ www.thelaurelsnursery.co.uk
**Contact:** Peter or Sylvia Kellett
**Opening Times:** 0800-1600 Mon-Fri, 0900-1200 Sat, Sun by appt. only.
**Min Mail Order UK:** £20.00
**Cat. Cost:** Free
**Credit Cards:** None
**Specialities:** Open ground & container ornamental trees, shrubs & climbers incl. birch, beech & *Wisteria*.
**Notes:** Mail order of small *Wisteria* only. Also sells wholesale.
**Map Ref:** S, C5 **OS Grid Ref:** TQ815313

**SLay** **LAYHAM GARDEN CENTRE & NURSERY** ⊠ ♿
Lower Road, Staple, Nr Canterbury, Kent,
CT3 1LH
Ⓣ (01304) 813267
Ⓕ (01304) 814007
Ⓔ layham@gcstaple.fsnet.co.uk
Ⓦ www.layhamgardencentre.co.uk
**Contact:** Ellen Wessel
**Opening Times:** 0900-1700 7 days.
**Min Mail Order UK:** Nmc
**Min Mail Order EU:** £25.00 + p&p
**Cat. Cost:** Free
**Credit Cards:** Visa Switch MasterCard
**Specialities:** Roses, herbaceous, shrubs, trees & hedging plants.
**Notes:** Also sells wholesale.
**Map Ref:** S, C6 **OS Grid Ref:** TR276567

**SLBF** **LITTLE BROOK FUCHSIAS** ♿
Ash Green Lane West, Ash Green,
Nr Aldershot, Hampshire, GU12 6HL
Ⓣ (01252) 329731
Ⓔ carol.gubler@business.ntl.com
Ⓦ www.littlebrookfuchsias.co.uk
**Contact:** Carol Gubler
**Opening Times:** 0900-1700 Wed-Sun 1st Jan-1st Jul.
**Cat. Cost:** 50p + Sae
**Credit Cards:** None
**Specialities:** Fuchsias, old & new.
**Map Ref:** S, C3

**SLdr** **LODER PLANTS** ⊠ ✈ ♠ € ♿
Market Garden, Lower Beeding, West Sussex,
RH13 6PP
Ⓣ (01403) 891412
Ⓔ sales@rhododendrons.com
Ⓦ www.rhododendrons.com
**Contact:** Chris Loder

**Opening Times:** 1000-1600 Mon-Sat, please ring first so we can give you our undivided attention.
**Min Mail Order UK:** Nmc
**Min Mail Order EU:** £100.00 + p&p
**Cat. Cost:** 2 × 1st class
**Credit Cards:** Switch MasterCard Visa
**Specialities:** Rhododendrons & azaleas in all sizes. *Camellia* & *Hydrangea*.
**Notes:** Also sells wholesale.
**Map Ref:** S, C3

**SLim** **LIME CROSS NURSERY** ♿ ◆
Herstmonceux, Hailsham, East Sussex, BN27 4RS
Ⓣ (01323) 833229
Ⓕ (01323) 833944
Ⓔ LimeCross@aol.com
Ⓦ www.Limecross.co.uk
**Contact:** Jonathan Tate, Anita Green
**Opening Times:** 0830-1700 Mon-Sat & 1000-1600 Sun.
**Cat. Cost:** 3 × 1st class
**Credit Cards:** Visa MasterCard Delta Switch
**Specialities:** Conifers, trees & shrubs, climbers.
**Notes:** Also sells wholesale.
**Map Ref:** S, D4 **OS Grid Ref:** TQ642125

**SLon** **LONGSTOCK PARK NURSERY** ⊠ ♿
Longstock, Stockbridge, Hampshire, SO20 6EH
Ⓣ (01264) 810894
Ⓕ (01264) 810924
Ⓔ longstocknursery@leckfordestate.co.uk
Ⓦ www.longstocknursery.co.uk
**Contact:** Peter Moore
**Opening Times:** 0830-1630 Mon-Sat all year excl. Xmas & New Year, & 1100-1700 Sun Mar-Oct, 1000-1600 Sun, Nov-Feb.
**Min Mail Order UK:** Nmc
**Cat. Cost:** None issued. Lists of *Buddleja*, *Penstemon*, roses & fruit can be emailed or sent for 1 × 1st class.
**Credit Cards:** All major credit/debit cards
**Specialities:** A wide range, over 2000 varieties, of trees, shrubs, perennials, climbers, aquatics & ferns. Nat. Collections of *Buddleja* & *Clematis viticella*.
**Notes:** Mail order for *Buddleja* only.
**Map Ref:** S, C2 **OS Grid Ref:** SO365389

**SLPl** **LANDSCAPE PLANTS** ⊠ ✈ ♿
Cattamount, Grafty Green, Maidstone, Kent, ME17 2AP
Ⓣ (01622) 850245
Ⓕ (01622) 858063
Ⓔ landscapeplants@aol.com
**Contact:** Tom La Dell
**Opening Times:** 0800-1600 Mon-Fri, by appt. only.
**Min Mail Order UK:** £100.00 + p&p
**Min Mail Order EU:** £200.00 + p&p
**Cat. Cost:** 2 × 1st class
**Credit Cards:** None
**Specialities:** Garden & landscape shrubs & perennials.
**Notes:** Also sells wholesale.
**Map Ref:** S, C5 **OS Grid Ref:** TQ772468

**SMac** **MACGREGORS PLANTS FOR SHADE** ⊠
Carters Clay Road, Lockerley, Romsey, Hampshire, SO51 0GL
Ⓣ (01794) 340256
Ⓜ 07802 751606
Ⓔ plants@macgregors-shadeplants.co.uk
Ⓦ www.macgregors-shadeplants.co.uk
**Contact:** Irene & Stuart Bowron
**Opening Times:** By appt. only. Please phone before travelling to make arrangements. Occasional nursery events & garden open days, details on website.
**Min Mail Order UK:** Nmc
**Cat. Cost:** Online only.
**Credit Cards:** MasterCard Visa
**Specialities:** Less usual plants for all types of shade. Available in small numbers.
**Notes:** Mail order usually restricted to small numbers sent by 24hr carrier. Other arrangements by negotiation.
**Map Ref:** S, C2 **OS Grid Ref:** SU308239

**SMad** **MADRONA NURSERY** ⊠ 🛈 € ♿
Pluckley Road, Bethersden, Kent, TN26 3DD
Ⓣ (01233) 820100
Ⓕ (01233) 820091
Ⓔ madrona@fsmail.net
Ⓦ www.madrona.co.uk
**Contact:** Liam MacKenzie
**Opening Times:** 1000-1700 Sat-Tue 10th Mar-28th Oct. Closed 4th-17th Aug.
**Min Mail Order UK:** Nmc
**Cat. Cost:** Free
**Credit Cards:** All major credit/debit cards
**Specialities:** Unusual shrubs, conifers & perennials. Eryngiums, *Pseudopanax*.
**Map Ref:** S, C5 **OS Grid Ref:** TQ918419

**SMDP** **MARCUS DANCER PLANTS** ⊠ 🛈 ♿
Kilcreggan, Alderholt Road, Sandleheath, Fordingbridge, Hampshire, SP6 1PT
Ⓣ (01425) 652747

| KEY | | |
|---|---|---|
| | ⊠ Mail order to UK or EU | Delivers to shows |
| | ✈ Exports beyond EU | € Euro accepted |
| | ♿ Accessible by wheelchair | ◆ See Display advertisement |

Ⓔ marcus.dancer@btopenworld.com
Ⓦ clematisplants.co.uk
**Contact:** Marcus Dancer
**Opening Times:** By appointment only.
**Cat. Cost:** 2 × 1st class.
**Credit Cards:** None
**Specialities:** Wide range of *Clematis*, smaller range of *Daphne*. Some varieties available in small quantities only.
**Notes:** Mail order plants in 9cm pots when available. Contact nursery for details.
**Map Ref:** S, D1

**SMeo** **MEON VALLEY PLANTS**
Broadhanger Farm, Froxfield,
Nr Petersfield, Hampshire,
GU32 1DW
Ⓜ 07818 088019
Ⓔ info@meonvalleyplants.co.uk
Ⓦ www.meonvalleyplants.co.uk
**Contact:** Camilla Moreton
**Opening Times:** By appt. only.
**Cat. Cost:** 2 × 1st class for list.
**Credit Cards:** None
**Specialities:** Unusual bulbs, perennials & grasses. Many plants produced in small quantities.
**Map Ref:** S, C2 **OS Grid Ref:** SU713259

**SMHT** **MOUNT HARRY TREES** € ◆
Offham, Lewes, East Sussex,
BN7 3QW
Ⓣ (01273) 474456
Ⓕ (01273) 474266
Ⓔ mountharry@btopenworld.com
**Contact:** A Renton
**Opening Times:** By appt.
**Cat. Cost:** 1 × 1st class
**Credit Cards:** None
**Specialities:** Deciduous trees, specialising in heavy-standard to semi-mature sizes.
**Map Ref:** S, D4 **OS Grid Ref:** TQ313913

**SMHy** **MARCHANTS HARDY PLANTS** €
2 Marchants Cottages, Mill Lane,
Laughton, East Sussex,
BN8 6AJ
Ⓣ (01323) 811737
Ⓕ (01323) 811737
**Contact:** Graham Gough
**Opening Times:** 0930-1730 Wed-Sat, 21st Mar-13th Oct 2007.
**Cat. Cost:** 6 × 2nd class
**Specialities:** Uncommon herbaceous perennials. *Agapanthus*, *Kniphofia*, *Sedum*, choice grasses, *Miscanthus*, *Molinia*.
**Map Ref:** S, D4 **OS Grid Ref:** TQ506119

**SMrm** **MERRIMENTS GARDENS**
Hawkhurst Road, Hurst Green, East Sussex,
TN19 7RA
Ⓣ (01580) 860666
Ⓕ (01580) 860324
Ⓔ info@merriments.co.uk
Ⓦ www.merriments.co.uk
**Contact:** Taryn Cook
**Opening Times:** 0930-1730 Mon-Sat, 1030-1730 Sun (or dusk in winter).
**Cat. Cost:** Online only
**Credit Cards:** Visa Access American Express
**Specialities:** Unusual, wide-range of special roses. Tender & hardy perennials. Seasonal shrubs.
**Map Ref:** S, C4

**SMrs** **MRS MITCHELL'S KITCHEN & GARDEN** €
2 Warren Farm Cottages, The Warren,
West Tytherley, Salisbury, Wiltshire,
SP5 1LU
Ⓣ (01980) 863101
Ⓔ julianm05@aol.com
Ⓦ www.mrsmitchellskitchenandgarden.co.uk
**Contact:** Louise Mitchell
**Opening Times:** 1000-1700 Thu, Fri & some Sat, Apr-mid-Oct. Check web or phone to confirm weekly opening times.
**Cat. Cost:** Online only.
**Credit Cards:** None
**Specialities:** Family-run nursery stocking less usual cottage garden plants, especially hardy geraniums, oriental poppies, *Phlox*, *Echinacea*, heleniums, *Rudbeckia* & Michaelmas daisies. Some items in small quantities. Conversion to peat-free in progress.
**Notes:** Despite postal designation, nursery is in Hampshire. Accessible, but difficult, for wheelchairs because of deep gravel.
**Map Ref:** S, C2 **OS Grid Ref:** SU261333

**SOWG** **THE OLD WALLED GARDEN** ⊠ €
Oxonhoath, Hadlow, Kent, TN11 9SS
Ⓣ (01732) 810012
Ⓕ (01732) 810856
Ⓔ HeatherAngrave@aol.com
Ⓦ www.theoldwalledgarden.co.uk
**Contact:** John & Heather Angrave
**Opening Times:** 0900-1700 Mon-Sat. Sun by appt.
**Min Mail Order UK:** Nmc
**Cat. Cost:** 4 × 1st class
**Credit Cards:** All major credit/debit cards
**Specialities:** Many rare & unusual shrubs. Wide range of conservatory plants esp. Australian. Nat. Collection of *Callistemon*.
**Map Ref:** S, C4

**SPad** **PADDOCK PLANTS** ⊠ ⌂
The Paddock, Upper Toothill Road, Rownhams, Southampton, Hampshire, SO16 8AL
Ⓣ (023) 8073 9912
Ⓔ rob@paddockplants.co.uk
Ⓦ www.paddockplants.co.uk
**Contact:** Robert Courtney
**Opening Times:** By appt. only. Please telephone in advance.
**Min Mail Order UK:** Nmc
**Cat. Cost:** Free
**Credit Cards:** None
**Specialities:** Family-run nursery offering interesting range of perennials, grasses, ferns & shrubs, incl. some more unusual varieties. Some varieties grown in small quantities.
**Notes:** Online descriptive catalogue & ordering. Local delivery by our own transport.

**SPav** **PAVILION PLANTS** ⊠
18 Pavilion Road, Worthing, West Sussex, BN14 7EF
Ⓣ (01903) 821338
Ⓔ rewrew18@hotmail.com
**Contact:** Andrew Muggeridge
**Opening Times:** Please phone for details.
**Min Mail Order UK:** Nmc
**Cat. Cost:** 4 × 1st class
**Credit Cards:** None
**Specialities:** Perennials and bulbs. *Digitalis.*
**Notes:** Also sells wholesale.
**Map Ref:** S, D3

**SPer** **PERRYHILL NURSERIES LTD** ⊠ ⌂ ♿
Hartfield, East Sussex, TN7 4JP
Ⓣ (01892) 770377
Ⓕ (01892) 770929
Ⓔ sales@perryhillnurseries.co.uk
Ⓦ www.perryhillnurseries.co.uk
**Contact:** P J Chapman
**Opening Times:** 0900-1700 7 days 1st Mar-31st Oct. 0900-1630 1st Nov-28th Feb.
**Min Mail Order UK:** Nmc
**Cat. Cost:** £2.00 or online.
**Credit Cards:** Maestro Visa Access MasterCard
**Specialities:** Wide range of trees, shrubs, conifers, *Rhododendron* etc. Over 1300 herbaceous varieties, over 500 rose varieties.
**Notes:** Will deliver to small number of non-RHS shows. Mail order despatch depends on size & weight of plants.
**Map Ref:** S, C4 **OS Grid Ref:** TQ480375

**SPet** **PETTET'S NURSERY** ⊠ ⌂ € ♿
Poison Cross, Eastry, Sandwich, Kent, CT13 0EA
Ⓣ (01304) 613869
Ⓕ (01304) 613869
Ⓔ terry@pettetsnursery.fsnet.co.uk
Ⓦ www.pettetsnursery.co.uk
**Contact:** T & E H P Pettet
**Opening Times:** 0900-1700 daily Mar-Jul. 1000-1600 Aug-Oct weekdays only.
**Min Mail Order UK:** £10.00
**Min Mail Order EU:** £20.00
**Credit Cards:** None
**Specialities:** Climbers, shrubs, herbaceous perennials, alpines, pelargoniums, fuchsias.
**Notes:** Mail order Oct-Mar only. Also sells wholesale.
**Map Ref:** S, C6

**SPhx** **PHOENIX PERENNIAL PLANTS** ⌂ ♿
Paice Lane, Medstead, Alton, Hampshire, GU34 5PR
Ⓣ (01420) 560695
Ⓕ (01420) 563640
Ⓔ GreenFarmPlants.Marina.Christopher@Care4free.net
**Contact:** Marina Christopher
**Opening Times:** 1000-1800 Thu, Fri & Sat, 22nd Mar-20th Oct 2007.
**Cat. Cost:** 4 × 1st class
**Credit Cards:** All major credit/debit cards
**Specialities:** Perennials, many uncommon. *Sanguisorba, Thalictrum, Achillea, Eryngium, Monarda, Phlox, Verbascum*, centaureas, bulbs, grasses & late-flowering perennials.
**Notes:** Co-located with Select Seeds SSss.
**Map Ref:** S, C2 **OS Grid Ref:** SU657362

**SPin** **JOHN AND LYNSEY'S PLANTS**
2 Hillside Cottages, Trampers Lane, North Boarhunt, Fareham, Hampshire, PO17 6DA
Ⓣ (01329) 832786
**Contact:** Mrs Lynsey Pink
**Opening Times:** By appt. only. Open under NGS 1400-1800 Sun 16th Sep 2007.
**Cat. Cost:** None issued
**Credit Cards:** None
**Specialities:** Mainly *Salvia* with a wide range of other unusual perennials. Stock available in small quantities only, we will be happy to propagate to order. Nat. Collection of *Salvia* species.
**Notes:** Garden design & consultation service also available.
**Map Ref:** S, D2 **OS Grid Ref:** SU603109

KEY
⊠ Mail order to UK or EU ⌂ Delivers to shows
✈ Exports beyond EU € Euro accepted
♿ Accessible by wheelchair ◆ See Display advertisement

S

**SPla** **PLAXTOL NURSERIES** ⊠ ♿
The Spoute, Plaxtol, Sevenoaks, Kent,
TN15 0QR
Ⓣ (01732) 810550
Ⓕ (01732) 810149
Ⓔ alan@plaxtol-nurseries.co.uk
Ⓦ www.plaxtol-nurseries.co.uk
**Contact:** Alan Harvey
**Opening Times:** 1000-1700 7 days. Closed 2 weeks from Xmas Eve.
**Min Mail Order UK:** Nmc
**Min Mail Order EU:** £30.00 + p&p
**Cat. Cost:** 2 × 1st class
**Credit Cards:** All major credit/debit cards
**Specialities:** Hardy shrubs & herbaceous esp. for flower arrangers. Old-fashioned roses, ferns & climbers.
**Map Ref:** S, C4 **OS Grid Ref:** TQ611535

S

**SPlb** **PLANTBASE** € ♿
Sleepers Stile Road, Cousley Wood,
Wadhurst, East Sussex,
TN5 6QX
Ⓜ 07967 601064
Ⓔ graham@plantbase.freeserve.co.uk
**Contact:** Graham Blunt
**Opening Times:** 1000-1700, 7 days all year (winter by appt.).
**Cat. Cost:** 64p stamp
**Credit Cards:** None
**Specialities:** Wide range of alpines, perennials, shrubs, climbers, waterside plants, herbs, Australasian shrubs & South African plants.
**Map Ref:** S, C5

**SPoG** **THE POTTED GARDEN NURSERY**
Ashford Road, Bearsted, Maidstone, Kent,
ME14 4NH
Ⓣ (01622) 737801
Ⓔ pottedgarden@btconnect.com
Ⓦ www.thepottedgarden.co.uk
**Contact:** Any staff member
**Opening Times:** 0900-1730 (dusk in winter) 7 days. Xmas period opening times on website or answerphone. (Closed Xmas Day & Boxing Day.)
**Credit Cards:** All major credit/debit cards
**Map Ref:** S, C5

**SPol** **POLLIE'S PERENNIALS AND DAYLILY NURSERY** ⊠ ♿
Lodore, Mount Pleasant Lane,
Sway, Lymington, Hampshire,
SO41 8LS
Ⓣ (01590) 682577
Ⓕ (01590) 682577
Ⓔ terry@maasz.fsnet.co.uk
Ⓦ www.polliesdaylilies.co.uk
**Contact:** Pollie Maasz
**Opening Times:** 0930-1730 w/ends only during the daylily season mid-May to mid-Aug. Other times by appt. only.
**Min Mail Order UK:** £10.00
**Cat. Cost:** 2 × 1st class
**Credit Cards:** None
**Specialities:** *Hemerocallis*, also less commonly available hardy perennials. Stock available in small quantities only. Nat. Collection of Spider & Unusual Form *Hemerocallis*. 1300+ different cvs can be viewed, late Jun-mid Sep.
**Notes:** Mail order daylilies only.
**Map Ref:** S, D2

**SPop** **POPS PLANTS** ⊠ ✈ ⌂ €
Pops Cottage, Barford Lane,
Downton, Salisbury, Wiltshire,
SP5 3PZ
Ⓣ (01725) 511421
Ⓔ mail@popsplants
Ⓦ www.popsplants.com
**Contact:** G Dawson or L Roberts
**Opening Times:** By appt. only.
**Min Mail Order UK:** Contact nursery for details.
**Min Mail Order EU:** Contact nursery for details.
**Cat. Cost:** Contact nursery for details.
**Credit Cards:** Online only.
**Specialities:** *Primula auricula*. Some varieties in ltd. numbers. Nat. Collection of Show, Alpine & Double Auriculas.

**SPur** **PURE PLANTS**
Blackboys Nursery, Blackboys, Uckfield, East Sussex, TN22 5LS
Ⓣ (01825) 890858
Ⓕ (01825) 890878
Ⓦ www.pureplants.com
**Contact:** Brian Fidler
**Opening Times:** 0900-1700 Tue-Sat. Closed Sun & Mon except B/hol Sun 1000-1600 & B/hol Mon 0900-1700.
**Cat. Cost:** 2 × 1st class
**Credit Cards:** All major credit/debit cards
**Specialities:** Trees, shrubs, herbaceous, grasses & ferns. Many unusual varieties offered.
**Map Ref:** S, C4 **OS Grid Ref:** TQ515206

**SReu** **G REUTHE LTD** ⊠
Crown Point Nursery, Sevenoaks Road,
Ightham, Nr Sevenoaks, Kent,
TN15 0HB
Ⓣ (01732) 810694
Ⓕ (01732) 862166
Ⓔ reuthe@hotmail.co.uk
**Contact:** C & P Tomlin

**Opening Times:** 0900-1600 Thu-Sat. 1000-1600 Sun & B/hols Apr & May only, occasionally in Jun, please check. Closed Jan, Jul & Aug.
**Min Mail Order UK:** £30.00 + p&p
**Min Mail Order EU:** £500.00
**Cat. Cost:** £2.50
**Credit Cards:** Visa Access
**Specialities:** Rhododendrons & azaleas, trees, shrubs & climbers.
**Notes:** Mail order certain plants only to EU.

SRGP **Rosie's Garden Plants** ⊠ ✈ ⌂
Rochester Road, Aylesford, Kent,
ME20 7EB
Ⓣ (01622) 715777
Ⓜ 07740 696277
Ⓕ (01622) 715777
Ⓔ jcaviolet@aol.com
Ⓦ www.rosiesgardenplants.biz
**Contact:** J C Aviolet
**Opening Times:** Check website for new opening times.
**Min Mail Order UK:** Nmc
**Min Mail Order EU:** Nmc
**Cat. Cost:** Online only.
**Credit Cards:** Visa MasterCard Switch
**Specialities:** Hardy *Geranium*, *Buddleja* & *Aster*. 'Named' herbaceous & shrubs.
**Map Ref:** S, C4 **OS Grid Ref:** TQ737598

SRiF **Riverside Fuchsias** ⊠ ✈ ⌂ € ♿
Gravel Road, Sutton-at-Hone, Dartford, Kent,
DA4 9HQ
Ⓣ (01322) 863891
Ⓕ (01322) 863891
Ⓔ riverside_fuchsias@btopenworld.com
Ⓦ www.riversidefuchsias.pwp.blueyonder.co.uk/
**Contact:** George & Nellie Puddefoot
**Opening Times:** 0900-1700, Tue, Wed, Fri, Sat & Sun.
**Min Mail Order UK:** £1.50 per plant, 10 plants min. order.
**Min Mail Order EU:** €3.00
**Cat. Cost:** 3 × 1st class
**Credit Cards:** All major credit/debit cards
**Specialities:** *Fuchsia*. Nat. Collection holder.
**Notes:** Also sells wholesale.
**Map Ref:** S, B4

SRiv **River Garden Nurseries** ⊠ ⌂ € ♿ ◆
Troutbeck, Otford, Sevenoaks, Kent,
TN14 5PH
Ⓣ (01959) 525588
Ⓕ (01959) 525810
Ⓔ box@river-garden.co.uk
Ⓦ www.river-garden.co.uk
**Contact:** Jenny Alban Davies
**Opening Times:** By appt. only.
**Min Mail Order UK:** £10.00 + p&p
**Min Mail Order EU:** £50.00 + p&p
**Cat. Cost:** 2 × 1st class
**Credit Cards:** All major credit/debit cards
**Specialities:** *Buxus* species, cultivars & hedging. *Buxus* topiary.
**Notes:** Also sells wholesale.
**Map Ref:** S, C4 **OS Grid Ref:** TQ523593

SRkn **Rapkyns Nursery** ⌂ ♿
(Office) Brinkwells, School Lane,
Hadlow Down, East Sussex,
TN22 4HY
Ⓣ (01825) 830065
Ⓜ 07771 916933
Ⓕ (01825) 830065
**Contact:** Steven & Fiona Moore
**Opening Times:** 1000-1700 Tue, Thu & Fri, Mar-Oct incl.
**Cat. Cost:** 2 × 1st class
**Credit Cards:** None
**Specialities:** Unusual shrubs, perennials & climbers. Azaleas, campanulas, *Ceanothus*, geraniums, lavenders, lobelias, *Clematis*, penstemons & grasses. New collections of *Phormium*, *Phygelius*, *Agastache*, *Anemone*, *Heuchera*, *Heucherella* & salvias.
**Notes:** Nursery at Scotsford Farm, Street End Lane, Broad Oak. Heathfield, TN21 8UB. Also sells wholesale.
**Map Ref:** S, C4 **OS Grid Ref:** TQ604248

SRms **Rumsey Gardens** ⊠ ♿ ◆
117 Drift Road, Clanfield, Waterlooville,
Hampshire, PO8 0PD
Ⓣ (023) 9259 3367
Ⓔ info@rumsey-gardens.co.uk
Ⓦ www.rumsey-gardens.co.uk
**Contact:** Mrs M A Giles
**Opening Times:** 0900-1700 Mon-Sat & 1000-1700 Sun & B/hols. Closed Sun Nov-Feb.
**Min Mail Order UK:** Nmc
**Min Mail Order EU:** £15.00
**Cat. Cost:** Online only.
**Credit Cards:** Visa MasterCard Switch
**Specialities:** Wide general range. Herbaceous, alpines, heathers & ferns. Nat. & International Collection of *Cotoneaster*.
**Map Ref:** S, D2

S

KEY
⊠ Mail order to UK or EU ⌂ Delivers to shows
✈ Exports beyond EU € Euro accepted
♿ Accessible by wheelchair ◆ See Display advertisement

**SRos** **Rosewood Daylilies** ⊠
70 Deansway Avenue, Sturry, Nr Canterbury, Kent, CT2 0NN
Ⓣ (01227) 711071
Ⓕ (01227) 711071
Ⓔ Rosewoodgdns@aol.com
**Contact:** Chris Searle
**Opening Times:** By appt. only. Please phone.
**Min Mail Order UK:** Nmc
**Cat. Cost:** 2 × 1st class
**Credit Cards:** None
**Specialities:** *Hemerocallis*, mainly newer American varieties. *Agapanthus*.
**Map Ref:** S, C5

**SRot** **Rotherview Nursery** ⊠ ♁ € ♿
Ivy House Lane, Three Oaks, Hastings, East Sussex, TN35 4NP
Ⓣ (01424) 756228
Ⓔ rotherview@btinternet.com
Ⓦ www.rotherview.com
**Contact:** Ray & Wendy Bates
**Opening Times:** 1000-1700 Mar-Oct, 1000-1530 Nov-Feb, 7 days.
**Min Mail Order UK:** £10.00 + p&p
**Min Mail Order EU:** £20.00 + p&p
**Cat. Cost:** 4 × 1st class
**Credit Cards:** All major credit/debit cards
**Specialities:** Alpines.
**Notes:** Nursery is on same site as Coghurst Camellias. Also sells wholesale.
**Map Ref:** S, D5

**SSea** **Seale Nurseries** ♿ ◆
Seale Lane, Seale, Farnham, Surrey, GU10 1LD
Ⓣ (01252) 782410
**Contact:** David & Catherine May
**Opening Times:** 1000-1600 Tue-Sat incl. Other times by appt. Closed 25th Dec-mid Jan.
**Cat. Cost:** None issued.
**Credit Cards:** Visa Switch Access Delta
**Specialities:** Roses & *Pelargonium*. Some varieties in short supply, please phone first.
**Map Ref:** S, C3 **OS Grid Ref:** SU887477

**SSpi** **Spinners Garden** € ♿
School Lane, Boldre, Lymington, Hampshire, SO41 5QE
Ⓣ (01590) 673347
**Contact:** Peter Chappell
**Opening Times:** 1000-1700 Tue-Sat. By appt. Dec & Jan.
**Cat. Cost:** Sae for plant list.
**Credit Cards:** None
**Specialities:** Less common trees & shrubs esp. *Acer*, *Magnolia*, species & lace-cap *Hydrangea*. Bog & woodland plants, especially trilliums.
**Map Ref:** S, D2 **OS Grid Ref:** SZ323981

**SSss** **Select Seeds** ⊠ ♁ ♿
Paice Lane, Medstead, Nr Alton, Hampshire, GU34 5PR
Ⓣ (01420) 560695
Ⓕ (01420) 563640
Ⓔ GreenFarmPlants.Marina.Christopher@Care4free.net
**Contact:** Marina Christopher
**Opening Times:** Not open. Mail order only.
**Min Mail Order UK:** £10.00
**Cat. Cost:** 3 × 1st class
**Credit Cards:** All major credit/debit cards
**Specialities:** Seeds. *Aconitum*, *Eryngium*, *Thalictrum*, *Sanguisorba* & *Angelica*.
**Notes:** Co-located with Phoenix Perennial Plants SPhx.
**Map Ref:** S, C2 **OS Grid Ref:** SU657362

**SSta** **Starborough Nursery** ⊠ ♿
Starborough Road, Marsh Green, Edenbridge, Kent, TN8 5RB
Ⓣ (01732) 865614
Ⓕ (01732) 862166
Ⓔ starborough@hotmail.co.uk
**Contact:** C & P Tomlin
**Opening Times:** 0900-1600 Mon-Sat (closed Wed & Sun). Closed Jan, Jul & Aug.
**Min Mail Order UK:** £30.00 + p&p
**Min Mail Order EU:** £500.00
**Cat. Cost:** £2.50
**Credit Cards:** Visa Access
**Specialities:** Rare and unusual shrubs especially *Daphne*, *Acer*, rhododendrons & azaleas, *Magnolia* & *Hamamelis*.
**Notes:** Certain plants only to EU.

**SSth** **Southease Plants** ♿
Corner Cottage, Southease, Nr Lewes, East Sussex, BN7 3HX
Ⓣ (01273) 513681
Ⓜ 07791 856206
Ⓕ (01273) 513681
**Contact:** Adrian Orchard
**Opening Times:** 1100-1700 Wed-Sat, 1400-1700 Sun & by appt.
**Cat. Cost:** 2 × 1st class
**Credit Cards:** None
**Specialities:** A small nursery concentrating on hellebores, species & hybrids, grown on the nursery from seed collected from selected plants or obtained from specialist growers. Ltd. quantities.
**Map Ref:** S, D4 **OS Grid Ref:** TQ422052

SSto **Stone Cross Garden Centre** ♿ ◆
Rattle Road, Pevensey, Sussex, BN24 5EB
Ⓣ (01323) 763250
Ⓕ (01323) 763195
Ⓔ gardencentre@stone-cross-nurseries.co.uk
Ⓦ www.stone-cross-nurseries.co.uk
**Contact:** Mrs J Birch
**Opening Times:** 0830-1730 Mon-Sat & 1000-1600 Sun & B/hols.
**Cat. Cost:** None issued
**Credit Cards:** Visa Access Switch
**Specialities:** *Hebe* & *Clematis*, evergreen shrubs. Lime tolerant & coastal shrubs & plants.
**Notes:** Also sells wholesale
**Map Ref:** S, D4 **OS Grid Ref:** 6104

SSvw **Southview Nurseries** ⊠ ⌂
Chequers Lane, Eversley Cross, Hook, Hampshire, RG27 0NT
Ⓣ (0118) 9732206
Ⓕ (0118) 9736160
Ⓔ Mark@Trenear.wanadoo.co.uk
Ⓦ www.southviewnurseries.co.uk
**Contact:** Mark & Elaine Trenear
**Opening Times:** Mail order only. Orders for collection by prior arrangement.
**Min Mail Order UK:** Nmc
**Cat. Cost:** Free
**Credit Cards:** None
**Specialities:** Unusual hardy plants, specialising in old-fashioned pinks & period plants. Nat. Collection of Old Pinks. Pinks collection open in June. Please ring for details.
**Notes:** Orders by prior arrangement only.
**Map Ref:** S, C3

SSwd **Springwood Nursery** ⊠
5 Southview Drive, Uckfield, East Sussex, TN22 1TA
Ⓜ 07760 152587
Ⓔ springwood.nurserysx@tiscali.co.uk
Ⓦ SpringwoodNurserySussex.co.uk
**Contact:** Kevin Clift
**Opening Times:** Mail order only. Open by appt. only.
**Min Mail Order UK:** Nmc
**Credit Cards:** None
**Specialities:** *Hedychium*. Some plants available in small quantities.
**Notes:** Also sells wholesale.

STes **Test Valley Nursery** ⊠ ⌂ €
Stockbridge Road, Timsbury, Romsey, Hampshire, SO51 0NG
Ⓣ (01794) 368881
Ⓔ julia@testvalleynursery.co.uk
Ⓦ www.testvalleynursery.co.uk
**Contact:** Julia Benn
**Opening Times:** 1000-1700 Tue-Sun Mar-Oct, or by appt.
**Min Mail Order UK:** Nmc.
**Cat. Cost:** 3 × 1st class
**Credit Cards:** All major credit/debit cards
**Specialities:** Large range of herbaceous perennials, incl. unusual & new varieties. Some varieties available in small quantities only. Phone first to avoid disappointment.
**Notes:** Mail order Oct-Mar only.
**Map Ref:** S, C2

STil **Tile Barn Nursery** ⊠ ✈ ⌂ €
Standen Street, Iden Green, Benenden, Kent, TN17 4LB
Ⓣ (01580) 240221
Ⓕ (01580) 240221
Ⓔ tilebarn.nursery@virgin.net
Ⓦ www.tilebarn-cyclamen.co.uk
**Contact:** Peter Moore
**Opening Times:** 0900-1700 Wed-Sat.
**Min Mail Order UK:** £10.00 + p&p
**Min Mail Order EU:** £25.00 + p&p
**Cat. Cost:** Sae
**Credit Cards:** None
**Specialities:** *Cyclamen* species.
**Notes:** Also sells wholesale.
**Map Ref:** S, C5 **OS Grid Ref:** TQ805301

STre **Peter Trenear** ⊠ ♿
Chantreyland, Chequers Lane, Eversley Cross, Hampshire, RG27 0NX
Ⓣ (0118) 9732300
Ⓔ peter@babytrees.co.uk
Ⓦ www.babytrees.co.uk
**Contact:** Peter Trenear
**Opening Times:** 0900-1630 Mon-Sat.
**Min Mail Order UK:** £5.00 + p&p
**Cat. Cost:** 1 × 1st class
**Credit Cards:** None
**Specialities:** Trees, shrubs, conifers, bonsai & *Pinus*.
**Map Ref:** S, C3 **OS Grid Ref:** SU795612

STrG **Terrace Gardener** ⊠ €
Meadow View, Hildenbrook Farm, Riding Lane, Hildenbrook, Kent, TN11 9JN
Ⓣ (01732) 832762
Ⓔ johan@terracegardener.com
Ⓦ www.terracegardener.co.uk

KEY
⊠ Mail order to UK or EU ⌂ Delivers to shows
✈ Exports beyond EU € Euro accepted
♿ Accessible by wheelchair ◆ See Display advertisement

S

**Contact:** Johan Hall
**Opening Times:** Not open. Mail order only, incl. online & by phone. Telephone orders 0800-1700 Mon-Fri.
**Min Mail Order UK:** Nmc
**Cat. Cost:** Free
**Credit Cards:** All major credit/debit cards
**Specialities:** Mediterranean trees & plants. Container gardening. Architectural & hardy exotics.

SUsu **USUAL & UNUSUAL PLANTS** ⌂ €
Onslow House, Magham Down, Hailsham, East Sussex, BN27 1PL
Ⓣ (01323) 840967
Ⓕ (01323) 844725
Ⓔ jennie@uuplants.co.uk
Ⓦ www.uuplants.co.uk
**Contact:** Jennie Maillard
**Opening Times:** 0930-1730 Wed-Sat, 17th Mar-16th Oct. Other times strictly by appt. only.
**Cat. Cost:** Online only.
**Credit Cards:** None
**Specialities:** Small quantities of a wide variety of unusual garden-worthy perennials esp. *Erysimum*, *Euphorbia*, hardy *Geranium*, *Salvia* & grasses.

S

SVic **VICTORIANA NURSERY GARDENS** ⊠ ♿
Challock, Ashford, Kent, TN25 4DG
Ⓣ (01233) 740529
Ⓕ (01233) 740030
Ⓔ info@victoriana.ws
Ⓦ www.victoriana.ws
**Contact:** Stephen Shirley
**Opening Times:** 0930-1630 (or dusk) Mon-Fri, 1030-1630 Sat. (1030-1630 Sun in summer months.)
**Min Mail Order UK:** £3.95
**Cat. Cost:** Free or online.
**Credit Cards:** Delta MasterCard Visa Switch
**Specialities:** *Fuchsia*, 600+ varieties. Also vegetable plants, seeds, fruit trees & bushes.
**Map Ref:** S, C5 **OS Grid Ref:** TR018501

SVil **THE VILLAGE NURSERIES** ⌂ € ♿
Sinnocks, West Chiltington, Pulborough, West Sussex, RH20 2JX
Ⓣ (01798) 813040
Ⓕ (01798) 817240
Ⓔ villagenurseries@btconnect.com
Ⓦ www.village-nurseries.co.uk
**Contact:** Peter Manfield
**Opening Times:** 0900-1800 or dusk, 7 days.
**Cat. Cost:** None issued
**Credit Cards:** All major credit/debit cards
**Specialities:** Extensive selection of hardy perennials, plus wide range of seasonal patio & bedding plants. Many plants grown in biodegradable pots.
**Map Ref:** S, D3 **OS Grid Ref:** TQ095182

SWal **WALLACE PLANTS** ⌂
Lewes Road Nursery, Lewes Road, Laughton, East Sussex, BN8 6BN
Ⓣ (01323) 811729
Ⓔ sjk@wallaceplants.fsnet.co.uk
Ⓦ www.wallaceplants.fsnet.co.uk
**Contact:** Simon Wallace
**Opening Times:** 0930-1800 7 days, incl. B/hols, Mar-Sep, 0930-1600 Oct-Feb.
**Cat. Cost:** 3 × 1st class
**Credit Cards:** None
**Specialities:** Ornamental grasses, *Hebe*s, herbaceous/perennials, salvias, penstemons & choice, rare & unusual plants.
**Map Ref:** S, D4 **OS Grid Ref:** TQ513126

SWat **WATER MEADOW NURSERY** ⊠ ⊠ ⌂ ♿
Cheriton, Nr Alresford, Hampshire, SO24 0QB
Ⓣ (01962) 771895
Ⓕ (01962) 771895
Ⓔ plantaholic@onetel.com
Ⓦ www.plantaholic.co.uk
**Contact:** Mrs Sandy Worth
**Opening Times:** 1000-1700 Wed-Sat Mar-Jul or by appt.
**Min Mail Order UK:** £10.00 + p&p
**Min Mail Order EU:** £50.00 + p&p
**Cat. Cost:** 6 × 1st class or £2.00 cheque.
**Credit Cards:** All major credit/debit cards
**Specialities:** Water lilies, extensive water garden plants, unusual herbaceous perennials, aromatic herbs & wildflowers. New Super Poppy Range. Nat. Collection of *Papaver orientale* group.
**Notes:** Mail order by 24 hour courier service only. Also sells wholesale.
**Map Ref:** S, C2

SWCr **WYCH CROSS NURSERIES** ♿
Wych Cross, Forest Row, East Sussex, RH18 5JW
Ⓣ (01342) 822705
Ⓕ (01342) 825329
Ⓔ roses@wychcross.co.uk
Ⓦ www.wychcross.co.uk
**Contact:** J Paisley
**Opening Times:** 0900-1730 Mon-Sat.
**Cat. Cost:** Free
**Credit Cards:** All major credit/debit cards
**Specialities:** Roses.
**Map Ref:** S, C4 **OS Grid Ref:** TQ420320

SWvt **Wolverton Plants Ltd** € ♿ ◆
Wolverton Common, Tadley, Hampshire, RG26 5RU
Ⓣ (01635) 298453
Ⓕ (01635) 299075
Ⓔ Julian@wolvertonplants.co.uk
Ⓦ www.wolvertonplants.co.uk
**Contact:** Julian Jones
**Opening Times:** 0900-1800 (or dusk Nov-Feb), 7 days. Closed Xmas/New Year.
**Cat. Cost:** Online only.
**Credit Cards:** All major credit/debit cards
**Notes:** Also sells wholesale.
**Map Ref:** S, C2 **OS Grid Ref:** SU555589

## Wales and the West

WAbb **Abbey Dore Court Garden** € ♿
Abbey Dore Court, Abbey Dore, Herefordshire, HR2 0AD
Ⓣ (01981) 240419
Ⓕ (01981) 240419
Ⓦ www.abbeydorecourt.co.uk
**Contact:** Mrs C Ward
**Opening Times:** 1100-1730 1st Apr-30th Sep. Closed Mon, Wed & Fri. Open B/hol Mons.
**Cat. Cost:** None issued
**Credit Cards:** None
**Specialities:** Mainly hardy perennials, many unusual, which may be seen growing in the garden. *Astrantia*, *Crocosmia*, *Helleborus*, *Paeonia*, *Pulmonaria* & *Sedum*.
**Map Ref:** W, C4 **OS Grid Ref:** SO388308

WAbe **Aberconwy Nursery** ⛫ ♿
Graig, Glan Conwy, Colwyn Bay, Conwy, LL28 5TL
Ⓣ (01492) 580875
**Contact:** Dr & Mrs K G Lever
**Opening Times:** 1000-1700 Tue-Sun mid-Feb-mid-Oct.
**Cat. Cost:** 2 × 2nd class
**Credit Cards:** Visa MasterCard
**Specialities:** Alpines, including specialist varieties, esp. autumn gentians, *Saxifraga* & dwarf ericaceous. Shrubs & woodland plants incl. *Helleborus* & smaller ferns.
**Map Ref:** W, A3 **OS Grid Ref:** SH799744

WAct **Acton Beauchamp Roses** ⊠ ✈
Acton Beauchamp, Worcestershire, WR6 5AE
Ⓣ (01531) 640433
Ⓕ (01531) 640802
Ⓔ info@actonbeaurose.co.uk
Ⓦ www.actonbeaurose.co.uk
**Contact:** Lindsay Bousfield
**Opening Times:** 1400-1700 Tue-Sat Apr-Oct, 1000-1700 B/hol Mon. 1400-1700 Thu-Sat, Nov-Mar.
**Min Mail Order UK:** Nmc
**Min Mail Order EU:** Nmc
**Cat. Cost:** 3 × 1st class
**Credit Cards:** Maestro Solo Visa MasterCard
**Specialities:** Species roses, old roses, modern shrub, English, climbers, ramblers & ground-cover roses.
**Map Ref:** W, C4 **OS Grid Ref:** SO683492

WAln **L A Allen** ⊠
Windy Ridge, Cerrigwibber, Llandrindod Wells, Powys, LD1 5NY
Ⓔ lesallen2006@yahoo.co.uk
**Contact:** L A Allen
**Opening Times:** By prior appt.
**Min Mail Order UK:** Nmc
**Min Mail Order EU:** Nmc
**Cat. Cost:** 4 × 1st class
**Credit Cards:** None
**Specialities:** Nat. Collection of *Primula auricula*. Type: alpine auricula, show edged, show self, doubles, stripes. Surplus plants from the Collection so available in small quantities. Occasionally only 1 or 2 available of some cvs.
**Notes:** Also sells wholesale.

WAlt **Alternative Plants** ⊠
The Brackens, Yorkley Wood, Nr Lydney, Gloucestershire, GL15 4TU
Ⓣ (01594) 562457
Ⓔ alternativeplants@tiscali.co.uk
Ⓦ alternativeplants.co.uk
**Contact:** Mrs Rosemary Castle
**Opening Times:** Mail order only.
**Min Mail Order UK:** £10.00
**Min Mail Order EU:** £20.00
**Cat. Cost:** 3 × 1st class
**Credit Cards:** None
**Specialities:** Unusual native plants. Small stocks, spring/autumn supply.

WAul **Aulden Farm** ⊠ ⛫ ♿
Aulden, Leominster, Herefordshire, HR6 0JT
Ⓣ (01568) 720129
Ⓔ pf@auldenfarm.co.uk
Ⓦ www.auldenfarm.co.uk
**Contact:** Alun & Jill Whitehead

| KEY | | |
|---|---|---|
| | ⊠ Mail order to UK or EU | ⛫ Delivers to shows |
| | ✈ Exports beyond EU | € Euro accepted |
| | ♿ Accessible by wheelchair | ◆ See Display advertisement |

**Opening Times:** 1000-1700 Tue & Thu Apr-Aug. Thu only in Mar & Sep. Other times by appt. Please phone.
**Min Mail Order UK:** Nmc
**Min Mail Order EU:** £20.00
**Cat. Cost:** 2 × 1st class
**Credit Cards:** Paypal
**Specialities:** Hardy herbaceous perennials, with a special interest in *Hemerocallis* & *Iris*.
**Notes:** Mail order for *Hemerocallis* & *Iris* only.
**Map Ref:** W, C4 **OS Grid Ref:** SO462548

**WBIS** **British Iris Society** ⊠
Aulden Farm, Aulden, Leominster, Herefordshire, HR6 0JT
Ⓣ (01568) 720129
Ⓔ alun@britishirissociety.org.uk
Ⓦ www.britishirissociety.org.uk
**Contact:** Alun Whitehead
**Min Mail Order UK:** Nmc
**Min Mail Order EU:** Nmc
**Cat. Cost:** Plant list free but membership required.
**Credit Cards:** None
**Specialities:** *Iris*.
**Notes:** Plants available to members. Please apply for membership.

W

**WBod** **Bodnant Garden Nursery Ltd** ⊠ ♿
Tal-y-Cafn, Colwyn Bay, Caernarfonshire, LL28 5RE
Ⓣ (01492) 650731
Ⓕ (01492) 650863
Ⓔ sales@bodnant-plants.co.uk
Ⓦ www.bodnant-plants.co.uk
**Contact:** Stephen Dixon
**Opening Times:** All year.
**Min Mail Order UK:** Nmc
**Cat. Cost:** £2.50 cost refundable with 1st order.
**Credit Cards:** Visa MasterCard Switch Connect
**Specialities:** *Rhododendron*, *Camellia*, *Magnolia*. Wide range of unusual trees and shrubs.
**Map Ref:** W, A3 **OS Grid Ref:** SH809723

**WBor** **Bordervale Plants** ♿
Nantyderi, Sandy Lane, Ystradowen, Cowbridge, Vale of Glamorgan, CF71 7SX
Ⓣ (01446) 774036
Ⓦ www.bordervale.co.uk
**Contact:** Claire E Jenkins
**Opening Times:** 1000-1700 Fri-Sun & B/hols Mar-early Oct. Other times by appt.
**Cat. Cost:** 2 × 1st class large sae or online.
**Credit Cards:** None
**Specialities:** Unusual herbaceous perennials, trees & shrubs, as well as cottage garden plants, many displayed in the 2 acre garden.
**Notes:** Garden open for NGS & Red Cross. See website for details.
**Map Ref:** W, D3 **OS Grid Ref:** ST022776

**WBou** **Bouts Cottage Nurseries** ⊠ €
Bouts Lane, Inkberrow, Worcestershire, WR7 4HP
Ⓣ (01386) 792923
Ⓦ www.boutsviolas.co.uk
**Contact:** M & S Roberts
**Opening Times:** Strictly by appt. only.
**Min Mail Order UK:** Nmc
**Min Mail Order EU:** Nmc
**Cat. Cost:** 1st class sae.
**Credit Cards:** None
**Specialities:** *Viola*.

**WBrE** **Bron Eifion Nursery** ⊠ €
Bron Eifion, Criccieth, Caernarfonshire, LL52 0SA
Ⓣ (01766) 522890
Ⓔ gardencottage@talktalk.net
**Contact:** Suzanne Evans
**Opening Times:** 1000-dusk 7 days 1st Mar-31st Oct. 1st Nov-29th Feb by appt. only.
**Min Mail Order UK:** £30.00 + p&p
**Min Mail Order EU:** £50.00 + p&p
**Cat. Cost:** None issued.
**Credit Cards:** None
**Specialities:** *Kalmia*, *Daphne*, *Embothrium*, plants for coastal regions & wide and interesting range of hardy plants.
**Map Ref:** W, B2

**WBrk** **Brockamin Plants** ♿
Brockamin, Old Hills, Callow End, Worcestershire, WR2 4TQ
Ⓣ (01905) 830370
Ⓔ dickstonebrockamin@tinyworld.co.uk
**Contact:** Margaret Stone
**Opening Times:** By appt. only.
**Cat. Cost:** Free.
**Credit Cards:** None
**Specialities:** Hardy perennials, especially hardy geraniums and some asters. Stock available in small quantities only.
**Map Ref:** W, C5 **OS Grid Ref:** SO830488

**WBuc** **Bucknell Nurseries**
Bucknell, Shropshire, SY7 0EL
Ⓣ (01547) 530606
Ⓕ (01547) 530699
**Contact:** A N Coull
**Opening Times:** 0800-1700 Mon-Fri & 1000-1300 Sat.
**Cat. Cost:** Free
**Credit Cards:** None

**Specialities:** Bare-rooted hedging conifers & forest trees.
**Notes:** Also sells wholesale.
**Map Ref:** W, C4 **OS Grid Ref:** SO356736

**W**BVN **Banwy Valley Nursery** ⊠ ♿
Foel, Llangadfan, Nr Welshpool, Powys, SY21 0PT
Ⓣ (01938) 820281
Ⓕ (01938) 820281
Ⓔ syd@banwnursery.co.uk
Ⓦ www.banwnursery.co.uk
**Contact:** Syd Luck
**Opening Times:** 1000-1700 Tue-Sun. Open B/hols.
**Min Mail Order UK:** Nmc
**Cat. Cost:** 2 × 1st class or via email
**Credit Cards:** All major credit/debit cards
**Specialities:** Perennials, shrubs, incl. climbers, ornamental & fruit trees. Ever expanding range of magnolias & rhododendrons. All grown on the nursery.
**Notes:** Large specimens not available by mail order.
**Map Ref:** W, B3 **OS Grid Ref:** SH993107

**W**CAu **Claire Austin Hardy Plants** ⊠ ✈ ♿
Edgebolton, Shawbury, Shrewsbury, Shropshire, SY4 4EL
Ⓣ (01939) 251173
Ⓕ (01939) 251311
Ⓔ enquiries@claireaustin-hardyplants.co.uk
Ⓦ www.claireaustin-hardyplants.co.uk
**Contact:** Claire Austin
**Opening Times:** 0900-1700 Mon-Sat, 1000-1600 Sun. Closed Xmas to New Year.
**Min Mail Order UK:** Nmc
**Min Mail Order EU:** £50.00 + p&p
**Cat. Cost:** UK £3.50, Europe €5.00
**Credit Cards:** MasterCard Visa Switch
**Specialities:** *Paeonia*, *Iris*, *Hemerocallis* & hardy plants. Nat. Collections of Bearded *Iris* & Hybrid Herbaceous *Paeonia*.
**Notes:** Exports tree peonies only beyond EU.
**Map Ref:** W, B4

**W**CCa **Claines Canna Collection** ⊠ €
197 Northwick Road, Claines, Worcester, Worcestershire, WR3 7EJ
Ⓣ (01905) 456459
Ⓜ 07798 8150
Ⓕ (01905) 458713
Ⓔ mdalebo@clainescanna.co.uk
Ⓦ www.clainescanna.co.uk
**Contact:** Malcolm Dalebo
**Opening Times:** W/ends only by appt.
**Min Mail Order UK:** Nmc
**Min Mail Order EU:** Nmc
**Cat. Cost:** Free or online.
**Credit Cards:** Paypal
**Specialities:** *Canna.*
**Notes:** Also sells wholesale.

**W**CEl **Celyn Vale Eucalyptus Nurseries** ⊠ ✈
Carrog, Corwen, Merioneth, LL21 9LD
Ⓣ (01490) 430671
Ⓕ (01490) 430671
Ⓔ info@eucalyptus.co.uk
Ⓦ www.eucalyptus.co.uk
**Contact:** Andrew McConnell & Paul Yoxall
**Opening Times:** 0900-1600 Mon-Fri Jan-Nov. Please phone first outside these days.
**Min Mail Order UK:** 3 plants + p&p
**Min Mail Order EU:** 3 plants + p&p
**Cat. Cost:** 2 × 1st class
**Credit Cards:** All major credit/debit cards
**Specialities:** Hardy *Eucalyptus* & *Acacia.*
**Notes:** Also sells wholesale.
**Map Ref:** W, A3 **OS Grid Ref:** SJ116452

**W**CFE **Charles F Ellis** ⊠ €
(Office) Barn House, Wormington, Nr Broadway, Worcestershire, WR12 7NL
Ⓣ (01386) 584077 (nursery)
Ⓕ (01386) 584491
Ⓔ info@ellisplants.co.uk
Ⓦ www.ellisplants.co.uk
**Contact:** Charles Ellis
**Opening Times:** 1000-1600 7 days 1st Apr-30th Sep. Other times by appt.
**Min Mail Order UK:** Nmc
**Cat. Cost:** None issued.
**Credit Cards:** None
**Specialities:** Wide range of more unusual shrubs, conifers & climbers.
**Notes:** Nursery is at Oak Piece Farm Nursery, Stanton, near Broadway.
**Map Ref:** W, C5

**W**CHb **The Cottage Herbery** ⌂
Mill House, Boraston, Nr Tenbury Wells, Worcestershire, WR15 8LZ
Ⓣ (01584) 781575
Ⓕ (01584) 781483
Ⓦ www.thecottageherbery.co.uk
**Contact:** K & R Hurst
**Opening Times:** By appt. only. Order collection service available.
**Cat. Cost:** 6 × 1st class

KEY
⊠ Mail order to UK or EU ⌂ Delivers to shows
✈ Exports beyond EU € Euro accepted
♿ Accessible by wheelchair ◆ See Display advertisement

**Credit Cards:** None
**Specialities:** Over 600 varieties of herbs. Aromatic & scented foliage plants, esp. *Monarda*, *Rosmarinus*, *Campanula*, alliums & seeds. Soil Assoc. licence no. G6475.
**Notes:** Group visits & courses, lectures & talks. Sae for list or see website.

**WChG** **CHENNELS GATE GARDENS & NURSERY** ♿
Eardisley, Herefordshire, HR3 6LT
Ⓣ (01544) 327288
**Contact:** Mark Dawson
**Opening Times:** 1000-1700 7 days Mar-Oct.
**Cat. Cost:** None issued.
**Credit Cards:** None
**Specialities:** Interesting & unusual cottage garden plants, grasses, hedging & shrubs.
**Map Ref:** W, C4

W

**WCLn** **COUNTRY LANE NURSERIES** ♿
Plwmp, Llandysul, Ceredigion,
SA44 6HU
Ⓣ (01239) 851015
Ⓜ 07976 411884
Ⓕ (01239) 858921
Ⓔ Theresa.Glover@btinternet.com
**Contact:** Theresa Glover
**Opening Times:** 1000-1700 Wed-Sun, Easter-end of Sep. Other times please phone first.
**Cat. Cost:** 2 × 1st sae for plant list.
**Specialities:** Good range of unusual hardy perennials and shrubs, incl. large range of moisture-loving & bog plants.
**Notes:** Also sells wholesale. Home-reared, pure-breed poultry & waterfowl to view & for sale.
**Map Ref:** W, C2 **OS Grid Ref:** SN364511

**WClo** **CLOSE NURSERY** ♿
Shipton-Moyne Road, Tetbury,
Gloucestershire, GL8 8PJ
Ⓣ (01666) 505021
Ⓔ lindastead@tiscali
**Contact:** P Stead
**Opening Times:** 0900-1700 Mon-Sat, 1000-1700 Sun.
**Cat. Cost:** None issued.
**Credit Cards:** All major credit/debit cards
**Specialities:** Herbaceous.
**Map Ref:** W, D5 **OS Grid Ref:** ST884918

**WCor** **CORSESIDE NURSERY** ☒
Angle, Pembrokeshire,
SA71 5AA
Ⓣ (01646) 641505
Ⓔ corsesidenursery@btinternet.com
**Contact:** Sandra Williams
**Opening Times:** 1000-1600, 7 days. Open all year. Gardens open 3 times a year, or by appt.
**Min Mail Order UK:** Nmc
**Cat. Cost:** Online only.
**Credit Cards:** None
**Specialities:** Coastal hardy shrubs, perennials and succulents. *Lanpranthus* & *Aeonium*. All stock seed-raised or from cuttings/division. Specialist advice by appt.
**Notes:** Also sells wholesale
**Map Ref:** W, D1 **OS Grid Ref:**

**WCot** **COTSWOLD GARDEN FLOWERS** ☒ €
Sands Lane, Badsey, Evesham, Worcestershire,
WR11 7EZ
Ⓣ nursery (01386) 833849:
mail order (01386) 422829
Ⓕ nursery (01386) 49844
Ⓔ info@cgf.net
Ⓦ www.cgf.net
**Contact:** Bob Brown/Vicky Parkhouse
**Opening Times:** 0900-1730 Mon-Fri all year. 1000-1730 Sat & Sun Mar-Sep. Sat & Sun Oct-Feb by appt.
**Min Mail Order UK:** Nmc
**Min Mail Order EU:** Nmc
**Cat. Cost:** £1.50 or 6 × 1st class.
**Credit Cards:** MasterCard Access Visa Switch
**Specialities:** A very wide range of easy & unusual perennials. Nat. Collection of *Lysimachia*.
**Notes:** Also sells wholesale.
**Map Ref:** W, C5 **OS Grid Ref:** SP077426

**WCra** **CRANESBILL NURSERY** ☒ ♿
White Cottage, Stock Green,
Nr Redditch, Worcestershire,
B96 6SZ
Ⓣ (01386) 792414
Ⓕ (01386) 792280
Ⓔ cranesbilluk@aol.com
Ⓦ www.cranesbillnursery.com
**Contact:** Mrs S M Bates
**Opening Times:** 1000-1700 19th Mar-30th Sep. Closed Wed & Thu. Aug by appt. only. Open most w/ends.
**Min Mail Order UK:** Nmc
**Min Mail Order EU:** Nmc
**Cat. Cost:** 4 × 1st class
**Credit Cards:** All major credit/debit cards
**Specialities:** Hardy geraniums & other herbaceous plants.
**Map Ref:** W, C5 **OS Grid Ref:** 975585

**WCre** **CRESCENT PLANTS** ☒ ♿
Stoney Cross, Marden, Hereford,
HR1 3EW
Ⓣ (01432) 880262

Ⓕ (01432) 880262
Ⓔ june@auriculas.co.uk
Ⓦ www.auriculas.co.uk
**Contact:** June Poole
**Opening Times:** Open by appt. Please phone.
**Min Mail Order UK:** Nmc
**Min Mail Order EU:** Nmc
**Cat. Cost:** Free
**Credit Cards:** All major credit/debit cards. Payment by Paypal online.
**Specialities:** Named varieties of *Primula auricula* incl. show, alpine, double, striped & border types.
**Notes:** Orders dispatched post free.
**Map Ref:** W, C4 **OS Grid Ref:** SO525477

WCru **CRûG FARM PLANTS** ⊠ ♿ ◆
Griffith's Crossing, Nr Caernarfon, Gwynedd, LL55 1TU
Ⓣ (01248) 670232
Ⓔ info@crug-farm.co.uk
Ⓦ www.crug-farm.co.uk
**Contact:** B and S Wynn-Jones
**Opening Times:** 1000-1700 Thu-Sun last Sat Feb to last Sun Jun, plus B/hols, then Thu-Sat until last Sat in Sep.
**Min Mail Order UK:** Nmc
**Cat. Cost:** 3 × 2nd class or online.
**Credit Cards:** All major credit/debit cards
**Specialities:** Shade plants, climbers, species *Hydrangea*, *Araliaceae*, rare trees & shrubs, *Convallariaceae*, herbaceous & bulbous incl. self-collected new introductions from the Far East & the Americas. Nat. Collections. of *Coriaria*, *Paris* & *Polygonatum*.
**Notes:** Delivery by overnight carrier.
**Map Ref:** W, A2 **OS Grid Ref:** SH509652

WDib **DIBLEY'S NURSERIES** ⊠ ⌂ € ♿ ◆
Llanelidan, Ruthin, Denbighshire, LL15 2LG
Ⓣ (01978) 790677
Ⓕ (01978) 790668
Ⓔ sales@dibleys.com
Ⓦ www.dibleys.com
**Contact:** R Dibley
**Opening Times:** 1000-1700 7 days Mar-Oct.
**Min Mail Order UK:** Nmc
**Min Mail Order EU:** Nmc
**Cat. Cost:** Free
**Credit Cards:** Visa Access Switch Electron Solo
**Specialities:** *Streptocarpus*, *Columnea*, *Solenostemon* & other gesneriads & *Begonia*. Nat. Collection of *Streptocarpus*.
**Notes:** Also sells wholesale.
**Map Ref:** W, A3

WDin **DINGLE NURSERIES** ⌂ ♿ ◆
Welshpool, Powys, SY21 9JD
Ⓣ (01938) 555145
Ⓕ (01938) 555778
Ⓔ jill@dinglenurseries.co.uk
Ⓦ www.dinglenurseries.co.uk
**Contact:** Jill Rock
**Opening Times:** 0900-1700, 7 days.
**Cat. Cost:** Free plant list
**Credit Cards:** MasterCard Switch EuroCard, Delta Visa
**Specialities:** Largest range of trees & shrubs in Wales. Wide seasonal selection of garden plants incl. roses, herbaceous perennials, conifers & barerooted forestry, hedging & fruit. All sizes incl. many mature specimens.
**Notes:** Also sells wholesale
**Map Ref:** W, B4 **OS Grid Ref:** SJ196082

WDyf **DYFFRYN NURSERIES** ⊠ € ♿
Home Farm, Dyffryn, Cardiff, CF5 6JU
Ⓣ (02920) 592085
Ⓕ (02920) 593462
Ⓔ sales@dyffryn-nurseries.co.uk
Ⓦ www.dyffryn-nurseries.co.uk
**Contact:** Victoria Hardaker
**Opening Times:** 0800-1600 Mon-Fri, 1100-1600 Sat & Sun.
**Min Mail Order UK:** £25.00
**Min Mail Order EU:** £25.00
**Cat. Cost:** Information on request
**Credit Cards:** MasterCard Access Switch Delta Visa
**Specialities:** Native & exotic mature, hardy specimen & architectural plants.
**Notes:** Also sells wholesale.
**Map Ref:** W, D3

WDyG **DYFFRYN GWYDDNO NURSERY**
Dyffryn Farm, Lampeter Velfrey, Narberth, Pembrokeshire, SA67 8UN
Ⓣ (01834) 861684
Ⓔ sally.polson@virgin.net
Ⓦ www.pembrokeshireplants.co.uk
**Contact:** Mrs S L Polson
**Opening Times:** By appt. only.
**Credit Cards:** None
**Specialities:** Eclectic, yet wide-ranging, from tender salvias & grasses to bog. Peat-free & principled. Plants available in small quantities only. Bamboos. *Bamboo* collection open by appt. in aid of NGS.

KEY
⊠ Mail order to UK or EU ⌂ Delivers to shows
✈ Exports beyond EU € Euro accepted
♿ Accessible by wheelchair ◆ See Display advertisement

**Notes:** Also sells wholesale.
**Map Ref:** W, D2 **OS Grid Ref:** SR138148

WEas **Eastgrove Cottage Garden Nursery** ♿
Sankyns Green, Nr Shrawley, Little Witley, Worcestershire, WR6 6LQ
Ⓣ (01299) 896389
Ⓦ www.eastgrove.co.uk
**Contact:** Malcolm & Carol Skinner
**Opening Times:** 1400-1700 Thu, Fri, Sat 26th Apr-14th Jul, plus May B/hol Sun & Mon. Closed throughout Aug. 1400-1700 Thu, Fri, Sat 6th Sep-6th Oct.
**Cat. Cost:** Online only.
**Credit Cards:** None
**Specialities:** Unique cottage garden & arboretum. Many varieties of *Viola*, *Iris*, *Dianthus* & *Aquilegia*, plus a wide range of old favourites & many unusual plants. RHS Partnership garden with 2 acres of arboretum plus grass labyrinth.
**Map Ref:** W, C5 **OS Grid Ref:** SO795644

W

WFar **Farmyard Nurseries** ✉ ✈ ♿ ◆
Llandysul, Ceridigion, SA44 4RL
Ⓣ (01559) 363389 or (01267) 220259
Ⓕ (01559) 362200
Ⓔ richard@farmyardnurseries.co.uk
Ⓦ www.farmyardnurseries.co.uk
**Contact:** Richard Bramley
**Opening Times:** 1000-1700 7 days excl. Xmas, Boxing & New Year's Day.
**Min Mail Order UK:** Nmc
**Min Mail Order EU:** Nmc
**Cat. Cost:** 4 × 1st class
**Credit Cards:** Visa Switch MasterCard
**Specialities:** Excellent general range esp. *Helleborus*, *Hosta*, *Tricyrtis* & *Schizostylis*, plus shrubs, trees, climbers, alpines & esp. herbaceous. Nat. Collection of *Tricyrtis*.
**Notes:** Also sells wholesale.
**Map Ref:** W, C2 **OS Grid Ref:** SN421406

WFFs **Fabulous Fuchsias**
The Martins, Stanley Hill, Bosbury, Nr Ledbury, Herefordshire, HR8 1HE
Ⓣ (01531) 640298
Ⓔ afuchsia@excite.com
**Contact:** Angela Thompson
**Opening Times:** By appt. only. Sells at local plant fairs.
**Cat. Cost:** 3 × 1st class
**Credit Cards:** None
**Specialities:** *Fuchsia*: hardy, bush, trailing, species, triphyllas, unusual varieties, many available in small quantities only.

WFib **Fibrex Nurseries Ltd** ✉ ✈ ⌂
Honeybourne Road, Pebworth, Stratford-on-Avon, Warwickshire, CV37 8XP
Ⓣ (01789) 720788
Ⓕ (01789) 721162
Ⓔ sales@fibrex.co.uk
Ⓦ www.fibrex.co.uk
**Contact:** U Key-Davis & R L Godard-Key
**Opening Times:** 0900-1700 Mon-Fri 1st Mar-31st Aug. 0900-1600 Mon-Fri 1st Sep-28th Feb. 1030-1600 Sat & Sun 17th Feb-29th Jul. Closed last 2 weeks Dec & 1st week Jan. Closed Easter Sun & Aug B/hol Mon.
**Min Mail Order UK:** £10.00 + p&p
**Min Mail Order EU:** £20.00 + p&p
**Cat. Cost:** 2 × 1st class
**Credit Cards:** Switch MasterCard Visa
**Specialities:** *Hedera*, ferns, *Pelargonium* & *Helleborus*. National Collections of *Pelargonium* & *Hedera*. Plant collections subject to time of year, please check by phone.
**Notes:** Restricted wheelchair access. Also sells wholesale.

WFoF **Flowers of the Field**
Field Farm, Weobley, Herefordshire, HR4 8QJ
Ⓣ (01544) 318262
Ⓕ (01544) 318262
Ⓔ info@flowersofthefield.co.uk
Ⓦ www.flowersofthefield.co.uk
**Contact:** Kathy Davies
**Opening Times:** 0900-1900 7 days.
**Cat. Cost:** 2 × 1st class
**Credit Cards:** None
**Specialities:** Traditional & unusual perennials, grasses, shrubs, trees & herbs. Oriental lilies & freesias for cutting.
**Notes:** Nursery partially accessible for wheelchairs. Also sells wholesale.
**Map Ref:** W, C4

WFuv **Fuchsiavale Nurseries** ✉ ⌂ ♿
Worcester Road, Torton, Kidderminster, Worcestershire, DY11 7SB
Ⓣ (01299) 251162
Ⓕ (01299) 251256
Ⓔ helen@fuchsiavale.co.uk
Ⓦ www.fuchsiavale.co.uk
**Contact:** Helen Andre
**Opening Times:** 0900-1700 Mon-Sat, Apr-Aug. 1000-1600 Mon-Sat, Jan-Mar & Sep-Dec. 1000-1600 Sun & B/hols all year.
**Min Mail Order UK:** £9.00 (6 plants @ £1.50 incl. p&p)
**Min Mail Order EU:** £9.00 + p&p
**Cat. Cost:** Free

**Credit Cards:** All major credit/debit cards
**Specialities:** *Fuchsia*. A good range of shrubs, perennials & trees also available.
**Map Ref:** W, C5 **OS Grid Ref:** SO843723

**W**Gob **The Gobbett Nursery** ⊠
Farlow, Kidderminster, Worcestershire, DY14 8TD
Ⓣ (01746) 718647
Ⓕ (01746) 718647
Ⓔ christine.link@lineone.net
Ⓦ www.thegobbettnursery.co.uk
**Contact:** C H Link
**Opening Times:** 1030-1700, Mon-Sat.
**Min Mail Order UK:** £10.00
**Cat. Cost:** 3 × 1st class.
**Credit Cards:** None
**Specialities:** *Syringa*, *Magnolia*, *Camellia* & *Cornus*. Some varieties available in small quantities only.
**Map Ref:** W, B4 **OS Grid Ref:** SO648811

**W**Gor **Gordon's Nursery** ⊠ ♠ ♿
1 Cefnpennar Cottages, Cefnpennar, Mountain Ash, Mid-Glamorgan, CF45 4EE
Ⓣ (01443) 474593
Ⓕ (01443) 475835
Ⓔ sales@gordonsnursery.co.uk
Ⓦ www.gordonsnursery.co.uk
**Contact:** D A Gordon
**Opening Times:** 1000-1800 7 days Mar-Jun. 1000-1700 7 days Jul-Oct. 1100-1600 weekends only Nov & Feb. Closed Dec-Jan.
**Min Mail Order UK:** Nmc
**Cat. Cost:** 3 × 1st class
**Credit Cards:** All major credit/debit cards
**Specialities:** Shrubs, perennials, alpines & dwarf conifers.
**Notes:** Mail order only available in some cases, please check for conditions in catalogue.
**Map Ref:** W, D3 **OS Grid Ref:** SO037012

**W**GwG **Gwynfor Growers** ⊠ ♠ ♿
Gwynfor, Pontgarreg, Llangranog, Llandysul, Ceredigion, SA44 6AU
Ⓣ (01239) 654151
Ⓔ info@gwynfor.co.uk
Ⓦ www.gwynfor.co.uk
**Contact:** Steve & Angie Hipkin
**Opening Times:** 1000 to sunset Wed, Thu & Sun, all year round.
**Min Mail Order UK:** Nmc
**Cat. Cost:** 4 × 1st class, free by email.
**Credit Cards:** None
**Specialities:** Plants to intrigue & delight the gardener, incl. heritage Welsh apple varieties, scented shrubs & ground cover.
**Notes:** Plants also available at Aberystwyth & Lampeter Farmers' Markets.
**Map Ref:** W, C2 **OS Grid Ref:** SN331536

**W**Hal **Hall Farm Nursery** ⊠ ♠ €
Vicarage Lane, Kinnerley, Nr Oswestry, Shropshire, SY10 8DH
Ⓣ (01691) 682135
Ⓕ (01691) 682135
Ⓔ hallfarmnursery@ukonline.co.uk
Ⓦ www.hallfarmnursery.co.uk
**Contact:** Christine & Nick Ffoulkes-Jones
**Opening Times:** 1000-1700 Tue-Sat 1st Mar-31st Oct 2007.
**Min Mail Order UK:** £20.00
**Cat. Cost:** 4 × 1st class
**Credit Cards:** Visa MasterCard Electron Maestro
**Specialities:** Unusual herbaceous plants, grasses, bog plants & pool marginals, late-flowering perennials, foliage plants.
**Notes:** Nursery partially accessible for wheelchairs.
**Map Ref:** W, B4 **OS Grid Ref:** SJ333209

**W**Har **Harley Nursery** ♿
Harley, Shropshire, SY5 6LN
Ⓣ (01952) 510241
Ⓕ (01952) 510570
Ⓔ njmurphy@hotmail.co.uk
**Contact:** Duncan Murphy, Moira Murphy & Nicholas Murphy
**Opening Times:** 0900-1730 Mon-Sat, 1000-1700 Sun & B/hols. Winter hours 0900-1700 Sun & B/hols.
**Cat. Cost:** 2 × 1st class
**Credit Cards:** All major credit/debit cards
**Specialities:** Wide range of ornamental & fruit trees. Own grown shrubs, climbers, wide range of hedging plants. Conservation & wildlife plants & native trees a speciality.
**Map Ref:** W, B4

**W**HCG **Hunts Court Garden & Nursery** ♿
North Nibley, Dursley, Gloucestershire, GL11 6DZ
Ⓣ (01453) 547440
Ⓕ (01453) 549944
Ⓔ keith@huntscourt.fsnet.co.uk
**Contact:** T K & M M Marshall
**Opening Times:** 0900-1230 & 1345-1700 Tue-Sat excl. Aug, nursery & garden. Also by appt. See NGS for Sun openings.

KEY
⊠ Mail order to UK or EU ♠ Delivers to shows
✈ Exports beyond EU € Euro accepted
♿ Accessible by wheelchair ◆ See Display advertisement

W

**Cat. Cost:** 5 × 2nd class
**Credit Cards:** None
**Specialities:** Old roses species & climbers. Hardy *Geranium*, *Penstemon* & unusual shrubs.
**Map Ref:** W, D4

WHCr **HERGEST CROFT GARDENS**
Kington, Herefordshire,
HR5 3EG
Ⓣ (01544) 230160
Ⓕ (01544) 232031
Ⓔ gardens@hergest.co.uk
Ⓦ www.hergest.co.uk
**Contact:** Stephen Lloyd
**Opening Times:** 1200-1730, 7 days, Apr-Oct.
**Cat. Cost:** None issued
**Credit Cards:** All major credit/debit cards
**Specialities:** *Acer*, *Betula* & unusual woody plants.
**Notes:** Limited wheelchair access.

W

WHer **THE HERB GARDEN & HISTORICAL PLANT NURSERY** ⊠
Ty Capel Pensarn, Pentre Berw,
Anglesey, Gwynedd,
LL60 6LG
Ⓣ (01248) 422208
Ⓜ 07751 583958
Ⓕ (01248) 422208
Ⓦ www.HistoricalPlants.co.uk
**Contact:** Corinne & David Tremaine-Stevenson
**Opening Times:** By appt. only.
**Min Mail Order UK:** £15.00 + p&p
**Min Mail Order EU:** £50.00 + p&p sterling only.
**Cat. Cost:** List £2.50
**Credit Cards:** None
**Specialities:** Rarer herbs, rare natives & wild flowers; rare & unusual & historical perennials & old roses.
**Map Ref:** W, A2

WHil **HILLVIEW HARDY PLANTS** ⊠ ⊠ ⌂ € ♿ ◆
(off B4176), Worfield, Nr Bridgnorth,
Shropshire, WV15 5NT
Ⓣ (01746) 716454
Ⓕ (01746) 716454
Ⓔ hillview@themutual.net
Ⓦ www.hillviewhardyplants.com
**Contact:** Ingrid, John & Sarah Millington
**Opening Times:** 0900-1700 Mon-Sat Mar-mid Oct. At other times, please phone first.
**Min Mail Order UK:** £15.00 + p&p
**Min Mail Order EU:** £15.00 + p&p
**Cat. Cost:** 5 × 2nd class
**Credit Cards:** All major credit/debit cards
**Specialities:** Choice herbaceous perennials incl. *Acanthus* & *Acanthaceae*, *Aquilegia*, *Auricula*, *Primula*, *Canna*, *Crocosmia*, *Eucomis*, *Ixia*, South African bulbs. Nat Collection of *Acanthus*.
**Notes:** Also sells wholesale.
**Map Ref:** W, B4 **OS Grid Ref:** SO772969

WHlf **HAYLOFT PLANTS** ⊠
Manor Farm, Pensham, Pershore,
Worcestershire, WR10 3HB
Ⓣ (01386) 554440
Ⓕ (01386) 553833
Ⓔ info@hayloftplants.co.uk
Ⓦ www.hayloftplants.co.uk
**Contact:** Yvonne Walker
**Opening Times:** Not open. Mail order only.
**Min Mail Order UK:** Nmc
**Min Mail Order EU:** Nmc
**Cat. Cost:** Free
**Credit Cards:** All major credit/debit cards

WHoo **HOO HOUSE NURSERY** € ♿ ◆
Hoo House, Gloucester Road, Tewkesbury,
Gloucestershire, GL20 7DA
Ⓣ (01684) 293389
Ⓕ (01684) 293389
Ⓔ nursery@hoohouse.co.uk
Ⓦ www.hoohouse.plus.com
**Contact:** Robin & Julie Ritchie
**Opening Times:** 1000-1700 Mon-Sat, 1100-1700 Sun.
**Cat. Cost:** 3 × 1st class
**Credit Cards:** None
**Specialities:** Wide range of herbaceous & alpines – many unusual, incl. *Aster*, *Papaver*, *Geranium* & *Penstemon*. Nat. Collections. of *Platycodon* & *Gentiana asclepiadea* cvs.
**Notes:** Also sells wholesale.
**Map Ref:** W, C5 **OS Grid Ref:** SO893293

WHrl **HARRELLS HARDY PLANTS** ⊠
(Office) 15 Coxlea Close, Evesham,
Worcestershire, WR11 4JS
Ⓣ (01386) 443077
Ⓕ (01386) 443852
Ⓔ enicklin@evesham11.fsnet.co.uk
Ⓦ www.harrellshardyplants.co.uk
**Contact:** Liz Nicklin & Kate Phillips
**Opening Times:** 1000-1200 Sun Mar-Nov. Other times by appt. Please phone.
**Min Mail Order UK:** Nmc.
**Cat. Cost:** 3 × 1st class
**Credit Cards:** None
**Specialities:** Display gardens showcase wide range of hardy perennials, esp. *Hemerocallis* & grasses.

**Notes:** Nursery located off Rudge Rd, Evesham. Please phone for directions or see catalogue. Partial wheelchair access. Mail order Nov-Mar only.
**Map Ref:** W, C5 **OS Grid Ref:** SP033443

WIvy **IVYCROFT PLANTS** ⊠ € ♿
Upper Ivington, Leominster, Herefordshire, HR6 0JN
Ⓣ (01568) 720344
Ⓔ rogerandsue@ivycroft.freeserve.co.uk
Ⓦ www.ivycroft.freeserve.co.uk
**Contact:** Roger Norman
**Opening Times:** 0900-1600 Thu Feb & Apr-Sep. Other times by appt., please phone.
**Min Mail Order UK:** Nmc
**Min Mail Order EU:** Nmc
**Cat. Cost:** 2 × 1st class
**Credit Cards:** None
**Specialities:** *Cyclamen*, *Galanthus*, *Salix*, alpines, herbaceous & ferns.
**Notes:** Mail order Feb/Mar & Jul/Aug, *Galanthus* & *Salix* in winter only.
**Map Ref:** W, C4 **OS Grid Ref:** SO464562

WJas **PAUL JASPER TREES** ⊠
The Lighthouse, Bridge Street, Leominster, Herefordshire, HR6 8DX
Ⓕ (01568) 616499 for orders.
Ⓔ enquiries@jaspertrees.co.uk
Ⓦ www.jaspertrees.co.uk
**Contact:** Paul Jasper
**Opening Times:** Not open. Mail order only.
**Min Mail Order UK:** £40.00 + p&p
**Cat. Cost:** Online only. Regular catalogue updates on website.
**Credit Cards:** None
**Specialities:** Full range of fruit & ornamental trees. Over 100 modern and traditional apple varieties + 220 others all direct from the grower. Many unusual varieties of *Malus domestica*.
**Notes:** Also sells wholesale.

WJek **JEKKA'S HERB FARM** ⊠ ⛺ ♿
Rose Cottage, Shellards Lane, Alveston, Bristol, BS35 3SY
Ⓣ (01454) 418878
Ⓕ (01454) 411988
Ⓔ farm@jekkasherbfarm.com
Ⓦ www.jekkasherbfarm.com
**Contact:** Jekka McVicar
**Opening Times:** 4 times a year. Please check website for dates.
**Min Mail Order UK:** £15 plants
**Min Mail Order EU:** Seeds only to the EU.
**Cat. Cost:** 4 × 1st class
**Credit Cards:** Visa MasterCard Delta Switch Maestro
**Specialities:** Culinary, medicinal, aromatic, decorative herbs. Soil Association licensed herb farm.
**Map Ref:** W, D4

WKif **KIFTSGATE COURT GARDENS** ♿
Kiftsgate Court, Chipping Camden, Gloucestershire, GL55 6LW
Ⓣ (01386) 438777
Ⓕ (01386) 438777
Ⓔ kiftsgte@aol.com
Ⓦ www.kiftsgate.co.uk
**Contact:** Mrs J Chambers
**Opening Times:** 1200-1800 Sat-Wed, May, Jun & Jul. 1400-1800 Sun, Mon-Wed, Apr, Aug, Sep.
**Cat. Cost:** None issued
**Credit Cards:** All major credit/debit cards, except American Express
**Specialities:** Small range of unusual plants.
**Map Ref:** W, C5 **OS Grid Ref:** SP170430

W

WLav **THE LAVENDER GARDEN** ⊠ ⛺ €
Ashcroft Nurseries, Nr Ozleworth, Kingscote, Tetbury, Gloucestershire, GL8 8YF
Ⓣ (01453) 860356 or 549286
Ⓜ 07837 582943
Ⓔ Andrew007Bullock@aol.com
Ⓦ www.TheLavenderG.co.uk
**Contact:** Andrew Bullock
**Opening Times:** 1100-1700 Sat & Sun. Weekdays variable, please phone. 1st Nov-1st Mar by appt. only.
**Min Mail Order UK:** £50.00 + p&p
**Min Mail Order EU:** £50.00 + p&p
**Cat. Cost:** 2 × 1st class
**Credit Cards:** None
**Specialities:** *Lavandula*, *Buddleja*, plants to attract butterflies. Herbs, wildflowers. Nat. Collection of *Buddleja*.
**Notes:** Also sells wholesale.
**Map Ref:** W, D5 **OS Grid Ref:** ST798948

WLeb **LEBA ORCHARD – GREEN'S LEAVES** ⊠ ⛺ ♿
Lea Bailey, Nr Ross-on-Wye, Herefordshire, HR9 5TY
Ⓣ (01989) 750303
Ⓜ 07890 413036
**Contact:** Paul Green
**Opening Times:** By appt. only, w/ends preferred.
**Min Mail Order UK:** £10.00 + p&p
**Cat. Cost:** 4 × 2nd class

KEY
⊠ Mail order to UK or EU ⛺ Delivers to shows
✈ Exports beyond EU € Euro accepted
♿ Accessible by wheelchair ◆ See Display advertisement

**Credit Cards:** None
**Specialities:** Ornamental grasses, sedges & phormiums. Increasing range of rare & choice shrubs, also some perennials.
**Notes:** Also sells wholesale.
**Map Ref:** W, C4

**WLHH** **LAWTON HALL HERBS**
Lawton Hall, Eardisland, Herefordshire, HR6 9AX
Ⓣ (01568) 709215
Ⓔ herbs@lawtonhall.co.uk
Ⓦ www.LawtonHall.co.uk
**Contact:** Alexandra Fox
**Opening Times:** 1030-1730 Tue-Sat. For other times please check first.
**Cat. Cost:** Available by email only.
**Credit Cards:** None
**Specialities:** Herbs, culinary, aromatic & medicinal. Herb & wild flower seeds.
**Notes:** Herb gardens & shop.
**Map Ref:** W, C4 **OS Grid Ref:** SO445595

W

**WMAq** **MEREBROOK WATER PLANTS** ⊠ ♿
Merebrook Farm, Hanley Swan, Worcestershire, WR8 0DX
Ⓣ (01684) 310950
Ⓔ enquiries@pondplants.co.uk
Ⓦ www.pondplants.co.uk
**Contact:** Roger Kings & Biddi Kings
**Opening Times:** 1000-1600 1st Apr-31st Jul. Aug-Mar by appt. Closed Sun & Wed.
**Min Mail Order UK:** Nmc
**Min Mail Order EU:** £25.00
**Cat. Cost:** Free or online.
**Credit Cards:** All major credit/debit cards
**Specialities:** *Nymphaea*, Louisiana irises & other aquatic plants. International Waterlily & Water Gardening Soc. accredited collection. Extensive display gardens open to the public (no charge).
**Map Ref:** W, C5 **OS Grid Ref:** SO802425

**WMnd** **MYND HARDY PLANTS** ⊠
Delbury Hall Estate, Diddlebury, Craven Arms, Shropshire, SY7 9DH
Ⓜ 07812 689155
Ⓕ 08717 142892
Ⓔ sales@myndplants.co.uk
Ⓦ www.myndplants.co.uk
**Contact:** Steve Adams
**Opening Times:** 1000-1700 Mon, Wed-Sat, closed Tues, 1100-1700 Sun, Mar-end Sep. Other times phone for appt.
**Min Mail Order UK:** £10.00 + p&p
**Min Mail Order EU:** £10.00 + p&p
**Cat. Cost:** 4 × 2nd class
**Credit Cards:** All major credit/debit cards
**Specialities:** Herbaceous plants.
**Notes:** Also sells wholesale.
**Map Ref:** W, B4 **OS Grid Ref:** SO510852

**WMoo** **MOORLAND COTTAGE PLANTS** ⊠ ♿
Rhyd-y-Groes, Brynberian, Crymych, Pembrokeshire, SA41 3TT
Ⓣ (01239) 891363
Ⓔ jenny@moorlandcottageplants.co.uk
Ⓦ www.moorlandcottageplants.co.uk
**Contact:** Jennifer Matthews
**Opening Times:** 1030-1730 daily excl. Wed end Feb-end Sep. Display garden open for NGS from mid-May.
**Min Mail Order UK:** See cat. for details.
**Cat. Cost:** 4 × 1st class
**Credit Cards:** None
**Specialities:** Traditional & unusual hardy perennials. Many garden-worthy rarities. Cottage garden plants; ferns & many shade plants; moisture lovers; ornamental grasses & bamboos; colourful ground cover.
**Map Ref:** W, C2 **OS Grid Ref:** SN091343

**WMou** **MOUNT PLEASANT TREES** €
Rockhampton, Berkeley, Gloucestershire, GL13 9DU
Ⓣ (01454) 260348
**Contact:** P & G Locke
**Opening Times:** By appt. only.
**Cat. Cost:** 3 × 2nd class
**Credit Cards:** None
**Specialities:** Wide range of trees for forestry, hedging, woodlands & gardens esp. *Populus*, *Platanus* & *Salix*.
**Notes:** Also sells wholesale.

**WNHG** **NEW HOPE GARDENS** ⊠
Batch Farm, Cockshutford, Craven Arms, Shropshire, SY7 9DY
Ⓣ (01746) 712898
Ⓔ Newhopegardensmz@aol.com
Ⓦ www.newhopegardens.com
**Contact:** Mark Zenick
**Opening Times:** Not open. Mail order only.
**Min Mail Order UK:** Nmc
**Cat. Cost:** Online only. Plant list on request.
**Credit Cards:** Paypal
**Specialities:** American bred, British grown, *Hemerocallis*. Ships bare-rooted plants.

**WOld** **OLD COURT NURSERIES** ⊠ € ♿
Colwall, Nr Malvern, Worcestershire, WR13 6QE
Ⓣ (01684) 540416
Ⓔ paulpicton@btinternet.com
Ⓦ www.autumnasters.co.uk
**Contact:** Paul & Meriel Picton

**Opening Times:** 1330-1700 Fri-Sun, May-Oct. 1100-1700 7 days, 1st week Sep-2nd week Oct.
**Min Mail Order UK:** Nmc
**Min Mail Order EU:** Nmc
**Cat. Cost:** 1 × 1st class
**Credit Cards:** None
**Specialities:** Nat. Collection of Michaelmas Daisies. Herbaceous perennials.
**Notes:** Mail order for *Aster* only.
**Map Ref:** W, C4 **OS Grid Ref:** SO759430

**W**Orn **Ornamental Tree Nurseries** ⊠ ♿
Broomy Hill Gardens, Cobnash, Kingsland, Herefordshire, HR6 9QZ
Ⓣ (01568) 708016
Ⓕ (01568) 709022
Ⓔ enquiries@ornamental-trees.co.uk
Ⓦ www.ornamental-trees.co.uk
**Contact:** Russell Mills
**Opening Times:** 0900-1800 Mon-Sat. 1000-1600 Sun.
**Min Mail Order UK:** £9.95
**Cat. Cost:** 3 × 1st class
**Credit Cards:** All major credit/debit cards
**Specialities:** Ornamental trees. Fruit trees.
**Notes:** Also sells wholesale.
**Map Ref:** W, C4

**W**Out **Out of the Common Way** ⊠ ⛟ €
(Office) Penhyddgan, Boduan, Pwllheli, Gwynedd, LL53 8YH
Ⓣ (01758) 721577 (Office), (01407) 720431 (Nursery)
Ⓔ jo.davidson@virgin.net
**Contact:** Joanna Davidson (nursery) Margaret Mason (office & mail order)
**Opening Times:** By arrangement.
**Min Mail Order UK:** Nmc
**Min Mail Order EU:** Nmc
**Cat. Cost:** A5 sae letter rate postage.
**Credit Cards:** None
**Specialities:** Labiates, esp. *Nepeta* & *Salvia*. *Aster*, *Geranium* & *Crocosmia*. Some plants propagated in small quantities only. Will propagate salvias to order.
**Notes:** Nursery is at Pandy Treban, Bryngwran, Anglesey. Partially accessible for wheelchairs.
**Map Ref:** W, A2 **OS Grid Ref:** SH370778

**W**OVN **The Old Vicarage Nursery** ⊠
Lucton, Leominster, Herefordshire, HR6 9PN
Ⓣ (01568) 780538
Ⓕ (01568) 780818
**Contact:** Mrs R M Flake
**Opening Times:** Most days. Please phone first if making a special journey.
**Min Mail Order UK:** Nmc
**Cat. Cost:** None issued.
**Credit Cards:** None
**Specialities:** Roses: old roses; climbers & ramblers; species & ground cover. *Euphorbia* & half-hardy *Salvia*.
**Map Ref:** W, C4

**W**Pat **Chris Pattison** ⊠ € ♿
Brookend, Pendock, Gloucestershire, GL19 3PL
Ⓣ (01531) 650480
Ⓕ (01531) 650480
Ⓔ cp@chris-pattison.co.uk
Ⓦ www.chris-pattison.co.uk
**Contact:** Chris Pattison
**Opening Times:** 0900-1700 Mon-Fri. W/ends by appt. only.
**Min Mail Order UK:** £10.00 + p&p
**Cat. Cost:** 3 × 1st class
**Credit Cards:** None
**Specialities:** Choice rare shrubs & alpines. Grafted stock esp. Japanese maples & liquidambars. Wide range of *Viburnum*, & dwarf/miniature trees & shrubs.
**Notes:** Mail order Nov-Feb only. Also sells wholesale.
**Map Ref:** W, C5 **OS Grid Ref:** SO781327

**W**PBF **P & B Fuchsias** ⊠ ⛟ € ♿
Maes y Gwaelod, Penclawdd Road, Penclawdd, Swansea, West Glamorgan, SA4 3RB
Ⓣ (01792) 851669
Ⓔ sales@gower-fuchsias.co.uk
Ⓦ www.gower-fuchsias.co.uk
**Contact:** Paul Fisher
**Opening Times:** 0900-1800 7 days 1 Mar-30 Sep.
**Min Mail Order UK:** £10.00 (6 plants) incl. p&p
**Cat. Cost:** 3 × 1st class
**Credit Cards:** None
**Specialities:** Fuchsias. Hybrid & species.
**Notes:** Cuttings only available Mar-May. Very ltd. quantities of each.
**Map Ref:** W, D3

**W**Pen **Penpergwm Plants** ♿
Penpergwm Lodge, Abergavenny, Monmouthshire, NP7 9AS
Ⓣ (01873) 840422/840208
Ⓔ boyle@penpergwm.co.uk

KEY
⊠ Mail order to UK or EU ⛟ Delivers to shows
☒ Exports beyond EU € Euro accepted
♿ Accessible by wheelchair ◆ See Display advertisement

W

Ⓦ www.penplants.com
**Contact:** Mrs J Kerr/Mrs S Boyle
**Opening Times:** 1400-1800 Thu-Sun, 29th Mar-23rd Sep 2007.
**Cat. Cost:** 2 × 1st class
**Credit Cards:** None
**Specialities:** Hardy perennials.
**Map Ref:** W, D4 **OS Grid Ref:** SO335104

**WPer** **PERHILL NURSERIES** ⊠ € ♿
Worcester Road,
Great Witley, Worcestershire,
WR6 6JT
Ⓣ (01299) 896329
Ⓕ (01299) 896990
Ⓔ PerhillP@aol.com
Ⓦ www.perhillplants.co.uk
**Contact:** Duncan Straw
**Opening Times:** 0900-1700 Mon-Sat, 1000-1600 Sun, 1st Feb-31st Jul. 0900-1700 Mon-Fri, 1st Aug-31st Jan.
**Min Mail Order UK:** Nmc
**Min Mail Order EU:** £10.00
**Cat. Cost:** 6 × 2nd class
**Credit Cards:** All major credit/debit cards
**Specialities:** 2500+ varieties of rare, unusual alpines & herbaceous perennials incl. *Penstemon*, *Campanula*, *Salvia*, *Thymus*, herbs, *Veronica*.
**Notes:** Also sells wholesale.
**Map Ref:** W, C4 **OS Grid Ref:** SO763656

W

**WPGP** **PAN-GLOBAL PLANTS** ♿
The Walled Garden, Frampton Court,
Frampton-on-Severn,
Gloucestershire,
GL2 7EX
Ⓣ (01452) 741641
Ⓜ 07801 275138
Ⓕ (01453) 768858
Ⓔ info@panglobalplants.com
Ⓦ www.panglobalplants.com
**Contact:** Nick Macer
**Opening Times:** 1100-1700 Wed-Sun 1st Feb-31st Oct. Also B/hols. Closed 2nd Sun in Sep. Winter months by appt., please phone first.
**Cat. Cost:** 6 × 1st class
**Credit Cards:** Maestro MasterCard Visa Solo Delta
**Specialities:** A plantsman's nursery offering a wide selection of rare & desirable trees, ornamental trees, shrubs, herbaceous, bamboos, exotics, climbers, ferns etc. Specialities incl. *Magnolia*, *Hydrangea* & *Bamboo*.
**Map Ref:** W, D5

**WPic** **THE PICTON CASTLE TRUST NURSERY** ♿
Picton Castle, Haverfordwest, Pembrokeshire,
SA62 4AS
Ⓣ (01437) 751326
Ⓕ (01437) 751326
Ⓔ pct@pictoncastle.freeserve.co.uk
Ⓦ www.pictoncastle.co.uk
**Contact:** D L Pryse Lloyd
**Opening Times:** 1030-1700 7 days except Mon Apr-Sep. Other times by arrangement.
**Cat. Cost:** 1 × 1st class
**Credit Cards:** None
**Specialities:** *Rhododendron*. Myrtle and relatives. Woodland & unusual shrubs. Nursery attached to 40 acre woodland garden.
**Map Ref:** W, D2 **OS Grid Ref:** SN011135

**WPnn** **THE PERENNIAL NURSERY** ⊠
Rhosygilwen, Llanrhian Road, St Davids,
Pembrokeshire, SA62 6DB
Ⓣ (01437) 721954
Ⓦ www.droughttolerantplants.co.uk
**Contact:** Mrs Philipa Symons
**Opening Times:** 1030-1730 Mar-Oct. Nov-Feb by appt.
**Min Mail Order UK:** Nmc
**Min Mail Order EU:** Nmc
**Specialities:** Herbaceous perennials & alpines. Tender perennials. Coastal plants. Herbs.
**Map Ref:** W, C1 **OS Grid Ref:** SM775292

**WPnP** **PENLAN PERENNIALS** ⊠ ✈ ⌂ € ♿
Penlan Farm, Penrhiwpal, Llandysul,
Ceredigion, SA44 5QH
Ⓣ (01239) 851244
Ⓜ 07857 675312
Ⓕ (01239) 851244
Ⓔ rcain@penlanperennials.co.uk
Ⓦ www.penlanperennials.co.uk
**Contact:** Richard & Jane Cain
**Opening Times:** 0930-1730 Fri-Sun & B/hols 1st Mar-30th Jun only. Jul-Feb by appt.
**Min Mail Order UK:** Nmc
**Min Mail Order EU:** Nmc
**Cat. Cost:** Online, or sae for CD-ROM
**Credit Cards:** All major credit/debit cards
**Specialities:** Aquatic, marginal & bog plants. Shade-loving & woodland perennials, ferns & grasses, all grown peat-free.
**Notes:** Mail order all year, next day delivery. Secure online web ordering.
**Map Ref:** W, C2 **OS Grid Ref:** SN344457

**WPrP** **PRIME PERENNIALS** ⊠ ⌂
Llety Moel, Rhos-y-Garth, Llanilar,
Nr Aberystwyth, Ceredigion, SY23 4SG
Ⓣ (01974) 241505
Ⓜ 07891 333656

Ⓔ liz@prime-perennials.co.uk
Ⓦ www.prime-perennials.co.uk
**Contact:** Elizabeth Powney
**Opening Times:** Open by appt. only.
**Min Mail Order UK:** Nmc
**Min Mail Order EU:** £12.00
**Cat. Cost:** 4 × 1st class
**Credit Cards:** None
**Specialities:** Specialist growers of rare, unusual & obscure perennials, ferns, bulbs & grasses. Some plants in small quantities. Peat free. Grown 650ft above sea level. National Coll. of *Tulbaghia*.
**Notes:** Mail order all year.
**Map Ref:** W, C3

**WPtf** **PANTYFOD GARDEN NURSERY** ☒ ♿
Llandewi Brefi, Tregaron, Ceredigion, SY25 6PE
Ⓣ (01570) 493564
Ⓕ (01570) 493585
Ⓔ sales@pantyfodgarden.co.uk
Ⓦ www.pantyfodgarden.co.uk
**Contact:** Susan Rowe
**Opening Times:** Nursery closed for refurbishment during 2007, except by prior arrangement.
**Min Mail Order UK:** Nmc
**Min Mail Order EU:** Nmc
**Cat. Cost:** Online only.
**Credit Cards:** All major credit/debit cards accepted online only.
**Specialities:** Hardy geraniums, unusual hardy perennials, black plants, woodland plants, plants for moist soil, all grown largely peat-free. Many plants available in small quantities. Nursery at 950ft with spectacular views.
**Map Ref:** W, C3 **OS Grid Ref:** SN654540

**WRai** **RAILS END NURSERY**
Back Lane, Ashton under Hill, Evesham, Worcestershire, WR11 7RG
Ⓣ (01386) 881884
Ⓕ (01386) 881407
Ⓔ salski@quinweb.net
Ⓦ www.ashtonunderhill.org.uk/business/railsend
**Contact:** Sally Skinner
**Opening Times:** 1000-1700 7 days, mid-Feb-end Oct. Nov-Jan by appt. only.
**Cat. Cost:** Free. Also online.
**Credit Cards:** All major credit/debit cards
**Specialities:** Family-run nursery, specialising in hardy herbaceous perennials, with an extending range of the unusual. All stock in small quantities.
**Notes:** Partially accessible for wheelchair users.
**Map Ref:** W, C5 **OS Grid Ref:** SO999375

**WRha** **RHANDIRMWYN PLANTS**
2 Tremcelynog, Rhandirmwyn, Nr Llandovery, Carmarthenshire, SA20 0NU
Ⓣ (01550) 760220
Ⓔ Sarafox3@hotmail.co.uk
**Contact:** Sara Fox/Thomas Sheppard
**Opening Times:** Open most days, but please ring first to avoid disappointment.
**Credit Cards:** None
**Specialities:** 1000+ varieties & species incl. aquilegias, campanulas, chrysanthemums, digitalis, geraniums, geums, *Lychnis*, *Mentha*, *Monarda*, *Origanum*, primulas, *Rosmarinus*, salvias & violas. Stock ltd. in quantity but not variety!
**Map Ref:** W, C3 **OS Grid Ref:** SN796428

**WRHF** **RED HOUSE FARM** ♿
Flying Horse Lane, Bradley Green, Nr Redditch, Worcestershire, B96 6QT
Ⓣ (01527) 821269
Ⓕ (01527) 821674
Ⓔ contact@redhousefarmgardenandnursery.co.uk
Ⓦ www.redhousefarmgardenandnursery.co.uk
**Contact:** Mrs Maureen Weaver
**Opening Times:** 0900-1700 Mon-Sat all year. 1000-1700 Sun & B/Hols.
**Cat. Cost:** 2 × 1st class
**Credit Cards:** None
**Map Ref:** W, C5 **OS Grid Ref:** SO986623

**WRic** **RICKARDS FERNS LTD** ☒ ✈ € ◆
(office) Carreg y Fedwen, Sling, Tregarth, Bangor, Gwynedd, LL57 4RP
Ⓣ (01248) 600385
Ⓕ (01248) 600385
Ⓔ info@rickardsferns.co.uk
Ⓦ www.rickardsferns.co.uk
**Contact:** Richard Hayward & Ben Kettle
**Opening Times:** 1000-1700 7 days, 1st Mar-31st Oct. Other times by appt.
**Min Mail Order UK:** £30.00 + p&p
**Min Mail Order EU:** £50.00 + p&p
**Cat. Cost:** Online or 5 × 1st class or 6 × 2nd class.
**Credit Cards:** All major credit/debit cards
**Specialities:** Ferns, incl. tree ferns.
**Notes:** Also sells wholesale. Nursery located at Lon Rallt, Pentir, Bangor LL57 4RP
**Map Ref:** W, A3 **OS Grid Ref:** GR592667

KEY
☒ Mail order to UK or EU — Delivers to shows
✈ Exports beyond EU — € Euro accepted
♿ Accessible by wheelchair — ◆ See Display advertisement

W

**WRos** **Rosemary's Farmhouse Nursery** ♿
Llwyn-y-moel-gau, Llanfihangel, Llanfyllin, Montgomeryshire, SY22 5JE
Ⓣ (01691) 648196
Ⓕ (01691) 648196
Ⓔ rosemary@farmhouse-nursery.wanadoo.co.uk
**Contact:** Rosemary Pryce
**Opening Times:** 1000-1700 most days all year, but advisable to phone to confirm.
**Cat. Cost:** None issued.
**Credit Cards:** None
**Specialities:** Unusual perennials & ornamental grasses. Hardy geraniums. The garden is planted as display & to encourage wildlife, butterflies & many birds.
**Notes:** Finalist, Nursery Retailer of the Year 2006.
**Map Ref:** W, B3 **OS Grid Ref:** SJ083149

**WRou** **Roualeyn Nurseries** ♿
Trefriw, Conwy, LL27 0SX
Ⓣ (01492) 640548
Ⓕ (01492) 640548
Ⓔ roualeynnursery@btinternet.com
**Contact:** Doug Jones
**Opening Times:** 1000-1700 weekdays 1st Mar-31st Aug, 1000-1600 Sat, Sun & B/hols.
**Cat. Cost:** 2 × 1st class.
**Credit Cards:** None
**Specialities:** Fuchsias, incl. species.
**Map Ref:** W, A3 **OS Grid Ref:** SH632778

**WSFF** **Saith Ffynnon Farm** ⊠ € ♿ ◆
Whitford, Holywell, Flintshire, CH8 9EQ
Ⓣ (01352) 711198
Ⓕ (01352) 716777
Ⓔ jan@7wells.org
Ⓦ www.7wells.co.uk
**Contact:** Jan Miller
**Opening Times:** By appt. only.
**Min Mail Order UK:** Nmc
**Min Mail Order EU:** Nmc
**Cat. Cost:** Online or 2 × 1st class.
**Credit Cards:** All major credit/debit cards accepted online only.
**Specialities:** Plants and seeds to attract butterflies and moths. Natural Dye plants. Nat. Collection of *Eupatorium* (Provisional). Stock available in small quantities unless ordered well in advance.
**Notes:** Percentage of profits go to Butterfly Conservation. Also sells wholesale.
**Map Ref:** W, A3 **OS Grid Ref:** SJ154775

**WSHC** **Stone House Cottage Nurseries** ♿
Stone, Nr Kidderminster, Worcestershire, DY10 4BG
Ⓣ (01562) 69902
Ⓔ louisa@shcn.co.uk
Ⓦ www.shcn.co.uk
**Contact:** L N Arbuthnott
**Opening Times:** 1000-1700 Wed-Sat. By appt. only mid Sep-mid Mar.
**Cat. Cost:** Sae
**Credit Cards:** None
**Specialities:** Small general range esp. wall shrubs, climbers & unusual plants.
**Map Ref:** W, C5 **OS Grid Ref:** SO863750

**WShi** **Shipton Bulbs** ⊠ €
Y Felin, Henllan Amgoed, Whitland, Carmarthenshire, SA34 0SL
Ⓣ (01994) 240125
Ⓕ (01994) 241180
Ⓔ bluebell@zoo.co.uk
Ⓦ www.bluebellbulbs.co.uk
**Contact:** John Shipton & Alison Foot
**Opening Times:** By appt. only.
**Min Mail Order UK:** Nmc
**Min Mail Order EU:** Nmc
**Cat. Cost:** Sae
**Credit Cards:** None
**Specialities:** Native British bulbs, & bulbs & plants for naturalising.
**Map Ref:** W, D2 **OS Grid Ref:** SN188207

**WSSs** **Shropshire Sarracenias** ⊠ ✈ € ♿
5 Field Close, Malinslee, Telford, Shropshire, TF4 2EH
Ⓣ (01952) 501598
Ⓔ mike@carnivorousplants.uk.com
Ⓦ www.carnivorousplants.uk.com
**Contact:** Mike King
**Opening Times:** By appt. only.
**Min Mail Order UK:** Nmc
**Min Mail Order EU:** Nmc
**Cat. Cost:** 2 × 1st class
**Credit Cards:** Paypal
**Specialities:** *Sarracenia. Dionaea muscipula* & forms. Some stock available in small quantities only. Nat. Collections of *Sarracenia* & *Dionaea*.
**Map Ref:** W, B4 **OS Grid Ref:** SJ689085

**WSuV** **Sunnybank Vine Nursery (National Vine Collection)** ⊠ ✈
King Street, Ewyas Harold, Rowlestone, Herefordshire, HR2 OEE
Ⓣ (01981) 240256
Ⓔ vinenursery@hotmail.com
Ⓦ vinenursery.netfirms.com
**Contact:** B R Edwards
**Opening Times:** Not open. Mail order only.
**Min Mail Order UK:** £8.00 incl. p&p
**Min Mail Order EU:** £13.00 incl. p&p
**Cat. Cost:** Free.

**Credit Cards:** None
**Specialities:** Vines. National Collection of *Vitis vinifera* (hardy, incl. dessert & wine).
**Notes:** EU sales by arrangement.

WTan **TAN-Y-LLYN NURSERIES** ⊠
Meifod, Powys, SY22 6YB
Ⓣ (01938) 500370
Ⓔ info@tanyllyn.the-nursery.co.uk
Ⓦ www.tanyllyn.the-nursery.co.uk
**Contact:** Callum Johnston
**Opening Times:** 1000-1700 Tue-Fri Mar-Jun and at other times by appt.
**Min Mail Order UK:** Nmc
**Cat. Cost:** 2 × 1st class
**Credit Cards:** None
**Specialities:** Herbs, alpines, perennials.
**Notes:** Also sells wholesale.
**Map Ref:** W, B3 **OS Grid Ref:** SJ167125

WThu **THUYA ALPINE NURSERY** ⊠
Glebelands, Hartpury, Gloucestershire, GL19 3BW
Ⓣ (01452) 700548
**Contact:** S W Bond
**Opening Times:** 1000-dusk Sat & Bank hol. 1100-dusk Sun, Weekdays appt. advised.
**Min Mail Order UK:** £4.00 + p&p
**Min Mail Order EU:** £10.00 + p&p
**Cat. Cost:** 4 × 2nd class
**Credit Cards:** None
**Specialities:** Wide and changing range including rarities, available in smallish numbers.
**Notes:** Partially accessible for wheelchair users.
**Map Ref:** W, C5

WTin **TINPENNY PLANTS** ♿
Tinpenny Farm, Fiddington, Tewkesbury, Gloucestershire, GL20 7BJ
Ⓣ (01684) 292668
Ⓔ plants@tinpenny.plus.com
**Contact:** Elaine Horton
**Opening Times:** 1200-1700 Tue-Thu or by appt. Nov & Dec appt. only.
**Cat. Cost:** None issued.
**Credit Cards:** None
**Specialities:** Wide range of hardy garden-worthy plants esp. *Helleborus*, *Iris* & *Sempervivum*. Small nursery will propagate to order rare plants from own stock. Small quantities only of some plants.
**Map Ref:** W, C5 **OS Grid Ref:** SO919318

WTou **TOUCHWOOD PLANTS** ⊠ ✈ ⌂
4 Clyne Valley Cottages, Killay, Swansea, West Glamorgan, SA2 7DU
Ⓣ (01792) 522443
Ⓔ Carrie.Thomas@ntlworld.com
Ⓦ www.touchwoodplants.co.uk
**Contact:** Carrie Thomas
**Opening Times:** Most reasonable days/times. Please phone first.
**Min Mail Order UK:** Nmc
**Cat. Cost:** 2 × 1st class.
**Credit Cards:** Paypal
**Specialities:** Seeds & plants. Nat. Collection of *Aquilegia vulgaris* cvs & hybrids. Plant stocks held in small quantities. Main stock is seed. Garden & *Aquilegia* Collection open.
**Notes:** Plants sent bare-rooted at relevant times of the year. Exports seeds only beyond UK.
**Map Ref:** W, D3 **OS Grid Ref:** SS600924

WVal **VALE SEEDS AND BULBS** ⊠ ✈ €
(Office) 3 Common Road, Evesham, Worcestershire, WR11 4PU
Ⓜ 07792 753112
Ⓕ (01386) 761603
Ⓔ sales@hippeastrums.co.uk
Ⓦ www.hippeastrums.co.uk
**Contact:** Andy Houghton & Junius des Brisay
**Opening Times:** Not open. Mail order only.
**Min Mail Order UK:** Nmc
**Min Mail Order EU:** Nmc
**Cat. Cost:** Free by email.
**Credit Cards:** Paypal
**Specialities:** *Hippeastrum* both species & hybrids. *Clivia* both species & hybrid, available as plants & seeds.
**Notes:** Also sells wholesale.

WViv **VIV MARSH POSTAL PLANTS** ⊠
Walford Heath, Shrewsbury, Shropshire, SY4 2HT
Ⓣ (01939) 291475
Ⓔ mail@PostalPlants.co.uk
Ⓦ www.PostalPlants.co.uk
**Contact:** Mr Viv Marsh
**Opening Times:** Selected w/ends in spring & autumn. Please phone for details. Other times by appt. only.
**Min Mail Order UK:** £30.00 plant value
**Min Mail Order EU:** £30.00 plant value
**Cat. Cost:** 5 × 1st class (£1 refund on first order). Also online.
**Credit Cards:** Visa MasterCard Switch Electron Maestro

KEY
⊠ Mail order to UK or EU ⌂ Delivers to shows
✈ Exports beyond EU € Euro accepted
♿ Accessible by wheelchair ◆ See Display advertisement

**Specialities:** Specialists in *Alstroemeria* & *Lathyrus*.
**Notes:** Wheelchair access with assistance. No disabled toilet.
**Map Ref:** W, B4 **OS Grid Ref:** SJ446198

**WWeb** **Webbs of Wychbold** € ♿ ◆
Wychbold, Droitwich, Worcestershire, WR9 0DG
Ⓣ (01527) 860000
Ⓕ (01527) 861284
Ⓔ gardenplants@webbsofwychbold.co.uk
Ⓦ www.webbsofwychbold.co.uk
**Contact:** Garden Plants Dept
**Opening Times:** 0900-1800 Mon-Fri winter. 0900-2000 Mon-Fri summer. 0900-1800 Sat & 1030-1630 Sun all year. Closed Xmas Day, Boxing Day & Easter Sun.
**Cat. Cost:** None issued
**Credit Cards:** All major credit/debit cards
**Specialities:** Hardy trees & shrubs, climbers, conifers, alpines, heathers, herbaceous, herbs, roses, fruit & aquatics. Nat. Collection of Shrubby *Potentilla*.
**Map Ref:** W, C5

**W**

**WWEG** **World's End Garden Nursery** ⌂ € ♿ ◆
Moseley Road, Hallow, Worcester, Worcestershire, WR2 6NJ
Ⓣ (01905) 640977
Ⓕ (01905) 641373
Ⓔ garden@robinpearce.co.uk
Ⓦ www.worldsendgarden.co.uk
**Contact:** Kristina & Robin Pearce
**Opening Times:** 1030-1700 Tue-Sat, Apr-Oct. Other times by appt.
**Cat. Cost:** Online or 4 × 1st class.
**Credit Cards:** All major credit/debit cards
**Specialities:** Wide range of herbaceous perennials, ferns & ornamental grasses. Display garden featuring *Hosta*, *Geum* & ferns.
**Notes:** Also sells wholesale.
**Map Ref:** W, C5 **OS Grid Ref:** SO815597

**WWFP** **Whitehall Farmhouse Plants** ⊠ ⌂
Sevenhampton, Cheltenham, Gloucestershire, GL54 5TL
Ⓣ (01242) 820772
Ⓜ 07711 021034
Ⓕ (01242) 821226
Ⓔ info@wfplants.co.uk
Ⓦ www.wfplants.co.uk
**Contact:** Victoria Logue
**Opening Times:** By appt. only.
**Min Mail Order UK:** Nmc
**Cat. Cost:** 2 × 1st class
**Credit Cards:** None
**Specialities:** A small nursery producing a range of interesting & easy hardy perennials for the garden. Some plants held in small quantities only.
**Map Ref:** W, C5 **OS Grid Ref:** SP018229

**WWHy** **Welsh Holly** ⊠ € ♿
Llyn-y-gors, Tenby Road, St Clears, Carmarthenshire, SA33 4JP
Ⓣ (01994) 231789
Ⓕ (01994) 231789
Ⓔ info@welsh-holly.co.uk
Ⓦ www.welsh-holly.co.uk
**Contact:** Philip Lanc
**Opening Times:** By appt. only.
**Min Mail Order UK:** Nmc
**Min Mail Order EU:** Nmc
**Cat. Cost:** 2 × 1st class
**Credit Cards:** None
**Specialities:** Hollies. Limited stock of less common plants.
**Notes:** Also sells wholesale.

**WWlt** **Wollerton Old Hall Garden** ♿
Wollerton, Market Drayton, Shropshire, TF9 3NA
Ⓣ (01630) 685760
Ⓕ (01630) 685583
Ⓔ info@wollertonoldhallgarden.com
Ⓦ www.wollertonoldhallgarden.com
**Contact:** Mr John Jenkins
**Opening Times:** 1200-1700 Fri, Sun & B/hols Easter-end Sep.
**Cat. Cost:** None issued
**Credit Cards:** All major credit/debit cards
**Specialities:** Perennials, hardy & half-hardy.
**Map Ref:** W, B4 **OS Grid Ref:** SJ624296

**WWpP** **Waterpump Plants** ⊠
Waterpump Farm, Ryeford, Ross-on-Wye, Herefordshire, HR9 7PU
Ⓣ (01989) 750177
Ⓔ liz.sugden2.@btinternet.com
**Contact:** Mrs E Sugden
**Opening Times:** Order collection service available.
**Min Mail Order UK:** £15.00
**Cat. Cost:** 4 × 1st class
**Credit Cards:** None
**Specialities:** Hardy geraniums. Small nursery with limited stock, will propagate to order.
**Map Ref:** W, C4 **OS Grid Ref:** SO642226

**WWst** **Westonbirt Plants** ⊠ ☒ €
9 Westonbirt Close, Worcester, WR5 3RX
Ⓣ (01905) 350429 (answerphone)
Ⓔ office@westonbirtplants.co.uk

Ⓦ www.westonbirtplants.co.uk
**Contact:** Garry Dickerson
**Opening Times:** Not open. Mail order only.
**Min Mail Order UK:** Nmc
**Min Mail Order EU:** Nmc
**Cat. Cost:** 3 × 1st class
**Credit Cards:** None
**Specialities:** *Iris*, *Fritillaria*, *Erythronium*, particular interest in Juno *Iris* species, + *Crocus*, *Corydalis*, *Lilium*, *Arisaema*, *Trillium*, *Arum* & tulip species. Woodland plants & hardy orchids, esp. *Calanthe* & *Cypripedium*. Many rare plants in ltd. numbers.

## ABROAD

XBlo **TABLE BAY VIEW NURSERY** ⊠ ✈ €
(Office) 60 Molteno Road, Oranjezicht, Cape Town 8001, South Africa
Ⓣ 00 27 21 683 5108
Ⓕ 00 27 21 683 5108
Ⓔ info@tablebayviewnursery.co.za
**Contact:** Terence Bloch
**Opening Times:** Mail order only. No personal callers.
**Min Mail Order UK:** £15.00 + p&p
**Min Mail Order EU:** £15.00
**Cat. Cost:** £3.40 (postal order)
**Credit Cards:** None
**Specialities:** Tropical & sub-tropical ornamental & fruiting plants.
**Notes:** Due to high local bank charges, can no longer accept foreign bank cheques only undated postal orders.

XBTW **B & T WORLD SEEDS** ⊠ ✈ €
Paguignan, 34210 Aigues-Vives, France
Ⓣ 00 33 (0) 4689 12963
Ⓕ 00 33 (0) 4689 13039
Ⓔ le@b-and-t-world-seeds.com
Ⓦ www.b-and-t-world-seeds.com
**Contact:** Lesley Sleigh
**Opening Times:** Not open. Mail order only.
**Min Mail Order UK:** £14.00 inc. carriage
**Min Mail Order EU:** £14.00 inc. carriage
**Cat. Cost:** £10 Europe, £14 elsewhere.
**Credit Cards:** Visa MasterCard
**Specialities:** Master list contains over 30,000 items. 700 sub-lists available.
**Notes:** Exports seed only. Catalogue/botanical reference system available on CD Rom. SeedyRom (TM) catalogue £20 worldwide. Also sells wholesale.

XFro **FROSCH EXCLUSIVE PERENNIALS** ⊠ ✈ €
Zielgelstadelweg 5, D-83623 Dietramszell-Lochen, Germany
Ⓣ 00 49 172 842 2050
Ⓕ 00 49 8027 9049975
Ⓔ info@cypripedium.de
Ⓦ www.cypripedium.de
**Contact:** Michael Weinert
**Opening Times:** Not open. Mail order only. Orders taken between 0700-2200 hours.
**Min Mail Order UK:** £350.00 + p&p
**Min Mail Order EU:** £350.00 + p&p
**Cat. Cost:** Online only.
**Credit Cards:** None
**Specialities:** *Cypripedium* hybrids. Hardy orchids.
**Notes:** Also sells wholesale.

XPde **PÉPINIÈRE DE L'ÎLE** ⊠ €
Keranroux, 22870, Ile de Brehat, France
Ⓣ 00 33 (0)2 96 200384
Ⓜ 06861 28609
Ⓕ 00 33 (0)2 96 200384
Ⓔ contact@pepiniere-brehat.com
Ⓦ www.pepiniere-brehat.com
**Contact:** Laurence Blasco & Charles Blasco
**Opening Times:** 1400-1800 spring & summer. Other times by appt. incl. Aug.
**Min Mail Order UK:** Nmc
**Min Mail Order EU:** Nmc
**Cat. Cost:** €6.00
**Credit Cards:** None
**Specialities:** *Agapanthus* & *Echium*. Plants from South Africa.

X

KEY
⊠ Mail order to UK or EU — Delivers to shows
✈ Exports beyond EU — € Euro accepted
♿ Accessible by wheelchair — ◆ See Display advertisement

# NURSERY INDEX BY NAME

Nurseries that are included in the *RHS Plant Finder* for the first time this year (or have been reintroduced) are marked in **bold type**. Full details of the nurseries will be found in **Nursery Details by Code** on page 816. For a key to the geographical codes, see the start of **Nurseries**.

| | |
|---|---|
| Kevin Hughes Plants | SKHP |
| Hull Farm | EHul |
| Hunts Court Garden & Nursery | WHCG |
| Hydon Nurseries | LHyd |
| Hydrangea Haven | SHyH |
| I.M.B. Plants | LIMB |
| Iden Croft Herbs | SIde |
| Imberhorne Lane Nursery | SImb |
| W E Th. Ingwersen Ltd | SIng |
| The Iris Garden | CIri |
| Iris of Sissinghurst | SIri |
| **Isle of Wight Lavender** | **SIoW** |
| Ivycroft Plants | WIvy |
| Jackson's Nurseries | MJac |
| Jasmine Cottage Gardens | CJas |
| Paul Jasper Trees | WJas |
| Jekka's Herb Farm | WJek |
| **Jo's Garden Enterprise** | **GJos** |
| John and Lynsey's Plants | SPin |
| John Ray Nursery | EJRN |
| **John Smith & Son** | **MSmi** |
| Vic Johnstone and Claire Wilson | SJoh |
| C & K Jones | MJon |
| Jungle Seeds and Gardens | MJnS |
| Kayes Garden Nursery | MKay |
| Keepers Nursery | SKee |
| Kelways Ltd | CKel |
| Kenwith Nursery (Gordon Haddow) | CKen |
| Kevock Garden Plants & Flowers | GKev |
| Kiftsgate Court Gardens | WKif |
| **Kirkdale Nursery** | **GKir** |
| Knoll Gardens | CKno |
| Kobakoba | CKob |
| L W Plants | LLWP |
| Ladybird Garden Nursery | ILad |
| Landford Trees | CLnd |
| Landlife Wildflowers Ltd | NLan |
| Landscape Plants | SLPl |
| Lane End Nursery | MLan |
| Laneside Alpines | NLAp |
| Langley Boxwood Nursery Ltd | SLan |
| Langthorns Plantery | ELan |
| Larch Cottage Nurseries | NLar |
| Larkspur Nursery | ELar |
| Laurel Farm Herbs | ELau |
| The Laurels Nursery | SLau |
| The Lavender Garden | WLav |
| **Lawton Hall Herbs** | **WLHH** |
| Layham Garden Centre & Nursery | SLay |
| Lea Rhododendron Gardens Ltd | MLea |
| Leatherbritches Kitchen Garden & Nursery | MLBr |
| Leba Orchard - Green's Leaves | WLeb |
| Leeds Lavender | NLLv |
| Brian Lewington | SBLw |
| Lilies Water Gardens | LLWG |
| Lime Cross Nursery | SLim |
| Lisdoonan Herbs | ILis |
| Little Brook Fuchsias | SLBF |
| Little Heath Farm (UK) (formerly Two Jays Alpines) | LLHF |
| Lochlands (HRB Ltd) | GLld |
| C S Lockyer (Fuchsias) | CLoc |
| Loder Plants | SLdr |
| Lodge Farm Plants & Wildflowers | MLod |
| Lodge Lane Nursery & Gardens | MLLN |
| Long Acre Plants | CLAP |
| Long House Plants | ELon |
| Longstock Park Nursery | SLon |
| Longstone Hardy Plants Nursery | MLHP |
| Lower Severalls Nursery | CSev |
| Lulworth Plants | MLul |
| Lydford Alpine Nursery | CLyd |
| M & M Plants | CMMP |
| M G H Nurseries | IMGH |
| S M McArd (Seeds) | EMcA |
| Elizabeth MacGregor | GMac |
| MacGregors Plants for Shade | SMac |
| Macpennys Nurseries | CMac |
| Macplants | GMaP |
| Madrona Nursery | SMad |
| **Majestic Trees** | **LMaj** |
| Mallet Court Nursery | CMCN |
| Marchants Hardy Plants | SMHy |
| Marcus Dancer Plants | SMDP |
| Lesley Marshall | EMar |
| Marshall's Malmaison | EMal |
| Marwood Hill Gardens | CMHG |
| The Mead Nursery | CMea |
| Meadow Cottage Plants | CMCo |
| Meadows Nursery | CMdw |
| Mendip Bonsai Studio | CMen |
| Mendle Nursery | NMen |
| Meon Valley Plants | SMeo |
| Merebrook Water Plants | WMAq |
| Merriments Gardens | SMrm |
| Mickfield Hostas | EMic |
| Mickfield Watergarden Centre Ltd | EMFW |
| Mill Cottage Plants | CMil |
| Mill Race Garden Centre | EMil |
| Millais Nurseries | LMil |
| **Millfield Nurseries** | **MMiN** |
| Miniature Bulbs - The Warren Estate | NMin |
| Mires Beck Nursery | NMir |
| **Monita House Garden** | **CMoH** |
| Monksilver Nursery | EMon |
| Moor Monkton Nurseries | NMoo |
| Moorland Cottage Plants | WMoo |
| Morehavens | LMor |
| Morton Hall Gardens | MMHG |
| **Mount Harry Trees** | **SMHT** |
| Mount Pleasant Trees | WMou |
| Mozart House Nursery Garden | MMoz |
| **Mrs Mitchell's Kitchen & Garden** | **SMrs** |
| Mucklestone Nurseries | MMuc |
| Ken Muir Ltd | EMui |
| **Muncaster Castle** | **NMun** |

| | |
|---|---|
| Rose Cottage Plants | ERCP |
| Roseholme Nursery | ERos |
| Roseland House Nursery | CRHN |
| Rosemary's Farmhouse Nursery | WRos |
| Rosewood Daylilies | SRos |
| Rosie's Garden Plants | SRGP |
| Rotherview Nursery | SRot |
| Roualeyn Nurseries | WRou |
| **Rowden Gardens** | **CRow** |
| Rumsey Gardens | SRms |
| Ryal Nursery | NRya |
| S & S Perennials | MSSP |
| St Bridget Nurseries Ltd | CSBt |
| **St Clare Nursery** | **EStC** |
| Saith Ffynnon Farm | WSFF |
| Salley Gardens | MSal |
| Sampford Shrubs | CSam |
| Scawsby Hall Nurseries | NScw |
| Scented Roses | CSRo |
| Scott's Wildflowers | NSco |
| Seaforde Gardens | ISea |
| Seagate Irises | ESgI |
| Seale Nurseries | SSea |
| Seaside Nursery | ISsi |
| Second Nature Plant Nursery | CSNP |
| **The Secret Garden** | **GSec** |
| **Secret Seeds** | **CSec** |
| Seeds by Size | LSee |
| Select Seeds | SSss |
| Sherston Parva Nursery | CSPN |
| Sherwood Cottage | CSdC |
| Shipton Bulbs | WShi |
| Showglads | MSGs |
| Shropshire Sarracenias | WSSs |
| Shrubland Park Nurseries | EShb |
| **Silver Dale Nurseries** | **CSil** |
| Simpson's Seeds Ltd | CSim |
| Slack Top Nurseries | NSla |
| Slipps Garden Centre | CSli |
| Smart Plants | MTPN |
| Snape Cottage | CSna |
| South West Carnivorous Plants | CSWC |
| Southease Plants | SSth |
| Southon Plants | LSou |
| Southview Nurseries | SSvw |
| Special Plants | CSpe |
| Spinners Garden | SSpi |
| Spring Reach Nursery | LSRN |
| Springwood Nursery | SSwd |
| Springwood Pleiones | NSpr |
| Starborough Nursery | SSta |
| **Station House Nurseries** | **MSHN** |
| Steventon Road Nurseries | MSte |
| Stillingfleet Lodge Nurseries | NSti |
| **Stone Cross Garden Centre** | **SSto** |
| Stone House Cottage Nurseries | WSHC |
| Stone Lane Gardens | CSto |
| **Stonyford Cottage Nursery** | **MSCN** |
| Stuckey's Alpines | CStu |
| Style Roses | ESty |
| Brian & Pearl Sulman | ESul |
| Summerdale Garden Nursery | NSum |
| Sunnybank Vine Nursery (National Vine Collection) | WSuV |
| Sunnyside Plants | CSsd |
| Suttons Seeds | CSut |
| Swallows Nursery | MSwo |
| **Sweet Knowle Aquatics** | **MSKA** |
| **Swines Meadow Garden Centre** | **ESwi** |
| Table Bay View Nursery | XBlo |
| Tan-y-Llyn Nurseries | WTan |
| Shirley Tasker | NShi |
| Tavistock Herb Nursery | NTHB |
| **Taylors Clematis Nursery** | **NTay** |
| Terrace Gardener | STrG |
| Test Valley Nursery | STes |
| Thorncroft Clematis Nursery | ETho |
| Thornhayes Nursery | CTho |
| A & A Thorp | MTho |
| Thuya Alpine Nursery | WThu |
| Tile Barn Nursery | STil |
| Timpany Nurseries & Gardens | ITim |
| Tinpenny Plants | WTin |
| Tissington Nursery | MTis |
| Todd's Botanics | ETod |
| Toobees Exotics | LToo |
| **Touchwood Plants** | **WTou** |
| Trecanna Nursery | CTca |
| Tregothnan Nursery | CTrG |
| **Tregrehan Garden** | **CTgr** |
| Trehane Camellia Nursery | CTrh |
| Peter Trenear | STre |
| **Treseders** | **CTsd** |
| Trevena Cross Nurseries | CTrC |
| Triscombe Nurseries | CTri |
| Edwin Tucker & Sons | CTuc |
| J Tweedie Fruit Trees | GTwe |
| **Urban Jungle** | **EUJe** |
| **Usual & Unusual Plants** | **SUsu** |
| Uzumara Orchids | GUzu |
| **Vale Seeds and Bulbs** | **WVal** |
| The Vernon Geranium Nursery | LVER |
| The Vicarage Garden | NVic |
| Victoriana Nursery Gardens | SVic |
| The Village Nurseries | SVil |
| Viv Marsh Postal Plants | WViv |
| Wallace Plants | SWal |
| Walled Garden Nursery | CWGN |
| The Walled Garden | EWll |
| Walnut Tree Garden Nursery | EWTr |
| Wanborough Herb Nursery | CWan |
| Ward Fuchsias | MWar |
| The Water Garden | CWat |
| Water Meadow Nursery | SWat |
| Waterperry Gardens Ltd | MWat |
| Waterpump Plants | WWpP |

# SPECIALIST NURSERIES

Nurseries have classified themselves under the following headings where they *exclusively* or *predominantly* supply this range of plants. Plant groups are set out in alphabetical order. Refer to **Nursery Details by Code** on page 816 for details of the nurseries whose codes are listed under the plant group which interests you. See page 813 for a fuller explanation.

## ACID LOVING PLANTS

CBcs, CDMG, CMen, CTrh, CWri, EECP, EHea, GGal, GGar, GGGa, GLld, IMGH, IPen, LHyd, LMil, MBar, MCri, MGos, MLea, MMuc, MYeo, NHar, NHim, NMun, SCam, SCog, SHea, SLdr, SOWG, SReu, SSta, WAbe, WBod, WRic, WThu

## ALPINE/ROCK PLANTS

CFul, CGra, CLyd, CNic, CPBP, CStu, CWat, CWil, CWon, EAlp, EBur, ECho, ECot, EDAr, EEls, EPot, GKev, IBal, IPen, MACG, MOne, NBro, NHar, NLAp, NMin, NNew, NPol, NRya, NSla, NWCA, SCog, SIng, SKHP, SPop, SRot, WAbe, WGor, WHoo, WThu

## AQUATIC PLANTS

CBen, CRow, CWat, EHon, EMFW, LLWG, LPBA, MSKA, NSco, SLon, SWat, WMAq, WPnP, WRic, XBlo

## BAMBOOS

CAgr, CDTJ, CEnt, EAmu, EExo, EFul, ENBC, EPla, ESwi, ETod, GBin, LEdu, LPal, MBrN, MJnS, MMoz, MMuc, MWhi, MWht, NGdn, NPal, SAPC, SArc, SBig, WDyG, WPGP

## BRITISH WILD FLOWERS

CHby, CNic, COld, CRea, EBWF, GBar, GPoy, GPWP, MHer, MLod, MSal, NMir, NSco, NTHB, SECG, SHdy, SIde, SWat, WAlt, WHer, WLHH, WSFF, WShi

## BULBOUS PLANTS

CAvo, CBro, CFFs, CGrW, CQua, CStu, CTca, CWoo, ECho, EFam, EMui, EPot, ERCP, ERos, IHer, MCri, MPoH, MSHN, MSSP, NFir, NMin, NOaD, SPhx, WPrP, WShi, WWst

## CACTI & SUCCULENTS

CFwr, CPhi, CTrC, EGln, EShb, LSou, LToo, MAga, NCro, NOaD, SCac, SChr, WCor

## CARNIVOROUS PLANTS

CHew, CSWC, EECP, MYeo, SHmp, WSSs

## CHALK-LOVING PLANTS

CSpe, EFam, EGoo, LSRN, SAll, SJoh, SMHT, SMrs, SSss, SSvw

## CLIMBERS

CPou, CRHN, CSPN, CTri, CWGN, ELan, ESCh, ETho, LFol, LSRN, MGos, MPet, NBea, NMun, NTay, SBra, SDea, SLau, SLim, SMDP, WCru, WFib, WSHC, WTou

## COASTAL PLANTS

CBod, CCCN, CHrt, CMHG, CPne, CTrC, CWCL, EBWF, GGal, GGar, IBal, ISsi, SAft, SAPC, SChr, SDea, WBod, WCor, WPnn

## CONIFERS

CDHC, CKen, CLnd, CMen, CRob, CTho, ECho, EOrn, LCon, LLin, MACG, MBar, MPkF, SLim, WGor, WMou, WThu

## CONSERVATORY PLANTS

CBrP, CCCN, CKob, CRHN, CSec, CSpe, EABi, EBak, EBls, EEls, EGln, EOHP, EShb, ESul, GFai, LHyd, LToo, MAga, MJnS, MNew, NFir, SHaC, SOWG, WRic, XBlo

## DROUGHT-TOLERANT

CKno, CPne, EAlp, ECha, EFam, EGln, EGoo, EHoe, ETod, LLWG, LLWP, LPal, MAga, MHrb, NHoy, SAft, SDow, SIde, SIoW, SJoh, SKHP, SPhx, SUsu, WCor, WHil, WJek, WPnn

## FERNS

CDTJ, CFwr, CLAP, CRWN, CWCL, ECha, EExo, EFer, EMon, GBin, IBal, MMoz, NMyG, SApp, SHmp, WAbe, WFib, WMoo, WPnP, WRic

## FRUIT

CAgr, CCAT, CCVT, CTho, CTri, ECrN, EMui, GTwe, IFFs, LBuc, LEdu, MCoo, MLod, SBmr, SCmr, SCrf, SDea, SKee, WHar, WJas, WSuV, XBlo

## GRASSES

CBod, CDMG, CKno, CPuk, CWCL, EAlp, EBWF, ECha, EGle, EHoe, ELan, EMon, EPla, EPPr, EPyc, EWsh, GAuc, GBin, GCal, IFoB, LEdu, LFox, LLWP, LSRN, MBar, MBrN, MMoz, MNrw, MWhi, NBro, NGdn,

NOak, NSti, SAft, SApp, SHDw, SPhx, SSss, SUsu, SWal, WHal, WLeb, WMoo, WPGP, WPrP

### Hedging

CCVT, CLnd, CTrC, CTrG, CTri, ECrN, EMac, ERom, ISsi, LBuc, LCon, MCoo, MHrb, NBee, SAft, SBLw, SDow, SECG, SHHo, SLan, SRiv, WBuc, WHar, WLav, WMou, WOrn, WWeb, WWHy

### Herbs

CArn, CBod, CHby, COld, CPbn, CSev, CWan, ECot, ELau, EOHP, GBar, GPoy, GPWP, ILis, LFol, LLWP, LMor, MHer, MHrb, MSal, NGHP, NLLv, NTHB, SDow, SHDw, SIde, SWat, WCHb, WJek, WLav, WLHH

### Marginal/Bog Plants

CBen, CDMG, CDWL, CLAP, CMHG, COld, CRow, CWat, EHoe, EHon, EMFW, GKev, IPen, LLWG, LPBA, MMuc, MSKA, MYeo, NCot, NHim, NMun, NSco, SHaC, WHal, WMoo, WPnP, WSFF, WShi

### Orchids

CBur, CLAP, CRea, EFEx, GUzu, LBut, MNew, NEqu, NLAp, NSpr, SHdy, WHer, WWst, XFro

### Organic

CAbx, CBdw, CBgR, CDMG, CHby, COld, CSec, CSRo, CTca, CTuc, EFer, GBar, GPoy, GPWP, ILis, LEdu, LLWP, MLod, MSal, MYeo, NPol, NTHB, SOWG, SPav, WCHb, WCor, WGwG, WJek, WPnP, WSFF, WShi

### Ornamental Trees

CBcs, CBdw, CCVT, CDul, CEnd, CLnd, CMen, CPMA, CSto, CTho, CTri, CWon, ECot, ECrN, EGFP, ELan, EMac, EMui, EPla, ERom, GAuc, GFor, GGal, IMGH, LBuc, LHyd, MGos, MPkF, NBea, NBee, NPal, SBir, SBLw, SBmr, SCrf, SHBN, SHHo, SLan, SLau, SLim, SLon, SMHT, SSta, WBod, WBuc, WCru, WHar, WJas, WMou, WOrn, WPGP, WWHy

### Palms

CDTJ, CKob, CPHo, EAmu, EExo, ESwi, ETod, LPal, LPJP, NPal, SArc, SBig, SChr

### Peat Free

CAbx, CBgR, CBre, CElw, CHby, CKob, CLAP, CMdw, CMea, CNic, CPom, CRHN, CRWN, CSam, CSec, CSev, CSNP, CSRo, CSsd, CTca, CTho, CTsd, EAro, EBla, EBWF, ECrN, EGoo, EHig, ELau, EMal, EPts, GPoy, ILis, LEdu, LLWP, MBNS, MCri, MLHP, MMoz, MPhe, MSal, MWgw, MWhi, NGby, NPol, NSco, SAft, SBch, SECG, SHHo, SMDP, SPav, SRiF, STes, WCHb, WCor, WDyG, WGwG, WHoo, WJek, WPic, WPnP, WPrP, WRha, WSFF, WShi

### Period Plants

CArn, CKel, CSna, CWGr, EBls, EKMF, IHer, ILis, NMin, SAll, SPop, SSvw, WAct, WFuv, WHer

### Propagate to Order

CAbx, CArn, CBnk, CCAT, CCCN, CElw, CFir, CKel, CLAP, CMdw, CMen, CPMA, CPne, CSev, CTsd, CWGr, CWon, CWVF, EAlp, EBla, EBls, ECho, ECrN, EECP, EEls, EFer, EFul, EGFP, EHrv, EPla, EPyc, EQua, ERhR, EShb, ESul, GBuc, GFai, GGal, GWWP, IGor, ILis, LHyd, LLWP, LMil, MLHP, MLod, MMoz, MSHN, MYeo, NBPN, NChi, NCot, NCro, NHoy, NLLv, NPol, NSco, NShi, NTHB, SAga, SBch, SCam, SDea, SECG, SHDw, SHea, SHyH, SJoh, SLau, SLdr, SLon, SMDP, SPav, SPol, SPop, SRiF, STes, SWat, WAct, WDyG, WFFs, WHer, WHil, WJek, WLav, WOrn, WPBF, WPnP, WPrP, WRic, WSFF, WSSs, WTin, WWHy, XBlo

### Roses

CPou, CSRo, EBls, ECnt, ESty, GCoc, IDic, ISsi, LFol, LGod, MAus, MGan, MHav, SLay, SLon, SSea, SWCr, WAct

### Seed

CDob, CHby, CKno, CRea, CSec, CSpe, CSut, CTuc, EMcA, GAuc, GPoy, LSee, MPet, MPoH, MSal, NChl, NGHP, NPol, NRob, SAft, SAll, SECG, SSss, WJek, WTou, XBTW

### Specimen Sized Plants

CArn, CBdn, CBen, CCCN, CCVT, CDTJ, CKel, CPMA, CRob, CTho, CTrG, CWon, EAmu, EBla, ECot, ECrN, EECP, EExo, EFer, EHrv, EKMF, EQua, ERom, EShb, ESwi, ETod, GAuc, GLld, IMGH, LBuc, LHyd, LMil, MAga, MBrN, MGos, MLea, MMoz, MMuc, MNew, MPhe, MYeo, NCro, NHim, NHoy, NPal, NPol, SAPC, SArc, SBig, SBLw, SCam, SHHo, SHmp, SHyH, SLan, SLdr, SLon, SReu, SRiF, SSta, SWat, WCru, WHer, WJek, WOrn, WPat, WRic, WWeb

### Topiary

ERom, SHHo, SLan, SRiv, WWeb

### Tropical Plants

CCCN, CKob, CPHo, EAmu, EShb, ESwi, EUJe, LToo, MJnS, MNew, SAPC, SArc, SBig, SHaC, SKHP, SOWG, WCru, XBlo

# INDEX MAP

The maps on the following pages show the approximate location of the nurseries whose details are listed in this directory.

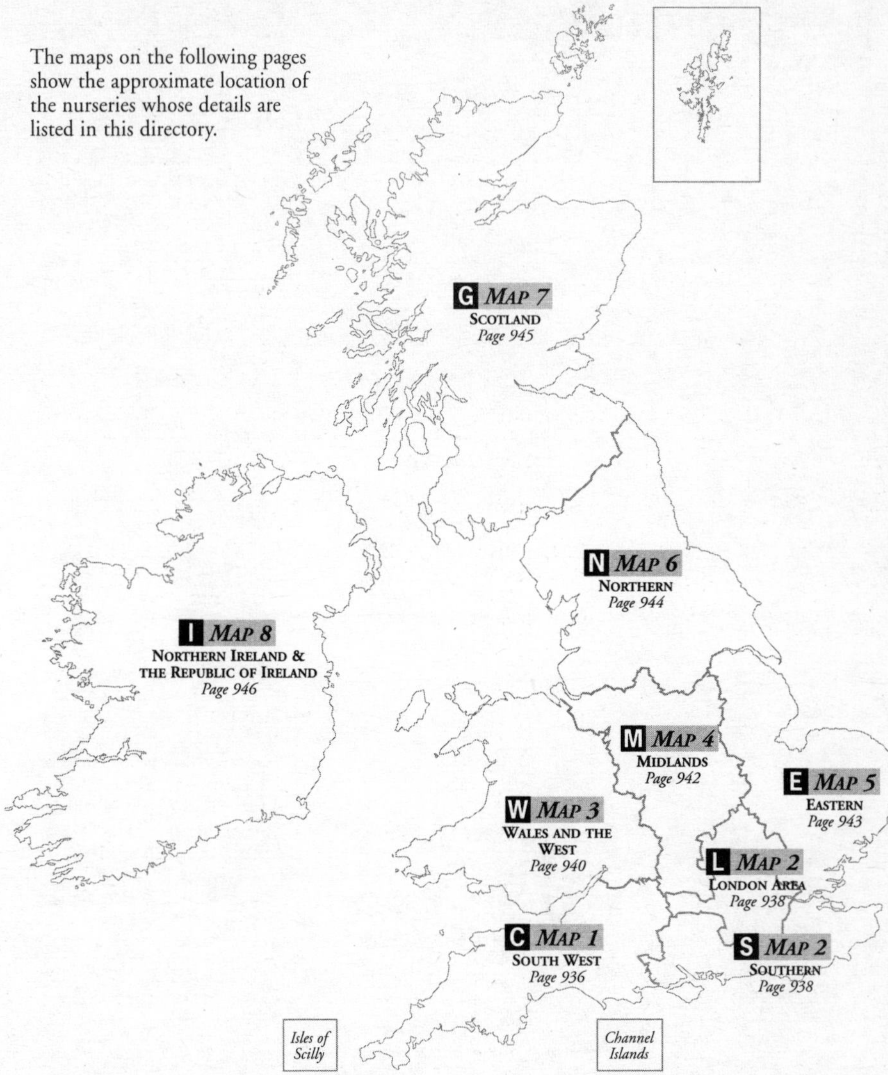


KEY

CHEx Details of nurseries with letter Codes in boxes are given in the Nursery Details by Code Index starting on page 816.

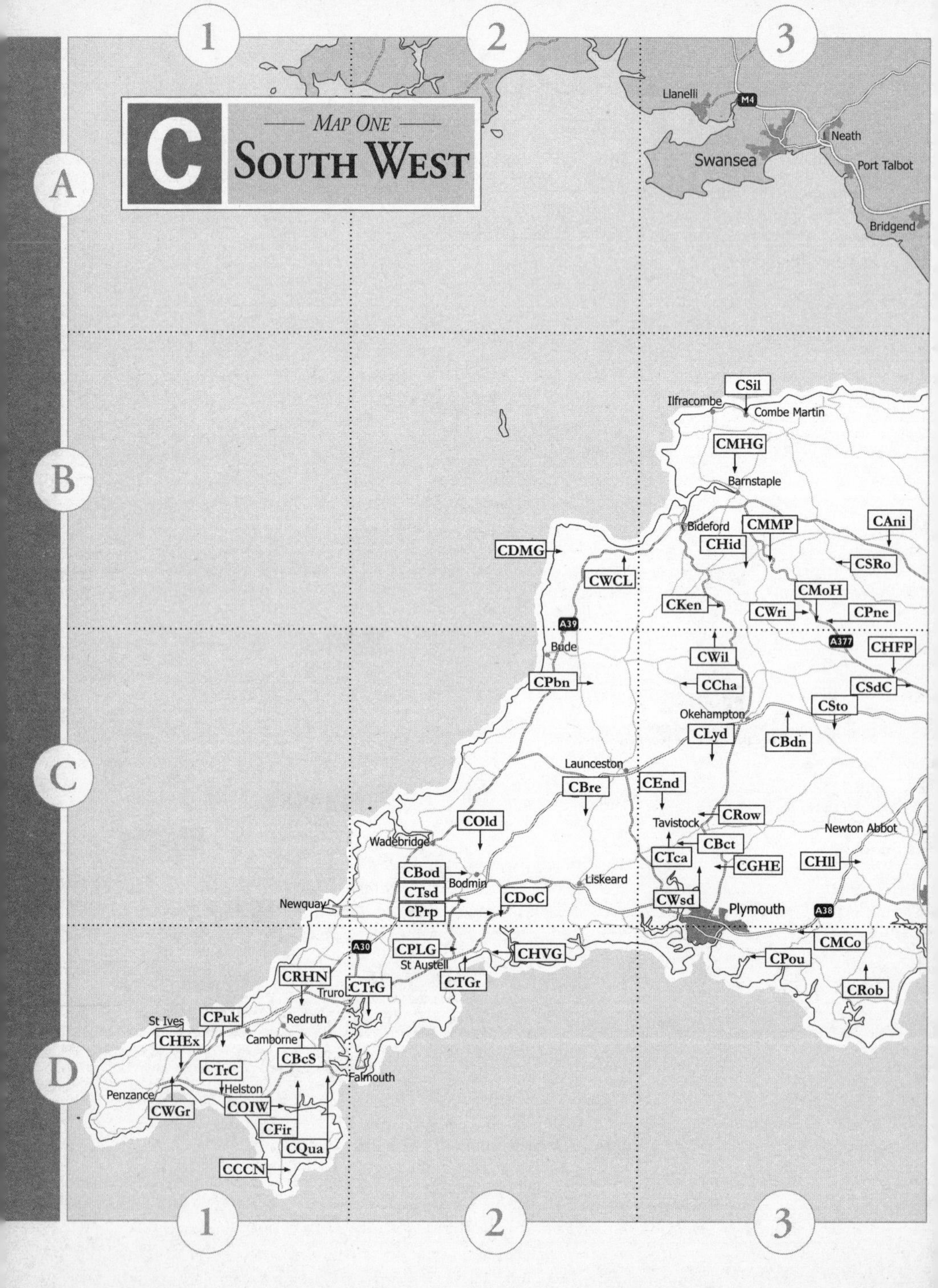
C
MAP ONE
SOUTH WEST
1
2
3
A
B
C
D
Llanelli
M4
Neath
Swansea
Port Talbot
Bridgend
CSil
Ilfracombe
Combe Martin
CMHG
Barnstaple
Bideford
CMMP
CAni
CDMG
CHid
CSRo
CWCL
CMoH
CKen
CWri
CPne
A39
A377
CHFP
Bude
CWil
CPbn
CCha
CSdC
Okehampton
CSto
CLyd
CBdn
Launceston
CBre
CEnd
COld
CRow
Tavistock
Newton Abbot
Wadebridge
CBct
CTca
CGHE
CHll
CBod
Bodmin
CTsd
Liskeard
CDoC
Newquay
CPrp
CWsd
Plymouth
A38
A30
CPLG
CHVG
CMCo
St Austell
CPou
CRHN
CTGr
Truro
CTrG
CRob
St Ives
CPuk
Redruth
CHEx
Camborne
CBcS
CTrC
Falmouth
Penzance
Helston
CWGr
COIW
CFir
CQua
CCCN

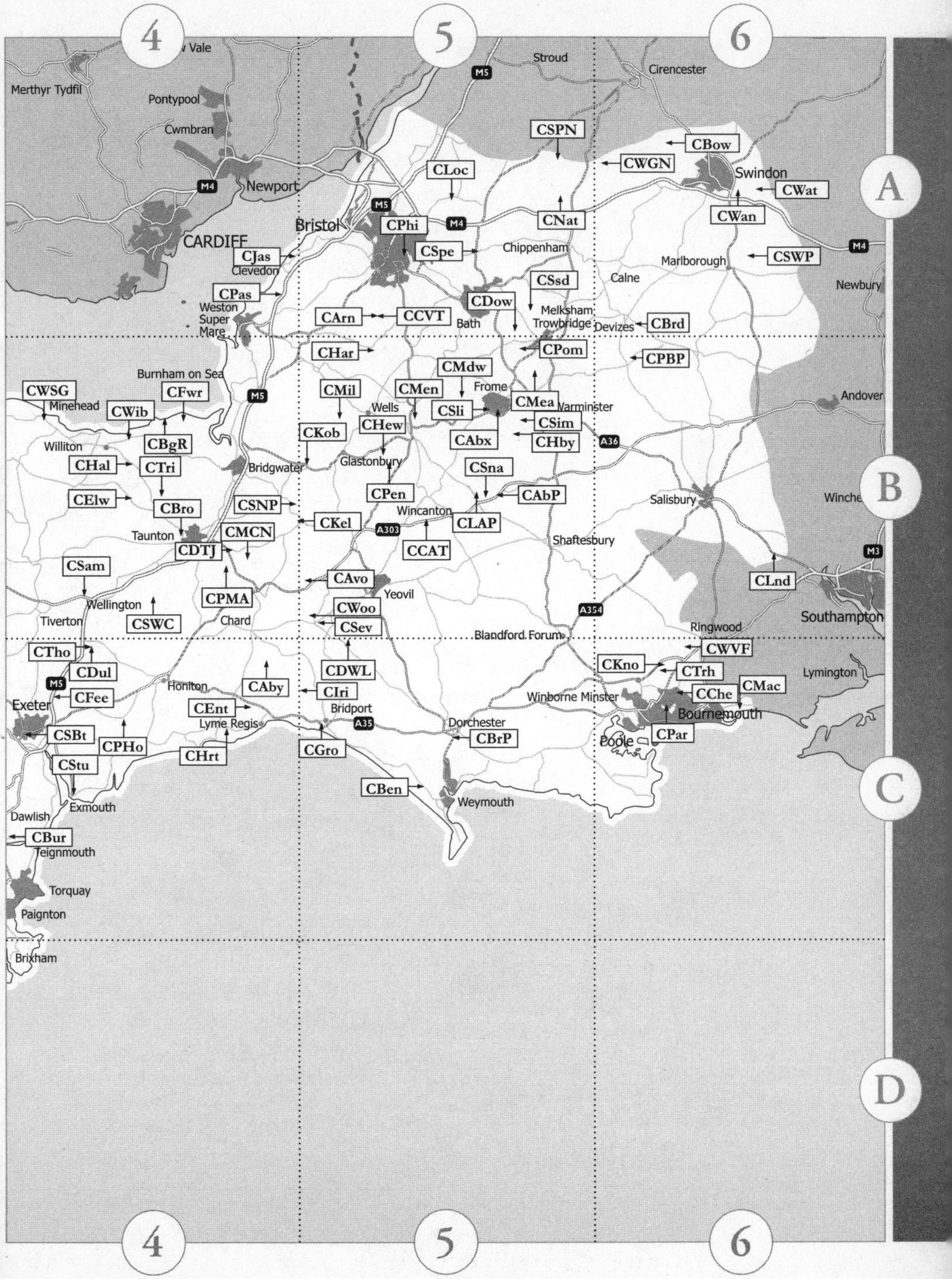
4
5
6
A
B
C
D
Merthyr Tydfil
Pontypool
Cwmbran
Newport
M4
CARDIFF
Bristol
M5
Stroud
Cirencester
Swindon
CSPN
CBow
CWGN
CLoc
CWat
CPhi
M4
CNat
CWan
CJas
Clevedon
CSpe
Chippenham
Marlborough
CSWP
CPas
Weston
Super
Mare
CSsd
Calne
Newbury
CDow
Melksham
Trowbridge
Devizes
CBrd
CArn
CCVT
Bath
CHar
CPom
CPBP
CMdw
Burnham on Sea
CWSG
Minehead
CWib
CFwr
CMil
CMen
Frome
CMea
Warminster
Andover
Wells
CSli
CSim
CKob
CHew
CAbx
CHby
A36
Williton
CBgR
CHal
CTri
Bridgwater
Glastonbury
CSna
CPen
CAbP
CElw
CBro
CSNP
Wincanton
Salisbury
Winche
CKel
A303
CLAP
Taunton
CMCN
CDTJ
CCAT
Shaftesbury
CSam
CAvo
M3
CLnd
Yeovil
Wellington
CPMA
CWoo
Southampton
Tiverton
CSWC
Chard
A354
CSev
Ringwood
Blandford Forum
CWVF
CTho
CDul
CKno
CTrh
Lymington
CDWL
CMac
Honiton
Exeter
CFee
CAby
CIri
Winborne Minster
CChe
CEnt
Bridport
Bournemouth
Lyme Regis
A35
Dorchester
CSBt
CPHo
CHrt
CGro
CBrP
Poole
CPar
CStu
CBen
Weymouth
Exmouth
Dawlish
CBur
Teignmouth
Torquay
Paignton
Brixham

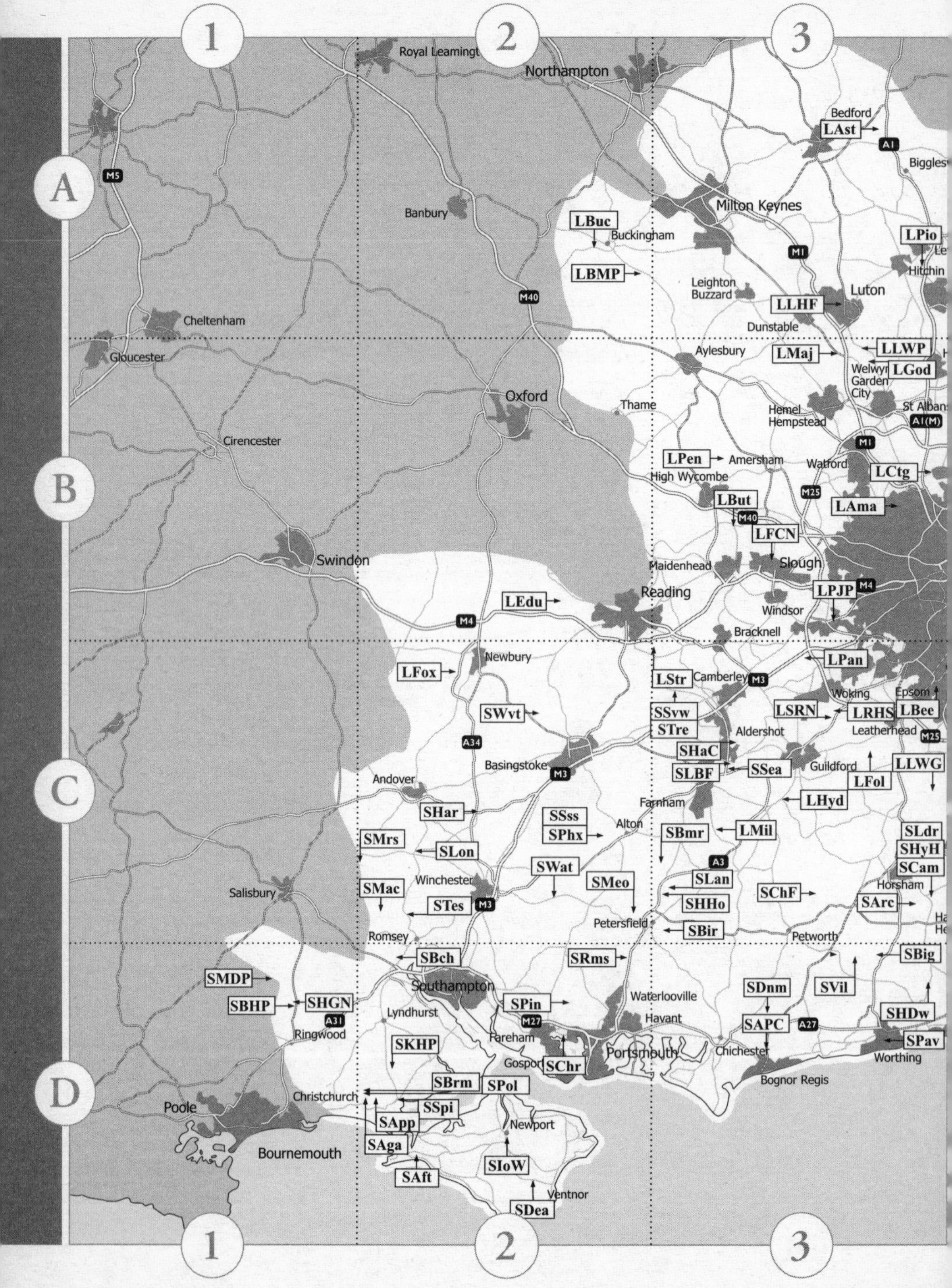
1
2
3
A
B
C
D
Royal Leamingt
Northampton
Bedford
LAst
A1
Biggles
M5
Banbury
Milton Keynes
LBuc
Buckingham
LPio
Le
Hitchin
M1
LBMP
Leighton Buzzard
Luton
M40
LLHF
Cheltenham
Dunstable
Gloucester
Aylesbury
LMaj
LLWP
Welwyn Garden City
LGod
Oxford
Thame
Hemel Hempstead
St Albans
A1(M)
Cirencester
LPen
Amersham
Watford
High Wycombe
LCtg
M25
LBut
LAma
M40
LFCN
Swindon
Maidenhead
Slough
LPJP
M4
Reading
LEdu
Windsor
M4
Bracknell
Newbury
LPan
LFox
LStr
Camberley
M3
Woking
Epsom
SWvt
SSvw
STre
LSRN
LRHS
LBee
Aldershot
Leatherhead
M25
A34
SHaC
Basingstoke
M3
SLBF
SSea
Guildford
LLWG
Andover
LFol
Farnham
LHyd
SHar
SSss
SPhx
Alton
SBmr
LMil
SLdr
SMrs
SHyH
SLon
SWat
A3
SCam
Winchester
SLan
SMac
SMeo
SChF
Horsham
Salisbury
M3
STes
SHHo
SArc
Petersfield
SBir
Romsey
Petworth
SBch
SRms
SBig
SMDP
Southampton
Waterlooville
SDnm
SVil
SBHP
SHGN
SPin
Lyndhurst
Havant
SHDw
A31
M27
SAPC
A27
Ringwood
Fareham
SPav
SKHP
Portsmouth
Chichester
Worthing
Gosport
SChr
Bognor Regis
SBrm
SPol
Christchurch
SSpi
Poole
SApp
Newport
SAga
Bournemouth
SIoW
SAft
Ventnor
SDea

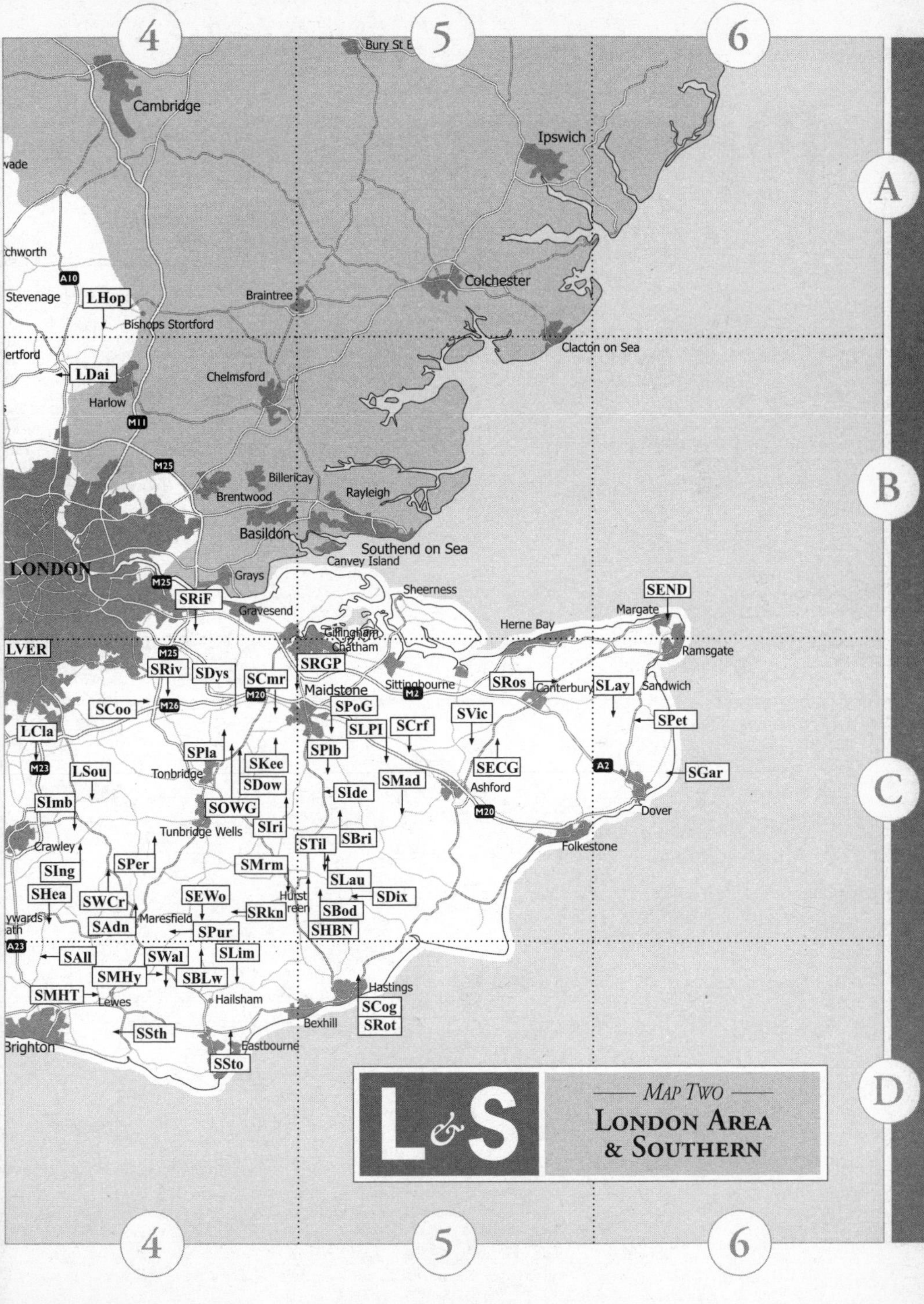

4
5
6
A
B
C
D
Bury St E
Cambridge
Ipswich
wade
chworth
A10
Stevenage
LHop
Bishops Stortford
Braintree
Colchester
Clacton on Sea
ertford
LDai
Harlow
Chelmsford
M11
M25
Billericay
Brentwood
Rayleigh
Basildon
Southend on Sea
Canvey Island
LONDON
Grays
M25
SRiF
Gravesend
Sheerness
SEND
Margate
Herne Bay
Gillingham
Chatham
Ramsgate
LVER
M25
SRiv
SDys
SCmr
SRGP
M20
Maidstone
Sittingbourne
M2
SRos
Canterbury
SLay
Sandwich
SCoo
M26
SPoG
SVic
SPet
LCla
SLPI
SCrf
M23
SPla
SPlb
SECG
A2
SGar
LSou
Tonbridge
SKee
SMad
Ashford
SDow
SIde
SImb
SOWG
M20
Dover
SIri
Tunbridge Wells
SBri
Crawley
STil
Folkestone
SIng
SPer
SMrm
SLau
SHea
SWCr
SEWo
Hurst
reen
SDix
ywards
ath
SAdn
Maresfield
SRkn
SBod
SPur
SHBN
A23
SAll
SWal
SLim
SMHy
SBLw
SMHT
Lewes
Hailsham
Hastings
SCog
SRot
Bexhill
SSth
Brighton
Eastbourne
SSto
L&S
MAP TWO
LONDON AREA
& SOUTHERN

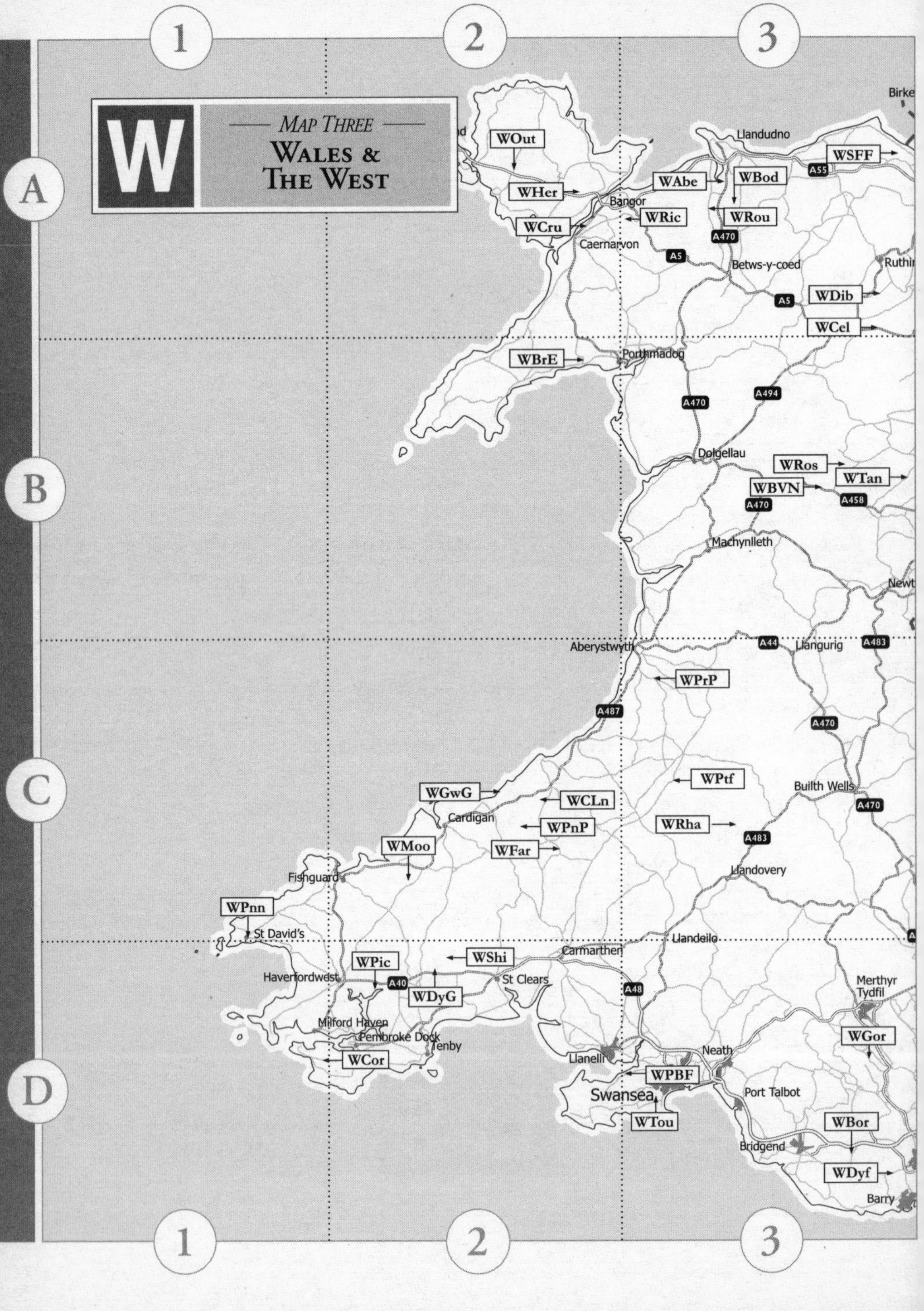
W
Map Three
Wales & The West
1
2
3
A
B
C
D
WOut
WHer
WCru
WAbe
WBod
WRic
WRou
WSFF
WDib
WCel
WBrE
WRos
WTan
WBVN
WPrP
WPtf
WGwG
WCLn
WPnP
WRha
WMoo
WFar
WPnn
WPic
WShi
WDyG
WCor
WPBF
WTou
WGor
WBor
WDyf
Llandudno
Bangor
Caernarvon
Betws-y-coed
Porthmadog
Dolgellau
Machynlleth
Aberystwyth
Llangurig
Builth Wells
Cardigan
Fishguard
St David's
Llandovery
Llandeilo
Carmarthen
Haverfordwest
St Clears
Milford Haven
Pembroke Dock
Tenby
Llanelli
Swansea
Neath
Port Talbot
Merthyr Tydfil
Bridgend
Barry
A55
A470
A5
A494
A458
A44
A483
A487
A40
A48

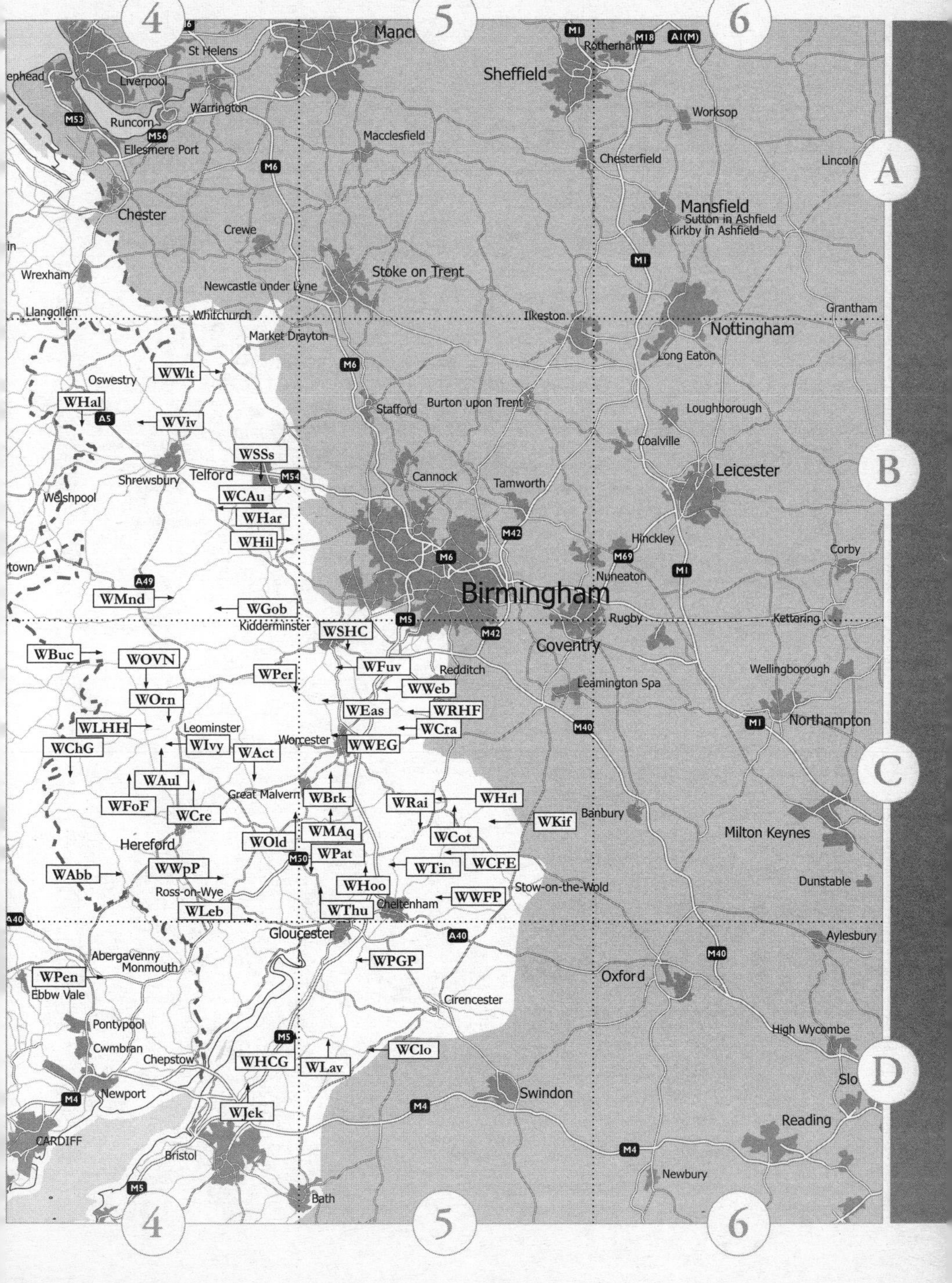
4
5
6
A
B
C
D
St Helens
Manc
Liverpool
Warrington
Runcorn
Ellesmere Port
Chester
Crewe
Wrexham
Llangollen
Whitchurch
Macclesfield
Sheffield
Rotherham
Worksop
Chesterfield
Lincoln
Mansfield
Sutton in Ashfield
Kirkby in Ashfield
Stoke on Trent
Newcastle under Lyne
Ilkeston
Nottingham
Grantham
Market Drayton
Long Eaton
Oswestry
Stafford
Burton upon Trent
Loughborough
Coalville
Leicester
Shrewsbury
Telford
Welshpool
Cannock
Tamworth
Hinckley
Nuneaton
Corby
Birmingham
Rugby
Kettering
Kidderminster
Coventry
Redditch
Wellingborough
Leamington Spa
Northampton
Leominster
Worcester
Great Malvern
Banbury
Milton Keynes
Hereford
Ross-on-Wye
Cheltenham
Stow-on-the-Wold
Dunstable
Gloucester
Aylesbury
Abergavenny
Monmouth
Ebbw Vale
Oxford
Cirencester
Pontypool
Cwmbran
Chepstow
High Wycombe
Newport
Swindon
Slo
Reading
CARDIFF
Bristol
Newbury
Bath
M6
M1
M18
A1(M)
M53
M56
A5
M54
M42
M69
A49
M5
M40
M50
A40
M4
WWlt
WHal
WViv
WSSs
WCAu
WHar
WHil
WMnd
WGob
WSHC
WBuc
WOVN
WPer
WFuv
WWeb
WOrn
WEas
WRHF
WLHH
WCra
WChG
WIvy
WAct
WWEG
WAul
WBrk
WFoF
WCre
WRai
WHrl
WKif
WMAq
WOld
WCot
WPat
WTin
WCFE
WAbb
WWpP
WHoo
WWFP
WLeb
WThu
WPGP
WPen
WHCG
WLav
WClo
WJek

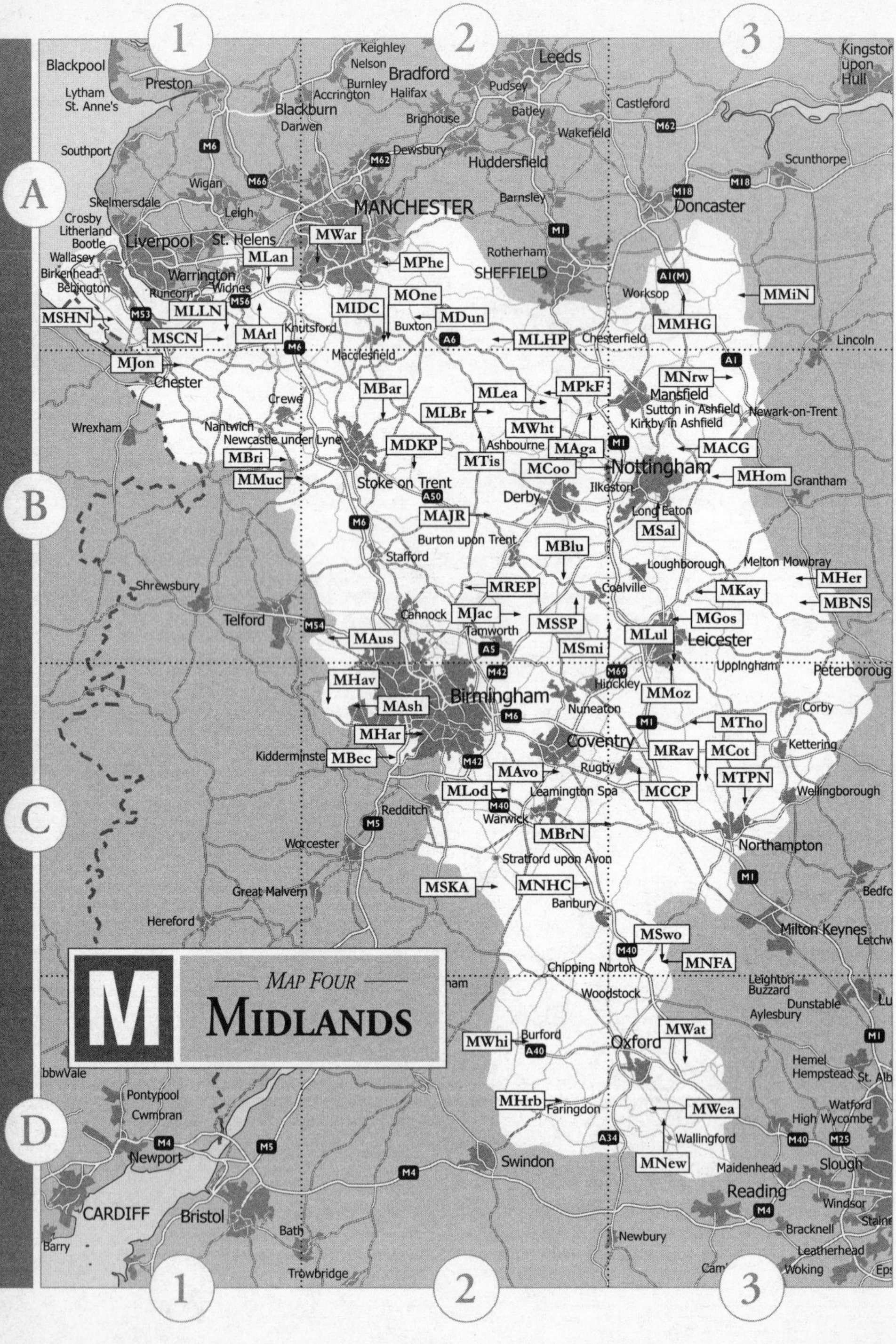
1
2
3
A
B
C
D
Map Four
M
Midlands
Blackpool
Preston
Lytham
St. Anne's
Southport
Keighley
Nelson
Burnley
Accrington
Blackburn
Darwen
Bradford
Halifax
Brighouse
Leeds
Pudsey
Batley
Wakefield
Castleford
Kingston upon Hull
Dewsbury
Huddersfield
Scunthorpe
Wigan
Skelmersdale
Leigh
MANCHESTER
Barnsley
Doncaster
Crosby
Litherland
Bootle
Liverpool
St. Helens
Wallasey
Birkenhead
Bebington
Warrington
Runcorn
Widnes
Rotherham
SHEFFIELD
Worksop
Knutsford
Buxton
Macclesfield
Chesterfield
Lincoln
Chester
Crewe
Wrexham
Nantwich
Newcastle under Lyne
Mansfield
Sutton in Ashfield
Kirkby in Ashfield
Newark-on-Trent
Ashbourne
Nottingham
Grantham
Stoke on Trent
Derby
Ilkeston
Long Eaton
Burton upon Trent
Stafford
Loughborough
Melton Mowbray
Shrewsbury
Coalville
Telford
Cannock
Tamworth
Leicester
Uppingham
Peterborough
Hinckley
Birmingham
Nuneaton
Corby
Coventry
Kettering
Kidderminster
Rugby
Leamington Spa
Wellingborough
Redditch
Warwick
Northampton
Worcester
Stratford upon Avon
Great Malvern
Banbury
Bedford
Hereford
Milton Keynes
Letchworth
Chipping Norton
Leighton Buzzard
Woodstock
Dunstable
Aylesbury
Burford
Oxford
Hemel Hempstead
St. Albans
Ebbw Vale
Pontypool
Cwmbran
Faringdon
Watford
High Wycombe
Newport
Wallingford
Swindon
Maidenhead
Slough
Reading
CARDIFF
Bristol
Windsor
Bath
Barry
Bracknell
Newbury
Leatherhead
Trowbridge
Woking
M6
M62
M66
M1
M18
A1(M)
A1
M53
M56
A6
A50
M54
A5
M42
M69
M5
M40
M4
A40
A34
M25
MWar
MLan
MPhe
MOne
MIDC
MDun
MLLN
MSHN
MSCN
MArl
MLHP
MMHG
MMiN
MJon
MBar
MLea
MPkF
MNrw
MLBr
MWht
MAga
MACG
MDKP
MTis
MCoo
MHom
MBri
MMuc
MAJR
MSal
MBlu
MREP
MHer
MKay
MBNS
MJac
MSSP
MGos
MAus
MSmi
MLul
MHav
MAsh
MMoz
MTho
MHar
MRav
MCot
MBec
MAvo
MTPN
MLod
MCCP
MBrN
MSKA
MNHC
MSwo
MNFA
MWat
MWhi
MHrb
MWea
MNew

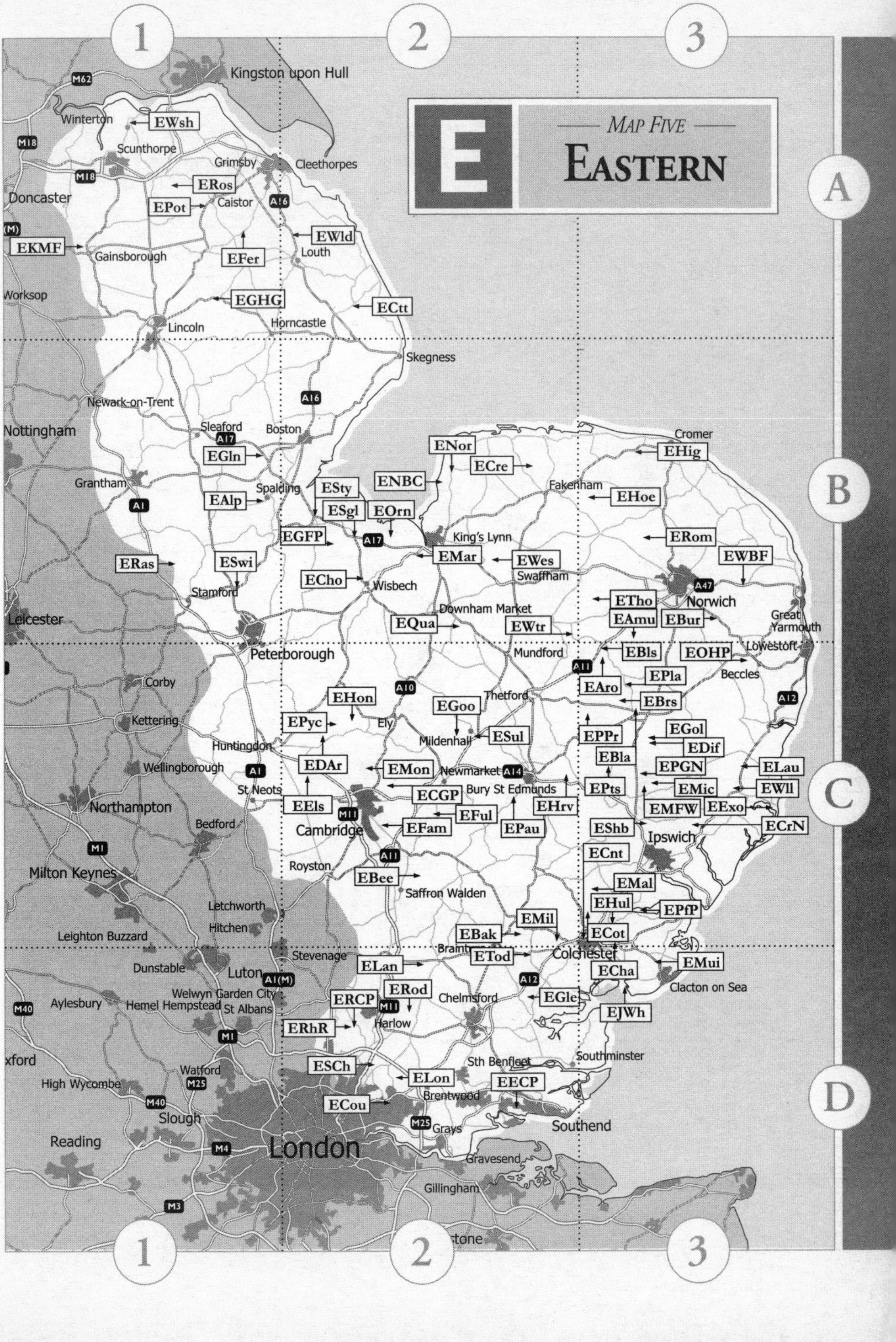
E
MAP FIVE
EASTERN
1
2
3
A
B
C
D
Kingston upon Hull
Winterton
EWsh
Scunthorpe
Grimsby
Cleethorpes
ERos
Doncaster
EPot
Caistor
EWld
Louth
EKMF
Gainsborough
EFer
Worksop
EGHG
ECtt
Lincoln
Horncastle
Skegness
Newark-on-Trent
Nottingham
Sleaford
Boston
EGln
Grantham
Spalding
ESty
ENor
ECre
Cromer
EHig
ENBC
Fakenham
EHoe
EAlp
ESgl
EOrn
EGFP
King's Lynn
ERom
ERas
ESwi
EMar
EWes
Swaffham
EWBF
Stamford
ECho
Wisbech
ETho
Norwich
Leicester
Downham Market
EAmu
EBur
Great Yarmouth
EQua
EWtr
Peterborough
Mundford
EBls
EOHP
Lowestoft
EPla
Beccles
Corby
EHon
EAro
Thetford
EBrs
EGoo
Kettering
EPyc
Ely
Mildenhall
ESul
EPPr
EGol
EDif
Huntingdon
EBla
EPGN
ELau
Wellingborough
EDAr
EMon
Newmarket
St Neots
ECGP
Bury St Edmunds
EPts
EMic
EWll
Northampton
EEls
EHrv
EMFW
EExo
EFul
Bedford
Cambridge
EFam
EPau
EShb
ECrN
Ipswich
Milton Keynes
Royston
ECnt
EBee
Saffron Walden
EMal
Letchworth
EHul
EPfP
Hitchen
EMil
Leighton Buzzard
EBak
ECot
Braintree
Colchester
Stevenage
ETod
EMui
Dunstable
Luton
ELan
ECha
Clacton on Sea
Welwyn Garden City
ERod
Aylesbury
Hemel Hempstead
St Albans
ERCP
Chelmsford
EGle
EJWh
ERhR
Harlow
Southminster
xford
Watford
ESCh
Sth Benfleet
High Wycombe
ELon
EECP
Brentwood
ECou
Slough
Southend
Grays
Reading
London
Gravesend
Gillingham
stone
M62
M18
A16
A17
A1
A47
A10
A12
A14
A11
M11
A1(M)
M1
M40
M25
M4
M3

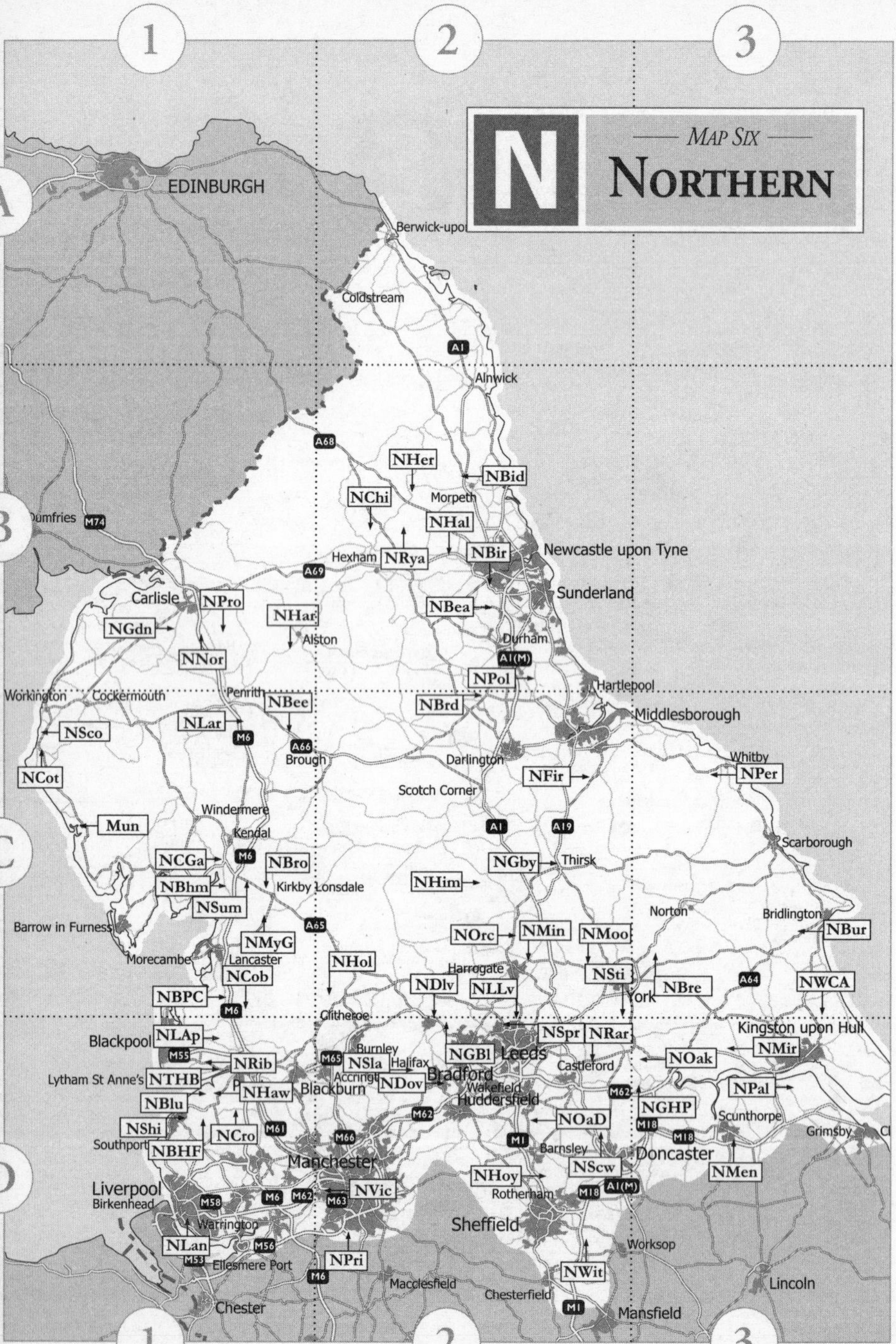
1
2
3
A
B
C
D
N
MAP SIX
NORTHERN
EDINBURGH
Berwick-upo
Coldstream
A1
Alnwick
A68
NHer
NBid
NChi
Morpeth
Dumfries
M74
NHal
Hexham
NRya
NBir
Newcastle upon Tyne
A69
Sunderland
Carlisle
NPro
NHar
NBea
NGdn
Alston
Durham
NNor
A1(M)
NPol
Hartlepool
Workington
Cockermouth
Penrith
NBee
NBrd
Middlesborough
NLar
M6
NSco
A66
Brough
Darlington
Whitby
NCot
NFir
NPer
Scotch Corner
Windermere
Mun
A1
A19
Kendal
Scarborough
NCGa
M6
NBro
NGby
Thirsk
NBhm
Kirkby Lonsdale
NHim
NSum
Norton
Bridlington
Barrow in Furness
A65
NOrc
NMin
NMoo
NBur
NMyG
Morecambe
Lancaster
NHol
Harrogate
NCob
NSti
A64
NWCA
NBPC
NDlv
NLLv
York
NBre
M6
Clitheroe
Kingston upon Hull
Blackpool
NLAp
NSpr
NRar
M55
Burnley
NGBl
Leeds
NOak
NMir
M65
NSla
Halifax
Castleford
Lytham St Anne's
NTHB
NRib
Accringt
Bradford
NPal
NHaw
Blackburn
NDov
Wakefield
M62
NBlu
Huddersfield
NGHP
Scunthorpe
M62
NOaD
NShi
NCro
M61
M18
Grimsby
Southport
NBHF
M66
M1
Barnsley
M18
Manchester
Doncaster
NScw
NMen
Liverpool
NHoy
Birkenhead
M58
M6
M62
M63
NVic
Rotherham
M18
A1(M)
Warrington
Sheffield
NLan
M56
Worksop
M53
Ellesmere Port
NPri
M6
NWit
Macclesfield
Chesterfield
Lincoln
Chester
M1
Mansfield
1
2
3

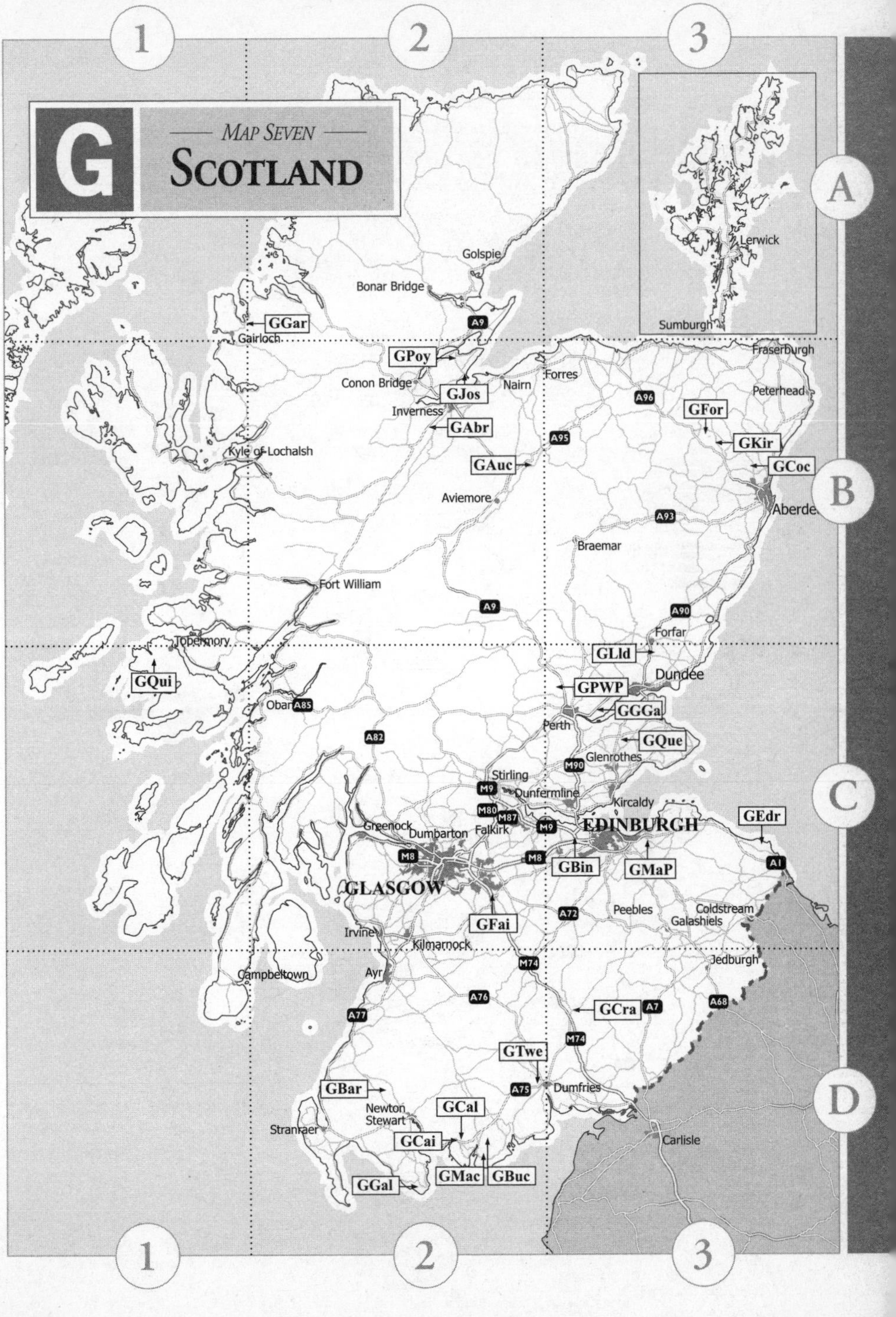
1
2
3
G
MAP SEVEN
SCOTLAND
A
B
C
D
Lerwick
Sumburgh
Golspie
Bonar Bridge
A9
GGar
Gairloch
GPoy
Fraserburgh
Conon Bridge
GJos
Nairn
Forres
Peterhead
Inverness
A96
GFor
GAbr
GKir
A95
Kyle of Lochalsh
GAuc
GCoc
Aviemore
Aberde
A93
Braemar
Fort William
A9
A90
Forfar
Tobermory
GLld
Dundee
GQui
GPWP
Oban
A85
GGGa
Perth
A82
GQue
Glenrothes
M90
Stirling
M9
Dunfermline
Kircaldy
M80
M87
M9
EDINBURGH
GEdr
Greenock
Dumbarton
Falkirk
M8
M8
GBin
GMaP
A1
GLASGOW
GFai
A72
Peebles
Coldstream
Galashiels
Irvine
Kilmarnock
Jedburgh
Campbeltown
Ayr
M74
A76
GCra
A7
A68
A77
M74
GTwe
GBar
A75
Dumfries
Newton
Stewart
GCal
Stranraer
GCai
Carlisle
GMac
GBuc
GGal
1
2
3

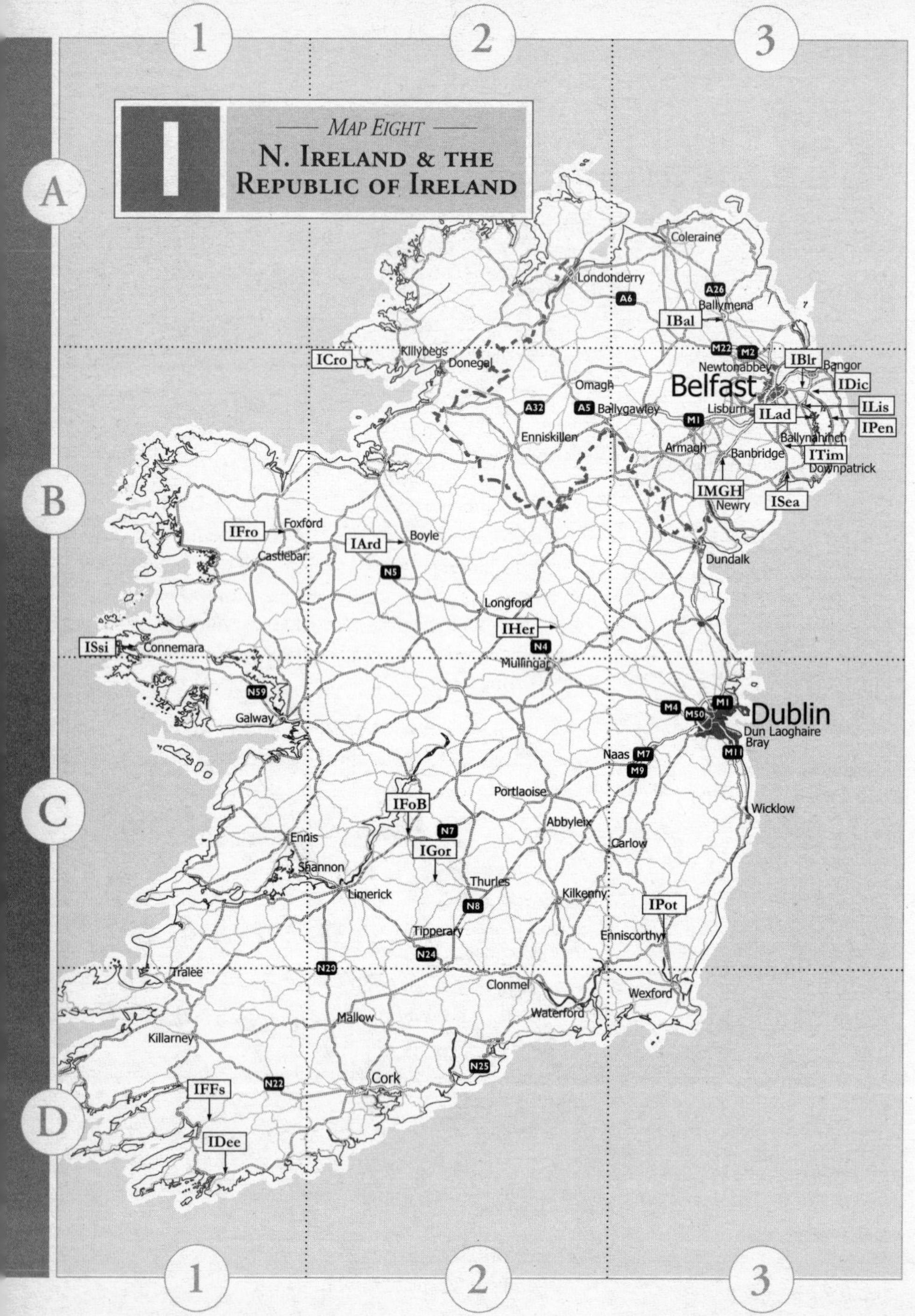

MAP EIGHT
I
N. IRELAND & THE REPUBLIC OF IRELAND
1
2
3
A
B
C
D
Coleraine
Londonderry
A26
A6
Ballymena
IBal
M22
M2
ICro
Killybegs
Donegal
IBlr
Bangor
Newtonabbey
IDic
Belfast
Omagh
A32
A5
Ballygawley
Lisburn
ILad
ILis
M1
IPen
Enniskillen
Armagh
Ballynahinch
Banbridge
ITim
Downpatrick
IMGH
Newry
ISea
IFro
Foxford
IArd
Boyle
Castlebar
N5
Dundalk
Longford
IHer
ISsi
Connemara
N4
Mullingar
N59
M4
M1
M50
Dublin
Galway
Dun Laoghaire
Bray
Naas
M7
M11
M9
Portlaoise
IFoB
Wicklow
N7
Abbyleix
Ennis
IGor
Carlow
Shannon
Thurles
Limerick
Kilkenny
N8
IPot
Tipperary
Enniscorthy
N24
N20
Tralee
Clonmel
Wexford
Mallow
Waterford
Killarney
N25
Cork
N22
IFFs
IDee
1
2
3

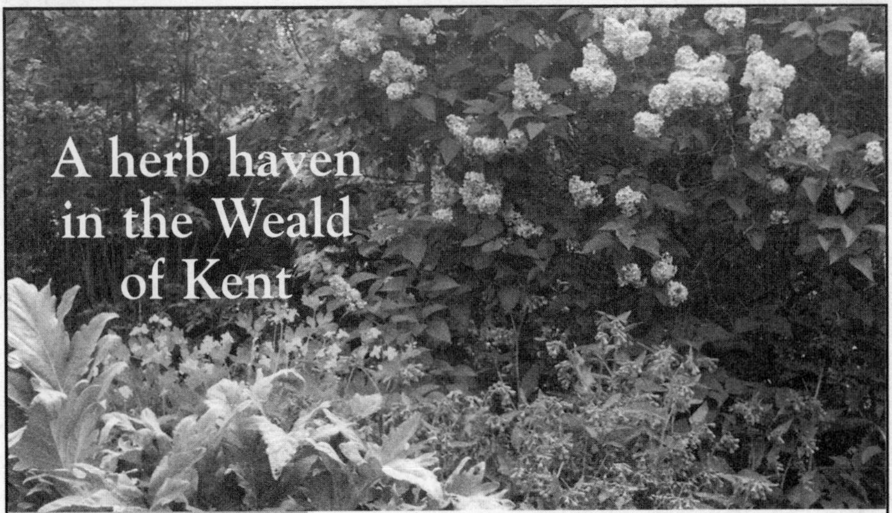
A herb haven
in the Weald
of Kent

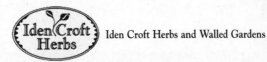

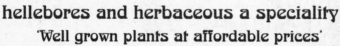

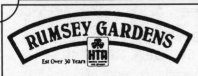

# INDEX OF ADVERTISERS

# RHS Show Awards 2006

*RHS Plant Finder* nurseries that were awarded RHS medals at the three major RHS Shows in 2006

## Chelsea Gold

Jacques Amand International
Avon Bulbs
Peter Beales Roses
Bowden Hostas
Burncoose Nurseries
Burnham Nurseries
The Cottage Herbary
Dibley's Nurseries
Downderry Nursery
Fernwood Nursery
Hampshire Carnivorous Plants
Hardy's Cottage Garden Plants
Harveys Garden Plants
Jekka's Herb Farm
Knoll Gardens
The Romantic Garden
South West Carnivorous Plants
Brian & Pearl Sulman

## Chelsea Silver-Gilt

Claire Austin Hardy Plants
David Austin Roses Ltd
Barnsdale Gardens
Broadleigh Gardens
Sheila Chapman Clematis
D'Arcy & Everest
Kobakoba
Mendip Bonsai Studio
Millais Nurseries
Potash Nursery
Rhodes & Rockliffe
Roualeyn Nurseries
Thorncroft Clematis
Westcountry Nurseries

## Chelsea Silver-Gilt Hogg

Ken Muir Ltd

## Chelsea Silver-Gilt Knightian

W Robinson & Sons Ltd

## Chelsea Silver

Choice Landscapes
Foxgrove Plants
Isle of Wight Lavender
Kelways Ltd
C S Lockyer (Fuchsias)
Pops Plants

## Chelsea Silver Grenfell

David Austin Roses Ltd

## Chelsea Bronze

Fibrex Nurseries Ltd
Fuchsiavale Nurseries

## Hampton Court Gold

Blacksmiths Cottage Nursery
Sheila Chapman Clematis
Dibleys's Nurseries
Downderry Nursery
Fir Trees Pelargonium Nursery (& **Most Creative Exhibit**)
Goldbrook Plants
Hampshire Carnivorous Plants
Jekka's Herb Farm
Mendip Bonsai Studio
Park Green Nurseries
Potash Nursery
Roualeyn Nurseries
South West Carnivorous Plants
Brian & Pearl Sulman

## Hampton Court Silver-Gilt

Allwood Bros
Jacques Amand International
Avon Bulbs
Big Plant Nursery
Culm View Nursery
Dibley's Nurseries
Fernwood Nursery
Fibrex Nurseries Ltd

Foxgrove Plants
Hardy's Cottage Garden Plants
Harveys Garden Plants
Hopleys Plants Ltd
C S Lockyer (Fuchsias)
P W Plants
Rotherview Nursery

### Winchester Growers Ltd

Hampton Court Silver-Gilt Hogg
Ken Muir Ltd

### Hampton Court Silver

Burncoose Nurseries
Burnham Nurseries
Hoyland Plant Centre
W E Th. Ingwersen Ltd
Isle of Wight Lavender
Mallet Court Nursery

### Hampton Court Silver Knightian

Highdown Nursery

### Hampton Court Bronze

Claire Austin Hardy Plants
Hillview Hardy Plants
Pioneer Nursery

### Hampton Court Festival of Roses Gold

David Austin Roses Ltd

### Hampton Court Festival of Roses Silver-Gilt

Peter Beales Roses
Henry Street Nursery

### Hampton Court Festival of Roses Silver

C & K Jones
Style Roses

### Hampton Court Festival of Roses Bronze

Seale Nurseries

### Tatton Gold

Cath's Garden Plants
Croston Cactus
Dibley's Nurseries
Edrom Nurseries
Farmyard Nurseries
Fernwood Nursery
Fir Trees Pelargonium Nursery
Mary Green
Hall Farm Nursery
Hampshire Carnivorous Plants
Jekka's Herb Farm
Elizabeth MacGregor
Mendip Bonsai Studio
Park Green Nurseries
Poppy Heads Ltd
W Robinson & Sons Ltd
Roualeyn Nurseries
South West Carnivorous Plants
Brian & Pearl Sulman

### Tatton Silver-Gilt

Bluebell Arboretum & Nursery
Burncoose Nurseries
Culm View Nursery
D'Arcy & Everest
Foxgrove Plants
Hardy's Cottage Garden Plants
Holden Clough Nursery
Hoyand Plant Centre
C S Lockyer (Fuchsias)
Pennard Plants
Shirley Tasker
Taylors Clematis Nursery

### Tatton Silver

Bridge End Nurseries
Broadleigh Gardens
Brownthwaite Hardy Plants
Cairnsmore Nursery
Sheila Chapman Clematis
Fibrex Nurseries Ltd
Green Garden Herbs
Hartside Nursery Garden
Harveys Garden Plants
Mallet Court Nursery
Oak Tree Nursery
Packhorse Farm Nursery
Passiflora, National Collection
Potash Nursery
White Cottage Alpines

### Tatton Bronze

Fuchsiavale Nurseries
Mickfield Hostas
ProudPlants
Rickards Ferns Ltd

# *The* HARDY PLANT SOCIETY

## MEMBERSHIP APPLICATION FOR 2007

The Annual Subscriptions are:
Single **£13.00** per year (one member)
Joint **£15.00** per year (two members at the same address)

• Subscriptions are renewable annually on **1 January**.
• Subscriptions of members joining after 1 October are valid until the end of the following year.
• Overseas members are requested to pay in pounds sterling by International Money Order or by credit card. An optional charge of £10.00 is made for airmail postage outside Western Europe of all literature, if preferred.

Please fill in the details in BLOCK CAPITALS, tear off this form and send it with your payment to the Administrator or telephone the Administrator with details of your credit card.

**Please tick the type of membership required**

☐ Single £13.00 per year (one member)
☐ Joint £15.00 per year (two members at one address)
☐ Airmail postage £10.00 per year (optional for members outside Western Europe)

NAME/S ..............................................................................................

ADDRESS ..............................................................................................

..............................................................................................

.................................................. POST CODE ..............................................

TELEPHONE NUMBER ..............................................................................

E-mail ..............................................................................................

I enclose a cheque/postal order* payable to **THE HARDY PLANT SOCIETY** (in pounds sterling ONLY) for £.........

**OR**
Please debit my Visa/Master Card* by the sum of £ .............
(* delete as required)

CARD NUMBER ☐☐☐☐ ☐☐☐☐ ☐☐☐☐ ☐☐☐☐

EXPIRY DATE ☐☐☐☐

Name as embossed on card ..............................................................

Signature ..............................................................

***Please print your name and address clearly, tear out the page and send it to The Administrator at the address overleaf***

The Hardy Plant Society is a Registered Charity, number 208080

PLANT HERITAGE

NCCPG

# THE NATIONAL PLANT COLLECTIONS®

## National Council for the Conservation of Plants & Gardens

Patron: HRH The Prince of Wales

### The Lost Garden of Britain

**We have a long history of gardening, plant collecting and breeding in the British Isles so our gardens contain an amazing diversity of plants. Due to the imperatives of marketing and fashion, the desire for 'new' varieties and the practicalities of bulk cultivation, many plants unique to British gardens have been lost. This diversity is important as a genetic resource for the future and as a cultural link to the past.**

### What is The National Council for the Conservation of Plants & Gardens?

The NCCPG's mission is to conserve, document and make available this resource for the benefit of horticulture, education and science. The main conservation vehicle is the National Plant Collection® scheme where individuals or organisations undertake to preserve a group of related plants in trust for the future. Our 40 local groups across Britain support the administration of the scheme, the collection holders and propagate rare plants; working to promote the conservation of cultivated plants.

### Who are the National Plant Collection® Holders?

Collection holders come from every sector of horticulture, amateur and professional. Almost half of the existing 660 National Collections are in private ownership and include allotments, back gardens and large estates. 121 collections are found in nurseries, which range from large commercial concerns to the small specialist grower. 57 local authorities are involved in the scheme, including Sir Harold Hillier Gardens & Arboretum (Hampshire County Council) and Leeds City Council. Universities, agricultural colleges, schools, arboreta and botanic gardens all add to the diversity, and there are also a number of collections on properties belonging to English Heritage, The National Trust and The National Trust for Scotland.

*Please see overleaf for Membership Application Form*

### What do Collection Holders do?

Collection holders subscribe to the scheme's ideals and stringent regulations. As well as protecting the living plants in their chosen group, they also work on areas including education, scientific research and nomenclature, with the common aim of conserving cultivated plants.

### How can you Help the Plant Heritage?

You can play your part in supporting plant conservation by becoming a member of NCCPG. Regular journals will keep you informed of how your support is helping to save our plant biodiversity. Through your local group you can play a more active role in plant conservation working with collection holders, attending talks, plant sales, local horticultural shows and nursery visits.

### How to Join:

**Please contact**
**Membership**
**NCCPG National Office**
**RHS Garden, Wisley**
**Woking, Surrey**
**GU23 6QP**

**Tel: 01483 211465**
**Fax: 01483 212404**
**E-mail: membership@nccpg.org.uk**
**Website: www.nccpg.com**

***'The NCCPG seeks to conserve, document, promote and make available Britain and Ireland's rich biodiversity of garden plants for the benefit of everyone through horticulture, education and science'***

**National Council for the Conservation of Plants & Gardens**

# Membership Application Form

Please complete and detach this form enclosing your payment and send to: Membership, NCCPG, The Stable Courtyard, Wisley Garden, Woking, Surrey GU23 6QP.

PLANT HER[ITAGE] NCCPG

## How to Join

**By post:** complete form and send to theabove address

**On line:** www.nccpg.com

## Annual Subscription Rates

*(please tick relevant boxes)*

- ☐ Individual UK **£20**
- ☐ Joint UK **£34** (two people at same address)
- ☐ Student (up to age 25 in full time education) **£5**
- ☐ Gardening clubs and non-commercial groups **£30**
- ☐ Corporate **£55**
- ☐ Friend ______________________ **(min £100)**

Friends make annual donations in support of our work (in addition to the membership fee)

- ☐ Please send me information on legacies
- ☐ Please send me information on becoming a Collection Holder
- ☐ I would like to make an additional donation of ________ towards the conservation work of NCCPG

## Please complete in CAPITALS

Title ______ First Name ______________________

Last Name ______________________

Date of Birth ______________________

Address ______________________

______________________

______________________ Postcode ______________________

Daytime Telephone ______________________

Email ______________________

*giftaid it* **Gift Aid Declaration: Are you a UK taxpayer? If you are, we can claim 28% from the government on your subscription at no extra cost to you.**

☐ I would like the National Council for the Conservation of Plants & Gardens to reclaim the tax on any membership subscription or donation that I make/have made since 6th April 2000 and all subscriptions and donations I make in the future, until I notify you otherwise. I have paid an amount of UK income tax or capital gains tax equal to any tax reclaimed. (Remember that if you receive a company pension, income tax may well be paid at source.)

## Instruction to your Bank or Building Society to pay by Direct Debit

DIRECT Debit

Please fill in the form and send to:
**Membership, NCCPG, The Stable Courtyard, Wisley Garden, Woking, Surrey GU23 6QP.**

Originators Identification Numb[er]

**9 7 4 2 1 2**

**Name and full postal address of your Bank or Building Socie[ty]**

To: The Manager ______________________

Bank/Building Societ[y]

Address ______________________

______________________

______________________

Postcode

Name(s) of Account Holder

Branch Sort Code

Bank/Building Society account number

Reference No. (NCCPG use only)

**Instruction to your Bank or Building Society**
Please pay the NCCPG Direct Debits from the account detailed in the instructi[on] subject to the safeguards assured by the Direct Debit Guarantee. I understa[nd] that this instruction may remain with the NCCPG and if so, details will be passe[d] electronically to my Bank/Building Society.

Signature(s)

Date / /

Banks and Building Societies may not accept Direct Debit Instructions for some types of accoun[t]

## Payment by Credit or Debit card (Excluding American Express/Diners)

**Card No:**

**Issue No** *(Switch only)* **Security code**

**Start Date** / **Expiry Date** /

**Bank Name** ______________________

**Name on Card** ______________________

**Signature** **Date**

**Payment by cheque:** Please make sterling cheques payable to **NCCPG.**



**National Council for the Conservation of Plants and Gardens**
The Stable Courtyard, Wisley Garden, Woking, Surrey GU23 6QP. **T** 01483 211465 **F** 01483 212404 **E** membership@nccpg.org.uk **W** www.nccpg.com

Company Registration No. 2222953. Registered charity No.1004009